Saint Joseph Edition of

The New Catholic Bible

Our Lord and Savior Jesus Christ

Saint Joseph Edition of

THE NEW CATHOLIC BIBLE

Translated from the Original Languages

WITH MANY HELPS FOR BIBLE READING

• Learning about Your Bible • Historical Survey of the Lands of the Bible
• Over 60 Photographs, Illustrations, Charts, and Maps of the Holy Land
• Bible Dictionary • Doctrinal Bible Index • The Sunday Gospels
• All Footnotes and Cross-References Keyed in Text
• Over 30 Self-Explaining Maps in Context

C.B. P.C.

CATHOLIC BOOK PUBLISHING CORP.
NEW JERSEY

OLD TESTAMENT

NIHIL OBSTAT: Most Rev. Fr. Gerardo R. Tapiador
Censor Librorum

IMPRIMATUR: ✠ Pablo Virgilio S. David, DD
Chairman, Episcopal Commission on the Biblical Apostolate
April 15, 2013

RESCRIPT

In accord with Canon 825, par. 1 of the Code of Canon Law, the Catholic Bishops' Conference of the Philippines hereby approves for publication *The Old Testament Books of the St. Joseph New Catholic Bible,* published by Catholic Book Publishing Corporation. This translation of the Old Testament is intended for private use and study only and may never be used for liturgical purposes.

NEW TESTAMENT

NIHIL OBSTAT: Fr. Oscar Alunday, SVD
Censor Librorum

IMPRIMATUR: ✠ Arturo M. Bastes, SVD, DD
Chairman, Episcopal Commission on the Biblical Apostolate
May 15, 2007

RESCRIPT

In accord with Canon 825, par. 1 of the Code of Canon Law, the Catholic Bishops' Conference of the Philippines hereby approves for publication *The New Testament Books of the St. Joseph New Catholic Bible,* published by Catholic Book Publishing Corporation. This translation of the New Testament is intended for private use and study only and may never be used for liturgical purposes.

(T-614)

Printed in India 23 TP 1

catholicbookpublishing.com

PREFACE

In the words of the *Catechism of the Catholic Church*, "And such is the force and power of the Word of God that it can serve the Church as her support and vigor and the children of the Church as strength for their faith, food for the soul, and a pure and lasting font of spiritual life." Hence, "access to Sacred Scripture ought to be open wide to the Christian faithful" (no. 131).

Hence, in the life of Christians there can never be too many translations of the Bible. It is a well-known fact that different translations are able to bring out nuances of meaning specific to each one. The Scriptures are so full of meaning that we can rightly say no single translation will do it justice.

Accordingly, it has become customary for Christians to make use of many translations of the sacred books in order to discover the riches of the Bible and pray with its text. In doing so, they are carrying out the recommendation of the Bishops of the United States:

"What is most necessary of all is that we begin . . . to meet with Christ as he speaks to us through the liturgical rites and the inspired word of Scripture. This should best start with the use of the primal form of 'mental prayer' or 'meditation,' traditionally known as . . . 'praying the Bible'" (*The Use of the Vernacular at Mass*, no. 1).

Following the highly acclaimed publication of the *New Catholic Bible* version of *The Psalms* in 2002 and *The New Testament* in 2015, this translation of the *New Catholic Bible* has been accomplished by the same board of highly qualified Scripture scholars under the direction of Rev. Jude Winkler, OFM Conv., S.S.L. They were committed to render as perfectly as possible a translation of literal or formal equivalence. Numerous translations were consulted and decisions were made by consensus according to accepted principles of textual criticism.

With a deep desire to be faithful to God's inspired words, the translators used the best available Hebrew and Greek texts to achieve a dignified and accurate version of the sacred text in language that is clear and meaningful to today's readers.

With multiple cross-references to other Scripture texts and extensive explanatory footnotes that reflect the most current consensus of Catholic scholarship, the *New Catholic Bible* is a translation that can be trusted to provide the reader with a prayerful and fulfilling Bible experience suitable for private devotion and study.

A ST. JOSEPH EDITION

Therefore, we have thought it worthwhile to make available a Catholic translation of the Bible in the renowned and exclusive format of our St. Joseph Editions of Bibles and Missals. The St. Joseph Edition is an editorial system developed over a span of fifty years. It consists in a series of features intended to ensure that a text (particularly a biblical or liturgical text) is user friendly, leading to greater readability and easier understanding.

The textual features or format in the present case are a large readable typeface, additional headings and subheadings, and a full measure extension for long lines of poetry that clearly indicates when a line has a runover. It also includes general introductions to both the Old Testament and the New Testament as well as introductions to each Book, copious cross-references, and pastoral notes or footnotes. For greater clarity and convenience, the footnotes and cross-references are printed at the bottom of each page and cross-indexed in the text itself.

An asterisk (*) in the text indicates that there is a footnote to the text in question. Each footnote is in turn clearly marked with the number of the chapter and verse to which it pertains. Similarly, a lightface superior italic letter [(a)] in the text indicates that there is a cross-reference to a particular verse or verses. The reference itself is also clearly marked with the same letter. Hence, the reader is always aware of a helpful footnote or cross-reference simply by reading the text.

OTHER FEATURES OF THIS EDITION

The *New Catholic Bible* offers a host of other helpful features. Some editions include a handy edge-marking Index and in most editions the words of Christ are in red.

Perhaps most important of all is a series of self-explaining maps showing key events and areas in the Bible, each placed near the text that it concerns. In this way, the reader is kept abreast of the history of salvation without needlessly turning to some other part of the book. In addition, extensive historical and biblical background material is provided in "The Lands of the Bible" and "Learning about Your Bible."

A series of photographs of important archaeological finds offers much light on the Testaments and provides impartial confirmation of the events present therein. Finally, the Bible Dictionary and the Doctrinal Bible Index help to bring the Sacred Scriptures into the very life and worship of each reader.

We trust that this new translation of the Bible will lead many into a better understanding of the Holy Books and a fuller knowledge of their principal author, the Triune God, and their primary protagonist, Jesus Christ, the Incarnate Word.

CATHOLIC BOOK PUBLISHING CORP.

CONTENTS

THE OLD TESTAMENT

THE NEW TESTAMENT

APPENDIX

LIST OF MAPS

The Old Testament

The New Testament

LIST OF PHOTOGRAPHS

The Old Testament

The New Testament

"Let them remember that prayer should accompany the reading of Sacred Scripture, so that God and human beings may talk together."

(Second Vatican Council:
Dogmatic Constitution on Divine Revelation, no. 25)

Prayer to the Holy Spirit

Come, Holy Spirit,
fill the hearts of your faithful.
And kindle in them the fire of your love.

A partial indulgence. *Enchiridion Indulgentiarum*, 1986 edition, no. 62

A *partial indulgence* is granted to the Christian faithful who read sacred scripture with the veneration due God's word and as a form of spiritual reading. The indulgence will be a *plenary* one when such reading is done for at least one-half hour.

(*Enchiridion Indulgentiarum*, 1986 edition, no. 50)

LEARNING ABOUT YOUR BIBLE

The Bible is a series of books written under the inspiration of the Holy Spirit between 1200 B.C. and around A.D. 100. They were produced in a number of different forms of literature (historical accounts, poetry, letters, parables, sayings, etc.). They were written in various languages: Hebrew, Aramaic, and Greek. They present different ideas about who God is and what God wants of us. Yet, these books, which we call Sacred Scripture, form a single message that we call the Word of God. The Letter to the Hebrews tells us that this Word is so powerful that it is like a two-edged sword that can separate bone from sinew. How was this collection put together? Who wrote its individual sections? Why? When? Etc.?

The Authors of the Pentateuch

The oldest portions of the Bible are cultic hymns which celebrate momentous events in Israel's history, e.g., Ex 15, which celebrates Israel's deliverance at the Red Sea. These hymns were probably sung at shrines to commemorate how God acted in Israel's history and to instruct the next generation about who their God was.

These hymns, however, were not enough once the Israelites conquered the land flowing with milk and honey. The nation needed an explanation as to how they had arrived at this point. Thus, a first school of authors wrote the story of God and Israel from the creation of the world up to the present day (ca 950 B.C.). These authors were called the Yahwists (for they tended to use the name "Yahweh" whenever they referred to God). Their stories are highly anthropomorphic and speak of the importance of Judah and Jerusalem and the monarchy. When they wrote of the primitive beginnings of the world (Gen 1–11), they borrowed ideas from other cultures to express their beliefs (e.g., God shaping Adam out of mud or clay, the flood, etc.). When they spoke of the patriarchal period (Gen 12–50), they depended upon stories passed down at various shrines scattered throughout the land (which would explain why some stories are doublets, once attributed to one patriarch and later to another). For more recent events, they depended upon the memory of the people and their storytellers and whatever chronicles existed at that time.

A century later, ca 850 B.C., another school of writers arose in the northern kingdom of Israel (for by now the ten northern tribes had broken away from the two southern tribes). These were called the Elohists, for they used the word "Elohim" when they spoke about God. They had a more spiritualized view of God. They centered their narratives on the exploits of the northern heroes: the prophets (e.g., Elijah and Elisha). Some of their stories repeat previously told Yahwist stories. The Elohist version was either placed side by side with the older Yahwist version or they were intertwined.

This process was repeated again some three hundred years later (ca 550 B.C.) when the Priestly school arose while the Jews lived in exile in Babylon. They emphasized the importance of ritual and law in order to preserve Jewish identity for a people living in exile.

Finally, there was a fourth source for the Pentateuch: the Deuteronomists. They take their name from the book of Deuteronomy which had been found in the temple around 622 B.C. Their writings speak of how things should have happened in Israel's history (e.g., wiping out all pagans from the land so that Israel would no longer be tempted by them to turn against Yahweh). The Deuteronomists often also edited materials written before their times, often reshaping the message to better reflect their point of view.

Sometime after the Exile in Babylon (587–539 B.C.), the books that we call the Pentateuch (the first five books of the Bible) were put together in the shape we now find them. They were called the Torah (a word that can also refer to the law of Israel) and they became the core of what Israel believed about God and his relationship with the people of Israel.

The Prophets

Given the complicated history of the writing and editing of the Pentateuch, it should be no surprise that the books of the prophets did not have a simple development. Some of the books of the prophets were written by disciples of the prophets (e.g., Amos and Hosea). Others seem to have been produced by the prophet himself or his secretary (e.g., Jeremiah and Ezekiel). Some books of the prophets are actually amalgamations of the prophecies of different prophets from different eras (e.g., Isaiah and Zechariah). One of the books of the prophets, Daniel, is probably not even a prophecy in its classical definition, for it is more a series of parables and apocalyptic visions, which supposedly occurred during the Babylonian Exile but which were actually written during the Maccabean rebellion (ca 165 B.C.).

The prophets use various techniques to proclaim their messages. There are visions, oracle statements (as if the sayings came from the mouth of God), poems, parables, prophetic actions. Frequently, while the prophets were addressing their own times, the Holy Spirit gave another, more profound meaning to their words and actions that foretold later events, especially the coming of the Messiah.

While one could speak of prophets in the days of Saul and David, (e.g., Nathan) and the next century (Elijah and Elisha), the classical age of prophets began around 750 B.C. and ran to around 445 B.C., the era of Ezra and Nehemiah and the closing of the age of prophecy.

Wisdom Literature

A third form of Old Testament literature is Wisdom Literature. Originally, this was a collection of folk sayings put together to instruct princes on how to govern their people (e.g., Prov 10ff). In later Old Testament times, the concept changed. Around 300 B.C., Judaism began to be influenced by Greek philosophical ideas which emphasized the transcendence of God. If God was the uncreated Creator who had nothing to do with the material world, then there had to be some intermediary to communicate God's will to us and our needs to God. Jewish people began to speak of God's attributes as this type of intermediary (e.g., God's holiness, Spirit, etc.). The most frequently used attribute was God's wisdom. It was portrayed as a woman (modeled after the Egyptian goddess Ma'at) which sought to instruct the ignorant and to lead them in God's ways (e.g., Prov 1–9, Sir 24).

The last Old Testament book to be written was probably the Book of Wisdom, written as late as 50 B.C.

The Psalms

The Book of Wisdom literature that has had the greatest influence upon Israel and the Church over the centuries is the Book of Psalms. It has been used in the liturgy of the temple/synagogue as well as of Christian communities ever since the Psalms were written (over a period of some 1,000 years).

One can identify various forms of literature in the Psalms: wisdom, lamentation, hymns, regal or Messianic, historic, etc. They often depend upon parallelism (repeating the same idea with similar or identical words to add emphasis) for this is one of the most important techniques in Hebrew poetry. Many of the more subtle forms of poetic structure (alliteration, rhythm, etc.) are difficult to reproduce in modern language translations.

The Languages of the Old Testament

Most of the Old Testament was written in Hebrew. One can often determine when a particular passage was written by the grammatical forms or the borrowed words from other languages (e.g., Aramaic, Persian, Greek) because Hebrew, like all languages, evolved over the centuries.

A few chapters of the books of Daniel and Ezra were written in Aramaic, the language that was spoken by most Jews after the Babylonian Exile.

Beginning with that exile, more and more Jews lived outside of Israel. Many of them spoke Greek as their mother tongue. This is why a Greek translation of the Hebrew Bible, called the Septuagint, was sponsored. This translation was used by Greek-speaking Jews until the end of the first century A.D. and continues to be used by Christians, especially the Orthodox, until this day.

In the last centuries before the birth of Jesus, certain books were written in Greek: 1 and 2 Maccabees, Judith, Tobit, Baruch, Wisdom, and The Wisdom of Ben Sira (although a Hebrew original text for Sirach has now been found). These Greek books were excluded from the canon of the Hebrew Bible by a decision issued by a gathering of rabbis in Jamnia around A.D. 85. Most Christians continued to consider these books to be a part of the Bible. These books became controversial in the days of Martin Luther, who argued that Christians should not use the rabbis' canon and who excluded them from his Bible (hence the difference between the Catholic and the Protestant Old Testament).

The Qumran Documents

When these texts are translated into modern languages, scholars work from the original languages in which they were written. That is difficult for the Old Testament, though, for the texts were mostly written in Hebrew and Aramaic. Early Christians tended not to conserve those manuscripts for they used the Greek and later, the Latin translations. The Hebrew manuscripts were conserved by the Jewish rabbis. In the sixth to the tenth centuries, the rabbis decided to produce a critical edition of the Hebrew Bible called the Masoretic text (this is when they added vowels to the text, for previously, the Hebrew text had been written only with consonants). After they finished, they destroyed all the older manuscripts to avoid confusion. How could we now be sure that the Hebrew Masoretic text was accurate?

Over the past century, archaeologists have discovered a number of Hebrew manuscripts that date back to the first and second centuries B.C. In 1896, they discovered a geniza, a storage room for old scrolls, in a synagogue in Cairo, Egypt.

Then, in 1947, they discovered the Dead Sea Scrolls at Qumran which contained numerous manuscripts of the original Hebrew text. These, and other more recent discoveries, have proven that the Masoretic text is essentially accurate.

Intertestamental Literature

These discoveries have also uncovered a number of books that were written in Old Testament times but never included in the canon. These include the Book of Jubilees and the Testament of the Twelve Patriarchs as well as numerous apocalyptic books. While they are very interesting and provide us with background material on the era just before the birth of Jesus, they were never considered to be part of the Bible.

The New Testament

Like the Old Testament, the New Testament was produced over a number of years, although nothing like the 1,000 years that it took for the books of the Old Testament to be written.

The first part of the New Testament to be written was the letters of St. Paul. Over the centuries, 14 letters have been attributed to St. Paul. Modern scholars are fairly certain that he wrote at least 7 of them: 1 Thessalonians, 1 and 2 Corinthians, Galatians, Philemon, Philippians and Romans. More questionable but still possible are 2 Thessalonians, Colossians, and Ephesians. Highly improbable are 1 and 2 Timothy and Titus. Finally, Hebrews is certainly not written by Paul.

Paul's first letter was probably 1 Thessalonians written around A.D. 50–51. He died around A.D. 67. He wrote to console, instruct, encourage, correct, etc. Following the Jewish custom of copying and sharing letters from important rabbis, the communities that received his letters quickly shared them with other Christian communities. By the end of the first century A.D., we have evidence of collections of Paul's letters having been made.

Paul was not the only apostle who wrote letters. Peter, James, Jude, and John all have letters that have been attributed to them (although we doubt that all these letters were actually written by them).

Furthermore, there is the Letter to the Hebrews. It is difficult to date this letter, but it was probably written sometime between A.D. 70–80 by an anonymous author. More a treatise than a letter, it calls upon the early Jewish-Christian community to embrace Christ totally and give up some of their Jewish practices.

All of these letters (with the exception of Philemon) were intended for public consumption. They would have been read alongside readings taken from the Old Testament, even if they had not yet acquired the stature of "Sacred Scripture," something that did not occur until the second century A.D. The public use of these books during the liturgy was, in fact, one of the criteria for these letters and the other books of the New Testament to be considered to be canonical. The three main criteria were that they had to have apostolic origin, be used in the liturgy, and be used throughout the Christian Churches scattered in all Europe, Asia, and Africa.

The Four Gospels

The essential core of the New Testament is the four Gospels. Each of the Gospels has its own unique character for each evangelist attempted to share the Jesus story in a way that would respond to the needs of his community.

Scholars believe that the first Gospel written was Mark. It was written around A.D. 70 by John Mark, a disciple of Peter, in Rome for a community that was undergoing persecution.

Mark patched his Gospel together by combining a series of sources: miracle stories, sayings, parables, independent narratives, a passion narrative, etc. The main characteristic of this Gospel is its frankness. Mark presents the story with all its flaws visible, as if he were producing the home videos of Jesus' ministry. At times ungrammatical and filled with clumsy transitions, it nevertheless presents a profound picture of Jesus who fully embraces our humanity even while he remains the Son of God.

The next two Gospels were written in the next decade, ca A.D. 80–85. They were Matthew and Luke.

Matthew's Gospel was written for a Jewish-Christian community that was being persecuted by Jewish authorities. It presents Jesus as the fulfillment of Jewish expectations, the Messiah whom Yahweh sent. It quotes the Old Testament extensively, and in it, Jesus teaches that he has not come to abolish the law but rather to fulfill it.

There is an ancient tradition that Matthew the apostle actually wrote the first Gospel in Aramaic. This is why the Gospel of Matthew is always the first Gospel found in the New Testament. The difficulty with this tradition is that the present Gospel of Matthew seems to have been written in Greek and it also seems to borrow from material found in Mark. It is possible that Matthew the apostle did produce a short document in Aramaic (possibly a collection of the sayings of Jesus) before the Gospel of Mark was written. Then, around A.D. 80, a second author used that document, the material found in Mark, and his own sources to produce the Gospel we know today as the Gospel of Matthew. Thus, Matthew the apostle would have written the first document about Jesus in Aramaic, but it was probably not a full Gospel, only a collection of sayings.

The other Gospel produced at this time was Luke. According to tradition, Luke was a physician, a Gentile-Christian, and a disciple of Paul. He produced both the Gospel of Luke and the Acts of the Apostles for a Gentile-Christian and Gentile audience. His portrait of Jesus is one filled with compassion. Jesus reaches out to the Anawim (the poor ones of Yahweh). They were the people who recognized their brokenness (the poor, sinners, foreigners, women, etc.) and therefore, embraced Jesus and his message.

Both Matthew and Luke contain a story of the infancy of Jesus. Mark, the first Gospel, did not. It began with Jesus' baptism in the Jordan by John the Baptist. A group of heretics called the adoptionists argued that this was when Yahweh had adopted Jesus as his Son. This is why Matthew and Luke show that Jesus was already God's Son when he was conceived. The last Gospel, John, would take that argument one step further and speak of Jesus already being God's Son "in the beginning."

Matthew, Mark, and Luke are collectively called the Synoptic Gospels. The word "synoptic" comes from two Greek words which mean "with" and "eye," implying that they saw their material from one eye, or one point of view, for they are so similar in the way they present their material.

The Gospel of John

The Gospel which is not synoptic, which sees the material from a different point of view, is the Gospel of John. It was probably written around A.D. 90 and was produced by a community founded by the Beloved Disciple. It emphasizes the divinity of Jesus who is in charge at all times, even during his passion and death. The cross is Jesus' hour of glory, that moment when Jesus most clearly reveals how much God loves us. The Gospel is filled with intense symbolism, so much so, that St. Augustine once said it was shallow enough for a child to play in and profound enough for an elephant to swim in.

Other Johannine Writings

The three letters of John are products of this same community (although probably not the same author). They speak of the fact that Jesus was truly human and truly divine, thus attacking docetism, a heresy which denied that God could have taken on our human flesh).

Finally, the Book of Revelation is attributed to John. Written around A.D. 96, it is the only entirely apocalyptic book in the New Testament canon. It speaks of the need to give witness to Jesus and his Word while we await the fulfillment of history and the end of times.

The New Testament Canon

Already by the end of the second century A.D., most of the books that we know as the New Testament were included in a list of inspired books. The books that entered the canon the latest were the Letter to the Hebrews (because of its uncertain authorship) and the Book of Revelation (because it was so unusual).

There were other books written around this time which were debated but not included in the canon (for they failed to meet one or more of the three criteria for inclusion in the canon). These include the Pastor of Hermes, the Didache, the Letter of Clement to the Corinthians, etc. Like the intertestamental books of the Old Testament, they provide a valuable insight into the beliefs of the infant Christian Church.

Still other books written, in general, a bit later were also not included, but this time because they were considered to be heretical. Among these are the Gnostic writings. Gnosticism was a heresy that denied the goodness of the material world and thus, Jesus' humanity. These writings present Jesus as a divine teacher who has as little as possible to do with the created world. Many of these documents were only recently discovered for their texts were often destroyed since the Church considered them to be erroneous and even dangerous.

The Language of the New Testament

All the books of the New Testament (with the possible exception of an early collection of Aramaic sayings put together by the apostle Matthew) were written in Greek. The particular form of Greek used was called "koine," which was the common Greek spoken by the ordinary people. These writings were intended for the simple people who constituted most of the early Christian community.

The Relationship between the Old Testament and the New Testament

How does the Old Testament and the Old Covenant relate to the New Testament and the New Covenant? Some early Christians argued that the Old Testament was obsolete and that its influences upon the New Testament should be discarded. But the mainline Church has argued that the Old Testament was a preparation for the coming of Jesus and the New Testament. The New Covenant does not replace the Old Covenant, it fulfills it. Many texts in the New Testament, in fact, either quote or allude to passages taken from the Old Testament to show how Jesus' mission and especially his suffering, death, and resurrection were foretold by the Old Testament.

At the same time, one must remember that while the revelation of the Old Testament was inspired by the Holy Spirit, it was nevertheless filtered through the cultural expectations of an ancient people. This is why we needed Jesus to come into the world: to reveal clearly who God is and what God wants of us.

Translating the Bible

Throughout the centuries, the Bible has continuously been translated into the vernacular. The Greek Septuagint (the Greek translation of the Hebrew Bible) and the Vulgate (St. Jerome's translation of the Bible into Latin) are early examples of this effort. Some vernacular translations used these two early translations, the Septuagint and the Vulgate, as their base texts, producing translations of translations. Pope Pius XII, in his encyclical *Divino Afflante Spiritu*, emphasized the importance of translating from the original languages (Hebrew, Aramaic, and Greek). Recent archaeological discoveries (e.g., at Ugarit and Ebla) have aided scholars in their effort to understand better ancient texts that are sometimes a bit obscure.

Scripture and Tradition

Sacred Scripture was produced by a believing community. The Holy Spirit acted through Israel and the early Church community to produce authors who wrote down the books we call Sacred Scripture. Yet, the Holy Spirit also works through the Church to reveal God's truth through her interpretation of Sacred Scriptures (a responsibility given to her by the Holy Spirit) and through tradition (another form of God's revelation). This is why we should read Scripture in the context of our Catholic community (lest our individual interpretation not be evaluated in light of the Holy Spirit's guidance through the magisterium of the Church) and why we should not discount beliefs because they are "only tradition" (for God also works through tradition).

Reading Sacred Scripture Today

Given this rich and profound history, how does one begin to read Sacred Scripture today?

First of all, it is always best for a Catholic to read from an approved Catholic translation. While translations produced by other Christian traditions have the same basic text, there are sometimes particular translations of certain phrases which could imply other theological positions. Furthermore, many other Christian translations do not contain all of the books of the Old Testament that we, Catholics, consider to be canonical (i.e., the Greek books).

Pray to the Holy Spirit. Reading the Bible is not like reading history or poetry. It is a faith journey and the Holy Spirit should be our guide.

Begin with one of the easier books. Some of the books, e.g., Leviticus and the Book of Revelation, are difficult to understand and could discourage one in one's attempt. A suggestion might be to start with the Gospel being used in that particular liturgical year. Thus, one will hear those readings both in one's personal reading and in the liturgy.

There is no rush to finish the Bible. There are one and two year programs to read the whole Bible, but they often leave one feeling that it has all been a blur.

Some spiritual directors suggest reading a little in the morning and a little in the evening. When getting up in the morning, place the Bible on the pillow. That way one can't go to bed without reading at least a verse or two. When going to bed, one can place the Bible on one's shoes. That way one can't get dressed without reading a verse or two.

Underline, highlight, write notes in the margins of the page, write down verses, etc.—to remember the passage throughout the day.

Some people study the Bible by examining the texts used at Mass on Sunday and on weekdays. The texts are arranged in such a way that one will cover almost every verse of the Bible within its two-year cycle for weekdays and three-year cycle for Sundays.

One could join a Bible Study group. The best groups are those which include reading Scripture, prayer, study, and spiritual sharing so that it is both an intellectual and a faith-sharing experience. It is preferable to join a Catholic group, but if that is not possible, then many mainline Christian groups have similar understandings of Scripture (although their understandings of hierarchy and sacraments will often be different).

Most of all, keep to it. Reading the Bible is not always easy, but its ultimate reward is an encounter with the Word of God that will transform our hearts and change our lives.

THE LANDS OF THE BIBLE

A Brief Survey of Peoples, Kingdoms, and Major Events

1. THE ANCIENT NEAR EAST

EGYPT

3200–1800 Before Christ

Egypt had thirty dynasties

ca 3200 **Predynastic period:** Two kingdoms: the kingdom of the Delta with its capital at Buto; the kingdom of Upper Egypt with its capital at Nekhen.

ca 2900 **I Dynasty:** rules Egypt for about 100 years.

ca 2800 **II Dynasty:** with its residence near Memphis. Rules Egypt for about 200 years.

ca 2600 **III Dynasty:** Old Memphite Kingdom. It rules Egypt for about 50 years and erects the first pyramid.

ca 2550 **IV Dynasty:** signals the apogee of the Memphite Empire. The largest pyramids are constructed. Rules Egypt for about 100 years.

2450 **V Dynasty:** worship of the *Sun* god predominates. Rules Egypt for about 100 years.

2350 **VI Dynasty:** marks the end of the Memphite Kingdom. Rules Egypt for about 150 years.

2200 **VII Dynasty:** seems never to have existed: 70 kings in 70 days.

2200 **VIII Dynasty:** finds Egypt divided into three kingdoms: the Delta, Middle Egypt, and Upper Egypt.

2150 **IX–X–XI Dynasties:** battle for the unification of Egypt. With the XI Dynasty begins the *Middle Theban Kingdom.*

2000 **XII Dynasty:** Egypt reaches the apogee of its history. It invades Palestine and Syria. Rules Egypt for about 200 years. Classic period of literary Egyptian language.

1800 **XIII Dynasty:** marks the decline of Egypt.

MESOPOTAMIA

3200–1800 Before Christ

The Sumerian Empire was made up of the first people of the Ancient Middle East. It had a very high culture and remained in power for more than 1000 years.

ca 3200 **Jemdet Nasr period:** at the time of Uruk IV. An era of the expansion and irradiation of the Sumerian culture.

ca 2900 **Mesilim period:** dominated by the Lagash dynasties (I, II, III).

ca 2650 **I Ur Dynasty period:** an era of struggle for power between the cities of Lagash and Ur. Lugalzaggisi tries to establish a Sumerian Kingdom united to the Uruk capital; but his efforts fail.

ca 2350 **Akkadian period:** an age of great expansion. Sargon I unites all Mesopotamia under one kingdom: Akkadians and Sumerians become one people.

2200 **Gutian period:** transformation of the entire Sumerian culture. The king begins to have himself called "god." Sumerian customs, languages and strategies are repressed.

ca 2000 **III Ur Dynasty period:** new political and cultural predominance on the part of Sumerians. The efforts of King Ur-nammu make this the most prosperous kingdom of Sumer; Sumerians and Akkadians become reconciled.

ca 1800 The Sumerian Empire disappears with the foundation of the first Babylonian kingdom.

EGYPT

1800–330 Before Christ

1750 **XIV–XV–XVI Dynasties:** period of the Hyksos. Occupation of Egypt.

1600 **XVII–XVIII Dynasties: New Theban Kingdom:** battles against the Hyksos—Ahmose I occupies Palestine—Thutmose I conquers Syria—Thutmose III wins the Battle of Megiddo.

1315 **XIX Dynasty:** Seti I defeats the Hittites at Kedesh—Rameses II again invades Palestine and Syria—Oppression of the Hebrews—Exodus of the Hebrews.

ca 1200 **XX Dynasty:** with capital at Thebes—Rameses III battles against the "Sea Peoples."

ca 1050 **XXI Dynasty:** with capital at Tanis—New decline of Egypt.

ca 950 **XXII Dynasty:** influence of Egypt over all of Palestine—Sheshonk I (the biblical Shishak).

ca 800 **XXIII Dynasty:** with capital at Bubastis. Egypt is broken up into little states.

ca 730 **XXIV Dynasty:** founded by Tefnakht and Bocchoris.

ca 715 **XXV Dynasty:** Nubian, founded by the Ethiopian Shabaka: unifies the Egyptian Empire.

ca 650 **XXVI Dynasty:** with capital at Sais (Saitic period). Neco invades Palestine and conquers Mari.

ca 500 **XXVII Dynasty:** the dynasty of the Persians, from Cambyses to Darius II who govern Egypt as a province of the Persian Empire.

ca 450 **XXVIII Dynasty:** constituted by the Egyptian Amyrtaeus. Battles Persian domination in Egypt.

ca 400 **XXIX Dynasty:** founded by Nepherites I.

ca 360 **XXX Dynasty:** founded by Nectanebo I, enjoys some prosperity until the Persians with Artaxerxes III reconquer Egypt in 342. It is the last indigenous Dynasty. The Persian domination under the XXXI Dynasty lasts only a short time since in 332, Alexander the Great puts an end to Pharaonic civilization.

ASSYRIA

1830–330 Before Christ

ca 1830 **Assyria** is ruled by a strong indigenous dynasty (Sargon I).

ca 1750 Assyria comes under an Amorite dynasty (Shamshi-adad I) and then forms part of the Empire of Hammurabi.

ca 1700 Assyria continued to rise in power during the rule of Bel-Ban: further defeating the Amorites and Babylonians

ca 1500 Rise of the **Hurite Kingdom of Mitanni** which subjugates even Assyria.

ca 1400 The **Kingdom of Mitanni** becomes a vassal of the Hittites.

1266 **Shalmaneser I** proclaims himself king of Assyria.

ca 1112 **Tiglath-pileser I** founds the Assyrian power and extends its dominion from the Persian Gulf to the Mediterranean.

883 **Ashurnasirpal II** extends the empire into northern Mesopotamia.

858 **Shalmaneser III** attacks the Arameans of Damascus, the small states of Phoenicia and Israel.

745 **Tiglath-pileser III** intervenes in the war of Damascus and Israel against Judah and reduces them to vassal states.

726 **Shalmaneser V** besieges Samaria.

721 **Sargon II** destroys the kingdom of Israel and deports its inhabitants.

704 **Sennacherib** lays siege to Jerusalem and devastates Babylonia.

680 **Esarhaddon** lifts Assyria's power to its height.

668 **Ashurbanipal:** rules over the most splendid period of Assyrian art and culture.

625–612 Decline of the Assyrian Kingdom and fall of Nineveh.

BABYLONIA

1830–330 Before Christ

ca 1830 **Start of I Dynasty** (Babylonian-Amorite) with capital at Babel.

ca 1750 **Babylonia reaches the apogee** of its greatness with king Hammurabi. His dominion extends over all of Mesopotamia and part of Assyria and Elam.

ca 1700 **II Babylonian Dynasty:** called that of the "Land of the Sea" (that is, near the foci of the Tigris and Euphrates).

ca 1500 **III Babylonian Dynasty:** made up of the Kassites stemming from the Iranian highland.

ca 1112 **New Babylonian Dynasty:** Nebuchadnezzar I delivers Babylonia from the Elamite invasion.

ca 900 Decline in the political power of Babylonia, which falls under the hegemony of Assyria, while retaining autonomous dynasties.

745 The king of Assyria also assumes the title of king of Babylonia.

605 **Nabopolassar** captures Nineveh and initiates the Neo-Babylonian Empire (or Chaldean Empire).

538 **Nebuchadnezzar II** subjugates and then destroys the kingdom of Judah (598–587).
End of the Chaldean Empire under Nabonidas and Balthasar.

PERSIAN

559–333 Before Christ

559	**Cyrus** the Great
529	**Cambyses**
521	**Darius I** Hystaspis
485	**Xerxes I** (Ahasuerus in the Book of Esther)
464	**Artaxerxes I**
424	**Xerxes II**
424	**Darius II**
404	**Artaxerxes II**
385	**Artaxerxes III**
337	**Arses**
335–330	**Darius III** Codoman
333	**Empire of Alexander the Great**

EGYPT

Alexander the Great to 30 Before Christ

333–323 Kingdom of Alexander the Great in Egypt.
With the death of Alexander the Great, in Egypt a new Hellenistic Dynasty begins: that of the Lagids with capital at Alexandria. It is composed of nine kings.

ca 305 **Ptolemy I Soter:** noble Macedonian, rules Egypt for almost 20 years.

ca 285 **Ptolemy II Philadelphus:** son of Soter. Literature and the arts flourish; he rules Egypt for almost 35 years.

ca 246 **Ptolemy III Euergetes:** son of Philadelphus. He undertakes an expedition in Syria, but internal troubles in Egypt oblige him to abandon his effort.

ca 221 **Ptolemy IV Philopator:** son of Euergetes. He resumes the war in Syria and defeats the adversary king at Raphia in 217.

ca 203 **Ptolemy V Epiphanes:** son of Philopator. He becomes his father's successor at the age of five.

SYRIA – MESOPOTAMIA

Alexander the Great to 30 Before Christ

332–323 Kingdom of Alexander the Great in all Asia.
At the death of Alexander the Great, in Syria the Hellenistic Dynasty of the Seleucids is begun with capital at Antioch.

ca 312 **Seleucus I Nicator:** founds the Seleucid Dynasty. He dies by assassination.

ca 280 **Antiochus I Soter:** son of Nicator. He leaves his power to his son.

ca 261 **Antiochus II Theos:** before dying names his firstborn as his heir.

ca 246 **Seleucus II Callinicus:** undergoes the third Syrian War.

ca 226 **Seleucus III Ceraunus:** son of Callinicus. Accomplishes nothing of note.

ca 223 **Antiochus III (the Great):** brother of Ceraunus; defeated by the Romans; leaves his kingdom in great poverty.

ca 180 **Ptolemy VI Philometor:** son of Epiphanes. Since he is very young, he governs under the tutelage of his mother.

ca 145 **Ptolemy VII Physcon:** brother of the preceding, also called Euergetes II; succeeds his brother who has been taken prisoner by Antiochus IV.

ca 116 **Ptolemy VIII (Soter II) Lathyrus:** has a most difficult life.

ca 108 **Ptolemy IX (Alexander I) Auletes:** illegitimate son of the preceding.

ca 51 At the death of Auletes, Cleopatra VII ascends the throne. Protected by Julius Caesar and later by Antony; she kills herself after Antony's defeat at Actium (31); Egypt becomes a Roman province.

ca 187 **Seleucus IV Philopator:** son of the preceding; has an insignificant reign.

ca 175 **Antiochus IV Epiphanes:** brother of Philopator. Hostile to the Hebrews, he initiates the first religious persecution. He dies during a military expedition in Persia (164).

ca 164 **Antiochus V Eupator:** succeeds his father at the age of twelve and rules for two years as a mere instrument of Lysias.

ca 161 **Demetrius I Soter:** son of Seleucus IV; dies fighting Alexander Balas.

ca 150 **Alexander Balas:** usurper, succeeds Demetrius I. Obliged to flee, he is killed.

ca 145 **Demetrius II Nicator:** son of Demetrius I; is taken prisoner by the Parthians.

ca 145 **Antiochus VI:** son of Alexander Balas; usurps the kingdom while Demetrius is in prison.

ca 138 **Antiochus VII Sidetes:** brother of Demetrius II; conquers Gazara, Joppa, Acre; he despoils Jerusalem and is killed by the Parthians.

ca 129 **Demetrius II:** returns to power after his imprisonment.

ca 125 **Antiochus VIII Gryphus:** brother of Demetrius II; is killed by Heraclone.

ca 113 **Antiochus IX Cyzicenus.**

The list of Seleucids goes on. It constitutes one continuous struggle on the part of pretenders to the throne who are ever ready to extend themselves in neighboring lands but inept to defend their own territory from foreign kings and petty local rulers: they fight only for their own personal and family honor, not for the good of their country.

This struggle goes on until the year 65 B.C. when Pompey eliminates the last Seleucid, Antiochus XIII, and declares Syria a Roman province.

II. THE HEBREW PEOPLE

I. FROM ABRAHAM TO MOSES

(Gen 12–25)

ca 1850 **Abraham** sets out from Ur; he probably follows the "royal road." This route is most likely: Ur—central Mesopotamia—western bank of the Euphrates—Hit—Abu Kamal—Haran. He remains at Haran until the death of his father Terah.

From Haran through the Euphrates Valley, he sets out for Aleppo. From Aleppo, he approaches the mountains of Anti-Lebanon, passes through Damascus, crosses the Jordan and heads for the Valley of Shechem. From there he goes to Hebron. In Canaan Abraham and his clan—about 300—dig wells, erect altars and acquire land.

Encountering a great famine in Canaan, Abraham goes to Egypt. Leaving Egypt, he returns in stages to Bethel, where he and his nephew Lot separate. Lot goes down the Jordan Valley as far as Sodom and to the south of the Dead Sea. Abraham remains in the terebinth of Mamre. From here Abraham goes forth with his followers to defeat the kings of the East who have sacked Sodom and carried off Lot. On his return, he is blessed by Melchizedek, priest and king of Salem (Jerusalem).

During his stay at Mamre, Abraham travels into the Negeb, to Gerar and Beer-sheba. Abraham's offering of Isaac takes place on Mt. Moriah, identified with the site of the temple at Jerusalem. Immediately after the offering, Abraham returns to his home in Hebron.

Sarah dies at Hebron and is buried at Machpelah which Abraham acquires as a tomb for his wife and his other dead. Abraham dies and is buried next to Sarah.

ca 1630 As a result of a prolonged famine, the "house of Israel" emigrates to Egypt: Joseph, son of Jacob, plays a large role in this emigration. The Israelites settle in the land of Goshen, also called the "land of Rameses" and remain there for about 400 years. During this lengthy period, the "house of Israel" increases ethnically through the annexation of Asiatic Semites who come to Egypt for various reasons. The XIX Dynasty (1315–1224), especially Pharaohs Seti I and Rameses II, constitute the oppressors of the "house of Israel."

II. FROM EGYPT TO THE PROMISED LAND

(Gen 25–50; Ex 1–18; Num 33)

ca 1230 The most probable date for the Exodus of the Hebrews from Egypt is about the year 1230 B.C. The most probable route seems as follows: Rameses—Succoth—Etham—Bitter Lakes—Desert of Etham—Marah—Elim—Dophkah—Rephidim—Mt. Sinai—Kibrath-hattaavah—Hazeroth—Rithmah—Rimmon-perez—Libnah—Rissah—Makheloth—Hashmonah—Kadesh-barnea—Hor-haggidgad—Jotbathah—Abronah—Ezion-geber—Punon—Oboth—Iye-abarim. After many wanderings and battles, the "house of Israel" reaches Mt. Nebo. From there the Lord shows Moses the "Promised Land." Having accomplished his great mission, Moses dies on Mt. Nebo.

III. FROM JOSHUA TO THE JUDGES

(Jos 1–24)

ca 1200 After the Transjordan has been conquered by Moses, Joshua—his successor—crosses the Jordan and conquers Jericho; he defeats the confederated kingdom of Jerusalem, Hebron, Yarmuth, Lachish and Debir; he extends the Israelite conquests to the whole territory between Gaza and Kadesh-barnea; he conquers central and northern Palestine.

ca 1190 After conquering Palestine, Joshua proceeds to the partitioning of the Cisjordan, since the Transjordan has already been divided by Moses among the tribes of Reuben, Gad, and the half-tribe of Manasseh. Joshua dies when he is about 120 years old. The "house of Israel," divided into twelve tribes, is harassed by various enemies: the Philistines, Moabites, and Ammonites.

IV. THE SERIES OF 12 JUDGES

(Jdg 1–21)

(an asterisk indicates the 6 "minor" Judges)

ca 1130 1) **Othniel** is the first Judge of Israel and the only one from the tribe of Judah. He delivers his people from the oppression of a king of Aram (or Edom). This gives Israel 40 years of peace.

2) **Ehud,** from the tribe of Benjamin. He slays Eglon, king of Moab, assuring peace in that region for 80 years.

3) * **Shamgar** is active at the time of Samson. He saves his people from an attack of the Philistines.

4) **Barak,** from the tribe of Naphtali, is driven by the prophetess Deborah to confront and defeat Sisera, general of the Canaanite army, oppressor of the Israelites.

5) **Gideon,** from the tribe of Manasseh, delivers his people from the Midianites, invaders and oppressors of Israel.

Abimelech, son of Gideon, commits many cruelties; he kills his brothers and proclaims himself king at Shechem, but after three years he perishes while battling against his rebelling subjects. He does not have the charisma of a judge nor does he save his people, but he is the first person who in tyrannical fashion seeks to introduce the monarchy in Israel.

6) * **Tola,** from the tribe of Issachar, rules Israel for 23 years.

7) * **Jair,** from the region of Gilead, rules Israel for 22 years.

8) **Jepthah,** from Gilead, one of the greatest warriors; he conquers the Ammonites and rules Israel for six years.

9) * **Ibzan,** probably from the tribe of Zebulun; he rules Israel for seven years.

10) * **Elon,** from the tribe of Zebulun; he judges Israel for ten years.

11) * **Abdon,** from the territory of Ephraim; he rules Israel for eight years.

12) **Samson,** from the tribe of Dan, inflicts grave losses on the Philistines. He is famous for his outstanding feats, and rules Israel for 20 years.

Samuel, from the tribe of Levi, although his history is not in the Book of Judges, is really the last of the Judges. He leads his people back to the worship of the true God: he fights and defeats the Philistines; he anoints Saul, as the first king of Israel, and then David, destining him for the kingdom (1 Sam 1–16).

V. THE THREE KINGS OF ALL ISRAEL

(1 Sam 13–31; 2 Sam 1–24;
1 Ki 1–11)

ca 1020 1) **Saul** is the first king of Israel —he wars against its enemies: Moabites, Ammonites, Edomites, the kings of Zobah, the Philistines. He dies by his own hand on Mt. Gelboa after reigning for 20 years.

1000 2) **David** is consecrated king of Judah and Hebron. For seven years he fights against the survivors of the house of Saul and finally becomes king of all Israel. He makes Jerusalem the capital. David wars against the Philistines in the lowlands of the hills of Judah and confines them to three nearby cities; he reconquers all of the territory of Canaan in the "Promised Land" and also subjugates the Ammonites, Moabites, and Edomites. After reigning 40 years, old and close to death, David names Solomon his successor.

970 3) **Solomon** provides for the safety of his throne; he eliminates his competitors and rules his people in a benevolent manner. He builds the temple-palace complex and completes the construction by which the place of the temple and the palace is united to the "city of David." Solomon's private life signals a progressive moral decline; he forms a harem for himself of foreign and idolatrous women; to please them, he builds pagan temples in Jerusalem.
At his death, the great kingdom splits into two rural states: the kingdom of Israel, with its capital at Shechem, formed by the northern tribes; the kingdom of Judah, with its capital at Jerusalem, formed by the southern tribes.

THE TWO KINGDOMS

(1 Ki 12–22; 2 Ki 1–25)

930–722 Before Christ

JUDAH

930–913 **Rehoboam** is the first king; he reinforces the kingdom with many constructions. He distributes the principal fortified cities among his sons and always resides at Jerusalem. He undergoes the invasion of the Pharaoh Sheshonk (1 Ki 14:21-31; 2 Chr 11:1—12:16).

913–911 **Abijam** wars against Jeroboam. He is buried in the city of David (1 Ki 15:1-8).

911–870 **Asa** removes all the idols fashioned by his predecessors; he repels the assaults of Baasha, king of Israel (1 Ki 15:9-23).

870–849 **Jehoshaphat** is zealous for religion, weak in confrontations, and unfortunate in politics; he lets himself be drawn by Ahab—his relative—against Damascus and against Moab (1 Ki 22:41-51).

849–843 **Jehoram** marries Athaliah, daughter of Ahab. The Edomites rebel against the yoke of Judah; the Philistines make incursion against him (2 Ki 8:16-24).

843 **Ahaziah** goes with Joram of Israel to fight against the Arameans; he is killed there by Jehu (2 Ki 9:14-30).

ISRAEL

930–910 **Jeroboam I** is the first king of Israel. He erects his capital at Shechem and then at Penuel in Transjordan. He establishes the worship of the "golden calf" at Bethel and Dan, effecting a religious schism (1 Ki 11:26ff; 12:1—14:20).

910–909 **Nadab,** son of Jeroboam, is slain by Baasha while he is besieging Gibbethon (1 Ki 15:25-31).

909–886 **Baasha** transfers the capital to Tirzah, seven miles from Shechem. An impious king, he suffers the extermination of his entire family (1 Ki 15:28; 16:1-7).

886–885 **Elah,** in a drunken state, is slain by his general **Zimri,** who then commits suicide after only seven days of rule (1 Ki 16:8-20).

885–874 **Omri** founds Samaria and transfers the capital of the kingdom to it. He is one of the most representative figures of Israel (1 Ki 16:21-28).

874–853 **Ahab,** son of Omri, repels the invasion of the king of Damascus. After marrying Jezebel, daughter of the king of Sidon, he allows her to introduce the worship of Baal into Israel. He is killed in a war against the Arameans (1 Ki 16:29-34; 18; 20:1—22:40).

853–852 **Ahaziah,** following the example of his parents, worships Baal, provoking God's wrath (1 Ki 22:52; 2 Ki 1:1-17).

852–843 **Joram,** the other son of Ahab, takes part in the war against Moab and against the king of Damascus.
The prophet Elisha overthrows the wicked dynasty of the Omrides and consecrates Jehu (2 Ki 3–8).

843–838 **Athaliah,** queen mother, has the entire royal line murdered (except Joash, a year-old baby); she fanatically propagates the worship of Baal until she is killed seven years later by a usurper whom she placed on the throne of Joash who is still young (2 Ki 11; 2 Chr 22:10; 23:15).

838–800 **Joash** reorganizes the administration of the temple; he delivers himself from the attacks of the king of Damascus with a large contribution. He is killed while descending from his place at Milo (2 Ki 11–12; 2 Chr 22–24).

800–785 **Amaziah** succumbs to the king of Israel; he is killed in a plot (2 Ki 14:1-21).

785–742 **Uzziah (Azariah)** restores and fortifies Jerusalem; builds up agriculture; reconquers the Negeb and the Philistine plain and controls Edom. Stricken by leprosy, he retires to private life (2 Ki 15; 2 Chr 26).

742–735 **Jotham** defeats the Ammonites and builds the upper gate of the temple of Jerusalem. Under his rule the prophet Isaiah begins his prophetic ministry (2 Ki 15; 2 Chr 27).

735–716 **Ahaz** uses gifts to buy the aid of the king of Assyria against the kings of Damascus and of Israel, plotting to harm Judah. He introduces polytheistic worship, institutes religious and political slavery, tramples justice and oppresses the poor to pay the Assyrians (2 Ki 16; 2 Chr 28).

843–816 **Jehu** has the kings of Israel and Judah killed as well as all the descendants of Ahab; he extirpates the worship of Baal; his kingdom is dismembered by the king of Damascus (2 Ki 9–11).

816–801 **Jehoahaz,** defeated by the king of Damascus, loses part of his territory; toward the end of his rule, thanks to the Lord's help, he regains the whole kingdom of Israel (2 Ki 13:19).

801–786 **Joash** defeats the king of Damascus three times; he obtains victories over Judah (2 Ki 13:10-24).

786–746 **Jeroboam II** gives back to the kingdom of Israel its ancient boundaries, reconquering the Transjordan; he increases the richness and power of the kingdom. Under his long rule, Israel reaches its greatest political and territorial power (2 Ki 14:23-29).

746 **Zechariah** rules for 6 months, and is assassinated by Shallum (2 Ki 15:8-12).

746–745 **Shallum,** murderer of Zechariah and friend of Damascus; rules only for one year (2 Ki 15:13-16).

745–737 **Menahem** marches against Shallum and kills him; he pays a large amount to Assyria and succeeds in strengthening the kingdom (2 Ki 15:17-22).

737–736 **Pekahiah,** after a very short reign is killed by his official Pekah (2 Ki 15:23-26).

736–732 **Pekah** is responsible for the fact that the kingdom of Israel is reduced solely to the territories of Ephraim and western Manasseh (2 Ki 15:27-31).

732–724 **Hoshea** plots against his predecessor, is imprisoned by the Assyrians, who invade Samaria. After three years, the kingdom of Israel comes to an end (722) (2 Ki 17).

THE SINGLE KINGDOM OF JUDAH

721–587/6 Before Christ

716–687 **Hezekiah** roots out pagan worship and strengthens the State. Sennacherib, king of Assyria, invades Judea and menaces Jerusalem. Hezekiah firmly retains his power; an unforeseen calamity forces Sennacherib to abandon the kingdom of Judah. Hezekiah effects a literary renascence, accomplishes magnificent civil engineering works, and excavates the tunnel destined to bring the waters of Ain Sitti Maryam Gibron to the pool of Siloam built by him (2 Ki 18; 2 Chr 29–32; Isa 36–39).

687 **Manasseh** is the most impious of all Judah's kings. He grants the most favor to foreign cults; he shows himself almost always as a loyal and servile vassal of the Assyrians. He is deported into Babylonia in chains, he is repentant and entirely submissive after a period in prison and is relocated on the throne of Judah by the Assyrian king (2 Ki 21; 2 Chr 33).

642–640 **Amon** follows in his father's footsteps and is killed, in his home, as a result of a plot on the part of his dependents (2 Ki 21:19-26).

640–609 **Josiah,** son of Amon, initiates a radical religious reform; he repairs the temple of God and destroys every sign of idolatry. Opposing a military expedition of Neco, king of Egypt, he is killed in battle (2 Ki 22–23; 2 Chr 34–35).

609 **Jehoahaz II,** son of Josiah, elected as king of Judah by the people, is taken prisoner by Neco into Egypt, where he dies (2 Ki 23; 2 Chr 36; Jer 22).

609–598 **Jehoiakim,** the other son of Josiah, rules as a tyrant; he protects the pagan resurgence; he persecutes and kills the prophets; he revolts against the late Babylonian kingdom and dies before Nebuchadnezzar's army reaches Jerusalem (2 Ki 24; Jer 22).

597 **Jehoiachin (called Jeconiah),** son of Jehoiakim, after reigning only three months, is deported to Babylon by Nebuchadnezzar (2 Ki 24; 2 Chr 36).

597–587/6 **Zedekiah,** another son of Josiah, is the last king of Judah. Nebuchadnezzar besieges and destroys Jerusalem; he deports king and people into exile. The kingdom of Judah becomes a Babylonian province (2 Ki 24:18—25:30).

FROM THE BABYLONIAN EXILE TO JUDAS MACCABEUS

(2 Ki 24–25; Ezr 1–10; Neh 1–10)

ca 587–538 **Babylonian captivity** of the Hebrews.

ca 538–515 **The Hebrews** return from the exile and begin the reconstruction of the temple.

ca 445 **Nehemiah** is sent to Jerusalem and reconstructs the walls of the holy city.

? 458 ? 398 **Ezra** is sent to Jerusalem and establishes the observance of the Mosaic Law.

ca 332 **Alexander the Great** conquers Palestine.

ca 305–285 **The Ptolemies** hold dominion over Palestine.

ca 199 **The Seleucid kingdom** occupies Palestine.

ca 168 **Antiochus IV Epiphanes** proclaims the abolition of the Judaic religion and dedicates the temple of Jerusalem to Olympian Zeus.

THE MACCABEAN DYNASTY

(1 Mac 1–16; 2 Mac 8–15)

167–134 Before Christ

Judas Maccabeus, the principal hero of the Jewish revolt against the yoke of Antiochus IV Epiphanes, gives his name to the Maccabean dynasty. It is composed of members of the family of the priest Mattathias.

ca 167–165 **Mattathias,** and his sons, from Modein begin the Jewish revolt against Antiochus IV Epiphanes, fierce enemy of the Jews.

ca 165–160 **At the death of Mattathias, Judas Maccabeus,** his third-born, takes over the waging of the war. He dies on the field of battle.

ca 160–142 **Jonathan,** fifth son of Mattathias, is acknowledged as high priest and leader of the Jews. He begins the struggle against Bacchides. He combats Apollonius and defeats him. Attracted by peace proposals, Jonathan goes to Ptolemais to meet Trypho; but as soon as he arrives, he is taken prisoner and killed.

ca 142–134 **Simon Maccabeus,** brother of Jonathan, assumes leadership of the Jews. He wrests Judean independence from Demetrius II. He combats Antiochus VII, defeating him by means of his son John. It turns out to be the final victory of the valorous and aged Simon. He is betrayed and slain during a banquet by a certain Ptolemy, governor of Jericho.

THE HASMONEAN DYNASTY

134–36 Before Christ

The Maccabean dynasty is succeeded by the dynasty of the Hasmoneans, descendants of Simon Maccabeus. The Hasmonean dynasty is composed of seven rulers who are also high priests (Hyrcanus II during the reign of Alexander).

134–104 **John Hyrcanus I,** son of Simon Maccabeus, initiates the Hasmonean dynasty. He is an able military man who combats Ptolemy (the slayer of Simon) and Antiochus VII. His reign is a very prosperous one.

104–103 **Aristobulus I Judah,** firstborn son of John Hyrcanus, successor to his father. He annexes to Judah part of the territory of Iturea.

103–76 **Alexander Jannaeus,** son of John Hyrcanus I, succeeds his brother Aristobulus I. He is the first one of his dynasty to use the title of king. Bold and intransigent, and dedicated to adventurous expeditions, he dies in battle.

76–67 **Alexandra Salome,** wife of Aristobulus I, seems to have been an ideal ruler.

67–63 **Aristobulus II,** son of Alexander Jannaeus; leads a very adventurous life and is poisoned to death. The civil war that he undertakes against Hyrcanus II provokes the intervention of Pompey (63 B.C.) after the latter's conquest of Syria for the Romans (65 B.C.).

63–40 **Hyrcanus II,** son of Alexander Jannaeus; timid and slothful by nature, is forced, after only three months, to resign in favor of his brother Aristobulus II; but he is then named ethnarch of the Jews by the Romans.

40–36 **Antigonus,** son of Aristobulus II, is the last Hasmonean king. He lives in continuous fighting with the pretender to the throne, Herod. The latter becomes king by the will of Antony and Cleopatra, and brings about the decapitation of Antigonus by the Romans.

FROM HEROD THE GREAT TO HADRIAN

39–4 Before Christ

39–4 B.C. **Herod the Great,** governor of Galilee, is proclaimed king of the Jews by Rome. Herod takes Joppa, conquers Medeba, besieges Jerusalem and captures it after a three-month siege; occupies Samaria and has the temple rebuilt. He dies at Jericho and is buried in the fortress of Herodium near Bethlehem.

Year of Rome 747–748 **BIRTH OF JESUS CHRIST IN THE CITY OF BETHLEHEM**

Year of Rome 754 BEGINNING OF THE CHRISTIAN ERA (A.D.)

4 B.C.–A.D. 6 **Archelaus,** son of Herod the Great and Malthace, the Samaritan, succeeds his father with the title of ethnarch of Judea, Idumea, and Samaria. It is a rule without glory. He rules for ten years: from 4 B.C.–A.D. 6. He is then deposed by the Romans and sent into exile.

4 B.C.–A.D. 39 **Herod Antipas,** son of Herod the Great and Malthace, becomes tetrarch of Galilee and Perea with his capital at Sepphoris, four miles from Nazareth, and later at Tiberias, which he constructs. He is not a wise king. Called a "fox" by Jesus, and reproached repeatedly by John the Baptist for his incestuous adultery, he is sent into exile by Caligula and dies. His tetrarchy, with that of Philip, passes over to Herod Agrippa I.

4 B.C.–A.D. 34 **Philip,** son of Herod the Great and Cleopatra of Jerusalem, becomes tetrarch of Batanea, Gaulanitis, Trachonitis, Auranitis, and Ituraea. He lives a peaceful and prosperous life. After 37 years of rule, he dies childless.

A.D. 6–41 **Judea** becomes part of the Roman province of Syria but is ruled by a Roman Procurator with his seat at the seaport of Caesarea and with an official residence at Jerusalem.

A.D. 41–44 **Herod Agrippa I,** nephew of Herod and Mariamne, by favor of Claudius becomes king of Judea and of the lands that had belonged to Herod the Great.

A.D. 44–66 **All of Palestine** becomes, at the death of Agrippa I, a Roman province, administered by a Procurator.

FROM THE BIRTH OF JESUS TO THE JEWISH WAR

(Mt; Mk; Lk; Jn; Acts)

7–6 B.C. **Jesus Christ is born** in Bethlehem during the reign of Herod the Great at the time of the census of Quirinius.

A.D. 5–6 **At the age of twelve** Jesus is taken to Jerusalem and speaks with the rabbis in the temple. Then he returns home to Nazareth until his public ministry.

27 **John the Baptist** begins his ministry of preaching repentance in the wilderness of Judea, and as a precursor of the Messiah calls upon the Jews to undergo baptism in the Jordan.

Jesus is baptized by John and begins to proclaim in Galilee the near advent of the kingdom of God. He gathers a group of disciples around him.

28 **Jesus goes to Jerusalem** for the Feast of the Passover.

29 **John the Baptist is imprisoned** as a dangerous agitator for having denounced Herod Antipas's marriage to Herodias, his half-brother's wife.

Shortly before the Passover Jesus multiplies the loaves and promises the Eucharist.

Jesus again goes to Jerusalem for the Feasts of Tabernacles and Dedication.

30 **Jesus enters Jerusalem in triumph** amidst a public demonstration acclaiming him as the Messiah.

At the time of the Passover Jesus is betrayed by one of his disciples, arraigned as a pretender to the Jewish throne and instigator of revolt against Rome, and condemned by Pontius Pilate to be crucified. Afterward, he rises again on the third day.

The Holy Spirit is poured out on the disciples, and the first community of the Church is born.

35 **Martyrdom of Stephen,** one of the first seven Hellenist deacons.

37 **Conversion of Saul** on the road to Damascus (to persecute the growing Christian Church); retreat to Arabia and then Damascus.

45 **Paul's first missionary journey:** Cyprus, Antioch in Pisidia, Lystra, and back to Antioch.

49 **Council of Jerusalem:** at the insistence of Paul the converts from paganism are exempted from the Mosaic Law.

50–52 **Paul's second missionary journey:** Lystra, Phrygia, Galatia, Philippi, Thessalonica, and Athens.

52–58 **Paul's third missionary journey:** he visits the same cities as the second journey and stays at Ephesus for three years, laying plans for another missionary journey.

61–63 **Paul is imprisoned** at Rome, then set free. Possibly he visits Spain.

63 or 67 **Martyrdom of Peter** at Rome.

67 **Martyrdom of Paul** at Rome.

THE JEWISH WAR

Date A.D. 44–66 After the death of Herod Agrippa I in 44, Judea is ruled by Roman procurators. Their cruelties and excesses stimulate the fervent nationalism and messianic expectations of the people and revolt against Rome.

1. THE WAR IN GALILEE

66–70 **The Jewish War:** Nero entrusts Vespasian with the task of bringing the Jews into complete subjection. **Vespasian** sets out from Antioch and joins the Roman army at Ptolemais (Acco) in the spring of 67.

At the same time, from Alexandria Titus goes to meet his father at Ptolemais. In April 67, the Roman army under the command of Trajan and Titus occupies Sephhoris, Gadara, Jotbathah, Jaffa, Tiberias, Tarichaea (Magdala), Gischala (Safed), Tabor, and Gamala. In October 67, all Galilee is conquered by the Romans.

2. THE WAR IN PEREA AND JUDEA

In June 67, a Roman legion goes up to Mount Gerizim to put down a rebellion of the Samaritans.

In May 68, Vespasian conquers Perea.

In May 69, Vespasian occupies all the cities around Jerusalem: Gophna, Akrabattene, Bethel, Ephraim, and Hebron.

In December 69, Vespasian is elected Emperor of Rome (after the turbulent year that sees three emperors succeed Nero: **Galba, Otho, and Vitellius**). He entrusts his son Titus with the task of ending the war in Judea and returns to Rome.

3. CONQUEST OF JERUSALEM

In March 70, Titus surrounds the whole city of Jerusalem:

a) **he places part of the army** north of Jerusalem in the region of Gabaa (Tel-el-Ful);

b) **he places another part** on Mount Scopus;

c) **he encamps the X Legion** on Mount Olivet;

d) **he sets up his camp** in front of the Psephinus Tower, at the corner of the Third Wall;

e) **he lets part of the troops pass** and places it at the Hippicus Tower.

Then the battle begins. After fifteen days of fierce fighting, on May 25, 70, the Romans take the Third Wall, batter it to the ground, and enter the quarter of Bezetha. Titus places his command in the region of Gareb.

Since Jewish resistance continues to be fierce, Titus builds a wall about ten feet high around the city, following the route: Gareb, Bezetha, Mount Olivet, Kidron Valley, Valley of Gehenna, Abu Tor, and coming back to Gareb. The length is about $4^1/_2$ miles.

When the construction is finished, Titus attacks the Fortress Antonia, and on July 15, 70, the fortress falls into the hands of the Romans, who raze it to the ground.

Next comes the temple. The struggle is fierce. But, on August 9, 70, the temple goes up in flames, and the banners of the Roman legionnaires are raised in front of the Eastern Gate. In this circumstance, Titus is proclaimed "emperor."

4. THE SECOND REVOLT

In 135, after the second Jewish revolt is put down with blood (132–135), the Emperor Hadrian rebuilds Jerusalem as a Roman colony.

Aelia Capitolina: on the temple area a statue of Jupiter is erected. Entrance to the city is prohibited to all Jews under penalty of death.

The prophecy of Jesus is fulfilled to the letter: "Jerusalem will be trampled underfoot by the Gentiles until the times of the Gentiles have been fulfilled" (Lk 21:24).

The ancient name of Judea is changed to that of **Palestine Syria.**

ABBREVIATIONS OF BOOKS OF THE BIBLE

Acts—Acts of the Apostles
Am—Amos
Bar—Baruch
1 Chr—1 Chronicles
2 Chr—2 Chronicles
Col—Colossians
1 Cor—1 Corinthians
2 Cor—2 Corinthians
Dan—Daniel
Deut—Deuteronomy
Eccl—Ecclesiastes
Eph—Ephesians
Est—Esther
Ex—Exodus
Ezek—Ezekiel
Ezr—Ezra
Gal—Galatians
Gen—Genesis
Hab—Habakkuk
Hag—Haggai
Heb—Hebrews
Hos—Hosea
Isa—Isaiah
Jas—James
Jdg—Judges
Jer—Jeremiah
Jn—John
1 Jn—1 John
2 Jn—2 John
3 Jn—3 John
Job—Job
Joel—Joel
Jon—Jonah
Jos—Joshua
Jud—Judith
Jude—Jude
1 Ki—1 Kings
2 Ki—2 Kings
Lam—Lamentations
Lev—Leviticus
Lk—Luke
1 Mac—1 Maccabees
2 Mac—2 Maccabees
Mal—Malachi
Mic—Micah
Mk—Mark
Mt—Matthew
Nah—Nahum
Neh—Nehemiah
Num—Numbers
Ob—Obadiah
1 Pet—1 Peter
2 Pet—2 Peter
Phil—Philippians
Philem—Philemon
Prov—Proverbs
Ps(s)—Psalms
Rev—Revelation
Rom—Romans
Ru—Ruth
1 Sam—1 Samuel
2 Sam—2 Samuel
Sir—Wisdom of Ben Sira
Song—Song of Songs
1 Thes—1 Thessalonians
2 Thes—2 Thessalonians
1 Tim—1 Timothy
2 Tim—2 Timothy
Tit—Titus
Tob—Tobit
Wis—Wisdom
Zec—Zechariah
Zep—Zephaniah

NOTE: For greater clarity and convenience, the footnotes and cross-references are printed at the bottom of each page and cross-indexed in the text itself. An *asterisk* (*) in the text indicates that there is a footnote to the text in question. Each footnote is in turn clearly marked with the number of the chapter and verse to which it pertains. Similarly, a *superior letter* ([a]) in the text indicates that there is a cross-reference to a particular verse. The reference itself is also clearly marked with the same letter. Hence, the reader is always aware of a footnote or cross-reference simply *by reading the text.*

[ ] Indicates a gloss
/ = Divides verse
// = Parallel

SIMPLE KEY TO REFERENCES

Gen 1:1 refers to the Book of Genesis, chapter 1, verse 1.
Gen 1:1a refers to the Book of Genesis, chapter 1, the first part of the verse.
Gen 1:1f refers to the Book of Genesis, chapter 1, verse 1, and the following verse (2).
Gen 1:1-10 refers to the Book of Genesis, chapter 1, verses 1 to 10 inclusive.
Gen 1:1-10, 14 refers to the Book of Genesis, chapter 1, verses 1 to 10 inclusive and verse 14.
Gen 1:1—2:3 refers to the Book of Genesis, chapter 1, verse 1, to chapter 2, verse 3 inclusive.
Gen 1:1; 2:3 refers to the Book of Genesis, chapter 1, verse 1, and chapter 2, verse 3.

Acknowledgments: The section on "Learning about Your Bible" has been prepared by Rev. Jude Winkler, OFM Conv. The panoramic view of "The Lands of the Bible" has been adapted with permission from the book *Atlante Biblico* by Giacomo Pesce, C.P. The maps have been adapted with permission from the books *Sagrada Biblia* published by Editorial Regina and *Atlas Historique de l'Ancien Testament* published by Spes.

THE
OLD TESTAMENT

GENERAL INTRODUCTION TO THE OLD TESTAMENT

The Old Testament Bible contains three main types of literature.

A first, extensive group of books, after a short introduction on the origin of the world and the human race, is concerned with events in the history of the Hebrew people, from its distant beginnings down almost to the threshold of the New Testament. Two different bodies of writings belong to this first group: the Pentateuch and the Historical Books. The latter are in turn subdivided into four sections:

1. The work of the Deuteronomist, includes the Books of Joshua, Judges, Ruth, Samuel (2 books), and Kings (2 books). The name "Historical Books" is often applied only to this section.

2. The work of the Chronicler, which includes the two Books of Chronicles, along with Ezra and Nehemiah.

3. Three stories of hope: Tobit, Esther, and Judith.

4. The two Books of Maccabees.

A second group consists of those books which are almost completely in the form of poetry and are therefore called, the Poetic Books. Since, however, they also deal chiefly with doctrinal or sapiential subjects, they are also called the Didactic Books or the Sapiential Books. Among these, the Psalms and the Book of Job are outstanding as poetry. The third group is made up of writings that bring together the oracles of the prophets of the Jewish people, and sometimes the events of the prophets' lives.

The reader is referred to the introductions of the individual books. Here, in an introduction intended to facilitate understanding of the Old Testament as a whole, I shall limit myself to highlighting the salient moments of Jewish history (which is divided into two clearly distinct periods, by the Assyro-Babylonian deportation) in its relation to the formation of the sacred books.

I. PREHISTORY

The account of the origin and formation of the Hebrew people is preceded by eleven chapters which have for their purpose to locate this people within the universal history of the human race, which is examined from its beginnings. It is these early stories that come to people's minds when they think of the Bible: creation, Adam and Eve, Cain and Abel, the Tower of Babel, Noah and the flood. Rightly so, for these introductory texts have a special significance. What is this significance?

The stories surely do not claim to be history as we would write history today. Rather, these descriptions of the foundation of the world describe our human vocation and also the essential elements of the human drama; they describe that which is the deepest reality of creatures and their history and which is the result of events that really happened. They describe our relation to God as the result of creation (a relation that we can never set aside), sin and death, the scandal of our divisions, our responsibility and our freedom, the fact that we are called to salvation.

The tradition puts these stories together, using images current in the mythologies of the neighboring peoples; but it has known how to transform these in a radical way by placing the emphasis—and here is its originality—on faith in a single God and on an authentic picture of the human being as it comes from the hands of God.

II. THE MAJOR MOMENTS IN THE HISTORY OF ISRAEL

Down to the End of the Monarchy

Before the Formation of the Monarchic State

Within the historical evolution of the Near East, the events and actions of Israel begin to emerge as the history of a particular human group at the time of Abraham (ca. 1850 B.C.). Its unique character will be revealed with ever increasing clarity until it is established as a political entity under King David (ca. 1010–970 B.C.).

The Cycle of the Patriarchs

We find no clear witness outside the Bible to the history of these distant ancestors. The tradition concerning this history gives a picture of a nomadic life that mirrors to a great extent what we know from other sources; they are therefore credible, at least in this respect, in the eyes of the critical historian. Legend certainly plays a part, but it is only ornamentation of a substance made up of authentic recollections. Ancient civilizations, before the age of writing, had a relish for story-telling that is being lost today; the stories were faithfully handed on thanks to fixed modes of expression.

The great ancestors put their mark on Israel's special destiny; they were the ones who launched its adventure with God. They stand out as incomparable human beings, and yet they are not divinized but are shown as having their weaknesses. Some stories enable us to see that there were divergent or superimposed traditions regarding certain events. Each tradition was perhaps connected originally with one of the many early sanctuaries built throughout the country; it was recited there at the time of worship. In this way memories were kept alive among the people, who venerated them as a communal possession. The final editor tried to unify these traditions without, however, always removing the signs that show them being cobbled together and the contradictions in details.

A first main idea strikes us in this ancient history: the God of the patriarchs is shown as having a personal relationship with those human beings; he is present in human history. He is a personal God, a God who commits himself and to whom human beings commit themselves in turn. It is not without reason that the Bible speaks constantly of "the God of Abraham, Isaac, and Jacob."

Abraham: the father of the Hebrew people, the point of departure of their vocation. Jacob, also called Israel: the founding father of the twelve tribes; for this reason his name, rather than that of Abraham, who was the father of other peoples as well, becomes the symbol of a common membership, a bond of union amid all the vicissitudes that will scatter this people in the course of the centuries down to today. Isaac: between Abraham and Jacob, becomes somewhat less prominent; he is the man who passes on the blessing of God.

The next personage to emerge after Jacob is Joseph, whose surprising fate gave rise to a wonderful narrative that is rich in psychology and teaching, very edifying, and a finely constructed piece of literature.

Whether or not the tribes really and directly descended from Abraham and Jacob, and whether or not they were all in Egypt, it is certain that only later on did they acquire their clear characteristic features. Secular documents have little to tell us about their origin, and historians can give only vague bits of information. This is of little importance. The day would come when they recognized their solidarity and the fact that despite their divisions, they shared one and the same vocation.

The Work of Moses

The first five books of the Bible, that is, the Pentateuch or Law, are attributed to Moses. Today, however, critics are able to show that the final redaction of these texts occurred at a much later date. Moses nonetheless remains the most prestigious of the prophets and at the same time the humblest of believers. He was also the founder of the people and the one who gave organization to newly-born Israel. No one else has ever played so important a role. It is with good reason, then, that the fundamental work, the constitutional charter of Israel, is attributed to him. Besides, except for Jesus, has the history of humanity ever known a greater mystic who has taught human beings to recognize God and his jealous demands?

It may be argued whether this leader led all the tribes through the wilderness (between 1250–1200 B.C.) or only the most important ones, and whether the signs and miracles attributed to him have perhaps been exaggerated. There is no doubt, however, that in his time the oppressed people were set free. This period will be a constant point of reference, because it was the period in which the people discovered God and entered into his plan.

The Law that is attributed to Moses created the customs of the people; it strengthened their faith in the one God amid a polytheistic world; it gave them their worship and their social life. Observance of it was not a constricting noose but a way of spiritual growth; it forged their spiritual attitudes and formed their consciences.

The Settlement in Canaan

This important period in Israel's history is still rather obscure. The Bible has preserved the memory of a great conquest but also accounts of endless guerilla warfare. As a result, the Book of Judges does not fully back up the grandiose pictures of the Book of Joshua. This period was close to the heart of Israel, because it was the period in which they were given the land; this people loved its country as the place to which God had linked his blessings and his presence. The land, promised and given, will in time become the symbol of the kingdom of God and finally of the heavenly homeland.

The conquest was followed by a no less obscure period during which the tribes remained independent, without a common leader, with the result that there was real anarchy. During this period, the confession of faith in the one God of the patriarchs entailed a demand, the significance of which it is difficult for us to grasp, for while people obeyed the God of Israel, they also feared the vengeance of other divinities who were thought of as having been defeated in the war of conquest but still installed in neighboring countries.

Furthermore, the people found themselves threatened with strangulation, because other invaders made their appearance during the same period and sought to gain for themselves part of the territory of Canaan. Among these were the well-armed and well-organized Philistines. Sudden attacks caused Israel to throw itself entirely on the Lord when everything seemed lost; thus, there were surprising revivals, but these were followed by periods of great disorder.

The Period of the Organized States

Birth and Consolidation of the Monarchy

The twelve tribes were divided into two groups, a northern and a southern. Unity was achieved only episodically, and even then it was only partial. When dangers and wars arose, it was necessary to organize the people if they wanted to survive, but if they appointed a leader, were they not perhaps mocking God, the sole king of Israel, and usurping his place? Nonetheless, a central organization under a king slowly took shape. Samuel, a prophet and the last of the judges, anointed Saul as king at God's command. But this reign left a tragic and unhappy memory. David, on the other hand, whom God put in the place of the rejected Saul, succeeded brilliantly and led Israel not only from war to independence and sovereignty but also to dominion over neighboring peoples. He also gave it its capital, Jerusalem. The incomparable splendor of the reign of Solomon, the next king, who gave the nation its magnificent temple, was seductive, but those who saw farther, discovered the gnawing worm already at work. In fact, human greatness caused forgetfulness of God; the way was being paved for an age of compromises, and Israel's endemic sickness, idolatry, found a place even within the royal family. Solomon's prestige rivaled, indeed, that of the mighty of his time, but should Israel become a people like others?

Political Decline

For over eighty years David, and then Solomon, were able by their personal authority to overcome the forces of division that kept North and South in opposition. But immediately after these two kings, each section claimed autonomy and sought to establish its own unity. The life of the little kingdom of Judah was centered in the one temple of Jerusalem. This focus was important, because it helped to strengthen faith in the one God. The kingdom of Israel (the North), on the other hand, had several sanctuaries, especially those at Shechem, Dan, and Bethel. The South remained faithful to the line of David down to the deportation; this was the Messianic line. The North, on the contrary, experienced crises among its rulers and palace revolts; several dynasties usurped power, one after another. Idolatry was a temptation to all of them and was fostered by the kings, often for political motives. There were, of course, also periods of fidelity; the teaching of the priests and the message of the prophets did not fail to recall the conditions of the covenant. The true prophets, the "guardians of the covenant," were challenged, but they were also listened to, as we know from the fact that their writings have been preserved.

The two states were increasingly caught in the vise of the great powers and were tossed about in conflicts, first between Egypt and Assyria and later between Egypt and Babylon. Samaria, the capital of Israel, fell in 721 B.C., and the people were deported to Nineveh. Judah, well defended on its hills, was sheltered by its distance from the routes of the armies and resisted for over a century, but it finally fell to the blows of the Babylonians in 587 B.C.

The Period of the Prophets

This period of decline was also the period of the prophets. Prophetism was a multiform movement. Entire groups devoted themselves to the cultivation of ecstasy; these were the official prophets, who spoke as the king desired. There were also authentic prophets, exceptional men who rose up to speak in the name of God; in the midst of the turmoil in Israel, they held fast to the indispensable values of the covenant and the human conscience. Thanks to them, human thought and faith in God made gigantic and definitive progress. In the North, Elijah and Elisha rose up as champions of God against the kings and also made themselves feared by their power as wonder-workers. In the South, the first two "major" prophets, Isaiah and Jeremiah, were close to the kings; they also left us their poems, as did the men in both kingdoms whom we call the "minor" prophets: Amos, Hosea, Micah, and others.

The Stages in the Redaction of the Books

The books that recount the history of Israel down to the fall of the monarchy, and especially the Pentateuch, are a mosaic of fragments in different genres and from different periods, all of them brought together in a degree of unity. Before the books took shape, shorter literary units had been formed in the course of the centuries; in these units earlier texts of varied origin were brought together for a variety of reasons. Prior to the period when anything was written down, there was oral tradition that preserved both the ancient prose material and the even more ancient poetic material.

Thus this part of the Old Testament, which is the fundamental part and the part whose historical coherence is of greater importance, is already the reflection of a tradition and an interpretation that had been revised several times over and the texts that had been worked on until they achieved their present form. Here are the main stages of this journey, as the scholars have been able to reconstruct them:

1. In the early period of the monarchy the ancient traditions, written and oral, were collected and integrated with testimonies and the stories of more recent events. The Yahwist and Elohist traditions, as well as the early annals for the reigns of Saul and David, were already established in the tenth and ninth centuries before Christ.

2. Beginning in the eighth century B.C., we enter a second stage of literary formation. This period marked the beginning of the activity of the prophets, who in their preaching reflected anew, and in a deeper way, on the preceding revelation as seen in the light of the contemporary religious and social condition of the people.

3. The seventh century saw the writing down of the substance of Deuteronomy, which presented the divine law anew on the basis of both ancient traditions and the theology preached by the prophets. The earlier historical narratives were reinterpreted in the light of all this.

4. In the sixth and fifth centuries B.C., the painful experience of exile led to a new rethinking of the entire historical and religious experience of Israel, this time by priestly circles that enriched the collections already written down with contributions from their own traditions as brought up to date with the fruits of their present thinking.

There is reason to think that our Old Testament text, at least for the first group of writings (from Genesis to the Books of Kings, inclusive) was already complete toward the beginning of the fourth century B.C.

III. FROM THE EXILE TO THE COMING OF JESUS CHRIST

The knowledge people usually have of the history of the chosen people ends, for practical purposes, with the Exile. After that, the only thing we know is the wonderful deeds of Daniel and the Maccabees, which stick up like islands in a vast sea of ignorance. In fact, for many Christians, the period from the restoration of Israel to the coming of Jesus is unimportant, a parenthesis or time of waiting in God's plan; it is the obscure and unimportant end of the Old Testament.

The reality is quite different. If the major prophets were silent during this period (and this was no small trial for believers), some voices were raised at the beginning of it, and they were strong voices, those of the last minor prophets: Obadiah, Haggai, Zechariah, Malachi. Above all, however, this was the period in which the priests and the scribes (students of the law) devoted themselves to a deeper understanding of the faith and the formation of spiritual movements. This period also bore the mark of another decisive experience: the Hebrews who returned from the Exile were forever cured of their recurring inclination to idolatry. It was not that they had ceased to come in contact with the pagan world; on the contrary, they were forced to see it close at hand in the daily life of their communities. But, far from allowing themselves to be absorbed by the surrounding culture—a very attractive culture!— their thinking and faith underwent a development and perhaps an adaptation, but one that led to a deepening of their own original values. A time of very great testing still lay ahead, but they would have the strength to struggle heroically in remaining faithful to monotheism and their heritage from their forebears. As a result, the faith in the time of Jesus would no longer be identical with the pre-Exilic faith; it would be the new and vigorous faith now known as "Judaism."

This period was, then, anything but a rather inglorious ending to a prestigious past! In fact, even if we look only at the duration of this period, we will see how inappropriate the term "epilogue" is. This period occupied almost six centuries, or as many as Israel had lived in the Promised Land after settling there. More importantly, it was these centuries that in God's plan proximately prepared the Old Testament to open itself to the New, in which everything would begin anew and be transformed. This is why it was precisely during this period that the Old Testament Bible as we know it today took shape. It is from this period that there dates not only the final redaction of the historical sections, already compiled during the preceding period, and the definitive redaction of the Psalms, but also the composition of almost all of the rest of the Old Testament (the Prophets in large measure; more or less the entire Sapiential part; and the remaining Historical Books). Let us try, then, to describe the life and more important events of these centuries.

The Exile

Allusions in the Prophets and many Psalms help us understand somewhat the lot of the exiles; they also help us understand their overflowing joy as they returned after 538 B.C. In addition, the general history of this period provides information on the lot of deported populations.

We today have not grown up with a religion that is tied to a country, a monarchy, or a single temple; it is, therefore, difficult for us to imagine what a torment exile was for the surviving Jews of the Kingdom of Judah. In addition to the harsh personal experience of deprivation, the Exile meant the total ruin of a people to the point that they were uprooted and their worship suppressed.

It is true that deported populations were gradually able to settle down. Although important individuals suffered the darkness of Babylonian prisons, the majority of the exiles did not have to live in the camps which the word "deportation" suggests to us. They were, nonetheless, always far from the Promised Land, deprived of their sanctuary, and without a recognized religious and political structure; in short, they were scattered and in disarray. In these circumstances, it took a great deal of daring to believe that, despite everything, the story of this people had not come to an end and that Israel still had its mission of bearing witness to God in the midst of the nations. Yet this was precisely the claim of the deported prophets (Ezekiel), spiritual persons, and priests; all the signs said otherwise, but the faith was now strengthened by what had happened.

It can be said, in fact, that in Exile Israel discovered new spiritual origins. It finally realized that God's plan was not dependent on the political fate of an earthly kingdom. Now that structures had been destroyed, God's word and law could touch hearts more deeply. Suffering was purifying. Israel recognized that its lot was the fulfillment of divine threats, a chastisement it had deserved, and it turned to the Lord with sincerity and with a greater depth and stability than before. In face of its conquerors who sang the glories of their gods, it cried out the nothingness of all idols. Yahweh would not accept the place he was invited to take in the procession of pagan divinities. The fear had been that the scattering of the chosen people would destroy their spiritual self-awareness and their unity; instead, they found their true unity, that given by faith and hope.

The Restoration

In 539 B.C., an unexpected and unforeseeable radical change occurred: the Persian empire replaced the Babylonian in control of the Middle East. Cyrus, the new master, who is presented in the second part of Isaiah as God's chosen instrument, gave proof of an unexpected tolerance toward the religion and customs of each ethnic group. All dreams were now permissible; songs were already improvised for the caravans that would cross the desert in a new exodus, an exodus more splendid than that of long ago. What hope-filled days! The reality was to be less impressive. Persian policy did indeed provide for organizing the return of deported peoples and the rebuilding of their sanctuaries, but Israel was not to experience a national restoration. It would not regain its independence and would remain for good under the control, even if often a benevolent control, of one or another foreign power. Israel would have to find some other basis than earthly political structures for its life and its specific religious vocation.

The exiles returned in a number of caravans that were formed at intervals. The returnees were for the most part members of the tribes of Judah and Benjamin, the families of which had lived at one time in Jerusalem and the surrounding territories; they came with their priests and Levites. The other tribes, which had cut themselves off after the death of Solomon in 931 B.C., had been in exile since 721 B.C., and after almost two centuries, were now widely scattered. Foreign populations had taken up residence in Samaria from the end of the eighth century B.C. on and formed a new ethnic group. The northern part of Palestine, too, displayed a medley of peoples, so much so that the land of Jesus' infancy and early public ministry came to be called "Galilee of the nations," that is, of the pagans.

The "little remnant" of survivors organized themselves with difficulty. Jerusalem was entirely in ruins; commercial activities and trade were not renewed, since the returnees preferred to settle in the surrounding area where at least the fruits of the earth were not lacking. The temple was rebuilt between 520 and 515 B.C., but only seventy years later the walls would need repair and Nehemiah would almost have to use force to accomplish the repopulation of the city. This rebuilding of the temple and the city was a modest, difficult task, but a courageous one. The Books of Ezra and Nehemiah contain the evidence for it.

The exiles who did not return organized into groups in foreign territory, chiefly in Babylonia and Egypt. Since they had no religious reasons for remaining attached to their new country, they would be more mobile and able to migrate. Thus, especially during the period of Greek domination, groups of Jews scattered across the Mediterranean world; wherever they went, they occupied a quarter of a city and opened a synagogue. They did, however, retain ties with Jerusalem, to which they went at times on pilgrimage.

Greek and Roman Domination

The regime of the Persians, who had authorized the restoration of a Jewish province, ended two centuries later, as unexpectedly as it had begun. This marked a second step taken by Providence, which was preparing the way for the coming of Christianity. The East had done its work; it was now the turn first of the Greeks and then of the Romans; in the future the task would be entrusted to all the nations. One name stands out at the beginning of this new upheaval: Alexander the Great. The Bible hardly mentions him, and then only long after the event (see 1 Mac 1:1). But the young conqueror filled the world with astonishment at his rapid victories. The countries along the Nile and the Euphrates now entered into the political and cultural life of the Mediterranean world; a common mentality spread abroad.

Alexander did not have time to enjoy his vast conquest, for he met death in Babylon in 323 B.C. His generals competed for power. Of importance for the biblical story were the dynasty of the Lagids or Ptolemies, who gained control of Egypt, and the dynasty of the Seleucids, who took possession of Syria, Asia Minor, and Persia. In 319 B.C., Judea was under the relatively peaceful control of the Ptolemies, but at the beginning of the second century B.C., the situation changed rapidly. In 198 B.C., Antiochus III defeated Egypt at Panion in Palestine, and Judea entered the orbit of the Seleucids. The new monarch brought his state to its greatest heights, but the generals of Rome were already taking to the roads of the East. The king had to accept burdensome conditions of peace: sending his own sons as hostages to Rome, handing over Asia Minor, and paying an enormous tribute. There is an echo of this in the biblical episode of Heliodorus (2 Mac 3).

The reign of Antiochus IV Epiphanes was marked by a Draconian policy of cultural and economic assimilation. In his vision everything had to submit to the Greek way of life. Fears for his own threatened reign are not enough to explain the arrogance of which he has left the memory; if we look at the money he coined we see that he was increasingly bent on his own divinization. From 167–164 B.C. he profaned the temple and launched a violent religious persecution, which in turn gave rise to the glorious revolt of the Maccabees. His successors, one after another, struggled for power and for the favor of the petty kings whom they sought to control; a period of intrigues returned, and the end of the first Book of Maccabees gives some examples of these.

As a result, the little province of Judea enjoyed for some decades a sufficiently stable autonomy and even enlarged its domain; it was ruled by high priests of Maccabean descent, who before the end of the second century B.C. also took the title of king. But unity and independence were uncertain possessions. Some religious groups deliberately distanced themselves from the policy of the priests; the confusing of spiritual charge and civil sovereignty was not without its dangers for the faith and for freedom and represented a step backward. The more forward-looking religious groups based their teaching solely on reverence for God and his law; these were the Hasids ("faithful ones"), from whom came the Pharisees, and the Essenes, who distanced themselves in an even more systematic way and whose thought and way of life have been revealed to us in the Dead Sea scrolls. Those who aligned themselves with the priesthood would be the opportunists of a later date: the Sadducees. The success of the religious movements among the people testified in its own way to the fact that the spiritual vitality of Judaism was no longer linked to the political lot of the nation.

Distant Rome was winning respect for its aristocratic regime; this great western power was capable of bringing pressure to bear on the Greek kingdoms.

The Jews, and especially the Maccabees, had sought alliances with it since the second century B.C. But a hundred years later the legions imposed Roman rule on the entire Mediterranean basin and ended the anarchy in the various states. Pompey intervened in Palestine. There he found Jerusalem in a state of revolt; religious and political factions were tearing at each other; different segments of the population were engaged in a terrible war. As if the faith were no longer an issue in these events, no book of the Bible has preserved the memory of those sad and shameful days. Pompey captured Jerusalem in 63 B.C.

Cynical schemers were subsequently able to take power locally; history has preserved the name of the despot known as Herod the Great (37–4 B.C.). He thought to win the gratitude of the Jews by rebuilding the temple with some magnificence. A few decades later Judea would be governed by procurators sent directly from Rome; the fact that one of them, Pontius Pilate, played a central part in the trial of Jesus saved him from being forgotten. Judea lived in a state of tension between the demands of the occupying ruler and expectations of rebellion. The Pharisees and the religious leaders known as the scribes were close to the people. Others pursued impossible political dreams; as the result of one of their revolts, the Jewish state would disappear for good in A.D. 70.

Meanwhile, however, Judaism had put down spiritual roots sufficiently deep for it to live on independently of the land and the temple, even though it would always look back to these with nostalgia.

The Communities

The community of Judea fulfilled a function of its own until its disappearance in the second destruction of Jerusalem in A.D. 70.

For almost six centuries, this Jewish community, more than any other, regarded itself as the guardian responsible for the faith and the prayer (see the Psalms), the vocation and the hope of Israel. Established in the land of the forefathers, which was always looked upon as the Promised Land, and with the temple as its center, led by the priests and instructed by the teachers of the law, this community made it its aim to ensure the permanence of the Jewish inheritance. This explains its care in preserving the priceless historical, prophetic, and sapiential writings that had been handed down, and in relating the understanding of these to the contemporary situation, as well as its assiduous production of new writings, in the form, above all, of meditations on its privileged history and on Israel's law, and of attempts to deepen and develop its understanding of these (Chronicles, Tobit, Job, Qohelet, Song of Songs, and, although not accepted into the Jewish Bible, Ben Sirach).

For three and a half centuries, down to the time of the Maccabees (177 B.C.), the Judean community sheltered itself against the upheavals in the world. Rather insensitive to universalist and missionary ideas (see, in contrast, the Book of Job), it waited instead for the day on which all peoples would give recognition to Jerusalem and would come there as pilgrims. But beginning in the second century B.C. this community was called upon to give an example of fidelity during the first religious persecution known to history. At that time, groups of its most selfless members were able to answer this unexpected demand with the heroism of martyrs and the victorious resistance of warriors, who gave new life to the ancient stories of the wars of the Lord that were their inspiration. Rightly would a new and glorious page in the history of Israel soon be written (first Book of Maccabees).

It was precisely from this community, in the midst of which it arose, that newborn Christianity would separate itself; it would be Paul, a Jew of the Diaspora, who would most vehemently proclaim the universality of salvation independently of the law, the nation, the land, and the sanctuary. James, on the other hand, a Christian of Jerusalem, would have more difficulty in following the lead of Paul.

Many communities scattered throughout Palestine preserved their ties to Jerusalem. The Samaritan community, on the other hand, remained suspect.

As we saw, the Samaritan community represented a mixed population. It had also opposed the restoration of Jerusalem and had built its own separate place of worship. The religious schism of Samaria was complete in the third century B.C.; from then on, the Samaritans would be viewed as heretics and are so seen in New Testament times. A small community of Samaritans has existed down to our own day.

The communities scattered throughout the world reflected the movement and fate of the populations with which they were mingled. They spread abroad especially during the Hellenistic period, a time of city-building and cultural renewal. Some of these Jewish communities built temples at Elephantine and Leontopolis (Egypt), but on the whole the communities retained their connections with Jerusalem and remained firm in the faith of their fathers, even if they wrote in Greek, the common language of the Mediterranean basin.

Their literary works bear witness to a desire for dialogue with the pagan world, an aspiration to be recognized as heirs of a great culture. It was in these exchanges that the missionary concern began to strengthen.

But these communities also experienced suspicion, ill-will, persecution, and plundering. In fact, they astonished others by their special way of life, their religion, and their law.

We do not know why they were unwilling to enter the life of the cities by including their God in the pantheon, where all the divinities could co-exist peacefully.

The authors of Judith, Esther, Daniel, Wisdom, and Maccabees II have in mind these cities that were tempted from time to time either to turn in on themselves or to let themselves be assimilated by tenacious and irresistible cultural movements. These cities also gathered up and translated into Greek the ancient biblical writings. This literary activity was especially intense in Alexandria, the city founded by Alexander the Great during his Egyptian campaign. The Greek version of the Hebrew originals is known as the Septuagint (the "seventy," i.e., translators). Its importance is inestimable because it made the Bible accessible to the vast Hellenistic world; it is the Bible that would be cited by the various New Testament writers, and all Christian communities outside of Palestine would take it as the foundational scriptures. In addition to the writings that had found a place in the Bible, a number of others were composed: commentaries on biblical history and teaching, applications, edifying stories, and so on, that bear witness to an intense spiritual and Messianic movement marked by a profound religious fidelity.

Scattered believers lived in expectation of a new gathering in Jerusalem, where all peoples would at last be reunited.

The answer to this hope was the event that took place on the Christian Pentecost.

Meanwhile, these communities spread throughout the world the knowledge of a single God and the expectation of a universal salvation. They served as a basis, throughout the cultural world of the Mediterranean, for the Christian mission that would actively propagate this mission of salvation, while identifying it with the new covenant of Calvary that had replaced the covenant of Sinai.

יהוה

BOOKS OF THE OLD TESTAMENT

THE PENTATEUCH

This, Israel's fundamental book, which it called the Torah (means Law), has five parts (whence the Greek name "Pentateuch" means "five sections"):

Genesis: the book describing the origin both of the world and of the Israelite people.

Exodus: the story of the departure from Egypt.

Leviticus: primarily, the rules for worship, the exercise of which is entrusted to the tribe of Levi.

Numbers (the book of censuses): the Law governing the organization of the people.

Deuteronomy (or "Second Law"): primarily a prophetic appeal for fidelity to the Law and for a conversion of heart.

In the form in which we now know it, the Pentateuch was, it seems, compiled around the second half of the fifth century B.C., but its roots are deep in the most remote past of Israel.

For a long time, the Hebrews, like all nomadic peoples, transmitted orally the traditions, laws, and customs of their people. In their substance the stories, even though revised and expanded, went back to real events. Subsequent generations completed, and adapted to new situations, the laws set down by Moses when he was organizing the people of God. Memories and traditions achieved a fixed form especially at the sanctuaries, that is, ancient centers of worship that kept the memory especially of events that had taken place there (Bethel, Shechem, Mizpah, etc.), and in liturgical formulas (songs, etc.) that were used at various religious festivals. Finally, in the period of the monarchy, the stability that this brought promoted literary activity. Starting in the tenth century, the "Yahwist" collection took form in Jerusalem; the "Elohist" collection arose a little later in the northern kingdom of Israel; then, in the eighth and seventh centuries, as a result of the activity of the Prophets, the "book" and discourses of Deuteronomy took shape; finally, during the Exile (sixth century), the Jewish priests, using criteria of their own, gave a new version of the laws and history of Israel (the "Priestly" tradition).

The Pentateuch arose out of this collection of traditions; this accounts for the various codes of laws that repeat one another and for the two versions of stories. Each tradition in fact has its own leading ideas, its own religious emphases, its own style. The first or "Yahwist" gives God the proper name "Yahweh"* from the outset. It seeks to give an answer to the major problems that all human beings raise, and stresses above all that the Lord

---

*Out of respect, this name was not pronounced when the sacred text was read but gave way to the word *Adonai*, "my lord." In keeping with this tradition, the present translation does not print the word "Yahweh" but indicates its presence in the original text by the term "LORD" printed by an initial capital letter followed by small capital letters.

has linked himself in a special way to the heirs of Abraham. Its style is lively, and it depicts God in human garb in order to bring out the point that he is close to human beings and loves them.

The "Elohist" tradition is more restrained; it calls God "Elohim," a common noun for "divinity." It depicts him as more demanding, emphasizes his superiority, and separates him to a greater extent from human beings: he speaks to them in dreams or through the mediation of the angels.

The "Priestly" tradition, for its part, likes numbers and genealogies; each stage of history (Noah, Abraham, Moses) is accompanied by a new covenant; it is concerned above all with laws and cultic institutions. Even the stories told bear the mark of this legalism; the account of creation, for example, aims at giving a basis for the law of the Sabbath; the covenant with Abraham finds expression in the sign of circumcision.

We shall leave aside for the moment the "Deuteronomic" tradition, which gave rise to a special book.

"In the beginning God created the heavens and the earth" *(Gen 1:1)*.

THE BOOK OF GENESIS

The Origins of the World and of the People of God

The Book of Genesis is made up of contributions from three sources, the Yahwist, the Elohist, and the Priestly, these contributions being intermingled even within one and the same episode. Despite this, the book has a unity, because the Priestly tradition has given it an organic structure. The story of the origins (chs. 1–11) and the story of the Patriarchs (chs. 12–50) are clearly distinguished.

The work first of all gives an imaginative account of creation and the first sin. Here, elements from ancient tradition are used in sketching a broad picture of the origins; various sections explain how evil, suffering, and death entered the world through the sin of the first man; the promise of salvation makes clear from the outset what the meaning of the entire biblical story will be. The priest who seems to have compiled these pages makes use of increasingly more focused genealogies in order to show the continuity of the creation of Adam and the obscure beginnings of the human race with the beginnings of Israel. Creation thus appears as the first act in the history of the salvation of humankind.

Contemporary advances in the study of the history, laws, and ways of life of the ancient East assure us that the popular stories about the Patriarchs are based on truthful living memories that were transmitted with the intention of being faithful. The sacred writers thus hark back to the distant past in order to show that the Creator has established special bonds with Israel. In the persons of their ancestors this people has enjoyed the preferential favor of God, who has chosen them for a special mission on behalf of the entire human race and has also promised them a land to live in.

This love-inspired plan is accepted by Abraham with a faith that stands up to every test, but the Lord is also able to entrust his promise even to a sinner like Jacob in order to show that his predilection is unmerited. He is thus able to turn to his own purposes a reprehensible crime like that of Joseph's brothers. In short, the second part of the book corresponds with the first: in order to save guilty humankind God enters history and links himself, for a specific period, to a particular people, choosing Abraham rather than Lot, Isaac rather than Ishmael, Jacob rather than Esau. The day will come, however, when all nations will be blessed in Abraham.

The promises stated in the Book of Genesis find their fulfillment in Christ and the Church. Jesus will be born of the line of Abraham, but he exists even before Abraham, because he is the beloved Son of the Father, the second and new Adam who comes to save what the first Adam had lost. The Church of Easter begins the new creation, but the chosen people of the new covenant are the spiritual descendants of Abraham the believer and are journeying toward the new Promised Land, the kingdom of heaven. The story of the Patriarchs is our story.

The Book of Genesis may be divided as follows:

- *I: Origin of the World and Humankind (1:1—11:32)*
  - *A: Creation and the Fall (1:1—3:24)*
  - *B: The Reign of Sin (4:1—5:32)*
  - *C: Death and Resurrection of God's Work (6:1—9:17)*
  - *D: A World of Diverse Peoples (9:18—11:32)*
- *II: Origin of the People of God (12:1—50:26)*
  - *A: Abraham, Man of Faith (12:1—25:18)*
  - *B: Jacob, the Sinner Who Redeems Himself (25:19—36:43)*
  - *C: Joseph, the Suffering Righteous One (37:1—50:26)*

I: ORIGIN OF THE WORLD AND HUMANKIND*

A: Creation and the Fall

CHAPTER 1

Origin of the Universe.* 1 In the beginning
God created the heavens and the
earth.*[a] 2 The earth was formless and
barren, and darkness covered the
abyss while the Spirit of God hovered
over the waters.[b]
3 God said, "Let there be light!" And there
was light.[c] 4 God saw that the light was
good, and he separated the light from
the darkness.[d] 5 And he called the light
day, and he called the darkness night.
This was the evening and the morning
of the first day.[e]
6 God said, "Let there be a firmament in
the midst of the waters to separate one
set of waters from the other." *[f] 7 God
separated the firmament from the waters, those waters that are under the
firmament from those that are above
the firmament. And it was so.[g] 8 God
called the firmament the heavens.
This was the evening and the morning
of the second day.[h]
9 God said, "Let the waters that are under
the heavens be gathered into one
place and let a dry place appear." And
it was so.[i] 10 God called the dry place
the land, and the gathered waters he
called the sea. And God saw that it
was good.[j]
11 God said, "Let the land bring forth
plants, those that produce seeds and
fruit trees that have seeds inside of the

a Gen 2:1, 4; 2 Mac 7:28; Job 38—39; Pss 8:5; 90:2; 104:2; Wis 11:17; Sir 16:24; Jer 10:12; Acts 14:15; Col 1:16f; Heb 1:2f; 3:4; 11:3; Rev 4:11.—b Gen 2:6; Job 33:4; Ps 104:30; Isa 32:15; Jer 4:23.—c 2 Cor 4:6; 1 Jn 1:5-7.—d Pss 104:31; 119:68; Jer 31:35.—e Ps 74:16.—f Isa 44:24; 2 Pet 3:5.—g Prov 8:27f; 2 Pet 3:5.—h Job 9:8; 37:18; Pss 19:1; 104:2; Isa 40:22; Jer 10:12; Zec 12:1.—i Job 38:8; Ps 33:7; Jer 5:22.—j Job 38:8; Pss 33:7; 90:2; 95:5.

1:1—11:32 The description of the origins of the universe and of mankind is not based on human testimony but is the fruit of reflection that was inspired by God and directed by him over the centuries. The Lord is the supreme master of the universe; he has from eternity formed a plan for the salvation of all the peoples of the earth. Mankind was brought to ruin by its own sin; the sin of Adam disfigured the divine work, but God loves mankind and, in order to lead it to salvation, chooses for himself a special people.

1:1—2:4a This majestic song in rhythmical prose was composed, it seems, in the priestly circles of Israel, perhaps after the Exile. It reflects the naive ideas of that time on the physical structure of the world: the heavens, for example, are imagined to be a solid vault in which the stars are set. The biblical text is akin to ancient Babylonian stories, now known to us, but it rises far above them. Here, everything that exists is the work of a single God; it takes only his word to create the universe. The Spirit, that is, the "breath," of God presides over creation. A day will come when, through the Spirit on Pentecost, God will give rise to the new creation, the new humankind that is reborn in Christ (2 Cor 5:17).

1:1 The story of creation is not intended as a scientific theory about the origins of the universe and human beings; it takes as its starting point ideas current in that part of the world and intends to teach certain fundamental and perennial truths about God as one, transcendent, existing prior to the universe, and about human beings as his creatures.

1:6 The ancient Semites viewed the heavens as a vault made of a solid material—the firmament—which holds back the waters above and separates them from the waters below; from openings in it—the floodgates (see Gen 7:11)—the flood will pour down.

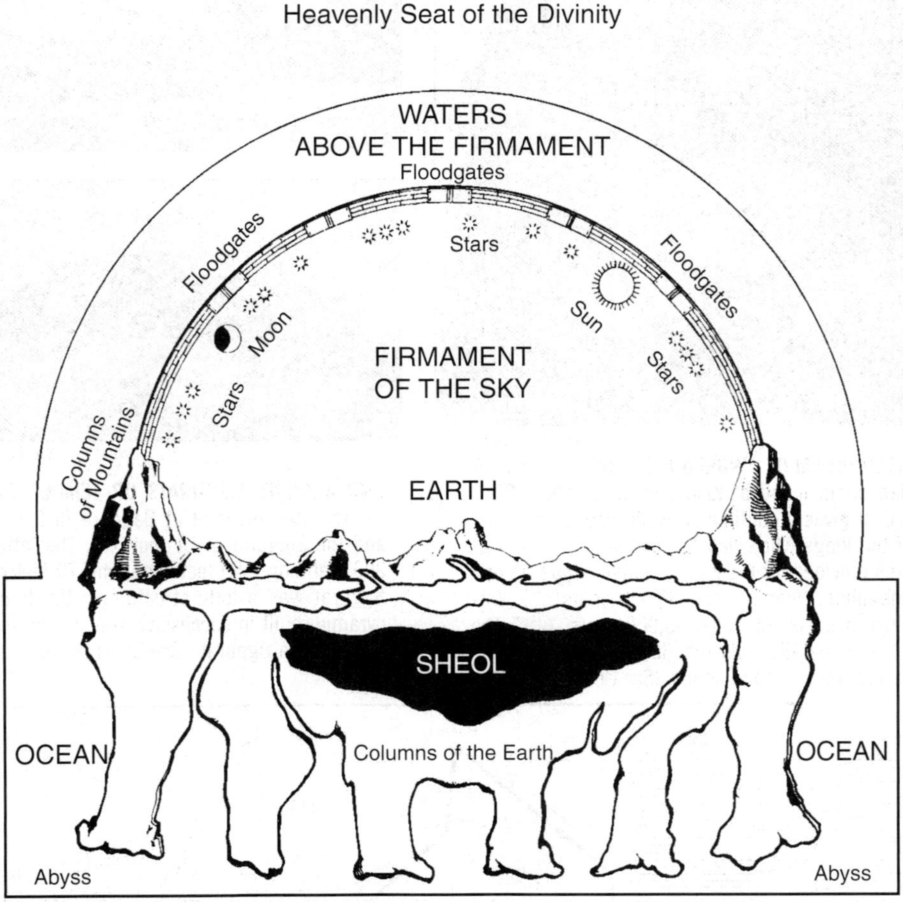

THE WORLD OF THE HEBREWS

THE WORLD OF THE HEBREWS — Graphic representation of the Hebrew conception of the world. God's heavenly seat rests above the superior waters. Below these waters lies the firmament or sky which resembles an overturned bowl and is supported by columns. Through the openings (floodgates) in its vault the superior waters fall down upon the earth in the form of rain or snow. The earth is a platform resting on columns and surrounded by waters, the seas. Underneath the columns lie the inferior waters. In the depths of the earth is Sheol, the home of the dead (also called the netherworld). This was the same prescientific concept of the universe as that held by the Hebrews' pagan neighbors.

Ashmolean Museum

WELD PRISM OF "WORLD HISTORY" — A Sumerian prism found at Kish and dated about 2000 B.C. It gives an outline of world history and a list of ten kings who ruled before the flood. The figures provided for the kings mentioned are beyond imagining: "Alagar ruled 36,000 years...." "Dumuzi, a shepherd, ruled 36,000 years. . . ." The biblical parallel of the long-lived Patriarchs seems sober by comparison. (See Gen 5:1-32.)

Dr. S. H. Horn

TWO ANCIENT ZIGGURATS OR TEMPLE TOWERS — The step pyramid at Saqqara in Egypt (top) and the Ziggurat at Ur (bottom). The latter was 200 feet long, 150 feet wide, and 70 feet high. A ziggurat was a lofty structure in the form of a pyramid, built in successive stages. The Tower of Babel was a ziggurat. (See Gen 11:1-9.)

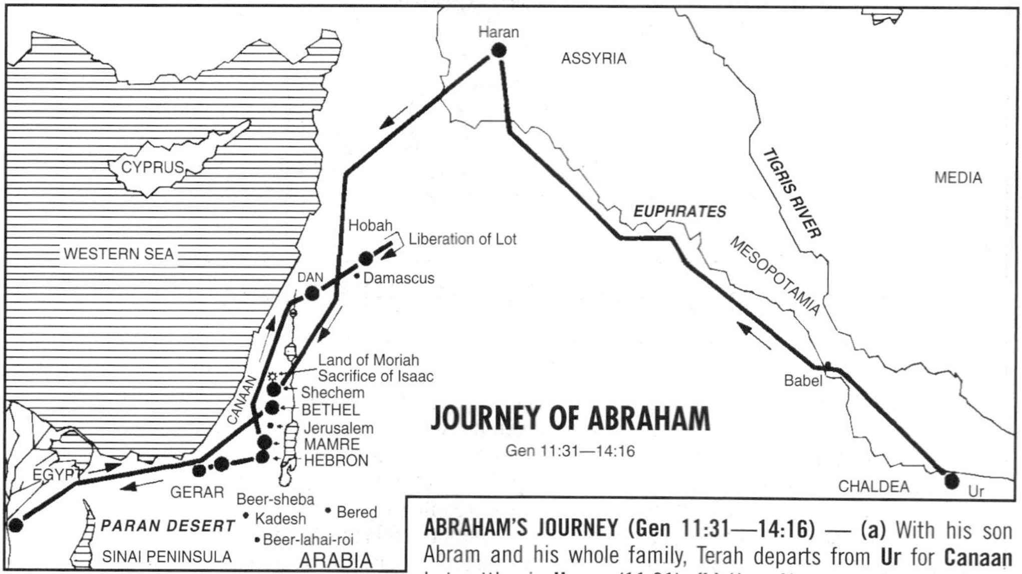

ABRAHAM'S JOURNEY (Gen 11:31—14:16) — **(a)** With his son Abram and his whole family, Terah departs from **Ur** for **Canaan** but settles in **Haran** (11:31). **(b)** Here Abram receives the Lord's call and starts out for **Canaan** (12:1-5). **(c)** At **Shechem** the Lord promises to give this land to Abram's descendants (12:6-7). **(d)** Between **Bethel** and Ai Abram builds an altar to the Lord and then journeys to the Negeb. A famine drives him into **Egypt** (12:8-20). **(e)** On his return to **Bethel,** he separates from Lot who settles near Sodom. Abram settles near the terebinth of Mamre, which is at **Hebron** (13:1-8). **(f)** When the kings of the Pentapolis capture Lot and his household (see Map opposite p. 24), Abraham overtakes and defeats them at **Dan** and pursues them as far as **Hobah,** north of **Damascus** (14:12-16).

fruit they bear, each according to its
own kind." And it was so.[k] 12 The land
brought forth plants, each according
to its kind, and trees that have fruit
with seeds inside of them, each ac-
cording to its kind. God saw that they
were good. 13 This was the evening and
the morning of the third day.
14 God said, "Let there be lights in the fir-
mament of the heavens to separate
the day from the night; let them be
markers to separate seasons and
days and years,[l] 15 and let them be
lights in the firmament of the heav-
ens to give light to the earth." And it
was so. 16 God made the two great
lights, the greater light to rule over
the day and the lesser light to rule
over the night, and he also made the
stars.[m] 17 God placed them in the fir-
mament of the heavens to light the
earth 18 and to rule over the day and
the night and to separate light from
darkness. And God saw that it was
good.[n] 19 This was the evening and
the morning of the fourth day.
20 God said, "Let the waters be filled with
living creatures and let birds fly
above the earth in the firmament of
the heavens."[o] 21 God created the
great sea creatures and all the other
creatures that fill the waters, each ac-
cording to its kind, and all the birds
that fly in the sky, each according to
its kind.[p] 22 God blessed them saying,
"Be fruitful and multiply and fill the
waters of the sea, and let the birds
multiply upon the earth."[q] 23 And this
was the evening and the morning of
the fifth day.
24 God said, "Let the earth bring forth living
creatures each according to its kind:
cattle and reptiles and wild animals,
each according to its kind." And it was
so.[r] 25 God made the savage beasts ac-
cording to their kind and the cattle ac-
cording to their kind and all of the
reptiles according to their kind. And
God saw that it was good.[s]
26 [t] And God said, "Let us * make man in our
image and likeness, and let them have
dominion over the fish of the sea and
over the birds of the sky and over the
cattle and over all the wild animals and
reptiles that crawl upon the earth."
27 God created mankind in his image, in the
image of God he created them, male
and female he created them.
28 God blessed them and told them,
"Be fruitful and multiply, and fill the
earth; subdue it and have dominion
over the fish of the seas and over the
birds of the air and over every living
creature that moves upon the earth."[u]
29 [v] And God said, "Behold, I give
you every plant that produces seeds
upon the earth and every tree that has
fruit with its seed inside of it: these
shall be your food. 30 And I give all
green plants to every wild animal and
to all the birds of the air and to all
creatures that move upon the surface
of the earth and that have the breath of
life in them." And it was so.
31 God saw all that he had made, and
behold, it was very good. This was the
evening and the morning of the sixth
day.[w]

CHAPTER 2

1 This is how the heavens and the
earth and everything in them were
made.[x]

2 * God completed his work on the seventh
day and on the seventh day he rested
from all of his work.[y] 3 God blessed
the seventh day and he consecrated
it, for on it he rested from all the
work he had done when he created all
things.[z]

4 This was the origin of the heavens and
the earth when they were first created.

k Ps 104:14.—l Job 26:10; Ps 19:1f; Bar 3:33.—m Deut 4:19; Ps 136:7ff; Wis 13:2ff; Jer 31:35.—n Jer 33:20, 25.—o Job 12:7-10.—p Job 3:8; 7:12; Pss 74:13; 148:7; Isa 27:1; Ezek 32:2.—q Gen 8:17.—r Sir 16:27f; Bar 3:32.—s Jer 27:5.—t 26f: Gen 5:1, 3; 9:6; Pss 8:6f; 103:14; 119:73; Wis 2:23; 10:2; Sir 17:1, 3f; Jas 3:7; 1 Cor 11:7; Eph 4:24; Col 3:10; Mt 19:4; Mk 10:6.—u Gen 8:17; 9:1; 33:5; Jos 24:3; Pss 8:7-10; 115:16; 127:3-5; Wis 9:2.—v 29f: Gen 9:3; Deut 12:15; Ps 104:14f.—w 1 Tim 4:4.—x Isa 45:12; Jn 1:3.—y Ex 20:9ff; 31:17; Heb 4:4, 10.—z Ex 20:11; Deut 5:14; Neh 9:14.

1:26 *Let us:* the plural "*us*" here is not a plural of majesty (this does not exist in Hebrew) but rather shows the divine process of deliberation as a consultation of God with himself (or with the angels?). When Isaiah describes the divine majesty (6:8), he too feels the need of using the plural; the same in Gen 3:22.

2:2-3 The model of a week that the Priestly account uses in describing the divine creation is meant to teach that the pattern of days of work followed by rest on the seventh day originates in the will of God himself.

Origin of Human Beings.* When the LORD
God made the earth and the heavens, [a]
5 there were not yet any plants of the field
nor had any herbs sprouted in the field,
for the LORD God had not yet made it
rain upon the earth and there was no one
to till the soil. [b] 6 He made a mist rise out
of the ground to water the whole surface
of the earth. 7 Then the LORD God
formed man * out of the dust of the earth
and he breathed his breath of life into his
nostrils and man became a living crea-
ture. [c]
8 And the LORD God planted a garden in
Eden, * in the east, and he put the man he
had formed there. [d] 9 The LORD God made
all sorts of beautiful and nourishing trees
sprout out of the earth, among which was
the tree of life * in the middle of the gar-
den and the tree of the knowledge of good
and evil. [e]
10 A river flowed out of Eden to water
the garden; then it divided into four
tributaries. [f] 11 * The first river was called
the Pishon. It waters the whole land of
Havilah where one can find gold, 12 and
the gold of that land is good. One can also
find bdellium and onyx in that land. [g]
13 The second river is the Gihon. [h] It flows
in the land of Ethiopia. 14 The third river is
the Tigris. It flows to the east of the land
of Asshur. The fourth river is the Eu-
phrates. [i]
15 The LORD God took the man and
placed him in the Garden of Eden so that
he might work it and care for it. [j] 16 The
LORD God told the man, "You can eat of
any of the trees in the garden, [k] 17 but you
must never eat from the tree of the knowl-
edge of good and evil. If you were to eat
from it, you would surely die." [l]
18 * And the LORD God said, "It is not
good for the man to be alone.* I wish to
make another creature who will be like
him." [m]
19 The LORD God therefore formed every
sort of wild animal and all the birds of the
air and he brought them before the man to
see what he would name them.* Whatever
the man called each living creature, that
was the name that it would bear. 20 The
man gave names to every type of animal,
all the birds of the air and all the wild ani-
mals, but the man could not find anything
that was like him.
21 The LORD God therefore caused the
man to fall into a deep sleep. He took
one of his ribs and replaced it with

a Job 38:8-11.—b Job 38:28; Ps 65:10f; Jer 10:13.—c Gen 3:19; 18:27; Tob 8:6; Job 34:15; Pss 103:14; 104:29f; Eccl 3:20; 12:7; Wis 7:1; Sir 33:10; 1 Cor 15:45.—d Isa 51:3; Ezek 31:9.—e Gen 3:22; Prov 3:18; Rev 2:7; 22:2, 14.—f Num 24:6; Ps 46:5; Ezek 47:5.—g Num 11:7.—h Sir 24:25.—i Ex 23:31; Num 22:5.—j Sir 7:15.—k Ps 104:14.—l Gen 3:2f; Rom 6:23.—m Tob 8:6; Sir 36:30; 1 Cor 11:9; 1 Tim 2:13.

2:4b-25 The preceding section (Gen 1:1—2:4a) is to be interpreted as a rethinking of certain aspects of creation and an integration, into a systematic and much broader vision, of what had already been set down in the following story, which is older. This Yahwist account of origins is a single piece that is subdivided into chapters 2, 3, and 4. In its literary form it follows the structure of Sumerian-Babylonian hymns that sing of the origins of civilization, but in its content it is truly religious and completely independent of those mythologies. It expresses, in popular language, a theology of the greatest richness and depth.

God is here called by his proper name, Yahweh, the name under which he reveals himself to his people, Israel; he alone, and no one else, is the maker of the entire world.

Man has need of a collaborator, and God provides this. Woman will be by her nature far superior to the animals, which however will provide help to her and the man. The man exercises dominion over them, while man and woman are made for each other and will achieve their purpose each through the other. This law that God has written into the nature of human beings is the basis for the unity of the couple in marriage, which establishes a single human entity that is no longer divisible into parts. Jesus will reaffirm this exigency (Mt 19:3-8) and St. Paul will remind Christian spouses that their union contributes to actuating in time an unsuspected spiritual reality, namely, the fruitful union of Christ and the Church, in which children of God are born (Eph 5:31-32).

The story of creation is meant to say what kind of beings men and women are and what their origin is, but it does not go into detail on the way in which they were created; it does not specify whether God formed man and woman by direct action or through the cooperation of natural forces that took very long periods to accomplish their work. At the same time, the story emphasizes the fact that the material being is animated by a higher vital principle that is not a product of nature but is infused by God himself. Finally, in describing the unity of the couple formed by the Creator the story proclaims that the human species is one.

2:7 *Man*, in Hebrew *adam*, is the common name of the human species; only beginning in Gen 4:25 and 5:1 will it be regarded as the proper name of the first male. Here and in 3:19, 23, the author connects it with Hebrew *adama*, "earth." This is not a scientific etymology but a popular one, based on assonance. In fact, it seems that *adam* derives from Sumerian *ada-mu*, "my father." His companion, too, is initially called "woman" and receives the proper name "Eve" only from Gen 3:20 on. It seems that this name, *haua* in Hebrew, derives from Sumerian *ama*, "mother."

2:8 *Eden* is derived from Sumerian *edin*, which means a level, steppe-like, desert region. The *garden* occupies an eastern section of it; this word, too, *gan* in Hebrew, is properly Sumerian and means a watered and cultivated piece of land. It was translated into Greek as *paradeisos*, "garden," giving rise to the name "earthly paradise."

2:9 The *tree of life* symbolizes the possibility of becoming immortal that was granted as an unmerited gift to human beings, although these were by nature subject to death (Gen 3:22). The *tree of the knowledge of good and evil* symbolizes the attribute proper to the Creator, by reason of which God is the foundation of the moral order. The first couple attempt to usurp this attribute (Gen 3:5, 22), desiring to decide for themselves what is good and evil for them.

2:11-13 The *Pishon* and the *Gihon* are completely unknown; if Gen 10:20 is taken into account, *Havilah* would be in Arabia.

2:18-25 This is the only full account of the creation of woman in ancient Near Eastern literature.

2:18 *Not good . . . to be alone:* without female companionship and a partner in reproduction, the man could not fully realize his humanity.

2:19 *Name them:* this was the man's first act of dominion over the creatures around him.

flesh.[n] 22 The LORD God then formed a
woman out of the rib that he had taken
from the man. He brought her before the
man.
23 The man said,

"This one is bone of my bones
and flesh of my flesh. *
She shall be called woman
because she was taken from man."

24 This is why a man leaves his father and
his mother * and joins with a wife, and the
two become one flesh.[o]
25 Now the man and the woman were
naked, but they did not feel any shame.[p]

CHAPTER 3

Origin of Evil. 1 * The serpent * was the
most clever of all the wild animals that
the LORD God had made. It said to the
woman, "Is it true that God told you not
to eat of any of the trees in the
garden?"[q]
2 The woman answered the serpent,
"We may eat of the fruit of the trees in the
garden, 3 but as for the fruit of the tree in
the midst of the garden, God said that we
must not eat it, nor even touch it, lest we
die."[r]
4 [s] But the serpent said to the woman,
"Certainly you shall not die! 5 God knows
that when you eat from it, your eyes will
be opened, and you will become like God,
knowing that which is good and that
which is evil."
6 The woman saw that the tree was good
for food and pleasing to look at and desir-
able for imparting wisdom. She took some
fruit and ate it. Then she gave some to her
husband who was with her, and he also ate
it.[t] 7 Their eyes were opened and they real-
ized that they were naked. They took fig
leaves and sewed them together, making
themselves a covering.
8 They then heard the LORD God walk-
ing in the garden toward the evening. The
man and his wife hid themselves from the
LORD God amongst the trees of the gar-
den.[u] 9 But the LORD God called out to the
man and said to him, "Where were
you?"[v]
10 He answered, "I heard you walking in
the garden and I was afraid because I was
naked, so I hid myself."[w]
11 He said, "Who let you know that you
were naked? Have you eaten from the tree
from which I commanded you not to eat?"
12 The man answered, "The woman
whom you put here with me, she gave me
some fruit from the tree and I ate it."
13 The LORD God said to the woman,
"What have you done?"
The woman answered, "The serpent
tricked me and I ate it."[x]
14 The LORD God said to the serpent, *

"Because you have done this, you will
be the most cursed
of all the animals
and of all the wild beasts.

n Sir 17:1; 1 Cor 11:8f; 1 Tim 2:13.—o Mt 19:5; Mk 10:7; 1 Cor 7:10f; Eph 5:31.—p Isa 47:3.—q Job 1:7; 2:2; 2 Cor 11:3; Rev 12:9; 20:2.—r Gen 2:17; Rom 6:23.—s 4f: Wis 2:24; Sir 25:13; Isa 14:14; Jn 8:44; 2 Cor 11:3.—t Gen 3:22; 1 Tim 2:14.—u Jer 23:24.—v 1 Ki 19:9, 13.—w Ex 19:16; Deut 5:5.—x 2 Cor 11:3.

2:23 *Bone of my bones and flesh of my flesh:* a common Semitic way of expressing consanguinity (Gen 29:14) or membership in the same tribe or even simply in the same people (2 Sam 5:1; 19:13-14) or the same city (Jdg 9:2). Here it means that the woman has the same nature as the man; she alone can make possible the love that characterizes the matrimonial bond. The words *she shall be called woman*, etc., can be understood only in light of the assonance in the original text: Hebrew, *isha*, "woman," seems to be the feminine form of *ish*, "man" in the sense of "male" (*adam* refers to man as including both man and woman, i.e., possessing the nature common to all human beings).

2:24 *Leaves his father and his mother:* instead of remaining under the protective custody of his parents, a man leaves them and, with his wife, establishes a new family unit. *Joins . . . one flesh:* the divine intention for husband and wife was monogamy. Together they were to form an inseparable union, of which "one flesh" is both a sign and an expression.

3:1-4 When human beings reject union with God, the source of being and good, they must inevitably perish. This is the meaning of the tragedy that overwhelms the human condition. Envious of human beings and their happiness, another being, like them a creature, urges them to doubt the divine word, thereby putting out the light of their faith. The biblical tradition will call this other being the "adversary" and "the father of lies" (Wis 2:24; Jn 8:44; Rev 12:9). Our author, anxious to combat pagan nature-centered cults that used the serpent as a symbol and strongly attracted the Israelites, presents the adversary under the form of a serpent.

Despite the victory of evil a hope dawns, a light in which the Christian tradition sees the Savior being already announced, a Savior with whom Mary, model of womanhood, is especially associated. The Lord does not abandon fallen humankind that has barred itself from the paradise of friendship with God; but it will have to struggle to win back its happiness.

3:1 The Semitic world attributed superhuman qualities to the *serpent:* the sacred serpent, the divine serpent, symbol of the divinities of the vegetative realm, protector of sanctuaries and borders, symbol of the way, guardian of life-giving plants, effective in divining the future and in black and diabolic magic. The sacred writer speaks of him instead as one of the *animals that the LORD God had made*, but also as *the most clever of all [of them]*; the connection with magic makes the serpent an appropriate symbol of activities directed against God; in addition, the serpent's special way of entering in a hidden manner and striking by surprise makes it an appropriate and instructive image of the tempter.

3:14 The biblical tradition uses the *serpent* to represent Satan; the divine punishment is aimed at the demon. *On your belly you shall crawl and you shall eat dust* is a customary Semitic way of describing enemies defeated in battle and compelled to acknowledge the power of their conqueror (see Ps 72:9; Isa 49:23; Mic 7:17).

On your belly you shall crawl
and you shall eat dust
for all the days of your life.[y]
15 I will establish hostility
between you and the woman,
between your line and her line.
Her offspring will crush your head
and you will bruise his heel." *[z]

16 To the woman he said,

"I will multiply your sufferings in childbirth;
with pain you shall bear your children.
You shall desire your husband,
but he shall lord it over you."[a]

17 To the man he said, "Because you listened to the voice of your wife and you ate from the tree from which I had commanded you not to eat,

"Cursed be the soil because of you!
With effort you shall obtain food
all the days of your life.[b]
18 Thorns and thistles shall it bring forth for you,
and you shall eat of the plants of the field.[c]
19 You shall have to sweat
to eat your bread
until the day when you return to the earth,
for from it you were drawn.
You are dust,
and unto dust you shall return."[d]

20 The man called his wife Eve, for she was the mother of all those who lived.
21 The LORD God made clothing for the man and woman out of animal skins and he clothed them. 22 The LORD God said, "Behold, man has become like one of us, for he has knowledge of that which is good and that which is evil. Now, we must prevent him from reaching out and taking the fruit of the tree of life lest he eat it and live forever."[e] 23 The LORD God cast him out of the Garden of Eden; henceforth he was to labor tilling the soil from which he had come.
24 When he expelled him, he placed cherubim * to the east of the Garden of Eden with flaming swords to keep watch over the way to the tree of life.[f]

B: The Reign of Sin*

CHAPTER 4

Hostility toward One's Neighbor.* 1 Adam was intimate with Eve his wife and she conceived and bore a son named Cain. She said, "I have obtained a son from the LORD." 2 Next she bore another child named Abel. Abel was a shepherd of flocks and Cain tilled the soil.
3 Some time later Cain offered the fruit of the earth as a sacrifice to the LORD,[g]
4 and Abel offered the firstborn of his flock and their fat offerings. The LORD was pleased with Abel and his offering,[h] 5 but he was not pleased with Cain and his offering. Cain was very angry and his countenance fell.
6 The LORD therefore said to Cain, "Why are you angry and why has your countenance fallen?[i] 7 If you do what is right, will you not be able to hold up your head? But if you do what is wrong, sin is crouching at your door. It seeks to dominate you, but you can overcome it."[j]
8 Cain said to his brother Abel, "Let us go out into the fields." While they were walking in the fields, Cain attacked his brother Abel and killed him.[k] 9 Then the LORD asked Cain, "Where is Abel, your brother?" He answered, "I do not know. Am I to be my brother's keeper?"

y Isa 65:25; Mic 7:17; Rev 12:9.—z Isa 7:14; 9:5; Rom 16:20; 1 Jn 3:8; Rev 12:17.—a 1 Cor 11:3; Eph 5:22f; 1 Tim 2:12.—b Gen 5:29; Rom 5:12; 8:20; Heb 6:8.—c Job 31:40; Ps 104:14; Isa 5:6; Heb 6:8.—d Gen 2:7; Job 10:9; 34:15; Pss 90:3; 103:14; Eccl 3:20; 12:7; Wis 15:8; Sir 10:9; 17:2; Rom 5:12; 1 Cor 15:21; Heb 9:27.—e Gen 2:9; Rev 22:2, 14.—f Ex 25:18-22; 1 Sam 4:4; 2 Ki 19:15.—g Lev 2:1f; Isa 43:23; Jer 41:5.—h Ex 34:19; Heb 11:4.—i Jon 4:4.—j Sir 7:1; Jude 11.—k Wis 10:3; Mt 23:35; Lk 11:51; 1 Jn 3:12; Jude 11.

3:15 This verse has traditionally been regarded as the protoevangelium, the first announcement of the salvation of the human race. The *offspring* of the woman refers to the human race but at a higher level to Jesus Christ who is source and cause of the common victory. Consequently, the *woman*, while certainly signifying Eve, the mother of the human race, refers at a higher level to Mary, the mother of Jesus and the new Eve.

3:24 The *cherubim* and the *flaming swords* symbolize the divine prohibition. In fact, the mythical winged *colossi*, half animal, half human, that stood guard at palaces, temples, and thrones of gods and kings in ancient Mesopotamia (known there as *karibu*; in the Bible see Ex 25:20; 1 Ki 6:27; Ezek 10:14), as well as the lightning represented in the form of flames or a wavy sword on stones marking the borders of territories, meant that access to the place in question was forbidden to profane persons and defended by the gods.

4:1—5:32 The story of Cain and Abel, in which agriculture and shepherding are already developed practices, may be an episode from the Neolithic Age, when the human race was already widespread. It is not impossible that Cain was the founder of the Kenites, a tribe allied with the Hebrews (Jdg 1:16; etc.). The Yahwist author would have chosen this known and important incident and moved it back to the time of the early ancestors in order to stress the point that there is a direct passage from breaking with God to breaking with the neighbor.

Thus sin multiplies and gradually becomes a power that tends to overwhelm the human race. But history will always be governed by two distinct forces: God and human beings, and God does not allow the wicked to gain exclusive control of the world.

4:1-15 Chapter 4 is also from the Yahwist source. Sin kills not only the sinner but the innocent.

10 The LORD told him, "What have you
done? Your brother's blood cries out to
me from the soil.[l] 11 Now may you be
cursed far from the soil that drank the
blood of your brother that you have
shed.[m] 12 When you till the soil, it shall not
be fruitful for you. You shall be a fugitive
and wanderer upon the earth."
13 Cain told the LORD, "My punishment
is too great to bear! 14 Behold, you are
banishing me from the soil this day. I will
have to hide far from you. I will be a fugi-
tive and wanderer upon the earth and
whoever meets me will be able to kill me."
15 But the LORD told him, "Not so! Who-
ever kills Cain will suffer a sevenfold
vengeance." The LORD placed a mark*
upon Cain, so that no one who might
meet him would strike him.

Descendants of the Murderer.* 16 Cain left
the presence of the LORD and lived in the
land of Nod,* which lies to the east of Eden.
17 Cain was intimate with his wife, and
she conceived and bore Enoch. He be-
came the founder of a city, which he
named after his son, Enoch. 18 To Enoch
was born Irad. Irad was the father of
Mehujael. Mehujael was the father
of Methusael. Methusael was the father of
Lamech.
19 Lamech had two wives: one named
Adah and the other named Zillah.
20 * Adah bore Jabal, who was the forefa-
ther of those who live in tents and herd
cattle. 21 His brother was named Jubal.
He was the forefather of those who play
the lyre and the flute. 22 Zillah bore
Tubalcain, the forger, and forefather of
those who forge things made of bronze
and iron. The sister of Tubalcain was
Naamah.
23 Lamech said to his wives,

"Adah and Zillah, listen to my voice;
wives of Lamech, lend an ear to what
I say.
I have killed a man for wounding me
and a boy, for bruising me.
24 If Cain received a vengeance of seven-
fold,
Lamech will receive one of seventy-
sevenfold."

First Stages of the History of Salvation.*
25 Adam was once again intimate with his
wife, and she bore a son who was named
Seth.* She said, "God has granted me an-
other child to take the place of Abel whom
Cain killed."
26 Seth also had a son who was named
Enosh. It was at this time that people began
to call upon the name of the LORD.[n]

CHAPTER 5

1 This is the book of genealogy for
Adam. When God created man, he made
him in the likeness of God;[o] 2 male and fe-
male he created them. He blessed them
and named them "human."
3[p] Adam was one hundred and thirty
years old when he had a son in his likeness,
who was named Seth.[q] 4 After he had Seth,
Adam lived another eight hundred years
and had other sons and daughters. 5 Adam
lived for nine hundred and thirty years, and
then he died.

---

l Ex 21:12; Num 35:33; Deut 21:7, 9; Pss 9:13; 106:38; Heb 12:24; Rev 6:9f.—m Deut 27:24.—n 1 Ki 18:24; 1 Chr 1:1; Ps 116:17; Joel 2:32; Zep 3:9; Lk 3:38.—o Gen 1:27; Wis 2:23; Sir 17:1; 1 Cor 11:7; Jas 3:9.—p 3-32: 1 Chr 1:1-4; Lk 3:36ff.—q Gen 4:25.

4:15 The *mark* is not a sign of disgrace but a sign of belonging to a clan and of the protection this ensures.

4:16-24 A very ancient tribal document. The tribe of Cain is connected with the origin of an inhabited area and with the legendary first practitioners of three trades associated with nomads. Moreover, Lamech, their father, is supposed to have begun the practice of polygamy and to have been noted for his savage and unbridled vendettas. In the eyes of the sacred writer, the passage shows that the progress of civilization cannot prevent a frightening moral regression.

4:16 *Land of Nod* or region of foreigners; *Nôd, nad,* is the fugitive and foreigner. Its geographical location has not been determined.

4:20-22 Shepherds, musicians, and smiths, three types of nomads, are traced back to three ancestors whose names point to their trades: *Jabal* (*ybl*, to lead), *Jubal* (*yôbel*, trumpet), and *Tubalcain.* (The Tubal were a people of the north, the land of metals, Gen 10:2; in other Semitic languages *kain* is a "*smith*").

4:25—5:32 God responds to human sin by seeing to it that life prevails over death. The section contains two parallel passages. The first, and shorter (4:25-26), concludes the Yahwist story of the origins. The void left by Abel is filled by Seth, the new founder of the people of God. Enosh, son of Seth, is the first to know the Lord under the ineffable name of Yahweh, which will later be revealed to the Israelites (Ex 3:14-15). The other passage (Gen 5:1-32), from the Priestly tradition, links up with chapter 1. The image of God, which was imprinted in the first human beings, has not been completely destroyed by sin but passes on in some manner to their descendants (see Gen 9:6). The extraordinary ages reached by these individuals have a symbolic value, but the meaning is obscure to us; the ancient lists of Sumerian-Babylonian kings likewise assign them very great lengths of life.

One of the patriarchs, Enoch, seems privileged: he is placed seventh in the list and has a much shorter life than the others, but the number of his years is a perfect number, that of the days in a solar year. The writer emphasizes his holiness and describes his end in a mysterious fashion, not saying that he died. All this suggests that the righteous are ripe for a higher destiny.

4:25 *Who was named Seth:* Hebrew, *Shet,* is explained by its assonance with the Hebrew verb, *shat,* which means "[God] has placed" (i.e., "has granted").

6 Seth was one hundred and five years old when he had Enosh. 7 After he had Enosh, he lived another eight hundred and seven years and had other sons and daughters. 8 Seth lived for nine hundred and twelve years, and then he died.

9 Enosh was ninety years old when he had Kenan. 10 After he had Kenan, Enosh lived another eight hundred and fifteen years and had other sons and daughters. 11 Enosh lived for nine hundred and five years, and then he died.

12 Kenan was seventy years old when he had Mahalalel. 13 After he had Mahalalel, he lived another eight hundred and forty years and had other sons and daughters. 14 Kenan lived for nine hundred and ten years, and then he died.

15 Mahalalel was sixty-five years old when he had Jared. 16 After he had Jared, he lived another eight hundred and thirty years and had other sons and daughters. 17 Mahalalel lived for eight hundred and ninety-five years, and then he died.

18 Jared was one hundred and sixty-two years old when he had Enoch. 19 After he had Enoch, he lived another eight hundred years and had other sons and daughters. 20 Jared lived for nine hundred and sixty-two years, and then he died.

21 Enoch was sixty-five years old when he had Methuselah. 22 Enoch walked with God.* After he had Methuselah, he lived another three hundred years and had other sons and daughters. 23 Enoch lived for three hundred and sixty-five years. 24 Enoch then walked with God and was no more for he was with God.[r]

25 Methuselah was one hundred and eighty-seven years old when he had Lamech. 26 After he had Lamech, he lived another seven hundred and eighty-two years and had other sons and daughters. 27 Methuselah lived for nine hundred and sixty-nine years, and then he died.

28 Lamech was one hundred eighty-two years old when he had a son. 29 He named him Noah, saying, "This one shall be a consolation for the work and labor that we must endure because the LORD has cursed the soil."[s] 30 After he had Noah, Lamech lived another five hundred ninety-five years and had other sons and daughters. 31 Lamech lived for seven hundred and seventy-seven years, and then he died. 32 Noah was five hundred years old when he had Shem, Ham, and Japheth.[t]

C: Death and Resurrection of God's Work*

CHAPTER 6

Widespread Perversion.* 1 When men began to multiply upon the earth, and they began to have daughters, 2 the sons of God saw that the daughters of men were beautiful and they married as many of them as they wanted.[u] 3 The LORD therefore said, "My spirit will not remain in them forever, for they are flesh and the length of their lives will be one hundred and twenty years."[v]

4 There were giants upon the earth at this time, as well as afterward. They were the children of the sons of God who married the daughters of men. These were the heroes of times past, men of renown.[w]

5 The LORD saw that the wickedness of men upon the earth was great, and that every plan that their hearts conceived was nothing but evil.[x] 6 The LORD regretted that he had made man upon the earth and his heart was grieved.[y] 7 The LORD said, "I will obliterate man, whom I created, from the earth. Together with man I will eliminate all the cattle and reptiles

r 2 Ki 2:1, 11; Pss 49:16; 73:24; 89:49; Wis 4:10f; Sir 44:16; 49:14; Heb 11:5.—s Gen 4:17ff.—t Gen 6:10; 10:1.—u Job 1:6; Mt 24:38; Lk 17:26f.—v Job 10:9; 34:14; Pss 78:39; 103:14; Isa 40:6; 57:16; Gal 5:16f; 1 Pet 3:20.—w Wis 14:6; Bar 3:26.—5:22 6:1—9:17 6:1-8 x Ps 14:1-3.—y Ex 32:14; 1 Sam 15:11, 35; 2 Sam 24:16; Isa 63:10; Jer 18:7-10; Eph 4:30.

5:22 *Walked with God:* he was morally and religiously perfect.

6:1—9:17 The entire biblical tradition presents the flood as an historical event (Wis 10:4; Sir 44:17-18; Mt 24:37-39; 1 Pet 3:20; etc.), but apart from popular texts no information was available for describing the material event.

It is from these popular texts that the external elements of the story come: the structure of the ark, the duration and extent of the flood, and so on, which are not part of the historico-religious message of the writer but serve in the composition of a vivid story. As a result, the Yahwist and Elohist traditions could differ in marginal aspects that are more picturesque in the one and more detailed in the other.

Humankind is renewed in the person of Noah. In the Christian tradition he is a figure of Christ, the one true righteous man, who remained untouched by the spread of sin and then, rising unharmed from death, became the source of resurrection for humankind.

6:1-8 The passage is from the Yahwist tradition. The writer seems to be using two fragments of ancient popular traditions (vv. 1-2, 4). The striking element in this chapter is the fact that human beings have gone so far in personal disintegration that they are no longer capable of thinking anything but evil (v. 5), so that any hope of recovery is morally impossible.

The tragic anthropomorphism seen in the divine regret highlights the power of evil, which is capable of destroying the work of the Creator; but the annihilation planned is the decision of the supreme Good, which is always the sole judge of its own plans (see Jer 18:1-12) and cannot allow the definitive victory of evil.

and the birds of the air, for I regret having
made them." 8 But Noah found favor with
the LORD. [z]

Salvation through the Righteous.* 9 This is
the story of Noah. Noah was a just and
blameless man at that time and he walked
with God. [a] 10 Noah had three sons: Shem,
Ham, and Japheth. 11 But the earth was
corrupt in God's sight and filled with vio-
lence. [b] 12 God saw that the earth was cor-
rupt, for every person on the earth was
perverse in what he did. [c]

13 God therefore said to Noah, "I have
decided to end everything, for they have
filled the earth with their violence. Be-
hold, I will destroy the entire creation. [d]
14 Build an ark* of gopher wood and di-
vide the ark into compartments and caulk
it with bitumen inside and out. 15 This is
how you shall make it: the ark will be
three hundred cubits long, fifty wide, and
thirty high. 16 Make a roof on the ark one
cubit high. * Place a door in the side of the
ark. Make it with three decks: lower, mid-
dle, and higher.

17 "Behold, I will send a flood. The wa-
ters shall cover the earth to destroy the
life of everything under the skies that has
the breath of life in it. Everything on the
earth shall perish. [e] 18 But I will establish a
covenant with you.

"Go into the ark, you and your sons,
your wife, and the wives of your sons. [f]
19 Bring into the ark two of everything
that lives, of all flesh. Bring a male and
female of each species into the ark to
save them. 20 Bring two birds of each
species, two animals of each species,
and two reptiles of each species with you
to save them. 21 As for you, gather every
type of food and take it with you. It shall
nourish both you and them."

22 Noah did all of this, exactly as God
had commanded him.

CHAPTER 7

1 The LORD said to Noah, "Enter into
the ark with your entire family, for I
have seen that you, of all this genera-
tion, are just in my sight. [g] 2 You are to
take seven pairs of each type of clean
animal with you, male and female. You
are to take one pair of each type of un-
clean animal with you, male and female.
3 You are also to take seven pairs of birds
of the air, male and female, with you, so
that you may save every species of ani-
mal upon the earth. [h] 4 In seven days I
will make it begin to rain upon the
earth, and it will rain for forty days and
forty nights. I will destroy from the face
of the earth every living creature I have
made." [i]

5 Noah did all that the LORD had com-
manded him to do.

End of the Sinful World.* 6 Noah was six
hundred years old when the flood began
and the waters covered the earth. 7 Noah

z Ru 2:2, 10, 13; Lk 1:30; Acts 7:46.—a Wis 10:4; Sir 44:17.—b Job 22:15ff; Pss 7:9; 73:6.—c Ps 14:1-3.—d Job 34:15; Sir 40:9f; 44:17; Jer 44:11, 27; Mt 24:37ff.—e Gen 7:4, 21; Ps 29:10; 2 Pet 2:5.—f Gen 9:9; Pss 25:10; 74:20; 106:45; Wis 14:6; Heb 11:7; 1 Pet 3:20.—g Wis 10:4; Sir 44:17; Ezek 14:14; 2 Pet 2:5.—h Gen 6:20.—i Gen 6:17; 8:2; 2 Pet 2:5.

6:9—7:5 The first part of the following passage (6:9-22) is from the Priestly tradition and links up with the end of chapter 5. First, in three verses (6:11-13), it uses the language of corruption and violence to summarize the entire history of sin and the decree of condemnation, both of which have been described in a more diffuse way in the Yahwist tradition. This is followed by the order to build the ark, which is found only in the Priestly version, and finally the announcement of the flood with the command to enter the ark. This passage from the Priestly tradition is followed by a repetition of the command to enter the ark and of the announcement of the flood from the Yahwist tradition (7:1-5). Note the difference of the two traditions when it comes to the number of animals brought into the ark: the Yahwist account, more popular in character, presupposes that in those very ancient times a distinction was already made between clean and unclean animals, whereas in fact the distinction was of later origin and codified in the Mosaic Law.

The New Testament praises the faith of Noah (Heb 11:7) and speaks of the harm done his contemporaries by their unbelief, because they were unable to accept the impulse to conversion that came from him as he was building the ark (1 Pet 3:20).

6:14 *Ark*, in Hebrew *teba*, is probably connected with the Egyptian, *teb(t)*, basket, sarcophagus, and perhaps with the Akkadian, *tabu*, the processional boat of the gods, or with Akkadian, *elippu tibitu*, a kind of boat. The same word is used in Ex 2:3, 5 for the basket in which Moses was saved.

6:16 A cubit was about 50 cm or one and a half feet. The ark was about 156 meters long, 26 meters wide, and 15 meters high (440 x 72 x 44 feet). It was a floating parallelepiped of about 55,000 or 60,000 cubic meters (82,000 or 90,000 cubic feet).

7:6-24 In this section the entrance into the ark and the description of the flood are repeated, first in the Yahwist version with inserts from the Priestly tradition (vv. 1-12) and then in the Priestly version with inserts from the Yahwist tradition (vv. 13-20); finally, there is a description of the effects of the flood that draws on both traditions (vv. 21-24). In the Yahwist tradition the flood is simply a torrential rain that continues for forty days (vv. 4, 12; 8:2b), while in the Priestly account, in keeping with the cosmic vision in Genesis 1:1-10, the waters are loosed both from the subterranean ocean and from the heavenly ocean (7:11; 8:2a).

According to the ideas of the ancients, in creating the world God separated the earth from the waters by creating the solid heavenly vault that divided the oceanic mass (the "abyss") into an upper part beyond the heavens and a lower, earthly part, and by then commanding the lower waters to retreat, allowing the dry land to emerge. At this point, then, the lower, subterranean waters invade the earth anew through springs, while passages ("floodgates") open in the heavenly vault and allow the upper waters to pour down. Thus God causes some effects of his creative work to cease. The waters that submerge the highest mountains on earth and destroy humankind and the animals effect a return of the universe to its primitive condition; the process is an image of the cosmic dimensions that sin, the rejection of God, has.

went into the ark with his sons, his wife,
and the wives of his sons to escape from
the waters of the flood.[j] 8 The clean ani-
mals and the unclean animals, the birds,
and the creatures that creep on the
ground* 9 entered the ark two by two,
male and female, along with Noah, just as
the LORD had commanded.[k] 10 After seven
days, the waters of the flood covered the
earth; 11 this happened in the six hun-
dredth year of the life of Noah, in the sec-
ond month, the seventeenth day of the
month. On that very day the springs of the
great abyss and the floodgates of the heav-
ens opened.* 12 The rains fell upon the
earth for forty days and forty nights.
13 That day Noah and his sons Shem,
Ham, and Japheth entered the ark along
with the wife of Noah and the three wives of
his sons. 14 They entered along with all living
creatures according to their kind, all cattle
according to their kind, all creeping crea-
tures according to their kind, and all birds
according to their kind. 15 They went into the
ark with Noah, two by two, every creature
that had breath in it. 16 Those that came, male
and female of every type of flesh, entered the
ark as God had commanded. The LORD
closed the door after them.
17 The flood lasted for forty days. The wa-
ters rose and lifted the ark off the earth as they
increased. 18 The waters continued to swell
and increased greatly on the earth until the
ark floated upon the waters. 19 The waters rose
more and more on the earth and covered all
the highest mountains that are under the
heavens. 20 The waters were fifteen cubits over
the tops of the mountains that they covered.
21 [l] Every living creature that moves upon
the earth, every bird, cattle, wild animal,
and creature that crawls upon the earth,
and every single person on dry land died.
22 Every creature on dry land that had the
breath of life in its nostrils died.
23 This is how every living creature on
earth was slain, every human being and
every animal, every reptile and every bird
of the air. They were blotted out of the
earth, and only Noah and those who were
with him in the ark survived.*
24 The waters covered the earth for one
hundred and fifty days.

CHAPTER 8

The New Creation.* 1 God remembered
Noah and all the wild and farm animals
that were with him in the ark. God made a
wind blow upon the earth, and the waters
began to recede. 2 The springs of the abyss
and the windows of the heavens were
closed, and the rains from the heavens
ceased. 3 The waters slowly receded from
the earth. At the end of one hundred and
fifty days they had greatly diminished. 4 In
the seventh month, the seventeenth day of
the month, the ark came to rest on Mount
Ararat.* 5 The waters continued to recede
until the tenth month. In the tenth month,
the first day of the month, the tops of the
mountains came into view.
6 After forty days had gone by, Noah
opened the window that he had made in the
ark 7 and released a raven to see if the wa-
ters had completely dried up. It flew back
and forth until the waters upon the earth
dried up. 8 Noah then released a dove, to see
if the waters had drained from the surface
of the earth, 9 but the dove, not finding any
place to land, returned to the ark (for the
waters still covered the surface of the earth).

j Wis 14:6; 1 Pet 3:20; 2 Pet 2:5.—k Gen 6:19.—l 21ff: Job 22:16; Mt 24:39; Lk 17:27; 2 Pet 3:6.

7:8 This verse, which seems to be the work of the final editor, brings the Yahwist source, which distinguishes between clean and unclean animals, into harmony with the Priestly source, which has the animals in pairs.

7:11 According to the calendar used in the Priestly story of the flood, the year is divided into twelve months of about thirty days each, depending always on the cycle of the moon. The first month, equivalent to Nisan, is the month of the first lunar cycle in the spring (March-April).

7:23 The flood prefigures the final judgment (Mt 24:37-41) and salvation through baptism (1 Pet 3:20-21).

8:1—9:7 The first five verses, on the withdrawal of the waters, are from the Priestly tradition with a short Yahwist insert, while the section on the raven and the dove is Yahwist. The sending of a bird to find solid land was a custom of ancient mariners and also occurs in Mesopotamian stories of the flood. The following section, on the departure from the ark, is again Priestly and is in continuity with chapter 9, which is from the same source, whereas 8:21-22 on sacrifice and the divine decision are Yahwist.

God does not allow evil to conquer him but defeats it by preparing a new world. With Noah, the second father of humankind, everything begins again: nature takes up its laws again and human beings rediscover their rights. However, sin had destroyed the harmony that existed in the beginning. Human beings enter into conflict with the animals and with one another. The prohibition of shedding blood and the punishment for murderers are intended to remind all that life belongs to God alone. The Lord concludes a new covenant with human beings but engages only himself; he has decided to be patient and allow freedom to go to its very limits. This ancient story of the covenant defines God's attitude toward all humankind. The universal covenant that Jesus will seal with his blood bears witness to the astounding greatness of God's love for human beings (see Jn 3:16).

8:4 *Ararat* (cuneiform texts have *Urartu*) has been variously identified: the northeast region of Lake Van; the mountains of Kurdistan; the Lubar mountains, near Zagros, close to the Nisir of the Gilgamesh myth.

He reached out and caught the dove and
brought it back into the ark.
10 After waiting another seven days, he
once again released the dove from the ark.
11 It returned to him toward the evening. In
its beak it had a sprig from an olive tree.
Noah understood that the waters had re-
ceded from the earth. 12 He waited another
seven days and then released the dove. It
did not return to him.
13 In the six hundred and first year of
Noah's life, in the first month, the first day
of the month, the waters dried up upon the
earth. Noah removed the covering from the
ark and, behold, the surface of the earth was
dry. 14 In the second month, the twenty-sev-
enth day of the month, the entire surface of
the earth was dry.
15 God commanded Noah, 16 "Leave the
ark, you and your wife, your sons and their
wives. 17 Take all the animals of every
species with you, birds, cattle, all the reptiles
that crawl upon the earth, take them all
with you. Let them spread out upon the
earth. May they be fruitful and multiply
upon the earth." [m]
18 Noah left the ark with his sons, his wife,
and his sons' wives.
19 All the living creatures and all the wild
animals, all the birds and all the reptiles
that crawl upon the earth, each according to
its kind, all left the ark.
20 Noah built an altar to the LORD, took
every kind of clean animal and some of
every kind of clean bird, and he offered
them as burnt offerings upon the altar. [n]
21 The LORD smelled the pleasant odor
and said to himself, "I will never again curse
the land because of humankind, for the in-
stinct of every human heart is evil from its
youth. I will never again destroy every living
creature. [o]

22 "As long as the earth endures,
seedtime and harvest,
cold and heat,
summer and winter,
day and night
shall not cease." [p]

CHAPTER 9

1 God blessed Noah and his sons and told
them, "Be fruitful and multiply and fill the
earth. [q] 2 * Fear and dread of you will come
upon every wild animal and every bird of
the air, everything that crawls upon the
earth and all the fish of the sea; they will be
under your dominion.
3 "Whatever moves and has life will be
used for your food. I give you all these
things, just as I have already given you
every green plant. [r] 4 * Only do not eat flesh
along with its life, that is, with its blood. [s]
5 For your blood, that is, your life, I will re-
quire an accounting. I will require it of
every living creature, and I will require it of
every human in regard to other humans,
each person for his brother. [t]

6 "Whoever spills human blood,
that person's blood will be shed;
for in the image of God
has God made man. [u]

7 And as for you, be fruitful and multiply;
become numerous upon the earth and have
dominion over it." [v]

Covenant of Mercy.* 8 God said to Noah
and his sons, 9 "As for me, I will establish
my covenant with you and your descen-
dants after you, [w] 10 with every living crea-
ture along with you—the birds, tame and
wild animals, and with all the animals
which left the ark. 11 I will establish my
covenant with you: never again will all
living creatures be cut off by the waters of a
flood, nor will the earth be laid waste by a
flood again." [x]
12 God said, "This will be a sign of the
covenant that I establish between me and
you and every living creature for all genera-
tions. 13 I will place my rainbow in the

m Gen 1:22, 28.—n Gen 12:7f; 22:2, 13; Ex 10:25; Lev 1:3; Jdg 6:26; 1 Sam 20:29.—o Sir 44:18; Isa 54:9; Rom 7:18.—p Jer 33:20, 25.—q Gen 1:22, 28; 8:17; Jas 3:7.—r Gen 1:29f; Deut 12:15.—s Lev 7:26f; 17:12; Deut 12:16, 23; 1 Sam 14:33; Ezek 33:25; Acts 15:20.—t Gen 4:10f; Ex 21:12; 1 Ki 2:32.—u Gen 1:26f; Lev 24:17; Num 35:33; Jas 3:9.—v Gen 1:28; 8:17; 9:2.—w Gen 6:18.—x Sir 44:18; Isa 54:9; Hos 6:7.

9:2-3 All this is simply a popular image for describing the complete happiness God had intended for humankind in the state of innocence. Verse 3 makes clear that the eating of meat is part of God's general plan for the created world.

9:4-6 In the popular Semitic view blood is the seat of the vital principle; it is not, however, a product of matter but is infused into it by God. Therefore, the blood belongs in its entirety to God, and in a special way the blood of human beings, made as they are in the image of God, who is their protector and avenger.

9:8-17 God's intention as enunciated in the Yahwist tradition (8:21-22) is rethought in this Priestly passage as a covenant between God and Noah, analogous to that which will later be established between God and Abraham (Gen 15; 17) and then between God and the Israelite people (Ex 19–24). The imagery brings out the unqualified steadfastness of the divine intention. The Covenant is freely made on God's part, that is, it does not depend on the future behavior of human beings, for the Lord does not ask Noah to fulfill any particular requirement.

clouds and it will be a sign of the covenant
between me and the earth.[y] 14 When I
gather the clouds over the earth, the rain-
bow will appear in the clouds. 15 I will re-
member my covenant between me and you
and with every living creature of every
kind, that water and flood shall never again
destroy all flesh.[z] 16 The rainbow will be in
the clouds and I will look upon it and re-
member the eternal covenant between
God and every living creature of every
kind that is found upon the earth."[a]
17 God said to Noah, "This is a sign of
the covenant that I am establishing be-
tween myself and every creature upon the
earth."

D: A World of Diverse Peoples*

The Return of Sin.* 18 The sons of Noah
who left the ark were Shem, Ham, and
Japheth. Ham was the father of the peo-
ple of Canaan.[b] 19 These were the three
sons of Noah, and from these came all the
people on the earth.
20 Now Noah tilled the soil, and he was
the first to plant grape vines. 21 He drank
some of the wine and he became drunk
and lay uncovered inside his tent.[c]
22 Ham, the father of the Canaanites, saw
his father lying naked, and he mentioned
it to his two brothers who were standing
outside.* 23 Shem and Japheth took a robe
and, holding it in back of them, walked
backward toward him and covered their
father with it. Having faced backward,
they did not see their father naked.
24 When Noah woke up from his
drunken slumber, he learned what his
youngest son had done to him. 25 Because
of this, he said,

"Cursed be Canaan!
A slave of slaves
shall he be to his brothers!"*[d]

26 *And he continued,

"Blessed be the LORD, the God of
Shem,
and let Canaan be his slave!
27 May God enlarge Japheth
so that he dwells in the land of
Shem;
and let Canaan be his slave!"

28 After the flood, Noah lived for three
hundred and fifty years. 29 In all, Noah
lived for nine hundred and fifty years, and
then he died.

CHAPTER 10

The Human Family.* 1 These are the de-
scendants of the sons of Noah: Shem,

y Sir 43:12; Ezek 1:28; Rev 4:3, 10.—z Gen 8:1; Ex 2:24; 6:5; 34:10; Lev 26:42, 45; Pss 89:35; 103:18; Isa 54:9.—a 2 Sam 7:13; 23:5; Ps 105:9f; Isa 9:7; 54:10; Jer 31:31-34; Heb 13:20.—b Gen 5:32; 10:1.—c Lam 4:21; Heb 2:15.—d Deut 27:16; Jos 9:27; Jdg 1:28, 30; 1 Ki 9:20f; Wis 12:11.

9:18—11:32 God has blessed the new creation, and the earth is repopulated. At the heart of this humankind, which is divided and marked by sin, is the towering figure of Abraham. It is upon him that the Lord has affixed his choice as the forerunner through whom the salvation of human beings will take place.

9:18-29 The story is from the Yahwist tradition. After the second creation, as after the first, we read the story of a sin, a condemnation, and a prophecy of hope. This last is connected with chapter 12 and the call of Abraham.

9:22 This is not a sexual sin but an abuse of power; the sons make themselves the superiors and judges of their father, who is humiliated and dishonored. To the Hebrews drunkenness is wanton, dishonorable, and humiliating; it provokes ridicule, leads to idolatry, incites violence, causes injustice and poverty, and makes persons subject to their enemies. It is unseemly especially for the leaders of nations. Clothing, then, in addition to being a means of decency, expresses the dignity of the person and his or her social position. When naked (Gen 3:7), Adam and Eve are deprived of glory and grace; the garments of skin with which God clothes them (Gen 3:21) are symbolic of their hope of being clothed again in their lost dignity.

9:25 According to the Semitic mentality, the blessings and curses of the Patriarchs (generally) are regarded as efficacious and able to determine the lot of the tribe represented by each Patriarch. For this reason, popular stories connected events or characteristics of a human group with blessings or curses uttered by an ancestor. In the present story Noah curses Canaan and therefore the Canaanites. The Canaanites were to be supplanted by the Hebrews in the conquest of the Promised Land. The Phoenicians, too, were Canaanites (see Gen 10:15-19; Jdg 1:31).

9:26-27 A great numerical and territorial expansion is announced for the descendants of Japheth; there is a play on the resemblance in sound between this ancestor's name and the verb meaning "to open," "to enlarge."

10:1-32 For the ancient Semites, a person's genealogy was not a strictly historical document, but a juridical one, meant to show the transmission of rights. For this reason, physical generation often serves as an image pointing to a legal generation, as, for example, adoption. The genealogical tree had, of course, to be composed of historical persons so as to determine a juridical succession.

The genealogy of peoples or cities is an image derived from the preceding and can signify ties of derivation or affinity between one people and another on the ethnic, geographical, historical, political, sociological, cultural, and other planes. Since the whole matter was flexible and since we are dealing only with an image, it is obvious that one and the same people could locate themselves, from different points of view, in various genealogical lineages, including some far removed from modern-day scientific genealogies.

On the basis of historical and geographical data, the Priestly tradition, here incorporating Yahwist features, in this chapter compiles a genealogical tree for peoples known in the second millennium B.C. The picture, in which an historical and religious intention is at work, asserts the substantial unity of the human race, which is divided into various peoples and languages. All human beings are brothers and sisters, sons and daughters of the same Creator God and heirs of his blessings, and all are meant to be saved.

Given its purpose, the picture does not provide a basis for resolving the anthropological question of monogenism or polygenism, nor the historical question of the extent of the flood. In this "list of peoples" the Semites come in last place because the writer takes them as his starting point for the continuation of his story, while from this point on the descendants of Japheth and Ham cease to be of direct concern to the biblical story.

Ham and Japheth, to whom sons were born after the flood.

2 [e] The sons of Japheth were Gomer, Magog, Madai, Javan, Tubal, Meschech, and Tiras.[f]

3 The sons of Gomer were Ashkenaz, Riphath, and Togarmah.

4 The sons of Javan were Elishah, Tarshish, the Kittim, and the Rodanim.

5 From these came the peoples of the islands and their territories, each clan in the nations with their own language.

6 The sons of Ham were Cush, Mizraim, Put, and Canaan.

7 The sons of Cush were Seba, Havilah, Sabtah, Raamah, and Sabteca.

The sons of Raamah were Sheba and Dedan.

8 Cush gave birth to Nimrod. He was the first of the mighty ones upon the earth. 9 He was a great hunter before the LORD, for it is said, "Just like Nimrod, a great hunter before the LORD." 10 The beginning of his kingdom was Babel, Erech, and Accad, all of them in the land of Shinar. 11 From that land he went to Asshur where he built Nineveh, Rehoboth-ir, Calah, 12 and Resen between Nineveh and Calah, which is the main city.

13 [g] Mizraim gave birth to the Ludim, Anamim, Lehabim, Naphtuhim, 14 Pathrusim, Casluhim, and Caphtorim (from whom came the Philistines).

15 Canaan gave birth to Sidon, his firstborn, and Heth, 16 and the Jebusites, the Amorites, the Girgashites, 17 the Hivites, the Arkites, the Sinites, 18 the Arvadites, the Zemarites, and the Hamathites.

Afterward the clans of the Canaanites spread outward. 19 The boundaries of the Canaanites stretch from Sidon in the area of Gerar up to Gaza, and then go toward Sodom, Gomorrah, Admah, and Zeboiim, up to Lasha.

20 These were the sons of Ham according to their clans and their languages, in their various territories and according to their peoples.

21 Shem, the ancestor of all of the sons of Eber and the older brother of Japheth, also had children.

22 [h] The sons of Shem were Elam, Asshur, Arpachshad, Lud, and Aram.

23 The sons of Aram were Uz, Hul, Gether, and Mash.

24 Arpachshad gave birth to Shelah, and Shelah gave birth to Eber. 25 Eber had two sons: one named Peleg (for in his days the earth was divided) and the other named Joktan.

26 Joktan gave birth to Almodad, Sheleph, Hazarmaveth, Jerah, 27 Hadoram, Uzal, Diklah, 28 Obal, Abimael, Sheba, 29 Ophir, Havilah, and Jobab. All these were the sons of Joktan.

30 They lived in the mountain region in the east, from Mesha on toward Sephar.

31 These were the sons of Shem according to their clans and their languages, in their various territories and according to their languages.

32 These were the families of the sons of Noah in their various generations and clans. These divided up to become all the nations on the earth after the flood.

CHAPTER 11

An Attempt at Unity.* 1 The whole world had only one language, everyone using the same words. 2 Migrating from the east, men came upon a plain in the land of Shinar where they settled.[i]

3 They said to each other, "Come, let us make bricks and bake them in a fire." These bricks were what they used instead of stone, and bitumen in place of cement.*

e 2-8: 1 Chr 1:5-10.—f Ezek 38:2.—g 13-18: 1 Chr 1:11-16. —h 22-29: 1 Chr 1:17-23.—i Gen 10:10.

11:1-9 After having presented in the list of peoples what might be called the mission field of the People of God, the biblical narrative dwells on a fundamental aspect of this field, one that is always alive in the various human groups, namely, the insistent need for unity. The passage, from the Yahwist source, makes use of an ancient popular story that seems to copy in an ironic way Mesopotamian texts on the dedication of its well-known temple towers.

The story concerns a migrating people who come down from the mountains into a vast plain and feel the need of establishing a city center with a skyscraper tower that will guarantee the maintenance of their unity. *Make a name for ourselves* means to establish a power that will foster their cohesion and their own political identity. But, as happens in human undertakings, a moment comes in which intentions diverge, so that the unity of the people is broken, as if they were speaking different languages. The tradition sees in this occurrence an explicit manifestation of God, the author of human nature. The direction events take always depends on God.

11:3 *Bricks . . . instead of stone, and bitumen in place of cement:* stone and cement were used as building materials in Canaan. Stone was scarce in Mesopotamia, however, so bricks and bitumen were used (as indicated by archaeological excavations).

4 Then they said, "Come, let us build a city and a tower so high that it touches the heavens.* We shall make a name for ourselves and not be scattered all throughout the earth."[j]

5 But the LORD came down and saw the city and the tower that these men were building. 6 The LORD said, "Behold, they are a single people and they have only one language. This is only the beginning of what they will do. Now nothing that they think up will be impossible for them. 7 Let us go down and confuse their language so that they will not understand each other when they speak."

8 The LORD scattered them over the whole earth* and they ceased building their city. 9 This is why it is called Babel,* for there the LORD confused everyone's language. It was also from there that the LORD scattered people over the whole earth.

Genealogy of Abraham.* 10 [k] The descendants of Shem are as follow:

Shem was one hundred years old when he had Arpachshad two years after the flood. 11 Shem, after he had Arpachshad, lived another five hundred years and had other sons and daughters.

12 Arpachshad was thirty-five years old when he had Shelah. 13 Arpachshad, after he had Shelah, lived another four hundred and three years and had other sons and daughters.

14 Shelah was thirty years old when he had Eber. 15 Shelah, after he had Eber, lived another four hundred and three years and had other sons and daughters.

16 Eber was thirty-four years old when he had Peleg. 17 Eber, after he had Peleg, lived another four hundred and thirty years and had other sons and daughters.

18 Peleg was thirty years old when he had Reu. 19 Peleg, after he had Reu, lived another two hundred and nine years and had other sons and daughters.

20 Reu was thirty-two years old when he had Serug. 21 Reu, after he had Serug, lived another two hundred and seven years and had other sons and daughters.

22 Serug was thirty years old when he had Nahor. 23 Serug, after he had Nahor, lived another two hundred years and had other sons and daughters.

24 Nahor was twenty-nine years old when he had Terah. 25 Nahor, after he had Terah, lived one hundred and nineteen years and had other sons and daughters.

26 Terah was seventy years old when he had Abram, Nahor, and Haran.[l]

27 These are the descendants of Terah.

Terah had Abram, Nahor, and Haran. Haran had Lot.[m] 28 Haran then died in the presence of his father Terah in the land of his birth, in Ur of the Chaldeans.*[n] 29 Abram and Nahor both married. The wife of Abram was Sarai, and the wife of Nahor was Milcah who was a daughter of Haran (the father of Milcah and Iscah).[o] 30 Sarai was barren and did not have any children.[p]

31 Then Terah took Abram, his son, and Lot, the son of Haran, and Sarai, his daughter-in-law and the wife of Abram his son, and he left Ur of the Chaldeans to go to the land of Canaan. They went as far as Haran where they settled.*[q]

j Job 20:6; Ps 44:12; Jer 31:10; 51:53; Ezek 6:8.—k 10-26: 1 Chr 1:24-27; Lk 3:34ff.—l Jos 24:2; 1 Chr 1:27.—m Gen 12:4; 13:1, 5, 8, 12; Lk 17:28; 2 Pet 2:7.—n Gen 15:7; Neh 9:7; Job 1:17; 16:11; Ezek 23:23; Acts 7:4.—o Gen 17:15; 20:12.—p Gen 16:1; 1 Sam 1:5; Lk 1:7, 36.—q Jos 24:3; Neh 9:7; Jud 5:6-9; Acts 7:4.

11:4 *Tower so high that it touches the heavens:* this is a direct reference to the most important temple tower (ziggurat) found in Babylon, which goes by the name of "the house that lifts high its head." Scholars regard the ziggurats of Babylonia as the earliest skyscrapers.

11:8 *Scattered them over the whole earth:* God countered their prideful rebellion at its very origin. They had chosen to settle, but he forced them to scatter. This account relates how it was that the families of the earth were separated, "each clan in the nations with their own language" (Gen 10:5) and were "divided up to become all the nations on the earth after the flood" (Gen 10:32).

11:9 *Babel* (i.e., Babylonia), according to a popular etymology, meant "gate of god" or "gate of the gods." The sacred writer, having told of the failure of the human undertaking (and the failure also of the gods who wanted to be worshiped on the Mesopotamian towers), asks us to read the name "Babel" as a reminder of that failure: he suggests a connection with the root *bll,* "to confuse," from which the form *balbel* and then, by contraction, *babel,* would supposedly be derived.

11:10-32 These verses are from the Priestly tradition, a continuation of the genealogy begun in chapter 5, except for verses 28-30, which are Yahwist. Beginning perhaps with Arpachshad, named as son of Shem, the list of names here is a real genealogy, a document of the family of Abraham; only the numbers continue to be symbolic and conventional, without any strictly historical value. Abraham comes from a seminomadic family or clan that has settled in the city of Ur, at that time on the shores of the Persian Gulf and already rich and powerful, especially in the 21st and 20th centuries B.C.

Abraham and his family travel up the valley of the Euphrates and settle in upper Mesopotamia. The period of these events may be around 1850 B.C.

11:28 *Ur of the Chaldeans:* Ur was an ancient city of the Sumerians in southern Mesopotamia as well as a populous and prosperous one. In this case, the phrase is an anachronism, because the Chaldeans were not known to history until some thousand years after Abraham.

11:31 Abraham traveled along the Euphrates to Haran, a trading town in northern Mesopotamia or Syria. This was the best route from which to reach Canaan and bypass the great desert with its people and animals (see Gen 12:4; Acts 7:2-4).

32 Terah lived to be two hundred and five
years old. Terah died in Haran.

II: ORIGIN OF THE PEOPLE OF GOD*

A: Abraham, Man of Faith*

CHAPTER 12

"Leave Your Country [and] Your People."*
1 The LORD said to Abram, "Leave your
country, your people, and the house of your
father, and go to the land to which I will
lead you. [r]

2 "I will make of you a great people
and I will bless you.
I will make your name great
and it will become a blessing. [s]
3 I will bless those who bless you
and curse those who curse you.
And through you
all the nations on the earth shall be
blessed." [t]

4 [u] Abram therefore departed, just as the
LORD had ordered him. Lot went along
with him. Abram was seventy-five years old
when he left Haran. 5 Abram took his wife
Sarai, Lot, the son of his brother, and all the
possessions that they had accumulated in
Haran, and all the people whom they had
acquired in Haran, and left for the land of
Canaan. Thus, they arrived in the land of
Canaan.
6 Abram traveled through the land until
he arrived at Shechem near the oak of
Moreh. In those days the Canaanites lived
in that land. [v] 7 The LORD appeared to
Abram and said to him, "I will give this
land to your descendants." Abram there-
fore built an altar there to the LORD who
had appeared to him. [w]
8 From there he traveled into the moun-
tain region to the east of Bethel and he
pitched his tent so that Bethel was to the
west and Ai was to his east. There he built
an altar to the LORD and called upon the
name of the LORD. [x] 9 Then Abram set out
again, gradually traveling toward the
Negeb. *

Abram a Refugee in Egypt.* 10 There was a
famine in the land and Abram went down
to Egypt to stay there for a time, for the
famine was very serious in the land. [y] 11 But,
when he was about to enter Egypt, he said
to Sarai, his wife, "Look, I realize that you
are a very beautiful woman. 12 When the
Egyptians see you, they will think, 'She is his
wife,' and they will kill me, leaving you alive.
13 Therefore, say that you are my sister, so
that they will treat me well and let me live
because of you." [z]
14 When Abram arrived in Egypt, the
Egyptians saw that his wife was very beau-
tiful. 15 The stewards of Pharaoh saw her
and told Pharaoh how beautiful she was.
They took the woman and brought her to
the house of Pharaoh. 16 Because of her
they treated Abram well. He received flocks
and herds, male and female slaves, female
donkeys, and camels.
17 But the LORD struck Pharaoh and his
household with terrible plagues because of
Sarai, the wife of Abram. [a] 18 Therefore,
Pharaoh summoned Abram and said to
him, "What have you done to me? Why did
you not tell me that she was your wife?
19 Why did you say, 'She is my sister,' so that
I ended up taking her as my wife? Here is
your wife; take her and leave!" 20 Then
Pharaoh entrusted him to some men who
accompanied him to the borders along with
his wife and all his belongings.

CHAPTER 13

Growth in Faith. 1 From Egypt Abram
traveled to the Negeb along with his wife

r Acts 7:3; Heb 11:8.—s Gen 17:6; Sir 44:20; Rom 4:17-22.—t Gen 18:18; 22:18; Acts 3:25; Gal 3:8.—u 4f: Gen 11:31; Jos 24:3; Acts 7:4.—v Heb 11:9.—w Ex 33:1; Deut 34:4; Acts 7:5.—x Gen 4:26; 8:20.—y Gen 26:1.—z Gen 20:12f; 26:7.—a Ps 105:14.

12:1—50:26 The second part of Genesis gathers and arranges the memories that Israel has preserved regarding its distant origins (which can be dated to between the 19th and 17th centuries B.C.). These memories reduce to a few essential traits the life of the ancestors of the chosen people.

12:1—25:18 God has never abandoned the human race that he created; the universe and nature speak of him to human beings (Wis 13; Rom 1:20), but the human conscience, blinded by self-centeredness and pride, reaches out to him only in a groping way (Acts 17:27).

This is the reason why God enters our history, chooses Abraham, forms a people for himself, progressively reveals himself to them, and remotely prepares them to welcome someday the true descendants of Abraham, Christ the Savior and the Church. Abraham is the father and model of believers (Gal 3; Rom 4) because he promptly responds to the voice of God.

12:1-9 Chapters 12–13 are from the Yahwist tradition. We do not know how the true God made himself known to the heart of Abraham.

It is certain that the Israelite tradition, diligent in safeguarding the memory of the Patriarch, has preserved the knowledge that his ancestors were pagans (Jos 24:2) and that at a certain moment Abraham's family came to know the true God and abandoned the religion of their fathers (Jud 5:7-8).

12:9 *Negeb:* the desert region south of Palestine.

12:10-20 Having followed the Lord's lead, Abraham encounters a famine. The momentary temptation would be to return to his home, but Abraham respects God's command and takes refuge in another country. However, the Patriarch is human and concerned for his life. The expedient he chooses is not a lie because Sarai is in fact his half-sister (see Gen 20:12).

and all his belongings. Lot was with him.[b]
2 Abram was very rich, having many ani-
mals, silver, and gold.[c]
3 He then gradually made his way from
the Negeb to Bethel, up to the place where
he had previously encamped between
Bethel and Ai. 4 This was the place where
he had built an altar and called upon the
name of the LORD.[d]
5 Lot, who traveled with Abram, also had
many flocks and herds and tents. 6 The area
where they were was not rich enough for
them to dwell together, for they had too
many possessions for them to live in the
same camp. 7 Because of this a quarrel
arose between the herdsmen of Abram and
those of Lot. (At that time the Canaanites
and the Perizzites lived in that land.)
8 Abram said to Lot, "Let us not have
strife between you and me, between my
herdsmen and yours, for we are relatives.*
9 Does not the entire land lie before you?
You should separate from me. If you wish
to go to the left, I will go to the right; if you
wish to go to the right, I will go to the left."
10 Lot looked around and saw that the
Jordan Valley was fertile and there was
water everywhere. (This was before the
LORD destroyed Sodom and Gomorrah.)
It was as beautiful as the garden of the
LORD, like the land of Egypt, all the way
down to Zoar. 11 So Lot chose the Jordan
Valley for himself, and he moved his tents
to the east. Thus, they separated from
each other. 12 Abram dwelt in the land of
Canaan and Lot dwelt in the cities of the
valley and pitched his tents near Sodom.
13 The inhabitants of Sodom were per-
verse and committed many sins against
the LORD.[e]
14 The LORD spoke to Abram after Lot
had separated from him saying, "Lift up
your eyes from where you are and look
around to the north and south, to the east
and the west.[f] 15 Everything that you see I
will give to you and your descendants for-
ever.[g] 16 I will make your descendants like
the dust of the earth. If one could count all
of the dust of the earth, then that person
would be able to count all your descen-
dants.[h] 17 Rise and travel throughout the
land, for I will give it to you."
18 Abram moved his camp and dwelt
near the Oak of Mamre at Hebron. He built
an altar to the LORD there.[i]

CHAPTER 14

Lot's Captivity and Rescue.* 1 When Am-
raphel was king of Shinar, Arioch king of
Ellasar, Chedorlaomer king of Elam, and
Tidal king of Goiim, 2 there was a war be-
tween them and Bera, king of Sodom, Bir-
sha, king of Gomorrah, Shinab, king of
Admah, Shemeber, king of Zeboiim, and
the king of Bela (that is, Zoar). 3 All the lat-
ter kings gathered in the Valley of Siddim,
that is, the Dead Sea. 4 For twelve years
they were vassals of Chedorlaomer, but in
the thirteenth year they rebelled against
him.
5 In the fourteenth year Chedorlaomer
and the kings allied with him arrived and
defeated the Rephaim in Ashteroth-kar-
naim, the Zuzim in Ham, the Emim in
Shaveh-kiriathaim 6 and the Horites on
Mount Seir as far as El-paran, which bor-
ders the desert.[j] 7 They then changed direc-
tion and came to En-mishpat (that is,
Kedesh), and they plundered the land of the
Amalekites as well the Amorites who lived
in Hazazon-tamar.
8 The king of Sodom, the king of Gomor-
rah, the king of Admah, the king of Ze-
boiim, and the king of Bela, that is, Zoar,
went out to the Valley of Siddim and did
battle with them, 9 with Chedorlaomer, king
of Elam, Tidal, king of Goiim, Amraphel,
king of Shinar, and Arioch, king of Ellasar.
There were four kings against five. 10 Now
the Valley of Siddim was full of bitumen
pools. When the kings of Sodom and Go-
morrah fled, they fell into these pools. The
others fled into the mountains. 11 The four
kings took all the possessions and provi-
sions of Sodom and Gomorrah and left.
12 They also captured Lot, the son of the
brother of Abram, and all his possessions
(for he lived in Sodom).[k]
13 One of those who escaped captivity
came and reported this to Abram the He-
brew who was camped at the Oak of
Mamre the Amorite, the brother of Eshcol
and Aner, who were Abram's allies. 14 When
Abram heard that his relative had been

b Gen 12:9.—c Ps 112:1ff; Prov 10:22.—d Gen 12:8.—e Gen 18:20; Ezek 16:49f; 2 Pet 2:6ff; Jude 7.—f Gen 28:14.—g Gen 12:7; Mt 5:5; Lk 1:55; Acts 7:5; Gal 3:16.—h Gen 22:17; Num 23:10.—i Gen 14:13.—j Deut 2:12.—k Gen 13:10ff.

13:8 Lot is the son of Haran, Abraham's brother (Gen 11:27, 31); the degree of kinship does not prevent Abraham and Lot being called *brothers* in some translations.

14:1-16 Chapter 14, which is perhaps from a special source, locates the life of Abraham within the history of the ancient East.

taken prisoner, he organized the armed
men who had been born to his household.
There were three hundred and eighteen
of them. They gave chase as far as Dan.
15 He divided his forces and his servants,
and defeated them during the night, fol-
lowing them all the way to Hobah, to the
north of Damascus. 16 He recovered the
booty and also Lot, his relative, and his
possessions, as well as the women and the
other people.

Meeting with Melchizedek near Jerusalem.*
17 When Abram returned after defeating
Chedorlaomer and the kings who were
with him, the king of Sodom met him in
the Valley of Shaveh, that is, the Valley of
the King.
18 Melchizedek, the king of Salem,* of-
fered bread and wine. As a priest of God
Most High,[l] 19 he blessed Abram with
these words,

"Blessed be Abram by God Most High,
Creator of the heavens and the
earth.
20 And blessed be God Most High
who has delivered your enemy into
your hands."

Then Abram gave him a tithe of all he had
taken.
21 The king of Sodom said to Abram,
"Give me the people; you take the booty."
22 But Abram said to the king of Sodom,
"I have sworn to the LORD, God Most High,
Creator of the heavens and the earth,*
23 that I would not take anything for myself,
not even a thread or a sandal strap, lest you
be able to say, 'I have enriched Abram.' 24 I
want nothing for myself other than what my
servants have already eaten. As for the men
who have accompanied me, Eshcol, Aner,
and Mamre, they can take their own
shares."

CHAPTER 15

The Covenant Guarantee of the Promise.*
1 Some time later the LORD communi-
cated these words to Abram in a vision,

"Do not fear, Abram.
I am your shield;
your reward shall be very great."

2 Abram answered, "My Lord GOD,
what will you give me? I will pass away
without children and my heir will be
Eliezer of Damascus." 3 Abram continued,
"Behold, you have not given me descen-
dants, and my servant will be my heir."
4 Then the word of the LORD came unto
him, "He will not be your heir; your own
child will be your heir."[m] 5 Then he led
him outside and told him, "Look into the
heavens and count the stars, if you can
count them. Such," he continued, "will
your descendants be."[n]

l Ps 110:4; Heb 5:6, 10; 7:1.—m Gen 17:16.—n Gen 22:17; 28:14; Ex 32:13; Deut 1:10; Sir 44:21; Rom 4:18; Heb 11:21.

14:17-24 It is not impossible that Melchizedek, the Canaanite priest of the supreme god El had found faith in the true God (see Vatican II, *Lumen gentium*, no. 16). His offering of bread and wine was undoubtedly a sacrifice of thanksgiving (also known as a communion sacrifice), in which the gifts offered to the divinity were then divided among those present and consumed, to signify that human beings are called to table fellowship with God.

According to Hebrew exegetes, these two personages prefigure David, descendant of Abraham and distant successor of Melchizedek on the throne of Jerusalem. In blessing Abraham, Melchizedek was blessing David, the instrument of God's conquests, who after conquering Jerusalem made it the center of worship of the Lord (2 Sam 6). At the same time, in paying homage to Melchizedek, Abraham was paying homage to Jerusalem, the city that the Lord would choose as his own dwelling and that from that time forward would worship the true God. It is clear that these visions needed to be broadened. According to Ps 110:4, Melchizedek prefigures Christ, a descendant of David, because only in this new David will kingship and priesthood be united again as they were long ago in Melchizedek; moreover, Christ will have an everlasting priesthood, different from the hereditary priesthood that began with Aaron. The Letter to the Hebrews, chapter 7, will explain the message of the psalm, saying that, since tithes are paid to a superior, Abraham's action was one of homage to a priesthood higher than the Israelite temple priesthood. Behind the veil of the ancient priest-king we are therefore to discern the person of Christ, who in virtue of his own sacrifice that will be completed in Jerusalem is the true source of the blessing bestowed on Abraham, that is, his victory and liberation of prisoners (see a similar observation in 1 Cor 10:4) and all the victories of the people of God. For this reason the Christian tradition sees in Melchizedek's sacrifice of bread and wine (see the First Eucharistic Prayer of the Mass, the Roman Canon) a sign and prediction of the Eucharist, which is the thanksgiving for the redemption wrought by Christ and a pledge of victory for believers who remain in union with him.

14:18 *Salem,* according to the entire Jewish tradition, is none other than Jerusalem (Ps 76:3). This very old Canaanite city was already inhabited before 3000 B.C. and is explicitly mentioned in Egyptian texts beginning with the start of the 19th century B.C. *God Most High:* in Hebrew, *El-Elyon,* a compound name made up of two Phoenician-Canaanite names for the supreme divinity; the writer sees in Melchizedek a worshiper of the true God.

14:22 A form of solemn oath.

15:1-21 This chapter begins the contributions of the Elohist tradition, which frequently, as here, is fused with the Yahwist tradition. Twice, at different moments (vv. 1, 7), God reminds Abraham of his promises, but the latter complains privately to him that he has as yet received no fruit from them. At the divine confirmation Abraham renews his faith and the Lord acknowledges him as righteous. St. Paul will conclude from this that human beings attain to the life of grace not through works they have done but because they believe (Gal 3:5-9).

Using the image of a smoking flame, an habitual symbol of the power and mystery of God, the latter himself carries out the ancient rite of passing between the parts of the sacrificial victims. Abraham is not asked to join in this passage but is simply present to the vision; the reason for this is that the covenant is a completely free act of God.

6 Abraham believed the LORD, who
credited it to him as righteousness. *[o]
7 And he said, "I am the LORD who
brought you out of Ur of the Chaldeans to
take possession of this land." [p]
8 He answered, "O Lord GOD, how will I
know that I am to possess it?"
9 He said, "Take a three-year-old heifer, a
three-year-old she-goat, a three-year-old
ram, a turtledove, and a young pigeon." [q]
10 He took all these animals and split
them in two and placed each half opposite
the other (except for the birds). 11 Birds of
prey landed upon the carcasses, but
Abram chased them away.
12 As the sun was setting, a trance fell
upon Abram, and a fearful darkness de-
scended upon him. 13 The LORD said to
Abram, "Know that your descendants
shall be foreigners in a land that is not
their own. They shall be made slaves and
oppressed for four hundred years. [r] 14 But
I will execute my judgment upon the na-
tion that they will have served. They will
leave it with great riches. [s] 15 As for you,
you will go in peace to your fathers, and
you will be buried at a happy old age. 16 In
the fourth generation they will return
here, for the iniquity of the Amorites has
not yet come to full measure." [t]
17 When the sun set, it was dark, and a
smoking brazier and a flaming torch
passed between the carcasses of the ani-
mals that had been split in two. * 18 On that
day the LORD made a covenant with
Abram, "To your descendants I will give
this land, from the river of Egypt to the
great river, the Euphrates, [u] 19 [v] the dwelling
place of the Kenites, the Kenizzites, the
Kadmonites, 20 the Hittites, the Perizzites,
the Rephaim, 21 the Amorites, the Canaan-
ites, the Girgashites, and the Jebusites."

CHAPTER 16

Abram's Son Ishmael.* 1 Now Sarai, the
wife of Abram, did not have any chil-
dren. She had an Egyptian slave named
Hagar. [w] 2 Sarai said to Abram, "Behold,
the LORD has kept me from having chil-
dren; sleep with my slave. Maybe I can
have children through her."
Abram did what Sarai had told him to
do. [x] 3 Thus, ten years after Abram had
begun to live in the land of Canaan, Sarai,
the wife of Abram, took Hagar the Egyp-
tian, her slave, and gave her to Abram her
husband as a wife. 4 He slept with Hagar,
and she became pregnant.
But once she realized that she was preg-
nant, she no longer treated her mistress
with respect. [y] 5 [z] Therefore, Sarai said to
Abram, "May this affront fall upon you! I
gave you my maid to embrace, but when
she realized that she was pregnant, she
stopped treating me with respect. Let the
LORD judge between you and me."
6 Abram said to Sarai, "Behold, your
slave is in your hands. Do with her as you
see fit." Sarai then maltreated her so
much that Hagar ran away.
7 The angel of the LORD * found her
near a spring in the desert. The spring
was on the road to Shur. [a] 8 The angel said
to her, "Hagar, slave of Sarai, where have
you come from and where are you going?"
She answered, "I am running away from
my mistress Sarai."
9 The angel of the LORD said to her,
"Return to your mistress and be obedient
to her." 10 The angel of the LORD contin-
ued, "I will multiply the number of your
descendants so much that you will not be
able to count them." [b]

---

o 1 Mac 2:52; Ps 106:31; Rom 4:3, 9, 22; Gal 3:6f; Jas 2:23.—p Gen 11:31; 12:1; Ex 32:13; Neh 9:7f; Acts 7:2f.—q Lev 1:14.—r Ex 12:40; Num 20:15; Jud 5:9f; Isa 52:4; Acts 13:20; Gal 3:17.—s Ex 3:8, 21f.—t 1 Ki 21:26.—u Ex 32:13; Neh 9:8; Ps 105:9; Sir 44:21.—v 19f: Deut 7:1.—w Gen 11:30; Lk 1:7, 36; Gal 4:24f.—x Gen 21:8f; Gal 4:22.—y 1 Sam 1:6; Prov 30:23.—z 5-16: Gen 21:10-19.—a Ex 15:22.—b Gen 13:16; 17:20; 21:13, 18; 25:12-18.

15:6 *Righteousness* in its general sense means the attitude with which human beings submit to the plans of God so that God the Savior can fulfill in them his purpose of freeing them from sin and rendering them righteous. St. Paul (Rom 4; Gal 3:5-9) and St. James (Jas 2:20-23) will explain the value of Abraham's faith and righteousness: he becomes righteous in virtue of his faith, even before submitting to the ritual practice of circumcision (see Gen 17), which will be the outward sign of a faith that is to be lived interiorly. Faith, however, is not simply the acceptance of a theoretical truth; it is a principle of action that calls for a certain kind of behavior, without which the faith would be illusory and crippled (see Deut 6:25; 24:13; etc.).

15:17 This ancient covenant rite signified that the contracting parties called down on themselves the bloody fate of the animals if they violated the solemn commitment they had accepted (see Jer 34:18-20). The flame or lightning flashes express omnipotence; the smoke or darkness signifies the mystery of God that is inaccessible to the human gaze.

16:1-16 The passage is Yahwist with additions from the Priestly tradition. By personal choice Abraham is monogamous and ready to die without sons rather than show disrespect to his wife Sarai (see Gen 15:2-3).

He does, however, yield to Sarai's insistence that he follow an ancient practice that was acceptable in cases of barrenness and found a place in Mesopotamian codes of law.

16:7 *The angel of the LORD:* in these ancient stories this is a conventional way of signifying sensible manifestations of God himself, "the God of the Vision" (v. 13).

11 The angel of the LORD added,

“Behold, you are pregnant:
you will bear a son
and call him Ishmael,
for the LORD has listened to you in your distress.
12 He will be a wild donkey of a man;
his hand will be against all
and the hands of all will be against him.
He will be opposed to all of his brothers.” [c]

13 Hagar gave a name to the LORD who had spoken to her, “You are the God of the Vision.”* Therefore, she said, “Here I remained alive after having received this vision.” 14 Because of this, the well is called Beer-lahai-roi. It is between Kedesh and Bered. [d]

15 Hagar gave birth to Abram’s son. Abram named the son whom Hagar had borne Ishmael. [e] 16 Abram was eighty-six years old when Hagar gave birth to Ishmael.

CHAPTER 17

The Covenant and Its Sign.* 1 When Abram was ninety-nine years old, the LORD appeared to him and said, “I am God Almighty.* Walk before me and be blameless. [f] 2 I will establish my covenant between me and you and I will multiply you greatly.” [g]

3 Abram immediately fell down upon his face. God said to him, 4 “On my part, behold, my covenant with you: you will be the father of many nations. [h] 5 You will no longer be called Abram, but Abraham, for I will make you the father of many nations.* [i] 6 I will make you very, very fruitful. I will make nations come from you, and you shall give birth to kings. 7 I will establish my covenant with you for all generations. It will be an eternal covenant. I will be your God and the God of your descendants after you. [j] 8 I will give you and your descendants after you this land where you are now an alien. All of the land of Canaan shall be your eternal possession. I will be your God.” [k]

9 God said to Abraham, “On your part, you must observe my covenant, you and your descendants after you, for all time. 10 This is my covenant that you must observe, a covenant between me and your descendants after you: every male among you must be circumcised. [l] 11 You shall circumcise the flesh of the male member. This shall be the sign of the covenant between me and you. [m] 12 Whenever baby boys are eight days old, they will be circumcised, whether they are your own children or the children of those whom you bought and who are foreigners and not of your bloodline. [n] 13 You must circumcise those who are born in your house and those who are bought by you. Thus, my covenant will be marked in your flesh as an eternal covenant. 14 The male who is not circumcised, the one whose flesh of his member is not circumcised, is to be cut off from his people. He will have violated my covenant.”

c Gen 21:20; 25:18.—d Gen 24:62.—e Gen 16:2; Gal 4:22.—f Gen 35:11; Ex 6:3.—g Gen 12:2; 13:16; Ex 32:13.—h Gen 15:18; Sir 44:21; Rom 4:17.—i Neh 9:7.—j Ex 6:7; Lev 26:9; Ps 105:42; Lk 1:72f; Gal 3:16; Heb 13:20; Rev 21:7.—k Ex 6:4; 32:13; Deut 1:8; 14:2; Lk 1:55; Acts 7:5.—l Gen 21:4; Lev 12:3; Jos 3:5, 7; Jn 7:22; Acts 7:8; Rom 4:11.—m Sir 44:20.—n Lev 12:3; Lk 1:59; 2:21.

16:13 *The God of the Vision:* in Hebrew, *El-Roi.* Hagar was amazed that she remained alive after seeing God—in contrast to the ancient belief that a person died upon seeing God (see Gen 32:31; Ex 20:19; Deut 4:33; Jdg 13:22).

17:1-27 Chapter 17 is simply the Priestly version of the story that has been already told in chapter 15 (the covenant) and will be told in the first half of chapter 18 (the promise of Isaac). Along with the Priestly version of the promises the present chapter gives a more developed idea of the covenant. As will become clear from subsequent biblical revelation, God’s promises to human beings contain an unqualified and unmerited part and a conditional part; the absolute aspect is seen in the covenant with Abraham, the conditional part in the covenant at Sinai, which will involve bilateral commitments (Ex 19–24).

The point that is special to this chapter is the theme of circumcision as a constitutive sign of entrance into the covenant. This practice was widespread among various eastern peoples as an initiation into adulthood or marriage and was regarded as a sacrificial act. Since the reason for the existence of the people of Israel and therefore of their religion was to prepare for the future descendants who are the recipients of the promises (see 18:19), it is understandable that the people’s consecration to God should be celebrated with a sign that is connected with generation; thus it was appropriate for them to make this custom their own. But it is a sign that entails a mission. When Israel becomes content to practice the rite while forgetting its meaning, the Prophets will remind it of the demand for fidelity: the rite is valueless without the disposition of the heart (Jer 4:4; Ezek 44:7). Paul goes further and teaches that this external religious mark is now obsolete, for we are saved henceforth by Jesus Christ; in him we receive the baptism that brings us into the new covenant; circumcision was only a prefiguration of baptism (Gal 5:6; Phil 3:3; Col 2:11-12).

17:1 *God Almighty:* in Hebrew, *El-Shaddai,* an ancient divine name from the period of the patriarchs (see Ex 6:3), retained chiefly in the Priestly tradition. The literal meaning is probably “The God of the Mountain,” referring to the widespread idea that the dwelling of the divinity was on the high mountains. In the Septuagint *El-Shaddai* is usually translated by the Greek word, *pantokrator,* “ruler of all,” while the Latin translations preferred *omnipotens,* “almighty,” which seems less valid.

17:5 In the Semitic vision of things, when one person changes the name of another, the former is asserting power over the latter and guiding his destiny. Here “Abraham” is explained by assonance with *ab hamôn,* “father of a multitude,” or *ab rab hamôn,* “father of a great multitude.”

15 God also said to Abraham, "As for Sarai, your wife, she will no longer be called Sarai, but rather Sarah. 16 I will bless her and I will give you and her a son. I will bless her so that she shall become the mother of nations; kings of peoples shall descend from her." [o]

17 Abraham bowed down to the earth and laughed* when he thought, "Shall a man who is one hundred years old have a son? And Sarah, who is ninety years old, can she give birth?" [p] 18 Abraham said to God, "If only Ishmael might live in your presence!"

19 But God said, "No, but Sarah, your wife, shall bear you a son, and you shall name him Isaac. I will establish my covenant with him as an eternal covenant, that I will be his God and the God of his descendants after him. [q] 20 As for Ishmael, I have heard you. Behold, I will bless him and make him fruitful and very, very numerous. Twelve princes shall come from him and I will make him a great nation. [r] 21 But I will establish my covenant with Isaac. Sarah shall give birth to him by this time next year." [s] 22 God thus finished speaking to Abraham, and rising into the heavens, he left him.

23 Abraham therefore took Ishmael his son and all those born into his house and all those whom he had bought—all the males belonging to the household of Abraham—and he circumcised the flesh of their foreskins that same day, as the LORD had commanded him. 24 Abraham was ninety-nine years old when he had the flesh of his foreskin circumcised. [t] 25 Ishmael, his son, was thirteen years old when the flesh of his foreskin was circumcised. 26 Abraham and his son Ishmael were circumcised that same day. 27 And all the men of his household, those born in his house and those foreigners bought with money, were circumcised with him.

CHAPTER 18

God Becomes a Guest.* 1 The LORD appeared to Abraham at the Oak of Mamre while he was sitting at the entrance to his tent during the hottest part of the day. [u] 2 He looked up and saw three men standing nearby. As soon as he saw them, he ran to meet them from the entrance of his tent and bowed down to the ground, [v] 3 saying, "My lord, if I have found favor with you, please do not pass on without stopping to visit your servant. 4 Let some water be brought so that you may wash your feet. Make yourselves comfortable under this tree. 5 Let me go and prepare a bit of food that you may refresh yourselves. Afterward, you can go on your way. It is for this that you have come to visit your servant."

They answered, "Do as you have said."

6 So Abraham hurried into the tent and said to Sarah, "Quick, take three seahs* of fine flour, knead it, and make it into rolls."

7 He ran to the herd, took a choice calf, and gave it to his servant, who quickly prepared it. 8 He then took curds* and milk, as well as the veal that had been prepared, and he placed them before his guests. And he stood by them under the tree while they ate.

9 They then said, "Where is Sarah, your wife?" He answered, "She is in the tent." 10 The LORD* said, "I will return this way a year from now, and by that time Sarah, your wife, will have a son." Sarah was listening at the entrance to the tent, just behind him. [w] 11 Abraham and Sarah were old, advanced in years. Sarah no longer had her monthly periods. [x] 12 Sarah therefore laughed to herself and said, "After I am withered and my husband is old, will I now have this pleasure?"

13 But the LORD said to Abraham, "Why is Sarah laughing and saying, 'Can I really give birth now that I am so old?' 14 Is anything impossible to the LORD? I will return to you at the appointed time, one year from now, and Sarah will have a son." [y] 15 Sarah denied laughing, saying, "I did not laugh," because she was afraid. But he said, "Yes, you did laugh."

o Gen 18:10; Gal 4:23.—p Rom 4:19; Heb 11:11f.—q Gen 11:30; 21:2; Ex 32:13; Sir 44:22.—r Gen 21:13, 18; 25:12-16.—s Gen 18:14; 21:2; 26:2-5; Ex 34:10; Rom 9:7.—t Gen 17:10; Rom 4:11.—u Gen 12:7; Acts 7:2.—v 2 Ki 4:16; Rom 9:9; Heb 13:1f.—w Gen 17:19; 21:1.—x Gen 17:17; Rom 4:19; Heb 11:11f.—y Job 42:2; Isa 40:29; 50:2; 51:9; Jer 32:17, 27; Mt 19:26; Mk 10:27; Lk 1:37; 18:27; Rom 4:21.

17:17 *Abraham . . . laughed:* here, in the Priestly tradition, Abraham prostrates himself in adoration and laughs, not out of disbelief (since he is performing an act of worship) but out of amazement at such a paradoxical announcement: the whole idea is too much for him to dare hope for it, and he declares himself satisfied if Ishmael, his son, can inherit the divine promises.

18:1-15 Chapters 18–19 are from the Yahwist tradition and might be entitled "The meaning of the covenant." Three individuals appear before Abraham; he receives them with an act of homage. "He saw three but worshiped the One," said the Fathers of the Church, who saw here a prefiguration of the Trinity.

18:6 *Three seahs:* a dry measure that equaled about one ephah.

18:8 *Curds:* a kind of soft cheese.

18:10 *The LORD:* literally, "he."

The "Friend" of God.* 16 The men rose up
and went along to look down upon Sodom
from on high while Abraham accompa-
nied them to show them the way. 17 The
LORD said, "Should I keep hidden from
Abraham what I am about to do,[z] 18 for
Abraham shall become a great and power-
ful nation and all of the nations of the
earth shall be blessed through him?[a] 19 I
chose him so that he would instruct his
sons and his family after him to observe
the ways of the LORD and to act with jus-
tice and righteousness so that the LORD
might fulfill what he has promised to
Abraham."[b]
20 Therefore, the LORD said, "The cry
against Sodom and Gomorrah is too great
and their sin is very grave.[c] 21 I am going
to descend to see if they have really done
all the evil that has cried out to me. I want
to know this!"
22 While the two men departed and jour-
neyed toward Sodom, Abraham remained
standing before the LORD. 23 Abraham ap-
proached him and said to him, "Is it true
that you will destroy the just along with
the wicked? 24 What if there are fifty righ-
teous people in the city? Will you really de-
stroy it? Will you not spare it for the sake
of the fifty righteous people that you found
there?[d] 25 Far be it from you to make the
righteous die along with the wicked, so
that the righteous would have the same
fate as the wicked. Far be it from you! Is it
possible that the judge of the whole earth
does not practice justice?"[e] 26 The LORD
answered, "If I find fifty righteous people
living in the city of Sodom, for their sake I
will spare the city."
27 Abraham spoke again, "Look how I
dare to speak with my Lord, I who am dust
and ashes.[f] 28 What if there are five fewer
than fifty righteous people, will you destroy
the entire city because of those five?"
He answered, "I will not destroy it if I
find forty-five there."
29 Abraham spoke again and said, "What
if you find forty there?" He answered, "I
will not do it, for the sake of those forty."
30 And again he said, "Let my Lord not
grow impatient with me if I continue to
speak; what if thirty are found there?" He
answered, "I will not do it if I find thirty
there." 31 Once again he said, "Look how I
dare to talk to my Lord! What if you find
twenty there?" He said, "I will not destroy
it, for the sake of those twenty."
32 Yet again he said, "My Lord, do not
grow impatient if I speak still another time;
what if ten are found there?" He answered,
"I will not destroy it, for the sake of the
ten."[g] 33 When the LORD had finished
speaking with Abraham, he went on his
way, and Abraham returned to his tent.

CHAPTER 19

Revelation of God the Judge.* 1 The two an-
gels arrived in Sodom toward the evening.
Lot was seated at the gate to Sodom. As
soon as he saw them, Lot got up and went
over to them and bowed down to the
ground. 2 He said, "My lords, come to the
house of your servant. Pass the night, wash
your feet, and then, in the morning, you
can go on your way."
They answered, "No, we will spend the
night in the town square."[h]
3 But he insisted so much that they went
with him to his house. He prepared a ban-
quet for them, making unleavened bread,*
and they ate their meal. 4 [i] But before they
went to bed, the men of the city, the inhabi-
tants of Sodom, gathered around the
house, the young and the old, all of them
without exception. 5 They called out to Lot
and said, "Where are those men who are
staying with you tonight? Make them come
out to us so that we can know them!"*
6 Lot went out to them at the door and,
after closing the door behind himself,
7 said, "No, my brothers, do not do this evil
thing! 8 Listen, I have two daughters who
have not yet known a man; let me bring

z Gen 19:24; Job 1:16; Ps 107:34; Am 3:7.—a Gen 12:2; Lk 1:55; Gal 3:8.—b Gen 17:19.—c Gen 19:13; Isa 3:9; Lk 17:28; Jude 1, 7.—d Jer 5:1.—e Deut 32:4; Job 8:3, 20; 34:10; Wis 12:15.—f Sir 10:9; 17:27.—g Jer 5:1; Ezek 22:30.—h Wis 10:6; Sir 16:8; Ezek 16:50; Heb 13:1f.—i 4-9: Jdg 19:22-25; Jude 1, 7.

18:16-33 For the first time in the Bible God's justice is questioned; trusting in the Lord, Abraham begins to try to bend it. The sacred writer, like his contemporaries, is convinced that members of one and the same group have a joint responsibility as well as the same destiny, but he thinks that ten righteous persons can save an entire city. The prophets Jeremiah (Jer 5:1) and Ezekiel (Ezek 22:30) will claim that a single righteous person is enough. Abraham, however, does not feel able to push his request any further; perhaps there were no truly righteous persons in the city.

19:1-29 The story probably reflects memories of fires in naphtha deposits in this region and of earthquakes that caused collapses in the area south of the Dead Sea. It also draws on legends created by the popular imagination that had been struck by the desolate landscape there, with its sulfur-infected air and its odd blocks of salt in the shape of statues.

19:3 *Unleavened bread* could be prepared more quickly than bread that had to rise.

19:5 Homosexuality, which was widespread among the Canaanites, was sternly prohibited by the Mosaic Law (Lev 18:22, 24; 20:13, 23; Jdg 19:22).

them outside and you can do whatever
you want with them. Just do not do any-
thing to these men, for they have entered
under the shelter of my roof."
9 But they answered, "Move out of the
way. This one has come into our midst as
a foreigner and he would dare to judge us!
Now we are going to treat you even worse
than them." And they so violently pushed
against Lot that they almost broke open
the door.[j] 10 But the men inside reached
out and pulled Lot inside the house, clos-
ing the door. 11 They struck all of those
who were standing outside the door with
blindness so that none of them could find
the door.
12 The men then said to Lot, "Who else
do you have here? Your sons-in-law, your
sons, and your daughters, and anyone
that you have in the city, bring them out
of this place[k] 13 for we are ready to de-
stroy this place. The complaint raised
against them before the LORD is great,
and the LORD has sent us to destroy it."[l]
14 Lot left to speak to his sons-in-law,
the men who were to marry his daugh-
ters, and he said, "Get up, let us go from
this place, for the LORD is about to de-
stroy the city." But his sons-in-law
thought he was joking.[m]
15 As dawn was breaking, the angels
urged Lot on, saying, "Get up, take your
wife and the two daughters who are here
and leave before you are caught up in the
punishment of this city."
16 Lot hesitated, but the men took him
by the hand, along with his wife and his
two daughters. They showed him the
mercy of the LORD by bringing him out
and leading him out of the city. 17 After
they had led him out, one of them said,
"Flee for your life. Do not look back and
do not stop while you are still in the val-
ley. Flee to the mountains lest you be
swept away."[n]
18 But Lot replied, "No, my lord!
19 Look, your servant has found favor in
your sight, and now you have shown even
greater mercy to me by saving my life.
Yet, I will not be able to flee to the moun-
tains to keep the disaster from overtaking
me. I will die. 20 Look at this city ahead. It
is close enough for me to reach, and it is
so small! Let me flee there. It is such a
small place. That way my life will be
saved."
21 He answered, "Behold, I will grant
you even this, that I will not destroy the
city of which you have spoken. 22 Hurry,
flee there because I cannot do anything
until you have arrived." For this reason
the city is called Zoar.[o]
23 The sun was rising when Lot arrived
in Zoar. 24 The LORD then rained sulfur
and fire from the heavens upon Sodom
and Gomorrah.[p] 25 He destroyed these
cities and the entire valley and all the in-
habitants of the cities and even the plants
in the soil.[q] 26 But the wife of Lot looked
back, and she became a pillar of salt.[r]
27 Abraham went out early in the
morning to the place where he had been
with the LORD. 28 He looked down from
the height on Sodom and Gomorrah and
the entire extension of the valley, and he
saw smoke rising out of the earth, like the
smoke coming out of a furnace.[s]
29 Thus God, who destroyed the cities of
the valley, remembered Abraham and
had Lot flee from the disaster, while he
destroyed the cities in which Lot had been
living.
Degeneration of Lot's Children.* 30 Lot
then left Zoar and went to live in the
mountains together with his two daugh-
ters, for they were afraid to stay in Zoar.
He lived in a cave with his two daughters.
31 The older one said to the younger one,
"Our father is getting old and there is no
one in this territory to marry us as hap-
pens all over the earth. 32 Come, we will
give wine to our father and then lie with
him; thus we will provide descendants for
our father."
33 That night they gave wine to their
father, and the older sister laid with her
father. He did not realize what was hap-
pening, not even when she lay down or
when she got out of bed. 34 The next day
the older sister said to the younger, "Be-

j Gen 13:12; 2 Pet 2:7f.—k 2 Pet 2:7-9.—l Isa 1:7, 9; Zep 2:9; Lk 17:29.—m Ex 19:21; Num 16:21; Jer 5:12; Lk 17:28; Rev 18:4.—n Wis 10:6; Mt 24:16.—o Wis 10:6.—p Pss 9:7; 11:6; 107:34; Wis 10:7; Isa 1:9; 13:19; 30:33; Jer 49:18; Lam 4:6; Am 4:11; Mt 10:15; Lk 17:29; 2 Pet 2:6.—q Deut 29:22; Jer 50:40; Am 4:11.—r Wis 10:7; Lk 17:32.—s Rev 9:2; 14:10f.

19:30-38 Since it was regarded as a dishonor and a curse not to have children, the daughters, being without husbands, make up for their state by a primitive makeshift. It is in this way that the story explains the origin of the Moabites and Ammonites, neighbors and enemies of Israel, who are remembered as being the fruit of the cursed cities. The condemnation of incest is implicit in the story, not only because it was condemned by the laws of Mesopotamia and the conscience of the time but also because Lot is made drunk in order to prevent his resistance (see also Lev 18:7).

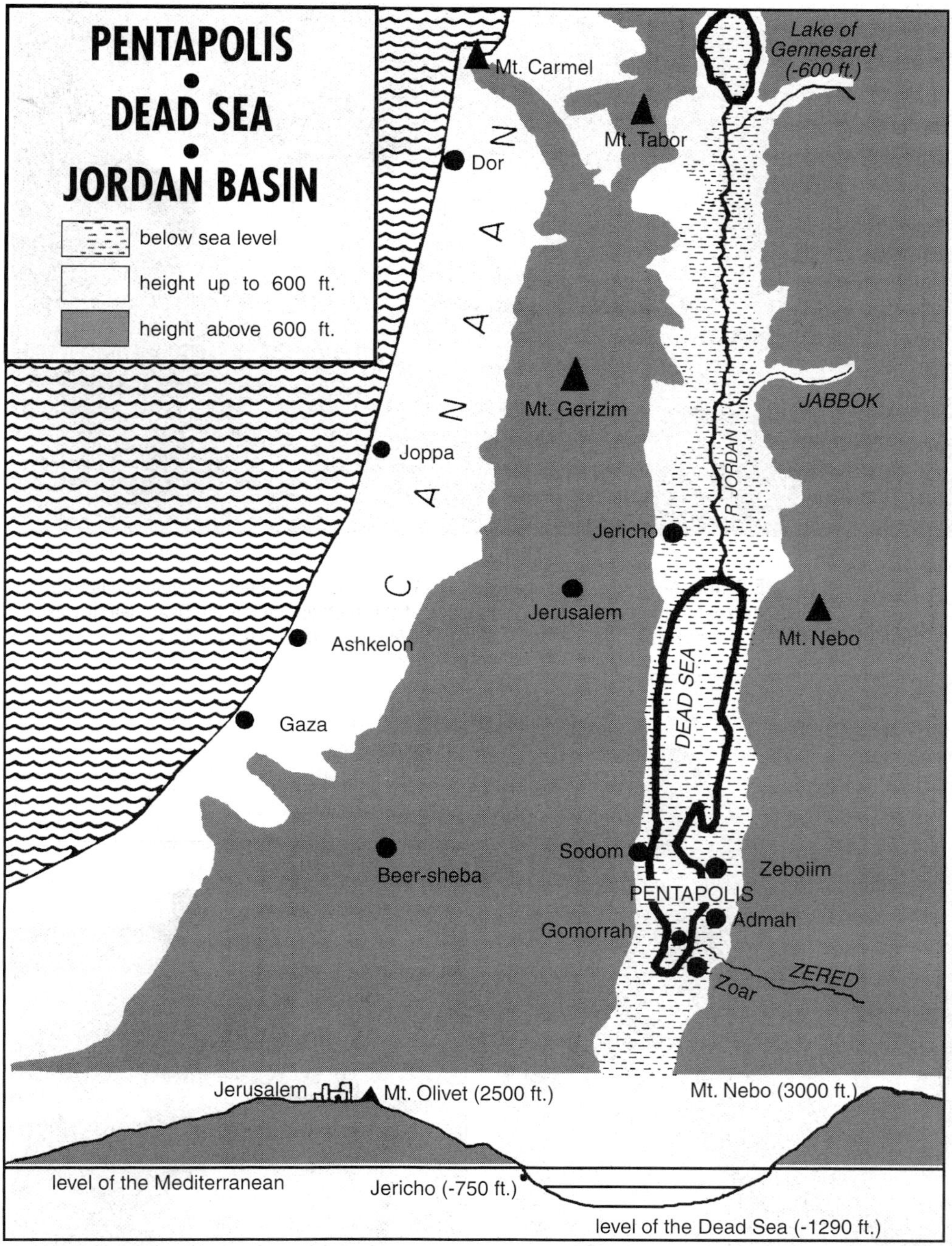

PENTAPOLIS — Five cities **(Sodom, Gomorrah, Zeboiim, Admah,** and **Zoar)** located on a fertile plain near the Dead Sea at the time of Abraham (ca 2000 B.C.). Lot and his family were captured by the kings of these cities and saved by Abraham who on his return was blessed by Melchizedek (Gen 14:12-24). The cities were punished for their sins by a cataclysmic destruction (Gen 19:24-29).

THE DEAD SEA — An inland lake 53 miles long and $2^3/_4$ to 10 miles wide fed by the Jordan. The lowest body of water on the earth's surface, 1290 feet below sea level, it is also called the "Valley of Siddim" (Gen 14:3), "Sea in the Arabah" (Deut 3:17), and "Eastern Sea" (Ezek 47:18).

Matson Photo Service

THE CITIES OF THE PLAIN — This is the probable site of the "Cities of the Plain": Sodom, Gomorrah, Admah, Zeboiim and Zoar. On the right are the salt slabs at the southern end of the Dead Sea. It was from the conquerors of these cities that Lot was delivered by Abraham. (See Gen 14:1-17.)

Matson Photo Service

COLOSSAL SALT SLABS — These colossal salt slabs are located in the cliffs of Jebel Usdum (the Hill of Sodom) at the southern end of the Dead Sea. It was probably here that the city of Sodom was situated before its destruction when Lot's wife was turned into a "pillar of salt." (See Gen 19:23-29.)

Matson Photo Service

THE WELL OF THE OATH — The importance of wells in some regions of Palestine made them more important than land and led to frequent disputes. This well in Beer-sheba is believed to be the "well of the oath" where Abraham made a pact with Abimelech, showing that in accord with ancient custom the well which he had dug was his property. (See Gen 21:27-32.)

hold, yesterday I slept with my father. Let
us make him drink wine tonight as well
and you can sleep with him. Thus, we will
provide descendants for our father."
35 That night as well they made their father
drink wine, and the younger sister slept
with him. He did not realize what had
happened, not even when she lay down or
when she got out of bed.

36 Thus, the two daughters of Lot con-
ceived children for their father. 37 The
older sister gave birth to a son whom she
called Moab, "from my father." He is the
forefather of the present-day Moabites.[t]
38 The younger sister also gave birth to a
son, and she called him Ben Ammi, "son
of my people." He is the forefather of the
present-day Ammonites.[u]

CHAPTER 20

God Corrects His Faithful Ones.* 1 Abra-
ham broke camp and traveled into the
Negeb, settling between Kedesh and Shur.
He was dwelling in Gerar. 2 Abraham had
said that Sarah, his wife, was his sister.
Therefore, Abimelech, king of Gerar, sent
to take Sarah for himself.

3 But God visited Abimelech during the
night in a dream and said to him, "Behold,
you are about to die because the woman
you have taken belongs to her husband."

4 Abimelech, who had not yet ap-
proached her, said, "My Lord, would you
destroy an innocent nation? 5 Did he not
tell me, 'She is my sister'? And did she not
also say, 'He is my brother'? I did this with
a pure conscience and in all innocence."

6 God answered him in the dream, "I
know that you acted with a good con-
science when you did this. I prevented you
from sinning against me. That is why I
kept you from touching her. 7 Now give the
woman back to this man. He is a prophet.
He will intercede for you, and you will live.
But if you do not restore her, know that
you and everyone with you will die."

8 Abimelech got up early in the morning
and summoned all his servants to whom
he recounted all these things. The men
were terrified. 9 Then Abimelech sum-
moned Abraham and told him, "What
have you done to us? What did I do to you
that you have subjected me and my king-
dom to such a great sin? You have done
things to me that you really should not
have done." 10 Then Abimelech asked
Abraham, "What were you afraid of that
you acted this way?"

11 Abraham answered, "I said to myself,
'Certainly there will be no fear of God* in
this place, and they will kill me because of
my wife.' 12 Besides, she is really my sister,
the daughter of my father, but not the
daughter of my mother; and she became
my wife.[v] 13 When God made me wander
from my father's homeland, I said to her,
'Please do me this favor. Wherever we go,
say that I am your brother.' "

14 Abimelech took flocks and herds,
male and female slaves, and he gave them
to Abraham, and he also gave back his
wife Sarah. 15 Furthermore, Abimelech
said, "Look around at my land; go and live
wherever you please!"

16 To Sarah he said, "Behold, I have
given two thousand shekels of silver to
your brother. May that repay you for what
has happened to you. Thus, your honor
will be totally preserved."

17 Abraham prayed to God and God
healed Abimelech, his wife, and his maid-
servants so that they could once more
have children. 18 For the LORD had ren-
dered all the women in the household of
Abimelech sterile because of Sarah, the
wife of Abraham.

CHAPTER 21

The Promised Son.* 1 The LORD visited
Sarah, as he had said he would. The LORD
fulfilled what he had promised to Sarah.[w]
2 Sarah conceived and bore a son to Abra-
ham in his old age at the very time that
the LORD had established.[x] 3 Abraham
named the son whom Sarah bore Isaac.[y]
4 Abraham circumcised his son Isaac when
he was eight days old, as God had com-

t Deut 2:9.—u Deut 2:19.—v Gen 12:13.—w Gen 17:19; 18:10; Gal 4:23; Heb 11:11.—x Gal 4:22; Heb 11:11.—y Mt 1:2; Lk 3:34.

20:1-18 This episode, the first that is surely from the Elohist tradition, seems to be another version of the incident already recorded in 12:10-20; among other reasons for saying this, it is not in its proper place, since it must have happened at an earlier time when Sarah was not yet expecting a son. The depiction of Sarah as Abraham's half-sister is a sign of the historical character of the story; the community of Israel would not have invented for the Patriarch a marriage that the Mosaic Law forbade as incestuous (Lev 18:9; 20:17).

20:11 *Fear of God:* a conventional phrase equivalent to "true religion." "Fear" in this phrase has the sense of reverential trust in God that includes commitment to his revealed will (word).

21:1-7 Isaac, who is born by the divine will even though nature is not up to the task, symbolizes the fact that salvation, which is foretold in his person, is not the work of human beings but entirely a gift of the Lord. The passage represents a fusion of the three sources.

manded him to do.[z] 5 Abraham was one
hundred years old when his son Isaac was
born.
6 Sarah said, "God has given me a rea-
son to laugh out loud. All will smile be-
cause of me."[a] 7 She then said, "Who
would have ever said to Abraham, 'Sarah
will nurse sons'? Yet I have borne him a
son in his old age."

Ishmael Is Sent Away.* 8 Isaac grew and
was weaned. On the day that he was
weaned, Abraham threw a great banquet.
9 But Sarah saw the son of Hagar the
Egyptian, the one whom she had borne to
Abraham, playing with* her son Isaac.
10 She said to Abraham, "Send this slave
and her son away, for the son of this slave
must not be an heir together with my son
Isaac."[b]
11 This greatly distressed Abraham for
he was concerned for his son. 12 But God
said to Abraham, "Do not let this matter
with your son and the slave woman dis-
tress you. Listen to what Sarah tells you.
Listen to her voice, for it is through Isaac
that descendants will bear your name.[c]
13 But I will also make the son of the slave
woman become a great nation, for he is
your son."
14 Abraham arose early in the morning
and gave Hagar bread and a skin of water,
placing them on her back. He entrusted
the child to her and sent her away. They
left and wandered in the desert of Beer-
sheba.
15 When they used up all the water in
the skin, she placed the child under a bush
16 and went and sat down opposite him,
about the distance of a bowshot. She said,
"I do not want to see the child die." She
sat opposite him and began to sob.
17 But God heard the voice of the child,
and the angel of God called upon Hagar
from the heavens and said, "What is the
matter, Hagar? Do not fear because God
has heard the voice of the child from
where he lies.[d] 18 Get up, take the child,
and hold him by the hand because I will
make a great nation of him."
19 God opened her eyes, and she was
able to see a spring of water. She went
over to it and filled the skin and gave the
child some water to drink.
20 God was with the child, and he grew
and lived in the desert and became an
archer. 21 He lived in the desert of Paran,
and his mother found him a wife in the
land of Egypt.

First Link with the Promised Land.* 22 At
that time, Abimelech along with Phicol,
the commander of his army, came and
said to Abraham, "God is with you in ev-
erything that you do. 23 Therefore, swear by
God that you will not act deceitfully with
me or with my sons or my descendants. As
I have been friendly to you, so too, you will
be friendly with me and with the land in
which you have dwelt as a guest."
24 Abraham answered, "I swear it."
25 But Abraham complained to Abim-
elech about a well that the servants of
Abimelech had seized. 26 Abimelech said,
"I do not know who did this thing. You
never told me about this and I did not hear
about it until today."
27 So Abraham took some sheep and cat-
tle and gave them to Abimelech, and the
two of them made a covenant. 28 Abraham
set apart seven fat lambs. 29 Abimelech
said to Abraham, "What is the meaning of
the seven lambs that you have set aside?"
30 He answered, "Please take these seven
lambs from me, and let them be a sign to
you that I dug this well." 31 Because of this
the place is called Beer-sheba (the well of
the seven), for they both swore an oath
there. 32 After the covenant had been con-
cluded at Beer-sheba, Abimelech and Phi-
col, the commander of his army, left and
returned to the land of the Philistines.
33 Abraham planted a tamarisk at Beer-
sheba, and there he called upon the name
of the LORD, the Eternal God.[e] 34 Abraham
dwelt in the land of the Philistines for
many years.

z Gen 17:10f; Acts 7:8.—a Gen 17:17.—b Jdg 11:2; Gal 4:30.—c Rom 9:7; Heb 11:18.—d Gen 16:7.—e Gen 4:26; Ex 15:18; Deut 32:40; 33:27; Job 36:26; Pss 10:16; 45:7; 90:2; 93:2; 103:19; 146:10; Isa 40:28; Jer 10:10; Hab 1:12; 3:6; Heb 13:8.

21:8-21 The two stories that follow are from the Elohist tradition. According to a number of critics, the first story is another version of the Yahwist-Priestly story in 16:4-16. It is to be noted, among other things, that Ishmael is here shown as a boy, while at the period here indicated he would have been an adolescent.

St. Paul uses the incident as an argument that the new Covenant replaces the old (Gal 4:21-31).

21:9 *Playing with:* this can also be translated as mocking. According to the later Jewish tradition, the word here refers to immoral or idolatrous practices on the part of Ishmael ("mocking" in the sense of Gen 39:14, 17); St. Paul, however, interprets it as meaning persecution (Gal 4:29), perhaps resulting from envy.

21:22-34 Two popular traditions are fused to explain the name "Beer-sheba": one explains it as meaning "well of the oath," the other as "well of the seven," that is, the seven lambs that the Patriarch gives the master of the territory as a guarantee of the agreement between them.

CHAPTER 22

Sacrifice of the Son.* 1 Some time later God tested Abraham. He said to him, "Abraham, Abraham!" He replied, "Here I am!"[f]

2 God said, "Take your son, your only son, the one you love, Isaac, and go to the land of Moriah * and offer him as a burnt offering on the mountain that I will show you."[g]

3 Abraham rose early in the morning, saddled a donkey, and took two servants and his son Isaac with him. He also took the wood for the burnt offering and set out toward the place about which God had spoken. 4 On the third day, Abraham looked up and saw that place from a distance. 5 Abraham said to his servants, "Stay here with the donkey. I and the boy will go over there. We will worship and then we will return to you." 6 Abraham took the wood for the burnt offering and loaded it upon his son Isaac. He himself carried the fire and the knife. They then set out together. 7 Isaac turned to his father Abraham and said, "My father!"

He answered, "Here I am, my son."

He continued, "Here are the fire and the wood, but where is the lamb for the burnt offering?"

8 Abraham answered, "God himself will provide the lamb for the burnt offering, my son!" And the two of them went on together.

9 They then arrived at the place of which God had spoken. There Abraham built an altar and piled up the wood. He tied up his son Isaac and placed him upon the altar so that he was lying upon the wood.[h] 10 Then Abraham reached out and took the knife to kill his son.[i] 11 But the angel of the LORD called out from heaven and said, "Abraham! Abraham!"

He answered, "Here I am."

12 The angel said, "Do not reach out your hand against the boy! Do not harm him in any way! Now I know that you fear God and you have not even withheld your son, your only son, from me."[j]

13 Abraham looked up and saw a ram that had its horns caught in a bush. Abraham took the ram and offered it as a burnt offering instead of his son.

14 Abraham called that place, "The LORD will provide," for he said, "On the mountain the LORD provided."

15 The angel of the LORD called Abraham from heaven again 16 [k] and said, "I swear by my own self, thus says the LORD: because you have done this and did not withhold your son from me, your only son, 17 I will bless you with every blessing and I will make your descendants very numerous, like the stars of the heavens or the sand on the shore of the sea. Your descendants shall take possession of the cities of your enemies.[l] 18 All the nations of the earth shall be blessed through your descendants, because you have obeyed my command."[m]

19 Abraham returned to his servants, and together they set out toward Beer-sheba, where Abraham made his dwelling.

Children of Abraham's Brother.* 20 Afterward, Abraham received this news: "Behold, Milcah has borne sons to your brother Nahor: 21 Uz the firstborn, Buz his brother, Kemuel (the father of Aram), 22 Chesed, Hazo, Pildash, Jidlaph, and Bethuel." 23 Bethuel became the father of Rebekah. Milcah gave birth to these eight sons for Nahor, the brother of Abraham. 24 His concubine, Reumah, also bore Tebah, Gaham, Tahash, and Maacah.

---

f Sir 44:20.—g 2 Chr 3:1; 1 Mac 2:52; Heb 11:17; 1 Jn 4:9.—h Jas 2:21.—i Wis 10:5.—j Jn 3:16; Rom 8:32; 1 Jn 4:9.—k 16f: Gen 15:5; Ex 32:13; Am 6:8; Lk 1:73; Rom 4:13; Heb 6:13f; 11:12.—l Gen 24:60; Hos 2:1.—m Gen 12:3; 18:18; 26:4; Ps 105:8-9; Sir 44:21; Acts 3:25; Gal 3:16.

22:1-24 This story is likewise from the Elohist tradition. After successes there is an unexpected new test. Trusting in God's word, Abraham has left everything, reached the land promised to his descendants, and waited patiently for the birth of a son. His sole treasure to this point has been his faith; it is only because of this that God has blessed him. Now he receives the order to sacrifice his very faith and hope, but he does not allow these to waver. The inexplicable thing is not that God should ask him to sacrifice a son, even though this is a harsh blow to his fatherly heart; for the religious outlook of that country allowed this deplorable form of worship (Jdg 11:30-39; 2 Ki 3:27; 16:3; 21:6). The apparent absurdity is that he must sacrifice the very thing for which he heretofore lived, the son for whose sake God had asked him to sacrifice every other good.

God himself has supplied the victim for the sacrifice. The ram given to Abraham was only a temporary victim. Another Father really sacrificed his own Son for the sake of humankind (Rom 8:32), perhaps on the very same mountain (2 Chr 3:1); then he won him back in the resurrection. It is only in virtue of this divine sacrifice, rather than of the faith of Abraham, that the Lord can give the Patriarch his great promises.

The conclusion of the incident prepares the way for a firm condemnation of the Canaanite practice of sacrificing children (see Deut 12:29-31; 18:10-12; Jer 7:31-33; 19:1-13). Above all, however, it exemplifies the result of every true sacrifice: God restores to his faithful, as the fruit of their faith, the freely given gift that they had surrendered in order to show that the Lord came first for them.

22:2 *Moriah* is also the mountain on which the Temple of Jerusalem will be built (2 Chr 3:1).

22:20-24 The passage is Yahwist. This genealogy is in continuity with Gen 11:29 and introduces the events that follow.

CHAPTER 23

Tomb of the Patriarch.* 1 Sarah lived to be
one hundred and twenty-seven years old.
2 She died at Kiriath-arba, that is Hebron,
in the land of Canaan. Abraham went in to
mourn for Sarah and he wept for her.
3 Abraham then left the body of his
loved one and said to the Hittites, 4 "I am a
foreigner and I sojourn among you. Sell
me a piece of land here for a grave. In that
way I can carry the body there and bury
it."[n]
5 The Hittites answered, 6 "Hear us, my
lord. You are a prince of God living in our
midst. Bury your dead one in the best of
our tombs. No one among us will prevent
you from burying your dead in your
tomb."
7 Then Abraham got up and bowed
down before the people of the land, the
Hittites, 8 and said to them, "If it is your
will that I take my deceased and bury her,
listen to me and convince Ephron, the son
of Zohar, 9 to give me the cave of Mach-
pelah, which is found at the edge of his
field. Let him sell it to me at its full price
so that it may be my burial place in your
land."
10 Now Ephron was seated among the
Hittites. Ephron the Hittite answered
Abraham in the hearing of the Hittites at
the entrance to the gate of the city. He
said, 11 "Hear me, my lord. I will give you
the field along with the cave. In the pres-
ence of the sons of my people, I give it to
you. Bury your dead."
12 Abraham bowed down to him before
the people of the land. 13 He spoke to
Ephron in the hearing of the people of the
land and said, "If only you would please
listen to me, I will pay you for the price of
the field. Accept it from me, so that I may
bury my dead there."
14 Ephron said to Abraham, 15 "Hear
me, my lord. A field with a value of four
hundred silver shekels,* what is that be-
tween me and you? Bury your dead there."
16 Abraham accepted Ephron's terms.
He paid Ephron the price that had been
mentioned in the hearing of the Hittites,
namely, four hundred silver shekels of the
current market weight.[o]
17 [p] The field of Ephron was at Mach-
pelah facing Mamre. The field and the
cave found there and all the trees in the
field and within the boundaries of the
field, 18 all these became the property of
Abraham in the presence of the Hittites at
the entrance to the gate of the city. 19 After-
ward, Abraham buried Sarah, his wife, in
the cave of the field of Machpelah facing
Mamre (that is Hebron), in the land of
Canaan. 20 The field and the cave passed
from the Hittites to Abraham as his burial
plot.

CHAPTER 24

The Marriage of Isaac.* 1 Abraham was
now old, well advanced in years, and the
LORD had blessed him in everything.
2 [q] Abraham said to his servant, the oldest
of his household, who supervised his prop-
erty, "Place your hand under my thigh*
3 and swear to the LORD, the God of heaven
and the God of the earth, that you will not
get a wife for my son from the daughters
of the Canaanites among whom we live.[r]
4 Rather, go to my homeland, to my family,
and choose a wife for my son Isaac."
5 The servant asked him, "If the woman
does not wish to follow me to this land,
should I take your son back to the land
from which you came?"
6 Abraham answered him, "Never take
my son back there! 7 The LORD, the God of
heaven and the God of the earth, who
called me out from the house of my father
and the land of my birth, spoke to me and
promised, 'To your descendants I will give
this land.' He himself will send an angel
before you so that you can find a wife for
my son.[s] 8 If the woman does not wish to
follow you, you will be absolved of the oath
you have made to me. Only, you must not
take my son back there." 9 The servant
placed his hand under the thigh of Abra-

n Gen 33:19; Ex 2:22; Lev 25:23; Pss 39:13; 105:12; 119:19; Acts 7:16; Heb 11:9.—o 2 Sam 24:24; Jer 32:9; Acts 7:16.—p 17f: Gen 49:29f.—q 2f: Gen 47:29.—r Gen 24:37; 28:1f; Jdg 14:3; Tob 4:12; 2 Cor 6:14-17.—s Gen 12:7; Ex 6:8; Tob 5:17; Rom 4:13; Gal 3:16.

23:1-20 This lively and picturesque passage is from the Priestly tradition.

23:15 *Four hundred silver shekels* are equivalent to about 5 kilograms of silver.

24:1-67 This Yahwist story is important for the People of God. It is not a good thing for the recipient of the promises to marry a Canaanite woman; since during the early years children are in the care of their mother, such a woman's ties to a corrupt people would do harm to God's work. A young woman from the man's own stock is much preferable.

24:2 *Under my thigh:* a euphemism for touching the genitals; to do this is to ask God, the author of life, to be witness to the oath.

ham, his master, and he swore an oath to
him concerning these things.
10 The servant took ten of his master's
camels along with all kinds of different
precious objects and he set out and went
to Aram-naharaim,* to the city of Nahor.
11 He rested the camels outside of the city,
near the well, at evening time when the
women would go out to draw water.
12 He said, "O LORD, God of my master
Abraham, grant me success today and be
gracious to my master Abraham! 13 Be-
hold, I am in front of the well and the
young women of the town are coming out
to draw water. 14 That young woman to
whom I say, 'Lower your jug and let me
drink,' and she responds, 'Drink, and I will
give your camels some water too,' let her
be the one you have chosen for Isaac, your
servant. By this I will know that you have
acted kindly to my master."
15 He barely finished speaking when Re-
bekah, who was the daughter of Bethuel,
the son of Milcah, who was the wife of
Abraham's brother Nahor, came out
with a jug on her shoulder.[t] 16 The young
woman was very pretty and a virgin,
never having slept with a man. She went
down to the well and filled her jug and
came back up.
17 The servant hurried up to her and
said, "Please give me some of the water
from your jug."
18 She answered, "Drink, my lord," and
quickly lowered the jug unto her hand and
gave him some water to drink.
19 When she had finished letting him
drink, she said, "I will draw water for your
camels as well, until they have finished
drinking." 20 She quickly emptied her jug
in the water trough and ran off to draw
more water from the well until all the
camels had drunk from it. 21 The man
watched in silence to see whether or not
the LORD would grant success to this
quest.
22 When the camels had finished drink-
ing, he took a gold ring weighing half a
shekel and fastened it to her nose, and he
placed upon her wrists two golden
bracelets that weighed ten shekels. 23 Then
he said, "Whose daughter are you? Tell
me. Do you have room in your house for
us to pass the night?"
24 She answered, "I am the daughter of
Bethuel, the son whom Milcah bore to
Nahor." 25 She added, "We have plenty of
hay and forage and also a place where you
can sleep tonight."
26 The man knelt and bowed down to
the LORD 27 and said, "Blessed be the
LORD, God of my master Abraham, who
has not ceased being generous and faithful
to my master. As for me, the LORD has
guided me along the way to the house of
the brother of my master."
28 The young woman ran and reported
all these things to her mother's household.
29 Now Rebekah had a brother named
Laban, and Laban rushed out to the man
at the well.[u] 30 In fact, as soon as he saw
the nose ring and the bracelets on the
wrists of his sister and heard what Re-
bekah, his sister, said, "This is what that
man told me," he went to the man who
was still standing alongside the camels at
the well. 31 He said, "Come, blessed one of
the LORD! Why are you still standing out
here when I have already prepared the
house for you and a place for your
camels?"
32 The man went into the house while
his camels were unloaded and given hay
and forage. Water was brought to wash his
feet and those of his men. 33 Then food
was placed in front of him, but he said, "I
will not eat until I have said what I must
say."
They answered, "Of course!"
34 He said, "I am the servant of Abra-
ham. 35 The LORD has greatly blessed my
master, and he has become powerful. He
has given him flocks and herds, silver and
gold, male and female slaves, camels and
donkeys. 36 Sarah, the wife of my master,
gave birth to a son when he was already
old, and he has given all his possessions to
him. 37 My master has made me swear an
oath. He said, 'You must not take a wife
for my son from among the daughters of
the Canaanites among whom we live.
38 You must go to the house of my father,
to my kin, to take a wife for my son.' 39 I
said to my master, 'What if the woman
will not follow me?'
40 "He answered, 'The LORD, in whose
presence I walk, will send an angel with
you and will assure the success of your

t Gen 22:23.—u Gen 27:43.

24:10 *Aram-naharaim:* "Land of the Two Rivers" (i.e., upper Mesopotamia), where Haran, residence of Abraham's relatives, was located (Gen 11:31).

journey. In this way, you will be able to
take a wife for my son from my kin and
the house of my father.[v] 41 By going to my
kin you will have fulfilled your oath. If they
do not give her to you, you will have ful-
filled your oath.'
42 "And so today I arrived at the well and
said, 'LORD, God of my master Abraham, if
you are going to grant success to this jour-
ney I am making, 43 since I am standing
near the well, grant that when a young
woman comes out to draw water and to
whom I say, "Give me a little water from
your jar to drink," 44 and she answers,
"Drink some, and I will draw water for
your camels," this will be the wife that the
LORD has chosen for the son of my master.'
45 "I had not even finished thinking this
when Rebekah came out with a jug on her
shoulder. She went to the well and drew
water. When I said to her, 'Please give me
some to drink,' 46 she immediately lowered
the jug and said, 'Drink, and I will give
your camels water to drink as well.' I drank
and she even gave my camels water to
drink.
47 "I asked her, 'Whose daughter are
you?'
"She answered, 'I am the daughter of
Bethuel, the son of Milcah who bore a son
to Nahor.'
"I put the ring on her nose and the
bracelets on her wrists. 48 Then I knelt and
bowed down to the LORD and blessed the
LORD, the God of my master Abraham,
who had guided me along the right path to
find the daughter of the brother of my
master to be the wife of my master's son.
49 Now, if you intend to act kindly and loy-
ally toward my master, let me know. If not,
let me know as well, so that I may search
elsewhere."
50 Laban and Bethuel then answered,
"This is from the LORD; there is nothing we
can say.[w] 51 Here is Rebekah; take her and
go so that she may be the wife of the son of
your master, just as the LORD has in-
structed you."
52 When the servant of Abraham heard
these words, he fell down to the earth be-
fore the LORD. 53 The servant then brought
out silver and gold ornaments and articles
of clothing and gave them to Rebekah. He
gave precious gifts to her brother and
mother as well. 54 He and his men then ate
and drank and slept the night. When he
rose in the morning, he said, "Let me go to
my master."[x]
55 But the brother and mother said, "Let
the girl remain with us for a little time, ten
days or so, and afterward you can go on
your way."
56 He answered them, "Do not delay me,
now that the LORD has granted success to
my journey. Let me leave and go to my
master."
57 They therefore said, "Let us call the girl
and ask her." 58 So they called Rebekah and
said to her, "Do you wish to leave with this
man?"
She answered, "I do."
59 They therefore allowed Rebekah and
her nurse to leave with Abraham's servant
and his men. 60 They blessed Rebekah and
told her,

"May you, our sister,
become thousands upon thousands,
and may your descendants conquer
the gates of their enemies."[y]

61 Thus, Rebekah and her nurse got up,
mounted their camels, and followed the ser-
vant. He took Rebekah with him and left.
62 Meanwhile Isaac was returning from
the well of Beer-lahai-roi and was dwelling
in the territory of the Negeb.[z] 63 Isaac went
out toward evening. He was looking out
over the countryside when he saw camels
arriving. 64 Rebekah also looked up and saw
Isaac, and she got down off her camel.
65 She said to the servant, "Who is that man
who is coming through the fields toward
us?"
The servant answered, "It is my master."
She took her veil* and covered herself.
66 The servant told Isaac everything that
had happened. 67 Isaac then brought Re-
bekah into the tent that had been his
mother's. He married Rebekah and loved
her. So Isaac found comfort after the death
of his mother.

CHAPTER 25

Other Children of Abraham.* 1 [a] Abraham
took another wife named Keturah. 2 She

v Tob 5:17; 10:13.—w Tob 7:12; Ps 118:23.—x Tob 7:14; 8:20.—y Gen 22:17; Ps 127:5.—z Gen 16:13f; 25:11.—a 1-4: 1 Chr 1:32f.

24:65 *She took her veil:* a betrothed woman did not remove her veil until the wedding night (see Gen 29:23-25).

25:1-6 The description shows that the other peoples are not without ties to the patriarch Abraham. In the future, the Midianites and the Sabeans will be named as representatives of pagans who convert (Ps 72:10; Isa 60:6).

gave birth to Zimran, Jokshan, Medan,
Midian, Ishbak, and Shuah. 3 Jokshan was
the father of Sheba and Dedan. Dedan
was the father of the Asshurim, Le-
tushim, and Leummim.[b] 4 The sons of
Midian were Ephah, Epher, Hanoch,
Abida, and Eldaah. All of these were the
sons of Keturah.

5 Abraham gave all his possessions to
Isaac. 6 As for the sons of the concubines
whom Abraham had, he gave them gifts
and, while he was still alive, sent them far
away from his son Isaac eastward, to live
in the east country.

Death of Abraham.* 7 Abraham lived for
one hundred and seventy-five years. 8 Then
Abraham breathed his last and died at a
good old age after a full life; and he was re-
united with his ancestors. 9 His sons Isaac
and Ishmael buried him in the cave of
Machpelah in the field of Ephron, the son
of Zohar the Hittite, near Mamre.[c] 10 This
was the field that he had bought from the
Hittites. There Abraham was buried near
his wife Sarah. 11 After the death of Abra-
ham, God blessed his son Isaac, and Isaac
lived near the Beer-lahai-roi.

Descendants and Death of Ishmael.*
12 These are the descendants of Ishmael,
the son of Abraham, whose mother was
Hagar the Egyptian, Sarah's slave.

13 [d] These are the names of the sons of
Ishmael in order of birth. The firstborn of
Ishmael was Nebaioth. He then had Kedar,
Adbeel, Mibsam,[e] 14 Mishma, Dumah,
Massa, 15 Hadad, Tema, Jetur, Naphish,
and Kedemah. 16 These are the Ishmaelites
and these are their names by their towns
and their camps. They were twelve
princes, each a prince of his own tribe.[f]
17 Ishmael lived for one hundred and seven
years. He then died and was reunited with
his ancestors. 18 They lived between Havi-
lah and Shur (which lies on the side of the
border of Egypt in the direction of Asshur),
and each of them held his own * against all
his kin.[g]

B: Jacob, the Sinner Who Redeems Himself*

Isaac's Two Sons.* 19 These are the de-
scendants of Isaac, the son of Abraham.

Abraham was the father of Isaac.
20 Isaac was forty years old when he mar-
ried Rebekah, the daughter of Bethuel the
Aramean of Paddan-aram and the sister
of Laban the Aramean.[h]

21 Isaac prayed to the LORD for his wife,
since she was barren. The LORD heard
him, and thus his wife became pregnant.
22 The sons fought with each other in the
womb, and she exclaimed, "If this is so,
why go on living?" She went to consult the
LORD. 23 The LORD answered her,

"Two nations are in your womb,
  and two peoples born of you shall be divided.
One shall be stronger than the other,
  and the older shall serve the younger."[i]

24 When the time came for her to give
birth, there were twins in her womb.[j]
25 The firstborn was red and totally cov-
ered with hair. So he was named Esau.
26 Immediately afterward, his brother was
born, holding on to the heel of Esau. So he
was named Jacob. Isaac was sixty years old
when they were born.[k]

27 The children grew up, and Esau be-
came an expert hunter, a man who lived in

b Isa 21:13.—c Gen 23:3-20.—d 13-16: 1 Chr 1:29ff.—e Isa 60:7.—f Gen 17:20.—g Gen 16:12.—h Gen 24:66.—i Gen 27:29; Num 24:18; Mal 1:2-5; Rom 9:11f.—j Hos 12:3; Lk 1:57; 2:6.—k Mt 1:2.

25:7-11 This short account is from the Priestly tradition.

25:12-18 This summary in the Priestly style is an appendix that completes the story of Abraham; from this moment on, the line of Ishmael disappears from the biblical history. According to God's promises, the descendants of Hagar are numerous and scattered. The names of the sons of Ishmael are the names of twelve nomadic tribes of northern Arabia; they show a demographic strength equal to that of the twelve tribes of Israel, for in this area they are heirs of the same blessing.

25:18 *Held his own:* this may also be translated "in opposition to," thus showing the fulfillment of the prediction found in Gen 16:12.

25:19—36:43 In the structure of Genesis the story of Isaac is absorbed into the more distinctive stories of his father Abraham and his son Jacob. The only free-standing section is chapter 26, which has for its subject the handing on to Isaac of the divine promises and blessings. We hear in the chapter an echo of the religious spirit of Abraham (25:21; 26:25; 28:1-4), and we observe also Isaac's weakness in preferring one son to the other (25:28). On the whole, the information given in Genesis is too sparse to give us a knowledge of Isaac's personality.

Jacob, the immediate founder of the twelve tribes of Israel, will be the outward sign of their unity. In his story, there are, first, two distinct cycles concerning his years as a young man: a Palestinian cycle involving Jacob and Esau (25:19-34; then chs. 27–28; later, 30–31) and a Mesopotamian cycle involving Jacob and Laban, which is inserted into the former. These are followed by the story of Jacob and his sons (from ch. 34 to the end of the Book), with an insert on the posterity of Esau (ch. 36). But within this third cycle the figure of Joseph occupies a predominant place; the events involving him form a story apart (chs. 37, 39–47), although at the end his story and that of the family merge.

25:19-34 The Lord, faithful to his word, grants Rebekah, who like Sarah is barren, the gift of motherhood. Twins are born and God prefers the younger and makes him the heir of the promise (see Mal 1:2-3; Rom 9:10-16). The point here is not personal salvation but a mission to be carried out in this life for the formation of God's people. The free choices of the Lord do not mean any injustice toward those who are not called.

the open country.[l] Jacob, on the other
hand, was a quiet man, who stayed among
the tents. 28 Isaac loved Esau, for he enjoyed
the taste of wild game, while Rebekah loved
Jacob.
29 One day Jacob cooked a lentil stew.
Esau came in from the countryside and he
was exhausted. 30 He said to Jacob, "Let me
eat a little of that red soup, for I am fam-
ished." (This is why he was also called
Edom. *)
31 Jacob said, "First sell me your rights as
firstborn."[m]
32 Esau answered, "I am about to die;
what good will my rights as firstborn be?"
33 Jacob told him, "Swear it right now." He
swore an oath and sold his rights as first-
born to Jacob.[n]
34 Then Jacob gave Esau some bread and
some lentil soup. He ate and drank. Then
he got up and left. This is how Esau de-
spised his birthright.

CHAPTER 26

Isaac Inherits the Blessing. 1 *[o] A second
famine came upon the land (after the first
famine in the days of Abraham). Isaac trav-
eled to Gerar to Abimelech, the king of the
Philistines.[p] 2 The LORD appeared to him
and said, "Do not go down into Egypt; live
in the land to which I will direct you. 3 Re-
main in that land for a while and I will be
with you and bless you. I will give all these
lands to you and your descendants and ful-
fill the promise I made to Abraham your
father.[q] 4 I will make your descendants as
numerous as the stars of the heavens and I
will give them all these lands. All the na-
tions on the earth will be blessed through
your descendants,[r] 5 for Abraham listened
to my voice and observed that which I
ordered: my commandments, my ordi-
nances and my laws." 6 Isaac thus dwelt in
Gerar.
7 The men of that place asked him about
his wife, and he said, "She is my sister," for
he was afraid to say, "She is my wife,"
thinking that the men of that place would
kill him because Rebekah was very beauti-
ful.
8 He had been there for quite some time
when Abimelech, the king of the Philis-
tines, came to the window and saw Isaac
caressing his wife Rebekah. 9 Abimelech
called to Isaac and said, "Surely, she is your
wife. Why did you say, 'She is my sister'?"
Isaac answered him, "Because I thought
I might be killed on her account!"
10 Abimelech continued, "What have you
done to us? It would have been easy for one
of the people to lie with your wife and that
would have brought sin upon us."
11 Hence, Abimelech gave this order to all
the people, "Whoever touches this man or
his wife will be put to death!"
12 Isaac planted a crop in a land and that
year he reaped a hundredfold. The LORD
had thus blessed him. 13 [s] He became im-
portant and continued to prosper until he
was very rich. 14 He possessed great flocks
and herds and slaves, and the Philistines
began to become jealous of him.

The Dispute over Wells. 15 [t] The Philistines
stopped up and filled in with dirt all the
wells that the servants of his father had dug
in the days of his father Abraham.
16 Abimelech said to Isaac, "Leave us, for
you are much mightier than we are."
17 Isaac went away from there, and
camped in the Valley of Gerar and dwelt
there. 18 Isaac returned to dig wells that the
servants of his father Abraham had dug
and that the Philistines had stopped up
after the death of Abraham. He gave them
the same names as his father had given
them.
19 The servants of Isaac dug in the valley
and found a well of living waters. 20 But the
shepherds of Gerar quarreled with the
shepherds of Isaac saying, "The water is
ours!" He therefore called the well Esek *
because they had quarreled with him.
21 They dug another well, but they quar-
reled over this one as well, and he called it
Sitnah. * 22 He thus moved away from there
and dug another well over which they did
not quarrel. He called it Rehoboth * and
said, "Now the LORD has given us room so
that we might prosper in the land."

l Gen 27:6f.—m Deut 21:17.—n Heb 12:16.—o 1-14: Gen 12:10-20.—p Gen 12:1-2.—q Gen 12:7; 15:18; Ex 32:13; Ps 105:8-9; Sir 44:22; Heb 11:9.—r Gen 12:3; 22:17f; 28:14; Ex 32:13.—s 13f: Job 1:3.—t 15-24: Gen 21:25-31.

25:30 *Edom* means "red" in Hebrew.

26:1-33 The promises and blessings given to Abraham are continued for his son Isaac. The same Yahwist that had transmitted the episode of Abraham in Egypt (Gen 12:10-20) narrates a similar one for his son, but with greater reticence and moral sensitivity. In the idiom of the time, cousins, such as Isaac and Rebekah were, called each other brothers and sisters. The inhabitants of the area were not, properly speaking, Philistines, since the latter immigrated only later on (13th century B.C.); these inhabitants were the Canaanites, who preceded the Philistines.

26:20 *Esek:* i.e., "Challenge."

26:21 *Sitnah:* i.e., "Opposition."

26:22 *Rehoboth:* i.e., "Room Enough."

23 From there he went to Beer-sheba.
24 That night the LORD appeared to him and
said, "I am the God of Abraham, your
father. Do not fear for I am with you. I will
bless you and multiply your descendants on
account of Abraham, my servant." [u]
25 He built an altar there and called upon
the name of the LORD. He pitched his tent
there, and his servants dug a well.

The Covenant with Abimelech. 26 [v] Abim-
elech traveled from Gerar with Ahuzzath
his friend and Phicol, the commander of his
army, to see Isaac. 27 Isaac said to them,
"Why have you come to me, for you hate
me and have sent me away from your
midst?"
28 They answered him, "We have seen
that the LORD is with you and we have said,
'Let there be an oath between us, between
you and us. Let us make a covenant with
you 29 that you will not do anything against
us, as we have not molested you but were
always good to you and let you go away in
peace.' You are now a man blessed by the
LORD."
30 He prepared a meal for them and they
ate and drank. 31 Rising early in the morn-
ing, they swore an oath to each other. Then
Isaac bade them farewell, and they went
away in peace.
32 That very day the servants of Isaac ar-
rived and informed him about the well that
they had dug saying, "We have found
water." 33 He called the well Shibah.* This
is the city called Beer-sheba today.

Esau's Hittite Wives.* 34 [w] When Esau was
forty years old he married Judith, the
daughter of Beeri the Hittite, and Base-
math, the daughter of Elon the Hittite.
35 They were a source of bitterness to Isaac
and Rebekah.

CHAPTER 27

Jacob Supplants His Brother.* 1 Isaac had
grown old, and his eyes had failed so much
that he could no longer see. He called his
older son, Esau, and said to him, "My
son."
He answered, "Here I am."
2 He continued, "See, I am old and do
not know when I will die. 3 Take your
weapons, your quiver and your bow, and
go out into the countryside and hunt for
some wild game for me. 4 Then prepare
me a plate of delicious meat and bring it
to me to eat, so that I may bless you before
I die."
5 Rebekah overheard Isaac speaking to
his son Esau. When Esau went out into the
countryside to hunt game and to bring it
home, [x] 6 Rebekah said to her son Jacob,
"Behold, I have heard your father speak-
ing to your brother Esau. 7 He said, 'Bring
me some game and prepare me a plate to
eat it so that I may give you the LORD's
blessing before I die.' 8 Now, my son, obey
my instructions: 9 Go immediately to the
flock and take two choice kids. I will pre-
pare them to make a plate for your father
just the way he likes it. 10 Then you can
carry it to your father to eat, so that he
may bless you before he dies."
11 Jacob answered Rebekah his mother,
"You know that my brother Esau is hairy,
while my skin is smooth. [y] 12 My father
might touch me and realize that I am
playing a trick on him and place a curse
on me instead of a blessing."
13 But his mother said, "Let that curse
fall on me, my son! Only obey me and go
and bring the kid goats."
14 He went to get them and brought
them back to his mother, and his mother
prepared them to make a meal the way his
father liked it. 15 Rebekah then took the
best clothes of her older son, Esau, which
were in the house with her. She put them
on her younger son, Jacob. 16 She put the
skins of the kid goats on the smooth parts
of his arms and neck. 17 Then she gave the
meal that she had prepared to her son
Jacob.
18 He went to his father and said, "My
father." He answered, "Here I am. Who
are you, my son?"
19 Jacob said to his father, "I am Esau,
your firstborn. I have done everything you
ordered. Please get up, sit down, and eat
the game so that you may bless me."
20 Isaac said to his son, "How did you
prepare it so quickly, my son?" He an-

u Gen 46:3.—v 26-33: Gen 21:22-31; Prov 16:7.—w 34f: Gen 27:46.—x Gen 25:28.—y Gen 25:25.

26:33 *Shibah:* i.e., "Oath of Seven." *Beer-sheba:* i.e., "Well of the Oath" or "Well of Seven."

26:34f These verses are from the Priestly source.

27:1-40 It had to be made clear that God chose Israel in a free and unmerited act and not because of human merits: all are sinners and salvation is a gift of his love (Rom 3:23-24).

As for the substitution of one person for another, this should not be judged by modern standards. The ancients thought that sacred acts like blessings had an immediate and irrevocable effect; when Isaac is told of the deception, he ratifies what has been done (vv. 33, 37).

swered, "The LORD placed the game right in front of me."

21 Then Isaac said, "Draw near and let me touch you, my son, so that I may know if you are really my son Esau or not."

22 Jacob drew near, and Isaac, his father, touched him and said, "The voice is the voice of Jacob, but the arms are the arms of Esau." 23 He did not recognize him, because his arms were hairy like the arms of his brother Esau, and he blessed him. 24 Then he said to him one more time, "Are you really my son Esau?" He answered, "I am."

25 He said, "Bring me the game to eat, my son, so that I can bless you."

Jacob served him the meal and Isaac ate; and he brought him wine and he drank. 26 Then his father Isaac told him, "Draw near and kiss me, my son."

27 He drew near and kissed him. Isaac smelled the scent of his clothes and he blessed him, saying,

"This is the scent of my son
like the scent of the fields
that the LORD has blessed. [z]
28 God grant you dew from the heavens
and the riches of the earth
and an abundance of grain and wine. [a]
29 May the peoples serve you,
and may the nations bow down before you.
May you be lord over your brothers,
and may your mother's sons bow down to you.
May the one who curses you be cursed
and the one who blesses you be blessed." [b]

30 Isaac had just finished blessing Jacob, and Jacob had just left his father, when Esau, his brother, arrived from the hunt. 31 He also prepared a meal and brought it to his father and said to him, "Rise, my father, and eat the wild game of your son, so that you may bless me."

32 His father Isaac said to him, "Who are you?"

He answered, "I am your firstborn son, Esau."

33 Isaac was seized by a violent trembling and said, "Then who was it who prepared the wild game and brought it to me? I ate it all before you arrived, and I blessed him; and the blessing will remain with him."

34 When Esau heard the words of his father, he shrieked and let out a bitter cry. He said to his father, "Bless me too, my father." 35 He answered, "Your brother came here with trickery and received your blessing."

36 He then said, "He has been well named Jacob,* for he has supplanted me twice. He already took away my birthright and now he has taken my blessing." He added, "Do you not have a blessing left for me?" [c]

37 Isaac answered Esau and said, "Behold, I have made him your lord and I have given him his brothers as his servants. He is to be maintained with grain and wine. What can I do for you, my son?"

38 Esau told his father, "Do you only have one blessing, my father? Bless me too, my father!" But Isaac was silent, and Esau cried out aloud. [d]

39 Finally Isaac spoke and said,

"Behold, far from the riches of the earth
shall your dwelling be
and far from the dew of the heavens. [e]
40 You shall live by the sword
and serve your brother.
But then, when you have dominion,
you shall break the yoke from your neck." [f]

Jacob Flees to Mesopotamia.* 41 Esau hated Jacob on account of the blessing that his father had given him. Esau thought, "The time to mourn my father is drawing near; then I will kill my brother Jacob." [g]

42 When Rebekah was told what Esau, her older son, had said, she called Jacob, her younger son, and said, "Esau your brother wants to get even with you by killing you. 43 So obey me, my son. Rise, and flee to Haran, to my brother Laban. 44 Remain with him for some time, till your brother's anger has calmed. 45 When the fury of your brother is soothed and he has forgotten what you did to him, I will send for you to bring you back from there. Why should I be deprived of the two of you in a single day?"

---

z Ps 65:10-14; Heb 11:20.—a Deut 33:13; 2 Sam 1:21; Prov 3:20; Isa 26:19; Hos 14:5; Hag 1:10; Zec 8:12.—b Gen 25:23; 49:8; Num 24:9.—c Gen 25:26, 29-34; Hos 12:4.—d Heb 12:17.—e Heb 11:20.—f 2 Ki 8:20, 22; 2 Chr 21:8.—g Wis 10:10; Ob 10.

27:36 *Jacob:* i.e., "He grasps the heel" (figuratively, "He deceives").

27:41-46 Wrongdoing is followed by atonement.

46 Rebekah said to Isaac, "I despise my
life because of those Hittite women. If
Jacob were to take a wife from among the
Hittites, from among the daughters of the
land, what good would life be to me?" [h]

CHAPTER 28

1 Isaac called to Jacob and blessed him
and gave him this command: "You must
not take a wife from among the daughters
of Canaan. [i] 2 Up, go to Paddan-aram, to
the house of Bethuel, the father of your
mother, and take a wife from there, from
among the daughters of Laban, the brother
of your mother. [j] 3 May God Almighty bless
you; may he make you fruitful and multiply
you, so that you become a multitude of
people. [k] 4 May he give you the blessing of
Abraham, to you and your descendants, so
that you may possess the land in which you
have dwelt as an alien, the land that God
gave to Abraham." [l] 5 Thus, Isaac sent
Jacob away. He went to Paddan-aram, to
Laban, the son of Bethuel the Aramean,
and the brother of Rebekah, the mother of
Jacob and Esau. [m]

6 Esau saw that Isaac had blessed Jacob
and had sent him to Paddan-aram to find
a wife, and that when he had blessed him,
he had commanded him, "You must not
take a wife from among the Canaanites."
7 Jacob obeyed his father and mother and
left for Paddan-aram. 8 Esau then under-
stood that Isaac disapproved of the
daughters of Canaan. 9 He therefore went
to Ishmael and, besides the wives he al-
ready had, he took as wife Mahalath, the
daughter of Abraham's son Ishmael and
the sister of Nebaioth. [n]

Jacob's Dream at Bethel.* 10 Jacob left from
Beer-sheba and traveled toward Haran.
11 He came upon a certain place and spent
the night there for the sun was setting. He
took a stone and used it as a pillow and
slept in that place. 12 He had a dream.
There was a ladder resting on the earth
with its top reaching to heaven. The angels
of God were ascending and descending
upon it. [o]

13 And the LORD stood before him and
said, "I am the LORD, the God of Abraham
your father and the God of Isaac. The land
on which you are lying shall be given to you
and your descendants. [p] 14 Your descen-
dants shall be like the dust of the earth and
shall extend to the west and the east, the
north and the south. All the nations of the
earth shall be blessed through you and
through your descendants. [q] 15 I am with
you and I will protect you wherever you go.
I will make you return to this country, for I
will not abandon you without having done
all that I have promised you." [r]

16 Jacob woke from sleep and said, "Truly,
the LORD is in this place, and I did not know
it." 17 He was filled with fear and said, "How
terrible this place is! This is truly the house
of God, this is the gate to heaven." [s]

18 In the morning Jacob arose early, took
the rock that he had used as a pillow, and
erected it as a pillar pouring oil on top of it. [t]
19 He named the place Bethel, * [u] although
the city had previously been called Luz.

20 Jacob made a vow, "If God remains
with me and protects me in this journey
that I am making and gives me bread to eat
and clothes to cover me, 21 and if I return in
peace to my father's house, the LORD will be
my God. 22 This stone that I am erecting as
a pillar shall be a shrine to God. I will offer
you one-tenth of everything that you give
me."

CHAPTER 29

The Wedding for Which Jacob Slaved.*
1 Jacob set out on his journey and traveled

h Gen 26:34f.—i Gen 24:3f; 26:35.—j Gen 17:1f, 4f; 25:20.—k Gen 48:16; Num 6:24; Ru 2:4; Pss 129:8; 134:3; Jer 31:23.—l Ex 32:13.—m Jud 8:26.—n Gen 36:2f.—o Jn 1:51.—p Deut 1:8; Mic 7:20.—q Gen 12:3; 13:14f; 15:5f; 18:18; 22:17f; 26:4; Deut 19:8; Sir 44:21.—r Gen 31:3; Neh 4:14; Pss 12:6, 8f; 105:10.—s Ex 3:5; 19:21; Jos 5:15; 1 Chr 22:1; 2 Chr 3:1; Ps 68:25, 36.—t Gen 31:13; 35:14f.—u Gen 35:6; 48:3; Jos 18:13; Jdg 1:23.

28:10-22 God does not delay in giving the refugee signs of his goodwill toward him, and the Mesopotamian period of Jacob's life is set between two important theophanies (the second is in 32:25-31). Upon him is to be built the ladder that he saw in a vision and that unites earth with heaven. The Mesopotamian temple towers were monuments of this kind; by means of them human beings expressed their dream of making the divinity come down to them. Jacob honors the place of the unexpected vision; it will become a sanctuary visited by people until it begins to rival the official sanctuary in Jerusalem (1 Ki 12:26-32; etc.). Jesus Christ, a descendant of Jacob, will tell his first apostles that the heavens will open and that the ladder of the vision is becoming a reality in his person (Jn 1:51). Our liturgy makes the patriarch's exclamation (Gen 28:17) its own when it celebrates the dedication of a church, which is the sign of the Christian community that prolongs the presence of the Savior on earth.

28:19 *Bethel:* i.e., "House of God."

29:1-30 The bride was veiled throughout the entire wedding ceremony, which ended only in the darkness of the night—thus the possibility of deception. In this case, again, the substitution of one person for another is not to be judged by our standards, especially since the intentional presence of many people (v. 22) must have compelled Jacob to accept what had been done. Polygamy was not a difficulty for him, since he was following the practice of nomads, whereas Abraham had been monogamous in accord with the spirit of his native Babylonian environment. Marriage with two sisters would later be prohibited by Israelite law (Lev 18:18); this is an indication of the historicity of the story.

to the lands of the east.[v] 2 He saw a well in
the countryside and three flocks of sheep
lying beside it. The flocks would drink at
this well, but the stone over the mouth of
the well was very large.[w] 3 When all the
flocks were gathered there, the shepherds
would roll the stone from the mouth of the
well and the sheep would drink there. They
would then replace the stone over the
mouth of the well.
4 Jacob said to them, "My brothers,
where are you from?" They said, "We are
from Haran."
5 He said to them, "Do you know Laban,
the son of Nahor?"
They said, "We know him."[x]
6 He said to them, "Is he well?"
They answered, "Yes, and here comes
his daughter Rachel with his flock."
7 He continued, "It is still early; it is not
yet the time to gather the sheep together.
Give the sheep something to drink and
then go and pasture them."
8 They said, "We cannot until all the
flocks are gathered together. Then we will
roll the stone away from the mouth of the
well and have the flocks drink."
9 He was still speaking with them when
Rachel arrived with her father's sheep, for
she was a shepherd. 10 When Jacob saw
Rachel, the daughter of his uncle Laban,
together with the sheep of his uncle Laban,
he got up and rolled the stone away from
the mouth of the well and gave water to the
sheep of his uncle Laban. 11 Jacob then
kissed Rachel and wept aloud. 12 He re-
vealed to Rachel that he was a relative of
her father, for he was the son of Rebekah.
So she ran to tell her father.
13 When Laban heard about Jacob, the
son of his sister, he ran to meet him. He
embraced him, kissed him, and brought
him to his house. Jacob told Laban all
about what had happened to him. 14 Laban
said to him, "You are my own flesh and
blood."
Jacob lived with him for a month.
15 Then Laban said to him, "Just because
you are my relative, should you be working
for me without a salary? Tell me what you
want as your salary."
16 Now Laban had two daughters. The
older was named Leah and the younger
was named Rachel. 17 Leah had sad* eyes,
while Rachel was very beautiful and lovely.
18 Because of this, Jacob loved Rachel. He
therefore said, "I will serve you for seven
years for Rachel, your younger daughter."
19 Laban answered, "I prefer to give her
to you rather than to a stranger. Stay with
me." 20 So Jacob served him for seven
years for Rachel. He was so in love with
her that it seemed only a few days.[y]
21 Then Jacob said to Laban, "Give me
my wife, for my time of service is com-
pleted and I wish to marry her."
22 Laban gathered all the men of that
place and threw a banquet. 23 When it was
the evening, he took his daughter Leah
and brought her to him and he married
her. 24 Laban gave his own slave Zilpah to
his daughter Leah as a slave.
25 When morning came, behold, it was
Leah! Jacob said to Laban, "What have
you done! Did I not serve you for Rachel?
Why have you tricked me?"
26 Laban answered, "It is not the cus-
tom in our land to give the younger one
before the older one. 27 Finish the bridal
week with this one; then I will give you
the other as well if you will serve me for
another seven years."[z]
28 Jacob did this. He finished the bridal
week with Leah, and then Laban gave
him Rachel as his wife. 29 Laban gave his
own slave Bilhah to his daughter Rachel
as a slave. 30 Jacob slept with Rachel, and
he loved Rachel more than Leah. So he
served his uncle for another seven years.[a]
The Children of Jacob.* 31 Now the LORD,
seeing that Leah was being overlooked,
opened her womb while Rachel re-
mained barren. 32 Leah conceived and
bore a son whom she named Reuben, for
she said, "The LORD has seen my humili-
ation; surely my husband will love me
now."[b]
33 Then she conceived another son and
said, "The LORD has heard that I was ig-
nored and he has given me this one as
well." She named him Simeon.
34 She conceived again and bore a son
and said, "This time my husband will
show me affection, for I have borne three
sons for him." Because of this she named
him Levi.

v Wis 10:10.—w Gen 24:11f.—x Tob 7:4.—y Hos 12:13.—z Hos 12:13.—a Deut 21:15ff.—b Gen 49:3.

29:17 *Sad:* the word can also mean "delicate."

29:31—30:24 Jacob had many sons, but Israelite tradition counts only twelve of them, including the last born, Benjamin (Gen 35:18), and regards them as the ancestors of the twelve tribes that make up the chosen people.

35 She conceived once again and bore a
son and said, "This time I will praise the
LORD." For this she named him Judah.
Then she stopped having children. [c]

CHAPTER 30

1 Rachel, seeing that it had not been
granted to her to bear sons to Jacob, be-
came jealous of her sister and said to
Jacob, "Give me sons, or I shall die!" [d]
2 Jacob was irritated with Rachel and
said, "Am I God? He is the one who did
not grant you the fruit of the womb." [e]
3 She answered, "Here is my servant
Bilhah; sleep with her so that she may
give birth upon my knees * and I also may
have offspring through her." [f]
4 She gave her slave Bilhah to Jacob as
a wife, and he slept with her. 5 Bilhah con-
ceived and bore a son to Jacob. 6 Rachel
said, "God has been just to me and has
also listened to my voice, giving me a
son." Because of this she named him
Dan.
7 Bilhah, the slave of Rachel, conceived
a second time and bore another son to
Jacob. 8 Rachel said, "I have undergone a
great struggle with my sister and I have
won." Because of this she named him
Naphtali.
9 Leah, seeing that she had ceased bear-
ing children, took her slave Zilpah and
gave her as a wife to Jacob. 10 Zilpah, the
slave of Leah, bore Jacob a son. 11 Leah
said, "What good luck!" And she named
him Gad.
12 Zilpah, the slave of Leah, bore a sec-
ond son to Jacob. 13 Leah said, "What joy!
The women shall call me truly happy."
Therefore, she named him Asher.
14 Around the time of the wheat har-
vest, Reuben found some mandrakes, *
and he brought them to his mother Leah.
Rachel said to Leah, "Give me a little of
your son's mandrakes."
15 But Leah answered, "Is it not enough
that you have taken away my husband?
Why do you want to take away my son's
mandrakes as well?" Rachel answered,
"Then he can lie with you tonight in ex-
change for your son's mandrakes."
16 That night, when Jacob arrived from
the fields, Leah went out to him and said
to him, "You must sleep with me because
I paid for the right to have you with my
son's mandrakes." Thus, he slept with her
that night. 17 God heard Leah, and she
conceived and bore a fifth son to Jacob.
18 Leah said, "God has rewarded me for
having given my slave to my husband."
This is why she named him Issachar.
19 Leah conceived and bore a sixth son
to Jacob. 20 Leah said, "God gave me a
beautiful gift. This time my husband will
prefer me because I have borne him six
sons." She therefore named him Zebulun.
21 She then bore a daughter and named
her Dinah.
22 God also remembered Rachel. He lis-
tened to her and opened her womb. 23 She
conceived and bore a son and said, "God
has removed my dishonor." [g] 24 She
named him Joseph saying, "May the LORD
grant me another son."

Jacob's Means of Becoming Prosperous.*

25 After Rachel had borne Joseph, Jacob
said to Laban, "Let me go and return to
my homeland. 26 Give me my wives, for
whom I have served you, and my chil-
dren, so that I can leave. You know how I
served you."
27 Laban said to him, "If I have found
favor with you, please stay, for through
divination I have come to know that the
LORD has blessed me because of you."
28 He added, "Establish your salary and I
will give it to you."
29 He answered, "You know how I served
you and how your possessions have multi-
plied through my work. 30 What little you
had before I arrived has grown beyond
measure, and the LORD has blessed you
since my arrival. But now, when will I be
able to work for myself as well?"
31 Laban then said, "What must I do for
you?" Jacob answered, "You do not have
to do anything if you will do the following
for me. I will return to pasture your flock
and watch over it. 32 Today I will pass
through all the animals. I will separate
every dark animal from among the sheep

---

c Mt 1:2; Lk 3:33.—d Prov 30:16.—e 2 Ki 5:7.—f Gen 16:2ff.—g Lk 1:25.

30:3 *Upon my knees:* after birth a father customarily took a child on his lap to indicate it was his. Rachel appeals to this custom to show that Bilhah's child is hers.

30:14 *Mandrakes:* the ancients regarded the mandrake or mandragora as an aphrodisiac and capable of promoting pregnancy.

30:25-43 For a long time, Laban has exploited the services of his nephew; now, despite their agreement, he deprives him of the speckled sheep and dark-colored goats to prevent him from obtaining a flock for himself. But Jacob has a trick or two up his sleeve.

and every goat that is spotted or speckled. This will be my salary. 33 In the future, let my honesty answer for me. When you come to verify my salary, every animal that is not speckled or spotted from among the goats and those that are not dark from among the sheep, if you find them with me, will be considered to have been robbed."

34 Laban said, "Good, let it be as you have said." 35 That day he removed the speckled and spotted he-goats and the speckled and spotted she-goats, all of those that had some white on them, and every sheep that was a dark color. He placed the flock in the care of his sons, 36 and he determined that there should be a distance of a three days' journey by camel from Jacob's flock. Jacob cared for the rest of Laban's flock.

37 But Jacob took fresh shoots of poplar, almond, and plane trees, and he made white * stripes in them by peeling the bark back down to the white core of the shoots. 38 He then took the shoots from which he had peeled the bark and he placed them in the channels, that is, in the watering troughs where the animals came to drink. They were placed where the animals could see them, and the animals mated when they came to drink. 39 Thus, the animals mated in the sight of the shoots, and the goats had kids that were streaked, speckled, and spotted. *

40 As for the sheep, Jacob separated them and had them face the animals that were streaked or fully dark of the flock of Laban. He put his own flock in a separate place; he did not put them together with Laban's flock. 41 Every once in a while, the healthier animals mated, and Jacob would put the shoots in the trough where the animals could see them, so that they would mate in the sight of the shoots. 42 When the animals were weak, he did not put them there. Thus, the weak animals belonged to Laban, and those that were healthy belonged to Jacob. 43 He grew rich beyond measure and possessed great numbers of flocks, male and female slaves, and camels and donkeys.

CHAPTER 31

Jacob Flees from Laban.* 1 Jacob came to know what the sons of Laban were saying: "Jacob is taking what belonged to our father, and he has gotten all his wealth from what belonged to our father." 2 And Jacob saw that Laban's attitude toward him had changed.

3 Then the LORD said to Jacob, "Return to the land of your fathers, to your homeland, and I will be with you." [h]

4 So Jacob sent for Rachel and Leah who were in the fields with the flocks 5 and he told them, "I see that your father's attitude to me is not like it was before. Still, the God of my father is with me. 6 You yourselves know that I have served your father with all my strength, 7 while your father has cheated and changed my salary ten times. But God did not let him harm me. [i] 8 If he said, 'The speckled animals will be your salary,' then all the animals born were speckled. If he said, 'The streaked animals will be your salary,' then all the animals born were streaked. 9 Thus, God took back your father's animals and gave them to me.

10 "Once, when the animals were in heat, I had a dream. I looked out and saw that the he-goats that were streaked, speckled, and mottled were ready to breed. 11 The angel of God said to me in the dream, 'Jacob!' I answered, 'Here I am.' 12 He continued, 'Look up and see: all the goats that are ready to breed are streaked, speckled, and mottled because I saw what Laban has done to you. 13 I am the God of Bethel, where you anointed a pillar and where you made an oath to me. Now, rise, leave this country, and return to your homeland.' " [j]

14 Rachel and Leah answered, "Do we still have property or an inheritance in the house of our father? 15 Are we not considered to be outsiders by him? He sold us and then used up our money. 16 All those things that God has taken from our father belong to us and to our children. Do what God has told you to do." [k]

17 Jacob got up, placed his children and his wives on camels, 18 and led all the ani-

h Gen 26:3; 28:15; 32:10.—i Jud 8:26.—j Gen 28:18-22.—k Wis 10:10f.

30:37 *Poplar . . . white:* the Hebrew terms for these words are puns on the name Laban. As Jacob had gotten the best of Esau (whose other name, Edom, means "red") by means of red stew (Gen 25:30), so he now tries to get the best of Laban (whose name means "white") by means of white branches. In effect, Jacob is using Laban's own tactic (deception) against him.

30:39 Jacob's scheme works—but only because of God's intervention (see Jacob's own admission in Gen 31:9), not because of Jacob's superstition.

31:1-21 Stemming from a different source, this account endeavors to show that Jacob is right in his quarrels with Laban; God himself has made him prosper. Overflowing with riches, Jacob judges it more prudent to put an end to their deteriorating relations, after having rallied his wives to his cause.

mals away. He took all his possessions with him, including the animals that he acquired in Paddan-aram, in order to return to Isaac, his father, in the land of Canaan.

19 When Laban had gone to shear the sheep, Rachel stole the household idols *[l] that belonged to her father. 20 Jacob sneaked away from Laban the Aramean, not letting him know that he was about to flee.[m] 21 This way he was able to go with all his possessions. He rose, crossed the river,* and traveled toward the mountains of Gilead.

Laban Pursues Jacob.* 22 On the third day, Laban was told that Jacob had fled. 23 He took his kinsmen with him and followed him for seven days. He caught up to him in the mountains of Gilead. 24 Then God came to Laban the Aramean in a dream by night and said to him, "Be careful not to do anything to Jacob, not a thing!"[n]

25 Laban therefore went and caught up to Jacob. Now Jacob had pitched his tents in the mountains, and Laban and his kinsmen were also camped in the mountains of Gilead. 26 Laban said to Jacob, "What have you done? You sneaked away and carried off my daughters as if they were prisoners of war! 27 Why did you secretly flee away and cheat me? Why did you not let me know? I would have given you a celebration with songs and the music of the tambourines and the harp. 28 You did not let me kiss my grandsons and my daughters. This was surely a foolish thing that you have done. 29 Realize that I could harm you, but the God of your father spoke to me last night. He forbade me to do anything to Jacob, not a thing. 30 I realize that you left because you were homesick for the house of your father, but why have you robbed my household idols?"

31 Jacob answered Laban and said, "I was afraid, and I thought that you would take your daughters back with force. 32 But as for whoever you find has taken your household idols, he will be put to death. With our relatives looking on, see if you can find anything belonging to you and take it." Jacob did not know that Rachel had robbed them.

33 Laban entered Jacob's tent and then the tent of Leah and the tent of the two slaves, but he did not find anything. Then he went out from Leah's tent and entered Rachel's tent. 34 Now Rachel had taken the idols and had placed them under a camel's saddle and had then sat upon it. Laban searched throughout the whole tent and did not find them.[o]

35 She said to her father, "Please do not be offended, my lord, if I cannot rise in your presence, but I am having my monthly time."* Laban therefore searched in the entire tent and did not find the idols.

36 Jacob was angry now and scolded Laban saying, "What crime have I committed, what sin did I do that you followed me? 37 Now that you have searched all my possessions, what have you found that belongs to you? Place it before me and your relatives and let it serve as evidence for or against me.

38 "I spent twenty years with you. None of your sheep or goats ever miscarried. I never ate any of the rams of your flock. 39 I never brought you an animal that had been injured by a wild beast. I made good for the loss myself. You held me responsible for whatever was robbed during the day and for whatever was robbed during the night.[p] 40 By day I was burnt by the sun and by night I suffered from the cold, and I spent many sleepless nights. 41 Twenty years I was with you. I served you fourteen years for your two daughters and six years for your flocks, and you changed my salary ten times. 42 If the God of my father, the God of Abraham, and the Terror of Isaac, had not been with me, you would have sent me away with nothing. But God saw my affliction and the work of my hands, and last night he was my judge."[q]

43 Laban then answered Jacob and said, "These daughters are my daughters and these grandsons are my grandsons. These

l Jdg 17:5; 1 Sam 19:13; 2 Ki 23:24; Hos 3:4.—m Gen 27:36.—n Wis 10:12.—o Gen 31:19; Lev 15:19f.—p Ex 22:12.—q Gen 31:24, 29.

31:19 *Household idols* (Hebrew, *teraphim*) were small statues of divinities worshiped by the family (see v. 30). They belonged by right to the principal heir.

31:21 *The river* was the Euphrates. *Gilead* is the mountainous region east of the Jordan.

31:22-54 The greedy uncle pursues Jacob in anger, but Rachel saves the situation through guile and Jacob takes offense at Laban's bad faith. The latter finally resigns himself to deal with Jacob, and an agreement is concluded concerning the relations and the pasture rights between Aram and Israel in the Transjordan. Thus, an account, which is not lacking in humor, justifies once again the rightness of Jacob—and of Israel.

31:35 *I am having my monthly time:* in later times, anything a menstruating woman sat on was considered ritually unclean (Lev 15:20). Rachel, too, had become a deceiver.

cattle are my cattle, and all you see is
mine. What could I do to you today and to
these daughters and to the children whom
they have brought into the world? 44 Come,
let us make a covenant between me and
you, and let it be a witness between me
and you."
45 Jacob took a stone and erected it as a
pillar.[r] 46 Then he said to his relatives,
"Collect some stones," and they took
stones and made a mound out of them.
They then ate sitting upon the mound.
47 Laban called it Jegar-sahadutha, while
Jacob called it Galeed.
48 Laban said, "Let this mound be today
a witness between me and you." Because
of this he called it Galeed 49 and also Miz-
pah, because he said, "May the LORD keep
watch between me and you when we will
no longer see each other.* 50 If you mis-
treat my daughters and take other wives
besides my daughters, be warned that God
will be a judge between you and me."
51 Laban continued and said to Jacob,
"Behold this mound and this pillar that I
have erected between me and you. 52 Let
this mound be a witness, and this pillar be
a witness, that I will not cross over past
this mound to do you harm and that you
will not cross over past this mound and
this pillar to do me harm. 53 The God of
Abraham and the God of Nahor be a judge
between us."
Jacob swore an oath by the name of the
Terror of his father Isaac. 54 Then he of-
fered a sacrifice on the mountain and in-
vited his relatives to eat with him. They
ate and spent the night on the mountain.

CHAPTER 32

1 Laban rose early in the morning,
kissed his grandsons and daughters, and
blessed them. Then he left and returned
home.
Jacob Prepares To Meet Esau.* 2 As Jacob
continued his journey, angels of God ap-
peared to him. 3 When Jacob saw them he
said, "This is the encampment of God,"
and he called the place Mahanaim. 4 Then
Jacob sent some messengers ahead to his
brother Esau in the land of Seir, the coun-
try of Edom.[s] 5 He gave them this com-
mand, "Say to my lord Esau, 'Thus says
your servant Jacob, I have sojourned with
Laban and I remained there until now. 6 I
have come to own oxen, donkeys, flocks,
male and female slaves. I am sending my
lord this information to seek his favor.'"
7 The messengers returned to Jacob say-
ing, "We went to your brother Esau. Now
he is coming to meet you and he has four
hundred men with him." 8 Jacob was terri-
bly afraid and filled with anxiety. He di-
vided the men of his camp into two groups
along with the flocks, the herds, and the
camels. 9 He thought, "If Esau were to
come to one group and destroy it, the other
would be safe."
10 Jacob said, "God of my father Abra-
ham and God of my father Isaac, LORD,
who told me, 'Return to your land, to your
homeland, and I will bless you,'[t] 11 I am
not worthy of the goodness and faithful-
ness that you have shown your servant.
When I passed over the Jordan I had noth-
ing but my staff, and now I have become
so rich that I could establish two camps.
12 Save me from the hands of my brother
Esau because I am afraid of him. Let him
not come and kill all of us, even the moth-
ers and children.[u] 13 Besides, you said, 'I
will make you prosper and I will make
your descendants like the sand of the sea,
so numerous that you cannot count
them.'"
14 Jacob spent the night there. Then he
selected the following gifts from among his
possessions for his brother Esau: 15 two
hundred she-goats and twenty he-goats,
two hundred ewes and twenty rams,
16 thirty nursing camels and their young,
forty cows and ten bulls, twenty female
donkeys and ten male donkeys. 17 He en-
trusted them to his servants, in separate
groups, and told them, "Go ahead of me
and leave some space between the groups."
18 He gave this order to the first group,
"When you meet Esau, my brother, and he

r Gen 28:22; 35:14.—s Gen 36:6.—t Gen 31:3.—u Gen 28:14; 48:16; Heb 11:12.

31:49 *May . . . other:* the so-called Mizpah benediction, which in context is in fact a denunciation or curse.

32:2-22 The way that Jacob has taken obliges him to go through the territory of the Edomites, and the suspicious Esau has undoubtedly not yet digested the wicked trick that his brother has played on him (Gen 27:1-45). According to the traditions, Jacob takes measures to save half of his caravan in case of a struggle or to disarm the hatred by gifts; the prayer that the author places on his lips provides the key to his story. Despite his unworthiness, Jacob is the heir of the promises; that is why the Lord protects him and heaps favors upon him. The adventures of the hero as well as those of the chosen people (Ex 3:11; Deut 7:7f) verify a law of the action of God who causes his power to appear through the weakness of human beings.

asks you, 'To whom do you belong? Where are you going? Who owns all these animals that you are driving?' [19] you are to answer, 'They belong to your servant Jacob. They are a gift for my lord Esau. And Jacob himself is behind us.' "

[20] He gave the same order to the second group and the third and all the other groups: "These are the words that you shall say to Esau when you meet him. [21] Tell him, 'Your servant Jacob is coming behind us.' " He was thinking, "The gifts that I am sending will calm him down, and then I will come before him. Maybe he will greet me kindly." [22] Thus, the gifts went ahead of him, while he spent the night in the camp.

A Mysterious Struggle.* [23] During the night Jacob arose, took his two wives, his two slaves, and his eleven sons and crossed over the ford of the Jabbok. [24] He took them, crossed over the brook and carried over all his possessions. [25] So Jacob remained alone, and a man wrestled with him until the dawn. [26] Seeing that he could not beat him, the man struck Jacob at the hip joint. Jacob's hip joint became dislocated while he continued to fight with him. [v] [27] The man said, "Let me go because it is dawn."

Jacob answered, "I will not let go of you until you will have blessed me."

[28] The man asked, "What is your name?" [w]

He answered, "Jacob."

[29] The man then said, "Your name will no longer be Jacob, but Israel* because you have wrestled with God and with man and have won."

[30] Jacob said to him, "Give me your name." He answered, "Why are you asking my name?" And then he blessed him. [31] Jacob called the place Peniel* because he said, "I have seen God face to face, and I am still alive." [x]

[32] The sun rose and Jacob left Penuel limping. [33] This is why Israelites to this day do not eat the sinew of the thigh, because the man had struck Jacob's hip joint and the sinew shrank.

CHAPTER 33

Reconciliation of the Two Brothers.* [1] Jacob looked up and saw Esau arrive, accompanied by four hundred men. He therefore divided up his sons among Leah, Rachel, and the two slaves. [2] He had the slaves and their children lead the way, and in back of them Leah and her sons, and then Rachel and Joseph. [3] He walked ahead of them and bowed to the ground seven times as he was approaching his brother.

[4] But Esau ran up to him, embraced him, threw his arms around his neck, and kissed him and wept. [5] Raising his eyes, he saw the women and the children and said, "To whom do these belong?"

He answered, "They are my sons whom God has graciously given to his servant."

[6] The slaves and their children came forward and bowed down. [7] Then Leah and her children came forward and bowed down. Finally, Rachel and Joseph came forward and bowed down.

[8] Esau asked again, "What is all this caravan that I have come across?"

He answered, "So that I might find favor in your sight, my lord."

[9] Esau said, "I have enough of my own possessions, brother; let these things be for you."

[10] But Jacob said, "No, if I have found favor in your sight, accept this gift from my hands. For it is for this that I have come into your presence as one would come into the presence of God, and you have received me favorably. [11] Accept this blessing that I give you, for God has been generous to me and I have enough." This is the way he insisted, and Esau accepted.

v Wis 10:12; Hos 12:4.—w Gen 35:10; 1 Ki 18:31.—x Jdg 13:22.

32:23-33 After the twenty years in Mesopotamia that were meant to purify him and straighten him out, Jacob is ready at last to begin his life as Patriarch of God's people in the Promised Land. In the stranger who wrestles with him at the ford of the Jabbok without revealing his name, Jacob recognizes the Lord and compels him to give his blessing. This is a confirmation of the patriarchal blessing that he had received from his father (Gen 27:27-29; 28:3-4) and also from the Lord (Gen 28:13-15) when he was beginning his journey abroad. Here the blessing is accompanied by the giving of a new name, an action that indicates a special act of taking possession: from this moment on Jacob will truly be God's man, who along with the name receives his special mission in life. From now on we see a man who has gradually learned to live by faith (see vv. 10-13, etc.).

32:29 *Israel:* the real etymology is uncertain; it may mean "God is mighty" or "God shows himself mighty." Here, however, the popular etymology is given: "He has shown his strength by wrestling with God" (see also Hos 12:4-5).

32:31 *Peniel:* a variant of *Penuel*, a town north of the Jabbok in Gilead (Jdg 8:8f, 17). *I have seen God face to face:* apart from the present context, this means to present oneself before God in the sanctuary with offerings for worship (see Deut 16:16).

33:1-20 Later on Jacob goes to the town of Shechem, in the center of Palestine, where he buys a plot of land and there sets up an altar to God as Lord of his own clan. According to tradition, this is the second property of the Patriarchs in the Promised Land; it will become an important sanctuary in the life of Israel (see Jos 8:30-35; 22:1-27; 1 Ki 12:1, 25; etc.).

12 Then Esau said, "Let us break camp
and set out; I will travel in front of you."
13 But Jacob answered, "My lord knows
that the children are delicate and that
my flocks and herds are burdened with
young ones. If they were to be pushed
even one day, the entire flock would
surely die. 14 Let my lord pass on ahead
of your servant, while I stay here going
slowly, at the pace of the animals that
will go ahead of me and at the pace of the
children, until I eventually reach my lord
in Seir."
15 Esau said, "I could at least leave a
part of my people with you!"
Jacob answered, "But why? Let me
only find favor in your sight, my lord!"
16 Thus, that same day, Esau departed
for Seir. 17 Jacob instead traveled to Suc-
coth where he built a house for himself
and made huts for his flock. This is why
he called the place Succoth.
18 When Jacob returned from Paddan-
aram, he arrived in peace at the city of
Shechem, which is in the land of Canaan,
and he camped in front of the city.[y] 19 He
bought the portion of land where he was
camped for one hundred pieces of silver
from the sons of Hamor, Shechem's
father.[z] 20 There he built an altar and
called it, El-Elohe-Israel, which means
El, the God of Israel.[a]

CHAPTER 34

The Incident at Shechem.* 1 Dinah, the
daughter whom Leah had borne for Jacob,
went out to see the young women of the
country. 2 When Shechem, the son of
Hamor the Hivite, the prince of the land,
saw her, he seized her and laid with her and
defiled her. 3 He was deeply attracted to
Dinah, the daughter of Jacob. He loved the
young woman and spoke comforting words
to her. 4 Then he said to Hamor, his father,
"Arrange for me to take this woman as a
wife."[b]
5 When Jacob learned that Dinah, his
daughter, had been defiled, his sons were in
the countryside with the animals. So he re-
mained silent until they returned.
6 Hamor, the father of Shechem, came to
Jacob to speak to him. 7 When the sons of
Jacob returned from the countryside, they
heard what had happened. They were furi-
ous and very indignant because he had done
this outrage in Israel, sleeping with a daugh-
ter of Jacob. One did not do these things![c]
8 Hamor said to them, "Shechem, my
son, is in love with your daughter. Please
give her to him in marriage. 9 Why not in-
termarry with us?* You give us your
daughters, and you can take our daughters
for yourselves. 10 You can live with us, and
the land will be at your disposal. Reside
here, move about freely, and buy prop-
erty."
11 Shechem said to Dinah's father and
her brothers, "Tell me what I can give you
in order to find favor in your sight. 12 You
can even raise my bridal price greatly and
the value of the due gifts. I will give you
whatever you ask. Only give me the young
woman as my wife."
13 The sons of Jacob answered Shechem
and his father Hamor deceitfully, for they
had dishonored their sister Dinah. 14 They
told them, "We cannot do this; we cannot
give our sister to a man who is not circum-
cised. This would dishonor us. 15 We will
only grant your request if you become like
us, if all of you circumcise your male
members. 16 Then we will give you our
daughters, and you can give us yours. We
will live with you, and we can become a
single people. 17 But if you will not listen to
our proposal concerning circumcising
yourselves, then we will take our daughter
and go away."
18 Their words pleased Hamor and
Shechem, the son of Hamor. 19 The young
man did not waste any time in doing this
thing, for he loved the daughter of Jacob.
He was also the most honored member of
the household of his father. 20 Hamor and
his son Shechem therefore went to the
gate of the city and spoke to the men of the
city, saying, 21 "These men are peaceful.
Let them live with us in the land and move
about freely. There is ample space in every
direction. We can take their daughters for
wives and we can give them ours. 22 But

y Gen 12:6; Jn 4:6.—z Jos 24:32; Jn 4:5; Acts 7:16.—a Jdg 6:24.—b Deut 21:14; 2 Sam 13:14.—c 2 Sam 13:12.

34:1-31 The incident does serious harm to the clan, which may in its turn suffer a harsh vendetta or be expelled from the Promised Land. For this reason, Simeon and Levi will suffer the consequences when Jacob decides on his successors (Gen 49:5-7). The story combines the Yahwist and Elohist traditions.

34:9 *Intermarry with us:* the Canaanites wanted to absorb Israel (see v. 16) in order to benefit from the blessings Jacob had received from the Lord (both his offspring and his possessions—vv. 21-23). This was a danger Israel constantly faced from other peoples and nations—either absorption or hostility, both of which are perpetual threats to the people of God.

there is one condition before these men will agree to live with us to become a single people: that we circumcise each of our males as they themselves are circumcised. 23 Would not their herds, their riches, and all their animals then be ours? Let us agree to their proposal, and they will then live with us."

24 All those who were near the gate of the city listened to Hamor and his son Shechem. All the men, everyone who had access to the gate of the city, had themselves circumcised.

25 On the third day, when they were still sore, two of the sons of Jacob, Simeon and Levi, * the brothers of Dinah, took swords, entered the city boldly, and killed all the men.[d] 26 They put Hamor and his son Shechem to the sword, took Dinah out of the house of Shechem, and left.[e] 27 The other sons of Jacob came upon the bodies and sacked the city because their sister had been dishonored. 28 They took their flocks and their herds, their donkeys and whatever they had in the city and in the countryside. 29 They carried off all their possessions as booty, sacking whatever was in their houses.[f]

30 Jacob said to Simeon and Levi, "You have placed me in a very difficult situation, making me hateful to the inhabitants of this land, to the Canaanites and the Perizzites, and I only have a few men with me. They will unite against me, and defeat me, and annihilate me and my household."

31 But they answered, "Should our sister be treated as a harlot?"

CHAPTER 35

Jacob Returns to Bethel.* 1 God said to Jacob, "Rise up, go to Bethel, and live there. Build an altar to the God who appeared to you when you fled from Esau, your brother, in that place."[g]

2 Jacob said to his family and to those who were with him, "Throw away the foreign gods that you have with you. Purify yourselves and change your clothes.[h] 3 Let us arise and go to Bethel where I will build an altar to the God who delivered me at the time of my distress and who has been with me along the way that I have traveled." 4 They gave Jacob all the foreign gods in their possession and the earrings they had in their ears. Jacob left them under the oak near Shechem.[i] 5 They then journeyed on, and a great terror came upon the people who lived in that area, so they did not pursue the sons of Jacob.[j]

6 Jacob and all the people who were with him arrived in Luz, that is, Bethel, which is in the land of Canaan.[k] 7 Here he built an altar and called the place El-Bethel, because God had revealed himself there, when he had fled from his brother.[l]

8 Deborah, the nurse of Rebekah, died there, and she was buried below Bethel, beneath an oak. This is why that place is called the Weeping Oak.

9 God appeared another time to Jacob, when he returned from Paddan-aram, and he blessed him. 10 God said to him,

"Your name is Jacob.
You shall no longer be called Jacob,
but Israel shall be your name."

Thus, he was called Israel.[m]

11 God said to him,

"I am God Almighty.
Be fruitful and become numerous.
People and assemblies of people shall come from you.
Kings shall come forth from your loins.
12 The country that I have given to Abraham and Isaac
I will give to you;
and to your descendants after you
I will give this land."[n]

13 Then God departed from him, in the place where he had spoken to him.

14 Jacob erected a pillar where God had spoken to him, a stone pillar upon which he poured a libation of oil.[o] 15 Jacob called

d Gen 49:6.—e Jud 9:2.—f Jud 9:3f.—g Gen 28:12f.—h Gen 31:19, 34; Ex 19:10; Jos 24:23; 1 Sam 7:3.—i Ex 32:3; 35:22; Jdg 8:24; Prov 25:12.—j Ex 15:16; 23:27; Deut 2:25; Jos 2:9; 1 Sam 7:10; 14:15; Ps 9:20; Isa 19:17; Zec 14:13.—k Gen 28:19; Jos 18:13; Jdg 1:22f.—l Gen 28:12f.—m 1 Ki 18:31; 2 Ki 17:34.—n Ex 32:13; Heb 11:9.—o Gen 28:18; 31:45.

34:25 *Simeon and Levi:* because they slaughtered the men of Shechem, their own descendants would be scattered far and wide. *Brothers of Dinah:* all three were children of Leah (Gen 29:33-34; 30:21). *Killed all the men:* Shechem's crime, serious as it was, hardly warranted such brutal and extensive retaliation (see vv. 27-29).

35:1-15 The Patriarch seems to be fleeing a threat of reprisal by the Shechemites (v. 5). Possibly he is also making a pilgrimage to his origins. In any case, this return to Bethel takes on a religious meaning: it is there that the Lord revealed himself to Jacob and there that he renewed his promises. The Patriarch and his family cleanse themselves and give up their pagan practices to affirm their faith in the one God to whom they wish to render homage; the Lord brooks no rivals in human hearts. This constitutes a first stable establishment of the People of God in the Holy Land.

the place where God had spoken to him
Bethel.

Jacob Endures Painful Times.* 16 They then
departed from Bethel. They were a short
distance outside of Ephrath when Rachel
went into labor and she suffered great dis-
tress. 17 When her pains were most severe,
the midwife said to her, "Do not fear, for it is
another son!" 18 With her last breath, for she
was dying, she called him Ben-oni, * the son
of my sorrow, but his father called him Ben-
jamin.

19 Rachel died and was buried on the
road to Ephrath, that is, Bethlehem.[p]
20 Jacob erected a pillar on the tomb. That
monument to Rachel can be seen to this
day.

21 Israel moved on and pitched his tent on
the other side of Migdal-eder. 22 While Israel
lived in that country, Reuben slept with Bil-
hah, the concubine of his father, and Israel
came to know about it.[q]

The Twelve Sons of Jacob.* Jacob had twelve
sons.

23 The sons of Leah:
Reuben, Jacob's firstborn,
Simeon, Levi, Judah,
Issachar and Zebulun.
24 The sons of Rachel:
Joseph and Benjamin.
25 The sons of Bilhah, the slave of Rachel:
Dan and Naphtali.
26 The sons of Zilpah, the slave of Leah:
Gad and Asher.

These were the sons of Jacob who were
born in Paddan-aram.

Death of Isaac.* 27 Jacob came to his father
Isaac at Mamre, at Kiriath-arba, that is He-
bron, where Abraham and Isaac had so-
journed. 28 Isaac lived for one hundred and
eighty years. 29 Isaac then breathed his last.
He died and was reunited with his people at
a ripe old age. His sons Esau and Jacob
buried him.

CHAPTER 36

List of the Clans Established in Edom.*
1 These are the descendants of Esau, that is,
of Edom.

2 Esau married women from the daugh-
ters of the Canaanites: Adah, the daughter of
Elon the Hittite, Oholibamah, the daughter
of Anah, who was the son of Zibeon the
Hivite,[r] 3 and Basemath, the daughter of Ish-
mael and the sister of Nebaioth.

4 Adah bore Eliphaz to Esau, and Base-
math bore Reuel.[s] 5 Oholibamah bore
Jeush, Jalam, and Korah. These were the
sons of Esau who were born in the land of
Canaan.[t]

6 Esau took his wives and sons and
daughters and all the people who were in
his household, his flocks and all his ani-
mals and all his possessions that he ac-
quired in the land of Canaan, and he went
into the land of Seir, far from his brother
Jacob.[u] 7 Their possessions, in fact, were
too extensive for them to live together,
and the land in which they were living
could not sustain the grazing of all their
animals. 8 Esau thus dwelt in the moun-
tains of Seir.[v] Now Esau is Edom.

9 These are the descendants of Esau, the
father of the Edomites, in the mountains of
Seir.

10 These are the names of the sons of Esau:
Eliphaz, the son of Adah who was
the wife of Esau, and Reuel, the
son of Basemath who was the wife
of Esau.
11 The sons of Eliphaz:
Teman, Omar, Zepho, Gatam, and
Kenaz.[w]

p Gen 48:7; 1 Sam 10:2; Mic 5:1-2.—q Gen 49:4; 1 Chr 5:1.—r Gen 26:34.—s 1 Chr 1:35.—t 1 Chr 1:35.—u Gen 32:4.—v Deut 2:4f; Jos 24:4.—w 2 Chr 1:36.

35:16-22 Rachel, Jacob's preferred wife, dies while giving birth to a son; later, he learns that his eldest son Reuben has committed a grave outrage against him. Thus, Jacob continues to expiate his sin.

35:18 *Ben-oni* means "Son of my sorrow." Jacob changes it to *Benjamin,* "Son of the right hand," that is, of good omen. This time, the popular etymology agrees with the scientific. But originally the name "son of the right hand" seems to have been inspired by geography: the right hand is the south, because the Semites oriented themselves by looking eastward to where the sun rises; therefore "Benjamin" means "son of the south."

35:22b-26 Jacob's twelve sons represent all the chosen people born of Abraham now established in the Holy Land. This list will be found frequently in the Bible.

35:27-29 The aged and taciturn Isaac seemed close to death when he blessed Jacob to the detriment of Esau (ch. 27). Here the Priestly tradition reports his death later and seems to know nothing about the rivalry between the two brothers.

36:1-43 The author has grouped together—without attempting to harmonize them in any way—teachings of diverse origins concerning the Edomites, that is, the line of Esau (v. 9ff) and the clans of the region of Seir that it occupied (v. 20ff). Deuteronomy affirms that the descendants of Esau replaced the indigenous peoples (Deut 2:12); rather both peoples seem to have been joined together: Esau marries a Horite (36:20) and one of his sons takes a concubine (vv. 12, 22). The Priestly tradition gave other names to the women of Esau (Gen 26:34; 28:9; see 36:1-5); it does this to explain in a different way the separation of Jacob and his brother (36:7; see Gen 33:12-17). But all these divergences are of little importance: it is solely a question of situating a fraternal people with respect to the people of Israel whom God has set apart for the salvation of humankind.

12 Eliphaz, the son of Esau, had a concubine named Timna, who bore Amalek to Eliphaz. These were the sons of Ada, the wife of Esau.
13 These are the sons of Reuel:
Nahath, Zerah, Shammah, and Mizzah. These were the sons of Basemath, the wife of Esau.[x]
14 These are the sons of Oholibamah, the wife of Esau, the daughter of Anah, who was the son of Zibeon, whom she bore to Esau:
Jeush, Jalam, and Korah.[y]

15 These are the leaders of the clans of Esau's descendants:
The sons of Eliphaz, the firstborn of Esau:
Teman, Omar, Zepho, and Kenaz,[z]
16 Korah, Gatam, and Amalek, all of them leaders of their clans. These were the leaders of the clans of Eliphaz in the land of Edom; they were the sons of Adah.
17 These are the sons of Reuel, Esau's son:
Nahath, Zerah, Shammah, and Mizzah, all of them leaders of their clans. These were the leaders of the clans of Reuel in the land of Edom; they were the sons of Basemath,[a] Esau's wife.
18 These are the sons of Oholibamah, Esau's wife:
Jeush, Jalam, and Korah, all of them leaders of their clans. These were the leaders of the clans borne to Oholibamah, the daughter of Anah and Esau's wife.
19 Such are the sons of Esau, that is Edom, and such are the leaders of the clans.
20 [b] These are the sons of Seir the Hittite who were living in the land:
Lotan, Shobal, Zibeon, Anah,
21 Dishon, Ezer, and Dishan. These were the leaders of the clans of the Horites, the sons of Seir in the land of Edom.
22 [c] The sons of Lotan:
Hori and Hemam. Lotan's sister was Timna.
23 The sons of Shobal:
Alvan, Mahanath, Ebal, Shepho, and Onam.
24 The sons of Zibeon:
Aiah and Anah. This is the Anah who found the hot springs in the desert when he was tending the donkeys of his father Zibeon.
25 The children of Anah:
Dishon and Oholibamah, the daughter of Anah.
26 The sons of Dishon:
Hemdan, Eshban, Ithran, and Cheran.
27 The sons of Ezer:
Bilhan, Zaavan, and Akan.
28 The sons of Dishan:
Uz and Aran.
29 These are the leaders of the clans of the Horites:
Lotan, Shobal, Zibeon, Anah,
30 Dishon, Ezer, and Dishan. These were all chiefs of the clans of the Horites, each according to their clans in the land of Seir.
31 [d] These are the kings who ruled in the land of Edom before the kings of Israel ruled over them:
32 Bela, the son of Beor, reigned in Edom, and his city was called Dinhabah.
33 Bela died and his son Jobab, the son of Zerah of Bozrah, reigned in his place.
34 Jobab died and Husham of the land of the Temanites reigned in his place.
35 Husham died and Hadad, the son of Bedad, who defeated the Midianites in the steppe of Moab, reigned in his place. His city was called Avith.
36 Hadad died and Samlah of Masrekah reigned in his place.
37 Samlah died and Shaul of Rehoboth by the River ruled in his place.
38 Shaul died and Baal-hanan, the son of Achbor, reigned in his place.
39 Baal-hanan, son of Achbor, died and Hadar reigned in his place. His city was called Pau. His wife's name was Mehetabel. She was the daughter of Matred from Mezahab.
40 These are the names of the leaders of Esau according to their clans, their lands, and their names:
Timna, Alvah, Jetheth,
41 Oholibamah, Elah, Pinon,
42 Kenaz, Teman, Mibzar,
43 Magdiel and Iram. These were the leaders of Edom according to their dwelling places in the lands that they occupied.

x 1 Chr 1:37.—y 1 Chr 1:35.—z Ex 15:15.—a 1 Chr 1:37.—b 20f: 1 Chr 1:38.—c 22-28: 1 Chr 1:39-42.—d 31-43: 1 Chr 1:43-54.

This was Esau, the father of the
Edomites.

C: Joseph, the Suffering, Righteous One*

CHAPTER 37

Hated by His Brothers.* 1 Jacob dwelt in
the land where his father had sojourned,
the land of Canaan.
2 This is the story of the descendants of
Jacob.
Joseph was seventeen years old and
tended the flocks with his brothers. He was
young and stayed with the sons of Bilhah
and the sons of Zilpah, the wives of his
father. Now Joseph told his father bad re-
ports about them.
3 Israel loved Joseph more than all his
other sons because he was the son of his
old age, and he had a long tunic made for
him. 4 His brothers, seeing that their
father loved him most of all his sons,
hated him and could not speak peaceably
with him.
5 Now Joseph had a dream and told it to
his brothers, which made them hate him
all the more.[e] 6 He told them, "Listen to
this dream that I had. 7 We were tying
sheaves of grain in the fields, and my sheaf
rose up and stood straight, while your
sheaves came around and bowed before
mine."
8 His brothers said, "Would you like to
reign over us and be our master?" And
they hated him all the more because of his
dream and for what he had told them.[f]
9 He had another dream and told it to
his brothers saying, "I had another dream;
listen. The sun and the moon and eleven
stars bowed down before me."
10 He told it to his father and brothers,
and his father scolded him and said,
"What type of dream is this? Must I and
your mother and your brothers bow down
to the ground in front of you?" 11 His
brothers were jealous of him, but his
father kept these things in mind.
Sold as a Slave.* 12 His brothers went out
to pasture the flocks of their father at
Shechem. 13 Israel said to Joseph, "You
know that your brothers have gone to pas-
ture at Shechem. Come, I wish to send you
to them."
He answered, "Here I am."
14 He said, "Go to see how things are
going for your brothers and the animals,
then return and tell me." He had him leave
from the Valley of Hebron and travel to
Shechem.[g]
15 As Joseph was wandering through the
fields, he found a man who asked him,
"For whom are you looking?"
16 He answered, "I am looking for my
brothers. Tell me how to find where they
are pasturing their flocks."
17 That man said, "They pulled up their
camp from here and I heard them say, 'Let
us go to Dothan.' "
Joseph therefore went in search of his
brothers, and he found them in Dothan.
18 They saw him from a distance, and, be-
fore he could draw close to them, they
plotted to put him to death.[h]
19 They said to one another, "Here
comes the dreamer. 20 Come, let us kill

e Gen 42:9.—f Gen 50:17.—g Gen 13:18.—h 1 Sam 19:11; 2 Chr 24:21; Pss 31:14, 21; 37:12, 32; Mt 12:14; Mk 14:1; Acts 23:12.

37:1—50:26 Under the rule of the Hyksos, who had come from Asia Minor (ca. 1750–1560 B.C.), Semites who had immigrated with them into Lower Egypt would fill high offices. The events of Joseph's life seem to fit better into a somewhat later period, at the beginning of the 18th dynasty (16th century B.C.), when it was still possible for Asiatics to hold high offices in Egypt. Joseph, who has been given the position of viceroy, finds himself charged with saving the people from famine and then with settling his own people in Goshen, a fertile region on the edges of the delta. The story, which belongs in the sapiential genre, combines contributions from the Yahwist and Elohist sources to bring to light the providential aspects hidden in the mystery of the suffering righteous man (Gen 45:4-13; 50:19-21).

It is evident that the Lord does not intervene openly but through the interplay of circumstances and the more or less upright behavior of individuals, but he does provide for the well-being of the vast human family by using the activity of those whom he has chosen; he even uses their sin to save them. The narrator has all the sons of Jacob going down into Egypt; as the ancestors of the twelve tribes they prepare the way, in a suitable environment, for the growth of the chosen people, which will, at the proper time, enter the Promised Land.

37:1-11 The story brings out the three reasons that feed a growing hatred in Joseph's brothers: his reporting of stories about them, their father's predilection for him, and his dreams. The *long tunic* is a princely garment, quite different from the short coat worn by shepherds, and Jacob was seriously imprudent in thus differentiating among his sons. As for the dreams, the Bible warns that these are most often vain (Deut 13:2-4; Jer 29:8-9); sometimes God does use them to make himself known to human beings (Num 12:6), but he alone explains their meaning (Gen 40:8; 41:16). Joseph will later on show that he himself possesses this special prophetic charism.

37:12-36 Some textual obscurities have led many critics to see in this passage the fusion of two different versions. In the Yahwist version the cause of the hatred would be the father's predilection; the Yahwist tradition, which had its center in Jerusalem and in the tribe of Judah, would be focusing on the doings of its own people. In the Elohist version, however, the hatred would be caused by the dreams. In narrating a complex event the storytellers may concentrate on one element rather than another, but this does not prevent both versions from being substantially true.

Joseph, who is hated and sold through no fault of his own, suffers the consequences of the error of his father, who is unable to control his own feelings, and of the baseness of his brothers who, like so many people, are hostile to the voice of a prophet.

Joseph will be a type of the Lamb of God who takes upon himself the sins of the world (1 Pet 2:24).

him and throw him in some cistern. We
will say, 'A wild animal devoured him.'
Then we will see what becomes of his
dreams." [i]
21 But Reuben heard this and wanted to
save him from their hands. He said, "Let
us not take his life." 22 Then he said to
them, "Do not spill his blood. Throw him
into this cistern in the desert, but do not
lay your hands upon him." He intended to
save him from their hands and restore
him to their father. [j]
23 When Joseph reached his brothers,
they stripped him of his tunic, the long
tunic that he wore. 24 They took him and
cast him into a dry cistern.
25 They then sat down to eat. When they
looked up, they saw a caravan of Ish-
maelites from Gilead with camels laden
with gums, balm, and myrrh. It was carry-
ing these things to Egypt. [k]
26 Judah said to his brothers, "What
would we gain if we killed our brother and
concealed his blood? [l] 27 Come, let us sell
him to the Ishmaelites. This way, we will
not have laid hands on him, for he is our
brother and our flesh." His brothers
agreed with him.
28 Now some Ishmaelite traders passed
by, and his brothers pulled Joseph up out
of the cistern and sold Joseph to the Ish-
maelites for twenty pieces of silver. Thus
Joseph was brought into Egypt. [m]
29 When Reuben returned to the cistern,
he found that Joseph was no longer there.
He ripped his garments, 30 and he returned
to his brothers and said, "The boy is gone!
Where can I turn?"
31 They took Joseph's tunic, slaughtered a
goat, and dipped the tunic in its blood.
32 They then sent their father the long tunic
and dispatched this message, "We have
found this; do you know if this is your son's
tunic?"
33 He recognized it and said, "It is my
son's tunic! A wild animal has devoured
him. Joseph has been torn to pieces." [n]
34 Then Jacob ripped his clothes, put
sackcloth on his loins, and mourned his
son for many days. 35 All his sons and his
daughters came to console him, but he did
not want to be consoled. He said, "No! I
wish to go down into the netherworld
mourning my son!" Thus did his father
weep for him. [o]
36 Meanwhile, the Midianites sold Joseph
in Egypt to Potiphar, a counselor of Phar-
aoh and a commander of the guard. [p]

CHAPTER 38

The Sons of Judah.* 1 At that time Judah
set out from his brothers and made camp
with a man named Hirah, an Adullamite.
2 Here Judah saw the daughter of a Ca-
naanite man named Shua, and he took her
as a wife and slept with her. [q] 3 She con-
ceived and bore a son and named him Er.
4 She conceived another time and bore a
son and named him Onan. 5 She bore still
another son and named him Shelah. She
was in Chezib when she gave birth to
him. [r]
6 Judah took a wife for his firstborn son
Er, and her name was Tamar. 7 But Er, the
firstborn of Judah, did things that were
wicked in the sight of the LORD, and the
LORD caused him to die. [s]
8 Judah then said to Onan, "Marry the
wife of your brother to fulfill the duty of a
brother-in-law to her and to assure de-
scendants for your brother." * [t] 9 But Onan
knew that the child would not have been
considered to be his own. Every time that
he slept with the wife of his brother, he
spilled his seed on the ground so that he
would not have to give his brother a son. *

i Gen 44:28.—j Gen 42:22.—k Gen 43:11.—l Job 16:18.—m Ps 105:17; Wis 10:13; Acts 7:9.—n Gen 44:28.—o Gen 42:38.—p Ps 105:17.—q 1 Chr 2:3.—r 1 Chr 4:21.—s 1 Chr 2:3.—t Deut 25:5; Mt 22:24; Mk 12:19; Lk 20:28.

38:1-30 In contrast to the innocent Joseph, who is struck down by the evil deeds of others, stand the moral troubles of the House of Judah, which, in combination with the corruption and violence of the other brothers, make it resemble a flower that is beaten down by a storm. It is, however, to the credit of Judah, who had suggested the selling of Joseph (Gen 37:26-27), that he later redeems himself by offering himself as a slave in the place of Benjamin in order to spare his father suffering that might prove fatal.

The present story gives the juridical reason why Perez, an ancestor of David (Ru 4:18, 22), is regarded as Judah's firstborn son; it is an application, although an abnormal one, of the law of the levirate, which is of very ancient origin; it was already followed by the Assyrians and Hittites and was later adopted by Israel (Deut 25:5-10). The detail about the birth of the twins (Gen 38:28-30) seems to point to a usurpation in favor of Perez. But above and beyond the juridical considerations, we have here the disconcerting choices of the Lord. When his time comes, Joseph will enjoy the rights of a firstborn in the inheritance of his father (Gen 48–49), but the Messiah will be the descendant of Judah and Tamar by way of Perez. God does not prefer the most worthy, and he uses sinners in weaving the web of salvation.

38:8 This verse describes "the law of the levirate" (from the Latin, *levir*, meaning "brother-in-law), which was decreed in Deuteronomy (25:5-6) and constituted a legal obligation in Israel (see Mt 22:24).

38:9 The law of the levirate required that in marrying Tamar, widow of Er, Onan should provide the dead man with a posterity. His sin is twofold: against social justice and Tamar, by deliberately and unlawfully preventing primogeniture, and against marriage, by frustrating its purposes.

10 This greatly displeased the LORD, and
the LORD caused him to die, too.
11 Thereupon Judah said to his daugh-
ter-in-law Tamar, "Return to the house of
your father as a widow until my son She-
lah will have grown up." For he thought,
"Let him not die like his brothers." So
Tamar went and returned to the house of
her father.
12 Quite some time later the daughter of
Shua, the wife of Judah, died. When Judah
had finished his time of mourning, he
went to Timnah to the sheep shearers.
Hirah, the Adullamite, went with him.
13 Tamar was told, "Your father-in-law
has gone to Timnah, to the sheep shearers
of his flock." 14 Tamar took off her clothes
of mourning, put on a veil, and com-
pletely covered herself. Then she went and
sat at the gate to Enaim, which is on the
road to Timnah. She realized that Shelah
had already grown up, but she had not yet
been given to him in marriage. * [u]
15 * Judah saw her and thought that she
was a prostitute, for she had covered her
face. 16 He headed over to her and said,
"Let me sleep with you." He did not know
that this was his daughter-in-law.
She said, "What will you give me to
sleep with me?"
17 He said, "I will send a goat from the
flock."
She said, "Will you give me a pledge to
hold until you will have sent it?"
18 "What pledge shall I give you?" he
asked.
"Your signet ring, your cord, and the
staff in your hand."
He gave them to her and slept with her,
and she conceived. 19 Then she got up and
left. She took off her veil and put her
clothes of mourning back on.
20 Judah sent his friend the Adullamite
with the goat to claim the pledge from the
woman, but he could not find her. 21 He
asked the men of that place, "Where is the
temple prostitute who was in Enaim
alongside the road?"
They answered, "There has never been
a temple prostitute there." [v]
22 So he returned to Judah and said, "I
did not find her. Even the men of that
place said, 'There has never been a temple
prostitute there.' "
23 Judah said, "Let her keep them.
Otherwise we will become a laughing-
stock. After all, I sent her the goat, but you
could not find her."
24 About three months later, Judah was
brought the following news: "Tamar, your
daughter-in-law, played the harlot and
she is also pregnant from her harlotry."
Judah said, "Let her be brought out and
burned!"
25 She had already been brought out
when she sent this message to her father-
in-law: "The man to whom these objects
belong is the father of the child." She con-
tinued, "Do you know to whom this signet
ring, cord, and staff belong?"
26 Judah recognized them and said, "She
is innocent and I am guilty, for I did not
give her my son Shelah." And he did not
sleep with her again.
27 When her time to give birth arrived, it
was discovered that she had twins in her
womb. [w] 28 While she was giving birth, one
of them put out his hand; so the midwife
took a scarlet thread and tied it to the
hand saying, "This one came out first."
29 But, when he pulled his hand back, his
brother came out. She said, "What a
breach you have opened for yourself!" [x] He
was named Perez. 30 Then his brother, who
had the scarlet thread tied around his
hand, [y] came out. He was named Zerah.

CHAPTER 39

Joseph, Blessed of God.* 1 When Joseph
was brought down into Egypt, Potiphar, a
counselor of Pharaoh and the commander

u Prov 7:10.—v Lev 19:29; Deut 22:21; 2 Ki 23:7; Hos 4:14.—w 1 Chr 2:4.—x Ru 4:12; Mt 1:3; Lk 3:33.—y Num 26:20; 1 Chr 2:4; Mt 1:3.

38:14 Tamar wants her right to children respected, no matter what the cost; Judah was preventing her from exercising this right (see v. 26).

38:15-24 We might question why Judah was so open about his relations with a prostitute yet ready to put his daughter-in-law to death for being one. The answer lies in the place of women in that time and place. The most important task of women was to bear children to perpetuate the family line. In order to ensure that the children really belonged to the husband, the bride was expected to be a virgin and to refrain from having relations with anyone but her husband. If a wife became an adulteress, she risked the penalty of death. There were, however, some women who did not belong to any man. They could be temple prostitutes supported by offerings or common harlots supported by the men who sought them out. The children of such women were nobody's heirs, and the men who used their services did not adulterate anyone's bloodlines. In opposition to such a secular outlook Scripture enhances the status of women (Gen 1:27f; 2:23) and strongly condemns prostitution (Lev 19:29).

39:1-6 Joseph becomes the majordomo of the captain of the guard, in which capacity he is a model of honor, fidelity, and constancy. He is living proof of the words of St. Paul that "God makes all things work together for good for those who love him" (Rom 8:28).

of the guard, an Egyptian, bought him from the Ishmaelites who had brought him down there.

2 The LORD was with Joseph and he prospered. He remained in the house of the Egyptian, his master.[z] 3 His master realized that the LORD was with him and that whatever he undertook prospered.[a] 4 Thus Joseph found favor with him and became his personal attendant. Potiphar even placed him in charge of his household and he entrusted him with all his possessions.[b] 5 From the moment that he was made overseer and entrusted with his possessions, the LORD blessed the household of the Egyptian because of Joseph, and the blessing of the LORD was upon all that Potiphar had, whether in the house or out in the fields. 6 He entrusted Joseph with all that he had and he did not concern himself with anything other than the food he ate.

The Righteous One Calumniated.* Now Joseph was handsome and good-looking. 7 After some time, the wife of his master set her eyes upon Joseph and said to him, "Sleep with me!"

8 But he refused and said to the wife of his master, "Look, my lord does not worry about anything in his house and he has entrusted me with all his possessions. 9 He has no more authority in this house than I do. He has not kept anything from me but you, for you are his wife. How could I ever do this evil thing and sin against God?" 10 Although she spoke every day to Joseph, he would not agree to sleep with her or even to be near her.[c]

11 One day he entered the house to do his work, but none of the servants was around. 12 She took hold of his tunic saying, "Sleep with me!" But he left his tunic in her hands and ran out of the house.

13 Seeing that he had left his tunic in her hands and that he had fled outside, 14 she called out to the servants and told them, "Look, this Hebrew has been brought into the house to mock us! He came in to lie with me, but I screamed out loud. 15 As soon as he heard me raise my voice and call out, he left his tunic with me and ran out of the house."

16 She left the tunic lying next to her until her master came home. 17 Then she told him these same things: "That Hebrew servant, whom you brought to our house, seized me to insult me. 18 But as soon as I cried out and shouted, he left his tunic next to me and ran out of the house."

19 When the master heard the story his wife told him, saying, "This is what your servant has done to me," he became very angry. 20 He seized Joseph and put him into the prison where they held royal prisoners.[d]

21 But the LORD was with Joseph. He showed him kindness and caused him to find favor with the chief jailer.[e] 22 The chief jailer entrusted all the prisoners to Joseph. Whatever had to be done there, he did it. 23 The chief jailer did not have to worry about any of those things that were entrusted to Joseph, for the LORD was with him and made whatever he did prosper.

CHAPTER 40

A Prophet in Suffering.* 1 Some time later, the cupbearer of the king of Egypt and the baker of the king of Egypt offended their master. 2 Pharaoh was angry with his two eunuchs, the chief cupbearer and the chief baker, 3 and he put them in prison in the care of the captain of the guard in the prison where Joseph was being held. 4 The captain of the guard assigned Joseph to their service. They thus remained in prison for a while.

5 Now, the same night, the cupbearer and the baker of the king of Egypt, who were in prison, both had a dream, each one having his own dream that had its own meaning.

6 The next morning Joseph came to them and saw that they were troubled. 7 He asked the eunuchs of Pharaoh who were with him in prison, in the house of his master, "Why are you so sad today?"

8 They said, "We had a dream, but no one can interpret it."

Joseph said to them, "Does not God have the power of interpreting? Tell your dreams to me."[f]

9 The chief cupbearer told his dream to Joseph and said, "In my dream I was

z 1 Sam 3:19; 10:7; 2 Sam 5:10; 2 Ki 18:7; Acts 7:9.—a 1 Sam 18:14; 2 Ki 18:7; 2 Chr 20:20; Pss 1:3; 128:2; Isa 33:6.—b Dan 1:19.—c 1 Mac 2:53.—d Ps 105:18.—e Acts 7:9f.—f Gen 41:16, 25, 28, 32; Deut 29:29; Dan 2:22, 28, 47.

39:6b-23 Despite the powerful temptation, the young man remains heroically faithful to the word given to his master no matter what the cost. And God comes to his aid as he does to all those who love him in adversity as well as in success.

40:1-23 The ancients regarded dreams as a way in which the divinity came in contact with human beings and revealed the future; God alone, however, could make known the meaning of these dreams.

standing in front of a vine 10 on which there
were three branches. As soon as it
sprouted, the flowers bloomed, and it
brought forth clusters of grapes. 11 I was
holding Pharaoh's cup in my hand. I took
the grapes and squeezed their juice into
Pharaoh's cup. I then gave Pharaoh the
cup."

12 Joseph told him, "Here is the interpre-
tation. The three branches are three days.
13 In three days, Pharaoh will lift up your
head and restore you to your office, and
you will give Pharaoh his cup just as you
once did when you were his cupbearer.
14 When you are happy again, please re-
member that I was with you. Do me this
favor: speak of me to Pharaoh and get me
out of here. 15 I was unjustly carried away
from the land of the Hebrews, and even
here I have done nothing for which I should
have been placed in this dungeon."

16 The chief baker, seeing that Joseph had
given a favorable interpretation, said to
him, "As for me, in my dream I was stand-
ing with three baskets of white bread on
my head. 17 In the baskets on my head were
all different kinds of food for Pharaoh that
would be prepared by a baker. But birds
ate the food from the baskets that I had on
my head."

18 Joseph answered and said, "Here is the
interpretation: the three baskets are three
days. 19 In three days, Pharaoh will lift off
your head and have you impaled; and the
birds will eat away your flesh."

20 Three days later, it was the birthday of
Pharaoh, and there was a banquet for all
his ministers. He lifted up the head of the
chief cupbearer and lifted off the head of
the chief baker before all his ministers.
21 He restored the chief cupbearer to his of-
fice as cupbearer, so that he would hand
the cup to Pharaoh. 22 He had the chief
baker impaled, just as Joseph had said in
his interpretation.

23 But the cupbearer did not remember
Joseph; he forgot him.

CHAPTER 41

Messenger of Salvation.* 1 Two years later,
Pharaoh had a dream in which he was
alongside the Nile. 2 Seven cows came out
of the Nile, beautiful and fat, and they
began to graze in the reed grass.[g] 3 Then
seven other cows came up out of the Nile
after them. They were ugly and thin, and
they stopped alongside the first cows on
the shore of the Nile. 4 The ugly and thin
cows devoured the seven beautiful and fat
cows. Then Pharaoh woke up.

5 He fell back asleep and had a second
dream. There were seven heads of grain on
one stalk, fat and healthy. 6 But seven
empty heads, shriveled by the east wind,
sprouted up after them. 7 The seven empty
heads swallowed the seven fat and healthy
heads. Then Pharaoh woke up; it had been
a dream.

8 In the morning, he was very troubled
and he summoned all the magicians and
wise men in Egypt. Pharaoh told them his
dream, but no one knew how to interpret it
for him.

9 The cupbearer spoke to Pharaoh,
"Today I remember that I have done some-
thing wrong. 10 Pharaoh was angry with his
servants and had sent me and the chief
baker into prison in the care of the captain
of the guard. 11 We both had dreams the
same night, but each of us had his own
dream with its own meaning. 12 There was
a young Hebrew there with us, a slave of
the captain of the guard. We told him our
dreams, and he interpreted them, giving
each of us an explanation for his dream.[h]
13 Just what he predicted came true: I was
restored to my office, and the other man
was impaled."

14 Pharaoh therefore summoned Joseph,
and they quickly brought him out of the
dungeon. He shaved and changed his
clothes and was brought to Pharaoh.[i]
15 Pharaoh said to Joseph, "I had a dream
and no one can interpret it. Now I have
heard it said that you can hear a dream
and immediately interpret it."

16 Joseph answered Pharaoh, "Not I, but
God will give Pharaoh a favorable an-
swer."[j]

17 Pharaoh said to Joseph, "In my dream
I was on the Nile riverbank. 18 Seven fat
and beautiful cows came out of the Nile
and they began to graze on the reed grass.
19 Then seven other cows came out after
them. They were poor and sickly and thin,
I had never seen any as ugly in all of Egypt.
20 The thin and ugly cows devoured the

g Ex 2:3; Job 33:15.—h Dan 1:17.—i Ps 105:20.—j Gen 40:8.

41:1-36 Joseph here represents the divine wisdom (Wis 10:14), which is far more effective than the efforts of the soothsayers; God alone knows the meaning of events because he alone is master of them.

seven fat cows.* 21 Even after they had eaten them, you still could not see that they had eaten anything. They were still as ugly as they had been before. Then I woke up.

22 "I then had a dream in which seven heads of grain sprouted on a single stalk. They were fat and good. 23 But seven dry heads, empty and shriveled by the east wind, sprouted after them. 24 The empty heads of grain swallowed the seven good heads. I told this to the magicians, but none of them could explain it to me."

25 Joseph said to Pharaoh, "Pharaoh's dreams are actually one dream. God has revealed to Pharaoh what he is about to do. 26 The seven beautiful cows are seven years, and the seven beautiful heads of grain are seven years. It is a single dream. 27 The seven thin and ugly cows that came up after them are seven years and the seven empty heads, withered by the east wind, are seven years. There will be seven years of famine.

28 "It is just as I have told Pharaoh. God has revealed to Pharaoh what he is about to do. 29 There will soon be seven years of great abundance in the land of Egypt. 30 Then the seven years after these will be seven years of famine. The years of abundance will be forgotten in the land of Egypt, and famine will ravage the land. 31 It will be forgotten that there was abundance in the land, for the famine that will follow will be very severe. 32 As for the fact that the dream was repeated twice, this means that God has decided the matter and God is hastening to fulfill it.

33 "Pharaoh should seek and find an intelligent and wise man and place him in charge of the land of Egypt. 34 Pharaoh should also appoint overseers in the land to collect a fifth of the produce of the land during the years of abundance. 35 They should collect all the food in these good years that are about to take place. They will gather the grain under the authority of Pharaoh and place it in granaries in the cities. 36 This food will serve as a reserve in the land for the seven years of famine that will come upon the land of Egypt. Thus, the land will not be devastated during the famine."

Joseph Is Made Viceroy of Egypt.*

37 Pharaoh and all his ministers were pleased with this.[k] 38 Pharaoh said to his ministers, "Could we find another man like this, in whom one finds the Spirit of God?"

39 So Pharaoh said to Joseph, "Since God has revealed all this to you, there is surely no one as intelligent or as wise as you. 40 You shall be in charge of my house. You shall have authority over all my people. Only the throne shall outrank you."[l]

41 Then Pharaoh said to Joseph, "Behold, I have made you ruler of the entire land of Egypt." 42 *Pharaoh took the ring off his finger and placed it on the finger of Joseph. He dressed him in clothes made of the finest linen and placed a gold chain around his neck.[m] 43 He had him ride in the chariot of his vizier, and before him they cried, "Make way!" He made him ruler of the entire land of Egypt.

44 Then Pharaoh said to Joseph, "I am Pharaoh, but without your permission no one can raise a hand or a foot in the entire land of Egypt."[n] 45 And Pharaoh named Joseph Zaphenath-peneah. He gave him Asenath, the daughter of Potiphera, a priest of On,* as his wife. Joseph went throughout the entire land of Egypt.

46 Joseph was thirty years old when he was brought before Pharaoh, the king of Egypt. Joseph left the presence of Pharaoh and traveled throughout the entire land of Egypt. 47 During the seven years of abundance the land was very fertile. 48 He collected all the food of these seven years when there was abundance in the land of Egypt. He placed the food in the cities, that is, in every city he deposited the food of the surrounding countryside. 49 Joseph gathered as much grain as the sand of the sea, enormous quantities. There was so much that it could no longer be measured, for it was beyond measure.

k Acts 7:10.—l 1 Mac 2:53; Ps 105:21; Wis 10:14; Acts 7:10.—m Est 3:10; 8:2, 8, 10.—n Ps 105:21f.

41:20 For the Egyptians the cow was a symbol of Hator, goddess of fertility, protector of the Nile, and goddess of the "Great Wave," that is, the ocean. Seven cows symbolized Osiris, inventor of agriculture and of the seven-year cycle (the people had linked the alternate flooding of the Nile and drought with the seven-year cycle). It was believed that during a famine, animals and human beings devoured one another, in a meeting of death with hunger.

41:37-49 God's Providence has turned the situation in Joseph's favor. Invested as prime minister in the most pure Egyptian tradition, Joseph now presides over the destiny of the country to which he was sold as a slave.

41:42-45 The ring, fine linen robes, and gold neck-chain are the insignia of authority; they may also be seen on monuments. *"Make way!":* Hebrew, *Abrech,* which may also mean "Kneel down!" and be a command to show supreme honor. *Zaphenath-peneah:* the meaning of the name is obscure; perhaps it means "God says: He is alive" or "He who explains hidden things."

41:45 *On:* i.e., Heliopolis.

The Great Famine.* 50 Joseph had two sons
in the years that preceded the famine.
They were born to Asenath, the daughter
of Potiphera, the priest of On.[o] 51 Joseph
called the firstborn Manasseh for, he said,
"God has made me forget all my difficul-
ties and my father's entire family." 52 He
named the second son Ephraim for, he
said, "God has made me prosper in the
land of my affliction."
53 The seven years of abundance in the
land of Egypt ended, 54 and the seven years
of famine began, just as Joseph had pre-
dicted. There was famine over the whole
earth, but there was food in Egypt.[p]
55 Then the whole land of Egypt began to
feel the hunger, and the people cried out to
Pharaoh to have food. Pharaoh said to all
the Egyptians, "Go to Joseph, and do what-
ever he tells you."
56 The famine spread throughout the en-
tire land. So Joseph opened up the store-
houses in which he had placed the grain,
and he sold it to the Egyptians. The famine
kept getting worse in Egypt. 57 People came
to Egypt from every country to buy grain
from Joseph, for the famine was severe
over the whole earth.

CHAPTER 42

The Sons of Jacob Seek Food in Egypt.*
1 When Jacob heard that there was grain in
Egypt, he said to his sons, "Why are you
standing around looking at each other?"
2 He continued, "Behold, I have heard that
there is grain in Egypt. Go down there and
buy some for us, so that we may stay alive
and not die."[q]
3 So ten brothers of Joseph went down to
buy grain in Egypt. 4 But Jacob did not
send Joseph's brother Benjamin with the
others, for he said, "Some misfortune
might befall him." 5 The sons of Israel,
therefore, arrived to buy grain along with
all the others who had also come, for there
was famine in Canaan.[r]
6 Joseph had authority over the land,
and he sold grain to all the people of the
land. Therefore, the brothers of Joseph
came to him and bowed down to the
earth.[s] 7 Joseph saw his brothers and rec-
ognized them, but he hid his identity from
them. He spoke harshly and said, "Where
do you come from?"
They answered, "From the land of
Canaan to buy food."
8 Joseph recognized his brothers, but
they did not recognize him. 9 Joseph re-
membered the dreams he had concerning
them, and he said to them, "You are spies.
You have come to see the nakedness of the
land."[t]
10 They answered, "No, my lord, your
servants have come to buy food. 11 We are
all sons of one man. We are honest. Your
servants are not spies."
12 But he said to them, "No, you have
come to spy out the nakedness of the
land."
13 They said, "Your servants are twelve
in all. We are brothers, sons of one man
from the land of Canaan. The youngest is
now with his father, and one is no more."[u]
14 Joseph said to them, "Things are just
as I have said: you are spies. 15 This is how
you shall be put to the test. By the life of
Pharaoh, you shall not leave here until
your youngest brother has arrived. 16 Send
one of your number to bring your brother;
the rest will remain as prisoners. You will
thus be put to the test concerning what
you have said, to see if you have told the
truth. If not, by the life of Pharaoh, you
are spies." 17 And he then held them in
prison for three days.
18 On the third day, Joseph said to them,
"Do this and you shall live, for I fear
God![v] 19 If you are honest, then leave one
of your brothers in prison and go to bring
the grain to ease the hunger of your
household. 20 Then bring me your
youngest brother. In this way, your words
will be seen to be true and you will not
die." They agreed.[w]
21 They said among themselves, "Surely
this terrible thing has come upon us be-
cause of our brother. We saw his torment
when he begged us, and we did not listen
to him. That is why this trouble has come
upon us."[x]
22 Reuben spoke to them, "Did I not tell
you not to sin against the boy? But you re-

o Gen 46:20; 48:5.—p Ps 105:16; Acts 7:11.—q Acts 7:12.—r Jud 5:10; Acts 7:11.—s Ps 105:21.—t Gen 37:5.—u Gen 44:20.—v Lev 25:43.—w Gen 43:5.—x Gen 37:18-27.

41:50-57 Joseph's foresight and adroit administration avert a disaster in Egypt and turn the country into the granary of the Near East.

42:1-24 Joseph's dreams (Gen 37:5-11) are fulfilled: without knowing it, his brothers prostrate themselves at his feet. In a moving scene in which he feigns severity and hides his feelings, Joseph leads them to bare their guilt in having sold their brother as a slave. The rhythm of the account demands the lengthy suspense in these chapters, which might seem at times to be deliberately cruel.

fused to listen. Now we will pay for his
blood."[y] 23 They did not know that Joseph
understood them because he was using an
interpreter.
24 He walked away from them and cried.
Then he returned and spoke with them. He
selected Simeon and had him placed in
chains while they were watching.

The Sons of Jacob Return to Canaan.*
25 Joseph gave orders that their sacks be
filled with grain, and that each one's
money be placed in his sack, and that they
be given provisions for their journey. This
was done for them.[z] 26 Then they loaded
the grain on their donkeys and departed.
27 At their night encampment, one of
them opened his sack to take out forage for
his donkey and saw his money lying at the
mouth of the sack. 28 He told his brothers,
"My money has been returned to me.
Look, it was in my sack."

Their hearts sank, and they began to
shake, saying to one another, "What is this
that God has done to us?"
29 When they reached their father Jacob
in the land of Canaan, they told him every-
thing that had happened to them. 30 "That
man who is the lord of the land spoke
harshly to us and placed us in prison as
spies of the land. 31 We told him, 'We are
honest men, not spies! 32 We are twelve
brothers, sons of one father. One is no
more, and the youngest is at home with
our father in the land of Canaan.'
33 "But the man who is lord of the land
answered us, 'This is how I shall know if
you are honest: leave one of your brothers
here with me, take the grain you need for
your household, and go. 34 Then bring your
youngest brother back to me. In that way I
shall know that you are not spies, but that
you are honest. I will return your brother
and you will have the freedom of the
land.' "
35 As they emptied their sacks, each one
found his money bag in his sack. When
they and their father saw their money
bags, they were filled with fear. 36 And their
father Jacob said, "You have taken away
my sons. Joseph is no more, and Simeon is
no more, and now you would like to take
away Benjamin. Everything is against me!"
37 Reuben said to his father, "You can kill
my two sons if we do not bring him back to
you. Entrust him to me, and I will bring
him back."
38 But he answered, "My son shall not go
down there with you because his brother is
dead and he alone remains. If something
bad were to happen to him during the jour-
ney that you were making, you would make
these gray hairs go down into the nether-
world."[a]

CHAPTER 43

The Sons of Jacob Set Out Again for Egypt.*
1 The famine continued to grow more se-
vere in the land. 2 When they had finished
eating the grain that they had brought
from Egypt, their father said to them,
"Return there to buy a little more food
for us."
3 But Judah said to him, "That man
told us harshly, 'You shall not come into
my presence if you do not have your
brother with you.'[b] 4 If you are willing to
let us leave with our brother, then we will
go down there and buy grain. 5 But if you
will not let him leave, we will not go be-
cause of what that man told us: 'You shall
not come into my presence if you do not
have your brother with you.' "[c]
6 Israel said, "Why have you done this
evil thing to me, to let that man know
that you had another brother?"
7 They answered, "That man interro-
gated us, demanding to know about us
and our family: 'Is your father still alive?
Do you have some other brothers?' and
we answered his questions. How could we
know that he would have said, 'Bring your
brother here' ?"
8 Judah said to Israel his father, "Let the
young one come with me. We will leave
immediately, so that we might live and not
die, we, you, and our children.[d] 9 I will
make myself the pledge for him. You will
receive him from my hand. If I do not
bring him back to you, I will bear this guilt
in your eyes all my life.[e] 10 If you had not
hesitated, we could have already gone
there and back twice by now."

y Gen 37:22.—z Mt 5:44; Rom 12:17, 20.—a Gen 37:35.—b Gen 44:23.—c Gen 42:20.—d Gen 42:37; Ps 33:18f.—e Gen 44:32.

42:25-38 The sons of Jacob wend their way home in sadness. Simeon has been retained as a hostage, the viceroy demands Benjamin, and the gold of the payment is stashed in the sacks. One would be worried over less.

43:1-14 With deep sadness of soul, the Patriarch gives in to the desire of the demanding viceroy and consents to let his youngest son go to Egypt. The difference between the traditions, along the lines already noted, reappears here: according to the Elohist it was Reuben who offered himself as surety (Gen 42:37); in the Yahwist story it is Judah who once more takes the lead (43:8-10).

11 Israel their father answered, "If this is
the way it is, do it. Pack your bags with the
choice products of the land to give to that
man as a gift: some balsam, a bit of honey,
resin, gum, pistachio nuts, and almonds.[f]
12 Take double the amount of money with
you. Take back the money that you found
in the mouth of your sacks; maybe there
was a mistake. 13 Take your brother as well;
leave and return to that man. 14 May God
Almighty help you to find mercy with that
man so that he will release your other
brother and Benjamin. As for me, if I
must mourn my children, I will do so."

The Sons of Jacob Are Guests of Joseph.*
15 The men therefore took the gifts, double
the money, and Benjamin and left. They
went down to Egypt and presented them-
selves to Joseph. 16 When Joseph saw Ben-
jamin with them, he said to his head
steward: "Bring these men into the house.
Slaughter an animal and prepare it. They
are to eat the noonday meal with me."

17 The steward did what Joseph had
ordered and brought the men into his
house. 18 They were worried when they
were brought into Joseph's house and they
said, "He brought us here because of the
money that was placed back in our sacks
the other time. They are going to fall upon
us and make us slaves and take our don-
keys as well."[g]

19 So they approached Joseph's head
steward and spoke to him at the entrance
to the house 20 saying, "My lord, we came
one other time to buy provisions.[h] 21 When
we arrived at the place where we spent the
night, we opened our sacks and each one
discovered his money in the mouth of the
sack. It was the exact amount of money we
had brought. But we have brought it back[i]
22 and we brought some other money as
well to buy more food. We do not know
who placed our money in the sacks."

23 But he told them, "Be at peace! Do
not fear! Your God and the God of your fa-
thers placed riches in your sacks. I re-
ceived your money." And he brought
Simeon to them.

24 The steward led the men into Joseph's
house, and gave them water to wash their
feet, and provided forage for their donkeys.
25 They prepared their gifts while they
waited for Joseph to arrive at noon, for they
knew that they were to eat in that place.

26 When Joseph arrived, they presented
to him the gifts that they had with them,
and they bowed their faces to the ground
before him. 27 He asked them how they
were and said, "How is your aged father,
the one about whom you have spoken? Is
he still alive?"[j]

28 They answered, "Your servant, our
father, is well, and he is still alive," and
they knelt and bowed down.

29 Looking up, he saw Benjamin, his
brother, the son of his mother, and said, "Is
this your youngest brother about whom
you have spoken?" He added, "God bless
you, my son!"[k] 30 Joseph went out in a rush,
for he was deeply moved at seeing his
brother and he was close to tears. He went
into his room and wept there.

31 Then he washed his face, went out,
and, controlling his emotions, ordered,
"Serve the meal."

32 He was served separately, then his
brothers, and then the Egyptians, for
Egyptians cannot eat with Hebrews. It
would be an abomination for them. 33 He
sat them before himself from the firstborn
to the youngest, each in the order of his
birth. They looked at each other with awe.
34 He served them a portion taken from
his own table, but the portion he gave to
Benjamin was five times larger than that
given to all the others. They then drank
with him until they were lighthearted.

CHAPTER 44

**Benjamin Is Condemned To Remain in
Egypt.*** 1 Joseph then gave this order to the
head steward of his house, "Fill these
men's sacks with as much food as they
can carry and place each man's money in
the mouth of his sack. 2 Also place my cup,
my silver cup, in the mouth of the sack of
the youngest along with the money for
their grain." And he did as Joseph had
ordered.

3 When morning dawned the men set
out with their donkeys. 4 They had just left
the city and were not far off when Joseph

f Gen 45:23.—g Lev 26:36; Job 15:21; Wis 17:10.—h Gen 42:3.—i Gen 42:27f.—j Tob 7:4.—k Gen 42:13.

43:15-34 After the misadventures of the first visit, the sons of Jacob are hard put to believe the kindness with which they are being treated, and they are reassured only at the banquet that is offered to them.

44:1-34 The author arranges his story very effectively. The sons of Jacob cannot doubt that an evil fate will befall the youngest of them. Will Judah's moving discourse touch the heart of the viceroy? The drama abounds.

said to the head steward of his house, "Up, follow the men. When you reach them, tell them, 'Why have you paid back evil for good? 5 Is this not the cup that my lord uses for drinking and to tell the future? Why have you done this evil thing?' "[l]

6 He reached them and repeated these words to them. 7 They told him, "Why is my lord saying these things? Far be it from your servants to do such a thing! 8 We brought the money that we found in the mouth of the sacks back from the land of Canaan. How could we steal the silver or gold from the house of your master? 9 Whichever of your servants is found with it will be put to death, and we will also become the slaves of your master."

10 He answered, "Very well, it will be as you have said. Whoever is found with it will be my slave; the others will be innocent."

11 Each one hurried to unload his sack and open it. 12 The steward searched from the oldest to the youngest. The cup was found in Benjamin's sack. 13 At this, they tore their clothes. Then each one loaded up his donkey, and they returned to the city.

14 When Judah and his brothers came to the house of Joseph, they found him still there; so they threw themselves on the ground in front of him. 15 Joseph told them, "What have you done? Did you not know that a man like me could cast a spell to find out the truth?"[m]

16 Judah said, "What will we say to our lord? What can we say? How can we justify ourselves? God has uncovered the iniquity of your servants. Let us be slaves of my lord, we and the one with whom the cup was found." 17 He answered them, "Far be it from me to do this! The man with whom the cup was found, he will be my slave. As for you, return in peace to your father."

18 But Judah came before him and said, "My lord, let your servant please speak a word in the ear of my lord. Let your anger not burn against your servant, for you are as great as Pharaoh himself. 19 My lord asked his servants, 'Do you have a father or a brother?' 20 We told my lord, 'We have an aged father and a younger brother who was born in his old age. His brother is dead, and he is the only remaining son of his mother, and his father loves him.'[n]

21 "You said to your servants, 'Bring him here to me, so that I can see him with my own eyes.' 22 We told my lord, 'The young one cannot leave his father; if he were to leave his father he would die.' 23 But you said to your servants, 'If your younger brother does not come down here with you, you shall not see my face.'[o] 24 When we returned to your servant, my father, we told him the words of my lord.

25 "Our father said, 'Return to buy a little more food for us.' 26 We answered, 'We cannot return down there if our younger brother does not go down with us. Otherwise, we will not be admitted into the presence of that man, if our younger brother is not with us.'

27 "Your servant, my father, said, 'You know that my wife bore me two sons. 28 One left me, and I said, "Surely he has been torn to pieces," and I have not seen him since.[p] 29 If you carry away this one and something were to happen to him, you would make this gray head go down with sorrow into the netherworld.'

30 "Now, when I go back to your servant, my father, and the young one is not with me (for the life of one is bound to the other), 31 he will surely die as soon as he sees that the young one is not with me. Thus, your servants will have made the gray head of your servant, our father, go down into the netherworld. 32 Your servant made himself a pledge for the young one with my father: 'If I do not bring him back to you, I will bear this guilt before you all my life.'[q]

33 "Let your servant remain as the slave of my lord instead of the young one. Let the young one return back with his brothers. 34 How could I return to my father without having the young one with me? I could not bear to see the evil that I will have done to my father."

CHAPTER 45

Joseph Reveals Himself to His Brothers and Manifests God's Plan.* 1 Joseph could no longer control himself in front of all of his

l Deut 18:10.—m Gen 30:27.—n Gen 42:13.—o Gen 43:3.—p Gen 37:20, 33.—q Gen 43:9.

45:1-20 Here at last is the denouement. This scene of the brothers' reunion magnifies the benevolence of Joseph. Far from avenging himself on his brothers, he pardons them for having sold him. His words are a recognition of God's Providence whose action in favor of his faithful ones Joseph discovers in the unfolding of his own adventures. And in preparation for the great epic of the Exodus it was necessary that Israel should settle in Egypt, as Pharaoh now invites them to do.

attendants and he cried out, "Let every-
one leave my presence!" Thus no one was
there when Joseph revealed himself to his
brothers. 2 He cried out so loudly that all
the Egyptians heard him, and the news
reached Pharaoh's palace.
3 [r] Joseph said to his brothers, "I am
Joseph! Is my father still alive?" But his
brothers could not respond for they were
dumbfounded at his presence.
4 Joseph said to his brothers, "Come
close to me!" They approached him, and
he said to them, "I am Joseph, your
brother, whom you sold into Egypt. 5 But
do not be grieved and do not be angry
with yourselves for having sold me down
here, for God sent me here before you to
save your lives. [s] 6 The famine has already
lasted two years in the land, and there are
another five years in which there will be
neither plowing nor reaping. 7 God sent
me here before you, to preserve a rem-
nant for you on the earth and to save your
lives by a great deliverance.
8 "It was not you who sent me here, but
God. He made me a father to Pharaoh,
lord over his whole household, and ruler
of all the land of Egypt. [t]
9 "Hurry, go up to my father and tell
him, 'Thus says your son Joseph, "God has
made me lord over all of Egypt. Come
down here to me and do not delay. [u] 10 You
will live in the land of Goshen * and stay
near me, you and your sons and the sons
of your sons, your flocks and your herds,
and all your possessions. 11 There I will
give you provisions, for there will still be
five more years to this famine, lest your
family fall into poverty, you, and your
family, and all you possess." '
12 "Your own eyes have seen it and the
eyes of my brother Benjamin have seen it:
it is I who speak to you. 13 Tell my father
all the glory that I have in Egypt and what
you have seen. Hurry to bring my father
down here."
14 He threw himself on the neck of Ben-
jamin and cried. Benjamin also cried hold-
ing on to his neck. 15 He then kissed all his
brothers and cried, holding them to him-
self. Afterward, his brothers spoke to him.
16 In the house of Pharaoh they heard
the report: "The brothers of Joseph have
arrived." This pleased Pharaoh and his
ministers. 17 Pharaoh said to Joseph: "Tell
your brothers, 'Do this: load up your ani-
mals, leave, and go to the land of Canaan.
18 Then bring your father and your fami-
lies and come to me. I will give you the
best of the land of Egypt, and you will eat
the finest products of the land.' [v]
19 "As for you, give them this command:
'Do this: take wagons with you from the
land of Egypt for your children and your
wives. Bring your father and come. 20 Do
not be concerned about your possessions,
for the best of everything in the land of
Egypt shall be yours.' "

The Sons of Jacob Return Home Again.*
21 This is what the sons of Israel did.
Joseph gave them wagons as Pharaoh
ordered, and he gave them provisions for
their journey. 22 He gave all of them fresh
clothing, but he gave Benjamin three hun-
dred shekels of silver and five sets of
clothes. 23 He also sent his father ten don-
keys loaded with products of Egypt and
ten donkeys loaded with grain, bread, and
other food for their father's trip. 24 He then
sent his brothers off and, while they were
leaving, he said to them, "Do not fight
during the journey."
25 They left Egypt and returned to the
land of Canaan, to their father Jacob,
26 and immediately told him, "Joseph is
alive; he is the ruler over the whole land of
Egypt!" But his heart was cold, for he
could not believe them. 27 When they told
him all the things Joseph had said to them
and when he saw the wagons that Joseph
had sent to bring him, their father's spirit
revived. 28 Israel said, "Enough! Joseph,
my son, is alive. I will go to see him before
I die!"

CHAPTER 46

Jacob Goes to Egypt. 1 * Israel set out
with all that he had and arrived at Beer-
sheba where he offered a sacrifice to the
God of his father Isaac.

r 3f: Acts 7:13.—s Gen 50:20; Job 10:12; Ps 107:17.—t Gen 45:5; Est 4:14.—u Acts 7:14.—v Acts 7:14.

45:10 *Goshen:* a region suitable for stock-rearing. For religious and legal reasons the Egyptians detested shepherds (the Hyksos; see Gen 46:34). The Hebrews will win positions of power and great wealth (vv. 18, 20; 47:6).

45:21-28 In contrast with the anxiety of the first return, it is a triumphal caravan that comes home to Canaan where the sons of Jacob go to fetch their aged father.

46:1-7 One last time, the Lord manifests himself and renews his promise to the Patriarchs: the sojourn into Egypt is only a stage; already we get a glimpse of the Exodus, the birth of the people of Israel. This account invites all believers to discover the plan of God in a most astounding history and in their own lives.

2 God appeared to Israel in a vision during
the night saying, "Jacob, Jacob." He an-
swered, "Here I am."
3 He continued, "I am God, the God of
your father. Do not fear to go down into
Egypt, for down there I will make a great
people of you.[w] 4 I will go down with you into
Egypt, and I will surely make you return.
Joseph will close your eyes."
5 Jacob left Beer-sheba, and the sons of Is-
rael put their father, their children, and their
wives into the wagons that Pharaoh had sent
to carry them. 6 They took with them their
animals and all the possessions that they had
acquired in the land of Canaan. Thus, Jacob
and all his descendants went to Egypt.[x] 7 He
brought his sons and grandsons, his daugh-
ters and granddaughters, and all his descen-
dants with him into Egypt.

8 These are the names of the sons of Israel
who entered Egypt: Jacob and his sons.

Reuben the firstborn of Jacob.[y]
9 The sons of Reuben:
Hanoch, Pallu, Hezron, and Carmi.[z]
10 The sons of Simeon:
Nemuel, Jamin, Ohad, Jachin, Zohar, and Shaul, the son of a Canaanite woman.[a]
11 The sons of Levi:
Gershon, Kohath, and Merari.[b]
12 The sons of Judah:
Er, Onan, Shelah, Perez, and Zerah, (but Er and Onan died in the land of Canaan).
The sons of Perez:
Hezron and Hamul.[c]
13 The sons of Issachar:
Tola, Puah, Jashub, and Shimron.[d]
14 The sons of Zebulun:
Sered, Elon, and Jahleel.[e]
15 These were the sons whom Leah bore
to Jacob in Paddan-aram, together with
their daughter Dinah. The total number of
her sons and daughters was thirty-three.[f]

16 The sons of Gad:
Zephon, Haggi, Shuni, Ezbon, Eri, Arod, and Areli.
17 The sons of Asher:
Imnah, Ishvah, Ishvi, Beriah, and their sister Serah.
The sons of Beriah:
Heber and Malchiel.[g]

18 These were the sons of Zilpah, whom
Laban had given to his daughter Leah. She
bore them to Jacob: sixteen in all.

19 The sons of Rachel, the wife of Jacob:
Joseph and Benjamin.
20 Ephraim[h] and Manasseh were born to Joseph in Egypt. They were the sons of Asenath, the daughter of Potiphera, the priest of On.*
21 The sons of Benjamin:
Bela, Becher, Ashbel, Gera, Naaman, Ahiram, Shupham, Hupham, and Ard.[i]
22 These were the sons Rachel bore to
Jacob—fourteen in all.

23 The son of Dan:
Hushim.[j]
24 The sons of Naphtali:
Jahzeel, Guni, Jezer, and Shillem.[k]
25 These were the sons of Bilhah whom
Laban gave to his daughter Rachel. She
bore them to Jacob: seven in all.

26 All those who entered with Jacob into
Egypt were his offspring. Not counting the
wives of the sons of Jacob there were sixty-
six in all.[l] 27 Two sons were born to Joseph
in Egypt. The members of the family of
Jacob who went to Egypt were seventy.[m]

Joseph and Pharaoh Welcome Jacob.*
28 Jacob sent Judah to Joseph ahead of the
rest so that he might give instructions in
Goshen before his arrival. When they ar-
rived in the land of Goshen, 29 Joseph made
his chariot ready and went up into Goshen
to greet Israel, his father. As soon as he saw
him, he threw himself around his neck and
wept for a long time holding on to his neck.
30 Israel said to Joseph, "Let me die, now
that I have seen your face, that you are
still alive."
31 Joseph said to his brothers and to the
family of his father, "I am going to inform

w Gen 12:2; 28:13; Ex 1:7.—x Ex 1:12; Jos 24:4; Jud 5:10; Acts 7:15.—y Ex 1:2.—z Ex 6:14; Num 26:5; 1 Chr 5:3.—a Ex 6:15; Num 26:12; 1 Chr 4:24.—b Ex 6:16; Num 3:17; 26:57; 1 Chr 6:1.—c Gen 38:3-10, 29f; Num 26:19; 1 Chr 2:5.—d Num 26:23f; 1 Chr 7:1.—e Num 26:26.—f Num 26:15f.—g Num 26:44; 1 Chr 7:30f.—h Gen 41:50; Num 26:28, 35.—i Num 26:38; 1 Chr 7:6; 8:1-4.—j Num 26:42.—k Num 26:48f; 1 Chr 7:13.—l Ex 1:5.—m Ex 1:5; Deut 10:22; Acts 7:14.

46:20 *On:* i.e., Heliopolis.
46:28—47:12 With the favor of the sovereign of Egypt cleverly orchestrated by Joseph, the children of Israel can establish themselves in the region to the east of the Nile delta without mingling with the Egyptians (46:34), not far from the frontier. They can then start out more easily at the time of the Exodus! By the play of circumstances, Providence has provided for everything.

Pharaoh and to tell him, 'My brothers and
the family of my father, who were in the
land of Canaan, have come to be with me.
[32] These men were shepherds of flocks and
they tended herds. They have brought
their flocks, their herds, and all their pos-
sessions.' [33] When Pharaoh summons you
and asks you what you do for a living,
[34] you should answer, 'Your servants have
been men who care for cattle from their
youth until now, just as our fathers did.'
This is so that you can dwell in the land of
Goshen." For all shepherds of flocks are an
abomination to the Egyptians. [n]

CHAPTER 47

[1] Joseph went to inform Pharaoh, saying
to him, "My father and my brothers with
their flocks and herds and with all their
possessions have come from the land of
Canaan. They are now in the land of
Goshen." [2] He selected five of his brothers
and presented them to Pharaoh.
[3] Pharaoh said to his brothers, "What
work do you do?"
They answered Pharaoh, "We shepherd
the flocks of your servants, just as our fa-
thers did." [4] They went on to tell Pharaoh,
"We came to sojourn in this land because
there were no more pastures for the flocks
of your servants. The famine is terrible in
the land of Canaan. Please allow your ser-
vants to dwell in the land of Goshen." [o]
[5] Pharaoh said to Joseph, "Your father
and your brothers have come to you. [6] The
land of Egypt is at your disposition. Have
your father and your brothers settle in the
best of the land. Let them dwell in the
land of Goshen. If you know any of them
as able men, place them in charge of my
cattle."
[7] Joseph then introduced Jacob, his
father, and presented him to Pharaoh.
After Jacob had blessed Pharaoh, [8] Phar-
aoh asked him, "How old are you?"
[9] Jacob answered Pharaoh, "One hun-
dred and thirty are the years of my so-
journing. Few and sad are the years of my
life, and I have not reached the number of
years that my fathers lived in their life
journey." [10] Then Jacob blessed Pharaoh
and withdrew from his presence.
[11] Joseph settled his father and his
brothers and gave them property in
Egypt, in the best part of the land, in the
territory of Rameses, as Pharaoh had
commanded. [p] [12] Joseph provided for his
father, his brothers, and all the family of
his father, as much bread as was needed
for each person.

Joseph's Administration.* [13] Now there
was no bread in the whole land, for the
famine was very severe. The land of Egypt
and the land of Canaan wasted away be-
cause of the famine. [14] Joseph collected all
the money there was in the land of Egypt
and in the land of Canaan for the grain
that they were buying. Joseph sent this
money to Pharaoh. [15] When the money of
the land of Egypt and the land of Canaan
was gone, all the Egyptians came to
Joseph and said, "Give us bread! Why
should we die while you are watching? We
do not have any more money."
[16] Joseph answered, "If you do not have
any more money, give me your animals
and I will give you bread in exchange for
the animals." [17] They therefore brought
their animals to Joseph, and Joseph gave
them bread in exchange for their horses
and sheep, their oxen and their donkeys.
That year he fed them with bread in ex-
change for their animals.
[18] That year having ended, they came to
him the next year and said to him, "We
will not hide from my lord that our money
is gone and our animals now belong to my
lord. We have nothing for my lord except
our own bodies and our land. [19] Why
should we die with you looking on, we and
our land? Buy us and our land in exchange
for bread, and we will become servants to
Pharaoh, we and our land. But give us
something to plant so that we live and not
die and the land not become a desert."
[20] Joseph acquired all the land of Egypt
for Pharaoh, because the Egyptians sold
their fields on account of the famine that
weighed upon them. Thus the land be-
came Pharaoh's property. [21] As to the peo-
ple, he moved them into the cities from
one end to the other of the borders of
Egypt. [22] Only the property which be-
longed to the priests was not bought, for
the priests had a fixed allotment given to

n Gen 45:10.—o Ex 23:9.—p Gen 45:10, 18; Ex 1:11; 12:37; Num 33:3, 5.

47:13-26 At the time of the New Empire (16th century B.C.), the greater part of the Egyptian farmers did not possess land; they were farmers of Pharaoh. To better illustrate Joseph's competency, the author gives him credit for this regulation about the land, which surprised the nomadic Israelites.

them by Pharaoh, and they ate the allot-
ment that Pharaoh had given them. This
is why they did not sell their land.
23 Joseph said to the people, "See, today
I have acquired you and your land for
Pharaoh. Here is seed, sow the land. 24 But
when you harvest it, you will give a fifth of
it to Pharaoh and four-fifths will be for
you to sow the fields and feed yourselves
and those who are in your household and
to feed your children."
25 They answered, "You have saved our
lives! Let us only find favor before my lord
and we will be servants of Pharaoh."
26 Joseph made a law that is still in force
up until this day for the land of Egypt, that
a one-fifth portion must be given to
Pharaoh. Only the land of the priests does
not belong to Pharaoh.
Final Dispositions of Jacob. 27 The Is-
raelites settled in the land of Egypt, in the
territory of Goshen. They had possessions
and were fruitful and became very nu-
merous. [q]
28 Jacob lived in the land of Egypt for
seventeen years and he lived for a total of
one hundred and forty-seven years. [r]
29 When the day of his death drew near,
Israel summoned his son Joseph and told
him, "If I have found favor in your sight,
place your hand under my thigh and deal
with me kindly and faithfully. Do not bury
me in Egypt. 30 When I lie with my fathers,
carry me from Egypt and bury me in their
tomb." [s]
31 "I will do as you say," he replied.
But Jacob demanded, "Swear it to me."
He answered, "I swear it." And he swore
it. Then Israel sank back on his pillow.

CHAPTER 48

Jacob Adopts and Blesses Joseph's Sons.*
1 Some time later, Joseph was told, "Be-
hold, your father is ill." So he brought his
two sons Manasseh and Ephraim with
him. 2 When Jacob was told, "Behold your
son Joseph is here for you," Israel sum-
moned his strength and sat up in bed.
3 [t] Jacob said to Joseph, "God Almighty
appeared to me in Luz, in the land of
Canaan, and blessed me, 4 saying to me,
'Behold, I will make you fruitful. I will mul-
tiply you and make you become a multi-
tude of peoples, and I will give this land to
your descendants after you as an eternal
possession.'
5 "Now the two sons born to you in the
land of Egypt before I arrived to be with
you in Egypt are mine. Ephraim and Ma-
nasseh will be mine just like Reuben and
Simeon. 6 The sons that you will have after
these, they will be yours. They will be called
by the name of their brothers in their in-
heritance. 7 As for me, while I was arriving
from Paddan, Rachel, your mother, died in
the land of Canaan while we were in jour-
ney, not too far on the road from Ephrath.
We buried her on the road to Ephrath, that
is, Bethlehem." [u]
8 Then Israel saw the sons of Joseph and
said, "Who are these?"
9 Joseph said to his father, "They are the
sons whom God has given me here."
Israel said, "Bring them to me so that I
can bless them."
10 The eyes of Israel were dim in his old
age. He could no longer see. Joseph ap-
proached him, kissed him, and embraced
him. 11 Israel said to Joseph, "I did not be-
lieve that I would see you face to face, and
now, behold, God has granted me even to
see your children."
12 Joseph took them off his knees and
bowed his face to the ground. 13 Then he
placed the two of them, Ephraim on the
left hand of Israel and Manasseh on the
right hand of Israel, and he brought them
to him. 14 But Israel took his right hand and
put it on the head of Ephraim, who was the
younger of the two, and the left hand he
put on the head of Manasseh, crossing his
arms, although Manasseh was the first-
born.
15 Then he blessed Joseph,

"God, before whom my fathers
Abraham and Isaac walked,
God who has been my shepherd
again and again until this day, [v]
16 the Angel who has freed me from every
evil,
bless these young ones!
Let my name be remembered through
them

q Ex 1:7.—r Ps 105:23.—s Gen 50:5.—t 3f: Gen 28:12-15.—
u Gen 35:19.—v Heb 11:21.

48:1-22 In Israel, there was no tribe of Joseph, but two tribes bore the name of his eldest sons Ephraim and Manasseh; the tribe of Ephraim was the stronger one and had become the leader of the tribes that revolted (1 Ki 11:26-31) and formed the northern kingdom after the schism of 931 B.C. The present passage wishes to explain in advance this rupture of the political and religious unity. It contains bits and pieces of diverse traditions.

and the name of my fathers
Abraham and Isaac
and let them be multiplied greatly
upon the earth." [w]

17 Joseph saw that his father had placed
his right hand on the head of Ephraim and
that this was wrong. He took the hand of
his father to remove it from the head of
Ephraim and put it on Manasseh's head.
18 He said to his father, "Not like this, my
father, this is the firstborn. Place your right
hand on his head."

19 But his father refused and said, "I
know, my son, I know. He will also become
a people, he will also be great, but his
younger brother will be greater than he
and his descendants will become a multi-
tude of nations." 20 He blessed them that
day,

"By you Israel shall pronounce bless-
ings saying,
'May God make you like Ephraim and
like Manasseh.'"

He thus put Ephraim before Manasseh. [x]

21 Israel then said to Joseph, "Behold, I
am ready to die, but God will be with you
and will bring you back to the land of your
fathers. 22 As for me, I give to you, more
than to your brothers, a mountain ridge
that I won from the hands of the Amorites
with sword and bow." [y]

CHAPTER 49

Jacob's Predictions for His Sons.* 1 Jacob
then summoned his sons and said,
"Gather together so that I can tell you
what will happen to you in future days.

2 "Gather and listen, sons of Jacob,
listen to Israel, your father.

3 "Reuben, you are the firstborn,
my strength and the firstfruit of my might,
excelling in dignity and excelling in power.
4 Unstable as water, you shall not have preeminence
because you invaded your father's bed
and defiled my couch
upon which you climbed. [z]

5 "Simeon and Levi are brothers;
their swords are implements of violence.
6 Let my soul not come into their council
nor my heart into their assembly,
for they have killed men with anger
and they maimed oxen as they pleased. [a]
7 Cursed be their anger, for it is fierce,
and their wrath, for it is cruel.
I will divide them in Jacob
and disperse them in Israel.

8 "Judah, your brothers shall praise you.
Your hand shall be on the neck of your enemies.
The sons of your father shall bow down before you.
9 A young lion is Judah.
From the prey, my son, you have turned.
He crouches like a lion,
and like a lioness;
who dares to rouse him? [b]
10 The scepter shall not depart from Judah
nor the mace from between his feet,
until it comes to whom it belongs,
and the obedience of the peoples is his. [c]
11 He tethers his colt to the vine,
and to a choice vine the colt of his donkey.

w Isa 44:22f; 49:7; 63:9; Am 9:12; Acts 15:17.—x Heb 11:21.—y Jos 17:14, 17f; Jn 4:5.—z Gen 35:22; 1 Chr 5:1f.—a Gen 34:25.—b 1 Chr 5:2.—c Num 24:17, 19; 1 Chr 5:2; 28:4; Pss 60:9; 108:9; Zec 10:11; Mt 2:6.

49:1-28 A metric composition from the Yahwist source that specifies the characteristics of the various tribes of Israel; in it can be recognized essential parts and subsidiary parts, and there is no reason for denying that the substance of the discourse really goes back to Jacob. The theme of Judah's preeminence receives an unexpected development. After the beginning of the poem, which confirms the rejection of Reuben and the condemnation of Simeon and Levi for the faults of which we already know, the words concerning Judah, the fourth son, take the form not of a blessing but of a prophetic oracle (vv. 8-12). Judah will enjoy a supremacy over his brothers and also victory over his enemies; he will be strong as a lion that returns from its prey and commands respect from all; he will retain the royal scepter until the moment when he passes it to its true owner, who will be a universal sovereign; this will be followed by a period of great prosperity. This means that Judah's sovereignty will be vicarious and temporary; but the true owner of the scepter will be from the same tribe because the enthusiastic praise of Judah would be inexplicable if his task were simply to prepare for the reign of a foreigner. The prophecy will be fulfilled in the reign of the House of David, which is to be followed by the Messianic reign that successive Prophets will describe. The prophecies concerning the other sons of Jacob are by their nature subsidiary.

From this point on, two facts are to be noted. The promises that God makes to a single person are no longer of the type "I will make of you a great people," for in the sons of Jacob this "great people" is already a reality, and the single person is no longer the father of the entire people of God; the blessings promised to the Patriarchs will rather be what the whole community expects. The new promises, on the other hand, look to the interior of the community and announce a particular person who will carry out the functions of a sovereign: he will lead the people to the victory predicted from Genesis 3:15 on, and he will make a reality the universal blessing already announced to the Patriarchs (Gen 12:3; etc.). In the second place, these promises are dissociated from primogeniture: the choice of Judah foreshadows that of David, the last of his brothers (1 Sam 16:1-13).

He washes his garments in wine,
and in the blood of the grapes his clothes.
12 His eyes are darker than wine,
and his teeth whiter than milk.

13 "Zebulun shall dwell along the sea,
and he shall be a haven to ships
and shall border upon Sidon.

14 "Issachar is a strong-boned donkey
crouching between two saddlebags.
15 He saw that his resting place was good
and his land was pleasant
so he bent down his shoulder to bear the burden
and became a toiling servant.

16 "Dan shall judge his people
as one of the tribes of Israel.
17 Dan will be like a serpent by the wayside,
an adder by the path,
that bites the heels of horses
and its horsemen fall backward.

18 "I hope in your salvation, O LORD.

19 "Gad shall be attacked by raiders,
but he shall raid them in return.

20 "Asher's food is rich,
and he shall provide delicacies for the king.

21 "Naphtali is a doe let loose;
he brings forth beautiful words.

22 "Joseph is a fruitful vine,
a fruitful vine near a spring,
whose branches run over the wall.
23 They have grieved him and attacked him,
archers have persecuted him,
24 but his bow is strong,
and the hands of his arms were made strong
by the hands of the Mighty One of Jacob,
because of the Shepherd, the Rock of Israel.
25 From the God of your father who helps you
and God Almighty
who blesses you with blessings from the heavens above,
blessings of the deep that lie below,
blessings of breasts and womb.
26 The blessings of your father,
are mighty beyond the blessings of the eternal mountains,
the boundaries of the everlasting hills;
may they come upon the head of Joseph
upon the crown of the head of the prince among his brothers.

27 "Benjamin is a ravenous wolf.
In the morning he devours his prey;
in the evening he divides his spoil."

28 All these make up the twelve tribes of
Israel. This is what their father told them,
blessing them. He blessed each one with
his own blessing.

The Death of Jacob. 29 Then he gave this
command: "I am about to be reunited
with my ancestors. Bury me with my fa-
thers in the cave in the field of Ephron
the Hittite, 30 in the cave that is found
in the field of Machpelah facing Mamre
in the land of Canaan. This is the cave
that Abraham bought with the field of
Ephron the Hittite, as his burial ground.[d]
31 There they buried Abraham and Sarah
his wife, there they buried Isaac and Re-
bekah his wife, and there they buried
Leah. 32 The field and the cave in it used
to belong to the Hittites."
33 When Jacob had finished giving this
command to his sons, he drew back his feet
into the bed and breathed his last and was
reunited with his ancestors.

CHAPTER 50

1 Joseph threw himself on the face of
his father. He wept upon him and kissed
him. 2 Then Joseph ordered his doctors to
embalm Israel. 3 This took forty days, the
time it takes to embalm. The Egyptians
mourned for him for seventy days.
4 When the days of mourning were over,
Joseph spoke to the household of Pharaoh.
He said, "If I have found favor in your
sight, I wish to speak these words into the
ears of Pharaoh: 5 My father made me take
an oath: 'Behold, I am about to die. Bury
me in the tomb I prepared for myself in the
land of Canaan.' May I go to bury my
father and return?"[e]
6 Pharaoh answered, "Go and bury your
father as you have vowed to do."
7 Joseph went to bury his father, and all
the ministers of Pharaoh, the elders of
his household, and all the elders of the
land of Egypt, 8 as well as the household
of Joseph and his brothers and the house-

d Gen 23:17.—e Gen 47:30.

hold of his father went with him. Only
the children, flocks, and herds were left
in the land of Goshen. 9 Even the war
chariots and the charioteers formed an
imposing caravan.
10 When they arrived at the threshing
floor of Atad, which is on the other side of
the Jordan, they performed a great and
solemn ritual mourning, and Joseph did
seven days of mourning for his father.
11 The Canaanites living in that land saw
the mourning at the threshing floor of
Atad and said, "It is a solemn funeral for
the Egyptians." Because of this they called
the place Abel-mizraim, and it is on the
other side of the Jordan.
12 Jacob's sons did what he had com-
manded them to do for him. 13 They
brought him into the land of Canaan and
buried him in the cave of the field of
Machpelah, the field that Abraham had
bought from Ephron the Hittite to be his
burial place and that faces Mamre.[f]
14 After he had buried his father, Joseph
returned to Egypt together with his
brothers and those who had gone with
him to bury his father.

Joseph's Mission and His Death.* 15 Now
the brothers of Joseph began to be afraid
because their father was dead, and they
said, "Who knows if Joseph will not treat
us like enemies and pay us back for the
evil things we have done to him?" 16 So
they sent word to Joseph, saying, "Your
father, before he died, gave this com-
mand: 17 'Say to Joseph: Forgive the of-
fense of your brothers and their sin for
the evil that they have done against you.
Forgive the trespass of the servants of the
God of your father.'" Joseph cried while
they were speaking to him.
18 His brothers went up and bowed to the
ground before him and said, "Behold your
slaves."
19 But Joseph said to them, "Do not
fear. Am I God?[g] 20 You intended to do
evil to me, but God decided to make it
serve a good, to fulfill that which today
has come true: to keep alive a numerous
people.[h] 21 Therefore, do not fear. I will
provide food for you and your children."
In this way, he consoled them and encour-
aged them.[i]
22 Joseph and the family of his father lived
in Egypt. He lived for one hundred and ten
years. 23 Thus, Joseph saw the sons of
Ephraim up to the third generation and also
the sons of Machir, the son of Manasseh,
who was born upon the knees of Joseph.[j]
24 Then Joseph said to his brothers, "I am
about to die, but God will come to visit you
and will bring you out of this land to the
land that he promised with an oath to
Abraham, to Isaac, and to Jacob.[k] 25 Joseph
had the sons of Israel swear an oath saying,
"God will surely come to visit you, and then
you are to carry my bones away with you."[l]
26 Joseph died when he was one hundred
and ten years old. He was embalmed and
placed in a coffin in Egypt.*[m]

---

f Gen 23:16; Acts 7:16.—g Gen 30:2; Ex 32:34; Rom 12:19; Heb 10:30.—h Gen 45:5.—i Gen 47:12.—j Num 32:39; Jos 17:1.—k Ex 3:8; Jos 24:32; Heb 11:22.—l Ex 13:19; Heb 11:22.—m Sir 49:15.

50:15-26 Secretly, Providence has woven the tissue of this history of Joseph. It was necessary that in the adventure readied for the sons of Jacob all Israel should go to Egypt. It is urgent for the Lord to intervene and make the children of Israel his people and to lead them into the Promised Land.

50:26 Thus ends the story of the origins of the Patriarchs. The points of departure for the Book of Exodus are laid. The first elements of the People of God are now in Egypt, whence they must one day return to the land promised to Abraham, the land of the Patriarchs, that of the tomb of ancestors, so that it may become the land of the People of God.

"Moses stretched out his hand. . . . the LORD caused the sea to move back. . . .
The children of Israel entered the sea on dry land" *(Ex 14:21-22).*

THE BOOK OF EXODUS
God Sets His People Free

The Book of Exodus expresses the faith of the Israelites, who, generation after generation, passed on the story of how the Lord remembered the promise he had made to Abraham their father: how he brought his oppressed people out of Egypt, renewed his Covenant with them, and led them into the Promised Land. This explains why the intervention of God, indicated by countless miracles, ultimately took the step concerning the concrete circumstances of the liberation and the stage in the wilderness. Thus, the Book of Exodus constitutes the act of Israel's birth and the mirror in which the people of God contemplates itself in order to understand its destiny.

Various traditions, often difficult to distinguish clearly and that had already served in the composition of the Book of Genesis, tell of the events that marked the beginning of the history of the Jewish people. But the work in which these traditions are combined possesses a genuine unity, for its aim is less to recover the details of those events than to bring out their meaning. Scholars locate the events in either the 15th or the 13th century B.C.

The Covenant, which is the focal point of the Jewish religion, is also the vital center of the book. It is expressed in a formula that sums up the relationship between Israel and God: the Lord delivers Israel from slavery and offers it freedom in order that it may agree to live in fidelity to his word.

The Ten Commandments and the many precepts that apply them to the countless situations of life have for their purpose to help Israel truly become what it is: a people chosen by the Lord and devoted to his interests.

The Exodus proves, therefore, to be the ideal period in the relationship of God and Israel, the time of their first love, of their betrothal, to use the wonderful image of the Prophets (Hosea, Jeremiah, Ezekiel).

It is also a time of testing, for the passage through the wilderness to the promised but distant land is a very difficult one; the Israelites are tempted to turn back, and more than once they forget him who has given them their freedom. But the Lord, a God of kindness, forgives them over and over.

The dominant figure in the Book is Moses. Chosen to be an intermediary and given the privilege of intimacy with God, he leads the people, organizes them by giving them their first laws and customs, and brings them into the covenant. He is one of the greatest personages in the political life and above all in the spirituality of the Old Testament and, beyond a doubt, of world history.

The Bible often bids us go back and meditate on the Exodus. The Psalms allude to it. Deuteronomy (chs. 1–11) brings out the spiritual meaning of the adventure in the wilderness. The second part of Isaiah (chs. 40–55) sings of the joy Israel experiences in its certainty that during its return from the Exile the miracles of the Exodus will be repeated. In a lengthy meditation on this story the Book of Wisdom (chs. 10–19) finds Divine Wisdom at work.

In the New Testament Jesus Christ is the new Moses who is to lead the new People of God, the Church, to the new Promised Land. He is the rock from which water springs to slake the thirst of believers; he is the true dwelling of God in the midst of humanity; he is the Passover lamb who with his blood redeems his people and seals the new and everlasting Covenant between humanity and the Father.

Christians too are set free from the slavery of sin by the water of Baptism without any merit on their part, and they go forward in the light of the Risen One toward the Kingdom of the Father. They too encounter trials and temptations, but the Eucharist is there like the manna to nourish them and sustain their journey. If they should stumble, they know that the God of the Covenant offers them forgiveness. Hence, the entire spiritual adventure of the baptized, like that of the Church, is already inscribed in the pages of the Book of Exodus.

The Book of Exodus may be divided as follows:

- *I: The Children of Israel in Egypt (1:1—12:28)*
  - *A: Oppression of the Israelites (1:1-22)*
  - *B: The Liberator Raised Up by God (2:1-25)*
  - *C: The Burning Bush (3:1—7:7)*
  - *D: The Plagues of Egypt (7:8—11:10)*
  - *E: The Passover (12:1-28)*
- *II: The Exodus from Egypt and the Journey to Sinai (12:29—18:27)*
  - *A: Departure from Egypt (12:29—15:21)*
  - *B: The Journey through the Wilderness (15:22—18:27)*
- *III: The Covenant at Mount Sinai (19:1—24:18)*
  - *A: The Covenant and the Ten Commandments (19:1—20:21)*
  - *B: The Book of the Covenant (20:22—24:11)*
  - *C: Moses on the Mountain: The Regulation of Worship (24:12-18)*
- *IV: Instruction on the Sanctuary and Its Ministers (25:1—31:18)*
- *V: The Golden Calf and the Renewal of the Covenant (32:1—34:35)*
- *VI: The Construction and Furnishing of the Sanctuary (35:1—40:38)*

I: THE CHILDREN OF ISRAEL IN EGYPT*

A: Oppression of the Israelites*

CHAPTER 1

1 * These are the names of the children of
Israel who entered Egypt with Joseph, each
of them arriving with his family: [a]
2 * Reuben, Simeon, Levi, and Judah,
3 Issachar, Zebulun, and Benjamin, 4 Dan
and Naphtali, Gad and Asher. 5 The total
number of those born to Jacob was seventy. *
Joseph was already in Egypt. [b]

6 * Now Joseph died and then all his
brothers and all that generation. 7 The chil-
dren of Israel multiplied and grew numer-
ous and very powerful and filled the land.

Harsh Condition of the Children of Israel.
8 * [c] Then a new king arose in Egypt who had
not known Joseph. 9 He said to his people,
"Behold, the children of Israel are very
numerous and more powerful than we are.
10 Let us deal wisely with them lest they con-
tinue to multiply. Otherwise, if there were a
war, they would join our enemies and battle
against us and then escape from the land."

11 So taskmasters were set over the chil-
dren of Israel to wear them down with
forced labor. They built the supply cities * of
Pithom and Raameses for Pharaoh. [d] 12 But
the more they were oppressed, the more
they multiplied and grew beyond measure.
The Egyptians began to dread the presence
of the children of Israel 13 and therefore put
them to work, treating them harshly. 14 They
made their lives difficult and forced them to
make clay bricks and to do all kinds of work
in the fields. They forced them to do every
type of harsh work.

Command to the Midwives. 15 The king of
Egypt said to the midwives of the Hebrews,
one of whom was named Shiphrah and the
other named Puah, 16 "When you assist the
Hebrew women who are in labor, look at
the child while it is still on the birthing stool.
If it is a boy, kill it. If it is a girl, you can let it
live." 17 But the midwives feared God. They
did not do what the king of Egypt had
ordered them to do. They let the babies
live. [e]

18 The king of Egypt summoned the mid-
wives and said to them, "Why have you
done this and let the babies live?" 19 The
midwives answered Pharaoh, "The Hebrew
women are not like the Egyptians. They are
full of life. Before the midwife arrives, they
have already given birth."

20 God blessed the midwives. The people
grew and became very numerous. 21 God
gave the midwives numerous families
because they had feared God. 22 Pharaoh
therefore gave this command to all of his
people: "Every male son who is born to the
Hebrews is to be thrown into the Nile, but
let the girl babies live." [f]

---

a Gen 46:5.—b Gen 46:27; Deut 10:22; Acts 7:14.—c 8ff: 2 Chr 18:14; Acts 7:18.—d Deut 26:6; 2 Chr 10:18.—e Job 1:1.—f Acts 7:19.

1:1—12:36 In this section, the Bible counterposes two peoples—the people of Pharaoh, who are cruel and oppressive, and the children of Israel, who are sorely oppressed. However, the more the latter are oppressed, the stronger they become. In their struggle to leave Egypt, the children of Israel will slowly become aware that they are a people chosen by God and set free to carry out an important task.

In carefully planning and preparing the salvation of the whole human race, the God of supreme love, by a special dispensation, chose for himself a people to whom he might entrust his promises. First, he entered into a Covenant with Abraham (see Gen 15:18) and, through Moses, with the people of Israel (see Ex 24:8). To this people that he acquired for himself, he so manifested himself through words and deeds as the one true and living God that Israel came to know by experience the ways of God with human beings, and with God himself speaking to them through the mouth of the Prophets, Israel daily gained a deeper and clearer understanding of his ways and made them more widely known among the nations (see Pss 22:28-29; 96:1-3; Isa 2:1-4; Jer 3:17).

1:1-22 Scholars calculate that about three centuries separated the death of Joseph, with which Genesis ends, and the Exodus of the Hebrew people. From this lengthy period the Bible singles out only two facts that are important for linking the past with the coming religious history of Israel.

1:1-7 The children of Israel flourish in Egypt, fulfilling the promise God had made to the Patriarchs (Gen 12; 17; etc.). They lived in Egypt 430 years (see Ex 12:40). We pass from the story of the great ancestors to that of a people.

1:2-4 The sons of Jacob are given here according to their respective mothers (see Gen 29:31; 30:20; 35:16-26).

1:5 *Seventy:* Gen 46:27; Deut 10:22 have the same number. The Greek translation, however, and a manuscript from Qumran have "seventy-five," as does Acts 7:14. The extra five persons are the descendants of Ephraim and Manasseh; they are mentioned in the Greek translation of Gen 46:27.

1:6-7 Scholars estimate that it was more than 200 years from the death of Joseph to the advent of the *new king.*

1:8-22 The Pharaoh, probably Rameses II (1298–1232 B.C.), becomes worried when he sees the proliferation of the Hebrews and takes various measures to exterminate this race and doubtless other Asiatic populations. The children of Israel who left Egypt are said to number 600,000, "not including children" (Ex 12:37). Works of the kind that the Hebrews are compelled to do are illustrated in Egyptian paintings of that period, even if these do not picture actual groups of the Patriarchs' descendants.

1:11 *Supply cities* is a military term (see 1 Ki 9:19). Pithom and Rameses are in the eastern part of the Nile Delta; Rameses is identified with either Tanis or El Qantara. *Pharaoh:* a royal title rather than a personal name.

B: The Liberator Raised Up by God

CHAPTER 2

Moses Is Saved.* 1 There was a certain man
from the tribe of Levi who took a daughter
of the tribe of Levi as his wife.[g] 2 The
woman conceived and bore a son. She saw
that he was handsome and she hid him for
three months. 3 But, not being able to hide
him any longer, she took a basket made of
papyrus, caulked it with bitumen and pitch,
and placed the baby in it and lay it among
the reeds growing on the riverbank of the
Nile. 4 The baby's sister* hid herself so that
she could watch what would happen from a
distance.[h]

5 Pharaoh's daughter went down to the
Nile to bathe while her attendants walked
along the riverbank. They saw the basket
among the reeds and sent a slave to fetch it.
6 They opened it and saw the baby. It was a
small baby boy who was crying. They had
compassion on it and said, "This is a
Hebrew baby."

7 The sister of the baby said to Pharaoh's
daughter, "Shall I go to call a wet nurse
from among the Hebrew women to feed the
child for you?"

8 "Go," said Pharaoh's daughter. The girl
went and called the baby's mother.
9 Pharaoh's daughter said to her, "Take this
baby with you and feed it for me. I will pay
you." The woman took the baby and fed it.
10 When the baby was grown, she brought it
to Pharaoh's daughter. He became a son to
her and she named him Moses, saying, "I
have saved him from the water." *[i]

Moses Flees to Midian.*[j] 11 One day Moses,
having grown up,* went out to his brethren
and saw how they were oppressed. He
noticed an Egyptian strike a Hebrew, one of
his brethren. 12 Looking around, he did not
see anyone, so he struck and killed the
Egyptian and buried him in the sand. 13 The
next day he went out again and, seeing two
Hebrews fighting, said to the one who was
in the wrong, "Why did you hit your broth-
er?" 14 He answered, "Who has made you
head and judge over us? Are you thinking of
killing me like you killed the Egyptian?"
Moses was afraid and thought, "Certainly
this thing is known." 15 Pharaoh heard about
it and sought to put Moses to death. Moses
fled from Pharaoh and traveled to the land
of Midian* where he sat down by a well.[k]

16 A priest of Midian had seven daughters.
They came to draw water to fill the trough
and give water to their father's flocks. 17 But
some shepherds arrived and chased them
away. Moses got up and defended them and
gave their animals something to drink.
18 They returned to their father Reuel* who
said to them, "Why are you back so soon
today?" 19 They answered, "An Egyptian
delivered us out of the hands of the shep-
herds. He drew water for us and gave water
to the flock to drink." 20 He said to his
daughters, "Where is he? Why did you leave
him there? Invite him to eat with us."
21 Moses agreed to live with that man, who
gave him his daughter Zipporah as a wife.
22 She bore him a son and he named his son
Gershom for he said, "I am a stranger in a
strange land." *[l]

God Does Not Forget the Covenant.* 23 And it
came to pass that the king of Egypt died.
The Israelites groaned because of their slav-
ery, and they cried out. The cry of their
bondage rose up to God.[m] 24 God heard
their cry and remembered his covenant
with Abraham, with Isaac, and with Jacob.[n]
25 God took note of the children of Israel and
acknowledged their need.

g Ex 6:20; Num 26:59; Lk 20:28.—h Num 26:59.—i Acts 7:21; Heb 11:24.—j 11-14: 2 Sam 21:18; Acts 7:23-28.—k 1 Mac 2:28; Mt 12:14; Acts 7:29; Heb 11:27.—l Ex 18:3-4.—m Ex 3:7, 9; Deut 26:7; Jas 5:4.—n Ex 6:5; Pss 105:8f; 106:44f; Lk 1:72; Acts 7:34.

2:1-10 In an account filled with charm, the narrator is pleased to show that God toys with obstacles and makes them serve his plan of salvation. The education in letters that Moses receives from the Egyptian court will be a great help in his mission.

2:4 *The baby's sister:* i.e., Miriam (see Ex 15:21).

2:10 Assonance links *Mosheh,* the Hebrew form of Moses, and the verb *mashah,* "to draw out."

2:11-22 Endangered by his defense of the children of his race, Moses is fearful and flees to the wilderness east of the Gulf of Aqaba. This episode prepares him for the difficulties to come (see Ex 18).

2:11 *Moses, having grown up:* according to Acts 7:23, almost forty years had now passed (see Ex 7:7).

2:15 *Midian,* which was south of Edom and east of the Gulf of Aqaba or Gulf of Elana, was inhabited by nomadic tribes.

2:18 It was perhaps different traditions that gave Moses' father-in-law different names: *Reuel* (here and in Num 10:29); *Jethro* (Ex 3:1; 4:18; 18:1). *Hobab* seems to be rather Moses' brother-in-law (Num 10:29; Jdg 4:11). The Hebrew terms for degrees of kinship do not have a very precise meaning.

2:22 Some Greek and Latin MSS add here a passage apparently from Ex 18:4: "and the other [son] named Eliezer, for he had said, 'The God of my father has come to my assistance and has freed me from the sword of Pharaoh.' "

2:23-25 God remembers his Covenant. Such will also be the case in all the moments when Israel will find itself in distress. *Covenant with Abraham:* see Gen 15:17-18; 17:7. *With Isaac:* see Gen 17:19; 26:24. *With Jacob:* see Gen 35:11-12.

THE EXODUS FROM EGYPT (ca 1320 B.C.: Ex 12:37—15:21) — **(a)** The Israelites set out from **Rameses** for **Succoth** with their livestock (12:37). **(b)** God does not lead them by way of the Philistines' land, but by the desert near the **Red Sea.** They set out from **Succoth** and encamp at **Etham** on the edge of the desert (13:17-20). **(c)** Following God's command, the people encamp before **Pi-hahiroth,** between **Migdol** and the sea, in front of **Baal-zephon.** There the Egyptians overtake them (14:1-9). **(d)** The Lord sweeps the seas with a strong east wind throughout the night and turns it into dry land. The Israelites cross over but when the Egyptians try to follow the waters flow back over them (14:21-31).

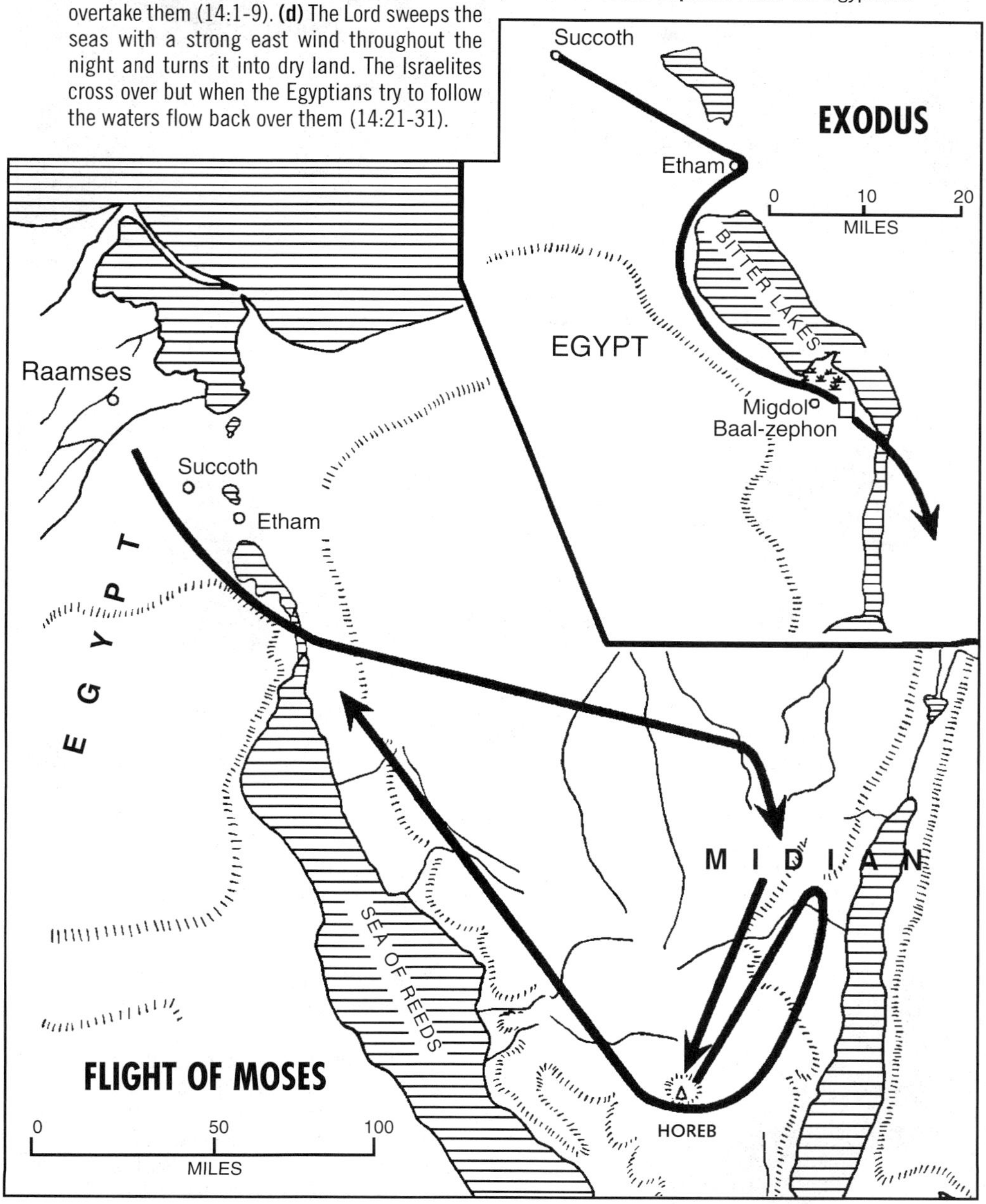

THE FLIGHT OF MOSES (Ex 1:1—12:36) — **(a)** Oppression of Israel in Egypt; the people build the store-cities of **Pithom** and **Rameses;** birth of Moses and his flight into **Midian** (1:1—2:25). **(b)** On the mountain of God, **Horeb,** the Lord appears to Moses, reveals the Divine Name ("I AM WHO AM") to him, and gives him the mission of delivering Israel (3:1—4:17). **(c)** Moses returns from **Midian,** and at God's command sets out for **Egypt;** at the **mountain of God,** he meets his brother Aaron and both return to **Egypt** (4:18-31). **(d)** Moses before Pharaoh: the ten plagues; permission to leave Egypt (5:1—12:36).

Metropolitan Museum of Art

BRICKMAKING IN EGYPT — A scene from the tomb of a famous Egyptian Vizier (1470–1445 B.C.), showing brickmaking in Egypt. Workmen with hoes knead clay moistened with water; other laborers carry material to two brickmakers. At this very time the Hebrews were slaving at this same occupation under the harsh Egyptian taskmasters. (See Ex 1:11-14.)

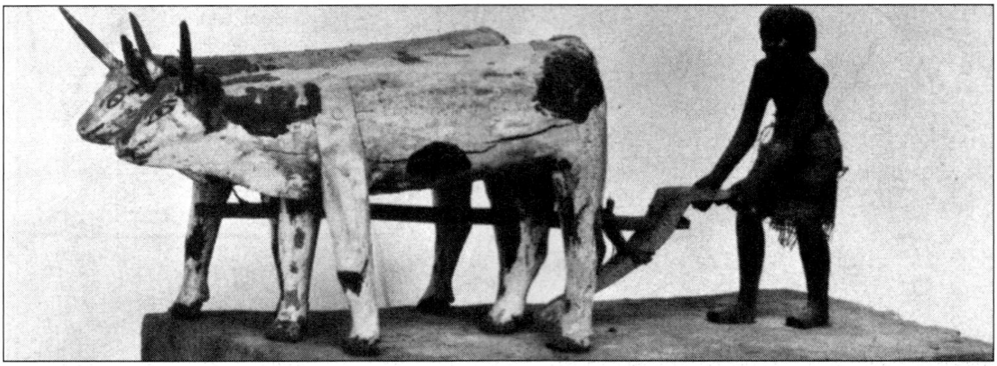

British Museum

FIELD WORK IN EGYPT — A plowman guides a two-handed plow drawn by two oxen. A bar or tongue is attached to the plow enabling the oxen to draw it along. A bar placed on the necks of the oxen just behind the long horns serves as a yoke. Plowing fields was no doubt one of the "kinds of field work" to which the Hebrews were subjected by their Egyptian masters. (See Ex 1:14.)

British Museum

BULL-CALF OF EGYPTIAN GOD APIS — Calf worship is known to have been part of the religious worship of all ancient Semitic peoples. The bronze bull Apis was worshiped at Memphis (Egypt) as sacred to Ptah (Hephaestus), principal god of the city. The golden calf later set up by the Hebrews in the desert may have been patterned after such a statue. (See Ex 32:4.) However, the golden calves set up several hundred years later at Bethel and Dan by Jeroboam (1 Ki 12:29) were most likely patterned after the bull-worship of their Semitic kin in Palestine; for example, among the Canaanites the bull was associated with various deities as the symbol of vital energy and strength.

C: The Burning Bush*

CHAPTER 3

The Call of Moses.* 1 Moses was tending the
flock of Jethro, his father-in-law, the priest
of Midian. He led the animals across the
desert and came to Horeb,* the mountain
of God. 2 [o] The angel of the LORD* appeared
to him in the flames of a fire burning in the
midst of a bush. He observed it and, behold,
the bush glowed with fire but was not con-
sumed. 3 Moses said, "I wish to draw near to
observe this wondrous thing and see why
this bush does not burn up."
4 The LORD saw that he was approaching
to see God and he called out from the bush,
"Moses, Moses." He answered, "Here I
am." [p] 5 He continued, "Do not approach.
Take your sandals off your feet, for the place
where you are standing is holy ground." [q]
6 He said, "I am the God of your ancestors,
the God of Abraham, the God of Isaac, and
the God of Jacob." Moses covered his face
because he was afraid to look at God.* [r]
7 The LORD said, "I have seen the misery
of my people in Egypt and I have heard
their cry because of their taskmasters. I
know about their sufferings. 8 [s] I have come
down to free them out of the hands of the
Egyptians and to lead them from that land
to a land that is beautiful and spacious, to a
land flowing with milk and honey,* the
place where the Canaanites, the Hittites,
the Amorites, the Perizzites, the Hivites,
and the Jebusites are found. 9 The cry of the
Israelites has come up to me and I myself
have seen the oppression with which the
Egyptians torment them. 10 Now go! I send
you to Pharaoh. Lead my people, the
Israelites, from Egypt."
11 Moses said to God, "Who am I to go to
Pharaoh to lead the children of Israel out of
Egypt?" 12 He answered, "I am with you.
Behold, this is proof that I have sent you,
when you will lead the people from Egypt,
you will serve God on this mountain."

God Reveals His Name.* 13 Moses said to
God, "If I come to the children of Israel and
say to them, 'The God of your ancestors
sent me to you,' but they say to me, 'What is
his name,' what should I say to them?"
14 God said to Moses, "I AM WHO I AM."*
Then he said, "You will say to the children of
Israel, 'I AM sent me to you.' " 15 God also
said to Moses, "You will say to the children
of Israel, 'The LORD, the God of your ances-
tors, the God of Abraham, the God of Isaac,
and the God of Jacob, sent me to you.' This
is my name forever. This is the title with
which I will be remembered from one gen-
eration to the next." [t]

Moses Is Invested with His Mission.*
16 "Go, gather the elders of Israel and tell
them, 'The LORD, the God of your ancestors,
has appeared to me,* the God of Abraham,
of Isaac, and of Jacob, saying, "I have seen
you and what is done to you in Egypt. 17 I
have said, 'I will make them go out from
the humiliation of Egypt to the land of the
Canaanites, the Hittites, the Amorites, the
Perizzites, the Hivites, and the Jebusites, to a
land flowing with milk and honey.' " '
18 "They will listen to your voice. You and
the elders of Israel will go to the king of

o 2-10: Mk 12:26; Acts 7:30-35.—p Acts 9:10.—q Jos 5:15; Acts 7:33.—r Ex 4:5; Mt 22:32; Mk 12:26; Lk 20:37; Acts 7:32; Rev 6:15.—s 8f: Gen 15:19ff.—t Ex 6:6; Pss 135:13; 145:13.

3:1—7:6 This grand text has always appealed to the most religious Jews and Christians. To those who strive to deepen their sense of their existence before God, the flaming fire and the Divine Name reveal the extent to which the Lord surpasses all that he has created but also how his love brings him close to human beings in order to lead them toward their destiny.

3:1-12 It is when Moses least expects it that he is called by God. The mystery of the fire that burns without being consumed astounds him. It is then that he discovers the sign of the presence and the devouring love of the Lord who so surpasses the creature that the latter feels crushed. But God keeps himself present in human history. Resolved to deliver his people, he chooses to have need of a man in order to manifest the divine power by giving him a mission to complete that is beyond human powers. History is about to take a new turn.

3:1 *Horeb:* i.e., another name for "Sinai."

3:2 *Angel of the LORD:* an expression that signifies God himself (see Gen 16:7).

3:6 Moses' action is based on the long held belief that no one can see God and live (see Gen 32:30).

3:8 *Land flowing with milk and honey:* an expression used by Eastern peoples to signify fertility (the terms are taken from the world of shepherds); the Pentateuch often uses the phrase to mean the Promised Land.

3:13-15 In Semitic thought, for a person to reveal his name to someone was equivalent to putting himself in that person's power. When the Lord of Israel describes himself as "He who is" (Yahweh), as the One who is there for his people, he is refusing to manifest himself completely, while at the same time revealing himself to be the living God who is always present in the midst of his people and involved with them. In the same way, Jesus will reassure his Apostles at the time of his leaving them: "I am with you always" (Mt 28:20).

3:14 *I AM WHO I AM:* later, as a show of awe and respect, the title *Adonai,* "my LORD," would be used.

3:16-22 Moses, entrusted with his mission, is to announce that God is preparing to have his people leave Egypt despite Pharaoh's refusal to let them go.

3:16 *Appeared to me:* to the Israelites this means that Moses has received special recognition from the Lord and his words are to be heeded. *Elders:* a title given to those who traditionally spoke for the children of Israel.

Egypt and tell him, 'The LORD, the God of the Hebrews, has appeared to us. Let us make a three days' journey into the desert to make a sacrifice to the LORD, our God.' [u] 19 I know that the king of Egypt will not permit you to leave unless he is forced. 20 I will therefore stretch out my hand and strike Egypt with all kinds of wonders that I will work in their midst. Afterward, they will let you go. [v]

21 "I will make this people find favor in the sight of the Egyptians. When you leave, you will not leave empty-handed. 22 Every woman will ask her neighbor and those living in her house for silver and gold and clothing, and you will put them on your sons and daughters. You will plunder the Egyptians."

CHAPTER 4

Moses Is Encouraged and Receives the Gift of Working Prodigies.* 1 Moses answered, "Behold, they will not believe me nor listen to my voice. They will say, 'The LORD has not appeared to you.' " 2 The LORD said to him, "What is in your hand?" He answered, "A staff." 3 The LORD said, "Throw it to the ground." He threw the staff to the ground, and it became a serpent, and Moses retreated away from it. [w] 4 The LORD said to Moses, "Reach out and take it by its tail." He reached out and took it, and it became a staff again in his hand. 5 "This is so that they will believe that the LORD, the God of their ancestors, the God of Abraham, the God of Isaac, and the God of Jacob, has appeared to you."

6 The LORD continued, "Place your hand inside your tunic." He placed his hand in his tunic and then drew it out. Behold, his hand was covered with leprosy and was white as the snow.* 7 The LORD said, "Put your hand back in your tunic." He put his hand back in the tunic and drew it out again. Behold, it was once again like the rest of his flesh. 8 "If they will not believe you and heed the first sign, then they will believe the message of the second. 9 If they do not believe either of the signs and will not listen to you, take some water from the Nile and pour it on dry ground. The water you take from the Nile will become blood on the ground." [x]

Aaron, Spokesman for Moses. 10 Moses said to the LORD, "My Lord, I am not eloquent. I have never been so in the past nor now that you have begun to speak to your servant. I am slow of speech and tongue." [y] 11 The LORD told him, "Who has made man with a mouth? Who can make him mute or deaf, seeing or blind? Is it not I, the LORD? 12 Now go! I will be with your mouth and supervise what you are to say." 13 Moses said, "Forgive me, my Lord, but please send someone else." 14 The LORD became angry with Moses and said to him, "Do you not have a brother, Aaron, a Levite. I know that he can speak well. He is now on his way here to meet you. When he sees you, his heart will rejoice.* 15 [z] You will speak to him and place the words he is to say in his mouth. I will be with you and with him while you speak and I will tell you what you are to do. 16 He will speak to the people for you. It will be as if he is your mouth and you are his God. [a] 17 Take this staff in your hand and perform the signs with it."

Moses Returns to Egypt.* 18 Moses left and returned to Jethro, his father-in-law, and told him, "Let me leave and return to my brothers who are in Egypt to see if they are still alive." Jethro said to Moses, "Go in peace." 19 The LORD said to Moses in Midian, "Go, return to Egypt, for those who sought to kill you are dead." 20 Moses took his wife and his sons, placed them on a donkey, and returned to the land of Egypt. Moses held the staff of God in his hand.

21 The LORD said to Moses, "When you return to Egypt, see that you do all the signs that I have placed in your hand in the presence of Pharaoh. But I will harden his heart and he will not let my people go. 22 You will say to Pharaoh, 'Thus says the LORD: "Israel is my firstborn son. [b] 23 I have told you to let my son go so that he might serve me, but you have refused to let him leave. Therefore, I will kill your firstborn son." ' " [c]

u Ex 5:3; Acts 28:28.—v Isa 19:22; Acts 7:36.—w Ex 7:10; Jn 3:14.—x Ex 7:17, 19f.—y Ex 6:12; Mk 7:37; Lk 17:5.—z 15f: Ex 7:1-2.—a Acts 21:39.—b Sir 36:17; 2 Pet 1:17.—c Ex 11:5; 12:29; Ps 105:36.

4:1-9 The Lord gives his help to those whom he sends to testify in his name. With the coming of Aaron on the scene, the work of the priestly line is inaugurated.

4:6 Moses is given a staff and leprous hand from God as visible evidence to show Pharaoh that he was from God.

4:14 This verse indicates one of the functions of Aaron as priest.

4:18-26 Moses returns to Egypt, and it is obvious that Pharaoh's obstinacy must be overcome, an obstinacy that the author—in keeping with the ancient mentality—attributes to God without occupying himself about human liberty. It is thus a way of saying that the Lord arranges events to bring about his plan.

24* On the way, when they were camped
for the night, the LORD came and tried to
kill Moses. 25 Zipporah took a flint knife and
cut the foreskin of her son and with it
touched Moses' feet and said, "You are now
my spouse of blood." 26 Then God let him go.
She said "spouse of blood" because of the
circumcision.

Moses Makes Contact with His People.*
27 The LORD said to Aaron, "Go meet Moses
in the desert." He went and met Moses on
the mountain of God and kissed him.
28 Moses told Aaron all the words that God
had sent him to say and about all the signs
that he had commanded him to do.
29 Then Moses and Aaron went and assem-
bled the elders of the children of Israel.
30 Aaron spoke to the people, telling them
all the words that the LORD had spoken to
Moses and performing the signs before the
people. 31 The people believed when they
heard that the LORD had visited the chil-
dren of Israel and had seen their affliction.
They knelt down in worship. [d]

CHAPTER 5*

First Audience of Moses with Pharaoh.
1 Afterward, Moses and Aaron went to
Pharaoh and proclaimed to him, "Thus
says the LORD, the God of Israel: 'Let my
people go so that they might celebrate a
feast in the desert.' " 2 Pharaoh answered,
"Who is the LORD that I should listen to his
voice and let Israel leave? I do not know the
LORD, and I will not let Israel leave." 3 They
said, "The God of the Hebrews has
appeared to us. Let us leave for a journey of
three days into the desert to celebrate a sac-
rifice to the LORD, our God, lest he punish
us with plague or the sword." [e]

4 The king of Egypt said to them, "Why,
Moses and Aaron, do you take the people
away from their work? Return to your
work." 5 Pharaoh added, "Behold how
numerous the people of the land are. Would
you have them rest from their labors?"

6 On that day, Pharaoh gave this order to
the taskmasters of the people and to his
overseers:* 7 "Do not give any more straw*
for making bricks to the people as you pre-
viously have. Let them get their own straw.
8 But you must demand that they make the
same number of bricks as before, without
any reduction. They are lazy. That is why
they are protesting, 'We wish to leave, we
must sacrifice to our God.' 9 Let more work
be laid upon them so that they keep busy
and not pay attention to lies."

10 The taskmasters of the people and the
overseers went out and spoke to the people:
"Pharaoh has ordered, 'I will not give you
straw. 11 You can go and gather it for your-
selves wherever you can find it, but your
work must not decline.' "

12 The people scattered all throughout
Egypt to gather stubble for straw. 13 But the
taskmasters urged them on saying, "Finish
your work, your daily quota, just as when
you were given straw."

Complaint of the Overseers. 14 The overseers
of the children of Israel, whom the taskmas-
ters of Pharaoh had placed over them, beat
them saying, "Why have you not finished
your number of bricks today and yesterday
like you did before?"

15 The overseers of the children of Israel
came to Pharaoh and appealed to him say-
ing, "Why do you treat your servants like
this? 16 You have not given straw to your ser-
vants, but you tell them to make bricks. Your
servants are beaten and it is the fault of your
own people." 17 He answered, "You are lazy,
lazy! This is why you say, 'We want to leave;
we must sacrifice to the LORD.' 18 Now go,
work! You will not be given straw, but you
will produce the same number of bricks."

19 The overseers of the children of Israel
saw that they were in trouble when they
were told, "Do not lower the daily number
of bricks." 20 Upon leaving Pharaoh, they
met Moses and Aaron who were waiting for
them. 21 They said, "The LORD look upon
you and judge, for you have made us hateful
to Pharaoh and his ministers. You placed
the sword in their hands to kill us."

---

d Jos 1:17.—e Ex 3:18; 8:27.

4:24-26 *The LORD came and tried to kill Moses:* the reference may be to an incident similar to that described in Gen 32:25-33. Moses' wife circumcises the boy and with his foreskin "touches [the] feet" (i.e., the genitals) of Moses. This seems intended as a rite that replaces circumcision, which Moses had not undergone. *Spouse of blood:* perhaps signifies "protected by the blood."

4:27-31 Moses makes contact with his people and awakens in them the hope of liberation.

5:1—6:1 The first meeting with Pharaoh results in a worsening of conditions for the enslaved Israelites. This result might seem to be a failure of the divine plan, but several interventions will be needed to advance the plan.

5:6 *Taskmasters . . . overseers:* the former were Egyptians with authority over the Israelites; the latter were most likely appointed by the Israelites themselves.

5:7 *Straw* was mixed with clay to give greater cohesiveness to the unbaked bricks.

Renewal of God's Promise. 22 Moses turned
again to the LORD and said, "My Lord, why
have you treated this people so badly? Why
did you send me? 23 From the time that
I went to Pharaoh to speak to him in your
name, he has treated this people harshly
and you have not done anything to free your
people."

CHAPTER 6

1 The LORD said to Moses, "Now you will
see what I am about to do to Pharaoh. With
a mighty hand he will let them go. With a
mighty hand he will drive them out of his
land."

Another Account of Moses' Call. 2 * God
spoke to Moses and told him, "I am the
LORD. 3 I appeared to Abraham, Isaac, and
Jacob as God the all-powerful, but I did not
reveal my name, the LORD, to them.[f] 4 I
established a covenant with them to give
them the land of Canaan, that land where
they dwelt as aliens.[g]

5 "And now I have heard the groaning of
the children of Israel in their bondage to the
Egyptians and I have remembered my
covenant. 6 Therefore, say to the children of
Israel, 'I am the LORD. I will bring you out
from your forced labor to the Egyptians. I
will free you from their slavery and liberate
you with an outstretched arm* and with
mighty acts of judgment. 7 I will take you as
my people, and I will be your God. You will
know that I am the LORD, your God, who
will bring you out from your forced labor to
the Egyptians.[h] 8 I will bring you into the
land that I swore with an oath I would give
to Abraham, to Isaac, and to Jacob, and I
will give it to you as an inheritance, for I am
the LORD.'"

9 Moses said these things to the children
of Israel, but they did not listen to him, for
they were at the limits of their endurance
because of their harsh slavery.*

10 The LORD said to Moses: 11 "Go to speak
with Pharaoh, the king of Egypt, so that he
will let the children of Israel leave his land."
12 But Moses said these things in God's pres-
ence, "Behold, the children of Israel have
not listened to me; how could Pharaoh lis-
ten to me, for I am a man of unskilled
speech?"[i]

13 The LORD spoke to Moses and Aaron
and gave them orders for the children of
Israel and for Pharaoh, king of Egypt, to let
the children of Israel leave the land of Egypt.

Genealogy of Moses and Aaron. 14 These are
the heads of their families. The sons of
Reuben, the firstborn of Israel, were
Hanoch, Pallu, Hezron, and Carmi. These
are the families of Reuben.[j] 15 The sons of
Simeon were Jemuel, Jamin, Ohad, Jachin,
Zohar, and Shaul, the son of the Canaanite
woman. These are the families of Simeon.

16 These are the names of the sons of Levi
according to their generations: Gershon,
Kohath, and Merari. Levi lived to be one
hundred and thirty-seven years old.[k]

17 The sons of Gershon, by their clans,
were Libni and Shimei.[l]

18 The sons of Kohath were Amram, Izhar,
Hebron, and Uzziel. Kohath lived to be one
hundred and thirty-three years old.[m]

19 The sons of Merari were Mahli and
Mushi. These are the families of Levi
according to their generations.[n]

20 Amram took Jochebed as his wife. She
was his father's sister. She bore Aaron and
Moses and Miriam. Amram lived to be one
hundred and thirty-seven years old.[o]

21 The sons of Izhar were Korah, Nepheg,
and Zichri.

22 The sons of Uzziel were Mishael,
Elzaphan, and Sithri.

23 Aaron took Elisheba, the daughter of
Amminadab and the sister of Nahshon, as
his wife. She bore Nadab, Abihu, Eleazar,
and Ithamar.[p]

24 The sons of Korah were Assir, Elkanah,
and Abiasaph. These are the families of the
Korahites.

25 Eleazar, the son of Aaron, took a daugh-
ter of Putiel, as a wife. She bore him
Phinehas. These are the heads of the ances-
tral clans of Levi.

---

f Gen 17:1; 35:11; Eph 3:5.—g Gen 15:18; 17:4-8; Acts 13:19.—h Lev 26:12.—i Ex 4:10; 6:30.—j Ex 46:9; Gen 46:9; Num 26:5f; 1 Chr 5:3.—k Ex 6:20; Num 3:17; 1 Chr 6:1; 23:6.—l Num 3:21; 1 Chr 6:2; 23:7.—m Num 3:27; 1 Chr 6:18; 23:12.—n Ex 6:16; Num 3:20; Ezr 8:19; 1 Chr 6:14; 23:21.—o Num 26:59.—p Gen 25:20; Ru 4:19f; 1 Chr 2:10.

6:2—7:7 The passage is from a Priestly tradition and dwells on the point that Moses and Aaron belong to the priestly family. After the doubt expressed in Ex 5:22, the redactor of the Book of Exodus seeks to reaffirm that Moses remains the chosen one of God to save his people.

6:6 *Outstretched arm:* this expression, like "mighty hand" in verse 1, suggests the power with which God intervenes.

6:9 Moses' words of encouragement fell on deaf ears. As the conditions of the children of Israel worsened, their spirits were crushed.

26 These are the Aaron and the Moses to whom the LORD said, "Bring the children of Israel out from the land of Egypt according to their hosts."

27 They told Pharaoh, the king of Egypt, to let the children of Israel leave Egypt. They are Moses and Aaron.

Moses and Aaron before Pharaoh. 28 This is what happened when the LORD spoke to Moses in the land of Egypt. 29 The LORD said to Moses, "I am the LORD! Tell Pharaoh, king of Egypt, what I say to you." 30 Moses spoke in the presence of the LORD, "Behold, I am a poor speaker, how will Pharaoh listen to me?"

CHAPTER 7

1 The LORD said to Moses, "Look, I have made you like a God to Pharaoh; Aaron will be your prophet.* 2 You will tell him what I have commanded you. Aaron, your brother, will tell Pharaoh to permit the children of Israel to leave his land. 3 But I will harden Pharaoh's heart and I will multiply my signs and wonders in the land of Egypt. 4 Pharaoh will not listen to you, and I will lay my hand upon Egypt and I will make my hosts leave Egypt, the children of Israel, with great acts of judgment.

5 "The Egyptians will know that I am the LORD, when I stretch out my hand against Egypt and bring the children of Israel out from their midst."

6 Moses and Aaron did what the LORD had commanded them to do. 7 Moses was eighty years old and Aaron was eighty-three years old when they spoke to Pharaoh.

D: The Plagues of Egypt*

Aaron's Staff Turned into a Snake. 8 The LORD said to Moses and Aaron, 9 "When Pharaoh says to you, 'Prove yourself by performing a wondrous deed,' you will say to Aaron, 'Take your staff and throw it in front of Pharaoh and it will become a serpent.' "[q] 10 Moses and Aaron then went to Pharaoh and did what the LORD had commanded them to do. Aaron threw his staff in front of Pharaoh and his servants, and it became a serpent. 11 Pharaoh gathered the wise men and sorcerers and even the magicians of Egypt. With their magic they did the same thing.[r] 12 Each one threw his staff and the staffs became serpents, but the staff of Aaron swallowed up their staffs. 13 Yet the heart of Pharaoh was hardened, and he did not listen to them, just as the LORD had predicted.

First Plague: Water Turned into Blood.* 14 The LORD said to Moses, "The heart of Pharaoh is hardened. He refuses to let the people go. 15 Go to Pharaoh in the morning when he goes out to the water and stand in front of him on the Nile riverbank and take the staff in your hand that was changed into a serpent. 16 Then you will tell him, The LORD, the God of the Hebrews, has sent me to tell you, 'Let my people go so that they can serve me in the desert. Up to now you have not obeyed.' 17 [s]The LORD says, 'By this you will know that I am the LORD. Behold, I will strike the waters of the Nile with the staff that I have in my hand, and they will change into blood. 18 The fish in the Nile will die, and the Nile will become putrid so that the Egyptians will not be able to drink from the Nile." ' "

19 The LORD said to Moses, "Command Aaron, 'Take your staff and stretch out your hand over the waters of Egypt, over their rivers, their canals, their ponds, and over all their supplies of water. They will turn into blood and there will be blood in all of the land of Egypt, even in their wood and stone jars.' "[t]

20 Moses and Aaron did what the LORD had commanded. Aaron raised his staff and struck the waters of the Nile in the sight of Pharaoh and his servants. All the waters of the Nile changed into blood. 21 The fish in the Nile died, and the Nile became putrid, so that the Egyptians could not drink the water. There was blood in the entire land of

q Ex 4:3; Jdg 6:13.—r Ex 4:2; 2 Tim 3:8.—s 17-21: Ex 4:9; Pss 78:44; 105:29; Wis 11:5-7; 19:19.—t Ex 10:12; Num 3:40.

7:1 A *prophet* is one who speaks in the name of another (here: Moses).

7:8—11:10 Bits from various traditions are skillfully combined to show the gradual hardening of Pharaoh and the increasing misfortunes that this brings upon Egypt. The ten "plagues" have for their purpose to show the character of the God in whose name Moses bids Pharaoh to release the Hebrews, but whom the proud "son of the sun" claims he does not know (Ex 5:2). This God is mightier than all the magicians of Egypt; he can command every creature, and his power extends not only to Israel but to the land of the Nile and its inhabitants.

These very colorful narratives profile the struggle between the Lord and the forces of evil. Pharaoh personifies the human freedom that is opposed to the divine plan but that God makes use of to realize his plan. We should not be surprised that tradition has systematized and amplified these events to better manifest the greatness and power of the Lord.

7:14-24 Moses appears as a prophet; he is the Lord's spokesperson.

Egypt. 22 But the magicians of Egypt, with
their magic, did the same thing. The heart
of Pharaoh was hardened and he did not lis-
ten to them, just as the LORD had predict-
ed.* 23 Pharaoh turned his back on them
and went into his house and did not even
pay attention to these things. 24 All the
Egyptians dug along the Nile to find water
to drink because they could not drink the
water in the Nile.

Second Plague: The Frogs. 25 Seven days
passed after the LORD had struck the Nile.
26 *[u] The LORD said to Moses, "Go to speak
to Pharaoh, 'Thus says the LORD, "Let my
people go to serve me. 27 If you refuse to let
them go, then I will strike your land with
frogs. 28 The Nile will swarm with frogs. They
will come out and go into your houses, into
the rooms where you sleep and up on your
beds, into the houses of your ministers and
your people, even into your ovens and your
kneading bowls. 29 The frogs will come out
and climb over you and your ministers." ' "

CHAPTER 8

1 The LORD said to Moses, "Command
Aaron: 'Stretch out your hand with your
staff over the waters, over the canals and
pools, and make frogs come out all over the
land of Egypt.' "

2 Aaron extended his hand over the
waters of Egypt and frogs came out and
covered the land of Egypt. 3 But the magi-
cians, with their magic, did the same thing
and made frogs to come up out all over the
land of Egypt.

4 Pharaoh had Moses and Aaron sum-
moned and said, "Pray to the LORD to take
the frogs away from me, and my people and
I will let the people go to sacrifice to the
LORD."

5 Moses said to Pharaoh, "Do me the
honor of telling me when I should pray for
you and your ministers and your people, to
free you and your house from frogs, so that
they only remain in the waters of the Nile."

6 He answered, "Tomorrow." Then Moses
said, "As you say. In order that you may
know that there is no equal to the LORD, our
God, 7 the frogs will leave your house and
those of your servants and of your people,
remaining only in the Nile."

8 Moses and Aaron left Pharaoh, and
Moses beseeched the LORD concerning the
frogs that he had sent against Pharaoh.
9 The LORD did as Moses had said and the
frogs died in the houses, in the courtyards,
and in the fields. 10 They piled them up in
heaps and the land stank. 11 But Pharaoh
saw that there was a moment of relief, and
he became stubborn and did not listen to
them, just as the LORD had predicted.

Third Plague: The Gnats.* 12 [v] Then the LORD
said to Moses, "Command Aaron, 'Stretch
out your staff and strike the dust of the
earth. It will change into gnats* in all the
land of Egypt.' " 13 This is what he did.
Aaron stretched out his hand with his staff,
struck the dust of the earth, and there were
gnats on man and beast. All the dust of the
earth changed into gnats throughout Egypt.
14 The magicians did the same thing with
their magic to produce gnats, but they were
not able to do it. The gnats were on man and
beast. [w] 15 The magicians said to Pharaoh,
"It is the finger of God." But the heart of
Pharaoh was so hardened that he did not
listen, just as the LORD had predicted.

Fourth Plague: The Flies.* 16 The LORD
said to Moses, "Get up early tomorrow and
present yourself to Pharaoh when he goes
down to the water. You are to tell him, 'Thus
says the LORD, "Let my people go so that
they can serve me! 17 If you do not let my
people go, then I will send flies* upon you,
upon your ministers, upon your people, and
upon your houses. The houses of Egypt will
be filled with flies, and even the ground on
which they stand will be filled with them.
18 But on that day I will set apart the land of
Goshen where my people live. There will be
no flies there, so that you will know that I,
the LORD, am in the land. 19 Thus I will
establish a difference between my people
and your people. This sign will happen
tomorrow." ' "

20 This is what the LORD did. A huge
swarm of flies flew into the house of

u 26-29: Ex 8:7; Pss 78:45; 105:30.—v 12f: Ps 105:31; Wis 19:10.—w Ex 7:22; Wis 17:7.

7:22 God allowed the magicians to imitate Moses who turned the Nile into blood, but did not have the power to reverse the miracle (i.e., change the blood into water).

7:26—8:11 The power of the God of Israel begins to impress Pharaoh.

8:12-15 For the first time, the magicians cannot compete with the Lord and recognize his presence.

8:12, 17 *Gnats, flies:* the type of bothersome insects that caused so much distress is not certain.

8:16-28 The power of God becomes more evident from the fact that he preserves Israel from the plague that he inflicts upon the Egyptians.

Pharaoh, the houses of his ministers, and all
over the land of Egypt. The area was devas-
tated because of the flies. [x]
21 Pharaoh summoned Moses and Aaron
and said, "Go and sacrifice to your God in
the land."
22 But Moses answered, "It would not
work, for the sacrifice that we are going to
make to the LORD, our God, is an abomina-
tion to the Egyptians. Could we perform a
sacrifice that is an abomination to the
Egyptians in their sight? Would they not
stone us?* 23 We will go into the desert, a
three days' journey, and that is where we
will sacrifice to the LORD, our God, just as
he has ordered us."
24 So Pharaoh answered, "I will let you go
and you can sacrifice to the LORD in the
desert. Only do not go too far and pray for
me." [y]
25 Moses answered, "I will leave you and
pray to the LORD. Tomorrow the flies will
depart from Pharaoh, from his ministers,
and from the people. Pharaoh, however,
must not deceive us by not letting the people
go to perform their sacrifice to the LORD."
26 Moses left Pharaoh and prayed to the
LORD. 27 The LORD did as Moses said, and
the flies departed from Pharaoh, from his
ministers, and from his people. There was
not even one left. 28 But Pharaoh became
stubborn and once again would not let the
people go.

CHAPTER 9

Fifth Plague: The Pestilence on Livestock.
1 The LORD said to Moses, "Go to Pharaoh
and tell him, 'Thus says the LORD, the God
of the Hebrews: "Let my people go so that
they can serve me. 2 If you refuse to permit
them to leave and you continue to hinder
them, 3 the hand of the LORD will come
upon your animals in the fields: upon the
horses, the donkeys, the camels, upon your
herds and flocks, with a horrible plague.
4 But the LORD will distinguish between the
animals of Israel and those of the Egyp-
tians, so that none of those that belong to
the children of Israel will die." ' "
5 The LORD established the date saying,
"Tomorrow the LORD will accomplish this
thing in the land." * 6 The next day, the LORD
accomplished this thing. All the animals in
Egypt died, but the animals of the children
of Israel did not die, not even one of them. [z]
7 Pharaoh sent men to find out, and not one
of the animals of Israel was dead. But the
heart of Pharaoh remained hardened, and
he would not let the people go.

Sixth Plague: The Boils.* 8 The LORD said to
Moses and Aaron: "Take two handfuls of
ashes from the furnace. Moses is to throw
them into the air in front of Pharaoh. 9 It
will become a fine powder that will spread
throughout the whole land and will produce
running sores upon the people and the ani-
mals throughout the land of Egypt." 10 They
therefore took ashes from the furnace and
stood before Pharaoh. Moses threw them
into the air, and they produced running
sores on people and animals. 11 The magi-
cians could not stand in the presence of
Moses because of the sores that had struck
them as well as all the Egyptians. 12 But the
LORD caused Pharaoh's heart to be hard-
ened. He did not listen to them, as the LORD
had predicted to Moses.

Seventh Plague: The Hail.* 13 The LORD said
to Moses, "Get up early in the morning and
present yourself to Pharaoh and proclaim,
'Thus says the LORD, the God of the
Hebrews, "Let my people go so that they
can serve me! 14 This time I will send all of
my plagues against you, against your minis-
ters, and against all your people, so that you
may know that there is no one like me upon
the whole earth. 15 By now I could have
stretched out my hand and struck you and
your people with plagues that would have
wiped you off the face of the earth. 16 In-
stead, I let you live to show you my power
and so that my name might be proclaimed
all throughout the earth. [a] 17 Will you still
oppose my people and not let them leave?
18 Behold, I will send a terribly violent hail
tomorrow at this time as has never been
seen in Egypt from the day it was founded
until today. 19 Send word to gather your ani-

---

x Pss 78:45; 105:31; Wis 16:9.—y Ex 9:28; Acts 8:24.—z Ex 9:7; Ps 78:48.—a Ps 106:8; Rom 9:17.

8:22 The Egyptians would not have endured seeing the Hebrews sacrifice animals that they, the Egyptians, regarded as sacred.

9:5 God personally performs the miracle without Moses or Aaron or any staff. This should have been a persuasive event for Pharaoh to change his heart but he remains hardened.

9:8-12 This time the magicians are eliminated not without humor: in their turn they are victims of the wonder worked by Moses.

9:13-35 The God of Israel wants to be recognized and served as Lord of the whole earth. Pharaoh acknowledges his sin but his heart remains unchanged.

mals and whatever is in the field into a safe
shelter. Hail will fall upon all the people and
upon all the animals that are in open coun-
tryside and that have not been brought into
shelter, and they will die." ' "
20 Some of the ministers of Pharaoh
feared the LORD and brought their slaves
and their animals into shelter.* 21 Others
did not take the words of the LORD to heart,
and they left their slaves and their animals
in the open countryside.
22 The LORD said to Moses, "Stretch your
hand out toward the heavens. Let there be
hail in all the land of Egypt, upon people,
upon animals, and upon the plants of the
field throughout the land of Egypt."
23 [b] Moses stretched his staff toward the
heavens, and the LORD sent thunder and
hail. Lightning struck the earth, and the
LORD made hail rain down upon the land of
Egypt. 24 There was hail and lightning in the
midst of the hail. The hail was so violent that
nothing like it had ever been seen in the
entire land of Egypt from the day it had
become a nation. 25 The hail struck every
person and animal that was in the open
countryside throughout the land of Egypt.
The hail also struck the plants in the field
and splintered every tree in the open coun-
tryside. 26 Only the land of Goshen, where
the children of Israel lived, had no hail.
27 Pharaoh summoned Moses and Aaron
and said to them, "This time I have sinned.
The LORD is right. I and my people are
guilty. 28 Pray to the LORD to stop the thun-
der and hail. I will let you leave. You need not
stay any longer." [c] 29 Moses answered him,
"When I leave the city, I will stretch out my
hands toward the LORD. The thunder will
cease, and the hail will end, so that you may
know that the earth belongs to the LORD.
30 But as for you and your ministers, I know
that you still do not fear the LORD God."
31 The linen and barley was ruined,
because the barley was in the ear and the
flax was flowering. [d] 32 But the wheat and
the rye and the spelt were not harmed for
they have a later season.
33 Moses left Pharaoh and the city. He
extended his hand toward the LORD. The
thunder and the hail stopped, and the rain
no longer poured down upon the land.
34 Pharaoh saw that the rain had stopped, as
had the hail and the thunder, but he contin-
ued to sin and be stubborn, together with
his ministers. 35 The heart of Pharaoh was
hardened and he did not let the children of
Israel leave, as the LORD had predicted
through Moses.

CHAPTER 10

Eighth Plague: The Locusts.* 1 Then the
LORD said to Moses, "Go to Pharaoh, for I
have hardened his heart and the hearts of his
ministers so that I may perform these signs in
their midst 2 and so that you can tell your sons
and grandsons how I dealt with the Egyptians
and the signs I worked in their midst so that
they may know that I am the LORD." [e]
3 Moses and Aaron went to Pharaoh and
told him, "The LORD, the God of the
Hebrews, says, 'How long will you refuse to
submit to me? Let my people go so that they
may serve me. 4 If you refuse to let my peo-
ple go, behold, I will send locusts upon your
land. 5 They will cover the entire country so
that you cannot even see the soil. They will
devour what is left, whatever survived the
hail, and they will devour every tree that
grows in your fields. 6 They will fill your
house, the houses of all your ministers and
the houses of all the Egyptians, so many
that even your fathers never saw so many,
nor the fathers of your fathers, from when
they came into this land until today.' " He
turned and left Pharaoh.
7 The ministers of Pharaoh said to him,
"How long will he be a snare to us? Let this
people go to serve the LORD, their God.
Otherwise Egypt may be ruined."
8 Moses and Aaron were summoned to
Pharaoh who said to them, "Go, serve the
LORD, your God. But who will leave with
you?" [f] 9 Moses said, "We will go with our
young and our old, with our sons and our
daughters, with our animals and our flocks,
so that we can celebrate a feast of the LORD."
10 * Pharaoh answered, "The LORD be
with you, if I let you and your children leave.
Clearly you have an evil project in mind.
11 No! Have only the men go with you and

b 23f: Pss 78:47; 105:32f; Rev 8:7.—c Ex 8:24; Acts 8:22.—d Jud 8:2; Prov 31:13.—e Deut 6:20ff; Ezek 15:7.—f Ex 12:31.

9:20 Some of Pharaoh's ministers acknowledge the power of God and take action to protect their slaves and animals from the predicted hail storm.

10:1-20 By remaining obstinate, Pharaoh furnishes God with the occasion to multiply his wonders and show that he is really the Lord.

10:10-11 Pharaoh does not trust the Hebrews and wants to keep the women and children in Egypt as hostages.

serve the LORD. That is what you want."
They then went out from Pharaoh.
12 [g] The LORD said to Moses, "Stretch out
your hand over the land of Egypt to send
locusts. Let them come down upon the land
of Egypt to eat every plant that the hail
spared." 13 Moses extended his staff over the
land of Egypt, and the LORD sent an east
wind over the land all that day and all that
night. By the morning, the east wind had
brought the locusts. 14 The locusts swarmed
over the whole land of Egypt and settled on
every part of the territory of Egypt. It was
very serious, so bad that it had never been as
bad before nor would it ever be as bad again
in the future. 15 They covered the whole land
so that the land was darkened. They de-
voured every plant in the land and every fruit
tree that the hail had spared. Not a green leaf
remained upon the trees or the plants in the
field throughout the land of Egypt.

16 Pharaoh quickly summoned Moses and
Aaron and said, "I have sinned against the
LORD, your God, and against you. 17 But
now once again forgive my sin and pray to
the LORD, your God, so that he may turn
aside this death from me." [h]

18 Moses left Pharaoh and prayed to the
LORD. 19 The LORD changed the direction of
the wind and made a strong wind blow from
the sea. It carried the locusts away and blew
them into the Red Sea. There was not one
locust left in all the land of Egypt. 20 But the
LORD hardened the heart of Pharaoh, and
he did not let the children of Israel leave.

Ninth Plague: The Darkness.* 21 The LORD
said to Moses, "Stretch out your hand
toward the heavens. Darkness will come
upon the land of Egypt, so dark that one can
feel it."

22 Moses stretched out out his hand toward
the heavens. Darkness came upon the land
of Egypt for three days. [i] 23 People could not
see each other, and for three days no one
could move around. But there was light
where the children of Israel were living.*

24 Pharaoh summoned Moses and said,
"Leave, and serve the LORD. Take your
babies with you. Only leave your flocks and
herds here."

25 Moses answered, "You must also grant
us sacrifices and burnt offerings that we will
offer to the LORD, our God. 26 Our animals,
too, must leave with us; not even a hoof will
be left behind. We must choose the sacrifi-
cial victims that we will offer to the LORD,
our God, from among them, and we will not
know how to serve the LORD until we will
have arrived in that place." 27 But the LORD
hardened the heart of Pharaoh who would
not let them go. 28 Pharaoh therefore said to
Moses, "Leave me! Make sure that you
never see me again, for the next time you
see my face, you will die." 29 Moses said,
"You have spoken well, for I will not see
your face again."

CHAPTER 11

Announcement of the Death of the Firstborn.*
1 The LORD said to Moses, "I will send still
another plague against Pharaoh and Egypt.
Afterward, he will let you go from here. He
will let you leave without restrictions. In
fact, he will chase you out.

2 [j] "Therefore, tell the people that each
man should ask from his neighbor and each
woman should ask from her neighbor
objects of silver and objects of gold."

3 The LORD caused the people to find
favor in the sight of the Egyptians. Moses,
too, was a man who was highly regarded in
the land of Egypt, both by the ministers of
Pharaoh and by the people. [k]

4 Moses then said, "Thus says the LORD,
'Around midnight I will go forth through
Egypt. [l] 5 [m] Every firstborn in the land of
Egypt will die, from the firstborn of
Pharaoh who sits upon the throne all the
way to the firstborn of the slaves who
work at the mill,* even the firstborn of
the animals. 6 A great lament will rise up
in all the land of Egypt such as will never
be repeated again. 7 But not even a dog
will growl against the children of Israel,
neither against humans nor animals, so
that you may know that the LORD makes
a distinction between Egypt and Israel.

---

g 12ff: Ex 14:26; Pss 78:46; 105:34f.—h 2 Chr 6:25; 2 Cor 12:12.—i Ps 105:28; Acts 9:9.—j 2f: Ex 3:21f; 12:35f; 2 Chr 35:6.—k Ex 3:21; 12:36.—l Ex 12:12.—m 5f: Ex 12:29f; Num 8:17.

10:21-29 Is this the rupture between Moses and Pharaoh? All Moses' warnings have remained without effect.

10:23 The Israelites were spared the destructive effects of the plagues, whereas the Egyptians had a foretaste of what hell is like. We have the assurance of God's faithfulness to those who remain faithful to God (see Deut 7:6).

11:1-10 This decisive blow to Pharaoh will result in his expelling Israel.

11:5 The female slave *at the mill* was assigned to operate the mill in the house. *Even the firstborn of the animals:* because these, like the firstborn of humans, were firstfruits belonging to the divinity; see Ex 13:2.

8 All these servants of yours will come
down to me and bow down in front of me
saying, "May you and all the people who fol-
low you leave." After that I will leave.' "[n]

Moses grew angry and left Pharaoh.

9 But the LORD had said to Moses,
"Pharaoh will not listen to you. Therefore, I
will multiply my signs in the land of Egypt."

10 Moses and Aaron did all these signs
before Pharaoh, but the LORD had so hard-
ened the heart of Pharaoh that he would not
let the children of Israel leave his land.

E: The Passover

CHAPTER 12

Preparations for the Passover.* 1 The LORD
said to Moses and Aaron in the land of
Egypt, 2 [o] "This month shall be the begin-
ning of months for you; it shall be your first
month of the year.* 3 Speak to the whole
community of Israel and say, 'The tenth of
this month each person shall obtain a lamb
for each family, one for each household. 4 If
the family is too small to eat the lamb, they
should join with their neighbors, based on
the number of people. Figure the lamb
according to how much each person can
eat. 5 Your lamb should be without blem-
ish,* male, a year old. You can choose either
a sheep or a goat. 6 Keep it until the four-
teenth day of this month. Then the whole
community of Israel shall slaughter it in the
evening.[p] 7 Take a bit of its blood, put it on
the two doorposts and upon the lintel of
every house in which it is to be eaten. 8 That
night eat its meat roasted. Eat it with
unleavened bread and bitter herbs. 9 Do not
eat it raw or boiled in water, but only roast-
ed with the head, legs, and inner organs.
10 Do not let any of it be kept until the morn-
ing. Whatever is left over in the morning
shall be burned in the fire. 11 This is how you
shall eat it, with your loins girt and sandals
on your feet and a staff in your hand. Eat
it quickly. It is the Passover* of the LORD.

12 " 'On that night I will pass over the land
of Egypt and strike the firstborn of the land
of Egypt, both human and animal, to render
justice against all the gods of Egypt. I am the
LORD.[q] 13 The blood on your houses shall be
the sign that you are inside. I will see the
blood and pass over. There shall be no plague
for you when I strike the land of Egypt.[r]

Preparations for the Unleavened Bread.
14 * " 'This day shall be a memorial for you.
You shall celebrate it as a feast of the LORD.
From generation to generation, let there be
an ordinance that you celebrate this feast.
15 For seven days you shall eat unleavened
bread. On the first day you shall dispose of
all leaven from your house. Whoever eats
leavened goods from the first day til the sev-
enth shall be cut off from Israel. 16 On the
first day you shall hold a sacred assembly
and another on the seventh day. On those
days you shall not work. You shall only pre-
pare what is to be eaten by everyone.

17 " 'You shall observe the custom of
unleavened bread, for on this same day I
brought out your hosts from the land of
Egypt. You shall observe this day from gen-
eration to generation as an eternal ordi-
nance.[s] 18 In the first month, the fourteenth
day of the month, in the evening, you shall
eat unleavened bread until the twenty-first
of the month, in the evening.[t] 19 For seven
days leavened bread shall not be found in
your house, for whoever eats leavened
bread shall be cut off from the community
of Israel, whether it be a foreigner or a

n Ex 12:31ff; Acts 22:18.—o 2-20: Lev 23:5-8; Num 9:2-5; 28:16ff; Deut 16:1-8; 2 Chr 30:2.—p Num 9:1-3; 28:8.—q Num 33:4; Ps 78:51; Ezek 5:15.—r Ex 12:23; Heb 11:28.—s Ex 13:3; Deut 16:3.—t Lev 23:6.

12:1-13 Passover was already being celebrated in the period when the Hebrews were pastoral nomads and used to offer the firstfruits of the flock. The blood poured on the posts of the tent was to protect those living in it. Once this ancient spring festival was connected with the departure from Egypt, it would commemorate the deliverance effected by God.

The Passover was essentially sacrificial from the beginning. Added to this was the meal (v. 11) and the urgency in which it was to be held because of the circumstances it commemorated: there is no time for seasoning anything (v. 9); neither is any other food to be eaten with it except for the bread and desert herbs; and the people are to be in traveling dress—standing, wearing sandals, and holding a staff—indicating that they are on a journey to the true Promised Land. Jesus chose to institute the Eucharist in the context of the Passover meal and to be crucified during Passover. He thus becomes the true Passover lamb, whose blood is shed for the salvation of all humankind.

12:2 This is the month of Abib, of the ripe ears of corn (see Ex 13:4). It would later be called Nisan (March-April).

12:5 The words *without blemish* are translated as *absque macula* (spotless) in the Vulgate; hence the widely used expression "spotless Lamb" for Jesus, the Passover lamb prefigured by the Jewish practice.

12:11 *Passover:* Hebrew, *pesah*, "passage"; that is, the Lord passed by, leaving untouched the houses marked with blood. The etymology of the Hebrew word is disputed.

12:14-30 The Feast of Unleavened Bread was an agricultural feast at which the new harvest was dedicated to the divinity. When the Hebrews settled in Canaan, they adopted this feast and amalgamated it with Passover. The biblical tradition connects it with the Exodus of the Hebrew people; therefore, it finds a place in this book, where it has become a pure commemoration.

native of the land. 20 You shall not eat leav-
ened bread; in all your houses you shall eat
unleavened bread.' "

Celebration of the Passover. 21 Moses sum-
moned all the elders of Israel and told
them, "Go and obtain a lamb for each fam-
ily and slaughter it for the Passover.*
22 Take a bunch of hyssop* and dip it into
the blood in the bowl and sprinkle the blood
from the bowl on the lintel and the two
doorposts. None of you shall go outside until
the morning. 23 The LORD will pass over to
strike the Egyptians. He will see the blood
on the lintel and on the two doorposts. The
LORD will, therefore, pass over the door and
will not allow the destroyer to enter into
your house to strike anyone there.*

24 "You shall observe this command as a
fixed rite for yourselves and your children
forever. 25 When you will have entered into
the land that the LORD will give you, as he
promised, you shall observe this rite.
26 [u] When your children ask you, 'What does
this rite of yours mean,' 27 you shall tell
them, 'It is the sacrifice of the Passover of
the LORD, who passed over the houses of the
children of Israel in Egypt when he struck
the Egyptians and spared our houses.' "

The people knelt down and worshiped.
28 Then the children of Israel went and did
exactly what the LORD had ordered Moses
and Aaron.

II: THE EXODUS FROM EGYPT AND THE JOURNEY TO SINAI

A: Departure from Egypt

Tenth Plague: The Death of the Firstborn.*
29 [v] At midnight the LORD slew every first-
born in the land of Egypt, from the firstborn
of Pharaoh who sat upon the throne to the
firstborn of the prisoners being held in dun-
geons, all the firstborn, both human and ani-
mal. 30 Pharaoh got up during the night along
with his ministers and all the Egyptians, and
a loud cry arose out of Egypt, for every house
had someone who had died.

Permission to Depart. 31 * Pharaoh sum-
moned Moses and Aaron during the night
and said, "Arise and leave my people, you
and the children of Israel! Go and serve the
LORD as you have said. 32 Take your herds
and your flocks, as you have said, and leave.
Bless me, too."

33 The Egyptians urged on the people to
drive them out of the land quickly, for they
said, "We are all about to die." 34 The people
took their unleavened dough with them, plac-
ing their kneading bowls wrapped in their
cloaks on their shoulders. 35 [w] The children of
Israel carried out Moses' order and had the
Egyptians give them objects of silver and gold
and clothes. 36 The LORD had inclined the
Egyptians favorably toward the people so that
they gave them whatever they requested. So,
they plundered the Egyptians.

Departure from Egypt. 37 The children of
Israel traveled from Rameses to Succoth.
There were six hundred thousand men on
foot, not counting children.[x] 38 There was
also a large crowd of people of mixed ances-
try with them, together with large numbers
of flocks and herds. 39 They baked the dough
that they had carried with them from Egypt
as cakes of unleavened bread for it had not
been leavened. They had been hurried out of
Egypt and had not had time to hesitate nor
to prepare provisions for the journey.

40 The children of Israel had lived in Egypt
for four hundred and thirty years.[y] 41 At the
end of four hundred and thirty years, exact-
ly to the day, all the hosts of the LORD went
up out of Egypt. 42 This was a night of vigil
unto the LORD, for bringing them out of the
land of Egypt. Hence, it must be a night of
vigil in honor of the LORD for all the children
of Israel, from one generation to the next.

Ordinances for the Passover.* 43 The LORD
said to Moses and Aaron, "These are the
ordinances for the Passover:

u 26f: Ex 13:8, 14; Deut 6:20f; Jos 4:6-7.—v 29f: Ex 11:4ff; 13:15; Pss 78:51; 105:36; 136:10; Wis 18:10-16.—w 35f: Ex 3:21f; 11:2f; Ps 105:37f.—x Gen 47:11; Num 33:3ff.—y Ex 12:41; Gen 15:13.

12:21 The reference is to the Passover lamb (Mt 26:17; 1 Cor 5:7)

12:22 *Hyssop:* was an aromatic plant used in purification rites.

12:23 The destroying angel, charged with inflicting punishment; see 1 Cor 10:10; Heb 11:28.

12:29-30 This time Egypt cannot remain indifferent to the misfortune that has come upon it.

12:31-42 This is the memorable night during which the Lord kept watch in order to deliver his people from slavery. With a view to magnifying the divine intervention, Israelite piety obviously exaggerated the numbers involved; historical fact has been transformed into liturgical story. For Christians, the Easter vigil will sing of the deliverance brought by Christ.

12:43-51 The traditional ritual (vv. 1-14) is supplemented by further arrangements that suppose the Hebrews to be already settled in Canaan.

"No foreigner may eat it. 44 As for each slave bought with money, you shall circumcise him so that he may eat it. 45 The foreigner and the hired laborer cannot eat it.

46 "It must be eaten in one house. One may not carry the meat outside of the house, and none of its bones is to be broken.* [z] 47 [a] All the community of Israel shall celebrate it.

48 "If a foreigner dwells among you and wishes to celebrate the Passover of the LORD, let each man in his household be circumcised. Then let him draw near to celebrate and he will be like a native of the land. But no one who is uncircumcised can eat it. 49 The same law will be binding on the native and the foreigner who is living in your midst."

50 All the children of Israel did just as the LORD had commanded Moses and Aaron. 51 On that very day the LORD brought Israel out of the land of Egypt, organized according to their hosts.

CHAPTER 13

Sign and Memorial. 1 * The LORD spoke to Moses, 2 "Consecrate each firstborn to me, whatever opens the womb in Israel, whether human or animal; it belongs to me." [b]

3 [c] Moses said to the people, "Remember this day on which you came out of Egypt, your place of slavery. The LORD brought you out from there with a mighty hand. Therefore, do not eat what has been leavened. 4 This day you came out is in the month of Abib. 5 When the LORD brings you to the land of the Canaanites, the Hittites, the Amorites, the Hivites, and the Jebusites, that he swore to your fathers to give you, a land flowing with milk and honey, you shall celebrate this rite in this month.

6 "For seven days you shall eat unleavened bread, and on the seventh you shall celebrate a feast in honor of the LORD. 7 For seven days you shall eat unleavened bread, and there shall be nothing leavened with you. There shall be no leaven in all of your territory. 8 On that day you shall teach your son: 'This is because of what the LORD did for me when he brought me out of Egypt.' 9 And it shall be a sign on your hand and a memorial before your eyes so that the law of the LORD may be upon your lips. With a mighty hand the LORD brought you out of Egypt.* [d] 10 You shall celebrate this rite at this time every year.

11 "When the LORD brings you to the land of the Canaanites, as he promised you and your fathers, and he will have given it to you as a possession, 12 [e] you shall dedicate each firstborn from the womb to the LORD. All male firstborn of your animals belong to the LORD. 13 You shall redeem every firstborn donkey with a lamb.* If you do not redeem it, you shall break its neck. You shall redeem each firstborn son from among his brothers.

14 "When your son asks you, 'What is the meaning of this,' you shall answer, 'With a mighty arm the LORD brought us out of the land of Egypt, our place of slavery. 15 When Pharaoh was stubborn and would not let us go, the LORD slew the firstborn in the land of Egypt, the firstborn of human and animal. Because of this I sacrifice the firstborn male from every womb to the LORD, and I redeem the firstborn of my sons.' 16 This shall be a sign on your hand and a memorial before your eyes, to remember that the LORD brought us out of Egypt with a mighty hand." [f]

The LORD Went before Them.* 17 When Pharaoh let the people leave, God did not guide them on the road through the land of the Philistines, even though it was shorter, for God thought, "Otherwise the people, seeing they would have to fight, may change their minds and return to Egypt." 18 God guided the people along the desert road toward the Red Sea. The children of Israel, well armed, left the land of Egypt.

19 Moses took the bones of Joseph along with him, for Joseph had solemnly sworn

z Lev 7:6; Num 9:12; Jn 19:36.—a 47f: Num 9:14.—b Ex 13:12-15; Num 8:17.—c 3-10: Ex 12:2-20; Mt 26:17.—d Ex 13:14, 16; Deut 6:8; 11:18.—e 12-15: Ex 13:2; 22:29f; 34:19f; Lev 24:9; Num 3:12f, 45; 8:16; 18:15; Deut 15:19.—f Ex 13:9; Acts 13:17.

12:46 This detail of the rite is fulfilled in Jesus: Jn 19:36.

13:1-6 The practice of offering the firstborn to God and of eating unleavened bread soon provided Israel with an opportunity of passing on to later generations the religious lesson learned from the events: namely, that what God did in the beginning he continues to do for his people.

13:9 Sign and memorial were understood in a material way. See Deut 6:8; 11:18; Mt 23:5 on the phylacteries worn on forehead or arm.

13:13 A donkey could not be offered in sacrifice (see Ex 34:19-20).

13:17-22 As he had promised, God led his people along the road of freedom. The account also seeks to explain why Israel had to journey for so many years in the desert. They do not follow the way of the sea, parallel to the road leading through Sile (modern El Qantara), along which there were wells and Egyptian forts; instead they travel the caravan route through the Sinai.

the children of Israel, saying, "Surely God
will come to visit you, and when he does you
must carry away my bones."[g]

[20] They left Succoth and camped in
Etham on the edge of the desert. [21] [h] The
LORD went before them as a pillar of cloud
during the day to guide them on their way,
and as a column of fire during the night to
give them light, so that they could travel day
and night. [22] During the day the pillar of
cloud never disappeared from the sight of
the people, nor did the column of fire dur-
ing the night.

CHAPTER 14

"I Will Display My Glory against Pharaoh."*
[1] The LORD said to Moses, [2] "Order the chil-
dren of Israel to turn around and camp in
front of Pi-hahiroth between Migdol and the
sea, in front of Baal-zephon. You shall camp
in front of it by the sea.[i] [3] Pharaoh will think
that the children of Israel are wandering
through the land because the desert has
blocked them in. [4] I shall harden the heart of
Pharaoh, and he will follow them. I will dis-
play my glory against Pharaoh and all his
army, so that the Egyptians will know that I
am the LORD." This is what they did.

[5] [j] When the king of Egypt was told that
the people had fled, the heart of Pharaoh
and his ministers was turned against the
people. They said, "What have we done in
letting Israel leave so that they will no
longer serve us?" [6] He prepared his chariot
and took his soldiers with him.

[7] Pharaoh took six hundred choice chari-
ots and all the other chariots of Egypt with
warriors on each of them. [8] The LORD hard-
ened the heart of Pharaoh, the king of Egypt,
who then pursued the children of Israel while
they were marching away in triumph. [9] The
Egyptians followed and caught up with them
while they were camped near the sea. All the
horses and chariots of Pharaoh, his horse-
men and his army were near Pi-hahiroth,
before Baal-zephon.

[10] When Pharaoh approached, the children
of Israel looked up and saw that the
Egyptians were marching after them. The
children of Israel were terrified and called
upon the LORD. [11] They said to Moses, "Why
did you bring us out to the desert to die? Was
it because there were not enough graves in
Egypt? What have you done bringing us out
of Egypt? [12] Did we not tell you in Egypt, 'Let
us stay here and serve the Egyptians?' It is
better for us to serve than for us to die in the
desert?"

[13] Moses answered, "Do not be afraid. Be
strong, and you will see the salvation that the
LORD will work for you today, for you will
never again see the Egyptians that you see
today.[k] [14] The LORD will battle for you. Be
calm!"

The Children of Israel Cross the Red Sea.*
[15] The LORD said to Moses, "Why do they cry
out to me? Order the children of Israel to set
out again. [16] You are to lift up your staff,
stretch out your hand over the sea, and divide
it so that the children of Israel may pass
through the midst of the sea on dry land. [17] I
will harden the heart of the Egyptians so that
they will enter after them. I will display my
glory against Pharaoh and all his army,
against his chariots and his horsemen. [18] The
Egyptians will know that I am the LORD when
I display my glory against Pharaoh, against
his chariots and his horsemen."[l]

[19] The angel of God, who had gone in front
of Israel's camp, now moved and went in
back of them. The pillar of cloud also moved
from their front to their back. [20] They were,
therefore, between the camps of the
Egyptians and the children of Israel. The
cloud was dark for the former group, while it
lit up the night for the other. Thus, one group
could not approach the other throughout the
night.

[21] [m] Moses stretched out his hand over the
sea. During the night the LORD caused the
sea to move back with a strong east wind,
producing dry ground. The waters split in
two. [22] The children of Israel entered the sea
on dry land, while the waters formed a wall
on their right and their left. [23] The Egyptians
pursued them with all the horses of Pharaoh,
his chariots, and his horsemen. They entered
after them in the midst of the sea. [24] Just

g Gen 50:25; Jos 24:32.—h 21f: Ex 40:38; Num 9:15-22; Deut 1:33; Neh 9:12, 19; Pss 78:14; 105:39; Wis 10:17.—i Ex 14:9; Num 33:7f.—j 5-8: Wis 19:3; 1 Mac 4:9.—k Ex 20:20; Zep 3:16; Jn 14:27.—l Ex 14:17; Ezek 30:26.—m 21f: Ex 14:16; 15:19; Gen 8:1; Pss 66:6; 78:13; 136:13f; Wis 10:18; 19:7f; Isa 63:12f; Heb 11:29.

14:1-14 As the Master of history, the Lord makes use of even his enemies to accomplish his plan of salvation.

14:15-31 At last, the chosen people throw off their bondage by traversing the waters on dry feet thanks to God who fights for them. Israel could do no less than acknowledge its liberator. God wrests his people from the imminent catastrophe. Tradition seized upon this event and multiplied and exaggerated its details in order to magnify a feat that gave glory to God. History has become epic.

before dawn the LORD of the column of fire and cloud looked upon the camp of the Egyptians and threw them into confusion.
25 He clogged the wheels of their chariots so that they could hardly move. The Egyptians said, "Let us flee from the children of Israel for the LORD is fighting with them against the Egyptians."

26 The LORD said to Moses, "Stretch out your hand over the sea. The waters will flow back upon the Egyptians, upon their chariots and their horsemen."

27 Moses stretched out his hand over the sea. At dawn the sea flowed back to its normal depth. While the Egyptians were fleeing right into it, the LORD overthrew them in the
midst of the sea. 28 [n] The waters flowed back and covered the chariots and the horsemen of the whole army of Pharaoh. Not a single one of those who had entered the sea to follow the children of Israel escaped.

29 The children of Israel had walked in the midst of the sea on dry land, the water forming walls on the right and the left. [o]
30 On that day the LORD saved Israel from the hands of the Egyptians, and Israel saw the Egyptians lying dead on the shores of the sea.
31 Israel saw the mighty hand that the LORD had extended against Egypt. The people feared the LORD and believed in him and in his servant Moses. [p]

CHAPTER 15

The Song of Moses and Miriam.* 1 Moses and the children of Israel therefore sang this song to the LORD:

"I will sing in honor of the LORD, for he is gloriously triumphant,
horse and horseman he has cast into the sea.
2 My strength and my song is the LORD,
for he has saved me.
He is my God, and I wish to praise him,
the God of my father, and I wish to exalt him. [q]
3 "The LORD is a warrior,
LORD is his name.
4 He has cast Pharaoh's chariots and his army into the sea.
His choice troops were drowned in the Red Sea.
5 The depths covered them
and they sank like a stone. [r]
6 "Your right hand, O LORD, is glorious in its power.
Your right hand, O LORD, has destroyed the enemy. [s]
7 With the greatness of your majesty you have overthrown those who rose up against you.
You sent forth your anger and it devoured them like straw.
8 At the breath of your nostrils, the waters piled up.
The flood waters piled up and stood like a mound;
the deep waters congealed in the midst of the sea.
9 "The enemy had said, 'I will pursue and overtake them.
I will divide the spoil, and my passion will be satisfied on them.
I will draw my sword, and my hand will destroy them.'
10 You blew your wind, and the sea covered them.
Like lead they sank in the mighty waters.
11 "Who is like you among the gods, O LORD?
Who is like you, majestic in holiness,
awesome in praise, doing wonders?
12 You extended your right hand
and the earth swallowed them.
13 "In your mercy you guided the people you had redeemed.
You guided them with strength to your holy dwelling. [t]
14 The people will hear and be afraid.
Anguish will seize the inhabitants of Philistia.
15 The leaders of Edom tremble,
the mighty ones of Moab are gripped with fear,
all the inhabitants of Canaan melt away.
16 [u] Fear and terror fall upon them.
The greatness of your arm makes them still as stone,

n 28f: Ex 15:19; Deut 11:4; Ps 106:11.—o Ex 15:19.—p 2 Sam 6:9; Ps 106:12; Wis 10:20.—q Ps 118:14; Sir 51:12; Isa 12:2.—r Neh 9:11; Ps 106:11.—s Ex 6:1; Ps 24:8.—t Ps 78:52.—u 16f: Ps 78:53ff; Isa 19:17.

15:1-21 Although this hymn is here put into the mouth of the leader, it shows the extent to which the biblical poets were determined to magnify the wonders that accompanied the crossing of the Red Sea (see Ps 106:9; Wis 19:6-9). The refrain attributed to Miriam, Moses' sister (Ex 15:21), may be regarded as the seed out of which the poem grew; it was later expanded (vv. 4-5, 8) and subsequently completed, for the song also in fact extols the journey to the Promised Land (vv. 13-16) and the building of the Temple (v. 17), both of which were other signs of God's merciful presence in the midst of his people.

University Museum

RAMESES II: PHARAOH OF THE OPPRESSION — A stele found at Beth-shan shows Rameses II (1290–1223 B.C.) of Egypt before the god Amon-Re. Between the two figures are vessels, probably booty offered to the god. At the bottom are name-rings of foes of the king surmounted by the upper parts of the body and a bound captive. Many scholars believe that Rameses II is the Pharaoh of the Oppression. Included in the inscriptions on the stele is the phrase that "he built up [the city of] Rameses with Asiatic Semitic (Hebrew) slaves." (See Ex 1:11.)

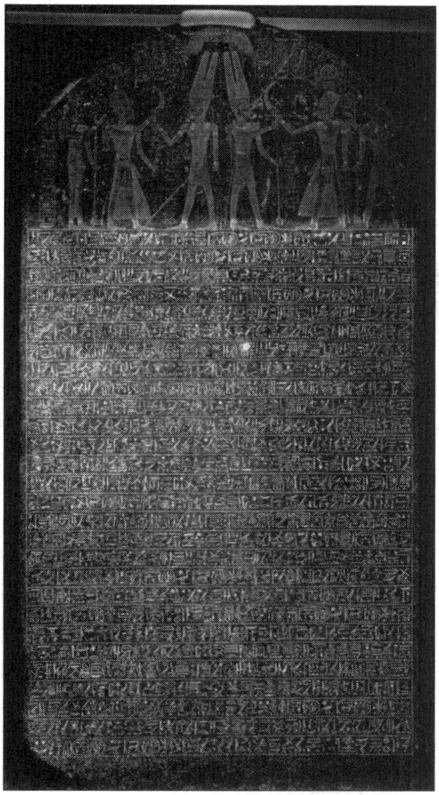

Cairo Museum

"ISRAEL TABLET" OF PHARAOH MERNEPTAH— Famous tablet found at Thebes dating to the fifth year (1218 B.C.) of the Pharaoh Merneptah, son of Ramesses II, who claims a decisive victory over the Israelites. Merneptah is regarded as the Pharaoh of the Exodus. (See Ex 5–13.)

Cairo Museum

LOWER PART OF "ISRAEL TABLET"— This part of the Merneptah stele bears the only contemporary reference to "Israel" in inscriptions of this period. The name Israel has been set off in a box.

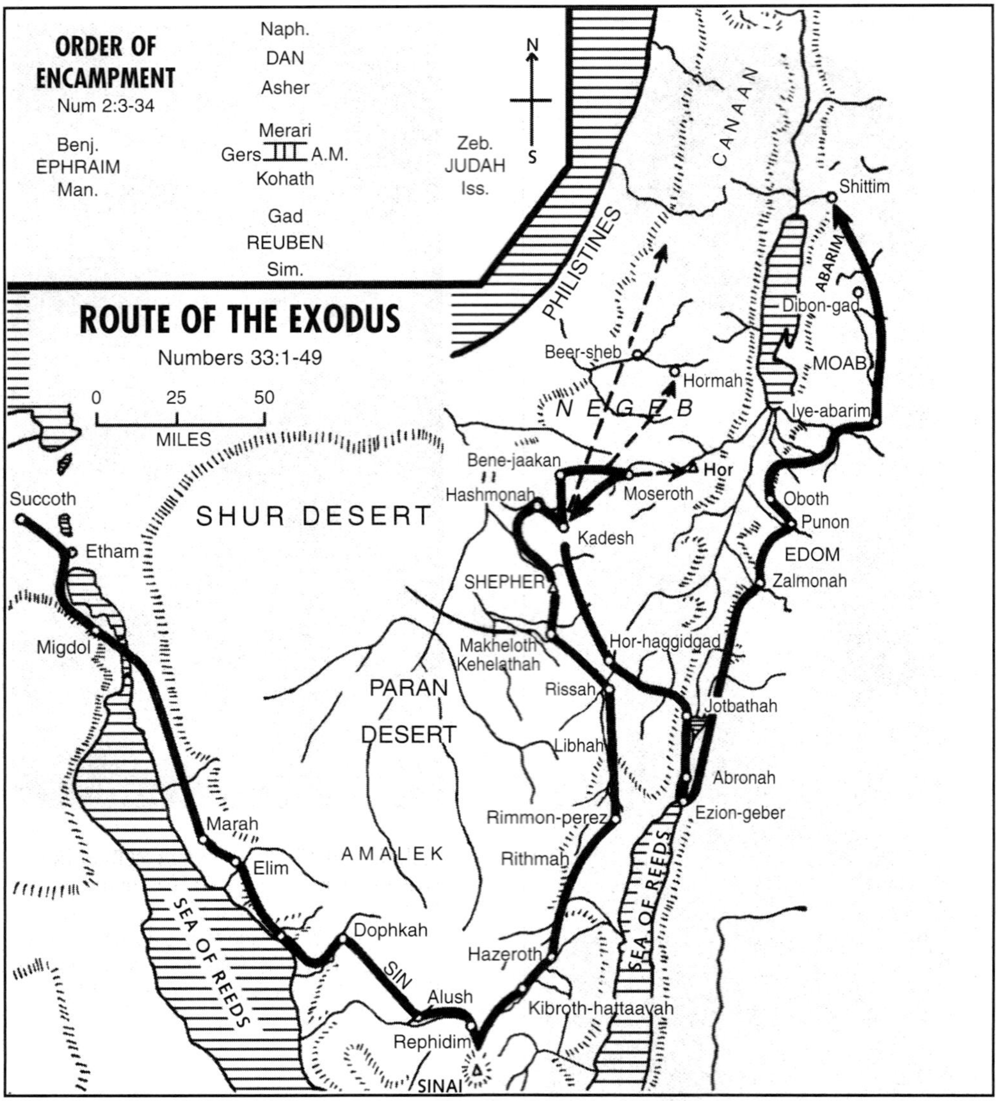

ROUTE OF THE EXODUS (Num 33:1-49) — **(a)** From **Egypt** to **Sinai:** Departure from Rameses. Encampments at Succoth, Etham (Pi-hahiroth opposite Baal-zephon), Migdol, Marah, Elim, stopping place near the Red Sea, in the desert of Sin, Dophkah, Alush, Rephidim, Sinai desert (Num 33:11-15) **(b) From Sinai to Kadesh:** Encampments at Kibroth-hattaavah, Hazeroth, Rithmah, Rimmon-perez, Libnah, Rissah, Kehelathah, Mount Shepher, Haradah, Makheloth, Tahath, Terah, Mithkah, Hashmonah; they encamp in the desert of Zin, that is, Kadesh (Num 33:16-30). **(c) Near Kadesh:** Encampments at Moseroth, Bene-jaakan, Mount Hor (Deut 10:6: Bene-jaakan, Moserah) where Aaron dies (Num 33:30-38). **(d) From Kadesh to the frontier of Moab:** Hor-haggidgad (Deut 10:6 Gudgedah), Jotbathah, Abronah, Ezion-geber, Zalmonah, Punon, Oboth, Iye-abarim (Num 33:37-44). **(e) From the frontier of Moab to the Jordan:** Starting from Iye-abarim they encamp at Dibon-gad, Almon-diblathaim, in the Abarim Mountains, and on the plains of Moab, near the Jordan at Jericho, between Beth-jeshimoth and Abel-shittim in the plains of Moab (Num 33:45-49). **(f) Order of encampment:** Cf. schema. **(g) Order of march:** army of Judah — Gershon and Merari with the tabernacle. — Army of Reuben — Kohathites with the holy things — army of Ephraim — army of Dan.

until your people have passed over,
O LORD,
until your people whom you have acquired have passed over.
17 You will bring them in and plant them
on the mountain of your inheritance,
in the place that you have prepared for your dwelling, O LORD,
the sanctuary that your own hands have founded.
18 The LORD reigns forever and ever."

19 When the horses of Pharaoh, his chariots,
and his horsemen went into the sea, the LORD
brought the waters of the sea back upon them,
while the children of Israel walked through
the midst of the sea on dry ground. [v]
20 Miriam the prophetess, the sister of Aaron,
took a tambourine in her hand, and all the
other women came out after her playing their
tambourines and dancing. 21 Miriam led them
in the refrain:

"Sing to the LORD for he is wondrously triumphant;
horse and horsemen he has cast into the sea." [w]

B: The Journey through the Wilderness*

The Waters of Marah and Elim. 22 Moses led
the children of Israel away from the Red Sea,
and they traveled toward the Desert of Shur.
They walked three days into the desert and
they did not find water. 23 They arrived at
Marah, but they could not drink the waters
of Marah for they were bitter. That is why the
place was called Marah.* 24 So the people
murmured against Moses, saying, "What
will we drink?" 25 He called upon the LORD,
who showed him a tree. When he cast it into
the water, it became sweet. [x]

The LORD made a statute and an ordinance for them there and put them to the
test. 26 He said, "If you listen to the voice of
the LORD, your God, and you do what is right
in his sight, if you listen to his ordinances and
observe all of his laws, I will not bring upon
you any of the diseases that I brought upon
the Egyptians, for I am the LORD, who heals
you."

27 Then they arrived at Elim where there
were twelve springs of water and seventy
palm trees. Here they camped near the
waters. [y]

CHAPTER 16*

Manna and Quail. 1 The entire community of
the children of Israel set out from Elim and
came to the Desert of Sin, which is found
between Elim and the Sinai on the fifteenth
day of the second month after they left the
land of Egypt. 2 In the desert the entire community of the children of Israel murmured
against Moses and Aaron. 3 The children of
Israel said to them, "Would that the hand of
the LORD had killed us in the land of Egypt
where we were seated by our pots filled with
meat and where we had more than enough
bread to eat. Instead you brought us out into
this desert to slay the whole assembly with
hunger."

4 The LORD said to Moses, "Behold, I am
about to rain bread down from the heavens
for you. The people should go out each day to
collect the amount they need for that day so
that I might test them to see whether they
follow my law or not. [z] 5 But on the sixth day,
when they are gathering what they will bring
home, they are to collect double what they
collect on the other days."

6 [a] Moses and Aaron said this to the children of Israel: "This evening you will know
that the LORD brought you out of the land of
Egypt, 7 and tomorrow morning you will see
the glory of the LORD, for he has heard your
murmuring against him. For what are we,
that you murmur against us?" 8 Moses also
said, "When the LORD gives you meat to eat
in the evening and bread to fill you in the
morning, it will be because the LORD has
heard the murmuring that you utter against
him. What are we, after all? Your murmur-

v Ex 14:21-29; 15:1.—w Ex 15:1; Jer 20:13.—x 2 Ki 2:21; Sir 38:5.—y Num 33:9.—z 1 Ki 11:38; Pss 78:24f; 105:40; Jn 6:31f, 58; 1 Cor 10:3.—a 6f: Ex 16:12; Prov 19:3; Phil 2:14.

15:22—18:27 The Hebrews journey through a desolate and hostile land that puts them in a sullen mood. God does not cease to multiply benefits in their favor. They thus represent the Church, the New People of God, who pursues her terrestrial march sustained by the Lord despite the failings of his children. It is in this long passage that the unity of Israel is forged and that it acquires its fundamental religious conceptions.

15:23 The Hebrew word *mar* means "bitter," "bitterness" (see Ru 1:20).

16:1-36 Despite all that God has already done for them, the Hebrews would rather grumble than hope. When one is lost in the desert, slavery seems less harsh than adventure, and the remembrance of the food of Egypt, even though little, makes one forget the Promised Land flowing with milk and honey. God meets the needs of his people, but in requiring them to be satisfied with daily "bread," he seeks to test the degree of their trust in him and bring them to the realization that everything in their lives depends on him (Deut 8:2-3). Jesus, too, will deliberately experience hunger in the wilderness (Mt 4:2) and will say that his body is the true bread come down from heaven (Jn 6:31-33).

ings are not against us, but against the LORD."

9 Moses said to Aaron, "Give this command to the whole community of Israel: 'Draw near to the presence of the LORD, for he has heard your murmurings.' "[b] 10 While Aaron spoke to the entire community of the children of Israel, they turned toward the desert and, behold, the glory of the LORD appeared in the clouds.

11 The LORD said to Moses, 12 "I have heard the murmurings of the children of Israel. Say this to them: 'At dusk you will eat meat, and in the morning you will have your fill of bread. You will know that I am the LORD, your God.' "

13 In the evening quail rose up and covered the camp. In the morning there was a layer of dew on the ground around the camp.[c] 14 The layer of dew evaporated, and on the surface of the desert there was something small and flaky, as small as hoarfrost on the ground. 15 The children of Israel saw it and said to one another, "What is it?"* because they did not know what it was. Moses said to them, "It is the bread that the LORD has given us as food.[d]

16 "This is what the LORD commands: 'Collect as much as each person can eat, an omer* per person. Let every person take as much as needed for the people living with him, for as many as there are in his tent.' "

17 This is what the children of Israel did. Some collected quite a bit and others much less. 18 They measured it with the omer. Those who had collected more did not have too much, while those who collected less did not have too little. They had collected just as much as each person could eat.[e]

19 Then Moses said to them, "Nothing should be left till the morning." 20 However, some did not obey Moses and saved a bit of it until the morning, but it grew rancid and had worms. Moses was angry with them.

21 They therefore collected it each morning, as much as each one would eat. When the sun warmed up, it melted away.

22 On the sixth day, they collected double the amount of bread, two omers for each person. All the leaders of the community came to tell Moses, 23 * and he said to them, "This is what the LORD ordered: 'Tomorrow is the Sabbath, a day of rest consecrated to the LORD. Bake what you have to bake, and boil what you have to boil. All that is left over should be stored until the morning.' "[f] 24 They preserved it until the morning, as Moses had ordered, and it did not go rancid, nor did they find worms in it.

25 Moses said, "Eat it today, because it is the Sabbath in honor of the LORD. Today you will not find it in the fields. 26 Six days you will collect it, but the seventh day is the Sabbath. There will be none on that day."

27 On the seventh day some of the people went out to collect it, but they did not find any. 28 Therefore, the LORD said to Moses, "How long will you refuse to obey my commands and my laws? 29 See that the LORD had given you the Sabbath. This is why he has given you two days worth of bread on the sixth day. Let every person stay where he is. No one is to go out on the seventh day to the place where they find it."

30 The people, therefore, rested on the seventh day.

31 The children of Israel called it manna. It was like coriander seed and was white. It tasted like wafers made from honey.[g] 32 Moses said, "This is what the LORD has ordered: 'Fill an omer and conserve it for your descendants so that they can see the bread that I gave you to eat in the desert, when I brought you out of the land of Egypt.' "

33 Moses, therefore, said to Aaron, "Take a jar and put a full omer of manna in it. Place it before the LORD and preserve it for your descendants." 34 Aaron did what the LORD had commanded Moses to do, he placed it in front of the Testimony,* to preserve it. 35 The children of Israel ate manna for forty years, until they arrived in an inhabited land. They ate the manna, therefore, until they arrived at the borders of Canaan.[h] 36 [The omer is one-tenth of an ephah.]

---

b Job 5:11; Jas 4:10.—c Ex 8:2; Num 11:31; Ps 78:27f.—d Deut 8:3; Mk 1:27.—e Ex 16:21; 2 Cor 8:15.—f Gen 2:3.—g Num 11:7; Rev 10:10.—h Jos 5:12; Jn 6:31.

16:15 The Hebrew word *man hu, What is it?* is a popular etymology of the word "manna" (see v. 31). On the Sinai peninsula the tamarisk exudes a substance resembling the biblical manna as described here. This does not make the Divine intervention any less extraordinary or eliminate the symbolic link with the Eucharist.

16:16 *Omer:* a measure equal to about four and a half liters. The sacred writer himself feels the need of explaining it (v. 36).

16:23-26 Keeping the Sabbath as a day consecrated to the Lord (see Gen 2:3) was already being practiced before the Lord's command in Ex 20:8-11 to keep it holy. The children of Israel were to avoid unnecessary work (i.e., collecting manna) and rest on the seventh day. Then, as now, people disregarded his words and did as they pleased.

16:34 *Testimony:* the tablets containing the Ten Words, to be described later on. See Ex 25:16; 31:18.

CHAPTER 17

Water from the Rock.* 1 The entire community of Israel pulled up their camp in the Desert of Sin and, as the LORD commanded, they moved by stages to their camp in Rephidim.[i] But there was no water for the people to drink. 2[j] The people protested against Moses, saying, "Give us water to drink." Moses said to them, "Why are you protesting against me? Why are you putting the LORD to the test?"

3 The people suffered from thirst because there was no water, so they murmured against Moses and said, "Why did you make us leave Egypt to die of thirst along with our children and our animals?" 4 Moses called upon the help of the LORD saying, "What will I do for this people? Only a little more and they will stone me."

5[k] The LORD said to Moses, "Walk in front of the people and bring some of the elders of Israel with you. Take the staff with which you struck the Nile in your hand and go! 6 Behold, I will stand before you on the rock at Horeb. You will strike the rock, and water will come out for the people to drink." Moses did this in the sight of the elders of Israel. 7 They called this place Massah* and Meribah, because the children of Israel had protested and had put the LORD to the test, saying, "Is the LORD in our midst or not?"[l]

While Moses Prays, the Amalekites* Are Defeated.* 8 Amalek came and fought against Israel in Rephidim.[m] 9 Moses said to Joshua, "Choose some men for us and go out to fight against Amalek. Tomorrow I will stand on the top of the hill with the staff of God in my hand." 10 Joshua did all that Moses had commanded him to do and he fought against Amalek while Moses, Aaron, and Hur stood on the top of the hill. 11 When Moses lifted his hands, Israel was stronger, but when he lowered them, Amalek was stronger. 12 Moses' hands grew heavy as he tired, so they took a stone and placed it under him as a stool. Aaron and Hur stood on either side and held up his hands. Thus, his hands were held steady until the sun set. 13 Joshua defeated Amalek and its people, putting them to the sword.

14 The LORD said to Moses, "Write this as a memorial in a book and recite it to Joshua: I will totally cancel the memory of Amalek from under the heavens."[n]

15 Moses built an altar, and he named it, "The LORD is my banner," 16 and he said, "A hand is raised upon the throne of the LORD that there will be war against Amalek from one generation to the next."

CHAPTER 18

Moses Visited by His Father-in-Law.* 1 Jethro, the priest of Midian and the father-in-law of Moses, came to know what God had done for Moses and for Israel, his people, and how the LORD had brought Israel out of Egypt.

2 Jethro brought Zipporah, the wife of Moses, with him, for he had sent her back to him, 3 and also her two sons. One son was named Gershom, for he had said, "I am a stranger in a strange land,"[o] 4 and the other named Eliezer, for he had said, "The God of my father has come to my assistance and has freed me from the sword of Pharaoh."

5 Jethro, Moses' father-in-law, and the sons and wife of Moses came to him in the desert where he was camped, near the mountain of God. 6 He had it announced to Moses, "It is I, Jethro, your father-in-law. I have come with your wife and your two sons."

7 Moses went out to meet his father-in-law. He bowed before him and kissed him. They inquired about each other's health, and then went into their tent. 8 Moses told his father-in-law what the LORD had done to Pharaoh and the Egyptians for the children of Israel, and also about all the difficulties that they had encountered during their journey, and from which the LORD had delivered them.

9 Jethro rejoiced over all the blessings that the LORD had shown to Israel when he liber-

i Num 33:12ff.—j 2-7: Num 20:2-13; Mt 4:7.—k 5f: Num 20:11; Deut 8:15; Pss 78:15f; 105:41; Wis 11:4; Isa 43:20; 48:21.—l Ps 95:8f; Heb 3:7-11.—m Deut 25:17; 1 Sam 15:2.—n Ex 24:4; Num 24:20; Deut 25:19; 1 Sam 15:3, 20.—o Ex 2:22; Jdg 18:30; 1 Chr 23:15.

17:1-7 Even though they are frequently helped by the Lord, the Hebrews are distrustful of him. The Psalmist has placed the blame for this on bad faith (Ps 95:8-9). God meets their challenge by slaking their thirst with a miracle that left its mark on Israelite piety (Deut 8:15; Ps 114:8). Some rabbis later imagined that the rock accompanied the people through the wilderness; Paul echoes this tradition (1 Cor 10:4), and John alludes to it (Jn 7:37-38).

17:7 *Massah* means "test," and *Meribah* "quarrel."

17:8-16 This account will allow the future generations to find assurance in the face of hostile peoples.

17:8 *Amalekites:* an ancient Arab people, located between Palestine and Egypt (see Gen 36:12).

18:1-12 This passage is probably not in its correct place, since it says that the meeting took place near Mount Sinai. It is part of traditions according to which all links were not broken between the pagan peoples and the God of Israel.

ated it from the hands of the Egyptians.[p]
10 Jethro said, "Blessed be the LORD, who
freed you from the hands of the Egyptians
and from the hands of Pharaoh. He deliv-
ered this people from the hands of the
Egyptians. 11 Now I know that the LORD is the
greatest of all gods because of what he has
done to the Egyptians. He delivered them
from their hands when they acted arro-
gantly."

12 Jethro, the father-in-law of Moses,
offered a burnt offering and sacrificed to
God. Aaron and all the elders of Israel came
and ate a banquet with the father-in-law of
Moses before God.

Moses Institutes the Judges.* 13 The next day
Moses sat in judgment over the people of
Israel. All the people stood before Moses
from morning until the evening.[q] 14 Jethro,
seeing what he was doing for the people, said
to him, "What is this that you do for the peo-
ple? Why do you sit in judgment alone, while
the people stand before you from morning
until evening?"

15 Moses answered his father-in-law,
"Because the people come to me to inquire
the will of God.[r] 16 When they have some
question, they come to me and I judge the
matter between them and let them know the
statutes of God and his laws."

17 The father-in-law of Moses told him,
"What you are doing is no good. 18 You will
surely wear yourself out, you and the people
with you, because this job is too difficult for
you. You cannot do it alone.[s] 19 Now, listen to
me. I wish to give you some advice, and God
be with you. You must act as the people's rep-
resentative before God and bring their cases
before him. 20 You will explain the decrees
and the laws to them. You will direct them
along the way that they should go and teach
the things that they must do. 21 You will also
choose virtuous men who fear God from
among the people, honest men who are not
filled with greed, and you will make them
leaders of thousands, hundreds, fifties, and
tens.[t] 22 They must judge the people at all
times. When there is an important matter,
they will refer it to you, but they will judge all
the minor issues. Thus, they will lighten the
burden upon you, for they will carry it with
you. 23 If you do this thing and if God com-
mands this of you, then you will be able to
continue and this people will arrive in peace
at its destination."

24 Moses listened to his father-in-law's
suggestion, and he did what he had sug-
gested that he do. 25 Moses chose capable
men from among all the men of Israel,
and he appointed them as leaders of the
people, as leaders of groups of thousands,
hundreds, fifties, and tens. 26 They judged
the people at all times. When there was a
difficult matter, they referred it to Moses,
but they themselves judged all the minor
issues. 27 Then Moses let his father-in-law
depart, and Jethro returned to his own
country.

III: THE COVENANT AT MOUNT SINAI

A: The Covenant and the Ten Commandments*

CHAPTER 19

God Proposes His Covenant.* 1 [u] Three
months to the day after the children of
Israel left the land of Egypt, they arrived in
the Sinai Desert. 2 They left the camp at
Rephidim and arrived in the Desert of
Sinai. There Israel camped in front of the
mountain.

3 Moses climbed up to meet God, and the
LORD called out to him from the mountain,
saying, "You will say this to the house of
Jacob and announce it to the children of
Israel: 4 'You yourselves have seen what I did
to the Egyptians and how I lifted you up on
eagles' wings and brought you here to me.[v]
5 Now, if you will obey my voice and keep my
covenant, you will be my own possession
from among all the peoples, for the entire
earth is mine. 6 You will be a kingdom of

p Lk 1:68.—q Isa 11:2-4; 28:6; Acts 28:23.—r Num 9:8.—s Num 11:14; Sir 13:2.—t Ex 18:25; Deut 1:15; 16:18; Acts 6:3.—u 1f: Ex 16:1; Num 33:15.—v Deut 32:11; Isa 40:31.

18:13-27 Set free, Israel becomes an autonomous people that requires them to be organized. Through the counsel of Jethro and his wise advice to Moses, the Midianite people serve as a model for them.

19:1—20:21 The entire past of Israel converges on the event at Sinai. The call of Abraham and the deliverance from the Egyptian yoke show God's intention to his people. The time has come for that people to respond to the divine preferences. The Covenant is not a contract between equals, in which offer and response are on the same level; rather, the initiative is entirely the Lord's. Israel does, however, have an obligation to agree to the "salvation" offered to it and to express a desire to commit itself to fidelity to the law of the Lord. The text of the Covenant will be Israel's religious and social constitution.

19:1-9 The Hebrews have reached the southern part of the Sinai peninsula; it is the imposing countryside dominated by this summit that serves as a backdrop for their meeting with God. In submitting themselves to the Lord, they will become a consecrated people. Thus, the People of God is truly born of the Sinaitic Covenant.

priests and a holy nation for me.' These are the words you will speak to Israel." *

7 Moses went and summoned the elders of the people and told them what the LORD had commanded him. 8 All the people answered together and said, "We will do what the LORD has said." Then Moses returned to the LORD and told him what the people had said.

9 The LORD said to Moses, "Behold, I am about to approach you in a thick cloud so that the people will hear when I speak to you and always believe in you." [w]

The LORD Descends on Sinai. 10 The LORD said to Moses, "Go to the people and consecrate them today and tomorrow. Have them wash their clothes 11 and have them ready for the third day, for on the third day the LORD will come down upon Mount Sinai to visit all the people.

12 [x] "You shall establish a boundary around it, saying, 'Take heed not to climb up the mountain or even touch its base. Whoever touches the mountain will be put to death.'

13 "No hand must touch that person, however, for he must be stoned or shot with an arrow. Whether it be a human or an animal, he is not to live. They can come up the mountain only when you blow the trumpet."

14 Moses went down the mountain to the people. He consecrated the people and had them wash their clothes. 15 Then he said to the people, "Be ready in three days' time. Abstain from sexual relations."

The Great Theophany. 16 [y] On the third day, as morning dawned, there was thunder, lightning, a dense cloud on the mountain, and the sound of loud trumpets. All the people in the camp were filled with fear.

17 Moses brought the people out of the camp to meet God. They stood on foot at the base of the mountain.

18 Mount Sinai was wrapped in smoke, for the LORD had descended upon it in fire and the smoke rose up like the smoke of a furnace. The entire mountain trembled. 19 The sound of the trumpet grew louder and louder. Moses spoke and God responded with the sound of thunder.

20 The LORD thus descended upon Mount Sinai, on the mountain peak, and he called out to Moses upon the mountain peak. Moses went up the mountain.

21 The LORD said to Moses, "Go down and warn the people not to break through to gaze upon the LORD; otherwise many will die. [z]

22 "Let the priests consecrate themselves before they approach the LORD. Otherwise the LORD will burst forth upon them."

23 Moses said to the LORD, "The people cannot climb up Mount Sinai, for you yourself have warned us saying, 'Establish a boundary around the mountain and declare it to be holy.' " [a]

24 The LORD told him, "Go, descend, then come back up with Aaron. But the priests and the people are not to break through to climb up to the LORD. Otherwise, he will burst forth against them."

25 Moses went down and spoke to the people.

CHAPTER 20

The Ten Commandments.* 1 God spoke all these words:

2 [b] "I am the LORD, your God, who brought you out of the land of Egypt, out of that place of slavery. 3 You shall not have other gods instead of me. 4 You shall not make idols or any image of things that are in the heavens above or that are upon the earth or that are in the waters under the earth. [c] 5 You shall not bow before them nor shall you serve them. I, the LORD, am your God, a jealous God, who punishes the sins of fathers upon their sons until the third and fourth generations of those who hate me, 6 but I will show my favor for a thousand generations of those who love me and observe my commandments.

7 "You shall not take the name of the LORD, your God, in vain, for the LORD will not leave unpunished those who use his name in vain. [d]

8 [e] "Remember the Sabbath and keep it holy. 9 Six days you shall labor and do your

w Ex 20:21; 24:15-18; Num 12:5.—x 12f: Ex 19:23; 34:3; Heb 12:18f.—y 16ff: Ex 24:16; Deut 4:10ff.—z Ex 3:5.—a Ex 19:12.—b 2-17: Deut 5:6-21; Rom 13:9.—c Ex 34:17; Lev 26:1; Deut 4:15-19; 5:8; 27:15.—d Lev 19:12; 24:16; Deut 5:11.—e 8ff: Ex 23:12; 31:13-16; 34:21; 35:2; Lev 23:3; Deut 5:12.

19:6 A people taken from among the nations and consecrated to God (Isa 61:6; 1 Pet 2:5-9; Rev 1:6)

20:1-17 The Decalogue ("Ten Words") is the basic law of the Covenant (there is a different version of the Decalogue in Deut 5:6-21). In fact, these *words* state consequences of commitment rather than laws: they show the result of denying God as Lord and deliverer (v. 2), as contrasted with belonging to the one true God. The prophets and Jesus will remind their hearers of the same requirement: the acknowledgment in the whole of one's life that salvation is from the Lord.

work, 10 but the seventh day is the Sabbath in honor of the LORD your God. You shall not do any work, neither you, nor your son, nor your daughter, nor your male slave, nor your female slave, nor your animals, nor the foreigner who dwells with you. 11 The LORD made the heavens and the earth and the seas and that which is in them in six days, but he rested the seventh day. Thus, the LORD blessed the Sabbath and declared it to be sacred.

12 [f] "Honor your father and your mother so that your days may be lengthened in the land that the LORD your God, will give you.

13 "You shall not kill.

14 "You shall not commit adultery.

15 "You shall not steal.

16 "You shall not give false witness against your neighbor.

17 "You shall not covet your neighbor's house. You shall not covet your neighbor's wife, nor his male slave, nor his female slave, nor his oxen, nor his donkey, nor anything that belongs to your neighbor."

Moses, Intermediary of the Covenant. 18 [g] All the people heard the thunder and saw the lightning. They heard the sound of the trumpet and saw the mountain smoking. They were filled with fear and kept their distance.

19 They said to Moses, "You speak to us and we will listen, but do not let God speak to us or we will die."

20 Moses spoke to the people saying, "Do not be afraid. God has come to put you to the test so that you may always be filled with fear of him and not sin."

21 The people kept their distance while Moses approached the dark cloud where God was found.

B: The Book of the Covenant*

Norms for Constructing an Altar to the LORD. 22 The LORD said to Moses, "Speak to the children of Israel: 'You have seen that I have spoken to you from the heavens. 23 Do not make gods from silver or from gold instead of me. You will not make them for yourselves. [h]

24 " 'Make an altar for me in the land and upon it offer your burnt offerings and your communion sacrifices, your sheep and your oxen. In all the places where I cause my name to be remembered, I will come to you and bless you. [i]

25 " 'If you make an altar out of stone for me, do not build it out of cut stone. If you use a chisel upon it, it will be considered to be unclean. 26 Do not go up to the altar by steps, lest your nakedness be seen.'* [j]

CHAPTER 21

Laws Concerning Slaves. 1 "These are the decrees that you will set before them.

2 [k] "When you buy a Hebrew slave, he will serve you for six years and in the seventh year he will go free, without paying anything.* 3 If he entered into slavery unmarried, he will go out alone. If he is married, then his wife will go with him. 4 If his master has given him a wife and she has had sons or daughters, the woman and her children will be the property of the master and he will go out alone.

5 "If the slave says, 'I love my master, my wife, and my children, and I do not want to go free,' 6 then the master will bring him before God. He will bring him to a door or a doorpost and will bore a hole in his ear with an awl. He will be his slave forever.

7 "When a man sells his daughter* as a slave, she will not go free as the male slaves do. 8 If she does not please her master who has taken her as a concubine, she will be allowed to be redeemed. But he cannot sell her to foreigners, for he has acted faithlessly to her. 9 If he wishes to give her as a concubine to his own son, he will treat her like a daughter. 10 If he takes another for himself, he will not withhold her food, her clothes, or her marriage rights. 11 If he does not give her these things, then she can go away without having to pay the price of her redemption.

f 12-16: Deut 5:16; Mt 19:18f; Mk 10:19; Lk 18:20; Rom 13:9.—g 18-21: Ex 19:18; Deut 4:11; 5:22-27; 18:16; Heb 12:18f.—h Ex 20:3f; Hos 13:4.—i Deut 12:5, 11; 14:23; 16:6; Jdg 21:4.—j Deut 27:5; Jos 8:31; Acts 24:6.—k 2-6: Lev 25:39ff; Deut 15:12-18; Jer 34:14; Mt 10:24.

20:22—24:11 This set of laws was probably promulgated at a later time than the Decalogue, since it supposes a people leading a settled, sedentary life. Perhaps it was given during the halt in the wilderness before Israel entered Canaan. The laws are concrete applications of the first commandment.

20:26 The one offering sacrifice would probably be wearing a simple loincloth, after the manner of the Egyptians, and would therefore risk indecent exposure.

21:2 God did not forbid slavery, but he clearly wanted to set limits on it. Perpetual slavery would not be tolerated.

21:7 *When a man sells his daughter:* this would seem to be inconceivable and not a subject to receive consideration. The author of life and of these decrees was aware of the evil that his people were capable of and so he employed preventative measures.

Different Cases of the Penalty of Death.
12 [l] "Whoever strikes a man causing his death
will be put to death. 13 However, if the man
did not lie in wait, but he met him by chance,
there will be a place where he can flee for
refuge.

14 "But when a person kills a neighbor with
premeditation, he shall be dragged away
from my altar to be put to death.

15 "Whoever strikes a mother or a father
will be put to death.

16 "Whoever kidnaps a man and either sells
him or has him still in his possession, shall be
put to death. [m]

17 "Whoever curses his father or his moth-
er shall be put to death.

Punishments for Personal Injury.* 18 "When
people are fighting and one of them injures
the other with a stone or with a fist, and this
does not kill the other but causes a serious
injury, 19 and yet the injured party is able to
walk around with a staff, then the one who
struck the blow shall be held to be innocent.
He must, however, pay the victim for the
time he lost on account of the injury and he
must pay for his medical care.

20 "When a man strikes his male or female
slave with a staff and kills that slave, he shall
surely be punished. 21 But if the slave lives for
a day or two, the slave-owner shall not be
punished, for the slave is his property.

22 [n] "When some men fight and injure a
pregnant woman so that she loses her child,
but there is no other damage, they will be
fined as much as the husband of the woman
decides. They will pay in the presence of a
judge. 23 But if further harm results, they will
pay a life for a life, [o] 24 an eye for an eye, a
tooth for a tooth, a hand for a hand, a foot for
a foot, 25 a burning for a burning, a wound for
a wound, a bruise for a bruise.

26 "When a man strikes the eye of his male
slave or his female slave and blinds the slave,
he will free the slave because of the eye. 27 If
he breaks a tooth of his male slave or his
female slave, he will free the slave to com-
pensate for the tooth.

Animals: Injuries and Thefts. 28 "If an ox gores
a man or a woman and that person dies, the
ox is to be stoned and its meat is not to be
eaten, but the owner of the ox will be consid-
ered to be innocent. [p] 29 However, if the ox
had already gored someone before and the
owner had been warned, yet failed to keep it
penned up, and if the ox gores another man
or a woman and that person dies, then the ox
is to be stoned and the owner is to be put to
death.

30 "If, however, a fine is imposed, he can
pay it to redeem his life, as much as has been
required. 31 This will also be the procedure if
a son or a daughter is gored.

32 "If an ox gores a male or female slave,
the master of the slave will be paid thirty
shekels of silver, and the ox is to be stoned.

33 "If someone leaves a cistern uncovered
or digs a cistern and does not cover it, and an
ox or a donkey falls into it, 34 the owner of the
cistern must make restitution and pay the
owner of the animal. The dead animal will
be his.

35 "If someone's ox gores another person's
ox and that ox dies, then they will sell the live
ox and divide its price between them, and
they will also divide the dead ox. [q] 36 But if it
is known that the ox had already gored oth-
ers and its owner had not confined it, then he
must pay ox for ox, and the dead animal will
be his.

37 "If a man steals an ox or a sheep and
then kills it or sells it, he shall pay back five
oxen for an ox and four sheep for a sheep. [r]

CHAPTER 22

1 "If a thief is surprised while he is breaking
in and is struck and dies, then there is no
bloodguilt for the striker. 2 But if the sun has
already risen on him, there would be blood-
guilt for the striker.

"A thief must surely pay restitution. If he
has nothing with which he can pay, then he is
to be sold to pay for his theft.

3 "If he is found with the animals he
robbed and they are still alive, whether
they be oxen or donkeys or sheep, he is to
repay double. [s]

Offenses Regarding Compensation. 4 "If
someone uses a field or a vineyard as a pas-
ture and lets his animals graze in someone
else's field, then he must repay that person
with the best of his field and the best of his
vineyard.

---

l 12ff: Lev 24:17; Num 35:15-29; Deut 4:41f; 19:2-5; 2 Sam 1:15.—m Deut 24:7.—n 22-25: Lev 24:18-21; 27:13; Deut 19:21; Mt 5:38.—o Lev 24:19-20.—p Gen 9:5.—q Acts 2:45.—r Ex 22:3; 2 Sam 12:6.—s Ex 21:37.

21:18-27 These penalties have for their purpose to prevent abuse of the private vendetta. Seen in this perspective, the law of retaliation is a model of justice for that period.

5 “If a fire breaks out and it spreads to the
thornbushes so that it burns the stacked
grain or the standing grain or the field itself,
the person who started the fire must make
restitution.*

6 “If someone entrusts his neighbor with
silver or goods for safekeeping, and there is a
robbery in that house and the thief is caught,
the thief shall pay back double. 7 If the thief is
not caught, the master of the house is to be
brought before the judges to swear that he
has not laid hands on the property of his
neighbor.

8 “Whatever the transgression, whether it
be about an ox or a sheep or clothes or any
other lost property about which a person has
said, ‘This is mine,’ the case of both parties
will be brought before the judges. Whoever
the judges find guilty shall pay back double to
his neighbor.

9 “If someone entrusts his neighbor with
a donkey or an ox or a sheep or any other
animal, and that animal dies or is injured
or stolen with no witnesses, 10 then an oath
to the LORD shall be taken between the two
parties declaring that the one entrusted
with the animal did not lay hands on his
neighbor’s property. The owner of the
property shall accept this and there shall
be no restitution. 11 But if it was stolen
while he was present, then he will make
restitution to its owner. 12 If it was torn to
pieces, let him bring the pieces as evi-
dence and he shall not pay restitution.[t]

13 “If someone borrows anything from a
neighbor and it is hurt or dies when the
owner is not there, he shall pay full restitu-
tion. 14 But if the owner is there, he shall not
have to pay restitution. If the animal was
hired, then its loss is the price of its hire.

Moral and Religious Regulations. 15 [u] “If a
man seduces a virgin who is not betrothed
and lies with her, he shall pay a dowry for her
and will make her his wife. 16 If her father
refuses to give her to him, he must give him
the normal amount of dowry paid for a vir-
gin.*

17 “You shall not allow a witch to live.

18 “Whoever lies with an animal must die.[v]
19 Whoever offers a sacrifice to any other god
besides the LORD will be annihilated.

20 [w] “You shall not mistreat or oppress the
foreigner, for you were foreigners in the land
of Egypt.

21 “You shall not oppress the widow or the
orphan. 22 If you mistreat them and they cry
out to me for help, I will surely hear their cry,
23 and my fury will burn and I will put you to
death by the sword. Your wives will be wid-
ows and your children will be orphans.

24 [x] “If you lend money to any of the poor
among my people, you will not act as a
creditor toward him nor will you take any
interest.

25 “If you take your neighbor’s mantle as a
pledge, you shall restore it to him at sunset,
26 for it is his covering. It is the cloak for his
body. What else would cover him when he
sleeps? Otherwise, when he cries out to me,
I will listen to his cry, for I am compas-
sionate.*

27 “You shall not blaspheme God nor curse
the leader of your people.[y]

28 “You shall not delay to make offerings
from your harvest and your vintage. You
shall give your firstborn from among your
sons to me. 29 You shall do the same with
your oxen and your sheep. Seven days it shall
remain with its mother, and on the eighth
day you shall give it to me.[z]

30 “You shall be men consecrated to me. So
do not eat the flesh of any beast that has been
torn to pieces in the countryside; you shall
throw it to the dogs.

CHAPTER 23

A Righteous and Fraternal People. 1 [a] “You
shall not utter a false report. Do not join
hands with the guilty to be an unjust witness.
2 Neither shall you follow the multitude in
doing evil nor shall you testify in a suit in
order to agree with the multitude and thus
falsify justice.

3 “You shall not even show partiality
toward a weak man in a lawsuit.

t Gen 31:39; Lev 17:15.—u 15f: Deut 22:28f.—v Lev 18:23; 20:15; Deut 27:21.—w 20-23: Ex 23:9; Lev 19:33f; Deut 10:18f; 24:17f; 27:19; Ps 94:6; Zec 7:10.—x 24-26: Lev 25: 35-38; Deut 23:19f; 24:10-13; Ezek 18:7f, 17f; Lk 6:34.—y Lev 24:11, 15; Acts 23:5.—z Ex 13:2; 34:19; Lev 22:27; Num 3:13; Deut 15:19.—a 1f: Deut 19:16ff.

22:5 Some translations are more definitive in describing the quality of the payback (i.e., it should err on the side of being generous).

22:16 The customary gift according to Deut 22:29 would be fifty shekels. A dowry is still part of the betrothal process in mid-eastern countries.

22:26 *I am compassionate:* God’s mercy and kindness go beyond the poor, the widow, and the orphan. His grace falls on the good and the undeserving. All we can do is gratefully accept this unmerited gift and respond with loving praise and thanks.

4 * "When you encounter the lost ox or
donkey of your enemy, you shall bring it back
to him. 5 When you see your enemy's donkey
lying helpless under its burden, you shall
refrain from leaving him alone. You must
help him to release it.

6 "You shall not pervert justice for a needy
person who turns to you in a dispute.

7 "Keep far away from falsehoods. Do not
slay the innocent or the just, for I will not
acquit the wicked.

8 "Do not accept gifts, for gifts blind the
clear-sighted and pervert the cause of the
righteous. [b]

9 "Do not oppress those who are sojourners,
for you know the life of the sojourner because
you yourselves were sojourners in the land of
Egypt.

10 [c] "For six years you shall sow the land
and you shall harvest its produce, 11 but in
the seventh year you shall let it rest and lie
fallow so that the needy of your people may
eat of it. Whatever is left, let the beasts of the
field eat it. You shall do likewise with your
vineyards and your olive groves. 12 For six
days you shall do your work, but on the
seventh day you shall rest so that your ox and
your donkey may rest, as well as the sons of
your female slaves and your sojourners.

13 "You shall take heed of all that I have
said to you. Do not mention the names of
other gods, nor let them be heard on your
lips.

Feasts and Rites To Be Observed. 14 [d] "Three
times a year you shall celebrate a feast in my
honor. *

15 "You shall observe the Feast of Unleav-
ened Bread. You must eat unleavened
products for seven days, as I have commanded
you, at the appointed time in the month of
Abib, for in that month I brought you out of
the land of Egypt. You will not appear before
me empty-handed.

16 "You shall also observe the Harvest
Feast of the firstfruits of that which you have
sown in the fields as well as the Feast of
Ingathering at the end of the year when you
gather the fruit of your labor in the fields.

17 "Three times a year all your men shall
appear before the LORD God.

18 [e] "You shall not offer the blood of my sac-
rifice with leavened bread, nor shall you
allow the fat of my feast to remain till the
morning.

19 "You shall bring the best of the firstfruits
of your soil to the house of the LORD, your
God. You shall not cook a kid goat in its
mother's milk. *

**Promises and Instructions for Entering into
Canaan.*** 20 "Behold, I will send an angel
before you to protect you on your way and to
bring you to the place that I have prepared. [f]
21 Pay heed to him and listen to his voice and
do not rebel against him for he will not pardon
your transgression since my name is in him.
22 If you listen to his voice and do what I will
tell you, I will be an enemy to your enemies
and an adversary to your adversaries.

23 [g] "When my angel goes before you and
leads you to the Hittites, the Perizzites, the
Canaanites, the Hivites, and the Jebusites, I
will destroy them. 24 You shall not bow down
to their gods nor serve them. You shall not do
what they do, but rather you shall demolish
and break their sacred pillars to pieces.

25 "You shall serve the LORD, your God. He
will bless your bread and water and take
away sickness from your midst. 26 There will
be no woman in your land who miscarries or
who is sterile. I will make you arrive at the
full count of your days.

27 [h] "I will send my terror before you and
throw into confusion all the peoples among
whom you will come. I will make your
enemies turn their backs and flee.

28 "I will send hornets ahead of you and
they will drive out the Hivites, the
Canaanites, and the Hittites from before you.
29 I will not drive them out from before you in
a single year lest the country remain deserted

---

b Deut 16:19; 27:25; Eccl 7:7; Ezek 22:12.—c 10f: Lev 25:3-7; Neh 10:31.—d 14-17: Ex 34:18, 22f; Lev 23:1-44; Deut 16:1-17; Zec 14:16.—e 18f: Ex 23:18; 34:25f.—f Ex 14:19; 23:20; 32:34; 33:2.—g 23f: Ex 34:10-16; Gen 24:7; Num 33:51f; Deut 7:24ff; Jdg 6:10.—h 27ff: Deut 2:25; 7:20ff; Jos 24:12.

23:4-5 Every one is to be treated the same (see Deut 22:1-4). Jesus is the example par excellence in showing others what it means to "Love your enemies" (Mt 5:44).

23:14 The feasts are those of the springtime (Unleavened Bread—Passover; see Ex 12:1, 11), of the summer (Feast of Weeks or Pentecost: 34:22), and of autumn (harvest festivals or Booths: Lev 23:34-43; Deut 16:13). (See Ex 34:18-23; Num 28–29; Deut 16:1-16.)

23:19 Cooking a young goat in its mother's milk was a pagan custom of the Canaanites.

23:20-33 Faithful service of the Lord was a condition for the entrance of the chosen people into the Promised Land. They would have to avoid defilement by other forms of worship and therefore by the peoples who practiced these. This is the context for understanding the laws regarding extermination and the anathema that were promulgated against foreigners; these laws were not applied to the letter (see Jos 6:17).

and the wild beasts multiply against you.
30 Little by little I will drive them out before
you until you have many sons to occupy the
land.
31 "I will establish your borders from the
Red Sea up to the sea of the Philistines, and
from the desert to the river. I will deliver the
inhabitants of the land into your hands and I
will drive them out from before you. 32 [i] But
you must not make a covenant with them or
their gods. 33 They are no longer to live in
your land. Otherwise, they would make you
sin against me, for you would serve their
gods and that would be a trap for you."

CHAPTER 24

The People of God Ratify the Covenant.* 1 He
said to Moses, "Come up to the LORD, you
and Aaron, Nadab, and Abihu, and seventy
of the elders of Israel, and worship from afar.
2 Moses alone shall approach the LORD, but
the others shall not draw near and the people
shall not go up with him."
3 Moses went to tell the people all the
words of the LORD and all the ordinances. All
the people answered together and said, "We
will keep all the commands that the LORD
has given." [j]
4 Moses wrote down all the words of the
LORD. Then he rose early in the morning and
built an altar at the foot of the mountain with
twelve pillars for the twelve tribes of Israel.
5 [k] He sent some of the young men of Israel to
offer burnt offerings and to sacrifice young
bulls as peace offerings to the LORD.
6 Moses took half of the blood and placed it
in bowls and the other half of the blood he
poured out on the altar. 7 He then took the
book of the covenant and read it in the pres-
ence of the people. They said, "All that the
LORD has commanded, we will do and obey."
8 Moses took the blood and sprinkled it on
the people saying, "Behold, the blood of the
covenant that the LORD has made with you
in accordance with all these words."
9 Then Moses went up with Aaron, Nadab,
Abihu, and the seventy elders of Israel.
10 They saw the God of Israel. Under his feet
was a pavement that looked as if it were
made from sapphires, shining like the very
heavens. 11 He did not stretch out his hand
against the nobles of the sons of Israel; they
saw God and yet they continued to eat and
drink.

C: Moses on the Mountain: The Regulation of Worship*

Moses Ascends the Mountain of God. 12 The
LORD said to Moses, "Climb up to me on the
mountain and remain there. I will give you
stone tablets with the laws and command-
ments that I have written for their instruc-
tion." [l]
13 Then Moses went up with Joshua, his
assistant, and they climbed the mountain of
God. 14 He told the elders, "Remain here to
wait for us until we return to you. Aaron and
Hur are here with you. Whoever has any con-
cern can bring it to them."
15 Moses then climbed up the mountain,
and clouds covered the mountain.
16 The glory of the LORD* settled upon
Mount Sinai, and clouds covered it for seven
days. On the seventh day he called to Moses
from out of the cloud. [m]
17 The glory of the LORD appeared to the
children of Israel to be a consuming fire on
the mountaintop. 18 Moses entered into the
midst of the cloud and climbed up the
mountain. He remained on the mountain for
forty days and forty nights. [n]

IV: INSTRUCTION ON THE SANCTUARY AND ITS MINISTERS

CHAPTER 25

**Moses Receives the Command to Establish a
Sanctuary.** 1 [o] The LORD said to Moses, 2 "Tell

---

i 32f: Ex 34:12-16; Deut 7:2ff; Jos 23:16.—j Ex 19:8; Jos 24:24.—k 5-8: Ezek 43:18; Heb 9:18ff.—l Ex 31:18; 32:15f; Deut 5:22; 10:4.—m Ex 40:34; Sir 45:4.—n Ex 19:18; 2 Mac 2:8; Heb 12:18.—o 1-7: Ex 35:4-9, 20-29; 36:3.

24:1-11 The ritual used in sealing the agreement shows the understanding of the contracting parties: God, who is represented by the altar, and the people share the same blood, which is a symbol of life. A clear prefiguration of the new and definitive covenant that will be sealed with the blood of Jesus (Mt 26:28).

24:12—31:18 The leader of the chosen people receives the favor of a lengthy and intimate meeting with the Lord. The tradition deriving from the priestly caste links to this episode an extensive set of ordinances (vv. 24:12—31:18) having to do with the sanctuary and the objects used in worship. This tradition uses recollections of ancient religious practices of the wilderness period and adapts them, in the conviction that the God of the covenant is present in the midst of his people in a particular way that must be respected because he has willed it. The tradition therefore projects on to the tent in the wilderness the later organization of the Jerusalem temple and the liturgy celebrated there. At the same time, it expresses the hope of an ideal future in which the holy people will devote themselves unreservedly to praising their Lord (see Ezek 40–48).

24:16 In the Priestly tradition *the glory of the LORD* (see Ex 16:10) is the manifestation of the divine presence. See 33:18, where a great theophany is described.

the children of Israel to gather an offering for me. Let each one raise up as an offering what his heart tells him is right. 3 This is what you shall gather from them: gold, silver, and bronze, 4 blue, purple, and scarlet cloth, fine linen, goats' hair, 5 rams' skins dyed red, sheep skins, acacia wood, 6 oil for the lamps, balsam for anointing oil and for fragrant incense, 7 onyx stones and stones for setting in the ephod and the breastplate.

8 [p] "They are to build a sanctuary for me and I will live in their midst. 9 Build it just as I will show you, following the pattern of the tabernacle and the pattern of all its furniture.

The Ark of the Covenant. 10 [q] "They are to make an Ark out of acacia wood. It is to be two and a half cubits long, one and a half cubits wide, and one and a half cubits high.* 11 You are to cover it with gold inside and out, and they are to put a gold molding on it. 12 You are to cast four golden rings for it and attach them to its four legs, two rings on one side and two rings on the other. 13 You are to make poles out of acacia wood and cover them with gold. 14 You shall put the poles into the rings on the two sides of the Ark so that you may carry the Ark with them. 15 The poles must remain in the rings of the Ark; they are not to be taken out of them.

16 "You will place the Testimony that I will give you in the Ark.

17 "You shall make a seat* of atonement of pure gold. It shall be two and a half cubits long and one and a half cubits wide. 18 You will make two cherubim* out of gold. Make them as hammered works, placing them on the two sides of the seat of atonement.

19 "Make one cherubim at one end and the other cherubim at the other end. Make the cherubim all of one piece at the two ends of the seat of atonement. 20 The cherubim shall have two wings spread out covering the seat of atonement. They shall be facing each other, and the faces of the cherubim will be turned toward the seat of atonement.

21 "You will place the seat of atonement on top of the Ark and place the Testimony that I will give you inside the Ark.

22 "I will meet you there. I will speak with you from the seat of atonement that is between the two cherubim upon the Ark of Testimony concerning all that I will command the children of Israel.

The Table of the Bread Offered to God. 23 [r] "You are to make a table of acacia wood, two cubits long, one cubit wide, and one and a half cubits high. 24 Cover it with pure gold and place a molding of gold upon it. 25 Make a frame one handbreath wide and place a molding of gold around it. 26 You shall also make four golden rings for it and place them at the four corners that are on its four legs. 27 Place the rings alongside the borders to hold the poles used in carrying the table.

28 "Make the poles out of acacia wood, cover them in gold, and carry the table with them. 29 Also make dishes and plates and flagons and jars out of pure gold to pour out libations. 30 Set the bread of the Presence on the table before me always. [s]

The Golden Lampstand. 31 [t] "You shall also make a lampstand of pure gold and hammer it out.

"Its base and shaft; its bowls and knobs and flowers shall be of one piece. 32 Six of the branches of the lampstand shall come out of its sides, three from one side of the lampstand and three from the other side of the lampstand. 33 On one branch there shall be three cups shaped like almond blossoms, with bud and flower. Also there shall be three cups shaped like almond blossoms, with bud and flower, on the next branch—and similarly for all six branches that rise out of the lampstand.

34 "On the shaft of the lampstand there shall be four cups shaped like almond blossoms with their bud and flower. 35 One bud shall be under the first set of two branches coming out of it, and one bud under the second set of two branches coming out of it, and one bud under the third set of two branches coming out of it, for there are six branches coming out of it. 36 The buds and their respective branches must be one piece with

p 8f: Ex 26:1-30; 36:8-38; Heb 8:5.—q 10-22: Ex 37:1-9; Heb 9:1-5.—r 23-30: Ex 25:23; 37:10-16.—s Lev 24:5ff; Num 4:7.—t 31-40: Ex 37:17-24; Heb 8:5.

25:10 The Ark is a rectangular chest. A *cubit* measures about 20 inches.

25:17 *Seat:* Hebrew, *kapporet*, from the root *kaphar*, "to cover" but also "to make expiation, wipe away." The rites of the great "day of expiation" were performed on this seat of the Ark (see Lev 16:11-16; Heb 9:5).

25:18 The *cherubim* correspond to the Babylonian *karibu*, half animals, half human beings, who guarded the gates of temples and palaces. The two at the ends of the atonement cover on the Ark of the Covenant have been regarded as representations of supernatural beings that are ministers of God. Yahweh sits between the cherubim (1 Sam 4:4; 2 Sam 6:2; 2 Ki 19:15; Pss 80:2; 99:1). Solomon will place two cherubim in the holiest room of the temple, beside the Ark (1 Ki 6:23-28). The chariot of God is drawn by four cherubim (Ezek 1; 10). See also Gen 3:24; Ps 18:11.

the lampstand, and the whole made from
one piece of pure gold that has been beaten
into shape.
37 "You shall then make seven lamps for
the lampstand and set them on the lamp-
stand to shed light in front of it.[u] 38 Its
snuffers and their trays are to be made of
pure gold.
39 "Use a talent* of pure gold for making
the lampstand and all of its accessories.
40 "See that you make them according to
the model that I have shown you on the
mountain.[v]

CHAPTER 26

The Tabernacle. 1 [w] "As for the tabernacle,
you shall make it out of ten curtains of fine
twisted linen, blue and purple and scarlet,
with cherubim sewn on them by skillful
craftsmen.* 2 The curtains shall be twenty-
eight cubits long and four cubits wide, each
curtain being the same size. 3 Five curtains
shall be joined together, and the other five
curtains shall be joined together. 4 Make
loops of blue cloth on the outside edge of the
first set, and likewise loops on the outside
edge of the second set. 5 Make fifty loops in
the first set and make fifty loops in the edge
of the second set. The loops should be sym-
metrical.[x] 6 Then make fifty golden clasps
and attach the sets of curtains to each other
to form the tabernacle.
7 "You shall then make curtains of goats
hair to build a tent over the tabernacle,
eleven curtains in all. 8 The curtains shall be
thirty cubits long and four cubits wide. Each
curtain shall be the same size. 9 You shall join
five of the curtains on one side and six cur-
tains on the other side. Fold back the sixth
curtain to double it over on the front of the
tent. 10 You shall make fifty loops in the out-
side edge of the first set, and fifty loops in the
edge of the second set. 11 You shall make fifty
bronze clasps and put the clasps into the
loops to join the tent together and make it a
single structure.
12 "The overlapping part of the curtain, the
half curtain that is left over, shall hang over
the back of the tabernacle. 13 The cubit that is
left over on the one side, like the cubit that is
left over on the other side, of what is remain-
ing in the length of the curtain of the tent,
shall hang over the two sides of the taberna-
cle to cover one side and the other.
14 "You shall make a covering for the tent
out of rams' skins dyed red, and over it shall
be a covering of sheep skin.

The Linear Structure of the Tabernacle.
15 [y] "You shall make upright frames for the
tent of acacia wood. 16 Each board shall be
ten cubits long and one and a half cubits
wide. 17 Each board shall have two joints in it
to fit them together. All the boards of the
tabernacle are to be made this way. 18 This is
how you shall make all the boards for the
tabernacle, twenty boards being on the
southern side. 19 You shall also make forty sil-
ver bases for the twenty boards, two bases for
each of the joints on one board, and two
bases for each of the joints on the next board.
20 On the second side of the tabernacle,
toward the north, there shall be twenty
boards 21 as well as their forty silver bases,
two bases under one board, and two bases
under the next board. 22 For the rear of the
tabernacle facing the west you shall make
six boards, 23 and two boards for the cor-
ners of the tabernacle in the rear. 24 They
shall be doubled together below and like-
wise joined together above into one ring.
The two of them will form two corners.
25 Thus, there shall be eight boards with
their silver bases, sixteen bases in all, with
two bases under one board and two bases
under the next board.
26 "You shall also make bars of acacia
wood, five for the boards of one side of the
tabernacle 27 and five bars for the boards for
the other side of the tabernacle and five bars
for the boards of the rear, toward the west.
28 The middle bar shall pass half way up the
boards, reaching from end to end. 29 Cover
the boards with gold, and make their rings
gold in which the bars are inserted, and also
cover the bars in gold.
30 "You shall build the tabernacle accord-
ing to the plan that you were shown on the
mountain.

u Lev 24:2ff; Num 8:2.—v Acts 7:44; Heb 8:5.—w 1-14: Ex 36:8-19; 40:19.—x Ex 36:12.—y 15-30: Ex 25:5; 36:20-34.

25:39 A *talent* weighed over 75 pounds.

26:1 It is not easy to picture the exact shape of the *tabernacle* or dwelling (in Latin, *tabernaculum,* "tent"), even though it is described in such detail.

It seems to be a structure that could be disassembled, something like a Bedouin tent, about 16 feet wide, 16 feet long, and 16 feet high.

Inside, the curtain (v. 31) separates "The Holy Place" from "the Most Holy Place," where the throne of God stood in darkness. See Lev 16; Mk 15:38; Heb 6:19; 9:6-14.

The Inner Veil. 31 z "You shall make a veil of blue and purple and scarlet cloth and fine twisted linen, with cherubim sewn upon it by skillful craftsmen. 32 You shall hang it on four columns of acacia wood covered in gold, with hooks of gold and standing upon four bases of silver. 33 Hang the veil from the clasps, and place the Ark of Testimony inside the veil. The veil shall serve you as the separation between the Holy and the Holy of Holies. 34 Place the seat of atonement on the Ark of Testimony in the Holy of Holies. 35 Set the table outside of the veil and the lampstand opposite the table on the south side of the tabernacle. You are to put the table on the north side.

The Entry Curtain. 36 "You shall make a curtain for the door to the tent of blue and purple and scarlet cloth and fine twisted linen that is covered with embroidery. 37 You shall make five columns of acacia wood covered in gold for the curtain. Their hooks are to be made out of gold and you shall cast five bronze bases.

CHAPTER 27

Altar of Burnt Offering. 1 a "You shall make an altar out of acacia wood. It is to be five cubits long and five cubits wide. The altar shall be square and be three cubits high. 2 Make horns* for its four corners and the horns and altar are one piece. You shall then cover it with bronze. 3 Fashion vessels to take away its ashes, as well as shovels, and basins, and forks, and fire pans. All of its utensils are to be made of bronze. 4 Make a grating for it, a network of bronze. Upon the net you shall fashion four rings made of bronze at its four corners. 5 Set it under the edge of the altar so that the net will hang halfway down the altar. 6 You shall also make poles for the altar. They shall be made of acacia wood covered with bronze. 7 The poles are to be placed through the rings, so that they are on either side of the altar for carrying it. 8 Make the altar with boards, hollow in the middle. It is to be made just as was shown to you on the mountain.

The Courtyard. 9 b "You shall make a courtyard* for the tabernacle. On the south side there shall be a drape of fine twisted linen, one hundred cubits long, to form the first side. 10 There are to be twenty columns with twenty bronze bases. The hooks of the pillars and their rings are to be made of silver.

11 "Likewise on the north side, there must be a drape one hundred cubits long, its twenty pillars with their twenty bronze bases. The hooks of the pillars and their rings are to be made of silver. 12 Along the width of the courtyard on the west side there shall be fifty cubits of drapes with ten columns and ten bases. 13 The width of the courtyard on the east side shall be fifty cubits. 14 On one side there are to be fifteen cubits of drapes with three columns and three bases, 15 and on the other side there are to be fifteen cubits of drapes with three columns and three bases.

16 "For the gate of the courtyard there shall be a curtain twenty cubits long, made of blue and purple and scarlet cloth and fine twisted linen with four columns and their four bases. 17 All the columns around the courtyard are to be filleted with silver. Their hooks shall be made of silver and their bases of bronze. 18 The length of the courtyard must be one hundred cubits, the width fifty, and the height five cubits, made of fine twisted linen with the bases made of bronze. 19 All the utensils of the tabernacle for whatever use and all the pegs of the courtyard are to be made of bronze.

The Oil for the Lampstand. 20 c "You shall order the children of Israel to obtain pure oil pressed from olives for the light, so that a lamp may burn continually. 21 It shall be in the meeting tent* outside the veil that is in front of the Testimony. Aaron and his sons shall tend it from evening until morning so that it may be before the LORD. This is a statute for the children of Israel throughout all their generations.

CHAPTER 28

The Priestly Vestments. 1 d "Have Aaron, your brother, and his sons approach you. Take them from among the children of Israel to be your priests: Aaron and Nadab, Abihu, Eleazar, and Ithamar, his sons. 2 You shall

z 31-37: Ex 36:35-38.—a 1-8: Ex 35:16; 38:1-7.—b 9-19: Ex 38:9-20; Ezek 40:14.—c 20f: Lev 24:1-4; Num 18:5.—d 1-5: Ex 39:1; 2 Chr 29:21; Sir 45:7.

27:2 The *horns* are protuberances at the four corners of the altar. They are especially holy: they are to be smeared with the blood of victims (see Ex 29:12), like the horns of the altar of incense (Ex 30:10). Anyone touching them could claim asylum (1 Ki 1:50; 2:28).

27:9 The *courtyard* is the sacred space around the sanctuary that was as far as the Israelites could enter; only priests were permitted beyond it and into the tabernacle space. Even the courtyard was limited in how many people could enter at one time.

27:21 The *meeting tent* is another term for the tabernacle, the place where God and his people meet.

make sacred vestments for Aaron, your brother, for glory and beauty. 3 Speak to all the most expert artisans, those to whom I have given a spirit of wisdom, and they shall prepare vestments for Aaron, for his consecration, so that he might exercise his priesthood in my honor.

4 "These are the vestments that they shall make: the breastplate and the ephod,* a robe, a checkered colored coat, a turban, and a sash. They will make sacred vestments for Aaron your brother and for his sons so that they may exercise their priesthood in my honor. 5 They must use gold, blue, purple, and scarlet cloth and linen.

The Ephod. 6 [e] "They shall make the ephod with gold, blue, purple, and scarlet material and fine linen, the work of skillful craftsmen. 7 It will have two shoulder pieces attached to its two ends so that it may be joined together. 8 The skillfully woven band to bind it together shall be placed over it and be of the same quality and materials: blue, purple, and scarlet cloth and fine twisted linen.

9 "Take two pieces of onyx and engrave the names of the children of Israel on them. 10 Put six of their names on the first stone, and the other six names on the second piece, written in order of their birth. 11 Engrave the names of the children of Israel on the two stones as an engraver engraves a signet ring. Insert them into settings of gold filigree. 12 Set the two stones on the shoulder pieces of the ephod, as stones of remembrance for the children of Israel. Thus, Aaron shall carry the names upon his shoulders* before the LORD, as a memorial. 13 [f] Also make settings of gold filigree 14 and two chains of pure gold that are twisted like cords. Then attach the chains to the settings.

The Breastplate. 15 [g] "You shall make a breastplate of judgment with skilled craftsmanship, the same as was used on the ephod. Make it of gold, blue, purple, and scarlet cloth and fine twisted linen. 16 It is to be square and doubled over, a span in length and a span in width. 17 Then cover it with settings of precious stones arranged in four rows. The first row shall have a ruby, a topaz, and an emerald. 18 The second row shall have a turquoise, a sapphire, and a diamond. 19 The third row shall have a jacinth, an agate, and an amethyst. 20 The fourth row shall have a beryl, an onyx, and a jasper. Mount them in gold filigree settings. 21 The stones shall correspond to the names of the children of Israel. There are to be twelve, standing for their names, each with engravings like that of a signet ring, each of them corresponding to a name of one of the twelve tribes.

22 "On the breastplate make chains of pure gold in the shape of twisted cords. 23 On the breastplate also make two golden rings and place the two rings at the edges of the breastplate.

24 "Attach the two golden chains to the two golden rings on the edges of the breastplate. 25 As for the two other ends of the chains, attach them to two filigree settings and fasten them to the front part of the shoulder pieces of the ephod. 26 Make two golden rings and place them at the two edges of the breastplate, on the inside edge next to the ephod. 27 Make another two golden rings and place them on the two shoulder pieces of the ephod, at their bottom on the front side, next to the place where it is attached to the skillfully woven band of the ephod. 28 Tie the rings of the breastplate to the rings on the ephod with a cord of blue material so that it may lie upon the skillfully woven band of the ephod and so that the breastplate may not pull away from the ephod.

29 "Thus Aaron shall carry the names of the children of Israel over his heart on the breastplate of judgment whenever he enters the sanctuary. This will serve as a memorial before the LORD forever. 30 Put the Urim and the Thummim inside the breastplate of judgment so that they will be over Aaron's heart whenever he enters into the presence of the LORD.* Aaron will forever bear the judgment of the children of Israel over his heart whenever he enters into the presence of the LORD. [h]

---

e 6-12: Ex 39:2-7; Lev 8:7.—f 13f: Ex 28:14, 22, 25; 39:15, 18; Sir 45:8-14.—g 15-21: Ex 26:31; 39:15-21.—h Ex 29:5; Lev 8:8.

28:4 The etymology of *ephod* is uncertain. The word signifies three different things: (a) the *ephod* worn in divination, that is, in consulting Yahweh (1 Sam 2:28); (b) the "ephod bad" ("linen ephod"), worn by ministers of worship (1 Sam 2:18); and (c) the "ephod of the high priest," a kind of cloth mounted on a belt with shoulder straps and with the breastplate of decision attached to it (see Ex 28:15ff).

28:12 *Carry the names upon his shoulders:* this is to signify to all of Israel that Aaron as the high priest represents all the people before God (see also v. 29).

28:30 On the breastplate were two small objects used in divination, that is, in a primitive practice aimed at discovering the divine will (see 1 Sam 14:41). The detailed description has for its purpose to bring out the splendor of the temple liturgy.

Other Priestly Vestments. [31] [i] "Make the robe for the ephod all in blue [32] with an opening in the middle for the head, with a woven border around the opening, like the opening of a garment, so that it may not be torn. [33] On its hem you shall design pomegranates of blue and purple and scarlet cloth, and fine twisted linen, all around its hem, with bells of gold between them [34] so that there shall be a golden bell* and a pomegranate alternating all around the hem of the robe. [35] Aaron must wear it when he ministers as priest, and one will hear the sound it makes when he enters the sanctuary, into the presence of the LORD, and when he leaves it, lest he die.

[36] "You are to make a plate of pure gold and engrave 'Holy to the LORD' on it as one engraves a signet ring. [37] Attach it with a blue cord to the front part of the turban.[j] [38] It will be on Aaron's forehead, so that Aaron may carry the weight of whatever guilt the children of Israel may incur in the holy things, when they consecrate their holy offerings. He will always wear it on his forehead so that they may be pleasing to the LORD.

[39] [k] "Weave the checkered tunic of fine linen and make a turban of fine linen and a sash embroidered with needlework. [40] Make tunics and sashes for the sons of Aaron as well as caps for them to give them honor and renown. [41] Put these garments on Aaron, your brother, and his sons. Then anoint them and ordain them and consecrate them, so that they may serve as priests in my honor.

[42] "Make linen undergarments to cover their nakedness. They must reach from their hips to their thighs. [43] Aaron and his sons will put them on whenever they enter into the meeting tent or when they approach the altar to minister in the sanctuary, so that they may not incur guilt and die. This shall be a perpetual statute for him and his offspring forever.

CHAPTER 29

Consecration of the Priests. [1] [l] "You shall observe this rite to consecrate them as my priests: Take a bull and two rams without defect, [2] and unleavened bread, unleavened cakes mixed with oil, and unleavened wafers with oil spread on them. You shall make them of fine wheat flour. [3] Put them in one basket and bring them and offer them together with the young bull and the two rams.

[4] "Then have Aaron and his sons approach the entrance to the meeting tent and wash them with water.[m] [5] Take the garments and clothe Aaron in the tunic, the robe of the ephod, the ephod, and the breastplate. Wrap the skillfully woven band of the ephod around him. [6] Place the turban on his head and put the holy crown over the turban. [7] Then pour the anointing oil on his head and anoint him.

[8] "As for his sons, make them draw near and clothe them in their tunics, [9] wrap their sashes around them, and tie their caps on them. They will participate in the priesthood by an eternal statute. This is how you shall consecrate Aaron and his sons.[n]

The Offering of the Sacrifices. [10] [o] "Then have the young bull brought in front of the meeting tent. Aaron and his sons shall lay their hands on its head. [11] Kill the bull before the LORD, at the entrance to the meeting tent. [12] Take part of its blood and with a finger put it on the horns of the altar. The rest of the blood shall be poured out at the base of the altar.

[13] "Take the fat that surrounds its entrails, the lobe of the liver, the two kidneys and the fat that surrounds them, and burn them as a sacrifice on the altar. [14] But the meat of the bull, its skin and its dung, you must burn outside the camp. It is a sin offering.[p]

[15] "Then take one of the rams. Aaron and his sons shall lay their hands on its head. [16] Kill the ram and gather its blood and pour it around the altar. [17] Cut the ram into pieces. Wash the entrails and the legs and put them with the pieces and the head. [18] Then burn the entire ram on the altar. It is a pleasing fragrance* to the LORD, a burnt offering to the LORD.

[19] "Take the second ram. Aaron and his sons shall lay their hands on its head, [20] and you shall kill it. Take part of its blood and

i 31-35: Ex 39:20ff; Sir 45:10.—j Ex 39:31; Lev 8:9; Num 15:38.—k 39-43: Ex 39:27ff; Lev 8:7.—l 1-8: Ex 28:40ff; Lev 8:1-9.—m Ex 40:12; Lev 8:6.—n Ex 31:10; Lev 8:13.—o 10-26: Lev 8:2, 14-30.—p Lev 9:11; Heb 13:11.

28:34 *A golden bell:* the sound of the bells alerted the people that the high priest Aaron was present in the sanctuary. Although they could not enter into the Holy Place, worshipers could join their prayers with his.

29:18 *A pleasing fragrance:* an anthropomorphism expressing the idea that the Lord accepts the sacrifice (see Gen 8:21; Lev 1:9; Num 28:2). *Burnt offering:* a sacrifice in which the entire animal is burned.

place it on the right ear lobe of Aaron and the
right ear lobes of his sons, on the thumbs of
their right hands and on the big toes of their
right feet. Then pour out the blood around
the altar. 21 Take some of the blood on the
altar and some anointing oil and sprinkle
Aaron and his vestments, the sons of Aaron
and their vestments. Thus, he shall be conse-
crated with his vestments together with his
sons and their vestments.

22 "Take the fat of the ram: the tail, the fat
that covers the entrails, the lobe of the liver,
the two kidneys and their fat, and the right
thigh, for it is a ram of consecration. 23 Also
take a round loaf of bread, a cake of bread
mixed with oil, and an unleavened wafer
from the basket of unleavened breads
placed before the altar. 24 Put all of it into
the hands of Aaron and the hands of his
sons. They shall wave it as an offering
before the LORD.* 25 Take everything from
their hands and burn it on the altar. It
shall be a pleasant fragrance to the LORD,
a burnt offering to the LORD.

26 "Take the breast of the ram of Aaron's
consecration and wave it as an offering
before the LORD. It shall be your portion.
27 [q] Consecrate the breast of the wave offering
and the thigh of the offering and wave it. It is
offered from the ram of the consecration,
and it is for Aaron and his sons. 28 It is to
belong to Aaron and his sons as the portion
reserved to them. This shall be an eternal
statute for the children of Israel. It will be the
priests' portion to be offered by the children
of Israel from their peace offerings, an offer-
ing unto the LORD.

The Transmission of the Sacred Vestments.
29 "The sacred vestments of Aaron shall
belong to his sons after him. They shall be
anointed and consecrated in them.[r] 30 Those
descendants of Aaron who succeed him in
the priesthood and who enter into the meet-
ing tent to minister in the sanctuary shall
wear these vestments for seven days.

The Sacred Food of the Priests. 31 [s] "Take the
ram of consecration and cook its meat in a
holy place. 32 At the entrance to the meeting
tent, Aaron and his sons shall eat the meat of
the ram and the bread of the basket. 33 They
shall eat those things with which atonement
was obtained. No outsider can eat them, for
they are holy things. 34 If any of the meat of
consecration or the bread is left over in the
morning, you shall burn whatever is left over
with fire; it shall not be eaten, for it is holy.
35 Do to Aaron and to his sons what I have
commanded you to do. For seven days you
shall consecrate them.

The Consecrated Altar and the Daily Sacrifice.
36 [t] "For each of seven days you shall offer a
young bull as a sin offering for atonement.
You shall also make a sin offering for the
atonement for the altar, and shall anoint it to
consecrate it. 37 For seven days you shall
make atonement for the altar and conse-
crate it. It shall thus become a most holy
thing, and whatever touches the altar will
become holy.*

38 [u] "Now this is what you shall offer up on
the altar every day and forever: two lambs, a
year old. 39 You shall offer one of these lambs
in the morning and the second lamb in the
evening. 40 With the first lamb you shall offer
a tenth of a measure of fine flour mixed with
a fourth of a hin of olive oil and a fourth of a
hin of wine as a libation. 41 Offer the second
lamb in the evening with the same offering
and libation as in the morning. It will be a
pleasant fragrance to the LORD, a burnt
offering to the LORD.

42 "It shall be a perpetual burnt offering
throughout all your generations at the
entrance to the meeting tent, in the presence
of the LORD, where I will meet you to speak
with you.

43 "I will meet with the children of Israel in
this place that will be consecrated to my
glory.[v] 44 I will consecrate the meeting tent
and the altar. I will also consecrate Aaron
and his sons to be my priests. 45 I will live in
the midst of the children of Israel and I will
be their God. 46 They shall know that I am the
LORD, their God, who brought them out of
the land of Egypt so that I, the LORD, their
God, might live in their midst.

CHAPTER 30

The Altar of Incense. 1 [w] "You shall build an
altar upon which to burn incense. Make it of
acacia wood, 2 one cubit long and one cubit

q 27f: Lev 7:31-34; 10:14f; Num 18:18f; Deut 18:3.—r Ex 40:13; Num 20:26, 28.—s 31-34: Lev 7:15; 8:31f.—t 36f: Ex 40:10; Lev 8:11.—u 38-42: Num 28:3-8; Ezek 46:13.—v Ex 25:22; 30:6.—w 1-5: Ex 30:2; 37:25-28.

29:24 See Lev 7:30. The object sacrificed was several times passed over the altar and then drawn back, in order to express the idea of an offering being made to God.

29:37 Just as those who ministered had to be cleansed and make atonement before offering worship, so too, the altar must be sanctified so that anything that touched it was holy.

wide. It shall be square, and two cubits high; and its horns shall all be one piece with it. 3 Cover its top, its sides, and its horns with pure gold, and make a gold molding around it. 4 You shall also make two golden rings below its molding on its two sides. Place them on opposite sides. They shall be used to insert poles with which to carry it. 5 You shall make the poles out of acacia wood and cover them with gold. 6 And you shall place the altar in front of the veil that hides the Ark of Testimony, in front of the seat of atonement that is upon it, where I will meet you.[x]

7 "Aaron shall burn fragrant incense upon the altar. He shall burn it each morning when he trims the lamps, 8 and also in the evening when he refills the lamps. There shall be perpetual incense before the LORD throughout all your generations. 9 Do not offer any unholy incense upon it, nor burnt offerings nor sacrifices nor libations. 10 Once a year Aaron shall perform an atonement ritual upon it, upon its horns. He shall make atonement upon it with the blood of your sin offering once a year throughout all your generations. It is something most holy to the LORD."[y]

The Temple Tax. 11 The LORD spoke to Moses and said, 12 "When you take a census of the number of the children of Israel, each man will offer a ransom for his life to the LORD, when you number them, lest there be a plague among them when you number them. 13 Each person counted in the census will give half a shekel according to the measure of the shekel of the sanctuary (a shekel is twenty gerahs). The half shekel will be an offering to the LORD. 14 Everyone who is counted in the census, from twenty years old and up, will give the LORD's offering. 15 The rich will not give more and the poor will not give less than half a shekel, when you give the LORD's offering, in order to ransom your life. 16 You shall take the money of this ransom of the children of Israel and designate it for the needs of the meeting tent. It shall be a memorial before the LORD for the children of Israel, for the ransom of your lives."[z]

The Basin for Washing. 17 The LORD said to Moses, 18 "You shall make a basin out of bronze, with a base of bronze, for ablutions. Place it between the meeting tent and the altar and fill it with water. 19 [a] Aaron and his sons shall wash their hands and their feet in it.* 20 When they enter the meeting tent, they shall perform an ablution with water, lest they die. Thus, whenever they approach the altar to minister, to burn an offering unto the LORD with fire, 21 they shall wash their hands and their feet so that they might not die. This shall be a perpetual statute for him and his sons, for all their generations."

The Anointing Oil. 22 The LORD said to Moses, 23 "Take the finest spices: five hundred shekels of flowing myrrh, half that amount of sweet-smelling cinnamon, namely two hundred and fifty shekels of it, two hundred and fifty shekels of aromatic cane, 24 five hundred shekels of cassia, all according to the shekel of the sanctuary, and a hin of olive oil. 25 Make a holy anointing oil out of them using the craft of the perfumer who blends oils. It shall be a holy anointing oil.[b] 26 With it you are to anoint the meeting tent, the Ark of Testimony, 27 the table and all its accessories, the lampstand and its accessories, the altar of incense, 28 the altar of burnt offerings and all of its accessories, and the basin and its base. 29 You shall consecrate these things, and they shall become most holy. Whatever touches them will be holy.

30 "You shall also anoint Aaron and his sons and consecrate them so that they may serve me as priests.[c] 31 Say to the children of Israel: 'This shall be my holy anointing oil for all your generations. 32 You shall not pour it out on anyone's body, nor shall you make anything else like it. It is holy, and it shall be holy to you.'

33 "Anyone who makes anything like it, or who pours it on an outsider, shall be cut off from his people."

The Incense. 34 [d] The LORD said to Moses, "Gather sweet spices, gum of stacte, onycha, resin of galbanum, equal measures of sweet spices and pure frankincense, 35 and make an incense using the skill of the perfumer. It is to be salted, pure and holy. 36 Beat some of it very fine and put it before the Testimony in the meeting tent where I shall meet with you. It shall be most holy to you.

37 "You shall not make for yourselves anything like this incense according to its com-

x Ex 25:21; 40:26.—y Lev 16:18.—z Ex 38:25; Num 18:26. —a 19ff: Ex 40:12, 31f.—b Ex 30:35; 37:29.—c Ex 29:7; Lev 8:12; Ps 133:2.—d 34ff: Ex 25:6; 37:29; Lev 6:12.

30:19 Cleansing before worship was so important that failure to be properly washed before entering the tent was tantamount to a death sentence for priests. We can take from this the necessity of preparing ourselves (i.e., confessing our sin), before we celebrate Eucharist. We do this as a community with the Penitential Act.

position. You shall consider it to be holy to the LORD. 38 Whoever makes anything like it to use for its sweet odor shall be cut off from his people."

CHAPTER 31

The Choice of Craftsmen for the Tabernacle. 1 [e]The LORD spoke to Moses and said to him, 2 "Behold, I have chosen Bezalel, the son of Uri, the son of Hur, of the tribe of Judah. 3 I have filled him with the Spirit of God* so that he possesses wisdom, understanding, knowledge, and is expert in every kind of craft 4 to design artistic works in gold, silver, and bronze, 5 to know how to cut stones for settings and how to carve wood. He is expert in every craft. 6 And behold, I have sent Oholiab, the son of Ahisamach, of the tribe of Dan to him. I have also given all skillful men their ability, so that they may make all that I have commanded you to make: 7 the meeting tent, the Ark of Testimony, the seat of atonement over it, and all the accessories of the tent, 8 the table with its accessories, the pure lampstand and its accessories, the altar of incense, 9 the altar of burnt offerings with all of its accessories, the basin and its base, 10 the finely crafted vestments, the sacred vestments for Aaron and the vestments for his sons, for their priestly ministry, 11 the oil of anointing, and the fragrant incense for the sanctuary. They shall produce all that I have commanded you."

The Sabbath.* 12 [f]The LORD said to Moses, 13 "Say to the children of Israel, 'You shall observe my Sabbaths, for the Sabbath is a sign between me and you for all your generations, so that you may know that I am the LORD, who makes you holy.

14 " 'Therefore, you shall observe the Sabbath, for it is holy to you. Whoever profanes it shall be put to death. Whoever works on that day shall be cut off from his people. 15 Six days you shall work, but the seventh day is a Sabbath of sacred rest for you, holy to the LORD. Whoever works on the Sabbath shall be put to death. 16 The children of Israel shall observe the Sabbath, celebrating the Sabbath throughout their generations as a perpetual covenant. 17 This is a perpetual sign between me and the children of Israel, for the LORD made the heavens and the earth in six days, but on the seventh he ceased and rested.' "

Moses Receives the Tablets of the Law. 18 When the LORD had finished speaking with Moses on Mount Sinai, he gave him the two tablets of Testimony, the stone tablets, written with the finger of God.[g]

V: THE GOLDEN CALF AND THE RENEWAL OF THE COVENANT

CHAPTER 32

The Golden Calf. 1 When the people saw that Moses delayed coming down the mountain, they gathered around Aaron and told him, "Make a god to walk before us, because we do not know what has happened to Moses, the one who brought us out of the land of Egypt."[h]

2 Aaron answered them, "Take the gold earrings off your wives and sons and daughters and bring them to me." 3 All the people took off their gold earrings and brought them to Aaron. 4 He took the gold from their hands and fashioned it with a chisel and made a molten calf.* They said, "Behold your God, O Israel, who brought you out of the land of Egypt."[i] 5 Seeing this, Aaron built an altar before the calf and proclaimed, "Tomorrow shall be a feast in honor of the LORD." 6 The following day they rose early, offered burnt offerings, and brought peace offerings. The people sat down and ate and drank. They then rose to divert themselves.

7 [j]The LORD said to Moses, "Leave, go down, because your people, whom you brought out of the land of Egypt, have become perverse. 8 They have quickly departed from the way that I have commanded them. They have made a molten calf for themselves, and have bowed down before it. They have offered sacrifices and said,

e 1-6: Ex 35:30-35.—f 12-17: Ex 20:8-11; 35:1-3; Deut 5:12.—g Ex 24:12; 32:15f; Deut 4:13; 5:22.—h Ex 14:11; 32:23; Acts 7:40.—i Ex 32:8; Deut 9:16; 1 Ki 12:28.—j 7f: Deut 9:12, 16; Ps 78:36.

31:3 *Filled him with the Spirit of God:* the Master Craftsman himself provides his ministers with gifts that enable them to design and construct places of worship. Here the Spirit of God filled Bezalel and others with the ability to build the meeting tent as his dwelling among the children of Israel.

31:12-17 This section is a departure from the preceding text concerning official worship, but inserted here lest the people forget the importance of rest from work (i.e., setting aside a day that is holy unto the Lord).

32:4 *Molten calf:* under Aaron's direction the people fashioned an idolatrous image of a bull. He tried to turn them back to the Lord by building an altar before it. The Israelites were forbidden to use any graven images and would be punished for their idolatry.

'Behold your God, Israel, who brought you out of the land of Egypt.' "

[9] The LORD also said to Moses, "I have observed this people, and I have seen that it is a stubborn people. [10] Now let me be, so that my rage can blaze out against them and destroy them. I will then make you a great nation."

The Prayer of Moses. [11] [k] But Moses entreated the LORD, his God, and said, "Why, O LORD, will you let your rage blaze out against your people, whom you brought out of the land of Egypt with great power and a mighty hand? [12] Why should the Egyptians be able to say about them, 'He brought them out for evil purposes, to kill them in the mountains and to consume them from the face of the earth'? Turn back your wrath and change your mind about harming your people. [13] Remember Abraham, Isaac, and Israel, your servants, to whom you swore by yourself and said, 'I will make your descendants as numerous as the stars of the heavens. All this land, of which I have spoken, I will give to your descendants as their possession forever.' " [l] [14] Then the LORD changed his mind and decided not to harm his people.

Moses Shatters the Tablets of the Law. [15] Moses left and went down the mountain with the two tablets of Testimony in his hands, tablets written on both sides. They were written on one side and the other. [m] [16] The tablets were made by God, and the writing on them was God's writing.

[17] Joshua heard the noise of the people as they shouted, and he cried out to Moses, "There are battle sounds coming from the camp!" [18] But Moses answered, "It is not the shout of victory, nor the sound of defeat. It is the sound of singing that I hear."

[19] When they drew near the camp, he saw the calf and the dancing. Moses became very angry. He flung down the tablets, breaking them to pieces at the foot of the mountain. [n] [20] He then seized the calf that they had made and burned it with fire. He ground it down until it was a powder and scattered it on water that he made the children of Israel drink.

The Zeal of the Levites. [21] Moses said to Aaron, "What has this people done to you that you have brought such a great sin upon them?" [22] But Aaron answered, "Let my lord not be angry, for you know this people and that they are set on evil. [23] They said to me, 'Make a god to walk before us, because we do not know what has happened to Moses, the man who brought us out of the land of Egypt.' [24] I said to them, 'Whoever has gold, take it off.' They gave it to me, and I threw it in the fire, and out came this calf."

[25] Moses saw that the people had lost control of themselves (for Aaron had let them run so wild that their enemies mocked them). [26] [o] So he stood at the gate to the camp and said, "Whoever is for the LORD, come to me!" All the sons of Levi gathered around him. [27] He cried out to them, "Thus says the LORD, the God of Israel: Each man strap a sword to his side. Then pass back and forth in the camp from one gate to another and slay your brother, your companion, and your neighbor."

[28] The sons of Levi did as Moses had commanded them. On that day three thousand men from among the people perished. [29] Moses then said, "Today you have consecrated yourself to the service of the LORD, each one at the cost of his son or his brother, that he might bestow a blessing upon you this day."

Moses Intercedes for His People. [30] [p] The next day Moses said to the people, "You have committed a great sin. Today I will climb up to the LORD. Perhaps I will obtain pardon for your sin."

[31] Moses returned to the LORD and said, "This people has committed a great sin. They made a god out of gold for themselves.* [32] But now, if you will, pardon their sin—if not, I pray, blot me out of the book that you have written."*

[33] The LORD said to Moses, "I will blot out of my book only him who has sinned against me. [34] Now go, lead the people to the place about which I told you. Behold, my angel will go before you. But on the day of reckoning, I will punish them for their sin."

[35] The LORD smote his people because they had made the calf that Aaron had fashioned.

k 11f: Num 14:13ff; Deut 9:28.—l Gen 16:10; 22:16f.—m Ex 24:12; Deut 9:15.—n Ex 34:1; Deut 9:16f.—o 26-29: Deut 33:8f; Ps 99:8.—p 30-34: Ps 99:6; Rom 2:5; 9:3.

32:31 Moses interceded with God for the wrongdoing of the Israelites and God forgave them. It is clear, however, that there are consequences that remain for both Moses and the people due to their sinfulness.

32:32 The book of life, in which are written the names of the elect, that is, the multitude of the predestined. See Isa 4:3; Rev 3:5.

CHAPTER 33

The Israelites Are Ordered To Depart. [1] The LORD said to Moses, "Get up and leave this place, you and the people whom I brought out of the land of Egypt, to go to the land that I have promised with an oath to Abraham, to Isaac, and to Jacob, saying, 'To your descendants I will give it.' [2] I will send an angel before you to drive out the Canaanites, Amorites, Hittites, Perizzites, Hivites, and Jebusites.[q] [3] Go up to the land flowing with milk and honey. But I will not go up in your midst, lest I destroy you along the way, for you are an obstinate people."

[4] The people heard this sad news and they mourned. No one put on his ornaments.

[5] The LORD said to Moses, "Say this to the children of Israel, 'You are an obstinate people. If I were to go up with you for a single moment, I would surely destroy you. Now, take off your ornaments so that I may know what to do with you.' "

[6] The children of Israel stripped themselves of their ornaments, from Mount Horeb onward.

A Provisional Tent for the Colloquy between God and Moses. [7] Moses took the tent and pitched it quite a distance outside of the camp, calling it the meeting tent. Anyone who sought the LORD would go to the meeting tent that was outside the camp.*[r] [8] Whenever Moses went out to the tent, all the people rose up and each one stood in the door to his tent. They watched Moses pass by until he entered the tent. [9] When Moses entered the tent, a column of cloud descended and remained at the entrance to the tent, and the LORD spoke with Moses. [10] The whole people saw the column of cloud that stood at the entrance to the tent, and they all got up and worshiped at the doors to their tents. [11] Thus the LORD spoke to Moses face to face, as a man speaks to his friend. He then returned to the camp while his servant Joshua, son of Nun, a young man, did not leave the tent.*[s]

The Prayer of Moses. [12] Moses said to the LORD, "Behold, you commanded me, 'Bring up this people,' but you did not tell me whom you would send with me. You even said, 'I know you by name,* and you have found favor with me.'[t] [13] Now, therefore, I beseech you, if I have found favor with you, show me your ways, so that I may know you and stay in your favor. Keep in mind that this people is your people."

[14] The LORD answered, "I will walk with you and give you rest." [15] Moses replied, "If you will not go with us, then do not make us go up from here, [16] for how will it then be known if I have found favor with you, I and your people? Is it not in your journeying with us, with me and your people, that we are marked out as being distinct from all the other peoples who are upon the face of the earth?"

[17] The LORD said to Moses, "I will also do this very thing that you have said, for you have found favor with me and I know you by name."

[18] So Moses said to him, "Show me your glory!"

[19] He answered, "I will make all my splendor pass in front of you and I will proclaim my name, the LORD, before you. I will show favor to those to whom I show favor and I will have mercy on those on whom I have mercy."[u] [20] He continued, "But you cannot see my face, for no one can see my face and live." [21] And the LORD continued, "There is a place near me. You will stand upon the rock. [22] When my glory passes by, I will place you in the cleft of the rock and cover you with my hand until I will have passed by. [23] Then I will take away my hand and you will see my back, but you cannot see my face."

CHAPTER 34

The New Tablets of the Law. [1] The LORD said to Moses, "Cut two stone tablets like the first ones. I will write on these tablets the words that were on the first tablets, the ones you broke.[v] [2] Be ready in the morning. Tomorrow morning you must climb up Mount Sinai and remain on the summit of the mountain with me. [3] No one is to climb up with you. No one

q Ex 23:23; Num 32:39.—r Ex 29:42f; Num 2:2.—s Num 12:8; Deut 34:10; Sir 45:4-6.—t Ex 32:34; 2 Chr 1:10.—u Deut 32:3; Rom 9:15.—v Ex 31:18; Deut 10:1f.

33:7 Moses took a large tent and erected it outside the camp as a provisional place of meeting with the Lord and as a tribunal, while the definitive tent was being erected, that is, the tabernacle or tent of meeting (see Ex 40:2), which was to stand in the midst of the camp (Num 2:2).

33:11 Moses meets the Lord face to face: this account is from a different source than the one in verse 20, which says that it is impossible for even Moses to see the face of God. The sacred writer is not concerned to harmonize the two divergent traditions.

33:12 The phrase, *know you by name*, signifies special love and protection.

should be on the summit of the mountain
nor anywhere on the mountain. Even the
flocks and the herds are not to graze in front
of that mountain."

4 Moses cut two tablets of stone like the
first ones. He arose early in the morning and
climbed up Mount Sinai, as the LORD had
commanded him, with the two stone tablets
in his hands.

The LORD Shows Himself to Moses. 5 The LORD
came down in a cloud and stood with him
there and proclaimed the name of the LORD.
6 [w] The LORD passed in front of him pro-
claiming, "The LORD, the LORD, a compas-
sionate and gracious God, slow to anger and
abounding in steadfast love and fidelity, 7 who
shows mercy to thousands. He forgives iniq-
uity and transgression and sin, but will by no
means forgive the iniquity of the fathers, vis-
iting it upon their sons and their sons' sons, to
the third and fourth generation."

8 Moses quickly bowed down to the ground
and worshiped. 9 He said, "If I have found
favor with you, my LORD, let the LORD walk
in our midst. Yet, it is an obstinate people.
Pardon our iniquity and sin and take us for
your own inheritance."

A New Book of the Law.* 10 The LORD said,
"Behold, I am going to establish a covenant
with you. I will perform marvelous deeds
before all your people, things that have never
been done before anywhere on the earth or
among any people. All the people in whose
midst you dwell will see the work of the
LORD, for it is a wondrous thing that I will do
with you.

11 "Observe what I command you today. I
will drive out the Amorites, Canaanites,
Hittites, Perizzites, Hivites, and Jebusites.
12 [x] Take care not to make any covenants with
the inhabitants of the land that you are
about to enter, lest it become a snare to you.
13 You are to tear down their altars, smash
their pillars, and cut down their sacred
trees.* 14 You must not worship any other
god, for the LORD is called Jealous, for he is a
jealous God.

15 "Do not make a covenant with the people
of that land lest, when they commit fornica-
tion for their gods and perform sacrifices to
their gods, they invite you and you eat of their
sacrifice.* 16 Do not take their daughters as
wives for your sons lest, when their daughters
commit fornication to their gods, they cause
your sons to commit fornication with their
gods as well.

17 "Do not make any molten gods for your-
selves. [y]

18 "Observe the Feast of Unleavened Bread.
For seven days eat unleavened bread at the
appointed time in the month of Abib, for it
was in the month of Abib that you came out
of Egypt.

19 [z] "Every creature that is the firstborn
from its mother's womb belongs to me: every
firstborn bull, every firstborn cattle and
sheep. 20 The firstborn of a donkey will be
redeemed with a lamb. If you do not redeem
it, you are to break its neck. All of your first-
born sons are to be redeemed.

"None is to appear before me empty-
handed.

21 "For six days you may work, but on the
seventh you must rest. Even during plowing
season and the harvest, you must rest. [a]

22 "You shall celebrate the Feast of Weeks,
that is, the firstfruits of the wheat harvest,
and also the Harvest Feast at the year's end.

23 "Three times a year all your men will
appear before the LORD God, the God of
Israel, 24 for I will cast out your enemies
before you and enlarge your borders. Neither
will any man desire your land, when you go
up three times a year to appear before the
LORD, your God. 25 [b] You shall not sacrifice
the blood of my sacrificial victim with leav-
ened bread, neither shall you let the sacrifi-
cial victim of the Passover remain until the
morning.

26 "You will bring the best of the firstfruits of
the land to the house of the LORD, your God.

"You shall not cook a kid goat in its moth-
er's milk."

---

w 6f: Ex 20:5f; Num 14:18; Deut 5:9f; Jer 32:18; Jon 4:2.—x 12-16: Ex 20:5; 23:32f; Deut 7:1-5; 12:2f.—y Ex 20:3; Lev 19:4.—z 19f: Ex 13:2, 12f; Lev 27:26.—a Ex 20:9f; 35:2.—b 25f: Ex 23:18f; Deut 16:4.

34:10-28 After their first false step the chosen people had to make a serious commitment to live according to the renewed covenant. As a remembrance of this event, the Yahwist tradition has preserved for us this new Decalogue, which is probably to be associated with the point at which Israel became sedentary and had to struggle with the nature cults of Canaan; this would account for the emphasis on taking part in the liturgical celebrations.

34:13 In the Canaanite religion the *pillars*, Hebrew, *massebot*, were symbols of the male god; their cult is condemned; see also Ex 23:24; Lev 26:1; Deut 7:5; 12:3; 16:22; Hos 3:4; 10:1; Mic 5:12. The *sacred trees* (Hebrew, *asherah*) were a symbol of the female goddess of love and fertility (Astarte).

34:15 As compared to the worship of Yahweh, which is likened to a legitimate marriage, the worship of false gods is described as prostitution. See Ezek 16; 23; Hos 1–3; Rev 17.

27 The LORD said to Moses, "Write down these words, for in accordance with them I have established a covenant with you and with Israel."

28 Moses remained with the LORD for forty days and forty nights without eating bread or drinking water. And he wrote the words of the covenant, the Ten Commandments, on the tablets.[c]

The Radiant Face of Moses.* 29 When Moses went down from Mount Sinai, he had the two tablets of Testimony in his hands, while he descended the mountain. He did not know that the skin of his face had become radiant, for he had been speaking with the LORD. 30 But when Aaron and all the children of Israel saw Moses and that the skin of his face had become radiant, they were afraid to approach him. 31 Moses therefore called to them, to Aaron and all the heads of the community, and they went over to him. Moses spoke to them. 32 All the children of Israel then drew near after them, and he commanded them to do all that the LORD had told him on Mount Sinai. 33 [d] When Moses was finished speaking to them, he put on a veil to cover his face. 34 Whenever Moses came before the LORD to speak with him, Moses took off the veil until he went outside. When he went outside, he told the children of Israel all that had been commanded them. 35 The children of Israel saw that the skin of his face had become radiant. Then he put the veil on over his face again, until he went in to speak with the LORD again.

VI: THE CONSTRUCTION AND FURNISHING OF THE SANCTUARY*

CHAPTER 35

Sabbath Regulations. 1 [e] Moses assembled the whole community of the children of Israel and said to them, "These are the things that the LORD has commanded you to do: 2 For six days you shall work, but the seventh shall be a holy day for you, a day of absolute rest, sacred to the LORD. Whoever works on that day shall be put to death. 3 You shall light no fires on the Sabbath in all of your dwellings."

Materials for the Tabernacle. 4 Moses told the whole community of the children of Israel, "This is what the LORD has commanded you to do: 5 [f] Take up an offering from among yourselves for the LORD. Whoever is generous, let him bring the offering to the LORD: gold, silver, and bronze, 6 blue, purple, and scarlet material, fine twisted linen, goat hair, 7 rams' skins dyed red, sheep skins, acacia wood, 8 oil for lamps, balsam for anointing, and oil for fragrant incense, 9 onyx stones and stones for setting in the ephod and the breastplate.

10 [g] "All the artisans among you shall come and make what the LORD has commanded: 11 the tabernacle, its tent, its covering, its hooks, its boards, its bars, its pillars, its bases; 12 the Ark and its poles, the seat of atonement, and the veil of the screen; 13 the table with its poles and all its accessories, the bread of the Presence; 14 the lampstand that provides light and its accessories, the lamps, and the oil for light; 15 the altar of incense with its poles, the anointing oil, and the fragrant incense; the screen for the door at the entrance to the tabernacle; 16 the altar of burnt offerings with its bronze grate, its poles, and all its accessories; the basin and its base; 17 the drapes for the courtyard, their columns, and their bases, and the screen for the gate of the courtyard; 18 the pegs for the tabernacle and the pegs for the courtyard and their cords; 19 the carefully prepared cloths for ministering in the sanctuary, the sacred vestments for Aaron the priest and the vestments for his sons to exercise their priesthood."

20 All the community of the children of Israel left the presence of Moses. 21 Then those whose hearts were stirred and whose spirits moved them came and brought the LORD's offerings to be used for the construction of the meeting tent and for all its service and for the sacred vestments. 22 [h] Men and women came forward, those whose hearts were willing, and they brought brooches and earrings and rings and armlets, all kinds of

c Ex 24:18; Deut 9:9, 18; 10:2, 4; Mt 4:2.—d 33f: 2 Cor 3:13, 16.—e 1-3: Ex 31:13-17; Lk 13:14.—f 5-9: Ex 25:2-7; 30:14.—g 10-19: Ex 31:6-11.—h 22-28: Ex 25:3-7; 39:1.

34:29-35 The face of Moses reflected the glory of God. The verb *qaran*, "to be radiant," is like the noun *qoren*, "horn." This explains why the verb was translated as "horns" in the Latin Vulgate and became part of the tradition. Paul refers to this passage when he reminds Christians of their transformation into the image of God (2 Cor 3:7-8, 18).

35:1—40:38 Thanks to Moses, Israel is restored to God's favor; this is therefore the period of the building of a sanctuary in order to ensure the presence of God in the midst of his people. This final part of the Book of Exodus looks back to and repeats almost verbatim the instructions given earlier (chs. 25–31).

golden objects, and each man dedicated his gold unto the LORD.

[23] All those who had blue or purple or scarlet cloth, or fine linen, or goat hair, or rams' skins dyed red, or sheep skins brought them. [24] Those who could make an offering of silver or bronze offered it to the LORD. Likewise, those who had acacia wood for some purpose brought it.

[25] Furthermore, all the skilled women spun with their hands and brought the blue, purple, and scarlet cloth and the fine linen they had spun. [26] All the women whose hearts were moved by wisdom spun goat hair. [27] The leaders brought onyx stones and stones for setting in the ephod and the breastplate, [28] balsam and oil for light, oil of anointing, and fragrant incense. [29] Thus, all the men and women whose hearts moved them to bring something for the construction that the LORD had commanded them to build through Moses brought it. The children of Israel brought their freewill offerings to the LORD.

The Artisans. [30] [i] Moses said to the children of Israel, "Behold, the LORD has summoned Bezalel, the son of Uri, the son of Hur, of the tribe of Judah, by name. [31] He has filled him with the Spirit of God, with wisdom, with intelligence, with knowledge, and with ability in every type of craft, [32] to design artistic works in gold, silver, and bronze, [33] to know how to cut stones for settings and how to carve wood. He is expert in every craft. [34] He has inspired him to teach, both him and Oholiab, the son of Ahisamach of the tribe of Dan. [35] He has filled them with the skill needed to do the work of the engraver, the designer, and the embroiderer, to work with blue and purple and scarlet cloth and fine linen, and to weave. They can do the work of any craftsman or designer.

CHAPTER 36

[1] [j] "Bezalel, Oholiab, and all the skilled craftsmen whom the LORD has gifted with wisdom and intelligence to know how to do any work in the construction of the sanctuary are to do everything just as the LORD has commanded."

Magnificence of the Gifts. [2] Moses summoned Bezalel, Oholiab, and all the skilled craftsmen in whose hearts the LORD had placed wisdom, everyone whose heart moved him to come to do the work. [3] They received from Moses all the offerings that the children of Israel had brought for the construction of the sanctuary. But every morning they continued to bring more offerings. [4] All the craftsmen who were building the sanctuary left the work they were doing [5] and came to Moses and said, "The people are bringing more than is needed for the work that the LORD has commanded."

[6] Moses, therefore, commanded and had proclaimed in the camp, "Let neither man nor woman bring anything more for the construction of the sanctuary." He thus stopped the people from bringing more offerings, [7] for what the people had already given was sufficient, and indeed even more than enough for the work.

The Curtains. [8] [k] All the craftsmen among them made the tabernacle with its ten curtains of twisted linen, blue, purple, and scarlet cloth, and cherubim skillfully crafted. [9] Each curtain was twenty-eight cubits long and four cubits wide. All the curtains were the same size. [10] Five of the curtains were joined to one another, and the other five curtains were joined to one another. [11] Loops of blue cloth were made on the outside edge of the first set, and likewise on the outside edge of the second set. [12] Fifty loops were made in the first set and fifty loops in the edge of the second set. The loops were symmetrical. [13] Then fifty gold clasps were made and attached the sets of curtains to each other to form the tabernacle.

[14] Curtains of goat hair were made to build a tent over the tabernacle — eleven altogether. [15] The curtains were thirty cubits long and four cubits wide; all eleven curtains were the same size. [16] Five of the curtains were joined on one side and six curtains on the other side. [17] Fifty loops were made in the outside edge of the first set, and fifty loops in the edge of the second set. [18] Fifty bronze clasps were made to join the tent together and make it a single structure. [19] Then a covering was made for the tent of rams' skins dyed red, and over it a covering of sheep skin.

The Boards. [20] [l] Upright frames were made of acacia wood for the tent. [21] Each board was ten cubits long and one and a half cubits wide. [22] Each board had two joints to fit them

i 30-35: Ex 31:1-6.—j 1f: Ex 31:1, 6; 35:35.—k 8-19: Ex 26:1-14; 36:17.—l 20-34: Ex 26:15-19.

together. This is how all the boards of the tabernacle were made. [23] Thus twenty boards were made for the south side of the tabernacle [24] and forty silver bases under the twenty boards, two bases for each of the two joints on each board. [25] Twenty boards were made for the other side of the tabernacle, the north side, [26] along with their forty bases of silver, two bases under one board and two bases under the next board. [27] For the rear of the tabernacle facing toward the west six boards were made. [28] Two boards formed the corner of the tabernacle in the rear. [29] They were doubled together below and joined together above into one ring. The two of them formed the two corners. [30] There were thus eight boards with their silver bases, sixteen bases, two bases under one board and two bases under the next board.

[31] Also made were bars out of acacia wood: five bars for the boards of one side of the tabernacle [32] and five boards for the other side of the tabernacle and five bars for the boards of the rear, toward the west. [33] The middle bar was made to pass half way up the boards, running from end to end. [34] The boards were covered with gold, and rings were made in which the bars were inserted out of gold; the bars were also covered in gold.

The Inner Veil and the Entry Curtain. [35] [m] The veil was made of blue and purple and scarlet cloth and fine twisted linen. Cherubim were made in the cloth, the work of skillful craftsmen. [36] Four columns were made for it out of acacia wood and covered in gold. The hooks were also made of gold and their four bases were made of silver.

[37] A screen was made for the door to the tent out of blue and purple and scarlet cloth and fine twisted linen, covered with embroidery. [38] Five columns were made for the screen with their hooks. The columns and their hooks were covered in gold and their five bases were made out of bronze.

CHAPTER 37

The Ark of the Covenant. [1] [n] Bezalel made the Ark out of acacia wood. It was two cubits and a half long, one and a half cubits wide, and one and a half cubits high. [2] He covered it with pure gold, inside and out, and put a gold molding on it. [3] He cast four golden rings for it and attached them to its four legs, two rings on one side and two rings on the other side. [4] He made poles out of acacia wood and covered them with gold. [5] He put the poles into the rings on the two sides of the Ark so that they might carry the Ark with them.

[6] He made the seat of atonement of pure gold. It was two and a half cubits long and one and a half cubits wide. [7] He made two cherubim out of gold. They were hammered works for the two sides of the seat of atonement, [8] one cherub on one side and one cherub on the other side. He made the cherubim all of one piece at the two ends of the seat of atonement. [9] The cherubim had two wings spreading out, covering the seat of atonement. They were facing one another and the faces of the cherubim were turned toward the seat of atonement.

The Table of the Bread for the Offering. [10] [o] He made a table out of acacia wood. It was two cubits long, one cubit wide, and one and a half cubits high. [11] It was covered in pure gold and had a molding of gold. [12] He made a frame a handswidth wide and placed a molding of gold around it. [13] He made four golden rings and placed them at the four corners that are its four legs. [14] The rings were alongside the borders and held the poles used to carry the table. [15] He made poles out of acacia wood and covered them in gold. [16] He also made the accessories for the table: dishes and plates and flagons and jars to pour out libations. He made them out of pure gold.

The Golden Lampstand. [17] [p] He made a lampstand out of pure gold. It was a hammered work. Its base and its shaft and its bowls and knobs and flowers were all one piece. [18] Six of the branches of the lampstand came out of its sides: three from one side of the lampstand and three from the other side of the lampstand. [19] There were three cups shaped like almond blossoms, with bud and flower, on one branch. And there were three cups shaped like almond blossoms, with bud and flower, on the next branch. Thus, there were six branches that rose out of the lampstand. [20] The shaft of the lampstand had four cups shaped like almond blossoms with bud and flower. [21] One bud was under the first set of two branches coming out of it, and one bud under the second set of two branches coming out of it, and one bud under the third set of

m 35-38: Ex 26:31-37; 2 Chr 3:14.—n 1-9: Ex 25:10-22; 37:28.—o 10-16: Ex 25:23-30; 38:5-7.—p 17-24: Ex 25:31-39; Num 8:4.

two branches coming out of it. Thus, there were six branches coming out of the lampstand. 22 The buds and their respective branches were all of one piece. All of it was one piece of pure gold that had been beaten into shape. 23 He made seven lamps, their snuffers and their trays out of pure gold. 24 The lampstand and all of its accessories required a talent of pure gold.

The Altar of Incense. 25 [q] He made an altar for burning incense out of acacia wood. It was one cubit long and one cubit wide; it was a square. It was two cubits high and its horns were all one piece with it. 26 Its top, its sides, and its horns were covered with pure gold and it had a gold molding around it. 27 He made two golden rings below its molding on its two sides. They were on opposite sides and were used to insert poles with which it could be carried. 28 He made the poles out of acacia wood and covered them with gold. 29 He prepared the sacred oil of anointing and the pure fragrant incense to burn, making use of the skills of the perfumer. [r]

CHAPTER 38

The Altar of Burnt Offering. 1 [s] He made an altar out of acacia wood. It was five cubits long and five cubits wide and three cubits high. 2 It had horns on its four corners and they were all one piece with it. It was covered with bronze. 3 He also made the accessories for the altar: vessels to take away its ashes, shovels, basins, forks, and firepans. All of its utensils were made out of bronze. 4 He made a grating for the altar, a network of bronze. He placed it under the edge of the altar so that the net hung halfway down the altar. 5 He made four rings of bronze and placed them at the four corners of the bronze grating so that poles could be inserted. 6 He made poles out of acacia wood and covered them with bronze. 7 He placed the poles through the rings on the sides of the altar so it could be carried. He made the altar out of boards, hollow in the middle.

The Basin for Washing. 8 He made the basin of bronze and its base of bronze from the mirrors* of the women who ministered at the door to the meeting tent.

The Courtyard. 9 [t] He made the courtyard. On the south side of the courtyard there was a drape of fine twisted linen, one hundred cubits long. 10 There were twenty columns with twenty bronze bases. The hooks of the pillars and their rings were made out of silver. 11 Likewise on the north side there was a drape one hundred cubits long. There were twenty columns with twenty bronze bases. The hooks of the pillars and their rings were made out of silver. 12 On the west side there were fifty cubits of drapes with ten columns and ten bases. The hooks of the pillars and their rings were made out of silver. 13 On the east side there were fifty cubits. 14 There was fifteen cubits of draping with three columns and three bases on one side. 15 On the other side of the entrance to the courtyard, there was fifteen cubits of draping with three columns and three bases. 16 All of the drapes that formed the courtyard were made of fine twisted linen. 17 The bases of the columns were made out of bronze. The hooks of the columns and the rings were made out of silver. The overlaying of their capitals and the columns of the courtyard were filleted with silver.

18 The screen for the entrance to the courtyard was made of needlework of blue, purple, and scarlet cloth and fine twisted linen. It was twenty cubits long and five cubits high, that is, wide, like the drapes of the courtyard. 19 It had four columns with their four bases out of bronze. Their hooks and the overlaying of their capitals and their bars were made out of silver. 20 All the pegs of the tabernacle and of the surrounding courtyard were made out of bronze.

The Materials Used.* 21 These are the expenses for the tabernacle, the dwelling place of the Testimony, that Moses ordered the Levites to calculate under the direction of Ithamar, the son of Aaron the priest. 22 [u] Bezalel, the son of Uri, the son of Hur, of the tribe of Judah, completed what the LORD had commanded Moses to do. 23 He did this together with Oholiab, the son of Ahisamach, of the tribe of Dan, who was an engraver and a skillful craftsman, and a weaver of blue, purple, and scarlet cloth and fine twisted linen.

q 25-28: Ex 25:5; 30:1-5.—r Ex 30:23ff, 34ff.—s 1-7: Ex 27:1-8; 2 Chr 1:5.—t 9-20: Ex 27:9-19; 38:15.—u 22f: Ex 31:2, 6; 35:30, 34; 36:1; 2 Chr 1:5.

38:8 In antiquity *mirrors* were made of polished bronze.

38:21-31 According to the account, a ton of gold and five tons of silver were used; the figures are certainly exaggerated in order to make the point that there is no such thing as too much beauty when it comes to honoring the presence of God in the midst of humanity.

[24] All the gold that was used in the work—
that is, for all the work of the sanctuary,
which was the gold from the offering—was
twenty-nine talents and seven hundred and
thirty shekels, measured by the shekel of the
sanctuary. [25] The silver of the assembly was
measured to be one hundred talents and one
thousand seven hundred and seventy-five
shekels, measured by the shekel of the sanc-
tuary. [v] [26] Every person who was counted in
the census twenty years old and up gave a
bekah, which is worth a half-shekel accord-
ing to the measure of the sanctuary. There
were six hundred and three thousand, five
hundred and fifty men. [w] [27] The one hundred
talents were used to make the bases of the
sanctuary and the bases for the veil. One
hundred talents were used for the one hun-
dred bases, or one talent for each base. [28] The
one thousand seven hundred and seventy-
five shekels were used for the hooks for the
pillars, and for overlaying and filleting their
tops. [29] The bronze presented in the offering
amounted to seventy talents and two thou-
sand four hundred shekels. [30] With it were
made the bases for the entrance to the meet-
ing tent, the altar of bronze with the netting
of bronze, and all the accessories for the
altar, [31] the bases for the courtyard, the bases
for the gate to the courtyard, and all the pegs
of the tabernacle and all the pegs of the sur-
rounding courtyard.

CHAPTER 39

The Priestly Vestments. [1] With the blue, pur-
ple, and scarlet cloth were made the finely
woven vestments for ministering in the sanc-
tuary, as well as the sacred vestments for
Aaron as the LORD had commanded
Moses. [x]

The Ephod. [2] [y] He made the ephod of gold
and blue, purple, and scarlet cloth and fine
twisted linen. [3] The gold was beaten into fine
plates and cut into wires and was interwoven
into the blue, purple, and scarlet cloth and
the linen with skilled craftsmanship. [4] Two
shoulder pieces were made for the ephod
that were attached to its two ends so that it
might be joined together. [5] The skillfully
woven band to bind it together that was
placed over it was of the same workmanship
and the same materials, of gold, blue, purple,
and scarlet cloth and twisted linen, as the
LORD had commanded Moses.

[6] The onyx stones were prepared and set
into settings of gold filigree. They were
engraved with the names of the children of
Israel, like an engraver engraves a signet
ring. [7] The two stones were set on the shoul-
der pieces of the ephod as stones of remem-
brance for the children of Israel, as the LORD
had commanded Moses.

The Breastplate. [8] [z] He made the breastplate
like the ephod, with fine workmanship. It was
made of gold, blue, purple and scarlet cloth
and fine twisted linen. [9] It was square and
doubled over, a span in length and a span in
width. [10] They covered it with settings of pre-
cious stones arranged in four rows. The first
row had a ruby, a topaz, and an emerald.
[11] The second row had a turquoise, a sap-
phire, and a diamond. [12] The third row had a
jacinth, an agate, and an amethyst. [13] The
fourth row had a beryl, an onyx, and a jasper.
They were set in gold filigree settings. [14] The
stones corresponded to the names of the
children of Israel. There were twelve, stand-
ing for their names. They were engraved like
the engraving of a signet ring, each name
corresponding to a name of one of the twelve
tribes.

[15] [a] They made chains of pure gold on the
breastplate in the shape of twisted cords.
[16] They also made two filigree settings of gold
and two golden rings and placed the two
rings at the two edges of the breastplate.
[17] They attached the two golden chains to the
two rings at the edges of the breastplate.
[18] They attached the other ends of the chains
to the two filigree settings and they thus
attached it to the front part of the shoulder
pieces of the ephod. [19] They made two other
golden rings and placed them on the two
edges of the breastplate, on its inside edge,
next to the ephod. [20] They made two other
golden rings and placed them on the two
shoulder pieces of the ephod, at their bottom
on the front side, next to the place where it is
attached to the skillfully woven band of the
ephod.

Other Priestly Vestments. [21] They then tied
the breastplate with its rings to the rings of
the ephod with a cord of blue material so
that it might lie upon the skillfully woven
band of the ephod and that the breastplate
might not pull away from the ephod, as the
LORD had commanded Moses.

---

v Lev 27:25.—w Num 1:46; 26:2.—x Ex 31:10; 35:19.—y 2-10: Ex 28:6-12; 39:21.—z 8-14: Ex 28:4, 15-21.—a 15-21: Ex 25:7; 28:14.

The Robe. 22 He made a robe of the ephod all in blue 23 with an opening in the middle and a woven border around the opening so that it might not be torn. 24 They made a design of pomegranates on the hem of the garment with blue, purple, and scarlet cloth and fine twisted linen. 25 They also made bells out of pure gold and placed the bells in between the pomegranates all around the hem of the robe. 26 There was a bell and a pomegranate, a bell and a pomegranate, around the hem of the robe used for ministering, as the LORD had commanded Moses.

Other Vestments. 27 [b] They also wove tunics from fine linen for Aaron and his sons, 28 a turban of fine linen, caps of fine linen, and undergarments of fine twisted linen, 29 and a sash of fine twisted linen, of blue, purple, and scarlet cloth, embroidered with fine needlework, as the LORD had commanded Moses.

The Turban. 30 [c] They made the plate of the holy crown out of pure gold and they wrote on it as an engraver would engrave a signet ring, "Holy to the LORD." 31 They attached it with a blue cord to the front part of the turban, as the LORD had commanded Moses.

Moses Inspects the Tabernacle. 32 Thus, all of the work of the tabernacle, of the tent of meeting, was finished. The children of Israel had done everything just as the LORD had commanded Moses. 33 They then brought the tabernacle to Moses, the tent and all its accessories, its clasps, boards, bars, columns, and bases, 34 the covering of rams' skins dyed red, the covering of sheep skins, the veil of the screen; 35 the Ark of Testimony with its poles, and the seat of atonement, 36 the table with all its accessories and the bread of the Presence, 37 the lampstand made of pure gold with its lamps, that is, the lamps that were to be placed on top of it, with all its accessories, the oil for light, 38 the altar of gold, the oil of anointing, the fragrant incense; the screen for the entrance to the tent, 39 the altar of bronze with its bronze grating, its poles and all its accessories, the basin and its base, 40 the drapes for the courtyard, their columns, their bases, and the screen for the gate to the courtyard, their cords, their pegs, and all the utensils for ministering in the tabernacle, for the meeting tent; 41 the finely woven vestments for ministering in the sanctuary, the holy vestments for Aaron the priest, and the vestments for his sons in their priestly ministry. 42 Whatever the LORD had commanded Moses, this is how the children of Israel did all their work. 43 Moses examined all the work, and behold, it was done as the LORD had commanded. So Moses blessed them.

CHAPTER 40

God Commands Moses To Consecrate the Tabernacle and the Priests. 1 Then the LORD spoke to Moses and said to him, 2 [d] "On the first day of the first month you shall set up the tabernacle, the meeting tent. 3 [e] Put the Ark of Testimony inside, and in front of the Ark hang the veil. 4 Bring in the table and arrange its accessories. Then bring in the lampstand and put on its lamps. 5 Place the altar of gold for incense before the Ark of Testimony and set up the screen at the entrance to the tent.

6 "Set the altar of burnt offerings in front of the entrance to the tabernacle, the meeting tent. 7 Place the basin between the meeting tent and the altar, and pour water into it. 8 Set up the courtyard all around, and put up the screen for the entrance to the courtyard.

9 [f] "Take the oil of anointing and anoint the tabernacle and everything in it. Consecrate it and all its furnishings, and it will become holy. 10 Also anoint the altar of burnt offerings and all its accessories. Consecrate the altar, and it will become most holy. 11 Also anoint the basin and its base and consecrate them.

12 [g] "Then have Aaron and his sons approach the entrance to the meeting tent and wash them with water. 13 Put the holy vestments on Aaron and anoint him and consecrate him so that he might serve me as a priest. 14 Also have his sons approach and put their tunics on them. 15 Anoint them, like their father, so that they might exercise my priesthood. In this way their anointing will confer upon them an eternal priesthood, for all their generations."

Moses Carries Out the Orders Received from God. 16 Moses did everything as the LORD had commanded him. 17 Thus, in the second year, the first day of the first month, the tabernacle was set up. 18 Moses erected the tabernacle. He laid its bases and set up its boards. He

b 27ff: Ex 28:39-42; 35:35.—c 30f: Ex 28:36f.—d 2-8: Ex 26:18; 40:16-33.—e 3ff: Ex 26:33ff; 40:3.—f 9ff: Ex 30:26-29; Lev 8:30.—g 12-15: Ex 28:41; 29:4-9; Lev 8:1-13.

fixed the bars and raised the columns.
19 He then extended the tent over the
tabernacle and over that he placed the cov-
ering for the tent, just as the LORD had
commanded him.

20 [h] He took the Testimony and placed it
inside the Ark. He attached the poles to the
Ark and put the seat of atonement on the
Ark. 21 He then placed the Ark in the taber-
nacle, setting up the veil as a screen and
hanging it in front of the Testimony, just as
the LORD had commanded Moses.

22 Moses placed the table in the meeting
tent, on the north side of the tabernacle, out-
side the veil. 23 He set up rows of bread upon
it before the LORD, just as the LORD had
commanded him. [i]

24 He set up the lampstand in the meeting
tent, opposite the table, on the south side of
the tabernacle. 25 He placed the lamps on it
before the LORD, just as the LORD had com-
manded him.

26 Moses then placed the golden altar in
the meeting tent, in front of the veil, 27 and
he burned fragrant incense upon it, just as
the LORD had commanded him. 28 He
placed the screen at the entrance to the
tabernacle.

29 He then placed the altar of burnt offer-
ing at the entrance to the tabernacle, the
meeting tent, and he offered burnt offerings
and grain offerings upon it, just as the LORD
had commanded him.

30 [j] He placed the basin between the meet-
ing tent and the altar and he put water in it
for ablutions. 31 Moses, Aaron, and his sons
then washed their hands and their feet with
it. 32 Whenever they entered the meeting tent
and approached the altar, they washed
themselves, as the LORD had commanded
Moses.

33 Finally, Moses erected the courtyard
around the tabernacle and the altar and put
up the screen to the entrance of the court-
yard. Thus Moses finished the work.

The Glory of God Fills the Tabernacle.
34 [k] Then a cloud covered the tent and the
glory of the LORD filled the tabernacle.*
35 Moses could not enter the meeting tent,
for the cloud had settled upon it and the
glory of the LORD filled the tabernacle.

The Guiding Cloud. 36 Throughout their
journeys, whenever the cloud would be
taken up and leave the tabernacle, the
children of Israel would break camp. 37 If
the cloud did not go up, they did not leave
until it had gone up. 38 Throughout their
journeys the cloud of the LORD remained
in the tabernacle during the day, and dur-
ing the night there was a fire in it, visible
to all the households of Israel.

h 20ff: Ex 25:16, 21; 26:33ff; 2 Chr 5:7.—i Ex 25:30; Lev 24:5-6.—j 30ff: Ex 30:18ff.—k 34-38: Ex 24:16; Num 9:15-22.

40:34 The Lord takes possession of the tent in the wilderness as he will later of Solomon's temple (1 Ki 8:10-11).

"Aaron is to place it [the lamp] . . . in the tent of meeting, burning it from evening to morning before the LORD forever" *(Lev 24:3).*

THE BOOK OF LEVITICUS

The Formation of a Holy People

When we finish reading Exodus, we would like to continue on with the story of the journey of the Hebrews through the wilderness after their halt at Sinai. Instead, we come upon a lengthy collection of laws.

Modern critics agree that during the Babylonian Exile some priests (of the tribe of Levi) collected and made part of their final text the liturgical books that had taken shape in the course of time: a ritual for sacrifices, another for the investiture of priests, a set of norms for distinguishing clean from unclean; at some later point, they added the "Law of Holiness" (chs. 17–26). It is this body of material that makes up the Book of Leviticus. The various components are not all from the same period: some prescriptions date from the time of Moses and even earlier; in other instances the editors adapt ancient rites to their own present religious concerns. The Law of Holiness, which probably dates from the last years of the monarchy (end of the seventh century) reflects the viewpoints of the Jerusalem priesthood and stands in contrast to the viewpoints found in Deuteronomy, which was published during the same period.

All the laws systematized in Leviticus are regarded as expressing God's will. They impose on the chosen people a common religious behavior by which this people will show themselves to be the people of the Sinai covenant. The Lord has delivered his own from the land of Egypt and he now expects them to acknowledge his presence and render him the worship due to him.

Sacrifice, which takes numerous forms, is the essential act of worship. It signifies that the children of Israel hand over themselves and their possessions to him who is their supreme protector. It unites them to their God and, by winning his forgiveness, restores this union when sin has broken it. In short, through sacrifice God saves and sanctifies his people. Israel is a priestly people; the priests in their actions symbolize the worship of an entire people.

In addition to moral and liturgical precepts, Leviticus lists various, sometimes quite detailed regulations meant to decide which objects and things hinder a person from drawing near to what is sacred, even though no moral fault might be involved; it was thought that these objects had a baleful power. Like the neighboring peoples, the children of Israel had their prohibitions, but even through these taboos, which were standard in this ancient civilization, they came to know the holiness of God, which is so strongly asserted throughout this book and which came to pervade their entire existence.

In summary, despite the arid lists, the laws that make up Leviticus reveal in their own way that God wills to save the whole person; that nothing in human life is without relevance to holiness; and that holiness is wholly and entirely dependent on God's initiative.

If readers will be patient enough to read all the pages of this book, tedious though these often are (especially due to the incessant repetition of the same formulas; but that was characteristic of Oriental legislation), they will be able to penetrate, by way of formulas and rites long since obsolete, to the heart of Israel's religious consciousness. As Christians, these readers will also be able to better understand the value of the sacrifice through which Jesus Christ saved the human race by giving his life for it.

The Book of Leviticus may be divided as follows:

- *I: A Ritual for Sacrifices (1:1—7:38)*
  - *A: Regulations for the Children of Israel (1:1—6:7)*
  - *B: Regulations for the Priests (6:8—7:38)*
- *II: Consecration of the Priesthood (8:1—10:20)*
- *III: Norms Concerning Ritual Purity (11:1—16:34)*
- *IV: The Law of Holiness (17:1—26:46)*
- *V: Redemptive Offerings (27:1-34)*

I: A RITUAL FOR SACRIFICES*

A: Regulations for the Children of Israel

CHAPTER 1

Burnt Offerings.* 1 The LORD spoke to
Moses from the meeting tent and said to
him,* [a] 2 “Speak to the children of Israel and
tell them: When any one of you brings an
offering to the LORD, you shall bring your
animal from the herd or the flock. 3 If the
offering is a burnt offering from the herd, let
him offer a male without defect. He shall
offer it at the entrance to the meeting tent,
that it might be pleasing to the LORD. [b] 4 He
shall lay his hand on the head of the burnt
offering, and it will be accepted for atone-
ment on his behalf. [c] 5 He shall kill the young
bull before the LORD, and the priests, the
sons of Aaron, shall take its blood and sprin-
kle it on the altar that is at the entrance to the
meeting tent.* 6 He shall skin the burnt offer-
ing and cut it into pieces. 7 The sons of Aaron,
the priests shall set a fire on the altar and

a Num 7:89.—b Lev 12:6; Ex 12:5.—c Lev 3:2, 8, 13; 4:15; 8:14, 22; 16:21; Ex 29:10, 15.

1:1—7:38 Different kinds of sacrifice were offered to the Lord in the Jerusalem temple. In them we find customs inherited from the period when the Hebrews lived a semi-nomadic way of life, as well as rites regularly practiced in Mesopotamia, Egypt, and especially in the land of Canaan. But the Israelite faith was able to purify the practices from all these influences and use them for the glory of the one true God (chs. 1–7).

1:1-17 The burnt offering as the perfect form of homage to God: the victim, which was without blemish, was entirely consumed in fire, that is, removed from the material universe so as to enter the world of God. The owner of the victim offered it, through the mediation of priests, as *a pleasing fragrance to the LORD*, an ancient Eastern expression which the Bible uses to signify that God accepts the victim (Gen 8:21). The pouring of the blood expressed the offering of the life.

1:1 Although these laws were composed long after Moses lived, the direct address form that is used throughout Leviticus implies that the laws embody the essence of what God taught him and wants the children of Israel to know.

1:5 *Meeting tent:* the tabernacle or sacred place where God met with the children of Israel.

arrange the wood upon the fire. [8] Then the sons of Aaron, the priests shall place the pieces of the animal, and its head and its fat, on the burning wood upon the altar. [9] He shall wash the entrails and the legs with water. Then the priest shall burn all of it on the altar as a burnt offering, a pleasing fragrance to the LORD. [d]

[10] "If the burnt offering is from the flock, a sheep or a goat, he shall offer a male without defect. [11] He shall slay it on the northern side of the altar before the LORD. The priests, the sons of Aaron, shall sprinkle its blood around the altar. [12] He shall cut it into pieces, and the priest shall take them, together with its head and its fat, and lay them upon the wood which is burning upon the altar. [13] He shall wash the entrails and the legs with water, and then the priest shall burn all of it on the altar as a burnt offering, a pleasing fragrance to the LORD.

[14] "If the burnt offering to the LORD consists of birds,* then let him bring his offering of turtledoves or young pigeons. [e] [15] The priest shall bring them to the altar and wring off their heads. He shall burn them upon the altar, but their blood is to be drained out on the side of the altar. [f] [16] He shall tear out their crops with their feathers and toss them to the east side of the altar, the place where the ashes are kept. [17] He shall split the birds into two halves holding on to their wings, but he shall not separate the pieces. Then the priest shall burn them on the burning wood upon the altar. It is a burnt offering, a pleasing fragrance to the LORD.

CHAPTER 2

Grain Offerings.* [1] "When anyone brings a grain offering as a sacrifice to the LORD, it is to be an offering of fine flour. He shall pour oil upon it and put incense on it [2] and bring it to the sons of Aaron, the priests. He shall take a handful of the flour and the oil and all of the incense. The priest shall burn it on the altar as a memorial portion, a burnt offering, a pleasing fragrance to the LORD.* [g] [3] The rest of the grain offering will be for Aaron and his sons, the most holy part* of the burnt offering to the LORD. [h]

[4] "When someone brings a cereal offering that has been baked in the oven, it is to be unleavened cakes made of fine flour mixed with oil or unleavened wafers sprinkled with oil. [5] If your cereal offering was prepared on the griddle, it is to be made of fine flour that has been mixed with oil. [i] [6] You shall break it into pieces and pour oil on it. It is a cereal offering. [7] If the cereal offering was prepared in a pan, it is to be made of fine flour with oil. [8] You shall bring your cereal offering made of these things to the priest who will bring it to the altar. [9] Then the priest shall take the memorial portion from the cereal offering and burn it on the altar. It will be a burnt offering, a pleasing fragrance to the LORD. [10] The rest of the cereal offering will be for Aaron and his sons. It is the most holy part of the burnt offering to the LORD.

[11] "None of the cereal offerings that you offer to the LORD will be leavened, for you are not to make burnt offerings of leaven or honey* to the LORD. [j] [12] As to the offering of firstfruits, you may bring them to the LORD, but you are not to bring them to the altar as a pleasing fragrance. [13] You are to season all of your cereal offerings with salt. You shall not permit your cereal offerings to be offered without the salt of your covenant.* You shall bring salt with all of your offerings. [k]

[14] "If you offer a cereal offering of firstfruits to the LORD, you shall offer the cereal offering of firstfruits in the form of crushed grain from newly ripened heads of grain that have been parched with fire. [15] You shall pour oil on it, and place incense upon it. It is a cereal offering. [16] Then the priest shall burn a part of the grain and of the oil and all of the incense as the memorial portion of the offering. It is a burnt offering to the LORD.

d Lev 3:5, 14-16; Ex 29:18.—e Lev 5:7; 12:8; 15:14; Lk 2:24.—f Lev 5:8; 9:12.—g Lev 6:15.—h Ex 29:24; Sir 7:31; 1 Cor 9:13.—i Num 15:9; 1 Chr 23:29.—j Lev 6:16f; 22:22; Ex 29:25; 34:25; 1 Cor 5:7; Gal 5:9.—k Num 18:19; Ezek 43:24.

1:14 *Birds:* for those who could not afford more costly sacrifices, doves or pigeons would suffice.

2:1-16 This chapter deals with the offering no longer of animals but of food; in addition, one section is addressed to priests. No yeast was allowed because it would corrupt the food.

2:2 The memorial portion was the part more suited to emitting a pleasing fragrance as it was burned; the ascent of the aroma was meant to make God mindful of the offerer.

2:3 *Most holy part:* this was the part of the people's offering reserved for the priests who were not to share it with family members and only eat it in the sanctuary.

2:11 *Honey:* not to be used in sacrifice, as was anything leavened, because it fermented quickly and was used in cultic practice.

2:13 *Salt of your covenant:* salt was required to be sprinkled by the priests on the offerings of the people, and was also used in making the incense for the sanctuary. Giving salt or consuming salt with others is a symbol of friendship, hence, the association with a covenant.

CHAPTER 3

Peace Offerings.* 1 "If the offering is a peace offering, if someone offers a young cow, whether it be male or female, it is to be without defect. He shall offer it to the LORD. [l] 2 He shall lay his hand on the head of the offering and slay it at the entrance to the meeting tent. The sons of Aaron, the priests, shall sprinkle its blood around the altar. [m] 3 From the peace offering he shall offer up the following as a burnt offering to the LORD: the fat above and surrounding the entrails, [n] 4 the two kidneys and their fat, the fat around the loins, and the lobe of the liver that he will detach along with the kidneys. 5 The sons of Aaron shall burn it on the altar, on the burnt offering* that is on the burning wood. It is a burnt offering, a pleasing fragrance to the LORD. [o]

6 "If one's peace offering to the LORD is from the flock, whether it be male or female, it is to be without defect. 7 If he presents a lamb as an offering, he shall offer it before the LORD. 8 He shall lay his hand on the head of the victim and slay it in front of the meeting tent. The sons of Aaron shall sprinkle its blood around the altar. 9 From the peace offering he shall offer up the following as a burnt offering to the LORD: the fat, the entire fat of the tail, cutting it away from the end of the backbone, the fat around the entrails and all that is above them, 10 the two kidneys with their fat and the fat around the loins, and the lobe of the liver that he will detach along with the kidneys. 11 Then the priest shall burn them on the altar as food offered up to the LORD by fire.

12 "If his offering is a goat, he shall offer it before the LORD. 13 He shall lay his hand on its head and slay it in front of the meeting tent. The sons of Aaron will sprinkle its blood around the altar. 14 From it he will offer up the following as a burnt offering to the LORD: the fat covering and above its entrails, 15 its two kidneys with their fat, the fat around the loins, and the lobe of the liver that he will detach along with the kidneys. 16 Then the priest shall burn them on the altar as food offered to the LORD by fire. All fat belongs to the LORD.

17 "It will be a perpetual statute throughout all your generations in all of your dwellings: you must not eat fat or blood." [p]

CHAPTER 4*

Sin Offerings.* 1 The LORD said to Moses, 2 "Speak to the children of Israel and say: If anyone unknowingly sins against one of the commandments of the LORD, doing one of the things he was not supposed to do, [q]

For an Anointed Priest. 3 "if it be an anointed priest who has sinned, thus bringing guilt upon the people, let him offer up a young bull without defect as a sin offering to the LORD. 4 He shall bring the young bull before the LORD at the entrance to the meeting tent, and will lay his hand on the head of the young bull and slay it before the LORD. 5 The priest who has been anointed shall take the blood of the young bull and carry it into the meeting tent. 6 He will dip his finger into the blood and sprinkle some of the blood seven times before the LORD in front of the sanctuary veil. 7 The priest shall put some of the blood on the horns of the altar of incense which is before the LORD in the meeting tent. He shall pour out the rest of the blood at the base of the altar of burnt offerings which is at the entrance to the meeting tent. [r] 8 He shall take all of the fat that is around the entrails and all the fat that is above, 9 the two kidneys and their fat, the fat around the loins, and the

l Lev 7:29; 22:21.—m Lev 1:4; Ex 29:10.—n Lev 4:8; Ex 29:13, 22.—o Lev 2:2; 6:8.—p Lev 7:26; 17:10-14; Gen 9:4; Deut 12:16, 23; 15:23.—q Lev 4:27; 5:15, 17; Num 15:22-29.—r Lev 8:15; 9:9; 16:18; Ex 29:12; Num 19:4.

3:1-17 The fat and the blood, which were connected with the mystery of life, were reserved for the Lord, the absolute master of life itself; the better morsels were reserved for the priests, and the remainder was taken by the offerer to be eaten by his family. By means of this sacred meal, the believer entered into a communion with the divinity; the sacrifice was therefore called a *peace offering*. It could be offered either in thanksgiving or in petition. This kind of sacrifice was celebrated on every sacred solemnity.

3:5 *On the burnt offering:* the daily presentation of peace offerings was ritually prescribed to be placed on top of the burnt offerings signifying fellowship with God and the priest.

4:1-35 Anyone who sinned unintentionally became unclean. To atone for the defect a sacrifice was offered; this rule held for everyone, but the offering varied according to the character of the guilty party. A sin of the high priest, who was leader of the people of God, especially after the Exile, rested on the entire community; consequently, the expiation for it was celebrated in a solemn fashion. The blood rite, the expiatory value of which will be seen further on (ch. 17), was the central point of the sacrifice; for the sins of the high priest as well as for the sins of the community, the blood was poured out inside the sanctuary. What remained of the victim was consumed by fire outside the encampment; the priests, being themselves sinners, had no right to eat of this sacred offering, since the sacrifice was for the entire community (v. 12). This type of sacrifice makes clear the ritual aspect of the fault, that is, it reflects a more primitive and less interior concept of sin.

4:1-2 Whereas burnt offerings, cereal offerings, and peace offerings were voluntary acts of worship, atonement for sins committed unintentionally was mandatory and usually involved faults concerning worship. As soon as one became aware of such a fault, one was required to bring a sin offering to the Lord. For those who were unaware of a fault, an annual Day of Atonement provided reconciliation for sins that had not been atoned for.

lobe of the liver that he will detach along with the kidneys. 10 He shall do just as he does with the ox of the sacrifice of a peace offering. He shall burn it all upon the altar of burnt offerings. 11 But as to the skin of the young bull, the meat with its head, the entrails, the legs and the dung, 12 that is, the young bull, he shall carry it outside of the camp to a pure place,* where they throw the ashes. He shall burn it upon a wood fire, in the place where they throw the ashes.

For the Whole Assembly. 13 "If the whole assembly of Israel unknowingly commits a sin, for the thing was not clear to them, and they do one of the things that they were commanded by the LORD not to do and they incur guilt,[s] 14 when they realize their sin, the assembly shall offer as a sin offering a young bull and bring it in front of the meeting tent. 15 The elders of the community shall lay their hands on the head of the young bull and they shall slay it before the LORD. 16 The priest who has been anointed shall take the blood of the young bull inside of the tent of meeting. 17 The priest shall dip his finger in the blood and sprinkle the blood seven times before the LORD in front of the veil. 18 He shall put some of the blood on the horns of the altar of incense which is before the LORD in the meeting tent. He will pour the rest of the blood at the base of the altar of burnt offerings which is at the entrance to the meeting tent. 19 He shall take all of its fat and burn it on the altar. 20 He shall perform the same ceremony with this young bull as with the offering of a sin offering: all done the same way. The priest shall make atonement for them, and they will be forgiven.* 21 Then he shall carry the young bull outside the camp and burn it as he burned the first young bull. It is a sin offering for the assembly.

For a Leader. 22 "When a leader has sinned, unknowingly doing any one of the things that the LORD God has commanded not to do, and he is guilty, 23 when he comes to know of the sin that he has committed, he shall bring as an offering a kid he-goat without defect. 24 He shall lay his hand on the head of the goat and slay it in the place where they slay burnt offerings before the LORD. It is a sin offering. 25 The priest shall take the blood of the sin offering with his finger and he shall put it on the horns of the altar of burnt offerings. He shall pour the rest of the blood at the base of the altar of burnt offerings. 26 He shall then burn every fat part on the altar like the fat of a peace offering. The priest shall make atonement for his sin and he shall be forgiven.[t]

For the Common People. 27 "If any of the common people has unknowingly sinned, doing any one of the things that the LORD has commanded them not to do, and he is guilty,[u] 28 when he comes to know of the sin that he has committed, he shall bring a she-goat as an offering, without defect, for the sin that he has committed. 29 He shall lay his hand on the head of the sin offering and slay it in the place of burnt offerings. 30 The priest shall take a bit of its blood with his finger and place it on the horns of the altar of burnt offerings. He shall then pour out the rest of the blood at the base of the altar. 31 He shall take out all of the fat parts, as one takes out all of the fat parts of a peace offering, and the priest shall burn them on the altar, a pleasing fragrance in honor of the LORD. The priest will make atonement for him and he shall be forgiven. 32 If he brings a lamb as a sin offering, he is to bring a female without defect. 33 He shall lay his hand on the head of the sin offering and he shall slay it in the place of burnt offerings. 34 The priest shall take a bit of the blood of the sin offering with his finger and he shall place it on the horns of the altar of burnt offerings. He shall then pour out the rest of the blood at the base of the altar. 35 He shall take out all of the fat parts, as one takes out the fat parts of a lamb in a peace offering, and he shall burn them on the altar upon the burnt offerings in honor of the LORD. The priest shall make atonement for him and the sin that he committed and he shall be forgiven.

CHAPTER 5

Other Ways to Atone. 1 "If anyone sins in that he heard a call to testify and he is a witness, having seen or heard of the matter, and he does not make it known, then he shall bear his guilt.[v] 2 Or if anyone touches any unclean thing, whether it be the carcass of an unclean animal or the carcass of unclean cattle or the carcass of any unclean creeping thing, even if

s Lev 4:22; Num 15:24-26.—t Lev 4:31; 6:7.—u Lev 5:17; Num 15:27.—v Prov 29:24.

4:12 *Pure place:* this was a place that was considered to be ritually clean and was not concerned with dirt or physical cleanliness.

4:20 *Will be forgiven:* this phrase, emphasizing God's forgiveness, is repeated numerous times in this section and reinforces the repeated assurance of God's mercy needed by all God's children throughout the ages.

he did not know it, he shall be unclean and be held guilty.[w] 3 Or if he touches human uncleanness,* of whatever type of uncleanness one might touch and become unclean, and he did not know it, when he comes to know of it he shall be guilty. 4 Or if someone rashly lets an oath slip from his lips, to do evil or to do good, in anything by which a person who swears a rash oath, and he does not realize it, when he comes to know it, he shall be guilty for any one of these things.[x] 5 Therefore, when someone is guilty of any one of these things, he shall confess the sin he has committed. 6 He shall bring a guilt offering to the LORD for the sin that he has committed: a female goat or sheep from the flock as a sin offering. The priest shall make atonement for him and for his sin.

7 "If someone cannot afford a lamb, then he shall bring as his guilt offering to the LORD two turtledoves or two pigeons for the sin that he has committed. One will be for a sin offering and the other will be a burnt offering.[y] 8 He shall bring them to the priest who shall offer the first for the sin offering. He will wring its head from its neck, but he will not rip it apart. 9 He shall sprinkle some of the blood of the sin offering on the sides of the altar, while the rest he shall pour out at the base of the altar. This is a sin offering. 10 The other bird will be offered as a burnt offering, following the normal procedure. Thus the priest shall make atonement for him, for the sin he has committed, and he shall be forgiven.

11 "But if he cannot afford two turtledoves or two young pigeons, let him bring a tenth of an ephah* of fine flour for his sin offering, as the offering for the sin he has committed. He shall not put any oil or incense upon it, for it is a sin offering. 12 He shall bring the flour to the priest who will take a handful of it as a memorial portion, burning it upon the altar, on the burnt offerings to the LORD. It is a sin offering. 13 Thus the priest shall make atonement for the sin he has committed in any one of these things and he shall be forgiven. The rest of the offering will be for the priest, as with the cereal offering."[z]

Guilt Offerings.* 14 And the LORD said to Moses, 15 "If anyone commits a trespass against God and unknowingly sins against any of the holy things of the LORD, then he shall bring his guilt offering to the LORD. He shall bring a ram from the flock, without defect, for a guilt offering. It is to be worth a certain number of shekels of silver according to the measure of the shekel of the sanctuary. 16 He shall make amends for having sinned against the holy thing, and he shall add a fifth to its value and give it to the priest. The priest shall make atonement for him with the ram of the guilt offering, and he will be forgiven. 17 When someone sins and does any of the things that the LORD has forbidden, even if he does not realize he did it, he has still committed an offense and must bear his guilt.[a] 18 He shall bring a ram without defect from the flock that is the value of the price of a guilt offering. The priest shall make atonement for the sin which he unknowingly committed and he shall be forgiven. 19 It is a guilt offering, for he was certainly guilty before the LORD."

CHAPTER 6

Daily Sacrifices.* 1 The LORD said to Moses, 2 "If anyone sins against the LORD by lying to a neighbor concerning a deposit or a security entrusted to him, or by robbery, or by defrauding a neighbor,[b] 3 or by finding something that was lost and lying about it and swearing a false oath, in any of these things that men do, and thereby sin, 4 when someone sins this way and has become guilty, he shall restore the stolen property that he took, or what he obtained through violence, or the deposit that was entrusted to him, or the lost object that he found, 5 or anything about which he falsely swore an oath. He shall add a fifth to it and give it to the person to whom it belongs on the day of his guilt offering. 6 He shall bring a guilt

w Lev 5:17; 11:24, 31, 39; 15:1-33.—x Jdg 11:30f; 1 Sam 14:24; Mk 6:23; Acts 23:12.—y Lev 12:8; Lk 2:24.—z Lev 4:26, 35; 7:5.—a Lev 4:2; 1 Jn 3:4.—b Lev 6:2; Ex 22:7.

5:3 *Human uncleanness:* a large part of Israelite ritual is based on the notions of pure and impure that affected the fitness of the person to enter the sanctuary for worship.

They are cultic rather than ethical determinations. In the New Testament, Jesus' interpretation of cleanliness went beyond the rigidity imposed by the Pharisees on exterior performance to address the person's interior disposition.

5:11 An *ephah* is a dry measure equal to approximately half a bushel.

5:14-19 This section along with the priestly regulations detailed in chapter 7 concern the *guilt offering.* Although sometimes used interchangeably with "sin offering," guilt offerings applied in those instances where restitution was required to be made.

6:1-7 Sacrifices were offered twice a day in the Jerusalem temple, at sunrise and sunset. It was a duty of the priests to keep the fire going constantly, signifying that worship should never cease.

offering to the priest, a ram without defect
from the flock which is the value of the price
of a guilt offering. 7 The priest shall make
atonement for him before the LORD and he
shall be forgiven of any of the things a person
may do and thereby become guilty."

B: Regulations for the Priests

Instructions for Burnt Offerings. 8 The LORD
said to Moses, 9 "Command Aaron and his
sons, saying: This is the law for burnt offer-
ings. The burnt offering is to remain on the
hearth of the altar all night, until the morn-
ing. The fire on the altar will be kept burning.
10 The priest shall wear his linen garment
and have his linen undergarments over his
flesh. He shall collect the ashes to which the
fire has reduced the burnt offering on the
altar and he will place them beside the altar.
11 Then he will take off those clothes and put
on others and carry the ashes outside the
camp to a clean place. 12 The fire on the altar
will be kept burning; it will not be extin-
guished. The priest shall burn wood on it
every morning, and he shall lay burnt offer-
ings on it and burn the fat of the peace offer-
ings upon it. 13 The fire must always be kept
burning on the altar. It must never go out.

For Cereal Offerings. 14 "This is the law con-
cerning cereal offerings. The sons of Aaron
shall offer them to the LORD in front of the
altar. 15 The priest will take a handful of fine
flour from it with the oil and all of the incense
that is on the offering, and he shall burn all of
it on the altar as a memorial portion, a pleas-
ing fragrance to the LORD. 16 Aaron and his
sons will eat whatever is left over from the
cereal offering. They will eat it unleavened, in
a holy place, in the courtyard of the meeting
tent. 17 It must not be baked with leaven. I
have assigned it to them as their portion of
my offerings by fire. It is a most holy thing,
like the sin offerings and the guilt offerings.
18 Every male from among the children of
Aaron may eat it. This will be a perpetual
statute for all of your generations concerning
the LORD's offerings by fire. Whoever touches
them shall be holy."* [c]

19 The LORD said to Moses, 20 "Aaron and
his sons are to make the following offerings
to the LORD on the day that they are anoint-
ed: a tenth of an ephah of fine flour as a reg-
ular cereal offering, half in the morning and
half in the evening. [d] 21 It will be prepared in
a pan with oil. You will bring it well mixed, in
baked pieces, like a cereal offering. It shall be
a pleasing fragrance to the LORD. [e] 22 That
priest from among the sons of Aaron who is
anointed to succeed him shall also make this
offering. It is a perpetual statute. It shall all
be burned in honor of the LORD. 23 Every
cereal offering made by a priest shall be
burned. It cannot be eaten." [f]

For Sin Offerings. 24 The LORD said to
Moses, 25 "Speak to Aaron and his sons and
tell them the following: 'This is the law for sin
offerings. The animal being offered for the sin
offering shall be slain in the place where
burnt offerings are slain, before the LORD. It
is most holy. 26 The priest who offered it as a
sin offering shall eat it in a holy place, in the
courtyard of the meeting tent.* 27 Whatever
touches the meat shall be holy. If some of the
blood is spattered on some clothing, the
clothing on which it is spattered shall be
washed in a holy place. 28 The earthen vessel
in which it is boiled is to be broken. If it has
been cooked in a bronze vessel, that will be
scoured and rinsed in water. 29 Every male of
the priestly family may eat it; it is a most holy
thing. 30 But no sin offering will be eaten
when its blood was brought into the meeting
tent to make atonement in the sanctuary. It
will be entirely burned in fire.

CHAPTER 7

For Guilt Offerings. 1 " 'This is the law for
guilt offerings. It is most holy. [g] 2 The guilt
offering will be slain where the burnt offer-
ings are slain. He is to sprinkle its blood
around the altar. [h] 3 [i] He shall offer all of its
fat: its fat tail, the fat that covers its entrails,
4 the two kidneys with their fat, the fat
around the loins, and the lobe of the liver that
he will detach along with the kidneys. 5 The
priest shall burn all of this on the altar as a
burnt offering to the LORD. It is a guilt offer-
ing. 6 All of the males of the priestly family
may eat it. They shall eat it in a holy place. It
is most holy. 7 The guilt offering is like the sin
offering. The same law applies for both. It
belongs to the priest who makes atonement
with it. 8 The priest shall also have the skin of
any burnt offering he makes for anyone.

---

c Lev 6:29; Num 18:10.—d Lev 5:11.—e Lev 2:5; 7:12.—f Lev 6:23.—g Lev 5:7, 15.—h Lev 1:11; 5:16.—i 3-5: Lev 3:4, 15; 7:5; Ex 29:13.

6:18 Whatever is offered to God is transformed and becomes holy. This applies to persons, places, and material things.

6:26 The sacrifice is only effective if the priest eats the meat that has been made holy through the sacrifice.

9 Every cereal offering baked in an oven, or prepared on a pan or a grill, shall belong to the priest who has offered it.[j] 10 Every cereal offering that is mixed with oil or is dry shall belong to all of the sons of Aaron, to all alike.[k]

For Peace Offerings. 11 * " 'This is the law for peace offerings that he shall offer unto the LORD. 12 If he is offering it as a sacrifice of thanksgiving, he shall offer unleavened cakes mixed with oil, and unleavened wafers with oil sprinkled on them, and fried cakes of fine flour mixed with oil together with his thanksgiving offering. 13 Besides these he shall also offer leavened bread with the sacrifice of thanksgiving of his peace offerings. 14 From them he shall offer one cake as a wave offering to the LORD. It will belong to the priest who sprinkled the blood of the peace offering. 15 [l] The meat from the thanksgiving sacrifice must be eaten on the same day that it was offered. Nothing is be left over until the morning. 16 But if the offering is a vow offering or a freewill offering, it is be eaten on the day that it was offered, and the leftovers must be eaten the next day. 17 Whatever is still left over until the third day must be burned in the fire. 18 If someone eats the meat of a peace offering on the third day, the offering shall not be pleasing. It shall be of no benefit to the person who offered it. It shall be an abomination, and whoever eats of it shall bear the guilt of his iniquity. 19 Any meat that has come into contact with something unclean is not to be eaten. It is to be burned in the fire. All who are clean may eat the meat of a peace offering, 20 but the person who is unclean and who eats the meat of the peace offering to the LORD is to be cut off * from his people. 21 If anyone touches anything unclean, whether it be the uncleanness of a person or an unclean animal or any abominable, unclean thing and that person then eats the meat of the sacrifice of the peace offering, he shall be cut off from his people.' "

Things Forbidden. 22 The LORD spoke again to Moses saying, 23 "Speak to the children of Israel and tell them: do not eat the fat of an ox or a sheep or a goat.[m] 24 The fat of an animal that dies a natural death or an animal that has been torn apart by a wild animal can be used for any function, only it is not to be eaten.[n] 25 Whoever eats the fat of an animal that has been offered to the LORD in fire will be cut off from his people. 26 You are not to eat blood in any of your dwellings, whether it be blood from a bird or from any other animal. 27 Whoever eats any animal's blood shall be cut off from his people."

Portions for the Priests. 28 And the LORD spoke to Moses saying, 29 "Speak to the children of Israel and tell them, 'Whoever offers the sacrifice of a peace offering to the LORD shall bring the offering of the sacrifice of the peace offering. 30 * He shall bring the offering to be made by fire to the LORD in his own hands. He shall bring the fat together with the breast, the breast that shall be waved before the LORD as a wave offering. 31 The priest shall burn the fat upon the altar, but the breast will be for Aaron and his sons.[o] 32 He will also give the right shoulder of the sacrifice of his peace offering as a wave offering to the priest. 33 The son of Aaron who offers the blood and the fat of the peace offering will receive the right shoulder as his portion. 34 I have taken the breast of the wave offering and the right shoulder that is offered from the sacrifices of the peace offerings of the children of Israel, and I have given them to Aaron the priest and his sons. This is an eternal statute for the children of Israel.[p]

35 " 'This is the portion consecrated to Aaron and the portion consecrated to his sons from the offerings made by fire to the LORD. They will receive them on the day that they present them ministering unto the LORD. 36 On the day that he anointed them, the LORD commanded that the children of Israel give this to them. It is a statute from one generation to the next.' " 37 These are the statutes concerning the burnt offerings, the grain offerings, the sin offerings, the guilt offerings and the consecration of the sacrifice of the peace offerings. 38 The LORD gave these commands to Moses on Mount Sinai on the day that he commanded the children of Israel to offer their oblations to the LORD when they were in the Desert of Sin.

---

j Lev 2:3-10; Num 6:20; 18:9; Ezek 44:29.—k Lev 2:14f.—l 15-18: Lev 7:16; 19:6f.—m Lev 3:17.—n Lev 22:8; Ex 22:31.—o Ex 29:26.—p Lev 10:14-16; Ex 29:27f; Jos 11:19.

7:11-36 This section gives additional regulations for peace offerings that was begun in chapter 3, specifically regarding the thanksgiving sacrifice for deliverance from illnesses, death, and other serious problems (see Pss 27:6; 50:14; 107:22; 116:17).

7:20 *Cut off:* the offender is banished from the community of God and in some cases executed (see Lev 18:29).

7:30-32 *Wave offering:* the breast and right shoulder of the peace offering were held aloft as a special presentation to the Lord (see Ex 29:26f; Num 6:20).

II: CONSECRATION OF THE PRIESTHOOD*

CHAPTER 8*

Priestly Consecration. 1 [q]The LORD spoke to
Moses saying, 2 "Bring Aaron and his sons
together with their garments,* the oil of
anointing, a young bull for a sin offering, two
rams, and a basket of unleavened bread 3 and
gather the whole assembly together at the
entrance to the tent of meeting." 4 Moses did
as the LORD had commanded and the com-
munity was gathered together at the
entrance to the tent of meeting. 5 Moses said
to the community, "This is what the LORD
has commanded."

6 Moses had Aaron and his sons draw near
and he washed them with water. 7 [r]Then he
put his coat on him and bound him with his
sash. He put the ephod on him and bound
him in the skillfully woven band of the ephod,
wrapping it around him. 8 He put his breast-
plate on him, and in the breastplate he
placed the Urim and the Thummim. 9 Then
he placed the turban on his head, and on the
front of the turban he placed the golden
plate, the holy crown, as the LORD had com-
manded Moses.

10 Then Moses then took the oil of anoin-
ting, and he anointed and consecrated the
tabernacle and everything that was in it. [s]
11 He sprinkled some of it upon the altar
seven times, anointing the altar and all of its
accessories, as well as the basin and its base,
to consecrate them. 12 He poured the oil of
anointing on the head of Aaron and anointed
Aaron, consecrating him. [t] 13 Then Moses
had the sons of Aaron draw near and he
clothed them in their tunics. He bound them
with their sashes and put their caps on their
heads, as the LORD had commanded Moses.

The Sin Offering. 14 He then had the
young bull of the sin offering brought to
him, and he had Aaron and his sons place
their hands on the head of the young bull
of the sin offering. 15 Moses slew it, took
some of its blood, and with his finger put
some of it on the horns around the altar to
purify it. He poured the rest of the blood at
the base of the altar and consecrated it,
making atonement for it. [u]

16 [v]He took all of the fat that was around
the entrails, the lobe of the liver, the two kid-
neys with their fat, and Moses burned all of
them upon the altar. 17 But the young bull, its
skin, its meat, and its manure were burned in
a fire outside of the camp, as the LORD had
commanded Moses.

The Burnt Offering. 18 He brought the ram
for the burnt offering and he had Aaron and
his sons place their hands on the head of the
ram. 19 Moses slew it and sprinkled its blood
around the altar. 20 He cut the ram into
pieces and he burned the head, its pieces,
and the fat. 21 After he had washed its entrails
and its legs with water, he burned the entire
ram upon the altar, a burnt offering making
a pleasant fragrance, a sacrifice by fire in
honor of the LORD, as the LORD had com-
manded Moses.

The Ram of Consecration. 22 Then he
brought the second ram, the ram of conse-
cration. Aaron and his sons placed their
hands on the head of the ram. 23 Moses slew
it and took its blood and placed it on the right
ear lobe of Aaron and the thumb of his right
hand and the big toe of his right foot.* [w]
24 Moses had the sons of Aaron approach
him and he put some of the blood on their
right ear lobes, on the thumbs of their right
hands, and on the big toes of their right feet.
He poured the rest of the blood around the
altar. 25 He took the fat, the tail, the fat
around its entrails, the lobe of the liver, the
kidneys with their fat, and the right thigh.
26 He took an unleavened bread, a cake of
bread with oil, and a wafer from the basket of
unleavened bread that was before the LORD.
He placed them on the fat and the right
thigh. 27 He placed all of these things in the
hands of Aaron and in the hands of his sons

q 1-36: Ex 29:1-46.—r 7ff: Ex 29:5; Sir 45:8-13.—s Ex 30:26; 40:9.—t Ex 40:13; Sir 45:15.—u Lev 4:7; 16:18; Heb 9:22.—v 16f: Lev 3:4; 4:8-11; 9:10.—w Lev 14:14; Ex 29:20.

8:1—10:20 It was thought that the liturgy of the temple faithfully reproduced the forms of worship celebrated in the wilderness in the tent of meeting. That is why the prescriptions of this ritual (chs. 8–10) were directly linked to the origin of Israelite worship at the foot of Sinai. These prescriptions highlight the importance of the priesthood, of which the people became conscious through the offering of sacrifices, and also the authority exercised by the Aaronic priesthood.

8:1-36 The candidates, who had been chosen by the Lord, were vested in their sacred robes and anointed with oil. Then three different sacrifices were offered: a sacrifice for sin, a burnt offering, an investiture sacrifice. This last rite was a real priestly consecration of Aaron and his sons for the carrying out of their ministry, although this consecration did not confer any supernatural power, as it does in the priesthood of Christ.

8:2 *Their garments:* a detailed description of the priest's clothing is given, including the ephod—an apron-like garment of fine linen and gold thread—worn by Aaron, the high priest. Simpler garments were worn by other priests.

8:23 In consecrating Aaron, Moses places some of the blood on his extremities to indicate his total consecration to God.

and they waved this wave offering before the
LORD. 28 Moses took them out of their hands
and burned them on the altar upon the
burnt offerings. This is the sacrifice of conse-
cration, a pleasant fragrance, a sacrifice
consumed by fire in honor of the LORD.
29 Then Moses took the breast of the ram
and waved it as a wave offering before the
LORD. It was Moses' portion of the ram of
consecration, as the LORD had commanded
Moses.

30 Moses took the oil of anointing and
some of the blood that was on the altar and
he sprinkled them upon Aaron and his
clothes, and upon his sons and their clothes.
Thus he consecrated Aaron and his clothes
and his sons and their clothes. 31 Moses said
to Aaron and his sons, "Cook the meat at
the entrance to the meeting tent and eat it
with the bread that is in the basket of con-
secration, as I commanded saying, 'Aaron
and his sons will eat it.' 32 Whatever is left
over from the meat and the bread is to be
burned in a fire. 33 * You are not to go out
from the entrance of the tent of meeting for
seven days, until the days of your consecra-
tion are complete, for it will take seven days
to consecrate you. 34 What was done today
was what the LORD commanded so that an
atonement might be made for you. 35 You
shall remain for seven days at the entrance
to the tent of meeting, day and night,
observing the commandment of the LORD,
lest you die, for thus I was commanded."
36 Aaron and his sons did what the LORD
had commanded through Moses.

CHAPTER 9*

The Priests' Offering. 1 The eighth day*
Moses summoned Aaron, his sons, and the
elders of Israel 2 and said to Aaron, "Take a
young male calf for a sin offering and a ram
for a burnt offering. Both are to be without
defect. Offer them to the LORD. 3 Say to the
children of Israel, 'Bring a kid goat as a sin
offering, a calf and a lamb, both one-year-
old, without defect, for a burnt offering, 4 a
bull and a ram for a peace offering, to burn
them before the LORD, and a cereal offering
mixed with oil, for today the LORD shall
appear to you.' "

5 They brought them to the meeting tent as
Moses had commanded. The whole commu-
nity approached and stood before the LORD.
6 * Moses said, "Behold, this is what the LORD
has commanded. Do it, and the glory of the
LORD shall appear."

7 Moses said to Aaron, "Come to the altar.
Offer your sin offering and your burnt offer-
ing and make atonement for yourself and for
your people. Present the people's offering
and make atonement for them, as the LORD
has commanded." [x]

8 Aaron therefore drew near the altar and
slew the calf of the sin offering, the offering
for himself. 9 His sons brought the blood to
him and he dipped his finger in it and put it
on the horns of the altar, pouring the rest of
the blood out at the base of the altar. 10 They
burned the fat, the kidneys, and the lobe
of the liver of the sin offering on the altar, as
the LORD had commanded Moses. 11 They
burned the meat and the skin on a fire out-
side of the camp. 12 They then slew the burnt
offering. The sons of Aaron brought the blood
to him and he sprinkled it around the altar.
13 They also brought the burnt offering to
him. It was cut into pieces. He burned the
pieces and the head upon the altar. 14 He
washed the entrails and the legs and burned
them upon the burnt offering on top of the
altar.

The People's Offering. 15 They then present-
ed the offering of the people. They brought
the goat of the sin offering for the people.
They slew it and offered it as a sin offering, as
they had done with the first one. 16 After this
they offered the second burnt offering
according to custom.

17 They then presented the cereal offering.
They took a handful and burned it upon the
altar beside the morning burnt offering.
18 They slew the bull and the ram of the peace
offering of the people. The sons of Aaron
brought the blood and they poured it around
the altar. 19 [y] They brought the fat parts of the
bull and the ram: the tail, the fat around the
entrails, the kidneys, and the lobe of the liver.
20 They placed the fat upon the breasts. He

x Lev 16:3-5.—y 19f: Lev 3:3ff; 8:16.

8:33-35 Strict rules regulated the consecration of the priests, who are not to leave the sanctuary for seven days under penalty of death. This follows the rites described in Ex 29:30, 35-37.

9:1-24 According to Leviticus, the essential role of priests was the conduct of worship; they offered sacrifices in order that the glory of God might be manifested, that is, in order that the Lord might make his presence known among his people, now purified of their sins. Only in passing is it said, a little further on (chs. 10–11), that the priests also had to teach the law.

9:1 *Eighth day:* this completes the time for full consecration of the priests.

9:6-21 It is now Aaron and his sons who will perform the ritual sacrifices for the people instead of Moses.

burned them upon the altar. 21 Aaron waved
the breasts and the right thigh as a wave
offering before the LORD, in the manner that
Moses had commanded. [z]

The LORD's Glory Revealed. 22 * Aaron, rais-
ing his hands toward the people, blessed
them, and, after he had sacrificed the sin
offering, the burnt offering, and the peace
offering, descended from the altar. 23 Moses
and Aaron entered the meeting tent. They
then went out and blessed the people, and
the glory of the LORD appeared to all the
people. [a] 24 A fire came out from the pres-
ence of the LORD and it consumed the burnt
offering and the fat upon the altar. All the
people saw this. They cried out and fell upon
their faces. [b]

CHAPTER 10

The Death of Nadab and Abihu. 1 * Now
Nadab and Abihu, the sons of Aaron, each
took his censer. They put fire and incense
into them and offered unholy fire before the
LORD, not as he had prescribed for them. [c]
2 But a fire came out from the presence of
the LORD and it devoured them and they
died before the LORD. [d] 3 Moses therefore
said to Aaron, "This is what the LORD has
said, 'I will show myself to be holy to those
who draw near to me and I will be glorified
before all of the people.'" Aaron therefore
remained silent. [e] 4 Moses called Mishael
and Elzaphan, the sons of Uzziel, the uncle
of Aaron, and told them, "Come here and
carry away your relatives from the sanctu-
ary. Take them outside of the camp." 5 They
drew near and carried them and their
tunics away outside of the camp, as Moses
had told them.

6 To Aaron, to Eleazar and Ithamar, his
sons, Moses said, "Do not uncover the hair of
your heads nor rend your garments, lest you
die and lest the wrath of the LORD come
upon the entire community. But let your
brothers, the whole household of Israel,
mourn the burning that the LORD kindled. * [f]
7 Do not go out from the entrance of the
meeting tent lest you die, for the oil of
anointing of the LORD is upon you." They did
what Moses told them.

Prohibition against Wine. 8 The LORD said to
Aaron, 9 "Do not drink wine or strong drink
when you are to enter the tent of meeting,
neither you nor your sons, lest you die. This
will be a statute forever throughout all of
your generations. 10 * This is so that you can
distinguish between what is holy and un-
holy, and between what is unclean and
clean, [g] 11 so that you can teach the children
of Israel all of the statutes that the LORD gave
through Moses."

Consuming Holy Things. 12 Then Moses said
to Aaron and to Eleazar and Ithamar, the
surviving sons of Aaron, "Take what is left
over from the cereal offering after part has
been offered by fire to the LORD, and eat it
unleavened near the altar, for it is most
holy. [h] 13 You must eat it in a holy place, for it
is the part assigned to you and to your sons
from the sacrifices offered by fire in honor of
the LORD, for thus I have been commanded.
14 [i] The breast of the wave offering and the
thigh that has been offered will also be eaten
by you, your sons, and your daughters, in a
clean place, for they have been assigned to
you as your portion and your sons' portion
from the peace offerings of the children of
Israel.

15 "They will take the thigh that is offered
and the breast that is a wave offering togeth-
er with the fat parts that are to be burned,
and they will wave them as a wave offering
before the LORD. This will be your portion
and your sons' portion as your right forever,
just as the LORD has commanded."

16 Now Moses diligently inquired about the
goat of the sin offering and found out that it
had been burned. He was angry with Eleazar
and Ithamar, the surviving sons of Aaron. He
said, 17 "Why have you not eaten the sacrifice
of the sin offering in a holy place, for it a most
holy thing? It was given to you to bear the
iniquity of the community, to make atone-
ment before the LORD. [j] 18 Behold, the blood
of the offering was not brought inside of the
sanctuary. You should have eaten it in the
sanctuary as I ordered you." 19 Aaron said to
Moses, "Behold, today they brought their sin

z Lev 7:31f; 8:29.—a Ex 39:47; Num 16:19.—b Jdg 13:20; 1 Ki 18:38; 2 Chr 7:1.—c Lev 16:1; Ex 24:1; Num 3:4; 26:61; 1 Chr 24:2.—d Num 16:35.—e Lev 21:6, 21; Ezek 28:25.—f Lev 21:1, 10.—g Lev 11:47; 20:25; 1 Ki 3:9; Ezek 22:26; 44:23.—h Lev 6:14, 16.—i 14f: Lev 7:34; Ezek 44:29.—j Lev 6:18f; Ex 29:38.

9:22-23 After Aaron's three-fold benediction (see Num 6:23-26) a dual blessing from Aaron and Moses is given.

10:1-2 Aaron's older sons die before the Lord because of their use of profane embers, *unholy fire*. This is another incidence of the Lord's fire that he used to consume the burnt offerings in Lev 9:24.

10:6 Unkempt hair and torn clothing were the signs of mourning.

10:10-11 *Between what is holy and unholy:* keeping the sacred apart from the profane was strictly maintained by the priests.

offering and their burnt offering before the
LORD. After these things have happened to
me, should I have eaten the sacrifice of the
sin offering? Would this have been pleasing to
the LORD?" 20 When Moses heard this, he was
satisfied.

III: NORMS CONCERNING RITUAL PURITY*

CHAPTER 11

Clean and Unclean Animals. 1 * The LORD
said to Moses and to Aaron, 2 "Tell the chil-
dren of Israel: These are the animals that you
may eat from among all the animals upon
the earth. 3 [k] You may eat any animal that
has a cloven hoof and that eats its cud.
4 From among those animals that chew their
cud and have cloven hoofs, you shall not eat
the following: camels, for it chews its cud but
does not have a divided hoof, so it will be
considered to be unclean; 5 the rock badger,
for it chews its cud but does not have a divid-
ed hoof, so it will be considered to be
unclean; 6 the hare, for it chews its cud but
does not have a divided hoof, so it will be
considered to be unclean; 7 the pig, for its
hoof is divided and is cloven hoofed, but it
does not chew its cud, so it will be considered
to be unclean. 8 You shall not eat their meat
nor shall you touch their carcasses. They will
be considered to be unclean.

9 "These are the animals that you may eat
that live in the water: you may eat anything
that has fins and scales in the seas or the
rivers. 10 But all the animals that move
through the water, whether seas or rivers,
that do not have fins or scales will be consid-
ered to be an abomination.

11 "They will be an abomination for you.
You shall not eat their meat and you shall
consider their carcasses to be an abomina-
tion. 12 Everything in the water that does not
have fins and scales will be an abomination
for you.

13 "Among birds the following will be con-
sidered to be an abomination; they will not
be eaten for they are an abomination: the
eagle, the bearded vulture and the osprey,
14 the vulture and every type of falcon,
15 every type of raven, 16 the ostrich, the
nighthawk, the sea gull, and every type of
hawk, 17 the owl, the cormorant, the ibis,
18 the swan, the pelican, the carrion vulture,
19 the stork, every kind of heron, the hoopoe,
and the bat.

20 "All winged creatures that crawl upon
four legs will be considered to be an abomi-
nation for you. 21 Yet from among the insects
that walk upon all fours, you may eat those
that have two legs above their feet to jump
upon the earth. 22 Therefore, you may eat the
following: all kinds of locusts, every kind of
bald locust, every kind of grasshopper, and
every kind of cricket. 23 But every other flying
insect that has four feet will be considered to
be an abomination.

24 "By these you shall become unclean,
whoever touches their carcasses shall be
unclean until the evening 25 and whoever car-
ries their carcasses must wash his clothes
and shall be unclean until the evening. 26 You
shall consider every animal to be unclean
that has undivided hoofs and does not chew
its cud. Whoever touches them shall be
unclean. 27 Every animal that walks upon all
fours and walks upon its paws will be unclean
to you. Whoever touches their carcasses shall
be considered to be unclean until the
evening. 28 Whoever carries their carcasses
must wash his clothes and shall be consid-
ered to be unclean until the evening. These
animals will be considered to be unclean.

29 * "These are the animals that crawl upon
the earth that will be considered to be
unclean: the weasel, the mouse, every kind of
tortoise, 30 the gecko, the crocodile, the
lizard, the snail, and the chameleon. 31 These
creeping things will be unclean for you.
Whoever touches their dead bodies will be
considered to be unclean until the evening.
32 Anything upon which one of these falls
when it is dead will be considered to be
unclean, whether it be a wooden vessel or
clothing or a skin or a sack, no matter what it
is made of. It is to be washed in water and
will be considered to be unclean until the
evening. Then it will be clean. 33 If one of
them falls into an earthen vessel, whatever it
contains, it will be considered to be unclean,

k 3-47: Deut 14:3-21.

11:1—16:34 Lacking as they did a knowledge of many of the secrets of nature, the ancients imagined hidden forces that were stronger than those of human beings and could do them harm. It was from this remote past that Israel inherited many prohibitions for their daily lives (chs. 11–16).

11:1—12:8 The animals forbidden were all those that were consecrated to pagan divinities or whose flesh excited repugnance. In classifying the animals that are listed, the author relies on more or less accurate observation (see also Deut 14:3ff); some of the animals are difficult to identify. The distinction between clean and unclean was abolished by Christian revelation (Mk 7:14, 23; Acts 10:9-16).

11:29-43 The prescriptions listed are also to be regarded as hygienic measures.

and it will be broken. 34 Any food upon which water falls will be considered to be unclean. Any liquid that can be drunk in any vessel will be considered to be unclean. 35 Everything upon which any part of their carcass falls will be considered to be unclean. Ovens and stoves will be smashed. They are unclean, and will be held to be unclean by you. 36 But a spring or a cistern where water is stored will be clean. Whoever touches their carcasses shall be unclean. 37 If any part of their carcasses falls upon seed for sowing, it will still be clean. 38 But if water falls on the seed and part of their carcasses falls on it, it is unclean to you.

39 "If an animal dies that was intended for food, whoever touches its carcass shall be unclean until the evening. 40 Whoever eats some of its carcass shall wash his clothes and shall be unclean until the evening. Whoever picks up its carcass shall wash his clothes and shall be unclean until the evening. [l]

41 "Every creeping thing that crawls upon the earth will be an abomination. It will not be eaten. 42 Everything that goes about upon its belly, and everything that goes about upon on all four legs, and everything that has many feet, hence, any of the creeping things that crawl upon the earth, are not to be eaten, for they are an abomination. 43 [m] You shall not make yourselves abominable with any of the creeping things that crawl, nor shall you defile yourselves because of them, lest you make yourselves unclean.

44 * "I am the LORD, your God. Consecrate yourselves and be holy for I am holy.* You will not defile yourselves with any of the creeping things that crawl upon the earth. [n] 45 I am the LORD who brought you out of the land of Egypt to be your God. Therefore, be holy, for I am holy.

46 "This is the law concerning animals and birds and every living creature that moves in the water and everything that crawls upon the earth, 47 so that you might know the difference between that which is unclean and that which is clean, between the animals that you can eat and those that you should not eat." [o]

CHAPTER 12

Purification after Childbirth.* 1 The LORD said to Moses, "Say to the children of Israel: 2 When a woman becomes pregnant and gives birth to a male child, she shall be considered to be unclean for seven days, just as when she menstruates. [p] 3 On the eighth day the flesh of his foreskin will be circumcised. [q] 4 Then she shall continue for thirty-three days in the blood of her purifying. She shall not touch any holy thing nor shall she enter into the sanctuary until the days of her purification are complete. 5 But if she gives birth to a girl, she shall be unclean for two weeks as during her menstruation. She shall continue in the blood of her purifying for sixty-six days.*

6 "When the days of her purification for a son or a daughter are complete, she shall bring a year-old lamb as a burnt offering and a pigeon or a turtledove as a sin offering to the priest at the entrance to the meeting tent. [r] 7 He shall offer it before the LORD and make atonement for her. She shall be cleansed from the flow of her blood. This is the law for a woman who has borne a male or female child. 8 If she cannot afford to offer a lamb, she shall offer two turtledoves or two young pigeons, one for a burnt offering and the other for a sin offering. The priest shall make atonement for her and she shall be clean."* [s]

CHAPTER 13

Infections of the Skin. 1 * The LORD said to Moses and to Aaron, 2 "When someone has a

l Lev 11:25; 17:15; 22:8.—m 43f: Lev 11:42; 20:25f.—n Lev 19:2; 20:7, 26; Mt 5:48; 1 Pet 1:16.—o Lev 10:10; Ezek 44:23.—p Lev 15:19; Num 19:22.—q Gen 17:12; Lk 1:59; Jn 7:22.—r Lev 5:7; Lk 2:22.—s Lev 1:14; 15:29; Lk 2:24.

11:44-47 These verses give the deeper reason for the criteria of clean and unclean: the Lord had delivered his people from Egyptian slavery so that they might acknowledge and worship him as the only true God. Animals that crawled along the ground did not enjoy a good reputation; in fact, the serpent, which was venerated by pagans, was regarded from the outset as an instrument of evil (Gen 3).

11:44 *Be holy for I am holy:* the central and repeated theme of Leviticus is holiness. The children of Israel are totally dedicated to God and to be like him because of what he has done for his people (see Mt 5:48).

12:1-8 It was thought that any woman bearing a child lost some of her vital energy; she would recover it by means of rites uniting her to God, the source of all life. Even the mother of Jesus would submit to this law of Leviticus (Lk 2:22-38).

12:5 This prescription shows the inferiority of women in the mind of the ancient East.

12:8 Allowance is made for those too poor to provide the prescribed offering following childbirth; doves or pigeons will suffice (see Lev 1:14).

13:1—14:57 These infectious diseases are the subject of detailed prescriptions that had for their purpose to safeguard the community. Leprosy, which was both repugnant and contagious, was especially feared; since it was the sign of a corruption, it rendered unclean anyone who contracted it. It was often regarded as a punishment from God (Num 12:10; 2 Chr 26:19-21). The priests, who were charged with diagnosing the sickness, had drawn up a list of primitive rites in keeping with their obligation of safeguarding the people from any blemish that might exclude them from worship (see Mk 1:44; Lk 17:14).

swelling or a scab or a spot on his skin, and it
turns out to be leprosy, then he shall be
brought to the priest Aaron or one of his sons
who is a priest.[t] 3 The priest shall examine
the diseased spot on his skin. If the hair of the
diseased spot has become white and the sore
seems to be deeper than the surface of the
skin, then the disease is leprosy. When the
priest has examined it, he shall pronounce
him unclean. 4 But if the spot on his skin is
white and is not deeper than the skin and the
hair on it has not become white, the priest
shall quarantine the person with the sore for
seven days. 5 On the seventh day the priest
shall examine that person again. If he sees
that the sore has not changed, and the sore
has not spread, he shall quarantine that per-
son for another seven days. 6 The priest shall
examine that person again on the seventh
day. If the sore has darkened, and the sore
has not spread, then the priest shall declare
that person clean. It was only a scab. He
shall wash his clothes and shall be consid-
ered to be clean. 7 But if the scab spreads
after the priest has examined him and
declared him to be clean, then he must be
examined by the priest again. 8 The priest
shall examine it, and if the sore has spread,
the priest shall pronounce him to be
unclean for it is leprosy.

9 "When a person has a leprous sore, he
shall be brought to the priest 10 and the priest
shall examine him. If there is a white bump
on the skin and the hair on it has turned
white, and there is tender, raw flesh on the
bump, 11 then it is a chronic leprosy of the
skin of his body. The priest shall declare him
unclean, but he shall not quarantine him for
he is unclean. 12 If the leprosy breaks out
upon the skin so that the leprosy covers all of
the skin of the diseased person wherever the
priest examined him, from head to foot,
13 then the priest shall examine the person
whose flesh is covered with leprosy. He shall
declare him clean when it has all turned
white, for he is clean. 14 But when some raw
skin appears on him, he shall be held to be
unclean. 15 The priest, when he sees the raw
skin, shall declare him unclean. The raw skin
is unclean; it is leprosy. 16 But if the raw skin
becomes white, then he shall come before
the priest 17 and the priest shall examine him.
If he sees that the sore has turned white, the
priest shall declare the person with the sore
to be clean, for he is clean.

18 "When someone has a boil on the skin
that has healed, 19 and then a whitish-red
bump or spot appears where the boil was, he
shall show it to the priest. 20 The priest shall
examine it. If he sees that it is deeper than
the skin and the hair has turned white, then
the priest shall declare him to be unclean. It
is a leprous sore that has broken out from the
boil. 21 But if the priest, upon examining it,
sees that it does not have white hair and it is
not deeper than the skin, but rather it is a bit
darker, then the priest shall quarantine him
for seven days. 22 If it spreads over the skin,
then the priest shall declare him to be
unclean, for the spot is leprous. 23 But if the
spot stays put and does not spread, then it is
a scar from the boil and the priest shall
declare him to be clean.

24 "When someone has a burn, and the raw
burn becomes a reddish-white spot, 25 then
the priest shall examine it. If the hair of the
spot has turned white and it appears to be
deeper than the skin, then it is leprosy. It has
broken out of the burn. The priest shall
declare him unclean, for it is a leprous sore.
26 But if the priest examines it and there is no
white hair on the spot and it is not deeper
than the skin, but is a bit darker, then the
priest shall quarantine him for seven days.
27 On the seventh day the priest shall exam-
ine him again. If it has spread over the skin,
then the priest shall pronounce him to be
unclean. It is a leprous sore. 28 But if the spot
has remained where it was and it has not
spread on the skin, but it is somewhat dark-
er, then it is only the swelling of a burn. The
priest shall declare him to be clean, because
it is only the scar from a burn.

29 "When a man or a woman has a sore on
the head or the beard, 30 the priest will exam-
ine the sore. If it is deeper than the skin and
the hair on it is yellow and thin, then the
priest shall pronounce it to be unclean. It is
the scab of leprosy of the head or the beard.
31 But if the priest examines the scab and it is
not deeper than the skin and there is no black
hair on it, then the priest shall quarantine the
person with the scab for seven days. 32 On the
seventh day the priest shall examine the sore.
If the scab has not spread and there is no
yellow hair on it, and the scab does not appear
to be deeper than the skin, 33 then the man
shall be shaven, but the scab is not to be
shaved. He is to be quarantined another seven

t Lev 13:28; Deut 24:8.

days. 34 On the seventh day the priest shall
examine the scab. If the scab has not spread
on the skin and it does not appear to be deep-
er than the skin, then the priest shall declare
him to be clean. He shall wash his clothes, for
he is clean. 35 But if the scab spreads after
his cleansing, 36 the priest shall examine
him. If the scab has spread, the priest need
not look for yellow hair. He is unclean. 37 But
if, from his viewpoint, the scab has not
grown larger and black hair has grown upon
it, then the scab is clean. The priest shall
declare him clean. 38 When a man or a
woman has white spots on the skin of the
body, 39 the priest shall examine that per-
son. If the spots on the skin of the body are
dull white, it is only a skin rash. The person
is clean.

40 "When a man has lost the hair on his
head and he is bald, he is clean. 41 If he has
lost the hair from the front of his head, and
he has a bald forehead, he is clean. 42 But if
there is a white reddish sore on his bald head
or his bald forehead, it is leprosy that has
broken out on his bald head or his bald fore-
head. 43 The priest shall examine him. If the
swollen sore on his bald head or his bald fore-
head is reddish-white, looking like leprosy on
the skin, 44 then he has leprosy and he is
unclean. The priest shall declare him unclean
because of the sore on his head.

45 * "Anyone who is infected with leprosy
shall wear torn clothes, his head is to be
uncovered, and he is to cover his moustache.
He shall cry out, 'Unclean, unclean!' 46 As
long as he is infected, he shall be utterly
unclean. He will live alone; his dwelling shall
be outside of the camp. [u]

Infections in Fabrics. 47 "When a garment
has a leprous mark on it, whether it be a
woolen garment or a linen garment, 48 whether
it is in the weave or the knit of the wool or the
linen, or if it is a skin or anything made of a
skin, 49 if there is a green or red spot on the
garment or the skin, whether in the weave or
the knit or on anything made of skin, it is to be
considered a mark of leprosy and it is to be
shown to the priest. 50 The priest shall look at
the spot, and shall secure that thing that is
infected for seven days. 51 He shall examine the
mark on the seventh day. If the spot on the gar-
ment has spread, whether it be in the weave
or the knit, or on the skin or on anything that
is made of skin, then the spot is an active lep-
rosy. It is unclean. 52 He shall burn the gar-
ment, whether the spot is in the weave or the
knit, whether it is made of wool or linen or is
anything made of skin. It has an active lep-
rosy, and it shall be burned in the fire. 53 But
if the priest examines it and the spot has not
spread on the garment, either in the weave
or the knit or on anything made of skin,
54 then the priest shall order that the thing
with the mark be washed,* and he shall
secure it for seven more days. 55 The priest
shall examine the thing with the spot after
it has been washed. If the color of the spot
has not changed, even if it has not spread, it
is unclean. It shall be burned in the fire
whether the bare spot is on the inside or
outside. 56 If the priest examines the gar-
ment and the spot has faded after the
washing, then he shall tear it out of the gar-
ment, whether it be made of skin or woven
or knitted. 57 But if it reappears on the gar-
ment, whether in the weave or the knit or
on anything made of skin, it is spreading.
Whatever is infected shall be burned in the
fire. 58 The garment, whether of weave or
knit or anything made of skin, that has
been washed and no longer has the spot,
shall be washed a second time and it will
then be clean. 59 These are the statutes con-
cerning infections of leprosy upon gar-
ments, whether woolen or linen, woven or
knitted, or on anything made of skin, on
how to declare it clean or to declare it
unclean." [v]

CHAPTER 14

Purification of Skin Diseases. 1 The LORD
spoke to Moses saying, 2 "This is the law for
the day of the cleansing of a person with lep-
rosy, when he is brought to the priest: [w] 3 The
priest is to go outside of the camp and exam-
ine him. If the priest discovers that the sores
of leprosy on the leper have been healed, 4 the
priest will order that two live, clean birds,
cedar wood, scarlet yarn, and hyssop be
brought to the person who is to be cleansed. [x]
5 The priest shall order that one of the birds
be killed over fresh water that is in a clay pot.
6 He is to take the live bird and dip the cedar

u Lev 23:29; Num 5:2; 12:14f; 2 Ki 15:5; Lk 17:12.—v Lev 13:47; 14:54.—w Lev 13:9; Mt 8:4; Mk 1:44; Lk 5:14.—x Num 19:6; Heb 9:19.

13:45-46 The leper had to wear a sign of mourning, such as torn clothing and uncombed hair, so that he might be recognized and relegated to the fringes of the community. These unfortunate people were still suffering this cruel lot in gospel times (Mt 8:1-4; Mk 1:40-45; Lk 5:12-16; 17:11-19).

13:54 *Washed:* it is not surprising that even in ancient times the treatment for disorders involved cleansing with water.

wood, the scarlet yarn, the hyssop, and the
live bird in the blood of the bird that was
killed over the fresh water. 7 He shall sprin-
kle the one who is to be declared cleansed
seven times. He will then release the live
bird in the open fields. 8 The person who is
being cleansed shall wash his clothes, shave
off all his hair, and wash himself with water.
He will then be considered to be clean.
Thereafter he may come into the camp, but
he shall stay outside of his tent for seven
days. 9 On the seventh day he shall shave off
all of his hair. He must shave the hair off his
head, his beard, his eyebrows, and the rest
of his hair. He shall wash his clothes and
bathe himself in water, and he shall then be
clean.

10 "On the eighth day he shall take two
male lambs without blemish and one ewe
lamb, a year old, without blemish, and
three-tenths of a portion of fine flour mixed
with oil for a cereal offering, and a log mea-
sure of oil. 11 The priest who will purify the
man to be made clean shall present him
and these things before the LORD at the
entrance to the tent of meeting. 12 The priest
shall take one of the lambs and offer it along
with the log measure of oil. This shall be a
guilt offering. He shall wave them as a wave
offering before the LORD. 13 He shall slay the
lamb in the same place that he is going to
slay the sin offering and the burnt offering,
in the sanctuary, for the sin offering belongs
to the priest just like the guilt offering. It is
most holy. 14 * The priest shall take some of
the blood of the guilt offering and put it on
the right ear lobe of the one who is being
cleansed, as well as on the thumb of his
right hand and the big toe of his right foot.[y]
15 The priest shall take some oil from the log
measure of oil and pour it into the palm of
his own left hand. 16 The priest shall dip his
right finger into the oil that is in his left hand.
With his finger he shall sprinkle the oil seven
times before the LORD. 17 The priest shall
take the rest of the oil in his hand and put it
on the right ear lobe of the one who is being
cleansed, and upon the thumb of his right
hand, and upon the big toe of his right foot,
and upon the blood of the guilt offering. 18 He
shall pour the rest of the oil that is in his hand
upon the head of the one who is being
cleansed. The priest shall make atonement
for him before the LORD. 19 The priest shall
then offer the sin offering and make atone-
ment for the uncleanness of the one who is
being cleansed. Afterward he shall slay the
burnt offering. 20 The priest shall offer the
burnt offering and the cereal offering upon
the altar. The priest shall make atonement
for him, and he shall be clean.

A Poor Person's Offerings. 21 "If he is poor
and cannot afford all this, then he shall bring
one lamb for a guilt offering to be waved, to
make atonement for him, and one-tenth a
measure of fine flour mixed with oil for a
cereal offering, and a log measure of oil,
22 and two turtledoves or two young pigeons,
whichever he is able to obtain. One will be for
a sin offering, and the other will be for a
burnt offering. 23 He shall bring them to the
priest on the eighth day of his cleansing,
at the entrance to the tent of meeting before
the LORD. 24 The priest shall take the lamb of
the guilt offering and the log measure of oil,
and the priest shall wave them as a wave
offering before the LORD. 25 He shall slay the
lamb of the guilt offering. The priest shall
take the blood of the guilt offering and put it
on the right ear lobe of the one who is being
cleansed, and upon the thumb of his right
hand, and upon the big toe of his right foot.
26 The priest shall pour the oil into the palm
of his own left hand. 27 The priest shall dip
his right finger into the oil that is in his left
hand. He shall sprinkle the oil with his fin-
ger seven times before the LORD. 28 The
priest shall take the rest of the oil that is in
his hand and put it on the right ear lobe of
the one who is being cleansed, and upon the
thumb of his right hand, and upon the big
toe of his right foot, upon the places that he
put the blood of the guilt offering. 29 He shall
pour the rest of the oil in his hand upon the
head of the one who is being cleansed. The
priest shall make atonement for him before
the LORD. 30 He shall offer one of the turtle-
doves or one of the young pigeons, whichev-
er he is able to obtain. 31 Whatever he has,
one of them will be offered as a sin offering
and the other as a burnt offering together
with the cereal offering. The priest shall
make atonement before the LORD for the
one who is being cleansed.

32 "This is the law for the person who has
leprosy and who cannot afford the things
that are needed for cleansing."

y Lev 8:23f; Ex 29:20.

14:14-17 Applying the blood of the guilt offering to the person's extremities by the priest indicated cleansing of the whole person. This mirrors the total consecration of Aaron to God by Moses in Lev 8:23.

Treatment of Skin Infections in Houses. 33 The
LORD said to Moses and Aaron, 34 "When you
come into the land of Canaan that I am giv-
ing to you as a possession, and I send the
infection of leprosy upon a house in the land
of your possession, [z] 35 the owner of the house
will come and speak to the priest saying, 'It
seems as if there is an infection in the house.'
36 The priest shall then order that they empty
out the house before he enters to examine
the infection, lest all that is within the house
be declared unclean. When they have fin-
ished, the priest shall go in to examine the
house. 37 He shall look at the infection, and if
the infection on the walls of the house is a
green or red spot, and if it seems to be deep-
er than the surface, 38 then the priest will go
out of the door of the house, and he shall
close up the house for seven days. 39 On the
seventh day the priest shall come back and
see if the infection has spread on the walls of
the house. 40 The priest shall then command
that they take the stones from the place that
is infected and they shall throw them outside
the city into an unclean place. 41 He shall
have the entire inside of the house scraped.
They are to throw the plaster that they
scraped off into a place outside the city, in an
unclean place. 42 They shall take other stones
and put them where the first stones were,
and they shall take other plaster and plaster
the house.

43 "If the infection in the house breaks out
again, after they have taken away the stones
and scraped the house and plastered it,
44 then the priest shall come and examine it.
If the infection in the house has spread, then
it is an active leprosy in the house and it is
unclean. 45 He shall break down the house.
All the stones and wood and plaster of the
house will be carried outside of the city to an
unclean place. 46 Furthermore, the person
who enters the house while it is closed will be
unclean until the evening. 47 He who lies
down in the house shall wash his clothes, and
he who eats in the house shall wash his
clothes.

48 "But if the priest comes and examines it,
and the infection in the house has not spread
after it has been replastered, then the priest
shall declare it to be clean, for the infection
has been cured. 49 He shall obtain two birds,
cedar wood, scarlet yarn, and hyssop to ritu-
ally purify the house. 50 He shall kill one of the
birds over fresh water that is in a clay pot.
51 Then he shall take the cedar wood, the
scarlet yarn, the hyssop, and the live bird,
and he shall dip them into the blood of the
slain bird and into the fresh water, and sprin-
kle the house seven times. 52 He shall purify
the house with the bird's blood, the fresh
water, the live bird, the cedar wood, the hys-
sop, and the scarlet yarn. 53 Then he shall
release the live bird in an open field outside
of the city. Thus he shall have made atone-
ment for the house, and it shall be clean.

54 "These are the statutes concerning all
types of sores of leprosy and scabs, 55 for in-
fections upon garments and houses, [a] 56 for
swollen spots, rashes, and bright spots, 57 to
decide whether something is unclean or
clean. This is the law concerning leprosy."

CHAPTER 15*

Personal Uncleanness. 1 The LORD said to
Moses and Aaron, 2 "Speak to the children of
Israel and say to them, 'When any man has a
bodily discharge, that discharge is unclean. [b]
3 This bodily discharge shall make him
unclean whether it is running or it has
stopped. His discharge shall make him
unclean. 4 Every bed upon which he lies when
he has a discharge shall be unclean, as shall
everything upon which he is sitting.
5 Whoever touches his bed will wash his
clothes and bathe in water and he shall be
unclean until the evening. 6 Whoever sits on
anything upon which the man with the dis-
charge sat shall wash his clothes and bathe in
water and shall be unclean until the evening.
7 Whoever touches a man who has had a dis-
charge shall wash his clothes and bathe in
water and shall be unclean until the evening.
8 If someone who has a discharge spits on
someone who is clean, that person shall wash
his clothes and bathe in water and shall be
unclean until the evening. 9 Everything that a
man who has a discharge rides upon shall be
unclean. 10 Whoever touches anything that
was under him shall be unclean until the
evening, and whoever carries those things
must wash his clothes and bathe in water
and he shall be unclean until the evening.
11 Whoever is touched by a man with a dis-
charge who has not rinsed his hands in water
shall wash his clothes and bathe in water and
shall be unclean until the evening. 12 Any clay

---

z Gen 17:8; Num 32:22.—a Lev 13:47-58.—b Lev 15:3; Num 5:2.

15:1-33 God is the master of life. For this reason, everything having to do with fertility and genital activity has an element of mystery and sacredness and acquires a religious value.

vessel that is touched by someone with a discharge shall be broken, and any wooden utensil shall be washed.

13 " 'When a man has been cleansed* from his discharge, he shall count off seven days from his cleansing. He shall wash his clothes and bathe himself in running water, and he shall be clean. 14 On the eighth day he shall take two turtledoves or two young pigeons and come before the LORD, at the entrance to the tent of meeting, and he shall give them to the priest. 15 The priest shall then offer them, one as a sin offering and one as a burnt offering. The priest shall make atonement for him before the LORD for his discharge.

16 " 'If any man has an emission of semen, he shall wash his whole body with water and he shall be unclean until the evening. 17 If any semen falls on any garment or on any skin, it is to be washed with water and it shall be unclean until the evening.[c]

18 " 'When a woman lies with a man and they have sex, they shall both bathe with water and they shall be unclean until the evening.

19 " 'If a woman has a discharge and the discharge from her body is blood, then she shall be impure for seven days, and whoever touches her shall be unclean until the evening.[d] 20 Everything upon which she lies during her menstrual impurity shall be unclean, and everything upon which she sits shall be unclean. 21 Whoever touches her bed shall wash his clothes and bathe in water and shall be unclean until the evening. 22 Whoever touches anything upon which she sat shall wash his clothes and bathe in water and shall be unclean until the evening. 23 Whoever touches anything that was on her bed or on something upon which she sat shall be unclean until the evening. 24 If any man lies with her so that her impurity is upon him, he shall be unclean for seven days and any bed upon which he lies shall be unclean.[e]

25 " 'If a woman has a discharge of blood for many days outside of the normal time of her impurity, or if it runs beyond the time of her impurity, then all the days when she has an unclean discharge shall be the same as the days of her menstrual impurity. She shall be unclean.[f] 26 Every bed upon which she lies all during the time of her discharge shall be for her like the bed of her impurity. Everything upon which she sits shall be unclean, just like the uncleanness of her time of menstrual impurity. 27 Whoever touches these things shall be unclean. He shall wash his clothes and bathe in water and shall be unclean until the evening.

28 " 'But if she is cleansed of her discharge, then she shall wait for seven days, and she shall then be clean. 29 On the eighth day, she shall take two turtledoves or two young pigeons and she shall bring them to the priest at the entrance to the tent of meeting. 30 The priest shall offer one as a sin offering and the other as a burnt offering. The priest shall make atonement for her before the LORD for her impure discharge.

31 " 'Thus you will keep the children of Israel from their uncleanness, lest they die* in their uncleanness when they defile my tabernacle that is in their midst.[g] 32 This is the law for anyone who has a discharge or who has an emission of semen and is therefore unclean 33 and for the woman who is having her menstrual discharge, and for someone having a discharge, whether man or woman, and for the man who lies with a woman who is unclean.' "

CHAPTER 16*

The Day of Atonement. 1 The LORD spoke to Moses after the two sons of Aaron died, after they came before the LORD. 2 The LORD said to Moses, "Tell Aaron your brother that he should not come into the sanctuary, inside of the veil, before the seat of atonement that is on the Ark whenever he wants, lest he die, for

c Deut 23:11ff.—d Lev 12:2, 5; Num 19:22.—e Lev 18:19.—f Mt 9:20; Mk 5:25; Lk 8:43.—g Lev 5:2; 22:9; Num 19:13.

15:13 *Cleansed:* God is the one who heals the person; the priest attests to the work done by God and ritually purifies the person.

15:31 *Lest they die:* the importance of atonement to be made by the priest on behalf of anyone considered unclean according to the impure discharges in chapter 15. Through ritual cleansing the person is restored physically, but most importantly spiritually.

16:1-34 Once a year, the high priest entered alone into the innermost part of the sanctuary and with the blood sprinkled the propitiatory, that is, the costly covering that contained the Ark of the Covenant and that symbolized the seat of God. The purpose of this rite was to expiate the uncleannesses with which the children of Israel had stained God's dwelling and to renew the personal relationship which the covenant at Sinai had established between God and his people.

The ceremony of atonement also continued a primitive Semitic practice: a goat was taken out into the wilderness, that is, into infertile and wretched land, and was let go there, not as an offering to a demon, Azazel (the word appears in the Hebrew text) but in order to get rid of the sins of which the animal was the symbolic bearer.

The Letter to the Hebrews recalls this liturgy in order to assert that Christ fulfilled in a definitive way what was done on the Day of Atonement; that is, he took upon himself the sins of the world and made expiation for them by means of his own blood (Heb 9:6-14).

I will appear in the cloud over the seat of atonement.[h] 3 Aaron is to come into the sanctuary with a young bull for a sin offering and a ram for a burnt offering. 4 He shall put on the holy linen tunic and the linen undergarments. He shall wrap the linen sash around himself and put on the linen turban. He shall put these holy garments on after he has washed his body with water. 5 He shall take two kid goats as a sin offering and one ram as a burnt offering from the assembly of the children of Israel.[i]

6 "Aaron shall offer the young bull as a sin offering for himself, making atonement for himself and his household. 7 He shall then take the two goats and bring them before the LORD, at the entrance to the tent of meeting. 8 Aaron shall cast lots for the two goats, designating one goat for the LORD and the other one for the scapegoat.* 9 Aaron shall take the goat upon which the LORD's lot fell and shall offer it as a sin offering. 10 But the goat upon which the lot fell to be the scapegoat shall be presented alive before the LORD, to make atonement upon it, and to send it out into the wilderness as the scapegoat.

11 "Aaron shall bring the young bull of the sin offering that is for himself and make atonement for himself and for his household. He shall slay the young bull as a sin offering for himself.* 12 Then he shall take a censer full of burning coals from the fire on the altar before the LORD. His hands are to be full of finely ground sweet incense. He shall bring these inside the veil. 13 He shall put the incense on the fire before the LORD, so that the cloud of incense might cover the seat of atonement that is on the Testimony, lest he die. 14 He shall take some of the blood from the young bull, and shall sprinkle it with his finger upon the east part of the seat of atonement. Seven times he shall sprinkle some of the blood with his finger in front of the seat of atonement.[j]

15 "He shall then slay the goat of the sin offering for the people and he shall bring its blood inside the veil. He shall do the same thing with this blood as he did with the blood of the young bull. He shall sprinkle it on the seat of atonement and in front of the seat of atonement. 16 Thus he shall make atonement for the sanctuary, for the uncleanness of the children of Israel, for their transgressions, and for all their sins. This is what he shall do for the tent of meeting that resides in the midst of their uncleanness. 17 No one is to be inside of the tent of meeting when he enters to make atonement in the sanctuary, until the time that he exits, so that he can make atonement for himself and for his household and for all of the assembly of Israel. 18 He shall go to the altar that is before the LORD and he shall make atonement for it. He shall take some of the blood of the young bull and some of the blood of the goat and he shall put it on the horns around the altar.[k] 19 He shall sprinkle the blood upon it with his finger seven times, cleansing it and purifying it from the uncleanness of the children of Israel.

The Scapegoat. 20 "When he has finished making an atonement for the sanctuary, and for the tent of meeting, and for the altar, he shall bring out the live goat. 21 Aaron shall lay both of his hands upon the head of the live goat and confess all of the iniquities of the children of Israel over it, and all of their transgressions, and all of their sins, putting them upon the head of the goat. The goat shall then be sent away, led by the hand of a man appointed to lead it into the wilderness.* [l] 22 The goat shall bear all of their iniquities into an isolated place. The man shall release it into the wilderness.[m]

23 "Aaron shall then enter the tent of meeting and take off the linen garments that he put on when he entered the sanctuary, and he shall leave them there. 24 He shall wash himself in a holy place and put on his normal clothes. He shall then come out and offer his burnt offering and the burnt offering of the people to make atonement for himself and for the people. 25 He shall burn the fat of the sin offering upon the altar.

26 "The man who led the scapegoat away shall wash his clothes and bathe himself with water, and then he can enter the camp. 27 The young bull of the sin offering and the goat of the sin offering, whose blood was brought

h Heb 9:6-12.—i Lev 4:13; Num 29:11.—j Num 19:4; Heb 9:13, 25.—k Lev 4:7; Ex 30:10; Ezek 43:20.—l Lev 5:5; 2 Cor 5:21.—m Isa 53:11-12; Jn 1:29; 1 Pet 2:24; 1 Jn 3:5.

16:8 The Hebrew text has "azazel" for *scapegoat.* This was the name of a demon which the ancient Hebrews and the Canaanites believed dwelled in the barren wilderness, that is, in a place where God did not exercise his fructifying activity.

16:11 In order for Aaron to be an acceptable minister for the people in the sanctuary, he himself had to be ritually cleansed (see Heb 5:1-3).

16:21 Aaron transferred the sins of the people by laying both hands on the sacrificial animal, thereby winning atonement for their transgressions.

into the sanctuary to make atonement, must be carried outside of the camp and burned with fire. This includes its hide, its meat, and its dung.[n] [28] The man who burned them shall wash his clothes and bathe himself with water, and then he can come into the camp.

The Fast. [29] "This will be a statute for you forever. On the tenth day of the seventh month, you must humble your spirits and do no work, whether it is a countryman or an alien dwelling among you*[o] [30] for that is the day that the priest shall make atonement for you, to cleanse you of your sins before the LORD, so that you may be clean. [31] It will be a Sabbath rest, and you will humble your spirits. This is a statute forever. [32] The priest who is anointed and consecrated to succeed his father as priest shall make atonement. He shall wear the sacred linen garments. [33] He shall make atonement for the sanctuary, for the tent of meeting, and for the altar. He shall make atonement for the priest and all the assembly of the people. [34] This shall be an everlasting statute for you, to make atonement for the children of Israel for all of their sins once a year." Moses did as the LORD had commanded him.[p]

IV: THE LAW OF HOLINESS*

CHAPTER 17

Sacredness of Blood. [1] * The LORD spoke to Moses, saying, [2] "Speak to Aaron and to his sons and to the children of Israel and say to them, 'This is what the LORD has commanded: [3] Whichever man of the house of Israel slays an ox or a lamb or a goat, either slaying it inside the camp or outside of it, [4] and does not bring it to the entrance of the tent of meeting, nor offers it to the LORD before the tabernacle of the LORD, that man shall be guilty of its blood, the blood that he shed, and that man shall be cut off from among his people.[q] [5] This is to stop the children of Israel from offering their sacrifices in the open fields, and so that they bring them unto the LORD at the entrance to the tent of meeting, to the priest, to offer peace offerings unto the LORD. [6] The priest shall sprinkle the blood upon the altar of the LORD at the entrance to the tent of meeting. He shall burn the fat as a sweet fragrance to the LORD. [7] They shall no longer offer their sacrifices to the demons* with whom they have prostituted themselves. This shall be a statute for them through all their generations.'[r]

[8] "You shall say this to them, 'Whoever from the house of Israel or from among the aliens living in your midst offers a burnt offering or a sacrifice, [9] and does not bring it to the entrance of the tent of meeting to offer it to the LORD, that person will be cut off from among his people. [10] * Whoever from the house of Israel or from among the aliens living in your midst eats anything with blood, I will set my face against that person and he shall be cut off from among his people.[s] [11] The life of all flesh is found in its blood. I have given it to you to make atonement for your life upon the altar. Blood is to make atonement for one's life.'[t] [12] Therefore, I told the children of Israel, 'No one of you shall eat blood, nor shall the alien living among you eat blood.'

[13] "Whoever from among the children of Israel or from among the aliens living in your midst hunts or catches a beast or a bird that can be eaten, let him pour out its blood and cover it with dust[u] [14] for it is the life of all flesh. The blood is its life. Therefore, I said to the children of Israel, 'You will eat no blood of any flesh, for the life of all flesh is in the blood. Whoever eats it will be cut off.' [15] Whoever eats a beast that died by itself, or that was torn asunder by beasts, whether he be a native or an alien, shall wash his clothes and bathe in water and he shall be unclean until the evening. Then he shall be clean.[v] [16] But if he does not wash or bathe, then he shall bear his guilt."

n Lev 4:12; Heb 13:11.—o Lev 23:27, 32; Num 29:7.—p Ex 30:10; Heb 9:7, 25.—q Deut 12:5ff.—r Ex 34:15; Deut 32:17; 1 Cor 10:20.—s Lev 3:17; 6:23.—t Gen 9:4; Deut 12:23.—u Deut 12:15-16.—v Lev 11:39f; 22:8; Deut 14:21.

16:29 This is the only place in the Old Testament where a penance is required before offering sacrifice.

17:1—27:34 In the final years of the monarchy, the priests of Jerusalem made a collection (chs. 17–27) of very ancient prescriptions, in order to remind the Jews that they were called to live a holy life. During and after the Exile, some priests reworked this collection in order to bring it into conformity with the perspectives of the priestly tradition of their day. In response to the pressure of pagan cults, this tradition emphasized the holiness of God and placed him above every creature and every false divinity.

17:1-9 Too often the Jews offered sacrifices to the fancied divinities of the rural areas (v. 7). Like Deut 12:2-7, the Law of Holiness combats idolatry and requires that sacrifices be offered only in the Jerusalem temple, symbolized here by the wilderness tent and regarded as the only place of true worship.

17:7 The Hebrew word translated *demons* means "goats." The reference seems to be to tutelary spirits in animal form that frequented deserted and desolate places; one such would be the *scapegoat* of Lev 16:8. See Isa 13:21; 34:14.

17:10-16 For the ancients blood was the symbol of life, and life belonged to God alone. Therefore, blood was not to serve as a food (see Acts 15:20, 29).

CHAPTER 18*

Sexual Conduct. 1 The LORD spoke again to Moses saying, 2 "Speak to the children of Israel and say to them: 'I am the LORD, your God.* 3 You shall not do things like they did in Egypt, where you dwelt, nor shall you do things like they do in Canaan, where I am bringing you. You shall not do these things, nor shall you follow their ordinances.* 4 You shall observe my statutes, and you shall keep my ordinances, walking in them. I am the LORD, your God. 5 You shall keep my ordinances and my statutes. He who obeys them shall live by them. I am the LORD, your God.[w]

6 " 'None of you is to be intimate with any of your close relatives, to uncover their nakedness. I am the LORD. 7 [x]You shall not uncover the nakedness of your father or your mother. She is your mother; you shall not uncover her nakedness. 8 You shall not uncover the nakedness of your father's wife, for her nakedness is like your father's own nakedness.[y] 9 You shall not uncover the nakedness of your sister, whether she be the daughter of your father or the daughter of your mother, whether she be born in your household or elsewhere. 10 You shall not uncover the nakedness of your son's daughter nor shall you uncover the nakedness of your daughter's daughter, for their nakedness is like your own nakedness. 11 You shall not uncover the nakedness of the daughter of your father's wife, the daughter born of your father. She is your sister, you shall not uncover her nakedness. 12 [z]You shall not uncover the nakedness of your father's sister. She is your father's close relation. 13 You shall not uncover the nakedness of your mother's sister. She is your mother's close relation. 14 You shall not uncover the nakedness of your father's brother. You shall not be intimate with his wife; she is your aunt.[a] 15 You shall not uncover the nakedness of your daughter-in-law. She is your son's wife; you shall not uncover her nakedness. 16 You shall not uncover the nakedness of your brother's wife. Her nakedness is like your brother's nakedness.*[b] 17 You shall not uncover the nakedness of both a woman and her daughter. Nor shall you uncover the nakedness of her son's daughter nor her daughter's daughter. They are her close relations. It would be shameful. 18 You shall not take the sister of your wife while she is still alive, uncovering her nakedness. They would be rivals.

19 " 'You shall not approach a woman to uncover her nakedness during her menstrual impurity. 20 You shall not have sex with your neighbor's wife, defiling both her and yourself. 21 You shall not offer any of your children to Molech.*[c] You shall not profane the name of your God. I am the LORD. 22 You shall not have sex with a man as you would with a woman. It is an abomination.[d] 23 Nor shall you have sex with any animal, defiling yourself. Nor shall any woman have sex with an animal. It is perverse.[e]

24 " 'You shall not defile yourself by doing any of these things, for the pagans have defiled themselves by all of these things. I am casting them out before you. 25 Because of this the land is defiled, and I will punish its iniquity. The land will vomit out its inhabitants. 26 Therefore, you shall observe my statutes and my ordinances. You shall not commit any abominations, neither anyone from your own nation nor any aliens who dwell among you. 27 The men of the land that lies before you have committed all of these abominations, and the land is defiled. 28 Otherwise the land will vomit you out, too, when you defile it, like it vomited out the pagans before you. 29 Whoever commits any of these abominations shall be cut off from among their people. 30 Therefore, you shall keep my ordinances, and you shall not do any of these abominable things, such as the things that were done before you, lest you defile yourself. I am the LORD, your God.' "[f]

---

w 1 Ki 2:3; Gal 3:12.—x 7-16: Lev 20:11-21.—y Lev 18:12; Deut 23:1; 27:20; 1 Cor 5:1.—z 12f: Lev 18:6; 20:19.—a Lev 20:20.—b Lev 20:21; Mt 14:3f; Mk 6:18.—c Lev 19:12; 20:2-5; Deut 18:10; 2 Ki 16:3; 21:6.—d Lev 20:13; Rom 1:27.—e Lev 20:15f; Ex 22:18; Deut 27:21.—f Lev 19:4; 20:23; Deut 18:9.

18:1-30 Marriage and sexual union with a close relative, adultery, homosexual activity, and bestiality are prohibited, with an emphasis not only on the human motives but also on the religious motive for the prohibition: such actions are an abomination to God. The law also condemns sacrifices of children; the latter were offered to win the protection of the divinities of Canaan (v. 21).

18:2 *I am the LORD, your God:* lest the children of Israel forget who is behind the extensive laws and regulations, this phrase occurs almost fifty times in chapters 18–26.

18:3 The Lord's call to holiness explicitly and repeatedly admonishes the children of Israel from any type of pagan behavior.

18:16 *Your brother's wife:* the prohibition against sexual relations with a brother's widow was qualified in Deut 25:5-6 to allow marriage when there was no male heir. In the New Testament, Herod's disregard for this law incurs the condemnation of John the Baptist (see Mt 14:4; Mk 6:18).

18:21 *Molech* was a pagan divinity of the underworld and connected with fire. See Lev 20:1-5.

CHAPTER 19

Behavior Pleasing to the LORD. 1 The LORD
spoke to Moses, saying, 2 "Speak to all the
assembly of the children of Israel and say: Be
holy, for I am holy. I am the LORD, your
God.[g] 3 Every man shall honor his father and
his mother, and keep my Sabbaths. I am the
LORD, your God.[h]

4 "Do not worship idols, nor make molten
gods for yourselves. I am the LORD, your
God.[i] 5 When you sacrifice a peace offering
to the LORD, you shall do it so that it will be
acceptable. 6 You shall eat it either on the
same day or on the next day. Whatever is
left over until the third day should be
burned in fire. 7 If you were to eat it on the
third day, it would be an abomination. It
would not be accepted.[j] 8 Therefore, every-
one who eats it shall bear his iniquity,
because he shall have profaned something
holy to the LORD. That person shall be cut
off from among his people.

9 * "When you gather the harvest of your
land, do not reap the corners of your field nor
gather the gleanings of your harvest.[k] 10 You
shall not glean your vineyard, nor shall you
gather all the grapes of your vineyard. You
shall leave them for the poor and the alien. I
am the LORD, your God.

11 "You are not to steal, nor should you
deceive nor lie to one another.[l] 12 Nor shall
you swear a false oath by my name, nor shall
you profane my name. I am your God, the
LORD.[m]

13 "You shall not defraud your neighbor,
nor shall you rob him. You shall not keep the
wages of the person you have hired all night,
until the morning.[n] 14 You shall not curse the
deaf, nor shall you put a stumbling block
before the blind, for you shall fear your God.
I am the LORD.

15 "You shall not commit any injustice in
judging the poor, nor shall you show partial-
ity to the mighty. You shall judge your neigh-
bor with righteousness.[o] 16 You are not to
spread slander among your people, nor shall
you act against the life of your neighbor. I am
the LORD.

17 "You shall not hate your brother in your
heart, nor shall you rebuke your brother in
any way, lest you bear sin because of him.[p]
18 You shall not seek vengeance nor bear a
grudge against the children of your people.
You shall love your neighbor as yourself.* I
am the LORD.[q]

19 "Obey my ordinances. Do not keep one
type of cattle with another. Do not sow a field
with seed that is mixed. Do not wear clothes
made both of wool and linen.

20 "If a man has sex with a slave girl who is
betrothed and belongs to another man, and
she has not been redeemed nor has she been
given her freedom, she shall be scourged, but
they shall not be put to death for she was not
free. 21 He shall bring his guilt offering to the
LORD, to the entrance of the tent of meeting,
a ram as a guilt offering. 22 The priest shall
make atonement for him before the LORD,
for the sin he has committed, with the ram of
the guilt offering. He shall be forgiven for the
sin that he has committed.

23 "When you come into the land and have
planted all kinds of trees, you shall leave its
fruit unharvested* for three years. It is not to
be eaten. 24 But the fourth year all of its fruit
will be holy, a praise offering to the LORD.
25 In the fifth year you can eat its fruit. Thus,
it will yield more richly for you. I am the
LORD, your God.

26 "You must not eat anything with blood in
it. You must not practice magic or cast
spells.[r] 27 * You must not trim the hair on the
side of your head, nor must you clip the
edges of your beard.[s] 28 You shall not slash
your skin to mourn the dead, nor shall you
have any tattoos. I am the LORD.

29 "Do not prostitute your daughter, forc-
ing her to commit fornication, lest the land
become adulterous and the land be full of
lewdness. 30 You will observe my Sabbaths
and respect my sanctuary. I am the LORD.[t]

---

g Lev 11:44; Mt 5:48; Jas 1:4; 1 Pet 1:16.—h Ex 20:12; Eph 6:2.—i Lev 26:1; Ex 20:3-5; 34:17; Deut 27:15; Ps 81:10; Bar 6:72.—j Lev 7:18.—k Lev 23:22; Deut 24:19ff; Ru 2:2.—l Ex 20:15f; Mt 19:18.—m Ex 20:7; Deut 5:11; Mt 5:33.—n Deut 24:14f; Mk 10:19.—o Ex 23:2f; Deut 1:17; 16:19; Ps 82:2; Prov 24:23; Zec 7:9.—p Mt 5:44; 18:15; Lk 17:3; Gal 6:1; 1 Jn 3:14.—q Mt 5:43f; 19:19; 22:39; Mk 12:31; Rom 13:9; Gal 5:14; Jas 2:8.—r Lev 3:17; Deut 18:10; 2 Ki 17:17; 21:6; 2 Chr 33:6; Acts 15:20.—s Lev 21:5; Deut 14:1.—t Lev 26:2; Ex 20:8; Deut 5:12.

19:9-10 Gleaning was an Israelite custom that provided for the poor and the strangers (see Ru 2).

19:18 *Love your neighbor as yourself:* a neighbor was not only those who lived close by but all those who one came in contact with. It is a central tenet of both Judaism and Christianity firmly espoused by Christ himself (Mt 22:39; Mk 12:31; Lk 10:27). The Old Testament teaching on loving your neighbor was extended to "love your enemies" in Mt 5:43-48; Lk 6:27-36.

19:23 *Unharvested* is "uncircumcised" in Hebrew. The reference is certainly to an ancient agricultural practice that was given a religious meaning through a comparison with circumcision.

19:27-28, 31 Pagan rites, prohibited for Hebrews (see 1 Ki 18:28; Zec 13:6).

31 “Do not consult mediums or seek after wizards, to be defiled by them. I am the LORD, your God.[u]

32 “You will stand up in the presence of those with gray hair, and honor the presence of those who are old, and you will fear your God. I am the LORD.

33 “If an alien dwells in your land, you will not harass him.[v] 34 You will treat the alien who dwells among you just as you would the person who was born among you. You shall love him as yourself, for you were once aliens in the land of Egypt. I am the LORD, your God.[w]

35 “You shall not cheat in measuring lengths or weights or volumes. 36 You will use honest scales, honest weights, an honest ephah, and an honest hin.* I am the LORD, your God, who brought you out of the land of Egypt.[x] 37 Therefore, you will observe all of my statutes and my decrees, and follow them. I am the LORD.”

CHAPTER 20*

Consequences of Forbidden Behavior. 1 The LORD said to Moses, 2 “Say again to the children of Israel: ‘Whoever among you sacrifices his child to Molech, whether he be of the children of Israel or of the aliens dwelling in your land, must be put to death. The people of the land will stone him.*[y] 3 I will set my face against that man, and cut him off from among his people, for he has sacrificed his child to Molech, defiling my sanctuary and profaning my holy name.[z] 4 If the people of the land ignore the fact that a man has sacrificed his child to Molech, and they do not kill him, 5 then I will set my face against that man and against his people, and I will cut him off, and I will cut off from their people all who go whoring after him, all those who whore after Molech.

6 “ ‘I will turn my face against that person who consults mediums and wizards, and I will cut him off from among his people.[a] 7 Consecrate yourselves and be holy, for I am the LORD, your God. 8 You shall observe my statutes and obey them. I am the LORD who consecrates you.[b]

9 “ ‘Everyone who curses his father or his mother must be put to death. He who curses his father or his mother* is guilty of his blood.[c] 10 When a man commits adultery with his neighbor’s wife, the adulterer and the adulteress must be put to death.[d] 11 The man who sleeps with his father’s wife has uncovered the nakedness of his father. They must be put to death; their blood is upon their own heads.[e] 12 If a man sleeps with his daughter-in-law, both of them must be put to death. They have done something perverse and their blood is upon their own heads.[f] 13 If a man has sex with another man, like one would have sex with a woman, both of them must be put to death. Their blood is upon their own heads.[g] 14 It is lewd for a man to marry a woman and her mother. Both he and they are to be burned with fire so that there might not be any lewdness among you.[h] 15 If a man has sex with an animal, he must die. You shall also slay the animal.[i] 16 If a woman approaches an animal to have sex with it, you shall kill both the woman and the animal. They must be put to death, for their blood is upon their own heads. 17 If a man marries his sister, his father’s daughter or his mother’s daughter, and he sees her nakedness and she sees his nakedness, it is shameful. They shall be cut off from their people, for he uncovered his sister’s nakedness and he shall bear his guilt.*[j]

18 “ ‘If a man has sex with a woman during her menstrual time, they shall have uncovered her flow of blood, and they shall both be cut off from among their people.[k] 19 You shall not uncover the nakedness of your mother’s sister or your father’s sister, for someone who uncovers a close relation shall

---

u Lev 20:6, 27; Deut 18:11; Isa 8:19; Jer 27:14.—v Ex 22:20; 23:9; Jer 22:3; Mal 3:5; Zec 7:10.—w Deut 10:19; Gal 5:14.—x Deut 25:13, 15; Prov 11:1; 16:11; 20:10; Ezek 45:10.—y Lev 18:21; Num 15:35.—z Ezek 23:39; 36:21.—a Lev 19:31; Deut 18:10.—b Lev 11:44; 19:2; 1 Pet 1:16.—c Ex 21:17; Prov 20:20; Mt 15:4; Mk 7:10; Lk 18:20.—d Lev 18:20; Ex 20:14; Deut 22:22; Jn 8:5.—e Lev 18:7f.—f Lev 18:15.—g Lev 18:22; Rom 1:27.—h Lev 18:17; Deut 27:23.—i Lev 20:16; Ex 22:18; Deut 27:21.—j Lev 18:9; Num 15:30; Deut 27:22.—k Lev 15:24; 18:19.

19:36 *Hin:* a liquid measure.

20:1-27 Those who disobeyed the prohibitions mandated by the law (many of these are listed in chapter 18) were severely punished: either condemned to death or expelled from the community. The severity is explained by the ways of that time; it shows how deeply rooted in the cultural environment of that period was the demand that drove Israel to protect itself from the pagan customs with which it was in constant contact: the holy God wanted his chosen people to be holy. Despite the conclusion (vv. 22-24), this legislation supposes that the Hebrews were already settled in the land of Canaan.

20:2 Such pagan practices as sacrificing children to Molech had found their way into Israel (2 Ki 16:3).

20:9 *Curses his father or his mother:* a death penalty for cursing a parent seems extreme, even under Levitical law. It is probable that this would be intended for serious and repeated offenses as described in Deut 21:20-21.

20:17 This is the only instance of public punishment.

bear his guilt.[l] [20] A man shall not have sex with his uncle's wife, for he shall have laid bare his uncle's nakedness. They shall bear their guilt and die childless. [21] It is unclean for a man to marry his brother's wife for he shall have uncovered his brother's nakedness. They shall be childless.

[22] " 'You shall therefore observe all of my statutes and ordinances and obey them, so that the land to which I am bringing you to dwell in will not vomit you out. [23] You shall not follow the ways of the nations that I cast out before you for having done all these things that I abhorred.[m] [24] But I have said to you, "You will inherit their land. I will give it to you to be your own, a land flowing with milk and honey. I am the LORD, your God, who chose you from among all people."[n] [25] You shall therefore distinguish between clean animals and unclean, between unclean birds and clean, so that you shall not make yourselves detestable by any animal or bird or anything that creeps on the ground that I indicated as being unclean.[o] [26] You shall be holy, for I, the LORD, am holy. I have chosen you from among all people that you shall be mine.[p]

[27] " 'A man or a woman who is a medium or a wizard must be put to death. You will stone them with stones, for their blood is upon their heads.' "[q]

CHAPTER 21

Regulations for Priests. [1] The LORD said to Moses, "Speak to the priests, the sons of Aaron, and say to them: 'No one shall become unclean by touching a dead person*[r] [2] except for a close relative, his mother, his father, his son, his daughter, his brother, [3] or his unmarried sister, who is near to him, for she has no husband. For these he can become unclean. [4] But he is not to become unclean for people related by marriage, becoming unclean for them.

[5] " 'Priests must not shave their heads bald nor trim their beards nor shall they cut their flesh.*[s] [6] They shall be holy to their God, and they are not to profane the name of their God, for they present offerings made by fire to the LORD, the food of their God. Therefore, they will be holy. [7] They are not to marry a prostitute or a woman who has been defiled, nor are they to marry a woman who has been divorced by her husband, for he is holy to his God.*[t] [8] You shall therefore consecrate him, for he offers the bread of your God. He will be holy to you, for I, the LORD, who sanctify you, am holy.

[9] " 'If the daughter of any priest defiles herself by playing the whore, thus defiling her father, then she is to be burned with fire.

[10] " 'The priest who is the most important from among his brothers, upon whose head was poured the oil of anointing, and who was consecrated to wear the garments, he is not to uncover his head or rend his garments [11] nor shall he make himself unclean by touching any dead body, even that of his own father or mother. [12] He shall not leave the sanctuary nor desecrate the sanctuary of his God, for the consecration of the oil of anointing of his God is on him. I am the LORD.[u] [13] He shall marry a woman who is a virgin. [14] He shall not marry a widow or a divorced woman or a woman who has defiled herself by fornication. Rather, he is to marry a virgin from his own people[v] [15] so that he not profane his posterity among his people. I am the LORD, who sanctifies him.' "

Priestly Defects. [16] The LORD spoke to Moses saying, [17] "Speak to Aaron saying: 'Any of your descendants who has a defect is not to draw near to offer the bread of his God. [18] No one who has a defect shall approach, whether he be blind or lame, disfigured or deformed,[w] [19] or if he has a crippled foot or hand, [20] or if he be hunchbacked or dwarfed, or if he has an eye defect, or a scab or sore or damaged testicles. [21] No descendant of Aaron the priest who has a defect shall draw near to present offerings made by fire to the LORD. He who has a blemish shall not come to offer the bread of his God [22] for the bread of his God is most holy. He can eat what is holy, [23] but he shall not enter inside the veil* or approach the

l Lev 18:12f; 19:8.—m Lev 18:30; Rom 12:2.—n Ex 3:8, 17; 6:8; Jer 11:5.—o Lev 11:2-47; Deut 14:4-20.—p Lev 7:21; 11:44; Ex 19:6; 1 Pet 1:16.—q Lev 19:31; Ex 22:17; Deut 18:11.—r Num 19:16; Ezek 44:25.—s Lev 19:27; Ezek 44:20.—t Ezek 44:22.—u Lev 10:7; Ex 29:7.—v Ezek 44:22.—w Lev 22:19ff; Deut 23:1.

21:1 Any contact with a dead person, even entering the place where there was a dead body, rendered a priest unclean. Close relatives, as described in verses 2-3 were exempt from this prohibition, but restrictions for the high priest made even this forbidden (vv. 11-12).

21:5 *Cut their flesh:* the pagan custom of defiling their body as a sign of mourning was not to be tolerated among the priests.

21:7 Regulations concerning marriage partners were stricter for the high priest and required that he marry a virgin (vv. 13-14), whereas it was highly recommended for other priests.

21:23 *Inside the veil:* physical imperfections prevented a priest from entering the sanctuary in order not to profane it.

altar because of his defect, lest he defile the
sanctuary. I am the LORD, who makes them
holy.' "
24 Moses said this to Aaron and to his sons
and to all of the children of Israel.

CHAPTER 22

Protecting What Is Sanctified. 1 The LORD
spoke to Moses saying, 2 "Tell Aaron and his
son to treat the holy things of the children of
Israel with respect so that they not profane
my holy name by those things that they have
consecrated to me. I am the LORD.
3 "Say to them: Any of your descendants
who approaches these holy things that the
children of Israel have consecrated to the
LORD while he is unclean, that person will be
cut off from my presence. I am the LORD.
4 "Any descendant who is a leper or who
has a discharge shall not eat of the holy
things until he is clean. Whoever touches
anything made unclean by contact with a
dead person or who has had an emission of
semen [x] 5 or whoever touches any creeping
thing that can make him unclean, or touch-
es a man whose uncleanness he acquires,
whatever the source of uncleanness,[y] 6 if
someone touches one such a person, then he
shall be unclean until the evening, and he
shall not eat of the holy things unless he
bathes himself with water.[z] 7 When the sun
sets, he shall be clean. He can then eat the
holy things, for it is his food. 8 He shall not
eat anything that died on its own or was torn
apart by wild beasts, thereby defiling him-
self. I am the LORD.[a] 9 They shall therefore
observe my statutes lest they become guilty
and die when they profane it. I am the LORD,
who sanctifies them.*
10 "No foreigner can eat the holy things. No
guest of the priest or hired hand can eat the
holy things.[b] 11 But if the priest buys a slave,
the slave can eat it, and if a slave is born to his
household, he can eat his food. 12 If a priest's
daughter marries an outsider, she cannot eat
an offering of the holy things. 13 But if a
priest's daughter is a widow or divorced and
she has no children, and she has returned to
her father's household as when she was
young, she can eat from her father's portion
of food, but no outsider is to eat of it. 14 If
someone eats some of the holy things by
accident, he is to add a fifth to its value and
give the holy thing to the priest.[c] 15 They
must not profane the holy things of the chil-
dren of Israel that they offer to the LORD[d]
16 lest they bear the guilt of their trespass
when they eat their holy things. I am the
LORD, who consecrates them."
Acceptable Offerings. 17 * The LORD spoke to
Moses, saying, 18 "Speak to Aaron and to his
sons and to all the children of Israel saying: If
anyone from the house of Israel or from
among the aliens living in Israel presents a
burnt offering as a votive offering or a free-
will offering to the LORD, 19 it must be a male
without blemish from among the cattle or
the sheep or the goats, for you to be found
acceptable.[e] 20 You shall offer nothing with a
defect; it shall not be acceptable for you.[f] 21 If
someone offers a peace offering as the fulfill-
ment of a vow or as a free-will offering,
whether it be from the cattle or the sheep, it
must be perfect to be acceptable. It must
have no defect.[g] 22 You shall not offer any-
thing that is blind or injured or maimed, or
anything with sores or scabs or scales. You
shall not use these as an offering to the LORD
by fire, on the altar to the LORD. 23 You can
offer a young bull or a lamb that has any
parts that are in excess or lacking as a free-
will offering, but it is not acceptable for a
votive offering. 24 You shall not offer anything
that is bruised or crushed or broken or cut to
the LORD. You shall not make this type of
offering in your land. 25 You shall not offer
food from a foreigner's hand to your God. All
of these things have their corruption in them
and their blemishes in them; they are not
acceptable for you."
26 The LORD spoke to Moses, saying,
27 "When a young bull or a sheep or a goat is
brought as an offering, you shall leave it for
seven days with its mother. On the eighth
day, it shall be acceptable as an offering
made by fire to the LORD.[h] 28 You are not to
kill a cow or ewe with its young on the same
day. 29 When you offer a sacrifice of thanks-
giving* to the LORD, you are to do it in the

x Lev 7:20; 15:16; Ex 29:33.—y Lev 11:24-43; Hag 2:13.—z Num 19:8; Heb 10:22.—a Lev 17:15; Deut 14:21; Ezek 44:31.—b Ex 29:33; Mt 12:4.—c Lev 5:16; 27:13, 15.—d Lev 19:8; Num 18:32.—e Lev 1:3, 10; Ezek 46:13.—f Lev 3:1; Deut 15:21; 17:1; Mal 1:8, 14.—g Lev 3:1, 6; Num 6:14.—h Lev 22:25; Ex 22:29.

22:9 Although many of the laws regarding cleanness were the same for the priests and other people, the penalties for the priests who were defiled were very harsh (see chs. 11–14).

22:17-25 This section clearly shows that physical imperfections disqualified any animal, or thing that approached the altar, just as it did the priest as seen in chapter 21.

22:29 *Sacrifice of thanksgiving:* unlike a fellowship offering that could be eaten the following day (Lev 7:16), the thanksgiving offering had to be consumed on the same day.

correct manner. 30 You shall eat it on the day
that you offer it; none of it is to be left over
until the next day. I am the LORD.[i] 31 You
shall observe my commandments and obey
them. I am the LORD.

32 "You shall not profane my holy name,
for I am to be hallowed among the children
of Israel. I am the LORD who hallows you,
33 who brought you out of the land of Egypt
to be your God. I am the LORD."

CHAPTER 23*

Holy Days. 1 The LORD spoke to Moses, say-
ing, 2 "Speak to the children of Israel and say
to them: These are the feasts of the LORD on
which you shall proclaim holy assemblies,
these are my feasts:

3 * "For six days work can be done, but the
seventh is a Sabbath of rest, a holy assembly.
You will do no work on it; it is a Sabbath of
the LORD in all of your dwellings.[j] 4 These are
the feasts of the LORD, holy assemblies that
you shall proclaim at their appointed time.[k]

Passover. 5 * "The evening of the four-
teenth day of the first month is the LORD's
Passover.[l] 6 The fifteenth day of the same
month is the Feast of Unleavened Bread to
the LORD. You are to eat unleavened bread
for seven days.[m] 7 On the first day you are to
have a holy assembly. No heavy labor is to
be done on that day. 8 You will make an
offering by fire to the LORD for seven days.
On the seventh day you are to have a holy
assembly. No heavy labor is to be done on
that day."

9 * The LORD spoke to Moses, saying,
10 "Speak to the children of Israel and say to
them: When you enter the land that I am giv-
ing you, and you collect the harvest, you are
to bring an omer measure of the firstfruits of
your harvest to the priest. 11 He shall wave
the omer before the LORD so that it might be
acceptable for you. The priest shall wave it on
the day after the Sabbath. 12 On the day that
you wave the omer, you shall offer a one-
year-old male lamb without blemish as a
burnt offering to the LORD. 13 Its grain offer-
ing is to be two-tenths of an omer of fine flour
mixed with oil, an offering made by fire to
the LORD, a pleasing fragrance. Bring a
fourth of a hin of wine as a drink offering.
14 You are not to eat bread or roasted grain or
the green heads of grain until that day that
you have brought your offering to your God.
This is a statute from one generation to the
next in all of your dwellings.

Pentecost.* 15 "You shall count off for your-
selves seven complete Sabbaths from the day
after the Sabbath when you brought your
omer as a wave offering.[n] 16 On the day after
the seventh Sabbath, having counted fifty
days, you shall offer a new cereal offering to
the LORD.[o] 17 You shall bring out from your
dwellings loaves of bread as wave offerings
that have been made with two-tenths of an
ephah of fine flour. They are to be baked with
leaven. They are the firstfruits to the LORD.
18 Along with the bread you shall offer seven
lambs without blemish and one young bull
and two rams as burnt offerings to the LORD.
Together with the cereal offerings and the
drink offerings, you are to make an offering
by fire, a pleasing fragrance to the LORD.
19 You shall sacrifice one of the kid goats as a
sin offering and you shall sacrifice two of the
one-year-old lambs as a peace offering.[p]
20 The priest shall wave them together with
the bread of the firstfruits as a wave offering
to the LORD, with two holy lambs. They shall
be an offering to the LORD for the priest.
21 You shall proclaim on that day that there is
to be a holy assembly. You are not to do any
heavy labor. This shall be a statute forever in
all of your dwellings, from one generation to
the next.

22 "When you collect the harvest of your
land, you shall not gather it right up to the
corners of the field, nor shall you gather up
the gleanings of your harvest. You shall leave
them for the poor and the alien. I am the
LORD, your God."

i Lev 7:15; 19:6.—j Ex 20:8-11; 23:12; 34:21; 35:2; Deut 5:12-15; Lk 13:14.—k Ex 23:14-19; Num 9:3.—l Num 9:2f; 28:16; Deut 16:1.—m Ex 12:18; 13:3, 10; 23:15; 34:18; Ezek 45:21.—n Ex 34:22; Num 28:26; Deut 16:9; Jos 5:11.—o Num 28:26; Acts 2:1.—p Lev 4:23; Num 28:30.

23:1-44 The solemnities marking the liturgical life of the Jewish people were connected with the events of the Exodus from Egypt; the solemnities were occasions for the renewal of their fidelity to the covenant. These assemblies of the people gave rise to traditions and were always joyous occasions. The Books of Numbers (chs. 28–29) and Deuteronomy (chs. 12–16) renew, explain in greater detail, and complete the regulations governing the liturgical life of Israel.

23:3-4 The Sabbath rest is in imitation of the Creator (Gen 3:2) and signifies that Israel is a free people.

23:5-8 Passover had its origin in ancient springtime festivals but now commemorated the preparations made for the deliverance of the people (Ex 12).

23:9-14 At Passover the firstfruits of the barley harvest were offered to God.

23:15-22 The Feast of Weeks, later called Pentecost, was an agricultural feast that had been instituted to thank the Lord for his blessings (Num 28:26-31); it then became the Feast of the Covenant.

New Year's Day.* [23] The LORD said to Moses, [24] "Speak to the children of Israel saying: On the first day of the seventh month you shall observe a Sabbath, a memorial with the blowing of trumpets, a holy assembly. [25] You shall do no heavy labor. You shall make an offering by fire to the LORD."

Day of Atonement.* [26] The LORD spoke to Moses, saying, [27] "The tenth day of the seventh month shall be a Day of Atonement. You shall have a holy assembly and you shall humble yourselves. You shall make an offering by fire to the LORD. [q] [28] You shall not work on this day, for it is a Day of Atonement, to make atonement for you before the LORD, your God. [29] Whoever does not humble himself that day shall be cut off from among his people. [30] I will destroy whoever does any work on that day from among his people. [31] You shall do absolutely no work. This shall be a statute forever from one generation to the next in all of your dwellings. [32] It shall be a Sabbath of rest for you. You shall humble yourselves on the evening of the ninth of the month. You shall celebrate your Sabbath from that evening until the next."

Feast of Booths.* [33] The LORD said to Moses, [34] "Speak to the children of Israel, saying: The fifteenth day of the seventh month shall be the LORD's Feast of Booths, for seven days. [r] [35] On the first day you shall have a holy assembly. You shall do no heavy labor. [36] For seven days you shall make an offering by fire to the LORD. On the eighth day you shall hold a holy assembly and you shall make an offering by fire to the LORD. It is a holy assembly, and you shall do no heavy labor. [37] These are the feasts of the LORD on which you shall proclaim holy assemblies, making a burnt offering to the LORD, and offering up a cereal offering, a sacrifice, and a drink offering, each on its own day, [38] in addition to the Sabbaths of the LORD, your gifts, your vows, and all of the free-will offerings that you give to the LORD. [39] On the fifteenth day of the seventh month, when you have gathered in the fruit of the land, you shall celebrate a feast to the LORD for seven days. On the first day there will be a Sabbath rest, and on the eighth day there will be a Sabbath rest. [s] [40] On the first day you shall gather for yourselves the shoots of the healthy trees, fronds from the palm trees, branches from the leafy trees, and willows from the brook, and you shall rejoice before the LORD, your God, for seven days. [41] You shall observe it as a feast of the LORD for seven days each year. This is a statute forever, from one generation to the next, that you shall celebrate in the seventh month. [42] You shall dwell in tents for seven days. All native-born Israelites shall dwell in tents [43] so that all of your generations may know that I made the children of Israel dwell in tents when I brought them out of the land of Egypt. I am the LORD, your God." [t]

[44] This is how Moses described the feasts of the LORD to the children of Israel.

CHAPTER 24

The Sanctuary Lamp. [1] * The LORD spoke to Moses, saying, [2] "Command the children of Israel to bring you pure oil of pressed olives for the lamp, that the light might burn continually. [u] [3] Aaron is to place it outside of the veil of the Testimony, in the tent of meeting, burning it from evening to morning before the LORD forever. This shall be a statute forever, from one generation to the next. [4] He shall place the lamps upon the pure golden lampstand, before the LORD forever.

The Bread Offering. [5] "You shall take fine flour and bake twelve cakes, two-tenths of an ephah in each cake. [v] [6] You shall set them in two rows, six cakes to a row, on the pure golden table before the LORD. [7] You shall sprinkle pure frankincense* upon each row, on the bread, so that it might be a memorial offering made by fire to the LORD. [8] Every Sabbath he shall set it in order before the LORD forever. It is an everlasting covenant for the children of Israel. [w] [9] It belongs to Aaron and his sons who are to eat it in a holy place, for it is a most holy part of his portion of the offerings made by fire to the LORD. This is a statute forever."

---

q Lev 16:29f; 25:9; Num 29:7.—r Num 29:12; Deut 16:13; Ezr 3:4; 2 Mac 1:9, 18; Jn 7:2.—s Ex 23:16; Num 29:12; Deut 16:13.—t Deut 31:10-13; Neh 8:14.—u Ex 27:20f; Num 8:2.—v Lev 14:10; Ex 25:30; 1 Ki 7:48; 2 Chr 4:19; 13:11; Heb 9:2.—w Ex 25:30; 1 Chr 9:32.

23:23-25 This feast was a survival of rural customs and was more popular than the religious New Year in spring that was part of the Levitical calendar.

23:26-32 See Lev 16:16. The ceremony showed traces of archaic rites, but it testified to a profound sense of sin.

23:33-44 A remembrance of the Exodus period was combined with the annual popular feast of thanksgiving for the harvest.

24:1-9 The meaning of this twofold rite was that God is always present among his people and that worship should be uninterrupted.

24:7 *Pure frankincense:* the sprinkling of incense did not relate to flavoring for the bread but was burned as a memorial offering alongside it.

Consequences of Blasphemy.* 10 The son of an Israelite woman, whose father was an Egyptian, went out among the children of Israel, and this son of the Israelite woman got into a fight with an Israelite man. 11 The son of the Israelite woman blasphemed the name of the LORD and cursed. They brought him to Moses. His mother's name was Shelomith, the daughter of Dibri, of the tribe of Dan. 12 They put him under guard until the will of the LORD might be revealed to them.[x] 13 The LORD spoke to Moses saying, 14 "Bring the one who has cursed outside of the camp. Let everyone who heard him lay their hands upon his head, and let all the assembly stone him. 15 You shall speak to the children of Israel saying, 'Whoever curses his God shall bear his guilt. 16 He who blasphemes the name of the LORD must be put to death. All of the assembly shall stone him, the alien as well as the native born. He who blasphemes the LORD shall be put to death.*[y]

17 " 'He who kills any man must be put to death.[z] 18 He who kills an animal shall make restitution for it, an animal for an animal.[a] 19 When a man wounds a neighbor, whatever he has done shall be done to him: 20 broken bone for broken bone, eye for an eye, tooth for a tooth. In whatever way he wounded another, so it shall be done to him.[b] 21 He who kills an animal shall make restitution and he who kills a man shall be put to death. 22 You shall have one set of laws for both the alien and for the native born. I am the LORD, your God.' "[c]

23 Moses told the children of Israel that they should bring the man who had cursed outside of the camp and stone him to death. The children of Israel did as the LORD had commanded Moses.[d]

CHAPTER 25

Year of the Sabbath. 1 * The LORD spoke to Moses on Mount Sinai, saying, 2 "Speak to the children of Israel saying to them: When you come into the land that I am giving you, the land is to keep a Sabbath to the LORD. 3 You shall sow the fields for six years and you shall prune the vineyard and harvest its fruit for six years,[e] 4 but the seventh year will be a Sabbath of rest to the LORD. It is a Sabbath to the LORD. You shall neither sow your field nor prune your vineyard.[f] 5 You shall not harvest whatever grows on its own, nor shall you gather the grapes of your undressed vines. It is a year of rest for the land. 6 During this Sabbath the land will provide food for you, for you and your servant, and your maid, and your hired hand, and your alien who dwells with you, 7 and for your cattle and your animals in the land. All of your produce will be for food.

The Year of Jubilee. 8 * "You shall count seven Sabbaths of years for yourselves, seven times seven years, and your span of seven times seven years will be forty-nine years. 9 You shall blow the trumpet of the Jubilee on the tenth day of the seventh month, on the Day of Atonement you shall blow the trumpet throughout the land. 10 You shall consecrate the fiftieth year, and proclaim liberty throughout the whole land to all of its inhabitants. It will be a Jubilee for you. Each of you shall return to his own property, and each shall return to his own clan.[g] 11 The fiftieth year shall be a Jubilee for you. You shall not sow nor reap. You shall not reap what grows on its own, and you shall not gather grapes from the undressed vines. 12 It is a Jubilee and it is to be holy for you. You shall eat only what comes directly from the fields.

13 "In the Jubilee Year you shall return each man to his property. 14 If you sell some merchandise to your neighbor, or you buy something from your neighbor, you shall not take advantage of one another. 15 You shall buy from your neighbor based on the number of years since the Jubilee. He is to sell to you based on the number of years left for har-

x Num 15:34.—y 1 Ki 21:10, Dan 3:96; Mt 26:65f; Jn 10:33.—z Gen 9:5f; Ex 21:12, 14; Num 35:31; Deut 19:11f.—a Ex 21:33f; Deut 19:21.—b Ex 21:24; Deut 19:21; Mt 5:38.—c Lev 19:34; Ex 12:49; Num 15:16.—d Num 15:35f; Acts 7:57f.—e Ex 23:10f.—f Lev 25:20ff; 1 Mac 6:49, 53.—g Num 36:4; Ezek 46:17; Lk 4:19.

24:10-23 This story of an incident that occurred in the wilderness not only shows that blasphemy must be punished but also provides an opportunity for recalling the law of talion (Deut 19:21), although this passage does not properly belong in this liturgical context. This severe legislation represented progress for society in that period, since it prevented excessive vendettas. See Ex 21:18-26. But the Gospel will go further (Mt 5:38-43).

24:16 Of all the transgressions, it is not certain why blasphemy was handled this way; perhaps to bind such a serious sin against God.

25:1-17 Every seven years the soil was to be allowed to rest (see Ex 23:10-13); this was a way of reminding the people that the earth belongs to the Lord. When Israel had become an agricultural society, it was tempted to think of itself as self-sufficient.

25:8-17 The Jubilee of the fiftieth year began with the sounding of trumpets or *yobel*, hence its name. This institution was closely connected with the sabbatical year and had for its purpose to ensure the vigorous maintenance of the structures on which Jewish society was based: the clan and the family estate. The text was composed during the Exile and reflects an abiding ideal rather than an actual practice.

vesting crops.[h] 16 If the number of years left is
greater, you shall increase the price paid, but
if the number of years is smaller, then you
shall decrease the price paid, for it is the
number of harvests that he is selling you.
17 You shall not wrong one another, for you
shall fear your God. I am the LORD, your God.

18 "You shall observe my statutes and
keep my ordinances and obey them in order
to live securely in the land. 19 The land shall
yield its fruit, and you shall eat your fill, and
dwell in the land securely. 20 If you should
say, 'What will we eat the seventh year, for
we are not sowing nor are we gathering our
increase,'[i] 21 then I will send my blessing
upon you in the sixth year so that the crops
are abundant enough for three years. 22 You
shall sow in the eighth year, but you shall
still be eating old fruit until the ninth year.
You shall be eating old fruit until its fruit
comes in.

Redemption of the Land. 23 * "The land will
not be permanently sold, for the land belongs
to me and you are my aliens and tenants.
24 In all the land that you possess, you shall
provide a redemption for the land. 25 If your
brother becomes impoverished and sells
part of his property, then his next of kin shall
come and redeem it. He shall redeem what
his brother has sold.*[j] 26 If there is no one
else to redeem it and the man himself can
redeem it, 27 then let him calculate the num-
ber of years since the sale, and let him pay for
the remaining years to the man to whom he
sold it, so that he can return to his property.
28 But if he is not able to get it back, then what
he sold shall remain in the possession of the
one who bought it until the Jubilee Year. It
shall revert to him in the Jubilee, so that he
can return to his property.

29 "If a man sells his home in a walled city,
then he can redeem it any time within one
year. He can redeem it for a year from the
time he sold it. 30 But if he has not redeemed
it within the period of one year, then the
house within the walled city shall belong to
the person who bought it forever, from one
generation to the next. It shall not revert
during the Jubilee Year. 31 Houses in villages
that have no walls around them shall be
treated just like fields in the countryside.
They can be redeemed, and they shall revert
in the Jubilee Year. 32 This does not apply to
the cities of the Levites, for the Levites can
redeem their possessions, their houses in the
cities, at any time. 33 Whenever a person buys
a house in the city from the Levites, what was
sold will revert in the Jubilee Year, for the
houses in the cities of the Levites are their
possession among the children of Israel.
34 But the fields at the edge of the city cannot
be sold, for that is their perpetual posses-
sion.[k]

35 "If a brother becomes poor and is unable
to support himself, then you shall help him,
letting him live with you as though he were a
guest or a lodger. 36 Do not practice usury or
ask for interest, but fear God, letting your
brother live with you. 37 You shall not charge
interest if you lend him money, nor offer him
food for profit.[l] 38 I am the LORD, your God,
who brought you out of the land of Egypt to
give you the land of Canaan, to be your God.

39 "If your brother becomes poor and sells
himself to you, you shall not make him serve
you as a slave.[m] 40 Treat him as a hired ser-
vant or a guest. He is to serve you only until
the Jubilee Year.* 41 He shall then leave you,
he and his children, and he shall return to his
own family and return to the property
owned by his fathers. 42 For you are my ser-
vants, whom I brought out of the land of
Egypt. You are not to be sold as slaves 43 or
treated harshly. Fear your God.

44 "You can have pagan male and female
slaves from the nations around you. You can
buy them, male and female slaves. 45 Fur-
thermore, you can buy the children of the
aliens living in your land, even those who
were born in your land. They shall be your
property. 46 Your children shall inherit them
after you die, for your slaves are property to
be inherited forever. But you shall not treat
your brethren, the children of Israel, with
this type of harshness.[n]

47 "If an alien or foreigner has grown rich
and one of your brethren becomes poor and
sells himself to the alien or foreigner living in
your midst or to a member of that foreigner's

h Lev 27:18, 23.—i Mt 6:25, 31; Lk 12:22, 29.—j Ru 2:20; 4:4, 6; Jer 32:7f.—k Num 35:3; Ezek 45:4.—l Ex 22:24.—m Ex 21:2; Deut 15:12.—n Isa 14:1f.

25:23-34 The earth belongs to God alone. Given this principle, regulations follow that complete and make the norms of the Jubilee Year more specific; their purpose is to protect the poor.

25:25 A relative is needed to buy back land for the family. This rule prevailed when Boaz rescued Ruth and Naomi (Ru 4:1-4). He was also willing to marry Ruth and support them (Ru 4:9-10).

25:40 This verse represents progress as compared with the Code of the Covenant (Ex 21:2).

family, 48 that person can be redeemed. One of his relatives can redeem him. 49 His uncle or his cousin or any of his relatives can redeem him, or if he is able, he can redeem himself. 50 He should reckon the time from when he bought him until the Jubilee Year with the buyer. The price of redemption will be based upon the number of years and the amount a hired servant would be paid. 51 If there are still a number of years, then he will pay a larger share of the price for which he was bought. 52 If only a few years remain until the Jubilee Year, he will calculate the redemption that he will give him according to that number of years. 53 He is to be treated like a hired servant that one would employ a year at a time. You are not to treat him harshly. 54 Even if he is not redeemed in any of these ways, he will be freed during the Jubilee Year, he and his children with him. 55 The children of Israel are my servants.* They are my servants, whom I brought out of the land of Egypt. I am the LORD, your God.

CHAPTER 26*

Rewards of Obedience. 1 "Do not make idols or carved images. Do not set up stone images in your land before which you bow down. I am the LORD, your God.[o] 2 Observe my Sabbaths and stand in awe before my sanctuary. I am the LORD. 3 Follow my statutes and keep my commandments and obey them.* 4 Then I will give you rain in its proper season and the yield of the land shall increase and the trees of the field shall bear their fruit.[p] 5 Your threshing shall continue even until your grape harvest, and the grape harvest shall continue until the time for planting. You shall eat your fill of your bread, and dwell securely in your land. 6 I will grant peace in the land. You shall lie down, fearing nothing. I will rid the land of savage beasts, and the sword will not pass through your land. 7 You shall pursue your enemies, and they shall fall by the sword before you. 8 Five of you shall chase a hundred, and a hundred of you ten thousand, and you shall put them to flight. Your enemies shall fall by the sword before you.[q] 9 I will look with favor upon you, and make you fruitful, and cause you to multiply, and establish my covenant with you. 10 You shall still be eating the old harvest and shall have to clean out the old because of the new.[r] 11 [s] I will establish my tabernacle among you, and my soul will not reject you. 12 * I will walk in your midst and I will be your God and you will be my people. 13 I am the LORD, your God, who brought you forth from the land of Egypt so that you would no longer be their slaves. I have broken the bonds of your yoke and brought you out with your heads held high.

Consequences of Disobedience. 14 "But if you do not listen to me and do not keep these commandments 15 and if you despise my statutes and hate my ordinances, failing to observe my commandments and breaking my covenant, 16 then I will do this to you: I will visit terror upon you, and consumption and fever that will destroy your eyesight and break your hearts. You shall plant your seeds in vain, and your enemies shall eat it. 17 I will set my face against you so that you are slain by your enemies. Those who hate you shall rule over you, and you shall flee even though no one is pursuing you.[t]

18 "Then, if you still do not obey me, I will punish you seven times as much for your sins. 19 I shall break down your stubborn pride. I shall make your skies like iron and your earth like brass. 20 Your strength shall be spent in vain, for your land will not yield its produce and the trees of the land shall not yield their fruit.

21 "If you continue to be hostile to me and will not obey me, I will bring plagues upon you, seven times greater than your sins. 22 I will also send wild animals into your midst. They shall carry off your children and cut down your cattle. They shall cause your numbers to decrease and your highways shall become desolate. 23 If you do not accept my correction through these things and you walk in opposition to me, 24 [u] then I will also walk in opposition to you and I will punish you seven times more than your sins. 25 I will bring a sword upon you that will execute vengeance for my covenant. When you are gathered together in your cities, I will send a

o Ex 20:4; Num 33:52; Deut 5:8; Ezek 20:7.—p Deut 11:14; Pss 68:9; 85:13.—q Deut 32:30; Jos 23:10.—r Lev 25:22; Joel 12:24.—s 11f: Ex 29:45; Ezek 37:26ff; Mt 28:20; 2 Cor 6:16.—t Deut 28:25; Ezek 15:7.—u 24f: Ex 9:3; Jer 2:30; Ezek 14:17; 21:14.

25:55 *Servants:* rather than a demeaning title, servant reflected the covenantal relationship established between Israel's God and his people.

26:1-46 This Law of Holiness will be completed in Deuteronomy (ch. 28): God shows his approval of the behavior of those who belong to him.

26:3 The promise of blessings of bountiful harvests from the land depends on obeying the Lord's commands.

26:12-13 Additional covenantal terminology that is associated with Hos 2:1f, 25.

plague upon you and you shall be delivered
into the hand of the enemy. 26 When I have
cut off your supply of bread, then ten women
shall bake bread in the same oven. They shall
deliver your measure of bread. You shall eat
it, but not be satisfied.[v]

27 "But if after all of this you still will not
obey me but walk in opposition to me, 28 then
I will walk in opposition to you in my fury. I
will punish you seven times more than your
sins. 29 You shall eat the flesh of your sons,
and you shall eat the flesh of your daughters.
30 I will destroy your high places and cut
down your idols. I will cast your bodies upon
the remains of your idols, and I will loathe
you.[w] 31 I will lay your cities waste and bring
desolation upon your sanctuaries. I will not
delight in your fragrant aromas. 32 I will lay
waste the land, and your enemies will dwell
there.[x] 33 I will scatter you among the pagans
and pull out my sword against you. Your land
shall be desolate and your cities shall be laid
waste. 34 The land shall be pleased with its
Sabbaths while it is desolate and you are
dwelling in the land of your enemies. The
land shall then rest and enjoy its Sabbaths.[y]
35 It shall rest as long as it lies desolate,
because it did not rest during your Sabbaths
when you dwelt in it.

36 "As for those of you who are left, I will
make their hearts so timid in the land of
their enemies that the sound of a blowing leaf
will put them to flight. They shall flee as
though fleeing from a sword. They shall fall
down when no one is chasing them. 37 They
shall fall all over one another as if before a
sword, even though no one is chasing them.
You shall not have the strength to stand
before your enemies. 38 You shall die among
the pagans, the land of your enemies will
devour you.

39 "Those of you who are left will pine away
in their iniquity in the land of their enemies,
and also because of the iniquity of their
fathers. They shall pine away with them.[z]
40 * If they confess their iniquity and the iniq-
uity of their fathers, the trespasses that they
committed against me, and that they acted
in opposition to me, 41 so that I walked in
opposition to them, and brought them into
the land of their enemies, if then their uncir-
cumcised hearts be humbled and they
accept the punishment for their sins, 42 then I
will remember my covenant with Jacob and
my covenant with Isaac and my covenant
with Abraham. These I will remember, and I
will remember the land.[a] 43 For the land will
have been abandoned by them, and will
enjoy its Sabbaths while it lies desolate when
they are no longer there. They shall accept
the punishment for their iniquity, for they
despised my ordinances and their souls
loathed my statutes. 44 Yet in spite of all of
that, when they are in the land of their ene-
mies, I will not reject them, nor will I loathe
them, utterly destroying them, and thus
breaking my covenant with them. I am the
LORD, their God. 45 For their sake I will
remember the covenant I made with their
ancestors whom I brought forth out of the
land of Egypt in the sight of the pagans so
that I might be their God. I am the LORD."[b]

46 These are the statutes and the ordi-
nances and the laws that the LORD estab-
lished through Moses between himself and
the children of Israel on Mount Sinai.

V: REDEMPTIVE OFFERINGS*

CHAPTER 27

Offerings and Dedications. 1 * The LORD
spoke to Moses, saying, 2 "Speak to the chil-
dren of Israel saying to them: When a person
makes a special vow to dedicate people to the
LORD by giving the equivalent sum of money,
3 you shall establish the value of a male from
twenty to sixty years old as being fifty shekels
of silver, according to the measure of the
sanctuary,* 4 and if it is a woman, then the
value is thirty shekels. 5 If the person is from
five years old to twenty years old, then the
estimated value of the person is twenty
shekels for a male and ten shekels for a
female. 6 If the person be from one month old
to five years old, then the estimation of the
value of a male is five shekels and the esti-

v Isa 9:19; 55:2; Ezek 4:16; 5:16; 14:13; Mic 6:14.—w Ex 22:23; 2 Chr 34:3-4, 7; Ezek 6:3-6; Mic 5:10.—x 1 Ki 9:8; Jer 9:11; 18:16; 19:8; 25:18; Ezek 5:15.—y Lev 25:2; 2 Chr 36:21.—z Num 14:18; Ezek 4:17; 24:23; 33:10.—a Gen 9:15; Ex 6:5; 2 Ki 13:23; Ps 106:45.—b Gen 17:7; Deut 4:31.

26:40-45 In addition to obedience (26:3), the repentance of the people assures the fidelity of God to the covenant.

27:1-34 This juridical supplement, which may seem dry as dust, provides norms useful in avoiding the exploitation of persons and things consecrated to God.

27:1-8 Men were always regarded as taking priority over women, since the latter were considered inferior to them.

27:3 A (silver) shekel was worth a gram of gold and was divided into twenty *gerahs*. The *measure of the sanctuary* was either a specimen kept in the sanctuary or a shekel of greater value. In the ancient Orient women "were worth less"; this was a sign of their inferiority to men.

mation of the value of a female is three shekels. 7 If a person is sixty years old or older, the estimation of the value of a male is fifteen shekels and the estimation of the value of a female is ten shekels. 8 But if anyone is too poor to pay the estimated value, then he will present himself before the priest and the priest will make an estimation based on the ability of the person vowing to pay. The priest will establish the value.

9 "If he brings an animal as an offering to the LORD, then everything that he has given to the LORD will be holy. 10 He should not exchange it, a good one for a bad one or a bad one for a good one. If he should substitute one animal for another, then both the original and the substitution become holy. 11 If it is an unclean animal, one that a person cannot offer to the LORD, then he will bring the animal before the priest 12 and the priest will determine whether it is good or bad and the priest will give an estimation of its value. This is how it will be established. 13 If the owner wishes to redeem it, he shall add a fifth to your estimation of its value.[c]

14 "If a man sets apart his house as something holy to the LORD, the priest shall make an estimation of it, whether it is good or bad, and the priest shall establish its value. This is how it shall be established. 15 If he desires to redeem the house that he has set apart, he shall add a fifth to its estimated value, and then it shall be his. 16 If a man sets apart a piece of his property to the LORD, then your estimation of its value shall be based on the seed that it takes to sow it, a homer* of barley being valued at fifty shekels of silver. 17 If he sets the field apart at the beginning of the Jubilee Year, this shall be your evaluation. 18 But if he sets apart the field after the Jubilee Year, the priest shall determine the value according to the number of years remaining until the Jubilee Year, and thus the evaluation shall be adjusted.[d] 19 If he wishes to redeem the field that he had set apart, then he shall add a fifth to your evaluation and it shall be his. 20 But if he does not redeem the field, or if he sold the field to another person, then it is not to be redeemed anymore, 21 but when the field is released in the Jubilee Year, it shall be holy to the LORD. It will be treated like a priest's field, and it shall be their property.

22 "If a man sets apart a field that he bought, a field that is not his family's inheritance, dedicating it* to the LORD, 23 then the priest shall make an estimation of its value from then until the Jubilee Year, and the man shall pay the estimation that day as something holy to the LORD. 24 In the Jubilee Year the field shall be returned to the one from whom it was bought, the one whose land it was.[e]

25 "Every estimation is determined according to the shekel of the sanctuary, twenty gerahs* to the shekel.

Offerings Not Redeemable.* 26 "No one shall dedicate the firstborn of an animal, for the firstborn already belongs to the LORD, whether it be an ox or a sheep, it belongs to the LORD.[f] 27 If it is an unclean animal, then he shall redeem it based on its evaluation and add a fifth to its value. If it is not redeemed, then it should be sold for its established value.

28 "But nothing that a person owns and is put under the ban for the LORD, be it man or animal or ancestral property, can be sold or redeemed. Everything set aside is most holy to the LORD. 29 No person under the ban can be redeemed. He must be put to death.

30 "Everything that belongs to the tithe of the land, be it the seed of the land or the fruit of the tree, belongs to the LORD. It is holy to the LORD.[g] 31 If someone wants to redeem his tithes, he shall add one-fifth to its value. 32 As to the tithes of the herd or the flock, of everything passing under the herdsman's staff, the tenth to pass shall be holy to the LORD. 33 He shall not investigate to see if it is good or bad, nor shall he exchange it for another. If he exchanges it, then the first animal and its substitute shall both be holy and are not to be redeemed." 34 These are the commandments that the LORD gave to Moses for the children of Israel on Mount Sinai.[h]

c Lev 27:14; Num 5:7.—d Lev 25:15f, 27.—e Lev 25:10, 28, 41; Ezek 46:17.—f Ex 13:2; Num 3:13.—g Lev 3:16; Num 18:21, 24; 2 Chr 31:5f, 12; Mal 3:8, 10.—h Ex 31:18.

27:16 A *homer* contains about 200 liters, and is equal to 10 ephahs.

27:22 *Dedicating it:* anything that was made anathema or forbidden (Hebrew, *herem*) was solemnly consecrated to God, without reservation and irrevocably; no one could profit by what had thus been consecrated. See Deut 13:14-16; 20:10-15; also Jos 7:1-21.

27:25 A *gerah* was the smallest unit of weight: six grains.

27:26-34 It is obviously impossible to consecrate to God what is his by right, nor, generally speaking, can it be bought back. This is true of what is anathema or "dedicated" to God: according to a practice inherited from the holy war, that which is consecrated to the Lord in this unqualified fashion must be destroyed, or else (in the perspective adopted by a less warlike mentality) must be reserved exclusively for the priests (Jos 6:17).

"Then Moses lifted up his arm and he struck the rock with his staff twice. Water came gushing out, and the community and their animals drank" *(Num 20:11).*

THE BOOK OF NUMBERS

In the Wilderness, toward the Promised Land

The title "Numbers" directs the reader's attention to the several censuses contained in the Book. The Hebrew title is more accurate: "In the wilderness," for the Book in fact narrates an important stage in the history of God's people: its forty-year sojourn in the wilderness that ends with the beginning of the conquest of the Promised Land.

The focus of the text is the incidents and institutions that marked this lengthy journey, but it incorporates these into a reflection on the religious meaning of the events and the time in the wilderness.

The outline that is adopted simplifies the historical reality, for in fact all the tribes did not follow the same itinerary, and the legislative prescriptions recorded do not all date from the period in the wilderness. It is true enough that the story is always based on recollections and practices from the time when the Hebrews were living in a semi-nomad state in the Negeb (southern Palestine) or in the Transjordan; but these recollections and practices were continually meditated on, retold, and interpreted over a period of centuries by a living tradition, before finding their present place in the great picture of sacred history that was drawn after the Exile by an editor who belonged to the Priestly tradition.

The people are described as a well-organized army, lined up behind their leaders and standards, ready to prove themselves capable of a holy war. But, more importantly, the people are seen as "the assembly of the Lord*" (Num 16:3); God dwells in the midst of the people and manifests his presence and activity by means of the cloud, the Ark of the Covenant, and, above all, his servant Moses. This assembly, with its priests and Levites who are in charge of worship, its Nazirites who are consecrated to God, and its faithful, is an image of another "assembly* *of the LORD," namely, the Church, the new people of God, within which the Spirit assigns various functions and responsibilities. Thus the Book of Numbers, despite its tedious stretches, helps us meditate on the Church, the liturgy, the priesthood, the consecrated life, and the responsibilities shared by all.*

The journey in the wilderness serves as a framework and occasion for describing the spiritual itinerary of the people of God. It is God who sets them on their way, sustains them, guides them, makes them retreat, and obtains water and food for them.

But the people are regretful when they remember Egypt, and they often rebel. Their sin slows their progress and calls down punishments. They must achieve conversion and purification (and the priesthood is given to them precisely so that they can do this more readily); they will not be able to enter the Promised Land until they are completely renewed.

This is why the Book of Numbers has always been esteemed by those desirous of knowing the ways of spiritual progress. From this point of view, it will always be a valuable guide.

The Book of Numbers may be divided as follows:

- *I: The Census and the Preparation to Depart from Sinai (1:1—10:10)*
- *II: Forty Years in the Wilderness (10:11—25:18)*
- *III: The Second Census and the Plan to Enter the Promised Land (26:1—36:13)*

I: THE CENSUS AND THE PREPARATION TO DEPART FROM SINAI*

CHAPTER 1

The Census. 1 The LORD spoke to Moses in the Sinai Desert in the tent of meeting on the first day of the second month of the second year after they left the land of Egypt, saying,* 2 [a] "Take a census of the community of the people of Israel, arranging them by their families, by their clans, listing every single man by name. 3 You and Aaron will count them, company by company, each one who is twenty years and older and is able to go to war in Israel. 4 A man from every tribe,* the head of his clan, will accompany you.

Assistants to Moses Named. 5 [b] "These are the names of the men who will accompany you: from the tribe of Reuben, Elizur, the son of Shedeur; 6 from the tribe of Simeon, Shelumiel, the son of Zurishaddai; 7 from the tribe of Judah, Nahshon, the son of Amminadab;[c] 8 from the tribe of Issachar, Nathanel, the son of Zuar; 9 from the tribe of Zebulun, Eliab, the son of Helon; 10 from the son of Joseph, from the tribe of Ephraim, Elishama, the son of Ammihud, and from the tribe of Manasseh, Gamaliel, the son of Pedahzur; 11 from the tribe of Benjamin, Abidan, the son of Gideoni;[d] 12 from Dan, Ahiezer, the son of Ammishaddai; 13 from Asher, Pagiel, the son of Ochran; 14 from Gad, Eliasaph, the son of Reuel; 15 from Naphtali, Ahira, the son of Enan." 16 These were the ones summoned from the assembly, the leaders of their tribes. They were the heads of the clans of Israel.[e]

17 Moses and Aaron took the men who had been named 18 and on the first day of the second month they gathered together the entire community who registered themselves by families, by the name of their fathers' households. The men twenty years and older were listed according to their names, one by one, 19 as the LORD had commanded Moses. And so he counted them in the Sinai Desert.

---

a 2f: Num 26:2.—b 5-15: Num 10:14-28.—c Ru 4:20.—d Ps 68:28.—e Ex 18:21, 25.

1:1—2:34 The final editor of the Book has somewhat exaggerated the figures, undoubtedly in order to highlight the extraordinary fecundity of the people of the promise (Gen 13:16). Perhaps he was also mistaken about the meaning of the Hebrew word translated as "thousand": at the time of the Exodus the word did not mean "thousand" but referred to the small contingent of men that each clan had to supply in time of war.

1:1 From the first verse of this book to the very last, it is Moses in his role as prophet—spokesperson of the Lord—that is emphasized time and again. Moses' unique position is described in Num 12:6-8.

1:4 *A man from every tribe:* appointing one man from each tribe to assist Moses and Aaron fostered a community spirit and a fair and accurate count.

The Count of the Twelve Tribes. [20] Thus the members of the tribe of Reuben, the oldest son of Israel, who were twenty years or older and who were fit to bear arms were listed by name according to their clans and families, one by one.[f] [21] The number of men in the tribe of Reuben was forty-six thousand, five hundred.

[22] The members of the tribe of Simeon who were twenty years or older and who were fit to bear arms were listed by name according to their clans and families, one by one. [23] The number of men in the tribe of Simeon was fifty-nine thousand, three hundred.

[24] The members of the tribe of Gad who were twenty years or older and who were fit to bear arms were listed by name according to their clans and families. [25] The number of men in the tribe of Gad was forty-five thousand, six hundred fifty.

[26] The members of the tribe of Judah who were twenty years or older and who were fit to bear arms were listed by name according to their clans and families. [27] The number of men in the tribe of Judah was seventy-four thousand, six hundred.

[28] The members of the tribe of Issachar who were twenty years or older and who were fit to bear arms were listed by name according to their clans and families. [29] The number of men in the tribe of Issachar was fifty-four thousand, four hundred.

[30] The members of the tribe of Zebulun who were twenty years or older and who were fit to bear arms were listed by name according to their clans and families. [31] The number of men in the tribe of Zebulun was fifty-seven thousand, four hundred.

[32] The sons of Joseph include the members of the tribe of Ephraim who were twenty years or older and who were fit to bear arms. They were listed by name according to their clans and families. [33] The number of men in the tribe of Ephraim was forty thousand, five hundred.

[34] There are also the members of the tribe of Manasseh who were twenty years or older and who were fit to bear arms. They were listed by name according to their clans and families. [35] The number of men in the tribe of Manasseh was thirty-two thousand, two hundred.

[36] The members of the tribe of Benjamin who were twenty years or older and who were fit to bear arms were listed by name according to their clans and families. [37] The number of men in the tribe of Benjamin was thirty-five thousand, four hundred.

[38] The members of the tribe of Dan who were twenty years or older and who were fit to bear arms were listed by name according to their clans and families. [39] The number of men in the tribe of Dan was sixty-two thousand, seven hundred.

[40] The members of the tribe of Asher who were twenty years or older and who were fit to bear arms were listed by name according to their clans and families, one by one. [41] The number of men in the tribe of Asher was forty-one thousand, five hundred.

[42] The members of the tribe of Naphtali who were twenty years or older and who were fit to bear arms were listed by name according to their clans and families, one by one. [43] The number of men in the tribe of Naphtali was fifty-three thousand, four hundred.

[44] This was the number of men counted by Moses and Aaron and the twelve leaders, each representing his ancestral clan. [45] The total number of the people of Israel who were listed according to their clan who were twenty years or older and fit to bear arms in Israel [46] was six hundred and three thousand, five hundred and fifty.

Responsibility of the Levites. [47] The families of the tribe of Levi, however, were not counted with the rest of them*[g] [48] for the LORD had said to Moses, [49] "You are not to take a census of the tribe of Levi, nor are you to include them in the census of the people of Israel. [50] You will assign the Levites responsibility over the tent of the tabernacle and over all of its vessels and over all of the things that belong to it. They will carry the tabernacle and all of its vessels. They will care for it and they will camp around the tabernacle.[h] [51] When the tabernacle is to be moved, the Levites will take it down. When it is to be erected, the Levites will set it up. Anyone else who approaches it must be put to death.

[52] "Each of the Israelites will pitch his tent within his own camp, alongside his own standard, each in his own company, [53] but

f Rev 7:5.—g Num 2:33.—h Num 3:5-8.

1:47 The tribe of Levi, the Levites, was responsible for worship and would not be counted for military purposes.

the Levites will camp around the tabernacle of the Testimony so that no wrath come upon the community of the people of Israel. The Levites will keep guard over the tabernacle of the Testimony."[i] 54 This is what the people of Israel did. They did everything that the LORD had commanded Moses.

CHAPTER 2*

Placement of the Tribal Camps. 1 The LORD spoke to Moses and Aaron, saying, 2 "Every Israelite will camp by their own standard, alongside the emblems of their father's household. They will camp some distance from the tent of meeting.[j]

3 "On the east side, toward the rising of the sun, will be the standard of the camp of Judah arranged by their companies. The leader of the tribe of Judah is Nahshon, the son of Amminadab. 4 His forces numbered seventy-four thousand, six hundred. 5 The tribe of Issachar will camp next to him. The leader of the tribe of Issachar is Nethanel, the son of Zuar. 6 His forces numbered fifty-four thousand, four hundred. 7 Then there is the tribe of Zebulun. The leader of the tribe of Zebulun is Eliab, the son of Helon. 8 His forces numbered fifty-seven thousand, four hundred. 9 The whole camp of Judah, by their companies, numbered one hundred eighty-six thousand, four hundred. They are to set out first on the march.

10 "On the south side of the camp is the standard of the camp of Reuben, arranged by their companies. The leader of the tribe of Reuben is Elizur, the son of Shedeur. 11 His forces numbered forty-six thousand, five hundred. 12 The tribe of Simeon will camp next to him. The leader of the tribe of Simeon is Shelumiel, the son of Zurushaddai. 13 His forces numbered fifty-nine thousand, three hundred. 14 Then there is the tribe of Gad. The leader of the tribe of Gad is Eliasaph, the son of Reuel. 15 His forces numbered forty-five thousand, six hundred fifty. 16 The whole camp of Reuben, by their companies, numbered one hundred fifty-one thousand, four hundred fifty. They are to be the second to set out on the march.

17 "Then the tent of meeting will set out, with the camp of the Levites in the middle of the other camps whenever they set up camp. This is how they are to set out, each man located under his own standards.

18 "On the west side of the camp is the standard of the camp of Ephraim, arranged by their companies. The leader of the tribe of Ephraim is Elishama, the son of Ammihud. 19 His forces numbered forty thousand, five hundred. 20 The tribe of Manasseh will camp next to him. The leader of the tribe of Manasseh is Gamaliel, the son of Pedahzur. 21 His forces numbered thirty-two thousand, two hundred. 22 Then comes the tribe of Benjamin. The leader of the tribe of Benjamin is Abidan, the son of Gideoni. 23 His forces numbered thirty-five thousand, five hundred. 24 The whole camp of Ephraim, by their companies, numbered one hundred eight thousand, one hundred. They are to be the third to set out on the march.

25 "On the north side of the camp is the standard of the camp of Dan, arranged by their companies. The leader of the tribe of Dan is Ahiezer, the son of Ammishaddai. 26 His forces numbered sixty-two thousand, seven hundred. 27 The tribe of Asher will camp next to him. The leader of the tribe of Asher is Pagiel, the son of Ochran. 28 His forces numbered forty-one thousand, five hundred. 29 Then comes the tribe of Naphtali. The leader of the tribe of Naphtali is Ahira, the son of Enan. 30 His forces numbered fifty-three thousand, four hundred. 31 The whole camp of Dan, by their companies, numbered one hundred fifty-seven thousand, six hundred. They are to march last with their standards."

32 [k] These were the people of Israel who were counted. There were six hundred three thousand, five hundred and fifty counted in their camps, in their companies, 33 but the Levites were not counted along with the people of Israel, as the LORD had commanded Moses. 34 The people of Israel did everything as the LORD had commanded Moses* by encamping under their standards and by the way they set out, each going with his clan and his family.

---

i Num 18:2-4.—j Num 1:52.—k 32f: Num 1:46-49.

2:1-34 The Hebrew people are seen here as a liturgical assembly that is hierarchically arranged, being organized in increasingly sacral concentric circles around the Dwelling of the holy God. The numbers from chapter 1 are repeated, as are the names of leaders.

2:34 *Did everything as the LORD had commanded Moses:* the subject of strict obedience shown by the people of Israel in Num 1:54 is repeated here and greatly contrasts with their later rebellion.

CHAPTER 3

Aaron's Offspring. 1 * These are the descendants of Aaron and Moses on the day that the LORD spoke to Moses on Mount Sinai. 2 These are the names of the sons of Aaron: the oldest was Nadab, and then there were Abihu and Eleazar and Ithamar.[l] 3 These are the names of the sons of Aaron, the priests who were anointed and consecrated to minister in the priesthood. 4 Nadab and Abihu died before the LORD when they offered unclean fire to the LORD in the Sinai Desert. They had no children. Eleazar and Ithamar ministered as priests in the presence of their father Aaron.[m]

The Tribe of Levi. 5 The LORD spoke to Moses, saying, 6 "Gather the tribe of Levi and have them stand before Aaron the priest so that they can minister to him.[n] 7 They will serve him and serve the whole assembly standing before the tent of meeting, ministering to the needs of the tabernacle. 8 They will take care of all of the furnishings of the tent of meeting and attend to the needs of the people of Israel as they minister in the tabernacle. 9 You will give the Levites to Aaron and his sons; they are dedicated to him from among the people of Israel.[o] 10 You will appoint Aaron and his sons, and they will serve as priests. Anyone else who draws near is to be put to death."

11 * The LORD spoke to Moses, saying, 12 [p] "Behold, I have taken the Levites from among the people of Israel as a substitute for the firstborn of the people of Israel, those who opened the womb. The Levites will be my own, 13 for every firstborn has belonged to me from the day that I slew all the firstborn in the land of Egypt. I have set apart all the firstborn as my own in Israel, both human and animal. They will be mine. I am the LORD."

Counting the Levites. 14 The LORD spoke to Moses in the Sinai Desert, saying, 15 "Count the sons of Levi by clan, by family. Count every male one month old and older."

16 So Moses counted them, as the word of the LORD had commanded * him. 17 [q] These are the names of the sons of Levi: Gershon, Kohath and Merari. * 18 These are the names of the sons of Gershon by their families: Libni and Shimei. 19 The sons of Kohath by their families were Amram, Izhar, Hebron, and Uzziel. 20 The sons of Merari by the families were Mahli and Mushi. These are the families of the Levites according to their clan.

21 From Gershon came the family of the Libnites and the family of the Shimeites. These are the families of the Gershonites. 22 They counted them, all males one month old and older, and they numbered seven thousand, five hundred. 23 The clan of the Gershonites were to camp behind the tabernacle to the west. 24 Eliasaph, the son of Lael, was the leader of the clan of the Gershonites. 25 [r] In the tent of meeting the sons of Gershon had responsibility for the care of the tabernacle, the tent with its covering, the screen for the entrance to the tent of meeting, 26 the curtains for the courtyard, the screen for the entrance to the courtyard that surrounds the tabernacle and the altar, its cords, and everything that had to be done with these.

27 From Kohath came the family of the Amramites, the family of the Izharites, the family of the Hebronites, and the family of the Uzzielites. These are the families of the Kohathites. 28 They counted them, all males one month old and older, and they numbered eight thousand, three hundred, ministering to the needs of the sanctuary. 29 The clan of the Kohathites were to camp on the south side of the tabernacle. 30 Elizaphan, the son of Uzziel, was the leader of the clan of the Kohathites. 31 Their responsibility was for the Ark, the table, the lampstand, the altars, the vessels of the sanctuary, the screen, and everything that had to be done with these.[s]

---

l Ex 6:23.—m Lev 10:2, 6; 1 Chr 24:2.—n 1 Chr 15:1-2.—o Num 8:19.—p 12-13: Num 8:16-18; Ex 13:2, 12.—q 17-20: Num 26:57; Gen 46:11; Ex 6:16-19; 1 Chr 6:1.—r 25-26: Ex 26:36; 27:9.—s Ex 25:10.

3:1—4:49 In the tribe of Levi, which is to be at the spiritual service of the community, a distinction exists between the priests, whose office it is to offer sacrifice, and the "Levites," who are to provide material services. Historically, however, this distinction dates only from the time of King Josiah (640–609 B.C.) and would become definitive only after the return from the Exile.

3:11-51 The Levites, being consecrated to the service of God, take the place of the firstborn of the entire people, those who have belonged to God ever since the Passover when the people were delivered from Egypt and the destroying angel spared their firstborn from slaughter (Ex 12:23).

3:16 *As the word of the LORD had commanded:* Moses' commitment to the Lord is firm and without exception.

3:17 See Ex 6:16-25. By omitting mention of Aaron and his family, the editor, a priest, means to underscore the superiority of the priests, who are not to be numbered among the simple Levites.

32 Eleazar, the son of Aaron the priest, was to be the supervisor of the leaders of the Levites. He was to oversee those who had the responsibility to care for the needs of the sanctuary.

33 From Merari came the family of the Mahlites, and the family of the Mushites. These are the families of Merari. 34 They counted them, all males one month old and older, and they numbered six thousand, two hundred. 35 Zuriel, the son of Abihail, was the leader of the clan of Merari. They were to camp on the north side of the tabernacle. 36 Their responsibility was for the boards of the tabernacle, and its bars, its pillars, its sockets and all of their parts, [t] 37 the pillars around the courtyard, and their pins, and their cords.

38 Finally, Moses, Aaron and his sons camped in front of the tabernacle on its east side, in front of the tent of meeting and eastward. They kept watch over the sanctuary, keeping the people of Israel and any other person from coming near, under penalty of death.

39 The total number of the Levites who were counted by Moses and Aaron at the command of the LORD, everyone in their families who was one month old and older, was twenty-two thousand.

Redemption of the Firstborn. 40 The LORD said to Moses, "Count all the firstborn males of the people of Israel, those one month old and older, and make a list of their names. 41 The Levites will be a substitute for me in place of the firstborn of the people of Israel. I am the LORD. The cattle of the Levites will be a substitute for the firstborn of the cattle of the people of Israel."

42 Moses counted all of the firstborn of the people of Israel as the LORD had commanded him 43 and he listed all the firstborn males by name, those one month old and older. They numbered twenty-two thousand, two hundred seventy-three.

44 The LORD spoke to Moses, saying, 45 "Take the Levites as a substitute for all the firstborn of the people of Israel, and the cattle of the Levites as a substitute for their cattle. The Levites are mine. I am the LORD."

46 Those who were to be redeemed among the firstborn of the people of Israel, not counting the Levites, numbered two hundred seventy-three. 47 "You will take five shekels for each person according to the shekel of the sanctuary, that is, twenty gerahs for each shekel [u] 48 and give the money to Aaron and his sons to redeem those who are in excess among them."

49 Moses took the redemption money for those who were in excess, above the number of those redeemed by the Levites. 50 He received the money for the firstborn of the people of Israel, one thousand three hundred and sixty-five shekels, according to the shekel of the sanctuary. 51 Moses gave the redemption money to Aaron and his sons as the LORD had commanded Moses by the word of the LORD.

CHAPTER 4

Delineation of Duties. 1 The LORD spoke to Moses and Aaron, saying, 2 "Count the number of the Kohathites from among the sons of Levi by their clans and their families. 3 Count all the men from thirty to fifty years old who go in to minister in the tent of meeting. * [v]

4 "This is the ministry of the Kohathites in the tent of meeting: tending to the most holy things. 5 When the camp is being moved, Aaron and his sons will take down the veil and cover the Ark of Testimony with it. 6 They are then to put on the sheep skins, cover it with a blue cloth, and put the poles in place. * 7 They will spread a blue cloth over the table for the shewbread. On it they will place the dishes and spoons and bowls and jars for the drink offerings. The bread of offering will remain on it. 8 Over these they will spread a scarlet cloth and cover it with sheep skins. You will then put the poles in it. 9 They are to take a blue cloth and cover the lampstand used for the light, its lamps, its tongs, its snuffers, and all of its oil dishes, all the things used in its ministry. 10 They will put it and all of its vessels within a hide of sheep skin and they will put it upon a litter. 11 They will spread a blue cloth upon the golden altar and cover it with a covering of sheep skins and put its poles in it. * [w] 12 Then they are to take all the implements with which they minister in the sanctuary, and

t Ex 26:15.—u Num 18:16; Ex 30:13; Lev 27:25.—v Num 8:24; 1 Chr 23:3, 24, 27.—w Ex 30:1-6.

4:3 This was the period during which the Levites served God in the temple of King David (see 1 Chr 23:3). The length of the period varies in different passages (see Num 8:24-25; Ezr 3:8). The institution certainly evolved.

4:6 For these objects used in worship, see Ex 35–38.

4:11 The gold altar is the altar of incense (Ex 30:1-10).

they are to cover them with a blue cloth and
with a covering of sheep skin and put them
on a litter. 13 They are to empty all the
ashes * out from the altar and spread a pur-
ple cloth on it. 14 They are to put all the uten-
sils with which they minister upon it, the
censers, the forks, the shovels, and the
basins. They are to take all of the utensils
with which they minister and spread a sheep
skin upon them. They will also put in its
poles.

15 "When Aaron and his sons have finished
covering the sanctuary and all of the vessels
of the sanctuary, when the camp is ready to
set out, the Kohathites will come forward to
carry it, but they will not touch anything that
is holy, lest they die. These things in the tent
of meeting are the responsibility of the
Kohathites.[x]

16 "Eleazar, the son of Aaron, has the
responsibility for the oil for the light, the
sweet incense, the daily meat offering, and
the oil for anointing. He shall also oversee
care for the tabernacle and everything in it,
the sanctuary and its vessels."

17 The LORD spoke to Moses and Aaron,
saying, 18 "Do not let the clan of the
Kohathites be cut off from among the
Levites. 19 Do these things for them so that
they may live. Otherwise they will die when
they come near to the most holy things.
Aaron and his sons will go and appoint each
one of them to their ministry and their
responsibilities, 20 only they are not to go in
and watch while the holy things are being
covered, lest they die."

21 The LORD spoke to Moses, saying,
22 "Count the number of the sons of Gershon
by their clans and their families. 23 Count all
the men from thirty to fifty years old who go
in to minister in the tent of meeting. 24 This
is the ministry of the clan of the Gershonites,
their service and responsibility. 25 They will
carry the curtains of the tabernacle and the
tent of meeting with its covering, the cover-
ing of sheep skin that is over it, the screen for
the entrance to the tent of meeting, 26 the
curtains for the courtyard, the screen for the
entrance to the courtyard that surrounds
the tabernacle and the altar, their cords, and
all of their accessories. They will do all that
needs to be done with these things. 27 All the
service of the Gershonites, what they are to
carry and what they are to do, will be under
the direction of Aaron and his sons. You are
to assign them responsibility for what they
are to carry. 28 These things in the tent of
meeting are the responsibility of the families
of the Gershonites. Their service will be
under the direction of Ithamar, the son of
Aaron the priest.

29 "Count the number of the Merarites by
their clans and their families. 30 Count all the
men from thirty to fifty years old who go in
to minister in the tent of meeting. 31 This is
their responsibility and service for the tent
of meeting: the boards of the tabernacle with
their bars, their pillars, their sockets,[y] 32 the
pillars surrounding the courtyard, their
sockets, their pins, their cords, and all their
accessories. You will assign the things that
they are charged to carry by name. 33 This is
the service of the clan of the Merarites. All of
their service in the tent of meeting will be
under the direction of Ithamar, the son of
Aaron, the priest."

Counting the Adult Levites. 34 Moses and
Aaron and the leaders of the assembly
counted the Kohathites by family and by
clan, 35 those who were from thirty to fifty
years old and who went in to minister in the
service of the tent of meeting. 36 By families
there were two thousand, seven hundred
and fifty. 37 This was the number of those in
the families of the Kohathites who minis-
tered in the tent of meeting, whom Moses
and Aaron counted, fulfilling the command-
ment of the LORD given to Moses.

38 The sons of Gershon were counted by
families and clan 39 counting those who were
from thirty years old to fifty years old and
who went in to minister in the service of the
tent of meeting. 40 Counted by family and
clan, there were two thousand, six hundred
and thirty of them. 41 This was the number of
the families of the sons of Gershon, all of
whom served in the tent of meeting, whom
Moses and Aaron counted, fulfilling the
commandment of the LORD.

42 The Merarites were counted by families
and clan, 43 those who were from thirty years
old to fifty years old and who went in to min-
ister in the service of the tent of meeting.
44 Counted by families, there were three
thousand, two hundred of them. 45 This was
the number of the families of the Merarites
whom Moses and Aaron counted, fulfilling

x Lev 16:13; 2 Sam 6:7.—y Num 3:36-37.

4:13 *Empty all the ashes:* the altar of holocausts. See Ex 27:1-8.

the commandment of the LORD given to
Moses.

46 Moses and Aaron and the leaders of
Israel counted all of the Levites according to
families and clans 47 who were from thirty
years old to fifty years old, everyone who
could enter to do the work of ministry and
who served carrying the tent of meeting.
48 There were eight thousand, five hundred
and eighty of them. 49 They were counted as
the LORD had commanded Moses, counting
all of those dedicated for service and carry-
ing, just as the LORD had commanded
Moses.

CHAPTER 5

Purifying the Camp. 1 The LORD spoke to
Moses, saying, 2 "Command the people of
Israel to expel from the camp every leper
and everyone who has a discharge and
everyone who is unclean because they
touched the dead.[z] 3 You will expel both men
and women from the camp. You will put
them out so that they do not make the camp
unclean, for I dwell in their midst."[a] 4 The
people of Israel did this, putting them out-
side of the camp. The Israelites did what the
LORD had instructed Moses.

Making Recompense.* [b] 5 The LORD spoke
to Moses, saying, 6 "Say to the people of
Israel, 'When a man or a woman sins in any
way, that person has been unfaithful to the
LORD and will be considered to be guilty.
7 He will confess the sin that he has commit-
ted. He will recompense his trespass, taking
the full amount and one-fifth more and give
it to the person against whom he has com-
mitted this offense. 8 But if the person
offended has no kinsmen who could receive
the recompense for the trespass, then let the
trespass be paid to the LORD, to the priest,
besides the ram that is being used to obtain
his atonement. 9 Every offering of holy
things that the people of Israel bring to the
priest will belong to him.[c] 10 Everyone's gift
of holy things will belong to him; whatever is
given to the priest belongs to him.' "

The Test of Unfaithfulness.* 11 The LORD
spoke to Moses, saying, 12 "Speak to the peo-
ple of Israel and say to them, 'If any man's
wife goes astray and is unfaithful to him,
13 and a man has sex with her, and this is hid-
den from her husband, and she is defiled but
keeps it a secret since there are no witnesses
and she was not caught in the act,[d] 14 and if
a spirit of jealousy comes upon him, and he
is jealous of his wife because she has defiled
herself, or if a spirit of jealousy comes upon
him and he is jealous of her even though she
has not defiled herself, 15 then he will take his
wife to the priest. He will also bring an offer-
ing for her, a tenth of an ephah of barley
meal in which he has not poured oil nor put
frankincense. This is a jealousy offering. *

16 " 'The priest will bring her and have her
stand before the LORD. 17 The priest will put
some holy water in a clay vessel and he will
put some of the dust from the floor of the
sanctuary into the water. 18 The priest will
have the woman stand before the LORD. He
will uncover her hair and he will place the
jealousy memorial offering in her hands. The
priest will hold the bitter water that brings
on a curse in his hands. 19 The priest will
have the woman swear an oath saying, "If no
other man has slept with you and if you have
not gone astray, becoming defiled while
married to your husband, then you will be
free from the curse that this bitter water
causes. 20 But if you have gone astray while
married to your husband, becoming defiled,
and you have had sex with someone other
than your husband," 21 (at this point the
priest will have the woman swear an oath to
curse herself, and the priest will say to the
woman) "then may the LORD make you a
curse and a blight among your people. May
the LORD make your loins rot and your
womb swell; * 22 this water that brings on a
curse will descend to your womb causing it
to swell and your loins to rot." The woman
will then say, "Amen, amen."[e] 23 The priest
will write these curses in a book and blot

z Num 19:11-16; Lev 13:45-46.—a Lev 26:12; 2 Cor 6:16.—b 5-7: Lev 5:15-25.—c Deut 18:3-4.—d Ex 20:14; Lev 18:20.—e Ps 109:18.

5:5-10 This section mirrors the punishment for personal wrongs given in Lev 15, but extends it to include those wronged who have no kinsmen, in which case restitution would be made directly to the priest.

5:11-31 Where there was suspicion but no proof, recourse was to divine judgment, the manner of which is prescribed by the biblical lawgiver. This kind of judgment, though adapted somewhat, goes back to a practice followed in antiquity, especially in Babylon. Even though the present text protects the wife from violence inflicted by a jealous husband, it also shows woman's condition of inferiority: in this humiliating situation the woman is presumed guilty, whereas no such provision is made in the case of an adulterous husband. The Gospels take a far different view (Mt 19:9; Jn 8:1-11)!

5:15, 18 *Jealousy offering:* a grain offering that was meant to encourage the wrongdoer to reflect on their sin.

5:21 *Your loins rot and your womb swell:* this was a terrible curse on a woman whose worth was determined by her ability to conceive and bear a child.

them out with the bitter water. 24 He will have the woman drink the bitter water that brings on the curse. The water that brings on the curse will enter her and will become bitter. 25 The priest will then take the jealousy offering out of the woman's hand and wave the offering before the LORD and offer it upon the altar. 26 The priest will take a handful of the offering as the memorial offering and will burn it upon the altar. After that he will have the woman drink the water.[f] 27 When he has made her drink the water, if she has defiled herself and been unfaithful to her husband, the curse in the water will enter her and be bitter and will cause her womb to swell and her loins to rot.[g] 28 But if the woman has not defiled herself and she is clean, then she will be unharmed and will conceive children.

29 " 'This is the law of jealousy, when a wife goes astray while married to her husband and becomes defiled 30 or when the spirit of jealousy comes upon him and he is jealous of his wife. He will bring his wife before the LORD and the priest will fulfill all the prescriptions of this law upon her. 31 The man will be free from guilt, but the woman will bear her guilt.' "

CHAPTER 6

Nazirite Laws.* 1 The LORD spoke to Moses, saying, 2 "Speak to the people of Israel and say to them, 'If a man or a woman dedicates himself or herself with a vow, a Nazirite vow to dedicate himself or herself unto the LORD, 3 [h]that person will abstain from wine and strong drink. He will not drink any vinegar made from wine or from strong drink, nor will he drink any grape juice, nor will he eat grapes or raisins. 4 He is not to eat anything that comes from the vine, not even the seeds or the skins as long as he is a Nazirite. 5 No razor will touch his head all throughout the time of his vow. He is to be holy until the days of his vow have been completed. He will let the hair on his head grow long. 6 He is not to approach any dead body during the entire period of his vow to the LORD. 7 He is not to make himself unclean even for his father or mother if they were to die, nor his brother or sister, for the consecration of God is upon his head. 8 He is to be holy to the LORD all the days of his vow.

9 " 'But if someone were to die suddenly in his presence and defile his consecrated head, he is to shave his head on the day of his cleansing and he will shave it again on the seventh day. 10 Then on the eighth day he will bring two turtledoves or two young pigeons to the priest at the entrance to the tent of meeting. 11 The priest will offer one of them as a sin offering and the other as a burnt offering making atonement for the uncleanness caused by the dead person. On that same day he is to consecrate his head* 12 and he will dedicate his days of consecration unto the LORD. He will bring a year-old male lamb as a guilt offering. The days that preceded this incident will not count, however, for his dedicated head had been defiled.

13 " 'This is the law concerning Nazirites when the time of their dedication is completed. He is to be brought to the entrance to the tent of meeting.[i] 14 He will bring a year-old male lamb without defect unto the LORD as a burnt offering, and a one-year-old ewe lamb without defect for a sin offering, and a one-year-old ram without defect as a peace offering 15 and a basket of unleavened bread made from fine flour mixed with oil, and unleavened wafers of bread with oil spread on them, and a cereal offering, and a drink offering. 16 The priest will bring them before the LORD and he will offer his sin offering and his burnt offering. 17 He will offer the ram as the sacrifice of a peace offering unto the LORD together with the basket of unleavened bread. The priest will also offer the cereal offering and the drink offering. 18 The Nazirite will shave his head at the entrance to the tent of meeting. He will take the hair that grew during the period when he was vowed and put it on the fire under the sacrifice of the peace offering. 19 The priest will take a shoulder of the ram that has been boiled, and an unleavened cake out of the basket, and an unleavened wafer, and he will put them into the hands of the Nazirite who has shaved off the hair of his vow. 20 The priest will wave them as a wave offering

f Lev 5:12.—g Jer 29:18; 42:18.—h 3-5: Lev 10:9; Jdg 13:5.—i Lev 14:11; Acts 21:23.

6:1-21 A Nazirite is a person consecrated to God by a vow. Samson was one (Jdg 13:5), as was the prophet Samuel (1 Sam 1:11); in the New Testament, perhaps John the Baptist (Lk 1:15) and Jesus himself (Mt 2:23) were Nazirites.

This state as a consecrated person is often mentioned in the Bible, but it underwent an evolution: initially it was regarded as a permanent gift but in the period in which the Book of Numbers was edited, it had become a temporary choice (see Acts 18:18; 21:23f, 26).

6:11 The guilt here is purely legal.

before the LORD. It is holy and will belong to
the priest, along with the breast of the wave
offering and the thigh that was presented.
After this the Nazirite can drink wine.[j]
21 This is the law of the Nazirite who has
vowed his offering unto the LORD for his con-
secration (apart from what else he can
afford). He must fulfill what he has vowed to
do by the Nazirite law.' "

The Priests' Blessing.* 22 The LORD spoke to
Moses, saying, 23 "Speak to Aaron and his
sons, saying, 'This is how you will bless the
people of Israel, saying to them,

24 [k] " ' "The LORD bless you and keep you.
25 The LORD shine his face upon you and
be gracious to you.
26 The LORD look upon you kindly and give
you peace." ' *

27 They will invoke my name upon the people
of Israel, and I will bless them."

CHAPTER 7

Tribal Offerings. 1 * The day that Moses
completed setting up the tabernacle, he
anointed it and consecrated it and all of its
furnishings, including the altar and all of its
utensils. He anointed and consecrated
them.[l] 2 The leaders of Israel, the heads of
the clans, and the leaders of the tribes that
had been counted in the census, made their
offerings. 3 They brought their offerings
before the LORD: six covered wagons and
twelve oxen. There was a wagon for each two
leaders, and an oxen for each of them. They
brought them before the tabernacle.

4 The LORD spoke to Moses, saying,
5 "Accept these things from them so that
they might be used in the service of the tent
of meeting. Give them to the Levites, each
according to his responsibility." 6 Moses took
the wagons and the oxen and gave them to
the Levites. 7 [m] He gave two wagons and four
oxen to the Gershonites for their responsi-
bilities. 8 He also gave four wagons and eight
oxen to the Merarites for their responsibili-
ties. They were under the direction of
Ithamar, the son of Aaron the priest. 9 None
of them were given to the Kohathites, for it
was their job to carry their portion of the
tabernacle upon their shoulders.[n]

10 The leaders also presented offerings to
commemorate the dedication of the altar on
the day that it was anointed. The leaders
placed their offerings before the altar. 11 The
LORD said to Moses, "Let each of the leaders
present his offering for the dedication of the
altar on successive days."

12 Nahshon, the son of Amminadab of the
tribe of Judah, presented his offering on the
first day. 13 His offering was one silver dish
that weighed one hundred and thirty shekels
and one bowl weighing seventy shekels, both
calculated according to the shekel of the
sanctuary. Both vessels were filled with fine
flour mixed with oil for a grain offering.
14 He also brought one gold pan weighing ten
shekels, filled with incense, 15 one young bull,
one young ram, one year-old male lamb for
a burnt offering, 16 one male goat for a sin
offering, 17 and two oxen, five rams, and five
year-old male lambs for a peace offering.
This was the offering of Nahshon, the son of
Amminadab.

18 Nethanel, the son of Zuar, the leader of
the people of Issachar, brought his offering
on the second day. 19 His offering was one sil-
ver dish that weighed one hundred and thir-
ty shekels and one bowl weighing seventy
shekels, both calculated according to the
shekel of the sanctuary. Both vessels were
filled with fine flour mixed with oil for a
grain offering. 20 He also brought one gold
pan weighing ten shekels, filled with incense,
21 one young bull, one young ram, one year-
old male lamb for a burnt offering, 22 one
male goat for a sin offering, 23 and two oxen,
five rams, and five year-old male lambs for a
peace offering. This was the offering of
Nethanel, the son of Zuar.

24 Eliab, the son of Helon, the leader of the
people of Zebulun, presented on the third
day 25 his offering of one silver dish that
weighed one hundred and thirty shekels and
one bowl weighing seventy shekels, both cal-
culated according to the shekel of the sanc-
tuary. Both vessels were filled with fine flour

j Lev 7:28-34.—k 24-27: Ps 4:6-7; Jn 14:27.—l Ex 40:17.—m 7-8: Num 4:24-33.—n Num 4:4-15.

6:22-27 *Invoke my name upon the people of Israel* means to make God benevolently present among the people. It is understandable that this text should have been adopted in the recent liturgical reform as an (optional) amplification of the blessing that the priest gives when he dismisses the people at the end of the Mass.

6:26 *Give you peace:* the Hebrew word is *shalom* and expresses a state of unanimity that can only be found through the Lord.

7:1—9:14 According to the Book of Exodus (Ex 40:17), these preparations were made a month before the census that is recorded at the beginning of the Book of Numbers. Evidently, the biblical author makes free use, in accordance with his own perspective, of the records available to him in the various traditions.

mixed with oil for a grain offering. 26 He also brought one gold pan weighing ten shekels, filled with incense, 27 one young bull, one young ram, one year-old male lamb for a burnt offering, 28 one male goat for a sin offering, 29 and two oxen, five rams, and five year-old male lambs for a peace offering. This was the offering of Eliab, the son of Helon.

30 Elizur, the son of Shedeur, the leader of the people of Reuben, presented on the fourth day 31 his offering of one silver dish that weighed one hundred and thirty shekels and one bowl weighing seventy shekels, both calculated according to the shekel of the sanctuary. Both vessels were filled with fine flour mixed with oil for a grain offering. 32 He also brought one gold pan weighing ten shekels, filled with incense, 33 one young bull, one young ram, one year-old male lamb for a burnt offering, 34 one male goat for a sin offering, 35 and two oxen, five rams, and five year-old male lambs for a peace offering. This was the offering of Elizur, the son of Shedeur.

36 Shelumiel, the son of Zurishaddai, the leader of the people of Simeon, presented on the fifth day 37 his offering of one silver dish that weighed one hundred and thirty shekels and one bowl weighing seventy shekels, both calculated according to the shekel of the sanctuary. Both vessels were filled with fine flour mixed with oil for a grain offering. 38 He also brought one gold pan weighing ten shekels, filled with incense, 39 one young bull, one young ram, one year-old male lamb for a burnt offering, 40 one male goat for a sin offering, 41 and two oxen, five rams, and five year-old male lambs for a peace offering. This was the offering of Shelumiel, the son of Zurishaddai.

42 Eliasaph, the son of Reuel, the leader of the people of Gad, presented on the sixth day 43 his offering of one silver dish that weighed one hundred and thirty shekels and one bowl weighing seventy shekels, both calculated according to the shekel of the sanctuary. Both vessels were filled with fine flour mixed with oil for a grain offering. 44 He also brought one gold pan weighing ten shekels, filled with incense, 45 one young bull, one young ram, one year-old male lamb for a burnt offering, 46 one male goat for a sin offering, 47 and two oxen, five rams, and five year-old male lambs for a peace offering. This was the offering of Eliasaph, the son of Reuel.

48 Elishama, the son of Ammihud, the leader of the people of Ephraim, presented on the seventh day 49 his offering of one silver dish that weighed one hundred and thirty shekels and one bowl weighing seventy shekels, both calculated according to the shekel of the sanctuary. Both vessels were filled with fine flour mixed with oil for a grain offering. 50 He also brought one gold pan weighing ten shekels, filled with incense, 51 one young bull, one young ram, one year-old male lamb for a burnt offering, 52 one male goat for a sin offering, 53 and two oxen, five rams, and five year-old male lambs for a peace offering. This was the offering of Elishama, the son of Ammihud.

54 Gamaliel, the son of Pedahzur, the leader of the people of Manasseh, presented on the eighth day 55 his offering of one silver dish that weighed one hundred and thirty shekels and one bowl weighing seventy shekels, both calculated according to the shekel of the sanctuary. Both vessels were filled with fine flour mixed with oil for a grain offering. 56 He also brought one gold pan weighing ten shekels, filled with incense, 57 one young bull, one young ram, one year-old male lamb for a burnt offering, 58 one male goat for a sin offering, 59 and two oxen, five rams, and five year-old male lambs for a peace offering. This was the offering of Gamaliel, the son of Pedahzur.

60 Abidan, the son of Gideoni, the leader of the people of Benjamin, presented on the ninth day 61 his offering of one silver dish that weighed one hundred and thirty shekels and one bowl weighing seventy shekels, both calculated according to the shekel of the sanctuary. Both vessels were filled with fine flour mixed with oil for a grain offering. 62 He also brought one gold pan weighing ten shekels, filled with incense, 63 one young bull, one young ram, one year-old male lamb for a burnt offering, 64 one male goat for a sin offering, 65 and two oxen, five rams, and five year-old male lambs for a peace offering. This was the offering of Abidan, the son of Gideoni.

66 Ahiezer, the son of Ammishaddai, the leader of the people of Dan, presented on the tenth day 67 his offering of one silver dish that weighed one hundred and thirty shekels and one bowl weighing seventy shekels, both cal-

culated according to the shekel of the sanctuary. Both vessels were filled with fine flour mixed with oil for a grain offering. [68] He also brought one gold pan weighing ten shekels, filled with incense, [69] one young bull, one young ram, one year-old male lamb for a burnt offering, [70] one male goat for a sin offering, [71] and two oxen, five rams, and five year-old male lambs for a peace offering. This was the offering of Ahiezer, the son of Ammishaddai.

[72] Pagiel, the son of Ochran, the leader of the people of Asher, presented on the eleventh day [73] his offering of one silver dish that weighed one hundred and thirty shekels and one bowl weighing seventy shekels, both calculated according to the shekel of the sanctuary. Both vessels were filled with fine flour mixed with oil for a grain offering. [74] He also brought one gold pan weighing ten shekels, filled with incense, [75] one young bull, one young ram, one-year-old male lamb for a burnt offering, [76] one male goat for a sin offering, [77] and two oxen, five rams, and five year-old male lambs for a peace offering. This was the offering of Pagiel, the son of Ochran.

[78] Ahira, the son of Enan, the leader of the people of Naphtali, presented on the twelfth day [79] his offering of one silver dish that weighed one hundred and thirty shekels and one bowl weighing seventy shekels, both calculated according to the shekel of the sanctuary. Both vessels were filled with fine flour mixed with oil for a grain offering. [80] He also brought one gold pan weighing ten shekels, filled with incense, [81] one young bull, one young ram, one year-old male lamb for a burnt offering, [82] one male goat for a sin offering, [83] and two oxen, five rams, and five year-old male lambs for a peace offering. This was the offering of Ahira, the son of Enan.

[84] This was the dedication offering from the leaders of Israel for the altar on the day that it was anointed: twelve silver dishes, twelve silver bowls and twelve gold pans. [85] Each silver dish weighed one hundred and thirty shekels and each silver bowl seventy shekels. All the silver vessels together weighed two thousand and four hundred shekels, calculated according to the shekel of the sanctuary. [86] The twelve gold pans full of incense weighed ten shekels each, calculated according to the shekel of the sanctuary. All together the gold pans weighed one hundred and twenty shekels. [87] There were twelve bull oxen for the burnt offering as well as twelve rams and twelve year-old male lambs with their grain offering, and there were twelve rams for the sin offering. [88] There were twenty-four bull oxen for the peace offering as well as sixty rams and sixty year-old male lambs. This was the dedication offering after it was anointed.

[89] When Moses had gone into the tent of meeting to speak with him, he heard a voice coming from above the mercy seat and between the two cherubim on the Ark of the Covenant speaking to him. So he spoke to him.* [o]

CHAPTER 8

The Lampstand. [1] The LORD spoke to Moses, saying, [2] "Speak to Aaron and say to him, 'When you set up the lamps, the seven lamps are to shine to the front of the lampstand.' " [p] [3] Aaron did this. He set up the lamps so that they faced forward on the lampstand, just as the LORD had commanded Moses. [4] This is how the lampstand was made: it was made from hammered gold from its base to its blossoms. The lampstand was made according to the pattern that the LORD had shown to Moses. [q]

Purifying the Levites. [5] The LORD said to Moses, [6] "Separate the Levites from the other people of Israel and purify them.* [7] Do the following to purify them: Sprinkle the water of expiation upon them, and have them shave their entire body and wash their clothes. This will purify them. [r] [8] Let them take a young bull and its cereal offering of fine flour mixed with oil. You shall also take another young bull for a sin offering. [9] You shall present the Levites before the tent of meeting. You shall also gather together the whole assembly of the people of Israel. [10] You shall present the Levites before the LORD, and all the people of Israel will lay their hands upon the Levites.* [11] Then Aaron will

o Ex 25:22; Pss 80:1; 99:1.—p Ex 25:37; Lev 24:2, 4.—q Ex 25:31-40.—r Num 19:9; Lev 14:9.

7:89 After a lengthy and repetitious listing of the precious gifts from the leaders of the 12 tribes, the chapter concludes with a highpoint: the presence of the Lord filling the tabernacle.

8:6 *Purify them:* through a complex ritual (see Ex 29) the priests were made holy whereas the Levites were cleansed for ministry.

8:10 The laying on of hands does not bestow any special power on the Levites, but makes of them an offering in the name of the people.

present the Levites to the LORD as a wave offering of the people of Israel so that they may carry out the work of the LORD. 12 The Levites will lay their hands upon the heads of the young bulls. You will offer one as a sin offering and the other as a burnt offering to the LORD to make atonement for the Levites.

13 "You shall have the Levites stand before Aaron and his sons to present them as a wave offering to the LORD. 14 Thus you will separate the Levites from the people of Israel, and the Levites will be mine.[s] 15 After this the Levites can go in and serve the needs of the tent of meeting, when you have purified them and offered them as a wave offering. 16 They are to be wholly dedicated to me from among the people of Israel. I have reserved them for myself as a substitute for all those who open the womb, the firstborn of the people of Israel. 17 All the firstborn of the people of Israel belong to me, both human and animal. I sanctified them to myself on the day that I killed every firstborn in the land of Egypt. 18 But I have taken the Levites as a substitute for all the firstborn of the people of Israel. 19 I have given the Levites as a gift to Aaron and his sons from among the people of Israel, to perform the work of the people of Israel in the tent of meeting and to make atonement for the people of Israel, so that no plague may come upon the people of Israel when the people of Israel approach near the sanctuary."[t]

20 So Moses and Aaron and all the assembly of the people of Israel did to the Levites what God had commanded Moses concerning the Levites, that is what the people of Israel did to them. 21 The Levites purified themselves and washed their clothes. Aaron presented them as a wave offering to the LORD, and made atonement for them to purify them. 22 Then the Levites went in and performed the work of the tent of meeting under the authority of Aaron and his sons. They did to the Levites the things that the LORD had commanded Moses concerning them.

23 The LORD spoke to Moses, saying, 24 "The Levites will go in to perform the work of the tent of meeting from the age of twenty-five years old.[u] 25 Then, when they are fifty years old, they will stop performing that service. They will work no more. 26 They may assist their brothers in carrying out the duties of the tent of meeting, but they themselves are not to perform that work. This is how you will establish the responsibilities of the Levites."

CHAPTER 9

Observing the Passover. 1 The LORD spoke to Moses in the Sinai Desert in the first month of the second year after they had come out of the land of Egypt. He said, 2 "Let the people of Israel celebrate the Passover at its appointed time. 3 You will celebrate it at its appointed time, on the fourteenth day of this month, at sunset. You will observe it in accordance with all its statutes; you shall follow all of its ordinances."[v] 4 So Moses told the people of Israel that they should observe the Passover. 5 They celebrated Passover on the sunset of the fourteenth day of the month in the Sinai Desert. The people of Israel did everything that the LORD had commanded Moses.

6 Now there were some men who had become unclean by touching a dead body, and they could not observe the Passover on that day. They came to Moses and Aaron on that day 7 and they said, "We are unclean because we touched a dead person's body. Why are we prohibited from presenting an offering to the LORD at its appointed time with the rest of the people of Israel?"

8 Moses said to them, "Stand here, and I will listen to what the LORD commands concerning your situation." 9 The LORD spoke to Moses, saying, 10 "Speak to the people of Israel, saying, 'If any of you or your descendants is unclean because that person comes into contact with a dead body or he is on a journey and is far away, that person shall still observe[*] the Passover of the LORD. 11 You will celebrate it the fourteenth day of the second month, you will eat it with unleavened bread and bitter herbs. 12 You shall not leave any leftovers until the morning, nor shall you break any of its bones. You will observe it according to the ordinances of the Passover of the LORD.[w]

13 " 'But if some person is ritually clean and is not off on a journey and that person refuses to observe the Passover, let that person be cut off from among his people. He did

---

s Num 3:12, 45.—t Num 3:9-10.—u Num 4:3.—v Ex 12:6; Lev 23:5-8.—w Ex 12:46; Jn 19:36.

9:10 *That person shall still observe:* though unclean, the Lord mercifully provided an alternate day to celebrate the Passover, evidencing his justice and his mercy.

not bring his offerings at the appointed time, so he will bear his sin.

[14] " 'If a foreigner* dwelling among you wants to observe the Passover of the LORD, let him do so according to the ordinances of the Passover and according to its ceremonies. There is one set of ordinances for those who are foreigners and for those who were born in the land.' " [x]

Journeying by the Cloud. [15] Now on the day that the tabernacle was set up, the cloud covered the tabernacle, the tent of meeting. From evening until morning it appeared in the form of fire. [y] [16] The cloud covered it by day and fire by night. [17] Whenever the cloud was lifted up from the tabernacle, the people of Israel would journey out. The people of Israel would then settle and pitch their tent in the place where the cloud would descend.

[18] The people of Israel would journey at the command of the LORD, and they would camp at the command of the LORD. As long as the cloud hovered over the tabernacle, they would stay where they were. [z] [19] Even when the cloud hovered over the tabernacle for several days, the people of Israel would observe the command of the LORD and they would not journey out. [20] At times the cloud would hover over the tabernacle for a few days. They stayed where they were in accordance with the command of the LORD, and they journeyed out in accordance with the command of the LORD. [21] Other times, the cloud would hover from evening until morning, and then the cloud would be lifted up in the morning. They would then journey out. Whether it was by day or by night that the cloud lifted off, it was then that they would journey out. [22] Whether it was two days or a month or a year that the cloud hovered over the tabernacle, the people of Israel would remain where they were. When it was lifted up, then they would journey out. [23] At the command of the LORD, they stayed where they were and at the command of the LORD they journeyed out. They observed the bidding of the LORD,* in accordance with the commands of the LORD received through Moses.

CHAPTER 10

Sounding the Trumpets. [1] The LORD said to Moses, [2] "Make two trumpets for yourself. Make them from hammered silver. Use them for summoning the assembly and for breaking camp. [3] When they are sounded, the whole assembly will gather before you at the entrance to the tent of meeting. [4] If only one is sounded, the leaders, the heads of the clans of Israel, are to assemble before you. [5] When the advance is sounded, the camps that lie on the east side will set out. [6] With the second blast of the trumpet, the camps that lie to the south side will set out. The trumpet blast will signal their setting out. [7] To gather together the assembly, sound the trumpets but not with the same signal.

[8] "The sons of Aaron, the priests, will sound the trumpets. This is to be an everlasting ordinance throughout all your generations. [a] [9] When you go into battle against an enemy who is oppressing you in your own land, sound a blast on the trumpets. Then you will be remembered by the LORD, your God, and you will be saved. [10] Also, at times of rejoicing, your solemn feasts and your new moon celebrations, you are to sound the trumpets over the burnt offerings and the peace offerings. They will be a memorial for you to your God. I am the LORD, your God." [b]

II: FORTY YEARS IN THE WILDERNESS*

Departure from Sinai. [11]* On the twentieth day of the second month of the second year, the cloud was lifted up from the tabernacle of the Testimony. [12] The people of Israel set out from the Sinai Desert and traveled until the cloud came to rest in the Desert of Paran.*

[13] They set out this first time in accord with the command of the LORD received through Moses. [14] The standard of the camp of the tribe of Judah went out first by their companies. Nahshon, the son of

x Ex 12:48-49.—y Ex 13:21; Neh 9:12, 19.—z 1 Cor 10:1.—a Num 31:6.—b Num 29:1; Ps 81:3-5.

9:14 *A foreigner:* a requirement to participate in the Passover celebration is to be circumcised.

9:23 *They observed the bidding of the LORD:* as in previous chapters that stress the obedience of the people, their eventual disobedience (ch. 11) is in marked contrast.

10:11—21:35 In this section, the Book of Numbers takes up the story begun in the Book of Exodus. As the Hebrews journey through the wilderness, they suffer and rebel, thereby bringing down divine punishment on themselves. The Church, the new Israel, is subject to analogous vicissitudes in the course of its history.

10:11-36 So orderly an advance has the appearance more of a liturgical procession than of a movement of nomads; it is reminiscent of the solemn transfers of the Ark under David and Solomon (2 Sam 6:12f; 1 Ki 8:3f).

10:12 The Desert of Paran is northeast of the Sinai.

Amminadab, was leader of its company.[c] 15 Nethanel, the son of Zuar, was the leader of the company of the tribe of Issachar. 16 Eliab, the son of Helon, was the leader of the company of the tribe of Zebulun. 17 The tabernacle was then taken down, and the Gershonites and the Merarites who carried the tabernacle set out. 18 The standard of the camp of the tribe of Reuben set forth next. Elizur, the son of Shedeur, was the leader of its company. 19 Shelumiel, the son of Zurishaddai, was the leader of the company of the tribe of Simeon. 20 Eliasaph, the son of Reuel, was the leader of the company of the tribe of Gad. 21 Then the Kohathites set forth carrying the sanctuary. The tabernacle was to be set up when they arrived. 22 The standard of the camp of the tribe of Ephraim came next. Elishama, the son of Ammihud, was the leader of its company. 23 Gamaliel, the son of Pedahzur, was the leader of the company of the tribe of Manasseh. 24 Abidan, the son of Gideoni, was the leader of the company of the tribe of Benjamin.

25 Finally, behind all of the other camps, the standard of the camp of the tribe of Dan set out. Ahiezer, the son of Ammishaddai, was the leader of its company. 26 Pagiel, the son of Ochran, was the leader of the company of the tribe of Asher. 27 Ahira, the son of Enan, was the leader of the company of the tribe of Naphtali. 28 This was the order of the companies of the people of Israel as they set out.

Plea to Hobab. 29 Moses said to Hobab, the son of Reuel the Midianite, Moses' father-in-law, "We are setting out for the place that the LORD said, 'I will give it to you.' Come with us and we will treat you well, for the LORD has promised good things to Israel."[d] 30 But he said to him, "I will not go, rather I will leave for my own land and my own people." 31 But he said, "Please do not leave us. You know where we should camp in the desert, and you could look out for us. 32 If you come with us, then whatever good things the LORD bestows upon us, we will share them with you."

Into the Wilderness. 33 They traveled a three days' journey from the mountain of the LORD, and the Ark of the Covenant went before them throughout the three days' journey, searching out a resting place for them.[e] 34 The cloud of the LORD was over them by day when they set out from the camp. 35 Whenever the Ark set forth, Moses would say,

"Rise up, O LORD, let your enemies be scattered.
Let those who hate you flee before you."*

36 Whenever it rested he said,

"Return, O LORD, to the thousands upon thousands of Israel."

CHAPTER 11

The People of Israel Complain. 1 The people complained about their hardships and the LORD heard and his anger flared up. Then the fire of the LORD burned up the outskirts of the camp.[f] 2 The people cried out to Moses, and Moses prayed to the LORD and the fire was quenched. 3 He named that place Taberah,* for the fire of the LORD had burned in their midst.

4 Now the rabble* among them fell victim to their desires again, and the people of Israel said, "Who will give us meat to eat?[g] 5 [h] We remember the fish we ate freely in Egypt, along with the cucumbers, the melons, the leeks, the onions, and the garlic. 6 But now our strength is fading away, all we ever see is this manna." 7 Manna had the shape of coriander seed and it looked like resin.[i] 8 The people would go around gathering it, and then they would grind it in a mill or beat it in a mortar. They cooked it in a pot or made it into cakes. It tasted something like fresh olive oil. 9 The manna would come down when the dew settled upon the camp at night.[j]

10 Moses heard the people weeping, each family at the entrance to their tent. The LORD became exceedingly angry, and Moses was greatly displeased. 11 Moses said to the LORD, "Why are you torturing your servant? Have I not found favor in your sight, that you would burden me with this whole people? 12 Did I conceive this entire people? Did I give birth to them that you should say to me,

c Num 2:3-9.—d Ex 2:18; Jdg 4:11.—e Deut 1:33.—f Num 14:2; Deut 9:22.—g Ex 16:3; Ps 78:18.—h 5-6: Num 21:5; Ex 16:3.—i Ex 16:14, 31.—j Ex 16:13; Ps 78:23-25.

10:35 A bit of liturgy (see Ps 68:1; Isa 33:3).

11:3 *Taberah* seems to mean "place of pasture," but the sacred writer here connects it with a similar root that means "to burn." According to Deut 9:22f, this spot was in the area of Kadesh.

11:4 *Rabble:* this group incited those who were close to the Lord by pointing out all the negatives. As with many groups, the most vocal often set the mood and actions of the masses.

'Carry them in your arms like a nurse car-
ries a small child to the land that I have
promised to their ancestors?' [13] Where can I
get enough meat to give to all this people, for
they cry to me saying, 'Give us meat to eat!'
[14] I cannot carry this entire people by myself;
they are too burdensome for me. [15] If this is
the way that you are going to treat me, and
if I have found favor in your sight, then
please put me to death right now so I do not
have to keep looking upon my misery."

[16] But the LORD said to Moses, "Bring me
seventy men from among the elders of
Israel whom you know to be elders and
leaders of the people. Bring them to the tent
of meeting, and have them stand there with
yourself. [17] I will come down and speak to
you there. I will take some of the Spirit that
is upon you and put it upon them. They will
carry the burden of the people with you, so
that you do not have to carry it alone.[k]
[18] Say to the people, 'Consecrate yourselves,
for tomorrow you will eat meat. You cried
out in the hearing of the LORD, saying,
"Who will give us meat to eat? We were bet-
ter off when we were in Egypt." Now the
LORD will give you meat, and you will eat it.
[19] You will not eat it for just one day, nor for
two days, nor for five days, nor for ten days,
nor for twenty days. [20] You will eat it for a
whole month, until your faces overflow with
it, and you become sick of it, for you have
despised the LORD who is among you and
whom you have confronted crying out,
"Why did we come out of Egypt?" ' "

[21] But Moses said, "I am standing among
six hundred thousand people on foot, and
you have said, 'I will give them meat to eat
for an entire month?' [22] Shall the flocks and
herds be slaughtered to satisfy their
desires? Will all of the fish of the sea be
gathered together to fill them?" [23] The
LORD answered Moses, "Is the LORD's
power limited? Now you will see whether
my word will be fulfilled or not."

Seventy Elders. [24] So Moses went out and
proclaimed the words of the LORD to the
people. He brought seventy of the elders of
the people and placed them around the
tabernacle. [25] Then the LORD came down in
a cloud and spoke to him. He took some of
the Spirit that was upon him and placed it
upon the seventy elders. When the Spirit
descended upon them, they began to proph-
esy,* although they did not do so again.[l]

[26] But two men had remained in the
camp. One was named Eldad, and the other
was named Medad. The Spirit descended
upon them. They had been on the list, but
they had not gone out to the tabernacle.
They began to prophesy in the camp. [27] A
young man ran and informed Moses, say-
ing, "Eldad and Medad are prophesying in
the camp." [28] Joshua, the son of Nun, who
had been an aide to Moses since he was
young, said, "My lord Moses, stop them."
[29] But Moses said to him, "Are you jealous
for me? Would that all of the LORD's people
were prophets, that the LORD would put his
Spirit upon them!" [30] Moses then returned
to the camp, he and the elders of Israel.

[31] Now a wind came forth from the LORD,
and it brought quail from the sea, making
them fall near the camp. They were all
around the camp, a day's journey on one
side and a day's journey on the other side.
They were piled up on the surface of the
land two cubits high.[m]

[32] The people stayed up all day, and all
night, and all the next day gathering the
quail. The least that any of them gathered
was ten homers. They spread them out for
themselves all around the camp. [33] But
while the meat was still between their teeth
and they were still chewing on it, the anger
of the LORD arose against the people and
the LORD struck the people with a horrible
plague.[n] [34] This is why that place was called
Kibroth-hattaavah,* because they buried
the people who had fallen victim to their
desires there.[o] [35] From Kibroth-hattaavah
the people traveled to Hazeroth and they
camped there.

CHAPTER 12

Miriam and Aaron Oppose Moses. [1] Miriam*
and Aaron criticized Moses because of the
Ethiopian woman whom he had married, for
he had married an Ethiopian woman. [2] They

k 1 Sam 10:6; 2 Ki 2:9.—l 1 Sam 10:9-13; Acts 2:17-18.—m Ex 16:13; Ps 78:26-28.—n Ps 78:30-31.—o Deut 9:22.

11:25 *They began to prophesy:* the prophetic gift in this case seems to be limited in time and power, but it allowed the seventy elders to be established as spiritual leaders.

11:34 At one time *Kibroth-hattaavah* certainly meant "grave of the Ta'avah" (i.e., a tribe). A different etymology, "graves of craving," allows the sacred writer to highlight the moral significance of the incident. According to Deut 9:23, the place was near Kadesh.

12:1 *Miriam* is the sister of Moses; the Ethiopian is Zipporah, a Midianite (Ex 2:21). In Israelite thinking, marriage with a foreign woman was cause for a family to lose the gift of prophecy.

said, "Has the LORD only spoken through Moses? Has he not also spoken through us?" And the LORD heard this.

[3] Now Moses was very humble, more so than anyone else upon the face of the earth.[p] [4] Suddenly the LORD spoke to Moses and Aaron and Miriam, saying, "Come out, you three, from the tent of meeting." And the three of them came out. [5] The LORD came down in a pillar of cloud and stood at the entrance to the tabernacle and summoned Aaron and Miriam, and they both came forward. [6] * He said, "Hear now my words:

"If anyone among you is a prophet,
I, the LORD, make myself known to him in a vision,
I speak to him in a dream.[q]
7 [r] It is not that way with Moses,
who is entrusted with all my household.
8 I speak to him face to face,
clearly, and not in riddles.
He beholds the very form of the LORD.

Why then were you not afraid to criticize my servant Moses?" [9] Then the anger of the LORD blazed against them, and he departed.

Miriam's Punishment. [10] When the cloud lifted up off of the tabernacle, there stood Miriam, leprous, white as snow. Aaron turned toward Miriam and saw that she was a leper.[s] [11] Aaron said to Moses, "Please, my lord, do not hold the sin against us that we have so foolishly committed! [12] Let her not be like a stillborn child who comes forth from its mother's womb with its flesh half eaten away." [13] Moses cried out to the LORD, "O God, I beseech you, heal her!" [14] The LORD replied to Moses, "If her father had only spit in her face, would she not have been shamed for seven days? Confine her outside of the camp for seven days. After that, let her be received back in."[t]

[15] So Miriam was confined outside of the camp for seven days. The people did not move on until Miriam was brought back in.

[16] After this, the people left Hazeroth and they camped in the Desert of Paran.

CHAPTER 13

Twelve Scouts. [1] * The LORD spoke to Moses, saying, [2] "Send some men out to explore the land of Canaan that I am giving to the people of Israel. Send one of the leaders from each of the ancestral tribes."

[3] [u] So Moses sent them out from the Desert of Paran by command of the LORD, each of them being one of the heads of the people of Israel. [4] These are their names:

from the tribe of Reuben there was Shammua, the son of Zaccur;
5 from the tribe of Simeon there was Shaphat, the son of Hori;
6 from the tribe of Judah there was Caleb, the son of Jephunneh;
7 from the tribe of Issachar there was Igal, the son of Joseph;
8 from the tribe of Ephraim there was Hoshea, the son of Nun;
9 from the tribe of Benjamin there was Palti, the son of Raphu;
10 from the tribe of Zebulun there was Gaddiel, the son of Sodi;
11 from the tribe of Joseph, that is, from the tribe of Manasseh, there was Gaddi, the son of Susi;
12 from the tribe of Dan there was Ammiel, the son of Gemalli;
13 from the tribe of Asher there was Sethur, the son of Michael;
14 from the tribe of Naphtali there was Nahbi, the son of Vophsi;
15 and from the tribe of Gad there was Geuel, the son of Machi.

[16] These are the names of those whom Moses sent to explore the land. Moses gave Hoshea, the son of Nun, the name Joshua.

[17] Moses sent them to explore the land of Canaan. He said to them, "Go up into the Negeb,* then go up into the hill country. [18] See what the land is like. Discover whether the people who live there are strong or weak, few or many. [19] How is the land upon which they are living, is it good or bad? How are the cities in which they dwell, are they open camps or fortified? [20] How is the land, is it fertile or poor? Are there trees or not? Try to bring back some of the fruit of the land" (for it was the season of the first ripe grapes).

[21] So they went up and explored the land, from the Desert of Zin up to Rehob, near the

p Sir 45:4; Mt 11:29.—q Gen 15:1; 46:2; 1 Ki 3:5.—r 7-8: Ex 33:11; Heb 3:2, 5.—s Deut 24:9.—t Lev 13:4-6; Deut 25:9.—u 3-33: Deut 1:20-29.

12:6-8 The poetic form emphasizes the solemn nature of the words that single out Moses as the only prophet worthy of God's trust.

13:1—14:45 Using various ancient traditions (Jos 14:6; 15:13; Jdg 1:10), the author tells of how Moses attempts to enter Canaan from the south.

13:17 The *Negeb* is the region in southern Palestine.

entrance to Lebo-hamath.* 22 They went up
into the Negeb and came to Hebron where
Ahiman, Sheshai, and Talmai, descendants
of Anak dwelt. (Now Hebron was built seven
years before Zoan in Egypt.)[v] 23 Then they
came to the Valley of Eshcol.* There they cut
down a branch with a single cluster of
grapes. Two men carried it on a pole. They
also brought along some pomegranates and
figs. 24 That place was called the Valley of
Eschol because of the cluster of grapes that
the people of Israel cut there.

The Scouts' Report. 25 They returned from
exploring the land at the end of forty days.
26 They left and went back to Moses and
Aaron and the whole assembly of the people
of Israel that was camped in Kadesh in the
Desert of Paran. They brought back a report
to them and showed the whole assembly the
fruit of the land.

27 Then they told Moses, "We went into the
land into which you sent us, and it truly flows
with milk and honey. This is its fruit.[w]
28 However, a powerful people dwells in that
land, and the cities are highly fortified.
Furthermore, we even saw the descendants
of Anak there. 29 The Amalekites live in the
land of the Negeb, and the Hittites, the
Jebusites, and the Amorites live in the hill
country. The Canaanites live by the sea and
along the banks of the Jordan."

30 Then Caleb quieted the people who were
standing before Moses and he said, "Let us
go at once to take possession of it, for we shall
surely conquer it." 31 But the men who had
gone up with him said, "We will not be able
to go up against the people for they are sure-
ly stronger than we are." 32 Thus, they
brought a negative report of the land which
they had explored for the people of Israel
saying, "The land which we went through to
explore is a land that devours its inhabitants.
All the people we saw in it were immense.[x]
33 We saw giants there, the descendants of
Anak (the Anak come from the Nephilim).
We felt as if we were only grasshoppers, and
we seemed like that to them."*

CHAPTER 14

The People Rebel. 1 * The whole assembly
cried out and wept loudly that night. 2 All the
people of Israel grumbled against Moses
and Aaron. The whole assembly said to
them, "Would that we would have died in
Egypt, or we had died in this desert![y] 3 Why
did the LORD bring us into this land so that
we fall by the sword? Our wives and our chil-
dren will be taken as plunder! Would it not
be better for us to return to Egypt?" 4 They
said to one another, "Let us choose a leader
who will take us back to Egypt."

5 Moses and Aaron fell on their faces
before the whole assembly of the people of
Israel gathered there. 6 Joshua, the son of
Nun, and Caleb, the son of Jephunneh, who
had spied out the land, tore their clothes.
7 They spoke to the entire assembly of the
people of Israel saying, "The land we passed
through and explored is a tremendously
good land.[z] 8 If the LORD is pleased with us,
he will lead us into that land and give it to us,
a land flowing with milk and honey. 9 Only do
not rebel against the LORD, nor be afraid of
the people of the land, for we will devour
them. Their protection is gone, and the LORD
is with us. Do not fear them!"[a]

The LORD's Response. 10 But the whole
assembly decided to stone them. Then the
glory of the LORD appeared in the tent of
meeting in front of all of the people of Israel.
11 The LORD said to Moses, "How long will
this people despise me? How long before
they trust me, in spite of all the signs that I
have performed in their midst?[b] 12 I will strike
them down with a plague and I will destroy
them. Then I will make a nation arise from
you that is greater and mightier than they
are."*[c]

13 But Moses said to the LORD, "The
Egyptians will hear about it, for by your
power you brought this people out from their
midst.[d] 14 They will report it to the people of
this land. They have heard that you, O LORD,
are in the midst of this people, for you, O
LORD, are seen face to face. Your cloud stands
over them, and you go before them as a cloud

v Jos 11:21; 15:14.—w Ex 3:8; Deut 1:25.—x Deut 1:28; Jos 14:8.—y Ex 16:3.—z Num 13:27; Deut 1:25.—a Deut 7:18.—b Pss 78:22; 106:24.—c Ex 32:10.—d Ex 32:11-14; Ps 106:23.

13:21 *Lebo-hamath* was near Lebanon. The sacred writer sees the exploration as extending to the ideal border in the north; in fact, the places explored were far more limited.

13:23 The *Valley of Eshcol* is near Hebron in southern Canaan. *Eshcol* means "cluster."

13:33 The spies' false report transmits their own fear and distrust of the Lord and sets the scene for the community's rebellion.

14:1-4 The ungrateful ones in the community, incited by the faithless spies, turn against the Lord dismissing all that he has done for them and preferring death to trusting in his promise.

14:12 The Lord's wrath is short lived. No sooner does he threaten to destroy the rebellious lot, then he promises for a second time since the Exodus to raise up a faithful people.

by day and as a pillar of fire by night. 15 Now if
you kill this people as if it were a single man,
then the nations that have heard of your fame
will say, 16 'The LORD was not able to bring
this people into the land that he promised
them, so he killed them in the wilderness.'[e]
17 Therefore, my LORD, show your great
power, for as you have declared, 18 'The LORD
is slow to anger and abounding in mercy, for-
giving sin and rebellion. Yet he does not leave
the guilty unpunished, visiting the iniquity of
the father upon the sons to the third and
fourth generation.'[f] 19 By your great mercy, I
beseech you, forgive this people, just as you
have forgiven this people ever since they left
Egypt until now."

20 The LORD answered, "I have forgiven
them, just as you have asked. 21 But assuredly,
just as I live and the glory of the LORD fills the
whole earth, 22 [g] because this entire people has
witnessed my glory and the miracles that I
performed in Egypt and in the wilderness,
and yet they have put me to the test these ten
times and have not heeded my voice, 23 none
of them will see the land that I promised to
their fathers. None of those who despised me
will see it. 24 But I will bring my servant Caleb
into the land that he entered because he has a
different spirit and wholeheartedly follows
me. His descendants will inherit it. 25 Turn
back tomorrow and set out for the wilderness
along the route to the Red Sea for the
Amalekites and the Canaanites are living in
the valley."

26 The LORD spoke to Moses and Aaron,
saying, 27 "How long will this wicked assembly
grumble against me? I have heard the com-
plaints of the people of Israel that they grum-
ble against me.[h] 28 So I declare to them: As I
live, says the LORD, I will make the things you
have said in my hearing happen: 29 your dead
bodies will fall to the ground in this wilder-
ness. None of you who are twenty years or
older and who have complained about me[i]
30 will enter the land in which I swore I would
make you dwell except for Caleb, the son of
Jephunneh, and Joshua, the son of Nun.
31 However, as for your little ones whom you
said would become plunder, I will bring them
in and they will come to know the land that
you have despised. 32 But your dead bodies
will fall to the ground in this wilderness.
33 Your children will wander in this wilderness
for forty years, and they will bear the burden
of your unfaithfulness, until your dead bodies
lie in the wilderness. 34 The number of days
that you explored the land was forty, and
there will be one year for each day. You will
bear the burden of your sins for forty years
and you will come to know my rejection.*[j] 35 I,
the LORD, have proclaimed this. I will surely
do this to this evil assembly that has gathered
together against me. In this wilderness they
will come to an end, there they will die."

36 The men whom Moses sent to explore
the land, and who, when they returned, incit-
ed the assembly to complain against him by
giving an evil report concerning the land,
37 those men who brought the evil report con-
cerning the land were struck down by a
plague before the LORD. 38 Of the men who
went to explore the land, Joshua, the son of
Nun, and Caleb, the son of Jephunneh, sur-
vived.

Doomed Invasion. 39 When Moses reported
these sayings to all the people of Israel, the
people mourned bitterly. 40 [k] They rose up
early the next morning and went to the top of
the mountain and said, "Here we are! We
have sinned, but we are ready to go up to the
place that the LORD has promised." 41 But
Moses said, "Why are you now disobeying the
command of the LORD? This will not succeed.
42 Do not go up, for the LORD is not with you.
You will be defeated by your enemies. 43 The
Amalekites and the Canaanites are there in
front of you. You will fall by the sword, because
you turned away from the LORD. The LORD
will not be with you." 44 In their presumption,
they went up into the high hill country, but the
Ark of the Covenant of the LORD and Moses
did not go out from the camp. 45 The
Amalekites and the Canaanites who lived in
the hill country came down and attacked
them and drove them back to Hormah.

CHAPTER 15

Additional Offerings. 1 The LORD spoke to
Moses, saying, 2 "Speak to the people of
Israel and say to them: 'When you come into
the land of your dwelling that I will give you
3 and you make an offering by fire to the
LORD, either a burnt offering or a sacrifice,
whether to fulfill a vow or as a freewill offer-
ing or on your appointed feast days, whether

e Ex 32:12; Deut 9:28.—f Ex 34:6-7; Ps 103:8.—g 22-23: Deut 1:34-35; Ps 95:11.—h Ex 16:12.—i Num 1:46; Heb 3:17; 1 Cor 10:5.—j Num 13:25; Ps 95:10.—k 40-45: Deut 1:41-44.

14:34 The Lord metes out punishment on the unfaithful people, condemning them to die in the desert as they had wished.

it be from the herd or the flock, in order to
make a pleasing fragrance to the LORD,
4 then the person bringing his offering to the
LORD should bring a cereal offering of a
tenth of an ephah of fine flour mixed with a
fourth of a hin of oil.*[l] 5 With each burnt
offering or sacrifice of a lamb you are to
make a drink offering of a quarter of a hin of
wine. 6 For a ram, you are to make a cereal
offering of two-tenths of an ephah of fine
flour mixed with a third of a hin of oil, 7 and
for a drink offering you are to offer a third of
a hin of wine, a pleasing fragrance to the
LORD.

8 " 'When you prepare a young bull as a
burnt offering or a sacrifice, whether to ful-
fill a vow or to make a peace offering to the
LORD, 9 you will offer a cereal offering of
three-tenths of an ephah of fine flour, mixed
with half a hin of oil along with the young
bull, 10 and you will bring a drink offering of
half a hin of wine. It will be an offering made
by fire, a pleasing fragrance to the LORD.
11 Each young bull or each ram, each lamb
or each kid goat is to be prepared in this way.
12 Whatever number you prepare, you shall
do this with each one.

13 " 'All who were born in the land will do
things this way when they present an offer-
ing by fire, a pleasing fragrance to the LORD.
14 If there is a foreigner living among you or
a person living among you for generations,
and he wishes to make an offering by fire, a
pleasing fragrance to the LORD, let him do it
as you have done it. 15 For the community,
there is one ordinance for you and for the
foreigner living in your midst, it is a perpet-
ual ordinance for all your generations. Thus,
you and the foreigner are the same before
the LORD. 16 The same laws and statutes
apply to you and the foreigner who is living
in your midst.' "

17 The LORD spoke to Moses, saying,
18 "Speak to the people of Israel and tell
them, 'When you enter into the land to
which I am bringing you, 19 then when you
eat the food of the land, you shall lift up an
offering to the LORD. 20 You shall lift up a
cake from the first* of your dough as an
offering just as you present an offering from
your threshing floor. 21 You shall give an
offering to the LORD from the first of your
dough for all your generations.[m]

Atonement Offerings. 22 " 'If by mistake you
have not observed all the commandments
that the LORD proclaimed through Moses,
23 all that the LORD commanded through
Moses, from the day that the LORD gave the
commandments and onward through all
your generations, 24 this is what will be done:
if the action was committed unintentionally
and without the knowledge of the assembly,
then the whole assembly is to offer up one
young bull as a burnt offering, a pleasing fra-
grance to the LORD, along with its cereal and
drink offerings, according to custom, as well
as one kid goat as a sin offering. 25 The priest
shall make atonement for the whole assem-
bly of the people of Israel, and it will be for-
given them, for it was unintentional. They
will have brought a sacrifice by fire to the
LORD, a sin offering to the LORD for their
mistake.[n] 26 All of the assembly of the people
of Israel and even the foreigner living among
them shall be forgiven, for all the people par-
ticipated in the mistake.

27 [o] " 'If a person sins unintentionally, then
he is to offer up a year-old she-goat as a sin
offering. 28 The priest is to make atonement
before the LORD for the one who has sinned
unintentionally. When atonement has been
made for him, he will be forgiven. 29 You
shall have one law for those who sin unin-
tentionally, whether they were born among
the people of Israel or they are foreigners liv-
ing in your midst.

30 " 'But if someone does anything defiant-
ly, whether he be native born or a foreigner,
then that person blasphemes the LORD and
is to be cut off from among his people.
31 Because he has despised the word of the
LORD and has broken his commandment, let
that person be completely cut off, and let his
guilt remain upon him.' "

Sabbath-breaker Punished.* 32 Now, while
the people of Israel were in the desert, they
came upon a man gathering wood on the
Sabbath.[p] 33 Those who found him gathering
wood brought him to Moses and Aaron and
to the whole assembly 34 and they put him
under guard, for it had not yet been estab-

---

l Lev 23:13.—m Num 18:26.—n Lev 4:20.—o 27-28: Lev 4:27-28.—p Ex 31:14-15; 35:2-3.

15:4 About four and a half liters of flour in about six and a half liters of oil.

15:20 *Lift up a cake from the first:* taking the first of the grain to make a cake for the Lord reflects the rule of firstfruits. Everything belongs to the Lord and the best is offered back to him in thanksgiving.

15:32-36 This fault is punished by death because it represents contempt of God, who has made his children a free people (Ex 20:8-11).

lished what was to be done to him.[q] [35] Then the LORD said to Moses, "Surely the man is to be put to death! Let the whole assembly stone him outside of the camp!" [36] So the whole assembly took him outside of the camp, and they stoned him to death, as the LORD had commanded Moses.

Tassels on Garments.* [37] The LORD spoke to Moses, saying, [38] "Speak to the people of Israel and tell them to have tassels on the corners of their garments throughout all their generations. Let them put a blue cord on the tassels of each corner.[r] [39] When you look at the tassels, you will remember the commandments of the LORD and keep them. Thus you will not prostitute yourselves by following after the lusts in your own heart or your own eyes. [40] Then you will remember to obey all the commandments and you will be holy to your God. [41] I am the LORD, your God, who brought you out of the land of Egypt to be your God. I am the LORD, your God."[s]

CHAPTER 16

Korah's Rebellion. [1] Korah, the son of Izhar, the son of Kohath, the son of Levi, and some Reubenites, Dathan and Abiram, the sons of Eliab, and On, the son of Peleth took action [2] and rose up against Moses. With them were some of the people of Israel, two hundred fifty leaders of the assembly, well known in the assembly and men of renown. [3] They gathered together against Moses and Aaron and said to them, "You have gone too far! The whole assembly is holy, every one of them, and the LORD is in their midst. Why, then, do you exalt yourselves above the assembly of the LORD?" *[t]

[4] When Moses heard this he fell on his face [5] and he spoke to Korah and his company, saying, "Tomorrow the LORD will reveal who belongs to him and who is holy when he allows him to approach him. He will allow the one whom he has chosen to approach him. [6] Do this: you and Korah and all his followers are to take censers [7] before the LORD tomorrow and put fire and incense in them. The man whom the LORD chooses shall be the holy one. You have gone too far, you Levites!"

[8] Then Moses said to Korah, "Hear now, you Levites, [9] is it not enough that the God of Israel has set you apart from the assembly of Israel to bring you onto himself, to minister in the tabernacle of the LORD, and to stand before the assembly serving them?[u] [10] He has brought you and all your brethren, the Levites, onto himself, and still you seek the priesthood too? [11] For this you and all your company have gathered together against the LORD. Who is Aaron that you should complain about him?"

Rebellion of Dathan and Abiram. [12] Then Moses summoned Dathan and Abiram, the sons of Eliab. They responded, "We will not come up! [13] Is it not enough that you brought us out of a land flowing with milk and honey to kill us in the desert? Now you are going to make yourself a prince over us? [14] Indeed, you have not brought us into a land flowing with milk and honey, nor have you given us an inheritance of fields and vineyards. Are you going to gouge out the eyes of these men? No, we will not come up!"

[15] Moses was very angry and said to the LORD, "Do not accept their offering. I have not taken one donkey from them, nor have I harmed any of them."[v] [16] Then Moses said to Korah, "You and your company are to appear before the LORD tomorrow, you, and them, and Aaron. [17] Each of you is to bring your censer and put incense in it. Each of you is to bring his censer before the LORD, two hundred and fifty censers. You and Aaron will also each bring a censer." [18] * So each took his own censer, put fire and incense in them, and stood at the entrance to the tent of meeting along with Moses and Aaron. [19] The whole assembly gathered against them at the entrance to the tent of meeting, and the glory of the LORD appeared to the whole assembly.

[20] The LORD spoke to Moses and Aaron, saying, [21] "Move away from this assembly so that I can destroy them at once." [22] But Moses and Aaron fell down upon their faces and said, "O God, O God of the spirits of all flesh,* will you be angry with the whole

q Lev 24:12.—r Deut 22:12; Mt 23:5.—s Ex 20:2; Lev 22:33.—t Ex 19:6; Ps 106:16.—u Deut 10:8.—v 1 Sam 12:3.

15:37-41 These tassels are not simply ornaments but a symbol that calls to mind the commandments of God. That is why Jews attach so much importance to them (Mt 9:20; 23:5).

16:3 Several different rebellions are combined in this section. The one that is most prominent is based on Korah's accusation against Moses and Aaron of abusing their roles as spiritual leaders.

16:18-21 Korah and 250 false priests who stood with Moses and Aaron with fire in their censers at the tent of meeting are fittingly put to death by the Lord's fire (perhaps lightning).

16:22 *God of the spirits of all flesh:* the Creator of every living being.

assembly because of the sin of one per-
son?”[w]
23 Then the LORD spoke to Moses, saying,
24 “Speak to the assembly, saying, ‘Draw
back from the dwellings of Korah, Dathan,
and Abiram.’ ”

Punishment of Dathan and Abiram. 25 Then
Moses got up and went to Dathan and
Abiram, followed by the elders of Israel.
26 He spoke to the assembly, saying, “Draw
back from the tents of these wicked men,
and do not touch anything that belongs to
them, or else you will be swept away in all
their sin.” 27 So they backed away from the
dwellings of Korah, Dathan, and Abiram.
Dathan and Abiram came out and stood in
the entranceway of their tents along with
their wives, their sons, and their little ones.
28 Moses said, “By this you shall know that
the LORD sent me to do all these things, for
they are not of my own doing.[x] 29 If these
men end up dying a natural death and are
visited by every person’s fate, then the LORD
has not sent me. 30 But if the LORD creates
something new and the earth opens up and
swallows them and all that belongs to them
and they go down alive into Sheol,* then you
will understand that they have treated the
LORD with contempt.”

31[y] As soon as he finished saying these
things, the ground split apart underneath
them. 32 The earth opened up its mouth and
swallowed them and their households as
well as the men who were with Korah and all
their possessions. 33 So they and all that
belonged to them went down alive into
Sheol and the earth closed over them. They
perished from the assembly. 34 All of Israel
that had gathered around them fled at their
outcry for they said, “The earth might swal-
low us up too!” 35 Fire came out from the
LORD and swallowed up the two hundred
and fifty who had offered incense.

36 The LORD spoke to Moses, saying,
37 “Speak to Eleazar, the son of Aaron the
priest, and have him gather up the censers*
from the blaze for they are holy. Scatter the
burning coals over there. 38 The censers of
these sinners will bear witness against them.
Hammer them into sheets to cover the altar,
for they have been presented to the LORD
and they are therefore holy. They will be a
warning to the people of Israel.”

39 Eleazar took the bronze censers with
which the men who had been destroyed by
fire had made their offering, and they ham-
mered them into sheets to cover the altar.
40 They were to be a reminder to the people
of Israel that no one other than a descendant
of Aaron was to draw near to offer incense to
the LORD lest what happened to Korah and
his company happen to them. He did this as
the LORD had commanded him through
Moses.

41 The very next day the whole assembly of
the people of Israel grumbled against Moses
and Aaron saying, “You have killed the
LORD’s people.” 42 When the assembly had
gathered in opposition to Moses and Aaron,
they looked up toward the tent of meeting
and, behold, the cloud covered it and the
glory of the LORD appeared.

43 Moses and Aaron stood in front of the
tent of meeting 44 and the LORD spoke to
Moses, saying, 45 “Stand away from this
assembly so that I can quickly put an end to
them.” Then they fell down on their faces.
46 Moses said to Aaron, “Take a censer and
put fire from the altar in it and put incense
in it. Go out quickly to the assembly to make
atonement for them, for anger has gone out
from the LORD and the plague has begun.”[z]

47 So Aaron did what Moses had com-
manded him and he ran out into the midst
of the assembly. The plague had already
begun among the people. He put in incense
and made atonement for the people. 48 He
stood between the dead and the living, and
the plague halted. 49 There were fourteen
thousand and seven hundred who died in
the plague (not counting those who died on
account of Korah). 50 Then Aaron returned
to Moses at the entrance to the tent of meet-
ing for the plague had been halted.

CHAPTER 17

Aaron’s Staff.* 1 The LORD spoke to Moses,
saying, 2 “Speak to the people of Israel and
take one staff from the leaders of each of the
ancestral tribes, and write each of their

w Gen 18:16; Job 12:10.—x Ex 3:12; Jn 2:11.—y Num 26:10; Ps 106:17-18.—z Wis 18:20-21; Ps 106:29.

16:30 *Sheol:* the dwelling place of the dead, where, according to the ancient idea of things, all the dead, without any distinction between the good and the wicked, lead a minimal kind of existence, as though they were shadows of themselves. Only as the Christian era draws near will teaching on the afterlife become clearer.

16:37 *Gather up the censers:* the bronze censers of the deceased sinful priests were hammered together into sheets for the altar as a reminder of their evil ways.

17:1-13 The word translated *staff* means both “staff of command” and “genealogical tree.”

names on the twelve staffs. 3 Write Aaron's name upon the staff of Levi, for there is one staff for the leader of each of the ancestral tribes. 4 You are to lay them in the tent of meeting in front of the Testimony where I meet with you.[a] 5 The staff of the man whom I choose will blossom. Thus I will bring an end to the grumblings of the people of Israel against you." 6 Moses spoke to the people of Israel, and all of the leaders gave him one staff each, one for each of the twelve ancestral tribes, and the staff of Aaron was among the other staffs. 7 So Moses placed the staffs before the LORD in the tent of meeting.

8 The next day, Moses went into the tent of meeting. The staff of Aaron of the tribe of Levi had blossomed and brought forth buds.* It was blooming and producing almonds. 9 Moses brought all of the staffs from before the LORD out to the people of Israel. They looked at them, and each man took his staff.

10 The LORD said to Moses, "Bring Aaron's staff before the Testimony to be kept as a warning to the rebels. This should end their grumblings against me, so that they may not have to die."[b] 11 Moses did this. He did as the LORD had commanded him. 12 Then the people of Israel spoke to Moses saying, "We are dying, we are lost! We are all lost! 13 Anyone who approaches the tabernacle of the LORD will die. Are we going to die?"

CHAPTER 18

Sanctuary and Altar Duties. 1 The LORD said to Aaron, "You and your sons and your family with you will bear guilt for offenses against the sanctuary, while you and your sons will bear guilt for offenses against your priesthood.[c] 2 Bring your brothers from the Levites, your ancestral tribe, with you. Let them join with you and serve you when you and your sons are before the tent of Testimony. 3 They will attend to your duties and all the duties of the tent, but they must not come near the vessels of the sanctuary or the altar, lest they die and you also die. 4 They will join you and attend to the duties of the tent of meeting, for every service in the tabernacle. Let no one else approach you.

5 "You will attend to the duties of the sanctuary and the duties of the altar so that no wrath come upon the people of Israel. 6 It is I, myself, who have selected your brothers, the Levites, from among the people of Israel as a gift to you, dedicated to the LORD, to serve in the tent of meeting.[d] 7 Only you and your sons can serve as priests for everything concerning the altar and whatever is inside the veil, and you will serve. I am giving you the service of the priesthood as a gift. Anyone else who comes near will be put to death." *

Priests' Share of Offerings. 8 The LORD spoke to Aaron: "I have given you responsibility over all my offerings, over all the sacred things of the people of Israel. I have given these things to you and your sons as a portion, a perpetual allotment.[e] 9 This shall be yours from among the most holy things dedicated by fire: all of their oblations, all of their cereal offerings, all of their sin offerings and all of their guilt offerings. These things that they offer to me will be most holy to you and your sons. 10 You will eat it in a Most Holy Place. Every male will eat it. It will be holy for you.

11 "This also is yours: the offering of their gifts along with the wave offerings of the people of Israel. I have given them to you and your sons and daughters as your portion forever. Everyone who is pure in your household can eat it.[f] 12 [g] I have given to you all of the best of the oil and the best of the wine and of the wheat and their firstfruits that they offer to the LORD. 13 The first ripe fruits of all that is in the land that they bring to the LORD shall be yours. Everyone who is pure in your household can eat it.

14 "Everything that is dedicated* to the LORD will be yours. 15 Everything that opens the womb of all flesh that they bring to the LORD, whether man or beast, shall be yours. Nevertheless, you will redeem the firstborn son and you will redeem the firstborn male of impure animals.[h] 16 When they are a month old, you shall redeem them at the redemption price of five shekels of silver, calculated according to the shekel of the sanc-

a Ex 25:22.—b Heb 9:4.—c Heb 7:25.—d Num 3:9-10.—e Lev 6:18.—f Ex 29:27-28.—g 12-13: Ex 23:19; Deut 18:4.—h Ex 13:2.

17:8 *The staff . . . had blossomed and brought forth buds:* as the Lord intended, Aaron's staff exceeded the others in fruitfulness and was a clear sign of God's choice of Aaron and his sons as true priests.

18:7 The Lord is very clear concerning who may and may not serve at the altar and required death for any impostors and for the priests they served.

18:14 *Dedicated:* refers to a vow to destroy something as a way of consecrating objects and persons to God, while the destroyer derives no advantage from them.

tuary, which weighs twenty gerahs. 17 You are not to redeem the firstborn of the cattle or the firstborn of the sheep or the firstborn of the goats, for they are holy. Sprinkle their blood upon the altar and burn their fat as an offering made by fire, a pleasing fragrance to the Lord. 18 Their meat shall be yours, as well as the breast of the wave offering and the right thigh. These are yours. 19 All of the offerings of the holy things that the people of Israel bring to the Lord, I have given them to you and your sons and your daughters with you as an ordinance forever. This is a covenant of salt forever between the Lord and you and your descendants with you." *

20 The Lord spoke to Aaron, "You will have no inheritance in their land, nor will you have any portion among them. I am your portion and your inheritance among the people of Israel. [i]

Tithes Owed to the Levites. 21 "I give the Levites all the tithes in Israel, an inheritance for the work that they perform in serving in the tent of meeting. 22 From now on the people of Israel must not approach the tent of meeting lest they sin and die. 23 The Levites will do the work of the tent of meeting. They will bear responsibility for offenses against it. This is an everlasting ordinance for all your generations. They will receive no inheritance from among the people of Israel. 24 I have given the Levites an inheritance of the tithes that the people of Israel present as an offering to the Lord. This is why I have said to them, 'They will have no inheritance among the people of Israel.' "

Tithes Paid by the Levites.* 25 The Lord spoke to Moses, saying, 26 "Speak to the Levites and say to them, 'When you receive a tithe from the people of Israel which I give you as an inheritance, you are to present a tithe of the tithe as the Lord's offering. [j] 27 Your offering will be reckoned to you as grain from the threshing floor or as produce from the winepress. 28 You shall present an offering to the Lord from all your tithes that you receive from the people of Israel; you will give the Lord's offering to Aaron the priest from them. 29 The Lord's offering will come from the best and the holiest portion of all the gifts that you offer up.' 30 Therefore, you will say to them, 'When you have lifted up the best of it, the rest will be apportioned to the Levites as the produce of the threshing floor and the produce of the winepress. 31 You can eat it anywhere, you and your households, as your reward for your service in the tent of meeting. 32 You will bear no guilt in this when you offer up the best of it, nor will you defile the holy gifts of Israel, lest you die.' "

CHAPTER 19

The Red Heifer. 1 The Lord spoke to Moses and Aaron, saying, 2 "This is a statute of the law which the Lord has commanded saying, 'Tell the people of Israel to bring you an unblemished red heifer that has no defect and upon which a yoke has never been placed. [k] 3 You will give it to Eleazar the priest. Take it outside of the camp and slaughter it in front of him. 4 Eleazar the priest is to dip his finger in the blood and sprinkle its blood seven times directly in front of the tent of meeting. 5 Then the heifer will be burned before him; its skin, its meat, its blood, and its dung will be burned. 6 The priest is to take cedar wood, hyssop, and scarlet wool and throw them upon the burning heifer. 7 The priest is then to wash his clothes and bathe himself. He can then enter the camp, but he will be unclean until the evening. 8 The man who burns it must also wash his clothes in water and bathe in water, but he, too, will be unclean until the evening. 9 A man who is clean is to gather up the ashes from the heifer and place them in a clean place outside of the camp. They will be kept by the assembly of the people of Israel for the water of purification, for removal of sin. [l] 10 The man who gathers the ashes of the heifer will wash his clothes, and he will be unclean until the evening. This is the way it will be for the people of Israel and the foreigner dwelling among them, a statute forever.

Water of Purification. 11 " 'Whoever touches a person's dead body will be unclean for seven days. 12 He will purify himself with the water on the third day, and on the seventh day he will be clean; but if he does not cleanse himself on the third day, then he will

---

i Deut 10:9; 12:12; 18:1-2; Jos 13:33; Ezek 44:28.—j Neh 10:38.—k Deut 21:3.—l Heb 9:13.

18:19 The choicest meat and produce offered to the Lord belonged to the priests and their families. The *covenant of salt* refers to the unbreakable contract that accompanies a covenant promise.

18:25-32 As recipients of the Lord's tithe, the Levites were responsible to tithe the best part of theirs to Aaron as an offering to the Lord along with a tenth of their income.

not be clean on the seventh day. 13 Whoever
touches a dead body, the body of someone
who died and then does not purify himself
defiles the tabernacle of the LORD. That per-
son shall be cut off from Israel. He will be
unclean because the water of purification
was not sprinkled upon him; he will be
unclean.[m]

14 " 'This is the law for when a man dies
inside of a tent. Everyone who comes inside
the tent and everything that is in the tent will
be unclean for seven days. 15 Every open
uncovered container will be unclean.
16 Anyone who is out in the open fields and
touches someone who has been killed with a
sword, or a dead body, or a bone of a person,
or a grave, that person will be unclean for
seven days.

17 * " 'For the unclean, take the ashes from
the burnt purification from sin and put
them into a vessel and pour fresh water over
them. 18 Then a person who is clean will dip
hyssop into the water and sprinkle it upon
the tent and upon its belongings and upon
all the people who were there, upon anyone
who touched a bone, or a person who was
killed, or a dead body, or a grave. 19 The
clean person will sprinkle the unclean on
the third day and on the seventh day. On the
seventh day he will purify himself. He will
wash his clothes and bathe himself in water,
and then he will be clean in the evening.[n]
20 But the man who is unclean and does not
purify himself will be cut off from the
assembly because he has defiled the sanctu-
ary of the LORD. The water of purification
was not sprinkled upon him and he is
unclean. 21 It will be an everlasting statute
that the one who sprinkles the water of
purification will wash his clothes. The one
who touches the water of purification will
be unclean until the evening. 22 Whatever
the unclean person touches will be unclean,
and the person who touches it will be
unclean until the evening.' "

CHAPTER 20

Death of Miriam. 1 * The people of Israel,
the whole assembly, came into the Desert
of Zin in the first month,* and the people
stayed in Kadesh. It was there that Miriam
died and was buried.

The Need for Water. 2 The community had
no water, and they gathered together
against Moses and Aaron.[o] 3 They argued
with Moses and said, "Would that we would
have died when our brothers fell before the
LORD. 4 Why have you brought the assem-
bly of the LORD into this wilderness so that
we die here, both we and our cattle? 5 Why
have you made us come out of Egypt to this
evil place? It has no grain, or figs, or vines,
or pomegranates. There is no water to
drink!"

Moses and Aaron Sin. 6 Moses and Aaron
went from in front of the assembly to the
entrance of the tent of meeting. They fell
upon their faces, and the glory of the LORD
appeared to them.

7 The LORD spoke to Moses, saying,
8 "Take the staff, and you and Aaron your
brother are to gather the assembly togeth-
er. Speak to the rock in their sight and it
will pour forth water. You will bring forth
water from the rock for the assembly and
their animals to drink."

9 Moses took the staff from before the
LORD, as he had been commanded. 10 Then
Moses and Aaron gathered the assembly
before the rock and he said to them, "Hear
now, you rebels! Must we bring forth water
out of this rock for you?"[p] 11 * Then Moses
lifted up his arm and he struck the rock
with his staff twice. Water came gushing
out, and the community and their animals
drank.[q]

12 But the LORD said to Moses and Aaron,
"Because you have not trusted and hal-
lowed me in the eyes of the people of Israel,
you will not lead this community into the
land that I have given them. 13 This is the

m Lev 15:31.—n Ezek 36:25.—o Ex 17:1.—p Ex 17:5-6; Ps 106:32-33.—q Ps 78:16; 1 Cor 10:4.

19:17-21 Throughout history water has been used for cleansing in religious ceremonies. Here is a detailed account of water being used in a cleansing ritual to purify persons who have come into contact with dead bodies. In the New Testament (Heb 9:13-14), the cleansing power of the blood of Christ is the ultimate means of being made clean.

20:1-13 God will rebuke Moses for not having faith, probably because his act of striking the rock with his staff may have looked too much like an act of magic. But it may also be that the editor was taking into account other traditions of which traces can be found in the Bible (Ex 17; Deut 1:37; Ps 106:32), in order to conceal a greater act of distrust on the part of the head of the community. The rock is an image for God and a symbol of Christ (Ps 18:2; Jn 7:38; 1 Cor 10:4).

20:1 *First month:* according to verses 22-29, this chapter covers the last of the 40 years in the desert after the Exodus. By this time there would have been a complete turnover of those 20 years and older who had been in the desert for the whole time.

20:11-12 The miraculous issue of water from the rock is accomplished by Moses apart from the Lord's instruction to speak to the rock. Moses is immediately chastised for his disobedience—both he and Aaron being denied entrance into the Promised Land.

water of Meribah, because the people of Israel quarreled with the LORD, and he showed himself to be bold among them."*[r]

Israel Denied Passage.* 14 Moses sent messengers from Kadesh to the king of Edom saying, "Thus says Israel, your brother, 'You know all the hardships that have come upon us. 15 Our ancestors went down to Egypt and lived there for many years. The Egyptians mistreated us and our fathers. 16 When we cried out, he heard our voice and sent an angel to bring us out of Egypt. We are now in Kadesh, a town at the edge of your territory.[s] 17 Please, let us pass through your land. We will not walk through the vineyards nor drink from the wells. We will pass along the King's Highway, and we will not turn to the right nor to the left until we have crossed over your borders.' "

18 But Edom said, "You will not pass through. Otherwise, I will come out against you with the sword."

19 The people of Israel replied, "We will go along the main road. If my cattle drink from your water, I will pay for it. Only let me pass through on foot, nothing else." 20 But he said, "You will not pass through." Edom came out against the people with a great and powerful force. 21 Since Edom refused to let Israel pass through its territory, Israel turned away from it.

The Death of Aaron. 22 When they left Kadesh, the whole assembly of the people of Israel came to Mount Hor.[t] 23 The LORD spoke to Moses and Aaron at Mount Hor near the border of Edom and said, 24 "Aaron is going to be gathered to his people.* He will not enter the land that I have promised to the people of Israel because you disobeyed my command at the waters of Meribah. 25[u] Take Aaron and his son Eleazar up Mount Hor. 26 Take Aaron's garments off and put them on Eleazar, his son. Aaron is to be gathered to his people; he will die there."

27 So Moses did as the LORD had commanded. They went up Mount Hor in the sight of the assembly. 28 Moses removed Aaron's garments and he put them upon Eleazar, his son. Aaron died on top of the mountain, and Moses and Eleazar then came down the mountain.[v] 29 The whole assembly learned that Aaron had died. The whole house of Israel mourned for Aaron for thirty days.

CHAPTER 21

Israel Destroys Arad. 1 When the Canaanite king Arad (who lived in the Negeb) heard that Israel was coming along the road to Atharim, he attacked the people of Israel and took some of them prisoner.[w] 2* Israel made a vow to the LORD saying, "If you will deliver this people into our hands, then we will utterly destroy their cities!"[x] 3 The LORD listened to the plea of Israel and delivered up the Canaanites. They totally destroyed them and their cities, therefore the place is called Hormah.

The Bronze Serpent.* 4 They traveled from Mount Hor along the way to the Red Sea in order to bypass the land of Edom, but the people became discouraged along the way. 5 The people spoke against God and Moses, saying, "Why have you brought us out of Egypt to have us die in the desert. There is no bread, no water, and we loathe this miserable food." *[y]

6 The LORD sent seraph* serpents among the people. They bit the people, and many of the people of Israel died.[z] 7 The people came to Moses and said, "We have sinned, for we have spoken against the LORD and against you. Pray to the LORD so that he might save us from the serpents." So Moses prayed for the people. 8 The LORD said to Moses, "Make a seraph serpent and put it upon a pole. Whoever has been bitten and looks upon it will live." 9 So Moses made a bronze serpent and put it upon a pole. If someone had been bitten by a serpent and he looked up at the bronze serpent, he lived.[a]

r Num 27:14; Ex 17:7.—s Ex 2:23; 23:20.—t Num 33:37.—u 25-26: Deut 32:50.—v Num 33:38; Ex 29:29.—w Num 33:40; Jdg 1:16.—x Jos 6:17.—y Num 11:6; Ex 16:3.—z Deut 8:15; 1 Cor 10:9.—a 2 Ki 18:4; Jn 3:14-15.

20:13 Hebrew allows the word *Meribah* and the word meaning *quarrel* to be interchanged.

20:14-21 According to the Fathers of the Church, the king of Edom is a prefiguration of those who do not accept the gospel.

20:24 *Gathered to his people:* this phrase indicated Aaron's impending death. Both he and Moses having rebelled against God (v. 12) would die.

21:2-3 *Hormah* means "dedicated to destruction." The entire booty taken in war is destroyed as an act of homage to God. See Num 18:14; Jos 6:7.

21:4-9 *The bronze serpent,* a sign of repentance and forgiveness, will be used by Jesus as a prefiguration of his own being lifted up on the cross (Jn 3:14).

21:5 *We loathe this miserable food:* this statement showed more than a distaste for the manna that the Lord had provided and that had been the brunt of ongoing complaints by the people. While they were rejecting the Lord's physical nourishment, they were turning away from his gift of grace.

21:6 *Seraph:* the Hebrew for a type of poisonous viper. The etymology suggests "fiery one," "burning one."

The Move to Moab. 10 The people of Israel
moved on and camped in Oboth. [b] 11 They
left Oboth and camped in Iye-abarim in
the desert that lie to the east of Moab.
12 From there they moved on and camped
in the Valley of Zered. 13 They then moved
on from there and camped on the other
side of the Arnon in the desert that
extends from the boundary of the Amo-
rites. The Arnon is the boundary of Moab,
the border between Moab and the
Amorites. 14 Thus, it is written in the Book
of Wars of the LORD,

"Waheb in Suphah,
and the wadis of the Arnon,
15 and the slope of the wadis
that extend to the site of Ar,
that lies along the boundary of Moab."

16 From there they continued on to Beer,
which is where the LORD spoke to Moses say-
ing, "Gather up the people and I will give
them water."

17 Then Israel sang this song,

"Spring up, O well! Sing to it!
18 The well which the leaders dug,
which the nobles of the people sank,
with the scepter and with their staves."

From the desert they continued on to
Mattanah, 19 and from Mattanah to Nahaliel,
from Nahaliel to Bamoth, 20 and from
Bamoth to the valley in the land of Moab
which is on the heights of the Pisgah over-
looking the wasteland.

Victory over Sihon and Og.* 21 Israel sent
messengers to Sihon, king of the Amorites,
saying, 22 "Let us pass through your land. We
will not wander into the fields nor into the
vineyards. We will not drink water from any
well. We will pass along the King's Highway
until we have crossed over your borders."

23 But Sihon would not allow Israel to
cross over his border. Sihon gathered all of
his people and marched out into the desert
against Israel. He went out to Jahaz and
fought with Israel. [c]

24 But Israel put him to the sword and
occupied his land from the Arnon to the
Jabbok up to the Ammonite territory (for the
boundary with the Ammonites was fortified).
25 Israel captured all of these cities, and Israel
settled in all of the cities of the Amorites, in
Heshbon and in all of its surrounding villages.
26 Heshbon was the city of Sihon, king of the
Amorites, for he had fought with the former
king of Moab, conquering all of his lands up
to the Arnon. 27 * This is why those who speak
in proverbs say,

"Come to Heshbon, let it be built.
Let Sihon's city be restored.
28 For fire went out from Heshbon,
a flame from the city of Sihon.
It devoured Ar of Moab,
the lords of the heights of the Arnon. [d]
29 Woe to you, Moab.
You have perished, O people of Che-
mosh. *
He has given up his sons as fugitives,
his daughters as captives to Sihon,
the king of the Amorites.
30 But we have shot at them,
Heshbon has perished even as far as
Dibon.
We have laid them waste up to Nophah,
which extends to the Medeba."

31 So Israel settled in the land of the
Amorites. 32 Moses sent out spies to Jazer,
and they captured those villages, driving out
the Amorites who lived there. 33 They then
turned and went along the road to Bashan. *
Og, the king of Bashan, went out with all his
people to battle them in Edrei.

34 The LORD said to Moses, "Do not be
afraid of him, for I have delivered him and
all his people and land into your hands. You
will do to him what you did to Sihon, the
king of the Amorites, who dwelt in Hesh-
bon." [e] 35 So they killed him and his sons and
all of his people until there was not a single
one alive, and they conquered his land.

CHAPTER 22*

1 * Then the people of Israel traveled to the
plains of Moab and camped along the
Jordan across from Jericho.

---

b Num 33:43.—c Deut 2:32; Jdg 11:20.—d Jer 48:45-46.—e Deut 3:2; Ps 136:17-22.

21:21-35 God fights alongside his people; nothing can resist him. These incidents will remain as exemplars for Israel and will be repeatedly extolled in national songs (see Pss 135:11; 136:10-20).

21:27ff An ancient Amorite song of victory, taken over by the Israelites.

21:29 *Chemosh* is the god of the Moabites. See Jdg 11:24; 1 Ki 11:7.

21:33 *Bashan:* a region on the border between present day Syria and Jordan. *Og:* a legendary giant; see Deut 3:11.

22:1-41 Arms were unable to halt the progress of the people of God. *Balak*, king of Moab, seeks to mobilize magical powers against them. In order to bring down a curse upon Israel, he calls upon the famous *Balaam*, a man of upright conscience who acts in good faith; but the soothsayer can only submit to God, who is more powerful than any sorcery.

22:1-21 The account vividly describes negotiations and an agreement on the practice known as incubation, which consisted in consulting the divinity through dreams. For the biblical editor there is only one God; it must therefore be none other than he who responds to the consulting soothsayer.

Balak Summons Balaam. 2 Now Balak, the
son of Zippor, had seen everything that
Israel had done to the Amorites,[f] 3 and
Moab was terrified because there were so
many people, and Moab was filled with
dread of the people of Israel. 4 Moab said to
the elders of Midian, "This mob will lick up
everything around us just like an ox licks up
grass in the pasture."

Balak, the son of Zippor, was the king of
the Moabites at this time. 5 He sent messen-
gers to Pethor which is near the river* in his
native land, to Balaam, the son of Beor, to
summon him. He said, "Behold, a people
has come out of Egypt and they cover the
surface of the earth. They are now living
opposite me. 6 Please come now and curse
this people for me for they are too powerful
for me. Maybe then I will be able to defeat
them and drive them out of the land. I know
well that whomever you bless is blessed, and
whomever you curse is cursed."

7 The elders of Moab and the elders of
Midian left, carrying the fee for the divina-
tion in their hands. They came to Balaam,
and they told him what Balak had said.[g]
8 He said to them, "Spend the night here,
and I will bring you the answer the LORD
gives me." So the leaders of Moab stayed
with Balaam. 9 God came to Balaam and
said, "Who are these men with you?"
10 Balaam said to God, "Balak, the son of
Zippor, the king of Moab, sent for me, say-
ing, 11 'Behold, a people has come out of
Egypt who now covers the face of the earth.
Now come and curse them for me. Perhaps
I will be able to defeat them and drive them
away.' " 12 But God said to Balaam, "Do not
go with them. Do not curse the people, for
they are blessed." *

13 The next morning Balaam arose and
said to Balak's representatives, "Go back to
your country, for the LORD refuses to allow
me to go with you."

14 The leaders of Moab returned and said
to Balak, "Balaam refused to come with us."
15 So Balak sent some more leaders, even
more distinguished than the others. 16 They
came to Balaam and said to him, "Thus says
Balak, the son of Zippor: 'Please, let nothing
keep you from coming to me 17 for I will
honor you greatly, and I will do whatever you
ask of me. Please come and curse this peo-
ple.' " 18 Balaam answered and said to the
servants of Balak: "If Balak were to grant
me his house full of silver and gold, I could
not do anything, small or great, contrary to
the word of the LORD, my God.[h] 19 But now,
please stay here this night as well, so that I
may know what the LORD says to me." 20 God
came to Balaam at night and said to him, "If
these men have come to summon you, rise
up and go with them, but do only what I tell
you."

Balaam's Donkey. 21 Balaam arose in the
morning and saddled his donkey and went
with the leaders of Moab. 22 But God grew
very angry because he had gone, and so an
angel of the LORD blocked his path on the
roadway. He was riding on a donkey and his
two servants were with him. 23 The donkey
saw the angel of the LORD* standing in the
roadway with his drawn sword in his hand,
and the donkey left the roadway and wan-
dered into the field. Balaam beat the donkey
to force it back onto the roadway.

24 Then an angel of the LORD stood in the
narrow pathway in the vineyards, walls
standing on either side. 25 When the donkey
saw the angel of the LORD, it pressed so close
to the wall that it crushed Balaam's foot
against it, so he beat it again. 26 Then the
angel of the LORD moved on ahead and
stood in a narrow place that had no room to
turn either to the right or to the left. 27 When
the donkey saw the angel of the LORD, it lay
down under Balaam who became angry and
beat it with a staff.

28 The LORD opened the donkey's mouth
and it said to Balaam, "What have I done to
you that you have beaten me these three
times?"[i] 29 Balaam answered the donkey,
"You have made a fool of me. If I had a
sword in my hand, I would kill you right
now!" 30 The donkey said to Balaam, "Am I
not your donkey, which you have always rid-
den, even til today? Have I ever done this to
you before?" He said, "No." 31 Then the LORD
opened Balaam's eyes and he saw the angel
of the LORD standing in the roadway with a
drawn sword in his hand. He bowed down
and fell flat on his face. 32 The angel of the
LORD said to him, "Why have you beaten

f Deut 23:5; Jos 24:9; Neh 13:2.—g 1 Sam 9:7.—h Num 24:13.—i 2 Pet 2:16.

22:5 The *river* is the Euphrates.

22:12 *They are blessed:* the people of Israel were under God's protection as promised to Abraham (see Gen 12:2-3) their Father.

22:23 *The donkey saw the angel of the LORD:* Balaam's magical powers did not go as far as his dumb beast's sensitivity in recognizing the messenger of the Lord.

your donkey these three times? Behold, I have come out to oppose you for the path before you is wrong. 33 The donkey saw me and turned away from me these three times. Otherwise, I would surely have killed you, but it I would have spared."

34 Balaam said to the angel of the LORD, "I have sinned. I did not realize that you were standing there opposing my way. If I have displeased you, then I will go back." 35 The angel of the LORD said to Balaam, "Go with the men, but say only what I tell you." So Balaam went with the leaders to Balak.

36 When Balak heard that Balaam was coming, he went out to Moab to meet him, a city which is on the Arnon border, at the farthest edge of his territory. 37 Balak said to Balaam, "Did I not summon you urgently? Why have you not come to me? Am I not able to reward you?" 38 Balaam said to Balak, "Behold, I have come to you now. Do I have any power to say anything? I will only speak the word that God puts in my mouth."[j]

39 Balaam went with Balak, and they arrived in Kiriath-huzoth. 40 Balak sacrificed oxen and sheep, and sent some of its meat to Balaam and the leaders who were with him. 41 The next day Balak took Balaam and brought him up to Bamoth-baal so that he might see the outposts of the people.

CHAPTER 23

Balaam's First Oracle. 1 * Balaam said to Balak, "Build me seven altars here, and prepare seven oxen and seven rams for me." 2 Balak did what Balaam had told him to do. Then Balak and Balaam offered a young bull and a ram on each altar. 3 Balaam said to Balak, "Stand by your offerings, and I will go off a bit. Perhaps the LORD will come to visit me. I will tell you whatever he reveals to me." He then went off to a high place.

4 God visited Balaam. He said, "I have prepared seven altars and I have offered a young bull and a ram upon each altar." 5 The LORD put a message in Balaam's mouth and said, "Return to Balak and proclaim this."

6 So he returned to him and found him standing by his sacrifice, he and the leaders of Moab. 7 Then he proclaimed his oracle:

"Balak has brought me from Aram,
the king of Moab from the eastern mountains saying,
'Come, and curse Jacob,
come and denounce Israel!'[k]
8 How shall I curse those
whom God has not cursed,
how shall I denounce
those whom the LORD
has not denounced? *
9 From the top of the rocks I see him,
from the hills I behold him.
Behold, a people dwelling alone,
not counted among the nations.
10 Who can count the dust of Jacob,
or number one-fourth of Israel?
Let me die the death of the righteous,
let my end be like his."

11 Then Balak said to Balaam, "What have you done to me? I brought you to curse my enemies, but you have bountifully blessed them." 12 But he answered, "Must I not proclaim what the LORD has put into my mouth?"

Balaam's Second Oracle. 13 Then Balak said to him, "Please come with me to another place. There you will be able to see them, but only their outposts; you will not see all of them. You can curse them for me from there."

14 So he brought him to the field of Zophim, to the top of Pisgah. He built seven altars, and he offered a young bull and a ram on each altar. 15 He said to Balak, "Stand here by your offering, and I will meet the LORD over there." 16 The LORD visited Balaam and put a word in his mouth saying, "Go back again to Balak and proclaim this."

17 He returned to him. He was standing by his offering, he and the leaders of Moab with him. Balak said to him, "What has the LORD said?" 18 He took up his oracle and said,

"Arise, Balak, and hear;
listen to me, son of Zippor!
19 God is not human, that he should lie,*
or the son of man, that he should change his mind.
Does he speak and then not act,
does he promise and then not fulfill it?[l]

j Jer 1:9.—*k* Num 22:6.—*l* 1 Sam 15:29; Mal 3:6; Rom 11:29.

23:1—24:25 The story of Balaam is told here chiefly in order to bring in the oracles of blessing. What is reported here is certainly very ancient traditions, comparable to the blessings of Jacob (Gen 49) and of Moses (Deut 33).

23:8 Balaam cannot do what Balak asks of him because God is protecting his people. None of Balaam's tricks can negate God's blessing on them.

23:19 *God is not human, that he should lie:* Balaam's lack of integrity and honesty are far removed from the steadfast mercy and goodness of God.

20 Behold, I have received a blessing;
he has blessed, and I cannot change it.
21 No misfortune is seen in Jacob,
no misery is seen in Israel.
The LORD, their God, is with them;
the shout of a king is among them.
22 God has brought them out of Egypt;
they are as strong as a wild ox.[m]
23 There is truly no sorcery against Jacob,
nor any divination against Israel.
Now it will be said of Jacob and Israel,
'What God has done!'
24 Behold, a people rises up like a lioness,
like a young lion it lifts itself up.
It will not lie down again until it eats the prey
and drinks the blood of the slain."[n]

25 Then Balak said to Balaam, "Then do
not either curse them in any way or bless
them in any way!" 26 But Balaam answered
Balak saying, "Did I not tell you: 'All that
the LORD says I must do!' "

Balaam's Third Oracle. 27 Balak said to
Balaam, "Please come, I will take you to an-
other place. Perhaps God will allow you to
curse them for me here." 28 Then Balak
brought Balaam to the top of Peor, to a
place that faced Jeshimon. 29 Balaam said to
Balak, "Build me seven altars here, and
prepare seven young bulls and seven rams
for me." 30 Balak did what Balaam had told
him to do, and he offered a young bull and a
ram on each of the altars.

CHAPTER 24

1 When Balaam saw that it pleased the
LORD to bless Israel, he did not go to seek
omens as he did before, but rather faced the
wilderness. 2 Balaam raised his eyes and he
saw Israel camped tribe by tribe. The Spirit
of God came upon him* 3 and he took up his
oracle:

"The oracle of Balaam, the son of Beor,
the oracle of one whose eye is opened.*
4 The oracle of one who hears the words of God,
who sees a vision of the Almighty;
who falls down, with eyes wide open.
5 How pleasant are your tents, O Jacob,
and your dwelling places, O Israel.[o]
6 Like valleys they spread out,
like gardens beside a river;
like aloes that the LORD has planted,
like cedars beside the waters;
7 like water that pours forth from buckets,
their seed will be mighty waters.
Their king will be higher than Agag,*
their kingdom will be exalted.
8 God has brought them forth from Egypt,
their strength is that of the wild ox.
They will devour nations,
they will break the bones of their enemies,
they will pierce them through with their arrows.[p]
9 He crouches down, he lay down like a lion; who dare rouse him?
Blessed is the one who blesses him,
but cursed is the one who curses him."[q]

10 Balak became enraged at Balaam.
Balak clasped his hands together and said
to Balaam, "I summoned you to curse my
enemies, but you have blessed them these
three times. 11 Now then, leave and go
home. I told you that I would reward you
richly, but the LORD has kept you from
being paid."

12 But Balaam said to Balak, "Did I not
tell your messengers who sent for me, 13 'If
Balak were to give me a house full of silver
and gold, I could not go beyond the word of
the LORD on my own either for good or for
bad. Whatever the LORD proclaims, that I
must speak!'[r] 14 Now I am going back to my
own people; come, allow me to let you know
what this people will do to your people in
the future."

Balaam's Fourth Oracle. 15 So he took up the
oracle and said,

"Balaam, the son of Beor,
the man whose eyes are open says,
16 The oracle of he
who has heard the words of God,
who has knowledge of the Most High,
who sees the vision of the Almighty,
who falls down with his eyes open:
17 * I see him, but not now.

m Num 24:8.—n Gen 49:9; Deut 33:20.—o Isa 54:2-3.—p Num 23:22.—q Gen 12:3; 27:29.—r Num 22:18.

24:2 *The Spirit of God came upon him:* the unusual wording here suggests that God has intervened and will use Balaam for his purposes.

24:3 *One whose eye is opened:* one who scrutinizes the secrets of God.

24:7 *Agag:* the king of the Amalekites, whom Saul will conquer (1 Sam 15:8).

24:17-19 This star, the sign of a hero sent by God, heralds King David, in keeping with the ancient promises made to Judah (Gen 49:10); this hero was expected to make subjects of the peoples who were Israel's neighbors. But behind this conqueror can be seen the glorious Messiah, Jesus Son of David (Mt 2:2; Rev 22:16).

I behold him, but not near.
A star comes forth from Jacob,
and a scepter rises out of Israel.
He will crush the brow of Moab,
he will destroy the children of Seth.[s]
18 Edom* will become a possession,
and Seir also will become a possession
of its enemies,
but Israel will grow strong.
19 A ruler will come out of Jacob,
he will destroy the remnant of the city."

20 He then looked toward Amalek and said,

"Amalek was the first of the nations,
but he will be the last until he perishes."[t]

21 He looked upon the Kenites* and took up
his oracle and said,

"Strong is your dwelling place,
and your nest is in the rock;
22 but Kain will be consumed.
How long until Asshur* carries you away
as a captive?"

23 He continued his oracle saying,

"Alas, who can live when God does this?
24 Ships will come from Kittim,
and will humble Asshur and Eber.
They, too, will face destruction."[u]

25 Then Balaam got up and went home,
and Balak also went his way.

CHAPTER 25

Israel Worships Baal of Peor. 1 While Israel
dwelt in Shittim,* the people began to play
the harlot with the daughters of Moab.
2 They invited the people to sacrifice to their
gods. The people ate and worshiped their
gods.[v] 3 So Israel yoked himself to Baal * of
Peor. The LORD grew angry at Israel[w] 4 and
the LORD said to Moses, "Take all of the lead-
ers of the people and hang them before the
LORD in broad daylight* so that the rage of
the LORD turns away from Israel."

5 So Moses said to the judges of Israel,
"Each of you is to kill those who joined
themselves to Baal of Peor."

6 Then one of the people of Israel came
and brought a Midianite woman to his rela-
tives before the eyes of Moses and before the
eyes of the whole assembly of the people of
Israel who were weeping at the entrance to
the tent of meeting.

Phinehas' Zeal for God. 7 When Phinehas,
the son of Eleazar, the son of Aaron the
priest, saw this, he got up and left the assem-
bly, taking a spear in his hand.[x] 8 He followed
the Israelite into the tent. He then drove it
through both of them, through the Israelite
and into the woman's stomach. This is how
the plague among the people of Israel was
stopped. 9 Yet, twenty-four thousand died*
in the plague.

10 The LORD said to Moses, 11 "Phinehas,
the son of Eleazar, the son of Aaron the
priest, has calmed my anger at the people of
Israel. He was zealous for my sake among
them so that I not consume the people of
Israel in my zeal. 12[y] Therefore, say, 'I estab-
lish my covenant of peace with him. 13 He
will have it, and his descendants after him,
as a covenant for an everlasting priesthood.
He was zealous for his God, and he made
atonement for the people of Israel.' "

14 Now the name of the Israelite who was
slain along with the Midianite woman was
Zimri, the son of Salu, a leader of the ances-
tral tribe of the Simeonites. 15 The name of
the Midianite woman who was killed was
Cozbi, the daughter of Zur, a tribal leader of
an ancestral tribe of Midian.

Downfall of the Midianites. 16 Then the LORD
spoke to Moses, saying, 17[z] "Harass the
Midianites and slay them 18 for they ha-
rassed you with their schemes when they
seduced you in the affair at Peor and in the
affair of Cozbi, the daughter of the leader of
Midian, their sister who was slain on the day
of the plague because of Peor."

III: THE SECOND CENSUS AND THE PLAN TO ENTER THE PROMISED LAND

CHAPTER 26

The Second Census. 1 After the plague, the
LORD spoke to Moses and to Eleazar, the

s Gen 49:10; 2 Sam 8:2.—t Ex 17:8, 14; 1 Sam 15:3.—u Dan 11:30.—v Ex 34:15-16; 1 Cor 10:20.—w Deut 4:3; Ps 106:28.—x Ps 106:30.—y 12-13: Ex 32:25-28; Ps 106:31; Ezek 44:15.—z 17-18: Num 31:2-12.

24:18 *Edom:* in the Negeb, the desert in southern Palestine.

24:21 *Kenites:* nomads of southern Palestine.

24:22 *Asshur:* the tribe of the Asshurites (Gen 25:3), rather than the Assyrians.

25:1 *Shittim:* opposite Jericho, on the other side of the Jordan. See Jos 2:1.

25:3 *Baal:* means "Lord" and was the generic name for the divinities of the Canaanites. See Num 31:16; Deut 4:3; 1 Cor 10:8.

25:4 *Hang them before the LORD in broad daylight:* a public display of those who had sinned might dissuade others from straying.

25:9 *Twenty-four thousand died:* the worship of Baal had a devastating effect on the people of Israel. The numbers are corroborated in the decrease from the first census to the second (see Num 1:44-46; 26:51).

priest, saying, 2 "Take a census of the whole assembly of the people of Israel by their father's house, those twenty years and older, all of those who are fit to bear arms." [a]

3 Moses and Eleazar spoke with them in the plain of Moab near the Jordan, across from Jericho, saying, 4 "Take a census of those twenty years and older, as the LORD commanded Moses, of all the people of Israel who came forth from the land of Egypt."

5 [b] Reuben was the firstborn son of Israel. The sons of Reuben were: Hanoch, of the Hanochite clan; Pallu, of the Palluite clan; 6 Hezron, of the Hezronite clan; Carmi, of the Carmite clan. 7 These were the clans of Reuben. Those counted numbered forty-three thousand, seven hundred and thirty.

8 The son of Pallu was Eliab. 9 The sons of Eliab were Nemuel, Dathan, and Abiram. These are the Dathan and Abiram who were the community leaders who rebelled against Moses and Aaron. They were companions of Korah when they rebelled against the LORD. 10 The earth opened its mouth and swallowed them together with Korah, whose followers died when fire devoured two hundred and fifty men; they served as a warning. [c] 11 The descendants of Korah, however, did not die out.

12 The sons of Simeon by their clans were: Nemuel, of the Nemuelite clan; Jamin, of the Jaminite clan; Jachin, of the Jachinite clan; 13 Zerah, of the Zerahite clan; and Shaul, of the Shaulite clan. 14 These were the clans of Simeon. There were twenty-two thousand, two hundred of them.*

15 The sons of Gad by their clans were: Zephon, of the Zephonite clan; Haggi, of the Haggite clan; Shuni, of the Shunite clan; 16 Ozni, of the Oznite clan; Eri, of the Erite clan; 17 Arod, of the Arodite clan; and Areli, of the Arelite clan. 18 These were the clans of Gad. There were forty thousand, five hundred of them.

19 The sons of Judah: Er and Onan (but Er and Onan died in the land of Canaan). [d] 20 The sons of Judah by their clans were: Shelah, of the Shelahite clan; Perez,* of the Perezite clan; and Zerah, of the Zerahite clan. 21 The sons of Perez were: Hezron, of the Hezronite clan; and Hamul, of the Hamulite clan. 22 These were the clans of Judah. There were seventy-six thousand, five hundred of them.

23 The sons of Issachar by their clans were: Tola, of the Tolaite clan; Puvah, of the Puvahite clan; 24 Jashub, of the Jashubite clan; and Shimron, of the Shimronite clan. 25 These were the clans of Issachar. There were sixty-four thousand, three hundred of them.

26 The sons of Zebulun by their clans were: Sered, of the Seredite clan; Elon, of the Elonite clan; and Jahleel, of the Jahleelite clan. 27 These were the clans of Zebulun. There were sixty thousand, five hundred of them.

28 The sons of Joseph by their clans through Manasseh and Ephraim were: 29 the sons of Manasseh: Machir, of the Machirite clan (Machir was the father of Gilead); Gilead, of the Gileadites. 30 These were the sons of Gilead: Iezer, of the Iezerite clan; Helek, of the Helekite clan; [e] 31 Asriel, of the Asrielite clan; Shechem, of the Shechemite clan; 32 Shemida, of the Shemidaite clan; and Hepher, of the Hepherite clan. 33 (Zelophehad, the son of Hepher, had no sons, only daughters. The name of the daughters of Zelophehad were: Mahlah, Noah, Hoglah, Milcah, and Tirzah.) 34 These were the clans of Manasseh. There were fifty-two thousand, five hundred of them.

35 The sons of Ephraim by their clans were: Shuthelah, of the Shuthelahite clan; Becher, of the Becherite clan; and Tahan, of the Tahanite clan. 36 These were the sons of Shuthelah: Eran, of the Eranite clan. 37 These were the clans of Ephraim. There were thirty-two thousand, five hundred of them. These were the descendants of Joseph by their clans.

38 The sons of Benjamin by their clans were: Bela, of the Belaite clan; Ashbel, of the Ashbelite clan; Ahiram, of the Ahiramite clan; 39 Shupham, of the Shuphamite clan; and Hupham, of the Huphamite clan. 40 The sons of Bela were Ard and Naaman: Ard, of the Ardite clan; and Naaman, of the Naamite clan. 41 These were the clans of Benjamin. There were forty-five thousand, six hundred of them.

a Num 1:2.—b 5-6: Ex 6:14; 1 Chr 5:3.—c Num 16:32.—d Gen 38:7; 46:12.—e Jos 17:2; 1 Chr 7:14-19.

26:14 *Twenty-two thousand, . . . of them:* the sons of Simeon in the first census numbered 59,300 (Num 1:22-23). Thirty-eight years later in the second census there is a loss of 37,100 representing the biggest loss of all the tribes. It is possible that most of those who died in the plague (Num 25:9) were from Simeon.

26:20 *Perez:* the Davidic line from which Jesus came would be through Perez (see Mt 1:3).

[42] The sons of Dan by their clans were: Shuham, of the Shuhamite clan. These were the clans of Dan. [43] The only clan was of the Shuhamites. There were sixty-four thousand, four hundred of them.

[44] The sons of Asher by their clans were: Imnah, of the Imnite clan; Ishvi, of the Ishvite clan; and Beriah, of the Beriite clan. [45] The descendants of Beriah were: Heber, of the Heberite clan and Malchiel, of the Malchielite clan. [46] Asher also had a daughter named Serah.* [47] These were the clans of Asher. There were fifty-three thousand, four hundred of them.

[48] The sons of Naphtali by their clans were: Jahzeel, of the Jahzeelite clan; Guni, of the Gunite clan; [49] Jezer, of the Jezerite clan; and Shillem, of the Shillemite clan. [50] These were the clans of Naphtali. There were forty-five thousand, four hundred of them.

[51] The total number of people of Israel was six hundred and one thousand, seven hundred and thirty.

Land Allotments. [52] The LORD then spoke to Moses, saying, [53] "The land is to be allotted unto these as an inheritance based on the number of those inscribed.[f] [54] To the larger group you will give a larger inheritance, to the smaller group you will give a smaller inheritance. Every clan will be given an inheritance according to its size. [55] But the land will be divided by lot; they will inherit it according to the number of the names of their ancestral tribes. [56] Each inheritance will be distributed by lot, to the larger and smaller groups."

The Levite Census. [57] *These were the Levites who were counted by their clans: Gershon, of the Gershonite clan; Kohath, of the Kohathite clan; and Merari, of the Merarite clan.* [58] These were also Levite clans: the Libnite clan; the Hebronite clan; the Mahlite clan; the Mushite clan; and the Kohathite clan. Kohath became the father of Amram. [59] The name of Amram's wife was Jochebed, the daughter of Levi, who was born to Levi in Egypt. She bore Aaron, Moses, and their sister Miriam to Amram. [60] To Aaron were born Nadab, Abihu, Eleazar, and Ithamar. [61] Nadab and Abihu died when they offered unclean fire before the LORD.[g] [62] The total number of all the males one month old and older was twenty-three thousand. They were not counted among the people of Israel because no inheritance was given to them among the people of Israel.

[63] These were the figures of the people of Israel counted by Moses and Eleazar the priest in the plain of Moab near the Jordan, across from Jericho. [64] There was not a single person among the people of Israel whom Moses and Aaron had counted in the Sinai Desert. [65] The LORD said of them: "They will surely die in the wilderness." There were none of them left except for Caleb, the son of Jephunneh, and Joshua, the son of Nun.[h]

CHAPTER 27

Zelophehad's Daughters.* [1] The daughters of Zelophehad, the son of Hepher, the son of Gilead, the son of Machir, the son of Manasseh, the son of Joseph came forward. The names of the daughters were Mahlah, Noah, Hoglah, Milcah, and Tirzah.[i] [2] They stood before Moses and Eleazar, the priest, and the leaders and all the assembly at the entrance to the tent of meeting. They said, [3] "Our father died in the desert, but he was not in the band of those who conspired together with Korah against the LORD. He died on account of his own sin. He had no sons. [4] Why should the name of our father perish from his clan because he did not have a son? Give us property among our father's kinsmen."

[5] So Moses brought their case before the LORD. [6] The LORD spoke to Moses, saying, [7] "What Zelophehad's daughters are saying is just. You surely must give them property as an inheritance among their father's kinsmen, and you must turn their father's inheritance over to them.[j] [8] Say to the people of Israel, 'If a man dies and leaves no son, then turn over his inheritance to his daughter. [9] If he has no daughter, then turn over his inheritance to his brothers. [10] If he has no brothers, then give his inheritance to his father's brothers. [11] If the father has no brothers, you

f Jos 11:23.—g Num 3:4; Lev 10:1-2.—h Num 14:28-29; 1 Cor 10:5-6.—i Num 26:33; Jos 17:3.—j Num 36:2.

26:46 *A daughter named Serah:* among all of the sons listed, Serah is the only daughter mentioned.

26:57-58 The two lists of Levite clans are not identical. They come from different traditions, the second being certainly the older. An attempt is made to reconcile them in 1 Chr 6:1-14.

26:57 The Levites have their own census as they did in the first counting (see ch. 3).

27:1-11 The fact that women engage in this type of bargaining concerning their rights of inheritance through their dead father is extraordinary for this time.

will give his inheritance to his nearest kinsman in his clan so that he might possess it. This will be a statute and an ordinance for the people of Israel, as the LORD commanded Moses.' "

Joshua Commissioned by Moses. 12 The LORD said to Moses, "Go up onto Mount Abarim and look upon the land that I have given to the people of Israel.[k] 13 After you have seen it, you will be gathered to your people, as Aaron your brother was, 14 for in the Desert of Zin, in the strife over the water with the assembly, you both disobeyed my command to treat me as holy before their eyes."[l] (This is the water of Meribah in Kadesh, in the Desert of Zin.)

15 Moses spoke to the LORD, saying, 16 "May the LORD, the God of the spirits of all flesh, place a man over the assembly 17 who will go out and come in before them, and who will lead them out and bring them in, so that the assembly of the LORD might not be like sheep without a shepherd." *[m] 18 So the LORD said to Moses, "Take Joshua, the son of Nun, a man in whom the Spirit is found, and lay your hand upon him.[n] 19 Have him stand before Eleazar the priest and before the whole assembly and commission him in their sight. 20 Give him some of your authority, so that the assembly of the people of Israel might obey. 21 He will stand before Eleazar, the priest, who will inquire for him before the LORD with the judgment of the Urim. At his word they will go out, and at his word they will come in, he and all the people of Israel with him, the whole assembly." *[o]

22 So Moses did as the LORD had commanded him. He took Joshua and brought him before Eleazar the priest and the whole assembly. 23 He laid his hand upon him and commissioned him, as the LORD had commanded through Moses.

CHAPTER 28

Daily Offerings. 1 * The LORD spoke to Moses, saying, 2 "Command the people of Israel and say to them, 'You will be careful to present my offering in its proper time, my food for my offerings made by fire, a pleasant fragrance.' 3 You will say to them, 'This is the offering that you will make by fire to the LORD: two male year-old lambs that are without defect. They are each day's regular burnt offering. *[p] 4 You will offer one lamb in the morning, and you will offer the other lamb in the evening 5 along with one-tenth of an ephah of fine flour mixed with one-fourth of a hin of pressed oil as a cereal offering. 6 This is the regular burnt offering which was established on Mount Sinai as a pleasing fragrance, an offering made by fire to the LORD. 7 Its drink offering is to be a fourth of a hin for each lamb. You will pour out the strong wine as a drink offering to the LORD in the sanctuary. 8 The other lamb will be offered in the evening with the same cereal offering as in the morning and the drink offering. You will offer it as an offering made by fire, a pleasing fragrance to the LORD.

Sabbath Offerings. 9 " 'On the Sabbath offer two male year-old lambs that are without defect, two-tenths of an ephah of fine flour mixed with oil as a cereal offering, and its drink offering.[q] 10 The burnt offering for each Sabbath is in addition to the regular burnt offerings and their drink offerings.

Monthly Offerings. 11 " 'At the beginnings of your months, you will offer a burnt offering to the LORD: two young bulls, one ram, and seven male year-old lambs that are without defect[r] 12 along with three-tenths of an ephah of fine flour mixed with oil as a cereal offering for each young bull, two-tenths of an ephah of fine flour mixed with oil as a cereal offering for each ram, 13 and one-tenth of an ephah of fine flour mixed with oil as a cereal offering for each lamb. This will be a burnt offering, a pleasing fragrance, an offering made by fire to the LORD. 14 The drink offering will be half a hin of wine for each young bull, a third of a hin for each ram, and a fourth of a hin for each lamb. This is the burnt offering to be made each new moon* throughout the year. 15 Besides the regular burnt offerings with their drink offerings, one kid goat is to be offered to the LORD as a sin offering.

k Deut 32:49.—l Num 20:12; Deut 32:51.—m 1 Ki 22:17; Ezek 34:5; Mt 9:36.—n Deut 34:9.—o Ex 28:30.—p Ex 29:38.—q Mt 12:5.—r Isa 1:13; Am 8:5.

27:17 Joshua will have authority to make all decisions that are useful in directing the advance of the people.

27:21 Although Joshua is appointed as successor to Moses (Deut 34:9), it is clear that he does not have the direct line to the Lord that Moses enjoyed.

28:1—29:39 These regulations complete those of Leviticus (chs. 1-7; 23) and the Book of Ezekiel (ch. 45); they describe the post-Exilic liturgy, the one that Jesus would later celebrate.

28:3 *Regular burnt offering:* referred to the daily offering, whereas there were additional offerings on the Sabbath (see vv. 9-10).

28:14 *New moon:* coincides with the offerings made at the beginning of each month.

At Passover.* [16] " 'The Passover of the LORD
is to be celebrated on the fourteenth day of
the first month.[s] [17] The fifteenth day of this
month is a feast, unleavened bread is to be
eaten for seven days. [18] On the first day you
will have a sacred assembly, you are not to do
any heavy labor.[t] [19] Present an offering made
by fire of two young bulls, one ram, and seven
male year-old lambs to the LORD. They are to
be without defect. [20] Their grain offering will
be fine flour mixed with oil. You will offer
three-tenths of an ephah for a young bull and
two-tenths of an ephah for a ram. [21] You will
offer one-tenth of an ephah for each of the
seven lambs [22] and one goat as a sin offering
to make your atonement. [23] You will offer
these in addition to the morning burnt offer-
ing, which is the regular burnt offering.
[24] This is the way that you will offer the food
of the offering made by fire each day for
seven days, a pleasing fragrance to the LORD.
It is offered in addition to the regular burnt
offerings and their drink offerings. [25] On the
seventh day you will have a holy assembly;
you are not to do any heavy labor.

Pentecost.* [26] " 'On the day of the first-
fruits,* when you bring a new cereal offering
to the LORD for the Feast of Weeks, you are to
have a holy assembly; you are not to do any
heavy labor.[u] [27] You will present a burnt
offering as a pleasing fragrance to the LORD
of two young bulls, one ram, and seven male
year-old lambs [28] along with their grain offer-
ings of fine flour mixed with oil: three-tenths
of an ephah for each young bull, two-tenths
of an ephah for each ram, [29] and a tenth of an
ephah for each of the seven lambs, [30] along
with one kid goat to make your atonement.
[31] They are to be without defect. [32] You will
present them in addition to the regular burnt
offerings along with their cereal offerings
and their drink offerings.

CHAPTER 29

Feast of Trumpets.* [1] " 'On the first day of
the seventh month you will have a holy
assembly. You are not to do any heavy labor.
It is a day for you to sound the trumpets.[v]
[2] You will offer a pleasing fragrance to the
LORD, a burnt offering of one young bull, one
ram, and seven male year-old lambs with-
out defect. [3] The cereal offering is to be fine
flour mixed with oil: three-tenths of an
ephah for a young bull, two-tenths of an
ephah for a ram, [4] and a tenth of an ephah
for each of the seven lambs. [5] The sin offer-
ing is one kid goat to make your atonement.
[6] These are in addition to the monthly and
daily burnt offerings along with their cereal
offerings and their drink offerings, according
to custom. They are offerings made by fire, a
pleasing fragrance to the LORD.

Day of Atonement. [7] " 'On the tenth day of
the seventh month you are to have a holy
assembly. You are to humble yourselves and
are not to do any heavy labor.*[w] [8] You will
present a burnt offering to the LORD as a
pleasing fragrance: one young bull, one ram,
and seven male year-old lambs, without
defect. [9] Their grain offering is to be fine
flour mixed with oil: three-tenths of an
ephah for the young bull, two-tenths of
an ephah for the one ram, [10] and a tenth of
an ephah for each of the seven lambs. [11] The
sin offering is one kid goat. This is in addition
to the sin offering of atonement and the reg-
ular burnt offerings with their cereal and
drink offerings.

Feast of Tabernacles.* [12] " 'On the fifteenth
day of the seventh month you are to have a
holy assembly. You are not to do any heavy
labor. You are to celebrate a feast of the
LORD for seven days.[x] [13] Present an offering
made by fire as a pleasing fragrance to the
LORD: thirteen young bulls, two rams, and
fourteen male year-old lambs. They are to be
without defect. [14] Their cereal offering is to
be fine flour mixed with oil: three-tenths of
an ephah for each of the thirteen young
bulls, two-tenths of an ephah for each of the

s Ex 12:18; Lev 23:5; Deut 16:1.—t Ex 12:16; Lev 23:7.—u Ex 23:16; 34:22; Lev 23:10.—v Num 10:10; Lev 23:24.—w Lev 16:29; 23:26-32.—x Lev 23:33-35.

28:16-25 Passover, which was long combined with the Feast of Unleavened Bread (Greek, *azymes*; see Ex 12), is the first major feast of the year (the year in this case begins in the spring).

28:26-32 Pentecost, which comes seven weeks after Passover, celebrates the harvest and commemorates God's self-revelation on Sinai after the departure from Egypt (see Lev 23:15-21).

28:26 *Day of the firstfruits:* usually referred to as the Feast of Weeks.

29:1-6 At one time, the first day of the first month of autumn became New Year's Day for the Israelites. The Feast of Trumpets was instituted during the period when the year began in the autumn. The sounding of the trumpet (ram's horn) is most often mentioned in the post-Exilic period.

29:7 The Feast of Trumpets prepares the people for fasting from work and food on the Day of Atonement, a time of reparation for the sins of the people.

29:12-40 The Feast of Tabernacles is a feast both of thanksgiving for the harvest and of commemoration of the period in the wilderness. This is the reason why the Israelites spend the eight days of this solemnity living in huts or tents (i.e., tabernacles). The number of sacrifices offered shows the importance of the feast, which was the most popular in Israel (see Lev 23:33-34; Jn 7:2).

two rams, 15 and a tenth of an ephah for each of the fourteen lambs. 16 The sin offering is one kid goat. This is in addition to the regular burnt offerings along with their cereal and drink offerings.

17 " 'On the second day offer twelve young bulls, two rams, and fourteen male year-old lambs without defect. 18 The cereal offering and the drink offering for the young bulls, rams, and lambs will be in the customary number. 19 The sin offering is one kid goat. This is in addition to the regular burnt offerings along with their cereal and drink offerings.

20 " 'Then on the third day offer eleven young bulls, two rams, and fourteen male year-old lambs, without defect. 21 The cereal offering and the drink offering for the young bulls, rams, and lambs will be in the customary number. 22 The sin offering is one kid goat. This is in addition to the regular burnt offerings along with their cereal and drink offerings.

23 " 'Then on the fourth day offer ten young bulls, two rams, and fourteen male year-old lambs, without defect. 24 The cereal offering and the drink offering for the young bulls, rams, and lambs will be in the customary number. 25 The sin offering is one kid goat. This is in addition to the regular burnt offerings along with their cereal and drink offerings.

26 " 'Then on the fifth day offer nine young bulls, two rams, and fourteen male year-old lambs, without defect. 27 The cereal offering and the drink offering for the young bulls, rams, and lambs will be in the customary number. 28 The sin offering is one kid goat. This is in addition to the regular burnt offerings along with their cereal and drink offerings.[y]

29 " 'Then on the sixth day offer eight young bulls, two rams, and fourteen male year-old lambs, without defect. 30 The cereal offering and the drink offering for the young bulls, rams, and lambs will be in the customary number. 31 The sin offering is one kid goat. This is in addition to the regular burnt offerings along with their cereal and drink offerings.

32 " 'Then on the seventh day offer seven young bulls, two rams, and fourteen male year-old lambs, without defect. 33 The cereal offering and the drink offering for the young bulls, rams, and lambs will be in the customary number. 34 The sin offering is one kid goat. This is in addition to the regular burnt offerings along with their cereal and drink offerings.

35 " 'On the eighth day you are to have a holy assembly. You are not to do any heavy labor.[z] 36 You are to present a burnt offering, an offering made by fire, a pleasing fragrance to the LORD: one young bull, one ram, and seven male year-old lambs, without defect. 37 The cereal offering and the drink offering for the young bull, ram, and lambs will be in the customary number. 38 The sin offering is one kid goat. This is in addition to the regular burnt offerings along with their cereal and drink offerings.

39 " 'You will present these to the LORD on your appointed feast days, in addition to your vow offerings, your free-will offerings, your cereal offerings, your drink offerings, and your peace offerings.' "

40 Moses spoke to the people of Israel, just as the LORD had commanded Moses. *

CHAPTER 30

Vows to the LORD and Others. 1 * Then Moses spoke to the leaders of the ancestral tribes of Israel, saying, "This is what the LORD commands: 2 When a person makes a vow to the LORD, or swears an oath to bind himself to some commitment, he is not to break his promise. He will do everything just as he said he would.

3 * "When a young woman who is still in her father's house makes a vow to the LORD, or swears an oath to bind herself to some commitment,[a] 4 and her father hears about her vow and her commitment made by oath and he says nothing to her, then all her vows and all the oaths by which she bound herself will be valid. 5 But if her father forbids it on the day that he hears about it, then none of her vows and the oaths with which she bound herself will be valid. The LORD will

y Num 28-30.—z Lev 23:36; Jn 7:37.—a Deut 23:22-24; Eccl 5:3-4; Ps 50:14.

29:40 The recitation of these events by Moses was necessary to show his obedience to the Lord even as his power was being transferred to Joshua.

30:1-2 A vow is a freely made commitment to do something more and better than the law requires and to do it out of pure love of God; once pronounced, it obliges in conscience before God.

30:3-8 This section specified the father's and husband's ability to override a woman's vow. Not only was this customary in Eastern cultures in biblical times but carried forward into modern times. Jesus' actions in the New Testament urge simplicity regarding oaths (Mt 5:33-37).

release her because her father has forbidden
her to do it.
6 “If she marries after she has made a vow
or a rash statement from her mouth by
which she has bound herself 7 and her hus-
band hears about it, and he says nothing to
her on the day that he hears about it, then
her vows and the oaths with which she
bound herself will be valid. 8 But if her hus-
band forbids it on the day that he hears
about it, then he makes void the vows she
has made and the rash statements from her
mouth by which she has bound herself. The
LORD will release her.[b]
9 “Any vow or obligation made by a widow
or a divorced woman by which she bound
herself will be binding. 10 If she made the vow
while she was in her husband’s house or
swore an oath to bind herself to some com-
mitment 11 and her husband heard about it
and said nothing to her and did not forbid it,
then all her vows and all the oaths with which
she bound herself will be valid. 12 But if her
husband forbids it on the day that he hears
about it, then whatever proceeded out of her
mouth concerning her vows or the oaths by
which she bound herself will not be valid. Her
husband makes them void and the LORD will
release her. 13 Her husband can let stand or
make void any vow or oath by which she
bound herself to humble herself. 14 But if her
husband says nothing to her from day to day,
then he confirms all her vows and all her
oaths. He has confirmed them because he
said nothing to her on the day that he heard
about it. 15 But if he makes them void after he
has heard about them, then he will bear her
guilt.”
16 These are the statutes that the LORD
commanded Moses concerning a husband
and his wife, and between a father and his
young daughter still living in her father’s
house.

CHAPTER 31

Israel Battles the Midianites.* 1 The LORD
spoke to Moses, saying, 2 “Take vengeance
upon the Midianites for the people of Israel.
After that, you will be gathered to your peo-
ple.”
3 Moses spoke to the people, saying, “Arm
some of your men for war so that they might
go out against the Midianites to execute the
LORD’s vengeance upon Midian. 4 Send a
thousand men to war from each of the tribes
of Israel.”
5 So they set aside a thousand from each
tribe of Israel, twelve thousand armed for
battle. 6 Moses sent them out to battle, a
thousand from each tribe, along with Eleazar
the priest. He took the vessels of the sanctu-
ary and the trumpets for the alarm in his
hands. 7 They battled against the Midianites,
as the LORD had commanded Moses, killing
all of the males. 8 They killed the kings of
Midian: Evi, Rekem, Zur, Hur, and Reba,
the five kings of Midian, along with the oth-
ers they killed. They also killed Balaam, the
son of Beor, with the sword.[c]
9 The people of Israel took captive the
women of Midian and their little ones and
all their cattle and all their flocks and all
their goods. 10 They also burned down all the
cities in which they dwelt and all their
fortresses. 11 They took all the booty and all
the spoils, both of man and beast[d] 12 and
brought the captives, the spoils, and the
booty to Moses and to Eleazar the priest and
to the assembly of the people of Israel at the
camp on the plain of Moab which is near the
Jordan, across from Jericho.
13 Moses, Eleazar the priest, and all the
leaders of the assembly met them outside of
the camp. 14 Moses was angry with the offi-
cers of the army, the captains of the thou-
sands and the captains of the hundreds, who
had returned from battle. 15 Moses said to
them, “Have you spared all the women?
16 These are the ones who caused the people
of Israel to follow the advice of Balaam, to
trespass against the LORD in the affair of
Peor, causing a plague among the assembly
of the LORD.[e] 17 Now kill every boy and kill
every woman who has slept with a man,
18 but save the girls for yourselves who have
not yet slept with a man.

Purification after Battle.* 19 “Any of you who
has killed a person and anyone who has
touched any of those who have been killed
must stay outside of the camp for seven
days. You are to purify yourself and your
captives on the third and the seventh days.

b Gen 3:16.—c Jos 13:21-22.—d Deut 20:14.—e Num 25:1-9; 2 Pet 2:15; Rev 2:14.

31:1-18 The story of God’s judgment on the Midianites certainly exaggerates some incidents in the campaign in the Transjordan. The massacre does not spare even the women: the prostitution of the sons of Israel at Baal of Peor (ch. 25) has left a humiliating memory. We must not apply the standard of our gospel morality to these practices of a remote age.

31:19-24 The cleansing ritual for anyone who engaged in battle for the Lord extended beyond the person to all things involved.

20 Purify all of your clothes as well as all of your
leather goods and everything made from goat
hair and everything made from wood."
21 Then Eleazar said to the men of war
who had gone into battle: "This is a statute of
the law which the LORD has commanded
Moses: 22 gold, silver, brass, iron, tin, lead,
23 and anything else that can withstand fire
will be pure if you pass it through fire.
However, it must also be purified with the
water of purification. Whatever cannot with-
stand fire must pass through water. 24 You
will wash your clothes on the seventh day,
and you will be pure, and you can then enter
the camp."[f]

Dividing the Spoils. 25 The LORD spoke to
Moses, saying, 26 * "You, Eleazar the priest,
and the leaders of the fathers' households
are to count the booty, both of man and of
beast. 27 Divide the booty into two parts,
between those who took part in the war, who
went out to battle, and all of the assembly.
28 Establish a share for the LORD from the
men of war who went out into battle: one out
of five hundred, of the people, of the cattle, of
the donkeys, and of the sheep.
29 "Take it from their half and give it to
Eleazar the priest as an offering to the LORD.
30 "From the half share that belongs to the
people of Israel, take one out of every fifty, of
people, of the cattle, of the donkeys, of the
sheep, and of all the animals. Give them to
the Levites who have responsibility over the
sanctuary of the LORD."
31 Moses and Eleazar the priest did as the
LORD had commanded Moses. 32 The booty
remaining from the spoils that the men of
war captured was six hundred seventy-five
thousand sheep, 33 seventy-two thousand
cattle, 34 sixty-one thousand donkeys, 35 and
thirty-two thousand girls who had never
slept with a man.
36 The half share for those who went out to
fight was three hundred thirty-seven thou-
sand, five hundred sheep, 37 of which the
share for the LORD was six hundred seventy-
five; 38 thirty-six thousand cattle, of which
the share for the LORD was seventy-two;
39 thirty thousand five hundred donkeys, of
which the share for the LORD was sixty-one;
40 and sixteen thousand people, of which the
share for the LORD was thirty-two.
41 Moses gave the share that was the
LORD's offering to Eleazar the priest, as the
LORD had commanded Moses.
42 The half share of the people of Israel,
which Moses had divided from that which
belonged to the men who had gone to war,
43 that is, the assembly's half was three hun-
dred thirty-seven thousand, five hundred
sheep; 44 thirty-six thousand cattle; 45 thirty
thousand, five hundred donkeys; 46 and six-
teen thousand people. 47 From the Israelite
half share, Moses took one part for every
fifty from man and beast and gave it to the
Levites who were responsible for the sanctu-
ary, as the LORD had commanded Moses.
48 The officers of the army, the captains of
the thousands, and the captains of the hun-
dreds, came to Moses. 49 They said to Moses,
"Your servants have counted the men of war
who are under our care, not missing one of
them. 50 We have therefore brought an offer-
ing to the LORD from what each man has
taken from the gold jewelry, the chains, the
bracelets, rings, earrings, and necklaces, to
make atonement for ourselves before the
LORD."[g]
51 Moses and Eleazar the priest took the
gold from them, all crafted jewelry. 52 The
entire gold offering that the captains of the
thousands and the captains of the hundreds
offered to the LORD was sixteen thousand,
seven hundred and fifty shekels. 53 (Each of
the men of war had taken booty for himself.)
54 Moses and Eleazar the priest took the gold
from the captains of the thousands and the
captains of the hundreds and brought it to
the tent of meeting as a memorial for the
people of Israel before the LORD.

CHAPTER 32

Settling in Transjordan. 1 The Reubenites
and the Gadites* had very large herds and
flocks. They saw that the lands of Jazer and
Gilead were suitable for herds and flocks,[h]
2 so the Gadites and the Reubenites came
and spoke to Moses and Eleazar the priest
and the leaders of the assembly saying,
3 "Ataroth, Dibon, Jazer, Nimrah, Heshbon,
Elealeh, Sebam, Nebo, and Beon, 4 the land
that the LORD has conquered before the peo-
ple of Israel, are lands suitable for herds and

f Lev 11:25.—g Ex 30:16.—h Num 21:32; Ex 12:38.

31:26-35 Precise rules are to be followed in dividing the spoils of war and equal provision was to be made for those who fought and those who remained in the community. In addition, a portion was to be dedicated to the Lord in the sanctuary.

32:1 *Reubenites and the Gadites:* these two tribes seek permission to remain in the fertile area of the Transjordan instead of crossing with the other tribes.

flocks, and your servants have herds and flocks." [5] They continued, "If we have found favor in your sight, then let this land be given to your servants as a possession. Do not bring us over the Jordan."

Moses' Response. [6] Moses said to the Gadites and the Reubenites, "Shall your brothers go to war while you rest here? [7] Why are you discouraging the people of Israel from going over into the land that the LORD has given them? [8] [i] This is what your fathers did when I sent them out from Kadesh-barnea to see the land. [9] When they went up into the Valley of Eshcol and saw the land, they discouraged the people of Israel so that they did not enter into the land that the LORD had given them. [10] [j] The LORD's anger blazed on that day and he swore, [11] 'None of those who are twenty years and older and who came out of Egypt will see the land that I promised to Abraham, to Isaac, and to Jacob, for they have not followed me wholeheartedly. [12] Only Caleb, the son of Jephunneh, the Kenizzite, and Joshua, the son of Nun, will see it for they followed the LORD wholeheartedly.' [k] [13] The LORD's anger blazed against Israel and he made them wander in the desert for forty years until the entire generation that had done evil in the sight of the LORD was consumed. [14] Now, you brood of sinful men have risen up to take your fathers' place, adding to the LORD's blazing anger against Israel. [15] If you turn away from him again, he will leave you in the desert and you will have destroyed this entire people." [l]

Another Request. [16] So they came up to him and said, "Let us build enclosures here for our herds and flocks and cities for our little ones. [17] We will still arm ourselves, going before the people of Israel, to bring them into their dwelling place. Our little ones will be sheltered from the inhabitants of the land in the fortified cities. [m] [18] [n] We will not return to our homes until every Israelite has received his inheritance. [19] We will not take an inheritance on the other side of the Jordan, for it has fallen to us to have an inheritance on this side of the Jordan, on the east."

Settlement Reached. [20] Then Moses said to them, "You are to do this: arm yourselves for the LORD's war, [21] and have all your armed men go over the Jordan before the LORD until he has driven out his enemies before him [22] and the land is subdued before the LORD. Then after this, you can return and be blameless before the LORD and before Israel. This land will be your possession before the LORD. [o] [23] But if you do not do this, then you will have sinned against the LORD, and be sure, your sin will catch up with you. [24] Build your cities for your little ones and your enclosures for your sheep, but then do what you have promised to do."

[25] The Gadites and the Reubenites said to Moses, "Your servants will do as our lord commands. [26] Our children and our wives, our flocks and our herds will remain here in the cities of Gilead. [p] [27] But your servants will cross over, every one of them armed for battle, to fight, as my lord has proposed."

[28] Moses gave orders to Eleazar the priest, Joshua the son of Nun, and the leaders of the ancestral tribes of the people of Israel. [29] Moses said to them, "If the Gadites and the Reubenites cross over the Jordan, every man armed for battle before the LORD, and the land is subdued before you, then you will give them the land of Gilead as a possession. [30] However, if they do not cross over armed, then they will have a possession among you in the land of Canaan."

[31] The Gadites and the Reubenites answered, saying, "We will do what the LORD has said to your servants. [32] We will cross over armed before the LORD into the land of Canaan. The possession of our inheritance will remain on this side of the Jordan." *

[33] So Moses gave to the Gadites and the Reubenites and to half of the tribe of Manasseh, the son of Joseph, the kingdom of Sihon, king of the Amorites, and the kingdom of Og, the king of Bashan; he gave the land and its cities with their territory and the cities of the surrounding countryside. [q] [34] The Gadites built Dibon, Ataroth, Aroer, [35] Atroth-shophan, Jazer, Jogbehah, [36] Beth-nimrah, and Beth-haran as fortified cities with sheepfolds for the sheep.

[37] The Reubenites built Heshbon, Elealeh, Kiriathaim, [38] Nebo, Baal-meon* (whose

---

i 8-9: Num 13:3, 27-33; Deut 1:22.—j 10-11: Deut 1:34-35.—k Num 14:24, 30; Deut 1:36.—l Deut 30:17-18.—m Deut 3:18; Jos 4:12-13.—n 18-19: Jos 13:8; 22:4.—o Deut 3:12-20.—p Jos 1:14.—q Num 21:24; Deut 3:12-17; Jos 12:1-6.

32:32 To retain order and responsibility among the tribes, the leaders of Gad and Reuben promise to serve in the Lord's army while leaving their women, children, and livestock behind.

32:38 *Nebo, Baal-meon:* the phrase in parenthesis that follows indicates that these two cities that carried the names of foreign gods should be changed.

names were changed) and Sibmah. They
gave other names to the cities that they built.
39 The Machirites who were from
Manasseh went to Gilead and took it, driv-
ing out the Amorites who were in it. 40 So
Moses gave Gilead to Machir, the son of
Manasseh, and he dwelt there.[r] 41 Jair, the
son of Manasseh, went and took its small
towns and called them Havvoth-jair.[s]
42 Then Nobah went and took Kenath and its
villages. He called it Nobah after himself.

CHAPTER 33

Stages of Israel's Journey.* 1 These are the
journeys of the people of Israel who came
out of the land of Egypt with their armies
under the leadership of Moses and Aaron.
2 At the command of the LORD, Moses
recorded the stages of their journeys. These
are their journeys by stages: 3 the people of
Israel left Rameses on the fifteenth day of
the first month, the day after Passover. They
went out triumphantly in the sight of the
Egyptians.[t] 4 This was while the Egyptians
were burying their firstborn whom the LORD
had slain. The LORD also executed judgment
upon their gods.
5 The people of Israel set out from
Rameses, and they camped in Succoth.
6 They set out from Succoth and they
camped in Etham, which is on the fringes of
the desert. 7 They left Etham and turned
back to Pi-hahiroth, to the east of Baal-
zephon. They camped near Migdol.[u] 8 They
left Pi-hahiroth and crossed over through
the midst of the sea into the desert. They
traveled for three days in the Desert of
Etham, camping in Marah. 9 They left
Marah and came to Elim. There are twelve
springs and seventy palm trees there, so they
camped there.[v] 10 They left Elim and
camped by the Red Sea.
11 They left the Red Sea and camped in the
Desert of Sin. 12 They left the Desert of Sin
and camped in Dophkah. 13 They left
Dophkah and camped in Alush. 14 They left
Alush and camped in Rephidim.[w] (There
was no water there for the people to drink.)
15 They left Rephidim and camped in the
Sinai Desert.[x] 16 They left the Sinai Desert
and camped in Kibroth-hattaavah. 17 They
left Kibroth-hattaavah and camped in
Hazeroth. 18 They left Hazeroth and camped
in Rithmah. 19 They left Rithmah and
camped in Rimmon-perez. 20 They left
Rimmon-perez and camped in Libnah.
21 They left Libnah and camped in Rissah.
22 They left Rissah and camped in
Kehelathah. 23 They left Kehelathah and
camped at Mount Shepher. 24 They left
Mount Shepher and camped in Haradah.
25 They left Haradah and camped in
Makheloth. 26 They left Makheloth and
camped in Tahath. 27 They left Tahath
and camped in Terah. 28 They left Terah and
camped in Mithkah. 29 They left Mithkah
and camped in Hashmonah. 30 They left
Hashmonah and camped in Moseroth.
31 They left Moseroth and camped in Bene-
jaakan. 32 They left Bene-jaakan and camped
in Hor-haggidgad. 33 They left Hor-hag-
gidgad and camped in Jotbathah.[y] 34 They
left Jotbathah and camped in Abronah.
35 They left Abronah and camped in Ezion-
geber.* 36[z] They left Ezion-geber and
camped in Kadesh, which is in the Desert of
Zin. 37 They left Kadesh and camped at
Mount Hor, on the border of Edom.
38 Then Aaron the priest went up Mount
Hor following the LORD's command. He died
there in the fortieth year after the people of
Israel came out of Egypt, on the first day of
the fifth month.[a] 39 Aaron was one hundred
and twenty-three years old when he died on
Mount Hor.
40 The Canaanite king of Arad who dwelt
in the Negeb in the land of Canaan heard
that the people of Israel were coming.
41 They left Mount Hor and camped in
Zalmonah. 42 They left Zalmonah and
camped in Punon. 43 They left Punon
and camped in Oboth. 44 They left Punon and
camped in Iye-abarim on the border of
Moab. 45 They left Iye-abarim, and camped
in Dibon-gad. 46 They left Dibon-gad and
camped in Almon-diblathaim. 47 They left
Almon-diblathaim and camped in the moun-
tains of Abarim near Nebo. 48 They left the
mountains of Abarim and camped in the
plain of Moab near the Jordan, across from
Jericho. 49 There on the plain of Moab they

r Deut 3:15.—s Deut 3:14; Jos 13:30.—t Ex 12:37; 14:8.—u Ex 14:2, 9.—v Ex 15:27; 16:1.—w Ex 17:1-7.—x Num 11:35; Ex 19:1.—y Deut 10:7.—z 36-37: Num 20:1, 22.—a Num 20:25-28; Deut 32:50.

33:1-49 At the time when the Hebrews were about to settle down in arable lands, it was found useful to make a record of the wilderness journey. Such is the purpose of this schematized list of forty stages, which are a reminder of the forty previous years of nomadic life.

33:35 *Ezion-geber* is the modern Elath on the Gulf of Aqaba.

camped near the Jordan from Beth-jeshimoth to Abel-shittim.

Possession and Division of Canaan. [50] On the plain of Moab near the Jordan, across from Jericho, the LORD spoke to Moses, saying, [51] "Speak to the people of Israel and say to them, 'When you cross the Jordan into the land of Canaan [52] drive out the inhabitants of the land before you. Destroy all of their carved images* and all of their cast idols. Demolish all of their high places.[b] [53] Take possession of the land and live in it, for I have given you the land to possess. [54] Distribute the land by lot among your families. Give a larger inheritance to those that are larger and a smaller inheritance to those that are smaller. Wherever the lot falls, give it to them. Distribute it according to your ancestral tribes.[c] [55] But if you do not drive out the inhabitants of the land, then those whom you leave will become splinters in your eyes and thorns in your sides. They will harass you in the land in which you dwell. And I will do to you what I meant to do to them.' "[d]

CHAPTER 34

Canaan's Boundaries. [1] The LORD spoke to Moses, saying, [2] "Command the people of Israel and say to them, 'When you come into the land of Canaan, this is the land that will fall to you as an inheritance: the land of Canaan to its borders.

[3] " 'Your southern section will run from the Desert of Zin along the border of Edom. Your southern border will be along the eastern coast of the Salt Sea.[e] [4] Your border in the south will extend from the Ascent of Akrabbim on to Zin, and then passing on the south of Kadesh-barnea on to Hazar-addar and Azmon. [5] From Azmon the border will stretch to the Wadi of Egypt,* ending where it enters the sea.[f]

[6] " 'Your western border will be the great sea. This will be your western border.

[7] " 'Your northern border will run from the great sea to Mount Hor. [8] From Mount Hor it will run to the Pass of Hamath. The border will then run to Zedad. [9] The border will continue on to Ziphron and it will end at Hazar-enan. This will be your northern border.

[10][g] " 'Your eastern border will run from Hazar-enan to Shepham. [11] The border will run down from Shepham to Riblah on the eastern side of Ain. The border will run down until it reaches the eastern shore of the Sea of Chinnereth.* [12] The border will run down along the Jordan until it enters the Salt Sea. This will be your land, with your borders on every side.' "

[13] Moses commanded the people of Israel, saying, "This is the land that you will inherit by lot, as the LORD commanded. Give it to the nine and one-half tribes. [14] The tribe of the Reubenites, according to their ancestral tribe, has received their inheritance. The tribe of the Gadites, according to their ancestral tribe, as well as the half-tribe of Manasseh, have received their inheritance. [15] The two and one-half tribes have received their inheritance across the Jordan, opposite Jericho, to the east, toward the direction of sunrise."

Appointed Leaders.* [16] The LORD spoke to Moses, saying, [17] "The names of the men who will divide the land for you are: Eleazar the priest and Joshua, the son of Nun. [18] You will choose one leader from each tribe to divide the land for inheritance.[h] [19] These are the names of the men: from the tribe of Judah: Caleb, the son of Jephunneh; [20] from the tribe of Simeon: Samuel, the son of Ammihud; [21] from the tribe of Benjamin: Elidad, the son of Chislon; [22] from the tribe of Dan, a leader: Bukki, the son of Jogli; [23] from the tribe of Joseph, from the tribe of Manasseh, a leader: Hanniel, the son of Ephod; [24] from the tribe of Ephraim, a leader: Kemuel, the son of Shiphtan; [25] from the tribe of Zebulun, a leader: Elizaphan, the son of Parnach; [26] from the tribe of Issachar, a leader: Paltiel, the son of Azzan; [27] from the tribe of Asher, a leader: Ahihud, the son of Shelomi; [28] from the tribe of Naphtali, a leader: Pedahel, the son of Ammihud." [29] These are the ones whom the LORD commanded to divide the inheritance of the people of Israel in the land of Canaan.

b Lev 26:1; Deut 7:2-5.—c Num 26:53-56.—d Jos 23:13; Jdg 2:3; Ps 106:36.—e Jos 15:1-3.—f Gen 15:18; Jos 15:4.—g 10-11: Deut 3:17; Jos 15:5; 2 Ki 23:33.—h Num 1:4.

33:52 *Destroy all of their carved images:* just as Israel had conquered the Midianites and eradicated their pagan symbols, the same fate now fell on the land of Canaan.

34:5 The *Wadi of Egypt* was the border between Egypt and Palestine. The *sea* is the Mediterranean.

34:11 *Sea of Chinnereth:* the Lake of Tiberias/Gennesaret, which a people of non-sailors might consider a "sea." Also called the Sea of Galilee.

34:16-29 The new leaders would assist Joshua and Eleazar in the division of the land among the ten tribes entering Canaan.

CHAPTER 35

The Levites' Share. 1 The LORD spoke to Moses in the plain of Moab near the Jordan, across from Jericho, saying, 2 "Command the people of Israel to give cities to the Levites from the inheritance that they will possess. Also give the Levites pastures around the cities.[i] 3 They are to have cities in which they can dwell as well as pastures for their cattle, their flocks, and all their other animals. 4 The pastures that you will give the Levites around the cities will extend one thousand cubits* from the city wall.

5 "Outside of the city, measure two thousand cubits on the east side, two thousand cubits on the south side, two thousand cubits on the west side, and two thousand cubits on the north side, with the city in the middle. This will be the pastures for the city.

6 "Six of the cities that you give to the Levites will be established as cities of refuge to which a person who has killed another can flee. In addition, there are to be another forty-two cities.[j] 7 In all you will give the Levites forty-eight cities along with their pastures. 8 The cities that you will give the Levites from the possession of Israel will be given according to the inheritance that they have inherited. Those who have more will give more and those who have less will give less."

Cities of Refuge. 9 The LORD said to Moses, 10 "Speak to the people of Israel and say to them, 'When you cross the Jordan into the land of Canaan, 11 choose cities that will be your cities of refuge to which a person who has accidentally killed another person can flee.[k] 12 These will be cities of refuge from the kinsman avenger* so that the killer will not die until he has received judgment before the assembly. 13 These six cities that you give will be your cities of refuge. 14 Give three cities across the Jordan and give three cities in the land of Canaan to be your cities of refuge. 15 These six cities will be a refuge for the people of Israel, for foreigners, and for foreigners dwelling among them, to which a person who has killed accidentally can flee.

Treatment of Murderers. 16 " 'If someone strikes another with an iron object to kill him, then he is a murderer. The murderer will be put to death.[l] 17 If someone strikes another with a stone in his hand to kill him, then he is a murderer. The murderer will be put to death. 18 If someone strikes another with a wooden object in his hand to kill him, then he is a murderer. The murderer will be put to death. 19 The kinsman avenger of blood will kill him. When he meets the murderer, he will put him to death. 20 If anyone pushes another person out of hatred or lays in wait and throws something at him in order to kill him,[m] 21 or if with bitterness he strikes someone with his hand in order to kill him, then that person will be put to death, for he is a murderer. The kinsman avenger of blood will kill the murderer when he meets him.

22 " 'But if someone without bitterness pushes another person or throws something at him without his lying in wait, 23 or he has a deadly stone object and he does not see the other, but drops it on him causing him to die, and he was not an enemy nor was he seeking to harm the other person, 24 then the assembly will judge between the killer and the kinsman avenger of blood according to these ordinances: 25 the assembly will save the killer from the hands of the kinsman avenger of blood. The assembly will send him back to the city of refuge to which he fled. He will live in it until the death of the high priest who was anointed with holy oil.[n]

26 " 'But if the killer at any time crosses over the boundary of the city of refuge to which he has fled, 27 and the kinsman avenger of blood finds him outside of the boundary of the city of refuge, and the kinsman avenger of blood kills the killer, he will not be considered to have blood guilt. 28 He should have remained in the city of refuge until the death of the high priest. After the death of the high priest, the killer can return to the land of his possession. 29 These things will be a statute and an ordinance for you for all of your generations and in all of your dwellings.

30 " 'If a person kills another, the murderer will be put to death upon the testimony of witnesses. But no one is to be put to death on

---

i Lev 25:32-34; Jos 14:3-4.—j Deut 4:41-43; Jos 20:2-9.—k Ex 21:13; Deut 19:1-13.—l Ex 21:12; Lev 24:17.—m Ex 21:14.—n Jos 20:6.

35:4 *Cubits:* Hebrew for feet. A cubit was about a half-meter.

35:12 The *avenger* (Hebrew, *goel*) is the closest relative of the victim; it is up to him to see justice done (see v. 19; Gen 4:15; 9:6; Deut 19:12; 2 Sam 14:11). He is also the authorized protector of his relatives; in particular, he must prevent the alienation of their properties (see Lev 25:23-25; Ru 4:3ff). By extension, God will be called "the *goel* of Israel" (Ps 18:14; Isa 41:14; Jer 50:34). A *goel* is basically a protector.

the testimony of a single witness.[o] 31 You are
not to accept a ransom for the murderer
who is guilty of death; he is to be put to
death. 32 You are not to take a ransom from
someone who has fled to his city of refuge
who wants to return to live in the land before
the death of the priest.

33 " 'You are not to pollute the land in
which you live, for blood pollutes the land,
and the land cannot be cleansed of the blood
that is shed upon it except through the blood
of the person who shed it. 34 You are not to
pollute the land in which you dwell, for I
dwell in it; I, the LORD, dwell among the peo-
ple of Israel.' "[p]

CHAPTER 36

The Daughters of Zelophehad. 1 [q]The family
heads of the clan of Gilead, the son of
Machir, the son of Manasseh, who were from
the clans of the descendants of Joseph, came
and spoke before Moses, before the leaders,
and before the family heads of the people of
Israel. 2 They said, "When the LORD com-
manded my lord to give the land as an inher-
itance by lot to the people of Israel, the LORD
commanded my lord to give the inheritance
of our brother Zelophehad to his daughters.
3 If they marry members of another Isra-
elite tribe, then the inheritance of our ances-
tral tribe will be added to the inheritance of
the tribe into which they have married. It
will be taken from the portion of our inher-
itance. 4 During the Jubilee of the people of
Israel their inheritance will be added to the
inheritance of the tribe into which they were
received. Thus, their inheritance will be
taken away from the inheritance of our
ancestral tribe."

5 Moses commanded the people of Israel
according to the word of the LORD, saying,
"The tribe of Joseph is correct in what they
have said. 6 This is what the LORD has com-
manded concerning the daughters of
Zelophehad: 'Let them marry whomever
they wish, only they are to marry within the
ancestral tribe of their father. 7 Thus, no
inheritance among the people of Israel will
be transferred from one tribe to another.
The people of Israel will hold on to the inher-
itance of their ancestral tribe. 8 Every
daughter who comes into the possession of
an inheritance of any tribe among the peo-
ple of Israel will marry someone from the
family of the tribe of her father. This way,
each Israelite will inherit the inheritance of
his fathers.[r] 9 No inheritance will pass from
one tribe to another. Each Israelite tribe is to
keep its own inheritance.' "

10 Zelophehad's daughters did as the
LORD had commanded Moses.* 11 Zelo-
phehad's daughters, Mahlah, Tirzah,
Hoglah, Milcah, and Noah, married their
cousins on their father's side. 12 They mar-
ried within the clans of the tribe of
Manasseh, the son of Joseph. Their inheri-
tance remained within their clan and their
tribe. 13 These are the commandments and
the ordinances that the LORD commanded
the people of Israel through Moses while
they were in the plain of Moab, near the
Jordan, across from Jericho.

---

o Deut 17:6; 19:15; Mt 18:16; 2 Cor 13:1.—p Ex 29:45; Lev 18:24-25.—q 1-2: Num 27:1-11; Jos 17:3-4.—r 1 Chr 23:22

36:10 Zelophehad's daughters remain obedient to the Lord's commands and are rewarded with their due inheritance. This concludes the book on a positive note.

"This is the blessing that Moses . . . gave to the Israelites before his death" *(Deut 33:1).*

THE BOOK OF DEUTERONOMY

The Covenant: Gift of Life and Requirement for Life

Beginning in the ninth century, Israel passed through a serious crisis: seduced by the prestige of neighboring nations, it gave itself increasingly to pagan practices. To meet this danger, movements of resistance in the name of God arose: reforms imposed by kings (Jehoshaphat, Jehu, Hezekiah, and others), decisive interventions by prophets, return to the traditions shaped by the priests, and the thinking and educational work of the "sages."

All these currents meet in the present Book, to which the Septuagint gives the name "Deuteronomy" or "Second Law" (in the Hebrew Bible the title is derived from the first words of the Book, as is the case with the other Books of the Pentateuch).

The book was composed by a Levite of the northern kingdom, probably around the eighth century, and has for its purpose not the reform of institutions but the conversion of hearts and the education of the people in fidelity to the covenant. After it had been forgotten for a while, King Josiah solemnly promulgated it in 622 B.C. as the document that would serve as the basis for a great movement of religious reform (see 2 Ki 22–23).

Ever since the time of Moses the Levite priests had constantly preached the covenant and had specified and adapted its requirements. Under their direction the people had regularly renewed their commitments to it in solemn celebrations. It is these liturgical texts and these sermons that are the basis of the Book. But the Book also draws upon the teaching of the prophets and the writings of the sages; it profits from memories of the conquest of Palestine and of God's holy wars; it also shows familiarity with the collections of laws put together by the Levites. In short, it summarizes all the riches of Israel's traditions (that is why the Book is put on the lips of Moses), while at the same time adapting them to a new situation. Though fundamentally tradi-

tional, Deuteronomy fully accepts the new political and economic conditions of the life of its time. It is a Book that uses the whip but also knows how to speak to the heart.

The exhortation is full of warmth when it introduces a theology of fidelity and infidelity into the sermons of Moses.

Deuteronomy allows us to understand just what it means to be the people of God and to grasp both the riches and the exigencies of the covenant that unites this people to God. The covenant is an unmerited gift and an urgent summons to which a response must be given in the midst of concrete reality.

Thus Deuteronomy constantly calls the believer back to basic attitudes: an ever deeper faith, a love of God that excludes all compromise, a joyous service of God, a real and optimistic acceptance of earthly realities, and a strength capable of overcoming.

Between the end of the seventh century and the early decades of the next (from Josiah to the morrow of the fall of Jerusalem) the great historical work was published that includes the books of Joshua, Judges, Samuel, and Kings. This collection is based on Deuteronomy, which serves as its doctrinal foundation. Historical memories are inserted into a religious outlook that is characteristic of the Deuteronomistic school: fidelity is the way to salvation, infidelity debases the people and leads them to destruction. As in the Book of Deuteronomy, Jerusalem has a central place in worship and in the dramatic history of Israel. Our text, in its original edition, was therefore parallel to this collection of books and provided the theological framework for long stretches of history.

During the Exile, the Book was revised because it had to be adapted to an entirely new situation; thus a second edition allowed new applications. Finally, after the Exile, the Book was incorporated into the Pentateuch, and stories were added to it for which there had been no room in Numbers.

The Book of Deuteronomy may be divided as follows:

I: Moses' First Address (1:1—4:43)
II: Moses' Second Address (4:44—28:69)
A: The Covenant with Israel (4:44—11:32)
B: The Deuteronomic Code (12:1—28:69)
III: Moses' Third Address (29:1—33:29)
IV: The Death of Moses (34:1-12)

I: MOSES' FIRST ADDRESS*

CHAPTER 1

Introduction. 1 * These are the words that Moses spoke to the whole of Israel on the desert side of the Jordan, in the Arabah,* opposite Suph, between Paran, Tophel, Laban, Hazeroth, and Dizahab. 2 This was an eleven days' journey from Horeb* to Kadesh-barnea by way of the highlands of Seir.
3 On the first day of the eleventh month of the fortieth year, Moses told the Israelites all that the LORD had commanded him to say to them.* 4 This was after he had killed

1:1—4:43 As it reflects on its past, Israel understands how everything has come to it from God.

1:1—3:29 The reflections are put on the lips of Moses and presented as his spiritual testament. In them reference is made to many incidents already recounted, especially in Numbers.

1:1 *Arabah:* the depression between the Red Sea and the southern stretches of the Jordan. *Suph:* the Suphah of Num 21:14. *Dizahab:* the modern el-Dhaibet. The Desert of *Paran:* the modern Gebel-et-Tih (see Num 10:12). *Laban* and *Hazeroth:* see Num 33:17-20. *Tophel:* perhaps the modern et-Tafileh.

1:2 *Horeb* or Sinai; *Seir:* in the Negeb or desert in southern Palestine. *Kadesh-barnea:* in southern Palestine, the modern Am Qedeis.

1:3 The date given is that of the death of Moses and his farewell address.

Sihon, the king of the Amorites who lived in
Heshbon, and Og, the king of Bashan, who
lived in Ashtaroth and Edrei.* [a]

Command to Leave Horeb. 5 On the eastern
side of the Jordan, in the land of Moab,
Moses began to explain this law, saying,
6 The LORD, our God, spoke to us at
Horeb, saying, "You have stayed at this
mountain long enough. 7 Go and proceed
into the hill country of the Amorites, into all
the territory neighboring the Arabah, into
the hill country and the lowlands, into the
Negeb and the seacoast, the land of the
Canaanites and Lebanon, as far as the great
river, the River Euphrates. 8 Behold, I have
given you the land. Go in and take posses-
sion of the land that the LORD promised he
would give to your fathers, to Abraham,
Isaac, Jacob, and their descendants after
them." [b]

Appointment of Leaders. 9 At that time I
said to you, "I am not able to carry the bur-
den of leading you all by myself. [c] 10 The
LORD, your God, has multiplied you and now
you are as numerous as the stars in the
heavens. [d] 11 May the LORD, the God of your
fathers, multiply you a thousand times over
and bless you, as he has promised you.
12 How can I handle your problems and your
burdens and your disputes all by myself?
13 Choose some wise, prudent, and respected
men from your tribesmen, and I will appoint
them as your leaders."

14 They answered, saying, "It would be
good to do what you suggested." 15 So I took
the leading men of your tribes, wise and
respected men, and made them your lead-
ers, captains of the thousands, and captains
of the hundreds, and captains of the fifties
and the tens, as your tribal officials. 16 [e] At
that time I instructed your judges, "Listen to
the disputes among your brethren and judge
them justly, whether between a man and his
fellow countryman or even the foreigner
who is with him.* 17 Do not show partiality
in judging; listen to both the lowly and the
great. Do not be afraid of anyone, for judg-
ment belongs to God. Bring me any case
that is too difficult for you and I will hear it."
18 At that time I instructed you concerning
everything that you were to do.

Twelve Explorers. 19 Then, as the LORD, our
God, had commanded us, we set out from
Horeb. We passed through the great and ter-
rible wilderness that you have seen up into
the hill country of the Amorites, coming to
Kadesh-barnea. [f] 20 I said to you, "Come up
into the hill country of the Amorites that the
LORD, our God, is giving to us. 21 Look! The
LORD, your God, has given the land to you.
Go up and take possession of it, as the LORD,
the God of your fathers, has instructed you.
Do not be afraid or discouraged." [g]

22 All of you came to me and said, "Let us
send men ahead of ourselves to explore the
land. They can bring a report back to us as to
which way we should travel and as to what
cities we will encounter."

23 This seemed to be a very good idea to
me. I chose twelve of your men, one from
each tribe. 24 They left and went up into the
hill country and reached the Valley of Eshcol
which they explored. 25 They gathered some
of the fruit of the land and brought it down
to us, reporting, "The land that the LORD,
our God, has given us is good."

The People Rebel. 26 [h] But you were unwill-
ing to go up. You defied the command of the
LORD, your God. 27 You complained in your
tents and said, "It is because the LORD hates
us that he brought us out of the land of Egypt
to deliver us into the hands of the Amorites
so they might destroy us. 28 Why should we
go up? Our brothers have frightened us by
saying, 'The people are larger and taller than
we are. The cities have great walls that reach
up into the heavens. Moreover, there are the
sons of the Anakim,* we have seen them
there.' " [i]

29 But I said to them, "Do not be afraid of
them! 30 The LORD, your God, marches
before you. He will fight for you, just as he
did on your behalf in Egypt, as you your-
selves have seen. 31 You saw how the LORD,
your God, carried you all throughout your
journey in the wilderness, just as a man car-
ries his son, until you arrived in this place." [j]
32 Yet, in spite of this, you did not trust the
LORD, your God. 33 He went ahead of you on

a Num 21:21-35.— b Gen 12:7; 15:18; 17:8; 28:13.—c Ex 18:13f; Num 11:14.—d Deut 10:22; Gen 15:5; 22:17.—e 16-17: Deut 16:18; Lev 19:15; Jas 2:9.—f Deut 8:15; Num 13:26.—g Jos 1:6, 9.—h 26-27: Deut 9:23; Num 14:1-4.—i Deut 9:1-2; Num 13:28, 31-33.—j Deut 3:22; Ex 14:14; Hos 11:1.

1:4 See chapters 2–3; Num 21:21-35.

1:16 A foreigner can have a permanent residence among the Israelites; he is free but cannot possess property; his situation is precarious, but there are many laws that protect him. The Israelite view of foreigners is already a positive step in the direction of universalism.

1:28 *Anakim:* ancient inhabitants of Palestine whom legend transformed into terrifying giants (see Deut 2:10-11).

your journey, as fire by night to search out a
place for you to pitch your tents and as cloud
by day to show you the path by which you
should travel.[k]
[34]When the LORD heard your words, he
became angry and swore, [35]"Not one of
these men from this evil generation will see
the good land that I promised to give to your
fathers [36]except for Caleb, the son of Je-
phunneh. He will see it, and I will give him
and his children the land upon which he has
set foot, for he has wholeheartedly followed
the LORD."
[37]The LORD grew angry with me because
of you and said, "You are not going to enter
it either.[l] [38]Joshua, the son of Nun, who
assists you, will enter it. Encourage him, for
he will bring Israel in to inherit it.
[39]Furthermore, your children whom you
said would be taken captive, those who do
not yet know the difference between good
and evil, they will enter it. I will give it to
them, and they will take possession of it.
[40]But as for you, turn back and set out
toward the wilderness along the route to the
Red Sea."
[41][m]Then you replied and said to me, "We
have sinned against the LORD. We will go up
and fight as the LORD, our God, has com-
manded us." So every one of you put on your
weapons, thinking it would be easy to go up
into the hill country.
[42]The LORD said to me, "Say to them, 'Do
not go up, nor fight. Otherwise you will be
slain by your enemies.' " [43]So I spoke to you,
but you would not listen to me. You defied
the command of the LORD and arrogantly
went up into the hill country. [44]The
Amorites who dwell in that hill country
came out against you and chased you like
bees, beating you down from Seir all the way
to Hormah.[n] [45]You came back and wept
before the LORD, but the LORD would not
pay attention to your voice nor give ear to
you. [46]So you stayed in Kadesh for a long
time, all the days that you spent there.

CHAPTER 2

The People Travel North. [1]Then we turned
back and set out for the wilderness along the
route to the Red Sea, as the LORD had
instructed me. We traveled around the high-
lands of Seir for many days.
[2]Then the LORD spoke to me, saying,
[3]"You have been going around these high-
lands long enough. Turn to the north [4]and
command the people: 'You are to pass
through the territory of your kin, the chil-
dren of Esau,* who dwell in Seir. They will
be afraid of you, so be very careful.[o] [5]Do not
provoke them, for I will not give you any of
their land, not even a single foot, for I have
given Esau possession of the highlands of
Seir.[p] [6]You are to purchase your food with
silver, and you will also purchase your drink-
ing water with silver. [7]The LORD, your God,
has blessed you in all your undertakings, and
he has watched over your journey through
this great wilderness these forty years. The
LORD, your God, has been with you, and you
have lacked for nothing.' "[q]
[8]So we went on, bypassing our kin, the
children of Esau, who dwell in Seir. We
turned from the Arabah road that comes up
from Elath and Ezion-geber and traveled
along the desert road of Moab.
Bypassing Moab. [9]Then the LORD said to
me, "Do not provoke the Moabites nor fight
with them, for I will not give you their land
as a possession. I have given the Ar to the
children of Lot as a possession."[r] [10][s](The
Emim lived there in days of old, they were a
great and numerous people, as tall as the
Anakim. [11]Like the Anakim they were con-
sidered to be Rephaim, but the Moabites
called them the Emim. [12]The Horites lived
in Seir in days of old, but the children of
Esau drove them out from before them-
selves and destroyed them, settling where
they had lived, just as Israel did in the land
that the LORD had given them to possess.)
[13]"Now rise up and cross the Valley of the
Zered." So we crossed the Valley of the
Zered. [14]It was thirty-eight years from when
we left Kadesh-barnea until when we
crossed over the Valley of the Zered. During
this time the entire generation of men of war
perished in the camp, as the LORD had
sworn to them. [15]For the hand of the LORD
was set against them, to wipe them out from
the camp until they were consumed.[t] [16]And
so the men of war among the people per-
ished.

k Ex 13:21; Num 10:33-34.—l Deut 3:26; 4:21; Num 20:12; Ps 106:32.—m 41-46: Num 14:39-45.—n Ps 118:12.—o Num 20:14-18.—p Gen 36:8; Jos 24:4.—q Deut 8:2-5.—r Gen 19:36-37; Num 21:28.—s 10ff: Gen 14:5; Num 13:22, 33.—t Num 14:29; Ps 106:26.

2:4 *Esau* (Edom) has allowed Israel to pass through and given it a welcome (v. 29; 23:8). A different version of the facts is given in Num 20:18.

Bypassing Ammon. 17 Then the LORD spoke
to me, saying, 18 "Today you will cross over
the Ar,* the boundary of Moab. 19 When you
come up against the Ammonites, do not
harass nor provoke them, for I will not give
you the land of the Ammonites as a posses-
sion. I have given it to the children of Lot as a
possession."[u] 20 (It is considered to be the
land of the Rephaim, for the Rephaim lived
in it in days of old, but the Ammonites call
them Zamzummin. 21 They were a great and
numerous people, as tall as the Anakim, but
the LORD destroyed them before them. They
drove them out and settled in their place.
22 He had done the same for the children of
Esau in Seir when he destroyed the Horites
before them. They drove them out and live
where they had lived to the present.[v] 23 The
Avvim, who lived in villages up to Gaza,*
were destroyed by the Caphtorim who came
from Caphtor. They dwell in their place.)[w]

Defeat of Sihon. 24 "Rise, set out and cross
over the Valley of the Arnon. I have given
Sihon the Amorite, the king of Heshbon, and
his land into your hands. Start to occupy it
and do battle with him. 25 From today on I
will place terror and fear of you in all of the
nations under the heavens. Whoever hears
about you will tremble and be in anguish
because of you."

26 [x] I sent messengers from the Desert of
Kedemoth to Sihon, the king of Heshbon,
with words of peace saying, 27 "Let me pass
through your land. I will travel on the road,
and I will not turn either to the right or the
left. 28 You can sell us food for silver so that we
might eat, and water for silver so that we
might drink, only let me pass through on
foot. 29 This is what the descendants of Esau
who live in Seir and the Moabites who live in
Ar did for me. Then I will pass over the
Jordan into the land that the LORD, our God,
has given us." 30 But Sihon, the king of
Heshbon, would not let us pass through, for
the LORD had hardened his spirit and made
his heart stubborn so that he might deliver
him into your hands, as he has today.[y]

31 Then the LORD said to me, "I have
begun to deliver Sihon and his land to you.
Now begin to take it, so that you may inher-
it his land." 32 Then Sihon came out against
us, he and all his people, to give battle at
Jahaz. 33 The LORD, our God, delivered him
over to us. We killed him and his sons and all
his people. 34 [z] It was then that we captured
all of his cities and completely wiped out
the men, the women, and the children of all
the cities.* We left nothing alive 35 except
for the cattle that we took as pillage along
with the spoils from the cities that we cap-
tured. 36 There was not a city that was too
strong for us, from Aroer on the shore of
the Arnon River and the city that is in the
valley, all the way up to Gilead. The LORD,
our God, delivered everything into our
hands.[a] 37 But as the LORD, our God, had
commanded, you did not enter the land of
the Ammonites, nor the land along the River
Jabbok, nor the cities in the hill country.

CHAPTER 3

Defeat of Og. 1 Next we turned and went up
the road to Bashan, and Og, the king of
Bashan, came out against us, he and all his
people, to give battle at Edrei.[b] 2 But the
LORD said to me, "Do not fear him, for I will
deliver him and all his people and his land
into your hands. You will do the same thing to
him that you did to Sihon, the king of the
Amorites, who lived in Heshbon." 3 The
LORD, our God, delivered Og, the king of
Bashan, and all his people into our hands. We
continued to attack them until there was not
a single survivor left. 4 This was when we cap-
tured all of his cities. There was not a single
city that we did not take from them, sixty in
all, the entire region of the Argob, the king-
dom of Og of Bashan. 5 All of these cities
were fortified with high walls, gates, and
bars. There were also a great number of
unfortified cities. 6 [c] We totally destroyed
them, just as we had destroyed Sihon, the
king of Heshbon, wiping out the men,
women, and children from every city. 7 But
we took all the cattle and spoils of the cities as
pillage.

8 This was when we took the land of two of
the kings of the Amorites from their hands,
land on the east of the Jordan, from the

u Gen 19:36-38.—v Gen 14:6; 36:8.—w Gen 10:14; Am 9:7.—x 26ff: Deut 20:10; Num 21–25; Jdg 11:19-22.—y Ex 4:21; Num 21:23.—z 34f: Deut 3:6; 7:2; Jos 8:27; 10:40.—a Deut 3:12-13; Ps 44:3.—b Num 21:33-35; Ps 136:18, 20.—c 6-7: Deut 2:24, 34; Jos 10:40.

2:18 *Ar:* a Moabite city that gave its name to the entire land; perhaps to be identified with Khirbet-rabba.

2:23 *Gaza:* a stronghold of the Philistines (see Am 9:7), who had entered Palestine in the thirteenth/twelfth century B.C.; *Caphtor* (Egyptian, *Keftiu*): Crete and the islands and coasts of the eastern Mediterranean.

2:34 Destruction, or anathema, was a way of completely consecrating something to the divinity. Deuteronomy makes it a means of preserving the people. See Deut 7:2.

Arnon River to Mount Hermon. 9 (The
Sidonians call Hermon Siron, while the
Amorites call it Senir.) 10 This included all of
the cities of the plain and all of Gilead and all
of Bashan, up to Salecah and Edrei, cities in
the kingdom of Og of Bashan. 11 (Og was the
last of the remnant of the Rephaim. His bed
was made of iron, and it was nine cubits long
and four cubits wide. It is now in Rabbah of
the Ammonites.)* [d]

Distribution of Conquered Lands. 12 From the
land that we occupied at this time, I gave the
Reubenites and the Gadites the land begin-
ning at Aroer on the Arnon River and half of
the hill country of Gilead as well as its cities. [e]
13 I gave the rest of Gilead and all of Bashan,
the kingdom of Og, to the half-tribe of
Manasseh. (This was the whole region of
Argob with all of Bashan, and it was known
as the land of the Rephaim. 14 The clan of Jair,
the son of Manasseh, took the entire region of
Argob up to the borders with the Geshurites
and the Maacathites. They named it after
themselves, so that Bashan is known as
Havvoth-jair until the present.) [f] 15* I gave
Gilead to Machir. 16 I gave the Reubenites
and the Gadites the land that stretched from
Gilead up to the Arnon River (with the cen-
ter of the valley being the boundary) and on
to the Jabbok River, the border with the
Ammonites. 17 Its border on the west was the
Jordan in the Arabah, from the Kinnereth
down to the Sea in the Arabah, the Salt Sea,
at the foot of the slopes of the Pisgah.

18 [g] At that time I commanded you, "The
LORD, your God, has given you this land to
possess. Have all of the armed men pass over
in front of their brethren, the Israelites,
armed for battle. 19 But your wives and your
children and your cattle (for I know that you
have many cattle) can remain in your cities
that I have given you. 20 It will be this way
until the LORD gives rest to your brothers as
he already has to you, so that they also come
to possess the land that the LORD, your God,
has given them on the other side of the
Jordan. Then, each of you can return to the
property that I have given you."

21 Then I commanded Joshua, "You have
seen with your own eyes what the LORD, your
God, has done to these two kings. This is what
the LORD will do to any kingdom that you
might encounter.* 22 Do not be afraid of
them, for the LORD, your God, will fight for
you." [h]

Moses Forbidden to Enter Jordan. 23 [i] At that
time I pleaded with the LORD, 24 "O LORD
God, you have begun to show your servant
your greatness and your strong arm. What
God in heaven or on earth can do such deeds
and mighty works as yours? 25 Please let me
cross over and see the bounteous land that is
on the other side of the Jordan, the hill coun-
try and the Lebanon."

26 But the LORD was angry with me
because of you* and would not listen to me.
The LORD said to me, "Enough! Do not speak
to me about this anymore. 27 Climb up to the
top of Pisgah and look to the west, the north,
the south, and the east and see it with your
own eyes, for you shall not cross over this
Jordan. 28 But give orders to Joshua and
encourage and strengthen him, for he is to
lead this people across and he will give them
the land that you see as an inheritance." [j]
29 So we remained in the valley opposite
Beth-peor.

CHAPTER 4

Benefits of Obedience. 1 Now listen, O
Israel, to the statutes and the ordinances
that I am teaching you to observe so that you
might live and go in and take possession of
the land that the LORD, the God of your
fathers, is giving you. [k] 2* You will not add to
what I command you, nor will you take away
from it, so that you might observe the com-
mandments of the LORD, your God, that I
am giving you. [l] 3 Your own eyes have seen
what the LORD did because of Baal-peor, for
the LORD, your God, wiped out from all of
those who followed Baal-peor from your
midst. [m] 4 But every one of you who clung to
the LORD, your God, is alive today.

d Deut 2:11; Gen 14:5; Jos 12:4.—e Deut 2:36; Num 32:32-38; Jos 13:8-13.—f Num 32:41; Jdg 10:3-5; 1 Chr 2:22.—g 18-20: Num 32:20; Jos 1:12-14; 4:12; 22:1-4.—h Deut 1:30; Ex 14:14.—i 23-29: Num 27:12-23.—j Deut 1:38; 31:3, 7; Num 27:18-23.—k Deut 5:1, 33; 6:1; 8:1; 11:8-9; 30:16.—l Jos 1:7; Rev 22:18-19.—m Num 25:4; Ps 106:28-29.

3:11 The bed seems more like a tomb. The description may refer to a geological or archaeological discovery: perhaps one of the dolmens to be seen in the region of Amman. This verse, like verse 9 above, verses 13b-14a below, and, earlier, 2:20-23, is a kind of explanatory note inserted in the discourse, of which it is not a part.

3:15-16 This assignment of land to the tribes refers to a period earlier than that in verses 12-13.

3:21 Drawing attention to the past victories of the Israelites is the Lord's way of encouraging them to trust that he will continue to be their stronghold against the Canaanites.

3:26 *Because of you:* Moses points his finger outward for his inability to enter the Promised Land. There are conflicting passages as to who is to blame (see Deut 32:51; Num 20:12).

4:2-3 Observing God's laws in their entirety secures for us the fullness of life.

5 Behold, I have taught you statutes and
ordinances just as the LORD, my God, com-
manded me, so that you might enter into the
land into which you are going and take pos-
session of it. 6 Carefully observe them, for
the nations will consider this is your wisdom
and your understanding. They will hear all
these statutes and say, "Truly this great
nation is a wise and understanding people." [n]
7 [o] For what nation is as great as we are?
Who has God as near to them, as the LORD,
our God, is whenever we call upon him?
8 What nation is so great that it has statutes
and ordinances as righteous as this law that
I set before you today?

9 Only be careful and watch yourselves
closely lest you ever forget the things that
your eyes have seen or you let them slip out
of your mind. Teach them to your children
and your children's children, [p] 10 especially
about the day that you stood before the
LORD, your God, in Horeb, when the LORD
said to me, "Assemble the people before me
so that I might let them hear my words.
They will thus learn to fear me all the days
that they live upon the earth, and they will
be able to teach their children." 11 [q] You ap-
proached and stood at the base of the moun-
tain. The mountain blazed with flames
reaching the very heavens, and it was cov-
ered with dark clouds and thick darkness.
12 The LORD spoke to you from the midst of
the fire. You heard the sound of words, but
you did not see a form. There was only a
voice. 13 He proclaimed his covenant to you
which he ordered you to fulfill, the Ten Com-
mandments, that he wrote upon two tablets
of stone. 14 The LORD then commanded me
to teach you the statutes and ordinances so
that you might observe them in the land that
you were crossing over to possess.

Pitfalls of Idolatry. 15 Therefore, guard your-
selves carefully, for you did not see any kind
of form when the LORD spoke to you on
Horeb from the midst of the fire. 16 Do not
become perverse and make an idol for your-
selves of any shape or likeness, whether male
or female, [r] 17 whether it be a land animal or
a bird that flies in the skies, 18 or like some-
thing that crawls on the ground or a fish in
the waters beneath the earth. 19 When you
look up into the skies and you see the sun
and the moon and stars, all the hosts of
heaven, do not be enticed to worship and
serve the things that the LORD, your God,
has assigned to every other nation under the
heavens. [s] 20 But as for you, the LORD has
chosen you and taken you out from the iron
furnace,* out of Egypt, to be a people who
are his own possession, as you are today. [t]

21 The LORD was angry with me because of
you and he swore that I would not cross over
the Jordan nor enter the fertile land that the
LORD, your God, has given to you as an
inheritance. [u] 22 I must die in this land; I will
not cross over the Jordan. But you will cross
over and take possession of this fertile land.
23 Therefore, keep guard over yourselves, lest
you forget the covenant that the LORD, your
God, has made with you and you make an
idol in the form of anything that the LORD,
your God, has prohibited. 24 The LORD, your
God, is a consuming fire and a jealous God. [v]

25 When you have borne children and
grandchildren and have dwelt in the land for
a long time, if you then become corrupt and
make any kind of idol, doing what is evil in
the sight of the LORD, your God, and provok-
ing him to anger, 26 I will call upon the heav-
ens and the earth to give witness against you
on that day so that you might be utterly
obliterated from the land that you are cross-
ing over the Jordan to possess. You will not
remain there long, but you will be totally
wiped out.

27 The LORD will scatter you among the
nations and only a few of you will survive
among the foreign peoples where the LORD
has led you. [w] 28 There you will serve gods,
the work of human hands, made of wood
and stone, which cannot see nor hear nor eat
nor smell. [x]

The LORD Is God. 29 But if you seek the
LORD, your God, and you strive with all your
heart and your soul, you will find him
there. [y] 30 When you are in distress and all of
these things happen to you in the future, you
are to return to the LORD,* your God, and
obey his voice, 31 and he will not abandon

n Deut 30:19; 32:46; Job 28:28; 2 Tim 3:15.—o 7-8: 2 Sam 7:23; Pss 46:1; 145:18; 147:19; 148:14.—p Deut 6:7; 11:19-21; 31:12; Ps 78:5-6.—q 11-13: Ex 19:18—20:22.—r Deut 5:8; Ex 20:4; Rom 1:23.—s Deut 17:3; Job 31:26; Wis 13:2.—t 1 Ki 8:51; Jer 11:4.—u Deut 1:37; Num 20:12.—v Deut 6:15; 9:3; Ex 24:17; Isa 33:14; Heb 12:29.—w Deut 28:62; Lev 26:14-19.—x Deut 28:64; Ps 115:4-5; Isa 44:17-20.—y Isa 55:6; Jer 29:13-14; Hos 5:15.

4:20 *Iron furnace:* referring to Egypt by this term implies the spiritual cleansing "by fire" that the Israelites encountered there. Also used in 1 Ki 8:51 and Jer 11:4.

4:30 *Return to the LORD:* reconciliation and restoration of our relationship with the Lord, then as now, hinges on the sinner's repentance.

you, nor destroy you nor forget the covenant
that he made with your fathers, confirming
it to them by oath, for the LORD, your God, is
a merciful God. [z]

32 Ask now about the days of old, the for-
mer times. From the day that God created
humans upon the earth, inquire from one
end of the heavens to the other, has anything
so great ever happened or has anything like
it been heard of? 33 Has any other people
heard the voice of God speak from the midst
of the flame, as you heard, and still live? [a]
34 Did God ever go and lead one nation from
the midst of another nation by trials, signs,
wonders, and battle, with a mighty hand and
an outstretched arm, with great and won-
drous deeds, all things that the LORD, your
God, did for you in Egypt before your very
eyes?

35 You were shown these things so that you
might come to know that the LORD is God;
there is no other besides him. [b] 36 He had you
hear his voice from out of the heavens so
that he might instruct you. He showed you
his great fire upon the earth so that you
might hear his voice from the midst of the
flames. 37 It was because he loved your
fathers and had chosen their descendants
after them that he brought you out of Egypt
before him by his great strength. 38 He drove
out greater and more powerful nations
before you so that he might bring you into
their land to give it to you as an inheritance,
just as it is today.

39 So today acknowledge it and take it to
heart that the LORD is God in the heavens
above and on the earth below. There is no
other. [c] 40 You shall obey his statutes and the
commandments that I give you today, so
that all may go well with you and your chil-
dren after you, and that you may live long in
the land that the LORD, your God, has given
you for all time.

Cities of Refuge. 41 [d] Then Moses set aside
three cities on the east of the Jordan 42 to
which anyone who unintentionally killed
another person with whom he had not pre-
viously been at enmity might flee. He could
flee to one of these cities and save his life.
43 They were Bezer,* on the desert plateau,
for the Reubenites, and Ramoth in Gilead
for the Gadites, and Golan in Bashan for the
men of Manasseh.

II: MOSES' SECOND ADDRESS

A: The Covenant with Israel*

Introduction. 44 This is the law that Moses
set before the Israelites. 45 These are the stip-
ulations, the statutes, and the judgments
that Moses declared to the Israelites when
they came out of Egypt 46 [e] and they were
dwelling in the valley near Beth-peor on the
east of the Jordan, in the land of Sihon, the
king of the Amorites, who lived in Heshbon,
and who was defeated by Moses and the
Israelites when they came out of Egypt.
47 They took possession of his land and also
the land of Og, the king of Bashan, the two
kings of the Amorites who reigned on the
east side of the Jordan. 48 This land extended
from Aroer, that is on the bank of the Arnon
River, up to Mount Sion (that is Hermon).
49 It included all of the plain on the east side
of the Jordan up to the Sea in the Arabah, at
the foot of the slopes of Pisgah.

CHAPTER 5

The Ten Commandments.* 1 Moses then
summoned all of the Israelites and said to
them, "Hear, O Israel, the statutes and the
decrees that I proclaim in your hearing
today. Learn them and carefully observe
them. 2 The LORD, our God, made a
covenant with us at Horeb. [f] 3 The LORD did
not make this covenant with our fathers, but
with those of us who are still alive and pres-
ent today. 4 The LORD spoke with you face to
face on the mountain from the midst of the
flame. [g]

5 "I stood between you and the LORD at
that time, declaring the word of the LORD to
you, for you were afraid and did not go up
the mountain because of the fire. He said, 6 'I

z Deut 31:8; Ex 34:6-7.—a Deut 5:24, 26; Ex 20:22.—b Ex 20:3; Isa 43:10.—c Jos 2:11.—d 41-43: Deut 19:1-13; Ex 21:13; Num 35:10-28.—e 46-49: Deut 2:26—3:29.—f Ex 19:5.—g Num 12:8; 14:14.

4:43 *Bezer:* perhaps Umm el-Aniad, to the east of Mount Nebo; *Ramoth:* perhaps Tell Ramit, east of the Jordan between the Jabbok and Yarmuk Rivers; *Golan:* perhaps Sahem el-Giolan, east of the Lake of Gennesaret.

4:44—11:32 This discourse existed, in great part, in the first edition of the book. The author hides behind the authority of Moses as he urges Israel to live the covenant to the full.

5:1-21 These covenant statutes, which we have already met in Ex 20:1-16, were recited by the Israelites during liturgical assemblies. They contain the word of God and show the people the way they must follow at all times; they are the basis of the morality of both the Old Testament and the gospel and represent fundamental norms of a human ethics. Comparable lists are found in 27:15-26; Ex 34:11-26; Lev 19:1-4, 11-18; but these are less general than the Decalogue.

am the LORD, your God, who brought you
out of the land of Egypt, out from the land of
slavery.[h] 7 You shall have no god other than
me. 8 You shall not make any idols in the
form of anything that dwells in the heavens
above or on the earth below or even in the
waters below the land.[i] 9 You shall not pros-
trate yourself to them nor worship them. I,
the LORD, your God, am a jealous God. I visit
the iniquity of the fathers upon their chil-
dren to the third and fourth generations of
those who hate me, 10 but I will show mercy
to the thousandth generation on those who
love me and observe my commandments.[j]
11 " 'You shall not take the name of the
LORD, your God, in vain, for the LORD will
not consider blameless those who take his
name in vain.[k]
12 " 'You shall observe the Sabbath by
keeping it holy, as the LORD, your God, has
commanded you. 13 You are to labor on six
days, doing all of your work then. 14 The sev-
enth day is the Sabbath of the LORD, your
God. You shall not do any work, neither you,
nor your son, nor your daughter, nor your
manservant, nor your maidservant, nor
your ox, nor your ass, nor your cattle, nor
even the foreigner living in your town. Thus
your manservant and maidservant can rest
as well.[l] 15 Remember that you were once a
slave in the land of Egypt. The LORD, your
God, brought you out from there with a
mighty hand and an outstretched arm.
Therefore, the LORD, your God, has com-
manded you to observe the Sabbath day.*
16 " 'Honor your father and your mother,
as the LORD, your God, has commanded
you,* so that you might have a long life and
things might go well with you in the land
that the LORD, your God, has given you.[m]
17 " 'You shall not murder.[n] 18 You shall
not commit adultery.[o] 19 You shall not
steal.[p] 20 You shall not bear false witness
against your neighbor.[q] 21 You shall not
desire your neighbor's wife. Nor shall you
desire your neighbor's house or land, or
his manservant or his maidservant, or his
ox or ass or anything that belongs to your
neighbor.' "[r]

Moses at Sinai. 22 These are the things that
the LORD proclaimed in a loud voice to your
whole assembly on the mountain from the
midst of the flame, out of the cloud and the
deep darkness, this and nothing more. He
then wrote them on two stone tablets and
gave them to me.[s] 23 When you heard the
voice coming out of the darkness, while
the mountain was blazing with fire,* all of
the leaders of your tribes and your elders
drew near to me.
24 You said, "The LORD, our God, has
shown us his glory and his majesty. We have
heard his voice coming forth from out of the
fire. Today we have seen that a man can live
even if God were to speak to him. 25 But now,
why should we die, for this great fire will
consume us if we listen anymore to the voice
of the LORD, our God? We will surely die.[t]
26 For what mortal has ever heard the voice
of the living God speaking out from the
midst of the flames, as we have, and contin-
ued to live? 27 You approach him and listen
to all that the LORD, our God, will say to you.
Then you can tell us all that the LORD, our
God, said to you. We will listen and obey."
28 The LORD heard what you said to me,
and the LORD said to me, "I have heard what
this people has said to you. Everything that
they said is acceptable. 29 Oh, that they
would have fear of me in their hearts and
they would observe all of my command-
ments always. Then things would go well
with them and their children forever.[u] 30 Go
tell them, 'Go back to your tents.' 31 But you,
stay here with me, so that I can pass on to
you all of the commandments and statutes
and decrees that you are to teach them so
that they might observe them in the land
that I am giving to them to possess.
32 Therefore, be careful to observe what the
LORD, your God, has commanded of you. Do
not turn away from it to the right nor the
left.[v] 33 Continue in all of the ways that the

h Ex 20:2-17; Ps 81:11.—i Deut 4:15-18; Lev 26:1.—j Ex 34:7; Jer 32:18.—k Deut 10:20; Ex 20:7; Lev 19:12; Ps 139:20.—l Gen 2:2; Jer 17:21, 24; Mt 12:2; Mk 2:27.—m Ex 21:17; Lev 19:3; Mt 15:4; 19:19; Mk 7:10; 10:19; Lk 18:20.—n Gen 9:6; Ex 20:13; Mt 5:21-22; Mk 10:19; Lk 18:20; Jas 2:11.—o Ex 20:14; Lev 20:10; Mt 5:27-30; 19:19; Mk 7:10; Lk 18:20; Jas 2:11.—p Ex 20:15; 22:1-3; Lev 19:11; Mt 19:19; Mk 10:19; Rom 13:9.—q Ex 20:16; 23:1; Ps 5:6-10; Mt 19:18; Lk 18:20.—r Rom 7:7; 13:9.—s Deut 4:13; Ex 24:12; 31:18.—t Deut 18:16; Ex 20:18-19; Heb 12:19.—u Deut 4:40; Ps 81:13; Isa 48:18.—v Deut 17:20; 28:14; Jos 1:7.

5:15 Like Passover (Deut 16:1-8), the Sabbath celebrates the deliverance of the people. In like manner, for Christians, Sunday commemorates the resurrection of Christ and their deliverance from sin. The day is a testimony to freedom.

5:16 *As the LORD, your God, has commanded you:* this phrase is worth repeating to give credence to what is expected of the Israelites and occurs many times throughout Deuteronomy.

5:23 *The mountain was blazing with fire:* whether the fire was symbolic or real, the association of fire with God's presence confirms for the Israelites the Lord's power to destroy.

LORD, your God, has commanded you. Continue in them so that you may live and prosper and that you may long dwell on the land of your inheritance."[w]

CHAPTER 6

1 These are the commands, statutes, and decrees that the LORD, your God, directed me to teach you so that you might observe them in the land to which you are going as your inheritance. 2 Thus, you will fear the LORD, your God, and observe the statutes and commandments that I give you—you, and your children, and your children's children—all the days of your life, so that you might live a long time.[x]

3 Hear, O Israel, and be careful to obey so that you might prosper and multiply greatly in a land flowing with milk and honey, just as the LORD, the God of your fathers, has promised you.

The Law of Love.* 4[y] Hear, O Israel, the LORD, our God, is LORD alone. 5 You shall love the LORD, your God, with all your heart, and with all your soul, and with all your might. 6 You shall keep these things that I command you today in your heart. 7 Teach them to your children. You shall talk of them when you are sitting in your home, and when you are walking along the way, and when you lie down and when you rise up. 8 * Bind them as a reminder upon your hand, and wear them as a pendant between your eyes 9 Write them on the doorframes of your houses and your gates.

Loyalty to the LORD. 10 *[z] When the LORD, your God, will have brought you into the land that he promised to your forefathers, to Abraham and Isaac and Jacob, that he would give to you, a land with large and pleasant cities that you did not build 11 with houses filled with all kinds of good things that you did not provide, wells that you did not dig, and vineyards and olive trees that you did not plant. When you have eaten your fill of them, 12 be sure not to forget the LORD who brought you out of the land of Egypt, from the land of slavery.

13 Fear the LORD, your God, and serve him. Swear oaths with his name. 14 You shall not seek after other gods, the gods of the peoples around you 15 for the LORD, your God, who lives among you is a jealous God.* Beware lest the anger of the LORD, your God, be kindled and he wipe you off of the face of the earth.

16 You shall not tempt the LORD,* your God, as you tempted him at Massah.[a] 17 You shall take heed to observe the commandments of the LORD, your God, and the decrees and statutes that he has given to you. 18 Do what the LORD regards as right and good so that things will go well with you and that you might enter in and take possession of the good land that the LORD promised to your fathers, 19 being able to cast out all of your enemies from before you, just as the LORD has promised.

Instructing Children. 20 In the future when your son asks you, "What is the meaning of the decrees and statutes and ordinances that the LORD, our God, has commanded of you,"[b] 21 you are to tell your son, "We were slaves to Pharaoh in Egypt, but the LORD brought us out of Egypt with a mighty hand. 22 The LORD performed signs and wonders in our sight, great and terrible things, that he imposed upon Egypt and upon Pharaoh and upon all of his household. 23 He brought us out from there so that he might bring us into and give to us the land that he promised to our fathers.

24 "The LORD commanded us to observe all of these statutes and to fear the LORD, our God, so that we might always prosper and be kept alive, even as we are today. 25 If we are diligent in observing all of these commandments before the LORD, our God, as he commanded of us, then this will be our righteousness."[c]

---

w Deut 4:40.—x Deut 4:9; 10:12, 13; Ex 20:20.—y 4-5: Deut 4:35, 39; Isa 44:6; Mk 12:29; 1 Cor 8:4.—z 10-12: Deut 8:10; Jos 24:13.—a Ex 17:1-7; Mt 4:7; Lk 4:12.—b Ex 10:2; 13:14.—c Deut 24:13; Pss 103:18; 119:34; Rom 10:5.

6:4-9 A classic passage that to this very day has been the prayer of Jews (the *Shema*) and their creed. It is a profession of faith in only one God, a faith that lays claim to the whole of the human person. Jesus will say: "The first is . . . . There is no other commandment greater than these" (Mk 12:28-31 and parallels).

6:8-9 These verses, like the preceding, are meant metaphorically (see Ex 13:9, 16); they were later interpreted literally. Verses 4-9 were written on parchment, placed in a wooden or metal box, and attached to the forehead and the back of the hands (phylacteries: see Mt 23:5). They were also attached to the doorposts at a man's height.

6:10-25 We can see, from the end of this passage, the profound meaning of "righteousness" in the Bible: it is a religious uprightness that takes the form of doing God's will in one's life.

6:15 *Jealous God:* a God who loves with a total and exclusive love. See Deut 4:24; 5:9.

6:16 To *tempt the LORD* or "test him" means to not trust in him (Ex 17:1-7; Num 14:22; Pss 78:41; 95:9; 106:13-14).

CHAPTER 7

Destroying the Nations. [1] * When the LORD, your God, has brought you into the land that you are entering to take possession of and he has driven out many nations before you, the Hittites, the Girgashites, the Amorites, the Canaanites, the Perizzites, the Hivites, and the Jebusites, seven nations in all, each larger and stronger than you are[d] [2] and when the LORD, your God, will have delivered them over to you and you will have defeated them, you are to wipe them out. You are not to make a covenant with them or show them any mercy. [3] * Do not intermarry with them. Do not give your daughters to their sons nor take their daughters for your sons. [4] They would turn your sons away from serving me to serve other gods and the anger of the LORD would be kindled against you and destroy you in an instant.

[5] This is what you are to do to them: you are to destroy their altars, tear down their sacred images, cut down their sacred groves, and burn up their idols in fire. [6] You are a people holy to the LORD, your God. The LORD, your God, has chosen you from among all the peoples in the world to be his own, a treasured possession.[e] [7] The LORD did not delight in you because you were more numerous than these other peoples, for you are actually the least numerous of all people. [8] It was because the LORD loved you and was keeping the promise that he had sworn to your fathers that the LORD brought you out with a mighty hand and redeemed you from the hand of Pharaoh, the king of Egypt, from the land of your slavery.

[9] Keep in mind, therefore, that the LORD, your God, is God. He is a faithful God who keeps his covenant of mercy to the thousandth generation toward those who love him and observe his commandments.[f] [10] But upon those who hate him, he will avenge himself face to face, wiping them out. He will not delay in avenging himself face to face with those who hate him.* [11] Therefore, be careful to observe the commandments, statutes, and decrees that I give you today.

Blessings of the Covenant. [12] If you obey these decrees and carefully observe them, then the LORD, your God, will preserve his covenant of mercy with you, as he promised to your forefathers. [13] He will love you and bless you and multiply you. He will bless the fruit of your womb and the crops on your land, your grain, your wine and your oil, as well as the calves of your herds and the lambs of your flocks, in the land that he promised to your forefathers to give to you. [14] You will be more greatly blessed * than any other people. None of your men or women will be childless, none of your cattle will be without young.[g] [15] The LORD will protect you from all illnesses. He will not inflict upon you any of the terrible diseases that you encountered in Egypt, but rather he will send them upon everyone who hates you. [16] You must annihilate all of the people whom the LORD, your God, delivers over to you. Do not look with pity upon them; do not serve their gods, for this would be a snare for you. [17] * You should say to yourselves, "These nations were stronger than we were. How did we ever drive them out?" [18] Do not be afraid of them. Remember what the LORD, your God, did to Pharaoh and to the whole of Egypt. [19] You saw with your own eyes the tremendous trials, signs, and wonders, how with a mighty hand and an outstretched arm the LORD, your God, brought you out. The LORD, your God, will do the same things to all of those people of whom you are afraid. [20] The LORD, your God, will destroy them by sending hornets into the midst of those who survived and are hiding. [21] Do not be afraid of them, for the LORD, your God, who is among you, is a great and awesome God. [22] Little by little the LORD, your God, will drive out those nations before you. You will not be able

d Gen 10:16-17; 15:19-21; Ex 3:8; Jos 3:10.—e Deut 14:2; 26:18; Ex 19:5-6; Ps 135:4; 1 Pet 2:9.—f Deut 4:39; 5:9-10; Neh 1:5; Pss 89:1-2; 33:4; 1 Cor 1:9.—g Ex 23:26.

7:1-16 By slaughtering its enemies, Israel safeguards itself against the danger of being absorbed by the pagan world around it. When God began the education of his people, he could not immediately require them to rise above the rough and brutal practices of the age.

Deuteronomy provides other examples of such barbaric customs. It does indeed urge an unyielding resistance to the attractions of paganism, but it prescribes that the separation be accomplished in a fairly peaceful way.

7:3-4 *Do not intermarry:* the challenge, then as now, is to remain faithful to the one, true God in marriage.

7:10 Each individual is personally responsible before God, as Ezekiel will later say in vigorous language (Ezek 18).

7:14 *More greatly blessed:* loving and obeying the Lord reaps fruitful benefits, whether materially or more importantly, as gifts of peace, hope, and joy in the face of trials.

7:17-26 This passage suggests that the region was not conquered as quickly as we might be led to think by the Book of Joshua, which simplifies the events. Israel could not settle in a wilderness; the anathema or law of destruction was therefore mitigated and never applied as systematically as some passages claim (see Jos 6:14-16).

to eliminate them immediately, lest the wild animals around you multiply too much.[h] 23 The LORD, your God, will hand them over to you, throwing them into a great confusion until they are totally wiped out. 24 He will deliver kings into your hands, and you will wipe out their names from under the heavens. No one will be able to stand up to you. You will destroy them.[i]

25 You are to burn the idols of their gods in the fire. Do not seek after the gold or the silver that covers them, nor take it for yourselves, lest it become a snare for you. It is an abomination to the LORD, your God. 26 Nor should you bring an abomination into your house, or you, like it, will be set aside for destruction. Loathe and detest it, for it is something that is cursed.

CHAPTER 8

The LORD's Kindness. 1 * Be diligent in observing all of the commandments that I am giving you today, so that you might live and multiply, and so that you might enter and take possession of the land that the LORD promised to your fathers. 2 Remember how the LORD, your God, guided your path through the wilderness for these forty years, abasing you and testing you so that he might know what was in your heart, whether or not you would observe his commandments. 3 He brought you low, allowing you to suffer from hunger. He then fed you with manna, something with which your fathers were not familiar, so that you might come to know that man does not live by bread alone,* but man lives by every word that comes forth from the mouth of the LORD.[j]

4 Throughout these forty years your clothing did not wear out nor did your feet swell. 5 Thus you could understand that the LORD, your God, was disciplining you, just like a father disciplines his son.[k] 6 Therefore, observe the commandments of the LORD, your God. Walk in his ways and fear him. 7 The LORD, your God, is bringing you into a good land, a land filled with brooks, fountains, and springs that rush forth from the valleys and the hills. 8 It is a land of wheat and barley, of vines, fig trees and pomegranates, a land with olive oil and honey. 9 It is a land in which you will not lack bread to eat; you will not lack anything at all. It is a land whose stones are iron and out of whose hills you can dig copper.

Warning about Prosperity. 10 When you have eaten your fill and are satisfied, then praise the LORD, your God, for the good land that he has given you. 11 Take heed not to forget the LORD, your God, by not observing his commandments, decrees, and statutes that I have given you today. 12 Otherwise, when you have eaten your fill and you have built fine houses and are living in them 13 and your herds and your flocks have grown large, and your silver and your gold have multiplied, in fact all that you own has multiplied, 14 then your heart might become proud and you will forget the LORD, your God, who brought you out of the land of Egypt, the land of your slavery. 15 He led you through a vast and terrible wilderness where there were snakes and fiery scorpions and thirst, where when there was no water he brought water forth from the hard rock for you.[l] 16 He gave you manna to eat in the wilderness, something with which your fathers were not familiar, to abase you and to test you, so that later on it might go well with you.

17 * You might think to yourself, "It is through my strength and the might of my own hand that I have acquired this wealth." 18 But remember the LORD, your God, for it is he who has given you the ability to acquire this wealth so that he might confirm the covenant that he made with your fathers, which is still in force today.[m] 19 But if you forget the LORD, your God, and follow after other gods, serving and worshiping them, then I swear to you today that you will surely perish. 20 You will perish just like the nations that the LORD crushed in your sight, for you would not have been attentive to the voice of the LORD, your God.

CHAPTER 9

Israel's Good Fortune. 1 Hear, O Israel, today you are going to pass over the Jordan

h Ex 23:29-30.—i Deut 11:25; Jos 1:5; 6:2; 12:7-24.—j Ex 16:11-36; Mt 4:4; Lk 4:4.—k Deut 4:36; Prov 3:11-12; Heb 12:6.—l Deut 1:19; 32:13; Ex 17:6; Num 20:11; 21:6; Ps 114:8.—m Deut 26:10; Prov 10:22; Hos 2:8.

8:1—10:11 In order to bring out other more profound and less obvious aspects of the covenant, Deuteronomy applies a method in use throughout the Bible. It reflects on the events of the sacred history which the people have experienced.

8:3 *Man does not live by bread alone:* the assurance of God's care for his people goes beyond their physical needs. Jesus used these words to confront Satan when he was being tempted (Mt 4:4), with certain belief in God's power to sustain those who love him.

8:17-19 These verses sum up the theology of fidelity that is characteristic of Deuteronomy.

to dispossess nations more powerful than you are which have large cities whose walls reach up into the heavens. [2] The people are strong and tall, descendants of the Anakim. You know all about them, for you have heard it said, "Who can stand up against the Anakim?" [n]

[3] Understand, therefore, that the LORD, your God, is crossing over ahead of you like a devouring fire today. He will destroy them and bring them low before you. Therefore, you will be able to drive them out and annihilate them quickly, just as the LORD has promised you. [4] After the LORD, your God, has driven them out before you, do not say to yourself, "It was because of my righteousness that the LORD brought me in to take possession of this land." It is because of the wickedness of the nations that the LORD is going to drive them out before you. [o] [5] It is not because of your righteousness or the sincerity of your heart that you are going to take possession of their land. Rather, it is because of the wickedness of these nations that the LORD, your God, will drive them out before you, fulfilling the promise that he made to your fathers, to Abraham, Isaac, and Jacob. [6] Understand, therefore, that it is not because of your righteousness that the LORD, your God, is giving you this good land to possess, for you are a stiff-necked* people.

The Golden Calf. [7] Remember, and never forget, how you angered the LORD, your God, in the wilderness from the day that you left the land of Egypt until the day that you arrived here. You have always been rebellious. [p] [8] At Horeb you made the LORD so angry that the LORD was angry enough to destroy you. [9] When I went up the mountain to receive the stone tablets, the tablets of the covenant that the LORD had made with you, I stayed up upon the mountain for forty days and forty nights, neither eating food nor drinking water. [10] The LORD gave me two stone tablets on which the finger of God had written all of the things that the LORD had said to you on the mountain from the midst of the flames on the day of the assembly. [11] At the end of forty days and forty nights, the LORD gave me two stone tablets, the tablets of the covenant. [12] Then the LORD said to me, "Arise, hurry down, for your people whom you brought forth out of Egypt has become perverse. They have quickly turned aside from the path that I had directed them to follow and they have made a molten image for themselves."

[13] Furthermore, the LORD also said to me, "I have observed this people, and they are indeed a stiff-necked people. [14] Leave me alone, so I can destroy them and blot out their name from under the heavens. I will make you a greater and more numerous nation than they are." [q]

[15] So I turned and climbed down the mountain that was blazing with fire, carrying the two tablets of the covenant in my two hands. [16] I looked out, and behold, you had sinned against the LORD, your God. You had made a molten calf for yourselves. How quickly you had turned away from the path in which the LORD had directed you. [17] I took the two tablets and with my two hands cast them down and broke them before your eyes. [18] Then I fell prostrate before the LORD for forty days and for forty nights.* I did not eat food nor did I drink water on account of all the sins you had committed, doing what was so evil in the sight of the LORD that you provoked him to anger. [19] I feared the anger and the wrath of the LORD, for he was angry enough at you to destroy you. Yet, the LORD once again listened to me. [r]

[20] The LORD was angry enough at Aaron to kill him, but I also prayed for Aaron at the same time. [21] I took that sinful thing, the calf that you had made, and I burned it in the fire. I crushed it and ground it so fine that it was like a powder, and I threw that powder into the stream that came down from the mountain. [22] You also angered the LORD at Taberah, at Massah, and at Kibroth-hattaavah. [s] [23] Then when the LORD sent you forth from Kadesh-barnea, saying to you, "Go up and take possession of the land that I have given to you," you despised the command of the LORD, your God. You did not trust him nor listen to his voice. [24] You have despised the LORD from the first day that I knew you.

[25] I fell down and lay prostrate before the LORD for forty days and forty nights because

---

n Num 13:22, 28; Jos 11:21-22.—o Deut 8:17; Lev 18: 23-30.—p Deut 8:2; 31:27; Ex 14:11.—q Deut 29:20; Ex 32:10; Num 14:12.—r Deut 10:10; Ex 34:10.—s Ex 17:7; Num 11: 1-34.

9:6 *Stiff-necked:* "hardheaded" people with closed hearts (see also 10:16).

9:18 *Forty days and for forty nights:* Moses' perseverance in prayer for Aaron and the Israelites (see also v. 25) saved them from destruction.

the LORD said that he was going to destroy
you. [26] I prayed to the LORD and said, "O
LORD, God, do not destroy your people, your
own inheritance, whom you redeemed by
your great power, and whom you brought
forth out of Egypt with a mighty hand. [t]
[27] Remember your servants Abraham,
Isaac, and Jacob. Do not consider the stub-
bornness of this people nor the wickedness
of their sin. [28] Otherwise, the people of the
land from which you brought them will say,
'The LORD brought them out and put them
to death in the desert because he was not
able to bring them into the land that he had
promised them and also because he hated
them.' [29] Yet, they are your people and your
inheritance, whom you brought out with
your great power and your outstretched
arm."

CHAPTER 10

The Stone Tablets. [1] The LORD then also
told me, "Carve out two stone tablets like
the first ones, and come up to me on the
mountain. You are also to make an Ark out
of wood. [2] I will engrave the words that had
been on the first tablets that you broke on
these tablets. Then you are to place them in
the Ark." [u]

[3] I made an Ark out of acacia wood and
carved out two tablets like the first ones and
climbed up the mountain with the two
tablets in my hands. [4] He wrote on the
tablets what he had written on the previous
ones, the ten commandments that the LORD
had proclaimed to you on the mountain
from the midst of the flames on the day of
the assembly. The LORD then gave them to
me. [5] I climbed down the mountain and
placed the tablets in the Ark that I had
made, as the LORD had commanded, and
they are still there today. [v]

[6] The Israelites traveled from the wells of
Bene-jaakan to Moserah.* There Aaron
died, and he was buried there. Eleazer, his
son, succeeded him as priest. [7] From there
they traveled to Gudgodah, and from
Gudgodah to Jotbathah, a land filled with
streams of water. [8] It was at this time that
the LORD set aside the tribe of Levi to carry
the Ark of the Covenant, to stand before the
LORD to minister to him, and to pronounce
blessings in his name, as they do until the
present. [w] [9] That is why the Levites have no
share in the inheritance with their brethren;
the LORD is their inheritance, as the LORD,
your God, promised them.

[10] Once again I stayed on the mountain for
forty days and forty nights, like the first
time, and the LORD heard me once again, for
the LORD decided not to destroy you. [x] [11] The
LORD said to me, "Rise up, proceed on your
journey ahead of the people so that they
might go in and take possession of the land
that I promised to their fathers to give
them."

God's Steadfast Love. [12] * And so now, O
Israel, what does the LORD, your God,
require of you but to fear the LORD, your
God, to walk in all of his ways, to love him, to
serve the LORD, your God, with all your
heart and all your soul, [y] [13] and to observe
the commandments and the statutes that I
am giving you today for your own good.
[14] Indeed the heavens and the highest heav-
ens* belong to the LORD, your God, as well
as the earth and all that is in it, [z] [15] yet the
LORD's sole delight was in your fathers. He
loved them so much that he chose you, their
descendants, above every other nation,
which is still true today.

[16] Therefore, circumcise the foreskin of
your hearts, and stop being stiff-necked,*
[17] for the LORD, your God, is the God of gods
and the LORD of lords, a great God, mighty
and awesome, who does not show partiality
nor take a bribe. [a] [18] He ensures justice for
the orphan and the widow, and demon-
strates his love for the foreigner by giving
him food and clothing. [b] [19] So now, show your
love to the foreigner, for you were once for-
eigners in the land of Egypt. [c]

[20] You shall fear the LORD, your God, and
you shall serve him and hold fast to him,
taking your oaths by his name. [d] [21] He is your

t Ex 32:11-13; Num 14:13.—u Deut 4:13; Ex 25:16, 21.—v Ex 40:20; 1 Ki 8:9.—w Deut 18:5; Num 3:6; 16:9.—x Ex 33:17.—y Deut 5:33; 6:13; Pss 100:2; 119:2; Mic 6:8.—z 1 Ki 8:27; Neh 9:6; Pss 115:16; 148:4.—a Jos 22:22; Ps 136:2-3; Acts 10:34; Rev 19:16.—b Ex 22:22; Ps 68:5-6.—c Deut 24:19; Lev 19:34; Ezek 47:22.—d Deut 11:22; Mt 4:10.

10:6 *Moserah:* the Moseroth of Num 33:30, about fifteen kilometers east of Kadesh. According to the priestly tradition, Aaron died on Mount Hor (Deut 32:50; Num 20:22; 33:38). Perhaps the two names, Moserah and Hor, refer to the same area.

10:12—11:1 A recapitulation brings out what the covenant involves for Israel as God's beloved. The points highlighted are the interior religious attitude, the demands of love and justice, and care for the needy and even for foreigners.

10:14 *The highest heavens:* literally, "the heavens of the heavens."

10:16 See Jer 4:4. The rite of circumcision of the flesh is worthless without a conversion of heart. This thought will recur often, as will that of the stiff neck; see the exclamation of Stephen in Acts 7:51: "You stiff-necked people, with uncircumcised hearts!"

glory, and he is your God. He has performed great and awesome wonders for you, deeds he performed before your very eyes. [22] Seventy of your ancestors went down into Egypt. Now the LORD, your God, has multiplied you so that you are as numerous as the stars in the sky. [e]

CHAPTER 11

God's Mighty Deeds. [1] You shall love the LORD, your God, and observe his ordinances, his statutes, his decrees, and his commandments always. [2] Remember this day, for I am now not speaking with your children, who did not experience the discipline of the LORD, your God, his majesty, his mighty hand and outstretched arm, [3] and the signs and deeds he did in Egypt to Pharaoh, the king of Egypt, and to the whole land, [4] what he did to the army of Egypt, to its horses and chariots, how he caused the waters of the Red Sea to flow over them as they pursued you, for the LORD brought a lasting destruction upon them, [f] [5] and what he did for you in the wilderness until you arrived here, [6] and what he did to Dathan and Abiram, the sons of Eliab the Reubenite, how he opened a hole in the ground right in the midst of the Israelites that swallowed them up, them and their households and their tents and all of their possessions. [7] You have seen with your own eyes all of these great deeds that the LORD has done.

[8] Therefore, keep all of the commandments that I give you today so that you may be strong and go in and take possession of the land that you are going over to possess [g] [9] and so that the LORD may prolong your life in the land that the LORD promised to give to your forefathers and their descendants, a land flowing with milk and honey.

[10] The land that you are entering to take possession of is not like the land of Egypt out of which you have come. There you planted your seeds and watered the plants by hand,* like you would in a vegetable garden. [11] The land that you are entering to take possession of is a land of hills and valleys that obtains its water from the rain of the skies. [h] [12] It is a land that the LORD, your God, cares for, the LORD, your God, continuously keeps his eyes on it, from the beginning of the year until the end of the year.

[13] * If you carefully observe the commandments that I give you today, to love the LORD, your God, and to serve him with all your heart and soul, [14] then he will provide the rain upon the land in its proper season, the fall rains and the spring rains, so that you can harvest your grain, your wine, and your oil. [i] [15] I will provide grass in your field for your cattle, so that you may eat until you are full.

[16] Only be careful not to let yourself be enticed, turning away and serving other gods, worshiping them. [j] [17] Then the LORD's anger would lash out against you. He would shut up the heavens so that there would be no rain, no produce from the land. Beware lest you soon perish in the good land that the LORD is giving you. [k]

Rewards of Faithfulness. [18] Fix these words in your heart and your soul, bind them as a reminder upon your hand, and wear them as a pendant between your eyes. [19] You are to teach them to your children. You shall talk of them when you are sitting in your home, and when you are walking along the way, and when you lie down and when you rise up. [l] [20] You are to write them on the doorframes of your houses and your gates [21] so that your days and the days of your children will be multiplied in the land that the LORD promised to give them, lasting as long as the heavens cover the earth. [m]

[22] If you are careful in observing all of these commandments that I give you, loving the LORD, your God, and walking in all of his ways and holding fast to him, [23] then the LORD will drive out all of these nations from before you. You will dispossess nations that are larger and stronger than you are. [24] Everywhere that your feet touch the ground shall be yours, from the desert and Lebanon, from the river, the River Euphrates, up to the western sea, this will all be your land. * [n] [25] No one will be able to stand up to you. The LORD, your God, as he promised you, he has put fear and dread of you upon everyone in the land, wherever you go.

Blessing and Curse. [26] Behold, I set before you today a blessing and a curse. [o] [27] There

e Deut 1:10; Gen 46:27.—f Ex 14:27-28; 15:1.—g Deut 31:6; Jos 1:6-7.—h Deut 8:7.—i Deut 28:12; Jer 5:24; Joel 2:23.—j Deut 4:9; 8:19; 29:18.—k Deut 4:26; Lev 26:20; 1 Ki 8:35.—l Deut 4:9-10; 6:7.—m Ps 89:29; Prov 3:2.—n Deut 1:7; Jos 1:3.—o Deut 30:1, 19; Lev 26:14-17.

11:10 *Watered the plants by hand:* that is, by scooping out channels that allow the water to reach the seed.

11:13-15 In this section, Moses shifts between the first and third person, speaking as a prophet and then for the Lord.

11:24 Israel never extended to these borders; they serve rather as an ideal. See Pss 72:8.

will be a blessing if you obey the commandments of the LORD, your God, that I give you today. 28 There will be a curse if you do not obey the commandments of the LORD, your God, and you turn from the way that I command you today and you seek after other gods whom you have previously not known. 29 When the LORD, your God, has brought you into the land that you are entering to possess, you are to proclaim a blessing on Mount Gerizim and a curse on Mount Ebal.[p] 30 (Are they not on the other side of the Jordan, toward the setting of the sun, in the land of the Canaanites who live in the Arabah near Gilgal, beside the terebinth of Moreh?) *[q] 31 You are to cross over the Jordan and enter in it and take possession of the land that the LORD, your God, has given you. When you have taken possession of it and are living in it, 32 then you are to observe all of the statutes and decrees that I have placed before you today.

B: The Deuteronomic Code*

CHAPTER 12

One Place of Worship. 1 *These are the statutes and the decrees that you must be careful to observe in the land that the LORD, the God of your fathers, has given you as an inheritance for the whole time that you live upon the earth.[r] 2 [s] You must totally destroy all the places where the nations that you shall dispossess served their gods, whether they be on the high mountains or upon the hills or under every green tree. 3 You are to overturn their altars and break their sacred pillars. You must burn their wooden idols in fires, you must cut down their carved idols and obliterate their names from that place. 4 This is not the way that you are to worship the LORD, your God.

5 You are to seek out the place that the LORD, your God, has chosen from among all the tribes to be where you shall place his name and establish his dwelling. This is where you are to go[t] 6 to bring your burnt offering, your sacrifices, your tithes, your wave offerings, what you have vowed to give as a freewill offering, and the firstborn from your herds and flocks.[u] 7 There you and your families will eat before the LORD, your God, and you shall rejoice at everything you have put your hand to, for the LORD, your God, will have blessed you. 8 You are not to do things the way we do them today, that each person does as he sees fit,[v] 9 for you have not yet come to your resting place, the inheritance that the LORD, your God, is giving you. 10 But when you cross the Jordan and live in the land that the LORD, your God, is giving to you as an inheritance, a place where he will give you peace from all the enemies who surround you so that you can live in safety,[w] 11 then you shall bring everything that I command you to the place that the LORD, your God, will have chosen for the dwelling place of his name: your burnt offerings, your sacrifices, your tithes, your wave offerings, and all of your choice vow offerings that you have vowed onto the LORD. 12 You and your sons and daughters, your menservants and your maidservants, and the Levite who lives in your town (for he has no claim to your inheritance) will rejoice before the LORD, your God.

13 [x] Make sure that you do not offer burnt offerings any place you might happen to see, 14 but you are to offer burnt offerings in the place that the LORD will choose in one of your tribes. There you are to fulfill all that I command you to do.

Permissible Slaughter. 15 Nevertheless, you can slaughter animals and eat meat within your town gates with the blessing that the LORD, your God, gives you, as much as you desire. The clean and the unclean may eat of it, the gazelle and the roebuck alike. 16 Only you are not to consume its blood;

p Deut 27:12-13; Jos 8:30-35.—q Gen 12:6; Jos 4:19.—r Deut 4:9-10.—s 2-3: Deut 7:5; Num 33:51-52; 1 Ki 14:23; 2 Ki 17:10; Jer 2:20.—t 2 Sam 7:13; 1 Ki 8:16-21, 29-30.—u Deut 14:22ff; Lev 1:3-17; 27:30.—v Jdg 17:6.—w Lev 25:18; Ps 4:8.—x 13-14: Jos 22:10-34.

11:30 *The terebinth of Moreh* were at Shechem, the modern Tell Balatah; the road to the place starts at Galgala and runs westward.

12:1—28:69 By means of its liturgy the people of God seek to establish a lifegiving relationship with God. Deuteronomy does not mean to suppress all other liturgical activity; the point is that worship must express the faith of the entire people. It is enough that any deviations be avoided and that every trace of pagan practices be rejected.

12:1—13:1 In the sanctuaries that had been built in various parts of the country the ceremonies were often contaminated by the Canaanite religion. To get rid of these pagan deviations and to strengthen the religious and political unity of the people, Deuteronomy requires the suppression of these sanctuaries, some of which had played an important role in Israel's past, even though they had originally been pagan. This centralization of worship in the place determined by God, namely, the Jerusalem temple, goes back probably to the time of the great reform of King Josiah at the end of the seventh century (2 Ki 22–23), but it is here attributed to Moses, who had inspired Israel's life of worship. As a result of this centralization, certain everyday actions such as the slaughtering of animals, which had hitherto been done at the sanctuaries, would be done by each individual at home and would therefore no longer have a sacral character (Deut 12:15).

you are to pour it on the ground as if it were water.*[y]

[17] You are not to eat the following things within your town gates: the tithe of the grain, wine, and oil, the firstborn of the herds or flocks, any of the vow offerings you have offered with a vow, any freewill offering and any wave offering. [18] You are to eat these before the LORD, your God, in the place that the LORD, your God, will have chosen, you and your son and your daughter, your manservant and your maidservant, and the Levite who lives in your town. You are to rejoice before the LORD, your God, in all of your undertakings.

[19] Take heed not to forsake the Levite for as long as you live in the land.[z] [20] When the LORD, your God, enlarges your boundaries, as he has promised that he will do, and you say to yourself, "I am going to eat some meat,"* because you feel like eating some meat, you can eat as much meat as you desire.

[21] If the place that the LORD, your God, will have chosen to put his name is too far from where you are living, you can kill any animal from the herd or the flock that the LORD has given you, just as I have instructed you. You can eat as much as you want of it within your town gates.[a] [22] You can eat them like you would eat the gazelle or the roebuck. Both the unclean and the clean can eat of it. [23] Only be careful that you do not consume the blood, for the blood is its life. You are not to eat the life with the meat. [24] You are not to consume the blood; you are to pour it on the ground as if it were water. [25] You are not to eat it, so that things may turn out well for you and your children after you, for you will be doing the right thing from the LORD's point of view.[b]

[26] Take your consecrated things and whatever you have vowed to give, and go to the place that the LORD has chosen. [27] Present your burnt offerings, both the meat and the blood, on the altar of the LORD, your God. You are to pour the blood out on the altar of the LORD, your God, but you can eat the meat. [28] Take heed to observe all of the things that I have commanded you, that things may go well with you and your children forever, when you do what is right and good in the sight of the LORD, your God. [29] The LORD, your God, will cut down the nations of the place where you are going before you so that you can dispossess them. When you take their place and settle in their land [30] and they have been destroyed before you, be careful not to be ensnared by asking questions about their gods such as, "How did these nations serve their gods? We should do the same thing as they did." [31] You shall not do these things to the LORD, your God. They have worshiped their gods with every kind of abomination that the LORD hates. They have even offered their sons and daughters as burnt sacrifices to their gods.[c]

CHAPTER 13

Punishing False Prophets. [1] Do whatever I command you to do. Do not add anything to it, nor ignore anything from it.

[2] If a prophet or one who foretells the future through dreams arises among you and performs some miraculous sign or wonder[d] [3] and that miraculous sign or wonder occurs, and he says to you, "Let us seek after other gods which we have not previously known and serve them,"[e] [4] you are not to listen to the words of that prophet or dreamer of dreams.* The LORD, your God, is testing you to see whether you love the LORD, your God, with all your heart and your soul.[f] [5] It is the LORD, your God, whom you are to follow. You must fear him and observe his commandments and obey what he tells you and serve him and hold fast to him. [6] But that prophet or the one who told the future through dreams is to be put to death for he counseled you to turn away from the LORD, your God, who brought you out of the land of Egypt and redeemed you from the land of slavery. He was driving you away from the way that the LORD, your God, had ordered must be your path. You must purge this evil from your midst.[g]

[7] *Even if your brother, the son of your mother, or your son, or your daughter, or your wife, or your closest friend secretly

y Gen 9:4; Lev 17:10-12.—z Deut 14:27.—a Deut 14:24.—b Deut 4:40; 13:18.—c Deut 9:5; 18:10; Lev 18:21.—d Mt 24:24; Mk 13:22.—e Deut 18:20; Jer 23:32.—f Deut 6:5; Ps 119:2.—g Deut 17:2-7; Jer 28:16; 29:32.

12:16 Blood is life and belongs to God (see v. 23; Gen 9:4).

12:20 *Eat some meat:* this indicates the freedom to choose to eat meat when the people entered Canaan instead of only the manna they were forced to eat in the wilderness.

13:4 *Dreamer of dreams:* this admonition to avoid false prophets does not discount the possibility of genuine revelations proceeding from dreams (see Gen 20:3, 6; 37:5, 9; Mt 1:20).

13:7-9 Like Jesus, who was tempted by his friend Peter (see Mt 16:21-23), we must also be vigilant and strong against temptation especially from those closest to us.

tempts you saying, "Let us go and serve other gods whom neither you nor your forefathers have known," [8] the gods of the people living around us, whether they be near or far, wherever they are upon the whole face of the earth, [9] you are not to agree to do this with him or even listen to him. You must show him no pity, you should not spare or conceal him. [10] [h] You must put him to death. You must be the first to lay hands on him to put him to death, and then all of the people after you. [11] Stone him to death! He sought to turn you away from the LORD, your God, who brought you out of the land of Egypt, out of the land of slavery. [12] Then all of Israel will hear of this and be filled with fear, and no one will ever do such an evil thing again in your midst.

[13] If you hear it said that in one of the cities that the LORD, your God, has given you to live in [14] there are evil men who have come out from among you and who have misled the inhabitants of the city saying, "Let us go and serve other gods whom we have not previously known," [i] [15] then you will inquire, and probe, and investigate it thoroughly. If it is clearly proven that this detestable thing has been done among you, [j] [16] you are to put the inhabitants of that city to the sword and you are to demolish it. Destroy everything in it, even killing the cattle with the edge of the sword. [k] [17] Gather all of the plunder from it in the middle of its streets, and burn the city and all the spoil in it to the ground. It is to be like a burnt offering to the LORD, your God. It is to remain a ruin forever, never to be rebuilt. [l] [18] You are not to hold on to any of those cursed things, so that the LORD may turn from his fierce anger and show you mercy. He will have compassion on you, and make you numerous, as he promised your fathers, [m] [19] for you will have heeded the voice of the LORD, your God, and observed all of the commandments that I gave you today and done what the LORD, your God, considered to be right.

CHAPTER 14

[1] You are the children of the LORD, your God. Do not slash yourselves nor shave the front of your heads on account of the dead.* [n] [2] You are a people who are holy to the LORD, your God, and the LORD has picked you out from among all the peoples on the earth to be a chosen people.

Clean and Unclean Food.* [3] You are not to eat any abominable thing. [4] These are the animals that you can eat: the ox, the sheep, the goat, [o] [5] the gazelle, the roebuck, the deer, the wild goat, the antelope, the wild ox, and the mountain sheep. [6] Every animal that has a cleft hoof, its hoof is divided in two parts, and that chews its cud is an animal that you can eat. [7] However, there are animals that chew their cud, or that have a cleft hoof that you cannot eat: the camel, the hare, and the rock badger, for they chew their cud but do not have a cleft hoof, so they are unclean for you. [8] Likewise, pigs have a cleft hoof, but they do not chew their cud, so they are unclean for you. You are not to eat their meat, nor even touch their dead carcasses. [p]

[9] You can eat any water creature that has fins and scales; those you can eat. [10] Whatever does not have fins or scales, you are not to eat. It is unclean for you.

[11] You can eat any clean bird. [12] These are the birds you shall not eat: the eagle, the bearded vulture, the osprey, [13] the hawk, the kite, any type of vulture, [q] [14] any kind of raven, [15] the owl, the night hawk, the gull, any type of falcon, [16] the little owl, the great owl, the barn owl, [17] the desert owl, the carrion vulture, the cormorant, [18] the stork, any type of heron, the hoopoe, and the bat. [19] Every type of flying insect is unclean for you. You shall not eat it, [r] [20] but you can eat any type of clean bird.

[21] Do not eat anything that died on its own. You can give it to a foreigner who is living in your town, and he can eat it, or you can sell it to a foreigner. But you are a people who are holy to the LORD, your God. You shall not eat a kid goat boiled in its mother's milk.* [s]

Tithes. [22] * Each year you are to tithe the yield of your seed that has grown in the

h 10-11: Deut 21:21.—i Jdg 19:22; 1 Jn 2:19.—j Isa 24:6; Zec 8:13.—k Jos 6:24; 8:28; Isa 7:16; 17:1.—l Deut 7:26; Ezek 26:14.—m Deut 12:25, 28.—n Lev 21:5; Ps 82:67; Rom 8:16.—o Lev 11:2-23; Acts 10:14.—p Lev 5:2; 11:26-27.—q Isa 34:15.—r Lev 11:20.—s Ex 23:19; 34:26; Lev 17:15; Ezek 44:31.—t Gen 28:22; Lev 27:30; Num 18:21.

14:1 A prohibition of some traditional pagan practices.

14:3-21 One would "be a slave" of alien gods if one were to eat animals consecrated to them. The law prohibits this (Ex 34:15). The list includes some other animals that are excluded either by custom or for reasons of hygiene.

14:21 Cooking a kid in its mother's milk was a pagan Canaanite practice.

14:22-27 This description of a tithe is different from that given in Num 18:21-24 and probably replaced the earlier law.

field.[t] 23 This is what you shall eat in the
presence of the LORD, your God, in the place
that he has established that his name be
placed: the tithe of your grain, wine, and oil,
the firstborn of your herd and flock. This will
be a lesson to fear the LORD, your God,
always. 24 [u] If the distance is so great that you
cannot carry it to the place that the LORD,
your God, has chosen to set his name, and
the LORD, your God, has blessed you, 25 then
you shall exchange it for money, and carry
the money to the place that the LORD, your
God, has chosen. 26 You can use that money
to buy whatever you wish, oxen, or sheep, or
wine, or strong drink, whatever you wish. You
and your family will consume it in the pres-
ence of the LORD, your God, and you will
rejoice.

27 You are not to neglect the Levite who
lives in your town, for he has no portion or
inheritance among you.[v] 28 * Every third
year you are to bring all of your tithes from
your produce for that year, and you will
deposit them in your town. 29 The Levite,
who has no portion nor inheritance among
you, the foreigner, the orphan, and the widow
who live in your town will consume it until
they are full. Thus, the LORD, your God, will
bless you in every endeavor you pursue.[w]

CHAPTER 15

Goodwill to the Poor. 1 * At the end of every
seven years you are to cancel debts.[x] 2 This
is how you are to do it. Everyone who has
made a loan to his neighbor will forgive the
debt. He will not require payment from his
neighbor nor his brother, for the LORD's par-
don of debts has been proclaimed. 3 You may
require payment from a foreigner, but you
must forgive the debt that your brother
owes.[y] 4 There should be no poor among
you, for the LORD will greatly bless you in the
land that the LORD, your God, has given you
to possess as an inheritance, 5 but only if you
carefully heed the voice of the LORD, your
God, and observe all of the commandments
that I give you today.[z] 6 The LORD, your God,
will bless you as he promised you. You will
lend to many nations, but borrow from
none. You shall rule over many nations, but
none shall rule over you.

7 If there is a poor man among you in the
towns of the land that the LORD, your God,
has given you, do not harden your heart nor
be stingy with your poor brother.[a] 8 Be gener-
ous with him, lending him what he needs,
whatever it is he needs.[b] 9 Be careful not to
harbor the evil thought in your mind, "The
seventh year, the time for canceling debts, is
near." Do not show bad will toward your poor
brother and end up giving him nothing. He
might appeal to the LORD, and it would be
your sin. 10 You must give to him, and you
should not have a grudging heart when you
give to him. The LORD, your God, will bless
you in all the endeavors that you undertake
because of what you have given.[c] 11 There will
always be poor people in the land. Therefore,
I command you, "Be generous to your poor
brother and the needy in your land."[d]

Freeing Slaves. 12 [e] If a fellow Hebrew man
or woman sells himself to you and serves for
six years, then in the seventh year you are to
set him free. * 13 When you release him, you
are not to send him away empty-handed.
14 Provide him generously from your flock,
your threshing floor, your winepress. Give to
him in the same way that the LORD, your
God, has blessed you. 15 Remember that you
were slaves in the land of Egypt, and the
LORD, your God, redeemed you. Therefore, I
give you this command today.

16 But if your slave says to you, "I do not
want to leave you," because he loves you and
your family and is well off with you, 17 then
take an awl and push it through his ear lobe
into the door. He will then be your slave for-
ever. You are to do the same with your maid-
servants as well. 18 Do not consider it to be a
hardship to set your slave free. You received
twice as much from him in the six years as
you would have from a hired hand, and the
LORD, your God, will bless you in all of your
undertakings.

The Firstborn. 19 Set apart for the LORD,
your God, the firstborn male from your
herds and your flocks. Do not set the first-

u 24-26: Mk 11:15; Jn 2:13-14.—v Deut 12:12-19; Num 18:20.—w Ps 41:2; Prov 22:9; Mal 3:10.—x Deut 31:10; Lev 25:1-55; Neh 10:31.—y Deut 15:2; 23:20.—z Deut 28:1; Ex 15:26.—a Mt 26:11; 1 Jn 3:17.—b Lev 25—35; Ps 37:21-22; Prov 19:17; Mt 5:42; Lk 6:34.—c 2 Cor 9:5-7.—d Mt 26:11; Mk 14:7; Jn 12:8.—e 12-18: Ex 21:2-11; Jer 34:8-22.

14:28-29 Never forgotten by the Lord, the orphan, foreigner, and widow were remembered in a special way by the Israelites every three years by a tithe on all the year's produce.

15:1-18 Note that God regards as done to himself what is done, be it good or evil, to the poor, and that this principle is frequently applied in Deuteronomy (14:29; 24:15) and throughout the Bible (1 Jn 4:17-21) and will be set in a new perspective by Jesus (Mt 25:35-45).

15:12 Women here have the same right as men; this marks progress over Ex 21:1-6.

born of your oxen to work, nor shear the
firstborn of your sheep.[f] 20 Each year you
and your family are to eat them before the
LORD, your God, in the place that the LORD
has chosen. 21 [g] If an animal has any blemish,
or is lame, or blind, or has any serious flaw,
you are not to sacrifice it to the LORD, your
God. 22 You can eat it within your own
towns. * The clean and the unclean can eat it,
as if it were a gazelle or a roebuck. 23 But you
must not consume its blood, you are to pour
it out on the ground as if it were water.

CHAPTER 16

Feast of the Passover. 1 * Observe the
month of Abib,* and celebrate the Passover
of the LORD, your God, for in the month of
Abib the LORD, your God, brought you forth
from Egypt during the night.[h] 2 Make a
Passover sacrifice from your flock or your
herd to the LORD, your God, in the place
where the LORD has chosen to place his
name. 3 Do not eat leavened bread, but eat
unleavened bread for seven days. This is the
bread of affliction, for you had to leave the
land of Egypt in haste. Thus, all of your life
you will remember the day that you came
forth from Egypt.[i] 4 There should be no leav-
ened bread in your entire land for seven
days. Do not let any of the meat of the sacri-
fice that was made on the first evening
remain until the next morning. 5 * You are
not to make the Passover sacrifice in any of
the towns that the LORD, your God, has
given you. 6 Do it only in the place that the
LORD, your God, has chosen to place his
name. You will make the Passover sacrifice
in the evening, when the sun goes down, at
the time when you went forth out of Egypt.
7 Roast the lamb and eat it in the place that
the LORD, your God, will choose. Then, in the
morning, return to your homes. 8 For six
days you are to eat unleavened bread. Then,
on the seventh day, you will hold a solemn
assembly to the LORD, your God, and you
are to do no heavy labor.[j]

Feast of Weeks. 9 [k] Count off seven weeks
from the time that you put the sickle to the
standing grain. You are to count off seven
weeks, 10 and then you will celebrate the
Feast of Weeks to the LORD, your God, mak-
ing a freewill offering in proportion to how
much the LORD, your God, has blessed you.
11 You and your son and your daughter, your
manservant and your maidservant, the
Levite who lives in your town, the foreigner,
the orphan, and the widow are all to rejoice
in the place that the LORD, your God, has
chosen to place his name. 12 Remember that
you were slaves in Egypt and carefully
observe these statutes.

Feast of Booths. 13 Celebrate the Feast of
Booths for seven days after you have gath-
ered the produce of your threshing floor and
your winepress. 14 Be joyful at the feast, you
and your son and your daughter, your
manservant and your maidservant, as well
as the Levite, the orphans, and the widows
who live in your town. 15 For seven days you
are to celebrate the feast to the LORD, your
God, in the place that the LORD will choose,
for the LORD, your God, has blessed you with
all your harvest and all of the works of your
hands. Therefore, you must surely rejoice.[l]

16 Three times a year all of your men
must appear before the LORD, your God, in
the place that he will choose: the Feast of
Unleavened Bread, the Feast of Weeks, and
the Feast of Booths. You are not to appear
before the LORD empty-handed.[m] 17 Each
of you is to bring a gift that is proportion-
ate to how much the LORD, your God, has
blessed you.

Justice. 18 * Appoint judges and officials
for each of your tribes in every town that the
LORD, your God, gives you. They are to
judge the people fairly.[n] 19 Do not pervert
justice nor show partiality. Do not accept a
bribe, for a bribe blinds the eyes of the wise
and twists the words of the righteous.[o]

---

f Ex 13:2; Lev 27:26; Num 18:15-18.—g 21-23: Lev 22:25; Mal 1:8.—h Ex 12:2; 2 Ki 23:21; Mt 26:17-29.—i Ex 12:8, 39; 34:18.—j Lev 23:8, 36; Lk 2:41; 22:7.—k 9-12: Ex 23:16; Lev 23:15; Num 28:26.—l Lev 23:36-42; Pss 4:7; 28:7.—m Ex 23:14-17; Ezr 3:4; Neh 8:14.—n Ex 18:13-26; 2 Chr 19:5-11.—o Prov 17:23; 18:5; Jn 7:24; Jas 2:9.

15:22 *Within your own towns:* because this is not a cultic meal.

16:1-17 The three annual pilgrimages which bring all the people together at the sanctuary are a high point in the liturgical life of Israel. The Feast of Weeks (later called the Feast of Pentecost) and the Feast of Tabernacles are agricultural festivals at which God is thanked for his blessings, whereas Passover and the Feast of Unleavened Bread (now combined into one) commemorate the deliverance from Egypt (Ex 12:1-20; 13:6-7; 23:15; 34:25; Lev 23).

16:1 *Abib:* the month of "the spikes [of grain]," corresponds to March–April.

16:5-6 The celebration of Passover at the sanctuary and not in the family home is a deuteronomic innovation that would be preserved only among the Samaritans.

16:18—20:20 The institutions that used to protect the life of Israel as a nation have now disappeared, but the spirit with which Deuteronomy tries to inspire them has not lost any of its value: the people of God will always be obligated to live the covenant in the setting of a concrete human society.

[20] Seek justice, so that you may live in and
inherit the land that the LORD, your God, has
given you.

False Worship. [21] Do not plant any sacred
grove beside the altar that you will build to
the LORD, your God. [22] Do not set up any
sacred pillar, for the LORD, your God, hates
these things. [p]

CHAPTER 17

[1] You shall not sacrifice an ox or a sheep
that has any blemish or any defect* whatso-
ever to the LORD, your God, for that would
be an abomination to the LORD, your God.
[2] If any man or woman is discovered in any
of the towns that the LORD, your God, has
given you who does what is evil in the sight
of the LORD, your God, transgressing his
covenant, [q] [3] going over and serving and wor-
shiping other gods, whether it be the sun or
the moon or any of the host of heaven, some-
thing that I have forbidden, [4] and you are
told about it, and you hear of it, then you
shall carefully check into it. If it is true, then
an abomination has been committed in
Israel; [5] you are to bring that man or woman
who has done this evil thing to the town
gates, and you shall stone that man or
woman to death.

[6] A person can be put to death upon the
testimony of two or three witnesses; a per-
son is not to be put to death upon the testi-
mony of a single witness. [r] [7] The witnesses
will be the first to raise their hand against
him to put him to death, then all of the peo-
ple will raise their hands against him, in
order to purge this evil from your midst.

Judges. [8] [s] If cases come before you that
are too difficult to judge, whether concern-
ing bloodshed, or lawsuits, or assault, then
take them to the place that the LORD, your
God, will choose. [9] Go to the priests, the
Levites, and the judge whose term it is, and
consult with them. They will give you a ver-
dict. [10] You must proceed according to the
verdict that they will have given you at the
place that the LORD will choose. Do every-
thing that they tell you to do. [11] Act accord-
ing to the law that they teach you and the
judgment that they render. Do not turn
away from the sentence that they pro-
nounce, either to the right or the left. [12] The
man who acts presumptuously by not obey-
ing either the priest who stands before the
LORD, your God, to minister there, or the
judge, is to die. In this way you will purge the
evil from Israel.* [t] [13] All the people will hear
of it and be filled with fear; they will not act
presumptuously anymore.

A Suitable King. [14] When you enter the land
that the LORD, your God, has given you and
you take possession of it and dwell there and
you say, "I will set a king over me like all the
other nations that surround me," [u] [15] you can
indeed have a king whom the LORD, your
God, will choose. You will make one of your
brethren your king, you are not to choose a
foreigner as king who is not one of your
brethren. [v] [16] He must not build up a large
stable for himself, and he must not send
people back to Egypt to procure a large sta-
ble, for the LORD has said that you are not to
return that way again. [w] [17] He should also
not have many wives, lest his heart be
turned astray. He must not accumulate
large sums of silver or gold. [18] When he takes
the throne of his kingdom, he is to write a
copy of the law that is entrusted to the
priests, the Levites for himself on a scroll. [x]
[19] [y] He should read it every day of his life so
that he can learn to fear the LORD, his God,
and to observe all the words of these laws
and statutes, fulfilling them. [20] In this way he
will not consider himself to be better than
his brethren in his heart, and he will not turn
away from the commandments to the right
or the left. He and his descendants will thus
reign a long time in the kingdom of Israel.

CHAPTER 18

[1] The priests who are Levites,* in fact, the
whole tribe of Levi, will have no portion nor
inheritance with Israel. They can eat from
the burnt offerings made to the LORD, that is
their inheritance. [2] They will have no inheri-
tance among their brethren; the LORD is
their inheritance, as he has promised them. [z]

p 1 Ki 14:15; 2 Ki 17:16; 21:3; 2 Chr 33:3.—q Jos 7:11, 15; Jdg 2:20; Jer 34:18.—r Num 35:30; Mt 18:16; 2 Cor 13:1.—s 8-9: Ex 18:13-26; 2 Chr 19:8-10; Ezek 44:24.—t Num 15:30; 1 Cor 5:13.—u 1 Sam 8:5, 19-20.—v 1 Sam 9:16; 10:24; Jer 30:21.—w 1 Ki 4:26; 10:26-29; Isa 2:7.—x Jos 8:32; 1 Sam 10:25.—y 19-20: Jos 1:8; 2 Sam 7:12-16; 1 Ki 2:4; Ps 132: 11-18.—z Num 18:20; Jos 13:14.

17:1 *Any blemish or any defect:* a recurring theme (see Lev 3:6; 22:19) that insists on setting aside only the best animals to sacrifice to the Lord.

17:12 According to the established court system, the children of Israel are bound to obey both the high priest in matters of religion and the judge in secular matters.

18:1 *The priests who are Levites:* an expression characteristic of Deuteronomy (17:9, 18; 21:5; 24:8; 27:9; 31:9). See the distinction between priests and simple Levites in Num 18. In Deuteronomy all the Levites are priests.

3 This is the portion due to the priest from
the people who offer a sacrifice of either an
ox or a sheep: the shoulder, the jowl, and the
inner organs. 4 You will give them the first-
fruits of the grain, the wine, and the oil, as
well as the first sheering of the sheep [a] 5 for
the LORD, your God, has chosen him and his
sons out of all of the tribes to minister in the
LORD's name forever. [b] 6 If any Levite in all of
Israel moves from his town where he had
been living and he desires to go to the place
that the LORD will choose, 7 then he may
minister in the name of the LORD, his God,
like all his fellow Levites who serve there in
the presence of the LORD. 8 He will be given
an equal share in their benefits in addition to
the proceeds from the sale of his inheri-
tance. [c]

Forbidden Practices. 9 When you enter the
land that the LORD, your God, is giving you,
you are not to learn to perform the abomi-
nations that those nations do. 10 [d] Let no one
among you offer his son or his daughter as a
burnt offering, or practice divination, or
interpret omens, or practice witchcraft,*
11 or cast spells, or act as a medium, or act as
a wizard, or seek oracles from the dead.
12 Whoever does any of these things is an
abomination to the LORD. It is because of
these abominations that the LORD, your
God, is driving them out before you.

13 You are to be blameless before the
LORD, your God. 14 These nations that you
are dispossessing listened to those who prac-
tice witchcraft and the diviners. It is not to
be that way among you, for the LORD, your
God, does not permit it.

Prophets. 15 The LORD, your God, will raise
up from among your countrymen a prophet
who will do what I have done for you, and you
will listen to him. [e] 16 This is just as you asked
the LORD, your God, at Horeb on the day of
the assembly when you said, "Let me not
hear the voice of the LORD, my God, any-
more, nor look upon this great fire, lest I die."
17 The LORD said to me, "They have spoken
well. 18 I will raise up a prophet from among
their countrymen who will be like you. I will
place my words in his mouth, and he will tell
them all that I command him. [f] 19 I myself will
call to account whoever does not heed my
words that he will proclaim in my name. [g]
20 [h] But if a prophet presumes to proclaim
something in my name that I have not said to
him, or he speaks in the names of other gods,
that prophet is to be put to death." 21 You
might say to yourself, "How can we know that
the LORD did not speak the message?" 22 If
what the prophet proclaims in the name of
the LORD is not true and it does not happen,
then the message was not proclaimed by the
LORD. The prophet has spoken presumptu-
ously, you should not fear him.*

CHAPTER 19

Cities of Refuge. 1 When the LORD, your
God, has destroyed the nations whose land
he is giving you, when you have driven them
out and you are dwelling in their cities and
houses, 2 * then set aside three cities in the
land that the LORD, your God, is giving you
to possess. 3 Build roads to them, and divide
the land that the LORD, your God, is giving
you as an inheritance into three parts so that
anyone who has killed another can flee to
them. 4 This is the regulation concerning the
one who has killed another and flees there to
save his life: one who kills his neighbor unin-
tentionally, who did not previously bear him
ill will, [i] 5 for example, when a man goes into
the woods with his neighbor to cut wood,
and as he is swinging the ax to cut down a
tree, and the head of the ax flies off and kills
the neighbor. That man may flee to one of
the cities to save his life. 6 Otherwise, the rel-
ative who seeks blood vengeance might seek
him out while he is still blind with rage, and
if the distance be too great he would then be
able to catch up with him and kill him even
though he did not really deserve to die since
he did not bear the man any previous ill
will. * [j] 7 This is why I command you to set
aside three cities for yourselves.

8 If the LORD, your God, adds to your ter-
ritory, as he promised to do to your ances-

---

a Ex 22:29; Num 18:12; 2 Chr 31:5.—b Deut 10:8; Ex 28:1; Jer 33:18.—c Num 18:24; 2 Chr 31:4; Neh 12:44, 47.—d 10-11: Ex 22:18; Lev 18:21; 19:31; 1 Sam 28:7-19.—e Lk 9:35; Jn 1:21, 45; Acts 3:22; 7:37.—f Ex 4:10-16; Isa 51:4, 16; Jn 4:25-26.—g Jer 11:21-23; Acts 3:23.—h 20-22: Deut 13:2-6; 1 Ki 22:1-40; Jer 14:13-16; 23:9-40; 28:1-17.—i Num 35:15.—j Num 35:12.

18:10 In preparing God's chosen people to enter the Promised Land, they are warned against adopting heathen practices. Instead, they are to put their full trust in the one true God.

18:22 Then, as now, discerning the true from the false prophet is necessary and simple. If what the prophet proclaims does not happen, they are not of the Lord, and these false prophets were subject to capital punishment.

19:2-13 As described in Num 35:7-34 six cities of refuge were to be designated for those guilty of the accidental death of another person. In this section, Moses speaks specifically about the three cities to be built in Canaan, west of the Jordan.

19:6 The victim's closest relative is the one appointed to kill the murderer (Hebrew, *goel:* see Num 35:12).

tors, and he gives you all the land that he promised to give to your fathers,[k] 9 for you have carefully observed all the commandments that I have given you today, to love the LORD, your God, and always walk in his ways, then you will set aside another three cities beside the first three. 10 Do this so that innocent blood not be shed in the land that the LORD, your God, is giving you as an inheritance. Thus, you will not be guilty of bloodshed. 11 But if a man bears ill will toward his neighbor and lies in wait for him, and jumps out at him and grievously wounds him so that he dies, and then he flees to one of these cities, 12 the elders of his town will send after him, bring him back, and hand him over to the relative who seeks blood vengeance so that he might be put to death. 13 Show him no pity. You must purge the guilt of shedding innocent blood from your midst so that things may go well with you.

Removing Landmarks. 14 Do not move your neighbor's boundary stone that was set up long ago to mark your inheritance in the land that the LORD, your God, has given you to possess.[l]

Witnesses. 15 One witness is not enough to convict someone of any crime or any offense that he might have committed. The matter is to be decided by the testimony of two or three witnesses.[m] 16 If a false witness arises to accuse another of a crime,[n] 17 the two men involved in the dispute must stand in the presence of the LORD before the priests and judges who are fulfilling their term. 18 The judges must make a thorough investigation. If a witness proves to be a liar, having falsely testified against another, 19 then whatever would have been done to the other is to be done to him. You must purge this evil from your midst.[o] 20 The rest of the people will hear of this and be filled with fear and no one will ever do such an evil thing in your midst again. 21 Show no pity: a life for a life,* an eye for an eye, a tooth for a tooth, a hand for a hand, and a foot for a foot.[p]

CHAPTER 20

Rules of Battle. 1 When you go out to fight your enemies and you see horses and chariots and more troops than you have, do not be afraid of them on account of the LORD, your God, who brought you up out of the land of Egypt. 2 When you are about to go into battle, have the priest approach and speak to the people. 3 He is to say to them, "Hear, O Israel, you are about to go into battle today against your enemies. Do not be fainthearted or afraid. Do not tremble or panic before them. 4 The LORD, your God, goes forth with you to fight against your enemies to deliver you."[q] 5 The officers will then say to the people: "If anyone has built a house and not yet dedicated it, he is to go home lest he die in battle and another dedicate it. 6 And if anyone has planted a vineyard and has not yet enjoyed its fruit, let him go home lest he die in battle and another eat its fruit.[r] 7 And if anyone has become betrothed to a woman and has not yet married her, let him go home lest he die in battle and another marry her."* 8 Even then the officers will say to the people, "If anyone is fearful or fainthearted, let him go home lest his brethren become fainthearted as well."[s]

9 When the officers have finished speaking to the people, they are to appoint commanders to lead the people. 10 [t] When you approach a city to do battle with it, offer it terms of peace. 11 If they accept your terms of peace and open their gates to you, then all the people who live there shall be subject to forced labor done on your behalf. 12 If they refuse your terms of peace, then you will do battle with them, besieging that city. 13 When the LORD, your God, delivers it into your hands, you shall put every man in it to death. 14 The women, the children, the cattle, and everything else in the city will be plunder to you. You may take as your own the spoil of your enemies that the LORD, your God, has delivered over to you.[u]

15 This is how you are to deal with all the distant cities, the cities that do not belong to these nations. 16 But in these cities that the LORD, your God, is giving you as an inheritance, you are not to leave anything alive.[v] 17 Wipe them out, the Hittites, the Amorites, the Canaanites, the Perizzites, the Hivites, and the Jebusites, just as the LORD, your

k Gen 15:18-21; 28:14; Ex 23:31; 34:24.—l Job 24:2; Prov 22:28; 23:10; Hos 5:10.—m Num 35:30; Mt 18:16; 2 Cor 13:1.—n Ex 23:1; Ps 27:12; Prov 6:19.—o Prov 19:5, 9.—p Ex 21:23-25; Lev 24:19-20; Mt 5:38.—q Deut 1:30; Ex 14:14; Pss 44:7; 144:10.—r Jer 31:5; 1 Cor 9:7.—s Jdg 7:3.—t 10-11: Jos 9:23-27; 2 Sam 10:19.—u Num 31:7, 9, 11; Jos 8:2; 22:8.—v Ex 23:31-33; Num 21:2-3; Jos 11:14.

19:21 *A life for a life:* although the law of retribution is extreme, the law was meant to avoid injustice and to ensure a penalty equal to the crime.

20:7 An exemption to serve in the military was allowed for an engaged man so that he would have the time after the marriage to have children and thereby ensure the family inheritance.

God, has commanded you. [18] Otherwise they will teach you to perform the abominations that they practice when they worship their gods, and you would be sinning against the LORD, your God. [w]

Preserving Trees. [19] When you besiege a city and it lasts a long time, and you do battle with it and capture it, do not cut down its trees with an ax, for you can eat their fruit. Do not cut them down! Are trees in the field like people that you would lay siege to them? [20] However, you can cut down those trees that are not fruit trees to use on the siegeworks until the city you are fighting falls. [x]

CHAPTER 21

Sacrifice for Untraceable Killing. [1] * If the body of a dead man is found lying on the ground of the land that the LORD, your God, has given you to possess, and it is not known who killed him, [2] have your elders and judges go out and measure the distance from the body to the neighboring towns. [3] [y] The elders of the town that is nearest to the body are to take a heifer that has never worked nor worn a yoke. [4] The elders of that town will then lead it down to a valley with a flowing stream that has not been plowed nor planted. In that valley they are to slit the heifer's throat. [5] The priests, the sons of Levi, will then come forward, for the LORD, your God, has chosen them to minister to him and to pronounce blessings in the name of the LORD and to decide all disputes and cases of assault. [6] The elders of the town that is nearest to the body will wash their hands * over the heifer whose throat had been slit in the valley, [7] and they will proclaim, "Our hands have not shed this blood, nor have our eyes seen it shed. [8] Accept this atonement for your people Israel, O LORD, whom you have redeemed, and do not hold your people responsible for the shedding of innocent blood." This shall atone for the bloodshed. [z] [9] In this way you will have purged yourself of the guilt of shedding innocent blood, since you will have done what is right in the sight of the LORD.

Marrying a Female Captive. [10] When you go to war against your enemies and the LORD, your God, delivers them into your hands and you take them captive, [a] [11] if you see a beautiful woman among them and you desire her, you can take her as your wife. [12] Bring her into your house, and have her shave her head and trim her nails [b] [13] and have her throw out the clothes she was wearing when she was taken captive. She is to live in your house for a full month and mourn her father and her mother. Then you may go to her and be her husband and she will be your wife. [c] [14] If you are not pleased with her, you are to let her go wherever she wishes. You are not to sell her or treat her like a slave, for you have already humbled her.

Law of the Firstborn.* [15] If a man has two wives, and he loves one and dislikes the other, and they both bear him children, both the one who is loved and the one who is disliked, and the son of the one who is disliked is the firstborn, [16] then when he gives his inheritance to his sons, he is not to give the rights of the firstborn to the son of the woman he loves in preference to the true firstborn, the son of the woman he dislikes. [17] He must acknowledge the son of the woman whom he disliked as the firstborn, giving him a double portion of everything that he owned. That son is the first sign of his strength, and the right of firstborn belongs to him. [d]

Punishing a Rebellious Son. [18] If someone has a stubborn and rebellious son who will not listen to his father or his mother, and will not heed them even when he is disciplined, [e] [19] then his father and mother are to take hold of him and bring him out to the elders at the town gate. [20] They are to say to the town elders, "This son of ours is stubborn and rebellious. He will not listen to us. He is a glutton and a drunkard." [f] [21] Then all the men of that town will stone him to death. You must purge the evil from your midst. All of Israel will hear of it and be filled with fear. [g]

Burying a Criminal.* [22] If a man guilty of a capital offense is put to death and his body is

w Ex 23:33; 34:16.—x Jer 6:6.—y 3-4: Num 19:2-3.—z Num 35:33.—a Jos 21:44; 1 Ki 8:46; 1 Chr 9:1.—b Lev 14:8, 9; Num 6:9; 8:7.—c Ps 45:10.—d Gen 49:3-4; 1 Chr 5:12.—e Ps 78:8; Isa 30:1; Jer 5:23.—f Prov 23:20-21; 28:7; Lk 7:34.—g Deut 13:5, 6, 11; Lev 20:2.

21:1—26:19 The final section of the Deuteronomic law brings together prescriptions that cannot be reduced to any order; they deal with all sorts of matters and have fairly diverse origins. Two more clearly defined groups can, however, be distinguished: laws regarding the family and social norms.

21:6 *Wash their hands:* in cases where the one responsible for taking someone's life cannot be found, the community can offer sacrifice to obtain forgiveness while maintaining their innocence.

21:15-17 While Scripture in no way condones polygamy, recognition of the firstborn's rights of inheritance are here defined when a man has more than one wife and children from them.

21:22-23 This is why the body of Jesus was buried before nightfall (Jn 19:31). See the application of the entire passage to Jesus in Gal 3:13.

hanging from a tree,[h] 23 you are not to leave his body on the tree overnight. Be sure to bury him that day, for anyone who is hung from a tree is under God's curse. You must not desecrate the land that the LORD, your God, is giving you as an inheritance.[i]

CHAPTER 22

Helping Your Neighbor. 1 If you see your neighbor's ox or sheep straying away, do not ignore it, but take it back to your neighbor. 2 If your neighbor does not live nearby or you do not know whose animal it is, take it to your own home and keep it there until your neighbor comes looking for it. Then give it back to him. 3 You are to do the same if you find his donkey or his cloak or anything that your neighbor loses. You are not to ignore it. 4 If you see your neighbor's donkey or ox fall on the road, do not ignore it. Help him to get it up again.[j]

Incidental Rules. 5 A woman is not to wear a man's clothing, nor is a man to wear a woman's clothing. The LORD, your God, detests all who do such things.*

6 [k] If you come across a bird's nest with young ones or eggs along the way, either in a tree or lying on the ground, and the mother bird is sitting upon the young ones or the eggs, do not take the mother with the young. 7 You can take the young ones, but let the mother go, so that things may go well with you and you may live a long life.

8 When you build a new house, place a parapet around your roof so that you do not bring blood guilt upon your house if anyone should fall from it.

9 You should not plant two different types of seed in your vineyard. If you do, the fruit of the seed you planted and the fruit in your vineyard will both be defiled.[l]

10 Do not plow with an ox and a donkey yoked together.

11 Do not wear clothing made of wool and linen woven together.

12 You are to make fringes on the four corners of the garment with which you cover yourself.*[m]

Rules for Sexual Relationships. 13 If a man takes a woman and has sex with her, but then he grows to hate her 14 and he charges her with shameful deeds and publicly defames her name saying, "I married this woman, but when I approached her I discovered that she was not a virgin," 15 have the father and mother of the young woman give proof of the young woman's virginity to the elders at the town gate.*[n] 16 The young woman's father will say to the elders, "I gave my daughter to this man to be his wife, and he has grown to hate her. 17 Now he has slandered her saying, 'I discovered that your daughter was not a virgin.' Here is proof of my daughter's virginity." They will then spread the cloth out before the elders. 18 The elders will take the man and punish him.[o] 19 They will fine him one hundred shekels of silver and give them to the father of the young woman because this man defamed the name of one of the virgins of Israel. She will continue to be his wife, and he cannot divorce her as long as he lives. 20 If, however, the charge is true and there is no proof of the young woman's virginity, 21 she is to be brought to the door of her father's house and there the men of the town will stone her to death. She did a disgraceful thing in Israel, committing fornication in her father's house. You must purge this evil from your midst.*[p]

22 If a man is discovered sleeping with another man's wife, both the man who slept with the woman and the woman must be put to death. You must purge the evil from Israel.[q]

23 If a man encounters a young woman who is betrothed to another man and he sleeps with her, 24 you shall take both of them to the city gate and stone them to death, the young woman because she was inside of the city and did not cry out, and the man because he violated his neighbor's wife. You must purge the evil from among you.

25 But if a man encounters a young woman betrothed to another man in the countryside and he overcomes her and has sex with her, then only the man who has done this is to die. 26 Do nothing to the young woman, for

h Mt 26:66; Mk 14:64; Acts 23:29.—i Jos 8:29; 10:27; Jn 19:31; Gal 3:13.—j Ex 23:4-5; 1 Cor 9:9.—k 6-7: Lev 22:28.—l Lev 19:19.—m Num 15:37-41; Mt 23:5.—n Deut 22:19.—o Deut 1:9-18; Ex 18:21-22.—p Gen 34:7; 2 Sam 13:12.—q Lev 20:10; Ezek 16:38-40; Jn 8:3-5.

22:5 Syrian and Canaanite practices, perhaps connected with sacral prostitution.

22:12 See Num 15:37. The law was still in force in the time of Christ (Mt 9:20).

22:15 The blanket or bedsheet used during the first night of marriage; the parents carefully preserved it.

22:21 An unfaithful fiancée is regarded as an adulteress, because a betrothal had the juridical effects of marriage.

she has not committed a sin deserving
death. This matter is just like when a man
attacks and murders his neighbor, 27 for the
man found the young woman in the coun-
tryside, and though the betrothed might
have screamed out, there was no one there
to rescue her.

28 [r] If a man encounters a young woman
who is a virgin but she is not betrothed, and
he overcomes her and has sex with her and
they are discovered, 29 he must pay the
young woman's father fifty shekels of silver.
He must marry the young woman, for he
has violated her, and he can never divorce
her for as long as he lives.

CHAPTER 23

1 A man shall not marry his father's wife;
he is not to dishonor his father's bed.* [s]

Membership Exclusions. 2 No one who has
been emasculated by crushing or cutting
can enter the assembly of the LORD.* 3 No
one who is illegitimate* can enter the
assembly of the LORD, nor can his descen-
dants to the tenth generation enter the
assembly of the LORD. [t] 4 No Ammonite or
Moabite can enter the assembly of the LORD,
even their descendants to the tenth genera-
tion cannot enter the assembly of the LORD [u]
5 for they did not greet you with bread and
water as you were on your way when you
came forth out of Egypt. They hired Balaam,
the son of Beor who came from Pethor in
Mesopotamia to curse you. 6 However, the
LORD, your God, would not listen to Balaam.
The LORD, your God, turned a curse upon
you into a blessing, for the LORD, your God,
loved you. 7 Do not establish a treaty of
friendship with them as long as you live. [v]

8 Do not detest an Edomite, for he is your
brother. Do not detest an Egyptian, for you
lived as a foreigner in his land. 9 The third
generation of children born to them can
enter the assembly of the LORD.

Camp Sanitation. 10 When you are
encamped against your enemies, stay away
from everything that is impure. 11 [w] If one of
your men among you is unclean because of
a nocturnal emission, let him move outside
of the camp. He is not to enter the camp.
12 When evening arrives, he is to wash him-
self with water, and he can come back inside
of the camp.

13 Designate a place outside of the camp
where you can go to relieve yourself. 14 You
shall have an implement with your equip-
ment so that when you relieve yourself, you
can dig a hole and cover over your excre-
ment.

15 The LORD, your God, walks among you
in your camp to protect you and to deliver
your enemies up to you, so your camp must
be holy, lest he see something unclean
among you and turn away from you.

Incidental Rules. 16 If a slave has taken
refuge from his master with you, you are not
to hand him over to his master. 17 Let him
live with you wherever he chooses, in what-
ever town he chooses. You are not to oppress
him.

18 No Israelite woman is to become a
sacred prostitute, nor is an Israelite man to
be a sacred prostitute. [x] 19 You are not to
bring the wages of a female prostitute or a
male prostitute* into the shrine of the LORD,
your God, to pay for any vow. Both of these
are abominations to the LORD, your God.

20 * [y] Do not charge your brother interest,
whether it be on money or food or anything
else that could earn interest. 21 You can
charge a foreigner interest, but you cannot
charge a brother interest. For this you will be
blessed by the LORD, your God, in everything
that you undertake in the land that you are
entering to possess.

22 If you make a vow to the LORD, your
God, do not be lax in paying it off, for the
LORD, your God, will certainly require it of
you, and you would be guilty of a sin. [z]
23 [a] But if you fail to make a vow, there is no
sin. 24 Whatever your lips utter, you must do,
for you have vowed a freewill offering to the
LORD, your God, with your own mouth.

25 If you enter your neighbor's vineyard,
you can eat as many grapes as you want, but

r 28-29: Ex 22:16-17.—s Lev 18:8; 1 Cor 5:1.—t Zec 9:6.—u Num 22:5, 6.—v Ezr 9:12; Dan 4:27.—w 11-12: Lev 15:16-17.—x 1 Ki 14:24; 2 Ki 23:7; Job 36:14.—y 20-21: Ex 22:25; Lev 25:35-37; Isa 24:20.—z Ps 50:14; Mt 5:33-34.—a 23-24: 1 Sam 1:11; Pss 56:12-13; 66:13-15; Eccl 5:3-5.

23:1 *Dishonor his father's bed:* literally, "lift the hem of his father's blanket." "To stretch the hem (of a blanket)" over a woman meant to marry her; "to lift the hem (of the blanket)" meant to attack the conjugal rights of another over a woman.

23:2 According to some scholars, this mutilation may have indicated that person now belonged to a Canaanite divinity.

23:3 *One who is illegitimate:* a person who had a foreigner for one of his parents.

23:19 *Male prostitute:* probably in a pagan temple.

23:20-21 Charging interest on a loan was regarded as usury down to modern times.

you are not to put any in a basket. 26 If you enter your neighbor's grain fields, you can pluck the kernels with your hands, but you are not to take a sickle to your neighbor's standing grain.[b]

CHAPTER 24

Marriage Laws. 1 *[c] If a man marries a woman, and after they are married she becomes displeasing to him because he has discovered something indecent about her, and he writes a bill of divorce and puts it in her hand, and he sends her forth from his house, 2 then after she has left his house, she can become the wife of another man. 3 If this second husband is displeased with her and writes her a bill of divorce and he puts it in her hand and he sends her forth from his house, or if the second man who took her to be his wife should die, 4 then her first husband who had sent her away cannot take her back to be his wife again, for she has been defiled. This would be an abomination to the LORD. You shall not cause the sin to come upon the land that the LORD, your God, is giving to you as an inheritance.

5 If a man has recently been married, he is not to go off to battle nor have any other duty laid on him. He will be free to stay at home for one year so that he can bring happiness to the wife whom he has married.

Additional Laws. 6 Do not take a lower or upper millstone as a pledge against a debt, for that would mean that you were taking the man's livelihood as a pledge.*

7 If anyone kidnaps one of his fellow Israelites, mistreating him and selling him, then that kidnapper is to be put to death, and you shall purge the evil from your midst.[d]

8 During an outbreak of leprosy, take heed to observe and carefully fulfill all that the priests, the Levites, tell you to do. Observe what they command of you and do it. 9 Remember what the LORD, your God, did to Miriam on the way after you came up out of Egypt.[e]

10 Be willing to lend your brother anything, and do not go to his house to obtain his pledge against the loan. 11 Stand outside his house, and the man to whom you made the loan will bring the pledge out to you. 12 If a man is poor, you are not to keep his pledge overnight. 13 You are to return his pledge to him when the sun goes down so that he can sleep in his own garment and bless you. This is righteous to the LORD, your God.

14 [f] You shall not oppress a hired hand who is poor and needy, whether he be one of your brethren or a foreigner who lives on the land within your town gates. 15 You are to give him his wages on the same day before the sun goes down, for he is poor and he has his heart set on it. Otherwise he might cry out against you to the LORD and it would be your sin.

16 Fathers are not to be put to death in the place of their sons, nor are sons to be put to death in place of their fathers. Each man is to be put to death for his own sin.[g]

17 You are not to pervert justice toward a foreigner or an orphan, nor are you to take a widow's garment as a pledge against a loan.[h] 18 Remember that you were once a slave in Egypt and the LORD, your God, redeemed you from there. This is why I command you to do this.

19 When you reap a harvest in the field and you miss a sheaf of grain, do not turn around to take it. Leave it for the foreigner, the orphan, and the widow. Then you will be blessed by the LORD, your God, in all of your undertakings.[i] 20 [j] When you beat your olive trees, do not go back over the branches a second time. Leave it for the foreigner, the orphan, and the widow. 21 When you harvest grapes in your vineyard, do not go back over it a second time. Leave it for the foreigner, the orphan, and the widow. 22 Remember that you were once a slave in the land of Egypt. This is why I command you to do this.

CHAPTER 25

Restricted Punishment. 1 If there is a dispute between men and they take it to court for the judges to decide, let them proclaim as innocent the righteous and as guilty the wrongdoer.[k] 2 If the guilty man deserves to be beaten, then the judge will have him lay

b Mt 12:1; Mk 2:23; Lk 6:1.—c 1-4: Jer 3:1; Mt 5:31-32; 19:3-9.—d Deut 19:19; Ex 21:16.—e Num 12:10-15.—f 14-15: Lev 19:13; Sir 34:26-27; Jas 5:4; Mt 20:8.—g 2 Ki 14:6; 2 Chr 25:4; Jer 31:29-30.—h Ex 22:22; Job 6:27; Ps 10:18.—i Lev 19:9; Ezek 47:22; Zec 7:10.—j 20-22: Lev 19:10; Ru 2:1-23.—k Ex 22:9; 1 Ki 8:32; Acts 23:3.

24:1-14 Divorce, like polygamy (see Deut 21:15), was customary at that period, and in both cases the law simply reduced the drawbacks, without approving the practices (see Mt 19:7-9).

24:6 Since the millstone was a tool absolutely necessary for ensuring a steady supply of food, it could not be taken away to pay off a debt.

down and beaten in front of him, giving him the number of lashes that his crime deserves. [3] He can be given up to forty lashes, but no more than that, for if he is given more than that, your brother might be shamed in your sight. [l]

[4] Do not muzzle an ox when it is treading out the grain.* [m]

Family Marriage.* [5] If brothers are living together, and one of them dies without having a son, then the widow of the deceased is not to marry outside of the family. Her husband's brother will take her as his wife and thus perform the duty of her husband's brother. [n] [6] The first son will bear the name of the deceased brother, so his name not be extinguished in Israel. [o] [7] However, if the man does not want to marry his brother's wife, let the brother's wife go to the elders of the town at the gate and say, "My husband's brother refuses to ensure the continuance of his brother in Israel. He will not perform the duty expected of a husband's brother." [8] Then the elders of the town will summon him and speak to him. If he continues to say, "I will not marry her," [9] then the brother's widow will come up to him in the presence of the elders, take off one of his shoes from his feet, and spit in his face saying, "This is what a man deserves who will not build a house for his brother." [p] [10] His family will be known as "the family of the unsandaled one" in Israel.

Incidental Rules. [11] If two men are fighting, and the wife of one of them comes forward to try to rescue her husband from the man who is beating him, and she reaches out and grabs him by his private parts, [12] you shall cut off her hand. You are to show her no pity.

[13] [q] You are not to have two different weights in your sack, one heavy and the other one light.

[14] You are not to have two different measures in your house, one large and the other one small.

[15] You must have accurate and honest weights and measures, so that you may live a long time in the land that the LORD, your God, has given you, [16] for anyone who does these things, who deals with others dishonestly, is an abomination to the LORD, your God.

[17] Remember what the Amalekites did to you as you were on your way when you came forth from the land of Egypt.* [18] They met you along the way and waylaid those who were lagging when you were weary and worn out. They had no fear of God. [r] [19] When the LORD, your God, gives you rest from all of the enemies who surround you in the land that the LORD, your God, is giving to you to possess as an inheritance, you shall blot out the memory of the Amalekites from under the heavens. Do not forget! [s]

CHAPTER 26

Thanksgiving for God's Gifts. [1] When you have entered the land that the LORD, your God, is giving to you as an inheritance and you have taken possession of it and are dwelling in it, [2] you shall take the firstfruits of the produce of the earth in the land that the LORD, your God, is giving you, and you shall put them in a basket. You shall then bring them to the place that the LORD, your God, has chosen as a dwelling place for his name. [t] [3] Go to the priest then in office and say, "I declare today to the LORD, your God, that I have come into the land that the LORD promised to our fathers to give us." [4] The priest will then take the basket out of your hand and set it down in front of the altar of the LORD, your God. [5] You shall declare before the LORD, your God, "My father was a wandering Aramean,* and he went down into Egypt with a few people and he dwelt there becoming a great nation, powerful and numerous. [u] [6] [v] The Egyptians mistreated us, afflicted us and forced us to do hard labor. [7] We cried out to the LORD, the God of our fathers, and the LORD heard our voice and took notice of our affliction, labor, and oppression. [8] The LORD brought us forth out of Egypt with a mighty hand and an out-

l Mt 27:26; Jn 19:1; 2 Cor 11:24.—m Prov 12:10; 1 Cor 9:9; 1 Tim 5:18.—n Mt 22:24; Mk 12:19; Lk 20:28.—o Gen 38:9; Ru 4:10.—p Num 12:14; Ru 4:7, 11; Job 30:10.—q 13-16: Lev 19:35-36; Prov 11:1; 20:23; Ezek 45:10; Mic 6:11.—r Ps 36:2; Rom 3:18.—s Ex 17:14; 33:14.—t Ex 22:29; 23:19; Tob 1:6-7.—u Gen 46:5-7, 26-27; Acts 7:14-15.—v 6-7: Ex 1:8-22; 2:23-25; Num 20:15-16.

25:4 Threshing was done in the east with the help of animals. St. Paul applies this precept in 1 Cor 9:9 and 1 Tim 5:18 in explaining why those who live for the altar should live from the altar.

25:5-10 The levirate (from Latin, *levir*, "husband's brother") was a common practice among many Eastern peoples (including the Assyrians and Hittites) and had for its purpose to ensure a posterity and, with this, the stability of inherited property (see the case proposed to Jesus by the Sadducees in Mt 22:23-26).

25:17 Amalek had violated the laws of the desert. He will be punished by Saul (1 Sam 15).

26:5 *A wandering Aramean:* likely a reference to Jacob and to the patriarchs from Aram-naharaim (see Gen 24:10; 25:20; 31:20).

stretched arm, with terrifying and awesome signs and wonders. 9 He brought us to this place and gave us a land, this land that is flowing with milk and honey. [w] 10 Now I have brought the firstfruits of the land that you, O LORD, have given me." Then place it before the LORD, your God, and worship the LORD, your God. 11 You and the Levites and the foreigner who lives with you will rejoice over every good thing that the LORD, your God, has given to you and your household.

12 When you have finished setting aside a tenth of the produce every third year, you are to give it to the Levite, the foreigner, the orphan, and the widow who live in your town so that they might eat it and be satisfied. [x] 13 Then you will declare before the LORD, your God, "I have brought these dedicated things from my house and have given them to the Levite, the foreigner, the orphan, and the widow, just as you commanded me. I have not violated your commandments, nor have I forgotten them. [y] 14 I have not eaten any of it while I was in mourning, nor did I remove any of it while I was unclean. I did not offer any of it to the dead. I have harkened to the voice of the LORD, my God, and have done everything that you have commanded me.* [z] 15 Look down from the heavens, your holy dwelling place, and bless the people of Israel and the land that you have given us as you had promised to our fathers, a land that is flowing with milk and honey." [a]

Covenant with God. 16 The LORD, your God, commands you today to observe these statutes and decrees. Carefully fulfill them with all of your heart and all of your soul. 17 You have solemnly declared today that the LORD is your God and that you will walk in his ways, that you will observe his statutes, commandments, and decrees, and that you will obey him, 18 and the LORD has solemnly promised you today that you will be his chosen people, as he had promised, and that you are to observe all of his commandments. 19 He will raise you up above every other nation in praise, fame, and honor. You will be a holy people* to the LORD, your God, as he has promised. [b]

CHAPTER 27

Altar on Mount Ebal.* 1 * Moses and the elders of Israel said to the people: Observe all of the commandments that I give you today. 2 [c] When you cross over the Jordan into the land that the LORD, your God, has given you, set up some large stones for yourselves and plaster them over. 3 When you cross over to enter the land that the LORD, your God, has promised you, a land flowing with milk and honey, just as the LORD, the God of your fathers, has promised you, write all of these laws on them. 4 When you have crossed over the Jordan, I command you today, you are to set them up on Mount Ebal and plaster them over. 5 [d] Build an altar there to the LORD, your God, an altar of stone. Do not use any iron tool upon them. 6 Build an altar of unhewn stones there to the LORD, your God. You shall offer your burnt offerings to the LORD, your God, there. 7 You are also to offer up peace offerings and eat them there, rejoicing in the presence of the LORD, your God. 8 You will write all of the words of the law upon these stones in a very clear manner.

9 Then Moses and the priests, the Levites, said to all of Israel: Take heed, O Israel, and listen, for today you have become the people of the LORD, your God. 10 Obey the command of the LORD, your God, and observe the commandments and the statutes that I give you today.

11 On the same day Moses said to the people: 12 When you cross over the Jordan, these are the ones who will stand on Mount Gerizim to bless the people: Simeon, Levi, Judah, Issachar, Joseph, and Benjamin. [e] 13 These are the ones who will stand on Mount Ebal to pronounce curses: Reuben, Gad, Asher, Zebulun, Dan, and Naphtali.

The Twelve Curses.* 14 The Levites will proclaim to all of the people of Israel,

15 "Cursed be the person who carves or casts an idol, an abomination to the LORD,

w Ex 3:8.—x Deut 14:28-29; Heb 7:5, 9.—y Ps 119:141, 153.—z Lev 7:20.—a 1 Ki 8:39, 43, 49; Ps 102:19; Isa 63:15.—b Ps 148:14; Isa 62:7; Zep 3:20.—c 2-3: Jos 8:30-32; 1 Sam 7:12.—d 5-7: Ex 20:24-25.—e Gen 35:18; Jos 8:33-35.

26:14 An allusion to the funeral banquets held by pagans in honor of the gods of vegetation.

26:19 *A holy people:* God raised up the children of Israel to a place of respect and the envy of others, set apart in a unique relationship to himself. Members of the Church today are called to glorify God as the ancient Israelites did.

27:1—30:20 In new discourses, usually called the third (27:1—28:68) and fourth (28:69—30:1), Moses dictates the regulations and ceremonies that are to mark the beginning of observance of the law on entrance into Palestine.

27:1-13 The carrying out of these orders is described in Jos 8:30-32.

27:14-26 For the carrying out of these prescriptions see Jos 8:33-35.

the work of human hands, and sets it up in
secret." Then all of the people will proclaim,
"Amen." *[f] 16 "Cursed is the one who dis-
honors father or mother." All of the people
will proclaim, "Amen."

17 "Cursed is the one who moves a neigh-
bor's boundary stone." All of the people will
proclaim, "Amen."

18 "Cursed is the one who leads a blind
person astray on the road." All of the people
will proclaim, "Amen." [g]

19 "Cursed is the one who withholds justice
from the foreigner, the orphan, or the
widow." All of the people will proclaim,
"Amen."

20 "Cursed is the man who sleeps with his
father's wife, dishonoring his father's bed."
All the people will proclaim, "Amen." [h]

21 "Cursed is the one who has sex with an
animal." All the people will proclaim,
"Amen." 22 "Cursed is the man who sleeps
with his sister, either the daughter of his
father or the daughter of his mother." All the
people will proclaim, "Amen." [i]

23 "Cursed is the man who sleeps with his
mother-in-law." All of the people will pro-
claim, "Amen." [j]

24 "Cursed is the one who kills a neighbor
in secret." All of the people will proclaim,
"Amen." [k]

25 "Cursed is the one who accepts a bribe
to kill an innocent person." All the people
will proclaim, "Amen."

26 "Cursed is the one who does not uphold
the words of this law and observe them." All
the people will proclaim, "Amen." [l]

CHAPTER 28

Blessings for Those Who Obey. 1 If you heed
the voice of the LORD, your God, and you
carefully observe all of the commandments
that I have given you today, then the LORD,
your God, will lift you up above all the other
nations upon the earth. 2 All of these bless-
ings shall come upon you and accompany
you if you obey the voice of the LORD, your
God. 3 You shall be blessed in the city, and
you shall be blessed in the countryside.
4 Your offspring shall be blessed, along with
your crops, and the young of your livestock,
the calves of your herds, and the lambs of
your flocks. [m] 5 Your basket and your knead-
ing trough shall be blessed. 6 You shall be
blessed when you enter and when you leave.
7 The LORD will grant that the enemies who
rise up against you will be defeated by you.
They shall come at you from one direction,
but they shall flee away from you in seven
different directions. *[n] 8 The LORD will send a
blessing upon your barns and everything
that you undertake. The LORD, your God, will
bless you in the land that he has given you.

9 The LORD will establish you as his own
holy people, as he solemnly promised you, if
you observe the commandments of the
LORD, your God, and walk in his ways.
10 Then all of the people upon the earth shall
see that you are called by the name of the
LORD, and they shall fear you. [o] 11 The LORD
will grant you great prosperity,* including
your offspring, the young of your livestock,
and the crops that come from the ground, in
the land that the LORD promised your ances-
tors to give to you. 12 The LORD will open up
the storehouse of his bounty in the heavens
for you, giving rain to the land in its proper
season and blessing all of your undertakings.
You shall lend to many nations, but you shall
borrow from none. 13 The LORD will make
you the head, not the tail, on top and not on
the bottom, if you heed the commandments
of the LORD, your God, that I give you today
and you observe them. 14 Do not turn aside
from any of the things that I command you
today, neither to the right nor to the left,
seeking after other gods to serve them.

Curses on Those Who Disobey. 15 If you do
not obey the voice of the LORD, your God,
carefully observing all his commandments
and statutes that I give you today, then all
these curses shall come upon you and over-
whelm you. [p] 16 You shall be cursed in the
city, and you shall be cursed in the country-
side. 17 Your basket and your kneading
trough shall be cursed. 18 Your offspring shall
be cursed, along with your crops, the calves
of your herds, and the lambs of your flocks.

---

f Ex 20:4, 23; Ps 115:4-8; Wis 14:8; 1 Cor 14:16.—g Lev 19:14.—h Gen 49:4; Lev 18:7-8; 20:11.—i Ex 22:18; Lev 18:23; 20:15-16.—j Lev 20:14.—k Deut 5:17; Ex 21:12; Num 35:30-31.—l Ps 119:21; Jer 11:3; Gal 3:10.—m Gen 49:25; Ex 23:26; Ps 107:38; Prov 10:22.—n Lev 26:6-8, 17; 2 Chr 6:34.—o 2 Chr 7:14; Isa 61:9; Acts 15:17.—p Bar 1:20; Dan 9:11; Mal 2:2.

27:15 *Amen:* "so be it!" The Hebrew word passed into Christian use.

28:7 *One direction . . . seven different directions:* the Lord assures the Israelites that even when the enemy pursues them as a united force, they will be overcome and flee in many groups.

28:11 *Grant you great prosperity:* along with the promise of plenty from the Lord, comes the responsibility to share with those who are in need.

19 You shall be cursed when you enter and
when you leave. 20 The LORD will send curs-
es, confusion, and vexation upon you in all of
your undertakings until you are destroyed
and come to sudden ruin on account of the
wickedness of what you have done by forsak-
ing me.

Illness and Deprivation. 21 [q] The LORD will
cover you with diseases until you are wiped
out from the land to which you are going to
possess. 22 The LORD will strike you with
consumption, with fever, with inflamma-
tions, with scorching heat, with drought,
with blight, and mildew. These will plague
you until you perish. 23 The heavens over
your head shall be like bronze, while the
ground under you shall be like iron. 24 The
LORD will turn the rains into dust and pow-
der. It shall pour down upon you from the
heavens until you cease to exist. 25 The LORD
will cause you to be defeated by your ene-
mies. You shall go out toward them in one
direction, but you shall flee away in seven
different directions. You shall be considered
to be a thing of horror to all of the nations
upon the earth. 26 Your bodies shall be food
for the birds of the air and the beasts of the
fields, and there shall be no one to frighten
them away. [r] 27 The LORD will strike you
with the boils of Egypt, and tumors, scab
and itching sores, from which you cannot be
healed. 28 The LORD will strike you with
mental illness, blindness, and dementia.
29 At noon you shall grope around like a
blind man in the darkness. Nothing you do
shall prosper, and you shall be beset by rob-
bers all the time, and there shall be no one
to rescue you. 30 The woman to whom you
are betrothed shall be seized by another
man who shall ravish her. You shall not be
able to live in the house that you have built,
and you shall not taste the fruit of the vine-
yard you have planted. 31 Your ox shall be
slaughtered before your eyes, but you shall
not get to eat any of it. Your donkey shall be
stolen away from you and not returned.
Your sheep shall be given over to your ene-
mies, and there shall be no one to rescue
you. 32 Your sons and your daughters shall
be given to another people, and you shall
wear out your eyes looking for them all day
long, powerless to lift a finger on their
behalf. 33 A people whom you do not know
shall devour all of the produce of the land
and of your work. You shall know nothing
but crushing oppression all of your days. [s]
34 What your eyes behold shall drive you
insane. 35 The LORD will strike you with
painful boils that cannot be healed on your
knees and your legs, spreading from the
soles of your feet to the top of your head.

A Place of Exile. 36 The LORD will bring you
and the king you have placed over your-
selves to a nation unknown to you or your
fathers. There you shall serve other gods,
gods made from wood and stone. 37 You
shall become an object of horror and a
byword among all the nations to which the
LORD will bring you.

Fruitless Labor. 38 You shall sow much seed
in your fields, but you shall harvest little, for
the locusts shall devour it. 39 You shall plant
and care for vineyards, but you shall not
drink its wine or gather its grapes, for the
worms will eat it. 40 You shall have olive
trees throughout your land, but you shall
not have olive oil, for the olives will drop off.
41 You shall have sons and daughters, but
you shall not enjoy them, for they shall go
off into captivity. 42 Locusts shall consume
your trees and the produce of your land.
43 The foreigner who is living with you shall
rise higher and higher, but you shall sink
lower and lower. 44 He shall lend to you, but
you shall not lend to him. He shall be the
head, and you shall be the tail.

45 All of these curses shall come upon you.
They shall pursue and overtake you until
you have been destroyed, for you did not
obey the voice of the LORD, your God, and
observe the commandments and statutes
that he gave you. 46 This shall be a sign and a
wonder to you and your descendants forev-
er,* 47 for you shall not have served the
LORD, your God, joyfully and gladly in a time
of prosperity. 48 Therefore, you shall serve
the enemies that the LORD sends against you
in hunger and thirst, in nakedness and dire
poverty. He will place an iron yoke upon
your neck until he has destroyed you. [t]

Invasion and Destruction. 49 The LORD will
bring a nation against you from far away,
from the ends of the earth. A nation whose
language you do not understand shall swoop
down like an eagle, 50 a fierce nation without
respect for the old or pity for the young.

q 21-22: Lev 26:25; Jer 24:10; Am 4:9-10.—r Ps 79:2; Isa 18:6; Jer 7:33; 34:20.—s Jer 5:15-17; Ezek 24:4ff.—t Jer 28:13-14; Lam 1:14; 4:4.

28:46 The punishment will be a warning to future generations.

51 They shall devour the young of your cattle and the produce of your land until you have been destroyed. They will leave you no grain, wine, oil, or calves in your herds, or lambs in your flocks, until you have been annihilated. 52 They shall lay siege to all of your towns until all of the high fortified walls in which you place your trust have fallen down. He will besiege you in your towns all throughout your land, all throughout your land that the LORD, your God, has given you. 53 [u] Because of the hunger and the suffering that your enemies bring upon you during the siege, you shall eat your own children, your sons and your daughters, whom the LORD, your God, has given you. 54 Even the most gentle and most sensitive among you shall treat his brother or the wife whom he loves or his surviving children poorly. 55 He shall not give any of them the flesh of the children that he is eating. He shall have nothing left because of the siege and the suffering the enemy has inflicted upon you in all of your cities. 56 The most gentle and sensitive woman among you, so gentle and sensitive that she would not step upon the ground with the soles of her feet, shall be hostile to the husband whom she loves and her own son and daughter. 57 She shall eat the afterbirth from her womb and the children she bears secretly because of hunger during the siege and the distress that your enemy shall inflict upon you in your cities.

Plagues. 58 If you do not carefully observe the words of the law that are written in this book, and do not revere this glorious and awesome name, the LORD, your God, 59 then the LORD will send these fearful plagues upon you and your descendants, harsh and prolonged disasters, wretched and lingering illnesses. 60 He will bring upon you all the illness that Egypt dreaded, and they will persist among you. 61 The LORD will also bring upon you every type of illness and disaster that is not recorded in this book until you shall have been annihilated. 62 You who were once as numerous as the stars in the heavens shall only be left with a few survivors, because you did not obey the voice of the LORD, your God. [v]

Punishment and Exile. 63 Just as it pleased the LORD to make you prosper and to multiply your numbers, so it will please him to ruin and destroy you. You shall be uprooted from the land that you are entering to possess. 64 The LORD will scatter you among every people, from one end of the earth to the other. There you shall worship other gods whom neither you nor your fathers knew, gods made of wood and stone. 65 Among these nations you shall find no rest, no repose for the soles of your feet. There the LORD will give you an anxious heart, weary eyes, and a spirit of despair. [w] 66 You shall live with constant doubt, filled with dread day and night, never sure of your life. 67 In the morning you shall say, "I wish it were evening." In the evening you shall say, "I wish it were morning." This will be because of the terrors in your heart and dread at what your eyes will have seen. 68 The LORD will send you back to Egypt on ships, making a journey that I said you would never make again. You shall offer yourselves for sale there to your enemies as male and female slaves, but no one shall buy you.

69 These are the terms of the covenant that the LORD commanded Moses to make with the Israelites in the land of Moab, in addition to the covenant he made with them at Horeb.

III: MOSES' THIRD ADDRESS

CHAPTER 29

Recalling Past Blessings. 1 Moses summoned all of the Israelites and said to them, You have seen with your own eyes all that the LORD did for you in Egypt, to Pharaoh and to his officials and to the entire land. 2 With your own eyes you have seen those great trials, the miraculous signs, and great wonders, 3 * but until now the LORD has not yet given you a heart that understands or eyes that see or ears that hear. [x] 4 During the forty years that I led you in the desert, your clothes did nor tatter, nor did the sandals on your feet wear out. 5 You ate no bread and drank no wine or strong drink. I did this so that you might know that I am the LORD, your God. 6 When you reached this place, Sihon, the king of Heshbon, and Og, the king of Bashan, came out to fight against us, but we defeated them. 7 We took their land and gave it as an inheritance to the tribe of

u 53-57: Lev 26:29; 2 Ki 6:28-29; Lam 2:20.—v Deut 1:10; 10:22; Jer 42:2.—w Lev 26:16, 36; Job 11:20; Lam 1:3; Hos 9:17.—x Isa 6:10; Acts 28:26, 27; Eph 4:18.

29:3-4 Even the most overwhelming occurrences are not enough to rouse belief unless God gives the grace to believe.

Reuben, the tribe of Gad, and half of the tribe of Manasseh.[y]

Exhortation To Be Faithful. 8 Therefore, carefully heed the words of this covenant and observe them, so that you might prosper in all that you do. 9 Today all of you are standing before the LORD, your God: the leaders of your tribes and your elders, your chief men and all of the men of Israel 10 together with your little ones, your wives, as well as the foreigners who live in your camp and who cut your firewood and draw your water.[z] 11 You are entering into a covenant with the LORD, your God, and into his oath that the LORD, your God, is making with you today. 12 Today he is making you his people so that he might be your God, as he promised you and swore under oath with your fathers Abraham, Isaac, and Jacob. 13 I am not making this covenant, this oath, only with you 14 who are standing here with us before the LORD, your God, but also with those who are not here today. 15 You know how we lived in the land of Egypt and how we passed through various nations on the way here. 16 You saw their abominations in their midst, idols of wood and stone, silver and gold. 17 Make sure that there is no man, nor woman, nor clan, nor tribe whose heart turns away from the LORD, our God, today to go and serve the gods of these nations; make sure there is no root among you that bears bitterness or wormwood. 18 Let no one who hears this curse bless himself in his heart saying, "I have peace in my heart because of the cleverness of my thoughts," as though he could sweep away both watered and dry soil.* [a] 19 The LORD will not forgive, for his wrath and his zeal will burn out against that man. All the curses that are written in this book will descend upon him, and the LORD will blot his name from under the heavens.[b] 20 The LORD will single him out from all the tribes of Israel for disaster, all of the curses of the covenant that are written in this book of the law.

Punishment for Unfaithfulness. 21 Your descendants in later generations and foreigners from distant lands will see all of the carnage that has come upon the land and the diseases with which the LORD has afflicted it. 22 [c] The whole land will be a burning waste of brimstone and salt. Nothing will be planted there, nothing will sprout up, no vegetation will grow there. It will be like the destruction of Sodom, Gomorrah, Admah, and Zeboim which the LORD destroyed in his anger and his wrath.

23 All the nations will ask, "Why has the LORD done these things to this land? Why this furious, terrible anger?" 24 The answer will be, "Because they have forsaken their covenant with the LORD, the God of their fathers, that he made with them when he brought them up out of the land of Egypt. 25 They went off and served other gods, worshiping gods that they did not know, gods that he had not given to them.[d] 26 Therefore, the LORD's anger raged against this land, bringing down upon it all the curses that are written in this book. 27 In anger and wrath the LORD uprooted them out of the land; with great indignation he cast them out into another land where they still are today."[e] 28 To the LORD, our God, belongs the mystery,* but these things have been revealed to us and to our children so that we may observe all of the words of this law.[f]

CHAPTER 30

God's Forgiveness and Blessing. 1 When all of these blessings and curses come upon you that I have set before you and you call them to mind wherever you are dispersed among all of the nations, 2 and you and your children return to the LORD, your God, and you obey his voice in all that I command you today with all your heart and all your soul, 3 then the LORD, your God, will have compassion on you in your captivity, and he will bring you back, gathering you from all the nations where the LORD, your God, has scattered you.[g] 4 The LORD, your God, will gather and fetch you back, even if your exiles are in the outermost parts of the heavens.[h] 5 The LORD, your God, will bring you into the land that your ancestors possessed so that you might possess it, and he will make you more prosperous and numerous than your ancestors. 6 The LORD, your God, will circumcise

---

y Num 32:32-33; Ps 135:12.—z Jos 9:21, 23, 27.—a Pss 36:2; 49:18; Heb 12:15.—b Ex 32:33; Pss 74:1; 79:5; Rev 3:5.—c 22-24: Gen 19:24; 1 Ki 9:8-9; Jer 22:8-9.—d Deut 4:19; 2 Ki 17:23; 2 Chr 36:21.—e 1 Ki 14:15; 2 Chr 7:20; Prov 2:22; Jer 12:14.—f Jn 5:39; Acts 1:7; 17:11; 2 Tim 3:16.—g Jer 24:6-7; 29:14; Ezek 16:53; 39:25.—h Neh 1:9; Isa 43:5-7; Jer 31:8, 10.

29:18 *Sweep away both watered and dry soil:* this expression used natural events to describe the results of God's wrath indicating that those who turned away from the Lord would bring hardship on the good soil (watered) and bad (dry) alike.

29:28 *Mystery:* refers to what we cannot know and need not know. Our job is to listen to God and keep his law.

your heart and the hearts of your offspring
so that you might love the LORD, your God,
with all your heart and all your soul, and
that you might live. [7] The LORD, your God,
will cause all of these curses to come upon
your enemies and those who hated and per-
secuted you. [i] [8] You shall once again obey the
voice of the LORD and observe all of his com-
mandments that I have given you today.
[9] The LORD, your God, will make you boun-
tiful in all of your undertakings, your off-
spring, your livestock, and the produce from
your land; the LORD will take as much
delight in bringing you prosperity as the
LORD delighted in your fathers [j] [10] if you obey
the voice of the LORD and observe his com-
mandments and his statutes that are written
in this book of the law, if you turn to the
LORD, your God, with your whole heart and
your whole soul.

[11] * This commandment that I give you
today is not too difficult for you, nor is it too
distant from you. [12] It is not in the heavens
that you should say, "Who will go up into the
heavens to bring it down to us so that we
might hear it and observe it?" [k] [13] Nor is it
beyond the sea that you should say, "Who
will cross over the sea to bring it to us so that
we might hear it and observe it?" [l] [14] No, the
word is very near to you, it is in your heart
and in your mouth, so that you might do it.

Israel's Choice. [15] See, I have set before you
today life and good, and death and evil. [m] [16] If
you obey the command that I give you today,
to love the LORD, your God, and to walk in
his ways, and to observe his command-
ments, statutes, and decrees, then you will
live and multiply, and the LORD, your God,
will bless you in the land that you are enter-
ing to possess. [n]

[17] But if your hearts turn away so that you
will not listen, and you are drawn away to
worship other gods and to serve them,
[18] then, as I swear to you today, you will sure-
ly perish. You will not live a long time in the
land that you are crossing over the Jordan to
enter and to possess.

[19] I call upon the heavens and the earth to
witness today that I have set before you life
and death, blessings and curses. Choose life,
so that you and your descendants might live
[20] loving the LORD, your God, obeying his
voice, and holding on to him, for he is life
and length of days to you, and so that you
might dwell in the land that the LORD
promised to give to your fathers, to Abra-
ham, Isaac, and Jacob. [o]

CHAPTER 31

The Appointment of Joshua. [1] Moses contin-
ued to speak these words to all of Israel,
[2] and he said to them: I am one hundred and
twenty years old today. I am no longer able
to go about freely. * The LORD has told me,
"You will not go over this Jordan." [p] [3] The
LORD, your God, himself will go over before
you. He will destroy all of these nations
before you so that you might dispossess
them. Joshua will lead you over, as the LORD
has decreed. [4] The LORD will do to them
what he did to Sihon and Og, the kings of
the Amorites, and to their land, when he
destroyed them. [q] [5] The LORD will deliver
them up to you so that you can do to them
everything that I ordered you to do. [6] Be
strong and courageous. Do not be afraid or
terrified of them, for the LORD, your God, is
going forth with you. He will never leave you
or abandon you. [r]

[7] Then Moses summoned Joshua and
said to him before all of the Israelites, "Be
strong and courageous, for you must go
with this people into the land that the
LORD, their God, promised their fathers to
give to them. You will give it to them as an
inheritance. [8] Do not be afraid or dismayed,
the LORD will go before you; he will not fail
or forsake you."

The Reading of the Law. [9] Then Moses
wrote down this law and he handed it over
to the priests, the Levites, who carried the
Ark of the Covenant of the LORD, and to all
of the elders of Israel. [10] Moses commanded
them, saying, "At the end of every seven
years, the feast of canceling debts, the Feast
of Booths, [11] when all of Israel comes before
the LORD in the place that he has chosen,
you are to proclaim it in the hearing of all of
Israel. [s] [12] Gather together the people, the
men, the women, the children, and the for-

---

i Deut 7:15; Gen 12:3.—j Deut 28:4, 11; 30:2; Jer 1:10; 32:41.—k Prov 30:4; Rom 10:6-8.—l Job 28:14; Rom 10:7.—m Prov 10:16; 11:19; 12:29; Job 36:11; Jer 21:8.—n Deut 4:1; Neh 9:29.—o Ps 37:3; Jn 5:26; 11:25; Acts 17:28.—p Ex 7:7; Num 20:12; 27:18-19.—q Num 21:21-35.—r Jos 10:25; Ps 94:14; Mt 28:20; Heb 13:5.—s Jos 8:34-35; 2 Ki 23:2.

30:11-14 The word of God is accessible to all people forever in Scripture, so that all might accept it with an open and willing heart.

31:2 *Go about freely:* despite his advanced years, Moses was not physically or mentally disabled (Deut 34:7). His movement was restricted by God who denied Moses' crossing over into Canaan.

eigner who lives in your towns, so that they
might hear it and learn to fear the LORD,
your God, so they might carefully observe
the words of this law. 13 Their children, who
do not yet know it, must hear it and learn
to fear the LORD, your God, the whole time
that you are living in the land that you are
crossing over the Jordan to enter and pos-
sess."

Commissioning Joshua. 14 [t] The LORD said
to Moses, "Behold, the day is approaching
when you will die. Summon Joshua and
present yourselves before the tent of meet-
ing so that I can commission him." * Moses
and Joshua went and presented them-
selves at the tent of meeting. 15 The LORD
appeared at the tent in a pillar of cloud,
and the pillar of cloud stood over the
entrance to the tent.

Predicting Israel's Rebellion. 16 The LORD
said to Moses, "You will soon sleep with your
fathers, but this people will rise up and pros-
titute themselves with foreign gods from the
land that they are entering. They will forsake
and break the covenant that I have made
with them. [u] 17 On the day that I become
angry with them and forsake them, I will
hide my face from them, and they will be
consumed. Many disasters and difficulties
will fall upon them. On that day they will say,
'Have these disasters happened to us
because our God is not with us?' [v] 18 I will
certainly hide my face that day on account
of all their wickedness in turning to other
gods. 19 Now write this song and teach it to
the Israelites. Put it in their mouths, so that
this song can be a witness for me against the
Israelites. 20 When I brought them into the
land flowing with milk and honey, the land
that I promised to their fathers, and when
they ate their fill and flourished, they will
turn to other gods and serve them, rejecting
me and breaking my covenant. [w] 21 When
many disasters and difficulties come upon
them, this song will testify against them,
because it will not be forgotten by their
descendants. I know their inclinations even
before I bring them into the land that I
promised them by oath." [x]

22 So Moses wrote down this song that day,
and he taught it to the Israelites. 23 The LORD
commissioned Joshua, the son of Nun, say-
ing to him, "Be strong and courageous for
you will lead the Israelites into the land that
I promised them, and I will be with you."

24 * When Moses had entirely finished
writing the words of this law in a book, [y]
25 Moses gave a command to the Levites who
carry the Ark of the Covenant of the LORD,
26 "Take this book of the law and put it beside
the Ark of the Covenant of the LORD, your
God, so that it can bear witness against you
27 for I know how rebellious and stiff-necked
you are. If you rebel against the LORD while
I am still alive and with you, how much
more so will you be after my death. 28 Gather
all the elders of your tribes and your officials
before me so that I can proclaim these
words in their hearing and call upon the
heavens and the earth to give witness
against them. [z] 29 I know that after my death
you will be totally perverse. You will turn
away from the way that I have commanded
of you. In days to come disasters will shower
down upon you because you will have done
what is evil in the sight of the LORD, provok-
ing him to anger through the works of your
hands."

30 Moses then recited in the hearing of the
Israelites the words of this entire song.

CHAPTER 32

1 * Give ear, O heavens, while I speak;
Listen, O earth, to the words of my
mouth.
2 Let my teaching fall down like rain,
and my words descend like the dew.
Like rain upon the sprouts,
and like showers upon the grass.
3 I will proclaim the name of the LORD,
Oh, praise the greatness of our God.
4 He is a rock, his deeds are perfect,
and all of his ways are just.
He is a God of truth who does no wrong;
he is just and upright. [a]
5 They have corrupted themselves,
on account of their defect they are no
longer his children,

t 14-15: Ex 33:9-11; Num 27:13.—u Ex 34:15; Jdg 2:11; 10:6, 13.—v Jdg 2:14; Ps 104:29, 40; Mic 3:4.—w Ps 16:4; Jer 13:25; Dan 3:28.—x 1 Chr 28:9; Hos 5:3.—y Deut 17:18; 2 Ki 22:8.—z Job 20:27; Isa 26:21.—a Ps 92:15; Isa 17:10; Hab 1:12; Rev 15:3.

31:14 This verse is to be connected with verse 23 (see Jos 1:1-9).

31:24-26 Upon completing the writing of the law, Moses instructed the priests to place it beside the Ark of the Covenant, designating its sacredness.

32:1-43 In order to make clear the sins that imperil the covenant, this song puts Israel through the mill in proper order. It is a hymn to the greatness of God, who is the strength of his people. It repeats the solemn admonitions of Moses and his successors.

they are a perverse and crooked generation.
6 Is this the way to repay the LORD,
O foolish and stupid people?
Is he not your father, who created you?
Has he not made you and established you?
7 Remember the days of old,
consider the years of past generations,
Ask your fathers, they will tell you,
your elders, they will inform you.
8 When the Most High divided the inheritance among the nations,
when he separated the sons of men,
he established the boundaries of the nations
according to the number of the sons of God. [b]
9 The LORD's own portion was his people,
Jacob his allotted inheritance.
10 He found him in a desert land,
a waste and howling wilderness.
He shielded him, he instructed him;
He guarded him as the apple of his eye.
11 Like an eagle that awakens its nest,
and hovers over its young,
he spread his wings and snatched him,
bearing him up on his pinions.
12 The LORD alone led him,
there was no foreign god with him. [c]
13 He made him ride on the heights of the earth,
he ate from the produce of the fields;
he had him suck honey from the rock,
and oil from the flinty rock,
14 curds from the herds and milk from the flocks,
fat lambs and rams,
herds of bulls of Bashan and goats,
the finest of the wheat,
from the blood of the grapes you drank wine.
15 But Jeshurun* grew fat and desirous,
sated with food; he became heavy and obese.
He abandoned God who had made him,
and rejected the rock of his salvation. [d]
16 They provoked him with foreign gods,
and angered him with abominations.
17 They sacrificed to demons that are not really gods,
to foreign gods that they had not known,
newly invented gods,
gods whom your fathers did not fear.
18 You deserted the rock who formed you;
you forgot God, who fathered you.
19 When the LORD saw it, he despised them;
his sons and his daughters frustrated him.
20 He said, "I will hide my face from them
and watch to see how they end,
for they are a perverse generation,
children who are unfaithful.
21 They have made me jealous by what is not a god,
angered me with their worthless things;
I will make them jealous of those who are not a people,
I will anger them with a foolish nation.
22 My anger has kindled fire to flame,
it burns down to the lowest level of Sheol,*
it devours the earth and its produce,
it ignites the foundation of the mountains. [e]
23 I will pile disasters upon them,
and use up my arrows against them.
24 I will send a wasting famine against them,
consuming pestilence and bitter destruction;
I will send the fangs of wild beasts
and the venom of the serpents that crawl in the dust.
25 Outside the sword will leave them childless,
inside there will be only terror.
Upon the young man and the virgin,
the infant and the old gray-haired man.
26 I said, 'I will scatter them
and wipe out remembrance of them from among humans,'
27 except that I dreaded the taunt of the enemy,
lest the foe misunderstand and say,
'Our hand has triumphed;
the LORD has not done this!' " [f]
28 They are a nation without sense,
there is no understanding in them.
29 If only they were wise and would understand this,
and consider how they will end.

b Ps 74:17; Acts 17:26.—**c** Ex 15:13; Isa 43:12.—**d** Isa 44:2; Jer 5:28; Ezek 14:5.—**e** Ps 18:7-8; Jer 15:14; Lam 4:11.—**f** Ps 74:18; Isa 10:13.

32:15 *Jeshurun*: i.e., Israel.

32:22 *Burns . . . to the lowest level of Sheol:* Sheol is the abode of all the dead and known in the New Testament as Hades where only the wicked dead repose.

30 How could one man put a thousand to flight,
or two drive away ten thousand,
unless the rock had delivered them,
and the LORD given them up?
31 For their rock is not like our rock,
even our enemies would judge it so.
32 Their vine comes from the vine stock of Sodom,*
and from the fields of Gomorrah.
Their grapes are filled with poison,
their clusters with bitterness.
33 Their wine is the venom of serpents,
the cruel venom of cobras.
34 Is this not stored away with me,
sealed up in my treasury? [g]
35 Vengeance is mine, and recompense.
Their foot will slip in due time,
for the day of destruction is at hand,
and their doom hastens upon them.
36 The LORD will judge his people,
he will have compassion on his servants
when he sees that their power is spent
and there are none who remain, slave or free.
37 He will say, "Where are their gods,
the rock in whom they trusted?
38 Who ate the fat of their offerings,
and drank their wine libations?
Let them arise and help you
and be your protection.
39 See now that I, I am he,
there is no other god besides me.
It is I who put to death and give life,
it is I who wound and heal.
No one can deliver you from out of my hand. [h]
40 I lift my hand up to the heavens,
and I swear, as I live forever,
41 I will sharpen my glistening sword;
my hand will seize onto justice.
I will render vengeance on my enemies;
I will repay those who hate me.
42 I will make my arrows drunk with blood,
and my sword will devour flesh,
the blood of the slain and the captives,
the heads of the enemy leaders."
43 Rejoice, O nations, with his people,
bow to him, all you gods
for he will avenge the blood of his servants
and take vengeance upon his foes,
but he will be merciful to his land and his people. [i]

44 Then Moses came and proclaimed all of
the words of this song in the hearing of the
people, he and Joshua, the son of Nun.

Moses' Last Appeal. 45 * When Moses fin-
ished saying all these things to all of the
Israelites, 46 he said to them, "Take to heart
all of the words that I bear witness to in your
midst today and that I command your chil-
dren to obey, observing all of the words of
this law. 47 This is not a light matter for you;
it is your very life. This will prolong your
days in the land that you are crossing over
the Jordan to possess."

Moses Dies on Mount Nebo. 48 That same
day the LORD said to Moses, 49 "Climb up
Mount Abarim, Mount Nebo, that is in the
land of Moab opposite Jericho, and look out
over the land that I am giving to the Israelites
as a possession. [j] 50 Then you will die on the
mountain that you have ascended, and you
will be gathered home to your people, just as
your brother Aaron died on Mount Hor and
was gathered home to his people [k] 51 because
you broke faith with me before the Israelites
at the waters of Meribath-kadesh in the
Desert of Zin; you did not uphold my holiness
in the midst of the Israelites. [l] 52 Therefore,
you shall only behold the land from a dis-
tance, you shall not enter into the land that I
am giving to the Israelites."

CHAPTER 33

Moses Blesses the Tribes. 1 This is the bless-
ing that Moses, the man of God, gave to the
Israelites before his death. [m] 2 * He said:

The LORD came from Sinai
and rose up over them from Seir;
he shone forth from Mount Paran.
He came for them with thousands upon thousands of his holy ones

g Job 14:17; Jer 2:22; Hos 13:12.—h Job 5:18; Ps 50:22; Isa 41:4; 43:10; Hos 6:1-2.—i Ps 85:1; Rom 15:10; Rev 6:10; 19:2.—j Lev 14:34; Num 27:12-14.—k Gen 25:8; Num 33:38-39.—l Ex 17:1-7; Num 20:1-13; 27:14; Ps 106:32-33; Ezek 47:19.—m Jos 14:6; 1 Sam 2:27; Ps 90:1.

32:32 *The vine stock of Sodom:* Israel's enemies had come from sinful ancestors and their actions were evil (i.e., "filled with poison").

32:45-52 After a final appeal for fidelity, Moses hears repeated the prohibition against his entering the Promised Land (3:26-28). We do not know for sure what the fault of Moses and Aaron was; perhaps it was that they seemed to attribute a miracle to themselves (Num 20:12).

33:2-5, 26-29 This ancient war hymn, dating from the time of the conquest, exalts the Lord who has accompanied his people from Sinai to the Jordan; like all texts inspired by the idea of the holy war (Deut 7:17-26; 9:1-13), this one urges trust in the power of the Lord.

with a flaming fire blazing in his right hand for them.
3 Truly, he loves the people;
all of his holy ones are in his hands.
They followed in your steps
and received your words.
4 Moses commanded a law,
an inheritance for the assembly of Jacob. [n]
5 He was king in Jeshurun*
when he gathered the heads of the people,
brought together the tribes of Israel.
6 Let Reuben* live, and not die;
let his men be not a few.

7 This is the blessing for Judah, he said:

Hear, O LORD, the call of Judah,
and bring him onto his people;
let his hands be enough for him,
and be a help against his enemies.

8 Concerning Levi, he said:

Let your Thummim* and your Urim
be with your holy one
whom you tested at Massah,
and with whom you contended at the waters of Meribah, [o]
9 who said of his father and his mother,
"I have not seen them,"
nor does he acknowledge his brother
or even know his own children.
They guarded the words of your covenant and observed it.
10 [p] He teaches your decrees to Jacob
and your law to Israel.
He offers incense before your altar
and whole burnt offerings on it.
11 Bless his skills in his undertakings, O LORD.
Strike those who rise up against him,
so they might never rise up again.

12 Concerning Benjamin, he said:

O beloved of the LORD,
may he dwell in safety beside him;
may he shelter him the entire day long,
and may he dwell between his shoulders.*

13 Concerning Joseph, he said:

His land is blessed by the LORD
with choice things from the heavens,
and with what lies deep below,
14 with the precious fruits of the sun,
the rich produce of the moon,
15 with the finest produce of the ancient mountains,
and the abundance of the everlasting hills,
16 with the most precious gifts of the earth and its fullness,
with his pleasures that are found in the bushes.
May these blessings come upon the head of Joseph,
upon the crown of the head of the one who was different from his brothers.
17 As with the firstborn of his ox, majesty is his;
and his horns are like the horns of the wild ox;
with them he will push the peoples together to the ends of the earth.
They are the thousands upon thousands of Ephraim,
and the thousands of Manasseh. [q]

18 Concerning Zebulun, he said:

Rejoice Zebulun, who lives outdoors,
and Issachar, who dwells in your tents.
19 You will summon the people to the mountain;
there they will offer righteous sacrifices.
They will feast on the abundance of the seas,
on the treasures hidden in the sands. [r]

20 Concerning Gad, he said:

Blessed be he who expands Gad's territory.
He lives like a lion, tearing at an arm or a head.
21 He chose the best portion for himself;
the ruler's part was reserved for him.
He practiced the righteousness of the LORD,
and his judgments concerning Israel.

22 Concerning Dan, he said:

Dan is a lion's cub springing forth from Bashan.

23 Concerning Naphtali, he said:

---

n Ps 119:111; Jn 1:17; 7:19.—o Ex 28:30; Lev 8:8; 1 Sam 14:41-42.—p 10-11: Ex 30:7; 2 Sam 24:23; 2 Ki 17:27-28; Mal 2:4-9.—q Num 23:22; Ps 44:5.—r Ps 4:5; Isa 2:3.

33:5 *Jeshurun:* a term of endearment for Israel.

33:6 *Reuben* was soon absorbed by Gad.

33:8 *Thummim...Urim:* dice used for casting lots on the ephod of the high priest (Ex 28:30). The Levites had shown themselves outstanding in fidelity to God (Ex 32:26-29).

33:12 The Ark had often stayed with the tribe of Benjamin.

Naphtali abounds with favor;
he is filled with the blessing of the LORD.
He will take his inheritance in the south, toward the sea.*

24 Concerning Asher, he said:

Most blessed of sons is Asher,
may he be favored by his brothers,
may he bathe his feet in oil.[s]
25 Your bolts will be iron and bronze,
your strength last as long as your days.
26 There is none like the God of Jeshurun,
who rides in the heavens to help you,
and on the clouds in majesty.[t]
27 The eternal God is a refuge,
below are everlasting arms.*
He will drive out your enemy from before you,
and proclaim, "Destroy him!"[u]
28 Israel dwells in safety,
and the spring of Jacob in security,
in a land of grain and wine,
where the heavens drop down dew.
29 Blessed are you, O Israel,
for who can be compared with you,
a people saved by the LORD,
who is the shield of your assistance
and the sword of your majesty.
Your enemies will cringe before you,
and you will walk upon their heights.[v]

IV: THE DEATH OF MOSES

CHAPTER 34*

1 Moses climbed up from the plains of
Moab to Mount Nebo,* the peak of Pisgah,
that is opposite Jericho. The LORD showed
him the entire land, from Gilead to Dan,
2 as
well as all of Naphtali, the land of Ephraim
and Manasseh, and all of the land of Judah
up to the western sea,[w]
3 the Negeb, the district of the Valley of Jericho, the city of
palms, up to Zoar.[x]
4 Then the LORD said to
him, "This is the land that I promised to
Abraham, Isaac, and Jacob when I said, 'I
will give it to your descendants.' I have let
you see it with your own eyes, but you are
not going to cross over into it."

5 Moses, the servant of the LORD, died in
the land of Moab, as the LORD had foretold.[y]
6 He buried him* in the land of Moab,
in the valley opposite Beth-peor, but up to
the present no one knows where his grave
is.[z]
7 Moses was one hundred and twenty
years old when he died. His eyesight was not
weak, nor was his strength diminished.

8 The Israelites grieved for Moses on the
plains of Moab for thirty days, until the prescribed period of weeping and mourning for
Moses was over.

9 Now Joshua, the son of Nun, was filled
with a spirit of wisdom, for Moses had laid
his hands upon him. The Israelites obeyed
him and did what the LORD had commanded Moses.[a]

10 Never again has a prophet arisen in
Israel like Moses who knew the LORD face to
face,[b]
11 [c] who performed such miraculous
signs and wonders that the LORD had sent
him to do in the land of Egypt, to Pharaoh
and to his officials and to his entire land.
12 No one has had his mighty power or performed the great and terrible deeds that he
did in the sight of all of Israel.

---

s Gen 49:20; Job 29:6.—t Ex 15:7-11; Pss 18:10; 68:33; 104:3.—u Jos 24:8; Ps 90:1; Isa 40:28.—v Deut 4:7; 2 Sam 22:3, 45; Pss 1:1; 66:3.—w Ex 23:31.—x Gen 12:9; Jdg 1:16; 2 Chr 28:15.—y Num 12:7; Jos 1:1-2; Mal 4:4.—z Deut 3:29; Jude 9.—a Num 27:18-23; Isa 11:2; Acts 6:6.—b Ex 33:11; Num 12:6-8; Acts 3:22-23.—c 11-12: Ex 4:21; 7:1, 8-12; Heb 3:1-6.

33:23 *Toward the sea:* most likely it is the Lake of Gennesaret; *south* refers to southern Galilee.

33:27 *Everlasting arms:* words of comfort and protection for the Israelites as they settle in Canaan.

34:1-12 The story is told with restraint, for the Bible rejects any cult of personality. No one will know where Moses is buried; his tomb, unlike that of the patriarchs, will remain unknown. A life of unparalleled intimacy with God was Moses' personal privilege (see Ex 33:11; Num 12:7-8).

34:1 *Nebo* is 2,700 feet high, *Pisgah* 3,067 feet; they are 2 miles distant from each other.

34:6 *He buried him:* we are not told precisely where. Apparently the burial of Moses was not a communal event, but personally taken care of by God.

THE HISTORICAL BOOKS

These Books tell the story of Israel's entrance into the land promised it by God and of its life there. In other words, it is the story of the great gift which the Lord gave to the children of Abraham and which they lost by their failure to respond to God's love for them. The dramatic events follow swiftly on one another over the course of a little more than six centuries; the story was handed on by witnesses who played a direct part in it or who were able to assess, in the light of later developments, events whose consequence they were still experiencing. The final editors, who did their work after the Exile (see the General Introduction), belonged in all likelihood to the Deuteronomistic school, as judged by the comments and reflections scattered throughout these Books.

This is a story in which the greatness of the events (the conquest of the territory, the establishment of a monarchical state) and of individuals (Samuel, Saul, David, Solomon, etc.) is almost equaled by their misfortunes. When read with the eyes of faith it becomes a continual dialogue between God and his people, a centuries-long contrasting back-and-forth between fidelity and infidelity that is repeated from each generation to the next.

These pages cannot leave the reader indifferent. They make us reflect on the present-day people of God; they ask insistently an urgent question: "What about you? Are you faithful?"

It is obvious, however, that texts coming down to us from an age and a civilization so different from ours will display aspects that may rub us the wrong way. Even more, some passages may even scandalize us. In some pages of Joshua and Judges, for example, whole populations are mercilessly exterminated, and the destroyers boast of it. But we would be wrong were we to be scandalized; what we are witnessing is the human conscience at a less developed stage, when the value of every human life, of the human person as such, was not yet clearly understood. Moreover, the victims of these savage practices did not react as we do; rather they found them to be normal and were ready to inflict them in turn on others. Progress will be made, a little at a time, and legislation will accept humanitarian concerns; but we must not be too impatient. The Bible is a book describing the education of a people; it displays therefore the progress typically made under a good teacher.

We feel a greater difficulty when we read that God himself commands the radical extirpation of peoples conquered by the Hebrews (the anathema). But we must bear in mind, first of all, that the authors and editors were quite ready to attribute the decisions of the people directly to God; their habitual way of speaking highlights God, the ultimate cause of all things, without stopping at immediate causes, whether natural or moral. Secondly, it emerges from some passages that the exterminations were less systematic than we might think; simplification, however, is an element in the literary genre. Above all, we must note that foreigners were not exterminated simply because they were foreigners (in fact, there is a rather frequent insistence, in God's name, on respect for other peoples), but because contact with idolatrous peoples and their immoral customs was a great danger to Israel; a radical separation from other religions was a necessity, and at that time peoples were identified with their religions. That this was so is shown by the fact that down to the Exile, Israel was incapable of resisting the powerful attraction of the idolatry around them. Nor, finally, should we pay insufficient heed to the fact that the exterminations are frequently presented as punishments for immorality.

"When the people heard the sound of the trumpets and the people let out a great shout, the wall collapsed, . . . and they took the city [Jericho]" *(Jos 6:20).*

THE BOOK OF JOSHUA

God Delivers the Land to His People

When researchers excavate the remains of ancient cities in Palestine, they discover traces of destruction and fire at a level that corresponds approximately to the 13th century B.C.: a civilization collapsed under pressure from new populations that were trying to establish themselves in the country. This was the period in which the Hebrews made their way to the land of Canaan.

In the eyes of the Hebrews, it was God who gave the victory to the tribes that were advancing into this new land. At ancient sanctuaries, generation handed on to generation stories that praised various salient moments in this conquest. Then, in the time of King Josiah (seventh century B.C.), during the fervent religious reform that had been initiated by the discovery of Deuteronomy, these ancient traditions were combined in order to display the wonderful unfolding of sacred history. Was not the conquest of Palestine a supremely important event in God's plan for his people? Beginning with the promise made to Abraham, the entire story is directed toward the gift of the land (Gen 12:1-7; 13:14-15; 17:8). It is precisely the conquest of Palestine that the Book of Joshua celebrates in epic style.

The work takes its name from Moses' successor; he is in fact the agent through whom God presides over the new destinies of his people at this decisive time (Jos 1:1-5; 3:7; 4:14; 11:15; 24:29). It is as God's deputy that Joshua directs the conquest, organizes the division of the land, and calls for the covenant. His very name means "God saves."

On every page this epic extols the initiative of God in saving his people; it reflects the unity and fidelity of Israel in the land given to it by the Lord. Its message is relevant even for us: ever faithful to his plan, God is leading all of us together to the true promised land of his kingdom (Heb 4), and it is still a Joshua (Jesus) who is bringing us into it. And by entering into the new covenant with us, he demands our fidelity to him, the only true God.

The exhortations to perseverance and fidelity that are contained in this Book quicken our sense of responsibility as Christians in the midst of the world and involved in the mission of the Church, the new people of God. We are called by the Lord and must be people who today choose him.

The Book of Joshua may be divided as follows:

I: The Conquest of the Promised Land (1:1—12:24)
II: The Division of the Land among the Tribes (13:1—21:45)
III: The Return of the Eastern Tribes and Joshua's Farewell (22:1—24:33)

I: THE CONQUEST OF THE PROMISED LAND*

CHAPTER 1

Assurance of Divine Aid. 1 After the death
of Moses, the servant of the LORD, the
LORD spoke to Joshua, the son of Nun, the
assistant of Moses, saying, 2 * "Moses my
servant is dead. Rise, therefore, and cross
over this Jordan, you and all of this people,
to the land that I am giving to them, the
people of Israel. [a] 3 [b] Every place that you
set your feet down, I have given to you, as
I promised to Moses. 4 Your territory will
extend from the Desert of Lebanon as far
as the great river, the River Euphrates, all
of the land of the Hittites, and as far as the
great sea on the west. 5 No one will be able
to withstand you, all the days of your life. I
will treat you just as I treated Moses, for I
will never forsake nor abandon you. [c] 6 So
be strong and take courage, for you will
lead these people to inherit the land that I
promised to their forefathers to give
them. 7 Only be strong and take courage.
Be careful to observe the entire law that
my servant Moses gave to you. Do not
turn away from it to the right or to the left,
so that you might prosper wherever you
go. 8 Do not let this book of the law be
absent from your mouth; meditate upon it
day and night, so that you might carefully
observe everything that is written in it.
Then you will prosper and be successful. [d]
9 I have given you a command. Be strong
and brave, do not be afraid nor dismayed.
I, the LORD, your God, will be with you
wherever you go." [e]

The Tribes beyond the Jordan. 10 So Joshua
gave a command to the leaders of the people
saying, 11 "Pass through the camp and give
orders to the people saying, 'Prepare three

a Num 12:7-8.—b 3f: Gen 15:18; Deut 11:24-25.—c Deut 7:24; 31:8; Heb 13:5.—d Ps 1:1-3.—e Deut 31:7f.

1:1—12:24 These ancient traditions are brought together in a magnificent comprehensive picture that plays down, without completely suppressing, the difficulties of the guerilla war and of the slow penetration of the tribes as they advance in a loose fashion. The editor does not intend to write a detailed diary of these events; he shows God at work clearing the country for his people who are wholly taken up with fighting. In the miraculous crossing of the Jordan and capture of Jericho and in later wonders during the conquest, Israel will always see the most obvious signs of God's saving intervention.

It is to be noted, however, that the extermination (the anathema) of Canaanite populations was far from being total; some groups were brought into subjection, others assimilated. Moreover, Israel understands the anathema to be connected with its vocation to the faithful service of the one God: amid the attractions of paganism they must remain vigilant for their independence and keep their faith and worship free of any contamination. According to the authors of this book, fidelity and infidelity always bring in their wake successes and failures in the course of the conquest and throughout history. From this outlook we ought to derive a reminder not to let our faith be contaminated by the new idols of our age.

1:2-9 The opening section establishes Joshua as a capable leader and successor to Moses in conquering the new land of Canaan. The Lord prepares Joshua for victory by demanding obedience to God's law.

days' worth of provisions for yourselves, for within three days you are going to cross over this Jordan in order to take possession of the land that the LORD, your God, has given to you as an inheritance.' " 12 Joshua then said to the Reubenites and the Gadites and to half of the tribe of Manasseh,*[f] 13 "Remember what Moses, the servant of the LORD, commanded you, saying, 'The LORD, your God, has given you a place of rest,* he is giving you this land.' 14 Your wives, your little ones, and your livestock are to remain on the land that Moses gave you on the far side of the Jordan, but all of your brave warriors will pass over armed, marching before your brethren to help them. 15 You shall remain there until the LORD gives rest to your brethren as well, and they too take possession of the land that the LORD, your God, has given them. Then you will come back to the land of your inheritance and take possession of it, the land that Moses, the servant of the LORD, gave you on the east of the Jordan, in the direction of the sunrise."[g] 16 They answered Joshua saying, "We will do whatever you command us to do, and we will go wherever you send us. 17 We will obey you just as we obeyed Moses in everything. May the LORD, your God, be with you just as he was with Moses. 18 Whoever rebels against your commands and does not obey whatever you command them to do will be put to death. Only be strong and brave."

CHAPTER 2*

Rahab Saves the Spies.* 1 Joshua, the son of Nun, secretly dispatched two spies from Shittim.* He told them, "Go reconnoiter the land, especially Jericho." They went and they came to the house of a prostitute named Rahab, where they stayed.[h] 2 The king of Jericho was told, "Look, some Israelites came here tonight to spy throughout the land." 3 The king of Jericho sent a message to Rahab saying, "Bring out the men who have come to you and entered your house, for they are here to spy through the whole countryside." 4 But the woman had taken the two spies and she had hidden them. She said, "The men came to me, but I did not know where they were coming from. 5 When it was time to close the gates at dusk, they left. I do not know where they went. Chase after the men quickly, you may catch up with them." 6 She had really taken them up on the roof and hidden them under stalks of flax* that she had laid out on the roof. 7 The men set out after them on the road that leads to the fords of the Jordan. The gate was shut as soon as the pursuers had gone out after them.

8 Before they went to sleep, she came up on the roof 9 and said to the men, "I know that the LORD has given you this land. We are terrified and all the inhabitants of the land are trembling at your approach.[i] 10 We have heard how the LORD dried up the water of the Red Sea before you when you came up out of Egypt, and what you did to the two kings of the Amorites, Sihon and Og, on the other side of the Jordan, how you annihilated them.[j] 11 When we heard about this, our hearts grew faint and everyone's courage failed because of you, for the LORD, your God is God in the heavens above and on the earth below.[k] 12 Now, I beg you, swear to the LORD that since I showed you kindness, you will also show kindness to my father's household. Give me a pledge of your fidelity. 13 Spare my father and my mother, my brothers and my sisters, and all their households, saving us from sure death." 14 The men answered her, "Our lives for your lives. If you do not inform on what we are doing, then we will treat you kindly and faithfully when the LORD has given us the land."

15 She let them down by a rope through the window, for the house in which she lived was built upon the city wall. 16 She said to them, "Go into the hills so that the pursuers will not find you. Hide there for three days until the pursuers shall have returned here. Then you can go on your way." 17 The men said to her, "We will not be bound to the

f Num 32:6, 20; Deut 3:18.—g Jos 22:1-4.—h Mt 1:5; Jas 2:25.—i Ex 15:15f; 23:27; Deut 2:25.—j Jos 4:23; Ex 14:21; Num 21:24, 33-35.—k Jos 5:1; Deut 4:39.

1:12 These are the three tribes that had occupied the territories east of the Jordan after the defeat of Sihon and Og, kings in the Transjordan area (see Num 32).

1:13 *A place of rest:* these would be welcome words for a people who relied on God's promise made to their ancestors.

2:1—4:18 The crossing of the Jordan is here a miracle of no less importance than the crossing of the Red Sea.

2:1-21 Because of the aid which Rahab gives to the scouts, she will escape the disaster in Jericho. The profession of faith in the irresistible action of the God of Israel that is placed on her lips (vv. 9-11) will cause her to be cited for her exemplary faith (Heb 11; Jas 2:25) and win her a place in the genealogy of Jesus (Mt 1:5), for she will have been given a place in Israel and then will have given birth to Boaz (see Jos 6:25; Mt 1:5).

2:1 *Shittim:* a place east of the Jordan (see Num 33:49).

2:6 *Stalks of flax:* because of its height (3–4 ft.), it made an excellent hiding place when stacked on the rooftop to dry in preparation for making linen cloth.

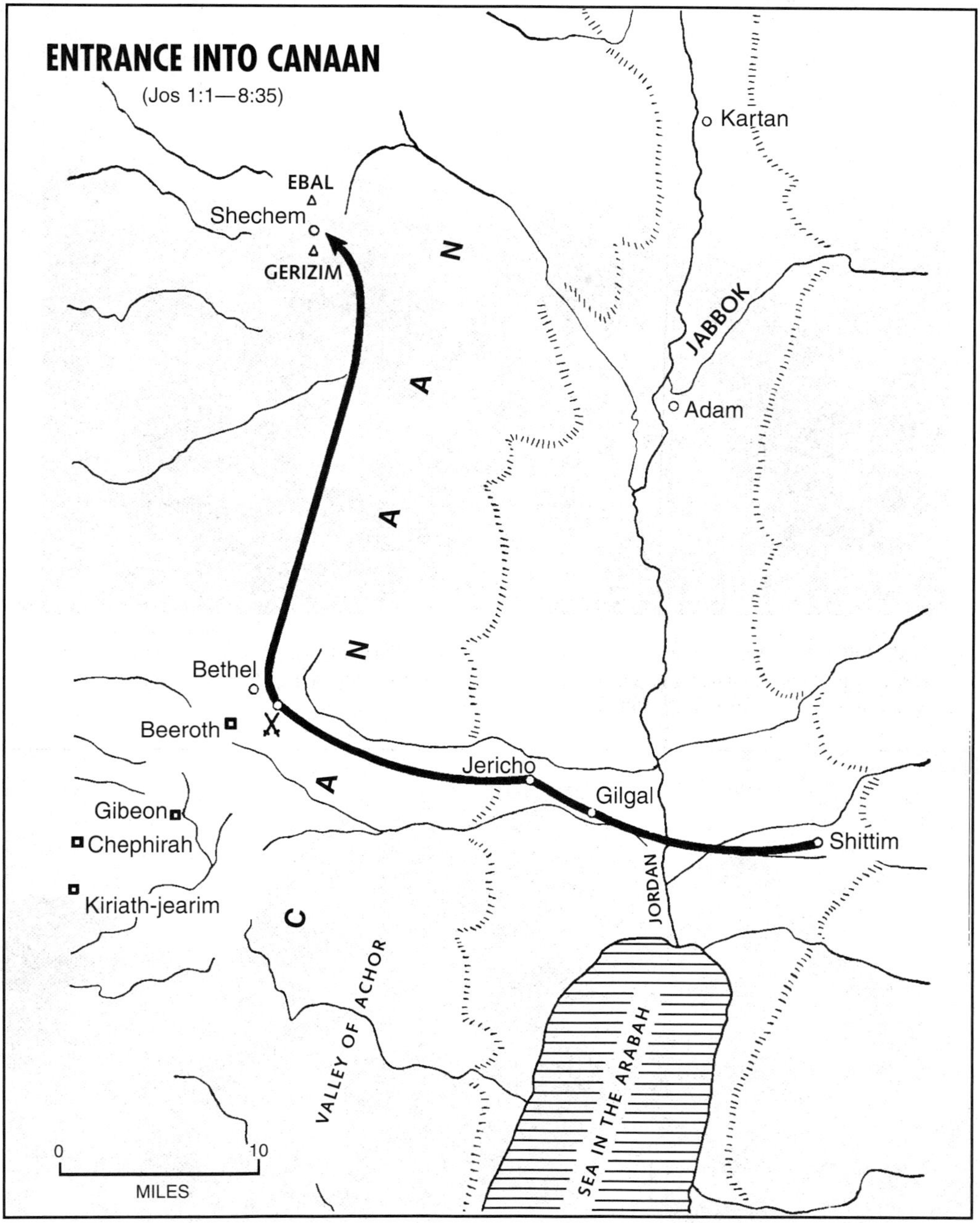

ENTRANCE INTO CANAAN (1220 – 1200 B.C.: Jos 1:1—8:35) — **(a)** At **Shittim** Joshua makes plans for passage across the **Jordan.** He sends spies to **Jericho** (1:1—2:4). **(b)** At the **Jordan:** the entry into the Promised Land marks the end of the Exodus. Joshua leaves **Shittim** with all the Israelites and crosses the Jordan opposite **Jericho** and camps at **Gilgal,** to the east of **Jericho** where the people celebrate the Passover (3:1—4:19). **(c)** At **Jericho,** the town is taken after seven days of siege (5:13—6:27). **(d)** At **Ai,** the Israelites are defeated by the people of Ai and driven back from the city. A violation of the anathema by Achan, who is stoned in the **Valley of Achor.** Joshua captures **Ai** by an ambush between **Bethel** and **Ai,** to the west of the town (7:2—8:28). **(e)** At **Shechem,** confirmation of the covenant takes place (8:30-35).

Matson Photo Service

DESERT OF SIN — Modern Debbet er-Ramleh, the most likely site of the desert (whose name was probably derived from the moon-god Sin) through which the Hebrews passed on their way from Egypt to Mount Sinai. (See Ex 16:1; 17:1; Num 33:11-12.)

Matson Photo Service

TRADITIONAL MOUNT SINAI — A modern shepherd tends his flock before the rugged slopes of Jebel Musa, one of the four possible sites (the others are Mount Serbal, Jebel Hallal, and Mount Seir). Mount Sinai was the location for the theophany of the Lord and the giving of the law. (See Ex 19:3.)

promise that you made us swear [18] unless, when we enter the land, you have a scarlet cord tied to the window from which you let us down, and unless you have brought your father, and your mother, and your brothers, and all of your father's household into your house. [19] Whoever goes outside of the doors of your house will be responsible for his own death, we will not be at fault. But whoever is in the house with you, it will be our responsibility if anyone lays a hand on him. [20] However, if you inform on what we are doing, then we will not be bound to the promise that you made us swear." [21] She said, "Let it be as you have said." She sent them away, and they departed. She then tied a scarlet cord to the window.

The Spies Report to Joshua. [22] They left, and went into the hills where they remained for three days until the pursuers had returned. The pursuers had searched all along that way, but had not found them. [23] * The two men then went back home. They came down from the hills and forded the river, coming to Joshua, the son of Nun. They told him everything that had happened to them. [24] They said to Joshua, "Surely the LORD has delivered the entire land into our hands, for all of the people in the land are overcome with fear of us."

CHAPTER 3

Instructions before the Crossing. [1] Joshua and all of the Israelites rose early the next morning and set out for Shittim, arriving at the Jordan where they camped before they crossed over it. [l] [2] Three days later the leaders of the people passed through the camp [3] giving orders to the people saying, "When you see the priests and Levites carrying the Ark of the LORD, your God, set out from where you are and follow after it. [4] Maintain a distance of about two thousand cubits* between it and yourselves; do not approach it too closely. Thus you will know the way you are to go, for you have never passed this way before." [5] Joshua said to the priests, "Consecrate yourselves, for tomorrow the LORD will perform wondrous deeds in your midst." * [m] [6] Joshua also said to the priests, "Pick up the Ark of the Covenant and pass on in front of the people." So they picked up the Ark of the Covenant and went on ahead of the people.

[7] The LORD said to Joshua, "Today I will begin to exalt you in the eyes of all of Israel, so that they may know that I will treat you the same way that I treated Moses. [n] [8] Say to the priests who are carrying the Ark of the Covenant: 'Approach the edge of the water and stand in the Jordan.' " [9] Joshua instructed the Israelites, "Come here and listen to the words of the LORD, your God." [10] Joshua continued, "This is how you will know that there is a living God among you who will drive out the Canaanites,* the Hittites, the Hivites, the Perizzites, the Girgashites, the Amorites, and the Jebusites from before you. [o] [11] Behold, the Ark of the Covenant of the LORD of all the earth will pass before you into the Jordan. [12] Choose twelve men from out of the tribes of Israel, one man from each tribe. [p] [13] * As soon as the priests who are carrying the Ark of the LORD, the LORD of the whole earth, set their feet down in the water, the waters of the Jordan will stop flowing downstream and will mount up in a heap." [q]

Crossing over the Jordan. [14] When the people broke camp to cross over the Jordan, the priests carrying the Ark of the Covenant went on ahead of them. [15] Now the Jordan was at its flood stage during the entire harvest season, but as soon as the priests carrying the Ark stepped into the Jordan, [16] the waters from upstream stopped flowing. They stood up in a mound quite a distance

l Jos 2:1.—m Jos 7:13; Ex 19:10.—n Jos 4:14.—o Ex 33:2; Deut 7:1.—p Jos 4:2, 4.—q Ex 15:8; Ps 78:13.

2:23-24 Joshua was among those sent out 39 years earlier on a spy mission and had encouraged the Israelites to remain steadfast in following God's plan (Num 13–14). To avoid any controversy, however, Joshua kept this spy mission a secret from the people.

3:4 *Cubits:* a measure of length in Hebrew; a cubit was about 50 cm. Two thousand cubits or a thousand yards was the distance of a Sabbath walk, that is, of the walk permitted to Hebrews on the Sabbath; this limitation symbolized the respect due to the divine transcendence.

3:5 See Ex 19:10, 15. The consecration or purification consisted in washing one's clothes and being sexually continent.

3:10 A list of the peoples living in the land of Canaan (present-day Palestine and Lebanon): *Canaanites:* the oldest inhabitants of the country; *Hittites:* a people from Anatolia who had settled in Syria and were of non-Semitic origin; *Hivites:* a non-Semitic people on whom we have no information; *Perizzites:* these, as the etymology of their name indicates, are inhabitants of open villages; *Girgashites:* people on whom we have no information; *Amorites:* in around the 20th century B.C. they were living in the area of the middle Euphrates, where they found the kingdom of Mari and the first Babylonian dynasty; in around the 15th century B.C., they would settle in Syria and then push southward; *Jebusites:* the inhabitants of Jerusalem.

3:13-17 Crossing the Jordan River to enter the Promised Land through God's parting of the water correlates to the crossing of the Red Sea (Ex 14) to leave Egypt. God was with them then and is with them now. The evidence of the Lord's mighty power restored their confidence and enhanced their reputation among their enemies.

away, at a town called Adam, near Zarethan. The waters that were flowing downstream to the Arabah (the Salt Sea) disappeared entirely, so the people were able to cross over the Jordan.[r] 17 The priests who were carrying the Ark of the Covenant of the LORD were standing on dry ground right in the middle of the Jordan. All of the Israelites passed over on dry ground until the entire people had crossed over the Jordan.[s]

CHAPTER 4

The Twelve Memorial Stones. 1 When the entire people had passed over the Jordan, the LORD spoke to Joshua, saying, 2 "Choose twelve men from among the people, one from each of the tribes,[t] 3 and tell them to take twelve stones from the bed of the Jordan where the priests had been standing, and to carry them over with you, depositing them at the place where you will be camping this evening."

4 So Joshua called the twelve men together whom the Israelites had chosen, one man from each tribe, 5 and Joshua said to them, "Cross over in front of the Ark of the LORD, your God, into the middle of the Jordan and have each man place a rock on his shoulder, one for each of the tribes of the Israelites. 6 * These will serve as a reminder for you when, in the future, your children ask, 'What is the meaning of these stones?'[u] 7 you will answer them, 'The waters of the Jordan stopped flowing before the Ark of the Covenant of the LORD. When it crossed the Jordan, the waters of the Jordan ceased to flow.' These stones will be a memorial to the Israelites forever."

8 The Israelites did just what Joshua had commanded them to do. They picked up twelve stones from the Jordan's riverbed, just as the LORD had instructed Joshua to do, one for each of the tribes of the Israelites, and they brought them out to the place where they were camping that night and they laid them down there. 9 Joshua set up the twelve stones that had been in the Jordan's riverbed, where the priests carrying the Ark of the Covenant had been standing. They are still there today.

10 Now the priests who were carrying the Ark stood in the middle of the Jordan until everything that the LORD had directed Joshua to tell the people had been done, the things that Moses had ordered Joshua to do. The people hurried over, 11 and when all the people had completed the crossing, the Ark of the LORD passed over, and the priests crossed over in front of the people. 12 The men of Reuben, the men of Gad, and the men of one of the halves of the tribe of Manasseh passed in front of the Israelites, clad in battle gear, as Moses had instructed them to do.[v] 13 About forty thousand men clad in battle gear passed over before the LORD into the plains of Jericho to do battle. 14 That day the LORD exalted Joshua before all of Israel. They revered him as long as he lived, even as they had revered Moses.

15 The LORD then said to Joshua, 16 "Tell the priests who are carrying the Ark of Testimony* to come up out of the Jordan." 17 So Joshua commanded the priests, "Come up out of the Jordan." 18 So the priests, carrying the Ark of the Covenant of the LORD, came up out of the Jordan. As soon as the priests' feet touched dry land, the waters of the Jordan returned back to their place, flowing at flood stage as they had before.

19 * The people came up out of the Jordan on the tenth day of the first month,* and they camped at Gilgal to the east of Jericho.[w] 20 Joshua erected the twelve stones that had been taken out of the Jordan at Gilgal. 21 He said to the Israelites, "In the future when your children ask their fathers, 'What is the meaning of these stones?' 22 tell your children, 'Israel crossed over the Jordan on dry land.' 23 The LORD, your God, dried up the waters of the Jordan before you until you could cross over, just as the LORD, your God, had dried up the Red Sea before us until we had crossed over it.[x] 24 He did this so that everyone upon the earth might know that

r Pss 66:6; 74:15; 114:3.—s Jos 4:7, 22; Ex 14:21, 29.—t Jos 3:12.—u Ex 12:26; 13:14; Deut 6:20.—v Num 32:17.—w Ex 12:2-3.—x Ex 14:21.

4:6-7 *What is the meaning of these stones?:* the Israelites were taught about God's plan and reminded of his faithfulness by seeing the stones and repeating the stories connected to them. This continues with the question and response at the Passover meal each year.

4:16 *Ark of Testimony:* an infrequently used name for the Ark of the Covenant (see Ex 25:22; 31:7; Num 4:5), derived from the fact that the Testimony, that is, the tablets of the Decalogue, was kept in the Ark.

4:19—5:15 Like the deliverance from Egypt, the crossing of the Jordan shows all future generations the power God exercises in saving his people. The first great sanctuary in Palestine will preserve the sacred tradition regarding this miracle. The author places two supremely important events during the stay at Gilgal: the circumcision of the entire male population (see Gen 17) and the Feast of Passover.

4:19 *On the tenth day of the first month:* that is, a few days before Passover (see 5:10).

the hand of the LORD is mighty and so that
you might always fear the LORD, your God."

CHAPTER 5

The Circumcision at Gilgal. 1 When all of the
Amorite kings on the west side of the Jordan
and all of the Canaanite kings who lived
along the coast heard that the LORD had
dried up the waters of the Jordan before the
Israelites until they had passed over it, they
grew fainthearted and they no longer had
the courage to face the Israelites.

2 * It was at that time that the LORD said to
Joshua, "Make flint knives for yourself and
circumcise the Israelites again."[y] 3 So
Joshua made flint knives and circumcised
the Israelites at Gibeath-haaraloth. 4 This is
the reason why Joshua had to perform this
circumcision. All of the men who had come
out of Egypt, all of the fighting men, had
died in the wilderness on their way from
Egypt.[z] 5 All of the men who had come out
had been circumcised, but all of those who
had been born in the wilderness on the way
from Egypt had not been circumcised. 6 The
Israelites had spent forty years in the wilder-
ness until all of the fighting men who had
come out of Egypt and who had not obeyed
the command of the LORD had died. The
LORD had sworn to them that they would
not see the land that he had promised to
their fathers to give us, a land flowing with
milk and honey.[a] 7 It was their children,
whom he had raised up in their stead, whom
Joshua circumcised, for they were still un-
circumcised because they had not been
circumcised on the way. 8 When he had fin-
ished circumcising the whole nation, they
remained where they were until they recov-
ered. 9 Then the LORD said to Joshua, "Today
I have removed the reproach of Egypt from
you." So this site has been called Gilgal up to
the present.

10 * On the evening of the fourteenth day of
the month, while they were camped at
Gilgal on the plains of Jericho, the Israelites
celebrated Passover.[b] 11 The day after
Passover, the very next day, they ate some of
the produce of the land: unleavened bread
and parched grain. 12 The manna stopped
the day after they had eaten the produce of
the land. There was no more manna for the
Israelites, but that same year they ate the
produce of the land of Canaan.[c]

Worship at Jericho.* 13 As Joshua drew near
Jericho, he looked up and saw a man stand-
ing in front of him with a drawn sword in his
hand. Joshua went up to him and said to
him, "Are you for us or for our adver-
saries?"[d] 14 He answered, "Neither. I, the
commander of the army of the LORD, have
now arrived." Joshua fell to the ground, face
first, and worshiped him. He said, "What
does my lord bid of his servant?" 15 The
commander of the army of the LORD said to
Joshua, "Take your shoes off your feet, for
the place where you are standing is holy
ground." Joshua did this.[e]

CHAPTER 6*

Jericho Overtaken. 1 Now Jericho was shut
up tight on account of the people of Israel,
none went out and none came in. 2 The
LORD said to Joshua, "Behold, I have given
Jericho, its king, and its mighty warriors into
your hands.[f] 3 Your soldiers are to march all
around the city once, doing that for six days.
4 Seven priests will carry seven trumpets
made from ram's horns in front of the Ark.
On the seventh day you are to march
around the city seven times while the priests
blow their trumpets.*[g] 5 Then they will

y Gen 17:9-10; Ex 4:24-26.—z Num 14:29; 26:64f; Deut 2:14; 1 Cor 10:5.—a Num 14:29-35; Deut 2:7; Heb 3:11, 17.—b Ex 12:6, 8; Num 9:3-5.—c Ex 16:35.—d Gen 18:2; 32:22-24; Ex 23:20-23.—e Ex 3:5.—f Deut 7:24.—g Num 10:8.

5:2-9 Circumcision was required of those who would celebrate the Passover, according to the prescriptions in Ex 12:43-48.

5:10-12 The celebration of Passover, the memorial of God's intervention for the salvation of his people, accompanies the decisive moments in the history of Israel. Thus it marks the moment of the departure from Egypt (Ex 12–13), the moment of the departure from Sinai (Num 9), and now the moment when Israel enters into possession of the Promised Land. It paves the way for the celebration of the Christian Passover, the center and memorial of all the blessings that the sacrifice of Christ, the Lamb of the new Passover, immolated for the salvation of all, has brought to humanity. With the celebration of Joshua's Passover the manna ceases, signifying that the journey in the wilderness has ended (see Ex 16).

5:13-15 The Bible has preserved only fragments of a mysterious ancient story, inspired perhaps by the story of God's appearance to Moses in the burning bush (Ex 3) and intended to signify a solemn confirmation of Joshua's mission as leader of the conquest. He showed his respect and subordination to God by taking off his shoes.

6:1-27 The entire ceremonial that precedes the fall of Jericho gives the event the character of a liturgical action rather than of a conquest; God is at work in giving the Promised Land to his people, just as he was at the crossing of the Jordan. The account is therefore not to be taken literally but as giving religious expression to a real intervention of God, whatever the manner of this intervention may have been. The story combines two different traditions that cannot be fully harmonized. One describes a procession accompanied by the playing of trumpets; the other says that the war shout was uttered after seven processional circlings of the city made in silence.

6:4 Such trumpets were weapons of war, intended to frighten the enemy (see Jdg 7:8-20) or to direct military operations (2 Sam 2:28; 20:22; Neh 4:12-14), but they were also used in some religious ceremonies, where they were accompanied by acclamations (Lev 25:9; 2 Chr 15:14).

make a long blast on the ram's horns. As
soon as you hear the sound of the trumpet,
have all of the people give a great shout. The
walls will fall down, and the people will go on
up, every man in a straight line."

6 So Joshua, the son of Nun, summoned
the priests and said to them, "Take up the
Ark of the Covenant. Have seven priests
holding trumpets made from rams' horns
precede the Ark of the LORD." 7 He gave the
command to the people, "Advance! March
around the city with the armed soldiers
walking in front of the Ark of the LORD."
8 When Joshua finished speaking to the peo-
ple, the seven priests carrying trumpets
made from rams' horns walked in front of
the LORD and moved forward, blowing their
trumpets, and the Ark of the LORD followed
them. 9 The armed soldiers marched in
front of the priests who were blowing their
trumpets, and a rear guard followed the Ark.
The whole time the trumpets were being
blown. 10 But Joshua commanded the peo-
ple, "Do not shout or raise your voices. Do
not say a thing until the day I tell you to
shout. Then you are to shout."

11 So he had the Ark of the LORD carried
around the city once. They then went back
into the camp where they spent the night.
12 Joshua rose early the next morning, and
the priests took the Ark of the LORD. 13 The
seven priests carrying the trumpets made
from rams' horns went ahead of the Ark of
the LORD, blowing on their trumpets as they
went. The armed soldiers marched in front
of them, and a rear guard followed the Ark of
the LORD, with the trumpets being blown the
whole time. 14 Thus they went around the city
once on the second day, and then they
returned to the camp. They did this for six
days in a row.

15 On the seventh day they rose at day-
break and went around the city seven times
just as they had before, but that day they
went around the city seven times. 16 On the
seventh time around when the priests blew
their trumpets, Joshua commanded the peo-
ple, "Shout out, for the LORD has given you
the city. 17 [h] The city and all that is in it are
devoted * to the LORD. Only Rahab the pros-
titute shall live, she and all who are in her
household, for she hid the spies whom we
sent there. 18 But avoid those things that are
dedicated, lest you call a curse on yourself
when you take something that is dedicated
and you bring a curse and destruction upon
the camp of Israel. 19 All the silver and gold
and objects of bronze and iron are dedicated
to the LORD. They must go into the treasury
of the LORD."

20 The people shouted and the priests blew
their trumpets. When the people heard the
sound of the trumpets and the people let out
a great shout, the wall collapsed, and each
man went up in a straight line and they took
the city. [i] 21 They wiped out everything that
was in the city, men and women, young and
old, ox and sheep and donkey, by the edge of
the sword.

Rahab's Family Spared. 22 [j] But Joshua said
to the two men who had spied out the coun-
tryside, "Go to the harlot's house and bring
her out to me, her and everyone who is with
her, just as you promised her that you would
do." 23 So the young men who had done the
spying brought out Rahab, her father, her
mother, her brothers, and everyone whom
she had with her. They brought out the entire
family and left them outside of the camp of
Israel. 24 They then burned the entire city
with everything that was in it. Only the silver
and gold, and the objects of bronze and iron
were put into the treasury in the house of the
LORD. 25 But Joshua spared Rahab the pros-
titute, along with her father's household,
and all that she owned because she had hid
the spies whom Joshua had sent. She lives
among the Israelites up to the present.

26 Joshua then said, "May the man who
attempts to rebuild this city, Jericho, be
cursed by the LORD. May he lose his first-
born* if he lays its foundation, may he lose
his youngest if he sets up its gates." [k] 27 The
LORD was with Joshua, and his reputation
became known throughout the land.

CHAPTER 7

Israelites Defeated at Ai. 1 * The Israelites,
however, acted treacherously with regard to

h 17f: Jos 2:4; 7:1; Deut 13:18; 20:17.—i 2 Mac 12:15; Heb 11:30.—j 22-23: Jos 2:13-14; Heb 11:31.—k 1 Ki 16:34.

6:17 *Devoted:* a reference to the anathema (i.e., consecrated to God), by which inhabitants and animals were condemned to destruction; the warriors were obliged not to take any booty; any precious objects were reserved for the sanctuary. In this case, the anathema has the character of simple destruction rather than of a complete offering to God.

6:26 *Lose his firstborn:* this is fulfilled in 1 Ki 16:34 when Jericho is rebuilt by a man whose son subsequently dies.

7:1—8:9 The cruel measures taken in this primitive war emphasize the condition required for God's help, namely, unconditional obedience and the sacrifice of personal desires. Observe that *Ai* means "ruin"; the account bears the mark of this.

those things that had been dedicated.
Achan, the son of Carmi, the son of Zabdi,
the son of Zerah, of the tribe of Judah, took
some of the dedicated things for himself.
The LORD's anger blazed forth against the
Israelites.[l] 2 Joshua sent some men from
Jericho to Ai, which is near Beth-aven, to the
east of Bethel. He said to them, "Go up and
take a look at the countryside," so the men
went up and investigated Ai. 3 They returned
and said to Joshua, "You should not send the
entire nation there, only send about two or
three thousand men against Ai to conquer
it. You should not bother the whole nation,
for there are not that many of them. 4 So
about three thousand men went up there,
and they had to flee from before the men of
Ai. 5 The men of Ai killed about thirty-six of
them when they chased them from their
gates all the way down to Shebarim. They
killed them as they ran down the slopes, and
the people's courage melted away like water.

6 Joshua tore his clothes and threw himself
face down on the earth in front of the Ark of
the LORD, remaining there until the evening.
The elders of Israel did the same, tossing
dust upon their heads.[m] 7 * Joshua said,
"Alas, O LORD, why did you bring this peo-
ple across the Jordan just to deliver us into
the hands of the Amorites so they could
destroy us? It would have been better if we
had stayed on the other side of the Jordan.
8 O Lord, what can I say, now that Israel has
fled before its enemies? 9 The Canaanites
and all of the other inhabitants of the land
will surely hear about this. They will sur-
round us and wipe out remembrance of our
name from the earth. What would happen to
the grandeur of your name?"[n]

10 The LORD said to Joshua, "Stand up!
What are you doing on your face? 11 Israel
has sinned. They have violated my covenant
that I commanded them to observe. They
have taken some of the dedicated things for
themselves. They have stolen, they have lied,
they have placed these things together with
their own property. 12 This is why the
Israelites could not stand up to their ene-
mies. They turned their backs and fled
because they were under a curse. I will not
be with you anymore unless you wipe out
those who are cursed from your midst.
13 Arise, consecrate the people. Tell them,
'Sanctify yourselves in preparation for
tomorrow. Thus says the LORD, the God of
Israel: "There are things that have been ded-
icated in your midst, O Israel. You will not be
able to stand up to your enemies until you
remove the dedicated things from your
midst."[o] 14 In the morning you will present
yourselves tribe by tribe. The tribe that the
LORD chooses will present itself clan by clan.
The clan that the LORD chooses will present
itself family by family. The family that the
LORD chooses will present itself person by
person. * 15 That person who has taken dedi-
cated things will be thrown into the flames,
he and all that he owns. He has violated the
covenant of the LORD and he has done a dis-
graceful thing in Israel.' "

Achan's Guilt and Punishment. 16 Early the
next morning Joshua had the people of
Israel come forward by their tribes, and
Judah was chosen. 17 The clans of Judah then
came forward, and the clan of the Zerahites
was chosen. The clan of the Zerahites came
forward family by family, and the family of
Zabdi was chosen.[p] 18 The family came for-
ward person by person, and Achan, the son
of Carmi, the son of Zabdi, the son of Zerah,
of the tribe of Judah was chosen.

19 Joshua said to Achan, "My son, give
glory to the LORD, the God of Israel, and
make your confession to him. Tell me now
what you have done, do not hide it from
me."[q] 20 Achan answered Joshua, "I have
truly sinned against the LORD, the God of
Israel, for this is what I have done. 21 I spot-
ted among the spoils a good garment made
in Babylonia,* and two hundred silver
shekels, and a bar of gold weighing fifty
shekels. I coveted them so I took them. They
are hidden in my tent, with the silver buried
underneath it."

22 Joshua sent some runners to the tent,
and there it was in the tent, with the silver
buried underneath it. 23 They took it out of
the tent and brought it to Joshua and to all
of the Israelites, laying it out before the

l Jos 6:17-19; 1 Chr 2:7.—m Job 2:12.—n Ex 32:12; Deut 9:28.—o Jos 3:5; Lev 20:7; 1 Sam 16:5.—p Num 26:20.—q Jer 13:16; Jn 9:24.

7:7-9 This informal and heartfelt prayer reveals Joshua's confusion in the light of defeat. His resort to persuasive questioning of God reveals his weakness and fear (i.e., humanity).

7:14 Tribes, which are subdivisions of nomadic societies, are made up of a number of clans; clans are made up of a number of families that descend from a common ancestor and are united by ties of blood; a family is made up of relatives living together, the head of it having juridical and religious authority.

7:21 *Babylonia:* the Hebrew has "Shinar," a region of Mesopotamia, but here standing for Babylonia, which was noted for its wealth.

LORD. [24] * Joshua, together with all of Israel, took Achan, the son of Zerah, along with the silver, the garment, and the bar of gold, his sons and his daughters, his oxen, donkeys and sheep, his tent and all his other property to the Valley of Achor. [25] Joshua said, "Why have you brought this calamity upon us? The LORD will bring a calamity down upon you today." Then all of the Israelites stoned him, and after they stoned the rest of them, they threw them in the fire. [r] [26] They piled up a great mound of stones over Achan that is still there to the present. The fierce anger of the LORD was thus quenched. This is why this site is called the Valley of Achor to this day. [s]

CHAPTER 8

Joshua Conquers Ai. [1] The LORD said to Joshua, "Do not be afraid or discouraged! Arise and take all of your soldiers with you, going up to Ai. See that I have given the king of Ai, and his people, and his city, and his land into your hands. [t] [2] You shall treat Ai and its king just like you did Jericho, except that you can take its plunder and cattle for yourselves. Set up an ambush for them behind the city." [u]

[3] So Joshua and all of the soldiers went up to Ai. Joshua selected thirty thousand of the strongest and most courageous and sent them out by night,* [4] commanding them, "Set up an ambush for them behind the city. Stay fairly close to the city, and be alert! [5] I will go with everyone who is with me and we will approach near the city. When they come out against us like they did before, we will flee before them. [6] They will chase after us until we have drawn them away from the city, for they will say to themselves, 'They are fleeing away from us just like the first time.' When we flee from them, [7] you are to spring out of the ambush and take the city. The LORD, your God, will deliver it into your hands. [8] When you have taken the city, set it on fire. Do what the LORD has commanded you to do! See, you now have my orders."

[9] Joshua sent them off, and they went into their ambush, lying in wait between Bethel and Ai, on the western side of Ai. Joshua spent the night with his people. [10] Early the next morning Joshua mustered the people, and he and the elders* of Israel marched off before them to Ai. [11] All of the soldiers who were with him went up and approached the city, drawing up in front of it. They pitched camp on the northern side of Ai, with the valley lying between them and Ai. [12] He had taken about five thousand men and set them up in an ambush between Bethel and Ai, on the western side of the city. [13] All the soldiers were thus ready, those who were on the northern side of the city and those lying in wait on the western side of the city. That night Joshua went down into the valley. [14] When the king of Ai saw this, he and all the men from the city rose early and went out to do battle with Israel at a fixed place in the plain. He did not know about the ambush that was lying in wait for him behind the city. [15] Joshua and all the Israelites were driven back before them, and they fled in the direction of the desert. [16] All of the men of Ai were summoned to pursue them. They followed after Joshua, and thus were drawn away from the city. [17] Every single man in Ai and Bethel went out after the Israelites. They left the city open and pursued the Israelites.

[18] The LORD then said to Joshua, "Stretch out the spear in your hand toward Ai, for I will deliver it into your hands." So Joshua stretched out the spear in his hands toward the city. [v] [19] As soon as he stretched out his hand, the men who were hiding in ambush rose from their place and rushed forward. They entered into the city and captured it, quickly setting it on fire. [20] The men from Ai looked back, and they saw smoke rising up into the sky from the city. There was no possibility of fleeing in any direction, for the people who had fled into the desert turned back upon their pursuers. [21] Joshua and all of the Israelites saw that those who had been in ambush had taken the city and that smoke was rising up from the city, so they turned and attacked the men from Ai. [22] The others also came out of the city against them, so that they were caught in the middle between two Israelite forces. They cut them down; none of them escaped or survived [w] [23] except

r Jos 6:18; Deut 13:17; 1 Chr 2:7.—s Deut 13:17; Hos 2:15.—t Jos 1:9; Deut 1:21.—u Deut 20:14.—v Ex 14:16; 17:9.—w Deut 7:2.

7:24-26 As head of the family Achan brings all of them down because of his disobedience. His entire family is eradicated and everything that belongs to him is destroyed. The Israelites understand this punishment to be appropriate to the sin of betrayal of the Lord.

8:3 A victory at Ai, a stronghold of the Canaanites, was important to the Israelites' confidence—that they were forgiven and their repentance was acknowledged by the Lord. It was also strategically important for the Canaanite kings to know that God was protecting the Israelites once again.

8:10 *Elders:* the leaders who formed a kind of aristocracy. In war they led their fellow tribesmen and in time of peace administered justice (Ex 18:13-26).

for the king of Ai, whom they captured alive and brought to Joshua.

[24] When the Israelites had finished killing all of those who lived in Ai, in the fields, and in the wilderness where they had chased them, putting all of them to the edge of the sword, all of the Israelites returned to Ai and put everyone in it to death by the sword. [25] Twelve thousand men and women were slain that day, all of those who lived in Ai. [26] Joshua did not pull back the hand that held the outstretched spear until he had wiped out everyone who had lived in Ai.[x] [27] The Israelites carried off the cattle and plunder from the city as booty for themselves, as the LORD had instructed Joshua. [28] Joshua burned Ai, leaving it a heap of ruins, and it remains desolate to this very day.[y] [29] He hung the king of Ai from a tree until that evening. When the sun was setting, Joshua ordered that they should take his body down from the tree and toss it down at the entrance to the city gate. They piled a large mound of stones on it, which is still there today.

The Altar on Mount Ebal.* [30] Joshua then built an altar on Mount Ebal to the LORD, the God of Israel [31] as Moses, the servant of the LORD, had commanded the Israelites to do in the book of the law. Moses had written, "It is to be an altar of unhewn stones that no one has touched with iron tools." They offered burnt offerings to the LORD there, and also sacrificed peace offerings.[z] [32] There, in front of all of the Israelites, he copied on the stones the law that Moses had written. [33] All of the Israelites, including their elders, their officials, and their judges were standing on either side of the Ark. They were facing the priests, the Levites who carry the Ark of the Covenant of the LORD. There were both the foreigners and the native born. Half of the people stood in front of Mount Gerizim, and half of the people stood in front of Mount Ebal, just as Moses, the servant of the LORD, had previously commanded, so that they might bless the people of Israel.

[34] Afterward he read all of the words of the law along with its blessings and curses, just as all of it is written in the book of the law.[a] [35] Joshua read every single word that Moses had commanded before the whole assembly of Israel, along with the women, the little ones, and the foreigners who were living with them.

CHAPTER 9*

United against Israel. [1] When all of the kings on that side of the Jordan heard about these things; those who were in the hill country, those on the western slopes, and those along the coast to the great sea, all the way up to Lebanon, the Hittites, the Amorites, the Canaanites, the Perizzites, the Hivites and the Jebusites;[b] [2] they gathered together as one to fight against Joshua and the Israelites.

Plot of the Gibeonites. [3] But the inhabitants of Gibeon heard what Joshua had done to Jericho and Ai[c] [4] and they devised a cunning plot. They prepared provisions, collecting them and putting them into old sacks upon their donkeys, along with old wineskins that were torn and mended. [5] They put old mended sandals on their feet, and dressed in old clothing, making sure that all of their provisions were dried out and crumbling. [6] They came to Joshua at the camp in Gilgal and said to him and to the people of Israel, "We have come here from a distant country, so make a covenant with us."[d] [7] The Israelites said to the Hivites, "Maybe you actually live among us, how could we make a covenant with you?" [8] They then said to Joshua, "We are your servants." Joshua said to them, "Who are you, and where do you come from?" [9] They said to him, "We, your servants, come from a very distant land because of the name of the LORD, your God. We have heard reports about him and everything that he did in Egypt [10] and everything that he did to the two kings of the Amorites on the other side of the Jordan; Sihon, the king of Heshbon, and Og, the king of Bashan, who dwelt at Ashtaroth. [11] Our elders and everyone who dwells in our land said to us, 'Take some provisions for the journey and go to meet with them and say to them, "We are your servants, so please make a covenant with us." ' [12] Here is our bread. It was still hot from the oven when we took it out of our houses on the day we set out to come to you. Look at it now, it is dry and crumbling. [13] These wineskins were new

---

x Ex 17:11-13.—y Jos 7:26; Deut 13:16.—z Ex 20:24f; Deut 27:5f.—a Deut 31:11; Neh 8:2f.—b Jos 3:10; Deut 1:7.—c Jos 6:21; 8:24-25; 11:19.—d Ex 23:32; Deut 7:2.

8:30-35 Gathered on Mount Ebal, near Shechem, the tribes have their first celebration in the Promised Land, in keeping with the order given them through the mouth of Moses (Deut 27). This celebration with its proclamation of blessings and curses is an element in the renewal of the covenant (Deut 28).

9:1-27 Another piece of evidence that the anathema was not carried out as systematically as some passages would seem to suggest.

when we filled them. Look at them now, they are falling apart. These clothes and our shoes have become old because of the very long journey that we have made."

[14] The Israelites partook of some of their provisions, but they did not ask the counsel of the LORD. *[e] [15] Joshua made peace with them; he made a covenant with them, permitting them to live. The leaders of the assembly also swore an oath to them.

Punishment of the Gibeonites. [16] Three days after they had made a covenant with them, they heard that they were actually neighbors, and that they were living in their land. [17] The Israelites went out and arrived at their cities three days later. Their cities were Gibeon, Chephirah, Beeroth, and Kiriath-jearim. [18] But the Israelites did not kill them, for the leaders of the assembly had made an oath to them by the LORD, the God of Israel. Everyone in the assembly, however, grumbled against their leaders. [19] All of the leaders said to the assembly, "We have made an oath to them by the LORD, the God of Israel, so now we cannot touch them. [20] This is what we will do to them. We will let them live, lest wrath come upon us because of the oath we swore to them." [21] So the leaders said to them, "Let them live. They will cut firewood and draw water for the whole assembly of Israel, just as the leaders promised them."[f]

[22] Joshua then summoned them and he said to them, "You have deceived us by telling us that you came from a distant land when you actually live in our midst. [23] Now, therefore, you will be cursed, you shall always be slaves, cutting firewood and drawing water for the house of my God."

[24] They answered Joshua, "Your servants were informed on how the LORD, your God, commanded Moses, his servant, to give you all the land and to kill all of the inhabitants in the land ahead of you. We truly feared for our lives, for you would have done this thing.[g] [25] So therefore, we are in your hands. Do whatever you consider to be right to us." [26] And so this is what he did to them: he rescued them out of the hands of the Israelites so that they did not kill them, [27] but Joshua established them that day as the ones who would cut firewood and draw water for the assembly and for the altar of the LORD in the place that he would choose, which they still do today.[h]

CHAPTER 10

Conspiracy against Gibeon. [1] * Now Adoni-zedek, the king of Jerusalem, heard that Joshua had taken Ai and had totally destroyed it, doing to Ai and its king what he had already done to Jericho and its king, and also how the inhabitants of Gibeon had made peace with Israel and were living near them.[i] [2] He and his people were shocked, for Gibeon was one of the larger cities, large enough to be one of the royal cities. It was larger than Ai, and all its men were mighty warriors. [3] Adoni-zedek appealed to Hoham, the king of Hebron, Piram, the king of Jarmuth, Japhia, the king of Lachish, and Debir, the king of Eglon, saying, [4] "Come up and assist me with an attack on Gibeon, for it has made peace with Joshua and the Israelites."

[5] The five kings of the Amorites, the king of Jerusalem, the king of Hebron, the king of Jarmuth, the king of Lachish, and the king of Eglon, and all of their armies went up and encamped outside of Gibeon to attack it. [6] The Gibeonites sent a message to Joshua who was in his camp at Gilgal saying, "Do not abandon your servants! Come up quickly to us and save us. All of the kings of the Amorites who live in the hill country have gathered forces against us."[j]

Joshua Rescues Gibeon. [7] So Joshua and all of his fighting men went up along with his most valiant warriors. [8] The LORD said to Joshua, "Do not be afraid of them. I have delivered them into your hands. Not one of them will be able to withstand you." [9] Joshua marched from Gilgal all night and took them by surprise. [10] The LORD routed them before Israel. They killed many at Gibeon, chasing after them on the road leading up to Beth-horon, slaying them all the way up to Azekah and Makkedah. [11] As they were fleeing before the Israelites on the road from Beth-horon to

e Num 27:21.—f Deut 29:11.—g Ex 23:27f; Deut 7:1f.—h Deut 12:5.—i Jos 8:26-29; 9:15.—j Jos 9:6.

9:14 By not seeking God's guidance in dealing with the Canaanites, the Israelites would be bound by vows that should not have been made and stuck with an alliance that did not benefit them.

10:1—12:24 A tradition worthy of being celebrated in an epic poem tells how the miracle of the hailstones and of the sun halting brought victory to Israel during a memorable battle. With this tradition is combined a systematic and simplified description of the conquest of southern and northern Palestine. Yet other passages in the Book of Joshua (Jos 13:1-6; 14:6-13; 15:13-19; 17:12, 16) and the entire Book of Judges record an often slow penetration of the country by tribes that were scattered and sometimes even in conflict with one another.

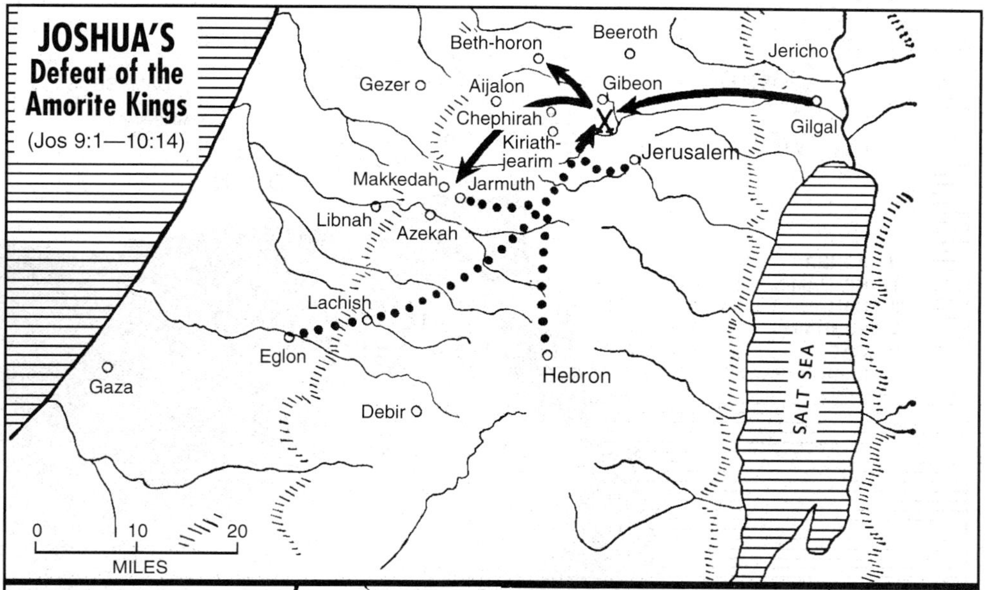

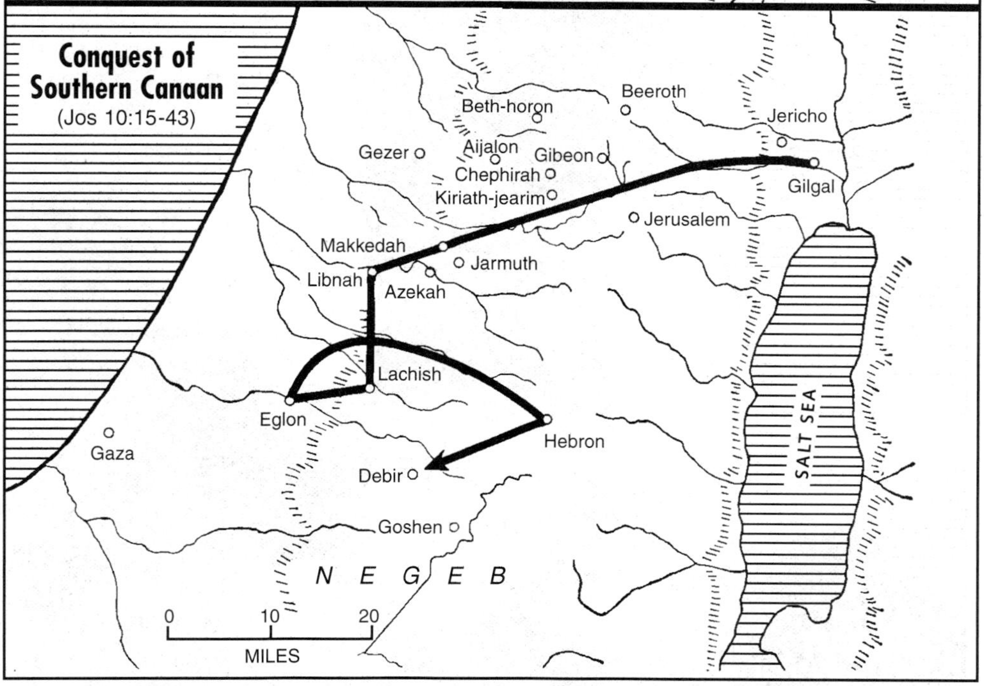

DEFEAT OF THE AMORITE KINGS (Jos 9:1—10:14) — **(a)** At **Gilgal** the Gibeonites trick Joshua into an alliance. Their cities of **Gibeon, Chephirah, Beeroth,** and **Kiriath-jearim** are spared (9:1-27). **(b)** The five kings of the Amorites, the kings of **Jerusalem, Hebron, Jarmuth, Lachish,** and **Eglon,** lay siege to **Gibeon** which asks Joshua for help (10:1-6). **(c)** From **Gilgal** Joshua goes to **Gibeon** and in the famous battle of the "sun stood still" slaughters the Amorites, chasing them by the way of ascent of **Beth-horon** and as far as **Azekah** and **Makkedah** (10:7-14).

CONQUEST OF SOUTHERN CANAAN (Jos 10:15-43) — **(b)** If **Gilgal** to **Lachish:** Joshua returns to **Gilgal,** then goes back to capture the kings who had hidden in the caves of **Makkedah.** Joshua takes **Makkedah, Libnah, Lachish,** and defeats the king of **Gezer** who had gone to the aid of Lachish. Then he takes **Eglon, Hebron,** and **Debir** (10:15-43).

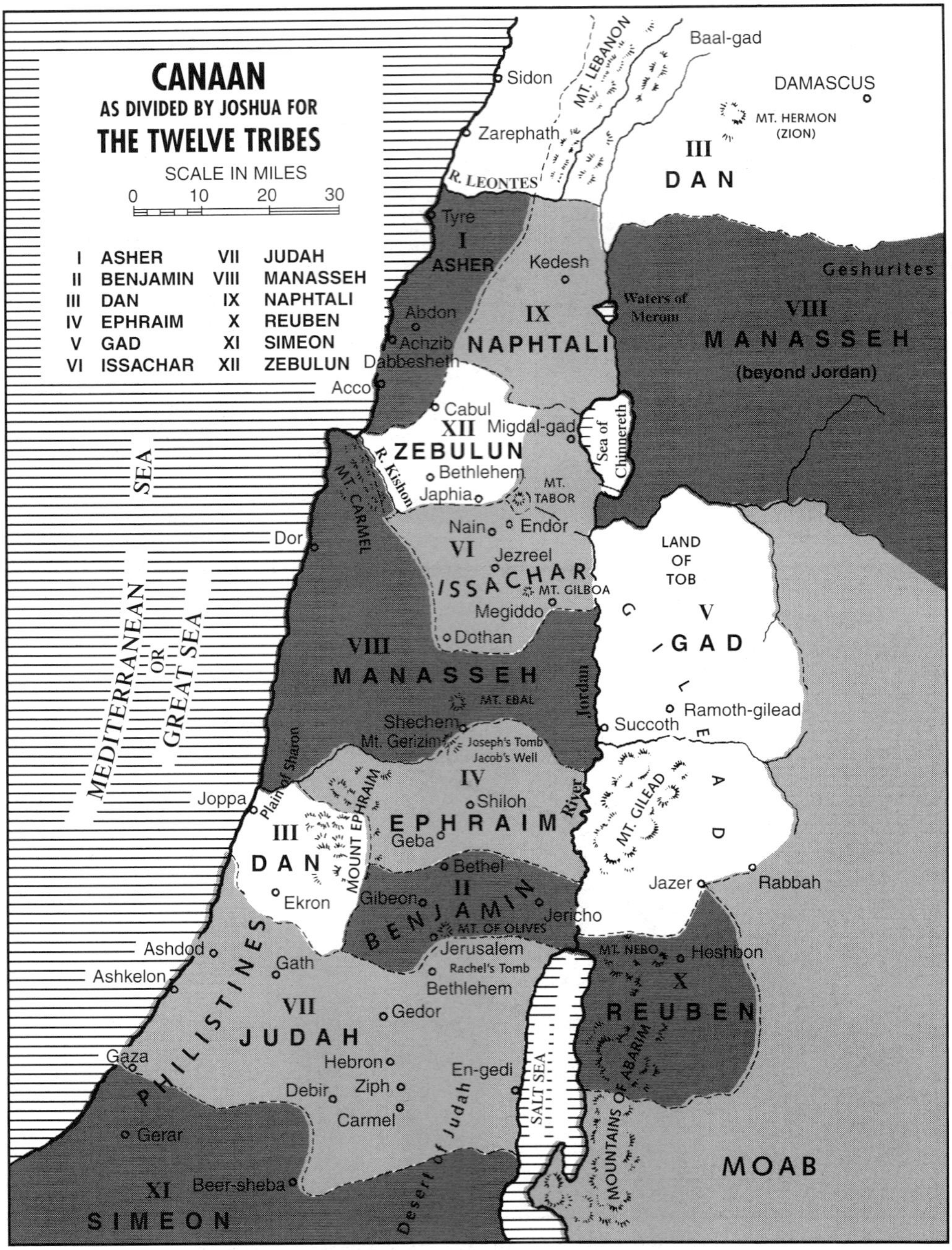

CANAAN AS DIVIDED BY JOSHUA FOR THE TWELVE TRIBES (Jos 13–19) — **(a) Judah** consists of about eighty towns in the south (15:1-12). **(b)** Southward of it in the **Negeb** is **Simeon** with seventeen towns (19:1-19). **(c)** North of Judah lies **Benjamin** with twenty-six towns (18:11-28). **(d) Dan** is at first north of Judah and west of Benjamin but later part of the tribe migrates northward and settles near Leshem, henceforth called **Dan** (19:40-48; Jdg 18). **(e) Ephraim** occupies the center of the country (16:5-9). **(f)** Half of **Manasseh** lies north of Ephraim (17:1-13) and the other half in the northern part of the country east of the Jordan (13:29-31). **(g)** Around the plain of Esdraelon lies **Issachar** (19:17-23). **(h)** West of the Sea of Chinnereth belongs to **Zebulun** (19:10-16). **(i) Asher** lies along the maritime plain of Galilee (19:24-31). **(j) Naphtali** occupies the northernmost part of the country (19:32-39). **(k)** South of the district east of Jordan dwells **Reuben** (13:15-23). **(l)** North of Reuben lies **Gad** (13:24-28).

Azekah, the LORD hurled down large hail-
stones upon them, so that more of them were
killed by the hailstones than had been killed
by the swords of the Israelites.[k]

12 On the day that the LORD delivered the
Amorites up to the Israelites, Joshua spoke
to the LORD in front of the Israelites saying,
"O Sun, stand still over Gibeon, O moon,
over the valley of Aijalon." 13 So the sun stood
still and the moon stopped until the nation
had taken vengeance upon their enemies. Is
this not written about in the Book of
Jashar? * The sun stood still in the middle of
the sky and delayed going down for a full
day.[l] 14 There had never before been a day
like this, and never will be again, a day when
the LORD listened to the voice of a man, for
the LORD fought for Israel. 15 Joshua and
all the Israelites with him then returned to
the camp in Gilgal.

Five Kings Executed. 16 These five kings fled
and hid themselves in a cave at Makkedah.
17 Joshua was told, "The five kings have been
found hidden in a cave at Makkedah."
18 Joshua said, "Roll large stones over the
mouth of the cave and assign men to guard
it, 19 but do not stay there yourselves. You
must chase after your enemies and attack
them in the rear. Do not allow them to enter
into their cities, for the LORD, your God, has
delivered them over into your hands."
20 When the Israelites had finished all but
wiping them out, and those few who
remained had slipped into fortified cities,
21 all the people returned safely to Joshua at
the camp in Makkedah. No one uttered a
sound against the Israelites.

22 Joshua said, "Open the mouth of the
cave, and bring those five kings out of the
cave to me."[m] 23 So they brought those five
kings out of the cave to him: the king of
Jerusalem, the king of Hebron, the king of
Jarmuth, the king of Lachish, and the king
of Eglon. 24 When they had brought those
five kings to Joshua, Joshua summoned all of
the men of Israel and said to the leaders of
the army who had gone out with him,
"Come here and put your feet on the necks
of these kings." * So they drew near and put
their feet on their necks. 25 Joshua said to
them, "Do not fear or be dismayed. Be
strong and courageous. This is what the
LORD will do to all of your enemies against
whom you are going to fight." 26 Joshua then
struck and killed them, hanging them from
five trees. They were left hanging from the
trees until the evening.[n] 27 At sunset Joshua
ordered that they be taken down from the
trees and cast into the cave where they had
been hiding. They placed large stones at the
mouth of the cave that are still there today.
28 That same day Joshua conquered Mak-
kedah. He put it and its king to the sword,
wiping out all of them. He did not leave any
survivors. He treated the king of Makkedah
the same way he had treated the king of
Jericho.[o]

The Conquest of Southern Canaan. 29 Joshua
and all the Israelites then moved on from
Makkedah to Libnah, and once there they
attacked Libnah. 30 The LORD handed it and
its king over into the hands of the Israelites.
They put everyone in it to the sword. He left
no survivors. He treated its king the same
way he had treated the king of Jericho.

31 Joshua and all of the Israelites then trav-
eled from Libnah to Lachish, making camp
outside of it and attacking it. 32 The LORD
handed Lachish over* into the hands of the
Israelites who took it on the second day.
They put everyone in it to the sword, just as
they had done at Libnah.

33 Horam, the king of Gezer, had come up
to assist Lachish. Joshua defeated him and
his army, leaving no survivors. 34 Joshua and
all of the Israelites then traveled from
Lachish to Eglon. They camped outside of it
and attacked it. 35 They captured it that
same day, putting everyone in it to the
sword. He totally wiped it out, just as he had
done at Lachish.

36 Joshua and all of the Israelites went up
from Eglon to Hebron and attacked it.
37 They took it and put everyone to the
sword, including its king, its dependent
towns, and all of its inhabitants. He totally
destroyed it and killed everyone in it, just as
he had done at Eglon.

38 Then Joshua and all of the Israelites
turned back to Debir and attacked it. 39 He
took it and its king and all of its dependent

---

k Job 38:22; Ps 18:13f.—l Isa 38:8.—m Deut 7:24.—n Jos 8:29.—o Jos 6:21.

10:13 *The Book of Jashar:* an ancient collection of poems (see 2 Sam 1:18) that is now lost.

10:24 *Put your feet on the necks of these kings:* this was a common demonstration of power among the military that announced to all who were victorious in battle. Here it is the Lord's triumph over the proud kings that is being proclaimed.

10:32 *The LORD handed . . . over:* the author repeatedly notes that each victory of the Israelite army comes from God.

towns. He put them all to the sword. He totally destroyed it and killed everyone in it. He left no survivors. He treated Debir and its king the same way he had treated Hebron and also Libnah and its king.

40 So Joshua struck down the entire land, the hill country, the Negeb, the western slopes and the mountain slopes and all of their kings. He left no survivors, just as the LORD, the God of Israel, had commanded.[p] 41 Joshua conquered from Kadesh-barnea up to Gaza, and the whole territory of Goshen up to Gibeon. 42 Joshua captured all of these kings and all of their lands in one campaign because the LORD, the God of Israel, was fighting for Israel. 43 Then Joshua and all of the Israelites returned to the camp at Gilgal.

CHAPTER 11

Conquest of the North. 1 When Jabin, the king of Hazor, heard about this, he sent to Jobab, the king of Madon, to the king of Shimron, to the king of Achshaph, 2 to the kings from the north who lived in the mountains, in the Arabah south of Chinneroth, in the western slopes, and in the highlands in Naphath-dor in the west,[q] 3 to the Canaanites who lived in the east and the west, to the Amorites, the Hittites, the Perizzites, the Jebusites who lived in the mountains, and to the Hivites who lived below Hermon in the land of Mizpah. 4 They went out along with all of their armies. There were as many of them as there is sand on the shore of the sea, along with a very large number of horses and chariots. 5 When all of these kings gathered together, they went and camped around the waters of Merom to do battle with Israel.

6 The LORD said to Joshua, "Do not be afraid of them, for tomorrow, around this time, I will deliver all of them up to be slain by Israel. You are to hamstring their horses and burn their chariots." 7 Joshua and the whole army with him surprised them at the waters of Merom and attacked them. 8 The LORD delivered them into the hands of the Israelites who defeated them and pursued them to Greater Sidon, to Misrephoth-maim and to the valley of Mizpah in the east. They continued to slay them until there were no survivors.[r] 9 Joshua did as the LORD had directed: the horses were hamstrung and the chariots were burned.

10 Joshua then turned back to Hazor and he captured it, putting its king to the sword. (Hazor had been at the head of all of those kingdoms.) 11 They also put everyone in it to the sword. They totally destroyed it, not leaving any survivors, and they burned Hazor to the ground. 12 Joshua captured all of these cities and their kings and he put them to the sword. He totally destroyed them, as the LORD had commanded Moses, his servant.[s] 13 But as for the cities built upon mounds, Israel did not burn any of them except for Hazor which Joshua burned. 14 The Israelites carried off the cattle and the spoils from these cities for themselves, but they put every person to the sword, totally destroying them and not leaving any survivors. 15 Whatever the LORD had commanded Moses is what Moses commanded Joshua, and Joshua did these things. He left nothing undone* from everything that the LORD had commanded Moses.[t]

Joshua's Conquests as Ordered by Moses. 16 Joshua conquered the entire land: the hill country, the Negeb, the whole of Goshen, the western slopes, the Arabah, and the mountains of Israel with their foothills, 17 from Mount Halak and the uplands toward Seir, up to Baal-gad in the Valley of Lebanon beneath Mount Hermon. He captured all of their kings and he struck them down, putting them to death.

18 Joshua waged war upon all of these kings for a long time.* 19 The Israelites conquered them all in battle. They did not make a covenant of peace with any city except with the Hivites who lived in Gibeon.[u] 20 It was the LORD himself who had hardened their hearts so that they fought against Israel and thus he might totally wipe them out, exterminating them without mercy, as the LORD had commanded Moses to do.[v]

21 It was at that time that Joshua went and crushed the Anakim* from the mountain country, from Hebron, from Debir, from Anab, from all of the hill country of Judah, and from all of the hill country of Israel.

p Deut 1:7; 20:16f.—q Jos 12:3f; Deut 7:1.—r Jos 13:6.—s Deut 7:2; 20:16f.—t Jos 1:7; Ex 34:11; Deut 7:2.—u Jos 9:3ff.—v Deut 2:30; 20:16-17.

11:15 *He left nothing undone:* Joshua's completion of God's plan begun by his servant Moses rests on his obedience in fulfilling every command issued by Moses.

11:18 The actual conquest of most of Canaan was spread out over seven years.

11:21 *Anakim:* these were the people described as giants by the Israelite spies whose reported findings about the Promised Land struck fear into the Israelites. Now they were ready to put aside their fear and pursue the enemy.

Joshua totally wiped them out along with
their cities.[w] 22 No Anakim were left in the
land of the Israelites. The only ones who sur-
vived lived in Gaza, Gath, and Ashdod. 23 So
Joshua conquered the entire land just as the
LORD had directed Moses to do. Joshua gave
it to Israel following their tribal divisions, and
there was a respite from fighting in the land.[x]

CHAPTER 12*

Conquered Kings East of the Jordan. 1 These
are the kings of the land that the Israelites
conquered and of which they took posses-
sion on the other side of the Jordan, from the
Arnon River up to Mount Hermon, includ-
ing the entire eastern side of the Arabah.[y]
2 There was Sihon, the king of the Amorites,
who lived in Heshbon and ruled from Aroer
which lay on the banks of the Arnon River.
The middle of the river up to the Jabbok
River formed the boundary with the
Ammonites. This included half of Gilead.
3 He also ruled over the eastern Arabah
from the Sea of Chinnereth to the Sea of
Arabah (the Salt Sea), the road to Beth-
jeshimoth and southward below the slopes
of the Pisgah.[z] 4 There was also Og, the
king of Bashan and its territory. He was the
last of the Rephaim,* and he lived in Ash-
taroth and Edrei, 5 and reigned over Mount
Hermon, over Salecah, and over all of
Bashan up to the boundary with the
Geshurites and the Maachathites, as well
as half of Gilead, up to the boundary with
Sihon, the king of Heshbon.* 6 Moses, the
servant of the LORD, and the Israelites con-
quered them. Moses, the servant of the
LORD, gave them into the possession of
the Reubenites, the Gadites, and one of the
halves of the tribe of Manasseh.[a]

Kings Conquered West of the Jordan.
7 These are the kings of the land that Joshua
and the Israelites conquered on this side of
the Jordan, the western side, from Baal-gad
in the Valley of Lebanon up to Mount Halak
and the uplands toward Seir. Joshua gave it
into the possession of the tribes of Israel
according to their tribal divisions. 8 There
was the hill country, the western slope, the
Arabah, the mountain slopes, the desert,
and the Negeb which belonged to the
Hittites, the Amorites, the Canaanites, the
Perizzites, the Hivites, and the Jebusites.
9 [b] There was one king from Jericho, there
was one king from Ai (which is near Bethel);
10 there was one king from Jerusalem; there
was one king from Hebron; 11 there was one
king from Jarmuth; there was one king from
Lachish; 12 there was one king from Eglon;
there was one king from Gezer;[c] 13 there was
one king from Debir; there was one king
from Geder;[d] 14 there was one king from
Hormah; there was one king from Arad;
15 there was one king from Libnah; there was
one king from Adullam; 16 there was one
king from Makkedah; there was one king
from Bethel; 17 there was one king from
Tappuah; there was one king from Hepher;
18 there was one king from Aphek; there was
one king from Lasharon; 19 there was one
king from Madon; there was one king from
Hazor; 20 there was one king from Shimron
Meron; there was one king from Achshaph;
21 there was one king from Taanach; there
was one king from Megiddo; 22 there was one
king from Kedesh; there was one king from
Jokneam in Carmel; 23 there was one king in
Dor (in Naphath-dor); there was one king of
the nations in Gilgal; 24 there was one king in
Tirzah. There were thirty-one kings in all.[e]

II: THE DIVISION OF THE LAND AMONG THE TRIBES*

CHAPTER 13

The Division Commanded by the LORD.
1 When Joshua had grown old and was well
advanced in years, the LORD said to him,
"You have grown old, and there is still quite
a bit of the land that you must conquer.*[f]
2 This is the part of the land that still
remains: the territory of the Philistines and
all of Geshur 3 from Sihor which lay near
Egypt, to the territory of Ekron in the north
(all of which is Canaanite). This is the terri-

w Num 13:33; Deut 9:2.—x Num 34:2f; Jdg 3:11; Heb 4:8.—y Deut 3:8-9.—z Jos 11:2; 13:20.—a Num 32:33.—b 9ff: Jos 6:2; 8:29.—c Jos 10:33.—d Jos 10:38-39.—e Deut 7:24.—f Jos 14:10; 23:1.

12:1-24 The conquered cities and their rulers were systematically overtaken by Joshua to the east and west of the Jordan River.

12:4 *Rephaim:* a legendary people to whom imposing monuments were attributed.

12:5 Peoples of the region, living on the southern slopes of Mount Hermon.

13:1—22:34 In the way in which they were distributed throughout Palestine and in their life there (chs. 13–22), the tribes saw the fulfillment of a promise and plan of God.

The special situation of the tribe of Levi is noteworthy. The editor several times emphasizes the point that this tribe is dedicated to the conduct of worship: the Lord is their portion.

13:1 Although Joshua was well over 80 years of age, the Lord continued to use him to fulfill his plan begun by Moses 40 years before.

tory of the five lords of the Philistines: of the
Gazathites, of the Ashdodthites, of the Ash-
kalonites, of the Gittites, of the Ekronites,
that is, the Avites.[g] 4 From the south, it
includes all of the land of the Canaanites
and Mearah, that belongs to the Sidonians,
up to Aphek, to the boundary with the
Amorites, 5 and it includes the land of the
Gebalites and all of Lebanon to the east,
from Baal-gad beneath Mount Hermon up
to the entrance to Lebo-hamath. 6 There are
also all of the inhabitants of the hill country
from Lebanon up to Misrephoth-maim, that
is, the land of the Sidonians. I myself will
drive them out before the Israelites. You are
to divide it among the Israelites as an inher-
itance as I have commanded you.[h] 7 Divide
this land as an inheritance among the nine
tribes and one-half of the tribe of Manasseh."

The Eastern Tribes. 8 The other half, the
Reubenites and the Gadites, had already
received their inheritance from Moses on
the other side of the Jordan, to the east.
Moses, the servant of God, gave it to them.[i]
9 It began at Aroer on the banks of the Arnon
River, from the city itself which is in the mid-
dle of the river, and it included the whole
plain of Medeba as far as Dibon, 10 all of the
cities of Sihon, the king of the Amorites, who
reigned in Heshbon, up to the boundary with
the Ammonites, 11 Gilead, the territory of
the Geshurites and the Maachathites, all of
Mount Hermon, all of Bashan up to Salecah,
12 and all of the kingdom of Og in Bashan
who reigned in Ashtaroth and Edrei (he was
the last of the Rephaim). Moses defeated
them and cast them out.[j]

13 The Israelites did not cast out the
Geshurites or the Maachathites. The Gesh-
urites and the Maachathites dwell among
the Israelites up to the present.*

14 He did not give any inheritance to the
tribe of Levi. The burnt offerings made to
the LORD, the God of Israel, are their inher-
itance, as he had told them.[k]

The Tribe of Reuben. 15 Moses had given an
inheritance to the Reubenites dividing it
according to their clans. 16 Their territory
included Aroer on the banks of the Arnon
River, from the city itself which is in the
middle of the river, as well as the whole plain
of Medeba, 17 Heshbon and all of its depen-
dent towns in the plain: Dibon, Bamoth-
baal, Beth-baal-meon, 18 Jahaz, Kedemoth,
Mephaath, 19 Kiriathaim, Sibmah, Zereth-
shahar on the mountain of the valley,
20 Beth-peor, the slopes of the Pisgah, and
Beth-jeshimoth. 21 These were all the cities
of the plain, the entire kingdom of Sihon, the
king of the Amorites, who reigned in
Heshbon. Moses had struck him down along
with the princes of Midian: Evi, Rekem, Zur,
Hur, and Reba, who were princes of Sihon
dwelling in that land.[l] 22 Among those who
were slain was also Balaam, the son of Beor,
whom the Israelites put to the sword.[m]
23 The boundary of the Reubenites was the
banks of the Jordan. These towns and vil-
lages are the inheritance of the Reubenites,
divided according to its clans.

The Tribe of Gad. 24 Moses gave an inheri-
tance to the Gadites, dividing it according to
their clans. 25 It included the territory of
Jezer, all of the cities of Gilead, and half of
the land of the Ammonites that ran from
Aroer near Rabbah 26 and Heshbon to
Ramath-mizpeh and Betonim, and from
Mahanaim to the boundary of Debir, 27 and
Beth-haram, Beth-nimrah, Succoth, and
Zaphon in the valley, and the rest of the
kingdom of Sihon, the king of Heshbon, with
the boundary running along the banks of
the Jordan up to the shores of the Sea of
Chinnereth (on the eastern side of the
Jordan). 28 These cities and towns were the
inheritance of the Gadites, divided accord-
ing to its clans.

The Half-tribe of Manasseh. 29 This is what
Moses gave to one of the halves of the tribe
of Manasseh, that is, the tribe of half of the
descendants of Manasseh, divided accord-
ing to its clans. 30 The territory started in
Mahanaim and included all of Bashan, the
entire territory of Og, the king of Bashan,
and all of the town in Jair in Bashan, sixty
towns in all,[n] 31 as well as half of Gilead, and
Ashtaroth and Edrei, the royal cities of Og in
Bashan. This was for the descendants of
Machir, the son of Manasseh, for one-half of
the descendants of the Machirites, divided
according to its clans.

32 These are the inheritances that Moses
distributed in the plains of Moab on the
other side of the Jordan, to the east of
Jericho. 33 But Moses did not give an inheri-

g Deut 2:23; Jdg 3:3.—h Jos 11:8.—i Jos 12:1ff; Num 32:33.—j Num 21:24; Deut 3:11.—k Num 18:20ff; Deut 18:1-2.—l Num 31:8; Deut 3:10.—m Num 31:8.—n Num 32:41.

13:13 Because the Israelites did not drive out the people in the lands they occupied, they will continue to wage battle against their pagan customs and culture.

tance to the tribe of Levi. The LORD, the God of Israel, was their inheritance, just as he had told them.[o]

CHAPTER 14

1 These are the inheritances that the Israelites received in the land of Canaan. Eleazar, the priest, and Joshua, the son of Nun, and the leaders of the ancestral tribes distributed it to them.[p] 2 The inheritance of the nine and one-half tribes was divided by lot just as the LORD had commanded Moses.[q] 3 Moses had given the inheritance to the two and one-half tribes on the other side of the Jordan. The Levites were not given an inheritance among them.[r]

4 The descendants of Joseph belonged to two tribes: Manasseh and Ephraim. The Levites were not given an inheritance in the land, only cities in which they could dwell along with their pastures for their herds and their flocks.[s] 5 The Israelites divided the land just as the LORD had commanded Moses.*

Caleb's Inheritance. 6 The Judahites came to Joshua in Gilgal, and Caleb, the son of Jephunneh, the Kenizzite, and said to him, "You know what the LORD said to Moses, the man of God, about me and you at Kadesh-barnea. 7 I was forty years old when Moses, the servant of God, sent me out from Kadesh-barnea to explore the land. I brought him back a report that expressed what I felt, 8 but my brethren who went up with me caused the hearts of the people to melt with fear. I, however, followed the LORD, my God, wholeheartedly.[t] 9 On that day Moses made an oath stating, 'The land upon which your feet have walked will be your inheritance and that of your children forever, for you have wholeheartedly followed the LORD, my God.' 10 The LORD has kept me alive these forty-five years since the LORD said this to Moses while the Israelites were wandering in the wilderness, as he promised. I am now eighty-five years old.[u] 11 I am just as strong today as on the day that Moses sent me out. I am just as vigorous in going out to fight as I was then. 12 Therefore, give me the hill country just as the LORD promised on that day. You yourself heard that day how the Anakim were there, and that their cities were large and well fortified, but if the LORD is with me, then I will be able to drive them out, just as the LORD has promised."[v]

13 Joshua blessed Caleb, the son of Jephunneh, and gave him Hebron as his inheritance. 14 Hebron has belonged to Caleb, the son of Jephunneh, the Kenizzite, as an inheritance ever since because he wholeheartedly followed the LORD, the God of Israel.[w] 15 (Hebron used to be called Kiriath-arba. It was named after Arba, the greatest of the Anakim.)

There was then a respite from fighting in the land.

CHAPTER 15

The Tribe of Judah. 1 The allotment for the tribe of the Judahites, divided according to its clans, extended to the boundary with Edom, down to the Desert of Zin in the extreme southern regions.[x] 2 Their southern boundary lie on the bay at the southern end of the Salt Sea. 3 It continued south of Akrabbim on to Zin, going up to the south of Kadesh-barnea past Hebron, up to Addar and it curved around to Karka. 4 It then passed along to Azmon out to the Wadi of Egypt, the border being on the sea. This shall be your southern boundary.[y] 5 The eastern boundary was the Salt Sea as far as the mouth of the Jordan.

The boundary of the northern quarter began at the bay of the sea at the mouth of the Jordan. 6 The boundary ran up to Beth-hoglah and passed to the north of Beth-arabah, and then it ran up to the stone of Bohan, the son of Reuben.[z] 7 The boundary then went up to Debir from the Valley of Achor, and then northward, in the direction of Gilgal that faces the Pass of Adummim on the south side of the river. The boundary then passed along the waters of En-shemesh until they flow out at En-rogel.[a] 8 The boundary then runs along the Valley of Ben-hinnom to the south of the Jebusite city (that is, Jerusalem). From there the boundary climbs up to the top of the mountain that lies to the west of the Hinnom Valley at the northern end of the Valley of Rephaim. 9 The boundary then runs from the top of the hill down to the spring of the waters of Nephtoah, going along to the cities of Mount

---

o Num 18:20; Deut 10:9.—p Num 34:17.—q Num 26:55.—r Jos 13:14; Num 32:33.—s Gen 48:5.—t Num 13:31-32; 14:24.—u Num 14:30.—v Jos 11:21-22; Num 13:33.—w Jos 22:6.—x Num 34:3-4.—y Num 34:5.—z Jos 18:18-19.—a Jos 7:26.

14:5 The division of the land by casting lots as commanded to Moses by the Lord (v. 2) was carried out exactly by his successor Joshua.

Ephron, continuing down to Baalah (that is,
Kiriath-jearim).[b] [10] The boundary then
curves westward from Baalah to Mount
Seir, running along the northern slopes of
Mount Jearim (that is, Chesalon), down to
Beth-shemesh and over to Timnah. [11] The
boundary runs along the northern slopes of
Ekron, passing on to Shikkeron, running
along Mount Baalah and reaching up to
Jabneel. This boundary ends at the sea.
[12] The western boundary lies along the shore
of the Great Sea.* This is the boundary that
runs around the Judahites according to their
clans.

Conquest by Caleb. [13] Joshua gave Caleb,
the son of Jephunneh, an inheritance among
the Judahites, as the LORD had commanded:
Kiriath-arba, that is, Hebron. (Arba was the
forefather of the Anak.)[c] [14] Caleb drove the
three Anakim out from it, that is Sheshai,
Ahiman, and Talmai. They were descen-
dants of Anak.[d] [15] From there he marched
out against the people living in Debir. (Debir
was previously called Kiriath-sepher.)[e]
[16] * Caleb said, "I will give my daughter
Achsah in marriage to the man who attacks
and captures Kiriath-sepher." [17] Othniel, the
son of Kenaz, the brother of Caleb, captured
it, so he gave him his daughter Achsah in
marriage. [18] One day she went up to him and
she urged him to ask her father for a field.
When she got off her donkey, Caleb said to
her, "What can I do for you?" [19] She
answered, "Please do me a favor. Since you
have already given me land in the Negeb,
give me some springs as well." He gave her
the upper springs and the lower springs.

The Cities of Judah. [20] This is the inheri-
tance of the Judahites, divided according to
its clans. [21] The cities at the edge of the land
of the Judahites in the direction of the
boundary with Edom in the south were:
Kabzeel, Eder, Jagur,[f] [22] Kinah, Dimonah,
Adadah, [23] Kedesh, Hazor, Ithnan, [24] Ziph,
Telem, Bealoth, [25] Hazor-hadattah, Kerioth-
hezron (that is, Hazor), [26] Amam, Shema,
Moladah, [27] Hazar-gaddah, Heshmon, Beth-
pelet, [28] Hazar-shual, Beersheba, Biziothiah,
[29] Baalah, Iim, Ezem, [30] Eltolad, Chesil,
Hormah, [31] Ziklag, Madmannah, Sansan-
nah, [32] Lebaoth, Shilhim, Ain, and Rimmon.
All together there were twenty-nine cities
along with the towns dependent upon them.

[33] On the western slopes there were:
Eshtaol, Zorah, Ashnah,[g] [34] Zanoah, En-gan-
nim, Tappuah, Enam, [35] Jarmuth, Adullam,
Socoh, Azekah, [36] Shaaraim, Adithaim, and
Gederah (that is, Gederothaim). There were
fourteen of these cities along with their
dependent towns. [37] There were also Zenan,
Hadashah, Migdal-gad, [38] Dilean, Mizpeh,
Joktheel, [39] Lachish, Bozkath, Eglon, [40] Cab-
bon, Lahmas, Chitlish, [41] Gederoth, Beth-
dagon, Naamah, and Makkedah. There were
sixteen of these cities along with their depen-
dent towns. [42] There were also Libnah, Ether,
Ashan, [43] Iphtah, Ashnah, Nezib, [44] Keilah,
Achzib, and Mareshah. There were nine of
these cities along with their dependent towns.
[45] There was also Ekron with its dependent
towns, [46] and the territory between Ekron
and the sea, near Ashdod, with all of their
dependent towns. [47] There was Ashdod along
with its dependent towns and villages, as well
as Gaza along with its dependent towns and
villages, all the way to the Wadi of Egypt and
the coast of the Great Sea.

[48] In the mountains there were Shamir,
Jattir, Socoh, [49] Dannah, Kiriath-sannah
(that is, Debir), [50] Anab, Eshtemoh, Anim,
[51] Goshen, Holon, and Giloh. There were
eleven of these cities along with their depen-
dent towns. [52] There were also Arab,
Dumah, Eshan, [53] Janim, Beth-tappuah,
Aphekah, [54] Humtah, Kiriath-arba (that is,
Hebron), and Zior. There were nine of these
cities along with their dependent towns.
[55] There were also Maon, Carmel, Ziph,
Juttah, [56] Jezreel, Jokdeam, Zanoah, [57] Kain,
Gibbeah, and Timnah. There were ten of
these cities along with their dependent
towns. [58] There were also Halhul, Beth-zur,
Gedor, [59] Maarath, Beth-anoth, and Eltekon.
There were six of these cities, along with
their dependent towns. [60] There were also
Kiriath-baal (that is, Kiriath-jearim) and
Rabbah. There were two of these cities along
with their dependent towns.[h]

[61] In the wilderness there were Beth-
arabah, Middin, Secacah, [62] Nibshan, the
City of Salt, and En-gedi. There were six of
these cities, along with their dependent
towns. [63] The Judahites could not drive out

b Jos 18:15.—c Jdg 1:10.—d Jos 11:21; Num 13:22; Jdg 1:20.—e Jos 10:38.—f Gen 35:21; 2 Sam 23:20.—g Jdg 13:25; 16:31.—h Jos 18:14.

15:12 *The Great Sea:* the Mediterranean.

15:16-19 In addition to winning the hand of Caleb's daughter Achsah in marriage, Othniel will become the first of the minor judges of Israel after Joshua's death (Jdg 1:13; 3:7-11).

the Jebusites, the people who were living in
Jerusalem. The Jebusites live in Jerusalem
among the Judahites up to the present.[i]

CHAPTER 16

The Tribe of Ephraim. 1 * The allotment for
the descendants of Joseph ran from the
Jordan by Jericho, east of the waters of
Jericho, and ran up into the hill country of
Bethel. 2 It went from Bethel (that is, Luz)
over to the boundary of the Arkites in
Ataroth. 3 It then descended westward to the
territory of the Japhletites up to the territory
of lower Beth-horon and on to Gezer, ending
at the sea.[j] 4 Manasseh and Ephraim, the
sons of Joseph, received their inheritance.

5 This is the territory of the Ephraimites,
divided according to its clans. The boundary
of the inheritance went from Ataroth-addar
in the east to upper Beth-horon[k] 6 and it
continued on to the sea. From Micmethath
in the north it curved eastward to Taanath-
shiloh, passing by it to the east of Janoah. 7 It
went down from Janoah to Ataroth and
Naarah, arriving at Jericho and then ending
at the Jordan. 8 From Tappuah the boundary
reached westward to the Kanah River and
from there it went to the sea. This was the
inheritance of the tribe of the Ephraimites,
divided according to its clans.[l] 9 It included
all of the cities that were set aside for the
Ephraimites in the inheritance of the
Manassehites, the cities and their dependent
towns. 10 They did not drive out the
Canaanites who were living in Gezer. The
Canaanites live among the Ephraimites up
to the present and they serve them doing
forced labor.[m]

CHAPTER 17

The Tribe of Manasseh. 1 This was the allot-
ment for the tribe of Manasseh, who was the
firstborn of Joseph, that is, of Machir, who
was the firstborn of Manasseh, and he was
also the father of the Gileadites because he
had received Gilead and Bashan since he
was a mighty warrior.[n] 2 This was the allot-
ment for the rest of the Manassehites, the
clans of the descendants of Abiezer, Helek,
Asriel, Shechem, Hepher, and Shemida.
These are the other male descendants of
Manasseh, the son of Joseph, according to
their clans.

3 *[o] Now Zelophehad, the son of Hepher,
the son of Gilead, the son of Machir, the son
of Manasseh had no sons, only daughters.
These are the names of his daughters:
Mahlah, Noah, Hoglah, Milcah, and Tirzah.
4 They went to Eleazar, the priest, to Joshua,
the son of Nun, and the elders and said, "The
LORD commanded Moses to give us an
inheritance among our brothers." He there-
fore gave them an inheritance among the
brothers of their father, just as the LORD had
commanded.

5 Manasseh's portion consisted of ten
parcels of land besides Gilead and Bashan,
which were on the east side of the Jordan,
6 for the daughters of Manasseh received an
inheritance along with the sons. The land of
Gilead belonged to the rest of the descen-
dants of Manasseh. 7 The territory of the
Manassehites ran from Asher to Micmethath
east of Shechem. The boundary then ran
south from there, so it included the people
living at En-tappuah. 8 (Manasseh had
received the land around Tappuah, which
lay on the boundary with Manasseh, but
Tappuah itself belonged to the Ephraim-
ites.) 9 The boundary then continued on
south to the Wadi Kanah. There were some
towns that belonged to Ephraim among the
towns of Manasseh, but Manasseh's bound-
ary ran along the north side of the river,
ending at the sea. 10 To the south, the land
belonged to Ephraim, while to the north the
land belonged to Manasseh. Its boundary
ended at the sea, bordering Asher on the
north and Issachar on the east.

11 Within Asher and Issachar, Manasseh
also possessed Beth-shan and the towns that
were dependent upon it, Ibleam and the
towns dependent upon it, the inhabitants of
Dor and the towns dependent upon it, the
inhabitants of Endor and the towns depen-
dent upon it, the inhabitants of Taanach and
the towns dependent upon it, and the inhab-
itants of Megiddo and the towns dependent
upon it. (These are three mountainous
areas.)[p]

---

i Jdg 1:21; 2 Sam 5:6.—j Jos 10:10; 18:13.—k Jos 18:13.—l Jos 17:8-9.—m Jdg 1:29; 1 Ki 9:16.—n Gen 50:23; Deut 3:15.—o Num 27:1-7.—p 1 Chr 7:29.

16:1—17:18 None of the 12 tribes is named for Joseph, the eldest of Jacob's sons. Instead, the largest and most ideal area is reserved for Joseph's two sons Ephraim and Manasseh.

17:3-4 The unusual situation of Israelite women inheriting property is carried out by Joshua in accordance with the law instituted by Moses at God's command (Num 27:1-11). Zelophehad's daughters reaped the benefits of this new law and set a precedent for future women.

[12] Yet, the Manassehites were not able to
occupy these cities, for the Canaanites were
determined to continue to live in that land.
[13] When the Israelites grew stronger, they
did subject the Canaanites to forced labor,
but they did not drive them out completely.
[14] * The descendants of Joseph said to
Joshua, "Why have you given us only one
allotment, one portion as our inheritance.
We are quite numerous, for the LORD has
blessed us." [q] [15] But Joshua answered them,
"If you are too numerous for the hill country
of Ephraim, then go up into the forest and
clear land for yourselves in the land of the
Perizzites and the Rephaim." [16] The descen-
dants of Joseph replied, "The hill country is
too small for us, and the Canaanites who live
in the plains have iron chariots, both the
ones living in Beth-shean and the towns
dependent upon it and those living in the
Valley of Jezreel." [r] [17] Joshua said to the
descendants of Joseph, to Ephraim and
Manasseh, "You are a numerous and very
powerful people. You will have more than
one allotment. [18] The forested hill country
will also be yours. Cut it down, and it will be
yours right to its fringes. The Canaanites
might have iron chariots and be strong, but
you can drive them out."

CHAPTER 18

[1] * The whole assembly of the Israelites
gathered together at Shiloh and they set up
the tent of meeting there. The land had been
brought under their control, [s] [2] but there
were still seven tribes among the Israelites
who had not yet received their inheritance.

Inheritance for the Remaining Seven Tribes.
[3] Joshua said to the Israelites, "How long will
you wait before you go in to take possession
of the land that the LORD, the God of your
fathers, has given you? [4] Choose three men
from each of your tribes. I will send them to
arise and go through the land, describing it
according to each of their inheritances. They
will then return to me. [5] They will divide it
into seven portions. Judah will continue to
live in its territory to the south, and the
descendants of Joseph will continue to live in
their territory to the north. [t] [6] You will write
down a description of the seven portions of
the land and bring it to me. I will cast lots for
you here before the LORD, our God. [7] The
Levites will have no portion among you, for
the priesthood of the LORD is their inheri-
tance. Gad, Reuben, and one of the halves of
the tribe of Manasseh have already received
their inheritance on the other side of the
Jordan, to the east, from Moses, the servant
of the LORD." [u]

[8] So the men arose and went on their way.
Joshua commanded them to write a
description of the land saying, "Go and trav-
el through the land, writing a description of
it. Return to me here so that I can cast lots
for you before the LORD in Shiloh."

[9] The men traveled through the land, writ-
ing a description of its cities, divided into
seven portions, in a book. They then came
back to Joshua in the camp at Shiloh.
[10] Joshua cast lots for them in Shiloh before
the LORD. Joshua divided the land among
the Israelites there, dividing it according to
their allotments. [v]

The Tribe of Benjamin. [11] The lot for the
tribe of Benjamin, divided according to its
clans, was selected. The territory for their
allotment lay between the Judahites and the
descendants of Joseph. [12] * On the north
their boundary started at the Jordan, going
up the northern slope of Jericho and out
west into the hill country until it exited in
the Desert of Beth-aven. [13] From there the
boundary traveled on toward Luz, passing
on the southern side of Luz (that is, Bethel).
The boundary then ran down to Ataroth-
addar, near the hill that lay to the south of
Lower Beth-horon. [14] From the hill that lay
facing Beth-horon on the south, the bound-
ary extended around the west side to the
south. It ended at Kiriath-baal (that is,
Kiriath-jearim), a city of Judahites. This was
the western side. [w]

[15] The southern side of the boundary
began at the outskirts of Kiriath-jearim and
extended to the west, reaching the spring of
the water of Nephtoah. [16] The boundary
extended to the foot of the hill that lay over

q Gen 48:19-22; Num 26:34-37.—r Jdg 1:19; 4:3.—s Jos 19:51.—t Jos 15:1—17:18.—u Jos 13:8, 33.—v Jos 19:51.—w Jos 15:9.

17:14-18 Here we see the real damage that ensued in Ephraim and Manasseh because they had not driven out the Canaanites from the land. Rather than simply hand over more land to them because of what was occupied, Joshua insisted that they prove themselves worthy.

18:1-2 The conquest of the promised land was not yet complete—seven tribes had not been assigned their land. But it seemed that the time was appropriate to move the Israelite center of worship from Gilgal to Shiloh.

18:12-20 The narrow strip of land inherited by the Benjaminites lay between the land of the two most powerful tribes of Judah and Ephraim.

the Valley of Ben-hinnom, north of the Valley of Rephaim. It continued through the Valley of Hinnom on the southern slope of the city of the Jebusites until it reached En-rogel.[x] 17 It then passed on north to En-shemesh, continued on to Geliloth which faced the Pass of Adummim, and ran up to the stone of Bohan, the son of Reuben. 18 It continued along the northern slope of the Arabah, continuing down into the Arabah itself. 19 The boundary then passed along the northern side of Beth-hoglah, ending at the northern bay of the Salt Sea which is at the southern part of the Jordan. This was their southern boundary. 20 The Jordan was their boundary on the east. This was the inheritance of the Benjaminites with the boundaries that surround it, divided according to its clans.

21 The cities of the tribe of the Benjaminites, divided according to its clans, were: Jericho, Beth-hoglah, Emek-keziz, 22 Beth-arabah, Zemaraim, Bethel, 23 Avvim, Parah, Ophrah, 24 Chephar-ammoni, Ophni, and Geba. There were twelve cities, along with their dependent towns. 25 There were also Gibeon, Ramah, Beeroth, 26 Mizpah, Chephirah, Mozah, 27 Rekem, Irpeel, Taralah, 28 Zela, Haeleph, Jebus (that is, Jerusalem), Gibeah, and Kiriath. There were fourteen cities with their dependent towns. This was the inheritance of the Benjaminites, divided according to its clans.

CHAPTER 19

The Tribe of Simeon.* 1 The second lot chosen was for Simeon, the tribe of the Simeonites, divided according to its clans. Their inheritance lay within the inheritance of the Judahites. 2 Their inheritance included: Beer-sheba (that is, Sheba), Moladah, 3 Hazar-shual, Balah, Ezem, 4 Eltolad, Bethul, Hormah, 5 Ziklag, Beth-marcaboth, Hazar-susah,[y] 6 Beth-lebaoth, and Sharuhen. There were thirteen of these cities along with the towns dependent upon them. 7 There were also Ain, Rimmon, Ether, and Ashan. There were four of these cities, along with the towns dependent upon them. 8 There were also all of the villages around these cities up to Baalath-beer (that is, Ramoth-negeb). This was the inheritance of the tribe of Simeon, divided according to its clans. 9 The inheritance of the Simeonites was taken from the portion allotted to the Judahites, for Judah's portion was too large for what they needed. Therefore, the Simeonites received their portion inside of their inheritance.

The Tribe of Zebulun. 10 The third lot chosen was for the Zebulunites, divided according to its clans. The boundary of their inheritance extended to Sarid. 11 It ran westward to Mareal up to Dabbesheth, extending up to the river in front of Jokneam. 12 Going eastward from Sarid, in the direction of the sunrise, it ran to the territory of Chisloth-tabor and then went on to Daberath, arriving in Japhia. 13 From there it continued eastward to Gath-hepher and Eth-kazim. It went out to Rimmon and turned toward Neah. 14 There the boundary went around the north side of Hannathon, ending in the Valley of Iphtahel. 15 It included Kattath, Nahalal, Shimron, Idalah, and Bethlehem. There were twelve cities along with the towns dependent upon them.[z] 16 These cities and villages were the inheritance of the Zebulunites, divided according to its clans.

The Tribe of Issachar. 17 The fourth lot chosen was for the Issacharites, divided according to its clans. 18 Within their boundaries were: Jezreel, Chesulloth, Shunem, 19 Hapharaim, Shion, Anaharath, 20 Rabbith, Kishion, Ebez, 21 Remeth, En-gannim, En-haddah, and Beth-pazzez. 22 The boundary passed Tabor, Shahazumah, and Beth-shemesh, ending at the Jordan. There were sixteen cities along with the towns dependent upon them. 23 These cities and these villages were the inheritance of the tribe of Issachar, divided according to its clans.

The Tribe of Asher. 24 The fifth lot chosen was for the Asherites. 25 Within their boundaries were: Helkath, Hali, Beten, Achshaph, 26 Allammelech, Amad, and Mishal. On its western side the boundary passed Carmel and Shihor-libnath. 27 It turned toward the sunrise, passing Beth-dagon, arriving at Zebulun and the Valley of Iphtahel. From there it went north to Beth-emek and Neiel, passing by Cabul on the left. 28 [a] It ran on to Abdon, Rehob, Hammon, and Kanah, extending to Greater Sidon. 29 The boundary then turned toward Ramah, and ran to the fortified city of Tyre. It turned toward Hosah, ending at the sea in the area around

x 2 Ki 23:10.—y 1 Sam 30:1.—z Mic 5:2.—a 28-30: Jdg 1:31.

19:1-9 The lot chosen for Simeon lay within Judah. Neither leader would argue with this, since it was clear that it was God who was assigning them.

Achzib. 30 It included Ummah, Acco, Aphek,
and Rehob. There were twenty-two cities
along with the towns dependent upon them.
31 These cities and villages were the inheri-
tance of the tribe of Asher, divided accord-
ing to its clans.

The Tribe of Naphtali. 32 The sixth lot cho-
sen was for the Naphtalites, divided
according to its clans. 33 Their boundary
went from Heleph and the large tree at
Zaanannim to Adami-nekeb, Jabneel,
Lakkum, and ended at the Jordan. 34 To the
west it went through Aznoth-tabor, arriv-
ing at Hukkok. It passed Zebulun on its
southern side, Asher on its western side,
and the Jordan in the direction of the sun-
rise. 35 Its fortified cities included: Ziddim,
Zer, Hammath, Rakkath, Chinnereth,
36 Adamah, Ramah, Hazor, 37 Kedesh,
Edrei, En-hazor, 38 Yiron, Migdalel, Horem,
Beth-anath, and Beth-shemesh. There
were nineteen cities along with the towns
dependent upon them. 39 These cities and
villages were the inheritance of the tribe of
Naphtali, divided according to its clans.

The Tribe of Dan. 40 The seventh lot chosen
was for the Danites, divided according to its
clans. 41 Within the boundaries of their
inheritance were: Zorah, Eshtaol, Ir-
shemesh, 42 Shaalabbin, Aijalon, Ithlah, [b]
43 Elon, Timnah, Ekron, 44 Eltekoh, Gib-
bethon, Baalath, 45 Jehud, Bene-berak,
Gath-rimmon, 46 Me-jarkon, and Rakkon,
along with the area in front of Joppa. 47 (But
the territory of the Danites was outside of
this area. The Danites went up to fight
against Leshem. They conquered it and put
it to the sword. They took possession of it
and dwelt there. They renamed Leshem
Dan after the name of Dan, their forefa-
ther.) [c] 48 These were the cities and the vil-
lages of the inheritance of the tribe of Dan,
divided according to its clans.

49 * When they finished dividing the land
into its allotted portions, the Israelites gave
an inheritance among themselves to Joshua,
the son of Nun 50 as the LORD had com-
manded. They gave him the city he had
requested: Timnah-serah in the hill country
of Ephraim. He built a city and settled
there. [d]

51 These are the inheritances that were
divided up by lot at Shiloh in the presence of
the LORD at the entrance to the tent of meet-
ing by Eleazar, the priest, by Joshua, the son
of Nun, and by the leaders of the ancestral
tribes of the Israelites. This concluded the
process of dividing up the land.

CHAPTER 20

The Cities of Refuge.* 1 The LORD then said
to Joshua, 2 "Speak to the Israelites and say,
'Choose refuge cities for yourselves, just as I
told you to do through Moses. [e] 3 This way
anyone who kills another accidentally or
unintentionally can flee there and take
refuge from the relative who seeks blood
vengeance. 4 When he flees to one of those
cities, he is to stand at the entrance to the
city gate and state his case in the hearing of
the elders of the city. They will then let him
enter the city, and they are to give him a
place where he can live with them. 5 If the
relative who seeks blood vengeance pursues
him, they are not to surrender the man who
killed another into his hands, for he killed his
neighbor unintentionally and he had not
previously shown him any enmity. 6 He will
continue to live in that city until he stands
trial before the assembly, and until the death
of the high priest who is then in office. At
that point the man who killed another can
go back to his own city, to his home, to the
city from which he had fled.' "

7 So they set apart Kadesh in Galilee in the
hill country of Naphtali, Shechem in the hill
country of Ephraim, and Kiriath-arba (that
is, Hebron) in the hill country of Judah. [f]
8 On the other side of the Jordan, to the east
of Jericho, they set aside Bezer in the wilder-
ness upon the plateau of the tribe of Reuben,
Ramoth in Gilead among the tribe of Gad,
and Golan in Bashan among the tribe of
Manasseh. [g] 9 These cities were designated so
that any Israelite or foreigner who lived
among them and who accidentally killed
another person might flee there, so that he
would not be killed by the relative who seeks
blood vengeance before he could stand trial
before the assembly.

---

b Jdg 1:35.—c Jdg 18:27-31.—d Jos 24:30; Jdg 2:9.—e Num 35:6-34; Deut 4:41; 19:2-3.—f Jos 21:9-16; 1 Chr 6:76; Lk 1:39.—g Jos 21:27, 36, 38.

19:49-50 After the boundaries for each tribe had been assigned, marking their areas of responsibility and avoiding conflicts over the choicest locations, Joshua, as the Lord had commanded, was awarded the city that he had requested for his obedient service to God's people.

20:1-9 God had prepared the Israelites to function well in their new land through his instructions to Moses many years earlier. The laws that required the establishment of "cities of refuge"—for someone who committed an unintentional murder—are detailed in Num 35:9-28; Deut 19:1-13.

CHAPTER 21

The Levitical Cities. 1 Now the leaders of the
ancestral clans of the Levites came to
Eleazar, the priest, Joshua, the son of Nun,
and the leaders of the ancestral tribes of the
Israelites 2 at Shiloh in the land of Canaan
and they said to them, "The LORD com-
manded through Moses that you give us
cities in which we can live and have pastures
for our cattle." * [h] 3 So the Israelites gave the
Levites cities and pastures out of their own
inheritance as the LORD had commanded.
4 The first lot chosen was for the Kohathites,
divided according to its families. Now the
Levites were the descendants of Aaron the
priest, and they were allotted thirteen cities
out of the inheritance of the tribes of Judah,
Simeon, and Benjamin. 5 The rest of the
descendants of Kohath were allotted ten
cities from the inheritance of the clans of the
tribes of Ephraim, Dan, and one of the halves
of the tribe of Manasseh. 6 The descendants
of Gershom were allotted thirteen cities
from the inheritance of the clans of the
tribes of Issachar, Asher, Naphtali, and the
half of the tribe of Manasseh that was living
in Bashan. 7 The descendants of Merari,
divided according to its families, were allot-
ted twelve cities from the inheritance of the
tribes of Reuben, Gad, and Zebulun. 8 This is
how the Israelites gave the Levites their cities
with their pastures, just as the LORD had
commanded through Moses.

9 These are the names of the cities that
were given from the tribe of the Judahites
and the tribe of the Simeonites. 10 (These
cities were given to the descendants of
Aaron who came from the Kohathite clan
because their lot was the first chosen.)
11 They were given Kiriath-arba (that is,
Hebron; Arba was the forefather of Anak)
and its surrounding pastures in the hill
country of Judah, [i] 12 but the fields belong-
ing to the city and the towns surrounding
it had already been given to Caleb, the son
of Jephunneh, as his possession. 13 So the
descendants of Aaron the priest were
given Hebron (which was a city of refuge
for someone who had killed another per-
son) and its pastures, Libnah and its pas-
tures, 14 Jattir and its pastures, Eshtemoa
and its pastures, 15 Holon and its pastures,
Debir and its pastures, 16 Ain and its pas-
tures, Juttah and its pastures, and Beth-
shemesh and its pastures. Thus, there
were nine cities from those two tribes.
17 From the tribe of Benjamin they were
given Gibeon and its pastures, Geba and
its pastures, 18 Anathoth and its pastures,
and Almon and its pastures. Thus, there
were four cities. [j] 19 In total, there were
thirteen cities with their pastures for the
descendants of Aaron the priest.

Cities of the Other Kohathites. 20 As for the
rest of the Kohathite families of the Levites,
these Kohathites were allotted cities out of
the inheritance of Ephraim. 21 In the hill
country of Ephraim they were given
Shechem (which was a city of refuge for
someone who had killed another person)
and its pastures, Gezer and its pastures,
22 Kibzaim with its pastures, and Beth-
horon with its pastures. Thus, there were
four cities. 23 From the tribe of Dan they
were given Elteke and its pastures, Gib-
bethon and its pastures, 24 Aijalon with its
pastures, and Gath-rimmon with its pas-
tures. Thus, there were four cities.

25 From one of the halves of the tribe of
Manasseh they were given Taanach with its
pastures, and Gath-rimmon with its pas-
tures. Thus, there were two cities. 26 In total,
there were ten cities with their pastures that
were given to the rest of the Kohathites.

The Cities of the Gershonites. [k] 27 The
Levite's clans of the Gershonites were given
from the other half-tribe of Manasseh, Golan
in Bashan (which was a city of refuge for
someone who had killed another) and its pas-
tures, and Ashtaroth and its pastures. Thus,
there were two cities. 28 From the tribe of
Issachar they were given Kishion and its pas-
tures, Daberath and its pastures, 29 Jarmuth
and its pastures, and En-gannim and its pas-
tures. Thus, there were four cities. 30 From the
tribe of Asher they were given Mishal with its
pastures, Abdon with its pastures, 31 Helkath
with its pastures, and Rehob with its pas-
tures. Thus, there were four cities. 32 From the
tribe of Naphtali they were given Kedesh in
Galilee (which was a city of refuge for some-
one who had killed another) and its pastures,
Hammath and its pastures, and Kartan and
its pastures. Thus, there were three cities. 33 In

h Num 35:1-2; 1 Chr 6:54.—i Jos 15:13; 1 Chr 6:55.—j 1 Chr 6:60; Jer 1:1.—k 27-33: 1 Chr 6:56-61.

21:2 In order that the Levites could minister to all the Israelites (Num 35:1-8) they were given special property rights in many of the cities occupied by the different tribes, thus making it possible for the people to have ready access to their priests.

total, there were thirteen cities with their pastures for the Gershonite families.

The Cities of the Merarites. 34 [l] The Merarite families (the rest of the Levites) were given from the tribe of Zebulun, Jokneam with its pastures, Kartah with its pastures, 35 Dimnah with its pastures, and Nahalal with its pastures. Thus, there were four cities. 36 From the tribe of Reuben they were given Bezer with its pastures, Jahaz with its pastures, 37 Kedemoth with its pastures, and Mephaath and its pastures. Thus, there were four cities. 38 From the tribe of Gad they were given Ramoth in Gilead (which was a city of refuge for someone who had killed another) and its pastures, Mahanaim and its pastures, 39 Heshbon and its pastures, and Jazer with its pastures. Thus, there were four cities. 40 In total, there were twelve cities allotted to the families of the Merarites (the rest of the Levites).

41 In all, there were forty-eight cities together with their pastures for the Levites within the land in the possession of the Israelites. [m] 42 Each of these cities has pastures surrounding it; this was true of all of the cities.

43 * [n] Thus the LORD gave Israel the entire land that he had promised to give to their fathers. They took possession of it and dwelt there. 44 The LORD then gave them rest on every side, just as he had promised their fathers. Not one of their enemies could stand up to them. The LORD had delivered all of their enemies into their hands. 45 None of the good things that the LORD had promised to the house of Israel failed to take place. It all came true. [o]

III: THE RETURN OF THE EASTERN TRIBES AND JOSHUA'S FAREWELL

CHAPTER 22

Dismissal of the Tribes. 1 Joshua then summoned the Reubenites, the Gadites, and one of the halves of the tribe of Manasseh 2 and he said to them, "You have done all that Moses, the servant of the LORD, commanded you to do, and you have obeyed me in everything. 3 For a long time now, right up to this very day, you have not deserted your brothers. You have fulfilled the task that the LORD, your God, gave you. 4 Now that the LORD, your God, has given your brothers the rest that he had promised them, you can return to your homes in the land that Moses, the servant of the LORD, gave you as a possession on the other side of the Jordan. [p] 5 Take heed to follow the commandments and the laws that Moses, the servant of the LORD, gave you: to love the LORD, your God, and to walk in his ways and to observe his commandments, holding fast to him and serving him with all your heart and all your soul." * [q]

6 Joshua then blessed them and sent them away, and they returned to their homes.

7 (Moses had given Bashan to one of the halves of the tribe of Manasseh, while Joshua gave the other half some land among their brothers on the western side of the Jordan.) When Joshua sent them to their homes, he blessed them [r] 8 saying, "Return to your homes with your great wealth: your numerous cattle as well as silver, gold, bronze, and iron, and your numerous garments. Divide the spoils from your enemies among your brethren." *

9 So the Reubenites, the Gadites, and one of the halves of the tribe of Manasseh left the Israelites at Shiloh, in the land of Canaan, to travel to the land of Gilead, the land they were to possess. They were given possession of it by the word of the LORD through Moses. [s]

The Altar across the Jordan. 10 When they arrived at Geliloth near the Jordan, the Reubenites, the Gadites, and one of the halves of the tribe of Manasseh built an altar there beside the Jordan. It was an impressive altar, something to see.

11 The Israelites then heard that the Reubenites, the Gadites, and one of the halves of the tribe of Manasseh had built an altar at Geliloth, on the border of Canaan, on the Israelite side of the Jordan. [t] 12 The Israelites heard about this and the whole

l 34-38: 1 Chr 6:22-66.—m Num 35:7.—n 43ff: Gen 13:15; Deut 11:31.—o Jos 23:14-15.—p Num 32:18; Deut 3:20.—q Deut 6:6, 17; 10:12.—r Jos 17:5; Num 32:33.—s Jos 18:1; Num 32:1, 26, 29.—t Deut 13:12-14.

21:43—22:34 Now that the land has been conquered and the distribution of it made, the tribes begin a more sedentary life. Israel enters into a period of peaceful possession, although the definitive settlement means a serious task for each territory (see the Book of Judges).

22:5 Considering that the Israelites had for so many years been preoccupied with the physical side of life, Joshua takes this opportunity to restate the need for them to make love of God and obedience to his commandments the primary focus of their lives.

22:8 In Joshua's parting blessing to the tribes he reminds them to share the spoils of victory with their less fortunate brothers and sisters.

assembly of the Israelites gathered together
at Shiloh to go and attack them.
13 The Israelites sent Phinehas, the son of
Eleazar the priest, to the Reubenites, the
Gadites, and one of the halves of the tribe of
Manasseh in the land of Gilead.[u] 14 With him
they sent ten leaders, a leader for each of the
tribes of Israel, each one the head of an ances-
tral clan among the divisions of Israel. 15 They
came to the Reubenites, the Gadites, and one
of the halves of the tribe of Manasseh in the
land of Gilead and they said to them, 16 "Thus
says the whole assembly of the LORD: What is
this treachery that you have committed
against the God of Israel, turning away from
the LORD this day by building an altar for
yourselves so that you might rebel against the
LORD? 17 Is the iniquity that was committed
at Peor not enough for us? We have not been
fully purified from it up to the present even
though there was a plague in the assembly of
the LORD.[v] 18 Why do you turn away from fol-
lowing the LORD today? If today you rebel
against the LORD, then tomorrow his anger
will rage against the whole assembly of Israel.
19 If the land in your possession is unclean,
then cross over to the land in the possession
of the LORD where the tabernacle of the LORD
is kept. You can share it with us. Only, do not
rebel against the LORD, and do not rebel
against us by building an altar other than the
altar to the LORD, our God. 20 When Achan,
the son of Zerah, committed a sin in regard
to the things that had been dedicated, did not
wrath come upon the whole assembly of
Israel? That man was not the only one who
perished because of his sin."[w]

21 So the Reubenites, the Gadites, and one
of the halves of the tribe of Manasseh replied
to the leaders of the divisions of Israel,
22 "The God of gods, the LORD! The God of
gods, the LORD! He knows! Let Israel know
as well! If this has been an act of rebellion or
treachery against the LORD, then may we
not be saved today.[x] 23 If we have built an
altar to turn away from the LORD, or to offer
burnt offerings or grain offerings, or to
make peace offerings on it, may the LORD
himself call us to account! 24 No! We did this
thing for fear that sometime in the future
your descendants might say to our descen-
dants, 'What do you have to do with the
LORD, the God of Israel? 25 The LORD has
made the Jordan a boundary between you
and us, you Reubenites and Gadites. You
have no share in the LORD.' Then your
descendants would have caused our descen-
dants to stop fearing the LORD. 26 This is why
we said to ourselves, 'Let us prepare for it
and build an altar, but not for burnt offer-
ings or sacrifices.' 27 Let it be a witness
between ourselves and yourselves as well as
for the generations that come after us so
that we might continue in the service of the
LORD, offering burnt offerings and sacrifices
and peace offerings before him. This way, in
the future, your descendants will not be able
to say to our descendants, 'You have no
share in the LORD.'[y] 28 We said to ourselves,
'If they ever say this to us or to our descen-
dants in the future, we will be able to tell
them to look at the copy of the LORD's altar
that was built by our fathers. It was not for
burnt offerings or sacrifices, but to serve as
a witness between ourselves and yourselves.
29 God forbid that we should rebel against
the LORD and turn away from the LORD
today by building an altar for burnt offer-
ings, grain offerings, and sacrifices in any
place other than the altar to the LORD, our
God, that stands in front of his tabernacle."[z]

30 When Phinehas the priest and the lead-
ers of the assembly, the leaders of the divi-
sions of Israel, heard what the Reubenites
and the Gadites, and the Manassehites said,
it greatly pleased them. 31 Phinehas, the son
of Eleazar the priest, said to the Reubenites,
the Gadites, and to the Manassehites,
"Today we are sure that the LORD is with us,
for you have not acted unfaithfully against
the LORD in this matter. You have now res-
cued the Israelites out of the hand of the
LORD."

32 Then Phinehas, the son of Eleazar the
priest, and the leaders returned from
the Reubenites and the Gadites in Gilead to
the land of Canaan, to the Israelites, and
they brought them a report. 33 The report
greatly pleased the Israelites and they
praised God. The Israelites decided not to
go up against the Reubenites and the
Gadites to fight them and destroy the land
in which they dwelt. 34 The Reubenites and
the Gadites gave the altar this name: A wit-
ness between us that the LORD is God.* [a]

u Ex 6:25; Num 25:7, 11.—**v** Num 25:1-9.—**w** Jos 7:1.—**x** Deut 12:1-2.—**y** Jos 24:27; Ex 27:1-8.—**z** Deut 12:13f.—**a** Gen 31:47-49.

22:34 *A witness between us that the LORD is God:* the name given by the Reubenite and Gadite tribes to the altar they built to dispel any notion of friction between the people on either side of the Jordan. It was a sign to all the Israelites and to future generations that they worshiped the same God.

CHAPTER 23*

Joshua's Final Discourse. 1 Quite some time
later, after the LORD had given Israel rest
from all of its surrounding enemies, and
when Joshua had grown old and was well
advanced in years, [b] 2 Joshua summoned all
of Israel including its leaders and officials,
their judges and their officers, and he said to
them, "I am now an old man, well advanced
in years [c] 3 and you have seen all that the
LORD, your God, has done to all of these
nations on your behalf, for the LORD, your
God, has fought for you. 4 I have divided up by
lot these remaining nations as an inheritance
for your tribes, all the nations that I have con-
quered between the Jordan and the Great
Sea to the west. [d] 5 The LORD, your God,
himself will drive them out before you. He
will push them out of your sight so that you
can take possession of the land that the
LORD, your God, has promised you. 6 Be
most courageous, and be careful to observe
everything that is written in the Book of the
Law of Moses. Do not turn away from it to
the right or the left. [e] 7 Avoid associating with
these nations that still remain among you.
Do not mention the names of their gods; do
not swear by them. Do not serve them; do
not worship them. [f] 8 Hold fast to the
LORD, your God,* as you have done up to
the present. 9 The LORD has driven out
great and powerful nations from before
you. To this day no one has been able to
stand up against you. 10 Just one of you has
been able to route a thousand, because the
LORD, your God, has fought for you, just as he
promised you that he would do. [g] 11 So be very
careful to love the LORD, your God.

12 * "But if you were to turn away and you
were to ally yourselves with the survivors of
the nations that remain here, and you were to
intermarry with them, and you were to asso-
ciate with them, [h] 13 then you should know for
sure that the LORD, your God, will no longer
drive out these nations before you. They will
be like snares and traps to you, as if they were
scourges upon your backs and thorns in your
eyes, until you finally vanish from this good
land that the LORD, your God, has given you. [i]

14 "I am now about to go the way of all upon
the earth. You know very well in your hearts
and your souls that not one of the good things
that the LORD, your God, promised you has
failed to take place. Every promise has been
fulfilled, not one of them has been broken.
15 Just as all the good things that the LORD,
your God, has promised you have come true,
so the LORD could bring upon you all the evil
that he has threatened until he has wiped you
out from this good land that the LORD, your
God, has given you. [j] 16 If you transgress the
covenant that the LORD, your God, has com-
manded you to observe, and you go and serve
other gods and worship them, then the
LORD's anger will blaze out against you. You
will quickly perish from the good land that
the LORD, your God, has given you."

CHAPTER 24*

Renewing the Covenant. 1 Joshua then gath-
ered all of the tribes of Israel at Shechem.
He summoned the elders of Israel along
with their leaders, their judges, and their
officers, and they presented themselves
before God. 2 Joshua said to all of the people,
"Thus says the LORD, the God of Israel: Your
fathers dwelt on the other side of the river in
times of old, including Terah, the father of
Abraham and the father of Nahor, and they
served other gods. [k] 3 Then I took Abraham
from the other side of the river and I led him
all through the land of Canaan. I multiplied
his descendants, giving him Isaac. [l] 4 I gave
Jacob and Esau to Isaac. I gave Mount Seir
to Esau to possess, but Jacob and his chil-
dren went down to Egypt. [m]

5 "I sent Moses and Aaron and I plagued
Egypt with what I did in their midst. After-
ward, I brought you out. 6 Then I brought
your fathers out of Egypt. You came to the
sea, and the Egyptians pursued your fathers

b Jos 13:1; 21:44.—c Jos 24:1; Deut 29:10.—d Jos 13:2-7; 14:2; Ps 78:55.—e Jos 1:7; Deut 5:32.—f Ex 20:5; Deut 7:2ff; Ps 16:4.—g Lev 26:8; Deut 3:22.—h Ex 34:15f; Deut 7:3.—i Ex 23:33; Num 33:55.—j Lev 26:14ff; Deut 28:15ff.—k Gen 11:27-32.—l Gen 12:1; Acts 7:2ff.—m Gen 25:25-26; 36:8; 46:6-7.

23:1-16 From the testament of Joshua (as from the discourse of Moses in Deuteronomy) Israel understands that its history is the work of the Lord. The land has been given to it because it is God's people, but if it compromises with pagan customs and forms of worship it will suffer the loss of its inheritance.

23:8 *Hold fast to the LORD, your God:* these words are the essence of Joshua's lifelong commitment to God and his absolute rule of life for others to follow.

23:12-14 The question of intermarriage and the dire predictions that are made here are not in any way a contrast to the actions of a loving and merciful God who wants what is truly best for his children. Would that these words were heeded so much pain and suffering could have been avoided.

24:1-28 The covenant at Shechem, which is connected with the beginning of the settlement in Palestine is a decisive moment for the political and religious destiny of the people. The plenary assembly of tribes chooses the covenant contracted at Sinai and the law of God that flows from it as its definitive constitution. The dramatic account of this choice of God is one of the greatest of religious texts.

with chariots and horsemen into the Red
Sea. 7 They cried to the LORD, and he caused
darkness to descend between you and the
Egyptians. He brought the sea down upon
them, and it covered them. Your own eyes
have seen what I did in Egypt. You then dwelt
in the wilderness for a long time. [n] 8 I brought
you to the land of the Amorites who lived on
the other side of the Jordan. They fought
against you, and I gave them up into your
hands so that you might take possession of
the land, and I crushed them before you.
9 Then Balak, the son of Zippor, the king of
Moab, rose up and fought against Israel. He
sent for and summoned Balaam, the son of
Beor, to curse you, [o] 10 but I would not listen
to Balaam. He therefore blessed you, and so
I delivered you out of his hands. 11 You
crossed over the Jordan and arrived at
Jericho. The men of Jericho fought against
you along with the Amorites, the Perizzites,
the Canaanites, the Hittites, the Girgashites,
the Hivites, and the Jebusites. I delivered
them into your hands. [p] 12 I sent hornets
before you to drive them out before you,
including the two kings of the Amorites. It
was not your sword or your bow that did it. [q]
13 I gave you a land on which you did not
labor, I gave you cities which you had not
built, and you dwell in them. You eat the fruit
of vineyards and olive trees that you did not
plant. [r] 14 Therefore, you must fear the LORD
and serve him with sincerity and fidelity. Put
aside the gods that your fathers served on
the other side of the river and in Egypt. Serve
the LORD. [s] 15 If it seems wrong to you to
serve the LORD, then today you must choose
whom you will serve, whether it be the gods
that your fathers served on the other side of
the river, or the gods of the Amorites who
dwell in the land. As for me and my house-
hold, we will serve the LORD." [t]

16 * The people said, "God forbid that we
should abandon the LORD to serve other
gods. 17 It was the LORD, our God, who
brought us and our fathers out of the land of
Egypt, the land of our bondage. He per-
formed great wonders in our sight. He pre-
served us all along the journey that we made,
and among all the people through whom we
passed. 18 The LORD drove out all the people
before us, even the Amorites who dwelt in
the land. We will serve the LORD, for he is our
God."

19 But Joshua said to the people, "You can-
not serve the LORD, for he is a holy God. He
is a jealous God, he will not forgive your sins
or your transgressions. [u] 20 If you turn away
from the LORD to serve foreign gods, then he
will turn away from you. He will punish you
and wipe you out, even after the good that he
has done for you."

21 The people said to Joshua, "No! We will
serve the LORD." 22 Then Joshua said to the
people, "You will serve as your own witness-
es that you have chosen to serve the LORD."
They answered, "We are witnesses." 23 He
continued, "Then put away the foreign gods
from among you. Bend your heart to the
LORD, the God of Israel." 24 The people said
to Joshua, "We will serve the LORD, our God,
and obey his voice." [v]

25 So Joshua made a covenant with the
people that day. He established statutes and
ordinances for them in Shechem. 26 Joshua
wrote these words in the book of the law of
God. He took a large stone and set it up there
under the oak that is in the sanctuary of the
LORD. 27 Joshua said to all the people, "This
stone will be a witness for us. It has heard all
of the words that the LORD spoke to us. It will
therefore be a witness for you, lest you deny
your God." 28 Joshua then sent the people
away, each to his own inheritance.

The Death of Joshua. 29 After this happened,
Joshua, the son of Nun, died. He was one
hundred and ten years old. 30 They buried
him within his own inheritance in Timnath-
serah in the hill country of Ephraim, north of
Mount Gaash. 31 Israel served the LORD dur-
ing Joshua's entire lifetime, and during the
lifetime of the elders who survived Joshua,
for they had known all of the works that the
LORD had performed on Israel's behalf.
32 The bones of Joseph, that the Israelites had
brought up out of Egypt, were buried in
Shechem in the parcel of land that Jacob had
bought for one hundred pieces of silver from
the sons of Hamor, who himself was the
father of Shechem. It was an inheritance for
the descendants of Joseph. 33 Eleazar, the
son of Aaron, then died. They buried him at
Gibeah, the place that Phinehas, his son, had
been given in the hill country of Ephraim.

---

n Ex 14:19-31; Num 14:33.—o Num 22:2-5.—p Jos 3:16f; 6:1.—q Ex 23:28; Deut 7:20; Ps 44:3.—r Deut 6:10-11.—s Deut 10:12-13; 1 Sam 12:24.—t Deut 30:15ff; Ru 1:15; 1 Ki 18:21.—u Ex 20:5; 23:21; 34:14; Lev 19:2.—v Ex 19:8; 24:3, 7; Deut 5:27.

24:16-18, 24 Fervent words of fidelity are spoken by the people in defense of their covenant with the Lord. Soon, however, they will be charged with breaking their contract with him (Jdg 2:2-3).

"When the angel of the LORD appeared, he said, 'The LORD is with you, O mighty warrior. . . . Go in your might and rescue Israel'" *(Jdg 6:12ff)*.

THE BOOK OF JUDGES

The Formation of a People

This "book of meditation," which is painted in such brilliant colors, is made up of events that left their mark on the destiny and faith of Israel and for this reason could not be forgotten. While the initial conquest of the Promised Land had left glorious memories, other less glorious but no less important ones were kept for later generations.

The chroniclers do not have a unified vision in which to locate these accounts; rather they tell a series of brief stories composed at different periods, then revised, completed, and corrected by later authors. The core of the book is made up of recollections of the "judges." These personages were evidently not all occupied, like Deborah under the palm tree (4:5), in listening to disputants; they were rather heroes who appeared here and there, now in one tribe, now in another, with the task of restoring unity, rooting out disorders, and defending a single tribe or the entire community of Israel in time of danger. Many of these inspired leaders perhaps played only a limited role. The epic episodes told about them are lights shed on the difficult life of the tribes before the establishment of the monarchy. They are the oldest material in the book.

But in the final redaction, the undertakings of these individuals are set in a framework of the religious thought of the Deuteronomistic school: the brief periods when Israel is oppressed can only be due to its infidelity and especially to its idolatry; then its wretched state causes it to turn to God, who on each occasion sends a savior. At the death of the latter, Israel falls back into sin, and the cycle is repeated (see 1:1-3, 6; 10:6-18).

One of the interesting things in Judges, then, is to see the great difficulties the Hebrews had to meet with as they began their life in Palestine.

They had to battle continually with the inhabitants of the land and with hostile neighbors; split up into tribes as they were, they found it difficult to turn themselves into a nation. Above all, they allowed themselves to be caught in the seductive snare of the pagan worship of Canaan.

These precious memories, the special flavor of which is caught to an exceptional degree in the story, shed light in their own way on the history of the people of God. The authors, moreover, realized this and sought, above all else, to give expression to a meaning that would be of permanent value.

In fact, in this people that had to struggle so hard, we already see the destiny of the Christian people, whose fragile faith is exposed to the threats and allurements of so many forms of idolatry.

In addition, however, the Book of Judges teaches us, by way of ups and downs that are at first sight rather dismaying, that the Lord is present and guiding his people.

Is this not for us a stimulus to hope?

Why? Because Jesus is with the Church, even though his presence is often embodied in weak human natures.

The Book of Judges may be divided as follows:

I: The Israelites Fail to Conquer Canaan (1:1—3:6)
II: The Period of the Judges (3:7—16:31)
III: Appendices: Stories of Dan and Benjamin (17:1—21:25)

I: THE ISRAELITES FAIL TO CONQUER CANAAN*

CHAPTER 1

Conquests by Judah and Simeon. 1 After
Joshua died, the Israelites asked the LORD,
"Who will be the first among us to go up to
fight against the Canaanites?" [a] 2 The LORD
said, "Judah will go up for, behold, I have
delivered the land into his hands." 3 Judah
said to Simeon, his brother, "Come up with
me into my allotted portion and we will fight
against the Canaanites together, and I will
then go up into your allotted portion." So
Simeon went up with him. [b]

4 Judah went up and the LORD delivered
the Canaanites and the Perizzites into their
hands. They slew ten thousand of them at
Bezek. 5 They came across Adoni-bezek at
Bezek and fought against him, and they
defeated the Canaanites and the Perizzites. [c]
6 Adoni-bezek fled away, but they chased
after him and caught him, cutting off his
thumbs and his big toes. 7 Adoni-bezek said,
"Seventy kings who had their thumbs and
big toes cut off used to scrounge for their
meals under my table. God has paid me
back for what I have done." They brought
him to Jerusalem, and he died there.

8 The Judahites fought against Jerusalem
and they captured it, putting it to the sword
and setting the city on fire.* [d] 9 After this,
the Judahites went down to fight against the
Canaanites living in the hill country, the
Negeb, and the western slopes. 10 They
advanced against the Canaanites living in
Hebron (which had previously been called
Kiriath-arba). They defeated Sheshai,
Ahiman, and Talmai. [e] 11 From there they
marched against the people who were living
in Debir (which had previously been called
Kiriath-sepher).

---

a Num 27:21.—b Jdg 1:17; Jos 19:1.—c Jos 10:1.—d Jos 15:63.—e Jos 15:13-17.

1:1—3:6 With each tribe fighting on its own behalf, the tribes of Israel establish themselves with difficulty in Canaan and often can do no better than coexist with the pagan populations that have been there from time immemorial.

1:8 Jerusalem will in fact be captured only in the time of David and he named it for himself, "The City of David" (2 Sam 5:6-9).

12 Caleb said, "I will give my daughter
Achsah as a wife to whomever attacks and
captures Kiriath-sepher." 13 Othniel, the son
of Kenaz, the younger brother of Caleb cap-
tured it, and he gave him Achsah his daugh-
ter in marriage.[f]

14 When she came to be with him, she
urged him to ask her father for a field. As she
got off her donkey, Caleb asked her, "What
can I do for you?" 15 She answered, "Please
do me a favor. You have given me land in the
Negeb. Please also give me some springs of
water." So Caleb gave her the upper springs
and the lower springs.

16 The Kenites, the descendants of Moses'
father-in-law, traveled to the City of Palms
with the Judahites to live in the Desert of
Judah, the Negeb, near Arad. They went and
settled there among the people.* [g] 17 Judah
and his brother Simeon went out against the
Canaanites living in Zephath. They con-
quered it, totally demolishing it. This is why
the city is now called Hormah. [h] 18 Judah cap-
tured Gaza with its territory, Ashkelon with
its territory, and Ekron with its territory.

19 The LORD was with Judah. They occu-
pied the hill country, but they could not drive
out the inhabitants of the plain because they
had iron chariots.* [i] 20 They gave Hebron to
Caleb, as Moses had decreed, driving the
three sons of Anak out from it.

21 The Benjaminites could not drive out
the Jebusites from Jerusalem, and the
Jebusites have continued to live with the
Benjaminites up to the present.[j]

22 The descendants of Joseph* attacked
Bethel, and the LORD was with them. 23 The
descendants of Joseph had first sent up spies
against Bethel. (Its name had previously
been Luz.) [k] 24 The spies saw a man coming
out of the city and said to him, "If you show
us an entranceway into the city, we will be
merciful to you." 25 He showed them an
entranceway into the city, and they put the
city to the sword, but they let the man and
his entire family go free. 26 The man traveled
to the land of the Hittites and he built a city
there that he called Luz, which is its name up
to the present.

Forced Labor. 27 Manasseh did not drive
out the inhabitants of Beth-shean and the
towns dependent upon it, Taanach and the
towns dependent upon it, Dor and the towns
dependent upon it, Ibleam and the towns
dependent upon it, or Megiddo and the
towns dependent upon it, for the Canaanites
were determined to live in those places. [l]
28 But when Israel became strong, it subject-
ed the Canaanites to forced labor, although
it did not completely drive them out.

29 Nor did Ephraim drive the Canaanites
out who lived in Gezer, and the Canaanites
continue to live among them in Gezer. [m]

30 Nor did Zebulun drive out the inhabi-
tants of Kitron or the inhabitants of Nahalol.
The Canaanites continue to live among
them, and they have been subjected to
forced labor.

31 Nor did Asher drive out the inhabitants
of Acco, nor the inhabitants of Sidon, nor
Ahlab, Achzib, nor Helbah, nor Aphik, nor
Rehob, 32 and so the Asherites continue to
live among the Canaanites, the inhabitants
of the land, because they did not drive them
out.

33 Nor did Naphtali drive out the inhabi-
tants of Beth-shemesh, nor the inhabitants
of Beth-anath. They continue to dwell
among the Canaanites, the inhabitants of
the land. Nevertheless, the inhabitants of
Beth-shemesh and Beth-anath were subject-
ed to forced labor.

34 The Amorites forced the Danites to con-
tinue to live in the hill country; they would
not permit them to come down into the
plain. [n] 35 The Amorites were also deter-
mined to continue to live on Mount Heres, in
Aijalon and in Shaalbim, but when the
descendants of Joseph grew powerful, they
subjected them to forced labor. 36 The
Amorite boundary ran from Akrabbim up to
Sela and beyond.

CHAPTER 2

The Israelites Break the Covenant.* 1 An
angel of the LORD went up from Gilgal to

f Jdg 3:9.—g Jdg 3:13; 4:11, 17; Deut 34:3.—h Num 21:3.—i Jos 17:16.—j Jos 15:63; 2 Sam 5:6.—k Gen 28:19—l Jos 17:11-13.—m Jos 16:10.—n Jos 19:47.

1:16 Moses' father-in-law is Hobab (Jdg 4:11); but the actual degree of kinship of Hobab with Moses is doubtful (see Ex 2:18). Num 10:29ff tells of Moses' invitation to Hobab (here identified as son of Reuel) to join the Israelites.

1:19 In many instances the Israelites are able to overcome a more powerful enemy, but in this case a more superior army will prevail, forcing the Israelites to live among them.

1:22 *The descendants of Joseph:* the author is referring to the tribes of Ephraim and Manasseh.

2:1-5 The explanation given by the angels offers a religious interpretation of Israel's failures; this is a later reflection by the Deuteronomist redactor as he attempts to understand the reason for the failures.

Bochim* and said, "I brought you up from out of the land of Egypt and led you to the land that I had promised your fathers saying, 'I will never break my covenant with you. 2 Make no covenant with the people of this land. Break down their altars.' But you have disobeyed me. Why have you done this?[o] 3 Now I proclaim to you that I will not drive them out from before you. They will be like thorns in your sides, and their gods will become a snare to you."[p] 4 When the angel of the LORD said these things to the Israelites, the people wept out loud. 5 They named that place Bochim, and they offered sacrifices to the LORD there.

The Death of Joshua. 6 After Joshua had dismissed the people, the Israelites all went to their inheritances and they took possession of the land.[q] 7 The people served the LORD during Joshua's lifetime and the lifetimes of the elders who survived Joshua and who had seen all of the great things that the LORD had done for Israel. 8 Joshua, the son of Nun, the servant of the LORD, died at the age of one hundred and ten. 9 They buried him within the land that was his inheritance, at Timnath-heres, in the hill country of Ephraim, to the north of Mount Gaash.

Infidelity of the People. 10 When that whole generation had been gathered home to their fathers, another generation arose after them that did not know the LORD* or the works that he had done for Israel.[r] 11 *[s] The Israelites did what was evil in the sight of the LORD, serving the Baals. 12 They abandoned the LORD, the God of their fathers, who had brought them out from the land of Egypt. They followed other gods, the gods of the people who lived around them, and they worshiped them. This provoked the LORD's anger 13 because they had abandoned him to serve Baal and the Astartes. 14 The LORD's anger blazed out against Israel, and he delivered them into the hands of raiders who plundered them. He sold them into the hands of their enemies living around them so that they could not stand up to them anymore. 15 Whenever they went out, the hand of the LORD was against them to defeat them, just as the LORD had told them, for the LORD had promised this to them. They therefore suffered terribly.

Deliverance through Judges. 16 However, the LORD raised up judges who delivered them out of the hands of those raiders.[t] 17 Yet, they would not listen to the judges, and they prostituted themselves after other gods, worshiping them. They quickly turned away from the way in which their fathers had walked, that of obeying the commandments of the LORD. They did not do this. 18 When the LORD raised up judges, the LORD was with the judge. He delivered them out of the hands of their enemies as long as the judge lived, for the LORD had mercy on them when they groaned under those who oppressed and afflicted them.

19 But when the judge died,* they turned back and became even worse than their fathers, following other gods, serving and worshiping them. They would not abandon their selfish, stubborn ways.[u] 20 So the anger of the LORD blazed out against Israel and he said, "Because this people has sinned against the covenant that I gave to their fathers and they have not heeded my voice, 21 I will no longer drive out any of the nations before them that were left when Joshua died.[v] 22 Thus, I will test Israel, to see whether or not they will keep to the way of the LORD, walking in it as their fathers did."[w] 23 The LORD therefore left those nations there, not hurrying to drive them out, nor delivering them into Joshua's hands.

CHAPTER 3

1 Now these are the nations that the LORD left to put Israel to the test through them (that is, all of those who had not experienced the wars in Canaan). 2 This was so that the descendants of the Israelites might learn about war, for up to that time they had not yet experienced it. 3 They were the five lords of the Philistines, all of the Canaanites, the Sidonians, and the Hivites who were living in the mountains of Lebanon between Mount

o Ex 23:32; 34:12-13.—p Deut 7:16; Jos 23:13; Ps 106:36.—q Jos 24:28.—r 1 Sam 2:12; Ps 81:12.—s 11-14: Jdg 3:7, 12; 4:1-2; 6:1; 8:33; 10:6-8.—t Jdg 6:6; Ps 106:43-45.—u Jdg 3:12; 4:1; 8:33.—v Jos 23:13.—w Jdg 3:1, 4.

2:1 *Bochim:* Hebrew for "weeper." It was a sacred place near Gilgal.

2:10 *Did not know the LORD:* we may not know why the Israelites drifted from their spiritual roots, but we do know that a faithful remnant stayed faithful to the Lord.

2:11-13 *Baals:* lords, the gods of the country (2 Ki 17:24-33). "Baal and the Astartes" (often in the plural) is the designation frequently used in the Old Testament for the Canaanite divinities, Baal being the masculine, and Astarte, the goddess of love and fruitfulness; the name of the latter is often replaced by the Hebrew word *asherah*, meaning a pole (see Jdg 3:7; Ex 34:13).

2:19 *When the judge died:* a cycle of unfaithfulness to the Lord, followed by repentance and God's deliverance, marked the time of the judges who led the Israelites temporarily but effectively.

Baal-hermon and Lebo-hamath.[x] 4 They
were left there to put Israel to the test to see
whether they would obey the command-
ments of the LORD that the LORD had given
them through Moses.
5 The Israelites lived among the Canaan-
ites, the Hittites, the Amorites, the Periz-
zites, the Hivites, and the Jebusites.[y] 6 They
took their daughters to be their wives, they
gave their own daughters to their sons, and
they served their gods.[z]

II: THE PERIOD OF THE JUDGES

Othniel's Conquest.* 7 The Israelites did
what was evil in the sight of the LORD, for-
getting the LORD, their God, and serving the
Baals and the Asherahs.[a] 8 The anger of the
LORD blazed out against Israel, so he sold
them into the hands of Cushan-rishathaim,
the king of Aram-naharaim.* The Israelites
were subjected to Cushan-rishathaim for
eight years. 9 When the Israelites cried out to
the LORD, the LORD sent the Israelites a lib-
erator. It was Othniel, the son of Kenaz,
Caleb's younger brother, and he delivered
them. 10 The Spirit of the LORD* came upon
him, and he became a judge of Israel. He
went to war, and the LORD delivered
Cushan-rishathaim, the king of Aram-
naharaim, into his hands. His hand over-
powered Cushan-rishathaim.[b] 11 The land
was at peace for forty years, and then
Othniel, the son of Kenaz, died.
Ehud's Victory. 12 The Israelites once again
did what was evil in the sight of the LORD.
Because of the evil they had done in the sight
of the LORD, the LORD gave Eglon, the king of
Moab, power over Israel.[c] 13 He joined up
with the Ammonites and the Amalekites,
and they went and attacked Israel, conquer-
ing the City of Palms. 14 The Israelites were
subjects of Eglon, the king of Moab, for eigh-
teen years.
15 The Israelites cried out to the LORD, and
the LORD raised up a liberator for them. He
was Ehud, the son of Gera, the Benjaminite,
a left-handed man.* The Israelites sent him
with tribute to Eglon, the king of Moab.[d]
16 Ehud had made a double-edged sword
that was one foot* long, and he strapped it
on under his clothing on his right thigh. 17 He
brought the tribute to Eglon. Now Eglon was
a very fat man.[e] 18 When he had received the
tribute, he dismissed the people who were
carrying the tribute. 19 At the idols of Gilgal,
he turned back and said, "I have a secret
message for you, O king." He said, "Be
quiet," until all his attendants left him.
20 Ehud then approached him while he was
sitting alone in the upper room. Ehud said,
"I have a message from God for you." As he
got out of his seat,[f] 21 Ehud reached in with
his left hand, drew the sword out from his
right thigh, and stuck it into his stomach. 22 It
went in so far that even the handle of the
sword was covered over by fat, and he could
not draw the sword out from his stomach. In
fact, excrement came out.
23 When Ehud went out onto the porch, he
shut and locked the doors to the upper room
behind himself. 24 When he left, the servants
came back. They saw that the doors to the
upper room were locked, and they said, "He
must be relieving himself in the summer
chamber."[g] 25 They waited so long that they
became anxious, but he still did not open the
doors of the upper room. They took a key
and opened it, and they found their lord
dead on the ground.[h]
26 While they were waiting, Ehud was able
to escape. Passing beyond the idols, he hur-
ried to Seirah. 27 When he arrived, he blew a
trumpet in the hill country of Ephraim. The
Israelites went down with him from the hill
country of Ephraim, and he stood in front of
them. 28 He said, "Follow me, for the LORD
has delivered your enemies, the Moabites,
into your hands." They followed him, and
they captured the fords of the Jordan oppo-
site Moab, and they did not let anyone cross
over.[i] 29 They slew around ten thousand of

x Gen 10:14-17; Ex 3:8; Jos 13:2-5.—y Ex 3:8, 17; Jos 3:10; Ps 106:35.—z Ex 34:16; Deut 7:3-4.—a Deut 4:9; Pss 78:11, 42; 106:7.—b Num 11:25; 1 Sam 11:6; 1 Ki 18:46.—c Jdg 2:11, 14; 1 Sam 12:9.—d 1 Chr 12:2; Pss 68:29; 89:22; 107:13.—e Job 15:27; Ps 73:4.—f Neh 8:5; Am 3:15.—g 1 Sam 24:3.—h 2 Ki 2:17.—i Num 21:34; Deut 2:24; Jos 2:24.

3:7-11 The story of Othniel is typical of the way in which judges or "charismatic" leaders appeared on the scene: they were raised up by God in a difficult situation.

3:8 *Naharaim:* meaning two rivers and are the upper Tigris and the upper Euphrates (southern Syria).

3:10 *The Spirit of the LORD:* from the very beginning of scripture, God's Spirit in nature (Gen 1:2) and in individuals is given to do his will for the good of his people. Here Othniel is God's channel, as are other judges, Gideon (Jdg 6:34) and Jephthah (Jdg 11:29), and later King David (1 Sam 16:13). Jesus, too, is "filled with the Holy Spirit," (Lk 4:1), as is Elizabeth (Lk 1:41).

3:15 *Left-handed man:* this indicates how it was possible for Ehud to have access to his weapon that was concealed on his right thigh (3:21).

3:16 *Foot:* Hebrew, *gomed;* a measure mentioned only here; its value cannot be determined; usually translated as "cubit."

the Moabites that day, all of them robust and courageous warriors, and not one of them escaped. 30 Moab was vanquished that day under the hand of Israel, and there was peace in the land for eighty years.

Deliverance by Shamgar. 31 He was succeeded by Shamgar,[*] the son of Anath. He killed six hundred Philistines with an oxgoad, and he delivered Israel.

CHAPTER 4

Judges Deborah and Barak. 1 After Ehud died the Israelites once again did what was evil in the sight of the LORD. 2 The LORD sold them into the hands of Jabin, the king of Canaan, who reigned in Hazor. The commander of his army was Sisera who lived in Harosheth-haggoyim.[j] 3 The Israelites cried out to the LORD, for he had nine hundred iron chariots. He oppressed the Israelites terribly for twenty years.

4 Now Deborah, the wife of Lappidoth, a prophetess, was then a judge in Israel.[*] 5 She used to sit underneath the palm tree of Deborah between Ramah and Bethel in the hill country of Ephraim. The Israelites would come up to her for judgment there. 6 She summoned Barak, the son of Ahinoam, from Kadesh of Naphtali, and she said to him, "The LORD, the God of Israel, commands you, 'Go, take ten thousand men from Naphtali and Zebulun with yourself and march toward Mount Tabor.[*][k] 7 I will lure Sisera, the commander of Jabin's army, along with his chariots and his forces, to the Kishon River, and I will deliver him up into your hands.' "[l] 8 Barak said to her, "If you go with me, then I will go, but if you do not go with me, then I will not go." 9 She said, "Fine, I will go with you. But because of how you are doing this, it will not work out to your glory. The LORD will hand Sisera over into the hands of a woman." So Deborah rose up and went with Barak to Kedesh. 10 Barak had summoned Zebulun and Naphtali to Kedesh. Ten thousand men were under his command, and Deborah went up with him.[m]

11 Now Heber, the Kenite, had moved away from the Kenites, the descendants of Hobab, the father-in-law of Moses. He pitched his tent by the terebinth of Zaanannim, which is near Kedesh.

12 They reported to Sisera that Barak, the son of Abinoam, had gone up to Mount Tabor. 13 Sisera gathered together his nine hundred iron chariots and all of the men who were with him, and he traveled from Harosheth-haggoyim to the Wadi Kishon. 14 Deborah said to Barak, "Rise up, for this is the day that the LORD has delivered Sisera into your hands. Has the LORD not gone out before you?" So Barak went down Mount Tabor, followed by his men.[n]

15 The LORD routed Sisera before Barak at the edge of the sword along with all his chariots and all his troops. Sisera climbed down from his chariot and fled on foot.[o] 16 Barak pursued the chariots and the army as far as Harosheth-haggoyim. All of the troops of Sisera fell to the sword; there was not a survivor left among them.[p]

17 Sisera fled on foot to the tent of Jael, the wife of Heber the Kenite, for there was peace between Jabin, the king of Hazor, and Heber the Kenite. 18 Jael went out to greet Sisera. She said to him, "Come in, my lord, come right in. Do not be afraid." He came into the tent, and she covered him with a blanket. 19 He said to her, "Please give me a little water to drink for I am thirsty." She opened up a skin of milk, gave him some to drink, and covered him again.[q] 20 He told her, "Stand at the entrance to the tent. If anyone comes by and asks, 'Is there anyone here,' tell that person, 'No.' " 21 But Jael, Heber's wife, got a tent peg, she took a hammer in her hands, and she snuck up to him when he was in a deep sleep. She drove it through his temple into the ground, and he died.[*][r]

22 Barak passed by in pursuit of Sisera, and Jael came out to him and said to him, "Come in, I will show you the man you are looking for." He found Sisera dead, the peg through his temple. 23 On that day the LORD brought Jabin, the king of Canaan, into subjection to the Israelites.[s] 24 The hand of the

---

j Jos 11:1; 1 Sam 12:9; Ps 83:10.—k Heb 11:32.—l Jdg 5:21; 1 Ki 18:40; Ps 83:10.—m Jdg 5:18; Isa 41:2.—n Deut 9:3; Ps 68:7.—o Ex 14:24; Jos 10:10; 1 Sam 7:10.—p Ps 83:10.—q Jdg 5:25.—r Jdg 5:26; 1 Sam 26:8-9, 12.—s Neh 9:24; Pss 18:48; 44:3; 47:4

3:31 *Shamgar:* one of the "minor" judges. But the distinction between "major" and "minor" is due more to the lack of information about the "minor" judges than to the lesser importance of the individuals themselves.

4:4 Deborah is distinct among the judges as the only female and as one who could foretell the future. She apparently was held in high esteem and trust by the people she served.

4:6 *Tabor:* the point where the territories of Naphtali, Zebulon, and Issachar met. It would be the mountain on which Jesus was transfigured.

4:21 By killing Sisera, Jael disregarded the rules of hospitality that were normally extended to someone who entered another's tent and guaranteed their safety.

Israelites constantly grew stronger against Jabin, the king of Canaan, until they had crushed Jabin, the king of Canaan.

CHAPTER 5*

The Song of Deborah. 1 On that day Deborah and Barak, the son of Abinoam, sang,

2 "Israel's leaders led bravely,
the people followed gladly,
praise the LORD.
3 Hear, O kings; give ear, O princes,
for I, myself, will sing about the LORD;
I will sing praise to the LORD, the God of Israel.
4 LORD, when you went out from Seir,
when you marched out of the fields in Edom,
the earth trembled, and the heavens poured,
the clouds poured down water.* [t]
5 The mountains quaked before the LORD,
he who was on Sinai,
before the LORD, the God of Israel. [u]
6 In the days of Shamgar, the son of Anath,
in the days of Jael,
the highways were deserted,
travelers took winding paths.
7 Village life ceased in Israel,
it ceased until I, Deborah,
until I rose up as mother in Israel.*
8 When they chose new gods,
war showed up at the gates.
Not a shield nor a spear was to be found
among the forty thousand in Israel. [v]
9 My heart was with the leaders of Israel;
they offered themselves willingly with the people.
Bless the LORD.
10 Speak, you who ride on white donkeys,
who sit in judgment,
who walk along the ways.
11 Far from the noise of archers,
in the places where there is water,
there they shall recount the righteous deeds of the LORD,
his righteous deeds toward his villagers in Israel.
Then the people of the LORD will go down to the gates. [w]
12 Awake, awake, Deborah.
Awake, awake, sing a song.
Arise, O Barak,
and lead your captives away,
O son of Abinoam. [x]
13 Then the remnant of the nobles marched,
the people of the LORD came to me with the mighty.
14 Some came from Ephraim,
whose roots were in Amalek;
Benjamin was with your people who followed you.
From Machir* officers came down,
from Zebulun those who bear a commander's staff.
15 The princes of Issachar were with Deborah,
Issachar was with Barak;
he sent them into the valley under his command.
In the districts of Reuben
there were serious doubts. [y]
16 Why did you stay among the sheep folds
to hear the bleating of the flocks?
In the districts of Reuben
there were serious doubts.
17 Gilead remained beyond the Jordan.
Dan, why did he remain by the ships?
Asher remained by the seashore
and stayed in his coves.*
18 The people of Zebulun risked their lives,
as did Naphtali on the heights of the field.
19 Kings came and fought;
the kings of Canaan fought at Taanach
by the waters of Megiddo,
but they took no plunder, no silver. [z]
20 From the heavens the stars fought on;*
they fought against Sisera in their courses.

t Deut 33:2; Ps 68:8-9; Hab 3:6.—u Isa 64:1-3.—v Deut 32:17.—w 1 Sam 12:7; Mic 6:5.—x Pss 57:9; 68:19.—y Num 32:6.—z Jdg 4:13; Jos 11:5; Rev 16:16.

5:1-31 This song, composed in the enthusiasm of victory, testifies to the wonder roused in Israel by the feats of deliverance and by the Lord's intervention. It is one of the most beautiful pieces of ancient literature and of great historical value as well, since it gives a vivid portrayal of the varying reactions of the tribes to the undertaking.

5:4 The point of the imagery is that God came to the aid of his people with extraordinary assistance; his "coming" is concretized by mentioning areas of southern Palestine.

5:7 *As mother in Israel:* an endearment for Deborah, who judges her people with a woman's intuition, wisdom, and compassion.

5:14 *Machir:* the elder son of Manasseh; here he stands for the half-tribe of Manasseh west of the Jordan, as opposed to the eastern half in Gilead.

5:17 After receiving a territory west of Jerusalem, Dan pushed northward to the region of the sources of the Jordan (see chs. 17–18).

5:20 *The stars fought on:* God's army battled the enemy.

21 The Wadi Kishon swept them away;
the ancient wadi,
the Wadi Kishon. [a]
March on, O my soul, be strong.
22 Then the horses' hoof beats thundered,
galloping, galloping, go the mighty steeds.
23 'Curse Meroz,'* said the angel,
'bitterly curse those who live there.
They did not come to help the LORD,
to help the LORD against the mighty.'
24 You will be blessed above other women,
O Jael, wife of Heber, the Kenite;
you are blessed above other women who live in tents. [b]
25 He asked for water, and she gave him milk.
In a dish fit for royalty, she brought him cream.
26 [c] Her hand reached for a tent peg,
her right hand for a workman's hammer.
She struck Sisera; she crushed his head,
she pierced and bored through his temple.
27 He sank down to her feet,
fell down and lay there.
At her feet he sank and fell down;
where he sank, there he fell, dead!
28 Sisera's mother looked out through a window,
she cried from behind the lattice,
'Why is his chariot taking so long?
Why is the clatter of chariots so late in coming?' [d]
29 The wisest of her ladies answers her,
indeed, she keeps saying to herself,
30 'Are they having trouble finding and dividing the spoils?
A woman or two to each man,
colorful garments as plunder to Sisera,
the plunder of garments with colorful needlework,
colorful needlework for around the plunderer's neck?'
31 So may all of your enemies perish, O LORD,
may those who love him come forth like the mighty sun."

There was then peace in the land for forty years.

CHAPTER 6*

Gideon's Call. 1 * The Israelites once again
did what is evil in the sight of the LORD, so
the LORD delivered them into the hands of
Midian for seven years. 2 The hand of Midian
weighed heavy upon Israel, and because of
the Midianites, the Israelites prepared
refuges for themselves in mountain caverns,
caves, and strongholds. [e] 3 Whenever the
Israelites sowed their crops, the Midianites,
the Amalekites and other peoples from the
East would attack them. 4 They camped
against them and devastated the produce of
the land all the way up to Gaza. They did not
leave a living thing in Israel, not a sheep, nor
an ox, nor a donkey. [f] 5 They came up with
their livestock and their tents like swarms of
locusts. They and their camels were impossible to count; they invaded the land and laid it waste.

6 The Midianites oppressed Israel so terribly that the Israelites cried out to the LORD.
7 When the Israelites cried out to the
LORD on account of the Midianites, 8 the
LORD sent the Israelites a prophet* who said
to them, "Thus says the LORD, the God of
Israel, 'I brought you up from the land
of Egypt, bringing you forth from the land of
your slavery. [g] 9 I delivered you out of the
hands of the Egyptians, out of the hands of
everyone who oppressed you. I drove them
out before you and gave you their land. 10 I
said to you, "I am the LORD, your God. Do
not show reverence to the gods of the
Amorites in whose land you dwell." But you
did not listen to my voice.' "

11 The angel came and sat under the oak in
Ophrah* that belonged to Joash the
Abiezrite. It was there that Gideon, his son,
was threshing wheat in a winepress to hide
his activities from the Midianites. [h] 12 When
the angel of the LORD appeared, he said,

---

a Jdg 4:7; Jos 1:6; Ps 83:10.—b Jdg 4:17; Lk 1:42.—c 26-27: Jdg 4:21.—d Prov 7:6.—e 1 Sam 13:6; Jer 41:9; Heb 11:38.—f Lev 26:16; Deut 28:30, 51.—g Deut 18:15; 1 Ki 20:13, 22.—h Ru 2:17; 3:2; Joel 3:13; Heb 11:32.

5:23 *Meroz:* the residents of this area were apparently expected to take part in the battle and are condemned for not helping "the LORD against the mighty."

6:1—8:35 After establishing themselves in a territory and beginning to cultivate the fields, the Israelites are exposed to a twofold danger: sporadic raids by still nomadic neighbors from across the Jordan and assimilation by the native religions of the conquered country.

6:1-3 The *Midianites* were nomadic tribes who were descended from Midian, a son of Abraham and Keturah (Gen 25:2-4), and lived southeast of the Dead Sea. The *Amalekites* (see Num 24:20) lived to the southwest of that sea. The *peoples from the East* are the Arabs in the eastern Transjordan.

6:8 *Sent . . . a prophet:* throughout Scripture we hear that God sent prophets to warn and redirect those who had strayed the course. Some of them, as in this instance, remain unnamed.

6:11 *Ophrah:* a place belonging to the tribe of Manasseh.

"The LORD is with you, O mighty warrior."
[13] Gideon said to him, "O my LORD, if the
LORD is with us, then why has all of this hap-
pened to us? Where are all his wonders that
our fathers told us about when they said,
'Did the LORD not bring us up from Egypt?'
But now the LORD has abandoned us into the
hands of the Midianites." [14] The LORD looked
at him and said, "Go in your might and res-
cue Israel out of the hands of the Midianites.
Have I not sent you?" [15] But he said to him,
"O Lord, how can I save Israel. My clan is the
poorest in Manasseh, and I am the youngest
in my father's household." [i] [16] The LORD said
to him, "I will be with you,* and you will
strike down the Midianites as if they were
only one man." [j] [17] He answered him, "If I
truly have found favor in your sight, then
show me a sign that it is you speaking to me.
[18] Please do not leave here until I return to
you, bringing my offering that I will set
before you." He said, "I will wait here until
you come back."

[19] Gideon went off and prepared a kid goat
and unleavened bread made from an ephah
of flour. He put the meat in a basket and the
broth in a pot, and brought them out to lay
them down under the oak, presenting them
to him. [k] [20] The angel of God said, "Take the
meat and the unleavened bread and lay
them on this rock, then pour out the broth."
He did these things. [21] The angel of the LORD
stretched forth the end of the staff that was
in his hand, touching the meat and the
unleavened bread. Fire rose up from the rock
and consumed the meat and the unleavened
bread. Then the angel of the LORD vanished
from his sight. [l]

[22] When Gideon realized that it had been
the angel of the LORD, he said, "Alas, O Lord
GOD, for now I have seen the angel of the
LORD face to face." [23] But the angel of the
LORD said to him, "Peace be with you. Do
not be afraid; you will not die." [m] [24] Then
Gideon built an altar to the LORD there and
called it, "The LORD is peace." It is still in
Ophrah of the Abiezrites up to the present.

[25] * Now that same night the LORD said to
him, "Take your father's spare ox, the ox that
is seven years old. Break down the altar to
Baal that belongs to your father, and cut
down the Asherah that is beside it. [n] [26] Build
a proper altar to the LORD, your God, on top
of this rock. Offer up the spare ox as a burnt
offering, using the wood from the Asherah
you cut down."

[27] So Gideon took ten of his servants and
did what the LORD had told him to do.
Because he was afraid of his father's house-
hold and the men of the city, he could not do
it during the day; he did it at night.

[28] Early in the morning the men from the
city arose and saw the altar of Baal demol-
ished and the Asherah alongside of it cut
down. The spare ox had also been offered on
the newly built altar. [o] [29] They asked one
another, "Who has done this?" When they
carefully investigated it, they were told,
"Gideon, the son of Joash, did this." [30] The
men from the city told Joash, "Bring your son
out. He must die, because he demolished the
altar to Baal and he cut down the Asherah
that was alongside of it." [31] But Joash said to
all those who were confronting him, "Are you
going to defend Baal's cause? Are you trying
to save him? Whoever defends his cause will
be put to death by tomorrow morning. If he is
really a god, then he can fight for himself
when someone breaks down his altar."
[32] From that day on they called him
Jerubbaal, saying, "Let Baal fight with him,"
because he cast down his altar. [p]

[33] All of the Midianites, the Amalekites,
and the peoples from the east gathered
together. They crossed over the Jordan, and
camped in the Valley of Jezreel.

[34] The Spirit of the LORD came upon
Gideon, and he blew his trumpet, summon-
ing those who were in Abiezer to follow
him. * [q] [35] He sent messengers all throughout
Manasseh, summoning them to follow him.
He also sent messengers to Asher, Zebulun,
and Naphtali, so that they too gathered
around him.

[36] Gideon said to God, "If you intend to
save Israel by my hands, as you have told

i Ex 3:11; 1 Sam 9:21; Isa 60:22.—j Ex 3:12; Jos 1:5.—k Jdg 13:15; Gen 18:6-8; Lev 19:36.—l Ex 4:2; Lev 9:24.—m Gen 16:13; Deut 5:26; Dan 10:19.—n Jdg 2:13; Ex 34:13.—o 1 Ki 16:32; 2 Ki 10:27.—p Jdg 7:1; 1 Sam 12:11.—q Jdg 3:10; 1 Chr 12:18; 2 Chr 24:20.

6:16 *I will be with you:* Gideon received reassurance from the Lord with the same words said to Moses, Aaron, and others entrusted with leadership of the Israelites.

6:25-32 It seems that an Israelite was employed to guard the pagan sanctuary of the village. Idolatry does not, strictly speaking, mean the suppression of the worship of the Lord, but rather participation also in other forms of worship. In Canaan, the worship of the Baals, the divinities of fruitfulness and the harvest, seduced the Israelites once they too had become farmers.

6:34 Here is another reference to the divine empowerment of the ones God calls to lead his people. Although Gideon is promised victory over the Midianites, he still needs an outward sign from God (v. 37).

me, [37] then I will put a wool fleece on the floor. If there is dew on the fleece itself, but the ground around it is dry, then I will know that you are going to save Israel by my hands, as you said." [38] Gideon got up early the next morning. He squeezed the fleece, and dew flowed out of the fleece, producing a bowl full of water.

[39] Then Gideon said to God, "Do not be angry with me if I make this request. Let me test the fleece one more time. This time let the fleece remain dry and the ground all around it be covered with dew." [40] This is what God did that night. Only the fleece was dry, for there was dew on the ground that surrounded it.

CHAPTER 7

Midian's Defeat. [1] Early in the morning Jerubbaal (that is, Gideon) and all of the people who were with him camped at the well of Harod. The Midianite army was to the north of them, in the valley by the hill of Moreh.

[2] The LORD said to Gideon, "You have too many people with you for me to deliver over the Midianites into your hands. Otherwise, Israel might vaunt themselves against me saying, 'We have saved ourselves by our own efforts.' [r] [3] Announce to the people, 'Whoever is afraid and panicking, let him go back and leave Mount Gilead.' " Twenty-two thousand of the men left, and there were ten thousand left.

[4] Then the LORD said to Gideon, "There are still too many men. Bring them down to the water, and I will test them for you. Of whomever I say to you, 'This one will go with you,' that is the one who will go with you. Of whomever I say to you, 'This one will not go with you,' that one will not go with you." [s] [5] He brought the men down to the water. The LORD said to Gideon, "You will set apart everyone who laps up water like a dog from anyone who kneels down to drink." [6] There were three hundred men who lapped up water by holding their hands to their face. The rest of the men knelt down to drink their water. [7] The LORD said to Gideon, "I will save you through the three hundred men who lapped up their water. I will deliver the Midianites into your hands. Let everyone else go back home." * [8] So they took the other people's provisions, and they placed their trumpets in their hands. Gideon sent all the other Israelite men back to their homes, but he kept three hundred men with him.

The army of Midian was camped in the valley below them. [9] That same night the LORD said to him, "Rise up, go down against the army, for I have delivered them into your hands. [t] [10] Draw near them until you can hear what they are saying, [11] and then your hands will be strengthened so that you can descend upon the camp." So he and his servant Purah went down to the outskirts of the camp. [12] The Midianites, the Amalekites, and all of the other easterners were lying in the valley, as thick as locusts. There were so many camels that they could not be counted; there were as many of them as there is sand on the seashore. [u]

[13] Gideon arrived just as a man was telling his friend about a dream. He said, "I dreamed that a barley cake* came tumbling into the Midianite camp. It hit a tent so hard that it overturned and collapsed." [14] His friend said, "This can only be the sword of Gideon, the son of Joash, the Israelite. God has delivered Midian and its entire army into his hands."

[15] When Gideon heard the content of the dream and its interpretation, he worshiped. He returned to the army of Israel and said, "Rise up, for the LORD has delivered the army of Midian into your hands."

[16] He divided the three hundred men into three groups, and he placed trumpets and empty jars with torches inside them into each man's hands. [v] [17] He said to them, "Watch me. Do whatever I do. When we reach the edge of the camp, do whatever I do. [18] When I and all those who are with me blow our trumpets, then blow your trumpets all around the camp and shout out, 'For the LORD and for Gideon!' "

[19] Gideon and the three hundred men who were with him reached the edge of the camp at the beginning of the middle watch, just after they had changed the guard. They blew their trumpets and broke the jars that were in their hands. [20] The three groups blew their

r Deut 8:17; 2 Cor 4:7.—s 1 Sam 14:6.—t Jdg 1:2; Jos 2:24.—u Jdg 6:3-5; Num 13:29; Jos 11:4.—v Gen 14:15; 1 Sam 11:11; 2 Sam 18:2.

7:7 By reducing the army to such a small number, it would be apparent to all that the victory came from God and turn Gideon and his men back to the true God.

7:13 The *barley cake* symbolizes the Israelites, now poor sedentary farmers; the *tent* symbolizes the nomads (the Midianites).

trumpets and broke their jars, holding the torches in their left hands and the trumpets in their right hands. They blew their trumpets and cried out, "A sword for the LORD and for Gideon."[w]

[21] While each man stood in his place around the camp, the army ran away crying. [22] When the three hundred men blew their trumpets, the LORD caused each man to attack his fellow soldiers with his sword. The army fled to Beth-shittah, toward Zeredah, coming to the border of Abel-meholah near Tabbath.*

[23] The men of Israel from out of Naphtali, from out of Asher, and from out of Manasseh gathered together and pursued the Midianites.[x] [24] Gideon sent messengers all throughout the hill country of Ephraim who said, "Come down against the Midianites, and capture the fords of the Jordan at Beth-barah before they reach them." So all the men from Ephraim gathered together and captured the fords of the Jordan at Beth-barah. [25] They also captured Oreb and Zeeb, two of the princes of the Midianites. They killed Oreb upon the rock of Oreb, and they killed Zeeb at the winepress of Zeeb. They pursued the Midianites, and brought the heads of Oreb and Zeeb to Gideon who was alongside of the Jordan.[y]

CHAPTER 8

Gideon's Second Campaign. [1] The Ephraimites said to him, "Why have you treated us this way? Why did you not summon us when you went out to fight against the Midianites?" And they rebuked him severely. [2] He answered them, "What have I ever done that could be compared to what you have done? Are not the gleanings of the grapes in Ephraim better than the vintage of Abiezer? [3] God delivered Oreb and Zeeb, the princes of Midian, into your hands. What was I able to do compared with what you did?" Their anger against him calmed down when he said that.

[4] Gideon and the three hundred men with him came to and crossed over the Jordan, exhausted, but still in pursuit. [5] He said to the men of Succoth, "Give some bread to the men who are with me, for they are weary, and I am chasing after Zebah and Zalmunna, the kings of Midian."[z] [6] The princes of Succoth asked, "Do you already have the hands* of Zebah and Zalmunna in your possession? Why should we give bread to your soldiers?" [7] Gideon answered, "For this, when the LORD has delivered Zebah and Zalmunna into my hands, I will tear at your flesh with desert thorns and briars."

[8] He went up to Penuel and said the same thing to them. The men of Penuel answered him the same way that the men of Succoth had,[a] [9] so he said to the men of Penuel, "When I come back again in peace, I will tear down this tower."

[10] Now Zebah and Zalmunna were in Karkor, and they had their armies with them, fifteen thousand men. These were all that were left from the armies of the easterners, for some one hundred and twenty thousand swordsmen had fallen. [11] Gideon went up by the nomad route to the east of Nobah and Jogbehah and he fell upon the unsuspecting army. [12] Zebah and Zalmunna fled away, and he chased after the two kings of Midian and captured them. Zebah, Zalmunna and their entire army were routed.[b]

[13] Gideon, the son of Joash, then returned from the battle by the Pass of Heres. [14] He captured a young man from Succoth and questioned him. He wrote down the names of the seventy-seven princes and elders of Succoth for him. [15] He came to the men of Succoth and said, "Look at Zebah and Zalmunna, the ones about whom you taunted me when you said, 'Are Zebah and Zalmunna in your hands now that we should give bread to your weary men?'" [16] He picked out the elders of the city, and he taught the men of Succoth a lesson with desert thorns and briars. [17] He also smashed down the tower of Penuel and he killed the men of the city.

[18] Then he said to Zebah and Zalmunna, "Where are the men whom you killed at Tabor?" They replied, "Each one of them looked like you, like the son of a king."[c] [19] He said, "They were my brothers, the sons of my mother. I swear to God, if you had spared them, I would not kill you."

w Gen 15:17; Deut 32:41.—x Jdg 6:35; Jos 17:7.—y Jdg 8:3-4; Ps 83:12; Isa 10:26.—z Gen 33:17.—a Gen 32:30; 1 Ki 12:25.—b Ps 83:12.—c Jdg 4:6; Jos 19:22.

7:22 The noise created by the trumpets confused Gideon's enemies and caused them to attack one another.

8:6 *Have the hands:* in biblical times, those who were victorious in battle would cut off the hands of those slain in battle for trophies.

[20] Then he said to Jether,* his firstborn, "Stand up, kill them." But the young man did not draw his sword because he was afraid; he was still quite young. [21] Then Zebah and Zalmunna said, "Get up yourself and fall upon us! It takes the courage of a man." So Gideon stood up and killed Zebah and Zalmunna, and he took the ornaments off the necks of their camels.

[22] The Israelites said to Gideon, "Rule over us, you, and your son, and your grandson, for you have delivered us out of the hands of Midian." [d] [23] But Gideon said to them, "Neither I nor my son will rule over you. The LORD will rule over you!"

[24] Gideon continued, "I do have one request to make of you. Let each man give me an earring from his share of the plunder." (They had gold earrings, for they were Ishmaelites.) * [e] [25] They answered, "We would be glad to give them to you." They spread out a garment, and each man threw his earrings from the plunder onto it. [26] The weight of the golden earnings he had asked for was one thousand, seven hundred golden shekels, not counting the ornaments, the necklaces, the purple garments that had been worn by the kings of Midian, and the chains that had been on the necks of their camels.

[27] Gideon had the gold made into an ephod* which he placed in Ophrah, his hometown. All of Israel prostituted itself by worshiping it there, and it became a snare to Gideon and his household.[f] [28] This is how Midian was subjected to the Israelites, so that they did not lift up their heads again. During Gideon's lifetime there was peace in the land, for forty years. [g]

Abimelech, Son of Gideon. [29] Jerubbaal went to his home and lived there. [30] Gideon had seventy sons of his own, for he had many wives. [h] [31] His concubine* who lived in Shechem also had a son who was called Abimelech. [i] [32] Gideon, the son of Joash, lived to a good old age, and he was buried in the tomb of his father Joash in Ophrah of the Abiezrites.

[33] As soon as Gideon died, the Israelites turned again and prostituted themselves after the Baals. They set up Baal-berith* as their god [34] and the Israelites forgot that the LORD, their God, had delivered them out of the hands of their enemies who surrounded them.[j] [35] They also failed to respect the family of Jerubbaal (that is, Gideon) for all of the good things that he had done for Israel.

CHAPTER 9

[1] * Abimelech, the son of Jerubbaal, traveled to Shechem to see his mother's brothers, and he said to them and to all of his mother's clan,* [2] "Ask in the hearing of the men of Shechem, 'Which is better for you, that you have the seventy sons of Jerubbaal rule over you, or that you have one rule over you?' Remember that I am your flesh and blood." [3] When his mother's brothers proclaimed this in the hearing of the men of Shechem, they were inclined to agree with Abimelech about this matter, for they said, "He is our brother." [4] They gave him seventy shekels of silver from the temple of Baal-berith, and Abimelech used it to hire some worthless and reckless fellows who followed him. [5] Then he went to his father's house at Ophrah and he killed his brothers, the sons of Jerubbaal, seventy men, upon one stone. There was no one left except for Jotham, the son of Jerubbaal, the youngest, for he had hid himself. [6] All of the men in Shechem and Beth-millo assembled together and they went and made Abimelech king by the oak of the pillar that is in Shechem.

[7] When Jotham was told about it, he went and stood on top of Mount Gerizim and shouted out, "Listen to me, O men of Shechem, so that God might listen to you. [k] [8] Once the trees went out to anoint a king for themselves. They said to the olive tree, 'Reign over us.' [9] But the olive tree said to

d 1 Sam 8:5; Hos 13:10.—e Gen 35:4; 49:27.—f Jdg 17:5; 18:14; Ex 25:7; Jos 18:23.—g Ps 83:3.—h Jdg 9:2-5; 2 Ki 10:1.—i Jdg 9:1; 10:1; Gen 22:24; 2 Sam 11:21.—j Jdg 3:7; Deut 4:9; Neh 9:17.—k Deut 11:29; Jn 4:20.

8:20 *Jether:* Gideon's firstborn was wise to reject his father's request to kill the kings. His fear kept him from doing something that could have distinguished him but his youth made him an unacceptable assailant before the enemy.

8:24 *Ishmaelites:* traders whose name is derived from the tribe that descended from Ishmael, son of Abraham (Gen 16). The traders in their caravans (including the men) liked to wear earrings.

8:27 *Ephod:* either a kind of idol or, more probably, an ephod used in divination (see Ex 28:4) as in 1 Sam 2:28, although here it draws the people to illicit worship.

8:31 *Concubine:* a woman who was inferior to her husband's primary wife.

8:33 *Baal-berith:* Canaanite god worshiped as "lord of the covenant," and in Jdg 9:46 referred to as El-berith, "god of the covenant."

9:1-6 One of the sons of Gideon slaughters his rivals in order to win power. This is unlike his father who refused to start a monarchy.

9:1 The Canaanites predominate in Shechem. Abimelech's mother must have been a Canaanite woman, and Gaal (v. 26), a Canaanite.

them, 'Why should I give up my oil, with
which God and men are honored, to go and
hold sway over the trees?' 10 Then the trees
said to the fig tree, 'You come and reign over
us.' 11 But the fig tree said to them, 'Why
should I give up my sweetness and my good
fruit to go and hold sway over the trees?'
12 Then the trees said to the vine, 'You come
and reign over us.' 13 But the vine said to
them, 'Why should I give up my wine which
cheers both God and man* to go and hold
sway over the trees?' [l] 14 Then all of the trees
said to the bramble, 'You come and reign
over us.' 15 The bramble said to the trees, 'If
you truly intend to anoint me as your king,
then come, and take refuge in my shade. If
not, then let fire come out of the bramble
and consume the cedars of Lebanon.' [m]

16 "Now if you have truly and in all sincer-
ity made Abimelech king, if you have treated
Abimelech and his household well, dealing
with him as he deserved, 17 for my father
fought for you, he risked his life and deliv-
ered you out of the hands of Midian, 18 but
you have risen up against my father's house-
hold, killing his sons, seventy men on one
stone, and you have made Abimelech, the
son of his handmaid, as king of the men of
Shechem because he is your relative, 19 if you
have truly and in all sincerity dealt with
Jerubbaal and his household today, then
rejoice in Abimelech and let him also rejoice
in you. 20 But if not, then let fire come out of
Abimelech and consume the men of
Shechem and Beth-millo, and let fire come
out from the men of Shechem and Beth-
millo and consume Abimelech."

21 Jotham ran away and fled, going to Beer
where he remained, for he was afraid of
Abimelech his brother. 22 Now Abimelech
ruled over Israel for three years. 23 Then God
sent an evil spirit between Abimelech and
the men of Shechem, and the men of
Shechem dealt treacherously with Abim-
elech. [n] 24 This happened because of the vio-
lence that was done to the seventy sons of
Jerubbaal, so that their blood might be upon
Abimelech, their brother, and upon the men
of Shechem, who had assisted in killing his
brothers.

25 The men of Shechem sat in ambush
against him upon the mountain tops. They
robbed all of those who passed by on the
road, and Abimelech was told about it.
26 Now Gaal, the son of Ebed, arrived in
Shechem, and the men of Shechem trusted
him. 27 They went out into the fields and
gathered the grapes, treading them. They
threw a celebration and went in to the tem-
ple of their god, eating and drinking and
cursing Abimelech. 28 Then Gaal, the son of
Ebed, asked, "Who is Abimelech, and who is
Shechem, that we should serve him? Is he
not the son of Jerubbaal, and is not Zebul his
assistant? Serve the men of Hamor, the
father of Shechem. Why should we serve
him? [o] 29 I wish that the people were under
my authority, for then I would get rid of
Abimelech. I would say to Abimelech,
'Gather your army and come out!' "

30 Zebul, the ruler of the city, heard what
Gaal, the son of Ebed, had said and he grew
angry at him. 31 He secretly sent messengers
to Abimelech saying, "Gaal, the son of Ebed,
and his brethren have come to Shechem,
and they are stirring up the city against you.
32 You and your men should come up by
night and lie in wait in the fields. 33 In the
morning, at sunrise, advance on the city. He
and his men will come out against you, and
you can do whatever you see fit to them."

34 So Abimelech and all the men who were
with him arose, and they laid in wait near
Shechem during the night. They were divid-
ed into four companies. 35 Now Gaal, the son
of Ebed, had gone out and he was standing at
the entrance to the city just as Abimelech
and his men were coming out from their
hiding places. [p] 36 When Gaal saw them, he
said to Zebul, "Look, people are coming
down from the mountain tops." Zebul said to
him, "You are just seeing the shadows on the
mountain, they just look like men." 37 But
Gaal said, "Look, people are coming down
from Tabbur-haarez. Another company is
coming by way of the Diviner's Terebinth."
38 Then Zebul said to him, "Where is your
mouth now, you who said, 'Who is
Abimelech that we should serve him?' Are
these not the men whom you despised? So go
out, now, and fight them!"

39 Gaal went out with the men of Shechem
and they fought against Abimelech. 40 Abim-
elech chased after him, and he fled away
from him. A large number fell wounded at

---

l Gen 14:18; Eccl 2:3; Song 4:10.—m 1 Ki 5:15; Ps 29:5; Isa 30:2.—n 1 Sam 16:14; 18:10; 19:9; 1 Ki 22:22.—o Gen 33:19; 34:2; 1 Sam 25:10.—p Jos 2:5; Isa 28:15, 17; Jer 49:10.

9:13 *Cheers both God and man:* wine here goes beyond the social aspect as it is often used in worship.

the entrance to the city. 41 Abimelech dwelt
in Arumah, and Zebul expelled Gaal and his
brethren so that they could no longer live in
Shechem. 42 The next day the people went
out into the field, and they told Abimelech.
43 He took his men, divided them into three
companies, and lay in wait in the fields for
them. He kept watch, and when they came
out of the city, he rose up and attacked
them. 44 Abimelech and the company that
was with him rushed forward and stood in
the entranceway to the gate of the city; the
other two companies rushed upon the peo-
ple who were in the fields and killed them.
45 Abimelech fought against the city all day
long, and he captured the city and killed the
people who were there. He demolished the
city and sowed it with salt. [q]

46 When the men in the tower of
Shechem* heard about this, they entered
the stronghold in the temple of El-berith.
47 Abimelech was told that all the men from
the tower of Shechem were gathered togeth-
er, 48 so Abimelech and all the people who
were with him climbed up Mount Zalmon.
Abimelech took an ax in his hand and cut
down a branch from a tree, and he carried it
on his shoulder. He said to the people who
were with him, "Hurry up and do what I just
did." [r] 49 So each of the men cut a branch like
he had and they followed Abimelech. They
laid them next to the stronghold, and they
set fire to them so that all of the men in the
tower of Shechem died, a thousand men and
women.

50 Abimelech went off to Thebez. He
camped before Thebez and captured it. [s]
51 There was a strong tower in the city, so all
the men and women from the city fled there
and shut themselves in, climbing up to the top
of the tower. 52 So Abimelech came up to the
tower and fought against it. He approached
the door of the tower to set it on fire.

53 * A certain woman cast the upper part
of a millstone down upon Abimelech's head,
and it cracked his skull. 54 He called out
quickly to his young man, his armor-bearer,
and he said, "Draw out your sword and kill
me, so that they cannot say, 'A woman killed
him.' " His young man thrust him through,
and he died. [t] 55 When the Israelites saw that
Abimelech was dead, they left, each man
going home.

56 God repaid Abimelech for the wicked
thing that he had done against his father by
killing his seventy brothers. 57 The LORD
repaid all of the evil that the men of
Shechem had done upon their own heads,
for the curse of Jotham, the son of Jerubbaal,
came down upon them.

CHAPTER 10

Tola and Jair. 1 After Abimelech, a certain
Tola, the son of Puah, the son of Dodo, an
Issacharite, rose up to deliver Israel. He dwelt
in Shamir in the hill country of Ephraim. 2 He
was judge over Israel for twenty-three years,
and when he died, he was buried at Shamir.

3 After him Jair, the Gileadite, rose up and
he was judge over Israel for twenty-two years.
4 He had thirty sons who rode on thirty don-
keys, and they also possessed thirty towns.
These are called Havvoth-jair up to the pres-
ent, and they are in the land of Gilead. [u] 5 Jair
died and was buried in Kamon.

Israelites Subject to the Ammonites. 6 The
Israelites again did what was evil in the sight
of the LORD. They served the Baals and the
Ashtoreths, the gods of Syria, the gods of
Sidon, the gods of the Ammonites, and the
gods of the Philistines. They abandoned the
LORD and did not serve him. [v] 7 The anger of
the LORD blazed out against Israel, and he
sold them into the hands of the Philistines
and the hands of the Ammonites. 8 From that
year on they oppressed and afflicted them for
eighteen years, that is, all of the Israelites who
were on the other side of the Jordan in the
land of the Amorites, that is, in Gilead.

9 The Ammonites also crossed over the
Jordan to fight against Judah, against
Benjamin, and against the house of Ephra-
im, so that Israel was sorely distressed. 10 The
Israelites called upon the LORD saying, "We
have sinned against you because we have
abandoned our God and served the Baals." [w]

11 The LORD said to the Israelites, "When
the Egyptians, the Amorites, the Am-
monites, the Philistines, [x] 12 the Sidonians,
the Amalekites, and the Midianites op-
pressed you, and you cried out to me, did I

q Deut 29:23; Jer 17:6; 48:9; Ps 107:34.—r Ps 68:15.—s 2 Sam 11:21.—t 1 Sam 31:4; 2 Sam 1:9; 1 Chr 10:4.—u Num 32:41; 1 Ki 1:33.—v Jdg 2:11-13; Deut 32:15; Ezek 27:16.—w Ex 9:27; 1 Sam 12:8-10; Ps 32:5; Jer 3:25.—x Ex 14:30; Num 21:21.

9:46 *Tower of Shechem:* probably a village (tower) quite near Shechem, on Mount Gerizim.

9:53ff The indignity of being struck by a woman and the weapon she used was God's way of reducing Abimelech's stature and punishing him for murdering his brothers to gain power.

not save you from out of their hands? [13] But
you have abandoned me for other gods,
therefore I will not save you anymore. [y] [14] Go
and cry out to the gods that you have chosen.
Let them save you in the hour of your des-
peration."* [z]

[15] The Israelites said to the LORD, "We
have sinned. Do with us however you see fit,
but please rescue us today." [a] [16] They
removed their foreign gods from their midst,
and they served the LORD. Finally, he could
no longer bear Israel's misery.* [b] [17] The
Ammonites gathered together and they
camped in Gilead. The Israelites also gath-
ered together, and they camped at Mizpah.
[18] The people and the leaders of Gilead said
to one another, "Who will begin the battle
against the Ammonites? That man will be
the leader of all of those who live in Gilead."

CHAPTER 11

Jephthah. [1] Now Jephthah the Gileadite
was a mighty warrior, but he was the son of
a prostitute. Gilead was the father of
Jephthah. [2] Gilead's wife bore him sons, but
when his wife's sons grew up, they drove
Jephthah out and said to him, "You shall not
have an inheritance in our father's house, for
you are the son of another woman."

[3] Jephthah fled from his brothers and
dwelt in the land of Tob. Jephthah gathered
some worthless fellows around himself, and
they went out with him. [c]

[4] After some time, the Ammonites made
war against Israel. [5] When the Ammonites
fought against Israel, the elders of Israel
went to bring back Jephthah from the land of
Tob. [6] They said to Jephthah, "Come and be
our leader so that we can fight against the
Ammonites." [7] Jephthah said to the elders of
Gilead, "Did you not hate me and drive me
out of my father's house? Why have you
come to me now that you are in trouble?"
[8] The elders of Gilead said to Jephthah, "This
is why we have returned to you, so that you
can go with us and fight against the
Ammonites and be the leader of all of those
who live in Gilead." [d] [9] Jephthah said to the
elders of Gilead, "If you take me back to fight
against the Ammonites, and the LORD deliv-
ers them up to me, will I then be your
leader?" [10] The elders of Gilead answered,
"The LORD will be a witness between us if we
do not do what you have said." [e] [11] Jephthah
went with the elders of Gilead, and the peo-
ple made him their leader and commander.
Jephthah spoke all of his words before the
LORD at Mizpah.

[12] Jephthah sent messengers to the king of
the Ammonites asking, "What do you have
against us? Why have you come here to fight
in our land?" [13] The king of the Ammonites
said to the messengers of Jephthah, "It is
because Israel took away my land when
they came up out of Egypt. It is the land that
lies between the Arnon and the Jabbok, all
along the Jordan. Now, give it back to me
peacefully." [f] [14] Jephthah sent the messen-
gers back to the king of the Ammonites
[15] saying, "This is what Jephthah says, 'Israel
did not take away the land of the Moabites
nor the land of the Ammonites. [g] [16] When
they came up out of Egypt, the people of
Israel passed through the desert up to the
Red Sea and then on to Kadesh. [17] Israel
then sent messengers to the king of Edom
saying, "Please let me pass through your
land," but the king of Edom would not lis-
ten. The same thing happened when they
sent to the king of Moab; he would not
agree, so Israel remained in Kadesh.

[18] "'They then went through the desert,
skirting the land of Edom and the land of
Moab. Passing along on the eastern side of
Moab, they camped on the far side of the
Arnon. They did not cross over the border
with Moab, for the Arnon was the border
with Moab. [h]

[19] "'Then Israel sent messengers to Sihon,
the king of the Amorites, who reigned in
Heshbon. Israel said to him, "Please let us
pass through your land into our territory."
[20] But Sihon did not trust Israel enough to let
them pass through his land. Sihon and all of
his forces camped at Jahaz and fought
against Israel. [21] The LORD, the God of Israel,
delivered Sihon and all of his men into
Israel's hands. They defeated them, and so
Israel took possession of all of the land of the
Amorites who lived in that territory. [22] They
captured the entire land of the Amorites

y Deut 32:15; Jer 11:10; 13:10.—z Isa 44:17; Jer 2:28; 11:12; Hab 2:18.—a 1 Sam 3:18; 2 Sam 10:12; Job 1:21.—b Jos 24:23; Isa 63:9; Jer 18:8.—c 2 Sam 10:6, 8.—d Jdg 10:18.—e Gen 31:50; Mic 1:2; Jer 42:5.—f Num 21:24.—g Deut 2:9, 19.—h Deut 2:8; Num 20:21; 21:4.

10:14 Deeply distressed over their plight, the unfaithful Israelites were further humiliated when they realized how ineffective the false gods were in helping them.

10:16 Downtrodden and finally repentant, the Israelites turned once again to the true God who relented and delivered them through another judge named Jephthah. God's mercy is without end.

from the Arnon to the Jabbok, and from the
wilderness to the Jordan.
23 " 'Now since it was the LORD, the God of
Israel, who has driven the Amorites out
from before the people of Israel, who are you
that you should take it over? 24 Should you
not possess what Chemosh,* your god, has
given you to possess? Whatever the LORD,
our God, has given us to possess, we will pos-
sess it.[i]
25 " 'Are you any better than Balak, the son
of Zippor, the king of Moab? Did he ever
quarrel with Israel or fight against it?
26 Israel lived in Heshbon and the towns
dependent upon it, in Aroer and the towns
dependent upon it, and in all of the cities that
lie along the Arnon for three hundred years.
Why did you not take it back then? 27 I have
not wronged you, but you have done this evil
to me by attacking me. Let the LORD, the
judge, decide between the Israelites and the
Ammonites today.' "[j]
28 The king of the Ammonites did not heed
the message that Jephthah had sent him.
29 The Spirit of the LORD came upon
Jephthah. He crossed over into Gilead and
Manasseh, passing through Mizpah of
Gilead, and from Mizpah of Gilead he
advanced against the Ammonites.[k]

Jephthah's Vow.* 30 Jephthah made a vow to
the LORD saying, "If you deliver the
Ammonites into my hands, 31 then whatever
comes out of the doors of my house to meet
me when I come back in peace from the
Ammonites, I will surely offer it up to the
LORD as a burnt offering."
32 Jephthah went to fight the Ammonites,
and the LORD delivered them into his hands.
33 He devastated some twenty cities between
Aroer and up to near Minnith, as far away as
Abel-keramim. It was a total massacre, and
the Ammonites were subjected to the
Israelites.[l]
34 When Jephthah came back to Mizpah, to
his home, it was his daughter who came out
to meet him dancing and playing the tam-
bourines. (She was his only child, for beside
her there were no other sons or daughters.)
35 When he saw her, he tore his clothes and
said, "Woe is me, for my daughter has made
me miserable and wretched. I made a vow
to the LORD; I cannot break it."[m] 36 "My
father," she said, "you have made a vow to
the LORD. Do to me what you have vowed to
do, for the LORD has taken vengeance for you
upon your enemies, the Ammonites. 37 Only
let me do this one thing, my father," she con-
tinued, "may I roam around the hill country
to mourn my virginity, for I will never
marry." 38 He answered, "Go!" She and her
friends went into the hill country for two
months, mourning her virginity. 39 When the
two months were over, she returned to her
father. He did what he had promised in his
vow to do to her. She never knew any man.
This is why there is a custom in Israel 40 for
young women in Israel to mourn the daugh-
ter of Jephthah the Gileadite for four days
every year.

CHAPTER 12

Shibboleth Murders. 1 The Ephraimites
gathered together and they traveled north-
ward to Jephthah and they said, "Why did
you go out to fight against the Ammonites
and you did not summon us to go with you?
We are going to set your house on fire!"
2 Jephthah answered, "I and the people
who were with me fought a great battle
against the Ammonites, and although I sum-
moned you, you did not deliver me out of
their hands. 3 When I realized that you would
not help me, I put my life in my hands and
crossed over to fight against the Ammonites.
It is the LORD who delivered them into my
hands. Why have you come here today to
fight against me?"[n] 4 Jephthah then sum-
moned the Gileadites and they fought
against the Ephraimites. The Gileadites
struck down the Ephraimites, because the
Ephraimites had said, "You Gileadites are
nothing more than refugees from Ephraim
and Manasseh."[o]
5 The Gileadites captured the fords of the
Jordan that lead to Ephraim. When one of
the survivors of the Ephraimites said, "Let
us cross over," the Gileadites said to him,
"Are you an Ephraimite?" If he replied,
"No," 6 then they said to him, "Say
Shibboleth." If he said, "Sibboleth," because
he could not pronounce it correctly, they

i Num 21:29; Jos 3:10; 1 Ki 11:7.—j Gen 16:5; 18:25; 1 Sam 24:12, 15.—k Jdg 3:10; 1 Sam 11:6.—l Ezek 27:17.—m Num 30:2-3; Eccl 5:2, 4-5.—n Deut 20:4; 1 Sam 19:5; 28:21; Job 13:14.—o 1 Ki 17:1; Isa 9:21.

11:24 *Chemosh:* the principal god of the Moabites (Num 21:29).

11:30-40 The daughter of Jephthah was a victim of the practice of human sacrifice, which had been taken over from the Canaanite religions. The practice elicited indignant protests from the prophets (Jer 7:31; Ezek 16:21). The sacred writer lets it be seen that he disapproves of it (Jdg 11:40).

would seize him and kill him at the fords of the Jordan. At that time forty-two thousand Ephraimites were killed.

7 Jephthah was a judge over Israel for six years. Jephthah the Gileadite died, and he was buried in one of the cities of Gilead. [p]

Ibzan. 8 * After him, Ibzan of Bethlehem was a judge over Israel. [q] 9 He had thirty sons and thirty daughters. He gave his thirty daughters away in marriage to those outside of his clan, and he took in thirty young women from outside of his clan for his sons to marry. Ibzan was a judge over Israel for seven years. 10 When Ibzan died, he was buried in Bethlehem.

Elon. 11 After him, Elon the Zebulunite was a judge over Israel for ten years. 12 When Elon the Zebulunite died, he was buried in Aijalon of Zebulun. [r]

Abdon. 13 After him, Abdon, the son of Hillel, the Pirathonite was a judge over Israel. 14 He had forty sons and thirty grandsons who rode on seventy donkeys. He was a judge over Israel for eight years. [s] 15 When Adbon, the son of Hillel the Pirathonite, died, he was buried in Pirathon in the land of the Ephraimites in the hill country of the Amalekites.

CHAPTER 13

The Angel and Manoah. 1 * The Israelites once again did what was evil in the sight of the LORD. The LORD delivered them over into the hands of the Philistines for forty years.

2 There was a certain man from Zorah, named Manoah, who was a Danite. His wife was barren and childless. 3 The angel of the LORD appeared to the woman and said to her, "Behold, you are barren and childless, but you will conceive and have a son. [t] 4 Make sure you do not drink any wine or strong drink. Do not eat any unclean thing, 5 for you will conceive and have a son. No razor is ever to touch his head, for he will be a Nazirite,* one dedicated to God from the womb. He will begin the deliverance of Israel out of the hands of the Philistines."

6 The woman went and told her husband, "A man of God has visited me. He looked like an angel of God, truly wondrous. I did not ask him where he came from, nor did he tell me his name. [u] 7 He said to me, 'Behold, you will conceive and have a son. Do not drink any wine or strong drink. Do not eat anything unclean, for from the womb until the day he dies he will be a Nazirite of God.' " [v]

8 Manoah prayed to the LORD, "O LORD, let the man of God whom you sent to us visit us again so that he might teach us how to raise the child who is to be born."

9 God listened to Manoah, and the angel of God visited the woman again when she was out in the fields, but Manoah, her husband, was not with her. 10 The woman quickly ran to tell her husband, "Behold, the man who appeared to me the other day is here."

11 Manoah got up and followed his wife. When he came to the man, he said, "Are you the man who spoke to my wife?" He answered, "I am." 12 Manoah asked him, "When your words are fulfilled, how should we treat the child?" 13 The angel of the LORD said to Manoah, "Your wife must do the things I said to her. 14 She cannot eat any of the products of the vine nor drink any strong drink nor eat anything unclean. She is to do everything that I commanded her to do."

15 Manoah said to the angel of the LORD, "Would you please stay here until we prepare a kid goat for you?" 16 The angel of the LORD answered Manoah, "Even though you hold me here, I will not eat anything. If you prepare a burnt offering, offer it up to the LORD." (Manoah did not realize that it was an angel of the LORD.) 17 Manoah asked the angel of the LORD, "What is your name, so that we can honor you when these things happen?" [w] 18 * The angel of the LORD answered, "Why do you ask me my name? It is a mystery." [x]

p Jdg 10:2, 5; Heb 11:32.—q Gen 35:19.—r Jos 10:12.—s Jdg 10:4.—t 1 Sam 1:20; Lk 1:13.—u 1 Sam 2:27; 1 Ki 13:1; Ps 66:5; Mt 28:3.—v Lev 10:9; Jer 35:6.—w Gen 32:29.—x Isa 9:6.

12:8-15 The judgeships of Ibzan, Elon, and Abdon over the next 25 years are briefly mentioned. As we move further away from the Israelites' initial entry into the Promised Land, the less we hear of any spiritual leaders among them.

13:1—16:41 The Philistines, new arrivals in the region, acted as masters of southern Palestine. Israel was under the control of these well-armed warriors and could no longer do anything. The story of Samson brings together some episodes reflecting this situation, which would continue to have its tragic effects until the time of David.

13:5 *Nazirite:* one who was consecrated to God by a vow. Sometimes, like Samson and John the Baptist, the consecration pre-dated their birth. Prohibitions against wine and other vine products (Num 6:3), and against a shaved head (Num 6:5), had serious consequences for Samson later in his life.

13:18-19 *Mystery:* the angel's name is beyond knowing. Manoah dedicates his offering to the Lord who "did a wondrous thing."

19 Manoah took a young goat together with
a grain offering and he offered them up to
the LORD on a rock. He did a wondrous thing
as Manoah and his wife looked on. 20 As the
flames rose up from the altar into the heav-
ens, the angel of the LORD rose up from the
altar in the flames as Manoah and his wife
looked on. They fell prostrate on the
ground. [y]

21 When the angel of the LORD did not
appear again to Manoah and his wife,
Manoah realized that it had been an angel of
the LORD. 22 Manoah said to his wife, "We
will surely die, for we have seen God!" [z] 23 But
his wife answered, "If the LORD wanted to kill
us, then he would not have accepted the
burnt offering and the grain offering from
our hands, nor would he have revealed all of
these things, nor would he have told us these
things." [a]

24 The woman gave birth to a son whose
name was Samson. The child grew and the
LORD blessed him. [b] 25 The Spirit of the LORD
began to stir in him while he was in
Mahaneh-dan, between Zorah and Eshtaol.

CHAPTER 14

Samson's Marriage. 1 Samson went down to
Timnah and he saw a Philistine woman in
Timnah. 2 When he returned, he told his
father and his mother, "I have seen a woman
in Timnah, a Philistine. Arrange for her to
be my wife." 3 His father and his mother
answered, "Is there no maiden among your
relatives or your countrymen that you would
go to take a wife from among the uncircum-
cised Philistines?" But Samson said to his
father, "Get her for me, for she is the one I
want." [c] 4 (His father and his mother did not
know that this was the LORD's plan. He was
seeking an opportunity to oppose the
Philistines, for the Philistines were ruling
over Israel.)* [d]

5 Samson went down to Timnah with his
father and his mother. As they were
approaching the vineyards of Timnah, a
young roaring lion came toward them. 6 The
Spirit of the LORD rushed upon him, and he
tore it apart with his bare hands as if he were
tearing apart a young goat. He told his father
and his mother not to tell anyone what he
had done. [e]

7 They went down and talked with the
woman, and Samson liked her. 8 Sometime
later, when he went down to marry her, he
stepped off the road to look at the lion's car-
cass. There was a bee's nest and some honey
in the lion's carcass. 9 He took some of it in
his hands, and ate it along the way. When he
rejoined his father and his mother, he gave
them some to eat, but he did not tell them
that he had taken the honey from the carcass
of the lion.

10 His father went down to see the woman.
Samson prepared a feast there, as is the cus-
tom among young men. 11 When they met
him, they brought in thirty companions to
be with him. 12 Samson said to them, "I will
give you a riddle. If you can figure it out and
solve it for me during these seven days of cel-
ebration, I will give you thirty linen gar-
ments and thirty changes of clothing. [f] 13 If
you cannot solve it, then you will have to give
me thirty linen garments and thirty changes
of clothing." They answered him, "Tell us
your riddle. Let's hear it." 14 He told them,
"From out of the eater came forth some-
thing to eat, from out of the strong one came
something sweet." For three days they could
not figure out the riddle.

15 On the fourth day, they said to Samson's
wife, "Coax Samson to explain the riddle for
us, or else we will burn you and your father's
house. Did you invite us here to rob us?" [g]
16 Samson's wife came to him crying and she
said, "You hate me. You don't really love me.
You posed a riddle to my people, and you did
not explain it to me." He told her, "I have not
even explained it to my father or my moth-
er; why should I explain it to you?"

17 She cried before him for the entire seven
days of the celebration. On the seventh day
he finally told her, for she had worn him out,
and she explained the riddle to her people. [h]
18 On the seventh day, before sunset, the men
from the city said to him, "What is sweeter
than honey? What is stronger than a lion?"
He said to them, "You would not have fig-
ured out my riddle if you had not plowed
with my heifer." * 19 Then the Spirit of the
LORD rushed upon him. He went down to
Ashkelon and he killed thirty men there. He

y Lev 9:24.—z Jdg 6:22; Deut 5:26; Num 17:12.—a Ps 25:14.—b 1 Sam 3:19; Lk 1:80; Heb 11:32.—c Gen 24:3-4; Deut 7:3; 1 Sam 14:6.—d Jdg 13:1; Jos 11:20.—e Jdg 3:10; 13:25; 1 Sam 17:34-36.—f Num 12:8; Ezek 17:2.—g Jdg 16:5; Eccl 7:26.—h Est 1:5.

14:4 Although Samson is filled with the Spirit (Jdg 13:25) he is a sinful man who marries a heathen woman against God's will. The spiritual writer indicates that God will use this transgression to defeat the Philistines. This is the good news!

14:18 The riddle refers to the incident related in verses 8-9.

took their belongings and gave a change of clothing to those who had explained the riddle. Burning with rage, he went back to his father's home.[i] 20 Samson's wife was given to his friend who had been his best man.[j]

CHAPTER 15

Samson's Revenge on the Philistines. 1 Later on, during the wheat harvest, Samson visited his wife, bringing her a kid goat. He said, "I am going in to my wife's room," but her father would not let him go in. 2 The father said, "I was so sure that you hated her that I gave her to your friend. Her younger sister is prettier than she is. Please, take her instead." 3 But Samson said to them, "It is no longer my fault if I harm the Philistines."

4 Samson went out and caught three hundred foxes. He tied them together, tail to tail. He then fastened a torch between each pair of tails.[k] 5 He set the torches on fire and let them go into the Philistine's standing grain. It burned up both the standing grain and the stacks of grain, as well as the vineyards and the olive orchards.

6 When the Philistines asked, "Who did this," they were told, "It was Samson, the son-in-law of the Timnite. He did it because they took his wife and gave her to his friend." The Philistines therefore went and burned her and her father to death.[l] 7 Samson said to them, "Because you have done this, I will never stop getting my vengeance on you." 8 He struck them ruthlessly, slaughtering many of them. He then went down and dwelt in a fissure of the rock of Etam.[m]

9 The Philistines went up and camped in Judah, spreading out near Lehi. 10 The Judahites asked, "Why have you come to fight against us?" They answered, "To take Samson prisoner so that we can do to him what he did to us." 11 Three thousand men from Judah went down to the fissure of the rock of Etam and said to Samson, "Did you not know that the Philistines are ruling over us? What have you done to us?" He answered, "I just did to them what they did to me."[n] 12 They said to him, "We have come to take you prisoner and to deliver you over to the Philistines." He said to them, "Swear to me that you will not kill me yourselves." 13 They said, "No, but we will tie you up and hand you over to them. We will not kill you." So they bound him with two new ropes and led him away from the rock.

14 As he approached Lehi, the Philistines came toward him shouting. The Spirit of the LORD rushed upon him. The ropes that were around his arms became like charred flax, and the binding fell off of his hands.[o]

15 He found a fresh jawbone of a donkey, and he reached out and took it in his hand. He then killed one thousand men with it.[p] 16 Samson said,

"With the jawbone of a donkey,
  I have piled them up;
with the jawbone of a donkey,
  I have killed a thousand men."

17 When he finished speaking, he dropped the jawbone from out of his hand. The name of that place is Ramath-lehi.

18 Now he was very thirsty, so he called out to the LORD, "You have given this great victory through the hand of your servant. Must I now die of thirst and fall into the hands of the uncircumcised?"* 19 God split open a hollow place in Lehi, and water came out. When he drank it, his strength returned and his spirit was revived. The spring is called En-hakkore, and it is still in Lehi today.[q] 20 Samson was a judge over Israel for forty years during the days of the Philistines.

CHAPTER 16

Samson at Gaza. 1 One day Samson went to Gaza. He saw a prostitute there, and he had sex with her. 2 The people in Gaza were told, "Samson is here." They surrounded the place where he was staying, and they lay in wait for him all night at the city gate. They kept quiet all night, saying, "In the morning we will kill him." 3 Samson lay there until midnight, and then at midnight he got up and took hold of the city gates with its two posts. He lifted up the gates, put them on his shoulders, and carried them to the top of the hill that faces Hebron.[r]

Samson and Delilah. 4 Sometime later he fell in love with a woman who lived in the Valley of Sorek. Her name was Delilah. 5 The lords of the Philistines visited her and said, "Entice him and see if you can find out the source of his great strength and how we can

i Jdg 3:10; Jos 13:3; 1 Sam 11:6.—j Jdg 15:2; Jn 3:29.—k Song 2:15.—l Jdg 14:15; Gen 38:24.—m Isa 2:21.—n Jdg 14:4; Ps 106:40-42.—o Jos 2:6; 1 Sam 11:6.—p Lev 26:8; Jos 23:10.—q Gen 45:27; 1 Sam 30:12; Isa 40:29.—r Jos 10:36.

15:18 Samson acknowledges that the Lord is the source of his strength, and the victory belongs to God.

overpower him and tie him up and subdue
him. Each one of us will give you eleven hun-
dred pieces of silver." [s]

6 Delilah said to Samson, "Please tell me
the source of your great strength and how
you could be tied up and subdued." 7 Samson
answered her, "If anyone were to tie me up
with seven fresh bowstrings that have never
been dried, then I would become as weak as
everyone else." 8 The lords of the Philistines
brought her seven fresh bowstrings that had
not been dried, and she tied him up with
them. 9 There were some men hiding in the
room when she cried out to him, "Samson,
the Philistines are upon you." He broke the
thongs like a piece of string that snaps when
it is close to a flame. Thus, the secret of his
strength was not known.

10 Delilah then said to Samson, "You have
mocked me and lied to me. Please, tell me
now how you could be tied up." 11 He
answered, "If anyone were to bind me with
new ropes that had never been used, then I
would become as weak as everyone else."
12 So Delilah took new ropes and she bound
him and cried out, "Samson, the Philistines
are upon you," as the men were hiding in the
room. He broke them off of his arms as if
they were made of thread.

13 Delilah then said to Samson, "Until now
you have mocked me and lied to me. Tell
me, now, how you could be tied up." He
answered, "If you were to weave the seven
locks on my head into the loom, 14 and fas-
tened it with a pin, then I should become
weak, and be like any other man." Again she
cried out, "Samson, the Philistines are upon
you." He woke up from his sleep and pulled
away from the pin, the loom, and the web.

15 She said to him, "How can you say, 'I
love you,' when you hold back your love from
me. You have mocked me these three times;
you have not told me where your strength
lies." [t] 16 She wore him out by talking to him
day after day, and nagging him, until he was
tired to death, 17 so he told her everything.
He said to her, "No razor has ever touched
my head because I have been a Nazirite of
God from my mother's womb. If I were to be
shaved, then my strength would disappear
and I would become as weak as any other
man." [u]

18 When Delilah saw that he had told her
everything, she summoned the lords of the
Philistines saying, "Come back one more
time, for he has told me everything." The
lords of the Philistines came to her, the
money in their hands. 19 She had him fall
asleep upon her knees, and she summoned a
man to shave off the seven locks on his head.
Thus, she began to subdue him, and his
strength left him. [v] 20 She cried out, "Samson,
the Philistines are upon you." He woke up
from his sleep and said, "I will go out like the
previous times and shake myself free." He did
not know that the LORD had left him.* [w]

21 The Philistines seized him and gouged
out his eyes. They took him down to Gaza
and bound him in bronze shackles, setting
him to grind grain in prison. [x]

Samson's Revenge and Death. 22 The hair on
his head began to grow back after it had been
shaved off. 23 The lords of the Philistines
gathered to offer a great sacrifice to their
god Dagon.* They celebrated and said, "Our
god has delivered us from the hands of
Samson, our enemy." [y] 24 When the people
saw him, they praised their god saying, "Our
god has delivered our enemy into our hands,
the one who laid waste to our country and
killed so many of us." 25 While they were in
high spirits, they cried out, "Call out Samson
so that he can entertain us." They sum-
moned Samson out of the prison, and he
entertained them. They set him between the
pillars. [z] 26 Samson said to the boy who was
holding his hand, "Let me feel the pillars on
which the temple is set so I can lean against
them." 27 The temple was packed with men
and women, and all of the lords of the
Philistines were there as well. There were
also about three thousand men and women
upon the roof, watching while Samson was
amusing them.

28 Samson called out to the LORD and said,
"O LORD, please remember me. I beg you,
please strengthen me* this one more time so
that I might take vengeance upon the
Philistines for my two eyes." [a]

s Jdg 14:15; Jos 13:3.—t Jdg 14:16.—u Jdg 13:5; Mic 7:5.—v Prov 7:26-27.—w Jos 7:12; 1 Sam 16:14; 18:12.—x Job 31:10; Isa 47:2; Jer 47:1.—y 1 Sam 5:2; 1 Chr 10:10.—z Jdg 9:27; Est 1:10.—a Jdg 15:18; Jer 15:15.

16:20 *The LORD had left him:* cutting himself off from the power of the Lord by his sinful life, Samson is at the mercy of his enemies who blind him and make him a prisoner.

16:23 *Dagon:* a Babylonian divinity that was taken to Phoenicia and adopted by the Philistines.

16:28 *Remember me . . . strengthen me:* Samson repented and God graciously granted his wish so that he slew more Philistines through his death than in his lifetime.

29 Samson took hold of the two middle pillars upon which the temple was set. He braced himself against them, one with his right hand and one with his left hand. 30 Samson said, "Let me die with the Philistines." He pushed with all his might, and the house came crashing down upon the lords and upon all of the people. Thus, he killed more people with his death than he had killed during his life. 31 His brothers and all of his father's household went down to get him. They brought him back and buried him between Zorah and Eshtaol in the tomb of Manoah his father. He was a judge over Israel for twenty years.

III: APPENDICES: STORIES OF DAN AND BENJAMIN*

CHAPTER 17

Micah and the Levite. 1 There was a man named Micah in the hill country of Ephraim. 2 He said to his mother, "I have those eleven hundred pieces of silver that were stolen from you and over which you uttered a curse. I took them." His mother said, "May the LORD bless you, my son." [b] 3 He returned the eleven hundred silver pieces to his mother. His mother said, "I solemnly consecrate my silver to the LORD for my son to produce a molten image. I will give it back to you." [c]

4 When he returned the silver to his mother, his mother took two hundred pieces of silver and gave them to the silversmith, who made a molten image and a carved idol. They were placed in the house of Micah. 5 This Micah had a temple, and he made an ephod and a teraphim. He consecrated one of his sons as his priest. [d] 6 In those days Israel had no king,* and everyone did what in his own opinion he thought to be right.

7 There was a young man from Bethlehem in Judah. He was living among the clan of Judah.* [e] 8 The man left the city of Bethlehem in Judah to seek another place to live. On his way he came to the hill country of Ephraim, to the house of Micah. 9 Micah asked him, "Where do you come from?" He answered, "I am a Levite from Bethlehem in Judah, and I am seeking a place to live." 10 Micah said to him, "Live with me; you can be like a father and a priest to me. I will give you ten silver pieces a year along with your clothes and your food." So the Levite went in. [f]

11 The Levite was pleased to live with the man. It was as if the young man were one of his sons. 12 Micah consecrated the Levite, and the young man became Micah's priest, and he lived in his house. [g] 13 Micah said, "Now I know that the LORD will be good to me, for the Levite has become my priest." *

CHAPTER 18

The Danites Overtake Micah. 1 At that time, there was no king in Israel. In those days the tribe of the Danites were seeking a place* where they could dwell, because up to that time they had not yet come into their inheritance among the tribes of Israel. 2 The Danites sent out five men, one from each of its clans, brave warriors. They went out from Zorah and Eshtaol to investigate the land and to explore it. They said to them, "Go and explore the land."

They came to the hill country of Ephraim, to the house of Micah, and they stayed there. [h] 3 As they drew near the house of Micah, they heard the voice of the young Levite, so they turned in there and said to him, "Who brought you here? What are you doing in this place? Why are you here?" 4 He told them what Micah had done for him and said, "He hired me, and I am his priest." 5 Then they said to him, "Please inquire of God whether our journey will be successful." [i] 6 He replied, "Go in peace. The LORD is with you on your journey."

b Ru 2:20; 1 Sam 15:13; 2 Sam 2:5.—c Ex 20:4, 23; Lev 19:4.—d Gen 31:19; Isa 44:13; Ezek 8:10.—e Ru 1:1-2; Mic 5:1-2; Mt 2:1.—f Jdg 18:19; Gen 45:8.—g Jdg 18:4; Num 16:10.—h Gen 30:6; Num 21:32; Jos 2:1.—i Jdg 20:18; 1 Sam 14:18; 2 Sam 5:19.

17:1—18:31 The ancient traditions with which the Book of Judges ends were collected at a time when Jerusalem, capital of the Davidic dynasty, was also regarded as the only legitimate sanctuary of God. Every other place of worship, therefore, was suspect of separatism and impiety. Thus one of the chroniclers does not fail to give prominence to the following ancient story that presents in a somewhat flattering light, the origins of the sanctuary of Dan: it was founded in defiance of the traditional prohibition against any image of God (Deut 4:15f) and in the absence of any real authority that would later guarantee the legitimacy of religious practices.

17:6 *Israel had no king:* this lament, repeated in Jdg 18:1; 19:1; 21:25, indicates that the Book of Judges was written during the time of the monarchy and reiterates that lawlessness and cultic behavior were a continuing problem while there was no king among the Israelites.

17:7 The Levite's name, Jonathan, will be given later (Jdg 18:30).

17:13 Micah was hedging his bets when he appointed a Levite as his priest. God, however, would never condone Micah's sinful behavior and deceptive ways.

18:1 *Seeking a place:* the Danites' lack of faith and trust in God prevented them from taking possession of their rightful allotment (see Jdg 1:34); they are now looking to possess land elsewhere.

7 The five men left and came to Laish.
They saw that the people there were living in
safety, just like the Sidonians lived, quiet and
secure. There were no rulers in the land who
could shame them in anything. They were
quite far away from the Sidonians, and they
had no ties to anyone.

8 They came back to their brethren in
Zorah and Eshtaol, and their brethren said
to them, "What do you have to say?" 9 They
said, "Arise so that we can attack them. We
have seen the land, and it is truly very good.
Do not delay in going there so that you can
enter and take possession of the land.[j]
10 When you enter, you will find a people liv-
ing in security in a vast land. God has given
it into your hands. It is a place where you will
not lack anything upon the earth."

11 Six hundred men from the clans of the
Danites went out from Zorah and Eshtaol
dressed in battle gear. 12 They went up and
camped in Kiriath-jearim in Judah. (This is
why this place is called Mahaneh-dan up to
this day. It lies to the west of Kiriath-jearim.)
13 They went on from there to the hill coun-
try of Ephraim, coming to the house of
Micah.

14 The five men who had gone out to inves-
tigate the land around Laish said to their
brethren, "Do you know that in these houses
there are an ephod, teraphim, and a carved
molten image? What do you think we should
do?"[k] 15 They turned aside and went to the
house of the young Levite (the house of
Micah) and they greeted him. 16 The six hun-
dred armed men, the Danites, stood by the
entrance to the gate.

17 The five men who had gone out to inves-
tigate the land then arrived there. They took
the carved image, the ephod, the teraphim
and the molten image. The priest stood at the
entrance to the gate with the six hundred
men who were armed for war.[l] 18 When they
went into Micah's house and took the carved
image, the ephod, the teraphim and the
molten image, the priest asked them, "What
are you doing?" 19 They said to him, "Be
quiet! Put your hand over your mouth, and
come with us to be a father and a priest to us.
Is it better to be a father and a priest to one
man's household, or to be father and priest to
a tribe and a clan in Israel?"[m] 20 This pleased
the priest. He took the ephod, the teraphim,
and the carved image and traveled with those
people. 21 They then turned and departed,
with their children, their cattle, and their pos-
sessions in the front of the march.

22 When they had traveled some distance
from the house of Micah, the men who lived
in the houses near Micah's house overtook
the Danites. 23 When they shouted out, the
Danites turned and said to Micah, "What is
the matter with you, calling out such a
group?" 24 * He replied, "You took the gods
that I made and the priest, and then you went
on your way. What else do I have? How could
you say to me, 'What is the matter with
you?'" 25 The Danites said to him, "Keep
quiet, or these men could get angry, and you
and your household could lose their lives."
26 So the Danites continued on their journey.
When Micah saw that they were too strong
for him, he turned back and went home.[n]

27 They took away the things that Micah
had made and his priest, and they arrived in
Laish. This land was quiet, with people who
lived in security, and they put them to the
sword and burned the city down.[o] 28 There
was no one to deliver them, for Sidon was far
away and they had no allies. This happened
in the valley near Beth-rehob. They built a
city and dwelt there. 29 They named the city
Dan after their forefather who was called
Dan. He was the son of Israel. The city had
originally been called Laish.[p] 30 The Danites
set up the carved idol, and they chose
Jonathan, the son of Gershom, the son of
Moses, and his sons as priests to the Danites,
and they continued to serve until they were
exiled from the land. * 31 They maintained
the carved idol that Micah had made, and it
remained there the whole time that the
house of God was in Shiloh.

CHAPTER 19

The Levite's Concubine. 1 * In those days
there was no king in Israel, and there was a

j Num 13:30; 1 Ki 22:3.—k Jdg 17:4-5; Gen 31:19; Jos 19:47.—l Gen 31:19; Mic 5:13.—m Jdg 17:10; Job 13:5; 21:5; Isa 52:15.—n 2 Sam 3:39; Pss 18:18; 35:10.—o Gen 34:25; Num 31:10; Jos 19:47.—p Gen 14:14; Jos 19:47; 1 Ki 15:20.

18:24ff Micah finally admits to the complete loss of everything he foolishly valued, but even in his misery he does not repent and return to the true God.

18:30 Jonathan is therefore a descendant of Moses (Ex 2:22) and this is the reading in the Septuagint, whereas the Hebrew text has "Manasseh."

19:1—21:25 In the absence of a single, stable authority, the religious anarchy that divided the people was accompanied by a moral and political anarchy; the royalist tradition likes to stress this fact. The story exaggerates the memory of grudges and acts of cruelty.

certain Levite who lived on the far side of the
hill country of Ephraim who took a concu-
bine from Bethlehem of Judah. 2 His concu-
bine cheated on him and she returned to her
father's house in Bethlehem. She had been
there for four months 3 when her husband
rose up to go to her in order to convince her
to return to him. He took along his servant
and two donkeys.

She invited him into her father's house,
and when her father saw him, he was
pleased to meet him. 4 His father-in-law, the
young woman's father, urged him to stay
with him. He stayed with him for three days,
eating and drinking and sleeping there. 5 On
the fourth day they rose early in the morning
and were leaving. The woman's father said
to his son-in-law, "Fortify yourself with
something to eat, and then you can go on
your way." [q] 6 Both of them sat down and
they ate and drank together, and then the
young woman's father said to the man,
"Please, stay the night and enjoy yourself."
7 When the man rose up to go, his father-in-
law urged him to stay, so he slept there.
8 Early on the morning of the fifth day, the
young woman's father said, "Fortify your-
self, wait until the afternoon." So the both of
them ate together.

9 When the man got up to depart along with
the concubine and his servant, his father-in-
law, the young woman's father, said to him,
"Look, it is almost evening, stay the night
because the day is almost over. Stay here and
enjoy yourselves. You can get up early tomor-
row morning and be on your way home."
10 But the man would not stay the night. He
got up and left and went toward Jebus (that is,
Jerusalem) along with his two saddled don-
keys and his concubine. [r]

11 It was already late in the day when they
were passing by Jebus, so the servant said to
his master, "Come, let us stop at the city of the
Jebusites and stay for the night." 12 The master
said, "I will not stop at a foreign city whose
inhabitants are not Israelites. Let us continue
on to Gibeah." 13 He said to his servant, "We
will try to reach Gibeah or Ramah and spend
the night in one of those places." 14 They went
on, and the sun was setting as they
approached Gibeah in Benjamin. [s] 15 They
stopped there to spend the night in Gibeah.
They went in and sat in the city square, but no
one took them home for the night.

16 That evening an old man* came in from
working in the fields in the hill country of
Ephraim. He was living in Gibeah, and the
men of that place were Benjaminites. [t]
17 When he looked up and saw a traveler in
the city square, the old man said, "Where
are you going? Where have you come from?"
18 He answered, "We are on our way from
Bethlehem in Judah to the far side of the hill
country of Ephraim. I am from there. I had
gone to Bethlehem in Judah, but now I am
going to the house of the LORD. No one has
welcomed me into his home. 19 We have both
straw and fodder for our donkeys and bread
and wine for ourselves your servants—me,
your maidservant, and the young man who
is with me. We do not need anything." 20 The
old man said, "Peace be with you. Let me
supply whatever you need, only do not spend
the night in the city square." 21 So he took
them into his home and fed the donkeys. He
washed their feet, and they had something to
eat and drink. [u]

Abuse at Gibeah. 22 While they were enjoy-
ing themselves, certain men from the city
who were surely sons of Belial* surrounded
the house. They beat on the door and spoke
to the old man, the master of the house, say-
ing, "Bring out the man who entered your
house, so that we can know him." [v] 23 The
master of the house went out to them and
said to them: "No, my brothers, do not do
this evil thing. This man is a guest in my
house; do not do this disgraceful thing.
24 * Look, here is my virgin daughter and his
concubine. I will bring them out to you now.
You can abuse them, and do whatever you
want to them, but do not do such a vile thing
to this man." [w] 25 But the men would not lis-
ten to him. The man thrust his concubine
outside to them. They raped her and mal-
treated her all throughout the night, and in
the morning they let her go.

26 At daybreak the woman came to the
house where her master was staying and fell
down in the doorway. She remained there

q Gen 18:5.—r Gen 10:16; Jos 15:8; 1 Chr 11:4-5.—s Jos 15:57; 1 Sam 10:26; Isa 10:29.—t Ps 104:23.—u Gen 24:32-33; Lk 7:44.—v Gen 19:4-5; Deut 13:13; Rom 1:26-27.—w Gen 19:8; Deut 21:14.

19:16 *An old man:* since he was from the hill country of Ephraim, he was a compatriot of the Levite.

19:22 *Sons of Belial:* "Belial" (nothing); in the course of time it came to be used as a proper name for the power of evil, as in 2 Cor 6:15.

19:24-27 The despicable behavior and lack of moral integrity of the master and his guest is a blatant example of how low society had sunk without a religious leader to guide them.

until it was light. 27 Her master got up in the morning and opened the doors to the house to be on his way, and he found his concubine lying in the doorway to the house, her hands upon the threshold. 28 He said to her, "Get up. Let us be on our way," but there was no answer. The man then put her on his donkey and set out for home.

29 When he arrived home, he picked up a knife, took his concubine, and cut her body into twelve parts. He then sent it into each of the territories of Israel.[x] 30 Everyone who saw it said, "No one has ever done such a thing from the day that the Israelites came up out of Egypt until the present. Think about it. Take counsel. Tell us what to do."[y]

CHAPTER 20

The Israelites' Attack Plan. 1 All of the Israelites from Dan to Beer-sheba and from Gilead gathered together as one in an assembly before the LORD at Mizpah. 2 The leaders of all of the people of the tribes of Israel took their place in the assembly of the people of God, four hundred thousand soldiers armed with swords.

3 Now the Benjaminites heard that the Israelites had gone up to Mizpah. The Israelites said, "Tell us how this evil thing happened." 4 The Levite, the husband of the woman who had been killed, answered, "I and my concubine came into Gibeah of Benjamin to spend the night.[z] 5 The men of Gibeah rose up and surrounded me and the house during the night. They intended to kill me, and they raped my concubine until she died. 6 I took my concubine and cut her up into pieces, sending them to each region in the inheritance of Israel, for they had committed this lewd and disgraceful act in Israel. 7 Now, all of you Israelites, discuss it among yourselves and give your counsel here."

8 All of the people rose up as if they were one man and they said, "None of us will go home! No! None of us will return home! 9 This is what we are going to do to Gibeah. We will choose who will attack it by lot.[a] 10 We will take ten from every hundred in all of the tribes of Israel, and one hundred out of one thousand, and one thousand out of every ten thousand. We will also take provisions for the people. When they arrive at Gibeah in Benjamin, they will then pay for all the disgraceful things that they have done in Israel."

11 All of the men of Israel gathered together, united as if they were one man, and they went up against the city. 12 The tribes of Israel sent men all throughout the tribe of Benjamin saying, "What is this wicked thing that has been committed among you?[b] 13 Deliver up those sons of Belial, those men of Gibeah, so that we may put them to death and purge the evil from Israel." *

But the Benjaminites would not listen to what Israel had said. 14 The Benjaminites gathered together from out of the cities and they went to Gibeah to fight against the Israelites. 15 There were twenty-six thousand Benjaminites from the cities armed with swords, in addition to the seven hundred chosen men from Gibeah. 16 There were seven hundred chosen men among them who were left-handed. Each of them could sling a stone at a hair and never miss.

17 There were four hundred thousand men from Israel armed with swords (not counting the Benjaminites), each of them fighting men. 18 The Israelites went up to Bethel and sought counsel from God. They said, "Who among us should be the first to go up in battle against the Benjaminites?" The LORD answered, "Judah should go up first." *[c]

19 The next morning the Israelites rose up and camped outside of Gibeah.

War with the Benjaminites. 20 The Israelites went out to fight against Benjamin. The Israelites lined themselves up to fight at Gibeah. 21 The Benjaminites came out of Gibeah and that day they cut twenty-two thousand Israelites down to the ground. 22 But the Israelites encouraged one another and once again took the same positions for battle that they had taken the first day. 23 The Israelites went up and wept before the LORD until that evening, asking counsel of the LORD and saying, "Should we go up again to fight against the Benjaminites, our brothers?" The LORD answered, "Go up to fight them."[d]

24 So the Israelites approached the Benjaminites the second day. 25 When the

---

x Jdg 20:6; 1 Sam 11:7.—y Prov 13:10; Hos 9:9.—z Jos 15:57.—a Lev 16:8.—b Deut 13:14.—c Gen 49:10; Num 27:21; Jos 12:9.—d Jdg 18:5; Num 14:1; Jos 7:6.

20:13 An offer was put on the table by the Israelites that could have averted war with the Benjaminites, but in their hardness of heart they ignore it.

20:18 *Judah should go up first:* as in previous encounters with the enemy, the Israelites invoke the counsel of the Lord before battle—this time against their own brothers.

Benjaminites came out of Gibeah to fight
them the second day, they cut another eigh-
teen thousand Israelites down to the ground,
all of them armed with swords. [26] So all of the
Israelites, all of the people, went up to Bethel
and wept and sat there before the LORD, fast-
ing that entire day until evening. They sacri-
ficed burnt offerings and peace offerings
before the LORD. [e] [27] The Israelites asked
counsel of the LORD (for in those days the
Ark of the Covenant of God was kept there.
[28] Phinehas, the son of Eleazar, the son of
Aaron, ministered before it in those days.)
They said, "Shall we once again go out to do
battle against the Benjaminites, our brothers,
or shall we stop fighting?" The LORD
answered, "Go up, for tomorrow I will deliv-
er them into your hands." [f] [29] * Israel set an
ambush around Gibeah. [30] The Israelites
went up against the Benjaminites on the
third day lined up in front of Gibeah as they
had been the other times. [31] The Benjamin-
ites came out against those people, and they
were drawn away from the city. They began
to strike and kill the people as they had
before, so that thirty Israelites fell in the
highways, one leading up to Bethel, and the
other to Gibeah, and also in the fields.

[32] While the Benjaminites were saying to
themselves, "We are striking them down like
the other times," the Israelites were saying,
"Let us run away and draw them away from
the city and onto the highways." [33] All of the
Israelites rose up from their positions and
they lined up at Baal-tamar. In the mean-
time, those who were lying in ambush on the
western side of Gibeah charged forward.
[34] Ten thousand of the chosen men from out
of all of Israel attacked Gibeah. The fighting
was so heavy that they did not realize that
disaster was near. [35] The LORD defeated
Benjamin before Israel. The Israelites cut
down twenty-five thousand, one hundred
Benjaminites that day, all of them armed
with swords. [g]

[36] The Benjaminites then saw that they
were defeated. The Israelites had given way
before the Benjaminites, because they trusted
in the ambush that they had set near Gibeah.
[37] The men who had been in ambush made a
sudden rush toward Gibeah. The men in
ambush marched in and put the entire city to
the sword. [38] The Israelites had arranged with
those who were in ambush that they should
raise up flame and a great cloud of smoke
from out of the city. [39] The Israelites would
then turn around in the battle. [h]

The Benjaminites had begun to overcome
and kill the Israelites, about thirty of them,
and they were saying to themselves, "Surely
we are striking them down before us as we
did in the first battle." [40] When the flames
and the column of smoke began to rise up
out of the city, the Benjaminites looked back
and saw flames rising up into the heavens
from the city. [41] The Israelites turned on
them, and the Benjaminites were terrified,
for they realized that they faced disaster.
[42] They fled from before the Israelites, run-
ning toward the desert, but the fighting over-
took them. Those who were in the city came
out and cut them down there. [43] They sur-
rounded the Benjaminites, chased them,
and easily overran them near Gibeah, in the
direction of the sunrise. [44] Eighteen thousand
men from Benjamin fell, all of them brave
warriors. [i] [45] As they turned and fled toward
the desert up to the rock of Rimmon, they
cut down five thousand men along the high-
ways. They kept after them all the way to
Gidom, and killed another two thousand of
them. [j] [46] On that day, twenty-five thousand
men of Benjamin fell, all of them armed
with swords and all of them brave warriors.

[47] But six hundred men had fled into the
wilderness, to the rock of Rimmon, and they
stayed at the rock of Rimmon for four
months. [48] The Israelites went back to the
Benjaminites, putting all of the men from
their cities and their beasts and anything else
they found to the sword. They also burned
down all of their cities.

CHAPTER 21

Preserving the Tribe of Benjamin. [1] The
Israelites had sworn an oath at Mizpah say-
ing, "None of us will give his daughter in
marriage to a Benjaminite." [2] The people
went up to Bethel where they sat before God
until the evening. They raised up their voices
and wept bitterly. [3] They said, "O LORD, God
of Israel, why has this happened to Israel,
that today there should be one tribe missing
from Israel?"

e Ex 32:6; Lev 1:3; 2 Sam 12:21.—f Deut 18:5; Num 25:7; Jos 2:24.—g 1 Sam 9:21.—h Ps 78:9.—i 1 Sam 10:26; Ps 75:5.—j Jos 15:32.

20:29-48 Two similar stories, with a few small differences (vv. 29-36a; 36b-41), tell of a fratricidal struggle. It took three attempts for Israel to overcome the Benjaminites, finally using a strategy similar to one that was successful against Ai (Jos 8).

[4] Early the next morning the people built
an altar there and sacrificed burnt offerings
and offered peace offerings. [k] [5] The Israelites
said, "Who from all of the tribes did not
come up to the assembly of all of the tribes of
Israel before the LORD?" (They had made a
solemn oath that anyone who did not come
before the LORD at Mizpah was to be put to
death.) [6] The Israelites grieved for Benjamin,
their brother. They said, "Today one tribe is
cut off from Israel. [7] How shall we provide
wives for those who remain, since we have
sworn an oath to the LORD that we would not
give them our daughters as their wives?"

[8] Then they asked, "Which one of the
tribes has not come to the LORD at Mizpah?"
They found that no one from Jabesh-gilead
had come to the assembly. [l] [9] When they
counted the people, they realized that none
of the inhabitants of Jabesh-gilead were
there. [10] The assembly sent twelve thousand
brave fighting men there, giving them the
command, "Go and put the inhabitants of
Jabesh-gilead to the sword, including women
and children. [11] This is what you are to do.
Wipe out every man and every woman who
has slept with a man." [m] [12] They found four
hundred young women who had never slept
with a man among the inhabitants of
Jabesh-gilead. They brought them into the
camp in Shiloh which is in the land of
Canaan. [13] The whole assembly sent a mes-
sage to the Benjaminites who were at the
rock of Rimmon, summoning them in
peace. [n] [14] The Benjaminites then returned
and they were given wives from the women
of Jabesh-gilead who had been kept alive.
But there were not enough of them.

[15] * The people grieved for Benjamin
because the LORD had made a breach in the
tribes of Israel. [16] The elders in the assembly
said, "How are we going to provide wives for
the rest of them? For the women of Ben-
jamin have been annihilated." [17] They said,
"The Benjaminite survivors must have an
inheritance, so that a tribe of Israel will not
be blotted out. [18] We cannot give them our
daughters as wives, for the Israelites have
sworn an oath saying, 'Cursed be anyone
who gives a wife to Benjamin!' " [19] They
continued, "But look, there is an annual fes-
tival of the LORD in Shiloh, to the north of
Bethel and east of the road that runs from
Bethel to Shechem and on to the south of
Lebonah." [20] They instructed the Ben-
jaminites, "Go, lie in wait in the vineyards [o]
and stay on watch. [21] When the young
women of Shiloh come out dancing, rise up
out of the vineyards and each man can seize
a wife for himself from the young women of
Shiloh, and then return to Benjamin. [p]
[22] When their fathers and their brothers
complain to us, we will say, 'Please do us
this favor, for we did not take a wife for each
of them during the war. You are not guilty,
for you did not really give your women to
them.' "

[23] This is what the Benjaminites did. Each
man took a wife for himself from among the
young women who were dancing. They then
went and returned to their inheritance,
rebuilding the cities and dwelling in them. [q]
[24] The Israelites then left that place and each
man went to his own tribe, his own clan.
Each man returned to his own inheritance.
[25] In those days Israel had no king, and
everyone did what in his own opinion he
thought to be right. [r]

---

k Jdg 20:26; 2 Sam 24:25.—l 1 Sam 11:1; 2 Sam 2:4; 1 Chr 10:11.—m Num 31:17.—n Jdg 20:47; Jos 15:32.—o Jos 18:1; 1 Sam 1:3.—p Ex 15:20.—q Jdg 20:48; Jos 24:28.—r Deut 12:8.

21:15-17 Despite their vow to withhold their women in marriage to the Benjaminite survivors, the Israelites seek a resolution to prevent the extinction of the tribe.

Boaz met Ruth gleaning in his field *(Ru 2:3ff)*.

THE BOOK OF RUTH

A Foreign Woman, Ancestress of the Messiah

The royal house of David certainly retained the memory of a foreign woman, a convert, who, because of her filial devotion, had deserved to become part of the illustrious lineage from which the Messiah was to be born; this happened back in the time of the judges of Israel. This recollection was exploited in a pleasing way and turned into the Book of Ruth; its composition may be dated toward the end of the fifth century B.C. It represents, therefore, a simple family tradition that was introduced into the history of the chosen people and became part of the history of the salvation of humanity.

The facts are not told as though they were directly of concern to the history of Israel or bore witness to the action of God in the working out of his people's destiny. The touching idyll of Ruth resembles rather an edifying tale, like the stories of Tobit and Jonah.

Ruth is a woman of Moab, of a race that is rejected by Deuteronomy (23:4); she becomes a daughter of Israel and through the kind arrangement of God takes her place in the genealogy of King David. What a beautiful subject, and what a fine lesson!

The author, like the author of the Book of Jonah, seems to have been written in order to protest against an overly narrow nationalism. Is he perhaps criticizing the excessively severe measures taken, after the Exile, against marriages with foreign women, all as part of an effort to protect the Jewish community from contact with pagans (Ezr 9–10; Neh 13:1-3, 23-27)? Or the story may have in view an older but surely quite similar situation. In any case, it is not unimportant, is it, that a pagan woman of exemplary life should have been accepted as one of the ancestors of David and the Christ (Mt 1:3-5)? Compassion toward relatives, acceptance of strangers, and gratitude for the grace of faith that God granted a foreign woman: these are the rich and always relevant lessons of this Book.

CHAPTER 1*

Naomi's Life in Moab. [1] In the days of the
judges,* a famine broke out in the land. A
certain man from Bethlehem in Judah went
to live in the land of Moab along with his wife
and his two sons. [2] The man's name was
Elimelech and his wife was Naomi, and his
two sons were Mahlon and Chilion. They
were Ephrathites from Bethlehem in Judah.
They traveled to the land of Moab and dwelt
there. [a]
[3] Elimelech, Naomi's husband, died, and
she was left with her two sons. [4] They both
married Moabite women. The name of one
was Orpah, and the name of the other was
Ruth. When they had lived there for about
ten years,* [5] both Mahlon and Chilion died,
leaving the woman bereft of her husband
and two sons.
[6] * She set out with her two daughters-in-
law to return from the land of Moab, for in
Moab she had heard how the LORD had
come to the aid of his people, giving them
food to eat. [b] [7] She and her two daughters-in-
law set out from the place where they had
been living and took the road leading back to
the land of Judah. [8] Naomi said to her two
daughters-in-law, "Each of you should go
back to your mother's house. May the LORD
show you as much kindness as you have
shown to those who died and to me. [9] May
the LORD grant each of you consolation in
the home of a husband." She then kissed
them, and they wept aloud. [c] [10] They said to
her, "We will go with you back to your peo-
ple." [11] But Naomi replied, "Go back, my
daughters. Why would you go with me? Do I
still have any sons in my womb who might
become your husbands? [12] Go back, my
daughters. Go your way. I am too old even to
have a husband. Even if I thought that there
was still hope for me and I slept with a hus-
band tonight and gave birth to sons, [13] would
you wait for them to grow up? Would you
stay unmarried for them? No, my daughters,
for it greatly grieves me on your account
that the hand of the LORD has been raised
against me." [d]

Ruth Stays with Naomi. [14] They cried out
loud again, and Orpah kissed her mother-in-
law goodbye, but Ruth clung to her. [15] Then
she said, "Look, your sister-in-law has gone
back to her people and her gods. Follow your
sister-in-law." [16] But Ruth answered, "Please
do not insist on my leaving you or forsaking
you. Wherever you go I will go, and wherev-
er you live I will live. Your people will be my
people and your God will be my God.*
[17] Wherever you die, I will die and be buried
there. May the LORD do this to me and even
worse if anything other than death separates
me from you." [18] When she saw that she was
determined to go with her, she said no
more. [e]

Life in Bethlehem. [19] So they both traveled
on until they came to Bethlehem. When they
arrived in Bethlehem, there was a commo-
tion among all of the inhabitants of the city
on account of them. The women exclaimed,
"Is this Naomi?" [20] She told them, "Do not
call me Naomi, call me Mara. The Almighty
has made my life so very bitter. [f] [21] I went
away full, but the LORD has brought me back
empty. Why should you call me Naomi? The
LORD has brought witness against me; the
Almighty has afflicted me."
[22] So Naomi returned, and Ruth, the
Moabite, her daughter-in-law, went with her.
They left the land of Moab and they arrived
in Bethlehem at the beginning of the barley
harvest. [g]

CHAPTER 2

Ruth and Boaz. [1] * Naomi's husband had a
kinsman, a very wealthy man from the clan
of Elimelech, whose name was Boaz. [h]

a Gen 35:19; Jdg 3:30.—b Ex 4:31.—c Ru 3:1.—d Jdg 2:15; Ps 32:4.—e Acts 21:14.—f Ex 15:23; Job 6:4.—g Ru 2:23; Ex 9:31.—h Ru 3:2, 12; Mt 1:5.

1:1-22 The names seem to have been chosen as descriptions of the individuals: *Mahlon* (weakness) and *Chilion* (consumption) were destined to die young. *Ruth* means "the friend" (the companion); *Orpah* means "she who turned her back." The names thus sum up the destiny of the family. There is no reference here to the bad reputation of Moabite women (Num 25:1).

1:1 *In the days of the judges:* the author introduces the Book of Ruth by referring to a time in Israelite history that was marked by idolatry and sin. Naomi and Ruth's story of selfless commitment to God and each other is a shining light in otherwise dark circumstances.

1:4 The blending of the Israelites and Moabites was not encouraged but marriage was not forbidden as it was with the Canaanites.

1:6-22 In the blows of fate Naomi recognizes the hand of the Lord; but her faith is not strong enough for her to believe that her life can have any further meaning: Naomi (my sweetness) is henceforth Mara (bitterness).

1:16 This familiar passage occurring in song and used in religious wedding ceremonies to mark the faithful love and commitment pledged by the bride and groom has even deeper roots. Throughout time, God has chosen the most unlikely people to increase his kingdom. Ruth, a Moabite, worships the true God and is recognized and blessed for her faithfulness. She became a great-grandmother to King David and an ancestor of Jesus.

2:1-7 Ruth belongs to the class of poor people whom the law authorized to glean in fields that had been harvested. "You shall not . . . gather up the gleanings of your harvest. . . . leave them for the poor and the alien" (Lev 23:22; see Deut 24:19-22; Lev 19:9-10).

2 Ruth the Moabite said to Naomi, "Let me
go now to the field and glean ears of corn
after one in whose sight I might find favor."
So she said, "Go, my daughter."

3 She left and went and gleaned in the field
after the reapers. It happened that she
arrived at a portion of the field that belonged
to Boaz of the clan of Elimelech.* 4 Just then
Boaz arrived from Bethlehem and he said to
the reapers, "The LORD be with you." They
answered him, "The LORD bless you."[i]
5 Boaz asked his foreman of the harvesters,
"Whose young woman is this?" 6 The fore-
man of the harvesters answered, "The young
woman is a Moabite. She came back with
Naomi from the land of Moab.[j] 7 She said,
'Please let me glean and gather the sheaves
after the harvesters.' She arrived early this
morning and has continued working contin-
uously until now, except for a short rest in
the shelter."

8 So Boaz said to Ruth, "Listen to me, my
daughter. Do not go and glean in any other
field and do not go away from here. Stay
here with my servant girls. 9 Keep your eyes
on the field that they are reaping, and follow
after them. I have told the young men not to
bother you. When you are thirsty, go to the
water jars and drink from what the young
men have drawn." 10 She bowed down with
her face to the ground and said, "Why have
I, a foreigner, found favor in your sight that
you should take notice of me?" 11 But Boaz
answered her, "I have been informed of all
that you have done for your mother-in-law
since your husband died, how you left your
father and your mother and the land of your
birth and came to live with a people whom
you had not previously known.[k] 12 May the
LORD repay you for what you have done.
May you be richly rewarded by the LORD, the
God of Israel, under whose wings you have
taken refuge."*[l] 13 Then she said, "May I
continue to find favor in your sight, my lord.
You have comforted me and shown kindness
to your servant, even though I am not really
one of your servants."

14 At mealtime Boaz said to her, "Come
over here and have some bread and dip it
into the sour wine." She sat alongside the
reapers. He served her so much roasted
grain that she ate until she was full and there
was still some left over.

15 When she got up to glean, Boaz gave
orders to his men: "Even if she gathers
among the sheaves, do not reproach her.
16 Let some fall out from the bundles and
leave it there for her to glean, but do not
chastise her."

17 So she gleaned in the field until the
evening. She threshed out what she had
gleaned, and it amounted to an ephah of
barley. 18 She gathered it up and went back
into the city. She showed her mother-in-law
what she had gleaned, and she also brought
out and gave her what she had saved after
she was full. 19 Her mother-in-law asked her,
"Where did you glean today and where did
you work? May he who took notice of you be
blessed." She told her mother-in-law with
whom she had worked, "The name of the
man with whom I worked today is Boaz."
20 Naomi said to her daughter-in-law, "May
he be blessed by the LORD who has not with-
drawn his favor from the living nor the
dead." Then Naomi said to her, "The man is
one of our relatives, one of our closest rela-
tions."*[m] 21 Ruth the Moabite added, "He
said to me, 'You should stay close to my
young men until they have finished my har-
vest.' " 22 So Naomi said to Ruth, her daugh-
ter-in-law, "It is good for you to go out with
his servant girls, lest you be harmed in some
other field."

23 So Ruth stayed close to the servant girls
of Boaz to glean until the barley and the
wheat harvests were over, and she continued
to live with her mother-in-law.[n]

CHAPTER 3*

Naomi Instructs Ruth. 1 Then Naomi, her
mother-in-law, said to her, "My daughter,
should I not seek a home for you so that you
may find security?[o] 2 Is not Boaz, with
whose servant girls you were, our relative?

i Ps 129:8; Lk 1:28.—j Ru 1:22.—k Ru 1:14-17.—l 1 Sam 24:19; Ps 17:8.—m Gen 24:27; Prov 17:17.—n Deut 16:9.—o Ru 1:9.

2:3 Ruth was no stranger to hard work and her humility in gleaning was rewarded with the providential discovery of the field of Boaz, her kinsman.

2:12 *Under whose wings . . . taken refuge:* Ruth's apparent fidelity to the God of the Israelites is noted with admiration by Boaz.

2:20 Although Naomi wavered and complained during her worst trials, she never despaired of God's goodness. She now recognizes the hand of the Lord who has been at work and is providing for her and Ruth through Boaz's kindness.

3:1-18 Naomi, having lost her sons (Ru 1:5) and being too advanced in years to remarry, wants to apply the law of the levirate (Deut 25:5-6) in favor of her daughter-in-law. Boaz, asked to marry Ruth, admires her for her fidelity and is ready to carry out the duties of a kinsman redeemer toward her (Lev 25:25). There is, however, another who is a closer kinsman. This detail makes the story a more lively one.

Tonight he will be winnowing barley on the
threshing floor.[p] 3 Bathe and perfume your-
self and put on your best clothes. Go down to
the floor, but do not let him know you are
there until he has finished eating and drink-
ing. 4 When he lies down to sleep, note the
place where he is lying. Go and uncover his
feet and lie down. He will tell you what you
should do." 5 She said to her, "I will do what-
ever you say."

6 She went down to the floor and did every-
thing just as her mother-in-law had instruct-
ed her. 7 When Boaz had finished eating and
drinking and was feeling a bit merry, he went
over to lie down at the far end of the grain
pile. She quietly approached, uncovered his
feet and lay down.[q]

8 In the middle of the night, the man was
startled when he turned over and there was
a woman at his feet. 9 He said, "Who are
you?" She answered, "I am Ruth, your hand-
maid. Spread your covering* over your
handmaid, for you are my next of kin." 10 He
said, "May you be blessed by the LORD, my
daughter. This latter kindness you have
shown is greater than the former, for you
have not sought after the young men,
whether poor or rich. 11 Now, my daughter,
do not fear. I will give you whatever you ask,
for all of my people in the city know that you
are a virtuous woman. 12 It is true that we are
close relatives, but there is another relative
closer than I.[r] 13 Remain this night. When
morning comes, if he fulfills his duty as next
of kin, then good, let him do it. But if he will
not fulfill his duty as next of kin, then I will
fulfill that duty for you. I swear, as the LORD
lives. Now lie down until the morning."[s]

14 So she laid at his feet until the morning,
and she arose before it was possible to rec-
ognize another person. Then he said, "Do not
let it be known that a woman came to the
threshing floor." 15 He also said, "Bring over
your shawl and hold it open." As she held it,
he measured out six measures of barley and
laid it upon her. She then went into the city.

16 When she came to her mother-in-law,
she said, "How did it go, my daughter?" She
told her all that the man had done for her.
17 Then she said, "He gave me these six mea-
sures of barley, for he said to me, 'Do not go
to your mother-in-law empty-handed.' "
18 Then she said, "Wait here, my daughter,
until the matter has worked itself out, for the
man will not rest until he has brought it to a
conclusion today." *[t]

CHAPTER 4

Boaz Marries Ruth. 1 So Boaz went to the
city gate and sat down there. The relative of
whom Boaz had spoken was passing by, so
he said, "Come over here, my friend, and sit
down." So he came over and sat down.*[u]
2 He gathered ten of the elders of the city and
said, "Sit down," and they sat down.

3 Then he said to the next of kin, "Naomi
has come back from the land of Moab and is
selling the parcel of land that belonged to
our kinsman Elimelech. 4 I thought that I
would tell this to you. Buy it in the presence
of those who dwell here and in the presence
of the elders. If you intend to redeem it as
next of kin, then redeem it. If you do not
intend to redeem it, then tell me so that I can
know, for there is no one else besides you to
redeem the land, and then I am next in line."
He said, "I will redeem it."[v] 5 Then Boaz
said, "When you acquire the field, you also
receive the hand of Ruth the Moabite, the
wife of the deceased, to raise up the name of
the deceased for an inheritance." 6 But the
kinsman said, "I cannot redeem it for
myself, lest I endanger my own inheritance.
You can exercise my right of next of kin, for
I cannot redeem it."[w]

7 Now in those days in Israel it was the cus-
tom that when there was an act of redemp-
tion or of the exchange of lands, one man
would take off his sandal and give it to the
other in order to confirm the action. This
was an act of confirming actions in Israel.[x]
8 So the kinsman said to Boaz, "Buy it for
yourself," and he took off his sandal.

9 Boaz then said to the elders and to all the
people, "You are witnesses today that I have
bought from Naomi all that belonged to
Elimelech, and all that belonged to Chilion
and all that belonged to Mahlon. 10 More-
over, I have acquired Ruth, the Moabite, the
wife of Mahlon, to be my wife, to perpetuate
the name of the deceased for an inheritance

p Ru 2:1; Deut 25:5-10.—q Jdg 19:6, 22; 2 Sam 13:28.—r Ru 4:1.—s Ru 4:5.—t Ps 37:3-5.—u Ru 3:12.—v Lev 25:25.—w Ru 3:12-13.—x Deut 25:9.

3:9 *Spread your covering:* Ruth's invitation to Boaz was not immoral for it was customary for the nearest kin to fill this role (see Deut 25:5-10).

3:18 Naomi speaks confidently about Boaz's intentions because she knew what kind of man he was.

4:1 Boaz was well aware that he could find his relative at the city gate which was the center of activity and a place to conduct business.

so that the name of the deceased not disap-
pear from among his brethren nor from the
gates of his native place. You are witnesses
today."
11 All the people who were in the gateway
and the elders said, "We are witnesses. May
the LORD make the woman who is coming
into your home like Rachel and Leah, both of
whom built up the house of Israel. May you
prosper in Ephrathah and be renowned in
Bethlehem.[y] 12 May your home be like that
of Perez, whom Tamar bore to Judah,
because of the children that the LORD will
give you through this young woman."
13 So Boaz took Ruth and she became his
wife. He slept with her, and the LORD grant-
ed that she conceive, and she bore a son.
14[z] The women said to Naomi, "Blessed be
the LORD, who has not left you without a next
of kin; may his name be famous throughout
Israel.* 15 He will renew your life and sup-
port you in your old age. Your daughter-in-
law, who loves you and who is worth more
than seven sons to you, has borne him."
16 Naomi then took the child and laid him in
her lap. She became his nurse. 17 The neigh-
bor women gave him a name, saying, "A son
is born to Naomi." They called him Obed.*
He was the father of Jesse, the father of David.
18 * This is the genealogy of Perez: Perez was
the father of Hezron;[a] 19 Hezron was the
father of Ram; Ram was the father of
Amminadab; 20 Amminadab was the father of
Nahshon; Nahshon was the father of Salmon;
21 Salmon was the father of Boaz; Boaz was
the father of Obed; 22 Obed was the father of
Jesse; and Jesse was the father of David.

y Gen 29:31; 35:16-18.—z 14ff: Lk 1:58.—a Mt 1:3-6.

4:14 The good news about the birth of a son, "the redeemer of the family," as well as Ruth's devoted loyalty to Naomi is acknowledged publicly.

4:17 *Obed* means "servant (of God)."

4:18-22 This list seems to have been added by a different writer in order to emphasize the lesson of the Book of Ruth. When Matthew uses this list in constructing the genealogy of Jesus, he does not forget to introduce the name of Ruth the Moabite, because salvation is offered to all human beings (Mt 1:3-5).

"Whenever an evil spirit came upon Saul, David took a harp and played it. Saul revived and he felt better" *(1 Sam 16:23).*

THE FIRST BOOK OF SAMUEL

To Live in Love

The First Book of Samuel tells the history of Israel during the entire 11th century B.C.

The account begins with the presentation of two people of faith: Hannah, who was childless and entrusts her plight to the Lord, and Samuel, her son, who is dedicated to the service of the Lord as the last Judge of Israel.

The people of Israel demand a king for Israel so that they might be like other nations. One can hear the debate for and against the monarchy through these chapters. Samuel chooses Saul, who starts out well, but quickly sins against the Lord and is rejected.

Samuel is then sent to anoint David in his place. David enters the court of Saul (there are two versions as to how this happens) where he is widely popular. He is acclaimed as a great warrior, greater than Saul. This drives Saul to fits of murderous paranoia. He repeatedly tries to kill David. David, who on the other hand, refuses to harm Saul, is an anointed of the Lord. The Book closes with the death of Saul and his sons in battle and the beginning of the reign of David.

The First Book of Samuel may be divided as follows:

I: The Last Judges: Eli and Samuel (1:1—7:17)
II: The Inauguration of the Monarchy (8:1—12:25)
III: The Reign of Saul and the Introduction of David (13:1—31:13)

I: THE LAST JUDGES: ELI AND SAMUEL*

CHAPTER 1*

Elkanah's Pilgrimage to Shiloh. 1 There was
a certain man from Ramathaim-zophim,
from the hill country of Ephraim, whose
name was Elkanah, the son of Jeroham, the
son of Elihu, the son of Tohu, the son of
Zuph, an Ephraimite. [a] 2 He had two wives.
The name of one of them was Hannah, and
the name of the other was Peninnah.
Peninnah had children, but Hannah did not
have any children. [b] 3 This man would travel
from his city yearly to worship and to sacrifice to the LORD of hosts* in Shiloh. The two
sons of Eli, Hophni and Phinehas, were
priests there. [c]
4 When Elkanah performed his sacrifice,
he would give a portion of it to Peninnah his
wife and a portion each to all of her sons and
daughters, 5 but he would give a double portion to Hannah, for he loved her although the
LORD had left her barren. 6 Her rival* provoked her and made her miserable because
the LORD had left her barren. [d] 7 This went on
year after year. Whenever she went up to the
house of the LORD, she provoked her. This
made her weep, and she refused to eat.
8 Elkanah, her husband, said to her, "Hannah, why do you weep? Why are you not eating? Why are you so downhearted? Am I not
worth more than ten sons to you?" [e]
Hannah's Prayer. 9 Once, when they had finished eating and drinking in Shiloh, Hannah
stood up. Now Eli the priest was sitting upon
a chair by the doorpost of the temple of the
LORD. 10 She was greatly distressed and she
prayed to the LORD, weeping bitterly.* 11 She
made a vow saying, "O LORD of hosts, if you
will regard the troubles of your handmaid
and will remember me, and not forget your
handmaid, and you will give your handmaid
a son, then I will dedicate him to the LORD
for his entire life, and no razor* will ever
touch his head." [f]
12 As she continued to pray to the LORD, Eli
watched her mouth. 13 Hannah was praying
in her heart so that only her lips were moving, her voice could not be heard. Eli, therefore, thought that she was drunk. [g] 14 He said
to her, "How long are you going to stay
drunk? Get rid of your wine!" 15 Hannah
answered, "Oh no, my lord! I am a woman
who is deeply troubled. I have not been
drinking either wine or liquor. I have been
pouring out my soul to the LORD. [h] 16 Do not
account your handmaid to be a daughter of
Belial. I have been speaking out of the abundance of my difficulties and my grief."
17 Then Eli answered, "Go in peace. The God

a Jos 17:17-18; 1 Chr 6:19f.—b 1 Sam 1:7; Gen 4:19, Deut 21:15.—c Ex 10:26; Deut 16:16; Jdg 21:19; Lk 2:41.—d Gen 16:4f; Jdg 13:3; 1 Ki 16:7; Lk 23:10.—e Ru 4:15.—f Gen 28:20; Num 6:1-5; 30:9; Jdg 13:2-5; 16:17; Lk 1:13-15.—g 1 Sam 25:36; 1 Ki 8:54; Lk 3:21.—h Pss 25:21; 34:17; 42:4; Mt 15:22.

1:1—7:17 It is not by chance that Samuel gives his name to the entire book (with its two parts), for he receives a very special call and is chosen to be a prophet and leader in Israel. His main task will be to help the chosen people make the transition from a confederacy to a monarchy without losing, in the process, their direct and exclusive attachment to Yahweh, who will always be their sole Lord. The initial picture of Samuel occupies the first seven chapters.

1:1-28 As in the case of Isaac, Samson, and John the Baptist, a child given to a barren woman has a special destiny.

1:3 *LORD of hosts:* Hebrew, *Jahve seba'ot*. The meaning is that God is the God of all the creatures, heavenly and earthly, in the universe, and that these are regarded as a single well-ordered multitude of beings.

1:6 *Her rival:* Hannah, because of her inability to have a child, was considered a failure in Old Testament thinking. It was also permissible for Elkanah to divorce his wife who was barren, but he remained faithful to her. Peninnah filled the role of a second or co-wife, in Hebrew, *sara*.

1:10 Hannah showed her true colors by her faithfulness to the Lord. Rather than give up or complain about her fate she prayed in the midst of her great distress.

1:11 *No razor:* an external sign of consecration to God (see Jdg 16:17), after the fashion of the Nazirites (Num 6:5).

of Israel grant the request you have made of him." [18] She said, "Let your handmaid find favor in your sight." The woman then went her way and ate, and she was not downcast anymore.

[19] They arose early the next morning and worshiped before the LORD. They then went their way and came to their home in Ramah. Elkanah slept with Hannah, and the LORD remembered her.

The Birth of Samuel. [20] In time it came to pass that Hannah conceived and bore a son whom she named Samuel, saying, "For I have asked the LORD for him." [21] When Elkanah and his household went up to offer the annual sacrifice to the LORD and to fulfill his vow, [22] Hannah did not go. She said to her husband, "After the boy is weaned, I will take him and present him before the LORD, and he will dwell there forever." [i] [23] Elkanah, her husband, said to her, "Do what you think is best. Stay here until you have weaned him, only may the LORD bring his word to fulfillment." So the woman stayed there and nursed her son until she weaned him.

Samuel's Consecration. [24] When she had weaned him, she took him with herself along with a three-year-old bull, an ephah of flour, and a skin of wine. She brought him to the house of the LORD in Shiloh, although the child was still young. [25] After they sacrificed the bull, they brought the child to Eli. [26] * She said, "Oh my lord, as my soul lives, I am the woman who stood beside you praying to the LORD. [j] [27] I prayed for this child, and the LORD has granted the request that I made of him. [28] Therefore, I have dedicated him to the LORD. As long as he lives, he shall be dedicated to the LORD." So they worshiped the LORD there.

CHAPTER 2

1 * Then Hannah prayed and said,

"My heart rejoices in the LORD,
my horn is lifted high in the LORD.
My mouth boasts over my enemies,
for I rejoice in my salvation. [k]
2 There is no holy one like the LORD,
there is none beside you,
nor is there a rock like our God. [l]
3 * Do not talk so proudly
nor let arrogance come forth from your mouth,
for the LORD is a knowing God,
and by him actions are weighed. [m]

4 The bows of the mighty are broken,
the feeble are clothed in strength. [n]
5 The well-fed hire themselves out for bread,
and the hungry cease to hunger.
The barren has borne seven times,
while she who has many children grows faint. [o]

6 The LORD kills and brings to life.
He brings down to Sheol, and lifts up. [p]
7 The LORD makes poor and makes rich,
he humbles and he also exalts.
8 He raises the poor from the dust,
and from the refuse he lifts up the beggar,
To seat them among princes,
that they might inherit a throne of glory.

For the LORD's are the pillars of the earth,
and he has set the world upon them. [q]
9 He will guard the feet of his saints,
but the wicked will be cut off in the darkness,
for by strength none shall prevail.
10 Those who oppose the LORD will be shattered,
he will thunder against them from the heavens,
the LORD will judge the ends of the earth,
He will give strength to his king,
and exalt the horn of his anointed one." [r]

[11] Then Elkanah went home to Ramah, but the child ministered before the LORD under Eli the priest.

i 1 Sam 1:5; Ex 34:23; Lk 2:22.—j Gen 18:22; Lev 9:5; Ru 2:13; 1 Ki 3:26.—k Deut 8:14; 33:17; Est D:13; Pss 35:25; 106:19; Isa 61:10.—l Deut 32:4; 2 Sam 22:3; 23:3; Pss 18:2; 78:41; 144:1.—m 1 Ki 20:11; Pss 44:8; 75:5; Prov 27:1; Isa 16:6.—n Deut 33:25; Jdg 5:13; 8:21; 16:5; Pss 21:13; 33:16; 62:3; Isa 40:29.—o Jdg 13:2; Ru 4:15; Isa 54:1; Jer 15:10.—p Deut 32:39; Tob 3:10; 4:19; Job 5:11; 18:17; Pss 30:4; 119:50.—q Job 9:6; 10:9; 38:6; Pss 104:5; 113:8; 121:3; Prov 3:33.—r Gen 14:19; Pss 73:11; 98:9; 1 Cor 4:4.

1:26-28 True to her word, Hannah—without regrets—presented her son Samuel to Eli to serve God as she had promised (1:11). This heroic sacrifice was her tribute to the Lord, who had given him to Hannah in the first place.

2:1-10 This canticle was composed later on, but it suits the event described so well that Mary's Magnificat is largely inspired by it (Lk 1:46ff).

2:3-5 Hannah had no need to remonstrate with those (i.e., Peninnah) who had shown her disrespect because she knew God as the supreme judge and trusted in his divine justice.

The Sons of Eli.* 12 * Now Eli's sons were sons of Belial, they had no regard for the LORD. 13 [s] This is how the priests would deal with the people when anyone came to offer a sacrifice: the priest's servant would come with a three-pronged fork in his hand. 14 He would stick it in the pan, or kettle, or caldron, or pot. Everything that he would bring up with the fork was for the priest. This is how they treated all the Israelites who came up to Shiloh. 15 Even before the fat was burned, the priest's servant would come up to a man and say, "Give the priest some meat to roast. He will not take any boiled meat from you, only raw meat." 16 If the man said to him, "Let the fat be burned first, then you can take what you want," he would answer him, "No! Give it to me now, or I will take it by force." [t] 17 The young men's sin was very serious before the LORD, for they were treating the LORD's offering with contempt.

Hannah's Family Grows. 18 Samuel was ministering to the LORD, a boy wearing a linen ephod. * 19 His mother would make him a little robe and bring it to him each year when she came up with her husband to offer their yearly sacrifice. 20 Eli would bless Elkanah and his wife saying, "May the LORD grant you children from this woman in place of the one you have dedicated to the LORD." They then went home. [u] 21 The LORD was gracious to Hannah, and she conceived and bore three sons and two daughters. Young Samuel grew up in the presence of the LORD. [v]

Eli's Warning Ignored. 22 Now Eli was very old, and he heard about all the things that his sons were doing to the whole of Israel, how they lay with the woman who gathered at the entrance to the tent of meeting. 23 He said to them, "Why do you do these things? I have been hearing about your evil deeds from everyone. 24 No, my sons! It is an evil report that I hear among the LORD's people. 25 If one man sins against another, then a judge will judge him. If a man sins against God, who will intercede for him?" But they would not listen to their father's rebuke, for the LORD wanted to put them to death. *

26 Meanwhile young Samuel grew in stature and favor with the LORD and with men. [w]

The Punishment of Eli's Sons. 27 * Now a man of God came to Eli and said, "Thus says the LORD, 'Did I not clearly reveal myself to your father's house when they were in Egypt, in Pharaoh's house? 28 Did I not choose him from out of all of the tribes of Israel to be my priest, to go up to my altar, to burn incense, and to wear an ephod before me? Did I not give your father's house all of the burnt offerings of the Israelites? [x] 29 Why do you scorn my sacrifice and my offering that I have prescribed for my dwelling? Why do you honor your sons more than me by fattening yourselves on the choicest of the offerings of my people Israel?

30 [y] " 'Therefore,' says the LORD, the God of Israel, 'Even though I declared that you and your father's house would minister before me forever, now, far be it from me,' says the LORD. 'I will honor those who honor me, and those who despise me will be despised. 31 Behold, the days are coming when I will cut off your strength and the strength of your father's house, so that not a single old man remains in your house. 32 You will see the distress of my dwelling in spite of all that I have given Israel. In your house there will never again be an old man. 33 Everyone of you whom I do not cut off from my altar will be spared so that you can cry out your eyes and grieve your heart. All the descendants of your house will die in the prime of their life.

34 " 'This will be a sign for you of what will come upon your two sons, upon Hophni and Phinehas. They will both die on the same day. [z] 35 But I will raise up for myself a faith-

s 13-15: Ex 29:27f; Lev 1:8; 7:29-36; Deut 18:3; 2 Chr 8:14.—t Lev 3:3ff.—u 1 Chr 6:8.—v 1 Sam 3:19; Lk 2:40.—w 1 Pet 3:12.—x 1 Sam 23:9; 30:7f; Lev 1:7.—y 30f: 2 Sam 22:26; 1 Ki 2:27; 1 Chr 28:4; Ps 18:25.—z 1 Sam 4:11, 17.

2:12-36 The lengthy episode about the prophet explains why, in the time of Solomon, the high priesthood was transferred from Abiathar, a descendant of Eli, to Zadok (1 Ki 2:27-35). It also justifies the removal of various local sanctuaries from Levite control after the centralization of worship in Jerusalem (2 Ki 23:9) toward the end of the seventh century.

2:12-17 Under the law, Eli's sons, who were priests, had many advantages. They were, however, filled with greed and took more than their due, thereby undermining their position. Eli's failure to take action caused hardship for others and in the end destroyed his and his sons' relationship with God.

2:18 *Ephod:* a priestly garment that little Samuel was already wearing, although his was not made of the same precious material as the priests'.

2:25 *The LORD . . . put them to death:* because of their deception, sinfulness, and arrogance against God and the people they served, the Lord would no longer protect Eli's sons, and this led to their death.

2:27-32 The high priesthood, which, after Aaron, had belonged to his son Eleazar (Num 20:25-28), had been transferred to the line of the latter's younger brother, Ithamar (1 Chr 24:3), at a time and in a way not recorded in the Bible. The present prophecy will soon begin to be fulfilled in the killing of Ahimelech and the other priests of Nob (1 Sam 22:11-18, 20), although Abiathar, Ahimelech's son, will be saved on that occasion, only to be removed by Solomon.

ful priest who will do what is my in heart and
my mind. I will firmly establish his house,
and he will walk before my anointed for-
ever. 36 Whoever is left in your house will bow
down to him for a piece of silver or a loaf of
bread. He will say, "Please place me in one of
the priest's offices so that I might have a
piece of bread to eat." ' "[a]

CHAPTER 3

Samuel's Call.* 1 Young Samuel ministered
to the LORD under Eli. Now the word of the
LORD was rare in those days, there were not
many visions.[b] 2 At that time Eli, whose eye-
sight had begun to grow so weak so that he
could not see well anymore, was lying down
in his place. 3 The lamp of God had not yet
gone out, and Samuel was lying down in
the temple of the LORD where the Ark of
God was kept.*[c] 4 The LORD called out,
"Samuel." He answered, "Here I am." 5 He
ran to Eli and said, "Here I am, you called
me." He said, "I did not call you, go back and
lie down." He went and lay down.

6 The LORD called again, "Samuel."
Samuel got up and went to Eli and said,
"Here I am, you called me." He said, "I did
not call you, my son, lie down again." 7 Now
Samuel did not yet know the LORD, and the
word of the LORD had not yet been revealed
to him.[d]

8 The LORD called Samuel a third time. He
got up and went to Eli and said, "Here I am,
you called me." Then Eli realized that the
LORD had called him. 9 So Eli told Samuel,
"Go and lie down. If he calls you, say, 'Speak,
LORD, for your servant is listening.' " So he
went and lay down in his place.

10 Then the LORD came and stood and
called out as he had the other times,
"Samuel, Samuel." Samuel said, "Speak,
LORD, for your servant is listening." 11 The
LORD said to Samuel, "Behold, I am going to
do something in Israel that will cause the
ears of everyone who hears it to ring.[e] 12 On
that day I will bring against Eli all of the
things that I have proclaimed against his
house, from beginning to end. 13 I have told
him that I would judge his household forev-
er because of the sin about which he knew,
because his sons brought a curse upon them-
selves and he did not restrain them.[f]
14 Therefore, I have sworn to the house of Eli
that the guilt will never be atoned from Eli's
house by either sacrifice or offering."

15 Samuel lay down until the morning,
and then he opened the doors to the house
of the LORD. However, he was afraid to
reveal the vision to Eli, 16 but Eli called
Samuel and said, "Samuel, my son," and
he answered, "Here I am." 17 He said,
"What is it that the LORD said to you?
Please, do not hide it from me. May the
LORD do it to you* and even more if you
hide anything from me of all those things
that he said to you." 18 So Samuel told him
everything, hiding nothing from him. He
then said, "He is the LORD, let him do what
seems best to him."

Samuel the Prophet. 19 Samuel grew up,
and the LORD was with him and did not let
any of his words fall to the ground.[g] 20 All of
Israel, from Dan to Beer-sheba,* knew that
Samuel had been confirmed as a prophet of
the LORD.[h] 21 The LORD continued to appear
in Shiloh, for the LORD revealed himself to
Samuel in Shiloh through the word of the
LORD.

CHAPTER 4*

The Defeat of the Israelites. 1 * Samuel's
word came to all of Israel. Now the Israelites
went out to fight against the Philistines. They
were camped at Ebenezer, and the Philis-
tines were encamped in Aphek. 2 The
Philistines drew up in battle line against the
Israelites, and when they joined up in battle,
the Israelites were defeated by the Phil-
istines who killed about four thousand of
them on the battlefield.

3 When the soldiers came back into camp,
the elders of Israel asked, "Why has the

a 2 Ki 23:9; Rom 15:16.—b Ps 74:9; Ezek 13:3.—c Ex 25:22; 27:20f; Lev 24:2, 4.—d Mt 16:17.—e 2 Ki 21:12.—f 1 Sam 2:27-36; Isa 44:8; Rev 13:6.—g 1 Sam 2:21.—h Jos 8:33; Jdg 20:1; 2 Sam 24:2; 1 Ki 5:5.

3:1-18 Mysteriously touched by the Lord, whose call he does not initially recognize, the boy Samuel serves his apprenticeship as a prophet, learning to listen to and transmit the word of the Lord; he thus becomes the first in the long line of the prophets (see Jer 28:8).

3:3 The sacred lamp or candelabrum (Ex 27:20-21); in other words, it was still night.

3:17 *May the LORD do it to you:* a frequently occurring formula of petition. The evil predicted in the formula is specified in some passages.

3:20 *From Dan to Beer-sheba:* specifying the northernmost city, to the city of Beer-sheba in the south, emphasized that everyone in Israel was aware of Samuel's call to be a prophet.

4:1—7:1 This story of the Ark, which is now part of the Book of Samuel, had in all probability existed as an independent narrative; it is one episode in the wars between the tribes and the Philistines.

4:1-22 The Lord punishes the sin of the sons of Eli; the scales are weighed against them.

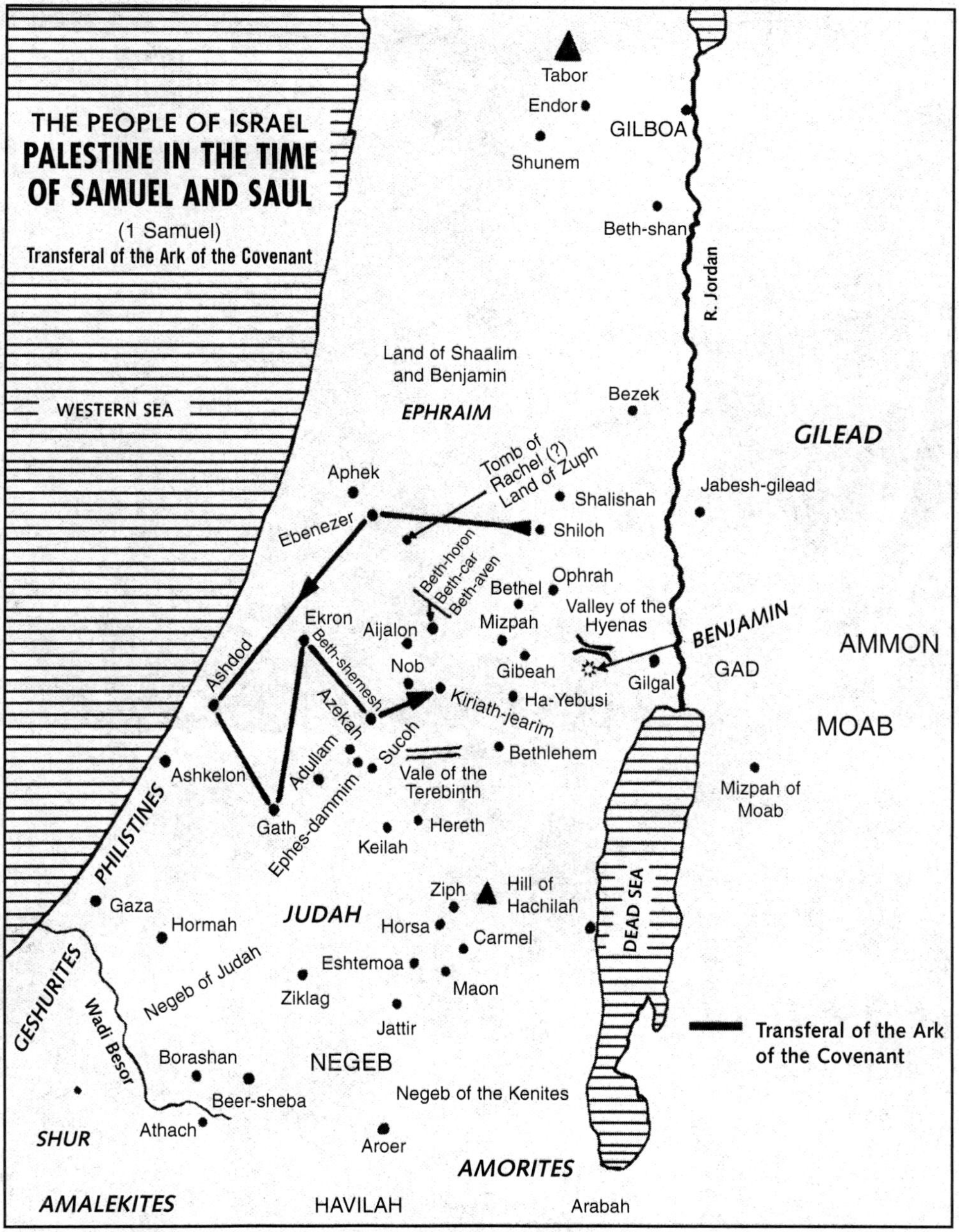

PALESTINE IN THE TIME OF SAMUEL AND SAUL (1 Sam 1–13) — **(a)** The period of the Judges ends with the fall of the sanctuary at **Shiloh** and the capture of the Ark of the Covenant under the onslaught of the Philistine invasions (ca 1050–1020 B.C.). **(b)** Self-supporting states emerge, each under the authority of its king, similar to the Canaanite kings found in **Ammon,** and **Moab** in Transjordan, and among the Arameans in Syria. **(c)** To ward off the **Philistines,** or "People of the Sea," who settle on the coastal plain of Canaan and set up a confederation of city-states **(Ashdod, Ashkelon, Gaza, Gath** and **Ekron),** the Ark is moved from **Shiloh** to lead the Hebrew armies. The Israelites are defeated and the Ark is captured (4:1-11). **(d)** The Philistines transfer the Ark in turn from **Ebenezer** to **Ashdod, Gath, Ekron,** and then return it to **Beth-shemesh.** From there it is taken to **Kiriath-jearim** with rejoicing (5:1—7:1). **(e)** The priestly prophet Samuel then anoints Saul as king of Israel (7:2—12:25).

Oriental Institute

PRISONERS FROM AMONG THE SEA PEOPLES (PHILISTINES) — This relief shows an Egyptian leading two prisoners to Rameses III (1195–1164 B.C.) who celebrates his victory over some Sea Peoples—probably part of the force that tried to invade Egypt but were repulsed in the great land and naval battle of 1191 B.C. The prisoners are wearing shackles suspended by a cord around the neck. To the left are more prisoners with arms bound at the back.

The Sea Peoples went on to settle in Palestine—the Thekels in the Sharon Plain and the Philistines in the Philistine Plain — farther south where their history became intertwined with that of the Hebrews. (See Jdg 3:31; 13-16; 1 Sam 4–6; 13f; 31:10; 2 Sam 5:22f; 8:1; etc.)

LORD brought defeat upon us today at the
hands of the Philistines? Let us go get the
Ark of the Covenant from Shiloh so that it
can go out before us and save us from the
hands of our enemies." [i]

The Ark Is Captured. 4 So the people sent to
Shiloh to bring the Ark of the Covenant of
the LORD of hosts who is enthroned between
the cherubim.* The two sons of Eli, Hophni
and Phinehas, were there with the Ark of the
Covenant of God. [j] 5 When the Ark of the
Covenant of the LORD came into the camp,
all of the Israelites raised such a loud shout
that it shook the earth.

6 When the Philistines heard the uproar,
they asked, "What is this great uproar in the
Hebrew camp?" When they found out that
the Ark of the LORD had come into the camp,
7 the Philistines became frightened. They
said, "A god has come into the camp!" They
said, "Woe to us, for nothing like this has
happened before. [k] 8 Woe to us! Who will
deliver us out of the hands of these mighty
gods? These are the gods who struck the
Egyptians with all kinds of plagues in the
desert. 9 Be strong. Act manfully, O Philis-
tines, or you will end up as slaves to the
Hebrews, just like they were to you. Act
manfully and fight!"

10 So the Philistines fought, and the
Israelites were defeated, and each man fled
to his own tent. The slaughter was great, for
Israel lost thirty thousand foot soldiers.
11 The Ark of God was captured and Eli's two
sons, Hophni and Phinehas, were killed. * [l]

The Death of Eli. 12 That same day a Ben-
jaminite ran from the battle line to Shiloh.
His clothes were torn and there was dust on
his head. [m] 13 He came upon Eli who was sit-
ting by the side of the road. He was watch-
ing, concerned about the Ark of God. When
the man entered the city and told them
what had happened, the entire city raised
up a cry.

14 When Eli heard the uproar, he said,
"What is the meaning of this outcry?" The
man hurried over and explained it to Eli.
15 Now Eli was ninety-eight years old, and his
eyesight was so poor that he could barely
see. [n] 16 The man said to Eli, "I am the one
who came from the battle. I escaped from
the battle today." He asked, "How did things
go, my son?" 17 The messenger answered,
"Israel has fled from before the Philistines,
and there has been a great slaughter. Your
two sons, Hophni and Phinehas, are dead,
and the Ark of God has been captured." 18 At
the mention of the Ark of God, he fell over
backwards off his seat beside the gate, and he
broke his neck and died, for he was a very old
man and quite heavy. He had been a judge*
of Israel for forty years.

19 * His daughter-in-law, the wife of Phin-
ehas, was pregnant. When she heard the
news that the Ark of God had been captured,
and that her father-in-law and her husband
were dead, she sunk to her knees and gave
birth, for she was overcome by her labor
pains. 20 As she was dying, the women who
were standing around her said to her, "Do
not fear, for you have borne a son." But she
gave no response, nor did she even look at
it. [o] 21 Then she named the child Ichabod, for
she said, "The glory of God has departed
from Israel," for the Ark of God had been
captured and also because of what had hap-
pened to her father-in-law and her husband.
22 For this she said, "The glory of God has
departed from Israel, for the Ark of God has
been captured." [p]

CHAPTER 5

Devastation Follows the Ark. 1 The Phil-
istines then took the Ark of God, transport-
ing it from Ebenezer to Ashdod. [q] 2 When the
Philistines took the Ark of God, they brought
it into the temple of Dagon* and set it along-
side of Dagon. 3 When the people of Ashdod
got up the next morning, they found Dagon
fallen down, with his face pressed to the
earth, in front of the Ark of the LORD. So they
picked Dagon up and put him back in his
place.

i Num 10:35.—j Ex 25:22.—k Jud 14:3.—l 1 Sam 2:34; 4:4, 11.—m Jos 7:6; 22:12; 2 Sam 1:2; Jer 7:12; 41:5.—n Gen 48:10; Isa 44:18.—o 1 Sam 14:3; 35:16ff.—p Ps 78:61.—q Jos 11:22; 1 Chr 13:6.

4:4 *Enthroned between the cherubim:* in the Old Testament, cherubim, part human and part beast, are distinct from angels. The golden cherubim on the Ark cover the propitiation (Ex 25:10-22). The Israelites believed that God's presence on the Ark would bring victory for Eli's sons, Hophni and Phinehas, in battle.

4:11 The battle was a total failure for Israel from the slaughter of men, the capture of the Ark of God, and the fulfillment of the prophecy that Eli's sons would die on the same day (1 Sam 2:34).

4:18 *Had been a judge:* in the sense that he had been the high priest; forty years is a round number signifying a generation.

4:19-22 This passage shows how the devastating losses for Israel overshadowed what otherwise would be a hopeful sign with the birth of Phinehas's son Ichabod.

5:2ff *Dagon:* the chief god of the Philistines, who worshiped many gods and who thought that the Ark would bring blessings to them as it did to the Israelites. They discovered that the power of the Ark was beyond their control.

4 When they rose again the next morning,
they found him fallen down again, with his
face pressed to the earth, in front of the Ark
of the LORD. His head and both of his hands
were cut off and lying in the threshold; all
that was left of Dagon was his torso. 5 This is
why to this day neither the priests of Dagon
nor anyone who enters the temple of Dagon
in Ashdod steps upon its threshold. 6 The
hand of the LORD bore down upon Ashdod.
He brought devastation to Ashdod and its
environs, striking the people with tumors.*[r]

7 * When the people of Ashdod saw what
was happening, they said, "We must not
keep the Ark of the God of Israel here with
us, for his hand bears down upon us and our
god Dagon." 8 They summoned the lords of
the Philistines and said to them, "What are
we to do with the Ark of the God of Israel?"
They answered, "Let the Ark of God be taken
to Gath." So they moved the Ark of the God
of Israel.

9 But after they moved it, the hand of the
LORD rose against that city, causing great
confusion there. He struck the people of that
city, both the young and the old, with
tumors. 10 They, therefore, sent the Ark of
God to Ekron. When the Ark of God was
approaching Ekron, the people of Ekron
cried out, "They are bringing the Ark of the
God of Israel here to kill us, too!"

11 So they summoned all of the lords of the
Philistines and told them, "Send the Ark of
the God of Israel back to its home, lest it kill
all of us. There is death and panic all through-
out the city, and the hand of God is bearing
down upon us heavily." [s] 12 The men who did
not die were stricken with tumors, and a cry
rose up from the city to the heavens.

CHAPTER 6

The Return of the Ark of God. 1 When the
Ark of the LORD had been held in Philistine
territory for seven months, 2 the Philistines
summoned the priests and diviners and
said, "What should we do with the Ark of the
LORD? Tell us how to send it back home."

3 They answered, "If you return the Ark of
the God of Israel, do not send it away empty-
handed. Rather, send a guilt offering to him.
Then you will be healed, and you will under-
stand why he continued to afflict you."*[t]
4 They then asked, "What sort of guilt offer-
ing should be made to him?" They answered,
"Send five golden tumors and five golden
mice, as many as the lords of the Philistines,
for the plague was on you all, lords included.
5 You should make offerings in the likeness of
tumors and in the likeness of the mice that
have been ravaging the land, and give glory
to the God of Israel. Perhaps he will ease up
on you, your gods, and your land.

6 "Why would you harden your hearts, like
the Egyptians and Pharaoh hardened their
hearts? When he dealt harshly with them,
did they not let them go, and they went their
way? [u]

7* "Prepare a cart drawn by two milk
cows that have calves but have never been
yoked. Hitch the cows to the cart, but take
the calves away, leading them home. [v] 8 Take
the Ark of the LORD and place it upon the
cart, and put the figures of gold that you are
sending back as a guilt offering in a box at its
side. Then send it off, and let it go its way.
9 Watch it, and if it goes up the road to its
own land, to Beth-shemesh, then it is clear
that he has brought this great woe upon us.
But if it does not, then we shall know that it
was not he who punished us, that it hap-
pened by chance."

The Ark at Beth-shemesh. 10 The men did
this. They took two milk cows and tied them
to a cart, shutting up their calves at home.
11 They then put the Ark of the LORD upon
the cart along with the box containing the
golden mice and the statues of the tumors.
12 The cows went straight up to Beth-
shemesh, sticking to the road and lowing as
they went along. They did not waver in their
course to the right nor the left. The lords of
the Philistines followed them as far as the
border with Beth-shemesh.

13 Now the people of Beth-shemesh were
harvesting their wheat in the valley when
they looked up and saw the Ark. They re-
joiced at what they saw. 14 The cart came
into the field of Joshua of Beth-shemesh, and

r 1 Sam 6:5; Jos 4:24; Ps 78:66; Acts 13:11.—s Jos 22:16; 24:23.—t Deut 7:15; Mt 8:8.—u Ex 7:14; 8:15; 9:34.—v Num 19:2; Deut 21:3; 2 Sam 6:3.

5:6 *Tumors:* i.e., plague, spread by rats (see 6:4); see also Ps 78:66.

5:7-11 The Philistine victory was short lived. Once they realized that the Ark was not helping them, they sought out ways to return it to the Israelites.

6:3 The Philistine priests and diviners responded to the Ark as they traditionally would in appeasing an angry god. Their guilt offering, however, was not in line with Levitical requirements.

6:7-12 This passage depicts another Philistine ploy to determine if the god of the Israelites was responsible for bringing them harm. God had his own reasons for showing them his power over the milk cows.

it stopped there by a large rock. The people
chopped up the wood from the cart and
offered up the milk cows as a burnt offering
to the LORD.[w] 15 The Levites lowered the Ark
down along with the box that contained the
objects made of gold and placed them on the
large rock. On that day the men of Beth-
shemesh offered burnt offerings and per-
formed sacrifices to the LORD.[x]

16 The five lords of the Philistines saw all of
this and returned to Ekron that same day.
17 The golden tumors that the Philistines
sent back as a guilt offering to the LORD were
for Ashdod, Gaza, Ashkelon, Gath, and
Ekron: one tumor for each city. 18 There
were as many golden mice as there were
cities under the rule of the five lords of the
Philistines, both the fortified cities and the
country villages. The large rock upon which
they set the Ark of the LORD is in the field of
Joshua of Beth-shemesh to this day.[y]

Punishment for Irreverence. 19 He slew some
of the men of Beth-shemesh because they
had looked into the Ark of the LORD. He slew
seventy of them.* The people raised up a
lamentation because the LORD had struck
the people with a great slaughter. 20 The men
of Beth-shemesh said, "Who is able to stand
before this holy LORD God? To whom should
we send it?" 21 They sent messengers to the
people of Kiriath-jearim saying, "The
Philistines have sent back the Ark of the
LORD. Come down and fetch it for your-
selves."

CHAPTER 7

1 Some men from Kiriath-jearim came
and took the Ark of the LORD away. They
brought it to the house of Abinadab on the
hill, and they consecrated Eleazar, his son, to
take care of the Ark of the LORD.

Samuel the Judge. 2 * The Ark remained at
Kiriath-jearim for a long time, for twenty
years. All of the people of Israel lamented
after the LORD.

3 Samuel said to all the people of Israel, "If
you intend to return to the LORD with your
whole heart, then rid yourselves of the for-
eign gods you have among you, the Astartes,
and commit your hearts to serve the LORD
alone, then he will deliver you out of the
hands of the Philistines."[z] 4 So the Israelites
threw away their Baals and Astartes,* and
served the LORD alone.

5 Samuel then said, "Assemble all of the
Israelites at Mizpah,* and I will intercede to
the LORD for you."[a] 6 When they had gath-
ered at Mizpah, they drew water and poured
it* before the LORD. They fasted that day and
confessed, "We have sinned against the
LORD." Now, Samuel was the judge of the
Israelites at Mizpah.[b]

Defeat of the Philistines. 7 When the
Philistines heard that the Israelites had
gathered at Mizpah, the lords of the
Philistines went up to attack them. When the
Israelites heard about this, they were afraid
of the Philistines. 8 The Israelites said to
Samuel, "Intercede for us unceasingly with
the LORD, our God, that he might deliver us
from the power of the Philistines."

9 [c] So Samuel took a suckling lamb and
offered it as a burnt offering to the LORD.
Samuel cried out to the LORD for the sake of
Israel, and the LORD heard him.

10 While Samuel was performing the sac-
rifice, the Philistines drew near to engage the
Israelites in combat. The LORD boomed with
a loud thunder that day, and the Philistines
panicked and they were defeated by the
Israelites. 11 The men of Israel rushed out
from Mizpah and pursued the Philistines.
They slaughtered them all the way to
Beth-car. 12 Samuel then took a stone and
set it up between Mizpah and Shen. He
called it "Ebenezer," saying "the LORD
helped us here."*

13 Thus the Philistines were defeated and
they no longer raided the territory of Israel.
The hand of the LORD was raised against the
Philistines as long as Samuel lived.[d] 14 The
towns that lay between Ekron and Gath that

w 2 Sam 24:21ff.—x Num 8:15; Deut 31:25.—y Gen 31:52; Jos 6:12; 24:26.—z 1 Sam 12:10, 20, 24; Jos 24:23; Jdg 6:6-10; 10:10-16.—a 1 Sam 10:17; Jdg 11:11; 20:1.—b Gen 24:45; Jdg 20:26; Ps 106:6; Lam 2:19.—c 9f: Lev 6:5; Jos 10:10; 2 Sam 22:14f; Sir 46:16ff.—d Gen 26:18; Jdg 3:30; 8:28; 11:33.

6:19 *He slew seventy of them:* here is another instance of God meting out the punishment he had promised for disobedience. God tried over and over again to bring back his people to his ways to avoid further retribution.

7:2-17 This story seems to have been written in the North for the purpose of exalting the person of Samuel by depicting him as the greatest of the judges of Israel and the deliverer of God's people.

7:4 *Baals and Astartes:* these are Canaanite gods whose union was believed to bring fertility to the earth.

7:5 *Mizpah:* a very significant place for the Israelites, considering that Samuel was appointed judge (7:6), and Saul, the first king of Israel, was presented to the people (10:17ff) there.

7:6 *Drew water and poured it:* pouring water on the ground before the Lord was symbolic of repentance for sin and a return to the Lord.

7:12 The Israelites set up a stone in gratitude for the Lord's help in rescuing them from the Philistines.

the Philistines had captured from Israel
were restored to the Israelites, and Israel
was able to deliver its borderlands from the
hands of the Philistines. There was even
peace between Israel and the Amorites.

15 Samuel continued to serve as the judge
of Israel throughout his entire lifetime.[e]
16 Each year he made a circuit among
Bethel, Gilgal, and Mizpah, judging Israel in
all of those places, 17 but he always returned
to Ramah, for that was his home, and he
judged Israel there, too. He built an altar to
Yahweh there.[f]

II: THE INAUGURATION OF THE MONARCHY*

CHAPTER 8

The People Request a King. 1 When Samuel
grew old, he appointed his sons as judges
over Israel. 2 The name of the older was Joel,
and the name of the younger was Abijah, and
they were judges at Beer-sheba. 3 The sons
did not walk in his ways. They sought dis-
honest gains, took bribes, and perverted jus-
tice.[g]

4 All of the elders of Israel gathered togeth-
er and came to Samuel at Ramah. 5[h] They
said to him, "You are now old, and your sons
are not following in your path. Appoint a
king over us, just like all the other nations
have."

6 It displeased Samuel when they said to
him, "Appoint a king over us," so Samuel
prayed to the LORD. 7[i] The LORD said to him,
"Listen to everything that the people have
requested of you. It is not you whom the peo-
ple have rejected, they have rejected me as
their king. 8 They have done this from the
day that I brought them up out of Egypt to
this very day. They have rejected me and
served other gods, just as they have rejected
you. 9 So grant their request, but warn them
solemnly and inform them what the king
who reigns over them will do."

The Rule of a King. 10 Samuel told the peo-
ple who were asking for a king everything
that the LORD had said. 11 He said, "This is
what the king who reigns over you will do. He
will take away your sons to serve him on his
chariots and his horses, and they will run in
front of his chariots.*[j] 12 He will appoint
some as commanders of groups of thou-
sands, and others as commanders of groups
of fifty. He will set some to plowing his fields
and reaping his harvests. Others will make
weapons and equipment for his chariots.[k]
13 He will take your daughters to be makers
of perfumes and cooks and bakers. 14 He will
take the best of your fields, vineyards, and
olive groves and he will give them to his
attendants. 15 He will take a tenth of your
grain harvest and the harvest of your vine-
yards and give it to his officials and his
attendants. 16 He will take your menservants
and your maidservants, the best of your cat-
tle and donkeys, and use them for his own
work. 17 He will take a tenth of your flocks,
and you, yourselves, will become his slaves.[l]
18 When that day comes, you will cry out for
help because of the king that you have cho-
sen, but on that day the LORD will not listen
to you."*

19 But the people refused to listen to
Samuel. They said, "No! We want a king over
us![m] 20 Then we will be like every other
nation, with a king to lead us and to go out
before us to fight in our battles."

21 When Samuel heard everything that the
people had said, he repeated it to the LORD.
22 So the LORD said to Samuel, "Listen to
them and appoint a king over them." Then
Samuel said to the men of Israel, "Let each
man go back to his own town."

CHAPTER 9

Saul and the Lost Donkeys. 1 There was a
certain man from Benjamin whose name
was Kish, the son of Abiel, the son of Zeror,
the son of Bechorath, the son of Aphiah. He
was a man of high standing in Benjamin.[n]
2 He had a son whose name was Saul. He
was a handsome young man, and there was
no one in Israel who was more handsome

e Jdg 3:10; 12:7, 9; 1 Ki 5:1.—f 1 Sam 7:17; 9:12; 14:35; 15:34; Jos 8:30.—g Ex 23:2, 8; Deut 16:19; Jdg 2:17.—h 5f: Deut 17:14f; Jos 13:1; Acts 13:21.—i 7f: 1 Sam 8:22; 12:1, 12f; Jdg 8:22f; 10:13; 1 Ki 9:9; 11:4.—j 1 Sam 10:25; Deut 17:14-20; 1 Ki 12:4.—k 2 Sam 18:1; 1 Ki 1:5.—l 1 Sam 17:8.—m 1 Sam 8:5; 10:19; 1 Ki 18:21.—n 1 Sam 14:51; Num 1:4; 1 Chr 8:33.

8:1—15:35 Israel needs a strong authority to deal with the Philistine threat. Neighboring peoples offer a model: monarchy. But does not having a king mean imitating the pagan nations and betraying the Lord, who is the only true king of his people? The conscience of Israel is disturbed; the passages we shall be reading here (revised by the author of the book) bear witness to this unease: some Israelites are in favor of a monarchy, others opposed to it.

8:11 *In front of his chariots:* as a sign of honor; this custom continued in the East down to modern times (2 Sam 15:1; 1 Ki 1:5).

8:18 Samuel, despite his many admonitions, could not convince the Israelites that they would regret their decision to appoint a king. He wanted them to recognize that in God alone would they find true peace and deliverance.

than he. He was also a head taller than any-
one else.[o] 3 Now the donkeys belonging to
Kish, the father of Saul, were lost, and Kish
said to Saul his son, "Take one of the ser-
vants with you and go up and look for the
donkeys." *

4 So he passed through the hill country of
Ephraim, in the area around Shalishah, but
he could not find them. Then he went into
the area around Shaalim, but they were not
there. He next passed into the land of the
Benjaminites, but they did not find them.

5 When they came to the land of Zuph,
Saul said to the servant who was with him,
"Come on, let us go back, lest my father stop
worrying about the donkeys and start wor-
rying about us." 6 But the servant replied,
"There is a man of God in this town. He is
highly respected, and everything that he says
comes true. Let us now go to him, perhaps
he can tell us where to go."[p]

7 [q] Saul said to his servant, "If we go, what
are we going to bring the man? We have used
up all of the food in our sacks. We have noth-
ing to give the man of God. What do we
have?" 8 The servant answered Saul, saying,
"I have a quarter of a shekel of silver. I will
give it to the man of God so that he can tell
us which way to go." 9 (In former days in
Israel, if someone wanted to ask something
of God, he would say, "Come, let us go to the
seer," for in those days prophets were called
seers.)[r] 10 So Saul said to his servant, "Good!
Let us go." They went into the town where
the man of God was living.

11 As they were going up the hill on the way
to the town, they met some young women
who were coming out to draw water. They
said to them, "Is the seer here?"[s] 12 They
answered, "He is. Hurry now, for he has just
arrived in the town today because the people
are offering a sacrifice on the heights. *[t]
13 Find him as soon as you enter the town
before he goes up to the heights to eat. The
people will not start to eat until he arrives,
for he must bless the sacrifice. Afterward,
those who are invited will eat. Go up now, for
right around now you should find him."

Saul Meets Samuel. 14 They went into the
town, and as they were entering the town,
Samuel was coming out toward them to go
up to the heights. 15 Now the day before Saul
arrived, the LORD had revealed this to
Samuel:[u] 16 "About this time tomorrow I
will send you a man from the land of
Benjamin. You will anoint him as leader over
my people Israel. He will deliver my people
out of the hands of the Philistines. I have
regarded my people, for their cry has risen
up to me."[v] 17 When Samuel saw Saul, the
LORD said to him, "This is the man of whom
I have spoken to you. He is to rule over my
people."

18 * Saul approached Samuel in the gate-
way and said to him, "Please tell me where
the seer's house is." 19 But Samuel answered
Saul, "I am the seer. Go up ahead of me to
the heights, for you will eat with me today. I
will let you go on your way tomorrow, and I
will make known to you all that is on your
mind. 20 As for the donkeys that were lost
three days ago, do not worry about them, for
they have been found. Is not all the desire of
Israel placed upon you and all your father's
family?" 21 But Saul answered, "Am I not a
Benjaminite, the smallest of the tribes in
Israel? Is not my family the least important
of the clans in the tribe of Benjamin? Why
are you saying this to me?"[w]

22 Then Samuel brought Saul and his ser-
vant into the hall, and he sat them down at
the head of those who had been invited;
there were about thirty in all. 23 Samuel said
to the cook, "Bring me the piece of meat that
I brought you, the portion I told you to set
aside." 24 The cook brought up the leg and
what was on it and set it in front of Saul. He
said, "Here is what I saved for you. Eat it,
because I set it aside for this moment from
when I first invited the guests." So Saul ate
with Samuel that day.

25 After they came down from the heights
into the town, he spoke to Saul on the roof of
his house. 26 They rose about daybreak, and
Samuel called up to Saul on the rooftop,
"Get up, and I will send you on your way."
Saul got up, and both he and Samuel went

o 1 Sam 10:23.—p 1 Sam 3:19.—q 7f: 1 Ki 14:3; 2 Ki 4:42; 5:15; 8:8f.—r Gen 25:22; Sir 46:15.—s Gen 24:11ff; Ex 2:16.—t 1 Sam 7:17; 16:2, 5; 20:6, 29; Deut 12:13; 1 Ki 3:2, 4.—u Acts 13:21.—v 1 Sam 10:1; Jos 11:6.—w 1 Sam 15:17; Jdg 20:15.

9:3 Since horses were not bred in Israel, donkeys were among the livestock of the wealthy (see Job 1:2-3; 42:12); they were the mounts used at that time.

9:12 The heights above the city were regarded as the place best suited for sacred gatherings (as a result, "high place" means "sacred place" unless otherwise indicated). In this passage the reference is to a communion sacrifice.

9:18-21 Saul was so consumed by his search for the lost donkeys that he blocked out the important events that God was preparing him for. Our own problems often prevent us from seeing how God is working in our lives.

outside together. 27 As they were coming to
the edge of the town, Samuel said to Saul,
"Tell your servant to go on ahead of us," and
he went on ahead. He continued, "You stay
here for a while, so that I can reveal the word
of God to you." [x]

CHAPTER 10

Saul Is Anointed. 1 Samuel took a flask of
oil, and he poured it upon his head. He
kissed him and said, "Has not the LORD
anointed you as leader over his inher-
itance?* [y] 2 When you leave me today, you
will encounter two men near the Tomb of
Rachel on the border of Benjamin. They will
say to you, 'The donkeys that you were look-
ing for have been found. Your father has
stopped worrying about the donkeys and has
begun to worry about you saying, "What
shall I do about my son?" ' [z]

3 "From there you are to continue on until
you arrive at the Terebinth of Tabor. Three
men who are on their way to God in Bethel
will meet you there. One will be bringing
three young goats, another three loaves of
bread, and the third a bottle of wine. 4 They
will greet you and give you two loaves of
bread. Take them from them.

Signs and Prophecies. 5 [a] "After that go to
Gibeath-elohim where there is a Philistine
outpost. As you approach the city, you will
meet a band of prophets coming down from
the high places with lyres, tambourines,
flutes, and harps being played before them.
They will be prophesying.* 6 The Spirit of
the LORD will rush upon you, and you will
prophesy with them, for you will be changed
into another person. [b] 7 Once these signs
occur, do whatever comes to hand, for God
is with you. 8 Precede me to Gilgal, and I will
come down to be with you and to offer burnt
offerings and to sacrifice peace offerings. You
are to wait for seven days until I come to you
and show you what to do." [c]

The Signs Fulfilled. 9 When Saul turned
around to leave Samuel, God changed his
heart. All those signs were fulfilled that day.
10 When they arrived at Gibeah, they were
met by a band of prophets. The Spirit of the
LORD rushed upon him and he prophesied
among them. [d] 11 When all of those who had
known him saw him prophesying among the
prophets, they said to one another, "What
has happened to the son of Kish? Is Saul also
one of the prophets?" [e] 12 A man who lived
there asked, "Who is their father?" This is
why it became a saying, "Is Saul also one of
the prophets?"

13 After Saul stopped prophesying, he
went up to the high places. 14 Saul's uncle
asked him and his servant, "Where have you
been?" He answered, "Looking for the don-
keys. When we realized that we could not
find them, we went to Samuel." 15 Saul's
uncle said, "Tell me what Samuel said to
you." 16 Saul said to his uncle, "He informed
us that the donkeys had been found." He did
not tell him about what Samuel had said
concerning the kingdom.

Saul Is Chosen King.* 17 Samuel sum-
moned the people of Israel to Mizpah. [f] 18 He
said to the Israelites, "Thus says the LORD,
the God of Israel, 'I brought Israel up from
Egypt and delivered them out of the hands of
the Egyptians and all of the nations that
oppressed you.' [g] 19 But today you have
rejected your God who himself delivers you
from all of your adversities and difficulties.
You have said to him, 'Appoint a king over
us.' Now present yourselves before the LORD
by tribes and by clans." [h]

20 When Samuel had all of the tribes of
Israel approach him, the tribe of Benjamin
was chosen by lot. 21 Then he had the tribe of
Benjamin approach him clan by clan, and
the clan of Matri was chosen. Finally Saul,
the son of Kish, was chosen. But when they
looked for him, he could not be found.
22 They then asked the LORD, "Has the man
arrived yet?" The LORD answered, "Yes, he
has hidden himself among the baggage." [i]
23 They ran and brought him back from
there. When he stood among the people he
was a head taller than any of them.

x Jdg 3:20.—y 1 Sam 9:16f; 24:7; Jdg 2:18; 9:9; 1 Ki 1:39; Acts 13:21.—z Jer 31:15; Mk 14:13.—a 5f: 1 Sam 13:3-4; 19:20f.—b 1 Sam 11:6; 16:13; 19:21; Jdg 13:25; 14:6, 19; 15:14; 2 Ki 3:15.—c 1 Sam 7:16; 13:8; Gen 7:10; Lev 3:1.—d 1 Sam 19:20-24; Num 11:25.—e 1 Sam 9:1; 19:20-21, 24; 1 Chr 26:28.—f 1 Sam 7:5; Jdg 20:1.—g Ex 4:22; 18:11; 20:2; Lev 11:45; 25:38; Num 15:41; 21:5; Deut 5:6; Jdg 6:8f.—h 1 Sam 8:5, 19; Jos 7:14.—i 1 Sam 30:24.

10:1 The pomp and circumstance associated with the crowning of an Israelite king also included an anointing that proclaimed the king not only ruler but God's representative as well. This was a reminder to him that his wisdom came from the Holy Spirit and not from himself.

10:5 Samuel's time saw the formation of guilds of prophets, that is, men dedicated to divine worship, in which they accompanied the rites with chants and music; they worked themselves up to a kind of ecstasy and even delirium (1 Sam 19:20-24).

10:17-27 Another account of Saul's investiture; the passage is in direct continuity with chapter 8.

24 Samuel said to all the people, "Do you see
whom the LORD has chosen? There is no one
else like him among the people." All the peo-
ple cried out, "Long live the king."[j]

25 Samuel instructed the people concern-
ing the ordinances of the kingdom. He wrote
this in a book and placed it before the LORD.
Then Samuel dismissed all of the people,
each to his own home.[k] 26 Saul also went
home to Gibeah, and he was accompanied
by a group of brave men whose hearts God
had touched.* 27 But some sons of Belial
said, "How can this one save us?" They held
him in contempt and brought him no gifts,
but he held his peace.

CHAPTER 11*

Victory over the Ammonites. 1 Nahash the
Ammonite went up and camped outside of
Jabesh-gilead. All of the men in Jabesh said
to Nahash, "Make a covenant with us and we
will be subject to you."[l] 2 But Nahash
answered, "I will only make a covenant with
you if I gouge out your right eyes* so that
you might bring shame upon all of Israel."[m]
3 The elders of Jabesh answered, "Give us a
reprieve of seven days so that we can send
messengers all throughout the territory of
Israel. If no one comes to save us, then we
will surrender to you."

4 When the messengers arrived at Gibeah,
Saul's city, and they proclaimed these things
in the hearing of the people, all the people
cried out and wept. 5 Saul was just then
coming back from the field behind his oxen,
and asked, "What is wrong that the people
are weeping?" So they told him what the
men from Jabesh had said.

6 When he heard this report, the Spirit of
the LORD rushed upon Saul and he burned
with rage.*[n] 7 He took a pair of oxen and
cut them into pieces. He sent them by mes-
sengers all throughout the territory of
Israel. He said, "Whoever does not follow
Saul and Samuel will have this done to his
oxen." The fear of the LORD came upon the
people so that they came out as if they were
one man.[o]

8 When Saul counted the Israelites who
were in Bezek, there were three hundred
thousand of them, and thirty thousand
from Judah. 9 They said to the messengers
who had come to them, "Say to the men of
Jabesh-gilead: 'Tomorrow, before the sun
warms up, you will have help.' " The messen-
gers went and reported this to the men of
Jabesh who were elated. 10 So the men of
Jabesh said, "Tomorrow we will surrender to
you, and you can do to us what you see fit."

11 The next day Saul divided his people
into three groups. During the morning
watch they attacked the camp of the
Ammonites and continued to strike them
down until the day was hot. Even those who
survived were scattered, so that not two of
them remained together.

Saul Proclaimed King. 12 The people said to
Samuel, "Who is it who asked, 'Is Saul to
reign over us?' Bring those men out so that
we can put them to death." 13 But Saul said,
"No one will be put to death today, for today
the LORD delivered Israel."[p] 14 Samuel said
to the people, "Come, let us go to Gilgal and
reaffirm the kingdom there." 15 All of the
people went to Gilgal, and they confirmed
Saul as king before the LORD in Gilgal. They
sacrificed peace offerings before the LORD,
and Saul and all of the Israelites greatly
rejoiced there.

CHAPTER 12*

Samuel's Innocence. 1 Samuel said to all of
Israel, "I have listened to everything you said
to me and I have appointed a king over you.[q]
2 Now you have a king leading you. I am old
and gray, and my sons are in your presence.
I have led you from the days of my youth up
to the present. 3 Behold, I testify against you
in the presence of the LORD and his anoint-
ed. Whose ox have I taken? Whose donkey
have I taken? Whom have I cheated? Whom
have I oppressed? From whose hands did I

j 2 Sam 16:16; 1 Ki 1:25, 39; 2 Ki 11:12.—k 1 Sam 8:11; Deut 17:14-20.—l 1 Sam 12:12; 31:11.—m 1 Ki 15:19.—n 1 Sam 16:13; Jdg 14:6, 19.—o 1 Ki 11:30.—p 2 Sam 19:23; 1 Pet 3:18.—q 1 Sam 8:7, 9, 22; Deut 17:14.

10:26 Before Saul was appointed king, the religious center of Israel was in Ramah, Samuel's home. When Saul returned to his hometown of Gibeah and set up shop there, the political center was separated from the religious center.

11:1-15 The final part of this section, in which Samuel is not even mentioned, comes from a different tradition about Saul's election; it speaks of his election as being reaffirmed and thus is made to harmonize with what has gone before.

11:2 *Gouge out your right eyes:* the shame of this was that it would render them unfit for military service.

11:6 *Burned with rage:* linking the Spirit of the Lord with Saul's anger confirms that justifiable anger can be used by God to right a wrong, in this case, to overcome those who were persecuting the Israelites.

12:1-25 Like Moses (Deut 29–31) and Joshua (Jos 24), at the moment of his retirement, Samuel reviews his life.

receive a bribe to close my eyes? I am willing
to restore it all to you." [r]
4 They answered, "You have not cheated
us nor have you oppressed us, nor have you
taken anything from anyone's hands." 5 So
Samuel said, "The LORD is a witness before
you, and the anointed is also a witness before
you, that you have not found anything in my
hands." They answered, "He is our witness."

Samuel's Review of the People. 6 Samuel
then said to the people, "It is the LORD who
appointed Moses and Aaron, and he brought
you up out of the land of Egypt. [s] 7 Now,
therefore, stay here, so that I can plead my
case with you before the LORD concerning all
of the righteous deeds that the LORD did on
your behalf and for your fathers.
8 "After Jacob went into Egypt, your
fathers cried out to the LORD, and the LORD
sent Moses and Aaron who brought your
fathers out of Egypt and led them here to
settle in this place. [t] 9 They forgot the LORD,
their God, so he sold them into the hands of
Sisera, the leader of Hazor's army, and into
the hands of the Philistines, and into the
hands of the king of Moab, who fought
against them. [u] 10 They cried out to the LORD
and said, 'We have sinned, for we have aban-
doned the LORD to serve the Baals and the
Astartes. Deliver us out of the hands of our
enemies, and we will serve you.' [v]
11 "Then the LORD sent Jerubbaal, Barak,
Jephthah, and Samuel. He rescued you out
of the hands of the enemies who surrounded
you so that you might live in safety. [w] 12 But
now when you saw that Nahash, the king of
the Ammonites, was attacking you, you said
to me, 'No! We want a king to rule over us,'
even though the LORD, your God, was your
king. [x]

Samuel's Farewell. 13 "Now, behold the king
you have chosen, the one whom you desired.
The LORD has given you a king. [y] 14 If you fear
the LORD and serve him and hearken to his
voice and do not rebel against the com-
mandment of God, and if both you and the
king who reigns over you follow the LORD,
your God, then fine. 15 But if you do not
hearken to the voice of the LORD and you
rebel against the commandment of the
LORD, then the hand of the LORD will be
against you as it was against your fathers.
16 "Now, therefore, stand here and see this
great thing that the LORD is doing before your
eyes. 17 Is it not now the season for the wheat
harvest? I will call upon the LORD to send
thunder and rain. Then you will perceive and
realize the great wickedness that you have
done before the LORD in asking for a king." * [z]

Samuel Intercedes on Behalf of the People.
18 Then Samuel called upon the LORD, and
the LORD sent thunder and rain that day. All
of the people were filled with fear of the
LORD and of Samuel. 19 All of the people said
to Samuel, "Pray to the LORD, your God, for
your servants that we might not die, for we
have added this to our other evil deeds, that
we asked for a king."
20 But Samuel said to the people, "Do not
be afraid. You have done all of this wicked-
ness, but you have not turned away from fol-
lowing the LORD. Serve the LORD with your
whole heart. 21 Do not turn aside after use-
less things that cannot be to your profit, nor
can they deliver you, for they are useless. [a]
22 The LORD will not abandon you because of
his great name,* for the LORD desired to
make you his people. [b]
23 "As for myself, far be it from me to sin
against the LORD by not praying for you. I
will instruct you in the way that is good and
right. 24 Only fear the LORD and serve him
faithfully with your whole heart, considering
the great things he has done for you.* 25 But
if you continue to do what is wicked, then
both you and your king will perish."

III: THE REIGN OF SAUL AND THE INTRODUCTION OF DAVID

CHAPTER 13

Saul's Unlawful Sacrifice. 1 Saul was thirty
years old when he began to reign, and he
ruled over Israel for forty-two years. 2 Saul
chose three thousand of the men of Israel for

r Ex 20:17; 23:8; Num 16:15; Deut 16:19; Sir 46:19.—s Jer 34:13; Mic 6:4.—t Gen 46:5, 8; Ex 1:11; 2:23ff; 15:25.—u Jdg 3:8, 12ff; 4:2f; 10:7; 13:1.—v 7:3f; Ex 15:25; Num 21:7.—w Jdg 6:14, 32; 11:1.—x 1 Sam 8:6f, 19; 11:1f; Jdg 8:23; 2 Sam 14:16.—y 1 Sam 8:7.—z Ex 9:23, 28ff; 1 Ki 18:1, 24.—a Deut 32:37ff; Tob 14:6; Isa 57:13.—b Ex 14:14; Jos 7:9; Jer 14:21; Dan 3:34.

12:17 Since this is the dry season in Israel, rainfall would clearly be a sign of God's intervention and displeasure with the people's insistence on having a king.

12:22 *Because of his great name:* the people of Israel shared a significant place in being chosen by God. Often in the Old Testament, the Lord is called upon to save his people from their sin, and although he will punish them, he will never abandon them.

12:24 Here Samuel reminds the people for the second time (see v. 7) to recall all the Lord has done for them.

himself. Two thousand were with Saul in
Michmash in the hill country of Bethel, and
one thousand were with Jonathan in Gibeah
in Benjamin. He sent the rest of the people to
their homes.

[3] Jonathan attacked an outpost of the
Philistines at Geba, and the Philistines heard
about it. Saul had trumpets blown all
throughout the land and proclaimed, "Let
the Hebrews hear!" [c] [4] All of Israel heard the
report: "Saul has attacked an outpost of the
Philistines, and now Israel has become
abhorrent to the Philistines." The people
were summoned to join Saul at Gilgal.

[5] The Philistines were assembled to fight
against Israel. They had thirty thousand
chariots,* six thousand charioteers, and so
many men that they seemed like the sand on
the shore of the sea. They went up and
camped outside of Michmash, to the east of
Beth-haven. [d] [6] When the men of Israel saw
that they were in trouble for the people were
being hard pressed, they hid themselves in
caves, in thickets, among the rocks, in cel-
lars, and in cisterns. [7] Some Hebrews even
crossed over the Jordan to the land of Gad
and Gilead.

Saul was still in Gilgal, and all of the peo-
ple who were following him trembled with
fear. [8] He waited for seven days, the time
period that Samuel had established, and yet
Samuel had not yet arrived. The people
began to drift away. [9] * So Saul said, "Bring
me the burnt offerings and the peace offer-
ings," and he offered up the burnt offerings.
[10] Just as he finished offering up the burnt
offering, Samuel arrived. Saul went out to
greet him. [11] Samuel asked him, "What
have you done?" Saul answered, "I did it
because the people were drifting away from
me, and you had not arrived at the estab-
lished time, and the Philistines were as-
sembled at Michmash. [12] I thought, 'The
Philistines are coming down against me at
Gilgal, and I have not yet made entreaty to
the LORD.' I felt compelled to offer up a
burnt offering."

[13] Samuel responded to Saul, "You have
acted foolheartedly, you have not observed
the command of the LORD, your God. If you
had, the LORD would have established your
reign over Israel forever. [e] [14] But now your
reign shall not endure because you have not
observed what the LORD commanded you.
The LORD has sought a man after his own
heart, and the LORD has appointed him as
leader over his people." [f]

Preparations for War. [15] Samuel got up and
left Gilgal for Gibeah in Benjamin. Saul
counted those who were with him, and there
were around six hundred men. [16] Saul, and
Jonathan his son, and the people who were
with him stayed in Gibeah in Benjamin,
while the Philistines camped outside of
Michmash.

[17] Raiders went out from the camp in
Michmash in three groups. One went toward
Ophrah into the land of Shual, [g] [18] another
went toward Beth-horon, and the third went
toward the border that lay over the Valley of
Zeboim near the desert.

[19] There were no blacksmiths in the land of
Israel for the Philistines had reasoned,
"Otherwise the Hebrews might make
swords or spears." [h] [20] So all of the Israelites
had to travel down to the Philistines to have
their plowshares, their hoes, their axes, and
their sickles sharpened. [21] The charge was
two-thirds of a shekel for the plowshares and
hoes, and one-third of a shekel for sharpen-
ing the axes and pointing the goads.* [22] This
is why on the day of the battle not a sword or
a spear was found in the hands of any of the
people who were with Saul and Jonathan;
only Saul and Jonathan, his son, had them.
[23] Now a force of Philistines had gone out to
the pass at Michmash. [i]

CHAPTER 14

Jonathan Defeats the Philistines. [1] * One day
Jonathan, Saul's son, said to his young
armor-bearer, "Come, let us cross over to
the other side to that outpost of Philistines,"
but he did not tell his father.

[2] Saul had remained in the upper part of
Gibeah under a pomegranate tree that is in
Migron. There were around six hundred
men with him. [3] Abijah, the son of Ahitub,

c 1 Sam 14:1-15; Jdg 3:27; 6:34; 10:11-12; 2 Sam 20:1f.—d Jos 11:4; Isa 10:28.—e Sir 15:20.—f 1 Sam 25:30; 2 Sam 7:15f; Ps 78:70; Dan 6:27; Acts 13:22.—g 1 Sam 14:15; 17:19; Jdg 8:32.—h Jdg 5:8.—i 1 Sam 14:15.

13:5 *Thirty thousand chariots:* some of the Greek translations render it as "three thousand."

13:9-12 Saul became impatient and took matters in his own hands by offering sacrifice himself, instead of waiting for a priest as prescribed by the law. His disobedience did not sit well with Samuel or with the Lord.

13:21 A very high price for this period.

14:1ff This section shows the declining nature of Saul's leadership as a result of his deteriorating relationship with God.

the brother of Ichabod, the son of Phinehas, the son of Eli, was the priest of the LORD in Shiloh, and he wore an ephod. Now, the people did not know that Jonathan had left.[j]

4 Along the passes through which Jonathan was traveling to go over to the Philistine outpost, there was a rocky cliff on one side and there was a rocky cliff on the other side. They were called Bozez and Seneh. 5 One of them faced the north toward Michmash, and the other faced the south toward Gibeah. 6 Jonathan said to his young armor-bearer, "Come on, let us cross over to that outpost of uncircumcised men. Perhaps the LORD will be with us, for nothing can keep the LORD from saving, whether it be by many or by few."[k] 7 His armor-bearer said to him, "Do what you have in mind, my heart is with you."

8 Jonathan said, "Let us cross over to those men and show ourselves to them. 9 If they say to us, 'Wait where you are until we come over to you,' then we will stay where we are and not go over to them. 10 But if they say, 'Come here to us,' then we will go, because the LORD has delivered them into our hands, and this is a sign to us."*[l]

11 So the two of them showed themselves to the Philistine force, and the Philistines said, "Look, the Hebrews are coming up out of the holes in which they have hidden themselves." 12 Then the men of that force said to Jonathan and his armor-bearer, "Come over to us and we will show you something." Jonathan said to his armor-bearer, "Come, follow me, for the LORD has delivered them into Israel's hands."

13 Jonathan climbed up using his hands and his feet, and his armor-bearer followed him. They fell before Jonathan, and his armor-bearer also put them to death after him. 14 That first time Jonathan and his armor-bearer slaughtered about twenty of them, all within half the area an ox could plow.

15 The army in the fields and all the people in the outposts and the raiding parties were seized with panic, and they were shaking so much that even the ground quaked, for it was a tremendous panic.[m]

16 Saul's watchmen in Gibeah of Benjamin saw the army melting away in all directions. 17 Saul said to the people who were with him, "Take stock and see who has left us." They took stock, and Jonathan and his armor-bearer were not there. 18 Saul said to Abijah, "Bring the Ark of God here" (for the Ark of God was then with the Israelites). 19 While Saul was talking with the priest, the noise that was rising up from the Philistine army kept getting louder. Saul said to the priest, "Withdraw your hand." 20 Then Saul and all the people who were with him assembled and went into battle. There was great confusion, each man attacking his neighbor with his sword.[n] 21 Furthermore, those Hebrews who had previously sided with the Philistines and who had gone up into their camp changed sides to be with the Israelites who were with Saul and Jonathan.

22 When all of the Israelites who had hid themselves in the hill country of Ephraim heard that the Philistines were fleeing, they joined them in battle, chasing closely after them.[o] 23 Thus the LORD saved Israel on that day, and the fighting continued on through Beth-haven.

Saul's Oath. 24 The men of Israel had been hard pressed that day, so Saul placed the people under an oath which said, "Whoever eats any food before this evening, before I have had the chance to seek vengeance upon my enemies, will be cursed," Therefore, no one ate anything.

25 All of them entered a woodland, and there was some honey on the ground. 26 When they entered the woods, they saw honey oozing out, but no one put his hand to his mouth because they feared the oath. 27 But Jonathan had not heard about the oath with which his father had bound the people, so he stuck out the end of the staff that was in his hand and he dipped it in the honeycomb. He then put his hand to his mouth, and his eyes brightened.

Jonathan's Violation of the Oath. 28 One of the men shouted out, "Your father has put the people under an oath saying, 'Whoever eats food today will be under a curse.'" By now, the people were faint. 29 Jonathan said, "My father has brought trouble into the land. Look how my eyes brightened up just

j 1 Sam 2:28; 4:21; 14:18; 23:9; 30:7.—k 1 Sam 14:17; 17:26, 36, 47; Sir 39:18; 1 Mac 3:19; Ps 21:6.—l Jdg 3:28; 12:3; Jer 31:7.—m Gen 41:56; Jdg 8:12.—n Jdg 7:22.—o 1 Sam 13:3; 17:2; 1 Ki 2:28.

14:10 *This is a sign to us:* Jonathan and his armor-bearer were no match for the Philistine army, but they trusted that God was with them and they were rewarded with a tremendous victory.

because I ate a little bit of this honey. 30 The
slaughter among the Philistines has not been
all that great. How much larger would it
have been today if the people had eaten
freely of their enemies' plunder that they had
found?"

31 That day they struck down the Philis-
tines from Michmash to Aijalon, and the
people were very weary. 32 The people
rushed upon the spoil, and took sheep, oxen,
and calves, and they slaughtered them upon
the ground. The people ate them along with
blood. [p]

33 They spoke to Saul saying, "Look, the
people are sinning against the LORD for they
are eating food with the blood still in it." He
said, "You have acted treacherously. Roll this
large rock over toward me." 34 Saul then
said, "Go among the people and say to them,
'Let each man bring his ox and his sheep to
me here. They can slay them here and eat
them. Do not sin against the LORD by eating
it with its blood still in it.'" Each man
brought his ox there, and they slaughtered
them there that night. 35 Saul built an altar
to the LORD. It was the first time that he built
an altar to the LORD. * [q]

Jonathan Is Saved from Death. 36 Saul said,
"Let us go down after the Philistines by night.
We can prey upon them until the morning
and not leave one of them alive." They said,
"Do whatever you think best," but the priest
approached and said, "Let us inquire of
God." 37 So Saul sought counsel from God
asking, "Shall I go down after the Philistines?
Will you deliver them into Israel's hands?"
But he did not answer that day.

38 So Saul said, "Let all of the leaders of
the people draw near so that we can know
and find out what sin has been committed
today. 39 As the LORD who delivers Israel
lives, even if it be Jonathan, my son, that man
will surely die." But none of the people
answered him.

40 He then said to all of Israel, "You stand
on one side, I and Jonathan my son will
stand on the other." The people said to Saul,
"Do what you think is best." [r] 41 Saul then
said to the LORD, the God of Israel, "Give me
the complete truth." Jonathan and Saul were
chosen by lot, but the people escaped. [s]
42 Saul said, "Cast lots to choose between me
and Jonathan, my son." Jonathan's lot was
chosen.

43 Saul said to Jonathan, "Tell me what you
have done." Jonathan told him, "I only tasted
a little honey with the end of my staff that
was in my hand. Must I now die?" 44 Saul
answered, "May God do this to me and even
more, for, Jonathan, you must surely die." [t]
45 But the people said to Saul, "Shall
Jonathan die, the one who brought about this
victory in Israel? Never! As the LORD lives,
not one hair from his head will fall to the
ground, for he did this today with God's
help." This is how the people rescued
Jonathan * that day, and he was not put to
death. [u]

Saul's Reign Summarized. 46 Saul returned
from his pursuit of the Philistines, and the
Philistines returned to their homes. 47 * Thus
Saul established his reign over Israel. He
fought against all of his surrounding ene-
mies, against Moab, against the Ammonites,
against Edom, against the kings of Zobah,
and against the Philistines. He punished
them on every side. [v] 48 He assembled an
army and struck down the Amalekites,
delivering Israel out of the hands of those
who plundered them.

49 Saul's sons were Jonathan, Ishvi, and
Malkishua. The older of his two daughters
was named Merab, and the younger was
named Michal. [w] 50 His wife's name was
Ahinoam, and she was the daughter of
Ahimaaz. The name of the commander of
his army was Abner, the son of Ner, who was
Saul's uncle. 51 Saul's father Kish and
Abner's father Ner were the sons of Abiel. [x]

52 There was bitter fighting against the
Philistines all throughout the days of Saul.
Whenever Saul saw a strong or brave man,
he took him into his service.

---

p 1 Sam 14:34; 15:14, 21; Lev 3:17; 7:26f; 17:10-14; Isa 34:7; Acts 15:20, 29.—q 1 Sam 7:17; Jdg 6:24.—r Deut 27:9; Jos 7:13ff.—s 1 Sam 25:24; 28:6; Ex 28:30.—t 1 Sam 3:17; 14:33; Ru 1:17.—u Jdg 15:18; 1 Ki 1:52; Acts 7:9.—v Jos 11:18; 2 Sam 1:22; 8:2-5.—w 1 Sam 18:17, 20, 25; 31:2; 1 Chr 8:33; 9:39; 10:2.—x 1 Sam 9:1; 14:51; 1 Chr 8:33.

14:35 Saul was late in giving honor to God for his kingship. He consistently made the mistake of relying on his own wits and approaching God as a last resort.

14:45 *The people rescued Jonathan:* Saul was more intent on saving his image than on killing Jonathan. The intervention of the people got him out of a bad spot so that he did not have to carry out his threat against Jonathan.

14:47-52 This is a piece of archival information, of which there will be further examples in the history of the kings. The present chronological notice is very positive in its evaluation of Saul's historical work as a whole and deserves credence. Verse 52 implies the beginnings of a standing army.

CHAPTER 15*

Saul's Disobedience. 1 Samuel said to Saul, "The LORD sent me to anoint you as king over his people Israel. Therefore, hearken to the sound of the words of the LORD. 2 Thus says the LORD of hosts: 'I will remember what the Amalekites did to Israel when they waylaid them as they were coming up out of Egypt.[y] 3 Go now, and attack Amalek. Wipe out everything that belongs to them. Do not spare any of them, kill men and women, children and infants, oxen and sheep, camels and donkeys.'"[z]

4 Saul summoned the people and counted them at Telaim. There were two hundred thousand soldiers and ten thousand men from Judah. 5 Saul went to the city of Amalek and set up an ambush in the valley.

6 Saul said to the Kenites, "Go away, leave the Amalekites, so that I not destroy you along with them. You were kind to all of the Israelites when they came up out of Egypt." So the Kenites moved away from the Amalekites.*[a]

7 Saul then struck down the Amalekites from Havilah down to Shur which lies to the east of Egypt. 8 He captured Agag, the king of the Amalekites alive, but he put all of the people to the sword. 9 Saul and the people spared Agag, all of the best of the sheep and oxen, the fat calves and lambs, everything that was good. Yet, everything that was weak and useless they totally destroyed.

Samuel Rebukes Saul. 10 The word of the LORD came to Samuel saying, 11 "I am sorry that I appointed Saul as king, for he has turned away from me by not observing my commandments." Samuel was disturbed, and he cried out to the LORD all that night. 12 Early in the morning, Samuel went out to meet Saul. Samuel was told, "Saul has gone to Carmel. He set up a monument there for himself, so he turned around and traveled on, going down to Gilgal."*

13 Samuel went to Saul, and Saul said to him, "May you be blessed. I have fulfilled the command of the LORD." 14 Samuel responded, "Then what is the bleating of the sheep in my ears, and the lowing of the oxen that I hear?" 15 Saul answered, "They have brought them from the Amalekites. The people spared the best of the sheep and oxen to sacrifice to the LORD, your God. We have totally destroyed the rest of it." 16 Samuel said to Saul, "Stop! I will tell you what the LORD said to me tonight." He said, "Keep speaking." 17 Samuel said, "Though you are little in your own opinion, are you not the leader of the tribes of Israel? Has the LORD not anointed you as king over Israel?[b] 18 The LORD sent you on a mission and said, 'Go, and completely destroy the sinners, the Amalekites. Fight against them until they are wiped out.' 19 Why did you not heed the voice of the LORD? Why did you pounce on the spoil, doing what was evil in the sight of the LORD?"[c]

20 Saul answered Samuel, "But I did hearken to the voice of the LORD. I went on the mission on which the LORD sent me. I have wiped out Agag, the king of Amalek, and the Amalekites. 21 The people took sheep and cattle from the plunder, the best of the dedicated things, to sacrifice them to the LORD, your God, in Gilgal."

22 * But Samuel replied, "Does the LORD delight in burnt offerings and sacrifices as much as in heeding the voice of the LORD? Behold, obedience is better than sacrifice, being attentive is better than the fat of rams.[d] 23 Rebellion is like the sin of witchcraft, arrogance like the evil of idolatry. Because you have rejected the word of the LORD, he has rejected you as king."

Saul Asks for Pardon. 24 Saul answered Samuel, "I have sinned against the command of the LORD and against your instruction because I was afraid of the people and I listened to their complaints. 25 Now, I beg you, forgive my sin and return with me, so that I can worship the LORD." 26 But Samuel said to Saul, "I will not go back with you because you have rejected the word of the LORD. The LORD has rejected you as king over Israel."[e]

27 As Samuel turned to leave, Saul grabbed on to the hem of his garment and

y Ex 17:8-10, 16; Deut 25:17ff.—z 1 Sam 17:35; 27:8; 30:17; Ex 17:16; Num 10:9; 24:20.—a Ex 6:11; Num 24:21; Deut 20:8.—b 1 Sam 9:21; 12:6; 1 Chr 27:16-22.—c 1 Sam 14:32; 28:18.—d Deut 12:27; Prov 21:3; Isa 34:6; Hos 6:6; Am 5:21-25; Mt 9:13; 12:7; Heb 10:9.—e 1 Sam 15:1; 16:1; 1 Ki 11:11, 30f.

15:1-35 This is an another version of Saul's faults; it took form in circles that did not know the other stories of Saul's rejection.

15:6 The Kenites were a semi-nomad people who were allied with Israel in the wilderness and during the conquest (Num 10:29; Jdg 1:16).

15:12 Again we see Saul's dishonor and disrespect for God by erecting a monument to himself. This is totally unlike his predecessors, Moses and Joshua, who put God first in all things.

15:22-23 A very important passage: the first of the prophets already proclaims the religion of the spirit that will subsequently be the subject of the writing prophets. Religious acts must be done out of obedience and love to be meaningful.

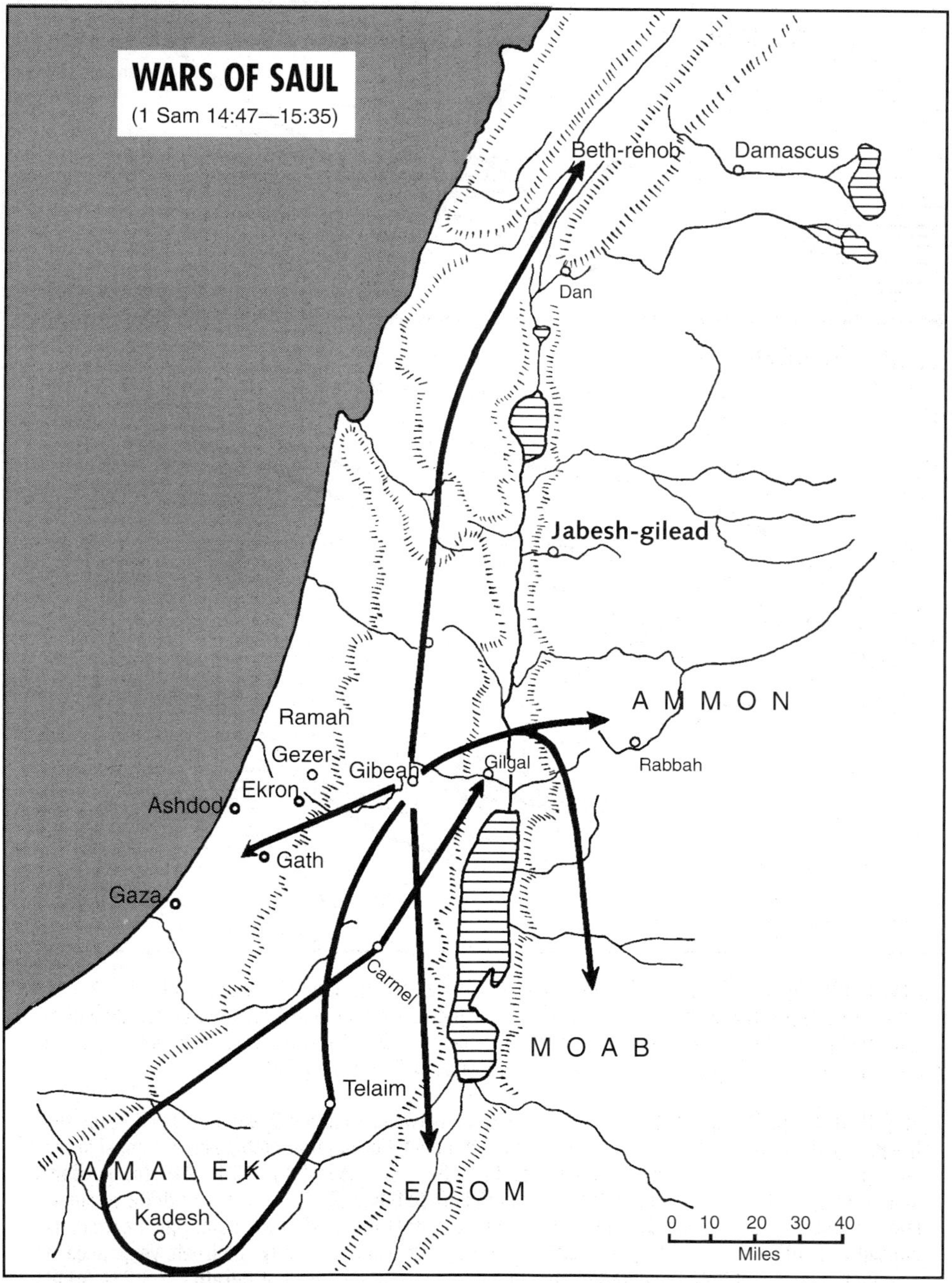

THE WARS OF SAUL (1 Sam 14:47—15:35) — **(a)** Saul becomes king of Israel and defeats all its surrounding enemies: **Moab, Ammon, Edom, Beth-rehob,** the king of Zobah, the Philistines, and the Amalekites (14:47). **(b)** Saul is told to strike **Amalek** and destroy everything and everybody in it. After reviewing his troops at **Telaim** he goes to the city of **Amalek** and prepares an ambush in the wadi. He defeats the Amalekites from Havilah as far as Shur but fails to carry out the ban (15:1-9). **(c)** At **Carmel** Saul raises a trophy in his honor (15:21). **(d)** At **Gilgal** Samuel reproaches Saul for disobeying the Lord, and Saul asks for pardon. After executing Agag, king of **Amalek**, Samuel goes to **Ramah** and Saul to **Gibeah**—and the two never meet again (15:13-15).

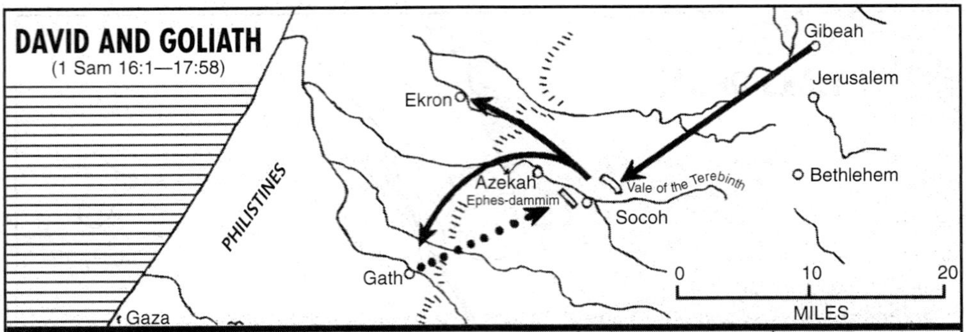

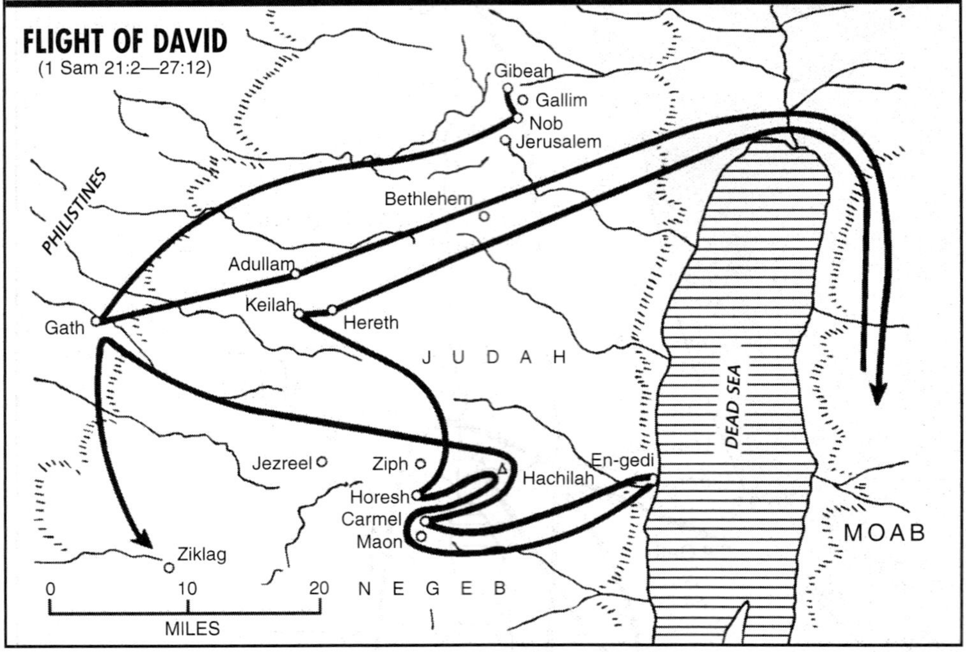

DAVID AND GOLIATH (1 Sam 16:1—17:58) — **(a)** At **Bethlehem** Samuel anoints David (16:13). **(b)** At the **Vale of the Terebinth** the Philistines encamp between **Socoh** and **Azekah** at **Ephes-dammim;** the Israelites on the opposite side. Individual battle between David and Goliath. The Israelites pursue the Philistines to the approaches of **Gath** and the gates of **Ekron** (17:1-54).

FLIGHT OF DAVID (1 Sam 18:1—27:12) — **(a)** Break between Saul and David, but David keeps the friendship of Jonathan (18:1—19:17). **(b)** At Ramah, David, fleeing, takes refuge near Samuel in the strongholds of the wilderness: Saul pursues him there unsuccessfully (19:18-24). **(c)** At **Nob,** Ahimelech gives the holy bread and the sword of Goliath to David (21:1-10). **(d)** At **Gath** David simulates madness before Achish, king of Gath (21:11-16). **(e)** At the Cave of Adullam, David surrounds himself with 400 men (22:1-2). **(f)** In **Moab,** David puts his family for safety at Mizpeh. Vengeance of Saul on the priests of Nob. David returns to Judah and hides in the forest of **Hereth** (22:3-23). **(g)** At **Keilah,** David defeats the Philistines there, and then sets out at random with 600 men (23:1-13). **(h)** In the **Desert of Ziph,** Saul pursues David, hidden in the forest, on the **Hill of Hachilah.** David renews the alliance with Jonathan, and withdraws to the **Desert of Maon.** Saul then goes to battle with the Philistines. **(i)** In the **Cave of En-gedi,** David spares Saul. Death of Samuel (24:1—25:1). **(j)** At **Carmel,** David seeks food from Nabal, and is insulted by him (25:2-43). **(k)** In the **Desert of Ziph** and at the **Hill of Hachilah,** David goes to the tent of Saul during the night and spares him. Saul returns to **Gibeah** (26:1-25). **(l)** Among the **Philistines,** Achish, king of **Gath,** gives **Ziklag** to David. From there, David makes excursions against the Geshurites and the Amalekites, and pretends that he has plundered the **Negeb** of Judah, of Jerahmeel, and of the Kenites (27:1-12).

tore it. 28 Samuel said to him, "The LORD has
torn away the kingdom of Israel from you
today. He has given it to one of your neigh-
bors, someone who is better than you. 29 He
who is the strength of Israel does not lie nor
does he repent, for he is not a man that he
should change his mind."[f]

30 He said, "I have sinned. Please honor
me before the elders of my people and before
Israel. Come back with me so that I might
worship the LORD, your God." 31 Samuel
went back with Saul, and Saul worshiped the
LORD.

Agag's Death. 32 Then Samuel said, "Bring
me Agag, the king of the Amalekites." Agag
came before him hesitantly, for Agag said,
"Surely the bitterness of death is past."
33 Then Samuel said, "As your sword made
women childless, so among women your
mother will be childless." Samuel then
hacked Agag to pieces before the LORD.[g]

34 After this Samuel traveled to Ramah,
and Saul went up to his house in Gibeah of
Saul. 35 Samuel did not go back to visit Saul
again until the day of his death, though
Samuel mourned for Saul. The LORD regret-
ted that he had appointed Saul as king over
Israel.

CHAPTER 16

1 The LORD said to Samuel, "How long will
you continue to mourn for Saul, for I have
rejected him as king over Israel. Fill your
horn with oil and go, I am sending you to
Jesse in Bethlehem. I have seen a king for
myself among his sons."[h] 2 But Samuel said,
"How can I go? Saul will hear about it and
kill me." The LORD said, "Take a heifer with
you and say, 'I am going to make a sacrifice
to the LORD.' 3 Invite Jesse to the sacrifice,
and I will let you know what you are to do.
You will anoint for me whomever I point out
to you."[i]

David Is Anointed as King. 4 Samuel did
what the LORD had said. When he arrived in
Bethlehem, the elders of the city came out to
him trembling with fear. They asked, "Do
you come in peace?" 5 Samuel answered,
"Yes. In peace I have come to make a sacri-
fice to the LORD. Purify yourselves and come
to the sacrifice with me." Then he purified
Jesse and his sons, and he invited them to the
sacrifice.[j]

6 When they arrived, he looked at Eliab
and said, "Surely his anointed one stands
before the LORD." 7 But the LORD said to
Samuel, "Do not consider his appearance or
how tall he stands, for the LORD has rejected
him. He does not see the way that men see,
for men look on the outward appearance,
but the LORD looks at the heart."[k]

8 [l] Jesse then summoned Abinadab and
had him pass in front of Samuel. He said,
"The LORD has not chosen this one either."
9 Then Jesse had Shammah pass by. He said,
"The LORD has not chosen this one either."
10 Jesse made his seven sons pass in front of
Samuel. Samuel said to Jesse, "The LORD
has not chosen these either."

11 Samuel asked Jesse, "Are these all of
the children?" He said, "There is still the
youngest; he is watching the sheep." Samuel
said to Jesse, "Send for him and fetch him.
We will not sit down until he has arrived."

12 And so he sent for and brought him. He
was ruddy, with a fine and handsome
appearance. The LORD said, "Rise up and
anoint him, for he is the one." 13 Samuel took
the horn of oil, and he anointed him in the
midst of his brothers. The Spirit of the LORD
rushed upon David from that day onward,
and Samuel then returned to Ramah.[m]

Saul's Armor-Bearer.* 14 * Now the Spirit of
the LORD had departed from Saul, and an
evil spirit oppressed him. * 15 Saul's servants
said to him, "Behold, an evil spirit from God
is troubling you. 16 Let our lord command
your servants to seek out someone who is
talented in playing the harp. When an evil
spirit from God descends upon you, he can
play and you will feel better."[n] 17 Saul said to
his servants, "Find someone for me who
plays well and bring him to me." 18 One of his
servants said, "I have seen a son of Jesse
from Bethlehem who is talented at playing.
He is strong and a brave warrior. He is pru-

f Num 23:19.—g Ex 21:23; Jer 2:30; 15:9; Mt 26:52.—h Jos 17:6; Ru 4:17-22; 1 Ki 1:39; 1 Chr 11:3.—i 1 Sam 9:16; 16:5.—j 1 Sam 9:12f; 16:2, 10; 20:26; Gen 31:54; Job 1:5.—k 1 Sam 10:23f; 1 Chr 28:9; Prov 15:11; Isa 10:33; Jn 8:15; Acts 1:24.—l 8ff: 1 Sam 17:12f; Gen 26:22; 47:7; 1 Chr 2:13ff.—m 1 Sam 10:6; 11:6; Jdg 3:10; Sir 46:13.—n 1 Sam 18:10; 19:9.

16:14—17:58 This passage gives two different accounts of David's entrance into the service of Saul. A first tradition describes David as the king's new minstrel. This tradition is interwoven with a second that tells of David's combat with Goliath. In this second tradition David goes off to see his brothers on the field of battle, and he is not presented to Saul until after his victory over Goliath.

16:14-23 One of the stories of David being selected for the king's service.

16:14 *An evil spirit oppressed him:* when the Spirit of the Lord departed from Saul, the emptiness was filled with a spirit that caused him to act erratically (i.e., attempt to murder David).

dent in his speech and handsome, and the
LORD is with him."[o] 19 * So Saul sent mes-
sengers to Jesse saying, "Send me David,
your son, who is tending the sheep."

20 Jesse took a donkey loaded with bread, a
skin of wine, and a young goat, and he sent
them with David, his son, to Saul.[p] 21 David
came to Saul and entered into his service.
He loved him very much, and he became his
armor-bearer.

22 Saul sent to Jesse saying, "Please let
David be in my service, for he has found
favor in my sight." 23 Whenever an evil spirit
came upon Saul, David took a harp and
played it. Saul revived and he felt better, and
the evil spirit would depart from him.

CHAPTER 17

David and Goliath. 1 The Philistines assem-
bled their armies, and they were gathered at
Socoh in Judah. They were camped between
Socoh and Azekah in Ephes-dammim.[q]
2 Saul and the Israelites gathered together
and camped in the Valley of Elah. They
arranged themselves in order for battle
against the Philistines. 3 The Philistines
stood on one side of a mountain, and Israel
stood on the mountainside facing them, with
the valley in between them.

4 Then a champion named Goliath of
Gath came forth out of the camp of the
Philistines. He was six cubits and a span
high.* 5 He wore a bronze helmet on his
head, and he wore armor, a coat of mail
weighing five thousand shekels of bronze.
6 On his legs he wore bronze leg armor, and
he had a bronze javelin slung on his back.
7 His spear shaft was like a weaver's beam,
and the head of the spear weighed six hun-
dred iron shekels. His shield-bearer walked
before him.[r]

8 He stood and cried out to the armies of
Israel, "Why do you come out arrayed in
battle line? Am I not a Philistine, and are you
not servants of Saul? Choose a man and
have him come down to me. 9 If he is able to
fight me and kill me, then we will become
your slaves. But if I defeat and kill him, then
you will be our slaves and serve us." 10 Then
the Philistine said, "I defy the armies of
Israel today. Give me a man so that we can
fight each other."

11 When Saul and all of Israel heard what
the Philistine said, they were dismayed and
terrified.

David Arrives in the Camp.* 12 Now David
was the son of Jesse from Bethlehem in
Judah, an Ephrathite. He had eight sons, and
in Saul's days he was already old and well on
in years.[s] 13 Jesse's three oldest sons had fol-
lowed Saul into battle. The names of the
three sons who had gone into battle were:
Eliab, the oldest, Abinadab, the second old-
est, and Shammah, the next oldest. 14 David
was the youngest. The three oldest followed
Saul. 15 David went back and forth to Saul
in order to tend to his father's sheep in
Bethlehem.[t]

16 For forty days, each morning and each
evening, the Philistine presented himself.

17 Jesse said to David, his son, "Take this
ephah of roasted grain and these ten loaves of
bread to your brothers. Rush this out to your
brothers' camp. 18 Also take along these ten
cheeses for the commander of their group of
one thousand. See how your brothers are far-
ing, and bring back news from them."

19 They and Saul and all of the men of
Israel were in the Valley of Elah fighting
against the Philistines. 20 David rose early
the next morning, left the sheep with some-
one to tend them, took the things and left as
Jesse had instructed him. He came to the
outskirts of the camp just as the army was
going forth into battle, shouting their war
cries.[u] 21 Israel and the Philistines were
lined up for battle, one army facing the
other. 22 David left his things in the care of
the keeper of supplies. He ran to the battle
line and came to his brothers whom he
greeted.[v]

23 As he was talking with them, Goliath of
Gath, the champion of the Philistines, came
forth from the Philistine lines, and he shout-
ed the same taunt, and David heard it.
24 When all the Israelites saw the man, they
ran away from him in great fear.

---

o 2 Sam 5:10; 17:8; Acts 18:24.—p 1 Sam 9:7f; 10:4, 16:1.—q Gen 26:14; Deut 2:32; 1 Ki 4:10.—r 2 Sam 21:19; 23:7; 1 Ki 10:14; 1 Chr 11:23; 20:5.—s 1 Sam 16:1, 10; Jdg 19:18; Ru 1:2; 1 Ki 1:1.—t 2 Sam 7:8; Ps 78:70-71.—u 1 Sam 26:5; Jos 3:1; 1 Chr 10:14; Isa 42:13.—v 1 Sam 25:13; Mt 28:9.

16:19-21 David is given an opportunity to learn firsthand the ways of leading the people from Saul, who apparently does not know that Samuel has already anointed David as the Lord instructed (v. 13).

17:4 *Six cubits and a span high:* Goliath is nearly ten feet tall and has powerful weapons in marked contrast to young David whose power comes from God.

17:12-31 As noted above, this story gives another version of David's entrance into the circle around Saul.

25 Now the Israelites had been saying, "Do
you see how this man keeps coming out?
Surely he comes out to defy Israel. The king
will give a great reward to the man who kills
him. He will even give him his daughter in
marriage, and he will exempt his father's
family from taxes in Israel."

26 David spoke to the men who were
standing by him saying, "What will be done
for the man who kills this Philistine and
removes this disgrace from Israel? Who is
this uncircumcised Philistine that he should
defy the armies of the living God?" * [w]
27 The
people answered him saying something like,
"This is what will be done for the man who
kills him."

28 When Eliab, David's oldest brother,
heard him speaking to the men, Eliab
became very angry at David. He said, "Why
have you come down here? With whom did
you leave those few sheep in the desert? I
know about your pride and the wickedness
of your heart, for you only came down here
to see the battle."
29 David answered, "What
have I done now? Was it not just a question?"

30 Then he turned away from him and
spoke to another man, asking the same
thing. The people answered him the same
way they had before.
31 When the words that
David had spoken were heard, they were
repeated to Saul who summoned him.

David Accepts the Challenge.
32 David said
to Saul, "Let no one lose heart on account of
him. Your servant will go out and fight with
this Philistine." [x]
33 Saul said to David, "You
cannot go out against the Philistine and fight
with him. You are only a boy, and he has been
a warrior since he was young."
34 [y] David said
to Saul, "Your servant has been tending his
father's sheep. When a lion or a bear would
come and carry a lamb away from the flock,
35 I would chase after it and strike it and res-
cue it from out of its mouth. When it would
rise up against me, I would seize it by its fur
and strike and kill it.
36 Your servant has
killed lion and bear. This uncircumcised
Philistine will be like one of them because he
has defied the army of the living God."

37 David continued, "The LORD who has de-
livered me from the paw of the lion and the
paw of the bear will deliver me out of the
hands of this Philistine." Saul then said to
David, "Go, and may the LORD be with you." [z]

David Prepares for the Encounter.
38 Saul
dressed David in his own armor. He put a
bronze helmet on his head and covered him
with a coat of mail.
39 David fastened his
sword over his armor, and he tried to walk
around in it, but he was not used to it. David
said to Saul, "No! I cannot walk in these,
because I am not used to them." David then
took them off.

40 He took his staff in his hand, and he
chose five smooth stones from out of the
stream. He put them in a pouch in his shep-
herd's bag, and with his sling in his hand, he
approached the Philistine.

David's Victory.
41 Meanwhile, the Philistine
drew nearer to David, his shield-bearer pre-
ceding him.
42 The Philistine looked David
over, and he held him in contempt, for he
was only a youth, ruddy, and handsome. [a]
43 The Philistine said to David, "Am I a dog,
that you come out to me with sticks?" The
Philistine cursed David by his gods.
44 The
Philistine said to David, "Come over to me,
and I will give your flesh to the birds of the
air and the beasts of the field." [b]
45 David said
to the Philistine, "You are coming against
me with sword, spear, and javelin. I am com-
ing against you in the name of the LORD of
hosts, the God of the armies of Israel, whom
you have defied.
46 The LORD will deliver you
into my hands today. I will strike you down
and take off your head. Today I will give the
bodies of the Philistine army to the birds of
the air and the beasts of the field. Thus,
everyone on the earth will know that there is
a God in Israel.
47 All of those who are gath-
ered in assembly here will know that it is not
by sword or spear that the LORD saves, for
the battle is the LORD's, and he will give you
over into our hands." [c]

48 When the Philistine got up and ap-
proached David, David ran quickly to meet
the Philistine in battle.
49 David reached into
his bag and pulled out a stone. He launched
it with the sling and struck the Philistine on
his forehead. The stone sunk into his fore-
head, and he fell face first to the earth.

50 David triumphed over the Philistine
with a sling and a stone. David struck down
the Philistine and killed him, even without

---

w 1 Sam 18:25; Jdg 15:18; 2 Ki 19:4; Isa 37:4.—x 2 Sam 17:10.—y 34f: Jdg 14:6; Sir 47:3; Isa 11:7.—z 2 Sam 22:3; 2 Chr 20:17; Prov 28:1.—a 1 Sam 16:12.—b Deut 28:26; Ps 79:2-3; Isa 18:6; Jer 15:3.—c 1 Sam 14:6, 10; Job 41:18; Ps 33:16.

17:26 David was not terrorized by Goliath's size as were most of the people. He was enraged that Goliath was defying God, and he trusted that God would win the victory over the Philistines.

carrying a sword in his hand.[d] 51 David ran over to the Philistine and stood over him. He took hold of his sword and drew it out from the sheath. He killed the Philistine and cut off his head with it.

The Philistines Flee. When the Philistines saw that their champion was dead, they fled. 52 The men of Israel and Judah rose up and shouted. They pursued the Philistines until they arrived at the entrance to Gath and the gates of Ekron. The Philistines who had been struck down were all along the Shaaraim road even up to Gath and Ekron.[e] 53 When the Israelites returned from chasing after the Philistines, they plundered their tents. 54 David took the head of the Philistine and brought it to Jerusalem, and he placed his armor in his tent.*

David Is Presented to Saul. 55 When Saul watched David go forth against the Philistine, he said to Abner, the commander of the army, "Whose son is this young man?" Abner answered, "As surely as you live, I do not know." 56 The king said, "Ask around whose son this young man is." 57 When David returned after having killed the Philistine, Abner took him and brought him before Saul, with David still holding the Philistine's head in his hand. 58 Saul said to him, "Whose son are you, young man?" David answered, "Your servant is the son of Jesse, the Bethlehemite."

CHAPTER 18

David and Jonathan. 1 When David finished speaking with Saul, David's soul was bonded with Jonathan's soul. Jonathan loved him more than he loved himself.[f] 2 From that day on, Saul would not permit him to return to his father's house.

3 Jonathan made a covenant with David, because he loved him more than he loved himself. 4 Jonathan took off the robe that he was wearing, and he gave it to David, even giving him his sword, his bow, and his belt.[g] 5 Whatever Saul sent David to do, he did it so wisely that he placed him in charge of warriors. This pleased all of the people, and even Saul's servants.

Saul's Jealousy. 6 When David returned after having struck down the Philistine, the women came out from the cities of Israel to greet King Saul with singing and dancing, with joyful songs, tambourines, and lutes.[h] 7 * As the women danced, they sang, "Saul has killed his thousands, and David has killed his ten thousands."[i] 8 Saul was very angry at this for the saying displeased him. He said, "They give David tens of thousands, and me they only give thousands. What else is he lacking but the kingdom?" 9 From that time on, Saul kept an eye on David.

10[j] The next morning an evil spirit from God rushed upon Saul, and he prophesied right inside of the house. David played on the harp, as he did every day. In the meantime, Saul had a javelin in his hand.* 11 Saul cast the javelin, saying to himself, "I will pin David to the wall," but David eluded him twice. 12 Saul feared David, for the LORD was with him, but he had departed from Saul.

13 Saul sent him away, giving him command over a thousand men. He would go out and come back publicly. 14 David prospered in everything he did, for the LORD was with him.[k] 15 When Saul saw that he was very successful, he grew to dread him. 16 But Israel and Judah loved David, for he went out and came back publicly.

David's Marriage. 17 Saul said to David, "Here is my oldest daughter, Merab, I will give her to you in marriage, only be a brave warrior and fight the LORD's battles." Saul thought, "It will not be by my hand, but let it be by the hands of the Philistines."[l] 18 David said to Saul, "Who am I? What is my life or my father's family worth in Israel that I should become the king's son-in-law?"* 19 When Saul's daughter Merab should have been given to David, she was given instead to Adriel, the Meholathite, as his wife.

20 Now Michal, Saul's daughter, loved David. When Saul was informed about this, he was pleased.[m] 21 Saul thought, "I will give her to him so that she might be a trap for him and so that the hands of the Philistines will be against him." Saul said to David, "You have a

d 1 Mac 4:30; Sir 47:4; Wis 18:22.—e 1 Sam 14:36; 1 Ki 2:40; 1 Chr 4:31; 1 Mac 3:11; Jer 50:4.—f 1 Sam 19:1-7; 20:17; 23:16; 2 Sam 1:26.—g 2 Sam 1:22.—h Ex 15:20f; Jdg 11:34; Jud 15:12-13.—i 1 Sam 18:8; 21:12; 29:5; Sir 47:6f.—j 10f: 1 Sam 16:14; 19:9f; 20:33; 22:6; 26:8.—k 2 Ki 18:7; 2 Chr 14:6.—l 1 Sam 14:49; 17:25; Sir 46:3.—m 1 Sam 14:49.

17:54 An anticipatory notice; see 2 Sam 5:6-9.

18:7-8 *Thousands, . . . ten thousands:* an example of a practice common in Hebrew poetry; it is inspired by the taste for parallelism.

18:10 The note on 1 Sam 16:14 explains the evil spirit that overcomes Saul.

18:18 In spite of David's success and popularity with the people, he remained humble and did not take advantage of Saul.

second chance to be my son-in-law." 22 Saul
ordered his servants, "Speak in confidence to
David saying, 'The king is pleased with you,
and all his servants love you. You should
become the king's son-in-law.'" 23 Saul's ser-
vants said these things to David, and David
answered, "Do you think it is a light matter to
become the king's son-in-law? I am only a
poor man and not highly esteemed."

24 Saul's servants told him, "David was
speaking about this thing." 25 Saul said, "This
is what you are to say to David, 'The king does
not want a dowry, he only wants one hundred
Philistine foreskins, so he might be avenged
on the king's enemies.'" Saul planned to have
David fall at the hands of the Philistines.*[n]
26 When his servants told David these things,
David was well-pleased to become the king's
son-in-law. Before the allotted time had
expired, 27 David went out with his men and
killed two hundred Philistines. David brought
their foreskins and presented the full number
to the king so that he might become the king's
son-in-law. So Saul gave him Michal, his
daughter, in marriage.

28 When Saul saw and realized that the
LORD was with David, and that Michal, his
daughter, loved him, 29 Saul dreaded him all
the more, and Saul was David's enemy for the
rest of his life. 30 The Philistine leaders con-
tinued to go out to battle, and whenever they
went out, David would encounter them with
more success than all of Saul's other ser-
vants, so that his name became well known.[o]

CHAPTER 19

Jonathan Defends David. 1 * Saul told his
son Jonathan and all his servants that they
should kill David, but Jonathan, Saul's son,
was very fond of David. 2 Jonathan informed
David about it saying, "Saul, my father, is
seeking to kill you. Be on your guard tomor-
row morning. Stay in some secret place and
hide there.[p] 3 I will go out and stand beside
my father in the field where you are. I will
speak to him about you, and I will tell you
what I discover."

4 Jonathan spoke well of David to his
father Saul. He said to him, "May the king
not wrong his servant David, for he has not
wronged you. What he has done has only
been to your benefit. 5 He risked his life when
he killed the Philistine. The LORD won a
great victory for all of Israel. You saw it and
you rejoiced. Why would you sin against
innocent blood by killing David for no rea-
son?"[q]

6 Saul listened to Jonathan, and Saul
swore, "As the LORD lives, he will not be
killed." 7 Jonathan then called David, and
Jonathan informed him about all these
things. Jonathan brought David to Saul, and
he was in his presence as he had been before.

8 War broke out again, and David went out
to fight against the Philistines. He struck
them down, slaughtering many, and they
fled from him.

David Is Saved by Michal. 9 [r] Now an evil
spirit from the LORD was upon Saul, and he
was sitting in his house, holding a javelin in
his hand while David was playing some
music. 10 Saul tried to pin David to the wall
with the javelin, but he eluded Saul, and he
drove the javelin into the wall. That night
David fled and escaped.

11 * Saul sent deputies to David's house to
watch for him and to kill him in the morn-
ing. Michal, David's wife, told him, "If you do
not save yourself tonight, you will be killed
tomorrow."[s] 12 So Michal lowered David
down through a window, and he fled and
escaped.[t]

13 Michal took a teraphim and laid it on
the bed, and she placed a goat's hair pillow
where his head would be, and she covered it
over with clothes.* 14 When Saul sent
deputies to seize David, she said, "He is
sick." 15 Saul sent the deputies back to look
for David saying, "Bring him back to me on
a litter so I can kill him." 16 When the
deputies arrived, they found the teraphim in
the bed with the pillow of goat's hair where
the head would be.

17 Saul said to Michal, "Why have you
deceived me by sending away my enemy so
that he could escape?" Michal said to Saul,
"He said to me, 'Let me go or I will kill you.'"

n 1 Sam 17:26; Gen 34:12; 1 Ki 2:1.—o 1 Sam 29:3-5; 1 Chr 14:2, 17; Lk 7:16-17.—p 1 Sam 23:17; 1 Mac 1:53; Sir 6:13; Jer 9:3; Jn 7:19-20.—q 1 Sam 17:55-56; Deut 19:10; Ps 119:109.—r 9f: 1 Sam 16:14; 18:10f; 2 Ki 6:32.—s 1 Sam 19:15; Jdg 16:2.—t Jos 2:15; Acts 9:25; 2 Cor 11:33.

18:25 That is, the king wants a hundred of his enemies slain; their sex is attested by the proof offered. Verse 27 speaks of "two hundred," but see 2 Sam 3:14. This barbarian practice was shared by other peoples.

19:1-7 This is one tradition about the intervention of David's friend Jonathan. Another will be found in chapter 20.

19:11-17 The incident probably occurred during the very night of the wedding, since the passage is in logical continuity with 1 Sam 18:27.

19:13 Since the idol was bald-headed, the goat's skin was needed to make it look like David.

David, Samuel, and Saul in Ramah. [18] When David had fled and made his escape, he went to Samuel in Ramah and told him everything that Saul had done to him. He and Samuel went to Naioth and they stayed there.

[19] Saul heard that David was in Naioth in Ramah. [20] * He sent deputies to capture David. They saw a band of prophets there prophesying, and Samuel was their leader. The Spirit of God rushed upon Saul's deputies, and they prophesied as well. [u] [21] Saul was told about it, and he sent other deputies, but they prophesied as well. A third time Saul sent deputies, but they also prophesied.

Saul and the Prophets. [22] Finally, he himself went to Ramah, and he came to the great well in Secu. He asked, "Where are Samuel and David?" Someone told him, "They are at Naioth in Ramah." [23] So he went to Naioth in Ramah, and the Spirit of God rushed upon him, too. He walked along, prophesying, until he arrived at Naioth. [24] He stripped off his clothes and he prophesied as he had in Samuel's presence. He laid down naked all that day and all that night. This is why they say, "Is Saul also one of the prophets?" [v]

CHAPTER 20

David and Jonathan's Friendship. [1] David fled from Naioth in Ramah and he went to Jonathan and said, "What have I done? What is my crime? How have I wronged your father that he is trying to take my life?" [w] [2] He answered him, "You will surely not die! Everything that my father does, whether it is important or insignificant, he confides to me. Why would my father hide this from me? It is just not so." [3] But David swore an oath saying, "Your father knows very well that you like me, so he said to himself, 'I will not let Jonathan know about it, lest he be grieved by it.' As the LORD lives and as you live, there is only one step between me and death."

[4] So Jonathan said to David, "Whatever you want me to do for you, I will do it." [5] David said to Jonathan, "Tomorrow is the new moon celebration,* and I am supposed to dine with the king. Let me go and hide myself in the field until the evening of the day after tomorrow. [x] [6] If your father should miss me, tell him, 'David begged me for permission to hurry to Bethlehem because they are offering an annual sacrifice there for the whole clan.' [7] If he says, 'That is fine,' then your servant is safe. But if he becomes very angry, you can be sure that he is plotting harm. [8] Deal kindly with your servant, for you have entered into a covenant before the LORD with your servant. If I am guilty, kill me yourself, why should you hand me over to your father?"

[9] Jonathan answered, "Never! If I knew for sure that my father was planning to harm you, would I not tell you?" [10] David asked Jonathan, "Who will tell me if your father's answer is harsh?" [y] [11] Jonathan said, "Come. Let us go out into the field." So they went out into the field together. [12] Jonathan said to David, "By the LORD, the God of Israel, by this time on the day after tomorrow, I will have sounded out my father. If he is well disposed toward David, will I not send word to you to let you know? [13] [z] Otherwise, may the LORD do this and more to Jonathan. But if my father wishes to harm you, I will send you away so that you can be safe. May the LORD be with you as he has been with my father. [14] Only will you not treat me with the LORD's kindness as long as I live, so that I not be killed? [15] Never cease being kind to my family, even when the LORD has eliminated all of David's enemies from the face of the earth."

[16] So Jonathan made a covenant with the house of David saying, "May the LORD take vengeance on all of David's enemies." [17] Jonathan made David swear again by his love for him, for he loved him more than he loved himself.

[18] Then Jonathan said to him, "Tomorrow is a new moon, and you will be missed because your seat will be empty. [19] The day after tomorrow, hurry down to the place where you hid yourself when this trouble began, and stay by the stone of Ezel. [a] [20] I will shoot three arrows off to the side of it, as if I were shooting at a target. [21] Then I will send a boy out saying, 'Go and find the arrows.' If

u 1 Sam 10:5f, 10; Num 11:25.—v 1 Sam 10:10ff; Gen 9:21.—w 1 Sam 27:4; Num 22:28.—x Num 10:10; 28:11-15; Ezr 3:5; Neh 10:34.—y 1 Sam 23:12.—z 13-16: 1 Sam 24:22f; 2 Sam 9:1-13; 21:7.—a 1 Sam 19:1-7; 20:18.

19:20-24 Although Saul is filled with jealousy over David's success, and this is clouding his judgment, he is still able to speak God's words. The gift of prophecy is given—not for his enhancement—but to communicate God's thoughts.

20:5 *The new moon celebration:* a time for the Israelites to gather socially to dedicate themselves anew to the Lord. They preferred to celebrate when the moon was not yet visible, as opposed to pagan worship that focused on the full moon, not on the Creator God.

I say to him, ‘Look, the arrows are on this side of you. Bring them,’ then, as the LORD lives, you are safe, there is no danger. 22 But if I say to the boy, ‘Look, the arrows are ahead of you,’ then go on your way, for the LORD is sending you. 23 The LORD is a witness between me and you forever in regard to the things about which we have spoken.”

David’s Absence. 24 So David hid himself in the field. When the new moon celebration began and the king sat down to eat, 25 the king sat in his usual place by the wall. Jonathan sat facing him, and Abner was sitting by Saul’s side, but David’s place was empty. 26 Saul did not say anything that day, because he thought, “Something must have happened to him so that he is impure, surely he is unclean.”* [b]

27 But the next day, the second day of the month, David’s place was still empty. Saul asked Jonathan, his son, “Why did the son of Jesse not come to eat yesterday nor today?” 28 Jonathan answered Saul, “David begged me for permission to go to Bethlehem. 29 He said to me, ‘Please let me go, for our family is offering a sacrifice in the city. My brother has told me to be there. If I have found favor with you, please, let me leave to go to see my brothers.’ This is why he has not come to the king’s table.” 30 Saul became angry at Jonathan and he said to him, “You son of a perverse and rebellious woman. I knew that you sided with the son of Jesse to your own shame and the shame of your mother’s nakedness. 31 For as long as the son of Jesse lives upon the earth, neither you nor your kingdom will be stable. Send for him and bring him to me, for he must die.”* 32 Jonathan answered Saul, his father, saying, “Why must he die? What has he done?” 33 Saul cast a javelin at him to kill him. Jonathan thus knew that his father intended to kill David. [c]

34 Jonathan was enraged and he got up from table. He did not eat on the second day of the month because he was angry at his father for the shameful way he had treated David.

Jonathan Warns David. 35 The next morning, Jonathan went out into the field at the time he had arranged with David. He had a small boy with him. 36 He said to the boy, “Run, find the arrows that I shoot.” The boy ran off, and he shot an arrow beyond him. 37 When the boy arrived at the place that Jonathan had shot the arrow, Jonathan said, “Is the arrow not ahead of you?” 38 Then Jonathan cried out to the boy, “Hurry, run, do not stop!” The boy picked up Jonathan’s arrows and returned to his master. 39 (The boy did not know anything about this, only Jonathan and David knew what was happening.)

40 Jonathan gave his weapons to his boy and said, “Go, carry them into the city.” 41 After the boy had left, David got up from the south side of the place, and he bowed down three times before him, face to the ground. They kissed one another, and they wept over one another, David more so. [d] 42 Jonathan said to David, “Go in peace, since we have both sworn in the name of the LORD saying, ‘May the LORD be between me and you, between my descendants and your descendants, forever.’ ” He got up and left, and Jonathan went back into the city.

CHAPTER 21

The Priest and the Holy Band. 1 David came to Nob, to Ahimelech the priest. Ahimelech was afraid when he encountered David and he said to him, “Why are you alone? Why is no one with you?” 2 David said to Ahimelech the priest, “The king sent me on some business, and he said to me, ‘Do not let anyone know anything about this task on which I am sending you or what I commanded you to do.’ I have sent my young men to such and such a place. [e] 3 Now, therefore, what do you have at hand? Give me five loaves of bread or whatever can be found.”

4 The priest answered David saying, “I do not have any regular bread at hand, but there is consecrated bread, if the young men have abstained from being with women.” [f] 5 David answered the priest saying, “We have assuredly abstained from being with women these three days since I set out. The young men’s gear is consecrated even on missions that are not consecrated. How much more is their gear consecrated today.”

---

b 1 Sam 16:5; Lev 7:20f; 15:1ff.—c 1 Sam 18:11; Jer 51:11.—d Gen 29:11; 50:1; Ru 1:14.—e 1 Sam 16:4; Isa 10:32; Mk 2:26.—f Lev 24:5, 9; Lk 9:13.

20:26 The meal that accompanied the festival of the new moon involved a sacrifice to God and required ritual purification (see Ex 19:10, Lev 15:16, Num 19:11-22). Without such a cleansing, David could not participate.

20:31 Saul continues to view David, son of Jesse, as the major impediment to the continuation of his dynasty. Jonathan, because of his love of God and David, bypasses any opportunity to prevent David from succeeding Saul (1 Sam 23:16-18).

6 So the priest gave him the consecrated bread, because there was no other bread than the shewbread. The shewbread had been removed from before the LORD and taken away when it was replaced by the hot bread.*

7 One of Saul's servants was there that day, detained before the LORD. His name was Doeg, the Edomite, and he was Saul's chief shepherd.[g]

Goliath's Sword. 8 David asked Ahimelech, "Do you have a spear or a sword at hand? I did not bring either my sword nor any other weapon because the king's mission had to be done in haste." 9 The priest answered, "The sword of Goliath, the Philistine whom you killed in the Valley of Elah, is here. It is wrapped in a cloth behind the ephod.* If you want it, take it, because it is the only one here." David said, "There is none like it, give it to me."

10 That day David rose up and fled because he was afraid of Saul. He went to Achish, the king of Gath.[h] 11 The servants of Achish said to him, "Is this not David, the king of the land? Is he not the one they sing about as they dance, 'Saul has killed his thousands, David has killed his ten thousands.' "

David Pretends Insanity. 12 David took these words to heart, and he was terrified of Achish, the king of Gath.[i] 13 He pretended to be out of his mind in front of them. While he was on his hands he would pound on the doors to the gate, and he would drool down his beard. 14 Achish said to his servants, "Look at the man! He is out of his mind! Why did you bring him to me? 15 Am I so in need of people who are out of their mind that you brought me this man who is acting so strange? Must this man come into my house?"

CHAPTER 22

David Flees. 1 David left and escaped to the cave of Adullam. When his brothers and all of his father's household heard, they went down to him there.[j] 2 Everyone who was in distress, everyone who was in debt, and everyone who was discontented gathered around him, and he became their leader. He had about four hundred men with him.*

3 From there, David traveled to Mizpah in Moab. He said to the king of Moab, "Please let my father and my mother stay with you until I know what God will do with me." 4 He brought them to the king of Moab, and they lived with him the whole time that David was in the stronghold.

5 But the prophet Gad said to David, "Do not stay in the stronghold.* Leave, and go to the land of Judah." David left and went into the forest of Hareth.[k]

Doeg Betrays Ahimelech. 6 Saul heard that David and his men had been discovered. Saul, holding a spear in his hand, was sitting in Gibeah under the tree of Ramah, and all of his servants were standing around him. 7 Saul said to his servants who were standing around him, "Hear now, you Benjaminites. Will each of you get fields and vineyards from the son of Jesse? Will you all be officers of thousands and officers of hundreds? 8 Is that why all of you have conspired against me? No one tells me when my son makes a covenant with the son of Jesse. None of you is concerned about me or tells me that my son has incited my servant to lie in wait for me today."[l]

9 But Doeg the Edomite, who was standing with Saul's servants, said, "I saw the son of Jesse go to Nob, to Ahimelech, the son of Ahitub. 10 Ahimelech inquired of the LORD for him, and he gave him provisions, and he gave him the sword of Goliath the Philistine."[m]

Saul Slays the Priests. 11 The king summoned Ahimelech, the son of Ahitub, the priest, as well as all of his father's family in Nob who were also priests. All of them came to the king. 12 He said, "Listen now, O son of Ahitub." He answered, "Here I am, my lord." 13 Saul said to him, "Why have you conspired with the son of Jesse against me? You gave

g Mt 12:3.—h 1 Sam 17:51; 1 Chr 21:30.—i 1 Sam 18:7; 29:5; 1 Ki 2:40.—j 2 Sam 23:13; 2 Mac 12:38; Ps 63; Mic 1:15.—k 2 Sam 24:11; 1 Mac 5:45; 6:5.—l 1 Sam 18:3; 23:18; Acts 13:22.—m 1 Sam 21:2-10; Ps 52.

21:6 Ahimelech disregarded the law to give the holy bread—meant only for the priests—to David and his men. This act of kindness upheld the higher law (Lev 19:18). Jesus would later echo the precedence of the law of charity in Mt 12:1-8; Lk 6:1-5.

21:9 *Ephod:* a vestment worn by a priest and apparently large enough to harbor Goliath's sword. We do not know how it came to be there or why David, who slew the giant many years before, did not know of its whereabouts.

22:2 David, himself a fugitive, gathers around him a motley crew of followers, who somehow remain faithful to him and who become military leaders and "mighty men" (2 Sam 23:8).

22:5 *Stronghold:* a safe place, most likely connected with the cave in verse 1.

him bread and a sword. You inquired of God whether he should lie in wait for me today."

14 Ahimelech answered the king, "Who among all of your servants is as faithful as David, the king's son-in-law, who goes about at your bidding, and who is respected in your house? 15 Was that the first time I inquired of the LORD for him? No! Let the king not accuse your servant or any of my father's family, for your servant knows absolutely nothing about any of this."

16 The king said, "You must die, Ahimelech, you and all of your father's family." 17 The king said to the guards who were standing around him, "Turn around and kill the priests of the LORD, for they are in league with David. They knew about his fleeing, and they did not tell me." But the king's servants would not stretch out their hands to fall upon the priests of the LORD. [n]

18 So the king said to Doeg, "You turn around and fall upon the priests." Doeg the Edomite turned around, and he fell upon the priests, killing eighty-five men who wore a linen ephod that day. 19 He put Nob, the city of the priests, to the sword: men, women, children and infants, oxen, donkeys, and sheep.

Abiathar Escapes. 20 Now one of the sons of Ahimelech, the son of Ahitub, escaped. He was named Abiathar, and he fled to David. [o] 21 Abiathar told David that Saul had killed the LORD's priests. 22 David said to Abiathar, "I knew that day, when I saw that Doeg the Edomite was there, that he would surely tell Saul. I have caused the death of everyone in your father's family. 23 Stay with me, and do not be afraid. The same man who seeks my life seeks your life as well, but you will be safe with me." *

CHAPTER 23

David Rescues Keilah. 1 Some people then spoke to David saying, "Look, the Philistines are attacking Keilah and they are robbing the threshing floors." [p] 2 David inquired of the LORD saying, "Shall I go to attack these Philistines?" The LORD said to David, "Go attack the Philistines and rescue Keilah." 3 David's men said to him, "Look, we are afraid here in Judah. How much more would we be if we went to Keilah to fight against the armies of the Philistines?" 4 David inquired of the LORD once again, and the LORD said, "Rise, go down to Keilah, for I will deliver the Philistines into your hands." [q]

5 David and his men went to Keilah and they fought with the Philistines. They slaughtered many of them, and they brought away their livestock. Thus David saved the inhabitants of Keilah.

6 When Abiathar, the son of Ahimelech, fled to David at Keilah, he went down with an ephod in his hand.

Saul Chases David. 7 * Saul was told that David had gone to Keilah. Saul said, "God has delivered him into my hands for he has trapped himself behind gates and bars." [r] 8 Then Saul assembled all of the people for war, to go down to Keilah and lay siege to David and his men.

9 David knew that Saul was plotting evil against him, so he said to Abiathar the priest, "Bring the ephod here." 10 David said, "O LORD, the God of Israel, your servant has truly heard that Saul is seeking to come to Keilah to destroy the city on account of me. [s] 11 Will the men of Keilah deliver me into his hands? Will Saul come down here as your servant has heard? O LORD, the God of Israel, I beg you to tell your servant." The LORD said, "He will come down." 12 Then David said, "Will the men of Keilah deliver me and my men into the hands of Saul?" The LORD answered, "They will deliver you over."

13 So David and his men (there were around six hundred of them) left Keilah and went wherever they could go. Saul heard that David had left Keilah, so he halted the pursuit.

14 David stayed in the wilderness strongholds, and he remained in the hill country of the Desert of Ziph. Saul sought him every single day, but God did not deliver him into his hands. 15 David realized that Saul was coming out to seek his life while he was in the Desert of Ziph at Horesh.

16 Jonathan, Saul's son, arose and went to David in Horesh and encouraged him in

---

n 1 Sam 21:7; Dan 2:14.—o 1 Sam 23:6; 30:7; 1 Ki 2:26f.—p Jos 15:44.—q 1 Sam 17:47; Ex 17:4-5; Jdg 20:28; Ps 28:1; Acts 22:10.—r 1 Sam 23:13; 2 Sam 5:19; 1 Chr 11:2.—s 1 Sam 23:12; Gen 19:13; Jer 34:2.

22:23 *You will be safe with me:* unlike Saul, who destroyed the priesthood, David takes Abiathar, the lone survivor, under his wing.

23:7ff Saul again misreads the signs as if God would orchestrate David's demise by presenting Saul with an opportunity to kill him. His behavior shows how out of touch with God's ways he has strayed.

God. 17 This is what he said to him, "Do not
be afraid, for the hand of Saul, my father, is
not going to find you. You will be the king
over Israel, and I will be next to you. Even
my father Saul knows that." [t] 18 The two of
them made a covenant before the LORD.
David stayed in the woods, and Jonathan
returned home.

19 The Ziphites then came up to Saul in
Gibeah saying, "Is David not hiding with us
in strongholds in the woods, on the hill of
Hachilah which is to the south of Jeshimon? [u]
20 Therefore, come down as you wish to, O
king, come down, and for our part we will
deliver him into the king's hands." 21 Saul
said, "May you be blessed by the LORD, for
you have had compassion on me. 22 Go,
please, and prepare yourselves. Investigate
and reconnoiter where he is hidden and find
out who has seen him there, for I have been
told that he is very clever. [v] 23 See, therefore,
and find out about all the places where he is
hiding, then come back to me with certain
information. Then I will go with you, and if
he is in the land, I will search for him all
throughout the thousands of Judah."

Escape from Saul. 24 They rose up and pre-
ceded Saul to Ziph. David and his men were
in the Desert of Maon, in the Arabah to the
south of Jeshimon. [w] 25 Saul and his men
were searching, and when David was told
about it, he went down to the rock and
stayed in the Desert of Maon. Saul heard
about this and pursued David in the Desert
of Maon.

26 Saul was on one side of the mountain,
and David and his men were on the other
side of the mountain. David, out of fear,
hurried to get away. Saul and his men were
trying to surround David and his men to
capture them.

27 A messenger came to Saul saying,
"Come quickly, for the Philistines have
invaded the land." 28 Saul broke off his pur-
suit of David and he left to fight against the
Philistines. This is why they called that place
the Rock of Escape.

CHAPTER 24

David Spares Saul's Life. 1 David went up
from there and dwelt in the strongholds of
En-gedi. [x] 2 When Saul returned from pursu-
ing after the Philistines, he was told, "David
is in the desert in En-gedi." 3 Saul took three
thousand chosen men from out of all of
Israel, and he went out and sought David
and his men on the rocks of the wild goats.

4 He came to the sheepfolds along the
way, and there was a cave there. Saul
entered it to relieve himself, and David and
his men stayed in the recesses of the cave. [y]
5 David's men said to him, "This is the day
that the LORD spoke of when he said, 'I will
deliver your enemy into your hands, you
may do to him as you see fit.' " David got up
and secretly cut off a corner of Saul's robe.
6 But David's conscience began to bother
him because he had cut off a corner of
Saul's robe. 7 He said to his men, "The LORD
forbid that I should do such a thing to my
lord, lifting my hand against the LORD's
anointed, for he is the LORD's anointed." [z]
8 * With these words David rebuked his ser-
vants, and he would not let them rise up
against Saul.

Saul rose from the cave and went on his
way. 9 David also arose and left the cave.
He cried out after Saul saying, "My lord,
the king." Saul looked back and saw David
bowed down, face to the ground, lying
prostrate. 10 David said to Saul, "Why do
you listen to men who say, 'David is trying
to harm you?' 11 Behold, you have seen for
yourself today how the LORD delivered you
into my hands in the cave. Some urged me
to kill you, but I spared you. I said, 'I will
not raise up my hand against my lord, for
he is an anointed one of the LORD.' 12 Look,
my father, see the corner of your robe in
my hand. I cut off the corner of your robe,
but I did not kill you. So see and under-
stand that I am not guilty of wrongdoing or
rebellion. I have not wronged you, but yet
you hunt me to take my life. [a] 13 May the
LORD be the judge between me and you.
May the LORD take my vengeance upon
you, but I will not raise my hand against
you. 14 As the old proverb states, 'Evil
deeds come from evil doers,' but I will not
raise my hand against you. [b] 15 Against
whom has the king of Israel come out?
Whom do you pursue? After a dead dog?
After a flea? 16 May the LORD be a judge

t 1 Sam 20:14-16; 2 Chr 18:3.—u 1 Sam 26:1-3; Ps 54.—v 1 Sam 19:17.—w 1 Sam 25:2-5; Jos 12:1; Mk 6:31-32.—x 1 Sam 23:14,19.—y Ps 57.—z 1 Sam 10:1; 31:4; 2 Sam 1:14.—a Jer 38:25-26; Rom 12:19.—b Mt 7:16.

24:8ff David shows an incredible degree of humility and restraint to the person who has done nothing to win his affection or respect. By continuing to honor God's anointed king despite his evil ways, he is ultimately submitting himself to God's authority.

and decide between me and you. May he
examine my cause and plead it; may he
deliver me out of your hands." [c]

Saul's Apology to David. 17 When David had
finished saying these things to Saul, Saul
said, "Is that your voice, my son, David?"
And Saul cried out and wept. 18 He said to
David, "You are more righteous than I am,
for you have treated me well, but I have
treated you poorly. 19 Today you have
revealed to me how you have treated me
well, for the LORD had delivered me into
your hands, but you did not kill me. [d]
20 When a man finds his enemy, does he
allow him to walk away unharmed? May the
LORD richly reward you for what you have
done to me today. [e] 21 Truly, now I know that
the kingdom of Israel will be firmly placed in
your hands. 22 Now swear to me by the LORD
that you will not cut off my descendants after
me, nor will you eliminate my name from
my father's family."

23 David swore an oath to Saul, and Saul
returned to his home. David and his men
went up into the stronghold.

CHAPTER 25

Death of Samuel. 1 Now Samuel died, and
all of Israel gathered to mourn for him.
They buried him at his home in Ramah.
David then went down into the Desert of
Paran. *[f]

Nabal and Abigail. 2 There was a certain
man from Maon who had property in
Carmel, for he was very wealthy. He owned
three thousand sheep and one thousand
goats, and he was shearing his sheep in
Carmel. [g] 3 His name was Nabal, and his
wife's name was Abigail. She was a good
woman, intelligent and beautiful, but her
husband, who was a Calebite, was difficult
and disagreeable in his dealings. [h]

4 While David was in the wilderness, he
heard that Nabal was shearing his sheep.
5 David sent ten young men, and David said
to the young men, "Go up to Carmel and
approach Nabal, greeting him in my name.
6 Say to him, 'May you have a long and pleas-
ant life, and may your household prosper,
and may all that you own multiply. [i] 7 I have
heard that you were shearing. When your
shepherds were with us, we did not harm
them nor did anything that belonged to
them go missing the whole time they were at
Carmel. 8 Ask your young men, and they will
tell you. Therefore, show your favor to these
young men, for we are here on a feast day.
Please give your servants and your son
David whatever comes to hand.' "

9 When David's young men arrived, they
said all of these things to Nabal in David's
name. Then they waited. 10 Nabal answered
David's servants, "Who is David? Who is the
son of Jesse? There are many slaves these
days who have run away from their masters.
11 Why should I take my bread and my water,
and the meat that I have butchered for my
shearers, and give them to men when I do
not even know from where they have come?"

12 David's young men turned and went on
their way. They came back and told him all
these things. 13 David said to his men, "Let
each man put on his sword." Each man put
on his sword, and David also put on his
sword. About four hundred men went up
with David while the other two hundred
remained with the supplies. [j]

14 One of the young men told Abigail,
Nabal's wife, "Behold, David sent messen-
gers into the wilderness to greet our master,
and he insulted them. 15 But they have treat-
ed us well, and they have not harmed us, nor
did anything go missing when we were wan-
dering about in the fields near them. 16 Night
and day, the whole time that we were with
them tending the sheep, they were like a wall
around us. 17 Now think about it and figure
out what you will do, for certain disaster is
awaiting our master and his entire house-
hold. He is a son of Belial, and no one can
speak to him."

18 Abigail acted quickly. She took two hun-
dred loaves of bread, two skins of wine, five
butchered sheep, five seahs of parched grain,
one hundred raisin cakes, and two hundred
fig cakes, and she loaded it all on donkeys. [k]
19 She then said to her servants, "Go on
ahead, I will follow you." But she did not tell
this to her husband.

20 As she was riding along on the donkey,
she went down into a mountain ravine, and
there was David and his men coming down

c 1 Sam 26:19; Pss 35:1ff; 43:1.—d 1 Sam 14:12; 26:23.—e Ru 2:12.—f 1 Sam 28:3; Gen 35:29; Sir 46:13-20.—g 1 Sam 23:24; Gen 26:13; 2 Chr 29:33.—h 1 Sam 27:3; Deut 1:35-36; Jos 14:6; 1 Chr 2:42.—i Lk 24:36.—j 1 Sam 17:39; 22:2.—k 2 Sam 16:1.

25:1 With the death of Samuel, the spiritual leader of the Israelites, a void existed that was not filled until David ascended the throne.

the other side, and she met them. 21 David had been saying, "Surely it was in vain that I watched over all of his things in the wilderness so that nothing that he owned went missing. He has paid me back evil for good. 22 May God do this to David, and even more, if by morning I have left alive even one male who belongs to him." [l]

23 When Abigail saw David, she quickly got off the donkey, and she fell down before David, bowing her face to the ground. 24 She fell at his feet and said, "Let the blame be upon me, my lord. Please permit your handmaid to speak to you, hear what your handmaid has to say to you.

25 "May my lord not pay attention to this man of Belial, Nabal. He is just like his name. His name means fool, and folly is his companion. But as for me, I, your handmaid, did not see the young men whom you sent.*

26 "Now, my lord, as the LORD lives and you live, the LORD has kept you from coming to shed blood and avenging yourself with your own hands. May your enemies and all who seek to harm my lord be like Nabal. [m] 27 Now, may this gift that your handmaid has brought my lord be given to the young men who follow my lord.

28 "I beg you, forgive your handmaid's offense, for the LORD will surely establish an enduring dynasty for my lord because he fights the LORD's battles. May no wrongdoing be found in you all of your days. 29 Even though someone should rise up to pursue you to seek your life, my lord's life will be bound in the bundle of life with the LORD, your God. He will launch out as from the pocket of a sling the lives of your enemies. [n]

30 "When the LORD has fulfilled all of the good things which he has said to you, my lord, and he has established you as ruler over Israel, 31 then there will have no staggering burden of guilt upon my lord's conscience for either having shed blood without cause or for my lord having sought his own revenge. When the LORD has brought my lord success, remember your handmaid." [o]

32 David then said to Abigail, "Blessed be the LORD, the God of Israel, who has sent you to meet me today. 33 May you be blessed for your good advice, for today you have prevented me from coming to shed blood and seeking vengeance for myself with my own hands. 34 For as surely as the LORD, the God of Israel lives, who kept me from harming you, if you had not hurried out to meet me, then by morning there would not have been even one male left to Nabal."

35 David accepted the things that she had brought him out of her hands. He said to her, "Return home in peace. See, I have listened to what you said and I have granted your request."

Nabal's Death. 36 When Abigail returned to Nabal, he was in his house feasting as if he were at a king's banquet. Nabal was in high spirits, for he was very drunk. She, therefore, did not tell him a thing until daybreak. 37 In the morning, when Nabal was no longer under the influence of the wine, his wife told him these things. His heart failed him, and he became like a stone. 38 About ten days later, the LORD struck Nabal down and he died. [p]

39 When David heard that Nabal was dead, he said, "Blessed be the LORD who has upheld my cause against Nabal for having treated me with scorn. He has kept his servant from wrongdoing, and the LORD has repaid Nabal's wrongdoing upon his own head."

David's Marriage to Abigail. David sent word to Abigail, asking her to be his wife. 40 David's servants came to Abigail in Carmel and they said to her, "David has sent us to you so that he could take you as his wife." 41 She bowed down with her face to the ground, and she said, "Behold your handmaid, a servant to wash the feet of my lord's servants." [q]

42 Abigail quickly got up and rode on a donkey, accompanied by five of her women. She followed David's messengers, and she became David's wife. 43 David also married Ahinoam of Jezreel, so both of them were his wives. 44 But Saul gave Michal, his daughter, David's wife, to Paltri, the son of Laish, who was from Gallim.

CHAPTER 26

David Spares Saul Again.* 1 Now the Ziphites came to Saul at Gibeah and said,

l 2 Sam 3:35; 1 Ki 16:11; 21:21; 2 Ki 9:8.—m Deut 20:4; 30:7; 2 Sam 3:3; 15:21; Isa 62:8.—n Ps 69:28; Jer 11:21-22; 38:16.—o Wis 11:13; Jer 14:21; 22:3; 1 Pet 3:16.—p 2 Chr 13:20; Acts 12:23.—q 1 Sam 28:14; Jn 13:5.

25:25 Abigail seems to know how to protect herself and her family and prudently separates her own lot from her husband Nabal by offering counsel to David.

26:1-25 These are not the same events as were related in chapter 24, but they are told for the same purpose: to highlight David's generosity and magnanimity.

"Is not David hiding himself on the hill of
Hachilah, opposite Jeshimon?" 2 Saul rose
up and went down into the Desert of Ziph.
He had three thousand of the chosen men of
Israel with him, and he sought David in the
Desert of Ziph. [r]

3 Saul camped by the road on the hill of
Hachilah, which is opposite Jeshimon. David
was staying in the desert, and he saw Saul
pursuing him in the desert. 4 David had sent
out spies and discovered that Saul had
indeed come. [s]

5 David arose and went to the place where
Saul was camped. David detected the place
where Saul was lying, alongside of Abner,
the son of Ner, the commander of his army.
Now Saul was lying within the fortifications,
and the people were encamped all around
him. 6 David said to Ahimelech the Hittite
and to Abishai, Joab's brother, the son of
Zeruiah, "Who will go down with me to
Saul in the camp?" Abishai said, "I will go
with you."

7 So David and Abishai went among the
people by night, and they found Saul asleep
within the fortifications, his spear stuck in
the ground near his head. Abner and the
people were lying all around him. [t] 8 Abishai
said to David, "God has delivered your
enemy into your hands today. Let me strike
him once, pinning him to the ground. I will
not have to strike him twice." 9 But David
said to Abishai, "Do no violence to him. Who
can stretch forth his hand against the LORD's
anointed and be guiltless?" 10 David contin-
ued, "As the LORD lives, the LORD himself
will strike him down. Either his time will
come, or he will simply die, or he will go into
battle and be killed. [u] 11 The LORD forbid that
I should stretch out my hand against the
LORD's anointed. Now take the spear that is
by his head and the water jar, and let us
leave."

12 David took the spear that was by Saul's
head and the water jar and they left. No one
had seen them, and no one knew about it,
nor did anyone wake up. They all kept sleep-
ing, for the LORD had caused them to fall
into a deep sleep. [v]

13 David then crossed over to the other
side, and he stood on the top of a distant hill,
so that there was quite a space between
them. 14 David cried out to the people and to
Abner, the son of Ner, "Will you not answer
me Abner?" Abner said, "Who are you that
you call out to the king?" 15 * David said to
Abner, "Are you not a man? Who is like you
in Israel? Why have you not kept guard over
your lord, the king? Someone came in to kill
the king, your lord. 16 You have not done well.
As the LORD lives, you deserve to die, for you
have not protected your master, the LORD's
anointed. Look around now for the king's
spear and the water jar that were at his
head."

17 Saul recognized David's voice, and he
said, "Is this the voice of my son David?"
David answered, "It is my voice, my lord, O
king." 18 He continued, "Why is my lord
chasing after his servant? What have I done?
What wrongdoing have I committed? [w]
19 Now may my lord, the king, listen to the
words of his servant. If the LORD has incited
you against me, may he now accept an offer-
ing. * If it was done by humans, may they be
cursed by the LORD. They have driven me
out of the LORD's inheritance, saying, 'Go
serve other gods.' 20 Do not let my blood fall
to the earth far from the presence of the
LORD. My king has come out to search for a
flea, like one who goes out to hunt a par-
tridge in the mountains."

21 Saul responded, "I have sinned. Come
back, David, my son, for I will not try to
harm you again because you considered my
life to be precious. I have played the fool and
made a terrible mistake." 22 David said,
"Here is the king's spear. Let one of your
young men come over and fetch it. 23 The
LORD rewards each man for his righteous-
ness and his faithfulness. The LORD deliv-
ered you into my hands today, but I would
not stretch out my hand against the LORD's
anointed. 24 May the LORD value my life as
much as I have valued your life today. May
he deliver me from all of my difficulties." [x]
25 Saul said to David, "May you be blessed
David, my son, for you will accomplish
many things and you will triumph." David
went his way, and Saul returned to his
home.

r 1 Sam 13:2; 27:1.—s Jos 2:1.—t 1 Sam 26:8, 12.—u 1 Sam 17:37; Jos 22:23; Ps 37:13.—v Gen 2:21; 15:12; Mt 26:45.—w Mic 2:1.—x Tob 13:5; Est C:30; Acts 20:24.

26:15ff Again David does not take advantage of the circumstances to kill Saul. By removing his water jar and sword and sparing Saul and Abner, David makes the point that he respects his undeserving earthly king and most of all his true King, God.

26:19 *An offering:* that is, may he be placated by a sacrifice.

CHAPTER 27

David's Flight to the Philistines. 1 * David thought to himself, "One of these days I will perish at Saul's hands. I might as well escape into the land of the Philistines. Saul will give up hope of catching me anywhere in the territory of Israel, and I will escape out of his hand."

2 David and his six hundred followers went over to Achish, the son of Maoch, the king of Gath.[y] 3 David stayed with Achish at Gath. Each man had his family with him, and David had his two wives: Ahinoam, the Jezreelite, and Abigail, Nabal's wife, of Carmel. 4 When Saul was told that David had fled to Gath, he did not go out after him anymore.

5 David said to Achish, "If I have found favor in your sight, then let me be given a place in one of your country towns to live. Why should your servant live in the royal city with you?" 6 That day Achish gave him Ziklag. Ziklag has belonged to the kings of Judah up to the present.[z] 7 David lived in the territory of the Philistines for one year and four months.[a]

David's Raids. 8 David and his men went up and raided the Geshurites, the Gezrites, and the Amalekites. (From the days of old these were the people who lived in the land running from Shur down to the land of Egypt.) 9 When David attacked a place, he did not leave a man or a woman alive. He took the sheep, oxen, donkeys, camels, and clothes, and he would then return to Achish.

10 * When Achish would ask, "Where have you gone raiding today," David would say to him, "To the south of Judah, or to the south of the Jerahmeelites, or to the south of the Kenites."[b]

11 David did not leave a man or a woman alive to bring them to Gath, for he thought they might say, "This is what David did." He did this the whole time that he was living among the Philistines. 12 Achish trusted David saying, "He has become so utterly hateful to his people, Israel, that he will be my servant forever."

CHAPTER 28

1 In those days the Philistines gathered together their armies to fight against Israel. Achish said to David, "Know that you and your men are to go out to battle with me." 2 David said to Achish, "Then you will know for sure what your servant can do." Achish said to David, "You will, therefore, be my bodyguard from now on."

3 Samuel was dead, and all of Israel had mourned for him and had buried him in Ramah, his own city. Saul had expelled mediums and wizards from out of the land.[c] 4 The Philistines assembled together and went and camped at Shunem. Saul gathered together all of Israel and they camped at Gilboa. 5 * When Saul saw the Philistine army, he was afraid, and his heart trembled. 6 Saul inquired of the LORD, but the LORD did not answer him in dreams, or by the Urim, or through the prophets.[d]

Saul and the Medium. 7 Saul said to his servants, "Find me a woman who is a medium so that I can go to her and inquire of her." His servants answered, "There is a woman who is a medium in Endor."[e] 8 Saul disguised himself, putting on other clothes. He went with two men, and they came to the woman by night. He said, "Please consult a spirit for me, bring up the one whose name I give you." 9 But the woman said to him, "You surely know what Saul has done, how he has expelled mediums and wizards out of the land. Why would you set a trap for my life, bringing on my death?" 10 Saul swore an oath to her by the LORD saying, "As the LORD lives, you will not be punished for this." 11 The woman asked, "Whom shall I bring up for you," and he answered, "Bring up Samuel for me."

Samuel Appears. 12 When the woman saw Samuel, she cried out in a loud voice, and the woman said to Saul, "Why have you deceived me, Saul?" 13 The king said to her, "Do not be afraid! What did you see?" She said to Saul, "I saw a spirit coming up from the earth." 14 He said to her, "What does he look like?" She said, "An old man wearing a robe came up." Saul realized that it was

y 1 Sam 21:11-16; 1 Ki 2:39.—z 1 Sam 30:1.—a 1 Sam 29:3.—b 1 Sam 30:14, 29; Num 24:21; 1 Chr 2:9, 25, 42.—c 1 Sam 25:1; Sir 46:20.—d 1 Sam 14:37, 41; Ex 28:30; Lev 8:8.—e Lev 19:31; 20:27; Deut 18:10ff; 1 Chr 10:13ff; Acts 16:16.

27:1—31:13 The text from here to the end of the Book is clearly divided into two sections. The first relates David's difficult situation that forces him into exile among the Philistines. The second contrasts Saul's situation: he is mastered by fear; God abandons him.

27:10-12 David's deception seems warranted considering Achish is not a friend to Israel, and David needs someplace to hide from Saul.

28:5ff Saul is so unnerved by the approach of the Philistine army and so removed from the guidance of the Lord, that he resorts to the occult for direction, going against his own prohibition.

Samuel, and he bowed down and prostrated his face to the ground.

[15] Samuel said to Saul, "Why have you bothered me by bringing me up?" Saul answered, "I am in great distress. The Philistines are fighting against me, and God has turned against me. He does not answer me anymore, either by prophets or by dreams. I have called upon you so that you can make known to me what I should do." [16] Samuel said, "Why do you question me now that the LORD has turned against you and has become your enemy?[f] [17] The LORD has done for himself exactly what he predicted through me. The LORD has ripped the kingdom out of your hand, and he has given it to your neighbor, to David. [18] You did not heed the voice of the LORD nor enact his fierce rage against Amalek. Therefore, the LORD has done this thing to you today.[g] [19] The LORD will hand over both you and Israel into the hands of the Philistines. Tomorrow you and your sons will be with me. The LORD will also deliver the army of Israel into the hands of the Philistines."[h]

The Medium Feeds Saul. [20] Saul fell full length upon the ground for he was terrified because of what Samuel had said. His strength was gone, for he had not eaten anything all day and night. [21] When the woman came up to Saul and saw that he was greatly troubled, she said to him, "Look, your handmaid has obeyed your command. I have taken my life in my hands when I did what you had ordered me to do. [22] Therefore, please heed the voice of your handmaid. Let me give you something to eat, and then you will have the strength to go on your way."[i] [23] * He refused and said, "I will not eat!"

But both his servants and the woman kept urging him, and he finally listened to them. He got up off the ground and sat on the couch. [24] The woman had a fatted calf in the house, and she quickly killed it. She took some flour, kneaded it, and baked it into loaves of unleavened bread. [25] She set it before Saul and his servants. They ate, and then they got up and went on their way that night.

CHAPTER 29

The Philistines Reject David. [1] The Philistines gathered all of their forces together at Aphek. The Israelites camped by the spring in Jezreel.[j] [2] The lords of the Philistines were marching along with their units of hundreds and thousands while David and his men were marching at the rear with Achish.

[3] The lords of the Philistines said, "What about these Hebrews?" Achish replied to the lords of the Philistines, "Is this not David, a servant of Saul, the king of the Israel? He has been with me these days, these years. I have found no fault in him since he came to me up until the present."[k]

[4] The lords of the Philistines were angry with him, and the lords of the Philistines said to him, "Send that man back, let him go back to the place where you have assigned him. Do not let him go into battle with us, lest he turn against us during the battle. What other way could he reconcile to his master if not with the heads of these men?[l] [5] Is this not the David of whom they sang while they were dancing, 'Saul has killed his thousands, and David has killed his ten thousands.' "

[6] So Achish summoned David and said, "As the LORD lives, you have been upright with me. You have done well in your going out and your coming back with your army. From the day you came to me up to the present, I have found nothing wrong in you. Nevertheless, the lords do not approve of you. [7] Therefore, go back, and leave in peace, so that you not displease the lords of the Philistines."

[8] David said to Achish, "But what have I done? As long as I have been with you, up until now, have you found anything in your servant that would explain why I am not able to go to fight against the enemies of my lord, the king?" [9] Achish answered David, "I consider you to be as good as an angel of God. Nevertheless, the lords of the Philistines have said, 'He will not go up with us into battle.' [10] Now, therefore, rise up early in the morning with your master's servants who have come with you. Get up at daybreak and depart."[m]

[11] David and his men arose in the morning, and they left for the land of the Philistines, and the Philistines went up to Jezreel.

f 1 Sam 15:27f; 2 Chr 12:5; Mt 19:17.—g 1 Sam 15:18f, 26; Deut 25:19.—h 1 Sam 31:2-6; Sir 46:20.—i Gen 18:5; 23:13.—j 1 Sam 4:1.—k 1 Sam 27:7.—l 1 Sam 29:9; 1 Chr 12:19f.—m 1 Chr 12:22.

28:23ff Saul could no longer hide from the terrible indictment against him. God's rejection has plummeted him into an abyss of despair, and he must be forced to eat.

CHAPTER 30

Ziklag Destroyed. 1 Three days later David and his men arrived in Ziklag. The Amalekites had invaded the Negeb and Ziklag; Ziklag was attacked and burned down.[n] 2 The women who were there, young and old, were taken captive. They did not kill any of them, but they carried them off and went on their way.

3 When David and his men arrived in Ziklag, they found it burned to the ground and their wives and their sons and their daughters had been taken captive. 4 David and his men with him wept out loud until they had no more strength to weep. 5 David's two wives, Ahinoam, the Jezreelite, and Abigail, the wife of Nabal of Carmel were also taken captive.[o]

6 David was greatly distressed because the people were talking about stoning him. Every single one of them was embittered because of his sons and his daughters, but David found strength in the LORD, his God.

7[p] David said to Abiathar the priest, the son of Ahimelech, "Bring the ephod out here." Abiathar brought the ephod out to David.* 8 David inquired of the LORD saying, "Shall I pursue after this raiding party? Will I overtake them?" He answered him, "Pursue, for you are sure to overtake them and succeed in the rescue."

David Pursues the Amalekites. 9 David and the six hundred men who were with him left and arrived at the Wadi Besor where some stayed behind, 10 for two hundred men stayed behind who were too exhausted to continue on over the Wadi Besor. David continued the pursuit with four hundred men.

11 They found an Egyptian in a field and they brought him to David. They gave him bread to eat and water to drink 12 as well as a piece of fig cake and two raisin cakes. When he had eaten, he revived, for he had not had anything to eat or any water to drink for three days and three nights. 13 David asked him, "To whom do you belong? Where are you from?" The young man answered, "Egypt. I am a slave to an Amalekite. My master abandoned me because I became sick three days ago. 14 We raided the south of the Cherethites, and the territory of Judah, and the south of Caleb, and we burned down Ziklag."[q] 15 David said to him, "Can you lead me to this raiding party?" He answered, "Swear to me by God that you will not kill me or hand me over to my master, and I will take you down to them."

16 He took him down, and they were scattered all over the countryside, eating, drinking, and dancing to celebrate the great plunder they had taken from the land of the Philistines and the land of Judah. 17 David fought them from dusk of that day until the next evening. None of them escaped except for four hundred young men who mounted their camels and fled away.[r]

18 David recovered everything that the Amalekites had carried away, and David rescued his two wives. 19 Nothing was missing, not young nor old, not sons nor daughters, not plunder nor anything that they had taken. David recovered it all. 20 David drove all of the flocks and herds before the livestock saying, "This is David's plunder."

Division of the Spoils. 21 David came to the two hundred men who were so weary that they could not follow and whom David had left behind at the Wadi Besor. They came out to meet David and the people who were with him. As David and the people drew near, he greeted them. 22 All of those who had gone with David but who were wicked men of Belial said, "None of them went with us, so we should not give them any of the spoil. Each of them can take his wife and children and depart." 23 David replied, "No, my brothers. You must not do that with what the LORD has given us. The LORD protected us and delivered over into our hands the raiding party that came out against us. 24 Who will listen to what you are saying? The share of the man who went down into battle will be the same as the share of the man who stayed with the supplies. They will be equal shares."[s] 25 He made this a statute and an ordinance in Israel from that day up until the present.[t]

26 When David arrived in Ziklag, he sent some of the spoils to the elders of Judah* who were his friends saying, "Behold, this is a gift from the spoils of the enemies of the

n 1 Sam 27:6, 10; Jos 8:19; 1 Chr 12:21.—o 1 Sam 27:3; 30:5; 2 Sam 2:2; 3:3.—p 7f: 1 Sam 2:28; 23:6; Ex 28:30; 1 Ki 1:42; 2:26.—q 1 Sam 27:10; 1 Ki 1:38; Ezek 25:16.—r 1 Sam 15:3; Jos 6:17; Jdg 7:12.—s 1 Sam 17:22; 25:13.—t Gen 47:26; Num 31:27.

30:7 David needed direction from God, but he did not have access to the tabernacle that was in Saul's territory. The ephod he requested might have contained the Urim and Thummim.

30:26 *The elders of Judah:* David is already exhibiting leadership qualities by making this positive gesture to the leaders of Judah, thereby, enhancing his position as the next king.

LORD." 27 He sent it to those who were in Bethel, to those who were in Ramoth-negeb, to those who were in Jattir, 28 to those who were in Aroer, to those who were in Siphmoth, to those who were in Eshtemoa, 29 to those who were in Rachal, to those who were in the cities of the Jerahmeelites, to those who were in the cities of the Kenites, [u] 30 to those who were in Hormah, to those who were in Borashan, to those who were in Athach, 31 to those who were in Hebron, and to those who were in all those places where David had roamed.

CHAPTER 31*

The Death of Saul. 1 Now the Philistines fought against Israel, and the Israelites fled before the Philistines, and many were killed at Mount Gilboa. 2 The Philistines pressed hard upon Saul and his sons. His sons, Jonathan, Abinadab, and Malchishua were killed by the Philistines. [v]

3 There was fierce fighting around Saul, and when the archers found their mark, they seriously wounded him. 4 Saul said to his armor-bearer, "Draw your sword and thrust it through me, lest these uncircumcised come and thrust me through and abuse me." But the armor-bearer would not do this for he was terrified. Saul, therefore, took his sword and fell upon it. [w] 5 When his armor-bearer saw that Saul was dead, he, too, fell upon his sword and died with him. [x]

6 So Saul and his three sons and his armor-bearer and all of his men died together on the same day. 7 When the Israelites on the other side of the valley and those on the other side of the Jordan saw that the Israelites had fled and that Saul and his sons were dead, they abandoned the cities, and the Philistines came and occupied them.

8 The next day the Philistines came out to strip the dead, and they found Saul and his three sons fallen on Mount Gilboa. 9 They cut off his head and stripped off his armor. They sent messengers throughout the land of the Philistines to proclaim the news in the temples of their idols and among the people. [y] 10 They put his armor in the temple of Astartes, and they fastened his body to the wall in Beth-shan.

Saul Is Buried.* 11 [z] When those living in Jabesh-gilead heard what the Philistines had done to Saul, 12 all of their brave men traveled during the night and took down the bodies of Saul and his sons from the wall of Beth-shan. They went to Jabesh where they cremated them. 13 They took their bones and they buried them under a tree in Jabesh, and they fasted for seven days. *

u 1 Sam 27:10; Jdg 1:16.—v 1 Sam 14:49; 28:19; 1 Chr 10:2f.—w Jdg 9:54; 1 Chr 10:4.—x 1 Sam 26:9; 2 Mac 14:42; Rom 6:8.—y 1 Sam 17:4, 54; 2 Sam 1:20; 1 Chr 10:9.—z 11ff: 1 Sam 11:1-11; Jdg 21:12; 2 Sam 2:4-7; 1 Chr 10:11.

31:1-13 2 Sam 1:5-10 gives a slightly different version.

31:11-13 Saul had rescued Jabesh (1 Sam 11:1-11). Cremation was forbidden, but is justified here because the decomposition of the corpses was far advanced. This is the only instance of cremation in the Bible.

31:13 The death of Saul exposed a bitter truth to the people, who believed that a king would bring them power and prestige. They now knew that having a bad king was far worse than having no king.

THE SECOND BOOK OF SAMUEL

Establishing a Kingdom for God

David, taken from his father's flocks, becomes the Lord's Anointed, the king of all Israel. He is a man endowed with all the natural gifts; he loves his people, his wives, his children; he retains a simplicity in his way of life. His reign leaves a decisive mark on the religious and political future of Israel. Himself an able politician and a matchless warrior, he wins the permanent freedom of his people from the Philistine yoke, and turns them into a sovereign nation as he united Judah and Israel under his rule. This unity will, however, be broken as early as the time of his second successor and will thenceforth be an abiding nostalgic ideal.

Amid the conflicts that accompany his attainment of power and amid the intrigues of those who aspire to succeed him, David, a deeply religious man, retains a simplicity of heart that pleases God. In every circumstance he recognizes God at work, and he struggles unceasingly to remain faithful to the Lord and to the mission which the Lord gives to his people. To understand David's extraordinary personality and also his limitations, we must take into account the customs and civilization of the time; in any case, his many examples of virtue have permanent value, and the Books of Kings will constantly refer to him as the prototype of the king who is a faithful servant of Yahweh. As far as the house of David is concerned, the entire story from this point on, as told here and in the Books of Kings, is paralleled and supplemented by the two Books of Chronicles.

The Second Book of Samuel may be divided as follows:

I: The Reign of David (2:8—20:26)
II: Appendices (21:1—24:25)

CHAPTER 1

The Report of Saul's Death. 1 Shortly after the death of Saul, David returned from defeating the Amalekites, and he stayed for two days in Ziklag.[a] 2 On the third day a man appeared from Saul's camp, with his clothes in tatters and dirt on his head. Upon coming into David's presence, he fell to the ground and paid him homage.

3 David asked him: "Where have you come from?" And he replied: "I have escaped from the Israelite camp." 4 David then inquired: "What has happened there? Tell me!" The man answered: "The soldiers fled from the battle, but many of them fell and died. Saul and his son Jonathan are also dead."

5 David then asked the young man who had brought the news: "How do you know that Saul and his son Jonathan are dead?" 6 [b] The young man replied: "By chance I happened to be on Mount Gilboa, and I beheld Saul leaning on his spear as the chariots and the horsemen were closing in on him. 7 When he happened to turn around and saw me, he summoned me to him. I said: 'Here I am.' 8 Saul then said to me: 'Who are you?' And I told him: 'I am an Amalekite.'[c] 9 Then he gave me this order: 'Come here, stand over me, and kill me. The throes of death have overcome me, yet I am still alive.'

10 "Therefore, I stood over him and slew him, for I knew that he could not possibly survive because of the wounds he had suffered. Then I removed the crown that was on his head and the armlet from his arm, and I have brought them here to you, my lord."

11 * Then David took hold of his clothes and tore them, and the men who were with him did the same.[d] 12 They mourned and wept, and they fasted until evening for Saul and his son Jonathan, as well as for the army of the LORD and the house of Israel, because they had fallen by the sword.

13 David then said to the young man who had brought him the report: "Where do you come from?" He answered: "I am the son of a resident alien, an Amalekite."[e] 14 David thereupon asked him: "How was it that you were not afraid to lift your hand to destroy the LORD's anointed?"[f]

15 Then David summoned one of his young soldiers and gave him this order: "Come here and strike him down!" The young man struck him down, and he died. 16 As he fell, David said to him: "Your blood be on your own head. You convicted yourself by your own testimony when you said: 'I killed the LORD's anointed.'"

Elegy for Saul and Jonathan. 17 David chanted the following lament over Saul and his son Jonathan, 18 and he ordered that this dirge over them be taught to the people of Judah. It is recorded in the Book of Jashar.[g]

19* "Your glory, O Israel, lies slain upon your heights.
How the mighty have fallen!
20 "Do not mention it in Gath
or proclaim it in the streets of Ashkelon.
Let not the daughters of the Philistines rejoice

a 1 Sam 30:17-20; 31:1-13; 1 Chr 12:1.—b 6-10: 2 Sam 4:10; 1 Sam 18:11; 31:1-4; 1 Chr 10:1-4, 8.—c Num 24:20; 1 Sam 30:13.—d 2 Sam 13:31; Jdg 11:35.—e Gen 29:4.—f 1 Sam 10:1; 24:7; Ps 105:15.—g Jos 10:13.

1:11-12 Despite King Saul's vindictive behavior toward David, upon hearing about the death of Saul and his friend Jonathan, David and his men showed their respect and sadness by fasting and mourning. David will be rewarded for his patient submission to God's will.

1:19-27 Here again we see the immense generosity of spirit that David displayed in spite of his struggles with Saul. A gifted musician, he composed a stirring song, known as "The Song of the Bow," for the king and his son.

and the daughters of the uncircumcised exult.[h]

21 "You mountains of Gilboa,
may no dew or rain fall upon you,
and may your fields not bring forth grain.
For there the shields of the warriors were tarnished,
and the shield of Saul is no longer anointed with oil.[i]

22 "From the blood of the slain,
from the flesh of the valiant,
The bow of Jonathan did not turn back,
nor did the sword of Saul return unbloodied.[j]

23 "Saul and Jonathan:
in life they were beloved and kind;
in death they were not separated.
They were swifter than eagles
and stronger than lions.

24 "O daughters of Israel, weep for Saul
who clothed you in scarlet and fine embroidery,
and who beautified your apparel with ornaments of gold.

25 "How the mighty have fallen in battle!
Jonathan lies slain upon your heights.

26 "I grieve for you, Jonathan my brother.
To me you were greatly beloved.
Your love for me was more wonderful
than the love of a woman.[k]

27 "The warriors have fallen,
and their weapons have been abandoned!"

CHAPTER 2

David Is Anointed King.* 1 After this, David
inquired of the LORD, asking: "Shall I go up
into one of the towns of Judah?" The LORD
replied to him: "Go up." Then David asked:
"To which one stall I go?" The LORD answered: "Hebron."

2 Therefore, David went up to Hebron with
his two wives, Ahinoam of Jezreel, and
Abigail, the widow of Nabal of Carmel.[l]
3 David also brought up the men who were
with him, along with their families, and they
settled in the towns of Hebron. Then the men
of Judah came to Hebron, and there they
anointed David as king of the house of
Judah.

4 When David received a report that the
men of Jabesh-gilead were the ones who had
buried Saul,[m] 5 he sent messengers to the
people of Jabesh-gilead to say to them: "May
you be blessed by the LORD for having done
this act of kindness to your lord Saul by
burying him. 6 Now may the LORD bestow his
love and faithfulness upon you. Moreover, I
too will treat you with kindness because you
have done this charitable deed. 7 Therefore,
have courage and be valiant, for even though
your lord, Saul, is dead, the house of Judah
has anointed me as their king."

I: THE REIGN OF DAVID

Ishbaal as King of Israel.* 8 Meanwhile the
commander of Saul's army, Abner, the son
of Ner, had taken Ishbaal, the son of Saul,
and brought him over to Mahanaim.[n]
9 There he made him king over Gilead, the
Ashurites, Jezreel, Ephraim, Benjamin, and
all Israel. 10 Ishbaal, the son of Saul, was forty
years old when he became king over Israel,
and he reigned for two years. However, the
house of Judah followed David. 11 The length
of time that David was in Hebron as king of
the house of Judah was seven years and six
months.[o]

Combat near Gibeon. 12 Abner, the son of
Ner, departed from Mahanaim with the servants of Ishbaal and went to Gibeon. 13 Joab,
the son of Zeruiah, also set forth with
David's servants and encountered them at
the pool of Gibeon. One group sat down on
one side of the pool, while the other group
sat on the opposite side.[p]

14 Then Abner suggested to Joab: "Let us
have the young men come forward and
engage in hand-to-hand combat before us."
Joab replied: "Let them come forward."
15 Therefore, they came forward and were
counted: twelve men from Benjamin for
Ishbaal, the son of Saul, and twelve of the
servants of David. 16 Each one grasped his
opponent by the head and thrust his sword
into his opponent's side. Thus they all fell

h Jdg 16:23; 1 Sam 6:17; 31:9; Mic 1:10.—i Gen 27:28.—j Deut 32:42; 1 Sam 14:47.—k 1 Sam 18:1; 20:17; 1 Mac 9:21.—l 1 Sam 25:42f; 30:5.—m 1 Sam 31:1ff; Jer 17:25.—n 1 Sam 14:50.—o 1 Ki 2:11; 1 Chr 3:4.—p 2 Sam 2:31; 1 Ki 1:7; 1 Chr 27:24.

2:1-7 The story seems to know nothing of the intervention of Samuel when he anointed the young David as king (1 Sam 16:13).

2:8-11 After King Saul's death the kingdom of Israel is split and Judah and Simeon align themselves with David. The remaining ten tribes are faithful to Saul's son Ishbaal. A lengthy war between the house of Saul and the house of David ensues.

down together. Therefore, that place, which is in Gibeon, was called the Field of Swords.

Death of Asahel. 17 On that day the battle was extremely fierce, and when it was finally over, Abner and the men of Israel were defeated by David's forces. 18 The three sons of Zeruiah were there—Joab, Abishai, and Asahel. Then Asahel, who was as fleet of foot as a wild gazelle,[q] 19 pursued Abner, turning neither to the left nor to the right as he followed him.

20 Abner looked back and said: "Is that you, Asahel?" He replied: "Yes, it is." 21 Abner then said to him: "Turn to your right or left, seize one of the young men, and take from him what is of value." However, Asahel had no intention of forsaking his pursuit.

22 Abner once again tried to dissuade him: "Cease your pursuit of me. Why should I strike you to the ground? How then could I look your brother Joab in the face?"[r] 23 Nevertheless Asahel refused to turn away. Therefore, Abner struck him in the stomach with the butt of his spear, and the spear protruded through his back. He fell there and died instantaneously.

All those who came to the place where Asahel had fallen and died came to a halt. 24 However, Joab and Abishai continued the pursuit of Abner until, as the sun was going down, they came to the hill of Ammah, which lies east of Giah on the road toward the wilderness of Gibeon.

Truce between Joab and Abner. 25 The Benjaminites rallied to the support of Abner, gathering in a tightly knit formation behind Abner and taking their stand at the top of a hill. 26 Then Abner called out to Joab: "Will this slaughter never end? Do you not realize how bitter the end will be? How long will it take before you order your people to cease from the pursuit of their brothers?"

27 Joab replied: "As God lives, if you had not spoken, the soldiers would not have relented in their pursuit of their brothers until morning." 28 Then Joab sounded the trumpet, and all the troops came to a halt. They abandoned their pursuit of the Israelites and did not engage in battle any further.

29 Abner and his men traveled all that night through the Arabah. Then they crossed the Jordan and continued their journey the entire morning until they came to Mahanaim.[s] 30 After returning from the pursuit of Abner, Joab gathered his people together and discovered that, aside from Asahel, nineteen other servants of David were missing. 31 However, the forces of David had killed three hundred and sixty Benjaminites, followers of Abner. 32 They took up Asahel and buried him in the tomb of his father at Bethlehem. Then Joab and his men marched throughout the night, and they reached Hebron at daybreak.

CHAPTER 3

1 A lengthy war ensued between the house of Saul and the house of David. As time went on, David grew steadily stronger, while the house of Saul became notably weaker.

Sons Born in Hebron.* 2 [t] Sons were born to David at Hebron. His firstborn was Amnon, whose mother was Ahinoam of Jezreel; 3 his second was Chileab, whose mother was Abigail, the widow of Nabal of Carmel; his third was Absalom, whose mother was Maacah, the daughter of Talmai, the king of Geshur;[u] 4 the fourth was Adonijah, whose mother was Haggith; the fifth was Shephatiah, the son of Abital;[v] 5 the sixth was Ithream, the son of David's wife Eglah. These were born to David in Hebron.

Ishbaal and Abner Quarrel. 6 During the war between the house of Saul and the house of David, Abner had gradually been gaining power in the house of Saul. 7 Now Saul had had a concubine whose name was Rizpah, the daughter of Aiah. And Ishbaal said to Abner: "Why have you slept with my father's concubine?"[w]

8 Abner became enraged at this insult of Ishbaal, and he said: "Am I nothing more than a dog's head in Judah? I have continued to be loyal to the house of your father Saul and to his brothers and friends, and I have not betrayed you into the hands of David. Yet now you charge me with a crime involving a woman.

9 "May God punish Abner severely, and inflict even greater ills, if I fail to accomplish

q Jdg 1:20; 1 Chr 2:16.—r 2 Sam 2:30; 3:16, 27f, 30; 1 Sam 17:57.—s Deut 2:8; 1 Sam 26:7.—t 2-5: 1 Sam 27:3; 1 Chr 3: 1-30; Zec 12:10.—u 2 Sam 13:37; 15:8.—v 1 Ki 1:5; 1 Chr 3:2.—w 2 Sam 21:8ff; Gen 22:24.

3:2-5 This list, which is completed further on (2 Sam 5:13-16), helps us identify the precise relationship of the personages in the stories that follow. The list names only the firstborn of each wife. Marital morality, which shows such progress in the later sapiential books, has not yet distanced itself from the pagan customs of the East.

for David what the LORD swore to him.[x] 10 I shall take the kingdom from the house of Saul and establish the throne of David over Israel and over Judah, from Dan to Beersheba."[y] 11 And Ishbaal did not dare to say another word in response, because he was afraid of him.

Abner and David Reconciled. 12 Abner sent messengers on his own behalf to say to David: "Who should control the land? If you come to an agreement with me, I will give you my support in bringing all Israel over to you." 13 * David replied: "Good! I will negotiate an agreement with you. However, I will impose one condition. You will not be allowed to appear in my presence unless you bring back Saul's daughter, Michal, when you come to see me."[z]

14 Then David also sent messengers to Ishbaal, the son of Saul, with this demand: "Return to me my wife Michal whom I espoused after paying the ransom of one hundred foreskins of the Philistines." 15 Therefore, Ishbaal summoned Michal and took her away from her husband Paltiel, the son of Laish.[a] 16 However, her husband, weeping copiously, followed her as far as Horonaim, at which time Abner commanded him: "Go back," and he returned home.

17 Abner then proceeded to confer with the elders of Israel. "For a long time now," he said, "you have wanted David to be your king. 18 Now is the time for you to make that wish a reality, for the LORD has said of David: 'By means of my servant David I will deliver my people Israel from the hand of the Philistines and from all their enemies.' " 19 Abner also spoke personally to the Benjaminites. After that he went to Hebron to notify David about everything that the people of Israel and the house of Benjamin had agreed to do.

20 When Abner, accompanied by twenty men, came to David at Hebron, David prepared a feast for Abner and the men who were with him. 21 Abner then said to David: "Allow me now to go and assemble all Israel for my lord the king, in order that they may make a covenant with you, and thus you will reign over all that your heart desires." Therefore, David dismissed Abner, who went away in peace.[b]

The Death of Abner. 22 Just then, David's men returned with Joab from a raid, bringing with them a large amount of plunder. By then Abner had been dismissed by David and was no longer in Hebron, for he had gone his way in peace. 23 When Joab and all of the soldiers with him arrived, Joab was informed that Abner, the son of Ner, had come to the king, and that the king had sent him on his way in peace.

24 Then Joab went to the king and said: "What have you done? Abner came to you. What motivated you to dismiss him and allow him to go away as an innocent man? 25 You must be aware that Abner, the son of Ner, came here with the purpose of deceiving you, in order to learn about your movements and to find out what you are doing."

26 When Joab left David's presence, he sent messengers to pursue Abner, and they brought him back from the cistern of Sirah. However, David knew nothing at all about this. 27 When Abner returned to Hebron, Joab pretended that he wanted to speak to him privately and took him aside at the city gate, where he stabbed him fatally in the stomach. Thus Abner died in retaliation for the murder of Asahel, the brother of Joab.[c]

28 Later, when David heard the news, he said: "Before the LORD, I and my kingdom are forever innocent of the blood of Abner, the son of Ner.[d] 29 May the guilt for this act fall on the head of Joab and his entire family. May the house of Joab never be unafflicted by men who suffer from running sores or leprosy or effeminacy or who are doomed to die by the sword or are in need of bread."[e] (30 Joel and his brother Abishai had murdered Abner because he had killed their brother Asahel at the battle of Gibeon.)

David Mourns Abner. 31 Then David said to Joab and all the people who were with him: "Tear off your clothes, put on sackcloth, and mourn over Abner." King David himself walked behind the bier.[f] 32 After they buried Abner at Hebron, the king wept aloud at the grave of Abner, and all the people also wept. 33 Then the king sang this lament for Abner:

x Ru 1:17; 1 Ki 2:32.—y 1 Sam 25:30; Jer 22:2.—z 1 Sam 18:20-27.—a Num 34:26; 1 Sam 25:43-44; 1 Chr 11:11.—b 2 Sam 2:14; 5:3.—c 1 Sam 18:22.—d 2 Sam 2:22f; Jn 18:36.—e Num 5:2.—f 2 Sam 21:10; 2 Ki 19:1.

3:13-15 The intricacies of forging alliances are apparent in David's diplomatic and shrewd plan to reunite all Israel and to win back his wife Michal.

"Why should Abner have died
the way a lawless brute dies?
34 Your hands were not bound,
your feet were not fettered
As one falls at the hands of the wicked,
you too have fallen."
And all the people continued to weep for
him.
35 After that, the people tried to persuade
David to eat something while it was still day,
but David swore: "May God deal with me
severely, and even more terribly, if I eat
bread or anything else prior to sunset."[g]
36 All the people took note of his pledge with
approval, just as everything that the king did
truly pleased them. 37 Therefore, on that day
the people and all Israel were fully convinced
that the king had no part in the killing of
Abner, the son of Ner.
38 Then the king said to his servants: "You
surely must realize that a prince and a great
warrior has fallen this day in Israel. 39 And
today, even though I have been anointed as
the king, I feel weak and powerless with the
realization that these men, the sons of
Zeruiah, are too strong for me. May the
LORD repay the evildoer as his evil crimes
deserve."[h]

CHAPTER 4

The Death of Ishbaal. 1 When Saul's son
Ishbaal heard that Abner had died at
Hebron, his courage failed him, and all Israel
was alarmed. 2 Ishbaal had two men who
served as captains of raiding parties; one
was named Baanah, and the other was
named Rechab. They were the sons of
Rimmon, a Benjaminite from Beeroth—for
Beeroth is regarded as being part of
Benjamin.[i] 3 The people of Beeroth had fled
to Gittaim, where they have remained as
aliens to this very day.[j]
4 Jonathan, the son of Saul, had a son
whose feet were crippled. He was five years
old when the news about Saul and Jonathan
came from Jezreel. His nurse picked him up
and fled, but in her haste to get away, the
young boy fell to the ground and became
lame. His name was Meribbaal. *[k]
5 The sons of Rimmon of Beeroth, Rechab
and Baanah, arrived at the house of Ishbaal
during the hottest part of the day while he
was taking his midday rest. 6 The woman
who was stationed at the door had fallen
asleep while she was sifting wheat. 7 There-
fore, Rechab and his brother quietly slipped
past her and entered the house, and when
they found him asleep on the couch in his
bedroom, they attacked and killed him and
cut off his head. Then they took his head and
traveled throughout the night by way of the
Arabah.
The Murder Avenged.* 8 When they arrived
in Hebron, they brought the head of Ishbaal
to David and said to the king: "Here is the
head of Ishbaal, the son of Saul, your enemy,
who sought your life. Thus has the LORD this
day avenged my lord the king on Saul and
his offspring."[l]
9 Then David replied to Rechab and his
brother Baanah, the sons of Rimmon the
Beerothite: "As the LORD lives, he who has
delivered me from every danger, 10 in Ziklag
I seized and ordered to be killed the man
who brought me word that Saul was dead.
That was how I rewarded him.[m] 11 How
much more then should I take such action
when wicked men have slain an innocent
man as he was lying on his bed in his house.
Should I not now exact vengeance on you for
shedding his blood and remove you from the
face of the earth?"
12 Therefore, at David's command, his
young soldiers killed them. Then they cut off
their hands and feet and hung their bodies
beside the pool at Hebron. However, they
took the head of Ishbaal and buried it in
Abner's grave at Hebron.[n]

CHAPTER 5

David as King of Israel. 1 *[o] Then all the
tribes of Israel came to David at Hebron and
said: "Listen to us. We are your own flesh and
blood. 2 In former days, when Saul was our

g Ru 1:17; 1 Ki 2:23.—h Ps 28:4; Wis 14:9; Isa 3:11.—i Jos 9:17f; Rom 11:1.—j Lev 18:26; Jos 18:25; Neh 11:33.—k 2 Sam 9:3; 19:25; 21:7.—l 1 Sam 24:5; 1 Chr 11:3; 12:24; Mk 6:28.—m 2 Sam 1:1, 6-10, 14, 16.—n Deut 21:22f; 1 Sam 31:10.—o 1ff: 2 Sam 19:13; 1 Sam 9:21; 1 Chr 11:1ff.

4:4 *Meribbaal*: in Hebrew Mephibosheth (see ch. 9).

4:8-12 As in the case of the messenger announcing Saul's death (2 Sam 1:1-16), David is not won over by Rechab and Baanah's murder of his rival Ishbaal. David's sense of justice demands severe punishment and dishonor for them while Ishbaal's remains are treated with respect.

5:1-12 Jerusalem, which had not belonged to either Judah or Israel, will be the sign of the nation's political unity and, quite soon, of its religious unity as well; it will be the symbol of God's presence in the midst of humanity. Both the Jewish and, later, the Christian traditions will meditate deeply on the mystery of Jerusalem; the Church will be seen as the new Jerusalem (Gal 4:26; Heb 12:22), the Jerusalem of the last times, which in turn prepares the way for the "Jerusalem that is to come" (see Rev 21).

king, you were the one who led the Israelites on their campaigns and brought them back. Moreover, the LORD said to you: 'You shall be the shepherd of my people Israel and be the ruler of Israel.' "[p] 3 Then all the elders of Israel came to David, the king of Hebron, and David made a covenant with them there before the LORD. After this they anointed David as king of Israel.[q]

4 David was thirty years old when he began to reign, and he reigned for forty years. 5 In Hebron he reigned over Judah for seven years and six months, and then in Jerusalem he reigned over all Israel and Judah for thirty-three years.[r]

Capture of Zion. 6 Then the king and his men marched to Jerusalem to attack the Jebusites who inhabited the land. These people said to David: "You will never come in here. Even the blind and the lame will stop you in your tracks." In this way they showed their contempt for David and his forces.[s]

7 *Despite their boast, David did take the stronghold of Zion, which is now known as the City of David. 8 David had said on that day: "All those who are eager to attack the Jebusites must scale the water shaft to attack the lame and the blind, the bitter enemies of David." Therefore, it is said: "The blind and the lame shall not enter the palace."[t]

9 David then took up residence in the stronghold and called it the City of David. After that, he constructed a wall around it from the Millo* inward.[u] 10 David steadily continued to grow more powerful, for the LORD, the God of hosts, was with him.[v]

11 [w] King Hiram of Tyre sent envoys to David with cedar wood, and he also supplied carpenters and stonemasons who built a palace for David. 12 Then David had no doubt at all that the LORD had established him as king of Israel and that he had exalted his kingdom for the sake of his people Israel.

David's Family in Jerusalem. 13 [x] After he departed from Hebron, David took more concubines and wives in Jerusalem, and more sons and daughters were born to him.* 14 These are the names of those children who were born to him in Jerusalem: Shammua, Shobab, Nathan, Solomon, 15 Ibhar, Elishua, Nepheg, Japhia, 16 Elishama, Eliada, and Eliphelet.

Rout of the Philistines.* 17 When the Philistines heard that David had been anointed king of Israel, they all went forth in search of him. When David learned of this, he sought refuge in the stronghold. 18 After the Philistines arrived and deployed their forces in the valley of Rephaim, 19 David inquired of the LORD: "Shall I go forth and attack the Philistines? Will you deliver them into my power?" The LORD replied to David: "Go forth and attack them! I shall deliver the Philistines into your hands."[y]

20 Therefore, David went forth to Baal-perazim and defeated them there. Then he said: "The LORD has broken through the battle lines of my enemies as though they had been breached by the flood waters of a river." That is why that place is called Baal-perazim. 21 The Philistines abandoned their idols there, and David and his men carried them away.[z]

22 However, the Philistines made another invasion and spread out in the Valley of Rephaim. 23 Then David once again consulted the LORD, who said: "Do not attack them from the front. Rather, encircle them from the rear and attack them in front of the balsam trees. 24 When you hear the sound of marching in the top of the balsam trees, advance immediately, for then you will know that the LORD has gone forth ahead of you to strike down the army of the Philistines."

25 David followed the instructions of the LORD, and he routed the Philistines from Gibeon all the way to Gezer.

CHAPTER 6

The Ark Brought to Jerusalem. 1 David again gathered all the chosen men of Israel, thirty thousand in all. 2 Then he set forth with his entire force to Baalah of Judah to bring up from there the Ark of God, which bears the

p Ex 6:13; Deut 17:15; 1 Sam 18:16.—q 1 Ki 1:45.—r 2 Sam 2:11; 1 Ki 2:11; 1 Chr 3:4.—s Jos 15:63; Jdg 1:19, 21; Isa 29:3.—t Lev 21:18; Mt 21:14f.—u 1 Ki 3:1; 9:24; 11:27.—v 1 Chr 11:9; Pss 78:70ff; 132:13; Lk 1:66.—w 11-25: 1 Chr 14:1-16; Tob 1:4.—x 13-16: 1 Chr 3:5-8; 14:3-7.—y 1 Sam 23:4.—z 1 Chr 14:12.

5:7-9 *Stronghold of Zion:* the name "Zion" continued in use and was extended to include the entire hill on which the temple would later be built (see 2 Sam 24:15-25; 2 Chr 3:1).

5:9 *Millo:* a supporting terrace or embankment, the precise form of which we do not know, formed the southern extremity of the City of David (see 1 Ki 9:15; 2 Chr 32:5).

5:13 David's love for God seems to have been matched by his love for women. Unfortunately, his many children later caused many problems for him and for Israel.

5:17-25 David had somewhat of an unholy alliance with the Philistines who turned against him when he was intent on uniting Israel. David's reliance on the Lord and obedience in following his instructions in attacking the Philistines was rewarded once again.

name of the LORD of hosts who is enthroned
above the cherubim. [a]

3 They placed the Ark of God on a new cart
and brought it forth from the house of
Abinadab, which stood on the hill. Uzzah
and Ahio, the sons of Abinadab, were guiding
the new cart. [b] 4 Uzzah walked alongside the
Ark of God, with Ahio walking in front.
5 David and the entire house of Israel danced
joyfully before the LORD with all their might,
singing to the accompaniment of lyres,
harps, tambourines, castanets, and cym-
bals. [c]

6 When they arrived at the threshing floor
of Nacon, Uzzah reached out his hand to the
Ark of God and steadied it because the oxen
were stumbling. 7 This aroused the LORD's
anger against Uzzah because of his irrever-
ent act, and he died there beside the Ark of
God. [d] 8 David became greatly upset because
the LORD had vented his anger against
Uzzah, and to this very day that place is
called Perez-uzzah.

9 David greatly feared the LORD that day,
and he said: "How can the Ark of the LORD
be placed in my care?" 10 Therefore, he de-
cided not to take the Ark of the LORD to be in
his care in the City of David. Instead he took
it to the house of Obed-edom the Gittite. [e]
11 The Ark of the LORD remained in the
house of Obed-edom the Gittite for three
months, and the LORD blessed Obed-edom
and his entire household. [f]

12 [g] When King David was informed that
the LORD had blessed the family of Obed-
edom and everything that belonged to him
because of the Ark of God, David went and
brought up the Ark of God from the house of
Obed-edom to the City of David amid great
rejoicing.

13 When the bearers of the Ark of the LORD
had advanced six steps, David sacrificed an
ox and a fattened calf. 14 * Then, girded with a
linen ephod, he danced before the LORD with
all his might, [h] 15 as he and all the Israelites
brought up the Ark of the LORD with shouts of
joy and the blowing of trumpets.

16 As the Ark of the LORD entered the City
of David, Michal, the daughter of Saul,
watched from a window. When she saw King
David leaping and whirling around before
the LORD, she despised him in her heart.

17 [i] They brought in the Ark of the LORD
and set it in its place inside the tent that
David had erected for it. Then David offered
burnt offerings and peace offerings in the
name of the LORD of hosts. 18 When he had
finished making these offerings, he blessed
the people in the name of the LORD of hosts.
19 Then he distributed food to all of the peo-
ple, both men and women, giving to each
person in the multitude a loaf of bread, a
portion of meat, and a raisin cake. Then all
the people returned to their homes.

20 When David returned to bless his house-
hold, Michal, the daughter of Saul, came out
to meet him. She said: "What an exhibition
the king of Israel has made of himself today,
exposing himself in the view of the slave girls
of his followers like any vulgarian who choos-
es to shamelessly expose himself before
them!" * [j]

21 David replied to Michal: "I was dancing
in gratitude for the LORD, not for them. The
LORD chose me instead of your father and
his entire family and appointed me as leader
over Israel, the people of the LORD. I shall
continue to dance before the LORD in grati-
tude, [k] 22 and I will demean myself even
more. I will be lowly in your esteem, but I
will be held in honor by those slave girls of
whom you speak."

23 Saul's daughter Michal had no children
to the day of her death.

CHAPTER 7

David's Concern for the Ark. 1 * When King
David was settled in his palace and the LORD
had granted him rest from all his enemies
surrounding him, [l] 2 he said to the prophet

---

a Ex 25:10; Jos 15:9; 1 Ki 2:26; Ps 132:8ff.—b 1 Sam 4:3f; 6:7f; 7:1; Dan 3:55.—c 2 Chr 29:25; Ezr 3:10; Pss 68:25f; 150:3-5.—d Deut 3:26; 1 Chr 13:11.—e 1 Chr 13:13.—f 2 Sam 6:10; Gen 39:5; 1 Chr 26:4.—g 12-23: 1 Ki 8:1; 1 Chr 15:1-29; Ps 24:7-10.—h 1 Sam 2:18.—i 17ff: Lev 1:1-17; 3:1-17; 1 Chr 16:1ff.—j 1 Sam 18:20; 1 Chr 16:43; Tob 14:9.—k Deut 27:7; 1 Sam 13:14; 15:28.—l 1 Ki 5:4; Sir 47:13.

6:14-15 Amid great pomp and circumstance and wearing a priestly vestment, King David leads the procession that would return the Ark to Jerusalem.

6:20 Saul's daughter Michal considers King David's exuberant display of joy undignified, but it does not dissuade him from his unbridled happiness and choice to freely praise God without restraint or fear of judgment.

7:1-16 David wants to build a "house," a temple, for the Lord, but the Lord turns things around: he promises that he will build a "house" for David, that is, that he will keep David's descendants forever on the throne of Israel; this marks the climax of the story of David. It is also one of the most important passages of the Bible: generation after generation, Israel will read and reread it (see Pss 89; 132); gradually its faith will glimpse the image of the "Son of David," the Messiah (Anointed One), who will save Israel and renew the universe, until the day when Jesus, the Christ (Anointed One) and Son of David, will come for the real fulfillment of this expectation.

Nathan: "Here I am, dwelling in a house of cedar, while the Ark of God dwells in a tent."[m] 3 Nathan replied to the king: "Do not hesitate to do whatever you have in mind, for the LORD is with you."[n]

4 However, that same night the word of the LORD came to Nathan: 5 "Go and tell my servant David: 'Thus says the LORD: "Are you determined to build a house for me to dwell in?[o] 6 I have not dwelled in a house from the day I brought the Israelites out of Egypt to this very day. I have been moving from place to place while living in a tent and a tabernacle. 7 In all of my travels everywhere among the Israelites, did I ever ask any of the judges whom I had appointed to shepherd my people Israel why they had never built me a house of cedar?" ' "

The LORD's Promises. 8 "Now then, this is what you are to say to my servant David: 'Thus says the LORD of hosts: "I was the one who took you from the pastures and your work of caring for the sheep to be the ruler of my people Israel.[p] 9 I have been with you wherever you went, and I have destroyed all of your enemies who dared to challenge you. Moreover, I intend to make your name as famous as the names of the greatest men on the earth.[q]

10 " ' "I also shall provide a place for my people Israel, and there I will plant them so that they may dwell there and never again be disturbed. Nor will the wicked afflict them anymore, as was the case formerly, 11 from the time that I appointed judges over my people Israel. I will grant you rest from all of your enemies.

" ' "Moreover, I, the LORD, promise that I will establish a royal house for you.[r] 12 *[s] And when it is time for you to be with your ancestors, I will designate as your heir one of your sons to succeed you, and I shall establish his kingdom forever. 13 It is he who will build a house in honor of my name, and I shall ensure that his royal throne will stand firm forever.

14 " ' "I shall be a father to him, and he will be my son. If he does wrong, I shall punish him as any father would do and not fail to inflict chastisements upon him.[t] 15 However, I will never withdraw my steadfast love from him as I withdrew it from Saul and shielded you from his vindictive plots.[u] 16 Your descendants and your kingdom will stand firm forever before me, and your throne shall endure forever." ' "[v]

17 Nathan then related all these promises and this entire revelation to David.

King David's Prayer. 18 Then King David went in and, sitting in the presence of the LORD, he said:

"Who am I, Lord GOD, and what is my lineage, that you have brought me this far?[w] 19 Yet you regarded this as too insignificant an honor, Lord GOD, for you have also deigned to extend your protective care to the house of your servant for a long time to come. Who can truly consider himself sufficiently worthy to be the recipient of such love, Lord GOD?

20 "What more can David say to you, Lord GOD, since you know everything about your servant? 21 For the sake of your promise and in accordance with the purpose you have in mind, you have decided to reveal all this to your servant.

22 "How great you are, Lord GOD! There is no one like you, and there is no God except you alone, as everything that we have heard confirms.[x] 23 And what other nation on earth can be compared to your people Israel, whom you sent forth to redeem for yourself from Egypt by awe-inspiring deeds as you drove out other nations and their gods.[y] 24 [z] You have established your people Israel as your own forever, and you, LORD, became their God.

25 "And now, LORD God, in regard to the promise that you have made concerning your servant and his house, do what you have promised, 26 so that your name will be exalted forever, and people will say: 'the LORD of hosts is the God of Israel,' and the house of your servant David will be established before you,[a] 27 since you, the LORD of

m 1 Chr 17:1.—n Ps 132:1-5; Lk 1:28.—o 1 Ki 5:17; 8:16, 27; 1 Chr 17:4, 7, 22:8; 28:3; Isa 66:1; Acts 7:48.—p 1 Sam 16:13; 17:15-20; 1 Chr 17:7; Ps 78:70f.—q Ps 89:23.—r 2 Sam 23:5; 1 Ki 2:4-24; Jn 14:2.—s 12ff: 1 Ki 5:19; 8:19; 1 Chr 17:12; 22:10; 28:6; Ps 89:5, 27f.—t 1 Chr 17:13.—u 1 Sam 13:14; 15:26; 2 Ki 19:34; 1 Chr 17:11-14; Ps 89:34.—v 1 Mac 2:57; Mic 5:3; Mk 11:10.—w 1 Chr 17:16.—x Ex 15:11; Deut 33:26; Jud 16:13; Jer 10:7.—y Deut 4:7, 34; 1 Chr 17:21; Est C:9.—z 24f: Ex 6:7; Deut 7:6; 26:17; 29:12; Isa 14:32.—a Sir 42:17.

7:12-16 The divine adoption of Solomon, one of whose descendants is the Messiah, will ensure the perpetuity of the kingdom, is a first ray of light on the divine sonship of Christ (see Heb 1:5). It is an impressive fact that while the kingdom of Israel, formed after Solomon's death, saw no less than eight changes of dynasty in a little more than two centuries (931–721 B.C.), the Davidic dynasty was the only one to rule in Judah for three and a half centuries (931–587 B.C.), even though it, too, was subject to palace conspiracies.

hosts, the God of Israel, made this revelation to your servant: 'I shall build a house for you.' Therefore, your servant has found the courage to offer this prayer to you.

28 "And now, Lord GOD, you are God, and your words are true. You have made this generous promise to your servant.* [b]
29 Therefore, bless the house of your servant, so that it may remain ever before you. For you, Lord GOD, have spoken, and with your blessing the house of your servant will be blessed forever."

CHAPTER 8

Summary of David's Wars. 1 A short time later, David attacked the Philistines and subdued them, and he also wrested Metheg-ammah from their control. 2 In addition he defeated the Moabites, after which he ordered them to lie on the ground and then measured them off with a length of cord. He measured two lengths of cord for those who were to be put to death, and one length for those who were to be spared. The Moabites then became David's subjects and brought him tribute. [c]

3 David also defeated King Hadadezer of Zobah, the son of Rehob, as he led an expedition to restore his dominion along the Euphrates River. [d] 4 David captured from him one thousand seven hundred horsemen and twenty thousand foot soldiers. He also hamstrung all but one hundred of the chariot horses. [e]

5 When the Arameans of Damascus came to the aid of King Hadadezer of Zobah, David killed twenty-two thousand men of the Arameans. 6 He then established garrisons among the Arameans of Damascus, and they became his subjects and brought him tribute.* The LORD brought David victory wherever he went.

7 David also took the gold shields that were carried by the guards of Hadadezer, and he brought them to Jerusalem. [f] 8 In addition, from Bethah and Berothai, towns belonging to Hadadezer, David removed an immense quantity of bronze.

9 When Tor, the king of Hamath, heard that David had defeated Hadadezer's entire army, 10 he sent his son Joram to King David to greet him and to congratulate him for having been victorious in his battle against Hadadezer, for Hadadezer had often been at war with Tor. Joram brought with him objects of silver, gold, and bronze. 11 These also King David consecrated to the LORD, as he had also done with the silver and gold he had taken from every nation he had conquered— [g] 12 from Edom and Moab, from the Ammonites and the Philistines, from Amalek, and from the spoil taken from King Hadadezer of Zoab, the son of Rehob.

13 David became even more greatly renowned when, on his return, he slew eighteen thousand Edomites in the Valley of Salt, [h] 14 after which he stationed garrisons throughout Edom. Thus all the Edomites became David's subjects. And the LORD continued to give victory to David wherever he went.

David's Officials. 15 [i] David reigned over all Israel, and he administered law and justice among all his people.* 16 Joab, the son of Zeruiah, was in command of the army. Jehoshaphat, the son of Ahilud, was in charge of the records. 17 Zadok, the son of Ahitub, and Ahimelech, the son of Abiathar, were priests. Seraiah was secretary. 18 Benaiah, the son of Jehoiada, was in command of the Cherethites and the Pelethites.* David's sons were priests. [j]

CHAPTER 9

David and Meribbaal.* 1 David inquired: "Is there anyone belonging to the family of Saul who is still alive, to whom I may show kindness for Jonathan's sake?" [k] 2 Now Saul's family had a servant whose name was Ziba, and he was summoned to appear before David. The king asked him: "Are you Ziba?" He replied: "I am at your service." [l]

b Num 23:19; 1 Ki 8:56; Jer 32:17; Jn 17:17.—c Gen 19:37; 1 Chr 18:2.—d 1 Ki 11:23.—e Jos 11:6, 9; 1 Chr 18:4; 2 Mac 12:20.—f 1 Ki 14:26; 1 Chr 18:7.—g 1 Chr 18:11; 2 Chr 31:6.—h 1 Sam 27:9; 2 Ki 14:7; 1 Chr 18:12.—i 15-18: 2 Sam 20:23-26.—j 2 Sam 15:18; 23:20; 1 Ki 1:38, 44.—k 1 Sam 18:1-4.—l 2 Sam 16:1-4.

7:28 David completes his intimate prayer of trust in God's promise of eternal blessings for him and his descendants.

8:6 *Tribute:* this tax on a conquered people was a way of recognizing and supporting those who were victorious in battle.

8:15 King David won the love and admiration of most people because of the fairness and respect that he practiced even when dealing with his enemies. This kind of justice reflects God's will and way as prescribed in Deut 16:18-20.

8:18 *Cherethites and the Pelethites:* foreign mercenaries who were the king's bodyguards.

9:1-13 What to make of a king who shows mercy and kindness to the enemy's descendants? King David searches out and finds the crippled grandson of Saul in a show of overwhelming generosity and goodness for no political or military benefit but to please God alone.

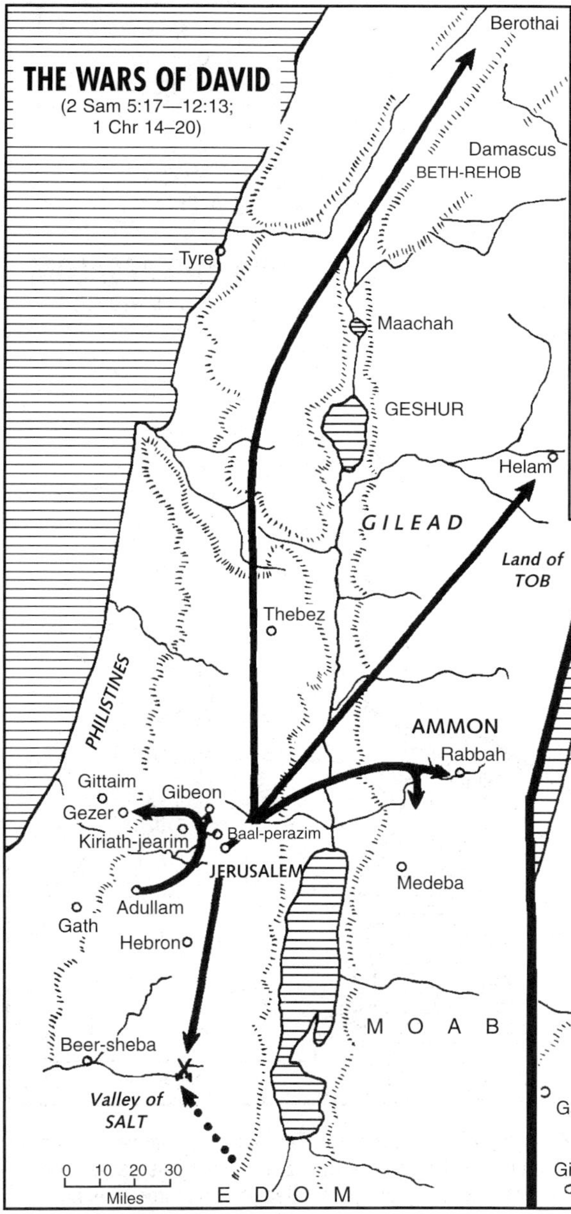

DAVID AND ISHBAAL (2 Sam 2:8—5:16) — **(a)** At **Mahanaim,** Abner, leader of Saul's army, establishes Ishbaal, son of Saul, as king over **Gilead,** the Asshurites, **Jezreel, Ephraim,** Benjamin, and all **Israel** (2:8-11). **(b)** At **Gibeon,** the servants of Ishbaal and those of David battle near the pool. Joab pursues Abner to the hill of Ammah which lies east of the valley toward the desert near **Geba** (2:11-24). **(c)** At **Mahanaim,** Abner retakes the city through the Valley of the Jordan. Later he is reconciled with David and killed by Joab. Death of Ishbaal (2:25—4:8). **(d)** At **Hebron,** David is acknowledged as king by all Israel. He captures **Jerusalem** and makes it his capital (5:1-16).

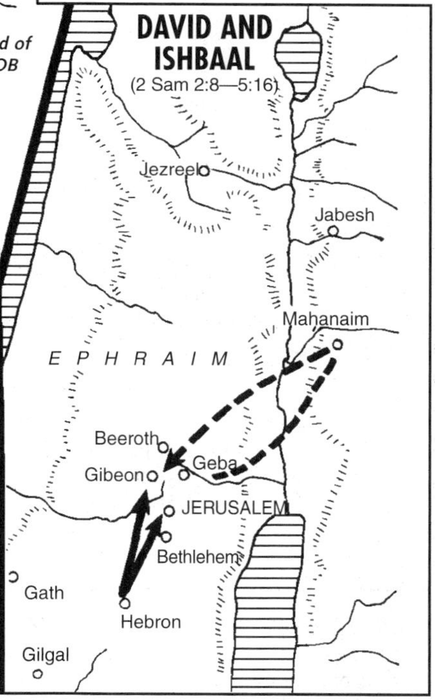

WARS OF DAVID (2 Sam 5:17—8:4; 10:1—12:13; 1 Chr 14–20) — **(a)** David makes war against the **Philistines.** From **Adullam,** David routs the Philistines twice in the Valley of Rephaim, first at **Baal-perazim,** and secondly from **Gibeon** to **Gezer.** Transferal of the Ark of the Covenant from **Kiriath-jearim** to **Jerusalem** (5:17—7:29). **(b)** David makes the Moabites pay tribute (8:1-2). **(c)** David defeats Hadadezer, king of Zobah, and the **Arameans** of Damascus who had come to his aid. He carries away a great quantity of bronze from Tebah and **Berothai.** The king of Hamath sends a message of friendship to David (8:3-12). **(d)** Defeated in the **Valley of Salt,** the **Edomites** become subjects of David (8:13-14). **(e)** In a first campaign, the Ammonites hire the Arameans of **Beth-rehob** and Zobah, the king of **Maacah** and his men, and the people of **Tob.** Joab divides his army in two and successively defeats the Arameans before **Medeba** and the Ammonites who hastened to return to their city. Joab spares **Rabbah,** capital of the Ammonites. David's sin and repentance (10:1—12:31). **(f)** Second campaign against Hadadezer, between the two Ammonite campaigns. David rallies all Israel, crosses the Jordan, and defeats the army of Hadadezer at Helam (1:15-19).

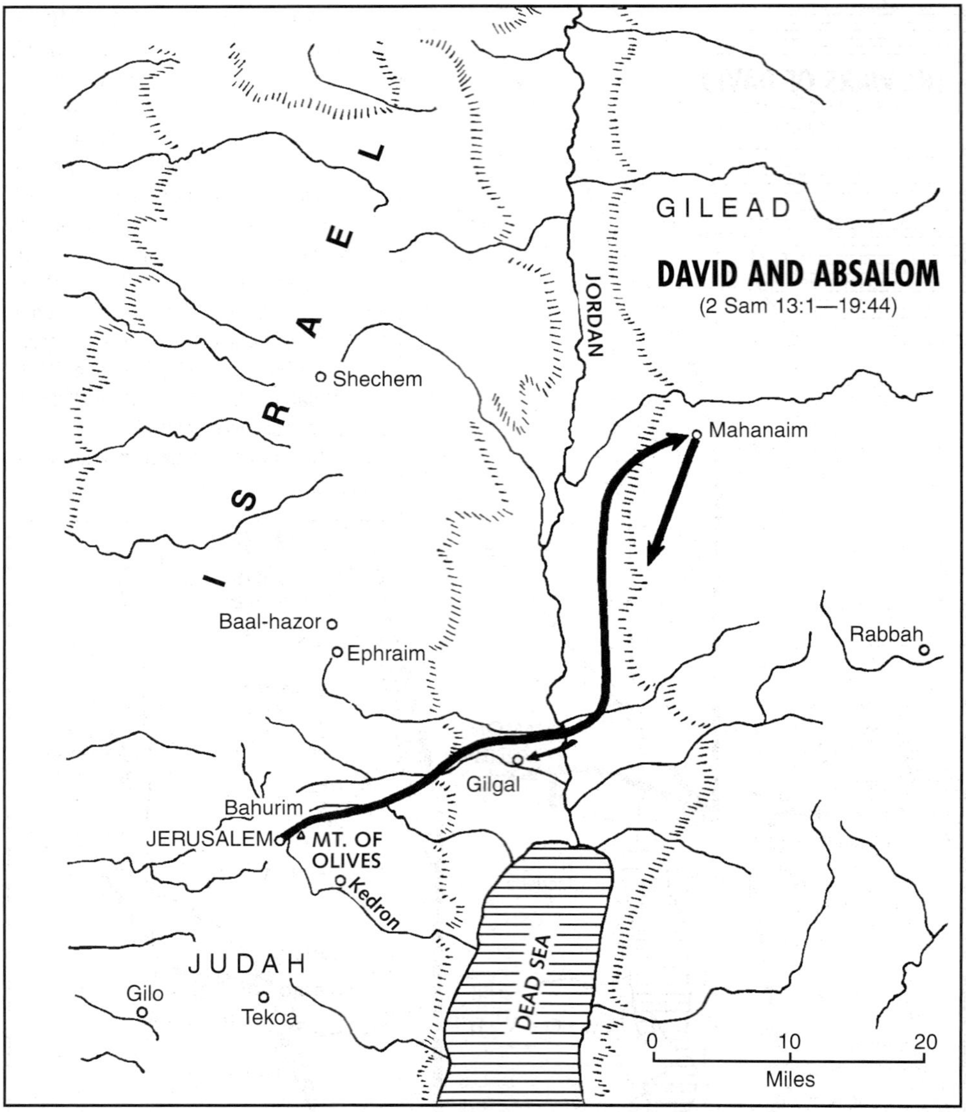

DAVID AND ABSALOM (2 Sam 13:1—19:44) — **(a)** At **Baal-hazor,** near **Ephraim,** Absalom has Amnon put to death, and for three years takes refuge with the king of Geshur. Subsequently he passes two years of disgrace in Jerusalem (chs. 13–14). **(b)** At Hebron, four years later, Absalom proclaims himself king. He sends for Ahithophel the Gilonite, David's counselor (15:1-12). **(c)** At **Jerusalem,** David, knowing himself to be in great danger, flees in the direction of the **Jordan,** accompanied by the Cherethites, Pelethites, and by the Ittai and the Gittites come from Gath (15:13-22). **(d)** At the **Kidron Brook,** David sends Zadok the priest, back to **Jerusalem** with the Ark (15:25-29). **(e)** At the **Mount of Olives,** he sends Hushai to Absalom to frustrate the projects of Ahithophel. After having mounted to the summit, David receives provisions from Ziba, servant of Meribbaal (15:30—16:4). **(f)** At **Bahurim,** Shimei insults David (16:5-14). **(g)** At **Jerusalem,** Hushai pretends to be on the side of Absalom and fights the proposition of Ahithophel who wishes to pursue David immediately. He causes David to avoid danger. The emissaries leave En-rogel and for a time hide themselves at **Bahurim** (16:15—17:23). **(h)** At **Mahanaim,** supporters from **Rabbah** and Lo-debar bring provisions and furniture to David, who musters the army but himself remains behind. The battle takes place in the forest near **Mahanaim.** Defeat and death of Absalom (17:24—18:15). **(i)** At **Gilgal,** the people of Judah come to meet the king who has come back from **Mahanaim.** David pardons Shimei. Meeting with Meribbaal. The king continues his journey with Chimham, son of Barzillai the Gileadite (18:6—19:44).

3 The king then asked: "Is there anyone
from Saul's family still alive to whom I may
show God's kindness?" "There is a son of
Jonathan who still remains," Ziba said to the
king. "His feet are crippled." [m] 4 Then the king
inquired: "Where is he?" Ziba answered: "He
is living in the house of Machir, the son of
Ammiel, at Lo-debar." [n]

5 Then King David sent for him and had
him brought from the house of Machir, the
son of Ammiel, at Lo-debar. 6 When
Meribbaal, the son of Jonathan and the
grandson of Saul, entered David's presence,
he fell on his face and did obeisance. David
said: "Meribbaal!" He replied: "I am your
servant."

7 David then said to him: "Do not be afraid.
I intend to show you great kindness for the
sake of your father Jonathan. I shall restore to
you all the lands that belonged to your grand-
father Saul, and you yourself shall always eat
at my table." 8 Meribbaal again prostrated
himself and said: "Of what importance is
your servant that you should look with kind-
ness upon a dead dog like me?" [o]

9 Then David summoned Saul's servant
Ziba and said to him: "I am turning over to
your master's grandson everything that
belonged to Saul and to his family. 10 You and
your sons and your servants shall cultivate
the land for him and bring in the harvest to
provide for your master's family to eat.
However, Meribbaal, your master's grand-
son, shall always eat at my table."

Ziba, who had fifteen sons and twenty ser-
vants, 11 said to the king: "Your servant shall
do everything that my lord the king has com-
manded him." Therefore, Meribbaal ate at
the king's table like one of the king's sons. [p]

12 Meribbaal had a young son whose
name was Mica. All the members of Ziba's
household became servants of Meribbaal. [q]
13 However, Meribbaal lived in Jerusalem
because he always ate at the king's table, for
he was crippled in both feet. [r]

CHAPTER 10

Insult of the Ammonites. 1 Sometime after-
ward the king of the Ammonites died, and
his son Hanun succeeded him as king.
2 David thought: "I will show Hanun, the son
of Nahash, the same loyalty that his father
showed to me." Then David sent a delegation
to console him at the loss of his father.

When David's envoys entered the country
of the Ammonites, 3 the Ammonite princes
said to their lord Hanun: "Do you truly
believe that David means to honor your
father just because he has sent envoys to
express their condolences to you? Is it not far
more likely that he has sent them to be spies
so that they may explore and reconnoiter the
city and thus be better prepared to over-
throw it?"

4 Thereupon Hanun seized David's
envoys, shaved off half of their beards, cut
away the lower half of their garments up to
their hips, and then sent them away.* [s]
5 When David was informed about how they
had been treated, he sent messengers to
meet them, for they were greatly humiliat-
ed, and to instruct them: "Remain in
Jericho until your beards have grown again,
and then return."

Ammonites Defeated. 6 When the Am-
monites realized that they had greatly
offended David, they sent envoys to hire the
Arameans of Beth-rehob and the Arameans
of Zobah to come to their support, twenty
thousand foot soldiers in number, as well as
one thousand men from the king of Maacah,
and twelve thousand men from Tob. [t]

7 When David learned about this, he sent
out Joab with his entire force of trained war-
riors. [u] 8 The Ammonites then came forth
and drew up in battle formation at the
entrance of their city gate, while the
Arameans of Zobah and Rehob and the men
of Tob and Maacah stayed some distance
away in the open country.

9 When Joab perceived that he would be
attacked both from the front and from the
rear, he chose the best of the troops of Israel
and arrayed them against the Arameans.
10 He put the rest of his forces in charge of his
brother Abishai and arrayed them against
the Ammonites.

11 Then Joab said: "If the Arameans are too
strong for me, then you must come to my
aid. However, if the Ammonites are too
strong for you, then I will come to help you.
12 Be brave! Let us fight courageously for the

m 2 Sam 4:4; 9:1.—n 2 Sam 9:5; 16:13; 17:27; Am 6:13.—o 2 Sam 16:9; Gen 23:12.—p 2 Sam 9:13; 19:29.—q 1 Chr 8:34.—r 2 Sam 21:7.—s 1 Chr 19:4; Isa 20:4.—t 2 Sam 8:3; 10:18; 1 Sam 14:47.—u 2 Sam 11:1.

10:4 A full beard was the mark of adulthood and authority for an Israelite male, and shaving David's men was grossly offensive and demanded retribution on the Ammonites.

sake of our people and for the cities of our
God. The LORD will do what he judges to be
best." [v]

13 Then Joab and the soldiers with him
moved forward into battle against the
Arameans and put them to flight. 14 When
the Ammonites saw that the Arameans had
fled, they likewise fled when they were con-
fronted by Abishai and withdrew into the
city. Then Joab ceased his attack against the
Ammonites and withdrew to Jerusalem.

Arameans Defeated. 15 [w] When the Ara-
means realized that they had been defeated
by Israel, they gathered their forces together.
16 Hadadezer sent messengers to summon
other Arameans who lived beyond the
Euphrates, and they came to Helam, with
Shobach, the commander of the army of
Hadadezer, at their head.

17 When David was informed of this, he
assembled all of the forces of Israel, crossed
the Jordan, and advanced to Helam. The
Arameans then drew up in battle formation
against David and fought with him. 18 How-
ever, they were compelled to flee from the
Israelite forces. David's men killed seven
hundred Arameans in chariots and forty
thousand foot soldiers. In addition, Sho-
bach, the general of their army, was serious-
ly wounded, and he died on the battlefield. [x]

19 When all of the kings who were vassals of
Hadadezer realized that they had been
defeated by Israel, they sued for peace with
the Israelites and became their subjects. As a
result, the Arameans were afraid to give any
further help to the Ammonites.

CHAPTER 11

David's Son. 1 With the onset of spring, the
time of year when kings go off to war, David
sent forth Joab along with his officers and
the entire Israelite army. They destroyed the
Ammonites and besieged Rabbah. However,
David himself remained in Jerusalem. [y]
2 One evening, when David arose from his
couch and walked about on the roof of his
palace, he saw from the roof a woman
bathing. She was very beautiful. 3 David
made inquiries about the woman, and he
was told: "That is Bathsheba, the daughter
of Eliam and the wife of Uriah the Hittite." [z]

4 David sent messengers to fetch her, and
when she came to him, he had relations with
her, just after she had purified herself from
her uncleanness. Then she returned home. [a]
5 The woman conceived, and she sent a mes-
sage to David: "I am pregnant."

6 Then David sent word to Joab: "Send me
Uriah the Hittite," and Joab did so. 7 When
Uriah returned, David asked him how Joab
and the troops were faring and how the war
was going. 8 Then David said to Uriah: "Go
down to your house and bathe your feet."
Uriah departed from the king's palace, and a
gift from the king was sent to his house. [b]

9 However, Uriah did not return to his
house, but rather he slept at the palace gate
with all the king's bodyguard. 10 Upon receiv-
ing the report that Uriah had not returned
home, David said to him: "You have just
arrived from a journey. Why didn't you go
down to your house?"

11 Uriah replied: "The Ark and Israel and
Judah are lodged in tents, and my master
Joab and your majesty's soldiers are en-
camped in the open fields. How then can I
feel comfortable to go to my house, to eat
and to drink and to sleep with my wife? As
the LORD lives, and as you yourself live, I
shall do no such thing." [c]

12 Then David said to Uriah: "Remain here
for one more day. Tomorrow I will send you
back." Therefore, Uriah remained that day in
Jerusalem. 13 On the following day David
invited Uriah to eat and drink with him and
caused him to become drunk. In the evening
he went outside to lie down and fall asleep
with the king's servants, but he did not go
down to his house.

14 In the morning David wrote a letter to
Joab and sent it to him in the care of Uriah.
15 In the letter he wrote: "Assign Uriah up
front where the fighting is fierce, and then
draw back from him so that he may be
struck down and die." [d]

16 As Joab was besieging the city, he sta-
tioned Uriah where he knew the enemy had
deployed its most valiant warriors. 17 When
the men of the city came forth and fought
against Joab, some of the soldiers of David
fell. Uriah the Hittite was also slain. [e]

18 Then Joab sent David a full account of
the battle, 19 and he instructed the messen-
ger: "When you have finished telling the king

v Deut 31:23; 1 Sam 3:18; 1 Chr 19:13.—w 15-19: 2 Sam 8:3-8; 1 Chr 19:19.—x 2 Sam 10:17; 1 Chr 19:18.—y 2 Sam 10:7; 1 Chr 20:1.—z 2 Sam 23:34, 39.—a Lev 12:2; 15:19, Prov 6:29.—b 2 Sam 11:12.—c 1 Sam 4:3f.—d 1 Ki 15:5.—e 2 Sam 11:21; Jud 6:12.

all the details about the fighting, [20] his anger
may be aroused and he may say to you: 'Why
did you go so close to the city to fight? Were
you not aware that they would shoot from
the wall? [21] Do you recall who killed Abim-
elech, the son of Jerubbaal? Was it not a
woman who dropped down a millstone on
him from the wall, resulting in his death at
Thebez? Why did you go so close to the wall?'
Then say to him: 'Your servant Uriah the
Hittite is also dead.' "[f]

[22] Therefore, the messenger set off, and on
his arrival he relayed to David everything
that Joab had instructed him to say. [23] He
told David: "Their men initially gained an
advantage over us, and they came forth to
fight against us in the open, but we drove
them back to the entrance of the gate.
[24] Then their archers shot down at your ser-
vants from the wall, and some of the king's
servants died. Your servant Uriah the Hittite
was also slain."

[25] David then said to the messenger: "This
is what you are to say to Joab: 'Do not let this
matter cause you any distress, for the sword
devours now one and now another. Press
your attack against the city and destroy it.'
That message should encourage him." *

[26] When the wife of Uriah was told that her
husband was dead, she mourned for him.
[27] Then, when the period of mourning was
over, David sent for her and brought her to
live in his palace. She became his wife and
bore him a son. However, the LORD was
greatly displeased at what David had done. [g]

CHAPTER 12

Nathan's Parable. [1] The LORD sent the
prophet Nathan to David, and when Nathan
arrived, he said to him: "There were two
men in a certain town. One was rich and the
other was poor. [h] [2] The rich man had flocks
and herds in great abundance, [3] but the poor
man had nothing at all except for one little
ewe lamb which he had bought. He cared for
it, and the lamb grew up with him and with
his children. It would share the little food he
had and drink from his cup and sleep in his
arms. It was like a daughter to him.

[4] "On one occasion the rich man wel-
comed a traveler into his house, but he had
no wish to take one animal from his flock or
herd to provide a meal for his guest. Instead
he took the poor man's ewe lamb and pre-
pared that for his visitor."

[5] On hearing this, David flew into a rage
against that man, and he said to Nathan: "As
the LORD lives, the man who has done this
deserves to die. [6] He must make fourfold
restitution* for the lamb, because he has
done this without showing the least bit of
pity." [i]

David's Punishment. [7] Then Nathan said to
David: "You are that man! Thus says the
LORD, the God of Israel: 'I anointed you king
of Israel, and I rescued you from the clutch-
es of Saul. [j] [8] I gave you your master's house
and your master's wives as your own. I also
gave you the house of Israel and the house of
Judah. And if that had not been sufficient, I
would have given you even more.

[9] " 'Why have you shown your lack of grat-
itude to the LORD by doing what is evil in his
sight? You have struck down Uriah the
Hittite with the sword and taken his wife to
be your own after having killed him with the
sword of the Ammonites. [k] [10] Now, therefore,
the sword shall never depart from your
house, since you have shown contempt for
me and have taken the wife of Uriah the
Hittite to be your wife.' [l]

[11] "Thus says the LORD: 'I will bring mis-
fortune upon you from within your own
house. Before your very eyes I shall take your
wives and give them to your neighbor, and
he shall lie with your wives in broad day-
light. [m] [12] You have done such deeds in secret,
but I will do them in broad daylight for all
Israel to see.' "

David's Repentance. [13] David said to
Nathan: "I have sinned against the LORD."
Nathan replied to David: "The LORD has
decided to forgive your sin. You shall not
die. [n] [14] However, since you have shown your
utter contempt for the LORD by this deed,
the child born to you will die."

[15] After Nathan returned home, the LORD
struck the child that the wife of Uriah had

f Jdg 9:50-54.—g Gen 20:3.—h Sir 47:1.—i Ex 21:37; Job 21:31; Lk 19:8.—j 1 Sam 16:13.—k 2 Sam 11:21.—l 2 Sam 13:28f; 18:14.—m Gen 26:10.—n 1 Ki 21:29; Ps 32:5; Sir 47:11; Lk 15:21.

11:25 David's offhanded way of dealing with Uriah's murder indicates that he has put his sinful desire before his relationship with God. He has lost his way and his heart was hardened against anyone and anything that interfered with his desire.

12:6 *Fourfold restitution:* although David doesn't yet admit to his sinfulness, he will be burdened with the death of four of his sons, Bathsheba's firstborn, and later Amnon, Absalom, and lastly Adonijah.

borne to David, and it fell gravely ill. 16 David,
therefore, pleaded with God for the child. He
maintained a strict fast, and throughout the
night he would lie on the ground. 17 The elders
of his household stood around him, urging
him to rise from the ground. However, he
refused to do so, nor would he take food with
them.

18 On the seventh day the child died, and
the servants of David were afraid to tell him
that the child was dead, for they said: "While
the child was alive, we spoke to him, but he
refused to listen to us. How then can we
inform him that the child is dead? He may do
something desperate." 19 However, David saw
that his servants were whispering among
themselves, and he realized that the child had
died. He asked the servants: "Is the child
dead?" They replied: "Yes, the child is dead."

20 David, thereupon, rose from the ground,
bathed and anointed himself, and changed
his clothes. He then went into the house of
the LORD and worshiped before he returned
to his own house. When he requested food,
they set it before him, and he ate. 21 His ser-
vants said to him: "Why are you acting in
this way? You fasted and wept for the child
while it was alive, but when the child died,
you got up and ate food."

22 David said: "While the child was still alive,
I fasted and wept, for I thought: 'Perhaps the
LORD will be merciful to me and allow the
child to live.'[o] 23 But now that he is dead, why
should I fast? Can I bring him back again? I
shall go to him, but he will not return to me."[p]

24 * David then proceeded to console his
wife Bathsheba. He went to her and slept
with her. As a result, she bore a son, whom
they named Solomon. The LORD loved him,
25 and he sent a message to the prophet
Nathan instructing him to name the child
Jedidiah according to the LORD's wish.

The Ammonite War Ends. 26 [q] Shortly there-
after, Joab attacked Rabbah of the Am-
monites and captured the royal city. 27 Then
Joab sent messengers to inform David: "I
have assaulted Rabbah and gained control
of the water supply. 28 Therefore, assemble
the rest of the soldiers, lay siege to the city,
and capture it. Otherwise I myself will
capture the city, and then it will be named
after me."

29 Without delay, David assembled the rest
of his soldiers and went to Rabbah, where he
assaulted the city and captured it. 30 He took
the crown of Milcom from his head.
Weighing a talent of gold and encrusted with
precious stones, it was placed on David's
head. He also carried out a tremendous
amount of spoil from the city.

31 Furthermore, David led away the city's
inhabitants and set them to work with saws
and iron picks and iron axes or assigned
them to toil at brickmaking. This was his
regular procedure in regard to all the Am-
monite towns. Then he and all of his soldiers
returned to Jerusalem.

CHAPTER 13

The Crime of Amnon. 1 Sometime later the
following events occurred. David's son
Absalom had a beautiful sister whose name
was Tamar, and David's son Amnon fell
madly in love with her.[r] 2 Amnon was
obsessed with her to the point that he
became ill because of his love for his sister
Tamar, since she was a virgin and Amnon
felt it was impossible for him even to
approach her.

3 However, Amnon had a friend whose
name was Jonadab. He was the son of
David's brother Shimeah, and he was an
extremely devious man.[s] 4 He asked
Amnon: "O son of the king, why do you
appear to be so depressed morning after
morning? Will you not tell me?" Amnon
replied: "I am in love with Tamar, the sister
of my brother Absalom."

5 Then Jonadab said to him: "Lie down on
your bed and pretend to be ill. When your
father comes to visit you, say to him: 'Please
let my sister come and give me something to
eat. Ask her to prepare the food in my pres-
ence for me to see and then eat it from her
hand.'" 6 And so Amnon lay down and pre-
tended to be ill. When the king came to visit
him, Amnon said: "Please let my sister
Tamar come and make some cakes before
my eyes so that I can receive some nourish-
ment from her hand."

7 Then David sent a message to Tamar in
the palace, saying: "Go to your brother
Amnon's house and prepare some food for
him." 8 Therefore, Tamar went to the house of

o Bar 1:5.—p Job 7:9.—q 26-31: 2 Sam 11:7; 1 Chr 20:
1-3.—r 2 Sam 3:2f; 1 Chr 3:9.—s 2 Sam 21:21; Gen 3:1.

12:24-25 The child's two names signify God's forgive-
ness. *Solomon* is connected with "shalom" (peace), and
Jedidiah means "loved by God."

her brother Amnon and found him lying in
bed. She took dough and kneaded it, made
some cakes while he watched, and baked the
cakes.

9 Then Tamar took the pan and set out the
cakes before him, but he refused to eat and
ordered everyone else to leave the room.
10 Thereupon, Amnon said to Tamar: "Bring
the food into the bedroom so that I may eat
from your hand." Therefore, Tamar took the
cakes she had made and brought them into
the bedroom to Amnon her brother.

11 However, when she offered them to him
to eat, he took hold of her and said: "Come to
bed with me, my sister." [t] 12 She answered
him: "No, my brother! Do not force me! Such
repulsive acts are not done in Israel. Do not
commit such a vile act! [u] 13 And as for me,
where could I go to hide my shame?
Moreover, you would be disgraced in Israel.
Therefore, I beg you to speak to the king. He
will not refuse you permission to marry me."

14 Despite her entreaty, he would not listen
to her. Rather, he overpowered her and
raped her. [v] 15 Then Amnon was seized with
intense hatred for her, a hatred that was far
greater than the love he had had for her. "Get
up and leave," he said. 16 But she answered:
"No, my brother. If you send me away, that
would be an even greater wrong* than the
other wrong you perpetrated against me."
However, he refused to listen to her.

17 Then Amnon summoned his personal
attendant and said: "Take this woman out of
my presence and bolt the door after her!"
18 She was wearing a long gown with sleeves,
for this is how the virgin daughters of the
king were clothed in those days. 19 Tamar put
ashes on her head and tore the long gown
that she was wearing. Then, putting her hand
on her head, she went away, weeping loudly. [w]

20 Her brother Absalom said to her: "Has
your brother Amnon been with you? Be
quiet now, my sister. He is your brother. Do
not take this to heart." Then Tamar, forlorn
and inconsolable, went to live in the house of
her brother Absalom.

21 * When King David learned about all
this, he became extremely angry. However,
he did not punish his son Amnon because he
was his firstborn and he loved him. 22 But
Absalom refused to say a single word to
Amnon, either good or bad, since he hated
Amnon because he had raped his sister
Tamar. [x]

Absalom's Plot. 23 Two years later, when
Absalom had sheepshearers at Baal-hazor,
near Ephraim, he invited all of the king's
sons. 24 Absalom went to the king and said:
"Your servant has summoned the sheep-
shearers to work. Will your majesty and his
retinue please come?" 25 The king replied:
"No, my son. If we all were to go, we would
prove to be a burden to you." Absalom con-
tinued to urge him, but the king still refused
to go, although he gave him his blessing.

26 Absalom then said: "If you will not come,
then please allow my brother Amnon to go
with us." The king replied: "Why should he go
with you?" 27 However, Absalom continued to
urge him, until finally the king allowed
Amnon and all the other princes to go.

28 [y] Absalom prepared a feast fit for a king,
and he instructed his servants: "Watch care-
fully! When Amnon is merry with wine and I
say to you: 'Strike down Amnon,' then slay
him. Do not be afraid. You will simply be
obeying my command. Be courageous and
act valiantly!"

The Death of Amnon. 29 When the servants
of Absalom did to Amnon as Absalom had
commanded, then all of the king's sons leapt
to their feet, mounted their mules, and fled.
30 While they were still on the road, a report
came to David that Absalom had slain all of
the king's sons and that not a single one of
them had survived. 31 The king stood up, tore
his garments, and threw himself on the
ground. All of his servants who were stand-
ing around him also tore their garments. [z]

32 However, Jonadab, the son of David's
brother Shimeah, said: "Let not my lord
think that all the young princes, the sons of
the king, have been killed. Amnon alone is
dead, for Absalom has been determined to
exact vengeance ever since the day that

t Gen 34:2.—u Lev 18:9; 20:17; Deut 27:22.—v Bar 2:5.—w Tob 3:1.—x Gen 37:4.—y 28f: Ru 2:15.—z 2 Sam 1:11; Jud 14:16.

13:16 *An even greater wrong:* rape was a terrible sin (Deut 22:28-29) and what Amnon did by rejecting Tamar only added to the seriousness of his wrongdoing. She would be unable to prove her innocence, and now that she was no longer a virgin, she had no chance of marrying.

13:21-22 David's righteous anger over Amnon's rape and betrayal of Tamar never resulted in punishment of his eldest son. One wonders if David's own indiscretion with Bathsheba colored his response. His ill feelings toward his son continued, and when Absalom seeks revenge and kills Amnon, David again side skirts the issue, once again demonstrating David's vulnerability and ineffectiveness as a family man.

Amnon raped his sister Tamar. 33 Therefore, my lord the king should not believe the report that all of the king's sons are dead. Only Amnon is dead."

34 Meanwhile Absalom had fled. When the man on sentry duty looked up, he saw a large group of people coming down the hill from the direction of Horonaim. Immediately he hastened to the king and reported: "I have seen men coming down the hill from Horonaim."

35 Jonadab said to the king: "Behold, the king's sons have returned, just as I said they would." 36 No sooner had he finished speaking than the king's sons arrived, weeping aloud. The king and all his servants also wept bitterly.

37 Absalom, who had taken flight, went to Talmai, the son of Ammihud, the king of Geshur, [a] 38 and he remained in Geshur for three years.

Efforts for Absalom's Return. 39 During all that time, David mourned over his son, but once he became reconciled to the death of Amnon, he yearned to be reconciled with Absalom.

CHAPTER 14

1 Joab, the son of Zeruiah, ascertained that the king, in his heart, longed for Absalom, 2 so he sent to Tekoa and had a wise woman brought from there. He said to her: "Pretend to be a mourner. Dress yourself in mourning garments and do not anoint yourself with oil. Simply pretend to be a woman who has been grieving for the dead for many days. 3 Then go to the king and speak to him as I instruct you." After that, Joab told her what she was to say.

4 When the woman of Tekoa approached the king, she fell prostrate to the ground in homage and said: "Please help me, O king." 5 [b] The king asked: "What can I do for you?" She replied: "As you can see I am a widow. My husband is dead. 6 Your servant had two sons, and they fought with one another in the field. There was no one around to separate them, and one of them struck the other and killed him.

7 "Now the entire family has risen against your servant and demanded: 'Give up the man who killed his brother, so that we can put him to death to atone for the life of the brother whom he killed. Thus we shall get rid of the heir as well.' Should they do this, they will extinguish my one remaining ember and leave my husband neither name nor posterity on the face of the earth." 8 The king said to the woman: "Return home. I myself shall issue orders on your behalf."

9 Then the woman of Tekoa said to the king: "My lord, let the guilt be on me and on my father's house. The king and his throne will be without guilt." 10 The king replied: "If anyone says something further that is threatening to you, have him brought to me, and he will never trouble you again." 11 * Then she said: "May the king keep the LORD, your God, in mind so that the avenger of blood will be prevented from killing any further and my son will not be destroyed." The king swore: "As surely as the LORD lives, not one hair of your son's head will fall to the ground." [c]

12 The woman continued further; "Please permit your servant to speak a further word to my lord the king." He replied: "Speak." 13 She said: "In pronouncing this verdict, has not the king condemned himself by devising something like this against the people of God, since you have refused to bring back your banished son? 14 We all must die. We are like water that is spilled on the ground and cannot be gathered up again. However, God does not take away a life. Rather, he devises ways that will enable us to avoid being estranged forever from him. [d]

15 "I have dared to speak in this way to your majesty because the people have intimidated me. I thought: 'Perhaps if I can speak to the king, he will grant the request of his servant. 16 He will surely listen to me and deliver his servant from the hands of those who seek to cut off both me and my son from God's inheritance.' 17 And I further thought: 'Perhaps the word of my lord the king will restore my peace of mind, for my lord the king is like an angel of God in discerning between good and evil.' May the LORD, your God, be with you." [e]

18 Then in reply the king said to the woman: "Do not be evasive in replying to the

a 2 Sam 15:8; 1 Chr 3:2.—b 5-7: Num 35:19; 2 Ki 4:1-2; 6:26f; Mt 21:33-38.—c 1 Sam 14:45; Acts 27:34.—d Job 7:9; 14:7-12; Ps 88:5, 11ff; Acts 13:34.—e 1 Sam 29:9.

14:11ff In carrying out Joab's instructions on behalf of King David's son, the woman from Tekoa wisely incorporates protection for herself. In modern terms, she was hedging her bets in case King David looked unkindly on her involvement with Joab's plan.

question I will now ask you." The woman answered: "Let my lord the king present his question." 19 Then the king asked: "Is not the hand of Joab behind you in all this?" The woman asserted: "As you live, my lord the king, no one can avoid being completely truthful in responding to what you ask. Yes, it was your servant Joab who instructed me and taught your servant all the things she was to say. 20 Your servant Joab did this to present the situation in a different light. But my lord has the wisdom of an angel of God and is fully aware of everything that happens in the land."

Absalom's Return. 21 Then the king said to Joab: "Very well. I grant this request. Go forth and bring back the young man Absalom." 22 Then Joab fell prostrate to the ground in homage and blessed the king, saying: "My lord the king, today your servant knows that I have found favor with you, since the king has granted his servant's request."

23 Then Joab set out immediately for Geshur and brought back Absalom to Jerusalem. 24 But the king said: "Let him go to his own house. He shall not come into my presence." Therefore, Absalom went to his own house and was not received by the king.[f]

25 In all Israel there was no one who was so highly praised for his beauty as Absalom, who did not have a single blemish from the sole of his foot to the top of his head.[g] 26 When he would cut the hair of his head—something he used to do at the close of every year because his hair became too heavy for him—the hair weighed two hundred shekels according to the royal standard. 27 To Absalom three sons were born, and also one daughter whose name was Tamar and who was truly beautiful.*[h]

Absalom Is Pardoned. 28 Absalom lived in Jerusalem for two years without coming into the king's presence. 29 Then Absalom summoned Joab, wishing to send him with a message to the king, but Joab refused to come. He then sent for him a second time, but Joab still refused to come. 30 Then Absalom instructed his servants: "Joab's field adjoins mine, and he has barley there. Go and set it on fire." Therefore, Absalom's servants set the field on fire.[i]

31 Then Joab went to Absalom's house and asked him: "Why have your servants set my field on fire?" 32 Absalom replied: "I sent word to you to come here so that I could send you to the king to give him this message from me: 'Why did you summon me to come back from Geshur. I believe that I would be better off if I were still there. Let me now appear before the king. If I am guilty of anything, let him kill me.' "

33 Joab then went before the king and reported this to him. Thereupon the king summoned Absalom, who came and prostrated himself before him, with his face to the ground. Then the king welcomed Absalom with a kiss.

CHAPTER 15

Absalom's Plot. 1 After this, Absalom provided himself with a chariot and horses and with fifty men to run on ahead of him.[j] 2 Absalom was accustomed to arise early and stand by the side of the road that led to the city gate. If someone had a lawsuit to bring before the king for judgment, Absalom would call out and ask him: "Which town do you come from?" and that person would answer: "Your servant is from one of the tribes of Israel."

3 Then Absalom would reply: "Your petition may be clearly valid and just, but there is no one who is authorized by the king to hear you." 4 He would further add: "If only I were appointed as judge in the land, then everyone who has a lawsuit or a claim to be arbitrated could come to me, and I would ensure that he would have his case judged fairly."[k]

5 Moreover, whenever a man came before him and prostrated himself, Absalom would stretch out his hand, embrace him, and kiss him. 6 By behaving in such a manner to every Israelite who approached the king to seek justice, Absalom captured the affectionate loyalty of the people.[l]

Conspiracy in Hebron. 7 After a period of four years had elapsed, Absalom said to the king: "Please allow me to go to Hebron so that I may fulfill the vow that I have made to the LORD. 8 For while I lived at Geshur in Aram, I made this vow: 'If the LORD ever brings me back to Jerusalem, then I shall

f 2 Sam 3:13.—g Isa 1:6.—h 2 Sam 18:18; Heb 11:23.—i Ex 9:31; Jdg 15:5.—j 1 Sam 8:11; 1 Ki 1:5.—k Ps 82:3.—l Rom 16:18.

14:27 Absalom gives tribute to his sister Tamar by naming his daughter after her. This also ensures that Amnon's wrongdoing will be remembered long after Absalom murders him.

worship the LORD in Hebron.' "[m] 9 The king
replied: "Depart in peace." Therefore, Ab-
salom arose and went to Hebron.

10 Then Absalom sent messengers
throughout all the tribes of Israel with this
message: "As soon as you hear the sound of
the trumpet, then shout: 'Absalom has
become king in Hebron.' "

11 Two hundred men had accompanied
Absalom from Jerusalem. They had been
invited as guests and had gone with him in
complete innocence, totally unaware of
what was going on. 12 Absalom also sent for
Ahithophel the Gilonite, who was David's
counselor, and asked him to come from his
town of Giloh to join him in offering the sac-
rifices. Thus the conspiracy grew in strength,
and Absalom's supporters continued to
increase in numbers.[n]

David Flees from Jerusalem. 13 A messenger
came to David with this report: "The men of
Israel have transferred their allegiance to
Absalom." 14 Upon hearing this, David said
to all of his officials who were with him in
Jerusalem: "Get ready to depart! If we do
not flee, then none of us will be able to
escape from Absalom. Depart as quickly as
you can, or he will soon overtake us and
inflict disaster upon us and put the city to
the sword." *[o]

15 The king's officials then replied: "What-
ever our lord the king decides, we are pre-
pared to follow your commands." 16 Then
the king set forth, followed by his entire
household, aside from ten concubines whom
he left behind to take care of the palace.[p]

17 As the king moved on, followed by all the
people, he halted at the last house, with the
officials at his side. 18 As he watched,
all the Cherethites and all the Pelethites and
all of the six hundred Gittites who had fol-
lowed him from Gath passed on before
him.[q]

David and Ittai. 19 Then the king said to Ittai
the Gittite: "Why should you also come with
us? Go back and stay with King Absalom.
For you are a foreigner, and in addition you
are also an exile from your own country.
20 You arrived only yesterday. How can I ask
you to wander about with us today when
truly I do not know where I am going? Go
back home, therefore, and take your coun-
trymen with you, and may the LORD grant
you his kindness and his faithful love."

21 However, Ittai replied to the king: "As
the LORD lives, and as my lord the king lives,
wherever my lord the king may be, whether
it means life or death, there your servant will
also be."[r]

22 David then said to Ittai: "Go ahead,
then, and march on!" Therefore, Ittai the
Gittite marched on with all his men and the
families that were with him. 23 Everyone in
the countryside wept aloud as the king and
all the people crossed the Wadi Kidron and
moved on toward the desert wilderness. *

David and the Priests. 24 Zadok was also
there, as well as all the Levites with him, as
they carried the Ark of the Covenant of God.
They set down the Ark of God beside
Abiathar until all those who were with them
had marched out of the city.

25 Then the king said to Zadok: "Take the
Ark of God back into the city. If I find favor
in the LORD's eyes, he will bring me back and
permit me to see both the Ark and the place
where it dwells. 26 But if he says: 'I am not
pleased with you,' then here I am. Let him do
with me as he sees fit."[s]

27 The king also said to Zadok the priest:
"Aren't you a seer? You and Abiathar can
return safely into the city with your sons,
your own son Ahimaaz, and Abiathar's son
Jonathan. 28 I shall wait at the fords of the
wilderness until I receive word from you."
29 Therefore, Zadok and Abiathar took the
Ark of God back to Jerusalem and remained
there.

30 David then ascended to the Mount of
Olives, weeping as he went, with his head
covered and walking barefoot. All the people
with him also covered their heads and wept
as they went.[t] 31 When it was revealed to
David that Ahithophel was among the con-
spirators with Absalom, he said: "O LORD, I
beg you to turn the counsel of Ahithophel
into folly."[u]

David and Hushai. 32 When David arrived at
the summit where God was worshiped,

m 2 Sam 13:37; Gen 28:20; Jn 4:21.—n 2 Sam 15:34; 16:23; Jos 15:51.—o 2 Sam 20:6; Lk 21:21.—p 2 Sam 16:21f; 20:3.—q 2 Sam 8:18; 20:7.—r Ru 1:16; 2 Ki 2:4.—s 1 Cor 10:5.—t 1 Chr 21:19; Mic 1:8.—u 2 Sam 16:23; 17:14, 23; Jdg 16:28.

15:14 What looks like cowardice in King David's decision to flee Jerusalem is more likely the wisdom and trust in God that has worked to his advantage in the past. Choosing his battles with confidence in the Lord's faithfulness will eventually bring him victory over Absalom.

15:23 The Kidron Valley lies between Jerusalem and Mount of Olives (see Jn 18:1).

Hushai the Archite came forth to meet him
with his tunic torn and with dirt upon his
head.[v] [33] David said to him: "If you come
with me, you will only be a burden to me.
[34] However, if you return to the city and say
to Absalom: 'I will be your servant, O king.
As I was formerly your father's servant, now
I will be your servant,' you will make it pos-
sible for me to frustrate the advice of
Ahithophel.[w]

[35] "The priests Zadok and Abiathar will be
with you there. Report to them everything
that you hear in the royal palace. [36] Their two
sons are there with them: Zadok's son
Ahimaaz, and Abiathar's son Jonathan.
Through them you shall send word to me of
everything you hear."

[37] So David's friend Hushai came into the
city just as Absalom was entering Jerusalem.

CHAPTER 16

David and Ziba. [1] When David had gone a
short distance beyond the summit, he was
met by Ziba, the servant of Meribbaal. Ziba
had with him a pair of saddled donkeys
laden with two hundred loaves of bread, one
hundred bunches of raisins, one hundred
bunches of summer fruits, and one skin of
wine.[x] [2] The king said to Ziba: "What are you
planning to do with these?" Ziba replied:
"The donkeys are for the king's family to ride
on, the bread and the fruit are for the sol-
diers to eat, and the wine is for those to drink
who fall exhausted in the desert."

[3] The king then asked: "And where is your
master's son?" Ziba replied: "He is staying in
Jerusalem, for he said: 'Today the house of
Israel will restore to me my father's king-
dom.' "[y] [4] Therefore, the king said to Ziba:
"Everything that belonged to Meribbaal is
yours." Then Ziba replied: "I humbly pay you
homage, my lord the king. May I always be
considered to be worthy of being granted
your favor."[z]

David and Shimei. [5] As King David was
nearing Horonaim, he was approached by a
man of the family of Saul. His name was
Shimei, the son of Gera, and he was cursing
as he drew near.[a] [6] He threw stones at David
and his servants, as well as at all the
people and the soldiers on his right and on
his left.

[7] As he cursed, Shimei shouted: "Get out,
get out, you murderous scoundrel! [8] The
LORD has repaid all of you for the blood of
the house of Saul whose sovereignty you
have stolen, and the LORD has given the king-
dom to your son Absalom. Now your
wickedness has caught up with you, for you
are a man of blood."[b]

[9] Then Abishai, the son of Zeruiah, said to
the king: "Why should this dead dog be
allowed to curse my lord the king? Let me go
over and behead him."[c] [10] However, the king
said: "What do you and I have in common,
you sons of Zeruiah? If he is cursing because
the LORD told him: 'Curse David,' who will
then dare to say: 'Why have you done so?' "[d]

[11] Then David said to Abishai and all his
servants: "If my own son who was conceived
from my loins is now seeking my life, how
much more understandable is it that this
Benjaminite is prepared to do so! Let him
alone, and let him curse, for the LORD has
instructed him to do so.[e] [12] Perhaps the
LORD will look upon my wretched condition
and grant me a blessing to repay me for the
curses that I have been forced to endure this
day."[f]

[13] Therefore, David and his men resumed
their journey, while Shimei kept abreast of
him on the opposite hillside, cursing as he
went and throwing stones and flinging dust
at him.[g] [14] When the king and all the people
with him reached the Jordan, they stopped
there to rest, for they were exhausted.

Absalom's Counselors.* [15] Meanwhile Absalom
and all of the Israelites entered Jerusalem,
and accompanying him was Ahithophel.
[16] Then Hushai the Archite, David's friend,
approached Absalom and said to him:
"Long live the king! Long live the king!"[h]

[17] Then Absalom asked Hushai: "Is this the
way you show loyalty to your friend?"
[18] Hushai replied to Absalom: "I intend to
follow the man whom the LORD and this
people and all the men of Israel have chosen,
and I will remain with him. [19] Besides, whom
should I serve if not his son? Just as I served
your father, so will I serve you."[i]

---

v 2 Sam 16:16; Est C:13.—w 2 Sam 16:19; Prov 11:14.—x 2 Sam 9:1-13; 1 Sam 25:18.—y 2 Sam 19:26f.—z Gen 27:29.—a 1 Ki 2:8.—b 2 Sam 19:5.—c 2 Sam 9:8; 19:23; 1 Sam 24:15; 26:6.—d 2 Sam 15:25f; Sir 33:12.—e 2 Sam 12:11; Jdg 3:15.—f 2 Ki 19:4; Ps 25:18.—g 2 Sam 19:19-24; 1 Ki 2:44.—h 2 Sam 15:32-37.—i 2 Sam 16:18.

16:15-23 Absalom takes up residence in Jerusalem and officially takes over his father's concubines, but this is a wicked act (see Gen 49:4). It is a mockery of David; Nathan had foretold this supreme humiliation as a consequence of his sin (2 Sam 12:11-12).

20 Then Absalom said to Ahithophel:
"Give us your counsel on what you think we
should do." 21 Ahithophel replied to Ab-
salom: "Go to your father's concubines
whom he left behind to take care of the
palace and have relations with them. As a
result, all Israel will hear that you have
greatly antagonized your father, and the
courage of all your supporters will be
strengthened." 22 Therefore, a tent was
pitched for Absalom upon the roof, and in
the sight of all Israel Absalom lay with his
father's concubines.[j]

Counsel of Ahithophel. 23 Now in those days
the counsel offered by Ahithophel was
regarded as counsel presented by God him-
self. And that was how the counsel of
Ahithophel was regarded by both David and
Absalom.[k]

CHAPTER 17

1 Ahithophel said to Absalom: "Let me
choose twelve thousand men, and I will set
forth in pursuit of David this very night. 2 I
plan to overtake him when he is weary and
discouraged and to throw him into a panic.
Then, when all the people who are with him
flee, I will strike down only the king.[l] 3 After
that, I will bring all the people back to you,
like a bride returning to her husband. You
are seeking the death of only one man. The
rest of the people will be unharmed."
4 Absalom and all the elders of Israel found
this plan to be satisfactory.

Counsel of Hushai. 5 Then Absalom said:
"Now also summon Hushai the Archite, and
let us hear what he has to say."[m] 6 When
Hushai arrived, Absalom said to him: "This
is what Ahithophel suggested. Shall we do as
he advises? If not, give us your ideas in this
regard."

7 Hushai replied to Absalom: "On this par-
ticular occasion Ahithophel has not offered
good advice." 8 Then he went on to say: "You
well know that your father and his men are
warriors and that they are as fierce as a bear
in the wilderness who has been robbed of her
cubs. In addition, your father is unsurpassed
in devising strategy, and he will not spend
the night with the troops.[n]

9 "You can be certain that even now he has
concealed himself in a cave or some other
place. And if some of our troops should be
slain during the first attack, the word will
quickly spread that the followers of Absalom
have been slaughtered. 10 Then even the
most valiant of our warriors, with courage
like that of a lion, will shrink away in fear. For
all Israel well knows that your father is a
warrior and that those who serve with him
are brave.[o]

11 "This is the advice that I offer to you.
Summon all Israel, from Dan to Beer-sheba,
to be gathered in support of you, and be at
their side as they march into battle. 12 When
we catch up with him, wherever he may be
found, we shall then attack him and descend
upon him as the dew falls upon the ground.
He will not survive, nor will any of those with
him. 13 And if he should withdraw into a
town, all Israel shall bring ropes into that
town, and we shall drag it down into a gorge
so that not even a single remnant of it can be
found there."

14 Then Absalom and all the Israelites
declared: "The counsel of Hushai the Archite
is superior to that of Ahithophel." For the
LORD had determined to frustrate the
shrewd advice of Ahithophel and thereby
bring disaster on Absalom.[p]

David Told of the Plan. 15 Then Hushai said
to the priests Zadok and Abiathar: "This is
the counsel that Ahithophel gave to Absalom
and the elders of Israel, and this is what I
advised. 16 Therefore, send a warning to
David without delay and tell him: 'Do not
spend the night at the fords in the desert, but
cross over as quickly as you can. Otherwise
the king and all the people with him may be
annihilated.' "[q]

17 Jonathan and Ahimaaz were waiting at
En-rogel. A servant girl used to go there and
report to them what was happening, and
then they would go and inform King David,
for they could not risk being seen entering
the city. 18 However, a young lad saw them
and informed Absalom. Therefore, the two
of them ran off quickly and went to the house
of a man in Horonaim. He had a cistern in
his courtyard, and they climbed down into it.

19 The man's wife then took a covering,
stretched it out over the cistern, and strewed
crushed grain on it so that nothing would be
noticed. 20 When the servants of Absalom
came to the woman at the house, they asked:

j 2 Sam 12:11f.—k 2 Sam 15:12; 17:23.—l 1 Ki 2:29.—m
2 Sam 16:20.—n Prov 17:12.—o Ex 15:3; Jos 2:11.—p 2 Sam
15:31; 1 Chr 27:33.—q 2 Sam 15:28.

"Where are Ahimaaz and Jonathan?" The woman replied: "They went by here a short while ago and went toward the water." They continued their pursuit, but when they found no sight of them, they returned to Jerusalem.[r]

21 After they had departed, the two men climbed out of the cistern and went to warn King David. "Leave immediately and cross the water quickly," they said, as they related to him how Ahithophel had decided to proceed against him. 22 Therefore, David and all of the people with him set out and crossed the Jordan. By dawn there was not a single one left who had not crossed to the opposite bank of the Jordan.

23 When Ahithophel realized that his advice had not been followed, he saddled his donkey and departed straight home to his own town. Then, having left detailed instructions to ensure the well-being of his family, he hanged himself. He died and was buried in his father's tomb.[s]

24 By the time that Absalom had crossed the Jordan with all the men of Israel, David had already reached Mahanaim. 25 Absalom had appointed Amasa to be commander of the army in Joab's place. Amasa was the son of a man called Ithra the Ishmaelite who had married Abigail, the daughter of Nahash and the sister of Joab's mother Zeruiah.[t] 26 The Israelites and Absalom encamped in the territory of Gilead.

27 When David came to Mahanaim, he was greeted by Shobi, the son of Nahash from Rabbah of the Ammonites, and Machir, the son of Ammiel from Lo-debar, and Barzillai the Gileadite from Rogelim.[u] 28 They brought bedding, basins, and earthen vessels, wheat, barley, flour, roasted grain, beans, lentils, 29 honey and curds, and cheese from the flocks and herds for David and the people with him to eat, as they said: "Your troops must have been hungry and thirsty and exhausted in the desert."

CHAPTER 18

Preparation for Battle. 1 David mustered the men who were with him, and he appointed commanders to be in charge of units of a thousand and units of a hundred.* 2 Then David divided his army into three groups: one under the command of Joab, another under the command of Abishai, the son of Zeruiah and the brother of Joab, and the third under the command of Ittai the Gittite. After that, the king said to the soldiers: "I myself will also march forth with you."[v]

3 However, the soldiers replied: "You must not come with us. If we are forced to flee, they will not be concerned about us, not even if half of us should die. However, you are worth ten thousand of us. It would be better if you remain in the city to supply whatever help we may need."

4 The king said to them: "I shall do whatever seems best to you." Then he stood beside the gate while all the soldiers marched out by hundreds and by thousands. 5 He also gave this order to Joab, Abishai, and Ittai: "For my sake, deal gently with the young man Absalom." And all of the soldiers heard the king give this directive to the commanders in regard to Absalom.

Defeat of Absalom. 6 Then the army marched into the field against Israel, and a battle was fought in the forest near Mahanaim.[w] 7 The Israelite forces were defeated there by the forces of David, and the casualties numbered twenty thousand men. 8 The battle spread over the entire countryside, and the forest claimed more victims that day than the sword.

Death of Absalom. 9 Meanwhile, Absalom, by chance, happened to encounter some of David's men. He was riding on his mule, and as it passed under the thick branches of a large oak, his head became caught in its branches, and he was left hanging in midair while the mule he had been riding continued on.[x] 10 Someone who had seen this reported to Joab: "I saw Absalom hanging from an oak."

11 Joab said to the man who had informed him: "If you actually saw him, why then did you not strike him to the ground then and there? I would have willingly given you ten pieces of silver and a belt."

12 However, the man replied to Joab: "Even if you were to weigh out a thousand shekels of silver and place them in the palm of my hand, I would not raise my hand against the king's son. For in our hearing the king charged you and Abishai and Ittai: 'Protect

r 1 Mac 4:5; Lk 9:53.—s 2 Sam 15:31; Ezr 2:1.—t 2 Sam 20:4-13; 1 Chr 18:15.—u 2 Sam 9:4,5; 1 Ki 2:7.—v Jud 14:2.—w Jos 17:18.—x 2 Sam 13:29.

18:1 In stark contrast to the ineffectual behavior David has recently adopted, he finally acts like the leader he had formerly been. This is the beginning of the end for Absalom.

the young man Absalom for my sake.'[y] 13 On
the other hand, if I had dealt treacherously
with Absalom and thereby placed my life in
jeopardy—and nothing is hidden from the
king—then you would have dissociated your-
self from me."[z]

14 Joab then answered him bluntly: "I can-
not waste my time arguing with you."
Thereupon he took three javelins in his hand
and thrust them into the heart of Absalom
while he was still alive, hanging in midair
from the oak tree.[a] 15 Then ten young men
who served as Joab's armor-bearers closed
in on Absalom, struck him, and killed him.

16 After that, Joab ordered the trumpet to
be sounded, and the soldiers ceased their
pursuit of Israel because he had ordered
them to halt.[b] 17 They picked up Absalom,
flung his body into a large pit in the forest,
and piled up a great mound of stones over
him. Meanwhile all the Israelites had fled to
their tents.[c]

18 During his lifetime Absalom had taken a
pillar and erected it for himself in the King's
Valley, for he said: "I have no son to perpetu-
ate the memory of my name." He named the
pillar after himself, and to the present day it
is still called Absalom's Monument.[d]

David Told of Absalom's Death. 19 Then
Ahimaaz, the son of Zadok, said to Joab:
"Grant me permission to take the good news
to the king that the Lord has delivered him
from the power of his enemies." 20 But Joab
replied: "Today you would not be the bearer
of good news. On some other day, you may
do so, but you shall not do so today, because
the king's son is dead."

21 Then Joab said to an Ethiopian: "Go
forth and report to the king what you have
witnessed." The Ethiopian bowed down
before Joab and ran off. 22 Then Ahimaaz, the
son of Zadok, again said to Joab: "Come what
may, allow me to run after the Ethiopian."

Joab replied: "My son, why do you wish to
go? You will not receive any reward for the
news you bring." 23 "Come what may," he
answered, "I want to run." Joab finally
relented, and he said: "I grant you leave to
depart." Then Ahimaaz sped off by way of
the plain of the Jordan and outran the
Ethiopian.

24 While David was sitting between the
inner and the outer wall, a sentry went up to
the roof of the gate by the wall, and when he
looked up, he saw a man running alone.
25 The sentry called down to the king and
reported this to him. "If he is alone," said the
king, "he has some news to tell us."

26 As the man continued to draw nearer,
the sentry beheld another man running, and
he shouted to the gatekeeper, saying: "Look!
Here comes another man running alone."
The king asserted: "He must also be bring-
ing good news."[e] 27 The sentry added: "The
first one runs just like Ahimaaz, the son of
Zadok." The king replied: "He is a good man,
and I feel certain that he comes with good
news to report."[f]

28 Then Ahimaaz called out to the king:
"All is well!" After that he prostrated himself
before the king with his face to the ground
and said: "Blessed be the LORD, your God,
for he has delivered up the men who rebelled
against my lord the king."

29 Thereupon the king asked: "Is all well
with the young man Absalom?" Ahimaaz
answered: "When the king's servant Joab
sent your servant forth, I was aware of a
great commotion, but I do not know what it
was all about." 30 The king said: "Stand off to
the side and wait over there." Therefore, he
stepped aside and remained there.

31 When the Ethiopian arrived, he said: "I
bring good news for my lord the king. For the
LORD has vindicated you this day, delivering
you from the power of all those who rebelled
against you." 32 Then the king asked the
Ethiopian: "Has all gone well with the young
man Absalom?" The Ethiopian answered:
"May the enemies of my lord the king and all
those who rise up to harm you share the fate
of that young man."[g]

33 Greatly shaken, the king went up to the
chamber over the gate, weeping incessantly.
And as he went, he cried out: "O my son
Absalom! My son! My son Absalom! If only I
had died instead of you, Absalom, my son,
my son!" *

CHAPTER 19

Joab Reproves David. 1 Word was brought
to Joab: "The king is weeping and mourning

---

y 1 Ki 2:28.—z Sir 22:26.—a 2 Sam 2:25-26; 12:10; 13:28f; Job 16:14.—b 2 Sam 2:28.—c Jos 7:26; 8:29.—d Gen 14:17; Jdg 16:29-30.—e 2 Sam 18:27.—f 2 Ki 9:20.—g 1 Sam 25:26.

18:33 David's lament over his son Absalom's death is the typical response of any loving parent. No matter how difficult the relationship has been, it is not natural for a child to predecease a parent, and in this case there is a lot of guilt and failure on David's part to explain Absalom's mistakes.

for Absalom."[h] 2 Therefore, that day's victory was turned into one of mourning for the entire army when the troops heard the report: "The king is grieving for his son."

3 The troops stole furtively into the city that day, much as soldiers steal in who are ashamed when they flee from a battle. 4 Meanwhile the king covered his face and cried out in a loud voice: "O my son Absalom! O Absalom, my son, my son!"

5 Then Joab came to the king's house and said to him: "Today you have caused all of your officers and servants to feel ashamed, humiliating those who saved your life today, and the lives of your sons and daughters, and the lives of your wives and concubines,[i] 6 by showing love for those who hate you and hatred for those who love you.

"You have made it perfectly clear that your commanders and soldiers mean nothing to you. I feel certain that if Absalom were still alive and all the rest of us were dead, then you would be pleased. 7 Therefore, get up, come out, and reassure your servants. I swear by the LORD that if you do not go out, not one man will be left with you by nightfall, and that will be worse for you than all the calamities you have endured from your youth until now."[j]

8 On hearing these words, the king arose and took his seat at the gate. When it was announced to the troops: "The king is sitting at the gate," they all assembled there before him.[k]

The Reconciliation. Meanwhile all the Israelites had fled to their homes. 9 However, throughout all the tribes of Israel, there was great dissension, and the people were arguing among themselves, saying: "The king delivered us from the clutches of our enemies and rescued us from the hands of the Philistines. But now he has fled from the country to escape from Absalom. 10 However, Absalom, whom we anointed to reign over us, has fallen in battle. Why, then, does no one offer the suggestion that we should restore the king to his palace?"

11 When King David learned of the debate that was ensuing throughout Israel, he sent this message to the priests Zadok and Abiathar: "Say to the elders of Judah: 'Why should you be the last to bring back the king to his palace? 12 You are my brothers, my own flesh and blood. Why then should you be the last to bring the king home?'

13 "And say to Amasa: 'Are you not my bone and my flesh? * May God deal with me in the most severe way possible if from now on you are not the commander of my army in place of Joab.' "[l] 14 With those words, David won over the hearts of all the men of Judah as though they were one man, and they sent this message to the king: "Return, both you and all who serve you."

David and Shimei. 15 When the king on his return reached the Jordan, the men of Judah came to Gilgal to greet him and escort him across the river.[m] 16 Shimei, the son of Gera the Benjaminite, from Horonaim, hurried down with the men of Judah to welcome King David.

17 Accompanying Shimei were one thousand men from Benjamin. Ziba, the servant of the house of Saul, together with his fifteen sons and twenty servants, hastened to the Jordan ahead of the king. 18 They crossed at the ford to transport the king's household and to do whatever the king requested.

When Shimei, the son of Gera, crossed the Jordan, he threw himself down before the king, 19 [n] and he said: "I entreat my lord not to hold me guilty or to remember how shamefully I behaved on the day my lord the king departed from Jerusalem. I beg you not to hold my guilt against me. 20 I humbly admit that I have sinned. Today I am the first of all the house of Joseph to come down to meet my lord the king."

21 However, Abishai, the son of Zeruiah, objected, saying: "Should not Shimei be put to death because he cursed the LORD's anointed?" 22 David replied: "Of what concern are my decisions to you, you sons of Zeruiah, that you have become my adversary? Should anyone be put to death this day in Israel? Am I not fully aware that today I am king of Israel?" 23 Then the king said to Shimei: "You shall not die," and he confirmed that with an oath.[o]

David and Meribbaal. 24 Meribbaal, the grandson of Saul, also came down to greet the king. He had not bathed his feet or

h Jdg 20:26.—i 2 Sam 15:30.—j Prov 14:28.—k 2 Sam 15:2.—l Gen 29:14.—m Jos 5:9.—n 19ff: 2 Sam 16:13; Ex 22:27; 1 Ki 2:8, 44.—o 2 Sam 16:9f; 1 Sam 11:13; 1 Ki 2:8, 42.

19:13 *My bone and my flesh:* David displays his keen sense of diplomacy in replacing Joab and appointing Amasa as his commander, thereby, effecting the union of the kingdom which is what David was all about.

trimmed his beard or washed his clothes from the day the king departed until the day he returned safely.

25 When he came from Jerusalem to meet the king, the king asked him: "Why did you not go with me, Meribbaal?"[p] 26 He said: "My lord the king, my servant betrayed me. Since your servant is lame, I said to him: 'Saddle a donkey for me so that I may ride on it and accompany the king.'

27 "However, he has slandered your servant to my lord the king. But I well know that your majesty is like an angel of God. Do what you judge to be best. 28 Although my father's entire family deserved to die at your majesty's hands, you placed me, your servant, among those who eat at your table. What right do I have to make any further appeals to the king?"[q]

29 However, the king said to him: "There is no necessity for you to say anything further. I have decided that you and Ziba shall divide the property equally." 30 Meribbaal replied to the king: "Let him take it all, inasmuch as my lord the king has arrived home safely."

David and Barzillai. 31 Barzillai the Gileadite had come down from Rogelim, and he accompanied the king to the Jordan, where he then planned to take leave of him. 32 Barzillai was quite elderly, eighty years old. He was the one who had provided for the king during David's stay at Mahanaim, for he was a very wealthy man.[r]

33 The king said to Barzillai: "Cross over with me and stay with me as my guest, and I will provide for you in Jerusalem." 34 But Barzillai replied to the king: "How many more years do I have to live, that I should go up with the king to Jerusalem? 35 I am now eighty years old. Can I distinguish between what is pleasant and what is not? Can your servant taste what he eats or what he drinks? Can I still hear the voices of men and women singing? Why then should your servant be an added burden to my lord the king?[s]

36 "Your servant will go a short distance across the Jordan with the king. That hardly makes me worthy to receive such a generous reward. 37 Please allow your servant to return to his own town and end his days there, near the graves of my father and my mother. But here is your servant Chimham. Let him cross over with my lord the king, and then do for him whatever you think is right."

38 The king replied: "Chimham shall cross over with me. I shall do for him whatever you wish, and whatever you request from me, I will do for you." 39 Thereupon all the people crossed the Jordan, and then the king also crossed over. After the king had kissed Barzillai and blessed him, Barzillai returned to his home.[t] 40 Then the king continued on his journey to Gilgal, accompanied by Chimham.

Israel and Judah Quarrel. All the people of Judah and half the people of Israel had escorted the king across the river. 41 Before long, all the men of Israel came to the king and complained: "Why have our brothers, the men of Judah, stolen you away and joined with all David's men in escorting the king and his household across the Jordan?" 42 Then all the men of Judah replied to the men of Israel: "We did so because the king is our close relative. What right do you have to complain about this? Have we eaten anything at the king's expense? Have we received any gifts from him?"

43 The men of Israel retorted to the men of Judah: "We have ten shares in the king. In addition, we have a greater claim than you do. Why do you continue to slight us? Were we not the first ones to suggest the possibility of bringing back the king?" However, the words of the men of Judah were even more vitriolic than the words of the men of Israel.[u]

CHAPTER 20

Sheba's Rebellion. 1 A trouble-making scoundrel named Sheba, the son of Bichri and a Benjaminite, happened to be there. He sounded the trumpet and cried out:

"We have no share in David,
nor any portion in the son of Jesse.
Every man to his tent, O Israel!"[v]

2 When they heard this, all the men of Israel deserted David to follow Sheba, the son of Bichri. However, the people of Judah maintained their loyalty to the king and followed him steadfastly all the way from the Jordan to Jerusalem.

3 When David returned to his palace in Jerusalem, he took the ten concubines whom he had left behind to look after the palace, and he put them in a house under guard. He

p 2 Sam 21:7.—q Zec 12:8.—r 2 Sam 17:27ff; 1 Ki 2:7; Ezr 2:61; Neh 7:63.—s Ps 90:10; Isa 21:11.—t Gen 45:15.—u 1 Ki 11:31.—v 1 Sam 13:3; 1 Ki 12:16.

provided for them, but he did not engage in relations with them. They were shut up in confinement until the day of their death, living as if they were widows.[w]

Amasa's Death. 4 Then the king said to Amasa: "Summon the men of Judah and order them to appear before me within three days."[x] 5 Amasa set out to summon the men of Judah, but his mission took longer than the time specified by the king.

6 Then David said to Abishai: "Sheba, son of Bichri, may very well prove to do greater damage to us than Absalom. Take your lord's servants and pursue him before he can reach any fortified towns and escape from us." 7 Therefore, Joab's forces, the Cherethites, the Pelethites, and all of the most skilled warriors marched out under the command of Abishai and left Jerusalem to pursue Sheba, son of Bichri.[y]

8 When they arrived at the large stone in Gibeon, Amasa came forth from the opposite direction to meet them. Joab was wearing his tunic, and over it was a belt with a sword in its sheath fastened at his waist. As he moved forward, the sword fell loose from his sheath. 9 Then Joab said to Amasa: "I trust that you are well, my brother." Having said that, Joab grasped Amasa's beard with his right hand as if to kiss him.

10 Amasa was not on his guard and failed to notice the sword in Joab's left hand. Joab struck him with it in the belly so that his entrails poured forth to the ground. He did not find it necessary to strike a second blow, since Amasa had died instantaneously. Then Joab set forth with his brother Abishai in pursuit of Sheba, son of Bichri.[z]

11 One of Joab's men stood on guard next to the body of Amasa, and he shouted: "Follow Joab, all those of you who favor Joab and support David!" 12 Meanwhile Amasa lay wallowing in his blood in the middle of the road, and the man who had exhorted all of his fellow soldiers to follow Joab saw that everyone was stopping to stare at the body. Therefore, he carried Amasa's body from the road and placed it in a field, with a garment covering the corpse.[a] 13 Once the body had been removed from the road, all the men moved on and followed Joab in pursuit of Sheba, son of Bichri.

Joab Pursues Sheba. 14 Sheba passed through all the tribes of Israel until he arrived at Abel-beth-maacah.* Shortly afterward, all of the Bichrites assembled and followed him into the town.[b] 15 Joab's forces then arrived and besieged him in Abel-beth-maacah. After they threw up a siege ramp against the town, all of Joab's forces began to batter the wall to throw it down.

16 *Suddenly a wise woman stood on the rampart and shouted from the town: "Listen! Listen! Tell Joab to come here so that I may speak with him." 17 When Joab approached her, the woman asked: "Are you Joab?" He answered: "I am." She continued: "Listen to what your maidservant has to say." He replied: "I am listening."

18 She then spoke as follows: "In the old days they used to say: 'Go to Abel if you wish to find the answer,' and in that way a matter would be settled. 19 This town prides itself on being one of the most peaceful and loyal in Israel. She is like a faithful mother, and yet you are seeking to destroy her. Why do you seek to devour the inheritance of the LORD?"[c]

20 Joab replied: "Not at all! Far be it from me to devour or to destroy anything. 21 That is not the case at all. However, a man from the hill country of Ephraim, named Sheba, son of Bichri, has rebelled against King David. If you surrender to us just this one man, I will withdraw from the town." The woman said to Joab: "His head will be thrown over the wall to you."

22 Then the woman went to confer with all the people, and they followed her advice, cutting off the head of Sheba, son of Bichri, and throwing it to Joab. Thereupon he sounded the trumpet, and all of his forces withdrew from the town, each to his own home while Joab returned to the king in Jerusalem.

David's Officials. 23 Joab was the commander of the entire army in Israel. Benaiah, son of Jehoiada, was in command

w 2 Sam 15:16; 16:20ff; Gen 38:26.—x 2 Sam 17:25; 19:14.—y 2 Sam 8:18.—z 2 Sam 3:27, 30; 1 Ki 2:5.—a Jud 9:3.—b Ezek 9:5.—c 2 Sam 21:3.

20:14 *Abel-beth-maacah:* a fortified town near Dan, in the far north of Israel.

20:16ff *A wise woman . . . shouted from the town:* this marks the second incidence in 2 Samuel of a wise woman taking on a traditional male role as spokesperson (see 2 Sam 14:1-20). Previously the wise woman from Tekoa interceded with King David at Joab's instruction. Now another woman speaks up of her own accord and is able to convince Joab to spare her town.

of the Cherethites and the Pelethites.[d] 24 Adoram was in charge of the forced labor. Jehoshaphat, son of Ahilud, was the recorder. 25 Sheva was the secretary. Zadok and Abiathar were priests.[e] 26 Ira the Jairite was also David's priest.

II: APPENDICES*

CHAPTER 21

Gibeonite Vengeance.* 1 During the reign of David there was a famine for three successive years. Therefore, David consulted the LORD, who said: "Saul and his family have incurred bloodguilt because he put the Gibeonites to death."[f] 2 Thereupon the king summoned the Gibeonites and conferred with them. (Now the Gibeonites were not Israelites; rather they were a remnant of the Amorites. Although the Israelites had sworn to spare them, Saul had sought to exterminate them in his zeal for the people of Israel and Judah.)[g]

3 David said to the Gibeonites: "What can I do for you? How shall I atone for our treatment of you so that you may bless the heritage of the LORD?" 4 The Gibeonites replied: "We have no right to demand silver or gold from Saul and his family, nor do we have the right to put anyone to death." "Then what do you want me to do for you?" asked David.[h]

5 They said to the king: "We cannot forget that man who destroyed us and planned to annihilate us so that we would never be able to have a place in the territory of Israel. 6 Please hand over to us seven of his male descendants, so that we may dismember them before the LORD at Gibeon on the mountain of the LORD." The king replied: "I will hand them over to you."[i]

7 However, the king spared Meribbaal, the son of Jonathan, son of Saul, because of the oath of the Lord that bound together David and Saul's son Jonathan.[j] 8 But the king took Armoni and Meribbaal, the two sons that Rizpah, the daughter of Aiah, had borne to Saul, and the five sons of Saul's daughter Merab whom she had borne to Adriel, the son of Barzillai of Meholah.[k] 9 He surrendered them into the hands of the Gibeonites, who dismembered them on the mountain before the LORD. All seven of them perished together. They were put to death during the first days of the harvest, just as the barley harvest was beginning.

10 Then Rizpah, the daughter of Aiah, took sackcloth and spread it out on a rock for herself, from the beginning of the harvest until the rain fell from the heavens upon the bodies. She kept the birds of the sky away from the bodies by day and the wild beasts by night.[l]

11 When David was informed about what Aiah's daughter Rizpah, the concubine of Saul, had done, 12 he went forth and took the bones of Saul and the bones of his son Jonathan from the people of Jabesh-gilead, who had absconded with them from the public square of Beth-shan, where the Philistines had hung them up after they had killed Saul on Gilboa.[m]

13 After David had removed from there the bones of Saul and the bones of his son Jonathan, he also gathered up the bones of those who had been slain and dismembered. 14 The bones of Saul and his son Jonathan were buried at Zela, in the territory of Benjamin, in the tomb of Saul's father Kish. After all of the king's commands had been carried out, God answered prayers that were offered up on behalf of the country.[n]

Exploits in Philistine Wars.* 15 Once again the Philistines went to war against Israel. David went down with his men to fight against the Philistines, but he began to grow weary. 16 Ishbi-benob one of the descendants of the Rephaim, whose bronze spear weighed three hundred shekels and who was wielding new weapons, boasted that he would have no difficulty in slaying David.

17 However, Abishai, the son of Zeruiah, came to David's rescue, attacking the Philistine and slaying him. Then David's men swore to him this oath: "Never again must you go forth with us to engage in battle, lest the lamp of Israel be extinguished."[o]

d 2 Sam 8:16ff; 23:20; 1 Chr 18:15, 17.—e 2 Sam 8:17f; 1 Chr 15:11.—f 2 Sam 24:13; Lk 4:25.—g Jos 9:3-27.—h Ps 49:7-9.—i Num 25:4.—j 2 Sam 9:6, 13; 1 Sam 18:3; 20:8ff, 15f, 42.—k 2 Sam 3:7.—l 2 Sam 3:31; 12:16.—m 1 Sam 31: 10-13.—n 2 Sam 24:25.—o 1 Ki 11:36; 15:4; 2 Ki 8:19; Ps 132:17.

21:1—24:25 A series of conjoined passages interrupts the history of the Davidic succession; the final act in this history will be found at the beginning of the First Book of Kings.

21:1-14 In accordance with the idea then current, that every misfortune is a result of sin, the famine is attributed to an atrocity of Saul. The descendants of the guilty person must, therefore, be put to death. Perhaps David takes the occasion to rid himself of some rivals; the son of Jonathan is spared (see 2 Sam 9:1ff).

21:15-22 A story that is epic and legendary in character.

[18] After this, war again broke out with the
Philistines in Gob. On that occasion,
Sibbecai of Husha killed Saph, one of the
Rephaim.[p] [19] [q] Shortly afterward there was
another battle with the Philistines at Gob,
and Elhanan, the son of Jair from Bethlehem
killed Goliath of Gath, the shaft of whose
spear was like a weaver's beam.

[20] There was yet another battle which took
place at Gath, where a giant appeared with
six fingers on each hand and six toes on each
foot—twenty-four in all. He too was
descended from the Rephaim. [21] When he
started to taunt Israel, Jonathan, the son of
David's brother Shimei, killed him.

[22] These four giants were descendants of
the Rephaim in Gath, and they fell at the
hands of David and his servants.

CHAPTER 22*

Song of Thanksgiving. [1] David sang to the
LORD the words of this song on the day when
the LORD delivered him from the hands of all
his enemies and from the hands of Saul.[r]
[2] [s] He sang:

"The LORD is my rock,
my fortress and my deliverer,
my God, my rock in whom I take refuge.
3 You are my shield and my saving strength,
my stronghold and my refuge,
my savior who delivers me from violence.[t]
4 I call upon the LORD
who is worthy of all praise;
then I shall be saved from my enemies.

5 The waves of death encompassed me,
and the destructive torrents assailed me.[u]
6 The bonds of Sheol enmeshed me;
the snares of death confronted me.
7 In my distress I called out to the LORD;
I called to my God for help.
From his temple he heard my voice,
and my cry to him reached his ears.

8 "The earth quaked and shook;
the foundations of the heavens trembled,
quaking because of his blazing anger.
9 Smoke rose from his nostrils,
while a devouring fire poured forth from his mouth
that kindled coals into flame.

10 "He parted the heavens and came down;
dark clouds lay under his feet.
11 He descended on the back of a cherub and flew,
soaring swiftly on the wings of the wind.[v]

12 "He used the darkness as his covering;
dense thunderclouds were his canopy.[w]
13 From the radiance before him
coals were kindled into burning fire.

14 "The LORD thundered from the heavens,
and the Most High caused his voice to resound.
15 He shot his arrows and scattered them;
he hurled forth his lightning bolts and routed them.

16 "Then the depths of the sea were exposed,
and the earth's foundations ware laid bare.
This occurred at the rebuke of the LORD,
at the blast of breath from his nostrils.[x]

17 "He reached down from on high and snatched me up;
he drew me out of the watery depths.[y]
18 He delivered me from my mighty enemy,
from my foes who were too powerful for me.

19 "They confronted me in my hour of calamity,
but the LORD came forward to support me.
20 He set me free in a spacious field;
he rescued me because he loves me.

21 "The LORD has rewarded me for my righteousness;
because my hands were pure he has recompensed me.
22* For I have kept the ways of the LORD
and have not followed the path of wickedness.

23 "His laws are clearly known to me,
and I have not failed to observe his decrees.
24 I was blameless in his sight,
and I kept myself free from sin.[z]

p 1 Chr 11:29; 20:4-8.—q 19f: 1 Sam 17:4, 7; 1 Chr 20:5.—r Ex 15:1; Ps 18:1.—s 2-51: Pss 18:3-51; 144:2.—t 1 Sam 2:1f; Isa 60:18.—u Ps 69:15.—v Ex 25:18; Ps 104:3.—w Eccl 11:3.—x Job 28:11.—y Ps 144:7; Mt 14:30f.—z Gen 6:9.

22:1-51 This passage and Ps 18 are essentially the same with a few differences. David's musical talents as composer and harpist are evident in this hymn of thanksgiving.

22:22-25 This section seems to deny David's sinfulness, but is more of a tribute to God's forgiveness and faithfulness (i.e., in God's eyes, all is forgiven and David is "whiter than snow;" Ps 51:7).

25 Therefore, the LORD has rewarded my righteousness,
the cleanness of my hands in his sight.
26 "To the faithful you show yourself faithful;
to the blameless you show yourself blameless.
27 To the pure you show yourself pure,
but to the perverse you show yourself to be shrewd.
28 Those who are humble you save,
but you ignore those who are haughty.
29 "You, O LORD, are my lamp;
my God will enlighten my darkness.
30 With your help I can storm a rampart;
with my God to aid me I can scale any wall.
31 The way of God is blameless;
the LORD's promise has proved true.
He is a shield to all
who take refuge in him. [a]
32 "For who is God except the LORD?
Who is a rock aside from our God?
33 The God who girds me with strength
has kept my feet free of obstacles.
34 This God has made my feet swift as a deer's
and set me securely on the heights. [b]
35 He trains my hands for war
so that my arms can bend a bow of bronze.
36 "You have given me the shield of salvation;
you stoop down to make me great.
37 You broaden the path for my steps,
and my feet have not slipped.
38 "I pursued my enemies and destroyed them;
I did not turn back until I made an end of them.
39 I crushed them completely and they did not rise;
they fell under my feet.
40 "You girded me with strength for the battle;
you subdued my assailants beneath me.
41 You caused my enemies to retreat before me,
and those who hated me I destroyed.
42 "They cried out for help,
but there was no one to save them.
They cried out to the LORD,
but he did not answer them. [c]
43 I ground them as fine as the dust of the earth;
I trampled them down like dust in the streets.
44 "You have delivered me from the strife of my people;
you made me the head of the nations;
a people I did not know became my subjects. [d]
45 Foreigners came forth cringing before me;
as soon as they heard of me, they obeyed me.
46 Having become disheartened,
they came forth trembling from their strongholds. [e]
47 "The LORD lives! Blessed be my rock.
Exalted be the God of my salvation
48 O God, you granted me vengeance
and subjected entire nations to me.
49 You freed me from my enemies
and exalted me above my adversaries,
delivering me from violent men. [f]
50 "For this I will praise you among the nations, O LORD,
and sing praise to your name. [g]
51 You have given great victories to your king,
and you have shown steadfast love to your anointed,
to David and his descendants forever."

CHAPTER 23

The Last Words of David* 1 These are the last words of David:

"The oracle of David, the son of Jesse,
the oracle of the man whom the Most High exalted,
the anointed of the God of Jacob
and the beloved of the Mighty One of Israel: [h]
2 "The Spirit of the LORD has spoken through me;
his word is on my tongue. [i]
3 The God of Israel has spoken;
the Rock of Israel has said of me:
'He who rules people justly,
who rules in the fear of God [j]
4 is like the morning light at sunrise
on a cloudless morning after rainfall

a Deut 32:4; Prov 30:5; Mt 5:48.—b Isa 33:16; Hab 3:19.—c Prov 1:28.—d Jer 1:10; Acts 12:11.—e Jer 5:22; Mic 7:17.—f 2 Tim 4:18.—g Ps 22:23; Rom 15:9.—h Num 24:16; 1 Ki 2:1-9; Sir 47:8.—i Ps 139:4; Isa 59:21; Jer 1:9.—j Ps 72:1-4; Sir 9:16.

23:1-7 This canticle is paired with the preceding chapter. It can be compared with the final words of Jacob (Gen 49) and Moses (Deut 33).

that causes the grass of the earth to
sparkle.'[k]

5 "My house stands firm with God,
for he has made an everlasting cov-
enant with me,
well ordered in all things and secure.
Will he not bring to fruition
my salvation and my every desire?[l]

6 "But the ungodly are all like thorns
that must be cast aside,
for they cannot be grasped by the
hand.[m]

7 No one dares to touch them
except with an iron bar or the shaft of
a spear,
and then only to consume them by
fire."

David's Warriors. 8 [n]These are the names of
David's warriors. Ishbaal, a Hachamonite,
was the leader of the Three. It was he who
brandished his spear over eight hundred
men and slew all of them at one time.

9 Next to him among the Three was
Eleazar, the son of Dodo the Ahohite. He was
with David at Pas-dammim when the
Philistines had assembled there for battle.
When the Israelites withdrew, 10 he stood his
ground and struck down the Philistines until
his hand became so stiff that he was unable to
release it from the sword. The LORD brought
about a great victory that day. Afterward the
people rallied around him, but only so that
they might be able to strip the dead.

11 Next to him was Shammah, the son of
Agee the Hararite. The Philistines had gath-
ered together at Lehi where there was a field
with an abundant crop of lentils. When the
Israelites fled upon being confronted by the
Philistines,[o] 12 Shammah took his stand in
the middle of the field, defended it, and cut
down the Philistines. Thus the LORD brought
about a great victory.

13 At the beginning of the harvest, three of
the Thirty went down to join David at the
cave of Adullam, while a band of Philistines
was encamped in the Valley of Rephaim.[p]
14 David was then in the stronghold, and
there was a garrison of Philistines in
Bethlehem.

15 One day David said longingly: "Oh, if
only someone would give me some water to
drink from the well that is by the gate of
Bethlehem!" 16 On hearing this, the Three
forced their way through the camp of the
Philistines, drew water from the well by the
gate of Bethlehem, and presented it to David.
However, he refused to drink it, and instead,
he poured it out to the LORD,[q] 17 saying: "The
LORD forbid that I should do this. How can I
drink the blood of the men who went forth to
obtain it and thereby placed their lives at
risk?" Therefore, he would not drink it.

18 Abishai, the brother of Joab and the son
of Zeruiah, was chief of the Thirty. It was he
who brandished his spear over three hun-
dred men whom he had killed. 19 He was the
most illustrious member of the Thirty and
he became their commander. However, he
never became one of the Three.

20 Benaiah of Kabzeel was the son of
Jehoiada and a valiant warrior who was
renowned for many great exploits. It was he
who slaughtered two of Moab's most
renowned warriors. On one occasion he also
lowered himself into a pit and killed a lion on
a day when snow had fallen.[r] 21 Further-
more, he was the one who slew an Egyptian,
a man of striking stature who was armed
with a spear. Benaiah went against him with
a club, wrested the spear from the
Egyptian's hand, and slew him with his own
spear. 22 Such exploits of Benaiah, the son of
Jehoiada, won for him a name among the
Thirty warriors. 23 Although he commanded
greater respect than the rest of the Thirty, he
was not equal to the Three. David appointed
him to be the commander of his bodyguard.

24 Among the Thirty were Asahel, the
brother of Joab; Elhanan, the son of Dodo,
from Bethlehem;[s] 25 Shammah from Harod;
Elika from Harod; 26 Helez from Beth-pelet;
Ira, the son of Ikkesh, from Tekoa; 27 Abiezer
from Anathoth; Mebunnai the Hushathite;[t]
28 Zalmon the Ahohite; Maharai from
Netophah; 29 Heled, the son of Baanah,
from Netophah; Ittai, the son of Ribai, from
Gibeah in Benjamin; 30 Benaiah from Pira-
thon; Hiddai from the torrents of Gaash;
31 Ali-albon from Beth-arabah; Azmaveth
from Bahurim; 32 Eliahba from Shaalbon;
the sons of Jashen; 33 Jonathan, the son
of Shammah, from Harar; Ahiam, the son of
Sharar, from Harar; 34 Eliphelet, the son of
Abishai, from Bath-maacah; Eliam, the son

k Jdg 5:31; Ps 72:6; Mt 13:43.—l 2 Sam 7:11,15f; Ps 89:30; Isa 55:3.—m Deut 13:14; Prov 12:21.—n 8-39: 1 Chr 27:1-15.—o Jdg 15:9.—p 1 Sam 22:1; Mic 1:15.—q 1 Chr 11:18.—r 2 Sam 8:18; 20:23; Jdg 14:6; 1 Ki 2:29f.—s 2 Sam 2:18-23; 1 Chr 11:26.—t 2 Sam 21:18; 1 Chr 27:12.

of Ahithophel, from Gilo;[u] 35 Hezro from Carmel; Paarai the Arbite; 36 Igal, the son of Nathan, from Zobah; Bani the Gadite; 37 Zelek the Ammonite; Nahari from Beeroth, the armor-bearer of Joab, the son of Zeruiah; 38 Ira the Ithrite; Gareb the Ithrite; 39 Uriah the Hittite—thirty-seven in all.[v]

CHAPTER 24*

Census of the People. 1 [w] Once again the anger of the LORD was aroused against Israel, and he incited David against them, saying: "Go forth and take a census of Israel and Judah." 2 Therefore, the king said to Joab and to all the army commanders who were with him: "Go throughout all the tribes of Israel from Dan to Beer-sheba and take a census of the people so that I may know how many there are."

3 Joab said to the king in response: "May the LORD, your God, increase the number of your people a hundredfold, and may the eyes of my lord the king live to see it. But why does my lord the king want to undertake this task?" 4 However, the king was determined to follow through on this enterprise, and he overruled Joab and the army commanders. Therefore, they departed from the presence of the king in order to take the census.

5 After crossing the Jordan, they began at Aroer and the town in the middle of the valley, and then they moved on toward Gad and Jazer.[x] 6 After that, they proceeded to Gilead and to Kadesh in the land of the Hittites. Next they came to Dan, and from Dan they cut across to Sidon 7 and arrived at the fortress of Tyre, moving on afterward to all the towns of the Hivites and Canaanites, and then to the Negeb of Judah, at Beer-sheba.[y]

8 Having traveled throughout the entire country, they returned to Jerusalem at the end of nine months and twenty days. 9 Joab then reported to the king the number of those who had been recorded in the census. In Israel there were eight hundred thousand men who were fit for military service, and in Judah there were five hundred thousand. *

The Pestilence. 10 However, after the census had been taken, David was stricken with remorse, and he said to the LORD: "I have committed a grievous sin in what I have done. I beseech you, LORD, to forgive the guilt of your servant, for I have acted very foolishly."[z] 11 When David arose the following morning, the word of the LORD had come to the prophet Gad, David's seer, saying: 12 "Go forth and say to David: 'This is the word of the LORD: "I offer you three alternatives." Choose one of them, and I will inflict it upon you." ' "

13 Therefore, Gad came to David and reported what the LORD had said. Then he asked him: "Which do you choose? Do you prefer three years of famine to afflict your land? Or do you prefer to take flight for three months while your enemies pursue you? Or do you prefer to have your land afflicted with three days of pestilence? Consider carefully the choices you have been offered and decide what answer I am to take back to the one who sent me."[a]

14 David said to Gad: "I am in a desperate plight. It is far better to fall into the hands of the LORD, for his mercy is great. Let me not fall into the hands of men." 15 Therefore, David chose the option of the pestilence. Then the LORD sent a pestilence throughout Israel from that morning until the appointed time, and seventy thousand of the people died, from Dan to Beer-sheba.

16 However, when the angel stretched forth his hand toward Jerusalem to destroy it, the LORD regretted the terrible calamity that he had approved, and he said to the angel who was afflicting the people: "That is enough! Stay your hand!" The angel of the LORD was then standing at the threshing floor of Araunah the Jebusite.[b] 17 When David saw the angel who was striking down the people, he said to the LORD: "I was the one who sinned. I was the one who acted wickedly. What have these sheep done? Let your hand fall upon me and my family."

Sacrifice of Atonement. 18 On that day Gad came to David and said to him: "Go up and erect an altar to the LORD on the threshing

u 1 Chr 11:36; 27:34.—v 2 Sam 11:3f; 12:9.—w 1-25: 1 Chr 21:1-27; 27:23.—x Deut 30:18; Jos 18:7.—y Gen 46:1; 2 Chr 28:18.—z Ex 10:17; 1 Sam 24:6; 1 Chr 21:7.—a 2 Sam 21:10; 1 Chr 21:18.—b Ex 12:23; 2 Ki 19:35; Ezek 9:8.

24:1-25 A parallel to the famine reported in chapter 21. In this case, the wicked act that causes it is the census taken of men capable of bearing arms and the reliance on this human might. In fact, God alone is master of life and of victory. In the understanding of the ancients, who did not distinguish between what God simply tolerates and what he commands, he gave the order for the famine. In fact, the first Book of Chronicles (ch. 21) substitutes the name Satan for that of the Lord. The underlying historical fact is difficult to explain.

24:9 The census result gave a population of about seven million, which was impossible. The numerical system used in the Bible often escapes us.

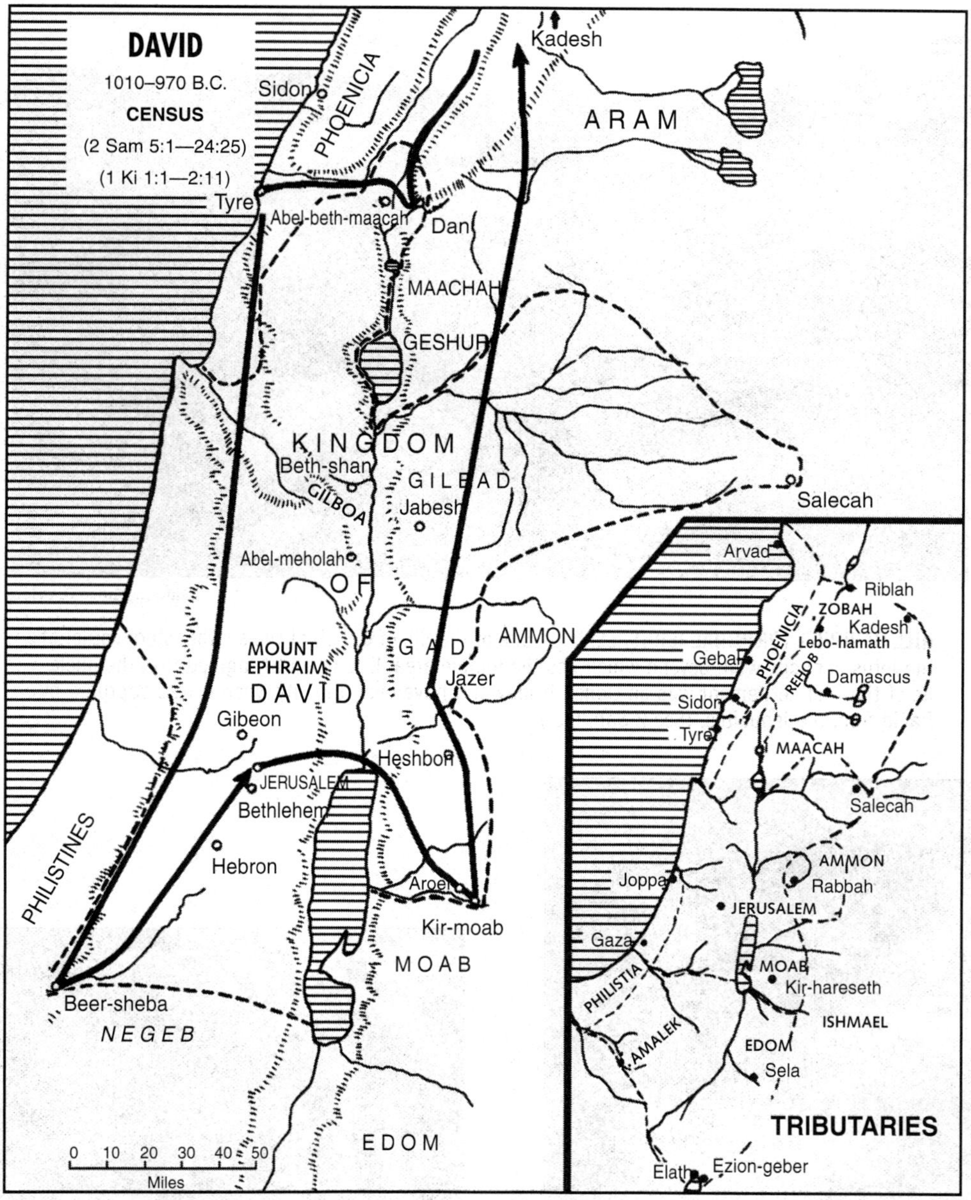

END OF THE REIGN OF DAVID (2 Sam 20–24; 1 Ki 1:1—2:11; 1 Chr 21–29) — (a) In the last years of his reign David combats the revolt of Sheba the Benjaminite (20:1-22) and the conspiracy of his son Adonijah (1 Ki 1–2). (2 Sam 20–24 and 1 Chr 21–29 here add other narratives of uncertain date: David expiates an injustice done to the Gibeonites by Saul. The brave men of David. Songs of David. Preparation for the construction of the Temple.) **(b)** The king tells Joab and the rulers of the army to take a **census** from **Dan** to **Beer-sheba.** Crossing the Jordan, they begin near **Aroer,** and go toward **Gad** and on to **Jazer.** They continue on to **Gilead** and to **Kadesh** in the land of the **Hittites;** they come to **Dan,** and turn to **Sidon,** going to the fortress of **Tyre** and to all cities of the **Hivites** and **Canaanites;** and ending up in the **Negeb of Judah** at **Beer-sheba.** They come to **Jerusalem** at the end of nine months and twenty days (24:1-9). **(c)** David's old age. Conspiracy of Adonijah. Solomon is solemnly crowned. Death of David after reigning for forty years: seven years at **Hebron** and thirty-three years at **Jerusalem** (2 Sam 24:10-25; 1 Ki 1:1—2:11).

Matson Photo Service

HILL OF OPHEL (ORIGINAL JERUSALEM) — Site of the Hill of Ophel, at the southeastern corner of the Jerusalem city wall, beyond which lies the temple area. It is generally agreed that the nucleus of the first settlement was on Ophel. It may still have been the city when it was captured by David from the Jebusites. (See 2 Sam 5:3.)

Matson Photo Service

EXCAVATIONS AT OPHEL — Site of the excavations at Ophel conducted in 1961, showing the city wall at the top. Excavators have found evidence of the foundation for a town in 3300 B.C. They also claim to have uncovered much of the second millennium ruins. This would make it the site captured by David and the one to which the Ark was brought. (See 2 Sam 7:12ff.)

Matson Photo Service

STRUCTURE RESEMBLING THE ARK OF THE COVENANT — Relief shows a structure on wheels found at Capernaum. It might resemble the Ark of the Covenant which was carried by the Hebrews into battle and by David into Jerusalem and has since disappeared into history. (See 2 Sam 7:12ff.)

floor of Araunah the Jebusite." [19] Therefore, David obeyed Gad's instructions and went up as the LORD had commanded.

[20] When Araunah looked down and beheld the king and his retinue coming toward him, he went forth and prostrated himself before the king with his face to the ground. [21] Then Araunah asked: "Why has my lord the king come to his servant?" David replied: "I have come to purchase the threshing floor from you in order to build an altar to the LORD so that the plague may be lifted from the people."

[22] [c] In reply, Araunah said to David: "I beseech my lord the king to take and offer up whatever he wishes. Here are the oxen for the burnt offering, as well as the threshing sledges and the yokes of the oxen for wood. [23] All this, O king, Araunah gives to the king." Then he added: "May the LORD, your God, look favorably upon your offering."

[24] However, the king said to Araunah: "No. I insist on paying you for this. Under no circumstances will I offer up to the LORD, my God, burnt offerings that cost me nothing." Therefore, David purchased the threshing floor and the oxen for fifty shekels of silver. *

[25] Then David built there an altar to the LORD and offered burnt offerings and peace offerings. After this, the LORD answered David's supplications for the land, and the plague was lifted from Israel. [d]

c 22f: 1 Sam 6:14; 1 Ki 19:21.—d 2 Sam 21:14; Gen 8:20; Ps 106:30.

24:24 The price is a small one. In 1 Chr 21:25 David pays 600 shekels of gold. The price is solely for the oxen and the threshing floor where David builds an altar.

THE BOOKS OF KINGS

From Glory to Destruction: Infidelity Spreads

Like the Books of Samuel, of which they are the continuation, the two Books of Kings are a single work in two parts that was probably composed after the capture of Jerusalem in 587 B.C. The editor, who is unknown to us, uses various documents to which he frequently refers the reader: the History of Solomon, the Annals of the Kings of Israel (or of the North), the Annals of the Kings of Judah, and others.

The Books of Samuel told of the rise of the monarchy from Saul to David, the latter being solidly established as king over the people of God.

The Books of Kings follow a descending curve: they begin with the reign of Solomon (970–931 B.C.), the most splendid in Israel's history, and end with the capture of Jerusalem and the deportation to Babylon. There is then no longer a king, or a capital, or a temple; the destruction is complete.

But during the four centuries covered by the two Books we meet the great names of Elijah and Elisha, some reforming kings, and the activity of such prophets as Isaiah. This point should be underscored in order to avoid a blanket pessimistic judgment of the history of Israel. Destruction came about by degrees: at the death of Solomon the North and the South split apart, leaving divided a country that David had united by great effort; in 721 B.C., the capital of the North, Samaria, is captured by the Assyrians, and the kingdom of "Israel" disappears. In 587 B.C., it is the turn of the kingdom of Judah. The story of Solomon and the story of his successors form the two parts into which the entire work is divided.

In the Books of Kings religious reflections become more numerous and more systematic in character than in the Books of Samuel.

The author pays special attention to the fate of Jerusalem and of the temple; his aim is to explain how Israel could have fallen so low.

Events, reflected on in the light of faith, show that the kings had turned the chosen people away from God.

Because the kings failed to trust in God and to be faithful to him, they were unable to continue in the line begun by David; they did not deserve the covenant, and they betrayed it.

This vision is rather oppressive. Sin is everywhere so deeply rooted and so commonplace that it is not possible to see how human beings, left to themselves, can rescue themselves from it; God himself must intervene and give a "new heart" (Jer 31:32f; 32:39f).

The Books lead the reader to reflect on the emptiness of earthly glories as the author of Ecclesiastes (2:1-11) will do later on when he recalls the splendors of Solomon.

The Books of Kings may be divided as follows:

I: The Reign of Solomon (1 Ki 1:1—11:43)
II: The Reign of Jeroboam (1 Ki 12:1—14:20)
III: Kings of Israel and Judah (1 Ki 14:21—16:34)
IV: Stories of Elijah and Ahab (1 Ki 17:1—2 Ki 1:18)
V: Stories of Elisha and Joram (2 Ki 2:1—13:25)
VI: Kings of Israel and Judah (2 Ki 14:1—17:41)
VII: Kingdom of Judah after 721 B.C. (2 Ki 18:1—25:30)

THE FIRST BOOK OF KINGS

I: THE REIGN OF SOLOMON

CHAPTER 1

Help for King David. 1 Now King David was
old, well on in years. They would cover him
up, but he could not get warm. 2 So his ser-
vants said to him, "My lord, the king, let a
young virgin be found for you to attend to
you and to care for you. She can lie alongside
of you so that my lord, the king, can keep
warm." 3 And so they searched for a beauti-
ful young woman all throughout the territo-
ry of Israel, and they found Abishag the
Shunamite, and they brought her to the
king.[a] 4 The young woman was very beauti-
ful, and she cared for the king. She served
the king, but he did not have intimate rela-
tions with her.

Adonijah's Plan. 5 Adonijah, the son of
Haggith, exulted himself saying, "I will be
king." He had his own chariots and horse-
men, and he had fifty men to run in front of
him.*[b] 6 His father never rebuked him by
saying, "Why have you done this?" He was
very handsome, and he had been born after
Absalom.

7 Adonijah conferred with Joab, the son of
Zeruiah, and with Abiathar the priest, and
they helped Adonijah and followed after
him. 8 But Zadok the priest, Benaiah, the son
of Jehoiada, Nathan the prophet, and Shimei
and Rei, David's brave warriors, did not side
with Adonijah.

9 * Adonijah sacrificed some sheep, oxen,
and fatted calves at the stone of Zoheleth in
En-rogel. He invited all of his brethren, the
king's sons, and all of the men of Judah, the
king's servants,[c] 10 but he did not invite
Nathan the prophet, Benaiah, the king's
brave men, or Solomon, his brother.

Solomon Becomes King. 11 Nathan, there-
fore, spoke to Bathsheba, Solomon's mother,
saying, "Have you not heard that Adonijah,
the son of Haggith, is reigning, and our lord
David does not know about it. 12 Come and
let me give you counsel, so that I may save
my own life and the life of your son Solomon.

13 "Go at once to King David and say to
him, 'Did not my lord, the king, make an
oath to your handmaid, saying, "Solomon,
your son, will reign after me and will sit
upon my throne? Why, then, is Adonijah

a 1 Ki 2:17; Est 2:2.—b Gen 26:14; 2 Sam 15:1.—c Gen 29:22; Zep 1:8.

1:5 See 2 Sam 3–4: Adonijah, David's fourth son, had become the eldest son and, therefore, pretender to the throne.

1:9-10 Adonijah was not the true successor to King David. It was Solomon who was chosen by God and having animal sacrifice would not legitimize his rule.

reigning?" 14 While you are still speaking with the king, I will arrive and confirm your words.' "

15 So Bathsheba went into the king's chamber. Now the king was very old, and Abishag the Shunamite served the king.* [d] 16 Bathsheba bowed down, paying obeisance to the king, and the king said, "What do you want?" 17 She said to him, "My lord, you made an oath to your handmaid by the LORD, your God, saying, 'Solomon, your son, will reign after me, and he will sit upon my throne.' 18 But now Adonijah is reigning, and my king does not know about it. 19 He has sacrificed many oxen, fatted calves, and sheep, and he has invited all of the king's sons, Abiathar the priest, and Joab the commander of the army, but he did not invite your servant Solomon.

20 "Now, my lord, the king, the eyes of all of Israel are upon you. They want you to tell them who will sit upon your throne, my lord, the king.* 21 Otherwise when my lord, the king, sleeps with his fathers, I and Solomon, my son, will be condemned."

22 While she was still speaking with the king, Nathan the prophet entered. 23 They announced to the king, "Nathan the prophet." He came before the king and bowed down with his face to the ground before the king. [e] 24 Nathan said, "Has my lord, the king, said, 'Adonijah will rule after me and he will sit upon my throne?' 25 Today he went down and sacrificed many oxen, fatted calves, and sheep, and he invited all of the king's sons, the captains of the army, and Abiathar the priest. They are eating and drinking with him, and they are saying, 'Long live King Adonijah!' 26 But he did not invite myself, your servant, Zadok the priest, Benaiah, the son of Jehoiada, nor Solomon, your servant. 27 Has my lord, the king, done this thing without informing your servant about who is to sit upon your throne after you, O lord, my king?"

28 Then King David said, "Summon Bathsheba." She came into the king's presence and stood before the king. 29 The king then swore an oath, saying, "As the LORD lives who has delivered me from all of my adversities, 30 and as I swore to you by the LORD, the God of Israel saying, 'Solomon, your son, will reign after me, and he will sit upon my throne in my place,' I will fulfill it today." 31 Bathsheba bowed down with her face to the ground and did obeisance saying, "May my lord, King David, live forever."

32 King David said, "Summon Zadok the priest, Nathan the prophet, and Benaiah, the son of Jehoiada, to me." They came before the king. 33 The king said to them, "Take your lord's servants and put Solomon, my son, on my own donkey and bring him to Gihon. 34 There, have Zadok the priest and Nathan the prophet anoint him as king over Israel. Sound your trumpet and proclaim, 'Long live King Solomon.' [f] 35 Then follow him back up so that he might come and sit upon my throne, for he will take my place as king. I have chosen him to be the king over Israel and Judah."

36 Benaiah, the son of Jehoiada, answered the king saying, "Amen! May the LORD, the God of my lord, the king, confirm it. 37 May the LORD be with Solomon just as he has been with my lord, the king. May he make his throne greater than the throne of my lord, king David."

38 So Zadok the priest, Nathan the prophet, Benaiah, the son of Jehoiada, the Cherethites, and the Pelethites went down. They had Solomon ride upon King David's donkey, and they brought him to Gihon. 39 Zadok the priest took a horn of oil out from the tabernacle and he anointed Solomon. They sounded the trumpet and all of the people proclaimed, "Long live, King Solomon." [g] 40 All of the people went up and joined his following, and they played upon flutes and so greatly rejoiced that the ground shook from the noise.

Adonijah Acknowledges Solomon. 41 Adonijah and all of those whom he had invited to be with him finished eating and heard it. When Joab heard the sound of the trumpet, he asked, "What is this uproar coming from the city?" 42 While he was still speaking, Jonathan, the son of Abiathar the priest arrived. Adonijah said, "Come in, for a brave man like you must bring good news."

---

d Jud 16:23.—e Acts 10:25.—f 1 Chr 24:6; Hos 5:8.—g 1 Sam 16:13.

1:15 The relationship between David and Bathsheba has changed dramatically since the adultery and murder that had started it. He is now an old man with another woman in her place, but she comes to intercede on behalf of her son Solomon.

1:20 Israel, unlike other nations during this period, was not bound by the law of primogeniture. Bathsheba is almost taunting King David with her words to force him to denounce Adonijah and to name Solomon as his successor. David has never opposed Adonijah but now needs to take a firm stand.

43 Jonathan answered Adonijah saying, "It is not so! Our Lord, king David, has made Solomon king. 44 The king sent him with Zadok the priest, Nathan the prophet, Benaiah, the son of Jehoiada, the Cherethites, and the Pelethites, 45 and Zadok, the priest, and Nathan the prophet anointed him in Gihon. They are coming up from there rejoicing so that the city resounds with it. This is the noise that you heard. 46 Moreover, Solomon is sitting upon the royal throne.

47 "The king's servants have come to bless our lord, King David, saying, 'May God make the name of Solomon greater than your name, and his throne than your throne.' The king then worshiped in his bed 48 and the king said, 'Blessed be the LORD, the God of Israel, who has allowed me to see with my own eyes the one who will sit upon my throne.' "

49 All of those whom Adonijah had invited became frightened, and they rose up and they each went his own way. 50 But Adonijah, because he feared Solomon, got up and went and took hold of the horns of the altar. *

51 Solomon was told, "Adonijah is afraid of King Solomon, for he has taken hold of the horns of the altar saying, 'Let King Solomon swear an oath to me today that he will not harm his servant.' " 52 Solomon replied, "If he shows himself to be a man of virtue, then not one of his hairs will fall to the ground. But if he proves to be wicked, he will die!"

53 So King Solomon sent and had him brought down from the altar. He came and bowed down to King Solomon, and Solomon said to him, "Go home."

CHAPTER 2

David's Parting Words before Death. 1 As David's death drew near, he instructed Solomon, his son, saying, 2 "I am going the way of all upon the earth. Be strong, and show yourself to be a man. 3 * Observe the ordinances of the LORD, your God, walking in his ways and keeping his statutes, his commandments, his ordinances, and what he witnessed in writing in the law of Moses. In this way you will prosper in whatever you do and wherever you go.[h] 4 The LORD will keep the promise he made about me saying, 'If your descendants heed their way and they walk before me faithfully with all of their heart and all of their soul, there will always be one of yours upon the throne of Israel.'[i]

5 * "Now, you know what Joab, the son of Zeruiah, did to me, what he did to the two commanders of the army of Israel, to Abner, the son of Ner, and Amasa, the son of Jether. He killed them, shedding their blood during peacetime as if it were a time of war. The blood of battle is upon the belt around his waist and the sandals upon his feet. 6 Deal with him as you think wise, but do not let his gray head go down into Sheol in peace. 7 Show kindness to the sons of Barzillai the Gileadite. Let them be among those who eat at your table, for they came to me when I fled from Absalom, your brother.[j]

8 "Now, you also have Shimei, the son of Gera, the Benjaminite from Bahurim. He cursed me terribly on the day I traveled to Mahanaim, yet he also came down to meet me at the Jordan. I swore an oath to him by the LORD saying, 'I will not put you to death by the sword.' 9 You should not let him go unpunished. You are a wise man; you will know what to do with him. Bring his gray head down to Sheol with blood."

10 David slept with his fathers, and he was buried in the City of David.[k] 11 David had reigned over Israel for forty years. He reigned in Hebron for seven years, and he reigned in Jerusalem for thirty-three years.[l]

Solomon Affirms His Power. 12 Then Solomon sat on the throne of David, his father, and his reign was firmly established.

13 Now Adonijah, the son of Haggith, came to Bathsheba, the mother of Solomon. She asked him, "Do you come in peace?" He answered, "In peace." 14 Then he added, "I have something to say to you." She said, "Speak." 15 He said, "You know that the kingdom was mine. All of Israel looked to me to reign. But things changed, and the kingdom is my brother's, for it is his from the LORD.

h Deut 11:22; 17:19; 29:8.—i Jos 22:5; 2 Sam 7:11-16; Ps 132:11f.—j Gen 33:10; 2 Sam 19:33ff.—k 2 Chr 12:16; Acts 2:29.—l 2 Sam 5:5; 1 Chr 3:4.

1:50 Adonijah invokes the right of asylum which the sanctuary and, especially the altar, was regarded as providing and which was regulated by the law (Ex 21:13-14).

2:3-4 King David advised Solomon to be true to the One who had promised him and his descendants to remain in power. This promise hinged on their obedience to the Lord and ultimately would be broken by their disobedience.

2:5-9 King David continues to share the political strategy that he has learned and that will enable Solomon to secure his throne. In modern terms: keep your friends close and your enemies closer. In some cases, it might be necessary to eliminate those who will not serve God.

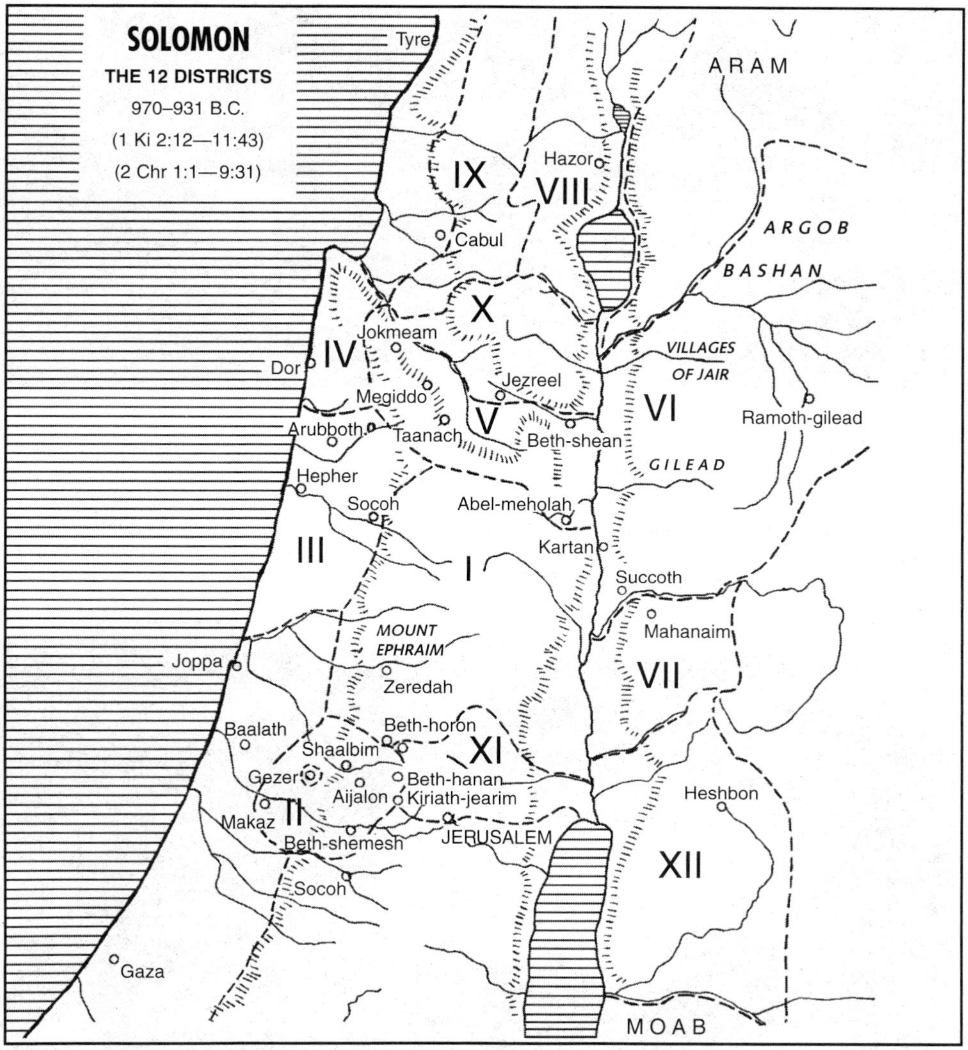

INTERIOR POLITICS (1 Ki 2:12—4:19; 2 Chr 1:1-18) — Solomon consolidates his power through the deaths of Adonijah, Joab, and Shimei, and the exile of Abiathar of Anathoth. The dream at Gibeon. He reorganizes the administration of the kingdom by establishing twelve districts and commissaries: (1) In the hill country of Ephraim. (2) At **Makaz, Shaalbim, Beth-shemesh,** Elon and **Beth-hanan.** (3) At **Arubboth, Socoh,** and the whole region of **Hepher.** (4) All the Naphath-dor. (5) **Taanach** and **Megiddo,** and beyond **Jokmeam**, and in all **Beth-shean,** and in the country around Zarethan below **Jezreel** from **Beth-shean** to **Abel-meholah.** (6) **Ramoth-gilead,** the **villages of Jair,** the district of **Argob,** which is in **Bashan,** sixty cities. (7) **Mahanaim.** (8) Naphtali. (9) Asher and along the rocky coast. (10) Issachar. (11) Benjamin. (12) The land of **Gilead**, the land of Sihon, king of the Amorites, and of Og, king of **Bashan**. Besides, there was one prefect in the king's own land (Judah) (4:8-19).

EXTERIOR POLITICS (1 Ki 4:20—11:43; 2 Chr 1:18—9:31). — **(a)** Solomon's rule extends from Tiphsah on the Euphrates to **Gaza** on the border of Egypt. He builds the temple, fortifies **Jerusalem, Hazor, Megiddo, Gezer, Beth-horon** the lower, Baalath, and Tamar in the wilderness (4:20—9:25). **(b)** At Ezion-geber near Elath he arms a fleet of ships which proceed to Ophir and bring back precious cargoes (9:26-28). **(c)** Egypt's Pharaoh gives him his daughter in marriage; the Queen of Sheba pays him a visit for a treaty of commerce (9:16; 10:1-13). **(d)** Hiram of **Tyre**, in exchange for his alliance, acquires an important part of the 9th district, twenty towns of the "Land of Galilee" (9:10-14). Hadad, Rezon, and Jeroboam rise up against Solomon (11:14-40).

Matson Photo Service

STABLES OF SOLOMON (RESTORED) — Partially restored model of Solomonic stables found at Megiddo. The stable consisted of five units, each accommodating about 24 horses. Each unit had a center passage flanked by rows of pillars serving as supports for the roof and as hitching posts. Mangers were between the pillars, and stalls for the horses were on each side of the central passageway. The capacity of the compound at Megiddo was about 450 horses and 150 chariots. Their date of construction is placed around 975–925 B.C. (See 1 Ki 9:15-19.)

Matson Photo Service

STABLES OF SOLOMON (RUINS) — Though no serious military operations found place in his reign, Solomon established himself in a position of strength by gathering a large chariot force. He designated certain cities as chariot cities: Megiddo, Taanach, Gezer, Hazor and others. His corps of chariots was stationed in them, probably numbering 1400 chariots, 4000 stalls for chariot horses, and 12,000 horses. Indication as to how this corps was raised is given in 1 Ki 10:28-29.

16 Now I beg one thing from you; do not deny
me." She said, "Speak." 17 He said, "Please
speak to Solomon the king, for he will not
refuse you, and ask him to give me Abishag
as a wife." 18 Bathsheba answered, "Very
well, I will speak to the king for you."

19 Bathsheba, therefore, went to King
Solomon to speak to him on behalf of
Adonijah. The king rose up to meet her and
bowed down to her. He sat down on his
throne, and had a throne placed for the
king's mother, so that she sat on his right
hand.* 20 She said, "I desire to make one
small request of you. Please do not deny
me." The king said to her, "Ask, my mother,
for I will not deny you." 21 She said, "Let
Abishag the Shunamite be given to Adonijah
your brother as a wife."

22 King Solomon answered his mother
saying, "Why do you request Abishag the
Shunamite for Adonijah? Why not ask for
the kingdom for him, for he is my older
brother? Ask it for him and for Abiathar the
priest, and for Joab, the son of Zeruiah."
23 Then King Solomon swore an oath by the
LORD saying, "May God do this to me and
more if Adonijah has not spoken this thing
at the cost of his life.[m] 24 Now, therefore, as
the LORD lives, who has confirmed me and
has set me upon the throne of David, my
father, and who has built a house for me as
he promised, this very day Adonijah will be
put to death." 25 So King Solomon sent
Benaiah, the son of Jehoiada, and he fell
upon him, so that he died.

26 The king said to Abiathar the priest, "Go
to Anathoth, to your own fields, for you real-
ly deserve to die now. I will not put you to
death, however, because you have carried
the Ark of the LORD, the God, before David,
my father, and because you suffered what-
ever my father suffered." 27 So Solomon
removed Abiathar as priest of the LORD, thus
fulfilling the word of the LORD which he had
spoken concerning the house of Eli in
Shiloh.[n]

m Ru 1:17; 1 Sam 14:44.—**n** 1 Sam 2:31.—**o** 1 Sam 20:42; 1 Chr 17:14; Ezek 33:4.

2:19 The king's mother had an official rank and special powers. She was known as the "Great Mother." For this reason her name is constantly given in the notices on the various kings.

2:31 Joab had a history of murdering those who threatened his position. As David's general, the blame ultimately rested with the King. Now Solomon wants to clear his father's name by transferring the guilt to the rightful place.

2:35 It is the king who appoints or replaces the high priest. The latter is one of his officials (2 Sam 8:17).

28 The news came to Joab (for Joab had
followed Adonijah although he had not fol-
lowed Absalom), and Joab fled to the taber-
nacle of the LORD and took hold of the horns
on the altar. 29 King Solomon was told,
"Joab has fled to the tabernacle of the LORD,
and he is by the altar." So Solomon sent
Benaiah, the son of Jehoiada, saying, "Go,
fall upon him."

30 Benaiah arrived at the tabernacle of the
LORD and said to him, "Thus says the king,
'Come out.'" He answered, "No, I will die
here!" Benaiah brought a report back to the
king saying, "This is what Joab said; this is
how he answered me." 31 So the king said to
him, "Do what he said, fall upon him and
bury him, so that you may remove the inno-
cent blood that Joab shed from me and the
house of my father.* 32 Thus the LORD will
bring the blood back upon his own head. He
struck down two men who were more righ-
teous and better than he: Abner, the son of
Ner, the commander of the army of Israel,
and Amasa, the son of Jether, the command-
er of the army of Judah. He slew them with
the sword, even though my father did not
know about it. 33 Their blood shall come back
upon the head of Joab and upon the heads of
his descendants forever. But there will be
peace forever from the LORD upon David,
upon his house, and upon his throne."[o]

34 So Benaiah, the son of Jehoiada, went up
and fell upon him and slew him and buried
him in his house in the desert. 35 The king
assigned Benaiah, the son of Jehoiada, as his
replacement to command the army, and the
king replaced Abiathar with Zadok the
priest.*

36 The king then sent for and summoned
Shimei and he said to him, "Build a house
for yourself in Jerusalem, but do not leave it
to go anywhere. 37 On the same day that
you cross over the Kidron Brook, know
that you will surely die, and your blood
will be upon your own head." 38 Shimei
said to the king, "What you have said is
good. Your servant will do what my lord,
the king, has said." Shimei dwelt in
Jerusalem for a long time.

39 Three years later, two of Shimei's slaves
ran away to Achish, the son of Maacah, the
king of Gath. Shimei was informed, "Look,
your slaves are in Gath." 40 Shimei rose up,
and saddled his donkey, and went to Achish
in Gath to search for his slaves. Shimei went

and brought his slaves back from Gath.
41 Solomon was told that Shimei had trav-
eled from Jerusalem to Gath and had come
back again. 42 The king sent for and sum-
moned Shimei and said to him, "Did I not
make an oath by the LORD and warn you,
saying, 'The day that you go forth and travel
anywhere, know that you will surely die?' You
answered me, 'The word that I have heard is
good.' 43 Why have you not observed the oath
of the LORD and the commandment that I
gave you?"

44 The king also said to Shimei, "You know
in your own heart about all of the evil that
you did to my father; therefore, the LORD will
requite your wickedness upon your own
head.[p] 45 But King Solomon will be blessed,
and the throne of David will be secure before
the LORD forever." 46 So the king gave a com-
mand to Benaiah, the son of Jehoiada, and
he went out and struck him down, and he
died. Thus the reign was firmly established in
the hands of Solomon. *

CHAPTER 3

Solomon Asks for Wisdom. 1 Solomon made
a marriage alliance with Pharaoh, the king
of Egypt, and he married Pharaoh's daugh-
ter. He brought her into the City of David
until he finished building his palace and the
temple of the LORD and the walls surround-
ing Jerusalem.[q]

2 * In the meantime, the people sacrificed
upon the high places, * for a temple to the
name of the LORD had not yet been built.
3 Solomon loved the LORD, walking in the
statutes of David his father, except that he
sacrificed and burned incense upon the high
places.

4 The king went to Gibeon to perform a
sacrifice there, for that was an important
high place. Solomon offered up one thou-
sand burnt offerings upon that altar.

5 The LORD appeared to Solomon that
night in a dream at Gibeon. God said, "Ask
me for whatever you want." 6 Solomon
answered, "You have shown great kindness
to your servant, David, my father, because
he walked before you in fidelity and righ-
teousness. His heart was upright before you.
You have even continued to show him this
great kindness by having given him a son to
sit upon his throne up to this very day.[r]
7 Now, O LORD, my God, you have estab-
lished your servant as king in the place of
David, my father, but I am only a small child
and do not know how to go out and come in.
8 Your servant is among the people you have
chosen, a great people. There are so many of
them that they cannot be numbered or
counted. 9 Therefore, give your servant a dis-
cerning heart to judge your people and to
distinguish between what is good and what is
bad, for who would be able to judge this, your
great people?"[s]

10 It pleased the LORD that Solomon had
asked for this. 11 God said to him, "Because
you have asked for this thing, and you have
not asked for a long life for yourself, or that
you be rich, or for the life of your enemies,
but you asked for understanding to discern
what is just, 12 behold, I am fulfilling your
request. I will give you such a wise and
understanding heart that there was never
anyone like you before your times, nor will
anyone like you rise up afterwards. *

13 "I will also give you those things for
which you did not ask, both riches and
honor, so that no other king will be like you
as long as you live.[t] 14 If you walk in my ways,
keeping my statutes and commandments,
just as David, your father, walked, then I will
prolong your life."

15 Solomon woke up, and it had been a
dream. He went to Jerusalem and stood
before the Ark of the Covenant of the LORD.
He offered up burnt offerings and peace
offerings, and he celebrated a feast with all
his servants.

Solomon's Wisdom. 16 Now two prostitutes
came to the king and stood before him.
17 One of the women said, "O my lord, I and
this woman live in the same house. I had a
child while this woman was in the house.

18 "Three days after I had my child, this
woman also had a child. We were there

p 2 Sam 16:5; Eccl 7:22.—q 1 Ki 7:8.—r 1 Ki 14:8; 2 Chr 1:8.—s 2 Chr 1:10; Jer 22:3.—t Gen 1:29; Wis 7:11; Mt 6:29.

2:46 Although he was very much like his father—a man of peace—Solomon followed his father's advice concerning his enemies (vv. 5-9) and had Joab, Shimei, and Adonijah killed in order to avoid more bloodshed.

3:2-15 The celebration of worship apart from the place where the Ark resided was not yet forbidden; the editor deplores it, however, because he could see from what happened that the practice had favored idolatry.

3:2 *High places:* continued a Canaanite practice; the worship of the Lord there was contaminated by the worship of Baal (Jdg 6:25f).

3:12 The Lord's overwhelming gratuitous response to Solomon's request for an understanding heart sets him apart forever and demonstrates the extent to which God blesses those who are faithful and serve with a clean heart.

together, and there was no one else with us in
the house, only the two of us. 19 This woman's
child died during the night because she
rolled over upon it. 20 She got up in the mid-
dle of the night, and she took my son from
my side while your servant was asleep. She
put him by her breast, and she put her dead
son by my breast. 21 When I got up the next
morning to nurse my son, he was dead. I
examined him carefully in the morning, and
behold, it was not the son whom I had
borne."

22 The other woman said, "No! My son is
the living one; your son is the dead one!" The
first woman said, "No! Your son is the dead
one, and my son is the living one!" They
argued this way before the king.

23 The king said, "The one says, 'This is my
son, the living one, and that is your son, the
dead one,' while the other one says, 'No!
Your son is dead, my son is alive.' " 24 The
king said, "Bring me a sword." So they
brought a sword to the king. 25 The king said,
"Divide the living child in two. Give one-half
to one of them, and one-half to the other."

26 The woman whose child was alive was
moved to compassion for her son and she
said to the king, "O my lord, give her the liv-
ing child. Do not kill him!" But the other
said, "Neither I nor you will have him. Cut
him in two!"

27 The king then said, "Give her the living
child. Do not kill him. She is his mother."
28 When all of Israel heard about how the
king had judged the case, they were filled
with awe toward the king. They realized that
he had the wisdom of God by the way he was
able to judge properly.

CHAPTER 4

Solomon's Wealth and Household. 1 King
Solomon reigned over all of Israel. 2 These
were his officials: Azariah, the son of Zadok,
was the priest; 3 Elihoreph and Ahijah, the
sons of Shisha, were the scribes; Jehosha-
phat, the son of Ahilud, kept the records;
4 Benaiah, the son of Jehoiada, was the com-
mander of the army; Zadok and Abiathar
were the priests; 5 Azariah, the son of
Nathan, was the director of the local officials;
Zabud, the son of Nathan, was the king's own
priest and advisor; 6 Ahishar was the major-
domo of the palace; and Adoniram, the son
of Abda, was in charge of forced labor.

7 Solomon had twelve local officials in
charge of all of Israel.* They provided food
for the king and his household. Each of them
was assigned to provide provisions for one
month each year. 8 These are their names:
Ben-hur, in the hill country of Ephraim;
9 Ben-deker, in Makaz, Shaalbim, Beth-
shemesh, and Elon-beth-hanan; 10 Ben-
hesed, in Arubboth (Socoh and all the lands
of Hepher belonged to it); 11 Ben-abinadab,
(who was married to Taphath, the daughter
of Solomon) in Naphath-dor; 12 Baana, the
son of Ahilud, in Taanach and Megiddo, and
in all of Beth-shean, which lie alongside of
Zarethan below Jezreel, running from Beth-
shean to Abel-meholah and on across to
Jokmeam; 13 Ben-geber, in Ramoth-gilead
(the towns of Jair, the son of Manasseh, in
Gilead were his as well as the region of
Argob in Bashan with its sixty large cities
fortified with bronze gate bars); 14 Ahinadab,
the son of Iddo, in Mahanaim; 15 Ahimaaz,
(who married Basemath, the daughter of
Solomon) in Naphtali; 16 Baana, the son of
Hushai, in Asher and Aloth; 17 Jehoshaphat,
the son of Paruah, in Issachar; 18 Shimei, the
son of Ela, in Benjamin; 19 and Geber,
the son of Uri, in Gilead (the land of Sihon,
the king of the Amorites, and of Og, the king
of Bashan). He was the only district official
in that territory.

20 The people of Judah and Israel were as
numerous as the sand on the shore of the
sea. They ate, and they drank, and they were
happy.[u] 21 Solomon ruled over all of the
kingdoms in the land that extended from the
river over to the land of the Philistines and
down to the border with Egypt. They
brought tribute and served Solomon for his
entire lifetime.

22 Each day's provision for Solomon
included thirty cors* of fine flour, sixty cors
of meal, 23 ten fat oxen, twenty pasture-fed
cattle, and one hundred sheep, in addition to
deer, gazelles, roebuck, and fatted fowl.

24 He ruled over all of this side of the river,
from Tiphsah to Gaza, over all of the kings
on this side of the river. He had peace on
every side.

---

u Gen 22:17; 32:12; Prov 14:28; Dan 3:36.

4:7 *All of Israel:* in actuality this applied to the northern tribes who were expected to provide more than Judah in the south to the monarchy. This, among other inequities, would lead to the dissolution of the kingdom (see 1 Ki 12:1-19).

4:22 *Cors:* the largest Hebrew measure of solid weight; it has been calculated as being equivalent to between two hundred and four hundred liters.

25 Judah and Israel lived in safety from
Dan to Beer-sheba, every man under his
own vine and under his own fig tree, during
the entire time of Solomon.[v] 26 Solomon
also had forty thousand stalls for his chariot
horses, and twelve thousand horsemen.

27 Those officials provided food for King
Solomon and for all of those who came to
King Solomon's table. Each one was
assigned his month, and they saw to it that
nothing was missing. 28 Each of them also
brought his quota of barley and straw for the
chariot horses and the other horses to the
assigned place.

The Wisdom of Solomon. 29 God granted
Solomon wisdom and understanding be-
yond measure, a largeness of heart that was
as abundant as the sand on the shore of the
sea. 30 The wisdom of Solomon was even
greater than that of the wisdom of all of the
men of the East and of the wisdom of Egypt.
31 He was wiser than any other person,
including Ethan the Ezrahite and Heman,
Chalcol, and Darda, the sons of Mahol. His
fame spread to all of the surrounding
nations. 32 He proclaimed three thousand
proverbs,* and he produced one thousand
and five songs. 33 He was able to discourse
upon trees, from the cedars of Lebanon even
to the hyssop that springs out of the wall. He
also spoke about animals and birds, reptiles
and fish. 34 Everyone came to hear the wis-
dom of Solomon, sent by kings from all over
the world who had heard about his wisdom.

CHAPTER 5

Temple Plans. 1 Hiram, the king of Tyre,
sent his servants to Solomon for he had
heard that he had been anointed as king in
his father's place, for Hiram had always been
a friend of David.* 2 Solomon sent to Hiram,
saying, 3 "You know that David, my father,
could not build a temple for the name of the
LORD, his God, because he had to fight bat-
tles on every side until the LORD placed
them under his feet. 4 Now the LORD, my
God, has given me rest on every side, so that
there are neither adversaries nor disasters.
5 I therefore intend to build a temple for the
name of the LORD, my God, as the LORD
foretold to David, my father, when he said,
'Your son whom I will establish to take your
place upon your throne will be the one who
will build a temple for my name.'[w] 6 Give
orders to cut cedars of Lebanon for me. My
servants will work alongside your servants,
and I will pay your servants whatever wage
you set. You know that we have no one
among us who is as skilled as the Sidonians
in cutting down trees."

7 When Hiram heard Solomon's message,
he rejoiced greatly. He said, "Blessed be the
LORD today, for he has given David a wise
son to rule over this great nation." 8 Hiram
sent word to Solomon, saying, "I have
received the message you sent me, and I will
do everything that you wish concerning the
cedar trees and fir trees. 9 [x] My servants will
haul them down from Lebanon to the sea,
and I will float them across the water by
rafts, bringing them to the place that you
establish for me. They will be broken apart
for you there, and you can take them away.
You, in turn, can fulfill my desire by provid-
ing food for my household."

10 So Hiram gave Solomon all the cedar
trees and fir trees that he desired, 11 and
Solomon gave Hiram twenty thousand cors
of wheat as food for his household and twen-
ty cors of pure oil. This is what Solomon gave
to Hiram every year. 12 The LORD gave
Solomon wisdom, just as he had promised
him. There was peace between Hiram and
Solomon, and they made a covenant with
each other.

13 * Then King Solomon raised up a labor
force from all of Israel, and the labor force
numbered thirty thousand men. 14 He sent
ten thousand of them each month to
Lebanon in shifts. They were in Lebanon for
one month, and then they were home for two
months. Adoniram was in charge of the
forced labor.

15 Solomon also had sixty thousand who
served as porters, and eighty thousand who
carved stone in the hill country. 16 In addi-
tion, Solomon had three thousand and three
hundred supervisors in charge of the work.
They directed the people who did the work.

v Isa 60:18; Mic 4:4.—w Jdg 20:1; Sir 47:12.—x 9-14: 2 Chr 9:23; Sir 47:16f.

4:32 *Three thousand proverbs:* many of Solomon's wise sayings are found in the Book of Proverbs, in the Song of Songs, and in Ecclesiastes.

5:1 *Friend of David:* Hiram's connection to David was more of a political than a social one. Solomon's continuation of the alliance is woven into the deals made between them for the construction of the temple.

5:13-14 King Solomon's wisdom was apparent in scheduling the workforce for monthly tours during the building of the temple. In this way, he was assured of a fresh supply of rested and willing workers. Solomon followed his father's advice concerning his enemies (vv. 5-9).

17 The king gave orders, and they prepared
huge, costly stones to lay the foundation of
the temple with hewn stones. 18 Thus
Solomon's workmen, and Hiram's work-
men, and the men of Gebal prepared the
timber and the stone for the construction of
the temple.

CHAPTER 6

Solomon Builds the Temple.* 1 And so he
began to build the temple of the LORD in the
four hundred and eighteenth year after the
Israelites came out of the land of Egypt, in
the fourth year of Solomon's reign over
Israel, in Ziv, the second month. *[y]

2 The temple that King Solomon built for
the LORD was sixty cubits long, twenty cubits
wide, and thirty cubits high. 3 The portico in
front of the main part of the temple was as
wide as the temple, that is, twenty cubits
wide. It extended ten cubits in front of the
temple. 4 He made windows with recessed
frames for the temple. 5 He built chambers
all around the outside walls of the main part
and the inner sanctuary of the temple in
which there were side rooms. 6 The lowest
chamber was five cubits wide, the middle
chamber was six cubits wide, and the third
level was seven cubits wide. He made narrow
ledges all around the temple so that nothing
had to be fastened to the walls of the temple.

7 Stone that had been made ready was
used in the building of the temple so that one
did not hear the sound of hammers or chis-
els or any other iron tool while the temple
was being built. *

8 The entrance for the lowest level was on
the right side of the temple. One went up by
stairs from there to the middle level, and
from the middle to the third level. 9 Thus he
built the temple and completed it by roofing
it with beams and cedar planks.

10 He built side rooms all along the temple.
They were five cubits high, and they were
attached to the temple with cedar beams.

11 The word of the LORD then came to
Solomon, 12 "As for this temple that you are
building, if you walk in my statutes and carry
out my ordinances and observe my com-
mandments, walking in them, then I will ful-
fill the promise I made to David, your father,
through you. [z] 13 I will dwell among the
Israelites and I will not abandon my people
Israel." [a]

14 Thus Solomon built the temple and
completed it. 15 He lined the inside walls of
the temple with cedar boards, covering the
temple from the floor to its ceiling. He cov-
ered the floor of the temple with fir planks.

16 He separated off twenty cubits at the
rear of the temple with cedar planks that ran
from the floor to the ceiling, making an inner
sanctuary, the Holy of Holies. 17 The part in
front of the temple sanctuary was forty
cubits long. 18 The inside of the temple was
covered with cedar carved with buds and
open flowers. Everything was covered in
cedar, and no stone could be seen.

19 He set up the inner sanctuary in the
temple as a place to set the Ark of the
Covenant of the LORD. 20 The inner sanctu-
ary was twenty cubits long, twenty cubits
wide, and twenty cubits high. It was covered
in pure gold, as was also the cedar altar.

21 Solomon covered the inside of the tem-
ple in pure gold. He stretched gold chains in
front of the inner sanctuary, and he covered
it in pure gold. 22 He covered the entire tem-
ple with gold until he had completed the
whole temple. He also covered the altar that
was in the inner sanctuary with gold.

23 He made two cherubim for the inner
sanctuary out of olive wood, each ten cubits
high. 24 The first wing of the cherub was five
cubits and the other wing was also five
cubits, making ten cubits from the tip of one
wing to the tip of the other. 25 The other
cherub was also ten cubits, for the two cheru-
bim were the same size and shape. 26 Each of
the cherubim was ten cubits high. 27 He set
the cherubim in the innermost room of the
temple. The wings of the cherubim were
spread out, so that the wing of one touched
one wall, while the wing of the other touched
the other wall, and their wings touched one
another in the middle of the room. 28 He cov-
ered the cherubim with gold.

---

y 2 Chr 3:1.—z 2 Sam 7:13; Ezek 20:19.—a Ex 29:45; Jos 1:5.

6:1-38 The sanctuary in the proper sense, built around 960 B.C., had the dimensions of one of our not very large churches; other structures were attached to it. But nothing more was needed to match the tabernacle built by Moses. Its grandeur came from the space around it, while the richness of the materials used ensured the desired magnificence.

6:1 The date has a religious rather than a historical significance. There is an equally long period between, on the one hand, the building of the tent in the wilderness and the building of the temple, and, on the other, the building of the temple and its rebuilding after the Exile. Each period counted twelve generations of high priests.

6:7 When Solomon had the temple built every detail was carefully planned and executed, including the respect that was shown to the Lord by cutting the stone at a distance from the building site to avoid undue noise.

29 He carved images of cherubim, palm trees, and open flowers on all of the walls around the temple, both in the inner and the outer rooms. 30 The floor of the temple was covered with gold, both in the inner and outer rooms.

31 He made doors of olive wood for the entrance to the sanctuary. It had a five-sided frame. 32 There were two olive wood doors, and upon them he carved images of cherubim, palm trees, and open flowers. He covered the cherubim and the palm trees with beaten gold.

33 In the same way he made four-sided frames out of olive wood for the entrance to the temple itself. 34 He also made two doors out of fir wood. Each of the doors had two folding panels. 35 He carved cherubim, palm trees, and open flowers upon them, and he carefully covered the carvings upon them with gold. 36 He built the inner court with three rows of hewn stone and then a row of cedar beams.

37 In the fourth year, the month of Ziv, the foundation of the temple of the LORD was laid. 38 In the eleventh year, the month of Bul, which is the eighth month, the temple was completely finished according to its plans. He needed seven years to build it. [b]

CHAPTER 7

Solomon's Palace. 1 * Now Solomon took thirteen years to completely finish building his own palace. 2 He built the palace out of Lebanon wood. It was one hundred cubits long, fifty cubits wide, and thirty cubits high. It was built upon four rows of cedar pillars, with cedar beams stretching out upon the pillars. 3 It was roofed with cedar that lay over the beams that rested on the pillars. There were forty-five beams, fifteen in a row. 4 Its windows were set high in the wall in sets of three, each set facing the other. 5 All of the doorways and windows had rectangular frames, with the windows facing each other in sets of three.

6 He made a hall of pillars. It was fifty cubits long and thirty cubits wide. There was a porch in front of it with other pillars and covered over by a canopy.

7 There was a throne room, the hall of justice, where he would sit in judgment. He covered it with cedar from floor to ceiling. 8 The palace in which he lived had another court inside the hall which had the same design. Solomon also built another palace like this hall for Pharaoh's daughter whom he wed. [c]

9 All of these, from the outside to the great courtyard, and from the foundations to the eaves, were built with costly stone that had been trimmed with saws on the inside and outside edges. 10 The foundations were laid with costly stones that were quite large, some being ten cubits and some eight cubits. 11 Above these were costly stone, cut to measure, and cedar beams.

12 The great courtyard was surrounded by three layers of cut stone and one layer of cedar beams, as was the inner courtyard of the temple of the LORD and its porch.

13 * King Solomon brought back Hiram from Tyre. 14 His mother was a widow from the tribe of Naphtali, and his father had been a craftsman from Tyre who worked in bronze. He was wise and knowledgeable and a skilled craftsman with all varieties of bronze work. He came to King Solomon and did all of his work.

15 [d] He cast two bronze pillars, each of them measured eighteen cubits high and twelve cubits in circumference.* 16 He also cast two bronze capitals to be set on the top of the pillars. Each of the capitals was five cubits high. 17 A network of chains decorated the capitals on top of the pillars, seven on each of the capitals. 18 He made two rows of pomegranates which covered the network upon the capitals on top of the pillars. He did this on each of the capitals. 19 The capitals on top of the pillars that were in the porch were in the shape of lilies, four cubits high. 20 Upon each of the capitals of the two pillars, on the outwardly curved surface between the network, there were two rows of pomegranates, two hundred in all. 21 He erected the pillars

b 1 Chr 28:6.—c 1 Ki 3:1; 2 Chr 8:11.—d 15f: 2 Ki 25:17; Jer 52:21-23; Ezek 40:49.

7:1-12 The royal palace was located south of the temple, to the right as one looked eastward. This location recalled that of the king in relation to the Lord (Ps 109:1): he has the place of honor; he is the Lord's representative among the people, his "messiah" or anointed one.

7:13-51 We are grateful that the text has preserved for us the name of the expert craftsman in bronze, a man of Tyre (but with a Hebrew mother) who was thought worthy of executing the king's great works. The "sea" (v. 23) is a great basin, containing the water for the priests' ablutions. The ten basins on the movable stands were needed for supplying the water, of which a great deal was used, especially for washing the space in front after the immolation of the victims. There are other passages having to do with the temple objects and their use (Ex 30:17; 37; 38; 2 Chr 3–4; Ezek 20–43).

7:15 The bronze was booty taken by David in war (1 Chr 18:8).

Matson Photo Service

TEMPLE OF SOLOMON (MODEL) — Dr. Conrad Schick's famous model of Solomon's temple. The temple consisted of three sections: (1) the Porch through which the temple was entered; (2) the Holy Place: 30 by 60 by 45 feet; (3) the Holy of Holies: a thirty foot cube overlaid with gold. It was built on a nine-foot high platform with ten steps in front. (See 1 Ki 6–7.)

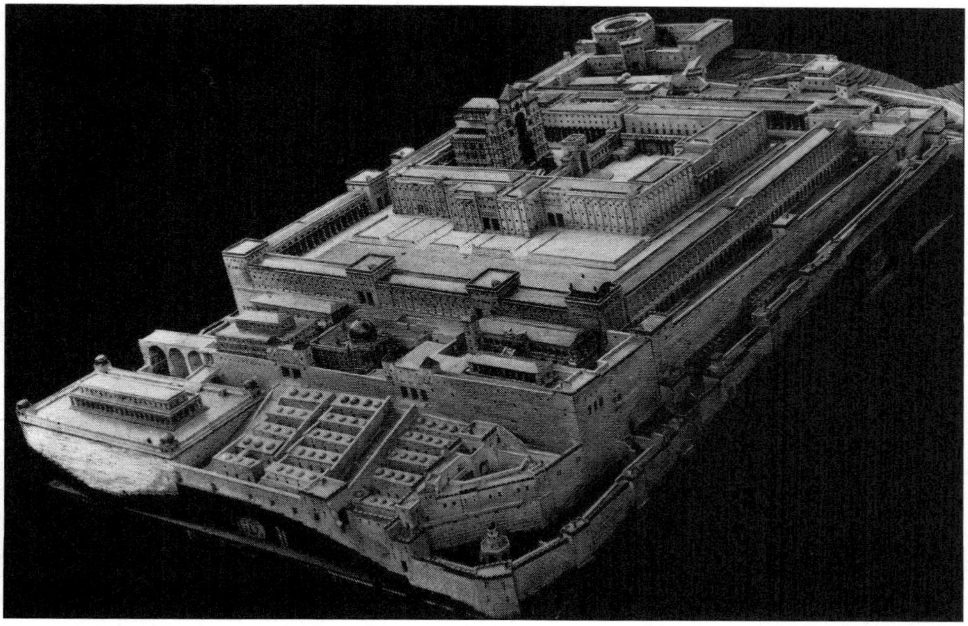

Matson Photo Service

ANOTHER VIEW OF TEMPLE OF SOLOMON — The majestic temple of Solomon and its environs (after Dr. Schick's model). This was the crowning achievement of the united Israelite Kingdom of David and Solomon. It took seven years and six months to build (see 1 Ki 6:37f). After standing for three centuries it was burned to the ground by the soldiers of Nebuchadnezzar in 587–586 B.C., after everything of value had been taken away. (See 2 Ki 25:9, 13-17.)

Oriental Institute

TEMPLE OVAL AT KHAFAJAH — Temple of neighboring peoples in the 3rd millennium. It covered an area of more than three-quarters of an acre and was founded on a bed of sand more than 8 meters thick. It is likely that such architecture from western Asia influenced the Hebrews as much as did the Phoenicians, who contributed architects and craftsmen to Solomon's temple. (See 1 Ki 5:6.)

Oriental Institute

INCENSE ALTAR FROM MEGIDDO — Small limestone altar with four projections at the top for burning incense found at Megiddo (10th-9th century B.C.). It is reminiscent of the altar in the temple which also had horns. (See 1 Ki 8:64.)

Oriental Institute

INCENSE ALTAR FROM SOUTH ARABIA — A square trough on four feet connected by rungs— an altar from South Arabia illustrating the influence that the land of the Queen of Sheba possibly exerted on the altar of Solomon's temple. (See 1 Ki10:1-13.)

in the porch of the temple. He erected the pillar on the right and called it Jachin, and he erected the pillar on the left and called it Boaz. 22 On the top of the pillars there was lily work. Thus, the work on the pillars was completed.

23 Then he made a molten sea, ten cubits from one edge to the other. It was five cubits high, and thirty cubits in circumference. 24 Under the brim of its circumference there were gourds, ten to a cubit. There were two rows of gourds all around the sea, the gourds having been cast when the rest of it was cast. 25 It stood upon twelve oxen, three facing to the north, three facing to the west, three facing to the south, and three facing to the east. The sea rested upon them, and their hindquarters were on the inside. 26 It was a handsbreadth thick, and its brim was like the brim of a cup, like a lily blossom. It held two thousand baths.

27 He also made ten bronze carts. Each cart was four cubits long, four cubits wide, and three cubits high. 28 This is how the carts were made. They had panels, and the panels were set in frames. 29 There were lions, oxen, and cherubim on the panels between the frames. On the top of the frames was a stand. Below the lions and the oxen there were embossed wreaths.

30 Each cart had four bronze wheels and bronze axles. There were supports for a basin at the four corners. The supports were cast with wreaths on either side. 31 The opening at the top of the cart was one cubit, and the opening was round, shaped like a pedestal, and it was one and a half cubits deep. There were carvings around the opening. The panels of the cart were square and not round.

32 The four wheels were under the panels, and the axles for the wheels were attached to the cart. Each wheel was one and a half cubits high. 33 The wheels were made like chariot wheels, with axles, rims, spokes, and hubs, all of which were made from cast metal.

34 Each cart had four handles, one on each corner, the handles being one piece with the cart. 35 There was a circular band a half a cubit high at the top of the cart. The supports and the panels were attached to the top of the cart. 36 He engraved cherubim, lions, and palm trees on the surface of the supports and the panels wherever he could, with wreaths all around them.

37 This is how he made the ten carts. They were all cast from one mold, so they were the same size and shape. 38 He then made ten bronze basins. Each basin held forty baths and was four cubits across. There was one basin for each of the ten carts.

39 He placed five of the stands at the right side of the temple, and five of the stands on the left side of the temple. He placed the sea on the right side of the temple, toward the southeast.

40 Hiram also made basins, and shovels, and bowls. Thus Hiram completed all of the work that he was doing for King Solomon for the temple of the LORD: 41 the two pillars, the two bowl-shaped capitals that were on the top of the two pillars, the two networks that covered the bowl-shaped capitals on top of the two pillars, 42 the four hundred pomegranates for the two networks, two rows of pomegranates for each of the networks that covered the two bowl-shaped capitals on top of the pillars,* 43 the ten carts, and the ten basins upon the carts, 44 one sea, and the twelve oxen under the sea, 45 the pots, the shovels, and the basins.

All of the utensils that Hiram made for King Solomon for the temple of the LORD were made from bright bronze. 46 The king cast them in the plain of the Jordan, in the clay ground that lie between Succoth and Zarethan. 47 Solomon did not weigh any of these utensils because there were too many of them; the weight of the bronze used in them was not determined.

48 Solomon also made all of the furnishings that were in the temple of the LORD: the golden altar; the golden table upon which they laid the shewbread;[e] 49 the lampstands made of pure gold, five on the right side and five on the left side; the flower work, the lamps, and the tongs, all made of gold; 50 the bowls, the snuffers, the sprinkling bowls, the spoons, and the censers, all made from pure gold; and the golden hinges for the inner sanctuary, the Holy of Holies, and for the doors of the main part of the temple.

51 When King Solomon had completed all of the work on the temple of the LORD, Solomon brought in the things that David, his father, had dedicated: the silver, the gold,

---

e 1 Ki 6:21; 2 Chr 4:19.

7:42 The decorative aspects of the building seem extremely ornate, but each of the chosen materials have significant symbolism. Pomegranates had adorned the tabernacle that Moses oversaw, and their abundant use was a sign of the beauty and holiness of the temple.

and the furnishings. He placed them in the treasury of the temple of the LORD. [f]

CHAPTER 8

Solomon Dedicates the Temple. 1 Solomon then assembled all of the elders of Israel, all of the heads of the tribes and the leaders of the ancestral clans of the Israelites. They came to King Solomon in Jerusalem in order to bring the Ark of the Covenant of the LORD out of the City of David, that is, Zion.

2 All of the men of Israel assembled before King Solomon at the festival during the month of Ethanim,* the seventh month. 3 When all of the elders of Israel had arrived, the priests took the Ark 4 and they brought the Ark of the LORD and the tent of meeting and all of the sacred furnishings that were in the tabernacle. The priests, and the Levites, 5 and King Solomon, and the entire assembly of Israel gathered with him in front of the Ark. They sacrificed so many sheep and oxen that they could not even be counted or numbered.

6 The priests then brought the Ark of the Covenant of the LORD to its place in the inner sanctuary of the temple, the Most Holy Place, underneath the wings of the cherubim. 7 The wings of the cherubim were spread out covering the place where the Ark was. The cherubim covered the Ark and its poles. 8 The poles stretched out so that one could see the ends of the poles in the Holy Place in front of the inner sanctuary, but one could not see them outside. They are still there up to the present. 9 There was nothing in the Ark except for the two stone tablets that Moses had placed in it at Horeb when the LORD made a covenant with the Israelites when they came out of the land of Egypt. [g]

10 When the priests came out of the Holy Place, a cloud filled the temple of the LORD. 11 The priests could not stand there to minister on account of the cloud, for the glory of the LORD had filled the temple of the LORD.

12 Then Solomon said, "The LORD said that he would live in thick darkness, [h] 13 but now I have built you a temple to dwell in, a place where you can abide forever."

14 The king then turned around to face the entire assembly of Israel, and he blessed the entire assembly of Israel who stood before him. 15 He said, "Blessed be the LORD, the God of Israel, who has fulfilled what he promised to my father, David, for he said, 16 'From the day that I brought my people Israel out of Egypt, I had not chosen a city from all of the tribes of Israel in which a temple for my name could be built, but I chose David to be the leader of my people Israel.'

17 "My father David desired to build a temple for the name of the LORD, the God of Israel, [i] 18 but the LORD said to my father David, 'You desired to build a temple for my name, and this desire of yours was good, 19 but you are not the one who will build the temple. Your son who comes forth from your body will build the temple for my name.' 20 The LORD has kept the promise that he made. I have been raised up in my father's stead to reign upon the throne of Israel, just as the LORD promised, and I have built a temple for the name of the LORD, the God of Israel. 21 I have provided a place for the Ark in which one finds the covenant of the LORD that he made with our fathers when he brought them out of the land of Egypt."

Solomon's Prayer.* 22 Solomon then stood before the altar of the LORD in front of the entire assembly of Israel, and he extended his hands to the heavens. 23 He said, "O LORD, the God of Israel, there is no God like you in the heavens above or on the earth below, who keeps a covenant of mercy with your servants who walk before you with all their heart. 24 You have kept your promise to your servant, David, my father. You spoke it with your own mouth, and with your own hand, you have fulfilled it today.

25 "And so now, O LORD, God of Israel, take heed of what you said to your servant, David, my father, when you said, 'You will not fail to have one who will sit before me on the throne of Israel, if only your children walk before me as you have walked before me.' [j] 26 Now, O God of Israel, let what you have said to your servant David, my father,

f 2 Sam 8:11; 2 Chr 5:1.—g Ex 34:4, 27; Deut 5:2; 2 Chr 5:10; Heb 9:4.—h 2 Chr 6:1; Ps 97:2.—i 2 Sam 7:5; 2 Chr 6:7, 10.—j 1 Ki 9:5; 2 Sam 7:12; 2 Chr 6:16.

8:2 *Ethanim:* a month in the Canaanite calendar that corresponded to the Hebrew seventh month (September-October). The greatest of the feasts was the Feast of Booths, that celebrated the passage from one year to another.

8:22-66 A prayer filled with faith and love. It gradually moves outward from the needs of the people to the dimensions of the world and touches in a very concrete way on difficult situations. Even if the section on the Exile was added after the possibility had become a reality, it is completely in the spirit of the prayer. In this liturgical supplication, which ends with a blessing, Solomon plays the role of a high priest—a privileged intermediary between the Lord and his people. The remainder, in its present form, is a model for the religious outlook of Israel.

come true. 27 But will God truly dwell upon
the earth? Behold, the heavens and the high-
est heavens could not contain you, how
much less this temple that I have built?

28 "Give heed to the prayer of your servant
and his supplication, O LORD, my God. Listen
to the cry and the prayer that your servant
makes before you today. 29 May your eyes be
wide open upon this temple night and day,
the place of which you said, 'My name will be
there.' Heed the prayer that your servant
makes for this place. 30 Hear the supplication
of your servant and your people Israel when
they pray for this place. Hear from your
dwelling place in heaven, and when you hear,
forgive.

31 "When a man wrongs his neighbor and
he is required to swear an oath, and he comes
to make the oath before your altar in this
temple, 32 then listen from heaven and act.
Judge between your servants, condemning
the evil one and bring down upon his head his
deeds. Prove innocent the righteous one, giv-
ing him what his righteousness deserves.

33 "When your people Israel have been
defeated by an enemy because they have
sinned against you, and they return to you
and confess your name, and they pray and
make supplication to you in this temple,
34 then listen from heaven and forgive the sin
of your people Israel, and bring them back to
the land that you gave to their fathers.

35 "When the heavens have been closed up
and there is no rain because they have sinned
against you, and they pray in this place and
they confess your name, and they turn from
their sin because you have punished them, [k]
36 then listen from heaven and forgive the sin
of your servants, your people Israel, so that
you might teach them the right path in which
they should walk, and send rain upon your
land which you have given to your people as
an inheritance.

37 "When there is famine in the land, or
pestilence, blight, mildew, locusts, or grass-
hoppers, or if their enemies besiege them in
the land of their cities, whatever plague or
sickness might occur, 38 and whatever prayer
or supplication is made by anyone, or by all of
your people Israel, because each person
knows the plague of his own heart, and he lifts
up his hands toward this temple, 39 then listen
from your heavenly dwelling place. Forgive,
and act, and give each person what his ways
deserve, for you know his heart, for you alone
know all human hearts, 40 so that they might
fear you all the days that they live in the land
that you gave our fathers.

41 "And as to the foreigner who does not
belong to your people Israel, but comes from
a distant land for your name's sake, [l] 42 for
they have heard about your great name and
your strong hand and your outstretched
arm, and he comes to this temple to pray,
43 listen from your heavenly dwelling place,
and do everything for which the foreigner
calls out to you. Then all of the people upon
the earth will know your name and fear you
just as your people Israel does, and that they
might know that the temple that I have built
is called by your name.

44 "When your people go out to battle
against their enemy wherever you send
them, and they pray to the LORD toward the
city that you have chosen and toward the
temple that I have built for your name,
45 then listen to their prayer and supplication
from heaven and maintain their cause.

46 "If they sin against you, for there is no
one who is sinless, and you are angry with
them so that they are delivered over to the
enemy and carried off as captives into
the land of their enemy, whether it be far or
near, [m] 47 and they have a change of heart in
the land where they have been carried off
into captivity, and they repent and they
make supplication to you in the land where
they have been carried off as captives, and
they say, 'We have sinned, we have done what
is wrong, and we have acted wickedly,' 48 and
if they turn back to you with all their heart
and all their soul in the land to which their
enemies took them as captives, and they
pray to you in the direction of the land that
you gave their fathers, and the city that you
have chosen, and the temple that I have built,
49 then listen to their prayer and their suppli-
cation from your heavenly dwelling place
and maintain their cause. 50 Forgive your
people who have sinned against you, all of the
offenses that they have committed against
you, and cause those who carried them off
into captivity to be filled with compassion.

51 "They are your people and your inheri-
tance whom you brought forth from Egypt,
from the midst of an iron-smelting furnace.
52 May your eyes be open to see the supplica-

k 2 Chr 6:26.—l Gen 17:12; 2 Chr 6:32.—m 2 Chr 6:36; Eccl 7:20; 1 Jn 1:8.

tion of your servant and the supplication of
your people Israel. Listen to them whenever
they call out to you, 53 for you separated your
inheritance from all the other people upon
the earth, as you declared through Moses
your servant, when you O LORD, my Lord,
brought our fathers out of Egypt."

54 When Solomon had finished saying all
of these prayers and supplications to the
LORD, he rose up from before the altar of the
LORD where he had been kneeling with his
hands lifted up to the heavens. [n] 55 He stood,
and he blessed the whole assembly of Israel
in a loud voice, saying, 56 "Praise be to the
LORD who has given rest to his people Israel
just as he promised. He has not failed to ful-
fill a single word of all the good promises
that he made through Moses his servant.

57 "May the LORD, our God, be with us, just
as he was with our fathers; may he not leave
us or abandon us. 58 May he turn our hearts
to him to walk in all of his ways and to
observe all of his commandments, his
statutes, and his ordinances which he com-
manded our fathers.

59 "May these words that I have prayed
before the LORD draw near to the LORD, our
God, both day and night. May he uphold the
cause of his servants and the cause of his
people Israel, responding to each day's
needs, 60 so that all the people upon the earth
might know that the LORD is God, there is no
other.

61 "Let your heart, therefore, be at peace
with the LORD, our God, by walking in his
statutes and observing his commandments,
as is true today."

62 Then the king and all of Israel with him
offered sacrifices before the LORD. 63 Solo-
mon offered up a sacrifice of peace offerings
to the LORD of twenty-two thousand oxen
and one hundred twenty-two thousand
sheep. This is how the king and all of the peo-
ple of Israel dedicated the temple of the
LORD.

64 That day the king consecrated the court
in front of the temple for burnt offerings,
grain offerings, and for the fat of peace offer-
ings because the bronze altar that was before
the LORD was too small for burnt offer-
ings, grain offerings, and the fat of peace
offerings. [o]

65 At that time Solomon celebrated before
the LORD, our God, with all of Israel, a great
assembly, people who came from the
entrance of Hamath down to the Wadi of
Egypt. It lasted seven days, and then anoth-
er seven days, fourteen days in all.* 66 The
next day he sent the people away. They
blessed the king and they went home, filled
with joy and glad of heart for all of the good
things that the LORD had done for David, his
servant, and Israel, his people.

CHAPTER 9

The LORD's Promise to Solomon. 1 When
Solomon had completed the construction of
the temple of the LORD and the royal palace,
Solomon had accomplished all that he
desired to do.

2 The LORD appeared to Solomon a sec-
ond time, as he had appeared to him at
Gibeon. [p] 3 The LORD said to him, "I have
heard your prayer and your supplication
that you made before me, and I have conse-
crated the temple that you built by establish-
ing my name there forever. My eyes and my
heart will always be there. 4 And as for you, if
you walk before me as David, your father,
walked, in integrity of heart and righteous-
ness, and you do all that I command you,
and you observe my statutes and my ordi-
nances, 5 then I will establish your royal
throne over Israel forever just as I promised
David, your father, when I said, 'You will not
fail to have one who will reign upon the
throne of Israel.' [q]

6 "But if your children turn away from me,
and they do not follow me nor do they
observe my commandments or my statutes
that I have set before you, and they go off to
serve other gods, and they worship them,
7 then I will cut Israel off from the land that
I have given them, and I will reject from my
sight this temple that I have consecrated for
my name. Israel will become a byword and a
laughingstock among all the nations. 8 Al-
though this temple is now exalted, everyone
who passes by it will be astonished and will
hiss at it, and they will say, 'Why has the LORD
done this to this land and to this temple?' [r]
9 Then they will answer, 'Because they aban-
doned the LORD, their God, who brought
their fathers forth from the land of Egypt.
They have embraced other gods, and they

n Dan 9:20.—o Ex 40:29; 2 Chr 7:7.—p 1 Ki 3:5; 11:9; Gen 12:7; 26:2; 2 Chr 7:12.—q 2 Sam 7:12-16; 2 Chr 6:16; 7:18.—r Deut 29:23; 2 Chr 7:21; Jer 22:8; 51:37.

8:65 The dedication of the temple coincided, as was noted above, with the Feast of Booths, which lasted seven days.

have worshiped them and served them. This
is why the LORD has brought all of these di-
sasters upon them.' "

Taking Account. 10 At the end of twenty
years during which Solomon built two build-
ings, the temple of the LORD and the royal
palace, 11 King Solomon gave twenty towns
that were in the land of Galilee to King
Hiram, the king of Tyre, who had provided
Solomon with all the cedar wood, fir, and
gold that he desired. 12 When King Hiram
traveled out from Tyre to inspect the towns
that Solomon had given him, he was not
pleased with them. 13 He said, "What kind of
cities have you given me, my brother?" He
has called the land Cabul up to the present
day. 14 Now Hiram had sent the king one
hundred twenty talents of gold.*

15 This is an account of the forced labor
that King Solomon raised in order to build
the temple of the LORD, his own palace,
Millo, the walls of Jerusalem, Hazor,
Megiddo, and Gezer.[s] 16 (Pharaoh, the king
of Egypt, had gone up and captured Gezer.
He burned it down and killed the Canaanites
who were living there. He gave it as a dowry
to his daughter, Solomon's wife. 17 Solomon
then rebuilt Gezer.) He also built lower
Beth-horon, 18 Baalath, and Tadmor in the
desert, all of which were within his land.
19 Solomon also had storage cities for provi-
sions, cities for his chariots, and cities for his
horses. Solomon built whatever he desired in
Jerusalem, Lebanon, and all the land that he
ruled.

20 All of the people who survived from
among the Amorites, the Hittites, the
Perizzites, the Hivites, and the Jebusites (for
these people were not Israelites), 21 that is,
their descendants who remained in the land
(for the Israelites had not been able to wipe
them out) were conscripted by Solomon to
serve as slave labor, as is still true today.

22 Solomon did not reduce the Israelites to
slavery. They were his fighting men, his offi-
cials, his princes, his captains, the com-
manders of his chariots, and his charioteers.
23 They were also the chief officials who were
in charge of Solomon's work projects. There
were five hundred and fifty of them, and they
supervised the men who did the work.
24 After Pharaoh's daughter came up to the
City of David, to the palace that he had built
for her, he then built Millo.

25 Three times a year* Solomon offered up
burnt offerings and peace offerings upon the
altar that he had built for the LORD. He also
burnt incense on the altar before the LORD,
and so he fulfilled his temple duties.[t] 26 King
Solomon built ships at Ezion-geber, which is
near Elath on the Red Sea in the land of
Edom. 27 Hiram sent some of his men who
were sailors, seafaring men who knew the
sea, to sail with Solomon's men. 28 They
sailed to Ophir* and brought back and
delivered to King Solomon four hundred
and twenty talents of gold.

CHAPTER 10

The Queen of Sheba's Visit.* 1 When the
Queen of Sheba heard about Solomon's rep-
utation, she came to test him with difficult
questions.*[u] 2 She came to Jerusalem with a
very large caravan, with camels carrying
spices and large quantities of gold and pre-
cious stones. When she arrived upon her visit
to Solomon, she told him everything that
was on her mind. 3 Solomon answered all of
her questions. There were no hidden things
that Solomon could not tell her.

4 When the Queen of Sheba saw all of
Solomon's wisdom, the palace that he had
built, 5 the food on his table, the assembly of
his servants, the attendance of his ministers
in their robes and their cupbearers, and the
way that he went up into the temple of the
LORD, she was overwhelmed. 6 She said to
the king, "The report that I heard in my own
land concerning your actions and your wis-
dom are true. 7 However, I could not believe
the report until I had come and seen it with
my own eyes. They did not tell me the half of
it. Your wisdom and your wealth exceed the
report that I heard. 8 Happy are your men

s 2 Sam 5:25; Jer 49:28.—t 2 Chr 8:1; Ezek 43:27.—u 2 Chr 9:1; Mt 12:42; Lk 11:31.

9:14 This was a considerable sum; even considering fluctuations in its value, it would be at least 5000 pounds that Hiram sent to Solomon.

9:25 *Three times a year:* on the great annual feasts of Unleavened Bread, Pentecost, and Booths (see Ex 23:4-19).

9:28 *Ophir:* a region rich in gold, probably on the western coast of Arabia.

10:1-13 Solomon's reputation drew foreign rulers. The prophet Isaiah (60:6) will use the memory of the visit of the Queen of Sheba (Arabia) to exalt Jerusalem as spiritual capital of all peoples in Messianic times; it is due to Isaiah that the queen plays a part in our Epiphany liturgy. Our Lord will also recall her in his comparison of himself and Solomon (Mt 12:42).

10:1 The kingdom of Sheba was located in the southeastern part of the Arabian peninsula (this explains our Lord's reference to the "queen of the south" in Mt 12:42; Lk 11:31); in fact, however, the visitor was probably the queen of a Sheban colony in northern Arabia.

and happy are these, your servants, who always stand before you and hear your wisdom. 9 Blessed be the LORD, your God, who delights in you, placing you upon the throne of Israel. The LORD of Israel has established you as king to exercise justice and righteousness because he has loved you forever."[v]

10 She then gave the king one hundred and twenty talents of gold, great quantities of spices, and precious stones. A more abundant quantity of spices never arrived than that which the Queen of Sheba gave to King Solomon.

11 Furthermore, the ships of Hiram that had brought the gold from Ophir also brought large quantities of almug wood and precious stones from Ophir. 12 The king made steps of almug wood for the temple of the LORD and for the king's palace as well as harps and stringed instruments for accompanying singers. Almug wood such as this has not arrived or been seen up to the present day.

13 King Solomon gave the Queen of Sheba whatever she desired. He gave her whatever she asked for in addition to what King Solomon had already given her. She then returned, going to her own country along with her servants.

Solomon's Wealth. 14 * The weight of the gold that Solomon would receive in a year was six hundred, sixty-six talents[w] 15 in addition to what he received from merchants and the profits from trade, as well as from the Arabian kings and the governors of the land.

16 King Solomon made two hundred shields from beaten gold. Each of the shields contained six hundred shekels of gold. 17 He also made three hundred shields from beaten gold. Three minas of gold went into each shield. The king placed them in the palace built with the wood of Lebanon. 18 The king also made an ivory throne and had it overlaid with fine gold. 19 The throne had six steps, and the back of the throne had a rounded top. On either side of the seat there were armrests, and there was a lion standing alongside each of the armrests. 20 There were twelve lions standing upon the six steps, with one on each side of the step. Nothing like this had ever been made in any other kingdom.

21 All of King Solomon's goblets were made of gold, and all of the other utensils in the palace made from Lebanon wood were also made from the finest gold. Nothing was made from silver, for it was not considered to be worth anything in Solomon's time.

22 The king also had ships of Tarshish at sea along with Hiram's ships. Once every three years the ships of Tarshish would return, bringing gold, silver, ivory, apes, and baboons with them. 23 King Solomon was greater in wealth and wisdom than all of the other kings on the earth.[x]

Solomon's Acclaim. 24 Everyone on the earth sought to visit Solomon to listen to his wisdom which God had placed in his heart. 25 Year after year, everyone brought him presents of things made from silver, things made from gold, garments, armor, spices, horses, and donkeys.

Solomon's Chariots and Horses. 26 Solomon collected chariots and horsemen. He had one thousand, four hundred chariots and twelve thousand horsemen. He stationed them in cities and with the king in Jerusalem.[y]

27 The king made silver as common as stones in Jerusalem. Cedar became as common as the sycamore that abounds in the Shephelah.* 28 Solomon brought horses from Egypt and Cilicia. The king's merchants bought them in Cilicia. 29 They imported chariots from Egypt that cost six hundred silver shekels and horses that cost one hundred and fifty. They also exported them to all of the Hittite and Aramean kings.

CHAPTER 11

Solomon's Wives and Idolatry. 1 * But King Solomon loved many foreign wives. In addition to Pharaoh's daughter, there were Moabite women, Ammonites, Edomites, Sidonians, and Hittites.[z] 2 These were from the nations about which the LORD had said to the Israelites, "You are not to go to them, nor are they to come to you, for they will surely turn your heart away to follow their gods." Solomon clung to them in love. 3 He had

v 1 Sam 25:32; Isa 9:6.—w 1 Ki 9:28; 2 Chr 9:13.—x 1 Ki 5:10; 2 Chr 9:22.—y 2 Chr 1:14; 9:25.—z 1 Ki 3:1; Deut 17:17; Sir 47:19f.

10:14ff God was generous to Solomon and rewarded him with enormous wealth and power because when presented with the opportunity, he had humbly asked for wisdom (1 Ki 3:13).

10:27 *Shephelah:* the hilly region between the mountains of Judea and the Mediterranean.

11:1ff For all his wisdom, Solomon's weakness for women is his downfall. He disregards God's command not to marry foreign women, and by aligning himself with so many heathen women, he eventually turns away from the true God.

seven hundred wives and three hundred con-
cubines, and his wives perverted his heart.
4 When Solomon grew old, his wives
turned his heart to serve other gods. His
heart did not rest in peace with the LORD, his
God, as the heart of David, his father, had.
5 He followed Ashtaroth, the goddess of the
Sidonians, and Moloch, the abomination of
the Ammonites. 6 Solomon did what was evil
in the sight of the LORD. He did not follow
after the LORD completely as his father
David had. 7 Solomon built a high place to
Chemosh, the abomination of the Moabites,
and to Moloch, the abomination of the
Ammonites, on a hillside that lies to the east
of Jerusalem. [a] 8 He did the same thing for all
of his foreign wives. He burned incense and
sacrificed to their gods.
9 * The LORD therefore became angry with
Solomon for he had turned his heart away
from the LORD, the God of Israel, who had
appeared to him twice, 10 and who had given
him a command concerning this very thing,
that he not follow after other gods, but he did
not observe what the LORD had command-
ed. 11 Therefore, the LORD said to Solomon,
"Because you have done this and you have
not observed my covenant and my statutes
that I had given to you, I will surely tear the
kingdom away from you and give it to your
servant.
12 "Nevertheless, I will not do this during
your days, for the sake of David, your father.
I will tear it out of the hands of your son. 13 I
will not tear the entire kingdom away. I will
give your son one tribe for the sake of David,
my servant, and for the sake of Jerusalem
which I have chosen."

Solomon's Adversaries. 14 The LORD raised
up an adversary to Solomon: Hadad, the
Edomite, who was a descendant of the kings
in Edom. 15 When David had been in Edom,
and Joab, the commander of the army, had
gone up to bury those who had been killed,
for every male had been killed in Edom [b]
16 (for Joab and all of Israel had remained
there for six months until they had killed
every male in Edom), 17 Hadad had fled into
Egypt along with certain Edomites who had
been his father's servants. Hadad was only a
little child. 18 They came up out of Midian to
Paran, and they took men with them from
Paran and went to Egypt, to Pharaoh, the
king of Egypt, who gave him a house and
provided him with provisions and gave him
some land.
19 Pharaoh liked Hadad so much that he
gave him the sister of his own wife to marry,
the sister of Queen Tahpenes. 20 The sister of
Tahpenes bore him a son named Genubath.
Tahpenes raised him in Pharaoh's house-
hold. Genubath belonged to Pharaoh's
household, as if he were one of Pharaoh's
sons.
21 While he was in Egypt, he heard that
David was now sleeping with his fathers and
that Joab, the commander of the army, was
dead. Hadad said to Pharaoh, "Let me leave
so that I might return to my own land." [c]
22 Pharaoh said to him, "What have you ever
been without that you seek to return to your
own land?" He answered, "Nothing, but let
me go anyway."
23 God also stirred up another adversary
against him, Rezon, the son of Eliada. He
had fled from his lord, Hadadezer, the king of
Zobah. 24 He gathered some men to himself
and became the leader of a band of them
when David conquered the forces of Zobah.
They traveled to Damascus and dwelt there,
reigning in Damascus. 25 He was an adver-
sary of Israel all through Solomon's time,
adding to the difficulties caused by Hadad.
He ruled in Aram and despised Israel.

Jeroboam's Kingship Predicted. 26 There was
a certain Jeroboam, the son of Nebat, who
was an Ephraimite from Zeredah. His moth-
er was a widow whose name was Zeruah. He
rebelled against the king. 27 This is how he
rebelled against the king: Solomon built
Millo and repaired the breaches in the wall of
the City of David, his father. 28 Jeroboam was
an impressive man, and when Solomon saw
that the young man was capable, he placed
him in charge of the whole component of
forced labor of the house of Joseph.
29 * When Jeroboam went out from
Jerusalem, he was met along the way by
Ahijah, the Shilonite, who was a prophet. He
was wearing a new garment, and the two of
them were alone in the field. 30 Ahijah

a 1 Ki 11:5.—b 1 Ki 11:16; 2 Sam 8:14.—c 2 Ki 14:20; 2 Chr 27:9.

11:9ff The slippery slope for Solomon into idolatry and sin took some time and several outright acts of disobedience on his part. Despite the warnings and threats from the Lord, he continued his downward spiral, losing God and everything he had been given in abundance.

11:29ff Jeroboam is given the heads up by the prophet Ahijah that he will inherit 10 of Israel's 12 tribes. Benjamin and Judah—often referred to as one tribe—would remain loyal to David—King Solomon's father.

grabbed the new garment that he was wearing and he tore it into twelve pieces. 31 He then said to Jeroboam, "Take ten pieces for yourself, for thus says the LORD, the God of Israel, 'Behold, I will tear the kingdom out of the hands of Solomon and I will give you ten tribes.[d] 32 One tribe will remain for the sake of my servant David and for the sake of the city of Jerusalem, which I have chosen from out of the tribes of Israel.

33 "'This is because he has abandoned me and he has worshiped Ashtaroth, the goddess of the Sidonians, Chemosh, the god of the Moabites, and Moloch, the god of the Ammonites. He has not walked in my paths, doing what was right in my sight by observing my statutes and ordinances as David, his father, did. 34 But I will not take the whole kingdom out of his hands. I will keep him as ruler all the days of his life for the sake of David, my servant, whom I chose, for he observed my commandments and my statutes, 35 but I will take it out of his son's hands. I will then give you ten of the tribes. 36 I will give one tribe to his son so that David, my servant, might have a light before me always in Jerusalem, the city that I have chosen for my name.[e]

37 "'I will take you, and you will reign over all that your heart desires. You will be the king over Israel. 38 If you listen to all that I have commanded you and you walk in my ways and you do what is right in my sight, observing my statutes and my commandments, as David, my servant, did, then I will be with you and I will build a secure dynasty for you just as I built one for David. I will give you Israel. 39 I will humble the descendants of David because of this, but not forever.' "

40 Solomon tried to kill Jeroboam, so Jeroboam rose and fled into Egypt, to Shishak, the king of Egypt. He stayed in Egypt until Solomon had died.[f]

Solomon's Death. 41 As for the rest of Solomon's deeds and the wisdom that he demonstrated, are they not written in the Book of the Acts of Solomon? 42 Solomon reigned in Jerusalem over all of Israel for forty years. 43 Solomon then slept with his fathers, and he was buried in the City of David, his father. Rehoboam, his son, then ruled in his stead.

II: THE REIGN OF JEROBOAM* *

CHAPTER 12

Revolt against Rehoboam. 1 Rehoboam went to Shechem, for all of Israel had gone to Shechem to make him king.[g] 2 When Jeroboam, the son of Nebat, heard about this in Egypt where he had fled from King Solomon, he returned from Egypt.

3 They sent for Jeroboam, and when he arrived, he and the whole assembly of Israel spoke to Rehoboam, saying, 4 "Your father made our yoke heavy. If you make our service and our heavy yoke lighter than the heavy load your father laid on us, then we will serve you." 5 Rehoboam answered, "Go away for three days, and then come back to me." So the people departed.

6 King Rehoboam consulted with the elders who had stood before Solomon, his father, during his lifetime. He said, "How do you advise me to answer this people, so that I can give them an answer?" 7 They answered him, "If you become a servant to this people today and you serve them and you give them a favorable answer, then they will be your servants forever."

8 But he ignored the advice that the elders had given him, and instead, he consulted with the young men who had grown up with him and who stood before him. 9 He asked them, "What advice do you give me so that we can give an answer to this people who have spoken to me, saying, 'Make the yoke lighter than that which your father laid upon us?' "[h]

10 The young men who had grown up with him answered, "Say the following to the people who said to you, 'Your father made our yoke heavy; will you lighten it for us?' Say this to them: 'My little finger is thicker than my father's waist! 11 My father laid a heavy yoke on you, but I will add to your yoke. My father chastised you with whips, but I will chastise you with scorpions.' "

d 1 Ki 12:15.—e 1 Ki 11:13; 15:4; 2 Chr 6:6.—f 2 Chr 10:2.—g 2 Chr 10:1; Neh 6:7.—h 2 Chr 10:9.

12:1—22:40 This section is continued in the second Book of Kings, down to chapter 17.

12:1—16:28 The division of the two kingdoms is represented as a judgment of God, but this is regularly the way the Bible speaks of every revolution and every war. Everything has to be paid for. The sins of Solomon, who had become a proud despot, and the ineptitude of his sons made the schism inevitable. After the division the two kingdoms had to reorganize, but the northern kingdom took a wrong path. The Books of Kings, however, are interested in the political history of the northern kingdom only to the extent that it influenced the religious history of the Israelite people.

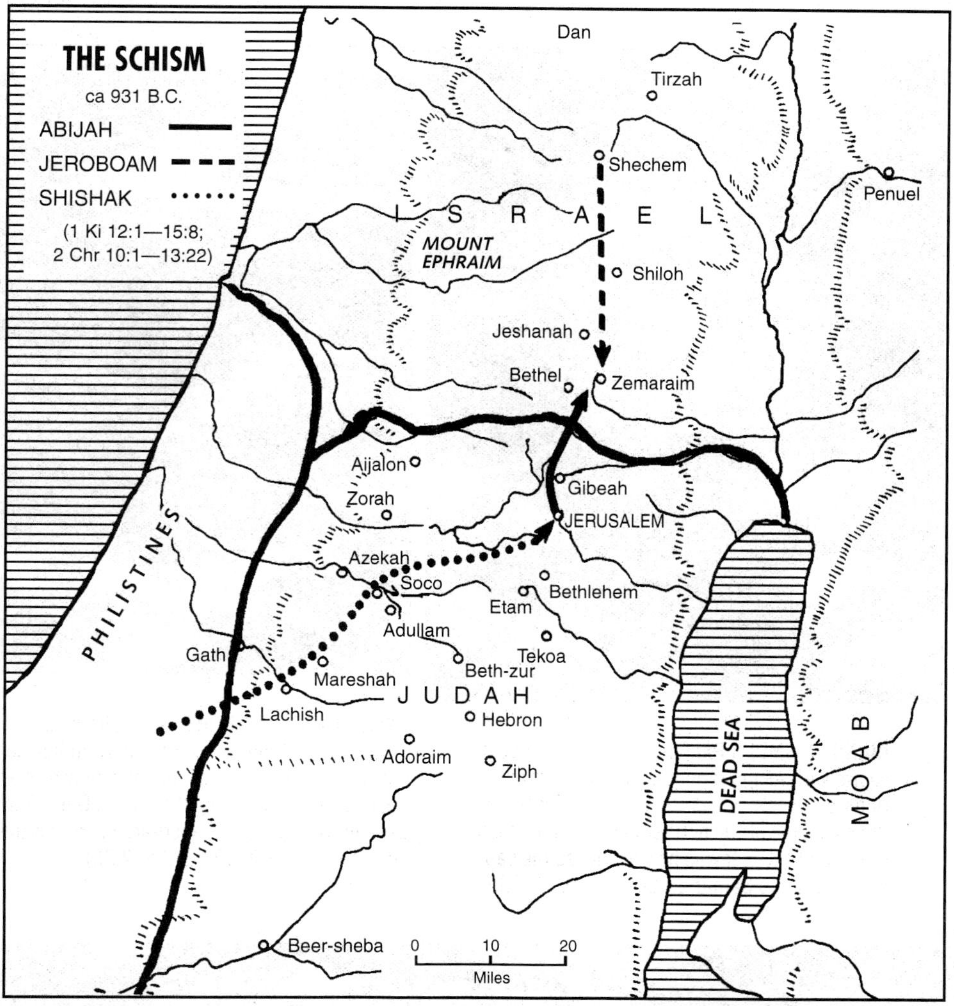

THE KINGDOM OF JUDAH

1. REHOBOAM (931–913 B.C.)

1 Ki 12:1—14:30; 2 Chr 10:1—12:16

THE KINGDOM OF ISRAEL

1. JEROBOAM (931–910 B.C.)

1 Ki 12:20—14:18

At **Shechem,** convocation of the people and revolt of the northern tribes.

(a) Rehoboam reigns over Judah and Benjamin. The prophet Shemaiah advises against any attempt at forced reunification (12:17-24). Rehoboam builds fortified cities: **Bethlehem, Etam, Tekoa, Beth-zur, Soco, Adullam, Gath, Mareshah, Ziph, Adoraim, Lachish, Azekah, Zorah, Aijalon, Hebron** (2 Chr 11:5-12). **(b)** Persecuted by Jeroboam, the priests, scattered in Israel, come to Jerusalem (2 Chr 11:13-17). **(c)** However, Sheshonk (Shishak), king of Egypt, invades Judah, pillages the temple and the royal palace (1 Ki 14:25-27).

(a) Returning from Egypt, Jeroboam is crowned king of Israel by the people of the dissident tribes (12:1-16). **(b)** He fortifies **Shechem** and **Penuel;** he institutes idolatrous worship at **Bethel** and **Dan** (12:25-32). A prophet from Judah condemns the altar at **Bethel.** The prophet Ahijah of **Shiloh** predicts the death of Abijah, son of Jeroboam (12:32—13:34).

2. ABIJAH (913–911 B.C.)

1 Ki 15:1-8; 2 Chr 13

War between Abijah and Jeroboam. The latter is defeated at Mount Zemaraim, in the highlands of Ephraim. Abijah annexes **Bethel, Jeshanah,** Ephron (2 Chr 13:1-21).

Matson Photo Service

RUINS OF OMRI'S PALACE — A series of open courts with rooms ranged about them from the ruins of Omri's palace in Samaria. Omri was the sixth king of the northern kingdom of Israel (886–874 B.C.). It was he who moved the capital of Israel to Samaria. (See 1 Ki 16:23-28.)

Matson Photo Service

EXCAVATIONS AT BETHEL — Walls of a house dating to the time of Joshua. Many archaeological confirmations of the biblical history of Bethel have been found. During the time of Omri, Bethel became the greatest sanctuary of the northern kingdom. (See 1 Ki 12:32; 2 Ki 2:2f.)

British Museum

ASSYRIAN KING ASHURBANIPAL HUNTING LIONS — King Ashurbanipal (883–859 B.C.) is shown hunting lions. The king and his driver stand in a chariot drawn by two horses as two footmen assist in the hunt. The chariot has six-spoked wheels and crossed quivers attached to the side. Ashurbanipal was the father of Shalmaneser III, who later exacted tribute from Jehu, and a contemporary of Omri. (See 1 Ki 16:23-28.)

12 Three days later Jeroboam and all of the
people returned to Rehoboam as the king
had decreed when he said, "Come back to
me in three days." 13 The king responded
harshly to the people. He ignored the coun-
sel that the elders had given him. 14 He said
to them what the young men had advised
him saying, "My father laid a heavy yoke on
you, but I will add to your yoke. My father
chastised you with whips, but I will chastise
you with scorpions."

15 Thus the king would not listen to the
people, for the LORD had brought this about
to fulfill what he said when the LORD spoke
through Ahijah the Shilonite to Jeroboam,
the son of Nebat. 16 When all of Israel real-
ized that the king would not listen to them,
the people answered the king, "What share
do we have in David? What inheritance do
we have in the son of Jesse? To your own
tents, O Israel. Look after your own house, O
David." So the people of Israel returned to
their homes.* [i]

17 Rehoboam still ruled over those Israel-
ites who were living in the cities of Judah.
18 King Rehoboam sent out Adoniram who
was in charge of the forced labor, but all of
Israel stoned him to death. King Rehoboam,
however, mounted his chariot and fled to
Jerusalem. 19 Israel has been in rebellion
against the house of David up to the present
day.[j]

20 When all of Israel heard that Jeroboam
had come back, they sent for him and sum-
moned him to an assembly. They made him
king over all of Israel. No one followed the
house of David except for the tribe of Judah.

21 When Rehoboam arrived in Jerusalem,
he assembled the entire house of Judah
along with the tribe of Benjamin, one hun-
dred and eighty thousand fighting men to
battle against the house of Israel and to
restore the kingdom to Rehoboam, the son
of Solomon. 22 But the word of God came to
Shemaiah, the man of God, saying, 23 "Speak
to Rehoboam, the son of Solomon, the king
of Judah, and to all of the house of Judah and
Benjamin, and to the rest of the people, say-
ing, 24 'Thus says the LORD, You are not to go
up or fight against your brothers, the Is-
raelites. Let each man return home, for this
thing is from me.' " They obeyed the word of
the LORD, and they turned around and left,
as the LORD had instructed.

25 Jeroboam built Shechem in the hill
country of Ephraim and he dwelt there. He
went out from there and built Penuel.

Jeroboam's Idolatry. 26 Jeroboam said to
himself, "The kingdom is going to return to
the house of David. 27 If this people goes up
to sacrifice in the temple of the LORD in
Jerusalem, the heart of this people will
return to their lord, to Rehoboam, the king
of Judah. They will kill me and they will
return to Rehoboam, the king of Judah."

28 The king sought counsel, and so he
made two golden calves.* [k] He said to them,
"It is too difficult for you to go up to
Jerusalem. Behold, your gods, O Israel,
which brought you up out of the land of
Egypt." 29 He placed one in Bethel, and he
placed the other in Dan.* 30 This thing
became a sin, for the people went to worship
before one of them, even to Dan.

31 He built shrines upon the high places,
and he appointed priests from the lowliest of
people who were not Levites.

32 He established a festival on the fifteenth
day of the eighth month like the one that was
celebrated in Judah, and he offered sacrifices
upon the altar. He did this in Bethel, offering
sacrifices to the calves that he had made. In
Bethel he also appointed priests for the high
places that he had made.

33 And so he established a festival for the
Israelites on the fifteenth day of the eighth
month, a date of his own choosing, and he
offered up a sacrifice on the altar he had
built in Bethel. He offered up a sacrifice and
burned incense on the altar.

CHAPTER 13

Prophetic Disobedience. 1 A man of God
came from Judah and went to Bethel, led by
the word of the LORD, and Jeroboam was
standing by the altar offering incense. 2 He
cried out the word of the LORD against the

---

i 2 Sam 20:1; 2 Chr 10:16.—j 2 Ki 17:23; 2 Chr 10:19.—k Ex 32:8; 2 Ki 17:36; Tob 1:5.

12:16 The kingdoms did not divide immediately, but between Solomon's demise and the actions of both Rehoboam and Jeroboam, the people do not have a leader strong or wise enough to keep them united.

12:28 *Two golden calves:* by setting up a new place of worship outside of Jerusalem, Jeroboam disregards God's rules of worship and starts his own religion separating the people both physically and spiritually from their true home. His efforts are doomed as were previous generations that worshiped golden calves (Ex 32).

12:29 That is, at the two opposite ends of the new state: Dan was near the headwaters of the Jordan; Bethel was on the road to Jerusalem.

altar saying, "O altar, O altar, thus says the
LORD, 'A son will be born to the house of
David by the name of Josiah. On you he will
sacrifice the priests of the high places who
now burn incense upon you. Human bones
will be burnt upon you.' "[*] [l]

3 That same day he gave a sign saying,
"This is a sign of what the LORD has pro-
claimed: The altar will be split in two and the
ashes on it will be poured out."

4 When the king heard the man of God
speaking against the altar in Bethel,
Jeroboam stretched out his hand from the
altar proclaiming, "Seize him!" The hand
that he stretched out toward him shriveled
up, and he could not pull it back again. 5 The
altar split apart and its ashes spilt out from
the altar, fulfilling the sign that the man of
God had proclaimed through the word of the
LORD.

6 The king said to the man of God,
"Intercede now to the LORD, your God, and
pray for me so that my hand might be made
well." The man of God interceded with the
LORD, and the king's hand was made well,
just like it was before.

7 The king said to the man of God, "Come
home with me and have something to eat,
and I will give you a gift." 8 But the man of
God said to the king, "Even if you were to
give me half of what belongs to you, I would
not go with you, nor would I eat bread or
drink water in this place. 9 I received a com-
mand by the word of the LORD, 'Do not eat
bread or drink water or return by the way
you came.' "[m] 10 He returned by another way,
and did not go back by the way that he had
come to Bethel.

Fate of a Disobedient Prophet.[*] 11 Now there
was an old prophet who lived in Bethel
whose sons came and told him all about the
things that the man of God had done in
Bethel that day. 12 They also told their father
what he had said to the king. Their father
asked them, "Which way did he go?" His
sons showed him the way on which the man
of God from Judah had gone. 13 He said to
his sons, "Saddle up the donkey for me."
They saddled up the donkey, and he rode
on it.

14 He rode after the man of God and found
him sitting under an oak tree and said to
him, "Are you the man of God who came
from Judah?" He answered, "I am." 15 So he
said to him, "Come home and eat with me."

16 He answered, "I cannot return nor can I
go with you. I cannot eat bread with you nor
drink water with you in that place. 17 The
word of the LORD told me, 'Do not eat bread
nor drink water there. Do not return by the
way which you came.' "

18 He said, "I am also a prophet like you.
An angel spoke the word of the LORD to me,
saying, 'Bring him back with you into your
house so that he can eat bread and drink
water.' " But he was lying.

19 The man of God returned with him and
he ate bread and drank water in his house.
20 While they were sitting at the table, the
word of the LORD came to the prophet who
brought him back. 21 He cried out to the man
of God who had come from Judah, "Thus
says the LORD: 'Because you defied the
mouth of the LORD and have not observed
the command that the LORD, your God,
commanded you, 22 but you came back and
ate bread and drank water in the place that I
told you not to eat bread nor drink water,
therefore your body will not be buried in the
tomb of your fathers.' "

23 When he had finished eating bread and
drinking, the prophet who had brought him
back saddled his donkey up for him. 24 On
the way, a lion came upon him and killed
him, and his body was thrown down upon
the road, with both the donkey and the lion
standing alongside of him.

25 Some of those who were passing by on
the road saw his body tossed down there,
and there was a lion standing by the body.
They came and reported it in the city where
the old prophet was living. 26 When the
prophet who had brought him back while he
was on his way heard about it, he said, "It is
the man of God who disobeyed the word of
the LORD. The LORD has delivered him over
to the lion who tore him to pieces and killed
him, just as the word of the LORD had
declared to him."

27 The prophet said to his sons, "Saddle up
the donkey for me," and they saddled it up.
28 They went out and found the body that
had been thrown down along the way, and

l 2 Ki 23:16; Isa 34:6.—m 1 Ki 13:17.

13:2 This prophecy is fulfilled in exactly the way it is given when Josiah kills the pagan priests on their altars (2 Ki 23:1-20).

13:11-34 This popular anecdote, which is part of the stories about the prophets, contains a lesson that goes beyond the incident itself: one must never disobey an order from God.

the donkey and the lion were standing along-
side of it. The lion had not eaten the body nor
had it attacked the donkey. [29] The prophet
picked up the body of the man of God and
put it upon the donkey. He brought it back to
the old prophet's city to mourn for him and
bury him. [30] Then he laid the body in his own
grave. They mourned over him saying, "Oh,
my brother!"

[31] After he buried him, he said to his sons,
"When I die, bury me in the grave where the
man of God is buried. Lay my bones along-
side of his. [n] [32] The thing that he proclaimed
by the word of the LORD against the altar in
Bethel and against all of the shrines on the
high places throughout the cities of Samaria
will certainly be fulfilled."

[33] Even after this, though, Jeroboam did
not turn away from his evil ways. Once again
he appointed priests for the high places from
the lowliest of people. He consecrated as
priests for the high places anyone who want-
ed to be consecrated. [34] This was the sin of
the house of Jeroboam * that caused it to be
cut off and wiped out from the face of the
earth.

CHAPTER 14

The LORD Condemns Jeroboam.* [1] It was at
that time that Abijah, the son of Jeroboam,
fell ill. [2] Jeroboam said to his wife, "Get up
and disguise yourself so that they cannot tell
that you are Jeroboam's wife, and then go to
Shiloh. Ahijah, the prophet, is there, the one
who told me that I would be king over this
people. [o] [3] Take ten loaves of bread with you
along with some cakes and a jar of honey
and go to him. He will tell you what will hap-
pen to the child."

[4] Jeroboam's wife did this. She got up and
went to Shiloh and entered the house of
Ahijah. Ahijah could no longer see, for his
eyes had grown dim because of his age. [5] But
the LORD said to Ahijah, "Behold, the wife of
Jeroboam is coming to ask something from
you concerning her son who is sick. This is
what you are to say to her."

When she arrived, she pretended she was
someone else. [6] When Ahijah heard the
sound of her feet as she came through the
door, he said, "Enter, O wife of Jeroboam.
Why do you pretend to be someone else? I
have been sent to you with heavy tidings. [7] Go
tell Jeroboam, 'Thus says the LORD, the God
of Israel: I have exalted you from among the
people, and I have made you the leader over
my people Israel. [8] I tore the kingdom away
from the house of David and gave it to you.
Yet, you have not been like my servant David
who observed my commandments and who
followed me with all of his heart, doing what
is right in my sight. [9] You have done more
evil than those who preceded you. You have
gone after and made other gods, molten
images, enraging me and casting me behind
your back. [10] Behold, I will bring evil down
upon the house of Jeroboam. I will cut off
from Jeroboam everyone who pees against
the wall, every bondsman and everyone who
is free in Israel. I will wipe out the remnant of
the house of Jeroboam as one burns up dung
until it is completely consumed. [p] [11] Those
who belong to Jeroboam and who die in the
city will be eaten by the dogs; those who die
in the fields will be eaten by the birds of the
air. The LORD has spoken.' [q]

[12] "As for you, get up and go home. The
moment that your feet enter the city, your
child will die. [13] All of Israel will mourn for
him and bury him. He is the only one who
comes from Jeroboam who will be placed in
a grave because he is the only one in the
house of Jeroboam in whom the LORD, the
God of Israel, has found anything good.

[14] "The LORD will raise up a king over
Israel for himself who on that day will cut off
the house of Jeroboam. What? Even now!
[15] The LORD will strike down Israel, just as a
reed is shaken in the water. He will uproot
Israel from out of this good land that he gave
to their fathers. He will scatter them beyond
the river because they have made their
wooden images, provoking the LORD to
anger. [16] He will give up Israel because of the
sins of Jeroboam, for he sinned and he
caused Israel to sin."

[17] Jeroboam's wife then got up and left and
came to Tirzah. When she arrived at the
threshold of the house, the child died.

---

n Gen 49:29; 2 Ki 23:17; Tob 4:3.—o 1 Ki 11:29; Jer 7:12.—
p 1 Ki 14:14; 15:29; 21:21.—q 1 Ki 16:4; 21:24; Isa 1:20.

13:34 *Sin of the house of Jeroboam:* appointing his own priests for worship was a serious sin—only those from the tribe of Levi could serve (Num 3:10). There could be no true worship for the people in the northern kingdom under these circumstances.

14:1-20 An elderly, blind prophet is compelled to curse the man whom he had chosen to be king at the Lord's order (see 11:29); this is the beginning of the henceforth frequent conflicts between men of God and the rulers of Israel. Jeroboam will serve, in the stories about his successors, as the example of a wicked king.

18 They buried him, and all of Israel
mourned for him, according to the word of
the LORD that he had spoken through Ahijah
the prophet, his servant.

19 The rest of the deeds of Jeroboam, how
he made war and how he reigned, are writ-
ten in the book of the chronicles of the kings
of Israel. 20 Jeroboam reigned for twenty-two
years, and then he slept with his fathers, and
his son Nadab reigned in his stead.

III: KINGS OF ISRAEL AND JUDAH

Rehoboam's Reign. 21 Rehoboam, the son
of Solomon, reigned in Judah. Rehoboam
was forty-one years old when he began to
reign, and he reigned for seventeen years in
Jerusalem, the city that the LORD had chosen
from out of all of the tribes of Israel to place
his name. His mother's name was Naamah,
and she was an Ammonite.[r]

22 Judah did what was evil in the sight of
the LORD.* With the sins that they commit-
ted which were worse than what their
fathers had done, they provoked the LORD to
jealousy. 23 They also set up high places for
themselves as well as sacred pillars and
Asherah everywhere and under every green
tree. 24 There were even male prostitutes in
the land. They did every abomination that
the nations had done which the LORD had
cast out before the Israelites.

25 In the fifth year of King Rehoboam,
Shishak, the king of Egypt, attacked Jeru-
salem. 26 He took away the treasures from
the temple of the LORD and the treasures out
of the royal palace. He took everything away,
including the gold shields that Solomon had
made.[s]

27 King Rehoboam made bronze shields to
replace them. He entrusted them into the
hands of the commanders of the guard who
watched over the entrance to the king's
palace. 28 The guards would carry them
whenever the king went into the temple of
the LORD. Afterwards, they would return
them to the guardroom.

29 As for the rest of the deeds of Reho-
boam and all that he did, are they not writ-
ten in the book of the chronicles of the kings
of Judah? * 30 There was war between Reho-
boam and Jeroboam during their entire
reigns. 31 Rehoboam slept with his fathers,
and he was buried with his fathers in the
City of David. His mother's name was
Naamah, and she was an Ammonite. Abijam,
his son, then reigned in his stead.

CHAPTER 15

Abijam's Reign. 1 In the eighteenth year of
the reign of King Jeroboam, the son of Nebat,
Abijam became the king of Judah.[t] 2 He
reigned in Jerusalem for three years. His
mother's name was Maacah, and she was
the daughter of Abishalom.

3 He committed all of the sins that his
father had committed before him. His heart
was not at peace with the LORD, his God, as
the heart of David, his father, had been. 4 In
spite of this, the LORD, his God, gave him a
lamp in Jerusalem for the sake of David,
raising up his son to succeed him and mak-
ing Jerusalem strong.* 5 He did this because
of David who had done what was right in the
sight of the LORD, and he had not turned
away from anything that he had been com-
manded throughout his entire life with the
exception of what happened with Uriah the
Hittite.[u] 6 There was war between Reho-
boam and Jeroboam during their entire
reign.

7 The rest of the deeds of Abijam and all
that he did, are they not written in the book
of the chronicles of the kings of Judah? There
was war between Abijam and Jeroboam.

8 Abijam slept with his fathers, and they
buried him in the City of David, and Asa, his
son then reigned in his stead.

Asa's Reign. 9 In the twentieth year of the
reign of Jeroboam as the king of Israel, Asa
became the king of Judah. 10 He reigned for
forty-one years in Jerusalem. His mother's
name was Maacah, the daughter of
Abishalom.

11 Asa did what was right in the sight of the
LORD, as his father David had. 12 He ex-

r 2 Chr 11:17; 12:13.—s 1 Ki 10:16; 2 Chr 12:9.—t 2 Chr 13:1f.—u Gen 26:5; 2 Sam 11:4; 2 Chr 29:2.

14:22 *Evil in the sight of the LORD:* Rehoboam's rule brought Judah to its knees. As the behavior of the people became depraved and they lost sight of God and worshiped idols, the glorious kingdom that Solomon had built crumbled and fell to foreign invaders (vv. 24-25), reducing the temple and palace to ruins.

14:29 The author of the Books of Kings shares the sources that were used: the Annals of the Kings of Judah in this verse; the Annals of the Kings of Israel (v. 19) and the History of Solomon (1 Ki 11:41). Although they probably existed in some form, they have never been found.

15:4 In various ways and despite the unfaithfulness of David's descendants, the Lord will bless them as a tribute to the goodness and faithfulness of David. God's mercy is a total gift and often without merit.

pelled the male prostitutes from the land,
and he removed all of the idols that his
father had made. 13 He also deposed his
mother Maacah as queen mother because
she had made an image of an Asherah. Asa
cut down her idol and burned it in the
Kidron Valley. 14 But he did not do away with
the high places. Nevertheless, Asa's heart
was at peace with the LORD all of his life.
15 He brought those things that his father
had dedicated and those things that he had
dedicated, silver, and gold, and vessels, into
the temple of the LORD.[v]

16 There was war between Asa and
Baasha, the king of Israel, during their entire
reigns. 17 Baasha, the king of Israel, attacked
Judah, and he fortified Ramah in order to
prevent anyone from going out or coming in
to the king of Judah.

18 Asa took all of the silver and all of the
gold that remained in the treasury of the
LORD's temple and the treasury of the royal
palace. He gave them to his servants and
King Asa sent them to Ben-hadad, the son of
Tabrimmon, the son of Hezion, the king of
Aram, who lived in Damascus, saying,
19 "Let there be a covenant between me and
you, between my father and your father.
Behold, I have sent you a gift of silver and
gold. Go, break your covenant with Baasha,
the king of Israel, so that he might pull back
from attacking me."

20 Ben-hadad agreed with King Asa, and
he sent the commanders of his army to
attack the cities of Israel. He conquered Ijon,
Dan, Abel-beth-maacah, as well as all of the
Chinnereth and the land of Naphtali.
21 When Baasha heard about this, he stopped
building Ramah and he dwelt in Tirzah.

22 King Asa then issued a proclamation to
all of Judah from which no one was exempt
that they should carry away the stones and
the timber that Baasha was using for the
construction of Ramah. King Asa used them
to build up Geba in Benjamin and Mizpah.

23 As for the rest of the deeds of Asa, all of
his achievements, and all that he did, and the
cities that he built, are they not written in the
book of the chronicles of the kings of Judah?
In his old age, he suffered from difficulties
with his feet.[w]

24 King Asa slept with his fathers, and he
was buried with his fathers in the City of
David, his father, and his son Jehoshaphat
reigned in his stead.

Nadab's Reign. 25 Nadab, the son of
Jeroboam, became the king of Israel in the
second year of the reign of Asa, the king of
Judah, and he reigned over Israel for two
years. 26 He did what was evil in the sight of
the LORD, and he walked in the way of his
father, in his sin, which he also caused Israel
to commit.

27 Baasha, the son of Ahijah, of the house of
Issachar, plotted against him, and Baasha
struck him down at Gibbethon, a Philistine
city, while Nadab and all of Israel were laying
siege to Gibbethon. 28 Baasha killed him in
the third year of the reign of Asa, the king of
Judah, and he reigned in his stead.

29 As soon as he began to reign, he struck
down all of Jeroboam's household. He did not
leave Jeroboam a single person who was still
breathing; he wiped them out. This fulfilled
what the LORD had said when he spoke
through Ahijah, the Shilonite[x] 30 because of
the sins that Jeroboam committed and
because he caused Israel to sin, provoking the
anger of the LORD, the God of Israel.*

31 As for the other deeds of Nadab and all
the other things that he did, are they not writ-
ten in the book of the chronicles of the kings
of Israel?

32 There was war between Asa and Baasha,
the king of Israel, during their entire reigns.*[y]

Baasha's Reign. 33 In the third year of the
reign of Asa, the king of Judah, Baasha, the
son of Ahijah, became the king over all of
Israel in Tirzah, and he reigned for twenty-
four years. 34 He did what was evil in the
sight of the LORD, walking in the ways of
Jeroboam, in his sin, which he also caused
Israel to commit.

CHAPTER 16

1 The word of the LORD then came to Jehu,
the son of Hanani, condemning Baasha: 2 "I
lifted you up out of the dust and appointed
you as ruler over my people Israel, but you
have walked in the ways of Jeroboam and
you have caused my people Israel to sin, pro-
voking my anger at their sins. 3 Therefore, I
will wipe out Baasha and the descendants of

v 1 Chr 29:5; Ezr 1:4; 1 Mac 4:49.—w 2 Chr 16:11.—x 1 Ki 14:10; 21:22; Jdg 9:45.—y 1 Ki 15:16.

15:30 In contrast to the mercy shown to David's descendants (v. 4), God shows no mercy to Jeroboam's household because he led his people into sin and away from the true God.

15:32 The verse repeats verse 16.

his house. I will make your house like the
house of Jeroboam, the son of Nebat.[z]
4 Those who belong to Baasha who die in the
city will be eaten by dogs, and those who
belong to him who die in the field will be
eaten by the birds of the air."

5 As for the other deeds of Baasha, what he
did, and his achievements, are they not writ-
ten in the book of the chronicles of the kings
of Israel?

6 Baasha slept with his fathers and was
buried in Tirzah. Elah, his son, reigned in his
stead.

Elah's Reign. 7 The word of the LORD came
through Jehu the prophet, the son of Hanani,
to condemn Baasha and his house for all the
evil he had done in the sight of the LORD. He
provoked him to anger through the deeds of
his hands, for he did the same things as the
house of Jeroboam and because he wiped
it out.

8 Elah, the son of Baasha, began to reign
over Israel in Tirzah during the twenty-sixth
year of the reign of Asa, the king of Judah, and
he reigned for two years.

9 Then Zimri, his servant and the com-
mander of half of his chariots, plotted
against him. He was in Tirzah, and he got
drunk in the house of Arza, the major-domo
of the palace in Tirzah. 10 Zimri entered and
struck him and killed him during the twen-
ty-seventh year of the reign of Asa, the king
of Judah, and he reigned in his stead.[a] 11 As
soon as he began to reign, he struck down all
of Baasha's household. He did not leave a
single person who pees against the wall,
whether he be one of his relatives or one of
his friends. 12 Zimri wiped out the entire
house of Baasha, in accordance with the
word of the LORD which condemned Baasha
through Jehu, the prophet. 13 This was
because of the sins of Baasha and the sins of
Elah, his son, and because they caused Israel
to sin, provoking the LORD, the God of Israel,
to anger over their worthless idols.

14 As to the other deeds of Elah and all that
he did, are they not written in the book of the
chronicles of the kings of Israel?

Zimri's Reign. 15 Zimri reigned in Tirzah for
seven days during the twenty-seventh year of
the reign of Asa, the king of Judah.

The people were camped near Gibbethon,
a Philistine city. 16 When the people camped
there heard, "Zimri had plotted against and
killed the king," they made Omri, the com-
mander of the army, king over all of Israel
that very day in the camp. 17 Omri and all of
Israel departed from Gibbethon and they
besieged Tirzah. 18 When Zimri saw that the
city had been captured, he went up into the
citadel of the king's palace and he set the
palace on fire around himself and he died.
19 This was because of the sins that he had
committed, doing what was evil in the sight
of the LORD and walking in the ways of
Jeroboam, in his sin, and causing Israel to sin.

20 As for the other deeds of Zimri, and the
conspiracy that he plotted, are they not writ-
ten in the book of the chronicles of the kings
of Israel?

Civil War. 21 The people of Israel were then
divided into two factions. Half of them fol-
lowed Tibni, the son of Ginath, as king, and
the other half followed Omri. 22 The people
who supported Omri defeated the people
who followed Tibni, the son of Ginath. Tibni
died, and Omri became the king.

Omri's Reign.* 23 It was during the thirty-
first year of the reign of Asa, the king of Judah,
that Omri began to reign over Israel. He
reigned for twelve years, six of them from
Tirzah.

24 He bought the hill of Samaria from
Shemer for two talents of silver, and he built
a city upon the hill and named it Samaria,
after Shemer, the owner of the hill.[b]

25 Omri did what was evil in the sight of the
LORD, worse than any of those who preceded
him. 26 He walked in the ways of Jeroboam,
the son of Nebat, in his sin, causing Israel to
sin, provoking the LORD, the God of Israel, to
anger over their worthless idols.

27 As to the other deeds of Omri, what he
did, and his accomplishments, are they not
written in the book of the chronicles of the
kings of Israel? 28 Omri slept with his fathers
and was buried in Samaria, and his son
Ahab reigned in his stead.

Ahab's Reign. 29 * Ahab, the son of Omri,
began to reign over Israel during the thirty-

z 1 Ki 21:22; Ezek 25:7.—a 2 Ki 9:31.—b 1 Ki 16:32.

16:23-28 Omri builds the capital city, Samaria, the destruction of which will mark the end of the northern kingdom in 721 B.C.

16:29—2 Kings 2:13 Into the story of the reign of Omri's son and successor (874–853 B.C.) a literary and religious masterpiece is inserted: the story of Elijah. In fact, the usual conclusion of the description of Ahab's reign is found in 1 Ki 22:39-40. There is general agreement that the majority of the stories about Elijah come from a tradition that originated in prophetic circles. These stories are noteworthy for their elegant style but are also distinguished by the nobility of the subject, for they extol one of the greatest men of God eighth year of the reign of Asa, the king of Judah. Ahab, the son of Omri, reigned over Israel in Samaria for twenty-two years.

30 Ahab, the son of Omri, did more evil in the sight of the LORD than any of those who preceded him. 31 As if it were not enough that he committed the sins of Jeroboam, the son of Nebat, he also married Jezebel, the daughter of Ethbaal, the king of the Sidonians, and he went after and served Baal and worshiped him.[c] 32 He set up an altar for Baal in the temple of Baal that he had built in Samaria. 33 Ahab also set up an Asherah, and Ahab did more to provoke the anger of the LORD, the God of Israel, than all of the kings of Israel who preceded him.

34 During his time, Hiel of Bethel rebuilt Jericho. He laid its foundation over Abiram, his eldest, and he built its gates over Segub, his youngest. This was just as the word of the LORD had foretold through Joshua, the son of Nun.*[d]

IV: STORIES OF ELIJAH AND AHAB

CHAPTER 17

Elijah Predicts a Drought. 1 * Now Elijah the Tishbite from Tishbe in Gilead said to Ahab, "As the LORD, the God of Israel, lives before whom I stand, there shall be no dew or rain these years except at my word."[e]

2 Then the word of the LORD came to him saying, 3 "Go forth from here and go eastward to the Wadi Kerith near the Jordan and hide there. 4 You can drink from the brook there, and I have commanded the ravens there to feed you." 5 So he went and did what the LORD had said, and he dwelt in the Wadi Kerith near the Jordan. 6 The ravens brought him bread and meat in the morning, and bread and meat in the evening, and he drank from the wadi.[f]

7 After some time the wadi dried up because there had been no rain in the land. 8 The word of the LORD came to him, saying, 9 "Arise and go to Zarephath* which belongs to Sidon and live there. I have commanded a woman there who is a widow to take care of you."

10 So he arose and went to Zarephath. When he arrived at the gate to the city, there was a woman there who was a widow. She was gathering sticks, and he called out to her and said, "Bring me a little water in a jar so that I can have something to drink."[g]

11 As she went to get it for him, he called out to her and said, "Please also bring me a bit of bread in your hand." 12 But she said to him, "As the LORD, your God, lives, I do not have any bread. I only have a handful of flour in a jar and a little bit of oil in a jug. I am gathering two sticks so that I can prepare it for myself and my son so that we can eat it and die."

13 Elijah said to her, "Do not be afraid. Go and do what you have said, but first make a small piece of bread and bring it to me. Afterwards, you can make some for yourself and your son. 14 For thus says the LORD, the God of Israel, 'The jar of flour will not be used up, the jug of oil will not go dry, up until the day that the LORD sends rain upon the earth.' "

15 She went and did what Elijah had told her to do. She, and he, and her household ate for a long time. 16 The jar of flour was not used up, and the jug of oil did not go dry, just as the word of the LORD had foretold through Elijah.

Elijah Restores Life to the Widow's Son.* 17 After these things happened, the son of the woman who owned the house fell ill. The illness was so severe that there was no breath left in him.

18 She said to Elijah, "What do I have to do with you, O man of God? Have you come to me to make me remember my sins,* and to put my son to death?" 19 He said to her, "Give me your son." He took him from her lap and carried him to the upper room, and he laid him upon his own bed. 20 He called out to the LORD, "O LORD, my God, have you

---

c Wis 14:22.—d Jos 6:26; 11:23.—e 2 Ki 1:3; Sir 48:3.—f Ex 16:35.—g Lk 4:26.

---

in the Old Testament. Elijah represents the entire prophetic movement, as Moses does the entire law. To say "Moses and Elijah" is to include everything that God revealed to human beings before the coming of Jesus Christ. This is why they accompany Jesus when he is introduced by the Father on Tabor (see Mt 17; Mk 7; Lk 9).

16:34 The two sons were the victims in a foundation sacrifice, according to ancient practice.

17:1-6 The name "Elijah" means "The Lord is my God" and really suits him: in the midst of a people who prostrate themselves before idols, the prophet is a champion of the living God. Elijah confronted Ahab by predicting the long drought that would not be remedied by worshiping Baal, but only through the power of the true God.

17:9 *Zarephath:* on the coast of Phoenicia, south of Sidon.

17:17-24 The first raising from the dead of which the Bible speaks is on behalf of a foreign woman (see Lk 4:25-26).

17:18 *Make me remember my sins:* it was not uncommon at the time for a parent to blame themselves for a child's disabilities. Elijah's ability to raise the widow's son from death was a sign to the people of God's power among them.

brought disaster upon the widow with
whom I am living by killing her son?"
21 He stretched himself out upon the boy
three times, and he cried out to the LORD
and said, "O LORD, my God, may this
child's life return to him." [h]

22 The LORD heard Elijah's voice, and the
child's life returned to him and he revived.
23 Elijah took the child and brought him
down from the upper chamber into the
house and handed him over to his mother
saying, "See, your son is alive." 24 The
woman said to Elijah, "Now I know that you
are a man of God, and that the word of God
that is in your mouth is true." [i]

CHAPTER 18

Elijah and Ahab. 1 Now after quite some
time, the word of the LORD came to Elijah in
the third year saying, "Go, show yourself to
Ahab, and I will send rain upon the earth."
2 Elijah went and showed himself to Ahab.
There was a severe famine in Samaria.

3 Ahab summoned Obadiah, the major-
domo of his household. (Now Obadiah
greatly feared the LORD. 4 When Jezebel cut
down the prophets of the LORD, Obadiah
took one hundred of the prophets and he hid
them by fifties in a cave, and he provided
them with bread and water.) 5 Ahab said to
Obadiah, "Go through the land where there
are springs of water and through all the
wadis. Perhaps you will find some green
grass for the horses and donkeys so that we
might not lose all of the animals."

6 They divided the land between them,
and they went through it. Ahab went in one
direction, and Obadiah went in the other
direction by himself. 7 As Obadiah was going
along, he met Elijah. He recognized him and
fell on his face and said, "Is that you, my
lord, Elijah?" 8 He said to him, "It is I. Go
and tell your lord: 'Behold, Elijah is here.' "

9 But he answered, "How have I sinned
that you would hand your servant over to
Ahab so that he will kill me? 10 As the LORD,
your God, lives, there is no land or kingdom
into which my lord has not sent to search for
you. When they said, 'he is not here,' he made
the kingdom and the nation swear an oath
that they could not find you. 11 And now you
are telling me, 'Go tell your lord: "Behold,
Elijah is here." ' 12 When I have left you, the
Spirit of the LORD will carry you off to some
unknown place. When I go and tell Ahab, and
he cannot find you, he will kill your servant
who has feared the LORD from my youth.
13 Has it not been reported to my lord what I
did when Jezebel killed the prophets of the
LORD, how I hid one hundred of the LORD's
prophets by fifties in a cave and provided
them with bread and water? [j] 14 But now you
are telling me, 'Go, tell your lord: "Behold,
Elijah is here." ' He will kill me."

15 Elijah answered, "As the LORD of hosts
before whom I stand lives, I will surely show
myself to him today."

16 So Obadiah went to Ahab and told him,
and Ahab went to meet Elijah. 17 When
Ahab saw Elijah, Ahab said to him, "Is that
you, O troubler of Israel?" 18 He answered,
"It is not I who have troubled Israel. It is you
and your father's household who have aban-
doned the commandments of the LORD and
have followed after Baal. 19 Now send word,
and gather together all of Israel for me on
Mount Carmel, along with four hundred
and fifty prophets of Baal and four hundred
prophets of Asherah, those who eat at Jeze-
bel's table."

Elijah Destroys the Evil Prophets. 20 So Ahab
sent word to all of the Israelites, and he gath-
ered together the prophets on Mount
Carmel. 21 Elijah approached all of the peo-
ple and said, "How long will you be stuck
between two points of view? If the LORD is
God, then follow him, but if it is Baal, then
follow him." But the people did not say a sin-
gle thing to him. * [k]

22 Elijah then said to the people, "I am the
only prophet of the LORD left, but there are
four hundred and fifty prophets of Baal.
23 Now give us two oxen. They can choose
which ox is theirs. Let them cut it up and lay
it on the wood, but do not set it on fire. I will
prepare the other ox and lay it on the wood,
but I will not set it on fire. 24 Call on the
name of your God, and I will call on the
name of the LORD. The God who answers
with fire, that is God." All of the people an-
swered, "You have spoken well."

25 So Elijah said to the prophets of Baal,
"You can be the first to choose one of the
oxen for yourselves and prepare it because

h 1 Ki 17:20; Eccl 12:7.—i Mk 15:39.—j 1 Ki 18:4; Mt 25:35.—k Ex 16:28; Jos 24:15.

18:21 Elijah saw that the people had succumbed to Baal worship by following Ahab and the false prophets, but he also knew that he could not be silent and he urged them to make a choice for the true God. The story of the drought is really a story of the war between good and evil.

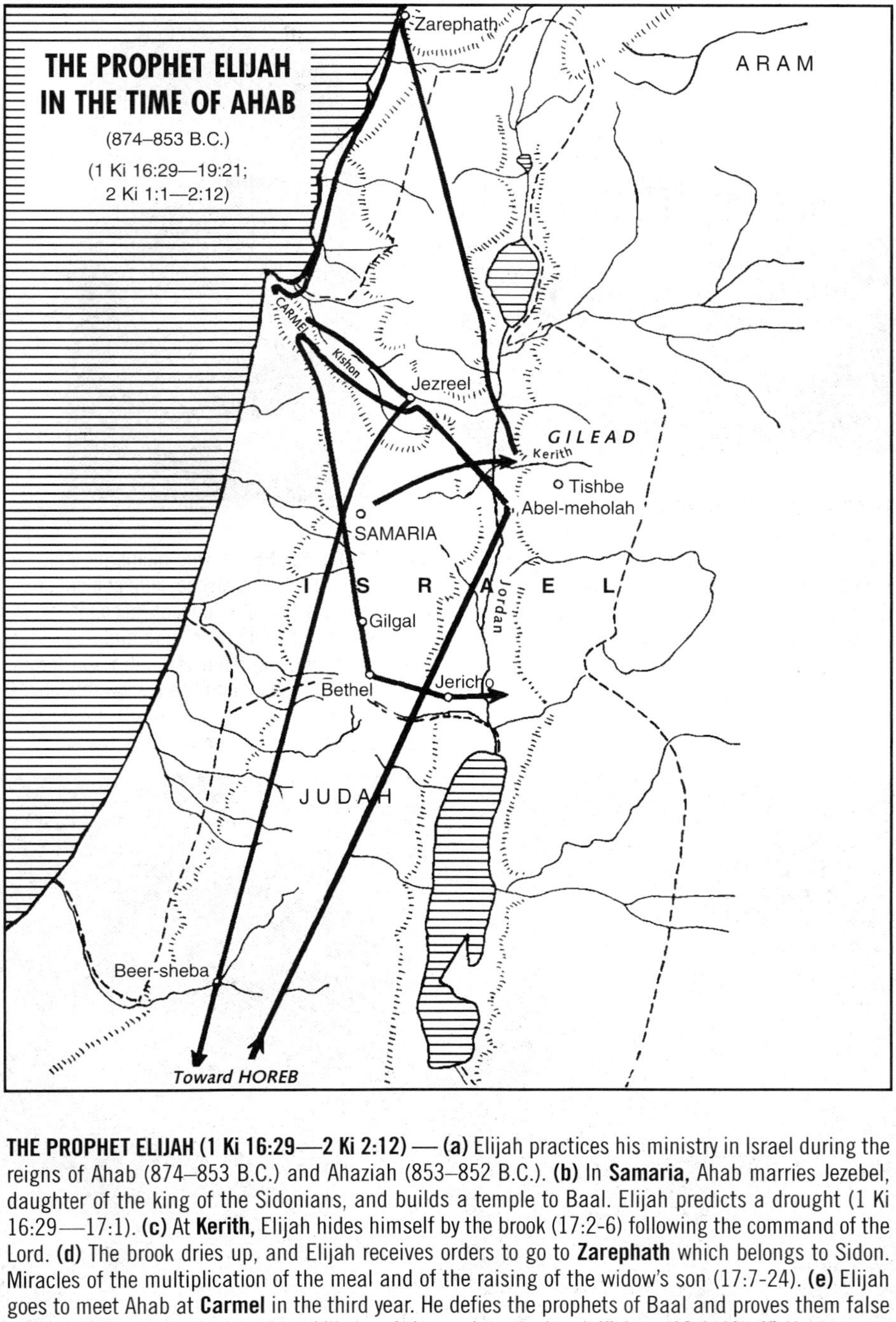

THE PROPHET ELIJAH (1 Ki 16:29—2 Ki 2:12) — **(a)** Elijah practices his ministry in Israel during the reigns of Ahab (874–853 B.C.) and Ahaziah (853–852 B.C.). **(b)** In **Samaria,** Ahab marries Jezebel, daughter of the king of the Sidonians, and builds a temple to Baal. Elijah predicts a drought (1 Ki 16:29—17:1). **(c)** At **Kerith,** Elijah hides himself by the brook (17:2-6) following the command of the Lord. **(d)** The brook dries up, and Elijah receives orders to go to **Zarephath** which belongs to Sidon. Miracles of the multiplication of the meal and of the raising of the widow's son (17:7-24). **(e)** Elijah goes to meet Ahab at **Carmel** in the third year. He defies the prophets of Baal and proves them false before all the people; he has them killed and thrown into the brook **Kishon** (18:1-40). **(f)** Having predicted rain, Elijah leaves for **Jezreel** with Ahab. Threatened by Jezebel, he flees to **Beer-sheba,** and from there to Mount Horeb. An angel comforts him (18:41—19:7). **(g)** At Mount Horeb, the Lord commands Elijah to go to the desert near Damascus. Elijah is told to anoint Hazael as king of **Aram,** Jehu as king of Israel, and Elisha of **Abel-meholah** as prophet in his place (19:8-18). **(h)** At **Abel-meholah,** he throws his cloak over Elisha (19:19-21). **(i)** At **Jezreel,** Elijah reprimands Ahab concerning the vineyard of Naboth (21:1-29). **(j)** "On a hilltop," Elijah receives the officers sent by Ahaziah, (2 Ki 1:9-21). **(k)** On his way from **Gilgal,** Elijah, accompanied by Elisha, passes through **Bethel** and **Jericho,** crosses the **Jordan,** and then is taken up into heaven (2 Ki 2:1-12).

Matson Photo Service

SITE OF ELIJAH'S VICTORY ON MOUNT CARMEL — A Carmelite convent now stands on the traditional site of Elijah's victory in the name of the Lord over the 450 prophets of Baal. As the aftermath of the victory, Baal was exposed as no god at all, the people again acknowledged the Lord as their God, the prophets of Baal were put to death, and Elijah was obliged to flee for his life from Jezebel's wrath. (See 1 Ki 18—19:3.)

Matson Photo Service

THE MOABITE STONE — This memorial stele erected about 840–820 B.C. by Mesha, king of Moab, parallels and complements the biblical account of Moab's enslavement to Israel under Ahab and its subsequent liberation during the reign of Ahab's son Joram. The stele states that Moab had been subjugated by "Omri, king of Israel, . . . and his son (Ahab)" to whom Mesha had been forced to pay tribute. (See Ki 3:4-27.)

British Museum

JEHU PAYING TRIBUTE TO SHALMANESER III — A detail from the Black Obelisk of Shalmaneser III of Assyria (859–824 B.C.) records the tribute of King "Jehu, son (successor) of Omri" in the year of his ascension (842 B.C.). It shows Jehu bowing before the Assyrian king. This is the only contemporary representation extant of an Israelite king. (See 2 Ki 9:1—10:33.)

you are more numerous. Call upon the
name of your gods, but do not set it on fire."
26 They took the ox that had been given
them, and they prepared it. They called upon
the name of Baal from the morning until
noontime. They said, "Hear us, O Baal." But
there was no voice, and no one answered.
They then leapt around on the altar they had
built. 27 At noon, Elijah mocked them and
said, "Cry out loud, for he is a god. He might
be meditating, or maybe he has gone aside.
Perhaps he is on a journey, or maybe he is
asleep and needs to be woken up."
28 So they cried out loud, and they slashed
themselves with knives and swords as was
their custom until blood gushed out from
their bodies. 29 In the afternoon they prophe-
sied until the time of the evening sacrifice, but
there was no voice, no answer, no one listened.
30 Elijah said to all the people, "Come over
here to me." So all the people went over to
him. He repaired the altar of God that had
been torn down. 31 Elijah took twelve stones,
the number of the tribes of the sons of Jacob
to whom the word of the LORD came saying,
"Your name will be Israel." 32 With the stones
he built an altar to the name of the LORD. He
dug a trench around the altar deep enough to
hold two measures of seed. 33 He piled up the
wood, and cut up the ox into pieces. He laid
them on the wood and said, "Fill four barrels
with water and pour them on the burnt sacri-
fice and the wood." 34 Then he said, "Do it a
second time," and they did it a second time.
Then he said, "Do it a third time," and they
did it a third time. 35 The water flowed around
the altar, and the water filled the trench.

36 * At the hour for the evening sacrifice,
Elijah the prophet drew near and said, "O
LORD, the God of Abraham, Isaac, and Israel,
let it be known today that you are the God of
Israel, and that I am your servant, and I have
done all of these things by your command.[l]
37 Answer me, O LORD, answer me so that
this people might know that you, O LORD, are
God, and that you are turning their hearts
back again."
38 The fire of the LORD fell down and con-
sumed the burnt offering as well as the wood,
the stones, the soil, and even the water that it
licked up from the trench. 39 When all of the
people saw this, they fell down upon their
faces and said, "The LORD is God; the LORD is
God!"
40 Elijah said to them, "Seize the prophets
of Baal; do not let one of them escape." They
seized them, and Elijah had them brought
down to the Wadi Kishon and killed them
there.[m]
41 Elijah said to Ahab, "Go, eat, and drink,
for I hear the sound of heavy rain." 42 Ahab
went to eat and drink, and Elijah climbed up
to the top of Carmel. He cast himself down to
the ground and placed his face between his
knees.
43 He said to his servant, "Go, now, and look
out toward the sea." He went and looked and
said, "There is nothing." Seven times he told
him, "Go again." 44 The seventh time he said,
"Behold, there is a small cloud like the shape
of a man's hand rising from out of the sea."
He said, "Go tell Ahab, 'Prepare your chariot
and go down before the rain stops you.' "
45 Meanwhile, the skies grew dark with
clouds, the wind rose up, and it poured. Ahab
rode off and went to Jezreel. 46 The hand of
the LORD was upon Elijah, and he girded up
his loins* and ran in front of Ahab to the
entrance of Jezreel.

CHAPTER 19

Elijah Flees to Horeb.* 1 Now Ahab told
Jezebel about everything that Elijah had
done, and all about how he had killed all of
the prophets by the sword. 2 Jezebel sent a
messenger to Elijah saying, "May the gods
do this to me and more if by this time
tomorrow I have not made your life like their
lives."
3 He rose up and fled for his life, going to
Beer-sheba in Judah, and he left his servant
there.[n] 4 He went a day's journey off into the

---

l Jer 14:22.—m 2 Chr 23:17.—n Gen 19:30; 21:31.

18:36-38 As on many occasions in the history of Israel, God intervenes with a sign that the people who have abandoned him cannot ignore in order to win them back. In this case, the fire of the Lord convinces them, and they follow Elijah's command to kill the prophets of Baal.

18:46 *Girded up his loins:* Elijah ran after Ahab, in this case, pulling up his clothes and securing them, so that he could run quickly into Jezreel so that the events of the ending of the drought and the killing of the evil prophets would be known there. Elijah also wanted to confront Ahab about his wrongdoing, just as Nathan had confronted David about Uriah (2 Sam 12:9).

19:1-18 Threatened with death, the prophet Elijah must flee and experiences a real agony that recalls that of Moses (Num 11); it also reminds us of the agony of Jesus, and like Jesus Elijah is strengthened by an angel. He then journeys to the mountain of the covenant. Here the Lord shows himself to be the supreme God by means of impressive phenomena, but he also shows himself to be close to his servant in the form of a light breeze; he strengthens Elijah and reconfirms him in his mission as defender of the faith. The forty-day journey of Elijah to Horeb has a place in the Lenten liturgy, as do Moses' forty days on Horeb.

desert. He came to a broom tree and sat
down under it, and he asked to die. He said,
"It is enough, O LORD, take away my life, for
I am no better than my fathers." [o]

5 As he lay there, he fell asleep under the
broom tree, and, behold, an angel touched
him and said, "Get up and eat!" 6 He looked
around, and by his head there was a piece of
bread that had been cooked on coals and a
jar of water. He ate and drank, and then he
laid down again.

7 The angel of the LORD touched him a sec-
ond time and said, "Get up and eat, because
the journey is too difficult for you." 8 He got
up, and ate and drank. Strengthened by that
food, he traveled for forty days and forty
nights to the mountain of God, Horeb. [p] 9 He
entered a cave and spent the night there. The
word of the LORD said to him, "What are you
doing here, Elijah?" 10 He answered, "I have
been zealous for the LORD, the God of hosts,
for the Israelites have forsaken your cov-
enant and torn down your altars and killed
your prophets by the sword. I am the only
survivor, and they are seeking to take my life
away."

11 He said, "Go out and stand on the
mountain before the LORD, for the LORD will
pass by." There was a powerful, strong wind
that tore the mountain apart and shattered
rocks before the LORD, but the LORD was not
in the wind. After the wind, there was an
earthquake, but the LORD was not in the
earthquake. [q] 12 After the earthquake, there
was a fire, but the LORD was not in the fire.
After the fire, there was a tiny whisper.

13 When Elijah heard it, he wrapped his
face in his mantle and went out and stood at
the entrance to the cave. The voice said to
him, "What are you doing here, Elijah?"
14 He answered, "I have been zealous for the
LORD, the God of hosts, for the Israelites
have forsaken your covenant and torn down
your altars and killed your prophets by the
sword. I am the only survivor, and they are
seeking to take my life away." [r]

15 The LORD said to him, "Go, return to
the Desert of Damascus. When you arrive
there, anoint Hazael as the king of Aram.
16 Also, anoint Jehu, the son of Nimshi, as
the king of Israel, and anoint Elisha, the son
of Shaphat from Abel Meholah as prophet
in your stead. [s] 17 Jehu will put to death
those who escape from the sword of Hazael,
and Elisha will put to death those who
escape from the sword of Jehu. 18 Yet, I have
prepared a remnant in Israel of seven thou-
sand,* none of whom have bent their knees
to Baal nor have any of their mouths kissed
him." [t]

Elisha Follows Elijah. 19 So Elijah left that
place and found the son of Shaphat who was
plowing with twelve yokes of oxen preceding
him (he was driving the twelfth pair him-
self), and he tossed his mantle on him.
20 Elisha left the oxen and ran after Elijah
and said, "Please let me kiss my father and
mother good-bye and then I will follow you."
But he said, "Go back, what have I done to
you?" [u]

21 He went back, and took a yoke of oxen
and killed them. He used the oxen's equip-
ment to boil their meat, and he gave it to the
people to eat. He then got up and followed
Elijah, ministering to him.*

CHAPTER 20

Ahab's Victory over the Arameans. 1 * Ben-
hadad, the king of Aram, gathered together
his entire army. He had thirty-two kings with
him along with their horses and chariots.
They went up and besieged Samaria, fight-
ing against it.

2 He sent messengers into the city, to
Ahab, the king of Israel, saying, "Thus says
Ben-hadad: 3 'Your silver and your gold are
mine, as are the best of your wives and your
children.' " 4 The king of Israel answered, "O
king, my lord, I and all that I own are yours."

5 The messengers came again and said,
"Thus says Ben-hadad: 'I have sent to you
demanding that you send me your silver and
your gold, your wives and your children.
6 Around this time tomorrow, I will send my
servants to you. They will search through
your palace and the houses of your servants.
They will take hold of whatever they like and
carry it away.' "

o 1 Ki 19:5; Jon 4:3.—p Ex 24:13; Deut 10:10.—q Job 37:6; Ezek 11:23.—r 2 Chr 34:4; 1 Mac 13:4; Rom 11:3.—s 2 Ki 3:11; 9:2.—t Rom 11:4.—u Lk 9:61.

19:18 *Seven thousand* is symbolic, indicating a large number. *Kissed,* in a literal sense, signifies "adore." "Adore" (Latin, *ad os,* meaning "to the mouth") derives from the practice of bringing another's hand to one's mouth as a sign of worship.

19:21 Elisha demonstrates his commitment to be Elijah's successor by killing his oxen (i.e., destroying his livelihood as a farmer).

20:1ff Since the kingdom was divided, Israel (north) had a series of sinful rulers who no longer were faithful to the Lord. During the next two centuries, both Judah (south) and Israel would suffer the consequences of their depravity and succumb to their enemies.

7 The king of Israel summoned all of the elders of the land and said, "See how this man is looking for trouble. He sent a message to me seeking my wives, my children, my silver, and my gold, and I did not deny it to him." 8 The elders and all of the people said to him, "Do not listen to him, do not agree!"

9 So he replied to the messengers of Ben-hadad, "Tell my lord, the king: 'Your servant will do everything that you demanded the first time, but I cannot do this thing.' " The messengers went away and brought him the answer.

10 Then Ben-hadad sent to him, saying, "May the gods do this to me and more if there is enough dust remaining from Samaria to give a handful to each of those who follow me." *

11 The king of Israel answered, "Say: 'He who is putting on his armor should not boast like someone who is taking it off.' " 12 He heard this message while he and the kings were drinking in the tents and he said to his servants, "Get ready!" So they prepared to attack the city.

13 In the meantime, a prophet came to Ahab, the king of Israel, and said, "Thus says the LORD: 'Do you see this enormous mob? Behold, I will deliver them into your hands today so that you might know that I am the LORD.' "[v] 14 Ahab said, "Who will do it?" He answered, "Thus says the LORD: 'The young officers from the provinces.' " He asked, "Who should start the battle?" He answered, "You!" *

15 So he summoned the young officers from the provinces, and there were two hundred and thirty-two of them. Then he counted all of the Israelites there, and there were seven thousand.

16 They set out at noon when Ben-hadad and the thirty-two kings who were helping him were getting drunk in their tents. 17 The young officers from the provinces went out first. Ben-hadad sent out men who told him, "The men from Samaria are advancing." 18 He said, "If they are coming out to make peace, take them alive, and even if they have come out to fight, take them alive."

19 And so the young officers from the provinces came out from the city, and the army followed after them. 20 Each of them killed his opponent, and the Arameans fled away with Israel pursuing them. Ben-hadad, the king of Aram, escaped on a horse with some of his horsemen.

21 The king of Israel went out and defeated the horsemen and the chariots, and he killed a large number of the Arameans. 22 Afterwards, the prophet came to the king of Israel and said, "Go and strengthen yourself, and see what must be done, for next spring the king of Aram will attack you again."

23 The servants of the king of Aram said to him, "Their gods are the gods of the hills. That is why they were stronger than we were. We should fight against them in the plain, and we will surely be stronger than they are. 24 Just do this, remove all of the kings from their command and replace them with the officers. 25 You must assemble an army as large as the army you lost, horse for horse and chariot for chariot. Then we will be able to fight against them in the plain. We will certainly be stronger than they are." He listened to their advice and followed it.

26 In the spring of the year, Ben-hadad assembled the Arameans and went to Aphek to fight against Israel. 27 When the Israelites were assembled and given provisions, they went out against them. The Israelites camped opposite them, and they looked like two little flocks of goats, while the Arameans covered the countryside.

28 The man of God arrived and spoke to the king of Israel, saying, "Thus says the LORD: 'The Arameans think that the LORD is the God of the hills but not the God of the lowlands. I will therefore deliver this enormous army into your hands, and thus you will know that I am the LORD.' "

29 They camped opposite one another for seven days, and then on the seventh day they joined in battle. The Israelites killed one hundred thousand of the Aramean infantry in one day. 30 The rest of them escaped into the city of Aphek, but a wall collapsed upon twenty-seven thousand of the survivors.

Ben-hadad fled into the city and hid in an inner room. 31 His servants said to him, "Behold, we have heard that the kings of the house of Israel are merciful kings. Please let us put sackcloth around our waists and

---

v 1 Ki 20:22; Ezek 11:10.

20:10 The meaning is: I will destroy Samaria so completely that not enough will be left of it to supply each soldier with a handful of dust.

20:14 The soldiers were at the disposition of each provincial prefect.

ropes around our heads and go out to the
king of Israel. Perhaps he will spare your
life." [w] 32 So they put sackcloth around their
waists and they put ropes around their
heads and they went out to the king of Israel
and said, "Ben-hadad said, 'Please let me
live.'" He answered, "Is he still alive? He is
my brother." *

33 The men were listening carefully and
they quickly took up his refrain, "Ben-hadad
is your brother!" He said, "Go and bring him
here." When Ben-hadad came out to him, he
had him join him in the chariot.

34 Ben-hadad said to him, "I will give back
the cities that my father took from your
father. You can set up marketplaces in Da-
mascus just like my father did in Samaria."
He answered, "I will release you on the basis
of this covenant." So he made a covenant
with him and released him.

Ahab Is Condemned by a Prophet.* 35 One of
the sons of the prophets, inspired by the
word of the LORD, said to his companion,
"Please strike me," but the man refused to
strike him. 36 So he said to him, "You have
not obeyed the voice of the LORD, so as soon
as you leave me, you will be killed by a lion."
As soon as he left him, a lion found him and
killed him. [x]

37 The prophet found another man and
said, "Please strike me." So the man struck
and wounded him. 38 The prophet left and
waited for the king along the road, disguising
himself with a bandage over his eyes.

39 As the king passed by, he cried out to the
king, "Your servant went out into the heat of
the battle. A man came over and brought a
man to me saying, 'Guard this man. If he
escapes, then you will pay a life for a life, or
else you will have to pay a talent of silver.'
40 While your servant was busy here and
there, he disappeared." The king of Israel
said to him, "That will be your judgment;
you have decided it for yourself." 41 He quick-
ly removed the bandage from his face, and
the king of Israel recognized that he was one
of the prophets. 42 He then said to him,
"Thus says the LORD: 'Because you have
released from your hands a man whom I
had designated for total destruction, your
life will stand for his life, your people for his
people.'" [y] 43 The king of Israel, therefore,
returned to his palace deeply troubled, and
he arrived in Samaria.

CHAPTER 21

Naboth's Vineyard. 1 After these things, it
happened that Naboth the Jezreelite had a
vineyard in Jezreel near the palace of Ahab,
the king of Samaria. 2 Ahab said to Naboth,
"Give me your vineyard so that I can use it
as a vegetable garden since it is next to my
palace. I will give you a better vineyard in its
place, or if you prefer, I will pay you its worth
in money." 3 But Naboth said to Ahab, "The
LORD forbid that I should give you the inher-
itance of my fathers."

4 * So Ahab entered his palace furious that
Naboth, the Jezreelite, had said to him, "I will
not give you the inheritance of my fathers."
He laid down upon his bed and turned his
face away, refusing to eat anything.

5 Jezebel his wife entered and said to him,
"Why is your spirit so depressed that you
refuse to eat anything?" 6 He said to her, "It
is because I spoke to Naboth the Jezreelite
and I said to him, 'Give me your vineyard in
exchange for money, or, if you like, I will give
you another vineyard for it.' But he
answered, 'I will not give you my vineyard.'"

7 Jezebel, his wife, said to him, "Do you not
reign over the kingdom of Israel? Get up and
eat something. Cheer up, and I will give you
the vineyard of Naboth the Jezreelite."

8 So she wrote some letters in Ahab's
name and sealed them with his seal and sent
the letters to the elders and the nobles who
lived in Naboth's city. 9 In the letters she
wrote, "Proclaim a fast, and have Naboth sit
in a prominent place among the people.
10 But place two sons of Belial opposite him
to bear false witness, saying, 'You blas-
phemed God and the king.' Then carry him
out and stone him to death." [z]

11 So the men in his city, the elders, and the
nobles who lived in his city did what had
been written in the letters that had been sent

w 2 Ki 19:1.—x 1 Ki 13:26.—y 1 Ki 13:21; 20:39.—z 1 Ki 21:13; Deut 19:15.

20:32 The reputation of the Hebrew kings for mercy is immediately confirmed by what happens. Sackcloth (Hebrew, *sak*, a bristly cloth) the same as "the cilice," from Latin, *cilicium*, a name given by the Romans. The word was derived from Cilicia, in Asia Minor, the best known of the places where the cloth was made.

20:35-43 The leniency shown to Ben-hadad was a political mistake, and one of the guild of prophets foretells its consequences by means of a parable involving a drastic action.

21:4ff The conspiracy that Ahab and Jezebel weave against the just and faithful Naboth confirms the depths they have sunk to. In their struggle for power and control, they will stop at nothing to get what they want.

to them. 12 They proclaimed a fast and had
Naboth sit in a prominent place among the
people. 13 Two men then came in, sons of
Belial, and they sat opposite him. The sons of
Belial bore witness before the people saying,
"Naboth blasphemed God and the king."
They carried him out of the city and they
stoned him to death.

14 They then sent word to Jezebel, saying,
"Naboth has been stoned to death." 15 As
soon as Jezebel heard that Naboth had been
stoned to death, Jezebel said to Ahab, "Get
up, and take possession of the vineyard that
Naboth the Jezreelite refused to sell you.
Naboth is no longer alive; he is dead."
16 When Ahab heard that Naboth was dead,
Ahab got up and went down to the vineyard
of Naboth the Jezreelite to take possession
of it.

17 The word of the LORD came to Elijah the
Tishbite, saying, 18 "Get up, and go down to
meet Ahab, the king of Israel, who is in
Samaria. He is now in the vineyard of
Naboth. He had gone down there to take
possession of it. 19 Then say to him, 'Thus
says the LORD: "Have you killed someone to
take possession of his property?"' Say to
him, 'Thus says the LORD: "In the place
where the dogs licked up the blood of
Naboth, the dogs will lick up your blood as
well."' "[a]

20 Ahab said to Elijah, "So you have found
me, my enemy." He answered, "I have found
you because you have sold yourself to do
what was evil in the sight of the LORD:
21 'Behold, I will bring disaster down upon
you. I will consume your descendants and I
will cut off from Ahab all of those who pee
against the wall, whether slave or free. 22 I
will make your house like the house of
Jeroboam, the son of Nebat, and like the
house of Baasha, the son of Ahijah, because
you have provoked me to anger and have
caused Israel to sin.' 23 And of Jezebel the
LORD says, 'The dogs will devour Jezebel by
the walls of Jezreel.'[b] 24 Those who belong to
Ahab and who die in the city will be eaten by
dogs, and those who die in the field will be
eaten by the birds of the air."

25 There was no one like Ahab who sold
himself to do what was evil in the sight of the
LORD, urged on by Jezebel, his wife. 26 He was
detestable in the way that he followed after
idols, just as the Amorites had whom the
LORD had cast out from before the Israelites.

27 When Ahab heard these things, he tore
his clothes, put on sackcloth, and fasted. He
lay in sackcloth, and went around in mourn-
ing. 28 The word of the LORD came to Elijah
the Tishbite, saying, 29 "Have you seen how
Ahab has humbled himself before me?
Because he has humbled himself before me,
I will not bring the disaster during his days.
I will bring disaster upon his house during
the days of his son."[c]

CHAPTER 22

Jehoshaphat Allies with Ahab. 1 For three
years there was no war between Aram and
Israel. 2 But in the third year, Jehoshaphat,
the king of Judah, came down to the king of
Israel. 3 The king of Israel said to his ser-
vants, "Do you know that Ramoth in Gilead
belongs to us? We have kept quiet and have
not taken it out of the hands of the king of
Aram." 4 He said to Jehoshaphat, "Will you
go to Ramoth-gilead to fight with me?"
Jehoshaphat said to the king of Israel, "I am
yours, and my people are your people, and
my horses are your horses."

5 Jehoshaphat said to the king of Israel,
"Inquire today concerning the word of the
LORD." 6 * The king of Israel gathered togeth-
er the prophets, four hundred of them, and
he said to them, "Shall I go up to fight at
Ramoth-gilead or shall I desist?" They
answered, "Go up, for the LORD will deliver it
into your hands."

7 But Jehoshaphat asked, "Is there not
another prophet of the LORD from whom
we can inquire?" 8 The king of Israel said to
Jehoshaphat, "There is still one man by
whom we can inquire of the LORD, but I
hate him, because he does not prophesy
good things for me, only evil. He is
Micaiah, the son of Imlah." Jehoshaphat
said, "Let the king not say this." 9 The king
of Israel summoned an officer and said to
him, "Rush over to Micaiah, the son of
Imlah."

10 Now the king of Israel and Jehoshaphat,
the king of Judah, were sitting upon their
thrones, wearing their robes, at a threshing
floor at the entrance to the gate of Samaria.

a 1 Ki 22:38; 2 Ki 1:4.—b 2 Ki 9:10; Jud 1:5.—c 2 Chr 12:12.

22:6f Elijah had the 450 prophets of Baal put to death (1 Ki 18:19); he did not kill all of the false prophets. Jehoshaphat's request for another prophet implies that he was rejecting the 400 remaining, but in the end, both he and Ahab listen to the heathen prophets.

All of the prophets were prophesying before
them. 11 Zedekiah, the son of Chenaanah,
made some iron horns for himself and said,
"Thus says the LORD: 'You will gore the
Arameans* with these until they are con-
sumed.' "[d] 12 All the prophets prophesied in
the same way, saying, "Go to Ramoth-gilead
and triumph! The LORD will deliver it into
the hands of the king."

Micaiah Prophesies Doom. 13 The messen-
ger who had gone to summon Micaiah said
to him, "Behold, the words of the prophets
are consistently favorable to the king. Let
your pronouncement be like their words and
speak favorably." 14 But Micaiah said, "As
the LORD lives, I will only say what the LORD
says to me."

15 When he arrived before the king and the
king said to Micaiah, "Shall we go to fight at
Ramoth-gilead or shall we desist," he
answered, "Go and triumph, for the LORD
will deliver it into the hands of the king."
16 But the king said to him, "How many
times do I have to warn you not to tell me
anything in the name of the LORD other than
what is true." 17 So he said, "I saw all of Israel
scattered upon the hills, as sheep without a
shepherd, and the LORD said, 'These have no
master, let them return to their homes in
peace.' "*

18 The king of Israel said to Jehoshaphat,
"Did I not tell you, he will not prophesy what
is good for me, only what is evil?"

19 He said, "Therefore, hear the word of
the LORD: I saw the LORD sitting upon his
throne, with all of the hosts of heaven stand-
ing on his right and his left.[e] 20 The LORD
said, 'Who will convince Ahab to go up to
Ramoth-gilead so that he might fall?' One
said one thing, another said another. 21 Then
a spirit came forth and stood before the
LORD and said, 'I will convince him.' 22 The
LORD said to him, 'How?' He said, 'I will go
out and put a lying spirit in the mouths of all
of his prophets.' He said, 'You must convince
him too, and you will succeed. Go and do it.'
23 Now therefore, the LORD has put a lying
spirit into the mouths of all of these
prophets. The LORD has spoken evil concern-
ing you."[f]

24 Then Zedekiah, the son of Chenaanah,
approached Micaiah and struck him on the
cheek. He said, "How did the Spirit of the
LORD depart from me to speak to you?"
25 Micaiah answered, "Behold, the day will
come when you will enter an inner chamber
to hide yourself."

26 The king of Israel said, "Seize Micaiah
and take him to Amon, the city leader, and to
Joash, the king's son 27 and say, 'Thus says the
king: Put this man in prison and feed him
with punishment rations of bread and give
him punishment rations of water to drink
until I return in safety.' " 28 Micaiah said, "If
you return in safety, then the LORD has not
spoken through me." He also added, "Listen,
all you people!"

Ahab's Death. 29 So the king of Israel and
Jehoshaphat, the king of Judah, went up to
Ramoth-gilead. 30 The king of Israel said to
Jehoshaphat, "I will go into battle disguised,
but you go into battle dressed in your robes."
So the king of Israel went into battle dis-
guised.

31 Now the king of Aram had commanded
the captains of his thirty-two chariots, "Do
not fight with the small nor the great; save
yourselves for the king of Israel."[g] 32 When
the captains of the chariots saw Jehosh-
aphat, they said, "This is certainly the king of
Israel." They turned to attack him, but when
Jehoshaphat cried out, 33 the captains of the
chariots realized that it was not the king of
Israel. They turned away from pursuing him.

34 But someone drew his bow, and by
chance he hit the king of Israel in the joints
of his armor. He said to his chariot driver,
"Turn around and carry me out of the bat-
tle, for I am wounded."* 35 As the battle
grew more savage that day, they propped
the king up in his chariot facing the
Arameans. The blood from his wound
dripped onto the floor of the chariot, and
that evening he died.[h]

36 As the sun was setting, there was a cry
that spread through the army: "Everyone to
his own city, everyone to his own land."
37 And so the king died and was brought to
Samaria, and they buried the king in
Samaria. 38 Someone washed out the chariot

d 2 Chr 18:10.—e 2 Chr 18:18; Isa 6:1.—f Ezek 14:9.—g 2 Ki 13:4.—h 1 Ki 20:42; 2 Chr 18:34.

22:11 *Gore the Arameans:* the symbolism here with horns represents the two kings Ahab and Jehoshaphat in their unified battle against a common enemy.

22:17 Micaiah's prophecy includes the reference to being without a shepherd and master which may be referring to the deaths of both Ahab and Jehoshaphat in battle.

22:34 All of Ahab's attempts to ensure his survival in battle are pointless. His disguise did not change the evil in his heart where God sees and judges a person. The random arrow that struck him was the ultimate punishment for his evil deeds.

at the pool in Samaria, and the dogs licked
up his blood while the prostitutes were
bathing. This fulfilled what the word of the
LORD had said.[i]

39 Are not the rest of the deeds of Ahab and
all that he did, the ivory house and all of the
cities that he built, are they not written in the
book of the chronicles of the kings of Israel?
40 Ahab slept with his fathers, and Ahaziah,
his son, reigned in his stead.

Jehoshaphat's Reign. 41 Jehoshaphat, the
king of Judah, began to reign during the
fourth year of the reign of Ahab, the king of
Israel. 42 Jehoshaphat was thirty-five years old
when he began to reign, and he reigned for
twenty-five years in Jerusalem. His mother's
name was Azubah, the daughter of Shilhi.
43 * He walked in the ways of Asa, his father.
He did not turn away from them, from doing
what was right in the sight of the LORD. Still,
he did not do away with the high places, and
the people offered sacrifices and burned
incense upon the high places.[j] 44 Jehoshaphat
made peace with the king of Israel.

45 Are not the rest of the deeds of Jehosha-
phat, his achievements, and how he fought,
are they not written in the book of the chron-
icles of the kings of Judah?

46 As to the rest of the sacred prostitutes
who remained in the days of Asa his father, he
expelled them from the land. 47 There was no
king in Edom, only a representative of the
king.

48 Jehoshaphat built merchant ships that
went to Ophir for gold, but in fact they never
sailed, for the ships sank at Ezion-geber.
49 Then Ahaziah, the son of Ahab, said to Je-
hoshaphat, "Let your servants go with my
servants in the ships." But Jehoshaphat would
not allow it.

50 Jehoshaphat slept with his fathers, and he
was buried in the City of David, his father,
and then Jehoram, his son, reigned in his
stead.

Ahaziah's Reign. 51 Ahaziah, the son of
Ahab, began to reign over Israel in Samaria
during the seventeenth year of the reign of
Jehoshaphat, the king of Judah. He reigned
over Israel for two years. 52 He did what was
evil in the sight of the LORD, and he walked
in the way of his father and in the way of his
mother, and in the way of Jeroboam, the son
of Nebat, who caused Israel to sin. 53 He
served Baal and worshiped him, and pro-
voked the LORD, the God of Israel to anger,
just as his father had.[k]

i 1 Ki 21:19.—j 2 Ki 21:21; Sir 48:22.—k 2 Ki 15:24; 23:15.

22:43ff Jehoshaphat's reign is a return to the Lord in many ways, but although he tried, he did not entirely eradicate the heathen shrines (see 2 Chr 20:33).

THE SECOND BOOK OF KINGS

CHAPTER 1

Ahaziah Consults Baal-zebub. 1 After Ahab's
death, Moab rebelled against Israel.[a]

2 Now Ahaziah had fallen down through
the lattice of his upper chamber in Samaria
and he was injured, so he sent messengers,
saying, "Go to Baal-zebub, the god of Ekron,
to inquire as to whether I will recover from
this illness or not." *

3 But the angel of the LORD said to Elijah
the Tishbite, "Arise, go up to meet the king of
Samaria's messengers and say to them, 'Is it
because there is no god in Israel that you are
going to make inquiry of Baal-zebub, the
god of Ekron?' 4 Therefore, thus says the
LORD: You shall not rise from the bed on
which you lie; you will surely die." Then
Elijah departed.

5 The messengers then returned to him. He
said to them, "Why have you come back?"
6 They answered him, "A man came up to
meet us and he said, 'Return to the king who
sent you and say: Thus says the LORD: Is it
because there is no god in Israel that you have
sent to make inquiry of Baal-zebub, the god
of Ekron? You shall not rise from the bed on
which you lie; you will surely die.' "

7 The king asked them, "What sort of man
was this who came up to meet you and who
said these words to you?" 8 They replied, "He
was wearing a garment made from hair *
and a leather belt around his waist." He said,
"It was Elijah the Tishbite!"

a 2 Sam 8:2.

1:2 Baal-zebub, "Lord of the flies," a distorted version of the name of the divinity Baal-zebul (Lord Prince; see Mt 10:25; 12:24).

1:8 *Garment made from hair:* this distinctive attire set Elijah apart as one who was committed to delivering God's hard messages to the king and other prophets, despite the rejection and loneliness that often resulted. In the New Testament, John the Baptist strikes a similar appearance and fate (Mt 3:4; Mk 6:17).

9 The king then sent a captain of fifty along
with his fifty men. He went up to him, and he
found him sitting on a hilltop. He said to
him, "O man of God, the king orders you,
'Come down!' " 10 Elijah answered the cap-
tain of the fifty men, saying, "If I am truly a
man of God, then let fire come down from
the heavens and consume you and your fifty
men." Fire then came down from the heav-
ens and it consumed him and his fifty men.[b]

11 He sent another captain of fifty along
with his fifty men. He said to him, "O man of
God, this is what the king says, 'Come down
at once!' " 12 Elijah answered them, "If I am
a man of God, then let fire come down from
the heavens and consume you and your fifty
men." Then God's fire came down from the
heavens and consumed him and his fifty
men.

13 And so a third time he sent a captain of
fifty along with his fifty men. The third cap-
tain of the fifty came and fell on his knees
before Elijah and pleaded with him saying,
"O man of God, please let my life and the
lives of these fifty men, your servants, be
considered to be precious in your sight.[c]
14 Behold, fire has come down from the
heavens, and it has consumed the previous
two captains of the fifty along with their fifty
men. Let my life be precious in your sight."

15 The angel of the LORD said to Elijah, "Go
down with him. Do not be afraid of him." So
he went down with him to the king. 16 He
said to the king, "Thus says the LORD: Is it
because there is no God in Israel of whom
you can inquire that you have sent messen-
gers to make inquiry of Baal-zebub, the god
of Ekron? Because of this, you shall not rise
from the bed on which you lie. You will sure-
ly die!"[d]

17 He died, fulfilling the word of the LORD
that Elijah had proclaimed. Because he had
no son, Joram reigned in his stead during the
second year of the reign of Jehoram, the son
of Jehoshaphat, the king of Judah. 18 As for
the rest of the deeds of Ahaziah, what he did,
are they not written in the book of the chron-
icles of the kings of Israel?

V: STORIES OF ELISHA AND JORAM

CHAPTER 2

Elijah Is Taken to Heaven. 1 * Elijah and
Elisha were traveling from Gilgal when the
LORD was about to take Elijah into heaven in
a whirlwind. 2 Elijah said to Elisha, "Wait
here, for the LORD has sent me to Bethel."
But Elisha answered, "As the LORD lives and
as you live, I will not leave you." So they went
down to Bethel.

3 The sons of the prophets came forth
from Bethel to Elisha and they said to him,
"Do you know that today is the day that the
LORD is going to take away your master who
is over you?" Elisha answered, "Yes, I know
it. Be quiet!"

4 Elijah then said to Elisha, "Please stay
here, for the LORD has sent me to Jericho."
But he answered, "As the LORD lives and as
you live, I will not leave you." So they went to
Jericho.

5 The sons of the prophets in Jericho came
to Elisha and said, "Do you know that today
is the day that the LORD is going to take away
your master who is over you?" He answered,
"Yes, I know. Be quiet!"

6 Elijah said to him, "Stay here, please, for
the LORD has sent me to the Jordan." He
answered, "As the LORD lives and as you live,
I will not leave you." So the two of them
went on.

7 Now fifty of the sons of the prophets went
out and watched from a distance as the two
of them stood at the Jordan. 8 Elijah took his
mantle and rolled it up. He struck the waters
with it, and they split apart, so the two of
them crossed over on dry ground.[e]

Elisha Succeeds Elijah. 9 After they had
crossed, Elijah said to Elisha, "Ask me for
whatever you want before I am taken away."
Elisha said, "Let me please have a double
portion* of your spirit."[f] 10 He answered,
"You have asked for something that is diffi-
cult. If you see me taken away from you, then
it will be yours. If not, then it will not be so."

11 As they were walking along talking, a
chariot of fire and horses of fire separated
them, and Elijah went up into the heavens in
a whirlwind.[g] 12 Elisha saw this and cried
out, "My father! My father! The chariot and
horsemen of Israel!" And then he could not

b Lev 10:1-2; 1 Ki 18:38; Lk 9:51-55.—c Ps 72:14.—d Sir 48:6.—e Ex 14:22, 29; Jos 3:14-17.—f Num 11:17; Deut 21:17.—g Gen 5:24; Ps 104:4.

2:1-13 Elisha will be the successor of the prophet who disappears in a mysterious manner; but according to Jewish tradition (Mal 3:23; Mt 17:12; Lk 1:17) Elijah will appear again when the Messiah comes.

2:9 *A double portion:* twice as much as to the other heirs of Elijah's spirit, in accordance with the law governing the firstborn (Deut 21:17).

see him anymore. He took hold of his clothes and tore them apart.*

13 He picked up the mantle of Elijah that had fallen off of him, and he went back and stood by the banks of the Jordan. 14 He took the mantle of Elijah that had fallen off of him, and he struck the waters and said, "Where is the LORD, the God of Elijah?" When Elisha struck the waters, they split apart and he crossed over.

15 The sons of the prophets from Jericho who had been watching said, "The spirit of Elijah has come to rest upon Elisha." They came out to meet him, and they bowed down to the ground before him.[h] 16 They said to him, "Behold, there are fifty strong men with your servants. Let them go out and search for your master. Perhaps the Spirit of the LORD has picked him up and set him down on a mountain or in some valley." But he answered, "Do not send them."[i]

17 They continued to insist until he became embarrassed and he said, "Send them." The fifty men searched for three days, but they did not find him.[j] 18 When they came back to him in Jericho where he was staying, he said to them, "Did I not tell you that you should not go?"

Healing the Water. 19 The men of the city said to Elisha, "Behold, this city is in a pleasant location, as my lord sees, but the water is bad and the ground is barren." 20 He said, "Bring me a new bowl, and put some salt in it." So they brought it to him. 21 He went out to the spring of water, and he threw the salt into it, saying, "Thus says the LORD: I have healed these waters. They shall never again produce death or make the land barren."[k] 22 The waters have remained healed up to the present day, just as Elisha had declared.

23 *From there he traveled to Bethel. As he was on his way, some little children came out of the city and they mocked him crying out, "Go away, baldy! Go away, baldy!"[l] 24 He turned around and stared at them. He cursed them in the name of the LORD. Two female bears came out from the woods and mauled the children, forty-two of them.

25 From there he went to Mount Carmel, and then he returned to Samaria.

CHAPTER 3

Joram's Campaign against Moab. 1 Joram, the son of Ahab, began to reign over Israel in Samaria in the eighteenth year of the reign of Jehoshaphat, the king of Judah, and he reigned for twelve years. 2 He did what was evil in the sight of the LORD, but not as bad as his father and his mother. He removed the idol of Baal that his father had made.[m] 3 Still, he clung to the sins of Jeroboam, the son of Nebat, causing Israel to sin. He did not turn away from them.

4 Mesha, the king of Moab, tended sheep. He had to give the king of Israel one hundred thousand lambs and the wool from one hundred thousand sheep. 5 When Ahab died, the king of Moab rebelled against the king of Israel.

6 King Joram went out from Samaria and he gathered together all of Israel. 7 He sent this message to Jehoshaphat, the king of Israel: "The king of Moab has rebelled against me. Will you not go out with me to fight against Moab?" He answered, "I will go. My people are your people, and my horses are your horses." 8 He said, "By which way should we go up?" He answered, "By way of the Desert of Edom."

9 The king of Israel went out with the king of Judah and the king of Edom. They wandered around for seven days, but there was no water for the army or the animals that followed them. 10 The king of Israel said, "What? Has the LORD called three kings together only to hand them over into the hands of Moab?" 11 Jehoshaphat asked, "Is there not a prophet of the LORD so that we can inquire of the LORD through him?" A servant of the king of Israel answered, "There is Elisha, the son of Shaphat. He used to pour water onto the hands of Elijah."*[n] 12 Jehoshaphat said, "The word of the LORD is with him."

So the king of Israel and Jehoshaphat and the king of Edom went down to him. 13 But Elisha said to the king of Israel, "What do you and I have to do with each other? Go to

h 1 Sam 10:5.—i 1 Ki 18:12; Acts 8:39.—j Heb 11:5.—k Ex 15:25.—l 2 Chr 30:10; Job 19:18; Ps 31:18.—m 1 Ki 16:30-32. —n 1 Ki 22:7.

2:12 The same will be said in connection with Elisha himself (2 Ki 13:14); the meaning is that Elijah was worth an entire army in Israel's defense.

2:23-24 *Go away, baldy!:* the age of Elisha's taunters is questionable, but their message is clear: "We don't want to hear about your God or any condemnation of our gods." Elisha's cursing did not bring the bears, but the Lord heard his cry and punished them for their idolatry and disbelief.

3:11 *Pour water onto the hands of Elijah:* the recommendation of Elisha, a prophet who might have served Elijah, was affirmed by Jehoshaphat to the kings of Edom and Israel in their search for a prophet of the Lord.

the prophets of your father and your mother." The king of Israel said, "No, the LORD called together these three kings to deliver them into the hands of Moab." 14 Elisha said, "As the LORD of hosts lives before whom I stand, if it were not for the presence of Jehoshaphat, the king of Judah, I would not even look at you or take notice of you. 15 Now, bring a harpist to me." While the harpist was playing, the hand of the LORD came upon him.[o] 16 He said, "Thus says the LORD: Fill this valley with ditches. 17 For thus says the LORD: You will see neither wind nor rain, but this valley will fill up with water for you and your animals to drink. 18 This will be easy for the LORD, and he will also hand over the Moabites into your hands. 19 You will overthrow every fortified city and every larger city. You will cut down every good tree, stop up every well, and scatter stones in every good field."[p]

20 In the morning while they were offering a sacrifice, water came flowing from Edom. The land was filled with water. 21 The Moabites heard that the kings were coming to fight against them, and they gathered together everyone who was old enough to put on armor and older and they stationed them on the border.

22 When they got up in the morning, the sun was shining on the water, and the Moabites saw that the water on the other side was as red as blood.* 23 They said, "This is blood. Surely the kings have attacked and killed one another. To the spoil, Moab!"

24 When they arrived at the camp of Israel, the Israelites rose up and defeated the Moabites who fled before them. They pushed forward, cutting down the Moabites. 25 They then destroyed the cities, and each cast his stone onto a good piece of land, filling it in. They stopped up all of the wells, and they cut down all of the good trees. But they left the stones of Kir-hareseth, although the slingers surrounded and attacked it.[q]

26 When the king of Moab saw that the battle was too fierce for him, he took seven hundred swordsmen with him to break through to the king of Edom, but they could not. 27 They took his oldest son who would have reigned in his stead, and they offered him up as a burnt offering upon the wall. They were furious at Israel. They departed and returned to their own land.[r]

CHAPTER 4

The Widow's Oil. 1 * Now the wife of one of the sons of the prophets cried out to Elisha, saying, "Your servant, my husband, is dead, and you know that your servant lived in fear of the LORD. His creditor is coming to take away his two sons to be his slaves." 2 Elisha said, "What can I do for you? Tell me, what do you have at home?" She answered, "Your servant has nothing at home except for a flask of oil."[s] 3 He said, "Go around and borrow jars from all of your neighbors. Empty jars, and not too few of them. 4 Then go inside, and shut the door behind you and your sons. Fill all of those jars, and when a jar is full, set it to the side."

5 So she left him, and she shut the door behind her and her sons who had brought her jars, and she kept pouring. 6 When all of the jars were full, she said to her son, "Bring me another jar." He said, "There are no more jars," and then the oil stopped flowing.

7 She went and recounted it to the man of God, and he said, "Go and sell the oil and pay your debt. You and your children can live on what is left over."

Elisha and the Shunammite.* 8 One day Elisha traveled to Shunem.* There was an important woman there, and she insisted that he stop to eat. Whenever he passed by there, he would stop to eat.[t]

9 She said to her husband, "Behold, this man who often visits us is a holy man of God. 10 We should prepare a small room on the roof, and place a bed, a table, a chair, and a lamp in it for him. Then he can stay there when he visits us."[u]

11 One day he arrived, and he went into the room to lie down. 12 He said to Gehazi, his servant, "Call the Shunammite." So he called her, and she stood before him. 13 He said to him, "Say to her, 'You have put yourself through all this trouble for us. What could be done for you? Should we speak to the king or the commander of the army for

o Ezek 1:3.—p Deut 20:19.—q Isa 16:7.—r Jdg 11:30-31; Mic 6:7.—s 1 Ki 17:12.—t Jos 19:18.—u Mt 10:41.

3:22 A mirage caused by the rays of the rising sun on the desert, or else a coloring due to the ocher or red clay that was so plentiful as to give the region its name (Edom means "red").

4:1ff This chapter recounts God's mercy and power in providing for the needs of the faithful. God uses Elisha to help the widow in debt, to restore life to the dead boy, to purify food, and to feed one hundred men.

4:8-37 The story is very like the one told of Elijah (1 Ki 17:17-24).

4:8 *Shunem:* at the foot of Little Hermon in northern Israel.

you?' " She answered, "I dwell among my own people."

14 He said, "Then what can be done for her?" Gehazi answered, "She and her husband are old, and they have no children." 15 Elisha said, "Summon her." He called her and she stood in the doorway. 16 He said, "You will embrace a son around this time next year." She said, "No, my lord, O man of God. Do not lie to your servant." [v]

17 The woman became pregnant, and she had a son that time the next year, just as Elisha had predicted. 18 The child grew up, and one day he went out to his father who was with the reapers. [w] 19 He said to his father, "My head! My head!" He said to a young man, "Carry him to his mother." 20 He picked him up and brought him to his mother. He sat on her lap until noon when he died.

21 She went up and laid him on the bed belonging to the man of God. She closed him in the room and went out. 22 She called to her husband and said, "Please send me one of the young men and one of the donkeys so that I can hurry to the man of God and return." 23 He said, "Why would you go today? It is not a new moon or the Sabbath." But she said, "It is all right." *

24 She saddled the donkey and said to her servant, "Lead on, and do not slow down for me unless I tell you." 25 So she departed and came to the man of God on Mount Carmel.

When the man of God saw her from a distance, he said to Gehazi his servant, "Behold, it is the Shunammite. 26 Run to her and say to her, 'Is everything all right? Is your husband well? Is your child well?' " She answered, "It is all right."

27 When she reached the man of God on the mountain, she took hold of his feet. Gehazi approached to push her away, but the man of God said, "Leave her alone. Her spirit is in despair, but the LORD had hidden it from me and did not tell me."

28 She said, "Did I ask for a son from my lord? Did I not say, 'Do not lie to me.' "

29 Elisha said to Gehazi, "Gird up your loins, and take my staff in your hands, and go! If you meet anyone, do not greet him. And if anyone greets you, do not answer. Lay my staff upon the child's face." * 30 But the boy's mother said, "As the LORD lives and as you live, I will not leave you." So he got up and followed her.

31 Gehazi went on before them, and he laid the staff upon the child's face, but there was no sound or response. He went out to meet him, and he said to him, "The child did not wake up."

32 When Elisha arrived at the house, the child was lying dead upon his bed. 33 He went in, and he shut the door on the two of them, and then he prayed to the LORD. 34 He got up and lay upon the child, mouth to mouth, eyes to eyes, and hands to hands. He stretched himself out upon the child, and the child's flesh grew warm. 35 He turned and walked back and forth in the room, and then he went and stretched himself out again. The boy sneezed seven times, and then the boy opened his eyes. [x]

36 Elisha called for Gehazi, and he said, "Call this Shunammite." He called her, and she came, and he said to her, "Take your son." 37 She came in and bowed down, falling to the ground at Elisha's feet. She then took her son and left. [y]

Poisoned Stew. 38 Elisha returned to Gilgal, and there was a famine in the land. The sons of the prophets were sitting in front of him, and he said to his servant, "Set up the large pot and cook some soup for the sons of the prophets."

39 One of them went out into the field to gather some herbs and he found a wild vine. He picked the wild gourds, filling his cloak. He cut them up into the pot of soup, although no one knew what they were.

40 When they poured out the soup for the men to eat, and they began to eat the soup, they cried out, "O man of God, there is death in the pot." And they could not eat it.

41 He said, "Bring some flour." He threw it into the pot and said, "Pour it out for the people to eat." And there was nothing harmful in the pot. [z]

Multiplication of Loaves. 42 A man came from Baal-shalishah, and he brought the man of God twenty loaves of barley bread from the firstfruits along with some heads of grain. He said, "Give it to the people so that they might eat." 43 His servant said, "What? Should I place this before one hundred men?" But he said again, "Give it to the peo-

v Gen 18:9-15.—w Ru 2:3.—x Jos 6:15; Heb 11:35.—y 1 Ki 17:23.—z Ex 15:25; 2 Ki 2:21.

4:23 It was customary to approach the prophets on festival days (see 1 Sam 20:5).

4:29 The sign of an urgent mission (see Lk 10:4). Easterners are, even today, very formal, and even the simplest greeting takes time.

ple to eat, for thus says the LORD: They will
eat, and there will be some left over." [a]
44 He set it before them, and they ate, and
there was some left over, just as the LORD
had predicted.

CHAPTER 5

Cure of Naaman. 1 * There was a certain
Naaman, who was the commander of the
army of the king of Aram. He was an honor-
able man, highly esteemed by his master,
because it was through him that the LORD
had delivered Aram. He was a brave soldier,
but he had leprosy.
2 Aramean raiders had gone out into the
land of Israel and had taken a young girl cap-
tive who served Naaman's wife. 3 She said to
her mistress, "If only my lord would present
himself to the prophet who is in Samaria. He
would cure him of his leprosy."
4 He went to his lord and said, "This is
what the young girl from the land of Israel
said."
5 The king of Aram said, "Go! I will send a
letter to the king of Israel."
He went on his way, taking with him ten
talents of silver, six thousand pieces of gold,
and ten changes of clothing. 6 He brought the
letter to the king of Israel which said, "With
this letter I am sending you my servant
Naaman so that you might cure him of his
leprosy."
7 When the king of Israel read the letter, he
tore his clothes and said, "Am I God, with
the power to kill and give life, that he sends
me a man to heal him of his leprosy? Think
of it, see how he is seeking a quarrel with
me." [b]
8 When Elisha, the man of God, heard that
the king of Israel had torn his clothes, he sent
to the king, saying, "Why have you torn your
clothes? Let him come to me so that he
might know that there is a prophet in Israel."
9 So Naaman went with his horses and his
chariot, and he stood at the door to Elisha's
house. 10 Elisha sent a messenger to him,
saying, "Go, wash seven times in the Jordan,
and your skin will be restored, and you will
be clean." [c]
11 But Naaman went away angry and said,
"Behold, I thought he would surely come out
to me and stand and call upon the name of
the LORD, his God, and wave his hand over
the place and heal the leprosy. 12 Are not the
Abana and the Pharpar, the rivers of
Damascus, better than all of the rivers of
Israel? Could I not wash in them and be
made clean?"
So he turned away and left in a rage. 13 His
servants approached him and spoke to him
saying, "My father, if the prophet had told
you to do something difficult, would you not
have done it? How much more should you
do it when he said, 'Wash and be made
clean.' "
14 He went down and he bathed himself in
the Jordan seven times as the man of God
had instructed him to do. His skin became
like the skin of a little child, and he was
clean. [d]
15 He and all of his attendants returned to
the man of God. He came and he stood
before him and said, "Behold, I now know
that there is no God upon the earth except in
Israel. Please accept a gift from your ser-
vant." [e] 16 He answered, "As the LORD lives
before whom I stand, I will not accept it."
Even though he urged him to take it, he
refused. *
17 * Naaman said, "If not, then let your ser-
vant be given two donkey loads of dirt, for
your servant will never again offer burnt
offerings or sacrifices to any other god but
the LORD. 18 Only may the LORD forgive me
this one thing: When my master enters the
temple of Rimmon to worship there, and he
leans on my hand and I also bow down in the
temple of Rimmon, may the LORD forgive
your servant this thing."
19 He said to him, "Go in peace." He left
and traveled a little way. 20 But Gehazi, the
servant of Elisha, the man of God, said,

a Mt 14:20; Lk 9:13; Jn 6:12.—b Gen 30:2; Deut 32:39; 1 Sam 2:6; Jn 5:21.—c Jn 9:7.—d Job 33:25; Lk 4:27.—e Jos 2:11; Dan 2:47.

5:1-17 The story is highly instructive (see Lk 4:27). The episode of the bathing has been seen as prefigurative of baptism, the waters of which cleanse from sin. Naaman was probably suffering from a simple skin disease; otherwise he would have been kept apart as a leper.

5:16 Given the time and place, the prophet's disinterestedness is admirable. He anticipates the command of Jesus to the apostles that they should not take pay for their ministry (Mt 10:8). Elijah's action stands out even more clearly in contrast to his servant, who is so greedy that he is willing even to slander his master (vv. 20-21).

5:17-19 Rimmon or Hadad-rimmon was the principal divinity of Damascus (Zec 12:11). Naaman asks for a little earth from the land of the true God in order to make for himself a sacred place in which he may pray. He thereby becomes a model for converted pagans. But he is faced with a difficult matter of conscience and he asks that he not be forbidden outward participation in the false worship that is forced upon him. The prophet leaves the convert in his state of good faith, without expressly giving his approval.

"Behold, my master has spared Naaman the
Aramean by not accepting from his hands
what he brought. As the LORD lives, I will run
after him and take something from him."
21 So Gehazi followed Naaman. When
Naaman saw him running after him, he got
off the chariot to greet him and he said, "Is
all well?" 22 He answered, "All is well. My
master sent me, saying, 'Two young men
from among the sons of the prophets have
now come to me from the hill country of
Ephraim. Please give them a talent of silver
and two changes of clothing.' "
23 Naaman said, "Please take two talents."
He urged it on him, and he bound up two tal-
ents of silver in two bags along with two
changes of clothing. He entrusted it to two of
his servants who carried it before him.
24 When he came to the tower, he took it from
their hands and he placed it in the house. He
then dismissed the men and they left.
25 He went in and stood before his master.
Elisha said to him, "Where are you coming
from, Gehazi?" He answered, "Your servant
has not gone anywhere." 26 He said to him,
"Was not my spirit with you when the man
got off of his chariot to meet you? Is this now
the time to receive money, or clothing, or
olive orchards, or vineyards, or sheep, or
oxen, or menservants, or maidservants?
27 On account of this, Naaman's leprosy will
cling to you and your descendants forever."
He went out from his presence, and he was a
leper, as white as snow.

CHAPTER 6

Finding the Lost Ax. 1 The sons of the
prophets came to Elisha and said, "Look, the
place where we meet with you is too small.
2 Let us go to the Jordan. Each of us can take
a pole, and we can make a place for our-
selves there." He answered, "Go."
3 One of them said, "Will you please go
with your servants." He answered, "I will go."
4 He went with them and they came to the
Jordan and began to cut down trees.
5 One of the men was cutting down a tree,
but the iron ax head fell into the water. He
cried out, "Woe is me, master, for it was
borrowed." 6 The man of God asked,
"Where did it fall?" So he showed him the
place. He cut down a stick and tossed it
there, and it made the iron float. 7 He said,
"Pick it up." So he stretched out his hand
and grabbed it.

Aramean Ambush. 8 Now the king of Aram
was fighting against Israel. He conferred
with his servants saying, "I will set up my
camp over there."
9 The man of God sent word to the king of
Israel, saying, "Beware of passing by that
place, for the Arameans have gone down
there." 10 The king of Israel sent men to the
place that the man of God had indicated. He
warned him and saved him more than once
or twice.
11 The king of Aram was enraged at this,
and he summoned his servants and said,
"Will you not let me know which of us has
sided with the king of Israel?" 12 One of his
servants answered, "No one, my lord, O
king. It is Elisha, the prophet who is in Israel,
who tells the king of Israel whatever you say
in your bed chamber."
13 He said, "Go find out where he is so
that I can send and capture him." He was
told, "He is in Dothan." *[f] 14 He sent hors-
es and chariots and a large army there.
They arrived at night and surrounded the
city.
15 Early the next morning, when the ser-
vant of the man of God got up and went
out, behold, he saw an army with horses
and chariots surrounding the city. His ser-
vant said to him, "Oh, my lord, what shall
we do?" 16 He answered, "Do not be afraid.
There are more with us than with them." [g]
17 Then Elisha prayed, "O LORD, open his
eyes so that he might see." The LORD opened
the young man's eyes, and he looked, and
behold, the hill was covered with horses and
chariots and fire all around Elisha. [h]
18 As they came down toward him, Elisha
prayed to the LORD, "Strike this people with
blindness." They were stricken with blind-
ness, as Elisha had said. 19 Then Elisha said
to them, "This is not the way, and this is not
the city. Follow me, and I will bring you to
the man whom you are seeking." He led
them to Samaria.
20 When they entered Samaria, Elisha
said, "Open the eyes of these men, O LORD,
so that they might see." The LORD opened
their eyes and they saw that they were in the
middle of Samaria.

f Gen 37:17.—g Ps 55:19; Rom 8:31.—h 2 Ki 2:11; Ps 68:18.

6:13 *Dothan:* 18 km north of Samaria (see Gen 37:17; Jud 3:9).

21 When the king of Israel saw them, he
said to Elisha, "Shall I kill them, my father?
Shall I kill them?" 22 He answered, "Do not
kill them! Would you kill someone whom you
had taken with the sword or the bow? Give
them bread and water so that they can eat
and drink and go back to their master."

23 He prepared a great feast for them, and
when they finished eating and drinking, he
sent them away, and they returned to their
master. No more Aramean raiding parties
came into the land of Israel.

24 Sometime later, Ben-hadad, the king of
Aram, assembled his whole army and he
went up and laid siege to Samaria. 25 There
was a terrible famine in Samaria, and they
continued the siege until a donkey's head
sold for eighty shekels of silver, and a quarter
of a kab of dove's dung sold for five shekels of
silver.

26 * As the king of Israel was passing by on
the wall, a woman cried out to him, "Help
me, my lord, O king." 27 He said, "If the LORD
does not help you, where can I get help for
you? From the threshing floor? From the
winepress?"

28 The king said to her, "What do you
want?" She said, "This woman said to me,
'Give me your son, so that we can eat him
today. We can eat my son tomorrow.' 29 So we
cooked my son and we ate him. The next day
I said to her, 'Give me your son so that we
can eat him,' but she hid her son." [i]

30 When the king heard the woman's
words, he tore his clothes. As he walked
along on the wall, the people looked up and
they saw that he was wearing sackcloth
underneath his clothes. 31 He said, "May
God do this to me and more if the head of
Elisha, the son of Shaphat, remains on his
body today."

32 Elisha was sitting in his house, and the
elders were sitting with him. The king sent a
man to him, but even before the messenger
arrived, he said to the elders, "Do you not
see how he has sent this son of a murderer to
cut off my head? Look, when the messenger
arrives, shut and bar the door against him. Is
not the sound of his master's feet behind
him?" [j]

33 As he was still talking, the messenger
came down to him. He said, "This disaster is
from the LORD. Why should I wait for the
LORD any longer?"

CHAPTER 7

1 Elisha said, "Listen to the word of the
LORD for thus says the LORD: By this time
tomorrow a seah* of flour will sell for a
shekel and two seahs of barley will sell for a
shekel in the gates of Samaria." 2 An officer
on whose arm the king was leaning said to
the man of God, "Behold, even if the LORD
were to make windows in the heavens, how
could this happen." He answered, "Behold,
your eyes will see it, but you will not eat any
of it." [k]

Lepers at the Gate. 3 There were four lepers
at the entrance to the city gate, and they said
to one another, "Why are we sitting here
until we die?* [l] 4 If we say, 'Let us go into
the city,' there is famine in the city. We would
die there. If we continue to sit here, we will
die just the same. Let us go and surrender to
the army of the Arameans. If they let us live,
then we will live, but if they kill us, then we
will die."

5 At dusk they got up and went into the
camp of the Arameans. When they arrived
at the edge of the Aramean camp, they did
not find anyone. 6 The LORD had made the
Aramean army hear the sound of chariots
and the sound of horses and the sound of a
large army. They said to one another, "The
king of Israel has paid the Hittite kings and
the Egyptian kings to attack us." 7 They
arose at dusk and fled, abandoning their
tents, their horses, and their donkeys, leav-
ing their camp as it was. They fled for their
lives. [m]

8 These lepers reached the edge of the
camp, and they entered one of the tents
where they ate and drank and carried away
silver, gold, and clothing. They went off and
hid it, and they then entered another tent
and carried off things from it as well. They
went and hid those things.

9 They then said to one another, "What we
are doing today is not right. It is a day of
good news, and we are keeping it to our-
selves. If we wait until the morning, will we

i Lev 26:27-29; Deut 28:52-57.—j Ezek 8:1.—k Ps 78:23; Mal 3:10.—l Lev 13:46.—m Ps 48:4-6; Prov 28:1.

6:26ff The king of Israel was aware of the extreme measures that the famine in Samaria had wrought (i.e., women eating their children). He knew that it was a result of the people's unfaithfulness to the true God and was predicted in Deut 28:49-57.

7:1 *Seah:* about 15 liters; the low price reflects the end of the famine.

7:3 Lepers had to remain apart (Lev 13:46); they are at the gate because the countryside is overrun by the enemy. It will be by means of these outcasts that God rescues the city.

not be punished? Come on, let us go and
inform the king's household."
10 So they went and called out to the city
gatekeeper, saying, "We have come from the
Aramean camp, and there was no one there,
not a sound from anyone. Yet, the horses are
tied up, and the donkeys are tied up, and the
tents are the way they were."
11 The gatekeepers shouted out the news,
and it was heard in the king's palace. 12 The
king got up during the night and he said to
his servants, "I will explain to you what the
Arameans have done to us. They knew that
we were hungry, so they left the camp and
hid in the field, saying, 'When they come out
from the city, we will catch them alive and
take the city.' "[n]
13 One of his servants said, "Let some men
take five of the horses that are left in the city.
Their fate will be the same as the rest of the
Israelites who are left here, for the rest of the
Israelites are doomed as well. Let us send
them to see."
End of the Siege. 14 The king chose two
chariots with their horses, and he sent them
after the Aramean army saying, "Go and
see!" 15 They followed them to the Jordan,
and all along the way they found garments
and equipment that the Arameans had
thrown away in their haste. The messengers
returned and reported it to the king.
16 The people went out and they plundered
the tents of the Arameans. A seah of flour
sold for one shekel, and two seahs of barley
sold for one shekel, as the LORD had said.
17 Now the king had placed the officer on
whose arm he leaned in charge of the gate,
and the people trampled him in the gateway,
as the man of God had foretold when the
king had visited him.
18 And so what the man of God had said to
the king came true, for he said, "Two seahs of
barley will sell for a shekel, and a seah of
flour will sell for a shekel at this time tomor-
row in the gates of Samaria." 19 The officer
had said to the man of God, "Behold, even if
the LORD were to make windows in the heav-
ens, how could this happen," and he had
answered, "Behold, your eyes will see it, but
you will not eat any of it." 20 This is exactly
what happened, for the people trampled him
in the gateway and he died.

CHAPTER 8

Famine Predicted. 1 Now Elisha spoke to the
woman whose son he had restored to life,
saying, "You and your household must get
up and go to dwell wherever you can, for the
LORD has called a famine down upon the
land, and it will last for seven years."[o]
2 The woman rose up and did what the
man of God had told her to do. She and her
household went and dwelt in the land of the
Philistines for seven years. 3 At the end of
seven years, the woman returned from the
land of the Philistines. She went to the king
and begged for her house and her land.
4 The king had been talking to Gehazi, the
servant of the man of God, and he had said,
"Please tell me all of the great things that
Elisha has done." 5 Just as he was recount-
ing to the king how he had restored a dead
body to life, the woman whose son he had
restored to life beseeched the king for her
house and her land. Gehazi said, "My lord,
O king, this is the woman whose son Elisha
restored to life."
6 The king questioned the woman about it,
and she told him about it. The king assigned
an official for her case, saying, "Restore
everything to her, including the produce
from the field from the day she left the land
up until the present."
Ben-hadad's Death Foretold. 7 Elisha went
to Damascus, to Ben-hadad, the king of the
Arameans, who was ill. He was told, "The
man of God has come here."
8 The king said to Hazael, "Take a present
with you and go and meet the man of God.
Inquire of the LORD through him, asking,
'Will I recover from this illness?' "[p]
9 Hazael went to meet him, and he took a
present of forty camel loads of the finest
products of Damascus with him. He stood
before him and said, "Ben-hadad the king
of Aram, has sent me to you, saying, 'Will
I recover from this illness?' " 10 Elisha
answered, "Go and say to him, 'You will
surely recover,' for the LORD has revealed to
me that he will surely die." *
11 He continued to stare at him until he
became embarrassed. The man of God then
began to weep. 12 Hazael asked, "Why is my
lord weeping?" He answered, "Because I

n 2 Ki 6:25-29; Jos 8:4.—o Ru 1:1; Ps 105:16.—p 1 Ki 14:1-3.

8:10 That is, he will die, but not of his present disease; he would have recovered, had he not been killed.

know what harm you will do to the Israelites. You will burn down their strongholds, you will put their young men to the sword, you will dash their children to the ground, and you will rip open their pregnant women." [q]
13 Hazael said, "But how could your servant, who is nothing more than a dog,* do such a great thing?" Elisha answered, "The LORD has revealed to me that you will be the king of Aram."

14 He left Elisha and went back to his master who said to him, "What did Elisha say to you?" He answered, "He told me that you will surely recover." 15 The next day he took a thick cloth and soaked it in water. He placed it over the king's face, so that he died. Hazael then reigned in his stead.

Reign of Joram of Judah. 16 In the fifth year of the reign of Joram, the son of Ahab, the king of Israel, when Jehoshaphat was the king of Judah, Joram, the son of Jehoshaphat, began to reign over Judah. 17 He was thirty-two years old when he began to reign, and he reigned for eight years in Jerusalem. 18 He walked in the ways of the kings of Israel, as the house of Ahab had, for the daughter of Ahab was his wife. He did what was evil in the sight of the LORD. 19 Yet, the LORD would not destroy Judah for the sake of David, his servant, for he had promised to give a light to him and his children forever. [r]

20 During his reign, Edom rebelled against Judah and set up their own king. 21 Joram went to Zair with all of his chariots. He rose up during the night and attacked the Edomites who had surrounded him. The captains of his chariots and his army fled back home. 22 Edom has been in a state of rebellion against Judah up to the present. Libnah rebelled at the same time. [s]

23 As for the other deeds of Joram, what he did, are they not written in the book of the chronicles of the kings of Judah?

24 Joram slept with his fathers, and he was buried with his fathers in the City of David, and Ahaziah, his son, reigned in his stead.

Ahaziah Rules Judah. 25 Ahaziah, the son of Joram, began to reign as the king of Judah during the twelfth year of the reign of Joram, the son of Ahab, the king of Israel.
26 Ahaziah was twenty-two years old when he began to reign, and he reigned in Jerusalem for one year. His mother's name was Athaliah. She was the daughter of Omri, the king of Israel.* 27 He walked in the ways of the house of Ahab and did what was evil in the sight of the LORD, as the house of Ahab had, for he was the son-in-law of the house of Ahab.

28 He went to war against Hazael, the king of Aram, at Ramoth-gilead along with Joram, the son of Ahab. The Arameans wounded Joram. [t] 29 Joram returned to Jezreel to recover from the wounds he had received from the Arameans at Ramoth when he fought against Hazael, the king of the Arameans.

Ahaziah, the son of Joram, the king of Judah, went down to visit Joram, the son of Ahab, in Jezreel because he was ill.

CHAPTER 9

Anointing of Jehu. 1 Elisha the prophet summoned one of the sons of the prophets and said to him, "Gird up your loins and carry this flask of oil to Ramoth-gilead.*
2 When you arrive there, search for Jehu, the son of Jehoshaphat, the son of Nimshi. Go to him, and separate him from his companions, bringing him to an inner chamber.
3 Take the flask of oil and pour it on his head, saying, 'Thus says the LORD: I have anointed you as king over Israel.' Then open the door and flee, do not wait around." [u]

4 So the young man, the prophet, went to Ramoth-gilead. 5 When he arrived, the commanders of the army were sitting around. He said, "I have a message for you, commander." Jehu said, "For which of us?" He answered, "For you, commander."

6 Jehu got up and went into the house. He poured the oil on his head and said, "Thus says the LORD, the God of Israel: 'I have anointed you as king over the people of the LORD, over Israel. 7 You are to wipe out the house of Ahab, your master, and take vengeance for the blood of my servants, the prophets, and the blood of all of the servants

q Ps 137:9; Hos 13:16; Am 1:13.—r 2 Sam 7:12-16; Rev 21:23.—s Gen 27:40.—t Deut 4:43; 2 Chr 22:6, 7.—u 1 Ki 19:16.

8:13 *Nothing more than a dog:* this seemingly derogatory designation might be Hazael's way of declaring his powerlessness to commit the atrocities that Elisha forecasts.

8:26 Athaliah, whether the daughter or granddaughter of Omri (see v. 18), acted much as her evil parents Ahab and Jezebel did. After her son Ahaziah is killed in battle, Athaliah wipes out all the male descendants and rules as queen (see 2 Ki 11:1).

9:1 Elisha carries out the third commission given to Elijah (1 Ki 19:16). He does it through the agency of one of the sons—that is, disciples—of the prophets; as Elisha's envoy, he shares his authority.

of the LORD that Jezebel has shed.[v] 8 The
entire house of Ahab must perish. Everyone
who pees against the wall in Israel who
belongs to Ahab must be cut off, whether he
be slave or free. 9 I will make the house of
Ahab like the house of Jeroboam, the son of
Nebat, and like the house of Baasha, the son
of Ahijah.[w] 10 And as for Jezebel, the dogs
will devour her on the Jezreel plot of ground.
No one will bury her.' " Then he opened the
door and fled.

11 When Jehu came outside to the servants
of his lord, one of them said to him, "Is
everything all right? Why did this madman*
come to visit you?" He answered, "You know
the man and the things he says." 12 They said,
"That is not true. Tell us now what he said."
Jehu said, "He said this to me, 'Thus says the
LORD: I have anointed you as king over
Israel.' "

13 Each of them quickly took his cloak and
put it under him upon the stairs. They blew
the trumpets and proclaimed, "Jehu is
king!" *[x]

The Murder of Joram. 14 So Jehu, the son of
Jehoshaphat, the son of Nimshi, plotted
against Joram.

Joram and all of Israel had been defending
Ramoth-gilead against Hazael, the king of
Aram, 15 but Joram had returned to Jezreel
to recover from the wounds he had received
from the Arameans when he fought against
Hazael, the king of Aram. Jehu said, "If
this is what you want, then prevent anyone
from leaving the city and going to Jezreel to
report it."

16 Jehu then got in his chariot and rode to
Jezreel, for that was where Joram was stay-
ing. Ahaziah, the king of Judah, had also
gone down to visit Joram.

17 When the watchman upon the tower in
Jezreel observed Jehu's forces arriving, he
said, "I see a company." Joram said, "Get a
horseman and send him out to meet them.
Let him say, 'Do you come in peace?' " 18 The
horseman went to meet them and said, "Thus
says the king: 'Do you come in peace?' " Jehu
answered, "What do you have to do with
peace? Fall in behind me." The watchman
said, "The messenger has reached them, but
he is not coming back."

19 He sent out a second horseman who
came to them and said, "Thus says the king:
'Do you come in peace?' " Jehu answered,
"What do you have to do with peace? Fall in
behind me."

20 The watchman reported, "He has
reached them, but he is not coming back.
The one who is driving is driving like Jehu,
the son of Nimshi, for he is driving furiously."
21 Joram said, "Prepare my chariot."

When his chariot had been made ready,
Joram, the king of Israel, and Ahaziah, the
king of Judah, each drove out with his chari-
ot against Jehu. They encountered him at the
plot of Naboth, the Jezreelite. 22 When Joram
saw that it was Jehu, he said, "Do you come
in peace?" Jehu answered, "How can there
be peace as long as the idolatries and witch-
crafts of Jezebel, your mother, continue to
multiply?"[y]

23 Joram turned and fled, and he cried out
to Ahaziah, "It is treachery, O Ahaziah!"
24 Jehu drew back his bow and struck Joram
between his shoulders. The arrow pierced his
heart, and he sunk down in his chariot.

25 * Jehu said to Bidkar, his captain, "Pick
him up and throw him down in the plot that
belonged to Naboth, the Jezreelite. Remem-
ber how you and I were riding together
behind Ahab, his father, when the LORD pro-
claimed this prophecy against him. 26 'As
surely as yesterday I saw the blood of Naboth
and his sons,' says the LORD, 'I will repay you
upon this plot,' says the LORD. Therefore,
take him and throw him down upon this
plot, in accordance with the word of the
LORD."

Death of Ahaziah. 27 When Ahaziah, the
king of Judah, saw this, he fled on the road to
Beth-haggan. Jehu followed after him, shout-
ing, "Kill him too!" They wounded him on
the way up to Gur, which is by Ibleam. He
escaped to Megiddo, but he died there.[z]
28 His servants took him by chariot to
Jerusalem, and they buried him in the tomb
of his fathers in the City of David. 29 Ahaziah
had begun to reign over Judah in the
eleventh year of the reign of Joram, the son
of Ahab.

Death of Jezebel. 30 Jehu then went to
Jezreel. When Jezebel heard, she painted her

v Deut 32:35-43.—w 1 Ki 14:10; 16:3-5.—x 2 Sam 15:10; Mt 21:7-8.—y 1 Ki 18:19; Rev 2:20.—z Jdg 1:27; 2 Chr 22:9.

9:11 *Madman:* so named because of the ecstatic manifestations that often accompanied prophetic inspiration.

9:13 They make a kind of throne for him with the means at hand; in like manner, the crowd will offer royal honors to Jesus on Palm Sunday (Mt 21:8).

9:25-26 An account that is independent of 1 Ki 21; the slaying of Naboth's son is a new element in the story.

face and fixed her hair, and she leaned out
the window.[a] 31 When Jehu entered the gate,
she said, "Do you come in peace, Zimri, you
murderer of your master?"

32 He looked up at the window and said,
"Who is on my side? Who?" Two or three
eunuchs looked down to him. 33 He said,
"Throw her down!" They threw her down
so that her blood sprinkled on the wall and
on the horses as they trampled her down.

34 He went in and ate and drank and said,
"Go now, and bury that accursed woman,
for she is the daughter of a king." 35 When
they went out to bury her, all they found
was her skull, her feet, and the palms of her
hands. 36 They went back and told him. He
said, "This is the word of the LORD which he
spoke through his servant, Elijah, the
Tishbite, when he said, 'The dogs will eat
the flesh of Jezebel on the plot in Jezreel.[b]
37 Jezebel's body will be like dung spread
over the surface of the field on the plot in
Jezreel so that no one will be able to say:
This is Jezebel.' "

CHAPTER 10

The Killing of Ahab's Descendants. 1 Now
there were seventy sons of Ahab in Samaria,
so Jehu wrote letters that he sent to
Samaria, to the officials of Jezreel, to the
elders and the guardians of Ahab's children,
saying,*[c] 2 "As soon as you receive this let-
ter, for your master's sons are with you and
you have chariots and horses and a fortified
city and armor, 3 choose the best and most
worthy of your master's sons and set him
upon his father's throne, and fight for your
master."

4 They were terrified and said, "If two
kings could not resist him, then how could
we resist him?" 5 The major-domo of the
palace who was in charge of the city, the
elders, and the guardians sent to Jehu, say-
ing, "We are your servants. We will do what-
ever you tell us. We will not appoint anyone
as king; we will do as you see fit."[d]

6 He wrote them a second letter, saying, "If
you are with me and willing to obey me, then
take off the heads* of these men, the sons of
Ahab, and bring them to me in Jezreel by
this time tomorrow."

There were seventy sons of the king who
were being raised by the leading citizens of
the city. 7 When they received the letter, they
slew the king's sons, seventy of them, and
they put their heads in baskets and sent
them to Jezreel.

8 When the messenger arrived, he told
him, "We have brought the heads of the
king's sons." He said, "Put them in two piles
at the entrance to the gates until the morn-
ing."

9 The next morning, he went out and stood
before all the people and said to them, "You
are innocent! I plotted against my master
and killed him, but who killed all of these?
10 Know then that not a word of the LORD
which the LORD spoke against the house of
Ahab will fall to the ground. The LORD has
fulfilled what he said through his servant
Elijah."[e]

11 So Jehu killed all of those who remained
from the house of Ahab in Jezreel, all his
chief men, all of his relatives, and all of his
priests, so that none of them were left alive.[f]

Ahaziah's Kinsmen. 12 He then rose up and
left and went to Samaria. On the way, at
Beth-eked of the shepherds, 13 Jehu met the
brothers of Ahaziah, the king of Judah. He
said, "Who are you?" They answered, "We
are the brothers of Ahaziah. We are going
down to greet the sons of the king and the
sons of the queen mother." 14 He said, "Take
them alive!" They took them alive and they
slew them at the well of Beth-eked, forty-two
of them. He did not leave any of them alive.

15 When he left there, he encountered
Jehonadab, the son of Rechab, who came out
to meet him. He greeted him and said, "Is
your heart right? Is your heart with my
heart?" Jehonadab answered, "It is." He said,
"If it is, give me your hand." He gave him his
hand, and he took him up into his chariot.[g]
16 He said, "Come with me, and see my zeal
for the LORD." So they had him ride in his
chariot. 17 When he arrived in Samaria, he
killed all of those who were left of Ahab in
Samaria until he had wiped them out, fulfill-
ing what the LORD had said when he spoke
through Elijah.

Baal's Temple Destroyed. 18 Jehu then gath-
ered together all of the people and said to

a Jer 4:30; Ezek 23:40.—b 1 Ki 21:23.—c Jdg 8:30.—d Jos 9:8.—e 1 Ki 21:19-29.—f Job 18:19; Hos 1:4.—g 1 Ki 20:33; 1 Chr 2:55; Jer 35:1-19.

10:1 The number seventy signifies the totality of Ahab's sons (Gen 46:27; Jdg 8:30). In addition, "son" has a broad meaning in Hebrew and may therefore signify all the kinsmen with a right of succession.

10:6 *Heads:* a deliberately ambiguous word (it can mean "heads" in the literal sense, or "principal ones"), so that Jehu can say he had not given the order to kill (v. 9).

them, "Ahab only served Baal a little, but
Jehu will serve him a lot.[h] 19 Summon all of
the prophets of Baal to me, all of his ser-
vants, and all of his priests. Let no one be
missing, for I am going to offer a great sacri-
fice to Baal. Whoever is missing will not live."
Jehu did this as a trick so that he might put
to death those who worshiped Baal.[i] 20 Jehu
said, "Proclaim a solemn assembly for
Baal." And they proclaimed it.

21 Jehu sent throughout all of Israel, and all
of the worshipers of Baal came. There was
not a single one of them who did not come.
The temple of Baal was full from one end to
the other. 22 He said to the person who was in
charge of the wardrobe, "Bring forth the
vestments for all of the worshipers of Baal."
So he brought forth vestments for them.*

23 Then Jehu and Jehonadab, the son of
Rechab, went to the temple of Baal. He said
to the worshipers of Baal, "Look around and
see that there are no servants of the LORD
here, only worshipers of Baal." 24 They went
in to offer sacrifices and burnt offerings.

Jehu posted eighty men and said, "If any of
the men whom I have placed in your hands
escapes, it will be your life for his life." 25 As
soon as he had finished offering up the burnt
offerings, Jehu said to the guards and the
captains, "Go in and slay them. Let no one
escape." They put them to the sword. The
guards and the captains then cast them out,
and they entered the inner shrine of the tem-
ple of Baal. 26 They brought the sacred pil-
lars out from the temple of Baal and they
burned them. 27 They smashed the idol of
Baal, and they tore down the temple of Baal
and made it into a refuse dump, which it is
up to the present.[j] 28 Thus, Jehu destroyed
Baal throughout Israel.

Death of Jehu. 29 However, Jehu did not
turn away from the sins of Jeroboam, the son
of Nebat, who caused Israel to sin, that is, fol-
lowing the golden calves in Bethel and Dan.[k]

30 The LORD said to Jehu, "Because you
have done what was right in my sight, doing
everything that was in my heart to the house
of Ahab, your sons to the fourth generation
will sit upon the throne of Israel."

31 But Jehu did not take heed to walk in the
ways of the LORD, the God of Israel, with all
his heart, nor did he turn away from the sins
of Jeroboam who caused Israel to sin.[l]
32 Therefore, the LORD began to cut off parts
of Israel, and Hazael conquered them
throughout all of the territory of Israel[m] 33 to
the east of the Jordan: all of the land of
Gilead, that is, Gad, Reuben, and Manasseh,
from Aroer which is near the Arnon River,
including Gilead and Bashan.

34 Now the rest of the deeds of Jehu, and all
that he did, and his accomplishments, are
they not written in the book of the chronicles
of the kings of Israel?

35 Jehu slept with his fathers and they
buried him in Samaria. Jehoahaz, his son,
then reigned in his stead. 36 Jehu reigned
over Israel in Samaria for a period of twen-
ty-eight years.

CHAPTER 11

The Rule of Athaliah. 1 When Athaliah, the
mother of Ahaziah, saw that her son was
dead, she killed all of the royal heirs. 2 But
Jehosheba, the daughter of King Joram, the
sister of Ahaziah, took Joash, the son of
Ahaziah, and secreted him away from the
king's sons who were being murdered. They
hid him and his nurse from Athaliah in the
bed chamber so that he might not die.[n]

3 He was hidden with her for six years in
the temple of the LORD, and Athaliah reigned
over the land. 4 In the seventh year, Jehoiada
sent for and summoned the captains of the
hundreds, the Carites,* and the guards. He
brought them to the temple of the LORD. He
made a covenant with them and took an oath
from them in the temple of the LORD. Then he
showed them the king's son.

5 He commanded them, "This is what you
are to do: for the one-third of you who come
on duty on the Sabbath: a third of you are to
guard the king's palace;[o] 6 a third of you are
to be at the Sur Gate; and a third at the gate
behind the guard. Guard the palace. 7 For the
other two-thirds of you who come off duty on
the Sabbath and who keep guard in the tem-
ple of the LORD and the king's palace, 8 sur-
round the king, each man with his weapons in
his hand. Whoever approaches the ranks is to
be put to death. Be with the king when he
goes out and when he comes in."

9 The captains of the hundreds did every-
thing that Jehoiada, the priest, had com-

h Jdg 2:11; 1 Ki 16:30-33.—i 1 Ki 18:19, 40.—j Ezr 6:11; Dan 2:5; 3:29.—k 1 Ki 12:28-30.—l Deut 4:9; Prov 4:23.—m 2 Ki 8:12.—n Jdg 9:5.—o 1 Chr 9:25.

10:22 They changed their clothing as a preliminary purification for offering worship (see also Gen 35:2; Ex 19:10).

11:4 *Carites:* Hebrew, *Kari;* corresponds perhaps to the Cherethites of 1 Ki 1:38; they were the king's bodyguard.

manded. Each of them brought the men
who were coming on duty on the Sabbath as
well as those who were going off duty on the
Sabbath and they came to Jehoiada the
priest.

10 The priest gave the captains of the hun-
dreds the spears and the shields that had
belonged to King David and that were kept
in the temple of the LORD.[p] 11 The guards
stood with their weapons in their hands
from the southern side of the temple to the
northern side of the temple by the altar and
the temple, surrounding the king.

12 He brought the king's son out and put a
crown on him. He gave him the testimony,
and they proclaimed him as king and
anointed him, clapping their hands and pro-
claiming, "Long live the king!"[q]

13 When Athaliah heard the noise from the
guard and the people, she came to the peo-
ple in the temple of the LORD. 14 She looked
out and behold, the king was standing by a
pillar,* as was the custom, with the princes
and the trumpeters standing by the king. All
the people of the land rejoiced and blew the
trumpets.

Athaliah tore her clothes and cried out,
"Treason! Treason!" 15 Jehoiada the priest
commanded the captains of the hundreds
and the commanders of the army and said
to them, "Bring her out between the ranks,
and put to the sword anyone who follows
her." (This was because the priest had said
that she was not to be killed in the temple of
the LORD.)

16 They seized her as she passed by the
place where the horses enter the king's
palace. She was put to death there.

17 Jehoiada made a covenant* between the
LORD and the king and the people that they
would be the LORD's people. He also made
one between the king and the people.[r]

18 All of the people went into the temple of
Baal. They smashed to pieces his altars and
his images. They killed Mattan, the priest of
Baal, in front of the altars.

The priest then appointed guards for the
temple of the LORD.[s] 19 He took the captains
of the hundreds, the Carites, the guards, and
the people of the land with him and they
brought down the king from the temple of
the LORD and entered the royal palace by
way of the guards' gate. He then took his
place on the royal throne.

20 All of the people of the land rejoiced, and
the city was quiet, for Athaliah had been put
to the sword in the royal palace.

21 Joash was seven years old when he
began to reign.

CHAPTER 12

Reign of Joash. 1 Joash began to reign dur-
ing the seventh year of the reign of Jehu, and
he reigned for forty years in Jerusalem. His
mother's name was Zibiah, and she was
from Beer-sheba.

2 * Joash did what was right in the sight of
the LORD all of his days. Jehoiada, the priest,
instructed him. 3 However, he did not elimi-
nate the high places, and the people still sac-
rificed and burned incense on the high places.

4 Joash said to the priests, "Gather all of
the money that has been brought into the
temple of the LORD as a sacred offering, the
money from the census, the money from
personal vows, and all of the money that
each man saw fit to bring to the temple of
the LORD.[t] 5 Let the priests each take it
from their treasurers, and let them use it to
repair whatever damage they might find in
the temple."

6 In spite of this, in the twenty-third year of
the reign of King Joash, the priests had not
yet repaired the damage in the temple.
7 King Joash therefore summoned Jehoiada
the priest and the other priests and he said
to them, "Why have you not repaired the
damage in the temple? Take no more money
from the treasurers; hand it over for the
repair of the temple."

8 The priests agreed that they would take
no more money from the people and that
they, themselves, would not repair the dam-
age in the temple. 9 Jehoiada took a chest
and cut a hole in its lid. He placed it beside
the altar on the right side as one enters the
temple of the LORD. The priests who guard-

p 2 Sam 8:7.—q 1 Sam 10:24; Isa 55:12.—r 2 Ki 23:3; 2 Chr 23:3, 16.—s Deut 12:3.—t Ex 35:5, 29; 1 Chr 29:3-9.

11:14 *Standing by a pillar:* the king was awarded this special place in the temple court on feasts and Sabbaths near the altar for burnt offerings.

11:17 *Made a covenant:* this was not a new covenant but a renewal of the covenant made with the Lord over 100 years before as described in the Book of Deuteronomy that had been long forgotten and disregarded by the king and the people. Here there is a further reference to a second covenant between the king and the people.

12:2ff Joash was a good student and learned well from the faithful high priest Jehoiada. Unfortunately, Joash did not eliminate the practice of making sacrifices only in designated areas. This kept alive pagan customs that led the people away from the true God.

ed the door placed all of the money that was
brought into the temple of the LORD in it. [u]
10 When they saw that there was quite a bit of
money in the chest, the king's scribe and the
high priest would come. They would count
the money that was found in the temple of
the LORD, and they would put it in bags.

11 When the money had been counted,
they placed it in the hands of the supervisor
of the work being done on the temple of the
LORD. With it they paid those who were
working on the temple of the LORD: the car-
penters and the builders, 12 the masons, and
the stonecutters. It was also used to buy
wood and hewn stone that were used to
repair the damage in the temple of the
LORD, and for all of the expenses involved in
repairing the temple.

13 However, the money that was brought
into the temple of the LORD was not used to
make silver basins, nor snuffers, nor sprin-
kling bowls, nor trumpets, nor any utensils
made with gold, nor any utensils made with
silver. [v]

14 They gave it to the workmen who used it
to repair the temple of the LORD. 15 More-
over, they did not ask for an accounting from
the men into whose hands the money had
been deposited for the payment of the work-
men, for they acted honestly.*

16 The money from guilt offerings and
from sin offerings was not brought into the
temple of the LORD for it belonged to the
priests.* [w]

17 Hazael, the king of Aram, went up and
fought against Gath. He captured it, and
Hazael decided to go up to Jerusalem.

18 Joash, the king of Judah, took all of the
sacred things that had been dedicated by
Jehoshaphat, Jehoram, and Ahaziah, his
ancestors, the kings of Judah, and all of the
sacred things that he had dedicated, and all
of the gold that was found in the treasury of
the temple of the LORD and the royal palace,
and he sent it to Hazael, the king of Aram,
who then departed from Jerusalem. [x]

19 As for the other deeds of Joash, what he
did, are they not written in the book of the
chronicles of the kings of Judah?

20 Joash's servants plotted against him,
and they killed him at Beth-millo, on the
road going down to Silla. 21 His servants who
killed him were Jozacar, the son of Shim-
eath, and Jehozabad, the son of Shomer.

He died, and they buried him with his
fathers in the City of David. Amaziah, his
son, reigned in his stead.

CHAPTER 13

Reign of Jehoahaz of Israel. 1 Jehoahaz, the
son of Jehu, became the king over Israel in
Samaria in the twenty-third year of the reign
of Joash, the son of Ahaziah, the king of
Judah. He reigned for seventeen years.

2 He did what was evil in the sight of the
LORD, following the sins of Jeroboam, the
son of Nebat, who had caused Israel to sin.
He did not turn away from them. 3 The
LORD's anger blazed against Israel, and he
delivered them into the hands of Hazael,
the king of Aram, and into the hands of
Ben-hadad, the son of Hazael, throughout
his entire reign.

4 Jehoahaz then pleaded with the LORD,
and the LORD listened to him for he
observed the suffering of Israel which was
being oppressed by the king of Aram. [y] 5 The
LORD gave Israel a deliverer, and they
escaped from under the hand of the
Arameans. The Israelites were able to live in
their own homes as they had before.

6 But they did not turn away from the sins
of the house of Jeroboam who caused Israel
to sin. They continued to walk in them. An
Asherah continued to stand in Samaria. [z]

7 There was nothing left to Jehoahaz's men
except for fifty horsemen, ten chariots, and
ten thousand footmen. The king of Aram had
destroyed the rest of them, making them like
the dust that lies on the threshing floor.

8 As for the rest of the deeds of Jehoahaz,
and all that he did, and all his achievements,
are they not written in the book of the chron-
icles of the kings of Israel?

9 Jehoahaz slept with his fathers, and he
was buried in Samaria. Jehoash his son,
reigned in his stead.

Reign of Jehoash of Israel. 10 Jehoash, the
son of Jehoahaz, began to reign over Israel in
Samaria in the thirty-seventh year of the
reign of Joash, the king of Judah, and he
reigned for sixteen years.

u Mk 12:41; Lk 21:1.—v 1 Ki 7:48-51.—w Lev 5:14-19.—x 1 Ki 15:18.—y 2 Ki 14:26-27; Num 21:7-9; Ps 78:34.—z Ex 34:13; 1 Ki 16:33.

12:15 The honesty of these laymen is contrasted with the negligence of the priests whom they are replacing (vv. 7-8).

12:16 For a crime, that is, a sin against justice, and for sin generally, expiatory sacrifices were prescribed (Lev 4–5).

11 He did what was evil in the sight of the
LORD, and he did not turn away from the
sins of Jeroboam, the son of Nebat, who
caused Israel to sin, but he walked in them.

12 As for the rest of the deeds of Jehoash,
what he did, his achievements, and how he
fought against Amaziah, the king of Judah,
are they not written in the book of the chron-
icles of the kings of Israel? [a]

13 Jehoash slept with his fathers, and then
Jeroboam sat upon his throne. Jehoash was
buried in Samaria with the kings of Israel.

Elisha's Final Prophecy. 14 Now Elisha had
fallen sick with the illness from which he
died. Jehoash, the king of Israel, went down
to visit him and wept over him. He cried out,
"My father! My father! * The chariots and
horsemen of Israel!" [b]

15 Elisha said, "Bring a bow and arrows,"
so he brought a bow and arrows. 16 He said
to the king of Israel, "Take the bow in your
hands," so he took the bow in his hands.
Elisha then put his hands on the king's
hands. 17 He said, "Open the east window,"
and he opened it. Elisha said, "Shoot," and
he shot. He said, "The arrow of the deliver-
ance of the LORD! The arrow of the deliver-
ance from Aram! You will wipe out the
Aramean in Aphek, totally devouring
them." [c]

18 Then he said, "Take the arrows," and he
took them. He said to the king of Israel,
"Strike the ground," and he struck it three
times and then stopped.

19 The man of God was angry with him
and said, "You should have struck it five or
six times. Then you would have defeated
Aram until it was consumed. As it is now,
you will only defeat it three times."

20 Elisha then died and was buried.

Now Moabite raiders used to raid the land
during the spring. 21 Once while some people
were burying a man, they spotted a band of
raiders, and they cast the man's body into
Elisha's tomb. When the man's body touched
Elisha's bones, he came back to life and
stood up on his feet. [d]

22 Hazael, the king of Aram, oppressed
Israel all throughout the reign of Jehoahaz.
23 But the LORD was gracious to them and
had compassion upon them and showed
respect to them because of his covenant with
Abraham, Isaac, and Jacob. Up to the pres-
ent he had not yet destroyed them nor had
he cast them out of his presence.

24 Hazael, the king of Aram, then died, and
Ben-hadad, his son, reigned in his stead.

25 Then Jehoash, the son of Jehoahaz, re-
captured from the hands of Ben-hadad, the
son of Hazael, the cities that he had taken
from the hands of his father Jehoahaz.
Jehoash defeated him three times, and he
recaptured the cities of Israel.

VI: KINGS OF ISRAEL AND JUDAH

CHAPTER 14

Amaziah of Judah. 1 Amaziah, the son of
Joash, the king of Judah, began to reign dur-
ing the second year of the reign of Jehoash,
the son of Jehoahaz, the king of Israel. 2 He
was twenty-five years old when he began to
reign, and he reigned for twenty-nine years
in Jerusalem. His mother's name was
Jehoaddin, and she was from Jerusalem.

3 He did what was right in the sight of the
LORD, but not like David, his father. He did
everything like his father Joash had done.
4 He did not eliminate the high places, and
the people continued to sacrifice and burn
incense upon the high places.

5 As soon as the kingdom was firmly in
his hands, he killed the servants of his
father, the king. 6 He did not put to death
the sons of the murderers for it is written in
the book of the law of Moses, "You shall not
put the fathers to death on account of the
sons, nor shall you put to death the sons on
account of the fathers. Each man is to be
put to death for his own sins." * [e]

7 He slew ten thousand Edomites in the
Valley of Salt, and he captured Sela in battle.
He named it Joktheel, which is its name up
to the present. [f]

8 Amaziah sent messengers to Jehoash, the
son of Jehoahaz, the son of Jehu, the king of
Israel saying, "Come, let us meet face to
face." 9 Jehoash, the king of Israel, replied to
Amaziah, the king of Judah, saying, "A this-
tle in Lebanon sent to a cedar in Lebanon,
saying, 'Give your daughter to my son in
marriage.' A wild beast in Lebanon passed

a 2 Chr 25:17ff.—b 2 Ki 2:12.—c Jos 8:18; 1 Ki 20:26.—d Sir 48:14; Mt 27:52.—e Job 21:19-20; Ezek 18:4, 20.—f Jdg 1:36.

13:14 *My father! My father!:* Jehoash's lament on Elisha's passing is reminiscent of Elisha's words on the death of Elijah. Jehoash was mistaken in holding Elisha responsible for Israel's well-being instead of giving the acclamation to the Lord.

14:6 The principle set down here is repeated by Ezekiel (ch. 18).

by and trampled on the thistle.[g] 10 You have
defeated Edom, and now you have become
arrogant. Stay at home in your glory. Why
should you stir up trouble and cause the
downfall of yourself and of Judah as well?"
11 But Amaziah would not listen, so
Jehoash, the king of Israel, attacked him. He
and Amaziah, the king of Judah, met face to
face at Beth-shemesh in Judah. 12 Judah was
defeated by Israel, and each man fled to his
own tent.
13 Jehoash, the king of Israel, captured
Amaziah, the king of Judah, the son of
Jehoash, the son of Ahaziah, at Beth-
shemesh. He then went to Jerusalem and
broke down the walls of Jerusalem from the
Ephraim Gate up to the Corner Gate, a dis-
tance of four hundred cubits.[h] 14 He took all
of the gold and all of the silver and all of the
utensils from the temple of the LORD and
from the treasury of the royal palace. He also
took hostages and returned to Samaria.
15 As for the other deeds of Jehoash, what
he did, his achievements, and how he defeat-
ed Amaziah, the king of Judah, are they not
written in the book of the chronicles of the
kings of Israel?
16 Jehoash slept with his fathers, and he was
buried in Samaria with the kings of Israel,
and Jeroboam, his son, reigned in his stead.
17 Amaziah, the king of Judah, the son of
Joash, lived for another fifteen years after the
death of Jehoash, the son of Jehoahaz, the
king of Israel. 18 As for the other deeds of
Amaziah, are they not written in the book of
the chronicles of the kings of Judah?
19 They plotted against him in Jerusalem,
and he fled to Lachish. They sent for him in
Lachish and they killed him there. 20 They
brought him back by horse and they buried
him in Jerusalem with his fathers in the City
of David.
21 The people of Judah then took Azariah
who was sixteen years old, and they made
him king in the place of his father Amaziah.
22 He rebuilt Elath and restored it to Judah
after the king was sleeping with his fathers.

Jeroboam II of Israel.* 23 Jeroboam, the son
of Joash, became the king of Israel in
Samaria during the fifteenth year of the
reign of Amaziah, the son of Joash, the king
of Judah. He reigned for forty-one years.
24 He did what was evil in the sight of the
LORD, and he did not turn away from the
sins of Jeroboam, the son of Nebat, who
caused Israel to sin.
25 He restored the boundaries of Israel
from the entrance of Lebo-hamath to the
Sea of Arabah. This fulfilled the word of the
LORD, the God of Israel, that had been pro-
claimed by his servant Jonah, the son of
Amittai, the prophet from Gath-hepher.*[i]
26 The LORD saw how terribly everyone in
Israel was suffering, whether they were slave
or free, for there was no one to help them in
Israel. 27 He saved them by the hand of
Jeroboam, the son of Joash, for the LORD had
not said that he would blot out the name of
Israel from under the heavens.
28 As for the other deeds of Jeroboam, what
he did, his achievements, how he fought and
recovered Damascus and Hamath for Israel
which had previously belonged to Judah, are
they not written in the book of the chronicles
of the kings of Israel?
29 Jeroboam slept with his fathers, with the
kings of Israel, and Zechariah his son,
reigned in his stead.

CHAPTER 15

Azariah of Judah.* 1 Azariah, the son of
Amaziah, the king of Judah, began to reign
during the twenty-seventh year of the reign
of Jeroboam, the king of Israel. 2 He was six-
teen years old when he began to reign, and
he reigned for fifty-two years in Jerusalem.
His mother's name was Jecholiah who was
from Jerusalem.
3 He did what was right in the sight of the
LORD, doing everything as Amaziah, his
father, had done. 4 However, he did not elim-
inate the high places, and the people still
offered sacrifices and burned incense on the
high places.
5 The LORD struck down the king so that he
was a leper until the day of his death. He
lived in a separate house while Jotham, the
king's son, took charge of the palace and gov-
erned the people of the land.[j]

g Jdg 9:8-15.—h Neh 8:16; 2 Chr 25:23.—i Deut 3:17; Jon 1:1; Mt 12:39.—j 2 Chr 26:21; 27:1.

14:23-29 Amos and Hosea, one a native of Judah, the other of Israel, began their mission as prophets in the reign of Jeroboam II and in his territory.

14:25 In later times this Jonah is turned into the chief character of the Book of Jonah, among the minor prophets.

15:1-7 In the year in which King Amaziah died, Isaiah had the well-known vision in the temple that inaugurated his prophetic activity (Isa 6). In verses 13 and 30, Amaziah is called Uzziah; we do not know the reason for the double name.

6 As for the other deeds of Azariah, what
he did, are they not written in the book of the
chronicles of the kings of Judah?

7 Azariah slept with his fathers, and they
buried him with his fathers in the City of
David. Jotham, his son, then reigned in his
stead.

Zechariah of Israel. 8 Zechariah, the son of
Jeroboam, became the king of Israel in
Samaria during the thirty-eighth year of the
reign of Azariah, the king of Judah. He
reigned for six months.

9 He did what was evil in the sight of the
LORD, as his fathers had done. He did not
turn away from the sins of Jeroboam, the son
of Nebat, who caused Israel to sin.

10 Shallum, the son of Jabesh, plotted
against him. He attacked him in front of the
people and killed him, reigning in his stead.

11 The other deeds of Zechariah are writ-
ten in the book of the chronicles of the kings
of Israel. 12 This fulfilled the word of the
LORD that had been spoken to Jehu: "Your
sons to the fourth generation will sit upon
the throne of Israel."

Shallum of Israel. 13 Shallum, son of Jabesh,
began to reign during the thirty-ninth year
of the reign of Uzziah, the king of Judah, and
he reigned for a full month in Samaria.
14 Then Menahem, the son of Gadi, from
Tirzah, went up to Samaria. He attacked
Shallum, the son of Jabesh, in Samaria and
he killed him. He then reigned in his stead.

15 As for the rest of the deeds of Shallum,
and his plot, are they not written in the book
of the chronicles of the kings of Israel?

16 Menahem then started out from Tirzah,
and he attacked Tappuah and everyone in it
and its environs because they would not
open up its gates. He killed everyone in it,
even ripping open the bellies of the pregnant
women. [k]

Menahem of Israel. 17 Menahem, son of
Gadi, began to reign over Israel during the
thirty-ninth year of the reign of Azariah, the
king of Judah. He reigned in Samaria for ten
years.

18 He did what was evil in the sight of the
LORD. During his entire reign he did not turn
away from the sins of Jeroboam, the son of
Nebat, who caused Israel to sin.

19 Then Pul, the king of Assyria, attacked
Israel, and Menahem gave Pul one thousand
talents of silver so that he might have his
support and strengthen his hold upon the
kingdom. 20 Menahem took the money from
Israel. Every wealthy man had to give fifty
shekels of silver to be given to the king of
Assyria. The king of Assyria therefore with-
drew and did not remain in the land any
longer.

21 As for the other deeds of Menahem and
what he did, are they not written in the book
of the chronicles of the kings of Israel?

22 Menahem slept with his fathers, and
Pekahiah, his son, reigned in his stead.

Pekahiah of Israel. 23 Pekahiah, the son of
Menahem, began to reign over Israel in
Samaria during the fiftieth year of the reign
of Azariah, the king of Judah. He reigned for
two years.

24 He did what was evil in the sight of the
LORD. He did not turn away from the sins of
Jeroboam, the son of Nebat, who caused
Israel to sin.

25 Pekah, the son of Remaliah, one of his
captains, plotted against him. He attacked
him in Samaria, in the citadel of the royal
palace. Taking fifty Gileadites with him, he
killed him, Argob, and Arieh. He then
reigned in his stead.

26 The other deeds of Pekahiah and what
he did are written in the book of the chroni-
cles of the kings of Israel.

Pekah of Israel. 27 Pekah, the son of
Remaliah, began to reign over Israel in
Samaria during the fifty-second year of the
reign of Azariah, the king of Judah. He
reigned for twenty years.*

28 He did what was evil in the sight of the
LORD. He did not turn away from the sins of
Jeroboam, the son of Nebat, who caused
Israel to sin.

29 During the reign of Pekah, the king of
Israel, Tiglath-pileser, the king of Assyria
came and captured Ijon, Abel-beth-maacah,
Janoah, Kedesh, and Hazor. He captured
Gilead and Galilee, including all of the land
of Naphtali, and he took them captive into
Assyria. [l]

30 Then Hoshea, the son of Elah, plotted
against Pekah, the son of Remaliah. He
attacked him and killed him and reigned in
his stead during the twentieth year of the
reign of Jotham, the son of Uzziah.

---

k 1 Ki 4:24; Hos 13:16.—l 1 Chr 5:26; Jer 50:17.

15:27 The twenty-year reign ascribed to Pekah is not in line with dates assigned to his assassination by Hoshea and Hoshea's ascension to the throne and the dates of future rulers.

31 As for the rest of the deeds of Pekah and
what he did, they are written in the book of
the chronicles of the kings of Israel.

Jotham of Judah. 32 Jotham, the son of
Uzziah, the king of Judah, began to reign
during the second year of the reign of Pekah,
the son of Remaliah, the king of Israel. 33 He
was twenty-five years old when he began to
reign, and he reigned for sixteen years in
Jerusalem. His mother's name was Jerusha,
the daughter of Zadok.

34 He did what was right in the sight of the
LORD, everything just as his father Uzziah
had done. 35 The high places were not elimi-
nated, though, and the people continued to
offer sacrifices and burn incense on the high
places. He rebuilt the upper gate to the tem-
ple of the LORD.[m]

36 As for the other deeds of Jotham, what
he did, are they not written in the book of the
chronicles of the kings of Judah?

37 In those days, the LORD began to send
Rezin, the king of Aram, and Pekah, the son
of Remaliah, against Judah.

38 Jotham slept with his fathers, and he
was buried with his fathers in the City of
David, his father. Ahaz, his son, reigned in
his stead.

CHAPTER 16*

Ahaz of Judah. 1 Ahaz, the son of Jotham,
the king of Judah, began to reign during the
seventeenth year of the reign of Pekah, the
son of Remaliah. 2 Ahaz was twenty years
old when he began to reign, and he reigned
in Jerusalem for sixteen years.

He did not do what was right in the sight
of the LORD as David, his father, had done.
3 He walked in the ways of the kings of Israel,
even sacrificing his son in fire. He practiced
the abominations of the nations whom the
LORD had cast out before the Israelites.[n]
4 He performed sacrifices and burned
incense on the high places, on the hilltops,
and under every green tree.[o]

5 Then Rezin, the king of Aram, and
Pekah, the son of Remaliah, the king of
Israel, attacked Jerusalem. They besieged
Ahaz, but they could not defeat him. 6 It was
at this time that Rezin, the king of Aram,
reconquered Elath, and the Arameans drove
the Judahites out of Elath. The Edomites
then settled in Elath and they have dwelt
there up to the present.

7 Ahaz sent messengers to Tiglath-pileser,
the king of Assyria, saying, "I am your ser-
vant and your son. Come and save me from
the hands of the king of Aram and the hands
of the king of Israel who have risen up
against me."

8 Ahaz took the silver and the gold from
the temple of the LORD and the treasury of
the royal palace, and he sent it to the king of
Assyria as a gift. 9 The king of Assyria con-
sented to his request, and the king of Assyria
attacked Damascus and captured it. He
deported its people to Kir.

10 Then King Ahaz traveled to Damascus
to meet Tiglath-pileser, the king of Assyria.
He saw an altar in Damascus, and King
Ahaz sent Uriah the priest to Damascus to
make a drawing of the altar along with a
complete description of its construction.[p]
11 Uriah the priest built an altar according to
everything for which King Ahaz had sent
him to Damascus. Uriah finished it before
King Ahaz returned from Damascus.
12 When the king returned from Damascus,
the king saw the altar. The king approached
the altar and made an offering on it. 13 He
offered up burnt offerings and cereal offer-
ings. He poured out drink offerings and
sprinkled the blood of his peace offerings
upon the altar. 14 He brought the bronze
altar that was before the LORD from the
front of the temple, from between the altar
and the temple of the LORD, and he placed it
on the north side of the altar.[q]

15 King Ahaz gave orders to Uriah the
priest, saying, "Offer on the great altar the
morning burnt offerings and the evening
cereal offerings, the king's burnt offerings
and his cereal offerings, along with the burnt
offerings, cereal offerings, and drink offer-
ings of all of the people of the land. Sprinkle
the blood of the sacrifices on it, but I will use
the bronze altar when I make inquiries."
16 Uriah the priest did everything that King
Ahaz had commanded.

m 2 Chr 23:20.—n Lev 18:21; Deut 9:4; 12:31.—o Deut 12:2; Ezek 6:13.—p Isa 8:2.—q Ex 20:24; 2 Chr 4:1.

16:1-20 Despite efforts to force Ahaz into a coalition against Assyria, this king prefers to declare himself a vassal of the mighty Tiglath-pileser III. Some of his neighbors take advantage of his difficulties to rid themselves of his yoke. Inspired by what he has seen in other sanctuaries, Ahaz introduces deviant reforms into the temple. Isaiah will try in vain to communicate to Ahaz his own confidence in the Lord (Isa 6–7 and the prophecy of Immanuel). See also 2 Chr 28.

17 King Ahaz cut off the side panels and he removed the basins from the moveable carts, he removed the sea from the bronze oxen underneath it and he placed it on a stone base. 18 He took away the Sabbath canopy* that had been built on the temple and the royal entrance outside the temple of the LORD on account of the king of Assyria.

19 Now the rest of the deeds of Ahaz, what he did, are they not written in the book of the chronicles of the kings of Judah?

20 Ahaz slept with his fathers, and he was buried with his fathers in the City of David. Hezekiah, his son, reigned in his stead.

CHAPTER 17

Hoshea of Israel. 1 Hoshea, the son of Elah, began to reign over Israel in Samaria during the twelfth year of the reign of Ahaz, the king of Judah. 2 He did what was evil in the sight of the LORD, but not like the kings of Israel who preceded him.

3 Shalmaneser, the king of Assyria, attacked him, and Hoshea became his vassal and gave him tribute. [r] 4 The king of Assyria discovered that Hoshea was involved in a conspiracy, for he had sent messengers to the king of Egypt, and he had not given tribute to the king of Assyria as he had in previous years. The king of Assyria therefore shut him up, throwing him in prison. 5 * The king of Assyria occupied the entire land, and he went up to Samaria and besieged it for three years.

6 The king of Assyria captured Samaria in the ninth year of the reign of Hoshea. He carried Israel away into Assyria, settling them in Halah, near Habor, on the River Gozan, in the cities of the Medes. [s] 7 This happened because the Israelites had sinned against the LORD, their God, who had brought them out of the land of Egypt, from under the hand of Pharaoh, the king of Egypt. They had revered other gods 8 and they had walked in the statutes of the nations whom the LORD had cast out before them and that the kings of Israel had introduced.

9 The people of Israel secretly did what was wrong against the LORD, their God. They built high places for themselves in all of their cities, whether it be a simple watchtower or fortified city. 10 They set up pillars and Asherahs for themselves on every high hill and under every green tree. [t] 11 They burned incense on all of the high places like the nations whom the LORD had carried away before them. They did wicked things, provoking the anger of the LORD. 12 They served idols, of which the LORD had said to them, "You are not to do this thing."

13 The LORD had testified against Israel and against Judah through every prophet and every seer saying, "Turn from your evil ways. Keep my commandments and my statutes according to the law that I gave your fathers and which I sent you by my servants, the prophets." [u] 14 But they would not listen. They hardened their necks to make them just like the necks of their fathers who had not believed in the LORD, their God. [v] 15 They despised his statutes and his covenant that he had made with their fathers and the warnings by which he bore witness against them. They followed after vain idols, becoming foolish. They also followed after the nations that surrounded them, the ones of whom the LORD had told them that they should not do what they did. [w] 16 They abandoned the commandments of the LORD, their God, and they made molten images of two calves for themselves. They made Asherah, worshiped all the host of heaven, and served the Baals. * [x] 17 They burned their sons and their daughters in fire, and they practiced divination and sorcery. They sold themselves to do what was evil in the sight of the LORD and to provoke him to anger. [y]

18 The LORD was thus very angry with Israel. He removed them from out of his sight, so that there were none of them left except for the tribe of Judah. [z]

19 Judah did not keep the commandments of the LORD, their God, but they walked in the practices that Israel had introduced. 20 The LORD rejected all of the descendants of Israel, punishing them and delivering

r Hos 10:14.—s 1 Chr 5:26; Isa 42:24.—t Ex 34:12-14; Mic 5:14.—u Jer 25:5.—v Acts 7:51.—w Jdg 2:20; Ps 78:10.—x 1 Ki 12:28; 16:33; Isa 40:26.—y Deut 18:10-12; Rom 7:14.—z 2 Thes 1:9.

16:18 *Took away the Sabbath canopy:* as a vassal to Tiglath-pileser, the king of Assyria, King Ahaz made several religious concessions, such as building a new altar, to please him. Ahaz's political mistake allowed the Assyrian king to take God's place as leader in Judah.

17:5-23 The capital falls (721 B.C.) after a three-year siege. The northern kingdom now vanishes, and a page of Israel's history is turned, with no hope of going back. The simple record of the event in verses 5-6 is followed by a spiritual comment, the result of long meditation, which recalls countless pages of the prophetic literature. Another account of the tragic events in the north is given in 2 Ki 18:9-12.

17:16 The reference is to the golden calves in Dan and Bethel (1 Ki 12:28).

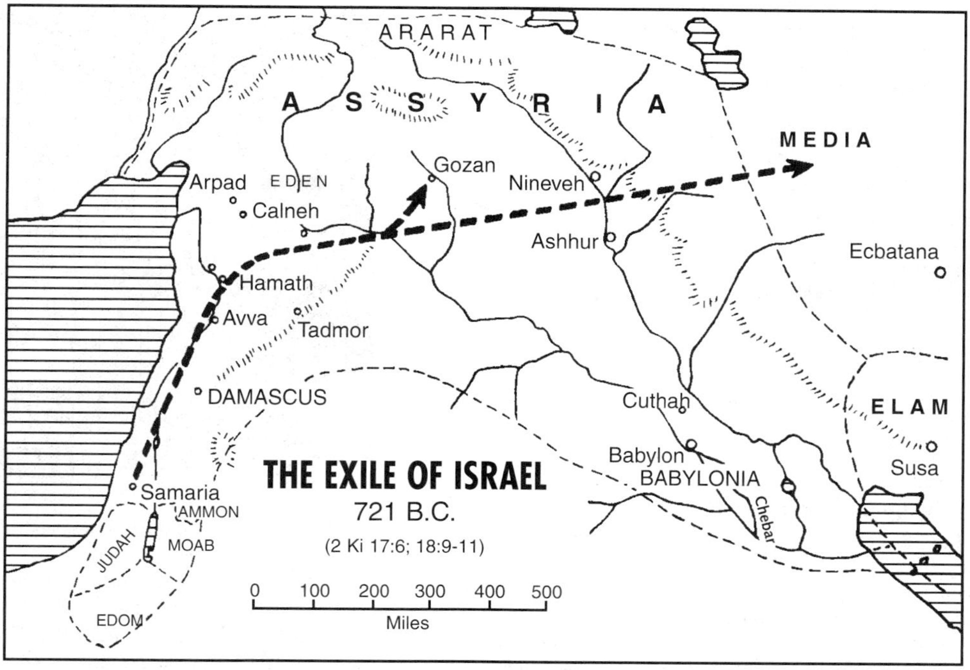

THE EXILE OF THE KINGDOM OF ISRAEL (721 B.C.: 2 Ki 17:6; 18:9-11) — **(a)** Shalmaneser V, king of Assyria, goes up against Hoshea who submits and pays tribute. However, Hoshea appeals to the king of Egypt and is cast into prison (2 Ki 17:1-4). **(b)** The king of Assyria occupies the whole land and besieges **Samaria** for three years. The city is finally captured by Sargon II, son of Shalmaneser in 721 B.C. (17:5-6). **(c)** The Israelites are deported to Halah at the Habor, a river of **Gozan,** and in the cities of **Media** (17:6).

Matson Photo Service

RUINS OF SAMARIA — On the left are the ruins of the old city gate of Samaria and on the right the ruins of the Grand Colonnade. Samaria, the capital of the northern kingdom, was set up like a fortress by Omri. When Ben-hadad II of Syria besieged Ahab there, he was unsuccessful; and in 724 B.C. when the Assyrians besieged it under Shalmaneser V (727–722 B.C.), it took them three years to overcome and finally destroy it under Sargon II (721–705 B.C.), his son, in 721 B.C. (See 1 Ki 20; 2 Ki 17:1-23.)

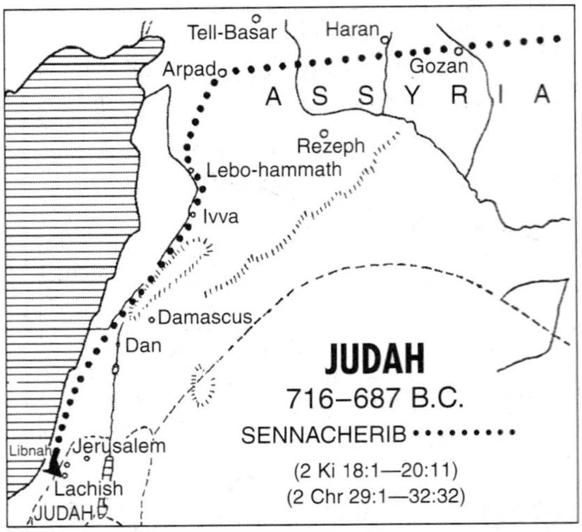

JUDAH UNDER SIEGE (2 Ki 18:1—20:11; Isa 36–37; 2 Chr 29–32) — (a) After purifying the temple and defeating the Philistines at Gaza, Hezekiah is attacked by Sennacherib fresh from victories in **Lebo-hamath** at **Arpad,** Sepharvaim, Hena, **Ivva,** and Samaria (2 Ki 18:8-27). **(b)** The Lord sends "an angel" driving Sennacherib to Nineveh (19:35-37) where he is killed by his sons and succeeded by his son, Esarhaddon (681 B.C.).

Oriental Museum

SARGON II BEFORE A GOD — Reconstructed wall painting showing Sargon II (721–705 B.C.) holding a mace and extending his fingers in supplication to his god who holds the rod and keys symbolizing authority. It was Sargon II who captured Samaria in 721 B.C. (See 2 Ki 18:7-12.)

British Museum

SENNACHERIB RECEIVING BOOTY FROM LACHISH — Stone relief from Nineveh showing Sennacherib of Assyria (704–681 B.C.) receiving prisoners and booty from the Canaanite city of Lachish. Sennacherib was the successor of Sargon II. Assyrian records (especially the Taylor Prism) give accounts of the campaigns he was waging in Palestine at the same time that he was attacking Jerusalem in 701 B.C. Though he did not take Jerusalem, he boasts that he "shut up Hezekiah like a bird in a cage." This corroborates the Bible account that the Lord delivered Jerusalem from Sennacherib. (See 2 Ki 18:13—19:17; 2 Chr 32:1-22; Isa 36:1—37:38.)

them into the hands of those who plundered
them until he had cast them out of his sight.
21 When he tore Israel away from the
house of David, they made Jeroboam, the
son of Nebat, their king. Jeroboam misled
Israel, causing them to turn away from fol-
lowing the LORD, making them commit a
great sin. [a] 22 The Israelites walked in all of
the sins that Jeroboam committed; they did
not turn away from them 23 until the LORD
had removed them from out of his sight as
he had predicted through all of his servants,
the prophets. Israel was exiled out of their
own land into Assyria where they are up
until the present.

Foreigners Deported to Samaria.* 24 The king
of Assyria brought people from Babylon,
Cuthah, Avva, Hamath, and Sepharvaim,
and he settled them in the cities of Samaria
to replace the Israelites. They took posses-
sion of Samaria and dwelt in its cities.
25 When they first began to dwell there,
they did not fear the LORD, so the LORD sent
lions among them which killed some of
them. 26 The king of Assyria was told, "The
nations that you deported and settled in the
cities of Samaria do not know the law of
the God of the land. This is why he sent lions
among them to kill them, because they did
not know the law of the God of the land."
27 The king of Assyria commanded,
"Carry one of the priests there whom you
deported. Let him go and dwell there to
teach them the law of the God of the land."
28 One of the priests whom they had car-
ried away from Samaria went and dwelt in
Bethel. He taught them how to fear the
LORD. 29 But all the nations still made their
own gods, and they placed their shrines on
the high places which the Samaritans had
made, each nation in their own cities where
they dwelt. 30 The men of Babylon made
Succoth-benoth, the men of Cuth made
Nergal, the men of Hamath made Ashima,
31 and the Avvites made Nibhaz and Tartak.
The Sepharvites burned their children in
fire to Adrammelech and Anammelech, the
gods of the Sepharvaim.
32 They also feared the LORD, and they
appointed priests for the high places from
their lowliest classes. They performed sacri-
fices for them in the shrines on the high
places. 33 So they feared the LORD but they
also served their own gods in the tradition of
the nations from which they had been carried
away. 34 Up to the present they still follow their
previous traditions. They do not fear the
LORD, and they do not observe the statutes or
the ordinances or the law or the command-
ment that the LORD had given to the children
of Jacob to whom he gave the name Israel. [b]
35 The LORD made a covenant with them
and ordered them, "You shall not fear other
gods,* nor shall you bow yourselves down to
them, nor shall you serve them, nor shall you
offer sacrifices to them. 36 You shall fear the
LORD who brought you up out of the land of
Egypt with great power and an outstretched
arm. You are to fear him, and you are to wor-
ship him, and you are to offer sacrifice to
him. [c] 37 You will always carefully observe the
statutes, the ordinances, the laws, and the
commandments that he wrote for you. You
are not to fear other gods. 38 You will not for-
get the covenant that I made with you, and
you are not to fear other gods. 39 You will fear
the LORD, your God. He will deliver you out
of the hands of all of your enemies."
40 However, they would not listen; they
practiced their previous traditions. 41 The
nations thus feared the LORD, but they also
served their graven images. Their children
and their grandchildren did what their
fathers had done, up to the present day.

VII: KINGDOM OF JUDAH AFTER 721 B.C.

CHAPTER 18

Hezekiah. 1 * Hezekiah, the son of Ahaz, the
king of Judah began to reign during the third
year of the reign of Hoshea, the son of Elah,
the king of Israel. 2 He began to reign when
he was twenty-five years old, and he reigned
for twenty-nine years in Jerusalem. His
mother's name was Abi, and she was the
daughter of Zechariah.

a 1 Ki 11:11.—b 1 Ki 18:31.—c Ex 6:6; Ps 136:12.

17:24-41 In accordance with Assyrian custom, the territory now largely deserted is repopulated by other peoples, who are taught to worship the Lord but who combine this with worship of the gods of their native lands. The resultant syncretism gives rise to the Samaritans, who will be regarded as heretics (Ezr 4:1-5; Sir 50:25), even in New Testament times (Jn 4:9, 20; 8:48; Acts 8:4-6; Lk 9:52; Mt 10:5). The mingling of the remaining Israelites with the newcomers was perhaps enough to explain the development.

17:35 *Not fear other gods:* from this point to verse 40, inclusive, the text picks up verse 23 and continues the reflection on the Israelites; the point is that they did not worship the Lord. Verse 41 refers again to the Samaritans.

18:1-8 Hezekiah's coming inaugurates a reign full of promise, for the new king is a true son of David, wholly devoted to the Lord. He is given four chapters (2 Chr 29–32) in Second Chronicles.

3 He did what was right in the sight of the
LORD, just as his father David had done. 4 He
eliminated the high places and he broke
down the pillars. He cut down the Asherah
and he broke into pieces the bronze serpent
that Moses had made, for up to those days
the Israelites had burned incense to it and
they called it Nehushtan. [d] 5 He trusted in
the LORD, the God of Israel, so much that
there was no one like him among all of the
kings of Judah who followed him or who
preceded him. 6 He held fast to the LORD,
and he did not depart from following after
him. He kept the commandments that the
LORD had given to Moses. 7 The LORD was
with him whenever he went forth and he
prospered.

He rebelled against the king of Assyria and
he refused to serve him. 8 He struck down the
Philistines as far as Gaza and its territory,
from its watchtower to its fortified city.

9 * In the fourth year of the reign of King
Hezekiah, which was the seventh year of the
reign of Hoshea, the son of Elah, the king of
Israel, Shalmaneser, the king of Assyria,
attacked Samaria and besieged it. 10 At the
end of three years he captured it. It was in
the sixth year of the reign of Hezekiah, which
was the ninth year of the reign of Hoshea, the
king of Israel, that Samaria was captured.

11 The king of Assyria deported Israel to
Assyria. He settled them in Halah, on the
Habor, the river of Gozan, and in the cities of
the Medes. [e] 12 This happened because they
did not listen to the voice of the LORD, their
God. They transgressed his covenant, every-
thing that Moses, the servant of the LORD,
had commanded. They would not listen nor
would they obey.

Invasion of Sennacherib. 13 Sennacherib, the
king of Assyria, came up against all of the
fortified cities of Judah, and he captured
them during the fourteenth year of the reign
of King Hezekiah. [f] 14 Hezekiah, the king of
Judah, sent a message to the king of Assyria
at Lachish saying, "I am guilty; withdraw
from me and I will pay any penalty you
decide." The king of Assyria required
Hezekiah, the king of Judah, to pay three
hundred talents of silver and thirty talents of
gold. 15 Hezekiah gave him all of the silver
that was to be found in the temple of the
LORD and the treasury of the royal palace.

16 It was at this time that Hezekiah
stripped the gold from the doors to the tem-
ple of the LORD and from the doorposts that
Hezekiah, the king of Judah, had overlaid. He
gave it to the king of Assyria. [g]

17 The king of Assyria sent the general, the
lord chamberlain, and the commander
along with a large army from Lachish to
King Hezekiah in Jerusalem. They went up
and came to Jerusalem. When they arrived,
they stood by the conduit of the upper pool
that is on the highway in the Fuller's Field.
18 They called out for the king, and Eliakim,
the son of Hilkiah, the major-domo, Sheb-
na, the scribe, Joah, the son of Asaph, who
kept the archives, came out to them. [h]

19 The commander said to them, "Say this
to Hezekiah: 'Thus says the great king, the
king of Assyria: What is the source of your
hope in which you trust? 20 You say (but they
are only empty words), "I have counsel and
strength for war!" Now, on whom do you rely
that makes you willing to rebel against me?
21 Behold, you have placed your confidence
upon the staff of this bruised reed, you trust
in Egypt, which, if someone were to lean on
it, it would pierce his hand, going through it.
That is what Pharaoh, the king of Egypt, is to
all who trust in him. [i] 22 But if you say to me,
"We trust in the LORD, our God," is he not
the one whose high places and altars
Hezekiah has eliminated, for he said to
Judah and Jerusalem, "You will worship
before this altar in Jerusalem." '

23 "Therefore, give your pledge to my lord,
the king of Assyria: I will give you two thou-
sand horses, if you are able to put riders on
them. 24 How could you repulse the least
important of my master's servants even
though you are trusting Egypt for chariots
and horsemen? 25 Was it apart from the
LORD I have now come up to destroy this
place? The LORD said to me, 'Go up to attack
this land and destroy it.' "

26 Then Eliakim, the son of Hilkiah,
Shebna, and Joah said to the commander,
"Please speak to your servants in Aramaic,
for we understand it. Please do not speak to

d 2 Chr 31:1; Isa 36:7; Wis 16:5-7; Jn 3:14.—e Isa 37:12.—f Isa 1:7; Mic 1:9.—g 2 Chr 29:3.—h Isa 22:15-25.—i Jer 25:15, 19; 37:7; Ezek 29:6.

18:9—19:7 Hezekiah is forced to pay tribute to Sennacherib, the powerful king of Assyria (704–681 B.C.). The conqueror from the east is not satisfied with this, however, and becomes threatening and overbearing. The section from 18:13 to 20:19 is repeated, with some variations in Isa 36–39. Isaiah is the prophet who strengthens Hezekiah's steadfastness and trust in God.

us in Hebrew when the people who are upon
the wall can hear it." *
27 But the commander said to them, "My
master has not sent me just to you and your
master to say these things, but to the men sit-
ting on the wall who may have to eat their
own dung and drink their own urine like you."
28 The commander then stood and cried
out in a loud voice in Hebrew, "Hear the
word of the great king of Assyria! 29 Thus
says the king: Do not let Hezekiah deceive
you. He cannot deliver you out of my hands.
30 Do not let Hezekiah convince you to trust
in the LORD, saying, 'The LORD will surely
deliver us; this city will not be delivered over
into the hands of the king of Assyria.' 31 Do
not listen to Hezekiah, for thus says the king
of Assyria: Make peace with me by paying
tribute. Then, come out and eat from your
own vines and from your own fig trees and
drink water from your own cistern 32 until I
take you away to a land which is like your
own, a land of grain and wine, a land of
bread and vineyards, a land of olive oil and
honey. Live, do not die.

"Do not listen to Hezekiah when he tries
to convince you saying, 'The LORD will deliv-
er us.' 33 Have the gods of any of the nations
delivered their land out of the hands of the
king of Assyria? 34 Where are the gods of
Hamath and Arpad? Where are the gods of
Shepharvaim, Henah, and Ivvah? Did they
rescue Samaria from out of my hands?
35 "Which of the gods from any of the
nations has delivered their land from out of
my hands? How could the LORD deliver
Jerusalem out of my hands?"
36 But the people remained silent and they
did not say a word to him, for the king had
commanded them, "You are not to answer
him."
37 Then Eliakim, the major-domo, Shebna
the scribe, and Joah, the son of Asaph, who
kept the archives, went to Hezekiah with
their torn clothes, and they told him what
the commander had said.

CHAPTER 19

Hezekiah and Isaiah. 1 When King Heze-
kiah heard this, he tore his clothes, put on
sackcloth, and went into the temple of the
LORD.
2 He sent Eliakim, the major-domo,
Shebna, the scribe, and all of the elders of
the priests, all wearing sackcloth, to Isaiah
the prophet, the son of Amoz. 3 They said to
him, "This is what Hezekiah says: Today is a
day of trouble and rebuke and disgrace, as
when children come to term but there is not
enough strength to deliver them. 4 Perhaps
the LORD, your God, will hear the words of
the commander whom the king of Assyria,
his master, has sent to taunt the living God.
Perhaps he will rebuke him for the words
which the LORD, your God, has heard.
Therefore, raise up a prayer for the survivors
who still remain." [j]
5 When King Hezekiah's servants came to
Isaiah, 6 Isaiah said to them, "This is what
you are to tell your master: Thus says the
LORD: Do not let the words you have heard,
the words by which the king of Assyria blas-
phemed me, do not let them frighten you.
7 Behold, I will send a spirit into him so that
when he hears a certain rumor, he will
return to his own land. I will have him cut
down by the sword in his own land." [k]
8 When the commander returned, he
heard that the king of Assyria had with-
drawn from Lachish and he found him in
Libnah. 9 He had heard a report concerning
Tirhakah, the king of Ethiopia, saying,
"Behold, he has come to fight against you."

So he once again sent messengers to
Hezekiah, saying, 10 "Say this to Hezekiah,
the king of Judah: 'Do not let your God in
whom you trust deceive you when he tells
you that Jerusalem will be delivered out of
the hands of the king of Assyria. 11 You have
heard what the king of Assyria has done to
every land, totally destroying them. Will you
then be delivered? 12 Did the gods of the
nations that were destroyed by my ancestors
deliver them, the gods of Gozan, Haran,
Rezeph, and the Edomites who were in Tel-
assar? 13 Where is the king of Hamath? The
king of Arpad? The king of the city of
Shepharvaim? Of Hena? Of Ivvah?' "
14 Hezekiah took the letter from the hand
of the messenger and he read it. He then
went to the temple of the LORD and he
spread it out before the LORD.
15 Hezekiah prayed to the LORD, saying, "O
LORD, God of Israel, who dwells between the
cherubim, you alone are the God of all of the
nations on the earth. You made the heavens
and the earth. [l] 16 Bend your ear, O LORD,

j Gen 45:7; 1 Sam 17:36.—k Ex 14:24; Jer 51:46.—l Ex 25:22; Jos 2:11.

18:26 Aramaic was beginning to be the language of international relations in the Middle East. The people understood only the Jewish language, that is, the Hebrew spoken in Jerusalem.

and hear. Open your eyes, O LORD, and see.
Hear the words that Sennacherib has sent to
taunt the living God. 17 It is true, O LORD,
that the kings of Assyria have destroyed the
nations and their lands. 18 They have cast
their gods into the flames, for they were not
really gods. They were only the work of
human hands, made from wood and stone.
19 Now, O LORD, our God, deliver us from out
of his hands so that all of the kingdoms upon
the earth might know that you, O LORD, are
the only God."[m]

Punishment of Sennacherib. 20 Isaiah, the
son of Amoz, then sent to Hezekiah, saying,
"Thus says the LORD, the God of Israel: 'I
have heard your prayer to me concerning
Sennacherib, the king of Assyria.'

21 * "This is the word that the LORD has
spoken about him:

"The virgin daughter of Zion
despises you and laughs at you.
The daughter of Jerusalem
tosses her head at you.
22 Whom have you taunted and blasphemed?
Against whom have you raised your voice
and lifted your eyes in pride?
Against the Holy One of Israel.
23 You have taunted the LORD through your messengers by saying,
'I have come up to the heights of the mountains
with many chariots, to the peaks of Lebanon.
I have cut down tall cedars,
choice fir trees.
I have entered its most remote stand,
its finest forests.
24 I have dug wells in foreign lands and drunk the water.
I have dried up the streams of Egypt
with the soles of my feet.'

25 "Have you not heard?
Long ago I established it,
in ancient times I planned it.
Now I have ordained that you break down
fortified cities into piles of ruins.
26 Their inhabitants, having lost their power,
have become dismayed and confounded.
They are like the grass in the field,
like a green plant,
like grass growing on the roof
that is scorched before it can grow.
27 But I know where you live,
your going out, your coming in,
and how you rage against me.
28 The face that you rage against
and your arrogance have reached my ears.
I will put a ring in your nose
and a bridle in your mouth.
I will force you to return the way by which you came.[n]

29 "This will be a sign for you:
This year you will eat what grows by itself,
and the next year you will eat what springs from that.
But in the third year you will sow and reap,
you will plant vineyards and eat its fruit.
30 Once more a remnant of Judah that has escaped
will take root below
and bear fruit above.
31 Out of Jerusalem a remnant will come,
out of Mount Zion survivors.
The zeal of the LORD of hosts will do this.

32 "Therefore, thus says the LORD
concerning the king of Assyria:
He will not enter this city,
nor will he shoot an arrow there.
He will not come before it with a shield,
nor will he cast up a siege-work against it.
33 He will return by the way he came,
but he will not enter the city, says the LORD,
34 I will defend this city and save it, for my own sake
and that of David, my servant."[o]

35 That night an angel of the LORD went out
and killed one hundred eighty-five thousand
of the Assyrians.[p] 36 Sennacherib, the king of
Assyria withdrew, departed, and returned to
Nineveh.

37 Once, when he was worshiping in the
temple of his god Nisroch, his sons Adrammelech
and Sharezer cut him down by the
sword. They escaped into the land of

m 1 Ki 18:36; Ps 83:18.—n Job 41:2; Ezek 29:4.—o 1 Ki 11:12-13.—p 2 Chr 32:21; Nah 3:3.

19:21-34 This psalm, repeated in Isa 37:22-35, expresses pride and speaks the language of hope.

Armenia, and Esarhaddon reigned in his stead.

CHAPTER 20

Hezekiah's Illness. 1 In those days Hezekiah fell ill, and his death was approaching. Isaiah, the son of Amoz, the prophet, came to him and said, "Thus says the LORD: Set your house in order, for you are to die, you will not survive."

2 Hezekiah turned his face to the wall and prayed, saying, 3 "Please remember, O LORD, how I walked before you in fidelity and with a perfect heart. I have done what was good in your sight." And Hezekiah wept bitterly.[q]

4 The word of the LORD came to Isaiah before he left the middle courtyard, saying, 5 "Return and tell Hezekiah, the leader of my people: Thus says the LORD, the God of David, your father: I have heard, I have seen your tears. I will heal you today, and the day after tomorrow you will go up to the temple of the LORD. 6 I will add fifteen years to your life. I will deliver you and this city out of the hands of the king of Assyria. I will defend this city for my own sake and that of David, my servant."

7 Isaiah said, "Prepare a fig poultice." They took it and laid it on the boil, and he recovered.

8 Hezekiah said to Isaiah, "What is the sign that the LORD will heal me, and on the day after tomorrow I will go up into the temple of the LORD?" 9 Isaiah answered, "This is the sign that you will receive from the LORD that the LORD is going to do what he said: shall the shade climb up ten stairs, or go down ten stairs?"

10 Hezekiah answered, "It is too easy for the shade to go down ten stairs. No, let the shade go back up ten stairs."

11 Isaiah the prophet cried out to the LORD, and he brought the shade back up the ten stairs that it had gone down on the stairway of Ahaz.

12 At that time Merodach-baladan, the son of Baladan, the king of Babylon, sent letters and a gift to Hezekiah for he had heard that Hezekiah was ill. 13 Hezekiah listened to them and showed them his entire treasure house, the silver, the gold, the spices, and the precious ointments as well as the armory in the treasury. There was nothing in his palace or his dominion that Hezekiah failed to show them.

14 Isaiah the prophet came to Hezekiah and said to him, "What did these men say to you? Where did they come from?" Hezekiah answered, "They came from a distant land, from Babylon." 15 He said, "What have they seen in your palace?" Hezekiah answered, "They have seen everything in my palace; they did not miss any of my treasures."

16 Isaiah the prophet said to Hezekiah, "Listen to the word of the LORD: 17 Behold, the days are coming when everything in your palace, everything that your ancestors collected up to the present, will be carried off to Babylon. Nothing will be left, nothing, says the LORD.[r] 18 Some of your sons who come forth from you, whom you begot, will be taken away. They will become eunuchs in the palace of the king of Babylon."

19 Hezekiah said to Isaiah, "The word of the LORD that you have spoken is good," for he thought, "Will there not be peace and security in my days?"

20 Now the rest of the deeds of Hezekiah, his achievements, and how he built a pool and a conduit* that brought water into the city, are they not written in the book of the chronicles of the kings of Judah?[s]

21 Hezekiah slept with his fathers, and Manasseh, his son, reigned in his stead.

CHAPTER 21

Reign of Manasseh. 1 Manasseh was twelve years old when he began to reign, and he reigned for fifty-five years in Jerusalem. His mother's name was Hephzibah.

2 He did what was evil in the sight of the LORD, practicing the abominations of the nations whom the LORD cast out before the Israelites. 3 He rebuilt the high places that Hezekiah, his father, had destroyed. He raised up altars to Baal, and he made an Asherah, just as Ahab, the king of Israel, had done. He also worshiped the hosts of heaven* and served them.[t] 4 He built altars in the temple of the LORD of which the LORD

q 1 Ki 2:4; 2 Chr 31:20; Neh 13:22.—r 2 Ki 24:13; Jer 52:17-23.—s 2 Chr 32:32; Neh 3:16.—t 1 Ki 16:31-33; Jdg 6:28.

20:20 *Conduit:* the tunnel from the pool or cistern of Siloam; it was explored in 1880. It was a justly famous piece of work, since it had to be bored through rock.

21:3 *Hosts of heaven:* worship of the stars had been introduced as a result of Judah's becoming a vassal of Assyria (see 2 Ki 17:16).

had stated, "I will place my name in Jerusalem." 5 He built altars for the hosts of heaven in the two courts of the temple of the LORD. 6 He burned his son in flames, practiced witchcraft, used divination, and cooperated with mediums and wizards. He did horrible things in the sight of the LORD, provoking the LORD to anger.[u] 7 He set up a carved image of the Asherah in the temple about which the LORD had said to David and to Solomon, his son, "In this temple and in Jerusalem, which I have chosen from out of the tribes of Israel, I will place my name forever,[v] 8 nor will I make the feet of Israel wander from the land that I have given to their fathers if only they will be careful to do everything that I have commanded them, everything according to the law that Moses, my servant, gave them."

9 But they would not listen, and Manasseh enticed them to do more evil than the nations that the LORD had destroyed before the Israelites had done.

10 The LORD therefore spoke through his servant, the prophets, saying, 11 "Manasseh, the king of Judah, has committed these abominations, doing worse things than the Amorites who preceded him, causing Judah to sin with his idols.[w] 12 Therefore, thus says the LORD, the God of Israel: Behold, I am bringing a terrible disaster upon Jerusalem and Judah that is so bad that the ears of those who hear about it will tingle. 13 * I will stretch out over Jerusalem the measuring line that I used against Samaria and the plumb line I used against the house of Ahab.[x] 14 I will wipe out Jerusalem as one wipes out a dish, wiping it out and turning it over. I will abandon the remnant of my inheritance, and I will deliver them into the hands of their enemies. They will be plunder and booty to all of their enemies 15 for they have done what is evil in my sight, provoking me to anger from the day that their fathers came forth from Egypt even up to the present day."

16 Manasseh had shed so much blood that it covered Jerusalem from one end to the other. He caused Judah to sin, doing what was evil in the sight of the LORD.[y]

17 As for the other deeds of Manasseh, what he did, and the sins that he committed, are they not written in the book of the chronicles of the kings of Judah?

18 Manasseh slept with his fathers, and he was buried in his palace gardens, the Garden of Uzza.

Reign of Amon. Amon, his son, then reigned in his stead. 19 Amon was twenty-two years old when he began to reign, and he reigned for two years in Jerusalem. His mother's name was Meshullemeth. She was the daughter of Haruz from Jotbah.

20 He did what was evil in the sight of the LORD, as his father Manasseh had done. 21 He walked in all of the ways of his father. He served the idols that his father had served, and he worshiped them. 22 He abandoned the LORD, the God of his fathers, and he did not walk in the ways of the LORD.

23 Amon's servants plotted against him, and they killed him in his own palace. 24 The people of the land then plotted against all of those who killed King Ahab, and the people of the land made Josiah, his son, king in his stead.

25 As for the other deeds of Amon, what he did, are they not written in the book of the chronicles of the kings of Judah?

26 He was buried in his own grave in the Garden of Uzza, and his son Josiah reigned in his stead.

CHAPTER 22

Reign of Josiah.* 1 Josiah was eight years old when he began to reign, and he reigned for thirty-one years in Jerusalem. His mother's name was Jedidah, and she was the daughter of Adaiah from Bozkath.

2 He did what was right in the sight of the LORD, and he walked in the ways of David, his father. He did not wander off to the right or to the left.

The Book of the Law.* 3 During the eighteenth year of the reign of King Josiah, the king sent Shaphan the scribe, the son of Azaliah, the son of Meshullam, to the tem-

u Lev 18:21; 19:26; Deut 18:10.—v 2 Sam 7:13; 1 Ki 8:29; 9:3; Jer 32:34.—w Gen 15:16; Ezek 18:12.—x Isa 34:11; Lam 2:8; Am 7:7-9.—y Pss 10:11; 94:7.

21:13-14 Two customary metaphors for expressing a fate: Jerusalem will be treated as Samaria had been. The dish is abandoned when everything on it has been removed.

22:1-2 Josiah, a new David and a new Hezekiah, is a king according to God's heart. The reader desiring to follow the religious developments and political vicissitudes of this final period of the kingdom of Judah should read the relevant passages in Jeremiah, which make known the positions taken by the prophet as events followed ever faster on one another. See also 2 Chr 34–35.

22:3-20 The Book is Deuteronomy, the "Second Law," which repeated the law of Moses while adapting it. More accurately, perhaps, the book is the central, legislative part of Deuteronomy, which in fact inspires the reform then effected by Josiah. It must have been hidden or lost, or in any case forgotten, during the wicked reign of Manasseh.

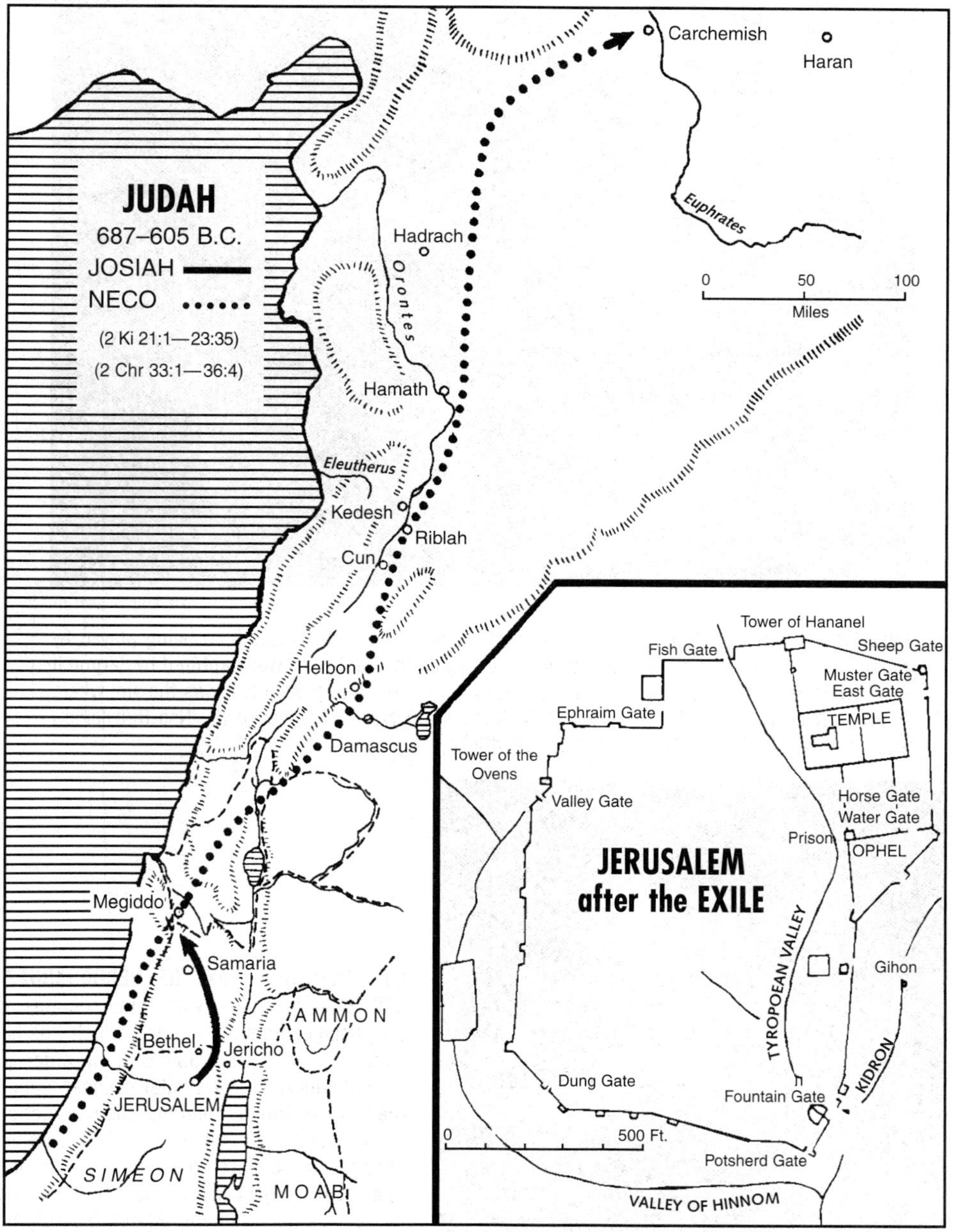

JUDAH UNDER JOSIAH (640–609 B.C.: 2 Ki 22:1—23:30; 2 Chr 34–35) — **(a)** Reign of justice. Discovery of the book of the law. Josiah orders the destruction of the idolatrous temples of **Bethel,** of the high places of **Samaria,** Manasseh, Ephraim, **Simeon,** Naphtali. Solemn celebrations of the Passover, and renewal of the covenant (22:1—23:27). **(b)** Neco, king of Egypt, crosses Palestine to come to the aid of the king of Assyria (Ashurbanipal) against the king of Babylon. Josiah confronts him on the plain of **Megiddo** and is killed there (23:28-30). **(c)** Jehoahaz succeeds Josiah and reigns only three months. Neco captures him at **Riblah,** puts him in exile in Egypt, and replaces him by Eliakim, to whom he gives the name of Jehoiakim (23:31-34). **(d)** In 605 B.C., the battle of **Carchemish** takes place in which Nebuchadnezzar defeats the Egyptians (Neco) and drives them back to **Hamath.**

British Museum

MUSICIANS FROM CARCHEMISH — The basalt relief shows a drum and horn being played by musicians of Carchemish. This important Hittite city on the Euphrates was captured by Sargon II in 717 B.C. (see Isa 10:9) and became the capital of an Assyrian province. It was the site where Pharaoh Neco was defeated in 605 B.C. by Nebuchadnezzar II, founder of the Neo-Babylonian empire (604–561 B.C.). (See 2 Chr 35:20; Jer 48:2.)

CYLINDER WITH TEXT OF NEBUCHADNEZZAR II — A cylinder with three columns of text, each containing 96 lines, which was inscribed shortly after 586 B.C. by order of Nebuchadnezzar II. A similar cylinder, called the Weidner Tablet, mentions the destruction of the land of Jerusalem in 597 B.C. Nebuchadnezzar boasts that he "encamped against the city of Judah and on the second day of the month Adar (March 15/16), he seized the city and captured the king. He appointed there a king of his own choice, received its heavy tribute and sent them to Babylon." All of this agrees perfectly with the Bible account. (See 2 Ki 24:10-17.)

University Museum

ple. He said,[z] 4 “Go up to Hilkiah, the high
priest. Have him count the money that the
doorkeepers have collected from the people
in the temple of the LORD. 5 Have him give it
to the supervisors of the workmen in the
temple of the LORD. Have them pay those
who are working to repair the damage in the
temple of the LORD: 6 the carpenters, the
builders, and the masons. Also have them
buy timber and hewn stone to repair the
temple. 7 They do not need to make an
accounting of the money that has been given
to them because they have acted honestly.”

8 Hilkiah, the high priest, said to Shaphan,
the scribe, “I have found the book of the law
in the temple of the LORD.” Hilkiah gave the
book to Shaphan who read it.[a]

9 Then Shaphan the scribe went to the king
and he brought the king a report saying,
“Your servants have gathered together the
money that has been collected in the temple,
and they have handed it over to the supervi-
sors of the workmen in the temple of the
LORD.” 10 Then Shaphan the scribe informed
the king, “Hilkiah the priest has given me a
book.” Shaphan read it in the presence of the
king.

11 When the king heard the words of the
book of the law, he tore his clothes. 12 King
Josiah gave orders to Hilkiah the priest,
Ahikam, the son of Shaphan, Achbor, the son
of Micaiah, Shaphan the scribe, and Asaiah,
the king’s servant, saying, 13 “Go and inquire
of the LORD for me and for all of the people
and for all of Judah about the words of the
book that had been found. The LORD’s anger
against us is great for our fathers have not
heeded the words of this book. They did not
do everything that is written in it concerning
us.”[b]

14 Hilkiah the priest, Ahikam, Achbor,
Shaphan, and Asaiah went to the prophetess
Huldah, the wife of Shallum, the guardian
of the wardrobe, the son of Tikvah, the son of
Harhas. She lived in the second district of
Jerusalem. They spoke with her. 15 She said
to them, “Thus says the LORD, the God of
Israel, go tell the man who sent you to me:
16 Thus says the LORD: Behold, I will bring
disaster upon this place and upon all of those
who live in it, everything that is in the book
that the king of Judah has read. 17 They have
forsaken me, and they have burned incense
to other gods, provoking me to anger with all
the deeds of their hands. My wrath will blaze
out against this place and it will not be
quenched.

18 “But as for the king of Judah who sent
you to inquire of the LORD, this is what you
will say to him: Thus says the LORD, the God
of Israel: As for the words that you have
heard, 19 because your heart was penitent
and you have humbled yourself before the
LORD when you heard how I spoke against
this place and against its inhabitants, that
they would become a desolation and a curse,
and you tore your clothes and you wept
before me, I have also heard you, says the
LORD.[c] 20 Therefore, I will gather you to your
fathers, and you will be gathered to your
grave in peace, so that you will not have to
look upon all of the evil that I will bring upon
this place with your own eyes.” They brought
the report back to the king.

CHAPTER 23

Josiah the Reformer. 1 The king then sent
and assembled all of the elders of Judah and
Jerusalem. 2 The king went up to the temple
of the LORD, and all of the men of Judah and
all the inhabitants of Jerusalem went with
him, including the priests, the prophets, and
all of the people, both the humble and the
important. He read aloud all of the words
from the book of the covenant that had been
found in the temple of the LORD.[d]

3 The king stood by the pillar, and he made
a covenant before the LORD to follow the
LORD and to observe his commandments,
his testimonies, and his statutes with all his
heart and all his soul, fulfilling the words of
this covenant that were written in this book.
All of the people joined in the covenant.

4 The king commanded Hilkiah the high
priest, and the priests of the second order,
and the doormen to carry out of the temple
of the LORD all of the utensils that had been
used for Baal, for Asherah, and for the heav-
enly host. He burned them outside of
Jerusalem in a field in the Kidron Valley, and
they took their ashes to Bethel.[e]

5 He expelled the pagan priests whom the
kings of Judah had appointed to burn
incense on the high places in the cities of
Judah and those that surrounded Je-
rusalem, those who had burned incense to
Baal, to the sun, the moon, the planets, and

z 2 Chr 34:8ff.—**a** Deut 31:24.—**b** 1 Sam 9:9.—**c** Lev 26:31; Isa 57:15; Jer 26:6.—**d** Ex 24:7; Deut 31:11.—**e** Sir 49:3.

to all of the hosts of heaven.[f] 6 He brought the Asherah out of the temple of the LORD, taking it outside of Jerusalem to the Kidron Valley. He smashed it to pieces, tossing its dust upon the graves of the common people.

7 He also tore down the quarters that housed the male prostitutes in the temple of the LORD, and where the women did the weavings for the Asherah.[g] 8 He brought all of the priests from the cities of Judah, and he desecrated all of the high places from Geba to Beer-sheba where the priests had burned incense. He demolished the shrines at the gates, at the entrance to the gate of Joshua, the leader of the city, which was to the left of the city gate. 9 Although the priests of the high places did not go up to the altar of the LORD, they did eat the unleavened bread with their brethren.

10 He desecrated Topheth* in the Valley of Ben-hinnom so that no one could sacrifice his son or daughter in fire to Molech.[h] 11 He removed the horses that the king of Judah had dedicated to the sun at the entrance to the temple of the LORD. They had been in the court near the room of the official Nathan-melech. He burned the chariots dedicated to the sun.

12 The king demolished the altars* that the kings of Judah had built on the roof near the upper room of Ahaz as well as the two altars that Manasseh had built in the two courts of the temple of the LORD. He broke them to pieces and cast them into the Kidron Valley.[i] 13 The king also desecrated the high places that were to the east of Jerusalem, that is, to the south of the Hill of Corruption which Solomon, the king of Israel, had dedicated to the Ashtaroth, the vile goddess of the Sidonians, to Chemosh, the vile god of the Moabites, and to Molech, the abomination of the Ammonites.

14 He smashed the sacred pillars and cut down the Asherah. He defiled these places with human bones. 15 He broke down the altar in Bethel, the altar and the high place that Jeroboam, the son of Nebat, who caused Israel to sin, had built. He burned the high place and crushed it to powder, and he also burned the Asherah.

16 Josiah looked around and when he saw that there were graves on the hillside, he sent for and removed the bones from the graves. He burned them upon the altar to defile it. This fulfilled the word of the LORD that the man of God had proclaimed through these words.

17 He then asked, "What is that monument that I see?" The men of the city told him, "It is the tomb of the man of God who came from Judah and proclaimed these things that you have done against the altar of Bethel." 18 He said, "Leave it alone! Do not let anyone disturb his bones!" So they left his bones and the bones of the prophet who had come from Samaria.

19 Josiah also removed all of the shrines of the high places in the cities of Samaria that the kings of Israel had established, thus provoking the LORD to anger, just as he had done at Bethel.[j]

20 Josiah killed all of the priests of the high places upon the altars and he burned human bones upon them. He then returned to Jerusalem.

21 The king then commanded all of the people saying, "Observe the Passover of the LORD, your God, according to what is written in this book of this covenant."[k] 22 Passover had not been observed from the days of the judges who governed Israel nor all throughout the days of the kings of Israel and the kings of Judah. 23 This Passover of the LORD was celebrated in Jerusalem in the eighteenth year of the reign of King Josiah.

24 Josiah also expelled the mediums and the wizards. He did away with the household gods, the idols, and all the other abominations that were to be found in the land of Judah and Jerusalem. He did this to fulfill the words of the law that were written in the book that Hilkiah the priest found in the temple of the LORD.[l]

25 There had never before been any king like him nor will there ever be one after him who turned to the LORD with all his heart and all his soul and all his might according to the law of Moses.[m]

26 In spite of this, the LORD did not turn away the heat of his fierce anger which raged against Judah because all of the things that Manasseh had done to provoke his anger.

f Jer 8:2.—g 1 Ki 14:24; Ezek 16:16.—h Lev 18:21; Isa 30:33; Jer 7:31.—i Jer 19:13; Zep 1:5.—j 2 Chr 34:6-7.—k Ex 12:3; Num 9:2.—l Gen 31:19; Deut 18:10-12.—m Sir 49:1-3; Jer 22:15.

23:10 *Topheth:* a crematory for the sacrifice of children.

23:12 *Altars:* dedicated to the astral divinities (see 2 Ki 21:3f; Jer 19:13; Zep 1:5).

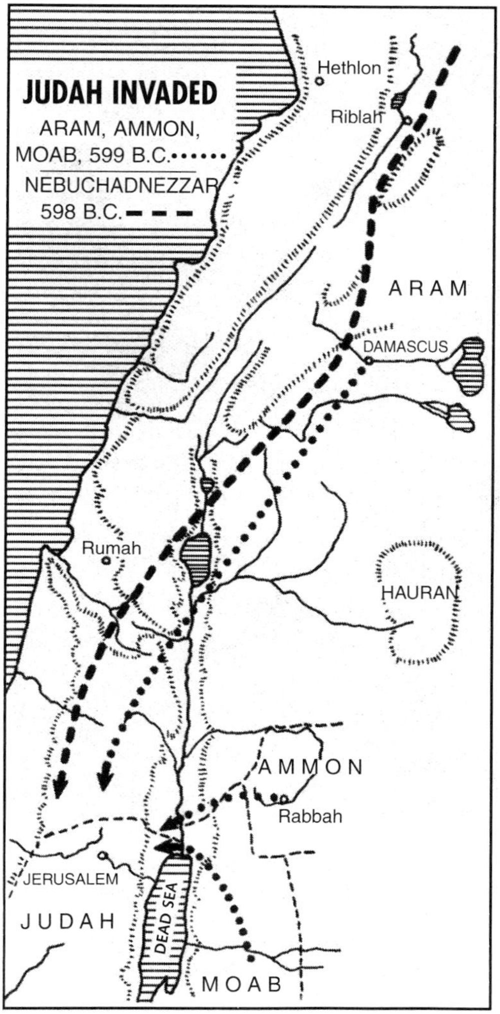

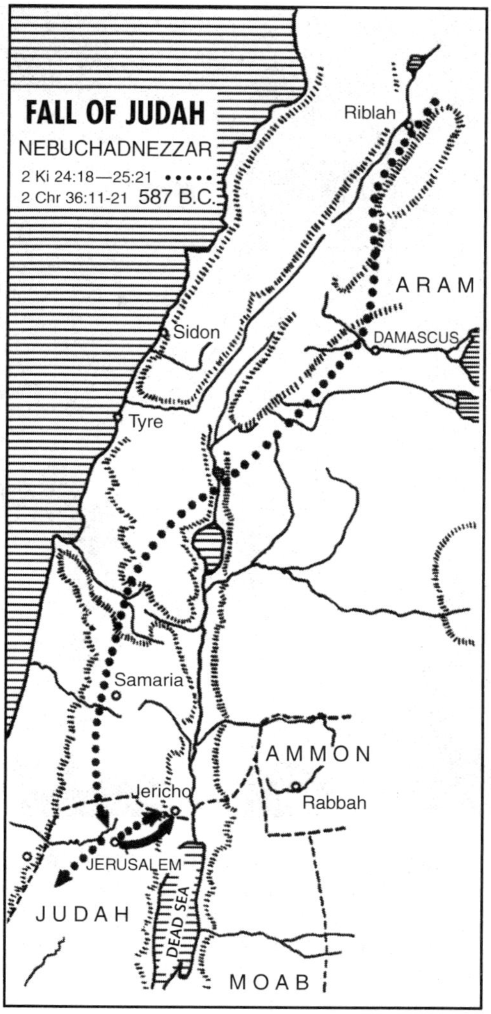

JUDAH INVADED (609–598 B.C.: 2 Ki 23:36—24:6; 2 Chr 36:5-8; Jer 26:36) — **(a)** Jehoiakim submits to Nebuchadnezzar and remains subjugated for three years (24:1). **(b)** Jeremiah prophesies the ruin of Jerusalem (Jer 26). **(c)** Jehoiakim attempts a revolt. But he sees his country invaded by the Chaldeans, the Syrians, the Moabites, and the Ammonites, encouraged by Nebuchadnezzar who is occupied elsewhere (2 Ki 24:2-3). **(d)** In 598 B.C., Jehoiachim becomes king and the first siege of Jerusalem, by Nebuchadnezzar, takes place. Jehoiachim goes there with all his family; he is deported into Babylon. His uncle Mattaniah is established as king under the name Zedekiah (24:8-17).

FALL OF JUDAH (587 B.C.: 2 Ki 24:18—25:21; 2 Chr 36:11-21) — **(a)** In 588 B.C., Zedekiah, counting on help from Hophra, king of Egypt, revolts against Assyria (2 Ki 24:18-20). Nebuchadnezzar once again comes down from Babylon and besieges Jerusalem. He lifts the siege temporarily while he goes off to defeat Hophra but returns and defeats Zedekiah at **Jericho.** He returns to Jerusalem and takes the city in 587 B.C., tears down its walls and carries off thousands of people into exile into **Babylon** (25:1-21). **(b)** The Jews in exile are comforted by the prophets Deutero-Isaiah and Ezekiel. **(c)** In 538 B.C., Cyrus the Mede captures Babylon and allows the exiles to start back for home under Zerubbabel (Ezr 1:1—2:10). **(d)** Over the next two hundred years, the Jewish commonwealth is reestablished (as part of the generally benevolent Persian Empire) with the aid, especially, of Nehemiah the court official and Ezra the scribe.

Oriental Museum

NEBUCHADNEZZAR'S BABYLON (RESTORED) — A view of ancient Babylon (restored according to Unger). Nebuchadnezzar wished to make it the most famous city of the world in his time; he built new canals and navigable waterways, erected magnificent buildings, and built extensive parks. Its size and splendor amazed all who saw it. It was to this city that the Israelites were exiled after Jerusalem was besieged by Nebuchadnezzar for eighteen months and destroyed in 587 B.C. (See 2 Ki 25.)

Oriental Museum

RUINS OF NEBUCHADNEZZAR'S PALACE — A view of the ruins of Nebuchadnezzar's palace at Babylon, along whose east side ran the sacred procession street, decorated with enameled tiles representing the dragon and the bull, to the Ishtar gate at the southeast corner. In 538 B.C., the Persian king, Cyrus the Great, conquered Babylon without encountering resistance and shortly afterward, the Hebrew exiles were allowed to return home. (See 2 Chr 36:22-23; Ezr 1:1-6.)

27 The LORD said, "I will remove Judah from
out of my sight just as I have removed Israel.
I will reject this city that I have chosen,
Jerusalem, and the temple of which I said:
My name will be there."

28 * As for all of the other deeds of Josiah,
what he did, are they not written in the book
of the chronicles of the kings of Judah?

29 During his reign, Pharaoh Neco, the
king of Egypt, traveled up to the Euphrates
River to give his assistance to the king of
Assyria. King Josiah attacked him. When
Pharaoh Neco saw him at Megiddo, he killed
him. [n] 30 His servants brought his dead body
back from Megiddo to Jerusalem and they
buried him in his own tomb.

The people of the land took Jehoahaz, the
son of Josiah, and they anointed him as king
in his father's stead.

Reign of Jehoahaz. 31 Jehoahaz was twenty-
three years old when he began to reign, and
he reigned for three months in Jerusalem.
His mother's name was Hamutal, and she
was the daughter of Jeremiah from Libnah.

32 He did what was evil in the sight of the
LORD, everything that his fathers had done.

33 Pharaoh Neco imprisoned him at
Riblah in the land of Hamath so that he
could not reign in Jerusalem. He imposed a
tribute upon the land of one hundred talents
of silver and a talent of gold. *

34 Pharaoh Neco appointed Eliakim, the
son of Josiah, as king in his father's stead. He
changed his name to Jehoiakim, and he took
Jehoahaz away when he returned to Egypt,
where he died.

35 Jehoiakim gave silver and gold to
Pharaoh, but he taxed the land to get the
money that Pharaoh had demanded. He
taxed the people of the land according to
their assessments for the silver and the gold
that he had to give to Pharaoh.

Reign of Jehoiakim. 36 Jehoiakim was twen-
ty-five years old when he began to reign, and
he reigned in Jerusalem for eleven years. His
mother's name was Zebidah, and she was
the daughter of Pedaiah from Rumah.

37 He did what was evil in the sight of the
LORD, everything that his fathers had done.

CHAPTER 24

1 * During his reign Nebuchadnezzar, the
king of Babylon, came up, and Jehoiakim
became his vassal for three years. He then
changed his path and rebelled against him.

2 The LORD sent bands of Chaldeans,
bands of Arameans, bands of Moabites, and
bands of Ammonites against him. They
attacked Judah to destroy it, fulfilling the
word of the LORD which he had spoken
through his servants, the prophets. [o] 3 This
surely came upon Judah at the command of
the LORD so that he might remove them
from out of his sight on account of the sins of
Manasseh and everything that he had done
4 and on account of the innocent blood that
he had shed, for he covered Jerusalem with
innocent blood, something that the LORD
would not forgive.

5 As for the rest of the deeds of Jehoiakim,
all that he did, are they not written in the
book of the chronicles of the kings of Judah?

6 Jehoiakim slept with his fathers, and
Jehoiachin, his son, reigned in his stead.

7 The king of Egypt did not come out of his
land anymore because the king of Babylon
had taken everything that belonged to him
all the way from the River of Egypt up to the
Euphrates River.

Reign of Jehoiachin.* 8 Jehoiachin was
eighteen years old when he began to reign,
and he reigned for three months in Jeru-
salem. His mother's name was Nehushta.
She was the daughter of Elnathan from
Jerusalem.

9 He did what was evil in the sight of the
LORD, everything that his fathers had done.
10 During his reign, the servants of Nebu-
chadnezzar, the king of Babylon, came up
to Jerusalem and the city was besieged. [p]
11 Nebuchadnezzar, the king of Babylon,
came to Jerusalem while his servants were
besieging it.

---

n 2 Chr 35:20; Zec 12:11.—o Jer 25:9; Hab 1:6.—p Dan 1:1-2.

23:28-37 After the threat from Assyria (which was attacked by the Babylonians and Medes in 616 B.C.; Nineveh fell in 612 B.C.), came the threat from Egypt. Josiah tried to stop the pharaoh as the latter was marching to the aid of Assyria; Josiah opposed him at Haran but it ended tragically (609 B.C.).

23:33 *Talent of gold:* this is an unusually small amount to be charged and is rendered in older translations as ten or one hundred talents.

24:1-7 Egyptian overlordship ceased after the battle of Carchemish (605 B.C.), which changed the map of the Middle East. Babylonia then came on the scene of history to execute the judgment of God. Indeed, according to the author, everything that happens has its source in the anger of God at the infidelity of the people; Jeremiah will describe this anger as seen through the prism of his own sensibilities. See in Jer 36 an incident in which Jehoiakim shows his contempt for the prophet.

24:8-17 King Jehoiachin pays for the rebellion of his father: he is deported along with the entire court and selected members of the population. The temple is sacked. This king's name is given as Jechoniah or Coniah in Jeremiah and in Mt 1:11-12.

12 Jehoiachin, the king of Judah, went out to
the king of Babylon, he, his mother, his ser-
vants, his princes, and his officials. The king
of Babylon carried him off during the eighth
year of his reign. 13 He carried off all of the
treasures from the temple of the LORD and
the treasures from the royal palace. He cut to
pieces all of the gold vessels that Solomon,
the king of Israel, had made for the temple of
the LORD, just as the LORD had foretold.[q]
14 He carried away all of Jerusalem and all of
its princes and all of its brave warriors. There
were ten thousand captives, and no crafts-
men or iron smiths remained, only the poor-
est of the people were left. 15 He carried
Jehoiachin off to Babylon along with the
king's mother, the king's wives, his officers,
and the important people of the land. He
carried them off into captivity in Babylon.[r]
16 The king of Babylon brought them into
captivity, all of the important people, seven
thousand of them, and the craftsmen and
iron smiths, one thousand of them, and all of
those who were strong and ready for war.

17 The king of Babylon made Mattaniah
king in his father's stead, and he changed his
name to Zedekiah.[s]

Reign of Zedekiah.* 18 Zedekiah was twenty-
one years old when he began to reign, and he
reigned for eleven years in Jerusalem. His
mother's name was Hamutal. She was the
daughter of Jeremiah from Libnah.[t]

19 He did what was evil in the sight of the
LORD, everything that Jehoiakim had done.
20 This happened to Jerusalem and Judah on
account of the anger of the LORD, and he cast
them out from his presence. Zedekiah then
rebelled against the king of Babylon.

CHAPTER 25

1 It was during the ninth year of his reign,
on the tenth day of the tenth month, that
Nebuchadnezzar, the king of Babylon, and
all his army came up against Jerusalem. He
camped and made siege-works all around
it.* 2 The city was under siege until the
eleventh year of the reign of King Zedekiah.
3 By the ninth day of the fourth month the
famine was so severe that there was no food
left for the people of the land.

4 There was a breach in the city wall, and
all of the warriors fled at night by way of the
gate between the two walls by the king's gar-
den, even though the Chaldeans surrounded
the city. They went toward the Arabah.[u]

5 The Chaldean army chased after them
and caught up with the king in the plains of
Jericho, scattering his entire army. 6 They
captured the king and brought him up to the
king of Babylon who was at Riblah where
he pronounced his judgment. 7 They killed
Zedekiah's sons before his eyes, and then
they put out his eyes, bound him in brass fet-
ters, and carried him off to Babylon.

Destruction of Jerusalem. 8 On the seventh
day of the fifth month of the nineteenth year
of the reign of Nebuchadnezzar, the king of
Babylon, Nebuzaradan, the captain of the
guard and a servant of the king of Babylon,
came up to Jerusalem. 9 He burned down the
temple of the LORD, the royal palace, all of
the buildings of Jerusalem. He burned down
every large building.[v] 10 All of the Chaldean
army that was with the captain of the guard
broke down all of the walls surrounding
Jerusalem. 11 Nebuzaradan, the captain of
the guard, carried off the rest of the people
who remained in the city, those who had
deserted to the king of Babylon, and the rest
of the multitude.

12 But the captain of the guard left the
poorest of the people who were to be vine-
dressers and herdsmen.

13 The Chaldeans broke into pieces the
bronze pillars in the temple of the LORD and
the bronze sea and its base in the temple of
the LORD. They carried the bronze off to
Babylon. 14 They took away the pots, the
shovels, the snuffers, the spoons, and all of
the bronze vessels that were used for min-
istry there.[w] 15 The captain of the guard also
took away the censers and the bowls, and
everything that was made with gold or silver.
16 One could not even measure the weight of
the bronze from all these things: the two pil-
lars, the sea, and its base that were made by
Solomon for the temple of the LORD.[x]
17 Each bronze pillar with its capital was
eighteen cubits tall. The capital was three

q Ezr 1:7; Isa 39:6.—r Est 2:6.—s Jer 1:3; 52:1.—t 2 Chr 36:11.—u Ps 144:14; Jer 39:4-7.—v Ps 74:3-8; Lam 4:11.—w Ezr 1:7.—x 1 Ki 7:47.

24:18-20 Zedekiah brings the sin of Judah to its completion and hastens the destruction of the country. The section from 24:18—25:30 is repeated as the conclusion of the Book of Jeremiah (ch. 52). In Jer 37–38, there is also a record of the meetings and conversation between the prophet (who urges the uselessness of resistance) and the king.

25:1 For the third time, the Babylonian army invaded Judah, destroying the temple and taking the people captive. Judah, like Israel, was unfaithful to God, who gave them many opportunities to turn back to him.

cubits high, along with a bronze network and pomegranates upon the capital. The other pillar was identical with its network.[y]

18 The captain of the guard took away Seraiah, the chief priest, Zephaniah, the second priest, as well as three of the doormen.
19 He also took the officer who was in charge of the fighting men out of the city as well as five of the king's advisors who were caught in the city. He took the scribe assigned to the leader of the army, the one who would muster the people of the land. He also took sixty of the people of the land who were found in the city.

20 Nebuzaradan, the captain of the guard, took them and brought them to the king of
Babylon in Riblah. 21 The king of Babylon struck them down and killed them in Riblah in the land of Hamath. Thus, Judah was carried away from their land into exile.

Gedaliah Governs Judah.* 22 As for the rest of the people who had remained in the land of Judah, Nebuchadnezzar, the king of Babylon, appointed Gedaliah, the son of Ahikam, the son of Shaphan, over them.

23 When all of the captains of the army (they and their men) heard that the king of Babylon had made Gedaliah governor, they came to Gedaliah in Mizpah. They were Ishmael, the son of Nethaniah, Johanan, the son of Kareah, Seraiah, the son of Tanhumeth the Netophathite, and Jaazaniah, the son of the Maachathite, and their men.

24 Gedaliah swore to them and to their men, saying to them, "Do not be afraid of the servants of the Chaldeans. Live in the land and serve the king of Babylon, and everything will be all right with you."

25 But during the seventh month, Ishmael, the son of Nethaniah, the son of Elishama, a member of the royal family, came with ten men and struck down Gedaliah. He died along with the Jews and Chaldeans who were with him in Mizpah.

26 All of the people then rose up, the small and the great, and the captains of the army, and they went to Egypt because they were afraid of the Chaldeans.

Jehoiachin's Release from Prison.* 27 In the thirty-seventh year of the captivity of Jehoiachin, the king of Judah, on the twenty-seventh day of the twelfth month, Evil-merodach who had become king that year, released Jehoiachin, the king of Judah, from
prison.[z] 28 He spoke kindly to him and he set him upon his throne which was above the thrones of the kings who were with him in
Babylon. 29 He changed his prison clothes, and he ate his meals with him for the rest of
his life. 30 He was given a regular allowance from the king, a portion for each day of the rest of his life.

y 1 Ki 7:15-22; Jer 52:21-23.—z Gen 40:13; Jer 52:31-34.

25:22-26 These painful incidents are told in detail in Jeremiah (Jer 40–42). Judah is now like "a desert that no one can cross" (Jer 9:12), since Babylonia does not introduce new inhabitants as Assyria had done in the case of Israel. But the wintry silence is preparing for the germination of new seed. This will produce a new people, one that has the law written in its heart and that will come to rebuild these ruins (Jer 31:33).

25:27-30 Evil-merodach succeeds his father, Nebuchadnezzar, in 561 B.C. and being a more humane man, takes pity on Jehoiachin, who has been in prison since 597 B.C. His treatment of the vassal king has been brilliantly confirmed by discoveries in 1940 that mention "Jaukinu, king of the land of Judah" as among those who receive supplies from the king's treasury.

THE FIRST BOOK OF CHRONICLES

A New Meditation on the History of Israel

A new "history of the people of God" begins with the two Books of Chronicles (in the Septuagint, the Greek translation of the Hebrew scriptures, these Books are entitled "Paralipomena," that is, "things left out," or complementary material). Understanding this will help us not be confused by the genealogies that open the Books and by the impression given that stories already told in the preceding Books of the Bible are being told once again. We shall see in a moment the profound originality of this work.

The Chronicler brings together a collection of data that are at times unconnected among themselves but, taken together, provide a unique religious vision that extends from Adam to the return from Exile.

The contents can be divided into four sections: (1) from Adam to David (1 Chr 1–9); (2) David as the one entrusted with the promise of the kingdom (1 Chr 10–29); (3) Solomon, builder of the temple (2 Chr 1–9); and (4) the descendants of David (2 Chr 10–36).

Why does the author go back over the past? We must bear in mind that he lived in the third century B.C. But since the Exile in the sixth century, Judea had lost its independence and the political importance it had had at one time. The Jews were now a small ethnic and religious minority, a community governed by a high priest and priests of the family of Zadok (1 Ki 3:25). The entire life of Israel was regulated by the law of Moses and organized around the rebuilt temple. In this community that was thus turned in on itself, worship took on a new life; feasts and pilgrimages regularly attracted crowds to Jerusalem.

The ideal, however, was far from being achieved. The priests were compromised by the links to the financial agents of the Ptolemies, who were the foreign masters of the country. The great mission of Israel was now but a memory or distant hope. The average Israelite was beginning to lose confidence in the seriousness of the divine promises. It was among the Levites and cantors that the faith remained most alive.

In all likelihood, the Chronicler belonged to this group. He has a good knowledge of the biblical writings that had already been collected and of other documents subsequently lost, and, of course, of the many oral traditions. His aim is to remind a people now in danger of indifference, that they have a divine destiny. In Israel's past he sees God slowly preparing, by his choices and interventions, for the establishment of his reign, and this from the very beginning of the world. He sees David as the central personage in this history. When the king was concerned to build a house, that is, a temple, did not God himself promise him a house and a posterity that would last forever? The kingdom was founded on the dynasty of David and on the temple in Jerusalem—that is the principal point of reference for this author. True enough, the power of the kings, who were too often unfaithful, disappeared at the Exile, and the pagans destroyed the temple. But God remained faithful to his promises, and after the Exile the temple was rebuilt, and the family of David again produced illustrious descendants. Despite, then, the modest character of Israel's present situation, all hopes were legitimate. It was precisely to revive the hopes of his people that the Chronicler composed his work; this work includes not only the two Books of Chronicles, but also the Books of Ezra and Nehemiah, which carry the story down to the period after the Exile and are meant to signal a new beginning. The Books of Chronicles themselves are concerned with the Davidic kingdom.

These Books, written to promote a vital liturgy and to preserve the Messianic hope, seem to be the fruit of patient labor. They are a religious meditation, a spiritual reflection, on the history of Israel, rather than a narrative. When he thinks it necessary, the author adapts and interprets the facts in order to better bring out his own thought. He wants to make clear how the plan of God is being carried out despite human resistance.

This work of a zealous writer is not permeated by any breath of poetry; the tone is meditative and didactic. And yet, the Chronicler left his mark on such writers as Sirach (see Sir 44–50) and the author of Wisdom (see Wis 10–19), as well as on such religious groups as the Pharisees and the Essenes. He certainly helped the best among the Jews to wait in faith and prepare for the coming Messiah.

The First Book of Chronicles may be divided as follows:

I: Genealogical Tables (1:1—9:34)
II: The History of David (9:35—29:30)

I: GENEALOGICAL TABLES*

CHAPTER 1

From Adam to Abraham. 1 * Adam, Seth,
Enosh, 2 Kenan, Mehalalel, Jared, 3 Enoch,
Methuselah, Lamech, Noah. [a]

4 The sons of Noah were Shem, Ham, and
Japheth.

5 * The sons of Japheth were Gomer,
Magog, Madai, Javan, Tubal, Meshech, and
Tiras. [b]

6 The sons of Gomer were Ashkenaz,
Riphath, and Togarmah.

7 The sons of Javan were Elishah, Tarshish,
Kittim, and Rodanim.

8 The sons of Ham were Cush, Mizraim,
Put, and Canaan.

9 The sons of Cush were Seba, Havilah,
Sabta, Raama, and Sabteca.

The sons of Raama were Sheba and
Dedan.

10 Cush was the father of Nimrod, and he
grew up to be a mighty warrior upon the
earth. [c]

11 Mizraim was the father of Ludim,
Anamim, Lehabim, Naphtuhim, 12 Path-
rusim, Casluhim, and Caphtorim (from
whom the Philistines came).

13 Canaan was the father of Sidon (his
firstborn), Heth, 14 the Jebusites, the Amo-
rites, the Girgashites, 15 the Hivites, the
Arkites, the Sinites, 16 the Arvadites, the
Zemarites, and the Hamathites.

17 The sons of Shem were Elam, Asshur,
Arpachshad, Lud, and Aram.

The sons of Aram were Uz, Hul, Gether,
and Mash. [d]

18 Arpachshad was the father of Shelah,
and Shelah was the father of Eber.

19 Eber had two sons: the name of one of
them was Peleg, for during his days the earth
was divided, and his brother's name was
Joktan.

20 Joktan was the father of Almodad,
Sheleph, Hazarmaveth, Jerah, 21 Hadoram,
Uzal, Diklah, 22 Ebal, Abimael, Sheba,
23 Ophir, Havilah, and Jobab. All of these
were the sons of Joktan.

24 Shem, Arpachshad, Shelah, [e] 25 Eber,
Peleg, Reu, 26 Serug, Nahor, Terah, 27 and
Abram that is, Abraham. [f]

From Abraham to Jacob.* 28 The sons of
Abraham were Isaac and Ishmael. [g] 29 These
are their descendants: the firstborn of
Ishmael was Nebaioth, then Kedar, Adbeel,
Mibsam, [h] 30 Mishma, Dumah, Massa, Ha-
dad, Tema, 31 Jetur, Naphish, and Kedemah.
These were the sons of Ishmael.

32 The sons of Keturah, Abraham's concu-
bine, were Zimran, Jokshan, Medan, Mid-
ian, Ishbak, and Shuah.

The sons of Jokshan were Sheba and
Dedan.

33 The sons of Midian were Ephah, Epher,
Hanoch, Abida, and Eldaah. These were all
descendants of Keturah.

34 Abraham was the father of Isaac. The
sons of Isaac were Esau and Israel. [i]

35 The sons of Esau were Eliphaz, Reuel,
Jeush, Jalam, and Korah.

36 The sons of Eliphaz were Teman, Omar,
Zepho, Gatam, and Kenaz, and by Timna
there was Amalek. [j]

37 The sons of Reuel were Nahath, Zerah,
Shammah, and Mizzah.

38 The sons of Seir were Lotan, Shobal,
Zibeon, Anah, Dishon, Ezer, and Dishan. [k]

39 The sons of Lotan were Hori and
Homam. Timna was Lotan's sister.

---

a Gen 4:24; Jude 14.—b Gen 10:2-4.—c Gen 10:8.—d Gen 10:22ff.—e Gen 11:10-26; Lk 3:34-36.—f Gen 17:5; Neh 9:7.—g Gal 4:22-23; Heb 11:11.—h Gen 25:13-16.—i Gen 21:2-3; 25:19; Mt 1:2; Acts 7:8.—j Gen 36:11.—k Gen 36:20-28.

1:1—9:34 The Book begins with a long list of names, genealogies and censuses, which bewilder the modern reader. But such lists are found elsewhere in the Bible, because in the view of the ancients, they give expression to a vision of history and the great connections that mark the plan of God; for this reason, the accuracy of the information conveyed is not essential. In like manner, Genesis establishes a continuity between Adam and Abraham as a way of locating the first patriarch in the trajectory of God's plan (see Gen 5; 11). The evangelists will endeavor to construct a genealogy of Jesus that goes back either to Abraham (Mt 1) or to Adam (Lk 3:23), in order to show that all of history was leading up to Jesus Christ. In the first nine chapters of Chronicles we will likewise find at work a theological conception of human history. Here are its main perspectives: all human beings are connected with one another by their common origin in Adam, but from among them God chose a people and, inseparable at the center of this people, King David and the priests. The king is the sign of the Messianic promises, while the priests are the guardians of the sanctuary wherein Israel meets God. In the author's eyes, all of humanity gravitates around God's will to establish his reign and his worship among us. Such is the author's grand vision, which is given learned expression in these endless lists.

1:1-4 This is the list in Gen 5.

1:5-7 The three sons of Noah populate the earth, but Shem is the origin of the privileged posterity that leads to Abraham and, through him, to the people of Israel.

1:28-54 Abraham is not only the founder of the Israelite people but from him and from his son Isaac come other peoples, brothers and sisters of Israel (hostile brethren in many instances). Recalled here, as secondary branches, are the Ishmaelites and the Edomites, and a short history of the latter is sketched.

40 The sons of Shobal were Alian, Mana-
hath, Ebal, Shepho, and Onam. The sons of
Zibeon were Aiah and Anah.

41 The son of Anah was Dishon.

The sons of Dishon were Hemdan, Esh-
ban, Ithran, and Cheran.

42 The sons of Ezer were Bilhan, Zaavan,
and Jaakan.

The sons of Dishan were Uz and Aran.

43 These were the kings who reigned in the
land of Edom before a king reigned over the
Israelites: Bela, the son of Beor, whose city
was named Dinhabah.[l] 44 When Bela died,
Jobab, the son of Zerah from Bozrah,
reigned in his stead.[m] 45 When Jobab died,
Husham from the land of the Temanites
reigned in his stead.[n] 46 When Husham died,
Hadad, the son of Bedad, who defeated
Midian in the land of Moab reigned in his
stead. His city was named Avith. 47 When
Hadad died, Samlah from Masrekah
reigned in his stead. 48 When Samlah died,
Shaul from Rehoboth on the river reigned in
his stead. 49 When Shaul died, Baal-hanan,
the son of Acbor, reigned in his stead.
50 When Baal-hanan died, Hadad reigned in
his stead. His city was named Pai, and his
wife's name was Mehetabel, the daughter of
Matred, the daughter of Mezehab. 51 Hadad
also died.

The chieftains of Edom were Timna,
Aliah, Jetheth, 52 Oholibamah, Elah, Pinon,
53 Kenaz, Teman, Mibzar, 54 Magdiel, and
Iram. These were the chieftains of Edom.

CHAPTER 2

1 These were the sons of Israel: Reuben,
Simeon, Levi, Judah, Issachar, Zebulun,*
2 Dan, Joseph, Benjamin, Naphtali, Gad, and
Asher.

Judah. 3 The sons of Judah were Er, Onan,
and Shelah. They were born to him by Shuah
the Canaanite. Er, the firstborn of Judah, did
what was evil in the sight of the LORD and he
slew him. 4 Tamar, his daughter-in-law, bore
him Perez and Zerah, so Judah had five sons
in all.[o]

5 The sons of Perez were Hezron and
Hamul.

6 The sons of Zerah were Zimri, Ethan,
Heman, Calcol, and Darda. There were five
of them in all.

7 The son of Carmi was Achar who trou-
bled Israel when he violated the ban.[p]

8 The son of Ethan was Azariah.

9 The sons of Hezron were Jerahmeel,
Ram, and Chelubai.[q]

10 Ram was the father of Amminadab, and
Amminadab was the father of Nahshon, the
leader of the Judahites.[r]

11 Nahshon was the father of Salma, and
Salma was the father of Boaz.

12 Boaz* was the father of Obed, and Obed
was the father of Jesse.

13 Jesse was the father of Eliab, his first-
born, and then Abinadab, his second,
Shimea, his third,[s] 14 Nethanel, his fourth,
Raddai, his fifth, 15 Ozem, his sixth, and
David, his seventh.

16 Their sisters were Zeruiah and Abigail.
The three sons of Zeruiah were Abishai,
Joab, and Asahel.[t]

17 Abigail bore Amasa, and Amasa's father
was Jether the Ishmaelite.

18 Caleb, the son of Hezron, had sons
through Azubah, his wife, and through
Jerioth. These were her sons: Jesher, Shobab,
and Ardon. 19 When Azubah died, Caleb
married Ephrath, who bore him Hur.

20 Hur was the father of Uri, and Uri was
the father of Bezalel.[u]

21 Afterwards, Hezron went to the daugh-
ter of Machir, the father of Gilead. He mar-
ried her when he was sixty years old, and she
bore him Segub.[v]

22 Segub was the father of Jair who ruled
twenty-three cities in Gilead.

23 Geshur and Aram captured Havvoth-
jair as well as Kenath with the towns depen-
dent upon it, sixty towns in all. All of these
were the sons of Machir, the father of
Gilead.[w]

l Gen 36:31-39.—m Isa 34:6; 63:1; Jer 49:13, 22.—n Job 2:11.—o Gen 38:13-30; Mt 1:3.—p Jos 7:1; 22:20.—q Mt 1:3.—r Ru 4:19-20.—s 1 Sam 16:6, 9.—t 2 Sam 2:18.—u Ex 24:14; 31:2; 2 Chr 1:5.—v Num 26:29; 27:1; Jos 13:31.—w Deut 3:14; Jos 13:30.

2:1 The chosen people emerge against the preceding background of human history. The chapters that follow are interested solely in the twelve tribes that are the origin of this people. The books of the Bible provide a number of lists of the tribes; there are differences, sometimes considerable, from list to list; the differences can be explained by reference to the various periods in which the documents were composed. Why these lists? In the unceasing effort to paint a picture of the people, a list represents a new awareness of the people's vocation. Here the author is recalling the past, not so much out of a concern for history as in the name of a hope: in a period in which no glory attaches to the people, he looks ahead to the rebuilding of the Israel of God.

2:12 *Boaz:* a kinsman of Naomi who married her daughter-in-law Ruth by exercising his rights under the levirate law (see Ru 2–4). Their son Obed was the grandfather of David.

24 After Hezron died in Caleb-ephrathah,
Abijah, Hezron's wife, bore him Ashhur, the
father of Tekoa.

25 The sons of Jerahmeel, the firstborn of
Hezron, were Ram, the firstborn, Bunah,
Oren, Ozem, and Ahijah.[x] 26 Jerahmeel had
another wife whose name was Atarah. She
was the mother of Onam.

27 The sons of Ram, the firstborn of
Jerahmeel, were Maaz, Jamin, and Eker.

28 The sons of Onam were Shammai and
Jada.

The sons of Shammai were Nadab and
Abishur.

29 The name of the wife of Abishur was
Abihail, and she bore him Ahban and Molid.

30 The sons of Nadab were Seled and
Appaim. Seled died without having any children.

31 The son of Appaim was Ishi, and the son
of Ishi was Sheshan, and the son of Sheshan
was Ahlai.

32 The sons of Jada, Shammai's brother,
were Jether and Jonathan. Jether died without having any children.

33 The sons of Jonathan were Peleth and
Zaza. These were the descendants of
Jerahmeel.

34 Now Sheshan had no sons, only daughters. He had an Egyptian slave whose name
was Jarha. 35 Sheshan gave his daughter to
Jarha his slave as a wife, and she bore him
Attai.

36 Attai was the father of Nathan, and
Nathan was the father of Zabad.[y]

37 Zabad was the father of Ephlal, and
Ephlal was the father of Obed.

38 Obed was the father of Jehu, and Jehu
was the father of Azariah.

39 Azariah was the father of Helez, and
Helez was the father of Eleasah.

40 Eleasah was the father of Sismai, and
Sismai was the father of Shallum.

41 Shallum was the father of Jekamiah, and
Jekamiah was the father of Elishama.

42 The son of Caleb, the brother of
Jerahmeel, was Mesha, his firstborn, who
was the father of Ziph. His son Mareshah
was the father of Hebron.

43 The sons of Hebron were Korah,
Tappuah, Rekem, and Shema.

44 Shema was the father of Raham, and
Raham was the father of Jorkeam.

Rekem was the father of Shammai.

45 Maon was the son of Shammai, and
Maon was the father of Beth-zur.[z]

46 Caleb's concubine, Ephah, bore him
Haran, Moza, and Gazez.

Haran was the father of Gazez.

47 The sons of Jahdai were Regem, Jotham,
Geshan, Pelet, Ephah, and Shaaph.

48 Caleb's concubine, Maacah, bore Sheber
and Tirhanah. 49 She also bore Shaaph, the
father of Madmannah, and Sheva, the father
of Machbenah and Gibea. Caleb's daughter
was Achsah.[a]

50 These were the descendants of Caleb.
The sons of Hur, the firstborn of Ephrathah,
were Shobal, the father of Kiriath-jearim,
51 Salma, the father of Bethlehem, and
Hareph, the father of Beth-gader.

52 The descendants of Shobal, the father
of Kiriath-jearim were Haroeh, half the
Manahathites, 53 and the clans of Kiriath-jearim: the Ithrites, the Puthites, the
Shumathites, and the Mishraites. From these
came the Zorathites and the Eshtaolites.[b]

54 The descendants of Salma were
Bethlehem, the Netophathites, Atroth-beth-joab, half of the Manahathites, the Zorites,[c]
55 and the clans of the scribes who dwelt in
Jabez: the Tirathites, the Shimeathites, and
the Sucathites. These are the Kenites who
came from Hammath, who was the father of
the house of Rechab.[d]

CHAPTER 3*

1 These were David's sons who were born
in Hebron: Amnon, the firstborn, the son of
Ahinoam of Jezreel; Daniel, the second, the
son of Abigail of Carmel;[e] 2 Absalom, the
third, the son of Maacah, the daughter of
Talmai, the king of Geshur; Adonijah, the
fourth, the son of Haggith; 3 Shephatiah, the
fifth, the son of Abital; Ithream, the sixth,
the son of Eglah. 4 These six were born in
Hebron where he reigned for seven years
and six months. He reigned for thirty-three
years in Jerusalem.[f]

x 1 Sam 27:10; Job 32:2.—y 1 Chr 11:41.—z Jos 15:55-58.—a Jos 15:16; Jdg 1:12.—b 2 Sam 23:38.—c Ezr 2:22; Neh 7:26; 12:28.—d Num 24:21; Jdg 1:16; 1 Sam 15:6.—e 2 Sam 3:2-3; Jos 15:56.—f 2 Sam 2:11; 5:5.

3:1-24 The history of Solomon and the other kings will come later in the work. The list of David's descendants is complete (whereas there are omissions in Mt 1:7-11). The list from the Exile onward (v. 17ff) has for its purpose to show the survival of the descendants of David; in fact, only the names of Shealtiel and Zerubbabel will appear in the genealogy of Jesus in Mt 1 (and Lk 3).

5 These were the children born in Jerusalem: Shimea, Shobab, Nathan, and Solomon. These four were from Bathsheba, the daughter of Ammiel.[g] 6 There were also Ibhar, Elishua, Eliphelet, 7 Nogah, Nepheg, Japhia, 8 Elishama, Eliada, and Eliphelet, nine of them in all. 9 These were the sons of David, not counting his sons by his concubines. Tamar* was their sister.[h]

10 * Solomon's son was Rehoboam, Abijah his son, Asa his son, Jehoshaphat his son,[i] 11 Joram his son, Ahaziah his son, Joash his son,[j] 12 Amaziah his son, Azariah his son, Jotham his son,[k] 13 Ahaz his son, Hezekiah his son, Manasseh his son,[l] 14 Amon his son, and Josiah his son.[m]

15 The sons of Josiah were Johanan his firstborn son, Jehoiakim, his second son, Zedekiah, his third son, and Shallum, his fourth son.

16 The successors of Josiah were Jehoiakim, his son Jehoiachin, and Zedekiah.[n]

17 The sons of Jehoiachin the captive were Shealtiel his son,[o] 18 Malchiram, Pedaiah, Shenazzar, Jekamiah, Hoshama, and Nedabiah.

19 The sons of Pedaiah were Zerubbabel and Shimei.*[p]

The children of Zerubbabel were Meshullam, Hananiah, Shelomith, their sister, 20 and five named Hashubah, Ohel, Berechiah, Hasadiah, and Jushab-hesed.

21 The descendants of Hananiah were Pelatiah, Jeshaiah, the sons of Rephaiah, the sons of Arnan, the sons of Obadiah, and the sons of Shecaniah.

22 The son of Shecaniah was Shemaiah, and the sons of Shemaiah were Hattush, Igal, Bariah, Neariah, and Shaphat. There were six of them.[q]

23 The sons of Neariah were Elioenai, Hizkiah, and Azrikam. There were three of them.

24 The sons of Elioenai were Hodaviah, Eliashib, Pelaiah, Akkub, Johanan, Delaiah, and Anani. There were seven of them.

CHAPTER 4

1 The descendants of Judah were Perez, Hezron, Carmi, Hur, and Shobal.[r]

2 Reaiah, the son of Shobal, was the father of Jahath, Jahath was the father of Ahumai and Lahad. These were the clans of the Zorathites.

3 These were the sons of Etam: Jezreel, Ishma, Idbash, and their sister Hazzelelponi.

4 Penuel was the father of Gedor, and Ezer the father of Hushah. These were the sons of Hur, the firstborn of Ephrathah, the father of Bethlehem.[s]

5 Ashur, the father of Tekoa, had two wives: Helah and Naarah. 6 Naarah bore him Ahuzzam, Hepher, Temeni, and Haahashtari. They were the sons of Naarah.

7 The sons of Helah were Zereth, Izhar, and Ethnan.

8 Koz was the father of Anub, Zobebah, and the clans of Aharhel, the son of Harum.

9 * Jabez was the most honorable of his brothers. His mother named him Jabez because she said, "I bore him with pain." 10 Jabez called upon the God of Israel saying, "Oh that you would bless me and enlarge my territory. May your hand be with me, and keep me from harm so that I might be free from grief." God granted what he requested.

11 Chelub, Shuhah's brother, was the father of Mehir, who was the father of Eshton.

12 Eshton was the father of Beth-rapha, Paseah, and Tehinnah, the father of Irnahash. These were the men of Recah.

13 The sons of Kenaz were Othniel* and Seraiah.

The sons of Othniel were Hathath and Meonothai.[t]

14 Meonothai was the father of Ophrah.

Seraiah was the father of Joab, the father of Geharashim, for they were craftsmen.[u]

15 The sons of Caleb, the son of Jephunneh were Ir, Elah, and Naam.

g 2 Sam 11:3.—h 2 Sam 13:1-2.—i 1 Ki 14:21-31; 2 Chr 12:16.—j 2 Ki 8:16-24; 2 Chr 21:1.—k Isa 1:1; Hos 1:1; Mic 1:1.—l 2 Ki 16:1-20; Jer 26:19.—m 2 Chr 33:21; Zep 1:1.—n 2 Ki 24:6, 8; Mt 1:11.—o Ezr 3:2; 5:2.—p Neh 7:7; Hag 1:1; 2:2; Zec 4:6.—q Ezr 8:2-3; Neh 3:29.—r Gen 38:29; 46:12; Num 26:21; Mt 1:3.—s Ru 4:11.—t Jos 15:17; Jdg 1:13.—u Neh 11:35.

3:9 *Tamar:* raped by her step-brother Amnon, son of David and Ahinoam, she was later vindicated by his murder by her full brother Absalom (2 Sam 13).

3:10-16 Solomon's progeny provided many rulers for the nation of Judah until its destruction by the Babylonians.

3:19 In Hag 1:1 and Ezek 3:2, Zerubbabel is the son of Shealtiel (see Mt 1:12; Lk 3:27); the present verse needs there-fore to be rearranged. The Septuagint replaces Pedaiah with Shealtiel.

4:9-10 The prayer of Jabez has been immortalized throughout history as a request for protection and rich blessings in this life.

4:13 *Othniel:* after winning Achsah as his wife by conquering Kiriath-sepher, he serves as the first judge of Israel (Jdg 1:9-15).

The son of Elah was Kenaz.

16 The sons of Jahallelel were Ziph, Ziphah, Tiria, and Asarel.

17 The sons of Ezrah were Jether, Mered, Epher, and Jalon. A wife of his gave birth to Miriam, Shammai, and Ishbah, the father of Eshtemoa.[v] 18 His wife was from Egypt, and she gave birth to Jered, the father of Gedor, Heber, the father of Soco, and Jekuthiel, the father of Zanoah. These were the sons of Bithiah, Pharaoh's daughter, whom Mered had married.

19 The sons of Hodiah's wife, the sister of Naham were the fathers of Keilah the Garmite and Eshtemoa the Maachathite.[w]

20 The sons of Shimon were Amnon, Rinnah, Ben-hanan, and Tilon.

The descendants of Ishi were Zoheth and Ben-zoheth.

21 The sons of Shelah, the son of Judah, were Er, the father of Lecah, Laadah, the father of Mareshah, and the clans of linen workers at Beth-ashbea, 22 Jokim, the men of Cozeba, Joash, and Saraph who ruled in Moab and Jashubi-lahem. These records are from ancient times. 23 They were potters who lived in Netaim and Gederah. They dwelt there and worked for the king.

Simeon. 24 The sons of Simeon were Nemuel, Jamin, Jarib, Zerah, and Shaul.[x] 25 Shallum was his son, Mibsam was his son, and Mishma was his son.

26 The descendants of Mishma were Hammuel, his son, Zaccur, his son, and Shimei, his son.

27 Shimei had sixteen sons and six daughters, but his brothers did not have many children so the whole clan did not become very large in Judah. 28 They lived in Beer-sheba, Moladah, Hazar-shual,[y] 29 Bilhah, Ezem, Tolad, 30 Bethuel, Hormah, Ziklag,[z] 31 Beth-marcaboth, Hazar-susim, Beth-biri, and Shaaraim. These were their cities up to the time of the reign of David. 32 Their dependent villages were Etam, Ain, Rimmon, Tochen, Ashan, five of them in all, 33 as well as all of the villages that surrounded these cities up to Baal. These were their settlements and their genealogies.

34 Meshobab, Jamlech, Joshah, the son of Amaziah, 35 Joel, Jehu, the son of Joshibiah, the son of Seraiah, the son of Asiel, 36 as well as Elioenai, Jaakobah, Jeshohaiah, Asaiah, Adiel, Jesimiel, Benaiah, 37 and Ziza, the son of Shiphi, the son of Allon, the son of Jedaiah, the son of Shimri, the son of Shemaiah— 38 these were the names of the leaders of their clans. Their families increased greatly. 39 They traveled toward the entrance of Gedor on the east side of the valley, to seek pastures for their flocks. 40 They found good, rich pastures and a spacious land that was quiet and peaceful. Some Hamites* had lived there from ancient times.[a]

41 The men whose names are written here arrived during the days of Hezekiah, the king of Judah. They attacked those living there as well as the Meunites who were found there. They wiped them out, as is still true today. They dwelt in their place for there were pastures for their flocks there.[b]

42 About five hundred of the Simeonites invaded the hill country of Seir led by Pelatiah, Neariah, Rephaiah, and Uzziel, the sons of Ishi. 43 They killed the rest of the Amalekites who had escaped, and they have lived there up to the present.

CHAPTER 5

Reuben. 1 The sons of Reuben, the firstborn of Israel (for he was the firstborn, but when he defiled his father's bed, his birthright was given to the sons of Joseph, the son of Israel. For this reason he could not be listed in the genealogy according to his birthright.[c] 2 Though Judah was the strongest of the brothers and a ruler came through him, the birthright belonged to Joseph.)[d]

3* The sons of Reuben, the firstborn of Israel, were Hanoch, Pallu, Hezron, and Carmi.[e]

4 The descendants of Joel were Shemaiah, his son, Gog, his son, Shimei, his son, 5 Micah, his son, Reaiah, his son, Baal, his son, 6 and Beerah, his son, whom Tiglath-pileser, the king of Assyria, carried off into exile. He was the leader of the Reubenites.[f]

7 These were their brethren by their clans, listed according to the generations of their genealogy. Jeiel, their leader, Zechariah, 8 and Bela, the son of Azaz, the son of

v 1 Sam 30:28.—w Deut 3:14; Jos 15:44.—x Gen 29:33; Ex 6:15; Num 26:12.—y Jos 19:2.—z Jos 15:31.—a Jdg 18: 7-10.—b 2 Ki 18:8; 2 Chr 29:1.—c Gen 29:32; 49:4; Deut 33:6.—d Mic 5:2; Mt 2:6.—e Gen 46:9; Ex 6:14; Num 26: 5-11.—f 2 Ki 15:29.

4:40 *Hamites:* non-Israelite inhabitants of southern Palestine; sometimes they are called "Egyptians" (see Gen 21:9).

5:3-5 The relations between the clan of Joel and the tribe of Reuben are not clarified.

Shema, the son of Joel. They dwelt in the
area that ran from Aroer to Nebo and Baal-
meon.[g] 9 To the east, they lived on the edge
of the desert that runs up to the Euphrates
River because their herds had grown
numerous in the land of Gilead. 10 During
the days of Saul they fought against the
Hagrites who fell at their hands. They lived
in their dwellings to the east of Gilead.[h]

Gad. 11 The Gadites lived alongside of
them in the land of Bashan up to Salecah.[i]
12 Joel was their leader, Shapham the next,
then Janai, Shaphat, and Bashan. 13 Their
brethren, by their ancestral clans, were
Michael, Meshullam, Sheba, Jorai, Jacan,
Zia, and Eber. There were seven of them
in all.

14 These were the sons of Abihail, the son of
Huri, the son of Jaroah, the son of Gilead, the
son of Michael, the son of Jeshishai, the son
of Jahdo, the son of Buz.

15 Ahi, the son of Abdiel, the son of Guni,
was the leader of the clan.

16 The Gadites lived in Gilead, in Bashan,
all of their villages, and all throughout the
pastures of Sharon. 17 All of these were
entered in the genealogies during the reigns
of Jotham, the king of Judah, and Jeroboam,
the king of Israel.

18 The Reubenites, the Gadites, and one-
half of the tribe of Manasseh had forty-four
thousand, seven hundred and sixty trained
warriors armed with shield, sword, and bow
who went out to battle. 19 They fought
against the Hagrites, Jetur, Naphish, and
Nodab. 20 They helped in fighting against
them, and the LORD delivered the Hagrites
and those who were with them into their
hands for they had cried out to God all
throughout the battle. He responded to
them because they had put their trust in
him.[j] 21 They seized their livestock: fifty
thousand camels, two hundred thousand
sheep, and two thousand donkeys. They also
took one hundred thousand captives.
22 Many others were killed, falling because it
was God's battle. They then dwelt there in
their place until the time of the Exile.[k]

The Half-tribe of Manasseh. 23 The one-half
of the tribe of Manasseh who dwelt in the
land of Bashan up to Baal-hermon, that is
Senir, or Mount Hermon, grew numerous.

24 These were the leaders of their ancestral
clans: Epher, Ishi, Eliel, Azriel, Jeremiah,
Hodaviah, and Jahdiel. They were brave war-
riors, famous, and the leaders of their ances-
tral clans, 25 but they betrayed the God of
their fathers, prostituting themselves with
the gods of the various peoples of the land
whom God had destroyed before them.[l]
26 Therefore the God of Israel stirred up the
spirit of Pul, the king of Assyria (that is, the
spirit of Tiglath-pileser, the king of Assyria).
He led away the Reubenites, the Gadites,
and one-half of the tribe of Manasseh and
brought them to Halah, Habor, Hara, and to
the Gozan River where they are up to the
present.

Levi. 27 * The sons of Levi were Gershon,
Kohath, and Merari.

28 The sons of Kohath were Amram, Izhar,
Hebron, and Uzziel.

29 The children of Amram were Aaron,
Moses, and Miriam.

The sons of Aaron were Nadab, Abihu,
Eleazar, and Ithamar.[m]

30 Eleazar was the father of Phinehas, and
Phinehas was the father of Abishua.

31 Abishua was the father of Bukki, and
Bukki was the father of Uzzi.

32 Uzzi was the father of Zerahiah, and
Zerahiah was the father of Meraioth.

33 Meraioth was the father of Amariah,
and Amariah was the father of Ahitub.

34 Ahitub was the father of Zadok, and
Zadok was the father of Ahimaaz.

35 Ahimaaz was the father of Azariah, and
Azariah was the father of Johanan.

36 Johanan was the father of Azariah. He
served as priest in the temple that Solomon
built in Jerusalem.

37 Azariah was the father of Amariah, and
Amariah was the father of Ahitub.

38 Ahitub was the father of Zadok, and
Zadok was the father of Shallum.

39 Shallum was the father of Hilkiah, and
Hilkiah was the father of Azariah.

40 Azariah was the father of Seraiah, and
Seraiah was the father of Jehozadak.

---

g Num 32:3; Jos 13:17; Jdg 11:26.—h Ps 83:6-7.—i Jos 13:11, 24-28.—j Deut 33:20-21; Ps 22:4-5.—k Jdg 3:2; 2 Ki 15:29; 2 Chr 6:34.—l Ex 34:15; 2 Ki 17:7.—m Ex 6:20.

5:27—6:66 The tribe of Levi comes at the center of these genealogical sketches. The Chronicler assigns great importance to the temple and its worship. In this post-Exilic period it is, in fact, the priestly class that keeps the people united and leads them. The information given here has to do with various aspects of the life and functions of the Levites. As the only tribe not to possess a territory, Levi very quickly lost any political role and was put in charge solely of the sanctuaries and, later, of the one temple in Jerusalem (see Num 3–4; 2 Ki 23).

41 Jehozadak was carried off when the LORD sent Judah and Jerusalem into exile by the hand of Nebuchadnezzar.

CHAPTER 6

1 The sons of Levi were Gershon, Kohath, and Merari.[n]

2 The names of the sons of Gershon were Libni and Shimei.[o]

3 The sons of Kohath were Amram, Izhar, Hebron, and Uzziel.[p]

4 The sons of Merari were Mahli and Mushi.[q]

These were the ancestral clans of the Levites. 5 From Gershon: Libni, his son, Jahath, his son, Zimmah, his son, 6 Joah, his son, Iddo, his son, Zerah, his son, and Jeatherai, his son.

7 The descendants of Kohath were Amminadab, his son, Korah, his son, Assir, his son, 8 Elkanah, his son, Ebiasaph, his son, Assir, his son,[r] 9 Tahath, his son, Uriel, his son, Uzziah, his son, and Shaul, his son.

10 The descendants of Elkanah were Amasai, Ahimoth, 11 Elkanah, his son, Zophai, his son, Nahath, his son, 12 Eliab, his son, Jeroham, his son, Elkanah, his son, and Samuel, his son. 13 The sons of Samuel were Joel, his firstborn, and Abijah, his second.

14 The descendants of Merari were: Mahli, Libni, his son, Shimei, his son, Uzzah, his son, 15 Shimea, his son, Haggiah, his son, and Asaiah, his son.[s]

16 These are the ones whom David assigned to sing in the shrine of the LORD after the Ark was placed there.* 17 Their ministry was to sing before the tabernacle, the tent of meeting, until Solomon built the temple of the LORD in Jerusalem. They also performed their other duties according to their responsibilities.

18 These are the men who served along with their children: from the Kohathites: Heman, the singer, the son of Joel, the son of Samuel, 19 the son of Elkanah, the son of Jeroham, the son of Eliel, the son of Toah, 20 the son of Zuph, the son of Elkanah, the son of Mahath, the son of Amasai, 21 the son of Elkanah, the son of Joel, the son of Azariah, the son of Zephaniah, 22 the son of Tahath, the son of Assir, the son of Ebiasaph, the son of Korah,[t] 23 the son of Izhar, the son of Kohath, the son of Levi, the son of Israel.

24 There was also his brother Asaph who served at his right side. Asaph, the son of Berechiah, the son of Shimea, 25 the son of Michael, the son of Baaseiah, the son of Malchijah, 26 the son of Ethni, the son of Zerah, the son of Adaiah, 27 the son of Ethan, the son of Zimmah, the son of Shimei,[u] 28 the son of Jahath, the son of Gershon, the son of Levi.

29 The Merarites, their brethren, served on his left: Ethan, the son of Kishi, the son of Abdi, the son of Malluch, 30 the son of Hashabiah, the son of Amaziah, the son of Hilkiah, 31 the son of Amzi, the son of Bani, the son of Shemer,[v] 32 the son of Mahli, the son of Mushi, the son of Merari, the son of Levi.

33 Their fellow Levites were appointed to various types of service in the tabernacle, the shrine of the LORD.[w] 34 But Aaron and his descendants were the ones who offered sacrifices on the altar for burnt offerings and the altar of incense. They also performed all of the work needed in the Holy of Holies where they made atonement for Israel in accordance with everything that Moses, the servant of God, had commanded.

35 These were the descendants of Aaron: Eleazar, his son, Phinehas, his son, Abishua, his son, 36 Bukki, his son, Uzzi, his son, Zerahiah, his son, 37 Meraioth, his son, Amariah, his son, Ahitub, his son, 38 Zadok, his son, and Ahimaaz, his son.

39 These were the sites assigned as their dwelling places throughout the land. They were assigned to the descendants of Aaron from the Kohathite clan because this was their allotment. 40 They were given Hebron in the land of Judah along with its surrounding pastures. 41 But the fields and the villages that surrounded the city were given to Caleb, the son of Jephunneh.

42 The descendants of Aaron were given Hebron (which was a city of refuge), Libnah with its pastures, Jattir, Eshtemoa with its pastures, 43 Hilen with its pastures, Debir with its pastures, 44 Ashan with its pastures, Jetta with its pastures, and Beth-shemesh with its pastures.

n Gen 46:11.—o Ex 6:17.—p Num 3:19; 26:59.—q Num 3:20; 26:58.—r Ex 6:24.—s 2 Chr 34:20.—t Ex 6:24.—u 1 Chr 2:6.—v Ezr 2:10.—w Num 3:6-7.

6:16 David, an accomplished musician and songwriter, appointed singers and gathered choirs to provide music for the temple to give glory and praise to the Lord.

45 From the tribe of Benjamin they were
given Gibeon with its pastures, Geba with its
pastures, Almon with its pastures, and
Anathoth with its pastures. There were thir-
teen cities for their clans.
46 The rest of the Kohathites were allotted
ten cities* from the clans of one-half of the
tribe of Manasseh. 47 The descendants of
Gershon, clan by clan, were allotted thirteen
cities from the tribe of Issachar, the tribe of
Asher, the tribe of Naphtali, and the part of
the tribe of Manasseh living in Bashan.
48 The descendants of Merari, clan by clan,
were allotted twelve cities from the tribe of
Reuben, the tribe of Gad, and the tribe of
Zebulun.
49 The Israelites gave the Levites these
cities along with their pastures. 50 They were
allotted these previously named cities from
the tribe of the Judahites, the tribe of
the Simeonites, and the tribe of the
Benjaminites.
51 Some of the remaining Kohathites were
given cities from the territory of the tribe of
Ephraim. 52 In the hill country of Ephraim
they were given Shechem (a city of refuge)
with its pastures, Gezer with its pastures,
53 Jokmeam with its pastures, Beth-horon
with its pastures, 54 Aijalon with its pastures,
and Gath-rimmon with its pastures.
55 The rest of the Kohathite clans were
given Aner with its pastures and Bileam
with its pastures from one-half of the tribe of
Manasseh.
56 The Gershonites were given the follow-
ing from the clan of one-half of the tribe of
Manasseh: Golan in Bashan with its pas-
tures, and Ashtaroth with its pastures.
57 From the tribe of Issachar they were
given Kedesh with its pastures, Daberath
with its pastures, 58 Ramoth with its pas-
tures, and Anem with its pastures.
59 From the tribe of Asher they were given
Mashal with its pastures, Abdon with its pas-
tures, 60 Hukok with its pastures, and Rehob
with its pastures.
61 From the tribe of Naphtali they were
given Kedesh in Galilee with its pastures,
Hammon with its pastures, and Kiriathaim
with its pastures.
62 The rest of the Merarites were given
Rimmon with its pastures, and Tabor with
its pastures from the tribe of Zebulun.
63 On the other side of the Jordan, to the
east of Jericho, they were given from the
tribe of Reuben: Bezer in the desert with its
pastures, Jahzah with its pastures, 64 Kede-
moth with its pastures, Mephaath with its
pastures.
65 From the tribe of Gad they were given
Ramoth in Gilead with its pastures,
Mahanaim with its pastures, 66 Heshbon
with its pastures, and Jazer with its pastures.

CHAPTER 7

Issachar. 1 The sons of Issachar were Tola,
Puah, Jashub, and Shimron. There were four
of them in all. [x]
2 The sons of Tola were Uzzi, Rephaiah,
Jeriel, Jahmai, Ibsam, and Shemuel, all lead-
ers of their ancestral clans. During the reign
of David, the descendants of Tola had twen-
ty-two thousand, six hundred brave warriors
in their generations.
3 The son of Uzzi was Izrahiah. The sons of
Izrahiah were Michael, Obadiah, Joel, and
Isshiah. All five of them were leaders.
4 According to the generations of their ances-
tral clans, they had thirty-six thousand war-
riors, for they had many wives and children.
5 There were eighty-seven thousand brave
warriors in all of their genealogies from
among the brethren who belonged to the
clans of Issachar.
Benjamin. 6 The sons of Benjamin were
Bela, Becher, and Jediael. There were three
of them in all. [y]
7 The sons of Bela were Ezbon, Uzzi,
Uzziel, Jerimoth, and Iri. They were the five
leaders of the ancestral clans. There were
twenty-two thousand and thirty-four brave
warriors according to their genealogies.
8 The sons of Becher were Zemirah, Joash,
Eliezer, Elioenai, Omri, Jeremoth, Abijah,
Anathoth, and Alemeth. All of these were
the sons of Becher. 9 These are the genealo-
gies of the leaders of the ancestral clans and
their twenty thousand, two hundred brave
warriors.
10 The son of Jediael was Bilhan. The
sons of Bilhan were Jeush, Benjamin,
Ehud, Chenaanah, Zethan, Tarshish, and
Ahishahar.

x Gen 46:13; Num 26:23.—y Gen 46:21; Num 26:38.

6:46 *Allotted ten cities:* **this method of assigning ownership was understood to be guided by God and therefore more fair than if left to the decision of an arbitrary person.**

11 All of the sons of Jediael were leaders
of the brave warriors, of whom there were
seventeen thousand, two hundred ready for
battle.

12 The Shuppites and the Huppites were
descendants of Ir, and the Hushim were
descendants of Dan.

Naphtali and Manasseh. 13 The sons of
Naphtali were Jahziel, Guni, Jezer, and
Shallum. They were descendants of Bilhah.

14 * The descendants of Manasseh includ-
ed Ashriel who was a descendant of his
Aramean concubine. She bore Machir, the
father of Gilead. [z]

15 Machir took a wife from among the
Huppites and the Shuppites. His sister's
name was Maacah. Another of his descen-
dants was Zelophehad who only had daugh-
ters.

16 Maacah, the wife of Machir, gave birth
to a son named Peresh. His brother's name
was Sheresh, and his sons were Ulam and
Rakem.

17 The son of Ulam was Bedan. These were
the descendants of Gilead, the son of Machir,
the son of Manasseh. [a]
18 His sister was
Hammolecheth. She gave birth to Ishhod,
Abiezer, and Mahlah.

19 The sons of Shemida were Ahian,
Shechem, Likhi, and Aniam.

Ephraim. 20 The descendants of Ephraim
were Shuthelah, Bered, his son, Tahath, his
son, Eleadah, his son, Tahath, his son,
21 Zabad, his son, and Shuthelah, his son.
Ezer and Elead were killed by men born in
the land of Gath when they led a raid to take
away their cattle.
22 Their father Ephraim
mourned for them for a long time, and his
relatives came to comfort him.
23 Then he
slept with his wife again, and she conceived
and bore a son whose name was Beriah
because misfortune had visited his family.*
24 His daughter was Sheerah. She built upper
and lower Beth-horon as well as Uzzen-
sheerah. [b]

25 Rephah was his son as well as Resheph.
There was Telah, his son, Tahan, his son,
26 Ladan, his son, Ammihud, his son, Elish-
ama, his son,
27 Nun, his son, and Joshua, his
son. [c]

28 Now their possessions and their dwelling
places included Bethel and the towns depen-
dent upon it, to the east Naaran, to the west
Gezer and the towns dependent upon it,
Shechem and the towns dependent upon
it, Ayyah and the towns dependent upon it.* [d]
29 Near the boundary with Manasseh there
were Beth-shean and the towns dependent
upon it, Taanach and the towns depen-
dent upon it, Megiddo and the towns
dependent upon it, and Dor with its towns.
The descendants of Joseph, the son of
Israel, dwelt in them. [e]

Asher. 30 The sons of Asher were Imnah,
Ishvah, Ishvi, Beriah, and their sister Serah. [f]

31 The sons of Beriah were Heber and
Malchiel, who was the father of Birzaith.

32 Heber was the father of Japhlet, Shomer,
Hotham, and their sister Shua.

33 The sons of Japhlet were Pasach,
Bimhal, and Ashvath. These were the chil-
dren of Japhlet.

34 The sons of Shomer were Ahi, Rohgah,
Jehubbah, and Aram.

35 The sons of his brother Hotham were
Zophah, Imna, Shelesh, and Amal.

36 The sons of Zophah were Suah, Har-
nepher, Shual, Beri, Imrah,
37 Bezer, Hod,
Shamma, Shilshah, Ithran, and Beera.

38 The sons of Jether were Jephunneh,
Pispa, and Ara.

39 The sons of Ulla were Arah, Hanniel,
and Rizia.

40 These were all the descendants of Asher,
the leaders of the ancestral clans, the mighty
brave warriors, and the main leaders. In
their genealogies there were twenty-six
thousand warriors ready for battle.

CHAPTER 8

Benjamin. 1 Benjamin was the father of
Bela, his firstborn, Ashbel, his second,
Aharah, his third, [g]
2 Nohah, his fourth, and
Rapha, his fifth.

---

z Gen 41:51; Num 26:30; Jos 17:1.—a 1 Sam 12:11.—b Jos 16:3, 5.—c Ex 17:9-14; 24:13.—d 1 Ki 9:16.—e Jos 17:11.—f Gen 46:17; Num 26:44-46.—g Gen 46:21; Num 26:38-44.

7:14-15 Manasseh had contacts with the Arameans (see Gen 31:46f). Machir was the half-tribe that dwelt across the Jordan (see Num 32:39f) and was certainly the older of the two half-tribes (see Jdg 5:14). The Huppites and Shuppites belonged to the tribe of Benjamin, while Jabesh in Gilead, a town in the territory of Manasseh, was allied with the Benjaminites (see Jdg 21:12).

7:23 The clan of Beriah later became part of Benjamin (see 8:13).

7:28 Shechem is usually placed in the tribe of Manasseh. In this passage, the Chronicler seems to be giving the name Ephraim to the combined tribes of Ephraim and Manasseh.

3 The sons of Bela were Addar, Gera, the
father of Ehud,* 4 Abishua, Naaman, Ahoah,
5 Gera, Shephuphan, and Huram. [h]

6 These were the sons of Ehud. They were
the leaders of the ancestral clans of those
who lived in Geba. They forced them to
move to Manahath: 7 Naaman, Ahijah, and
Gera, who forced them to move. He was the
father of Uzza and Ahihud.

8 Shaharaim had children in the land of
Moab after he sent away Hushim and Baara,
his wives. 9 Through Hodesh, his wife, he was
the father of Jobab, Zibia, Mesha, Malcam,
10 Jeuz, Sachia, and Mirmah. They were his
sons and leaders of the ancestral clans.

11 Through Hushim he was the father of
Abitub and Elpaal.

12 The sons of Elpaal were Eber, Misham,
Shemed, who built Ono and Lod and the
towns dependent upon them, [i] 13 Beriah, and
Shema. They were the leaders of the ances-
tral clans of those who lived in Aijalon and
who drove out the inhabitants of Gath. [j]

14 Ahio, Shashak, Jeremoth, 15 Zebadiah,
Arad, Eder, 16 Michael, Ispah, and Joha were
the sons of Beriah.

17 Zebadiah, Meshullam, Hizki, Heber,
18 Ishmerai, Izliah, and Jobab were the sons
of Elpaal.

19 Jakim, Zichri, Zabdi, 20 Elienai, Zillethai,
Eliel, 21 Adaiah, Beraiah, and Shimrath were
the sons of Shimei.

22 Ishpan, Eber, Eliel, 23 Abdon, Zichri,
Hanan, 24 Hananiah, Elam, Antothijah,
25 Iphdeiah, and Penuel were the sons of
Shashak.

26 Shamsherai, Shehariah, Athaliah,
27 Jaareshiah, Elijah, and Zichri were the
sons of Jeroham. 28 These were the leaders of
the ancestral clans by their leader. They
dwelt in Jerusalem.

29 Now the father of Gibeon, whose wife's
name was Maacah, lived in Gibeon.* [k] 30 His
firstborn son was Abdon, then Zur, Kish,
Baal, Nadab, 31 Gedor, Ahio, Zecheriah,
32 and Mikloth, who became the father of
Shimeah. They dwelt near their brethren in
Jerusalem, living with them.

33 Ner was the father of Kish, and Kish was
the father of Saul.

Saul was the father of Jonathan, Mal-
chishua, Abinadab, and Esh-baal. [l]

34 The son of Jonathan was Meri-baal, and
Meri-baal was the father of Micah. [m]

35 The sons of Micah were Pithon, Melech,
Tahrea, and Ahaz.

36 Ahaz was the father of Jehoaddah.
Jehoaddah was the father of Alemeth,
Azmaveth, and Zimri.

Zimri was the father of Moza.

37 Moza was the father of Binea, Raphah
was his son, Eleasah was his son, and Azel
was his son.

38 Azel had six sons whose names were
Azrikam, Bocheru, Ishmael, Sheariah, Oba-
diah, and Hanan. All of these were sons of
Azel.

39 The sons of Eshek, his brother, were
Ulam, his firstborn, Jeush, his second, and
Eliphelet, his third.

40 The sons of Ulam were brave warriors,
archers. They had many sons and grandsons,
one hundred and fifty in all. These were all of
the descendants of Benjamin. [n]

CHAPTER 9*

1 Thus all of Israel was recorded by its gen-
erations, for behold, it was inscribed in the
book of the kings of Israel.

Judah was carried away into Babylon for
its unfaithfulness. 2 The first inhabitants who
dwelt in their possessions in their cities were
the Israelites, the priests, the Levites, and the
temple slaves.* [o]

3 Among the Judahites who dwelt in
Jerusalem along with the Benjaminites,
Ephraimites, and Manassehites were: 4 Uthai,
the son of Ammihud, the son of Omri, the son
of Imri, the son of Bani, a descendant of
Perez, the son of Judah.

h Jdg 3:15.—i Neh 6:2; 7:37; 11:35; Ezr 2:33.—j Jos 10:12; 11:22.—k Jos 9:3.—l 1 Sam 9:1; 14:49; 28:19; 2 Sam 2:8.—m 2 Sam 4:4; 9:6, 12.—n Num 26:38.—o Jos 9:27; Ezr 2:70; Neh 11:3-22.

8:3 Ehud was the liberator of Israel from the Moabites; his story is in Jdg 3:15f.

8:29 According to what is said below in 1 Chr 21:29, the tabernacle was at Gibeon, before David moved it.

9:1-34 The genealogies end with a description of the population of Jerusalem at the return from Exile. After the Exile the religious restorers will more than ever regard Jerusalem as the holy city; it will become the symbol of the heavenly city that is awaited at the end of time. Other lists are given in Ezek 1; Neh 7; 11.

9:2 The reference is certainly to the descendants of slaves or foreigners who had long since been incorporated into Israel and assigned to subordinate cultic functions.

5 From the Shelanites there was Asaiah,
the firstborn, and his sons. 6 From the sons of
Zerah there was Jeuel and their brethren, six
hundred and ninety of them.

7 From the Benjaminites there were Sallu,
the son of Meshullam, the son of Hodaviah,
the son of Hassenuah, 8 Ibneiah, the son
of Jeroham, Elah, the son of Uzzi, the son
of Michri, and Meshullam, the son of
Shephatiah, the son of Reuel, the son of
Ibnijah, 9 along with their kinsmen, accord-
ing to their generations. There were nine
hundred fifty-six of them. All of these were
leaders of their ancestral clans.

10 From the priests there were Jedaiah,
Jehoiarib, Jachin, 11 and Azariah, the son
of Hilkiah, the son of Meshullam, the son of
Zadok, the son of Meraioth, the son of
Ahitub, the chief custodian of the temple.
12 There were also Adaiah, the son of
Jeroham, the son of Pashhur, the son of
Malchijah, and Maasai, the son of Adiel, the
son of Jahzerah, the son of Meshullam, the
son of Meshillemith, the son of Immer.[p]
13 Their brethren, who were the leaders of
the ancestral clans, included one thousand,
seven hundred and sixty men. They were all
capable men who were responsible for min-
istry in the temple of the LORD.

14 From the Levites there were Shemaiah,
the son of Hasshub, the son of Azrikam, the
son of Hashabiah, who was a Merarite.
15 There were Bakbakkar, Heresh, Galal, and
Mattaniah, the son of Mica, the son of Zichri,
the son of Asaph. 16 There were Obadiah, the
son of Shemaiah, the son of Galal, the son of
Jeduthun, and Berechiah, the son of Asa, the
son of Elkanah. They lived in the village of
the Netophathites.

17 The gatekeepers were Shallum, Akkub,
Talmon, Ahiman, and their brethren.
Shallum was their leader. 18 They have been
stationed at the king's gate on the east up to
the present day. They were the gatekeepers
of the Levites.

19 Shallum, the son of Kore, the son of
Ebiasaph, the son of Korah, and his brethren
from the ancestral clan of the Korahites
were the gatekeepers at the entrance to the
tabernacle just as their ancestors had been
the gatekeepers to the entrance of the
dwelling place of the LORD. 20 In former
days, Phinehas, the son of Eleazar, had been
their leader, and the LORD had been with
him.[q]

21 Zechariah, the son of Meshelemiah was
the gatekeeper at the entrance to the tent of
meeting. 22 There were two hundred and
twelve of those who had been chosen to be
gatekeepers. They are registered by their
family history in the villages. David and
Samuel the seer had assigned them to their
responsibilities. 23 They and their children
were responsible for guarding the gates of
the temple of the LORD (the shrine of the
tabernacle) by turns. 24 The gatekeepers
served in the four directions of the east, the
west, the north, and the south. 25 Their
brethren who lived in the villages would
come up to join them for a period of seven
days from time to time.[r]

26 There were four Levites who held the
office of chief gatekeepers. They were
responsible for the chambers and the trea-
suries of the temple of the LORD. 27 They
would spend the night stationed around the
temple of God because they were responsi-
ble for it, and then they would open it each
morning.[s]

28 Some of them were responsible for the
vessels used in the liturgy, and they would
count them when they were brought in and
taken out. 29 Others were assigned responsi-
bility for the furniture and all of the other
things used in the sanctuary as well as the
flour, wine, oil, incense, and spices. 30 Some
of the priests were responsible for mixing the
spices in the ointments.[t]

31 There was a certain Levite, Mattithiah,
the firstborn of Shallum the Korahite, who
was responsible for the baking of the bread.
32 Some of the Korahites, their brethren,
were in charge of preparing the shewbread
every Sabbath.[u]

33 Those who were singers, the leaders of
their ancestral clans of Levites, would stay in
the chambers. They were free from other
responsibilities, for they were busy working
day and night.[v]

34 These were all leaders of the ancestral
clans of the Levites, leaders according to
their generations, and they dwelt in
Jerusalem.

p Ezr 2:38; Neh 10:3; Jer 21:1.—q Ex 6:25; Num 25:7-13.—r 2 Ki 11:5.—s Num 3:38; Isa 22:22.—t Ex 30:20-33.—u Ex 25:30; Lev 24:5-8.—v Ps 134:1.

II: THE HISTORY OF DAVID*

Genealogy of Saul. 35 Jeiel, the father of Gibeon, dwelt in Gibeon. His wife's name was Maacah. 36 His firstborn was Abdon, then there were Zur, Kish, Baal, Ner, Nadab, 37 Gedor, Ahio, Zechariah, and Mikloth.

38 Mikloth was the father of Shimeam. They lived near their brethren, their brethren who lived in Jerusalem.

39 Ner was the father of Kish, and Kish was the father of Saul.

Saul was the father of Jonathan, Malchishua, Abinadab, and Esh-baal.[w]

40 The son of Jonathan was Merib-baal, who was the father of Micah.

41 The sons of Micah were Pithon, Melech, Tahrea, and Ahaz.

42 Ahaz was the father of Jarah, and Jarah was the father of Alemeth, Azmaveth, and Zimri.

Zimri was the father of Moza.

43 Moza was the father of Binea, Rephaiah was his son, Eleasah his son, and Azel his son.

44 Azel had six sons, and these are their names: Azrikam, Bocheru, Ishmael, Sheariah, Obadiah, and Hanan. They were the sons of Azel.

CHAPTER 10

Saul's Death and Burial. 1 Now the Philistines attacked Israel, and Israel fled from the Philistines. Many fell and were killed at Mount Gilboa. 2 The Philistines pursued Saul and his sons. The Philistines killed Jonathan, Abinadab, and Malchishua, the sons of Saul. 3 The fighting around Saul became fierce when the archers hit him. The archers wounded him. 4 Saul said to his armor-bearer, "Take out your sword and run me through lest these uncircumcised men come and mock me." But he was terrified, so Saul took out a sword and fell on it.[x] 5 When his armor-bearer saw that Saul was dead, he, too, fell on his sword and died. 6 Saul and his three sons died, and his whole household died with him.

7 When all the Israelites in the valley saw that they had fled and that Saul and his sons were dead, they abandoned their cities and fled. The Philistines came and occupied them.

8 The next day the Philistines came up to strip the dead, and they found Saul and his sons who had fallen on Mount Gilboa. 9 They stripped him, taking his head and his armor. They sent word throughout the surrounding land of the Philistines proclaiming the news among their idols and their people. 10 They placed his armor in the shrine of their gods, hanging his head in the shrine of Dagon.*[y]

11 When all the people in Jabesh-gilead heard about everything that the Philistines had done to Saul, 12 all of their brave men rose up and took away the body of Saul and the bodies of his sons. They brought them to Jabesh and buried their bones under the oak tree in Jabesh. They then fasted for seven days.[z]

13 * Saul died because of the transgressions that he had committed against the LORD, against the word of the LORD which he did not observe, for he even consulted with a medium to make inquiry.[a] 14 He did not inquire from the LORD. He slew him and turned the kingdom over to David, the son of Jesse.[b]

CHAPTER 11

David Becomes King. 1 * All of Israel gathered before David in Hebron and they said, "Behold, we are your bone and your flesh.[c] 2 Moreover, in times past, even when Saul

w 1 Sam 9:1.—x 1 Sam 31:4-7.—y Jdg 16:23.—z 2 Sam 2:5.—a Lev 19:31; Deut 18:9-14; 1 Sam 13:13; 15:23; 28:7.—b 1 Sam 15:28; 2 Sam 3:9-10.—c Gen 13:18.

9:35—29:30 The second part of the first Book of Chronicles is devoted entirely to David. The Chronicler takes much of his material from the Books of Samuel, but everything that made David so human and such a vivid personage is passed over in silence; there is nothing here of the lively youth, the friend of Jonathan, the hunted outlaw, the repentant and harshly-tested sinner, the man crushed by family tragedies and the intrigues of his successors. The Books of Samuel portray a heartrending drama; the Chronicler, on the contrary, draws a clear but austere picture. He prefers the serious side and emphasizes fundamental characteristics. Here, then, is, first of all, David as founder of the royal dignity; then David as establisher of the cult in Jerusalem; finally, and above all, David, depository of the divine promises.

10:10 *Shrine of Dagon:* with the victory of the Philistines over the Israelites, the armor and head of Saul were presented to their most important god. When the Philistines captured the Ark of the Covenant, they brought it to the temple of Dagon in Ashdod (1 Sam 5:1-5). It was finally destroyed by the Maccabees (1 Mac 10:84).

10:13-14 Instead of turning to God first, Saul bypassed God in favor of a medium. Eventually his disobedience and unfaithfulness brought God's wrath upon him.

11:1—12:40 The difficulties attending the succession to Saul and the period in which the power of David was limited to the southern tribes (2 Sam 2–4) are deliberately passed over. The new king chosen by God is immediately presented as the sole head of the entire people of Israel (see 12:24f).

was the king, you led Israel out and brought
them in. The LORD, your God, said to you,
'You will shepherd my people Israel. You will
be the ruler of my people Israel.' "[d] 3 When
all of the elders of Israel came to the king in
Hebron, he made a covenant before the
LORD with them at Hebron. They anointed
David as king over Israel, fulfilling the word
of the LORD that had been spoken by
Samuel.[e]

David Conquers Jerusalem. 4 David and all
of Israel went to Jerusalem, that is, Jebus.
The Jebusites were the inhabitants of that
land.[f] 5 The inhabitants of Jebus said to
David, "You will never enter." Nevertheless,
David captured the citadel of Zion, that is,
the City of David. 6 David had said,
"Whoever leads the attack on the Jebusites
will be the commander-in-chief." Joab, the
son of Zeruiah, led it so he became the com-
mander.[g]

7 David lived in the citadel, and thus it was
called the City of David. 8 He built up the city
around it, from Millo to the surrounding
walls. Joab repaired the rest of the city.[h]
9 David's power grew and grew, for the LORD
of hosts was with him.[i]

David's Brave Warriors. 10 These were the
leaders of David's brave warriors. They
made him and his kingdom strong, with all
of Israel making him king, according to the
word of the LORD about Israel. 11 * This is the
list of David's brave warriors: Ishbaal, a
Hachmonite, was the leader of the captains.
He raised up his spear against three hundred
men at one time and he slew them.

12 After him there was Eleazar, the son of
Dodo, who was one of the three mighty men.
13 He was with David at Pas-dammim when
the Philistines gathered there for battle. It
was a field that was planted with barley, and
the people fled before the Philistines.[j]
14 They took their stand in the middle of the
field. They defended it and slew the
Philistines, for the LORD brought about a
great deliverance.

15 Now three of the thirty captains came
down to the cave of Adullam to be with
David, while the army of the Philistines was
camped in the Valley of Rephaim.[k] 16 David
was in the stronghold, and there was a
Philistine outpost in Bethlehem. 17 David
longed for water so he said, "Oh that you
would give me some water to drink from the
well that is at the gate of Bethlehem." 18 The
Three broke through the lines of the Phil-
istine army and drew water from the well
at the gate to Bethlehem. They took it and
brought it to David, but David would not
drink it. He poured it out before the LORD.[l]
19 He said, "Far be it from me, my God, that
I should do such a thing, that I would drink
the blood of these men, for they risked their
lives to bring it back." Therefore, he would
not drink it.

These are the deeds of the Three brave
warriors. 20 Abishai, the brother of Joab, was
the leader of the Three. He raised up his
spear against three hundred men and he
slew them. He was the most famous of the
Three.[m] 21 He was twice as honored as the
Three, for he was their captain, even though
he was not one of the Three.

22 Benaiah, the son of Jehoiada, was a
brave warrior who performed many deeds.
He was from Kabzeel. He slew two of Moab's
mightiest men. He also descended into a pit
on a snowy day and killed a lion. 23 He also
slew a very tall Egyptian who was five cubits
tall. The Egyptian had a spear in his hand
that was as big as a weaver's beam. He
attacked him with his staff, and he snatched
the spear out of the Egyptian's hand and
slew him with his own spear. 24 These were
the deeds of Benaiah, the son of Jehoiada. He
was as famous as the Three Brave Warriors.
25 He was more greatly honored than any of
the Thirty,* but he did not belong to the
Three. David assigned him to be in charge of
his bodyguard.[n]

26 The brave warriors were: Asahel, the
brother of Joab; Elhanan, the son of Dodo
from Bethlehem; 27 Shammoth the Harorite;
Helez the Pelonite; 28 Ira, the son of Ikkesh
from Tekoa; Abiezer from Anathoth;
29 Sibbecai the Hushathite; Ilai the Ahohite;
30 Maharai the Netophathite; Heled, the son
of Baanah the Netophathite; 31 Ithai, the son
of Ribai from Gibeah in Benjamin; Benaiah
the Pirathonite; 32 Hurai, from the Wadi of
Gaash; Abiel the Arbathite; 33 Azmaveth the

---

d 1 Sam 18:5-6; Ps 78:71; Mt 2:6.—e 1 Sam 16:1-13; 2 Sam 2:4.—f Jos 15:8; Jdg 1:21.—g 2 Sam 8:16.—h 1 Ki 9:15; 11:27; 2 Chr 32:5.—i Est 9:4.—j 2 Sam 23:11-12.—k 2 Sam 5:18, 22; Isa 17:5.—l 2 Sam 23:16.—m 1 Sam 26:6-10; 2 Sam 16:9; 18:2.—n 2 Sam 8:18; 20:23.

11:11-12 *Three mighty men:* the Chronicler in this case only mentions two men, Ishbaal and Eleazar. However, we know from 2 Sam 23:11 that Shammah was the third.

11:25 *The Thirty:* these would be David's best military officers. The list of names in 2 Sam 23 differs somewhat from those given here.

Baharumite; Eliahba the Shaalbonite; 34 the
sons of Hashem the Gizonite; Jonathan, the
son of Shagee the Hararite; 35 Ahiam, the son
of Sacar the Hararite; Eliphal, the son of Ur;
36 Hepher the Mecherathite; Ahijah the
Pelonite; 37 Hezro the Carmelite; Naarai, the
son of Ezbai; 38 Joel, the brother of Nathan;
Mibhar, the son of Hagri; 39 Zelek the
Ammonite; Naharai the Berothite, the
armor-bearer of Joab, the son of Zeruiah;
40 Ira the Ithrite; Gareb the Ithrite; 41 Uriah
the Hittite; Zabad, the son of Ahlai; 42 Adina,
the son of Shiza the Reubenite, who was the
leader of the Reubenites and the Thirty with
him; 43 Hanan, the son of Maacah; Joshaphat
the Mithnite; 44 Uzzia the Ashterathite;
Shama and Jeiel, the sons of Hotham the
Aroerite; 45 Jediael, the son of Shimri; his
brother Joha the Tizite; 46 Eliel the Mahavite;
Jeribai and Joshaviah, the sons of Elnaam;
Ithmah the Moabite; 47 Eliel; Obed; and
Jaasiel the Mezobaite.

CHAPTER 12

David's First Followers. 1 These were the
men who came to David while he was at
Ziklag, a fugitive from Saul, the son of Kish.
They were the brave warriors who helped
him in battle. 2 They were armed with bows,
and they could sling stones or shoot arrows
from a bow with their right hand or their left.
They were kinsmen of Saul from Benjamin.[o]

3 Ahiezer was their leader, and then Joash,
who were the sons of Shemaah the Gibe-
athite. There were Jeziel and Pelet, the sons
of Azmaveth; Beracah; Jehu the Anathothite;
4 Ishmaiah the Gibeonite, a brave warrior
from among the Thirty and the leader of the
Thirty; Jeremiah; Jahaziel; Johanan; Jozabad
the Gederathite;[p] 5 Eluzai; Jerimoth; Beali-
ah; Shemariah; Shephatiah the Haruphite;
6 Elkanah; Isshiah; Azarel; Joezer; Jashobeam
the Korahite; 7 and Joelah and Zebadiah, the
sons of Jeroham from Gedor.

8 Some Gadites joined David in the wilder-
ness. They were brave men, warriors ready
for battle, able to handle the shield and the
spear. Their faces were as fierce as the faces
of lions, and they were as swift as gazelles
upon the mountains.[q] 9 Ezer was the first;
Obadiah was the second; Eliab was the third;
10 Mishmannah was the fourth; Jeremiah
was the fifth; 11 Attai was the sixth; Eliel was
the seventh; 12 Johanan was the eighth;
Elzabad was the ninth; 13 Jeremiah the tenth;
and Machbannai the eleventh. 14 These
Gadites were captains of the army. The
weakest of them was worth a hundred, the
strongest was worth a thousand.[r] 15 They
were crossing over the Jordan during the first
month when it was overflowing its banks,
and they put to flight everyone who was liv-
ing in the valleys to the east and the west.

16 Some other Benjaminites and Judahites
also went out to David in his stronghold.
17 David went out to meet them and he said
to them, "If you have come to me in peace,
to help me, then your heart will be one with
my heart. But if you are here to betray me to
my enemies even though my hands are inno-
cent, may the God of our fathers see it and
rebuke you."

18 The Spirit then came upon Amasai, the
leader of the captains, and he said,

"We are yours, David.
We will be with you, O son of Jesse.
May it go well with you,
and may it go well with those who help
you,
for your God will help you."

David received them and made them cap-
tains of his raiding parties.

19 Some men from Manasseh went over to
David when he went to the Philistines to
fight against Saul. He, however, did not help
them because the lords of the Philistines had
discussed it and sent him away saying, "It
would cost us our heads if he were to defect
to his master Saul."

20 These were the men of Manasseh who
went over to him in Ziklag: Adnah, Jozabad,
Jediael, Michael, Jozabad, Elihu, and Zil-
lethai. They were captains of the thousands
in Manasseh. 21 They helped David fight
against the raiding parties, and they were
brave warriors, all of them captains of the
army.

22 From that time on, more men would
arrive daily to help David until he had a
large army, like an army of God.*

Assembly at Hebron. 23 These are the num-
bers of the bands of those who came to
David in Hebron ready for battle. They
turned Saul's kingdom over to him, accord-
ing to the word of the LORD.

o Jdg 20:16.—p Jos 15:36.—q Gen 30:11; 2 Sam 2:18.—r Lev 26:8; Deut 32:30.

12:22 *Army of God:* David built a large and powerful army that won countless victories and indeed seemed to be on a higher plane than other military groups.

24 From Judah, there were six thousand,
eight hundred men bearing shield and spear,
ready for battle. 25 From Simeon there were
seven thousand, one hundred brave war-
riors, ready for battle. 26 From Levi there
were four thousand, six hundred men.
27 These included Jehoiada, the leader of the
Aaronites, and with him there were three
thousand, seven hundred men. 28 There was
Zadok, a young man who was a brave war-
rior, with twenty-two captains from his
father's household. 29 From Benjamin, Saul's
kinsmen, there were three thousand men,
most of whom had remained faithful to the
house of Saul until then. 30 From Ephraim
there were twenty thousand, eight hundred
brave warriors who were famous in their
ancestral clans. 31 There were eighteen thou-
sand men from one-half of the tribe of
Manasseh. They were designated by name to
go and make David king. 32 From Issachar
there were two hundred leaders with their
brethren under them. They understood well
the time and what Israel should do.* [s]
33 From Zebulun there were fifty thousand
experienced fighters ready to go into battle.
They had every different type of weapon,
and they were of undivided loyalty. 34 From
Naphtali there were one thousand captains
along with thirty-seven thousand men
armed with shield and spear. 35 From Dan
there were twenty-eight thousand, six hun-
dred men, ready for battle. 36 From Asher
there were forty thousand experienced fight-
ers ready for battle. 37 From the eastern side
of the Jordan, there were one hundred and
twenty thousand men armed with every dif-
ferent type of weapon from Reuben, Gad,
and one-half of the tribe of Manasseh.

38 All of these were well-trained fighting
men. They came to Hebron for they whole-
heartedly wanted to make David king over
all of Israel. The rest of Israel was in agree-
ment to make David king.* 39 They spent
three days eating and drinking with David
(for their brethren had provided provisions
for them). 40 Their neighbors from as far
away as Issachar, Zebulun, and Naphtali
brought food on their donkeys, camels,
mules, and oxen: plentiful supplies of flour,
fig cakes, raisin cakes, wine, oil, oxen, and
sheep, for joy had spread throughout Israel.

CHAPTER 13

The Ark Is Returned to Jerusalem. 1 * After
David consulted with the captains of the
thousands and the hundreds and with all of
the leaders, 2 he spoke to the assembly of
Israel, saying, "If you feel that this is good,
for the LORD, our God, has willed it, then let
us send messengers to the rest of our
brethren throughout the land of Israel,
including the priests and the Levites who are
in their cities and pastures, so that they can
come and join us. [t] 3 Let us bring the Ark of
God to where we are, for they did not make
inquiry at it during the reign of Saul."

4 The whole assembly said that they would
do this, for all of the people considered it to
be the right thing to do. 5 David assembled all
of Israel, from the Shihor* in Egypt up to
Lebo-hamath, to bring the Ark of God from
Kiriath-jearim. [u] 6 David and all of the
Israelites with him went to Baalah of Judah,
that is, Kiriath-jearim, to bring up from
there the Ark of God, the LORD, who dwells
between the cherubim where his name is
proclaimed. [v] 7 They carried the Ark of the
LORD on a new cart to the house of
Abinadab. Uzzah and Ahio drove the cart.
8 David and all of Israel played before the
LORD with all their might, singing and play-
ing on the harps, lyres, tambourines, cym-
bals, and trumpets.

9 When they came to the threshing floor of
Chidon, Uzzah reached out his hand to grab
the Ark because the oxen had stumbled.
10 The LORD's anger blazed against Uzzah,
and he struck him down because he had
touched the Ark.* He died there before the
LORD. 11 David was disturbed because of the
LORD's outburst against Uzzah, which is why
that place is called Perez-uzzah up to the
present day. [w]

s Est 1:13.—t Isa 37:4.—u Num 13:21; Jos 13:3; 1 Sam 6:21; 7:1.—v Ex 25:22; Jos 15:9; 2 Ki 19:15.—w Ps 7:11.

12:32 According to Hebrew tradition, the descendants of Issachar were experts in astronomy.

12:38 There was an extraordinary show of support for making David their king—both from the military (over 300,000) and general population.

13:1—16:43 The Chronicler highlights the installation of the Ark in Jerusalem as the first solemn religious act of his hero. In order to lend the event an exceptional grandeur, he imagines all Israel being solemnly summoned to participate in this triumphal action. The capital with its liturgy and its priesthood becomes the holy city of the people of God. The first civil and military activities of the reign (ch. 14) will be simply an interlude in this solemnity.

13:5 *Shihor:* usually called "the River of Egypt"; this marked the southern border of Palestine.

13:10 *Uzzah . . . touched the Ark:* in his fervent desire to protect the Ark, Uzzah, son of Shimei, disregarded the strict rules for moving it that were assigned by God to Moses (Num 4:5-15). His offense resulted in his immediate death.

12 David was afraid of the LORD that day,
saying, "How shall I bring the Ark of God to
myself?" 13 He did not take the Ark with him
into the City of David. He had it carried into
the house of Obed-edom the Gittite. 14 The
Ark of God remained with the family of
Obed-edom, in his house, for three months.
The LORD blessed the house of Obed-edom
and all that he owned. [x]

CHAPTER 14

David in Jerusalem. 1 Now Hiram, the king
of Tyre, sent messengers to David, along
with cedar wood, masons, and carpenters to
build him a palace. [y] 2 David knew that the
LORD had confirmed him as king over Israel
and that his kingdom had been highly exalted for the sake of his people Israel.

3 In Jerusalem David married more wives,
and he had more sons and daughters.
4 These were the names of the children who
were born to him there: Shammua, Shobab,
Nathan, Solomon, 5 Ibhar, Elishua, Elpelet,
6 Nogah, Nepheg, Japhia, 7 Elishama, Beeliada, and Eliphelet.

David's Victory over the Philistines. 8 When
the Philistines heard that David had been
anointed as king over all of Israel, all of the
Philistines went up to seek out David. David
heard about it and went out to meet them. [z]
9 The Philistines arrived and spread themselves out in the Valley of Rephaim.

10 David inquired of God, saying, "Shall I
go out against the Philistines? Will you deliver them into my hands?" The LORD
answered them, "Go up, I will deliver them
into your hands." *

11 They went up to Baal-perazim, and
there David defeated them. David said,
"God has broken my enemies by my hand,
just as when waters break forth." This is why
that place is called Baal-perazim. [a] 12 They
had left their gods there, and David gave an
order that they be burned in the fire. [b]

13 Still another time the Philistines came
and spread themselves out in the valley.
14 David inquired of God again, and God said
to him, "Do not attack them directly, but circle around them and attack them from
behind the balsam trees. 15 As soon as you
hear the sound of marching in the tops of the
balsam trees, go forth into battle, for God
has gone forth before you to strike down the
Philistines."

16 David did as God had commanded him,
and they struck down the army of the
Philistines from Gibeon all the way to Gezer.
17 David's fame spread throughout every
land, and the LORD caused all of the nations
to fear him. [c]

CHAPTER 15

Carrying the Ark to Jerusalem. 1 After
David had constructed buildings for himself in the City of David, he prepared a
place for the Ark of God, pitching a tent
for it.

2 David then said, "No one can carry the
Ark of God except the Levites. The LORD has
chosen them to carry the Ark of God and to
minister to him forever." [d]

3 David assembled all of Israel in Jerusalem to bring the Ark of the LORD to the
place that he had prepared for it. [e] 4 David
assembled the descendants of Aaron and the
Levites.

5 From the descendants of Kohath, there
were Uriel, their leader, and one hundred
and twenty of his brethren. 6 From the
descendants of Merari, there were Asaiah,
their leader, and two hundred and twenty of
his brethren. 7 From the descendants of
Gershon, there were Joel, their leader, and
one hundred and thirty of his brethren.
8 From the descendants of Elizaphan, there
were Shemaiah, their leader, and two hundred of his brethren. 9 From the descendants
of Hebron, there were Eliel, their leader, and
eighty of his brethren. 10 From the descendants of Uzziel, there were Amminadab,
their leader, and one hundred and twelve of
his brethren.

11 David summoned Zadok and Abiathar,
the priests, and Uriel, Asaiah, Joel, Shemaiah, Eliel, and Amminadab the Levites. [f]
12 He said to them, "You are the leaders of
the ancestral clans of the Levites. Sanctify
yourselves and your brethren so that you
might bring the Ark of the LORD, the
God of Israel, to the place that I have

x 1 Chr 26:4-5; 2 Sam 6:11.—y 2 Chr 2:3; Ezr 3:7; Hag 1:8.—z 2 Sam 5:17.—a Ps 94:16; Isa 28:21.—b Ex 32:20; Deut 7:5, 25.—c Deut 2:25; Jos 6:27; 2 Chr 26:8.—d Num 4:15; Deut 10:8; 31:25; 1 Sam 6:15; Ps 134:1.—e 2 Sam 6:15, 17.—f 1 Chr 12:27-28; 1 Sam 22:20.

14:10 The Chronicler's unabashed esteem for David comes through as he points out the wisdom of David, who always consulted the Lord before going into battle.

prepared for it.[g] 13 * It is because you did not
bring it up the first time that the LORD burst
forth against us, for we did not inquire of
him about the proper order."[h]

14 The priests and the Levites sanctified
themselves to bring up the Ark of the LORD,
the God of Israel. 15 The descendants of the
Levites carried the Ark of God by its poles on
their shoulders, as Moses had commanded,
according to the word of the LORD.[i]

16 David spoke to the leaders of the Levites
to appoint their brethren as singers, lifting
their voices up with joy, and accompanied by
music played on the lyres, harps, and cym-
bals.[j] 17 So the Levites appointed Heman,
the son of Joel, and one of his brethren,
Asaph, the son of Berechiah, and from
among the brethren of the Merarites, Ethan,
the son of Kushaiah.

18 With them, there were their brethren of
second rank: Zechariah, Uzziel, Shemira-
moth, Jehiel, Unni, Eliab, Benaaiah,
Maaseiah, Mattithiah, Eliphelehu, Mikneiah,
Obed-edom, and Jeiel, the gatekeepers.

19 The musicians Heman, Asaph, and
Ethan were to play upon bronze cymbals.
20 Zechariah, Uzziel, Shemiramoth, Jehiel,
Unni, Eliab, Maaseiah, and Benaiah were to
play the lyres according to Alamoth.
21 Matthithiah, Eliphelehu, Mikneiah, Obed-
edom, Jeiel, and Azaziah were to play upon
harps according to the Sheminith. 22 Chena-
niah, the leader of the Levites dedicated to
music, directed the music, for he was skillful
at it.

23 Berechiah and Elkanah were the gate-
keepers for the Ark. 24 Shebaniah, Joshaphat,
Nethanel, Amasai, Zechariah, Benaiah, and
Eliezer, the priests, were to blow the trum-
pets before the Ark of God. Obed-edom and
Jeiel were also gatekeepers for the Ark.[k]

The Ark Comes to Jerusalem. 25 David, the
elders of Israel, and the captains of the thou-
sands went to bring the Ark of the Covenant
of the LORD up from out of the house of
Obed-edom with joy.[l] 26 God helped the
Levites carry the Ark of the Covenant of the
LORD, and they sacrificed seven bulls and
seven rams. 27 David was dressed in a robe
made from fine linen, as were the Levites
who were carrying the Ark, the singers, and
Chenaniah, the director of the music. David
also wore a linen ephod.*[m] 28 All of Israel
brought up the Ark of the Covenant of the
LORD with shouting, to the sound of the
horn, the trumpets, and the cymbal, and
playing upon the harps and the lyres.[n]

29 As the Ark of the Covenant of the LORD
came to the City of David, Michal, the
daughter of Saul, was watching out the win-
dow. She saw King David dancing and play-
ing, and she despised him in her heart.

CHAPTER 16

1 They brought the Ark of God and placed
it inside of the tent that David had pitched
for it. They offered burnt sacrifices and
peace offerings before God.[o] 2 When David
had finished offering the burnt offerings and
the peace offerings, he blessed the people in
the name of the LORD. 3 He gave each man
and each woman in Israel one loaf of bread,
a piece of meat, and a cake of raisins.

The Levite Ministers. 4 He appointed some
of the Levites to minister before the Ark of
the LORD, to commemorate, to thank, and
to praise the LORD, the God of Israel.[p]
5 They were Asaph, the leader, Zechariah,
the next in charge, and Jeiel, Shemiramoth,
Jehiel, Mattithiah, Eliab, Benaiah, and
Obed-edom. They were to play upon the
lyres and the harps while Asaph was to play
upon the cymbals. 6 Benaiah and Jahaziel
were the priests who normally blew the
trumpets before the Ark of the Covenant of
the LORD.*

7 On that day David first gave Asaph and
his brethren this psalm of thanks to the
LORD:

8 * Give thanks to the LORD, call upon his
name;
make his deeds known among the
nations.[q]

9 Sing to him, praise him with song;
speak of all his wondrous deeds.

g 2 Chr 35:6.—h Lev 5:10; 1 Ki 8:4.—i Ex 25:10-22; 2 Chr 35:3.—j Ezr 2:41; Neh 11:23; Ps 68:25; Job 21:12.—k Num 10:8; Jos 6:4-8.—l 2 Chr 1:4; 5:2; Jer 3:16.—m 1 Sam 2:18; 2 Sam 6:14.—n 1 Ki 1:39; Zec 4:7.—o 2 Sam 6:17-19.—p Sir 47:9.—q Pss 105:1-15; 118:1.

15:13-15 Even with all his wisdom, David sometimes failed to follow God's instructions. Although returning the Ark to Israel was the right thing to do, David was careless in following the prescribed method and was unsuccessful until he was obedient to God's explicit instructions.

15:27 The Chronicler seems to want to clarify what had been said in 2 Sam 6:14; the ephod was of linen, but it was worn over a robe of fine linen.

16:6 The trumpets were to be blown only by priests; the cymbals of the leaders of the choirs set the rhythm.

16:8-36 The prayer is composed of sections of several Psalms (Pss 105:1-15; 96; 106:1, 47-48). The author's purpose is to provide a model for the Jerusalem liturgy.

10 Glory in his holy name,
let the hearts of those who seek the LORD rejoice.
11 Seek the LORD and his strength,
seek his face continually.
12 Remember the marvels he has done,
his wondrous deeds and the judgments of his mouth.
13 O descendants of Israel, his servant,
O children of Jacob, his chosen one.
14 He is the LORD, our God,
his judgments extend to all the earth. [r]
15 He always remembers his covenant,
the word he has commanded for a thousand generations,
16 which he made with Abraham,
the oath he swore to Isaac.
17 He confirmed it to Jacob as a decree,
to Israel as an eternal covenant,
18 saying, "I will give you the land of Canaan;
it will be your allotted inheritance."
19 When there were only a few of them,
few indeed, with foreigners among them,
20 they wandered from nation to nation,
from one kingdom to another people.
21 He did not let anyone oppress them,
for their sake he rebuked kings,
22 "Do not touch my anointed;
do no harm to my prophets." [s]
23 Sing to the LORD, all the earth,
proclaim his salvation from day to day.
24 Declare his glory among the nations,
among all nations, his marvelous deeds.
25 For great is the LORD, greatly to be praised;
he is to be feared more than all the other gods.
26 All the gods of the nations are idols,
but the LORD made the heavens.
27 Glory and honor are before him,
strength and joy in his dwelling place.
28 Give to the LORD, O families of nations,
give to the LORD glory and strength. [t]
29 Give to the LORD the glory due his name.
Bring an offering and come before him;
worship the LORD in holy attire.
30 Tremble before him, all the earth;
the world is firmly established, not to be moved.
31 Let the heavens be glad, and the earth rejoice;
let them say among the nations, "The LORD reigns."
32 Let the sea roar, and whatever fills it;
let the fields rejoice, and all that is in them.
33 The trees of the forest will sing out before the LORD,
for he comes to judge the earth.
34 Give thanks to the LORD, for he is good;
his mercy endures forever.
35 Shout forth, "Save us, O LORD, our savior;
gather us in and deliver us from the nations.
Then we will give thanks to your holy name,
we will glory in your praise."
36 Praise the LORD, the God of Israel,
forever and ever.
All the people said, "Amen! Praise the LORD!"

37 He left Asaph and his brethren there
before the Ark of the Covenant of the
LORD to minister before the Ark and to do
each day's required work. 38 He also left
Obed-edom and sixty-eight of his
brethren with them. Obed-edom, the son
of Jeduthun, and Hosah were the gate-
keepers.

39 He also left Zadok, the priest, and his
fellow priests before the tabernacle of the
LORD at the high place in Gibeon. [u] 40 He
was to offer the regular burnt offerings
upon the altar of burnt offerings, each
morning and each evening, just as it is
written in the law of the LORD which he
gave to Israel. [v] 41 With him there were
Heman and Jeduthun and the others who
had been chosen, who had been designat-
ed by name to give thanks to the LORD, for
his mercy endures forever. [w] 42 Heman and
Jeduthun were responsible for playing the
trumpets and the cymbals as well as the
other sacred musical instruments. The
sons of Jeduthun were gatekeepers.

43 Then all the people departed, each
returning home. David, too, went home to
bless his household. [x]

CHAPTER 17*

Nathan's Oracle. 1 After David had moved
into his palace, David said to Nathan the

r Isa 26:9.—s Gen 12:17; 20:3; Ex 7:15-18.—t Ps 29:1-2.—u 1 Ki 3:4; Jos 9:3-4.—v Ex 29:38; Num 28:3.—w 2 Chr 5:12-13; Ezr 3:11.—x 2 Sam 6:19-20.

17:1-27 At the center of the story of David (from which all the shadows have been removed) the Chronicler places the event that gives it meaning and that is recorded in 2 Sam 7:1-17. Being made ancestor and type of the future "Anointed One," the Messiah, David is given an unparalleled place in the history of salvation.

prophet, "Behold, I live in a house of cedar,
but the Ark of the Covenant of the LORD lives
under awnings."[y] 2 Nathan said to David,
"Do whatever you want to, for the LORD is
with you."

3 But that same night the word of the LORD
came to Nathan, saying, 4 "Go and tell David
my servant: Thus says the LORD, 'You are not
to build a house in which I will live. [z] 5 I have
not dwelt in a house from the time that I
brought Israel up from out of Egypt up to the
present day. I have traveled around from one
tent site to another. 6 In the whole time that I
have traveled around with Israel, have I ever
said to any of the judges of Israel whom I
commanded to shepherd my people, Why
have you not built me a house made from
cedar wood?'

7 "Now, therefore, tell my servant David:
Thus says the LORD of hosts, 'I took you from
the sheepfold, from following after the sheep,
to be the ruler over my people Israel. [a] 8 I
have been with you wherever you have gone,
and I have cut down all of your enemies from
before you. I have made your name famous,
as famous as the great men of the earth. 9 I
will establish a dwelling place for my people
Israel. I will plant them so that they might
dwell in their own place. They will not have
to move about anymore, nor shall the children
of wickedness oppress them as they
have done in the past, 10 from the time that
I commanded judges to be over my people
Israel. I will humble all of your enemies. [b]

" 'Furthermore, it is the LORD who will
build you a house. 11 When your days have
been fulfilled and you go to be with your
fathers, I will raise up your seed after you,
one of your sons,* and I will establish his
kingdom. 12 He will build a house for me,
and I will establish his throne forever. [c] 13 I
will be his father, and he will be my son. I
will not withdraw my mercy from him, as
I took it away from the one who preceded
you. * [d] 14 I will have him stand firm in my
house forever, and his throne will be established
forever.' "

15 Nathan reported this entire vision and
all of these words to David.

David's Prayer of Thanksgiving. 16 King
David then went in and sat before the LORD
and said, "Who am I, O LORD God, and what
is my household that you have brought me to
this point? 17 And as if there were a small
thing in your sight, O God, you have spoken
about the future of your servant's house. You
have looked upon me, treating me as one
who is highly exalted, O LORD God. 18 What
else could David say to you for honoring
your servant, for you know your servant
well? 19 O LORD, you have done this great
thing and revealed all these great things for
the sake of your servant and because you
have willed it. [e] 20 There is no one like you, O
LORD, and there is no other God but you, as
we have heard with our own ears. [f] 21 And
who is like your people Israel, the one nation
upon the earth whose God went forth to
redeem his own people, thus making a great
name for yourself, and who drove out
nations with great wonders from before your
people whom you redeemed out of Egypt.
22 You have granted that your people, Israel,
will be your own people forever, and you, O
LORD, will be their God. [g]

23 "O LORD, let the things that you have
spoken concerning your servant and his
household now be established forever, even
as you have promised. [h] 24 As it is established,
so will your name be forever great. It will be
said, 'The LORD of hosts is the God of Israel,
the God of Israel.' Let the household of
David, your servant, be established before
you forever. [i] 25 You, O God, have revealed to
your servant that you will build him a house.
This is why your servant has found it in his
heart to say this prayer before you. 26 O
LORD, you are God, and you have promised
this good thing to your servant. 27 Therefore,
may it please you to bless the house of your
servant so that it might be before you forever,
for you have blessed it, O LORD, and may
it be blessed forever." [j]

CHAPTER 18

David's Conquests. 1 * After this, David
defeated the Philistines. He subdued Gath
and took it and its dependent towns from the
Philistines.

y 2 Sam 5:11.—z 1 Chr 28:3.—a 1 Sam 16:11.—b Jdg 2:16.—c 1 Ki 5:5.—d Lk 1:32; 2 Cor 6:18; Heb 1:5.—e Isa 37:35.—f Sir 36:4.—g Ex 19:5-6.—h 1 Ki 8:25.—i Ps 46:7, 11.—j Pss 16:11; 21:6-7.

17:11 The prophet speaks here of *your seed . . . one of your sons*, while in 2 Sam 7:12 he speaks of "your heir . . . one of your sons," a direct reference to Solomon.

17:13 The words in 2 Sam 7:14: "If he does wrong, I shall punish him as any father would do and not fail to inflict chastisements upon him," are omitted here.

18:1—20:8 Combining the main accounts given of wars in 2 Sam 8; 10; 12; 21, the author composes a large-scale page of military history. His intention is to show how God blessed the man he had chosen as leader of his people.

2 He struck down Moab, and the Moabites
became David's vassals and brought him
tribute.[k]
3 The king defeated Hadadezer, the king of
Zobah up to Hamath when he went forth to
establish his power along the Euphrates
River. 4 David took one thousand chariots
from him, as well as seven thousand horse-
men, and twenty thousand foot soldiers.
David hamstrung the chariot horses, keep-
ing one hundred chariots for himself.[l]
5 When the Arameans of Damascus came
to help Hadadezer, the king of Zobah, David
killed twenty-two thousand of the Arameans.
6 David then stationed men in Damascus of
the Arameans, and the Arameans became
David's vassals, bringing him tribute. The
LORD guarded over David wherever he went.
7 David took the gold shields from Had-
adezer's servants, and he brought them to
Jerusalem. 8 He also brought large quantities
of bronze from Tibhath and Cun, Hadade-
zer's cities. Solomon used the bronze to
make the sea, the pillars, and vessels.[m]
9 When Tou, the king of Hamath, heard
how David had defeated the entire army of
Hadadezer, the king of Zobah, 10 he sent his
son Hadoram to King David to greet him
and bless him because he had fought against
Hadadezer and defeated him, for Hadadezer
was at war with Tou. He brought him objects
of gold, silver, and bronze.[n] 11 King David
dedicated them to the LORD along with
the gold and the silver that he had taken
from all the nations, from Edom, Moab, the
Ammonites, the Philistines, and from
Amalek.
12 In addition to this, Abishai, the son of
Zeruiah, killed eighteen thousand of the
Edomites in the Valley of Salt.[o] 13 He also
established outposts in Edom, so that all of
Edom became David's vassals. The LORD
guarded over David wherever he went.
14 David reigned over all of Israel, and he
gave judgment and justice to all of his peo-
ple. 15 Joab, the son of Zeruiah, was the com-
mander of the army, and Jehoshaphat, the
son of Ahilud, was the archivist.[p]
16 Zadok, the son of Ahitub, and Ahim-
elech, the son of Abiathar, were the priests,
and Shavsha was the scribe.[q] 17 Benaiah, the
son of Jehoiada, was in charge of the Cher-
ethites and the Pelethites, and David's sons
were the officials of the king.*[r]

CHAPTER 19

David's Battles with the Ammonites.
1 Sometime after this, Nahash, the king of
the Ammonites, died, and his son reigned in
his stead.[s] 2 David said, "I will show kindness
to Hanun, the son of Nahash, because his
father showed kindness to me." So David
sent emissaries to console him with regard
to his father. David's servants came to the
land of Ammon, to console Hanun.
3 The Ammonite nobles said to Hanun,
"Do you really think that David is honoring
your father by sending men to console you?
Do you not see that David has sent his ser-
vants to overthrow you and to spy out the
land?"[t] 4 Hanun, therefore, seized David's
servants, shaving them and cutting their
garments up to their hips. He then sent them
away.
5 Some men came in and told David about
what had happened to the men, so he sent
someone to meet them, for the men were
terribly embarrassed. The king told them,
"Wait at Jericho until your beards grow
back, and then return."
6 The Ammonites realized that they had
become abhorrent to David, so Hanun and
the Ammonites sent one thousand talents of
silver to hire chariots and horsemen from
Mesopotamia, Aram, and Zobah. 7 They
hired thirty-two thousand chariots for them-
selves along with the king of Maacah and his
people. They came and camped in front of
Medeba. The Ammonites also assembled
from out of their cities and went out to fight.
8 David heard about this, so he sent Joab
and his army of brave warriors out. 9 The
Ammonites came and arranged themselves
in battle line at the gate to the city while the
kings who had come with them stood in the
fields by themselves.
10 Joab saw that they were arranged in bat-
tle line both in front of him and behind him,
so he chose some of the best men in Israel
and placed them up against the Arameans.
11 He placed the rest of the people under the
command of Abishai, his brother, and they

k Num 21:29.—l Gen 49:6; Jos 11:6,9.—m 1 Ki 7:15, 23; 2 Chr 4:12, 15-16.—n 2 Sam 8:10.—o 1 Ki 11:15.—p 2 Sam 8:16.—q 2 Sam 8:17.—r 1 Sam 30:14.—s Gen 19:38; Jdg 10:17—11:33; Zep 2:8-11.—t 2 Sam 10:3.

18:17 In the parallel passage in 2 Sam 8:18, David's sons are described as priests. The Chronicler suppresses this bit of information. In his view, the priesthood is reserved exclusively to the descendants of Levi, a tribe to which King David did not belong. We see here a greater strictness in the conception of the priesthood.

lined up against the Ammonites.[u] 12 He said, "If the Arameans are too strong for me, then you help me, but if the Ammonites are too strong for you, then I will help you. 13 Be brave and let us be strong for our people and the cities of God. May the LORD do what he judges to be right."

14 Joab and the people who were with him drew up to fight against the Arameans, and they fled before him. 15 When the Ammonites saw that the Arameans were fleeing, they also fled before Abishai, his brother. They went into the city, and Joab returned to Jerusalem.

16 When the Arameans realized that they had been defeated by Israel, they sent messengers to summon the Arameans who lived beyond the river. Shophach, the commander of Hadadezer's army, led them.[v]

17 When David was told, he gathered all of Israel together and crossed over the Jordan. He came upon them and lined up for battle against them. David set up his troops, and they fought against him.

18 The Arameans fled from before David, and he slew seven thousand charioteers and forty thousand foot soldiers. He also killed Shophach, the commander of the army.

19 When Hadadezer's servants saw that they had been defeated by Israel, they made peace with David and became his vassals. The Arameans were no longer willing to help the Ammonites.

CHAPTER 20

1 In the spring of the year when kings go out to war, Joab led the army out, and he laid waste the land of the Ammonites. They came and besieged Rabbah while David stayed in Jerusalem. Joab defeated Rabbah and destroyed it.[w]

2 David took away their king's crown. It weighed one golden talent, and there were precious stones on it. It was set upon David's head. He also took away much spoil.

3 He also took away the people who were in it. He put them to work with saws, iron picks, and axes. David did this to all of the Ammonite cities. David and all the people then returned to Jerusalem.[x]

Battle with the Philistines. 4 Sometime after this, there was a war with the Philistines at Gezer. This was when Sibbecai the Hushathite killed Sippai, who was one of the Rephaim. They were subdued.[y]

5 There was another war with the Philistines, and Elhanan, the son of Jair, killed Lahmi, the brother of Goliath the Gittite. The staff of his spear was as large was a weaver's beam.[z]

6 There was war again at Gath where there was an enormous man who had six fingers on each hand and six toes on each foot, twenty-four fingers and toes in all. He was a Rephaim. 7 He taunted Israel, and Jonathan, the son of Shimea, David's brother, killed him. 8 These were born to the Rephaim in Gath, and they fell at David's hand and those of his servants.

CHAPTER 21

The Census and Plague. 1 Now Satan took his stand* against Israel, and he tempted David to take a census of Israel.[a]

2 David said to Joab and to the leaders of the people, "Go take a census of Israel from Beer-sheba to Dan. Bring the number to me so that I might know it."

3 Joab answered, "May the LORD multiply his people a hundred times over, but, my lord, the king, are these not my lord's servants? Why would my lord order this? Why would he bring this guilt upon Israel?"[b]

4 Nevertheless, the king was resolute with Joab. Joab departed and traveled all throughout Israel, and he then returned to Jerusalem. 5 Joab gave the total number of the people to David. In all of Israel there were one million one hundred thousand men who could draw the sword. In Judah there were four hundred and seventy thousand men who could draw the sword. 6 He did not count Levi or Benjamin, however, for Joab found the king's command to be detestable.[c]

7 God was greatly displeased at this, and he struck down Israel.

8 David said to God, "I have sinned grievously in doing this. I beg you now, take away the iniquity of your servant, for I have acted very foolishly."

---

u 1 Sam 26:6; 2 Sam 10:10.—v 2 Sam 10:15-16.—w Deut 3:11; Am 1:13-15.—x 2 Sam 12:31.—y Gen 14:5; Jos 10:33.—z 1 Sam 17:7.—a Zec 3:1-2.—b Deut 1:11.—c Num 1:49.

21:1 *Satan took his stand:* again the Chronicler colors David's behavior in a favorable light. Satan's presence takes the full responsibility for the decision to order a census off of David. It remains his choice, however, just as any temptation that we give in to. The census was sinful because it showed a lack of respect for God's power.

9 * The LORD then spoke to Gad, David's seer, saying, 10 "Go and speak to David saying: Thus says the LORD: 'I will offer you three options. Choose one of them so that I might do it to you.' "

11 Gad came to David and said, "Thus says the LORD: 'Choose for yourself 12 three years of famine, or three months of being defeated by your enemies, with the swords of your foes striking you down, or else three days of the sword of the LORD. Plague will be in the land, and the angel of the LORD will cause destruction all throughout the territory of Israel.' Think about the answer I should take back to him who sent me."

13 David said to Gad, "I am greatly distressed. Let me fall into the hands of the LORD, for his mercies are truly great. Let me not fall into human hands." [d]

14 So the LORD sent a plague upon Israel, and seventy thousand people fell because of it. 15 God also sent an angel to Jerusalem to destroy it. As he was destroying it, the LORD regretted the disaster, and he said to the destroying angel, "Enough! Hold back your hand!" [e]

Ornan's Threshing Floor. So the angel of the LORD stood by the threshing floor of Ornan, the Jebusite.

16 David looked up, and he saw the angel of the LORD standing between the earth and the heavens, holding a drawn sword in his hands that was stretched out over Jerusalem. David and the elders fell down upon their faces, clothed in sackcloth. * [f]

17 David said to God, "Was it not I who commanded the census of the people? I am the one who sinned, for I have truly done what was wrong. As for these sheep, what have they done? O LORD, my God, let your hand be against me and my father's household, but let your people not suffer from the plague."

18 The angel of the LORD then commanded Gad to tell David that David should go and set up an altar to the LORD on the threshing floor of Ornan, the Jebusite. [g] 19 So David went up as Gad, who spoke in the name of the LORD, had said.

20 Ornan turned around, and he saw the angel, and his four sons who were with him went and hid themselves while Ornan remained on the threshing floor.

21 David came to Ornan, and Ornan looked out and saw David. He went out from the threshing floor and bowed down with his face to the ground before David. 22 David said to Ornan, "Give me this place, the threshing floor, so that I can build an altar to the LORD on it. Sell it to me at full price so that the plague can be withdrawn from the people."

23 Ornan said to David, "Take it for yourself. Let my lord, the king, do what he sees fit. Behold, I will also give you the oxen for burnt offering and the instruments used for threshing for wood and wheat for the grain offering. I will give it all to you."

24 But King David said to Ornan, "No, I will surely pay you the full price. I will not take anything from you for the LORD, nor will I offer any burnt offering that did not cost me anything."

25 David gave Ornan the weight of six hundred shekels of gold for the site. 26 David then built an altar to the LORD there, and he offered burnt offerings and peace offerings. He called upon the LORD, and he answered him from heaven by sending fire upon the altar of the burnt offerings. [h]

27 The LORD gave the command to the angel, and he put his sword back in its sheath. 28 David then realized that the LORD had answered him at the threshing floor of Ornan the Jebusite, and he performed a sacrifice there.

29 At that time, the tabernacle of the LORD that Moses had made and the altar of burnt offerings were at the high place in Gibeon. 30 But David could not go in to make inquiry of God, for he was afraid of the sword of the angel of the LORD.

CHAPTER 22

1 Then David said, "This is the house of the LORD God, and this is the altar for the burnt offerings of Israel." [i]

Preparations for Building the Temple. 2 David ordered that all of the foreigners who were in the land of Israel be gathered together. He assigned them the task of serving as masons

d Pss 51:1; 130:4, 7.—e Gen 6:6; Ex 32:14.—f Num 14:5; Jos 7:6.—g 2 Chr 3:1.—h Lev 9:24; Jdg 6:21.—i Gen 28:17.

21:9—29:30 David is not the one who will build the temple. But the Chronicler wants to attribute to him at least the initiative in this undertaking. Thus the king makes careful preparations for the building, and Solomon simply executes his plans. David's liturgical work will mark the completion of the unity he is seeking, by bringing the entire people together in the one temple.

21:16 This verse, which is peculiar to the Chronicler, presupposes a new way of imagining the angels (see Dan 9:21; 2 Mac 10:29).

to prepare hewn stone to build the house of
God.[j] 3 David prepared quite a bit of iron for
the nails to be used in the doors, the gates,
and the joints. He also prepared so much
bronze that it could not be measured. 4 He
also had much cedar wood, for the
Sidonians of Tyre had brought much cedar
wood to David.[k]

5 David said, "Solomon, my son, is young
and inexperienced, and the house that will
be built for the LORD must be tremendously
magnificent, famous, and glorious through-
out every land. I will therefore make prepa-
rations for it now." So David made many
preparations before he died.

6 He then summoned Solomon, his son,
and he charged him to build a house for the
LORD, the God of Israel.[l] 7 David said to
Solomon, "My son, I wanted to build a house
for the name of the LORD, the God of Israel,[m]
8 but the word of the LORD came to me say-
ing, 'Because you have shed so much blood
and you have waged many wars, you will not
build a house for my name because you have
shed too much blood upon the earth before
me. 9 Behold, a son will be born to you who
will be a man of peace* and rest. I will give
him a respite from all of his surrounding
enemies, for his name will be Solomon. I will
give peace and quiet to Israel during his
reign.[n] 10 He is the one who will build a house
for my name. He will be my son, and I will be
his father. I will establish the throne of his
kingdom over Israel forever.'[o]

11 "Now, my son, the LORD will be with you.
You will prosper, and you will build a house
for the LORD, your God, as he has pro-
claimed. 12 May the LORD give you insight
and understanding when he sets you over
Israel so that you might observe the law of
the LORD, your God.[p] 13 You will prosper if
you carefully observe the statutes and the
ordinances that the LORD gave Moses for
Israel. Be strong and be brave. Do not be
afraid nor dismayed. 14 I have put myself to
the trouble of preparing the following for the
temple of the LORD: one hundred thousand
talents of gold, one million talents of silver,
so much bronze and iron that it could not
even be weighed, and an abundance of wood
and stone. You can now add to it.* 15 You
have many workmen: stonecutters, masons,
carpenters, and men who are skilled in every
type of craft.[q] 16 You cannot even count those
who can work with gold, silver, bronze, and
iron. So now be about it, and the LORD will
be with you."

Charge to the Leaders. 17 David command-
ed all of the leaders of Israel to assist
Solomon, his son, saying, 18 "Is not the LORD,
your God, with you? Has he not given you
rest on every side? He has placed the inhab-
itants of the land in your hand, and the land
has been subjected to the LORD and his peo-
ple.[r] 19 Now dedicate yourselves heart and
soul to seeking the LORD, your God. Rise up
and build a sanctuary for the LORD, your
God. Bring the Ark of the Covenant
of the LORD and the sacred vessels of God
into the temple that will be built for the
name of the LORD."

CHAPTER 23

The Levitical Classes. 1 * When David was
old and his years were complete, he made
Solomon, his son, king over Israel.[s] 2 He
gathered together all of the leaders of Israel
along with the priests and the Levites.

3 The Levites who were thirty years and
older were counted, and the total number of
them was thirty-eight thousand.[t] 4 David
appointed twenty-four thousand of them to
supervise the work on the temple of the
LORD, and another six thousand of them
were to be officials and judges. 5 Four thou-
sand of them were to be gatekeepers, and
four thousand were to praise the LORD upon
musical instruments about which David
said, "I made them to praise the LORD."[u]

6 David divided the Levites of Gershon,
Kohath, and Merari into groups.[v]

7 From the Gershonites there were Ladan
and Shimei. 8 The sons of Ladan were Jehiel,
the firstborn, Zetham, and Joel. There
were three in all. 9 * The sons of Shimei were
Shelomoth, Haziel, and Haran. There were
three of them in all. These were the leaders

j Ex 1:11; Deut 20:11.—k 2 Chr 2:9; Ezr 3:7.—l Acts 7:47.—m Deut 12:5, 11; 2 Sam 7:2.—n Jos 14:15; 1 Ki 4:20, 25.—o Heb 1:5.—p 1 Ki 3:9.—q 2 Sam 5:16.—r Jos 21:44; 23:1.—s 1 Ki 1:30.—t Num 4:3-49.—u Ps 92:3.—v Ex 6:16; Num 3:17; 26:57.

22:9 *Peace:* in Hebrew, *shalom*, which is here connected with the name "Solomon."

22:14 The numbers seem fantastic. They can be explained by the idealizing outlook of the Chronicler.

23:1-2 In the setting of a great assembly of all the leaders of Israel, whom David has brought together for the solemn proclamation of his successor, the author gives a description of the organization of worship (chs. 23–26), which is followed, due to an association of ideas, by a description of the civil organization (ch. 27).

23:9-10 The text is to some extent corrupt at this point.

of the ancestral clans of Ladan. 10 The sons of
Shimei were Jahath, Zizah, Jeush, and
Beriah. Shimei had four sons in all. 11 Jahath
was the leader, and Zizah was the second in
charge. Jeush and Beriah did not have many
sons, so they were reckoned as a single
ancestral clan.

12 The sons of Kohath were Amram, Izhar,
Hebron, and Uzziel. There were four of them
in all. [w]

13 The sons of Amram were Aaron and
Moses. Aaron was set apart to consecrate
the most holy things. He and his sons were to
burn incense before the LORD forever, and to
minister, and to proclaim blessings in his
name forever.

14 The sons of Moses, the man of God, were
included with the tribe of Levi. [x] 15 The sons
of Moses were Gershom and Eliezer.

16 Shubael was the son of Gershom, his
first. 17 Rehabiah was the son of Eliezer, his
first. Eliezer had no other sons, but Reha-
biah had a large number of sons.

18 Shelomith was the son of Izhar, his first-
born.

19 The sons of Hebron were Jeriah, his first-
born, Amariah, his second, Jahaziel, his
third, and Jekameam, his fourth.

20 The sons of Uzziel were Micah, his first-
born, and Isshiah, his second.

21 The sons of Merari were Mahli and
Mushi. The sons of Mahli were Eleazar and
Kish.

22 Eleazar died without having any sons, he
had only had daughters. The sons of Kish,
their relatives, married them. [y]

23 The sons of Mushi were Mahli, Eder, and
Jeremoth. There were three of them in all.

24 These were the descendants of Levi by
their ancestral clans, with the leaders of the
ancestral clans as they were registered by
name and counted. These are the ones who
could perform the work in the temple of the
LORD, twenty years old and older.* [z]

25 David did this because he said, "The
LORD, the God of Israel, had given his people
rest so that they might dwell in Jerusalem
forever. [a] 26 The Levites therefore no longer
have to carry the tabernacle or any of the
articles used in its service."

27 Thus, according to the last instructions
of David, the Levites who were twenty years
or older were counted. 28 Their responsibility
was to assist the sons of Aaron in the service
of the temple of the LORD, to be in charge of
the courtyard and the inner chambers, to
purify all of the holy things, and to fulfill
other tasks in the temple of the LORD. [b]
29 They were responsible for the shewbread,
for the flour for the cereal offerings, for the
unleavened loaves, for the baking and the
mixing, and for all the standards of mea-
surement and size. [c] 30 They were to stand
every morning to thank and praise the
LORD. They were to do the same every
evening. [d] 31 They were also to do this when-
ever burnt offerings were made to the LORD
on the Sabbath, on the new moons, and on
the appointed feasts, as they had been com-
manded to do regularly before the LORD, [e]
32 that they were to serve the tent of meeting
and be responsible for the sanctuary under
the direction of the descendants of Aaron,
their brethren, for the service of the temple
of the LORD. [f]

CHAPTER 24

The Priestly Classes. 1 These are the divi-
sions of Aaron.

The sons of Aaron were Nadab, Abihu,
Eleazar, and Ithamar. [g] 2 Nadab and Abihu
died before their father, and they did not
have any sons. Eleazar and Ithamar served
as priests. [h]

3 David, with the help of Zadok, a descen-
dant of Eleazar, and Ahimelech, a descen-
dant of Ithamar, divided them according to
the responsibilities of their service. [i]

4 A larger number of leaders was found
among the descendants of Eleazar than
among the descendants of Ithamar. This is
how they were divided: for the descendants
of Eleazar there were sixteen leaders of the
ancestral clans, and for the descendants of
Ithamar there were eight leaders of the
ancestral clans. 5 They divided them by lot,
for there were officials of the sanctuary* and
officials of God from among the descendants
of Eleazar and from among the descendants
of Ithamar. 6 Shemaiah, the son of Nethanel,

w Ex 6:18; Num 3:19.—x Deut 33:1.—y Num 36:8.—z 2 Chr 31:17; Ezr 3:8.—a Ps 132:13.—b 2 Chr 29:15; Neh 13:9; Mal 3:3.—c Lev 2:4-7.—d Ps 134:1.—e Isa 1:13, 14; Col 2:16.—f Num 3:6-9; Ezek 44:14.—g Ex 6:23; Num 3:2-4; Ezr 6:18.—h Lev 10:2.—i 2 Sam 8:17; 2 Chr 8:14.

23:24 *Twenty years old and older:* earlier in this chapter (v. 3) the minimum age of those who entered Levitical service was thirty. The lower age might have been David's way of attracting more candidates.

24:5 *Officials of the sanctuary:* carried out the functions of the temple (in the sanctuary); *officials of God:* worked in the annexes to the sanctuary.

the scribe, a Levite, recorded it in the pres-
ence of the king and the officials: Zadok the
priest and Ahimelech, the son of Abiathar,
and the leaders of the ancestral clans of the
priests and the Levites, one ancestral clan
being taken from Eleazar and then one from
Ithamar.
7 The first lot fell to Jehoiarib, the second
lot fell to Jedaiah, 8 the third lot fell to Harim,
the fourth lot fell to Seorim, 9 the fifth lot fell
to Malchijah, the sixth lot fell to Mijamin,
10 the seventh lot fell to Hakkoz, the eighth lot
fell to Abijah,[j] 11 the ninth lot fell to Jeshua,
the tenth lot fell to Shecaniah, 12 the eleventh
lot fell to Eliashib, the twelfth lot fell to
Jakim, 13 the thirteenth lot fell to Huppah,
the fourteenth lot fell to Ishbaal, 14 the fif-
teenth lot fell to Bilgah, the sixteenth lot fell
to Immer,[k] 15 the seventeenth lot fell to
Hezir, the eighteenth lot fell to Happizzez,
16 the nineteenth lot fell to Pethahiah, the
twentieth lot fell to Jehezkel, 17 the twenty-
first lot fell to Jachin, the twenty-second lot
fell to Gamul, 18 the twenty-third lot fell to
Delaiah, and the twenty-fourth lot fell to
Maaziah.
19 This was the appointed order of service
when they would come into the temple of the
LORD. This was according to the regulations
given by Aaron their ancestor as the LORD,
the God of Israel, had commanded.*

Other Levites. 20 As for the other descen-
dants of Levi, Shubael was the son of Am-
ram, and Jehdeiah was the son of Shubael.
21 The firstborn son of Rehabiah was Is-
shiah.
22 From the Izharites there was She-
lomoth.
Jahath was the son of Shelomoth.
23 The sons of Hebron were Jeriah, the
firstborn, Amariah, the second, Jahaziel, the
third, and Jekameam, the fourth.[l]
24 Micah was the son of Uzziel, and Shamir
was the son of Micah.
25 Isshiah was the brother of Micah.
Zechariah was the son of Isshiah.
26 The sons of Merari were Mahli and
Mushi and the descendants of his son
Uzziah.[m]
27 Among the descendants of Merari, there
was Jaaziah, whose sons were Beno,
Shoham, Zaccur, and Ibri.
28 From Mahli there was Eleazar who did
not have any sons.
29 From Kish, there was Jerahmeel, the son
of Kish.[n]
30 The sons of Mushi were Mahli, Eder, and
Jerimoth.
These were the Levites, according to their
ancestral clans. 31 They also cast lots, just as
their brethren, the descendants of Aaron,
had done. This was done before King David,
Zadok, Ahimelech, the leaders of the ances-
tral clans of the priests and the Levites. The
families of the oldest brother were treated
the same as those of the youngest.

CHAPTER 25

The Musicians. 1 David, together with the
captains of the army, set aside some of the
sons of Asaph, Heman, and Jeduthun who
were to prophesy* with harps, lyres, and
cymbals. This is the list of those engaged in
their ministry.[o]
2 From the sons of Asaph there were Zaccur,
Joseph, Nethaniah, and Asharelah. The sons of
Asaph were under the direction of Asaph who
prophesied at the command of the king.
3 From Jeduthun there were his sons
Gedaliah, Zeri, Jeshaiah, Shimei, Hasha-
biah, and Mattithiah. There were six of them
in all. They were under the direction of their
father Jeduthun who prophesied using the
harp to give thanks and praise to the LORD.[p]
4 From Heman there were his sons
Bukkiah, Mattaniah, Uzziel, Shubael, Jeri-
moth, Hananiah, Hanani, Eliathah, Giddalti,
Romamti-ezer, Joshbekashah, Mallothi,
Hothir, and Mahazioth. 5 These were all the
sons of Heman, the king's seer. They were
given the word of God to exalt him. God gave
Heman fourteen sons and three daughters.[q]
6 All of these were under the direction of their
father. They played music for the temple of
the LORD upon cymbals, lyres, and harps, for
the ministry of the temple of God. Asaph,
Jeduthun, and Heman were under the direc-
tion of the king.[r]

j Neh 12:4, 17; Lk 1:5.—k 1 Chr 9:18-24.—l Num 3:27.—m Ex 6:19.—n 1 Chr 23:22.—o 2 Chr 5:12; 35:15; Neh 11:17; Ezr 3:10.—p Gen 4:21; Ps 33:2.—q 2 Chr 35:15.—r 1 Chr 15:16, 19.

24:19 The turns of the ministers lasted a week, from one Sabbath to the next (see 2 Ki 11:9); this remained the practice until the destruction of the temple and the city in A.D. 70. See Lk 1:5, 8, 23.

25:1 *Prophesy:* i.e., they sang under inspiration, either like the prophets gathered in the guilds, who sang to the sound of musical instruments, or in the sense that they were the authors of inspired songs. See Pss 51; 74–84 (Asaph); 88 (Heman); 62 (Jeduthun).

7 Along with their brethren, all of whom
were trained and skilled in performing the
songs of the LORD, there were two hundred
and eighty-eight of them. 8 The young and
old, the teacher and the student all cast lots.

9 The first lot fell to Asaph, to the family of
Joseph; the second fell to Gedaliah, who
together with his brethren and sons num-
bered twelve; 10 the third lot fell to Zaccur,
who together with his sons and brethren
numbered twelve; 11 the fourth lot fell to
Izri, who together with his sons and his
brethren numbered twelve; 12 the fifth lot
fell to Nethaniah, who together with his sons
and relatives numbered twelve; 13 the sixth
lot fell to Bukkiah, who together with his
sons and relatives numbered twelve; 14 the
seventh lot fell to Jesarelah, who together
with his sons and relatives numbered
twelve; 15 the eighth lot fell to Jeshaiah, who
together with his sons and relatives num-
bered twelve; 16 the ninth lot fell to
Mattaniah, who together with his sons and
his relatives numbered twelve; 17 the tenth
lot fell to Shimei, who together with his sons
and his relatives numbered twelve; 18 the
eleventh lot fell to Uzziel, who together with
his sons and his relatives numbered twelve;
19 the twelfth lot fell to Hashabiah, who
together with his sons and his relatives
numbered twelve; 20 the thirteenth lot fell to
Shubael, who together with his sons and his
relatives numbered twelve; 21 the fourteenth
lot fell to Mattithiah, who together with his
sons and his relatives numbered twelve;
22 the fifteenth lot fell to Jeremoth, who
together with his sons and his relatives
numbered twelve; 23 the sixteenth lot fell to
Hananiah, who together with his sons and
his relatives numbered twelve; 24 the seven-
teenth lot fell to Joshbekashah, who togeth-
er with his sons and his relatives numbered
twelve; 25 the eighteenth lot fell to Hanani,
who together with his sons and his relatives
numbered twelve; 26 the nineteenth lot fell
to Mallothi, who together with his sons and
his relatives numbered twelve; 27 the twenti-
eth lot fell to Eliathah, who together with his
sons and his relatives numbered twelve;
28 the twenty-first lot fell to Hothir, who
together with his sons and his relatives
numbered twelve; 29 the twenty-second lot
fell to Giddalti, who together with his sons
and his relatives numbered twelve; 30 the
twenty-third lot fell to Mahazioth, who
together with his sons and his relatives
numbered twelve; 31 the twenty-fourth lot
fell to Romamti-ezer, who together with his
sons and his relatives numbered twelve.

CHAPTER 26

Classes of Gatekeepers. 1 These are the divi-
sions of the gatekeepers.

From the Korahites, there was Meshele-
miah, the son of Kore, one of the sons of
Abiasaph.[s] 2 The sons of Meshelemiah were
Zechariah, his firstborn, Jediael, his second,
Zebadiah, his third, Jathniel, his fourth,
3 Elam, his fifth, Jehohanan, his sixth, and
Eliehoenai, his seventh.

4 Obed-edom also had sons. They were
Shemaiah, his firstborn, Jehozabad, his sec-
ond, Joah, his third, Sachar, his fourth,
Nethanel, his fifth, 5 Ammiel, his sixth, Issa-
char, his seventh, and Peullethai, his eighth,
for God blessed Obed-edom.[t]

6 His son Shemaiah also had sons who
became the leaders of the ancestral clans
because they were most capable. 7 The sons
of Shemaiah were Othni, Rephael, Obed,
and Elzabad. His brethren Elihu and
Semachiah were also capable men. 8 All of
these were the descendants of Obed-edom.
They and their brethren were capable men,
strong enough to do their work. There were
sixty-two descendants of Obed-edom in all.

9 Meshelemiah had eighteen sons and rela-
tives who were capable men.

10 The sons of Hosah the Merarite were
Shimri, his firstborn (although he was not
really the firstborn, his father assigned him
the honor of firstborn),[u] 11 Hilkiah, the sec-
ond, Tebaliah, the third, and Zechariah, the
fourth. Hosah had thirteen sons and rela-
tives in all.

12 These were the divisions of the gatekeep-
ers according to their leaders. Their duties
were to minister in the temple of the LORD.
13 They cast lots for the gates, the young and
the old, according to their ancestral clans.

14 The lot for the East Gate fell to
Meshelemiah. They then cast lots for his son
Zechariah who was a wise counselor. His lot
came out, and the North Gate was allotted to
him. 15 The lot for the South Gate fell to
Obed-edom, and that for the storehouse fell
to his sons. 16 The lot for the West Gate and
the Shallecheth Gate on the upper road fell
to Shuppim and Hosah.

---

s 1 Chr 9:19; 2 Chr 8:14; 23:19; Neh 12:45.—**t** 2 Sam 6:10.—**u** Deut 21:16; 1 Chr 5:1.

There were guards alongside of guards.
17 Each day there were six Levites to the east.
Each day there were four to the north. Each
day there were four to the south, and there
were two at a time for the storehouse. 18 As
for the courtyard* to the west, there were
four on the roadway and two in the court-
yard itself.

19 These were the divisions for the gate-
keepers who were the descendants of Korah
and the descendants of Merari. [v]

Treasurers and Other Officials. 20 Their fel-
low Levites supervised the treasury of the
temple of God and the treasury of the dedi-
cated objects. [w] 21 The descendants of Ladan,
who were Gershonites through Ladan and
leaders of the ancestral clans of Ladan the
Gershonite were Jehiel, 22 with the sons of
Jehiel, who were Zetham and his brother
Joel. They were responsible for the treasury
of the temple of the LORD.

23 From the Amramites there were the
Izharites, the Hebronites, and the Uzzielites.

24 Shubael, a descendant of Gershom, who
was the son of Moses, was the supervisor of
the treasury.

25 His relatives through Eliezer were
Rehabiah, his son, Jeshaiah, his son, Joram,
his son, Zichri, his son, and Shelomith, his
son. 26 Shelomith and his brethren were
responsible for the treasury of the dedicated
objects. They had been dedicated by King
David, by the leaders of the ancestral clans,
by the captains of the thousands and the
hundreds, and by the captains of the army. [x]
27 Some of the spoils taken in battle had been
dedicated for the maintenance of the temple
of the LORD. 28 There were also all the things
that had been dedicated by Samuel the seer,
Saul, the son of Kish, Abner, the son of Ner,
and Joab, the son of Zeruiah. Whatever had
been dedicated was under the supervision of
Shelomith and his brethren.

Magistrates. 29 From the Izharites there
were Chenaniah and his sons who were
assigned responsibilities outside of the tem-
ple as officials and judges over Israel. [y]

30 From the Hebronites there were
Hashabiah and his relatives, one thousand
seven hundred capable men, who were offi-
cials on the west side of the Jordan for all of
the concerns involving the LORD and all of
the service to the king. [z]

31 From the Hebronites there was Jerijah,
who was the leader of the Hebronites accord-
ing to the generations of the ancestral clans.

In the fortieth year of the reign of David, a
search was made, and some of their capable
men were found in Jazer of Gilead. [a] 32 He
had two thousand seven hundred capable
men among his brethren who were the lead-
ers of the ancestral clans. King David made
them responsible for any concern of God or
any concern of the king among the
Reubenites, the Gadites, and among one-
half of the tribe of Manasseh.

CHAPTER 27

Commanders of the Army. 1 This is the list of
the leaders of the ancestral clans of the
Israelites, the captains of the thousands and
the hundreds, the officials who served the
king in anything concerning going out or
coming in as they were on duty from month
to month, all throughout the year. Each divi-
sion had twenty-four thousand men.

2 Ishbaal, the son of Zabdiel, was in charge
of the first division for the first month. There
were twenty-four thousand men in his divi-
sion. [b] 3 He was a descendant of Perez, and
he was the leader of all of the captains of the
army for the first month.

4 Dodai the Ahohite was in charge of the
division for the second month. There were
twenty-four thousand men in his division.

5 Benaiah, the son of Jehoiada, the priest,
was the third leader of the army for the third
month. He was the leader, and there were
twenty-four thousand men in his division.
6 This was the same Benaiah who was a
brave warrior from among the Thirty and
the leader of the Thirty. His son Ammizabad
was in charge of his division.

7 Asahel, the brother of Joab, was the
fourth for the fourth month. Zebadiah, his
son, succeeded him. There were twenty-four
thousand men in his division. [c]

8 Shamhuth the Zerahite was the fifth
leader for the fifth month. There were twen-
ty-four thousand men in his division.

9 Ira, the son of Ikkesh the Tekoite was the
sixth for the sixth month. There were twen-
ty-four thousand men in his division.

v Neh 7:1; Ezek 44:11.—w 1 Ki 7:51; 2 Chr 24:5.—x 2 Sam 8:11.—y Deut 17:8-13.—z Neh 11:15-16.—a Jos 13:25; 2 Sam 5:4.—b 2 Sam 23:8-30.—c 1 Chr 11:26.

26:18 *Courtyard:* perhaps a colonnade attached to the western part of the outer courtyard of the temple.

10 Hellez the Pelonite, an Ephraimite, was
the seventh for the seventh month. There
were twenty-four thousand men in his divi-
sion.
11 Sibbecai the Hushathite, a Zerahite, was
the eighth for the eighth month. There were
twenty-four thousand men in his division.
12 Abiezer the Anathothite, a Benjaminite,
was the ninth for the ninth month. There
were twenty-four thousand men in his divi-
sion.
13 Maharai the Netophathite, a Zerahite,
was the tenth for the tenth month. There
were twenty-four thousand men in his divi-
sion.
14 Benaiah the Pirathonite, an Ephraimite,
was the eleventh for the eleventh month.
There were twenty-four thousand men in his
division.
15 Heldai the Netophathite from the family
of Othniel was the twelfth for the twelfth
month. There were twenty-four thousand
men in his division.

Tribal Heads. 16 The leaders of the tribes of
Israel were: for the Reubenites: Eliezer, the
son of Zichri; for the Simeonites: Shepha-
tiah, the son of Maacah; 17 for the Levites:
Hashabiah, the son of Kemuel; for the
Aaronites: Zadok; 18 for the Judahites: Eliab,
the brother of David; for the Issacharites:
Omri, the son of Michael; 19 for the
Zebulunites: Ishmaiah, the son of Obadiah;
for the Naphtalites: Jeremoth, the son of
Azriel; 20 for the Ephraimites: Hoshea, the
son of Azaziah; for one-half of the tribe of
Manasseh: Joel, the son of Pedaiah; 21 for the
other half of the tribe of Manasseh in Gilead:
Iddo, the son of Zechariah; for the Ben-
jaminites: Jaasiel, the son of Abner; 22 and for
the Danites: Azarel, the son of Jeroham.
These were the leaders in charge of the
tribes of Israel.
23 David did not take stock of those who
were younger than twenty years old because
the LORD had said that Israel would increase
to be as many as the stars in the heavens. [d]
24 Joab, the son of Zeruiah, began to count
them, but he did not finish when wrath fell
upon Israel because of it. Therefore the num-
ber was not entered into the chronicles of
King David.

Administrators. 25 Azmaveth, the son of
Adiel, was responsible for the royal treasury.
Jonathan, the son of Uzziah, was in charge of
the storehouses in the fields, the cities, the
villages, and the watchtowers. 26 Ezri, the son
of Chelub, was in charge of the field work-
ers who farmed the land. 27 Shimei the
Ramathite was in charge of the vineyards.
Zabdi the Shiphmite was in charge of the
harvest from the vineyards for the wine cel-
lars. 28 Baal-hanan the Gederite was in
charge of the olive and sycamore trees on
the western slopes. Joash was in charge of
the olive oil supply in the cellars. [e] 29 Shitrai
the Sharonite was in charge of the grazing
herds in Sharon. Shaphat, the son of Adlai,
was in charge of the herds in the valleys. [f]
30 Obil the Ishmaelite was in charge of the
camels. Jehdeiah the Meronothite was in
charge of the donkeys. 31 Jaziz the Hagrite
was in charge of the flocks.
These were all officials in charge of King
David's possessions. 32 Jonathan, David's
uncle, was a counselor. He was an insightful
man, and he was a scribe. Jehiel, the son of
Hachamoni, was in charge of the king's sons.
33 Ahithophel was the king's counselor.
Hushai the Archite was the king's compan-
ion.* [g] 34 Ahithophel was succeeded by
Jehoiada, the son of Benaiah, and by
Abiathar.* Joab was the commander of the
king's army.

CHAPTER 28

Assembly at Jerusalem. 1 * David sum-
moned all the leaders of Israel, the leaders of
the tribes, the leaders of the divisions for the
service of the king, the captains of the thou-
sands, the captains of the hundreds, the
officials in charge of all the goods and pos-
sessions of the king and his sons, together
with the other officials, the mighty men, and
the brave warriors to Jerusalem. 2 King
David rose to his feet and said, "Listen to
me, my brethren, my people. I had my heart
set upon building a house to serve as a rest-
ing place for the Ark of the Covenant of the
LORD, the footstool of our God. I made
preparations for building it, [h] 3 but God said
to me, 'You will not build a house for my
name for you have been a man of war and
have shed blood.'

d Gen 12:2; 22:17.—e 1 Ki 10:27; 2 Chr 1:15.—f Isa 33:9; 35:2; 65:10.—g 2 Sam 15:12, 37.—h 2 Sam 7:2; Ps 132:7; Isa 60:13.

27:33 *The king's companion:* this must have been the title of a high ranking officer of the court.

27:34 *Abiathar:* the high priest then in office.

28:1—29:30 During a solemn liturgy David tells the people of his plans for the temple; he involves them all in the great work, and asks for God's help. This passage continues the account that was interrupted in 1 Chr 23:2.

4 “Yet, the LORD, the God of Israel, has
chosen me from my father’s entire house-
hold to be the king over Israel forever, and
from Judah he chose me as leader, from the
house of Judah, the household of my father
and the sons of my father. It pleased him to
make me king over all of Israel.[i] 5 From my
sons, from my many sons whom the LORD
has given me, the LORD has chosen
Solomon, my son, to sit upon the throne of
the kingdom of the LORD over Israel.[j] 6 He
said to me, ‘Solomon, your son, will build my
temple and my courts, for I have chosen him
to be my son, and I will be his father. 7 I will
establish his kingdom forever if he carefully
observes my commandments and my ordi-
nances, as they are doing today.’

8 “Now therefore, in the sight of all of Israel
and the assembly of the LORD and in the
hearing of our God, I charge you to carefully
observe all of the commandments of the
LORD, your God, so that you might possess
this good land and it might be an inheritance
for your descendants forever.[k]

9 “And you, Solomon, my son, know that
God is your father. Serve him with all your
heart and with a willing mind, for the LORD
searches every heart, and he understands
the ponderings of every thought. If you seek
him, you will find him, but if you abandon
him, then he will cast you off forever.[l] 10 Take
heed, now, that the LORD has chosen you to
build a temple as a sanctuary. Be strong and
do it.”

Temple Plans Given to Solomon. 11 David
then gave Solomon, his son, the plans for the
porch of the temple, its treasuries, its upper
chambers, its inner chambers, and the place
of the seat of mercy.*[m] 12 The plans included
everything that the Spirit had inspired con-
cerning the courtyards of the temple of the
LORD, all of the surrounding chambers, the
treasury of the temple of the LORD,
and the treasury for the dedicated objects.

13 He also told him about the divisions of
the priests and Levites, and for all of the
work to be done in the service of the temple
of the LORD, as well as, for all the vessels used
in the service of the temple of the LORD.

14 He gave the weight of the gold and all the
golden implements for the various forms of
service, and the weight of the silver in the
implements for the various forms of service.
15 He also told him the weight for the golden
lampstands and their lamps, the weight of
the gold for each of the lampstands and their
lamps, the weight of the silver for the lamp-
stands and their lamps, according to the use
of each of the lampstands.[n] 16 He told him
the weight of the gold for each of the tables
for the shewbread and likewise the weight
of the silver for the silver tables. 17 He told
him the weight of the pure gold for the forks,
the sprinkling bowls, and the pitchers, the
weight of gold for each of the basins, and the
weight of the silver for each of the silver dish-
es. 18 He told him the weight of the refined
gold for the altar of incense. He also gave
him the pattern for the chariot, that is, the
golden cherubim with outstretched wings
that covered the Ark of the Covenant of the
LORD.[o]

19 David said, “This is all in writing for the
hand of the LORD was upon me; he gave me
understanding of all of the details of the
plan.”

20 David also said to Solomon, his son, “Be
strong! Be brave! Do it! Do not be afraid or
discouraged, for the LORD, the God, my God,
is with you. He will not fail you nor will he
abandon you until you have finished all of
the work in service of the temple of the
LORD.[p] 21 Behold, the divisions for the
priests and the Levites for all of their service
in the temple of the LORD are completed,
and you will have at your disposition every
type of workman skillful in every craft. The
leaders and the people will obey your every
command.”

CHAPTER 29

Gifts for the Temple. 1 * King David then
said to the whole assembly, “My son,
Solomon, is the one whom God has chosen.
He is young and inexperienced, and the task
is great. This is not a palace for a human, but
it is for the LORD God.

2 “I have made preparations for the temple
of the LORD, my God, with all my resources:
the gold, the golden objects, the silver, the sil-
ver objects, the bronze, the bronze objects,

i Gen 49:8-12; 1 Sam 16:6-13.—j 1 Chr 3:1-9; Wis 9:7.—k Deut 4:5.—l 2 Chr 6:30; Jer 29:13.—m Ex 25:9; Acts 7:44; Heb 8:5.—n Ex 25:31-37.—o Ex 25:20-22; 30:1-10; 1 Ki 6:23-28.—p Jos 1:5-7; Hag 2:4.

28:11 The buildings and locus of the seat of mercy or place of atonement were the sanctuary and the Holy of Holies (place of the Ark and its cover, the seat of mercy, which is named because it played the most important role in the annual rite of atonement).

29:1-9 The numbers seem inflated here, as they were earlier (1 Chr 22:14); they are a way of bringing out the importance and high quality of the gifts.

the iron, the iron objects, the wood, the wood
objects, the stone, the onyx for settings, the
glistening stones of various colors, all types
of precious stones, and marble, all of them in
great quantities. [q]

3 “Moreover, in my devotion to the temple
of my God, I have given gold and silver from
my own possessions for the temple of my
God in addition to everything that I have
prepared for the holy temple. 4 This includes
three thousand talents of gold (gold of
Ophir) and seven thousand talents of refined
silver to be used for overlaying the walls of
the buildings. [r] 5 It is also for the gold and the
gold objects, the silver and the silver objects,
and all types of work to be done by the crafts-
men. Now, who is willing today to consecrate
himself to the LORD?” [s]

6 The leaders of the ancestral clans and the
tribes of Israel, the captains of the thousands
and the hundreds, and the supervisors of the
king’s work gave willingly. 7 They gave five
thousand talents and ten thousand darics*
of gold, ten thousand talents of silver, eigh-
teen thousand talents of bronze, and one
hundred thousand talents of iron. [t] 8 Any of
those who had found precious stones gave
them to the treasury of the temple of the
LORD through Jehiel the Gershonite. 9 The
people rejoiced because they had willingly
responded and had given with their whole
hearts to the LORD, and King David also
rejoiced greatly. [u]

10 * David praised the LORD in front of the
whole assembly, and David said:

“Blessed are you, O LORD,
the God of Israel,
our father forever and ever.

11 “Yours, O LORD, are greatness,
power, glory, strength, and majesty,
for everything in heaven and on earth is
yours.
Yours, O LORD, is the kingdom;
you are exalted as head over all. [v]

12 Wealth and honor are from you,
you reign over all.
In your hand are power and might;
it to is in your hand make great and to
give strength to all. [w]

13 Now, our God, we thank you,
and we praise your glorious name.

14 But who am I, and what are your people,
that we should be able to do this?
All things belong to you,
and everything that we have given you
is from your hand.

15 We are foreigners and aliens,
as all our fathers were before us.
Our days are like a shadow upon the
earth,
none of them abide. [x]

16 O LORD, our God,
all of this wealth that we have to build
a temple for you
and for your holy name is from your
hand,
and it all belongs to you.

17 I know, my God,
that you have tested my heart,
and that you are pleased with
the integrity of my heart.
I have willingly offered you all these
things.
And now I have seen your people who are
present here.
They joyfully and willingly make
this offering to you. [y]

18 O LORD, God of our fathers,
of Abraham, Isaac, and Jacob,
keep this desire in the inner thoughts
of your people forever,
and make their hearts loyal to you.

19 Give my son Solomon a pure heart
so that he might observe your com-
mandments, your ordinances, and
your statutes,
and do everything to build the temple
for which I have made provision.”

20 David then said to the whole assembly,
“Praise the LORD, your God!” The whole
assembly praised the LORD, the God of their
fathers. They bowed down their heads, and
they fell prostrate before the LORD and the
king.

21 On the next day they made sacrifices to
the LORD and offered burnt offerings to the
LORD: one thousand bulls, one thousand
rams, and one thousand lambs. There were
drink offerings and other sacrifices in abun-

q Ezr 1:4; Hag 2:8; Isa 54:11.—r 2 Chr 9:10; 1 Ki 9:28.—s Ex 25:2; 35:5-6.—t Ezr 2:69; Neh 7:70.—u 1 Ki 8:61; 2 Cor 9:7.—v Mt 6:13; 1 Tim 1:17; Rev 5:13.—w 2 Chr 1:12; Eccl 5:19; Rom 11:36.—x Job 14:2; Heb 11:13; Wis 2:5.—y Ps 139:23; Prov 15:11; 17:3; Jer 11:20.

29:7 *Darics:* evidently an anachronism, since darics were gold Persian coins.

29:10-20 The thanksgiving which the king offers in the name of the people is still one of the most beautiful of liturgical prayers.

dance for all of Israel. 22 They ate and drank
before the LORD that day with great joy.*
Then they acknowledged Solomon, the
son of David, as king a second time, and they
anointed him before the LORD to be ruler
and Zadok to be priest. 23 Solomon sat on the
throne of the LORD in the place of David, his
father. He prospered and everyone in Israel
obeyed him.[z] 24 All of the leaders and mighty
men and all of King David's sons paid obei-
sance to King Solomon. 25 The LORD exalted
Solomon greatly before all of Israel, and he
bestowed upon him majesty and royal digni-
ty as no king in Israel had ever had before
him.[a]
26 David, the son of Jesse, reigned over all
of Israel. 27 He ruled over Israel for forty
years. He reigned for seven years in Hebron,
and he reigned for thirty-three years in
Jerusalem.[b] 28 He died at a good, old age in
the fullness of his years. He had enjoyed
wealth and honor. Then Solomon, his son,
reigned in his stead.
29 * As for the other deeds of King David,
from the beginning to the end, they are writ-
ten in the Book of Samuel the Seer, the Book
of Nathan the Prophet, and in the Book of
Gad the Seer, 30 along with all of the details of
his reign and his might and his own times
and those of Israel and of all the kingdoms of
the other lands.

z Deut 17:18; 1 Ki 2:12.—a Jos 3:7; 1 Ki 10:7; Eccl 2:9.—b Gen 23:19; 2 Sam 5:4-5.

29:22 Solomon was David's choice to succeed him (1 Chr 23:1), and this is a public affirmation of his appointment.

29:29-30 It is of interest to know of the works used by the author, but they are unknown to us.

THE SECOND BOOK OF CHRONICLES

According to the author of Chronicles, David was the true founder of the temple liturgy: he planned everything but, when he died, everything was still only planned or sketched, and it was his son who continued the work and actually built the sanctuary in Jerusalem.

This work was decisive for the religious future of Israel. It is to this fact that the Chronicler is pleased to call our attention.

He says nothing about the sins of Solomon (his love of luxury, his many wives and concubines, his despotism, his tolerance of pagan cults in his harem), because he does not want to dim the glory of a reign which he seems to identify with the entirely pure glory of the new temple. The building and dedication of the temple are the high points of Solomon's reign, and it is upon these that future generations should meditate. And yet it was of this same prince that the author of the Book of Samuel was thinking when he drew an unflattering portrait of what a king would be (1 Sam 8:10-17). The Book of Exodus, beginning in chapter 35, also bears witness to the important place which Israel gave to its sanctuary.

From this point on, Chronicles runs parallel to the two Books of Kings, but limits itself to the Davidic kingdom of Jerusalem.

The Second Book of Chronicles may be divided as follows:

I: The Reign of Solomon (1:1—9:31)
II: The Monarchy before Hezekiah (10:1—27:9)
III: Reforms of Hezekiah and Josiah (28:1—35:27)
IV: The End of the Kingdom (36:1-23)

I: THE REIGN OF SOLOMON

CHAPTER 1

Solomon's Wisdom.* 1 Solomon, the son of David, strengthened his hold on the kingdom, for the LORD his God was with him and made him exceedingly powerful.

2 After summoning all Israel, Solomon addressed the commanders of units of thousands and hundreds, the judges, and all the leaders in Israel, the heads of families. 3 Then, accompanied by the entire assembly, he went to the high place at Gibeon where God's meeting tent was located, the tent that Moses, the servant of the LORD had made in the wilderness.[a] 4 However, David had brought up the Ark of the Covenant from Kiriath-jearim to the place that David had prepared for it, having pitched a tent for it in Jerusalem.

5 In addition, the bronze altar that Bezalel, the son of Hur, had made was also there in front of the tabernacle of the LORD, and Solomon and the assembly frequently consulted him.[b] 6 Solomon also offered one thousand burnt offerings upon the bronze altar which was at the meeting tent.

7 That night God appeared to Solomon and said to him: "Ask what you wish me to grant you." 8 Solomon replied to God: "You have shown great and faithful love to my father, and you have granted me the privilege of succeeding him as king. 9 O LORD God, let your promise to my father David now be fulfilled, for you have made me king over a people as numerous as the dust of the earth.[c] 10 Therefore, now grant me wisdom and knowledge to lead this people, for without your help who can rule this great people of yours?"[d]

11 Then God replied to Solomon: "Since this is your heart's desire and you have not asked for wealth or possessions or honor, or for the lives of those who are hostile to you, or even for a long life for yourself, but instead have asked for wisdom and knowledge for yourself so that you may govern my people over whom I have designated you to be king, 12 wisdom and knowledge will be granted to you. I will also give you riches, possessions, and glory such as no king before you has had and none after you shall be granted." *

Solomon's Wealth.* 13 Then Solomon returned to Jerusalem from the meeting tent to the high place at Gibeon, and he reigned as king over Israel. 14 He accumulated vast numbers of chariots and horses, amassing fourteen hundred chariots and twelve thousand horses. He stationed some in the chariot cities, and the rest with the king at Jerusalem.

15 In Jerusalem the king made silver and gold as common as stones, and he made cedars as plentiful as the sycamores in the lowlands.[e] 16 Solomon's horses were imported from Egypt and Cilicia, obtained by the king's traders from Cilicia at the prevailing price.[f] 17 The traders would import chariots from Egypt for six hundred shekels apiece, and horses from Cilicia for one hundred and fifty shekels apiece. They also exported them to all the kings of the Hittites and the Arameans.[g]

CHAPTER 2

Final Preparations for the Temple. 1 Solomon then resolved to build a house to honor the LORD as well as a palace for himself.[h] 2 Therefore, he conscripted seventy thousand men to carry the stone and eighty thousand men to serve as stonecutters, as well as three thousand six hundred men to oversee them.

3 Then Solomon sent this message to King Huram of Tyre: "Some time ago you dealt with my father David, sending him cedars to build a palace in which he would dwell. 4 Now I am preparing to build a house in honor of the LORD, my God, and to consecrate it to him so that fragrant incense can be burned before him, along with the perpetual display of the loaves of permanent offering, for burnt offerings morning and evening, and for the Sabbaths, the new moons, and the festivals of the LORD, our God, as is ordained forever for Israel.[i]

5 "The house that I intend to build must be large, since our God is greater than all other

a Lev 17:4; Jos 9:3-4.—b Ex 38:1-2; 1 Chr 2:20.—c Gen 12:2; 2 Sam 7:25; 1 Ki 8:25.—d Num 27:17; 2 Sam 5:2; Prov 8:15-16.—e Isa 60:5.—f 1 Ki 10:28.—g Song 1:9.—h Deut 12:5.—i Ex 30:7; Num 28:14.

1:1-12 The new king goes to the ancient sanctuary in Gibeon, where he venerates the tent of meeting, the "tabernacle" of God (1 Chr 16:39; Ex 27; 35).

1:12 We can surmise that Solomon was already wise in declaring his preference for wisdom and knowledge, and being given enormous wealth besides, shows the unmerited abundance of blessings that flow from the Lord when we choose rightly. Although all of these may be limited in this life, the love of the Lord is without end.

1:13-17 Solomon is conspicuous for his large number of war chariots. Even today impressive remains of royal stables are to be seen in the area of Megiddo.

gods.[j] 6 But who is really able to build a
house for him when the heavens, even the
highest heavens, cannot contain him? And
who am I to build a house for him, except as
a place to make offerings before him?[k]

7 "Therefore, now send me an artisan who
is highly skilled at working in gold, silver,
bronze, and iron, and in purple, crimson,
and blue fabrics, and who is expert in the art
of engraving. I want him to work with the
skilled craftsmen in Judah and Jerusalem
who were provided by my father David.
8 Also send me cedar, cypress, and juniper
timber from Lebanon, for I am well aware
that your servants are skilled in felling the
trees of Lebanon.

"My servants will work with your servants
9 in order to prepare for me a vast quantity
of timber, for the house that I intend to build
will be great in size and a marvel to behold.
10 Furthermore, I will provide for your ser-
vants the woodcutters who fell the trees,
twenty thousand kors of wheat, and twen-
ty thousand kors of barley, along with
twenty thousand measures of wine and
twenty thousand measures of oil."*

11 In a letter that he sent to King Solomon
in response, King Huram of Tyre replied:
"Because of the love that the LORD has for
his people, he has appointed you as their
king."[l] 12 Then Huram went on to say:
"Blessed be the LORD, the God of Israel, who
made heaven and earth. He has given King
David a wise son blessed with intelligence
and discernment who will build a house for
the LORD and a royal palace for himself.[m]

13 "I have now sent you Huram-abi,* a
skilled artisan and a man of intelligence.
14 He is the son of a Danite woman and of a
father from Tyre. He is skilled in the art of
working in gold, silver, bronze, iron, stone,
and wood, and in purple, crimson, and blue
fabrics and fine linen. He also is competent
to do all sorts of engraving and to execute
any design that may be assigned to him, in
collaboration with your own skilled crafts-
men and those of my lord David, your father.

15 "And now, let my lord send to his ser-
vants the wheat, barley, oil, and wine which
he has promised.[n] 16 We shall cut down all
the timber you need from Lebanon and float
it all down to you as rafts by sea to Joppa.
Then it will be your responsibility to trans-
port it to Jerusalem."[o]

17 Shortly thereafter Solomon took a cen-
sus of all the aliens who were residing in the
land of Israel, similar to the census that his
father David had taken. There were found to
be one hundred and fifty-three thousand six
hundred aliens. 18 Solomon designated sev-
enty thousand of them to be porters, eighty
thousand to be stonecutters in the hill coun-
try, and three thousand six hundred as over-
seers to ensure that the people were doing
the work assigned to them.

CHAPTER 3

Construction of the Temple. 1 * Then
Solomon began to build the temple of the
LORD in Jerusalem on Mount Moriah where
the LORD had appeared to his father David,
at the site that David had chosen, on the
threshing floor of Ornan the Jebusite.[p] 2 He
commenced building it on the second day of
the second month of the fourth year of his
reign.

3 These are the measurements specified
by Solomon for building the house of God.
According to the old standard of measure-
ment, its length was sixty cubits and its
width was twenty cubits.* 4 The vestibule
was twenty cubits long, spanning the entire
breadth of the house of God, and its height
was also twenty cubits.[q]

5 He overlaid the nave with cypress, which
he covered with fine gold and embossed with
palms and chains.[r] 6 He also adorned the
house beautifully with settings of precious
stones and with gold from Parvaim. 7 Then
he overlaid the house with gold, including its
beams, its thresholds, its walls, and its doors,
and he carved cherubim on the walls.

8 He also made the Holy of Holies. Its
length, corresponding to the width of the
house, was twenty cubits, and its width was
also twenty cubits. He overlaid all of it with

j 1 Chr 22:5; Ps 135:5.—k Jer 23:24.—l 1 Ki 10:9.—m Neh 9:6; Pss 33:6; 102:26.—n Ezr 3:7.—o Jos 19:46; Jon 1:3.—p 2 Sam 24:18; Acts 7:47.—q 1 Ki 6:3.—r 1 Ki 6:17; Ezek 40:16.

2:10 King Solomon had lofty ideas for building a temple worthy of the Lord and these amounts of wheat, barley, wine, and oil promised for the best materials are inflated accordingly. For a more realistic listing of what was offered for the wood, see the parallel passage in 1 Ki 5:11.

2:13-14 *Huram-abi:* "Huram" in 1 Ki 7:13; his mother is there said to be of the tribe of Naphtali.

3:1—5:1 The inmost place of the sanctuary had changed its name: it is no longer the place where David spoke to the priest, but the Most Holy Place, into which only the high priest entered once a year; a court of the temple was reserved for the priests.

3:3 In antiquity a cubit was about 52 cm (see Ezek 43:13).

six hundred talents of fine gold.[s] 9 The
weight of the gold nails was fifty shekels. He
also overlaid the upper chambers with gold.

10 For the Holy of Holies he made two
carved cherubim which were then overlaid
with gold. 11 The wings of the cherubim*
together had a total span of twenty cubits. A
wing of one cherub, five cubits in length,
extended to a wall of the building, while the
other wing reached out to meet a wing of
the other cherub. 12 Similarly, one wing of
the second cherub also extended five cubits
to touch the other wall of the building, while
its other wing reached out to meet a wing of
the first cherub.

13 The combined wings of these two cheru-
bim extended twenty cubits. They stood with
their feet on the ground, facing the nave.
14 Solomon also made the curtain* of pur-
ple, crimson, and blue fabrics and fine linen
and embroidered it with winged creatures.[t]

15 In front of the temple he erected two pil-
lars that totaled thirty-five cubits high, with
a capital measuring five cubits on the top of
each pillar.[u] 16 Next he made chains in the
form of a necklace and put them on the tops
of the pillars, and then he carved one hun-
dred pomegranates and attached them to
the chains. 17 Finally, he erected the pillars in
front of the temple, one on the right and the
other on the left. The one on the right he
called Jachin, and the one on the left he
called Boaz.

CHAPTER 4

1 Then Solomon made a bronze altar
twenty cubits long, twenty cubits wide, and
ten cubits high. 2 After that, he made the sea
of cast metal. It was circular in shape, ten
cubits from rim to rim, and five cubits high.[v]

3 Under the sea and completely encircling
the thirty cubits of its circumference there
was a ring of figures of oxen in two rows, ten
to the cubit. 4 It stood on twelve oxen, three
facing north, three facing west, three facing
south, and three facing east. The hindquar-
ters of each faced inward, and the sea was set
on them.[w] 5 It was a hand's breadth in thick-
ness, and its rim was like that of a cup—lily-
shaped. It could hold three thousand baths.*

6 He also made ten basins for washing,
placing five on the right and five on the left.
These were to be employed to rinse what
would be used for the burnt offerings.
However, the sea was for the priests to
wash in.

7 Then he made ten lampstands of gold as
prescribed and placed them in the temple,
five on the right side and five on the left.[x]
8 He also made ten tables and placed them in
the temple, five on the right and five on the
left, as well as one hundred basins of gold.*

9 Next he made the court of the priests and
the great courtyard with its gates. After he
had overlaid the doors with bronze,[y] 10 he
placed the sea off to the southeast on the
right-hand side of the temple.

11 Meanwhile Huram made the pots, the
shovels, and the basins. He thus completed
all the work he had undertaken for King
Solomon on the temple of God:[z] 12 the two
pillars, the bowls, and the two capitals that
were on the top of the pillars; the two sets of
filigree to cover the two bowls of the capitals
that were on the top of the pillars; 13 the four
hundred pomegranates for the two net-
works, with two rows of pomegranates for
each network, to cover two bowl-shaped cap-
itals surmounting the two pillars; 14 the ten
stands and the basins on the stands; 15 the
one sea and the twelve oxen that supported
it; 16 likewise the pots, the shovels, and the
basins—all of these articles Huram-abi
made of burnished bronze cast for King
Solomon for the house of the LORD.

17 Then the king had them cast in the
foundry between Succoth and Zeredah in
the plain of the Jordan.[a] 18 Solomon made all
these objects in great quantities, and as a
result, the weight of the bronze was not
determined.

19 Solomon had all of these articles made
for the LORD God: the golden altar, the tables
for the bread of the Presence,[b] 20 * the lamp-
stands and their lamps of pure gold to burn

s Ex 26:33.—t Gen 3:24; Ex 26:31; Mt 27:51; Heb 9:3.—u 1 Ki 7:15-20; Rev 3:12.—v Rev 4:6; 15:2.—w Ezek 48:30-34; Rev 21:13.—x Ex 25:31, 40; 1 Ki 7:49.—y 1 Ki 7:12.—z 1 Ki 7:14.—a Gen 33:17.—b 1 Ki 7:48-50; Ex 25:30.

3:11 *The cherubim:* a special category of mighty angels with well-defined functions.

3:14 *The curtain:* in fact, Solomon made a door (1 Ki 6:31) in place of the veil of which Ex 26:31 speaks.

4:5 *Baths:* a liquid measure equaling approximately 40 quarts. The number of baths stated in 1 Ki 7:26 is 2000.

4:8 The interior courtyard where the altar of holocausts was placed.

4:20-22 There is no such thing as too much gold when it came to building a permanent place for the Israelites to worship the Lord. This was a testimony to their great love and respect, and perhaps their guilt for worshiping idols. Later these detailed plans would be used to reconstruct the temple that would be destroyed by the Babylonians.

before the inner sanctuary as prescribed;
21 the flowers, the lamps, and the tongs of the
purest gold; 22 the snuffers, the bowls, the
ladles, and the firepans of pure gold. As for
the entrance to the temple, the inner doors
to the Most Holy Place and the doors to the
nave of the temple were of gold.

CHAPTER 5

Dedication of the Temple. 1 When all the
work that Solomon had done was complet-
ed, he brought in the treasures that his
father David had dedicated, and he deposit-
ed the silver, the gold, and all the vessels in
the treasuries of the house of God.

2 Then Solomon summoned the elders of
Israel, and all the heads of the tribes and the
princes of the families of Israel, to bring up
the Ark of the Covenant of the Lord from the
City of David, which is Zion.[c] 3 All the men
of Israel assembled before the king at the fes-
tival of the seventh month.

4 When all the elders of Israel had arrived,
the Levites lifted up the Ark, 5 and the priests
and the Levites carried it and the meeting
tent with all the sacred vessels that it con-
tained.[d] 6 King Solomon and the entire con-
gregation of Israel who were present with
him assembled before the Ark and sacrificed
so many sheep and oxen that they could not
be counted or reckoned.

7 Then the priests brought the Ark of the
Covenant of the LORD to its place in the
inner sanctuary of the temple, in the Most
Holy Place, underneath the wings of the
cherubim. 8 For the cherubim spread out
their wings over the place where the Ark
stood, so that they sheltered the Ark and its
poles.

9 The poles were so long that their ends
could be seen from the Holy Place in front of
the inner sanctuary, but they could not be
seen from outside. They are still there to this
very day.* 10 There was nothing inside the
Ark aside from the two tablets which Moses
had put there at Horeb when the LORD had
made a covenant with the people of Israel
after they had departed from Egypt.[e]

11 When the priests emerged from the
Holy Place—for all the priests who were
present had sanctified themselves without
regard to their divisions—12 all the Levitical
singers, Asaph, Heman, and Jeduthun, with
their sons and brothers, dressed themselves
in fine linen, with cymbals, lyres, and harps.
They were standing to the east of the altar
with one hundred and twenty priests, blow-
ing the trumpets.[f]

13 The trumpeters and the singers joined
in unison to offer praise and thanksgiving to
the LORD, and when the volume was raised,
with trumpets and cymbals and other musi-
cal instruments, in praise of the LORD:

"For he is good,
  for his steadfast love endures
    forever,"*

the temple was filled with the cloud of the
glory of the LORD, 14 and as a result of the
cloud the priests could not continue to
minister, for the glory of the LORD filled the
temple of God.

CHAPTER 6

1 Then Solomon said:

"The LORD has said
  that he has chosen to dwell in thick
    darkness.
2 I have built you a magnificent temple, O
    LORD,
  a dwelling place in which you may
    reside forever."

3 Then the king turned around and
blessed the entire assembly of Israelites as
they stood before him. 4 He said: "Blessed
be the LORD, the God of Israel, who has
fulfilled with his hand what he promised
with his mouth to my father David, when
he said: 5 'From the day I brought my peo-
ple out of the land of Egypt, I have not cho-
sen a city from any of the tribes of Israel in
which to have a temple built to honor my
name, nor did I choose any man to be the
ruler over my people Israel. 6 However,
now I have chosen Jerusalem, where I
shall be honored, and I have chosen David
to rule my people Israel.'[g]

7 "My father David was determined to
build a temple to honor the LORD, the God of
Israel. 8 However, the LORD said to him: 'In
wishing to build a temple in my honor, you
did well. 9 But nevertheless you shall not
build the temple. Rather, your son who shall

c 1 Ki 8:1-9; 2 Sam 6:12.—d Num 3:31; 1 Chr 15:2.—e Deut 10:2-5; Heb 9:4.—f 1 Ki 10:12; 1 Chr 9:33; Ps 68:25.—g Deut 12:5; Isa 14:1.

5:9 *Still there to this very day:* this statement in fact, is not correct, however, the Chronicler chose to copy it from sources that preceded the destruction of Solomon's temple.

5:13 *His steadfast love endures forever:* the refrain of Pss 118; 136.

be born to you shall be the one who will build the temple in my name.'

10 "Now the LORD has fulfilled his promise that he made. For I have succeeded my father David and taken his place on the throne of Israel, as the LORD foretold. In addition, I have built the temple to honor the name of the LORD, the God of Israel. 11 There I have installed the Ark containing the covenant of the LORD that he made with the people of Israel."

Solomon's Prayer.* 12 Then, in the presence of the whole assembly of Israel, Solomon stood before the altar of the LORD and spread out his hands. 13 Solomon had made a bronze platform, measuring five cubits long, five cubits wide, and three cubits high, which he directed to be placed in the center of the courtyard, and he stood on it. Then he knelt down* in the presence of the whole assembly of Israel and spread out his hands toward heaven.[h]

14 "LORD, God of Israel," he said, "there is no God like you in heaven or on earth, as you keep your covenant and show steadfast love to your servants who walk before you with all their heart. 15 You have kept the promise you made to my father David. Indeed, what you promised him with your words you have fulfilled by your deeds.

16 "And now, LORD, God of Israel, keep the promise you made to your servant David, my father, when you said: 'You shall never fail to have a successor to sit in my presence on the throne of Israel, provided that your sons are careful to keep to their ways and conform to my law, as you yourself have done.' 17 Therefore, O LORD, God of Israel, let this promise be confirmed which you promised to your servant David.

18 "And yet, will God indeed dwell with the people on earth? If the heavens and even the highest heavens cannot contain you, how much less this temple which I have built![i] 19 Look with kindness on your servant's prayer and his plea, O LORD, my God, heeding the cry and the prayer that your servant makes before you.

20 "May your eyes be forever on this house day and night, the place where you decreed that you would establish your name. Listen to the prayer that your servant offers in your presence. 21 Also hear the supplications of your servant and of your people Israel which they direct toward this place. Listen from your heavenly dwelling, and when you hear, grant us forgiveness.

22 "When anyone sins against his neighbor and is required to take an oath, and he comes forth and swears before your altar in this temple, 23 then listen from heaven and take the necessary action. Judge your servants, requiting the guilty person and holding him responsible for his conduct, but absolving the innocent person and rewarding him in accordance with his righteousness.[j]

24 "Should your people Israel sin against you and as a result be defeated by an enemy, but then return to you and confess your name and pray and plead to you in this temple, 25 listen to them and forgive the sin of your people Israel and then bring them back to the land that you gave to them and their ancestors.

26 "When the heavens are shut and there is no rain because your people have sinned against you, but then they pray toward this place, praise your name, and desist from sin because you have afflicted them, 27 listen to their pleas in heaven and forgive the sin of your servants and of your people Israel. Show them the path of righteousness along which they should walk and send down rain upon your land which you have given to your people as an inheritance.

28 "Should there be famine afflicting the land, or plague, or blight, or mildew, or locusts, or caterpillars, or should enemies besiege your people in any of their cities, or should plague or sickness befall them, 29 then mercifully listen to the prayer or supplication of everyone among your people Israel, each one knowing his own suffering and his own sorrows and stretching out his hands toward this temple. 30 Listen from heaven, your dwelling place, as you grant forgiveness and deal with each man according to his deeds, since you alone know what is in each person's heart.*[k] 31 As a result, the people will fear you and walk in your ways through-

h 1 Ki 8:54; Neh 8:4; Ps 95:6.—i Isa 40:22; Ps 11:4; Rev 21:3.—j Isa 3:11; 65:6; Mt 16:27.—k 1 Sam 2:3; Pss 7:9; 44:22; Prov 16:2; 17:3.

6:12-42 This is the beautiful prayer already read in 1 Ki 8:22-61. The ending has been shortened and replaced by some verses from Ps 132.

6:13 *He knelt down:* a significant show of love and respect for the Lord displayed by King Solomon. He is unafraid of breaking custom or of what others will say, just as his father David did when he danced before the Lord (2 Sam 6:14).

6:30 At this point in his prayer, Solomon shows his complete faith in God's justice and mercy, who alone knows what is in one's heart.

out all the days that they live in the land that
you gave to our ancestors.
32 "Likewise, when foreigners who do not
belong to your people Israel come from a
distant land because of your great name and
your mighty hand and your outstretched
arm, and they approach and pray in your
temple, 33 listen from heaven, your dwelling
place, and grant whatever they ask of you, in
order that all the peoples of the earth may
acknowledge your name and fear you, as do
your people Israel, and that they may know
that this house which I have built bears your
name.
34 "If your people go forth to engage in war
against their enemies, wherever you choose
to send them, and they pray to you, facing
toward this city that you have chosen and
toward this house that I have built to honor
your name, 35 then listen from heaven to
their prayer and their supplication, and
defend their cause.
36 "When your people sin against you—for
there is no one who does not sin—and in
your anger against them you deliver them
into the power of the enemy who will carry
them away captive to a land far or near,[l]
37 and then, later on, if they come to their
senses in the land to which they have been
taken as captives and they repent, entreating
you in the land of their captivity as they say:
'We have sinned and done wrong; we have
acted wickedly,' 38 and they repent with all
their heart and soul in the land of their cap-
tivity to which they have been taken, and
they pray, turning toward the land which you
gave to their ancestors, toward the city you
have chosen and the temple I have built to
honor your name, 39 then from heaven, your
dwelling place, hear their prayer and their
pleas, uphold their cause, and forgive your
people who have sinned against you.
40 "Now, O my God, let your eyes be open
and your ears be attentive to the prayer
offered in this place.

41 "Now rise up, O LORD God,
and go to your resting place,
you and the Ark of your might.
Let your priests, LORD God,
be clothed with your salvation,
and let your faithful ones
rejoice in your goodness.
42 O LORD God, do not reject your
anointed one.
Remember the faithful love of your
servant David."

CHAPTER 7

1 When Solomon had ended his prayer,
fire came down from heaven and consumed
the burnt offering and the sacrifices, after
which the glory of the LORD filled the tem-
ple. 2 The priests could not enter the house
of the LORD because the glory of the LORD
had filled it.[m]
3 When all the Israelites beheld the fire
descending and the glory of the LORD upon
the temple, they bowed down upon the pave-
ment with their faces to the ground. Then
they worshiped and gave thanks to the LORD,
saying:

"For he is good,
for his mercy endures forever."[n]

4 Then the king and all the people offered
sacrifices before the LORD. 5 King Solomon
offered as a sacrifice twenty-two thousand
oxen and one hundred and twenty thousand
sheep. Thus the king and all the people dedi-
cated the house of God.
The Dedication. 6 The priests stood at their
appointed posts, as did the Levites, with the
musical instruments for the LORD that King
David had made for giving thanks to the
LORD—for his love endures forever—when-
ever David used them to offer praise to their
accompaniment. Opposite them the priests
sounded their trumpets while all the
Israelites stood.* [o]
7 Then Solomon consecrated the middle
part of the court that lay in front of the house
of the LORD. There he presented the burnt
offerings and the fatty portions of the shared
offerings because the bronze altar which he
had made could not hold the burnt offering
and the grain offering and the fatty parts.[p]
8 After that Solomon, and all Israel with
him, a massive congregation, from Lebo-
hamath to the Wadi of Egypt, celebrated the
festival for seven days. 9 On the eighth day
they held a solemn assembly, inasmuch as
they had celebrated the dedication of the
altar for seven days.
10 On the twenty-third day of the seventh
month, Solomon sent the people back to

l Eccl 7:20; Jer 9:5; Rom 3:9.—m Ex 29:43; Deut 12:5, 11; 1 Ki 8:10-11.—n 2 Chr 5:13; Ps 136:1.—o Num 10:8; 1 Chr 15:16-21.—p 1 Ki 8:64.

7:6 The reference to the Psalms is clear. But on this point see the introduction to the Book of Psalms.

their homes rejoicing and happy in heart
because of all the wonderful things that the
LORD had granted to David, to Solomon,
and to his people Israel. 11 Solomon had
completed the house of the LORD and the
royal palace. Everything that he had been
determined to accomplish in the house of
the LORD and in his own house had been suc-
cessfully completed.

God's Warning to Solomon. 12 Then the
LORD appeared to Solomon during the night
and said to him: "I have heard your prayer,
and I have chosen this place for myself as a
house of sacrifice. 13 When I shut up the
heavens so that there is no rain, or com-
mand the locusts to devour the land, or send
a pestilence to overcome my people, 14 and if
then my people who bear my name humble
themselves and pray to me and seek my
presence as they turn from their wicked
ways, then I will hear them from heaven and
forgive their sins and restore their land. [q]

15 "Then my eyes will be open and my ears
will be attentive to the prayers that are
offered in this place. 16 For now I have chosen
and consecrated this house so that my name
may be there forever and my eyes and my
heart shall constantly be there.

17 "As for you, if you on your part live in
my presence as your father David lived,
doing everything that I have commanded
you and observing my laws and my decrees,
18 then I will establish your royal throne, as I
promised by a covenant with your father
David when I said: 'You shall never lack a
male successor of yours to rule over Israel.' [r]

19 "However, if you turn away and forsake
my laws and my commandments which I
have laid down for you, and then proceed to
serve other gods and worship them, 20 then I
will uproot the people from the land which I
have given them. I will cast from my sight
this temple which I have consecrated for my
name, cast it out of my sight, and make it
a byword and an object of ridicule for all
people.

21 "And in regard to this temple that was
once so exalted, everyone who passes by it
will be appalled at the sight and ask: 'Why
has the LORD allowed this to happen* to this
land and to this house?' [s] 22 Then others will
reply: 'Because the people abandoned the
LORD, the God of their fathers, who brought
them out of the land of Egypt. Instead, they
adopted other gods, whom they worshiped
and served. That is why the LORD has
brought all these disasters upon them.' "

CHAPTER 8

Solomon's Buildings. 1 * At the end of the
twenty years that Solomon had taken to
build the house of the LORD and his own
palace, 2 he rebuilt the cities that Huram had
given to him, and he settled the Israelites in
them.

3 Then Solomon went to Hamath-zobah
and captured it.* 4 After that he fortified
Tadmor* in the wilderness and all the stor-
age towns that he had built in Hamath. 5 He
also built Upper Beth-horon and Lower
Beth-horon, fortified cities with walls, gates,
and bars, [t] 6 and Baalath, all the supply cities
belonging to Solomon, and all the towns for
his chariots and for his cavalry and what-
ever else Solomon decided to build in
Jerusalem, in Lebanon, and throughout his
entire dominion.

7 All the people who still remained of the
Hittites, the Amorites, the Perizzites, the
Hivites, and the Jebusites who did not belong
to Israel [u]—8 that is, from their descendants
still surviving in the land, whom the people of
Israel had not destroyed—Solomon subject-
ed to forced labor, as is still the case today.*

9 However, Solomon did not use the peo-
ple of Israel as slaves for all the work he
wanted done. Rather, they were assigned as
soldiers and his officers, as well as the com-
manders of his soldiers and his cavalry.*
10 These served as King Solomon's officials,

q Num 6:27; Isa 55:7; Ezek 18:32.—r Jer 33:17, 21; 2 Sam 7:13; Mic 5:2.—s Deut 29:23-24; Jer 19:8.—t Jos 10:10; 1 Chr 7:24.—u Gen 10:16; Ezr 9:1.

7:21 *Allowed this to happen:* it's easier to accept that God punishes those who commit sinful acts, but thousands of years later good people continue to grapple with the question of unmerited hardship and random violence. Even Solomon's wisdom does not provide the answer to God's allowing will. Only faith will suffice.

8:1—9:31 The Lord prospers the undertakings of the man who built his temple. But the picture which the Chronicler sketches of the reign of Solomon is brighter than the reality. For a more concrete and less grandiloquent description of the facts, see the first Book of Kings.

8:3 See 1 Ki 9:11f. *Zobah* was an Aramean kingdom north of Damascus. "He went," like "he built," etc., means he had it done.

8:4 *Tadmor:* the Semitic name, still in use, for Palmyra, an oasis which is mentioned in an Assyrian inscription dating from a century before Solomon and which became famous in the third century A.D. In fact, however, the reference is clearly to Tamar, on the southern shore of the Dead Sea; see the parallel in 1 Ki 9:18.

8:8 *As is still the case today:* the expression is repeated elsewhere, showing that the author is using an ancient source.

8:9 The opening statement does not correspond to the facts (see 1 Ki 5:13), but attests to the Israelites' sense of being free people.

two hundred and fifty in number, who exer-
cised authority over the people.

Solomon's Piety. 11 Solomon brought the
daughter of Pharaoh up from the City of
David to the place that he had built for her,
for he said: "No wife of mine shall live in the
house of King David of Israel, for the places
that the Ark of the LORD has entered are
sacred."

12 Then Solomon sacrificed burnt offer-
ings to the LORD upon the altar of the LORD
that he had built in front of the portico, [v] 13 in
accordance with what was required for each
day, offerings in accordance with the law of
Moses for the Sabbaths, the new moons, and
the annual dedicated feasts—the Feast of
Unleavened Bread, the Feast of Weeks, and
the Feast of Booths. [w]

14 Following the ordinances of his father
David, Solomon designated the various divi-
sions of the priests for their service, and the
Levites for their offices of praise and ministry
alongside the priests as the duty of each day
required, and the gatekeepers designated for
specific gates, for such was the command of
David, the man of God. [x] 15 The instructions
that David had specified in regard to the
priests and Levites and also concerning the
treasuries were never disregarded.

16 Thus all of Solomon's work was accom-
plished, from the day that the foundation of
the house of the LORD was laid until the
house of the LORD was completed.

Solomon's Glory. 17 Then Solomon went to
Ezion-geber and Elath on the seacoast of
Edom, [y] 18 and Huram sent ships under the
command of his own officers and manned
by experienced seamen familiar with the
sea. They went to Ophir, together with the
servants of Solomon, and brought back from
there four hundred and fifty talents that they
presented to King Solomon.

CHAPTER 9

The Queen of Sheba. 1 When the Queen of
Sheba was informed about Solomon's repu-
tation, she came to Jerusalem to test him
with difficult questions. Arriving with a very
large retinue, and with camels bearing
spices, an immense quantity of gold, and
precious stones, she came to Solomon and
discussed everything she had on her mind. [z]
2 Solomon answered all of her questions.
There was nothing she asked that he was
unable to explain to her.

3 When the Queen of Sheba witnessed the
wisdom of Solomon, the palace he had built,
4 the food served at his table, the seating of
his ministers, the attendants and the ele-
gance of their clothing, the cupbearers in
their robes, and the burnt offerings that he
presented in the house of the LORD, it literal-
ly took her breath away.

5 Then she said to the king: "The reports I
heard in my own country about your accom-
plishments and your wisdom proved to be
true. 6 However, I did not believe those
reports to be accurate until I came and saw
all this with my own eyes. Moreover, I have
come to realize that I was not told even half
of the greatness of your wisdom. You far sur-
pass everything I had heard about you.

7 "How fortunate your people are! Happy
are these servants of yours who are continu-
ally attending you and listening to your wis-
dom! 8 Blessed is the LORD, your God, who
has taken such great delight in you and
placed you on his throne as king for the
LORD, your God. Because of the love of your
God for Israel and his desire to have Israel
endure forever, he has appointed you to be
their king so that you may ensure that justice
and righteousness will be maintained." [a]

9 Then she presented King Solomon with
one hundred and twenty talents of gold,
large quantities of spices, and precious
stones. There had never been spices previ-
ously to equal those that the Queen of Sheba
gave to King Solomon.

10 Besides all this, the servants of Huram
and the servants of Solomon who had
brought gold from Ophir also brought large
amounts of algum wood and precious stones.
11 From the algum wood the king made stairs
for the house of the LORD and for the king's
palace, as well as lyres and harps for the
singers. Nothing to match them had ever
been seen before in the land of Judah.

12 King Solomon gave the Queen of Sheba
everything she desired and requested, far
surpassing what she had brought to the king.
Then she departed with her servants and
journeyed back to her own land.

13 The weight of the gold that Solomon
received each year amounted to six hundred
and sixty-six talents of gold 14 in addition to
the tolls levied on merchants and what was

v 1 Ki 8:64.—w Ex 29:38; Num 28:9.—x 1 Chr 24:1; 25:1; 26:1.—y 1 Ki 9:26.—z 1 Ki 10:1-13; Mt 12:42; Lk 11:31.—a 1 Ki 2:12; 1 Chr 17:14.

collected from foreign trade. All the kings of
Arabia and the governors of the provinces
also brought gold and silver to Solomon.[b]
15 Moreover, King Solomon made two
hundred large shields of beaten gold, with six
hundred shekels of beaten gold going into
each shield, 16 and three hundred bucklers of
beaten gold, with three hundred shekels of
gold going into each buckler. The king stored
all these in the House of the Forest of
Lebanon.
17 King Solomon also made a large ivory
throne which he overlaid with pure gold.
18 The throne had six steps, and a footstool of
gold was fastened to it. There were armrests
on each side of the seat, with two lions stand-
ing beside the arms, 19 while twelve lions
stood on either side of the six steps. Nothing
like it had ever been made in any other
kingdom.
20 Furthermore, all of Solomon's drinking
vessels were of gold, and all the vessels of the
House of the Forest of Lebanon were made
of pure gold. Silver was not regarded as any-
thing of value in the days of King Solomon.
21 The king had a fleet of ships that sailed to
Tarshish with the servants of Huram. Once
every three years a fleet of ships from
Tarshish used to return with a cargo of gold,
silver, ivory, apes, and monkeys.
22 Thus King Solomon surpassed all the
kings of the earth in riches and in wisdom,[c]
23 and all the kings of the earth sought to con-
sult Solomon in order to hear from him the
wisdom that God had implanted in his
heart. 24 Moreover, every single one of those
kings brought a gift with him: objects of sil-
ver and gold, garments, weapons, spices,
horses, and mules in an annual tribute.[d]
25 Solomon had four thousand stalls for
horses and chariots, and twelve thousand
horses, which he stationed in the chariot
cities and with the king in Jerusalem.[e] 26 He
ruled over all the kings from the Euphrates
to the land of the Philistines and the border
of Egypt.[f]
27 King Solomon made silver as common
in Jerusalem as stone, and cedars as plentiful
as the sycamores of the foothills. 28 Horses
were imported for Solomon from Egypt and
from all the other countries.

The Death of Solomon. 29 The rest of the
acts of Solomon's reign, from first to last, are
recorded in the history of Nathan the
prophet, in the prophecy of Ahijah the
Shilonite, and, in the visions of Iddo the seer
concerning Jeroboam, the son of Nebat.*
30 Solomon reigned in Jerusalem over all
Israel for forty years. 31 Then he rested with
his ancestors and was buried in the city of his
father David. He was succeeded by his son
Rehoboam.

II: THE MONARCHY BEFORE HEZEKIAH

CHAPTER 10

The Kingdom Divided. 1 Rehoboam imme-
diately went to Shechem, for all Israel had
gone there. 2 When Jeroboam, the son of
Nebat, learned about this in Egypt, where he
had fled from King Solomon, he then
returned from Egypt.
3 The people thereupon summoned
Jeroboam, and he and all Israel came to
Rehoboam and said to him:[g] 4 "Your father
laid a heavy yoke upon us. However, if you
agree to lighten the harsh labor and the
heavy yoke that he imposed on us, we will
serve you." 5 Rehoboam replied to them:
"Come back to me again in three days, and
then I will inform you of my decision." On
hearing this, the people departed.
6 Then King Rehoboam sought the coun-
sel of the elders who had served as atten-
dants and advisors to his father Solomon
during his lifetime. He asked them: "What
answer do you advise me to give to this peo-
ple?"[h] 7 They replied: "If you will treat this
people with kindness and be fair in your
dealings with them, they will remain your
servants forever."[i]
8 However, Rehoboam rejected the advice
that the elders had given him and proceeded
to consult the young men who had grown up
with him and who now attended him. 9 He
said to them: "What reply do you advise me
to give to this people who have requested
that I lighten the yoke that my father
imposed on them?"
10 The young men who had grown up with
him replied: "This is the answer that you
should give to this people who said to you:
'Your father made our yoke heavy. We
implore you to lighten it for us.' Tell them:

b Jer 25:24.—c 2 Chr 1:12; 1 Ki 3:13.—d 2 Chr 32:23; Pss 45:13; 68:30; Isa 18:7.—e 1 Sam 8:11.—f Gen 15:18-21; 1 Ki 4:21; Ps 72:8-9.—g 1 Ki 12:3.—h 1 Ki 12:6; Job 8:8-9; 12:12.—i Prov 15:1.

9:29 The prophecy is the one made to Jeroboam (1 Ki 11:29f). Iddo was a prophet of whose activity and work we have no knowledge.

'My little finger is thicker than my father's loins. 11 Although my father laid a heavy yoke on you, I shall make it heavier. My father beat you with whips, but I will scourge you with scorpions.' "

12 On the third day, Jeroboam and all the people came to Rehoboam as the king had instructed them to do. 13 The king replied to them sharply, having rejected the advice which the elders had given him. 14 Rather, he followed the advice of the younger men and said: "My father laid a heavy yoke on you, but I will make it even heavier. My father beat you with whips, but I will scourge you with scorpions."

15 Thus the king did not listen to the people, for this turn of events was ordained by God so that the LORD might fulfill his word that he had spoken to Jeroboam, the son of Nebat, through Ahijah the Shilonite.

16 * When all Israel realized that the king would not listen to them, the people answered the king:

"What share have we in David?
We have no heritage in the son of Jesse.
Let all of you depart to your tents,
O Israel!
Look now to your own house,
O David!"

Then all Israel departed to their tents.[j] 17 Therefore, Rehoboam reigned over only those Israelites who lived in the towns of Judah.

18 When King Rehoboam sent forth Hadoram, the commander in charge of the forced labor, the Israelites stoned him to death. However, King Rehoboam managed to mount his chariot and flee to Jerusalem.[k] 19 Thus from that day to this, Israel has been in rebellion against the house of David.

CHAPTER 11

1 When Rehoboam reached Jerusalem, he mustered one hundred and eighty thousand chosen warriors of the house of Judah and Benjamin to fight against David and restore the kingdom to him. 2 However, this word of the LORD came to Shemaiah, the man of God: 3 "Say to Rehoboam, son of Solomon, king of Judah, and to all Israel in Judah and Benjamin: 4 'Thus says the LORD: You are not to march out to fight against your brothers. Return home, every single one of you, for this is my doing.' " Therefore, they obeyed the command of the LORD and turned back from their campaign against Jeroboam.

Rehoboam's Works. 5 Rehoboam took up residence in Jerusalem, and he built a number of fortified cities in Judah.[l] 6 He built up Bethlehem, Etam, Tekoa, 7 Beth-zur, Soco, Adullam, 8 Gath, Mareshah, Ziph, 9 Adoram, Lachish, Azekah, 10 Zorah, Aijalon, and Hebron. These were the fortified cities in Judah and Benjamin.

11 He then strengthened the defenses of these fortifications and stationed commanders in them, as well as supplies of food, oil, and wine. 12 He also supplied all the cities with large shields and spears of great strength. Thus he retained control of Judah and Benjamin.

Jeroboam's Priests. 13 The priests and the Levites throughout Israel placed themselves at Rehoboam's disposal. 14 Actually the Levites had abandoned their pasture lands and their holdings and had come to Judah and Jerusalem because Jeroboam and his sons had rejected their services as priests of the Lord.[m] 15 Jeroboam therefore appointed his own priests for the high places and for the satyrs and calves he had made.[n]

16 On the other hand, those who were determined to seek the LORD, the God of Israel, followed the Levites to Jerusalem to sacrifice to the LORD, the God of their ancestors. 17 They strengthened the kingdom of Judah, and for three years they made Rehoboam, the son of Solomon, secure, for they followed the example of David and Solomon for three years.

Rehoboam's Wives. 18 Rehoboam married Mahalath, who was the daughter of Jerimoth, the son of David, and whose mother was Abihail, the daughter of Eliab son of Jesse.[o] 19 She bore him sons: Jeush, Shemariah, and Zaham.

20 After her he married Maacah, the daughter of Absalom, who bore him Abijah, Attai, Ziza, and Shelomith. 21 Rehoboam loved Maacah, the daughter of Absalom, more than all his other wives and concubines. He had eighteen wives and sixty con-

j 2 Sam 20:1.—k 1 Ki 5:14.—l Jos 10:20.—m Num 35:2-5.—n 1 Ki 12:31; 13:33.—o 1 Sam 16:6.

10:16-19 King Rehoboam, son of Solomon, who had everything and lost it because of his inordinate desire for power and mistreatment of his people, is forced to flee and relinquish his kingdom.

cubines, and he fathered twenty-eight sons
and sixty daughters.[p]

22 Rehoboam appointed Abijah, the son of
Maacah, as the chief prince among his
brothers, inasmuch as he intended to make
him king. 23 He acted wisely by distributing
some of his sons throughout all the districts
of Judah and Benjamin in all the fortified
cities. He also gave them copious provisions
and obtained a number of wives for them.

CHAPTER 12

Rehoboam's Unfaithfulness. 1 After Reho-
boam's kingdom was firmly established and
he grew ever more powerful, he, and all
Israel* with him, abandoned the law of the
LORD. 2 In the fifth year of the reign of King
Rehoboam, because he and his people had
been unfaithful to the LORD, King Shishak of
Egypt attacked Jerusalem*[q] 3 with twelve
hundred chariots and sixty thousand horse-
men. In addition, he also brought with him
from Egypt a vast army beyond counting—
Libyans, Sukkites,* and Ethiopians.[r]

4 After Shishak had captured the fortified
cities of Judah and had arrived at the out-
skirts of Jerusalem, 5 the prophet Shemaiah
came to Rehoboam and the commanders of
Judah who had gathered at Jerusalem
because of Shishak, and he said to them:
"Thus says the LORD: 'You have abandoned
me, and therefore I have abandoned you to
the power of Shishak.' " 6 Then the officers of
Israel and the king humbled themselves and
said: "The LORD is just."[s]

7 When the LORD saw that they had hum-
bled themselves, this word of the LORD came
to Shemaiah: "Because they have humbled
themselves, I will not destroy them. Rather,
I will grant them some degree of deliver-
ance, and my wrath shall not be poured out
upon Jerusalem by the hand of Shishak.[t]
8 However, they shall become his servants, so
that they may come to understand the dif-
ference between serving me and serving the
rulers of other countries."

9 Therefore, Shishak, the king of Egypt,
attacked Jerusalem and carried away the
treasures of the house of the LORD as well as
the treasures of the king's palace. He seized
everything, including the shields of gold that
Solomon had made. 10 Therefore, King
Rehoboam made bronze shields to replace
them and entrusted them to the command-
ers of the guard on duty at the entrance of
the king's palace.

11 Whenever the king entered the house of
the LORD, the guards would accompany him,
bearing the shield and then afterward would
return them to the guardroom. 12 Because
Rehoboam had humbled himself, the anger
of the LORD was averted from him so as not
to destroy him completely, and the condi-
tions in Judah continued to improve.

13 Therefore, King Rehoboam strength-
ened his power in Jerusalem and continued
to reign. He was forty-one years old when he
first ascended the throne, and he reigned for
seventeen years in Jerusalem, the city in
which, out of all the tribes of Israel, the LORD
chose to be honored. His mother's name was
Naamah, an Ammonite.[u] 14 However, he fol-
lowed an evil path, for he had not truly
resolved to seek the LORD.

15 The events of Rehoboam's reign, from
beginning to end, are written in the records
of Shemaiah the prophet and of Iddo the
seer. There was continual warfare between
Rehoboam and Jeroboam. 16 Rehoboam
slept with his ancestors and was buried in
the City of David. His son Abijah succeeded
him as king.

CHAPTER 13

Abijah and Jeroboam Go to War. 1 In the
eighteenth year of King Jeroboam, Abijah
became king of Judah. 2 He reigned for three
years in Jerusalem. His mother's name was
Micaiah, the daughter of Uriel of Gibeah.

When war broke out between Abijah and
Jeroboam,* 3 Abijah prepared to engage in
battle with an army of valiant warriors com-
posed of four hundred thousand picked
men, while Jeroboam took the field against

p Deut 17:17.—q 1 Ki 14:25; 1 Chr 5:25.—r Isa 18:2; Dan 11:43.—s Ex 9:27; Ezr 9:15; Ps 11:7.—t 1 Ki 21:29; Jer 7:20; Ezek 5:13; Ps 78:38.—u Ex 20:24; Deut 12:5.

12:1 *All Israel:* that is, the people of God, not the "kingdom of Israel."

12:2 This campaign of Pharaoh Shishak (Sheshonk) is depicted on the walls of a temple at Karnak.

12:3 *Sukkites:* a people of east Africa; see the Suco of whom Strabo speaks, and the modern Suakim.

13:2 In 2 Chr 11:20 Maacah is the daughter of Absalom. Perhaps an error has crept into the text, but this explanation is not necessary. The Hebrew has no special word for grandfather/mother and grandson/daughter; instead it says "father of the father" or "son of the son" and often says simply "father" and "son." In any case, Maacah was not the daughter of Absalom, because we know that he had only one daughter, Tamar (2 Sam 14:27). In keeping with the same idiom, "mother" in 2 Chr 15:16 means "grandmother."

him with eight hundred thousand chosen
mighty warriors.
4 Then Abijah stood up on the slopes of
Mount Zemaraim in the hill country of
Ephraim and cried out: "Listen to me,
Jeroboam and all Israel![v] 5 Do you not know
that the LORD, the God of Israel, gave the
kingship over Israel to David and his sons for-
ever by a covenant of salt?[w] 6 Yet Jeroboam,
the son of Nebat, a servant of Solomon, the
son of David, rose up and rebelled against his
lord,[x] 7 and certain worthless scoundrels
gathered around him and proved to be too
strong for Rehoboam, the son of Solomon,
since at that time Rehoboam was far too
young and inexperienced and was unable to
withstand them.
8 "And now you believe that you can with-
stand the kingdom of the LORD that is in the
hands of David's descendants, you with your
multitude of supporters and the golden
calves that Jeroboam made as gods for you.
9 Have you not driven out the priests of the
LORD, the descendants of Aaron and the
Levites, and made priests of your own like
the peoples of foreign countries? Anyone
who comes with an offering of a young bull
and seven rams is automatically accepted as
a priest of these gods that are no gods.[y]
10 But as for us, the LORD is our God, and we
have not forsaken him. The priests who are
ministering to the LORD are descendants of
Aaron, and the Levites assist them. 11 Every
morning and evening they present burnt
offerings and fragrant incense to the LORD,
display the rows of bread on the table of pure
gold, and light the lamps on the golden
lampstand every evening. For we indeed
observe our responsibilities toward the
LORD, our God, but you have abandoned
him. 12 God is with us. He is our leader. His
priests with their trumpets are prepared to
sound the call to battle against you. O
Israelites, do not engage in conflict against
the LORD, the God of your ancestors, for you
will not succeed."[z]
13 Meanwhile Jeroboam had sent a detach-
ment of troops to attack them from behind.
His main force was stationed in front of the
forces of Judah, while the ambush lay behind
them. 14 When the men of Judah turned
around, they realized that they were sur-
rounded and that they had to engage in bat-
tle on both fronts. Then they cried out to the
LORD while the priests blew the trumpets.
15 After that, the men of Judah sounded their
battle cry, and when they shouted, God rout-
ed Jeroboam and all Israel before Abijah and
Judah. 16 The Israelites fled before the Ju-
dahites, and God delivered them into the
Judahites' hands.
17 Abijah and his army inflicted heavy loss-
es upon the Israelites. Five hundred thou-
sand picked men of Israel fell during the
battle. 18 The Israelites were thoroughly
defeated at that time by the forces of Judah,
because the Judahites relied on the LORD,
the God of their ancestors.[a] 19 Abijah pur-
sued Jeroboam and captured three cities
from him: Bethel with its dependencies,
Jeshanah with its dependencies, and Ephron
with its dependencies. 20 Jeroboam did not
regain his power during the reign of Abijah.
Finally the LORD struck him down, and he
died. 21 However, Abijah continued to grow
ever stronger. He married fourteen wives
and became the father of twenty-two sons
and sixteen daughters.

The Death of Abijah. 22 The rest of the acts
of Abijah's reign, what he did and what he
said, are recorded in the midrash of the
prophet Iddo. 23 Abijah rested with his
ancestors and was buried in the City of
David. His son Asa succeeded him, and dur-
ing his reign the country was at peace for ten
years.

CHAPTER 14

Asa the Reformer. 1 Asa did what was good
and righteous in the eyes of the LORD, his
God. 2 He destroyed the foreign altars and
the high places, smashed to pieces the
sacred pillars, and cut down the sacred
poles.[b] 3 He further commanded Judah to
seek the LORD, the God of their ancestors,
and to obey his laws and his command-
ments.
4 Throughout all the cities of Judah he
removed the high places and the incense
altars, and under him the kingdom was at
peace.[c] 5 He also built fortified cities in
Judah during those years of peace which the
LORD had granted. 6 Asa then said to Judah:
"Let us build up these cities and surround
them with walls, towers, gates, and bars. The
land is still ours because we have sought the
guidance of the LORD, our God, and he has

v Jos 18:21-22.—w Num 18:19; 2 Sam 7:11-13.—x 1 Ki 11:26.—y Ex 29:35-36; Jer 2:11; Gal 4:8.—z Num 10:8-9; Acts 5:39.—a 1 Chr 5:20; Ps 22:5.—b Ex 23:24; Jdg 2:2.—c 1 Ki 15:14; Isa 27:9; Ezek 6:4.

given us peace on every side." Therefore,
they built and prospered.

Zerah's Invasion. 7 Asa had an army of
three hundred thousand warriors from
Judah armed with shields and spears, and
two hundred and eighty thousand from
Benjamin armed with shields and bows. All
of them were mighty warriors. 8 * Zerah
the Ethiopian marched out against them
with an army of one million men and three
hundred chariots, and they advanced as far
as Mareshah. 9 Asa went forth, to confront
him, and the opposing armies drew up
their battle lines in the Valley of Zephathah
near Mareshah.

10 Asa then cried out to the LORD, his God,
saying: "LORD, there is no one else like you
to help the powerless against a mighty foe.
Come to our aid, O LORD, our God, for we
are relying upon you, and in your name we
are prepared to confront this horde. O
LORD, you are our God. Do not allow these
mere mortals to prevail against you." [d]
11 Then the LORD enabled Asa and Judah to
strike down the Ethiopians, and they fled.
12 Asa and his army followed in pursuit as
far as Gerar. The Ethiopians fell mortally
wounded until there were no survivors.
Then the army of Judah carried off a
tremendous amount of booty. [e]

13 Following that victory, the Judahites
destroyed all the cities around Gerar, for the
fear of the LORD had filled the people with
terror. Then they plundered all these villages
and carried off all the treasures that were of
great value. [f] 14 They also attacked the tents
of those who had livestock and carried away
great numbers of sheep and goats and
camels. After that they returned to Jeru-
salem.

CHAPTER 15

Cult Reform. 1 The Spirit of God then
came upon Azariah, the son of Oded. 2 He
went out to meet Asa and said to him:
"Listen to me, Asa, and all Judah and
Benjamin. The LORD is with you while you
are with him. If you seek him, he will permit
you to find him, but if you abandon him, he
will abandon you. [g] 3 For a long time Israel
was without a priest to impart teaching and
without the law. 4 However, when in their
distress they turned to the LORD, the God of
Israel, and sought him, he allowed them to
find him. [h]

5 "In those times it was not safe for anyone
to come or go, since all the inhabitants of the
land were afflicted with massive distur-
bances, 6 with nations being crushed by
other nations and cities by other cities, for
God troubled them with every kind of dis-
tress. [i] 7 But as for you, be strong and do not
be discouraged, for your work shall be
rewarded." [j]

8 When Asa heard these words and the
prophecy of Azariah, the son of Oded the
prophet, he became resolute in his courage
and ordered the removal of the abominable
idols throughout the land of Judah and
Benjamin as well as from the towns he had
captured in the hill country of Ephraim. He
also repaired the altar of the LORD which
stood in the vestibule of the house of the
LORD.

9 Then Asa assembled all the people of
Judah and Benjamin, as well as those from
Ephraim, Manasseh, and Simeon who were
residing among them, since great numbers
of people from Israel had deserted to him
when they came to realize that the LORD his
God was with him. 10 All the people assem-
bled at Jerusalem in the third month of the
fifteenth year of Asa's reign. 11 On that day
they sacrificed to the LORD seven hundred
oxen and seven thousand sheep from the
plunder they had brought back. 12 After
that, they entered into a covenant to seek
the LORD, the God of their fathers, with all
their heart and soul, 13 while asserting that
all those who refused to seek the LORD, the
God of Israel, were to be put to death,
whether young or old, whether man or
woman. [k]

14 Then all of them swore an oath to the
LORD with a loud voice and shouts of joy,
while the trumpets and the horns resound-
ed. 15 All Judah rejoiced over the oath, for
they had sworn with all their heart and had
sought the LORD with sincere desire. As a
result, the LORD had allowed himself to be
found by them, and he granted them peace
on every side.

d 1 Ki 8:44; Pss 60:13-14; 79:9.—e Gen 10:19; 2 Sam 22:38; Ps 44:3.—f Gen 35:5; Deut 2:25; 11:25.—g Jer 29:13; Hos 3:5; Jas 4:8.—h Deut 4:29.—i Isa 19:2; Mt 24:7; Mk 13:8; Lk 21:10.—j Jos 1:7, 9; Ps 18:21; Prov 14:14; Jer 31:16.—k Deut 13:9-16.

14:8-10 This incident is not documented in extrabiblical sources; since Zerah is not called a pharaoh or a king, he was probably a commander of hordes who came from Africa or Arabia, across the Sinai peninsula.

[16] King Asa even removed his mother Maacah from her position as queen mother because she had made an obscene image for the worship of Asherah. Asa cut it down, crushed it to powder, and burned it in the Kidron Valley.[l] [17] Although he did not remove the high places from Israel, Asa himself remained faithful throughout his life. [18] He brought into the house of God the votive gifts* of his father as well as his own votive gifts—silver, gold, and sacred vessels.

[19] There was no further warfare until the thirty-fifth year of the reign of Asa.

CHAPTER 16

Asa's Infidelity. [1] In the thirty-sixth year of the reign of King Asa, Baasha, the king of Israel, invaded Judah and fortified Ramah to prevent anyone from leaving or entering the kingdom of Asa, the king of Judah. [2] Asa then brought out silver and gold from the treasuries of the house of the LORD and of his own palace, and he sent it to Ben-hadad, the king of Aram, who resided in Damascus.

[3] "Let there be an alliance between the two of us," Asa said, "as there was between my father and your father. Behold, I am sending you silver and gold. In return, I am asking you to break your alliance with Baasha, the king of Israel, so that he will withdraw from me." [4] Ben-hadad approved the request of King Asa and sent the commanders of his armies against the towns of Israel. They ravaged Ijon, Dan, Abel-maim, and all of the store cities of Naphtali.[m]

[5] When Baasha heard this, he discontinued his plan to fortify Ramah, and he abandoned any further improvements. [6] Then King Asa ordered all the men of Judah to remove the stones of Ramah and its timber that Baasha had been using to fortify that place, and he used them instead to fortify Geba and Mizpah.

[7] At that time Hanani the seer came to King Asa of Judah and said to him: "Because you relied on the king of Aram and did not rely instead on the LORD, your God, the army of the king of Aram has escaped from your clutches.[n] [8] Did not the Ethiopians and the Libyans have a vast army with great numbers of chariots and cavalry? And yet, when you relied on the LORD, he delivered them into your hands. [9] For the eyes of the LORD range throughout all the earth to strengthen the hearts of those who are totally committed to him. You have acted foolishly in this instance, and from now on you will be forced to endure wars."[o] [10] Then Asa became enraged at what the seer had said, and he ordered Hanani to be imprisoned in the stocks. Furthermore, at the same time Asa treated some others of his people with great cruelty.

[11] The history of the reign of Asa, from beginning to end, is recorded in the book of the kings of Judah and Israel. [12] In the thirty-ninth year of his reign, Asa was gravely afflicted with severe disease in his feet. However, even during his illness he did not seek the help of the LORD but rather resorted to taking the advice of physicians.[p] [13] Then, in the forty-first year of his reign, he died and fell asleep with his ancestors. [14] They buried him in the tomb that he had hewn for himself in the City of David, having laid him on a bier that had been filled with spices and various kinds of perfumes. In addition they also kindled a very great fire in his honor.*[q]

CHAPTER 17

Zeal of Jehoshaphat for the Law. [1] Asa was succeeded as king by his son Jehoshaphat, and immediately thereafter he set out to strengthen his position against Israel. [2] He stationed forces in all the fortified cities of Judah, and he placed garrisons throughout Judah and in the cities of Ephraim which his father Asa had captured.

[3] The LORD was with Jehoshaphat* because he had followed the example of his father from his earliest years and did not consult the Baals.[r] [4] Rather, he sought the God of his father, observing his commandments, and refused to follow the practices of Israel. [5] As a result of this, the LORD made secure Jehoshaphat's control of the kingdom. All Judah brought gifts to Jehoshaphat, and his wealth and glory were exceedingly great.[s] [6] He took enormous pride in following the ways of the LORD, and he ordered the

---

l Ex 34:13; 2 Sam 15:23; 1 Ki 2:19.—m 1 Ki 15:20; 2 Ki 15:29.—n 2 Chr 13:18; 1 Ki 16:1.—o 1 Sam 13:13; Job 24:23; Prov 15:3; Zec 4:10.—p Ps 103:3; Jer 17:5-6.—q Gen 50:2; Jn 19:39-40.—r 1 Ki 22:43.—s 1 Sam 10:27.

15:18 *Votive gifts:* Asa's gifts were most likely the booty he and his father had secured from previous battles.

16:14 They burned aromatic plants.

17:3 *The LORD was with Jehoshaphat:* the Chronicler gives special mention to this king and to his successors, Hezekiah and Josiah.

removal of the high places and the sacred
poles from Judah.

[7] In the third year of his reign Jehoshaphat
sent his most learned officials—Ben-hail,
Obadiah, Zechariah, Nethanel, and Mica-
iah—to teach in the cities of Judah. [t] [8] * With
them he also sent the Levites—Shemaiah,
Nethaniah, Zebadiah, Asahel, Shemiramoth,
Jehonathan, Adonijah, and Tobijah. Accom-
panying those Levites were the priests
Elishama and Jehoram. [9] They taught in
Judah, having with them the book of the law
of the LORD. They traveled through all the
cities of Judah, instructing the people. [u]

The Power of Jehoshaphat. [10] The fear of the
LORD seized all the kingdoms of the coun-
tries surrounding Judah, and as a result, they
did not make war against Jehoshaphat.
[11] Some of the Philistines brought gifts to
Jehoshaphat, as well as silver as a tribute,
while the Arabs also brought him a flock of
seven thousand seven hundred rams and
seven thousand seven hundred he-goats.

[12] Jehoshaphat grew steadily more power-
ful. He built fortresses and storage cities in
Judah. [13] He also supervised great works in
the cities of Judah, and he stationed soldiers,
valiant warriors, in Jerusalem. [14] The sol-
diers were classified by ancestral houses. Of
Judah, the commanders of thousands:
Adnah was the highest-ranking commander,
with three hundred thousand mighty war-
riors. [15] Next in line under him was
Jehohanan the commander, with two hun-
dred and eighty thousand mighty warriors,
[16] and next to him was Amasiah, the son of
Zichri, who had volunteered for the service
of the LORD, with two hundred thousand
mighty warriors. [v]

[17] Of Benjamin: Eliada, a mighty warrior
with two hundred thousand men armed
with bow and shield, [18] and next in line to
him was Jehozabad with one hundred and
eighty thousand men equipped for war.
[19] These were the men in the service of the
king, apart from those whom the king had
stationed in fortified cities throughout all
Judah.

CHAPTER 18

Alliance with King Ahab. [1] When Jehosha-
phat had accumulated great wealth and
honor, he allied himself to Ahab by mar-
riage. [2] Some years later he went down to
visit Ahab in Samaria. Ahab slaughtered an
abundance of sheep and oxen for him and
his retinue, hoping also to persuade him to
join forces and attack Ramoth-gilead.

[3] King Ahab of Israel, therefore, asked Je-
hoshaphat, the king of Judah: "Will you join
me in attacking Ramoth-gilead?" Jehosh-
aphat replied: "I am united with you. My
people are your people. We will join you in
this war." [4] However, Jehoshaphat also said
to the king of Israel: "First let us consult the
word of the LORD." [w]

The Prophets. [5] Then the king of Israel
gathered the prophets together, four hun-
dred in number, and said to them: "Shall we
go forth to engage in battle against Ramoth-
gilead, or shall I refrain?" They replied: "Go
forth, for God will deliver it into the king's
power." [6] However, Jehoshaphat asked: "Is
there no other prophet of the LORD here
from whom we may seek guidance?"

[7] The king of Israel replied to Jehoshaphat:
"There is still one other prophet here
through whom we may seek the guidance of
the LORD. However, I hate him, because he
never prophesies anything that is favorable
for me, but only disaster. His name is
Micaiah, the son of Imlah." [8] Then the king of
Israel summoned a court official and said:
"Bring here quickly Micaiah, the son of
Imlah."

[9] The king of Israel and King Jehoshaphat
of Judah, arrayed in their robes, were seated
on their respective thrones at the entrance of
the gate of Samaria, and all the prophets
were prophesying before them. [x] [10] Zedekiah,
the son of Chenaanah, had made for himself
iron horns, and he said: "Thus says the LORD:
'With horns like these you shall gore the
Arameans until they are destroyed.' " [11] All of
the prophets were prophesying in the same
vein, saying: "Attack Ramoth-gilead and you
will triumph. The LORD will deliver it into
your hands."

[12] The messenger who had been sent to
summon Micaiah said to him: "Listen to
what I am telling you. What the prophets
have said is favorable to the king. I trust that
you will also deliver a favorable decision."
[13] However, Micaiah replied: "As the LORD

t Lev 10:11; Neh 8:7; Mal 2:7.—u Deut 6:4-9; Ezr 7:25.—v Jdg 5:2, 9.—w 1 Sam 23:2, 4, 9; 2 Sam 2:1.—x Ru 4:1.

17:8-9 Jehoshaphat was disturbed by the people's lack of knowledge about God, and he made it a priority to send learned men throughout Judah to educate them in the ways of the Lord.

lives, I can announce only what the LORD
instructs me to say."[y]

14 When the prophet arrived, the king
asked him: "Micaiah, shall we go up to attack
Ramoth-gilead, or shall I refrain?" Micaiah
replied: "Attack and triumph. They will be
delivered into your hands." 15 However, the
king said to him: "How many times must I
demand that you swear to tell me nothing
but the truth in the name of the LORD?"

16 Then Micaiah said:

"I saw all Israel scattered on the mountains,
like sheep without a shepherd.
And I heard the LORD say: 'These have no master;
let each one go home in peace.' "[z]

17 Then the king of Israel said to Jehosh-
aphat: "Did I not tell you that he would not
prophesy anything favorable about me, but
only whatever is unfavorable?"

18 However, Micaiah continued: "Listen
now to the word of the LORD. I saw the LORD
seated on his throne with all the host of
heaven sitting to his right and to his left.
19 The LORD asked: 'Who will entice King
Ahab of Israel so that he may go up and fall
at Ramoth-gilead?' Then one said one thing
and another said something in contradic-
tion, 20 until a spirit came forward and stood
before the LORD, saying: 'I will entice him.'
'How?' asked the LORD.

21 "The spirit replied: 'I will go forth and be
a lying spirit in the mouths of all his
prophets.' Then the LORD said: 'You shall
succeed in deceiving him. Go forth and do it.'
22 So now you will see that the LORD has put
a lying spirit in the mouths of these your
prophets. The LORD has decreed disaster for
you."* [a]

23 Then Zedekiah, the son of Chenaanah,
came up to Micaiah and struck him on the
cheek. After he had done so, he asked:
"Which way did the Spirit of the LORD pass
from me to speak to you?"[b] 24 Micaiah
replied: "You shall find out on the day when
you run from room to room in order to
hide."

25 The king of Israel then ordered that
Micaiah be seized and handed over to
Amon, the governor of the city, and to Joash,
the king's son, 26 and said: "Throw this man
into prison and give him only a meager por-
tion of bread and water until I return home
safely." 27 Micaiah retorted: "If you ever do
return safely, the LORD has not spoken
through me." Then he added: "Mark my
words, you peoples, all of you!"*

Ahab's Death. 28 The king of Israel and King
Jehoshaphat of Judah went up to Ramoth-
gilead. 29 The king of Israel said to Jehosh-
aphat: "I shall disguise myself when I go into
battle, while you wear your royal robes."
Therefore, the king of Israel disguised him-
self, and they went forth into battle.

30 Meanwhile the king of Aram had issued
this command to the captains of his chari-
ots: "Do not engage in battle with anyone,
whether small or great, except with the king
of Israel." 31 When the chariot commanders
saw Jehoshaphat, they shouted: "That is the
king of Israel," and they moved quickly to
attack him. However, when Jehoshaphat
cried out, the LORD came to his aid and drew
them away from him.

32 Once the chariot commanders realized
that he was not the king, they ceased their
pursuit of him. 33 However, one man drew
his bow at random, and without realizing it
he struck the king of Israel between the joints
of his armor. The king then ordered the driv-
er of his chariot: "Turn around and carry me
away from the fighting, for I am wounded."
34 The battle grew ever more fierce as the
day went on, and the king of Israel propped
himself up in his chariot facing the Ara-
means. He remained there until evening,
and at sunset he passed away.

CHAPTER 19

Jehoshaphat Rebuked. 1 When King Jehosh-
aphat of Judah returned in safety to his
palace in Jerusalem, 2 Jehu the seer, the son
of Hanani, went forth to meet him, and he
said to the king: "Should you help the wicked
and love those who hate the LORD? Because
of this, the wrath of the LORD will strike
you. [c] 3 Even so, some good can be found in
you, for you have removed the sacred poles
from the land and have set your heart on
seeking God."

---

y Num 22:18-20, 35.—z Num 27:17; 1 Chr 9:1.—a Job 12:16; Ezek 14:9.—b Jer 20:2; Mk 14:65; Acts 23:2.—c 1 Ki 16:1; Ps 139:21.

18:22 Ahab was easily deceived by the prophets who lied to him because instead of seeking God's truth, he went to those who told him only what he wanted to hear.

18:27 *Mark my words . . . all of you:* Micaiah's words also appear as the words of Micah the prophet (Mic 1:2) in the next century.

Jehoshaphat's Appointments. 4 Jehosha-
phat resided in Jerusalem, but he regularly
went forth among the people, from Beer-
sheba to the hill country of Ephraim, and
brought them back to the LORD, the God of
their ancestors. 5 He also appointed judges in
the land, in each of the fortified cities of
Judah. [d]
6 Jehoshaphat said to the judges: "Pay
careful attention to what you are doing. You
are to judge not on behalf of human beings
but on behalf of the LORD, who will be with
you when you pronounce sentence. 7 Now let
the fear of the LORD be upon you. Be careful
in your judgments, for the LORD, our God,
will not tolerate the perversion of justice, or
partiality, or the taking of bribes." [e]
8 Jehoshaphat also appointed some of the
Levites, priests, and heads of families in
Jerusalem to administer justice in the name
of the LORD and to settle disputes. 9 He gave
them this command: "You shall act at all
times in the fear of the LORD, in faithfulness,
and with your whole heart. [f] 10 Whenever a
case is brought before you from your kins-
men who live in other towns, whether in
regard to bloodshed or offenses against the
law or the commandments, statutes, or ordi-
nances, then you shall instruct them in such
a way that they do not incur guilt before the
LORD; and the wrath of the LORD will not
descend upon you and your kindred. [g]
11 Amariah, the chief priest, will be your
superior in all matters that concern the
LORD; and Zebadiah, the son of Ishmael, the
leader of the house of Judah, is your superi-
or in all matters that concern the king,*
while the Levites will serve as your officers.
Act firmly and with courage, and may the
LORD be with those on the side of the good."

CHAPTER 20

War against Edom. 1 A short time after-
ward, the Moabites and the Ammonites,
along with some of the Meunites,* came to
engage Jehoshaphat in battle. 2 The following
communiqué was sent to Jehoshaphat: "A
great multitude is coming forth against you
from Edom, from beyond the sea.* They are
already at Hazazon-tamar, that is, En-gedi."
3 Jehoshaphat was alarmed, and he hastened
to seek the guidance of the LORD, while pro-
claiming a fast throughout all Judah. 4 The
people of Judah assembled, to seek help from
the LORD, as they came from all the towns of
Judah to consult the LORD. [h]

Prayer of Jehoshaphat. 5 Jehoshaphat stood
up in the assembly of Judah and Jerusalem
in the house of the LORD before the new
court 6 and said: "O LORD, God of our
fathers, are you not the God in heaven, and
do you not rule over all the kingdoms of the
nations? In your hands are power and might,
and there is no one who can withstand you. [i]
7 Was it not you, our God, who drove out the
inhabitants of this land for your people Israel
and gave it forever to the descendants of
Abraham? 8 They have lived in it and have
built you a sanctuary there to honor your
name, saying: 9 'Should any disaster befall
us, whether the sword of judgment or war or
blood or pestilence or famine, we shall stand
before this temple that bears your name and
call out to you in our distress, and you will
hear our cries and save us.'
10 "But now, behold the Ammonites, the
Moabites, and the people of Mount Seir,
whom you would not permit the Israelites to
invade when they came from the land of
Egypt and whom they avoided and made no
attempt to destroy them. [j] 11 See how these
people repay us by coming forth to drive us
out of the possession you gave us as an inher-
itance. 12 O God will you not pass judgment
against them? For we are powerless against
this vast horde that is coming against us. We
do not know what to do, but our eyes are
turned toward you." [k]

Prophecy of Victory. 13 All the men of Judah
were standing before the LORD, with their
infants, their wives, and their children.
14 Then the Spirit of the LORD came upon
Jahaziel the son of Zechariah, son of Benai-
ah, son of Jeiel, son of Mattaniah, a Levite of
the sons of Asaph, in the midst of the
assembly.
15 Jahaziel said: "Listen attentively, all
Judah and you inhabitants of Jerusalem, and
King Jehoshaphat. Thus says the LORD to
you: 'Do not fear or lose heart at the sight of
this vast horde, for the battle is not yours but
God's. [l] 16 March down against them tomor-
row. They will be coming up by the ascent of

---

d Ex 18:26.—e Gen 18:25; Job 8:3; Rom 2:11; Col 3:25.—f 2 Sam 23:3.—g Deut 17:8.—h Jer 36:6.—i Deut 4:39; 1 Chr 29:12; Mt 6:9.—j Num 20:21; Deut 2:4-6, 18-19.—k Jdg 11:27; Ps 25:15; Mic 7:7.—l 1 Sam 17:47; Ps 92:8.

19:11 *Matters that concern the LORD* and *matters that concern the king:* a clear distinction was therefore made between religious authority and secular authority.

20:1 *Meunites:* a tribe of the Transjordan.

20:2 *The sea:* the Dead Sea.

Ziz, and you will encounter them at the end
of the gorge near the Desert of Jeruel. 17 You
will have no need to fight in this battle. Take
your position, stand firm, and behold the
victory of the Lord on your behalf, O Judah
and Jerusalem! Do not fear or be dismayed.
Go forth against them tomorrow, for the
LORD will be with you.' "

18 Then Jehoshaphat knelt down with his
face to the ground, and all Judah and the
inhabitants of Jerusalem fell down before
the LORD to worship him. 19 After that, the
Levites from among the Kohathites and
Korahites stood up and sang the praises of
the LORD, the God of Israel, with a powerful
voice.

Overcoming the Invaders. 20 Early the next
morning they rose and hastened to set out
for the wilderness of Tekoa. As they depart-
ed, Jehoshaphat stood up and said: "Listen
to me, Judah, and you inhabitants of
Jerusalem. Hold firmly to your faith in the
LORD, your God, and you will be secure.
Believe in his prophets and you will be suc-
cessful." [m]

21 After conferring with the people,
Jehoshaphat appointed some to sing to the
LORD and praise the splendor of his holiness
as they marched forth at the head of the
army:

"Give thanks to the LORD,
for his love endures forever."

22 At the moment they began their hymn
of praise, the LORD set an ambush against
the Ammonites, the Moabites, and the peo-
ple from Mount Seir who were invading
Judah. As a result, they were routed. 23 For
the Ammonites and the Moabites turned
against the people of Mount Seir and com-
pletely destroyed them. Then, when they had
finished off the inhabitants of Mount Seir,
they proceeded to destroy each other. [n]

24 When the warriors of Judah came to the
watchtower of the wilderness and looked
toward the multitude, what they beheld were
nothing but corpses lying on the ground. No
one had escaped. 25 Then, when Jehosha-
phat and his men came to collect the booty,
they found an immense number of livestock
as well as personal property, clothing, and
precious articles which they took for them-
selves until they were unable to carry any
more. They spent three days gathering the
booty because of its abundance.

26 On the fourth day they all assembled, in
the Valley of Berakah,* the name that it
bears to this day, because it was there that
they blessed the LORD. 27 Then all the people
of Judah and Jerusalem returned to
Jerusalem with joy, since the LORD had given
them reason to rejoice over their triumph
against their enemies.

28 They entered Jerusalem to the sound of
lyres, harps, and trumpets and went into the
house of the LORD. 29 The fear of God fell
upon all the kingdoms of the neighboring
countries when they heard that the LORD
had fought against the enemies of Israel.
30 And thereafter Jehoshaphat's kingdom
enjoyed peace, since God gave him rest on
every side.

Jehoshaphat's Many Deeds. 31 Thus Je-
hoshaphat reigned over Judah. He was thir-
ty-five years old when he became king, and
he reigned in Jerusalem for twenty-five
years. His mother's name was Azubah; she
was the daughter of Shilhi. 32 He followed the
example of his father Asa, and he did not
deviate from it, doing what was right in the
sight of the LORD. 33 However, the high places
were not abolished, and the people had not
as yet fixed their hearts on the God of their
fathers.*

34 The remainder of the acts of Jehosha-
phat, from first to last, are written in the
chronicles of Jehu, the son of Hanani,
which is included in the book of the kings of
Israel.* [o]

35 Later King Jehoshaphat of Judah allied
himself with King Ahaziah of Israel, who
was guilty of wicked deeds. 36 * Jehoshaphat
joined Ahaziah in the building of ships to sail
to Tarshish. The fleet was built at Ezion-
geber. 37 As a result, Eliezer, the son of
Dodavahu of Mareshah, then prophesied
against Jehoshaphat, saying: "Because you
have made an alliance with Ahaziah, the

m Isa 7:9; Prov 16:3.—n Jos 6:17; Ezek 38:21.—o 1 Ki 16:1, 7.

20:26 *Berakah:* the Hebrew word for "blessing" or "praise."

20:33 In 17:6, Jehoshaphat is said to have gotten rid of the high places. The discrepancy shows that the expressions used are not adequately nuanced; the meaning here is "not removed completely." There, the meaning is "removed, but not completely."

20:34 *Kings of Israel:* of the entire Hebrew people, including, therefore, events that took place in Judah.

20:36-37 The Hebrew speaks of "ships that could go to Tarshish." Tarshish was identified generally with the lands of the western Mediterranean. If we understand Tarshish as meaning any distant land, and "ships that could go to Tarshish" as meaning any ships capable of lengthy voyages, any contradiction disappears.

LORD will destroy what you have made." The
ships were wrecked, and they were never fit
to sail to Tarshish.

CHAPTER 21

1 * Jehoshaphat rested with his ancestors
and was buried with them in the City of
David. His son Jehoram succeeded him as
king.[p] 2 Jehoram's brothers, the sons of
Jehoshaphat, were Azariah, Jehiel, Zecha-
riah, Azariah, Michael, and Shephatiah. All
of these were sons of King Jehoshaphat of
Judah. 3 Their father gave them many gifts of
silver, gold, and other valuable possessions,
as well as fortified cities in Judah. However,
he bestowed the kingship upon Jehoram
because he was the firstborn.

The Evil Deeds of Jehoram. 4 When Jehoram
had firmly established himself on his father's
throne, he put all of his brothers to the sword
as well as some of the princes of Israel.[q] 5 He
was thirty-two years old when he ascended
the throne, and he reigned in Jerusalem for
eight years.

6 Jehoram followed the practices of the
kings of Israel as the house of Ahab had
done, for he had married one of Ahab's
daughters, and he did what was evil in the
eyes of the LORD. 7 However, the LORD was
not willing to destroy the house of David
because of the covenant that he had made
with David and because of his promise to
give him and his descendants a lamp for-
ever.[r]

8 During the reign of Jehoram, Edom
revolted against the rule of Judah and
appointed its own king. 9 Therefore, Jehoram
crossed over into Edom with his com-
manders and all his chariots. He set out dur-
ing the night and attacked the Edomites who
had surrounded him and his chariot com-
manders.

10 However, Edom has remained in rebel-
lion against the sovereignty of Judah to the
present day. Libnah revolted against the rule
of Jehoram at the same time because he had
forsaken the LORD, the God of his fathers,
11 and because he had established shrines in
the hill country of Judah, leading the inhabi-
tants of Jerusalem into idolatry and the peo-
ple of Judah into apostasy.

Retribution. 12 A letter came to Jehoram
from the prophet Elijah with this message:
"Thus says the LORD, the God of your father
David: 'You have not followed the example
of your father Jehoshaphat, nor of Asa, king
of Judah,*[s] 13 but have instead followed the
example of the kings of Israel and have led
Judah and the inhabitants of Jerusalem into
apostasy, just as the house of Ahab did. Also,
you have murdered your brothers, members
of your father's house, who were far more
worthy than you.

14 " 'Because of all this, the LORD will
cause a great affliction to affect your people,
your children, your wives, and all your prop-
erty. 15 Moreover, you yourself will suffer
greatly from a severe disease afflicting your
bowels that will eventually cause them to
protrude.' "

16 Then the LORD aroused against Jehoram
the hostility of the Philistines and of the
Arabs who dwelt near the Ethiopians.*
17 They attacked Judah, invaded it, and car-
ried away all the wealth that was found in the
king's palace, together with his sons and his
wives. Not a son was left to him except the
youngest, Jehoahaz.[t]

18 After all this the LORD struck down
Jehoram with an incurable disease of the
bowels. 19 In the course of time, after two
years had gone by, his bowels came forth as
a result of his disease, and he died in unbear-
able agony. His people did not bother to
make a funeral pyre for him as they had
done for his ancestors.

20 Jehoram was thirty-two years old when
he became king, and he reigned in Jerusalem
for eight years. He passed away with none of
the people exhibiting any sign of regret, and
he was buried in the City of David, although
not in the tombs of the kings.[u]

---

p 1 Ki 22:51.—q 1 Ki 2:12; Jdg 9:5.—r 2 Sam 7:13-15.—s 2 Ki 1:16-17.—t Joel 4:5.—u Jer 22:18, 28.

21:1—28:27 In less than a century after the separation of the two kingdoms, the faith had grown weak in Judah, and there was a relaxation of morals. Under the influence of the powerful neighbor to the north, pagan practices gradually infiltrated the land and Jerusalem, its capital. The temple and the priesthood were bastions that resisted and saved the "house" of David for a time. But in about 745 B.C., the Assyrians came to power; they would threaten the Lord even in his sanctuary. In telling this entire story, the pessimistic Chronicler emphasizes the special responsibility of the kings in Jerusalem.

21:12 Either Elijah was still alive, or he had already disappeared (his end in 2 Ki 2:1-11 precedes the story of Joram, but this is not a decisive argument). In the second case, Elijah may have had prophetic foresight of the future and have written his vision down with orders to make it known at the proper time.

21:16 These are the same people who paid tribute to his father (2 Chr 17:11); with the changed conduct of the sovereign, these relationships also changed.

CHAPTER 22

Ahaziah. [1] The people of Jerusalem then chose Jehoram's youngest son Ahaziah* as his successor, since the troops who had come into the camp with the Arabs had killed all the older sons. Thus Ahaziah, the son of Jehoram, reigned as King of Judah.

[2] Ahaziah was twenty-two years old when he ascended the throne, and he reigned in Jerusalem for one year. His mother's name was Athaliah, a granddaughter of Omri. [3] He too followed the ways of the house of Ahab, for his mother encouraged him to pursue evil practices. [v] [4] * To his own destruction he did what was evil in the sight of the LORD, as the house of Ahab had done, for after his father's death they became his advisors.

[5] Ahaziah even followed their advice when he made an alliance with Jehoram, the son of King Ahab of Israel, to make war against King Hazael of Aram, at Ramoth-gilead. In that conflict Jehoram was wounded by the Arameans. [6] As a result, Ahaziah, the son of Jehoram, king of Judah, went down to visit Jehoram, the son of Ahab, in Jezreel. [w]

[7] However, it was ordained by God that the visit of Ahaziah to Jehoram should be the occasion of his downfall. For when he arrived there, he went forth with Jehoram to meet Jehu, the son of Nimshi, whom the LORD had anointed to destroy the house of Ahab. [x] [8] While Jehu was executing judgment on the house of Ahab, he also encountered the officials of Judah and the sons of Ahaziah's brothers, and he killed them. [y]

[9] Then Jehu went forth in search of Ahaziah, and his men captured him while he was hiding in Samaria. They brought Ahaziah to Jehu, who put him to death. However, they buried him, for they said: "He was the grandson of Jehoshaphat who sought the LORD with all his heart." As a result, there was no one remaining from the house of Ahaziah who was strong enough to rule. [z]

[10] When Athaliah, the mother of Ahaziah, was told that her son was dead, she was determined to destroy all the royal offspring of the house of Judah. [11] However, Jehosheba, the daughter of King Jehoram, secretly took Joash, the son of Ahaziah, and stole him away from among the king's sons who were about to be killed, and she put him with his nurse in a bedroom.

In this way, Jehosheba, who was the daughter of King Jehoram and the wife of Jehoiada the priest, as well as a sister of Ahaziah, hid Joash from Athaliah so that she was unable to kill him. [12] Joash remained hidden with them in the house of God for six years while Athaliah reigned over the land.

CHAPTER 23

Athaliah Opposed. [1] In the seventh year Jehoiada bolstered his courage and entered into a covenant with regimental commanders: Azariah, son of Jehoram; Ishmael, son of Jehohanan; Azariah, son of Obed; Maaseiah, son of Adaiah; and Elishaphat, son of Zichri. [2] They went throughout Judah, gathering the Levites from all the cities of Judah as well as the heads of the families of Israel, and they came to Jerusalem.

[3] Then the whole assembly made a covenant with the king in the temple of God. Jehoiada said to them: "Here is the king's son! He will reign as king, as the LORD promised concerning the sons of David. [a] [4] This is what you must do: one-third of you, priests and Levites, who come on duty on the Sabbath, are to guard the gates. [5] Another third are to be assigned to the king's palace, and the final third are to be stationed at the Foundation Gate, while all the people shall be in the courts of the house of the LORD. [6] Allow no one to enter the house of the LORD except the priests and the Levites who are on duty. They may enter because they are holy, but all the other people must continue to observe the instructions of the LORD. [b] [7] The Levites shall station themselves by surrounding the king on all sides, each one with his weapon drawn, and anyone who tries to enter the temple is to be put to death. They must remain with the king wherever he goes."

[8] The Levites and all Judah did everything that the priest Jehoiada had commanded. Each one brought his own men, both those who came on duty on the Sabbath and those who were scheduled to go off duty, since Jehoiada the priest had not dismissed any of the divisions. [9] Then the priest handed over

v 2 Ki 8:27.—w 1 Ki 19:15; 2 Ki 8:13-15.—x 2 Ki 9:16.—y 2 Ki 10:13.—z Jdg 9:5.—a 2 Ki 11:17; 2 Sam 7:12.—b Zec 3:7.

22:1 *Ahaziah:* the Jehoahaz of 21:17 (Hebrew text). Both names have the same components, but in inverse order: "Yahweh supports."

22:4-5 Ahaziah aligned himself with the same crooked group that had advised his father Jehoram leading to his downfall and death.

to the captains the spears and the large and
small shields that belonged to King David
and that were stored in the house of God.
10 After that, Jehoiada the priest stationed
all the people, each one with a weapon in his
hand, from the south side to the north side of
the temple and around the altar, while form-
ing a circle around the king. 11 Then they
brought forth the king's son, placed the
crown on his head, presented him with the
covenant, and proclaimed him king. When
Jehoiada and his sons had anointed him,
they shouted: "Long live the king!" [c]
12 When Athaliah heard the shouts of the
people as they ran forth to proclaim him as
king, she went into the house of the LORD
where the people had assembled. 13 As she
looked on, she beheld the king standing by
his pillar* at the entrance, with the officers
and the trumpeters at the king's side, and
with the people of the land rejoicing and
blowing trumpets, while the singers with
their musical instruments were leading the
celebrations. Thereupon Athaliah tore her
clothes and cried out: "Treason! Treason!"
14 Immediately Jehoiada the priest gave
the following orders to the captains who
were in command of the troops: "Take her
outside between the ranks. If anyone tries to
follow her, put him to death by the sword!"
Then the priest made it clear: "Do not put
her to death in the temple of the LORD."
15 After that they seized her and brought her
to the entrance of the Horse Gate of the
palace, and there they put her to death. [d]
16 After that, Jehoiada made a covenant
between himself and all the people and the
king that they should be the LORD's people.
17 Then all the people went to the temple of
Baal and demolished it. They smashed its
altars and its images, and they killed
Mattan, the priest of Baal, in front of the
altars. 18 Jehoiada entrusted the supervision
of the temple of the LORD to the Levitical
priests whom David had designated to pre-
sent burnt offerings to the LORD, as pre-
scribed in the law of Moses, with singing and
rejoicing as David had ordained. 19 He also
stationed guards at the gates of the LORD's
temple to ensure that no one should enter
who was in any way unclean.
20 Then Jehoiada took with him the cap-
tains of units of a hundred, the nobles, the
governors of the people, and all the people of
the land and escorted the king down from
the house of the LORD. Entering the palace
through the Upper Gate, they seated the
king on the royal throne. [e] 21 All the people of
the land rejoiced, and the city was quiet and
serene after Athaliah had been put to death
by the sword.

CHAPTER 24

Temple Repairs.* 1 Joash was seven years
old when he became king, and he reigned for
forty years in Jerusalem. His mother's name
was Zibiah; she was from Beer-sheba. 2 Joash
did what was right in the eyes of the LORD as
long as Jehoiada was alive. 3 Jehoiada select-
ed two wives for him, and he became the
father of several sons and daughters.
4 Sometime later, Joash decided to restore
the temple of the LORD. 5 After he assembled
the priests and the Levites, he said to them:
"Go forth to all the towns of Judah and with-
out any delay collect the money that is due
each year so that we may make the annual
repairs that are necessary. See to it that you
act quickly." However, the Levites did not
hasten to proceed immediately. [f]
6 Therefore, the king summoned Jehoiada,
the chief priest, and asked him: "Why have
you not required the Levites to bring in from
Judah and Jerusalem the tax levied by
Moses, the servant of the LORD, and by the
assembly of Israel for the tent of the testi-
mony?" [g] 7 For the wicked Athaliah and her
sons had broken into the house of God and
had even given to the Baals the sacred rev-
enues of the temple of the LORD.
8 Therefore, the king ordered that a chest
be made and placed outside the gate of the
house of the LORD. 9 Then a proclamation
was made throughout Judah and Jerusalem
to bring to the LORD the tax which Moses,
the servant of God, had imposed on Israel
in the desert. 10 As a result, the officials and
all the people rejoiced, and they willingly
brought their contributions, depositing them
in the chest until it was filled. [h]

c Ex 25:16; Deut 17:18; 1 Sam 10:24.—d Neh 3:28; Jer 31:40.—e 2 Ki 15:35.—f Ex 30:16; Mt 17:24.—g Ex 38:21; Neh 10:33.—h Ex 25:2; 1 Chr 29:3, 6, 9.

23:13 *By his pillar:* a special place in the temple court designated for the king during the offerings made on feasts and Sabbaths.

24:1-16 King Joash repairs the temple; to this end, he sets up a system that will provide reliable aid for the maintenance of the sacred dwelling: a collection box to receive the offerings of the faithful, and a collection to be taken up throughout the country. After the Exile, this latter collection will become a regular tax on behalf of the sanctuary (see Mt 17:24), and will be demanded even of Jews in the Diaspora outside of Palestine.

[11] Whenever the chest was brought to the royal officials by the Levites, and it was evident that it contained a large amount of money, the king's secretary and the representative of the chief priest would come to empty it and then return the chest to its designated place. They did this day after day and collected money in great abundance. [12] Then the king and Jehoiada gave the money to those who were responsible for carrying out the work of the house of the LORD, and they also hired masons and carpenters to restore the house of the LORD, while workers skilled in iron and bronze devoted themselves to making all the necessary repairs.

[13] The laborers concentrated on their labor, and the repairs progressed steadily at their hands. They restored the house of God to its original state and strengthened it. [14] After they had completed their work, they brought the rest of the money to the king and Jehoiada, and it was used to make vessels for the house of the LORD, vessels for the services and for burnt offerings, and basins and other gold and silver utensils. They continually offered burnt offerings in the LORD's temple throughout the lifetime of Jehoiada.

[15] Jehoiada lived to a ripe old age. He was one hundred and thirty years old when he died. [16] He was buried with the kings in the City of David because of all the good he had done in Israel for God and his temple.

Apostasy of King Joash.* [17] After the death of Jehoiada, the officials came and paid homage to the king, and he listened to their advice. [18] Then they forsook the temple of the LORD, the God of their ancestors, and they began to worship the sacred poles and the idols. Because of their guilt, God's wrath descended upon Judah and Jerusalem.[i] [19] Although the LORD sent prophets to lead them back to him, they refused to listen.

[20] Then the Spirit of God took possession of Zechariah, the son of Jehoiada the priest. He stood up before the people and said to them: "Thus says the LORD: 'Why do you transgress the commands of the LORD so that you cannot prosper? Because you have abandoned the LORD, he has abandoned you.' "[j]

[21] However, they conspired against him, and at the king's order they stoned him to death in the court of the house of the LORD.[k] [22] Thus King Joash, forgetting the loyalty of Zechariah's father, Jehoiada, killed his son. As he was dying, he said: "May the LORD see this and call you to account."

Retribution. [23] At the turn of the year the Aramean army advanced against Joash. When they reached Judah and Jerusalem, they massacred all the leaders of the people and sent all their spoil to the king of Damascus. [24] Although the invading Aramean army had come with only a small force, the LORD delivered into their hands a very large army because they had abandoned the LORD, the God of their ancestors. Thus they executed judgment against Joash.[l]

[25] When the Arameans had withdrawn, leaving Joash severely wounded, his servants conspired against him to avenge the blood of the son of the priest Jehoiada, and they killed him on his bed. Thus he died, and they buried him in the City of David, but they did not bury him in the tombs of the kings.

[26] Those who conspired against him were Zabad, the son of Shimeath the Ammonite, and Jehozabad, the son of Shimrith, a Moabite.[m] [27] Accounts of his sons, of the many oracles against him, and of the rebuilding of the house of God are all recorded in the commentary of the book of kings. His son Amaziah succeeded him.

CHAPTER 25

Campaign in Edom. [1] Amaziah was twenty-five years old when he ascended the throne, and he reigned for twenty-nine years in Jerusalem. His mother was Jehoaddan from Jerusalem. [2] He did what was right in the sight of the LORD, although he did not do so wholeheartedly.

[3] As soon as the kingdom was firmly under his control, Amaziah put to death those servants who had murdered his father, the king. [4] However, he did not put their children to death, in obedience to what is written in the law, in the Book of Moses, where the LORD commanded: "Parents shall not be put to death for their children, nor shall children be put to death for their parents. Each one shall be put to death for his own sin."[n]

i Ex 34:13; Jos 24:20; Jer 17:2.—j Jdg 3:10; 1 Chr 12:18; Lk 11:51.—k Neh 9:26; Mt 23:35; Acts 7:58-59.—l Lev 26:25; Deut 28:25; Isa 10:5.—m 2 Ki 12:21.—n Deut 24:16; Num 26:10-11.

24:17-22 This particular odious assassination remained impressed on the memory of Israel, since it will still be mentioned in the Gospel (Mt 23:35).

5 Then Amaziah assembled the people of Judah and assigned them according to their ancestral houses under commanders of thousands and of hundreds for all Judah and Benjamin. He registered those who were twenty years old and upward and found that there were three hundred thousand men fit for service and capable of wielding spear and shield. 6 He also hired one hundred thousand valiant warriors from Israel for one hundred talents of silver.

7 However, a man of God came to him and said: "O king, do not permit the Israelite army to march with you, for the LORD is not with Israel or with any of the Ephraimites. 8 Rather, fight valiantly only with your own forces. Remember that God has the power to help you or to cause your defeat."

9 Amaziah then said to the man of God: "What shall I do about the one hundred talents that I paid for the Israelite troops?" The man of God replied: "The LORD can give you much more than that."[o] 10 Amaziah then dismissed the troops that had come to him from Ephraim and sent them home. That caused them to be infuriated with Judah, and they returned home seething with fierce resentment.

11 *Then Amaziah marshaled his courage and led out his army. They advanced to the Valley of Salt, and there they killed ten thousand men of Seir. 12 In addition, the men of Judah captured another ten thousand men alive. Bringing them to the top of a cliff, they threw them down so that they were all dashed to pieces.[p] 13 Meanwhile, the mercenaries whom Amaziah had sent back home, without allowing them to take part with him in the battle, raided the cities of Judah from Samaria to Beth-horon. They slaughtered three thousand people in those cities and carried off great quantities of plunder.

Infidelity of Amaziah. 14 On his return from his slaughter of the Edomites, Amaziah brought back with him the gods of the people of Seir. He set them up as his own gods, bowed down before them, and burned sacrifices to them.[q] 15 As a result, the LORD's anger was aroused by Amaziah, and he sent him a prophet who said to him: "Why have you resorted to gods who could not save their own people from your clutches?"

16 While he was still speaking, however, the king said to him: "Have we appointed you as a royal counselor? Stop right now, if you value your life!" Therefore the prophet stopped, but first he said: "I know that God has decided to destroy you for having done this and for not listening to my advice."

Retribution. 17 After King Amaziah of Judah consulted his advisors, he sent a message to Joash son of Jehoahaz, son of Jehu, the king of Israel, saying: "Come and let us meet face to face."

18 King Joash of Israel sent back this reply to King Amaziah of Judah: "The thistle on Lebanon sent a message to the cedar on Lebanon, saying: 'Give your daughter in marriage to my son.' However, the wild animal of Lebanon passed by and trampled down the thistle.[r] 19 You say to yourself: 'I have defeated Edom,' and now you are growing ever more boastful. Remain at home. Why should you get involved with potential disaster so that you fall and bring down Judah with you?"

20 However, Amaziah refused to listen, for God had resolved to hand them over because they had consulted the gods of Edom. 21 Therefore, King Joash of Israel marched forth, and he and King Amaziah of Judah faced one another in battle at Beth-shemesh which belongs to Judah. 22 There Judah was defeated by Israel, and everyone fled to his tent.

23 King Joash of Israel captured King Amaziah of Judah, son of Joash, son of Jehoahaz, at Beth-shemesh and brought him to Jerusalem. Then he demolished the wall of Jerusalem from the Ephraim Gate to the Corner Gate, a distance of four hundred cubits.[s] 24 After that he took away all the gold and silver and all the vessels he found in the house of God that had been in the care of Obed-edom, together with the treasures of the palace, as well as hostages. Then he returned to Samaria.

25 King Amaziah, son of Joash of Judah, lived for fifteen years after the death of King Joash, son of Jehoahaz of Israel. 26 The rest of the deeds of Amaziah's reign, from first to last, are recorded in the book of the kings of Judah and Israel.

27 From the time when Amaziah turned away from the LORD, a conspiracy was

o Deut 8:18; Prov 10:22.—p Ps 141:6; Ob 3.—q Ex 20:3; Isa 44:15.—r Jdg 9:8-15.—s 2 Ki 14:13; Neh 8:16; Jer 31:38.

25:11-12 *Valley of Salt:* south of the Dead Sea, in the territory of Edom (Seir); see 2 Sam 8:13. *A cliff:* a rock on which was subsequently built a city which bears that name (i.e., the modern Petra).

formed against him in Jerusalem, and he
fled to Lachish, where he was pursued and
murdered. 28 His body was conveyed on
horses to Jerusalem, and there he was buried
with his ancestors in the City of David.

CHAPTER 26

The Works of Uzziah. 1 * Then all the people
of Judah chose Uzziah, even though he was
only sixteen years old, and they made him
king as the successor to his father Amaziah.
2 It was he who rebuilt Elath and restored it
to Judah after the king had fallen asleep with
his ancestors.

3 Uzziah was sixteen years old when he
ascended the throne, and he reigned in
Jerusalem for fifty-two years. His mother's
name was Jecoliah; she was from Jerusalem.
4 He did what was right in the sight of the
LORD, just as his father Amaziah had done.
5 Furthermore, he consulted God through-
out the lifetime of Zechariah, who instructed
him in the fear of God. As long as he sought
the guidance of the LORD, God allowed him
to prosper. * [t]

6 Uzziah went forth and fought the
Philistines. He demolished the walls of Gath,
the walls of Jabneh, and the walls of Ashdod;
and he built cities in the territory of Ashdod,
and elsewhere among the Philistines. [u] 7 God
helped him against the Philistines, against
the Arabs who lived in Gur-baal, and against
the Meunites.

8 The Ammonites paid tribute to Uzziah,
and his fame spread as far as the borders of
Egypt, for he became ever more powerful. [v]
9 Moreover, Uzziah built towers in Jerusalem
at the Corner Gate, at the Valley Gate, and at
the Angle, and he fortified them. 10 He also
erected towers in the wilderness and dug
many cisterns, for he had large herds of cattle
both in the Shephelah and in the plain; and he
had farmers and vinedressers in the hills and
in the fertile lands, for he loved the soil.

11 Uzziah had a well-trained army ready to
engage in battles and divided into divisions
according to their numbers as specified by
the scribe Jeiel and the staff officer Ma-
aseiah, under the direction of Hananiah, one
of the king's commanders. 12 The total num-
ber of the heads of ancestral houses of
mighty warriors was two thousand six hun-
dred. 13 Under their command was an army
of three hundred and seven thousand five
hundred, a powerful force to help the king
against his enemies.

14 Uzziah provided for the entire army the
shields, spears, helmets, coats of armor,
bows, and slingstones. 15 In Jerusalem he also
had requisitioned machines, invented by
skilled workers, to be placed on the towers
and battlements for shooting arrows and
large stones. His fame spread far and wide,
for he was so miraculously gifted that he
became very powerful.

Pride and Punishment. 16 However, when Uz-
ziah continued to grow ever stronger, he also
was afflicted with pride, and that led to his
destruction. For he proved unfaithful to the
LORD his God by entering the temple of the
LORD to make an offering on the altar of in-
cense. [w] 17 Then the priest Azariah and eighty
priests of the LORD who were courageous men
followed him.

18 The priests confronted King Uzziah and
said to him: "It is not for you, Uzziah, to burn
incense to the LORD, but for the priests, the
descendants of Aaron, who are consecrated
to make offerings. Leave the sanctuary, for
you have done wrong, and you will no longer
share in the glory that comes from the LORD
God." [x] 19 Uzziah had a censer in his hand to
burn the incense, but while he showed his
intense anger to the priests, leprosy broke
out on his forehead, in the presence of the
priests in the house of the LORD, by the altar
of incense. [y]

20 When the chief priest, Azariah, and all
the other priests looked at Uzziah carefully
and saw that his forehead was leprous, they
quickly removed him from the temple; and
he himself was equally anxious to leave
because the LORD had afflicted him. 21 King
Uzziah remained a leper until the day of his
death, and because he was thus afflicted, he
dwelt while confined in a separate house,
since he was excluded from the house of the
LORD. His son Jotham was in charge of the
palace of the king, and he governed the peo-
ple of the land. [z]

22 The rest of the history of Uzziah, from
first to last, was written by the prophet
Isaiah, the son of Amoz. 23 Uzziah rested
with his ancestors and was buried with

t Dan 1:17.—u Isa 14:29; Jer 25:20; Am 1:8.—v Gen 19:38.—w Deut 32:15; 2 Ki 14:10.—x Ex 30:7-8; Num 16:39-40.—y 2 Ki 5:25-27.—z Lev 13:46; Num 5:2.

26:1ff See 2 Ki 14:21-22; 15:1-7, where Uzziah is called Azariah.

26:5 This Zechariah, of whom we know nothing, is distinct from the man of the same name in 2 Chr 24:21.

them, but in the field adjoining the royal tombs, for they said: "He is a leper." His son Jotham succeeded him as king.

CHAPTER 27

Jotham. 1 Jotham was twenty-five years old when he became king, and he reigned in Jerusalem for sixteen years. His mother was Jerusha, the daughter of Zadok.[a] 2 He did what was right in the sight of the LORD just as his father had done, although he did not enter the temple of the LORD. However, the people continued their corrupt practices.

3 Jotham built the upper gate of the house of the LORD, and he supervised the extensive construction on the wall of Ophel.*[b] 4 He also built towns in the hill country of Judah as well as forts and towers in the wooded areas.

5 Later Jotham went to war against the king of the Ammonites and defeated them. As a result, the Ammonites had to give him one hundred talents of silver, together with ten thousand kors of wheat and ten thousand kors of barley. The Ammonites also paid him the same amount in the second and third year afterward.[c] 6 Jotham became very powerful because he followed an unswerving course in the presence of the LORD, his God.

7 The rest of the acts of Jotham, all his wars and other projects, are recorded in the book of the kings of Israel and Judah.[d] 8 He was twenty-five years old when he ascended the throne, and he reigned for sixteen years in Jerusalem. 9 Jotham slept with his ancestors, and he was buried in the City of David. His son Ahaz succeeded him.

III: REFORMS OF HEZEKIAH AND JOSIAH

CHAPTER 28

The Impiety of Ahaz. 1 Ahaz was twenty years old when he ascended the throne, and he reigned in Jerusalem for sixteen years. Unlike what his ancestor David had done, he did not do what was right in the sight of the LORD. 2 Rather, he followed the example of the kings of Israel and even cast molten idols of the Baals.

3 Furthermore, Ahaz offered burnt sacrifices in the Valley of Ben-hinnom* and even went so far as to immolate his sons by fire according to the abominable practices of the nations whom the LORD had driven out before the Israelites.[e] 4 He offered sacrifices and burned incense on the high places, on the hills, and under every green tree.

Retribution. 5 Therefore, the LORD his God delivered him over into the hands of the king of Aram. After the Arameans defeated him, they took large numbers of captives and brought them to Damascus. He was also given over into the power of the king of Israel, who inflicted heavy casualties on him.*[f] 6 In a single day, Pekah, the son of Remaliah, killed one hundred and twenty thousand valiant warriors.

7 Zichri, an Ephraimite warrior, killed Maaseiah, the king's son, Azrikam, the commander of the palace, and Elkanah, who was second only to the king in authority. 8 The Israelites took captive from their kinsmen two hundred thousand women, sons and daughters. They also took immense quantities of booty from them and brought it all back to Samaria.

The Prophecy of Oded. 9 In Samaria there was a prophet of the LORD by the name of Oded. He went out to meet the army when it returned to Samaria, and he said: "It was because the LORD, the God of your fathers, was angry with Judah that he delivered them into your hands. However, you have slaughtered them with an intense rage that has reached up to heaven.[g]

10 "And now you have decided to force the people of Judah and Jerusalem to be your slaves. However, have you yourselves not been guilty of sins against the LORD, your God? 11 Now listen to me! Release the captives you have taken from your kinsmen, for the fierce anger of the LORD has been aroused against you."

12 On hearing this, some of the Ephraimite leaders—Azariah, son of Jehohanan; Berechiah, son of Meshillemoth; Jehizkiah, son of Shallum; and Amasa, son of Hadlai—confronted those who were returning from the war 13 and said to them: "Do not bring these captives here, for what you are proposing will only increase our sins and our guilt. For

a 2 Ki 15:32-35; 1 Chr 3:12.—b Neh 3:26.—c Gen 19:38.—d 2 Ki 15:36.—e Lev 18:21; 2 Ki 23:10; Jos 15:8.—f 2 Ki 16:5; Isa 7:1-9.—g Isa 10:5; Ezr 9:6; Rev 18:5.

27:3 *Ophel:* the southern spur of the temple mount.

28:3 *Ben-hinnom:* Gehenna, south and southwest of Jerusalem.

28:5 In the account of Ahaz, the Chronicler supplies many details peculiar to him.

our guilt is already substantial, and fierce anger threatens the security of Israel."

14 Therefore, in the presence of the officials and the entire assembly, the soldiers surrendered the captives and the booty. 15 Then those Ephraimite leaders proceeded to help those who had been led away captive. From the booty they clothed those who were naked. They gave them clothing and sandals and gave them food, drink, and healing balm. All those who were weak they mounted on donkeys and took them to their brethren in Jericho, the city of palm trees. Then they themselves returned to Samaria.[h]

Other Sins of Ahaz. 16 At that time King Ahaz sent a plea to the king of Assyria asking for help.[i] 17 The Edomites had once again invaded and defeated Judah, and carried away captives.[j]

18 Meanwhile, the Philistines had raided the towns in the foothills and the Negeb of Judah. They captured and occupied Beth-shemesh, Aijalon, and Gederoth, as well as Soco with its villages, Timnah with its villages, and Gimzo with its villages, and settled there. 19 For the LORD had brought Judah low because of Ahaz, king of Israel,* who had behaved without restraint in Judah and had proved to be totally unfaithful to the LORD.

20 After that, Tiglath-pileser, king of Assyria, came to Ahaz, but rather than assisting him, he oppressed him instead.[k] 21 Then Ahaz plundered the temple of the LORD, the palace of the king, and the house of his officials. He proceeded to give the plunder to the king of Assyria, but no help from him was forthcoming.

22 During this period of distress, King Ahaz became even more unfaithful to the LORD. 23 He proceeded to offer sacrifices to the gods of Damascus who had defeated him, thinking: "Since the gods of the king of Aram have supported them, I will sacrifice to them so that they may decide to help me." However, they only caused further disaster to him and to all of Israel.[l] 24 Then Ahaz gathered up the vessels of the house of God and broke them into pieces. After he shut up the doors of the house of the LORD he made altars for himself in every corner of Jerusalem.[m] 25 In every city of Judah he built high places to offer sacrifices to other gods, thus provoking the anger of the LORD, the God of his ancestors.

26 The rest of his deeds and all his activities, from first to last, are written in the book of the kings of Judah and Israel. 27 Ahaz slept with his ancestors, and he was buried in the city of Jerusalem, but he was not laid to rest in the tombs of the kings of Israel. His son Hezekiah succeeded him.

CHAPTER 29

Reforms of Hezekiah. 1 * Hezekiah was twenty-five years old when he became king, and he reigned in Jerusalem for twenty-nine years. His mother was Abijah, the daughter of Zechariah. 2 He did what was right in the eyes of the LORD, just as his ancestor David had done.

3 In the first month of the first year of his reign, he opened the doors of the temple of the LORD and repaired them.[n] 4 Next he brought in the priests and the Levites and assembled them in the square on the east. 5 Then he said to them: "Listen to me, you Levites. Sanctify yourselves first. Then sanctify the house of the LORD, the God of your ancestors, and remove the filth from the sanctuary. 6 For our ancestors were unfaithful and did what was evil in the sight of the LORD, our God. They abandoned him, turned away their faces from him, and turned their backs on him.[o] 7 They also shut the doors of the vestibule and extinguished the lamps, and they ceased to burn incense or present any burnt offerings in the sanctuary to the God of Israel.

8 "Therefore, the anger of the LORD fell upon Judah and Jerusalem, and he has made them an object of terror, astonishment, and derision, as you can see with your own eyes. 9 Our fathers have fallen by the sword, and our sons and daughters and our wives have been taken captive as a result. 10 Now I am determined to make a covenant with the God of Israel, in the hope that his fierce

h Deut 34:3; Prov 25:21; Lk 10:25-37.—i Ezek 23:12.—j Ps 137:7; Isa 34:5; Am 1:11.—k 2 Ki 15:29; 1 Chr 5:6; Isa 7:17; 8:7.—l Jer 44:17-18.—m 2 Ki 16:18.—n 2 Ki 18:16.—o Jer 2:27; Ezek 8:16; Dan 9:5-6.

28:19 *King of Israel:* Ahaz ruled the tribes of Judah and Benjamin, and the Chronicler refers to him often as the king of all the people, not only the northern kingdom.

29:1—35:27 Undermined in its foundations by paganism and threatened by the empires of the Assyrians and Chaldeans, the little kingdom of Judah is saved by its great prophets and good kings: Isaiah and Hezekiah in the eighth century, Jeremiah and Josiah in the seventh. The success was fairly temporary in both cases. Hezekiah was succeeded by Manasseh, who was the exact opposite of his father, and Josiah was succeeded by sons who brought on the final destruction.

anger may turn away from us.[p] [11] Therefore,
my sons, do not be negligent any longer, for
the LORD has chosen you to sit in his pres-
ence and to serve him, to be his ministers,
and to offer incense before him."

[12] The Levites immediately set to work:
from the sons of the Kohathites: Mahath, son
of Amasai, and Joel, son of Azariah; from the
sons of Merari: Kish, son of Abdi, and
Azariah, son of Jehallel; from the Gershon-
ites: Joah, son of Zimmah, and Eden, son of
Joah; [13] from the sons of Elizaphan: Shimri
and Jeuel; from the sons of Asaph: Zechariah
and Mattaniah; [14] from the sons of Heman:
Jehuel and Shimei; from the sons of
Jeduthun: Shemaiah and Uzziel. [15] They
gathered their brothers together and sancti-
fied themselves; then, in obedience to the
king's order in accordance with the LORD's
command, they proceeded to purify the
house of the LORD.

[16] The priests entered the inner part of the
LORD's house to cleanse it, and they brought
all the unclean things that they found in the
temple of the LORD and deposited them in
the court of the house of the LORD, where the
Levites collected them and carried them out
to the Kidron Valley. [17] They began the rites of
sanctification on the first day of the first
month, and on the eighth day of the month
they had arrived at the vestibule of the LORD.
Then for eight days they sanctified the LORD's
house, and on the sixteenth day of the first
month they had finished.

[18] Their work having been completed, they
went in to King Hezekiah and said: "We have
cleansed the entire house of the LORD, the
altar of burnt offering with all its utensils,
and the table for setting out the consecrated
bread with all its utensils. [19] We have
restored and consecrated all the articles that
King Ahaz had cast aside during his reign
because of his infidelity. They are now in
place before the altar of the LORD."

The Rite of Expiation. [20] King Hezekiah rose
early the next morning, assembled the offi-
cials of the city, and went up to the house of
the LORD. [21] They brought with them seven
bulls, seven rams, seven lambs, and seven
male goats as a sin offering for the kingdom,
for the sanctuary, and for Judah, and he
ordered the priests, the sons of Aaron, to
offer them on the altar of the LORD.[q]

[22] Therefore, after the city officials slaugh-
tered the bulls, the priests received the blood
and sprinkled it on the altar. Then the rams
were slaughtered, and, the priests sprinkled
the blood on the altar. After that, the lambs
were slaughtered, and the priests sprinkled
the blood on the altar.

[23] Finally the he-goats for the sin offering
were brought before the king and the assem-
bly, who laid their hands on them. [24] Then
the priests slaughtered them and used their
blood as a sin offering at the altar in order to
make atonement for all Israel. For the king
commanded that the burnt offering and the
sin offering should be made for all Israel.

[25] The king stationed the Levites in the
house of the LORD with cymbals, harps, and
lyres, according to the ordinance prescribed
by David, by Gad the king's seer, and by
Nathan the prophet. This commandment
was prescribed by the LORD through his
prophets. [26] The Levites were stationed with
the instruments of David while the priests
stood ready with the trumpets. [27] Then
Hezekiah commanded that the burnt offer-
ing be presented on the altar. And at the
moment when the burnt offering began, the
song to the LORD began also, to the accom-
paniment of the trumpets and the instru-
ments of King David of Israel.[r] [28] The entire
assembly bowed in worship while the singers
sang and the trumpeters sounded, all of this
continuing until the burnt offering had been
completed.

[29] When the burnt offering was finished,
the king and all those who were present with
him bowed down and worshiped. [30] King
Hezekiah and his officials commanded the
Levites to sing praises to the LORD in the
words of David and of the seer, Asaph. They
joyfully sang their praises, after which they
knelt down and prostrated themselves in
worship.

[31] Then Hezekiah issued this command:
"Now that you have consecrated yourselves
to the LORD, come forward and bring your
sacrifices and thank offerings to the house of
the LORD."

Therefore, the assembly brought sacrifices
and thank offerings, and all those who had
generous hearts brought burnt offerings.[s]
[32] The number of burnt offerings that the
assembly brought was seventy bulls, one hun-
dred rams, and two hundred lambs. All these
were designated as a burnt offering to the

p Num 25:4; Ezr 10:14.—q Lev 4:3-14.—r 1 Sam 16:16.—s Ex 25:2; 35:22; Heb 13:15-16.

LORD. 33 The consecrated offerings were six hundred bulls and three hundred sheep.

34 However, the priests were too few in number to be able to skin the burnt offerings. Therefore, their brethren the Levites were clearly more conscientious than the priests in sanctifying themselves. 35 In addition to a great number of burnt offerings, there was also the fat of the fellowship offerings and the libations for the burnt offerings. Thus the service of the house of the LORD was restored. 36 Then Hezekiah and all the people rejoiced over what God had done for the people and how suddenly all this had been completed.

CHAPTER 30*

Invitation to the Passover. 1 Hezekiah sent messengers to all Israel and Judah, and he also wrote letters to Ephraim and Manasseh, inviting them to come to the house of the LORD in Jerusalem to celebrate the Passover in honor of the LORD, the God of Israel. 2 * The king and his officials and the entire assembly in Jerusalem had agreed to celebrate the Passover in the second month, 3 having been unable to celebrate it at the proper time because the priests had not sanctified themselves in sufficient numbers and the people had not yet assembled in Jerusalem. [t]

4 The proposal was accepted by the king and all the assembly. 5 Therefore, they resolved to issue a proclamation throughout all Israel, from Dan to Beer-sheba, that the people should come to Jerusalem and celebrate the Passover in honor of the LORD, the God of Israel. For the feast had not been celebrated in large numbers in the manner prescribed. 6 Accordingly, couriers traveled throughout Israel and Judah with letters from the king and his officials, as the king had commanded, saying: "O people of Israel, return to the LORD, the God of Abraham, Isaac, and Israel, so that he may turn back to you, the remnant left from the hands of the kings of Assyria. 7 Do not be like your ancestors and your brothers who were unfaithful to the LORD, the God of their ancestors, so that he made them an object of horror, as you yourselves now see. [u] 8 Do not be stiff-necked as your ancestors were, but submit yourselves to the LORD and come to his sanctuary that he has consecrated forever, and serve the LORD, your God, so that his fierce anger may turn away from you. 9 For when you return to the LORD, your brothers and your children will be treated with compassion by their captors and return to this land. For the LORD, your God, is gracious and compassionate, and he will not turn his face away from you if you return to him." [v]

10 The couriers went from town to town in Ephraim and Manasseh, and as far as Zebulun, but the people scorned and mocked them. 11 Nevertheless a few people from Asher, Manasseh, and Zebulun humbled themselves and came to Jerusalem. 12 The hand of God was also on Judah to make the people of one mind to do what the king and the officials commanded in accordance with the word of the LORD.

The Passover Celebrated. 13 A huge crowd gathered together in Jerusalem to celebrate the Feast of Unleavened Bread in the second month. 14 They began their work by removing the altars that were in Jerusalem. Then they removed all the altars of incense and threw them into the Kidron Valley. [w]

15 On the fourteenth day of the second month they slaughtered the Passover lamb. Meanwhile, the priests and the Levites were ashamed; after they consecrated themselves, they brought burnt offerings to the temple of the LORD. 16 Then they took their accustomed places according to the law of Moses, the man of God, while the priests sprinkled the blood that they had received from the Levites.

17 Since many people in the assembly had not sanctified themselves, the Levites had to slaughter the Passover lambs for them to the LORD.* [x] 18 For a large number of people, mainly from Ephraim, Manasseh, Issachar, and Zebulun, had not cleansed themselves, but even so they ate the Passover contrary to what was prescribed.

t Num 9:6-13.—u Ps 78:8; Jer 11:10; Acts 7:51.—v 1 Ki 8:50; Isa 55:7; Jer 25:5; Ezek 33:11.—w 2 Sam 15:23.—x Ezr 6:20.

30:1-27 In 721 B.C., the northern kingdom was brought into submission and demolished by the Assyrians. Refugees streamed to Jerusalem and took part in the Jewish renewal. As a result, all Israel seemed invited to celebrate this solemn Passover. In writing this passage, the author, along with his contemporaries, dreams that he is seeing the liberation of his country and the return of the Jews scattered throughout the Mediterranean world.

30:2-3 The law allowed for this delay in celebrating the Passover (see Num 9:6-13).

30:17 The killing of the lamb was the prerogative of the head of each family (see Ex 12:3-6).

However, Hezekiah prayed for them, say-
ing: "May the good LORD grant pardon 19 to
all those who are determined to seek God,
the LORD, the God of their ancestors, even
though they have not been purified as holi-
ness requires." 20 The LORD listened to
Hezekiah and healed the people.[y]

21 With great rejoicing the Israelites who
were present in Jerusalem celebrated the
Feast of Unleavened Bread for seven days,
while the Levites and the priests day after
day praised the LORD with all their strength.
22 Hezekiah then spoke encouragingly to all
the Levites who had shown themselves to be
well skilled in the service of the LORD.
During the seven days of the festival the peo-
ple consumed their assigned portion of food,
sacrificing offerings of well-being and giving
thanks to the LORD, the God of their ances-
tors.

23 Then the entire assembly agreed to con-
tinue the festival for another seven days,
and they did so with joyous celebration.
24 Hezekiah, the king of Judah, contributed
to the assembly one thousand bulls and
seven thousand sheep, and the officials gave
to the assembly one thousand bulls and ten
thousand sheep, while the priests sanctified
themselves in great numbers. 25 The entire
assembly of Judah rejoiced, along with the
priests and the Levites and the resident
aliens who had come from Israel, as well as
the resident aliens who dwelt in Judah.
26 There was great rejoicing in Jerusalem, for
since the time of Solomon, the son of King
David of Israel, nothing of this magnitude
had been seen in Jerusalem. 27 Then the
priests and the Levites stood up and blessed
the people, and their voices were heard by
God when their prayer reached his holy
dwelling in heaven.[z]

CHAPTER 31

Reform of Worship. 1 When the festivities
had come to a close, all of the Israelites who
were present went forth to the towns of
Judah, smashed the sacred pillars, cut down
the sacred poles, and demolished the high
places and the altars throughout Judah and
Benjamin, as well as in Ephraim and
Manasseh, until they had destroyed them all.
Then all the Israelites returned to their var-
ious towns and their individual properties.

2 Hezekiah reestablished the priests and
the Levites into various divisions, assigning
to each priest and Levite his own specific
duty, whether in regard to holocausts or
peace offerings, to minister or to give thanks,
or to sing praises within the gates of the
LORD's dwelling.

3 The king provided from his own wealth a
portion from his possessions for holocausts
during the morning and evening as well as
on Sabbaths, new moons, and festivals, as
prescribed in the law of the LORD. 4 He also
commanded the people who lived in
Jerusalem to provide the portion due to the
priests and the Levites so that they might
devote themselves completely to the law of
the LORD.[a]

5 As soon as the command of the king had
been promulgated, the Israelites provided
an abundance of the firstfruits of grain, wine,
oil, honey, and all the other produce of the
fields; they brought in an abundant tithe of
everything. 6 The Israelites and Judeans who
lived in the towns of Judah also brought in a
tithe of their cattle and sheep and a tithe of
sacred gifts that had been consecrated to the
LORD, their God, laying them in heaps.[b]
7 They began to accumulate the heaps in the
third month, and they completed that task in
the seventh month.

8 When Hezekiah and his officials came
and beheld the heaps, they blessed the LORD
and his people Israel. 9 Then Hezekiah ques-
tioned the priests and the Levites about
those heaps. 10 The chief priest Azariah, who
was of the house of Zadok, replied: "Since
the people began to bring their contributions
to the house of the LORD, we have had
enough to eat, and much more in addition.
For the LORD has so greatly blessed his peo-
ple that a great amount is still left over."[c]

11 Then Hezekiah issued orders to prepare
storerooms in the house of the LORD. When
that task was completed, 12 the people faith-
fully brought in their contributions, their
tithes, and their consecrated gifts. The chief
officer in charge of the donations was
Conaniah the Levite, with his brother
Shimei as second in command. 13 Jehiel,
Azaziah, Nahath, Asahel, Jerimoth, Jozabad,
Eliel, Ismachiah, Mahath, and Benaiah were
appointed as supervisors under Conaniah
and his brother, Shimei, by the order of King
Hezekiah and Azariah, the chief officer of the
house of God.

---

y 2 Chr 6:20; Mal 3:20; Jas 5:16.—z Num 6:23; Deut 26:15; Ps 68:6.—a Num 18:8; Neh 13:10.—b Lev 27:30; Deut 14:28.—c Ex 36:5; 2 Sam 8:17; Mal 3:10.

14 Kore, the son of Imnah the Levite, and
the keeper of the east gate, was in charge of
the free-will offerings to God, with the
responsibility to apportion the contributions
made to God and the most sacred offerings.
15 Eden, Miniamin, Jeshua, Shemaiah,
Amariah, and Shecaniah faithfully assisted
him in the priestly cities and distributed the
portions to their kindred, old and young
alike, by divisions.* [d]

16 In addition, they distributed shares to
the males thirty years old and above who
would enter the house of the LORD to take
their part daily in the service, according to
their divisions as their office required. 17 The
priests were enrolled according to their
ancestral houses; the Levites who were twen-
ty years old and above were registered
according to their offices.

18 The priests were enrolled with all their
dependents—their little children, their
wives, their sons and their daughters, the
entire multitude—since in virtue of their
permanent standing they had to be faithful
in consecrating themselves. 19 As for the
descendants of Aaron, the priests, who lived
on the pasture lands belonging to their
towns, designated the men to distribute por-
tions to every male among the priests and to
everyone who was registered in the genealo-
gies of the Levites. [e]

20 Hezekiah did this throughout Judah,
doing what was good and right and faithful
in the eyes of the LORD, his God. [f] 21 Every-
thing that he undertook in the service of the
house of God, and in obedience to the law
and the commandments to seek his God, he
did with all his heart, and he prospered. [g]

CHAPTER 32

Invasion of Sennacherib. 1 After Hezekiah
had proved his fidelity by his deeds and his
acts of faithfulness, King Sennacherib of
Assyria invaded Judah and laid siege to the
fortified towns, intending to take them by
storm.

2 When Hezekiah realized that Sennach-
erib was determined to attack Jerusalem, [h]
3 he suggested to his officers and warriors
that they block up the springs of water that
were outside the city, and they supported his
plan. 4 Then a large number of people were
summoned to block up all the springs, as well
as the stream that flowed through that land,
saying: "Why should the kings of Assyria
come here and find an abundance of water?" [i]

5 Hezekiah next concentrated on strength-
ening his defenses. He repaired every breach
in the city wall that was broken down and
raised towers upon it. Then he built another
wall outside that first wall. He also strength-
ened the Millo of the City of David and gath-
ered large numbers of weapons and shields. [j]

6 Next Hezekiah appointed military com-
manders over the people, and after gathering
them together in his presence in the square
at the gate of the city, he spoke these words of
encouragement: 7 "Be strong and brave. Do
not have any fear or be discouraged when
confronted with the king of Assyria and the
vast horde that serves him. Remember that
there is one with us who is greater than any-
one who is with him. [k] 8 He has only human
strength, but we have the LORD, our God,
with us to help us and to fight our battles."
The people were greatly encouraged by the
words of King Hezekiah of Judah. [l]

Sennacherib's Threat. 9 After this, while
King Sennacherib of Assyria was besieging
Lachish with all his forces, he sent his repre-
sentatives to Jerusalem to deliver this mes-
sage to King Hezekiah of Judah and to all the
Judeans who were in Jerusalem: 10 "King
Sennacherib of Assyria has this to say: What
gives you the confidence to remain in
Jerusalem while it is under siege? [m] 11 Heze-
kiah is misleading you, condemning you to
die of famine and thirst, when he says: 'The
LORD, our God, will save us from the clutch-
es of the king of Assyria.' 12 Was it not the
same Hezekiah who removed the LORD's
shrines and altars and issued this command
to Judah and Jerusalem: 'You shall worship
before only one altar, and on that altar alone
you shall offer sacrifices'? 13 Are you not
aware what I and my ancestors have done to
all the peoples of other lands? Were the gods
of those nations able to save their lands from
my power? 14 Of all the gods of these nations
which my ancestors totally destroyed, was
there even one who was able to save his peo-
ple from my hand? How then will your God
be able to deliver you from my power?

d Jos 21:9-19.—e Lev 25:34; Num 35:2.—f 2 Ki 20:3.—g Deut 29:8; Ps 119:2.—h Jer 1:15.—i 2 Ki 18:17; Nah 3:14.—j Neh 2:17,18.—k Num 14:9; Deut 31:6; 2 Ki 6:16.—l Job 40:9; Ps 20:7; Jer 17:5.—m 2 Ki 18:19.

31:15 On the priestly cities, see Jos 21:9-19.

15 “Do not permit Hezekiah to deceive you or mislead you in this way, and do not believe him. How can you place your trust in him, since no god of any nation or kingdom has been able to save his people from my hand or from the hand of my ancestors? How much less will your God be able to save you from my clutches!” [n]

16 Sennacherib’s officials offered further negative comments against the Lord God and against his servant Hezekiah. 17 In addition, Sennacherib wrote letters filled with contemptuous remarks about the Lord, the God of Israel, saying: “Just as the gods of other nations could not rescue their people from my hands, so the God of Hezekiah will not be able to save his people from my power.”

18 Then the forces of Sennacherib shouted loudly in Hebrew to the people of Jerusalem who were stationed on the wall, trying to strike them with terror and fear, and thus hoping to be able to conquer the city. 19 They spoke of the God of Jerusalem as if he were in no way superior to any of the gods of the other peoples of the earth, simply the work of human hands. [o]

The Defeat of Sennacherib. 20 Then King Hezekiah and the prophet Isaiah, the son of Amoz, prayed and cried out to heaven. 21 Therefore, the Lord sent an angel who destroyed every valiant warrior, leader, and commander in the camp of the king of Assyria. As a result, Sennacherib returned in disgrace to his own land. When he entered the temple of his god, some of his sons slew him with the sword. [p]

22 Thus the Lord saved Hezekiah and the inhabitants of Jerusalem from the hands of Sennacherib and from the hands of all their enemies, affording them rest on every side. 23 Many people brought gifts to the Lord in Jerusalem and costly gifts to King Hezekiah of Judah. From that time onward he was held in high esteem by all nations.

Hezekiah’s Other Deeds. 24 In those days Hezekiah fell seriously ill. Then he prayed to the Lord, and the Lord answered him by granting him a sign. 25 However, Hezekiah was a proud man, and he failed to respond with gratitude for the kindness that the Lord had shown him. As a result, the wrath of the Lord fell upon him and upon Judah and Jerusalem. 26 But then Hezekiah humbled himself because of the pride of heart that he had exhibited, as did also the inhabitants of Jerusalem, so that the wrath of the Lord did not fall upon them during Hezekiah’s lifetime.

27 Hezekiah possessed great wealth and honor. He built for himself treasuries for his silver and gold, for his precious stones, for spices and shields and for all kinds of other costly things, 28 storehouses for the harvests of grain, new wine and oil, and stalls for all kinds of cattle and flocks of sheep. 29 He also built cities for himself, and he acquired flocks and herds in abundance, for God had given him very great possessions.

30 This same Hezekiah closed the upper outlet of the waters of Gihon and directed their course down to the west side of the City of David. In every respect he prospered in all his works, [q] 31 although when envoys were sent by the king of Babylon to ask him about the miraculous sign* that had occurred in the land, God left him to himself in order to test him and to discover what was in his heart.

32 The rest of the acts of Hezekiah and his pious works are recorded in the vision of the prophet Isaiah, the son of Amoz, in the book of the kings of Judah and Israel. 33 Hezekiah slept with his ancestors, and he was buried at the ascent to the tombs of the descendants of David. All Judah and the inhabitants of Jerusalem paid him honor at his death. His son Manasseh succeeded him as king.

CHAPTER 33

Manasseh’s Rule. 1 Manasseh was twelve years old when he ascended the throne, and he reigned for fifty-five years in Jerusalem. 2 He did what was evil in the sight of the Lord by following the abominable practices of the nations that the Lord had driven out in favor of the Israelites.

3 Manasseh rebuilt the high places that his father Hezekiah had torn down, erected altars to the Baals, made sacred poles, and prostrated himself before all the host of heaven and served them. 4 He built altars in the temple of the Lord about which the Lord had said: “My name shall be in Jerusalem forever.”

n Ex 5:2; Isa 37:10; Dan 3:15.—o Ps 115:4-8.—p Gen 19:13; 2 Ki 19:7; Isa 37:37-38.—q 1 Ki 1:33; 2 Ki 20:20.

32:31 *Miraculous sign:* this refers to the healing of the king, in verse 24.

5 Manasseh also built altars for all the host
of heaven* in the two courts of the house of
the LORD. 6 Further, he immolated his sons
by fire in the Valley of Ben-hinnom, prac-
ticed soothsaying, divination, and sorcery,
and had dealings with mediums and wiz-
ards. Thus he perpetrated great evil in the
sight of the LORD and aroused his anger.[r]

7 Manasseh took the carved image of the
idol that he had made and placed it in the
house of God, concerning which God had
said to David and to Solomon his son: "In
this house, and in Jerusalem, the city which I
chose out of all the tribes of Israel, I will
establish my name forever. 8 I will never
again allow the feet of Israel to be removed
from the land which I assigned to your
ancestors, provided that they are careful to
observe all that I commanded them in
regard to the entire law, the statutes, and the
ordinances given through Moses."

9 However, Manasseh led Judah and the
inhabitants of Jerusalem astray so that they
did far greater evil than the nations which
the LORD had destroyed in favor of the
Israelites.[s] 10 The LORD spoke to Manasseh
and his people, but they refused to listen.

Manasseh's Conversion. 11 Therefore, the
LORD brought against them the command-
ers of the army of the king of Assyria. They
took Manasseh captive with hooks, shackled
him with chains, and brought him to
Babylon.*[t] 12 In his distress, he entreated
the mercy of the LORD, his God, and hum-
bled himself greatly before the God of his
ancestors. 13 After praying to him, the LORD
was moved by his entreaty. Having accepted
his supplication, he restored him to his king-
dom in Jerusalem. Then Manasseh fully
understood that the LORD is indeed God.

14 Afterward, Manasseh built an outer wall
for the City of David, to the west of Gihon in
the valley, and he extended it up to the
entrance by the Fish Gate and encircling
Ophel, raising it to a great height. He also
stationed military commanders in all the
fortified towns of Judah.[u] 15 Furthermore,
he removed the foreign gods and the idol
from the house of the LORD, as well as all the
altars that he had built on the mountain of
the house of the LORD and in Jerusalem, and
he cast them outside the city.

16 Manasseh also restored the altar of the
LORD, and upon that altar he sacrificed
peace offerings and thanksgiving offerings,
while at the same time commanding Judah
to serve the LORD, the God of Israel.
17 Though the people continued to sacrifice
at the high places, they now did so only to the
LORD, their God.

18 The rest of the acts of Manasseh, his
prayer to his God, and the prophecies of the
seers* who spoke to him, in the name of
the LORD, the God of Israel, can be found in
the annals of the kings of Israel. 19 His prayer
and how God was moved by his entreaty, all
his sins and his infidelity, and the sites where
he built high places and set up sacred poles
and idols before he humbled himself, can be
found recorded in the chronicles of the
seers.* 20 Manasseh slept with his ancestors,
and he was buried in the garden of his
palace. His son Amon succeeded him.

Amon. 21 Amon was twenty-two years old
when he became king, and he reigned in
Jerusalem for two years. 22 He did what was
evil in the eyes of the LORD, just as his father
Manasseh had done. Amon sacrificed to all
the idols that his father Manasseh had
made, and he worshiped them.

23 Amon did not humble himself before
the LORD as his father Manasseh had done.
On the contrary, Amon only increased his
guilt.[v] 24 His servants conspired against him,
and they assassinated him in the palace.
25 However, the people of the land killed all
those who had conspired against King
Amon, and then they proclaimed his son
Josiah as his successor.

CHAPTER 34

The Reforms of Josiah. 1 Josiah was eight
years old when he ascended the throne, and
he reigned in Jerusalem for thirty-one years.
2 He did what was right in the eyes of the
LORD, and he followed in the ways of his

r Lev 18:21; Deut 18:10-11; 2 Ki 21:6.—s Jer 15:4; Ezek 5:7.—t Ps 107:10, 11; Isa 37:29.—u 1 Ki 1:33; Neh 3:3; 12:39; Zep 1:10.—v Ps 18:28; Prov 3:34.

33:5 *Host of heaven:* the reference is to the astral divinities of the pagan world, and especially of Babylonia.

33:11 We would expect the name of Nineveh, not of Babylon. Rather than suspecting some confusion, we should see a confirmation of the accurate information of the writer. Manasseh may in fact have gone to Babylon, for it is known that at that period the Assyrian sovereigns frequently stayed in Babylon, in whose fidelity, they had little confidence.

33:18 *The seers:* the prophets.

33:19 *Chronicles of the seers:* most Hebrew manuscripts read "Hozai," an unknown prophet. Perhaps the Uzza of 2 Ki 21:18 is meant. The prayer of Manasseh to his God is not the "prayer of Manasseh" that is contained in the extra-canonical appendix to the Latin Bible.

ancestor David, not deviating either to the
right or to the left.
3 In the eighth year of his reign, while he
was still a youth, Josiah began to seek the
God of his ancestor David, and in the twelfth
year he began to purge Judah and Jerusalem
of the high places, the sacred poles, and the
carved and the cast images.* 4 Then, in his
presence and following his instructions, he
oversaw the destruction of the altars of the
Baals, and the incense stands erected above
them were torn down. The sacred poles and
the carved and molten images were shat-
tered and beaten into dust, which was then
scattered over the tombs of those who had
sacrificed to them.[w] 5 Finally, the bones of
the priests he burned upon their altars. Thus
he purified Judah and Jerusalem.

6 In the towns of Manasseh, Ephraim, and
Simeon, and in the ruined villages as far as
Naphtali, 7 Josiah destroyed the altars,
crushed the sacred poles and the images into
powder, and demolished all the incense
altars throughout all the land of Israel. Then
he returned to Jerusalem.

The Temple Restored. 8 In the eighteenth
year of his reign, after he had purified the
land as well as the temple, Josiah sent
Shaphan, the son of Azaliah, Maaseiah, the
governor of the city, and Joah, the son of
Joahaz the recorder, to repair and restore
the house of the LORD, his God. 9 They came
to the high priest Hilkiah and delivered the
money that had been brought into the house
of God, which the Levites, the guardians of
the threshold, had collected from Manasseh,
Ephraim, and all the remnant of Israel, as
well as from all of Judah, Benjamin, and the
inhabitants of Jerusalem.[x]

10 They delivered the money to the master
workmen in the house of the LORD, and these
in turn used it to pay the workmen in the
LORD's house who were restoring and
repairing the temple. 11 They also gave
money to the carpenters and the builders to
purchase quarried stone, as well as timber
for the rafters and beams of the buildings
which the kings of Judah had permitted to
fall into disrepair.

12 The men worked conscientiously at
their tasks. Their overseers who directed the
work were Jahath and Obadiah, Levites of
the line of Merari, and Zechariah and
Meshullam, members of the Kohathites. The
Levites, all of them skilled in the art of play-
ing musical instruments, 13 were in charge of
the men who carried the burdens, and they
directed all the workers in every kind of
labor, while other Levites were secretaries,
officials, and gatekeepers.

Discovery of the Law. 14 When they brought
out the money that had been deposited in
the house of the LORD, the priest Hilkiah
found the book of the law of the LORD which
had been given through Moses. 15 Hilkiah
said to the secretary, Shaphan: "I have
found the book of the law in the house of
the LORD," and then he gave the book to
Shaphan.[y]

16 Shaphan brought the book to the king
and reported to him: "Your servants are
doing everything that has been entrusted to
them. 17 They have melted down the silver
that had been deposited in the house of the
LORD and have handed it over to the super-
visors and the workers." 18 Shaphan the sec-
retary also informed the king: "Hilkiah the
priest has handed over a book to me." Then
Shaphan proceeded to read extracts from
the book in the presence of the king.

19 When the king heard the words of the
law, he tore his garments.[z] 20 Then he issued
this command to Hilkiah, Ahikam, the son of
Shaphan, Abdon, the son of Micah, the sec-
retary, Shaphan, and the king's servant,
Asaiah: 21 "Go forth and inquire of the LORD
for me and for the remnant in Israel and in
Judah concerning the words of the book that
has been discovered. For the intense wrath of
the LORD that has been poured out on us is
great, because our ancestors did not observe
the LORD's command and do all that is writ-
ten in this book."

22 Therefore, Hilkiah and those others
whom the king had designated went to the
prophetess Huldah, the wife of Shallum, son
of Tokhath, son of Hasrah, the guardian of
the wardrobe, and consulted her at her
home in the Second Quarter of Jerusalem,
as they had been instructed. After they spoke
to her, 23 she replied: "Thus says the LORD,
the God of Israel: 'Tell the one who sent you
to me: 24 The LORD says: I am going to bring
disaster upon this place and upon its inhabi-

w Ex 32:20; Lev 26:30; 2 Ki 23:11.—x 2 Chr 24:8-9.—y 2 Ki 22:8; Ezr 7:6; Neh 8:1.—z Deut 28:3-68; Jos 7:6; Isa 37:1.

34:3 At the time of Josiah, it was not unusual for a male to undertake heavy responsibilities, and the Chronicler rightly places these reforms under him since he had early on put himself in God's hands.

tants—all the curses written in the book that
was read in the presence of the king of
Judah. [a] 25 Because they have abandoned me
and have burned incense to other gods,
thereby provoking my anger with all the
works of their hands, my wrath will be
poured out on this place and it will not be
quenched.'

26 "As for the king of Judah who sent you
to inquire of the LORD, give this response:
'Thus says the LORD, the God of Israel: In
regard to the words that you have heard,
27 since your heart was penitent and you
humbled yourself before God when you
heard his words spoken against this place
and its inhabitants and tore your garments
and wept before me, I in turn have listened,
declares the LORD. 28 I will gather you to
your ancestors, and you shall be taken to
your grave in peace. Your eyes will not live
to behold all the disaster that I will inflict
upon this place and its inhabitants.' " Then
the representatives of the king brought
back this answer to him.

Renewal of the Covenant.* 29 Thereupon,
after the king convened all the elders of
Judah and Jerusalem, 30 he went up to the
house of the LORD with all the men of Judah,
the inhabitants of Jerusalem, the priests and
the Levites, and all the people, both great
and small. In their hearing he read the entire
contents of the book of the covenant that was
discovered in the house of the LORD.

31 Then the king stood by his pillar and
entered into a covenant before the LORD to
obey him and keep his commandments, his
decrees, and his statutes with all his heart
and soul, and thus carry out the words of the
covenant that were written in this book. [b]
32 After that, he had all those in Jerusalem
and in Benjamin pledge their conformity to
the covenant of God, the God of their
fathers.

33 Josiah removed all the abominable idols
from the entire territory that belonged to
the people of Israel, and he made it a
requirement that all those who lived in Israel
must worship their God. Throughout his life-
time they did not turn away from following
the LORD, the God of their ancestors.

CHAPTER 35

The Passover. 1 Josiah then celebrated
the Passover to the LORD in Jerusalem,
with the Passover lamb being slaughtered
on the fourteenth day of the first month. [c]
2 He appointed the priests to their offices
and encouraged them to do their duty in
the service of the house of the LORD.

3 Josiah said to the Levites who instructed
all Israel and who ware consecrated to the
LORD: "Put the sacred Ark in the house built
by Solomon, son of David, king of Israel. You
no longer need to carry it on your shoulders.
Serve now the LORD, your God, and his peo-
ple Israel. [d] 4 Prepare yourselves by families
in your ancestral houses, following the direc-
tions written by King David of Israel and by
his son Solomon. [e]

5 "Take your positions in the sanctuary
according to the family divisions of the ances-
tral houses of your brethren, the laity, and let
there be one division of Levites for each fam-
ily division. 6 Slay the Passover lamb, sanctify
yourselves, and on behalf of your brethren
make preparations, doing what the LORD
commanded through Moses." [f]

7 Then Josiah contributed to the common
people, as Passover offerings for all those
who were present, a flock of thirty thousand
lambs and goats, in addition to three thou-
sand bulls. All these were from the king's
own property. 8 His officials also contri-
buted willingly to the people, to the priests,
and to the Levites. Hilkiah, Zechariah, and
Jehiel, the chief officers of the house of
God, gave to the priests for the Passover
offering two thousand six hundred lambs
and three hundred bulls. [g] 9 Conaniah, along
with his brothers Shemaiah and Nethanel,
and Hashabiah, Jehiel, and Jozabad, the
chiefs of the Levites, contributed on behalf
of the Levites for the Passover offerings five
thousand lambs and kids in addition to five
hundred bulls.

10 When the service had been arranged, the
priests stood in their places and the Levites in
their divisions, as the king had commanded.
11 The Passover lambs were slaughtered, and
the priests sprinkled the blood handed to
them while the Levites skinned the animals.

12 The Levites set aside the burnt offerings
so that they might distribute them according
to the subdivisions of the laity who would
then offer them to the LORD, as it is written
in the Book of Moses. They did the same
with the bulls. 13 Then they roasted the

a Prov 16:4; Isa 3:9; Jer 40:2.—b 2 Ki 11:17.—c Ex 12:6; Num 28:16.—d 2 Chr 5:7; Deut 33:10.—e 2 Chr 8:14; 1 Chr 9:10-13.—f Lev 11:44; Ezr 6:20.—g 1 Chr 29:3.

34:29-33 This great liturgy describes a kind of anticipation, the reunion of the Jewish community around the temple after the Exile.

Passover victim over an open fire as pre-
scribed, and they boiled the holy offerings in
pots, in cauldrons, and in pans, which they
then distributed quickly to all the people. [h]

14 Afterward they prepared the Passover
for themselves and for the priests, since the
priests, the descendants of Aaron, were kept
occupied until nightfall in offering holocausts
and the fatty portions. Therefore, the Levites
prepared the Passover for themselves and for
the priests, the descendants of Aaron. 15 The
singers, the descendants of Asaph, were in
their designated places in accordance with
the command laid down by David, and also
by Asaph, Heman, and the king's seer,
Jeduthun. The gatekeepers were stationed at
each gate. They did not need to leave their
stations, inasmuch as their brethren, the
Levites, made the preparations for them. [i]

16 Thus the entire service of the LORD was
arranged on that day in order to celebrate
the Passover and the Feast of Unleavened
Bread for seven days. 17 The people of Israel
who were present on that occasion kept the
Passover at that time, as well as the Feast of
Unleavened Bread, for seven days.

18 No Passover like this one had been
observed in Israel since the days of the
prophet Samuel, nor had any of the kings of
Israel ever celebrated a Passover as was kept
by Josiah, by the priests and the Levites, by
all the people of Judah and Israel who were
there, and by the inhabitants of Jerusalem. [j]
19 This Passover was celebrated in the eigh-
teenth year of the reign of Josiah.

Josiah's Reign Ends. 20 After all this had
occurred and Josiah had restored the tem-
ple, Neco, the king of Egypt, went forth to
attack Carchemish on the Euphrates, and
Josiah marched out to confront him. [k]
21 Neco then sent messengers to him to say:
"Why should you be concerned about me,
king of Judah? I have no intention of attack-
ing you. My quarrel is not with you but just
with those with whom I am at war. God has
commanded me to proceed without delay.
Therefore, do not oppose God, who is sup-
porting me, so that he will not destroy you."

22 However, Josiah had no intention of
yielding to Neco's request that came from
the mouth of God, but rather he engaged in
battle on the plain of Megiddo. 23 The
archers then shot King Josiah, and he com-
manded his servants: "Take me away, for I
am severely wounded."

24 Therefore, his servants removed him
from his own chariot and transferred him
with another chariot to Jerusalem, where he
died. He was buried in the tombs of his
ancestors, and all Judah and Jerusalem
mourned for him. 25 Jeremiah also com-
posed a lament* for Josiah, which is recited
to this day by all the male and female singers
in their dirges. These became a tradition in
Israel and can be found recorded in the
Book of Lamentations. [l]

26 The rest of the history of Josiah and his
pious deeds in accordance with what is writ-
ten in the law of the LORD, 27 and his acts,
from first to last, are recorded in the book of
the kings of Israel and Judah.

IV: THE END OF THE KINGDOM

CHAPTER 36*

Jehoahaz. 1 The people of the land then
took Jehoahaz, the son of Josiah, and made
him king in Jerusalem as the successor to his
father. 2 Jehoahaz was twenty-three years old
when he ascended the throne, and he
reigned for three months in Jerusalem.
3 Then Neco, the king of Egypt, deposed him
in Jerusalem and imposed a levy on Judah of
one hundred talents of silver and one talent
of gold. 4 Following that, the king of Egypt
made his brother Eliakim king over Judah
and Jerusalem and changed his name to
Jehoiakim, but Neco took his brother
Jehoahaz and had him brought to Egypt. [m]

Jehoiakim. 5 Jehoiakim was twenty-five
years old when he became king, and he
reigned for eleven years in Jerusalem. He did
what was evil in the eyes of the LORD his
God. 6 Nebuchadnezzar, the king of Bab-
ylon, then attacked him and bound him with
chains to take him to Babylon. 7 Nebuchad-
nezzar also carried away to Babylon some of
the vessels of the house of the LORD and
placed them in his palace in Babylon. [n]

8 The rest of the acts of Jehoiakim, the
detestable things that he did, and what hap-

h Ex 12:8-9; Lev 6:28; 1 Sam 2:13-15.—i 1 Chr 25:1; Neh 12:46; Ps 68:26.—j 2 Ki 23:21-23.—k 2 Ki 23:29; Isa 10:9; Jer 46:2.—l Jer 22:20; Lam 4:20.—m Jer 22:10-12; Ezek 19:4.—n Ezr 1:7; Jer 27:16; Dan 1:2.

35:25 *Lament:* these are not the Lamentations that occupy a Book of the Bible.

36:1-23 These kings simply make an appearance and are tossed about by events. The only personages who stand out in these hours of chaos are the prophets: Jeremiah and Baruch. Despite everything, they foretell that the faith has a future.

pened to him as a consequence, are written
in the book of the kings of Israel and Judah.
His son Jehoiachin succeeded him.

Jehoiachin. 9 Jehoiachin was eighteen years
old when he became king, and he reigned in
Jerusalem for three months and ten days. He
did evil in the sight of the LORD. 10 At the
turn of the year, King Nebuchadnezzar sent
for him and had him brought to Babylon,
along with the most precious vessels that
were in the temple of the LORD, and he
appointed his brother Zedekiah as king over
Judah and Jerusalem. [o]

Zedekiah. 11 Zedekiah was twenty-one
years old when he became king, and he
reigned for eleven years in Jerusalem. 12 He
did evil in the sight of the LORD his God,
and he did not humble himself before the
prophet Jeremiah, who revealed the word
of the LORD.

13 Zedekiah also rebelled against King
Nebuchadnezzar, who had compelled him to
take an oath in God's name. He became
stubborn and obstinate, and he refused to
return to the LORD, the God of Israel. [p]
14 Furthermore, all the leaders of Judah, the
priests, and the people became ever more
unfaithful, imitating all the shameful prac-
tices of the nations and defiling the temple of
the LORD which he himself had consecrated
in Jerusalem.

15 The LORD, the God of their ancestors,
unceasingly sent them word through his
messengers because he had compassion on
his people and on his dwelling place. [q]

16 However, they continued to ridicule the
messengers of God, despising his words and
scoffing at his prophets, until the wrath of
the LORD against his people became so fierce
that there was no remedy. [r]

17 Therefore, the LORD God brought up
against them the king of the Chaldeans, who
slew their young men with the sword in the
sanctuary and spared neither young man
nor maiden, neither the aged nor the feeble.
God gave them all into his power.

18 All the vessels of the house of God, both
large and small and all the treasures of the
LORD's house and of the king and his
princes—all these Nebuchadnezzar brought
to Babylon. 19 They set fire to the house of
God, demolished the walls of Jerusalem, and
burned all its palaces to the ground along
with its cherished possessions until every-
thing there of value was destroyed. [s]

20 In addition, Nebuchadnezzar deport-
ed to Babylon all those who had escaped
the sword, and they became servants to
him and to his sons until the Persians
came to power. 21 During the time that the
land lay desolate, it enjoyed its Sabbath
rests to fulfill the word of the LORD spoken
by Jeremiah: "Until the land has atoned
for its lost Sabbaths, it will lie fallow until
seventy years are fulfilled."

Decree of Cyrus.* 22 In the first year of
Cyrus, king of Persia, in fulfillment of the
word of the LORD spoken by Jeremiah, the
LORD inspired King Cyrus to issue this edict
throughout his kingdom, announced by a
herald and also stated in a written edict: [t]
23 "Thus says Cyrus, king of Persia: The
LORD, the God of heaven, has given me all
the kingdoms of the earth, and he has also
appointed me to build him a temple in
Jerusalem, which is in Judah. Therefore,
whoever among you belongs to his people,
may the LORD, his God be with him. Let him
go up!" [u]

---

o 2 Sam 11:1; 2 Ki 24:10-17; Isa 52:11; Jer 37:1.—p 2 Ki 24:20; Jer 52:4; Ezek 17:13.—q Jer 7:25; Zec 1:4; Mt 5:12.—r Ezr 5:12; Job 8:2; Prov 1:25; Mt 23:34-37.—s Jer 11:16; 17:27; Lam 4:11; Am 2:5.—t Ezr 1:1; Isa 44:28; Jer 25:12.—u Ezr 1:1; 7:13

36:22-23 Chronicles does not end with the tragic outcome (i.e., the deportation to Babylon). By adding the edict of Cyrus that authorizes the return to Jerusalem, the author makes it clear that the history of God's chosen people will continue; the sins of human beings cannot cause the cancellation of the divine plan of salvation. This short ending, so moving in its sobriety, is also the beginning of the Book of Ezra. This shows that the latter is by the same author.

"The LORD, the God of heaven, . . . has designated me to build him a house at Jerusalem in Judah" *(Ezr 1:2).*

THE BOOK OF EZRA

The Return from the Exile

The history thus far of the Jewish people, whom we last saw in the Exile, has revealed to us an Israel rather different from the Jewish community that we shall meet later on in the time of Jesus and the Gospels.

How was this different Israel formed?

The period of the restoration, which began in 538 B.C., is especially important for anyone who wishes to understand Judaism, the birth and basic orientations of which are told in the two Books known as Ezra and Nehemiah (1 and 2 Esdras in the Vulgate), from the names of the respective personages prominent in them.

In narrating the restoration of the Jewish community after its return from the Exile and thereby completing the grandiose picture of the "history of salvation" that was begun in the Books of Chronicles, the author had at his disposal first-order sources which he follows very closely: lists of the families that returned from the Exile, genealogical documents, royal decrees, administrative correspondence, and personal recollections. But his perspective is not that of a historian; his primary concern is to set forth a teaching regarding a community that still has its place in the plan of God, and to define the major aspects of Jewish life in so new a period of its history. In the interests of producing a clearer picture he does not restrict himself to a chronological order. This decision, along with the fact that, at that time, numbers were not used to distinguish sovereigns having the same name, creates an awkward situation for anyone attempting a historical reconstruction of the restoration period.

At the same time, however, the following represents a plausible reconstruction of the chronology. Beginning in 538 B.C. (edict of Cyrus), the first exiles return to Palestine under governor Sheshbazzar; later on, a second group is led by Zerubbabel and the priest Joshua.

These erect the altar of burnt offerings once again, reestablish the order of worship, and lay the foundations of the temple. The envy of their neighbors, however, forces the builders to interrupt their work.

Encouraged by the preaching of the prophets Haggai and Zechariah, the builders take up their work again in 520 B.C., although they still experience obstacles. Four years later, the temple is consecrated, and Passover is celebrated there (Ezr 1–6).

In 445 B.C., Nehemiah, a personal servant of King Artaxerxes I, arrived in Jerusalem with complete authorization to rebuild the walls. The work began and was carried to a successful conclusion, although the Samaritans opposed the project for a long time (Neh 6:12; 14; Ezr 4). But the wretched condition of the people had led to social disorders, which Nehemiah attempted to eliminate (Neh 5). He also managed to get a few people to come and build their own houses within the circle of the walls (chs. 7; 11). He then returned to his functions in Susa in 433 B.C. but reappeared in Jerusalem before the death of Artaxerxes (in 424 B.C.). During this second stay, he played a more direct part in the organization of the community and solved various problems: the presence of foreigners, the portions of the Levites, the Sabbath rest, and marriages with pagan women (ch. 13); finally, he compiled the norms of the covenant (ch. 10).

Around 398 B.C., Ezra, secretary for Jewish affairs at the court of Persia, came to Jerusalem and, in the name of Artaxerxes II, imposed the law of Moses as the law of the state. The community celebrated the Feast of Booths, sent away the foreign women, and confessed their sins; in this way, it ratified the law by its behavior. It was now that Judaism was born (Ezr 7–10; Neh 9). Even if events took place in a different order (Ezra, Nehemiah's collaborator, may have gone to Jerusalem under Artaxerxes I; if the king in his case was Artaxerxes II, Ezra was quite advanced in age), it would not greatly matter. The important thing is the deeper meaning of the events. These reveal a period of disillusionment, but also one not lacking in greatness. After the high hopes of deliverance that filled some exiles with so much enthusiasm (see Isa 40–55), Israel, now poor, weak, and sinful, saw its dream of restoring the monarchy vanish. But in its very poverty, it discovered that it was called to a more spiritual life. In its midst were prophets such as Haggai and Zechariah, who, along with Zerubbabel and Joshua, Nehemiah and Ezra, were the pioneers of this difficult restoration.

The main body of the liberated members of Israel settled in the land of their fathers, around Jerusalem. The history of salvation began anew: this is the great event the Chronicler wants to emphasize in these chapters in which he has assembled, around the personage of Ezra, passages regarding the quite different phases of the period following upon the Exile.

The Book of Ezra may be divided as follows:

- *I: The Return from the Exile (1:1—6:22)*
- *II: The Deeds of Ezra (7:1—10:44)*

I: THE RETURN FROM THE EXILE

CHAPTER 1

The Decree of Cyrus. 1 In the first year of
Cyrus, king of Persia, in order that the word
of the LORD spoken by Jeremiah might be
fulfilled, the LORD inspired King Cyrus of
Persia to issue the following proclamation
throughout his kingdom and also have it put
in writing: [a]

2 "King Cyrus of Persia says this: The
LORD, the God of heaven, has given to me all
the kingdoms of the earth, and in addition
he has designated me to build him a house
at Jerusalem in Judah. [b] 3 May God be with
all those among you who belong to his peo-
ple. * They are to go up to Jerusalem in
Judah and rebuild the house of the LORD, the
God of Israel, the God who is in Jerusalem.
4 And let everyone who has survived, and
who has settled down to reside in that locale,
be assisted by the people of that place with
silver and gold, with goods and livestock, in
addition to the voluntary offerings for the
house of God in Jerusalem."

5 Then the heads of the families of Judah
and Benjamin, as well as the priests and
Levites—all those whose spirit has been
aroused by God—prepared to go forth and
rebuild the house of God in Jerusalem. 6 All
of their neighbors assisted them with gifts of
every kind—silver and gold, goods and live-
stock, and many valuable gifts, in addition to
all of their free-will offerings.

7 Furthermore, King Cyrus himself hand-
ed over the vessels of the house of the LORD
that Nebuchadnezzar had carried away
from Jerusalem and placed them in the
temple of his gods. [c] 8 Cyrus, the king of
Persia, ordered them to be released into the
charge of Mithredath, the treasurer, who
made a complete inventory of them before
turning them over to Sheshbazzar, the
prince of Judah. *

9* This was the final inventory: thirty gold
dishes; one thousand silver dishes, in addi-
tion to twenty-nine others that had been
repaired; 10 thirty gold bowls; four hundred
and ten silver bowls; one thousand other
articles. 11 The final total of all the gold and
silver vessels was five thousand four hun-
dred. All these Sheshbazzar took with him
when he led the exiles back from Babylon to
Jerusalem.

CHAPTER 2

Census of the Province. 1 These were the
people of the province who returned from
the captivity of the exiles, those whom
Nebuchadnezzar, the king of Babylon, had
carried away to Babylon and who returned
to Jerusalem and Judah, each to his own
town. [d] 2 They were led back by Zerubbabel,
Jeshua, Nehemiah, Seraiah, Reelaiah, Mor-
decai, Bilshan, Mispar, Bigvai, Rehum, and
Baanah. *

The census of the men of the people of
Israel: 3 the sons of Parosh, two thousand
one hundred and seventy-two; 4 the sons of
Shephatiah, three hundred and seventy-two;
5 the sons of Arah, seven hundred and sev-
enty-five; 6 the sons of Pahath-moab, name-
ly the descendants of Jeshua and Joab, two
thousand eight hundred and twelve; 7 the
sons of Elam, one thousand two hundred
and fifty-four; 8 the sons of Zattu, nine hun-
dred and forty-five; 9 less the sons of Zaccai,
seven hundred and sixty; 10 the sons of Bani,
six hundred and forty-two; 11 the sons of
Bebai, six hundred and twenty-three; 12 the
sons of Azgad, one thousand two hundred
and twenty-two; 13 the sons of Adonikam, six
hundred and sixty-six; 14 the sons of Bigvai,
two thousand and fifty-six; 15 the sons of
Adin, four hundred and fifty-four; 16 the sons
of Ater, namely the descendants of Heze-
kiah, ninety-eight; 17 the sons of Bezai, three
hundred and twenty-three; 18 the sons of
Jorah, one hundred and twelve; 19 the sons of
Hashum, two hundred and twenty-three;
20 the sons of Gibeon, ninety-five; 21 the sons
of Bethlehem, one hundred and twenty-
three; 22 the sons of Netophah, fifty-six; 23 the
sons of Anathoth, one hundred and twenty-
eight; 24 the sons of Beth-azmaveth, forty-

a Ezr 5:13-17; 6:3-5; 2 Chr 36:22-23; Jer 25:11-12; 29:10-14.—b Isa 44:28; 45:13.—c 2 Ki 24:13; 25:13-16; 2 Chr 36:7-10.—d 2 Chr 36:20; Neh 7:73.

1:3 *Belong to his people:* it seems strange that someone who is not a Jew is entrusted with the responsibility to return God's people to their homeland. Cyrus, who ruled over what was formerly Assyria and Babylon offers immunity to the entire 12 tribes; however, his invitation to rebuild God's temple is only acknowledged by Judah and Benjamin.

1:8 *Sheshbazzar, the prince of Judah:* it is uncertain whether he and Zerubbabel are one and the same because of the custom of giving Babylonian names to Jews in exile. Both are identified as governors of Judah.

1:9-10 The numbers have perhaps been miscopied or are exaggerated.

2:2 The Nehemiah mentioned here is not the same one who will rebuild Jerusalem almost a century later, and Mordecai is not the person who is named in the Book of Esther.

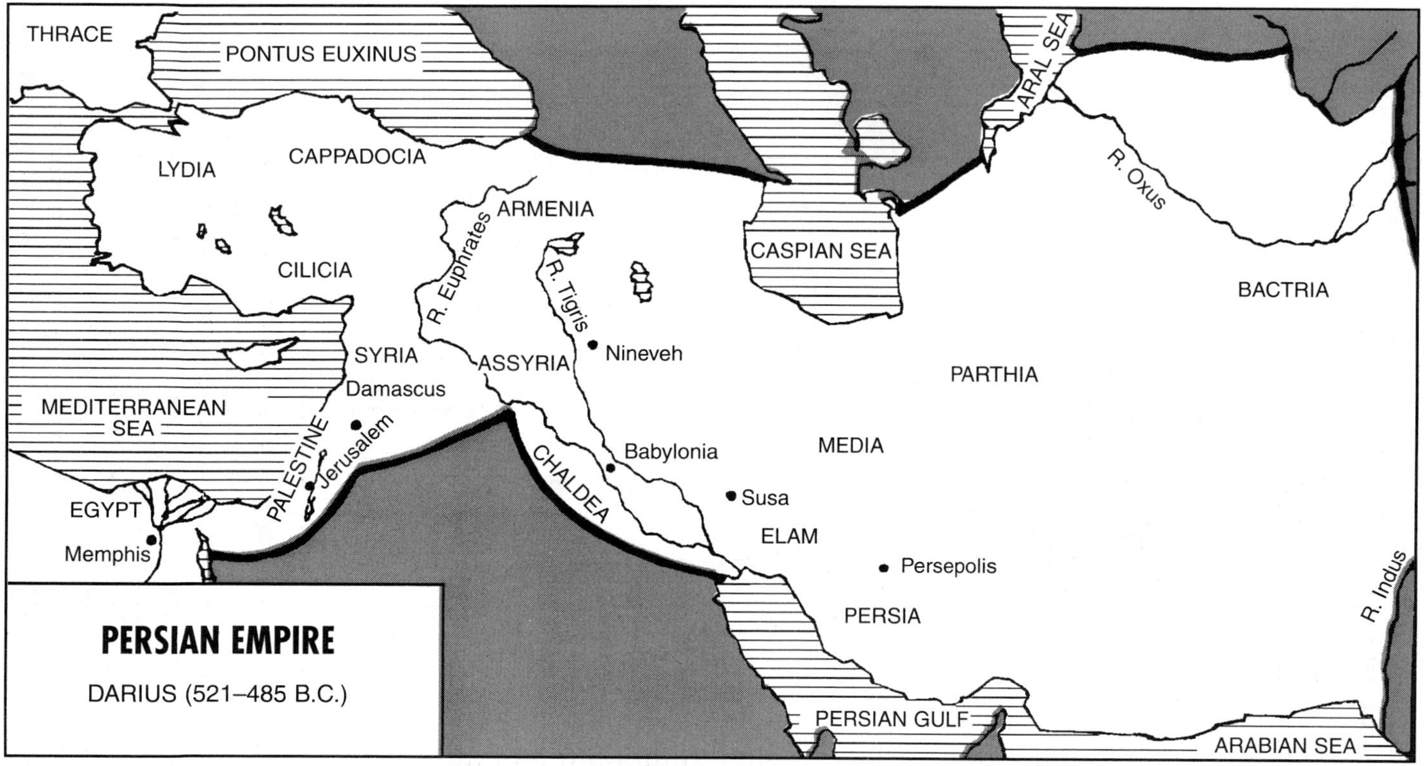

THE EXILE AND THE PERSIAN EMPIRE — **(a)** Cyrus, a petty prince of Anshan, a small district of **Elam,** rebels against Astyges his overlord and becomes king of the Medes in 550 B.C.; a few years later, Cyrus marches into Asia Minor and conquers Croesus, the fabulously wealthy king of Lybia (546 B.C.). **(b)** At this point, Deutero-Isaiah points to Cyrus as the instrument of Yahweh who will enable his people to return home and rebuild Jerusalem. **(c)** In 538 B.C., this hope is justified as Cyrus captures Babylon without waging a battle, overturns the Babylonian Empire, and reverses the policy of mass deportations by allowing the captives, including the Jews, to return to their lands and rebuild their temples. **(d)** Some of the exiles start immediately back for home under Zerubbabel (Ezr 1–2; 10), but many elect to remain in Babylon, continuing to practice their religion without sacrificial ritual, taking advantage of the opportunity for trade, and amassing riches instead of coping with the sterile soil of their fathers.

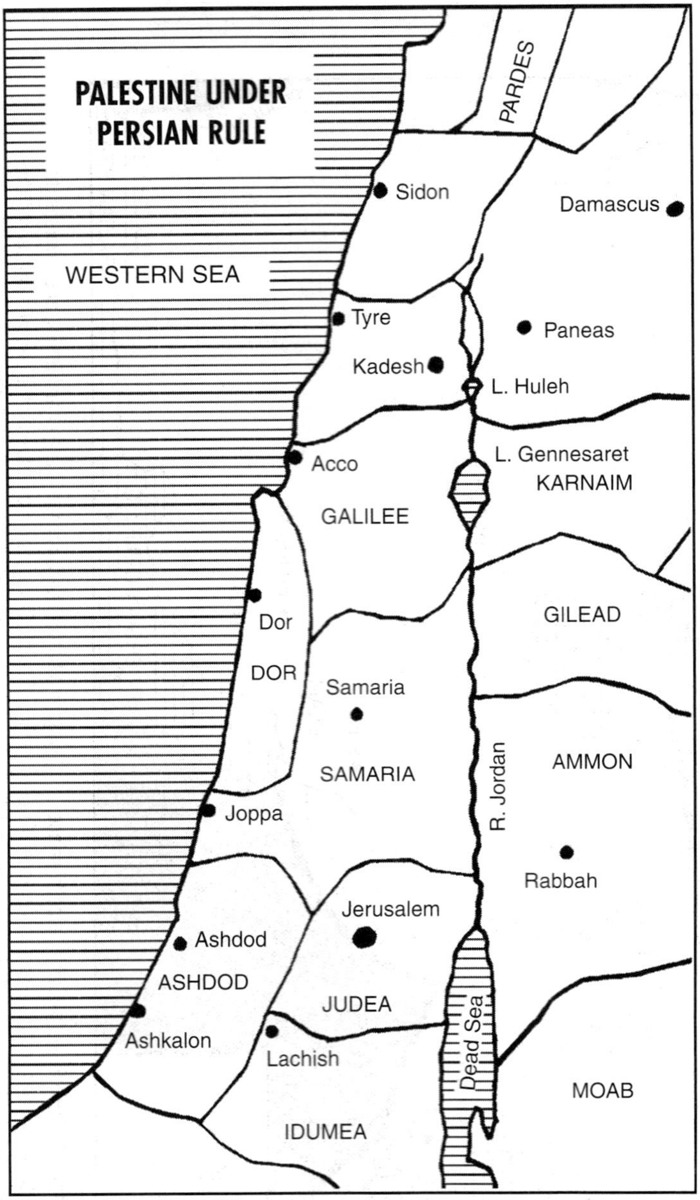

THE PERIOD OF RESTORATION UNDER PERSIAN DOMINATION (538–333 B.C.) — **(a)** During these next two hundred years, the Jewish community is established as part of the generally benevolent Persian Empire. A new community is formed out of a combination of the Judean peasants who had remained in Palestine and kept up their religion in an ignorant and superstitious way (Jer 41: 5ff) and the more intelligent of the religious devotees who had returned from the Exile where they had cherished the laws of the past and framed codes for the future. **(b)** In 538-515 B.C., the Jewish colony which occupies but a small territory about Jerusalem under Zerubbabel begins to construct the temple prompted by the leadership and inspiration of the prophets **Haggai** and **Zechariah.** **(c)** About 445 B.C., **Nehemiah** a court official of Artaxerxes I, secures the governorship of Judah and rebuilds the walls of the holy city; he reorganizes the Jewish community as distinct from the Samaritans (Neh 13; 28ff). **(d)** In 398 B.C., Ezra arrives in Jerusalem and establishes the observance of the Mosaic Law (Neh 8) and the renewal of the Covenant (Neh 9–10).

two; 25 the sons of Kiriath-jearim, Chephi-
rah, and Beeroth, seven hundred and forty-
three; 26 the sons of Ramah and Geba, six
hundred and twenty-one; 27 the sons of
Michmas, one hundred and twenty-two;
28 the sons of Bethel and Ai, two hundred
and twenty-three; 29 the sons of Nebo, fifty-
two; 30 the sons of Magbish, one hundred
and fifty-six; 31 the sons of the other Elam,
one thousand two hundred and fifty-four;
32 the sons of Harim, three hundred and
twenty; 33 the sons of Lod, Hadid and Ono,
seven hundred and twenty-five; 34 the sons of
Jericho, three hundred and forty-five; 35 the
sons of Senaah, three thousand six hundred
and thirty.

36 The priests: the sons of Jedaiah, who
were of the house of Jeshua, nine hundred
and seventy-three; 37 the sons of Immer, one
thousand and fifty-two; 38 the sons of
Pashhur, one thousand two hundred and
forty-seven; 39 the sons of Harim, one thou-
sand and seventeen.

40 The Levites: the sons of Jeshua,
Kadmiel, Binnui, and Hodaviah, seventy-
four.[e]

41 The singers: the sons of Asaph, one hun-
dred and twenty-eight.

42 The gatekeepers: the sons of Shallum,
the sons of Ater, the sons of Talmon, the
sons of Akkub, the sons of Hatita, the sons of
Shobai, one hundred and thirty-nine in all.

43 The temple slaves: the sons of Ziha, the
sons of Hasupha, the sons of Tabbaoth,
44 the sons of Keros, the sons of Siaha,
the sons of Padon, 45 the sons of Lebanah,
the sons of Hagabah, the sons of Akkub,
46 the sons of Hagab, the sons of Shamlai,
the sons of Hanan, 47 the sons of Giddel, the
sons of Gahar, the sons of Reaiah, 48 the sons
of Rezin, the sons of Nekoda, the sons of
Gazzam, 49 the sons of Uzza, the sons of
Paseah, the sons of Besai, 50 the sons
of Asnah, the sons of the Meunites, the sons
of the Nephusites, 51 the sons of Bakbuk, the
sons of Hakupha, the sons of Harhur, 52 the
sons of Bazluth, the sons of Mehida, the sons
of Harsha, 53 the sons of Barkos, the sons of
Sisera, the sons of Temah, 54 the sons of
Neziah, the sons of Hatipha.

55 The descendants of the slaves of
Solomon: the sons of Sotai, the sons of
Hassophereth, the sons of Peruda, 56 the sons
of Jaalah, the sons of Darkon, the sons of
Giddel, 57 the sons of Shephatiah, the sons of
Hattil, the sons of Pochereth-hazzebaim, the
sons of Ami. 58 The total of the temple slaves
and the descendants of Solomon's servants
numbered three hundred and ninety-two.

59 The following were those who returned
from Tel-melah, Tel-harsha, Cherub, Addan,
and Immer but were unable to prove that
their families and their ancestry were of
Israelite origin: 60 the sons of Delaiah, the
sons of Tobiah, the sons of Nekoda: six hun-
dred and fifty-two. 61 And also in regard to
the sons of the priests: the sons of Habaiah,
the sons of Hakkoz, the sons of Barzillai (he
had married one of the daughters of
Barzillai the Gileadite and became known
by his name). 62 These men had searched for
their names in the genealogical records *
but they were not to be found there. As a
result, they were excluded from the priest-
hood as unclean. 63 Consequently the gover-
nor * ordered them not to partake of the most
sacred food until a priest arrived to consult
the Urim and the Thummim.[f]

64 The entire assemblage numbered forty-
two thousand three hundred and sixty peo-
ple, 65 apart from their male and female
slaves, who numbered seven thousand three
hundred and thirty-seven, not including two
hundred male and female singers. 66 Their
horses numbered seven hundred and thirty-
six. In addition, their mules numbered two
hundred and forty-five, 67 their camels num-
bered four hundred and thirty-five, and
their donkeys numbered six thousand seven
hundred and twenty.

68 When they arrived at the house of the
LORD in Jerusalem, some of the heads of
families gave free-will offerings for the
rebuilding of the house of God on its original
site. 69 According to their resources they
donated sixty-one thousand gold drachmas,
five thousand silver minas, and one hundred
priestly robes. *

70 The priests, the Levites, and some of the
people settled in Jerusalem and its vicinity,
while the singers, the gatekeepers, and the

e Deut 18:6-7; Neh 12:24.—f Ex 28:30; Num 3:10; 16:39.

2:62 *Genealogical records:* during this time period, examining records was extremely important for many reasons. One must prove that they descended from Abraham to be considered a true Jew, and this allowed them to participate in full community life.

2:63 *Governor:* Sheshbazzar; see Ezr 1:8.

2:69 As generous as these donations were, fundraising for the new temple did not compare to the money that David raised for the building of Solomon's temple, and hence it would never compare to the splendor of the original temple.

temple servants lived in their towns, and all the rest of the Israelites settled in their towns.

CHAPTER 3

Restoration of the Altar. 1 When the seventh month came and the Israelites had settled in their towns, the people gathered in Jerusalem as a single entity. 2 Then Jeshua, the son of Jozadak, with his fellow priests, and Zerubbabel, the son of Shealtiel, with his brothers, set out to rebuild the altar of the God of Israel, in order to offer upon it the holocausts as prescribed in the law of Moses, the man of God.

3 Despite their fear of the peoples that surrounded them, they erected the altar on its former site, and upon it they presented burnt offerings to the LORD both morning and evening.[g] 4 They also celebrated the Feast of Booths as prescribed and offered the holocausts required for each day.

5 * In addition, they presented the regular burnt offerings and the sacrifices prescribed for the new moons and for the festivals sacred to the LORD, as well as all the free-will offerings made to the LORD. 6 From the first day of the seventh month they began to present burnt offerings to the LORD, even though the foundations of the temple of the LORD had not yet been laid.

Founding of the Temple. 7 Then money was contributed to the masons and the carpenters, while food, drink, and oil were given to the Sidonians and the Tyrians so that they could procure cedar trees and transport them from Lebanon by sea to Jaffa, permission for which was granted by King Cyrus of Persia.[h]

8 In the second month of the second year of their arrival at the house of God in Jerusalem, Zerubbabel, the son of Shealtiel, and Jeshua, the son of Jozadak, together with the rest of their brothers, the priests, the Levites, and all the people who had returned to Jerusalem from their captivity, began their project. 9 Jeshua, along with his sons and his brothers, together with Kadmiel and Binnui, the son of Henadad, and their sons and brethren, agreed to supervise the workers in the house of God.

10 When the builders had laid the foundation of the temple of the LORD, the priests in their robes with their trumpets, and the Levites, the sons of Asaph, with their cymbals, were stationed there to praise the LORD according to the ordinances established by King David of Israel.[i] 11 They chanted praise and offered thanksgiving to the LORD, singing:

"The LORD is good,
and everlasting is his faithful love
toward Israel."

Then all the people raised a great shout, praising the LORD because the foundation of the house of the LORD had been laid. *[j]

12 However, many of the priests and Levites and heads of families, elderly people who had seen the former house, wept loudly in sorrow when they beheld the foundations of this one, although many others shouted aloud for joy. 13 As a result, the people were unable to distinguish the clamor of the joyful shouts from the cries of those who were weeping. So great were the shouts and the cries that the sounds could be heard a long distance away.

CHAPTER 4

Samaritan Interference. 1 When the enemies of Judah and Benjamin heard that the returned exiles were in the process of building a temple to the LORD, the God of Israel, 2 they approached Zerubbabel and Jeshua and the heads of families and said: "Let us assist you as you build, for we reverence your God as you do, and we have been sacrificing to him ever since the days of King Esarhaddon of Assyria who brought us here."[k]

3 However, Zerubbabel, Jeshua, and the rest of the heads of Israelite families replied: "You shall have no share in the building of the house for our God. We alone shall build it for the LORD, the God of Israel, as King Cyrus of Persia has commanded us."

4 As a result, the people who lived around them became determined to discourage the people of Judah and to make them fearful of continuing to build. 5 Moreover, they also bribed officials to frustrate the plans of the

g Ex 29:39; Num 28:1-8.—h 1 Chr 22:4; 2 Chr 2:10-16.—i Ezr 5:16; 1 Chr 28:11-13.—j 1 Chr 16:34; Pss 24:7-10; 106:1; Isa 12:6.—k Ezr 4:7-10; Neh 4:1-13.

3:5-6 The returning exiles did not wait until the temple was rebuilt to make sacrifices to God because they realized their great need for God and how their disobedience had destroyed them.

3:11 See the psalms of thanksgiving (e.g., the whole of Ps 136).

people of Judah. This continued during the
remaining years of the reign of King Cyrus
of Persia and into the reign of King Darius
of Persia. *

Later Hostility. 6* At the beginning of the
reign of Ahasuerus, the people of the land
drew up an accusation against the inhabi-
tants of Judah and Jerusalem. 7 And later, in
the days of Artaxerxes of Persia, Mithredath
joined Tabeel and their other associates in
writing a letter to the king in Aramaic and
then translated.

8 After that, Rehum the governor and
Shimshai the secretary wrote a letter to King
Artaxerxes denouncing Jerusalem as follows:

9 "From Rehum the governor and Shim-
shai the secretary, and the rest of their asso-
ciates, the judges, the envoys, the officials,
the magistrates, and the governors over the
men from Tripolis, Persia, Erech, and Bab-
ylon, the Elamites in Susa, and 10 all the
other peoples whom the great and illustri-
ous Ashurbanipal deported and settled, in
the city of Samaria and in the rest of the
province of West-of-Euphrates." *

11 This is a copy of the letter that they sent
to him: "To King Artaxerxes, from your ser-
vants, the people of the province of Trans-
Euphrates: 12 The king has the right to know
that the Jews who came up from you to us
have arrived in Jerusalem and are in the
process of rebuilding this rebellious and
wicked city. They have restored the walls
and are repairing the foundations. [l] 13 Now
we wish to inform the king that if the city is
rebuilt and the walls are restored, they will
refuse to pay tribute, taxes, or tolls, causing
the royal revenues to be sharply reduced.

14 "Now, because we share the salt of the
palace, * we know that it is not right for us to
witness the king's dishonor. We therefore are
sending this information to the king 15 in
order that a search may be made in the
archives of your ancestors. In those archives
you will discover that this is a rebellious city
greatly troublesome to kings and provinces,
and that sedition has been stirred up within
its walls from the earliest times. That is why
this city was destroyed. 16 Therefore, we wish
to inform you, O king, that if this city is
rebuilt and its walls are raised up again, you
will be left without any territory in Trans-
Euphrates."

17 The king sent this reply: "To Rehum the
governor, to Shimshai the secretary, and to
the rest of their associates who reside in
Samaria and in the province of West-of-
Euphrates: Greetings!

18 "The letter you have sent to us has now
been accurately translated and been read in
my presence. 19 When an inquiry was made
at my command, it was discovered that this
city has frequently risen up against the kings
in the past, and that revolt and rebellion
were more than an occasional occurrence.
20 In addition, powerful kings have reigned in
Jerusalem and exercised authority over the
entire province of West-of-Euphrates while
exacting tribute, taxes, and tolls. [m]

21 "Therefore, now give orders that these
men must cease their work, and make it
clear that this city is not to be rebuilt until I
issue a decree to that effect. 22 And take care
that you do not act negligently in this
regard, lest the damage increase, to the
detriment of the royal house."

23 As soon as the text of the letter from
King Artaxerxes was read before Rehum the
governor, Shimshai the secretary, and their
colleagues, they traveled immediately to
Jerusalem and compelled the Jews by force
of arms to stop their work.

Rebuilding of the Temple. 24 Work on the
house of God in Jerusalem then ceased, and
it so remained until the second year of the
reign of King Darius of Persia. *

CHAPTER 5

1 Afterward, the prophets Haggai and
Zechariah, the son of Iddo, prophesied to
the Jews who were in Judah and Jerusalem
in the name of the God of Israel who was
over them. * [n] 2 Thereupon Zerubbabel, the
son of Shealtiel, and Jeshua, the son of
Jozadak, began again to rebuild the house of

---

l Ezr 5:3; Neh 1:3.—m 1 Ki 4:21; 1 Chr 18:3-4.—n Hag 1:1; Zec 1:1; 7:1.

4:5 Darius I (522—486 B.C.) included Syria and Palestine in his fifth satrapy (administrative province), known as the Satrapy Beyond the River (i.e., beyond the Euphrates). The account in verse 5 is taken up again in verse 24.

4:6-7 *Ahasuerus:* successor of Darius I, reigned from 486–465 B.C. He was succeeded by Artaxerxes I (465–424 B.C.).

4:10 The Aramaic text has Osnapper as the king's name, but he is probably the famous Ashurbanipal (668—626 B.C.), son of Esarhaddon (v. 2) and continuer of his policy.

4:14 *Share the salt of the palace:* they were supported and paid by the king, and therefore, under obligation to him.

4:24 Work on the temple was interrupted for as many as ten years and resumed about the year 520 B.C.

5:1 See the introductions to the Books of the prophets Haggai and Zechariah.

God in Jerusalem, and the prophets of God
were with them, giving them support.
3 At that time Tattenai, the governor of
West-of-Euphrates, Shethar-bozenai, and
their associates came to them and asked:
"Who has given you the authority to rebuild
this house and complete this structure?
4 What are the names of the men who are
constructing this building?" 5 However, the
eyes of their God continued to watch over
the elders of the Jews, and they were not
forced to stop until a report could reach
Darius and an official reply could then be
sent back in regard to this matter. [o]
6 This is a copy of the letter that Tattenai,
the governor of Trans-Euphrates, Shethar-
bozenai, and their associates sent to King
Darius. 7 This is the written report that they
forwarded to him:
"To King Darius: Our sincere greetings.
8 Let it be known to your majesty that we
went to the province of Judah and visited the
house of the great God. It is being rebuilt
with massive stones, and beams of timber
are being laid in the walls. The work is being
done diligently, and significant progress has
been made.
9 "We then questioned the elders, asking
them: 'Who gave you permission to build
this house and to finish this structure?' 10 We
also asked them their names for your infor-
mation so that we could record the names of
those who were their leaders.
11 "They gave us this answer: 'We are the
servants of the God of heaven and earth. We
are in the process of rebuilding the house
that was erected many years ago, a house
that a great king of Israel had built and
completed. 12 But because our ancestors
provoked the wrath of the God of heaven,
he delivered them into the power of
Nebuchadnezzar, the Chaldean king of
Babylon, who destroyed this temple and
deported the people to Babylon.
13 " 'However, King Cyrus of Babylon, * in
the first year of his reign, issued a decree
that this house of God should be rebuilt. [p]
14 Moreover, the gold and silver articles of
the house of God, which Nebuchadnezzar
had removed from the temple of Jerusalem
and brought into the temple of Babylon,
King Cyrus in turn removed from the tem-
ple of Babylon and ordered them to be
delivered into the hands of a man named
Sheshbazzar, whom he had appointed gov-
ernor. 15 He said to him: "Take these vessels.
Go forth and deposit them in the temple of
Jerusalem, and let the house of God be
rebuilt on its original site."
16 " 'Then this Sheshbazzar came and laid
the foundations of the house of God in
Jerusalem, and from that time until now it
has been under construction, and it is not
yet completed.' 17 Now, if it pleases the king,
order that a search be made in the royal
archives of Babylon to ascertain whether a
decree was issued by King Cyrus for the
rebuilding of this house of God in Jerusalem.
Then ask the king to convey his decision on
this matter to us."

CHAPTER 6

The Decree of Darius. 1 * After that, King
Darius issued an order to search the
archives where the documents were stored
in Babylon. 2 Eventually in the fortress of
Ecbatana, * a scroll was discovered with the
following text:
3 "In the first year of his reign, King Cyrus
issued this decree concerning the house of
God in Jerusalem: Let the house be rebuilt
as a place where sacrifices are offered and
burnt offerings are presented. Its height
shall be sixty cubits and its width sixty
cubits, 4 with three layers of massive stones
and one layer of timber. The cost is to be
defrayed by the royal treasury.
5 "Furthermore, the gold and silver ves-
sels of the house of God, which Nebuchad-
nezzar took from the temple in Jerusalem
and brought to Babylon, are to be given
back. Each one is to be returned to its prop-
er place in the temple in Jerusalem and
deposited in the house of God.
6 "Now you, Tattenai, governor of West-of-
Euphrates, and Shethar-bozenai, and your
associates, the officials in West-of-Euphrates,
keep away from that place. 7 Leave the gov-
ernor of the Jews and the elders of the Jews
alone so that they may continue to work on
that house of God. They are to rebuild it on
its former site.

---

o Ezr 4:24; 8:22; Ps 33:18.—p Ezr 1:1-8; 2 Chr 36:22.

5:13 *King Cyrus of Babylon:* Cyrus was previously referred to as king of Persia (Ezr 1:1) and now has extended his reign over Babylon as well. It is used here to signify the importance of the city where the Jews were held captive for over 70 years.

6:1-2 The reference is to the eastern regions of the empire.

6:2 *Ecbatana:* modern Hamadan (Iran); this was the capital of Media.

[8] "I have also issued a decree in regard to
your dealings with the elders of the Jews to
ensure the rebuilding of this house of God.
Let these men be repaid for their expenses,
in full and without delay, from the royal
revenue, the taxes of West-of-Euphrates.
[9] Whatever else is required—young bulls,
rams, and lambs for burnt offerings to the
God of heaven, wheat, salt, wine, and oil,
according to what the priests in Jerusalem
require—let that be given to them day by
day without fail, [10] so that they may offer
sacrifices that are acceptable to the God of
heaven and pray for the life of the king and
his sons.

[11] "Furthermore, I have issued a decree: if
anyone disobeys this order, a beam shall be
torn from his house. Then he is to be
impaled on it, and his house is to be reduced
to a pile of rubble. [12] May the God who has
established his name there overthrow every
king or people who may presume to change
or to destroy this temple in Jerusalem. I,
Darius, have issued this decree. Let it be
strictly obeyed."

The Work Completed. [13] Then Tattenai, the
governor of West-of-Euphrates, Shethar-
bozenai, and their associates fully carried
out the instructions sent to them by King
Darius, [14] and the elders of the Jews contin-
ued to make good progress with the rebuild-
ing. Supported by the prophesying of
Haggai the prophet and Zechariah, the son
of Iddo, they completed the reconstruction
in accordance with the command of the God
of Israel and the decrees of Cyrus, Darius,
and Artaxerxes, the king of Persia. [q]

[15] This temple was completed on the
twenty-third day of the month of Adar, in
the sixth year of the reign of King Darius.
[16] The Israelites—the priests, the Levites,
and the remainder of the exiles—celebrated
the dedication of this house of God with joy.
[17] For the dedication of this house of God
they offered one hundred bulls, two hundred
rams, and four hundred lambs, and, as a sin
offering for all Israel, twelve male goats, cor-
responding to the number of the tribes of
Israel. [18] Then they installed the priests in
their divisions and the Levites in their divi-
sions for the service of God in Jerusalem, as
prescribed in the Book of Moses.

The Passover. [19] The exiles celebrated the
Passover on the fourteenth day of the first
month. [r] [20] For both the priests and the
Levites had purified themselves, and they
were all ceremonially clean. The Levites sac-
rificed the Passover lamb for all the exiles
who had returned, for their brothers the
priests, and for themselves.

[21] Therefore, the Israelites who had
returned from exile, as well as those who
had separated themselves from the unclean
practices of their Gentile neighbors in order
to seek the Lord, the God of Israel, ate the
Passover lamb. [s] [22] For seven days they joy-
fully celebrated the Feast of Unleavened
Bread, for the LORD had given them cause
to rejoice by making the king of Assyria
change his attitude toward them, so that he
supported them in their work on the house
of God, the God of Israel. *

II: THE DEEDS OF EZRA*

CHAPTER 7

Ezra the Scribe. [1] After these occurrences,
during the reign of Artaxerxes, * king of
Persia, Ezra, the son of Seraiah, son of
Azariah, son of Hilkiah, [2] son of Shallum, son
of Zadok, son of Ahitub, [3] son of Amariah,
son of Azariah, son of Meraioth, [4] son of
Zerahiah, son of Uzzi, son of Bukki, [5] son of
Abishua, son of Phinehas, son of Eleazar,
son of the high priest Aaron—[6] this Ezra
came up from Babylon. He was a scribe who
was skilled in the law of Moses which was
given by the LORD, the God of Israel, and the

q Ezr 1:1; 5:1; Zec 4:9.—r Ex 12:1-20; Num 28:16.—s Ezr 9:1-15; Ex 19:10, 14.

6:22 The union of the feasts of Passover and Unleavened Bread had already taken place in the period of the Deuteronomic reform (622 B.C.; see Deut 16:1-8). The king of Persia is called king of Assyria inasmuch as he was heir to the Assyrian empire.

7:1—10:44 At the beginning of the fourth century, or even earlier, Ezra was concerned to create a solid organization of his countrymen who had again settled in Palestine, in order to protect them against pagan influences. In his person a new kind of biblical personage makes his appearance: the scribe. The scholar, as servant of the royal court, had existed since David's time, but now he becomes more important; as an expert in the law, he gradually replaces the priest (who henceforth deals almost exclusively with the ritual performance of worship) and becomes an influential personage. His often disturbing presence will be seen throughout the gospel story.

The main element in Ezra's reform has to do with the marriages of Jews to women of the local population and reaches the point of dismissing these foreign wives. To understand this resolution of the problem, we must look to the setting. Infidelity had brought the nation into exile; therefore only an intransigent fidelity could safeguard it against a new disaster. Furthermore, as the entire past showed, beginning with Solomon's harem, infidelity made its way in through mixed marriages.

7:1 *Artaxerxes:* this would seem to be Artaxerxes II (404–358 B.C.). Therefore, the seventh year of his reign is 398 B.C.

king granted him everything that he
requested, since the hand of the LORD God
was upon him.[t]

7 Ezra was accompanied to Jerusalem by a
number of Israelites, priests, Levites, singers,
gatekeepers, and temple slaves in the seventh
year of the reign of King Artaxerxes. 8 Ezra
arrived in Jerusalem in the fifth month of the
seventh year of the king's reign.

9 On the first day of the first month, Ezra
had ordered the departure from Babylon,
and he arrived in Jerusalem on the first day
of the fifth month, since the gracious hand of
his God was upon him. 10 For he had devot-
ed himself to the study and observance of
the law of the LORD so as to put that law into
practice and to teach its statutes and ordi-
nances in Israel.

The Decree of Artaxerxes. 11 This is a copy of
the letter that King Artaxerxes gave to Ezra
the priest-scribe, a scholar in matters per-
taining to the commandments and statutes
of the LORD for Israel: *

12 "Artaxerxes, king of kings, to Ezra the
priest-scribe, a scholar versed in the com-
mandments and statutes of the LORD for
Israel.[u] 13 I have issued a decree stating that
any of the people of Israel in my kingdom,
including their priests and Levites, who
freely choose to go up to Jerusalem with you
are free to do so. 14 For you are being sent by
the king and his seven counselors to make
inquiries as to how the law of your God in
which you are extremely knowledgeable is
being followed in Judah and Jerusalem.

15 "You are also to convey the silver and
gold which the king and his counselors have
voluntarily offered to the God of Israel
whose dwelling is in Jerusalem, 16 as well as
all the silver and gold which you may receive
throughout the province of Babylon and the
voluntary offerings that have been freely
contributed by the people and the priests for
the house of their God in Jerusalem.

17 "You must spend this money with
extreme care to purchase bulls, rams, and
lambs, as well as the cereal offerings and
libations, and sacrifice them on the altar of
the house of your God in Jerusalem. 18 As for
the remainder of the silver and gold, you
and your brothers may do whatever seems
best to you. 19 In the presence of the God of
Israel you are to deliver those vessels that
have been given to you for the service of the
house of your God. 20 As for whatever else is
required and you are obliged to supply for
the needs of the house of your God, you may
supply from the royal treasury.

21 "I, King Artaxerxes, have issued this
decree to all the treasurers of West-of-
Euphrates: Whatever the priest Ezra, the
scribe of the law of the God of heaven, may
request of you is to be provided to him
exactly, 22 up to one hundred talents of sil-
ver, one hundred kors of wheat, one hundred
baths of oil, and unlimited amounts of salt.
23 Let everything that the God of heaven
commands be carried out exactly for the
house of the God of heaven so that wrath
may not be inflicted upon the realm of the
king and his sons. 24 We also wish to make
clear to you that it is against the law to
impose a tribute, tax, or toll on any priests,
Levites, singers, gatekeepers, temple slaves,
or other servants of this house of God.

25 "As for you, Ezra, in accordance with
the wisdom of your God which you possess,
you are to appoint magistrates and judges *
to administer justice to all the people in
West-of-Euphrates—to all, that is, who know
the laws of your God. Furthermore, you are
to instruct all those who do not know these
laws.[v] 26 Whoever refuses to obey the law of
your God and the law of the king is to have
judgment be strictly executed, whether the
penalty be death, banishment, confiscation
of property, or imprisonment."

Ezra and His Companions. 27 Then Ezra
said: "Blessed be the LORD, the God of our
ancestors, who has influenced the heart of
the king in this way to glorify the house of
the LORD in Jerusalem, 28 and who permit-
ted me to be granted the faithful love of the
king and his counselors and all the most
powerful of the king's officials. Because the
hand of the LORD, my God was upon me, I
assembled those Israelite leaders to accom-
pany me." *

CHAPTER 8

1 These are the family heads and those
registered with them who set forth from
Babylon with me in the reign of King
Artaxerxes:

t Ezr 7:28; Neh 8:9, 13.—u Ezek 26:7; Dan 2:37.—v Ex 18:21, 25; Deut 16:18; Ps 37:30-31.

7:11 The document is written in Aramaic.

7:25 *Magistrates and judges:* those that acknowledge the religion of the Israelite people.

7:28 This prayer of thanks and praise is Ezra's way of completely acknowledging his dependence on God, without whom he would not have attained his state in life.

2 Of the sons of Phinehas: Gershom; of the
sons of Ithamar: Daniel; of the sons of
David: Hattush, 3 son of Shecaniah; of the
sons of Parosh: Zechariah, and with him one
hundred and fifty males were enrolled; 4 of
the sons of Pahath-moab: Eliehoenai, son of
Zerahiah, and with him two hundred males;
5 of the sons of Zattu: Shecaniah, son of
Jahaziel, and with him three hundred males;
6 of the sons of Adin: Ebed, son of Jonathan,
and with him fifty males; 7 of the sons of
Elam: Jeshaiah, son of Athaliah, and with
him seventy males; 8 of the sons of
Shephatiah: Zebadiah, son of Michael, and
with him eighty males; 9 of the sons of Joab:
Obadiah, son of Jehiel, and with him two
hundred and eighteen males; 10 of the sons of
Bani: Shelomith, son of Josiphiah, and with
him one hundred and sixty males; 11 of the
sons of Bebai: Zechariah, son of Bebai, and
with him twenty-eight males; 12 of the sons
of Azgad: Johanan, son of Hakkatan, and
with him one hundred and ten males; 13 of
the sons of Adonikam: the younger sons,
whose names were Eliphelet, Jeiel, and
Shemaiah, and with them sixty males; 14 of
the sons of Bigvai: Uthai and Zaccur, and
with them seventy males.

The Journey to Jerusalem. 15 I assembled
them by the river that flows to Ahava, and
we camped there for three days. During that
time I noticed the people and the priests,
but I was unable to discern any Levites.* [w]
16 Therefore, I summoned Eliezer, Ariel,
Shemaiah, Elnathan, Jarib, Elnathan,
Nathan, Zechariah, and Meshullam, who
were judicious men, 17 and sent them to
Iddo the leader at a place called Casiphia, in
order to procure for us ministers to serve in
the house of our God.

18 By the gracious providence of God they
sent to us Sherebiah, a wise man, one of the
sons of Mahli, son of Levi, son of Israel, with
his sons and kinsmen, eighteen men. 19 They
also sent us Hashabiah, and with him his
brother Jeshaiah of the descendants of
Merari with his kinsmen and their sons,
twenty men, 20 and two hundred and twenty
temple slaves whom David and the princes
had assigned to serve the Levites, all of them
enrolled by name.

21 Then I proclaimed a fast there by the
River Ahava, so that we might humble our-
selves before our God and pray that he
would grant a successful journey for our-
selves, our children, and all our posses-
sions. [x] 22 For I was ashamed to ask the king
for foot soldiers and cavalry to protect us
from enemies along the way, inasmuch as
we had said to the king: "The hand of our
God is upon all who seek his protection, but
his fierce wrath is against all who forsake
him." 23 Therefore, we fasted and prayed to
God to grant us a safe journey, and he
answered our prayer.

24 Then I selected twelve of the leading
priests, together with Sherebiah and
Hashabiah and ten of their kinsmen. 25 I
weighed out in their presence the silver, the
gold, and the utensils, the contributions
which the king, his advisors, his officials, and
all the Israelites present there had offered
for the house of our God.

26 I weighed out and handed over to them
six hundred and fifty talents * of silver, one
hundred silver vessels weighing two talents,
one hundred talents of gold, 27 twenty gold
bowls worth one thousand darics, and two
superb vessels of polished bronze, as pre-
cious as gold.

28 Then I said to them: "You are conse-
crated to the LORD, as are the utensils. The
silver and the gold are a free-will offering to
the LORD, the God of your fathers. 29 Guard
them carefully until you weigh them out to
the leading priests, the Levites, and the
heads of the families of Israel in Jerusalem
within the chambers of the house of the
LORD." 30 The priests and the Levites then
took charge of the silver, the gold, and the
sacred articles that had been weighed out to
be taken to the house of our God in
Jerusalem.

31 On the twelfth day of the first month we
set forth from the Ahava Canal to make our
journey to Jerusalem. The hand of God
remained to protect us from our enemies
and bandits along the way. 32 When we
arrived in Jerusalem, we rested for three
days.

33 On the fourth day, the silver, the gold,
and the vessels were weighed in the house of
God and presented to the priest Meremoth,

w Ezr 8:21, 31.—x 2 Chr 7:14; Ps 37:11.

8:15 Ezra's journey was delayed while he waited for more Levites to come forward to serve the people. In our current day, we seek and wait for those who will answer God's call to serve.

8:26 *Six hundred and fifty talents:* this would convert to about 25 tons of silver. Even a much smaller amount would have been difficult to transport.

the son of Uriah, who was accompanied by
Eleazar, the son of Phinehas and the Levites
Jozabad, the son of Jeshua, and Noadiah, the
son of Binnui. 34 Everything was counted
and weighed, and the total weight was
recorded at that time.

35 After that, those who had returned from
their captivity presented burnt offerings to
the God of Israel: twelve bulls for all Israel,
ninety-six rams, seventy-two lambs, and, as
a sin offering, twelve male goats. All these
were presented as a holocaust to the LORD.
36 They also delivered the king's instructions
to the royal satraps and to the governors in
West-of-Euphrates who then pledged their
support to the people and the house of God.

CHAPTER 9

Denunciation of Mixed Marriages. 1 After
these matters had been concluded, the lead-
ers approached me and said: "The people of
Israel, including the priests and the Levites,
have not kept themselves separated from
the neighboring peoples with their abom-
inable practices—the Canaanites, the Hit-
tites, the Perizzites, the Jebusites, the
Ammonites, the Moabites, the Egyptians,
and the Amorites.[y] 2 They have taken
women of these nations as wives for them-
selves and their sons, and as a result, they
have contaminated the holy race by such
unions. In this regard the leaders and the
magistrates have been the major offenders."

Ezra's Exhortation. 3 Upon hearing this
news, I tore my tunic and cloak, after which
I plucked hair from my beard and my head
and sat down in a complete stupor until the
evening sacrifice. 4 Then all those who trem-
bled with fear at the words of the God
of Israel gathered around me, while I sat
there appalled until the evening sacrifice.[z]
5 * However, at the time of the evening sacri-
fice, I arose from my stupor, with my cloak
and my mantle torn, and I fell to my knees
while stretching out my hands to the LORD.

6 Then I said: "O my God, I am too
ashamed and embarrassed to lift my face to
you, my God, because our iniquities have
increased until they have risen higher than
our heads, and our guilt has reached the
heavens. 7 From the time of our fathers until
now our guilt has been great, and because of
our iniquities we and our kings and our
priests have been handed over into the
power of foreign rulers and subjected to the
sword, to captivity, to pillage and disgrace,
as is the case today.

8 "But now, for a brief moment, the LORD,
our God has shown mercy to us by allowing
a remnant of us to escape and given us a sta-
ble home in his sanctuary, thereby bringing
light to our eyes and granting us some relief
in our bondage. 9 For we are slaves, but God
has not forgotten us in our state of slavery.
He has extended his faithful love to us and
turned the good will of the kings of Persia
toward us, while granting us new life to
rebuild the house of our God, restore its
ruins, and provide us with a wall of protec-
tion in Judah and Jerusalem.[a]

10 "But now, our God, what can we say
after all this? For we have abandoned your
commandments, 11 which you gave through
your servants, the prophets, when you said:
'The land that you are entering to possess is
a land polluted by the abominations of the
people of the country and their disgusting
practices that have filled it with their filth
from one end to the other. 12 Therefore, do
not give your daughters in marriage to their
sons or let their daughters marry your sons.
Nor must you seek peace with them or
enhance their prosperity. In this way you will
grow strong, enjoy the produce of the land,
and leave it as an inheritance to your chil-
dren forever.'[b]

13 "After all that has befallen us for our
evil deeds and our great guilt, you, O LORD,
have punished us less than our sins have
deserved and have allowed us to survive.
14 Shall we once again disobey your com-
mandments and intermarry with people
who engage in these loathsome practices?
Would you not be enraged with us to the
point that you would destroy us, leaving us
with neither remnant nor survivor? 15 O
LORD, God of Israel, you are righteous. We
survive only as a remnant. We come here
before you in our guilt. Because of this, none
of us can stand in your presence."[c]

CHAPTER 10

The People's Response. 1 While Ezra was
praying and acknowledging their guilt as he

---

y Gen 10:16; 19:37; Ex 23:23; Neh 9:2.—z Ezr 10:3; Isa 66:2, 5.—a Ex 1:14; Neh 9:36; Ps 106:46.—b Deut 7:3.—c Neh 9:8; Ps 130:3; Dan 9:7.

9:5-15 Ezra prays a prayer of repentance for the sins of the people. Although he is not guilty of these sins himself, he is saddened by them to the point of tears and moves them to be aware of the serious nature of their disobedience.

wept and prostrated himself in front of the
temple of God, a vast assemblage of men,
women, and children gathered around him
as the people wept profusely. 2 Then
Shecaniah, the son of Jehiel, one of the sons
of Elam, spoke up and said to Ezra: "We
have been unfaithful to our God by marry-
ing foreign women from the peoples of this
land. However, in spite of this, there is still
hope for Israel. 3 Let us now make a
covenant with our God to send away all
these wives and their children, in accor-
dance with the counsel of my lord and of
those who fear the commandments of our
God. Let it be done in accordance with the
law. *[d] 4 Rise up, then, for the matter is in
your hands. We will support you. Therefore,
have courage and take action!"

5 Then Ezra rose to his feet and put the
leading priests and Levites and all Israel
under oath to do what had been said. In uni-
son they took the oath. 6 Then Ezra departed
from his place before the house of God and
entered the room of Jehohanan, the son of
Eliashib, where he spent the night without
eating food or drinking water, because he was
in mourning over the betrayal by the exiles.

7 A proclamation was issued throughout
Judah and Jerusalem that all of the exiles
were to assemble in Jerusalem, 8 and that
those who failed to appear within three
days, as specified by the officials and the
elders, would forfeit their property and be
excluded from the assembly of the exiles.

9 All the men of Judah and Benjamin
gathered together in Jerusalem three days
later, on the twentieth day of the ninth
month. All the people sat down in the open
square before the house of God, greatly dis-
tressed because of the matter at hand and
because they had no shelter from the heavy
rain. 10 Then Ezra the priest stood up and
said to them: "You have been unfaithful in
marrying foreign wives, thus adding to
Israel's guilt. 11 Now confess to the LORD, the
God of your ancestors, and do his will.
Separate yourselves from the people of the
land and from foreign women."

12 Then all those who had assembled
replied loudly, saying in unison: "We shall do
as you say. 13 However, there are many peo-
ple here; it is the rainy season, and we can-
not stay out in the open. Besides, this is
something that cannot be resolved in one or
two days, since those of us who have sinned
in this regard comprise a vast number.

14 "Therefore, permit our officials to rep-
resent the entire community, and let all those
in our towns who have married foreign wives
present themselves at designated times,
accompanied by the elders and the judges for
each town, until the fierce anger of our God at
what has occurred has been turned away
from us."[e] 15 Only Jonathan, the son of
Asahel, and Jahzeiah, the son of Tikvah, sup-
ported by Meshullam and Shabbethai, the
Levites, opposed this proposal.*

The Guilty. 16 The exiles did as had been
proposed, while Ezra the priest selected
men who were family heads, representing
their families, each of them designated by
name. They met in sessions to examine the
matter, beginning with the first day of the
tenth month. 17 By the first day of the first
month they had passed judgment on all the
men who had married foreign women.

18 Among the members of priestly fami-
lies, the following were found to have mar-
ried foreign women: of the sons of Jeshua,
son of Jozadak, and his brothers: Maaseiah,
Eliezer, Jarib, and Gedaliah, 19 who pledged
to dismiss their wives, and their guilt offer-
ing was a ram from the flock for their guilt;

20 of the sons of Immer: Hanani and
Zebadiah; 21 of the sons of Harim: Ma-
aseiah, Elijah, Shemaiah, Jehiel, and Uz-
ziah; 22 of the sons of Pashhur: Elioenai,
Maaseiah, Ishmael, Nethanel, Jozabad, and
Elasah;

23 of the Levites: Jozabad, Shimei, Kelaiah
(also called Kelita), Pethahiah, Judah, and
Eliezer;[f]

24 of the singers: Eliashib, and of the gate-
keepers: Shallum, Telem, and Uri.

25 Among the Israelites: of the sons of
Parosh: Ramiah, Izziah, Malchijah, Mijamin,
Eleazar, Malchijah, and Benaiah; 26 of the
sons of Elam: Mattaniah, Zechariah, Jehiel,
Abdi, Jeremoth, and Elijah; 27 of the sons of
Zattu: Elioenai, Eliashib, Mattaniah,
Jeremoth, Zabad, and Aziza;

28 of the sons of Bebai: Jehohanan,
Hananiah, Zabbai, and Athlai; 29 of the sons

d Deut 7:2-3; Mt 5:32.—e Deut 13:18; 2 Chr 29:10.—f Neh 8:7; 11:16.

10:3 Although the idea of divorcing wives and children seems ungodly and extreme, it was significant in showing the attention to God's law that had been ignored by taking foreign wives in the first place.

10:15 Perhaps these opponents were afraid that the commission of inquiry would proceed too slowly, and they wanted more urgent measures taken.

of Bani: Meshullam, Malluch, Adaiah,
Jashub, Sheal, and Jeremoth; 30 of the sons of
Pahath-moab: Adna, Chelal, Benaiah,
Maaseiah, Mattaniah, Bezalel, Binnui, and
Manasseh;

31 of the sons of Harim: Eliezer, Isshijah,
Malchijah, Shemaiah, Shimeon, 32 Ben-
jamin, Malluch, and Shemariah; 33 of the
sons of Hashum: Mattenai, Mattattah,
Zabad, Eliphelet, Jeremai, Manasseh, and
Shimei; 34 of the sons of Bani: Maadai,
Amram, Uel 35 Benaiah, Bedaiah, Cheluhi,
36 Vaniah, Meremoth, Eliashib, 37 Mat-
taniah, Mattenai, and Jaasu; 38 of the sons of
Binnui: Shimei, 39 Shelemiah, Nathan, and
Adaiah; 40 of the sons of Zachai: Shashai,
Sharai, 41 Azarel, Shelemiah, Shemariah,
42 Shallum, Amariah, Joseph; 43 of the sons of
Nebo: Jeiel, Mattithiah, Zabad, Zebina,
Jaddai, Joel, Benaiah.

44 All these had married foreign woman
but sent them away with their children.

THE BOOK OF NEHEMIAH

Building the Community

The Book deals with more than one subject, but it has only one protagonist: Nehemiah, a zealous layman with a high rank in the Persian court.

The Chronicler introduces genealogies that come down even to later times, but the main part of the Book is taken from the memoirs of Nehemiah himself, who twice came from Susa to Jerusalem under Artaxerxes I: a first time in 445 B.C., when he remained for twelve years, and a second time shortly after (13:6).

The specific undertaking of this layman was to rebuild the walls of Jerusalem (chs.1–6) and to repopulate the abandoned city. In the course of the work, we see the beginnings of more fraternal relationships (ch. 5) and the community assembling to celebrate a solemn liturgy at which they learn the law and pledge themselves to observe it (chs. 8; 10).

The Book of Nehemiah may be divided as follows:

I: The Deeds of Nehemiah (1:1—7:73)

II: Promulgation of the Law (8:1—13:31)

I: THE DEEDS OF NEHEMIAH

CHAPTER 1

Nehemiah's Vocation. 1 The words of
Nehemiah, the son of Hacaliah.

In the month of Kislev, * in the twentieth
year, while I was in the citadel of Susa,
2 Hanani, one of my brothers, arrived with
some men from Judah. I asked them about
the Jews—those who had survived the cap-
tivity—and about Jerusalem.

3 They replied: "Those who survived the
captivity and remained in the province are
in dire distress and badly demoralized. The
wall of Jerusalem lies in ruins and its gates
have been destroyed by fire." 4 Upon hearing
this, I sat down and wept, * mourning for
several days while fasting and praying
before the God of heaven. [a]

5 Then I offered this prayer: "O LORD, God
of heaven, you are a great and awesome God
who keeps his covenant of steadfast love
with those who love him and obey his com-
mandments. 6 Let your ear be attentive and
your eyes open to heed the prayer of your
servant that I now offer to you day and night

a Ezr 9:3; Dan 9:3.

1:1 *Month of Kislev:* November–December. The twentieth year of the reign of Artaxerxes I was 445 B.C. Susa was one of the capitals used by the Persian kings. The others were Ecbatana, Persepolis, and Babylon.

1:4 *Sat down and wept:* there was much for Nehemiah to be saddened by in Jerusalem. Walls represented safety for the people against intruders and a sense of independence and strength. The Jews needed to rebuild to gain a sense of control but were prevented from doing so by a previous edict (Ezr 4:6-23).

in your presence on behalf of your servants,
the people of Israel. [b]

"I confess the sins that your servants, the
Israelites, have committed against you. I
and my family are equally guilty in this
regard. 7 We have offended you grievously
and failed to keep the commandments, the
statutes, and the laws you enjoined on your
servant Moses.

8 "Do not fail to remember the promise
you made to your servant Moses when you
said: 'If you are unfaithful, I shall scatter you
among the nations. 9 However, if you return
to me and obey my commandments and ful-
fill them, then I will gather even those
among you who have been scattered to the
farthest ends of the world and bring you
back to the place I have chosen as a dwelling
for my name.' [c]

10 "These are your servants, your people,
whom you have redeemed by your great
power and your strong hand. 11 O LORD, let
your ear be attentive to the humble prayer
of your servants who take delight in revering
your name. Grant that your servant will be
given success this day and win this man's
compassion"—for at that time I was cup-
bearer to the king. * [d]

CHAPTER 2

Appointment by the King. 1 In the month of
Nisan, in the twentieth year of King
Artaxerxes, since the wine was my responsi-
bility, I took the wine and gave it to the king.
Inasmuch as I had never before showed any
sign of sadness in his presence, * 2 the king
asked me: "Why do you look so depressed?
You clearly are not ill. This is the result of
your sadness of heart."

Despite the fact that I was greatly fearful,
3 I said to the king: "May your majesty live
forever! How can I possibly fail to be
depressed when the city where my ancestors
are buried lies in ruins and its gates have
been destroyed by fire?" 4 The king then said
to me: "What do you wish to request of me?"

Having first prayed to the God of
heaven, * 5 I said to the king: "If your
majesty approves and your servant has
found favor with you, I beg you to send me
to Judah, to the city where my ancestors are
buried, so that I can rebuild it." 6 Then the
king—with the queen sitting beside him—
said to me: "How long will your journey
take, and when will you return?" Once I had
given the king a specific date that was
acceptable to him, he approved my request.

7 Then I said to the king: "If it pleases the
king, let letters be given to me for the gover-
nors of West-of-Euphrates with orders to
grant me safe passage until I arrive in
Judah. [e] 8 I also request that you give me a
letter for Asaph, the keeper of the king's for-
est, directing that he give me timber for the
gates of the citadel adjoining the temple,
and for the wall of the city, and for the resi-
dence I will occupy." The king granted what
I requested, for the gracious hand of my
God was upon me. [f]

9 When I came to the governors of West-of-
Euphrates, I presented the king's letters to
them. The king had also sent an escort of
army officers and cavalry to accompany me.
10 However, when Sanballat * the Horonite
and Tobiah the Ammonite official heard this,
it displeased them greatly that someone had
come to seek the welfare of the Israelites.

Nehemiah Inspects the Wall. 11 * When I
arrived in Jerusalem, I rested there for three
days. 12 Then I set out by night with just a
few other men. I revealed to no one what my
God had inspired me to do for Jerusalem,
and I took no animal with me other than the
one I was riding.

13 I went forth by night through the Valley
Gate toward the Dragon Spring as far as the
Dung Gate, and I observed how the walls of
Jerusalem lay in ruins with its gates
destroyed by fire. [g] 14 I then passed over to
the Fountain Gate and the King's Pool, but
there was no room there for the animal I
was riding to continue.

---

b Deut 28:14-15; 2 Chr 6:40.—c Deut 12:5; Jer 29:11-14.—d Gen 40:21; Ps 118:25.—e Ezr 6:6; 8:36.—f Ezr 7:6; Eccl 2:5-6.—g Neh 1:3; 12:31.

1:11 *Cupbearer to the king:* one of the highest ranks at the royal court. It was Nehemiah's job to secure the safety and quality of the king's food and allowed him easy access to share his concerns about the Jews with the king.

2:1 *Sadness in his presence:* it was not considered wise to appear depressed before the king—no one in mourning clothes could even be in his presence. The king's questioning of Nehemiah about his appearance was a dangerous thing.

2:4 On many occasions in this short Book, we read that Nehemiah invoked God's assistance before speaking or acting. This shows his trust in God that was the fruit of his ongoing intimate relationship with him.

2:10 *Sanballat:* the governor of Samaria, called the "Horonite" from the city of Horonaim in the land of Moab (see Isa 15:5). Tobiah was in all probability a member of a family (the Tobiads) who in the third century B.C. would flourish in the region of the Ammonites.

2:11-20 Poets who experienced the disaster have preserved for us their deeply felt and horrified memory of the mass of stones and ruins that made the site of Jerusalem such a sad place (Pss 74; 79; Lam 1; 2; 5).

15 Therefore, I went up by way of the valley in the dark, examining the wall until I once again reached the Valley Gate and re-entered the city. 16 The officials did not know where I had gone or what I had been doing. I had not as yet disclosed anything to the Jews, neither to the priests, nor to the nobles, nor to the magistrates, nor to any of the other persons who were to be involved in the work. *

Rebuilding Jerusalem's Walls. 17 Then I said to them: "You now can realize the difficulty we face. Jerusalem lies in ruins, and its gates have been destroyed by fire. Therefore, we must rebuild the wall of Jerusalem so that we will no longer be looked upon as a disgrace." 18 Then I told them how God had been so extremely gracious to me, and I also revealed the encouragement that the king had given me. They replied: "Let us begin the rebuilding at once," and they undertook their work vigorously.

19 However when Sanballat the Horonite, Tobiah the Ammonite slave, and Geshem the Arab heard about this, they ridiculed and mocked us, saying: "What is this you are doing? Are you rebelling against the king?" [h] 20 In turn I gave them this answer: "The God of heaven will grant us success, and we his servants intend to start the rebuilding immediately. But as for you, you have no share in Jerusalem or any claim or historic right in Jerusalem."

CHAPTER 3

List of Builders. 1 * Eliashib the high priest then set to work with his fellow priests and rebuilt the Sheep Gate. They laid its beams and put the doors in place, after which they consecrated it as far as the Tower of the Hundred and the Tower of Hananel. [i] 2 The men of Jericho worked next to Eliashib, and Zaccur, the son of Imri, built next to them.

3 The sons of Hassenaah built the Fish Gate. They laid its beams and set up its doors, its bolts, and its bars. [j] 4 Meremoth, the son of Uriah, son of Hakkoz, carried out the necessary repairs next to them. Meshullam, the son of Berechiah, son of Meshezabel, was next to him, followed by Zadok, son of Baana.

5 Next to Zadok the Tekoites carried out the necessary repairs, although their nobles refused to demean themselves by helping their masters. 6 Joiada, the son of Paseah, and Meshullam, the son of Besodeiah, repaired the Old Gate, laying its beams and setting up its doors, its bolts, and its bars.

7 At their side were Melatiah the Gibeonite, Jadon the Meronothite, and the men of Gibeon and Mizpah who did the repairs under the jurisdiction of the governor of West-of-Euphrates. 8 Next to them the repair work was carried out by Uzziel, the son of Harhaiah, a member of the goldsmiths' guild, and at his side was Hananiah, a member of the perfumers' guild. They renovated the wall of Jerusalem as far as the Broad Wall of the public square.

9 Next to them the repairs were carried out by Rephaiah, the son of Hur, who was the ruler of half the district of Jerusalem. 10 At his side was Jedaiah, the son of Harumaph, who made the repairs opposite his own house. Next to him the repairs were carried out by Hattush, the son of Hashabneiah.

11 Malchijah, the son of Harim, and Hasshub, the son of Pahath-moab, repaired another section and the Tower of the Ovens. 12 Next to them, Shallum, the son of Hallohesh and ruler of the other half of the district of Jerusalem, carried out repairs with the help of his daughters. *

13 Hanun and the inhabitants of Zanoah repaired the Valley Gate. They rebuilt it and put its doors, its bolts, and its bars in place, and they also repaired a thousand cubits of the wall, as far as the Dung Gate. 14 The Dung Gate itself was repaired by Malchijah, the son of Rechab, the ruler of the district of Beth-haccherem; he rebuilt it and put the doors in place with their bolts and bars.

15 The Fountain Gate was repaired by Shallum, the son of Colhozeh, the ruler of the district of Mizpah; he rebuilt it, placed a roof over it, and put its doors in place with their bolts and their bars. He also built the wall of the Pool of Shelah that adjoined the king's garden, as far as the steps descending from the City of David. 16 After him,

h Neh 2:10.—i Neh 3:20; 13:28; Jer 31:38.—j Neh 12:39.

2:16 Nehemiah shows great wisdom by inspecting the walls at night and not sharing his mission with anyone until he was prepared to take action. He realized that opening the idea to others would cause controversy among the Jews and lose time that could be used better in completion of the task of rebuilding.

3:1ff It was necessary in a city as large as Jerusalem to have many gates for both military and trade reasons.

3:12 All the people of Jerusalem were involved in rebuilding the city walls, notwithstanding the women (i.e., Shallum's daughters).

Nehemiah, the son of Azbuk, ruler of half the
district of Beth-zur, made the repairs from a
point opposite the tomb of David as far as
the artificial pool and the House of the
Heroes.[k]

17 After him, repairs were carried out by
the Levites under the direction of Rehum,
the son of Bani. Next to him, Hashabiah, the
leader of half the district of Keilah, carried
out the repairs for his own district. 18 After
him, their kinsmen took charge of the
repairs, headed by Binnui, the son of
Henadad, leader of half the district of
Keilah.

19 Next to him was Ezer, the son of Jeshua,
leader of Mizpah, who repaired the adjoin-
ing section opposite the ascent to the
armory at the Angle. 20 After him, Baruch,
the son of Zabbai, repaired another section
from the Angle to the door of the house of
the high priest Eliashib.

21 After him, Meremoth, the son of Uriah,
son of Hakkoz, repaired another section,
from the door of the house of Eliashib to the
end of the house. 22 After him, repairs were
carried out by the priests who lived in the
district.

23 After them, Benjamin and Hasshub
carried out the repairs opposite their house,
and after them Azariah, son of Maaseiah,
son of Ananiah, did the repairs beside his
own house. 24 After him, Binnui, the son of
Henadad, repaired the adjoining sector
from the house of Azariah to the Angle and
the Corner.

25 After him, Palal, the son of Uzai, carried
out repairs in front of the Angle and the
tower projecting from the Upper Palace of
the king to the court of the guard. Next to
him, Pedaiah, the son of Parosh, carried out
the repairs 26 to a point opposite the Water
Gate on the east and the projecting tower.
27 After him the Tekoites repaired the adjoin-
ing section opposite the great projecting
tower as far as the wall of Ophel.

28 Above the Horse Gate the priests car-
ried out repairs, each one opposite his own
house. * 29 After them, Zadok, the son of
Immer, carried out the repairs opposite his
own house, and after him Shemaiah, the son
of Shecaniah, the keeper of the East Gate,
did the necessary repairs.[l]

30 After him, Hananiah, the son of
Shelamiah, and Hanun, the sixth son of
Zalaph, repaired a second section. After
him, Meshullam, the son of Berechiah,
made the necessary repairs opposite his liv-
ing quarters. 31 After him, Malchijah, a gold-
smith, made the needed repairs as far as the
house of the temple servants and of the mer-
chants opposite the Inspection Gate and as
far as the upper room at the Corner. 32 And
between the upper room at the Corner and
the Sheep Gate the goldsmiths and the mer-
chants carried out all the needed repairs.

Opposition from Judah's Foes. 33 When
Sanballat was informed that we were
rebuilding the wall, his anger was aroused,
and he was greatly enraged. He ridiculed the
Jews, 34 and in the presence of his compan-
ions and the army of Samaria he said:
"What are these feeble Jews doing? Will they
restore what has been damaged beyond
repair? Will they offer sacrifices? Will they be
able to complete their work in a single day?
Will they manage to refurbish the stones that
have been damaged and reduced to ashes?"
35 And Tobiah the Ammonite, who was stand-
ing beside Sanballat, added: "If a fox were to
climb on top of the stone wall they are build-
ing, it would crumble before them."

36 Then we prayed: "Listen to us, O our
God, for we are despised. Turn their insults
back upon their own heads. Let them
become objects of contempt in a land of cap-
tivity. 37 Do not pardon their wickedness or
allow their sins to be blotted out from your
sight, for they have insulted the builders to
their face."[m]

38 Meanwhile we continued to rebuild the
wall, which was soon completed all the way
around up to half its height, while the people
put their hearts into their work.

CHAPTER 4

1 When Sanballat and Tobiah and the
Arabs, the Ammonites, and the Ashdodites *
heard that the repairs to the walls of
Jerusalem were proceeding according to
plan and that the gaps were beginning to be
closed, they became infuriated.[n] 2 As a
result, they all plotted together to launch an
attack against Jerusalem and throw all of us

k 2 Ki 20:20; 2 Chr 16:14.—l Jer 19:2; Ezek 40:6.—m Jer 18:23.—n Neh 2:10; Ezr 4:1-5.

3:28 Nehemiah's plan was masterful in that everyone willing and able could participate. Here we read that each priest worked on the portion opposite their house ensuring good work being done without traveling a distance.

4:1 *Ashdodites:* the people of Ashdod were Philistines; 13:23 speaks of women of Ashdod who had married Jews.

into panic and confusion. 3 Therefore, we prayed to our God and posted guards against them day and night in an attempt to foil their plans.

4 Meanwhile, the Judahites were saying: "The strength of the laborers is beginning to falter, and the rubbish is so extensive that we will not be able to rebuild the wall." 5 However, our enemies, who were adamant in their belief that we would not know or see anything before they came into our midst, prepared to kill us and put a stop to the work.

6 When the Jews who lived near them came to us, they warned us ten times over: "Whichever way you turn, they will be prepared to attack us." 7 Therefore, I commanded men to position themselves in the lowest places behind the wall, and near them I stationed the people by families with their swords, spears, and bows.

8 After I made a thorough inspection, I addressed the nobles, the officials, and the rest of the people, saying: "Have no fear of them! Remember the LORD, who is great and awe-inspiring, and fight for your brothers, your sons, your daughters, your wives, and your homes." 9 When our enemies realized that we were forewarned and that God had thwarted their plans, they withdrew, and we all went back to the wall, each one to his particular task.

10 From that time on, however, half of my men did the construction work, while the other half posted themselves behind the whole house of Judah as they rebuilt the wall. 11 Those who carried the building materials did their work with one hand while holding a spear with the other.[o] 12 Moreover, every worker involved in the task of building had his sword strapped to his side at all times. In addition, a trumpeter stood beside me.

13 * I then said to the nobles, the officials, and the rest of the people: "Our work is extensive and spread out, and we are widely separated from each other along the wall. 14 Whenever you hear the sound of a trumpet, come to our side to support us immediately. Our God will fight for us."

15 Therefore, we continued to labor at the work, from the break of dawn until the stars came out. 16 At the same time I also told the people: "Let every man with his servant remain each night in Jerusalem, so that they may spend the night as a guard for us and be at work during the day." 17 Therefore, neither I, nor my brothers, nor my servants, nor any of the bodyguards who accompanied me ever took off our clothes. In addition, each one kept his spear in his right hand.

CHAPTER 5

Antisocial Conduct. 1 * Soon thereafter, there arose a great outcry from the common people and from their wives against their Jewish brothers.[p] 2 Some were vehement in their complaints that they were forced to pledge their sons and daughters in order to obtain grain so that they might eat and stay alive. 3 Others asserted that they were forced to mortgage their fields, their vineyards, and their houses in order to survive.

4 Furthermore, there were those who said: "We are being forced to borrow money on our fields and vineyards in order to pay the king's tax. 5 And although our flesh is identical to that of our kinsmen and our children are as good as theirs, we will have to subject our sons and daughters into slavery. Some of our daughters have already been enslaved, and our fields and our vineyards now belong to others."[q]

Nehemiah's Action. 6 When I heard these complaints and the cries of the people, I was extremely angry. 7 After having considered the various options, I threatened to bring charges against the nobles and the magistrates, accusing them of exacting interest from their own kinsmen.

Then I summoned a great assembly to deal with them, 8 and I said to them: "As far as it was humanly possible, we have bought back our fellow Jews who had been sold to foreigners. However, now you are selling your own brothers and thus forcing us to purchase them back." They remained silent, for they were unable to come up with a satisfactory reply.

9 Therefore, I said: "What you are doing is terribly wrong. Should you not walk in the fear of our God and make clear that you are not at all concerned with the taunts of the nations who are our enemies? 10 Moreover, I

o Ps 149:6.—p Deut 15:7; Jer 34:8-22.—q Lev 25:39; 2 Ki 4:1.

4:13-14 Nehemiah combined prayer with thoughtful safety precautions, constantly reminding the workers of their goal and of God's protection.

5:1ff It is one thing to be abused by outsiders; here, the enemies were fellow Jews who probably had returned under Zerubbabel (Ezr 1:2) and were now the social and financial elite who were taking advantage of the newly arrived.

myself, along with my brothers and my ser-
vants, have lent the people money and grain
without charge. Let us cease the custom of
usury.[r] 11 I also ask that you restore to them
this very day their fields, their vineyards,
their olive groves, and their houses, together
with the interest on the money, the grain, the
wine, and the oil that you have lent them."

12 They replied: "We will give it all back
and demand nothing more from them. We
will do just what you ask." I then summoned
the priests and made them swear to do what
they had promised. 13 I also shook out the
folds of my garment and said: "So may God
shake out from home and property every-
one who fails to adhere to this promise. May
every such man be shaken out and emp-
tied." *

All the assembled people said "Amen"
and praised the LORD, and they did as they
promised.

Nehemiah's Lack of Self-Interest. 14 More-
over, from the twentieth year that King
Artaxerxes appointed me to be their gover-
nor in the land of Judah until the thirty-
second year, neither I nor my brothers ate
the food allotted to the governor by the
king.[s] 15 On the other hand, the former gov-
ernors, my predecessors, had laid a heavy
burden on the people and exacted from
them forty shekels of silver each day for food
and wine, while their servants also
oppressed the people. However, because I
feared God, I did not act in this way.

16 Indeed, I devoted all my efforts to the
work on the wall, and I acquired no land,
while all my servants were gathered there
for the work. 17 Moreover, there sat at my
table guests who numbered one hundred
and fifty people, Jews and officials, as well as
those who came to us from the surrounding
nations.

18 Every day one ox, six choice sheep, and
some poultry were prepared for me, as well
as skins of wine in abundance every ten
days. Despite all this, I did not claim the gov-
ernor's food allowance because the people
had such a heavy burden of labor.

19 O my God, please remember me favor-
ably for all that I have done for this people.

CHAPTER 6

Plots against Nehemiah. 1 When it had been
reported to Sanballat, Tobiah, Geshem the
Arab, and the rest of our enemies that I had
rebuilt the wall and that not a single breach
was left in it (although up to that time I had
not set up the doors in the gates), 2 Sanballat
and Geshem sent me this message: "Come
here and confer with us in one of the villages
in the plain of Ono." Their intention was
clearly to do me harm.[t]

3 Therefore, I sent messengers to them
with this reply: "I am engaged in a great
project, and I cannot come down to you at
this particular time. Why should the work
come to a grinding halt while I leave it and
come down to you?" 4 They sent me the
same invitation four times, and on each
occasion I gave them the same reply.

5 Then, for the fifth time, Sanballat sent his
servant to me with the same message, but
this time in an unsealed letter. 6 In it was
written: "It has been reported among the
nations, and Geshem * confirms it, that you
and the Jews are planning a rebellion, that
this is the reason you are building the wall,
and that you are intending to become their
king. 7 We have also heard that you have
appointed prophets in Jerusalem to proclaim
you king. Needless to say, such rumors will be
brought to the attention of the king. So come
at once and let us discuss this together."

8 I sent the following reply to him: "No
such thing that you are suggesting has taken
place. It is all in your imagination." 9 They
all were trying to frighten us, hoping that we
would become lax in our work and the job
would not be completed. But instead I be-
came more determined than ever.

10 One day I went to the house of
Shemaiah, the son of Delaiah, son of
Mehetabel, who was confined to his house.
He said to me:

"Let us meet in the house of God
 inside the sanctuary,
 and let us lock the doors of the temple.
For men are coming to kill you;
 they are coming to kill you tonight."

11 However, I said: "Should a man like me
run away? Or should a man like me go into
the temple to save his life?"

12 Then I realized that God had not sent
Shemaiah to say this, but rather that Tobiah
and Sanballat had hired him. 13 He had been

r Ezek 18:13.—s Neh 13:6.—t 1 Chr 8:12.

5:13 *Shaken out and emptied:* a symbolic act and saying that Nehemiah pronounced as a curse on anyone who failed to keep the promise to forego usury and treat people justly.

6:6 *Geshem:* the Hebrew has Gashmu.

bribed to intimidate me and make me sin by
acting in this way. Then they could ruin my
reputation and discredit me.
14 Remember Tobiah and Sanballat, O my
God, according to those things they did, and
also the prophetess Noadiah and the rest of
the prophets whose purpose was to intimi-
date me. [u]

Conclusion of the Work. 15 The wall was fin-
ished on the twenty-fifth day of the month of
Elul. * It was completed in fifty-two days.
16 When all our enemies heard about this,
and all the surrounding nations were com-
pletely aware of what had been happening,
they realized that all this work had been
completed with the help of God. [v]
17 At the same time, however, the nobles of
Judah were sending many letters to Tobiah,
and in turn, letters from Tobiah kept coming
to them, 18 for many in Judah were bound to
him by oath, because he was the son-in-law
of Shecaniah, son of Arah, and his son
Jehohanan had married the daughter of
Meshullam, son of Berechiah. 19 They were
always praising Tobiah's good deeds in my
presence, and they reported my words to
him. Furthermore, Tobiah also sent letters
to me in an attempt at intimidation.

CHAPTER 7

1 When the wall had been rebuilt and I had
set the doors in place, and the gatekeepers,
the singers, and the Levites had been
appointed, 2 I put my brother Hanani in
charge of Jerusalem, and I appointed
Hananiah as the commander of the citadel,
for he was a trustworthy man and more
God-fearing than most.
3 I said to them: "The gates of Jerusalem
are not to be opened until the sun is hot, *
and when the sun begins to go down, have
the gatekeepers shut and bar the doors.
Appoint guards from among the inhabitants
of Jerusalem, some at their posts and others
in front of their own homes."

Census of the Province. 4 Now the city was
large and spacious, but there were few
inhabitants within it, and the houses had not
been rebuilt. 5 Then my God put it into my
mind to assemble the nobles, the magis-
trates, and the common people to be
enrolled by families. I also discovered the
genealogical record of those who had been
the first to come back. This is what I found
written in it:
6 These are the inhabitants of the province
who returned from the captivity of those
exiles whom King Nebuchadnezzar of
Babylon had carried away. Each returned to
his own town. [w] 7 They were the ones who
returned with Zerubbabel, Jeshua, Ne-
hemiah, Azariah, Raamiah, Nahamani,
Mordecai, Bilshan, Mispereth, Bigvai,
Nehum, and Baanah.
The number of the Israelite people: 8 the
sons of Parosh, two thousand one hundred
and seventy-two; 9 the sons of Shephatiah,
three hundred and seventy-two; 10 the sons
of Arah, six hundred and fifty-two; 11 the
sons of Pahath-moab who were sons of
Jeshua and Joab, two thousand eight hun-
dred and eighteen; 12 the sons of Elam, one
thousand two hundred and fifty-four; 13 the
sons of Zattu, eight hundred and forty-five;
14 the sons of Zaccai, seven hundred and
sixty; 15 the sons of Binnui, six hundred and
forty-eight; 16 the sons of Bebai, six hundred
and twenty-eight; 17 the sons of Azgad, two
thousand three hundred and twenty-two;
18 the sons of Adonikam, six hundred and
sixty-seven; 19 the sons of Bigvai, two thou-
sand and sixty-seven; 20 the sons of Adin, six
hundred and fifty-five; 21 the sons of Ater
who were sons of Hezekiah, ninety-eight;
22 the sons of Hashum, three hundred and
twenty-eight; 23 the sons of Bezai, three hun-
dred and twenty-four; 24 the sons of Hariph,
one hundred and twelve; 25 the sons of
Gibeon, ninety-five; 26 the men of Beth-
lehem and Netophah, one hundred and
eighty-eight; 27 the men of Anathoth, one
hundred and twenty-eight; 28 the men of
Beth-azmaveth, forty-two; 29 the men of
Kiriath-jearim, Chephirah, and Beeroth,
seven hundred and forty-three; 30 the men of
Ramah and Geba, six hundred and twenty-
one; 31 the men of Michmas, one hundred
and twenty-two; 32 the men of Bethel and Ai,
one hundred and twenty-three; 33 the men of
Nebo, fifty-two; 34 the sons of another Elam,
one thousand two hundred and fifty-four;
35 the sons of Harim, three hundred and

u Jer 23:9-40.—v Neh 4:1; Pss 118:22-23; 127:1.—w Ezr 2:1-70.

6:15 *Elul:* September–October. *Fifty-two days:* the work was certainly carried out very energetically by all the people, but we must remember that the destruction had not been total and that the rebuilding had not begun with Nehemiah (see the decree of Artaxerxes in Ezr 4:17-22).

7:3 *Sun is hot:* Nehemiah's unusually late opening for the city gates was a preventative measure against any enemy planning an attack before the people were fully awake.

twenty; 36 the sons of Jericho, three hundred
and forty-five; 37 the sons of Lod, Hadid, and
Ono, seven hundred and twenty-one; 38 the
sons of Senaah, three thousand nine hun-
dred and thirty.

39 The priests: the sons of Jedaiah, of the
house of Jeshua, nine hundred and seventy-
three; 40 the sons of Immer, one thousand
and fifty-two; 41 the sons of Pashhur, one
thousand two hundred and forty-seven;
42 the sons of Harim, one thousand and sev-
enteen.

43 The Levites: the sons of Jeshua and
Kadmiel of the descendants of Hodeviah,
seventy-four.

44 The singers: the sons of Asaph, one hun-
dred and forty-eight.

45 The gatekeepers: the sons of Shallum,
the sons of Ater, the sons of Talmon, the sons
of Akkub, the sons of Hatita, and the sons of
Shobai: one hundred and thirty-eight.

46 The temple slaves: the sons of Ziha, the
sons of Hasupha, the sons of Tabbaoth, 47 the
sons of Keros, the sons of Sia, the sons of
Padon, 48 the sons of Lebana, the sons of
Hagaba, the sons of Shalmai, 49 the sons
of Hanan, the sons of Giddel, the sons of
Gahar, 50 the sons of Reaiah, the sons
of Rezin, the sons of Nekoda, 51 the sons of
Gazzam, the sons of Uzza, the sons of
Paseah, 52 the sons of Besai, the sons of the
Meunites, the sons of the Nephusites, 53 the
sons of Bakbuk, the sons of Hakupha,
the sons of Harhur, 54 the sons of Bazlith,
the sons of Mehida, the sons of Harsha, 55 the
sons of Barkos, the sons of Sisera, the sons of
Temah, 56 the sons of Nezaiah, the sons of
Hatipha.

57 The descendants of the slaves of
Solomon: the sons of Sotai, the sons of
Sophereth, the sons of Perida, 58 the sons
of Jaala, the sons of Darkon, the sons of
Giddel, 59 the sons of Shephatiah, the sons of
Hattil, the sons of Pochereth-hazzebaim,
the sons of Amon. 60 The total of the temple
slaves and the sons of Solomon's slaves; three
hundred and ninety-two. [x]

61 The following were those who returned
from Tel-melah, Tel-harsha, Cherub, Addon,
and Immer but were unable to prove that
their families were of Israelite descent: *
62 the sons of Delaiah, the sons of Tobiah, and
the sons of Nekoda, numbering six hundred
and forty-two. 63 Also, among the priests:
the sons of Hobaiah, the sons of Hakkoz,
and the sons of Barzillai (he had married
one of the daughters of Barzillai the
Gileadite and adopted that name). 64 These
men had sought to find their entries among
those enrolled in the genealogies, but their
names were not able to be found there, and
as a result, they were excluded from the
priesthood as unclean. 65 Consequently, His
Excellency forbade them to partake of any of
the consecrated food until a priest appeared
who was able to consult the Urim and the
Thummim.

66 The entire assembly numbered forty-
two thousand three hundred and sixty, [y]
67 not including their male and female slaves,
of whom there were seven thousand three
hundred and thirty-seven, as well as two
hundred and forty-five male and female
singers. 68 They also had seven hundred and
thirty-six horses, two hundred and forty-five
mules, 69 four hundred and thirty-five
camels, and six thousand seven hundred and
twenty donkeys.

70 Some of the heads of families con-
tributed to the work. The governor gave to
the treasury one thousand drachmas of gold,
fifty bowls, and five hundred and thirty
priestly garments. 71 And some of the heads
of ancestral houses gave to the building fund
twenty thousand drachmas of gold and two
thousand two hundred minas of silver. 72 The
contributions of the rest of the people
amounted to twenty thousand gold drach-
mas, two thousand minas of silver, and sixty-
seven priestly garments.

73 The priests, the Levites, the gatekeepers,
the singers, and the temple servants, along
with some of the people and the rest of the
Israelites, took up residence in their own
towns.

II: PROMULGATION OF THE LAW

CHAPTER 8

Ezra Reads the Law. 1 * Now when the sev-
enth month came, and the Israelites had
settled in their towns, all the people assem-
bled together as a unit in the square in front
of the Water Gate. Then they asked Ezra the

---

x Ezr 2:58.—y Ezr 2:64-67.

7:61 *Prove . . . Israelite descent:* having proof of one's lineage as a descendant of Abraham (i.e., one of God's people) was of utmost importance.

8:1ff Ezra was the religious leader of the Israelites and a commanding presence to them. Nehemiah was a devoted layman who wielded a strong political and social influence on the Jews.

scribe to bring forth the Book of the Law of
Moses which the LORD had given to Israel. [z]
2 Accordingly, on the first day of the seventh
month, Ezra the priest brought the law
before the assembly, both men and women,
as well as all those old enough to compre-
hend what was said.

3 Facing the square in front of the Water
Gate, Ezra read from the book of the law
from dawn until noon in the presence of the
men and women as well as those who could
understand what was being said. All the peo-
ple listened attentively to the book of the
law. 4 Ezra the scribe stood on a wooden
platform that had been constructed for the
occasion, and beside him stood Mattithiah,
Shema, Anaiah, Uriah, Hilkiah, and
Maaseiah on his right hand, and Pedaiah,
Mishael, Malchijah, Hashum, Hashbad-
danah, Zechariah, and Meshullam on his
left.

5 Then Ezra opened the book in the sight
of all the people—for he was standing above
them. As soon as he opened it, all the people
rose to their feet. 6 Next he blessed the LORD,
the great God, and all the people lifted up
their hands as they answered, "Amen!
Amen!" Then they bowed their heads and
prostrated themselves before the LORD with
their face to the ground.

7 In addition, the Levites Jeshua, Bani,
Sherebiah, Jamin, Akkub, Shabbethai,
Hodiah, Maaseiah, Kelita, Azariah, Jozabad,
Hanan, and Pelaiah helped the people to
understand the law while the people
remained in their places. [a] 8 Ezra read plain-
ly from the book of the law of God, making
its meaning clear so that the people could
understand what was being said.

9 Then Nehemiah the governor, Ezra the
priest-scribe, and the Levites who were
instructing the people said to all the people:
"This day is holy to the LORD, your God. Do
not mourn, and do not weep." For all the
people were weeping as they heard the
words of the law. 10 Then Nehemiah added:
"You now may go. Eat rich food and drink
what is sweet. Moreover, send some of these
to those for whom nothing has been pre-
pared, for this day is holy to our LORD.
Furthermore, do not be grieved, for the joy
of the LORD is your strength." [b]

11 The Levites, thereupon, calmed all the
people, saying: "Be quiet, for this is a sacred
day. There is no reason for you to be sad-
dened." 12 Then all the people went off to eat
and drink, to distribute portions, and to cel-
ebrate with great rejoicing, since they had
come to comprehend the meaning of what
had been proclaimed to them.

The Feast of Booths. 13 On the second day
of the month, the family heads of all the peo-
ple, together with the priests and the
Levites, gathered around the scribe Ezra to
study the words of the law. 14 And written in
the law that the LORD had prescribed
through Moses, they found that the
Israelites were to live in booths * during the
feast of the seventh month. [c]

15 In addition, they were to issue this
proclamation and circulate it throughout
their towns and in Jerusalem: "Go forth into
the hills and bring branches of olive and wild
olive trees, and of myrtle, palm, and other
leafy trees to make booths, as the law pre-
scribes." 16 Therefore the people went out
and brought back branches to make shelters
for themselves, each on his own roof, and in
their courtyards and in the precincts of the
house of God, and in the square at the Water
Gate and in the square at the Gate of
Ephraim.

17 Therefore the whole community of
those who had returned from their captivity
made booths and lived in them, something
that the Israelites had not done from the
days of Joshua, the son of Nun, until that day,
and there was very great rejoicing. [d] 18 Each
day, from the first to the last day, Ezra read
from the book of the law of God. They cele-
brated the feast for seven days, and on the
eighth day, as prescribed, they held a solemn
assembly.

CHAPTER 9

Confession of the People. 1 On the twenty-
fourth day of this month, the Israelites,
wearing sackcloth and with their heads cov-
ered with dust, assembled together for a
fast. [e] 2 Then those of Israelite descent sepa-
rated themselves from all foreigners, after
which they stood up and confessed their sins
and the iniquities of their ancestors. *

z 2 Chr 34:15; Ezr 3:1; 7:6.—a Neh 10:10-13; Deut 33:10.—b Deut 26:11-13; Est 9:19.—c Lev 23:33-36; Ezek 45:25.—d 2 Chr 7:8; 30:21; 35:18.—e 1 Sam 4:12; Job 2:12; Dan 9:3.

8:14 *Live in booths:* after studying the law read by Ezra, the people heeded this instruction to remind themselves of God's protection while they wandered in the wilderness.

9:2 In addition to fasting and wearing sackcloth, the repentant Israelites made a public confession of their sins and that of their ancestors.

3 They next stood in their places and read
from the book of the law of the LORD, their
God, for a fourth part of the day, after which
they spent another quarter of the day in con-
fessing their sins and worshiping the LORD,
their God. 4 Standing on the platform of the
Levites were Jeshua, Binnui, Kadmiel,
Shebaniah, Bunni, Sherabiah, Bani, and
Chenani, and they cried aloud to the LORD,
their God.
5 Then the Levites, Jeshua, Kadmiel, Bani,
Hashabneiah, Sherebiah, Hodiah, Shebaniah,
and Pethahiah, said:

"Stand up and bless the LORD, your God
from everlasting to everlasting.
And blessed is your glorious name
that is exalted above all blessing and praise."

6 Then Ezra said:

"You alone are the LORD:
you have created the heavens,
the highest heavens with all their host,
the earth and all that is upon it,
the seas and all that is in them.
To all of them you gave life,
and the hosts of heaven worship you.[f]

7 "You are the LORD,
the God who chose Abram,
who brought him out from Ur of the Chaldeans
and changed his name to Abraham.
8 Finding that his heart was faithful,
you made a covenant with him
to give to his descendants
the land of the Canaanites,
Hittites, Amorites, Perizzites,
Jebusites, and Girgashites.
The promises of yours you fulfilled,
for you are just.[g]

9 "You beheld the misery of our ancestors in Egypt
and heard their cry at the Red Sea.[h]

10 "You performed signs and wonders against Pharaoh,
against all his servants and the people of his land.
Because you knew of the great arrogance
with which they treated our forefathers,
and you won renown for yourself
that has lasted even to this very day.
11 "You divided the sea before them,
and they passed through the sea on dry ground.
However, their pursuers you hurled into the depths
like a stone cast into turbulent waters.[i]
12 By a pillar of cloud you led them by day,
and by a pillar of fire during the night,
to light the way ahead of them
along which they were to follow.[j]

13 "You came down on Mount Sinai
and spoke with them from heaven.
You gave them regulations and laws
that are just and right,
statutes and commandments that are good.[k]
14 You made known to them your holy sabbath,
and through your servant Moses
you gave them commandments, statutes, and laws.

15 "You gave them bread from heaven
to ease their hunger,
and you brought forth water from a rock
to quench their thirst.
You also told them to enter
and take possession of the land
which you had solemnly sworn to give them.[l]

16 "However, they and our ancestors acted with arrogance;
they stubbornly refused to obey your commandments.
17 They refused to obey you
and no longer recalled the miracles
you had wrought among them.
In their obstinacy they became stiff-necked
and came to a decision
to return to their slavery in Egypt.
But because you are a forgiving God,
gracious and compassionate,
Slow to anger and rich in mercy,
you did not forsake them.[m]

18 "Even when they had cast for themselves
a calf out of molten metal
and proclaimed: 'Here is your God
who brought you up from Egypt,'
and were guilty of gross blasphemies,

f Deut 6:4; 2 Ki 19:15; Ps 103:21.—g Gen 15:18-19; Jos 21:43-45.—h Ex 2:23-24; 14:10-12.—i Ex 14:21; 15:5, 10.—j Ex 13:21-22.—k Ex 19:11, 18-20; Ps 19:7-9.—l Ex 16:4; 17:6; Deut 1:8; Jos 1:2-4.—m Ex 34:6; Num 14:4.

19 you in your great compassion [n]
did not abandon them in the wilderness.
The pillar of cloud never failed
to lead them on their journey by night,
nor did the pillar of fire fail by night
to light the way ahead of them
by which they were to go.

20 "You bestowed your good spirit on them
to give them understanding.
Your manna you did not withhold from their mouths,
and you gave them water in their thirst. [o]
21 For forty years you sustained them;
they lacked nothing in the wilderness.
Their clothes did not become worn,
and their feet did not become swollen.

22 "You gave them kingdoms and peoples,
allotting to them even the most remote frontiers.
They took possession of the land of King Sihon of Heshbon
and the land of King Og of Bashan. [p]
23 You made their children as numerous
as the stars of the heavens,
and you brought them into the land
which you had commanded their fathers to enter and possess.

24 "The sons entered and took possession of the land,
and you subdued the Canaanite inhabitants
and delivered them into your power,
their kings as well as the peoples of the land,
to deal with them as they pleased.
25 They captured fortified towns and fertile land;
they took possession of houses
filled with all kinds of good things,
cisterns already dug, vineyards,
olive groves, and fruit trees in abundance.
They ate and had their fill, grew fat,
and found delight in your great goodness. [q]

26 "Nevertheless they grew disobedient,
rebelled against you,
and cast your law behind their backs.
They also killed your prophets
who bore witness against them
to bring them back to you,
while they committed great blasphemies. [r]
27 Therefore, you delivered them
into the power of their enemies
who caused them to suffer greatly.
But when they would cry out to you
in the midst of their oppression,
from heaven you heard them,
and in your great compassion
you would send them saviors
to deliver them from the clutches
of their oppressors.

28 "However, after some respite,
they would resume their evil deeds,
and so the LORD abandoned them to their enemies
who then became their rulers.
When once again they appealed to you,
you heard them from heaven,
and because of your compassion
you rescued them on many occasions.
29 You solemnly warned them
in order to bring them back to your law.
However, they became arrogant
and refused to obey your commandments,
and they sinned against your ordinances
whose observance would bring life
to those who keep them.
Rather they stubbornly turned aside,
and in their obstinacy they refused to obey. [s]

30 "You were patient with them for many years
and warned them by your spirit
through the prophets.
However, when they continued to refuse to listen,
you put them at the mercy
of the people of other lands.
31 Yet even so, because of your great compassion,
you did not completely destroy them,
nor did you forsake them,
for you are a gracious and merciful God. [t]

32 "Therefore, O our God,
you are great, mighty, and awesome,
maintaining the covenant and your faithful love.

---

n Ex 32:4-8.—o Deut 2:7; Isa 63:11-14.—p Num 21:21-35; Deut 2:26-36.—q Deut 3:5; 6:10-11.—r 2 Chr 36:16; Ezek 16:15-21; Wis 2:10-20.—s Lev 18:5; Zec 7:11.—t Neh 9:17; Jer 4:27.

Do not treat lightly,
as something of little account,
these hardships that have afflicted us,
our kings, our princes, our priests,
our prophets and all your people,
from the days of the kings of Assyria
until this very day. [u]
33 You have treated us with justice
in everything that has happened to us,
for you have remained faithful to us
even though we have done wrong in
your eyes. [v]
34 "Our kings, our princes, our priests,
and our ancestors
did not keep your law,
nor did they pay attention to your commandments
or heed the warnings you gave them.
35 Even while they were in their own kingdom,
despite the abundant goodness
that you bestowed upon them,
and despite the wide and fertile land
that you lavished upon them,
they did not serve you
or renounce their evil deeds.
36 "But see, here we are slaves today,
slaves in this land
that you gave to our ancestors
so that we might savor its fruits
and all the good things it produces. *
37 All its abundant yield
is given to the kings
whom you have set over us
because of our sins.
They also rule over our bodies
and do as they please with our cattle;
therefore we are in great distress."

CHAPTER 10

The Agreement of the People. 1 In view of all
this, we intend to make a firm agreement in
writing. On the sealed document will appear
the signatures of our princes, our Levites,
and our priests.

2 Those whose names were on the sealed
document were, first of all, Nehemiah, the
son of Hacaliah, and Zedekiah. 3 Seraiah,
Azariah, Jeremiah, 4 Pashhur, Amariah,
Malchijah, 5 Hattush, Shebaniah, Malluch,
6 Harim, Meremoth, Obadiah, 7 Daniel,
Ginnethon, Baruch, 8 Meshullam, Abijah,
Mijamin, 9 Maaziah, Bilgai, and Shemaiah:
these are the priests. [w]

10 The Levites were Jeshua, son of Azaniah,
Binnui, of the sons of Henadad, Kadmiel,
11 and their kinsmen Shebaniah, Hodiah,
Kelita, Pelaiah, Hanan, 12 Mica, Rehob,
Hashabiah, 13 Zaccur, Sherebiah, Shebaniah,
14 Hodiah, Bani, and Beninu.

15 The leaders of the people were Parosh,
Pahath-moab, Elam, Zattu, Bani, 16 Bunni,
Azgad, Bebai, 17 Adonijah, Bigvai, Adin,
18 Ater, Hezekiah, Azzur, 19 Hodiah, Hashum, Bezai, 20 Hariph, Anathoth, Nebai,
21 Magpiash, Meshullam, Hezir, 22 Meshezabel, Zadok, Jaddua, 23 Pelatiah, Hanan,
Anaiah, 24 Hoshea, Hananiah, Hasshub,
25 Hallohesh, Pilha, Shobek, 26 Rehum,
Hashabnah, Maaseiah, 27 Ahijah, Hanan,
Anan, 28 Malluch, Harim, Baanah.

29 The rest of the people, the priests, the
Levites, the gatekeepers, the singers, the
temple servants, and all the others who had
separated themselves from the neighboring
peoples of the lands to adhere to the law of
God—their wives, their sons, their daughters, all who are capable of understanding—
30 have now joined their brothers, the nobles,
and with a solemn oath have sworn to follow
the law of God which was given through
Moses, the servant of God, and to observe
and obey all the commandments, the rules,
and the statutes of the LORD, our Lord.

31 We have agreed that we will not give our
daughters in marriage to the peoples of the
land or take their daughters for our sons. * [x]
32 Moreover, if the people of the country
bring any merchandise or grain to sell on the
sabbath day, we will not purchase it from
them on the sabbath or on a holy day. Also,
we will forego the crops of the seventh year
and cancel the debts of every person. [y]

33 We willingly assume these following
obligations for ourselves: we will give one-third of a shekel yearly for the service of the
house of our God: 34 for the loaves, for the
showbread, for the daily cereal offering, for
the daily holocaust, for the sacrifices on Sabbaths, new moons, and festivals, for the holy

u Isa 7:17-18; Lam 5.—v Jer 12:1; Dan 3:27; 9:14.—w Neh 7:43; 9:4.—x Deut 7:3; Ezr 9:1-3; 10:10-12.—y Neh 5:1-13; Ex 20:8; Lev 25:1-7.

9:36 The Israelites reoccupied the land that God had provided for them, but were still required to return part of their resources to a foreign king.

10:31 The topic of intermarriage is one of great importance for the Israelites' survival and strength. Every time the Israelites married foreigners, they got caught up in idolatrous practices, and hence, they suffered both personally and politically.

offerings, for sin offerings to make expiation
on behalf of Israel, and for all the duties of
the house of our God.

35 We have also cast lots among the priests,
the Levites, and the people for the wood
offering, so that it will be brought into the
house of our God by each family in turn, at
appointed times each year, to be burned on
the altar of the LORD, our God, as prescribed
in the law. 36 Furthermore, we pledge to
bring the firstfruits of our crops and of our
fruit trees.[z]

37 Also, as it is prescribed in the law, we will
bring to the house of our God, to the priests
who minister in the house of our God, the
firstborn of our children and of our animals,
including the firstborn of our flocks and
herds. 38 We will also bring the first batch of
our dough and our offerings of the fruit of
every tree, the wine, and the oil to the priests,
to the chambers of the house of our God, as
well as the tithes from our soil to the Levites,
for it is the Levites who collect the tithes in
all of our rural farming villages.[a]

39 An Aaronite priest must accompany the
Levites when they collect the tithes, and the
Levites are to bring one-tenth of the tithes to
the house of our God, to the storerooms of
the treasury.* 40 For the Israelites and the
Levites must bring the offerings of grain,
wine, and oil to the storerooms of the trea-
sury where the vessels of the sanctuary are
kept and where the ministering priests, the
gatekeepers, and the singers are lodged.
Under no circumstances shall we neglect the
house of our God.

CHAPTER 11

Repeopling of Jerusalem. 1 * The leaders of
the people took up residence in Jerusalem.
Therefore, the rest of the people cast lots.
One man out of ten was to reside in
Jerusalem, the holy city, while the other nine
were to remain in the surrounding towns.[b]
2 The people commended all those who will-
ingly agreed to live in Jerusalem.

The Residents in Jerusalem. 3 These are the
leaders of the province who lived in
Jerusalem. However, in the towns of Judah
all the others lived on their own property:
Israelites, priests, Levites, temple servants,
and the descendants of Solomon's servants.[c]

4 In Jerusalem there dwelt both the sons of
Judah and the sons of Benjamin. These were
the Judahites: Athaiah, the son of Uzziah,
son of Zechariah, son of Amariah, son of
Shephatiah, son of Mehallalel, of the descen-
dants of Perez; 5 Maaseiah, the son of
Baruch, son of Col-hozeh, son of Hazaiah,
son of Adaiah, son of Joiarib, son of
Zechariah, a descendent of Shelah. 6 The
total number of the sons of Perez who dwelt
in Jerusalem was four hundred and sixty-
eight valiant warriors.

7 These were the Benjaminites: Sallu, the
son of Meshullam, son of Joed, son of
Pedaiah, son of Kolaiah, son of Maaseiah,
son of Ithiel, son of Jeshaiah, 8 and his broth-
ers Gabbai and Sallai: nine hundred and
twenty-eight in number. 9 Joel, the son of
Zichri, was their chief, and Judah, the son of
Hassenuah, was second in charge of the city.

10 Among the priests were: Jedaiah, the
son of Joiarib, Jachin, 11 Seraiah, the son of
Hilkiah, son of Meshullam, son of Zadok,
son of Meraioth, son of Ahitub, supervisor of
the house of God, 12 and their kinsmen who
were responsible for the work in the temple:
eight hundred and twenty-two; Adaiah, the
son of Jeroham, son of Pelaliah, son of Amzi,
son of Zechariah, son of Pashhur, son of
Malchijah, 13 and his brethren, heads of fam-
ilies: two hundred and forty-two; Amashai,
the son of Azarel, son of Ahzai, son of
Meshillemoth, son of Immer, 14 and his
brethren, valiant warriors: one hundred and
twenty-eight. Their overseer was Zabdiel,
the son of Haggedolim.

15 Among the Levites were: Shemaiah, the
son of Hasshub, son of Azrikam, son of
Hashabiah, son of Bunni; 16 Shabbethai and
Jozabad, the Levitical leaders who were
responsible for the outside work of the house
of God; 17 Mattaniah, the son of Mica, son
of Zabdi, son of Asaph, director of the
psalms who led the prayer of thanksgiving,
and Bakbukiah, who ranked second among
his associates; finally, Abda, the son of
Shammua, son of Galal, son of Jeduthun.
18 The total number of the Levites in the holy
city was two hundred and eighty-four.

19 The gatekeepers were Akkub, Talmon,
and their associates, who kept watch at the

z Ex 13:1, 11-16; Deut 26:1-2.—a Lev 27:30; Num 18:21-32.—b Neh 7:4; 11:18.—c 1 Chr 9:2-34; Ezr 2:43-57.

10:39 The sum taken by the priests from the tithes to the Levites (see Num 18:25-28).

11:1-2 *One man out of ten:* not enough of the exiles willingly returned to Jerusalem; there were others who moved inside the city walls involuntarily by lottery.

gates. They numbered one hundred and seventy-two.[d]

[20] The rest of the Israelites, including the priests and the Levites, lived in all the other cities of Judah, each man on his inherited property. [21] However, the temple slaves lived on Ophel. Ziha and Gishpa were in charge of them.

[22] The chief officer of the Levites in Jerusalem was Uzzi, the son of Bani, son of Hashabiah, son of Mattaniah, son of Mica, of the descendants of Asaph, the singers appointed to the service of the house of God.[e] [23] For they were under the king's orders, and it was obligatory for them to fulfill those orders which regulated their daily activity. [24] Also, Pethahiah, the son of Meshezabel, a descendant of Zerah, the son of Judah, was the king's chief advisor in all matters that affected the people.

The Other Cities. [25] As for the villages with their surrounding fields, some of the people of Judah lived in Kiriath-arba and its villages, and Dibon and its villages, and Jekabzeel and its villages, [26] and in Jeshua, and in Moladah, and in Beth-pelet, [27] in Hazar-shual, and in Beer-sheba and its villages, [28] in Ziklag, in Meconah and its villages, [29] in En-rimmon, in Zorah, in Jarmuth, [30] in Zanoah and Adullam and their villages, Lachish and its fields, and Azekah and its villages. Thus they settled from Beer-sheba to the Valley of Hinnom.

[31] Some of the Benjaminites also lived in Geba, Michmash, Aija, Bethel with its villages, [32] Anathoth, Nob, Ananiah, [33] Hazor, Ramah, Gittaim, [34] Hadid, Zeboim, Neballat, [35] Lod, Ono, and the Valley of Artisans.

[36] Also, some divisions of the Levites in Judah settled in Benjamin.

CHAPTER 12

Priests and Levites under Zerubbabel. [1] These are the priests and the Levites who returned with Zerubbabel, the son of Shealtiel, and with Jeshua: Seraiah, Jeremiah, Ezra, [2] Amariah, Malluch, Hattush, [3] Shecaniah, Rehum, Meremoth, [4] Iddo, Ginnethon, Abijah, [5] Mijamin, Maadiah, Bilgah, [6] Shemaiah, Joiarib, Jedaiah, [7] Sallu, Amok, Hilkiah, and Jedaiah. These were the priestly heads and their brethren in the days of Jeshua.

[8] The Levites were Jeshua, Binnui, Kadmiel, Sherebiah, Judah, and Mattaniah, who with his brethren was in charge of the songs of thanksgiving. [9] Bakbukiah and Unno, their colleagues, stood opposite them during the service.

High Priests. [10] Jeshua was the father of Joiakim, Joiakim was the father of Eliashib, Eliashib was the father of Joiada, [11] Joiada was the father of Jonathan, and Jonathan was the father of Jaddua.

Priests and Levites under Joiakim. [12] In the days of Joiakim, these were the priests who were the heads of families: the family of Seraiah, Meraiah; of Jeremiah, Hananiah;[f] [13] of Ezra, Meshullam; of Amariah, Jehohanan; [14] of Malluch, Jonathan; of Shebaniah, Joseph; [15] of Harim, Adna; of Meremoth, Helkai; [16] of Iddo, Zechariah; of Ginnethon, Meshullam; [17] of Abijah, Zichri; of Miniamin and, of Moadiah, Piltai; [18] of Bilgah, Shammua; of Shemaiah, Jehonathan; [19] of Joiarib, Mattenai; of Jedaiah, Uzzi; [20] of Sallu, Kallai; of Amok, Eber; [21] of Hilkiah, Hashabiah; of Jedaiah, Nethanel.

[22] In the time of Eliashib, Joiada, Johanan, and Jaddua, the heads of the families of priests were registered in the Book of Chronicles, up to the reign of Darius the Persian. [23] The Levites, the heads of the ancestral houses, were registered in the Book of Chronicles, * up until the time of Johanan, the son of Eliashib.[g]

[24] The heads of the Levites were Hashabiah, Sherebiah, Jeshua, Binnui, Kadmiel, and their associates, while their brothers formed an alternate choir opposite them in fulfillment of the command of David, the man of God. [25] The alternate choir was composed of Mattaniah, Bakbukiah, and Obadiah. Meshullam, Talmon, and Akkub were the gatekeepers who guarded the storehouses at the gates. [26] All those mentioned above lived in the time of Joiakim, the son of Jeshua, son of Jozadak, as well as in the days of Nehemiah the governor and of Ezra the priest-scribe.

Dedication of the City Wall. [27] At the dedication of the wall of Jerusalem, the Levites were sought out wherever they had settled and were brought to Jerusalem to celebrate the dedication with joyful hymns of thanks-

d 2 Chr 27:3; 33:14.—e 2 Chr 20:14.—f Neh 10:3-9.—g Jos 10:13; 1 Chr 29:29.

12:23 *Chronicles:* the reference is not to the biblical book of this name.

giving and with songs to the accompani-
ment of cymbals, lyres, and harps.
28 The levitical singers were also assem-
bled from the region around Jerusalem,
from the villages of the Netophathites,
29 from Beth-gilgal and from the region of
Geba and Azmaveth, for the singers had
built for themselves settlements around
Jerusalem. 30 When the priests and the
Levites had purified themselves, they puri-
fied the people, the gates, and the wall.
31 I then commanded the leaders of Judah
to assemble on the top of the wall, and I
appointed two large choirs to give thanks.
The first of these went in procession to the
right along the top of the wall, toward the
Dung Gate. 32 Bringing up the rear were
Hoshaiah and half the leading men of Judah,
33 along with Azariah, Ezra, Meshullam,
34 Judah, Benjamin, Shemaiah, and Jere-
miah, 35 as well as some of the priests with
trumpets, and also Zechariah, the son of
Jonathan, son of Shemaiah, son of Mat-
taniah, son of Micaiah, son of Zaccur, son of
Asaph, 36 with his kinsmen Shemaiah,
Azarel, Milalai, Gilalai, Maai, Nethanel,
Judah, and Hanani, with the musical instru-
ments of David, the man of God. The scribe
Ezra walked at their head.
37 They walked past the Fountain Gate
and went straight up by the steps of the City
of David and continued along the top of the
wall, above the palace of David, as far as the
Water Gate on the east.
38 The second choir made its way to the
left. I and half of the leaders of the people
followed them along the top of the wall from
the Tower of the Ovens to the Broad Wall,
39 and past the Ephraim Gate, and over the
Old Gate, and by the Fish Gate and
the Tower of Hananel, and the Tower of the
Hundred to the Sheep Gate. Finally, they
came to a halt at the Prison Gate. [h]
40 Then the two choirs took their places in
the house of God. However, I had half of the
magistrates with me, 41 as well as the priests
Eliakim, Maaseiah, Minjamin, Micaiah,
Elioenai, Zechariah, and Hananiah with the
trumpets, 42 and Maaseiah, Shemaiah,
Eleazar, Uzzi, Jehohanan, Malchijah, Elam,
and Ezer. The singers sang loudly under the
direction of Jezrahiah.
43 There were great sacrifices offered on
that day, and the people rejoiced because
God had given them great joy. The women
and children rejoiced along with them, and
the joy of Jerusalem could be heard from a
great distance away.

Offerings for Priests and Levites.* 44 On that
occasion men were appointed to take charge
of the chambers that had been set aside for
the storerooms, the contributions, the first-
fruits, and the tithes, and to collect in them
those portions required by the law for the
priests and the Levites from the fields
belonging to them. For all Judah rejoiced in
its officiating priests and Levites, [i] 45 since
they, along with the singers and gatekeepers,
performed the service of their God and the
service of purification, as ordained accord-
ing to the rules laid down by David and his
son Solomon.
46 For since ancient times, from the days
of David and Asaph long ago, there had been
leaders for the singers and for the songs of
praise and thanksgiving to God. [j] 47 There-
fore, in the days of Zerubbabel and Nehe-
miah, all Israel regularly supplied the daily
portions for the singers and the gatekeepers
according to their daily needs. They present-
ed the consecrated contributions to the
Levites, and the Levites set apart the dedi-
cated portions to the sons of Aaron. [k]

CHAPTER 13*

Separation from Aliens. 1 On that day they
were reading aloud to the people from the
Book of Moses, and there it was found writ-
ten: "No Ammonite or Moabite should ever
be allowed to enter the assembly of God, [l]
2 since they had not come to welcome the
Israelites with food and water, but they
rather hired Balaam to curse them, even
though our God turned the curse into a
blessing." 3 When the people heard the law,
they excluded from Israel all those of foreign
descent. [m]

h 2 Ki 14:13; Jer 31:38.—i Lev 7:29-34; 1 Chr 23–24; 2 Chr 8:14.—j 1 Chr 25:1-7; 2 Chr 29:30.—k Num 18:21-29.—l Neh 13:23; Deut 23:3-5.—m Ezr 10:11.

12:44-47 In the view of the Chronicler, the acknowledged royal officials, Zerubbabel and Nehemiah, are the pioneers of a time of perfection in which the rights and dignity of the Levites are respected and the law is strictly observed. The author once again emphasizes the role of the Levites against the overly ex-clusive claims of the priests, who were more favorable to the Samaritans, though the latter had meanwhile become schismatics.

13:1-31 After Nehemiah had returned to his post at the court of Persia, many abuses crept into the Jewish community. He returns for the express purpose of repressing these abuses.

Reform in the Temple. 4 However, before
this, the priest Eliashib, * who had been
appointed to be in charge of the chambers of
the house of our God and who was a close
associate of Tobiah, 5 had provided for
Tobiah a large room in which previously had
been stored the grain offerings, the incense,
the temple vessels, the tithes of grain, wine,
and oil prescribed for the Levites, singers,
and gatekeepers, and the contributions for
the priests.

6 All this took place when I was away from
Jerusalem, for in the thirty-second year of
King Artaxerxes of Babylon, I had gone to
consult the king. Sometime later, however, I
asked the king for permission to leave, 7 and
after I returned to Jerusalem, I learned
about the evil thing that Eliashib had done
on behalf of Tobiah in providing him with a
room in the courts of the house of God.

8 I was extremely displeased, and in retal-
iation I threw all of Tobiah's household
goods out of the room. 9 After that, I gave
orders for the room to be purified, and also
commanded that the utensils of the house of
God be replaced, along with the grain offer-
ing and the frankincense.

10 In addition I discovered that the Levites
had not been receiving the portions that had
been assigned to them. As a result of this, the
Levites and the singers who had been con-
ducting the services had all withdrawn to
their farms. * 11 Then I remonstrated with
the magistrates, demanding: "Why has the
house of God been neglected?" After that, I
summoned back the Levites and once again
stationed them at their posts.

12 Then all Judah once again brought the
tithes of grain, wine, and oil to the store-
houses. 13 As supervisors of the storehouses
I appointed Shelemiah the priest, Zadok the
scribe, and Pedaiah, one of the Levites, and,
as their assistant, Hanan, the son of Zaccur,
son of Mattaniah, since they were regarded
as faithful, and their duty was to make the
distributions to their kinsmen.

14 Remember me for this, O my God, and
do not blot out from your memory the good
deeds that I have done for the house of my
God and its observances.

Sabbath Observances. 15 In those days I
observed men in Judah treading winepresses
on the Sabbath, and also bringing in sacks
of grain and loading them on their donkeys,
together with wine, grapes, figs, and every
other kind of merchandise into Jerusalem
on the Sabbath. I warned them not to sell
food on that day. [n] 16 In addition, Tyrians
who resided in Jerusalem were also bring-
ing in fish and every other kind of mer-
chandise and selling it to the Judahites on
the Sabbath.

17 Therefore, I rebuked the nobles of
Judah, saying to them: "What is this evil
thing you are doing in profaning the Sab-
bath? 18 Is not this exactly what your ances-
tors did, with the result that our God has
brought all this misery down upon us and
upon this city? And now you are adding to
the wrath that is befalling Israel by profan-
ing the Sabbath."

19 When the evening shadows were falling
on the gates of Jerusalem before the
Sabbath, I gave orders for the doors to be
shut, and I further directed that they were
not to be opened again until the Sabbath
was over. Furthermore, I stationed some of
my attendants at the gate to ensure that no
merchandise would be brought in on the
Sabbath day. *

20 On one or two occasions the merchants
and dealers in goods of all kinds spent the
night outside Jerusalem, 21 until I warned
them, saying: "Why are you spending the
night in front of the city wall? If you ever do
so again, I will not hesitate to lay hands on
you." From that time on, they did not return
on the Sabbath. 22 Then I ordered the
Levites to purify themselves and to act as
guards at the gates, in order that the
Sabbath day would be kept holy.

Remember this also in my favor, O my
God, and have mercy on me in accordance
with your great love and mercy. [o]

Mixed Marriages. 23 In those days also I saw
Jews who had married women from
Ashdod, Ammon, and Moab. [p] 24 Half of
their children spoke the language of Ashdod
or the language of one of the other peoples,
but none of them could speak the language
of the Jews.

25 Thereupon I reprimanded them and I
cursed them, beat some of them and pulled

n Neh 10:32; Ex 20:8-11.—o 1 Chr 15:12.—p Neh 10:31; 13:1-3; Ezr 9–10.

13:4 *Eliashib:* an enemy of Nehemiah (see 6:1).

13:10 Among the abuses that Nehemiah encountered was the failure of the people to support the priests, who had to suspend worship in order to support themselves by farming.

13:19 The Sabbath begins at dusk of the preceding day.

out their hair, and I made them swear in the
name of God: "You are not to give your
daughters in marriage to their sons or to
take away any of their daughters in marriage for your sons or for yourselves.
[26] "Did not King Solomon of Israel sin
because of such women? Among all the
nations there was no king like him. He was
loved by his God, and God made him king
over all Israel. Yet even he was led into sin*
by foreign women. [q] [27] Must we now hear
that you have committed this very grave
offense, breaking faith with our God by marrying foreign women?"
[28] One of the sons of Jehoiada, the son of
the high priest Eliashib, was the son-in-law
of Sanballat the Horonite. I drove him from
my presence.
[29] Remember them, O my God, because
they have defiled the priesthood and the
covenant of the priests and the Levites.
[30] Thus I cleansed them from everything
foreign, and I drew up the regulations for the
priests and the Levites, defining the duties of
their office. [31] I also provided for the deliver-
ies of wood at specific times and for the first-
fruits.

Remember this in my favor, O my God. [r]

q 1 Ki 11:1-8.—r Neh 10:35.

13:26 *Led into sin:* by using the legendary King Solomon as an example of the perils of marrying an unbeliever, Nehemiah reinforced his warning against intermarriage.

NARRATIVES OF HOPE

TOBIT, JUDITH, ESTHER

Times of great stress frequently give rise to the secret circulation of writings that announce the hope of the oppressed as well as the defeat of the oppressors and encourage religious, national, or ethnic fidelity. They present themselves as historical accounts, but upon reading them, one quickly realizes that the context is fictitious and the events are imaginary. Under the appearance of a page of history, a lesson for the present is proposed.

The three Books that follow—Tobit, Judith, Esther—belong to this category of writings: they simulate an account of the past in order to interpret the present. They are born in a moment when Israel feels threatened in its faith, vocation, and prayer-life by the hostility of a pagan world. In the wake of the Exile, Israel becomes ever more aware that the unity of the people will result not from a unique homeland but from a unique faith and a unique hope.

In the case of Tobit and Judith, we cannot arrive at the original Hebrew; while in the case of Esther, the Hebrew text is shorter than the Greek translation. And only Esther has become a part of the Bible of the Hebrews.

The Christian Church, which in its turn has experienced dispersion and persecution, has recognized the authentic inspiration not only of Tobit and Judith but also of the additions that are part of the Greek version of Esther.

The Protestant Churches, which returned to the Hebrew Bible, recognize only the shorter text of Esther.

THE BOOK OF TOBIT

The Mirror of the Hebrew Family

The Book of Tobit was composed in the third or second century B.C. with the purpose of preserving the traditional faith for the Jews who remained outside Palestine even after the return of many of them from the Exile. Centered around an Israelite deported to Nineveh by Shalmaneser (we are therefore in the eighth century), the account mentions a few captivating personages and, in particular, the son of one.

From the very beginning we know that the life of the protagonist of the account is exemplary; he is a faithful Jew who observes the law of Moses, and God rewards him for this absolute fidelity.

Despite appearances, the work does not narrate a real history. It was composed very artfully and imaginatively to edify the readers. We quickly become aware that the author is taking liberties with facts.

If we took the account literally, Tobit would have lived at least two centuries, and his son would have had to walk 180 miles in two days. This point, however, is of little import. The author, a sage, is concerned above all to paint the life of a just man for his readers. With this concrete illustration, he wishes to show that true wisdom, the way that leads to fidelity, consists in loving God and observing his commandments no matter what may occur. Herein lies the key to this Book.

The writer is able to instruct without annoying. His sense of the picturesque and his acuteness of observation contribute to make his work a literary jewel. It enchants us by evoking the family traditions of Israel; and long before the Gospel, it celebrates the nobility that characterizes marriage from the very beginnings: one husband and one wife.

According to the author, the just receive their recompense on earth; Christ had not yet come to illumine the complete dimension of human destiny. But to discover Providence in daily life and to overcome sorrowful situations by means of faith—as this Book invites us to do—are elements that form part of Christian existence.

The Bible has given us many pages about the covenant and about the requirements for the life of the people. It is touching to find, in an account closer to daily life, praise for the fidelity that is lived in the framework of family life, the meaning of almsgiving, respect for the dead, concern for purity, and the love of prayer.

The Latin text of the Vulgate, translated from the Hebrew and Aramaic by St. Jerome, has various differences and additions with respect to the text followed here, which is that of the Greek translation. Fragments of the original have been found in the Dead Sea Scrolls.

The Book of Tobit may be divided as follows:

- *I: The Suffering of the Righteous (1:3—3:17)*
  - *A: Tobit, a Righteous Man Put to the Test (1:3—3:6)*
  - *B: Sarah: Innocence Diabolically Offended (3:7-17)*
- *II: The Righteous Are Rewarded (4:1—12:22)*
  - *A: Tobit's Testament (4:1-21)*
  - *B: Tobiah's Journey (5:1—10:7)*
  - *C: The Return of Tobiah (10:8—12:22)*
- *III: Vision of the New Times (13:1—14:15)*
  - *A: The Canticle of Tobit (13:1-18)*
  - *B: Tobit's Prophecy (14:1-12a)*
  - *C: The Last Days of Tobiah (14:12b-15)*

CHAPTER 1

A Man Called Tobit. 1 This book relates the story of Tobit,* son of Tobiel, son of Hananiel, son of Aduel, son of Gabael of the family of Asiel, of the tribe of Naphtali. 2 During the reign of Shalmaneser,* king of Assyria, Tobit was taken into captivity from Thisbe, which is south of Kedesh Naphtali in Upper Galilee, above Hazor and some distance to the west of Asher, north of Phogor.[a]

I: THE SUFFERING OF THE RIGHTEOUS*

A: Tobit, a Righteous Man Put to the Test

A Model Israelite. 3 I, Tobit, have traveled along the paths of truth and righteousness throughout all the days of my life. I carried out many charitable deeds for my kindred and for those of my people who had been sent into exile with me to Nineveh in the country of the Assyrians. 4 While I was still a youth in my own country, the land of Israel, the whole tribe of my ancestor Naphtali had forsaken the house of David and Jerusalem, even though this city had been designated out of all the tribes of Israel, so that all those tribes might offer their sacrifices in the place where the temple, the dwelling place of God, had been constructed and consecrated for the enduring use of all future generations. 5 All my kindred and the entire house of my ancestor Naphtali used to offer sacrifice on all the mountains of Galilee to the calf that Jeroboam, king of Israel, had erected in Dan.[b]

6 I alone would frequently make the pilgrimage to Jerusalem for the festivals, in accordance with the everlasting decree prescribed for all Israel. I would hasten to Jerusalem with the firstfruits of the fields and the firstborn of the flocks, the tithes of the cattle, and the first shearings of the sheep.[c] 7 I would present these to the priests, the sons of Aaron, at the altar. To the Levites who were ministering at Jerusalem I would likewise give the tithes of grain, wine, olive oil, pomegranates, figs, and other fruits. In addition, for six consecutive years I would prepare a second tithe in money and bring it each year to disburse in Jerusalem.[d]

8 A third tithe I would distribute among orphans and widows as well as among the converts who were dwelling among the Israelites. Every third year when I brought this third tithe, we would consume it together in accordance with the decree prescribed in the law of Moses and with the commands of Deborah, the mother of my father Tobiel; for when my father died, I was left an orphan.

9 When I achieved manhood, I married a woman named Anna, who was of our own lineage, and she bore me a son whom I named Tobiah.

Tobit Deported and Persecuted. 10 * After the Exile to Assyria, I came to Nineveh as a captive. All the members of my kindred and of my people ate the food of pagans,[e] 11 but I conscientiously avoided doing so. 12 And because I remained faithful to God with my whole heart, 13 the Most High gave me favor and good standing with Shalmaneser, and I was entrusted with the task of purchasing everything he needed.[f] 14 Until his death I used to travel to Media to buy supplies for him there, and I deposited pouches of money worth ten talents in the care of my kinsman Gabael, son of Gabri, who lived at Rages, in Media. 15 However, when Shalmaneser died and his son Sennacherib* succeeded him as king, the roads into Media became dangerous, and so I could no longer travel there.

Courage in Burying the Dead. 16 During the reign of Shalmaneser I carried out many charitable deeds for my kindred and my people. 17 I would give my bread to the hungry and my clothing to those in need, and if I saw one of my people who died and had been cast outside the walls of Nineveh, I

a 2 Ki 17:3; 18:9ff.—b 1 Ki 12:26-32.—c Ex 23:14-17; 34:23; Deut 16:16.—d Num 18:12f, 24; Deut 14:22-29; 18:4f.—e Lev 11; Deut 14:3-21; Acts 15:29; 1 Cor 8:7ff.—f Dan 2:48f.

1:1 Note that though the account begins in the third person, from 1:3—3:6 it uses the first person. *Tobit* is short for *Tobiahu,* "God is my good."

1:2 *Shalmaneser* V (727–722 B.C.) was the Assyrian king who began the siege of Samaria, but it was Sargon II (722–705 B.C.) who captured it and took its inhabitants into exile.

1:3—3:17 Two sequences are juxtaposed. In two different places, two Israelites, two relatives, whose fidelity cannot be placed into doubt, are led to touch the depth of suffering. Even the Old Testament is aware, above all after the Exile, that suffering lies on the path of those who wish to serve God.

1:10-22 Without any concern for chronology, the author mixes up reigns. He wishes to stress that Tobit remains faithful in spite of any trials; he is an example offered for our meditation. The end of the passage relates to literature: Ahiqar, who is here characterized as a Hebrew and a cousin of Tobit, is the protagonist of the *Book* (or *Wisdom*) *of Ahiqar*, of Assyrian origin, preserved in various redactions and translations, which portrays him as conspicuous for wisdom and probity (see Tob 2:10; 11:18; 14:10; Jud 5:5).

1:15 *Sennacherib* (705–681 B.C.) was the son of Sargon (722–705 B.C.), but neither one was descended from Shalmaneser.

would bury that person.[g] 18 I also buried
those who were put to death by Sennacherib
when he fled from Judea during those days
of judgment that the king of heaven decreed
against him because of his blasphemies. In
his anger he slew many Israelites; but I
would steal their bodies and bury them, so
that Sennacherib would look for them in
vain. 19 But a certain citizen of Nineveh told
the king that I was the one who was burying
them in secret. When I learned that the king
was aware of what I was doing and that he
wanted to put me to death, I was overcome
with fear and fled. 20 Everything that I pos-
sessed was seized and confiscated for the
royal treasury. Nothing was left to me except
for my wife Anna and my son Tobiah.

21 However, less than forty days later the
king was murdered by two of his sons, who
then fled to the mountains of Ararat. His son
Esarhaddon, who succeeded him as king,
appointed Ahiqar, the son of my brother
Anael, to be in charge of all the revenues of
the kingdom, with control of the entire
administration.* [h] 22 Then Ahiqar took up
my cause, and I was allowed to return to
Nineveh. Ahiqar had been chief cupbearer,
keeper of the seal, administrator, and trea-
surer under Sennacherib, king of Assyria,
and so Esarhaddon had reappointed him.
He was a relative of mine—my nephew.[i]

CHAPTER 2

His Neighbors Deride Tobit's Generosity.

1 During the reign of Esarhaddon, therefore,
I returned home, and my wife Anna and my
son Tobiah were restored to me. At our festi-
val of Pentecost, the Feast of Weeks, an
excellent dinner was prepared for me, and I
reclined to eat.[j] 2 The table was set for me,
and an abundance of food was placed before
me. I said to my son Tobiah, "Go out, my
child, and find some poor man among our
people exiled here in Nineveh. If he is whole-
heartedly devoted to God, bring him back
with you to share my meal. I will wait for
you, my son, until you return."

3 And so Tobiah went out to search for
some poor person of our people. When he
returned, he said, "Father!" I replied, "What
is it, my son?" "Father," he answered, "one of
our people has been murdered and thrown
into the marketplace, and he is still lying
there strangled." 4 I sprang up at once, leav-
ing my dinner without having even tasted it;
and I removed the body from the market-
place and put it in one of the rooms until
sunset when I would be able to bury it.
5 When I returned, I bathed myself and ate
my dinner in sorrow,[k] 6 recalling the words
pronounced by the prophet Amos against
Bethel:

> "I will turn your religious feasts into
> mourning,
> and all your singing into weeping."[l]

7 And I wept. When the sun had set, I went
out, dug a grave, and buried him. 8 My
neighbors jeered at me, saying, "Is he still
unafraid? Once previously he had been
hunted down under the penalty of death for
this identical offense; yet here he is, after his
escape, once again burying the dead."

In the Heat of the Trial. 9 That same night,
after bathing, I went into the courtyard and
lay down to sleep by the courtyard wall, with
my face uncovered because of the heat. 10 * I
was not aware that sparrows were poised on
the wall above me. Their warm droppings fell
into my eyes, causing white patches to form,
and I had to go to the doctors for a cure. But
the more they treated my eyes with their
ointment, the more my vision was impaired
by the white patches, until at last I became
completely blind. For four years I remained
sightless. All my kindred grieved at my situa-
tion, and Ahiqar took care of me for two
years, until he departed for Elymais.* [m]

11 At that time my wife Anna used to earn
money by working in her rooms for pay-
ment, spinning wool and weaving cloth.

g Job 31:16-20.—h 2 Ki 19:37; 2 Chr 32:21; Sir 48:21; Isa 37:38; 2 Mac 8:19.—i Tob 11:18; 14:10.—j Ex 23:14; Lev 23:15-21; Num 28:26-31; Deut 16:9-12.—k Num 19:11-22.—l Am 8:10.—m Tob 11:18; 14:10.

1:21 The *Book of Ahiqar* speaks of him as a principal official of Sennacherib and Esarhaddon whom his ungrateful nephew caused to be condemned to death (see Tob 11:18; 14:10); but Ahiqar hid himself, regained his prominence, and punished his nephew.

2:10 *Elymais* was the Greek name for Elam, which lay between Persia and Babylonia.

2:10a At this point the Vulgate has an additional seven verses that begin as follows: "12 The Lord permitted that [Tobit] should undergo this trial so that his patience might be an example to his posterity, like the patience of holy Job. 13 For although he had always feared God from his infancy, and kept his commandments, he did not complain against God because the evil of blindness had befallen him. 14 Rather, he continued immovable in the fear of God, giving thanks to God all the days of his life. 15 For as the kings [i.e., fellow chieftains] taunted holy Job, so his relations and kindred mocked at Tobit's life, saying: 16 'Where is your hope, for which you gave alms and buried the dead?' 17 But Tobit rebuked them, saying, 'Do not speak this way; 18 for we are children of saints and we await that life that God will give to those who never lack faith in him.' "

12 When she delivered what she had made to
those who had ordered the work, they would
pay her. On the seventh day of the month
Dystros,* she completed a particular job of
weaving and delivered it to her employers.
They not only paid her the agreed-upon
wages in full but also gave her a young goat
for a meal. 13 When the goat entered my
house, it began to bleat. I called to my wife
and asked, "Where did you get this goat?
Perhaps it was stolen. Return it to its own-
ers. We have no right to eat anything stolen."
14 But she reassured me, "It was given to
me as a bonus in addition to my wages."
However, I did not believe her, and I insisted
that she return it to its owners. I became
very angry over this. She replied, "Where is
your almsgiving? Where are your good
deeds? Everyone can now see the kind of
person you really are!" [n]

CHAPTER 3

Tobit's Prayer. 1 With deep distress I
groaned and wept aloud. Then, sobbing, I
began to pray:

2 "You are just, O Lord,
and all your deeds are just.
All your ways are merciful and true;
you are the judge of the world. [o]
3 And now, O Lord, be mindful of me
and look upon me with favor.
Do not punish me for my sins
or for my unthinking offenses
or those of my ancestors. [p]

"They sinned against you
4 and did not obey your commandments.
Therefore, you have subjected us to pillage, captivity, and death,
to become the talk, the laughingstock, and the object of scorn,
of all the nations among which you have dispersed us. [q]

5 "And your many judgments are true
when you deal with me as my sins deserve
and those of my ancestors.
For we have not kept your commandments,
nor have we walked in truth in your sight.

6 "So now, deal with me as you wish;
command that my life be taken away from me
so that I may be removed from the face of the earth and once again become dust.
For it is better for me to die than to live,
because I have endured undeserved insults,
and I am engulfed in the deepest grief.

"Command, O Lord, that I be delivered from this affliction;
receive me into the eternal abode,*
and do not, O Lord, turn your face from me.
For it is better for me to die
than to endure a life of such unrelieved misery
and to be subjected to these insults." [r]

B: Sarah: Innocence Diabolically Offended*

Sarah's Misfortune. 7 * On the same day, at
Ecbatana in Media, it also happened that
Sarah, the daughter of Raguel,* had to
endure the insults of one of her father's
maids. 8 For she had been married to seven
husbands, but the wicked demon Asmodeus
had slain each of them before the marriage
had been consummated as is customary.
The servant girl said to her, "You are the one
who has slain your husbands! Behold, you
have already been given in marriage seven
times, but you have experienced no joy with
any of your husbands. 9 Just because your
husbands are dead is no reason to abuse us.

---

n Job 2:9.—o Pss 25:10; 119:137; Dan 3:27.—p Ex 34:6f.—q Deut 28:15; Bar 1:16-22; 2:4f; 3:8; Dan 9:5f.—r Num 11:15; 1 Ki 19:4; Job 7:15; Jon 4:3, 8.

2:12 The Macedonian month of *Dystros* corresponded to the Jewish month of Shebat (January–February). *For a meal:* literally, "for the hearth." The gift may have been given at the time of some feast in the spring like the Jewish Feast of Purim.

3:6 The author has Tobit use the words of Jonah who wanted to die because God had not destroyed the hated Ninevites (Jon 4:3, 8). In comparable circumstances, Moses (Num 11:15), Elijah (1 Ki 19:4), and Job (Job 7:15) also prayed for death. *Eternal abode:* a reference to Hades, the abode of the dead from which no one returns (Job 7:9-10; 14:12; Isa 26:14). The fuller revelation of a blessed immortality in the Book of Wisdom was still to come.

3:7-17 The story of Tobit is brusquely interrupted. In a second sequence, the author introduces a new and unexpected personage.

3:7-10 In the ancient East, sicknesses and sometimes even death were attributed to the wickedness of a demon, here called Asmodeus, "the destroyer" (even though he is not related to Asmadaeva, the worst demon of Avesta, the sacred book of the Persians).

3:7 *Raguel:* cousin of Tobit (see Tob 7:2). *Ecbatana* was the capital of the middle kingdom (the contemporary Hamadan in Iran).

Join them, and may we never live to see any son or daughter of yours!"

10 On that day, deeply distressed, she went in tears to an upper room in her father's house, intending to hang herself. But then she considered further, thinking: "Perhaps they will reproach my father, saying to him, 'You had only one beloved daughter, but because of her misfortune she hanged herself.' Thus I would cause my father in his old age to descend to Hades, overcome with sorrow. It would be far better for me not to hang myself but to beg the Lord to grant that I die so that I will no longer have to listen to these taunts."[s]

Sarah's Prayer. 11 * Then, with hands outstretched toward the window, she offered this prayer:

"Blessed are you, merciful God!
May your name be blessed forever,
and may all your works forever praise you.[t]

12 "And now, O Lord, I turn my face toward you
and raise my eyes to you.

13 Command that I be delivered from the earth,
never again to endure such reproaches.

14 "You know, O Master, that I am innocent
of an act of impurity with any man,

15 and that I have never dishonored my name
or the name of my father in this land of exile.

"I am the only child of my father,
and he has no other child to be his heir.
Neither does he have a close relative or other kindred as a potential bridegroom
for whom I should stay alive.
I have already suffered the loss of seven husbands.
Why then should I want to live any longer?
However, if it is not your will, O Lord, to take my life,
then look on me with pity
and never again permit me to hear these insults."

An Answer to Prayer. 16 * At that very moment the prayer of both these petitioners was heard in the glorious presence of God,
17 and Raphael* was sent to heal them both. He was to remove the white patches from Tobit's eyes so that he might once again behold God's light with his own eyes, and he was to give Sarah, the daughter of Raguel, in marriage to Tobiah, son of Tobit, and then free her from the wicked demon Asmodeus. For Tobiah had the right to claim her in marriage before any other suitor.

At the very moment that Tobit returned from the courtyard to his house, Sarah, the daughter of Raguel, descended from her upper room.[u]

II: THE RIGHTEOUS ARE REWARDED*

A: Tobit's Testament

CHAPTER 4

1 That same day Tobit remembered the money he had left in the custody of Gabael at Rages in Media,
2 and he said to himself, "I have now asked for death. Therefore, before I die, I should call my son Tobiah and

s Tob 6:15; Gen 37:35; 42:38; 44:29, 31.—t 1 Ki 8:44-45, 48-49; Pss 28:2; 134:2; Dan 6:11.—u Tob 4:12f; 6:12f; Gen 24:3f.

3:11-15 The Vulgate version of this prayer (vv. 13-23) is as follows: "[13] She said: 'Blessed is your name, O God of our fathers. When you are angry, you still show mercy, and in the time of tribulation you forgive the sins of those who call upon you. [14] To you, O Lord, I turn; on you my eyes are fixed. [15] I beg, O Lord, that you will loose me from the bond of this reproach, or else take me away from the earth. [16] You know, O Lord, that I have never lusted after any man and have kept my soul clean from shameful desire. [17] Neither have I frequented the company of the wanton nor cast my lot with the lovers of dalliance. [18] When I consented to take a husband, your law rather than my lust was my rule. [19] It seems that I was unworthy of the love of these men, or perhaps they were not worthy of my love. It may be that you were reserving me for another husband, [20] for your counsel is beyond human reach. [21] But this at least all your worshipers know: there was never a life of trials that did not have its crown; never a distress from which you could not save; never a punishment without a gateway to your mercy. [22] For you do not delight in our loss; rather, after a storm you bring a calm and after tears and weeping you fill us with rejoicing. [23] May your name, O God of Israel, be blessed forever.' "

3:16-17 Is the cry of the righteous who are afflicted heard by God? The author lets us in on the secret: God is neither indifferent nor absent; his Providence disposes everything for the good of those who love him. Through the intermediary of an angel, Raphael—that is, "God heals"—his Providence intervenes in favor of his two suffering children.

3:17 *Raphael:* an angel, whose name means "God heals."

4:1—12:22 We revisit Tobit with his preoccupations. Starting from this situation, the account is picked up. The author invites us to discover the Lord at work in the life of the righteous. Efficaciously and discreetly, Providence acts through a series of vicissitudes whose hero is Tobiah and that recall the history of the patriarchs.

tell him about this money." 3 * Therefore, he
summoned his son Tobiah and said to him,
"My son, when I die, give me a proper buri-
al. Honor your mother, and do not abandon
her during her lifetime. Do whatever pleas-
es her, and never grieve her in any way.[v]
4 Remember, my son, she endured many
risks for your sake while you were in her
womb. And when she dies, bury her beside
me in one grave.

5 "Be faithful to the Lord all the days of
your life, my son, and never succumb to the
desire to sin or to transgress his command-
ments. Do good works all the days of your
life, and do not walk in evil ways. 6 For if you
lead an honest life, you will be successful, as
will all those who live uprightly.* [w]

7 "Distribute alms from your possessions.
If you do not avert your gaze from anyone
who is poor, God will never turn his face
away from you.[x] 8 Your almsgiving should
be in proportion to your means. If you have
been blessed with great abundance, give
much; if you possess little, do not be afraid
to give even some of that.[y] 9 In this way you
will be accumulating for yourself a goodly
treasure for the day of adversity.[z] 10 For
almsgiving delivers the donor from death
and saves people from descending into dark-
ness. 11 Those who give alms have a worthy
offering in the presence of the Most High.[a]

12 "My son, avoid all forms of immorality.
Above all, choose a wife from among the lin-
eage of your ancestors. Do not marry any-
one who is not descended from your father's
tribe, for we are the descendants of the
prophets. Remember, my son, that Noah,
Abraham, Isaac, and Jacob, our ancestors
from of old, all took wives from their own
kindred. They were blessed in their children,
and their descendants will inherit the land.[b]
13 Therefore, my son, you too must love your
kindred; do not disdain them, the sons and
daughters of your people, and do not be too
proud to take a wife for yourself from
among them. Such pride results in ruin and
great anxiety. Idleness, too, leads to loss and
dire poverty, since idleness is the mother of
famine.

14 "Do not withhold until the following day
the wages of those who work for you, but pay
them at once. If you serve God, you will be
rewarded. Be cautious, my son, in every-
thing that you do, and let your behavior be
disciplined.[c] 15 Do not do to anyone what
you yourself hate.* Do not drink wine to
excess or allow drunkenness to become your
companion on your journey of life.[d]

16 "Share your food with the hungry and
your clothes with those who are in need of
them. Whatever you have in excess, give as
alms, and do so ungrudgingly.[e] 17 Gener-
ously provide bread and wine at the graves
of the just, but give nothing to sinners.*[f]

18 "Seek the advice of every wise person,
and do not ignore any useful counsel. 19 Bless
the Lord God at all times; ask him to guide
you along straight paths and to grant suc-
cess to all your plans and works. Pagan
nations lack such guidance, unless the Lord
himself who is the source of all good things
chooses to grant it. The Lord exalts those he
wills or casts them down even to the depths
of Hades. Finally, my son, remember these
precepts and never let them be effaced from
your heart.[g]

20 "And now, my son, I must tell you that I
have on deposit ten talents of silver in the
care of Gabael, son of Gabri, at Rages in
Media.* 21 Do not be afraid, my son, because
we have become poor. Great wealth is yours
if you fear God, avoid every kind of sin, and
do what is good in the sight of the Lord, your
God." [h]

v Ex 20:12; Prov 23:22; Sir 7:27.—w Tob 13:6; Jn 3:21; Eph 4:15.—x 7f: Tob 12:8ff; Deut 15:7f, 11; Prov 19:17; Sir 4:1-6; 14:13; Lk 14:13; 1 Jn 3:17.—y Sir 35:9.—z Mt 6:20f.—a Sir 3:30; 29:12.—b Tob 3:15, 17; 6:12; Gen 11:29, 31; 25:20; 28:1-4; 29:15-30; Ex 34:16; Deut 7:3; Jdg 14:3.—c Lev 19:13; Deut 24:15.—d Mt 7:12; Lk 6:31.—e Deut 15:10; Isa 58:7; Mt 25:35f; Lk 14:13; 2 Cor 9:7.—f Jer 16:7.—g Deut 4:6; Ps 119:10.—h Rom 8:17; 1 Tim 6:6ff.

4:3-19 A collection of ethical counsels that parallels those found in the Wisdom Books, especially Proverbs and Sirach, as well as in the wisdom literature of other nations and peoples of the ancient Near East: duties toward parents (vv. 3-4); prosperity resulting from a moral life (vv. 5-6); need of almsgiving and charity (vv. 7-11, 16-17); marriage within one's kindred (vv. 12-13); idleness and industry (v. 13); prompt payment of wages (v. 14); the golden rule in its negative form (v. 15a); temperance in drink (v. 15b); acceptance of good counsel (v. 18); and use of prayer (v. 19).

4:6 Before the fuller revelation of the Book of Wisdom and the New Testament concerning the retribution in the afterlife, the people of the Old Testament believed that virtue led to prosperity and sin brought about disaster (see Deut 28).

4:15 *Do not do to anyone what you yourself hate:* this is a negative formulation of the so-called Golden Rule concerning the relations with others and is found in almost all religions. Jesus gave it a positive formulation (see Mt 7:12; Lk 6:31).

4:17 The use of food and drink at the tomb of the dead is prohibited by Deuteronomy (Deut 26:14) because the tomb renders unclean whatever comes in contact with it (Num 19:11-19). Hence, this verse should be understood to mean bringing food and drink dinners of consolation to the home of the family of the deceased (see Jer 16:7).

4:20 *Rages in Media* lies within the vicinity of the present-day Tehran.

B: Tobiah's Journey

CHAPTER 5

A Welcome and Mysterious Guide. 1 Then
Tobiah replied to his father Tobit, "I will do
everything that you have commanded me,
father. 2 But how will I be able to retrieve the
money from him inasmuch as he does not
know me and I do not know him? What
proof can I give him so that he can recognize
me, trust me, and give me the money? And
furthermore, I do not know what roads I
must take to make this journey to Media."
3 Then Tobit answered his son Tobiah, "We
each signed a document that I divided into
two parts, one for each of us. I kept one part,
and I put the other part with the money.
Twenty years have now elapsed since I left
this money in his care. So now, my son, you
must find a trustworthy man who will
accompany you. We will pay him wages until
you return. But go and collect the money
from Gabael." *
4 So Tobiah went out to look for someone
who knew the way to Media and would be
willing to accompany him. Outside, he
encountered the angel Raphael standing in
front of him. Unaware that he was an angel
of God,[i] 5 Tobiah said to him, "Where do you
come from, young man?" "I am an Israelite,
one of your kindred," he replied. "I have
come here to look for work." Then Tobiah
said to him, "Do you know the way to
Media?"
6 "Yes," he answered. "I have been there
many times. I am familiar with all the
routes, and I know them well. I have often
traveled to Media where I used to stay with
Gabael, our kinsman who lives at Rages in
Media. It generally takes two full days* to
travel from Ecbatana to Rages, inasmuch as
Rages is situated in a mountainous area
while Ecbatana is in the middle of a plain."
7 Tobiah said to him "Wait for me, young
man, while I go inside and tell my father. I
need you to travel with me, and I shall pay
you for your time."[j] 8 He replied, "Very well,
I will wait for you, but do not be too long."
9 Tobiah went back inside to tell his father
Tobit what had transpired. He said to him,
"I have found a fellow Israelite to make the
journey with me." Tobit said, "Call the man
inside, my son, so that I may find out about
his family and ascertain to what tribe he
belongs, to ensure that he will be a trustwor-
thy traveling companion for you." Tobiah
went back outside and summoned him. He
said, "Young man, my father would like to
talk with you."
10 When Raphael entered the house, Tobit
greeted him first. When Raphael said,
"Joyous greetings to you," Tobit replied,
"What joy can I experience anymore? I am
blind. I can no longer see the light of heaven.
I live in darkness like the dead who no longer
see the light. Though still alive, I am dead for
all intents and purposes. I hear people speak
but I cannot see them." Raphael said, "Have
courage! God in his providence will restore
your sight. Have courage!"

Tobit then said, "My son Tobiah wishes to
go to Media. Will you accompany him as his
guide? I will pay your wages, brother." "Yes,"
he answered. "I can go with him. I am famil-
iar with all the roads, for I have often been to
Media. I have journeyed across all its plains
and mountains, and I know all its roads."
11 Tobit said, "Brother, tell me what family
and tribe you belong to." 12 Raphael asked,
"Why do you need to know my family and
my tribe? Are you seeking a family and a
tribe or a hired man to accompany your son
on his journey?" Tobit answered, "I want to
be quite sure whose son you are and what
your name is."[k]
13 Raphael replied, "I am Azariah,* son of
Hananiah the elder, one of your relatives."
14 Tobit said in answer, "Welcome! God save
you, brother. Do not be offended at me for
wanting to learn the truth about you and
your family. As it so happens, you are a rela-
tive, and of a good and noble lineage. I knew
Hananiah and Nathaniah, the two sons of
Shemaiah the elder. They used to go on pil-
grimage with me to Jerusalem, where we
would worship together. They never strayed
from the path of righteousness. Your kindred
are worthy people. You indeed come of good
stock. Welcome!"

i Heb 13:2.—j Tob 12:2.—k Jdg 13:17f.

5:3 It is thus a question of the receipt that Tobit received from Gabael and of a voucher whose two parts had to match at the moment of verification.

5:6 A detail that indicates a poor knowledge of geography. Far from taking only *two full days*, the 180-mile journey from Rages to Ecbatana took the army of Alexander the Great eleven days. All the author is interested in at this point is to show that Tobiah, aided by Raphael, had a practical knowledge of the area to which he was going.

5:13 The names are symbolic and express the mission of the angel: *Azariah* signifies "help of God"; *Hananiah*, "grace of God."

15 Then he added, "I will pay you a drach-
ma* a day and in addition allow you the
same expenses as those for my son. If you go
with my son, 16 I will even add a bonus to
your basic wages." Raphael replied, "I will go
with him, so have no fear. We will depart
from you in good health, and we will return
to you in good health, because the route is
safe." 17 Tobit said, "God bless you, brother."

Then Tobit called his son and said to him,
"My son, prepare everything you need for
the journey and set out with your kinsman.
May God in heaven protect both of you on
your journey there and return you to me
safe and sound, and may his angel accom-
pany you and ensure your safety, my son."

Tobiah's Leavetaking. Before departing on
his journey, Tobiah kissed his father and
mother. Tobit said to him, "Have a safe jour-
ney." 18 However, his mother began to weep,
and she said to Tobit, "Why must you send
my child away? Is he not the staff on whom
we lean as he supports us in whatever we
do? [l] 19 Do not pile money upon money.
Rather let it serve as a ransom for our son.
20 Let us be content with the life that the
Lord has provided for us."

21 "Do not worry," Tobit replied. "Our son
will depart from us in good health and will
return to us in good health. Your eyes will
see him on the day when he returns to you
safe and sound. 22 So banish such thoughts.
Do not be concerned about them, my sister.
A good angel will accompany him, his jour-
ney will be successful, and he will return to
us safe and sound." 23 Then she stopped
weeping.

CHAPTER 6

Catch of a Large Fish. 1 The youth left
together with the angel, 2 and the dog fol-
lowed them out of the house and accompa-
nied them. They journeyed until nightfall
and then camped beside the Tigris River.
3 When the youth went down to bathe his
feet in the river, a large fish leapt out of the
water and tried to swallow his foot. He cried
out, 4 but the angel said, "Take hold of the
fish and don't let it escape." The youth took
hold of the fish and pulled it to the shore.
5 The angel then said to him, "Cut the fish up
and take out its gall, heart, and liver. Keep
them with you, and throw out the entrails,
for the gall, heart, and liver can be used as
medicines." 6 The youth cut the fish up and
set aside the gall, heart, and liver. He broiled
and ate part of the fish, salting the rest so
that it could be used on the journey.
Afterward they continued their travels
together until they drew near to Media.

7 Then the youth posed this question to the
angel: "Brother Azariah, what medicinal
value can there be in the heart, liver, and gall
of the fish?" 8 * He replied, "As far as the
heart and liver are concerned, when you
burn them and the smoke rises in the pres-
ence of someone, man or woman, who is
afflicted by a demon or an evil spirit, that
affliction will disappear for good and will
never plague that person again. 9 As regards
the gall, if you anoint the eyes of someone
where white patches have appeared on them
and then blow on those patches, the eyes will
be healed."

Raphael's Counsels. 10 When they had
entered Media and were drawing near to
Ecbatana, 11 Raphael said to the youth,
"Brother Tobiah!" He answered, "Here I
am." Raphael went on: "Tonight we must
stay in the home of Raguel who is a relative
of yours. He has a daughter named Sarah,
12 but aside from her he has no other son or
daughter. Since you are her next of kin, you
above all others have the right to marry her
and to inherit her father's goods. This girl is
sensible, brave, and very beautiful, and her
father is a fine man." [m]

13 He continued: "Since you have the right
to marry her, listen to me, brother. Tonight
I will speak to her father and secure his
approval to have her betrothed to you. When
we return from Rages, we will hold her mar-
riage celebration. I know that Raguel has no
right to refuse your request or to betroth her
to another man without incurring the death
penalty as decreed in the Book of Moses. He
clearly understands that you above all other
men have the right to marry his daughter.

"So listen to me, brother. Tonight we will
speak about the girl and arrange for her to
be betrothed to you. And when we return
from Rages, we will take her with us and
bring her to your home."

---

l Tob 10:4.—m Tob 4:12f; Num 36:8.

5:15 A *drachma* was most likely a day's wage for an artisan. This type of contract for a journey by horseback with a guide remained in use in the East up to the introduction of the automobile.

6:8-9 See verse 17 and especially Tob 8:3; 11:4, 11f. The therapeutic powers of the entrails of fish were recognized by ancient medicine, but here, it is a question of the divine assistance through the medium of the angel.

[14] However, in reply to Raphael, Tobiah
said, "Brother Azariah, I have heard that
she has already been given in marriage
seven times, and that each of her husbands
died in the bridal chamber. The very night
that they entered her room, they died, and I
have heard people claim that it was a demon
who killed them. [15] Therefore, I am afraid.
The demon does not harm her because he
loves her, but he kills any man who tries to
approach her. I am my father's only son, and
if I should die, I fear that the resulting grief
would bring my father and mother to their
grave—and they have no other son to bury
them."[n]

[16] Raphael retorted, "Have you forgotten
your father's instructions to take a wife from
his family? Now listen to me, brother. Do not
worry about this demon. Take Sarah in mar-
riage. I know that this very night she will be
given to you in marriage. [17] When you enter
the bridal chamber, take some of the heart
and liver of the fish and place them on the
burning incense. [18] When the demon smells
the odor that will arise, he will flee, and
never again will he be seen near her.

"Then, before you go to bed with her, both of you must first stand up and pray. Beseech the Lord of heaven to grant you his mercy and protection. Do not be afraid; she was set apart for you before the world was created. You will save her, and she will go with you. Undoubtedly by her you will have children who will be like brothers to you. Do not worry!"

When Tobiah heard Raphael's words and learned that Sarah was his kinswoman, related through his father's lineage, he was filled with love for her, and his heart became set on her.*

CHAPTER 7

Raguel Welcomes His Guests. [1] As they
entered Ecbatana, Tobiah said, "Brother
Azariah, take me directly to our kinsman
Raguel." So he brought him to the house of
Raguel, where they found him sitting beside
his courtyard gate. They greeted him first,
and he replied, "Greetings to you, too, my
brothers. You are welcome, and I wish you
good health."

When he brought them into his house, [2] he
said to his wife Edna, "This young man truly
resembles my kinsman Tobit." [3] Then Edna
asked them, "Where are you from, broth-
ers?" They replied, "We belong to the
descendants of Naphtali, who are now in
exile at Nineveh." [4] "Do you know our kins-
man Tobit?" she asked, and they answered,
"Yes, we do." "Is he well?" she inquired.
[5] "He is alive and well," they replied, and
Tobiah added, "He is my father."

[6] Raguel leapt to his feet and, with tears in
his eyes, he kissed him, saying, [7] "God bless
you, my child. You are the son of a good and
noble father. But how tragic it is that such an
upright and charitable man has lost his
sight!" He then embraced his kinsman
Tobiah and wept. [8] His wife Edna also wept
for Tobit, as did their daughter Sarah.

Sarah Is Given in Marriage to Tobiah.
[9] Afterward Raguel slaughtered a ram from
the flock and gave them a warm welcome.
When they had bathed and reclined to eat,
Tobiah said to Raphael, "Brother Azariah,
please ask Raguel to give me my kinswoman
Sarah in marriage." [10] Raguel overheard this
and said to the young man, "Eat and drink
and be merry tonight, for no one else but
you, my brother, has the right to marry my
daughter Sarah. In any event, I do not have
the right to give her to anyone else, since you
are my closest relative.

"However, my son, I must frankly reveal
the truth to you. [11] I have previously given
her in marriage to seven of our kinsmen,
and they all died on their wedding night
when they entered her chamber. But for the
moment, my child, eat and drink, and may
the Lord show kindness in dealing with you
both." Tobiah answered, "I will neither eat
nor drink anything until you give me what is
mine."

Raguel said to him, "I will do so. She is yours, in accordance with what is prescribed in the Book of Moses, and heaven itself decrees that she be given to you. Take your kinswoman; from now on you belong to her and she belongs to you. She is given to you from today forever. May the Lord of heaven look upon you favorably tonight, my child, and grant you mercy and peace."

[12] Then Raguel summoned his daughter
Sarah, and when she came to him, he took

n Tob 3:10.

6:18 The Vulgate develops these concepts further: the angel instructs Tobiah to abstain for the first three nights; then to come together with his bride because of the desire for children more than the desire to follow the sexual impulse.

her by the hand* and gave her to Tobiah
with these words: "Take her as your wife in
accordance with the law and the decree
written in the Book of Moses. Take her and
bring her safe and sound to your father. And
may the God of heaven bless both of you
with peace and prosperity."[o] 13 Then, after
summoning her mother and instructing her
to bring him a scroll, he drew up and affixed
his seal to a marriage contract* stating that
he gave Sarah to Tobiah as his wife accord-
ing to the decree of the law of Moses.[p]
14 Afterward they began to eat and drink.

15 Later on, Raguel called his wife Edna and
said, "My sister, get the other room ready and
bring her there." 16 She went and made the
bed in the room as he had instructed and
brought Sarah there. After weeping over her,
she wiped away her tears and said, 17 "Have
courage, my daughter. May the Lord of heav-
en turn your grief to joy. Have courage, my
daughter." Then she departed.

CHAPTER 8

An Unusual Wedding Night. 1 When they
had finished eating and drinking and were
ready to retire, they escorted the young
man from the dining room to the bed-
room. 2 Then Tobiah recalled Raphael's
instructions. He removed the liver and
heart of the fish from the bag where he had
stored them, and he placed them on the
embers of the incense. 3 The odor of the
fish so repelled the demon that he fled to
Upper Egypt.* However, Raphael followed
him there and bound him hand and foot.
Then he returned at once.[q]

4 * When the girl's parents had left the
room and closed the door behind them,
Tobiah got out of bed and said to Sarah,
"Arise, my beloved. Let us pray and implore
our Lord to grant us his mercy and protec-
tion." 5 She got up, and they started to pray
and ask that they might be kept safe. Tobiah
began by saying:

"Blessed are you, O God of our ances-
tors;
may your name be praised forever and
ever.
Let the heavens and everything you have
created
praise you forever.[r]
6 You made Adam, and you provided him
with his wife Eve
to be his help and support,
and from these two the human race
has sprung.
You said, 'It is not good for the man to be
alone;
let us provide him with a helper like
himself.'[s]
7 And now I am taking this kinswoman as
my wife
not out of lust
but with sincere love.
Grant that she and I may obtain mercy
and that we may reach a happy old age
together."

8 Then together they said, "Amen, amen,"
9 and they slept through the night.

But Raguel arose and summoned his ser-
vants, and they went outside and dug a
grave, 10 for he said, "If Tobiah should die, we
will be subjected to ridicule and scorn."
11 When they had finished digging the grave,
Raguel went back into the house and sum-
moned his wife, 12 saying, "Send one of the
maids into the room to see whether Tobiah
is still alive. If he should be dead, let us bury
him so that no one will know anything about
it." 13 They summoned the maid, lit a lamp,
and opened the bedroom door. After the
maid went in and found them sound asleep
together, 14 she came out and informed
them that Tobiah was alive and that there
was nothing wrong. 15 Then Raguel blessed
the God of heaven with these words:

o Gen 24:50f.—p Tob 6:12.—q Mt 12:22-30, 43-45.—r Dan 3:26.—s Gen 2:18-23.

7:12 *Took her by the hand:* the Vulgate stipulates that the father should place the hand of his daughter in the hand of her spouse. This gesture is unknown to the Bible; used in the marriage ceremonies of Greeks and Romans, it has passed into the Christian rite. *God of heaven:* an expression of late post-Exilic times that intends to stress the sublime character and the power of God (see Dan 2:18-19, 37, etc.). *And . . . prosperity:* the Vulgate (Tob 7:15) gives a fuller blessing whose words have been included in the Nuptial Blessing in the marriage rite: "May the God of Abraham, the God of Isaac, and the God of Jacob be with you; may he join you together and fulfill his blessing in you."

7:13 *Marriage contract:* the Mosaic Law did not contemplate marriage certificates, but they were introduced by custom; examples of them are found in the fifth century B.C. among the Aramaic papyri of Elephantine.

8:3 *Upper Egypt:* possibly refers to the Sahara Desert. Infecund and therefore "cursed," deserts were believed to be the dwelling of demons (see Isa 13:21; Mt 4:1; 12:43). The bonds indicate that the devil has been rendered impotent.

8:4-6 The Vulgate reads (vv. 4-6): "4 Then Tobiah exhorted his bride: 'Sarah, arise and let us pray to God today, and tomorrow, and the next day. These three nights are set apart for our union with God. When the third night is over, we will be joined in one, you and I. 5 For we are the children of saints, and we must not be joined together like heathens who do not know God.' 6 So they both arose and prayed earnestly together that health might be given their union."

"Blessed are you, O God, with every pure blessing.
Let all your chosen ones bless you; let them bless you forever.
16 Blessed are you for having given me joy; that which I feared did not occur.
Rather you have dealt with us according to your great mercy.
17 Blessed are you for showing compassion
to two only children.
Be merciful to them, Master, and keep them safe;
allow them to live their lives fully
in happiness and in mercy."

18 Then he instructed his servants to fill in the grave before daybreak.

The Great Wedding Feast. 19 Having asked his wife to bake many loaves of bread, Raguel went out to his flock and selected two oxen and four rams and ordered them to be slaughtered. Thus they began to prepare for the feast.

20 Then he called Tobiah and swore an oath to him: "You shall not depart from here for fourteen days.* Rather, you shall stay here eating and drinking with me, and you shall bring joy to my daughter's heart after all the suffering she has endured. 21 Take at once half of everything I possess,* and then return with her safe and sound to your father. When my wife and I are dead, you will inherit the other half. Have courage, my son. I am your father and Edna is your mother, and now and forever we belong to you just as much as we belong to your wife. Have courage, my son."

CHAPTER 9

Tobiah Remembers His Primary Mission.* 1 Then Tobiah sent for Raphael. 2 "Brother Azariah," he said, "take four servants and two camels with you and leave for Rages. 3 Go to Gabael's house, give him the note of credit, and collect the money. Then invite him to come with you to the wedding celebration. 4 As you realize, my father must be counting the days, and if my return should be delayed by as little as a single day, he will be deeply grieved. You witnessed the oath that Raguel has sworn, and I cannot violate that oath."

5 * And so Raphael, together with the four servants and two camels, went to Rages in Media and lodged with Gabael. Raphael gave Gabael the note of credit, informed him about the marriage of Tobiah, son of Tobit, and invited him to the wedding feast. Gabael immediately arose and counted out to him the money bags with their seals still intact. Then they loaded them onto the camels.

6 The following morning they both arose early and set off to the wedding celebration. When they entered Raguel's house, they found Tobiah reclining at table. He jumped up and greeted Gabael, who wept and blessed him with these words: "Good and noble son of a father equally good and noble, upright and generous, may the Lord bestow the blessing of heaven on you and your wife, as well as on your wife's father and mother. Blessed be God, for I observe in Tobiah the very image of my cousin Tobit."*

CHAPTER 10

Anxiety of Tobiah's Parents.* 1 Meanwhile, every day Tobit continued to estimate the number of days Tobiah would need for the journey there and for the return trip. When that time had elapsed and still his son had not returned, 2 he said, "Is it possible that he has been detained there? Perhaps Gabael is dead and there is no one who is able to give him the money." 3 And he began to worry. 4 His wife Anna said, "My son has perished

---

8:20 *Fourteen days:* the duration of the festivities, which normally would take place in the house of the groom, is doubled from one week (see Gen 29:27; Jdg 14:12) to two. They will then be repeated according to custom (Tob 11:18).

8:21 *Half of everything I possess:* in contrast to the accounts of the patriarchs (Gen 24), the text here does not speak of a sum given by the fiancé to his betrothed's father; on the contrary, it is the latter who gives a dowry to his daughter.

9:1-6 Ever present, the benevolent guide acquitted himself on the journey to the satisfaction of everyone. Gabael's blessing (v. 6) constitutes one of the high points of Tobiah's trip.

9:5-6 It is interesting to note that *Gabael,* as is true of all the personages in this Book, except Asmodeus, the husband-slaying demon (Tob 8:7), turns out to be most gracious, honorable, and trustworthy.

9:6 Instead of this verse, the Vulgate (vv. 8-12) reads as follows: "[8] And when Gabelus entered Raguel's house, he found Tobiah sitting at the table; Tobiah leaped up and they embraced. Gabelus wept and blessed God [9] and said, 'The God of Israel bless you, because you are the son of a very good and just man, a true worshiper of God and giver of alms. [10] May a blessing come upon your wife and upon your parents. [11] And may you see your children and your children's children unto the third and fourth generation. May your seed be blessed by the God of Israel, who reigns forever and ever.' [12] And when all had said Amen, they began to feast; but the merry-making over this wedding was such as became God's worshipers."

10:1-7a There is feasting at Ecbatana, but at Nineveh, time has stopped. Overwhelmed by anxiety, the aged parents count the days. The author artfully handles the contrast and sketches one of the most moving scenes in the Book.

and is no longer among the living." And she
began to weep, and to mourn over her son,
saying,[t] 5 "Alas, my child, the light of my
eyes. Why did I permit you to make this jour-
ney?" [u]

6 However, Tobit continued to reassure
her: "Hush! Do not worry, my dear. He is all
right. Probably something unexpected has
happened to delay them. The man who is
accompanying him is trustworthy and one
of our kindred. So do not grieve for him, my
dear. He will be here soon."

7 But she retorted: "Let me alone and do
not try to deceive me! My child has per-
ished." Each day she would go out and
maintain her watch on the road her son had
taken, and she would listen to no one. At
sunset she would return home and mourn
and weep throughout the night, unable to
sleep. [v]

C: The Return of Tobiah

Tobiah Insists on Returning Home.* After the fourteen days for the wedding celebration that Raguel had sworn to hold for his daughter had come to an end, Tobiah approached him and said, "Now please let me depart, for I am positive that my father and mother do not believe that they will ever see me again. So I beseech you, father, that you allow me to return home now to my father Tobit. I have already explained to you the condition in which I left him."

8 Raguel replied, "My child, stay with me,
and I will send messengers to your father to
give him news of you." 9 But Tobiah insisted,
"No, I beg you to let me return home to my
father." 10 Without any further hesitation,
Raguel turned over to Tobiah Sarah his
bride, as well as half of all his possessions—
male and female slaves, oxen and sheep,
donkeys and camels, clothing, money, and
household goods. 11 Bidding them farewell,
he prepared to send them on their way.
Embracing Tobiah, he said, "Good-bye, my
son. Have a safe journey. May the Lord of
heaven grant prosperity to you and your
wife Sarah. Hopefully, before I die, I will be
able to see your children."

12 He then kissed his daughter Sarah and
said to her: "My daughter, honor your hus-
band's father and mother, since from now
on they are as much your parents as the
ones who gave you life. Depart in peace,
my daughter, and may I hear nothing but
good reports about you as long as I live."
After this, he bade good-bye to them and
let them go.

13 Then Edna said to Tobiah, "My child,
and beloved brother, may the Lord bring
you back home safely, and may I live long
enough to see the children born to you and
my daughter Sarah before I die. In the sight
of the Lord I entrust my daughter into your
keeping. Do not cause her suffering in any
day of your life. Go in peace, my child. From
now on I am your mother and Sarah is your
beloved wife. May we all have good fortune
for the rest of our lives." Then she kissed
them both and sent them away safe and
sound.

14 When Tobiah was ready to leave
Raguel's house, he was filled with happiness
and joy, and he blessed the Lord of heaven
and earth, the King of all that exists, for
ensuring the success of his journey. Finally
he blessed Raguel and his wife Edna, saying,
"May I honor you for the rest of my life."

CHAPTER 11

The Aged Tobit Recovers His Sight.* 1 As
they neared Kaserin, which is close to
Nineveh, 2 Raphael said, "You know your
father's condition when we departed. 3 Let
us hurry on ahead of your wife and pre-
pare the house while she and the others
journey on after us." 4 As they went on
together, Raphael then said to Tobiah,
"Have the fish gall ready at hand." And the
dog followed them.

5 Meanwhile Anna was sitting, watching
the road by which her son would come.
6 When she caught sight of his approach, she
said to his father, "Tobit, your son is coming,
and so is the man who served as his com-
panion."

7 Raphael said to Tobiah before he reached
his father, "I am sure that his eyes will be
opened. 8 Smear the fish gall on them. This
medicine will cause the white patches to
shrink and to peel away from his eyes. Then

t Tob 5:18.—u Tob 5:23.—v Gen 45:26.

10:7b-14 God has not yet accomplished his purpose, for Tobit's trial is still in progress. It is time for the final act to be played and the story to reach its conclusion. Tobiah takes leave of his parents-in-law and starts out for Nineveh with a joyful caravan.

11:1-18 The righteous Tobit recovers his sight as compensation for his faithfulness. The author's message has been delivered. Later, Jesus will proclaim: "Blessed are the pure of heart, for they will see God" (Mt 5:8).

your father will recover his sight, and once
again he will be able to see the light of day."
9 Then Anna ran forward and threw her
arms around her son. "Now I am ready to
die, my son," she said, "for I have seen you
once again." And she wept.[w] 10 Then Tobit
rose to his feet and came stumbling through
the courtyard gate. Tobiah went up to him
11 with the fish gall in his hand, and holding
him firmly he blew into his eyes, saying,
"Have courage, father!" 12 He next applied
the medicine to his eyes with great care,
13 and it made them sting. Then, with both
hands, he peeled off the white patches,
beginning at the corners of Tobit's eyes.
When Tobit saw his son, he threw his arms
around him, 14 and weeping, he exclaimed,
"I can see you, my son, the light of my eyes."
Then he said:

"Blessed be God,
  and blessed be his great name,
  and blessed be all his holy angels.
May his holy name be blessed
  throughout all the ages forevermore.
15 Although he afflicted me,
  he has had mercy on me,
  and now I see my son Tobiah."

Then Tobit went inside, rejoicing and praising
God with all his strength. Tobiah reported
to his father about the success of his
journey, saying that he had brought back the
money with him, that he had married Sarah,
the daughter of Raguel, and that Sarah would
soon arrive at their home, since she was not
far from the gates of Nineveh.[x]

16 Tobit went out to the gates of Nineveh to
meet his daughter-in-law, rejoicing and
praising God. When the people of Nineveh
observed him walking along vigorously
without anyone guiding him, they were
astonished. 17 Tobit related in their presence
how God had been merciful to him and
restored his sight. When he met Sarah, the
wife of his son Tobiah, he blessed her in these
words: "Welcome, my daughter. Blessed be
God who has sent you to us, my daughter.
Blessed are your father and mother. Blessed
is my son Tobiah. Blessed are you, my
daughter. Welcome now to your home, and
enter with joyfulness and in blessedness, my
daughter."

And so that was a day of joy for all the Jews
in Nineveh. 18 Ahiqar and his nephew Nadab
also came to share in Tobit's happiness. They
celebrated Tobiah's wedding feast for seven
days, and many gifts were given to him.

CHAPTER 12

God's Providence Revealed.* 1 After the wed-
ding celebrations had been completed, Tobit
summoned his son Tobiah and said to him,
"My son, it is time that you paid the wages
owed to the man who journeyed with you,
and in addition you should give him a bonus."
2 Tobiah replied, "Father, how much should I
pay him? I would not be averse to giving him
half of all the possessions he brought back
with me.[y] 3 He returned me to you safe and
sound, he cured my wife, he brought back the
money with me, and he healed you. How
much extra should I give him?"

4 Tobit answered, "It would only be just,
my son, for him to receive half of all that he
brought back." 5 So Tobiah called his com-
panion and said, "For your wages take half
of all that you brought back, and go in
peace."

6 ** Raphael called both men aside pri-
vately and said to them, "Bless God, and in
the presence of all the living praise him and
acknowledge all the good things he has done
for you. Bless and extol his name with hymns
of praise. Proclaim to all people the deeds of
God, and never cease to offer thanksgiving to
him. 7 The secret of a king should be con-
cealed, but the works of God should be pub-
licly proclaimed as they deserve. Do what is
good, and no evil will befall you.

8 "Prayer and fasting are worthy acts, but
better than these is almsgiving with justice.
A little with righteousness is better than
much with wickedness. It is better to give
alms than to hoard gold.*[z] 9 For almsgiving
saves us from death and purges every type
of sin. Those who give alms will enjoy a long
life,[a] 10 but those who commit sin and do evil
deeds are their own worst enemies.

w Gen 33:4; 45:14; 46:29f; Lk 15:20.—x Tob 13:2; Deut 32:39; 1 Sam 2:6.—y Tob 5:3, 7, 15f.—z Tob 4:7-11; Sir 29:8-13.—a Dan 4:24.

12:1-22 At the very hour of receiving his compensation, Tobiah's mysterious guide reveals his true identity: the angel Raphael. He is entrusted—as his name indicates—with soothing the pains of the righteous undergoing trials. In doing so, he is only God's instrument—it is the Lord who must be thanked.

12:6-10 Like a teacher of wisdom, Raphael now directs a brief exhortation to Tobit and his son—similar to the one Tobit addressed to his son in Tob 4:3-19.

12:6f These two verses reinforce the Jewish people's belief that praising God was the most important duty (see Isa 38:16-20).

12:8 Another translation is: "prayer with fasting is a good thing; but true almsgiving is worth more than both of these"; it is a way of speaking used in proverbs (see Sir 40:18-26).

11 "I will now tell you the entire truth;
nothing will be hidden from you. I have
already said to you that it is prudent to keep
a king's secret but that the works of God
should be publicly proclaimed as they
deserve. 12 I can now reveal to you, Tobit, that
when you and Sarah prayed, I was the one
who presented your supplications before the
Glory of the Lord, as well as when you buried
the dead.[b] 13 On the occasion when you did
not hesitate to get up and leave your dinner to
go and bury the dead man, 14 I was sent to test
you.* However, at the same time, God sent
me to heal you and your daughter-in-law
Sarah. 15 I am Raphael, one of the seven
angels who stand ready to enter before the
Glory of the Lord."*[c]

16 The two men were deeply shaken and
fell to the ground in fear. 17 But the angel
said to them, "Do not be afraid.* Peace be
with you. Praise God forevermore. 18 As for
me, when I came to you, the decision was
not in accord with my will but in accord with
the will of God. Therefore, continue to bless
him every day of your life and sing hymns of
praise to him. 19 When you thought that you
saw me eating, that was only a vision—I did
not eat anything. 20 Now raise yourselves
from the ground and give thanks to God. I
am about to ascend to him who sent me.
Make a written record of all these things
that have happened to you."[d]

21 He then ascended, and when they stood
up they could no longer see him. 22 They kept
blessing God by singing hymns of praise,
and they gave thanks to him for the mar-
velous deeds he had accomplished when an
angel of God had appeared to them.

III: VISION OF THE NEW TIMES

A: The Canticle of Tobit*

CHAPTER 13

Call for Conversion from Sin. 1 Then Tobit in
his joy composed this prayer:

"Blessed be God who lives forever,
for his kingdom endures throughout all ages.[e]
2 For he both punishes and forgives;
he consigns people to the depths of Hades
and brings them up from the great abyss.
Nothing can escape his hand.[f]

3 "Praise him, you Israelites, before the nations,
for though he has scattered you among them,
4 he has shown you his greatness even there.
Exalt him in the presence of every living creature,
for he is our Lord and our God;
he is our Father and our God forever.[g]
5 He will scourge you for your iniquities,
but he will again show his mercy to all of you.
He will gather you from all the nations
among whom you have been dispersed.[h]

6 "If you turn to him with all your heart and soul
to do what is right in his presence,
then he will turn to you
and will no longer hide his face from you.
So now consider what he has done for you
and shout your praises to him.
Bless the Lord of justice
and exalt the King of the ages.

"In the land of my exile I sing his praise
and make known his power and majesty to a sinful nation:
Turn back, you sinners, and be upright in your conduct before him;
perhaps he will then look upon you with favor
and show you mercy.[i]

7 "As for me, I exalt my God,
and my soul rejoices in the King of heaven.

b Job 33:23f; Acts 10:4; Rev 8:2.—c Lk 1:19; Rev 8:2.—d Jdg 13:20.—e Tob 3:11; 8:5, 15; 1 Chr 29:10.—f Tob 11:15; 13:9; Deut 32:39; 1 Sam 2:6; Wis 16:13.—g Isa 63:16; 64:8; Jer 3:4; Mt 6:9.—h Deut 30:3; Neh 1:9.—i Deut 30:2; 1 Tim 1:17.

12:14 *I was sent to test you:* God is frequently shown testing those faithful to him (e.g., Job 1–2).

12:15 See Rev 8:2. The Bible mentions only three names of angels: Raphael, Michael, and Gabriel. *Seven* is a number that indicates fullness and perfection.

12:17 *Do not be afraid:* compare Mt 28:5, 10.

13:1-18 Tobit's thanksgiving is expanded in a meditation on the work of God toward the people whom he has chosen and on the future of Jerusalem, the holy city, surpassing the framework of the family history.

8 Let all people declare his majesty
and sing his praises in Jerusalem.

9 "O Jerusalem, holy city,
he scourged you for the deeds of your hands,
but he will again show mercy on the children of the righteous.[j]

10 "Give thanks to the Lord for his goodness,
and bless the King of the ages,
so that his tabernacle may be rebuilt with joy within you.
May he offer comfort to all of your exiles,
and may he love all those within you who are in distress
for all generations to come.

The New Jerusalem, Light of the Nations

11 "A bright light will shine over all the regions of the earth;
many nations will come to you from afar,
drawn to your holy name, Lord God, from every corner of the earth,
bearing gifts in their hands for the King of heaven.
Generation after generation will give joyful praise to you,
and the name of your chosen city will endure forever through all ages.[k]
12 Accursed are all who speak a harsh word against you;[l]
accursed are all who destroy you
and pull down your walls,
all who overthrow your towers
and set your homes on fire;
but blessed forever are all those who rebuild you.

13 "Go, then, and rejoice over the children of the righteous,
for they will all be gathered together
and will praise the Lord of the ages.
14 Blessed are those who love you,
and blessed are those who rejoice in your prosperity.
Blessed are those who grieve over you
because of your afflictions.
For they will rejoice over you
and behold all your joy forever.[m]

15 "Praise the Lord, the great King, my soul;
16 Jerusalem will be rebuilt as his dwelling place for all ages.
How happy I shall be if a portion of my descendants survive
to witness your glory and praise the King of heaven.
The gates of Jerusalem will be constructed of sapphire and emerald,
and all your walls with precious stones.
The towers of Jerusalem will be built of gold,
and their battlements with pure gold.[n]
17 The streets of Jerusalem will be paved
with rubies and stones from Ophir.
18 The gates of Jerusalem will sing hymns of joy,
and all her houses shall cry out:
'Alleluia. Blessed be the God of Israel.
In you his holy name will be blessed forever.' "

B: Tobit's Prophecy

CHAPTER 14*

[1] So ended Tobit's words of praise. He died
peacefully at the age of one hundred and
twelve and was buried with much honor in
Nineveh. [2] He was sixty-two years old when
he lost his eyesight, and after he was cured
he lived a happy life, gave alms, and contin-
ually blessed God and proclaimed his great-
ness.

[3] Prior to his death, he summoned his son
Tobiah and Tobiah's seven sons, and issued
these instructions:[o] [4] "My son, take your
children and hasten to Media, for I believe
the word of God that Nahum spoke about
Nineveh. It will all take place. Everything
will happen to Assyria and Nineveh that was
spoken by the prophets of Israel sent by
God.[p] None of their words will be unfulfilled;
everything will occur at the appointed time.
You will be safer in Media than in Assyria or

j Tob 11:15; Isa 60; Mic 7:19; Rev 21.—k Isa 2:3f; 9:1; 49:6; 60:1; Mic 4:2; Zec 8:22.—l Bar 4:31f.—m Ps 122:6; Isa 66:10.—n Tob 14:5; Isa 54:11-13; 62:2; Rev 21:10-21.—o Gen 47:29f.—p Nah 2:2—3:19.

14:1-15 The end of the Book takes on an apocalyptic tone. Assyria, the persecutor of the chosen people, had already fallen some centuries previously. The author presents the event as a prophecy in the mouth of Tobit whom he makes a contemporary of this time past. In the destruction of empires, he sees a pledge of the power of God capable of restoring his people. Moreover, he also sees the future coming of new times: all the nations will be converted and the Israelites reunited in their homeland, the Holy Land definitively renewed. This is why Tobit counsels his descendants to follow the example of Ahiqar, the celebrated wise man of the East.

Babylon. For I know and believe that what-
ever God has said will be accomplished. Not
a single word of the prophecies will remain
unfulfilled.

"All of our kindred who dwell in Israel will
be scattered and carried off in exile out of
that good land. The whole territory of Israel,
even Samaria and Jerusalem, will be deso-
late. The temple of God there will be burned
to the ground, and for a period of time it will
be abandoned.* 5 However, God will once
again have mercy on them and bring them
back to the land of Israel. They will rebuild
the temple of God, but it will not be compa-
rable to the first one until the period when
the appointed times will come. Then they
will all return from their captivity and
rebuild Jerusalem in splendor. And the tem-
ple of God will be rebuilt there, as the
prophets of Israel have foretold.[q]

6 "All the nations of the entire world will
be converted and offer sincere worship to
God. They will all renounce their idols who
have deceitfully led them into error,[r] 7 and
with justice they will praise the eternal God.
All of the Israelites who are spared in those
days and remain firmly mindful of God will
be gathered together. They will go to
Jerusalem and dwell in safety forever in the
land of Abraham, which will be given over to
them. Those who sincerely love God will
rejoice, whereas those who are guilty of sin
and wickedness will disappear from the
earth.[s]

8 "Now, my children, I give you this injunc-
tion. Serve God faithfully and do what is
pleasing to him. Teach your children to do
what is right and to give alms, to be mindful
of God and at all times to bless his name sin-
cerely and with all their strength.

9 "So now, my son, depart from Nineveh;
do not remain here. 10 Once you have
buried your mother next to me, do not
spend even one more night within the con-
fines of this city, where the people are with-
out shame as they engage in wickedness
and deceit. Recall, my son, what Nadab*
did to Ahiqar who had raised him. While
still alive, Ahiqar was forced to hide in a
grave. However, God's justice did not allow
this disgraceful outrage to remain unpun-
ished, inasmuch as Ahiqar came out again
into the light of day, while Nadab descend-
ed into eternal darkness because of his
attempt on Ahiqar's life.

"Because Ahiqar gave alms, he managed
to escape the deadly trap that Nadab had set
for him. However, Nadab himself fell into
that trap and was destroyed.[t] 11 So, my chil-
dren, you can see what almsgiving accom-
plishes, as well as what wickedness does—it
leads to death. But now my breath fails me."

12 They placed him on his bed, where he
died, and he received an honorable burial.[u]

C: The Last Days of Tobiah

When his mother died, Tobiah buried her
beside his father. Then he and his wife and
children returned to Media and settled in
Ecbatana with his father-in-law Raguel.
13 He treated his wife's aging parents with
great care and respect, and later he buried
them in Ecbatana in Media.

Tobiah inherited the estate of Raguel as
well as that of his father Tobit. 14 Greatly
respected, he died at the age of one hundred
and seventeen. 15 Before his death he heard
of the destruction of Nineveh and witnessed
the exile of the city's inhabitants whom King
Cyaxares* of Media had taken captive.

Tobiah praised God for everything he had
inflicted on the inhabitants of Nineveh and
Assyria. Before his death he rejoiced over
the fate of Nineveh, and he blessed the Lord
God forever and ever. Amen.[v]

q Neh 12:27; Jer 31:38.—r Isa 60:1-4.—s Isa 60:21; Jer 32:37; Ezek 34:28; 37:25; 39:26.—t Tob 1:21f.—u Tob 4:4.—v Ps 137:8; Nah 1–3.

14:4 See Nah 2–3; and also Isa 10:12-19. Nineveh fell in 612 B.C. at the hands of the Medes and Babylonians; Samaria, in 721 B.C.; Jerusalem, in 587 B.C. Note that the action of the Book is situated during the apogee of the Assyrian Empire (middle of the seventh century B.C.).

14:10 *Nadab:* in the Book of Ahiqar, the protagonist is the chancellor for the Assyrian kings Sennacherib and Esarhaddon. As his successor, he grooms his adopted nephew, Nadab, but the latter schemes to have his uncle disgraced and put to death. Ahiqar seeks asylum in a friend's house and is ultimately vindicated when Nadab's treachery is uncovered. Nadab is cast into a dungeon where he meets his death. The reason behind Ahiqar's salvation was his almsgiving.

14:15 *Cyaxares* established the power of Media by teaming with Nabopolassar, king of Babylon, to subdue the power of Nineveh, which they destroyed in 612 B.C.

THE BOOK OF JUDITH

Invitation to Courage

After the story of a family delineated in the Book of Tobit, the Bible gives us a national drama in two parts. In the first, the fearsome armada of Holofernes imposes its domination over all peoples; the little Israelite nation is threatened and in danger of perishing. In the second, the situation is reversed; a hope of victory rises from the Jewish camp: the pious and wise Judith—that is, the "Jewess," who incarnates Israel's resistance and faith—triumphs over the coarseness of the general. God has saved his people.

The account is artfully set forth. Tension rises progressively; groups and personages oppose each other in clear contrast. Intervals of time are introduced, and the final confrontation takes place smoothly and safely. The account makes use of nocturnal scenes in a Middle Eastern decor, and the hymns and processions of Israel add an element of grandeur. Without question, the Book of Judith is a literary masterpiece.

But it must be seen as just that—a literary rather than a historical work. A few of its details can be explained by symbolic meaning. (Nebuchadnezzar is the name of the major enemy of the people of God, having destroyed the kingdom of Judah and its capital; he is made king of Assyria because that country brought about the destruction of the other kingdom, that of Israel.)

But the action in itself, clearly situated within the Persian epoch (see 16:10), and within a generation after the return from the Exile (see 4:3, 6; 8:18), cannot be connected with known historical events; Bethulia itself, placed within Samaria, is a new name. Indeed, the author does not wish to impart the record of past events to us; he intends only to draw attention to the religious meaning of the conflict that continually sets the People of God in opposition to the wicked.

Faithful to his covenant, the Lord does not abandon his children in their trials; he intervenes at the appointed hour to save them from their enemies. This recurring biblical theme is, however, set in motion in an apocalyptic tone that evokes in particular the great visions of Daniel. And, in fact, from the time of the prophets, the people were awaiting the day in which the pagan masses, representing the powers of evil, would mount an assault on the kingdom of God and be overcome in a way that could not be foreseen.

At the same time, the Book resembles the edifying stories so dear to the Jewish people of the last few centuries before the Christian era. Writing in Greek, the author makes use of an earlier Aramaic or Hebrew account about the deed of a local heroine, and he adapts it in the light of national events. At times he imitates ancient scenes from the life of the patriarchs and also recalls the accounts of the holy war with all their appendage of radical and cruel proceedings to which the ancients were accustomed.

Like the Books of the Maccabees and in the name of the religious traditions of Israel, this Book encourages resistance to the Greek paganism that seeks to impose itself on all peoples. Worthy of note is the total absence of references to Samaritans, even though the action takes place in Samaria (see 4:4); this is probably due to the idealistic reasons that govern the author's vision. However, the fact that the narrative concludes with a pilgrimage from Bethulia to Jerusalem would lead one to think that the author wishes to direct a severe and ironic lesson to the inhabitants of Israel as well as a call to come together in the face of a common foe.

While the Book of Judith is not among the major works of the Bible, it is not lacking in charm. The Church has drawn from it images and texts for liturgical prayer: what it teaches concerning the power and faithfulness of God, the unfolding of history, and the final victory of good is always relevant. Even though Judith scarcely mentions love, it remains for the modern reader a book of faith and hope.

The Book of Judith may be divided as follows:

I: The Assyrian Threat (1:1—3:10)
II: Campaign against Bethulia (4:1—7:32)
III: Deliverance through a Woman (8:1—13:20)
IV: Triumph of the People of God (14:1—16:20)
V: Epilogue (16:21-25)

I: THE ASSYRIAN THREAT*

A: Fall of the Empire of the Medes

CHAPTER 1*

War against the Medes. 1 It was the twelfth year of the reign of Nebuchadnezzar,* who ruled the Assyrians in the great city of Nineveh. During that period Arphaxad ruled over the Medes in Ecbatana,[a] 2 and he completely encircled this city with a wall constructed of hewn stones, each stone three cubits thick and six cubits long. The completed wall was seventy cubits high and fifty cubits thick. 3 At the city's gates he erected towers one hundred cubits high, with a thickness of sixty cubits at its foundations. 4 He made its gates seventy cubits high and forty cubits wide to enable his entire army to march out in a body with his infantry arrayed in proper rank.

5 In those days, King Nebuchadnezzar waged war against King Arphaxad in the vast plain of the district of Regau. 6 Coming to his support were all the inhabitants of the hill country, all who dwelt along the Euphrates, the Tigris, and the Hydaspes,* and from the plain, Arioch, king of the Elamites. Thus many nations banded together to confront the forces of the Cheleoud.[b]

Nebuchadnezzar's Message to Many Peoples. 7 Then Nebuchadnezzar, king of the Assyrians, sent messengers to all the inhabitants of Persia, and to all who lived in the west: those who dwelt in Cilicia and Damascus, Lebanon and Anti-lebanon, to all who lived along the seacoast, 8 to the peoples of Carmel and Gilead, Upper Galilee, and the great plain of Esdraelon, 9 to all those who were in Samaria and its towns, and beyond the Jordan as far as Jerusalem, Bethany, Chelous, Kadesh, and the River of Egypt, to Tahpanhes, Rameses, and the whole land of Goshen, 10 even beyond Tanis and Memphis, and to all the inhabitants of Egypt as far as the borders of Ethiopia. 11 However, the inhabitants of all those lands paid no heed to the summons of Nebuchadnezzar, king of the Assyrians, and refused to join forces with him for the campaign. They were not afraid of him, regarding him as just a man. They sent his envoys away empty-handed and in disgrace.

The Campaign against Arphaxad. 12 Then Nebuchadnezzar's anger was aroused against that entire region, and he swore by his throne and his kingdom to take revenge

a Gen 10:22.—b 1 Mac 6:1.

1:1—3:10 The author manipulates history, geography, and numbers, as in apocalyptic works, to impress the reader; in this gigantic and unequal combat, the fate of the party of God takes place.

1:1-16 Nebuchadnezzar personifies the power and haughtiness of those who dominate nations and combat the People of God. The name *Arphaxad*, a person unknown to history, is taken from Gen 10:22; the dimensions of the fortifications are exaggerated so as to give the impression of something colossal. The *forces of the Cheleoud* probably refers to the Chaldeans. The peoples are listed by enumerating the biblical names from one end to the other of the Near East. With the collapse of the Median Empire (in fact it was absorbed by the Persian Empire), the whole power of paganism lies in the hand of a single king. The public rejoicing is on a par with those after similar victories (Est 1:3-8; Dan 5).

1:1 *Nebuchadnezzar*, king of Babylonia (604–562 B.C.), was never called "king of Assyria" and did not reign at Nineveh, which had been destroyed in 612 B.C. by his father Nabopolassar. *Ecbatana* (modern-day Hamadan) was founded by the Mede Deioces. Some scholars believe that the Book's historical confusion (of which this is an example) is deliberate with the purpose of stamping the work as fiction.

1:6 *Hydaspes* is probably the result of a confusion with the well-known Hydaspes in India; it could refer to the Choaspes River, which flowed through Susa, or the Ulai, which flowed past it. The *Elamites* were found in the eastern province of the Persian Empire (see 1 Mac 6:1).

on all the territories of Cilicia, Damascus,
and Syria, and also to put to the sword all
the inhabitants of Moab, Ammon, the whole
of Judea, and everyone in Egypt, as far as the
coasts of the two seas.* [13] In the seventeenth
year he led his forces against King Arphaxad
and defeated him in battle. He routed the
whole army of Arphaxad, his entire cavalry
force, and all his chariots. [14] He occupied his
towns, and, advancing on Ecbatana, he
seized its towers, plundered its market-
places, and reduced its former splendor to
ruin. [15] He captured Arphaxad in the moun-
tain regions of Ragau and ran him through
with his spears, destroying him once and for
all. [16] Then he returned to Nineveh with all
who had joined forces with him, an
immense horde of warriors. There he and
his army rested and feasted for one hundred
and twenty days.[c]

B: The Western Campaign

CHAPTER 2

Council of War against the West. [1] In the
eighteenth year, on the twenty-second day
of the first month, there was a conference
in the palace of Nebuchadnezzar, king of
the Assyrians, about following through on
his threat of vengeance against the entire
region.* [2] Summoning all of his ministers
and nobles, he outlined to them his secret
plan and asserted his determination to
effect the total destruction of that entire
area. [3] They then decreed that all those
who had not responded to the king's sum-
mons were to be put to death.

[4] When he had completed his plan,
Nebuchadnezzar, king of the Assyrians,
summoned Holofernes,* the highest-rank-
ing general in his army, and second only to
him in power, and he said to him, [5] "Thus
says the great king, the lord of all the earth:
'Go forth from my presence and take with
you men of unquestioned valor, one hun-
dred and twenty thousand infantrymen and
twelve thousand cavalry.[d] [6] March against
all the peoples of the west because they
refused to comply with my command.
[7] Advise them to have earth and water
ready,* for I am moving against them in my
wrath and I will cover the entire extent of
their territory with the feet of my soldiers, to
whom I will deliver them to be plundered.
[8] Their wounded will fill their ravines and
wadis, and all of their rivers will be choked
to overflowing with their dead. [9] I will send
them away as exiles to the ends of the earth.

[10] " 'Therefore, go ahead of me and seize
all of their territory for me. Should they sur-
render to you, hold them for me until the
time comes for their punishment. [11] As for
those who resist, show them no mercy, but
hand them over to slaughter and plunder
throughout the entire region. [12] For as I
live,* and by my royal authority, what I have
spoken I will accomplish by my power. [13] Be
careful not to disobey a single word of your
lord, but carry out fully what I have com-
manded you—and do so without delay.' "

Campaign of Holofernes. [14] Leaving the pres-
ence of his lord, Holofernes summoned all
the commanders, generals, and officers of
the Assyrian army. [15] In compliance with the
orders of his lord, he mustered one hundred
and twenty thousand picked troops and
twelve thousand mounted archers, [16] and he
organized them in the regular battle forma-
tion. [17] He took along a vast number of
camels, donkeys, and mules to transport the
baggage, and innumerable sheep, oxen, and
goats for their food supply, [18] as well as
ample rations for every man, and a great
amount of gold and silver from the royal
palace.

[19] Then, in advance of King Nebuchad-
nezzar, he set out with his whole army on
the campaign to overrun the entire region to
the west with their chariots, cavalry, and
picked infantrymen. [20] Accompanying them
was a motley crowd like a swarm of locusts
or the dust particles of the earth—a multi-
tude too numerous to count.[e]

c Est 1:3f.—d 5f: Est D:13.—e Jdg 7:12; Joel 2:2-7.

1:12 *As far as the coasts of the two seas:* an obscure expression that may mean between the Dead Sea and the Mediterranean or between these two and the Red Sea.

2:1 The date is symbolic because Nebuchadnezzar destroyed Jerusalem and the temple in his eighteenth year (see Jer 51:12, 29).

2:4 *Holofernes* is a Persian name (as is *Bagoas* in Jud 12:11), and Artaxerxes III Ocho had two officers with those names. This indicates that in the author's mind, this Persian king was also symbolized by Nebuchadnezzar.

2:7 *To have earth and water ready:* a Persian way of speaking to indicate the provisions for troops that were moving through a country. In general, as we know from Greek historians, the Persians sought submission by pretending to offer earth and water.

2:12 *As I live:* this phrase usually indicates an oath on God's part (see Deut 32:40); thus, Nebuchadnezzar is putting himself on a par with divinity (see Jud 6:2). *By my royal authority:* literally, "by my hand"; after raising his hand against God and his people, Nebuchadnezzar is brought down by the "hand" of Judith (see Jud 9:9f; Isa 10:5-14).

C: Devastation of the Fertile Crescent*

Stages of the Campaign. 21 They set out from Nineveh, and after marching for three days they reached the plain of Bectileth. From Bectileth they moved ahead to encamp near the mountains that lie to the north of Upper Cilicia. 22 From there Holofernes advanced into the hill country with his entire force—infantry, cavalry, and chariots. 23 He ravaged Put and Lud and plundered all the Rassisites and the Ishmaelites on the border of the desert south of Chaldea.[f]

24 Then, following the Euphrates, he went through Mesopotamia and destroyed all the fortified cities along the Wadi Abron until he reached the sea. 25 He seized the territory of Cilicia and slaughtered everyone who offered him the slightest resistance. Then he proceeded to the southern borders of Japheth, facing Arabia. 26 He encircled the Midianites, set fire to their tents, and pillaged their sheepfolds. 27 Following that, he swooped down into the plain of Damascus at the time of the wheat harvest. He razed all their fields, destroyed their flocks and herds, sacked their towns, laid waste to their countryside, and slew all their young men by the sword.

28 Fear and dread of him seized all the inhabitants of the seacoast, those living in Sidon and Tyre and those located in Sur and Ocina as well as those found in Jamnia, while even the populations of Azotus and Ascalon were equally frightened of him.[g]

CHAPTER 3

Capitulation of the West. 1 Therefore, they sent envoys to him to sue for peace in these words: 2 "We, the servants of the great king, Nebuchadnezzar, lie prostrate before you. Do with us as you wish. 3 Our dwellings, all our territory, and all our wheat fields and our flocks and herds and all our encampments are yours to do with as you please. 4 Our towns and their inhabitants are also at your service; come and deal with them as you see fit."

5 After the envoys had been received by Holofernes and they told him all this, 6 he went down with his army to the seacoast and stationed garrisons in all the fortified towns, assigning picked men from them to serve as auxiliaries. 7 The people of these cities and all the inhabitants of the surrounding countryside welcomed him with garlands and dancing to the sound of tambourines.* 8 Despite this, he demolished all their sanctuaries and cut down their sacred groves, thereby carrying out his commission to destroy all the gods of the land so that all the nations would worship Nebuchadnezzar alone and that only he would be invoked as a god by people of every tongue and tribe.[h]
9 Finally, Holofernes advanced toward Esdraelon, in the neighborhood of Dothan, facing the great ridge of Judea. 10 He encamped between Geba* and Scythopolis and remained there for an entire month as he replenished the necessary supplies for his forces.

II: CAMPAIGN AGAINST BETHULIA

A: The Israelites Prepare To Resist*

CHAPTER 4

Defensive Preparations. 1 When the Israelites living in Judea heard of everything that Holofernes, the commander-in-chief of King Nebuchadnezzar, had done to the nations, and how he had pillaged and destroyed all their temples, 2 they were filled with unspeakable dread at his approach and greatly concerned over the fate of Jerusalem and of the temple of the LORD, their God.
3 For they had just returned from exile a short time before, and only recently had the

---

f Gen 10:22.—g Ex 15:15f.—h 2 Chr 17:6.

2:21—3:10 The forces of Holofernes arrive at the doors of Judea by outflanking the steppes of Syria from the north with a march that included a bizarre line of advance and stopping places, many of which are still unknown. This can only indicate that the author possessed little knowledge of local geography or had no interest in factual accuracy. The ultimate purpose of the conquistador is to demand from all the conquered peoples divine honors for his sovereign. Indeed, in Nebuchadnezzar, we see profiled the person of Antiochus IV Epiphanes, the second century B.C. persecutor of the Jews, who sought to impose his cult on them (Dan 11:36-37). The Assyrian and Babylonian kings did not demand divine honors; it all started with Alexander the Great.

3:7 This was the Greek manner of celebrating a victory, which reveals an author who was contemporary with the Hellenistic domination.

3:10 *Geba* may refer to the mountain range called "Gelboe," which had *Scythopolis* (the Greek name for Beth-shean mentioned in Jos 17:11) at its eastern end.

4:1-15 The very center of religious life, the temple, is threatened. The author clearly combines the remembrance of the Babylonian Exile and recent history. The whole fate of Israel depends on Bethulia, the unknown city that receives the mission to stop the invader. It is imagined as an inaccessible fortress that bars the way to Jerusalem. The name may have been selected because it evokes "Bethel," that is, the "house of God." The other localities seem to have been freely taken from the accounts of Joshua's conquests (Jos 6:1; 10:10; 11:1).

people of Judea been gathered together, with
the sacred vessels, the altar, and the temple
reconsecrated after their profanation.*
4 Therefore, they notified the entire region of
Samaria, Kona, Beth-horon, Belmain, and
Jericho, Choba and Aesora, and the Valley of
Salem. 5 The people of those areas estab-
lished outposts on the summits of the high
mountains, fortified their villages, and
stored up food supplies from the recently
harvested fields in preparation for war.

6 Joakim, the high priest in Jerusalem at
that time, wrote to the inhabitants of
Bethulia and Betomesthaim, which is oppo-
site Esdraelon, facing the plain near Dothan,
7 ordering them to occupy the mountain
passes, since they were the only means of
access to Judea. Since the narrow approach
would not allow more than two men to
advance abreast of each other, there would
be no difficulty in preventing the advance of
the attacking forces. 8 The Israelites carried
out the orders issued by Joakim, the high
priest, and by the senate* of the whole peo-
ple of Israel in session at Jerusalem.

Prayer and Penance. 9 At the same time, all
the men of Israel cried out to God with great
fervor, humbling themselves before him and
fasting. 10 They, together with their wives
and children, their livestock, and every resi-
dent alien, hired laborer, and slave, wrapped
themselves in sackcloth.[i] 11 And all the
Israelite men, women, and children living in
Jerusalem prostrated themselves in front of
the temple, and with ashes on their heads
they spread out their sackcloth before the
LORD. 12 They even draped the altar in sack-
cloth, and with one voice they prayed fer-
vently, imploring the God of Israel not to
allow their children to be carried off and
their wives to be taken captive, the towns
they had inherited to be destroyed, and their
temple to be profaned and desecrated for
the heathens to gloat over.[j]

13 The LORD heard their prayers and
looked kindly on them in their distress. For
the people fasted for many days throughout
Judea and before the temple of the LORD
Almighty in Jerusalem.[k] 14 Joakim the high
priest and all the priests stood in the pres-
ence of the LORD and ministered to him.
They wore sackcloth around their loins as
they offered the daily burnt offerings, the
votive offerings, and the freewill offerings of
the people. 15 With ashes on their turbans
they cried out to the LORD with all their
power, imploring him to look with favor on
the whole house of Israel.

B: A Council of War

CHAPTER 5

What People Is This? 1 Holofernes, the com-
mander-in-chief of the Assyrian army,
received the intelligence report that the
Israelites had prepared for war, blockading
the mountain passes, fortifying all the high
peaks, and establishing barricades in the
plains. 2 [l] Filled with rage, he summoned all
the princes of the Moabites, the generals of
the Ammonites, and the governors of the
coastal regions.* 3 "Tell me, you Canaan-
ites," he demanded, "what people is this that
dwells in the hill country? What towns do
they inhabit? How large is their army?
Whence do they derive their power and
strength? Who rules as their king and leads
their army? 4 Why have they alone, of all the
peoples of the west, refused to come and
meet with me?"

Discourse of Achior, the Good Pagan. 5 Then
Achior,* the leader of all the Ammonites,
said to him, "My lord, if it pleases you to
allow your servant to speak, I shall provide
you with the true facts about this people that
lives nearby in the mountain district.
Nothing that is untrue shall be spoken by the
lips of your servant.[m]

6 * "This people is composed of descen-
dants from the Chaldeans. 7 At one time
they settled in Mesopotamia because they
refused to follow the gods of their ancestors

---

i 10f: Joel 1:13f; 2:15ff; Jon 3:7f.—j Est 4:1f.—k Est 4:16.—l Deut 2:21.—m Jud 11:9-19.

4:3 See 1 Mac 4:36-61; 2 Mac 10:1-9. Against the chronology of things, the author places the return from the Exile and repopulation of Jerusalem (539–400 B.C.)—and apparently even the purification of the temple after the persecution of Antiochus IV Epiphanes—all within the lifetime of Nebuchadnezzar.

4:8 *Senate:* a post-Exilic institution. As for Joakim, see Neh 12:10.

5:2 This verse refers to petty local rulers.

5:5 *Achior:* is thought to have been fashioned after the celebrated sage Ahiqar mentioned in the Book of Tobit (Tob 1:21f; 2:10; 11:18; 14:10). The author has him give a summary of the history of Israel centered around the acts of God (see Pss 78; 105; 106; Wis 10; Ezek 16:20; Acts 7; see also the story of Balaam, Num 22–24). It prepares the ground for the words Judith will use to obtain Holofernes's attention (Jud 11:5-19).

5:6-9 Abraham originally came from Ur of the *Chaldeans* (Gen 11:28) and then migrated to Harran (Gen 11:31) in Aram-naharaim (Gen 24:10), which the Greeks named *Mesopotamia. The gods of their ancestors:* refers to the pagan gods that Abraham's father, Terah, and his relatives worshiped.

who lived in Chaldea.[n] 8 Since they had abandoned the ways of their ancestors and worshiped the God of heaven, the God they had come to know, they were banished from the presence of the gods of their forefathers. As a result, they fled to Mesopotamia, where they dwelt for a long time. 9 But their God commanded them to depart from the place where they were living and to migrate to Canaan.[o]

"They settled there and acquired great wealth in gold and silver and vast herds of livestock. 10 Later, when a severe famine afflicted the land of Canaan, they went down to Egypt, where they remained as long as food was available in abundance for them. There they grew into so great a multitude that their numbers could not be counted.[p] 11 So the king of Egypt turned against them and exploited them by forcing them to labor at brickmaking and reducing them to slavery.[q] 12 They besought their God, and he afflicted the whole land of Egypt with incurable plagues.

"When the Egyptians expelled them, 13 their God dried up the Red Sea before them[r] 14 and guided them along the route to Sinai and Kadesh-barnea. They drove out all the inhabitants of the desert, 15 settling in the land of the Amorites, and by their power they exterminated the entire population of Heshbon. Then they crossed over the Jordan and took possession of the whole hill country.[s] 16 They drove out before them the Canaanites, the Perizzites, the Jebusites, the Shechemites, and all the Gergesites, and they dwelt in the mountains for a long time.[t]

17 "As long as they did not sin before their God, they enjoyed prosperity, for their God who loathes wickedness was with them.[u] 18 However, whenever they strayed from the path he had prescribed for them, they suffered tremendous losses in many battles and were led away as captives to foreign countries. The temple of their God was razed to the ground, and their towns were occupied by their enemies.[v] 19 But now that they have returned to their God, they have come back from the lands where they had been scattered, have again taken possession of Jerusalem where their temple is located, and have settled in the mountain region that was uninhabited.

20 "So now, my lord and master, if this people has committed the fault of sinning against their God, and if we can ascertain the accuracy of this report, then we can go up and conquer them.[w] 21 But if they are a nation that is guiltless, then, my lord, it would be better for you to leave them alone, for their LORD and God will protect them, and we will then become the laughingstock of the whole world."

Reaction of the Pagans. 22 When Achior had finished with his recommendations, all the people crowding around the tent began to murmur. The officers of Holofernes and all the inhabitants of the seacoast and of Moab demanded that he be cut to bits. 23 "We are not afraid of the Israelites," they said. "They are a powerless people who are incapable of withstanding a strong attack. 24 Therefore, let us move forward, Lord Holofernes. Your great army will swallow them up."[x]

CHAPTER 6

Holofernes's Answer. 1 When the uproar of the crowd surrounding the council had subsided, Holofernes, the commander-in-chief of the Assyrian army, said to Achior in the presence of the whole contingent of the coastland peoples, of the Moabites, and of the Ammonite mercenaries: 2 "Who do you think you are, Achior, you and your Ephraimite mercenaries, to prophesy among us as you have done today and to attempt to convince us not to make war against the people of Israel because their God will protect them? What god is there besides Nebuchadnezzar? He will send his forces and wipe them off the face of the earth. Their God will not save them.[y]

3 "We, the servants of Nebuchadnezzar, will destroy them as easily as if they were one man. They will not be able to withstand the strength of our cavalry.[z] 4 We will tread them underfoot, their mountains will be drunk with their blood, and their plains will be filled with their corpses. They cannot possibly withstand us and will perish without a trace. Thus says King Nebuchadnezzar, lord of all the earth. He has spoken, and none of his words will prove to be unfulfilled.[a]

---

n Gen 11:31.—o Gen 11:31-12:5.—p Gen 42:1-5; 46:1-7; Ex 1:7.—q 11f: Ex 1:8-14; 5:4-21; 7:1-9.—r 13f: Ex 14:21f, 29.—s Num 21:21-32; Jos 2:10.—t Deut 7:1.—u 17f: Deut 28–30; Ps 106:40-46; Isa 59:2.—v 2 Ki 25.—w 20f: Jud 8:18ff; 11:10.—x Jud 6:2; 9:7; 16:2.—y Jud 3:8; 9:7; 2 Ki 18:32-35.—z Isa 36:18ff; 37:4, 16-20.—a Jud 6:17.

[5] "As for you, Achior, you Ammonite mercenary, you have said these things in a moment of perversity. Therefore, you will not see my face again from this day until I have taken revenge on this brood of fugitives from Egypt. [6] Then when I return, the sword of my army or the spear of my servants will pierce your sides, and you will fall among the wounded.[b] [7] My servants will now take you back into the hill country and leave you at one of the towns along the mountain passes. [8] You will not die until you perish together with them. [9] If you are truly confident that they will not fall into our hands, then there is no need for you to look so downcast. However, I have spoken, and none of my words will prove false in any respect."

Achior in Bethulia. [10] Then Holofernes ordered his servants who were standing by in his tent to seize Achior, transport him to Bethulia, and leave him for the Israelites. [11] And so the servants took him into custody and escorted him out of the camp into the plain, and from there into the hill country, until they arrived at the springs below Bethulia. [12] As soon as the men of the town saw them, they took up their weapons and ran out of the town to the top of the hill, and all the slingers prevented them from ascending by hurling stones on them. [13] Therefore, taking shelter below the hill, they bound Achior and left him lying at the foot of the hill. Then they returned to their master.

[14] When the Israelites came down from their town and found him, they untied him and led him into Bethulia. They brought him before the magistrates of the town, [15] who at that time were Uzziah, son of Micah of the tribe of Simeon, Chabris, son of Gothoniel, and Charmis, son of Melchiel. [16] Then they summoned all the elders of the town, and all the young men and women also hurried to the assembly. They had Achior stand in the midst of all the people, and Uzziah interrogated him about what had happened. [17] In reply he told them what had taken place at the council of Holofernes, what he himself had said in the presence of the Assyrian leaders, and all that Holofernes had boasted he would do to the house of Israel.

[18] On hearing this, the people fell prostrate in worship of God and cried out, [19] "O LORD, God of heaven, behold their arrogance. Have pity on our people in their humiliation, and look kindly this day on those who are consecrated* to you." [20] Then they reassured Achior and praised him warmly. [21] Uzziah brought him from the assembly to his home, where he gave a banquet for the elders. All that night they called upon the God of Israel for assistance.

C: Siege of Bethulia

CHAPTER 7

Holofernes's Maneuvers To Blockade Bethulia. [1] The following day Holofernes issued orders to his whole army and all the allies who had joined him to initiate action against Bethulia, seize the passes up into the hill country, and engage the Israelites in battle. [2] That same day their troops went into action, an army numbering one hundred and seventy thousand infantry and twelve thousand cavalry, not to mention the baggage train and the foot soldiers charged with its maintenance—an immense multitude. [3] They encamped in the valley near Bethulia close to the spring, and they spread out in breadth toward Dothan as far as Balbaim, and in length from Bethulia to Cyamon, which faces Esdraelon.

[4] When the Israelites caught sight of this vast force, they were greatly terrified. "These men will now devour the whole country," they said to one another. "Neither the high mountains nor the valleys nor the hills will ever be able to support their weight."[c] [5] Even so, they all took up their weapons, lit fires on their towers, and remained on guard throughout the night.

[6] On the second day Holofernes led out all his cavalry in full view of the Israelites in Bethulia. [7] He reconnoitered the approaches to the town and located the springs that were the source of their water supply. He seized these and stationed detachments of soldiers to guard them before he returned to his main force.

b Jud 5:22.—c 1 Mac 12:28f.

6:19 *Consecrated:* the holy people, set apart for the kingdom of God (see Ex 19:6; Dan 7:27; 8:24). The Vulgate (Jud 6:15) gives a longer form of this prayer: "O LORD, God of heaven and earth, behold their pride; see our lowliness and look favorably upon your holy ones. Show that you do not forsake those who trust in you, but that you bring low those who trust in themselves and glory in their own strength."

8 All the chieftains of the Edomites and all
the leaders of the Moabites, together with
the commanders of the coastal region,
jointly approached him. 9 "Please listen to
our suggestion, my lord," they said, "and
your army will not sustain a single loss.
10 These Israelites do not rely on their spears
but on the height of the mountains where
they dwell, for it is extremely difficult to
reach the peaks of the mountains.[d]
11 Therefore, my lord, do not employ a regu-
lar formation to attack them, and in this way
not a single one of your troops will be lost.

12 "Remain in your camp, and keep all
your troops there with you. Station some of
your soldiers to maintain control of the
spring flowing from the base of the moun-
tain, 13 since that is where all the people of
Bethulia obtain their water. When they start
dying of thirst, they will surrender their
town. Meanwhile, we and our troops will
ascend to the summits of the nearby moun-
tains and set up camp there to ensure that
not a single person will escape from that
town.[e] 14 They and their wives and children
will waste away with hunger, and even
before the sword strikes them their corpses
will be strewn in the streets of their town.
15 In this way you will make them pay dear-
ly for their defiance and their refusal to
receive you peacefully."

16 Their words pleased Holofernes and all
his attendants, and he gave orders for their
proposal to be carried out. 17 Accordingly,
the army of the Moabites moved forward,
together with five thousand Assyrians. They
encamped in the valley and seized the water
supply and the springs of the Israelites.
18 The Edomites and the Ammonites went
up and encamped in the hill country oppo-
site Dothan, and they sent some of their
forces to the southeast opposite Egrebel,
near Chusi, beside the Wadi Mochmur. The
remainder of the Assyrian army took up
positions in the plain; they filled the entire
countryside, forming an immense encamp-
ment with the great multitude of their tents
and supply trains.

The Israelites under Siege. 19 The Israelites
cried out to the LORD, their God, greatly dis-
heartened at the realization that their ene-
mies had surrounded them and cut off every
avenue of retreat. 20 For thirty-four days the
entire Assyrian army, with infantry, chari-
ots, and cavalry, kept them surrounded,
until all the water jars possessed by the
inhabitants of Bethulia were empty. 21 Their
cisterns were also running dry, so that there
was no day on which they had enough to
drink, and their drinking water began to be
rationed. 22 Their children fainted away, and
the women and young men grew weak with
thirst. They collapsed in the streets and the
gateways of the town, for they had no
strength left.

23 Then all the people, including the young
men, women, and children, gathered
around Uzziah and the rulers of the town.
They raised a great clamor of protest and
said in the presence of all the elders: 24 "May
God judge between you and us. You have
perpetrated a grave injustice on us by refus-
ing to sue for terms of peace with the
Assyrians. 25 Now we have no one to help us.
God has delivered us into their power, and
they will find us lying prostrate before them
from thirst and exhaustion. 26 Therefore, sur-
render to them even now. Deliver the entire
town as booty to the army of Holofernes and
to all his forces. 27 For it would be preferable
for us to be conquered by them. Even though
we would become their slaves, at least we
would be alive and not have to witness our
little ones dying before our eyes, and our
wives and children gasping their last breath.
28 By heaven and earth, and by our God, the
LORD of our ancestors, who is punishing us
for our own sins and those of our ancestors,
we adjure you to do this very day what we
have proposed."[f]

29 The entire assembly then wailed bitter
lamentations and called on the LORD God
with loud cries. 30 In response, Uzziah said
to them: "Have courage, my people! Let us
continue to hold out for five more days. By
that time the LORD, our God will show his
mercy toward us. He will not abandon us
completely. 31 At the end of that period, if
no help has reached us, I will do as you
say."[*] 32 Then he dismissed the men to
their posts, and they returned to the walls
and towers of their town. The women and
children were sent to their homes.
Throughout the town there was a sense of
impending doom.

---

d 1 Ki 20:23, 28; Ps 68:16.—e Ex 5:21.—f Jos 7:9.

7:31 It appears that Uzziah considers the town to be impregnable and is expecting help from Jerusalem or help from God in the form of a great rain that will fill all the cisterns of the town.

III: DELIVERANCE THROUGH A WOMAN

A: Judith the God-Fearer

CHAPTER 8

Pious, Beautiful, and Wealthy. 1 Now in those
days Judith learned about this situation.
She was the daughter of Merari, son of Ox,
son of Joseph, son of Oziel, son of Elkiah,
son of Ananias, son of Gideon, son of
Raphain, son of Ahitub, son of Elijah, son of
Hilkiah, son of Eliab, son of Nathanael, son
of Salamiel, son of Sarasdai, son of Simeon,
son of Israel.* 2 Her husband Manasseh,
who belonged to her own tribe and clan, had
died at the time of the barley harvest.
3 While he stood in the field supervising the
binding of the sheaves, he suffered sun-
stroke. He took to his bed and died in
Bethulia, his native city, and was buried
with his ancestors in the field between
Dothan and Balamon.

4 Judith remained home as a widow for
three years and four months. 5 She set up a
shelter for herself on the roof of her house,
wearing sackcloth around her waist and
dressed in mourning garb.[g] 6 She fasted all
the days of her widowhood except on the
Sabbath eve and the Sabbath itself, the day
before the new moon and the day of the new
moon, and the festivals and days of rejoicing
of the house of Israel.[h] 7 She was beautifully
formed and lovely to behold. Her husband
Manasseh had left her gold and silver, men
and women servants, livestock, and land,
and she oversaw this inheritance. 8 No one
had anything derogatory to say about her,
for she was a deeply God-fearing woman.

The Elders Reproached. 9 When Judith heard
about how the shortage had demoralized the
people and about the harsh words of bitter
complaint they had spoken against their
ruler, and she learned of all that Uzziah had
said to them in reply, as he had promised
them under oath to hand over the town to
the Assyrians at the end of five days, 10 she
dispatched her maid who was in charge of all
her possessions to ask Uzziah, Chabris, and
Charmis, the elders of the city, to visit her.
11 When they arrived, she said to them:

"Listen to me, rulers of the people of
Bethulia. You were wrong to speak to the
people as you did today, binding yourself by
an oath between God and you, vowing to
hand over the town to our enemies at the
end of five days unless the LORD comes to
our aid by that time. 12 What right do you
have to put God to the test this day, and to
set yourselves above him in the disposal of
human affairs?[i] 13 You are laying down con-
ditions for the LORD Almighty. Will you
never understand anything? 14 If you cannot
plumb the depths of the human heart or
comprehend the workings of the human
mind, how then can you fathom God who
has made all these things, discern his mind,
and understand his purposes?[j]

"No, my brothers, do not provoke the
anger of the LORD, our God. 15 For even if he
does not decide to come to our aid within
the next five days, he has the power to pro-
tect us at any time he pleases, or even to
destroy us in the presence of our enemies.
16 It is not your right to impose conditions
on the LORD, our God.

"God is not like a human being, to be
persuaded by threats,
or like a mere mortal, to be won over
by pleas.

17 "Therefore, while we await the deliver-
ance that is his to give, let us call upon him
to help us, and he will hear our cry if it
pleases him. 18 For in recent times and even
today there has not been a single tribe or
clan or district or town of ours that wor-
ships gods made with human hands, as was
the case in days gone by.[k] 19 It was due to
such conduct that our ancestors were hand-
ed over to the sword and pillage and were
utterly destroyed by our enemies.[l] 20 How-
ever, since we acknowledge no other god but
the LORD, we sustain the hope that he will
not desert us or any of our people.

21 "If we are captured, then all Judea will
fall, and our temple will be pillaged, and
God will make us pay with our blood for its
desecration. 22 The blame for the slaughter
and deportation of our kindred and the dev-
astation of our land he will lay on our heads
wherever among the nations we shall be
enslaved. We will be a source of mockery
and contempt in the eyes of our masters.
23 Our enslavement will not become a

g Jdg 3:20; 2 Ki 4:10.—h Lk 2:37.—i Job 38:2; 40:2, 7f; 42:3.—j Job 41:3; Prov 14:10; Wis 9:13; Isa 40:13; Rom 11:33f; 1 Cor 2:11.—k Jud 5:20f; 11:10.—l Pss 78:56f; 106:13f; Jer 7:16-20.

8:1 The third part of the Book begins. Through her name, this young widow incarnates the people of the covenant (Jud 16:3f).

source of eventual benefit to us, but the LORD, our God will use it to dishonor us.

24 “Therefore, my brothers, let us set an example for our kindred. Their very lives depend upon us, and the defense of the sanctuary, the temple, and the altar is our responsibility. 25 Despite all this, let us offer thanks to the LORD, our God, for he is putting us to the test as he did our ancestors.[m] 26 Remember how he dealt with Abraham, and how he tested Isaac, and what happened to Jacob in Syrian Mesopotamia while he was tending the sheep of Laban, his mother's brother. 27 The LORD did not subject them to these fiery ordeals for vengeance but to test their loyalty, and so has he done with us.[n] The LORD chastises those who worship him as a means of admonition.” *

The Elders' Accord. 28 Then Uzziah said to her: “Everything that you have said was spoken with a sincere heart, and there is no one who can deny your words. 29 Today has not been the first time that you have given evidence of your wisdom, for from your earliest years all the people have recognized your good sense and the right disposition of your heart. 30 However, the people were so parched with thirst that they led us to make this promise and to take an oath that cannot be broken. 31 But you are a God-fearing woman. Therefore, pray for us now, petitioning the LORD to send rain to fill our cisterns so that we shall no longer be faint with thirst.”

32 “Listen to me,” Judith said to them. “I intend to do something that will be remembered by our descendants through all future generations. 33 Be present at the town gate tonight to let me go out with my maid. Before the days have ended that have been designated by you to surrender the town to our enemies, the LORD will deliver Israel by my hand.

34 * “But do not question me about the plan I have in mind, for I will not reveal anything to you until I have accomplished what I intend to do.” 35 Uzziah and the rulers said to her, “Go in peace, and may the LORD God be with you to take vengeance on our enemies.” 36 Then they left her roof shelter and returned to their posts.

B: The Prayer of Judith*

CHAPTER 9

Tribal Memories. 1 Then Judith prostrated herself, strewed ashes on her head, and uncovered the sackcloth she was wearing. At the same time when the evening incense was being offered in the temple of God in Jerusalem, Judith besought the LORD in a loud voice:[o]

2 “O LORD, God of my ancestor Simeon,
you have armed him with a sword
so that he could exact vengeance on those foreigners
who had torn off a virgin's girdle to defile her,
exposed her thighs to cause her to be ashamed,
and violated her womb to dishonor her.
“Even though you had warned them,
‘This must not happen,’
they proceeded to do so. *[p]

3 As a result, you turned over their rulers
to be slaughtered,
and you covered with their blood
the bed that they had defiled with their treachery.
You struck down slaves as well as their princes,
even princes as they sat on their thrones.

4 You handed over their wives as booty
and sent their daughters into captivity,
and all the spoils you apportioned among your beloved sons
who had burned with zeal for you
and who in their abhorrence at the defilement of their kinswoman
called on you for help.

5 “O God, my God,
heed also the prayer of a widow.
You were the source of these events
and those that occurred before and those that followed.

m 25f: Gen 22:1-12.—n Deut 4:7.—o Ex 30:7f; Ps 141:2.—p Jud 6:15; Gen 34.

8:27 It is not bearing suffering and one's cross that makes people holy and dear to God but suffering with patience.

8:34-35 It was not a weak woman who was liberating the people, but God; and to move God to work his wonders, prayer was needed.

9:1-14 It is the hour of evening prayer. In union with the worshipers in the temple, Judith prostrates herself and addresses a long prayer to God (see Neh 9:5f; Tob 3:lf; 4:11f; Est 4:17f).

9:2 The virgin referred to was Dinah, daughter of Jacob, who was victimized by the Hivite Shechem (Gen 34:2). In revenge, Dinah's brothers, Simeon and Levi, persuaded Shechem and the men of his city into being circumcised and then slew them while they lay weak in bed (see Gen 34:13-29).

You have planned what is happening now
and what will occur in the future.
Whatever you devise comes to pass.[q]
6 The things you decide upon present themselves and proclaim:
'Here we are.'
All your ways are prepared in advance,
and your judgment is made with foreknowledge.[r]

Trust Only in God

7 "Here are the Assyrians,
a vast force, glorying in their horses and riders,
boasting of the strength of their foot soldiers,
and placing their trust in shield and spear, bow and sling.
They are not aware that you are the LORD
who obliterates wars;
the title of LORD is yours alone.[s]
8 "Shatter their strength with your power
and crush their might in your wrath.
For they are determined to desecrate your sanctuary
and to defile the tabernacle where your glorious name resides,
and with their swords to cut down the horns of your altar.
9 Take note of their arrogance
and bring down your wrath on their heads.
Give me, a widow,
the strength of hand to accomplish my plan.[t]
10* By the guile of my lips
strike down the slave together with the master,
the ruler together with the servant.
Shatter their arrogance
by the hand of a woman.
11 "Your strength does not lie in numbers
nor does your power depend upon strong men.
You are the God of the lowly,
the helper of the oppressed,
the support of the weak,
the protector of the forsaken,
the savior of those who have lost all hope.[u]
12 "Please, please, God of my forefather,
God of the heritage of Israel,
LORD of heaven and earth,
Creator of the waters,
king of all your creation,
hear my prayer.
13 Grant that my deceitful words may result
in the wounding and destruction of those
who have devised dire plans
against your covenant and against your temple,
against Mount Zion and the dwelling place your children have inherited.[v]
14 Let your whole nation and all its tribes clearly understand
that you are God,
the God of all power and might,
and that there is no other who protects the people of Israel
but you alone."

C: Judith Goes to War

CHAPTER 10

The Preparations. 1 When Judith had concluded her petition to the God of Israel and
had ended all these words, 2 she rose from the
ground where she had been lying prostrate,
summoned her maid, and went down into
the house, whose use she restricted only to
Sabbaths and feast days. 3 Removing the
sackcloth she had been wearing and laying
aside her widow's garb, she bathed her body
with water and anointed herself with precious perfumes. She arranged her hair, tied a
ribbon around it, and donned the festive
attire she was accustomed to wear when her
husband Manasseh was still alive.[w] 4 She put
sandals on her feet and arrayed herself with
anklets, bracelets, rings, earrings, and all her
jewelry. In this way she made herself beautiful enough to entice the eyes of all the men
who might see her.[x]
5 She gave her maid a skin of wine and a
flask of oil, and she filled a bag with roasted
grain, cakes of dried figs, bread, and cheese.

q Isa 44:7; Pss 115:3; 135:6.—r Job 38:35; Isa 46:9-13; Bar 3:35.—s 7f: Jud 5:23; 6:2; 16:2; Ps 33:16f.—t Ps 59:13-14.—u Jdg 7:4-7; 1 Sam 14:6.—v Jud 10:4; 11:20, 23; 16:6, 9; Est C:23f.—w Jud 8:6ff.—x Jud 9:13.

9:10-13 Judith proposes to captivate Holofernes with her beauty and then slay him. She could do this legitimately using guile and violence because Holofernes was waging war on Bethulia.

Wrapping up all these provisions, she gave them to the maid as well.[*][y]

[6] They then went out to the town gate of Bethulia, where they found Uzziah waiting with the elders of the city, Chabris and Charmis. [7] When they beheld Judith transformed in looks and dressed quite differently, they were amazed at her beauty and said to her, [8] "May the God of our ancestors grant his favor to you and crown your efforts with success, so that the Israelites may be glorified and Jerusalem may be exalted."

Judith bowed down to God. Then she said to them, [9] "Order that the town gate be opened for me so that I may go forth and carry out the things you have just said to me." They complied with her request and ordered the young men to open the gate for her. [10] When they had done so, Judith went out, accompanied by her maid. The men of the city continued to watch her until she went down the mountain and crossed the valley, at which point they lost sight of her.

In the Enemy Camp. [11] As the two women were proceeding straight across the valley, they were intercepted by an Assyrian patrol. [12] * The soldiers took Judith into custody and asked her, "To what people do you belong? Where have you come from, and where are you going?" "I am a daughter of the Hebrews," she replied, "and I am fleeing from them, because they are about to be delivered into your hands and become your prey. [13] I am on my way to see Holofernes, the commander-in-chief of your army, to give him a trustworthy intelligence report. I will show him a route by which he can gain control of the entire hill country without a single one of his men being either injured or slain."[z]

[14] As the soldiers listened to what she had to say, they gazed upon her face and marveled at her beauty. [15] "By coming down so promptly to see our master, you have saved your life," they said. "Go immediately to his tent. Some of us will escort you and present you to him. [16] When you are in his presence, do not be afraid. Just report to him what you have told us, and he will treat you well." [17] Then they detailed a hundred of their men to serve as an escort for her and her maid, and they brought them to the tent of Holofernes.

[18] When the news of her arrival spread through the tents of the camp, a crowd gathered around her as she stood outside the tent of Holofernes while he was being informed about her. [19] They were filled with admiration for her beauty, which caused them to feel a sense of wonder in respect to all the Israelites. They said to one another, "How can anyone despise these people who have women like this among them? It would be a wise move on our part not to leave a single one of their men alive, for if they get away, they will be able to beguile the entire world."

D: Judith Meets Holofernes

First Meeting. [20] Then the bodyguards of Holofernes and all of his attendants came out and escorted her into the tent. [21] Holofernes was reclining on his bed under a canopy of purple and gold decorated with emeralds and other precious stones. [22] When they announced her to him, he came to the entrance of the tent, with lamps of silver borne before him. [23] As Judith came into the presence of Holofernes and his attendants, they all marveled at the beauty of her face. She prostrated herself before him and paid him homage, but his attendants raised her up.

CHAPTER 11

[1] Then Holofernes said to her, "Have courage, woman! You have no reason to fear. I have never done harm to anyone who chose to serve Nebuchadnezzar, the king of the whole earth. [2] As for your people who dwell in the hill country, if they had not insulted me, I would never have raised my spear against them. They have brought this on themselves. [3] But now tell me why you have fled from them and have come over to us. In any case, you have guaranteed your safety by joining us. Have courage! You will survive this night and countless nights thereafter. [4] No one will harm you. On the contrary, you will be well treated, as is true of all the subjects of my lord, King Nebuchadnezzar."

[5] Judith replied, "Please listen to the words of your servant, and allow your handmaid to speak in your presence. I will utter no deceit-

y Jud 12:2; Est C:28.—z Jud 11:5f.

10:5 Judith brought food with her so as not to be made unclean by taking pagan food.

10:12-13 Judith's use of deceit here and in 11:5-19 is in accord with Old Testament morality (see Gen 27:1-25; 34:13-29; 37:32ff; Jos 2:1-7; Jdg 4:17-22).

ful untruth to my lord this night.[a] 6 If you fol-
low the advice of your handmaid, God will
grant success to your efforts, and my lord
will not fail to achieve any of his purposes.
7 By the life of Nebuchadnezzar, the king of
all the earth, and by the power of him who
has sent you to bring a sense of order to the
lives of all creatures! Not only do all people
serve him through you, but even the wild
beasts, the cattle, and the birds of the air as
a result of your power will live in the service
of Nebuchadnezzar and his entire house![b]
8 We have indeed heard of your wisdom and
cleverness. You are renowned everywhere
throughout the whole world as being unsur-
passed in ability anywhere in the kingdom, a
man of superior intellect and brilliant as a
military tactician.

9 [c] "We have also learned of Achior's
speech to your council. When the men of
Bethulia spared him, he told them every-
thing he had said to you. 10 Please do not
disregard his words, but keep them in mind,
for what he said is true. Our people cannot
be punished nor will the sword prevail over
them unless they sin against their God.[d]
11 But now, my lord, you will not experience
any defeat or failure, for sin has permeated
their lives and they are doomed to die.

12 "Since their food supply is exhausted
and their water is desperately low, they have
decided to slaughter their animals, and they
are determined to consume all the things
that God by his laws has forbidden them to
eat. 13 They have decided to eat the first-
fruits of the grain and the tithes of oil and
wine that they had consecrated and
reserved for the priests who minister in the
presence of our God in Jerusalem—things it
is unlawful for any layperson to so much as
touch.[e] 14 They have sent messengers to
Jerusalem to seek authorization from the
council of elders, since even the people
there have been doing these things. 15 On the
very day that authorization arrives and
they act upon it, they will be handed over to
you to be destroyed.

16 "When I, your servant, learned all this,
I fled from them. God has sent me to
accomplish with you such deeds that will
astonish people throughout the world
whenever they learn about them. 17 * [f] I,
your servant, am a God-fearing woman,
and I worship the God of heaven night and
day. Now, my lord, I ask your authorization
to remain with you. Every night your ser-
vant will go out into the valley and pray to
God. He will reveal to me when they have
committed their sinful acts. 18 Then I will
come and let you know, so that you may go
out with your whole army, and none of
them will be able to withstand you. 19 I will
guide you through Judea until you reach
Jerusalem, and there I will set up your
throne in the very center of the city. You will
drive them as if they were sheep without a
shepherd, and not even a dog will dare to
growl at you. I have been granted fore-
knowledge of this; it was revealed to me,
and I have been sent to proclaim it to you."

No Other Woman Is Her Equal! 20 Her words
pleased Holofernes and all his attendants.
They marveled at her wisdom and ex-
claimed,[g] 21 "No other woman from one end
of the earth to the other is her equal in
beauty and in wisdom of speech!" 22 Then
Holofernes said to her, "God has done well
in sending you ahead of your people so that
victory will be ours and destruction will be
the fate of those who have insulted my lord.
23 Not only are you beautiful to behold, but
you are eloquent in your wisdom. If you do
as you have promised, your God shall be my
God; furthermore, you shall dwell in the
palace of King Nebuchadnezzar and you
shall be renowned throughout the entire
world."[h]

CHAPTER 12

Judith's Conduct. 1 Then he commanded
them to bring her to the room where his sil-
ver dinnerware was kept, and he gave
orders that a table be set for her with some
of his own delicacies to eat and his own wine
to drink. 2 But Judith said, "I cannot partake
of these, in case doing so might cause me to
break our law. What I have brought with me
will be sufficient for my needs."[i] 3 "Should
your provisions run out," Holofernes asked
her, "where can we acquire more of the
same kind to replenish your supply? None
of your people are here with us." 4 Judith

a 5f: Jud 10:13.—b Jer 27:6; Bar 3:16f; Dan 2:38.—c 9f: Jud 5:5.—d Jud 5:21; 8:18.—e Deut 14:22.—f Jud 11:15.—g Jud 9:13.—h Jud 9:13.—i Jud 10:5; Est C:28; Dan 1:8.

11:17-20 Judith takes advantage of the idea of the pagans who believed in divine communications given as oracles in determinate places almost always at night, and says that she is going to receive the orders of her God outside the camp. She does this so as to have ease of flight once Holofernes is slain (see Jud 13:10).

replied, "As surely as you live, my lord, your
servant will not use up the supplies I have
with me before the LORD accomplishes by
my hand what he has foreordained."
[5]Then the attendants of Holofernes led
her into the tent, where she slept until mid-
night. Shortly before the morning watch she
arose [6]and sent this message to Holofernes:
"Please give orders, my lord, to allow your
servant to go out and pray." [7]Holofernes
commanded his guards not to restrict her
movements. She remained in the camp for
three days, going out each night to the Valley
of Bethulia and bathing in the spring of the
camp. [8]After bathing, she would implore
the LORD, the God of Israel, to guide her
way toward the triumph of his people.
[9]Then she would return, purified, to the
camp and remain in the tent until she took
her evening meal.

E: Judith Overcomes Holofernes

The Tragic Banquet. [10]On the fourth day
Holofernes held a banquet for his personal
attendants only. None of his army officers
was invited. [11]He said to Bagoas, the
eunuch in charge of his personal affairs,
"Go to the Hebrew woman who is in your
care and persuade her to come and join us
and to eat and drink in our company. [12]We
would be disgraced if we let such a woman
go without enjoying her favors. If we do not
seduce her, she will laugh us to scorn."
[13]So Bagoas left the presence of Holo-
fernes and approached Judith. "My fair
maiden," he said, "do not be reluctant to
come to my lord and enjoy the honor of his
company. Enjoy yourself, drink wine with
us, and behave today like one of the
Assyrian women who are in attendance at
the palace of Nebuchadnezzar." [14]"Who am
I to refuse my lord?" Judith replied. "I am
eager to do promptly whatever is pleasing
to him, and that will be a source of joy to me
until the day of my death."
[15]Thereupon she proceeded to adorn her-
self with her festive garments and all her
feminine finery. Her maid went ahead of
her and spread out on the ground for her in
front of Holofernes the fleece* she had
received from Bagoas on which she might
recline while dining. [16]Then Judith came in
and took her place. Holofernes was over-
come with desire for her, and his passion
was aroused. He had been waiting for an
opportunity to seduce her from the day he
had first laid eyes on her. [17]He said to her,
"Drink, and be merry with us!" [18]"I will
gladly do so, my lord," Judith replied, "for
today is the greatest day of my life." [19]Then
she took what her maid had prepared, and
she ate and drank in his presence. [20]Holo-
fernes was so enchanted with her that he
drank a great quantity of wine, more than
he had ever drunk on any one day in his
entire life.

CHAPTER 13

The Critical Moment. [1]When the hour grew
late, his attendants quickly withdrew.
Bagoas closed the tent from the outside and
excluded the attendants from the master's
presence. They withdrew to their beds, for
the banquet had lasted so long that they
were all exhausted.* [2]Judith was left alone in
the tent with Holofernes, who was sprawled
on his bed, completely intoxicated. [3]Judith
had instructed her maid to stand outside
the bedchamber and to wait for her to come
out, as was the case on the previous days.
She had said that she would be going out to
pray, and she explained this also to Bagoas.
Death of Holofernes. [4]When all had depart-
ed and no one of either great or minor
importance was left in the bedchamber,
Judith stood beside the bed of Holofernes
and silently uttered this prayer: "O LORD,
God of all power, look favorably in this hour
on what I am doing for the glory of
Jerusalem. [5]Now is the time to come to the
aid of your heritage and to carry out my
plan to crush the enemies who have risen
up against us."
[6]She then went to the bedpost near the
head of Holofernes and took the sword that
hung there. [7]She drew close to his bed,
grasped the hair of his head, and said, "Give
me strength this moment, O LORD, God of
Israel." [8]Then with all her might she struck
his neck twice and cut off his head.*[j] [9]Next

j Jdg 4:21.

12:15 *Fleece:* a carpet on which one could stretch out to eat according to custom in the East.

13:1 Everyone departed in order to leave Holofernes with Judith. Bagoas, who was the last to depart, closed the tent from the outside so that Judith could not exit. But Judith had left her maid outside in order to act as a lookout and to open the tent for her.

13:8 It was always legitimate to slay an enemy in war. At this time, the war was not between armies but between peoples, and the conquered peoples were slain or enslaved. Hence, it was licit for Judith to slay Holofernes, and even more so inasmuch as she represented the town of Bethulia and had received permission to do what she did from the town's authorities.

she rolled his body off the bed and pulled down the canopy from its posts. After this she came out and handed over the head of Holofernes to her maid, 10 who put it in the food pouch. The two of them then left the camp together, as they were accustomed to do when going out to pray.

Liberation Proclaimed. They passed through the camp, circled around the valley, and ascended the mountain to Bethulia. As they approached its gates, 11 Judith called out to the sentries from a distance, "Open up! Open the gate! God, our God, is with us, still exhibiting his power in Israel and his strength against our enemies. He has done so this very day."[k] 12 When the people of the town heard her voice, they hurried down to the town gate and summoned the elders. 13 All the people, of both high and low rank, came running, for it hardly seemed credible that she had returned safely. They opened the gate and welcomed the women, lighting a fire to provide light, and gathering around them.

14 Judith then cried out in a loud voice: "Praise God! Praise him! Praise God who has not withdrawn his mercy from the house of Israel but has destroyed our enemies by my hand this very night!"

15 Then she removed the head from the food pouch and held it up for them to see. "Behold the head of Holofernes," she said, "the commander-in-chief of the Assyrian army, and here is the canopy under which he lay in a drunken daze. The LORD has struck him down by the hand of a woman.[l] 16 As the LORD lives, who has protected me on my journey, I swear that it was my face that seduced him to his destruction, and that he committed no sinful act with me to cause my defilement or my disgrace."*

Blessed Are You above All Other Women!* 17 All the people were greatly astonished, and, bowing in worship to God, they spoke with a single voice: "Blessed are you, our God, for this day you have humiliated the enemies of your people." 18 Then Uzziah said to her:

"Blessed are you, daughter, by the Most High God,
above all other women on earth.
And blessed be the LORD God,
the Creator of heaven and earth,
under whose guidance you cut off
the head of the leader of our enemies.[m]
19 The hope that inspired you will never fade
from the memory of those who praise the power of God.
20 May God make your deed redound to your everlasting honor
and shower blessings upon you,
because you risked your life
when our nation was faced with annihilation,
and you averted our ruin,
walking uprightly before the LORD."

And all the people responded, "Amen! Amen!"

IV: TRIUMPH OF THE PEOPLE OF GOD

A: Response to the News of Holofernes's Death

CHAPTER 14

Judith's Counsel. 1 Then Judith said to them, "Listen to me, my friends. Take this head and hang it upon the parapet of your wall. 2 Then at daybreak, as soon as the sun rises, all of you should take up your weapons, and let all the able-bodied men march out of the city under the direction of a leader, as if you were about to march down to the plain to attack the Assyrian outpost. But do not go down. 3 Their soldiers will seize their weapons and go into the camp to rouse the commanders of the Assyrian army. When they rush to the tent of Holofernes and do not find him, panic will seize them and they will flee before you. 4 Then you and all who live within the borders of Israel will pursue them and cut them down in their tracks. 5 * But before you

k Ex 15:1-2; Pss 48:7-11; 68; 98:1-3.—l Jud 14:18.—m Jdg 5:24; Lk 1:28, 42.

13:16 The Vulgate (Jud 13:20-21) has a fuller text corresponding to this verse: "20 As the LORD is a living God, his angel has protected me on the way to Holofernes, during my stay there, and on my return. The LORD has not allowed his handmaid to be defiled but has brought me back to you without stain of sin, rejoicing over his victory, my escape, and your deliverance. 21 One and all, glorify him, for he is good, for his mercy endures forever" [see Ps 136:1].

13:17-20 The Liturgy has made use of this text to render homage to the Blessed Virgin Mary who with full knowledge faced the moral sufferings connected with her divine motherhood.

14:5-10 The courage of Achior the Ammonite is rewarded: he gives glory to the true God and is received in the holy community of Israel. In being converted, Achior begins to realize what awaits Israel: the salvation of non-Jews (Sir 36:1-3; Isa 60).

do all this, bring Achior the Ammonite to me so that he may see and recognize the man who treated the house of Israel with contempt and sent him to us as if to his death."

Achior Summoned. 6 Therefore, they summoned Achior from the house of Uzziah. When he came and saw the head of Holofernes held up by one of the men in the assembly of the people, he fell forward in a dead faint. 7 After they revived him, he threw himself at the feet of Judith and did homage to her. "Blessed are you in every tent in Judah," he said, "and the people of every nation who hear your name will be terror-stricken. 8 But now please tell me everything that you did during these days."

In the presence of the people Judith recounted all that she had done from the day she left until the very moment she began speaking to them. 9 When she had finished speaking, the people raised a great shout, and the town resounded with their cries of jubilation. 10 Upon seeing all that the God of Israel had done, Achior believed firmly in God. Therefore, he was circumcised, and he became a member of the community of Israel, as he is to the present day.[n]

Consternation in the Camp.* 11 At daybreak they hung the head of Holofernes on the wall. Then all the Israelite men took up their weapons and marched out in companies to the mountain passes. 12 When the Assyrians saw them, they sent word to their leaders, who immediately notified the generals and captains and all the other officers. 13 These in turn came to the tent of Holofernes and said to the steward in charge of all his personal affairs, "Wake up our master, for the slaves have had the audacity to come down to engage in battle against us, which will be their complete destruction."

14 Bagoas went in and knocked at the entry of the tent, thinking Holofernes was sleeping with Judith. 15 But when no one answered, he parted the curtains, entered the bedchamber, and found him sprawled on the floor, dead, with his head missing. 16 He burst forth with a great cry, weeping and groaning and shouting, and he tore his garments. 17 Then he went into the tent that Judith had occupied, and when he did not find her, he rushed out to the assembled troops and shouted: 18 "The slaves have tricked us! A single Hebrew woman has brought disgrace on the house of King Nebuchadnezzar! Look! Holofernes is lying on the ground, headless!"[o]

19 When the leaders of the Assyrian army heard these words, they tore their tunics and were greatly confounded. Loud cries and shouts arose in the camp.

CHAPTER 15

General Disbandment.* 1 When the men who were still in their tents learned what had happened, they were thrown into confusion. 2 Overcome with fear and trembling, they made no effort to band together in unity, but with one accord they all rushed out and fled by every road across the plain and through the mountains. 3 Those who had been stationed in the hills around Bethulia also took to flight. Then all the Israelite soldiers rushed out in pursuit of them.

4 Uzziah sent messengers to Betomasthaim, to Choba and Kona, and to the whole territory of Israel to inform them what had occurred and to urge all of them to attack the enemy and destroy them. 5 As soon as the Israelites heard the news, they all attacked the enemy with a unified spirit and cut them down all the way to Choba. Even the men from Jerusalem and the entire mountain region participated in the onslaught, for they too had been told of what had happened in the camp of the enemy. The men of Gilead and Galilee surrounded the flanks of the enemy and inflicted a great slaughter, even beyond Damascus and its borders.

6 The rest of the inhabitants of Bethulia fell on the camp of the Assyrians and plundered it, acquiring great riches. 7 And when the Israelites returned from the slaughter, they seized what remained. Even the villages and towns of the hill country and the plain acquired a great amount of booty, which was available in large quantities.[p]

n Ex 12:48.—o Jud 13:15; 16:5-9; Jdg 9:54.—p Est 9:5, 16.

14:11-19 Judith has proved right. Believing themselves attacked, the Assyrian soldiers run to get their arms. They already are treating the besieged people as slaves. However, a surprise awaits them: they discover the cadaver of the general-in-chief.

15:1-7 As at the time of Gideon, a divine terror sows panic in the camp of the enemies (Jdg 7:7-21). To the disbandment of the Assyrian army responds the regathering of the children of Israel: the effect is desired by the author.

B: Ceremonies of Thanksgiving

The Honor of Our People!* 8 Joakim the high priest and the elders of the Israelites who dwelt in Jerusalem came to witness for themselves the wonderful things that the LORD had done for Israel, and to meet Judith and offer her their congratulations.[q]
9 *When they came into her presence, they all blessed her with one accord and said to her:

"You are the glory of Jerusalem,
the surpassing pride of Israel,
the great honor of our people.
10 You have done all this with your own hand;
you have been the source of much good to Israel,
and God has approved what you have wrought.
May you be blessed by the LORD Almighty
forever and ever."

And all the people responded, "Amen!"
11 The entire populace looted the camp for thirty days. They presented Judith with the tent of Holofernes, all his silver dinnerware, his beds, his drinking vessels, and all his furniture. She accepted these gifts, harnessed her mules, hitched them to her wagons, and loaded the gifts on them.
12 All the women of Israel gathered to see her. They sang her praises and performed a dance in her honor. She took branches of ivy* in her hands and distributed them among the women around her,[r]
13 while she and those women crowned themselves with olive wreaths. Then, at the head of the procession, she led the women as they danced, while the men of Israel, in full armor, followed them, wearing garlands and singing hymns.

C: Judith's Hymn of Thanksgiving

14 In the presence of all Israel, Judith began this hymn of thanksgiving, and the people joined her in singing it:*

CHAPTER 16

1 "Break into song to my God with tambourines,
sing to the LORD with cymbals.
Offer to him a psalm of praise,
exalt him and invoke his name.[s]
2 For the LORD is a God who crushes warfare
and establishes his camp in the midst of his people;
he delivered me from the hands of my oppressors.[t]
3 "The Assyrian descended from the mountains of the north,
with myriads of his warriors he came.
Their troops choked the valleys
and their cavalry covered the hills.
4 He threatened to set my country aflame
and put my young men to the sword,
dash my infants to the ground,
seize my children as booty,
and carry off my virgins as spoil.
5 "But the LORD Almighty has thwarted them[u]
by the hand of a woman.
6 For their mighty one was not brought low by young men;
no titans* struck him down,
nor did tall giants assault him.
But Judith, the daughter of Merari,
overcame him by the beauty of her face.[v]
7 She laid aside her widow's garb
to raise up the oppressed in Israel.

q Isa 25:1.—r Ex 15:20f; Jdg 11:34; 1 Sam 18:6; Jer 31:4, 13.—s Pss 81:2f; 135:1ff; 149:1ff.—t Jud 5:23; 6:2; 9:7f; Ex 15:3; Pss 46:10; 68:30; 76:3.—u Jud 14:8.—v Jud 9:13.

15:8-13 The leaders come from Jerusalem to celebrate the victory whose architect was Judith. The feast is organized according to Greek custom. In the acclamation to Judith, the Church sees the announcement of salvation with which another woman is associated, and she applies its words to the Blessed Virgin Mary.

15:9-10 These verses are regularly applied to Mary, the Mother of God, by the Church, especially in her Liturgy. For example, they are found in Mass no. 43 of the new Masses of the Blessed Virgin Mary. This Mass commemorates Mary as the "handmaid of our redemption" because she is the handmaid of the Lord (see Lk 1:38).

This can be done because Judith was a type of Mary. Just as Judith courageously freed her people from the siege by Holofernes, so Mary in her warfare against the serpent, the ancient enemy (see Gen 3:15), brought blessings upon the people of Israel and upon the whole Church.

In the same way, Mary is also the prophetess of the redemption of Israel. Becoming the voice of her people, she magnified the Lord, because, mindful of his mercy, he had come to the rescue of his people by redeeming them from slavery to sin (Lk 1:46, 54-55).

Thus, the Church shows that Mary is a loving Mother, given to us by God in his mercy, one who cares unceasingly with a mother's love for all God's children in their need, breaking the chains of every form of captivity, so that we might enjoy full liberty of body and spirit.

15:12 *Branches of ivy:* a Greek custom found only in one other place in the Bible: 2 Mac 10:7. The Jews waved palm branches in times of rejoicing (Lev 23:40; Jn 12:13; Rev 7:9).

15:14 The hymn of Judith is regarded as one of the most beautiful examples of Hebrew poetry in its conciseness and vivacity.

16:6 *Titans* and *giants* were current terms derived from Greek mythology.

She anointed her face with perfume,
8 bound up her hair with a fillet,
and donned a linen gown to beguile him.
9 Her sandal attracted his gaze,
her beauty captivated his mind,
and the sword cut through his neck.[w]

10 "The Persians quaked at her audacity,
the Medes cowered at her daring.
11 When my lowly ones shouted, they were terrified;
when my weak ones cried out, they trembled,
and when they raised their voices, the enemy took to flight.
12 The sons of slave girls ran them through
and wounded them like the children of deserters;
they perished before the army of my LORD.[x]

13 "I will sing a new hymn to my God.
O LORD, you are great and glorious,
wonderful in strength, invincible.[y]
14 Let all your creatures serve you,
for you spoke and they were made.
You sent forth your spirit and they were created;
no one can resist your voice.[z]
15 The mountains are shaken to their foundations;
at your glance the rocks melt like wax.

"But to those who fear you
you still show compassion.[a]
16 The fragrant offering of a sacrifice is a small thing,
as is the fat of all burnt offerings in your sight,
but whoever fears the LORD is great forever.[b]

17 "Woe to the nations that rise up against my people.
The LORD Almighty will punish them
on the day of judgment.
He will send fire and worms into their flesh;
they shall weep with pain forever."[c]

D: Thanksgiving at Jerusalem

18 The people then went to worship God at Jerusalem. As soon as the people were purified, they presented their holocausts, their free-will offerings, and their gifts. 19 Judith presented to God as a votive offering all the possessions of Holofernes that the people had given to her, as well as the canopy that she had taken for herself from his bedchamber.[d] 20 For three months the people continued their celebration in Jerusalem before the sanctuary, and Judith stayed with them.

V: EPILOGUE

21 When those days ended, they all returned to their homes. Judith went to Bethulia and remained on her estate. For the rest of her life she was honored throughout the whole country. 22 Even though she received many proposals of marriage, she gave herself to no man from the time that her husband Manasseh died and was gathered to his ancestors. 23 Her reputation continued to grow as her years increased, and she lived in her husband's house until her death at the advanced age of one hundred and five. She set her maid free, died in Bethulia, and was buried in the cave where her husband Manasseh was interred.[e] 24 The house of Israel mourned her for seven days. Prior to her death she distributed her property to the close relatives of her husband Manasseh and to her own relatives.[f]

25 During the lifetime of Judith and for a long time after her death, no one again dared to threaten the Israelites.*[g]

w Jud 9:13.—x 1 Sam 31:4.—y Pss 86:10; 144:9; 147:5.—z Est C:2; Pss 33:9; 104:30; 148:5.—a Jdg 5:5; Pss 25:14; 97:5; 103:15.—b Ps 86:11; Sir 34:13-17.—c Jdg 5:31; Sir 7:17; Isa 66:24; Joel 4:1-4.—d Num 31:48-54; Deut 13:13-18.—e Gen 23:19; 49:29-32.—f 1 Sam 31:13; Sir 22:12.—g Jdg 3:11, 30; 5:31; 8:28.

16:25 The Book ends on the same note as the ending of some of the stories in the Book of Judges: during the lifetime of Judith and for a long time after her death, no one again dared to spread terror among the Israelites (see Jdg 3:11,30; 5:31; 8:28). The last part of the Book is also reminiscent of events in Judges. Bagoas's discovery of Holofernes's body recalls the discovery of Eglon (see Jdg 3:23-25); the fake attack by the Israelites recalls Gideon's ploy (see Jdg 7:16-22); and the person of Judith recalls Deborah and Jael (Jdg 4–5). The Book also recalls the pattern of the stories in Judges: (1) the people are afflicted; (2) they call upon the Lord; (3) the Lord sends them a judge; (4) they are favored with peace throughout the lifetime of the judge.

The Vulgate adds a note at the end of the chapter (v. 31) concerning the feast day on which Judith's victory is celebrated: "31 The day of festivity of this victory is received by the Hebrews in the number of their holy days, and is religiously observed by them from that day to this" [see Est 9:27f]. Although there is no evidence of this in the calendar, in Jewish folklore, the story of Judith is connected with the Feast of Hanukkah, the celebration of the purification of the temple at the time of the Maccabees (when the Book was most likely written). Some authors maintain that Judith was read in the synagogue at Hanukkah. Judith thus has a relation to Passover, Weeks, and Sukkoth.

THE BOOK OF ESTHER

For the Freedom of the Faith

An unknown author recounts how God makes use of a woman to set free his people whose existence is threatened by the all-powerful minister of a Persian king. The drama takes its point of departure from one of the episodes of the conflict, well known in ancient history, between the pagan world and the Jewish people—because of their religion and their customs.

Beautiful in its literary aspect, although a bit heavy-handed in its emphases, the account brings on stage vivacious personages with well-drawn features. They are representative types: Ahasuerus, the Eastern monarch; Haman, the high official and sworn enemy of the Jews; Mordecai, the ardent patriot; Esther, the worthy sister of the courageous heroines of the Bible. The author knows how to highlight contrasting situations, how to maintain tension, and bring about the resolution, all the while keeping the reader breathless.

Our author makes us relive, with much truth, the historical framework in which he chooses to have his drama take place: the time when the Persian Empire dominates the Near East. He seems to have composed his drama expressly to transform the Feast of "Purim" into a celebration of national independence, whereas it was originally probably nothing more than a great feast of spring.

Like the Books of Tobit and Judith, the Book of Esther is not a pure and simple novel; although the author takes much liberty in his dealings with history and geography, his sole intent is to instruct and edify.

Besides the Hebrew text, in which—something very curious—God is never named, there exist also Greek versions that add 107 verses and felicitous complements recognized by the Catholic Church as inspired writings. These are the parts indicated in this edition by letters (A–F), which emphasize the action of Providence more expressly.

Scholars tell us that A, C, D, and F were probably composed in Hebrew or Aramaic and were part of the Semitic text used by the Greek translator: B and E were probably composed in Greek. The postscript (F:11) indicates that A and F were part of the Semitic text when Lysimachus of Jerusalem composed his translation around 114 B.C. The date for B, C, D, and E is sometime before A.D. 93.

Following the line of the story of Joseph at Pharaoh's court or the deeds of Daniel at Nebuchadnezzar's court—if Daniel antedates it—the Book of Esther, composed in all likelihood between the third and the second century B.C., brings the Jewish people a message of consolation in accord with their tradition.

The dispersed communities, or the community held under political tutelage even in the Holy Land, encounter malevolence and, at times, persecution. Many await with impatience a national liberation or, at least, a time when the Jewish people will have importance amid the nations. If nothing else, they await the triumph of the faith.

It is expressly thinking of these situations that writings like the Book of Esther take up anew the ancient biblical theme of the reversal of circumstances. When all appears lost, God never abandons those who trust in him (Pss 118:8; 124:1) and observe his commandments (Ps 118).

The author insists on the value of spiritual means: prayer, fasting, and chastity, which characterize the spirituality of the age. Nationalism remains restrained, and God's vengeance prevails over his mercy when he intervenes in confrontations between nations.

In the crucible of suffering, there still remained to be discovered the whole vastness of God's goodness: Jesus would reveal that his call does not exclude any country or any race. But even now a message remains for us: the greatness of God in confrontations with the pride of people and nations and his concern for the oppressed. No earthly power is definitive, and we have the certainty that in one way or another, God is not indifferent to the action of human beings in the midst of the events of their time.

The Book of Esther may be divided as follows:

I: Prologue (A:1-17)
II: Esther Chosen as Queen (1:1—2:23)
III: Haman's Plot To Destroy the Jews (3:1-13; B:1-7; 3:14—4:8; B:8-9; 4:9-17; C:1—D:16; 5:1-14)
IV: Vindication of the Jews (6:1—8:12; E:1-24; 8:13—10:3)
V: Epilogue (F:1-11)

In his Latin translation of the Bible known as the Vulgate, Jerome placed the Greek additions (A–F) at the end of the Hebrew Book of Esther, and they were numbered consecutively when the Bible was divided into chapters and verses. The order of the Vulgate in relation to the order of the Greek text is as follows:

11:2-12; 12:1-6 = A:1-17 at the beginning of the Book
13:1-7 = B:1-7 after 3:13
13:8-18; 14:1-19; 15:4-9 = C:1—D:16 after 4:17
15:1-2 = B:8-9 after 4:8
16:1-24 = E:1-24 after 8:12
10:4-13; 11:1 = F:1-11 after 10:3

I: PROLOGUE

CHAPTER A*

Mordecai's Dream. 1 In the second year of the
reign of King Ahasuerus* the Great, on the
first day of Nisan, Mordecai, son of Jair, son of
Shimei, son of Kish, of the tribe of Benjamin,
had a dream.[a] 2 A Jew of exalted rank who
lived in the citadel of Susa,* he held high
office at the royal court. 3 He was also one of
the captives whom Nebuchadnezzar, king of
Babylon, had carried away from Jerusalem
with Jeconiah,* king of Judah.[b]
4 [c] His dream* was as follows. The earth
was filled with noise and tumult, peals of
thunder and an earthquake, and confused
turmoil. 5 Then two huge dragons appeared,
ready for combat. When they let loose with a
mighty roar, 6 every nation responded by
preparing to wage war against the righteous
people. 7 It was a day of darkness and gloom,
distress and tribulation, oppression and
great anguish upon the earth. 8 The righteous
people were greatly troubled, fearing the
evils that threatened them, and they prepared to die. 9 [d] Then they cried aloud to

a Est 2:5.—b Est 2:6; 2 Ki 24:15; 2 Chr 36:9-10; Jer 22:24ff; 24:1; 29:1-2.—c 4ff: Est F:2, 4ff.—d 9f: Est F:3.

A:1-17 Dreams or heavenly visions (Gen 40:8; 41:1; Dan 2:2, 19; 4:2, 16; 7–12) reveal a plan of God in the Bible. In the huge struggle between nations, God will intervene to save his chosen people. This section is from the Greek text, and immediately after the dream (Est A: 12-17) comes the plot uncovered by Mordecai. According to the Hebrew text, the plot was hatched when Esther was already queen. The text also speaks of recompense, which seems to contradict Est 6:1-3.

A:1 *King Ahasuerus:* Xerxes I (485–465 B.C.); son of Darius I, he ascended the throne in 485 B.C., defeated the Egyptians and Babylonians, but fell to the Greeks in 480–479 B.C., and was assassinated by his officials in 465 B.C. *Mordecai:* a Babylonian name based on the god Marduk. Mordecai's genealogy indicates opposition to Israel's enemy in accord with 1 Sam 15:7ff. There Saul, whose father's name was *Kish, of the tribe of Benjamin,* defeated Agag the Amalekite; in A:17, Haman is termed the son of an Agagite (i.e., a person from Agag, a territory adjacent to Media). *Shimei* was a Benjaminite who cursed David (2 Sam 16:5ff), and *Jair* was the minor judge, a Transjordanian Manassehite (Jdg 10:3). *Nisan:* the Babylonian month for March–April; all the month names in the book are of Babylonian derivation.

A:2 *Susa:* one of the two capitals of the Persian Empire under the Achaemenid kings, together with Persepolis, the summer royal palace.

A:3 *Jeconiah:* king of the southern kingdom of Judah (597 B.C.) also known as Jehoiachin (2 Ki 24:8-15). This verse dates Mordecai's captivity as 598 B.C.; verse 1 dates his dream 112 years later (484 B.C.). However, some are of the opinion that the text means Mordecai was a descendant of the group deported at that time.

A:4 The *dream* is interpreted in Est F:1-6.

God, and at their outcry a great river* overflowing with water appeared, with its source being a tiny spring. [10] Light flooded the earth as the sun rose, and the humble were exalted, and they devoured those who were regarded as honorable.

[11] After having this dream and seeing what God had decided to do, Mordecai awoke. That entire day, he meditated on it in his heart and sought to understand every last detail.*

Discovery of the Plot against the King. [12] [e] Mordecai was accustomed to take his rest in the royal courtyard, along with Bagathan and Thares, two of the king's eunuchs who guarded the court. [13] One day he heard them speaking together and, after inquiring about their purposes, learned that they meant to assassinate King Ahasuerus. He warned the king of their scheme, [14] and after the king had questioned the eunuchs and obtained their confession, he ordered them to be put to death. [15] The king had the details of this event recorded, and Mordecai also wrote an account of what had occurred. [16] [f] The king then rewarded Mordecai with a court appointment and gave him other gifts.*

[17] However, Haman, son of Hammedatha the Agagite, who was highly regarded by the king, began to look for an opportunity to harm Mordecai and his people to avenge the execution of the two eunuchs of the king.[g]

II: ESTHER CHOSEN AS QUEEN

CHAPTER 1

A Great Banquet.* [1] This took place in the days of Ahasuerus, the king who ruled over one hundred and twenty-seven provinces stretching from India to Ethiopia.* [2] At that time, King Ahasuerus was reigning from the royal throne of the citadel of Susa, [3] and in the third year of his reign, he threw a great banquet for all his nobles and officials.[h] The military commanders of Persia and Media were present, and so were the princes and the nobles of the provinces.

[4] For a full one hundred and eighty days the king showcased the wealth of his kingdom and the splendor and glory of his majesty. [5] When these days were over, he threw a banquet, lasting seven days, in the enclosed garden of his palace, for all the people, from the least to the greatest, who lived in the citadel of Susa.

[6] The garden had hangings of white and blue linen, fastened with cords of white linen and purple material to silver rings on marble pillars. Gold and silver couches were on the pavement, which was of porphyry, marble, mother-of-pearl, and other costly stones.[i] [7] Wine was served in golden goblets, each different from one another, and the royal wine was abundant, in keeping with the king's beneficence. [8] By the order of the king, there were no limits on the drinks. For he instructed all the wine stewards to give everyone whatever was requested.

Queen Vashti Deposed. [9] Meanwhile, in the king's royal palace, Queen Vashti* was giving a banquet for the women.

[10] On the seventh day, when King Ahasuerus was merry with wine, he summoned the seven eunuchs who were his personal servants—Mehuman, Biztha, Harbona, Bigtha, Abagtha, Zethar, and Carkas.[j] [11] He ordered them to bring the queen into his presence, wearing the royal crown, so he could show her off to the officials and all his guests, for she was lovely to look at. [12] But Queen Vashti refused to come at the official command issued through the eunuchs. This embarrassed the king and made him furious.

[13] Since it was his custom to consult experts in matters of law and justice, the king consulted with the wise men who understood the laws. [14] He summoned Carshena, Shethar, Admatha, Tarshish, Meres, Marsena, and Memucan, the seven

e 12-15: Est 2:21ff; 6:1ff.—f Est 6:3.—g Est 3:1-15; B:1-7; E:13.—h Jud 1:16.—i Ezek 23:41; Am 6:4.—j Dan 5:1.

A:9 The expressions *great river* and *tiny spring* refer to Esther (see F:3).

A:11 Mordecai is aware that the dream predicts God's action, but he does not yet grasp the interpretation given in Est F:1ff.

A:16 As the sequence of events in the Hebrew text shows, Mordecai was rewarded only at a later date (Est 2:22f; 6:3).

1:1-8 The extension of the power, luxuriousness of the palace, and weakness of morals correspond well with the reign of Ahasuerus, that is, Xerxes I (485–465 B.C.), the famous king defeated by Greece, of whom Herodotus says that he subsequently gave himself up to every type of debauchery. Liberal in the sphere of religion, he revised the ceremony to respect the customs of those invited (v. 8)—e.g., the Persian custom required guests to drink a certain amount of glasses of wine. However, St. Jerome thought Ahasuerus to be Artaxerxes II (405–362 B.C.), because the Greek text speaks constantly about "Artaxerxes," and Plutarch tells us that this monarch kept in his harem a number of women corresponding to the days of a year.

1:1 *From India to Ethiopia:* this phrase indicates the greatest extent of the Persian empire—that is, from western India to Upper Egypt—achieved under Darius the Great, who was the father of Ahasuerus.

1:9 *Queen Vashti:* according to Herodotus, the wife of Ahasuerus was Amestris, a Persian woman.

Persian and Median officials who had spe-
cial access to the king and were highest in
the kingdom.[k]
15 The king asked, "What does the law say
must be done about Queen Vashti, who dis-
obeyed the command of King Ahasuerus
issued through the eunuchs?"
16 It was Memucan, then, who replied in
the presence of the king and the nobles:
"Queen Vashti has wronged not only the
king but also all the nobles and peoples
throughout the provinces of King Ahas-
uerus. 17 For this behavior of the queen will
become known to all the women, and they
will disrespect their husbands and say, 'King
Ahasuerus commanded that Queen Vashti
enter his presence, but she refused to come.'
18 So this very day the Persian and Median
women of the nobility who have learned
about the queen's behavior will react
against the king's nobles in like manner,
resulting in no end of rancor and discord.
19 "Therefore, if it pleases the king, let him
issue a royal decree inscribed in the laws of
Persia and Media, which cannot be
repealed,* to the effect that Vashti is never-
more to enter the presence of King Ahas-
uerus and that her position be given to
someone more worthy than she is.[l] 20 Then
when the edict is published throughout his
vast domain, all the women will respect
their husbands, from the greatest to the
least."[m]
21 The king and his nobles found this
advice very acceptable, so the king acted
upon Memucan's words. 22 He sent dispatch-
es to all parts of the kingdom—to every
province in its own script and to each people
in its own language—proclaiming in each
people's tongue that every man should be
the master of his own house.*

CHAPTER 2

Esther Is Made Queen. 1 After a time, the
anger of King Ahasuerus abated, and he
began to think of what Vashti had done and
what he had decreed about her. 2 At this
point, the king's personal attendants sug-
gested, "Let a search be made to find beau-
tiful young virgins for the king. 3 Let the king
appoint commissioners in every province of
his kingdom to bring all those beautiful
young virgins into the harem at the citadel
of Susa. Let them be placed in the care of
Hegai, the king's eunuch who is in charge of
the women, and let them receive beauty
treatments. 4 Then let the girl who pleases
the king become queen in place of Vashti."
This advice pleased the king, and he acted
upon it.
5 Now there was in the citadel of Susa a
Jew from the tribe of Benjamin, named
Mordecai, son of Jair, the son of Shimei, the
son of Kish. 6 He had been carted off into
exile from Jerusalem by Nebuchadnezzar,
king of Babylon, among those taken captive
with Jeconiah, king of Judah.[n] 7 Mordecai
had a cousin named Hadassah,* whom he
had brought up because she had lost her
father and mother. She was also known as
Esther and was a beautiful young woman.
Mordecai had taken her as his own daughter
after her father and mother had died.[o]
8 When the king's order and edict had
been proclaimed, many young women were
brought to the citadel of Susa and placed in
the care of Hegai. Esther, too, was brought
to the royal palace in the care of Hegai, who
was in charge of the harem.[p] 9 She pleased
him and won his favor. So Hegai lost no time
in furnishing her with cosmetics and provi-
sions and in assigning her seven maids from
the king's palace while transferring her and
the maids into the best place in the harem.
10 Now on the counsel of Mordecai, Esther
did not mention her nationality or family to
anyone. 11 And every day Mordecai walked
back and forth in front of the courtyard of
the harem, seeking to learn how Esther was
and what was happening to her.
12 Before each girl's turn came when she
could visit King Ahasuerus, she must have
completed twelve months of prescribed
beauty treatments: six months with oil of
myrrh and another six with perfume and
cosmetics.[q] 13 When the girl went to visit the
king, she received whatever she requested to
take with her from the harem to the king's
royal palace. 14 She would go there in the

k Ezr 7:13-14.—l Est 8:5, 8; Dan 6:8f.—m Dan 3:4; 6:26.—n Est A:3; 2 Ki 24:15; 2 Chr 36:9f; Jer 22:24ff; 24:1; 29:1f.—o Est 2:15.—p Dan 1:3-20.—q Est 4:11.

1:19 *Laws . . . which cannot be repealed:* according to the historian Siculus, the idea of irrevocable laws existed at the time of Darius III (335–331 B.C.), the last king of Persia (see Est 8:8).

1:22 Among the many languages spoken in the Persian Empire, the principal ones were Persian, Aramaic, Babylonian, Egyptian, Elaite, Greek, and Phoenician, each of which had its own script.

2:7 *Hadassah:* in Hebrew signifies "myrtle"; *Esther* in Persian signifies "star" and is associated with the Babylonian goddess "Ishtar."

evening and in the morning would come
back to another part of the harem, which
was in the care of Shaazgaz, who was in
charge of the concubines. She would not
visit the king again unless he summoned her
by name. [r]

15 As for Esther, daughter of Abihail and
adopted daughter of Mordecai, when it
came time for her turn to visit the king, she
asked nothing more than what the royal
eunuch Hegai, who was in charge of the
harem, suggested. Nevertheless, she won
the admiration of all who saw her. 16 So, in
the seventh year of his reign, in the tenth
month, Tebeth,* Esther was brought to King
Ahasuerus in the royal palace.

17 The king loved Esther more than any of
the other women, and she won his favor and
approval more than any of the other virgins.
So he set a royal crown on her head and
made her queen in place of Vashti. 18 Then
the king gave a great banquet for all his
nobles and administrators to honor Esther.
He proclaimed a holiday* throughout the
provinces and gave gifts with royal liberality.

[Mordecai Uncovers a Conspiracy.* 19 [s] To
resume: When the virgins were assembled a
second time, Mordecai was sitting at the
king's gate, 20 and Esther had still not
revealed her family or nationality just as
Mordecai had instructed her. For she was
still following his advice as she had done
when he was bringing her up.

21 [t] During the time Mordecai spent at the
king's gate,* Bagathan and Thares, two of
the king's eunuchs who guarded the
entrance, became angry and plotted to kill
King Ahasuerus. 22 However, Mordecai
became aware of the plot and told Queen
Esther about it, and she informed the king
for Mordecai. 23 When the matter was inves-
tigated and proved to be true, both men
were hanged on a gibbet. All this was record-
ed in the book of the annals in the king's
presence.]

III: HAMAN'S PLOT TO DESTROY THE JEWS

CHAPTER 3

Mordecai Refuses To Honor Haman.* 1 Some-
time later, King Ahasuerus honored
Haman, son of Hammedatha, the Agagite,
giving him a higher rank and seating him
above all his royal nobles. [u] 2 All the royal
officials who were at the king's gate would
kneel down and render homage to Haman,
for that is what the king had ordered to be
done toward him. But Mordecai refused to
kneel and bow down to him. [v]

3 The other officials at the king's gate
asked Mordecai, "Why do you fail to obey
the king's command?" [w] 4 Day after day they
spoke to him about this, but he did not listen
to them. So they told Haman about it to
see whether Mordecai's explanation was
acceptable, for he had informed them that
he was a Jew.

5 When Haman realized that Mordecai
was not going to kneel down or pay him
homage, he became enraged. 6 Moreover, he
decided that it would not be enough to kill
only Mordecai; having learned who Morde-
cai's people were, he sought to destroy all the
Jews—Mordecai's people—in the kingdom
of Ahasuerus.

Edict against the Jews. 7 * In the twelfth year
of King Ahasuerus, in the first month, Nisan,
they cast the *pur*,* (that is, the lot) in the
presence of Haman. And the lot fell on the
thirteenth day of the month of Adar. [x]

8 Then Haman said to Ahasuerus, "There
is a certain race of people scattered among
the nations all over your empire who keep
themselves separate. They observe customs
that are not like those of any other people.

r Est 2:19f; 4:11, 16.—s 19f: Est 2:14.—t 21ff: Est A:12-15; 6:1ff.—u Est B:3; 5:11; E:11.—v Est C:5; 5:9, 13; 6:10, 12.—w Est 4:16.—x Est 9:24ff; F:10.

2:16 *Tebeth:* Persian name that corresponds to December–January.

2:18 *A holiday:* the Greek text reads: "remission of sins."

2:19-23 This is the Hebrew account of the plot already related in the Greek text (A:12-17). Although the text is corrupt, one thing is clear. After the distractions of the harem, the author wants to remind his readers of the main elements of the story up to this point: Mordecai's position, Esther's hidden nationality, Mordecai's unrewarded service, and the record of this in the royal annals.

2:21 *King's gate:* either an edifice (see Est 4:2-6; 5:8; 6:12) or determinate services of the court (see v. 9; 6:10). Excavations at Susa have unearthed rooms on both sides of the grandiose entrance to the royal palace. Hence, Mordecai can be thought to have been exercising watchful care over Esther or rendering royal service (see A:2).

3:1-6 Refusing to render to a minister the honors prescribed by the king, Mordecai exemplifies Jewish pride to the court mentality. In fact, such practices were normal in the East and even in Israel (1 Ki 1:23; 2 Ki 4:37). The Greek text will attach an idolatrous sense to this reverence requested before Haman (Est C:5-7), while the Hebrew text does not go this far.

3:7-11 The text mentions *pur*, a word that is Babylonian. Importance is attributed to it in order to make the connection with the Jewish Feast of Purim (Est 9:24-26).

3:7 *Pur:* Assyro-Babylonian term; the lot was used to establish the days that were auspicious (see Est 9:20ff). The month of Adar corresponds to February–March.

Moreover, they do not obey the king's laws, and it is not in the king's best interests to tolerate them.[y] 9 If it pleases the king, issue a decree to put them all to death, and I will deposit ten thousand talents into the royal treasury for those who bring it to pass."[z]

10 Therefore, the king removed the signet ring* from his finger and gave it to Haman, the son of Hammedatha, the Agagite, the enemy of the Jews.[a] 11 The king told him, "Keep the money, and do whatever you want with this race of people."

12 So on the thirteenth day of the first month, the royal secretaries were summoned, and at the dictation of Haman they wrote out—in the script of each province and in the language of each people *—an order to the king's satraps, the governors of every province, and the nobles of the various peoples.[b] This order was written in the name of King Ahasuerus himself and sealed with the royal signet ring. 13 This order was sent by couriers* to all the provinces to the effect that all Jews, young and old, including women and children, should be put to death, destroyed, wiped out in one day, the thirteenth day of the twelfth month, Adar, and their goods seized as spoil.[c]

CHAPTER B

A Copy of the Edict.* 1 This is the copy of the edict:

"King Ahasuerus the Great writes the following to the governors of the one hundred and twenty-seven provinces extending from India to Ethiopia and to their subordinate officials: 2 Having been established as the ruler of many nations and master of the entire world, it has always been my policy never to be overwhelmed with the arrogance of power but always to rule with fairness and kindness, so as to ensure for my subjects a life of tranquillity in this kingdom, with the assurance of safe passage for everyone within its borders and the restoration of the peace desired by all.[d]

3 "When I sought the counsel of my advisors as to how this goal might be achieved, Haman, whose sound judgment, unfailing devotion, and steadfast loyalty have enabled him to achieve a rank second only to mine in the kingdom, spoke up.[e] 4 He informed us that, mingled among all the races of the world, there is one hostile people whose laws are opposed to those of all other nations and who continually act in defiance of royal ordinances, so that the unification of the empire that we envision cannot be accomplished.[f]

5 "In the realization that this people stands uniquely alone in its continual hostility to all other nations, observes laws that are at complete variance with ours, and commits the most grievous of crimes, thereby undermining the stability of our government, 6 we hereby decree that all the persons designated to you in the letters written by Haman, who was appointed to safeguard our interests and who is a second father to us, shall, with their wives and children, be totally destroyed by the swords of their enemies, without any sign of mercy or pardon, on the fourteenth day* of the twelfth month, Adar, of the present year.[g] 7 In this way, when these people, whose treacherous opposition to us has been of long duration, have descended into the netherworld by a violent death in a single day, our kingdom will once again enjoy perpetual stability and peace."

(CHAPTER 3)

14 A copy of the text of the edict was to be issued as law in every province and made known to the people of every nationality so that they might be ready for that day. 15 The couriers went quickly by order of the king, and the edict was issued in the citadel of Susa. Then the king and Haman sat down to feast, but the city of Susa was perplexed.

y Est 3:13; B:4; Dan 3:8-12; Wis 2:14f.—z Est 7:4.—a Gen 41:42.—b Dan 3:4-7.—c Est B:6; 7:4.—d Est E:8f; Jud 2:5.—e Est 3:1; 5:11; E:11.—f Est 3:8.—g Est 3:13; 7:4; E:11ff.

3:10 *Signet ring:* a ring with a seal that was impressed on documents in order to give them authenticity.

3:12 *In the script of each province and in the language of each people:* omitted in the Greek. Ordinarily such official correspondence was written in Aramaic.

3:13 *Couriers:* created by Cyrus, galloped on the best steeds in Media. Haman hastens to send out the edict almost a year beforehand, since he knows the changeable character of the king; once sent out, the edict is immutable.

B:1-7 The Greek text opts to give this edict in full. It shows the official style but also the common accusations made by persecutors of the Jews (see Est 3:8; 4:12f; Jud 12:2; Wis 2:14-15; Dan 3:8-12).

B:6 *Fourteenth day:* the Hebrew text (Est 2:13) and the Greek text here do not agree on the day of the month specified by the king. In Est 9:15, 18 a two-day celebration is decreed, and the thirteenth, fourteenth, and fifteenth days of Adar are all mentioned.

CHAPTER 4

Mordecai Persuades Esther To Help. 1 When
Mordecai heard all that was going on, he tore
his clothes, put on sackcloth and ashes, and
went through the city wailing loudly and sor-
rowfully.[h] 2 But he came to a halt at the
entrance to the king's gate because no one
wearing sackcloth was allowed to go in.
3 (Similarly, in every province to which the
king's edict and order reached, the Jews went
into great mourning, with fasting, mourn-
ing, and weeping. Many put on sackcloth and
ashes.)

4 When Queen Esther's maids and
eunuchs went to her and told her about
Mordecai, she became deeply troubled. She
sent clothes for him to wear in place of the
sackcloth, but he refused to do so. 5 Esther
then called Hathach, one of the king's
eunuchs who had been assigned to her ser-
vice, and ordered him to find out what this
action of Mordecai meant and why it was
being done.

6 So Hathach went out to Mordecai in the
public square in front of the king's gate.
7 Mordecai told him everything that had
happened as well as the exact amount of sil-
ver that Haman had promised to put in the
royal treasury for the destruction of the Jews.
8 Mordecai also gave him a copy of the edict
that had been published in Susa, for the
annihilation of the Jews, to show and explain
to Esther. Hathach was to urge her to go into
the king's presence to plead for mercy and
intercede with him for her people.

8 * "Remember the days of your lowly
estate," Mordecai had Hathach say, "when
you were brought up in my charge; for
Haman, who stands next to the king, has
asked for our death. 9 Invoke the LORD and
speak to the king on our behalf; save us from
death."

9 Hathach went back to Esther and told
her what Mordecai had said. 10 Then she
gave him a message for Mordecai: 11 "All the
servants of the king and the people of the
royal provinces are aware that any man or
woman who approaches the king in the inner
palace without being summoned suffers
automatic death. The sole exception to this
rule is if the king extends to such a person the
golden scepter, which spares his life. Yet as
for me, I have not been summoned by the
king for thirty days."[i]

12 When Esther's words reached Morde-
cai, 13 he sent back this reply: "Do not imag-
ine that because you are in the king's palace
you alone of all the Jews will escape. 14 Even
if you remain silent now, relief and deliver-
ance for the Jews will arise from another
place;* but you and your father's family will
perish. And who knows? Perhaps it was for
just such a time as this that you obtained the
royal dignity."

15 Then Esther sent back this reply to
Mordecai: 16 "Go, and assemble all the Jews
who are in Susa, and fast for me. Do not eat
or drink for three days, night or day. My
maids and I will do the same thing. After
that, I will go to the king—against the law.
And if I perish, I perish!"[j]

17 Then Mordecai went away and carried
out all of Esther's instructions.

CHAPTER C

The Prayer of Mordecai. 1 * Calling to mind
everything that the LORD had done,
Mordecai prayed to him in these words:

2 "O LORD God, King and ruler of all
things, the entire universe is subject to your
power, and no one can thwart you in your
intention to save Israel.[k] 3 You made heav-
en and earth and every wonderful thing
under the firmament. 4 You are LORD of all,
and there is no one, O LORD, who can resist
you. 5 [l] Since you know all things, O LORD,
you realize that it was not because of inso-
lence or pride or a desire for glory that I so
acted in refusing to bow down to this
haughty Haman. 6 To ensure the salvation
of Israel, I would gladly have kissed the
soles of his feet. 7 But I acted in this way so
as not to place human glory above the glory
of God. I will not bow down to anyone but
you, my LORD, and I will not act in this way
out of pride.

h Jud 4:12.—i Est 2:14; D:12.—j Est C:12f.—k Ex 19:5; 2 Chr 20:6f; Jud 16:14; Isa 41:10-16.—l 5ff: Est 3:2; 5:9.

4:8-9 *Remember the days of your lowly estate . . . save us from death:* these verses belong to chapter B.

4:14 *From another place:* it is evident from the Greek additions in chapter C that this is a reference to God's intervention.

C:1—D:16 If the Hebrew text has avoided using the name of God, even though stressing the religious attitude of mourning and fasting, the Greek text gives free reign to the meditation of faith. The person of faith acts resolutely but counts on God for success. The prayers of Mordecai and Esther have an explicit religious tone to them. They speak of God as *LORD* and *King* and *LORD, God of Abraham.* They portray him as the Creator and Ruler of all things, who is just, brought his people out of Egypt, answers prayers, and is able to save them in the present.

8 "Now, LORD, my God and King, O God of Abraham, spare your people, for our enemies are determined to exterminate us and to destroy the inheritance that has been yours from times of old.[m] 9 Do not forsake your people whom you redeemed and brought out of Egypt for yourself.[n] 10 Hear my prayer and have mercy on your heritage. Turn our sorrow into joy so that we may live to sing praise to your name, O LORD. Do not silence the lips of those who praise you."[o]

11 And all the Israelites also cried aloud with all their strength, since death was before their eyes.

The Prayer of Esther. 12 [p] Queen Esther, too, was seized with great anguish and sought recourse from the LORD. 13 Removing her splendid robes, she put on garments of sadness and mourning. Instead of rich perfumes, she covered her head with dirt and ashes. She greatly mortified her body, and every part that she used to adorn elegantly, she now covered with her disheveled hair.

14 Then Esther prayed to the LORD, the God of Israel, and said: "O my LORD, you alone are our King. Come to my assistance, for I am alone and have no one to help me but you. 15 My life is in great danger.[q] 16 From my earliest days I was taught by my family that you, O LORD, chose Israel out of all the nations and our fathers from among all their forebearers, as an everlasting heritage, and that you have fulfilled all the promises you made to them.[r] 17 But now we have sinned against you, and you have handed us over to our enemies[s] 18 because we paid honor to their gods. You are just, O LORD.

19 "However, now our enemies are not satisfied with our bitter slavery. They have vowed to their idols 20 to annul the decree you have proclaimed and destroy your heritage, to silence the mouths of those who praise you and to destroy your altar and the glory of your house,* [t] 21 and instead, to open the mouths of the nations to praise their worthless idols and to offer an earthly king everlasting praise.

22 "O LORD, do not consign your scepter to gods who do not exist. Do not let our enemies exult in our downfall, but turn their designs against them and make an example of the chief of our persecutors. 23 Remember us, O LORD. Reveal yourself in this time of our tribulation, and give me courage, O King of gods and Master of every dominion. 24 Give me the power of persuasive speech when I face the lion and enable me to turn his heart to hatred of the one who is our enemy so that he and all those who share his feelings may perish.[u] 25 Save us by your arm and come to my aid, for I am alone and have no one on whom to rely but you, O LORD.

"You know all things. 26 You are fully aware that I hate the honors offered by the wicked and abhor the bed of the uncircumcised or of any alien. 27 You know the straits I am in. I loathe the symbol of my proud position that I wear on my head on days when I appear in public. I detest it as if it were an unclean rag, and I do not wear it on days when I am in private.[v] 28 I, your servant, have never eaten at Haman's table, nor have I attended any banquet of the king or drunk the wine of libations. 29 From the day I changed my state until now, I have experienced no joy except in you, O LORD, God of Abraham. 30 O God all-powerful, give heed to the pleas of those in despair. Deliver us from the power of the wicked and rescue me from my fear."

CHAPTER D

Esther Appears before the King. 1 * On the third day, having finished her prayers, Esther removed her penitential garments and arrayed herself in the splendor due to her state. 2 Thus beautifully adorned, she invoked the aid of God, who watches over and saves all, and took her two maids with her. 3 One of them provided gentle support for her, 4 while the other followed, bearing her train. 5 She was radiant in the splendor of her beauty, and her countenance was joyous as though permeated with love, but her heart was filled with fear. 6 She passed through one door after another and finally

m Ex 3:6.—n 1 Ki 8:51; Ps 33:12; Jer 10:16; Dan 9:26.—o Ps 6:5; Isa 38:18-20.—p 12f: Est 4:16.—q Est 4:16.—r Deut 4:20; 7:6; 9:29; 14:2; 26:18; 32:9.—s Jdg 2:12-14.—t Est C:10.—u Dan 11:26.—v Lev 15:19-30; Isa 64:5.

C:20 If the Hebrew people were destroyed, the divine promises would be annulled, especially the great promise of the Messiah who was to be born from that people. *House:* the temple, which had been rebuilt under Darius I, father of Xerxes I.

D:1-5 Anyone who entered the king's presence without his summons or permission was put to death, unless the king pardoned the intrusion (Est 4:11). Although Esther feared for her safety, she decided to enter the king's presence in order to avoid personal danger and to persuade the king to withdraw his edict against the Jews. She beautified her appearance as an aid in her quest.

stood in the presence of the king. He was
seated on his royal throne, clothed in all his
kingly regalia adorned with gold and pre-
cious stones, so that his appearance was ter-
rifying.
7 He looked up, and his face blazed with
anger when he saw her. The queen grew
faint, turned pale, and steadied herself
against the head of the maid who preceded
her. 8 Then God changed the king's mood
from anger to one of gentleness. In alarm he
sprang from his throne, held her in his arms
until she revived, and soothed her with com-
forting words. 9 "What is the matter,
Esther?" he said to her. "I am your husband.
Take courage. 10 You shall not die, for our
decree applies only to the common folk.
11 Come near!" 12 Then he raised his gold
scepter and, touching her neck with it,
embraced her and said: "Speak to me." [w]
13 She replied: "My lord, when I ap-
proached you, you looked like an angel of
God, and I was filled with fear at your majes-
tic presence. 14 You are wonderful, my lord,
and your face is enchanting." 15 As she said
this, she fell in a faint. 16 Then the king
became troubled as his attendants sought to
revive her.

CHAPTER 5

Esther's Request to the King. [1 * On the
third day, Esther donned her royal garments
and positioned herself in the inner courtyard
in front of the king's hall. The king was seated
on his royal throne in the hall, facing the
entrance. 2 When he spotted Queen Esther
standing in the courtyard, he made her wel-
come by holding out the golden scepter that
was in his hand. So Esther came near and
touched the top of the scepter.]
3 Then the king asked, "What is it, Queen
Esther? What is your request? Even if it
should be half of my kingdom,* it will be
given to you." [x]
4 "If it pleases the king," Esther replied, "I
would like you and Haman to be my guests
today at a banquet that I have prepared for
you."
5 Thereupon the king exclaimed, "Hurry,
bring Haman here so that we may do what
Esther wishes." With that, the king and
Haman went to Esther's banquet.
6 As they were drinking wine, the king
again asked Esther, "Now, what is your peti-
tion? It will be given you. And what is your
request? Even if it is up to half of my king-
dom, it will be granted." [y]
7 Esther replied, "My petition and my
request is this: 8 If I have found favor with the
king and if it pleases the king to grant my
petition and fulfill my request, let the king
and Haman come tomorrow to another ban-
quet that I will prepare for them. Then I will
answer the king's question."
Haman's Rage against Mordecai. 9 When
Haman left that day he was happy and in a
good mood. But when he caught sight of
Mordecai at the king's gate and noted that he
neither rose nor showed fear in his presence,
he was consumed with rage toward Morde-
cai. [z] 10 Nonetheless, he was able to control
himself and go home.

Then he invited his friends to his house
and asked his wife, Zeresh, to join them.
11 Haman boasted to them about his great
wealth, his many sons, and about the honor
the king had paid him by promoting him
above the other nobles and officials. [a]
12 "And even more than this," Haman added,
"Queen Esther invited me as the only one to
the banquet with the king today, and tomor-
row I am again invited to be her guest with
the king. 13 Yet I get no pleasure out of any of
this as long as I see that Jew Mordecai seat-
ed at the king's gate." [b]
14 Then his wife, Zeresh, and all his friends
suggested, "Why not have a gibbet set up,
fifty cubits high,* and in the morning ask the
king to have Mordecai hanged on it. Then go
to the banquet with the king and enjoy your-
self." Haman liked the idea, and he had the
gibbet built. [c]

IV: VINDICATION OF THE JEWS

CHAPTER 6

Mordecai Is Honored. 1 That night the king
found it difficult to sleep, so he ordered the
book of the chronicles of his reign to be
brought in and read to him. 2 During the
reading, the passage came up about Morde-
cai uncovering the plot to assassinate King

w Est 4:11.—x Est 5:6; 7:2; 9:12; Mk 6:23.—y Est 5:3.—z Est 3:2f; C:5ff; 6:10, 12.—a Est 3:1; B:3; E:11; 9:6-10.—b Est 3:2f; 6:10, 12.—c Est 6:4; 7:9f.

5:1-2 The Hebrew text in these verses is a condensed form of the account already given in the Greek text.

5:3 *Even . . . half of my kingdom:* a customary hyperbole (see Mk 6:23).

5:14 *Fifty cubits high:* the height of the gallows (seventy-five feet) is certainly a hyperbole for effect.

Ahasuerus on the part of Bagathan and Teresh, two of the royal eunuchs who guarded the doorway. [d]

3 The king asked, "How has Mordecai been honored and rewarded for this?"

The attendants said, "He has received neither honor nor reward." [e]

4 The king said, "Who is in the court?" Now Haman had just come into the outer court of the king's palace to speak to the king about hanging Mordecai on the gibbet that he had built for him. [f]

5 His attendants replied, "Haman is waiting in the court."

"Let him come in," the king said.

6 When Haman came in, the king asked him, "What should be done for the man whom the king wants to reward?"

Now Haman thought to himself, "What man would the king rather reward than me?" 7 So he replied to the king, "For the man whom the king wants to reward, 8 * let there be brought in the purple robe that the king wore and the horse that he rode when the royal crown was placed on his head. 9 Then let the robe and the horse be entrusted to one of the noblest of the king's officials. Let them robe the man the king wants to reward and lead him on the horse through the city streets, proclaiming before him, 'This is what is done for the man the king wants to reward.' " [g]

10 Then the king said to Haman, "Go, right away. Get the robe and the horse and do for Mordecai the Jew—who sits at the king's gate—what you have suggested. Do not leave out anything you have proposed." [h] 11 So Haman procured the robe and the horse. He put the robe on Mordecai and had him ride through the city streets, proclaiming, "This is what is done for the man the king wants to reward."

12 Afterward, Mordecai went back to the king's gate. Haman, however, hurried home, with his head covered * in grief 13 and told Zeresh his wife and all his friends what had befallen him. [i]

His friends and his wife, Zeresh, told him, "If Mordecai, before whom your downfall has started, is of the Jewish race, you will not be able to overcome him but will surely suffer defeat, because the living God is with him."

Haman Is Put to Death. 14 While they were still speaking, the king's eunuchs arrived and took Haman to the banquet Esther had prepared.

CHAPTER 7

1 So the king and Haman went to dine with Queen Esther. 2 And once again, on the second day as they were having wine, the king asked, "Queen Esther, what is your petition? It will be given you. What is your request? Even if it is for half my kingdom, it will be granted you." [j]

3 Queen Esther replied, "If I have found favor with you, O king, and if it pleases your majesty, grant me my life—this is my petition. And spare my people—this is my request. 4 [k] For I and my people have been handed over to destruction, slaughter, and extinction. If we had merely been sold as male and female slaves, I would have not said anything, because such distress would not be reason enough to disturb the king." *

5 Then King Ahasuerus asked Queen Esther, "Who is it and where is the one who has done such a thing?" [l]

6 Esther replied, "Our enemy is this wicked man Haman."

In terror, Haman faced the king and queen. 7 The king got up in a rage, left his wine, and went out into the palace garden. But Haman stayed behind to beg Queen Esther for his life, since he feared that the king had already decided his fate.

8 So Haman threw himself upon the couch on which Esther was reclining. At that very moment the king was just returning from the palace garden to the banquet hall. The king exclaimed: "Will he also violate the queen while she is with me in my own house?"

The words were scarcely out of the king's mouth when Haman's face was covered. 9 [m] Then Harbona, one of the eunuchs who attended the king, said, "There is a gibbet fifty cubits high at Haman's house. Haman

d Est A:12ff; 2:21ff.—e Est A:16.—f Est 5:14; 7:9f.—g Gen 41:42f; 1 Ki 1:33; Dan 5:29.—h Est 2:21; 3:2f; 5:13.—i Est 3:2f; 5:9, 13.—j Est 5:3.—k Est 3:13; B:6.—l Est 3:8f.—m 9f: Est 5:14; 6:4.

6:8-9 The honors are rendered according to the customs of the Persians and Assyrians. It was thought that clothes were imbued with the personality of those who wore them (the same as for Elijah in 2 Ki 2:8-13) and hence, to wear the king's clothes signified to share in the royal dignity. Ancient images show us the royal crown placed on the head of a horse.

6:12 *Head covered:* a sign of mourning (see 2 Sam 15:30; Jer 14:4).

7:4 Esther plays skillfully on the sentiments of the king and upon an ever-important subject: finances.

prepared it for Mordecai, who warned your majesty about the plot."

The king said, "Hang him on it." 10 So they hanged Haman on the gibbet he had prepared for Mordecai, and the king's anger cooled down.

CHAPTER 8

The King's Edict in Favor of the Jews. 1 That same day, King Ahasuerus gave Queen Esther all the property of Haman, the enemy of the Jews. And Mordecai was invited to come into the king's presence, for Esther revealed how he was related to her. 2 The king removed his signet ring, which he had taken back from Haman, and gave it to Mordecai. And Esther placed Mordecai in charge of Haman's property. [n]

3 Then Esther spoke with the king again, falling at his feet and weeping. She begged him to revoke the evil plot that Haman, the Agagite, had set up against the Jews. [o] 4 Then the king extended the golden scepter to Esther, and she arose and stood before him.

5 "If it pleases your majesty," she said, "and seems the right thing to do, and if I have found favor with you so that you love me, let an order be issued to overrule the letters that Haman, son of Hammedatha, the Agagite, devised and wrote for the destruction of the Jews in all the royal provinces. [p] 6 For how can I bear to see the evil that is about to fall on my people, and how can I behold the destruction of my race?"

7 King Ahasuerus then said to Queen Esther and to the Jew Mordecai, "Now that I have given Esther the property of Haman, and he has been hanged on the gibbet because he attacked the Jews, [q] 8 you may write another edict in the king's name on behalf of the Jews as seems best to you, and seal it with the king's signet ring—for no document that is written in the king's name and sealed with his ring can be revoked." *

9 Then on the twenty-third day of the third month, Sivan, the king's scribes were summoned. They wrote out all Mordecai's words to the Jews and to the satraps, governors, and nobles of the one hundred and twenty-seven provinces stretching from India to Ethiopia. These words were written in the script of each province and the language of each people and also in the script and language of the Jews. 10 Mordecai wrote in the name of King Ahasuerus, sealed the letters with the king's signet ring, and sent them via mounted couriers, riding speedy royal horses. 11 [r] The king's edict gave the Jews in every city the right to assemble and protect themselves as well as to destroy, kill, and annihilate, along with their wives and children, every armed group of any nation and province that should attack them, and to seize their goods as spoil. 12 The day appointed for the Jews to do this in all the provinces of King Ahasuerus was the thirteenth day of the twelfth month, Adar.

CHAPTER E

A Copy of the Edict.* 1 This is a copy of the edict:

"King Ahasuerus the Great to the governors of the one hundred and twenty-seven provinces extending from India to Ethiopia, and to all our loyal subjects: Greetings!

2 "Many people who have been the recipients of ever-increasing honors through the bountiful kindness of their benefactors tend to grow ever more arrogant. 3 Not only do they plot to injure our subjects but, as their power tends to increase their insolent behavior, they even begin to scheme against their very benefactors. 4 Not only do they make it impossible for others to experience gratitude, but they are so inundated in their own arrogance that the concept of goodness has become meaningless to them, and they even believe that they will escape the all-seeing God and his justice, which hates evil.

5 "In addition, it often happens that the deceitful schemes of friends who have been entrusted with the administration of public affairs 6 influence their benefactors to become unwitting accomplices of theirs in the shedding of innocent blood. Thus, the sincere desire of rulers to achieve only the good of their subjects is thwarted by deceitful trickery. 7 History is replete with stories of such evil, but never more so than at the

---

n Est 9:1; Prov 11:8; 26:27; Mt 7:2.—o Prov 13:22; Dan 2:48f.—p Est 1:19; 3:12.—q Est 8:2.—r 11f: Est 9:1-4.

8:8 The king cannot revoke a previous edict directly because of the irrevocable character of the laws of the Medes and Persians (Est 1:19; Dan 6:9). What he can do is empower Esther to issue a new edict in his name that makes the earlier edict ineffective (see Est 3:12-13).

E:1-24 The author of the Greek text attributes to Xerxes I the reflection that sages were more apt to make concerning the manner with which the affairs of the people are conducted and concerning the injustice that threatens the action of a man in power. He is fond of explaining in detail the freedom that the Jewish communities should enjoy and connects the Book of Esther with the Feast of Purim.

present when we examine the evil wrought in our midst through the criminal deeds of those officials who disgraced their office of authority by their wicked conduct. [8] [s] From this moment on we shall direct all of our efforts to ensure the peace and tranquillity of all our subjects in the kingdom, [9] revising our policies as necessary and giving equitable treatment in adjudicating matters that are brought before us.

[10] "In this regard, Haman, son of Hammedatha, a Macedonian* without a trace of Persian blood or of the kindness that is part of our heritage, was the recipient of our hospitality. [11] He so completely enjoyed the goodwill that we extend to all nations that we regarded him as our father before whom all should bow down, and we proclaimed him to rank second in line to the royal throne. [t] [12] However, unworthy of this dignity, Haman with unrestrained arrogance undertook to deprive us of our kingdom and our life. [13] By acts of deceit he insisted that it was essential for us to order the destruction of Mordecai, our savior and constant benefactor, and of Esther, our innocent royal consort, together with their whole race. [u] [14] By such measures he sought to render us vulnerable and to transfer the sovereignty now enjoyed by the Persians to the Macedonians.

[15] "However, we have determined that the Jews, who were marked for extermination by this thrice-wicked man, are no evildoers. On the contrary, they are governed by the most righteous laws [16] and are children of the Most High, the living God of sovereign majesty who has ensured for us as well as for our ancestors the continuing prosperity of our kingdom.

[17] "Therefore, I command you to ignore the letters sent by Haman, son of Hammedatha, [18] for he who wrote them has been hanged, together with his entire household, at the gates of Susa. God, the ruler of the universe, has inflicted upon him the punishment he so richly deserved. [v]

[19] "Instead, post copies of this letter in every public place and permit Jews to be governed by their own laws. [w] [20] Furthermore, ensure that on the day scheduled for their annihilation, the thirteenth day of the twelfth month, Adar, they will receive your aid to defend themselves against their assailants in a time of oppression. [21] For God, who rules over all things, has changed that day for his chosen people from a day of destruction to a day of joy. [22] And therefore you, too, must include among your commemorative feasts this day as one for rejoicing, [23] so that both today and in the future it may be for us and for all loyal Persians a memorial of deliverance and a reminder of destruction for those who plot against us.

[24] "Any city or province that does not observe this edict shall be mercilessly destroyed by fire and sword. It will be made unaccessible not only to all people, but also to wild animals and birds forever." [x]

(CHAPTER 8)

[13] A copy of the text of the edict to be issued as law in every province was made known among all peoples of every nationality so that the Jews might be ready on that day to avenge themselves on their enemies.*

[14] The couriers, riding the royal horses, sped forth in haste at the king's command. And the edict was also promulgated in the citadel of Susa.

[15] Mordecai departed from the king's presence vested in royal garments of blue and white, with a large crown of gold and purple robe of fine linen, and the city of Susa held a joyous celebration. [y] [16] For the Jews it was a time of happiness and joy, exaltation and triumph. [17] In every province and in every city, wherever the king's edict arrived, there was joy and gladness among the Jews, with banqueting and feasting. And many of the peoples of that land became Jewish, for they were seized with the fear of the Jews. [z]

CHAPTER 9

Triumph of the Jews. [1] * [a] On the thirteenth day of the twelfth month of Adar, the edict of the king was to become effective. It was on this day that the enemies of the Jews had

s 8f: Est B:2.—t Est B:3, 6.—u Est A:17.—v Est 7:10; 9:14.—w Ezr 7:25f.—x Est 9:1.—y Dan 5:7.—z Est 9:27.—a 1f: Est 8:11f; Gen 22:17.

E:10 *Macedonian:* used here and in E:14 possibly by a Hellenistic redactor who knew how much the Persians despised the Macedonians who eventually conquered them. Hence, Haman was viewed as the representation of all the irrational hatred against Jews who found themselves in a foreign environment.

8:13 See note on Est 9:1-15.

9:1-15 This episode of blood, in which facts and numbers are certainly exaggerated, illustrates an idea frequently found in the Bible: sooner or later justice is rendered for the oppressed. It is noteworthy that the author thinks of a limited retaliation and excludes plundering. The evolution of conscience takes from the whole Bible, and especially from the New Testament, a sense of God and a respect for persons that were not yet attained at this epoch.

expected to become masters of them. But in a role reversal it was the Jews who became masters of their enemies. 2 The Jews assembled in their cities in all the provinces of King Ahasuerus to attack those seeking their destruction. No one could withstand them, because the people of all the other nationalities were afraid of them. 3 Moreover, all of the provinces, the satraps, the governors and the king's administrators helped the Jews, out of fear of Mordecai. 4 Mordecai was powerful in the palace: his fame spread throughout the provinces, and his power kept on growing.

5 [b] The Jews overcame all their enemies with the sword, killing and destroying them, and did what they pleased to their enemies. 6 [c] In the citadel of Susa, they killed and destroyed five hundred men. 7 They also killed Parshandatha, Dalphon, Aspatha, 8 Porathai, Adalia, Aridatha, 9 Parmashta, Arisai, Aridai, and Vaizatha, 10 the ten sons of Haman, son of Hammedatha, the enemy of the Jews. However, they did not engage in plundering.[d]

11 On the same day, the number of those slain in the citadel of Susa was reported to the king. 12 He said to Queen Esther, "The Jews have killed and destroyed five hundred men and the ten sons of Haman in the citadel of Susa. But what must they have done in the other royal provinces! You shall again be granted whatever you ask, and whatever you request will be honored."

13 "If it pleases the king," Esther replied, "let the Jews in Susa be permitted again to carry out this day's edict tomorrow also, and let the ten sons of Haman be hanged on gibbets."

14 The king then gave an order that this should be done. An edict was issued in Susa, and they hanged the ten sons of Haman.[e] 15 The Jews in Susa came together on the fourteenth day of the month of Adar, and they put to death three hundred men in Susa. However, they did not engage in plundering.* [f]

16 Meanwhile, the other Jews who were in the king's provinces also assembled to protect themselves and to obtain rest from their enemies. They killed seventy-five thousand* of them, but they did not engage in plundering.[g] 17 This took place on the thirteenth day of the month of Adar, and on the fourteenth day of the month they rested and made it a day of feasting and joy.

18 The Jews in Susa, however, had assembled on the thirteenth and fourteenth of the month of Adar. On the fifteenth of the month they rested, and made it a day of feasting and joy.

19 That is why rural Jews, who live in villages, observe the fourteenth of the month of Adar as a day of feasting and rejoicing, a holiday on which they give presents to one another.[h] Instead, those who live in large cities celebrate the fifteenth of Adar as a day of feasting and joy and give presents to each other.*

The Feast of Purim.* 20 Mordecai recorded these events, and dispatched letters to all the Jews throughout the provinces of King Ahasuerus, to both those who were near and those who were far off. 21 He commanded them to celebrate every year the fourteenth and fifteenth days of the month of Adar, 22 as the time when the Jews succeeded in obtaining relief from their enemies and as the month when their sorrow was turned into joy and their mourning into a day of celebration. He wrote them to observe these days as days of feasting and rejoicing, sending food to one another and gifts to the poor.

23 So the Jews accepted all that Mordecai had written to them.[i] 24 [j] For Haman, son of Hammedatha, the Agagite, the enemy of the Jews, had hatched a plot to destroy them and had cast the *pur* (that is, the lot) for their defeat and destruction. 25 But when Esther entered the royal presence, the king gave written orders that the wicked scheme Haman had devised against the Jews should be turned against him instead and that he

b Ex 3:13; 9:15; Jud 15:6.—c 6-10: Est 5:11.—d Est 9:15; Jud 15:7, 11.—e Est 7:10; E:18.—f Est 9:10.—g Jud 15:6.—h Neh 8:10-12.—i Est 9:29.—j 24ff: Est 3:7; F:10.

9:15 This second massacre accounts for the two dates of the Purim celebration by Jews in Susa—thirteenth and fourteenth of Adar (see v. 18).

9:16 *Seventy-five thousand:* in the Greek version, the number is fifteen thousand. This too may be the result of a literary artifice as in the case of the gallows for Mordecai (see Est 5:14).

9:19 *Instead . . . other:* found only in the Greek.

9:20-32 Haman had cast the lot (*pur*) to decide to exterminate the Jews. The latter, providentially vindicated, must celebrate annually the anniversary day of this memorable fact. In reality, the true origin of this feast, which was to take place in February–March, is unknown. Probably these celebrations of the beginning of the year were not very religious at their origin and common to other people. But thanks to the Book of Esther, they have become for the Jewish communities a feast of their freedom. This feast began with a fast, and the Book of Esther was read in the synagogue stressing the maledictions against the enemies of Israel. Hence, popular feasts took place with well sprinkled meals and masked manifestations similar to a carnival.

and his sons should be hanged on gibbets.[k]
26 (Therefore, these days were called Purim,*
from the word *pur.*)

Because of everything mentioned in this
letter and because of what they had seen and
what they had experienced, 27 the Jews took
upon themselves, their descendants, and any
who should join them,* the inviolable obli-
gation to celebrate these two days every year
in the way prescribed and at the time ap-
pointed.[l]

28 These days were to be remembered in
every generation by every family, and in
every province and in every city. Moreover,
these days of Purim were never to fall into
disuse among the Jews, nor should their
memory die out among their descendants.[m]

29 Queen Esther, daughter of Abihail and of
Mordecai the Jew, wrote with complete
authority to confirm this second letter about
Purim. 30 [n]And Mordecai sent documents
about peace and security to all the Jews in
the one hundred and twenty-seven provinces
of Ahasuerus's kingdom. 31 Thus, there were
established, for their appointed time, these
days of Purim that Mordecai the Jew and
Queen Esther had designated for the Jews,
and as they had established for themselves
and for their race, the duty of fasting and
supplication. 32 Esther's decree confirmed
these rules concerning Purim, and it was
recorded in the book.

CHAPTER 10

The Greatness of Mordecai. 1 King Ahas-
uerus imposed tribute throughout the land
to its distant shores. 2 And all his acts of
power and might, as well as an account of the
greatness of Mordecai, whom the king pro-
moted, are set down in the book of the annals
of the kings of Media and Persia. 3 Mordecai
the Jew was second in rank to King
Ahasuerus, preeminent among the Jews, and
held in high esteem by his fellow Jews
because he worked for the good of his people
and was the herald of peace for his whole
race.[o]

V: EPILOGUE

CHAPTER F

Mordecai's Dream Fulfilled.* 1 [p]Then Mor-
decai said: "All this is God's doing, 2 for I
remember the dream I had about these
events, and not one of them has failed to
be fulfilled— 3 the tiny spring that became
a river, the light that shone, the sun, the
abundance of water. The river is Esther,
whom the king married and established as
queen. 4 The two dragons are Haman and
myself. 5 The nations are those who joined
together to extinguish the name of the
Jews. 6 And my nation is Israel who cried
to God for deliverance and was saved.

"The LORD has saved his people and deliv-
ered us from all these evils. God has per-
formed great signs and wonders such as have
never before occurred among the nations.
7 To accomplish this he prepared two lots,*
one for the people of God and one for all the
nations. 8 These lots were cast at the pre-
scribed hour and time, on the day of judg-
ment before God and all the nations. 9 And
God remembered his people and rendered a
verdict of justice in favor of his heritage.

10 "Therefore, they are to assemble with
joy and gladness before God and celebrate
these days in the month of Adar, on the
fourteenth and fifteenth of that month,
from generation to generation among his
people Israel forever."

A Postscript about Purim. 11 In the fourth
year* of the reign of Ptolemy and Cleopatra,
Dositheus, who said he was a priest and
Levite, and his son, Ptolemy, brought to
Egypt the preceding letter about Purim, say-
ing that it was genuine and had been trans-
lated by Lysimachus, son of Ptolemy, of the
community of Jerusalem.

k Est 6:5-13.—l Est 8:17; 9:21.—m Zec 2:15.—n Est 9:23-26.—o 2 Mac 15:14.—p 1-6: Est A:4-10

9:26 The Feast of *Purim* is still celebrated among the Jews. The thirteenth day is a fast and the Book of Esther is read; the fourteenth day, after a new reading from the Book of Esther, is spent joyously recalling and celebrating the divine benefits.

9:27 *Any who should join them:* that is, the proselytes, pagans converted to Judaism.

F:1-10 Historically, it is not very likely that a Jew could have carried out the high functions of Mordecai at the Persian court. He has such importance in the present Book that it could also be called "Mordecai the Jew." Hence, the Feast of Purim was at times known as Mordecai's Day (2 Mac 15:36).

F:7 *Two lots:* the Greek text here gives a more religious interpretation of Purim, speaking of lots prepared by God to ascertain the destiny of *the people of God* and that of *all the nations.* (See Est 3:7 for another explanation for the name of the feast.) Hence, we know that in 114 B.C. a Jewish community in Egypt received the Book of Esther from the established community in Judea, most likely in connection with the Feast of Purim of which the text speaks.

F:11 *Fourth year:* probably 114 B.C. There were three Ptolemys who had a wife called Cleopatra: Ptolemy VIII (114 B.C.), Ptolemy XII (77 B.C.), and Ptolemy XIV (48 B.C.). Most scholars favor the first here. *The preceding letter:* a reference to the entire Book of Esther, probably including some of the Additions as well.

Judas and his men "pray[ed] that the sin that had been committed [by their dead comrades] might be completely blotted out" *(2 Mac 12:42).*

THE FIRST BOOK OF MACCABEES

The Epic Story of a Resistance

The First Book of Maccabees was written in Hebrew by a Jew from Jerusalem, probably around the beginning of the first century before Christ. However, only translations are extant as well as the Greek text that provides faith for the Church. In his work, the author details almost half a century of Jewish history, from 175–134 B.C., that is, from the accession of Antiochus IV Epiphanes to the throne of Syria until the death of Simon Maccabeus.

A conscientious writer, he sets down the events according to their chronological order, except for a few particulars. Like the historiographers of antiquity, he selects his facts, loves to put them in a dramatic form, inflates the numbers, and places eloquent discourses on the lips of his heroes.

We will not reprove him if he takes some liberties when he transcribes archival letters and documents about which he probably knows nothing more than the essential content. To express his enthusiasm and his emotion, he turns poet.

However, his political tendencies render him partial: he has too much ingenuous admiration for the Romans (who will not hesitate to occupy Palestine without much regard!) and approves without reserve the champions of independence, his compatriots. By contrast, he is indignant against the undertakings of the kings of Syria and frequently treats them with excessive severity.

Despite this partisan position, he remains a serious and objective historian, reports what he has seen, and utilizes the testimonies of contemporaries and official documents. This historian is also a believer, convinced that Providence guides and sustains the unexpected rebirth of his people.

As is the case with the Book of Esther, God—out of respect—is never named; he is evoked by the word "Heaven." But it is he who favors the bold maneuvers of Judas and his brothers; it is he who brings about the victory. The allusions to the law, the temple, and the covenant, as well as the prayers of the combatants, bear witness to his presence.

In brief, the soul of this new holy war is the Lord. As in the time of Joshua and David, it is the covenant that is in question in this reconquest. The faith of Israel remains basically the same as of old, but it is expressed in a new way: the zeal for the Law, the worship at the temple, the horror of uncleanness, and the curses of the Gentiles; this is what characterizes these Jews of the second century B.C.

Moreover, the religious revolt in its beginnings is colored little by little with political ambitions. The author does not seem to be shaken by it, while certain religious movements are disturbed. This is perhaps the gravest lacuna in an interesting and human story that exudes heroism and combines the intransigence of faith with the passion for freedom.

The First Book of Maccabees may be divided a follows:

I: A Great Danger for the Faith (1:1-64)
II: The Great Days of the Resistance (2:1—6:63)
III: The Rise of the Hasmoneans (7:1—16:24)

I: A GREAT DANGER FOR THE FAITH

CHAPTER 1*

The Succession of Alexander the Great.*
1 [a]After Alexander of Macedon, the son of
Philip, had come from the land of Kittim*
and defeated Darius, the king of the Persians
and the Medes, he succeeded him as king, in
addition to his position as king of Greece. 2 He
engaged in many campaigns, captured
strongholds, and executed kings. 3 In his
advance to the ends of the earth, he plun-
dered countless nations. When the earth was
reduced to silence before him, his heart
swelled with pride and arrogance.* 4 He
recruited a very powerful army, and as
provinces, nations, and rulers were con-
quered by him, they became his tributaries.

5 However, when all this had been ac-
complished, Alexander became ill, and
he realized that his death was imminent.
6 Therefore, he summoned his officers, nobles
who had been brought up with him from his
youth, and he divided his kingdom among
them while he was still alive. 7 Then, in the
twelfth year* of his reign, Alexander died.

8 After that, his officers assumed power in
the kingdom, each in his own territory.
9 They all put on royal crowns after his
death, as did their heirs who succeeded
them for many years, inflicting great evils
on the world.

10 From these there sprang forth a wicked
offshoot, Antiochus Epiphanes, the son of
King Antiochus.[b] Previously he had been a
hostage in Rome. He began his reign in the
one hundred and thirty-seventh year of the
Greeks.*

Hellenism in Palestine.* 11 In those days
there emerged in Israel a group of rene-
gades who led many people astray, saying,
"Let us enter into an alliance with the
Gentiles around us. Many disasters have
come upon us since we separated ourselves
from them."[c] 12 This proposal received great

a 1-10: Dan 8:20ff; 11:3f, 21.—b 2 Mac 4:7.—c 2 Mac 4:9-17.

1:1-64 In the sixth century B.C., the Exile had endangered the existence of Israel as a nation. Out of this crisis, the national hope came forth purified: the vocation of Israel, reduced to a little protectorate, was not that of being a power but of remaining, above all, the people bearing witness to God. The crisis of the Maccabean period is more grave. For the first time, Israel is threatened as a spiritual family: it is the trial of hope.

1:1-10 The young Macedonian conqueror had formed an immense empire for himself (333–324 B.C.). He died prematurely, and his kingdom was divided among the generals who quarreled over his inheritance. Judea profited from the benevolence of the Lagids who ruled Egypt. However, at the beginning of the second century B.C., it became subjugated by the successors of Seleucus, the Seleucids, who ruled in Syria and spread Hellenism throughout the Middle East. With the advent of Antiochus IV Epiphanes in 175 B.C., the pressure reaches its zenith.

1:1 *Kittim:* designates primarily Cyprus but encompasses other foreign countries among which was Macedonia. *Greece* here designates the region of Asia Minor that had already been colonized by the Greeks for a long time.

1:3 After defeating the Persians, Alexander the Great reached the Indian Ocean.

1:7 *Twelfth year:* 334 B.C.

1:10 The year 137 of the Seleucid era corresponds to 175 B.C.

1:11-15 In order to unify his kingdom, the new monarch Antiochus IV Epiphanes imposed Greek customs everywhere. These were contradictory to the Jewish religious requirements, which were made precise from the end of the Exile. Nonetheless, the king could rely—especially at Jerusalem—on a current of opportunists favorable to Hellenism because of ambition or a desire for cultural integration: the clan of Jason whose members are termed *renegades*.

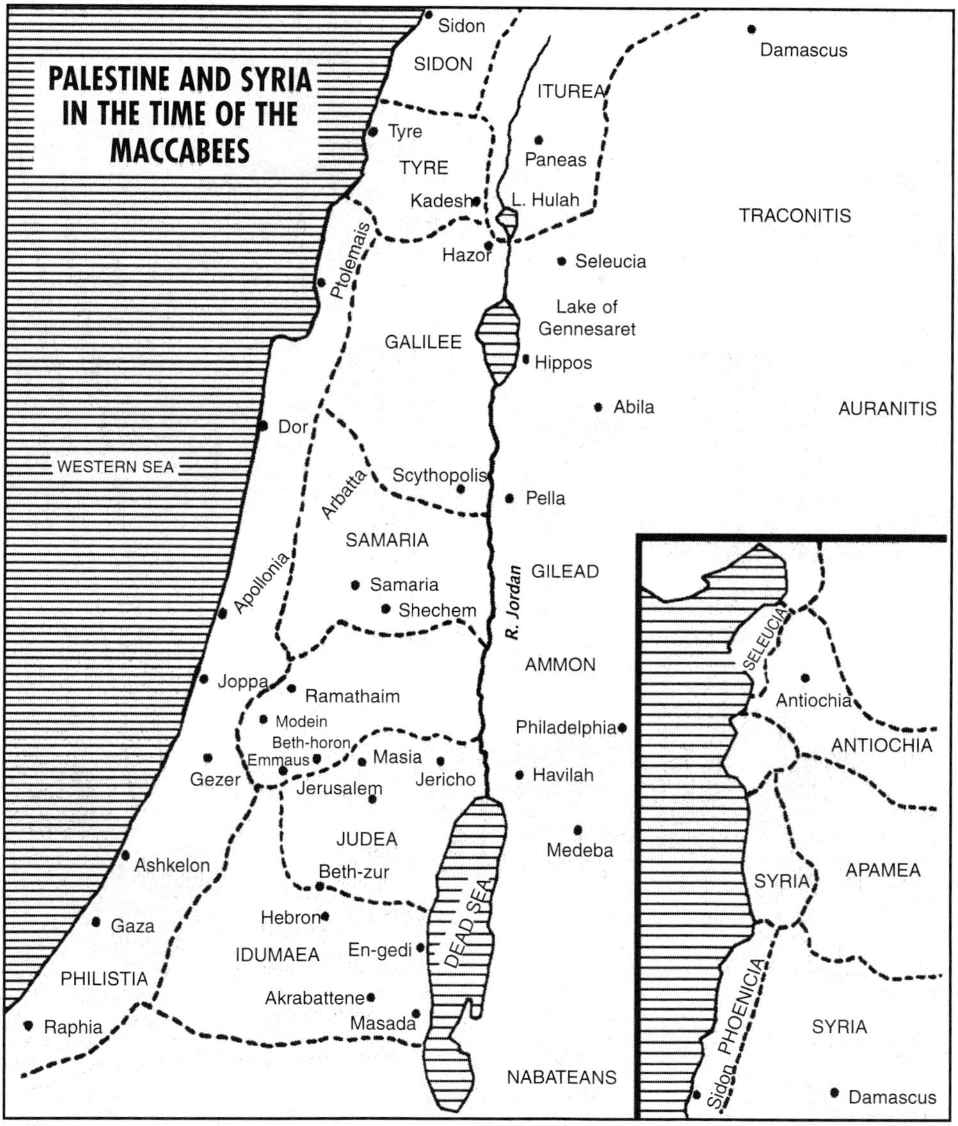

PALESTINE AND SYRIA IN THE TIME OF THE MACCABEES (166–63 B.C.: 1 Mac 1–16; 2 Mac 8–15) — **(a)** With their defeat by Alexander the Great at the Battle of Arbela (331 B.C.), the Persians lose not only their empire but also control over Palestine. After the death of Alexander, the Jews are ruled benevolently by the Egyptian Ptolemies for over one hundred years (323–198 B.C.). **(b)** The Seleucids, who have inherited the greater part of Alexander's empire, bring the Jews under their dominion again (198 B.C.), and Antiochus IV Epiphanes determines to compel the Jews to adopt the Greek religion and converts the temple to the worship of the Olympian Zeus (168 B.C.) (1 Mac 1). **(c)** The sons of the priest Mattathias (from **Modein**) organize a revolt under the leader Judas (called Maccabeus or "the Hammerer"). Judas cleanses the temple in 165 B.C., an event commemorated in the Jewish festival of Dedication (Hanukkah) before being killed in battle in 160 B.C. (3:1—9:22). **(d)** He is succeeded first by his brothers, Jonathan (160–142 B.C.) and then Simon (142–134 B.C.) who gains Jewish independence and establishes the Hasmonean dynasty, holding the high priesthood and the civil power (9:23—16:16). **(e)** John Hyrcanus I (134–104 B.C.) wins complete independence for the Jews and enlarges their territory to include **Samaria** and the Moabite region beyond the Jordan. **(f)** In 63 B.C., the Romans end Jewish independence, but allow the last two Hasmoneans to govern: Hyrcanus II (63–40 B.C.) and Antigonus (40–36 B.C.).

REMAINS OF THE TOMBS OF THE MACCABEES— View of what are thought to be the remains of the tombs of the Maccabees in Modein, a village in the Shephelah. It was here that Mattathias struck the first blow for Jewish religious freedom (21:28). It was here also that Simon built a splendid monument, in memory of his parents and brothers and the Jewish victory, which could be seen at sea and lasted 500 years. And it was here that Mattathias was buried together with his sons Judas and Jonathan. (See 2:70; 9:19; 13:25.)

ANTIOCH ON THE ORONTES — A view of Antioch on the Orontes, at the foot of Mount Silpius, capital of ancient Syria. This was the most famous of the sixteen Antiochs built by Seleucus Nicator (312–280 B.C.), founder of the Seleucid dynasty. The city was built up and beautified by Antiochus IV Epiphanes (175–163 B.C.) and served as his base. His policies of Hellenization incurred the bitter opposition of the Maccabees and ultimately led to Jewish independence from Syria under the Hasmonean dynasty which ruled Judea from 166–37 B.C. (See 1 Mac 1–2.)

popular support, 13 [d]and when some of the
people immediately thereafter approached
the king, he authorized them to introduce
the practices observed by the Gentiles.
14 Therefore, they built a gymnasium in
Jerusalem according to Gentile custom,
15 concealed the marks of their circumci-
sion, and abandoned the holy covenant.
Thus they allied themselves to the Gentiles
and sold themselves to the power of evil.[e]

The Temple of Jerusalem Is Sacked.* 16 Once
his kingdom had been firmly established,
Antiochus was determined to become king
of Egypt so that he might reign over both
kingdoms. 17 He invaded Egypt with a mas-
sive force of chariots, elephants, and caval-
ry, supported by a large fleet.[f] 18 When he
engaged Ptolemy, the king of Egypt, in bat-
tle, Ptolemy fled in fear before him, amidst
a great number of casualties. 19 The fortified
cities in the land of Egypt were captured,
and Antiochus plundered the kingdom.

20 After his return from his conquest of
Egypt in the year one hundred and forty-
three, Antiochus advanced upon Israel and
Jerusalem with a massive force.[g] 21 In his
arrogance he entered the sanctuary and
removed the golden altar, the lampstand for
the light with all its fixtures, 22 the table for
the loaves of offering, the libation cups and
bowls, the golden censers, the curtain, and
the crowns. He stripped off all the gold dec-
orations on the front of the temple, 23 and he
seized the silver and gold and precious ves-
sels and all the hidden treasures he could
find. 24 Taking all this, he returned to his own
country, having caused great bloodshed and
boasted arrogantly of what he had accom-
plished.[h]

25 There was great mourning throughout Israel,
26 and the rulers and the elders groaned.
Girls and young men wasted away,
and the beauty of the women waned.
27 Every bridegroom raised up laments,
and the bride sat mourning in her bridal chamber.[i]
28 The land trembled for its inhabitants,
and the entire house of Jacob was clothed in shame.

29 Two years later the king sent his chief
collector of tribute to the cities of Judah.
When he came to Jerusalem with a power-
ful force,[j] 30 he deceitfully addressed the
people there with sentiments of peace.
Once he had gained their confidence, he
suddenly launched a savage attack on the
city and exterminated many of the people
of Israel. 31 He plundered the city and set it
on fire. He demolished its dwellings and the
walls that encircled the city, 32 took the
women and children captive, and seized
the livestock. 33 Then they rebuilt the City of
David with a massive high wall and strong
towers,[k] and it became their citadel.*
34 There they stationed a sinful race of rene-
gades, who fortified themselves inside it,
35 storing up arms and provisions, and
depositing there the plunder they had col-
lected from Jerusalem. Thus they posed a
significant threat.

36 The citadel became an ambush against the sanctuary,
an evil adversary for Israel at all times.
37 They spilled innocent blood all around the sanctuary,
and even defiled the sanctuary itself.[l]
38 Because of them the inhabitants of Jerusalem fled,
and the city became a dwelling place of strangers.
She became estranged from her own offspring,
and her children abandoned her.
39 [m]Her sanctuary became as desolate as a desert;
her feasts were turned into mourning,
her sabbaths into reproach,
her honor into contempt.
40 Her dishonor was equal to her former glory,
and her exaltation was turned into mourning.

d 13ff: 2 Mac 4:7-17.—e 1 Cor 7:18.—f 2 Mac 5:1; Dan 11:25-28.—g 20-24: 2 Mac 5:11-21.—h 2 Mac 3:10.—i Lam 1:4.—j 29-32: 2 Mac 5:24ff.—k 1 Mac 6:18.—l Ps 79:1-3.—m 39f: Tob 2:6; Am 8:10.

1:16-40 This event took place in 169 B.C. The plunderer of the temple had great need of money after his first campaign in Egypt; after the second, he brutally occupied the city of Jerusalem. The arrogance of the king, who wanted to incarnate Zeus, impressed his contemporaries and especially the author of the Book of Daniel (Dan 7:8-25; 8:11-14; 9:27; 11:31,36; 12:11ff). The prince who makes himself a god and plays with the life of human beings becomes the type of the Antichrist (Rev 13:15).

1:33 The ancient Jebusite fortress defeated by David (see 2 Sam 5:7-9). This fortification, called Acra, will present the Maccabees with much work for them (see 1 Mac 6:18-32; 11:20-24; 13:49-51).

The Great Persecution.* 41 Then the king issued an edict to his whole kingdom that all of his subjects should become a united people, 42 with each nation abandoning its particular customs. All the Gentiles accepted the decree of the king, 43 and many among the Israelites adopted his religion, sacrificing to idols and profaning the Sabbath.

44 [n] The king also sent messengers to Jerusalem and the cities of Judah with edicts commanding them to adopt practices that were foreign to their country: 45 to prohibit holocausts, sacrifices, and libations in the sanctuary, to profane the Sabbaths and feast days, 46 to defile the temple and its priests, to build altars, temples, and shrines for idols,[o] 47 to sacrifice swine* and other unclean beasts, 48 to leave their sons uncircumcised, and to allow themselves to be defiled with every kind of impurity and abomination, 49 so that they would forget the law and change all their observances. 50 Anyone who refused to obey the command of the king was to be put to death.[p]

51 These were the terms of the edicts he issued throughout his kingdom. He appointed inspectors to supervise all the people, and he commanded all the towns of Judah to offer sacrifices, town by town. 52 Many of the people, abandoning the law, joined them and committed evil deeds in the land, 53 thereby driving Israel into hiding in every possible place of refuge.

54 On the fifteenth day of the month Chislev, in the year one hundred and forty-five, the king erected upon the altar of holocausts the abomination that causes desolation, and pagan altars were built in the surrounding towns of Judah.[q] 55 Incense was offered at the doors of the houses and in the streets. 56 Any scrolls of the law that were found were torn to pieces and destroyed by fire. 57 If any people were discovered in possession of a book of the covenant or acting in conformity with the law, they were condemned to death by the decree of the king.[r]

58 Month after month these wicked people used their power against any loyal Israelite found in the towns. 59 On the twenty-fifth day of each month they offered sacrifice on the altar erected on top of the altar of holocausts. 60 In accordance with the royal decree, any women who had their children circumcised were put to death,[s] 61 with their infants hung from their necks; also put to death were their families and those who had circumcised them.

62 Despite all this, many in Israel stood firm and were resolved in their hearts not to eat any unclean food. 63 They preferred to die rather than to be defiled by such food and profane the holy covenant, and they suffered death for their convictions.[t] 64 Great affliction was unleashed upon Israel.

II: THE GREAT DAYS OF THE RESISTANCE*

A: Resistance Begins: Mattathias (167–166 B.C.)

CHAPTER 2

Mattathias and His Sons. 1 In those days Mattathias,* son of John, son of Simeon, a priest of the family of Joarib, departed from Jerusalem and settled in Modein. 2 He had five sons: John, who was called Gaddi;[u] 3 Simon, who was called Thassi; 4 Judas, who was called Maccabeus;* 5 Eleazar, who was called Avaran; and Jonathan, who was called Apphus. 6 When he observed the sacrilegious acts that were being committed in Judah and Jerusalem, 7 * he said: "Alas! Why was I born to witness the ruin of my people and the ruin of the holy city, and to sit by idly while she has been delivered over to her enemies, and the sanctuary given into the hands of foreigners? [v]

8 "Her temple has become like a prison
 without honor,
9 her glorious vessels have been carried
 off as booty.

---

n 44-63: 2 Mac 6:1-11.—o 2 Mac 6:2; Dan 9:27.—p 2 Mac 6:18—7:41.—q 1 Mac 6:7; Dan 9:27; 11:31.—r 2 Mac 2:14.—s 60f: 2 Mac 6:10.—t 2 Mac 6:10.—u 1 Chr 9:10.—v Neh 11:1.

1:41-64 King Antiochus IV Epiphanes adds sacrileges as the zenith of his doings, erecting at the heart of the temple of Jerusalem, on the very altar of holocausts, an altar to Zeus, the great god of the pagans: this is the abomination that causes desolation (Dan 9:27; 11:31). We are in early December 167 B.C. The people of the covenant are obliged to choose: to become pagan or to suffer violence.

1:47 *Swine:* the pig was the unclean animal par excellence (see Lev 11:7; Deut 14:8).

2:1—6:63 Many Jews, above all the rich, collaborated with the established power. A family of priests (called the Hasmoneans after the name of their forefather) takes to the woods and soon gathers together a group of resisters.

2:1 *Mattathias* signifies "gift of Yahweh." *Joarib* was the head of the first priestly division (see 1 Chr 24:7). *Modein* was seventeen miles west of Jerusalem.

2:4 *Maccabeus* is thought to derive from a Hebrew word meaning "hammer."

2:7-13 Mattathias's lament takes its inspiration from ancient texts (Lam 2:11-21).

Her infants have been slaughtered in the streets,
her young men slain by the sword of the enemy.[w]
10 What nation has not usurped a share of her sovereignty
and carried off her possessions as plunder?
11 All her adornment has been stripped from her;
she who enjoyed freedom has now become a slave.
12 We see our sanctuary, and our beauty, and our glory now laid waste.
The Gentiles have defiled them.[x]
13 What now do we have to live for?"

14 Then Mattathias and his sons tore their garments, put on sackcloth, and engaged in great mourning.

A Righteous Anger. 15 The officers of the king who had been commissioned to enforce the apostasy came to the town of Modein to ensure that the sacrifices were being offered.
16 Many Israelites assembled around them, but Mattathias and his sons stood apart.
17[y] Then the officers of the king addressed Mattathias in these words: "You are a leader in this town, respected and influential, and you have the support of your sons and brothers. 18 Now be the first to come forward and obey the decree of the king, as all the Gentiles have done, as well as the citizens of Judah and the people who remain in Jerusalem. Then you and your sons will be counted among the Friends of the King,* and you and your sons will be honored with gold and silver and many other gifts."

19 However, Mattathias responded in a loud voice: "Even if every nation in the king's dominions obeys him, each one forsaking the religion of its fathers and agreeing to submit to the king's commands, 20 I and my sons and my brothers will continue to observe the covenant of our fathers.[z]
21 God forbid that we should ever forsake the law and its statutes. 22 We will not obey the king's commands or deviate from our religion to the right hand or to the left."

23 As he finished speaking, a Jew came forward in the sight of all to offer sacrifice on the altar in Modein, in accordance with the royal decree. 24 When Mattathias observed this, he became inflamed with zeal. His righteous anger aroused, he sprang forward and slaughtered him on the altar. 25 At the same time he also killed the officer of the king who was present to enforce the sacrifice, and he destroyed the altar. 26 In this way he demonstrated his zeal for the law, just as Phinehas had done with Zimri, the son of Salu.[a]

27 Then Mattathias advanced through the town, shouting: "Let everyone who is zealous for the law and who stands by the covenant come with me!" 28 Then he and his sons fled to the hills, leaving behind in the town everything that they possessed.[b] 29 Many of the people who desired to live in accordance with justice and the law went down to the desert* and settled there, 30 taking with them their sons, their wives, and their livestock, so oppressive were the sufferings that they had been forced to endure.

31 Shortly thereafter it was reported to the officers of the king and the forces stationed in Jerusalem, the City of David, that those who had refused to obey the king's edict had retreated to hiding places in the desert. 32[c] A large force set out in pursuit and caught up with them; they encamped opposite them and prepared to attack them on the Sabbath. 33 "Enough of this defiance!" they said. "Come out and obey the king's edict, and your lives will be spared."
34 "We will not come out," they replied, "nor will we do what the king commands and profane the Sabbath."

35 Then the enemy immediately launched an attack on them, 36 but they did not retaliate, neither hurling rocks nor barricading their hiding places. 37 They only said, "Let us all die in a state of innocence. Heaven and earth are our witnesses that you are massacring us without the slightest justification." 38 Therefore, the enemy attacked on the Sabbath and massacred them along with their wives, their children, and their livestock—one thousand persons in all.

Mattathias Organizes the Resistance.*
39 When Mattathias and his friends were

w Lam 2:11, 21.—x Ps 50:2; Lam 2:15.—y 17ff: Deut 13:6-11.—z Ex 19:8.—a 1 Mac 2:54.—b 2 Mac 5:27.—c 32-38: 2 Mac 6:11.

2:18 *Friends of the King*: an official court title; others were "Chief Friends and King's Kinsmen."

2:29 *The desert* refers to the wilderness of Judea, southward from Jerusalem and west of the Dead Sea, where one could easily find hiding places in grottoes and caves.

2:39-48 Mattathias is joined by the *Hasideans*, the "pious," a group of fervent Jews who would give rise to the Pharisees (and probably the Essenes). At first they had resisted passively (1 Mac 1:62f; 2:37), but now they turned to active resistance. They would later oppose the Maccabean movement as too political.

informed of this, they grieved deeply for
them. 40 "If we all do as our kindred have
done," they said to one another, "and refuse
to fight against the Gentiles in defense of our
lives and our traditions, they will soon wipe
us off the face of the earth." 41 On that day
they formulated this decision: "Let us fight
against anyone who attacks us on the
Sabbath, so that we will not all be killed, as
happened to our kindred who died in their
hiding places."

42 Soon thereafter they were joined by a
group of Hasideans, valiant warriors of
Israel, each one a stout defender of the law.
43 In addition, all those who were refugees
from the persecution joined up with them,
adding to their strength. 44 After organizing
an army, they struck down sinners in their
anger and renegades in their fury. Those who
escaped them fled to the Gentiles for safety.[d]
45 Mattathias and his friends marched
through the kingdom, destroying the pagan
altars 46 and forcibly circumcising all the
uncircumcised boys they found within the
borders of Israel. 47 They hunted down their
arrogant enemies, and their efforts pros-
pered under their direction. 48 Thus they
defended the law against the Gentiles and
their kings, and they did not allow the wicked
to emerge triumphant.

Last Words of Mattathias.* 49 When the time
drew near for Mattathias to die, he said to
his sons: "Arrogance and scorn have now
grown strong; this is an age of turmoil and
violent fury. 50 Therefore, my sons, be zeal-
ous for the law and be willing to give your
lives for the covenant of our ancestors.

51 "Remember the deeds that our ancestors performed in their generations,
and you shall win great honor and everlasting renown.
52 Was not Abraham found faithful when he was put to the test,
and it was reckoned to him as righteousness?[e]
53 Joseph, in the time of his distress, kept God's law,
and he became the lord of Egypt.[f]
54 Phinehas, our ancestor,* because of his burning zeal,
received the covenant of everlasting priesthood.[g]
55 Joshua, for carrying out his commission,
became a judge in Israel.[h]
56 Caleb, for his testimony in the assembly,
received an inheritance in the land.[i]
57 David, as a result of his mercy,
inherited the throne of an everlasting kingdom.[j]
58 Elijah, because of his burning zeal for the law,
was taken up into heaven.[k]
59 Hananiah, Azariah, and Mishael, for their faith,
were rescued from the flames.[l]
60 Daniel, for his innocence,
was rescued from the lions' jaws.[m]
61 Therefore, remember that from generation to generation
no one who hopes in him will be lacking in strength.
62 Do not fear the words of sinful people,
for their glory will turn to dung and worms.[n]
63 Today they are exalted, but tomorrow they are nowhere to be found
because they have returned to the dust,
and their grandiose schemes have come to naught.
64 My children, draw your courage and strength from the law,
for through it glory will be yours.[o]

65 "Here is your brother Simon who I know
is a man of sound judgment. Always listen to
him, for he will act as your father. 66 Judas
Maccabeus, a mighty warrior from his
youth, will be the commander of your army
and direct your battles against the peoples.
67 Enroll in your cause all who observe the
law, and in this way you will avenge the
wrongs perpetrated on your people. 68 Pay
back the Gentiles in full, and obey the pre-
cepts of the law."

69 Then he blessed them and was gathered
to his ancestors. 70 He died in the year one
hundred and forty-six and was buried in the

d Isa 63:3.—e Gen 15:6; 22:1ff.—f Gen 39:7-10; 41:39-43.—g Num 25:10-13; Sir 45:23ff.—h Jos 1:2, 5.—i Num 13:30; 14:6-9, 24; Jos 14:14.—j 2 Sam 2:3; 7:16.—k 1 Ki 19:10, 14; 2 Ki 2:11.—l Dan 3:50.—m Dan 6:23; 14:31-42.—n Ps 83:10.—o Deut 31:9; Jos 1:6f.

2:49-70 This literary and, in certain moments, poetical page takes its inspiration from ancient biblical accounts (Gen 49; Deut 33; 1 Ki 2:1-9) as well as recent ones such as the Book of Daniel.

2:54 *Phinehas, our ancestor:* by connecting Mattathias with the priest Phinehas, grandson of Aaron (Num 15:10-13), the author wishes to attest to the legitimacy of the priesthood of the Hasmoneans, which will later be contested.

tombs of his ancestors in Modein, and all Israel mourned him with great lamentation.*

B: The Holy War: Judas Maccabeus (166–161 B.C.)

CHAPTER 3

Eulogy of a Hero. [1]Then his son Judas, who was known as Maccabeus, took his place. [2]All his brothers and all who had allied themselves to his father gave him their support, and they enthusiastically continued to fight for Israel.

3 He enhanced the glory of his people,
and like a giant he put on his breastplate.
He girded himself with the armor of warfare,
engaging in battles and protecting the camp by his sword.[p]
4 In his exploits he was like a lion,
like a young lion roaring for prey.
5 He pursued and tracked down the wicked,
and he cast into the flames those who troubled his people.
6 The lawbreakers cowered with terror at his approach;
all evildoers were completely confounded.
Under his leadership deliverance was achieved,
7 as he caused many kings to become embittered,
but Jacob to be gladdened by his deeds;
and his memory is blessed forever.[q]
8 He marched through the towns of Judea,
destroying the apostates who dwelt there.
He turned away wrath from Israel,
9 and his renown spread to the ends of the earth,
as he saved those that were on the brink of perishing.

First Battles of Judas. [10]Then Apollonius* united the Gentiles with a large army from Samaria to wage war against Israel. [11]On learning this, Judas marched out to confront him, and he defeated and killed him. Many fell wounded, and those who survived took flight. [12]Then their spoils were seized. The sword of Apollonius was taken by Judas, who used it in his battles for the rest of his life.

[13]When Seron, the commander of the Assyrian army, learned that Judas had mustered a large force of faithful soldiers prepared for battle, [14]he said, "I will make a name for myself and win great renown in the kingdom if I defeat Judas and his followers who have shown such contempt for the king's edict." [15]And once again a large army of unbelievers banded together to help him exact vengeance on the Israelites.

[16]When he reached the ascent of Beth-horon,* Judas marched out to confront him with a small contingent. [17]However, when they observed the army that was gathered to do battle with them, his soldiers said to Judas, "How can we, as few as we are, fight against so great a multitude? Besides, we are faint with hunger, for we have eaten nothing all day." [18]But Judas replied, "It is easy for many to be defeated by a few. In the sight of Heaven,* there is no distinction between deliverance by many and deliverance by a few. [19]Victory in war does not depend upon the size of the fighting force, but rather upon the strength that comes from Heaven.[r] [20]Our enemies have come against us in a display of insolence and lawlessness to destroy us and our wives and our children, and to plunder us. [21]However, we are fighting in defense of our lives and our laws. [22]He himself * will crush them before our eyes; therefore, do not be afraid of them."[s]

[23]When he had finished speaking, he rushed suddenly against Seron and his army, and they were crushed before him. [24]He pursued them down the descent of Beth-horon as far as the plain. About eight

p 2 Mac 8:5.—q Prov 10:7; Wis 4:1.—r 1 Sam 14:6.—s Bar 6:22.

2:70 Mattathias died in 166 B.C., a year after the beginning of the revolt.

3:10 *Apollonius* is probably the same Mysian "collector of tribute" who the year before had carried out a great slaughter at Jerusalem, imposing Hellenism by force of arms (see 1 Mac 1:29-34). Inasmuch as he was a strategist from Samaria (and its governor, according to Josephus), we can understand how he could gather together a large army of Samaritans, whose enmity toward the Jews was long-established and deep-seated (see Ezr 4:1-5; Neh 4:1-2; 12:28).

3:16 *The ascent of Beth-horon:* a gorge that ran from the mountains of Judea to the coast. The town was about twelve miles from Jerusalem.

3:18 In late Judaism, it was customary to avoid naming Yahweh: at the time of the Persians, the expression "God of heaven" was used. In the period that interests us, the name *Heaven* is used in the same sense. This discretion was inspired by respect toward the one God.

3:22 *He himself:* this is another way of avoiding pronouncing the divine name.

hundred* of their men fell, and those who
survived fled to the country of the Philistines.[t]
25 As a result, Judas and his brothers began to
be feared, and terror seized the Gentiles all
around them. 26 His fame came to the atten-
tion of the king, and all the Gentiles talked
about Judas and his battles.

Syria Readies the Repression.* 27 When King
Antiochus learned about these develop-
ments, he was infuriated, and he ordered
the mobilization of all the forces of his king-
dom, a very powerful army.* 28 He withdrew
from his treasury enough money to provide
his soldiers with a year's pay in advance,
and he ordered them to be prepared for
action at a moment's notice. 29 Then he real-
ized that this expenditure had exhausted
the reserves in his treasury, and that the
revenues from the province had dwindled
as a result of the dissension and disaster he
had caused for his empire by abolishing the
laws that had been in effect from the earli-
est times. 30 He thus began to fear that, as
had happened on more than one occasion,
he would not have sufficient funds to cover
his normal expenses and the gifts that he
had been accustomed to distribute more
lavishly than had any of his predecessors on
the throne. 31 Greatly concerned, he decided
to go to Persia and levy tribute on those
provinces and in this manner raise a large
sum of money.

32 He therefore left Lysias, a distinguished
nobleman of royal lineage, in charge of the
king's affairs from the Euphrates River to
the Egyptian frontier, 33 and he also gave
him responsibility for the care of his son
Antiochus* until he returned. 34 He turned
over to him half of his army, together with
the elephants, and provided him with
detailed instructions about all that he want-
ed done. As for the inhabitants of Judea and
Jerusalem, 35 Lysias was to send an army
against them to crush and destroy the
power of Israel and the remnant of
Jerusalem, and to wipe out the memory of
them from the land. 36 Furthermore, he was
to settle foreigners throughout the territory
and to distribute their land by lot.

37 The king then took the remaining half of
his forces and set out from Antioch, his cap-
ital, in the year one hundred and forty-
seven. He crossed the Euphrates River and
advanced through the upper provinces.

38 [u] Lysias chose Ptolemy, the son of Dory-
menes, and Nicanor* and Gorgias, powerful
men among the Friends of the King,[v] 39 and
under their command he sent forty thou-
sand infantry and seven thousand cavalry to
invade the land of Judah and destroy it in
compliance with the king's orders. 40 Setting
out with all their forces, they reached the
plain in the region of Emmaus,* where they
pitched camp. 41 When the local merchants
heard the news of this army, they came to
the camp with a large amount of silver and
gold as well as fetters, seeking to purchase
the Israelites for slaves. In addition, forces
from Idumea and Philistia joined with
them.

The Triumph of Judas.* 42 Judas and his
brothers realized how critical their situation
had become, with opposing forces en-
camped within their territory. They also had
learned of the orders that the king had
issued for the total destruction of their peo-
ple. 43 Therefore, they said to one another,
"Let us restore the shattered fortunes of our
people and fight for our people and our
sanctuary."

44 They then gathered together in a full
assembly, both to prepare for battle and to
offer prayers and implore mercy and com-
passion.

45 Jerusalem was uninhabited like a wilder-
ness;

t Jos 10:10.—u 38-44: 2 Mac 8:8-15.—v 38: 1 Mac 7:26; 2 Mac 4:45; 8:8f; 10:14.

3:24 *About eight hundred:* scholars agree that the numbers in this Book are indicative rather than real. In accord with biblical usage, they serve as a barometer of the measure of the victory achieved or the importance of the battle waged rather than as an actual count of those involved.

3:27-41 The author certainly exaggerates the figures to indicate the importance of what is at stake and the courage of Judas. The parallel account in 2 Mac 8:8-11 is more toned down, while the Book of Judith evokes this event in the apocalyptic style (Jud 2).

3:27 It is natural for the author to have all the attention of Antiochus IV focus on Palestine. In reality, however, at that time he had to be seriously preoccupied with the situation in his far-off eastern provinces disturbed by disorders and threatened by the growing power of the Parthians.

3:33 *His son Antiochus:* Antiochus V Eupator (164–162 B.C.), who was only nine years old at the time.

3:38 *Nicanor* was the leader of another expedition against the Jews four years later and was ultimately slain by Judas (see 1 Mac 7:26-46).

3:40 *Emmaus:* this was not the Emmaus of Lk 24:13, but a town about twenty-five miles west of Jerusalem, which dominated the ways of access to it.

3:42-59 Preparations are made for a holy war by prayer and penitence (see 1 Sam 7:5). The Lord is implored, his word is consulted (see v. 48), and the law is more strictly observed, for it is from *Heaven*—that is, from God—that the outcome of the combat depends. The people are ready to risk everything in the cause of God, to save the temple and the nation.

not one of her children entered or
came out.
The sanctuary was trodden underfoot,
and foreigners had captured the
citadel,
which had become a lodging place for
the Gentiles.
Joy had vanished from Jacob;
the flute and the harp were silent.

46 [w] After assembling, they made their
way to Mizpah,* opposite Jerusalem,
because in former times Mizpah had been
a place of worship for Israel. 47 That day
they fasted, donned sackcloth, sprinkled
ashes on their heads, and tore their gar-
ments. 48 They unrolled the scroll of the law,
seeking therein the guidance for which the
Gentiles consulted the images of their gods.
49 They also carried with them the priestly
vestments and the firstfruits and the tithes,
and they brought forth the Nazirites* who
had completed the period of their vows.[x]
50 Then they cried aloud to Heaven: "What
shall we do with these people, and where
shall we take them?[y] 51 Your sanctuary has
been trampled underfoot and profaned,
and your priests mourn in humiliation.
52 And now the Gentiles have formed an
alliance to destroy us. You are well aware of
what fate they plan for us. 53 How will we be
able to withstand them if you do not come
to our aid?" 54 Then they sounded the trum-
pets and raised a great shout.

55 After this, Judas appointed leaders of the
people, in charge of thousands, hundreds,
fifties, and tens. 56 He ordered to return to
their homes those who were building houses,
those who were just married, those who were
planting vineyards, and those who were
afraid, in accordance with the provisions of
the law.[z] 57 Then the army marched out and
encamped to the south of Emmaus. 58 "Arm
yourselves and be brave," Judas instructed.
"In the morning be prepared to fight against
these Gentiles who have assembled against
us to destroy us and our sanctuary. 59 It is bet-
ter that we die in battle than that we witness
the misfortunes of our people and our sanc-
tuary.[a] Whatever Heaven wills, so will he do."

CHAPTER 4

The Battle of Emmaus.* 1 Gorgias took five
thousand infantry and a thousand picked
cavalry, and this detachment set out at night
2 in order to launch a surprise attack on the
camp of the Jews. Men from the citadel
served as his guides. 3 However, Judas
learned of their plan, and he and his soldiers
moved out to attack the royal forces at
Emmaus 4 while some of the troops were still
dispersed away from the camp. 5 When
Gorgias reached the camp of Judas by night,
therefore, he found no one there, and he
began to search for them in the mountains,
saying, "These men are fleeing from us."

6 At daybreak, Judas appeared in the plain
with three thousand men, although they
lacked the armor and the swords they would
have wished for. 7 They saw the camp of the
Gentiles with its strong fortifications, flanked
with cavalry, and a fighting force expert in
the art of warfare. 8 Judas said to those who
were with him: "Do not be afraid of their
superior numbers or panic when they attack.
9 Remember how our ancestors were saved
at the Red Sea when Pharaoh was pursuing
them with his forces.[b] 10 So now let us cry out
to Heaven, asking him to show us his favor, to
remember his covenant with our ancestors,
and to destroy this army confronting us
today.[c] 11 Then all the Gentiles will know that
there is one who redeems and saves Israel."[d]

12 When the foreigners looked up and saw
them advancing against them, 13 they came
out of their camp to engage in battle. Then
the men with Judas blew their trumpets,
14 and the fighting began. The Gentiles were
defeated and fled into the plain. 15 All those
who were in the rear fell by the sword, and
the rest were pursued as far as Gazara* and
the plains of Judea, to Azotus and Jamnia,
with about three thousand of them slain.

16 When Judas and his army broke off their
pursuit, he said to the people: 17 "Do not be
greedy for plunder, for we have yet another
battle ahead of us. 18 Gorgias and his army
are very close to us in the mountain area.

w 46ff: 1 Sam 7:5f; 2 Mac 8:16-23.—x Num 6:2-5.—y Est C:11.—z Deut 20:5-8; Jdg 7:3.—a 1 Mac 2:21f.—b Ex 14:21ff.—c 1 Mac 2:20-21.—d 2 Mac 1:27; Isa 49:26.

3:46 *Mizpah:* political and religious center (see Jdg 20:1-3; 1 Sam 7:12) about eight miles north of Jerusalem along the way to Samaria. From there one could see the temple of Jerusalem, which had been profaned.

3:49 *Nazirites:* see Num 6:1-21 and note.

4:1-25 Judas knows how to unite action and prayer. A remarkable tactician, he forces the adversary to divide his forces, then defeats him in a surprise attack, and pillages his camp. Once the victory is achieved, Judas and his men offer fervent thanksgiving to God (*Heaven*).

4:15 The pursuit took all directions: *Gazara*, or Gezer (Jos 21:21; 1 Ki 9:17), lay five miles northwest of Emmaus; *Judea* was to the far south; *Azotus*, or Ashdod, and *Jamnia*, were west and southwest.

Stand firm now against our enemies and defeat them. After that, you can safely take as much booty as you please."

[19] Just as Judas was finishing this speech, a detachment appeared, looking down from the mountain. [20] They could see that their army had been put to flight and that their camp was being burned. The smoke that could be clearly seen indicated what had occurred. [21] When they perceived this, they were very much afraid, and when they also beheld the army of Judas in the plain, ready for battle, [22] they all fled into the territory of the Philistines.

[23] Then Judas went back to plunder the camp, and they confiscated a great amount of gold and silver, violet and purple cloths, and magnificent treasures. [24] As they returned, they sang hymns of thanksgiving and praise to glorify Heaven, "for he is good, for his mercy endures forever." * [e] [25] Thus Israel experienced a great deliverance that day.

Victory over Lysias. [26] [f] Those foreigners who had managed to escape went to Lysias and reported to him everything that had occurred. [27] When he heard the news, he was greatly disturbed and disappointed, because his plots against Israel had not turned out as he had intended and in accordance with the command of the king.

[28] So the following year he mobilized sixty thousand picked infantry and five thousand cavalry to defeat them. [29] They marched into Idumea and encamped at Beth-zur.* Judas confronted them with ten thousand men, [30] and when he realized how strong their army was, he offered this prayer:

"Blessed are you, O Savior of Israel, who crushed the attack of the mighty warrior by the hand of your servant David and delivered the camp of the Philistines into the hands of Jonathan, the son of Saul, and of his armor-bearer.[g] [31] Deliver this army into the hands of your people Israel, and destroy the pride of the enemy in their troops and cavalry. [32] Fill them with fear, weaken the boldness of their strength, and let them quake at their own destruction. [33] Strike them down with the sword of those who love you, so that all who acknowledge your name will praise you with hymns."

[34] Then both sides entered into battle, and in the hand-to-hand combat five thousand of the army of Lysias were slain. [35] When Lysias saw his army being routed and the boldness of the soldiers of Judas who were prepared either to live or to die nobly, he withdrew to Antioch and began to recruit a force of mercenaries for a further invasion of Judea with an even larger army.

C: Restoration of the Temple*

[36] [h] Then Judas and his brothers said: "Behold, our enemies have been crushed; let us go up to purify the sanctuary and rededicate it." [37] And so the entire army assembled, and they went up to Mount Zion. [38] There they found the sanctuary desolate, the altar desecrated, the gates burned to the ground, the courts overgrown with weeds as in a thicket or on some mountain, and the chambers of the priests in ruins.[i] [39] Then they tore their garments and uttered loud cries of mourning; they sprinkled their heads with ashes [40] and fell prostrate, with their faces to the ground. And when the signal was given with the trumpets, they cried out to Heaven.

[41] Then Judas designated men to engage in combat with those in the citadel while he purified the sanctuary. [42] He appointed blameless priests who were devoted to the law; [43] these purified the sanctuary and carried off the stones of the Abomination to an unclean place. [44] They discussed what should be done about the altar of burnt offerings that had been desecrated,[j] [45] and they made the proper decision to demolish

---

e Ps 118:1ff, 29.—f 26-35: 2 Mac 11:1-2.—g 1 Sam 17:48ff.—h 36-59: 2 Mac 10:1-8.—i Ps 74:2-7.—j 1 Ki 8:64.

4:24 The victors intoned the great Hallel (Ps 118) in thanksgiving.

4:29 *Beth-zur:* ancient Canaanite city situated on an isolated height at the confines of Idumea about twenty miles south of Jerusalem on the road to Hebron. Fortified by Rehoboam (2 Chr 11:7), it had become in Maccabean times a key stronghold in the Judaic defense (see 1 Mac 4:61; 9:52; 11:65; 14:7-33; Jos 15:58).

4:36-61 After almost three and a half years of intense guerrilla fighting, the insurgents occupy Jerusalem. In the enthusiasm of the liberation, they put an end to the pagan profanation and reestablish the worship of God. This is the culminating moment of the Book. First the sanctuary had to be purified (see 2 Chr 29:3-17), the altar had to be rebuilt, and the constructions had to be restored. On December 14, 164 B.C., the sacrifice is celebrated. As in ancient times, the dedication is celebrated with the joyous participation of all the people. As a testimony of the times, however, is the fact that the sacred enclosure must be transformed into a fortress. This occurrence gives all their meaning to the struggles of the Jewish resistance; it is the reason why the author omits various preceding events that are recorded in 2 Mac 11:13—12:9, and records only afterward the death of Antiochus IV Epiphanes (1 Mac 6:1-17). A new feast is instituted: "Hanukkah," or consecration, celebrated in December, remains ever popular within Jewish families; it is also called the second Feast of Booths (Lev 23) or the Feast of Lights; it will be mentioned in the Gospel (Jn 10:22).

it so that it would not be a source of lasting
shame to them inasmuch as the Gentiles
had defiled it.*

Therefore, they tore down the altar [k] 46 and
stored the stones in a suitable place on the
temple hill until a prophet should appear on
the scene to determine what should be done
with them. 47 They took unhewn stones,
according to the law, and built a new altar
fashioned after the former one.[l] 48 They also
repaired the sanctuary and the interior of
the temple and purified the courts. 49 They
made new sacred vessels and brought the
lampstand, the altar of incense, and the table
into the temple.[m] 50 Then they burned
incense on the altar, and they lit the lamp on
the lampstands to illuminate the temple.[n]
51 Finally, they placed loaves of bread on the
table and hung the curtains, thereby bring-
ing to completion all of the work they had
undertaken.

52 Early in the morning on the twenty-fifth
day of the ninth month, that is, the month of
Chislev, in the year one hundred and forty-
eight, 53 they arose and offered sacrifice, in
accordance with the law, on the new altar of
burnt offerings that they had constructed.[o]
54 On the anniversary of the day on which the
Gentiles had desecrated it, on that very day it
was dedicated with hymns, harps, flutes, and
cymbals. 55 All the people prostrated them-
selves in adoration and praised Heaven, who
had granted success to their endeavors.

56 They celebrated the dedication of the
altar for eight days and joyfully offered burnt
offerings and sacrifices of praise and thanks-
giving. 57 They decorated the front of the tem-
ple with gold crowns and shields; they
restored the gates and the chambers for the
priests and furnished them with doors.
58 There was great rejoicing among the people
inasmuch as the disgrace inflicted by the
Gentiles had been removed. 59 Then Judas, his
brothers, and the entire congregation of
Israel decreed that the days marking the
rededication of the altar should be observed
with joy and gladness for eight days every
year on the anniversary, beginning on the
twenty-fifth day of the month Chislev.[p]

60 At that time they fortified Mount Zion,
encircling it with high walls and strong tow-
ers to prevent the Gentiles from coming and
trampling over it as they had done in the
past. 61 Judas stationed a garrison there to
guard it, and he also fortified Beth-zur so
that the people would have a stronghold fac-
ing Idumea.

D: New Military Operations*

CHAPTER 5

War against Nearby Tribes. 1 [q] When the
Gentiles in the surrounding area heard that
the altar had been rebuilt and the sanctuary
had been rededicated, they became greatly
angered. 2 They determined to destroy the
descendants of Jacob who were living in their
midst, and they began to persecute and mas-
sacre the people. 3 [r] Then Judas made war on
the descendants of Esau at Akrabattene* in
Idumea because they were besieging the
Israelites. He inflicted on them a massive
defeat, overcame them, and took their spoils.
4 He also remembered the wickedness of the
sons of Baean,* who had proved to be a snare
and a stumbling block to the people with their
ambushes on the roads. 5 Having blockaded
them in their towers, he vowed to effect their
total destruction. Then he set ablaze their
towers with all the people in them.[s] 6 Next, he
crossed over to attack the Ammonites,*
where he was confronted by a strong army
and a large crowd of people, with Timothy as
their leader. 7 He engaged in many battles
with them, and they were crushed and struck
down. 8 After capturing Jazer* and its vil-
lages, he returned to Judea.

Judas Called Upon for Help. 9 The Gentiles
in Gilead* banded together against the

k 1 Mac 6:7.—l Ex 20:25.—m Ex 25:23-39; 30:1-6.—n Ex 30:7ff.—o Ex 30:10; Ezek 43:18-27.—p Jn 10:22.—q 1f: 1 Mac 13:6.—r 3ff: 2 Mac 10:15-23.—s Jos 6:17.

4:45 From the time of Malachi, the prophets are silent in expectation of the Prophet *par excellence* (see Jn 1:21; Lk 7:16). This silence was one of the greatest trials for Judaism (see 1 Mac 9:27; 14:14; Pss 73:9; 76:9; Lam 2:9; Ezek 7:26): the expectation was that he would decide questions that had remained suspended (see v. 44: was it licit to utilize the altar that had been profaned by pagan sacrifices?). The interpretation of the law will henceforth be the task of the scribes.

5:1—6:63 Solidly established at Jerusalem, Judas undertakes military campaigns in the neighboring countries to liberate the faithful Jews and punish their persecutors. These punitive expeditions must have been carried out after the death of Antiochus IV Epiphanes (see 2 Mac 10:14-38).

5:3 *Akrabattene:* a region that was situated along the ancient border of Judea, southwest of the Dead Sea, and that rose from the depression to the middle of Idumea. Another possibility may be the zone of Acrabeta about eight miles southwest of Shechem.

5:4 *Baean:* probably a district in the Transjordan (Num 32:3).

5:6 *Ammonites:* a Semitic people located east of the Jordan.

5:8 *Jazer:* a town west of Ammon and fifteen miles north of Heshbon (Num 32:3).

5:9 *Gilead:* a region of the Transjordan, north of the territory inhabited by the Ammonites (which corresponds to the land around the modern Ammon).

Israelites who were living in their territory,
with the intention of destroying them.
However, the Israelites fled to the stronghold
of Dathema [10] and sent the following letter to
Judas and his brothers: "The Gentiles
around us have banded together to destroy
us, [11] and they are preparing to come and
seize this stronghold in which we have taken
refuge. Timothy is in command of their
army. [12] Please come immediately and res-
cue us from their clutches, for many of us
have already fallen. [13] All of our kindred who
dwelt among the Tobiads have been killed,
and the Gentiles have carried off their wives
and children, confiscated their property, and
slain about a thousand people there." [t]

[14] While the letter was still in the process
of being read, other messengers, with their
garments torn, arrived from Galilee with a
similar message, [15] reporting that the people
of Ptolemais, Tyre, and Sidon* had united
with the whole of Galilee of the Gentiles to
destroy them. [u] [16] When Judas and the peo-
ple heard these reports, they convened a
great assembly to determine what they
should do for their beleaguered kindred who
were under attack by their enemies.

[17] Judas said to his brother Simon,
"Choose as many troops as you need and go
forth to rescue your kindred in Galilee,
while my brother Jonathan and I will go to
Gilead."

[18] He left the remainder of his forces
under the command of Joseph, son of
Zechariah, and Azariah, a leader of the peo-
ple, to defend Judea. [19] "Take charge of these
people," he commanded them, "but do not
engage the Gentiles in battle until we come
back." [20] Simon was allotted three thousand
men for the march on Galilee, while eight
thousand men were assigned to Judas for
the march on Gilead.

Victories in Galilee and Gilead. [21] Simon
advanced into Galilee and engaged in many
battles with the Gentiles, who were crushed
before him. [22] He pursued them to the gate
of Ptolemais. About three thousand of the
Gentiles were slain, and he gathered their
spoils. [23] Then he took back with him the
Jews who were in Galilee and Arbatta,* with
their wives and children and all their pos-
sessions, and he brought them to Judea with
great rejoicing.

[24] [v] Meanwhile, Judas Maccabeus and his
brother Jonathan crossed the Jordan and
journeyed for three days through the desert.
[25] There they encountered some Nabateans*
who received them peacefully and reported
to them everything that had happened to
their kindred in Gilead: [26] "Many of them
have been surrounded in Bozrah, in Bosor
near Alema, in Chaspho, Maked, and
Carnaim"—all of these towns were large
and fortified—[27] "and some have been shut
up in the other towns of Gilead. The enemy
plans to attack and capture these strong-
holds tomorrow and to destroy all the peo-
ple inside them in a single day."

[28] Judas and his army immediately
changed direction, crossing the desert to
Bozrah. He captured the city, put the entire
male population to the sword, confiscated
all their possessions, and set the place on
fire. [29] During the night he led his army from
that place and journeyed to the stronghold
of Dathema. [30] At dawn they caught sight of
an innumerable horde who were bringing
forth ladders and engines of war to capture
the stronghold, and already beginning the
assault on those besieged. [31] When Judas
saw that the attack had begun and heard a
war cry rising to heaven from the city,
accompanied by trumpet blasts and loud
shouts, [32] he said to the men of his army:
"Fight this day for your kindred!"

[33] He advanced behind them with three
columns, sounding their trumpets and
shouting in prayer. [34] When the army of
Timothy realized that it was Maccabeus,
they fled before him. He inflicted a crushing
defeat on them, and about eight thousand of
their men fell that day. [35] Then he moved on
toward Alema and attacked and captured it.
He slew every male in it, plundered the town,
and set it afire. [36] From there he moved on
and took Chaspho, Maked, Bosor, and the
other cities of Gilead.

---

t 2 Mac 12:17.—u Isa 8:23.—v 24-36: 2 Mac 12:10-16.

5:15 *Ptolemais, Tyre, and Sidon:* three cities of the Phoenician coast, very famous in antiquity (Ptolemais, thus called by Ptolemy II in 261 B.C., was first known by the name Acco). Anti-Jewish hatred spreads in Palestine and especially in Galilee, which was inhabited from the most ancient times by a mixture of pagan populations (see 1 Ki 9:11); few Jews lived in *Galilee of the Gentiles* (Isa 9:1; Mt 4:15).

5:23 *Arbatta:* a site near the Sea of Galilee or the Arabah depression south of the Dead Sea (Deut 1:7; Jos 11:16).

5:25 *Nabateans:* a people of Arabic or Aramaic origin established southwest of Palestine; they became rich and powerful as caravaners moving commerce from the Persian Gulf to the Red Sea and controlling all of the Transjordan as far as Damascus. It was a Nabatean governor from whom St. Paul escaped about A.D. 38 (2 Cor 11:32f).

37 [w] After these things, Timothy gathered
another army and pitched camp opposite
Raphon, on the other side of the stream.
38 Judas sent men to reconnoiter their camp,
and they returned to him with this report:
"All the Gentiles in this area have come to
his support, encompassing a very large
force. 39 They have also hired Arab merce-
naries to assist them. They are encamped
across the stream and are prepared to
attack you." Judas therefore went forward to
engage them in battle.

40 As Judas and his army were approach-
ing the stream, Timothy said to the officers
of his forces, "If he crosses over to us first,
we shall not be able to resist him, and he will
surely defeat us.[x] 41 However, if he is fearful
and camps on the other side of the river, we
will cross over to him and defeat him."

42 When Judas reached the stream, he
stationed the scribes* of the people along-
side it and gave them this command, "Do
not allow anyone to encamp, but order
them all to enter the battle." 43 He himself
was the first one to cross over to the attack,
and his entire army followed him. The
Gentiles were crushed; at his approach
they threw down their arms and fled to the
temple* at Carnaim. 44 The Jews captured
that city and then burned down the temple
with all who were inside. Thus Carnaim
was captured, and no further resistance
was offered to Judas.[y]

45 Then Judas assembled all the Israelites
who dwelt in Gilead, both great and small,
with their wives and their children and their
possessions, an enormous company of peo-
ple, to escort them to the land of Judah.
46 [z] When they reached Ephron,* a large,
strongly fortified town situated along the
road, they discovered that it was impossible
to bypass it to either the right or the left; they
had no other option than to pass through it.
47 However, the inhabitants of the town barri-
caded the gates with stones and denied them
passage.[a] 48 Judas then conveyed to them the
following peaceful message: "We wish to pass
through your territory in order to reach our
own. No one will do you any harm. We will
simply pass through on foot." However, they
refused to open their gates to him.

49 Judas then issued an order that all of his
forces should remain where they were.
50 After they took up their positions, he led
them in an assault on that town the entire
day and all through the night, and it was
delivered into his hands. 51 After he put
every male to the sword, razed the town to
the ground, and plundered it, he marched
through it over the bodies of the dead.

52 Then they crossed the Jordan into the
extensive plain* opposite Beth-shan. 53 Judas
continued to rally the stragglers and to
encourage the people throughout the jour-
ney until they reached the land of Judah.
54 They ascended Mount Zion with joy and
gladness and offered burnt offerings because
they had returned safely without the loss of a
single person.

Israelite Commanders Defeated at Jamnia.
55 While Judas and Jonathan were in Gilead
and Simon their brother was in Galilee out-
side Ptolemais, 56 Joseph, son of Zechariah,
and Azariah, the commanders of the army,
heard about their valiant deeds and the
heroic battles that they had fought, 57 and
they said, "Let us also make a name for our-
selves by going out to fight against the
Gentiles in our area."

58 Therefore, they issued orders to the
forces under their command to march
against Jamnia. 59 Gorgias and his men came
out of the town to confront them in battle.
60 Joseph and Azariah were routed, and they
were pursued to the borders of Judea. On
that day about two thousand Israelites were
slain. 61 Thus the people suffered a massive
defeat because they had not heeded the
instructions of Judas and his brothers, but
instead attempted to match their brave
accomplishments. 62 However, they did not
belong to the family of those through whom
the deliverance of Israel was to be achieved.

The Israelites' Success over the Edomites and the Philistines. 63 The valiant Judas and
his brothers became greatly renowned
throughout Israel and among all the
Gentiles, wherever their name was heard,
64 and crowds thronged around them to offer

w 37-44: 2 Mac 12:20-26.—x 1 Sam 14:9f.—y 2 Mac 12:21.—z 46-54: 2 Mac 12:27-31.—a Num 20:17-21; 21:21-25.

5:42 *Scribes:* not the doctors of the law of whom the Gospels speak but officials with either civil or military positions, perhaps in charge of enrollment.

5:43 *Temple:* the temple dedicated to Atargatis, the Syrian fish goddess.

5:46 *Ephron:* modern Et-Taiyibeh, eight miles east of the Jordan, the road that descends from Gilead to the bridge over the Jordan. A large village atop a rocky peak.

5:52 *The extensive plain* lay between the Jordan and Mt. Gilboa. *Beth-shan* was located about eighteen miles south of the Sea of Galilee (see Jdg 1:27; 1 Ki 4:12).

them praise. [65]Then Judas and his brothers
went forth and attacked the descendants of
Esau in the country toward the south. He
conquered Hebron* and its villages, destroy-
ing its fortifications and burning down the
towers encircling it. [66]He then marched into
the land of the Philistines and passed
through Marisa. [67]On that day, several
priests who inadvisedly went out to fight in
their desire to prove their courage fell in bat-
tle. [68]Judas next turned toward Azotus in the
land of the Philistines. He destroyed their
altars and burned the statues of their gods,
plundered their towns, and then returned to
the land of Judah.

CHAPTER 6

Defeat and Death of Antiochus IV.* [1] [b]As King
Antiochus was going through the upper
provinces, he heard that Elymais,* a city in
Persia, was renowned for its wealth in silver
and gold, [2]and that its temple was very rich,
containing gold shields, breastplates, and
weapons left there by Alexander, the son of
Philip, the king of Macedon and the first to
reign over the Greeks. [3]Therefore, he jour-
neyed there in an attempt to capture and
plunder the city, but he was unsuccessful
because the people of the city had become
aware of his designs [4]and rose up in battle
against him. He was put to flight and had to
withdraw in great disappointment and
retreat toward Babylon.

[5]While he was still in Persia, a messenger
brought him the news that the armies that
had invaded the land of Judah had been rout-
ed, [6]that Lysias—who had advanced with a
massive force—had been put to flight by the
Israelites, that the Israelites had grown
increasingly strong as a result of the weapons,
equipment, and abundant spoils they had
captured from the armies they had destroyed,
[7]that they had pulled down the Abomination
he had built upon the altar in Jerusalem, and
that they had surrounded the sanctuary with
high walls as they had done in the past and
had fortified his city of Beth-zur. [c]

[8]When the king heard this report, he was
distraught and deeply shaken. Sick with
grief because his plans had failed, he
retreated to his bed. [9]He lay there for many
days, overwhelmed repeatedly with disap-
pointment,* and he realized that he was at
the point of death.

[10]Therefore, he summoned all his Friends
and said to them: "Sleep is gone from my
eyes, and my heart is overwhelmed with anx-
iety. [11]I have asked myself: 'Why have I been
brought to these depths of despair, inasmuch
as during my reign I was always kind and
greatly beloved?' [12]But now I recall the evil
deeds I perpetrated in Jerusalem in seizing
all its vessels of silver and gold and unjustifi-
ably ordering the extermination of the
inhabitants of Judah. [13]I am certain that this
is the reason why these misfortunes have
afflicted me, and why I am dying here of bit-
ter grief in a strange land."

[14]Then he summoned Philip, one of his
Friends, and appointed him ruler over his
entire kingdom. [15]He gave him his crown,
his robe, and his signet ring, entrusting him
with the authority to educate his son
Antiochus and train him to be king. [16]King
Antiochus died in Persia, in the year one
hundred and forty-nine.*

Judas Besieges the Citadel of Jerusalem.
[17]When Lysias learned that the king was dead,
he designated the king's son Antiochus,*
whom he had brought up from childhood, to
succeed him as king, and he gave him the
name Eupator. [d]

[18]Meanwhile, the men garrisoned in the
citadel were blockading the Israelites in the
sanctuary, taking advantage of every oppor-
tunity to harm them and thereby further
the cause of the Gentiles. [e] [19]Judas therefore

b 1-13: 2 Mac 1:12-17; 9:1-29.—c 1 Mac 1:54; 4:41ff, 60f.—d 2 Mac 10:10f.—e 1 Mac 1:33ff.

5:65 *Hebron:* the ancient city that David made the capital of his realm for seven years (2 Sam 2:11; 3:2; 5:5). Situated twenty miles south of Jerusalem, but always within the territory of the tribe of Judah, it subsequently fell into the hands of the Edomites.

6:1-16 The author portrays the death of Antiochus IV Epiphanes as happening *after* the purification of the temple and as the result of God's justice. In reality, it appears that the persecutor died in the autumn of 164 B.C., *before* the purification of the temple (1 Mac 4:36f). See note on v. 16.

6:1 *Elymais:* a city by this name is unknown; the name seems to refer to a mountainous chain of Persia, in ancient times more often known by the name Elam.

6:9 *Overwhelmed repeatedly with disappointment:* perhaps a type of insanity. According to 2 Mac 9:5-12, the king was afflicted with a repugnant physical illness.

6:16 *The year one hundred and forty-nine:* this date technically encompasses September 164 to October 163 B.C. According to a Seleucid list of kings, Antiochus died in November or December of 164 B.C.; the author of 2 Maccabees also implies that Antiochus died before the restoration of the temple at Jerusalem.

6:17 *The king's son Antiochus:* Antiochus V Eupator (that is, Antiochus "of a good father"), then about nine years old and under the guardianship of Lysias, who governed and waged wars in his name. He was put to death along with Lysias two years later when Demetrius, brother of Antiochus IV, came and claimed the kingship (see 1 Mac 7:1ff).

resolved to bring about their destruction,
and he mobilized all the people to besiege
them. [20]They assembled and stormed the
citadel in the year one hundred and fifty,
employing catapults and engines of war
whose construction he had ordered. [21]Some
of those besieged in the garrison escaped,
joined by some godless Israelites. [22]They
approached the king and said:

"How much longer are you going to delay
in your pursuit of justice and avenging our
comrades? [23]We were happy to serve your
father, to follow his instructions, and to obey
his commands. [24]As a result, our own kin-
dred have besieged the citadel and turned
against us. They have put to death as many of
us as they have been able to capture, and they
have plundered our property. [25]Furthermore
we are not the only ones against whom they
have taken action, for they have attacked all
the lands throughout your territory. [26]At
this very moment they are besieging the
citadel in Jerusalem, determined to capture
it, and they have fortified the sanctuary and
Beth-zur. [27]Unless you quickly make some
move to impede them, they will do far worse
things than these, and you will not be able to
stop them."

The Battle of Beth-zur. [28][f] The king became
enraged when he heard this, and he sum-
moned all his Friends, his generals, and the
commanders of his cavalry.[g] [29]He also
recruited mercenary forces from other
kingdoms and from the islands of the seas.
[30]His forces numbered one hundred thou-
sand foot soldiers, twenty thousand cavalry,
and thirty-two elephants trained for war.
[31]They advanced through Idumea and
besieged Beth-zur, continuing the attack for
many days. They also constructed engines of
war, but the defenders made a raid and set
them on fire, fighting courageously.

[32]Then Judas left the citadel and en-
camped at Beth-zechariah,* opposite the
camp of the king. [33]The king rose at day-
break, and after a forced march along the
road to Beth-zechariah, his forces drew up
in battle formation and sounded their trum-
pets. [34]The elephants were roused for battle
by being given a mixture of grapes and
mulberries to drink. [35]These beasts were
distributed among the phalanxes. With each
elephant there were stationed a thousand
men arrayed in coats of mail, with bronze
helmets. In addition, five hundred picked
cavalry were assigned to each beast. [36]They
anticipated every move made by the ele-
phant; wherever it went, they immediately
accompanied it, never leaving its side. [37]On
each elephant, for its protection, and fas-
tened to its back by a harness, was a strong
wooden tower that held four soldiers who
fought from that position, as well as an
Indian driver. [38]The rest of the cavalry were
stationed on either side of the army, so that
they could harass the enemy while being
protected by the phalanxes.

[39]When the sun shone on the gold and
bronze shields, the mountains blazed with
their reflection and gleamed like burning
torches. [40]Part of the king's army was sta-
tioned on the high hills, while others were
assembled in the plain. They advanced
steadily and in good order, [41]and seized all
who trembled as they heard the clamor
raised by this vast multitude as they marched
and by the clash of their arms, for their army
was a very large and powerful force.

[42]Judas and his army advanced to give
battle, and six hundred of the king's army
were slain. [43]Eleazar, called Avaran, noted
that one of the elephants was adorned with
royal armor. Since it was larger than all the
other beasts, he thought that the king must
be astride it,[h] [44]and he gave his life to save
his people and win for himself everlasting
renown. [45]He courageously charged toward
it through the midst of the phalanx, killing
men right and left, so that they fell back on
all sides at his approach. [46]He got in position
under the elephant and stabbed it from
below, slaying it. The beast fell to the ground
on top of him, and he died there.

[47]When the Jews saw the strength and
ferocity of the royal forces, they retreated
before them. [48][i] A part of the king's army
marched up to Jerusalem to attack them,
and the king encamped at both Judea and
Mount Zion. [49]He made terms of peace with
the people of Beth-zur, and they evacuated
the town, for they had no provisions there
that would enable them to withstand a siege,
since that was a sabbatical year* in the land.[j]

f 28-54: 2 Mac 13:1-23.—g 1 Mac 6:14.—h 2 Mac 13:15.—
i 48f: 2 Mac 13:22-23.—j Lev 25:2.

6:32 *Beth-zechariah* was located six miles from Beth-zur and ten miles southwest of Jerusalem.

6:49 *Sabbatical year:* every seventh year the land had to lie fallow (Ex 23:11; Lev 25:3-7); this is the only time that the application of the law is recorded. The year without a harvest was followed by a shortage of food.

[50]The king then occupied Beth-zur and stationed a garrison there to defend it.

[51]He besieged the sanctuary for many days, employing artillery, engines of war to hurl fire and stones, machines to shoot arrows, and catapults. [52]The Jews for their part set up machines of their own to counter theirs, and they continued the battle for many days. [53]However, there was no food in the storerooms because it was the sabbatical year, and those who had fled from the Gentiles and taken refuge in Judea had consumed the last of the reserves. [54]Only a few men remained in the sanctuary; the rest scattered to their own homes, for the famine proved too severe for them.

Offer of a Peace Treaty. [55] [k] Lysias heard that Philip, whom King Antiochus, prior to his death, had appointed to bring up his son Antiochus to be king, [56]had returned from Persia and Media with the forces that had accompanied the king, and that he was attempting to seize control of the government. [57]Therefore, he quickly gave orders to withdraw, saying to the king, to the commanders of the army, and to the soldiers, "Every day we are growing weaker, our provisions are running low, the place we are besieging is strong, and the affairs of the kingdom demand our attention.[l] [58]Let us now come to terms with these people and make peace with them and with their entire nation. [59]Let us grant them permission to live in accordance with their laws as they used to do, for it was on account of our abolition of these laws that they became angry and were provoked into doing all these things."

[60]This proposal met with the approval of the king and his commanders, and he presented the Jews with peace terms, which they accepted. [61]Therefore, the king and his commanders ratified the treaty by oath, and accordingly the Jews emerged from their stronghold. [62]However, when the king entered Mount Zion and saw how strongly the place was fortified, he broke the oath that he had sworn and gave orders to demolish the encircling wall. [63]Then he departed and returned in haste to Antioch. He found Philip in control of the city, but he engaged in battle against him and took the city by force.

III: THE RISE OF THE HASMONEANS

A: Judah Renews the Resistance

CHAPTER 7

Demetrius Becomes King.* [1] [m]In the year one hundred and fifty-one, Demetrius, the son of Seleucus, departed from home and, arriving with a few men at a town on the seacoast, began to rule there. [2]As he was entering the royal palace of his ancestors, his troops seized Antiochus and Lysias with the intention of handing them over to him. [3]However, when he was informed of this act, he said, "Keep them out of my sight." [4]The soldiers therefore executed them, and Demetrius ascended the royal throne.[n]

Alcimus Invents Intrigues for the New King. [5]Then all the renegades and godless men of Israel approached him, led by Alcimus* who had designs on the high priesthood. [6]They brought to the king this accusation against the people: "Judas and his brothers have killed all your Friends and have driven us out of our country. [7]Send a man whom you trust to go forth and inspect the devastation that Judas has wreaked on us and on the lands ruled by the king, and authorize him to punish him and all their allies."

[8]The king chose Bacchides, one of the Friends of the King, who was the governor of West-of-Euphrates, an influential personage in the kingdom, and a loyal supporter of the king. [9]He sent him and the godless Alcimus, whom he appointed as high priest, with orders to exact vengeance on the Israelites.[o] [10]They set out, and when they arrived with a large army in the land of Judah, they sent envoys to Judas and his brothers to suggest deceitful proposals of peace. [11]But the latter placed no trust in

k 55-63: 2 Mac 13:23-26.—l 2 Mac 11:13ff.—m 1-7: 2 Mac 14:1-11.—n Est 7:8.—o 1 Mac 7:5.

7:1-4 *Demetrius* I Soter (reigned 162–150 B.C.) was the *son of Seleucus* IV Philopator, elder brother of Antiochus IV Epiphanes and the lawful heir to the kingdom. When his father Seleucus had become king (1 Mac 1:10), he had been sent as a hostage to Rome to replace his uncle. Upon the death of his uncle, he petitioned the senate to be released, but to no avail. At the age of twenty-five he fled from Rome with a small group of men and landed in Tripolis, a *town on the seacoast.* With the aid of the Syrians he defeated his rival Antiochus V and had him put to death. His ascent to the throne rekindled the internal conflict that pitted the Hellenizing Jews and the party of the resistance against one another. The family of the Maccabees ended up getting the best of him.

7:5-6 *Alcimus:* he was not a member of the high priestly family but belonged to the Hellenizing party and was willing to help Demetrius. After the death of Menelaus (2 Mac 14:3), he became high priest and was confirmed by Demetrius. He caused more havoc on the Israelites than the Gentiles did (1 Mac 7:23).

their words, since they saw the immense force that had accompanied them.

[12]However, a group of scribes approached Alcimus and Bacchides to ask for just terms of peace. [13]The Hasideans were the first among the Israelites to request a peace agreement,[p] [14]for they said, "A priest of the line of Aaron has come with the army, and he will not be a party to any wrongful act." [15]Alcimus engaged in peace talks with them, and he swore this oath to them: "We will not attempt to injure you or your friends." [16]However, once he had gained their confidence, he arrested sixty of them and put them to death in one day, in fulfillment of the words of Scripture:

17 "They have scattered the bodies of your
faithful ones
and shed their blood round about
Jerusalem,
and there is no one to bury them."[q]

[18]Then fear and dread of them fell on the whole people. "There is no truth or justice among them," they said. "They have violated their agreement and their sworn oath."

[19]Bacchides then withdrew from Jerusalem and encamped at Beth-zaith,* where he ordered the arrest of many of those who had deserted to him, along with some of the people. He slaughtered them and cast them into an immense pit. [20]After that he placed Alcimus in charge of the province, leaving an army with him to give him support, while he himself went back to the king.

The War Springs Up Anew. [21]Alcimus used every means to continue in his role as high priest, [22]and all those who were reckoned as troublemakers rallied to his support. They gained control of the land of Judah and inflicted great damage on Israel. [23]When Judas saw all the wrongs that Alcimus and his supporters had inflicted on the Israelites, exceeding anything that the Gentiles had done, [24]he went throughout the territory of Judea, punishing those who had deserted and preventing them from gaining access to rural areas. [25]When Alcimus saw that Judas and his supporters were gaining considerable strength and realized that he would not be able to withstand them, he returned to the king and brought malicious charges against them.

Nicanor Is Entrusted with Putting Down the Insurgents. [26][r]Then the king sent Nicanor,* one of his most distinguished officers and a bitter enemy of Israel, with orders to destroy the people. [27]Having arrived in Jerusalem with a large force, he sent to Judas and his brothers this deceitful message couched in peaceful terms: [28]"Let there be no fighting between you and me. I shall come with a small escort to have a peaceful meeting with you."

[29]When he came to Judas, they greeted each other peaceably, but the enemy had made plans to kidnap Judas. [30]When Judas became aware that Nicanor's visit had a treacherous purpose, he became afraid and refused to meet him again.[s] [31]After Nicanor realized that his plot had been uncovered, he marched out to meet Judas in battle near Caphar-salama.* [32]About five hundred of Nicanor's men were slain; the rest fled to the City of David.

[33][t]After these events, Nicanor went up to Mount Zion. Some of the priests from the sanctuary and some of the elders of the people came out to greet him peaceably and to show him the burnt offering that was being offered for the king. [34]But he mocked and jeered at them, defiled them,* and spoke arrogantly, [35]swearing in his rage: "Unless Judas and his army are turned over to me immediately, I will burn this temple to the ground when I return victorious." Then he went off in great anger. [36][u]At this turn of events, the priests went in and stood tearfully before the altar and the sanctuary, saying: [37]"You have chosen this house to bear your name and to be a house of prayer and supplication for your people. [38]Exact vengeance on this man and his army, and let them fall by the sword. Remember their blasphemies and grant them no reprieve."

Judas Routs the Enemy. [39]Nicanor left Jerusalem and encamped at Beth-horon, where he was joined by an army from Syria.

p 1 Mac 2:42.—q Ps 79:1ff.—r 26f: 1 Mac 3:38; 2 Mac 8:9.—s 2 Mac 14:30.—t 33-38: 2 Mac 14:31-36.—u 36ff: Joel 2:17.

7:19 *Beth-zaith:* perhaps three miles north of Beth-zur and twelve miles south of Jerusalem or Bezetha, north of the temple area in Jerusalem.

7:26 *Nicanor* was, according to Josephus, one of the men who escaped from Rome with Demetrius. He is placed in a better and truer light by 2 Mac 14:17-25, and 2 Mac 14:26-30 shows that his friendship with Judas was eroded by the machinations of Alcimus.

7:31 *Caphar-salama:* a town about five miles northeast of Jerusalem.

7:34 *Defiled them:* he spat on them and made them legally defiled.

40 Meanwhile, Judas pitched camp in Adasa* with three thousand men, where he offered this prayer: 41 [v] "When the messengers from the king were guilty of blasphemy, your angel sent forth and struck down one hundred and eighty-five thousand of his men. 42 In the same way, crush this army before us today, so that everyone will come to know that Nicanor has spoken blasphemously against your sanctuary. Judge him according to his wickedness." [w]

43 The armies met in battle on the thirteenth of the month of Adar. Nicanor's army was crushed, and he himself was the first to fall in the battle. [x] 44 When his army saw that Nicanor had fallen, they threw down their arms and fled. 45 The Jews pursued them a day's journey, from Adasa as far as Gazara, sounding their trumpets in warning as they followed. 46 People emerged from all the surrounding villages of Judea and hemmed in Nicanor's forces, driving them back to confront their pursuers. They all fell by the sword, without a single one managing to escape.

47 Then the Jews collected the spoils and the booty. They cut off Nicanor's head and the right hand that he had stretched out so arrogantly, and they brought them to Jerusalem to be put on display there. 48 The people rejoiced greatly and celebrated that day as a great festival. 49 They decreed that this occasion was to be observed each year on the thirteenth day of Adar.* 50 And for a short time the land of Judah was at peace.

CHAPTER 8

The Prestige of Rome.* 1 Judas heard of the reputation of the Romans—how they were mighty men who favored all who joined themselves to them and made an alliance with all who came to them and were strong and powerful. 2 He had also been told of the battles they had fought and of the brave deeds that they had performed against the people of Gaul* as they conquered them and forced them to pay tribute, 3 and what they had done in the province of Spain, seizing the silver and gold mines there 4 and by their planning and persistence gaining control of the entire country even though it was considerably distant from their own. They also had subdued kings who had come against them from the ends of the earth,* crushing them and inflicting heavy losses on them, while the rest paid tribute to them every year.

5 Philip* and Perseus, the king of the Macedonians, and the others who had engaged in battle against them had been crushed by them and subjugated. 6 They had also defeated Antiochus the Great, the king of Asia, who had attacked them with one hundred and twenty elephants, and with cavalry and chariots and a very large army. 7 * They had taken him alive and imposed terms of surrender that obligated him and his successors to pay a substantial annual tribute, give hostages, 8 and surrender portions of his best provinces—the countries of India, Media, and Lydia—which they took from him and gave to King Eumenes. 9 When the Greeks devised a plan to attack and destroy them, 10 the Romans got wind of it and sent against them a single general.* In the ensuing battle many of the Greeks were wounded and fell, and the Romans took captive their wives and children, tore down their strongholds, and enslaved them, a status that they endure even to the present day. 11 All of

v 41f: 2 Mac 8:19; 15:22f; 2 Ki 18:17—19:37.—w Isa 37:36ff.—x 2 Mac 15:25-35.

7:40 *Adasa:* a town about seven miles from Beth-horon on the road to Jerusalem.

7:49 *The thirteenth day of Adar:* March 161 B.C. This feast came to be called Nicanor Day and was one of the days on which mourning was prohibited, but it was not celebrated for very long.

8:1-16 This Book must certainly have been redacted a long time before Jerusalem was captured by Pompey in 63 B.C. for then, Rome became an enemy. The eulogy of Rome in this chapter is given as one of the reasons why 1 Maccabees was not preserved by the Palestinian Jews of the century that followed.

8:2 *Gaul:* the text has Galatia, but it must be read as Cisalpine Gaul, which was defeated in 222 B.C. (the first great expansion of Rome outside the peninsular part of Italy), because, listed in chronological order are the subsequent conquests, beginning with the Iberian one that followed immediately upon the Gallican. However, the Romans also defeated the Galatians in 189 B.C.

8:4 *Against them from the ends of the earth* (that is, from the Straits of Gibraltar) had come Hannibal and then his brother Hasdrubal, Carthaginian leaders, in the Second Punic War: the latter was stopped and slain at Metaurus while the former, after clamorous initial successes, was beaten at Zama.

8:5 *Philip* V and *Perseus* were the last two kings of Macedonia, defeated respectively at Cynoscephalae in 197 B.C. and at Pydna in 168 B.C.

8:7-8 This is a question of the hard-fought Battle of Magnesia in 190 B.C., which opened Asia to Rome. However, the evident delight of the historian in the defeat suffered by the father of the persecutor of the Jews carries him away: Antiochus was not captured; he was forced to pay 15,000 talents. *India* and *Media* seem to be a copyist's error for Lydia and Mysia. *Eumenes* II (197–158 B.C.), king of Pergamum, was an ally of Rome who received much of Seleucid Asia Minor.

8:10 *A single general:* Lucius Mummio conquered the Achaean League at Leucopetra, destroyed Corinth and sold the inhabitants into slavery in 146 B.C. Hence, this is an anachronism of the author.

the other kingdoms and islands that opposed
them they destroyed and subjugated.

12 However, with their friends and those
who depended on them for protection, they
maintained strong ties of friendship. They
had subdued kings far and near, and all who
heard of their reputation were terrified of
them. 13 Those whom they wished to help
ascend to a throne became kings; those
whom they wished to depose were over-
thrown. As a result, they were greatly exalt-
ed. 14 Yet for all this not one of them ever put
on a crown or wore purple as an emblem of
authority. 15 They had built a senate house
where each day three hundred and twenty
senators deliberated on how best to achieve
the well-being of the people. 16 They entrust-
ed one man* each year to rule over them
and their dominions; all obeyed this one
man without any envy or jealousy.

Alliance with Rome. 17 Therefore, Judas
chose Eupolemus, son of John, son of Accos,
and Jason, son of Eleazar, and sent them to
Rome to make a treaty of friendship and
alliance,[y] 18 in the hope that in this way they
would escape the yoke, for they could clear-
ly see that the kingdom of the Greeks was
reducing Israel to a state of slavery. 19 Fol-
lowing a very lengthy journey to Rome, the
envoys entered the senate chamber and
spoke these words: 20 "Judas Maccabeus and
his brothers and the Jewish people have sent
us to conclude a treaty of alliance and peace
with you and to enroll ourselves as your
allies and friends." 21 This proposal pleased
the Romans, 22 and this is a copy of their
reply, which they inscribed on tablets of
bronze* and sent to Jerusalem, where it
would remain in the possession of the Jews
as a record of peace and alliance:[z]

23 "May good fortune attend the Romans
and the Jewish nation at sea and on land for-
ever. May sword and foe be far from them.
24 But if war should be instigated against
Rome or any of her allies throughout her
dominions, 25 the Jewish nation shall provide
them with their wholehearted support as the
occasion shall demand. 26 To the enemy that
instigates that war they shall not give or pro-
vide grain, arms, money, or ships. Thus have
the Romans decreed, and they shall fulfill
their obligations without receiving any rec-
ompense. 27 In the same way, if war should be
instigated against the nation of the Jews, the
Romans shall provide them with their
wholehearted support as the occasion shall
demand. 28 To the enemy that instigates that
war they shall not give grain, arms, money,
or ships. Thus have the Romans decreed, and
they shall fulfill their obligations without any
breach of faith. 29 In these terms the Romans
have made a treaty with the Jewish people.
30 Subsequently, if both parties should decide
to make any addition or deletion, they shall
have the authority to do so, and any such
addition or deletion that they make shall be
deemed valid.

31 "Concerning the wrongs that King De-
metrius is perpetrating against the Jewish
people, we have written to him as follows:
'Why have you made your yoke heavy upon
our friends and allies the Jews? 32 If they
have any further complaint to make against
you, we shall uphold their rights and make
war on you by land and sea.' "*

CHAPTER 9

The Heroic Death of Judas. 1 When De-
metrius heard that Nicanor and his army
had fallen in battle, he sent Bacchides and
Alcimus into the land of Judah for a second
time, and with them the right wing of his
army. 2 They took the road to Galilee and,
besieging Mesaloth in Arbela,* they cap-
tured it and killed many people. 3 In the first
month of the year one hundred and fifty-two
they encamped outside Jerusalem,* 4 and
from there they marched to Berea with
twenty thousand foot soldiers and two thou-
sand cavalry.

y 1 Mac 12:1f; 15:15-22; Ex 34:15; Isa 30:1-3.—z 1 Mac 14:18.

8:16 *One man:* in reality, there were two consuls, but only one went on far-off military expeditions. This may be the origin of the idea that there was only one ruler. In everything else they alternated governing every month. In any case, everything said about the Romans is arrived at by way of reputation.

8:22 Important documents were often inscribed on *tablets of bronze.*

8:32 The documentation is in the style of so many pacts concluded by the Romans, in particular very similar to the treaty concluded with the isle of Stampalia in 105 B.C. But verses 31-32 may come from other sources. The safe conduct accorded by the consul C. Fannio to the ambassadors who were returning has been preserved by the historian Flavius Josephus.

9:2 *They took the road . . . Arbela:* this is a reconstruction of the Greek text, which reads: "They took the road to Gilgal and camping opposite Mesaloth captured it" but makes no sense. For Gilgal was in the Jordan Valley close to Jericho while Arbela was a hill in Galilee; *Mesaloth* were caves overhanging a gorge west of the Sea of Tiberias.

9:3 That is, March–April of 160 B.C., a few weeks after the rout of Nicanor. Scholars have noted that the interval of time is too short for the Syrians to have been able to gather together a new army, but perhaps this may be explained by Bacchides's volatile nature.

5 Judas meanwhile had encamped at Elasa with three thousand picked men. 6 When his men saw the immense number of the enemy forces, they were greatly terrified, and many slipped away from the camp, until only eight hundred men remained.

7 When Judas realized that the battle was imminent and that his army was melting away, he became despondent, for he had no time to redeploy them. 8 But despite being disheartened, he said to those who remained, "Let us rise up and advance against the enemy. We may have sufficient strength to defeat them." 9 His men tried to dissuade him, saying, "We do not have the necessary strength. Let us save our own lives now and return to fight them when our kindred have joined up with us. Right now we are too few." 10 But Judas replied, "Far be it from us to do such a thing as to flee from them. If our time has come, let us die bravely for our kindred and leave no stain upon our honor." [a]

11 Then the army of Bacchides marched out from the camp and was arrayed in battle position. The cavalry was divided into two squadrons. The slingers and the archers went ahead of the army, and the most skilled warriors were in the front line. 12 Bacchides was on the right wing. The phalanx, flanked by the two squadrons, advanced to the sound of the trumpets, and the men with Judas also blew their trumpets. 13 The earth shook with the noise of the armies, and the battle raged from morning until evening. 14 Observing that Bacchides and the main strength of his army were on the right, Judas, with his most valiant men at his side, 15 drove back the right wing and pursued them as far as Mount Azotus.* 16 But when those on the left wing observed that the right wing had been crushed, they reversed direction and closely followed Judas and his men, attacking them from the rear. 17 The battle was fought desperately, and many on both sides fell. 18 Judas was among those who fell, and the rest fled.

19 Jonathan and Simon took their brother Judas and buried him in the tomb of their ancestors at Modein. 20 All Israel wept over him with great mourning for many days, saying, 21 "How tragically the mighty one has fallen, the savior of Israel!" [b] 22 The rest of the acts of Judas, the battles that he waged, the valorous deeds that he performed, and his greatness have not been recorded, for they were very numerous.

B: The Politics of Jonathan (160–143 B.C.)

Jonathan Succeeds Judas. 23 After the death of Judas, the renegades came out of hiding in all parts of Israel, and all the evildoers reappeared. 24 In those days there was a severe famine, and the country went over to their side. 25 Bacchides chose godless men to be in charge of the country. 26 These searched out and hunted down the friends of Judas and brought them to Bacchides, who took his revenge on them and mocked them. 27 There was great distress* in Israel, the likes of which had not been since the days when the prophets ceased to appear among them.

28 Then all the friends of Judas assembled and said to Jonathan, 29 "Since the death of your brother Judas there has been no one like him to lead us against our enemies and Bacchides, as well as against those of our own nation who are hostile to us. 30 Therefore, today we have chosen you to take his place as our ruler and our leader, and to fight our battle." 31 Thereupon Jonathan accepted the leadership in the place of his brother Judas.

Jonathan and Simon Retaliate. 32 When Bacchides learned of this, he made plans to kill Jonathan, 33 but Jonathan and his brother Simon and all who were with him heard about it, and they took refuge in the wilderness of Tekoa,* where they encamped by the waters of the pool of Asphar. 34 Bacchides learned of this on the Sabbath day, and he crossed the Jordan with his entire army.

35 Jonathan sent his brother* to act as leader of the multitude and to ask the Nabateans, with whom he was friendly, for permission to store with them the great quantity of baggage that they had brought with them. [c] 36 However, the sons of Jambri made a sortie from Medeba,* captured John, and carried off the baggage. 37 Some time afterward the news was reported to Jonathan and his brother Simon: "The sons

a 1 Mac 2:37; 2 Mac 7:5.—b 2 Sam 1:27.—c 1 Mac 5:25.

9:15 *Mount Azotus:* some think that this should read *mountain slopes* because of a scribal error confusing the word *ashdot* ("slopes") with *ashdod* ("Azotus").

9:27 *Great distress:* with respect to the distress of the Jews at the silence of the prophets, see 4:46.

9:33 *Tekoa* was the home of the prophet Amos (Am 1:1) about five miles from Bethlehem.

9:35 *His brother:* this was not Simon but John (v. 36).

9:36 *Medeba* was located northeast of the Dead Sea.

of Jambri are celebrating a great wedding, and with a large retinue they are escorting from Nadabath the daughter of one of the great nobles of Canaan." [38]Remembering how their brother John had been slain, they went up and hid themselves under the cover of a mountain.

[39]As they kept watch, they observed a tumultuous procession come into sight carrying a great amount of baggage. The bridegroom came forth, escorted by his fully armed friends and his kindred, to welcome the bridal party with tambourines and musicians. [40]The Jews sprang on them from their place of ambush and began to slay them. Many fell wounded, and the rest fled toward the mountain; and the Jews gathered up all their spoil. [41]Thus the wedding was turned into mourning and the sound of their music into lamentation.* [42]Having thereby gained revenge for the blood of their brother, the Jews returned to the marshes of the Jordan.

"Let Us . . . Fight for Our Lives." [43]When Bacchides heard of this, he came with a huge force to the banks of the Jordan on the Sabbath. [44]Then Jonathan said to those with him, "Let us get up now and fight for our lives, for today things have changed considerably from the way they used to be. [45]In front of us the battle awaits; behind us are the waters of the Jordan on one side and marshland and thickets on the other. There is no way out. [46]Cry out to Heaven that you may be saved from our enemies." [47]Once the battle had begun, Jonathan raised his arm to strike Bacchides, but Bacchides managed to elude him and escaped to the rear. [48]Jonathan then leapt into the Jordan and swam across to the other side with his men. However, the enemy did not pursue them across the Jordan. [49]On that day Bacchides lost about one thousand men.

Bacchides Builds Strongholds. [50]After returning to Jerusalem, Bacchides built strongholds in Judea with high walls, gates, and bars: the fortress in Jericho, Emmaus, Beth-horon, Bethel, Timnath, Pharathon, and Tephon, [51]and he stationed a garrison in each to harass Israel. [52]He also fortified the city of Beth-zur, Gazara, and the citadel, and in them he placed soldiers and stores of provisions. [53]He took the sons of the leading men of the country as hostages and placed them under guard in the citadel at Jerusalem.[d]

Alcimus Dies Paralyzed. [54]In the year one hundred and fifty-three, in the second month, Alcimus ordered the demolition of the wall of the inner court of the sanctuary, thereby destroying the work of the prophets.[e] [55]However, he had only begun the work of demolition when he suffered a stroke. His mouth was closed and he was paralyzed, unable to utter a word or give commands concerning his house. [56]Before much time had passed, he died in great agony. [57]On learning that Alcimus was dead, Bacchides returned to the king, and the land of Judah was left in peace for two years.

Bacchides Negotiates with Jonathan. [58]Then all the renegades gathered together in council. "Now is the time," they said, "with Jonathan and his people living in peace and security, for us to bring back Bacchides, and he will capture all of them in a single night." [59]Therefore, they went and consulted with him. [60]Bacchides set out with a large force, simultaneously sending letters secretly to all his allies in Judea that instructed them to seize Jonathan and his men. However, they were unable to do so because their plot became known, [61]and Jonathan and his men arrested about fifty of the ringleaders in this treacherous plan and put them to death.

[62]Then Jonathan withdrew with Simon and his companions to Bethbasi* in the desert. He rebuilt the fortifications that had been demolished and strengthened them. [63]When Bacchides learned of this, he assembled his entire army and sent instructions to his supporters in Judea. [64]Then he came and encamped opposite Bethbasi, and after constructing engines of war, he fought against it for many days.

[65]Leaving his brother Simon in the city, Jonathan went out into the country area accompanied by only a few men. [66]He struck down Odomera and his kindred and the people of Phasiron in their encampment, all of whom had been preparing to set out to join in the battle.* [67]Meanwhile, Simon and his forces made a sortie from the town and set fire to the engines of war. [68]Moving against Bacchides, they exerted such pressure that they inflicted a severe

d 1 Mac 10:9.—e Ezek 6:14.

9:41 This is a quotation from Am 8:10.
9:62 *Bethbasi* was a little southeast of Bethlehem.
9:66 It is a question of semi-nomadic tribes who resisted the recruitment of Jonathan.

defeat upon him. Inasmuch as his plans for a military assault had been frustrated, 69 Bacchides vented his anger on the renegades who had advised him to undertake this invasion. He slew many of them and then decided to return to his own land.

70 When Jonathan learned of this, he sent envoys to negotiate terms of peace with him and obtain the release of the captives. 71 Bacchides agreed to Jonathan's proposals and swore that he would never again try to cause him harm for the rest of his life. 72 He handed over the prisoners he had previously taken captive from the land of Judah. Then he returned to his own land and never again came into their territory.

73 Thus the sword ceased from Israel. Jonathan settled in Michmash,* from where he began to serve as judge for the people and to exile the renegades from Israel.

CHAPTER 10

Jonathan Is Named High Priest.* 1 In the year one hundred and sixty, Alexander Epiphanes,* the son of Antiochus, arrived by sea and occupied Ptolemais. The people there welcomed him, and he began to reign. 2 When King Demetrius heard of this, he assembled a very large army and marched out to engage him in battle. 3 Demetrius also sent a letter to Jonathan honoring him and expressing the desire for continued peace, 4 for he thought to himself, "Let us move first to make peace with him before he makes peace with Alexander against us, 5 recalling all the wrongs that we inflicted upon him and his brothers and his nation."

6 So Demetrius gave Jonathan the authority to raise an army and to procure arms and to designate himself as an ally; and he also ordered the hostages in the citadel to be released to him. 7 Thereupon Jonathan went to Jerusalem and read the letter to all the people and to those in the citadel. 8 They were all greatly frightened when they heard that the king had given him authority to raise an army. 9 They released the hostages to Jonathan, and he restored them to their parents.[f]

10 Jonathan then took up residence in Jerusalem and began to rebuild and restore the city. 11 He ordered those entrusted with the work to build the walls and to encircle Mount Zion with squared stones for its fortification, and this task was accomplished.

12 The foreigners who occupied the fortresses built by Bacchides abandoned them; 13 all of them deserted their posts and fled to their own lands. 14 Only in Beth-zur did some remain of those who had forsaken the law and the commandments, for it served as a place of refuge.

15 King Alexander was informed of all the proposals made by Demetrius to Jonathan, and he was also told of the battles that Jonathan and his brothers had fought, of the heroic deeds that they had accomplished, and of the hardships that they had endured. 16 His response was, "Shall we ever come across another man like him? Let us take steps to make him our friend and ally." 17 He therefore wrote a letter to him in these words:

18 "King Alexander sends greetings to his brother Jonathan. 19 We have heard that you are a mighty warrior and worthy to be our friend. 20 We have therefore appointed you today to be the high priest of your nation. You are also to have the title 'Friend of the King,' supporting our interests and maintaining friendly relations with us." In addition he sent him a purple robe and a crown of gold.[g]

21 Jonathan put on the sacred vestments in the seventh month of the year one hundred and sixty, at the Feast of Booths.* He also raised an army and procured a large supply of arms.

Political Turning Point. 22 When Demetrius learned of these developments, he was greatly distressed, and he said, 23 "How did we

f 1 Mac 9:53.—g 1 Mac 2:18.

9:73 *Michmash* was eight miles northeast of Jerusalem and well known because of the deed of Jonathan, the son of Saul (see 1 Sam 14:5-23). *Jonathan . . . began to serve as judge:* Jonathan acted as a natural leader, as the leaders of the Book of Judges had done.

10:1-21 Jonathan belongs to the priestly families that the biblical genealogies trace to Aaron, and our author considers his nomination on the part of the occupying prince to be normal. However, others will be more perplexed. Thus, the movement of the Asmodians will judge this fact as arbitrary and irregular, and the Essenes regard it as a true usurpation of the high priesthood and separate themselves from official Judaism. On the other hand, a descendant of the high priest Onias (see 2 Mac 3), Onias IV, will construct a Jewish temple at Leontopolis in Egypt. In any case, the new high priest has his mind above all on things of war and politics.

10:1 *Alexander* I *Epiphanes* came from Ephesus and claimed to be the son of Antiochus IV Epiphanes although his given name was Balas. He claimed the kingship in 150 B.C. and reigned until 145 B.C. The Roman senate recognized him—aided by the urging of Attalus II of Pergamum and by the fact that the Romans had not forgiven Demetrius for becoming king without permission.

10:21 *Jonathan . . . Feast of Booths:* Jonathan's tenure as high priest began around October 23–30, 152 B.C., after there had been no high priest in Jerusalem for seven years.

allow Alexander to get ahead of us in gaining
the friendship of the Jews and thus strength-
ening his position? 24 I too will write to them
in conciliatory terms and offer them honors
and gifts as an inducement to support me."
25 Therefore, he sent them this message:
"King Demetrius sends greetings to the
Jewish nation. 26 We have heard of how you
have honored our agreement with us and
have continued to maintain our friendship,
and that you have not transferred your alle-
giance to our enemies. At this news we
rejoice. 27 If you now continue to keep faith
with us, we will reward you handsomely for
what you do on our behalf, 28 granting you
numerous exemptions and bestowing gifts
on you.
29 [h] "I now free you and exempt all the
Jews from payments of tribute, from the tax
on salt, and from the crown levies.* 30 From
this day henceforth, I also renounce the
third of the grain harvest and the half of the
fruit harvest to which I am entitled. From
this day and for all time I will not collect
them from the land of Judah or from the
three districts annexed to it from Samaria.[i]
31 Jerusalem and its surroundings, its tithes
and its revenues, shall be sacred and free
from tax. 32 I also relinquish my authority
over the citadel in Jerusalem and transfer it
to the high priest, so that he may station
within it men of his own choosing to guard
it. 33 Every Jew carried off into captivity
from the land of Judah into any part of my
kingdom I set free without ransom, and all
their taxes, even those on their livestock, are
to be voided. 34 Let all feast days, Sabbaths,
new moon festivals, appointed days, and the
three days that precede and the three days
that follow a festival be days of exemption
and release for all the Jews in my kingdom.[j]
35 No one will have the authority to exact any
payment from them or to impose any bur-
den on them in any matter whatsoever.
36 "Thirty thousand Jews will be enrolled
in the king's army, and they will receive the
standard benefits given to all the forces of
the king. 37 Some of them will be stationed in
the major strongholds of the king; others
will be appointed to positions of trust in the
kingdom. Their officers and commanders
will be appointed from their own number,
and they will be allowed to observe their
own laws, as the king has commanded in the
land of Judah.
38 "As for the three districts that have been
annexed to Judea from the province of
Samaria, let them be so incorporated with
Judea that they will be considered to be
under one ruler and will obey no authority
other than the high priest. 39 Ptolemais and
the adjoining land I bestow as a gift to the
sanctuary in Jerusalem so that the neces-
sary expenses of the sanctuary may be
met.* 40 I also promise an annual grant of
fifteen thousand shekels out of the king's
revenues from appropriate places. 41 As for
the additional funds that the officials have
not paid as was done in previous years, they
shall henceforth be handed over for the
needs of the temple. 42 Furthermore, the five
thousand silver shekels that used to be taken
annually from the income of the temple will
no longer be collected, since these funds
belong to the priests who minister there.
43 "All who take refuge in the temple in
Jerusalem or in any of its precincts because
of money owed to the king or any other debt
will be released without any forfeiture of
property they possess in my kingdom. 44 The
cost of the rebuilding and restoration of the
structures of the sanctuary are to be taken
from the revenues of the king. 45 Likewise,
the cost of rebuilding the walls of Jerusalem
and fortifying it all around, and of rebuild-
ing the walls in Judea, are to be covered by
the royal revenues."
46 When Jonathan and the people heard
these proposals, they put no faith in them
and refused to accept them, for they
remembered the great evils that Demetrius
had perpetrated in Israel and the harsh
oppression he had inflicted on them. 47 They
favored Alexander, for he had been the first
to make peaceful overtures to them, and
they remained his allies throughout his life.
48 King Alexander assembled a great army
and encamped opposite Demetrius. 49 When
the two kings met in battle, the army of
Demetrius fled, and Alexander pursued
him and defeated his soldiers. 50 The battle
raged fiercely until sunset, and Demetrius
was killed on that day.

h 1 Mac 11:28f, 35.—i 1 Mac 11:28, 34.—j Num 28:11; Jud 8:6; Isa 1:13f.

10:29 The payment of *crown levies* was at first spontaneous but had now become a tax.

10:39 At that time Ptolemais was in the possession of Alexander Balas so that such a gift could provide the Jews with an incentive to side with Demetrius and achieve the effective possession of the city.

Alexander Allies Himself with Egypt.*
51 Alexander sent envoys to Ptolemy, the king
of Egypt, with this message: 52 "Now that I
have returned to my kingdom and taken my
seat on the throne of my ancestors and
established my rule by crushing Demetrius
and thereby gaining control of my country—
53 for I met him in battle, defeated him and
his army, and now occupy the throne of his
kingdom—54 let us therefore enter into an
alliance of friendship with one another. Give
me your daughter as my wife; as your son-
in-law, I will give gifts to you and to her that
are in keeping with your royal position."

55 King Ptolemy said in his reply: "Happy
was the day on which you returned to the
land of your ancestors and took your seat on
the throne of their kingdom. 56 I hereby agree
to your request, but please come to me at
Ptolemais so that we may meet each other,
and I will become your father-in-law, as you
have proposed."

57 In the year one hundred and sixty-two,
Ptolemy set out from Egypt with his daugh-
ter Cleopatra and came to Ptolemais,
58 where King Alexander met him. Ptolemy
gave him his daughter Cleopatra in mar-
riage, and their wedding was celebrated at
Ptolemais with great pomp, as is customary
with such royal occasions.

Jonathan Is Named Governor.* 59 King
Alexander then wrote to Jonathan, asking
him to come and meet him. 60 Jonathan went
amidst great pomp to Ptolemais, where he
met the two kings. He presented them and
their Friends with silver and gold and many
gifts and thus won their favor.[k] 61 Some trou-
blemaking renegades from Israel united
themselves in opposition to him, but the king
paid no heed to them. 62 Rather, he issued
orders that Jonathan should be divested of
his own garments and be clothed in royal
purple, and this was done. 63 The king then
seated him at his side and said to his officers,
"Accompany him to the center of the city
and proclaim that no one is to bring charges
against him on any matter or to make trou-
ble for him in any way."

64 [l] When his accusers observed the honor
that was paid to him in this proclamation
and saw him clothed in his purple robe, they
all fled. 65 The king also honored him by
enrolling him as one of his Chief Friends,
and he appointed him as commander and
governor of the province. 66 Then Jonathan
returned in peace and joy to Jerusalem.

Jonathan Defeats Apollonius. 67 In the year
one hundred and sixty-five, Demetrius,* the
son of Demetrius, came from Crete to the
land of his ancestors. 68 When King Alex-
ander learned of this, he was greatly dis-
turbed, and he returned to Antioch. 69 De-
metrius appointed Apollonius as governor of
Coelesyria,* and the latter assembled a
large force, encamped at Jamnia, and sent
the following message to Jonathan the high
priest: 70 "You are the only one who has seen
fit to rise up against us. Because of you, I
have been assailed by ridicule and brought
into disgrace. Why do you flaunt your
authority against us in the hill country? 71 If
you have such confidence in your forces,
come down to meet us in the plain, and there
we can test each other's strength. The power
of the cities is ready to support me. 72 Make
an inquiry to find out who I am and the iden-
tity of the others who are supporting me. You
will be told that you cannot make a stand
against us. Your ancestors were twice put to
flight in their own land. 73 Now you too will
not be able to withstand my cavalry and
such an army in the plain, where there is not
a stone or a pebble or a place to flee."

74 When Jonathan heard this message
from Apollonius, his spirit was aroused. He
set out from Jerusalem with ten thousand
picked men, and his brother Simon joined
him with reinforcements. 75 He encamped
outside Joppa, where the people of the city
had closed its gates against him because
Apollonius had a garrison there. 76 However,
when they began the siege, the people of the
city became terrified, and they opened the
gates, whereupon Jonathan took possession
of Joppa.

77 When Apollonius learned of this, he
assembled three thousand cavalry and a
large force of infantry. He marched to

k 1 Mac 2:18.—l 64f: 1 Mac 2:18; 11:27.

10:51-58 The new alliance is ratified in 150 B.C. at Ptolemais, a city that had remained half-Egyptian: the new king of Antioch married Cleopatra, the daughter of the king of Egypt. Cleopatra was about fifteen; she later married Demetrius II and still later his brother Antiochus VII.

10:59-66 Received with royal honors, the Hasmonean sees his civil and military powers confirmed. Already high priest, he can manage sword and thurible. This means going beyond the religious tradition of Israel and embarking on a perilous way that will render unpopular the Maccabean dynasty, in which the Herodian kings will insert themselves.

10:67 *Demetrius:* Demetrius II Nicator.

10:69 *Coelesyria* was the name of the valley between Lebanon and the Anti-Lebanon. Here it includes Palestine and indicates the whole western province of the Seleucid kingdom.

Azotus as though he were planning to march
through it, but at the same time he advanced
into the plain, confident in the strength of
such a large number of cavalry. 78 Jonathan
pursued him as far as Azotus, where the
armies engaged in battle. 79 Apollonius, how-
ever, had left a thousand cavalry concealed
behind them. 80 Jonathan realized that there
was an ambush behind him, for his army
was surrounded and showered with arrows
from morning until evening. 81 But his men
held their ground as Jonathan had ordered,
while the enemy's horses became weary.

82 At that point, when the cavalry was
exhausted, Simon led his forces forward and
engaged the enemy phalanx in battle.
Overwhelmed by him, they took to flight.
83 The horsemen scattered over the plain and
fled to Azotus, seeking refuge in Beth-dagon,
the temple of their idol. 84 [m] However, Jona-
than burned and plundered Azotus and its
surrounding villages, and he destroyed by
fire both the temple of Dagon and the men
who had taken refuge in it. 85 The number of
those who fell by the sword, together with
those who were burned to death, totaled
about eight thousand men. 86 Then Jonathan
left there and encamped outside Ashkelon,
and the people of that city came out to meet
him with great pomp. 87 He and his men then
returned to Jerusalem laden with a great
deal of booty.

88 When King Alexander heard of these
events, he conferred even greater honors on
Jonathan. 89 He sent him a gold buckle, which
it was customary to present to the King's
Kinsmen,* and he also gave him Ekron and
all its territory as a possession.

CHAPTER 11

Demetrius II Becomes King. 1 The king of
Egypt then gathered a huge army, as numer-
ous as the sands on the seashore, and also a
great fleet of ships. His purpose was to take
possession of Alexander's kingdom by sub-
terfuge and add it to his kingdom. 2 He set
out for Syria with protestations of peace,
and the people of the towns opened their
gates to him and went out to meet him. King
Alexander had commanded them to do so,
since Ptolemy was his father-in-law. 3 How-
ever, on entering the towns, Ptolemy
stationed troops as a garrison in each one.

4 When he reached Azotus, he was shown
the burnt-out temple of Dagon, Azotus and
its outlying areas demolished, corpses
strewn everywhere, and the charred remains
of those burned by Jonathan in the fighting
and stacked up in heaps along his route. [n] 5 In
an attempt to turn the king against
Jonathan, they explained to him what
Jonathan had done, but the king said noth-
ing. 6 Jonathan met the king with pomp at
Joppa, and they exchanged greetings and
spent the night there. 7 Jonathan accompa-
nied the king as far as the river called
Eleutherus,* and then he returned to Je-
rusalem.

8 King Ptolemy took possession of the cities
along the seacoast as far as Seleucia by the
sea,* and he continued to devise wicked plans
against Alexander. 9 He sent envoys to King
Demetrius, saying: "Come, let us make a pact
with each other. I will give you in marriage
my daughter whom Alexander has married,
and you will reign over the kingdom of your
father. 10 I regret that I gave my daughter to
him, for he has sought to kill me."* 11 He
made this deceitful accusation against
Alexander because he coveted his kingdom.
12 After taking his daughter away from him
and giving her to Demetrius, Ptolemy ended
his friendship with Alexander, and their
enmity became clearly manifest. 13 Then
Ptolemy entered Antioch and assumed the
crown of Asia in addition to the crown of
Egypt that he already possessed.

14 King Alexander was in Cilicia at that
time because the people of that region were
in revolt, 15 but when he was informed about
what was occurring, he marched against
Ptolemy, who opposed him with a strong
force and put him to flight. 16 Alexander fled
to Arabia to seek protection, and King
Ptolemy's triumph was complete 17 when
Zabdiel the Arab cut off Alexander's head
and sent it to Ptolemy. 18 However, three days

m 1 Mac 11:4; 1 Sam 5:2-5.—n 1 Mac 10:84.

10:89 *King's Kinsmen:* a title higher than that of "Friends of the King" (see 1 Mac 2:18). It referred to a more elevated class among the dignitaries of the Hellenistic courts. *Ekron* was an ancient Philistine city, about eight miles southeast of Jamnia, which had been given to Jonathan as a personal possession with taxes assigned to him (see 1 Sam 27:6).

11:7 *Eleutherus:* the northern limit of Coelesyria, which today is the northern border of Lebanon.

11:8 *Seleucia by the sea:* the main port for Antioch near the mouth of the Orontes.

11:10 *I regret . . . sought to kill me:* Flavius Josephus reports that a friend of Alexander called Ammonius had failed in an attempt to assassinate Ptolemy. Ptolemy seized the occasion to blame Alexander and claim the throne.

later King Ptolemy died, and his men in the fortified cities were killed by the inhabitants there. 19 Thus Demetrius became king in the year one hundred and sixty-seven.

Jonathan Makes a Pact with Demetrius. 20 At this juncture Jonathan mustered the men of Judea for an attack on the citadel in Jerusalem, and they set up a large number of engines of war to use against it. 21 However, some renegades who were traitors to their own nation went to the king and informed him that Jonathan was besieging the citadel. 22 When Demetrius heard this report, he was furious, and he immediately set out for Ptolemais. He also wrote to Jonathan, ordering him to end the siege and to meet him for a conference at Ptolemais as soon as possible.

23 When Jonathan heard this, he gave orders to continue the siege. Then, selecting some elders of Israel and priests to accompany him, he placed himself in jeopardy 24 by taking silver, gold, clothing, and numerous other gifts and journeying to Ptolemais, where by means of these gifts he won the favor of Demetrius. 25 Although some renegade Jews of his own nation brought charges against him, 26 the king treated him just as his predecessors had done and honored him in the presence of all his Friends. 27 He confirmed him in the high priesthood and in all the other positions of honor he had previously held, and he had him enrolled among his Chief Friends.

28 Jonathan asked the king to exempt Judea and the three districts* of Samaria from tribute, and promised him three hundred talents in return.[o] 29 The king consented and wrote the following letter to Jonathan about all these matters:

30[p] "King Demetrius sends greetings to his brother Jonathan and to the Jewish nation. 31 For your own information we are sending you a copy of the letter that we wrote to our kinsman Lasthenes* concerning you, as follows: 32 'King Demetrius sends greetings to his father Lasthenes. 33 Since the Jewish people are our friends and fulfill their obligations to us, we have decided to reward them. 34[q] Therefore, we confirm their possession of the territory of Judea and of the three districts of Aphairema, Lydda, and Ramathaim. These districts, with all their dependencies, were annexed to Judea from Samaria for the benefit of all those who offer sacrifices for us at Jerusalem instead of paying the royal taxes that the king formerly received from them every year from the crops of the land and the fruit of the trees. 35 From this day forward we also release them from the payment of other revenues that are due to us—that is, tithes, and tribute, the tax on the salt pits, and the crown taxes. 36 These provisions shall be irrevocable from this moment for all time. 37 Be sure, therefore, to have a copy of them made and given to Jonathan, so that it may be displayed in a conspicuous place on the holy mountain.' "

Jonathan's Forces Save Demetrius. 38 When King Demetrius saw that the country was at peace under his rule and that there was no opposition to him, he dismissed his forces, sending all of them to their own homes except for the foreign troops that he had recruited from the islands of the nations. As a result, all the soldiers who had served under his predecessors hated him. 39 Trypho, one of Alexander's former supporters, observed that all the soldiers were grumbling against Demetrius. He went to see Imalkue the Arab, who was bringing up Antiochus, Alexander's young son,[r] 40 and repeatedly urged him to hand over the boy to him so that he could become king in place of his father. During his stay there for many days, he also reported to Imalkue everything that Demetrius had done and the hatred that his soldiers felt toward him.

41 Meanwhile, Jonathan sent a report to King Demetrius asking that he withdraw his troops from the citadel in Jerusalem and from the strongholds, for they showed constant hostility toward Israel. 42 In reply, Demetrius sent this message back to Jonathan: "I will not only do this for you and your nation, but I will also confer great honor upon you and your nation whenever the opportunity presents itself. 43 In return, please do me the favor of sending men to fight for me, because all my troops have deserted."

o 1 Mac 10:29; 11:34.—p 30-37: 1 Mac 10:26-45.—q 34f: 1 Mac 10:29; 11:28.—r 1 Mac 12:39.

11:28 The *three districts* were already mentioned in 10:30, 38. They were previously part of Samaria and had been annexed to Judea (1 Mac 10:38); they are named in verse 34 below: Aphairema (the Ephrem of Jn 11:54, four miles northeast of Bethel), Lydda (the hometown of Aeneas, who was cured by Peter in Acts 9:32ff, ten miles southeast of Joppa) and Ramathaim (the Arimathea of the Gospels, e.g., Mt 27:57, nine miles northeast of Lydda).

11:31 *Lasthenes:* the architect of the victory of Demetrius who had commanded the troops gathered on the Aegean islands with which the kingdom had been reconquered.

44 Therefore, Jonathan sent three thou-
sand skilled fighting men to him at Antioch,
and when they reached the king, he was
delighted at their arrival, 45 for the people,
one hundred and twenty thousand strong,
had massed together in the center of the
city, intending to kill him. 46 However, the
king took refuge in the palace, while
the people seized control of the main
streets of the city and began to fight. 47 The
king then summoned the Jews to come to
his aid. They immediately rallied around
him and then spread out through the city.
On that day they killed about one hundred
thousand of its inhabitants, 48 after which
they set fire to the city and seized a great
amount of booty. Thus they saved the life of
the king.

49 When the people of the city realized that
the Jews had the city at their mercy, their
courage failed them, and they cried out to
the king, making this entreaty: 50 "Grant us
terms of peace, and order the Jews to stop
fighting against us and our city." They threw
down their arms and made peace. 51 The
Jews thus gained glory in the eyes of the king
and of all his subjects in the kingdom, and
they returned to Jerusalem with a great
amount of spoil.

52 However, when King Demetrius felt
secure on his royal throne and the land
was peaceful under his rule, 53 he broke all
the promises he had made and became
estranged from Jonathan. Instead of reward-
ing Jonathan for all the services he had ren-
dered him, he treated him very harshly.

Jonathan Enters the Service of Antiochus VI.
54 After this, Trypho returned, bringing with
him the young boy Antiochus,* who was
crowned king.[s] 55 All the soldiers that
Demetrius had discharged rallied to Anti-
ochus and fought against Demetrius, who
was routed and fled. 56 Trypho captured the
elephants and took control of Antioch.

57 Then the young Antiochus wrote to
Jonathan as follows: "I confirm you in the
high priesthood, place you in authority over
the four districts, and appoint you as one of
the King's Friends." 58 He also sent him a din-
ner service of gold plate and gave him the
right to drink from gold vessels, to dress in
royal purple, and to wear a gold buckle.[t]
59 He also appointed Jonathan's brother
Simon as governor of the region from the
Ladder of Tyre* to the frontiers of Egypt.

60 Jonathan then set out and traveled
through West-of-Euphrates* and its cities,
and the whole Syrian army rallied to his sup-
port. When he reached Ashkelon, the people
of the city received him with great honor.
61 From there he proceeded to Gaza, but the
people of Gaza closed their gates to him.
Therefore, he besieged Gaza, burning down
its suburbs and plundering them. 62 Then the
people of Gaza pleaded with Jonathan for
mercy, and he granted them peace, taking
the sons of their rulers as hostages and send-
ing them to Jerusalem. He then traveled
through the country as far as Damascus.

63 Jonathan heard that the generals of
Demetrius had arrived at Kadesh in Galilee
with a large army, intending to remove him
from office. 64 He went forth to confront
them, leaving his brother Simon in the
province. 65 Simon encamped opposite Beth-
zur, attacked it for many days, and blockad-
ed the inhabitants within it. 66 Finally, they
sued for peace, which he granted to them,
although he expelled them from the town,
took possession of it, and stationed a garri-
son there.

67 Meanwhile Jonathan and his army
encamped by the Lake of Gennesaret. Early
in the morning they marched to the Plain of
Hazor.* 68 There in the plain was the army of
the foreigners advancing to attack, having
first prepared an ambush against him in the
mountains. 69 While the main force made
a frontal attack, the troops in ambush
emerged from their place of concealment
and joined in the fighting. 70 All of the men
with Jonathan fled; not one of them was left
except for Mattathias, son of Absalom, and
Judas, son of Chalphi, the commanders of
the army. 71 Jonathan tore his clothes, threw
dust on his head, and prayed. 72 Then he
resumed the battle and completely routed

s 1 Mac 11:39; 12:39.—t 1 Mac 2:18.

11:54 This is *Antiochus* VI Epiphanes, son of Alexander Balas, reared by the Arabian sheik Imalkue (see 11:39-40). From 145–142 B.C., he was educated by Trypho, who was an intriguing personage, a representative of the court of Alexander Balas who successively took the sides of Ptolemy and then Demetrius II and ultimately decided to stir up the military revolt against Demetrius (v. 38f) in order to make his protégé king.

11:59 *Ladder of Tyre:* a locality ten miles south of Tyre, so called because the coastal road ascends the rock by means of a series of steps.

11:60 *West-of-Euphrates:* the territory of Palestine and Coelesyria (see 1 Mac 3:32; 7:8).

11:67 *Plain of Hazor:* the site of the ancient Canaanite city southwest of Lake Hulah and ten miles north of the Lake of Gennesaret (Jos 11:10).

the enemy, who took to flight. 73 When the
fugitives from Jonathan's army observed
this, they returned to his banner and joined
him in the pursuit of the enemy as far as
their camp in Kadesh, where they en-
camped. 74 About three thousand of the for-
eign troops fell on that day. Jonathan then
returned to Jerusalem.

CHAPTER 12

**Jonathan Renews Friendship with Rome and
Sparta.** 1 When Jonathan saw that the times
were favorable, he selected men to send to
Rome for the purpose of confirming and
renewing the treaty of friendship with the
Romans.[u] 2 He also sent letters to the same
effect to Sparta and elsewhere.

3 Upon reaching Rome, the envoys entered
the senate chamber and said, "The high
priest Jonathan and the Jewish people have
sent us to renew their treaty of friendship
and alliance with you." 4 The Romans pro-
vided them with letters that requested the
authorities in various locations to give the
envoys safe conduct to the land of Judah.

5 This is a copy of the letter that Jonathan
wrote to the Spartans: 6 * "Jonathan the high
priest, the senate of the nation, the priests,
and the rest of the Jewish people send greet-
ings to their brothers the Spartans. 7 Quite
some time ago a letter was sent to Onias*
the high priest from Arius your king, stating
that you are indeed our brothers, as the
attached copy shows.[v] 8 Onias welcomed the
envoy with honor and accepted the letter, on
which was set forth a clear declaration of
alliance and friendship. 9 Although we have
no need of such things, inasmuch as we have
as a source of encouragement the sacred
books* in our possession,[w] 10 we have decid-
ed to request the renewal of our pact of fam-
ily ties and friendship with you so that we
may not become estranged from you, for a
great many years have elapsed since you last
contacted us.

11 "We, for our part, remember you con-
stantly in the sacrifices we offer and in our
prayers at our festivals and on other
appointed days, for it is right and proper to
remember brothers.* 12 We rejoice in your
renown. 13 We ourselves, however, have en-
dured many trials and wars, and the kings in
our vicinity have been attacking us. 14 We did
not want to bother you and our other allies
and friends during these wars, 15 inasmuch
as we have the support of Heaven to help us.
Therefore, we were delivered from our ene-
mies, and they have been humbled. 16 And so
we have chosen Numenius, the son of
Antiochus, and Antipater, the son of Jason,
and we have sent them to the Romans to
renew our former pact of friendship and
alliance.[x] 17 We have also instructed them to
visit you and greet you and deliver this letter
about the renewal of our pact of family ties.
18 Please send us a reply to this letter."

19 This is a copy of the letter that was sent
to Onias: 20 [y] "Arius, the king of the Spartans,
sends greetings to Onias the high priest. 21 A
document has been uncovered that states
that the Spartans and the Jews are brothers,
both being descended from Abraham. 22 And
now that we have learned of this, we ask that
you write to us with news of your welfare.
23 We, on our part, affirm that your livestock
and your possessions belong to us and that
ours belong to you, and we are instructing
our envoys to give you a promise to this
effect."

Jonathan Thwarts the Syrian Offensive.
24 When Jonathan heard that the generals of
Demetrius had returned to wage war against
him with an even larger army than previous-
ly, 25 he set forth from Jerusalem and met
them in the region of Hamath,* thereby giv-
ing them no opportunity to invade his own
territory. 26 He sent spies into their camp
who returned and informed him that the
enemy was preparing to attack the Jews
that night. 27 Therefore, at sunset Jonathan
commanded his troops to remain awake
and fully armed throughout the night, pre-
pared for battle, and he stationed outposts
all around the camp. 28 When the enemy
learned that Jonathan and his men were
ready for battle, they were terrified, and their

u 1 Mac 8:17.—v 1 Mac 12:2-23; 2 Mac 5:9.—w Rom 15:4.—x 1 Mac 14:22; 15:15.—y 20-23: 1 Mac 12:6f.

12:6-18 The author transcribes the letter inserting a few teachings in it; indirectly, he reveals to us that the collection of the Scriptures (v. 9) is constituted.

12:7 The persons seem to be *Onias* I, high priest (323–290 B.C.), and Arius I, king of Sparta (309–265 B.C.), whose tasks coincided during the period from 309–300 B.C.

12:9 *Sacred books:* the law, the prophets, and other books mentioned in the prologue to Wisdom of Ben Sira (v. 1), after 132 B.C.

12:11 Despite the separatism practiced by the Jews, no law prohibited them from praying for other peoples, even Gentiles, for their rulers (see Jer 29:7; Ezr 6:10), and in particular for foreign sovereigns on whom Israel depended.

12:25 *Region of Hamath:* the Seleucid territory of Upper Syria northeast of Coelesyria and separated from it by the Eleutherus River. *His own territory:* Coelesyria, which was under Jonathan's command (1 Mac 11:59ff).

courage failed them. After lighting fires in
the camp, they then withdrew. 29 However,
Jonathan and his men were not aware of
their withdrawal until morning, for they saw
the fires burning. 30 Although Jonathan pur-
sued them, he was unable to overtake them,
for they had crossed the River Eleutherus.
31 And so, Jonathan turned aside to attack
the Arabs who are called Zabadeans,* and
he thoroughly routed them and engaged in
plunder. 32 Then he moved on to Damascus,
marching through that entire region.

33 Simon also set out and advanced as far
as Ashkelon and its neighboring strongholds.
He then turned toward Joppa and occupied
it, 34 for he had heard that its inhabitants
intended to hand over this stronghold to the
supporters of Demetrius, and he stationed a
garrison there to guard it.

**Jonathan Erects Fortifications in Jerusalem
and Judea.** 35 When Jonathan returned, he
convened the elders of the people and
secured their agreement to build strong-
holds in Judea, 36 to increase the height of the
walls in Jerusalem, and to erect a high barri-
er between the citadel and the city so that
the citadel would be isolated and its occu-
pants would be unable to engage in com-
merce with the city. 37 The people worked
together to rebuild the city. Part of the wall
above the valley to the east had collapsed,
and the quarter called Chaphenatha was
also repaired. 38 Simon meanwhile rebuilt
Adida in the Shephelah, and he strength-
ened its fortifications with gates and bars.

Jonathan Falls into the Hands of His Enemies.
39 Meanwhile, Trypho set his sights on
becoming king of Asia, assuming the crown,
and launching an attack on King Antiochus.[z]
40 However, he was afraid that Jonathan
would not allow him to do this and might
even resort to war to prevent him from
doing so. Therefore, he set out and marched
to Beth-shan, in the hope of seizing him and
putting him to death. 41 Jonathan marched
out to confront him with forty thousand
picked warriors and arrived at Beth-shan.

42 When Trypho saw that Jonathan was
confronting him with a large army, he was
hesitant about launching an attack against
him. 43 Instead he received him with honor,
commended him to all his Friends, and gave
him gifts. He also ordered his Friends and all
his soldiers to obey him as they would him-
self. 44 Then he said to Jonathan, "Why have
you put all your soldiers to so much trouble
when we are not at war? 45 Send them back
home after first choosing a few of them to
remain with you, and journey with me to
Ptolemais. I will hand it over to you together
with the other strongholds and the remain-
ing troops and all the officials, and then I will
depart for home. That was my purpose in
coming here."

46 Jonathan believed that he was being
truthful and did as he had suggested. He dis-
missed his forces, and they returned to the
land of Judah. 47 However, he kept three thou-
sand men with him, two thousand of whom
he left in Galilee while one thousand accom-
panied him. 48 But as soon as Jonathan
entered Ptolemais, the people of the city
closed the gates and seized him, and they
slew with the sword all those who had accom-
panied him.

49 Trypho sent soldiers and cavalry into
Galilee and the Great Plain* to destroy all of
Jonathan's men. 50 When these learned that
Jonathan had been captured and his forces
had been slaughtered, they encouraged one
another and marched in close formation,
ready for battle. 51 Their pursuers, realizing
that they were prepared to fight for their
lives, turned back. 52 Thus they all returned
home safely to the land of Judah. They
grieved over Jonathan and his companions
and were in great fear, and all Israel was
plunged into mourning.

53 All the surrounding nations were deter-
mined to destroy them. "They have no
leader or ally," they said. "Now let us attack
them and wipe out every memory of them
from all peoples."[a]

C: Simon Achieves Independence (143–134 B.C.)

CHAPTER 13

Simon Becomes Leader of Israel. 1 When
Simon heard that Trypho had assembled a
large army to invade and destroy the land of
Judah, 2 and he saw that the people were
trembling with fear, he went up to
Jerusalem. Assembling the people, 3 he
exhorted them in these words: "You your-
selves are fully aware of what I and my

z 1 Mac 11:39f, 54f.—a 1 Mac 5:2; 13:6.

12:31 *Zabadeans:* perhaps people northwest of Damascus.
12:49 *The Great Plain:* of Beth-shan (v. 41) where Jonathan's disbanded men remained.

brothers and the house of my father have
done for the laws and the sanctuary. You also
know about the battles we have fought and
the hardships we have endured. 4 As a result,
all of my brothers have perished for the sake
of Israel, and I alone am left. 5 Far be it from
me, then, to give priority to my own life in
any time of oppression, for I am not of any
greater worth than my brothers. 6 Rather, I
will avenge my nation and the sanctuary and
your wives and children, for all the nations
have united to destroy us because of their
hatred for us."[b]

7 These words rekindled the spirit of the
people, 8 and they replied by shouting, "You
are our leader in place of Judas and your
brother Jonathan. 9 Fight our battles, and we
will do whatever you tell us." 10 Therefore,
Simon assembled all the fighting men and
hurried to complete the walls of Jerusalem,
fortifying it on every side. 11 He sent
Jonathan, the son of Absalom, with a large
force to Joppa; Jonathan drove out the peo-
ple who were there and occupied the town.

Simon Prevents Trypho from Invading Judah.
12 Then Trypho departed from Ptolemais
with a large army to invade the land of
Judah, bringing Jonathan with him under
guard, 13 while Simon encamped in Adida,
opposite the plain. 14 When Trypho learned
that Simon had assumed the role of his
brother Jonathan and that he was prepared
to engage in battle with him, he sent envoys
to say to him, 15 "We are detaining your
brother Jonathan because of the money that
he owed to the royal treasury in connection
with the offices he held. 16 Send us a hundred
talents of silver, and two of his sons as
hostages to ensure that when he is set free he
will not revolt against us, and we will release
him."

17 Although Simon was positive that they
were speaking deceitfully to him, he had the
money and the boys brought to him, fearing
to provoke great hostility among the people,
who might say 18 that Jonathan perished
because Simon would not send Trypho the
money and the boys. 19 Therefore, he sent
both the boys and the one hundred talents,
but Trypho broke his word and refused to
release Jonathan. 20 Next, Trypho set out to
invade and ravage the country. He made a
detour along the road that leads to Adora,*
but Simon and his army kept marching
opposite him every place he went.

21 The men in the citadel sent messages to
Trypho, urging him to come to their aid by
way of the desert and to send them supplies.
22 Trypho prepared his entire cavalry force to
go, but that night it snowed so heavily that he
was unable to proceed. Therefore, he with-
drew into Gilead. 23 When he drew near to
Baskama,* he had Jonathan put to death
and buried him there. 24 Then Trypho
returned to his own country.

Jonathan's Funeral. 25 Simon sent for the
body of his brother Jonathan and buried him
in Modein, the city of his ancestors. 26 There
was great lamentation for him throughout
Israel, and the mourning lasted for many
days. 27 Over the tomb of his father and
brothers Simon erected a tall monument
that was visible from a great distance, com-
posed of polished stone back and front. 28 He
also erected seven pyramids, facing each
other, for his father and mother and four
brothers. 29 For the pyramids he devised an
elaborate setting of tall columns, surmount-
ed by trophies of armor as a perpetual
memorial, and next to the armor he placed
carved ships that could be seen by all who
sailed the sea. 30 This tomb, which he built at
Modein, remains to this day.

A New Political Autonomy.* 31 Trypho next
dealt treacherously with the young King
Antiochus. He killed him 32 and usurped his
position as king, claiming the crown of Asia
and inflicting great havoc on the country.
33 Meanwhile, Simon rebuilt the strongholds
of Judea, strengthening them with high tow-
ers, great walls, and bolted gates, and he
stocked the strongholds with provisions.
34 He also sent selected emissaries to King
Demetrius with a request that he grant tax
relief to the country, since Trypho had done
little else except plunder the land. 35 King
Demetrius responded favorably to his
request with the following letter:

36 "King Demetrius sends greetings to
Simon the high priest and the Friend of
Kings, and to the elders and the Jewish peo-
ple. 37 We have received the gold crown and
the palm branch that you sent, and we are

b 1 Mac 5:2; 12:53

13:20 *Adora* (or Adoram), five miles from Hebron (2 Chr 11:9).

13:23 *Baskama:* possibly northeast of the Sea of Galilee. *He had Jonathan put to death:* late in 143 or early in 142 B.C.

13:31-42 For the first time after the Exile (sixth century), despite the persistence of a few ties of vassalage, Israel rediscovers its political autonomy. This takes place in 142 B.C.

willing to enter into a treaty of peace with
you and to write to our officials with instruc-
tions to grant you an exemption from the
payment of tribute. [38]All of our previous
guarantees to you remain in force, and the
strongholds that you have built shall remain
in your possession. [39]We pardon any errors
or offenses committed up to now, and we
remit the crown tax that you owe. Moreover,
any other tax that formerly was collected in
Jerusalem is hereby canceled. [40]If any of you
are qualified to be enrolled in our service, let
them be enrolled. Let there be peace
between us."

[41]Thus in the year one hundred and sev-
enty, the yoke of the Gentiles was removed
from Israel, [42]and the people began to write
in their documents and contracts: "In the
first year of Simon, the great high priest,
commander and leader of the Jews."*

Simon Captures Gazara. [43]About that time,
Simon besieged Gazara* and surrounded it
with troops. He constructed a siege-
machine, and after he had brought it up to
the town, he opened a breach in one of the
towers and captured it.[c] [44]The men leapt
from the siege-machine into the city, and a
great tumult arose there. [45]The men of the
city, with their wives and children, mounted
the walls with their garments torn, and they
cried out loudly, imploring Simon to make
peace with them. [46]"Do not treat us as our
wickedness deserves," they said, "but
according to your mercy."

[47]Simon reached an agreement with
them and did not destroy them. However, he
expelled them from the city, and he purified
the houses that contained idols. Then he
entered the city with hymns and songs of
praise. [48]After removing everything from it
that was unclean, he settled there people
who observed the law. He also strengthened
its fortifications and built a residence for
himself.

The Citadel Surrenders.* [49]The occupants of
the citadel in Jerusalem were prevented
from coming out and going into the coun-
tryside to buy and sell. Thus they were in a
state of famine, and many of them died of
starvation. [50]Then they implored Simon to
make peace with them, and he granted their
request. Expelling them from the citadel, he
cleansed it of its defilement. [51]On the twen-
ty-third day of the second month, in the year
one hundred and seventy-one, the Jews
entered the citadel with shouting and the
waving of palm branches, to the accompani-
ment of lyres and cymbals and harps and
the singing of hymns and canticles, because
a great enemy of Israel had been destroyed.[d]
[52]Simon decreed that this day should be
observed each year with rejoicing. He also
strengthened the fortifications of the temple
hill alongside the citadel, and he took up res-
idence there with his men. [53]And since his
son John had now reached manhood, he
appointed him as commander of all the
forces, with his residence in Gazara.*

CHAPTER 14

Capture of Demetrius. [1]In the year one hun-
dred and seventy-two, King Demetrius
assembled his forces and marched into
Media to obtain support for his war against
Trypho.* [2]When Arsaces,* the king of Persia
and Media, heard that Demetrius had
invaded his territory, he sent one of his
generals to take him alive. [3]The general
marched forth and defeated the army of
Demetrius. He captured him and brought
him to Arsaces, who imprisoned him.

Glory of Simon*

4 The land was at peace all the days of
Simon,
who sought the good of his people.

c 2 Mac 10:32-38.—d 1 Mac 1:36.

13:42 The title of king is avoided, since it was regarded as reserved to the Davidic descendancy; only forty years later, however, the title will be assumed (Alexander Jannaeus, 103–76 B.C.).

13:43 *Gazara:* a key position in the Shephelah, fortified by Bacchides in 160 B.C.; see 1 Mac 9:52; a Greek inscription hostile to Simon has been found there. *Siege-machine:* a tower on wheels housing men with catapults and battering rams that could breach fortified walls.

13:49-53 The citadel in which Simon takes residence with his men will become the fortress Antonia. *Palm branches* signified victory (see 2 Mac 10:7).

13:53 Simon, the lone remaining son of Mattathias, calls upon his son who has already shown himself courageous in previous military actions. This son is *John* Hyrcanus who will succeed his father (see 1 Mac 16:1-3).

14:1 Some historians assign a later date to the invasion, opting for 138 B.C. (instead of 140 B.C.), the year in which Demetrius was captured. *Media* was west of Tehran and continued to be claimed by the Seleucids.

14:2 *Arsaces:* Arsaces VI, also known as Mithridates I, the Parthian king (171–138 B.C.). The Greeks and Macedonians in Persia and Babylonia had appealed to Demetrius for help because the Parthians had taken over both countries.

14:4-15 The author rediscovers his poetic inspiration to exalt the new hero. The traditional biblical images help him to sketch the picture of a time of peace and prosperity that announces the kingdom of the Messiah (Isa 9:1-5; Zec 3:10; 8:4f; 1 Ki 5:4f). The component reveals the religious soul of Israel in the second century B.C.: in it are reunited the ideal of poverty sung by the prophets (Zep 3:12; Ps 18:28) and the cultic legalistic ideal of the doctors of the temple (Pss 1; 118).

They were pleased at his rule
and with his magnificence throughout
his life.[e]
5 The crowning point of his glory was his
capture of the port of Joppa,
affording him a gateway to the isles of
the sea.
6 He enlarged the frontiers of his nation
and gained complete control of the
country.[f]
7 He took many captives
and conquered Gazara, Beth-zur, and
the citadel.
He cleansed the citadel of its defilement;
no one was able to withstand him.
8 The people farmed their land in peace;
the ground yielded its produce
and the trees of the plain their fruit.[g]
9 Old men sat in the squares;
all their conversation revolved around
their prosperity,
while the young men were arrayed in
splendid armor.[h]
10 He supplied the towns with food
and equipped them with fortifications
until his renown resounded to the ends
of the earth.
11 He established peace in the land,
and Israel was filled with great joy.[i]
12 All the people sat under their own vines
and fig trees,
and there was no one to make them
afraid.[j]
13 No one was left in the land to attack
them;
the kings in those days had been
crushed.
14 He gave help to the lowly among his
people
and was zealous for the law,
suppressing all the lawless and the
wicked.
15 He enhanced the splendor of the temple
and enriched it with many sacred ves-
sels.

Renewal of the Alliance with Rome and Sparta.
16 When the people heard in Rome and as
far away as Sparta that Jonathan had died,
they were deeply grieved.* 17 But when they
heard that his brother Simon had succeed-
ed him as high priest and that he was gov-
erning the country and the towns in it,
18 they wrote to him on bronze tablets to
renew the treaty of friendship and alliance
that they had established with his brothers,
Judas and Jonathan.[k] 19 The terms of the
treaty were read before the assembly in
Jerusalem.

20 This is a copy of the letter sent by the
Spartans: "The rulers and the citizens of
Sparta send greetings to Simon the high
priest and to the elders, the priests, and the
rest of the Jewish people, our brothers. 21 The
envoys you sent to our people have informed
us of your glory and fame, and we were over-
joyed to receive them. 22 We have made a
record of their report in the archives of our
public assembly, as follows: 'Numenius, the
son of Antiochus, and Antipater, the son of
Jason, have come to us to reaffirm their
friendship with us.[l] 23 The people have been
pleased to receive these men with honor and
to deposit a copy of their words in the public
archives so that the people of Sparta may
have a record of them. A copy of this docu-
ment has been made for Simon the high
priest.' "

24 After this, Simon sent Numenius to
Rome with a large gold shield weighing one
thousand minas, to confirm the alliance with
the Romans.[m]

Homage Rendered to Simon. 25 When the
people heard an account of these events,
they said, "How can we possibly thank
Simon and his sons? 26 He and his brothers
and the house of his father have stood firm
and repulsed the enemies of Israel, ensuring
the nation's freedom." Therefore, they
engraved an inscription on bronze tablets
and affixed them to pillars on Mount Zion.
27 *The following is a copy of the inscription:

"On the eighteenth day of Elul,* in the
year one hundred and seventy-two, the third
year of the high priesthood of Simon, 28 in
Asaramel, in a great assembly of the priests
and the people and the rulers of the nation
and the elders of the country, the following
resolution was approved:

e 1 Mac 3:3-9.—f Ex 34:24.—g Zec 8:41.—h Zec 8:4f.—i Lev 26:6.—j Mic 4:4; Zec 3:10.—k 1 Mac 8:22.—l 1 Mac 12:16; 15:15.—m 1 Mac 12:16; 15:15.

14:16 The embassy to Rome and Sparta took place soon after Simon's accession to power and the replies were received before Demetrius's expedition (vv. 1-3)—probably in 142 B.C.

14:27-47 The high priest held his office by divine appointment, indicated by descent from a particular family. But because there was no legitimate claimant, Simon was legitimized by a process known in ancient Israel (see Ex 19; 2 Ki 23; Ezr 10; Neh 9).

14:27 *Elul* is the sixth month of the year (the name is Babylonian but was used by the Jews after the Exile). Hence, we are in September of the year 140 B.C. *Asaramel:* a Hebrew word meaning "court of the people of God."

[29] " 'Because wars were a frequent occur-
rence in our country, Simon, the son of
Mattathias, a priest of the line of Joarib, and
his brothers have placed their lives in jeop-
ardy by confronting the enemies of their
nation, so that their sanctuary and the law
might be preserved, and in this way they
have brought great glory to their nation.[n]
[30] After Jonathan had rallied his nation and
become their high priest, he was gathered
to his ancestors. [31] When enemies resolved to
invade and to devastate their country and to
lay hands on their sanctuary, [32] Simon next
came forward to fight for his nation, spend-
ing a large portion of his personal wealth to
equip the soldiers of his nation and pay their
wages. [33] He fortified the towns of Judea,
including Beth-zur on the Judean frontier, a
location that had formerly been used by the
enemy to store their arms, and he stationed
there a garrison of Jewish soldiers. [34] He also
fortified Joppa by the sea and Gazara on the
border of Azotus, formerly occupied by the
enemy. He resettled Jews there and provided
them with everything that was necessary for
their restoration.

[35] " 'When the people recognized Simon's
loyalty and the glory that he was determined
to win for his nation, they made him their
leader and high priest because of everything
he had accomplished and for the loyalty and
justice he had maintained toward his nation,
as in every possible way he sought to exalt
his people.

[36] " 'In his time and under his leadership
the Gentiles were driven out of their country,
including those in the City of David in
Jerusalem who had built for themselves a
citadel from which they used to sally forth
and defile the environs of the sanctuary and
do grave damage to the state of its purity.
[37] He installed Jewish soldiers in this citadel
and fortified it for the greater security of the
land and the city, and he also heightened the
walls of Jerusalem. [38] As a result of all this,
King Demetrius confirmed him in the office
of high priest, [39] [o] made him one of his
Friends, and conferred the highest honors
on him. [40] For he had heard that the Romans
were addressing the Jews as friends and
allies and brothers, and that they had
received Simon's envoys with great honor.

[41] " 'The Jewish people and their priests
have therefore resolved that Simon is to be
their permanent leader and high priest until
a true prophet shall appear. [42] He is to act as
their governor and to have complete charge
of the sanctuary and its functions, and in
addition the supervision of the country, its
weapons, and its strongholds, [43] and is to be
obeyed by all the people. All contracts made
in the country are to be written in his name.
He shall be entitled to be clothed in royal
purple and to wear gold ornamentation.

[44] " 'None of the people or the priests are to
have the lawful authorization to nullify any
of these decisions, or to oppose any of his
commands, or to convene an assembly in
the country without his permission, or to be
clothed in royal purple or wear a gold
brooch. [45] Whoever acts in opposition to
these decisions or rejects any of them is to be
liable to punishment.

[46] " 'All of the people have agreed to grant
Simon the authority to act in accordance
with these decisions. [47] Simon has accepted
and has agreed to serve as high priest, to be
commander and ethnarch of the Jews and
the priests, and to be the protector of them
all.' "

[48] It was decreed that this inscription
should be engraved on bronze tablets and
placed in a conspicuous place in the pre-
cincts of the temple, [49] and that copies of it
were to be deposited in the treasury, where
they would be in the keeping of Simon and
his sons.

CHAPTER 15

Antiochus VII Recognizes Simon's Titles.
[1] Antiochus,* the son of King Demetrius,
sent a letter from the islands of the sea to
Simon, the priest and ethnarch of the Jews,
and to the entire nation. [2] It read as follows:

"King Antiochus sends greetings to
Simon, the priest and ethnarch of the Jews,
and to the Jewish nation. [3] Whereas certain
scoundrels have seized control of the king-
dom of my ancestors, I intend to assert my
claim to it so that I may restore it to its for-
mer state. I have recruited a large force of
mercenaries and have equipped warships.
[4] My intention is to land in my country and

n 1 Chr 24:7.—o 39f: 1 Mac 2:18.

15:1 *Antiochus* is Antiochus VII Sidetes (so-called because he was reared at Side in Pamphylia), son of Demetrius I, and younger brother of Demetrius II, currently a prisoner of the Parthians. At twenty years of age he left Rhodes to take his brother's place and drive out Trypho the usurper. He reigned from 138–129 B.C. After his brother's capture he married Cleopatra III (1 Mac 10:57f; 11:12).

take revenge on those who have ravaged my kingdom and laid waste many of its cities.

5 "Therefore, I now confirm all the tax exemptions that the kings who preceded me granted to you and any other privileges that they conferred upon you. 6 I authorize you to mint your own coinage as money for your country. 7 Jerusalem and its temple are to be free. All the weapons you have prepared and all the strongholds you have built and now occupy shall remain in your hands. 8 All debts you now owe to the royal treasury and any such future debts shall be canceled from this time forward forever. 9 When we again gain control of our kingdom, we shall bestow the highest possible honors on you and your nation and the temple, so that your glory will be manifest to the entire world."

Antiochus VII Besieges Trypho at Dor. 10 * In the year one hundred and seventy-four, Antiochus invaded the land of his ancestors, and all the troops rallied to him, leaving Trypho with only a few supporters. 11 With Antiochus in full pursuit, Trypho fled to Dor, which borders the sea, 12 for he now comprehended how desperate his situation was inasmuch as his troops had deserted him. 13 Antiochus encamped opposite Dor with one hundred and twenty thousand infantry and eight thousand cavalry. 14 He surrounded the town while his ships intensified the blockade from the sea. He thus put pressure on the town from land and sea, and he permitted no one to leave or to enter it.

Rome Issues an Edict in Favor of the Jews. 15 In the meantime, Numenius and his companions arrived from Rome with letters such as this addressed to the various kings and nations:[p]

16 * "Lucius, the consul of the Romans, sends greetings to King Ptolemy.[q] 17 Envoys from the Jews, our friends and allies, have come to us to renew our original treaty of friendship and alliance. They were sent by Simon the high priest and the Jewish people, 18 and they brought with them a gold shield weighing one thousand minas.[r] 19 Therefore, we have decided to write to various kings and countries with the edict that they are not to seek to harm them or to wage war against them or their cities or their country, and that they are not to enter into an alliance with those who war against them. 20 We have decided to accept the shield from them. 21 Therefore, if any rebels have fled to you from their country, you are to hand them over to Simon the high priest so that he may punish them according to their law."

22 The consul sent the same message to King Demetrius, to Attalus,* Ariarthes, and Arsaces, 23 and to the following countries: Sampsames, Sparta, Delos, Myndos, Sicyon, Caria, Samos, Pamphylia, Lycia, Halicarnassus, Rhodes, Phaselis, Cos, Side, Aradus, Gortyna, Cnidus, Cyprus, and Cyrene. 24 A copy of the letter was also sent to Simon the high priest.

Antiochus Gives Simon an Ultimatum. 25 King Antiochus besieged Dor for a second time, continuously assaulting it with his troops and the siege-machines he had constructed. He blockaded Trypho, preventing any movement either into or out of the town. 26 Simon sent to Antiochus two thousand picked men to support him together with silver and gold and a great amount of military equipment. 27 However, Antiochus refused to accept his aid. Instead, he broke all the agreements he had previously drawn up with Simon and became estranged from him.

28 Antiochus sent Athenobius, one of his Friends, to confer with Simon and say: "You are occupying Joppa and Gazara and the citadel in Jerusalem, cities that are part of my kingdom. 29 You have laid waste their territories, done immense damage to the country, and seized control of many places in my kingdom. 30 Therefore, either hand over the cities you have seized and relinquish the tribute money you have exacted from the places you have conquered beyond the frontier of Judea, 31 or else pay me five hundred talents of silver for the devastation you have caused and another five hundred talents to compensate for the tribute money of the cities. If you refuse to do this, we will come and make war on you."

p 1 Mac 8:17; 12:16; 14:22-24.—q 2 Mac 1:1.—r 1 Mac 14:24.

15:10-11 We are in 138 B.C. *Dor* is a fortified port city on the Mediterranean in the vicinity of Mount Carmel. It lost its importance when Herod the Great built the city of Caesarea eight miles to its south.

15:16-21 This letter brings the reader back (1 Mac 14:24). The circular is concerned with all the countries where there is a large Jewish community. This indicates that at the middle of the second century B.C. there were many Jews residing outside Palestine. *Lucius:* perhaps Lucius Caecilius Metellus, consul in 142 B.C. or Lucius Calpurnius Piso, consul in 140–139 B.C. *Ptolemy* VII Physcon reigned 145–116 B.C.

15:22 *Attalus:* Attalus II of Pergamum, who reigned 159–138 B.C. *Ariarthes:* Ariarthes V of Cappadocia, who reigned 162–130 B.C. *Arsaces:* see note on 14:2. *Delos* and the other localities were free states in Greece, the Greek isles, and Asia Minor. *Cyrene:* capital of Libya.

32 So Athenobius, the king's Friend, came to Jerusalem and was astounded upon observing the magnificence of Simon's court, the gold and silver vessels on his sideboard, and the rich display of his wealth.[s] When he delivered the king's message to him, 33 Simon said to him in reply:

"We have neither taken foreign land nor seized possession of the property of others. We have merely reclaimed our ancestral heritage that for a period of time had been unjustly seized by our enemies.[t] 34 Now that we have the opportunity, we fully intend to maintain possession of the heritage of our ancestors. 35 As regards Joppa and Gazara, which you demand, these towns were causing great damage among our people and in our land. However, we are willing to pay you one hundred talents for these cities."

36 Athenobius offered no response, but he returned to the king filled with wrath. When he reported to him what Simon had said and described the splendor of Simon and of everything he had seen, the king was enraged.

The Syrian Army Invades Judea.* 37 Meanwhile Trypho boarded a ship and escaped to Orthosia. 38 Then the king appointed Cendebeus as commander-in-chief of the coastal region and gave him infantry and cavalry forces. 39 He ordered him to deploy his troops against Judea, to rebuild Kedron* and fortify its gates, and to make war on the Jewish people while the king himself continued his pursuit of Trypho. 40 When Cendebeus arrived in Jamnia, he began to harass the people and to invade Judea, taking prisoners and slaying them. 41 He rebuilt Kedron and stationed cavalry and infantry there so that they could go forth and patrol the roads of Judea, as the king had ordered.

CHAPTER 16

Simon's Sons Repulse the Invader. 1 John then went up from Gazara and reported to Simon his father what Cendebeus was doing. 2 Simon summoned his two oldest sons, Judas and John, and said to them, "My brothers and I and my father's house have fought the battles of Israel from our youth until today, and on many occasions we were successful in saving Israel. 3 Now I am old, but by the mercy of Heaven you have achieved maturity. Take my place and my brother's, and go out and fight for our nation. And may the help of Heaven be with you."

4 John then selected twenty thousand of the country's infantry and cavalry, and they marched against Cendebeus. After spending the night at Modein, 5 they marched into the plain early in the morning, where a large force of infantry and cavalry was waiting to attack them, with a stream lying between the two armies. 6 John and his troops lined up in position facing them. When he realized that his soldiers were afraid to cross the stream, John himself crossed over first. On seeing this, his men followed him across. 7 Then he divided his army into two sections, with the cavalry centered between them, for the cavalry of the enemy were very numerous. 8 They sounded the trumpets, and Cendebeus and his army were put to flight. Many of them fell wounded, and the rest fled to the refuge in the stronghold. 9 Judas, the brother of John, fell wounded, but John pursued them until Cendebeus reached Kedron, which he had rebuilt. 10 When some of the enemy fled to the towers on the plain of Azotus, John set fire to these towers, and about two thousand of the enemy perished. He then returned safely to Judea.

Simon Assassinated by His Son-in-Law. 11 Ptolemy,* the son of Abubus, had been appointed governor of the plain of Jericho, and he possessed a great amount of silver and gold, 12 for he was the son-in-law of the high priest. 13 However, he became ambitious, determining to gain control of the country, and he therefore made treacherous plans to do away with Simon and his sons.

14 Simon, who was inspecting the towns of the country and attending to their needs, went down to Jericho with his sons Mattathias and Judas in the year one hundred and seventy-seven, in the eleventh month, which is the month of Shebat.* 15 The son of Abubus received them treacherously

s 1 Ki 10:4-5.—t Ex 23:30-31.

15:37-41 Upon Trypho's death, the king concerns himself with imposing his power. In 138 B.C., the war breaks out anew. *Orthosia:* a port between Tripoli and the Eleutherus River.

15:39 *Kedron:* a place southeast of Jamnia opposite the fortress of Gazara held by John Hyrcanus.

16:11 Concerning this *Ptolemy*, nothing is known except what is referred to him in this episode. The security of borders was very important. Simon entrusts the western borders to his son John and the eastern ones to his brother-in-law Ptolemy.

16:14 In February 134 B.C., *Shebat*, a name of Akkadian origin that was introduced into Jewish terminology after the Babylonian Exile, designated the eleventh month of the year.

at the small fortress called Dok,* which he had built. He entertained them at a sumptuous banquet, while his men were concealed in nearby hiding places. [16]When Simon and his sons were drunk, Ptolemy and his men rose up and seized their weapons. Rushing against Simon in the banquet hall, they killed him and his two sons and some of his servants. [17]By this act of vicious treachery he returned evil for good.

[18]Then Ptolemy wrote a report about his deed and forwarded it to the king, asking that troops be sent to aid him and that the country and its towns be placed under his rule. [19]He sent some troops to Gazara to do away with John, and he wrote letters to his military commanders inviting them to come to him so that he might reward them with silver, gold, and gifts. [20]He also sent other troops to seize control of Jerusalem and the temple mount. [21]However, someone ran ahead and reported to John at Gazara that his father and his brothers had been murdered and that Ptolemy was sending men to kill him too. [22]On hearing this, John was greatly shocked. When the men came to kill him, he had them arrested and put to death, for he had been forewarned of their mission to destroy him.

[23]The rest of the history of John* and his wars and the brave deeds that he performed, the walls he built, and the rest of his achievements [24]are recorded in the annals* of his high priesthood from the time when he succeeded his father as high priest.[u]

u 1 Mac 9:22.

16:15 *Dok* signifies in Aramaic a high place that lends itself to observation. It was three miles northwest of Jericho.

16:23 *John*, surnamed Hyrcanus, was high priest from 134–104 B.C. The Hasmonean dynasty was supplanted by Herod in 31 B.C. This verse and the succeeding one indicate that 1 Maccabees was completed only after his death.

16:24 The *annals* have been lost. The Book concludes in a similar fashion to the accounts of the kings of Israel (1 Ki 11:41; 2 Ki 10:34; 12:19; 20:20, etc.).

THE SECOND BOOK OF MACCABEES

Heroes of Faith

The Second Book of Maccabees is not the sequel to or the complement of the First. It deals with events that took place between 175–161 B.C., at the time of the great persecution.

We are at the beginning of the Jewish resistance, which the First Book of Maccabees presents in its entirety.

The second book was actually written before the first and does not depend on it in any way. It is differentiated from the latter above all by its style and religious sentiment and also by its recital of the facts. Its author seems to be a Jew of Alexandria who is writing, a little after 124 B.C., in Greek. He states that he is summarizing the much larger work of another Jew from the colony of Cyrene (North Africa), a certain Jason, about whom nothing is known.

The work is artfully composed. Each of its two principal parts (4:1—10:8 and 10:9—15:36) follows the same plan: the account of the battles and the testimony of the martyrs always conclude with a victory whose memorial must be celebrated every year. We are dealing with a book about history but also a sort of "golden legend" of the martyrs, victims of the persecution of Antiochus IV Epiphanes.

In effect, the author turns into a preacher and wishes to capture the imagination and sensitivity of the reader. He exalts the heroism of the Jews, exaggerates the cruelty of their enemies, whose forces and losses he inflates, realistically evokes the supplications, and sets about describing the heavenly manifestations that intervene to upset the events.

Behind this taste for the pathetic and the marvelous, which was dear to readers of that era, lies a very real concern for historical truth; but the author is more concerned with religion than with politics. His purpose is one of edifying his Alexandrian compatriots; he invites them to remain faithful to the temple of Jerusalem and to celebrate the Feast of the Dedication.

In the story that unfolds, this passionate believer sees God at work to chastise the conduct of human beings: evildoers and persecutors are always punished for their crimes. As for the righteous, the angels protect them and the saints intercede for them; if they suffer unto martyrdom, it is because they are certain that one day they will rise again and obtain a reward in another life. Up to that time, the Jewish faith had not yet reached such a point in the mystery of retribution and of the afterlife.

These teachings constitute a considerable enrichment for the theology of the Old Testament.

Taken up and developed in the New Testament, they have ensured the success of the Second Book of Maccabees in Christian circles.

The Second Book of Maccabees may be divided as follows:

I: Letters to the Jews in Egypt (1:1—2:32)
II: Heliodorus's Attempt to Profane the Temple (3:1-40)
III: Liberation of the Temple (4:1—10:8)
IV: The Acquisition of Religious Freedom (10:9—15:36)
V: Author's Epilogue (15:37-39)

I: LETTERS TO THE JEWS IN EGYPT*

CHAPTER 1

A: The First Letter (124 B.C.)*

1 The Jews in Jerusalem and those in the
land of Judea send greetings to their Jewish
kindred in Egypt and extend to them their
best wishes for peace. 2 May God grant you
prosperity and continue to remember his
covenant with Abraham, Isaac, and Jacob,
his faithful servants.[a] 3 May he give to all of
you a desire to worship him and to do his
will with a courageous heart and a well disposed spirit.[b] 4 May he open your mind to
his law and his commandments and bring
peace to your lives. 5 May he hear your
prayers and be propitious to you, and never
forsake you in a time of adversity. 6 Even at
this very moment we are offering prayers
for you here.
7 In the reign of Demetrius, in the year one
hundred and sixty-nine, we Jews wrote to
you during the period of persecution and
crisis that befell us during those years after
Jason and his followers had revolted against
the holy land and the kingdom,[c] 8 setting fire
to the temple gate and shedding innocent
blood. When we prayed to the Lord, our
prayer was heard. Hence, we presented sacrifices and offerings of grain, and we lit the
lamps and set out the loaves.[d] 9 We now
exhort you to observe the Feast of Booths in
the month of Chislev. 10 Dated in the year one
hundred and eighty-eight.

B: The Second Letter (164 B.C.)*

Tragic End of the Persecutor. The people of Jerusalem and Judea, the senate, and Judas send greetings and the wish for good health to Aristobulus,* the tutor to King Ptolemy

a Lev 26:42; Ps 106:45; Ezek 16:60.—b 1 Chr 28:9.—c 2 Mac 4:7-20.—d 1 Mac 4:38.

1:1—2:32 In the second century B.C., numerous Jews resided in Egypt where they formed characteristic communities. Greatly attached to Judaism, they maintained relations with Jerusalem. Two letters invite them to celebrate the Feast of the Dedication of the temple in Jerusalem. This is the reason why these letters are found at the beginning of the Second Book of Maccabees, wholly composed to exalt the temple and make the meaning of this feast comprehensible.

1:1-10a In 124 B.C., the Jews in Egypt were harassed by the authorities. The community of Jerusalem urged them to remain faithful, reminding them of the difficulties that they had experienced: trials at the time of Demetrius II (king of Syria, 145–139 B.C. and 129–125 B.C.) in 143 B.C. and apostasy of the high priest and persecutions between 174–164 B.C. From that time, the Feast of the Dedication (also called "Feast of Booths of December" because of its similarity with the Feast of Booths of October) was instituted by the leader of the Jewish resistance precisely when he had purified the temple of Jerusalem.

1:10b—2:18 This much longer letter was in reality to precede the first one because it was written in 164 B.C., a little before the temple was purified. It is addressed to Aristobulus, a Jew of Alexandria renowned for his commentary on the first five Books of the Bible and for his defense of Judaism. The document is complex and intermingles in the history of the time the legend that arose almost contemporaneously with the event. The author of the Second Book of Maccabees had no reason to exclude this amplification, which corresponded with the taste of his readers, who loved to find allegories either in history or in legend. He wished above all to invite them to celebrate the Feast of the Dedication of the year 164 B.C. (2 Mac 10:1-8; 1 Mac 4:36-59).

1:10 *Aristobulus:* a Jewish so-called philosopher of Alexandria, who was said to be a tutor of Ptolemy VI Philometor (180–145 B.C.) because he dedicated a book to the king showing that the Law and the Prophets were the source of the Greeks' wisdom and philosophy. *King Ptolemy:* Ptolemy VI Philometor, who is mentioned in 1 Mac 1:18; 10:51-59.

and a member of the family of anointed
priests,[e] and to the Jews in Egypt. 11 Since we
have been rescued by God from grave dan-
gers, we offer him our profuse thanks for
championing our cause against the king,*
12 [f]for it was he himself who drove out those
who fought against the holy city.

13 When their leader marched into Persia
with a force that was apparently invincible,
they were decimated in the temple of the
goddess Nanea* as the result of a deceitful
scheme engineered by the priests of Nanea.
14 *On the pretext of intending to marry the
goddess, Antiochus had come to the place
together with his Friends, with the purpose
of securing its many treasures as a dowry.
15 When the priests of Nanea had placed the
treasures on display, Antiochus with a few
attendants arrived at the temple precincts.
As soon as he entered the temple, the priests
locked him inside. 16 After opening a secret
trap door in the ceiling, they hurled stones at
the leader and his companions and struck
them down. Then they dismembered their
bodies and cut off their heads, throwing
them to the people outside.

17 Blessed in all respects be our God who
has delivered the godless to death.

The Legend of the Sacred Fire.* 18 We shall be
celebrating the purification of the temple on
the twenty-fifth day of the month Chislev,
and thus we thought it proper to give you
some information so that you too may cele-
brate the Feast of Booths and the feast of the
fire* that appeared when Nehemiah offered
sacrifices after he had rebuilt the temple and
the altar.

19 For when our ancestors were being led
in exile to Persia, the devout priests of that
period took some of the fire from the altar
and hid it secretly in the hollow of a dry cis-
tern, taking the necessary precautions to
ensure that the place of concealment was
unknown to anyone. 20 After many years
had elapsed, in God's good time Nehemiah,
having been commissioned by the king of
Persia, sent the descendants of the priests
who had hidden the fire to search for it.

21 When they reported to us that they had
not found fire but only a thick liquid,
Nehemiah ordered them to draw some out
and bring it to him. After the materials for
the sacrifice had been prepared, Nehemiah
instructed the priests to sprinkle the liquid
on the wood and what lay on it. 22 When this
had been done, and after the sun that had
been clouded over for a while began to
shine, a great fire blazed up to the astonish-
ment of everyone. 23 While the sacrifice was
being burned, the priests and all present
offered prayer—Jonathan leading, and the
rest responding, led by Nehemiah.

24 The prayer took the following form:
"Lord, Lord God, Creator of all things, awe-
inspiring and mighty, just and merciful, the
only true king and benefactor, 25 you alone
are gracious, just, almighty, and eternal, the
deliverer of Israel from every evil, the one
who designated our ancestors as your cho-
sen ones and consecrated them.[g] 26 Accept
this sacrifice on behalf of all your people
Israel, and protect and sanctify your her-
itage. 27 Gather together our dispersed peo-
ple, set free those who have been enslaved
by the Gentiles, look with favor on those
who are despised and detested, and let the
Gentiles realize that you are our God.[h]
28 Punish those who oppress us and treat us
with arrogance. 29 Plant your people in your
holy place, as Moses promised."[i]

30 Then the priests chanted hymns.
31 After the sacrifice had been consumed,
Nehemiah ordered that the remaining liq-
uid be poured upon large stones. 32 When
this was done, a flame blazed up, but its
light faded when confronted by the blazing
light from the altar. 33 When this occurrence
became known, it was reported to the king

e Lev 4:3; 16:32.—f 12-17: 1 Mac 6:1-13.—g Isa 45:21; Mt 19:17.—h Ps 106:47; Jn 7:35; Jas 1:1; 1 Pet 1:1.—i 2 Mac 2:18; Deut 30:3ff.

1:11f *The king:* Antiochus IV Epiphanes of Syria, the persecutor of the Jews. He perished in 164 B.C. while leading a Persian invasion.

1:13 *Nanea:* an oriental goddess who is similar to the Greek goddess Artemis.

1:14-17 The death of Antiochus IV is depicted in a different way in 2 Mac 9:1-29 and in still another way in 1 Mac 6:1-16. The writer of this letter seems to have written it immediately after hearing a rumor of the king's death—hence in 164 B.C.

1:18-36 The thick water that becomes fire is none other than unrefined petroleum (*naphtha,* v. 36). The Persians were familiar with it and used it to celebrate fire, which played a great part in their worship. Inspired by the reminders of the Exodus, this legendary anecdote wished to attest that the worship rendered to God in the temple of Jerusalem was to remain the legitimate liturgy established by Moses and by Solomon because it would allow the sacred fire to be miraculously kept burning (Lev 6:12-13).

1:18 *The feast of the fire:* fire and light are connected with the Feast of Hanukkah, which is celebrated with a nine-branched candlestick. There is a Talmudic tradition that a small amount of oil burned miraculously for a long time until new oil could be consecrated. *Nehemiah:* in reality, it was not Nehemiah who rebuilt the altar and the temple but Zerubbabel (see Ezr 3:2; 5:2); but the importance of Nehemiah's work was so great that tradition attributed to him everything that took place after the return of the first exiles.

of the Persians that, in the very place where
the exiled priests had hidden the fire, a liq-
uid had appeared that Nehemiah and his
companions had used to burn the sacrificial
offerings. [34]After the king had verified this
fact, he had the place enclosed and he
declared it to be sacred* [35]and he distrib-
uted a goodly portion of the revenues he
received from that place to the people he
appointed as custodians. [36]Nehemiah and
his companions called the liquid "neph-
thar," which means purification, but it is
more commonly called "naphtha."*

CHAPTER 2

Jeremiah Hides the Sacred Objects for Worship.* [1]According to the official records,
Jeremiah the prophet ordered those who
were being deported to take some of the fire
with them, in the way previously described.
[2]Then, after having given them the law, the
prophet cautioned them not to forget the
commandments of the Lord or to let their
thoughts be led astray by the sight of the
gold and silver statues and their ornamen-
tation.[j] [3]And with other similar admoni-
tions he urged them never to allow the law
to depart from their hearts.

[4][k]That same document also records that
the prophet, in obedience to a divine revela-
tion, issued orders that the tent and the Ark
should accompany him, and that he went
off to the mountain* that Moses had
ascended to view God's inheritance. [5]Upon
arriving there, Jeremiah found a cave-
dwelling where he placed the tent, the Ark,
and the altar of incense, after which he
blocked off the entrance. [6]Some of his com-
panions came up later with the intention of
marking out the path, but they were unable
to find it. [7]When Jeremiah learned of this,
he rebuked them. "This place shall remain
unknown," he declared, "until God gathers
his people together again and shows them
his mercy. [8]Then the Lord will once again
disclose these things, and the glory* of the
Lord will appear together with the cloud, as
it was revealed in the time of Moses and
when Solomon prayed that the place might
be solemnly consecrated."[l]

[9]It is further related how Solomon in his
wisdom offered a sacrifice to mark the ded-
ication and completion of the temple. [10]Just
as Moses had prayed to the Lord and fire
had come down from heaven and con-
sumed the sacrificial offerings, so also did
Solomon pray, and the fire came down and
consumed the burnt offerings.[m] [11]Moses
had said, "The sin offering was consumed in
the fire because it had not been eaten."[n]
[12]Solomon celebrated the feast in the same
way for a period of eight days.

Judas Reconstructs the Library of Israel. [13]In
addition to these things, it is also set forth in
the records and in the memoirs of
Nehemiah* how he founded a library to
house the chronicles of the kings, the writ-
ings of the prophets and David, and the
letters of the kings in regard to sacred offer-
ings. [14]Similarly, Judas* has also collected
for us all of the books that had been scat-
tered during the recent war, and these are
now in our possession.[o] [15]If you ever have
need of any of them, send messengers to
bring them to you.

All the Jews Celebrate the Dedication.
[16]Since we are about to celebrate the feast
of the purification of the temple, we are
writing to you with the request that you also
observe this feast.[p] [17]God has saved his
entire people and has restored to all of us
our heritage, the kingdom, the priesthood,
and the consecration, [18]as he promised
through the law. We have complete trust
that he will soon have mercy on us and
gather us together from everywhere under
heaven into his holy place, for he has res-
cued us from great evils and has purified
that place.[q]

j Bar 6:3-72.—k 4f: Deut 32:49; 34:1; Rev 11:19.—l Ex 24:16; 1 Ki 8:11.—m Lev 9:23f; 2 Chr 7:1.—n Lev 10:16-20.—o 1 Mac 1:57.—p 1 Ki 8:65f.—q Deut 30:3ff.

1:34 *Place enclosed . . . sacred:* places where miracles occurred were *enclosed* as *sacred.* The Persians regarded fire as holy.

1:36 The Greek word for petroleum (*naphtha*) is likened to a Semitic word that means "loosened" (probably *nephthar*).

2:1-12 This legend about Jeremiah has very little connection with the prophet known for his diatribes against those who placed their hopes in the temple instead of changing their ways. But tradition attributed to him various letters and recommendations for the time of the captivity. The legend is retold here to show why the temple was the legitimate place of worship even though it lacked the sacred tent, Ark, and altar.

2:4 *The mountain:* Nebo (see Deut 34:1).

2:8 The *glory* and the *cloud* symbolize the direct presence of God (Ex 16:10; Mk 9:2-8). The *place* is the temple of Jerusalem.

2:13 *Memoirs of Nehemiah:* these are not contained in the biblical Book of Nehemiah and are regarded as a lost apocryphal work. Although there is no record that Nehemiah *founded a library,* the Pentateuch was canonized in his time, and he may have collected the Books of Kings.

2:14 *Judas* Maccabeus may have *collected . . . all of the books* remaining after the destruction during the reign of Antiochus IV (see 1 Mac 1:56f).

C: Author's Preface*

19 This is the story dealing with Judas
Maccabeus and his brothers,[r] the purifica-
tion of the great temple, and the dedication
of the altar, 20 as well as the wars against
Antiochus Epiphanes* and his son Eupator,
21 and the heavenly apparitions* that were
seen by those who showed their heroism in
fighting bravely for the cause of Judaism.
Despite being severely outnumbered, they
seized the entire land and put to flight the
barbarian hordes, 22 regaining possession of
the temple renowned throughout the world
and liberating the city and reestablishing the
laws that were in danger of being abolished,
as the Lord bestowed his mercy and favor on
them. 23 All this, which has been set forth in
detail by Jason of Cyrene[s] in five volumes,
we shall attempt to condense into a single
book.*

24 Considering the flood of statistics and
the difficulty likely to be encountered by
those who begin to wade through the
immense amount of material involved in
these historical narratives, 25 we have aimed
to please those who desire easy reading, to
make it uncomplicated for those who wish to
commit facts to memory, and to turn out a
product that will be of profit to all. 26 For
those of us who have undertaken the labor of
such abridging, the task has been far from
easy but in truth one that involves sweat and
sleepless nights, 27 as would also be true of
someone who would find it no simple affair
to prepare a banquet that his guests will find
completely satisfying.[t] Nevertheless, in our
desire to win the gratitude of many, we will
gladly endure the drudgery involved in this
project, 28 leaving the responsibility as
regards the accuracy of details to the origi-
nal author and confining our efforts to pro-
ducing a summary outline.

29 Just as the architect of a new house must
be concerned with the construction as a
whole, while the one who undertakes its
painting and decoration has to consider only
what is needed for its adornment, so, I
believe, it is the case with us. 30 It is the duty
of the original historian to examine the
entire subject at hand and judge the accura-
cy of the details. 31 The person who makes an
adaptation must have the freedom to aim at
conciseness of expression and to reject any
exhaustive treatment of the subject matter.
32 Therefore, without any further comment,
we shall here begin our narrative, inasmuch
as it would be absurd to offer a lengthy pref-
ace to the history and cut short the history
itself.

II: HELIODORUS'S ATTEMPT TO PROFANE THE TEMPLE*

CHAPTER 3

Heliodorus Arrives in Jerusalem. 1 [u] While the
holy city enjoyed total peace and the laws
were strictly observed because of the piety of
the high priest Onias* and his abhorrence of
wickedness, 2 the kings themselves honored
the holy place and enhanced the glory of the
temple with the most magnificent gifts,
3 even to the extent that Seleucus,* the king
of Asia, defrayed from his own revenues all
the expenses required for sacrificial services.
4 However, a man named Simon,[v] of the
priestly line of Bilgah, who had been
appointed administrator of the temple,
became involved in a dispute with the high
priest about the regulation of the city mar-
ket. 5 When he realized that he could not get
the better of Onias, he went to Apollonius of
Tarsus, who at that time was the governor of
Coelesyria and Phoenicia, 6 and reported to
him that the treasury in Jerusalem was so
overflowing with untold riches that the total
amount of the wealth was beyond reckoning

r 1 Mac 2:2-5.—s 1 Mac 15:23; Acts 2:10.—t Sir 32:1-3.—u 1ff: 2 Mac 15:12.—v 2 Mac 4:23.

2:19-32 This surprising preface demonstrates quite well to what extent the word of God yields to the personality of the inspired authors. From the vast history at his disposal, the author records above all what gravitates around two events: the reestablishment of the cult by Judas Maccabeus and the victory over Nicanor; these two events have given rise to a feast.

2:20 *Wars against Antiochus Epiphanes:* see 2 Mac 4:7—10:9; *his son Eupator:* see 2 Mac 10:10—13:26.

2:21 *Apparitions:* authentic divine manifestations in contrast to Antiochus's vain title of "god manifest" (*Epiphanes*). *Judaism:* first known usage of this term, which sums up in itself all that characterized the Jews as a nation and as a religion (see 2 Mac 8:1; 14:38) and is here used in contrast with Hellenism (see 2 Mac 4:13).

2:23 Cyrene possessed a flourishing Jewish colony that was, however, under the influence of the more important colony at Alexandria. *Jason of Cyrene* is not mentioned in any ancient sources, and no work of his is extant. The author of Second Maccabees may have had an actual source or he may have used the literary tradition of antiquity of resting one's work on the authority of a purported source.

3:1-40 This legendary episode about Heliodorus is set forth to stress the inviolability of the temple of Jerusalem. It was only because of the people's sins that God later allowed it to incur profanation (see 2 Mac 5:17f).

3:1 *The high priest Onias:* Onias III, who was high priest from 196–175 B.C. and died in 171 B.C. Sirach 50:1-21 has high praise for his father Simon.

3:3 *Seleucus:* Seleucus IV Philopator (187–175 B.C.).

and completely out of proportion to the cost
of the sacrifices, and that it would be possi-
ble to have it all brought under the control of
the king.

Mission of Heliodorus. [7]When Apollonius
conferred with the king, he told him about
the riches that had been reported to him.
The king appointed Heliodorus, his chief
minister, and sent him forth with orders to
effect the confiscation of the reported
wealth. [8]Heliodorus immediately set forth,
ostensibly to make a tour of inspection of the
cities of Coelesyria and Phoenicia, but in
actuality to carry out the king's command.
[9]When he arrived in Jerusalem and had
been cordially received by the high priest of
the city, he told him about the information
that had been reported, disclosed the true
purpose of his visit, and asked if the allega-
tions were accurate.

[10]The high priest explained that some of
the money was set aside for the care of wid-
ows and orphans,[w] [11]and that the rest
belonged to Hyrcanus, the son of Tobias,* a
man who held a very prominent position. In
contrast to what the impious Simon had
alleged, the total sum amounted to four hun-
dred talents of silver and two hundred tal-
ents of gold.

[12]He further added that it would be com-
pletely out of the question to inflict injustice
upon those who had placed their trust in the
sanctity of the place and in the holiness and
inviolability of a temple venerated through-
out the entire world. [13]However, because of
the orders he had received from the king,
Heliodorus stated that he had no other
choice but to confiscate the money for the
royal treasury. [14]And so, on the day he had
designated for the purpose, he went in to
draw up an inventory of the funds.

Distress of the Faithful. There was immense
distress throughout the city. [15]The priests
prostrated themselves in their priestly vest-
ments before the altar and prayed to him in
heaven who had issued the law governing
deposits* to keep those funds intact for those
who had deposited them. [16]The appearance
of the high priest pierced the heart of every
beholder, for his expression and his changed
color disclosed the anguish of his soul.
[17]Terror and bodily trembling had over-
whelmed him, clearly indicating to those
who beheld him the pain lodged in his heart.

[18]People rushed forth from their houses in
crowds to make a public supplication
because of the profanation that was threat-
ening the holy place. [19]Women thronged the
streets girded with sackcloth under their
breasts. Maidens who had been secluded
indoors came running, some to the gates,
others to the walls, while still others leaned
out of windows, [20]all of them raising their
hands to heaven in supplication. [21]It was a
pitiful sight to observe the crowd lying pros-
trate and the agony of the high priest in his
great anguish.

A Heavenly Knight Stops Heliodorus. [22]While
the people were imploring the Lord
Almighty to allow the deposits to remain
safe and secure for those who had deposited
them in trust, [23]Heliodorus proceeded with
his appointed task. [24]But just as he arrived
with his bodyguards at the treasury, the
Lord of spirits and of all power caused so
great a manifestation that all those who had
been so bold as to accompany Heliodorus
became panic-stricken at the power of God
and collapsed in terror.

[25]For there appeared to them a horse
magnificently caparisoned, mounted by a
rider of terrifying mien. Charging furiously,
the horse attacked Heliodorus with its front
hooves. The rider was seen to be accoutred
entirely in golden armor. [26]Then two young
men, remarkably strong, strikingly beauti-
ful, and magnificently attired, also appeared
before him. Taking their stand on either side
of him, they flogged him unremittingly,
inflicting numerous blows on him.

[27]Suddenly he fell to the ground, en-
veloped in a great darkness. His men picked
him up and laid him on a stretcher. [28]This
man, who but a moment previously had
entered the treasury with a great retinue
and his entire bodyguard, now was carried
away utterly helpless, and those under his
command openly acknowledged the sover-
eign power of God.

[29]While he lay prostrate, without the
power of speech because of the divine inter-
vention and bereft of any hope of deliver-
ance, [30]the Jews praised the Lord for his
miraculous glorification of his holy place.
And the temple, which a short time before

w Deut 14:29.

3:11 *Hyrcanus, the son of Tobias:* a member of the Tobiad family of the Transjordan (Neh 2:10; 6:17ff; 13:4-8). His father was Joseph, whose mother was the sister of the high priest Onias II.

3:15 *Law governing deposits:* see Ex 22:7-15.

had been filled with terror and commotion,
was now overflowing with joy and gladness at
the manifestation of the Lord Almighty.

[31] Some of the companions of Heliodorus
quickly pleaded with Onias to entreat the
Most High to spare the life of the man who
was now breathing his last. [32] Fearful that
the king might suspect that Heliodorus had
met with foul play at the hands of the Jews,
the high priest offered a sacrifice for the
man's recovery. [33] While the high priest was
making a sacrifice of expiation, the same
young men again appeared to Heliodorus,
clad in the identical apparel, and stood
before him. "Be very grateful to the high
priest Onias," they said to him, "since it is
for his sake that the Lord has spared your
life. [34] Since you have been scourged by
Heaven, proclaim to all people the majestic
power of God." When they had said this,
they vanished.

The Gentile General Is Converted. [35] After
Heliodorus had offered a sacrifice to the
Lord and made very solemn vows to the
Lord who had spared his life, he took his
leave of Onias and marched off with his sol-
diers to return to the king. [36] He bore witness
to everyone about the miracles of the
supreme God that he had witnessed with his
own eyes.

[37] When the king asked Heliodorus what
sort of man would be suitable to send to
Jerusalem on some future occasion, he
replied: [38] "If you have an enemy or some-
one who has been a traitor to your govern-
ment, send him there. You will get him back
soundly flogged, if indeed he manages to
survive at all. Without question, there is
some peculiarly divine power about the
place. [39] He who has his dwelling in heaven
watches over that place himself and pro-
tects it, and he strikes down and destroys
those who come to do it harm." [40] This was
the outcome of the episode of Heliodorus
and the preservation of the treasury.

III: LIBERATION OF THE TEMPLE

A: Persecution of Antiochus IV and Success of Hellenism

CHAPTER 4

**The Superintendent of the Temple Disturbs the
Public Order.** [1] *The aforementioned Simon,
who had served as an informer about the
money against his country, began to make
slanderous accusations against Onias,
claiming that it was he who had incited
Heliodorus and thus had instigated these
wretched disorders. [2] He even had the effron-
tery to accuse of conspiracy against the gov-
ernment this man who was a benefactor of
the city, the protector of his compatriots, and
a zealous defender of the laws. [3] When
Simon's hostility reached such proportions
that murders were actually committed by
one of his agents, [4] Onias realized how dan-
gerous the situation had become and that
Apollonius, the son of Menestheus, the gov-
ernor of Coelesyria and Phoenicia, was
encouraging Simon in his evil ways.
[5] Therefore, he appealed to the king, not to
accuse his compatriots but rather as one
who had at heart the best interests, both
public and private, of all the people. [6] He saw
that, unless the king intervened, public order
could not exist and that Simon would persist
in his madness.

Hellenism in Jerusalem.* [7] When Seleucus*
died and Antiochus, who was called
Epiphanes, succeeded him on the throne,
Jason, the brother of Onias, obtained the
high priesthood by corrupt means.[x] [8] *In a
petition he promised the king three hundred
and sixty talents of silver, with eighty talents
from another source of revenue. [9] In addi-
tion, he committed himself to a payment of
a further one hundred and fifty talents if he
was given the authority to establish a gym-

x 2 Mac 1:7; 1 Mac 1:10.

4:1-16 Profiting from the rise of Hellenism and political instability, several plotters seek to further their careers.

4:7-22 Joshua, who writes his name according to the Greek, *Jason,* gathers around him the partisans of Hellenism and encourages and favors pagan ways, in particular, games with nude athletes. The author describes some aspects of these new ways of life: the gymnasium, center of physical as well as cultural education, ensures the athletic and military formation of youth; those who are most outstanding also wear the *Greek hat,* the wide-brimmed hat of Hermes, the pagan god of athletic events.

4:7 *Seleucus* IV Philopator was killed in 175 B.C. by his minister Heliodorus, the same person who had been sent to confiscate the goods of the temple. *Antiochus* IV, Seleucus's younger brother, heard of it while he was in Athens and returned to his country. With the aid of the Romans, he eliminated Heliodorus and took control of the government, trampling on the rights of his brother Demetrius, who was then being held at Rome as a hostage in the wake of the Battle of Magnesia in which Antiochus III the Great had been defeated by the Romans (see 1 Mac 7:1).

4:8-9 Jason promised an increased tribute; the usual amount seems to have been around 300 talents. He expected to recover the sum from the usual entries of his little administrative region (Judea) and from eventual taxes that he could impose once he became high priest. *Antiochians:* honorary citizens of Antioch, a Hellenistic city of the Seleucid Kingdom that had a corporation of such people who enjoyed political and commercial privileges.

nasium and a youth club to be affiliated with it, and to enroll the people of Jerusalem as Antiochians.[y]

[10] When the king gave his assent and Jason succeeded to the office, he immediately imposed the Greek way of life on his fellow Jews. [11] He set aside the royal concessions that had been granted to the Jews through the efforts of John—the father of that Eupolemus[z] who later was sent on an embassy to negotiate a treaty of friendship and alliance with the Romans—and, abolishing the institutions founded on the law, he introduced customs that ran contrary to it.*
[12] He quickly established a gymnasium*[a] at the very foot of the citadel itself, and he convinced the most noble of the young men to wear the Greek hat.

[13] As a result of the introduction of foreign customs, the craze for Hellenism became so intense because of the unrestricted wickedness of the ungodly bogus high priest* Jason
[14] that the priests no longer bothered to fulfill their duties at the altar. Disdaining the temple and neglecting the sacrifices, they would hasten to participate in the unlawful exercises as soon as they heard the signal for the discus-throwing. [15] They showed no respect for what their ancestors had regarded as honorable and placed the greatest value on what the Greeks honored above all else.
[16] *As a result, they ended up suffering great affliction, for the very people whose way of life they sought to emulate and whom they wished to imitate in every respect became their enemies and oppressors. [17] It is no light matter to violate the laws of God, as will become clear in due course.

[18] When the quinquennial games were being held at Tyre in the presence of the king, [19] the villainous Jason sent envoys chosen from among the Antiochian citizens from Jerusalem to bring there three hundred silver drachmas for the sacrifice to Hercules. However, those who were designated to carry the money considered it improper for this money to be used as a sacrifice, and they decided to expend it for some other purpose. [20] And so, the money intended by the sender to be used for the sacrifice to Hercules was in fact applied, at the suggestion of those who brought it, to the construction of triremes.*

[21] When Apollonius, the son of Menestheus, was sent to Egypt for the coronation of King Philometor,* Antiochus learned that Philometor had become hostile to his reign. Concerned about his own security, after arriving at Joppa he moved on to Jerusalem,
[22] where he was given a lavish welcome by Jason and the people of the city, who escorted him in with a torchlight procession and acclamations. After this, he led his army into Phoenicia.

Jason Supplanted by Menelaus. [23] Three years later,* Jason sent Menelaus, the brother of the previously mentioned Simon, to deliver money[b] to the king and to complete the negotiations on some important matters. [24] But when Menelaus was presented to the king, he flattered him with an air of authority and thereby secured the high priesthood for himself, outbidding Jason by three hundred talents of silver.* [25] He returned with the royal appointment, despite the fact that he possessed no qualification that made him worthy of the high priesthood. He had the temper of a cruel tyrant and the rage of a savage beast. [26] Then Jason, who had supplanted his own brother, was now himself supplanted by another man and driven out as a fugitive into the land of the Ammonites.

[27] Although Menelaus continued to hold the office of high priest, he failed to make any payments of the money he had promised to the king, despite the insistent demands for payment by Sostratus, the captain of the citadel, [28] who had the responsibility for the collection of revenues. As a result, both men were summoned to appear before the king. [29] Menelaus left his own brother Lysimachus as his deputy in the high priesthood, while Sostratus desig-

y 1 Mac 1:11-15.—z 1 Mac 8:17.—a 1 Mac 1:14.—b 2 Mac 4:8f.

4:11 Antiochus III had granted the Jews the right to govern themselves according to the law of Moses. Concerning Eupolemus's mission to Rome, see 1 Mac 8:17.

4:12 The *gymnasium* where the youth exercised in the nude was located in the Tyropoeon Valley to the east of the citadel—right next to the eastern side of the temple.

4:13 Jason is called a *bogus high priest* because he obtained the high priesthood by bribery and did not keep the Mosaic Law.

4:16f Forsaking the Torah only leads to disaster: see also 1 Ki 17:5-18; 2 Chr 36:11-21; Neh 9.

4:20 *Triremes:* vessels of war with three sections of oars.

4:21 *Philometor:* Ptolemy VI, in 172 B.C.

4:23 *Three years later:* not after the last event narrated (which represents an insertion) but three years after the naming of Jason as high priest. The *Simon* spoken of is the one who had provoked the intervention of Heliodorus to confiscate the treasury of the temple (see vv. 1, 4; 3:14).

4:24 Taking account of verse 8, the conclusion is that Menelaus obligated himself to send 740 talents.

nated Crates, the commander of the
Cypriots,* to act in his place.

Murder of the Saintly Onias.* 30 While these
events were taking place, the people of
Tarsus and Mallus rose in revolt because
their cities had been given as a present to
Antiochis, the king's concubine.* 31 There-
fore, the king hurriedly departed to resolve
the problem, leaving Andronicus, one of his
ministers, to act as his deputy. 32 Menelaus,
believing that he had been presented with a
favorable opportunity, stole some of the gold
vessels from the temple and gave them to
Andronicus. Some other vessels he had
already previously sold to Tyre and the
neighboring cities.

33 When Onias received irrefutable evi-
dence of these facts, he publicly denounced
him, after having first withdrawn to a place
of sanctuary at Daphne,* near Antioch.
34 Thereupon, Menelaus approached An-
dronicus privately and urged him to arrange
for the death of Onias. Andronicus came to
Onias and treacherously offered him sworn
pledges with right hands joined. Despite his
suspicions, Onias was persuaded to leave the
place of sanctuary,[c] whereupon Andronicus,
without any regard for justice, immediately
put him to death.

35 The unjust murder of this man resulted
in an outpouring of grief and outrage not
only among the Jews but among people from
many other nations as well. 36 When the king
returned from the region of Cilicia, the Jews
of the city protested to him about the inde-
fensible killing of Onias, and in this they were
joined by Greeks who shared their anger
about this criminal act.* 37 Antiochus was
deeply grieved and filled with pity, and he
wept as he recalled the prudence and exem-
plary conduct of the dead man. 38 Inflamed
with anger, he immediately stripped
Andronicus of his purple robe, tore off his
other garments, and then paraded him
throughout the city to that very place where
he had committed the outrageous deed
against Onias. At that spot he put the mur-
derer to death, and thus the Lord repaid him
with the punishment he deserved.

Disorders at Jerusalem. 39 Lysimachus, with
the connivance of Menelaus, had committed
many sacrilegious thefts in the city. When
this became common knowledge, and the
people heard that many gold vessels had
already been disposed of, they rose up in
protest against him. 40 When the crowds
became even more enraged and menacing,
Lysimachus armed about three thousand
men and launched an unjustified attack. The
troops were commanded by Auranus, a man
advanced in years and no less in folly.
41 When the people realized that Lysima-
chus was the instigator of this attack, some
picked up stones, others blocks of wood, still
others handfuls of ashes lying around, and
they flung them indiscriminately at
Lysimachus and his men. 42 As a result, they
wounded many of them, even killing a few,
and put all the rest to flight. The temple
plunderer himself they put to death near the
treasury.

Menelaus Maintains His Power. 43 Charges
were brought against Menelaus as a result of
this incident. 44 When the king came to Tyre,
three men sent by the senate pleaded their
case before him. 45 Menelaus, realizing that
the verdict would go against him, promised
Ptolemy,[d] the son of Dorymenes,* a sub-
stantial sum of money if he would win over
the king. 46 Ptolemy therefore took the king
aside into a colonnade, as though for a
breath of air, and persuaded him to change
his mind. 47 Menelaus, the cause of all the
trouble, the king acquitted of all the charges
against him. But he condemned to death
those unfortunate men who had brought
forward the accusations and who would
have been adjudged as innocent and set free
even if they had pleaded their case before
the Scythians.* 48 Therefore, those who had
pleaded the cause of the city, the people,
and the sacred vessels quickly incurred an
unjust punishment. 49 Some Tyrians were
actually so enraged by this crime that they
provided sumptuously for their funerals.
50 However, Menelaus, because of the greed
of those who held power, remained in office,
where he grew in wickedness and estab-

c 1 Ki 1:50; 2:28; 2 Ki 11:15.—d 2 Mac 8:8; 1 Mac 3:38.

4:29 The mercenaries who formed the garrison of Jerusalem were *Cypriots.*

4:30-38 This vile murder of 171 B.C. is an important date in the Jewish history of the second century.

4:30 The Seleucids gifted cities or provinces to members of their family as personal fiefs.

4:33 *Daphne:* located some five miles from Antioch, had a *place of sanctuary* dedicated to Apollo and Artemis.

4:36 In Antioch, from its very foundation, there existed a Jewish colony with special rights and privileges.

4:45 *Dorymenes:* fought for Ptolemy IV against Antiochus III. His son *Ptolemy* had been governor of Cyprus and deserted to Antiochus IV (see 2 Mac 10:12f).

4:47 *Scythians:* people who lived in present-day southern Russia and were known for their brutality.

lished himself as the chief plotter against his compatriots.

CHAPTER 5

Jason Dies Wretchedly in Exile. [1]About this time, Antiochus undertook his second expedition* against Egypt.[e] [2][f]It then happened that all over the city, for almost forty days, there were apparitions of horsemen clad in gold galloping through the air, companies fully armed with lances and drawn swords— [3]squadrons of cavalry in battle order, charges and counter-charges in this direction and that, with brandished shields, massed spears, and hurled javelins, and gold accoutrements and armor of all kinds glittering brightly. [4]Therefore, everyone prayed that these apparitions might prove to be a good omen.

[5]However, when a false rumor began to circulate that Antiochus had died, Jason* commandeered no fewer than a thousand men and launched a surprise attack on the city. When the defenders on the walls were driven back and the city was on the verge of being taken, Menelaus took refuge in the citadel. [6]Jason then embarked on a merciless slaughter of his compatriots, failing to comprehend that success against one's own kindred was the greatest of disasters, but rather imagining that he was winning trophies of victory over enemies, not over his own people. [7]However, he failed to seize control of the government. In the end, his treachery only resulted in disgrace for him, and once again he took refuge in the country of the Ammonites.

[8]At length Jason came to a miserable end. After being accused before Aretas,* the ruler of the Arabs, he fled from city to city, hounded by all, detested as a transgressor of the laws, and hated as the executioner of his country and his compatriots, until he was cast ashore in Egypt. [9]From there he crossed the sea to Sparta, where he hoped to obtain sanctuary because of the Spartans' kinship* with him. There, he who had sent into exile so many children of his homeland, died himself in exile.[g] [10]Furthermore, this man who had cast out so many to be unburied now had no one to mourn for him, with no funeral of any kind and no place in the tomb of his ancestors.*[h]

Antiochus IV Epiphanes Ravages the Temple.* [11]When news of what had happened reached the king, he came to the conclusion that Judea was in revolt. He therefore set out from Egypt, raging like a wild beast, and took the city by storm.[i] [12]He then ordered his soldiers to cut down mercilessly everyone they met and to slay those who fled to their houses. [13]There was the massacre of young and old, the extermination of women and children, and the slaughter of young girls and infants. [14]In the course of three days there were eighty thousand victims—forty thousand killed in hand-to-hand fighting and another forty sold into slavery.

[15]Not content with this, the king had the audacity to enter the holiest temple in the entire world, with Menelaus, who had become a traitor to the laws and to his country, serving as his guide. [16]The king laid his unclean hands on the sacred vessels, and with his profane hands he gathered up the votive offerings that other kings had made to enhance the glory and the honor of the holy place. [17]With an inflated opinion of himself, Antiochus failed to realize that the Lord had been angered for a time because of the sins committed by the inhabitants of the city, and that it was for this reason that he was disregarding the holy place.[j] [18]If it had not been the case that they were involved in many sinful acts, Antiochus would have been flogged and checked in his presumptuous act as soon as

e 1 Mac 1:17.—f 2f: 2 Mac 3:24ff; 10:29f; 11:8.—g 2 Mac 13:8; Wis 11:16; 12:23; Ezek 35:6.—h Ps 78:64; Jer 16:4, 6; 22:18f.—i 11-20: 1 Mac 1:20-24.—j 2 Mac 6:12-16; 7:16-19, 32-38.

5:1 *Second expedition:* the author does not mention the first expedition against Egypt by Antiochus in 169 B.C. (1 Mac 1:16-20) and seems to regard the coming of the Seleucid army into Palestine in 171 B.C. (2 Mac 4:21f) as the first expedition. He apparently combines the first pillage of Jerusalem in 169 B.C. after Antiochus's first expedition against Egypt (1 Mac 1:20-28; see 2 Mac 5:5ff) with the second pillage of the city two years later (167 B.C.) following the king's second expedition against Egypt in 168 B.C. (1 Mac 1:29-35; see 2 Mac 5:24ff).

5:5 *Jason:* brother of Onias III and claimant of the high priesthood (2 Mac 4:7-10). He was later supplanted by Menelaus and driven into the Transjordan by him (2 Mac 4:26).

5:8 *Aretas:* King Aretas I of the Nabateans (see 1 Mac 5:25).

5:9 *Spartans' kinship:* see 1 Mac 12:20f concerning this fictitious kinship between Jews and Spartans.

5:10 Remaining unburied constituted an infamous punishment for the Jews (see 1 Mac 7:17; Deut 28:26; Jer 7:33; 22:19).

5:11-20 Obstructed in Egypt by the Romans (see Dan 11:27-30), the Syrian king retaliates against the Jews. The number of the victims is inflated, and the author exaggerates the event as well: he adds to the massacre the pillage that preceded it by a year (169 B.C.). What is important is solely the lesson that he draws from it: Israel has brought misfortune upon itself by sinning against God.

he approached, just as had been the case
with Heliodorus, whom King Seleucus had
sent to inspect the treasury.

19 [k]However, the Lord had not chosen the
people for the sake of the holy place, but
the holy place for the sake of the people.*
20 Therefore, the holy place itself, having
shared in the misfortunes that afflicted the
people, afterward shared in their good for-
tune, and what had been abandoned by the
Almighty in his anger was restored again in
all its glory once the great Sovereign became
reconciled.

The Governor Mistreats the Jews. 21 Antio-
chus hurried back to Antioch, taking with
him eighteen hundred talents from the tem-
ple. He was so arrogant that, in his pride, he
thought he could sail on the land and tra-
verse the sea on foot. [l] 22 However, he left gov-
ernors behind to oppress the people: at
Jerusalem he left Philip, a Phrygian by
birth* and with a more barbarous nature
than the one who appointed him, 23 and, at
Mount Gerizim,* Andronicus; and in addi-
tion to these there was Menelaus who lord-
ed it over his compatriots worse than the
others did.

Such was Antiochus's animosity toward
the Jewish people, 24 [m]that he sent Ap-
ollonius,* the commander of the Mysians,
with an army of twenty-two thousand men,
with orders to slaughter all the adult men
and to sell the women and children into slav-
ery. 25 When this man arrived in Jerusalem,
he pretended to be peacefully disposed and
waited until the holy Sabbath day. Then,
finding the Jews abstaining from work, he
ordered his men to parade fully armed. 26 He
put to the sword all those who came out to
watch, and then he charged into the city with
his armed warriors and slaughtered a great
number of people.

27 However, Judas Maccabeus,* with about
nine others, escaped into the wilderness,
where he and his companions lived like wild
animals in the hills, eating nothing but what
grew wild there to avoid contracting defile-
ment. [n]

CHAPTER 6

Pagan Cults Are Installed. 1 [o]Not long after-
ward, the king sent an Athenian senator to
force the Jews to forsake the laws of their
ancestors and to live no longer in accor-
dance with the laws of God. 2 He was also
instructed to profane the temple in Jeru-
salem and dedicate it to Olympian Zeus,*
and to dedicate the sanctuary on Mount
Gerizim to Zeus the Hospitable, as had been
requested by the people who inhabited that
place. [p]

3 This evil onslaught harshly intensified
the grievous distress of the people. 4 The
Gentiles made the temple a center of
debauchery and licentious revelry, as they
used the sacred precincts for immoral plea-
sures with prostitutes and intercourse with
women.* They also brought into the temple
sacrificial offerings that were forbidden, [q] 5 so
that the altar was covered with abominable
offerings that were prohibited by the law.

6 No one was allowed to keep the Sabbath
or to observe the traditional feasts or even to
admit being a Jew. 7 Furthermore, on the
monthly celebration of the king's birthday,
the Jews were forcibly compelled to partake
of the sacrificial victims, and when the festi-
val of Dionysus* was celebrated, they were
forced to wear wreaths of ivy and to take
part in the procession honoring him.

8 At the suggestion of the citizens of
Ptolemais, a decree was issued to the neigh-
boring Greek cities* ordering them to adopt
the same policies toward the Jews, compel
them to partake of the sacrifices, 9 and put to

k 19f: 2 Mac 3:1ff; 1 Chr 17:9; Mk 2:27.—l 1 Mac 1:23f.—m 24ff: 1 Mac 1:29f.—n 1 Mac 2:28.—o 1-11: 1 Mac 1:44-63.—p 1 Mac 1:46; Dan 9:27.—q Eph 5:18; Tit 1:6; 1 Pet 4:3-4.

5:19 People are more important than even the most sacred institutions (see Mk 2:27).

5:22 *Philip, a Phrygian by birth:* this is the same person mentioned in 2 Mac 6:11; 8:8 but not Philip the regent mentioned in 2 Mac 9:29; 1 Mac 6:14.

5:23 *Mount Gerizim:* a mountain in Samaria near the city of Shechem; at its summit the Samaritans had built a schismatic temple that would be destroyed by John Hyrcanus in 128 B.C.

5:24 *Apollonius:* the commander of the Mysians mentioned in 2 Mac 3:5; 4:4; 1 Mac 1:29.

5:27 *Judas Maccabeus:* the third son of Mattathias, of the Hasmonean family (1 Mac 2:1-28). *Defilement* was contracted because of taking part in customs contrary to the Mosaic Law (see 2 Mac 4:11; 1 Mac 1:48, 63).

6:2 *Olympian Zeus:* he had his counterpart in the Syrian Baal-shomem ("the Lord of the heavens"), which the Jews translated as "the abomination that causes desolation" (1 Mac 1:54; Dan 11:31; 12:11).

6:4 The temple became the locale for immoral pursuits common to the fertility cults of the ancient Near East.

6:7 *The festival of Dionysus:* Dionysian festivals were celebrated in Greece on four occasions between December and March.

6:8 *Greek cities:* the cities that had adopted the Greek customs were numerous in the neighboring regions of Judea, among which were Ptolemais, Tyre, Joppa, Ashkelon, Gaza, Samaria, and Scythopolis. They contained numerous colonies of Jews who had to endure violent persecutions until the period when they were liberated by the Maccabees.

death those who refused to conform to
Greek customs. Thus it was clear that disas-
ter was imminent. 10 For example, two
women were brought to trial, charged with
having circumcised their children. They
were publicly paraded around the city with
their babies hanging at their breasts and
then hurled headlong from the city wall.[r]
11 Others who had assembled in some near-
by caves to observe the Sabbath secretly
were betrayed to Philip, and all were burned
to death together, since their piety kept them
from defending themselves in their respect
for the holiness of the day.[s]

Purpose of Divine Judgment.* 12 [t] Now I urge
those who read this book not to be disheart-
ened by such calamities but to realize that
these punishments were inflicted not for the
destruction but for the discipline of our peo-
ple. 13 Indeed, it is a sign of great benevolence
when sinners are punished promptly rather
than having their wrongful acts escape retri-
bution for a period of time. 14 In the case of
the other nations the Lord waits patiently to
punish them until they have reached the full
measure of their sins.[u] However, he does not
deal with us in this way, 15 choosing to inflict
punishment on us before our sins have
reached their height so that he will not have
to punish us more severely at that time.
16 Therefore, he never withdraws his mercy
from us. Although he disciplines us by some
misfortunes, he does not forsake his own
people. 17 Let these words suffice as a re-
minder. Now we must proceed with our nar-
rative.

B: Accounts of Martyrdom

Martyrdom of Eleazar. 18 Eleazar, one of the
foremost teachers of the law, a man of
advanced age and distinguished appear-
ance, was being forced to open his mouth to
eat pork.[v] 19 But he, preferring death with
honor rather than a life marked by defile-
ment, spat it out and voluntarily went up to
the torture rack, 20 as should be done by all
who have the courage to reject the food that
it is not lawful to eat, suppressing the natu-
ral desire to save their lives.

21 The officials in charge of this sacrile-
gious meal took the man aside privately
because of their long acquaintance with him
and urged him to bring meat of his own pro-
viding that he was permitted to eat, and to
pretend that he was eating the sacrificial
meat that had been commanded by the king.
22 In this way he would be saved from death
and be treated kindly as a result of their
long-standing friendship. 23 But, making an
honorable decision, worthy of his years and
of the dignity of his advanced age, and of the
gray hairs he had attained and worn with
distinction, and of his impeccable conduct
even from childhood, but worthy above all of
the holy law given by God, he told them to
dispatch him immediately to the abode of
the dead.

24 "At this stage of my life it would be ter-
ribly wrong to be a party to such a pre-
tense," he said, "for many young people
would be led to believe that at the age of
ninety Eleazar had conformed to a foreign
practice. 25 If I should engage in deceit for
the sake of living a brief moment longer,
they would be led astray by me, while I
would bring defilement and disgrace on my
old age. 26 For the moment I would avoid the
punishment of mortals, but alive or dead
I shall never escape the hands of the
Almighty.[w] 27 Therefore, by bravely forfeit-
ing my life now, I shall prove myself worthy
of my old age, 28 and I shall leave to the
young a noble example of how to die a good
death willingly and nobly for our revered
and holy laws."

With these words he went immediately to
the torture rack. 29 Those who a short time
before had been so kindly disposed toward
him now became hostile after this state-
ment that they regarded as sheer madness.
30 When he was at the point of death as the
result of the blows he had received, he
groaned aloud and said: "The Lord in his
holy knowledge clearly realizes that al-
though I could have escaped death, not only
am I enduring terrible sufferings in my
body from this scourging, but in my soul
I am gladly accepting these torments be-
cause of my awe of him."

31 In this way he died, and by his death he
left an example of courage and a model of
virtue not only for the young but for the
entire nation.

---

r 1 Mac 1:60f.—s 1 Mac 2:32-38.—t 12-16: 2 Mac 5:17; 7:16-19, 32-38.—u Wis 11:9f; 12:2, 22.—v Lev 11:7f; Heb 11:35.—w 2 Mac 7:29; Lk 12:4f; Heb 10:31; 1 Pet 3:14.

6:12-17 Israel's defeats are explained as God's corrective punishment for its sins, always followed by God's mercy (see Isa 54:7f; Ps 94:12-15).

CHAPTER 7

Martyrdom of Seven Brothers and Their Mother.* [1]It also happened that seven brothers were arrested together with their mother. The king tortured them with whips and scourges in an attempt to force them to eat pork, in violation of the law of God.[x] [2]One of the brothers, acting as a spokesman for the others, said, "What do you expect to achieve by questioning us? We are prepared to die rather than transgress the laws of our ancestors."

[3]The king became enraged and issued orders to have pans and caldrons heated. [4]After this was done without delay, he commanded that the tongue of their spokesman be cut out and that he be scalped and his hands and feet cut off while the rest of his brothers and his mother looked on. [5]When he had been rendered utterly helpless but still breathing, the king ordered him to be taken to the fire and fried in one of the pans. As the smoke from the pan began to spread, his mother and his brothers encouraged one another to die in a noble manner, with words such as these: [6] [y] "The Lord God is watching, and he cannot fail to have compassion on us, as Moses declared in his canticle when he asserted: 'He will have compassion on his servants.' "*

[7]When the first brother had died in this manner, they brought forward the second to be subjected to their cruel sport. After the skin and hair of his head had been stripped off, they asked him: "Will you eat some pork rather than have your body tortured limb by limb?" [8]Replying in the language of his ancestors, he said to them, "Never!" Therefore, he in turn underwent the same torture that the first had endured. [9]With his final breath, he said: "You accursed fiend, you may send us forth from this present life, but the King of the universe will raise us up* to life eternal, since it is because of our obedience to his laws that we are dying." [z]

[10]After him, the third brother bore the brunt of their cruel torture. In response to their demand, he immediately thrust forth his tongue and courageously stretched forth his hands [11]as he said: "It was from Heaven* that I received these. For the sake of his laws I disdain them. From him I hope to receive them again." [a] [12]Both the king and his attendants were astounded as they witnessed the courage of this young man and his complete indifference to suffering.

[13]After he had died they maltreated and tortured the fourth brother in the same way. [14]When he was at the point of death, he cried out: "It is far better to choose to die at the hands of men and rely on the promise of God of being raised again by him. But for you there will be no resurrection to life."

[15]They next brought forward the fifth brother and tortured him. [16] [b]Directing his gaze at the king, he said: "Even though you yourself are mortal, you have authority over other mortals, and thus you can do as you please. However, do not think that God has abandoned our nation. [17]Just wait and you will see how his mighty power will torment you and your descendants."

[18]After him they brought forward the sixth brother. When he was about to die, he said: "Do not have any vain delusions. We are suffering these torments deservedly because we have sinned against our God and brought these appalling events on ourselves. [19]However, do not think that you will avoid the consequences of having dared to contend with God." [c]

[20]Especially admirable and deserving of everlasting remembrance was the mother. Although she witnessed the deaths of her seven sons within the space of a single day, she endured it courageously because of her hope in the Lord. [21]Filled with a noble spirit that reinforced her womanly thoughts with manly courage, she encouraged each of them in the language of their ancestors: [22] [d]"I do not know how you came to being in my womb. It was not I who endowed you with breath and life, nor did I set in order the

x Jer 15:9.—y Deut 32:36.—z 2 Mac 12:44; 14:46.—a 2 Mac 12:43ff.—b 16-19: 2 Mac 5:17; 6:12-16.—c Acts 5:39.—d 22f: Job 10:8-12; Ps 139:13-15; Eccl 11:5.

7:1-42 Together with the story of Eleazar, this celebrated narrative belongs to a new category of writings: the "Acts of the Martyrs." These were designed to encourage the faithful during persecutions and became very popular in Christian circles. We should not expect too much historical precision. The author wishes to edify by insisting on the atrocity of the tortures and the heroism of those who suffer them. Together with the Book of Daniel (Dan 12:2-3) and the Book of Wisdom (Wis 3:1-5), here for the first time in the Old Testament, faith in the resurrection is affirmed, and this expectation is rooted in a profound conception of the creation of the Covenant (see vv. 18, 22-23, 33).

7:6 Literal citation of Deut 32:36 according to the Greek version (Septuagint).

7:9 *The King of the universe will raise us up:* belief in the resurrection of the body is clearly stated here and in verses 11, 14, 23, 29, 36 (see also 12:44; 14:46; Dan 12:2).

7:11 *Heaven:* a circumlocution for God, which is also used in verse 34.

elements that established the composition of your being.[e] 23 Therefore, the Creator of the universe who authored the beginning of human life and devised the origin of all things will, in his mercy, restore breath and life to you, since you have placed his law above concern for your own desires."

24 Antiochus felt that he was being treated with contempt and suspected that her words were insulting. Since the youngest brother was still alive, the king did not limit himself to an appeal with mere words. Indeed, he promised him on oath that if he would abandon the traditions of his ancestors, he would not only make him rich and happy but also enroll him as his Friend and appoint him to high office. 25 When the young man paid no heed to his proposals, the king made an appeal to his mother, urging her to advise her son to save his life. 26 After a great deal of encouraging on his part, she agreed to try to persuade him.

27 However, she flouted the king's wishes by saying to her son in their native language as she leaned close to him: "My son, have pity on me. I carried you in my womb for nine months, nursed you for three years, reared you, and provided for your needs up to this point in your life. 28 I beg you, my child, to look at the heavens and the earth and see everything that is in them. Reflect on the fact that God did not create them from things that already existed* and that the human race came into being in the same way. 29 Have no fear of this butcher. Prove yourself worthy of your brothers by accepting death, so that through the mercy of God I shall receive you back again along with them."

30 She had barely finished speaking when the young man said: "What are you waiting for? I will not obey the king's command. I choose rather to obey the ordinance of the law that was given to our ancestors through Moses. 31 However, you, who have devised every kind of evil against the Hebrews, will certainly not escape the hands of God. 32 [e] We are suffering as the result of our own sins, 33 and while our living Lord is angry with us for a brief time as he seeks to correct and discipline us, he will eventually be reconciled with his servants. 34 However, you, perfidious wretch, are the most wicked of all mortal beings. Do not allow yourself to be deluded by vain hopes when you raise your hand against the children of Heaven, 35 for you will not be able to escape from the judgment of the almighty and all-seeing God. 36 My brothers, after enduring a brief period of suffering, have now drunk of the waters of everlasting life in accordance with his covenant, but you, convicted by the judgment of God, will receive a richly warranted punishment for your arrogance.[f]

37 "I too, like my brothers, surrender my body and my life for the laws of our ancestors. I appeal to God not to delay in showing mercy to our nation and by trials and afflictions to cause you to confess that he alone is God. 38 Through me and my brothers may there be an end to the wrath of the Almighty* that has justifiably fallen on our entire nation."

39 On hearing this, the king became enraged and dealt with him even more cruelly than with the others because of his defiance. 40 [g] And so the young man, having placed all his trust in the Lord, died undefiled. 41 The mother was the last to die, after her sons had perished.

42 Let this account be sufficient to relate the facts of the sacrificial meals and the monstrous tortures.

C: Liberation of the Holy City and the Temple

CHAPTER 8

Judas Maccabeus Conducts Guerrilla Warfare. 1 [h] Meanwhile, Judas, who was also called Maccabeus, secretly entered the villages with his companions and enlisted in their ranks their kindred as well as others who had remained faithful to Judaism.* Having

e 32, 38: 2 Mac 5:17; 6:12-16.—f 2 Cor 4:17.—g 40f: Heb 11:35.—h 1-7: 2 Mac 5:27; 1 Mac 3:10-26.

7:28 *God did not create them from things that already existed:* this is the most precise affirmation of the whole Old Testament concerning the doctrine of the creation out of nothing. God made all things by his almighty will and his creative word (see Heb 11:3).

7:38 *An end to the wrath of the Almighty:* this was to be achieved by increasing the suffering of Israel to such an extent that God would be moved to intervene for them (see Deut 32:36; Jdg 2:18). The apocryphal Book of 4 Maccabees, on the other hand, attributes this end to the Maccabees atoning for Israel's sins by their death: "All people, even the torturers [of the Maccabees], marveled at their courage and endurance, and [the Maccabees] became the cause of the downfall of tyranny over their nation. By their endurance they conquered the tyrant, and thus their native land was cleansed through them" (4 Mac 1:11; see also 17:20-22).

8:1 The narrative interrupted in 2 Mac 5:27 is taken up again here (see 1 Mac 1:26-64).

assembled a force of about six thousand,
[2]they implored the Lord to look with favor
on his people who were being oppressed on
all sides; to have pity on the temple that was
being profaned by godless people; [3]to have
mercy on the city that was being destroyed
and about to be leveled to the ground; to
hearken to the blood that cried out to him;
[4]to remember the lawless slaughter of inno-
cent children and the blasphemous deeds
perpetrated against his name; and to mani-
fest his hatred of evil.

[5] [i]As soon as Maccabeus had organized his
army, the Gentiles found that they were
unable to withstand him, for the wrath of the
Lord had turned to compassion. [6]Attacking
towns and villages without warning, he
would set them on fire. He captured strate-
gic positions and inflicted heavy losses on the
enemy, [7]usually preferring the night as being
especially advantageous for such attacks. His
reputation for valor spread far and wide.

First Victory over Nicanor. [8]*When Philip*
noted that Judas was making steady
progress little by little and that his success-
ful excursions were becoming ever more
frequent, he wrote to Ptolemy, the governor
of Coelesyria and Phoenicia, asking for his
help in defending the royal interests. [j]
[9]Ptolemy immediately appointed Nicanor,
the son of Patroclus, one of the king's Chief
Friends, and dispatched him in command
of at least twenty thousand troops from
various nations to exterminate the entire
Jewish race. As his associate he appointed
Gorgias, a general of considerable military
experience in the skills of war. [k] [10]Nicanor's
intention was to raise the two thousand tal-
ents of tribute owed by the king to the
Romans* by selling into slavery the Jews
who were taken prisoner. [11]Therefore, he
immediately notified the coastal cities that
he was prepared to sell them Jewish slaves
at the rate of ninety slaves for a talent.
However, he did not reckon with the judg-
ment from the Almighty that was about to
overtake him.

[12]When Judas learned of Nicanor's
advance and informed his men about the
approach of the enemy's army, [13]those who
were cowardly or without faith in the justice
of God deserted and got away. [14]But the oth-
ers sold all of their remaining possessions
while at the same time beseeching the Lord
for the deliverance of those who had been
put up for sale by the godless Nicanor even
before he had so much as encountered
them—[15]and to do so, if not for their own
sake, then at least out of consideration for
the covenants made with their ancestors and
because they themselves bore his sacred and
majestic name.*

[16]Maccabeus assembled his forces, who
numbered about six thousand, and exhorted
them not to succumb to panic when con-
fronted by the enemy, nor to fear the vast
horde of Gentiles who were advancing to
attack them unjustly, but to fight bravely,
[17]keeping ever before their eyes the outrag-
es unlawfully perpetrated by the Gentiles
against the holy place and the cruel indigni-
ties inflicted on the city as well as the sub-
version of their ancestral way of life. [18]"They
may place their trust in their weapons and
their acts of daring," he said, "but we trust
in almighty God who is able with a mere nod
to strike down both those who are marching
against us and, if necessary, the entire
world." [l]

[19]He then proceeded to remind them of
the occasions when divine interventions
had aided their ancestors—how, in the time
of Sennacherib, one hundred and eighty-
five thousand of the enemy forces had per-
ished, [m] [20]and about the occasion of the
battle in Babylon* with the Galatians when
the Jewish forces numbered no more than
eight thousand, aided by four thousand
Macedonians, and how, when the Mace-
donians were hard pressed, those eight
thousand, with the help received from
Heaven, had destroyed one hundred and
twenty thousand of the enemy and gath-
ered a great amount of booty. [21]With words
such as these he roused their courage and

i 5ff: 1 Mac 3:3-9.—j 2 Mac 4:45; 1 Mac 3:38.—k 1 Mac 7:26.—l Ps 20:7.—m 2 Mac 15:22; 2 Ki 19:35; Isa 37:36.

8:8-29, 34ff See 1 Mac 3:38—4:24 for a parallel account of the campaign of Nicanor and Gorgias, with certain differences.

8:8 *Philip:* the one who had been left by Antiochus at Jerusalem as superintendent (see 2 Mac 5:22) with the powers of a local governor (see 2 Mac 6:11); Ptolemy was already remembered as the protector of Menelaus in the trial held at Tyre in the presence of Antiochus (2 Mac 4:45-46).

8:10 *Two thousand talents of tribute owed by the king to the Romans:* as a result of the defeat of Antiochus III at Magnesia in 189 B.C., the Seleucids were obligated to pay 15,000 talents in successive payments. In the epoch in which the narrated events took place, the Seleucids were, according to Livius (*History* 42:6), late in their payments.

8:15 These words express an idea taken from Dan 9:19 that frequently appears in later Jewish prayers.

8:20 *Battle in Babylon:* a battle fought by Antiochus III against the rebel Molo in Media about 220 B.C.

made them ready to die for their laws and
their country.

Then Judas divided his army into four sec-
tions, 22 placing his brothers, Simon, Joseph,*
and Jonathan, in command of one division
each and assigning them fifteen hundred
men apiece. 23 Next, he appointed Eleazar*
to read aloud from the holy book, and he
gave them the rallying cry, "The help of
God." Then, taking command of the first
division, he joined battle with Nicanor.[n]

24 With the Almighty as their ally, they
slaughtered more than nine thousand of the
enemy, wounded and disabled the greater
part of Nicanor's army, and put all of them
to flight. 25 They also appropriated the
money of those who had come to purchase
them as slaves. After pursuing the enemy for
a considerable time, 26 they were obliged to
return because of the lateness of the hour.
Since it was the day before the Sabbath, they
could not continue their pursuit. 27 *After
collecting the arms of the enemy and strip-
ping them of their spoils, they observed the
Sabbath, offering fervent praise and thanks-
giving to the Lord who had preserved them
to witness on that day this manifestation of
his compassion. 28 When the Sabbath was
over, they distributed some of the spoils to
the victims of the persecution and to the
widows and orphans.[o] The rest they divided
among themselves and their children.
29 After this had been done, they joined in
common supplication, beseeching the mer-
ciful Lord to be fully reconciled with his
servants.

Defeat of Timothy and Bacchides.* 30 They
also engaged in battle with the forces of
Timothy and Bacchides, killing more than
twenty thousand of them and gaining pos-
session of some very high strongholds. They
divided the immense amount of plunder,
giving half to the persecuted orphans and
widows and the aged, and keeping the
remaining half for themselves. 31 They care-
fully collected the weapons of the enemy
and stored them in strategic locations; the
rest of the spoils they carried to Jerusalem.
32 They put to death the commander of
Timothy's forces, a most wicked man who
had inflicted great suffering on the Jews.
33 During the victory celebrations in their
ancestral city, they burned those who had
set fire to the sacred gates, including
Callisthenes, who had taken refuge in a tiny
house. Thus he received due recompense
for his sacrilegious deeds.

Flight and Testimony of Nicanor.* 34 [p] The
accursed Nicanor, who villainously had
brought along a thousand merchants to buy
the Jewish captives, 35 having been humbled
with the help of the Lord by those whom he
regarded as worthless, threw off his magnif-
icent garments and fled across the country,
unaccompanied, like a runaway slave, until
he reached Antioch. His major accomplish-
ment had been to oversee the destruction of
his own army. 36 Thus the man who had
undertaken to secure tribute for the Romans
by taking as prisoners the people of Je-
rusalem now bore witness that the Jews had
a champion and that they were therefore
invulnerable because they followed the laws
set down by him.

CHAPTER 9

Antiochus Epiphanes Meets a Wretched End.*
1 [q] About that time it so happened that
Antiochus was leading an ignominious
retreat from the region of Persia. 2 He had
entered the city called Persepolis and
attempted to plunder the temple and gain
control of the city. However, the people
immediately rose up in armed defense and
repulsed Antiochus and his men, with the
result that Antiochus was put to flight by the
inhabitants and forced into a humiliating
retreat. 3 On his arrival in Ecbatana, he

---

n 1 Mac 3:48.—o 2 Mac 3:10; Num 31:27; 1 Sam 30:24.—p 34f: 2 Mac 8:23f; 1 Mac 7:26.—q 1-29: 2 Mac 1:12-17; 1 Mac 6:1-13.

8:22 *Joseph:* called John in 1 Mac 2:2; 9:36, 38. The story of Nicanor's defeat is interrupted here and resumed in verse 34. The author seeks to group together the defeats that the Syrians suffered on various occasions. For the battles against Timothy, see 2 Mac 12:10-25; 1 Mac 5:37-44; for those against Bacchides, see 1 Mac 7:8-20.

8:23 *Eleazar:* another brother, who was killed at Beth-zechariah (1 Mac 2:5; 6:43-46). *The help of God:* a motto prescribed also in the *War Scroll* of Qumran for one of the banners of a returning army.

8:27-29 The victory was taken as a sign of God's favor; however, the campaign was not yet over (6:12-16; 1 Mac 4:19-25).

8:30-33 See 1 Mac 5:37-44 for the account of a battle against Timothy at Raphon.

8:34-36 Nicanor's defeat bore testimony to the fact that God was with the Jews—as long as they obeyed his law.

9:1-29 This event of 164 B.C. is here narrated for the third time (see 2 Mac 1:11-17; 1 Mac 6:1-17). The author repeats it in order to keep together the various accounts of the punishment of the persecutors of the Jews, including accounts of Judas's campaigns in Idumea and the Transjordan (see 2 Mac 10:14-38; 1 Mac 5:1-51) and the first expedition of Lysias (see 2 Mac 11:1-15; 1 Mac 4:26-35). The appended letter, in all probability, was not written to the Jews but to the citizens of Antioch. The text of the *letter,* whose transcript was enclosed (v. 25), is not given.

learned what had happened to Nicanor and
to the forces of Timothy. 4 Bursting with
anger, he devised a plan to make the Jews
suffer for the injury inflicted by those who
had put him to flight. Therefore, he ordered
his charioteer to drive without stopping until
he completed his journey.

However, the judgment of Heaven rode
with him, since in his arrogance he declared,
"Once I arrive in Jerusalem, I will turn it
into a mass graveyard for Jews." 5 And so the
all-seeing Lord, the God of Israel, struck him
with an unseen but incurable blow. Hardly
had he spoken those words when he was
seized with excruciating pains in his bowels
and acute internal torment[r]—6 an entirely
suitable punishment for one who had inflict-
ed many barbarous torments on the bowels
of others. 7 Nevertheless, he did not in the
least diminish his insolent behavior. More
arrogant than ever and breathing fire in his
rage against the Jews, he gave orders to drive
even faster. As a result, he was hurled from
the lurching chariot, and the fall was so vio-
lent that every part of his body was racked
with pain.

8 Thus he who only a short time before had
in his superhuman arrogance believed that
he could command the waves of the sea, and
who imagined that he could weigh high
mountains on a scale, was thrown down to
the ground and had to be carried in a litter,
clearly manifesting to all the power of God.[s]
9 The body of this ungodly man swarmed
with worms, and while he was still alive suf-
fering agonizing torments, his flesh rotted
away, so that the entire army was sickened
by the stench of his decay.[t] 10 Only a short
time before, he had thought that he could
touch the stars of heaven. Now no one could
even bring himself to transport the man
because of his intolerable stench.[u]

11 Ultimately, broken in spirit, he began to
lose his excessive arrogance and to come to
his senses under the scourge of God, for he
was racked with incessant pain. 12 When
he no longer could endure his own stench, he
exclaimed: "It is right to be subject to God.
Mere mortals should never believe that they
are equal to God." 13 Then this vile wretch
made a vow to the Lord, who would no
longer have mercy on him, 14 that he would
publicly declare to be free the holy city
toward which he had been hurrying to level
it to the ground and transform it into a mass
graveyard; 15 that the Jews, whom he had not
deemed to be worthy of burial but fit only to
be thrown out with their children and eaten
by wild animals and birds, would all be
granted equality with the citizens of
Athens;* 16 that the holy temple that he had
previously plundered, he would now adorn
with the finest offerings, replace all the
sacred vessels many times over, and provide
from his own revenues the expenses in-
curred for the sacrifices. 17 In addition to all
this, he would become a Jew himself and
would visit every inhabited place to pro-
claim the glory of God.

18 However, when his sufferings did not
abate in any way, inasmuch as the judgment
of God had already justly befallen him, he
lost all hope for himself and wrote to the
Jews the following letter, in the form of a sup-
plication. This was its content:

19 * "To his worthy Jewish citizens Antio-
chus, their king and general, sends warm
greetings and good wishes for their health
and prosperity. 20 If you and your children
are well and your affairs are prospering as
you wish, I am delighted. As my hopes are
directed toward heaven, 21 I cherish affec-
tionate memories of your esteem and good-
will toward me. On my way back from the
region of Persia I was afflicted with a dis-
tressing illness, and therefore I have thought
it necessary to make provisions for the gen-
eral welfare of all. 22 Actually I do not despair
about my health, for I am confident that I
will completely recover from my illness.
23 However, I recall that whenever my father
made expeditions into the upper provinces,
he would designate his successor, 24 so that if
anything unforeseen should happen or some
troublesome rumor should begin to circu-
late, the people throughout the realm would
not be troubled, for they would know to
whom the government had been entrusted.
25 Moreover, I am fully aware that the neigh-
boring rulers, particularly those situated on

r Acts 12:20-23.—s Job 38:8-11; Ps 65:7-8; Isa 40:12.—t Acts 12:23.—u Isa 14:13-15.

9:15 Antiochus IV had lived for some time at Athens and had received a most favorable impression of it. Desiring to grant the Jews *equality with the citizens of Athens* implies wishing to make Jerusalem a "free city" and giving to all Jews the right to govern themselves with their own laws.

9:19-27 This letter is not a "supplication" as stated in verse 18. It is addressed to Jews loyal to the king and requests that they be loyal to his *son* Antiochus V, who is being appointed as his successor. It was probably a circular letter sent to the different peoples in the kingdom.

the frontiers of our kingdom, are ever on the
watch for opportunities and waiting to see
what will develop.

"Therefore, I have designated as king my
son Antiochus, whom I have often before
entrusted and commended to most of you
when I made hurried trips to the upper
provinces. I have sent to him a letter in
regard to this and enclose a transcript for
you. [26] I therefore urge and entreat each of
you to remember the public and private ser-
vices I have rendered to you and to continue
to manifest goodwill toward me and my son.
[27] I am confident that my son will follow my
policy of benevolence and kindness in his
relations with you."

[28] And so this murderer and blasphemer,
after enduring agonizing sufferings to match
those he had inflicted on others, died a
wretched death in the mountains of a for-
eign land. [29] His close friend Philip* brought
back the body. Then, fearing the son of
Antiochus, he withdrew into Egypt, to the
court of Ptolemy Philometor.

CHAPTER 10

**Judas Recovers Jerusalem and Purifies the
Temple.** [1] Under the guidance of the Lord,
Maccabeus and his companions recovered
the temple and the city,* [v] [2] destroying the
altars* erected by the Gentiles in the public
square and tearing down their sacred
precincts. [3] After they purified the sanctu-
ary,* they built another altar. Then, striking
fire from flints, they offered sacrifice for the
first time in two years, burning incense,
lighting lamps, and setting out the bread of
the Presence. [4] When they had done this,
they prostrated themselves and implored
the Lord never again to allow them to be
afflicted with such misfortunes, and, were
they ever to sin, to discipline them himself
with moderation rather than hand them
over to blasphemous and barbarous nations.

[5] The purification of the temple took place
on the very same day on which the temple
had been profaned by the Gentiles, that is,
the twenty-fifth day of the same month
Chislev. [6] The celebration and rejoicing last-
ed for eight days, in the manner of the Feast
of Booths, as they recalled how, only a short
time before, during the Feast of Booths, they
had been living like wild animals in the
mountains and caves. [7] And so, carrying
wands entwined with ivy, and leafy branches
and palm fronds, they offered hymns of
thanksgiving to him whose guiding hand had
enabled them to achieve the purification of
his holy place. [w] [8] They also decreed by a
public edict, ratified by vote, that the whole
Jewish nation should observe these days
every year.

IV: THE ACQUISITION OF RELIGIOUS FREEDOM*

A: The War against Lysias, Minister of Antiochus V

The Threat to Peace. [9] Such were the cir-
cumstances surrounding the death of An-
tiochus who was called Epiphanes. [x]
[10] Now we will relate what took place
under Antiochus Eupator, the son of that
godless man, and offer a brief summary
of the evils that resulted from his wars.
[11] When Eupator succeeded to the throne,
he appointed a man named Lysias* to be
in charge of the government as command-
er-in-chief of Coelesyria and Phoenicia.
[12] Ptolemy, [y] who was called Macron, had
taken the lead in treating the Jews fairly to
atone for the previous injustices that they
had suffered, and he endeavored to main-
tain peaceful relations with them. [13] As a
result, he was denounced before Eupator
by the King's Friends. He heard himself
called a traitor at every turn because he
had abandoned Cyprus, which Philometor
had entrusted to him, and had transferred
his allegiance to Antiochus Epiphanes.
Unable to command the respect due his

v 1-8: 1 Mac 4:36-59.—w 2 Mac 14:4; Lev 23:40; Jn 12:13.—x 2 Mac 2:20-21; 1 Mac 6:17.—y 2 Mac 8:8.

9:29 *Philip:* perhaps Antiochus V's guardian (see 1 Mac 6:14-15). Most likely he feared Lysias, viceroy in the west, rather than the *son of Antiochus*, who was a child; so he joined Syria's enemy, Ptolemy VI. According to Josephus, Philip took over the Seleucid government and was later killed.

10:1 The account is resumed now from 2 Mac 8:36. See the parallel account in 1 Mac 4:36-59.

10:2 *Destroying the altars:* they tore down the altars that had been used for pagan worship.

10:3 They *purified the sanctuary* by removing the desecrated stones (1 Mac 1:44-46). *Striking fire from flints:* no mention is made of the legends of 2 Mac 1:19—2:1 concerning fire. *Two years:* in reality, it was three and a half years from the time when worship had been interrupted.

10:9—15:36 A new persecutor comes forth. He is defeated, however, because he threatened the temple. And the people of God celebrate the victory. It is the second part of the Book and takes up the same schema as the first.

10:11 *Lysias* is, in fact, named here for the first time in this Book. On the other hand, in 1 Maccabees we find more abundant information about him beginning with 1 Mac 3:32f where he is left by Antiochus IV as tutor of his son.

office, he took poison and thereby ended his life.

Judas Punishes the Idumeans.* 14 When Gorgias became governor of the region, he hired a force of mercenaries and maintained a state of war with the Jews. 15[z] At the same time, the Idumeans,* who controlled some strategic fortresses, were harassing the Jews, as they welcomed fugitives from Jerusalem and made every effort to continue the war. 16 Maccabeus and his forces offered public prayers, entreating God to support their efforts, and then launched an assault against the Idumean strongholds.[a] 17 Attacking them energetically, they captured these vantage positions, driving off all who manned the walls, and slaughtered all those whom they encountered, killing no fewer than twenty thousand men.

18 At least nine thousand of the enemy took refuge in two exceedingly strong towers that were fully equipped to withstand a siege. 19 Maccabeus left behind Simon and Joseph, as well as Zacchaeus and his troops, comprising a force sufficient to besiege them, while he himself set out for zones where he was more urgently needed. 20 However, Simon's men were avaricious, and they allowed themselves to be bribed by some of those who were in the towers. After receiving seventy thousand drachmas, they permitted a number of them to slip away. 21 When Maccabeus was told what had happened, he assembled the leaders of the people and denounced those men for having sold their kindred for money by freeing their enemies to fight against them. 22 Then he executed them as traitors and immediately captured both towers. 23 Since he was successful in everything he undertook by force of arms, he slaughtered more than twenty thousand men in the two strongholds.

Judas Defeats Timothy and Captures Gezer.* 24 Timothy, who had been defeated by the Jews once before, now gathered an enormous force of mercenaries and considerable numbers of cavalry from Asia. Then he marched into Judea, intending to take it by storm. 25 At his approach, Maccabeus and his men made supplication to God, sprinkling dust upon their heads and girding their loins with sackcloth. 26 Prostrating themselves on the steps in front of the altar, they implored him to support them in their struggle, and, as the law states, to be an enemy to their enemies and an adversary to their adversaries.[b]

27 After their prayer, they took up their weapons and advanced a considerable distance from the city, coming to a halt when they were near the enemy. 28 Just as dawn was breaking, the two armies joined battle, the one having as a pledge of success and victory not only their own valor, but also their reliance on the Lord, whereas the other had only their own fury to sustain them in battle.

29[c] When the fighting reached its height, there appeared to the enemy from the heavens five magnificent men, each astride a horse with a golden bridle, and they placed themselves in the forefront of the Jews. 30 Surrounding Maccabeus and shielding him with their own armor, they kept him from being wounded. Meanwhile, they propelled arrows and thunderbolts at the enemy, leaving them confused and blinded so that they were thrown into complete disarray and routed. 31 Twenty thousand five hundred of their infantry were slain, in addition to six hundred cavalry.

32 Timothy himself fled to a strongly garrisoned citadel called Gazara,* where Chaereas was in command.[d] 33 For four days Maccabeus and his forces eagerly besieged the fortress, 34 while the men inside, their confidence buoyed by their belief in the security of the place, continued to taunt them with terrible blasphemies and abominable insults. 35 At daybreak on the fifth day, twenty young men in the army of Maccabeus, infuriated at the blasphemies, bravely stormed the wall and with savage fury, cut down everyone they encountered. 36 Others who came up in a similar way attacked the

z 15-23: 1 Mac 5:3ff.—a 2 Mac 8:23f.—b Ex 23:22.—c 29f: 2 Mac 3:24ff; 5:2f; 11:8.—d 1 Mac 13:43-48.

10:14-23 The numbers are not certain; they merely serve to emphasize the victory.

10:15 *Idumeans:* ancient people of Edom (descendants of Esau) located south of Judea, which after the Exile had also become established in Hebron. Their hostility toward the Hebrews was of ancient date (see Num 20:14-21; Jdg 11:17). This may be the same campaign mentioned in 1 Mac 5:1-3.

10:24-38 The sequence of events is not respected. Later on (2 Mac 12:2, 10, 18), we will encounter the Timothy who is killed in this episode, and Gezer will be truly conquered only at the hands of Simon after the death of Judas (1 Mac 13:43-48). All this is of no importance for the author: grouping together events (even though some occurred later), he constructs a eulogy in honor of his hero.

10:32 *Gazara:* mentioned much more often in 1 Maccabees (4:15; 9:52; 13:43, 53; 16:1), it is an ancient Canaanite city at the foot of the Judean mountains. According to another hypothesis, it should be read as Jazer as in 1 Mac 5:8.

defenders from the rear and set fire to the
towers while starting other fires in which the
blasphemers were burned alive. Still others
broke down the gates and let in the rest of the
troops, who then took possession of the city.
37 Timothy, who had hidden in a cistern, was
slain, along with his brother Chaereas, and
Apollophanes. 38 When they had accom-
plished all of these exploits, they offered
hymns of praise and thanksgiving to the
Lord who had shown such great kindness to
Israel and given them the victory.

CHAPTER 11

Lysias Must Deal with the Jews.* 1 [e] Very soon
after that, Lysias, the guardian and kinsman
of the king, who was in charge of the govern-
ment, became greatly angered at what had
occurred. 2 He mustered about eighty thou-
sand foot soldiers and all of his cavalry and
advanced against the Jews. His intent was to
make Jerusalem a settlement for Greeks, 3 to
levy a tax * on the temple as he did on the
shrines of other nations, and to put the office
of high priest up for sale every year. 4 He gave
no consideration whatsoever to the power of
God, for he was supremely confident in his
infantry numbering in the tens of thousands,
and in his thousands of cavalry and his
eighty elephants. 5 Therefore, he invaded
Judea, and when he reached Beth-zur, a for-
tified place about twenty miles distant from
Jerusalem, he launched a strong attack
against it.

6 When Maccabeus and his men were
informed that Lysias was besieging the
strongholds, they and all the people im-
plored the Lord with lamentations and tears
to send a good angel to deliver Israel. [f]
7 Maccabeus himself was the first to take up
arms, and he urged the others to join him in
risking their lives to save their fellow Jews.
Then they all resolutely set out together.
8 And while they were still near Jerusalem, a
horseman suddenly appeared at their head,
clothed in white and brandishing weapons of
gold. [g] 9 Together they united in praising their
merciful God, and they were so filled with a
spirit of courage that they were ready to
attack not only men, but even the most sav-
age beasts and walls of iron. 10 They advanced
in battle order with the aid of their heavenly
ally, for the Lord had shown mercy toward
them. 11 They charged like lions against the
enemy and laid low eleven thousand of
them, in addition to sixteen hundred caval-
ry, and the remaining forces they put to
flight. 12 Most of those who escaped were
wounded and without their weapons, and
Lysias himself escaped only by taking flight
in a cowardly manner.

13 [h] However, Lysias was not lacking in
intelligence, and as he reflected upon the
defeat he had experienced, he came to the
realization that the Hebrews were invinci-
ble because the all-powerful God fought
on their side. Therefore, he sent emissaries
to them 14 to convince them to settle
everything on terms that were fair to both
sides, and he promised to persuade the
king to be their friend. 15 Solicitous for the
common good, Maccabeus agreed to
everything that Lysias proposed, and the
king granted every request on behalf of the
Jews that Maccabeus submitted in writing
to Lysias.

Lysias Writes to the Jews. 16 This is the
tenor of the letter that Lysias wrote to the
Jews: "Lysias sends greetings to the Jewish
people. 17 John and Absalom, your envoys,
have delivered to me your signed commu-
nication and inquired about the matters
put forth in it. 18 Anything that required the
king's attention, I referred to him, and he
has agreed to whatever was possible. 19 If
you maintain your goodwill toward the
government, I will endeavor to promote
your well-being in the future. 20 As to what-
ever concerns the details of these matters, I
have authorized your envoys and my repre-
sentatives to confer with you. 21 Farewell.
The twenty-fourth day of Dioscorinthius, in
the year one hundred and forty-eight." *

Antiochus Eupator Writes to Lysias. 22 The
king's letter read as follows: "King Antio-
chus sends greetings to his brother Lysias.
23 Now that our father has taken his place
among the gods, we desire that the subjects
of our realm be left undisturbed in the con-
duct of their own affairs. 24 We have heard
that the Jews are opposed to our father's pol-

e 1-12: 1 Mac 4:25-35.—f Ex 23:20.—g 2 Mac 3:24ff; 5:2f; 10:29f.—h 13-33: 1 Mac 6:57-61.

11:1-15 Once again, the author confuses the date and exaggerates the numbers. In his accounts of war, a heavenly apparition symbolizes the help that Judas and his men receive from God. Lysias's flight evokes that of Nicanor (2 Mac 8:35). These ways of proceeding are deliberate.

11:3 *Levy a tax:* all temples were subjected to taxes, but the temple of Jerusalem had been exempted by Antiochus III.

11:21 *The year one hundred and forty-eight:* 164 B.C. *Dioscorinthius:* should read "Dioscorus," which corresponds to February–March.

icy concerning the adoption of Greek cus-
toms but rather prefer their own way of life
and request that they be permitted to
observe their own laws. 25 Accordingly, since
it is our will that this nation too should be
free from disturbance, we decree that their
temple shall be restored to them and that
they be allowed to live in accordance with
the customs of their ancestors. 26 Therefore,
please send them word of our pledges of
friendship so that, informed of our policy,
they may be reassured and go contentedly
about their business."

27 The king's letter to the people was in
these terms: "King Antiochus sends greet-
ings to the Jewish senate and to the rest of
the Jews. 28 If you are well, this is our wish. We
ourselves are also enjoying good health.
29 Menelaus* has informed us of your wish to
return home and attend to your own affairs.
30 Therefore, those who return by the thirti-
eth day of Xanthicus will have our pledge
that they will be permitted 31 to observe their
own dietary laws and other laws as former-
ly, and none of them will be molested in any
way for offenses committed as a result of
ignorance. 32 I am also sending Menelaus to
assure you. 33 Farewell. The fifteenth day of
Xanthicus in the year one hundred and
forty-eight." *

The Romans Write to the Jews. 34 The Ro-
mans also sent a letter to the Jews, which
read as follows: "Quintus Memmius and
Titus Manius, legates of the Romans, send
greetings to the Jewish people. 35 Whatever
Lysias, the kinsman of the king, has granted
you, we also approve. 36 In regard to those
matters that he has submitted to the king for
judgment, as soon as you have considered
them, send someone to us without delay that
we may make suitable proposals on your
behalf, for we are on our way to Antioch.
37 Therefore, do not lose any time in sending
messengers to us to inform us about your
opinions. 38 Farewell. The fifteenth day of
Xanthicus in the year one hundred and
forty-eight."

CHAPTER 12

Judas Punishes Joppa and Jamnia. 1 After
these agreements had been concluded,
Lysias returned to the king and the Jews
reapplied themselves to their farming.
2 However, some of the governors in the
region—Timothy and Apollonius, the son of
Gennaeus,* as well as Hieronymus and
Demophon, and Nicanor, the commander of
the Cyprians—would not allow the Jews to
live quietly and in peace.

3 The people of Joppa committed a partic-
ularly wicked atrocity: they invited the Jews
who lived among them, together with their
wives and children, to set out on boats that
they had provided. There was no indication
of any animosity toward the Jews.* 4 There
had been a public vote of the city in this
regard, and the Jews accepted, since they
suspected no treachery and wished to live in
peace. The people of Joppa took them out to
sea and drowned at least two hundred of
them.

5 As soon as Judas learned of this act of
cruelty perpetrated against his compatriots,
he issued orders to his men, 6 and after call-
ing upon God, the just judge,[i] he attacked
the murderers of his kindred. He set fire to
the harbor during a nighttime attack,
burned the boats, and put to the sword those
who had taken refuge there. 7 Then, because
the gates of the town were closed, he with-
drew, intending to return later and wipe out
the entire community of Joppa.

8 However, after learning that the people
of Jamnia planned to deal in the same way
with the Jews who lived among them, 9 he
attacked the Jamnians by night and set fire
to the harbor and the fleet, so that the glow
of the flames was visible as far off as Je-
rusalem, thirty miles away.*

Judas Intervenes in Galaad.* 10[j] When the
Jews had proceeded more than a mile from
there in their campaign against Timothy,
they were attacked by at least five thousand

---

i 2 Mac 12:41; Pss 7:12; 9:5, 8.—j 10-16: 1 Mac 5:24-36.

11:29 *Menelaus:* the high priest spoken of in 2 Mac 4:23-25; 5:15.

11:33 The date given here is the same as for the Romans' letter in verse 38, which cannot be the case. The king's letter must be related to the peace treaty of the Seleucid year 149, that is, 163 B.C. Some believe that the appearance of the month Xanthicus in the body of the letter (v. 30), as well as in the close, caused the date of the Romans' letter to be transferred to the king's letter.

12:2 *Apollonius, the son of Gennaeus:* distinct from the Apollonius mentioned in 2 Mac 4:21, who was the son of Menestheus. *Nicanor:* distinct from the general spoken of in 2 Mac 8:9; 14:2.

12:3 The enmity of the inhabitants of Joppa toward the Jews continues even after the death of Judas (see 1 Mac 10:75; 12:33f; 13:11).

12:9 *Thirty miles away:* the distance is approximated; from Jerusalem to the ancient port of Jamnia was a distance of some thirty-five miles.

12:10-16 This campaign, which has no connection with the preceding episode, is recounted with greater precision and coherence in 1 Mac 5:9-68.

Arab infantrymen supported by five hun-
dred horsemen. 11 After a fierce struggle,
Judas and his companions were victorious
with the help of God. The defeated nomads
begged Judas to make a pact of friendship
with them, and they promised to supply the
Jews with cattle and to help them in every
other way possible. 12 Realizing that they
might indeed be useful in many ways, Judas
agreed to make peace with them, and after
assurances of friendship had been ex-
changed, the Arabs withdrew to their tents.

13 Judas also attacked a town named
Caspin, which was fortified by earthworks
and ramparts and inhabited by a mixed
population of Gentiles. 14 Confident in the
strength of their walls and their stock of pro-
visions, the besieged treated Judas and his
men with contempt, insulting them and
uttering blasphemies and profanity. 15 How-
ever, Judas and his men invoked the great
Sovereign of the world who, without batter-
ing ram or engines of war, had overthrown
Jericho in the days of Joshua. Then they
stormed the wall with a savage assault.[k]
16 They captured the town by the will of God,
inflicting such an indescribable slaughter
that the adjoining lake, a quarter of a mile in
width, appeared to be overflowing with
blood.

The Battle of Carnaim. 17 [l]When they had
advanced from there about ninety-five
miles, they came to Charax, which was in-
habited by those Jews known as Toubiani.* [m]
18 However, they did not find Timothy in that
region, for by then he had departed from
there without accomplishing anything, aside
from leaving behind a very strong garrison
in one place. 19 But Dositheus and Sosipater,
two of the generals of Maccabeus, marched
out and destroyed the force that Timothy
had left behind in the stronghold, a force that
numbered more than ten thousand men.
20 Meanwhile, Maccabeus divided his army
into cohorts, with a commander in charge of
each cohort,* and hurried in pursuit of
Timothy, whose troops numbered one hun-
dred and twenty thousand infantry and
twenty-five hundred cavalry. 21 When Tim-
othy learned of the approach of Judas, he
sent off the women and the children and also
the baggage to a place called Carnaim,
which was hard to besiege and difficult to
approach because of the narrowness of the
passages of entry.

22 However, after the first cohort of Judas
appeared, the enemy was stricken with ter-
ror and fear at the manifestation of the All-
seeing One.[n] In headlong flight, they scat-
tered in every direction, so that frequently
they were injured by their own comrades
and run through by the points of their
swords. 23 Judas pressed the pursuit vigor-
ously, putting the sinners to the sword and
slaying as many as thirty thousand men.

24 Timothy himself fell into the hands of
Dositheus and Sosipater and their men, but
with considerable cunning, he begged them
to let him go unharmed, the reason being
that he had the parents and relatives of
many of them in his power and their fate was
in his hands. 25 When he made a solemn
pledge to return those hostages unharmed,
they set him free for the sake of saving their
kindred. 26 Judas then marched against Car-
naim and the temple of Atargatis,* where he
slaughtered twenty-five thousand people.

Judas Returns to Jerusalem. 27 [o]After the
defeat and destruction of these, he led his
army against Ephron, a fortified town where
Lysias dwelt with people of various national-
ities. Stalwart young men took up their posts
in defense of the walls and made a spirited
stand, while inside there were large supplies
of engines of war and missiles. 28 However,
the Jews, having invoked the Sovereign
whose power shatters the strength of his ene-
mies, gained control of the town and killed
about twenty-five thousand of the people
inside. 29 Then they set out from there and
pushed on to Scythopolis,* seventy-five
miles from Jerusalem. 30 But when the Jews
who lived there testified to the goodwill
that the people of Scythopolis had shown
them, and to their kind treatment of them
during times of misfortune, 31 Judas and
his men thanked them and exhorted them
to be well disposed to their race in the
future also. Finally, since the Feast of
Weeks* was close at hand, they proceeded
to Jerusalem.

k Jos 6:1-21.—l 17-26: 1 Mac 5:37-44.—m 1 Mac 5:13.—n 2 Mac 7:35; 9:5; 15:21; Sir 15:18.—o 27-31: 1 Mac 5:45-54.

12:17 *Toubiani:* Jews from the land of Tob (see 1 Mac 5:13).

12:20 *Commander in charge of each cohort:* that is, Dositheus over one and Sosipater over the other.

12:26 *Atargatis:* a Syrian goddess whose symbol was the body of a fish.

12:29 *Scythopolis:* the Greek name for Beth-shan (see 1 Mac 5:52).

12:31 *Feast of Weeks:* Greek name for Pentecost, so called because it was celebrated seven *weeks* after the Passover.

An Engagement That Ends Badly. [32]After the
Feast of Pentecost, they marched against
Gorgias, the governor of Idumea, [33]who con-
fronted them with three thousand foot sol-
diers and four hundred horsemen. [34]In the
course of the ensuing battle, a small number
of Jews lost their lives. [35]However, a man
named Dositheus, one of Bacenor's cavalry
forces* and an individual of great strength,
caught hold of Gorgias by his cloak and
forcibly dragged him along, intending to
take the accursed man alive. But a Thracian
horseman bore down on Dositheus and cut
off his arm at the shoulder, enabling Gorgias
to escape to Marisa.

[36]Meanwhile, inasmuch as Esdris and his
men were exhausted after engaging in battle
for a long time, Judas called upon the Lord
to show himself their ally and leader in the
battle. [37]Then, raising a battle cry in his
ancestral tongue, along with hymns, he
launched a surprise attack and put the
forces of Gorgias to flight. [38]Thereupon
Judas rallied his forces and advanced to the
town of Adullam. Inasmuch as the seventh
day of the week was at hand, they purified
themselves according to custom and kept
the Sabbath there.

The Sacrifice for the Dead.* [39]On the follow-
ing day, since the need had now become
urgent, Judas and his men went to collect the
bodies of those who had fallen and to bury
them with their kindred in their ancestral
tombs. [40]However, under the tunic of each of
the dead, they found amulets that were
sacred to the idols of Jamnia, which the law
forbids the Jews to wear. Thus it was clear to
everyone that this was the reason that these
men had been slain.[p] [41]And so they all
praised the acts of the Lord, the just judge
who reveals things that are hidden, [42]and
they turned to supplication, praying that the
sin that had been committed might be com-
pletely blotted out. The noble Judas exhorted
the people to keep themselves free from sin,
since they had seen with their own eyes what
had happened as a result of the sin of those
who had fallen.

[43]Then he took up a collection from all of
his soldiers, amounting to two thousand sil-
ver drachmas, and sent it to Jerusalem to
provide for an expiatory sacrifice. In doing
this, he acted in a suitable and honorable
way, guided by his belief in the resurrection.*
[44]For if he had not expected those who had
fallen to rise again, it would have been super-
fluous and foolish to pray for the dead.
[45]However, if he was focusing on the splendid
reward reserved for those whose death was
marked by godliness, his thought was holy
and devout. [46]Therefore, he had this expia-
tory sacrifice offered for the dead so that
they might be delivered from their sin.

CHAPTER 13

The End of Menelaus, the Renegade. [1]In the
year one hundred and forty-nine, Judas and
his men were informed that Antiochus
Eupator was advancing on Judea with a
large army, and that accompanying him was
Lysias, his guardian, who was in charge of
the government. [2][q]Additionally, they had a
Greek force consisting of one hundred and
ten thousand foot soldiers, five thousand
three hundred horsemen, twenty-two ele-
phants, and three hundred chariots armed
with scythes.*

[3]Menelaus also joined them, and with
considerable hypocrisy, he kept urging
Antiochus on, not for the sake of his coun-
try's welfare, but in the belief that he would
thereby become established in office. [4]How-
ever, the King of kings* stirred up the fury of
Antiochus against this scoundrel, and when
Lysias offered convincing evidence to the
king that Menelaus was to blame for all the
trouble, Antiochus ordered him to be taken
to Beroea and executed there in the custom-

p Deut 7:25.—q 1 Mac 6:30.

12:35 *One of Bacenor's cavalry forces:* some ancient witnesses to the text have "one of the Toubiani" (see v. 17). *Cloak:* a short cloak attached to the chest or a shoulder by a buckle. It was very common with officials of the Hellenistic armies. *Marisa:* ancient Canaanite city, about thirteen miles west of Hebron on the road that descends along the Philistine coast.

12:39-46 Judas has a sacrifice of expiation celebrated that God may pardon the sins of the dead. From the viewpoint of the faith, this passage is of great importance. First of all, it bears witness in an explicit manner to belief in the resurrection of the dead. Secondly, it gives weight to the conviction of the Church concerning a purification after death, that is, during that provisional condition in which the deceased—before living fully in God—expiate their sins and can be aided by the prayer of the living. Thirdly, the passage also offers testimony on behalf of the communion of saints, that is, that spiritual exchange that unites all the faithful with one another.

12:43 The ancient ritual (Lev 4:1-5, 13; 6:17-23) provided various forms of sacrifices of expiation according to the status of the persons and the gravity of the sin committed. In this case, it was two thousand silver drachmas.

13:2 *Chariots armed with scythes:* special chariots of war, equipped with sharp scythes featuring teeth of iron that were in use especially among the Persians.

13:4 *King of kings:* a new title in the Bible (which was taken from the title of the Persian kings) to indicate the absolute sovereignty of God even over the powerful of this world (see Deut 10:17; 1 Tim 6:15; Rev 17:14; 19:16). *Beroea* is the Greek name for Aleppo in Syria.

ary local manner.[r] 5 In that place there is a
tower seventy-five feet high, full of ashes,
with a rim encircling it that slopes down pre-
cipitously on all sides into the ashes.
6 Anyone found guilty of sacrilege, or any
other heinous crime, is taken to the top and
then hurled down to destruction. 7 Such was
the fate suffered by Menelaus,* the trans-
gressor of the law, as he died without even
being given the privilege of burial in the
ground. 8 His manner of death was eminent-
ly just, for he had committed innumerable
sins against the altar whose fire and ashes
were holy, and it was in ashes that he met his
death.

Judas Triumphs against the Syrians at Modein.
9 The king then advanced with savage arro-
gance, aiming to inflict on the Jews far worse
sufferings than they had experienced under
his father. 10 [s]When Judas learned of this, he
urged the people to call upon the Lord night
and day and to implore him to come to their
aid now more than ever before, 11 since they
were in danger of being deprived of their law,
their country, and the holy temple, and not
to allow them, just when they had begun to
revive, to once again fall into the hands of the
blasphemous Gentiles. 12 When they had all
joined in this petition and had implored the
merciful Lord unceasingly for three days
with weeping and fasting as they prostrated
themselves, Judas encouraged them and
ordered them to stand ready.

13 After consulting privately with the el-
ders, he decided not to wait for the king's
army to invade Judea and take possession of
the city, but to march forth and resolve mat-
ters with the help of God. 14 Thus, commit-
ting the outcome to the Creator of the world
and exhorting his soldiers to fight bravely to
the death for the law, the temple, the city, the
country, and their way of life, he pitched
camp near Modein.* 15 After giving his
troops the battle cry, "God's victory," he
made a nighttime attack on the king's pavil-
ion with a picked force of his bravest young
warriors and killed about two thousand of
the enemy in the camp, also slaying the lead
elephant and its driver.[t] 16 Eventually, they
filled the camp with terror and confusion
and then withdrew in triumph,* 17 just as
dawn was breaking. All this was achieved
through the help and protection that Judas
had received from the Lord.

Antiochus V Makes a Treaty with the Jews.
18 [u]The king, having had a taste of the dar-
ing of the Jews, resorted to strategy to cap-
ture their positions. 19 He advanced against
Beth-zur, a strong fortress of the Jews, but
he was checked, driven back, and defeated.
20 Judas then sent whatever supplies were
needed to the garrison, 21 but Rhodocus, a
soldier in the Jewish army, passed on secret
information* to the enemy. He was found
out, arrested, and imprisoned. 22 The king
negotiated with the inhabitants of Beth-zur
for a second time, offering and accepting
pledges of friendship. After withdrawing, he
then attacked Judas and his men but was
defeated.

23 Soon afterward, he received a report
that Philip,* who had been left in charge of
the government in Antioch, had rebelled.
Stunned by this news, he opened negotia-
tions with the Jews, agreed to their terms,
and swore to respect all their rights. Having
reached this agreement, he offered a sacri-
fice, honored the sanctuary, and made a
generous donation to the holy place. 24 He
received Maccabeus in a gracious manner
and left Hegemonides to serve as governor
of the region from Ptolemais to the territory
of the Gerrhenes.

25 When he thereupon went to Ptolemais,
the people of that city expressed their disap-
proval of the treaty in no uncertain terms,
and were so angered that they wanted to
annul its provisions. 26 However, Lysias
mounted the rostrum and made a reasoned
defense of the treaty that won them over,
calmed them down, and obtained their
goodwill. Then he departed for Antioch.

---

r 1 Tim 6:15; Rev 17:14; 19:16.—s 10-12: 2 Mac 8:29; 11:9; 1 Sam 7:6; Joel 2:12.—t 1 Mac 6:43-46.—u 18-23: 1 Mac 6: 48-53.

13:7 *Menelaus:* remained unburied, the ultimate punishment for dishonor, as was the case with the other sacrilegious high priest, Jason (see 5:10).

13:14 *Modein:* the home of the Maccabean family (see 1 Mac 2:1) on the western boundary of Judea. The area was well situated to prevent the passage of those who from the plains attempted to ascend to Jerusalem by the sole road that passed through very narrow mountain gorges.

13:16 *They . . . withdrew in triumph:* according to 1 Mac 6:47, they fled.

13:21 *Secret information:* most likely concerning the lack of food in the besieged city (see 1 Mac 6:49).

13:23 *Philip:* named by Antiochus IV, before his death, as universal regent of his kingdom and entrusted with preparing Antiochus V to rule. Lysias, seeing himself left out, hastened to proclaim Antiochus king and have himself named prime minister (see 1 Mac 6:15f). While Antiochus V and Lysias were carrying on a military campaign (see 2 Mac 13:1-22), Philip returned from Egypt to which he had fled and proceeded to occupy Antioch (1 Mac 6:55-63).

Such are the basic facts of the king's attack
and his subsequent retreat.

B: The War against Nicanor's Strategy

CHAPTER 14

Alcimus Plots Intrigues against the New King.
1 *v* Three years later, Judas and his followers
were informed that Demetrius, the son of
Seleucus, had sailed into the harbor of
Tripolis with a powerful army and a fleet,*
2 and that he had taken control of the coun-
try after having done away with Antiochus
and his guardian Lysias.

3 Now a man named Alcimus, a former
high priest who had willfully incurred defile-
ment at the time of the revolt, realized that
there was no possible way that his safety
could be assured or that he could again have
access to the holy altar. 4 *w* Therefore, he
went to King Demetrius about the year one
hundred and fifty-one and presented him
with a crown of gold and a palm branch, in
addition to some of the customary olive
branches from the temple. On that occasion,
he kept silent. 5 However, he found an oppor-
tunity to further his mad scheme when
Demetrius invited him to a meeting of the
council and questioned him about the dispo-
sitions and the intentions of the Jews. He
replied:

6 "Those Jews who are called Hasideans
and are led by Judas Maccabeus are war-
mongers who foment sedition and prevent
the kingdom from achieving a state of tran-
quility. 7 That is why, although I have been
deprived of my ancestral dignity—I am
referring to the high priesthood—I have now
come here, 8 first out of my genuine concern
for the interests of the king, and second,
because of my regard for my compatriots,
since our entire nation has been afflicted
severely because of the irresponsible con-
duct of these people I have mentioned.
9 When you have ascertained the truth of
these facts, O king, may it please you to
make provision for the welfare of our coun-
try and our oppressed people, exhibiting the
same gracious kindness that you extend to
all. 10 For as long as Judas remains alive, it
will be impossible for the state to enjoy the
condition of peace."

11 When he had said this, the rest of the
King's Friends, all of whom were hostile to
Judas, added further fuel to the fire, inflam-
ing the anger of Demetrius even more.

12 *x* The king immediately chose Nicanor,*
who had been in command of the elephants,
and appointed him as governor of Judea.
Then, he sent him forth 13 with orders to put
Judas to death, to disperse his followers, and
to install Alcimus as high priest of the great
temple.

14 The Gentiles throughout Judea, who had
fled from the attacks of Judas, now flocked to
join Nicanor, confident that the misfortunes
and calamities of the Jews would mean pros-
perity for themselves.

Nicanor Makes Peace with Judas. 15 *y* When
the Jews learned that Nicanor was ap-
proaching and that the Gentiles were rally-
ing to his support, they sprinkled dust over
themselves and prayed to him who had
established his people forever and who
always came to the aid of his heritage. 16 At
the command of their leader, they set out
from there immediately and confronted the
enemy at the village of Adasa.* 17 Simon, the
brother of Judas, engaged in battle with
Nicanor, but suffered a minor setback due
to the sudden appearance of the enemy.
18 However, when Nicanor heard of the brav-
ery exhibited by Judas and his men and how
courageously they always fought for their
country, he became reluctant to allow the
issue to be settled by bloodshed. 19 There-
fore, he sent Posidonius, Theodotus, and
Mattathias to negotiate a treaty of peace.

20 After a lengthy discussion of the terms,
each leader explained them to his troops,
and all were of one mind in favor of accept-
ing them. 21 On the day decided upon for the
respective leaders to meet privately, a chari-
ot came forward from each side, and thrones
were set in place. 22 Judas had posted armed
men at strategic points to prevent any sud-
den act of treachery on the part of the
enemy. In this way, the conference was held
without any complications.

v 1-11: 1 Mac 7:1-7.—w 4-11: 1 Mac 7:7, 25; 13:37.—x 12f: 2 Mac 8:9; 1 Mac 3:38f.—y 15-19: 1 Mac 7:26-32.

14:1 See 1 Mac 7:1. The events are taking place in the spring of 161 B.C.

14:12 *Nicanor:* the Syrian general who had directed the first great expedition against Judea at the time of Antiochus IV. During the reign of Antiochus V, he had dissociated himself from the politics of the prime minister Lysias and had gone to Rome where he joined Demetrius I and accompanied him in his escape from there and eventual acquisition of the throne.

14:16 *Adasa:* a name that occurs only here and whose location is disputed. In any case, it had to be north of, and not far away from, Jerusalem since it was in this area that the parallel events narrated in 1 Mac 7:26-50 took place.

[23]Nicanor stayed on in Jerusalem and did
nothing there that could be construed as a
hostile act. He sent away the crowds that had
rallied to him, [24]but he always kept Judas
close to him, for he became deeply attached*
to him. [25]He urged him to marry and have
children, and Judas did marry and settle
down to lead the quiet life of an ordinary cit-
izen.

Nicanor Moves Anew against Judas. [26]When
Alcimus* discovered the depth of the friend-
ship that these two men had for each other,
he went to Demetrius with a copy of the
treaty they had signed. He claimed that
Nicanor was engaged in treasonable activity
against the state, since he had appointed
Judas, a conspirator against the kingdom, to
be his successor. [27]Enraged by the slander-
ous charges of that villain, the king wrote to
Nicanor, expressing his displeasure with the
terms of the treaty and commanding him to
send Maccabeus as a prisoner to Antioch at
once.

[28]When this message reached Nicanor, he
was greatly upset, for he did not wish to
break his agreement with a man who had
done nothing wrong. [29]However, since there
was no possible way to flaunt the king's wish-
es, he waited for an opportunity to carry out
the order by means of some stratagem.
[30]But Maccabeus began to notice that
Nicanor was becoming much cooler in his
dealings with him and displaying unaccus-
tomed rudeness whenever they met, and he
surmised that such an attitude did not bode
well for him. Therefore, he gathered a large
number of his followers and went into hiding
from Nicanor.*

[31][z] When Nicanor became aware that he
had been cleverly outwitted by this man, he
went to the great and holy temple at the time
when the priests were offering the custom-
ary sacrifices and ordered them to surren-
der Judas. [32]When they declared under oath
that they did not know the whereabouts of
the wanted man, [33]he stretched out his right
hand toward the temple and swore this oath:
"If you do not hand over Judas to me as a
prisoner, I shall level this shrine of God to
the ground and destroy the altar, and on this
very spot, I will erect a splendid temple to
Dionysus."

[34]Having issued this threat, he then left,
whereupon the priests stretched out their
hands to heaven and prayed to the constant
defender of our nation in these words: [35]"O
Lord of all, though you are in need of noth-
ing, it has pleased you that there should be a
temple for your dwelling place among us.[a]
[36]Therefore, O Holy One, Lord of all holi-
ness, preserve forever undefiled this house
that has so recently been purified."

The Voluntary Sacrifice of Razis.* [37]A man
named Razis, one of the elders of Jerusalem,
was denounced to Nicanor. He deeply loved
his compatriots and was highly esteemed by
them, and he was known as the father of the
Jews because of his loyalty. [38]In the early
days of the revolt, he had been convicted of
practicing Judaism and had risked unhesi-
tatingly both life and limb in that cause.
[39]Nicanor, in his determination to demon-
strate his contempt for the Jews, sent more
than five hundred soldiers to arrest him,
[40]for he thought that by such an action he
would deliver a severe blow to the Jews.
[41]When the troops were on the point of cap-
turing the tower and were forcing open the
outer gate, they called for fire to burn down
the doors. Razis, finding himself surrounded
on all sides, turned his sword on himself,
[42]preferring to die nobly rather than fall into
the hands of evil men and suffer outrages
unworthy of his noble birth.

[43]However, in the heat of the struggle he
failed to hit his mark exactly. So while the
troops rushed in through the doors, he
quickly ran up to the top of the wall and
courageously threw himself down into the
crowd. [44]They quickly separated, and a
space opened, and he plunged into the
midst of the empty area they had vacated.
[45]Still breathing and inflamed with anger,
he picked himself up and ran through the
crowd, even though blood was gushing
from his severe wounds. [46]Then, standing
on a steep rock, with almost the last drop of
blood drained from his body, he tore out his
entrails with both hands and flung them
into the midst of the crowd, calling upon
the Lord of life and spirit to restore them to

z 31-36: 1 Mac 7:33-38.—a Acts 17:25.

14:24 *Deeply attached:* only for a while (see vv. 14:31-33).

14:26 Failing to obtain civil power, *Alcimus* feared that Judas would be made his *successor* as high priest.

14:30 The account is here completed with what is said in 1 Mac 7:30-32.

14:37-46 Razis's suicide, which in any other circumstance would be a crime, is here equivalent to the heroic act of a martyr and becomes a supreme appeal for divine justice. At the same time, it bears witness to Razis's faith in the resurrection.

him once again. This was the manner of his death.[b]

CHAPTER 15

Nicanor's Blasphemy. [1]When Nicanor was informed that Judas and his troops were in the region of Samaria, he made plans to attack them on their day of rest when there would be no risk.* [2]Those Jews who had been forced to accompany him pleaded: "Do not massacre them in so savage and barbaric a fashion. Show respect for the day that the All-seeing has exalted and sanctified above all other days." [3]At this, the thrice-accursed wretch asked if there was a sovereign in heaven who had commanded the observance of the Sabbath day.[c] [4]When the Jews declared, "The living Lord himself, the ruler in heaven, ordered us to keep holy the seventh day," [5]he replied, "And I am a sovereign on earth, and I command you to take up arms and carry out the king's business." Nevertheless, he did not succeed in carrying out his wicked plan.

Judas's Humble Trust Is Contrasted with Nicanor's Haughty Certainty.* [6]Nicanor, in his utter boastfulness and arrogance, had planned to erect a public monument of victory over Judas and his men. [7]However, Maccabeus remained confident, firm in his belief that he would receive help from the Lord. [8]He urged his troops to have no fear of the attack of the enemy but to keep in mind the help that they had received from Heaven in former times and to remain confident that victory would be theirs through the help of the Almighty. [9]He encouraged them by citing the Law and the Prophets,* and by reminding them of the struggles they had already survived in the past, he filled them with fresh enthusiasm.[d] [10]When he had stirred up their courage, he issued his orders, reminding them at the same time of the treachery of the Gentiles and their violation of oaths. [11]Having armed each of them not so much with the protection of shield and spear as with the confidence aroused by brave words, he encouraged all of them by relating a dream, a type of vision, that was worthy of belief.

[12]What he had seen was this: Onias, the former high priest, a good and noble man, modest in bearing, gentle in manner, eloquent in speech, and trained from childhood in every virtue, was praying with outstretched hands for the whole Jewish community.[e] [13]Next, in the same fashion, another man appeared, distinguished by his great age and dignity, an impressive air of majesty and extraordinary authority. [14]Onias then began to speak. "This is God's prophet Jeremiah," he said, "who loves the family of Israel and fervently prays for his people and the holy city." [15]Jeremiah stretched out his right hand and presented Judas with a gold sword. As he gave it to him, he said, [16]"Take this holy sword as a gift from God. With it you will crush your enemies."

Preparations for Combat.* [17]Encouraged by the noble words of Judas, which had the power to inspire valor and stir up courage in the hearts of the young, the Jews resolved not to delay but to bravely take the offensive and engage in hand-to-hand combat, inasmuch as their city, their holy things,* and their temple were in danger. [18]Their concern was not so much for their wives and children or their brothers and sisters and kindred as it was for the consecrated sanctuary.[f] [19]Those who remained in the city experienced a similar anxiety, for they were anxious about the battle that was about to take place in the open country.

[20]Everyone now awaited the moment of decision. The enemy was already mounting the attack, with their troops drawn up in battle formation, with their elephants deployed in strategic positions, and with the cavalry stationed on the flanks. [21]Observing the deployment of the troops, the variety of the

b 2 Mac 7:9ff.—c Ex 20:11; 1 Mac 7:34.—d 2 Mac 8:23; Mt 5:17; 7:12; 22:40; Acts 13:15; 26:22.—e 2 Mac 3:1ff.—f 1 Mac 4:36.

15:1 The Maccabees had decided to defend themselves even on the day of the Sabbath (see 1 Mac 2:32-41).

15:6-16 Judas expects little from armaments and everything from God; he also knows that he can rely on the prayer of the saints like the former high priest Onias III (see 2 Mac 3:1-40) and the prophet Jeremiah, who was regarded by the post-Exilic Jews as one of the greatest figures in their history (see 2 Mac 2:1; Mt 16:14). This concept is something new in the Old Testament—a clear belief in the intercession of the saints.

15:9 *The Law and the Prophets* were now regarded as Scripture and known as the "sacred books" (1 Mac 12:9). Not all the other Books had been collected at this time (see Prologue to Wisdom of Ben Sira: "the Law ..., the Prophets, and the rest of the Books").

15:17-24 North of Jerusalem, the pagan forces are deployed in impressive array. However, the Jews face them with the ardor that comes from heroic faith—with complete trust in God. Judas prays for a victory like the one that God granted the Jews over Sennacherib, the king of Assyria, in the time of Hezekiah (Isa 37:36; 2 Ki 19:35)—and his prayers are heard.

15:17 *Holy things:* the expression *ta hagia* usually designates the temple or the sanctuary. Here it seems obvious that it refers to religious institutions, to the laws on which the Jewish life was based.

weapons, and the savagery of the elephants, Maccabeus stretched out his hands toward heaven and called upon the Lord who works miracles, for he was well aware that it was not by force of arms but, as God himself decides, that victory is won by those who deserve it. 22 [g] His prayer was in these words:

"You, O Lord, sent your angel in the days of King Hezekiah of Judea, and he slew at least one hundred and eighty-five thousand men of Sennacherib's army. 23 Now, O Sovereign of the heavens, please send a good angel once again to go before us spreading terror and panic. 24 May these blasphemers who have come to attack your holy people be struck down by the might of your arm." With these words he brought his prayer to a close.

The Gentiles Are Defeated.* 25 [h] Nicanor and his forces advanced to the sound of trumpets and songs of battle, 26 but Judas and his troops countered by engaging the enemy with invocations and prayers. 27 Fighting with their hands and praying to God in their hearts, they cut down at least thirty-five thousand men and greatly rejoiced over this manifestation of God's power. 28 When the battle was over and they were joyfully departing, they recognized Nicanor lying dead in full armor. 29 Thereupon, they raised tumultuous shouts in their ancestral tongue in praise of the divine Sovereign.

30 Then Judas, who had devoted himself, body and soul, to the defense of his people and had maintained from his youth his love for his compatriots, ordered them to cut off Nicanor's head and his whole right arm and carry them to Jerusalem. 31 When he arrived there and had called the people together and stationed the priests before the altar, he sent for those in the citadel 32 and showed them the head of the vile Nicanor and the wretched blasphemer's arm that had been boastfully stretched out against the holy house of the Almighty. 33 He cut out the tongue of the godless Nicanor and swore that he would feed it piecemeal to the birds and hang up the rewards of his folly opposite the temple. 34 On hearing this, everyone looked to heaven and blessed the Lord for the manifestation of his divine power, saying, "Blessed be he who has preserved his own place from defilement."

35 Judas hung Nicanor's head from the citadel, a clear and evident sign to everyone of the help of the Lord.[i] 36 By public vote it was unanimously decreed never to allow that day to pass unobserved, but to celebrate it on the thirteenth day of the twelfth month, called Adar in Aramaic,* the eve of Mordecai's day.[j]

V: AUTHOR'S EPILOGUE

37 This, then, was the fate of Nicanor, and since that time, the city has remained in the possession of the Hebrews. Therefore, I will bring my own work to an end here too. 38 If it has been well written and to the point, that has been my purpose. If it is poorly done and mediocre, that is the best I can do. 39 For just as it is injurious to drink wine by itself or water by itself, whereas wine mixed with water produces a pleasant and delicious drink that enhances one's enjoyment, so a skillful style used in presenting a story will delight the ears of those who read the work. Let this, then, be the end.

g 22f: 2 Mac 8:19; 2 Ki 19:35; Isa 37:36; 1 Mac 7:40f.—h 25-36: 1 Mac 7:39-50.—i 1 Sam 31:9f.—j 1 Mac 7:49.

15:25-36 Two armies and two civilizations confront one another: the battle songs of the Greeks are answered by the prayers of the Jews. In all probability the author is distorting the historical fact; he wishes to stress that the victory goes to the people of God. Judas reserves for the impious the fate that was assigned to blasphemers. From now on Israel will joyfully celebrate the anniversary of that memorable day: "Nicanor's Day" instituted in February–March 160 B.C.

15:36 *Adar in Aramaic:* the last month of the Jewish year, corresponding approximately with our month of March. "Nicanor's Day" was celebrated until A.D. 70 (when the Romans destroyed the temple) together with the "feast of Mordecai," that is, Purim (Est 9:17-32).

THE SAPIENTIAL AND POETIC BOOKS

At this point a new section of the Old Testament Bible begins. The writings we have read thus far—the two groups of narrative works—were in prose, with passages in verse. From here on, the opposite will rather be the case: Books generally poetic in form, but with some passages in prose. This new section will likewise contain two groups of Books: the first by "poets and wisdom writers," and the second by the "Prophets."

The first group includes:

—*Job:* a lengthy dialogue in verse on the problem of suffering.

—*Psalms:* 150 metrical compositions by various authors and from various periods.

—*Proverbs:* a collection of several series of sayings and maxims in metrical form.

—*Ecclesiastes:* an inquiry, again in chiefly metrical form, into the meaning of life.

—*Song of Songs:* a lyric poem in the form largely of a dramatic action.

—*Wisdom:* a poetic meditation in a broad poetic form.

—*Wisdom of Ben Sira:* a carefully worked out metrical composition consisting of maxims and elevations.

In these Books one theme keeps recurring with typical frequency: the theme of wisdom, i.e., wisdom about living. This is why the Books are known as the "Sapiential Books," although the name applies more strictly to the last five of the seven (thus leaving the adjective "poetic" as a description of the first two). But the concept of wisdom is also abundantly present in Job, which is a lengthy inquiry into wisdom, while among the Psalms, which are chiefly lyrical, there are quite a few that display a sapiential trend and are therefore called "didactic."

Some remarks are called for on each of two elements: the formal or literary aspect, and the sapiential aspect or the content.

Hebrew Poetry

Verses in Hebrew poetry are composed of two (sometimes three or more) parts, which are called "stichs"—the second of them being in some way symmetrical with the first. This is the characteristic element in all Hebrew poetry and is called "parallelism." The parallelism can take any of three forms. One is *synonymy*, which is the most common form; here the same idea is repeated in different words (e.g., Ps 114:4: "The mountains skipped like rams, / the hills like lambs of the flock"; Ps 49:1: "Hear this, all you peoples; / listen carefully, all you inhabitants of the world").

A second is *antithesis*, with the contrast putting the same idea into relief (e.g., "A wise son brings joy to his father, / but a foolish son gives grief to his mother"—Prov 10:1); this is, consequently, the form most used in sententious sayings.

A third form, which lends itself to great variety, is a *parallelism in a broad sense*, when the second stich simply completes the first (e.g., Ps 3:5: "Whenever I cry aloud to the LORD, / he answers me from his holy mountain"). In this third form, then, each of the two stichs often presents part of the idea, so that the entire thought is given by the two together.

Thus, in the example given from *Proverbs*, the point is not that the good son gives joy to the father alone while the bad son gives grief to the mother alone, but rather that each of the two sons obviously brings joy or grief to the "parents." So too, in Psalm 92:3, "to proclaim [the LORD's] kindness in the morning / and [his] faithfulness during the night" means to extol the divine goodness all day long, or "night and day."

Although verses composed of two stichs are by far the most common, there are, as was said above, verses containing three or more stichs. In fact, the Psalter begins with a three-membered verse: "Blessed is the man / who does not walk in the counsel of the wicked, / nor stand in the way of sinners, / nor sit in the company of scoffers" (Ps 1:1). If we look closely, it seems clear that since "scoffers" is parallel to "wicked" and "sinners," it is a synonym for these, "scoffing" being a form of wickedness and sin.

Generally speaking, attention to parallelism is a great help for grasping the precise meaning of a passage. When we read: "O God, endow the king with your judgment, / the son of kings with your righteousness" (Ps 72:1), we will not think of two different persons for whom two different favors are being asked, but, at most, that the king in question belongs to a royal dynasty.

Scholars have not yet reached unanimity in regard to strophes; it is generally admitted that they exist, but in practice, it is not easy to distinguish them.

Reality and Life

The *Book of Proverbs* has preserved opinions and sayings from quite remote ages. We see this straight off, for the proverbs consist of short sentences that transmit a popular observation, for example, a truth embodying the common sense of peasants. Rather than develop some grand theory, these proverbs concentrate on everyday life.

The Teachings and the Challenges

With the coming of the monarchy in the tenth century B.C. and with the organization of political power and a stable administration, there was recognition that public functionaries included not only the priest, but also the prophet and the wise man (or sage). This last became the promoter of an accepted and developed education, a tradition of thought that sought to integrate scientific knowledge, moral ideas, and theological claims. Wisdom thus became governess and teacher, for the benefit especially of those in authority. It ought not to surprise us that all the sacred Books dealing with this wisdom claim Solomon as their author.

From that time on, there seem to have been schools in Israel. Teachers established the kind of environment in which all problems were discussed. They did not close themselves to the experience of other peoples, but assimilated it while modifying it in the interest of providing a way of life that was in conformity with the covenant. With even greater scrupulosity, they collected the sayings of the ancients, the old traditions.

They began by showing respect for existing things, by accepting reality, by humility in the face of human limitations. One thing above all else they inculcated:

fidelity to God and to the law that he had given to Israel as its special privilege. Observance of the law was the beginning and end of wisdom, so much so that not infrequently law and wisdom became interchangeable terms.

Then came the bitter experience of the Exile. The difficult return marked the beginning of a new era in a changed cultural setting. It is clear that Israelite wisdom, too, shows the marks of this change, and it does so by dealing with the pressing problems of human beings. This applies, first, to the *Book of Job*. Its unknown author has a wonderful ability to observe nature and describe the mysteries of the universe, but, first and foremost, this great poem issues a challenge: traditional answers to the tragedy of suffering are inadequate, and the whole problem must be debated.

Next, *Ecclesiastes* (or *Qoheleth*) is not satisfied with what is generally regarded as a good education; in the eyes of those who have the courage to think, that is, truly wise people, there is no answer that can remove the scandal of injustice, illness, and death. In the night of the spirit, one must submit to the mystery, remain faithful, and not deny certainties already achieved.

The Period of the Theologians

The way courageously taken by Job and Ecclesiastes must have been regarded as a perilous one by many. Toward the end of the Old Testament another more conservative and reassuring attack on the problems is made: the *Book of Ecclesiasticus*, today more usually known as *Wisdom of Ben Sira*. But the author's serenity and his love of the solid tradition that he greatly desires to hand on also have a specific purpose: to prevent the originality of Israel and, above all, its faith from being diluted amid the heterogeneity of pagan civilizations.

In the course of its development in Israel, wisdom becomes increasingly theological. As biblical literature reaches its close, the teachers of wisdom work out their spiritual and moral synthesis, determine their main positions within the totality of their knowledge, and set these down in major pieces of writing. A few decades before the Christian era, the *Book of Wisdom* sets forth answers regarding human destiny and the goal of history that were revolutionary in their time.

For these wise men, wisdom acquires new connotations. It is seen as a higher kind of understanding and as a gift of God. Wisdom is imagined as a person at God's side, a witness to his thoughts and to his plans to make these known to humanity. Wisdom is, as it were, a presence of God in the midst of human beings—a demanding presence, since to acknowledge wisdom means also to be converted.

The texts constantly speak of wisdom, but in reality it is God himself who is being set before the mind and free will of each individual. The theme is developed not only in *Wisdom* (ch. 7), but especially in *Proverbs* (chs. 1; 8–9), *Job* (ch. 28), and *Baruch* (ch. 3). As seen by Christians, the thinking of these sages foretells in a vague way the presence of Christ, the incarnate word of God, and the coming of the Spirit who acts in the hearts of men and women.

In this collection of reflective works, the *Song of Songs* also found a place. It is a song that celebrates the love between man and woman and, at the same time, a song of God's love for humanity. Is this not perhaps the more important thing for the human heart?

"When three of Job's friends heard of all the misfortunes that he had endured, each of them set out from his own home . . . to console and comfort him" *(Job 2:11).*

THE BOOK OF JOB

Human Suffering and Divine Justice

The Book of Job will never lose the important place it has so long held in world literature. Never has the question of human suffering and divine justice been so forcefully asked. In the face of this problem all the answers that have been given, even those of the religions, seem pretentious, empty, and false.

In our Christian Bible, Job comes at the head of the series of writings that makes up the Poetic and Sapiential Books, and indeed it is the masterpiece of this collection. It was composed after the Exile and, in all probability, in the fifth century. During that period the temple had been rebuilt (520–515 B.C.; Ezr 5–6) and the walls of Jerusalem had been restored (445 B.C.; Neh 2–3; 6).

The small Jewish community that had been brought together again and organized anew around some important personalities was coming back to life under the more or less liberal control of the Persian authorities. There were difficulties, and as the self-centeredness of the various classes expanded, the injustices and violence of a former time reappeared (Neh 5). The poor were oppressed, and the scandal was all the more serious since the poor were often the most religious and faithful sector of the people. Prophets intervened to remind people of the ideal (Isa 58–59) and to answer the objections of those who were suffering and asking "Where is the God of justice?" (Mal 2:17; 3:13-21). This is precisely the serious question raised by the Book of Job.

The unknown author was certainly a member of the educated circles of Jerusalem. In fact, at a time when Aramaic was becoming the everyday language of the people, this writer handled classical Hebrew with the greatest ease; his many references to matters having to do with Egypt would suggest that he had traveled in the region of the Nile; in any case, he seems to be informed about the situations, mentalities, and traditions of the vast Eastern world around him; perhaps he had read the ancient poems of Egypt and Babylonia that already raised the mystery of suffering (in Egypt, "The Dialogue of the Despairing"; in Babylonia, "The Poem of the Suffering Just Man").

But the source of his religious thought is to be looked for primarily in the tradition of Israel: in addition to the Books of the covenant and the Lord's promises to his people (Deut 28), the author has in mind the tragic life of the Prophet Jeremiah, who was the victim of unjust persecution. Then too, following the Prophet Ezekiel, he is convinced that each person is responsible for his actions, good or bad, and is no longer heir to the punishment due past generations (Ezek 18; 33:10-20). Jeremiah's experience and Ezekiel's thoughts raise pressing questions.

In the Book of Job, the man who speaks is profoundly religious but also shaken in his faith; he is no longer able to harmonize the most fundamental elements of traditional teaching (God is just and good) with realities that continually impinge on his consciousness (there are righteous persons who suffer and wicked persons who are happy). It may be thought that he had personally experienced the suffering of which he speaks so powerfully and in such detail, and that in the depths of his own tribulation he had repeated Jeremiah's question: "Why?" (Jer 12:1).

The Book of Job depicts the personal tragedy of a conscience faced with a God who remains silent and whose justice is not visible. It also reflects the drama of Hebrew thought in this fifth century in which the Poor of the Lord (the anawim*) find themselves plunged into an unexpected experience: disillusionment.*

They have been disillusioned at the national level, since the enthusiastic predictions of the Prophets have not been fulfilled (Isa 35; 54; 60–62); they have been no less deeply disillusioned in their individual lives, since their fidelity to God has not profited them and since every day brings evidence that happiness is not proportioned to merit or to virtue, despite what the devout disciples of the Prophet Ezekiel too readily claim. The faith of Israel finds itself in a blind alley; it gropes blindly for a God who has become more distant and more mysterious.

But God himself is guiding the painful search; his grace is sustaining Israel, purifying its faith, and preparing it through tribulation to receive an increase in light with the revelation of a life that does not reach its end on earth. It will be necessary to wait until the second century (Dan 12:2-3; 1 Mac 7) before this certainty prevails.

While this conviction, which becomes a central assertion of the New Testament (Mt 5–7; Jn 11:24-25), satisfies the sense of justice and the quest for a personal destiny, it does not resolve all the problems raised by the author of the Book of Job. Job's deeply human tragedy is that of every age, since it touches human beings in that which is most personal and instinctive in them: the dread of suffering. However, Jesus with his message and example answers even this, by revealing the value and meaning of suffering as a trial and by teaching us to accept it while retaining a limitless trust in God our Father (see Lk 23:46).

The Book is made up essentially of a lengthy poetic debate between Job, the suffering righteous man, and his friends, who stick to the traditional teaching. Accusation and defense, solemn assertions and lyrical outpourings are woven together in an endless dialogue. The author evidently sides with Job, and yet each of the dialoguing persons contributes a carefully constructed religious outlook. Among the chapters are extremely beautiful poetic compositions on the earthly human condition, the secrets of the universe, and the spectacle that is this world. The cry of suffering is heartrending, but it does not prevent pauses for admiration. In the dispute among human beings, Job seems to have the last word (see ch. 31). But in this context what good is it to be right?

At the end, the Lord intervenes. This is the mystical moment, and Job the man is unexpectedly gripped by wonder in the presence of God's greatness and rises above his anguished question. In silence he comes to a more adequate idea of divine justice and to a humble acceptance of the human condition.

There is also, however, the far better known story of Job, a popular story, written in prose, that frames the forty chapters of dramatic debate. It takes the form of a short prologue (the misfortunes of Job) and a short epilogue (the restoration of Job). But this story presents us with a rather different personage from the one who speaks in the lengthy oratorical jousts. Job in the story is a righteous man for whom trials are not a scandal but simply an occasion for showing God a perfect and disinterested submission; because of this attitude, he will find himself once again covered in blessings. Yet this is the story that the author uses to begin and end his drama.

Sometimes the only thing people remember from the entire book is the story just described which, in the style of early accounts in Genesis, emphasizes the patience of Job. But despite the naive freshness and religious value of this popular legend, we must move beyond it if we are to uncover the real intentions of the author in the beautiful passages of the dialogues. His thought is hidden at almost every point in the confrontation of the several personages, and it would be an oversimplification to condemn in advance all the interventions of Job's clumsy friends. Each sheds light on some aspect of the truth, but it is especially Job and, at the end, God's final summation (chs. 38–41) that reveal the depths of the author's thought and communicate to us the essentials of his message on human suffering and divine justice.

The Book of Job may be divided as follows:

I: Prologue: Job's Prosperity, Woes, and Resignation (1:1—2:13)
II: First Cycle of Speeches (3:1—14:22)
III: Second Cycle of Speeches (15:1—21:34)
IV: Third Cycle of Speeches (22:1—31:40)
V: The Four Speeches of Elihu (32:1—37:24)
VI: The Intervention of God (38:1—42:6)
VII: Epilogue: Job's Honor and Goods Are Restored (42:7-17)

I: PROLOGUE: JOB'S PROSPERITY, WOES, AND RESIGNATION*

CHAPTER 1

A Good and Righteous Man.* 1 Job, a good
and righteous man, lived in the land of Uz.
He feared God and shunned evil. [a] 2 He was
the father of seven sons and three daughters,
3 and he possessed seven thousand sheep,
three thousand camels, five hundred yoke of
oxen, and five hundred donkeys, in addition
to a large number of servants. Thus, he was
the greatest man throughout the entire East.
4 Job's sons had the custom of taking turns
hosting banquets in one another's house, and
they would invite their three sisters to eat and
drink with them. 5 And when each banquet
had been completed, Job would send for his
children and sanctify them, rising early in the
morning and sacrificing burnt offerings for
each of them. For Job said, "It could perhaps
have happened that my sons have sinned and
blasphemed against God in their hearts."
This was his regular custom. [b]

a Job 1:8; 28:28.—b 1 Ki 21:10, 13.

1:1—2:13 Job, a personage celebrated for his virtues and his misfortunes, is one of those nomadic or seminomadic leaders—"the people of the East"—who had a reputation for wisdom. He is not an Israelite but lives in the Arabian wilderness that surrounds southern Palestine. He belongs to a distant past as one of a trio of legendary figures celebrated in Israel—the others being Noah, the hero of the flood, and Daniel, the protagonist of the biblical book modeled after an earlier Phoenician king renowned for wisdom, right judgment, and true piety (Ezek 14:14-20).

1:1-5 Job represents the ideal righteous person according to the Old Covenant, one who is faithful to all the religious observances. God blesses him in his children and in his possessions.

**"Why Should Job Not Be a God-Fearing
Man?"*** 6 [c] One day the sons of God assem-
bled to present themselves before the LORD,
and Satan was with them. [d] 7 The LORD said
to Satan, "Where have you come from?"
Satan answered the LORD and said, "I have
been roaming the earth and going back and
forth in it." [e] 8 The LORD asked him, "Have
you paid any notice to my servant Job? You
will not find anyone like him on the entire
earth. He is a good and righteous man who
fears God and shuns evil."

9 Satan said in reply, "Why should Job not
be a God-fearing man? 10 You have safe-
guarded him and his family and all his pos-
sessions with your protection. You have
blessed every one of his undertakings, and
his flocks have continued to increase
throughout the land. [f] 11 But if you stretch
out your hand and strike all that he has, he
will surely curse you to your face." 12 The
LORD then said, "Very well. All that he has is
in your power. However, you may not lay a
hand upon him." So Satan went forth from
the presence of the LORD.

Messengers of Woe.* 13 One day when Job's
sons and daughters were feasting and drink-
ing wine in their eldest brother's house, 14 a
messenger came to Job and said, "While
your oxen were plowing and the donkeys
were grazing beside them, 15 the Sabeans *
swooped down on them and carried them
off, after first putting the herdsmen to the
sword. I alone have escaped to tell you." [g]

16 While he was speaking, another messen-
ger arrived and said, "The fire of God *
flashed from heaven, striking the sheep and
their shepherds and consuming them. I
alone have escaped to tell you."

17 While he was still speaking, another
messenger ran up and said, "Three bands of
Chaldeans * made a raid on the camels and
carried them off and slaughtered those who
were tending them. I alone have escaped to
tell you."

18 While he was still speaking, yet another
messenger came forth and said, "Your sons
and daughters were feasting and drinking
wine in their eldest brother's house. 19 Then
suddenly a powerful wind swept across the
desert. It struck the four corners of the
house, which collapsed upon the young peo-
ple, and they are all dead. I alone have
escaped to tell you."

Blessed Be the Name of the LORD.* 20 Then
Job arose, tore his cloak, and shaved his
head. He threw himself prostrate on the
ground [h] 21 and said:

"Naked I emerged from my mother's
womb,
and naked I will return.
The LORD gave, and the LORD has taken
away;
blessed be the name of the LORD." [i]

22 In all this, Job did not sin, nor did he
revile God. [j]

CHAPTER 2

**Have You Paid Any Notice to My Servant
Job?*** 1 On another occasion the sons of God
came forward to present themselves before
the LORD, and Satan accompanied them. [k]
2 The LORD said to Satan, "Where have you
come from?" Satan answered the LORD and
said, "I have been roaming the earth and
going back and forth in it."

3 The LORD said to Satan, "Have you paid
any notice to my servant Job? You will not
find anyone like him on the entire earth. He
is a good and righteous man who fears God
and shuns evil. He still maintains his integri-
ty, even though you incited me to ruin him
without the slightest justification." [l]

4 Satan answered the LORD, "Skin for
skin! * A man will surrender everything he

c 6ff: Job 2:1ff.—d 1 Ki 22:19; Lk 22:31; Rev 12:9.—e Mt 12:43; 1 Pet 5:8.—f Job 1:3; 1 Sam 25:16.—g Gen 10:7; Ezek 24:26.—h Gen 37:29; Jer 7:29; Mk 14:63.—i Ru 1:21; 1 Sam 2:7; Eccl 5:15; 1 Tim 6:7.—j Job 2:10; Prov 10:19.—k Job 1:6.—l Job 1:1, 8; 9:17; 27:5.

1:6-12 The ancient story imagines God as surrounded by his court of heavenly beings for a discussion of human destinies. Satan is one of these servants; as his name indicates, his role is that of a prosecutor who is hostile to this human being (see Zec 3:1). Later on, Satan (Greek, *diabolos*, devil) will be turned into God's principal adversary, the leader of the demons, and will be identified with the "serpent" of Gen 3:1.

1:13-19 Four times without respite the announcement of disaster takes place. The accounts are linked together and are given along the same lines in order to dramatize the catastrophe.

1:15 *Sabeans:* nomadic raiders from northern Arabia.

1:16 *Fire of God:* that is, lightning (see Num 11:1; 1 Ki 18:38; 2 Ki 1:12).

1:17 *Chaldeans:* Syrian nomads.

1:20-22 Submissive to God in misfortune, Job is the model of pure religion, bereft of any egotism. He already announces the ideal of the Gospel.

2:1-6 Human beings are great before God when they patiently accept trials, but it is when suffering touches their very lives that they give the final proof of their fidelity.

2:4 *Skin for skin:* a proverbial expression that probably originated in the willingness to barter one animal skin for another. Here it means that Job is bearing his suffering with patience solely to avoid more severe suffering and to gain more favors from God.

has to save his own life. 5 But now if you
stretch forth your hand and touch his bone
and his flesh, he will curse you to your face."
6 The LORD said to Satan, "He is in your
power, but you must spare his life."

Job Did Not Utter a Single Sinful Word.*
7 Therefore, when Satan left the LORD's pres-
ence, he afflicted Job with malignant sores
from the soles of his feet to the top of his
head. 8 Job took a potsherd to scrape himself
as he sat among the ashes. *

9 Then his wife said to him, "When will you
give up persisting in your integrity? Curse
God and die!" [m] 10 He replied, "You are talk-
ing like a foolish woman. If we accept good
things from God, should we not be willing to
accept sorrows as well?" In all this, Job did
not utter a single sinful word. [n]

The Three Friends.* 11 When three of Job's
friends heard of all the misfortunes that he had endured, each of them set out from his own home—Eliphaz the Temanite, Bildad the Shuhite, and Zophar the Naamathite. After they gathered together, they went forth to console and comfort him. *

12 However, when they first saw Job from a
distance, they could hardly recognize him, and they wept aloud, tore their cloaks, and threw dust into the air over their heads.
13 Then they sat there with him upon the
ground for seven days and seven nights. None of them spoke a word to him, for they could clearly see how greatly he was suffering.

II: FIRST CYCLE OF SPEECHES

A: Job Curses the Day He Was Born

CHAPTER 3

Perish the Day on Which I Was Born. 1 After
this, Job opened his mouth and cursed the
day of his birth. [o] 2 He said:

3 "Perish the day on which I was born
and the night it was said, 'A boy is born.' [p]
4 May that day turn to darkness; *
may God not take note of it from above,
and may light not shine upon it.
5 May gloom and heavy darkness claim it;
let clouds spread over it
and blackness eclipse its light.
6 May thick darkness overpower it;
let it not be numbered among the days of the year
or reckoned in the cycle of the months.
7 "May that night be barren;
let no cry of joy be heard during it.
8 Let those curse it who curse the sea
and are prepared to rouse Leviathan. * [q]
9 May the stars of its twilight be darkened;
let it wait in vain for daylight
and never behold the first rays of dawn,
10 because it refused to shut the doors
of the womb of my mother who bore me
and shield my eyes from sorrow.

Why Go On Living?*

11 "Why did I not die at birth,
perishing as I came forth from the womb? [r]
12 Why were there knees to receive me
or breasts for me to feed on?
13 "For now I would be lying in tranquility,
asleep and resting peacefully
14 with kings and counselors of the earth
who built palaces for themselves that now lie in ruins,
15 or with princes who possessed gold in abundance
and filled their homes with silver.

m Job 6:29; 2 Ki 6:33; 1 Thes 5:8.—n Job 1:22; Jas 1:12; 5:11.—o Jer 15:10.—p Jer 20:14-15; Mt 26:24.—q Job 10:18; 41:1, 10; Pss 74:14; 104:26.—r Job 3:10; 10:18f.

2:7-10 Afflicted with a kind of leprosy, the sick man goes to live away from inhabited places atop a pile of dusty refuse that had accumulated over the years at the entrance to the city. The intervention of his wife in the guise of a temptress (see Gen 3:6-12; Jdg 16:4ff; Tob 2:14) puts the finishing touch to the trial of Job. His faith becomes even more heroic.

2:8 Sitting among ashes was a sign of mourning.

2:11-13 In the presence of Job, disfigured by suffering, his friends make use of rites of penitence and sorrow in common use: loud weeping, tearing of cloaks, throwing dirt over one's head, and long silent prostration (see Gen 50:10; Jos 7:6; 2 Sam 1:2, 11; 3:31).

2:11 Teman, Shuh, and Naamath were in Arabia, a land noted at that time for its wise men (see Prov 30:1; Jer 49:7; Ob 8-9; Bar 3:22f).

3:4 *May that day turn to darkness:* in the beginning God had said: "Let there be light" (Gen 1:3). Now Job so to speak says: "Let there be darkness," negating God's creative act.

3:8 This is an allusion to those sorcerers who claimed to be able to make days unlucky and to upset the order of the world. *The sea:* another possible translation is: "days." *Leviathan:* here it symbolizes the dark forces in the primitive chaos that God conquered and relegated to the depths of the ocean (see Pss 74:14; 104:26; Isa 27:1; 51:9; Am 9:3). Other creatures have also been put forth for the Leviathan, e.g., a killer whale.

3:11-19 In his suffering, Job regrets that he ever lived and longs for the hereafter: a kind of sleep in which there is no longer any place for suffering or for the unjust inequalities of the human condition. This hereafter is not the grave but the netherworld, which is a great pit within the earth in which the dead, now only shadows of themselves, are gathered together.

16 Or why was I not laid in a grave like a stillborn child,
like an infant that had never seen the light?
17 "In death* the wicked are free from worldly troubles
and the weary find rest.
18 There the captives enjoy the solace of peace
without having to cringe at the voice of their masters.
19 The small and the great are there as equals,
and servants are free from their masters.

What Good Is Life?*

20 "Why is light given to those in misery
and life to those whose hearts are bitter,[s]
21 who long for death that never comes
and seek for it more than for hidden treasure,
22 who would rejoice to see the grave
and exult on reaching the tomb,
23 who are unable to find their way
and whom God has hemmed in on every side?*[t]
24 "Sighs are for me my only food,
and my groans pour forth like water.
25 Everything that I fear has afflicted me,
and whatever I dread befalls me.
26 I am unable to find peace of mind or tranquility;
troubles assail me, and I find no rest."[u]

B: Eliphaz's First Speech*

CHAPTER 4

Can You Recall Even One Innocent Person Who Perished?* 1 Then Eliphaz the Temanite responded:

2 "If one of us attempts to reason with you,
will you be offended?
Yet who can refrain from speaking?
3 Recall how you instructed many others
and strengthened their feeble hands.
4 Your words have supported those who were staggering,
and you have made firm their faltering knees.
5 "But now that adversity has befallen you,
you have grown impatient;
you are dismayed because it has troubled you.
6 Does not your piety give you confidence
and the integrity of your life offer you hope?[v]
7 Can you recall even one innocent person
who perished?
Where have the upright ever been destroyed?[w]
8 "My experience has been that those who plow iniquity and sow trouble
reap no other harvest.
9 At the breath of God they are destroyed;
at the blast of his anger they perish.[x]
10 Even though they are as fierce as lions,
their fangs will be broken off.
11 The lion perishes for lack of prey,
and the whelps of the lioness are abandoned.

Can a Human Being Appear Upright in the Presence of God?*

12 "A word was quietly brought to me;
a whisper of it reached my ears.
13 It was made known to me in nighttime visions
when sleep comes upon all men.
14 I was seized with terror and trembling
that caused all my bones to shake violently.[y]
15 A spirit brushed across my face,
causing the hairs on my body to bristle.
16 It then halted,
but I could not discern its shape.
An image was before my eyes,
and then I heard a voice whisper:[z]
17 " 'Can a human being appear upright in the presence of God?

s 1 Sam 1:10.—t Job 19:8; Prov 4:19; Isa 40:27; Jer 13:16.—u Job 7:4, 14; 27:9; Isa 48:22; Mt 11:28.—v Job 1:1, 9; Prov 3:26.—w Ps 37:25; 2 Pet 2:9.—x Ps 18:16; Isa 11:4; 2 Thes 2:8.—y Job 33:19; Ps 119:120.—z 1 Ki 19:12.

3:17 *In death:* literally, "there."

3:20-26 The author expands the debate and raises the fundamental question: Does life still have value for someone whom Providence has left without children?

3:23 Earlier in the Book, Job is said to have been in God's safekeeping (Job 1:10). Now Job feels that God has hemmed him in on every side, leaving him in turmoil (see v. 26).

4:1—5:27 Job's friends, who have not experienced suffering, try to shed light on Job's suffering by means of their teaching. Their arguments remain theoretical in the presence of Job's cry.

4:1-11 Eliphaz is certain that experience shows one thing—virtue is always rewarded, and impiety is always punished. And if Job can take advantage of a virtuous life, he must remain confident.

4:12-21 Thanks to a personal revelation, Eliphaz has understood this important truth: man is only dust and impurity before his Creator. He echoes a major revelation of the entire Bible.

Can a mortal seem pure before its Maker?
18 God places no trust in his servants,
and he finds fault even with his angels. * [a]
19 How much more will this be true of those who dwell in houses of clay,
whose foundation is in the dust
and who can be crushed as easily as a moth.
20 From morning to evening they are cut down;
they perish forever, with hardly a thought from anyone.
21 Their tent-pegs are plucked up,
and they die devoid of wisdom.'

CHAPTER 5

Resentment Slays the Fool*

1 "Call out now if you so wish.
Is there anyone who will reply?
To which of the holy ones * will you turn? [b]
2 Resentment slays the fool,
and envy brings death to the simpleton.
3 I have seen a fool enjoy success for a time,
but suddenly his house was cursed.

4 "His children are cut off from safety,
slaughtered at the gate * without a defender.
5 The hungry devour their harvest,
even that growing amid the thorns, *
and the thirsty pant for their wealth.
6 For misery does not grow out of the earth,
nor does trouble spring from the soil.
7 Rather, man breeds trouble for himself,
as surely as sparks * fly upward. [c]

I Would Appeal to God*

8 "If I were you, I would appeal to God
and present my case before him.
9 He performs deeds that are beyond understanding,
and wonders that cannot be counted.
10 He provides rain for the earth
and sends down water upon the fields.
11 He raises on high those who are lowly,
and those who mourn he lifts to safety. [d]

12 "He thwarts the schemes of the crafty
so that they do not achieve any success.
13 He traps the cunning in their intrigues
and throws their plans into disarray. [e]
14 They encounter darkness in the daytime
and grope their way at noon as if it were night.
15 But he saves the destitute from the sword
and rescues them from the hand of the mighty.
16 Therefore, the poor once again have hope,
and iniquity must shut its mouth.

Blessed Is the Man Whom God Reproves*

17 "Blessed is the man whom God * reproves.
Therefore, do not reject the discipline of the Almighty.
18 For even though he wounds, he also binds up;
he smites, but his hands also heal. [f]
19 He will deliver you from trouble six times,
and on the seventh * no evil will touch you.
20 In time of famine he will rescue you from death,
and in wartime from the thrust of the sword.

---

a 2 Pet 2:4; Jude 1:6.—b Job 15:15; Heb 12:1.—c Job 14:1; Gen 3:17; Pss 58:4; 90:10.—d 1 Sam 2:7-8; Isa 61:2; Jas 1:9.—e Isa 29:14; Jer 8:8; 1 Cor 3:19.—f Deut 32:39; Isa 57:15; Hos 6:1f.

4:18 See Job 15:15. Taking his inspiration possibly from ancient beliefs (see Gen 6:2-4), the author already sets forth imprecise bits of a theory concerning the fall of the angels, which will be developed in the apocalypses (see Rev 12:7-12).

5:1-7 In time of trial, prayer is of no avail if it expresses obstinacy and vexation. Man is the cause of his own unhappiness.

5:1 *The holy ones:* after the Exile, this referred to the heavenly spirits (see Job 15:15; Dan 4:10, 14, 20; 8:13; Zec 14:5). They were beginning to be regarded as powerful intercessors with God (see Job 33:23-24; Zec 1:12).

5:4 *At the gate:* the place of the city where normal business was conducted and justice was administered.

5:5 *Even . . . thorns:* an alternative reading is: "God snatches it out of their mouths."

5:7 *Sparks:* literally, "sons of Resheph." Resheph was a god of the Canaanites whose name came to be used in the Old Testament as a symbol of fire (Song 8:6), lightning bolts (Ps 78:48), and pestilence (Deut 32:24; Hab 3:5).

5:8-16 Like an announcement of the Magnificat (Lk 1:49-53), this poem sings of the power and goodness of God. Eliphaz here presents a remarkable conception of prayer while excluding all discussion of human beings with God.

5:17-27 The traditional teaching on trials loves to describe the new earthly happiness that is in store for the faithful.

5:17 *God:* the Hebrew text has *Shaddai,* which means "the powerful one" or, literally, "God of the mountains." It was a name given to God in the time of the Patriarchs (see Gen 17:1; 35:11; 48:3; Ex 6:3). The author uses this archaic name in order to situate Job in a distant past.

5:19 *Six times . . . on the seventh:* a literary device for indicating a very large number or even a totality (see Prov 6:16f; 30:15f; Am 1:3-13).

21 "You will be shielded from the scourge of the tongue,
and you will not fear calamity when it looms.
22 You will laugh at destruction and famine
and not be terrified by the beasts of the earth.
23 For you will have a covenant with the stones of the field
and live in peace with wild animals.[g]
24 You will know that your tent is secure,
and your household will be intact when you inspect it.
25 "You will know that your descendants will be numerous,
and your offspring like the grass of the earth.[h]
26 You will go to the grave at a ripe old age,
like sheaves gathered at the right time.
27 All this we have researched, and it is true.
Heed it, and apply it to yourself."

C: Job's First Response*

CHAPTER 6

Impetuous Words.* 1 Job then answered with these words:

2 "If only my anguish could be weighed
and my misfortune placed with it on the scales.[i]
3 They would then outweigh the sands of the sea—
hence, my words have been impetuous.
4 For the arrows of the Almighty* have pierced me,
and my spirit soaks in their poison;
God's terrors are aligned against me.[j]
5 "Does the wild donkey bray when it has grass?
Does an ox bellow when it has fodder?
6 Can tasteless food be eaten without salt?
Is there any flavor in the whites of eggs?
7 I refuse to even touch them;
they are like uncleanness in my food.

The Consolation of Death*

8 "Oh, that I might receive my request
and God would grant me what I hope for:
9 that it would please him to crush me,
cutting me off and ceasing to restrain his hand.
10 Such would be my consolation,
and I would exult in my unrelenting pain,
since I have never rebelled against the commands of the Holy One.[k]
11 "Do I have the strength to continue to wait?
And what future awaits me should I decide to be patient?
12 Is my strength the strength of stone?
Is my flesh made of bronze?
13 How can I summon up the energy to survive?
All possible solutions to my plight are beyond my reach.[l]

My Brethren Have Betrayed Me*

14 "One who despairs should have the support of his friends
even if he has forsaken the fear of the Almighty.[m]
15 But my brethren have proved to be as treacherous as a torrent,
like watercourses that suddenly run dry;
16 they turn dark with ice
and swell with the thawing of the snow,
17 but they dry up in the hot season,
and in the heat vanish from their beds.
18 "Caravans wander off from their course;
they go into the wilderness and perish.
19 The caravans of Tema search for water;
the travelers from Sheba* move forward in hope.
20 But despite their confidence they are doomed to disappointment;
they arrive there, only to be frustrated.

g Isa 28:15; Hos 2:18.—h Pss 72:16; 112:2; Isa 44:3-4; 48:19.—i Job 31:6; Prov 11:1; Dan 5:27.—j Job 31:23; Gen 17:1; Deut 32:23; Ps 88:15-18.—k Job 23:11; Ps 94:19; Jer 45:3.—l Job 26:2.—m 1 Sam 20:42; Ps 69:21; Zec 7:9.

6:1—7:21 Eliphaz's words, despite their spiritual beauty, have remained theoretical. Is there any recourse outside of God?

6:1-7 Anyone who is without affliction cannot measure another person's suffering. Just as a bow reaches an adversary, God's chastisements pierce hearts; they are as frightening as his poisonous arrows (Deut 32:23; Ps 38:3; Lam 3:12-15; Ezek 5:16).

6:4 The *arrows of the Almighty:* (the Hebrew has the archaic *Shaddai*); the trials sent by God (see note on Ps 38:3).

6:8-13 Job has reached the end of his strength and his patience, and now waits only for death. His only consolation is that he will have remained faithful to God to the end.

6:14-21 Friendship is a refreshing source, but for the sick it is as rare as a spring for a caravan in the wilderness.

6:19 *Tema . . . Sheba:* Arabian commercial centers.

21 In much the same way you have dealt with me;
you are stunned at my plight and are terrified.

Make Me Understand How I Have Been at Fault*

22 "Did I ever ask you to give me anything,
or to use your vast wealth to alleviate my travails,
23 or to rescue me from the hands of an oppressor,
or to ransom me from the power of ruthless men?
24 "Instruct me, and I will be silent;
make me understand how I have been at fault.
25 I can readily accept logical explanations,
but your arguments are without merit.
26 Do you think that your words should be embraced
whereas mine are so fragile that they can be borne away by a light breeze?
27 You would even cast lots for the fatherless
and sell your friend at a bargain price.
28 "Therefore, now I beg you to look at me,
for I will not lie to your face.
29 Consider what I have said,
and let no further injustice be inflicted upon me.[n]
30 Does evil issue forth from my lips?
Would I not realize it if I spoke untruthfully?

CHAPTER 7

A Life of Exhausting Service*

1 "Is not man's life on earth an exhausting one,
and are not his days like those of a hired laborer?[o]
2 Like a slave who sighs for the evening shade
and like a laborer who is bent upon his wages,
3 so have I been forced to endure months of futility,
and nights of grief have been inflicted on me.
4 "When I lie in bed, I wonder,
'When will the daylight come so that I may rise?'
But the night drags on,
and I toss restlessly until the dawn.
5 My body is infected with worms and scabs;
my skin is cracked and festering.[p]

My Life Is But a Breath*

6 "My days pass more swiftly than a weaver's shuttle,
and they come to an end without a glimmer of hope.
7 "Remember that my life is but a breath of wind;
my eyes will never again see happiness.[q]
8 The eye that now sees me will see me no more;
I will vanish before your very eyes.
9 As a cloud vanishes and is no more,
so the one who descends to the netherworld * will never come up again.[r]
10 He will never again return to his home,
nor will he be remembered anymore.[s]
11 "Therefore, I will not restrain my mouth.
I will speak out in my anguish of spirit,
and I will complain in the bitterness of my soul.
12 Am I a monster of the deep, or a sea serpent,
that you place me under guard? *
13 When I say, 'I will find comfort in my bed,
and my couch will soothe my complaints,'
14 you then frighten me with dreams
and terrify me with visions,
15 so that I would prefer to be strangled
and to endure death rather than my sufferings.

n Job 19:6; 27:6.—o Job 14:14; Lev 25:50; Isa 16:14.—p Job 17:14; 19:26; Isa 14:11.—q Gen 27:46; Pss 39:5-6, 12; 62:10; 78:39; 144:4.—r Job 10:21; 2 Sam 12:23.—s Pss 37:10; 103:16.

6:22-30 Job has a deep sense of his innocence. Hence, the pious proposals of his friends seem to him to be inconsiderate.

7:1-5 The lot of the sick seems to be one of exhausting service comprising interminable days and nights of suffering.

7:6-16 Regret for the happiness that has vanished too soon and fear of the netherworld haunt the sick man. He feels that he is, so to speak, hunted by God.

7:9 *Netherworld:* this is the first explicit allusion to the great subterranean pit where the dead are gathered together. Job speaks of it according to the opinion in his day. It is no longer the sojourn of repose (Job 3:13-19), but a place from which one "will never again return," or where one is separated from his home, his family, and even his God.

7:12 This is a very poetic and Semitic way of representing the dominion of God over the forces of the universe.

16 My life is ebbing away; I cannot live forever.
Leave me alone, for my days are but a breath.[t]

A Continual Testing*

17 "What is man, that you make so much of him
or pay him any mind?[u]
18 You examine him every morning
and test him every moment of the day.
19 "Will you never take your eyes from me,
or let me alone long enough to swallow my saliva?
20 If I have sinned, what harm have I done to you,
O watcher of humanity?
Why have you designated me to be your target?
Why have I become a burden to you?*[v]
21 Why do you not pardon my offenses
and forgive my iniquity?
For soon I will lie down in the dust;
you will search for me, but I will be no more."

D: Bildad's First Speech*

CHAPTER 8

Does God Pervert Justice?* 1 Then Bildad the Shuhite spoke up and said:

2 "How long will you say such things?
The words of your mouth are like a turbulent wind.
3 Does God pervert justice?[w]
Does the Almighty distort the truth?
4 If your children sinned against him,
he has delivered them into the power of their transgressions.
5 "If you yourself will now seek God
as one who is pure and upright
and make supplication to the Almighty,
6 then he will rouse himself on your behalf
and restore the prosperity of your house.
7 Your former state will seem inconsequential
in the light of your future prosperity.

Inquire Now of Former Generations

8 "Inquire now of former generations
and reflect on what their ancestors came to realize.[x]
9 For we are only born yesterday and know nothing,
since our days on earth are but a shadow.*[y]
10 Will they not instruct you and tell you,
and utter words out of their understanding?
11 "Can a papyrus flourish where there is no marsh?
Can reeds grow without water?
12 While yet green and not cut down,
they wither more quickly than any plant.
13 Such is the fate of all those who forget God;
thus the hope of the godless man will perish.
14 His confidence is only a thread,
his trust a spider's web.
15 If he leans against his house, it will begin to totter;
if he clings to it, it will not endure.
16 "At dawn he seems quite strong and virile,
like a plant whose young roots spread out over the garden.
17 His roots are entwined around a pile of stones;
he draws his strength from among the rocks.
18 But if someone uproots him from his place,
it will disown him, saying, 'I have never seen you.'
19 There he lies, rotting along the roadside,*
and others will sprout forth from the soil.
20 "Be assured, God will not reject a blameless person,

t 1 Ki 19:4; Ps 39:14.—u Pss 8:5; 144:3; Heb 2:6.—v Job 16:12.—w Gen 18:25; Rom 3:5.—x Deut 4:32; 32:7.—y 1 Chr 29:15; Pss 39:7; 102:12; 109:23; 144:4.

7:17-21 Unlike the psalmist (Pss 8:5; 139:13-14, 23-24), Job cannot rejoice at the special attention God pays to human beings. This divine scrutiny shakes his conviction of innocence.

7:20 *Burden to you:* many Hebrew manuscripts have: "burden to myself."

8:1-22 In defense of the views commonly accepted by wise men, Eliphaz had appealed to a personal revelation. Bildad will rely mainly on the tradition of the ancients.

8:1-7 God is just. Bildad recalls this truth and draws from it an unexpected explanation of his friend's misfortunes: could they be a punishment for the evil conduct of his children?

8:9 *Our days . . . are but a shadow:* this is a frequent theme in the Wisdom Books (see Job 14:2; 1 Chr 29:15; Pss 102:12; 144:4; Eccl 6:12; 8:13).

8:19 *There he lies, rotting along the roadside:* the meaning of the Hebrew is unclear. The Vulgate reading is: "This is the joy of his way."

nor will he grasp the hand of the wrongdoer.
21 He will yet fill your mouth with laughter
and your lips with joyful cries. [z]
22 Those who hate you will be covered with shame,
and the tent of the wicked will cease to exist."

E: Job's Second Response*

CHAPTER 9

The Irresistible Power of God.* 1 Job then answered with these words:
2 "Indeed, I realize that this is true,
but how can anyone claim to be righteous before God?
3 If someone wished to debate with him,
he could not answer him once in a thousand.
4 God is wise in heart and mighty in strength;
who then has resisted him and remained unscathed?

5 "He moves mountains without their realizing it
and overturns them in his anger.
6 He shakes the earth out of its place,
and makes its pillars tremble.
7 He commands the sun, and it does not rise;
he seals up the light of the stars.
8 He alone stretches out the heavens
and tramples upon the waves of the sea. [a]
9 He made the Bear and Orion,
the Pleiades * and the constellations of the South.

10 "God performs deeds that are beyond understanding
and marvels that cannot be numbered.
11 If he passes near me, I do not see him;
he moves on, imperceptible to me.
12 If he snatches something away, who can stop him?
Who will dare to ask him, 'What are you doing?'
13 God will not relent in his wrath;
the servants of Rahab lie prostrate at his feet. [b]

Even If I Am Innocent, How Can I Answer God?*

14 "How then can I possibly reply to him
or devise arguments to counter him?
15 Even if I am innocent, how can I answer him?
I can only plead that he have mercy on me. [c]

16 "Even if I summoned him and he responded,
I do not believe that he would listen to what I said.
17 He might crush me in a tempest
and multiply my wounds without cause.
18 He might leave me no opportunity to regain my breath
and fill me with bitterness.

19 "If it is a contest of strength,
I cannot compete with him.
If it is a matter of judgment,
who can summon him to present his evidence?
20 Even though I am innocent,
my own mouth might condemn me.
Even though I am blameless,
he might prove me guilty. [d]
21 But am I without blame?
I am no longer certain.
Life itself I despise.

22 "It is all the same; that is why I say,
'He destroys both the innocent and the wicked.' [e]
23 When a deadly scourge suddenly appears,
he mocks the despair of the innocent.
24 When the earth is given into the hands of the wicked,
he blindfolds the eyes of its judges. *

z Pss 107:22; 118:15; 126:2; Isa 35:6.—a Gen 1:1, 8f; Pss 77:20; 104:2; Isa 40:22.—b Pss 87:4; 89:11; Isa 30:7.—c Gen 18:25; Pss 50:6; 96:13.—d Job 9:15; 15:6.—e Job 10:7-8; Eccl 9:2f; Ezek 21:3.

9:1—10:22 Far from denying the justice of God, Job proclaims it in his turn, but he will focus attention on the mystery of this justice by emphasizing the fearful power of the Creator and his seeming hostility to the human beings who have come from his own hands.

9:1-13 This first hymn to God the Creator emphasizes the nothingness of human beings. The Book of Job shows a liking for these grandiose visions in which we find the ancient cosmology reflected: earth is like a building set on pillars that reach down into the abyss (v. 6); in the firmament God has set constellations that cannot all be identified with certainty (v. 9).

9:9 *Bear . . . Orion . . . Pleiades:* three constellations, whose creation by God was evidence of his overwhelming might. They reappear in Job 38:31-32, and the last two are found in Am 5:8.

9:14-24 Hounded by the desire to obtain justice, Job would like to come before God. But the heavy burden of the trial leads him to have doubts both about his own virtue and about the justice of God.

9:24 *Blindfolds the eyes of [the earth's] judges:* in our day, we portray Lady Justice as wearing a blindfold, meaning that she will be an impartial judge. Job accused God of blindfolding the judges of his time so that they would be oblivious to both crimes and innocence.

If it is not he who does so,
then who else is responsible?

There Is No Arbiter To Judge between God and Me

25 "My days pass more swiftly than a runner;
they fly away without any experience of happiness.[f]
26 They skim past like boats of papyrus,
like an eagle swooping upon its prey.
27 If I say, 'I will forget my complaints,
I will put on a cheerful face instead of a sad countenance,'
28 I will still dread my sufferings,
for I know that you will not hold me innocent.

29 "If I am to be condemned as guilty,
why then should I struggle in vain?
30 If I should wash myself with snow
and cleanse my hands with lye,
31 you would plunge me into a dung-filled ditch
so that even my clothes would abhor me.

32 "For God is not a man like me,
someone before whom I can plead my case
or whom I can confront in a court.[g]
33 There is no arbiter to judge between us
with the power to render a verdict,
34 someone who could remove God's rod from me
so that I would not shrink from him in terror.
35 Then I would speak out without fear of him,
for I know I am not what I am thought to be.

CHAPTER 10

Tell Me Why!*

1 "I loathe my very life;
therefore I will give free rein to my complaints
and speak out in the bitterness of my soul.[h]
2 I will say to God: 'Do not condemn me,
but simply let me know what is your charge against me.
3 Do you get any joy in oppressing me,
spurning the work of your own hands
while approving the schemes of the wicked?
4 " 'Do you have eyes of flesh?
Do you see as a mortal sees?
5 Are your days like those of a mortal,
or your years like those of a man,[i]
6 that you investigate my iniquity
and keep a record of my sins,
7 even though you know that I am innocent
and have no one to rescue me from your hand?[j]

I Realize What Was Your Intent*

8 " 'Your hands created and fashioned me;
will you now turn away and destroy me?
9 Remember that you fashioned me like clay;
will you now reduce me again to dust?[k]
10 Did you not pour me out like milk
and curdle me like cheese?
11 You clothed me with skin and flesh
and knit me together with bones and sinews.

12 " 'You have given me life and kindness,
and in your providence you have preserved my spirit.
13 Yet within your heart you had a secret plan,
and I realize what was your intent:
14 you would be watching me,
and if I sinned, you would not absolve me of my guilt.

15 " 'Woe to me if I should be wicked.
Even if I am righteous, I dare not lift up my head,
for I am filled with shame
and bent over with affliction.
16 Should I lift up my head, you hunt me like a proud lion,
confronting me time and again with your awesome power.
17 You renew your onslaughts against me,
your fury increasing incessantly
as fresh troops assail me wave after wave.

---

f Job 7:6-7; Ps 90:9-10.—g Job 9:3; Num 23:19; Eccl 6:10; Rom 9:20.—h Job 7:11, 16; Num 11:15.—i Job 36:26; Pss 90:4; 102:25.—j Deut 32:39; Ps 50:21.—k Job 4:19; 7:21; 33:6; Gen 3:19; Isa 29:16.

10:1-7 Job multiplies questions in attempting to achieve some understanding of God's conduct.

10:8-17 The question is posed: what relation exists between God's love and his justice on earth in regard to human beings?

Let Me Alone So That I May Have a Few Moments of Happiness

18 " 'Why did you bring me forth from the womb?
It would have been better if I had died before an eye had beheld me,[l]
19 and had been carried from the womb to the grave
as though I had never existed.
20 Do I not have but a few remaining days of life?
Let me alone so that I may have a few moments of happiness[m]
21 before I go to the place of no return,
to the land of gloom and darkness,
22 to the land of deepest night,
a land of gloom and disorder,
where even the light is like darkness.' "

F: Zophar's First Speech*

CHAPTER 11

God Recognizes the Deceitful. 1 Then Zophar the Naamathite responded:

2 "Should we allow this torrent of words to go unanswered?
Is a clever speaker always to be considered right?
3 Should your endless talk reduce others to silence?
When you mock, is no one allowed to refute you?
4 For you said, 'My judgments are irrefutable
and I am blameless in the sight of God.'
5 Oh, how I wish that God would speak
and open his lips to contradict your opinions
6 while revealing to you the secrets of wisdom,
which puts human intelligence to shame.
Thus, you might know
that God will call you to account for your sin.[n]
7 "Can you fathom the mysteries of God?
Can you attain to the perfection of the Almighty?[o]
8 It is higher than the heavens—what can you do?
It is deeper than the netherworld—what can you know?
9 Its measure is longer than the earth
and broader than the sea.

10 "If while passing by he decides to imprison you
or subject you to judgment, who can prevent him?
11 He surely recognizes the deceitful;
he will hardly ignore their iniquity.
12 An ignorant fool can no more gain understanding
than a wild donkey can be domesticated.

Stretch Out Your Hands toward God*

13 "However, if you will have a change of heart
and stretch out your hands toward him in prayer,[p]
14 if you banish all iniquity far away from you
and do not allow wickedness to penetrate your tent,
15 you will then be able to lift up your face in innocence;
you will be unwavering and without fear.
16 You will then forget your wretchedness,
remembering it only as flood waters gone by.

17 "Then your life will be brighter than noonday,
and its darkness will be like morning.[q]
18 You will be filled with confidence because there is hope;
you will look around and take your rest in safety.[r]
19 You will lie down without fearing anyone,
and many will seek your favor.
20 But the eyes of the wicked will fail;
for them all the ways of escape will be closed,
and all they can hope for is death."

l Job 3:10-11; Eccl 4:2; 7:1.—m Job 7:7, 16; 9:25; Ps 39:14; Eccl 6:12.—n Job 9:4; 15:5; Ezr 9:13.—o Job 5:9; Rom 11:33.—p Job 5:8, 17; 1 Sam 7:3; Ps 78:8.—q Pss 37:6; 112:4; Isa 58:8, 10.—r Lev 26:6; Pss 3:6; 4:9; 127:2; Prov 3:24.

11:1-20 Annoyed by Job's protestations of innocence, Zophar officially urges him to meditate on the mystery of the divine wisdom and be converted.

11:13-20 Prayer combined with a sincere conversion can obtain from God a complete reversal of a situation.

G: Job's Third Response*

CHAPTER 12

Wisdom Will Die with You.* 1 Job then answered with these words:

2 "Undoubtedly, you are the voice of the people,
and when you die, wisdom will die with you.
3 But I also have intelligence;
I am not inferior to you in this regard.
Who is ignorant of all these things?
4* "I have become a laughingstock to my friends,
I whom God would answer when I called upon him;
although I am innocent and just, he afflicted me.[s]
5 Those who live untroubled lives scorn the misfortunes of others,
the blows that strike those who are already staggering.
6 Yet the tents of robbers remain undisturbed,
and those who provoke God sleep securely
as well as those who make a god of their strength.*
7 "But ask the animals, and they will teach you;
ask the birds of the air, and they will inform you.
8 Ask the reptiles on earth, and they will instruct you,
or let the fish of the sea enlighten you.
9 Which of all these is unaware
that the hand of God has done this?
10 "In God's hand is the soul of every living thing
and the breath of all mankind.[t]
11 Does not the ear test words
as the palate tastes food?
12 Wisdom is found in the aged,
and long life nourishes understanding.

With God Are Wisdom and Power

13 "With God are wisdom and power;
wise counsel and understanding are his.[u]
14 If he tears down, no one can rebuild;
anyone he imprisons cannot gain freedom.[v]
15 If he holds back the waters, drought ensues;
if he releases them, the land is overwhelmed.
16 Strength and wisdom are his;
his too are the deceived and the deceivers.
17 "He deprives counselors of their wits
and makes fools of judges.
18 He looses the sashes of kings
and gives them only a waistcloth to cover their loins.*
19 He forces priests to walk barefoot
and overthrows those in positions of power.[w]
20 He silences the lips of trusted counselors
and deprives the aged of their power of discernment.
21 "He pours contempt on princes
and disarms the powerful.
22 He unveils mysteries long obscured in darkness
and brings their meaning to light.[x]
23 He makes nations great and then destroys them;
he enlarges nations and then reduces them to nothing.
24 He weakens the minds of the leaders of the earth
and leaves them to wander in a trackless waste.
25 They grope their way in the darkness without light,
staggering like drunken men.

CHAPTER 13

Be Silent—I Want To Question God*

1 "All this I have observed with my own eyes;

s Job 17:6; Gen 6:9; 38:23; Ps 91:15.—t Job 33:4; Gen 2:7; Num 16:22; Acts 17:28.—u Job 9:4; Prov 21:30; Jer 32:19; 1 Cor 1:24.—v Isa 25:2; Ezek 26:14; Rev 3:7.—w Job 19:9; Lk 1:52.—x Job 3:5; Ps 139:12; 1 Cor 4:5.

12:1—14:22 Turning his back on his friends, Job addresses his God directly and boldly asks him to justify his conduct.

12:1-12 Job observes a disturbing contrast between the misfortune of the righteous and the tranquility of robbers. The whole of creation is a witness of this drama.

12:4-5 The righteous who are afflicted even have to suffer the scorn of the impious: see Ps 22:7-22; Mt 27:39-43.

12:6 *As well as those who make a god of their strength:* the Hebrew is obscure. Other translations given are: "As well as those who bring their god in their hands," or "In what God provides by his hand."

12:18 The probable meaning of the second half of the verse is that God at times reduces kings to slavery.

13:1-16 Job believes that his friends are charlatans, incapable of finding a remedy for his sufferings. Job will do battle alone with God.

my ears have heard and understood it.
2 What you know, I also know;
I am not inferior to you in any way.[y]
3 But I only wish to speak with the Almighty
and to argue my case with God.
4 As for you, you are obscuring the truth with lies,
and the solutions you offer are all worthless.

5 "Oh, if only you would be completely silent!
For you, that would be regarded as wisdom.
6 Hear now my reasoning
and listen to the plea that issues from my lips.
7 Is it on God's behalf that you utter lies?
Is it in his defense that you speak deceitfully?
8 Will you show partiality for him
as you plead his case?

9 "Will you feel totally comfortable when he examines you?
Will you be able to deceive him as you deceive men?
10 If you show partiality, even though not flagrant,
he will surely rebuke you.
11 Will not his majesty frighten you
and the fear of him overcome you?
12 The ideas you propose are proverbs of ash;
your arguments are defenses of clay.[z]

13 "Be silent so that I may speak on my own behalf.
Then let what may come upon me.
14 I am taking my life in my own hands
and placing myself in jeopardy.
15 Perhaps he may slay me, but I have no other hope
than to defend my conduct before him.[a]
16 This will prove to be my salvation,
for the godless will not dare to come before him.

I Am Certain That I Will Be Vindicated*

17 "Therefore, listen carefully to my words
and give my defense a careful hearing.
18 I have prepared my case carefully,
and I am certain that I will be vindicated.
19 If anyone can make a valid case against me,
then I will be silent and die.[b]

20 "Only grant me two things, O God,
and then I will not hide myself from your face:
21 just withdraw your hand far from me,
and stop frightening me with your terrors.
22 Then summon me, and I will answer,
or let me speak first, and then you can reply.

23 "Of how many crimes and sins am I guilty?
Make known to me my faults and my transgressions.
24 Why do you hide your face*
and look upon me as your enemy?[c]
25 Will you harass a wind-blown leaf
and chase after dry chaff?

26 "For you have drawn up bitter charges against me
and caused me to suffer for the iniquities of my youth,
27 putting my feet in the stocks
and keeping a close watch on every step I take
as you trace all my footprints.
28 Thus, I waste away like rotting wood
or like a moth-eaten garment.

CHAPTER 14

Everyone Born of Woman . . . *

1 "Everyone born of woman
has life that is short and filled with troubles.
2 He blossoms like a flower and soon begins to wither;
as fleeting as a shadow, he does not endure.[d]

y Job 12:3; 15:9.—z Neh 4:2-3; Prov 10:6; Jer 17:15.—a Job 5:8; 7:6; 27:5; Prov 14:32; Isa 12:2.—b Job 9:15; 40:4; Isa 50:8; Rom 8:33.—c Job 16:9; 19:11; Deut 32:20; Ps 88:15.—d Job 4:20; 8:9; Pss 90:6; 102:12; 103:15; 109:23; 144:4; Jas 1:10.

13:17-28 Before beginning his legal case against God, Job asks for a decrease in his distress and more freedom for his defense.

13:24 *Hide your face:* a Semitic expression signifying that God is irritated (Ps 27:9) or indifferent (Pss 30:8; 104:28f), with consequent misfortune for human beings.

14:1-12 Thoroughly unclean, humans cannot attain true purity, i.e., moral perfection. This wretchedness is precisely their excuse before God. And if the universe can be shaken and then renewed, for humans there is no revival; they remain buried in death forever. Survival in the subterranean netherworld is nothing more than a diminished existence. Human beings thus hasten toward their end without hope. What reason is there for God to pursue them?

3 Is it upon a creature like this that you fix your gaze
and bring him before you to be judged?
4 "Can a man be found who has avoided defilement?
There is no such person.
5 The extent of his life has already been determined,
and the number of his months is known to you;
you have established the limits that he cannot pass.
6 Turn your gaze away from him and leave him alone
so that, like a hired laborer, he may complete his days.

7 "At least for a tree there is always hope:
if it is cut down, it may sprout once again,
and its new shoots may burst with life. [e]
8 Although its roots age in the earth
and its stump dies in the ground,
9 once it scents water it will begin to bud
and put forth branches like a sapling.

10 "But when a man dies, he remains lifeless;
what is his fate once he expires?
11 As occurs when the waters of a lake recede
or a river ceases to flow and runs dry,
12 so men lie down and never rise again;
until the heavens cease to exist, they will not awaken
or be stirred out of their slumber.

Hide Me in the Netherworld*

13 "How I wish you would hide me in the netherworld
and shelter me until your wrath has subsided
while designating a time to call me to mind.
14 If one who dies were permitted to live once again,
I would willingly endure all the days of my service
waiting for my relief to arrive.
15 You would call and I would answer you;
you would long to see once again the creature you have made. [f]
16 You would count my every step
but not watch for any evidence of sin in me.
17 You would store up all my transgressions in a bag,
and you would cover over my guilt.

18 "But as a mountain eventually falls
and a rock is removed from its place,
19 as the waters wear away the stones
and cloudbursts wash away the soil,
so you destroy the hope of man.
20 You crush him once for all and he disappears;
you alter his appearance and send him away.
21 If his sons are honored, he is unaware of it;
if they are disgraced, he does not know it.
22 He is cognizant only of the pains his flesh endures,
and he grieves for no one except himself." [g]

III: SECOND CYCLE OF SPEECHES*

A: Eliphaz's Second Speech*

CHAPTER 15

You in Fact Discredit Religion. 1 Then Eliphaz the Temanite responded:

2 "Would a wise man respond with empty arguments
and make himself a windbag? *
3 Would he fill his defense with pointless talk
and speeches that serve no purpose?

4 "You in fact discredit religion
and do away with devotion to God,
5 because your iniquity dictates what you say
and you choose to exhibit a deceitful tongue.
6 Your own mouth condemns you, not I;
your own lips testify against you. [h]

e Job 19:10; 24:20; Isa 11:1.—f Job 10:3; 13:22.—g Job 21:21; Ps 38:8; Isa 21:3; Jer 4:19.—h Job 9:15, 20; Mt 12:37; Lk 19:22.

14:13-22 An astounding proposition is put forth: Job desires to descend to the netherworld as in a provisional hiding place or refuge (Ps 139:7-12; Isa 26:20) to escape the divine wrath and wait there for the Lord to remember the *creature [he has] made* and grant him forgiveness. Job dreams of immortality and suffers because he no longer enjoys the friendship of his God.

15:1—21:34 In this second part of the debate, the friends of Job add nothing new, but their tone becomes more aggressive.

15:1-35 Eliphaz urges Job to reflect once again on the evil passions of human beings and on the fate of the wicked: after fleeting success, a time of remorse comes upon them and, soon after, the ruin of all their fortunes.

15:2 *And make himself a windbag:* literally, "and fill himself with a hot east wind," i.e., the sirocco that comes in from the desert.

Are You the Firstborn of the Human Race?*

7 "Are you the firstborn of the human race?
Did you come into existence before the hills?
8 Are you a member of God's inner council?
Do you have a monopoly on wisdom? [i]
9 What do you know that we do not know?
What insight do you have that we do not share?
10 We ourselves have age and gray hair on our side,
people who far surpass your father in years.

11 "Are the consolations that God offers insufficient for you,
words whispered gently in your ear?
12 Why do you allow your passions to erode your judgment,
and why do your eyes flash with anger
13 so that you vent your rage against God
and permit such words to escape your mouth?

14 [j] "What is man, that he should be without fault,
or one born of woman, that he should be righteous? [k]
15 If God places no trust in his holy ones *
and the heavens are not pure in his sight,
16 how much less is man, who is vile and corrupt
and drinks up iniquity like water?

Listen to Experience and Tradition*

17 "I will tell you; listen to me.
I will recount what I have seen,
18 what has been related by wise men
who have faithfully transmitted the teachings of their ancestors,
19 to whom alone the land was given,
and no foreigner passed among them.

20 "The wicked man suffers torment all his days,
and limited are the years allotted to the tyrant.
21 Terrifying sounds echo in his ears,
and even when times are peaceful, marauders swoop down on him.
22 He despairs of escaping the darkness
and realizes that he is destined for the sword.

23 "In his wandering, he serves as food for vultures
and knows the day of darkness is at hand.
24 Distress and anguish overwhelm him;
they overpower him like a king prepared to attack.

25 "Because he has lifted his hands against God
and acted in brazen defiance of the Almighty, [l]
26 rushing stubbornly against him
with his massive embossed shield, *
27 with his jowls heavy and gross
and his waist bulging with fat,
28 he will dwell in cities that lie in ruins,
in houses that have been abandoned
and are crumbling into a heap of rubble.

29 "He will no longer be wealthy and his riches will not endure;
no longer will his power prevail.
30 He will not escape the darkness;
intense heat will shrivel his roots,
and the wind will cause his blossoms to disappear.
31 Let him not deceive himself by trusting in what is worthless,
for he will be left bereft. [m]

32 "His palm trees will wither before their time,
and his branches will never again be green.
33 He will be like a vine that sheds unripe grapes,
like an olive tree casting off its blossoms.
34 For the company of the godless will be completely barren,
and fire will consume the tents of those who are venal. [n]
35 They conceive malice and breed evil,
and they give birth to deceit." [o]

---

i Job 11:7; 29:4; Wis 9:13; Isa 9:6; Rom 11:34.—j 14ff: Job 25:4ff.—k Job 14:1, 4; 2 Chr 6:36.—l Job 36:9; Pss 2:2f; 73:9; 75:6.—m Job 31:5; Isa 44:20; Mic 2:11; Mk 13:5.—n Job 8:13; 15:30; Ex 23:8.—o Job 4:8; 5:7; Ps 7:15; Isa 59:4.

15:7-16 Eliphaz disparages humans in order to better destroy all of Job's pretensions to justice.

15:15 *Holy ones:* i.e., the angels (see Job 5:1).

15:17-35 According to Eliphaz's experience, the wicked are ceaselessly pursued by anxiety and all kinds of nightmares; they receive their punishment even in this life.

15:26 This is an image of an Assyrian or Babylonian soldier who takes part in an assault while protected by a massive round shield.

B: Job's Fourth Response*

CHAPTER 16

If You Were in My Place . . . 1 Job then answered with these words:

2 "I have heard similar comments on many occasions;
what wretched comforters you all are!
3 When will you cease your endless flow of foolish words?
Or what sickness afflicts you that you never cease babbling?

4 "I could also rant on as you do,
if you were in my place.
I could exhaust you with my words
and shake my head at you.*
5 But I would offer words of encouragement,
and comfort from my lips would alleviate your pain.
6 When I speak, my suffering is not eased,
and if I remain silent, my pain does not stop.

You Have Risen Up as a Witness against Me*

7 "Truly, my pain has left me exhausted,
and you have devastated my entire family.
8 You have risen up as a witness against me;
my gaunt appearance offers clear testimony to my plight.
9 Your anger has caused you to assail me,
and you gnash your teeth against me.
My enemies lord it over me;
10 they open their mouths to mock me.
They strike me insolently on the cheek;
they have all joined in league against me.[p]

11 "God has left me as prey for the godless
and handed me over to the power of the wicked.
12 I was living at peace until he crushed me;
he seized me by the neck and broke me into pieces,
setting me up as a target.
13 His archers encompass me on every side;
he pierces my loins without mercy
and pours out my gall upon the ground.
14 He repeatedly bludgeons his way through my defenses
and rushes upon me like a warrior.

My Witness Is in Heaven*

15 "I have sewn sackcloth over my skin
and laid my forehead in the dust.
16 My face is red from incessant weeping,
and dark shadows ring my eyelids,
17 even though my hands are free of violence
and my prayer is pure.

18 "O earth, do not cover my blood;*
let my cries never cease to be heard.
19 Even now my witness is in heaven;
my defender is on high.[q]
20 Although my friends scorn me,
I pour out tears before God,
21 pleading that he may listen to me
as a person would listen to a neighbor.
22 For there are only a few years left to me
before I set forth on that journey
from which there is no return.

CHAPTER 17

Where Then Will My Hope Be?*

1 "My spirit is broken,
my days are numbered,
and the grave is ready to receive me.
2 I am surrounded by mockers who taunt me,
and my eyes dwell on their hostility.

3 "I call upon you to be a witness on my behalf,
for there is no one else to whom I can turn.
4 You have closed the minds of others to reason,
but surely you will not allow them to triumph.

5 "Like a man who invites others to dine with him,

---

p Job 30:12; Pss 22:13; 35:15, 21; Isa 50:6.—q Job 31:2; Gen 31:50; Ps 113:5f; Isa 33:5; Rom 1:9.

16:1—17:16 Seeing himself close to his end, Job again raises a heartrending lament so that this may serve before God as a powerful appeal to his justice.

16:4 Shaking the head signifies commiseration, scorn, or mockery (see Ps 22:8; Jer 48:27; Mt 27:39).

16:7-14 Job sees himself as summoned before the tribunal of God. The scene makes us think of the persecuted righteous person (Ps 22:13-14, 17; Isa 53:10-12) and the Passion of Jesus (Mt 26:60-68; Lk 22:37). God is transferred into a warrior, and he crushes his victim without pity (Lam 3:12-13).

16:15-22 Job, prostrate in suffering, rediscovers a little hope: his God can still hear him and become his defender.

16:18 *Cover my blood:* blood shed and not covered over is, as it were, a call for vengeance (see Gen 4:10-11; Isa 26:21; Ezek 24:7).

17:1-16 Job remains anxious: his strength declines, his solitude becomes more profound, and around him his misfortune provokes only mockery and scandal.

while the eyes of his children are failing, *
6 I have become a byword in every land,
someone people spit upon. [r]
7 My eyes have become increasingly blinded with grief,
and all my members have been reduced to a shadow.
8 * The righteous are appalled at this,
and the innocent are indignant at the wicked.
9 The upright continue to adhere to a righteous path,
and those whose hands are pure will grow stronger. [s]
10 "Even so, come forward, all of you, and continue your attack.
I will not find even one man among you who is wise.
11 My days have passed and my plans are foiled;
the strings of my heart have been severed.
12 My enemies would have me believe that night is day
and that the light will soon eradicate the darkness.
13 "If I foresee the netherworld as my dwelling,
if I spread out my bed in the darkness,
14 if I call the grave my father
and the worm my mother or my sister,
15 where then will my hope be,
and who can foresee any happiness for me? [t]
16 Will they accompany me to the netherworld?
Will we descend together into the dust?"

C: Bildad's Second Speech*

CHAPTER 18

The Light of the Wicked Is Extinguished.

1 Then Bildad the Shuhite responded:
2 "When will you cease this torrent of words?
Once you start to think rationally,
then we can have a sensible discussion.
3 Why do you treat us like animals
and regard us as ignorant?
4 In your anger you tear yourself to pieces,
but the earth will not be forsaken on your account,
nor will a single rock be moved from its place.
5 "The light of the wicked is extinguished,
and the flame of his fire no longer shines.
6 The light in his tent begins to fade
and the lamp above him is put out. [u]
7 His vigorous stride begins to falter
and his own plans fail miserably.
8 He rushes headlong into a net,
and his feet are ensnared.
9 "A trap seizes him by the heel,
leaving him unable to escape.
10 A noose lies hidden on the ground for him;
pitfalls lie across his path.
11 Terrors alarm him on every side,
hounding his every step. [v]
12 His strength is weakened by hunger,
and disaster awaits him on all sides.
13 "His skin is eaten away by disease;
the firstborn of death devours his limbs. *
14 He is dragged from the security of his tent
and carted off to the king of terrors. *
15 Anyone can live in his tent since it is no longer his;
brimstone * is scattered over his dwelling.
16 His roots dry up below,
and his branches wither above.
17 "All memory of him vanishes from the earth;
his name is quickly forgotten. [w]
18 He is thrust from light into darkness
and banished from the world.

r Job 17:2; 30:9; Num 12:14; 1 Ki 9:7.—s Job 22:30; 2 Sam 22:21; Ps 84:8; Prov 4:18.—t Job 7:6; Ps 31:22; Lam 3:18.—u Job 12:25; 21:17; Prov 24:20.—v Job 15:20-24; 27:20; Pss 31:14; 55:4; Isa 28:19; Jer 20:4.—w Deut 32:26; Ps 34:17; Prov 10:7.

17:5 This verse is a kind of proverb; i.e., those who concern themselves with others when everything is amiss in their own home are regarded as a joke by people.

17:8-9 These verses are directed at Job's three friends, false upright men who are indignant at Job's impiety and profit from his misery to bestow upon themselves a certificate of sainthood.

18:1-21 The wrath of Job has the result of provoking Bildad to impatience. In the divine order of the universe, he says, there is no place for the problem of Job, whose words constitute a blasphemy.

18:13 The ancients regarded illnesses as the children of death; the allusion here, then, is to very serious illness.

18:14 *King of terrors:* i.e., death. In various civilizations the ruler of the realm of the dead was called Nergal, Pluto, or Moloch (see Isa 57:9).

18:15 *Brimstone:* an element used to disinfect a tent and remove every trace of the occupant.

19 He leaves no offspring or posterity among his people;
there is no survivor where he once lived.
20 Inhabitants of the west are appalled at his fate,
while those of the east are struck with horror.
21 Such indeed is the dwelling of the impious;
such is the home of everyone who cares nothing for God."

D: Job's Fifth Response*

CHAPTER 19

God Has Wronged Me.* 1 Job then answered with these words:

2 "How much longer will you torment me
and oppress me with your words?
3 You have reproached me now ten times,
and you mistreat me shamelessly.
4 And even if it were true that I have erred,
the fault would be completely mine.

5 "If indeed you want to exalt yourselves above me
and use my humiliation against me,
6 know that God has wronged me
and cast his net over me.
7 Even when I protest that I have been wronged,
no one comes forward to support me,
and I receive no justice when I cry out for help. [x]

8 "He has blocked my path so that I cannot pass,
and he has shrouded my way in darkness.
9 He has deprived me of my honor
and removed the crown from my head. [y]
10 He assails me on every side until I succumb;
he has uprooted my hope like a tree.
11 He has inflamed his anger against me
and looks upon me as his enemy.
12 His troops move forward as a single force;
they have surrounded me with siegeworks
and encamped around my tent.

13 "He has caused my brethren to turn against me;
my friends are completely estranged from me. [z]
14 My relatives and my companions now ignore me,
and those who were guests in my house have forgotten me.
15 Even my serving girls regard me as a stranger;
I have become an alien in their eyes.
16 When I summon my servant, he does not respond,
no matter how much I plead with him.

17 "My wife finds my breath repulsive;
my stench is loathsome to my relatives.
18 Even young children despise me; *
when I approach, they turn their backs on me.
19 All of my dearest friends abhor me;
those I love have turned against me. [a]
20 I have become just skin and bones
and have escaped with only my gums. *

21 "Have pity on me, my friends, have pity on me,
for the hand of God has touched me.
22 Must you pursue me just as God does?
Will not my flesh ever be enough to satisfy you? *

I Know That My Redeemer Lives*

23 "How I wish that my words might be written down
and inscribed on a scroll! [b]

x Job 30:20, 24, 28; Ps 22:3; Hab 1:2-4.—y Job 12:17; Ps 89:40, 45.—z Job 6:13; 16:7; Pss 31:12; 38:12; 69:9; 88:19.—a Job 6:14; 19:13-14; Ps 55:13-15; Sir 6:8.—b Job 31:35; Ex 17:14; Ps 40:8.

19:1-29 Though persecuted by God and condemned by humans, Job remains certain that he will someday see his cause triumphant and God himself acting as his defender.

19:1-22 Job is not going to justify himself before his friends any longer; it is the justice of God and not his own that is at issue. Job lets forth an ardent lamentation, an appeal for pity.

19:18 *Even young children despise me:* this fact was a great embarrassment in a patriarchal society, which insisted that its elders be respected and honored (see Ex 20:12).

19:20 The translation of this verse is uncertain. Most commentators believe it means "I am nothing and possess nothing except my skin and bones."

19:22 To eat someone's flesh meant to mistreat him and especially to slander him (see Ps 27:2).

19:23-29 This is regarded as the best-known and most-beloved passage in the Book of Job as well as the culmination of Job's understanding of his situation and his relationship with God. At the end of his life, Job is convulsed by a cry of hope, which he utters like a challenge, and also by the prospect of meeting his God, whom he will really see with his own eyes (Job 42:5).

God is Job's defender; originally, a *goel* was a close relative of somebody slain, who had to avenge that relative's blood, raise up a posterity to the dead man's wife, and redeem his property. Job, therefore, expects a liberation.

The Vulgate Latin translation interpreted this as resurrection of the body after death. The direct meaning of the Hebrew text may be extended, in a Christian perspective, to include the resurrection, but the Book of Job does not perceive this so clearly.

24 How I wish that with an iron chisel and with lead
they were engraved in stone forever!

25 [c] "But I know that my Redeemer lives,
and that at the end he will stand upon the dust.
26 After my awakening, he will call me close to him,
and then from my own flesh I will see God.[d]
27 I will see him with my own eyes;
my eyes, not those of another, will behold him.
How my heart within me yearns for that moment!

28 "As for you who say,
'How we will persecute him,
for the root of the trouble lies in him,'
29 beware of the sword that is pointed toward you,
for the avenger of wickedness is the sword,
and then you will know that there is indeed a judgment."[e]

E: Zophar's Second Speech*

CHAPTER 20

The Joy of a Sinner Lasts Only for a Moment.

1 Then Zophar the Naamathite replied:

2 "The words you have spoken have caused me great distress,
and as a result, I am forced to reply.
3 I have been outraged by your censure,
but now a spirit beyond my understanding
provides me with the answers to rebuke you.

4 "Surely you must know that since time began
and man was first placed on the earth,
5 the triumph of the wicked has always been short-lived,
and the joy of the sinner lasts only for a moment.[f]
6 Even though in his pride he towers to the sky
and his head touches the clouds,
7 he is destined to perish forever like his own dung,*
and those who used to see him will ask:
'Where is he?'
8 He will fade away like a dream and never be found again;
he will vanish like a vision of the night.
9 The eyes that saw him will see him no more,
and his dwelling will not behold him any longer.

He Wolfs Down Riches and Then Vomits Them Up

10 "His children will seek the favor of the poor,
and his hands will be forced to return his wealth.[g]
11 The youthful vigor that once filled his body
will be stagnant with him in the earth.

12 "Though wickedness is sweet in his mouth
and he hides it under his tongue,
13 though he continues to keep it in his mouth
and is loath to let it go,
14 yet such food will turn sour in his stomach,
working inside him like the venom of asps.
15 He wolfs down riches and then vomits them up;
God forces him to disgorge them from his stomach.

16 "Such a person will suck the venom of asps;
the tongue of a viper will slay him.
17 He will see no streams of oil
or rivers flowing with honey and cream.*
18 He will be forced to restore his gains without enjoying them;
even though his wealth increased, he will derive no enjoyment.
19 For he has oppressed the poor and left them destitute,
seizing houses that he did not build.

20 "Since his avarice could never be satisfied,

c 25ff: Phil 3:20.—d Ps 17:15; Mt 5:8; 1 Cor 13:12; 1 Jn 3:2.—e Job 15:22; 27:13-23; Pss 1:5; 9:8; 58:12.—f Job 8:12-13; 21:13; Ps 37:35-36.—g Job 5:4; 27:14.

20:1-29 Job's anguished appeal does not move his friend Zophar. Zophar once more paints a picture of Job as a proud and wicked man on whom the wrath of God will soon descend.

20:7 *Dung:* a symbol of everything that is ephemeral and without value (see 1 Ki 14:10).

20:17 *Oil . . . honey and cream:* these were staple products of Palestine.

no amount of hoarding will save him.[h]
21 Since his greed was insatiable,
his prosperity will not endure.
22 When he possesses everything he desires,
his troubles will begin,
and the full force of misery will strike him down.[i]
23 "God will unleash the fury of his wrath against him
and rain down upon him a hail of arrows.
24 If he escapes a weapon of iron,
a bow of bronze will pierce him through.
25 The tip of the arrow will protrude from his body
and the glittering point will emerge from his bladder;
terrors will descend upon him.
26 "Unrelieved darkness is what awaits him;
a fire * that does not need to be fanned will devour him,
and anything left in his tent will be consumed.[j]
27 The heavens will lay bare his iniquity,
and the earth will rise up against him.
28 Flood waters will sweep away his house
like the torrents on the day of God's wrath.
29 This is the lot that God reserves for the wicked,
the heritage assigned to him by God."

F: Job's Sixth Response*

CHAPTER 21

The Very Thought of My Plight Fills Me with Horror.* 1 Job then answered with these words:
2 "Listen carefully to my words;
at the very least, grant me this consolation.[k]
3 Bear with me while I speak;
once I have finished, you may jeer.
4 "Is my complaint limited to my fellow men?
Do I not have good reason to be impatient?
5 If you consider my plight carefully,
you will have good reason to be appalled
and to place your hand over your mouth.
6 The very thought of it fills me with horror,
and my entire body shudders.

Why Do the Wicked Continue To Survive?*

7 "Why do the wicked continue to survive,
achieving old age and increasing in power?[l]
8 They behold their children established around them
and their descendants continuing to flourish.
9 Their households are secure, with no cause for fear;
the rod of God does not descend upon them.
10 Their bulls breed without fail;
their cows give birth without miscarriage.
11 "The wicked send forth children as a flock;
their little ones dance and frolic.
12 They sing to the sound of the tambourine and the harp
and rejoice at the playing of the flute.
13 They spend their days in prosperity
and go down to the netherworld in peace.

They Say to God, "Leave Us Alone!"

14 "Despite this, these people say to God,
'Leave us alone!
We do not want to learn your ways.
15 Who is the Almighty that we should serve him?
And what would we gain by praying to him?'[m]
16 Is not the prosperity of the wicked
the result of their own efforts,
since they have never sought God's help?[n]

h Prov 11:4; Eccl 5:9; Zep 1:18; Lk 12:20.—i Job 15:29; Jdg 2:15.—j Deut 32:22; Ps 21:9.—k Job 13:17; 21:34.—l Job 12:6; 21:13; Pss 37:35; 73:3-5; Eccl 8:14; Jer 12:1f; Hab 1:13.—m Job 5:2; Ps 73:11-13; Mt 7:7.—n Job 22:18; Ps 49:7-8.

20:26 *Fire:* i.e., lightning.

21:1-34 Looking beyond his own experience, Job thinks of the human condition as a whole. He is aware of how serious his claim is: he raises the problem of evil, and it is the very justice of God that seems to be in the wrong.

21:1-6 This new consciousness of the problem of evil overwhelms the author himself.

21:7-13 Job paints a picture of the scandalous success of the wicked: peace, riches, children, pleasures—nothing is lacking to this happiness that accompanies evildoers to their grave (see Jer 12:1-2).

How Often?*

17 "Yet, how often is the lamp of the wicked extinguished?
How often does calamity befall them
as God in his anger uses his retribution to repay them?
18 How often are they like straw blown away by the wind
or like chaff that the storm carries off?

What Concern Will He Have for His Family?*

19 "According to you, God stores up punishment for a man's children,
but the wicked should be the ones punished and requited for their evil. [o]
20 Let his own eyes witness the destruction of God
that his sins have earned,
and let him quaff the wrath* of the Almighty!
21 For what concern will he have for his family
once his allotted number of months has been completed?

All Are Consigned To Lie Down in the Earth

22 "Who can offer wisdom to God
when God judges those who are on high? [p]
23 One man passes away while enjoying vigorous health,
blessed with security and contentment;
24 his loins are full of vigor
and his bones are rich in marrow.
25 Another dies in bitterness of soul,
never having tasted happiness.
26 Both are consigned to lie down in the earth
and worms soon cover them.

Have You Never Questioned Travelers?

27 "Believe me, I know what your thoughts are,
as well as the arguments you will use to counter me.
28 You will say, 'Where now is the great lord's house?
Where is the tent in which the wicked man dwelled?'
29 Have you never questioned travelers?
Do you ever listen to the evidence they proffer?
30 They testify that the wicked man is saved from disaster
and is rescued before the day of wrath.
31 "Who will reproach him for his conduct
and repay him for the evil he has done?
32 When he is carried to the grave,
a watch is maintained over his tomb.
33 The clods of the valley are sweet to him; *
the remainder of mankind will follow him,
and those who preceded him are beyond counting.
34 How then can you possibly offer me any comfort
when your words lack any semblance of truth?"

IV: THIRD CYCLE OF SPEECHES*

A: Eliphaz's Third Speech

CHAPTER 22

Is God Punishing You for Your Piety?* 1 Then Eliphaz the Temanite responded:
2 "Can anyone be of the slightest interest to God,
even if that person is recognized for his wisdom? [q]
3 Does the Almighty derive any pleasure if you are righteous?
Does he profit if you lead a blameless life? [r]
4 Is he punishing you for your piety
and therefore will bring you to justice?

o Ex 20:5; Jer 31:29; Ezek 18:2; Jn 9:2.—p Job 35:11; Pss 82:1; 113:5; Rom 11:34.—q Job 7:17; Lk 17:10.—r Job 35:7; Ps 143:2.

21:17-18 People say that the happiness of the wicked is fragile and ephemeral. Job skeptically asks how often this is really the case.

21:19-21 The ancient principle of collective retribution said that children are punished for their parents' sins (Job 5:4; 20:10; Deut 5:9). Job no longer accepts this explanation. Job demands that each person be repaid according to his or her deeds.

21:20 *Let him quaff the wrath:* an allusion to the cup containing the wine of the divine wrath (see Isa 51:17; Jer 25:15; Rev 16:19).

21:33 *The clods of the valley are sweet to him:* this line recalls the ancient wish spoken to those who were buried: "May the earth rest lightly upon you" (*Sit tibi terra levis*).

22:1—31:40 In this third cycle of speeches, the debate on the human condition remains intense. Job gives a firm answer to the attacks of the three friends by protesting his innocence.

It is important to note that the biblical text itself has reached us in a corrupt form in some places; this makes it impossible to certify fully that the discourses are assigned to the right persons.

22:1-5 If God intervenes to punish anyone, it is only because justice demands it. Indeed, Job's situation is so lamentable that Eliphaz believes his fault must be especially grave.

5 Is not your wickedness great?
Is there any limit to your iniquities?

The Injustice Job Has Committed*

6 "You have exacted pledges from your brothers as security
and left them naked, stripped of their clothing. * [s]
7 To the thirsty you offered no water to drink,
and you withheld bread from those who were starving.
8 Should the land belong only to the powerful?
Are only those who are favored allowed to dwell in it?

9 "You have sent widows away empty-handed
and left orphans without any means of support. [t]
10 That is why snares surround you
and sudden terror causes you to cringe,
11 why light has turned to darkness, leaving you unable to see,
and flood waters envelop you.

The Unbelief of Job

12 "Does not God who dwells in the heights of the heavens
behold how lofty are the highest stars?
13 [u] Even so, you say, 'What does God know?
How can he possibly judge through such deep darkness?
14 He cannot possibly see through the thick clouds
as he roams through the vault of the heavens.'

15 "Will you still continue to follow the ancient way
that those who are wicked have trod?
16 They were snatched away before their time;
their foundations were swept away by a flood. *
17 They had said to God, 'Leave us alone!'
and thought, 'What can the Almighty do to us?'
18 "Yet it was he who filled their houses with good things,
even though his plans and theirs were diametrically opposed. [v]
19 The upright rejoice at witnessing such a spectacle,
and the innocent deride them:
20 'See how our enemies have been destroyed,
and what remained of their wealth has been consumed by fire.' *

If You Return to the Almighty . . .

21 "Come to terms with God and be reconciled.
In this way good fortune will come to you. [w]
22 Accept the instruction from his lips
and keep his words in your heart. *
23 If you return to the Almighty, you will be restored;
if you remove iniquity from your tent
24 and treat gold as if it were only dust
and the gold of Ophir * as pebbles from the stream,
25 then the Almighty himself will be your gold
and your precious silver.

26 "For then the Almighty will be your delight
and you will lift up your face to God.
27 You will pray to him and he will hear you,
and you will fulfill your vows. [x]
28 Whatever decision you make will be successful,
and light will shine along your path.
29 For God brings low the arrogant
while he saves the humble. [y]
30 He delivers anyone who is innocent;
if your hands are clean, you will be saved." [z]

s Job 24:3; Deut 24:6, 17; Ezek 18:12, 16.—t Job 24:21; 29:13; 31:18.—u 13ff: Pss 10:11; 73:11; 94:7; Isa 29:15; Ezek 8:12; 9:9.—v Job 12:6; 21:16.—w Job 8:7; Ps 34:9-18; Isa 27:5; Jer 9:24; Rom 5:1.—x Job 5:27; 33:26; Num 30:2; Ps 61:6; 91:15.—y Pss 18:28; 138:6; Prov 29:23; Mt 23:12; Jas 4:10; 1 Pet 5:5.—z Job 17:9; Ps 18:21, 25.

22:6-11 According to Eliphaz, Job's misfortunes are nothing but the punishment for his faults. In chapter 29, Job will deny the type of behavior of which Eliphaz is here accusing him.

22:6 *You have exacted pledges . . . stripped of their clothing:* sins that have been condemned by the Prophets (see Am 2:8).

22:16 An allusion to the flood (Gen 6–8).

22:20 *Fire:* moving beyond the allusion to the flood, the speaker expands his horizon to include a description of the destiny in store for all sinners.

22:22 Job responds to this verse in the next chapter (Job 23:12). *Keep his words in your heart:* see note on Ps 119:11.

22:24 *Ophir:* a section of Arabia, probably on the western coast, from which highly refined gold was imported (see 1 Ki 9:28; 10:11; Ps 45:10).

B: Job's Seventh Response

CHAPTER 23

If Only I Knew Where To Find God!* 1 Job then answered with these words:

2 "My complaint remains bitter;
despite my groans, God's hand lies heavy on me.
3 Oh, if only I knew where to find him
so that I might discover his dwelling.
4 I would present my case before him
and state arguments in my defense.

5 "Then I would learn what he would answer me,
and contemplate his words to me.
6 He would not use his power to contend with me;
he would only need to consider my arguments.
7 There an upright man could reason with him,
and I would receive a verdict of acquittal.

8* "But if I go to the east, he is not there;
if I go to the west, I cannot behold him.
9 When I seek him in the north, I cannot find him;
when I turn to the south, I catch no glimpse of him.

God Has Caused My Courage To Fail*

10 "And yet he is aware of everywhere I go;
if he were to test me, I would emerge like pure gold. [a]
11 My footsteps have not strayed from the path he established;
I have followed his way and never turned aside.
12 I have not strayed from the commandments of his lips;
I have treasured in my heart the words of his mouth.
13 But once he has made a decision, who can oppose him?
Whatever he desires, that he does. [b]
14 He will not turn aside from what he has planned for me,
as is true of all his other decrees.

15 "That is why I am in such fear of him;
whenever I think of him, I am terrified.
16 God has caused my courage to fail;
the Almighty has filled me with dread.
17 For darkness hides me from him,
and obscurity veils his presence from me.

CHAPTER 24

The Injustice Crying Out in the World*

1 "The actual day of judgment is known by the Almighty;
why does he not reveal it to his faithful? * [c]
2 Those who are wicked move boundary stones;
they seize flocks and pasture them.
3 They drive off the donkey belonging to the orphan;
they take away the widow's ox as security.
4 They push aside the needy off the road;
those who are destitute are forced into hiding.

5 "Like wild donkeys of the wilderness
the poor go forth at dawn
searching the wasteland for food
with which to feed their children.
6 In the fields they reap what is not theirs
and steal from the vineyards of the wicked.
7 Without clothing, they spend the night naked,
lacking anything to shelter them from the cold.
8 They are soaked by the mountain rain
and cling to the rocks as a source of shelter.

9 "The fatherless child is snatched from the breast
and carried off as a pledge of security. [d]

a Job 31:6; Pss 37:18; 66:10; 1 Pet 1:7.—b Job 10:13; 42:2; Pss 115:3; 135:6; Isa 14:24.—c Job 14:5; Acts 1:7.—d Job 29:12; Deut 24:17; Ps 14:4.

23:1-9 Contrary to what Eliphaz believes, Job does not wish to escape the hand of God. He asks only that he may encounter God in order to set his case before him and let God know that an honest man is in his presence. But God is far off and inaccessible (see Job 9:11-12; Ps 139:7-10).

23:8-9 No matter in which direction Job goes, he cannot find God; see, in contrast, the words of the psalmist in Ps 139:7-10.

23:10-17 God knows that Job is righteous and faithful. However, God does not make allowances for him. He has taken sides and acts with disquieting freedom; because of this, Job is troubled in his faith and filled with terror. It is the very expression of the "night" through which every mystic must pass.

24:1-17 Here, as in places elsewhere, the translations differ widely (but without any of them achieving a clear meaning) in an effort to correct an unintelligible original.

24:1 Job is eagerly, but vainly, looking for the moment when God will intervene as on the "day of the LORD," or day of judgment, foretold by the Prophets (see Am 5:18).

10 They go about their work naked, without clothing;
despite their hunger they carry the sheaves.
11 Along the pathways they press out the oil;
they tread the winepresses but themselves suffer thirst.
12 From the town the groans of the dying are heard,
and those who are wounded cry out for help,
yet God remains deaf to their prayer.

13 "There also are those who rebel against the light;
they are ignorant of its ways
and refuse to frequent its paths.[e]
14 When nightfall descends, the murderer arises
to slay the poor and the needy;
during the night he steals forth like a thief.

15 "The eye of the adulterer also waits eagerly for twilight,
thinking, 'No eye will see me.'[f]
16 In the darkness men break into houses,
but during the day they shut themselves in,
for they are strangers to daylight.
17 Deep darkness is morning to them;
they only feel comfortable amid the terrors of the night.

God Carefully Monitors the Conduct of the Mighty*

18 "Such men are debris on the surface of the water;
their portion in the land is accursed,
and no laborer will toil in their vineyards.
19 As drought and heat melt the snow,
so does the netherworld cause sinners to disappear.
20 The womb that shaped them remembers them no more,
and the worm sucks them dry.

21 "They maltreat the barren and childless woman
and show no kindness to the widow.
22 God may sustain the mighty through his strength,
but he carefully monitors their conduct.[g]
23 He grants them a sense of security,
but his eyes are fixed on their ways.
24 They are exalted for a while,
and then they are gone;
they wither and fade like a flower,
shriveling up like ears of grain.

25 "If all this is not true, who will prove me wrong
and show that my words are sheer nonsense?"

C: Bildad's Third Speech*

CHAPTER 25

God's Dominance Inspires Terror. 1 Then Bildad the Shuhite responded:

2 "Sovereignty and awe belong to God
who has established peace in his realm on high.
3 How can anyone number his forces? *
Upon whom does his light not arise?

4 "How then can any man be righteous in God's eyes?
How can one born of woman be regarded as virtuous?[h]
5 If in his eyes the moon is not bright
and the stars are not pure,
6 how much less is man, who is a maggot,
a son of man, who is a worm?"

D: Job's Eighth Response

CHAPTER 26

How Profuse Is the Advice You Suggest!*
1 Job then answered with these words:

2 "What a help you are to the helpless,
and what strength you are to the weak!
3 What good counsel you give to the ignorant!
How abundantly you have manifested wisdom!

---

e Isa 5:20; Jn 3:19f; Eph 5:8ff.—f Job 31:9.—g Job 9:4; 12:19.—h Job 4:17ff; 9:2; 14:4.

24:18-25 This passage unduly breaks into the speech. Some critics prefer to think that it was displaced when the texts were being transcribed and that it should be put after Job 27:23, which is likewise anomalous. The two passages, which fit together rather well, would then make up Zophar's third speech.

25:1-6 The course of the debate gives the author an opportunity to introduce a fine piece on the greatness of God. According to some critics, Job interrupts briefly (Job 26:1-4), and Bildad's speech continues in Job 26:5-14. In this interpretation, Job picks up his thread again in Job 27:1ff.

25:3 *Forces:* the angels and the stars.

26:1-4 Job appeals to irony once again in answer to Bildad: is it right to proclaim God's power to a dying man?

4 Who has helped you utter those words?
And whose spirit issued forth from your mouth? [i]

God's Mighty Works

5 "The dead below tremble with fright,
as do the waters and all their inhabitants. [j]
6 The netherworld * is laid bare before him,
and Abaddon lies uncovered.
7 "He stretches out the North * above the void
and suspends the earth on nothingness.
8 He encloses the waters in dense clouds,
yet the clouds are not torn asunder under their weight.
9 He veils the face of the full moon,
spreading his clouds beneath it.
10 "He has established the horizon on the surface of the waters
as the boundary between light and darkness. [k]
11 The pillars of the heavens shake,
stunned by the thunder of his voice.
12 By his power he churns up the sea,
and by his skill he smites Rahab. * [l]
13 By his breath the skies are cleared,
and by his hand he has pierced the fleeing serpent. * [m]
14 "These deeds are only a sample of what he has done,
and how faint is the whisper that we hear of him,
but who can possibly comprehend the thunder of his power?"

CHAPTER 27

I Maintain the Rightness of My Cause.* 1 Job then continued his discourse:
2 "I swear by the living God who has denied me justice,
and by the Almighty who has filled my soul with bitterness, [n]
3 that as long as I have a shred of life remaining in me
and the breath of God is in my nostrils,
4 never will my lips utter falsehood,
nor will my tongue be guilty of deceit.
5 "Never will I concede that you * are right;
until death I will not renounce my innocence.
6 I maintain the rightness of my cause;
my conscience does not reproach me for the life I have led. [o]
7 "Let my enemy meet the fate of the wicked
and my adversary face the doom of the unjust.
8 For what hope does a godless man have when he is cut off,
when God takes away his life? [p]
9 Will God pay heed to his cry
when disaster comes upon him?
10 Will he then take delight in the Almighty
and call upon him at all times?
11 "I will teach you about the power of God;
I will not conceal the designs of the Almighty.
12 Yet all of you have seen it yourselves;
how then can you waste your time with idle words?"

E: Zophar's Third Speech*

The Law of the Violent

13 "This is the fate that God allots for the wicked man,
the inheritance that the violent receive from the Almighty. [q]
14 Though numerous, his children are destined for the sword,
and his descendants will never have enough to eat.
15 His survivors will perish as a result of pestilence,
and their widows will not mourn for them.
16 "Even though he amasses silver like dust
and piles up clothes like clay,

i 1 Ki 22:24.—j Prov 9:18; Ps 139:8, 11-12.—k Job 38: 8-11; Gen 1:4; Prov 8:29.—l Job 9:13; 12:13; Ex 14:21.—m Job 9:8; Isa 27:1.—n Job 6:29; 34:5; Isa 40:27.—o Job 29:14; Pss 18:20-23; 119:121; Isa 59:17; Acts 24:16; Rom 2:15.—p Job 8:13; 11:20; Lk 12:20.—q Job 15:20; 20:4-29.

26:6 *Netherworld:* see note on Ps 6:6. *Abaddon:* a Hebrew word meaning "a place of destruction," which was used as another word for the netherworld (see Job 28:22; Rev 9:11).

26:7 *The North:* another word for the firmament (see note on Ps 48:3).

26:12 See the note on Job 7:12.

26:13 *Fleeing serpent:* i.e., Leviathan; see notes on Job 3:8; 7:12.

27:1-12 Job gives a moving and energetic protest of his innocence, calling God as a witness. Going beyond the framework of the protest, the text describes the silence of God with which the man who has turned away from him will one day have to cope.

27:5 *You:* this word is plural in the original, indicating that Job is now speaking to his three friends as a group.

27:13-23 Despite its location here, this passage does not seem attributable to Job. It fits better with Zophar's thinking because it picks up an idea he has already developed in his second speech: the punishment of the wicked (see Job 20:29); it fits rather well with Job 24:18-25.

17 it is the righteous who will wear those clothes
and the innocent who will divide the silver.
18 The house he builds is as flimsy as a cobweb
or like a shack that shelters the watchman.
19 He goes to bed a man of wealth for the final time;
he opens his eyes to find that it is all gone. [r]
20 "By day terror overtakes him,
and at night a whirlwind carries him away.
21 An east wind seizes him and he is gone;
it sweeps him far away from his home. *
22 It assails him without pity,
and he flees from its force that menaces him.
23 His downfall is acclaimed with joy,
and he is derided wherever he may be.

F: The Praise of Wisdom*

CHAPTER 28

Where Can Wisdom Be Found?*

1 "There are mines for silver
and places where gold is refined.
2 Iron is extracted from the earth
and copper is smelted from ore.
3 Miners penetrate the darkness;
they search to the farthest recesses
to discover the ore hidden in gloom and shadow.
4 They open shafts in uninhabited places,
swinging suspended, far away from anyone.
5 "While grain is coming forth from the earth above,
what lies beneath is ravaged by fire.
6 Its rocks are the enclosure for sapphires,
and there is gold contained in its dust.
7 No bird of prey knows the path there;
the eye of a falcon has not seen it.
8 Proud beasts have not trodden it;
no lion has ever passed over it.
9 "Man begins to assail the granite rock
and overturns the mountains at their foundations.
10 He cuts channels into the rocks,
and his eyes behold precious gems.
11 He explores the sources of the streams
and brings hidden riches to light.
12 But where can wisdom be found?
And where is the place of understanding? [s]

Wisdom Cannot Be Purchased*

13 "No one knows the way to it,
nor is it to be found in the land of the living.
14 The abyss declares, 'It is not in me.'
The sea says, 'I do not have it.'
15 It cannot be purchased with gold,
nor can its price be weighed out in silver. [t]
16 "It cannot be acquired with the gold of Ophir,
nor with precious onyx or sapphire.
17 Gold or crystal * cannot be compared to it,
nor can it be exchanged for vessels of gold.
18 Neither coral nor alabaster deserve to be mentioned;
the price of wisdom is beyond pearls.
19 Topaz from Ethiopia is worthless in comparison to it,
nor can it be valued in terms of pure gold.
20 "Where then is the source of wisdom?
Where is intelligence to be found?

God Alone Knows Where Wisdom Can Be Found*

21 "It cannot be seen by the eye of any living creature;
it is even concealed from the birds of the air.

r Job 3:13; 7:8; 24:24; Pss 49:18.—s Job 28:20, 23, 28; Prov 1:20; Eccl 7:24f.—t Job 28:17; Prov 3:14; 8:10f, 19; 16:16; Wis 7:7-11.

27:21 See note on Job 15:2.

28:1-28 This praise of wisdom breaks into the debate between Job and his friends. This passage is related to other important passages in other Books dealing with the same subject (Prov 8:22-36; Sir 24; Bar 3:9—4:4). Wisdom is imagined as a person who dwells with God and is consulted by him. It is an image of God's own thought, in comparison with which all human efforts to discover things seem trivial.

28:1-12 The exploitation of mines in the search for gold or precious stones has amazed people from antiquity and led them to use the contribution of slaves and prisoners in pursuit of this difficult work (v. 4). However, it is not by such searches that one can extract the secret of wisdom.

28:13-20 Wisdom is not found along the route of human discoveries; all the treasures of the world are of no avail in acquiring it.

28:17 *Crystal:* the text actually speaks of "glass," but in antiquity this was very rare and valuable.

28:21-28 God alone knows where wisdom is found. Indeed, she was the inspiration of his work of creation (Prov 8:22-31)!

22 Abaddon and the netherworld * admit,
'We have only heard rumors of it.'
23 u "God alone understands the path to wisdom;
he alone knows where it can be found.
24 For he can observe the farthest ends of the earth,
and he sees everything under the heavens. v
25 "When God regulated the force of the wind
and measured out the waters,
26 when he imposed a limit for the rain
and cleared a path for the thunderbolt,
27 then he saw wisdom and evaluated it,
established it and assessed it completely.
28 And then he declared to man:
'The fear of the LORD is wisdom,
and to turn from evil is understanding.' " w

G: Job's Final Speech: His Appeal to God

CHAPTER 29

The Happy Time. 1 * Then Job continued further with his solemn discourse, as he said:
2 "Oh, how I yearn for the months long gone
and for those days when God kept watch over me, x
3 when his lamp continued to shine above my head
and by his light I could walk through darkness.
4 "In those days I was in my prime,
and God protected my tent.
5 The Almighty was ever present at my side,
and my children were around me.
6 My feet were bathed in milk,
and the rocks poured forth streams of oil * for me.
7 "When I would go forth to the gate of the city *
and take my seat in the public square,
8 the young men would see me and withdraw,
and the old men would rise to their feet.
9 The nobles would refrain from speaking
and would place their hands over their mouths. y
10 The voices of the princes were silenced,
and their tongues stuck to the roof of their mouths.

People Praised My Works

11 "Whoever heard my words spoke favorably of me,
and those who saw me testified to my merit,
12 because I delivered the poor who appealed for help
and the orphan who had no one to protect him.
13 The blessing of the wretched was given to me,
and I caused the widow's heart to sing for joy.
14 "I put on righteousness as my garment;
justice was my cloak and my turban.
15 I was eyes to the blind
and feet to the lame.
16 I was a father to the needy,
and I defended the rights of the stranger.
17 I broke the fangs of the wicked
and snatched their prey from their teeth.
18 "Then I thought, 'I will die in honor
after having multiplied my days like grains of sand, *
19 with my roots spreading out to the waters
and the dew lying on my branches throughout the night.
20 My glory will be forever new
and the bow in my hand forever strong.' z
21 * "Men waited expectantly to hear my words
and listened in silence to my counsel.

u 23-27: Prov 8:22-31.—v Pss 33:13f; 66:7; Isa 11:12; Heb 4:13.—w Job 37:24; Ex 20:20; Deut 4:6; Ps 111:10; Prov 1:7; 9:10.—x Job 1:10; Jer 31:28; 44:27.—y Job 29:21; 31:21; Jdg 18:19.—z Job 30:11; Gen 49:24; Ps 18:35.

28:22 *Abaddon and the netherworld:* see note on Job 26:6.

29:1-25 Job reminisces about days of yesteryear and brilliantly evokes his success as a great Eastern chieftain. Happiness was with him. He made laws with a sovereign authority, and an entire people surrounded him with honor and respect. (Verses 21-25 are normally placed after v. 10, although we have kept them in their place.)

29:6 *Milk . . . oil:* see note on Job 20:17.

29:7 *Gate of the city:* the place where business was transacted and court cases were heard. Job used to take his *seat* there as a member of the city council.

29:18 *Grains of sand:* another possible translation is: "the phoenix"—a symbol of long life. The ancients regarded the phoenix as a bird that lived for centuries, then became consumed in flames, and finally arose from the ashes with new life.

29:21-25 These verses should be read after verse 10.

22 Once I had spoken, no one spoke further
but simply let my thoughts penetrate their minds.
23 They waited for me as for the rain,
with open mouths as though to drink in a spring shower.
24 "When I smiled at them, they were filled with gratitude,
and they were clearly strengthened because of the way I treated them. [a]
25 As their leader I told them which course to follow,
and I lived like a king among his troops,
or as a comforter of mourners.

CHAPTER 30

Now I Am the Laughingstock

1 "But now I am the laughingstock
of people who are younger than I,
people whose fathers I would not have considered fit
to put with the dogs guarding my flock. [b]
2 Of what use to me was the strength of their hands?
Their vigor had completely wasted away.
3 "Enfeebled by want and hunger,
they gnawed roots in the wilderness,
a gloomy place of dry and desolate ground.
4 They plucked saltwort and scrub for food,
and they ate the roots of the broom tree. *
5 Cast out from human society
and berated as thieves and pursued,
6 they were forced to live on the sides of ravines,
in holes in the ground, and in clefts of rock.
7 Among the bushes you could hear them braying,
huddled together under the nettles.
8 They are a vile and irresponsible brood,
driven as outcasts from society.
9 "And these are the ones who speak mockingly about me;
my name is a byword among them.
10 They abhor me and keep their distance from me;
they do not hesitate to spit in my face. [c]
11 And since God has loosened my bowspring * and humbled me,
they have ceased to have any restraint in my presence.
12 "The rabble attack in a mob on my right flank;
they lay snares for my feet
and raise their siege-ramps against me.
13 They advance through my crumbling defenses,
blocking every means of escape,
and no one restrains them.
14 They burst forward through a gaping breach
and advance in waves.
15 Terrors surround me on all sides;
my confidence disintegrates,
and my hope of deliverance vanishes like a cloud. [d]

God's Severity*

16 "And now my life has begun to ebb away;
my days are filled with grief and affliction.
17 During the night pain wracks my bones,
and I suffer from ceaseless throbbing that allows me no respite.
18 God seizes my garment violently,
grasping me by the collar of my tunic.
19 He has cast me into the mire,
and I am covered with dust and ashes.
20 "I cry out to you, O God, but you do not answer me;
I stand before you, but you barely take notice. [e]
21 You have turned with severity against me;
with your strong hand you persecute me.
22 You lift me up and place me at the mercy of the wind,
allowing me to be tossed about in the storm.
23 I know indeed that you will hand me over to death
and to the place appointed for every living mortal. [f]

---

a Num 6:25; Ps 89:15.—b Job 6:14; 12:4; 19:19.—c Job 17:6; 19:19; Deut 25:9; Mt 26:67.—d Job 3:25; 6:4; Ps 55:5f.—e Job 19:7; 1 Ki 8:52; Ps 22:3.—f Job 3:19; 2 Sam 14:14; Heb 9:27.

30:4 The foods mentioned here (*saltwort, scrub,* and *roots of the broom tree*) were the fare of those in extreme poverty.

30:11 *Loosened my bowspring:* i.e., done away with my strength.

30:16-23 Little by little Job comes back to his essential distress: the fierce hostility of a God who pursues him relentlessly. His faith survives but in a greatly wounded state.

Yet I Cannot Discover Why

24 "And yet should you not extend a hand
to someone who pleads with you for help?
25 Did I not shed tears over the plight of the unfortunate?
Was not my soul grieved for the destitute?
26 Yet when I hoped for good, only evil came;
when I looked for light, there was only darkness.
27 My inward parts are in constant pain,
and days of affliction torment me.
28 "I walk about dejected and without comfort;
I stand up in the assembly and cry for help. [g]
29 I have become a brother to the jackal
and a companion to the ostrich.
30 My skin has turned black and peels off my body,
and my bones are scorched by heat.
31 My harp has been tuned to dirges,
and my flute to the sounds of weeping.

CHAPTER 31

Let God Weigh Me on Honest Scales*

1 "I have made a covenant with my eyes
not to look with desire upon a virgin.
2 For what is man's lot prescribed by God above,
his inheritance from the Almighty on high?
3 Is it not destruction for the wicked
and disaster for wrongdoers?
4 Does not God see my ways
and number all my steps? [h]
5 "If I have walked in falsehood
or hastened my steps toward deceit,
6 let God weigh me on honest scales;
then he will know that I am blameless.

If My Steps Have Wandered . . .*

7 "If my steps have wandered from the path of righteousness,
or if my eyes have led my heart astray,
or if any stain has besmirched my hands,
8 then let someone else eat what I sow,
and let my crops be uprooted.
9 "If my heart has been enticed by a woman
and I have lain in wait at my neighbor's door,
10 then let my wife grind grain * for another
and let other men enjoy her.
11 For that would be a heinous crime
and judged as a criminal offense. [i]
12 It would be a fire that leads to Destruction *
until it consumes all my possessions completely. [j]
13 "If I have ever rejected the pleas of my male or female slaves
when they lodged a complaint against me,
14 what will I do when God confronts me?
What will I answer if he calls me to account? [k]
15 Did not he who formed me in the womb
also make them?
Did not the one God create all human beings? *
16 "Have I ignored the needs of the poor
or caused the eyes of widows to overflow with tears? [l]
17 Did I ever eat my bread alone
without sharing it with an orphan,
18 I whom God has reared like a father
and guided ever since I left my mother's womb?
19 "Have I ever seen a stranger in need of clothing,
or a poor wretch with nothing to cover him,
20 whose body has not blessed me
after being warmed with the fleece of my sheep?
21 Have I ever raised my hand against the innocent,
knowing that my friends would support me?
22 "If I have done any of these things,
then let my shoulder blade fall from my shoulder
and let my arm be torn from its socket.

---

g Job 17:14; 19:7; Ps 38:7; 43:2.—h Job 14:16; 2 Chr 16:9; Ps 139:3; Prov 5:21.—i Gen 38:24; Lev 20:10; Deut 22:22; Prov 6:32-33.—j Job 15:30; 26:6; 31:8.—k Job 33:5; Isa 10:3.—l Job 5:16; Jas 1:27.

31:1-6 If God recompenses everyone according to one's deserts, he must render justice to Job.

31:7-34 Using the traditional formula for cursing (Num 5:20-22), Job examines his life in all the fundamental areas of religion and the law. In his actions, intentions, and most secret feelings, he is without fault.

31:10 *Grind grain:* slaves were used for grinding grain.

31:12 *Destruction:* literally, "Abaddon"; see note on Job 26:6.

31:15 Some scholars believe that verses 38-40 of this chapter should be placed after this verse instead of in their accustomed spot.

23 For then the fear of God would overcome me
and I would be unable to stand in his presence.[m]
24 "Have I placed my faith in gold
and regarded it as my security?
25 Have I rejoiced in my great wealth
and the abundance of riches in my possession?
26 * Have I beheld the sun when it shone
and the moon moving in its splendor
27 and ever found my heart to be secretly enticed
so that I blew them a kiss in homage?
28 Any of these would be a serious offense,
for I would have been unfaithful to God above.[n]

29* "Have I ever rejoiced at the ruin of my enemy
or exulted when evil overtook him—[o]
30 I who would not allow my tongue to sin
by laying his life under a curse?
31 Have not those of my household said,
'Who has not eaten his meat and been sated?'
32 No stranger has ever had to spend the night in the street;
my door has always been open to the traveler.

33 "Have I ever concealed my transgressions as others do,
keeping my guilt buried within my breast,
34 because I feared the gossip that would ensue,
and I was terrified at the scorn of the multitude?
If so, then I would have remained silent
and not ventured out of doors.

May God Respond*

35* "Oh, if only I had someone to hear my defense
and my accuser would write out his indictment![p]
36 I would wear it on my shoulder
and place it on my head as a crown.
37 I would give him an account of my entire life,
and like a prince I would present myself before him.

Concluding Oath*

38 "If my land has cried out against me
and its furrows have joined in the weeping,
39 if I have eaten its produce without payment
and caused the death of its owners,
40 then let thistles grow instead of wheat
and noxious weeds instead of barley."
The words of Job are ended.

V: THE FOUR SPEECHES OF ELIHU*

CHAPTER 32

Elihu's Indignation Is Aroused.* 1 The three men then ceased to argue with Job because in his own eyes he was righteous.[q] 2 Then Elihu, the son of Barachel the Buzite,* of the family of Ram, became very angry. He was furious because Job believed that he was righteous and that God was in error. 3 And he was also angry at Job's three friends because they had never devised an answer to refute Job and thus had allowed God to appear to be wrong.[r]

4 While Job and his friends had been conversing, Elihu had refrained from addressing Job, since the three companions were older than he. 5 But when Elihu perceived that the three had no answer to offer, he could no longer contain his anger.

m Job 13:11; 30:15.—n Gen 38:24; Jos 24:27.—o Prov 17:5; 24:17; Ob 12.—p Job 13:3; 19:23; 23:3-7.—q Job 10:7; 13:18.—r Job 22:5; 32:12-13.

31:26-27 Job knows that to worship the sun or the moon is a sin (see Deut 4:19; 17:3; Ezek 8:16f), and he was careful not to do so. *Blew them a kiss:* a sign of respect that implied recognition of a divinity (the Latin word *adorare* ["adore"] came from *ad os* meaning "put the hand to the mouth"). Therefore, to blow a kiss to the stars meant to practice idolatry.

31:29-32 Job has never succumbed to gloating over enemies, which had been condemned by Moses (Ex 23:4f) and would later also be ruled out by Christ (Mt 5:43-47).

31:35-37 Job is ready to appear before God and certain to be able to refute every accusation in his presence.

31:35-36 The written indictment took the form of a lengthy papyrus scroll that Job would like to wear like a turban.

31:38-40 Job now offers a concluding oath to complete an earlier theme. He calls for a curse on his land if he has neglected social justice (see vv. 13-15). Some scholars place verses 38-40 after verse 15 in this chapter.

32:1—37:24 The speeches of Elihu (chs. 32–37), like the composition on wisdom (ch. 28), were probably added to the Book of Job in a second phase of the Book's history. The final editor was perhaps trying to soften the overly harsh positions put on the lips of Job. He tries to justify the intervention of this unexpected personage by saying that it was necessary to let the older men speak first. This champion of the rights of God adds little new except that he does a better job of situating suffering in the divine plan. When he has concluded his bit of eloquence, he is no longer mentioned.

32:1-5 Elihu's four poetic speeches are introduced by five prose verses written by the author.

32:2 *Buzite:* i.e., an inhabitant of the desert region of Buz in north Arabia (see Jer 25:23).

A: Elihu's First Speech

I Have Many Things To Say.* 6 Therefore Elihu, the son of Barachel the Buzite, began to speak.

"I am young in years,
and you are old.
Therefore, I held my tongue
and hesitated to express my opinion to you.
7 I thought, 'Age ought to speak;
many years will result in conveying wisdom.' [s]
8 "But it is the spirit in a man,
the breath of the Almighty,
that gives him understanding. [t]
9 It is not only the old who are wise;
it is not only the aged who understand what is right.
10 Therefore, I beg you to listen to me
and allow me to declare my opinion.
11 "I have been waiting to hear what you had to say,
and I listened attentively to your arguments
as each one of you chose your words with care.
12 I gave you my close attention,
but there is not one of you who has convicted Job
or refuted his statements.
13 Therefore, do not say, 'We have found wisdom;
let God confute him, not men!'
14 Job has not addressed his words to me;
therefore, I will not answer him in the way you have done.
15 "These three men are confounded and unable to respond;
words have failed them.
16 Am I then to wait because they do not speak,
but simply stand there, stuck for an answer?
17 I also will now have my say;
it is my turn to express my opinion.
18 For I have many things to say,
and the spirit within me forces me to speak. [u]
19 "I am ready to burst,
like a new wineskin with wine searching for a vent.
20 I must speak so that I may find relief;
I must open my lips and reply.
21 I will show no partiality to anyone,
nor will I use flattering words.
22 For I do not know how to flatter;
if I did, my Maker would soon do away with me.

CHAPTER 33

God Is Greater Than Any Human Being*

1 "Therefore, O Job, listen to my words
and pay careful attention to everything I have to say.
2 Behold, I have opened my mouth;
the words are on the tip of my tongue.
3 My words issue forth from an upright heart,
and my lips will be sincere in what I say.
4 The Spirit of God has made me,
and the breath of the Almighty gives me life. [v]
5 "Refute me if you are able to do so;
prepare your arguments and confront me.
6 In the sight of God I am just like you;
like you, I was formed from a piece of clay. [w]
7 Therefore, no fear of me should frighten you,
nor should you feel any pressure on my account.
8 "You have offered your defense in my presence,
and I have listened carefully to the words you spoke.
9 You said, 'I am pure and without sin;
I am clean, and there is no fault in me. [x]
10 Yet God continues to invent excuses against me
and regards me as his enemy.
11 He fastens my feet in shackles
and watches everything I do.'
12 "In regard to this, I tell you, you are completely wrong.

s Job 12:12; 2 Chr 10:6.—t Job 27:3; 33:4; Ps 119:34.—u Ps 39:4; 1 Cor 9:16.—v Job 10:3; 32:8; Gen 2:7.—w Job 4:19; Acts 14:15.—x Job 10:7; 13:18; 29:14; 34:5.

32:6-22 Right from the beginning of this lengthy monologue, Elihu opposes his wisdom to that of the ancients. Intelligence does not result from the short views of experience or tradition but from receiving inspiration from God (Wis 1:6; Sir 1:1-10; Isa 28:26; Dan 1:17). He does not hurl false accusations at Job as his friends did but uses Job's own words to criticize him (see Job 33:9-11; 34:5-6, 9; 35:2-3).

33:1-13 As far as Elihu is concerned, Job is too sure of himself. One cannot discuss things with God as an equal. In addition, Elihu correctly brings out that Job's perception of God as his enemy (v. 10; 13:24; 19:11) is wrong.

God is greater than any human being.[y]
13 Why then do you utter endless complaints
that he will not explain his decisions to you?

God Speaks in Many Ways*

14 "For God does speak, first in one way and then in another,
although we do not always perceive it.[z]
15 "In dreams and in visions of the night,
when deep sleep falls upon men
as they slumber on their beds,
16 God then opens their ears
and issues warnings that strike them with terror,
17 so that he may turn man away from evil
and check his pride.
18 In this way he spares his soul from the pit*
and his life from a violent death.
19 "Or again, he chastens him with pain upon his bed
and with unceasing agony in his bones,
20 so that he regards food with loathing
and rejects the choicest dishes.[a]
21 His flesh is so wasted away that it cannot be seen,
and his bones that once were invisible now begin to show.
22 His soul draws nearer to the pit
and his life to the abode of the dead.
23 "But then, if there should be an angel on his side,
one out of a thousand, a mediator,
to show him what is right for him
and expound God's righteousness to him,
24 he will take pity on him and say,
'Spare him from going down into the pit;
I have the ransom for his life.'
25 Then his flesh will regain its boyish freshness,
and he will return to the days of his youthful vigor.
26 "Then, if he entreats God to show him favor
and allow him to enter his presence with joy,[b]
27 he will affirm before everyone,
'I sinned and departed from the path of righteousness,
but God has not punished me as I deserved.
28 He spared my soul from descending into the pit,
and I will behold the light of life.'
29 "God indeed does all these things
again and again* for a man,
30 bringing back his soul from the pit
so that he may see the light of life.[c]
31 "Be attentive, Job, and listen to me;
be silent and I will speak.
32 If you have anything to say, then answer me;
speak, for I desire to justify you.
33 But if you have nothing to say, then listen to me;
be silent and I will teach you wisdom."

B: Elihu's Second Speech*

CHAPTER 34

Let Us Explore What Is Right.* 1 Then Elihu continued and said:
2 "Listen to my words, you wise men;
you men of learning, hear what I have to say.
3 For the ear tests the value of words
as the palate does with food.[d]
4 "Let us consider together what is right;
let us determine among ourselves what is good.
5 For Job has said, 'I am innocent,
but God has denied me justice;
6 I am in desperate straits
despite the fact that I have done no wrong.'
7 "Was there ever a man like Job
with his thirst for blasphemous charges,

y Ps 50:21; Eccl 7:20; Isa 55:8-9.—z Job 33:29; 40:5; Ps 62:12.—a Job 3:24; 6:7; Pss 102:5; 107:18.—b Job 22:26-29; Ps 50:15; Prov 8:35.—c Job 33:18; Pss 56:14; 107:20; Isa 38:17.—d Job 12:11.

33:14-33 When God manifests himself, human beings tremble with a salutary fear (Gen 20:3; 28:17). God also speaks through sickness, which could be transformed into the moment for inner renewal that leads to hope for the joy of a cure. An angel translates this language for humans and successfully intervenes for them before God.

33:18 *Pit:* i.e., the grave (see also vv. 22, 24, 28, 30).

33:29 *Again and again:* literally, "twice . . . three times" (see note on Job 5:19).

34:1-37 Elihu's thoughts become more spirited. He reaches the heart of the dispute: human suffering in the face of God's justice.

34:1-9 The entire problem lies herein. Elihu mounts a fiery defense of God.

8 who keeps company with evildoers
and travels with wicked men?
9 Did he not state that no one derives any benefit
by being pleasing to God? [e]

God Does Not Pervert Justice

10 "Therefore, listen to me like intelligent men.
Far be it from God to do evil; *
far be it from the Almighty to be unjust.
11 He requites everyone according to his deeds,
ensuring that he will receive what his conduct deserves. [f]
12 There can be no doubt that God will never do wrong;
the Almighty will not pervert justice.

13 "Did someone else entrust the world to his keeping?
Who but he established the whole world?
14 If he were to take back his Spirit to himself
and withdraw back into himself his breath,
15 all flesh would perish instantaneously
and mankind would turn again to dust. [g]

16 "If you have any semblance of intelligence, O Job,
pay attention to what I am saying.
17 How could an enemy of justice ever govern?
Would you dare to condemn the Righteous One, the Almighty,
18 who says to a king, 'You are a scoundrel,'
and to nobles, 'You are wicked men'?

19 "He shows no special respect to princes,
nor does he make any distinction between rich and poor,
for they are all the work of his hands. [h]
20 They die suddenly, without warning,
in the middle of the night;
at his touch the rich are no more,
and he removes the mighty without lifting a finger.

God's Eyes Observe the Ways of Humans

21 "For his eyes observe the ways of humans,
and he watches every step they take.
22 Nowhere is there darkness or gloom so dense
where evildoers may conceal themselves.
23 He forewarns no one when his time will come
to appear before God for judgment.
24 Without holding a trial he shatters the mighty
and establishes others in their place. [i]
25 Knowing the sinful deeds they do,
he overthrows them at night and they are crushed.

26 "He strikes them down for their crimes
while others look on,
27 because they have turned away from following him
and paid no heed to any of his ways.
28 But they caused the cries of the poor to reach him,
so that he heard the anguished appeal of the afflicted. [j]

29 "But if he remains silent and no one can condemn him,
and if he hides his face so that no one can behold him,
it is because he rules over nations and individuals
30 to prevent a godless man from ruling
and to set some wrongdoer free from affliction.

Job Is a Rebel to God*

31 "Suppose someone were to say to God,
'I was wrong, but I will not offend anymore;
32 instruct me how to avoid sin
so that I will not do it again.'
33 In your opinion, should God then punish such a person
because he rejected his laws?
For it is up to you to decide, not me;
therefore, please enlighten us.

34 "Men of intelligence will say to me,
and any wise listener will assert:
35 'Job speaks without knowledge; *
what he says lacks any intelligence.' [k]

e Job 9:22f, 30f; 21:15; Mal 3:14.—f Ps 62:13; Prov 24:12; Jer 32:19; Rom 2:6; 2 Cor 5:10; Rev 22:12.—g Job 10:9; Gen 3:19; Ps 90:4-10.—h Deut 10:17; 2 Chr 19:7; Rom 2:11; Eph 6:9; Col 3:25; 1 Pet 1:17.—i Job 12:19; Pss 2:9; 72:4.—j Job 5:15; 29:12; Ex 22:23; Jas 5:4.—k Job 35:16; 38:2.

34:10 *Far be it from God to do evil:* Elihu is answering a charge that God does evil, which Job in his frustration has intimated; for he has insisted that God is punishing him wrongfully and allowing evildoers to flourish (Job 24:1-12).

34:31-37 Exacerbated by his torment, Job has forgotten mercy and, in the view of Elihu, he speaks like a sinner who is entrenched in his rebellion.

34:35 *Job speaks without knowledge:* this theme is found also in God's first response (Job 38:2) and Job's final response (Job 42:3).

36 Would that Job be tried to the limit,
since his answers are those of the wicked.
37 For he is adding rebellion to his sin
by making an end of justice among us
and insulting God with abusive words."

C: Elihu's Third Speech*

CHAPTER 35

How Does Human Conduct Affect God?

1 Then Elihu continued his speech, saying:
2 "Do you think that you can defend your uprightness
by claiming that you are just before God? [l]
3 For you said: 'What does it mean to you?
Or what would you gain if I sinned?'
4 I will provide an answer for you
and your three friends as well.

5 "Look up to the skies and see;
observe the clouds towering above you.
6 If you sin, how can that affect God?
And if your offenses are multiplied,
how do you hurt him?
7 If you are righteous, what do you give him?
What does he receive from your hand? [m]
8 Your wickedness affects only someone like you,
and your righteousness affects only your fellow men.

No One Asks, "Where Is God?"

9 "People cry out under the weight of oppression;
they cry for help against the power of the mighty.
10 But not one of them asks, 'Where is God, my Maker,
who protects me during the night,
11 who gave us greater intelligence than the animals of the earth
and made us wiser than the birds of the air?'
12 Although they cry out, God does not answer
because of the pride of the wicked.

13 "But it is foolish to say that God does not hear
or that the Almighty does not pay attention.
14 Even though you do not see him,
he is aware of your plight,
and you must wait for his decision. [n]
15 But now, because God does not grow angry and punish
and because he allows transgressions to go unheeded,
16 Job gives vent to his anger with empty talk
and babbles a stream of utter nonsense." [o]

D: Elihu's Fourth Speech*

CHAPTER 36

God Renders Justice to the Afflicted.* 1 Elihu
then proceeded further and said:
2 "Be patient a little longer while I instruct you,
for I have more to say on God's behalf.
3 I will take my knowledge from afar
to support my assertion that my Master is just.
4 I promise that there will be no flaws in my arguments;
I come before you as a man of sound learning.

5 "God is mighty and does not recant;
he is great because of firmness of heart.
6 He does not let the wicked live on in all vigor
and renders justice to the afflicted. [p]
7 He does not withdraw his eyes from the righteous,
but he seats them forever with kings on the throne,
and they are exalted forever.

8 "He will also have sinners fettered with chains
and held fast by the bonds of affliction
9 after having denounced their conduct
and the sins of pride that they have committed.

l Job 32:2; 33:32.—m Job 22:3; 41:2; Lk 17:10; Rom 11:35.—n Job 9:11; 31:35; Ps 37:6.—o Job 34:35; 38:2; 42:3.—p Job 4:7; 34:26; Ps 72:4, 12f.

35:1-16 The silence of God is what upsets human beings. Is the Eternal One perhaps indifferent to human tragedies? Elihu looks for a different explanation: God is silent because unhappy human beings lack faith in their prayers, and they sin through pride. But the entire passage is obscure in its development.

36:1—37:24 With his usual excessive emphasis, Elihu repeats in his last discourse the main current beliefs on the justice and greatness of God: God does indeed reward the righteous and punish sinners (in direct contrast to Job's assertions). The text, which is often corrupt, does not allow us always to determine just what is proper to Elihu.

36:1-21 God's greatness consists in being just. He refutes the pretensions of the wicked and powerful and saves the poor. If Job could understand this, hope would arise in him. At times, the text speaks of poverty with the tone of the Gospel.

10 He opens their ears to correction,
commanding them to turn back from their evil ways.
11 "If they obey and once again serve him,
they will live out their days in prosperity,
and their years will pass pleasantly.
12 But if they do not obey him,
they will cross the river of death
and die as a result of their stubbornness.
13 Those whose hearts turn away from God rage against him,
and they do not cry for help when he chains them.
14 They die in the bloom of their youth
after a dissolute life.
15 But God rescues the suffering from their affliction,
employing their distress to instruct them.

16 "He also seeks to snatch you from torment.
When you were enjoying a life of comfort
with abundant riches and plenteous food,
17 you refused to bring the wicked to trial
or to uphold the rights of the orphan.
18 Beware lest abundance cloud your judgment
and that you not be corrupted by lavish gifts.
19 Bring the powerful to justice, not merely the poor,
those who are powerful, not only the weak.

20 "Do not long for the night
when you can drag people away from their homes.
21 Take care not to turn to evil;
that is why you are now being tested by affliction. [q]

God Is Truly Great*

22 "Behold, God is exalted in his power.
What teacher can equal him?
23 Who has prescribed the course he should follow?
Who can dare to say to him, 'You have done wrong'? [r]

24 "Therefore, remember to extol his work
which men have always praised in song.
25 All men can behold it,
admiring it from afar.
26 God is so great that he is beyond our understanding;
the number of his years is past counting.

27 "It is God who draws up drops of water
that he distills as rain to the streams.
28 His rain clouds pour down
and provide abundant water for mankind.

29 "Can anyone fathom how he spreads the clouds
as the carpeting of his tent?
30 Behold how he scatters his lightning
and covers the depths of the sea.
31 This is how he nourishes the nations,
providing food for them in abundance. [s]
32 He holds the lightning in his hands
and commands it to strike the designated mark.
33 His thunder warns us of his coming
as he prepares for combat against iniquity.

CHAPTER 37

1 "This also causes my heart to tremble
and to leap out of its place.
2 Listen to the thunder of God's voice
and the rumbling that comes forth from his mouth.
3 He sends it forth across the heavens,
along with his lightning to the ends of the earth.
4 Following this, there comes a roaring sound,
as God thunders with his majestic voice,
and he does not restrain his flashes of lightning
when his voice is heard.

5 "At God's command marvels come to pass;
he performs wonders beyond our ability to comprehend.
6 For he says to the snow, 'Fall upon the earth,'

q Job 36:8; Ps 66:18; Heb 11:25.—r Job 34:10; Isa 40:13; Rom 11:33-34.—s Job 37:13; Pss 104:14-15, 27-28; 145:15.

36:22—37:13 The sovereign wisdom of God radiates throughout the universe. In his hands, rain, tempest, and snow become calamities or benefits to accompany his justice in regard to human beings. This text is a lyrical chant of the power of God.

and to the rain shower, 'Turn into a heavy downpour.'
7 All human activity comes to a standstill
so that everyone may acknowledge his power.
8 Wild beasts return to their lairs
and take shelter in their dens.

9 "The tempest comes out of its chamber,
and the north winds bring bitter cold.
10 By the breath of God * ice is formed
and the surface of the waters becomes frozen. [t]
11 He weighs down the thick clouds with moisture,
and they scatter his lightning.
12 Following his command they blow about
over the face of the entire earth
to do whatever he directs.
13 Whether for correction of his people or for love,
he causes all this to happen. [u]

Reflect Upon the Marvelous Works of God

14 "Listen to my words, O Job;
stop and reflect upon the marvelous works of God.
15 Do you know how God controls the clouds,
or how he makes his lightning flash?
16 Do you know how the clouds are balanced,
the wondrous work of the one who is perfect in knowledge?
17 You who swelter in your stifling garments
when the earth lies still under the south wind,
18 can you, like him, spread out the skies,
hard as a mirror of cast metal? *

19 "Teach us, then, what we should say to him;
because of ignorance, we cannot present our case.
20 Do my words have any effect on him?
Is he informed of any man's commands?
21 Sometimes the light vanishes,
and the sky is overcast with clouds;
then the wind comes and sweeps them away.

22 * "Out of the north golden splendor comes forth,
and God is surrounded by awesome majesty. [v]
23 But the Almighty we cannot find;
he is unequaled in power and judgment,
and in his righteousness he will not violate justice.
24 Therefore, men revere him,
and all thoughtful men fear him." [w]

VI: THE INTERVENTION OF GOD*

A: The LORD's First Speech

CHAPTER 38

Gird Up Your Loins.* 1 Then from the heart of the storm the LORD answered Job:
2 "Who is this who obscures my intentions
with words devoid of knowledge?
3 Gird up your loins now like a man.
I will ask you questions,
and you will give me the answers. [x]

A1: The Mysteries of the Cosmos

Where Were You When I Laid the Earth's Foundations?

4 "Where were you when I laid the earth's foundations?
Tell me, if you have understanding.
5 Who determined its measurements? Do you know?
Who stretched out the measuring line over it?
6 What supports the pillars at its bases?
Who laid its cornerstone

t Job 38:29; Ps 147:17-18.—u Ex 9:22-23; 1 Sam 12:17-19.—v Ex 24:17; 1 Chr 19:11.—w Job 28:28; Isa 5:21; Mt 10:28.—x Job 40:2, 7; 42:4; Mk 11:29.

37:10 *Breath of God:* i.e., the wind.

37:18 *Hard as a mirror of cast metal:* see Deut 28:23 where this type of sky symbolizes unrelieved heat.

37:22-23 Elihu describes the advent of God, emphasizing both his power and his justice (see also Ps 48:3). He thus prepares Job for the appearance of God in the storm (chs. 38–41).

38:1—42:6 The Almighty comes in the storm. He is the Lord (Yahweh), the fearsome God of Sinai (Ex 19:16). The meeting both abashes and fascinates Job. God does not answer Job's irksome questions; the roles are reversed. The Lord presses him hard with his own questions. God does not defend himself, nor does he debate: he calls for adoration and silence. These chapters form part of the biblical songs of creation and are among the loftiest lyrical compositions of humankind. The wonders and secrets of the universe are evoked in splendid poetic images that are intended to give us a better insight into the inaccessibility of the mystery of God. And yet, Job has seen God. This man who has encountered God remains abashed. All his arguments have been immediately transcended; the only thing left is to make an act of unconditional faith.

38:1-3 *Gird up your loins:* it is God who calls Job to account for his pretensions. In the East, people tightened their belts and tucked up their garments in preparation for a struggle or for work (see Jer 1:17; Lk 12:35-37).

7 while the morning stars sang in unison
and the sons of God shouted for joy?[y]
8 "Who shut up the sea behind doors
when it burst forth from the womb,
9 when I made the clouds its garment
and wrapped it in thick darkness,
10 when I established bounds for it
and set its barred doors in place,
11 when I said, 'This far may you come, but
no farther;
here is where your proud waves must
halt'?[z]

Have You Ever Commanded the Morning?*

12 "During your entire life have you ever
commanded the morning to appear
or caused the dawn to rise in the east
13 so that it might grasp the ends of the
earth
and shake the wicked from its surface?
14 She turns it like clay under a seal
and dyes it as though it were a garment.
15 But light * is withheld from the wicked,
and their raised arm is broken.

Have You Ever Walked at the Bottom of the Abyss?

16 "Have you ever descended to the depths
of the sea
and walked at the bottom of the abyss?
17 Have the gates of death been revealed to
you
or have you seen the gates of the shadow of death?
18 Have you comprehended the vast expanse of the earth?
Tell me if you know all this.

19 "Can you point out the way to the
dwelling of light
and show the abode of darkness,
20 so that you may assign each to its designated boundary
and escort them on their homeward
paths?
21 Surely you must know this,
for you had already been born
and the years of your life are beyond
numbering!

Have You Entered the Place Where the Snow Is Stored?*

22* "Have you entered the place where the
snow is stored,
or seen the storehouses of the hail,
23 which I have reserved for times of distress,
for the times of war and battle?[a]
24 Can you show me the place where lightning is dispersed
or where the east wind is scattered over
the earth?

25 "Who has cut a channel for the downpour
of rain
and cleared a path for the thunderstorm
26 so that rain may fall on uninhabited
lands,
on the wilderness devoid of human life,
27 and thus reinvigorate the wastes and the
desolate land,
enabling grass to sprout on the thirsty
ground?

28 "Does the rain have a father?
Who has begotten the drops of dew?
29 Whose womb brings forth the ice?
Who gives birth to the frost of heaven,
30 causing a layer of stone to cover the
waters
and the surface of the earth to congeal?

Do You Know the Ordinances of the Heavens?

31 "Can you bind the chains of the Pleiades
or loosen the bonds of Orion?
32 Can you bring forth the constellations in
their season
or indicate which way to go to the
Bear * and its cubs?
33 Do you know the ordinances of the heavens?
Can you put into effect their rule on the
earth?[b]

34 "Can you raise up your voice to command the clouds
to envelop you in a deluge of rain?
35 Will flashes of lightning come forth at
your command
and say to you, 'Here we are'?

y Gen 1:16; Pss 19:2-5; 148:2-4.—z Job 38:8; Pss 65:8; 104:6-9.—a Jos 10:11; Isa 28:17; Ezek 13:11.—b Gen 1:16; Ps 148:6; Jer 31:35.

38:12-15 Each day the dawn comes to shake the earth, ridding it of the wicked as one shakes dust from a rug. The human race cannot help but stand in admiration.

38:15 *Light:* the uncertain light of night that favors evildoers (see Job 24:13; Isa 5:20).

38:22-30 Human beings cannot foresee or comprehend this play of natural forces; for the ancients, God seems to make sport of them and utilize them at his whim (Ex 9:18-26; Jos 10:11). As for us, we are better acquainted with the laws of nature, but the spectacle of the universe remains always a symbol of God's great freedom.

38:22-23 For hail as a divine weapon, see Gen 10:11; Ex 9:18-19; Isa 28:17; 30:30.

38:31-32 *Pleiades . . . Orion . . . Bear:* see note on Job 9:9.

36 Who has endowed the heart with wisdom
and given understanding to the mind? [c]
37 Who can number all the rain clouds
and empty the cisterns of the heavens
38 so that the dust solidifies into a thick mass
and the clods of earth cling together?

A2: The Astonishing World of the Animals*

The Lion and the Raven

39 "Can you hunt prey for the lioness
or satisfy the hunger of young lions
40 while they crouch in their dens
or lie in wait in the bushes?
41 Who provides the raven with prey
when its little ones cry out to God
in their need for sustenance? [d]

CHAPTER 39

The Mountain Goat and the Deer

1 "Do you know when the mountain goats give birth?
Have you ever observed deer in labor?
2 Can you accurately number the months that they carry their young
or know the time of their delivery
3 when they crouch down to give birth
and deliver their offspring?
4 Once their fawns grow strong and become independent,
they go forth on their own and do not return.

The Wild Donkey and the Wild Ox

5 "Who has given the wild donkey its freedom?
Who has untied its ropes?
6 I gave it the wastelands as its home
and the salt flats for its dwelling.
7 It scorns the noise of the city;
it is not forced to obey a driver's shouted order.
8 The mountains are the pasture over which it ranges
in search of any green foliage.

9 "Is the wild ox willing to serve you?
Will it stay by your manger during the night? [e]
10 Can you use ropes to harness its strength?
Will it harrow the furrows after you?
11 Can you depend upon its massive strength
to do your heavy work?
12 Can you rely upon it to return home
and bring your grain to your threshing floor?

The Ostrich and the Horse*

13 "The wings of an ostrich are ineffectual,
since its pinions and its plumage are scanty.
14 It leaves its eggs on the ground
and depends on the earth to warm them,
15 forgetting that a foot may crush them
or that a wild animal may trample upon them.
16 It cruelly disowns its young
as if they were not its own,
unconcerned if its labor has been wasted.
17 For God has denied it wisdom
and deprived it of understanding.
18 Yet with its swiftness of foot
it leaves both horse and rider in the dust.

19 "Do you give the horse its strength?
Have you clothed its neck with a mane?
20 Do you make it leap like a locust,
striking terror with its proud snorting?
21 It paws the plain jubilantly and prances
as it charges the battle line with all its strength.
22 It laughs at fear and is frightened of nothing;
it does not shy away when confronted with the sword.

23 "The quiver rattles at its side;
the spear and the javelin flash.
24 Trembling with eagerness it eats up the ground,
and when the trumpet sounds, there is no holding it back.
25 At each blast of the trumpet it cries 'Aha!'
From afar it scents the battle,
the shouts of the commanders, and the war cries. [f]

c Job 9:4; 32:8; Jas 1:5.—d Ps 147:9; Mt 6:26; Lk 12:24.—e Num 23:22.—f Jos 6:5; Ezek 36:2.

38:39—39:30 The animal world, too, is a bewildering world for human beings. God brings them before Job as he once did before Adam (Gen 2:19-20); however, his purpose now is to show not the power, but the weakness and ignorance of human beings: the life of the animals has secrets that elude the human grasp and depend on a higher wisdom.

39:13-25 The ostrich seems to be bizarre, lacking foresight, and hard on its little ones (Lam 4:3), but it has incomparable speed. Inexplicable is the bravery of the war horse, described here by a connoisseur and an artist.

The Hawk and the Eagle

26 "Did your wisdom enable the hawk to soar
as it spreads its wings toward the south?
27 Does the eagle soar aloft at your command
to build its nest on the lofty heights?
28 It dwells on the cliff in security,
spending its nights on a rocky crag.
29 From there it watches for its prey;
its eyes are able to behold it from afar.
30 Its young ones hungrily drink the blood;
wherever the slain are, it is there." [g]

CHAPTER 40

B: Job's Response to the LORD*

1 The LORD then said to Job:

2 "Will the one who finds fault with the Almighty respond?
Anyone who argues with God should state his case."

3 Job then answered the LORD and said:

4 "Since I am of little importance, how can I reply to you?
I will simply place my hand over my mouth.
5 Although I have spoken once, I will not answer;
I have spoken twice, but I will do so no more."

C: The LORD's Second Speech*

Unleash the Fury of Your Wrath.* 6 Then the
LORD addressed Job out of the whirlwind:

7 "Gird up your loins like a man.
I intend to put questions to you,
and you must give me your answers. [h]
8 Will you continue to deny that I am just?
Will you condemn me in order to justify yourself?
9 Do you have an arm like that of God?
Can your voice thunder as loudly as his?
10 "Display your majesty and grandeur;
array yourself with glory and splendor.
11 Unleash the fury of your wrath
and humble the haughty with a glance.
12 Look on all who are proud and shatter them;
strike down the wicked where they stand.
13 Bury all of them in the earth * together,
and shroud their faces in an unknown grave.
14 Then I in turn will acknowledge to you
that your own right hand is strong enough to save you. [i]

Behemoth . . . the First of God's Works*

15 "Look at Behemoth whom I made just as I made you;
it feeds on grass like an ox.
16 Yet what strength it has in its loins
and what power in the muscles of its body.
17 Its tail is as stiff as a cedar;
the sinews of its thighs are tightly knit.
18 Its bones are like tubes of bronze,
its limbs like rods of iron.

19 "It is the first of God's works;
only its Maker can control it with the sword.
20 The mountains provide it with food,
as do the wild animals that roam the hills.
21 It rests under the lotus trees
as it lies hidden among the reeds in the marsh.

22 "The lotus trees afford it shade,
and it is sheltered by the willows of the stream.
23 Even if the river becomes turbulent,
it does not become frightened;
it remains tranquil
even if the waters rise up to its mouth.
24 Who can blind its eyes and capture it
or pierce its nose with a trap?

Leviathan . . . the King of the Haughty*

25 "Can you catch Leviathan with a fishhook
or tie a rope around its tongue?

g Mt 24:28; Lk 17:37.—h Job 38:3.—i Ex 15:6, 12; Pss 20:7; 44:4; 60:7; 108:7; Isa 40:29; 41:10.

40:1-5 Human beings can argue forever, but when God speaks, a profound reverence seizes the believer. When forced to answer, Job retracts what he has said and ends his rebellion.

40:6—41:26 The author of this discourse knows how to use irony. Here God brings before Job two beasts of the Nile, both of them fearsome to humans but totally under God's control.

40:6-14 Despite appearances, God administers justice—something that Job cannot do. The implication is clear: Job should leave it to God's strong arm (see v. 9) to administer justice, which is also true for his own vindication (see v. 14).

40:13 *Earth:* literally, "dust," i.e., the netherworld, dark dwelling place of the dead.

40:15-24 *Behemoth:* i.e., the beast par excellence; here it refers to the hippopotamus who is impressive by its power; the other animals acknowledge its royalty.

40:25—41:26 The monster of chaos now becomes *Leviathan* (probably the crocodile), which is even more fearsome than Behemoth.

26 Can you put a rope through its nose
or pierce its jaw with a hook? *
27 Will it plead with you for mercy
and address you with gentle words?
28 Will it strike a bargain with you
that will make it your servant forever?
29 "Will you play with it as you would with a bird?
Will you put it on a leash to amuse your maidens?
30 Will traders bargain for it?
Will merchants divide it up?
31 Can you riddle its hide with harpoons
or its head with fishing spears?
32 If you ever should plan to lay a hand on it,
first think of the struggle that awaits you,
and then cease all such thoughts.

CHAPTER 41

1 "Any hope you have in this regard would be futile;
just the mere sight of it would convince you to retreat.
2 How ferocious it is when aroused!
No one could ever stand up to confront it. *
3 Who has attacked it and remained unscathed?
There has never been anyone under the heavens.
4 "Nor will I keep silence about its limbs,
or its strength, or its magnificent frame.[j]
5 Who can strip off its outer garment
or pierce the reinforced armor of its breastplate?
6 Who has ever managed to force open the doors of its mouth
and beheld the teeth that leave one in terror?
7 "Rows of shields adorn its back
and are tightly sealed together.
8 One presses so close to the next
that no air can pass between them.
9 Each is so joined, one to another,
that they hold fast and cannot be separated.
10 "When it sneezes, sprays of light* flash forth,
and its eyes are like the rays of the dawn.
11 Fiery torches emerge from its mouth
and sparks come flying out.
12 Smoke issues forth from its nostrils
as from a boiling pot on the fire.
13 Its breath sets coals ablaze,
and flames pour forth from its mouth.
14 "Strength resides in its neck,
causing terror to all who behold it.
15 The folds of its flesh are joined together,
firmly set in place and immovable.
16 Its heart is as hard as stone,
as unyielding as the lower millstone.
17 When it rears up, strong men become terrified,
and the waves of the sea retreat.
18 "Even though the sword reaches it,
there is no penetration,
nor is there with the spear, the dart, or the javelin.
19 It regards iron as straw
and bronze as rotting wood.
20 No arrow can force it to flee;
slingstones it regards as nothing but chaff.
21 To it a club is like a splinter,
and it laughs at the javelins that are hurled at it.
22 "Its lower parts are protected with jagged potsherds,
and it moves across the mire like a threshing sledge.
23 It causes the depths to boil like a cauldron;
it churns the sea like a pot of ointment.[k]
24 Behind it there is left a shining trail,
and in its wake the deep appears to be white-haired.
25 It has no equal upon the earth;
it is a creature that is utterly fearless.
26 It looks down upon all, even the highest;
it is king over all wild beasts."

j Job 39:11; 40:18.—k Ezek 32:2.

40:26 *Can you put a rope . . . hook?:* i.e., the treatment inflicted on prisoners at that time (see Ezek 29:4).

41:2 *Confront it:* some translate: "confront me."

41:10 *Light:* a vapor that gleams in the light of the sun. *Its eyes:* in Egyptian hieroglyphics, the irridescent red in the eye of the crocodile symbolizes the dawn.

CHAPTER 42

D: Job's Final Response*

Now I Have Seen You with My Own Eyes. 1 Job then answered the LORD in these words:

2 "I know that you can do all things
and that no plan you conceive can be thwarted. [l]
3 Because of my ignorance
I have spoken of things that I have not understood,
of things too wondrous for me to know. [m]
4 "You had said, 'Listen and let me speak.
I intend to put questions to you,
and you must give me your answers.'
5 I had heard of you only by hearsay,
but now that I have seen you with my own eyes,
6 I retract what I have said,
repenting in dust and ashes."

VII: EPILOGUE

JOB'S HONOR AND GOODS ARE RESTORED*

You Have Not Spoken About Me As You Should Have Done.* 7 After the LORD had finished speaking to Job, he said to Eliphaz the Temanite: "My anger is aroused against you and your two friends, for you have not spoken about me as you should, as my servant Job has. 8 Therefore, now take seven bulls and seven rams, and go to my servant Job, and offer up for yourselves a burnt offering. Then my servant Job will pray for you, and I will accept his prayer not to punish you severely, for you have not spoken about me as you should, as my servant Job has."

9 Therefore, Eliphaz the Temanite and Bildad the Shuhite and Zophar the Naamathite went forth and did what the LORD had commanded them. And the LORD accepted the intercession of Job.

God Restores the Prosperity of Job.*
10 Thereupon the LORD restored the prosperity of Job after he had prayed for his friends, and he enriched him with twice as much as he had possessed before. [n] 11 Then all his brothers and sisters came to him, as well as all his friends from former days. As they feasted with him in his house, they sympathized with him about his previous troubles, and they comforted him for all the misfortunes that the LORD had permitted to be inflicted upon him. Moreover, each of them gave him some money and a gold ring.

12 The LORD blessed the end of Job's life more than the beginning. He had fourteen thousand sheep, six thousand camels, a thousand yoke of oxen, and a thousand donkeys. [o] 13 He also fathered seven sons and three daughters. 14 He named the eldest daughter Jemimah, * the second Keziah, and the third Keren-happuch. 15 In the entire land there were no women as beautiful as Job's daughters, and their father gave them an inheritance along with their brothers. *

16 After this, Job lived for another one hundred and forty years, and he saw his children and his children's children to the fourth generation. 17 Then Job died at a very great age.

l Gen 18:14; Mt 19:26; Acts 4:28.—m Job 5:9; 38:2; Ps 139:6.—n Deut 30:3; Pss 85:2-4; 126:2-4; Jas 5:11.—o Job 1:3; 8:7; 42:10; Ezek 36:11.

42:1-6 Suffering is still mysterious, but Job humbles himself before God. He was wrong, posing as a judge in the name of too human an idea of God. He has now encountered God, i.e., he has had a new experience of God, a new perception of his mystery, and it has transformed him interiorly. Job can entrust himself with confidence to this God of infinite grandeur and unlimited power.

42:7-17 With Job's reply (vv. 1-6), the drama has come to an end, but the author does not want to leave his readers in ignorance of what became of the principal players. Here is the Lord's definitive judgment: the friends of Job are blameworthy, and Job, God's impatient but faithful servant, has the greatest blessings heaped upon him.

42:7-9 God conducts the trial of the three friends. Job's prayer will obtain pardon for them.

42:10-17 Job shows his greatness through his goodness, for he intercedes for those who have treated him harshly. Job recovers double what he previously had of honors, riches, posterity, length of life, and heaped-up possessions: all the rewards of the righteous, all the prosperity of the Patriarchs.

42:14 *Jemimah:* i.e., "dove." *Keziah:* i.e., "cassia" or "cinnamon." *Keren-happuch:* i.e., "eye cosmetic."

42:15 Normally, daughters received an inheritance only when there were no sons (see Num 27:1-11).

"You love righteousness and hate wickedness; therefore God, your God, has established you above your fellow kings by anointing you with the oil of gladness" *(Ps 45:8).*

THE BOOK OF PSALMS

An Incomparable Prayer Book

A Liturgical Anthology

*Many prayers and liturgical chants are scattered throughout the Bible, but the most substantial part of Israel's praise and petition is to be found in the one hundred and fifty poetical compositions called "Psalms" after their Greek name, with "Psalter" designating the entire collection (*psaltêrion, *the stringed instrument that accompanied the singing of the psalms). In Hebrew, on the other hand, the hymns, which form the most considerable part, have given the entire collection the name* Sefer Tehillim *(Book of Praises). The Psalter, in more or less its present form, was already available to the liturgical authorities in Jerusalem during the period of the second temple (third century B.C.).*

By analogy with the five Books of the Pentateuch (the Torah), the Psalter was divided, quite arbitrarily, into five books; this division seems to go back to the third century B.C. On the other hand, three main sections can be distinguished according to the name used for God ("the LORD," Yahweh, *in the first and third sections; "God,"* Elohim, *in the second); the three sections are Psalms 1–41, 42–89, and 90–150.*

There are also psalms that are part of less important pre-existing collections belonging to groups of cantors, such as those of Asaph (73–83) or Korah (42–50; 84–88), who had been charged with organizing the liturgical functions. In addition, the Psalter includes other distinguishable collections: the Pilgrim Psalms (120–134), Songs of the Kingdom (93–100), the Canticles of Zion and the Alleluia Hymns (113–119, 135–136, and 146–150).

More than one psalm already had a history and life of its own before being given its definitive text and definitive place in the Psalter as we now have it. In fact, some very ancient psalms were used and reread from century to century, adapted to new circumstances, and often revised (e.g., Pss 2; 110).

At the beginning of each psalm the Hebrew text provides some introductory notes that are still rather mysterious to us. These are the "superscriptions" or "titles." They indicate the presumed author of the psalm, the historical circumstances that supposedly inspired it, some instructions on the musical instruments to be used, and so on. Some critics think that these superscriptions are ancient, perhaps composed before the Exile; others think that they are much later additions, inserted when the collection had already been completed. In any case, rather than giving the objective meaning of the psalm, the superscription shows how it was understood and sung at a time far removed from its origin.

Many superscriptions attribute a given psalm to David (all those of the first Book, except for 32; and others). There is no doubt that the royal musician and poet who danced before the Ark and organized Israel's worship gave a decisive impulse to the liturgy and sacred songs, and that some of his compositions have been preserved (see 2 Sam 1:19-27; 23:1-7). Moreover, as head of Israel, David represented the entire people. Once the monarchy disappeared, he became, after the Exile, the model for believers and the type of the future Messiah, of the Jesus who would speak in the name of all the people and even of all humankind. For this reason, even if David did not himself compose any of the hundred and fifty psalms, at least in their present form (as some believe), the memory of him certainly inspired the cantors, who put his name over their own liturgical compositions.

Various Attitudes toward God

It is difficult to discern any particular order in the present sequence of the Psalter. Prayers of entreaty stand side by side with the most enthusiastic thanksgivings, just as in real life. The most that can be stated is that the burden of misfortune weighs more heavily in the first half of the Book, while praise becomes more sustained toward the end of it. In the commentary that follows, we try unobtrusively to suggest this rhythm.

Each psalm will therefore be viewed in itself without trying to establish any relationship of continuity. This does not mean that the Psalms cannot be grouped into some typical categories, depending on the ideas and emotions they express, on the liturgical needs they meet, and even on their rhythm and structure. Identification of the category to which a psalm belongs can contribute greatly to understanding it.*

The Hebrew name for the Psalter is "Book of Praises," and in fact there are many hymns of praise. The Alleluia psalms for the most part belong to this category. Another homogeneous group of psalms acclaims the Lord as King of the people and of the universe; these are the psalms of the kingdom, the Messianic hymns (47; 93; 96; 97; 98; 99; 145). Still another group voices the love of the people for Jerusalem, the mountain on which God dwells and on which the dynasty of its Messianic King is perpetuated; we call these the Canticles of Zion (24; 46; 48; 78; 84; 87; 122).

The songs of thanksgiving expressed wonder and gratitude. Petitions, complaints, and prayers of repentance and sorrow are perhaps the most frequent subjects of the Psalms. Some songs by unhappy singers became psalms of trust and gratitude (e.g., 13; 16; 22; 23; 31; 32; etc.).

The sapiential psalms are somewhat didactic in tone. The wise men in question endeavor to penetrate the riddle of life and unveil its meaning.

Finally, there are the royal psalms: songs and prayers that focus on the king and were perhaps used, at least initially, for the festival of consecration or the anniversary of enthronement. Like the psalms of the kingdom, in the course of time these were reread in a Messianic perspective. We should also note that some psalms turn the history of Israel into a prophecy in which the lessons of the past are solemnly proclaimed on the occasion of some great feast (78; 105; 106).

---

* The dating of the psalms given herein is approximative. Most scholars agree that dating them is very difficult and open to a great deal of discussion.

The External Form

Some psalms are acrostic or alphabetical; that is, their verses (or strophes) start with a word that begins with one of the twenty-two letters of the Hebrew alphabet (in alphabetical order). This device, like others common in poetry (rhyme, strophes, etc.), has for its purpose to heighten merit, but it can result in embarrassment from the viewpoint of artistic inspiration and literary perfection.

Hope Stimulated by Remembrance of the Past

The history of the Psalms is ongoing. It is true, of course, that the Psalter reflects the spiritual adventure of the ancient People of God, with its lights and shadows. But the Jewish tradition began at a quite early date to regard this Book as the herald of a unique religious experience that looked to the Messiah as witness and privileged beneficiary of the divine work of salvation. Thus the entire Psalter, which is a synthesis of the Old Testament in the form of poetry and prayer, becomes a Messianic prayer. The Christian tradition has therefore legitimately regarded it as also a prophecy and prefiguration of Jesus, who suffers before entering into his glory (Ps 22:19 and Jn 19:24; Ps 2:1-2 and Acts 4:25-27; etc.).

Because they had been used by Jesus and were fervently recited with new understanding by the first Christian community, which had emerged from Judaism, the Psalms automatically became the prayer of the Church, as they had been that of Israel; from that time on, they have been continually prayed by the Church. The new and spiritual Jerusalem sees partially realized in itself the glory of Zion, which the chosen people saw as still in the future.

There is no feast or celebration or reading of the word of God for which the Liturgy cannot find appropriate expressions or at least allusions in the Psalms. In praying the Psalms, the children of the Church express through these imperfect but irreplaceable songs from another age, the human and supernatural experience of sorrow and joy that they, the new People of God, also have as they travel toward the radiant goal of the history of the Church and humanity: "Zion, perfect in beauty," where "God shines forth" (Ps 50:2; Rev 21:2).

Calls for Vengeance?

At the same time, however, many of these songs are filled with curses and calls for vengeance, sometimes expressing a cruelty that is truly disconcerting (5:11; 31:18; 54:7; 83:14; 109:6f; 139:19f). We are dismayed to read: "Happy will he be who seizes your babies and smashes them against a rock!" (137:9). But we ought not be astonished by such language. The Psalms date from a time when the Gospel was not yet known; when placed on the lips of those being persecuted, they voice an urgent appeal for divine justice. (See notes on Ps 5:11; Ps 35.)

On the other hand, these vengeance psalms have a deeper meaning: at one time, they struck out against the enemies of the chosen people, the "heathen," that is, the enemies of God; today they give voice to a different hatred, that which Christians ought to have for the evil that Jesus intended to destroy by his death and against which Paul the apostle exhorts us to fight (Eph 6:11-13).

The Book of Psalms may be divided as follows:

Prologue: (1–2)
Book I: (3–41)
Book II: (42–72)
Book III: (73–89)
Book IV: (90–106)
Book V: (107–150)

PROLOGUE—PSALMS 1–2*

PSALM 1*

True Happiness

1 Blessed *is the man
who does not walk in the counsel of the wicked,
nor stand in the way of sinners,
nor sit in the company of scoffers. [a]
2 Rather, his delight is in the law of the LORD, *
and on that law he meditates day and night. [b]
3 He is like a tree planted near streams of water, [c]
which bears fruit in its season,
and whose leaves never wither. *
In the same way,
everything he does will prosper.
4 This is not true of the wicked,
for they are like chaff that the wind blows away. * [d]
5 Therefore, the wicked will not stand firm at the judgment, *
nor sinners in the assembly of the righteous. [e]
6 For the LORD watches over * the way of the righteous,
but the way of the wicked will perish. [f]

PSALM 2*

Universal Reign of the Messiah

1 Why do the nations rage
and the peoples devise futile plots? [g]

a Pss 10:2-11; 26:4-5, 9; 40:5; 51:15; 89:16; 128:4; Gen 49:6; Deut 33:29; Job 21:16; Prov 1:22; 4:18-19; Isa 28:14; Jer 15:17; Hos 7:5; Mt 7:13-14.—b Pss 112:1; 119:16, 35; Jos 1:8; Sir 39:1; Ezek 11:20; Rom 7:22.—c Pss 52:10; 92:13-15; Jer 17:8; Ezek 47:12.—d Pss 35:5; 83:14-16; Job 21:18; Isa 40:24; Jer 13:24.—e Pss 5:5; 35:18; 82:1; 111:1.—f Pss 37:18; 112:10; 121:5; Nah 1:7.—g Ps 21:12; Prov 24:2; Acts 4:25-28; Rev 11:18.

Pss 1—2 These first two psalms are regarded as a preface to the entire Psalter. Collections of psalms that were originally different were gradually regrouped to comprise the Psalter as we have it; the psalms attributed to David (3–41 and 51–72), the songs of Ascents (120–134), and the chants of the Hallel (105–107, 111–118, 135–150) constitute the most remarkable of these primary collections. But as presently arranged in our Bible, the Book of Psalms is divided like the Pentateuch (the first five Books of the Bible that are called the Law) into five unequal parts, each of which ends with a formula of acclamation.

Ps 1 At the entrance to the collection of the Psalms, we are immediately placed before a life-choice: God or nothingness. This option imposes itself on us throughout all the pages of the Bible. In the historical accounts, law codes, prophecies, prayers, and meditative texts, a line of division is set forth. It distinguishes between righteousness and impiety, self-reliance and faith, good and evil, wickedness and love. The words are varied and the experiences are numerous in order to bear witness to this rupture.

They mark a division between peoples, between individuals, and between the acts and projects of our lives. Appearances may produce change and daily contradict the faithful's overly naive dreams about prosperity; however, one fact remains: a life of righteousness and truth is a path of happiness, a path to God, whereas those who deaden their conscience for their own ends have no other future but ruin.

Every time a reader prays a psalm, he or she is forced to choose between the "two ways" (see Deut 30:15; Prov 4:18f; Jer 21:8), the difference between which is underscored by Jesus (see Mt 7:13; 25). The righteous are blessed for they are separated from sin, Bible-centered, and prosperous. Unlike them are the wicked who are doomed to judgment.

1:1 The Psalter begins by declaring the blessedness of the righteous (v. 1) and concludes by summoning all creation to praise God in heaven and on earth (Ps 150). Human beings are made for happiness, and the revealed moral law is oriented toward that happiness. *Blessed:* the happy state of life in fellowship with God, revering him and obeying his laws (see Pss 94:12; 112:1; 119:1f; 128:1; Prov 29:18). *Scoffers:* those who reject God and his law (see Prov 1:10-19).

1:2 *The law of the LORD:* either the first five Books of the Bible, known as the Torah (law), or divine instruction. *Meditates:* literally, "murmurs," i.e., assimilates the law of life that incarnates the presence of God and teaches the believer how to attain joyous intimacy with the Lord. Indeed, the law is a judgment of God and a happiness for human beings.

1:3 *Like a tree . . . never wither:* the righteous are able to withstand the rigors of life. Like a tree planted on fertile ground, they are able to enhance their spiritual life.

1:4 *Like chaff . . . blows away:* the wicked are completely powerless spiritually, for they are like chaff that is easily borne away, even by the slightest breeze.

1:5 At the judgment—either God's judgment of the wicked during life (see Pss 76:7f; 130:3; Ezr 9:15) or his judgment of them at the end of time (see Mal 3:2; Mt 25:31-46; Rev 6:17)—the wicked will bear the brunt of their misdeeds. *Righteous:* a name for the faithful People of God, i.e., those who reverence God and diligently strive to carry out his laws in every phase of their lives.

1:6 *Watches over:* the Lord takes an avid interest in their conduct (see Pss 31:7f; 37:18; Gen 18:19; Am 3:2; Nah 1:7). *The way of the wicked will perish:* a similar fate is set forth for the wicked in Ps 112:10: "the desires of the wicked will be fruitless." The theme of the two ways has already been found in Deut 30:15f and Jer 21:8; it will be taken up again in Prov 4:18f and Mt 7:13.

Ps 2 Although the surrounding peoples are rising up, the People of God are enthroning a new king; empowered by God's assistance, he shatters the coalition of their foes. This is the drama evoked in the present psalm, and it recurs more than once in the history of Israel. Thus, this poem found its place in a liturgy for royal consecration, for each king was a "messiah," that is, a man anointed with the sacred unction in the name of God. But the Prophets and the New Testament enlarged these perspectives. Hence, this ancient text evokes the whole drama of the world. It proclaims the sovereignty of God in the midst of the tumult of peoples and our human rebellions.

Behind the king of verse 6 can be glimpsed the Messiah (the Christ), a descendant of David and the Son of God, who will save his people (see Isa 9:5-6; Acts 4:25; 13:33; Heb 1:5). There is a premonition of the struggle that will take place at the end of time (see Ezek 38–39; Dan 12), a struggle already begun in the Passion of Jesus and in the persecutions of the Church (see Acts 4:25-28). But the psalm also expresses the hope of a final conversion of all the nations as they at last acknowledge the Lord (see Isa 45; Rev 19:15). God's plan will be achieved in the glory of the Messianic Kingdom.

2 The kings of the earth rise up,
and the princes conspire together
against the LORD
and against his Anointed One: * [h]
3 "Let us finally break their shackles
and cast away their chains from us." [i]
4 The one who is enthroned in heaven laughs;
the LORD mocks their plans. [j]
5 Then he rebukes them in his anger
and terrifies them in his wrath, saying, [k]
6 "I myself have anointed my king [l]
on Zion, my holy mountain." *
7 I will proclaim the decree * of the LORD:
He said to me, "You are my son;
this day I have begotten you." [m]
8 Simply make the request of me,
and I will give you the nations as your inheritance, [n]
and the ends of the earth as your possession. *
9 You will rule them with an iron scepter;
you will shatter them like a potter's vessel. * [o]
10 Therefore, O kings, pay heed;
take warning, O rulers of the earth. [p]
11 Serve the LORD with fear, and rejoice before him;
with trembling 12 bow down in homage * [q]
lest he become angry
and you perish from the way,
for his wrath can flare up in an instant.
Blessed are all those
who take refuge in him. [r]

BOOK I—PSALMS 3–41*

PSALM 3*

Trust in God in Time of Danger

1 A psalm of David. When he was fleeing from his son Absalom. [s]

2 O LORD, how great is the number of my enemies,
how many are those who rise up against me.
3 How numerous are the ones who say of me,
"He will not receive salvation from God." [t] *Selah**
4 But you, O LORD, are a shield to protect me;
you are my glory and the one who raises my head high. * [u]
5 Whenever I cry aloud to the LORD,
he answers me from his holy mountain. * [v] *Selah*
6 I lie down and sleep; [w]
I awaken again, for the LORD sustains me. *

h Pss 48:5; 83:6; Acts 4:25-26; Rev 19:19.—i Ps 149:8; 2 Sam 3:34; Job 36:8.—j Pss 37:13; 59:9; Prov 1:26; Wis 4:18; Isa 37:16; 40:15-17; 66:1.—k Pss 6:2; 21:10; 27:9; 38:1; 79:6; 90:7; 110:5.—l Pss 10:16; 24:10; 110:2.—m Pss 89:27f; 110:2-3; Isa 49:1; Lk 3:22; Heb 1:5; 6:5.—n Ps 22:28; Mt 21:38; Rev 2:26.—o Ps 110:5-6; Job 34:24; Jer 19:10; Rev 2:27; 12:5; 19:15.—p Ps 141:6; Prov 27:11; Wis 6:1.—q Pss 9:3; 34:10; 103:11.—r Pss 84:12; 146:5; Prov 16:20; Rev 6:16.—s 2 Sam 15:13ff.—t Pss 22:8; 71:11; Isa 36:15; 37:20.—u Pss 7:11; 18:3; 62:7-8; Gen 15:1; Deut 33:29; Isa 60:19.—v Ps 2:6.—w Pss 4:9; 17:15; Lev 26:6; Prov 3:24.

2:2 *Anointed One:* in Hebrew, *Mashiah* (whence the word "Messiah"), which in the Greek translation is *Christos;* it referred originally to the Davidic King but ultimately to Jesus Christ. This phrase has given rise to two titles of Jesus: "Messiah" from the Hebrew and "Christ" from the Greek. In Israel the power of office was bestowed by anointing both on kings (see Jdg 9:8; 1 Sam 9:16; 16:12f) and on high priests (see Lev 8:12; Num 3:3).

2:6 *Holy mountain:* reference to the site of the temple (see 2 Chr 3:4; 15:1; 33:15). Psalms 43:3; 46:5 have "holy mountain" and "holy place" respectively. Psalm 48:2 has "holy mountain" and Psalm 87:1 has "holy mountains."

2:7 *Decree:* this is nothing less than the prophecy of Nathan (see 2 Sam 7:14) applied to the Messiah by 1 Chr 17:13 (see Ps 89:27). Here the Messiah speaks after the rebels (v. 3) and after God who in an oracle (v. 6) has just enthroned him as King of Israel. He has also declared him his Son according to a formula familiar to the ancient Orient.

2:8 The Messiah's reign will be coextensive with that of God (see Isa 49:6; Dan 7:14). This verse is applied by Heb 1:5 (see Heb 5:5), then by tradition and the Liturgy, to the eternal generation of the Word.

2:9 The Book of Revelation applies this verse to Christ's triumphant reign (see Rev 12:5; 19:15).

2:12 *Bow down in homage:* another possible translation is: "honor the Son." *Blessed:* see note on Ps 1:1.

Pss 3–41 At the beginning of the Book we find a collection of psalms attributed to David. His life, replete with difficulties and brimming with confidence, was presented as an example: it inspired poems that David did not himself compose. One theme dominates the diversity of psalms that make up this first part: the innocent find themselves in the grip of the wicked. Hope is ceaselessly renewed as is torment: "My God, my God, why have you forsaken me?" (Ps 22:1). It is the trial of darkness; still one certitude remains: "You will fill me with joy in your presence" (Ps 16:11). Is not this the dialogue that takes place in the life of believers?

Ps 3 In time of great danger and anguish, the psalmist finds refuge in God as his shield (protector) and the one who fills him with courage. God answers his prayer and bestows peace and deliverance.

3:3 *Selah:* a word whose meaning is uncertain; possibly a musical term.

3:4 God will preserve the psalmist from dishonor and humiliation by means of his grace (see Pss 18:3; 27:5; 62:8; 110:5; Deut 33:29; Sir 11:12f).

3:5 *Holy Mountain:* see note on Ps 2:6.

3:6 This passage (see Prov 3:24) is applied by the Fathers of the Church to the dead and risen Christ.

7 Thus, I will not fear the multitudes
who have surrounded me on every side.[x]
8 Rise up, O LORD!
Rescue me, O my God!
You will strike all my enemies across the face *
and break the teeth of the wicked.[y]
9 Salvation comes from the LORD.
May your blessing be upon your people.[z] *Selah*

PSALM 4*

Joyful Confidence in God

1 For the director.* With stringed instruments. A psalm of David.
2 When I call upon you, answer me, O God,
you who uphold my rights.
When I was in distress, you set me free;
have pity on me and listen to my prayer.[a]
3 How long * will you people turn my glory into shame,
cherishing what is worthless and pursuing what is false?[b] *Selah*
4 Remember that the LORD wonderfully favors those who are faithful,*
and the LORD listens when I call out to him.[c]
5 * When you are angry, be careful not to sin;
reflect in silence
as you lie upon your beds.[d] *Selah*
6 Offer worthy sacrifices
and place your trust in the LORD.[e]
7 Many exclaim, "Who will show us better times!
Let the light of your face shine on * us, O LORD!"[f]
8 You have granted my heart * greater joy
than others experience when grain and wine abound.[g]
9 In peace I lie down and sleep,
for only with your help, O LORD,
can I rest secure.[h]

PSALM 5*

Morning Prayer for Divine Help

1 For the director.* With flutes. A psalm of David.
2 Listen to my words, O LORD;
pay heed to my sighs.[i]
3 Hear my cry for help,
my King and my God;
for to you I pray.[j]
4 O LORD, at daybreak * you hear my voice;
at daybreak I bring my petition before you
and await your reply.[k]

x Pss 23:4; 118:11; Job 11:15.—y Pss 6:5; 7:2; 58:7; Isa 25:9; Jer 42:11.—z Pss 27:1; 28:9; Isa 43:3; Jon 2:9; Rev 7:10.—a Pss 13:4; 27:7; 30:11; 118:5.—b Ps 62:4; Ex 16:7; 2 Ki 19:26; Jer 13:25.—c Ps 12:2; 1 Tim 4:7; 2 Pet 3:11.—d Ps 63:7; Dan 2:28; Eph 4:26.—e Pss 31:7; 51:21; Isa 26:4; Jn 14:1.—f Pss 31:17; 44:4; 67:2; 80:4; Num 6:25; Job 13:24; Dan 9:17.—g Isa 9:3; Acts 14:17.—h Ps 3:6; Lev 26:6.—i Pss 17:1; 40:2; 86:6; 130:1-2; Isa 35:10.—j Pss 44:5; 84:4.—k Wis 16:28; Isa 28:19; Ezek 46:13; Rom 8:19.

3:8 God treats the wicked like ferocious beasts whose jaws are shattered (see Pss 22:14f; 35:16; 58:7; Job 29:17; Ezek 22:25). The initial appeal reminds one of Jer 2:27. See notes on Pss 5:10; 35.

Ps 4 Those who are well established in life delude themselves by seeking happiness in riches and worldly vanities. The psalmist, rich in divine trust and joy, invites them to discover the price of God's friendship: "the light of [God's] face." This is an evening prayer (see vv. 5, 9), filled with desire for God; Christians move beyond its earthly perspectives. Prayer brings openness of heart, assurance of God's help, faith, divine approval, joy, and peace.

4:1 *For the director:* these words are thought to be a musical or liturgical notation.

4:3 *How long . . . ?:* see note on Ps 6:4.

4:4 *Those who are faithful:* one of several words (sometimes translated as "saints") for the People of God, who should be faithful to him (see Pss 12:2; 31:24; 32:6; 34:10). See also notes on Pss 16:3; 34:10.

4:5-6 One must fear to offend God but rather pray to him in the calm and silence of adoration. *When you are angry be careful not to sin:* these words are cited by Paul in Eph 4:26 with the sense that if anger takes hold of you, let it not lead you to act evilly—for there is such a thing as righteous anger (see Mk 3:5). *Beds:* can refer to the spot where one prostrated oneself to pray (see Ps 95:6; Sir 50:17), which is also suggested by the presence of the term *Selah*, or pause.

4:7 *Face shine on:* this image of benevolence and contentment (see Num 6:25; Prov 16:15; Dan 9:17) occurs frequently in the Psalter (see Pss 31:17; 67:2; 119:135; and especially note on Ps 13:2). The reading in the Septuagint and Vulgate is: "The light of your countenance, O LORD, is signed [or: imprinted] on us." It was interpreted as referring to the soul created in the image of God and regenerated by the baptismal character that makes a Christian a child of light (see Lk 16:8; Jn 12:36; 1 Thes 5:5; Eph 5:8).

4:8 *Heart:* the biblical center of the human spirit, which harbors a person's thoughts and emotions and gives rise to action.

Ps 5 This is a morning prayer (see v. 4) in which the psalmist prays for the Lord to hear his prayer and grant a sense of God's goodness and justice, bestow guidance, punish enemies, and bless the righteous. Broken by tribulation, the persecuted man appeals for the justice of God against his own enemies. Christians must spiritualize the call for vengeance, hating evil rather than those who do evil. To love God is to choose the cause of justice and bear the witness of a purified joy.

5:1 *For the director:* these words are thought to be a musical or liturgical notation.

5:4 *At daybreak:* the morning is the privileged moment for divine favors (see Pss 17:14f; 30:6; 46:6; 59:17). *I bring my petition:* other possible translations are: "I offer my vows" and "I prepare my offering."

5 For you are not a God who delights in
wickedness;
evil cannot remain in your presence. [l]
6 The arrogant shrink before your gaze;
you hate all who do evil. [m]
7 You destroy all who tell lies;
the LORD detests the violent and the
deceitful. [n]

8 But I will enter your house
because of your great kindness, *
and I will bow down in your holy
temple,
filled with awe of you. [o]
9 Lead me in your ways of righteousness,
O LORD,
for I am surrounded by enemies;
make your path straight before me. * [p]
10 For there is nothing trustworthy in their
mouth; * [q]
their heart devises treacherous
schemes.
Their throat is a wide open grave;
with their tongue they utter flattery.
11 Punish them, O God;
may their intrigues result in their
downfall. [r]
Cast them out because of their many
transgressions,
for they have rebelled against you. *
12 But may all who take refuge in you re-
joice;
may they shout for joy forever. [s]
Grant them your protection
so that those who love your name *
may rejoice in you.
13 Truly, you bless the righteous, O LORD;
you surround them with your goodwill
as with a shield. [t]

PSALM 6*

Evening Prayer for God's Mercy

1 For the director. * With stringed instru-
ments. "Upon the eighth." A psalm of David.
2 O LORD, do not rebuke me in your anger
or punish me in your wrath. [u]
3 Have mercy on me, O LORD, for I am tot-
tering;
help me, O LORD, for my body is in
agony. * [v]
4 My soul * is also filled with anguish.
But you, O LORD—how long? [w]
5 Turn, O LORD, and deliver my soul;
save me because of your kindness. *
6 For among the dead who remembers
you? [x]
In the netherworld who sings your
praises? *

---

l Ps 1:5; Prov 2:22.—m Ps 73:3; 2 Ki 19:32; Prov 8:13.—n Ps 101:7; Prov 6:17-19; Wis 14:9; Hab 1:13; Acts 5:3; Rev 21:8.—o Ps 138:2; 1 Ki 8:44; Dan 6:10; Jon 2:4.—p Ps 23:3; Prov 4:11; Isa 26:7; Jn 1:23.—q Ps 12:3; Prov 15:4; Jer 5:16; Rom 3:13.—r Pss 78:40; 141:10; Lam 1:5.—s Pss 33:1; 64:11; Rev 7:15-16.—t Pss 32:7; 35:2; 103:4; 112:3.—u Ps 38:2; Jer 10:24.—v Ps 61:3; Jer 17:14-15.—w Pss 13:2-3; 74:10; 79:5; 89:47.—x Pss 30:10; 88:11-13; 115:17; Eccl 9:10; Isa 38:18.

5:8 *Kindness:* Hebrew, *hesed;* this word denotes the sentiments that flow from a natural community, family, clan, or society (benevolence, favor). It is also the love of the covenant between the Lord and the community of Israel, regarded as his spouse and child. Finally, it includes the sentiments that are found in each of its members (grace and love on the part of the Lord, and piety on the part of the faithful). See also note on Ps 6:5.

5:9 *Make your path straight before me:* the Greek reads: "Make straight my way before you."

5:10 With *mouth, heart, throat,* and *tongue* they spread harm around. *Their throat is a wide open grave:* their words bring death to their hearers (see Jer 5:16)—a theme cited in Rom 3:13. *Heart:* see note on Ps 4:8.

5:11 This verse reminds us that the so-called imprecatory (or cursing) psalms (see note on Ps 35) have been a problem for Christians from the beginning of the use of the Psalter. Christ instructed Christians to pray for enemies (see Mt 5:44) and gave an example of this on the cross (see Lk 23:34). Yet the psalmists at times call for punishment (even of the most drastic kind) on enemies. Christians may look upon these statements as appeals for strict redress of evil in accord with the divine justice or direct them toward the enemies of their souls, the devil and his minions who are implacable foes of God.

5:12 *Your name:* a name usually designates the person, hence the Lord himself. See also note on Ps 8:2, 10.

Ps 6 This is the first of the so-called Penitential Psalms (6; 32; 38; 51; 102; 130; 143), a designation for psalms suitable for expressing repentance that goes back to the sixth century A.D. In affliction, the psalmist invokes the divine mercy, begs to be saved from death, confesses his wretchedness, and expresses faith in his own deliverance and his enemies' total abasement.

6:1 *For the director:* these words are thought to be a musical or liturgical notation. *Upon the eighth:* probably a musical term referring to an eight-stringed instrument.

6:3 *Body is in agony:* literally, "bones are shaken."

6:4 *Soul:* the Hebrew word, *nephesh,* usually means a person's life-giving breath, which disappears at death. It is thus applied to a person's very self as a living, conscious being ("my soul" equals "myself"). *How long?:* elliptical formula used in psalms of lamentation both in Babylonia and in Israel (see Pss 74:10; 80:5; 90:13; 94:3) to express anxiety over the divine aid that is late in coming.

6:5 *Kindness:* Hebrew, *hesed,* which may also be translated as "mercy" and refers to all that God promised to give to his people (see Deut 7:9, 12) through the Davidic dynasty (see Ps 89:25, 29, 34; 2 Sam 7:15; Isa 55:3). See also note on Ps 5:8.

6:6 The psalmist offers a motive for God to save him from death: it is the living who praise him. The netherworld was viewed as the place where the souls of the dead had a kind of shadowy existence, with no activity or lofty emotion. Just what that existence entailed at any given Old Testament period is difficult to gauge until the second century B.C. It is then that the sacred Books begin to speak more clearly about life after death (see Wis 3; Dan 12:1-3).

7 I am exhausted from my sighing;
every night I flood my bed with my tears,
and I soak my couch with my weeping.
8 My eyes grow dim because of my grief;
they are worn out * because of all my foes.[y]
9 Depart from me, all you evildoers, *
for the LORD has heard the sound of my weeping.[z]
10 The LORD has listened to my pleas;
the LORD has accepted my prayer.
11 All my enemies will be shamed and terrified;
they will flee in utter confusion. *[a]

PSALM 7*

Appeal to the Divine Judge

1 A plaintive song of David, which he sang to the LORD concerning Cush, * a Benjaminite.

2 O LORD, my God, I take refuge in you;
keep me safe from all my pursuers and deliver me,[b]
3 lest like a lion they tear me to pieces
and carry me off, with no one to rescue me.
4 O LORD, my God, if I have done this,
if my hands are stained with guilt,
5 if I have repaid a friend with treachery—
I who spared the lives of those who without cause were my enemies—*
6 then let my foe pursue and overtake me;
let him trample my life into the ground
and leave my honor in the dust.[c]
Selah
7 Rise up, O LORD, in your indignation;
rise against the fury of my enemies.
Rouse yourself for me,
and fulfill the judgment you have decreed.[d]
8 Let the peoples assemble in your presence
as you sit above them enthroned on high.
9 The LORD is the judge of the nations.
Therefore, pass judgment on me, O LORD, according to my righteousness,
according to my innocence, O Most High.
10 Put an end to the malice of the wicked
but continue to sustain the righteous,
O God of justice,
you who search minds and hearts. *[e]
11 God is a shield to me;
he saves those who are upright of heart.[f]
12 God is a just judge,
a God who expresses his indignation every day.
13 When a sinner refuses to repent,
God sharpens his sword,
and he bends and aims his bow.[g]
14 He has prepared deadly weapons for him
and made his arrows into fiery shafts.[h]
15 * Behold, he who conceives iniquity
and is pregnant with mischief
will give birth to lies.[i]
16 He digs a pit and makes it deep,
but he will fall into the trap he has made.[j]
17 His wickedness will recoil upon his own head,
and his violence will fall back on his own crown.

y Pss 31:10; 38:11; 40:13; 69:4; Job 16:78f; Isa 38:14.—z Pss 5:6; 119:115; 139:19; Mt 7:23; Lk 13:27.—a Pss 35:4, 26; 40:15; 71:13; 2 Ki 19:26.—b Pss 2:12; 3:8; 6:5; 11:1; 22:21; 31:2, 16; 119:86, 157, 161.—c Ps 143:3; Isa 10:6.—d Pss 9:5; 138:7.—e Pss 17:3; 26:2; 35:24; 43:1; 139:23; Wis 1:6; Jer 11:20; 17:10; 20:12; Rev 2:23.—f Ps 3:3; Job 33:3.—g Ps 11:2; Ezek 3:19.—h Ps 18:15; Isa 50:11.—i Job 15:35; Isa 59:4; Jas 1:15.—j Pss 9:16; 35:8; 57:7; 94:13; Prov 26:27; Eccl 10:8; Sir 27:26.

6:8 *Eyes grow dim . . . worn out:* a sign of failing strength (see Ps 38:11; 1 Sam 14:27, 29; Jer 14:6) or sorrow in affliction (see Pss 31:10; 88:10; Job 17:7; Lam 2:11) or dashed hopes (see Pss 69:4; 119:82, 123; Deut 28:32; Isa 38:14).

6:9 This apostrophe (taken up in Mt 7:23) has been prepared for by the end of verse 8. The enemies of the sick person, like the friends of Job, see in his trials a heavenly chastisement for hidden faults; they insult him and accuse him unjustly—a theme that is more developed elsewhere (see Pss 31; 35; 38; 69).

6:11 See notes on Pss 5:11; 35.

Ps 7 Falsely accused, the psalmist implores the divine assistance, affirms his innocence, invokes God's just judgment, and expresses limitless confidence in the punishment of his enemy as well as his own salvation, concluding with praise for God's righteousness.

7:1 *Cush* is not otherwise known, but as a Benjaminite he was probably a supporter of Saul. Hence, the psalm is associated with Saul's determined attempts on David's life.

7:5 *I who . . . enemies:* an alternative translation is: "and without cause have despoiled an enemy."

7:10 *Minds and hearts:* literally, "hearts and kidneys." These words were used as virtual synonyms (but "heart" most often) to refer to the innermost center of human life. To "search mind and heart" was a conventional expression for God's examination of a person's hidden character and motives (see Jer 11:20; 17:10; 20:12).

7:15-17 See notes on Pss 5:11; 35.

18 I will offer thanks to the LORD because of his righteousness,
and I will sing hymns of praise* to the name of the LORD Most High. [k]

PSALM 8*

The Majesty of God and the Dignity of Human Beings

1 For the director.* "Upon the *gittith*." A psalm of David.

2 O LORD, our Lord,
how glorious is your name* in all the earth!
You have exalted your majesty above the heavens.
3 Out of the mouths of newborn babes and infants*
you have brought forth praise
as a bulwark against your foes,
to silence the enemy and the avenger. [l]
4 When I look up at your heavens
that have been formed by your fingers,
the moon and the stars
that you set in place,
5 what is man that you are mindful of him, [m]
the son of man* that you care for him? [n]
6 You have made him a little less than the angels*
and crowned him with glory and honor.
7 You have given him dominion over the works of your hands [o]
and placed everything under his feet:
8 all sheep and oxen
as well as the beasts of the field,
9 the birds of the air, the fish of the sea,
and whatever swims in the paths of the sea.
10 O LORD, our Lord,
how glorious is your name in all the earth!

PSALMS 9–10*

PSALM 9*

Thanksgiving for the Triumph of Justice

1 For the director.* According to *Muth Labben*. A psalm of David.

2 I will offer praise to you, O LORD,
with my whole heart;
I will recount all your wondrous deeds.*
3 I will rejoice and exult in you;
I will sing praise to your name,*
O Most High.

k Pss 18:50; 30:5; 135:3; 146:2; Rom 15:11.—l Ps 143:12; Wis 10:21; Mt 21:16.—m Ps 144:3; Job 7:17.—n 1 Chr 29:14; Heb 2:6ff.—o Ps 19:2; Gen 1:26, 28; Wis 9:2; 1 Cor 15:27; Eph 1:22.

7:18 *I will offer thanks . . . and I will sing hymns of praise:* a vow to praise the Lord in keeping with the Israelite belief that praise must follow deliverance. The praise involved thank offerings and celebrating God's saving deed in the presence of others in the temple (see Ps 50:14f, 23). See also note on Ps 9:2. *Name:* see notes on Pss 5:12; 8:2.

Ps 8 In the midst of disconsolate supplications, here is a hymn that chants the splendor of God. But is not the best reflection of the divine majesty the grandeur of the human being? For the Lord has made this tiny being lost in the immensity of the world the crown of all creation. In the man "crowned with glory" Paul and the author of the Letter to the Hebrews see the glorified and risen Christ, who, while on earth, was for a time made lower than the heavenly creatures, the angels (see 1 Cor 15:25-27; Eph 1:22; Heb 2:5-9).

8:1 *For the director:* these words are thought to be a musical or liturgical notation. *Gittith:* possibly a musical instrument from the Philistine city of Gath, or else a song for the harvest and the winepress.

8:2, 10 *Name:* according to Semitic usage, this word designates the person with all its essential qualities. See also note on Ps 5:12.

8:3 *Out of the mouths of newborn babes and infants:* Jesus cites this passage with reference to the children who acclaim him on the day of his triumphal entry into Jerusalem (see Mt 21:16).

8:5 *Son of man:* a phrase used here and elsewhere as a synonym for human (see Ps 80:18; Ezek 2) and a sign of humility. Later it became a Messianic title in Daniel (7:13f) and Jewish apocryphal tradition (see 1 Enoch, 2 Esdras, and 2 Baruch). Eventually, Jesus made use of it to express his twofold destiny of suffering (see Mk 8:31; 9:13, 31; 10:33; 14:21) and of glory (see Mk 8:38; 12:36; 14:62).

8:6 *A little less than the angels:* that is, a little lower than the beings who comprise the heavenly court. The text for heavenly beings is *elohim*, that is, "God"; in effect, God created human beings in his own image and likeness. Some translate: "a little less than godlike"; and in Heb 2:9 this passage is said to be eminently fulfilled in Jesus Christ, the God-man. See also 1 Cor 15:27; Eph 1:22, where Paul applies to Christ the words "you have . . . placed everything under his feet" (v. 7).

Pss 9–10 In these psalms we are perhaps in the period of the return from the Exile, toward the end of the sixth century; the foreign occupiers and the people who had remained in Palestine regarded returning deportees as intruders and they mistreated them. This is the first alphabetical psalm; in the Masoretic Text it is divided into two psalms, while in the Greek Septuagint and Latin Vulgate Psalms 9 and 10 constitute one psalm. This accounts for the difference in the numbering of the psalms in these versions.

Ps 9 is predominantly praise of God for his royal blessings and glories, including deliverance from hostile nations, concluding with a short prayer for God's continuing righteous judgments (see v. 5) on the nations.

9:1 *For the director:* these words are thought to be a musical or liturgical notation. *According to Muth Labben:* nothing is known about these words.

9:2 The praise rendered to the Lord by the psalmists in the Psalter is customarily public praise for his goodness and glory as well as the saving acts he has performed on behalf of his people. Some have described such praise as the forerunner of the Gospel preaching in the New Testament. See also note on Ps 7:18.

9:3, 6, 11 *Name:* see note on Ps 5:12.

4 For my enemies have turned back;
in your presence they stumble and perish.
5 But you have upheld my just cause,
you who are seated on your throne as a righteous judge.

6 You have rebuked the nations and destroyed the wicked,
erasing their name forever and ever. [p]
7 The enemies have suffered endless ruin;
their cities have been utterly destroyed,
and not even their memory remains.

8 The LORD is enthroned forever;
he has established his throne for judgment.
9 He governs the world in righteousness
and judges the peoples with equity. [q]
10 The LORD is a refuge for the oppressed,
a refuge in times of distress. [r]
11 Those who revere your name place their trust in you,
for you never abandon those who seek you, O LORD.

12 Sing praise to the LORD enthroned in Zion; *
proclaim to the nations his wondrous deeds.
13 For the avenger of blood remembers them;
he does not ignore the cry of the afflicted. [s]

14 Have mercy on me, O LORD;
behold how my enemies afflict me,
you who save me from the gates of death. [t]
15 Then I will recount all your praises
and rejoice in your salvation
at the gates of the Daughter of Zion. *

16 * The nations have fallen into the pit they made;
their feet have been caught in the snare they laid.
17 The LORD has made himself known and rendered judgment;
the wicked are ensnared in the work of their own hands. [u]
Higgaion, * *Selah*

18 The wicked will depart into the netherworld,
all the nations that turned away from God.
19 But the needy will not be forgotten forever,
nor will the hope of the afflicted ever come to naught. [v]

20 Rise up, O LORD! Do not let man triumph;
let the nations be judged before you.
21 Strike them with fear, O LORD;
let the nations know that they are mere mortals. *Selah*

PSALM 10*

Prayer for Help against Oppressors

1 Why, O LORD, do you stand far off?
Why do you remain hidden in times of trouble?
2 In his arrogance the wicked hunts down the poor;
let him be ensnared by the schemes he has devised. [w]

3 The wicked boasts of his wicked desires;
he upholds the greedy and renounces the LORD. [x]
4 Filled with arrogance, he does not seek God,
but thinks, "God does not exist." * [y]
5 The wicked always seems to prosper;
your judgments are far from his mind,
and he scoffs at all those who oppose him.
6 He says in his heart, * "I will not be swayed;
I will never experience misfortune."

p Pss 37:10; 59:6; 105:14; Job 18:17; Isa 26:14.—q Pss 7:12; 96:10; 98:9.—r Pss 10:18; 37:39; Isa 25:4.—s Ps 10:17; Job 16:18.—t Num 10:9; Wis 16:13.—u Prov 5:22; Sir 27:26.—v Ps 25:3; Prov 23:18.—w Job 20:19; Isa 32:7.—x Pss 36:2; 49:7; 94:4; Jer 14:8.—y Pss 14:1b; 36:2; Job 22:13; Isa 29:15; Jer 5:12; Zep 1:12.

9:12 *Enthroned in Zion:* the Lord is enthroned not only in heaven (see Pss 2:4; 113:5) but also on earth—in the temple of Jerusalem from which he rules the world (see note on Ps 2:6; see also Ps 132:13).

9:15 *Daughter of Zion:* a personification of Jerusalem and its inhabitants in accord with ancient Near Eastern practice (see Pss 45:12; 137:8).

9:16-19 Under the Lord's just rule and in accord with the law of talion (see Ex 21:23-25; Lev 24:19f; Deut 19:21), the wicked who attack others are punished by the very actions they perform (see Ps 7:16). But the *needy* (v. 19), those who are attacked, will be saved by their trust in the Lord. Thus, God's honor and glory are vindicated when he judges and punishes the wicked.

9:17 *Higgaion:* probably a musical notation.

Ps 10 A prayer of one in trouble and seeking to be rescued, it explores the ways and motives of the wicked and calls on God the King to arise and defend the oppressed.

10:4 In denying the action of Providence the wicked in effect denies God (see Pss 10:13; 14:1b; 36:2f; Zep 1:12), who is some far-off personage (Ps 10:5).

10:6, 11, 13 *Heart:* see note on Ps 4:8.

7 His mouth is filled with curses, deceit,
and threats; *
his tongue breeds evil and malice. [z]
8 He lies in wait near the villages,
and from ambush he slays the innocent;
his eyes are on the watch for the helpless. [a]
9 He lies in wait like a lurking lion,
ready to strike the helpless;
he snares his victims,
seizing them in his net. [b]
10 He crouches and lies low,
and the poor are overwhelmed by his might.
11 He thinks in his heart,
"God has forgotten;
he hides his face and will never see
what is happening." [c]
12 Arise, O LORD! Lift up your hand,
O God!
Do not forget the afflicted.
13 Why should the wicked reject God
and say in his heart,
"He will not call me to account"?
14 But you note our troubles and our grief
so that you may resolve our difficulties. [d]
The helpless entrusts himself to you;
you are the recourse of the fatherless. [e]
15 Break the arms of the sinner and the evildoer;
seek out the wicked
until no more endure. *
16 *The LORD is King forever and ever;
the heathen will disappear from his land. [f]
17 You listen, O LORD, to the longings of the poor;
you strengthen their courage and heed
their prayers.
18 You ensure justice for the fatherless and
the oppressed
so that no one on earth may fill them
with terror. [g]

PSALM 11*

Unshakable Confidence in God

1 For the director. * Of David.
*In the LORD I take refuge.
How can you say to me,
"Flee like a bird to your mountains! [h]
2 For behold, the wicked are bending their bows
as they fit their arrows to the string
so that from the shadows
they can shoot at those who are upright. *[i]
3 If the foundations * are destroyed,
what can be done by those who are righteous?"
4 *The LORD is in his holy temple;
the LORD, whose throne is in heaven.
His eyes are fixed on the world;
his gaze examines everyone. [j]
5 The LORD tests the upright and the wicked;
he detests the lover of violence.

z Ps 73:8; Isa 32:7; Rom 3:14.—a Pss 11:2; 17:12; Job 24:14; Jer 5:26; Hos 6:9; Hab 3:14.—b Ps 17:12; Job 18:8; Prov 1:11; Jer 5:26.—c Pss 44:24; 64:5; 73:11; 94:7; Job 22:13; Ezek 9:9.—d Pss 22:12; 31:8; 56:9; 2 Ki 20:5; Isa 25:8; Rev 7:17.—e Pss 68:6; 82:3; 146:9; Ex 22:21-22; Deut 10:18; 33:29.—f Ps 145:13; Ex 15:18; Jer 10:10.—g Ps 146:9; Deut 10:18.—h Pss 7:2; 55:7; 91:3.—i Pss 7:14; 10:8; 37:14; 64:5; 2 Sam 22:35.—j Pss 14:2; 18:7; 27:4; 102:20; Deut 26:15; 1 Ki 8:48; Isa 66:1; Jon 2:8; Mic 1:2; Hab 2:20; Mt 5:34; 23:22.

10:7 *Curses, deceit, and threats:* this text, which contains the three most common weapons of the tongue in Israel's experience, is cited in Rom 3:14. *Curses* were believed to have real power over those upon whom they were leveled; *deceit* referred to slander and *threats* for evil purposes (see 1 Ki 21:8-15).

10:15 See notes on Pss 5:11; 35.

10:16-18 The Lord is the hope of the righteous (*the poor*) in a just world, for he is *King forever*. Because he is faithful to his covenant, he will defeat *the heathen* for he listens to the *longings of the poor* and establishes justice for them. Hence, *no one on earth* is to be feared.

Ps 11 This is a confession of confident trust in the Lord's righteous rule at a time when one's wicked adversaries seem to have the upper hand. Friends counsel flight to a mountain refuge to escape trouble, but the innocent psalmist stands fast, for the Lord protects those who seek asylum in his temple.

In praying this psalm, we should be mindful that although we can rely on God, we are never sure of ourselves. The Spirit of God is quick to help, but the "flesh," human nature, is weak—so much so that we must ask not to be put to the test (see Mt 26:41) and must flee from it if this is possible and permitted (see Mt 10:23).

11:1a *For the director:* these words are thought to be a musical or liturgical notation.

11:1b-3 The psalmist remains confident in the Lord even though he is under attack by the wicked and receives counsel from his advisers to flee.

11:2 The wicked are likened to archers setting traps; they are treacherous, furtive, and bent on maligning the upright and making them fall (see Pss 10:7-10; 37:14). *Those who are upright:* i.e., the righteous who know and love the Lord (see Pss 7:10; 36:11; 73:1).

11:3 The psalmist's advisers are concerned about the collapse of the *foundations* (i.e., the order of society; see Pss 75:4; 82:5; Ezek 30:4). This order has been established by the Lord at creation and is being maintained by him.

11:4-7 The psalmist relies on God, who is seated on his heavenly throne—a symbol of his royal rule and authority to judge (see Pss 9:8; 47:9)—and totally against those who love violence. At the right time, he will mete out to the wicked the judgment they deserve, and he will deliver the upright and grant them access to himself.

6 Upon the wicked he will rain down
fiery coals and brimstone; *
a scorching wind will be their allotted
portion. [k]
7 For the LORD is just
and he loves righteous deeds;
the upright will behold his face. *

PSALM 12*

Prayer against the Arrogance of Sinners

1 For the director. * "Upon the eighth." A psalm of David.

2 Help, O LORD, for there are no godly left;
the faithful have vanished from the
human race. [l]
3 Neighbors utter lies to each other;
they speak with flattering lips and
deceitful hearts. * [m]
4 May the LORD destroy all flattering lips
and every boastful tongue,
5 those who say, "We will prevail by our
tongues;
with our lips as our ally,
who can lord it over us?" [n]
6 "The poor have been oppressed,
and those who are needy groan.
Therefore, I will rise up now," says the
LORD;
"I will grant them the safety
for which they long." [o]
7 And the promises of the LORD are certain;
they are like silver refined in a furnace
and purified seven times. * [p]
8 * You, O LORD, will watch over us
and preserve us from this generation
forever.
9 For the wicked prowl on every side,
and what is vile is exalted by mankind.

PSALM 13*

Prayer of One in Sorrow

1 For the director. * A psalm of David.

2 How long, * O LORD—will you forget me
forever?
How long will you hide your face from
me? [q]
3 How long must I suffer anguish in my
soul
and sorrow in my heart * day and
night?
How long will my enemy lord it over me?
4 Look upon me, O LORD, my God, and
answer me;
enlighten my eyes, lest I sleep in death,
5 lest my enemy say, "I have defeated him,"
and my foes exult in my collapse. [r]
6 As for me, I trust in your kindness; *
my heart rejoices in your salvation.

---

k Pss 120:4; 140:11; Gen 19:24; 41:23, 27; Job 15:2; Prov 16:27; Isa 11:15; Ezek 10:2; 38:22; Rev 8:5; 20:10.—l Pss 14:3; 116:11; Isa 57:1; 59:15; Mic 7:2.—m Pss 28:3; 35:14; 55:22; Isa 59:3-4; Jer 9:8.—n Ps 31:19; Prov 18:21; Sir 5:3; Jas 3:6.—o Pss 34:7; 44:24f; Isa 33:10.—p Pss 18:31; 19:8; 2 Sam 22:31; Prov 30:5.—q Pss 6:4; 22:25; 42:10; 44:25; 77:8; 79:5; 89:47; 94:3; Deut 31:17; Isa 8:17; Lam 5:20.—r Pss 25:2; 38:17; 71:2.

11:6 *Fiery coals and brimstone:* an image of judgment taken from the destruction of Sodom and Gomorrah (see Gen 19:24; Deut 29:23; Ezek 38:22). *Scorching wind:* another image of judgment taken from the hot desert winds that blow over the Middle East and devastate the vegetation (see Isa 21:1; 40:7f; Jer 4:11). *Their allotted portion:* literally, "the portion of their cup." The cup that God gives people to drink is a symbol for their destiny (see Ps 16:5; Mt 20:22; 26:39; Rev 14:10).

11:7 *Behold his face:* an expression usually denoting access, especially to the king. Here the expression indicates access to the heavenly King, with reference to his presence at the temple (God's royal house on earth). It is legitimate for us to see in this text an allusion to ultimate access to the heavenly temple (see Pss 16:11; 17:15; 23:6; 140:14).

Ps 12 The psalmist, surrounded by the treachery and arrogance of sinners (see Mic 7:1-7), calls for help and is certain that God will judge them as their iniquity reaches its zenith. The words of the Lord can be fully relied on, whereas the boastful words of the adversaries are completely futile.

We Christians can make this supplication our own, for we feel deeply every disorder in the social realm. Eager for justice, we are outraged by every injustice, every disloyalty and fraud in social relations.

12:1 *For the director:* these words are thought to be a musical or liturgical notation. *Upon the eighth:* see note on Ps 6:1.

12:3 *Hearts:* see note on Ps 4:8.

12:7 *Purified seven times:* the number seven signified fullness or completeness; hence the phrase means "refined through and through." The words of the Lord are absolutely pure and true (see Pss 18:31; 19:8; Prov 30:5).

12:8-9 The psalmist voices his confidence that, although the wicked are at present lording it over the righteous, God will take care of the latter.

Ps 13 The suffering psalmist cries out to God in despair over his impending death and the triumph of his enemies. Suddenly (perhaps after a religious experience of some kind), his tone changes; he speaks from a heart brimming with complete trust in God and voices his joy and gratitude.

In praying this psalm, we can think of Christ in his abandonment on the cross and provisional defeat by death, in the face of his enemies' ephemeral success. We too experience the critical trial of God's silence and apparent absence. Far from weakening our confidence in God, this eventuality should strengthen it.

13:1 *For the director:* most likely a musical or liturgical notation.

13:2 *How long:* see note on Ps 6:4. *Hide your face:* when God hides his face, the righteous become concerned (see Pss 30:8; 104:29), for when God's face shines on people it brings deliverance and blessings (see Pss 31:17; 67:2; 80:4; 119:135).

13:3, 6 *Heart:* see note on Ps 4:8.

13:6 *Kindness:* see note on Ps 6:5.

7 I will sing to the LORD [s]
because he has been good to me.*

PSALM 14*

Corruption and Punishment of the Godless

1 For the director. * Of David.

The fool says in his heart,*
"There is no God."
People are depraved and their deeds are vile;
there is no one who does what is right. [t]

2 The LORD* looks down from heaven
upon the entire human race, [u]
to see if there are any who act with wisdom, [v]
if even a single one seeks God.

3 But they have all left the right path;
all alike are corrupt.
There is no one who does what is right,
not even one. * [w]

4 Have all these evildoers* no understanding?
They devour my people as they eat bread, [x]
and they never call upon the LORD. [y]

5 But later they will be filled with terror,
for God is on the side of the righteous. *

6 They sought to crush the hopes of the poor, *
but the LORD is their refuge.

7 Who will accomplish the salvation of Israel
that is to come out of Zion?*
When the LORD restores the fortunes of his people,
Jacob will rejoice and Israel will exult. [z]

PSALM 15*

The Righteous: Guests of God

1 A psalm of David.

O LORD, who may dwell in your sanctuary? [a]
Who may abide on your holy mountain? *

2 * The one who leads a blameless life
and does what is right,
who speaks the truth from the heart [b]
3 and does not slander anyone,
who does not harm a friend
and does not scorn a neighbor,
4 who looks with disdain on the wicked
but honors those who fear the LORD,
who abides by his oath,
no matter what the cost,

s Pss 7:18; 116:7.—t Pss 10:4; 36:2; Isa 32:6; Jer 5:12; Mic 7:2; Zep 1:12.—u Pss 11:4; 102:20; Job 41:34.—v 2b-4: Rom 3:10-12.—w Ps 12:2; 1 Sam 8:3.—x Pss 27:2; 53:5; Isa 9:11.—y Ps 79:6; Isa 65:1; Jer 10:25; Hos 7:7.—z Pss 85:2; 126:1.—a Ps 24:3-6; Isa 56:7; Mic 6:6-8.—b Ps 119:1; Eph 1:4.

13:7 The Septuagint and Vulgate add another line: "I will sing to the name of the LORD most high."

Ps 14 The psalmist envisions the world divided into "the fool[s]" (also termed "evildoers") and "the company of the righteous" (also termed "the poor" and "[God's] people"). Although the fools act as though there is no God and persecute the righteous, the psalmist is confident that God will eventually punish evildoers and reward the righteous. Psalm 53 is a somewhat revised duplicate of this psalm.

When Paul rereads this psalm, he will see in it a description of our sinful condition. No one is just in God's sight; we all need to be saved by Jesus Christ (Rom 3:10-25).

14:1a *For the director:* these words are thought to be a musical or liturgical notation.

14:1b Elsewhere the psalmists included themselves among those who are not righteous in God's eyes (see Pss 130:3; 143:2; see also 1 Ki 8:39; Job 9:2; Eccl 7:20). *Heart:* see note on Ps 4:8.

14:2 *The LORD:* in contrast with what "the fool" (v. 1b) thinks, the Lord is very much in evidence and has his eyes on the whole earth. *Seeks God:* see Ps 15 for a description of those who truly seek God.

14:3 After this verse, many Greek and Latin manuscripts add the Old Testament citations that were first combined in Rom 3:13-18.

14:4 *Evildoers:* live by the violence of their own doing rather than by reliance on the Lord (see Ps 10:2-4).

14:5 God is on the side of the righteous and, anytime he wishes, strikes sudden terror in the hearts of the wicked (see Deut 28:67; 1 Sam 14:15; 2 Chr 14:13; Job 3:25). *Righteous:* see note on Ps 1:5.

14:6 *Poor:* see note on Ps 22:27.

14:7 The righteous poor are identified with God's people. *Who will . . . Zion:* another possible translation is: "Oh, if only salvation for Israel / will come forth from Zion."

Ps 15 The psalmist presents a summary of moral conduct in the form of an instruction to those who have access to God at his temple (see Ps 24:3-6; Isa 33:14-16; Mic 6:6-8). He indicates that sanctity of life is necessary for those who wish to approach God and emphasizes the social virtues of justice and charity.

In praying this psalm, Christians keep in mind that by becoming man the Word has pitched his tent among us (see Jn 1:14), and in his body dwells the fullness of the divinity. In close contact and in profound communion with the body of Jesus, of whom she is the visible extension on earth, the Church constitutes the dwelling of God in the world (see 1 Cor 3:16f).

15:1 *Holy mountain:* an ancient designation for the temple, the place where God dwells upon the earth (see Pss 2:6; 3:5; 43:3; 48:2).

15:2-5 It is not sacrifices or ritual purity but moral righteousness that gives access to the Lord (see the basic covenantal law: Ex 20:1-17; see also Isa 1:10-17; 33:14-16; 58:6-10; Jer 7:2-7; Ezek 18:5-9; Hos 6:6; Am 5:14f, 21-24; Mic 6:6-8; Zec 7:9f; 8:16f). *Heart:* see note on Ps 4:8. *Those who fear the LORD:* a frequent expression in the Psalter (see, e.g., Ps 115:11), it refers to those who fear God and live in accordance with his will because of their reverence for him. Later it will take on a technical sense and refer to proselytes to Judaism not yet circumcised (see Acts 2:11; 10:2). *Interest on a loan:* laws dealing with interest on loans are found in Ex 22:24-27; Lev 25:35-37; Deut 15:7-11; 23:19f. In general, interest for profit was not to be charged to Israelites. Jesus went even further (see Lk 6:34f).

5 who does not charge interest on a loan
and refuses to accept a bribe against the innocent. [c]
Whoever does these things
will never fall.

PSALM 16*

God the Supreme Good

1 A *miktam* * of David.
Protect me, O God,
for in you I take refuge. [d]
2 I say to the LORD, "You are my Lord;
I have no good apart from you."
3 As for the saints * who are in the land,
they are the noble ones,
and in them there is all my delight.
4 Those who chase after other gods
only multiply their sorrows.
Never will I pour out libations of blood to them,
nor will I take up their names * on my lips.
5 O LORD, you are my allotted portion and my cup; *
you have made my lot secure. [e]
6 The boundary lines have established a pleasant site for me;
I have truly received a wonderful inheritance.
7 I bless the LORD who offers me counsel;
even during the night my heart instructs me.
8 I keep the LORD always before me,
for with him at my right hand
I will never fall. [f]
9 * Therefore, my heart is glad
and my soul rejoices;
my body too is filled with confidence.
10 For you will not abandon me to the netherworld
or allow your Holy One * to suffer corruption. [g]
11 You will show me the path to life;
you will fill me with joy in your presence
and everlasting delights at your right hand.

PSALM 17*

Prayer in Time of Persecution

1 A prayer of David.
Hear, O LORD, my call for justice;
give heed to my cry.
Listen to the prayer of my lips,
for they are free of deceit.
2 Let my vindication issue forth from you;
let your eyes discern what is right.
3 You have probed my heart *
and examined me throughout the night.
You have tested me
and found no malice in me,
for I have not sinned with my mouth. [h]

c Ex 22:24; 23:8; 1 Sam 8:3.—d Pss 2:12; 12:8; 25:20; 2 Pet 1:10.—e Pss 23:5; 73:26; Num 18:20; Deut 10:9; Sir 45:20-22; Lam 3:24.—f Pss 15:5; 73:23; 121:5; Acts 2:25-28.—g Pss 28:1; 30:4; 49:16; 86:13; Num 16:30; 2 Ki 19:22; Job 17:14; Hos 13:14; Jon 2:6; Acts 13:35.—h Pss 26:2; 139:23; Job 7:18; 23:10.

Ps 16 A prayer for safekeeping, pleading for the Lord's protection against the threat of death. It could also be called a psalm of trust. This psalm prepares the way for belief in an everlasting life with God. And it is easy to see how early Christian preachers could understand the final verses as a detailed prophecy of the Resurrection of Christ (Acts 2:24-28; 13:25).

This psalm is in a special way the prayer of those who have "chosen God" in one or other form of consecrated life. Rarely has the joy of a life lived in the presence of God been expressed with such enthusiasm. The wonder felt penetrates to the innermost being of the believer (that is, the "heart," which for the ancients was the seat of one's thoughts as well as desires and affections).

16:1 *Miktam:* its meaning is unknown. Some translate it as "song" or "poem"; others suggest that it means "in a low voice."

16:3 Another possible translation is: "As for the gods who are in the land / and the lofty ones, / I take no delight in them." *Saints:* i.e., the godly who live on earth as opposed to the angelic beings who are heavenly. See notes on Pss 4:4; 34:10.

16:4 *Take up their names:* that is, appeal to or worship them (see Jos 23:7).

16:5 *Cup:* a metaphor referring to what the host offers his guests to drink. To the righteous the Lord offers a cup of blessings (see Ps 23:5) or salvation (see Ps 116:13), but he makes the wicked drink from a cup of wrath (see Jer 25:15; Rev 14:10; 16:19).

16:9-11 The Lord, in whom the psalmist takes refuge, wills life for him (hence he has made known to him the path of life, v. 11) and will not abandon him to the grave, even though "heart and . . . flesh fail" (Ps 73:26). But implicit in these words of assurance (if not actually explicit) is the confidence that, with the Lord as his refuge, even the grave cannot rob him of life (see Pss 17:15; 73:24). If this could be said of David, how much more of David's promised Son! So Peter quotes verses 8-11 and declares that with these words David prophesied of Christ and his Resurrection (Acts 2:25-28; see Paul's similar use of v. 10b in Acts 13:35). *Heart:* see note on Ps 4:8.

16:10 *Holy One:* the reference is first of all to David, but the psalm is ultimately fulfilled in Christ.

Ps 17 Here again we have a picture of smug and pitiless people whose hearts are closed to the word of God as well as to the cry of the poor. The psalmist who endures their unjust accusations begs God to show forth his innocence and to punish his evil accusers. He is willing to leave earthly goods to them (v. 14) as long as he can rejoice in God's presence. Perhaps we can see in this desire for awakening, enlightened by God's face (v. 15), the burgeoning hope of the resurrection.

In praying this psalm, we should recall that in the Church (his Mystical Body) and in each Christian (as in a part of that Body), Jesus relives the mystery of his undeserved Passion and glorious Resurrection (see Acts 9:4f).

17:3 *Heart:* see note on Ps 4:8.

4 Despite what other people do,
I have been guided by the word of your lips *
and refrained from their acts of violence.
5 My steps have held fast to your paths;
my feet have not wavered. [i]
6 I call upon you, O God, for you will answer me.
Incline your ear to me and listen to my plea.
7 Show how wonderful is your kindness, *
you who save those who seek protection
by taking refuge at your right hand.
8 [j] Guard me as the apple of your eye;
hide me in the shadow of your wings *
9 [k] from the wicked who treat me with violence,
from deadly enemies who surround me.
10 There is no compassion in their hearts, *
and arrogance issues from their mouths.
11 They track me down and begin to close in,
watching for the chance to strike me down,
12 like a lion primed to attack its prey,
like a young lion lurking in hiding.
13 Rise up, O LORD, confront them, and cast them down; *
deliver me from the wicked by your sword.
14 With your hand, O LORD, snatch me from such people,
from the worldly whose reward is in this life. *
You satisfy the hunger of those you cherish;
their children have all they desire
and leave their wealth to their little ones.
15 But in my righteousness I will see your face; *
when I awaken, I will be blessed by beholding you. [l]

PSALM 18*

Thanksgiving for God's Help

1 [m] For the director.* Of David, the servant of the LORD. He sang to the LORD the words of this song after the LORD had rescued him from the clutches of all his enemies and from the hand of Saul. 2 He said:

I love you, O LORD, my strength,
3 O LORD, my rock, * my fortress, my deliverer.
My God is my rock in whom I take refuge,
my shield and the horn of my salvation,
my stronghold. [n]
4 I call upon the LORD, who is worthy of all praise;
and I am saved from my enemies.
5 The cords of death encompassed me,
and the torrents of destruction assailed me.

i Pss 18:37; 44:19; Job 23:11-12.—j 8-9: Pss 36:8; 57:2; 61:5; 63:8; 91:4; Deut 32:10; Ru 2:12; Prov 7:2; Zec 2:12; Mt 23:37.—k 9b-12: Pss 10:9; 22:13, 21; 35:17; 57:5; 58:7; Job 4:10-11.—l Pss 4:7; 31:17; 67:2; 73:25-26; 80:4; Num 6:25; Dan 9:17; Rev 22:4.—m 1-51: 2 Sam 22:1-51.—n Pss 3:4; 28:8; 31:2-4; 42:10; Gen 49:24; Deut 32:4; 1 Sam 2:1-2.

17:4 *Word of your lips:* God's revelation by which he made known the "paths" his faithful are to follow. *And refrained . . . violence:* an alternative translation is: "and kept the words of your law."

17:7 *Kindness:* see note on Ps 6:5.

17:8 *Apple of your eye . . . shadow of your wings:* conventional Hebrew metaphors for protection (see Deut 32:10; Prov 7:2; Isa 49:2).

17:10 *Hearts:* see note on Ps 4:8. *Arrogance . . . mouths:* see notes on Pss 5:11; 10:7.

17:13 *Cast them down:* see notes on Pss 5:11; 35.

17:14 *From the worldly . . . life:* or: "from mortals whose part in life is transitory." *You satisfy . . . little ones:* or: "With your treasures you fill their bellies; / their sons are enriched / and bequeath their abundance to their little ones."

17:15 *See your face:* see note on Ps 11:7. *When I awaken:* from the night of death; however, inasmuch as death is often compared to sleep (see Ps 76:6; Dan 12:1f), it may refer to a new awakening after death.

Ps 18 This song of David occurs also in 2 Sam 22 with minor variations. It is composed of an introduction (vv. 1-4), a conclusion (vv. 47-51), and three major divisions: (1) the Lord's deliverance of David from mortal enemies (vv. 5-20); (2) the moral grounds for the Lord's help (vv. 21-30); and (3) the Lord's help recounted (vv. 31-46).

Already emerging in this splendid psalm, which is both a song of thanksgiving and a song of victory, is the image of the King-Messiah, Jesus, born of the house of David and beloved Son of the Father; he will conquer the forces of evil. This poem is a festal song expressing wonder and thanksgiving and glorifying God.

To the extent that we can allow ourselves to be identified with Christ and become kings in him (see Ps 2), we can use this psalm to praise God the Father for the wonders that Paul celebrates in the hymn of the Letter to the Ephesians (1:3-15).

18:1 *For the director:* these words are thought to be a musical or liturgical notation.

18:3 *Rock:* a common symbol for God indicating his strength as a refuge or as a deliverer (see Pss 19:15; 31:3f; 42:10; 62:3, 8; 71:3; 73:26; 78:35; 89:27; 92:16; 94:22; 95:1; 144:1; Deut 32:15; Isa 17:10). See Jesus' use of the word in Mt 16:18. *Horn:* a symbol of strength (see Deut 33:17; Jer 48:25); it often had Messianic overtones (see Ps 132:17; Ezek 29:21).

6 The cords of the netherworld ensnared me,
and the snares of death * rose up before me. [o]
7 In my anguish I cried out to the LORD
and called to my God for help.
From his temple * he heard my voice,
and my cry to him reached his ears. [p]
8 * The earth swayed and rocked;
the foundations of the mountains shook, [q]
rocking because of his blazing anger.
9 Smoke poured forth from his nostrils,
while a scorching fire blazed out of his mouth
and kindled coals into flame.
10 He parted the heavens and came down;
dark clouds lay under his feet. [r]
11 He rode upon a cherub, *
soaring swiftly on the wings of the wind.
12 He used the darkness as his covering,
and dense thunderclouds as his canopy.
13 From the radiance before him thick clouds emerged,
spewing hail and flashes of fire. [s]
14 The LORD thundered from the heavens,
and the Most High let his voice be heard. [t]
15 He shot his arrows * and scattered them,
hurled his lightning bolts and routed them. [u]
16 Then the depths of the sea were exposed,
and the earth's foundations were laid bare,
at the rebuke of the LORD, *
at the blast of wind from his nostrils. [v]
17 He reached down from on high and snatched me up;
he drew me out of the watery depths. * [w]
18 He delivered me from my powerful enemy,
and from my foes, who were too strong for me.
19 They assailed me in the day of my misfortune,
but the LORD came forward to uphold me.
20 He led me forth into the open field;
he set me free because he was pleased with me.
21 The LORD has dealt with me according to my righteousness; *
because my hands were pure, he has rewarded me. [x]
22 For I have kept the ways of the LORD *
and refused to turn away from my God.
23 His laws are clearly known to me,
and I have not failed to observe his decrees.
24 I was blameless in his sight,
and I kept myself free of sin.
25 Therefore, the LORD has rewarded me according to my righteousness,
because of the cleanness of my hands in his eyes.
26 To the loyal, you show yourself to be loyal;
to the blameless, you show yourself to be blameless; [y]
27 to the pure, you show yourself to be pure;
but to the perverse, * you show yourself to be shrewd.
28 For you save the humble,
but you bring down the haughty. [z]

---

o Pss 88:8; 93:3-4; 116:3-4; Num 16:33f; Prov 13:14.—p Ps 30:3; Jon 2:2.—q Pss 97:3-4; 99:1; Jdg 5:4-5; Isa 64:1; Jer 10:10; Hab 3:9-11.—r Pss 50:3; 104:3; 144:5; Isa 63:19.—s Ps 104:3; Ex 13:21; 19:16; Deut 4:11.—t Pss 29; 77:19; Ex 19:19; 1 Sam 2:10; Job 36:29-30; 37:3-4.—u Ps 144:6; Deut 32:23; Wis 5:21; Rev 4:5.—v Ps 77:17; Ex 15:8; Isa 50:2; Zec 9:14.—w Ps 144:7; Ex 15:5; Prov 20:5.—x Ps 26:1; 1 Sam 26:23; 2 Chr 15:7; Job 22:30.—y Pss 31:24; 89:25; 125:4.—z Job 22:29; Prov 3:34; Mt 23:12.

18:6 *Cords of the netherworld . . . snares of death:* the psalmist had been in the grip of death and a prisoner of the grave (see Ps 116:3; Job 36:8).

18:7 *Temple:* God's heavenly dwelling where he is enthroned (see Pss 11:4; 113:5; Isa 6:1; 40:22).

18:8-16 In these powerful images the ancients sang of the presence and glory of God in creation and in events (see Pss 68:9f; 97:2-5; Ex 19:15-18; Jdg 5:4f; Job 36:29f; Isa 30:27f; Hab 3:3-15). The description gives a presentiment of the struggle at the end of time in which God triumphs.

18:11 *Cherub:* a winged being, represented at the entrance of Mesopotamian temples. Two cherubim stood on the Ark of the Covenant (see Ex 25:18; 1 Ki 6:23-28). God was regarded as enthroned on them (see Pss 80:2; 99:1) and riding upon the storm clouds (see Ps 104:3) or upon the cherubim.

18:15 *Arrows:* shafts of lightning (see Pss 77:18; 144:6; Hab 3:11).

18:16 The psalmist may be referring to the wondrous deed God accomplished at the Red Sea during the Exodus (see Ex 14:15-22).

18:17 *Watery depths:* symbols of great danger (see Pss 32:6; 40:3; 42:8; 66:12; 69:3, 15; 88:18; 130:1; Job 22:11; Isa 30:28; Jon 2:5f).

18:21 *Righteousness:* see note on Ps 1:5.

18:22 *Ways of the LORD:* see note on Ps 25:10.

18:27 God treats people the way they treat him and others. *The perverse:* those who stray from the straight way of the Lord. *Show yourself to be shrewd:* the Lord counters the evil acts of the wicked, one after the other.

29 You, O LORD, are light for my lamp; *
O my God, you make my darkness turn
to light. [a]
30 With your help I can storm a rampart;
with my God to aid me, I can scale any
wall.
31 The way of God is blameless,
and the LORD's promise proves true;
he is a shield to all
who flee to him for safety. [b]
32 Indeed, who is God except the LORD?
Who is the Rock besides our God? [c]
33 It is God who clothes me with strength
and makes my way blameless.
34 He gives me the swift feet of a deer
and places me securely on the heights. [d]
35 He trains my hands for war [e]
and my arms to bend a bow of bronze. *
36 You have given me the shield of your salvation;
your right hand sustains me,
and your goodness makes me great.
37 You broadened the path beneath me
so that my feet have never stumbled. [f]
38 I went after my enemies and overtook
them;
I did not turn back until they were
defeated.
39 When I knocked them down, they were
unable to rise;
they fell down at my feet.
40 You clothed me with strength for the
battle
and cast down my adversaries beneath
me.
41 You made my enemies retreat before me,
so that I could scatter those who hated
me.
42 They called for help, but there was no one
to deliver them;
they called to the LORD, but no answer
came.
43 I crushed them like fine dust before the
wind;
I trod on them like mud in the streets.
44 You delivered me from a people in rebellion,
and you placed me in charge of the
nations;
people I did not know have become my
subjects.
45 As soon as they heard me, they obeyed;
foreigners groveled before me.
46 Then they became disheartened
and came forth trembling from their
strongholds. [g]
47 The LORD lives! Blessed * be my Rock!
Exalted be God, my Savior! [h]
48 O God, you obtained vindication for me,
subjected nations under me, [i]
49 and freed me from my enemies.
You exalted me over my adversaries
and delivered me from the violent.
50 For this, O LORD, I will praise you among
the nations
and sing praise to your name. * [j]
51 You have bestowed great victories on
your king,
and you have shown kindness to your
anointed, *
to David and his descendants forever. [k]

PSALM 19*

God's Glory in Creation

1 For the director. * A psalm of David.
2 * The heavens proclaim the glory of God;
the firmament shows forth the work of
his hands. [l]

a Pss 27:1; 36:10; 43:3; 119:105; 132:17; Job 29:3; Mic 7:8.—b Pss 12:7; 77:14; Deut 32:4; Prov 30:5.—c Ps 35:10; Isa 44:8; 45:21.—d Deut 32:13; Isa 58:14; Hab 3:19.—e Ps 144:1; 2 Sam 22:35.—f Pss 17:5; 31:9; 66:9; Job 18:7.—g Mic 7:17; Heb 12:3.—h Pss 21:14; 144:1.—i Pss 20:7; 144:2.—j Pss 7:18; 9:12; 30:5; 57:10; 101:1; 108:2; 135:3; 146:2; Rom 15:9.—k Pss 89:5, 29-38; 144:10; 1 Sam 2:10; 2 Sam 23:1.—l Pss 8:1; 50:6; 89:6; 97:6; 147:4-5; 148:3-4; Gen 1:1-8; Isa 40:22; Rom 1:19-20.

18:29 *Light for my lamp:* a figure of life and happiness (see 1 Ki 11:36). *Light:* see note on Ps 27:1.

18:35 *Bow of bronze:* a bow difficult to bend that would shoot arrows with greater force.

18:47 *Blessed:* i.e., adored, praised, and thanked.

18:50 This text is cited by Paul (Rom 15:9) as a prediction of the conversion of the Gentiles. *Name:* see note on Ps 5:12.

18:51 *You have shown kindness to your anointed:* the Lord is mindful of his covenant with his anointed king and never ceases bestowing blessings upon him. This is even more true of the King and Anointed par excellence, Jesus Christ. *Kindness:* see note on Ps 6:5.

Ps 19 The universe is a hymn to the glory of the Lord, but this is even more true of the Mosaic Law. The silent revelation of creation is offered to all human beings, but the law, privilege of Israel, reveals to the hearts of believers God's perfection, justice, truth, and goodness and challenges them to imitate the divine life.

The ode to the sun in this psalm (vv. 5b-7) seems to be an imitation of a fragmentary Assyrian text in which the sun-god rises from the ocean and passes through the gates of the east to meet the goddess. The Christmas Liturgy uses this image to recall, in poetic language, the coming to earth of the Son of God.

By its splendor and vastness, the star-studded heavens teach us the glory, the splendor and infinite power, the prodigious artistry of the Father, the Son, and the Holy Spirit who work together in its continuous creation. The Law, perfect as far as its epoch and its place in the divine economy of salvation are concerned, was brought to its absolute perfection by Christ (see Mt 5:17).

19:1 *For the director:* these words are thought to be a musical or liturgical notation.

19:2-5b The heavens show forth the glory of their Creator to all peoples (see Ps 148:3).

3 One day imparts that message to the next,
and night conveys that knowledge to night.
4 All this occurs without speech or utterance;
no voice can be heard.
5 * Yet their message goes forth throughout the earth,
and their words to the ends of the world.
* In the heavens he has placed a tent for the sun,
6 which comes forth like a bridegroom from his wedding chamber,
rejoicing like an athlete who runs his course.
7 It rises from one end of the heavens,
and its circuit is completed at the other;
nothing can be hidden from its heat.

8 The law of the LORD is perfect,
affording refreshment to the soul.
The decree of the LORD is worthy of trust,
imparting wisdom to the simple. *[m]
9 The precepts of the LORD are right,
causing the heart * to rejoice.
The commands of the LORD are clear,
giving light to the eyes.
10 The fear of the LORD * is pure,
destined to endure forever.
The ordinances of the LORD are true,
and all of them are just.
11 They are even more precious than gold,
than an abundance of the purest gold;
they are also sweeter than honey[n]
that drips from the comb. *
12 * By these your servant is instructed;
obedience in following them will ensure a great reward.
13 But who can fully recognize his shortcomings?
Cleanse me of my hidden faults.
14 From willful sins preserve your servant;
never let them gain power over me.
Then I will be blameless
and innocent of serious sin.
15 Let the words of my mouth and the thoughts of my heart*
find favor in your sight,
O LORD, my Rock and my Redeemer.

PSALM 20*

Prayer in Praise of the Messiah King

1 For the director. * A psalm of David.
2 May the LORD answer you in times of trouble;
may the name * of the God of Jacob protect you.
3 May he send you help from the sanctuary
and grant you support from Zion. *[o]

m Pss 12:7; 93:5; 111:7; 119:130, 138, 144; Deut 4:6.—n Ps 119:72, 103, 127; 1 Sam 14:27; Job 22:24-25; Prov 8:10; Song 4:11; Sir 24:19; Ezek 3:3.—o Pss 30:10; 128:5; 134:3.

19:5ab Paul interprets this proclamation of the heavens as referring also to the proclamation of the Gospel (see Rom 10:18).

19:5c-7 The heavens are the divinely pitched tent for the lordly sun—widely worshiped in the ancient Near East (see Deut 4:19; 17:3; 2 Ki 23:5, 11; Jer 8:2; Ezek 8:16), but here a mere creature of God (as in Ps 136:8f; Gen 1:16). Of the created realm, the sun is the supreme metaphor of the glory of God (see Ps 84:12; Isa 60:19f), as it makes its daily triumphant sweep across the whole extent of the heavens and pours out its heat (felt presence) on every creature. The literature of the time applied to the sun the six synonyms for God's revelation in verses 8-11.

19:8 *The simple:* those who are inexperienced and hence childlike (see Ps 119:98-100; Prov 1:4); the New Testament shows that heavenly wisdom is a gift to "children," hidden from the worldly-wise (see Lk 10:21; 1 Cor 1:18ff; 2:8-10; 2 Tim 3:15).

19:9 *Heart:* see note on Ps 4:8.

19:10 *Fear of the LORD:* see note on Ps 15:2-5. In this case, some exegetes believe that the term "fear" should really be "word."

19:11 See Ps 119:103, 127. This entire hymn to the law is closely connected to the long Psalm 119.

19:12-14 The psalmist knows that God's commandments lead to life (see Deut 5:33). Yet he is also aware that like all human beings he is weak and imperfect. He may err unknowingly and need to seek forgiveness of *hidden faults* (v. 13; see Lev 5:2-4). However, *willful sins* (v. 14) are another matter; they cut one off from God and his people (see Num 15:30f). He prays to be preserved from them.

19:15 This meditation is presented to the Lord as a praise offering (see notes on Pss 7:18; 9:2; see also Pss 50:14; 104:33). *Heart:* see note on Ps 4:8. *Rock:* see note on Ps 18:3.

Ps 20 During a liturgy of prayer for the king just before he engages in battle with a powerful foe (2 Chr 20:6), the people (perhaps the assembled soldiers) pray for their king: is he not a "messiah," that is, an "anointed one" of the Lord (v. 7) and the head of the chosen people of the God of Jacob (v. 3)? A choir chants the petition (vv. 3-6) and a soloist (perhaps a Levite: see 2 Chr 20:14) responds (vv. 7-9); he announces assurance that the prayer will be heard, for Israel does not rely on the force of arms as its pagan neighbors do but on its God and Savior. Thus, the people already celebrate the coming triumph of the Lord.

In praying this psalm, we can ask the Father to grant the integral victory of Christ in his mystical members, just as he gained it in and for himself (see 1 Cor 15:22f). For the Father is the accomplisher of all things (see Rom 11:36).

20:1 *For the director:* these words are thought to be a musical or liturgical notation.

20:2, 6, 8 *Name:* see notes on Pss 5:12; 8:2, 10. *Protect you:* literally, "raise you to a high, safe place."

20:3 *Zion:* see note on Ps 9:12.

4 May he remember * all your sacrifices
and accept all your burnt offerings.
Selah

5 May he give you your heart's desire *
and grant you success in all your plans.

6 May we shout with joy over your victory
and lift up our banners in the name of our God. *
May the LORD grant your every request.

7 Now I know that the LORD will grant victory to his anointed; *
he will answer him from his holy heaven,
granting mighty victories with his right hand. [p]

8* Some trust in chariots, and some in horses, [q]
but we trust in the name of the LORD, our God.

9 They will collapse and fall,
but we will rise up and stand firm. [r]

10 O LORD, save the king,
and answer us when we call upon you.*

PSALM 21*

Thanksgiving for Messianic Blessings

1 For the director. * A psalm of David.

2 O LORD, the king rejoices in your strength;
your victories fill him with great joy. * [s]

3 You have granted him the desire of his heart *
and not withheld from him the request of his lips. *Selah*

4 You welcomed him with choice blessings *
and placed a crown of pure gold upon his head.

5 He asked you for life, and you gave it to him,
length of days forever and ever. * [t]

6 He has achieved great glory through your victory;
you have bestowed upon him splendor and majesty. *

7 You have conferred everlasting blessings * on him;
you gladdened him with the joy of your presence.

8 For the king places his trust in the LORD;
through the kindness * of the Most High he will not fall.

9* Your hand will lay hold of all your enemies;
your right hand will overcome all your foes.

p Pss 18:51; 28:8; 144:10; 1 Sam 2:10; Job 40:14; Hab 3:13.—q Ps 147:10-11; 1 Sam 17:45; 2 Chr 14:10; Prov 21:31; Isa 31:1; 36:9; 40:30-31; Hos 1:7.—r Ps 27:2; Isa 40:30; Jer 46:6.—s Ps 63:12; 1 Sam 2:10; 2 Sam 22:51.—t Pss 10:16; 45:18; 48:15; 133:3; 1 Ki 3:14; 2 Ki 20:1-7; Isa 38:1-20.

20:4 *Remember:* with God, remembering and acting go together (see Gen 8:1; Ex 2:24).

20:5 *Heart's desire:* see note on Ps 4:8.

20:6 *May we shout . . . name of our God:* see note on Ps 7:18. The Hebrew word for "victory" could also be translated as "salvation."

20:7 *His anointed:* i.e., the king of Israel (see Pss 2:2; 132:10); the divine help is his as intrinsic to his kingship (see Ps 18:51). See note on Ps 2:2.

20:8-9 The force of arms is useless in the face of the divine power. The Prophets were always against the use of horses and chariots in Israel, in imitation of the neighboring pagans (see Deut 17:16; Isa 31:1; Hos 1:7; Mic 5:10; Zec 12:4). The same affirmation occurs in Pss 33:16f; 147:10; Prov 21:31. A similar expression of confidence in the Lord rather than in human weaponry is made by David when facing Goliath (1 Sam 17:45-47).

20:10 The psalm ends in the same way as it began—with fervent prayers that the Lord will come to the aid of the king.

Ps 21 One would have a poor understanding of feasts if one did not allow chants to intermingle desires and reality. On a feast, the king appears to share the privileges of God: authority, long rule, and majesty, for the Lord has blessed and established him to save his people from their foes. The history of Israel will more than once give the lie to this ideal figure of the monarch. The Church sees therein the traits of Jesus Christ, King and Savior of the People of God; in him resides the blessing for the whole world. The psalm continued to be sung in Israel even when the kingship ended after the sixth century A.D.—but this time concerning a future Messianic King.

By a very simple spiritual transposition, this psalm enables us to sing of the divine blessings granted to Christ, especially his Resurrection, and to hope for his complete and decisive triumph over his enemies (the devil, sin, and death).

21:1 *For the director:* these words are thought to be a musical or liturgical notation.

21:2 King and people offer praise to the Lord for the victory that they have achieved over their foes through God's strength.

21:3 *Heart:* see note on Ps 4:8.

21:4 *You welcomed him with choice blessings:* as you once welcomed Abraham (see Gen 12:2) and Joseph (see Gen 48:20). *Placed a crown . . . upon his head:* alludes either to his own crown reinforcing his kingship after his victory or to the crown of the king that he had defeated (see 2 Sam 12:30). This verse is eminently applied to the Messiah (see Pss 45:4; 72:17; 2 Sam 7:29; 1 Chr 17:27).

21:5 The king asked the Lord for life and received *length of days forever and ever* (see 1 Ki 1:25, 31, 34, 39; Dan 2:4; 3:9).

21:6 *Glory . . . splendor and majesty:* like those of the heavenly King (see Ps 96:3).

21:7 *Everlasting blessings:* this phrase may refer to blessings of enduring value or an unending number of blessings. *Your presence:* God's favor, which is the greatest cause of joy inasmuch as it is the supreme blessing, leading to all others.

21:8 *Kindness:* see note on Ps 6:5.

21:9-13 The king's future victories are described as certain because of the Lord's action.

10 On the day when you appear, *
you will cast them into a fiery furnace.
The LORD's anger will engulf them,
and fire will consume them.
11 You will blot out their descendants from the earth
and rid the human race of their posterity. *
12 They have devised wicked schemes against you,
but, plot though they may, they will not succeed.
13 For you will force them to retreat
when you aim your bows at them.
14 Be exalted, O LORD, in your strength; *
we will sing and praise your power. [u]

PSALM 22*

Suffering and Triumph of the Messiah

1 For the director. * According to "The Deer of the Dawn." A psalm of David.
2 * My God, my God, why have you forsaken me?
Why have you paid no heed to my call for help,
to my cries of anguish? [v]
3 O my God, I cry by day, but you do not answer,
by night, but I am afforded no relief. * [w]
4 Yet you are enthroned as the Holy One;
you are the praise of Israel. [x]
5 Our ancestors placed their trust in you;
they trusted, and you gave them deliverance.
6 They cried out to you and were saved,
they trusted in you and were not put to shame. [y]
7 But I am a worm and not human, *
scorned by people and despised by my kinsmen. [z]
8 All who see me jeer at me;
they sneer in mockery and toss their heads: * [a]
9 "He relied on the LORD; [b]
let the LORD set him free.
Let the LORD deliver him,
if he loves him." *
10 * Yet you brought me out of the womb
and made me feel secure
upon my mother's breast.
11 I was entrusted to your care at my birth;
from my mother's womb, you have been my God. [c]
12 Do not remain aloof from me,
for trouble is near
and no one can help me. [d]
13 * Many bulls * are encircling me;
fierce bulls of Bashan are closing in on me.

---

u Pss 18:2, 47; 144:1; Num 10:35.—v Ps 10:1; Job 3:24; Isa 49:14; 54:7; Mt 27:46; Mk 15:34.—w Ps 42:4; Sir 2:10.—x Ps 71:22; Isa 6:3.—y Ps 25:3; Isa 49:23; Dan 3:39f; Rom 9:33.—z Ps 31:12; Isa 53:3.—a Pss 35:16; 109:25; Mt 27:39; Mk 15:29; Lk 23:36.—b Pss 71:11; 91:14; Wis 2:18-20; Mt 27:43.—c Ps 71:6; Gen 50:23; Isa 44:2; 46:3.—d Pss 35:22; 38:21; 40:14; 71:12; 2 Ki 14:26; Isa 41:28.

21:10 The expression *on the day when you appear*, (literally, "on the day of your face [judgment]" see Ps 34:17; Lam 4:16), and the mention of the *fire* are eschatological themes (see Ps 2:12; 2 Sam 23:7; Isa 30:33; Hos 7:7; Mal 3:19).

21:11 The foes of the king will have no descendants to make war on him.

21:14 The word *strength* in the concluding verse connects the theme with the opening verse: "O LORD, the king rejoices in your strength" (v. 2), and we will offer you our praise.

Ps 22 This psalm draws its inspiration from the "Songs of the Suffering Righteous Man (*or* Servant)" (Isa 52:13—53:12) and from the "Confessions of Jeremiah" (Jer 15:15; 17:15; 20:7); it ends, as they do, with the proclamation that the sufferings of the righteous man will restore life to humanity. Such a text seems planned, as it were, to become the prayer of Christ (Mk 15:34), and the Gospels have also singled out details from it that describe in advance the Passion of Jesus (e.g., Mt 27:35, 39, 43; Jn 19:23f, 28). The author of Hebrews even placed the words of verse 23 on the lips of Jesus (Heb 2:12). Indeed, no other psalm is so often quoted in the New Testament.

In praying this psalm, we can keep in mind that Christ continues to pray it through the Church and Christians, since he continues the mystery of his abandonment in his Mystical Body.

22:1 *For the director:* these words are thought to be a musical or liturgical notation. *According to "The Deer of the Dawn":* nothing is known about these words.

22:2-12 Why? The question erupts from the heart of a righteous man. Yesterday he was still enjoying God's favor as a son, but now he feels abandoned for no reason and afflicted with atrocious sufferings and made the laughingstock of freethinkers. Has God changed?

22:3 *But I am afforded no relief:* the Hebrew text is obscure here. Some translate: "by night, and am not silent."

22:7 *I am a worm and not human:* this passage clearly depicts the psalmist's sense of isolation (see Job 25:6; Isa 41:14).

22:8 *They sneer in mockery and toss their heads:* words and gestures of scorn, also indulged in by Christ's foes on Calvary (see Mt 27:39; Mk 15:29). See also note on Ps 5:10.

22:9 Cited in Mt 27:43. *If he loves him:* may be taken as "if God loves the sufferer" or "if the sufferer loves God."

22:10-11 After recalling what the Lord had been for Israel (vv. 4-6), the psalmist now recalls what the Lord has been for him. *I was entrusted to your care at my birth:* the father customarily acknowledged the newborn by taking it upon his knees (see Gen 50:23; Job 3:12).

22:13-22 Around the beleaguered man there arises a wave of hostility; he experiences in his flesh the whole of human sorrow. The images are delusive, and the cries become pathetic. Here is a man whose life is being taken away.

22:13-14, 17 *Bulls . . . lions . . . dogs:* these are metaphors for the enemies. *Bashan:* a land east of the Jordan that was noted for its good pasturage and the size and quality of its animals (see Deut 32:14; Ezek 39:18; Am 4:1).

14 They open wide their mouths against me
like ravening and roaring lions. [e]

15 My strength is trickling away like water,
and all my bones are dislocated.
My heart * has turned to wax
and melts within me.

16 My mouth is as dry as clayware,
and my tongue sticks to my jaw; *
you have laid me down in the dust of death.

17 A pack of dogs surrounds me;
a band of evildoers is closing in on me.
They have pierced my hands and my feet; *

18 I can count all my bones. * [f]
They stare at me and gloat;

19 they divide my garments among them,
and for my clothing they cast lots. * [g]

20 * But you, O LORD, do not remain aloof from me.
O my Strength, come quickly to my aid.

21 Deliver my soul from the sword,
my precious life from the grasp of the dogs.

22 Save me * from the lion's mouth
and from the horns of wild oxen. [h]

23 * I will proclaim your name to my family;
in the midst of the assembly I will praise you: * [i]

24 "You who fear the LORD, praise him.
All you descendants of Jacob,* give him glory.
Revere him, all you descendants of Israel.

25 For he has not scorned or disregarded
the wretched man in his suffering;
he has not hidden his face * from him
but has heeded his call for help."

26 I will offer my praise to you in the great assembly;
in the presence of those who fear him, I will fulfill my vows. *

27 * The poor * will eat and be filled;
those who seek the LORD will praise him:
"May your hearts live forever." [j]

28 All the ends of the earth
will remember and turn to the LORD.
All the families of the nations
will bow low before him. [k]

29 For kingly power belongs to the LORD;
he is the ruler of all the nations. [l]

30 All those who prosper on the earth will bow down before him;
all those who lie in the grave will kneel in homage.

31* But I will live for the LORD,

e Ps 17:12; Job 4:10; Ezek 22:25; Zep 3:3; 1 Pet 5:8.—f Ps 109:24; Mic 7:8.—g Lev 16:8; Mt 27:35; Mk 15:24; Lk 23:34; Jn 19:24.—h Pss 7:2-3; 17:12; 35:17; 57:5; 58:7; Job 4:10; 2 Tim 4:17.—i Pss 26:12; 35:18; 40:11; 68:27; 109:30; 149:1; 2 Sam 22:50; Heb 2:12.—j Pss 23:5; 69:34; 107:9.—k Pss 86:9; 102:23; Job 13:11; Isa 45:22; 52:10; Zec 14:16.—l Pss 47:8; 103:19; Ob 21; Zec 14:9.

22:15 *Bones . . . heart:* his combination of "bones" and "heart" (see note on Ps 4:8) was used to refer to the whole person (body and spirit) (see Ps 102:4; Prov 14:30; 15:30; Isa 66:14).

22:16 *My mouth . . . jaw:* see Jn 19:28 ("I thirst"). *The dust of death:* the netherworld, domain of the dead; the author is using the language of his day, as in Mesopotamian descriptions of the netherworld (see Job 7:9, 21).

22:17 *Pierced my hands and my feet:* his limbs are wounded by the dogs as he seeks to fend off their attacks (see also Isa 53:5; Zec 12:10; Jn 19:34). Although the phrase finds its complete fulfillment in Christ's crucifixion, it is not expressly used by the evangelists in the Passion account.

22:18 *I can count all my bones:* this could also be translated as "I must display all my bones." The meaning is that one is attacked and stripped of his garments (see v. 19).

22:19 Explicitly cited in Jn 19:24 as a prophecy fulfilled in the action of the soldiers who divided Christ's garments among them on Calvary.

22:20-22 The scene shifts as the beleaguered psalmist is led to confront the God of the Covenant. He thus recalls God's promises to be near his people and to protect them from all adversity. He throws himself on the Lord's mercy and is comforted.

22:22 *Save me:* an alternative translation is: "You have heard me." The psalmist knows he has been heard and will be delivered from death.

22:23-32 God reverses the righteous man's condition; his hope returns. In the temple, he celebrates his deliverance and offers a sacrifice of communion amidst the poor who love God. Then the perspective is enlarged even more. The whole earth gives thanks to God who rules the world and dispenses justice. The poor are called to the table of God, and the line of the righteous shall never be extinguished from the midst of human beings. Indeed, the passion of the righteous man has changed something in the human world. *Name:* see note on Ps 5:12.

22:23-25 The taunts of the psalmist's enemies are drowned out by the songs of God's faithful. The true *descendants of Jacob* are those who fear the Lord and seek him (see Ps 24:6).

22:25 *Not hidden his face:* a metaphor for God withdrawing from someone (see Pss 13:2; 27:9; 69:18; 88:15; 102:3; 143:7; Isa 8:17; Mic 3:4).

22:26 This verse affirms the importance of public worship by stressing the praise of God in the great assembly as well as the pledging of freewill offerings. Vows were often made in time of trial (see Pss 50:14; 61:9; 66:1f) and were implemented when God had effected deliverance from the trial (Ps 65:2f).

22:27-32 In an allusion to the Messianic Banquet (see Ps 23:5; Prov 9:1f; Isa 25:6; 55:1; 65:13), the psalmist describes a worldwide company of people from every state in life who will ultimately take up God's praise from age to age. It constitutes one of the grandest visions of the scope of the worshipers who will come to praise the saving acts of the Lord.

22:27 *The poor:* the *anawim,* originally the poor who depended on God for their livelihood; later, the humble, pious, and devout—those who hoped in God alone.

22:31-32 This is the more common translation (also found in the new Vulgate). An alternative translation is: "and those who cannot keep themselves alive. / Posterity will serve him; / future generations will be told about the Lord. / They will proclaim his righteousness / to a people yet unborn— / for he has done it."

and my descendants will serve him.
32 Future generations will be told about the Lord
so that they may proclaim to a people yet unborn [m]
the deliverance he has accomplished.

PSALM 23*

Prayer to the Good Shepherd

1 A psalm of David.
The LORD is my shepherd;
there is nothing I shall lack. [n]
2 He makes me lie down in green pastures; *
he leads me to tranquil streams.
3 He restores my soul, *
guiding me in paths of righteousness
so that his name may be glorified. [o]
4 Even though I wander
through the valley of the shadow of death, *
I will fear no evil,
for you are at my side,
with your rod and your staff
that comfort me. [p]
5 * You spread a table for me
in the presence of my enemies. [q]
You anoint my head with oil; *
my cup overflows. [r]
6 Only goodness and kindness * will follow me
all the days of my life,
and I will dwell in the house of the LORD
forever and ever. [s]

PSALM 24*

The LORD's Solemn Entry into Jerusalem

1 * A psalm of David.
The earth is the LORD's and everything in it, [t]
the world and all who live in it. *

m Pss 40:11; 48:14-15; 71:18; 78:6; 102:19; Isa 53:10; Lk 18:31; Eph 2:7.—n Pss 80:2; 95:7; 100:3; Gen 48:15; Deut 2:7; Ezek 34:2; Jn 10:11.—o Ps 115:1; Prov 4:11.—p Ps 107:14; Job 10:21; Isa 50:10.—q Pss 22:27; 63:6; 92:11.—r Pss 16:5; 116:13; Lk 7:46.—s Pss 27:4; 61:5; Neh 9:25.—t Pss 50:12; 89:12; Ex 9:29; Deut 10:14; Isa 66:1-2; 1 Cor 10:26.

Ps 23 This psalm is a profession of joyful trust in the Lord as the good Shepherd-King that has become one of the world's greatest prayers. The image of God in shepherd's garb has parallels in the Prophets (see Isa 40:11; Ezek 34:11-16) and will be the best known of the allegories in which Jesus speaks of himself (see Jn 10:11-18), so much so that the New Testament writers love to give him this title (see Heb 13:20; 1 Pet 2:25; Rev 7:17). The water, oil, and cup of wine of which the text speaks made Christians think of the Sacraments of initiation: Baptism, Confirmation, and Eucharist. As a result, the psalm used to be sung during the Easter Vigil by the newly baptized, who were filled with the joy of God.

In praying this psalm, we can dwell on the fact that the heavenly Father's love embraces us from eternity, preparing for us in Christ all kinds of spiritual blessings: election, adoption, redemption, incorporation into Christ (see Eph 1:3-14). He watches over us solicitously (see Mt 6:25-34) and follows us through the Good Shepherd who seeks out the straying sheep until he finds it again (see Lk 15).

23:2 *Green pastures:* a symbol for everything that makes life flourish. *Tranquil streams:* literally, "waters of resting places," waters that bring refreshment and well-being (see Isa 49:10).

23:3 *Restores my soul:* the Lord revitalizes the psalmist's spirit (see Ps 19:8; Ru 4:15; Prov 25:13; Lam 1:16). *Paths of righteousness:* paths that conform to the will of the Lord, the "right way."

23:4 *Valley of the shadow of death:* another possible translation is: "through the darkest valley." It refers to any situation that is death-threatening.

23:5-6 What was only a comparison used by the psalmist to indicate the happiness of those who dwell in the house of the Lord has become a wonderful reality in the New Covenant. God sets the table for all who as members of his Church seek rest and protection in the house of God during their pilgrimage. He gives them the Bread of Heaven and the cup of his love and the riches of his grace—Christ's Precious Blood and the anointing of the Spirit with his sevenfold gifts.

23:5 In the ancient Near East, covenants were frequently made at a meal (see Ps 41:10; Gen 31:54; Ob 7). *Anoint my head with oil:* reception customarily accorded to an honored guest at a banquet (see Lk 7:46; see also 2 Sam 12:20; Eccl 9:8; Dan 10:3). *Cup:* the same image is found in Pss 16:5; 75:9; 116:13. This verse indicates that the Messianic Banquet (see Ps 22:27) is reserved for the righteous; the wicked are excluded from it (see Isa 65:13f).

23:6 *Goodness and kindness:* the terms often refer to blessings of God's covenant with Israel; here they are personified (see Pss 25:21; 43:3; 79:8; 89:14). *Days of my life:* see Pss 27:4; 128:5. *Forever:* this word could mean "throughout the years." However, since even the pagan people surrounding Israel believed that human life continued after death in some kind of shadowy existence in the netherworld (see notes on Pss 11:7; 16:9-11), the word "forever" legitimately can be taken in its true sense.

Ps 24 A procession wends its way toward the temple; perhaps it bears the Ark of the Covenant to the holy place. Chants are expressed. They acclaim the Creator and thus recall the conditions for a true participation in worship: "clean hands and a pure heart" (vv. 3-6). At the entrance to the sanctuary, the cortege comes to a halt as the participants take time to meditate wonderingly about the presence of God. They must needs celebrate God the Vanquisher who takes possession of his holy dwelling; the titles given him (vv. 8-10) evoke the time when, represented by the Ark, the Lord would take his place at the head of the armies of Israel and lead them to victory (Num 10:35; Jos 6).

This psalm is well adapted to celebrating feasts of the Lord and to calling for the coming of his kingdom. It is also a psalm that makes demands, since it tells us of the conditions required for receiving the kingdom of God. The Church has always used this psalm in celebrating Christ's Ascension into the heavenly Jerusalem and into the sanctuary on high.

24:1-2 The Lord is proclaimed as the Creator, Sustainer, and Owner of the entire world. Therefore, he is worthy of the title "King of glory" (vv. 7-10). See Pss 29; 33:6-11; 89:6-19; 95:3-5; 104.

24:1 See Ps 89:12; Deut 10:14. This text is cited in 1 Cor 10:26.

2 For he founded it on the seas
and established * it on the rivers. [u]

3 Who may ascend the mountain of the LORD?
Who may stand in his holy place? [v]

4 One who has clean hands and a pure heart, *
who does not turn his mind to vanities
or swear an oath in order to deceive.

5 He will receive a blessing from the LORD
and vindication from God, his Savior.

6 This is the generation of those who seek him,
who seek the face of the God of Jacob. *Selah*

7 * Lift up your arches, O gates;
rise up, you ancient portals, *
so that the King of glory may come in. [w]

8 Who is this King of glory?
The LORD, strong and mighty,
the LORD, valiant in battle.

9 Lift up your arches, O gates,
rise up, you ancient portals,
so that the King of glory may come in.

10 Who is this King of glory?
The LORD of hosts: *
he is the King of glory. *Selah*

PSALM 25*

Prayer for Guidance and Help

1 * Of David.

To you, O LORD, I lift up my soul; [x]

2 in you, O my God, I trust. [y]
Do not let me be put to shame,
or permit my enemies to gloat over me.

3 No one who places his hope in you
will ever be put to shame,
but shame will be the lot of all
who break faith without justification. [z]

4 * Make your ways known to me, O LORD;
teach me your paths. [a]

5 Guide me in your truth and instruct me,
for you are God, my Savior,
and in you I hope all the day long.

6 Be mindful, O LORD, that mercy and kindness
have been yours from of old. [b]

7 Remember not the sins of my youth
or my many transgressions,
but remember me in your kindness,
for the sake of your goodness, O LORD. [c]

8 * Good and upright is the LORD;
therefore, he instructs sinners in his ways.

9 He guides the humble in what is right
and teaches them the path to follow.

10 The ways of the LORD * are kindness and truth
for those who keep his covenant and his decrees.

11 For the sake of your name, * O LORD,
pardon my iniquity, great though it be.

u Pss 75:4; 136:6; Gen 1:6; Isa 42:5.—v Pss 2:6; 15:1; 65:5.—w Ps 118:19-20; Ezek 44:2; Mal 3:1.—x Pss 86:4; 143:8.—y Ps 71:1.—z Ps 22:6; Isa 24:16; 49:23; Dan 3:40; 2 Tim 3:4-5.—a Pss 27:11; 86:11; 119:12, 35; 143:8, 10; Ex 33:13; Jn 14:6.—b Ps 98:3; Sir 51:8; Isa 63:7.—c Ps 106:4; Job 13:26; Isa 64:8.

24:2 *Founded . . . established:* a metaphor taken from the founding of a city. Extra-biblical records indicate that temples were regarded as microcosms of the created world; hence language applicable to temples was also applicable to the earth.

24:4 *Clean hands . . . pure heart:* those who do no evil and think no evil. Jesus said that the "pure of heart ... will see God" (Mt 5:8).

24:7-10 These verses speak of the arrival of the Lord, the King of glory, at his sanctuary in Zion after his victorious journey from Egypt. *The LORD of hosts* (v. 10), *the LORD, valiant in battle* (v. 8; see Ex 15:1-18), has routed his enemies and now comes in triumph to his own city (see Pss 46; 48; 76; 87).

24:7, 9 *Lift up your arches, O gates . . . you ancient portals:* the gates and doors are personified in accord with extra-biblical parallels.

24:10 *The LORD of hosts:* in Hebrew, *Yahweh Sabaoth*, sometimes translated as "the Lord of armies." The expression suggests, first of all, the God who leads the Israelite army, therefore the Almighty who is surrounded by angels and stars and who controls the cosmic forces; then the expression becomes simply a way of emphasizing the greatness and power of God. See also note on Ps 59:6.

Ps 25 One admires the inner quality of the righteous man who addresses himself to God in this alphabetical psalm. He does not believe that he is totally innocent. He takes false steps and deserves his wretchedness and his isolation because of his sins. His confession testifies to much uprightness and honesty. It is the attitude of a humble person who knows he is loved by God and trusts in him; he hopes to receive pardon, counsel, and assistance from the Lord. The theme of this beautiful prayer is given in the cry of hope in verses 1-2, which the Liturgy puts on the lips of Christians at the beginning of Advent.

In praying this psalm, we can dwell on the fact that in his unfailing love God is pleased to lead us back to the right path when we go astray and to keep us on it. Christ gives us salvation through the remission of sins (see Lk 1:77-79).

25:1-3 Prayer for relief from distress and the ensuing slander from one's foes.

25:4-7 Prayer for guidance and pardon. *Your ways:* that is, "your commandments" (see Pss 27:11; 86:11; 128:1; 143:8). *Kindness:* see note on Ps 6:5.

25:8-15 Trust in the Lord's covenant blessings.

25:10 *Ways of the LORD:* God's manner of dealing kindly with those who remain faithful to the covenant (see Pss 103:7; 138:5). See also Ps 85:10; Gen 32:10; Deut 33:9; and Paul's magnificent summary in Rom 8:28: "We know that God makes all things work together for good for those who love him."

25:11 *Name:* see note on Ps 5:12.

12 Who, then, is the man that fears the LORD? [d]
He will be shown the path he should choose. *
13 He will enjoy lasting prosperity, [e]
and his descendants will inherit the land. *
14 The LORD manifests himself to those who fear him, *
and he makes his covenant known to them.
15 My eyes are ever upon the LORD,
for he alone can free my feet from the snare. [f]

16 * Turn to me and have mercy on me,
for I am alone and afflicted. [g]
17 Relieve the anguish of my heart *
and free me from my distress.
18 Look upon my affliction and suffering,
and forgive all my sins.
19 Consider how numerous are my enemies,
and how fierce is their hatred of me.
20 Preserve my life and deliver me;
do not let me be put to shame,
for I seek refuge in you.
21 Let integrity and virtue preserve me,
for in you I place my hope.
22 Redeem* Israel, O God,
from all its troubles.

PSALM 26*

Prayer for the Righteous

1 Of David.

O LORD, come to my defense,
for I have lived a blameless life.
I have placed my trust in the LORD,
and never have I wavered in that regard. [h]
2 Test me, O LORD, and try me;
probe my heart and my mind. [i]
3 For your kindness * is before my eyes,
and I am constantly guided by your truth. [j]
4 I do not sit in the company of deceivers,
nor do I associate with hypocrites.
5 I abhor the assembly of the wicked,
and I refuse to associate with evildoers.
6 I wash my hands in innocence *
and join the procession around your altar, O LORD, [k]
7 giving voice to your praises
and proclaiming all your wondrous deeds. *
8 I love the house where you dwell, O LORD, [l]
the place where your glory resides. *
9 Do not sweep my soul away with sinners,
nor my life with those who thirst for blood, * [m]

d Ps 128:1; Job 1:8; Prov 19:23.—e Ps 37:9, 29; Isa 57:13; Mt 5:5.—f Pss 123:2; 141:8; 2 Chr 20:12; Heb 12:2.—g Pss 6:5; 86:16; 119:132; Num 6:25.—h Pss 15:2; 59:3; Heb 10:23.—i Pss 7:10; 17:3; 139:23; Jer 20:12.—j Pss 43:3; 86:11; 119:30.—k Ps 73:13; Deut 21:6-7; Mal 3:14; Mt 27:4.—l Pss 29:9; 63:3; 96:6; Ex 24:16; 25:8: 2 Chr 7:1; Isa 66:10.—m Pss 5:6; 28:3; 139:19.

25:12 *The path he should choose:* or "the path chosen for him."

25:13 *Inherit the land:* according to the teaching of the sages, God rewards the righteous here below by bestowing on them earthly goods that he withholds from the wicked (see Ps 37:9, 29; Prov 19:23). To this is added the returned exiles' hope for the enjoyment of the land of their ancestors (see Isa 57:13; 60:21; 65:9).

25:14 *The LORD manifests himself to those who fear him:* some translations have "The LORD manifests his secret to those who fear him," which is to be understood as divine intimacy and friendship (see Ps 73:28; Ex 33:11; Job 29:4; Prov 3:32; Jn 15:5) united with the understanding of divine things (see Jer 16:21; 31:34; Hos 6:6).

25:16-21 Renewed prayer for relief from distress and foes.

25:17 *Heart:* see note on Ps 4:8.

25:22 Concluding prayer on behalf of all God's people. *Redeem:* i.e., "deliver."

Ps 26 This psalm is a prayer for God's discerning mercies to spare his faithful servant from the death that overtakes the wicked. In the psalms of supplication, we often hear this protestation from those accused who call upon God to bear witness to their innocence. The prayer that we now read is perhaps that of a Levite, but certainly of a man who loves the life of the temple. He is very sure of his rectitude in the face of others' accusations. Possibly he is also quite conscious of the faults that everyone has in his life. He teaches us a great certainty: it is better to throw ourselves upon the judgment of God than to let ourselves be crushed by the judgment of others. This believer, who is at ease to praise the Lord in the temple, loves a clear and decided fidelity. Who would fail to be attracted by such a desire for uprightness and sincerity before God!

In praying this psalm, we can recall that since we share by faith and Baptism in the mystery of Christ dead and risen, our old self has been crucified with Christ so that the sinful body might be destroyed and we might cease to be enslaved by sin. Divested of our old nature and invested with the new nature of Christ who becomes all in all (see Col 3:9-11), we share in his holiness and irreproachable innocence before God, being purified from all injustice (see Rom 8:1; 1 Jn 1:9).

26:3 *Kindness:* see note on Ps 6:5.

26:6 *Wash my hands in innocence:* a liturgical action (see Ex 30:19, 21; 40:31f), which symbolized both inner and outer cleanliness (see Isa 1:16). Those who come to God must have "clean hands and a pure heart" (Ps 24:4). *Around your altar:* celebrating God's saving acts beside his altar was regarded as a public act of devotion in which assembled worshipers could be invited to participate (see Ps 43:5).

26:7 *Proclaiming . . . wondrous deeds:* see note on Ps 9:2.

26:8 *Where your glory resides:* the presence of God's glory meant the presence of God himself (see Ex 24:16; 33:22). His glory dwelt in the tabernacle (see Ex 40:35) and later in the temple (see 1 Ki 8:11). John 1:14 places that same presence in the Word made flesh who "dwelt among us."

26:9 A premature death was a divine chastisement (see Pss 5:7; 28:4; 55:24).

10 whose hands carry out evil schemes,
and whose right hands are full of bribes.
11 Rather, I choose to walk in innocence;[n]
redeem me and be merciful to me.[o]
12 My feet stand on level ground; *
in the full assembly I will bless the LORD.[p]

PSALM 27*

Trust in God, Our Light and Salvation

1 Of David.

The LORD is my light * and my salvation;
whom should I fear?
The LORD is the stronghold of my life;
of whom should I be afraid?[q]

2 When evildoers close in on me
to devour my flesh, *
it is they, my adversaries and enemies,
who stumble and fall.[r]
3 Even if an army encamps against me,
my heart * will not succumb to fear;
even if war breaks out against me,
I will not have my trust shaken.

4 There is only one thing I ask of the LORD,
just one thing I seek:
to dwell in the house of the LORD
all the days of my life,[s]
so that I may enjoy the beauty of the LORD *
and gaze on his temple.

5 For he will hide me in his shelter
in times of trouble.
He will conceal me under the cover of his tent *
and place me high upon a rock.[t]
6 Even now my head is raised high
above my enemies who surround me.
In his tent I will offer sacrifices * with joyous shouts;
I will sing and chant praise to the LORD.

7 O LORD, hear my voice when I cry out;
be merciful to me and answer me.
8 My heart * says of you,
"Seek his face."

It is your face, O LORD, that I seek;[u]
9 do not hide your face * from me.
Do not turn away your servant in anger,
you who have been my help.

Do not reject or forsake me,
O God, my Savior.
10 Even if my father and mother abandon me,[v]
the LORD will gather me up. *

11 Teach me your way,* O LORD,
and lead me along a level path
because of my enemies.[w]
12 Do not abandon me to the will of my adversaries,
for lying witnesses have risen against me,
breathing forth violence in their malice.

n Pss 73:13; 101:6.—o Pss 25:16; 31:6; 69:19; Jn 1:16.—p Pss 22:23; 35:18; 40:10; 52:11; 143:10; 149:1.—q Pss 9:10; 18:29; 36:10; 43:3; 56:5; Ex 15:2; 2 Sam 22:29; Isa 10:17; Mic 7:8.—r Pss 9:4; 14:4; Job 19:22; Rom 11:11.—s Pss 23:6; 42:3; 61:5; Lk 10:42.—t Pss 12:8; 17:8; 31:21; 40:3; Rev 7:15-16.—u Pss 24:6; 105:4; Hos 5:15.—v Isa 49:15; Jer 31:20; Hos 11:8.—w Pss 5:9; 25:4; 72:4; 86:11.

26:12 *Level ground:* where there is safety and no danger of falling. *Assembly:* worshiping at the sanctuary (as in Pss 1:5; 22:26; 35:18; 40:10f; 111:1; 149:1).

Ps 27 Although enemies or the difficulties of existence may be multiplied, the believer finds a sure refuge in God—such is the cry of trust that opens this psalm. Then the movement of the prayer deepens, becoming the search and avid desire for God. It is in the temple that one discovers the presence of the Lord in the sacrifice, chant, supplication, and the law. If such a search becomes necessary for life, will not God be present to his most forsaken and pressured servant?

In praying this psalm, we can place a similar confidence in God and the Lord Jesus, one capable of enabling us to overcome all adversity and death itself.

27:1 *The LORD is my light:* "light" often symbolizes happiness and well-being (see Pss 18:29; 36:10; 43:3; 97:11) or life and salvation (see Isa 9:2; 49:6; 58:8; Jer 13:16; Am 5:18-20), whose source is the Lord (see Isa 10:17; Mic 7:8f).

27:2 *To devour my flesh:* the psalmist's enemies are like rapacious beasts (see Pss 7:3; 17:12; 22:13f, 17); in the figurative sense, this refers to calumny (see Dan 3:8).

27:3 With the Lord as his stronghold and helper, the psalmist fears nothing—not even an army arrayed against him. So long as this strong union with God remains unbroken, the psalmist is secure. *Heart:* see note on Ps 4:8.

27:4 Tarrying in the house of the Lord is an expression and sign of spiritual union with God and intimacy with him. *Beauty of the LORD:* i.e., his goodness (see Ps 90:17).

27:5 *Shelter . . . tent:* references to the sanctuary of Jerusalem (see Rev 7:15f). See also Pss 31:21; 32:7; 61:5; 91:1.

27:6 *I will offer sacrifices:* see note on Ps 7:18.

27:8, 14 *Heart:* see note on Ps 4:8. *Seek his face:* an idiom meaning to commune with the Lord, originating in the custom of pilgrimages to sacred places (see Pss 24:6; 105:4; 2 Sam 21:1; Hos 5:15). It then took on the general sense of seeking to know the Lord, anticipate his desires, and live in his presence. In a word, to seek the Lord is to serve him faithfully (Deut 4:29-31).

27:9 *Hide your face:* see note on Ps 13:2.

27:10 Union with God gives confidence in prayer; and prayer is something that even the most devout person must do. Sirach says: "Pray in [the LORD's] presence" (17:25) and "Let nothing hinder you from promptly discharging your vows [i.e., your prayer]" (18:22).

27:11 *Your way:* God's manner of dealing kindly with those who remain faithful to the covenant by keeping his commandments (see Pss 86:11; 128:1; 143:8).

13 I am confident that I will behold the goodness of the LORD *
in the land of the living. [x]
14 Place your hope in the LORD:
be strong and courageous in your heart,
and place your hope in the LORD.

PSALM 28*

Thanksgiving for Supplications Heard

1 Of David.

To you I call out, O LORD, my Rock; *
do not turn a deaf ear to my cry. [y]
For if you remain silent,
I will be like those who go down to the pit. [z]
2 Hear my voice in supplication
as I plead for your help,
as I lift up my hands *
toward your Most Holy Place. [a]
3 Do not snatch me away with the wicked, [b]
with those whose deeds are evil,
who talk of peace to their neighbors
while treachery is in their hearts. * [c]
4 * Repay them as their deeds deserve
in accordance with the evil they inflict;
repay them for the works of their hands
and heap upon them what they justly deserve. [d]
5 Since they have paid no heed to the deeds of the LORD
or to the works of his hands,
he will strike them down
and refuse to restore them. [e]
6 Blessed * be the LORD,
for he has heard my cry of supplication.
7 The LORD is my strength and my shield;
my heart * places its trust in him.
He has helped me, and I exult;
then with my song I praise him.
8 The LORD is the strength of his people,
the refuge where his anointed one * finds salvation.
9 Save your people and bless your heritage;
be their shepherd * and sustain them forever.

PSALM 29*

God's Majesty in the Storm

1 A psalm of David.

Ascribe to the LORD, O mighty ones, *
ascribe to the LORD glory and might.

---

x Pss 31:19; 116:9; 142:6; 145:6; Isa 38:11.—y Ps 18:3; Prov 28:9.—z Pss 30:4; 88:5; 143:7; Deut 1:45; Prov 1:12; Jon 2:7.—a Pss 5:8; 134:2; 141:2; 1 Ki 8:48.—b Pss 26:9; 55:24; 139:19.—c Pss 12:3; 55:22; 62:5; Prov 26:24-28; Isa 1:15; 59:3-4; Jer 9:7.—d 2 Sam 3:39; Isa 3:11; Jer 50:29; 2 Tim 4:14; Rev 18:6; 22:12.—e Isa 5:12; 52:5; Am 6:5f.

27:13 *Goodness of the LORD:* the good things promised in the covenant with David (see 2 Sam 7:28). *Land of the living:* reference to this life or to the temple (see Pss 52:7; 116:9; Isa 38:11), where the God of life is present; the psalmist is speaking of the world of the living as opposed to the world of the dead.

Ps 28 The psalmist calls upon God and curses his persecutors; such vehemence indicates that he is close to the end of his strength. Deaf for a time, the Lord finally hears his servant; after anguish here is the thanksgiving. The concluding formula transforms the psalm into a prayer for Israel, the "anointed one," that is, the people consecrated (v. 8) to the service of God. Believers will one day refuse the sentiments of vengeance that spring up here from the experience of the oppressed psalmist; for God could not indistinctly combine honesty with wrongdoing.

In praying this psalm, we should keep in mind that in this life Christ does not normally answer our desire for escape or special privilege. He sends us out and immerses us in the world and its tribulations (see Jn 15:18—16:4; 17:18) after his election has drawn us out of it (see Jn 15:19). Yet we already foresee victory, for the same divine power that raised Christ from the dead will raise us also and lead our humanity into a state of glory (see Eph 1:17-20).

28:1 *Rock:* the Lord is the Rock, who gives strength and sustenance to his people and provides refuge for them (see Ps 18:3 and note). *Pit:* metaphor for the grave.

28:2 *Lift up my hands:* the usual posture for prayer (see Pss 63:5; 134:2; 141:2). *Most Holy Place:* the innermost part of the temple, the Holy of Holies, which contained the Ark of the Covenant and was looked upon as the place of God's presence on earth (see 1 Ki 6:16, 19-23; 8:6-8).

28:3 The psalmist prays that the Lord will deliver him from his adversities (see Ps 26:9-12) so that he will not be numbered with the wicked nor judged with them. *Hearts:* see note on Ps 4:8.

28:4-5 The wicked have not learned to respond to the Lord and his wondrous deeds in redemptive history (*the works of his hands*). Therefore, they will be judged according to *the works of their hands*. Justice requires that evil be removed so that its power will be completely voided. See notes on Pss 5:11; 35.

28:6 The psalmist gives praise to the Lord for having heard his prayer; this will result in righteous judgment and vindication. *Blessed:* see note on Ps 18:47.

28:7 No longer does the psalmist feel threatened to the point of despairing. He is overjoyed and jubilant because he knows that the Lord will come to his aid as his strength (see Ex 15:2) and his shield (see Ps 3:4). *Heart:* see note on Ps 4:8. *With my song I praise him:* see note on Ps 7:18.

28:8 *Anointed one:* here the reference seems to be to the entire people of God, which is consecrated to his service (see Ps 105:15; Ex 19:6; Hab 3:13). See also note on Ps 2:2.

28:9 *Be their shepherd:* a theme found also in Ps 80:2; Isa 40:11; Jer 31:10; Ezek 34; Mic 5:4. The Lord answered this prayer by sending the Good Shepherd, Jesus Christ (Jn 10:11, 14), who died for his sheep.

Ps 29 The psalmist sings a hymn of praise to the Lord, the King of creation, evoking his power and glory in the storm that terrifies the foes of Israel, while sparing the chosen people. He concludes by asking the Lord to give similar power to the king and to Israel.

We can pray this psalm in the knowledge that the voice of God has acquired a body in Christ Jesus, living Word of the Father. It calls upon all who are in heaven, on earth, and in the netherworld to attribute to Christ all glory and power, and to adore him alone.

29:1 *Mighty ones:* literally, "sons of God," which in the beginning probably referred to the pagan deities but later came to be understood as referring to the angels (see Pss 82:1; 89:7; Job 1:6). To eliminate the polytheistic meaning of the expression, the Septuagint and Vulgate added immediately after "mighty ones" the line "bring to the LORD the offspring of rams." This passage is sometimes applied to Israel, the son of God (see Ex 4:22; Deut 14:1; Acts 17:28).

2 Ascribe to the LORD the glory due to his name; *
worship the LORD in the splendor of his holiness.[f]

3[g] The voice of the LORD * echoes over the waters;
the God of glory thunders,
the LORD thunders over mighty waters.
4 The voice of the LORD is powerful;
the voice of the LORD is filled with majesty.

5 The voice of the LORD shatters the cedars;
the LORD shatters the cedars of Lebanon. *
6 He makes Lebanon skip like a calf,
and Sirion * like a young wild ox.

7 The voice of the LORD flashes forth
with bolts of lightning.
8 The voice of the LORD shakes the wilderness;
the LORD shakes the wilderness of Kadesh. *
9 The voice of the LORD batters the oaks
and strips the forests bare,
while in his temple all cry out, "Glory!" *

10 The LORD sits enthroned above the flood; *
the LORD is enthroned as king forever. [h]

11 May the LORD grant strength to his people.
May the LORD bless his people with peace. [i]

PSALM 30*

Thanksgiving for Deliverance from Death

1 A psalm. A song for the dedication of the temple. Of David.

2 I will exalt you, O LORD,
for you have raised me out of the depths *
and have not let my enemies exult over me.
3 O LORD, my God,
I called to you and you healed me. *
4 O LORD, you lifted me up from the netherworld; *
you saved me from sinking into the pit.[j]

5 Sing praise to the LORD, O you his saints; *
give thanks to his holy name.
6 For his anger lasts for only a moment,
while his goodwill endures for a lifetime.
Weeping may last throughout the night, *
but at daybreak there is rejoicing.

7 In time of good fortune, I said,
"Nothing can ever sway me." *

f Pss 68:35; 96:7-9; Deut 7:21; 1 Chr 16:29.—g 3-4: Pss 18:14; 46:7; 68:33; 77:19-20; 104:7; Ex 15:10; Job 37:4; Isa 30:30; Ezek 10:5.—h Gen 6–9; Isa 54:9; Bar 3:3.—i Pss 18:2-3; 28:8; 68:36; Isa 40:29; 41:10; 50:2; Dan 7:27.—j Ps 28:1; Num 16:33; 1 Sam 2:6; Jon 2:7.

29:2 *Name:* see note on Ps 5:12. *In the splendor of his holiness:* it probably refers to the priestly garments to be worn in the liturgy (see Ps 110:3), although it may also refer to God or to the sanctuary.

29:3 *The voice of the LORD:* this phrase appears seven times in imitation of the sound of thunder and symbolizes the power of God, the Lord of history as well as the Master of the elements, whose voice no one can resist (see Job 37:4f; Ezek 10:5).

29:5 *The cedars of Lebanon:* i.e., the strongest of all trees (see Isa 2:13).

29:6 *Sirion:* a Phoenician name for Mount Hermon in northern Palestine. The mountains there were originally given the general name of Lebanon.

29:8 *The wilderness of Kadesh:* probably a border location in southern Palestine; some believe it is a location north of Palestine near Lebanon and Mount Hermon.

29:9 The cry of *Glory!* takes place either in heaven (v. 2) or in the temple of Jerusalem whose liturgy echoes the heavenly praises.

29:10 *Enthroned above the flood:* a reference to God's control of the unruly primordial waters (see Gen 1:2, 6-10) or to his sending of the flood (see Gen 6:17), which was the first manifestation of the divine justice. Thus, the Lord will know how to make the cause of his people triumph (see Job 20:28; 22:16; Isa 24:18; 59:9ff).

Ps 30 This is a psalm of thanksgiving arising out of the experience of someone who was at death's door because of an illness, compounded by feelings of haughtiness in time of prosperity and despair in times of humiliation. The Lord listened to his cry and healed him; hence the psalmist calls for praise. This psalm came to be applied to Israel itself, especially in its experience of the Exile, and was chanted at the Feast of the Dedication of the Temple in commemoration of the purification of the temple in 164 B.C. (see Ezr 6:16; 1 Mac 4:36ff).

This psalm reminds us that while we await life eternal and union with Christ, the present life with its adversities offers us the opportunity to receive from the divine goodness a cure, various deliverances, and even spiritual resurrection.

30:2 *Out of the depths:* a common Old Testament phrase of extreme distress (see Pss 69:3, 16; 71:20; 88:6; 130:1; Lam 3:55; Jon 2:2) usually connected with the words "the grave" and "the pit."

30:3 *You healed me:* other passages that proclaim God as a healer are: Pss 103:3; 107:20; Hos 6:1; 7:1; 11:3; 14:5.

30:4 *Netherworld:* symbol for a life-threatening experience (see Ps 18:6; Jon 2:2). *Pit:* metaphor for the grave.

30:5 *Saints:* see note on Ps 16:3. *Name:* see note on Ps 5:12.

30:6 *Last throughout the night:* literally, "come in at evening to lodge," like a guest seeking a night's rest.

30:7 *In time of good fortune, I said, "Nothing can ever sway me":* security brings forgetfulness of God (see Deut 8:8-10; Hos 13:6; Prov 30:9). The secure psalmist spoke similar words to those of the wicked in Ps 10:6 and so lost the blessing promised to the righteous (see Ps 15:5).

8 O LORD, in your goodness
you established me as an impregnable mountain;
however, when you hid your face,
I was filled with terror. [k]

9 * To you, O LORD, I cried out,
and I implored my God for mercy:
10 "What advantage would my death provide
if I descend into the pit?
Can the dust praise you?
Can it proclaim your faithfulness?
11 Listen, O LORD, and have mercy on me;
O LORD, be my helper."

12 You have turned my mourning into dancing;
you have taken away my sackcloth *
and clothed me with joy. [l]
13 My heart * will therefore sing
in unceasing praise to you;
O LORD, my God,
I will praise you forever.

PSALM 31*

Prayer of Trust and Thanksgiving

1 For the director. * A psalm of David.

2 * [m] In you, O LORD, I have taken refuge;
let me never be put to shame;
in your righteousness deliver me.
3 Turn your ear to me,
and act quickly to save me.
Be to me a rock * of refuge,
a strong fortress to save me.

4 You are truly my rock and my fortress;
for the sake of your name, * lead and guide me. [n]
5 Deliver me from the snare that has been set for me,
for you are my refuge.
6 Into your hands I commend my spirit; *
you will redeem me, O LORD, God of truth. [o]

7 You hate those who cling to false idols,
but I put my trust in the LORD.
8 I will rejoice and exult in your kindness *
because you have witnessed my affliction
and have taken note of my anguish. [p]
9 You have not abandoned me into the power of the enemy;
rather, you have set my feet in the open.

10 * Have mercy on me, O LORD,
for I am in trouble.
My weeping is laying waste to my eyes
as well as my soul * and my body.
11 My life is consumed with sorrow
and my years with sighing.
My strength ebbs because of my misery,
and my bones are wasting away. [q]

12 I am an object of scorn
to all my enemies,
a loathsome sight to my neighbors,
and an object of dread to my friends.
When people catch sight of me outside,
they quickly turn away. [r]

13 I have passed out of their minds
like someone who has died;
I have become like a broken vessel. *
14 I have heard the hissing of many:
"There is terror on every side," *
as they conspire together against me
and plot to end my life.

15 But I place my trust in you, O LORD.
I say, "You are my God." [s]

k Ps 104:29; Deut 31:17.—l Ps 126:1-2; Est 9:22; Isa 61:3; Jer 31:13.—m 2-4: Pss 18:3; 71:1-2.—n Pss 9:9; 18:3; 71:3.—o Isa 45:19; Lk 23:46; Acts 7:59.—p Pss 10:14; 13:4; Lk 22:44.—q Pss 6:3; 32:3; 38:11; 73:26.—r Pss 25:19; 38:12; Job 19:13-19.—s Pss 4:6; 140:7; Isa 25:1.

30:9-11 In the stillness and inactivity of the pit, no one gives praise to God; the psalmist prays to be delivered so that he may rejoin those who worship the Lord (see Pss 6:6; 88:11-13; 115:17; Isa 38:18).

30:12 *Sackcloth:* a symbol of mourning (see Ps 35:13; Gen 37:34).

30:13 *Heart:* see note on Ps 4:8.

Ps 31 Faith, distress, and gratitude alternate in this prayer, evoking the "confessions" of the prophet Jeremiah, his dolorous destiny, and his intimacy with the Lord (Jer 17:14-18; 20:7-18). At the moment of death on the cross, Jesus will use this psalm to express his trusting abandonment to the Father (see Lk 23:46).

We should be mindful that God will often place us in a situation in which we can unite our voice to that of Christ in reciting this psalm, especially by letting us share his sufferings and making us become like him in death so that we may rise with him from the dead (see Phil 3:10f).

31:1 *For the director:* these words are thought to be a musical or liturgical notation.

31:2-9 No matter what may be the conflict in which we are enmeshed, God remains the one certitude. The images of the rock and the fortress attest to a serene and unshakable trust in God.

31:3 *Rock:* see note on Ps 18:3.

31:4 *Name:* see note on Ps 5:12.

31:6 *Into your hands I commend my spirit:* last words of Christ on the cross (see Lk 23:46) and St. Stephen (see Acts 7:59). *Spirit:* life itself.

31:8, 17, 22 *Kindness:* see note on Ps 6:5.

31:10-19 The prayer changes tone; after serenity comes a gasping cry. The stricken person is also one who is despised and rejected, an object of utter contempt by others. This is the despairing cry at times when we seem completely alone.

31:10 *Soul:* see note on Ps 6:4.

31:13 *Like a broken vessel:* a customary comparison for something that has been rendered useless (see Isa 30:14; Jer 19:11; 22:28).

31:14 *There is terror on every side:* a cry used when danger lurks (see Jer 6:25; 20:10; 46:5; 49:29).

16 My life is in your hands; *
deliver me from the power of my enemies,
from the clutches of those who pursue me.
17 Let your face shine * upon your servant;
save me in your kindness. [t]

18 * Do not let me be put to shame, O LORD,
for I have cried out to you.
Let the wicked be put to shame
and lie silent in the netherworld.
19 Let their lying lips be struck dumb,
lips that speak insolently against the righteous
with pride and contempt. [u]

20 * How great is your goodness, O LORD,
which you have stored up * for those who fear you
and which you bestow on those who take refuge in you,
in the presence of all the people.
21 You hide them in the safety of your presence
from those who conspire against them;
you keep them safe in your shelter,
far away from contentious tongues. [v]

22 Blessed * be the LORD,
for he has manifested his wondrous kindness to me
when I was under siege.
23 I had cried out in terror, [w]
"I have been cut off from your sight."
But you heard my plea
when I cried out to you for assistance.

24 Love the LORD, all his saints. *
The LORD protects his loyal servants,
but the arrogant he repays beyond measure.
25 Be strong and courageous in your hearts,
all you who place your hope in the LORD.

PSALM 32*

The Joy of Being Forgiven

1 Of David. A *maskil.* *
* Blessed is the one whose offense is forgiven,
whose sin is erased. [x]
2 Blessed is the one to whom the LORD charges no guilt
and in whose spirit there is no guile.

3 As long as I remained silent, *
my body wasted away
as the result of my groaning throughout the day. [y]
4 For day and night
your hand was heavy upon me;
my strength withered steadily
as though consumed by the summer heat. * *Selah*

5 Then I acknowledged my sin to you,
and I made no attempt to conceal my guilt.
I said, "I will confess my offenses * to the LORD,"
and you removed the guilt of my sin. [z]
Selah

t Pss 4:7; 67:2; Num 6:25.—u Pss 12:4; 120:2.—v Pss 27:5; 109:3; Rev 7:15.—w Ps 116:11; Jon 2:4.—x Ps 65:4; Prov 28:13; Isa 1:18; Hos 14:2; Rom 4:7-8.—y Pss 6:7; 31:11.—z Pss 38:19; 51:5; Job 31:33.

31:16 *My life is in your hands:* God is the ultimate master of every moment of everyone's life.

31:17 *Face shine:* see note on Ps 13:2.

31:18-19 See notes on Pss 5:11; 35.

31:20-25 A moment arrives when the believer experiences anew the power of God's presence. This holds good despite the mockery and false accusations of enemies, that is, the war of words that constitutes one of the greatest trials of our human relationships. Certain of God, the believer does not let himself become enmeshed in conflicts.

31:20 *Stored up:* the psalmist relies on the Lord who has stored up his goodness (his covenant promises) for his faithful ones.

31:22 *Blessed:* see note on Ps 18:47. *Kindness:* see note on Ps 4:8.

31:24 *Saints:* see notes on Pss 4:4; 16:3; and 34:10. *The arrogant:* often equal to the wicked, for the arrogant act as if they have no need of God and are a law to themselves (see Pss 10:2-11; 73:6; 94:2-7; Deut 8:14; Isa 2:17; Ezek 28:2, 5; Hos 13:6).

Ps 32 This is the second of the seven Penitential Psalms (6; 32; 38; 51; 102; 130; 143), a joyous testimony of gratitude for God's gift of forgiveness for those who confess their sins and follow the law of God. Instead of constantly pondering their sins, believers acknowledge their wretchedness before God and accept forgiveness and reconciliation. Their torment ceases, and a new person is born, overwhelmed by grace, confidence, and a sense of obedience.

In praying this psalm, we can focus not only on the happiness resulting from the forgiveness of particular sin but also on the more profound happiness obtained by the complete victory given us by God in Christ over sin under all its forms.

32:1a *Maskil:* this term cannot be given a precise translation; perhaps it means "teaching" or "training."

32:1b-2 Joyous declaration of the happiness of having one's sins forgiven by God (see Pss 65:5; 85:2; Job 31:33). This text is cited by Paul in Rom 4:7-8. *Blessed:* see note on Ps 1:1.

32:3 *I remained silent:* did not confess the sin before God. *Body:* literally, "bones."

32:4 According to St. Augustine, even before penitents acknowledge their sin, God hears the cry of their heart and pardons it because of their true contrition (see 2 Sam 12:13).

32:5 *Sin . . . guilt . . . offenses:* these are the three most common Hebrew words for evil thoughts and actions (see Ps 51:3-4; Isa 59:12).

6 Therefore, let everyone who is faithful pray to you
where you may be found. *
Even if great floods threaten, [a]
they will never reach him.
7 You are a place of refuge for me;
you preserve me from trouble
and surround me with songs of deliverance. * *Selah*
8 I will instruct you
and guide you in the way you should go;
I will counsel you
and keep my eyes upon you.
9 Do not behave without understanding
like a horse or a mule;
if its temper is not curbed with bit and bridle,
it will not come near you.
10 The wicked has a multitude of troubles,
but the man who trusts in the LORD
is surrounded by kindness. *
11 Be glad in the LORD and rejoice, you righteous;
shout for joy, all you upright of heart. * [b]

PSALM 33*

Praise of God's Providence

1 Rejoice in the LORD, you righteous;
it is fitting for the upright to praise him. [c]
2 Give thanks to the LORD on the harp;
offer praise to him on the ten-stringed lyre. [d]
3 Sing to him a new song; *
play skillfully on the strings with joyful shouts.
4 * For the word of the LORD is true,
and he is faithful in everything he does.
5 The LORD loves righteousness and justice; [e]
the earth is filled with his kindness.
6 The heavens were made by the word * of the LORD, [f]
and all their host by the breath of his mouth.
7 He gathers the waters of the sea as in a bowl; *
he places the deep in storehouses. [g]
8 Let all the earth fear the LORD;
let all the inhabitants of the world revere him. *
9 * For he spoke, and it came to be;
he commanded, and it stood firm. [h]
10 The LORD thwarts the plans of nations
and frustrates the designs of peoples.
11 But the plan of the LORD remains forever,
the designs of his heart for all generations. [i]
12 * Blessed is the nation whose God is the LORD,

a Pss 18:5; 69:14.—b Pss 33:1; 64:11; 92:2.—c Pss 5:12; 11:7; 32:11; 101:1; 147:1.—d 2-3: Pss 40:4; 92:4; 144:9; Rev 5:8.—e Pss 11:7; 119:64.—f Gen 2:1; Jn 1:1; Heb 11:3.—g Ps 78:13; Gen 1:9-10; Ex 15:8; Job 38:8.—h Ps 148:5; Gen 1:3f; Jud 16:14; Isa 48:13; Jn 1:3.—i Prov 19:21; Isa 40:8; 46:10.

32:6 The psalmist encourages the godly to draw near to God; even in the greatest adversities, the Lord will protect them. *Where . . . found:* another version is: "in time of distress." *Great floods:* symbol of grave danger (see note on Ps 18:17).

32:7 After receiving God's help, the psalmist will be surrounded by people celebrating this latest act of deliverance while he brings thank offerings.

32:10 *Kindness:* see note on Ps 6:5.

32:11 *Heart:* see note on Ps 4:8.

Ps 33 This psalm follows a classical pattern. First, the psalmist calls for praise to God. Then he proclaims praise for his great deeds: his word that created the three-tiered universe (vv. 4-9), his intervention in history when he chose his people from among the nations (vv. 10-12), and finally his powerful help for those who fear him (vv. 13-19). Thus, he contemplates God's work in creation, in the history of Israel, and in the lives of the righteous. The people acclaim Providence, whose wise plan is universal in its scope.

In Ephesians (Eph 1:9; 3:4f), Paul will explain this hidden plan of God that is carried to fulfillment in Christ's Passover in order that humankind may have life and the world may attain its goal.

33:3 *Sing to him a new song:* celebrate God's saving deed with a new song to make known his greatness to others and to give him praise (see Pss 7:18, and note; 40:4; 96:1; 98:1; 144:9; 149:1; Isa 42:10; Rev 5:9; 14:3).

33:4-5 The psalmist celebrates especially the perfections of the Lord. His nature and his self-revelation are in complete harmony; he is faithful (*true*) in everything that he does. He also loves righteousness and justice, i.e., he carries out his plans by his verdicts, rule, and covenant relationship with his people. Furthermore, his kindness is evident in his works on earth; he shows the same loyalty, constancy, and love toward the rest of creation that he shows to his people (v. 22). *Kindness:* see note on Ps 6:5.

33:6 The Fathers of the Church applied this verse to the Blessed Trinity: *LORD* = Father; *word* = Son; *breath* = Spirit. *All their host:* the stars of the sky were viewed as an army (see Neh 9:6; Isa 40:26; 45:12; Jer 33:22). See also note on Ps 24:10.

33:7 *He gathers the waters . . . as in a bowl:* God rules the dangerous waters so easily that it is like a person putting water into a bowl (see Ps 104:9; Gen 1:9f; Job 38:8-11; Prov 8:29; Jer 5:22).

33:8 The nations of the world feared many gods, each of whom reigned over the various heavenly bodies and over the land, sea, and sky. But the psalmist stresses that the Lord is the Creator-Ruler of the world and everything in it. Hence, he calls upon all nations and all peoples to fear the Lord because of his greatness and his goodness.

33:9-12 Whatever God spoke came into existence (see Heb 11:3). Everything reflects his wise rule. The nations are completely under his control (see Prov 19:21; 21:30; Isa 8:10; 19:17; 46:10f; Jer 29:11; Mic 4:12). God's providence works out his purposes. *Heart:* see note on Ps 4:8.

33:12-22 The psalmist now meditates on the election of God's people, after he has stressed the Lord's power and steadfast carrying out of his plans.

the people whom he has chosen as his heritage. *[j]
13 * The LORD gazes down from heaven
and beholds the entire human race.[k]
14 From his royal throne
he watches all who dwell on the earth.
15 He who has fashioned the hearts of them all
observes everything they do.

16 A king is not saved by a large army,
nor is a warrior delivered by great strength.
17 A horse offers false hope for victory;
despite its power it cannot save.

18 * But the eyes of the LORD are on those who fear him,
on those who trust in his kindness,
19 to deliver them from death
and to preserve their lives in time of famine.

20 * Our soul waits in hope for the LORD;
he is our help and our shield.[l]
21 Our hearts rejoice in him
because we trust in his holy name.
22 O LORD, let your kindness rest upon us,
for we have placed our hope in you.

PSALM 34*

Presence of God, Protector of the Righteous

1 Of David. When he pretended to be mad before Abimelech, who forced him to depart. *

2 * I will bless the LORD at all times;
his praise will be continually on my lips.[m]
3 My soul * will glory in the LORD;
let the lowly hear and be glad.
4 Magnify the LORD with me;
let us exalt his name together.

5 I sought the LORD, and he answered me;
he set me free from all my fears.
6 Look to him and you will be radiant;
your faces will never be covered with shame.
7 In my anguish * I cried out;
the LORD heard my plea,
and I was saved from all my troubles.

8 The angel of the LORD * encamps around those who fear God,
and he delivers them.[n]
9 Taste and see that the LORD is good;
blessed * is the man who takes refuge in him.[o]

10 Fear the LORD, * you his saints;
nothing is lacking for those who fear him.[p]
11 The powerful * suffer want and go hungry,
but those who seek the LORD want for no good thing.

---

j Ps 144:15; Ex 8:22; Deut 7:6.—k Ps 53:3; Job 34:21; Sir 15:19; Jer 16:17; 32:19.—l Pss 27:14; 28:7; 33:20; 115:9.—m Pss 71:6; 145:2; Eph 1:20; 1 Thes 5:18.—n Gen 16:7; Ex 14:19.—o Ps 2:12; 1 Pet 2:3.—p Deut 6:13; Prov 3:7.

33:12 The Lord freely chose his people as *his heritage* (see Pss 28:9; 74:2; 78:62, 71; 94:5, 14; 106:5, 40; Ex 19:5; Deut 4:20; 9:26, 29).

33:13-17 The Lord sees everything that happens on earth (vv. 13-15) and controls human destinies. *Hearts:* see note on Ps 4:8.

33:18-19 Success in any venture does not depend on earthly means but on God alone, who watches over his faithful and delivers them from death and every danger. *Eyes of the Lord:* a metaphor for the Lord's loving care. *Kindness:* see note on Ps 6:5.

33:20-22 The people respond by expressing a renewal of their covenant commitment. The Lord is their help and shield (see Pss 3:4; 28:7), and they trust in his holy name, with which they associate past acts of deliverance (see Ps 30:5). They promise to be submissive and abandon themselves to him as he works out his plans for the establishment of his kingdom and the renewal of the earth. *Soul:* see note on Ps 6:4. *Hearts:* see note on Ps 4:8. *Name:* see note on Ps 5:12. *Kindness:* see note on Ps 6:5.

Ps 34 This alphabetical psalm has two parts. The first voices thanksgiving for the solicitude with which God surrounds the righteous and the poor to deliver them from their anguish. Doubtless the psalmist has experienced this in life and gives his disciples the fruit of his experience. The second part takes the tone of an instruction (vv. 13-23): a sage invites the listeners to discover the path to happiness in the fear of the Lord.

The poorest of the poor and the wisest of the sages is Christ, and it is upon his lips that we can place this psalm after the example of John (Jn 19:36), numbering ourselves—in accord with the express indication of Peter (see 1 Pet 3:10-12)—among the children to whom he teaches the way of life and happiness. From the early days of Christianity this psalm served to teach those who were preparing for the Christian life and for Baptism (1 Pet 2:3).

34:1 The superscription refers to 1 Sam 21:11-15, but (probably as the result of a scribal error) erroneously substitutes Abimelech for Achish, King of Gath.

34:2-4 The praise of the Lord is continual, God-centered, and the response of a grateful heart—an offering that the Lord will never reject (see Ps 50:14-23; Hos 14:2; Heb 13:15). Its purpose is to acknowledge the Lord's greatness (see Pss 30:2; 69:31; 99:5; 107:32; 145:1). *Name:* see note on Ps 5:12.

34:3 *Soul:* see note on Ps 6:4.

34:7 *In my anguish:* literally, "this poor man." The word "poor" is usually applied to one who depends completely on God for his deliverance and his very life. See also note on Ps 22:27.

34:8 *Angel of the Lord:* i.e., the Lord's protection or the presence of God. However, such protection, although promised by the Lord (see Ps 91:11; Gen 32:2; 2 Ki 6:17; Mt 4:5f), is not automatic; it depends on one's allegiance to the covenant—the "fear of the LORD"—entailing the practices mentioned in verses 12-15.

34:9 This verse is applied to the Holy Eucharist by the Fathers of the Church and the Liturgy (see 1 Pet 2:3). *Blessed:* see note on Ps 1:1.

34:10 *Fear the Lord:* see note on Ps 15:2-5. *Saints:* that is, those consecrated to God and sharing in his holiness (see Ex 19:6; Lev 19:2; Num 16:3; Isa 4:3; Dan 8:24). See also notes on Pss 4:4; 16:3.

34:11 *Powerful:* literally, "lions"—fierce animals were symbols of people with power.

12 * Come, my children, * and listen to me;
I will teach you the fear of the LORD. [q]
13 Who among you delights in life [r]
and desires many years to enjoy prosperity? *
14 Then keep your tongue * from evil
and your lips from telling lies.
15 Shun evil and do good;
seek peace and pursue it. [s]
16 * The eyes of the LORD are on the righteous,
and his ears are open to their cry. [t]
17 The face of the LORD is turned against those who do evil,
to erase all memory of them from the earth.
18 * The righteous call out, and the LORD hears them;
he rescues them from all their troubles.
19 The LORD remains close to the brokenhearted,
and he saves those whose spirit is crushed.
20 * The misfortunes of the righteous man are many,
but the LORD delivers him * from all of them.
21 He watches with care over all his bones;
not a single one will be broken. [u]
22 * Evil will bring death to the wicked,
and those who hate the righteous will be condemned.
23 The LORD redeems the lives of those who serve him;
no one will be condemned who takes refuge in him.

PSALM 35*

Appeal for Help against Injustice

1 Of David.

Plead my cause, O LORD, with those who strive against me;
fight against those who fight against me.
2 Grasp your shield and buckler
and spring to my aid.
3 Brandish your spear and battle-ax
against those who pursue me.
Say to my soul, *
"I am your salvation."
4 May those who seek my life
suffer shame and disgrace.
May those who plan my downfall
be forced to retreat in disgrace. [v]
5 May they be like chaff flying in the wind, *

q Ps 66:16; Prov 1:8; 4:1.—r 13-17: 1 Pet 3:10-12.—s Ps 37:27; Mt 5:9; Heb 12:14.—t Ps 33:18; Mal 3:16.—u Jn 19:36.—v Pss 38:13; 40:15; 69:7; 70:3; 71:13; 83:17; Isa 45:16; Mal 2:9.

34:12-15 To gain wisdom entails two things: fearing the Lord and doing his will. The latter calls for integrity of language rather than deception (v. 14; see Jer 4:2), practicing good rather than evil (v. 15; see Ps 37:3, 27), and working for rather than against peace (vv. 15-16; see Ps 37:37; Mt 5:9; Rom 12:18; 14:19; Heb 12:14).

34:12 *Children:* a term (also translated as "simple" or "sons") for students in Wisdom literature (see Prov 1:22; 4:1; 8:32; Sir 3:1; 23:7).

34:13 This verse is found word for word in an Egyptian text of the 18th dynasty (tomb of Ai) (see 1 Pet 3:10f).

34:14 *Tongue:* see note on Ps 5:10.

34:16-17 The eyes and ears of the Lord are attuned to the righteous (see Ps 33:18), but the face of the Lord (see note on Ps 13:2) is against evildoers (see Lev 17:10; Jer 23:30; 1 Pet 3:10-12).

34:18-19 Compunction and humility are requirements for benefiting from the grace of salvation (see Ps 51:19; Mt 11:29f). The Lord hears the cry of the righteous (see Ps 145:19) and the brokenhearted (see Ps 147:3) and saves them from their afflictions.

34:20-21 No matter how many are the troubles of the righ-teous man, the Lord will deliver him (see Job 5:19; 2 Tim 3:11), protecting *all his bones,* a phrase representative of his whole being. *Not a single one will be broken:* John applies this text to Jesus on the cross as the righteous man par excellence. Hence, this text is regarded as a prophecy about Christ when he was crucified. Although it was the custom of the Romans to break the legs of a person they had crucified so that death would come more quickly, it was not carried out in this case and not one of Christ's bones was broken.

34:20 *Delivers him:* God promises to be our source of power, courage, and wisdom to help us through our troubles; at times he even chooses to take them away from us.

34:22-23 *The wicked* will perish in their own evil and *be condemned* (see Ps 9:16), but *the righteous* will be saved by the Lord (see Ex 6:6; Lk 1:68; Rev 14:3).

Ps 35 This is one of the so-called imprecatory (or cursing) psalms that call upon God to mete out justice to enemies (see vv. 24-26; Pss 3:8; 5:11; 6:10; 18:14-16; 28:4f; 31:18f; 37:2, 9-10, 15, 20, 35f; 40:15f; 54:7; 55:10, 16, 24; 58:8-12; 63:10-12; 64:8-10; 69:23-29; 71:13; 79:6, 12; 83:10-19; 129:5-8; 137:8-9; 139:19-22; 140:10-12; 141:10; 143:12). In their thirst for justice, the authors of these psalms use hyperbole (or overstatement) in order to move others to oppose sin and evil (see also note on Ps 5:11). In three successive waves, the frantic and indignant cry of the persecuted righteous man rises toward God; and three successive times the suppliant rediscovers hope. He is a man overwhelmed by the underhanded wickedness, betrayal, and calumnies of friends as well as the dark designs of adversaries. It reminds us once again of the evils suffered by the prophet Jeremiah (Jer 20:10-13), and we cannot refrain from thinking of the trial of Jesus before a tribunal bent on sending him to his death (Mt 26:57ff).

Christians are aware that the world continues to pursue Christ in the person of his disciples (see Mt 5:11; 10:17f; Jn 15:18-25), unjustly directing accusations and persecutions against them. Hence, the prayer formulated in this psalm must spring forth from the lips and hearts of the disciples united with their Master.

35:3 *Soul:* see note on Ps 6:4.

35:5 *Like chaff flying in the wind:* i.e., easily carried away. *Angel of the LORD:* see note on Ps 34:8.

with the angel of the LORD scattering them.[w]
6 May their way be shadowy and slippery,
with the angel of the LORD in pursuit.
7 Without cause they laid a net to trap me;
without cause they dug a pit to ensnare me.
8 May ruin come upon them unawares;
may the net they laid entrap them;
may they topple into the pit they dug.[x]
9 Then my soul * will rejoice in the LORD
and exult in his salvation.
10 My whole being * will say,
"O LORD, who is there like you?
You deliver those who are weak
from those who are too strong for them,
and you protect the poor and needy
from those who seek to exploit them."[y]
11 False witnesses step forward
and question me about things I do not know.
12 They give me back evil in place of good
and leave my soul in sorrow.[z]
13 Yet, when they were ill, I put on sackcloth *
and afflicted myself with fasting,
while I poured forth prayers from my heart.
14 I went about as though in grief,
as though for a friend or brother.
I bowed down in sorrow
as though lamenting for a mother.
15 But when I stumbled, they rejoiced and came together;
they came together and struck me unawares.
They slandered me without letup.
16 They mocked me with ever increasing fury
as they gnashed their teeth at me.
17 How long, * O LORD, will you look on?
Rescue me from these ravening beasts;
preserve my precious life from these lions.[a]
18 I will offer you thanks in the great assembly;
I will praise you amid the vast throng.[b]
19 Do not allow my treacherous enemies
to gloat over me;
do not permit those who hate me without reason *
to wink their eyes at me.[c]
20 * For they do not speak words of peace,
but they contrive deceitful words
to lead astray the peaceful in the land.[d]
21 They open wide their mouths shouting,
"Aha! Aha!
We have seen it with our own eyes."[e]
22 You have seen, O LORD; do not be silent.
O LORD, do not be far from me.[f]
23 Awaken and be diligent in my defense;
come to my aid, my God and my LORD.
24 * Defend me, O LORD, my God,
according to your righteousness,
and do not let them gloat over me.
25 Do not let them think,
"Aha! This is just what we wanted."
Do not let them say,
"We have swallowed him up."
26 Let all those who rejoice at my downfall
be put to shame and dismayed.
Let those who rise up arrogantly against me
be covered with shame and dishonor.
27 But let those who desire my vindication
shout for joy and be glad.
Let them cry out continually,
"Exalted be the LORD
who delights to see his servant in peace."
28 Then my tongue shall proclaim your righteousness
and sing your praise all the day long.[g]

w Pss 1:4; 34:8; 83:14; Job 21:18.—x Pss 7:16; 9:16; 57:7; Prov 26:27; Eccl 10:8; Sir 27:26; Isa 47:11; 1 Thes 5:3; 1 Jn 5:3.—y Pss 18:12; 51:10; 86:8; 89:7, 9; Ex 9:14; 15:11.—z Pss 27:12; 38:21-22; 109:5; Prov 17:13; Jer 18:20.—a Pss 6:4; 17:12; 22:22; 57:5; 58:7.—b Pss 22:23; 26:12; 40:11; 42:5; 149:1.—c Pss 9:14; 38:17; 69:5; Prov 6:13; Jn 15:25.—d Pss 38:13; 55:22; 120:6-7; Jer 9:7.—e Pss 40:16; 70:4; Lam 2:16; Ezek 25:3.—f Pss 10:1, 14; 22:12; 38:22; 109:1; Ex 3:7.—g Pss 5:9; 51:16; 71:15.

35:9 *Soul:* see note on Ps 6:4.

35:10 *My whole being:* literally, "all my bones." *Poor and needy:* see notes on Pss 22:27; 34:7.

35:13 *Sackcloth:* a symbol of mourning. *Fasting:* an act of mourning (see Ps 69:10). *Heart:* see note on Ps 4:8.

35:17 *How long. . . ?:* see note on Ps 6:4. *Lions:* a metaphor for enemies.

35:19 *Treacherous enemies . . . those who hate me without reason:* cited in Jn 15:25, since this psalm as well as Ps 69 was regarded by the New Testament authors as foreshadowing the Passion of Christ.

35:20-21 The enemies of the psalmist assail him and wrongly accuse him of some crime (see v. 11). These verses and verse 25 recall Ps 40:16; Lam 2:16; Ezek 25:3; 26:2; Hab 1:13.

35:24-26 See introduction above and note on Ps 5:11.

PSALM 36*

Human Weakness and Divine Goodness

1 For the director. * Of David the servant of the LORD.

2 Sin speaks to the wicked man in his heart; *
in his eyes there is no fear of God. [h]
3 He deludes himself with the idea
that his guilt will not be discovered and hated. *
4 The words his mouth utters are malicious and deceitful;
he has ceased to be wise and act uprightly.
5 Even when he lies on his bed, *
he is hatching evil plots.
He commits himself to a wicked course
and refuses to reject evil. [i]
6 * O LORD, your kindness extends to the heavens;
your faithfulness, to the skies. [j]
7 Your righteousness is like the mountains of God;
your judgments, like the mighty deep;
you sustain both humans and beasts, O LORD.
8 How precious, O God, is your kindness! *
People seek refuge in the shadow of your wings. [k]
9 They feast on the abundance of your house, * [l]
and you give them to drink from your delightful streams. [m]
10 For with you is the fountain of life, *
and by your light we see light. [n]
11 Continue to bestow your kindness * on those who know you,
and your saving justice on the upright of heart.
12 Let not the foot of the arrogant tread upon me,
nor the hand of the wicked drive me out.
13 Behold, the evildoers have fallen;
they are overthrown and unable to rise.

PSALM 37*

Fate of the Wicked and Reward of the Righteous

1 Of David.

Do not fume because of evildoers
or envy those who do wrong. [o]

h Prov 5:22; Jer 2:19; Hos 5:5; Rom 3:18.—**i** Pss 5:10; 144:8, 11; Prov 4:16; Mic 2:1.—**j** Pss 57:11; 71:19; 89:2.—**k** Pss 6:5; 17:8; 57:2.—**l** Pss 63:6; 65:5; Gen 2:8-10.—**m** Isa 55:1; Jn 4:14; Rev 22:1.—**n** Pss 4:7; 27:1; 80:4, 8, 20; 104:2; Isa 60:1, 19; Jer 2:13.—**o** Prov 3:31; 23:17; 24:1, 19; Mal 2:17; 3:14.

Ps 36 This psalm combines two contrasting pictures, which were perhaps separated at one time. On the one hand, there is a person destroyed by sin, whose heart holds no sentiment that is not turned to sin (vv. 2-5). On the other, there are creatures dedicated to God, that is, the righteous, who are peaceful and happy (vv. 6ff). These same traditional images of happiness will be found among the Prophets, suggestive of the ideal time for the installment of the future Messiah (Isa 12:2; 25:6; Jer 31:14; Ezek 47).

Christians know better than the psalmist that pride constitutes a maleficent force residing in all humans. In practice, it carries us inevitably along toward evil (see Rom 6:1-11). Through Christ, the Father preserves for us, his faithful, his salvation that shines continually upon us to render us holy and to defend us against outrages on the part of evil and the impious. The New Testament applies images from the second part of this psalm to Christ: light of humankind and inexhaustible wellspring of life (Jn 7:37f; 8:12; Rev 21:6).

36:1 *For the director:* these words are thought to be a musical or liturgical notation.

36:2 *Sin . . . heart:* an alternative translation is: "An oracle is within my heart / concerning the sinfulness of the wicked." *Heart:* see note on Ps 4:8. Paul cites this verse in Rom 3:18.

36:3 *His guilt will . . . be discovered and hated:* because it is an offense against God and hence punished by him.

36:5 *On his bed:* rather than meditating on God's law both day and night (Pss 1:2; 119:55), the wicked plots evil even on his bed.

36:6-7 *Your kindness . . . mighty deep:* God's influence reaches from one end of the world to the other and into every sphere. *Kindness:* see note on Ps 6:5.

36:8 *Kindness:* see note on Ps 6:5. *Shadow of your wings:* see note on Ps 17:8.

36:9 People rejoice together before the Lord. The image is of the abundance of meat from the sacrifices. This is already a prefiguration of the Messianic Banquet of which Jesus will speak, the "Supper of the Lamb" (Rev 19:9). *House:* the earth that provides food for all living creatures (see Pss 24:2; 104:14). *Streams:* the means by which God brings forth the rain out of his "storehouses" (Ps 33:7), which flow into the water sources on earth and give life to creatures.

36:10 *Fountain of life:* an expression to be taken in the widest possible sense as life implying prosperity, peace, and happiness (see Pss 46:5; 133:3; Isa 12:5; 55:1; Jer 2:13; 17:13; 31:12). In Proverbs this expression designates wisdom (Prov 13:14; 16:22; 18:4) and the fear of the Lord (14:27). The passage is applied to Christ, life and light of human beings (Jn 4:10, 14). *Light:* through God's loving kindness (see Pss 4:7; 31:17; 89:16; 97:11; Job 29:3) we enjoy fullness of life and well-being.

36:11 *Kindness:* see note on Ps 6:5. *Heart:* see note on Ps 4:8.

Ps 37 A peaceful, aged psalmist strings together, in alphabetical order, sayings about the opposing lots of the righteous and the wicked. It is a fine lesson in wisdom for those who grow angry at the successes of evildoers: their triumph is ephemeral. Experience and meditation on the word of God have revealed to this sage the happy destiny that the Lord has reserved for his friends; each of the righteous is called to enjoy the promises made to the people of Israel as a reward for their faithfulness: to dwell in the holy land in peace (vv. 3, 11).

The horizon remains limited to this world. Hence, it is a modest happiness if it were not irradiated by the nearness of the Lord and did not contain the still hidden promise of a love that cannot be extinguished, of an eternal joy.

Christ will reveal this infinite perspective: eternal happiness in the Kingdom of God, the true Promised Land, belongs to the poor, those who forgive and thirst for righteousness and peace (Mt 5).

2 They will wither quickly like the grass
and fade away like the green herb. * [p]
3 Put your trust in the LORD and do good,
that you may dwell in the land * and be secure. [q]
4 Take delight in the LORD,
and he will grant you what your heart * desires. [r]
5 Commit your way to the LORD;
place your trust in him, and he will act. [s]
6 He will make your righteousness shine like the dawn,
and the justice of your cause, like the noonday. * [t]
7 Wait quietly for the LORD
and be patient until he comes.
Do not fret over the man who prospers
because of his evil schemes.
8 Refrain from anger and turn away from wrath;
do not fret—it does nothing but harm.
9 For evildoers will be destroyed,
but those who wait for the LORD will inherit the land. * [u]
10 In a short while, the wicked will be no more;
no matter how diligently you search,
you will not be able to find him.
11 But the meek * will possess the land
and enjoy an abundance of peace. [v]
12 The wicked man plots against the righteous
and grinds his teeth at the sight of them.
13 But the LORD laughs at them,
knowing that their day * is approaching. [w]
14 The wicked draw their swords
and string their bows
to bring down the poor * and the needy
and to slaughter those who are upright. [x]
15 Their swords will enter their own hearts, *
and their bows will be shattered.
16 Preferable is the little that the righteous possess
than the great wealth of the wicked. [y]
17 For the power of the wicked will be overcome,
but the LORD protects the righteous.
18 The LORD looks after the lives of the upright, *
and their heritage will last forever.
19 They will not be confounded in times of evil,
and in days of famine they eat their fill.
20 But the wicked will perish,
all those who are enemies of the LORD.
Like the beauty of the meadows * they will wither away;
like smoke they will disappear. [z]
21 The wicked man borrows but neglects to repay,
whereas the righteous man is generous in giving.
22 For those blessed by the LORD will possess the land,
but those who are cursed will perish.
23 The LORD makes a man's steps secure [a]
when he approves of his conduct.
24 Even if he stumbles, he will never fall headlong,
for the LORD holds him by the hand. *
25 From my youth until my present old age,
I have never seen the righteous man abandoned

p Pss 90:6; 102:12; 103:15-16; Job 14:2; Jas 1:10.—q Ps 128:2; Deut 30:20; Ezek 34:14; Jn 10:9.—r Ps 21:3; Prov 10:24; Mt 6:33.—s Pss 4:6; 51:19; 55:23; Prov 3:5; 16:3.—t Ps 18:25; Wis 5:6; Isa 58:10.—u Pss 25:13; 101:8; 112:3-4; Prov 2:21; Isa 57:13.—v Lev 26:6; Num 14:24; Mt 5:5.—w Pss 2:4; 59:9; Wis 4:18; Ezek 12:23.—x Pss 11:2; 35:10; 57:5; 64:5.—y Prov 15:16; 16:8.—z Ps 34:22; Wis 5:14.—a Ps 147:11; Prov 20:24.

37:2 See notes on Pss 5:11; 35 (this also applies to vv. 9f, 15, 20, 35f).

37:3 *The land:* the Promised Land (Ps 25:13; Deut 16:20), which in the New Testament became a type of heaven (see Mt 5:3-12; Lk 6:20-26; Heb 11:9, 13-16). This word is also used in verses 9, 11, 22, 27, 29, 34.

37:4 *Heart:* see note on Ps 4:8.

37:6 *Dawn . . . noonday:* light and brightness symbolize truth, well-being, and happiness (see Job 22:28; Song 1:7; Wis 5:6).

37:9 Those who hope only in the Lord for their sustenance and their well-being (i.e., "the poor") will inherit the land, while those who bypass God and by wicked means try to take hold of it will come to naught (see notes on Pss 5:11; 35).

37:11 *The meek:* another word for the poor, those who count solely on God and follow his law (see Mt 5:5). Indeed, the promises of the Lord are only for the meek who depend solely on him (v. 9) and will enjoy an *abundance of peace.* "Peace" symbolizes the beneficence of the godly (see Ps 72:7) in contrast with the life of suffering (v. 12; see Ps 119:65f).

37:13 *Their day:* the time for their ultimate defeat, their death (see 1 Sam 26:10, where "his day" is translated as "his time").

37:14 *The poor:* see note on Ps 22:27.

37:15 *Hearts:* see note on Ps 4:8.

37:18 *Upright:* those who are God's faithful and obedient servants as was Abraham (see Gen 17:1).

37:20 *Beauty of the meadows:* the beauty of grass and flowers that comes and goes every year (see Pss 90:5f; 102:12; 103:15f; Job 14:2; Isa 40:6-8; Jas 1:10f).

37:24 See Prov 24:16.

or his children reduced to begging for bread. [b]
26 He is always compassionate and generous in lending,
and his children will be blessed. *
27 If you shun evil and do good, [c]
you will dwell in the land forever.
28 For the LORD loves the just, *
and he will not forsake his faithful ones.

Those who follow evil paths will be destroyed,
and the children of the wicked will be cut off,
29 whereas the righteous will inherit the land
and dwell in it forever. * [d]
30 * The mouth of the righteous man utters wisdom,
and his tongue speaks what is right. [e]
31 The law of his God is in his heart, [f]
and his steps do not waver.
32 * The wicked man keeps close watch on the righteous
and seeks an opportunity to kill him.
33 But the LORD will not abandon the righteous
to the power of the wicked,
nor will he allow him to be condemned
when he is brought to trial.
34 Wait for the LORD
and follow the path he has laid out;
then he will exalt you to inherit the land,
and you will see the destruction of the wicked. [g]
35 * I have seen a wicked man inflicting terror
and towering like a verdant tree. [h]
36 I passed by again, and he was gone;
I searched for him, but he was not to be found.
37 * Pay attention to the innocent and behold the upright,
for the man of peace will have a future. [i]
38 But the wicked will be completely destroyed,
and their children will be cut off.
39 * The salvation of the righteous is from the LORD;
he is their refuge in times of trouble. [j]
40 The LORD will help them and deliver them;
he will rescue them from the wicked and save them
because they flee to him for refuge.

PSALM 38*

Prayer of a Sinner in Great Peril

1 A psalm of David. For remembrance. *
2 O LORD, do not punish me in your anger
or chastise me in your wrath. [k]

b Job 4:7; Sir 2:10; Heb 13:5.—c Ps 34:15-16; Am 5:14; 3 Jn 11.—d Ps 25:13; Prov 2:21; Isa 34:17; 57:13.—e Ps 49:4; Prov 10:31.—f Ps 40:9; Deut 6:6; Isa 51:7; Jer 31:33.—g Pss 27:14; 31:25.—h Ps 92:8-9; Job 20:6-7; Isa 2:13; Ezek 31:10-11.—i Pss 11:7; 18:27; Prov 23:18; 24:14.—j Pss 3:9; 9:10; Isa 25:4.—k Pss 6:2; 39:12.

37:26 *Blessed:* see note on Ps 1:1.

37:28 The psalmist insists that the *LORD loves the just* (see Prov 2:8) who are *his faithful ones*, and he will never *forsake* them. Hence, Paul could say with complete confidence: "[Nothing] will be able to separate us from the love of God in Christ Jesus our Lord" (Rom 8:38f).

37:29 *The righteous will inherit the land and dwell in it forever* through their descendants (see Mt 5:5).

37:30-31 The wise man reveres the Lord and desires to do his will. God's law is written on his heart (see Ps 40:9; Deut 6:6; Isa 51:7; Jer 31:33; Ezek 36:27). He speaks wisely (see Ps 49:4) and establishes peace (see Ps 36:7). *Heart:* see note on Ps 4:8. *His steps do not waver:* from the way of the righteous (see 1:6).

37:32-33 The righteous need not fear the machinations of the *wicked*, for the Lord has promised to come to their assistance. He gave Canaan to Israel and the earth to all who love him (see Isa 65:17-25; 66:22; Rev 21:1).

37:35-36 God confounds the proud (see Job 20:6f; Isa 2:12; 14:13-15; Ezek 31:10f). *Verdant tree:* or "cedar of Lebanon."

37:37-38 The righteous have a bright future; the wicked have no future at all (see Prov 23:18; 24:14). *A future:* or "descendants."

37:39-40 The Lord is the protector of all who take *refuge* in him, all who call upon him for protection, deliverance, and victory (see Pss 9:10; 12:2; 34:7f).

Ps 38 The psalmist of this third Penitential Psalm (seven in all: Pss 6; 32; 38; 51; 102; 130; 143) is a man prostrated beneath the weight of his sickness and the vilification heaped on him by others, a man marked by the chastisement of God. He utters a suppliant and monotone plaint that seems as interminable as his suffering. Before God, he is pitiable, abandoned, and betrayed. This new Job (Job 6:4; 19:13-21) does not rebel. He thinks of himself as a sinner who deserves his lot and he suffers in silence, leveling neither recriminations nor imprecations against his adversaries. Indeed, hope stirs secretly in him.

The complete abandonment to God that is expressed here is also found in the third Lamentation (Lam 3:26-29) and in the Songs of the Servant of the Lord (see Isa 53:7). The Christian Liturgy sees in this man of sorrows an image of the Christ who was silent during his Passion.

In praying this psalm, we should look to ourselves, scrutinizing our lives and our consciences with a penetrating and impartial honesty, the better to discern the place of sin therein and the better to realize that we are and remain sinners (see Rom 7:14-20; 1 Jn 1:8f). This will in no way prevent us from begging God not to chastise us in his wrath but to save us as soon as possible from our afflictions and our foes.

38:1 *For remembrance:* the meaning is "For the memorial sacrifice" or "portion" (see Lev 2:2, 9, 16; 5:12; Isa 66:3); it occurs elsewhere only in Ps 70; an alternative translation is: "A petition."

3 For your arrows * have pierced me deeply,
and your hand has come down upon me. [l]
4 No portion of my body * has been unscathed
as a result of your anger;
my bones have become weak
as a result of my sins. [m]
5 My iniquities tower far above my head; *
they are a burden too heavy to bear. [n]
6 My wounds are fetid and fester
because of my folly.
7 I am bowed down and bent over,
as I spend each day in sorrow. [o]
8 My loins are filled with searing pain;
no part of my body * is unafflicted.
9 I am numb and completely crushed,
and I groan in anguish of heart. * [p]
10 O LORD, all my longing is known to you,
and my sighs are not hidden from you.
11 My heart throbs, and my strength is spent;
even the light has faded from my eyes. [q]
12 My friends and companions stay away from my affliction,
and my neighbors keep their distance.
13 Those who seek my life set traps;
those who wish me harm threaten violence
and plot treachery all day long. *
14 * But I am like a man who cannot hear,
like one who cannot open his mouth.
15 I am like one who hears nothing
and has no answer to offer.
16 I place my hope in you, O LORD;
you, O LORD, my God, will answer for me. [r]
17 For I prayed, "Never let them gloat over me
or exult should my foot slip."
18 I am at the point of exhaustion,
and my grief is with me constantly.
19 I acknowledge my iniquity,
and I sincerely grieve for my sin. [s]
20 * Numerous and strong are my enemies without cause;
many are those who hate me without good reason. *
21 Those who repay my good deeds with evil
oppose me because I follow a path of righteousness. [t]
22 Do not abandon me, O LORD;
my God, do not remain far from me. [u]
23 Come quickly to my aid,
O LORD, my Savior. [v]

PSALM 39*

The Brevity and Vanity of Life

1 For the director. * For Jeduthun. [w] A psalm of
David.
2 I said, "I will be careful of my behavior
so as not to sin with my tongue.

l Pss 31:11; 64:8; Job 6:4; 34:6; Lam 3:12; Ezek 5:16.—m Prov 3:8; Isa 1:5-6; 66:14.—n Pss 40:13; 65:3-4; Gen 4:13; Num 11:14; Ezr 9:6; Lk 11:46.—o Pss 35:14; 57:7.—p Pss 34:19; 102:4-6; Prov 17:22.—q Pss 6:8; 31:11; 88:10; Job 37:1.—r Pss 13:4; 27:14.—s Pss 32:5; 51:5; Lev 26:40.—t Pss 35:12; 109:5.—u Pss 10:1; 22:2, 12, 20; 27:9; 35:22.—v Pss 22:20; 40:14, 18.—w Pss 62:1; 77:1; 1 Chr 16:41; 25:1.

38:3 *Arrows:* i.e., the trials God has sent him (see Deut 32:23; Job 6:4; 34:6; Lam 3:12; Ezek 5:16).

38:4 *Body:* literally, "flesh." *Bones:* see note on Ps 34:20-21.

38:5 *My iniquities tower far above my head:* his guilt has resulted in both physical and psychological suffering.

38:8 *Body:* literally, "flesh."

38:9, 11 *Heart:* see note on Ps 4:8.

38:13 This passage recalls the fourth Song of the Servant (Isa 53:4, 7; see also Pss 31:11; 35:20; 37:32; 88:9; Job 12:4f; 19:13f).

38:14-17 Like a man deaf and dumb, the psalmist does not reply to those who slander him; he waits for the Lord to vindicate his cause.

38:20-21 Passage close to Pss 35:11; 109:3-5. Some Greek manuscripts and many versions add: "They have rejected me, the loved one, like some hideous corpse" (see Isa 14:19 Greek). This allusion to the crucified Christ is made even more explicit in the Coptic version by the words: "They have nailed my flesh."

38:20 *Hate me without good reason:* although the psalmist acknowledges that he sinned against the Lord, he protests his innocence of wrongdoing against his enemies (see note on Ps 35:19).

Ps 39 The psalmist is not a sage who reflects on existence but a man grappling with God. In the face of the blows that strike him, he realizes the total frailty of existence and even of life itself. He would like to cast out from his heart all intentions to rebel, but it is impossible for him to hold back his complaint any longer. A real faith in the resurrection is still absent and, apart from an intervention of God providing a new breath of life, everything seems a mockery. One thinks of the lucid reflections of Ecclesiastes 1:2.

This psalm reminds us that while doing our utmost to acquire and develop the eternal divine life in us, we must regard our bodily life as the highest good, the most precious natural talent entrusted to us by God for our vigilant concern and fruitful action. The heavenly Father himself watches over this life, assigning it food and drink (see Mt 6:25-34) and life itself (see Acts 17:25-28). Jesus himself watches over material life, looking after the hunger of the crowd (see Mt 15:32), curing the sick (Mt 4:23), and raising the dead (Mt 9:25). We must thus greatly value our life and seek to prolong it for the glory of God and our spiritual progress (see Phil 1:23-26). Christians too have this same feeling in times of great distress: without the Lord what value is there in life?

39:1 *For the director:* these words are thought to be a musical or liturgical notation. *Jeduthun:* he is believed to be one of the three men appointed choral directors by David (see 1 Chr 25:1). See note on Ps 89:1.

I will keep a muzzle on my mouth *
whenever the wicked are in my presence."
3 [x] I kept completely silent
and refrained from speech,
but my distress only increased.
4 My heart * smoldered within me,
and, as I pondered, my mind was inflamed,
and my tongue began to speak:
5 * "O LORD, let me know my end
and the number of days left to me;
show me how fleeting my life is.
6 You have allotted me a short span of days;
my life is as nothing in your sight;
human existence is a mere breath. [y]
Selah
7 Humans are nothing but a passing shadow;
the riches they amass are a mere breath,
and they do not know who will enjoy them. *
8 "So now, O LORD, what do I wait for?
My hope is in you.
9 Deliver me from all my sins;
do not subject me to the taunts of fools. *
10 "I was silent and did not open my mouth,
for it is you who have done it.
11 Remove your scourge from me;
I am crushed by the blows of your hand.
12 You rebuke and punish people for their sins;
like a moth you consume all their desires;
human existence is a mere puff of wind. *Selah*
13 * "Hear my prayer, O LORD;
do not be deaf to my cry
or ignore my weeping.
For I am a wayfarer * before you,
a nomad like all my ancestors. [z]
14 Turn your eyes away so that I may be glad
before I depart and am no more." *

PSALM 40*

Thanksgiving and Prayer for Help

1 For the director.* A psalm of David.
2 * I waited patiently for the LORD;
then he stooped down and heard my cry. [a]
3 He raised me up from the desolate pit,
out of the mire of the swamp;
he set my feet upon a rock,
giving me a firm footing. [b]
4 He put a new song * in my mouth,
a hymn of praise to our God.
Many will look on and be awestruck,
and they will place their trust in the LORD. [c]
5 Blessed * is the man
who places his trust in the LORD, [d]

x 3-4: Ps 37:1; Jer 20:9.—y Pss 62:10; 89:46; 90:9-10; 144:4; Gen 6:3; 47:9; Job 7:6, 16; 14:1; Prov 10:27; Eccl 6:12; Wis 2:5; Sir 18:8; Isa 65:20.—z Ps 119:19; Gen 23:4; Ex 12:48; Lev 25:23; 2 Ki 20:5; Heb 11:13; 1 Pet 2:11.—a Pss 6:10; 31:22; 34:16; 37:7; 116:1; 145:19; Lam 3:25.—b Pss 18:5; 28:1; 30:4; 69:3, 15-16; 88:5; Prov 1:12; Jer 38:6; Jon 2:6f.—c Ps 33:3; Rev 5:9.—d Pss 1:1; 34:9; Prov 16:20; Jer 17:7.

39:2 *Muzzle on my mouth:* to repress saying anything derogatory in the presence of the wicked.

39:4 *Heart:* see note on Ps 4:8.

39:5-7 The psalmist begs God to help him know and accept the brevity and vanity of life, a brevity and vanity stressed in other psalms (see Pss 62:10; 73:19; 90:10-11) and in Isa 40:17.

39:7 This passage is reminiscent of Ecclesiastes.

39:9 *Fools:* see notes on Ps 14:2-3.

39:13-14 The psalmist—a sinner and overcome with adversity—feels like a stranger in God's presence and in his world. Still, he has no doubts about belonging to the covenant community. So he begs the Lord to remove his judgment from him so that the psalmist may know joy once again.

39:13 *Wayfarer:* that is, one who is only a temporary sojourner on earth (see Lev 25:23: "The land belongs to me and you are my aliens and tenants"; see also Ps 119:19; 1 Pet 2:11).

39:14 *Am no more:* in the time of the psalmist there apparently was no idea of any resurrection, even a mitigated one in the netherworld (see note on Ps 6:6).

Ps 40 This psalm, one of the most engaging of the entire Psalter, is divided into two parts. The first (vv. 2-13) is a thanksgiving reminiscent of Jeremiah (Jer 7:22; 17:7; 31:33). The second (vv. 14-18) is a lament that appears also as Ps 70.

Every Christian (and the whole Church) can naturally recite this beautiful psalm in his or her own right as one really (though not yet completely) saved.

40:1 *For the director:* these words are thought to be a musical or liturgical notation.

40:2-12 The psalmist expresses a great hope in the Lord. No one knows God's goodness better than one who has experienced abandonment. Purified by trial, the psalmist welcomes God into the depths of his being, his life becomes a kind of inner offering, the only true sacrifice, and he joyfully bears witness to the Lord's righteousness, love, and truth. In reading this psalm, we get the impression of entering into the confidence of Christ himself, of divining his inner attitude toward the course of his action and above all toward his Passion. A few Greek translations have accentuated this resemblance even more; thus, the Letter to the Hebrews cites this psalm to make us understand the profound decision of Christ (Heb 10:5-10).

The best praise of God and the best sacrifice are the gift of one's heart and life. The Prophets often opposed ritual formalism and replaced it with the true religion that is internal (Isa 1:11; Jer 6:20; 31:33; Am 5:22; Hos 6:6). It is this experience to which the songs of the Suffering Servant bear witness (Isa 50:5; 53:10), which was also the experience of Christ.

40:4 *New song:* see note on Ps 33:3. *Many will look on:* see note on Ps 9:2.

40:5 *Blessed:* see note on Ps 1:1.

who does not follow the arrogant
or those who go astray after falsehoods.
6 How innumerable, O LORD, my God,
are the wonders you have worked;
no one can compare with you
in the plans you have made for us. [e]
I would proclaim them and recount them,
but there are far too many to enumerate. [f]
7 * Sacrifice and offering you did not desire,
but you have made my ears receptive. *
Burnt offerings and sin offerings
you did not demand. [g]
8 * Then I said, "Behold I come;
it is written of me in the scroll of the book.
9 To do your will, O God, is my delight;
your law is in my heart." * [h]
10 I have proclaimed your righteousness in the great assembly;
I did not seal my lips,
as you well know, O LORD. [i]
11 I have not concealed your righteousness within the depths of my heart;
I have spoken of your faithfulness and salvation.
I have not concealed your kindness and your truth
in the great assembly.
12 O LORD, do not withhold your mercy from me;
may your kindness * and your truth
keep me safe forever. [j]
13 I am surrounded by evils without number;
my sins have so engulfed me that I cannot see.
They outnumber the hairs on my head,
and my heart sinks within me. * [k]
14 * Be pleased, O LORD, to rescue me
O LORD, come quickly to my aid. [l]
15 * May all those who seek to take my life
endure shame and confusion.
May all those who desire my ruin
be turned back and humiliated. [m]
16 May those who cry out to me, "Aha, aha!" *
be overcome with shame and dismay. [n]
17 But may all who seek you
rejoice in you and be jubilant.
May those who love your salvation
cry out forever, "The LORD be magnified." [o]
18 Even though I am poor and needy, *
the LORD keeps me in his thoughts.
You are my help and my deliverer;
O my God, do not delay.

PSALM 41*

Trust in God in Sickness and Misfortune

1 For the director. * A psalm of David.
2 * Blessed is he who has concern for the weak;

e Ps 35:10; Deut 4:34.—f Pss 71:15; 75:1; 105:5; 136:4; 139:17-18; Deut 4:34.—g 7-9: Ps 51:18-19; Isa 1:11-15; 50:5; Jer 6:20; Hos 6:6; Am 5:22; Heb 10:5-7.—h Ps 37:31; Jn 4:34; 8:29.—i Pss 22:23, 32; 26:12; 35:18; 149:1; Jos 22:22.—j Ps 89:34; Zec 1:12.—k Pss 6:8; 38:4f, 11; 65:4; 69:5; Ezr 9:6.—l 14-18: Pss 70:2-6; 71:12.—m Pss 35:4, 26; 71:13; 1 Sam 20:1; Est 9:2.—n Ps 35:21, 25; Lam 2:16.—o Pss 35:27; 69:7, 33; 104:1; Deut 4:29; 1 Chr 28:9.

40:7-9 These verses are applied to Christ by Heb 10:5-10.

40:7 Obedience is better than sacrifice (see Pss 50:7-15; 51:18f; 69:32f; 1 Sam 15:22; Isa 1:10-20; Jer 7:22; Hos 6:6; Am 5:22-25; Mic 6:6-8; Acts 7:42f). *But you have made my ears receptive:* a variant reading from the Greek versions has: "but a body you have prepared for me," which was interpreted in a Messianic sense and applied to Christ (see Heb 10:5ff).

40:8-9 The psalmist presents himself to the Lord, submitting himself to whatever his Master may require (Heb 10:9). He presents himself as an offering to the Lord (see Rom 12:1f). *It is written of me in the scroll:* the scroll is the Torah or the Mosaic Law, transcribed on parchment scrolls. The alternative Greek reading is "with the scroll written for me," which suggests a Messianic sense.

40:9, 11, 13 *Heart:* see note on Ps 4:8.

40:12 *Kindness:* see note on Ps 6:5.

40:13 Hyperbolic statements expressing the intense nature of the sinner's sufferings (see Pss 6:8; 38:4f, 11; 69:5), which serve as a transition to the second part of the psalm.

40:14-18 Distress can remind a person of his attachment to sin. Is there any reason why people should vilify the person who acknowledges his faults? Realizing his attraction toward evil, the psalmist cries out to God, and the poor man rediscovers the joyous assurance that God thinks about him.

40:15-16 See notes on Pss 5:11; 35.

40:16 *Aha, aha!:* the mocking words of the psalmist's adversaries.

40:18 *Poor and needy:* see note on Ps 34:7. *My help and my deliverer:* the salvation promised to the faithful (see Isa 25:9), first conceived as natural with reference to the Exodus or the return from the Exile, was later conceived as spiritual without restriction of space or time (see, e.g., Pss 18:1; 19:15).

Ps 41 The psalmist is well aware that mercy is rarely given by human beings. In his illness, he received no mercy from others; instead his enemies gleefully engaged in malicious gossip about him and his coming death and even his friend betrayed him. However, the psalmist does not retaliate in kind; he turns to God for mercy, asking for a rich life with all his powers restored so that he can stand once again in the presence of the Lord.

In praying this psalm, we can recall that the entire psalm is applicable to Christ personally, with the exception of verse 5, which he can assume only in place of and in the role of his sinful members. Since Christ assures us of God's complete solicitude, we can recite this supplication on our account amid our earthly trials.

41:1 *For the director:* these words are thought to be a musical or liturgical notation.

41:2-4 The psalmist voices his confidence that the Lord will restore him to fullness of health and life because of the psalmist's regard for the weak. *Blessed . . . weak:* other psalms use the same designation ("Blessed") for those whom God favors (see Pss 32:1f; 34:9; 40:5; 65:5; see also note on Ps 1:1).

in time of trouble the LORD will deliver
him. [p]
3 The LORD will protect him and keep him
alive;
he will make him happy on earth
and not abandon him to the will of his
enemies.
4 The LORD will sustain him on his sickbed
and bring him back to health.
5 Once I prayed, "O LORD, have mercy on me;
heal me, for I have sinned * against
you.
6 In their malice my enemies say of me,
'When will he die and his name be forgotten?'
7 When someone comes to visit me,
he utters words without sincerity;
his heart * harbors slander,
and on departing he gives voice to it. [q]
8 "All my enemies whisper against me
and conjure up the worst in my regard.
9 'He has a fatal disease,' they say;
'he will never rise up from his sickbed.'
10 "Even my friend whom I trusted,
the one who dined at my table,
has risen up * against me. [r]
11 But you, O LORD, be merciful to me;
make me well * so that I may pay them
back."
12 By this I know that you are pleased with
me—
that my enemy fails to triumph over me.
13 Because of my innocence you uphold me
and let me stand in your presence forever.
14 Blessed * be the LORD, the God of Israel, [s]
forever and forever.
Amen and Amen.

BOOK II—PSALMS 42–72*

PSALM 42*

Prayer of Longing for God

1 For the director. * A *maskil* of the sons of
Korah.
2 [t] As a deer longs for running streams,
so my soul longs for you, O God. *
3 My soul * thirsts for God, the living God.
When shall I come to behold the face of
God? [u]

p Ps 25:17; Deut 14:29; Job 4:7-11; Prov 14:21.—q Pss 12:3; 31:12; 38:12-13; 88:9; 101:7; Job 19:13-19; Jer 20:10; Mt 5:11.—r Ps 55:14-15; Job 19:19; Mt 26:23; Lk 22:21; Jn 13:18.—s Pss 72:18f; 89:53; 106:48; 150:1-6; Neh 9:5; Dan 2:20.—t 2-3: Pss 36:10; 63:2; 84:3; 143:6; Deut 10:7; Isa 26:9; Joel 1:20; Jn 7:37.—u Pss 27:4; 63:2; 143:6; Jos 3:10; Mt 16:16; Rom 9:26.

41:5 *Sinned:* the psalmist acknowledges his sin and asks for forgiveness and healing—in keeping with the idea that sickness was a divine punishment for sin (see Ps 107:17; Job 32:3). In the cure of the man born blind, Jesus was to indicate that such was not the case (see Jn 9:2f).

41:7 *Heart:* see note on Ps 4:8.

41:10 This passage repeats a theme frequently developed (see Pss 31:12; 38:12; 55:15f; 88:9; Job 19:13; Jer 20:10; 38:22). It is cited by Jesus with reference to Judas (Jn 13:18) according to the sense of the Septuagint. *Risen up:* literally, "raised his heel."

41:11 *Make me well:* the fact that God heals the psalmist is in itself a judgment in his favor and against his adversaries, but paying them back is not part of God's judgment.

41:14 This doxology is not part of the psalm; it concludes the first of the five Books of the Psalter (see Pss 72:18f; 89:53; 106:48; 150). *Blessed:* see note on Ps 18:47.

Pss 42–72 The drama of the righteous confronted with the rise of evil terminated Book I of the Psalter. This conflict remains, but other themes come to the fore with greater insistence. Now the prayer often evinces a desire for God and to be far from human beings, oftentimes with a more mystical note added. At other times, crucial moments of history will appear to provoke alternatively both praise and supplication: the drama of the righteous remains—as that of the people. In short, in the psalms that follow, the collective aspect will be readily underlined.

Ps 42 This psalm, which really forms one with the next psalm, has a fascinating literary beauty but also expresses feeling of a rare kind. It is the lament of the exiled Levite combining nostalgia, distress, and fervent desire. Living in a foreign land, far from the temple of Jerusalem, the sole place where it was believed one would encounter God, the sacred ministers feel the Exile more deeply; the sanctuary is the only place where they find their happiness. They are the first to suffer the mockings of the pagans, who do not recognize the God to whom they have dedicated their lives. Three times the lament is voiced, and three times the chant that gives hope is also uttered, as the psalm vibrantly expresses the fervor for the temple, where the people flocked to celebrate the love and presence of God.

At the heart of this fervor we glimpse the deepest human yearning: the desire for God. It is this that here on earth inspires the candidates who seek to enter the Church, the "house of God," and we also place it on the lips of the dead who are waiting to be admitted into the new Jerusalem, the heavenly city of God. Consecrated men and women also recognize herein the movement of their souls. Is not this the sublime desire at the root of all human restlessness? Down the centuries Augustine has proclaimed: "Our hearts are restless until they rest in you."

42:1 *For the director:* these words are thought to be a musical or liturgical notation. *Maskil:* see note on Ps 32:1a. *Sons of Korah:* Levites (see 1 Chr 26:19). In Book II, seven psalms bear this inscription (Pss 42; 44–49) and four in Book III (Pss 84–85; 87–88).

42:2 *God:* from Pss 42 to 89, the ineffable tetragrammaton ("Yahweh") is generally replaced by "God" ("Elohim"), marking this as the "Elohist Psalter."

42:3 *Soul:* see note on Ps 6:4. *Living God:* see Deut 5:26. *Behold the face of God:* here the phrase is taken to mean God's personal presence (see Gen 33:10; Ex 10:28f). In other places the expression "see God" (or "see the face of God") indicates the presence of God in the temple (see Pss 11:7; 17:15; 63:3; Ex 24:10; 33:7-11; Job 33:26).

4 My tears have become my food
day and night, [v]
while people taunt me all day long, saying,
"Where is your God?" [w]
5 As I pour out my soul, [x]
I recall those times
when I journeyed with the multitude
and led them in procession to the house of God,
amid loud cries of joy and thanksgiving
on the part of the crowd keeping festival. [y]

6 Why are you so disheartened, O my soul?
Why do you sigh within me?
Place your hope in God,
for I will once again praise him,
my Savior and my God. *

7 My soul is disheartened within me;
therefore, I remember you
from the land of Jordan and Hermon,
from Mount Mizar. * [z]
8 The depths of the sea resound
in the roar of your waterfalls; *
all your waves and your breakers
sweep over me. [a]
9 During the day the LORD grants his kindness,
and at night his praise is with me,
a prayer to the living God. *

10 I say to God, my Rock, *
"Why have you forgotten me?
Why must I go about in mourning
while my enemy oppresses me?" [b]
11 It crushes my bones
when my foes taunt me,
jeering at me all day long,
"Where is your God?" *

12 Why are you so disheartened, O my soul?
Why do you sigh within me?
Place your hope in God;
for I will once again praise him,
my Savior and my God. *

PSALM 43*

Prayer To Worship God Anew

1 Grant me your justice, O God,
and plead my cause against a godless nation;
rescue me from those who are deceitful
and unjust. [c]
2 You, O God, are my refuge;
why have you rejected me?
Why must I go about in mourning,
while my enemy oppresses me?

3 Send forth your light and your truth; *
they will serve as my guide. [d]
Let them bring me to your holy mountain,
to the place of your dwelling. [e]
4 Then I will go to the altar of God,
to the God of my joy and delight,
and I will praise you * with the harp,
O God, my God.

v Pss 80:6; 102:10; Job 3:24.—w Pss 79:10; 115:2; Joel 2:17; Mic 7:10; Mal 2:17.—x 1 Sam 1:15; Lam 3:20.—y Pss 27:4; 55:15; 122:1, 4; Isa 30:29.—z Pss 43:5; 63:7; 77:12; Deut 3:8.—a Pss 18:5; 32:6; 69:3; 88:8; 124:4-5; Gen 1:2; 7:11; Jon 2:3.—b Pss 18:3, 33; 31:3-4; 35:14; 106:42; Job 20:19.—c Pss 109:2; 119:154.—d Pss 2:6; 18:29; 27:1; 36:10; 57:4; 2 Sam 15:25; Mic 7:8.—e Pss 2:6; 84:2-5; 122:1.

42:6 *Why . . . my God:* this refrain appears three times in this double psalm (vv. 6, 12; 43:5) and indicates that the two parts were originally one psalm (see note on v. 12).

42:7 *Mount Mizar:* not identified. The translation *from the land . . .* supposes a Levite exiled to the springs of the Jordan, at the foot of Mount Hermon. If we think of him as exiled in Babylon, the translation would be: "I will remember you / more than the land of the Jordan and Hermon, / than the lowly mountain [Zion]."

42:8 *The depths of the sea resound . . . your waterfalls:* the psalmist alludes to the "waterfalls" that carry God's waters from the "depths" above to the "depths" below (see note on Ps 36:9), bringing God's breakers sweeping over him (see Pss 69:2f; 88:8; Jon 2:3, 5). And God is involved in this danger of water toward the psalmist (see note on Ps 32:6)—he lets it happen.

42:9 Nonetheless, the psalmist is confident of God's kindness, and this sustains him (see note on Ps 6:5). *The living God:* some propose the translation: "the God of my life" and understand it as the "God who gives me life."

42:10 *Rock:* see note on Ps 18:3. *Why . . . ? Why . . . ?:* see note on Ps 6:4.

42:11 The psalmist has been abandoned by God to his godless enemies, who taunt him with the words *"Where is your God?"* He resembles a dying man, and his whole being (*bones*; see note on Ps 34:20-21) is distressed by his foes and by God's silence.

42:12 The refrain is voiced for the second time in this double-psalm (see v. 6, above) and will be repeated once more in Ps 43:5. This threefold refrain reflects the attitude of many of God's people during the Exile or any crisis situation. In such loneliness and alienation, faith is tried and leads to salvation. For hope is mindful of the Lord's glorious works of salvation and victory recounted in the sacred writings. See Mt 26:38 for the application of these words to Christ's agony in the Garden of Gethsemane.

Ps 43 The psalmist asks God for vindication so that he may be able to return to the temple and render him praise once again.

We can pray this psalm to augment our tranquil hope. We place our cause in God, who has sworn that he will obtain redress for us from our enemies (see Rom 12:19; Heb 10:30). He will enable us to journey toward the heavenly Jerusalem in the vast mobile column of his Church, the true liturgical procession and uninterrupted processional march that takes the elect to him (see Heb 10:19-22).

43:3 *Your light and your truth:* the psalmist personifies the divine attributes of light (see note on Ps 27:1) and truth (see Pss 25:5; 26:3; 40:11) and asks that they bring him safely to the temple. *Holy mountain:* see note on Ps 2:6.

43:4 *Altar of God . . . I will praise you:* see notes on Pss 7:18; 26:6.

5 Why are you so disheartened, O my soul?
Why do you sigh within me?
Place your hope in God;
for I will once again praise him,
my Savior and my God. *

PSALM 44*

Past Glory and Present Need of God's People

1 For the director. * A *maskil* of the sons of Korah.

2 * O God, we have heard with our ears,
our ancestors have told us,
of the deeds you performed in their days,
in the days of old.[f]
3 To establish them in the land,
you drove out the nations with your own hand;
you crushed the peoples
so that our ancestors could flourish.[g]
4 It was not their own swords that won them the land,
nor did their own arms make them victorious;[h]
rather, it was your right hand and your arm
and the light of your face, *
because you loved them.[i]
5 You are my * King and my God,
who bestowed victories upon Jacob.[j]
6 Through you we throw back our enemies;
through your name * we crush our assailants.
7 It is not in my bow that I trust,
nor can my sword ensure my victory.
8 It is you who saved us from our enemies;
you scattered in confusion those who hate us.
9 In God we boast the whole day long,
and we will praise your name forever.
Selah

10 * [k] But now you have rejected and humiliated us,[l]
and you no longer accompany our armies. *
11 You have forced us to retreat * before the enemy;
those who hate us plunder us unceasingly.[m]
12 You have handed us over like sheep to be slaughtered
and scattered us among the nations.[n]
13 You have sold your people for nothing,
receiving no gain from their sale.[o]
14 [p] You have subjected us to the contempt of our neighbors,
to the mockery and scorn of all who are near.
15 You have made us a byword to the nations;
the peoples shake their heads * at us.
16 All day long I am confronted by my disgrace,
and my face is covered with shame
17 as I hear the shouts of taunting and abuse
and see the hateful enemy seeking revenge.

18 All this has happened to us
even though we have not forgotten you
or been false to your covenant. *

f Ps 78:3; 2 Sam 7:22-23; 1 Chr 17:20.—g Pss 78:55; 80:10f; Acts 7:45.—h Deut 8:17f; Jos 24:12.—i Pss 4:7; 31:17; 67:2; 78:54; 80:4; Ex 15:16; Num 6:25; Dan 9:17; Hos 1:7.—j Pss 5:2; 21:6; 145:1.—k 10-27: Ps 89:39-52.—l Pss 60:12; 68:8.—m Lev 26:17; Deut 28:25; Jdg 2:14.—n Lev 26:33; Deut 28:64.—o Deut 32:30; Isa 52:3; Jer 15:13.—p 14-17: Pss 79:4; 80:7; 123:3-4; 2 Chr 29:8; Job 12:4; Dan 9:16.

43:5 See note on Ps 42:12.

Ps 44 In the history of Israel, times of joy and defeat alternate with one another. This hymn transmits the strong feeling of the people about the triumphs of bygone days and the defeat at hand. But they do not believe God can forget forever the people that he loves.

As the true "remnant" and the elite of God's servants, the Church very naturally uses this psalm of the remnant of Israel to beseech the Lord and Master to take pity on her in the severe trials that assail her. This national lamentation is a prayer for times when we feel overwhelmed by failure, uncertainty, and confusion.

44:1 *For the director:* these words are thought to be a musical or liturgical notation. *Maskil:* see note on Ps 32:1a. *Sons of Korah:* see note on Ps 42:1.

44:2-9 The liturgy of the Old Testament transmits with gratitude the memory of the great hours of the conquest. Isn't God the one who at that time was responsible for this people's victory? A hymn recalls these wondrous deeds.

44:4 *The light of your face:* see notes on Pss 4:7; 13:2.

44:5 *My:* this psalm is sung in the name of all Israel.

44:6, 9 *Name:* see note on Ps 5:12.

44:10-17 Only a lament can evoke the situation of that moment; we are doubtless at the time of the Exile, after 587 B.C. This prayer could have been utilized and adapted at other times of national calamity; thus, verses 18-23 make us think of the Maccabean period when Israel is conscious of being the faithful community that did not deserve persecution (167–164 B.C.); the people suffer for their faith rather than for punishment of sin. For Paul, this lament (v. 23) reflects the condition of Christians (Rom 8:36).

44:10 *You no longer accompany our armies:* as commander-in-chief (see Pss 60:12; 68:8; Ex 15:3; Jdg 5:4).

44:11 *You have forced us to retreat:* God is responsible for the defeats as well as the victories (v. 5) of Israel.

44:15 Since the People of God have been allowed by God to be conquered, plundered, scattered like sheep, and enslaved by their enemies, their name has been disgraced among the nations (see Deut 28:37; 1 Ki 9:7; Jer 24:10). *Shake their heads:* a gesture of scorn (see Ps 64:9).

44:18 Israel's present state is not the result of infidelity to God's Covenant (see Ex 19–24).

19 Our hearts * have not turned back,
nor have our feet wandered from your path.
20 Yet you have crushed us,
forced us to live among the jackals, *
and covered us with darkness. [q]
21 If we had forgotten the name * of our God
or lifted up our hands to a foreign god,
22 would not God have discovered it,
he who knows the secrets of the heart?
23 For your sake we are put to death all day long; [r]
we are treated like sheep destined to be slaughtered. *
24 Awake, O Lord. Why * do you sleep?
Rise up, and do not abandon us forever. [s]
25 Why do you hide your face *
and continue to ignore our misery and our sufferings? [t]
26 We have been brought down to the dust; [u]
our bodies cling to the ground. *
27 Rise up and come to our aid;
redeem us for the sake of your kindness. *

PSALM 45*

Nuptial Ode for the Messianic King

1 For the director. * According to "Lilies." A *maskil* of the sons of Korah. A love song.

2 * My heart * is moved by a noble theme
as I sing my poem to the king;
my tongue is like the pen of a skillful scribe.
3 You are the most handsome of men; *
grace has anointed your lips,
for God has blessed you forever. [v]
4 Gird your sword upon your thigh, O warrior,
and advance in splendor and majesty. [w]
5 Ride on triumphantly in truth, humility, and justice;
may your right hand perform wondrous deeds.
6 Your arrows are sharp;
nations will lie beneath your feet;
the enemies of the king will lose heart. *
7 [x] Your throne, O God, * will last forever and ever;

q Isa 34:13; Jer 9:10.—r Isa 53:7; Rom 8:36.—s Pss 10:1; 74:1; 77:8; 79:5; 83:2; 89:47.—t Pss 10:11; 13:2; 89:47; Job 13:24.—u Pss 7:6; 12:6; 26:11; 102:14; 119:25; Num 10:35.—v Song 5:10-16; Lk 4:22.—w Pss 21:6; 149:6.—x 7-8: Lam 5:19; Heb 1:8-9.

44:19 *Hearts:* see note on Ps 4:8. *Your path:* the path or way shown them by the Lord (see Ps 18:31).

44:20 *You have crushed us [and] forced us to live among the jackals:* i.e., relegated Israel to a place unfit for human beings (see Isa 13:22; Jer 9:11; 10:22). Another translation proposed is: "you crushed us as you did the sea monster." *Darkness:* they have been left without "light," which symbolizes the fruits of God's loving kindness (see note on Ps 36:10).

44:21 *Name:* see note on Ps 5:12. *Lifted up our hands:* the usual posture for prayer (see Ex 9:29), with palms turned upward.

44:23 In truth, Israel has suffered the hostility of the peoples because she has been the nation faithful to the Lord. Applying this verse to the Christian community (Rom 8:36), Paul is able to give it a positive slant because of Christ's victory through his Passion and Resurrection (Rom 8:37-39).

44:24 *Why . . . ?:* see note on Ps 6:4.

44:25 *Hide your face:* see note on Ps 13:2.

44:26 *Our bodies cling to the ground:* posture of those who are defeated, those at prayer, or those in affliction (see Pss 7:6; 119:25; Num 24:4; Deut 9:18).

44:27 *Kindness:* see note on Ps 6:5.

Ps 45 This unique psalm, probably composed for a royal wedding, opens with the dedication to the king, then lets the ceremony unfold before our eyes. First, it celebrates the monarchy, depicting it under the characteristics of a new David, the Anointed One already acclaimed by Isaiah (see Isa 9:5f; 11:3-5). He is a splendid war chief, a lieutenant of God who comes forth with a dazzling cortege; upon him rests the promise made to the House of David (see 2 Sam 7). Next it addresses and celebrates the queen—a foreigner (Ps 45: 11-18)—placed at the right hand of her royal spouse, richly adorned and heaped with gifts. She is ushered into the palace followed by her bridesmaids and offered an array of good wishes.

The psalm also reminds us of a different kind of marriage. The Prophets had spoken of God as espoused to his people (see Isa 62:5; Ezek 16:8f; Hos 2:16), a rich, though bold image. As Jews reread this beautiful lyric text, they had a presentiment of the covenant that the future Messiah was to establish and extend to include the pagan peoples. The Christian tradition finds in it a prediction of the marriage of Christ and the Church (Mt 9:15; 22:9; Jn 3:29; 2 Cor 11:5; Eph 5:22; Rev 19:9; 21:2), the new and definitive covenant that is extended to all peoples.

The Liturgy draws upon this psalm in celebrating the most impressive fulfillment of these mystical espousals: the Virgin Mary, Queen and Bride of the King, and those who, following her, have chosen Christ for their Bridegroom.

45:1 *For the director:* these words are thought to be a musical or liturgical notation. *According to "Lilies":* nothing is known about these words. *Maskil:* see note on Ps 32:1a. *Sons of Korah:* see note on Ps 42:1.

45:2-10 The poet addresses the King-Messiah and applies to him attributes of Yahweh (see Ps 145:4-7, 12f, etc.) and of Immanuel (see Isa 9:5f; 11:3-5). He is urged to conduct himself in such a way that his reign will be adorned even more splendidly than the wedding vestments he has on (Ps 45: 4-6). The best way he can do so is to make the glory of his kingdom consist in justice and righteousness (vv. 7-10).

45:2 *Heart:* see note on Ps 4:8.

45:3 *Most handsome of men:* so far above all other men was a king of that era regarded (see 1 Sam 9:2; 16:18) that he is akin to a god (see note on Ps 45:7). Older versions translated this phrase as "fairest among the sons of men." *Grace has anointed your lips:* see Prov 22:11; Eccl 10:12; see also Isa 50:4; Lk 4:22.

45:6 *Heart:* see note on Ps 4:8.

45:7 *O God:* a title of honor applied in the Bible to the Messiah (see Isa 9:6), as well as to the leaders and judges (see Ps 82:6), to Moses (see Ex 4:16; 7:1), to the spirit of Samuel (see 1 Sam 28:13), and to the House of David (see Zec 12:8). The fullest meaning of this description of the Davidic king is attained when it is applied to Christ (see Heb 1:8f).

the scepter of your kingdom will be a
scepter of justice.
8 You love righteousness and hate wickedness;
therefore God, your God, has established you above your fellow kings
by anointing you with the oil of gladness.
9 * All your robes are fragrant
with myrrh and aloes and cassia;
from palaces of ivory
stringed instruments bring joy to your heart.
10 Daughters of kings * are among your women in waiting;
at your right hand is your queen
adorned in gold of Ophir.
11 My daughter, listen carefully to my words
and follow them diligently.
Forget your people and your father's house; *
12 then the king will desire your beauty.
Since he is your lord,
13 bow down before him.
The Daughter of Tyre * will bring you gifts,
people of wealth will seek your favor.[y]
14[z] Within the palace the king's daughter is adorned
in robes threaded with gold.
15 In embroidered garments she is led to the king,
followed by her virgin companions,
who are also led to you.*
16 They are brought in with joy and gladness
as they enter the palace of the king.
17 Your * sons will take the place of your ancestors;[a]
you will make them princes in all the earth.
18 I will extol your name through all generations;
therefore, the nations will praise you forever and ever. *[b]

PSALM 46*

God, Refuge of His People

1 For the director. * A song of the sons of Korah. According to *alamoth.*
2 * God is our refuge and our strength,
a well-proved help in times of trouble. *[c]
3 Therefore, we will not be afraid, though
the earth be shaken

y Ps 72:10-11; Jos 19:29; 1 Ki 9:16; Isa 60:5f.—z 14-16: Isa 61:10; Ezek 16:10-13.—a Pss 68:28; 113:8; Gen 17:6; 35:11.—b Isa 60:15; 61:9; 62:2.—c Pss 9:10; 48:4; Isa 33:2; Jer 16:19; Joel 3:16.

45:9-10 The psalmist's descriptions and references of the preparations for the wedding ceremony—robes, spices, music, the royal daughters, and the royal bride—all emphasize the rightness of the moment and the anointing of this king, who is a son of David. God's blessing on him ensures the continuity of David's house in accord with God's promise (see 2 Sam 7:16). *Myrrh and aloes and cassia:* Oriental perfumes (see Gen 37:25; Ex 25:6; Song 1:13; 4:14). *From palaces of ivory:* see 1 Ki 22:39; Am 3:15; 6:4. *Heart:* see note on Ps 4:8.

45:10 *Daughters of kings:* in the allegorical sense, these are the pagan nations converted to the true God (see Song 1:3; 6:8; Isa 60:3f; 61:5) and admitted to his service (Ps 45:16). *Gold of Ophir:* the most prized kind of gold (see 1 Ki 9:28; 10:11; Job 22:24). The location of Ophir is not known; it is sometimes identified with the southern coast of Arabia or eastern Africa.

45:11 *Forget your people and your father's house:* all her concern should be with what follows, not with what went before; she is the queen and should be concerned with her husband the king.

45:13 The reward for joining God's people and for following the new way of life is exaltation among the nations. The people of Tyre—as well as other wealthy nations—will bring tribute to Jerusalem. Indeed, during Solomon's rule, precious gifts were brought to Jerusalem because of his great renown. *Daughter of Tyre:* the city of Tyre, famous for its wealth, which was the first foreign city to recognize the Davidic dynasty (see 2 Sam 5:11) and remained close to Solomon (see 1 Ki 5; 9:10-14, 26-28). See also note on Ps 9:15.

45:15 *To you:* i.e., to the king.

45:17 *Your:* i.e., the king's. *Earth:* or "land."

45:18 The psalmist sees the nations praising the Israelite king, i.e., especially the Messianic King. The Prophets had foretold that in the restoration the nations would bring him gifts to celebrate the dignity of the People of God among the nations. The Book of Revelation also mentions this aspect of the everlasting state: "The kings of the earth will bring their treasures.... The nations will come into it bringing their treasures and wealth" (Rev 21:24, 26). Filled with blessings (see Gen 17:6; 35:11), the new Zion will be glorious and sovereign (see Isa 60:15, 21; 61:9; 62:2, 7), especially in Messianic times.

Ps 46 This psalm exalts the power of the God of Israel, Master of nature and Ruler of both armies and peace. Upon a horizon of wars and cataclysms rises the city of Zion, peaceful and unshakable. God is in her, a refuge protecting her from all agitations, a river bringing her a richness of life. The psalm lets us relive the explosion of joy prompted by the defeat of the Assyrian armies in 701 B.C. (see 2 Ki 18:13—19:37; 2 Chr 32).

This great moment of the past allows the Prophets to designate in advance the drama at the end of time. Amidst the turmoil of nations, God intervenes to save his people, and the world is turned upside down before obtaining definitive peace. It is an image of the movement of history with its cataclysms and the hope of universal salvation.

In praying this psalm, we should recall that the new and eternal Jerusalem, our mother, is the Church (see Gal 4:26) to whom Christ guaranteed his perpetual protection that renders her indefectible.

46:1 *For the director:* these words are thought to be a musical or liturgical notation. *Sons of Korah:* see note on Ps 42:1. *Alamoth:* probably a musical term.

46:2-4 The divine presence in the temple guarantees the security of the holy city even though creation itself may seem to be falling apart (see Ps 104:6-9; Gen 1:9f).

46:2 *Help in times of trouble:* when people are in trouble, they feel the need of God's special protection (see Pss 22:20; 27:9; 40:14; 44:27; 63:8). They experience his presence especially when they go through a time of distress (see Ps 23:4). He is then very close to them (see Deut 4:7).

and the mountains tumble into the
depths of the sea, [d]
4 though its waters rage and seethe
and the mountains tremble at the
upheaval.
The LORD of hosts is with us;
the God of Jacob is our fortress. *
Selah
5 There is a river * whose streams bring joy
to the city of God,
the holy place where the Most High
dwells. [e]
6 God is in her midst; she will not be over-
come; [f]
God will help her at break of dawn. *
7 The nations are in tumult and kingdoms
fall;
when he raises his voice, * the earth
melts away. [g]
8 The LORD of hosts is with us;
the God of Jacob is our fortress.
Selah
9 Come and behold the works of the LORD,
the astonishing deeds he has wrought
on the earth. [h]
10 He puts an end to wars all over the earth; [i]
he breaks the bow and snaps the spear,
and he burns the shields with flames. *
11 "Be still and acknowledge that I am God,
exalted among the nations, [j]
exalted on the earth." *
12 The LORD of hosts is with us;
the God of Jacob is our fortress.
Selah

PSALM 47*

The LORD, King of All Nations

1 For the director. * A psalm of the sons of
Korah.
2 All you peoples, clap your hands, *
shout to God with cries of gladness. [k]
3 For the LORD, the Most High, is awe-
some;
he is the great King over all the
earth. [l]
4 He subdued nations under us
and brought peoples under our feet. [m]
5 He chose our inheritance for us,
the pride of Jacob, * whom he loved. [n]
Selah
6 * God has ascended amid shouts of joy;
the LORD, amid the sound of trum-
pets. [o]
7 Sing praises to God, sing praises;
sing praises to our King, sing praises.
8 [p] For God is the King of the entire earth;
sing hymns of praise to him.
9 God reigns over all the nations;
God is seated on his holy throne.
10 The princes of the nations assemble
with the people of the God of Abra-
ham;

d Pss 3:6; 93:3-4; 97:5; Job 9:5-6; Isa 24:18-20; 54:10.—e Pss 36:9; 48:2-3; 76:2.—f Deut 23:14; 2 Ki 19:35; Isa 17:14.—g Pss 2:1-5; 48:5-8; 76:7-9; Job 12:23; Isa 17:12-14.—h Pss 48:9-10; 66:5.—i Pss 37:15; 76:4; Isa 2:4; 39:9.—j Ps 48:11; Deut 32:39; Ezek 12:16.—k Pss 33:3; 89:16; Zep 3:14.—l Ps 95:3; Gen 14:18; Ex 15:18; Isa 24:23; 52:7.—m Pss 2:8; 18:40.—n Ps 16:6; Isa 58:14.—o Pss 24:8, 10; 68:19-20; 98:6; Num 23:21.—p 8-9: Pss 72:11; 93:1; 96:10; 97:1; 99:1; Jer 10:7; Zec 14:9; Col 3:16.

46:4 *The LORD of hosts is with us; / the God of Jacob is our fortress:* this comforting refrain occurs three times in the psalm—here and in vv. 8, 12 (although the Hebrew lacks it in v. 4). The first part (*The LORD . . . is with us*) is similar in structure and meaning to the name of the royal child in Isaiah: "Immanuel"—"God is with us" (Isa 7:14; 8:8, 10). *The LORD of hosts:* see note on Ps 24:10.

46:5 *River:* symbol of God's blessings; the symbolic waters (see Ps 36:9) that spring forth (see Ezek 47:1, 12; Joel 4:18; Zec 14:8) make the holy land fruitful, purify it (see Zec 13:1), and turn it into a new Eden (see Gen 2:10).

46:6 *At break of dawn:* the most favored time for attacks to be set in motion against cities but also for God's blessings (see Pss 17:15; 49:15; 101:8; Song 2:17; Isa 17:14). The psalm here most likely alludes to the retreat of Sennacherib's armies in 701 B.C. (see 2 Ki 19:35).

46:7 *His voice:* God's thunder (see Ps 104:7; Jer 25:30; Am 1:2). *The earth melts away:* under the heat of God's lightnings. But Israel has no need to fear any of these calamities.

46:10 This verse speaks of universal peace and anticipates the Messianic victory.

46:11 *Exalted . . . on the earth:* because of his wondrous deeds for his people, especially the Life, Passion, and Resurrection of Jesus Christ.

Ps 47 This psalm is concerned with the Feast of the New Year. The Ark is transported: "God has ascended . . ." and, during the procession, this chant of the kingdom (see note on Ps 93) goes forth. Israel proclaims the kingship of God (see Ex 15:18; Isa 52:7; Zep 3:15), who has handed over to his people the land of Canaan and the city of Jerusalem while also defeating the nearby peoples. The ancient chant remains, but it appears as a prelude to the Lord's reign over the whole universe (see Jer 10:7). The pagans will be converted and join God's people in acclaiming the only true King (see Ezr 6:21; Isa 19:23-25; 25:6; 60:11).

The Roman and Byzantine liturgies see in this text a psalm for the Ascension of Christ: Christ "has ascended amid shouts of joy" and "is seated on his holy throne" as Lord at the right hand of the Father; from there salvation is offered to all peoples (see Acts 2:34; Phil 2:9-11; Rev 5:7-9, 12f).

47:1 *For the director:* these words are thought to be a musical or liturgical notation. *Sons of Korah:* see note on Ps 42:1.

47:2 *Clap your hands:* a gesture used at occasions of great joy, e.g., at enthronements (see Ps 98:8; 2 Ki 11:12; Isa 55:12).

47:5 *Our inheritance . . . the pride of Jacob:* the Promised Land (see Gen 12:7; 17:8; Ex 3:8; Deut 1:8; Jer 3:18), which God gave Israel by a sovereign act.

47:6-7 God ascends liturgically to the temple in the Ark of the Covenant.

for the rulers * of the earth belong to
God, [q]
and he is exalted on high.

PSALM 48*

Thanksgiving for the Deliverance of God's People

1 A psalm of the sons of Korah. * A song.
2 Great is the LORD and worthy of high
praise [r]
in the city of our God.
His holy mountain, * 3 towering in its
beauty,
is the joy of the entire earth. [s]
Mount Zion, the true heights of the
north, * [t]
is the city of the great King.
4 God is in her citadels
and has revealed himself as her
fortress. *
5 * For the kings conspired together
and came onward in unison.
6 As soon as they beheld her, they were
astounded;
filled with panic, they fled. [u]
7 They were seized with trembling,
with pains like those of a woman in
labor, [v]
8 as though a wind from the east *
were breaking up the ships of Tarshish.
9 What we had heard,
we have now beheld for ourselves *
in the city of the LORD of hosts,
in the city of our God
that he established to endure forever.
Selah
10 O God, as we stand in the midst of your
temple,
we will meditate on your kindness. *
11 Like your name, * O God,
your praise extends to the ends of the
earth.
Your right hand is filled with righteous-
ness; [w]
12 let Mount Zion rejoice.
Let the towns of Judah exult
in your saving judgments. * [x]
13 * Walk around Zion; pass throughout her;
count the number of her towers.
14 Take careful note of her ramparts,
walk through her citadels,

q Ps 89:19; Ex 3:6; Ezr 6:21; Isa 2:2-4.—r Pss 86:10; 96:4; 135:5; 145:3; Jer 10:6.—s Ps 50:2; Lam 2:15; Ezek 16:14; Mt 5:35.—t Isa 14:13.—u Ex 15:16; Jdg 5:19.—v Ex 15:14; Job 4:14; Jer 4:31.—w Ps 113:3; Mal 1:11.—x Pss 97:8; 105:5; Deut 33:21.

47:10 In Messianic times, the reconciled peoples will form only one people with God's chosen ones. The covenant with Abraham (see Ps 105:6; Ex 3:6; Est C:2-5 [13:9-13]) will be extended to all humankind (see Ps 72:11; Gen 9:9; Isa 2:2; 45:20f; 56:6; Zec 8:20; 14:16). *Princes . . . rulers:* some suggest that these terms refer to the angelic spirits who watch over the nations (see Deut 32:8f; Dan 10:13).

Ps 48 With overflowing joy, this psalm sings of God and the holy city. All the glory of Jerusalem stems from the Lord who dwells, enveloped in mystery, in the temple on the hill in the heart of the city. From there he protects his people; he has even delivered this city from the assaults of the enemy. It is secure from the north (v. 3), east (v. 8), south (v. 11), and west (v. 14). There Israel encounters its God and gives him thanks. And from this dwelling of God, salvation, joy, and praise extend to all peoples and the whole universe. It is a grandiose vision; how can one not love this land of God in the midst of human beings!

To Christians, Zion stands for the Church of Jesus, soul of the world and sign of salvation for humankind, until all are gathered together into the kingdom of God, the heavenly Jerusalem (see Heb 12:22; Rev 14:1; 21:10-26).

48:1 *Sons of Korah:* see note on Ps 42:1.

48:2 *Holy mountain:* see note on Ps 2:6.

48:3 *The true heights of the north:* Zaphon. Mount Zaphon was in the far north, the home of the Canaanite storm-god Baal. The psalmist declares that, although Zion is only a small hill, it is higher than any other mountain because it is the home of the only true God (see Ps 68:16f).

48:4 The psalmist shows that Zion is impregnable not because of her walls but because of the fact that the Lord is present there as the strength of his people (see Pss 18:3; 122:7).

48:5-8 In recalling past defeats of Israel's enemies who attacked Zion, the psalmist may have in mind the victory over the Moab-Ammon coalition at the time of Jehoshaphat (see 2 Chr 20:22-28) or over the Assyrians at the time of Hezekiah (see 2 Ki 19:35f).

48:8 *East:* geographical allusion mentioned in the introduction. *Ships of Tarshish:* i.e., the most powerful ships, built for long voyages—like those that went as far as Tarshish, perhaps Tartessus in southern Spain (see 1 Ki 10:22).

48:9 *Heard . . . beheld for ourselves:* the psalmist may be referring to the glorious things that new pilgrims had heard about the beauty and awesomeness of the holy city and now beheld with their own eyes. He may also be referring to the things the pilgrims had heard from their ancestors about the security of the temple at Jerusalem (see Pss 44:2; 78:3) and now beheld for themselves. They became even more convinced of God's presence in Jerusalem ordering the world's events and working out the redemption of his people. *The LORD of hosts:* see note on Ps 24:10.

48:10 The godly meditate on God's mighty acts, taking comfort in, rejoicing in, and gratefully making offerings to the revelation of the perfections of the Lord. *Kindness:* see note on Ps 6:5.

48:11 *Name:* see note on Ps 5:12. *Right hand:* the reaction of praise is a positive response by the godly in contrast to the dread that befell the nations. The godly praise God from one end of the earth to another, declaring his righteousness, i.e., the Lord's victories and glorious work whose benefits his people share. That work is symbolized by his "right hand," which includes power, justice, righteousness, and love. As alluded to in the introduction to this psalm, "right hand" also has a connotation of "south" in Hebrew.

48:12 *Judgments:* God's actions in human affairs (see Ps 105:7; Isa 26:9), especially his victories over Israel's enemies (see Pss 98:8; 105:5; Deut 33:21).

48:13-14 The psalmist calls upon the people to walk around Jerusalem and see its great defenses (towers, ramparts, citadels). The physical defense system of Jerusalem may have been a symbol of a far greater strength—the protection of the Lord himself. Furthermore, inasmuch as the Lord was present in the temple at Jerusalem, defense of the city was an expression of loyalty to him.

so that you may recount for future generations[y]
15 that such is God;
our God forever and ever,
he will be our guide eternally. *

PSALM 49*

Deceptive Riches

1 For the director.* A psalm of the sons of Korah.

2 * Hear this, all you peoples;
listen carefully, all you inhabitants of the world,
3 whether lowborn or highborn,
rich and poor alike.

4 My mouth will speak words of wisdom,[z]
and the utterance of my heart* will give understanding.
5 I will listen carefully to a proverb,
and with the harp* I will interpret my riddle.

6 Why should I be afraid in evil times
when I am beset by the wickedness of my foes,*
7 those who place their trust in their wealth
and boast of the abundance of their riches?[a]
8 * For no one can ever redeem himself[b]
or pay a ransom to God for his release.
9 The price to ransom a life would be too costly;
no one would ever have enough
10 to enable him to live on forever
and avoid being consigned to the pit.

11 * For all can see that the wise die,
just as the foolish and the stupid also pass away,[c]
and all leave their wealth to others. *[d]
12 Their graves are their eternal homes,
their dwelling places for all generations,
even though they had named lands after themselves.
13 Despite his riches,
a man cannot escape death;[e]
he is like the beasts that perish. *

14 Such is the destiny of those who trust in themselves alone,
the fate of those who are pleased with their lot. * *Selah*
15 Like sheep* they are destined for the netherworld,
with death as their shepherd.

y Pss 22:31-32; 71:18; 78:6; 2 Sam 20:15; Isa 26:1; Lam 2:8.—z Pss 37:30; 78:2; Mt 13:35.—a Job 31:24; Prov 10:15; Jer 9:23.—b Job 33:24; Prov 11:4; Ezek 7:19; Mt 16:26.—c Pss 92:7; 94:8; Eccl 2:16.—d Ps 39:7; Sir 11:18-19; Lk 12:20.—e Job 14:2; Eccl 3:18-21; 2 Pet 2:12.

48:15 After seeing the well-nigh impregnable fortifications of Jerusalem, the people will feel more secure and better understand the greatness of the Lord, who protects his city and his people in accord with his promises; they will then recount it to their children and grandchildren. The Lord is their God forever, the great Shepherd-King (see note on Ps 23), who will continue to guide them *eternally* (literally, "till death").

Ps 49 The psalmist meditates on the vanity of riches and the problem of retribution (see Pss 37; 73), after introducing his discourse with a solemnity that is somewhat pretentious. He believes that he has the answer to the problems that torment many (though they are still far from experiencing the crisis of Job). Certainly, fortune is powerless to save the rich from the clutches of death, and no one can buy escape from death; on the contrary, the poor are "filled" because God pays for them what the rich cannot offer despite all their wealth.

The author also seems convinced that death cannot take away from him the divine friendship. The lot of the righteous cannot be the same as that of the wicked, for he suspects (without knowing how to imagine it) that the former will receive some kind of liberation at God's hand (v. 16).

In praying this psalm, we should be mindful that riches cannot assure our physical life and constitute an obstacle to our spiritual life. However, if we remain united with Christ, who has conquered death, we will rise with him (1 Cor 15:45f).

49:1 *For the director:* these words are thought to be a musical or liturgical notation. *Sons of Korah:* see note on Ps 42:1.

49:2-5 Solemn introduction: the first part (vv. 2-3) recalls the Prophets (see 1 Ki 22:28; Isa 34:1; Mic 1:2) and the second (vv. 4-5) recalls Ps 78:2; Job 33:4; 34:19; Prov 8:4f.

49:4 See Mt 12:34. *Heart:* see note on Ps 4:8.

49:5 The psalmist alludes to a kind of inspiration: since all wisdom is from God (see Job 28), he lent his ear to hear it; at the same time, he makes use of the *harp,* the instrument that accompanied prophesying (see 1 Sam 10:5f; 2 Ki 3:15).

49:6 The psalmist stresses that there is no reason to fear the wicked, for they place their trust in their wealth—which is powerless to save them from God (see vv. 8-10).

49:8-10 Wealth is useless to evade death; only God has the power to bring it about (see v. 16; 116:15; Job 33:24-26; Prov 11:4; Ezek 7:19; Mt 16:26; Rom 3:24). A wealthy person may live lavishly and give the impression that he will live forever. However, he too must at some point face death—which is a separation from the land of the living, from all life's comforts, and from social and economic advantages. *Pit:* a synonym for the netherworld (see Ps 16:10) that signifies death and perhaps retribution for evil done during life (see Ps 94:13).

49:11-12 Those who have amassed wealth for themselves (see Lk 12:20) or those who have rejected the voice of wisdom (see Prov 1:17f) are *the foolish and the stupid.* These have taken pains to ensure their memory by naming property after themselves but will be remembered only by the names engraved on their tombs (v. 12; see Isa 22:16). They will perish, forever bereft of their wealth.

49:11 A passage very close to Eccl 2:16 (see Pss 39:7; 92:7f).

49:13 The psalmist states that death is an inevitable part of earthly existence. He says nothing about life beyond death or the difference between human and animal life.

49:14 The psalmist does not condemn riches in themselves but only the attitude of self-sufficiency so often associated with wealth, which then leads to insensitivity, scheming, deception, and arrogance (see Jas 5:1-6) in both the rich and their followers.

49:15 *Like sheep:* death has become their shepherd, leading them to the grave. *They descend . . . waste away:* an alternative text is: "The upright will rule over them in the morning, / and their bodies will waste away." *In the morning:* the customary time for eschatological judgments and the triumph of the righteous (see Pss 17:15; 46:5; 101:8; Song 2:17; Isa 17:14).

They descend straight to the grave
where their bodies will waste away;
the netherworld will be their home.
16 But God will ransom me from the netherworld;
he will take me * to himself.[f] *Selah*
17 * Do not be afraid when someone becomes rich
and the splendor of his house increases.
18 When he dies, he will take nothing with him;[g]
his wealth will not accompany him below. *
19 Although during his lifetime he considered himself blessed:
"They will praise me because I have done well,"
20 he will end up joining the company of his ancestors
who will never again see the light. *[h]
21 Despite his riches,
a man who does not have wisdom
is like the beasts that perish. *

PSALM 50*

The Worship Acceptable to God

1 A psalm of Asaph. *
* The LORD, the God of gods, *
has spoken and summoned the earth
from the rising of the sun to its setting.[i]
2 From Zion, perfect in beauty,
God shines forth.[j]
3 Our God is coming, and he will not be silent;
he is preceded by a devouring fire,[k]
and a raging tempest surrounds him. *
4 He summons the heavens above
and the earth to judge his people:
5 "Gather before me my faithful servants
who made a covenant with me by sacrifice." *
6 The heavens proclaim his saving justice,
for God himself is the judge. *[l]
Selah
7 * "Listen, my people, and I will speak.
O Israel, I will testify against you.
I am God, your God.

f Pss 16:10; 73:24; 86:13; 103:4; 116:8; Gen 5:24.—g Ps 17:14; Eccl 5:15; Sir 11:18-19; 1 Tim 6:7.—h Gen 15:15; Job 10:21-22; 33:30.—i Ps 113:3; Deut 10:17; Jos 22:22.—j Pss 2:6; 48:3.—k Ps 97:3; Isa 42:14; Dan 7:10.—l Pss 19:2; 97:6; Gen 16:5; Job 9:15.

49:16 *Take me:* this is the same Hebrew verb that is used for God "taking up" his favored servants: Enoch (see Gen 5:24), Elijah (see 2 Ki 2:11f), and the righteous person (see Ps 73:24). The psalmist thus harbors the hope that God will rescue the righteous from the grave in some way. This hope will become stronger in Israel, as later Books show (see 2 Mac 7:9f; 12:44f; 14:46; Wis 2:23; 3:9; 6:19; Dan 12:2).

49:17-20 Faith enables the godly to avoid fearing anything that is transitory. Riches, splendor, and praise (garnered from self or from others) make no difference in the grave. Although wealth can protect one from the rigors of life, it is powerless against death, a place of utter darkness without even a ray of hope (*light*).

49:18 In contrast, God will glorify the righteous (see Pss 62:8; 73:24; 91:15; 1 Sam 2:30; Wis 3:7; 1 Tim 6:6-8).

49:20 See note on Ps 27:1.

49:21 The psalmist indicates that the godly who are wealthy are different from the senseless rich. Godly persons have understanding about riches as well as about their own mortality and about God, and they act accordingly.

Ps 50 This psalm takes the form of an indictment against God's people for the formalistic practice of their religion and a request for sacrifices of praise accompanied by obedience. It is divided into three parts: (1) the announcement of the Lord's arrival and the convening of the court (vv. 1-6); (2) the Lord's words of correction (vv. 7-15); (3) his rebuke for the wicked and promise of reward or punishment (vv. 16-23). The psalm itself may have been composed for a temple liturgy for reaffirming commitment to the covenant.

In praying this psalm, we should recall that Jesus also condemned formalism. Christ does not reproach us for our external worship, our beautiful liturgical celebrations, vows, oblations, or sacrifices. However, all these must truly reflect sentiments of profound religion—"a living sacrifice that is holy and acceptable to God" (Rom 12:1).

50:1a *Asaph:* probably a choral leader in the Jerusalem temple (see notes on Pss 73–89).

50:1b-6 The author knows how to conjure up the whole apparatus of a divine manifestation. God himself solemnly appears to challenge those who dishonor worship and the law and to recall for them the great demands of the covenant. Israel must realize that the God of Zion is the God of Sinai (see Ex 19:16-20). It is a picture of the Last Judgment.

50:1b *The LORD, the God of gods:* in Hebrew, a threefold formula for the divine name that can also be translated as: "The Mighty One, God, the LORD." It is found elsewhere only in Jos 22:22 (also see Deut 10:17). This psalm is notable for the seven names or other titles it uses for God (v. 1: *the God of gods* [or: The Mighty One], "God," "LORD"; v. 6: "judge"; v. 14: "Most High"; v. 21: "I am"; v. 22: "God"—alternative word, *Eloah*).

50:3 The Lord is the Ruler of the universe and his appearance is attended by phenomena calculated to create awe in his subjects: fire and a tempest. When he comes in judgment, he is like a consuming fire (see Deut 4:24; 9:3; Isa 66:16; Heb 12:29); in his anger, he may also storm like a tempest (see Isa 66:15).

50:5 Those consecrated to the Lord had made a covenant with him that was sealed by sacrifices (see Ex 24:4-8).

50:6 *Judge:* a title for God (see Ps 94:2; Gen 18:25; Jdg 11:27).

50:7-15 Pagans might have imagined that they owed food subsidies to their gods; the Lord has no need of our earthly goods, for everything belongs to him. This diatribe against purely external worship occurs often in the Bible, notably in the Prophets (see 1 Sam 15:22; 1 Chr 29:16-19; Isa 1:10-16; 29:13f; 58:1-8; Jer 6:20; 7:21; Hos 6:6; Joel 2:12; Mic 6:5-8; Zec 7:4-6; Mal 1:10) and is also found elsewhere in the Psalter (see Pss 40:7-9; 51:18f, etc.). The passages do not condemn sacrifices or worship in general, but only the formalism that is satisfied with performing external rites. We cannot bribe God; we can only acknowledge him by prayer and thanksgiving: this was the constant attitude of Jesus toward his Father. Truly religious persons are aware of their limitations; they await everything from God and realize that they owe him everything. The Gospel will lay a heavy emphasis on this teaching (see Mt 5:23; 12:7; Mk 12:33), and Paul will in turn repeat it in his instruction on worship in spirit (Rom 12:1; Phil 2:17; 3:3).

8 I do not rebuke you for your sacrifices,
for your burnt offerings are constantly before me.
9 "I will not accept a young bull from your homes
or goats from your folds. [m]
10 For all the living creatures of the forest are mine,
animals by the thousands on my hills.
11 I know every bird of the air,
and whatever moves in the fields belongs to me.
12 "If I were hungry, I would not tell you,
for the world is mine, and all that it holds. [n]
13 Do I eat the flesh of bulls
or drink the blood of goats?
14 "Offer to God a sacrifice of thanksgiving
and fulfill your vows to the Most High. [o]
15 Then if you cry out to me in time of trouble,
I will rescue you, and you will honor me." [p]
16 * But to the wicked God says:
"How can you recite my statutes
or profess my covenant on your lips?
17 For you loathe my instruction
and cast my words behind you.
18 "When you meet a thief, you join him;
you revel in the company of adulterers.
19 You employ your mouth for evil,
and your tongue frames deceit.
20 "You willingly speak against your brother
and slander the child of your own mother.
21 When you do such things, can I remain silent?
Do you think that I am * like you?
I will correct you
and set the charge before your face.
22 "Remember this, you who forget God, *
lest I tear you to pieces
and there be no one to rescue you.
23 He who offers a sacrifice of thanksgiving honors me;
to him who follows my way
I will show the salvation of God." [q]

PSALM 51*

The "Miserere": Repentance for Sin

1 For the director. * A psalm of David. 2 When
Nathan the prophet came to him after he had
sinned with Bathsheba. [r]

3 Have mercy on me, O God,
in accord with your kindness; *
in your abundant compassion
wipe away my offenses.
4 Wash me completely from my guilt,
and cleanse me from my sin.
5 For I am fully aware of my offense,
and my sin is ever before me. [s]

m Ps 69:32; Lev 1:5; Num 32:16; Am 5:21-22.—n Pss 24:1; 89:12; Ex 19:5; Deut 10:14; Jos 3:11; 1 Cor 10:26.—o Pss 27:6; 76:12; Hos 14:2; Heb 13:15.—p Pss 3:8; 4:2; 77:3; Isa 58:9.—q Pss 9:15; 91:16; 98:3; Isa 52:10.—r 2 Sam 12:1.—s Pss 32:5; 38:19; Isa 59:12; Ezek 6:9.

50:16-23 Another type of formalism is to have religion or the law on one's lips more than in one's heart and life. There is no authentic faith unless it includes a moral commitment and notably that of justice and respect toward others: "Not everyone who says to me, 'Lord, Lord,' will enter the kingdom of heaven, but only the one who does the will of my heavenly Father" (Mt 7:21).

50:21 *I am:* the formula that reveals the name of the Lord in the Old Testament (see Ex 3:14; Isa 41:4, 10, 14; 43:1-3, 10, 13). See notes on Mk 4:26; 6:50.

50:22 *God:* here the Hebrew is a relatively rare poetic word, *Eloah,* found frequently in Job (see also Pss 18:33; 139:19; Deut 32:15, 17; Hab 3:3).

Ps 51 This psalm, the "Miserere," the best known of the seven Penitential Psalms (Pss 6; 32; 38; 51; 102; 130; 143), is still the most authentic expression of our prayer as human beings. The kind of sincerity in the confession of sinfulness that it expresses requires a limitless trust in the mercy of God. Whether it voices the repentance of King David after his adultery (see 2 Sam 12:13) or that of the Jewish people after their return from the Exile during which they had become aware of their infidelity, the entreaty shows authentic repentance.

Men and women become conscious of the sin that alienates them from God (see Ezek 2:3; 16:43); evil plunges its roots deep within their being (see Jer 5:23; 7:24; 17:9; Ezek 36:26). A hasty forgiveness, an external purification, is not enough; it is the heart that must be transformed. God alone can effect this new creation and infuse a new Spirit (see Ezek 36:26). He allows sinners to come to their senses and humbly commit themselves to him again. He alone can answer the desire for complete renewal that is inscribed in a true request for forgiveness. Our thoughts turn immediately to Paul who movingly describes the dramatic situation of sinners (Rom 7:14ff) and then contrasts it with the exalted life of Christians who let themselves be led by the Holy Spirit (Rom 8).

Especially striking in this regard is verse 7 of this psalm: the individual—or the people—has been conceived in sin, begotten in guilt. The psalmist is surely not thinking of a sin of the mother that might infect the child, nor does the Old Testament consider the conjugal union to be sinful; by this exceptionally violent image the psalmist intends rather to convey the idea that the human being is born as a prisoner of a sinful environment.

All Christians—whether under the shock of some personal failing, under the, at times, searing impression of a life of mediocrity and nullity in God's eyes, or in union with the entire Church imploring the mercy of the Crucified upon the sinful world—have recited this psalm with its bubbling lyricism to express contrition and distress of soul, and to ask the Savior's mercy and their own inner renewal.

51:1 *For the director:* these words are thought to be a musical or liturgical notation. For the event referred to, see 2 Sam 11:1—12:25.

51:3 *Kindness:* see note on Ps 6:5. *Wipe away:* the psalmist pictures God keeping a record of a person's deeds on a scroll as earthly kings were wont to do (see Pss 56:9; 87:6; 130:3; 139:16; Ex 32:32f; Neh 13:14; Dan 7:10), and then wiping away the evil deeds when forgiveness is given.

6 Against you, you alone, * have I sinned;
I have done what is evil in your sight.

Therefore, you are right in accusing me
and just in passing judgment. [t]

7 Indeed, I was born in iniquity,
and in sin did my mother conceive me. * [u]

8 But you desire sincerity of heart; *
and you endow my innermost being with wisdom.

9 Sprinkle me with hyssop * so that I may be cleansed;
wash me until I am whiter than snow. [v]

10 Let me experience joy and gladness;
let the bones you have crushed exult.

11 Hide your face from my sins,
and wipe out all my offenses.

12 Create* in me a clean heart, O God,
and renew a resolute spirit within me. [w]

13 Do not cast me out from your presence
or take away from me your Holy Spirit. * [x]

14 Restore to me the joy of being saved,
and grant me the strength of a generous spirit.

15 I will teach your ways to the wicked,
and sinners will return to you.

16 Deliver me from bloodguilt, * O God,
the God of my salvation,
and I will proclaim your righteousness. [y]

17 O LORD, open my lips,
and my mouth will proclaim your praise.

18 For you take no delight in sacrifice;
if I were to make a burnt offering,
you would refuse to accept it. * [z]

19 My sacrifice, O God, is a broken spirit;
a contrite and humble heart, * O God,
you will not spurn.

20 * In your kindness, deal favorably with Zion;
build up the walls of Jerusalem. [a]

21 Then you will delight in righteous sacrifices,
in burnt offerings and whole oblations,
and young bulls will be offered on your altar.

PSALM 52*

Prayer for Help against Calumniators

1 For the director. * A *maskil* of David. 2 When
Doeg the Edomite went and told Saul, "David
has gone to the house of Ahimelech." [b]

t 1 Sam 15:24; Lk 15:21; Rom 3:4.—u Lev 5:2; Job 5:7; 14:4.—v Ex 12:22; Job 9:30; Isa 1:18; 44:22; Ezek 36:25; Heb 9:13-14.—w Pss 24:4; 78:37; Ezek 11:19; Eph 4:23-24.—x Wis 1:5; 9:17; Isa 57:15; 63:11f; Hag 2:5; Rom 8:9.—y Pss 25:5; 30:10; 35:28; 39:9.—z Pss 40:7; 50:8; 1 Sam 15:22; Isa 1:11-15; Hos 6:6; Am 5:21-22; Heb 10:5-7.—a Ps 147:2; Isa 58:12; Jer 31:4; Ezek 36:33.—b 1 Sam 21:7; 22:6ff.

51:6 *Against you, you alone:* the very essence of sin is that it constitutes an offense against God, even though it may also entail an offense against human beings. *Just in passing judgment:* permitted by God, sin calls for the intervention of his judgment (see Rom 3:4).

51:7 All human beings have a congenital inclination toward evil (see Gen 8:21; 1 Ki 8:46; Job 4:17; 14:4; 15:14; 25:4; Prov 20:9). God must take account of this situation, which is a mitigating circumstance, and show mercy. Later, the doctrine of original sin will be made explicit (see Rom 5:12f; Eph 2:3).

51:8 Despite his sins against God's teaching, the psalmist craves that teaching with his whole being; he wants to be among the wise who follow God's law, not the fools who reject it (see Ps 37:30f). *Heart:* see note on Ps 4:8.

51:9 *Hyssop:* a plant with many branchlets that is a convenient sprinkler, prescribed for sprinkling sacrificial blood or water for cleansing (see Ex 12:22; Lev 14:4; Num 19:18). *Whiter than snow:* purity beyond compare (see Isa 1:18; Dan 7:9; Rev 7:14; 19:14).

51:12 *Create:* verb reserved only for God (see Gen 1) and describing the act by which he brings into existence something new and wonderful (see Ex 34:10; Isa 48:7; 65:17; Jer 31:22). The justification of a sinner is the divine work par excellence (see Ezek 36:25f). *Heart:* see note on Ps 4:8.

51:13 *Holy Spirit:* the full phrase is found in the Old Testament only here and in Isa 63:10f, but the word "Spirit" alone is found throughout. It is by his Spirit that God creates (see Ps 104:30; Gen 1:2; Job 33:4) and redeems (see Isa 32:15; 44:3; 63:11, 14; Hag 2:5), inspires the Prophets (see Num 24:2f; 2 Sam 23:2; Neh 9:30; Isa 59:21; 61:1; Ezek 11:5; Mic 3:8; Zec 7:12) and directs their ministries (see 1 Ki 18:12; 2 Ki 2:16; Isa 48:16; Ezek 2:2; 3:14), prepares his servants for their given work (see Ex 31:3; Num 11:29; Jdg 3:10; 1 Sam 10:6; 16:13; Isa 11:2; 42:1), and bestows on his people a "new heart and . . . a new spirit," enabling them to live in accord with his will (see Ezek 36:26f).

51:16 *Bloodguilt:* the sin that brought about the death of an innocent man (see 2 Sam 12:5, 13) or the judgment passed upon a grave sin requiring the penalty of death (see Ezek 18:13).

51:18 See note on Ps 50:7-15.

51:19 *Broken spirit; a contrite and humble heart:* God is most pleased by a person who trusts in him despite trials of all sorts and who repents of sin and asks forgiveness. *Heart:* see note on Ps 4:8.

51:20-21 Scholars believe that these verses are a post-Exilic addition, made perhaps before the rebuilding of the walls of Jerusalem in 445 B.C. *Righteous sacrifices:* sacrifices that are not mere empty ritual but filled with praise and thanksgiving to God for his great works.

Ps 52 The psalmist indicates that a tragic end is reserved for arrogant cynicism and the perfidious tongue, while the righteous subsist, for they take refuge in God; they will have the happiness of living in the temple, i.e., in the presence of the Lord. This psalm constitutes one of the most violent indictments brought against wicked tongues; it resembles the wisdom psalms (see Pss 57:5; 59:8) and writings (Job 20).

In praying this psalm, we can dwell on the fact that Jesus teaches us to fear more than anything else those schemers who seek the death of our souls: the devil and the corruptive world, the givers of scandal (see 1 Jn 2:16; 1 Pet 5:8). The workers of evil know how to disguise themselves (see 2 Cor 11:15); by the power of Satan, they perform even lying works and use all the wicked deceptions of evil (see 2 Thes 2:9-12).

52:1-2 *For the director:* these words are thought to be a musical or liturgical notation. *Maskil:* see note on Ps 32:1a. For the event referred to, see 1 Sam 22:9f.

3 Why do you boast of your evil deeds,
you champion of malice? * [c]
All day long 4 you plot harm;
your tongue is like a sharpened razor,
you master of deceit.

5 * You love evil rather than good,
and lies rather than truthful speech. [d]
Selah

6 You wallow in destructive talk,
you tongue of deceit. [e]

7 * This is the reason why God will crush you
and destroy you once and for all.
He will snatch you from your tent *
and uproot you from the land of the living. [f] *Selah*

8 The righteous will see and be afraid;
they will mock him: [g]

9 "This is the man
who refused to accept God as his refuge.
Rather, he placed his trust in his abundant riches
and gathered strength by his crimes." [h]

10 * But I am like a green olive tree *
in the house of God.
I place my trust forever and ever
in the kindness of God. [i]

11 I will praise you forever
for what you have done, *
and in the presence of the saints
I will proclaim the goodness of your name. [j]

PSALM 53*

Foolishness of the Wicked

1 For the director. * According to *Mahalath.* A *maskil* of David.

2 * [k] The fool says in his heart,
"There is no God."
Such are depraved and their deeds are vile;
there is no one who does what is right. [l]

3 God looks down from heaven
upon the entire human race, [m]
[n] to see if there are any who act with wisdom,
if even a single one seeks God.

4 But they have all turned aside;
all alike are corrupt.
There is no one who does what is right,
not even one. [o]

5 Have all these evildoers no understanding?
They devour my people as they eat bread, [p]
and they never call out to God. [q]

c Pss 10:3; 12:4; 59:8; 120:2-3; Sir 51:3.—d Ps 58:4; Ex 10:10; 1 Sam 12:25; Jer 4:22; 9:5; Jn 3:19-20.—e Pss 5:10; 10:7; 109:2; 120:2-3; Prov 10:31; Jer 9:4.—f Pss 27:13; 28:5; 56:14; Deut 28:63; Job 18:14; 28:13; Prov 2:22; Isa 22:19; 38:11; Ezek 17:24.—g Pss 40:4; 44:15; 64:9; Job 22:19.—h Ps 49:7; 2 Sam 22:3; Job 31:24; Prov 11:28; Mk 10:23.—i Pss 1:3; 6:5; 13:6; 92:13-15; Jer 11:16; 17:8; Rev 11:4.—j Pss 22:23; 25:3; 26:12; 30:13; 35:18; 54:8; 149:1; Deut 7:6.—k 2-6a: Ps 14:2-6a.—l Pss 10:4; 36:2; 74:22; Isa 32:6; Jer 5:12; Mic 7:2; Zep 1:12.—m Pss 11:4; 102:20; Job 41:34.—n 3b-4: Rom 3:11-12.—o Ps 12:2; 1 Sam 8:3.—p Ps 27:2; Isa 9:11.—q Ps 79:6; Isa 65:1; Jer 10:25; Hos 7:7.

52:3 *You champion of malice:* the translation follows the Greek. The Hebrew has: "the kindness of God lasts all day long." The title is one of scorn; he is a champion only in his own mind, and God can easily put him in his place (see Isa 22:17).

52:5-6 The values of the wicked are distorted. He loves to think, speak, and do evil whenever he can profit from it (see v. 5; Mic 3:2). His entire being reflects the evil that is associated with the tongue (see Ps 120:2; Jas 3:1-12).

52:7-9 The wicked will be brought down by God while the righteous will subsist and mock them (see Ps 28:5; Job 18:14; Prov 2:22; Isa 22:17). The end of the wicked will be that of the foolish rich of Ps 49.

52:7 *Tent:* the earthly dwelling (see Job 18:14).

52:10-11 The godly or righteous stands in contrast to the "champion of malice" (v. 3). The latter relies on himself, does evil, and amasses ill-gotten riches and power; the Lord uproots him like a tree, turns him into a wanderer and destroys him like a building (v. 7). The godly relies on the Lord and is like a tree flourishing in the Lord's house. The "champion" boasts of his abilities; the godly praises the Lord for his wondrous works.

52:10 *Like a green olive tree:* symbol of a long and fruitful life inasmuch as it lives hundreds of years (see Pss 92:13-15; 128:3). *Kindness:* see note on Ps 6:5.

52:11 *I will praise you forever for what you have done:* a vow to praise the Lord for his punishing the wicked and saving the righteous (see Pss 13:6; 22:32; 31:23; 57:4) in keeping with the Israelite belief that praise must follow deliverance. The praise involved thank offerings and celebrating God's saving deed in the presence of others in the temple (see Ps 50:14f, 23). See also note on Ps 9:2. *Saints:* people of God who are and should be devoted to him (see note on Ps 4:4). *Name:* see note on Ps 5:12.

Ps 53 The psalmist stresses that when people banish God from their heart, they are led to renounce and exploit their neighbors. A generation turns away from God and erects injustice into a law, but the Lord of the poor and oppressed remains vigilant. The text reproduces Ps 14 with some variants: e.g., "God" is used for "the LORD" and verse 5 (which corresponds with vv. 5-6 of Ps 14) is different.

In praying this psalm, we can recall that all the attacks of spiritual or physical tyrants upon us are futile. Christ is with his faithful till the end of time, with the whole Church and with every Christian, to enable them to overcome all external and internal adversities. And without ceasing Christ offers to his Father, out of gratitude for deliverance, a sacrifice of thanksgiving—the Eucharist.

53:1 *For the director:* these words are thought to be a musical or liturgical notation. *Mahalath:* this word may signify a modulation indicating sadness. *Maskil:* see note on Ps 32:1a.

53:2-5 See notes on Ps 14:1b-4.

6 Later, they will be filled with terror,
and with good reason, *
although now they do not fear.
For God will scatter the bones
of those who attack you;
they will be put to shame,
for God has rejected them.

7 Who will bring about the salvation of Israel
that is to come out of Zion? *
When God restores the fortunes of his people,
Jacob will rejoice and Israel will exult. [r]

PSALM 54*

Prayer in Time of Danger

1 For the director. * On stringed instruments. A
maskil of David. 2 When the Ziphites came to
Saul and said, "David is hiding among us." [s]

3 O God, save me by your name; *
vindicate me by your power.
4 Hear my prayer, O God;
give ear to the words of my mouth.
5 Strangers * have risen against me;
those who are ruthless seek my life,
and they have no thought of God. [t]
Selah

6 Surely God is my helper;
the LORD is the one who sustains me. [u]
7 May their own evil recoil on my foes:
you who are faithful, destroy them. * [v]

8 * I will freely offer sacrifice to you,
and I will praise your name, O LORD,
for it is good.

9 For you have rescued me from all my troubles,
and my eyes have seen the downfall of my enemies. [w]

PSALM 55*

Prayer in Time of Betrayal by a Friend

1 For the director. * On stringed instruments. A
maskil of David.

2 * [x] Give ear to my prayer, O God,
do not ignore my supplication.
3 Listen to my cry and answer me,
for my troubles afford me no peace.

4 I am terrified by the shouts of the enemy
and the uproar of the wicked.
For they inflict troubles upon me,
and in their anger they revile me.

5 * My heart * is filled with anguish,
and I am beset by the terrors of death.
6 Fear and trembling overpower me;
horror overwhelms me.

7 I say, "If only I had wings like a dove
so that I could fly away and be at rest! [y]
8 I would flee away
and seek shelter in the wilderness. [z]
Selah

9 I would hurry to a place of refuge,
far from the savage wind and tempest."

r Pss 85:2; 126:1.—s 1 Sam 23:19; 26:1.—t Pss 18:49; 86:14.—u Pss 20:3; 118:7.—v Pss 94:23; 143:12.—w Pss 34:7; 58:10; 59:11; 91:8; 92:12; 112:8; 118:7.—x 2-3: Pss 5:2-3; 27:9; 86:6; 130:1-2; Lam 3:56; Jon 2:3.—y Pss 11:1; 91:4.—z 1 Sam 23:14; Jer 9:1; Rev 12:6.

53:6 This verse corresponds with the theme of Ps 14:6-7 that God crushes evildoers who attack his people, but the text is quite different. *Later . . . good reason:* an alternative translation is: "Then they were overcome with fear, / where there was no reason to fear." *Scatter the bones:* bodies left unburied (regarded as a horrible fate) in the wake of a devastating defeat—an allusion to Israel's divine deliverance from the siege of Sennacherib in 701 B.C. as a sign of what happens to all who attack God's people (see 2 Ki 19:35f; Isa 37:36f).

53:7 *Who will . . . Zion?:* another possible translation is: "Oh, if only salvation for Israel / would come forth from Zion."

Ps 54 The "name" stands for God himself, the Almighty One. To him the psalmist directs his supplication, from him help will come, and toward him will thanksgiving be extended. For Christians, the "name" is that of Jesus Christ, who saves those who invoke it (see Acts 2:21; Rom 10:9; 1 Cor 1:2). "There is no . . . other name under heaven given to men by which we can be saved" (Acts 4:12). The name "Jesus" means "God saves" (see Mt 1:21).

54:1-2 *For the director:* probably a musical or liturgical notation. *Maskil:* see note on Ps 32:1a. For the event in David's life, see 1 Sam 23:19.

54:3 The beleaguered psalmist summons God to give him justice (see Ps 17). *Name:* see note on Ps 5:12.

54:5 *Strangers:* probably a reference to the people of the Desert of Ziph (see 1 Sam 23:19). *They have no thought of God:* the same type of sinners as in Ps 53.

54:7 See notes on Pss 5:11; 35.

54:8-9 God and his faithful have the same enemies, whose defeat is a subject for joy and thanksgiving. *Praise your name:* see note on Ps 7:18.

Ps 55 The psalmist, a sensitive and pious Levite, interminably repeats his lament. Three times he describes his torment as the victim of calumny, distressed to see the holy city corrupted, and abandoned by his best friend. If only he could escape this misfortune that obsesses him! We are reminded of David in the wake of Absalom's rebellion against him (see 2 Sam 15–17) as well as of Jeremiah excoriated by his enemies (Jer 4:19; 5:1; 6:6; 9:1, 3, 7) and of Christ, the man of sorrows, betrayed by his friend (see Mt 26:21-23, 48-50).

This psalm is a prayer for days when we feel exhausted by the struggles of life, by the hostility of people and things, when we would like nothing more than to escape, to flee into some deserted spot and encounter nobody. However, the psalmist knows that only God's presence can free the heart imprisoned by suffering.

55:1 *For the director:* these words are thought to be a musical or liturgical notation. *Maskil:* see note on Ps 32:1a.

55:2-4 The psalmist begs God to listen to his plight.

55:5-9 So great is the physical danger and the mental anguish (see Pss 18:5f; 116:3) that the psalmist wishes he could run away from it all (see Jer 9:1-5).

55:5 *Heart:* see note on Ps 4:8.

10 *Restrain the wicked, O LORD, and confound their speech,*
for I see violence and strife in the city.
11 Day and night they make their rounds on its walls,
and within it are iniquity and malice.
12 Destruction is also in its midst;
oppression and treachery pervade its streets. [a]

13 *If it was an enemy who reviled me,
I could endure that.
If a foe had treated me with contempt,
I could manage to avoid him.
14 But it was you, one like myself,
a companion and a dear friend, [b]
15 with whom I engaged in pleasant conversation
as we walked with the festive throng
in the house of God.
16 Let death strike my enemies by surprise; [c]
let them descend alive to the netherworld,
for evil dwells in their homes
and in the depths of their hearts.*

17 *But I make my appeal to God,
and the LORD will save me.
18 Evening, morning, and noon*
I will cry out in my distress,
and he will hear my voice. [d]

19 *He will deliver me in peace and safety
from those who are arrayed against me,
even though there are many of them.
20 God will hear me and humiliate them,
he who has been enthroned forever.
Selah
For they neither change their ways
nor have any fear of God. [e]
21 My companion treats his friends harshly
and breaks his covenant.
22 His speech is smoother than butter,
but war is in his heart.
His words are more soothing than oil,
yet in reality they are drawn swords. [f]
23 Entrust your cares to the LORD,
and he will uphold you;*
he will never allow the righteous to waver. [g]
24 But you, O God, will send the wicked
down to the pit [h] of destruction;*
those who are bloodthirsty and treacherous
will not live out half their days.
But as for me,
I will put my trust in you. [i]

PSALM 56*

Boundless Trust in God

1 For the director.* According to *Yonath elem rehoqim*. A *miktam* of David. When the Philistines seized him at Gath. [j]

2 Be merciful to me, O God,
for people are trampling upon me;
all day long they keep up their attack.

a Ps 5:10; Jer 5:1; 6:6; Ezek 22:2; Hab 1:3; Zep 3:1.—b Ps 41:10; 2 Sam 15:12; Jer 9:3; Mt 26:21-24 par.—c Pss 49:15; 64:8; Num 16:33; Prov 1:12; Isa 5:14.—d Ps 141:2; Dan 6:11.—e Pss 29:10; 93:2; Deut 33:27; Bar 3:3.—f Pss 12:3; 28:3; 57:5; 62:5; 64:4; Prov 12:18; 26:24-28; Jer 9:7.—g Pss 18:37; 37:5; 112:6; Prov 3:5; 16:3; Mt 6:25; 1 Pet 5:7.—h Pss 9:16; 28:1; 30:4; 40:3; 73:18; 88:5; 143:7; Prov 1:12; Ezek 28:8; Jon 2:7.—i Pss 5:7; 25:2; 56:4; 130:5.—j 1 Sam 21:11; 24:3.

55:10-12 The psalmist issues an urgent call for God to come to his assistance.

55:10 See notes on Pss 5:11; 35. *Restrain . . . confound their speech:* possibly a reference to God's action at Babel (see Gen 11:5-9). Sins of the tongue, calumnies, false witness, and insults are often denounced in psalms of lamentation. *Violence . . . strife:* entities are personified here and in verse 11 *(iniquity . . . malice)*, and verses 10b-11 recall Jer 5:1; 6:6; 9:6; Ezek 22:2; Zep 3:1.

55:13-15 Doubtless, the betrayer is a Levite; the Targum identifies the false friend as Ahithophel (see Ps 44:11; 2 Sam 15:12). See also Mt 26:21-25.

55:16 The psalmist calls for the sudden, premature death of his enemies (see note on v. 10 above), which was the same as the punishment wished on one's enemies (see Pss 73:19; 102:25; Job 15:32; Prov 1:12; Isa 38:10; Jer 17:11), a punishment that overtook the rebellious band of Korah (see Num 16:32f). *Hearts:* (also v. 22). See note on Ps 4:8.

55:17-20 The psalmist believes that God will hear his prayer and come to his aid.

55:18 *Evening, morning, and noon:* the hours for prayer (see Dan 6:11f). The legal day begins at the setting of the sun ("evening").

55:19-24 The psalmist reflects once again on his friend's treachery and then puts his full trust in the Lord.

55:23 Text cited in 1 Pet 5:7 (see also Ps 121:2; Isa 50:10).

55:24 See note on verse 10 above. *Pit of destruction:* i.e., the grave.

Ps 56 A psalmist subjected to harassment appeals to the Lord to take note of the injustice he is undergoing. He calls for the judgment of God to come upon his persecutors; but, more importantly, a profound religious sense enables him to divine that the prayer and tears of human beings are precious in God's eyes. The spirit of this psalm resides in the refrain: a firm protestation of trust in the word of the Lord (vv. 5, 11-12) despite all the plots of humans. So strong is the psalmist's certitude on this point that it transforms his fervent prayer from a lament into a thanksgiving.

It is easy to place this psalm on the lips of Christ, for its themes are all found in the Passion: a plea for the Father's mercy, assaults of pagan tyrants, calumnies, plots and snares on the part of enemies, tears, cries of confidence, and a vow of thanksgiving. The psalm also provides Christians with a beautiful prayer of supplication in time of adversity, whether external or internal.

56:1 *For the director:* these words are thought to be a musical or liturgical notation. *According to Yonath elem rehoqim:* nothing is known about this phrase. *Miktam:* see note on Ps 16:1. For the event referred to, see 1 Sam 21:10-15.

3 My foes pursue me all day long,
with their forces too many to number.
4 When I am terrified,
I place my trust in you.
5 In God, whose word * I praise,
in God I place my trust and know no fear; [k]
what can people do to me? [l]
6 All day long they slander me;
their one thought is to bring evil upon me.
7 In groups they hide in ambush
and spy on my every step,
determined to take my life. [m]
8 Shall they escape in their iniquity?
Strike down the nations, O God, in your anger.
9 You have kept count of my wanderings
and stored my tears in your flask,
recording all these in your book. * [n]
10 My foes will turn back
when I call out to you.
Of this I am confident:
that God is on my side.
11 In God, whose word I praise—
in the LORD, whose word I praise—
12 in God I place my trust and know no fear;
what can people do to me?
13 I am bound, O God, by vows * to you,
and I will pay you my debt of gratitude. [o]
14 For you have delivered my life from death
and my feet from stumbling,
that I may walk in the presence of God *
in the light of the living.

PSALM 57*

Trust in God amid Suffering

1 For the director. * According to "Do not
destroy." A *miktam* of David. When he fled from
Saul into the cave. [p]

2 Have mercy on me, O God,
have mercy on me,
for in you my soul * takes refuge.
I will seek shelter in the shadow of your wings
until the time of danger has passed. [q]
3 I call out to God Most High,
to God who takes care of me. *
4 May he send his help from heaven to deliver me
and put to shame those who trample upon me; *Selah*
may God send his kindness * and his faithfulness.
5 I lie prostrate in the midst of lions
who are hungrily seeking human prey. [r]
Their teeth are spears and arrows,
and their tongues are razor-sharp swords. [s]
6 Be exalted, O God, above the heavens; [t]
let your glory shine over all the earth. *

k Pss 27:1; 52:11; 84:13; 130:5.—l Ps 118:6; Mt 10:28; Heb 13:6.—m Pss 59:4; 94:21; 140:5-6; Mk 3:6.—n Ps 10:14; 2 Ki 20:5; Isa 4:3; 25:8; Dan 7:10; Mal 3:16; Rev 7:17.—o Lev 7:11f; Num 30:3.—p 1 Sam 22:1.—q Pss 2:12; 17:8; 36:8.—r Pss 17:11-12; 22:22; 35:17; 58:7.—s Pss 11:2; 64:4; Prov 30:14.—t Pss 72:19; 102:16; Num 14:21.

56:5 *Word:* as in verse 11, God's "word" is the promise by which he committed himself to his faithful; this is a very familiar theme in the Psalter (see Pss 105:8-11; 119:42, 65; 130:5). *People:* (also in v. 12); literally, "flesh," representative of human frailty with respect to the divine power. People can indeed inflict pain, suffering, and death upon us, but they cannot rob us of our souls or our eternal future (see Ps 118:6; Heb 13:6). Jesus said: "Have no fear of those who kill the body but cannot kill the soul" (Mt 10:28); thus, we are to fear no one but God alone, who is also our helper.

56:9 God cares for his faithful and keeps a careful record of everything about them (see note on Ps 51:3)—even the tears they shed when they are in trouble. The theme of God's record is frequent (see, e.g., Ps 139:16; Job 19:23; Mal 3:16). Each tear of the righteous will be compensated (see 2 Ki 20:5; Isa 25:8; Rev 7:17). Indeed, Jesus indicated that God has such concern for us that he knows the number of hairs on our head (Mt 10:30).

56:13 *I am bound . . . by vows:* the psalmist is certain of being delivered and vows to make thanksgiving for it (see note on Ps 7:18).

56:14 *Walk in the presence of God:* an expression that indicates access to the heavenly King, with reference to his presence at the temple (God's royal house on earth). It is legitimate for us to see in this text an allusion to ultimate access to the heavenly temple (see Pss 16:11; 17:15; 23:6; 140:14). *Light of the living:* a happy life on earth (see note on Ps 36:9).

Ps 57 The psalmist pictures evildoers like lions tearing away at him and ravaging his reputation. It is altogether natural for him, then, to call upon God to come in power to chastise the enemy and establish his kingdom on earth. A second tableau ends the psalm: the believer sings of God's deliverance, which comes like a dawn in the midst of the night of danger. Part of this psalm is duplicated in Ps 108 (57:8-12 is the same as 108:2-6).

This supplication may be justly applied to Christ during his whole public life and Passion. Surrounded and attacked by his enemies, he seeks refuge in his Father, who cannot abandon him. It can also fittingly be applied to us who are constantly threatened by our spiritual enemies.

57:1 *For the director:* these words are thought to be a musical or liturgical notation. *According to "Do not destroy":* probably a note by an early scribe intended to prevent his manuscript from being discarded. *Miktam:* see note on Ps 16:1. For the event, see 1 Sam 24:1-3.

57:2 *My soul:* see note on Ps 6:4. *Shadow of your wings:* conventional Hebrew metaphor for protection; it may have been inspired by the wings of the cherubim spread over the Ark in the inner chamber of the temple (see 1 Ki 6:23-28).

57:3 *Who takes care of me:* an allusion to God's providence; other translations given are: "who puts an end to my troubles" and "who perfects his work in me."

57:4 *Kindness:* see note on Ps 6:5.

57:6 The psalmist asks that the kingdom of God may be manifested (see Ps 72:19; Num 14:21; 1 Chr 29:11; Isa 6:3; 33:10; Hab 2:14) by the deliverance of the faithful and the ruin of the wicked (see Pss 79:9; 102:16f; 138:5).

7 They set a trap for my feet,
and I was overcome with distress.
They dug a pit in my path,
but they themselves fell into it. [u]
Selah

8 * My heart * is steadfast, O God,
my heart is steadfast;
I will sing and chant your praise; [v]
9 awake, my soul!
Awake, lyre and harp!
I will awaken the dawn. * [w]

10 * I will give thanks to you among the peoples, O LORD;
I will sing your praises among the nations. [x]
11 For your kindness extends to the heavens;
your faithfulness, to the skies. [y]
12 Be exalted, O God, above the heavens;
let your glory radiate over all the earth.

PSALM 58*

The Judge of Unjust Rulers

1 For the director.* According to "Do not
destroy." A *miktam* of David.
2 O you rulers, * do you render justice?
Do you judge your people impartially? [z]

3 No! You devise wickedness in your hearts, *
and your hands bring about violence on the earth.
4 The wicked have gone astray right from the womb;
from birth these liars have taken the wrong path. *
5 Their venom is like that of a serpent;
they are as deaf as an asp that stops its ears
6 so as not to hear the voice of the charmer [a]
no matter how skillful the spells he casts. *

7 O God, break the teeth in their mouths;
tear out the fangs of these lions, O LORD. * [b]
8 * Cause them to vanish like water that drains off; [c]
make them wither like grass that is trampled. * [d]
9 Let them melt like a snail* that oozes into slime
or like a stillborn child that will never see the sun. [e]
10 Before they sprout thorns * like brambles or thistles,
may your whirlwind sweep them away. [f]

11 The righteous will rejoice
when he sees that justice has been done,

u Pss 7:16; 10:9; 140:5-6.—v Pss 108:2; 112:7.—w Pss 33:2; 39:9; Job 3:9; 38:12.—x Pss 9:12; 18:50; 30:5; 135:3; 146:2; 2 Sam 22:50; Rom 15:9.—y Pss 36:6; 71:19; 108:5.—z Ps 82:2; Deut 16:19; Prov 31:9.—a Pss 64:4; 140:4; Deut 18:11; 32:33; Eccl 10:11; Isa 3:3; Jer 8:17; Rom 3:13.—b Pss 3:8; 17:12; 22:22; 35:17.—c Job 11:16; Wis 16:29.—d Pss 37:2; 57:4; 90:5-6; 102:12; 103:15-16; Job 14:2; Isa 40:7.—e Num 12:12; Job 3:16; Eccl 6:3.—f Ps 118:12; Job 21:18; Hos 13:13; Nah 1:10.

57:8-12 These verses (with slight variations) are the same as verses 2-6 of Ps 108.

57:8 The psalmist is at peace because of his trust in the Lord. *Heart:* see note on Ps 4:8.

57:9 *Dawn:* personified as in Ps 139:9; Job 3:9; 38:12. The "night" (v. 5: "lie prostrate") symbolizes trials; deliverance comes with the "dawn" (see Ps 17:15).

57:10-11 A vow to offer ritual praise to the Lord for his goodness (see note on Ps 7:18). *Kindness:* see note on Ps 6:5.

Ps 58 This is one of the so-called imprecatory (or cursing) psalms (see note on Ps 35) that call upon God to mete out justice to enemies. In their thirst for justice, the authors of these psalms use hyperbole (or overstatement) in order to move others to oppose sin and evil. Such impassioned expressions may seem vengeful to a Western audience not used to the diatribes and curses of Easterners. And the joy exhibited over the justice to be meted out seems ferocious to us. However, we must realize above all that the psalmists were desiring only true justice, a justice that could not be derailed, denied, or mocked—because it was God's justice.

The psalmist and all Israel regard judges as well as rulers to be divine beings (see Pss 45:7; 82:6; Ex 21:6; Deut 19:17), for judging, like ruling, is a power of God. This psalm wars against those who pervert such a divine power.

The early Church applied this psalm to the trial of Jesus before the Sanhedrin (see Mt 26:57-68 par).

58:1 *For the director:* these words are thought to be a musical or liturgical notation. *According to "Do not destroy":* see note on Ps 57:1. *Miktam:* see note on Ps 16:1.

58:2 *Rulers:* literally, "gods": see introduction.

58:3 *Hearts:* see note on Ps 4:8.

58:4 The evil ways of the wicked (see Ps 10) are theirs from birth.

58:6 The roles of charmers and enchanters are frequently alluded to in the Old Testament (see Deut 18:11; Eccl 10:11; Isa 3:3; Jer 8:17).

58:7 The psalmist regards teeth as weapons of the mouths by which the wicked harass the righteous (see Ps 57:5), so he begs God to destroy them.

58:8-12 See notes on Pss 58; 35.

58:8b *Make them wither like grass that is trampled:* the meaning of the Hebrew is unclear. Another translation likens the psalmist's foes to archers who shoot blunted arrows. "When they ready the bow, let their arrows be blunted."

58:9 *Snail:* the ancients believed that snails dried up in the sun and evaporated.

58:10 The meaning of the Hebrew for this verse is uncertain. Another translation given is: "Before your pots can feel the heat of the thorns— / whether they be green or dry— / the wicked will be swept away." This accords with the fact that twigs from wild bushes (*thorns*) were used to start quick fires for cooking (see Ps 118:12; Eccl 7:6).

and he will bathe his feet
in the blood * of the wicked.[g]
12 Then the people will say,
"There is truly a reward for the righteous;
there is a God who dispenses justice on the earth."

PSALM 59*

Against Wicked Enemies

1 For the director.* According to "Do not destroy." A *miktam* of David. When Saul sent people to watch David's house in order to kill him.[h]

2 Rescue me, O my God, from my enemies;
defend me * against those who rise up against me.
3 Deliver me from those who do evil;
save me from the violence of the bloodthirsty.
4 They are lying in wait to take my life;
the powerful gather together against me.
For no offense or sin of mine, O LORD,
5 for no guilt of mine,
they stand ready to attack me.
Rise up to help me, and look on my plight;
6 you, LORD, God of hosts, * are the God of Israel.
Rouse yourself and punish all the nations;
show no mercy to these wicked deceivers. *Selah*
7 They return each evening,
snarling like dogs
as they prowl through the city.[i]
8 * See what spews from their mouths—
they spew forth from their lips,
and they assert, "Who is there to hear us?"
9 However, you laugh at them, O LORD;
you show your disdain for all the nations.[j]
10 * O my strength, I will keep watch for you,
for you, O God, are my fortress,
11 O God of mercy.
May God go before me
and allow me to have my way with my enemies.
12 Do not put them to death,
lest my people forget. *
Scatter them in your power
and bring them to their knees,
O LORD, our shield. *
13 For the sins of their mouths
and the words of their lips,
let them be trapped in their pride.
For the curses and lies they speak,[k]
14 put an end to them in your wrath;
put an end to them until they are no more.
Then it will be known to the ends of the earth
that God is the ruler over Jacob. *[l]
Selah

g Ps 68:24; Isa 63:1-6; Mal 3:18.—h 1 Sam 19:11.—i Pss 22:17; 55:11.—j Pss 2:4; 37:13; Prov 1:26; Wis 4:18.—k Ps 10:7; Prov 12:13; 18:7.—l Pss 46:9-11; 83:18-19; Ezek 5:13.

58:11 *Bathe his feet in the blood:* a vivid expression indicating complete victory over one's foes that was common in the Near East (see Ps 68:24; Isa 63:1-6).

Ps 59 The most realistic situation for this psalm is as follows: a believer, a Jewish group, or the whole people is exposed to persecution; it comes from forces that wish to impose paganism on the exiles or perhaps on Jerusalem itself. Like raging dogs that prowl the night in the cities of the East in search of prey, evil-intentioned persons attack the innocent victim with slander and curses, seeking to destroy his reputation and ultimately his life. The description is ferocious and the imprecation vehement and vengeful; but God will not tolerate lying and perfidy without end; the Almighty One cannot let himself be mocked, for his honor is at stake (v. 14).

We can pray this psalm to God and to Christ inserting our own name in all our temporal struggles, and even more in the bitter spiritual struggles we must constantly wage against our powerful spiritual enemies.

59:1 *For the director:* these words are thought to be a musical or liturgical notation. *According to "Do not destroy":* see note on Ps 57:1. *Miktam:* see note on Ps 16:1. The superscription imagines that the occasion for this psalm was the narrative in 1 Sam 19:11-17. Some believe it might have been when Jerusalem was under siege as at the time of Hezekiah (see 2 Ki 18:19), while others point to the time of Nehemiah (see Neh 4).

59:2 *Defend me:* literally, "lift me to a high, safe place."

59:6 *LORD, God of hosts:* an expression used first in 1 Sam 1:3 to designate the Lord as the sovereign over all powers in the universe—the God of all armies, both the heavenly army (see Ps 68:17; Deut 33:2; Jos 5:14; Hab 3:8) and the army of Israel (see 1 Sam 17:45). See also note on Ps 24:10. *God of Israel . . . punish all the nations:* seems to indicate an attack on Israel by the nations.

59:8-9 The wicked curse God as if he cannot see and hear and will not respond. But God laughs at them (see Pss 2:4; 37:13) and listens until the day of reckoning when the curses will fall back in judgment on the wicked themselves.

59:10-14 The psalmist asks God to put his foes to death, so that his people may not be seduced by them and so that the people will remember this particular saving act longer than they have remembered others (see Pss 78:11; 106:13).

59:12a-b Another translation possible is: "O God, put them to death, / so that they may not seduce my people."

59:12e *O LORD, our shield:* just as the king was regarded as the people's shield in ancient Israel (see Ps 84:10), so the Lord was called the Shield of his people (see Pss 7:11; 84:12; 89:19; 91:4; 115:9-11; Deut 33:29; Prov 30:5). Accordingly, the psalmist invokes this attribute of the Lord at this point.

59:14 God's punishment of the nations will show that God, the King of Israel (see Ps 24:1, 6; Isa 41:21ff; 63:19), is also the Master of the universe (see Pss 46:11f; 83:19).

15 * They return each evening,
snarling like dogs
as they prowl through the city.
16 They roam about searching for food,
and they growl if they do not have their fill.

17 But I will sing of your strength;
when morning dawns, I will proclaim your kindness. *
For you have been my fortress,
my refuge in times of trouble.
18 O my Strength, I will sing your praises,
for you, O God, are my fortress,
the God who shows me love. *

PSALM 60*

Prayer To End Wars

1 For the director. * According to "The Lily of
. . . ." A *miktam* of David (for teaching), 2 when he
fought against Aram-naharaim and Aram-
zobah; and when Joab, coming back, slew twelve
thousand Edomites in the Valley of Salt. [m]

3 O God, you have turned away from us
and left us defenseless.
Although your anger was aroused,
now come to our aid.
4 You shook the earth * and split it apart;
repair its cracks, for it continues to shake. [n]
5 You have inflicted hardships on your people; [o]
you have given us wine that made us stagger. *
6 But for those who fear you,
you have raised up a banner
to unfurl against the bow. * *Selah*
7 * With your right hand come to our aid and answer us
so that those you love may be delivered.

8 * God has promised from his sanctuary,
"In triumph I will apportion Shechem
and measure out the Valley of Succoth.
9 Gilead is mine, and Manasseh is mine;
Ephraim is my helmet, *
Judah is my scepter.
10 Moab is my washbasin; *
upon Edom I will plant my sandal;
over Philistia I will shout in triumph." [p]
11 * Who will lead me into the fortified city? *
Who will guide me into Edom?
12 Is it not you, O God, who have rejected us
and no longer go forth with our armies? [q]

m 2 Sam 8:2-3, 13; 1 Chr 18:2-3, 12.—n Pss 18:8; 75:4; 2 Chr 7:14; Isa 24:19.—o Pss 71:20; 75:9; Isa 51:17, 21-22; Jer 25:16; Zec 12:2.—p Ps 137:7; Deut 2:5; Ru 4:7-8; 2 Sam 8:1-2; Jer 49:7; Lam 4:21-22; Ezek 25:12-14.—q Pss 44:10; 68:8; Jos 7:12; Jdg 5:4-5; Isa 42:13.

59:15-18 The wicked wreak havoc like a pack of dogs, snarling and howling as they prowl about the city. The godly take courage in hearing of God's laughter (v. 9) and the assurance of his love (vv. 10-11). For the Lord is their strength and their fortress, who will deliver them from all their enemies and whom they will praise.

59:17 After the night of danger (vv. 7, 15), the psalmist will sing to God on the morning of deliverance (see notes on Ps 57; 57:9). *Kindness:* see note on Ps 6:5.

59:18 The psalmist vows to offer ritual praise for his deliverance (see note on Ps 7:18).

Ps 60 God responds to the supplication of the nation of Israel, which is suffering because it has neglected the covenant. The cry of a holy war sounds forth. God mobilizes Israel from one end to the other (vv. 8-9) to wreak judgment on enemy territory—one feels as if carried back to the time of the Exodus and the conquest of Canaan. After the Exile, this psalm could have been chanted during a penitential liturgy. Verses 7-14 are also found in Ps 108 as verses 7-14.

The military casualties and temporal disasters of ancient Israel typify the spiritual disasters that the Church, the new Israel, sometimes suffers. In union with Christ, her risen Head, the Church directs this supplication to the Father in critical moments of her history.

60:1-2 *For the director:* these words are thought to be a musical or liturgical notation. *According to "The Lily of . . .":* its meaning is unknown. *Miktam:* see note on Ps 16:1. The superscription refers to events that are found in 2 Sam 8:1; 1 Chr 18. However, the accounts make no mention of Edom or of the fact that David's forces met stiff resistance (vv. 3-5) and even a temporary defeat (v. 11f). The *Valley of Salt* is unknown (see 2 Sam 8:13).

60:4 *Shook the earth:* the defeat is likened to an earthquake, which is an apocalyptic characteristic (see Isa 24:20).

60:5 *Wine that made us stagger:* God has given them drink from the cup of the divine wrath (see Ps 75:9; Isa 51:17, 22; Jer 25:15) rather than the cup of the divine blessings (see Pss 16:5, including note; 23:5; 116:13).

60:6 *Bow:* symbol of the enemy, which relied on its bows.

60:7-14 These verses occur again as verses 7-14 of Ps 108.

60:8-10 The Lord gives his people an oracle of hope, reminding them of his promises that the earth is his and no enemy can stand against him. *Shechem* was west of the Jordan, and *Succoth* east of it; therefore, they indicated dominion over all of Palestine. Next are named four Israelite tribes; hence, there are three regions in all that must be reduced to subjection.

60:9 *Helmet:* a symbol of the strength exhibited by the tribe of Ephraim (see Deut 33:17; Jdg 7:24—8:3). *Scepter:* a symbol of the King-Messiah who had been promised from Judah (see Gen 49:10).

60:10 *Moab is my washbasin:* i.e., its people will do menial work for the Israelites (see Gen 18:4). *Plant my sandal:* an Eastern way of signifying possession.

60:11-14 The psalmist asks the Lord to lead him to victory even though the pain of defeat and God's apparent rejection are still with him. For he knows that the Lord remains with his people and will ensure a joyous and victorious outcome (see Pss 44:6; 118:15f).

60:11 *Fortified city:* doubtless Bozrah in Idumea (see Isa 34:6; 63:1; Am 1:12). It was from this inaccessible refuge that the Edomites sent incursions into Judea.

13 Grant us your help against our enemies,
for any human assistance is worthless.
14 With God's help we will be victorious,
for he will overwhelm our foes.

PSALM 61*

Prayer of One in Exile

1 For the director. * With stringed instruments. Of David.

2 O God, hear my cry
and listen to my prayer.
3 From the ends of the earth * I call to you,
with a heart that is fainting away;
set me high upon a rock.
4 For you are my refuge,
a tower of strength against the enemy. [r]
5 I will abide in your tent forever
and find refuge in the shelter of your wings. * [s] *Selah*
6 For you, O God, have heard my vows
and granted me the heritage of those who fear your name. *
7 * Add length of days to the life of the king;
may his years be prolonged for many generations. [t]
8 May he be enthroned in God's presence
forever, [u]
and may your kindness and faithfulness watch over him. [v]
9 Then I will sing praise to your name forever
as I fulfill my vows day after day. *

PSALM 62*

Trust in God Alone

1 For the director. * For Jeduthun. A psalm of David.

2 [w] In God alone is my soul * at rest;
it is from him that my salvation comes.
3 He alone is my rock and my salvation,
my fortress, so that I stand ever unshaken.
4 How long will you assault someone,
and all of you beat him down,
as if he were a leaning wall
or a tottering fence? *
5 They devise plots to dislodge me
from my place on high *
and delight in spreading lies about me.

---

r Pss 9:10; 46:2; 59:10; 62:8; Prov 18:10.—s Pss 15:1; 17:8; 36:8; 57:2; Deut 32:11; Mt 23:37.—t Ps 21:5; 1 Ki 3:14.—u Pss 72:5; 89:5.—v Pss 40:12; 85:11; 89:15, 25; Prov 20:28.—w 2-3, 6-7: Pss 18:3; 31:3-4; 42:10; 118:8; 146:3; Mic 7:7.

Ps 61 The psalmist, a Levite deported to Babylon along with the elite of the Jewish people in 598 B.C., voices his ardent desire to return to the holy city and resume his service in the temple. Added to this lament of the exiled Levite is a prayer for the king, probably on behalf of Zedekiah, the last to sit on the throne of David after the first deportation of 598 B.C. This prayer also calls upon the Messiah, who is to come from the royal line (see 2 Sam 7; 1 Chr 17:14), to reign forever, and whose coming Israel awaits.

This prayer beautifully expresses our hope as Christians. Sent by the Father and anointed by the Holy Spirit, Christ has become our Head, our guide and leader to the Father, provided we keep our eyes fixed on him by faith (see Acts 3:15; 5:31; Heb 2:10; 12:2). Long live Christ the King!

61:1 *For the director:* these words are thought to be a musical or liturgical notation.

61:3 *Ends of the earth:* the phrase can also be translated as "from the brink of the netherworld," i.e., the grave. *Heart:* see note on Ps 4:8. *Set me high upon a rock:* a reference to God's sanctuary (see Ps 27:5). Another translation is: "Lead me to the rock that is higher than I": a reference to God, the psalmist's "rock of refuge" (Pss 31:3; 71:3; see also Pss 18:3; 62:3, 7f; 94:22).

61:5 *Shelter of your wings:* see note on Ps 17:8.

61:6 The psalmist is certain of being heard (see Pss 56:14; 66:19) and resuming his functions (see Ps 16:5), for he is among those who fear God (see Mal 3:16). *Name:* see note on Ps 5:12.

61:7-8 As in Pss 85:11f; 89:15, 25, these personified divine attributes were thought to accompany the Messiah just as they protect the king (see Prov 20:28) or the simple Levite (see Ps 40:12). They were then applied to Christ, "Son of David," by the Fathers of the Church. The insistence on an eternal reign recalls the prophecy of Nathan (see 2 Sam 7:16; 1 Chr 17:14), which is frequently alluded to in the Psalter (see Pss 18:51; 45:18; 72:5, 17; 89:5; 132:12). *Kindness:* see note on Ps 6:5.

61:9 See note on Ps 7:18. To fulfill one's vows meant to make an offering or sacrifice promised to God, normally in a single ceremony. To do so *day after day* shows a commitment to a debt that could never be paid off or an awareness that God's blessings are new every morning. *Name:* see note on Ps 5:12.

Ps 62 This psalm recalls the malice of human beings (see Ps 4:3), the nothingness of creatures (see Ps 39:6f; Isa 40:15), the vanity of riches (see Ps 49:13; Prov 11:28; 27:24), and the impartiality of the heavenly Judge (see Pss 9:8f, 17; 11:7; 33:5; 140:13). It provides an unsurpassable lesson of wisdom and simple trust in God to those who are deeply hurt and deceived (see Ps 31). Human beings seek success in wickedness, falsehood, and violence. The believer knows the futility of this manner of acting; it is of no avail in the sight of God's judgment. Entirely different is the strength of the faithful: the Lord, who renders to each what they merit (Job 34:11; Prov 24:12; Sir 16:14; Ezek 18), will never fail them—and he is the only one who will never do so.

At the invitation of Christ and in union with him, we must learn to abandon ourselves to the heavenly Father in all the trials and difficulties of life and seek in him our rest and inner peace. We could thus recite this entire psalm to celebrate the wonderful fruits of this filial confidence and to exhort our life companions to practice similar abandonment.

62:1 *For the director:* these words are thought to be a musical or liturgical notation. *Jeduthun:* see note on Ps 39:1.

62:2 *Soul:* see note on Ps 6:4.

62:4 *Leaning wall . . . tottering fence:* metaphor for the psalmist's state of weakness—real (in God's eyes) or imagined (by his enemies).

62:5 *Place on high:* either a throne in the case of David or a place of safety such as a fortress on a cliff in the case of another psalmist. *Hearts:* see note on Ps 4:8.

They bless with their lips,
but they curse in their hearts. [x] *Selah*

6 In God alone be at rest, * O my soul;
it is from him that my hope comes.

7 He alone is my rock and my salvation,
my fortress, so that I stand unshaken.

8 My deliverance and my glory depend on God;
he is my mighty rock and my refuge. [y]

9 Trust in him at all times, my people,
and pour out your heart before him, *
for God is our refuge. *Selah*

10 Ordinary people are no more than a breath,
and the great are no more than a delusion.
When they are placed on scales all together,
they are lighter than air. * [z]

11 Do not place your trust in extortion,
and set no vain hopes in stolen goods;
no matter how greatly your wealth increases,
do not set your heart * on it. [a]

12 One thing God has revealed;
two things have I heard:
that power belongs to you, O God, [b]

13 and so does kindness, * O LORD.
You reward each person [c]
in accordance with his deeds.

PSALM 63*

Thirst for God

1 A psalm of David. When he was in the wilderness of Judah. * [d]

2 O God, you are my God,
for whom I have been searching earnestly. *
My soul yearns for you
and my body thirsts for you,
like the earth when it is parched,
arid and without water. [e]

3 I have gazed upon you in the sanctuary
so that I may behold your power * and your glory.

4 Your kindness * is a greater joy than life itself;
thus my lips will speak your praise.

5 I will bless you all my life;
with uplifted hands * I will call on your name.

6 My soul * will be satisfied as at a banquet
and with rejoicing lips my mouth will praise you.

---

x Pss 12:3; 28:3; 55:22; Prov 26:24-25.—y Ps 3:4; Isa 26:4; 60:19; Jer 3:23.—z Pss 39:6-7; 144:4; Job 7:16; Wis 2:15; Isa 40:15.—a Job 31:25; Eccl 5:9; Jer 17:11; Ezek 22:29; Mt 6:19-21, 24.—b Job 40:5; Rev 19:1.—c Pss 28:4; 31:24; 86:5; 2 Sam 3:39; Job 34:11; Jer 17:10; Mt 16:27; Rom 2:6; 2 Tim 4:14; Rev 22:12.—d 1 Sam 24; 2 Sam 15:23-28.—e Pss 36:8-10; 42:3; 84:3; 143:6; Isa 26:9.

62:6 *Be at rest:* see Pss 27:13f; 42:6, 12; 43:5.

62:9 *Pour out your heart before him:* a call for true prayer and meditation with God (see Lam 2:19). *Heart:* see note on Ps 4:8.

62:10 A reference to the manner of weighing precious objects; the lighter one would rise. On God's scale, the wicked are a puff of air. The image of the scale recurs in Job 31:6; Prov 16:2; 21:2; 24:12; Isa 40:15.

62:11 The Prophets inveighed against social crimes (see Isa 30:12; Ezek 22:29). The consequence was the recommendation to be detached from riches (see Job 27:12ff; 31:25; Eccl 5:8ff; Jer 17:11; Mt 6:19f, 24). *Heart:* see note on Ps 4:8.

62:13 The doctrine of personal retribution, taught by the Prophets, above all Ezekiel (see Ezek 18), is taken up by the sages and the psalmists (see Pss 28:4; 31:24; Job 34:11; Prov 24:12; Sir 16:13) and passes into the New Testament (see Mt 16:27; Rom 2:6; 2 Tim 4:14; Rev 2:23)—but only good deeds have eternal value. *Kindness:* see note on Ps 6:5.

Ps 63 A deported Levite thinks back to the time when he lived in the temple, close to God; in the silence of the night he meditates on those happy hours, the remembrance of which comforts him. And the desire rises in him and becomes more and more intense; already it is as if he is once again in the sanctuary with no other occupation than to offer unceasing praise to the One whose love surpasses every other good. In that time of deliverance the king will be filled with blessings by God while the oppressors will receive the severest of chastisements.

By its movement and style, this engaging prayer finds a place among the most beautiful psalms of longing (see Pss 42; 61; 73; 84). It enables us to rediscover—amid the difficulties of daily life and all that distracts us from the spiritual life—the longing for God, whose love is the only thing that makes life worth living. It can also serve as the song of the prodigal son (see Lk 15), enabling us to put into words the distress, hope, and penitence of the repentant sinner.

63:1 This superscription ascribes the psalm to a time when David was *in the wilderness of Judah* (see 1 Sam 24; 2 Sam 15:23-28; 16:2, 14; 17:16, 29).

63:2 *Earnestly:* literally, "in the morning" (see notes on Pss 57; 57:9). *My soul . . . my body:* i.e., my whole being.

63:3 The psalmist worships God, the Great King, who promised to dwell among his people—formerly in the Ark of the Covenant (see Pss 78:61; 132:8; 1 Sam 4:21) and now in the sanctuary where the psalmist envisions the Lord in all his *power* and *glory*.

63:4 *Kindness:* see note on Ps 6:5. For the Old Testament, the greatest good was earthly life; but God's kindness is better even than life.

63:5 *Uplifted hands:* the usual posture for prayer (see Ex 9:29, 33) with palms turned upward (see also Pss 44:21; 77:3; 88:10; 119:48; 143:6; 1 Ki 8:22; Ezr 9:5; Neh 8:6; 2 Mac 3:20). The lifting up of one's hands was also a symbol of dependence on and praise of the Lord (see Pss 28:2; 63:5; 1 Tim 2:8) *Name:* see note on Ps 5:12.

63:6 *Soul:* see note on Ps 6:4. *As at a banquet:* literally, "marrow and fat," the preferred meats of the Palestinian Arabs and a symbol of the best of foods (see Ps 36:9).

7 I think of you while I lie upon my bed, *
and I meditate on you during the watches of the night.
8 For you are my help,
and in the shadow of your wings I rejoice. *[f]
9 My soul clings tightly to you;
your right hand holds me fast.
10 * Those who seek my life will incur ruin;
they will sink down into the depths of the earth.
11 They will be slain by the sword
and their flesh will become food for jackals. *
12 But the king will rejoice in God;
all who swear by him * will exult,
for the mouths of liars will be silenced.[g]

PSALM 64*

Thanksgiving for God's Justice

1 For the director. * A psalm of David.
2 Listen, O God, to my cry of lament;
from the dreaded enemy preserve my life.
3 Protect me from the council of the wicked,
from the band of those who do evil.
4 They sharpen their tongues * like swords,
and they shoot forth their venomous words like arrows,[h]
5 while they attack the innocent from ambush,
shooting suddenly and without fear.
6 * They agree on their evil plan,
and they resolve to lay snares,
saying, "Who will see us?"
7 They plot evil schemes
and devise shrewd plots;
the thoughts of their hearts * are hidden.[i]
8 * However, God will shoot his arrows at them, *
and they will suddenly be struck down.[j]
9 Their own tongues will bring them down,
and all who see them will wag their heads. *[k]
10 * Then everyone will be in awe,
as they proclaim God's mighty deeds
and contemplate what he has done. *
11 The righteous will rejoice in the LORD
and take refuge in him;
all the upright in heart will praise him.[l]

---

f Pss 17:8; 27:9; 36:8; 118:7; Ru 2:12.—g Pss 21:2; 107:42; Deut 6:13; Isa 45:23; 48:1; Jer 12:16; Dan 13:43, 61; Zep 1:5.—h Pss 7:13; 11:2; 37:14; 55:22; 57:5; 58:7; Isa 49:2; Jer 9:2.—i Ps 140:3; Prov 6:14; Jer 11:20f.—j Pss 7:13-14; 38:3; Deut 32:42; Job 6:4; 34:6; Lam 6:12; Ezek 5:16.—k Pss 5:10-11; 44:15; 52:6; 59:13.—l Pss 5:12; 36:8; 57:2.

63:7 *Upon my bed:* during the night of darkness, the psalmist anxiously looks for the morning of God's deliverance (see notes on Pss 57; 57:9). *Watches of the night:* the night was divided into three watches, and if someone were aware of all three of them he was passing a sleepless night—in this case at prayer (see Ps 119:148; Lam 2:19).

63:8 See note on Ps 17:8.

63:10-12 See notes on Pss 5:11; 35.

63:10-11 The psalmist's enemies will lose their lives for having sought to kill him, and they will become *food for jackals,* i.e., they will remain unburied, a cause for shame (see note on Ps 53:6).

63:12 *All who swear by him:* to swear by the Lord signified devoted adherence to him (see Isa 45:23; 48:1; Zep 1:5). God will acquit his followers (see Deut 6:13; Jer 12:16; Dan 13:42, 60) but will chastise the wicked (see Ps 52:3-7).

Ps 64 The psalmist shows that the righteous are often defenseless before the cynicism of the machinations and calumnies to which they are prey. Those who weave their intrigues act in shadows and believe they are hidden from view. However, God sees everything, even secret human actions and designs. His judgment overtakes those who evade justice. Basing himself on the law of talion ("an eye for an eye"), the author imagines that, even here below, God will turn their evil against the wicked while publicly acquitting the righteous. Each life will be brought before the judgment of God; the righteous will find their joy in the Lord. Such is the lesson of the psalm, even though the ways of God follow a more mysterious course than its author yet suspected.

This psalm was applied to the Passion of Jesus by St. Augustine. It also finds a ready place in the prayer of the Church and the faithful who experience the physical and spiritual attacks of the world, the flesh, and the devil as we await the coming of Christ to dispense true justice (see Rev 19:1f).

64:1 *For the director:* these words are thought to be a musical or liturgical notation.

64:4 *Tongues:* see note on Ps 5:10.

64:6-7 These verses enlarge the portrait of the wicked set forth in verses 3-5; there the wicked are shown opposing the innocent, while here their common plotting is shown. The wicked lay snares to trap their victims (see Pss 35:7; 119:110; 140:6; 142:4; Deut 7:16; Prov 22:24f; Jer 7:9f).

64:7 *Hearts:* see note on Ps 4:8. *Hidden:* literally, "deep" (see Prov 18:4; 20:5).

64:8-10 See notes on Pss 5:11; 35.

64:8-9 God will turn on the wicked the harm they wanted to do to the psalmist, as demanded by the law of talion (see Pss 7:13f; 9:16f; 35:7f; 37:15; 59:13f; 140:10). He will shoot his arrows at them (see Ps 38:3; Deut 32:42). The shame they had intended to bring upon the godly will fall back upon themselves (see Pss 22:8; 52:7-9; 59:11; Jer 48:26).

64:9 *Wag their heads:* a common gesture of ridicule (see Pss 22:8; 44:15; 109:25; Jer 48:27).

64:10-11 The psalmist encourages all to proclaim and ponder the acts of God (see Ps 2:10; Isa 41:20) and to turn to him in adversity. He will vindicate his servants who are righteous (see Pss 7:11; 11:2-7), and they will be in a position to give him praise (see Ps 7:18).

64:10 The wicked asked derisively, "Who will see us?" (v. 6) and were unafraid of the consequences of their actions. But when all humanity sees the power of God, fear will come upon everyone.

PSALM 65*

Thanksgiving for Divine Blessings

1 For the director. * A psalm of David. A song.

2 It is fitting to offer praise to you, *
O God, in Zion.
To you our vows must be fulfilled,
3 for you answer our prayers.
To you all flesh must come,* [m]
4 burdened by its sinful deeds. [n]
Too heavy for us are our sins,
and only you can blot them out. *

5 Blessed * is the one whom you choose
and invite to dwell in your courts.
We will be filled with the good things of
your house,
of your holy temple.

6 Through your awesome deeds * of righteousness,
you respond to us, O God, our Savior;
you are the hope of all the ends of the
earth
and of the far-off islands. [o]

7 Clothed in your great power,
you hold the mountains in place. *
8 You quiet the roaring of the seas,
the turbulence of their waves, [p]
and the turmoil of the nations. * [q]

9 Those who dwell at the ends of the earth
are awestruck by your wonders. *
You call forth songs of joy
from sunrise and sunset.

10 You care for the earth and water it,
making it most fertile.
The streams of God * are filled with
water
to provide grain for its people. [r]
Thus, you prepare the earth for growth:
11 you water its furrows
and level its ridges;
you soften it with showers
and bless its yield. *

12 You crown the year with your bounty, *
and your tracks dispense fertility.
13 The pastures of the wilderness overflow,
and the hills are covered with rejoicing.
14 The meadows are clothed with flocks,
and the valleys are decked out with
grain;
in their joy they shout and sing together. * [s]

m Pss 22:28; 66:4; 86:9; Isa 66:23; Zec 14:16; Rev 15:4.—n Pss 32:1-2; 40:13; 78:38; 79:9; Isa 1:18; Heb 9:14.—o Ps 18:47; Isa 66:19.—p Pss 89:10; 93:3-4; 107:29; Job 26:12; 38:11; Mt 8:26.—q Isa 17:12.—r Ps 68:11; Lev 26:4; Isa 30:23, 25; Joel 2:22-23.—s Pss 72:16; 98:8; 144:13; Isa 44:23.

Ps 65 In Israel, the Harvest Feast (see Lev 23:29) directly follows the Day of Atonement (to which reference is made in Ps 65:4; see Lev 16). At this time the people celebrate a season of abundance. Joy and gratitude pervade this poem. At the beginning, there is a first acclamation to the Lord who dwells in Zion; in this privileged place God receives worship and dispenses pardon while the Levites are overwhelmed with joy and filled with grace. Then the horizon is expanded to include the very ends of the earth: the people praise the Master of the world whose exploits are proclaimed by all creation and history. Lastly, gratitude is offered for the huge harvest: the poet evokes the miracle that comes in the form of rain (for these regions ever threatened by drought); the springtime of Judea shines forth, and the country experiences a sumptuous rebirth.

The modern—scientific—way in which we look at the succession of the seasons and harvests need not deprive us of the wisdom of the ancients, which saw God at work and extolled his splendor and goodness. It is God who acts through the regular course of nature (see Mt 6:26, 30).

This psalm reminds us to offer God unceasing praise and thanksgiving (see Col 3:16f; Eph 5:19f).

65:1 *For the director:* these words are thought to be a musical or liturgical notation.

65:2 *It is fitting . . . praise to you:* another translation is: "Praise awaits you." The debt of giving praise to God is fulfilled when people carry out the vows they made in time of need (see note on Ps 7:18).

65:3 *To you all flesh must come:* i.e., all humankind will come to God. It recalls the universalism of the psalmists (see Pss 64:10; 66:1, 4, 8; 67:4-6) and of Isaiah (see Isa 17:12; 26:15; 66:19, 23).

65:4 *Blot them out:* or "make atonement for them." God forgives sins when his people repent and observe his rules for pardon (as he did for the Israelites who observed the Day of Atonement—see Lev 16:20-30).

65:5 *Blessed:* see note on Ps 1:1. *Good things of your house:* see note on Ps 36:9.

65:6 *Awesome deeds:* God's creative acts as reflected in the beauty and bounty of Nature and his saving acts as seen in the deliverance of Israel from Egypt and its establishment in the Promised Land (see Pss 106:22; 145:6; Deut 10:21; 2 Sam 7:23; Isa 64:3).

65:7 *Clothed in your great power, you hold the mountains in place:* the God of the psalmist is the Creator, the one who formed the mountains and continues to hold them in place (see Ps 93:1; Am 4:13).

65:8 Just as God tamed the turbulence of the primeval waters of chaos (see notes on Pss 32:6; 33:7), so he brings to an end the *turmoil of the nations* (see Isa 2:4f; 11:6-9; Mic 4:3f).

65:9 *Wonders:* the great saving acts of God indicated in note to verse 6.

65:10 *Streams of God:* the poet evokes the means by which God brings forth the rain out of his "storehouses" (Ps 33:7), which flow into the water sources on earth and give life to creatures (see Ps 46:5; Isa 33:21).

65:11 God sends both the "early" rain in the fall and the "latter" rain in the spring to water the ground and lead to abundant harvests—which he then blesses (see Deut 11:14; 28:12; Hos 6:3; Joel 2:23; Acts 14:17).

65:12 *Bounty:* literally, "goodness"; the reference is to both material and spiritual gifts, God's covenant promises. *Tracks:* God's royal chariot tours the heavens dispensing fertility throughout the earth (see Pss 18:11; 68:5; Deut 33:26; Isa 66:15; Am 9:13).

65:14 *In their joy they shout and sing together:* all creation joins in the praise of God for his goodness (see Pss 89:13; 96:11-13; 98:8f; 103:22; 145:10; 148:3f, 7-10; Job 38:7; Isa 44:23; 49:13; 55:12).

PSALM 66*

Thanksgiving for God's Deliverance

1 For the director. * A song. A psalm.
Shout joyfully to God, all the earth; *
2 sing to the glory of his name; *
offer to him glorious praise. [t]
3 [u] Say to God: "How awesome are your deeds!
Because of your great power,
your enemies grovel before you.
4 The whole earth bows down in worship before you,
singing praises to you,
singing praises to your name." *Selah*
5 Come and behold * the works of God,
the awesome deeds he has done for people.
6 He changed the sea into dry land;
they crossed the river * on foot.
There we rejoiced in him, [v]
7 for he rules forever by his power.
His eyes keep watch over the nations
so that the rebellious not exalt themselves. *Selah*
8 * Bless our God, all you peoples;
let the sound of his praise be heard.
9 For he has preserved our lives *
and has kept our feet from stumbling. [w]
10 For you, O God, have put us to the test;
you have purified us as silver is refined. [x]
11 * You allowed us to be snared in the net
and placed heavy burdens on our backs.
12 You let our captors ride over our heads, *
and we went through fire and water,
but now you have afforded us relief. [y]
13 * I will enter your house with burnt offerings
and carry out my vows to you,
14 the vows that my lips pronounced
and my mouth promised when I was in distress.
15 I will offer burnt offerings of fat animals
with the smoke of burning rams;
I will sacrifice to you bulls and goats. *Selah*
16 Come and listen, all you who fear God,
while I relate what he has done for me.
17 * I lifted up my voice in prayer to him;
his praise * was on my tongue.
18 * If I had harbored evil in my heart,
the LORD would not have listened.

t Pss 65:14; 79:9; Isa 44:23.—u 3-4: Pss 18:45; 81:16; Mic 7:17.—v Pss 74:15; 114:3; Gen 8:1; Ex 14:21f; Lev 23:40; Jos 3:14ff; Isa 44:27; 1 Cor 10:1.—w Pss 30:4; 91:12; 121:3; Deut 32:35; 1 Sam 2:9; Job 12:5; Prov 3:23.—x Ps 12:7; Ex 15:25; Isa 48:10; Dan 11:35; 12:10.—y Pss 32:6; 81:18; Isa 43:2; 51:22f.

Ps 66 This psalm is made up of two wholly autonomous parts: in the first, Israel praises God for his saving acts on its behalf, and in the second, an individual fulfills his vow to God for some favor. In its liturgy, Israel always contemplates anew the great days of the past: the Exodus from Egypt and the passage of the Jordan (v. 5). This does not constitute nostalgia for a past favor; yesterday's event is the sign of God's presence today. God always manifests himself as the savior of his people: now he delivers them from the distress of an invasion or possibly from the great trial of the Exile (vv. 8-11). A spirit of universalism pervades the first part of this poem: the whole earth is invited to proclaim the deliverances of God.

In the individual's prayer of thanksgiving, a man saved from a great trial comes to give praise by his offerings and his proclamation amidst his friends. The person who announces a deliverance at God's hands makes himself the spokesman of the community of believers.

This psalm is an apt reminder to offer God a fitting sacrifice of thanksgiving in the Eucharist. Such is the living sacrifice we offer God, placing ourselves in it as other living victims (see Rom 12:1) in order to thank him for the wonders accomplished in our souls, especially for our spiritual resurrection achieved in union with Christ's Resurrection (see Rom 6:5-8).

66:1a *For the director:* these words are thought to be a musical or liturgical notation.

66:1b *All the earth:* see note on Ps 65:3.

66:2 *Name:* see note on Ps 5:12.

66:5 *Come and behold:* in the eyes of the psalmist, God's saving acts are present and can be seen in the liturgical celebration in the temple.

66:6 *Sea . . . river:* the passages through the Red Sea (see Ex 14:1—15:21) and through the Jordan (see Jos 3:11—4:24) became typical of God's power and wondrous deeds in the history of Israel (see Ps 114:3; Isa 44:27; 50:2).

66:8-12 Praise for a new deliverance that God has worked on his people's behalf.

66:9 *Preserved our lives:* sometimes translated as "brought us to life," which accounts for the name "Resurrection Psalm" given this psalm in Greek and Latin manuscripts and its use in the Easter Liturgy.

66:11-12 The Israelites experienced imprisonment, slavery, and total defeat before being delivered by God and brought into a place of abundance (see Pss 18:20; 23:4-6; 119:45). The Lord does not permit his people to succumb to their trials (see Ps 37:24; 1 Cor 10:13) and rewards a persevering faith (see 1 Pet 1:7).

66:12 *You let our captors ride over our heads:* literally, "you let men mount our head," which suggests the ancient practice of victors in war placing their feet on the necks of their enemies as a sign of total subjugation (see Isa 51:23). *Fire and water:* conventional metaphors for the gravest of trials (see Pss 32:6; 81:8; Isa 43:2; 51:22f).

66:13-20 An individual fulfills the *vows* he promised to God when he was in trouble (see note on Ps 7:18; see also Pss 50:14; 116:17-19).

66:17-20 The psalmist's celebration of his deliverance includes a lament (*I lifted up my voice*, v. 17), a profession of commitment (*his praise was on my tongue*, v. 17), a protestation of innocence (*if I had harbored evil in my heart*, v. 18; see Pss 17:1f; 18:21f; 59:4f; Jn 9:31), and praise (*God truly did listen*, v. 19; see Pss 28:6; 31:22; 68:20, 36).

66:17 *I lifted up my voice . . . his praise:* prayer always entails praise in both the Old Testament and the New (see Phil 4:6; 1 Tim 2:1). Even while the psalmist was praying for help, he was also praising God for his goodness and mercy.

66:18-19 Because the psalmist acknowledged his sin, he was forgiven by God, and his prayer was heard. *Heart:* see note on Ps 4:8.

19 But God truly did listen,
and he was attentive to the words of my prayer.

20 Blessed * be God,
because he did not reject my prayer
or withhold his kindness from me.

PSALM 67*

Prayer That All May Worship God

1 For the director. * With stringed instruments. A psalm. A song.

2 O God, be gracious to us and bless us
and let your face shine upon us. * [z]
Selah

3 * Then your ways will be known on earth
and your salvation among all nations. [a]

4 Let the peoples praise you, O God;
let all the peoples praise you.

5 Let the nations rejoice and exult,
for you judge the peoples fairly
and guide the nations upon the earth. * [b]
Selah

6 Let the peoples praise you, O God;
let all the peoples praise you.

7 The earth has yielded its harvest;
God, our God, has blessed us. [c]

8 May God continue to bless us
and be revered to the ends of the earth.

PSALM 68*

Song of Victory

1 For the director. * A psalm of David. A song.

2 * May God rise up, and his enemies be scattered;
may his foes flee before him. [d]

3 As smoke is blown away in the wind,
so will they be blown away.
As wax melts away before a flame,
so will the wicked perish before God. [e]

4 But those who are righteous will rejoice;
they will exult before God,
crying out with great delight.

5 * Sing to God, sing praise to his name; *
exalt him who rides upon the clouds.

z Pss 4:7; 31:17; 44:4; 80:4; Num 6:24-26; Dan 9:17.—a Ps 98:2; Isa 40:5; 52:10; Jer 33:9.—b Pss 82:8; 98:9; 100:2-3.—c Ps 85:13; Gen 12:2; Lev 26:4; Isa 55:10; Ezek 34:27; Hos 2:23-24; Zec 8:12.—d Pss 12:6; 18:15; 89:11; 92:10; 132:8; 144:6; Num 10:35; Isa 17:13; 21:15; 33:3.—e Pss 9:4; 37:20; 97:5; Jud 16:15; Wis 5:14; Mic 1:4.

66:20 *Blessed:* see note on Ps 22:27. *Kindness:* see note on Ps 6:5.

Ps 67 This psalm recounts the assembly of the people for the Feast of the Harvest (see Ex 23:16; Lev 26:4) and their prayers of praise to God. They recall first all that he has done in Israel; the abundance of the fruits of the earth is like a new sign of his power and goodness. And more and more, they want the whole world to take part in this thanksgiving to God. The Lord is no longer merely the God of Israel; he is the Master and Judge of the whole world and all its peoples.

This psalm enables us to thank God for his material blessings on us. However, it also reminds us to ask God to continue to shower upon us his spiritual blessings so as to elicit admiration, envy, and divine praises even from nonbelievers.

67:1 *For the director:* these words are thought to be a musical or liturgical notation.

67:2 This verse was inspired by the priestly blessing (see Ps 31:17; Num 6:24-26). *Face shine upon us:* a radiant face is the sign of a joyous and benevolent heart (see Pss 4:7; 31:17; 44:4; 80:4; 119:135; see also note on Ps 13:2).

67:3-4 The history of the chosen people is a lesson that God gives to the pagan nations, enabling them to discover his power and goodness. They too are called to serve the one God and must join their praises to those of God's people. The refrain of the psalm (vv. 4, 6) insists on the universalism that the Prophets (see Jer 33:9), especially Second Isaiah, have impressed on the religious conscience of Israel. Many psalms bear witness to this spirit.

67:5 The psalmist prays that the nations may see the goodness of God's rule and respond with joy and praise (see Pss 98:4-6; 100:1).

Ps 68 This psalm may have been used in a processional liturgy celebrating the triumphal march of Israel's God to his sanctuary, possibly as part of the Feast of Booths or Tabernacles that included a procession of the tribes (vv. 25-28). With the words "May God rise up, . . ." the poet sets in motion the procession with the Ark, as at the time when it went before the marches of the people (v. 2; see Num 10:35). And he lets the whole history of Israel unfold before our eyes like a grand march of God, like his procession into the heart of Jerusalem. God rises, and the darkness dissipates; he takes the head of his people, and the adversaries are thrown into disorder. This epic poem assembles a series of allusive images, many of which remain obscure for us.

In this coming of God, however, we will recognize stirring moments in the destiny of Israel: the Exodus from Egypt and the divine manifestation at Sinai (vv. 8-9; see Ex 19:16), the wonders of the Exodus (vv. 10-11), the exploits of the Judges (vv. 12-15; see Book of Judges), the Conquest of Jerusalem (vv. 15-19), the sad fate of the criminal Ahab (v. 24; see 1 Ki 21:19), and the solemn Passover of Hezekiah who had reunited all the tribes of Israel (vv. 25-36; see 2 Chr 30), which foreshadowed the gathering in the holy city of the pagans who had finally come to render homage to the Lord of all nations.

The important thing in this psalm is not so much to grasp all the allusions as it is to let ourselves be carried along by the rhythm of the chant; we should listen to it as to a heroic march, as the glorious epic that draws Israel out of the atmosphere of everyday life. It is the ideal psalm for processions to the temple.

In the ascent of God, who rises to take possession of the sacred hill of Jerusalem, the apostle Paul sees the Ascension of Christ, who draws after him the redeemed people, the Church that is filled with the gifts of the Holy Spirit (v. 19; see Eph 4:8-11). When Christians sing this hymn, they recall the presence of God in the working out of the world's destiny and the march of humanity, which is continually called by God until it is made one again in glory.

68:1 *For the director:* these words are thought to be a musical or liturgical notation.

68:2-4 This first of nine parts prays that God will come at the head of his people to defeat their enemies and enter his sanctuary in triumph.

68:5-7 This second part calls for God to be praised as savior.

68:5 *Name:* see notes on Pss 5:12; 8:1. *Who rides upon the clouds:* the psalmist applies to Yahweh the image of the Canaanite storm-god Baal riding to battle on storm clouds; he thus stresses that Yahweh rather than Baal is the exalted God who makes the storm clouds his chariot (see v. 34; Pss 18:10f; 104:3; Deut 33:26; Isa 19:1; Hab 3:8; Mt 26:64).

Rejoice in the presence of this God
whose name is the LORD.[f]
6 *[g] The Father of orphans and the defender of widows:
such is God in his holy dwelling place.
7 He gives a home to those who are forsaken
and leads out prisoners amid chants of exultation,
while rebels are forced to live in an arid land.
8 *[h] O God, when you set out at the head of your people,
when you went marching through the wilderness, *Selah*
9 the earth quaked, *
and rain poured down from the heavens,
at the presence of God, the One of Sinai,
at the presence of God, the God of Israel.
10 * You poured down rain in abundance, O God,
and revived your exhausted inheritance.
11 It was there that your people settled;
and in your great goodness, O God,
you provided for those who were needy.
12 * The Lord issues the word, *
and a vast army proclaims good tidings:
13 "Kings and their armies are beating a hasty retreat;
even those who remained in camp are dividing up the spoils.[i]
14 "While you linger by the sheepfolds,
the wings of the dove are covered * with silver,
its feathers brilliant with shining gold."[j]
15 When the Almighty * routed the kings there,
it was like snow fallen upon Zalmon.
16 * The mountains of Bashan are God's mountains;
the mountains of Bashan are mighty peaks.
17 Why, O rugged mountains, do you gaze enviously
at the mountain * that God has chosen as his abode,
where the LORD himself will dwell forever?[k]
18 The chariots of God * are myriad,
thousands upon thousands;
the LORD has come down from Sinai
and entered into the holy place.
19 You ascended on high,
leading captives in your train;
you accepted slaves as tribute,
so that even rebels might dwell with the LORD God. *[l]

f Pss 7:18; 18:10; 104:3; Deut 33:26; Isa 19:1.—g 6-7: Pss 10:14; 25:16; 103:6; 146:7, 9; Ex 22:21; Bar 6:37.—h 8-9: Pss 44:10; 114:4, 7; Ex 13:21; Deut 33:2; Jdg 5:4-5; Heb 12:26.—i Jos 10:16; Jdg 5:19, 30.—j Gen 49:14; Jdg 5:16.—k Ps 132:13-14; Deut 12:5; Ezek 43:7.—l Pss 7:7; 47:6; Eph 4:8-10.

68:6-7 The Lord watches over the whole human race, acting on behalf of those who seek protection and vindication: the fatherless, the widows, the forsaken, and the exiles. His rule brings about justice out of injustice and vindication out of oppression (see Pss 10:14; 25:16; 79:11; 102:20f; 103:6; 146:9; Ex 22:21-23; Deut 10:18; Isa 61:1; Bar 6:37).

68:8-11 This third part recalls God's march at the head of his people from Egypt, through the Desert of Sinai, and into the Promised Land (see Ps 60:14; Ex 13:21; 19:16; Num 14:14; Deut 33:2; Hab 3:3).

68:9 *Earth quaked:* a reference to the "trembling" of Mount Sinai (see Ex 19:18). *Rain poured down from the heavens:* although there is no record of rain in the Sinai story, there is mention of "thunder, lightning, a dense cloud" (see Ex 19:16), which would usually indicate rain. In addition, rain is connected with the shaking of the earth (see Jdg 5:4).

68:10-11 These two verses evoke the miracles of the Exodus: the cloud (see Ex 13:21; Num 14:14), the manna and quail (see Ps 78:24f; Ex 16:4f), and the entrance into the Promised Land (v. 11: *it was there*).

68:12-15 This fourth part recalls the defeat of the Canaanite kings by God.

68:12 *Issues the word:* God foretells his victory over the Canaanites (see Ex 23:22f, 27f, 31; Deut 7:10-24; 11:23-25; Jos 1:2-6).

68:14 *Wings of the dove are covered:* even while in camp, before the battle, Israel (God's "dove": see Ps 74:19; Hos 7:11) is already assured of enjoying the booty (*silver* and *gold*) of the Canaanite kings, for God had guaranteed it (see Jos 2:8-11; 5:1; 6:16).

68:15 *Almighty:* the Hebrew is *Shaddai,* "the Mountain One." The name by which God revealed himself to the patriarchs was *El-Shaddai*: "God Almighty" (see Gen 17:1), which stressed God's power or his home in the mountains (see Ps 121:1). *Zalmon:* a mountain near Shechem (see Jdg 9:46-48) or a dark volcanic mountain in Bashan or Hauran east of the Sea of Galilee. It was known as the "dark one" in opposition to the "white one," Lebanon.

68:16-19 This fifth part celebrates the taking of Jerusalem to which God ascends and from which he will rule the world.

68:17 *The mountain:* Mount Zion, a little mount, which God has made the highest mountain because he has placed his temple there and dwells in it.

68:18 *Chariots of God:* the heavenly hosts (see Hab 3:8, 15), later termed "legions" by Jesus (see Mt 26:53). It may also refer to the heavenly chariots seen by Elisha (see 2 Ki 6:17) rather than the chariots of Solomon (see 1 Ki 10:26).

68:19 When God went up to his place of enthronement on Mount Zion (see Ps 47:6f), he had captives in his train and received gifts like a victor in battle. The apostle Paul applies this verse in its Greek translation to the ministry of the ascended Christ (Eph 4:8: "When he ascended to the heights, / he took prisoners into captivity / and gave gifts to men"). It assures all who believe in Christ that by trusting him they can overcome evil.

20 * Blessed be the LORD, day after day,
the God of our salvation, who carries
our burden. [m] *Selah*
21 Our God is a God who saves;
the LORD God delivers from death. *
22 God himself will smite the heads of his
enemies,
the hairy crowns of those who persist in
their sins. [n]
23 The LORD has said:
"I will bring them back even from
Bashan,
I will bring them back even from the
depths of the sea, *
24 so that you may bathe your feet in the
blood of your foes
and the tongues of your dogs may have
their share." * [o]
25 * Your procession, O God, comes into view,
the procession of my God and King
into the sanctuary.
26 The singers enter first,
with musicians trailing behind them,
while in their midst are the maidens
playing tambourines. * [p]
27 Bless God in the assembly;
the LORD, the source of Israel.
28 In the lead is Benjamin, the smallest in
number,
with the princes of Judah in a council,
as well as the princes of Zebulun and
Naphtali. [q]
29 * Marshal your power once again, O God,
the power of God that you have often
wielded for us.
30 For to your temple in Jerusalem
kings will come to you bearing gifts. *
31 Rebuke those wild beasts of the reeds, *
the herd of mighty bulls, the calves of
nations,
who bring bars of silver and prostrate
themselves;
rout the nations that delight in war.
32 Envoys will come from Egypt; [r]
Ethiopia will stretch out its hands to
God. * [s]
33 * Sing to God, all you kingdoms of the
earth;
sing the praises of the LORD, [t] *Selah*
34 who rides the ancient heavens above *
and speaks with his voice of thunder.
35 Acknowledge the power of God,
whose majesty is over Israel
and whose power is in the skies.
36 Awesome is God in his sanctuary,
the God of Israel, who gives power and
strength to his people. * [u]
Blessed be God!

m Pss 34:2; 145:2; Deut 32:11; Isa 46:3-4; 63:8.—n Ps 74:14; Deut 32:42.—o Ps 58:11; 1 Ki 21:19; 22:38; 2 Ki 9:36; Isa 63:1-6.—p Pss 81:3-4; 87:7; 149:3; 150:3-5; 2 Sam 6:5; Rev 18:22.—q Jdg 5:18; 1 Sam 9:21; Isa 9:1.—r Ezek 17:15; 29:2ff.—s Isa 18:7; 43:3; 45:14; Zep 3:10.—t Pss 7:18; 67:5; 138:4.—u Pss 18:2; 28:8; 29:11; Deut 7:21.

68:20-24 This sixth part offers joyous praise and the fervent hope that God's victories will continue.

68:21 *Delivers from death:* God delivers his faithful from the death inflicted on them by their enemies and also from the death that comes to all human beings (see notes on Pss 6:6; 11:7; 16:9-11; 17:15; 49:16; 73:23-26; 139:18; Job 19:23-29; Isa 26:19; Dan 12:2; see also 1 Cor 15).

68:23 *From Bashan . . . from the depths of the sea:* i.e., the heights and the depths, the farthest places to which enemies might flee.

68:24 A vivid expression indicating complete victory over one's foes that was common in the Near East (see Ps 58:11). It alludes to the predictions of Elijah (1 Ki 21:19f) about the death of Ahab (1 Ki 22:38), his son Joram, wounded at Ramoth Gilead and brought back to Jezreel (2 Ki 8:29; 9:15), and Jezebel (2 Ki 9:36).

68:25-28 This seventh part describes the procession as it approaches the temple and renews God's taking up residence there (see Pss 24; 47) in the presence of all Israel, both north and south. It also alludes to the Passover of Hezekiah in which all the tribes participated (see Ps 80:2f; 2 Chr 30:1ff; Isa 9:1).

68:26 *Tambourines:* instruments played especially after a victory in battle (see Ex 15:20; 1 Sam 10:5; 18:6; 2 Sam 6:5; Jer 31:4).

68:29-32 This eighth part gives the prayer that God may continue to rule over the enemies of his people and exact tribute from them.

68:30 The defeated nations, led by their kings, will bring tribute to the Lord who has established his majesty in his temple at Jerusalem (see Ps 76:12; Isa 18:7; 60:3-7; 66:20; Hag 2:7; Zec 2:11-13; 6:15; 8:21f; Rev 21:24).

68:31 The prayer contains a petition to strike the nations that will not submit to the Lord. *Wild beasts of the reeds:* the reference is to the crocodile, a symbol for Egypt (see Ezek 29:3), which in turn stands for all the hostile nations. *Herd of mighty bulls:* the "lords of nations" who oppress and seduce their peoples. *Bars of silver:* tribute from the foreign nations brought to Zion.

68:32 Egypt will submit, as will Ethiopia (i.e., the upper Nile region) who usually formed an alliance with Egypt (see Isa 18:1—19:15; 20:1-6).

68:33-36 This ninth part calls upon all nations to praise the God of Israel who dwells in the temple and acclaim him as the God of all nations (see Ps 47).

68:34 The words *who rides the ancient heavens above* indicate the Lord's majesty, for he rules the highest heavens (see Deut 10:14; 1 Ki 8:27). The thunder symbolizes the power and majesty of his rule (see Pss 18:14; 29:3) on behalf of his people (see Deut 33:26).

68:36 Although the Lord is awesome in his deeds (see Pss 47:3; 65:6; Ex 15:11; Deut 10:17; Rev 15:3f), he condescends to be present to his people in the sanctuary in order to aid them.

PSALM 69*

Cry of Anguish in Distress

1 For the director.* According to "Lilies." Of David.

2 * Save me, my God,
for the waters have risen to my neck. [v]
3 I am sinking in muddy depths
and can find no foothold.
I have fallen into deep waters,
and the floods * overwhelm me. [w]

4 I am exhausted from crying out;
my throat is parched.
My eyes have been worn out
searching for my God. [x]

5 More numerous than the hairs of my head
are those who hate me for no reason. *
Many are those who seek to destroy me,
and they are treacherous.
How can I restore
what I have not stolen? [y]

6 O God, you know how foolish I am;
my guilty deeds are not hidden from you. *
7 Do not allow those who hope in you
to be put to shame because of me,
O LORD of hosts.
Do not let those who seek you
suffer disgrace because of me,
O God of Israel. [z]

8 It is for your sake that I endure reproach
and that shame covers my face. [a]
9 I have become alienated from my brothers, *
a stranger to my mother's sons. [b]
10 Zeal for your house * consumes me,
and the insults directed at you fall on me. [c]

11 [d] When I mortified myself with fasting,
I exposed myself to scorn.
12 When I clothed myself in sackcloth,
I became a laughingstock.
13 Those who sit at the gate taunt me,
and drunkards make me the target of their ditties.

14 But I lift up my prayer to you, O LORD,
in the time of your favor. *
In your great kindness, O God,
respond to me with your certain help. [e]
15 [f] Draw me out of the mire,
and do not let me plunge any deeper.
Deliver me from my enemies
and from the deep waters.
16 Do not let the flood waters sweep over me,
or the depths swallow me up,
or the pit close its jaws around me.

17 Answer me, O LORD, for your kindness * is wonderful;
in your great compassion turn toward me.
18 Do not hide your face * from your servant;
answer me quickly, for I am in distress. [g]
19 Draw near to me and redeem me;
deliver me from my enemies.

v Pss 18:5; 32:6; 93:3-4; Job 22:11; Jon 2:5.—w Pss 40:3; 42:8; 124:4-5; Job 30:19.—x Pss 6:7; 25:15; 27:8; 119:82; 123:2; 141:8; Isa 38:14.—y Pss 35:19; 38:20; 40:13; Lam 3:52; Jn 15:25.—z Pss 25:3; 40:17.—a Ps 44:16; Jer 15:15.—b Pss 31:12; 38:12; Job 19:13-15; 53:3; Jn 7:5.—c Pss 89:51-52; 119:139; Jn 2:17; Rom 15:3.—d 11-13: Pss 35:13; 109:24-25; Job 30:9; Lam 3:14.—e Pss 32:6; 102:14; Isa 49:8; 2 Cor 6:2.—f 15-16: Pss 28:1; 30:4; 32:6; 40:3; 88:5; 144:7; Num 16:33; Prov 1:12.—g Pss 22:25; 50:15; 102:3; 143:7.

Ps 69 This Messianic psalm encompasses the laments of two different people in distress; the first may have been accused of thievery (v. 5), and the second may have been tormented because of his piety and derided for his faith. The swamp in which they are sinking and the waters by which they are engulfed are the images of the despair that afflicts a person facing death. The tragic state of the suppliants resembles that of the righteous person whom we have encountered in Ps 22 and who makes us think of the prophet Jeremiah (see Jer 15:15) and the Suffering Servant (see Isa 53:10). Their prayer, which appeals to God's justice as well as his compassion, concludes with a vast thanksgiving; the salvation that they await must be extended to all the lowly who rely only on God.

In their sufferings, Jesus sees his own suffering (Jn 15:25), and the evangelists have applied themselves to underscore this likeness (see Mt 27:46; Jn 2:17; 19:28; etc.). No psalm except Ps 22 is cited more often in the New Testament, a fact that led the Fathers of the Church to classify this psalm as Messianic.

69:1 *For the director:* these words are thought to be a musical or liturgical notation. *According to "Lilies":* nothing is known about this phrase.

69:2-3 *Waters . . . muddy depths . . . deep waters . . . floods:* a common means of indicating extreme distress (see note on Ps 30:2).

69:5 *Hate me for no reason:* see note on Ps 35:19. These words were completely fulfilled in the hatred his enemies had for Jesus (see Jn 15:25).

69:6 The psalmist admits his guilt, but he is innocent of the great crimes attributed to him by his enemies. This verse can be applied to Jesus only as an indication of the sins of the world that he took upon himself.

69:9 *I have become alienated from my brothers:* i.e., he is mocked by them; this text lies behind Jn 7:5, where Jesus' relatives ("brothers") do not believe in him.

69:10 *Zeal for your house:* cited in Jn 2:17 with reference to Jesus. *Insults directed at you:* cited in Rom 15:3 as an example of Jesus' selflessness.

69:14 *Time of your favor:* i.e., the special time when God is very near (see Ps 32:6; Isa 49:8; 61:2; 2 Cor 6:2). *Kindness:* see note on Ps 6:5.

69:17 *Kindness:* see note on Ps 6:5.

69:18 *Hide your face:* see note on Ps 13:2.

20 You know my reproach, my shame, and my dishonor;
all my oppressors are in your sight.
21 Insults have so broken my heart
that I am near the end of my strength.
I looked for compassion, but in vain,
for some consolers, but I found none. * h
22 They put gall in my food,
and in my thirst they gave me vinegar * to drink. i
23 * Let their table become a trap for them;
let their well-being become a snare. * j
24 Let their eyes dim so that they cannot see,
and let their limbs tremble constantly.
25 Vent your wrath on them,
and let your burning anger take hold of them.
26 Let their camp be left desolate; k
let there be no one to dwell in their tents. *
27 For they pursue the one you struck down
and tell of the pain of the one you hurt.
28 Charge them with crime after crime;
let them not share in your salvation.
29 Blot them out from the book of the living; *
do not number them among the upright. l
30 But I am filled with pain and suffering;
may your saving power, O God, raise me up.
31 * I will praise the name of God with a song
and glorify him with a hymn of thanksgiving.
32 This will gratify the LORD more than an ox
or a young bull with horns and hoofs: * m
33 "Let the poor * see this and rejoice;
let those who seek God take heart. n
34 For the LORD hears the needy
and does not turn his back on captives.
35 Let the heavens and the earth offer praise,
the seas and everything that moves therein."
36 For God will deliver Zion
and rebuild the cities of Judah. o
His people will live there and possess it;
37 his servants' children will inherit it,
and those who love his name will dwell there. p

PSALM 70*

Insistent Prayer for Divine Assistance

1 For the director. * Of David. For remembrance.

2 * q Make haste, O God, to rescue me;
O LORD, come quickly to my aid. r
3 * May all those who seek to take my life
endure shame and confusion.

h Ps 142:5; Job 6:14ff; Isa 63:5; Lam 1:2.—i Lam 3:15; Mt 27:34, 48; Mk 15:23; Lk 23:36; Jn 19:28-30.—j Job 18:10; Rom 11:9-10.—k Mt 23:38; Acts 1:20.—l Ps 139:16; Ex 32:32; Isa 4:3; Ezek 13:9; Dan 12:1; Mal 3:16; Rev 3:5; 20:12.—m Pss 40:7; 50:8-9, 14; 51:18; Isa 1:11-15; Hos 6:6; Am 5:21-22; Heb 10:5-8.—n Pss 22:27; 35:27; 70:5; 119:144.—o Ps 102:21-22; Isa 44:26; Ezek 36:10.—p Pss 25:13; 102:29; Isa 65:9.—q 2-6: Ps 40:14-18.—r Pss 22:20; 71:12.

69:21 *I looked for . . . consolers, but I found none:* see Job 6:14ff; 16:2; Lam 1:2; and in reference to Jesus, see Mt 26:40; Jn 16:32.

69:22 *Gall . . . vinegar:* the evangelists suggest that the sufferings of the psalmist as described in this verse foreshadowed the sufferings of Jesus on the cross (see Mt 27:34, 48; Mk 15:23; Lk 23:36; Jn 19:29).

69:23-29 Prayer for divine justice to prevail (see notes on Pss 5:11; 35).

69:23-24 These two verses are applied by Paul to the divine hardening of sinners' hearts that God allows (see Rom 11:9f). *Table:* a single tablecloth spread on the ground; hence the possibility of tripping over it.

69:26 Peter applies this verse to the replacement of Judas (see Acts 1:20).

69:29 *Book of the living:* a figurative expression denoting God's record of the righteous (see note on Ps 51:3). From the human point of view, individuals may be blotted out of that book, but from the divine point of view it contains only the names of the elect who will not be blotted out (see Phil 4:3; Rev 3:5; 13:8; 17:8; 20:15).

69:31-34 A vow to praise God for hearing his prayer (see note on Ps 7:18). *Name:* see note on Ps 5:12.

69:32 Prayer is worth more than the sacrifice of animals (see Pss 40:7; 50:13f; 51:18f), even the most perfect ones (see Lev 11:3; 1 Sam 1:24). See notes on Pss 40:7 and 50:7-15.

69:33 *Poor:* see note on Ps 22:27. *Heart:* see note on Ps 4:8.

Ps 70 The psalmist's cry is that of all who cannot endure suffering any longer and have no hope except in God. He calls upon God to come to his aid quickly. It is a slightly revised duplicate of Ps 40:14-18.

Every Christian (and the whole Church) can naturally recite this psalm in his or her own right as one really (though not yet completely) saved.

70:1 *For the director:* these words are thought to be a musical or liturgical notation. *For remembrance:* see note on Ps 38:1.

70:2-6 Distress can remind a person of his attachment to sin. Is there any reason why people should vilify the person who acknowledges his faults? Realizing his strong attraction toward evil, the psalmist cries out to God, and the poor man rediscovers with astonishment the joyous assurance that God thinks about him.

70:3-4 The psalmist prays for the downfall of his enemies, somewhat as Christians pray for the kingdom of God to come, which includes the petition that the Lord will come to vindicate his own and avenge the wrongs done by his enemies (see 2 Thes 1:5-10; see also notes on Pss 5:11; 35).

May all those who desire my ruin
be turned back and humiliated. [s]
4 May those who cry out to me, "Aha! Aha!" *
be forced to retreat in shame. [t]
5 But may all who seek you
rejoice in you and be jubilant.
May those who love your salvation
cry out forever, "May God be magnified." * [u]
6 As for me, I am poor and needy; *
hasten to my aid, O God.
You are my help and my deliverer;
O LORD, do not delay.

PSALM 71*

Prayer of the Righteous in Old Age

1 [v] In you, O LORD, I have taken refuge;
let me never be put to shame. [w]
2 In your righteousness rescue me and deliver me;
hear my plea and save me.
3 Be to me a rock of refuge
to which I can always go;
proclaim the order to save me,
for you are my rock and my fortress. [x]
4 O my God, rescue me from the hands of the impious,
from the grasp of cruel and ruthless foes. [y]
5 You, O LORD, are my hope,
my confidence, O God, from my youth.
6 I have relied upon you since birth,
and you have been my strength from my mother's womb;
my praise rises unceasingly to you. * [z]
7 I have become a portent to many, *
but you are my sure refuge.
8 My mouth is filled with your praises
as I relate your glory all day long.
9 Do not cast me off in my old age;
do not forsake me when my strength is completely spent.
10 For my enemies speak against me,
and those who seek my life plot together. [a]
11 They say: "God has abandoned him;
go after him and seize him,
for no one will come to his rescue."
12 O God, do not remain aloof from me;
come quickly to help me, O my God. [b]
13 Let those who accuse me
be put to shame and perish;
let those who are determined to harm me
incur contempt and disgrace. * [c]
14 But I will hope in you continually
and will render even more praise to you.
15 * My lips will proclaim your righteous deeds
and your salvation all day long, [d]
though I do not know their extent. *
16 I will speak of your mighty deeds, O Lord GOD,
and declare your righteousness, * yours alone.

s Pss 6:11; 35:4, 26; 71:13; 1 Sam 20:1; Est 9:2.—t Ps 35:21, 25; Lam 2:16.—u Pss 35:27; 69:7, 33; 104:1; Deut 4:29; 1 Chr 28:9.—v 1-3: Ps 31:2-4.—w Pss 22:6; 25:2; Deut 23:15; Ru 2:12.—x Pss 18:3; 28:8; 31:2-4.—y Ps 140:2; 2 Ki 19:19.—z Ps 22:11; Jer 17:14.—a Pss 3:2; 10:8; 22:8.—b Pss 22:20; 38:23.—c Pss 25:3; 35:4; 40:15; 70:3.—d Pss 35:28; 109:30.

70:4 *Aha! Aha!:* the mocking words of the psalmist's adversaries.

70:5 When the Lord works his deliverance, his people will rejoice in his salvation (see Ps 35:27) and give him praise.

70:6 *Poor and needy:* see note on Ps 34:7. *My help and my deliverer:* the salvation promised the faithful (see Isa 25:9), first conceived as natural with reference to the Exodus or the return from the Exile, was later conceived as spiritual without restriction of space or time (see Pss 18:3; 19:15).

Ps 71 Accustomed to being exposed to malevolence, an aged person, probably a cantor in the service of the temple, casts a look backward. From his childhood, every day of his long life he has endeavored to remain faithful to the Lord and to live in union with him; he has made praise of God his life companion. Profoundly confident, he begs God to come to his aid, resolute in his will to praise him with all his might. This lament resembles the "confessions" of the prophet Jeremiah (Jer 17:14-18) and could have been later applied to Israel itself. We could regard it as primarily a prayer of fidelity in difficult moments of old age; it is a fine prayer for the evening of life.

This supplication is appropriate for Christians in their temporal and spiritual trials, and even more on the lips of the Church who is looked upon by her enemies as old, failing, and vulnerable to receive the finishing blow.

71:6 *My praise . . . to you:* an alternative translation is: "my hope has always been in you."

71:7 *I have become a portent to many:* more by his trials (see Ps 31:12; Deut 28:46; Isa 52:14) than by the benefits received from God, for people are surprised to see a righteous person suffering.

71:13 A prayer for the divine justice to be done (see notes on Pss 5:11; 35).

71:15-18 A vow to offer praise to God for his help (see note on Ps 7:18).

71:15 The psalmist does not know the full extent of God's goodness toward him. For God's acts of *salvation,* consisting of his *mighty deeds* (v. 16) and *marvelous works* (v. 17), are too numerous to count (see Pss 40:6; 139:17f).

71:16 *Mighty deeds . . . righteousness:* God's "mighty deeds" on behalf of his people flow from his "righteousness"—and show forth that righteousness (see also v. 24). See also note on Ps 9:2.

17 O God, you have taught me from my youth,
and to this day I proclaim your marvelous works.
18 Now that I am old and my hair is gray,*
do not abandon me, O God,[e]
until I have extolled your might
to all the generations yet to come,[f]
your strength 19 and your righteousness, O God,
to the highest heavens.

You have done great things;[g]
O God, who is there who is like you?[h]
20 You have shown me many afflictions and hardships,
but you will once again revive me.
From the depths of the earth*
you will once again raise me up.
21 You will restore my honor
and console me once again.

22 Then I will also praise* you with the harp
for your faithfulness, O my God.
I will sing praises to you with the lyre,
O Holy One of Israel.
23 When I sing to you, my lips will rejoice,
and so will my soul, which you have redeemed.
24 All day long my tongue
will relate your righteousness.
For those who intended to do me harm
will suffer shame and disgrace.

PSALM 72*

The Kingdom of the Messiah

1 Of Solomon.
O God, endow the king with your judgment,
the son of kings with your righteousness.[i]
2 *He will govern your people fairly
and deal justly with your poor ones.[j]

3 The mountains will yield peace for the people,
and the hills, righteousness.[k]
4 He will defend the afflicted among the people,
save the children of the poor,
and overwhelm the oppressor.

5 He will reign as long as the sun,
as long as the moon, through all generations.[l]
6 He will descend like rain on the meadow,
like showers that water the earth.[m]
7 Justice will reign in his days,
and peace will abound
until the moon is no more.

8 His rule will extend from sea to sea,*
and from the river to the ends of the earth.[n]
9 His foes* will bow down before him,
and his enemies will lick the dust.[o]

10 The kings of Tarshish* and the Islands
will offer him tribute;
the kings of Sheba and Seba
will present him with gifts.[p]

---

e 1 Sam 12:2; Isa 46:4.—f Pss 22:31-32; 48:14-15; 145:4; Ex 9:16; Job 8:8.—g Pss 36:5; 72:18; Lk 1:49.—h Pss 35:10; 86:8.—i Pss 9:9; 99:4; Jer 23:5.—j Prov 31:8-9; Isa 9:6.—k Isa 45:8; 52:7; 55:12.—l Pss 61:8; 89:37-38; Jer 31:35.—m Deut 32:2; Isa 45:8; Hos 6:3.—n Ex 23:31; Deut 11:24; Zec 9:10.—o Isa 49:23; Mic 7:17.—p Ps 68:30; 1 Ki 10:1ff; Est 10:1; Isa 60:5-6.

71:17-18 *Youth . . . old and . . . gray:* this passage can be applied without difficulty to Israel to whom the Prophets apply images of youth (see Jer 2:2; Hos 2:15) and old age (see Isa 46:4; Hos 7:9; see also Ps 129:1f). *Might:* literally, "arm," a prophetic image (see Isa 51:9; 53:1), used often with respect to the miracles of the Exodus. This passage (see Pss 22:31f; 78:5f; 102:19) shows how conscious the psalmists were of being bearers of tradition.

71:20 *From the depths of the earth:* the realm of the dead, which is entered by the grave (see note on Ps 30:2).

71:22 *I will also praise:* a vow to praise God for his help (see note on Ps 7:18). *Holy One of Israel:* a frequent expression of the Book of Isaiah but used infrequently in the Psalter (see Pss 78:41; 89:19).

Ps 72 Only the expected Savior will fulfill all the hopes placed on the ideal leader described in this psalm, of whom the Prophets also speak (see Isa 9:7; 11:1-9; Jer 23:5f; 33:15f; Zec 9:9-17). The portrait bears more than one facet of King Solomon the Sage, but it is Messianic, i.e., it sketches a mysterious King who is to come. Promised a reign without end (v. 5), he will rescue the needy and poor from oppression and uphold their rights (vv. 12-14). He will establish definitive peace (v. 7), and the pagan nations that he subdues—even the most distant—will come to do homage to him (vv. 10-11). Finally, he will rule over the idealized Promised Land (v. 8) and transform it into a new heavenly paradise (vv. 6, 16).

Since Israel has never yielded to the temptation to make gods out of its kings, this king, too, is not divinized; the psalmist prays for him. This psalm is like a chart or mirror for a true reign in the name of God. It will be marked by the work of justice and peace, the effort for the deliverance of the poor and needy.

In proclaiming the Beatitudes, Jesus was to provide the authentic content of this perfect happiness that is promised for the reign of the Messiah. In the adoration of the Magi, Matthew (Mt 2:11) sees a visit from pagan kings who prostrate themselves at the feet of the promised Savior (vv. 10-11); hence, this psalm is read in the Liturgy during the Epiphany time.

72:2-3 Righteousness will rain down God's blessings on the people (see Pss 5:13; 65:10-14; 133:3; Lev 25:19; Deut 28:8).

72:8 *From sea to sea:* the Red Sea and the Mediterranean. The *river* is the Euphrates. Both details indicate the universality of the Messianic reign. *Ends of the earth:* an alternative translation is: "end of the land."

72:9 *His foes:* literally, "the Beast," a word referring to the tribes of the Arabian Desert, east of the Promised Land. *Lick the dust:* a sign of abject fear and defeat (see Mic 7:17).

72:10 All kings, whether near or far, will acknowledge the Messiah's rule. *Tarshish:* a seaport located in southern Spain, hence to the far west; *Sheba:* a city of southwest Arabia, hence to the far south; *Seba:* probably a region in modern Sudan, south of Egypt (see Gen 10:7; Isa 43:3). This verse is applied by Matthew to the visit of the Magi at Christ's birth (see Mt 2:11).

11 All kings will pay him homage,
and all nations will serve him. [q]

12 For he will save the poor who cry out
and the needy who have no one to help them.
13 He will have pity on the lowly and the poor;
the lives of the needy he will save. [r]
14 He will free them from oppression and violence,
for their blood is precious in his sight.

15 * Long may he live!
May the gold of Sheba be given to him.
May people pray for him unceasingly
and invoke blessings * on him all day long.

16 May grain abound throughout the land,
even growing abundantly on the mountain tops.
May its crops * be as plenteous as those of Lebanon, [s]
and may its people flourish like the grass of the field.

17 May his name * be blessed forever;
may it endure as long as the sun. [t]
May all peoples be blessed in him;
may all the nations proclaim his greatness. [u]

18 * Blessed be the LORD, the God of Israel,
who alone can perform such wondrous deeds. [v]

19 May his glorious name be blessed forever,
and may the whole world be filled with his glory.
Amen. Amen. [w]

20 The end of the psalms of David, son of Jesse. *

BOOK III—PSALMS 73–89*

PSALM 73*

False Happiness of the Wicked

1 A psalm of Asaph. *

God is truly good to the upright, *
to those who are pure in heart.

2 * But as for me, I nearly lost my balance; *
I was almost at the point of stumbling.
3 For I was filled with envy of the arrogant
when I perceived how the wicked prosper. [x]

---

q Ps 47:8; Ezr 1:2.—r Prov 31:9; Lk 10:33.—s Ps 4:8; Isa 27:6; Hos 14:6-8; Am 9:13.—t Ps 89:37.—u Gen 12:3; Zec 8:13.—v Pss 41:14; 89:53; 106:48; 150.—w Ps 57:6; Num 14:21; Hab 3:3.—x Ps 37:1; Job 9:24; 21:13; Prov 3:31; Jer 12:1; Mal 3:15.

72:15-17 The psalmist prays that the Messiah-King may enjoy a long and prosperous reign acknowledged by the whole world and be a blessing for all the nations.

72:15 *May people pray . . . and invoke blessings:* an obscure passage. As it is translated, it means: may the people pray for the Messiah, that he will benefit the poor with the treasures he has received, and may they bless and thank him. But Israel could also pray to ask God for a perfect Messiah and so offer vows for the extension of the Messianic kingdom (see Ps 61:8f). Hence, one could also translate: "He [the Messiah] will pray [intercede] for him [the poor] / and bless him" (see 1 Ki 8:14, 28).

72:16 Fertility of the land was one of the blessings of the Messianic age (see Hos 14:6f; Am 9:13). *May its crops . . . Lebanon:* may its crops possess the same vital power that the majestic cedars of Lebanon display.

72:17 *Name:* see note on Ps 5:12. *All peoples:* an echo of the promise to the patriarchs (see Gen 12:3; 18:18; 22:18; 26:4; 28:14).

72:18-19 This doxology is not part of the psalm; it concludes the second of the five Books of the Psalter (see Pss 41:14; 89:53; 106:48; 150). Praise of the Lord is the most profound religious attitude and ends every authentic prayer.

72:20 Colophon added by a redactor.

Pss 73–89 This third Book of the Psalter combines the collections of psalms of Asaph (probably a choral leader in the Jerusalem temple; see 1 Chr 25:2-6; 2 Chr 29:30) with the end of the Psalter of the Sons of Korah, which began in the second Book (Pss 42—49). The prayers are varied in accord with the experience of believers; we pass from the lament of the innocent to the exultation after victory. We read, by turns, canticles of Zion, chants of joy and hope, and historical retrospectives that often take the tone of great national lamentations. Each prayer expresses in a new way the longing for God and his salvation.

Ps 73 The psalmist is taken back by the prosperity of the wicked and the sufferings of the righteous (see Job; Eccl 7:15; Jer 12:1; Mal 3:15). Those who make sport of God seem to succeed in life much more than believers, and their example becomes a scandal for the righteous and the wise: what is the good of remaining faithful? Still he knows that no one should deny God. Tempted by doubt, the faithful psalmist reflects and seeks light in God's presence; in such a meditation, his faith deepens and a conviction imposes itself on him with new force: human glory has no tomorrow, but the friendship of God remains forever precious; it cannot end or deceive. The psalmist-sage who expresses himself here begins to suspect that the joy of being with the Lord could become eternal happiness (v. 24).

In times of trouble, at moments when people grow weary of being faithful, this psalm brings the grace of refreshment to the interior life.

73:1a *Asaph:* see notes on Pss 73–89.

73:1b *The upright:* literally, "Israel," i.e., the group of the "poor" (see v. 15; Pss 72:2ff; 149:4; 1 Mac 1:53; Isa 49:3, 13). *Pure in heart:* see note on Ps 24:4. *Heart:* see note on Ps 4:8.

73:2-3 Like many of the godly, the psalmist envied the prosperity of the wicked and their arrogance. Everything seemed to go well for them. They experienced "prosperity," i.e., well-being, full family life, and success in business. Hence, the psalmist was miserable, filled with self-pity and discontent with God's justice. But, although he almost lost his foothold on the "way" of the Lord, he righted himself with the help of the Lord, who sustains his saints (see Ps 37:23ff).

73:2 *I nearly lost my balance:* see note on Ps 37:30-31.

4 * They endure no painful suffering;
their bodies are healthy and well fed.
5 They are not plagued with burdens common to all;
the troubles of life do not afflict them.
6 So they wear arrogance like a necklace
and don violence like a robe.
7 Their callous hearts overflow with malice,
and their minds are completely taken up with evil plans. [y]
8 They mock and pour forth their malevolence;
in their haughtiness they threaten oppression. [z]
9 Their mouths rage against the heavens
while their tongues are never stilled on the earth.
10 * So the people blindly follow them
and find nothing offensive in their words. *
11 They say: "How does God know?
Does the Most High notice anything?" [a]
12 Such are the wicked,
as they pile up wealth, without any concerns.
13 * Is it in vain that I have kept my heart clean
and washed my hands in innocence? [b]
14 For I am stricken day after day
and punished every morning.
15 If I had decided, "I will speak like them,"
I would not have been true to your children. *
16 * When I tried to understand all this,
I found it too difficult for me,
17 until I entered the sanctuary of God *
and realized what their final end would be.
18 * Indeed, you set them on a slippery slope
and cast them headlong into utter ruin.
19 [c] How suddenly they are destroyed,
completely wiped out by terrors!
20 When you arise, O LORD,
you will dismiss them
as one discards a dream on awakening.
21 * When my heart was embittered
and my soul was deeply tormented,
22 I was stupid and unable to comprehend—
like a brute beast in your presence.
23 * Yet I am always with you;
you grasp me by the right hand. [d]
24 You guide me with your counsel,
and afterward you will receive me into glory. *
25 Whom do I have in heaven except you?
And besides you there is nothing else I desire on earth.

y Ps 17:10; Job 15:27.—z Pss 17:10; 41:6; Ezek 25:15; Col 3:8.—a Pss 10:11; 64:6; Job 22:13.—b Ps 26:6; Job 9:29-31; 21:14f; Mal 3:14.—c 19-20: Pss 49:14; 78:65; Job 20:8; Isa 29:8; 47:11.—d Pss 63:8; 121:5; Gen 48:13.

73:4-12 The psalmist describes the reasons that led the godly to envy the wicked. Evildoers seem to be carefree and unconcerned for the future. They have wealth and power and enjoy freedom of movement and speech. They appear untouched by life's frustrations: frailty, adversities, diseases, and hard labor. They disregard God and his laws with apparent impunity. They decree what can be done on earth and even what God can do in heaven. In short, it seems that God lets the wicked get away with their wickedness. *Hearts:* see note on Ps 4:8.

73:10-12 From the mistaken viewpoint of an afflicted person, the wicked enjoy power, glory, and prosperity without end.

73:10 The meaning of the Hebrew for this verse is unclear. Another translation is: "So the people turn to them / and find no fault in them."

73:13-14 The psalmist begins to have doubts about his effort to keep himself holy (see Pss 24:4; 119:9). He questions himself about the troubles and sufferings that he experiences while the wicked seem to have no such problems.

73:15 If he had expressed in public what he had been thinking, the psalmist would have denied the ancestral traditions and beliefs (see note on Ps 139:19-24) and betrayed the "poor." For the Lord is a father to Israel (Ex 4:22; Isa 63:16; Hos 11:1).

73:16-17 Understanding did not come to the psalmist until he entered into the *sanctuary of God.* There he regained his perspective in the light of God's greatness, glory, and majesty. He realized once again that the Lord is just and will judge the wicked in accord with their evil deeds.

73:17 *Sanctuary of God:* literally, "the divine sanctuaries." Rather than the temple (see Jer 51:51) where he would have been enlightened by God, or the divine mysteries (see Wis 2:22) in which he would have received revelation, this expression indicates the teaching contained in the Scriptures, the abode of wisdom (see Ps 119:130; Prov 9:1ff; Sir 39:1).

73:18-20 In reality, God makes the state of the wicked so precarious that they will not be stable but will vanish like the figures of a dream. The assurance of Scripture is that the wicked will incur sudden and complete judgment. They will be assailed by all kinds of terrors and death itself.

73:21-22 The psalmist stresses his former embittered state once again. In his grief he was irrational (see Ps 94:8) and not ruled by wisdom; he was like the fools who are compared to brute beasts (see Ps 49:13, 21; Isa 1:2f). He was assailed by doubt and mired in self-pity—but God used this experience to make him a better person and bring him closer to himself. *Heart:* see note on Ps 4:8.

73:23-26 The psalmist's experience of anguish is transformed into the joy of God's presence and his greatness. God protects him by holding his *right hand* (v. 23; see Ps 63:8; Isa 41:10, 13; 42:6; Jer 31:32), by strengthening his resolve (*rock,* v. 26; see Ps 18:3), and by taking care of all his needs (*portion,* v. 26; see Ps 16:5). God gives his servant wisdom and insight (*counsel*) as he journeys toward everlasting glory (v. 24; see Ps 32:8).

73:24 *Receive me into glory:* is it a question here of heavenly glory? The text does not make this clear. It states that God will preserve the righteous from a brutal and premature death and rehabilitate them (see Job 19:9; 29:18; 42:7), while he despises the wicked who will suddenly disappear (v. 18f). Nothing obliges us to give the verb "receive" a stronger meaning than in Pss 18:17 ("snatched me up") and 49:16 ("take"—see also note there) based on the assumption into heaven of Enoch (Gen 5:24; Sir 44:16) and Elijah (2 Ki 2:3; Sir 48:9). However, as in Ps 16:9f, the psalmist's fervor and the demands of his love for God lead him to long never to be separated from him; it constitutes a stage in the explicit belief in the resurrection, attested in Dan 12:2.

26 Even should my heart and my flesh * fail,
God is the rock of my heart
and my portion forever.
27 * But all those who are far from you will perish;
you destroy those who are unfaithful to you.
28 As for me, my happiness is to be near God,
and I have made the Lord GOD my refuge;
I will proclaim all your works *
at the gates of the Daughter of Zion.

PSALM 74*

Prayer in Time of Calamity

1 A *maskil* * of Asaph.

Why, O God, have you cast us off forever? [e]
Why * does your anger blaze forth
against the sheep of your pasture? [f]
2 Remember the people that you purchased long ago,
the tribe that you redeemed as your own possession, *
and Mount Zion that you chose as your dwelling. [g]
3 Direct now your steps * to the endless ruins,
toward the sanctuary destroyed by the enemy.
4 Your foes exulted triumphantly in the place of your assembly
and set up their memorial emblems.
5 They set upon it with their axes
as if it were a thicket of trees.
6 And then, with hatchets and hammers,
they bludgeoned all the carved work.
7 They set your sanctuary ablaze;
they razed and defiled the dwelling place of your name. * [h]
8 They said to themselves, "We will utterly crush them,"
and they burned every shrine of God in the land. *
9 Now we see no signs,
there are no longer any prophets,
and none of us knows how long this will last. * [i]
10 How long, O God, will the foe mock you?
Will the enemy blaspheme your name forever? * [j]
11 Why do you hold back your right hand?
Take it out from your robe and destroy them. *
12 Yet you, O God, are my King from of old,
working deeds of salvation throughout the earth.

e Pss 10:1; 43:2; 44:24; 77:8.—f Pss 79:13; 80:5; 95:7.—g Pss 68:17; 132:13; Ex 15:16; Deut 7:6; Isa 63:17; Jer 10:16; 51:19.—h Ps 79:1; Lev 20:3; Isa 64:10; Acts 21:28.—i Ps 77:9; Ex 4:17; Lam 2:9; Ezek 7:26.—j Pss 6:4; 80:4; 89:47.

73:26 *My heart and my flesh:* the whole being (see Ps 84:3). *Heart:* see note on Ps 4:8. *Portion:* as a Levite, the psalmist has the Lord for his portion (or inheritance) of the Promised Land, i.e., he lives off the tithes that the people present to the Lord (see Num 18:21-24; Deut 10:9; 18:1-8).

73:27-28 The psalmist now understands that all who are unfaithful to God must perish. Their judgment is a consequence not only of their failure to profess faith in God but also of their immoral and unjust practices.

73:28 *I will proclaim all your works:* the psalmist expresses the vow to praise the Lord's mercies (see note on Ps 7:18). At the gates of the *Daughter of Zion:* this phrase is added to the final line of the Septuagint. It is taken from Ps 9:15, which may be a liturgical adaptation.

Ps 74 This lamentation expresses the soul of a stricken people who feel abandoned even by God. The deportees who have returned from the Exile (538–529 B.C.), or else the Jews persecuted by Antiochus IV Epiphanes (167–164 B.C.), mourn over their sanctuary, which the pagans have profaned (see 2 Ki 25:9-12; Isa 64:10 for the former and 1 Mac 4:38; 2 Mac 1:8 for the latter). Has the Lord forgotten the covenant and the wonders he once accomplished to free his people (Ps 74:13-14), to sustain them in the journey through the wilderness, and to open the Promised Land for them (v. 15)?

Rightly, the past prevents the psalmist from despairing and enables him to believe in a better future. Israel has now lost all pretense of power; it is the community of the poor (vv. 19-21), conscious of its weakness; it is like the timid dove that God cannot abandon to the ferocity of the beasts (v. 19).

Prolonging Christ's presence and even identifying mysteriously with him, the Church is now God's people on earth (see 1 Pet 2:9f). She is also the earthly, visible temple of God, his city and the spiritual capital of the world (see 1 Cor 3:16; 1 Pet 2:4-6). Hence, her members can pray this psalm in trials when Christ seems to have delivered them over to persecution without end.

74:1a *Maskil:* see note on Ps 32:1a. *Asaph:* see notes on Pss 73–89.

74:1b *Why . . . ? Why . . . ?:* see note on Ps 6:4. *Forever:* figuratively speaking; it seemed like forever. *Sheep of your pasture:* see note on Ps 23.

74:2 In this time of great calamity, the psalmist begs God to recall his exploits at the Exodus, the Conquest, and the establishment of the temple. *You redeemed as your own possession:* see Deut 9:29.

74:3 The psalmist begs the Lord to hasten (*direct . . . steps*) to restore the sanctuary that the pagans have destroyed.

74:7, 10 *Name:* see note on Ps 5:12.

74:8 *Every shrine of God in the land:* i.e., shrines, whether legitimate or not (see 1 Ki 3:2; 2 Ki 18:4).

74:9 The people were used to asking the Prophets how long a divine punishment would last (see 2 Sam 24:13). In this case, they have had no miraculous signs of any kind, and the voice of the Prophets is absent as it has been for some time (see Ps 77:9; 1 Mac 4:46; 9:27; 14:41; Lam 2:9; Ezek 7:26).

74:10 Jeremiah had announced that there would be 70 years of exile (see Jer 25:11; 29:10), a round figure symbolizing a very long time (see Pss 6:4; 89:47).

74:11 To do battle, the warrior bared his arm from his garment (see Isa 52:10).

13 * By your power you split the sea in two [k]
and shattered the heads of the dragons
in the waters. [l]
14 You crushed the heads of Leviathan [m]
and gave him as food for the wild
beasts.
15 You opened up springs and torrents
and turned flowing rivers into dry
land. *
16 * Yours is the day, and yours also is the
night, [n]
for you set in place both sun and moon.
17 You fixed all the boundaries of the earth
and created both summer and winter.
18 * Remember, O LORD, how the enemy has
mocked you,
how a foolish people has blasphemed
your name.
19 Do not surrender the soul of your dove *
to wild beasts;
do not forget forever the life of your
poor.
20 Have regard for your covenant!
For the land is filled with darkness,
and the pastures are haunts of violence.
21 Do not let the oppressed turn back in
shame;
let the poor and needy * bless your
name.
22 Rise up, O God, and defend your cause;
remember how fools mock you all day
long.
23 Do not ignore the outbursts of your enemies,
the unceasing tumult of your foes.

PSALM 75*

God Is Judge of the World

1 For the director. * According to "Do not destroy!" A psalm of Asaph. A song.

2 We give thanks * to you, O God,
we give thanks to you.
For your wondrous deeds
declare that your name is near.
3 * You say, "When I receive the assembly,
I will judge with equity.
4 When the earth quakes, with all its inhabitants, [o]
it is I who will hold its pillars firm. *
Selah
5 * "I say to the arrogant, * 'Do not boast,'
and to the wicked, 'Do not lift up your
horns. [p]
6 Do not rebel against heaven
or speak with arrogance against the
Rock.' " * [q]

k Ps 89:10; Ex 14:21.—l Isa 27:1; 51:9-10; Ezek 29:3.—m Job 3:8; 41:1; Isa 27:1; Jer 50:39.—n 16-17: Ps 136:7-9; Gen 1:16.—o Pss 46:3f; 60:4; 93:1; 96:10; 104:5; 1 Sam 2:8; 2 Sam 22:8; Isa 24:19.—p Ps 5:6; 1 Sam 2:3; Zec 1:21.—q Ps 94:4; Job 15:25.

74:13-14 Allusion to the crossing of the Red Sea (see Ex 14:30) and the defeat of the Egyptians (see Isa 27:1; Ezek 29:3; 32:4). *Leviathan:* a mythological multi-headed monster of chaos; here it seems to stand especially for Egypt (for Egypt's crocodiles, see Job 40:25f).

74:15 Allusion to the miracles of the Exodus (see Ex 17:6; Num 20:11) and the crossing of the Jordan (see Jos 3:15f) where God's creative power is exercised (see Ps 89:11).

74:16-17 The psalmist indicates that God—in addition to having accomplished the Redemption of his people from Egypt (vv. 13-14)—is also the Creator who established the world. Thus, the clear implication is that God can establish his kingdom on earth in spite of all opposition.

74:18-21 The godly beg God to *remember* (see v. 2) the evil conduct of their oppressors (v. 19) who blaspheme his name and afflict his people. The Lord's name is sacred to them for it ensures that he will fulfill his covenant promises (see Ex 6:6-8). They ask him to come to their aid so that they will have reason to bless his name.

74:19 *Your dove:* a term of endearment for Israel (see Ps 68:14; Song 2:14; 5:2; 6:9; Hos 7:11; 11:11).

74:21 *Poor and needy:* see note on Ps 34:7. *Name:* see note on Ps 5:12.

Ps 75 This psalm has parallels to the song of Hannah (see 1 Sam 2:1-10). Freed from the Exile but always dependent on and pestered by those who had taken their place in the land, the People of God give thanks to the Lord. They know that in the end God will make right triumph on earth; the righteous will obtain glory, and the wicked will receive the chastisement they deserve. These oracles proclaim once again the reversal worked by true justice: the proud will be abased, and the humble will be lifted up.

We can pray this psalm with the same sentiments of the psalmist and apply the role of Judge to the risen Christ, to whom the Father has given it. We can proclaim the wondrous deeds of our Savior, who will come to save the righteous and punish the wicked on the last day.

75:1 *For the director:* thought to be a musical or liturgical notation. *According to "Do not destroy!":* see note on Ps 57:1. *Asaph:* see notes on Pss 73–89.

75:2 *Give thanks:* this is given in the form of praise (see Pss 7:18; 28:7; 30:13; 35:18). *Wondrous deeds:* see note on Ps 9:2. *Name:* see note on Ps 5:12.

75:3-6 This is a reassuring word from God, possibly through prophetic words already uttered by the Prophets (e.g., Isaiah in 2 Ki 19:21-34). *When I receive the assembly:* another possible translation is: "I choose the appointed time."

75:4 God is the Master of the moral order as well as the physical universe, and he keeps them stable (see Pss 93:1f; 96:10; 1 Sam 2:8) or makes them quake (see Ps 18:8; Job 26:11); no cataclysm escapes his will (see Pss 46:3f; 60:4), and he alone establishes the hour of the judgment (see Hab 2:3).

75:5-6 This passage recalls Ps 94:4; 1 Sam 2:3; Job 15:25f. The wicked are fools (see Pss 14:1; 94:7). The horn is the symbol of arrogant and aggressive force (see Pss 89:18; 92:11; Deut 33:17; 1 Ki 22:11); it will be broken (see Jer 48:25; Zec 2:1-4).

75:5 The Lord speaks to those who incite chaos and immorality: *the arrogant* and *the wicked* who live without God and his laws (see Pss 52:3; 73:3ff).

75:6 The wicked even dare to place themselves in direct opposition to God by *rebel[ling]*, i.e., raising their horns *against heaven* and speaking *with arrogance*, i.e., with outstretched neck—a common gesture of opposition.

7 * For judgment does not come from east or west,
nor from the wilderness or the mountains. * [r]
8 Rather, it is God who judges rightly, [s]
humbling one and exalting another. *
9 The LORD holds in his hand a cup
filled with foaming wine and richly spiced.
When he pours it out,
all the wicked * of the earth must drink; [t]
they will drain it down to the dregs.
10 As for me, I will proclaim this forever;
I will sing praises * to the God of Jacob.
11 "I will cut off all the horns of the wicked,
but the horns of the righteous * will be exalted." [u]

PSALM 76*

God, Defender of Zion

1 For the director. * With stringed instruments. A psalm of Asaph. A song.
2 * God is renowned in Judah;
his name is great in Israel. [v]
3 His tent has been established in Salem,
his dwelling place in Zion.
4 There he shattered the flashing arrows,
shields and swords and weapons of war. [w] *Selah*
5 * You are awesome and resplendent,
more majestic than the everlasting mountains.
6 The bold warriors lie plundered
and sleeping their last sleep. *
And not one of the men of war
can lift up his hands. [x]
7 At your rebuke, O God of Jacob,
both chariots and horses lie prostrate.
8 You indeed are awesome;
who can stand in your presence when your anger is aroused? [y]
9 You thundered your verdicts from the heavens;
the earth in its terror was silent
10 when you arose, O God, to judge,
to rescue all the afflicted of the land. * *Selah*

r Mt 24:23-27.—s Job 5:11; 1 Sam 2:7; Dan 2:21.—t Ps 60:5; Job 21:20; Prov 23:30; Isa 51:17, 21-22; Jer 25:15ff; Hab 2:16.—u Pss 89:18; 92:11; 112:9; 148:14.—v Ps 99:3; Hab 3:2.—w Pss 46:10; 48:4-8; 122:6-9; Ezek 39:9.—x Ps 13:4; Jdg 20:44; 2 Ki 19:35; Jer 51:39; Nah 3:18; Mt 9:24.—y Deut 7:21; 1 Sam 6:20; 1 Chr 16:25; Nah 1:6; Mal 3:2; Rev 6:17.

75:7-8 Concerning these first two verses of the response from earth (vv. 7-8), possibly by a Levite, see 1 Sam 2:7; Dan 2:21. The oracles against the nations envisaged such and such a power, in the north (see Zep 2:13), in the south (see Isa 30:6), or in the *wilderness* (Isa 21:1); other oracles were directed against the *mountains* of Israel (see Ezek 6:2; 36:1), or the forests of the south (see Ezek 21:2f). Here, the wilderness represents the south, and the mountains (Lebanon) stand for the north (see note on v. 7, below). As in Zec 1:16, the accent is placed on the universality of the divine judgment (see v. 9) on the day of the Lord (see Mt 24:23ff).

75:7 *For judgment does not come . . . the mountains:* another possible translation is: "No one from the east or the west / or from the wilderness can exalt a man." In other words, search where we may, there is no other arbiter but God; therefore, no earthly honor is anything but provisional. Furthermore, no one can escape God's judgment (see Ps 139); God will bring down anyone who exalts himself.

75:8 Indeed, judgment belongs to God alone, for he is sovereign in judgment and in redemption.

75:9 *All the wicked* will be vanquished by God. The image of the cup full of *foaming* and dizzying wine is taken from the Prophets (see Isa 51:17; Jer 25:15; 49:12; Lam 4:21; Ezek 23:31; Hab 2:15); it has already appeared in Ps 60:5 (see Job 21:20) and will reappear in Rev 14:10. See also note on Ps 16:5.

75:10 It is unclear who is speaking in this verse. It may be the Levite in his own name or as a representative of his people. *Sing praises:* see note on Ps 7:18. *Jacob:* i.e., Israel (see Gen 32:28).

75:11 This verse appears to be another word from the Lord to go with verses 2-5, above. He indicates that even if godlessness now triumphs and justice is subverted, at the end of time the Messiah will come to judge the nations in fulfillment of the promise about the victory of *the righteous.*

Ps 76 In 701 B.C., the mighty army of Sennacherib had camped beneath the walls of Jerusalem. One night the attacker suddenly lifted the siege. What mysterious terror did the Lord employ to put to rout the forces of that haughty ruler? It is the victory of God at Jerusalem; and in the holy city, God reveals himself through his triumphs (see 2 Ki 19:35). The memory of this event remained engraved in the minds of the people (see 2 Mac 8:19; Sir 48:21) and became the symbol for the salvation awaited by the poor, the remnant of God.

Like Ps 46, this hymn to the glory of Zion is doubtless inspired by that event; it restores the courage and hope of the exiles returning from Babylon after 538 B.C. The fearsome God prostrates the powerful of the world and saves the lowly. This confidence of the poor will continuously rise from the heart of humankind in protest against haughty dominators as an announcement of the judgment of God.

It is by the glorious Christ that God the Father dwells in and protects his new people, the Church. With this psalm, we can rightly celebrate our Savior, who is terrible for his enemies: the devil, sin, and death.

76:1 *For the director:* these words are thought to be a musical or liturgical notation. *Asaph:* see notes on Pss 73–89.

76:2-3 The Lord has chosen *Salem* (ancient name for Jerusalem; see Gen 14:18; Heb 7:1-3) as his royal city so that both the southern kingdom (*Judah*) and the northern kingdom (*Israel*) may gain reassurance that God is in their midst (see Ps 46).

76:5-11 Praise of God's mighty deed against the Assyrians and his judgment of evildoers.

76:6 *Last sleep:* allusion to the night of which 2 Ki 19:35 speaks (see Ps 13:5; Jer 51:39, 57; Nah 3:18).

76:10 *Rescue all the afflicted of the land:* the psalmist widens his perspectives to include not only the inhabitants of Zion, but also all the lowly who will be saved by God's defeat of the rulers and war leaders.

11 Human wrath only serves to praise you; *
those who survive your anger will cling to you.
12 * Make vows to the LORD, your God, and keep them;
let all the lands nearby
bring gifts to the Awesome One, [z]
13 who breaks the spirit of rulers
and inspires fear in the kings of the earth.

PSALM 77*

Lament and Consolation in Distress

1 For the director. * For Jeduthun. A psalm of Asaph.

2 * I cry aloud to God,
for when I cry out to God, he hears me. *
3 In the time of my distress I seek the LORD;
at night I stretch out my hands unceasingly,
and my soul refuses to be consoled. [a]

4 * I groan as I think of God;
my spirit grows faint as I meditate on him. [b] *Selah*

5 You keep my eyes from closing in sleep;
I am much too distraught to speak.

6 I reflect on the days of old
and recall the years long past.
7 At night I meditate in my heart, *
and as I reflect, my spirit questions: [c]

8 * "Will the LORD cast us off forever
and never again show us his favor? [d]
9 Has his kindness * vanished forever?
Has his promise ceased for all time?
10 Has God forgotten how to be merciful?
Has he shut up his compassion in anger?" *Selah*

11 * And I say: "This is my grief—
that the right hand * of the Most High has changed." [e]
12 I will remember the works of the LORD;
I will call to mind your wonders in the past. [f]
13 I will reflect on all your deeds
and ponder your wondrous works. *

14 O God, your way is holy. *
What god is as great as our God? [g]

z Ps 50:14; Num 30:3; Eccl 5:4-5.—a Pss 50:15; 88:2; Isa 26:16; Mt 2:18.—b Ps 6:3, 7; Jon 2:8.—c Ps 143:5; Deut 32:7.—d 8-10: Pss 13:2; 44:24; 74:1; 80:5; 89:47; 102:14; Lam 3:31.—e Pss 17:7; 18:36; Ex 15:6, 12.—f Ps 143:5; Num 14:1-4; Neh 9:17.—g Ps 18:31; Ex 15:11.

76:11 *Praise you:* everyone must give honor to the Most High—even those who rebel against the Lord and his kingdom must proclaim his honor and glory. When wrath leads men to do evil, it also leads to God's praise when he defeats them. The same theme is found in an alternative translation: "your wrath against men brings you praise"; in his wrath, he brings down the wicked and obtains praise from those he has thus rescued. Furthermore, God's wrath against evil is never exhausted. This should gain him the praise and fear of all peoples.

76:12-13 All people must respond wisely to the Lord. His covenant people must keep their *vows* to him. The Gentiles must offer homage to this *Awesome One* who rules over everyone, including kings.

Ps 77 During a difficult period that the people of Israel are experiencing after the return from the Exile, more than one fervent Israelite can think that God has abandoned his own. But the Lord does not act after the fashion of human beings: has he not from Egypt to Canaan, by means of the wonders of the Exodus (vv. 14-20), transformed a motley group of slaves into a people of his own?

The striking evocation of the passage through the Red Sea and the coming of God at Sinai enables the psalmist to rediscover the great certitude that God still guides his people. Such a certitude is present even when one must realize that God's ways are mysterious. Hope is reborn, purified by adversity and more unshakable than ever.

This psalm is a reminder of the Father's faithfulness toward Christ and calls us to remain faithful ourselves in times of distress and spiritual dryness. "Let us remain firm in the confession of our hope without wavering, for the one who made the promise is trustworthy" (Heb 10:23). We must imitate the ancients and, even more, Christ, by remaining faithful even in the darkest of times, for "we are not among those who draw back and are lost. Rather, we are among those who have faith and are saved" (Heb 10:39).

77:1 *For the director:* these words are thought to be a musical or liturgical notation. *Jeduthun:* see note on Ps 39:1. *Asaph:* see notes on Pss 73–89.

77:2-10 To the psalmist, God seems to have deserted his people; he no longer responds to appeals for help in time of distress and intense prayer.

77:2-3 The psalmist looked to God as the sole comforter of his distressed soul (see Gen 37:35; Jer 31:15). He cried out ceaselessly in prayer with hands outstretched—but remained uncomforted. *Soul:* see note on Ps 6:4.

77:4-7 Sleeplessness and dryness in prayer lead the psalmist's faith to be shaken, but he puts his mind on the origins of his people as God's people and attempts to rediscover hope (see Ps 119:52; Deut 32:7ff).

77:7 *Heart:* see note on Ps 4:8.

77:8-10 These verses follow the style of laments (see Pss 74:1; 89:47ff; Isa 63:15; Lam 3:21-24, 31ff). The prophetic word had ceased (see Ps 74:9); still God remained faithful to his promises, inscribed in the ancient writings on which the psalmist meditated endlessly (see Pss 1:2; 105:3ff) to convince himself that God had not changed in his love for his people (see Isa 49:14ff; Mal 3:6).

77:9 *Kindness:* see note on Ps 6:5.

77:11-21 The psalmist takes up the Book of History, so to speak, and meditates upon the great deeds of the Lord, the miracles he wrought in the past. He is so captivated by the reading that, in meditating on the glorious deeds that the Lord did for Israel in former times, he obtains peace of mind and forgets his present distress.

77:11 The psalmist remembers the years when God—by means of his *right hand*—provided strong guidance and protection for his people (see Pss 17:7; 18:35; Isa 41:10). And, he laments the loss of this protection once accorded them by their God.

77:13 The psalmist reflects on the Lord's *works* in their great variety—in creation, redemption, judgment, and salvation. See also note on Ps 9:2.

77:14 *Your way is holy:* see Ps 18:31; Deut 32:4. Another translation is: "your ways are seen in the sanctuary" (see Ps 63:3).

15 You are the God who works wonders;
you have displayed your might to the nations. [h]
16 With your strong arm you redeemed your people,
the descendants of Jacob and Joseph. * [i]
Selah

17 * When the waters * beheld you, O God,
when the waters beheld you, they writhed;
the very depths trembled. [j]
18 The clouds poured forth their water,
the skies thundered, [k]
your arrows * flashed back and forth.
19 The crash of your thunder resounded in the heavens;
your flashes of lightning lit up the world;
the earth trembled and shook. * [l]

20 Your path led through the sea,
your way, through the mighty waters,
though none could trace your footsteps. * [m]
21 You led your people like a flock
by the hand of Moses and Aaron. * [n]

PSALM 78*

God's Goodness in the Face of Ingratitude

1 A *maskil* * of Asaph.
* Give ear, my people, to my teaching;
pay attention to the words of my mouth.
2 I will open my mouth in parables * [o]
and expound the mysteries of the past.

3 * These things we have heard and know,
for our ancestors have related them to us. [p]
4 We will not conceal them from our children;
we will relate them to the next generation,
the glorious and powerful deeds of the Lord
and the wonders he has performed. [q]

5 He instituted a decree in Jacob
and established a law in Israel,
which he commanded our ancestors
to make known to their descendants, [r]
6 so that they would be known to future generations,
to children yet to be born.

---

h Pss 86:10; 89:7; Ex 3:20.—i Gen 46:26-27; Ex 6:6; Neh 1:10.—j Pss 18:16; 114:3; Nah 1:4; Hab 3:10.—k Pss 18:14-15; 29:3; 144:6; Deut 32:23; Job 37:3-4; Wis 5:21; Hab 3:11; Zec 9:14.—l Pss 18:8; 97:4; 99:1; Ex 19:16; Jdg 5:4-5; 2 Sam 22:13.—m Ex 14:22; Neh 9:11; Job 9:8; Wis 14:3; Isa 43:16; 51:10; Hab 3:15.—n Ps 78:52; Ex 4:16; 13:21; 15:20-21; Num 33:1; Isa 63:11-14; Hos 12:14; Mic 6:4.—o Ps 49:5; Mt 13:35; Lk 8:10.—p Pss 44:2; 145:4.—q Ex 10:2; Deut 4:9; Job 8:8; 15:18.—r Pss 19:8; 147:19; Deut 33:4.

77:16 *Descendants of Jacob and Joseph:* those who emigrated to Egypt (Jacob) and those who were born there (Joseph's sons) (see Ps 81:5ff; Gen 46:26f; 48:5).

77:17-20 The miracle of the crossing of the Red Sea is presented in a cosmic perspective, possibly to heighten the description of God's majesty in bringing his people from slavery to freedom, which led to the Passover. For Christians, the culminating miracle was God's deed in bringing Jesus from death to life after the crucifixion (see Mt 28:2; Eph 1:18-22), which led to the Christian Passover, Easter.

77:17 *The waters* are at the mercy of the Creator (see Pss 89:10; 93:3f; 104:7; 106:9; 114:3; Job 7:12; 38:10; Nah 1:4; Hab 3:10).

77:18 This verse is inspired by Hab 3:11. See also Pss 18:16; 68:9; 144:6. *Arrows:* i.e., lightning bolts.

77:19 This verse evokes the theophany at Sinai (see Ps 97:4; Ex 19:18).

77:20 See Neh 9:11; Wis 14:3; Isa 43:16; 51:10. God's action reveals his invisible presence as Shepherd and Savior (see Ps 78:52; Isa 63:11ff; Mic 6:4).

77:21 The conclusion to the thought expressed in verse 16: God led his people through the wilderness under the care of *Moses and Aaron.*

Ps 78 This lengthy sermon is given us as a lesson in wisdom: if the People of God wish to understand their destiny, they must reflect on their origins and meditate on the Exodus, which is a history of divine grace and human infidelity. In effect, their ancestors never responded with anything but ingratitude to the miracles that God multiplied for them. He rolls back the sea and brings water from a rock; the people already clamor for another prodigy (vv. 12-20). Filled with the manna and the quail, the people still murmur (vv. 23-30)! Then the Lord becomes angry and metes out punishment, but he soon grants pardon to them out of pity for their human weakness (vv. 31-39). On their behalf, he had also brought about the plagues (vv. 43-51), and guided them through the wilderness and into the Promised Land (vv. 52-56). Still, offenses multiplied; so he also resorted anew to chastisement. But ultimately, he reserved for his people the privileged holy place, Zion, and the shepherd after his own heart, David (vv. 59-72).

Thus, the psalm emphasizes the infidelity of Ephraim (the ancestor of the Samaritans), the choice of Judah, and the call of David. Its lesson is that in spite of the successive about-faces of the people, God accomplished his design.

Is this not also our history? To acknowledge God's love does not keep us from infidelities; at such times, the word of God challenges us but also brings pardon, and the Eucharist is given to sustain our steps. In Jesus, the new David and Good Shepherd, the People of God find a model and perfect guide to the new Promised Land, the heavenly Jerusalem, where the Father waits.

78:1a *Maskil:* see note on Ps 32:1a. *Asaph:* see notes on Pss 73–89.

78:1b-8 Remembrance of the great deeds of the Lord should serve to strengthen the people's faith in his power and fidelity. Thus, they will not forget what the Lord has done for their ancestors, which was a blessing for their descendants, and what God has demanded from his covenant people.

78:2 *Parables* in Hebrew means comparisons, or any sayings with deeper meaning, which are to be understood via the hidden comparison; in this case, the parable is the whole psalm. This passage is used by Mt 13:35 as a foreshadowing of Christ's teaching in parables (see also Ps 49:5; Ezek 17:2; 24:3).

78:3-5 *Israel* is the people of tradition (see Deut 4:9; 32:7; Job 8:8; 15:18; Isa 38:19; Joel 1:3); what its people hand down is, above all, the remembrance of the Exodus (see Ex 10:2; 13:14) and the covenant statutes (Deut 4:9-14; 6:20-25).

In turn they were to tell their children,[s]
7 so that they would place their trust in God,
and never forget his works
but keep his commandments.
8 Nor were they to imitate their ancestors,
a stubborn and rebellious generation,[t]
a generation whose heart * was not steadfast
and whose spirit was unfaithful to God.[u]

9 * The Ephraimites, who were skilled archers,
fled in terror on the day of battle. *
10 They failed to keep God's covenant
and refused to live in accord with his law.

11 They forgot the works he had done,
the wonders he had performed for them.
12 He worked marvels in the sight of their ancestors
in the land of Egypt, in the Plain of Zoan. *[v]
13 [w] He divided the sea so that they could pass,
heaping up the waters as a mound.[x]
14 He led them with a cloud by day,
and with the light of a fire by night.[y]

15 He split open rocks in the wilderness
and gave them water to drink from limitless depths.[z]
16 He brought forth streams from a rocky crag
and caused water to flow down in torrents.

17 * But they still sinned * against him,
rebelling against the Most High in the wilderness.[a]
18 They tested God's patience[b]
by demanding the food they craved. *
19 They railed against God, saying:
"Can God provide a banquet in the wilderness?[c]
20 Certainly when he struck the rock,
water gushed forth and the streams overflowed.
But can he also give us bread
or provide meat for his people?" *

21 [d] When the LORD heard this, he was filled with anger;
his fire blazed forth against Jacob,
and his wrath mounted against Israel,
22 because they had no faith in God
and put no trust in his saving might.

23 Yet he issued a command to the skies above
and opened the doors of the heavens.
24 He rained down manna for them to eat,
giving them the grain of heaven.[e]
25 Mere mortals ate the bread of angels; *
he sent them an abundance of provisions.

26 He made the east wind blow in the heavens
and brought forth the south wind in force.
27 He rained down meat upon them like dust,
winged birds like the sands on the seashore.
28 He let them fall within the camp,
all around their tents.

29 They ate and were completely satisfied,
for he had given them what they desired.
30 But when they did not curb their cravings,
even while the food was in their mouths,
31 the anger of God blazed up against them;
he slew their strongest warriors
and laid low the chosen of Israel.[f]

s Pss 22:31-32; 48:14-15; Deut 4:9; 6:7.—t Deut 31:27; 32:5; Isa 30:9.—u Ps 95:10; Num 14:34.—v Ps 106:7; Neh 9:17.—w 13-14: Pss 74:15; 136:13; Ex 14–15.—x Pss 66:6; 114:3; Ex 14:21-22; 15:8.—y Pss 99:7; 105:39; Ex 13:21; Wis 18:3.—z Pss 105:41; 114:8; Ex 17:1-7; Num 20:2-13; Deut 8:15; Wis 11:4; Isa 48:21; 1 Cor 10:4.—a Deut 9:7, 22; Ezek 20:13; Heb 3:16.—b Ps 106:14; Ex 16:2-36; 1 Cor 10:9.—c Ps 23:5; Num 21:5.—d 21f: Num 11; Deut 32:22; Heb 3:19.—e Ps 105:40; Ex 16:4, 13-15; Num 11:31ff; Deut 8:3; Wis 16:20; Jn 6:31.—f Num 14:29; Isa 10:16.

78:8 *Heart:* see note on Ps 4:8.

78:9-16 The psalmist stresses that the northern kingdom, in which Ephraim had the lead, has been unfaithful to the covenant (a theme of the prophets Amos and Hosea). It constitutes the last in a series of infidelities committed by Israel.

78:9 There is no record of flight from battle on the part of the Ephraimites; it may be a metaphor for Ephraim's failure to keep the covenant.

78:12 *Zoan:* a city in the Nile delta, capital of Egypt at the time of the Exodus.

78:17-31 The psalmist indicates that the Israelites rebelled against the Lord in the wilderness despite all kinds of marvels that he worked on their behalf. This led to the Lord's anger against them.

78:17 *Still sinned:* the psalmist has mentioned no sin, but because of the theme of water in verse 16, he is reminded of the people's murmuring over the lack of water at Marah (see Ex 15:24).

78:18 See Ex 16:2f.

78:20 See Ex 16:2f; Num 11:4.

78:25 *Bread of angels:* literally, "bread of mighty ones," which clearly refers to angels (see Ps 103:20; Wis 16:20; see also Jn 6:32, 50; 1 Cor 10:3). Psalm 105:40 speaks of "bread from heaven" (see Deut 8:3).

32 * Despite this, they continued to sin;
they put no faith in his wonders.
33 So he brought their days to an abrupt end
and cut off their years with sudden terror. *
34 When death afflicted them,
they sought him;
they searched eagerly for God. [g]
35 They remembered that God was their Rock, *
that God Most High was their Redeemer.
36 However, while they flattered him with their mouths
and lied to him with their tongues,
37 their hearts * were not right with him,
nor were they faithful to his covenant. [h]
38 Even so, he was compassionate toward them;
he forgave their guilt
and did not destroy them.
Time after time he held back his anger,
unwilling to stir up his rage. [i]
39 For he remembered that they were flesh,
like a breath of wind that does not return.
40 * How often they rebelled against him in the wilderness
and pained him in the wasteland.
41 Again and again they tested God's patience,
provoking the Holy One of Israel. *
42 They did not keep in mind his power
or the day when he delivered them from their oppressor, [j]
43 [k] when he manifested his wonders in Egypt
and his portents in the Plain of Zoan.
44 * He turned their rivers into blood;
they could not drink from their streams.
45 He sent swarms of flies that devoured them
and frogs that devastated them. [l]
46 He assigned their harvest to the caterpillars
and their produce to the locusts.
47 He destroyed their vines with hail
and their sycamore trees with frost. [m]
48 He exposed their cattle to hailstones
and their flocks to bolts of lightning. [n]
49 He sent upon them his blazing anger,
wrath, fury, and hostility,
a band of destroying angels. *
50 He gave his anger free rein;
he did not spare them from death
but delivered their lives to the plague.
51 He struck down all the firstborn in Egypt, [o]
the firstfruits of their manhood in the tents of Ham. *
52 Then he led forth his people like sheep
and guided them through the wilderness like a flock. [p]
53 He led them in safety, and they were not afraid,
while the sea engulfed their enemies. [q]
54 He brought them to his holy land,
to the mountain his right hand had purchased. [r]
55 He drove out the nations before them,
apportioning a heritage for each of them
and settling the tribes of Israel in their tents. *
56 * Even so, they put God to the test
and rebelled against the Most High,
refusing to observe his decrees.

g Num 21:7; Deut 32:15, 18; Isa 26:16.—h Ps 95:10; Isa 29:13; Hos 8:1.—i Ps 85:4; Ex 32:14; Num 14:20; Isa 48:9; Ezek 20:22; Hos 11:8-9.—j Ps 106:21; Jdg 3:7.—k 43f: Pss 105:27-36; 135:9; Ex 7:14—11:10; 12:29-36; Wis 16–18. —l Ps 105:31; Ex 8:2, 6f, 17, 24.—m 46-47: Pss 105:32-35; 147:17; Ex 9:23; Wis 16:16.—n Ex 9:3, 25.—o Pss 105:36; 135:8; 136:10; Ex 12:29.—p Pss 28:9; 77:21; Isa 66:11-14; Hos 12:14; Mic 6:4.—q Ps 106:10-11; Ex 14:26-28.—r Ps 44:4; Ex 15:17.

78:32-39 The people's infidelity to the Lord continued unabated throughout the entire sojourn in the wilderness (see Isa 26:16; 29:13; Hos 5:15; 8:1). However, the Lord tempered his punishment, for he knew they shared the inherent weakness of human beings (see Pss 65:4; 85:4; 103:13f; Ex 32:14; Num 14:20; 21:7ff; Isa 48:9; Ezek 20:22).

78:33 Nonetheless, the Lord decreed that the faithless generation of the Exodus would never set foot on the Promised Land (see Num 14:22f, 28-35).

78:35 *Rock:* see note on Ps 18:3.

78:37 *Hearts:* see note on Ps 4:8.

78:40-55 The Israelites continued to rebel against God in the wilderness. They failed to recall how he had delivered them from Egypt by such wonders as the plagues and the passage through the Red Sea. Nonetheless, the Lord went on to lead them to the conquest and settlement of the Promised Land.

78:41 *Holy One of Israel:* see note on Ps 71:22.

78:44-51 The psalmist is not concerned about a complete, chronological, and exact narrative of the plagues. He gives them in a different order and enumeration, while also omitting the third, fifth, sixth, and ninth (see Ex 7–12).

78:49 *Destroying angels:* the psalmist here generalizes the theme of the "destroyer" of the firstborn (see Ex 12:23), personifying the Lord's *wrath, fury, and hostility* as agents of his anger (see Ex 9:14; Deut 32:24; Job 20:23).

78:51 *Tents of Ham:* usually linked with Egypt (see Pss 105:23, 27; 106:21f; Gen 10:6).

78:55 The psalmist here summarizes the story of the Conquest told in Joshua.

78:56-64 This part, like its predecessors, begins with the remembrance of Israel's sins and evokes the time of Samuel and Saul in the Book of Judges. Because of the people's infidelity, God rejected Israel (see Jer 7:12ff).

57 They turned away and were disloyal like their ancestors;
they were as unreliable as a faulty bow.
58 They angered him with their high places *
and made him jealous with their idols. [s]
59 When God saw this, he became enraged
and rejected Israel totally. *
60 He forsook his dwelling in Shiloh, *
the tent where he dwelt among mortals. [t]
61 He surrendered his might into captivity
and his glory * into the hands of the enemy. [u]
62 He abandoned his people to the sword
and vented his wrath on his own heritage.
63 Fire devoured their young men,
and their maidens had no wedding song. [v]
64 Their priests fell by the sword,
and their widows sang no lamentation.
65 * Then the LORD awakened as from sleep,
like a warrior flushed from the effects of wine.
66 He struck his enemies and routed them,
inflicting perpetual shame on them.
67 He rejected the tent of Joseph
and did not choose the tribe of Ephraim.
68 Rather, he chose the tribe of Judah,
Mount Zion, * which he loved. [w]
69 He built his sanctuary like the high heavens,
and like the earth * that he founded forever.
70 He chose David * to be his servant
and took him from the sheepfolds. [x]
71 From tending sheep he brought him
to be the shepherd of his people Jacob,
of Israel, his heritage. [y]
72 He shepherded them with an unblemished heart
and guided them with a knowing hand. *

PSALM 79*

Prayer for Restoration

1 A psalm of Asaph. *
* O God, the nations have invaded your heritage;
they have profaned your holy temple
and turned Jerusalem into a heap of ruins. [z]
2 They have given the corpses of your servants
as food to the birds of the air,

s Ex 20:4; Deut 32:16, 21; Jdg 2:12.—t Jos 18:1, 8; 21:1f; Jdg 18:31; 1 Sam 1:3; Jer 7:12; 26:6; Ezek 8:6.—u Ps 132:8, 17; 1 Sam 4:11, 22; 2 Chr 6:41.—v Num 11:1; Deut 32:25; Jer 7:34.—w Pss 48:2; 50:2; 87:2; 108:9; Lam 2:15.—x Ps 89:21; 1 Sam 13:14; 2 Chr 6:6; Ezek 34:23; 37:24.—y Gen 37:2; 1 Sam 16:11-13; 2 Sam 7:8.—z 2 Ki 25:9-10; Neh 4:2; Jer 26:18; Lam 1:10.

78:58 *High places:* the Canaanites were accustomed to building altars to their gods on hills (high places), a custom followed by the Israelites who built altars to Yahweh on hills. However, this led to the adoption of pagan practices and idols by God's people. *Jealous:* see Ex 20:5 ("I . . . am . . . a jealous God.").

78:59 The psalmist is not speaking here of a permanent abandonment of Israel by God.

78:60 *Shiloh:* a shrine located in Ephraim (see Jdg 21: 19) that was the center of Israelite worship from the time of Joshua (see Jos 18:1, 8; 21:1f; Jdg 18:31; 1 Sam 1:3; Jer 7:12; 26:6). It was destroyed by the Philistines when the Ark of the Covenant was captured (see 1 Sam 4:1-11).

78:61 *His might . . . his glory:* the divine attributes of which the Ark of the Covenant was the symbol (see Ps 132:17; 1 Sam 4:19ff; 2 Chr 6:41).

78:65-72 After the Israelites had been cleansed by the divine chastisement, the Lord had mercy on them and fought by their side once more in vanquishing their enemies. But afterward, God chose Judah instead of Ephraim as the leading tribe, Mount Zion instead of Shiloh as the royal seat (the place of his sanctuary), and David instead of Saul as his king and regent. David is the ideal shepherd (see Ezek 34:23; 37:24), the Lord's anointed (see Ps 89:21), and the type of the Messiah to come (see Ps 110). What the Lord did for the people in the wilderness, David did in his name for the people of Judah.

78:68 *He chose . . . Mount Zion:* see Ps 132:11, 17.

78:69 *High heavens . . . earth:* the Lord built his sanctuary to last like the heavens and the earth (see note on Ps 24:2) and to reflect his glory as they do (see Pss 19:2; 29:9; 97:6).

78:70 *He chose David:* see Ps 132.

78:72 The Prophets regarded Israel, led by David, as the hope of God's people (see Ezek 34:23; 37:24; Mic 5:2)—fulfilled in Jesus (see Mt 2:6; Jn 10:11; Rev 7:17).

Ps 79 In this poem the psalmist is speaking of the darkest days of Israel's history: in 587 B.C., the Chaldeans captured and sacked Jerusalem; the neighboring Moabites and Edomites then attacked them as they were in their death-throes. Israel is aware now that it deserved to be punished for its infidelities, and it appeals to God's mercy. In this lamentation, the distress of the oppressed calls upon the Lord for redress. The pagans dishonor the divine name; this is tantamount to a defeat for the Lord. In avenging his own, God must first save his honor in the eyes of the world, and his people will be grateful to him. Such is the theme of this national lamentation.

Must vengeance be paid back seven times (i.e., in full measure) upon one's neighbors? Christ has told us to pardon seventy times seven (Mt 18:22)—so we cannot take this psalm literally. Still it remains a poignant appeal to God's mercy, an act of faith in the Lord when everything seems to be collapsing around us. We do not demand the total destruction of our enemies but a salutary punishment, in keeping with the divine justice, which brings evildoers low in order to pardon and save them.

79:1a *Asaph:* see notes on Pss 73–89.

79:1b-4 God's city and temple have been desecrated and so have his worshipers, whose dead bodies have been left unburied. *Saints:* see note on Ps 16:3.

the flesh of your saints
to the beasts of the earth. [a]
3 They have poured out their blood like water
all around Jerusalem,
and no one is left to bury them. * [b]
4 We have become the scorn of our neighbors, [c]
mocked and derided by those around us. *
5 * How long, O LORD? * Will you be angry forever?
How long will your rage continue to blaze like a fire? [d]
6 * Pour out your wrath on the nations
that refuse to acknowledge you,
on the kingdoms
that fail to call on your name. * [e]
7 For they have devoured Jacob
and ravaged his homeland.
8 Do not hold against us the sins of our ancestors;
let your mercy come quickly to meet us,
for we are in desperate straits. * [f]
9 * Help us, O God, our Savior,
for the glory of your name;
deliver us and wipe away our sins
for your name's sake. * [g]
10 Why should the nations ask,
"Where is their God?" [h]
Before our eyes make it clearly known among those nations
that you avenge * the blood of your servants. [i]
11 Let the groans of the captives come before you;
through your great power
save those who have been sentenced to death. * [j]
12 Repay our neighbors sevenfold * in their breasts, O LORD,
for the insults with which they taunted you. [k]
13 Then we, your people, the sheep of your pasture,
will offer thanks to you * forever;
from generation to generation
we will proclaim your praise.

PSALM 80*

Prayer for the Persecuted People

1 For the director. * According to "Lilies." *Eduth.* A psalm of Asaph.
2 * Listen to us, O shepherd of Israel, *
you who lead Joseph like a flock.
As you sit enthroned upon the cherubim,
shine forth [l]

a Ps 80:13-14; Deut 28:26; Jer 7:33.—b 1 Mac 7:17; Jer 14:16; 16:4; Zep 1:17.—c Pss 39:9; 44:14; 80:7; 123:3-4; Job 12:4; Ezek 6:14; Dan 9:16; Zep 2:8.—d Pss 13:2; 44:24; 74:1; 89:47; Deut 4:24.—e Ps 14:4; Sir 36:1-5; Jer 10:25.—f Pss 116:6; 142:7.—g Pss 25:11; 31:4; Ezek 20:44; 36:22.—h Pss 42:4; 115:2; Joel 2:17; Mal 2:17.—i Deut 32:43; Joel 3:2; Rev 6:10.—j Pss 79:11; 102:21; 126:1; Lk 4:18.—k Pss 12:7; 89:51-52; Gen 4:24; Isa 65:6-7; Jer 32:18.—l Pss 23:1-3; 77:21; 95:7; 100:3; Gen 48:15; Ex 25:22; 1 Sam 4:4; 2 Sam 6:2; Ezek 34:2; Mic 7:14.

79:2-3 *They have given . . . the flesh . . . to bury them:* these verses are cited freely in 1 Mac 7:17 in application to the massacre of sixty pious Jews in Jerusalem during the Maccabean wars.

79:4 A secular hostility opposed Israel to its neighbors, as is shown by the oracles of the Prophets against the nations (see Lam 3:45; Zep 2:8).

79:5-8 The divine justice cannot remain inactive in the case of such wickedness, which calls out for retribution.

79:5 *How long . . . ?:* see note on Ps 6:4. *Rage:* i.e., a jealous rage (see Ps 119:139; Nah 1:2). *Blaze like a fire:* see Deut 4:24; 6:15; Zep 1:18; 3:8.

79:6-7 Cited in Jer 10:25. Concerning the call for redress, see note on Ps 5:11.

79:6, 12 See notes on Pss 5:11; 35.

79:8 The exiles beg God to show mercy on them and not hold the sins of their ancestors against them (see 2 Ki 17:7-23; 23:26f; 24:3f; Dan 9:4-14).

79:9-13 The psalmist beseeches God to pardon Israel for his name's sake so that the Most High may no longer be dishonored and blasphemed by the nations. Then the People of God will praise him from generation to generation.

79:9 The divine pardon is always gratuitous; it is the effect of his mercy and love (see Ps 78:38; Ezek 20:44; 36:22; see also note on Ps 65:4).

79:10 *You avenge:* God is the avenger of blood in Israel (see Pss 18:48; 19:15; 58:11f; 94:1; 149:7; Deut 32:43).

79:11 *Captives . . . those who have been sentenced to death:* literally, "the sons of death," i.e., the exiles in Babylonia (see Ps 102:21) who are under threat of death if they seek to escape.

79:12 *Sevenfold:* a symbolic phrase meaning fullness or superabundance (see Ps 12:7; Gen 4:24; Lev 26:21).

79:13 *Offer thanks to you:* see note on Ps 7:18.

Ps 80 At the time of this psalmist, the northern kingdom of Israel and the southern kingdom of Judah have disappeared in turn (721 and 587 B.C.). For the time being, Israel will be nothing but a scattered flock, a ruined vineyard. Where can restoration come if not from God?

This psalm is well adapted to our prayer during Advent: so deep is our wretchedness that we await the coming of God; he alone can turn us to himself by his presence and lead us to conversion.

80:1 *For the director:* these words are thought to be a musical or liturgical notation. *According to "Lilies." Eduth:* nothing is known about this phrase. *Asaph:* see notes on Pss 73–89.

80:2-8 God is the Shepherd of Israel (see Isa 40:11; Jer 31:10; Ezek 34:31), and Jesus will call himself the Good Shepherd (see Jn 10). This image evokes profound links between Israel and God—affectionate solicitude on one side and confident belonging on the other. Hence, those who are in distress do not address an unknown and distant God.

80:2 *Shepherd of Israel:* see Pss 74:1; 77:21; 78:52, 71f; 79:13. *Joseph:* see note on Ps 77:16. *Cherubim:* see note on Ps 18:11.

3 over Ephraim,* Benjamin, and Manasseh.
Stir up your power
and come to save us.

4 [m]Restore us, O LORD of hosts;
let your face shine * upon us,
and we will be saved.

5 O LORD of hosts,*
how long will you be angry
at your people's prayers? [n]
6 You have fed them with the bread of tears
and made them drink tears beyond measure. [o]

7 You have made us an object of contention to our neighbors,
a source of mockery to our enemies. [p]

8 Restore us, O LORD of hosts;
let your face shine upon us,
and we will be saved.

9 *You brought a vine * out of Egypt;
you dispersed the nations and planted it.
10 You prepared the ground for it;
then it took root and filled the land.
11 The mountains were covered with its shade
and the cedars of God * with its shoots.
12 It sent out its boughs as far as the Sea,*
its shoots as far as the river.

13 *Why have you broken down its walls
so that all who pass by pluck its grapes? * [q]
14 The boars from the forest ravage it,
and wild beasts of the field feed on it. [r]

15 Turn once again to us, O LORD of hosts; *
look down from heaven and see;
take care of this vine,
16 this shoot * that your right hand has planted,
the son that you yourself made strong.

17 Let those who would burn it or cut it down
perish when confronted by your rebuke.
18 Let your hand rest upon the man at your right,*
the son of man that you yourself made strong.

19 Then we will never again turn away from you;
give us life and we will call upon your name.*

20 Restore us, O LORD of hosts;
let your face shine upon us,
and we will be saved.

PSALM 81*

Exhortation To Worship Worthily

1 For the director.* "Upon the *gittith*." Of Asaph.

2 Sing out your joy to God our strength;
shout aloud to the God of Jacob. * [s]

m 4, 8, 20: Pss 4:7; 31:17; 67:2; 85:5; Num 6:25; Jer 31:18.—n Pss 13:2; 44:24; 74:1; 79:5; 89:47; Deut 4:24; 29:20.—o Pss 42:4; 102:10.—p Pss 44:14; 79:4; 123:3-4; Job 12:4; Dan 9:16.—q Ps 89:41; Jer 12:7-13; 39:8.—r Jer 5:6; Hos 2:12.—s Pss 43:4; 66:1; 68:27; 81:2-3; 87:7; 149:3; 150:3-4; 2 Sam 6:14; Jud 16:1; Jer 31:4.

80:3 *Ephraim* and *Manasseh* were the two principal tribes of the northern kingdom, with which *Benjamin* was at times associated (see Num 2:18f). It was also in front of these three tribes that the Ark of the Covenant advanced during the sojourn from Sinai to the Promised Land (see Num 10:21-24).

80:4 *Let your face shine:* see notes on Pss 4:7; 13:2.

80:5 *LORD of hosts:* see note on Ps 59:6. *How long . . . ?:* see note on Ps 6:4.

80:9-17 Israel is God's magnificent garden whose ideal limits extend as far as the Euphrates ("river" of v. 12). God is like the vinedresser who cherishes his vine/vineyard and takes pleasure in it. How could he not be saddened to see it devastated (see Isa 5:1-7; 27:2-5; Jer 2:21; 12:10)? This image will pass into the New Testament (see Mt 20:1; 21:33-41; Jn 15:1-5).

80:9 *Vine:* a familiar allegory in the Prophets (see Isa 5:1; 27:2; Jer 2:21; 12:10; Ezek 17:6-8; 19:10-14; Hos 10:1; 14:7; Mic 7:1), as is that of the shepherd (see Ps 23:1; Gen 48:15; Ezek 34:11). See also Mt 20:1; Jn 15:1.

80:11 *Cedars of God:* cedars that were so huge, they were regarded as being planted by God.

80:12 *Sea:* i.e., Mediterranean; *River:* i.e., Euphrates.

80:13-20 The psalmist begs God to attend once again to his wasted vine then, the people will once again praise their savior.

80:13 *Why . . . ?:* see note on Ps 6:4.

80:15 *LORD of hosts:* see note on Ps 59:6.

80:16 *Shoot:* i.e., Israel. *Son:* i.e., Israel. The word may also be translated as "branch." Some versions omit verse 16b.

80:18 *Man at your right:* probably a reference to Israel, beloved son of the Lord (see Ex 4:22) or to the Davidic king who will lead the army in battle. Other suggestions put forth by scholars are Zerubbabel and Ezra, who presided over the restoration. *Son of man:* another word for "man" in the first half of this verse.

80:19 A vow to offer praise to God (see note on Ps 7:18).

Ps 81 The blasts of the trumpet call Israel to an assembly. The time is the full moon of September, the Feast of Booths or Tabernacles (see Num 10:10; Lev 23:34, 39-43). The covenant is renewed. At such a time, it is also important to rediscover the demands of fidelity. The psalmist, who is completely pervaded by the spirit of Deuteronomy, makes everyone aware of them. Let the people be on guard not to close their hearts to God. Today (v. 14), as yesterday (vv. 8, 12-13), the fidelity of God is checkmated by the infidelity of human beings.

In the last verse (v. 17) of this psalm, Christians cannot fail to be reminded of the blessings of the Eucharist in which we are filled with the "finest of wheat" (words found in the Mass texts of the Holy Thursday Evening Mass and the Easter Season), with bread that has become the Body and Blood, Soul, and Divinity of our Lord Jesus Christ. Each Eucharist is a renewal of the New Covenant, enabling us to relive the saving events of Christ's Passion and Resurrection. And in each Eucharist, we pledge ourselves to Christ by hearing and keeping his word proclaimed and by receiving his Body and Blood.

81:1 *For the director:* these words are thought to be a musical or liturgical notation. *Upon the gittith:* see note on Ps 8:1. *Asaph:* see notes on Pss 73–89.

81:2 *Jacob:* i.e., Israel (see Gen 32:28-29). Concerning the ritual "shout," see Ps 33:3.

3 Raise the chant and sound the tambourine;
play the pleasant harp and the lyre.
4 Sound the trumpet at the new moon,
and also at the full moon on the day of our Feast. * [t]
5 For this is a law in Israel,
a decree of the God of Jacob. [u]
6 He imposed this testimony on Joseph *
when he departed from the land of Egypt.
I now hear an unfamiliar voice:
7 "I lifted the burden from their shoulders; [v]
their hands put aside the laborer's basket. *
8 When you cried out to me in distress, I rescued you; *
from the thunderclouds I answered you;
I tested you at the waters of Meribah: [w]
Selah
9 " 'Listen to me, O my people, while I warn you.
O Israel, if only you would listen to me! [x]
10 You must not accept a foreign god in your presence; [y]
you must not bow down to an alien deity.
11 I am the LORD, your God,
who brought you up from the land of Egypt;
open your mouth * wide so that I may fill it.'
12 "But my people did not listen to my voice;
Israel refused to obey me. *
13 So I abandoned them to their stubborn hearts * [z]
and let them follow their own devices.
14 * "If only my people would listen to me,
if only Israel would walk in my ways, * [a]
15 I would quickly subdue their enemies
and raise my hand * against their foes. [b]
16 "Then those who hate the LORD * would tremble before him,
for their doom would last forever.
17 But Israel he would feed with the finest of wheat *
and fill them with honey from the rock." [c]

t Pss 81:4; 98:6; Ex 19:13; Lev 23:24; Num 10:9-10; 29:1; 31:6; Jos 6:4; 2 Ki 11:14; 1 Chr 15:28.—u Ex 23:14ff.—v Ex 1:14; 6:6; Isa 9:4.—w Ps 95:8; Ex 2:23ff; 17:7; 19:16; Num 20:13; 27:14; Deut 33:8.—x Ps 50:7; Ex 15:26; Isa 55:2-3.—y 10-11: Ex 20:2-6; Deut 5:6-10; Ezek 2:8.—z Jer 3:17; 7:24; Acts 7:42.—a Deut 5:29; Isa 48:18.—b Lev 26:7-8; Am 1:8.—c Ps 147:14; Ex 29:2; Deut 32:13-14; Ezek 16:19.

81:4 The first day of the lunar month (new moon) was for a long time celebrated as a feast (see 2 Ki 4:23; Isa 1:13; Hos 2:11; Am 8:5). Here it is a question of the beginning of the seventh month, long considered as the new year (see Lev 23:24; Num 29:1); on the following full moon (on the fifteenth of the month), the Feast of Tabernacles was celebrated (see Lev 23:34; Num 29:12), five days after the Day of Atonement (see Lev 16:29). It concluded the cycle of feasts that began with the Passover and Unleavened Bread six months before (see Ex 23:14-17; Lev 23; Deut 16:13-15). Every seventh year the covenant law was to be read to all the people (see Deut 31:9-13; Neh 8:2-15).

The purpose of the Feast of Tabernacles was to proclaim aloud the mighty deeds of the Lord in the history of salvation. During the feast, the assembly recalled God's wondrous works in Egypt.

81:6 *Joseph:* see note on Ps 77:16. *I now hear an unfamiliar voice:* the "voice" is the "thunder" of God's judgment against Egypt (v. 8). Some translate: "We heard a language we did not understand," and regard it as referring to the fact that the people were aliens in a foreign land (see Ps 114:1; Deut 28:49; 33:19). Some also regard this as a reference to inspiration.

81:7 *Burden . . . basket:* allusion to the forced labor that the Israelites had to endure in Egypt (see Ex 1:11-14).

81:8 *When you cried out . . . I rescued you:* see Ex 3:7-10; see also Ps 106:9; Ex 14:21, 24; 15:8, 10. *From the thunderclouds:* allusion to the theophany at Sinai (see Ex 19:16ff). *I tested you . . . Meribah:* see Ps 95:8; Ex 17:1-7.

81:11 The Lord challenges Israel to obey the first commandment of fidelity to God after the proclamation of the Exodus (see Ps 78:23-29; Deut 11:13-15; 28:1-4). *Open your mouth wide:* i.e., trust in the Lord alone for every need. *So that I may fill it:* as he did in the wilderness (see v. 17; Ps 78:23-29; see also Ps 37:3-4; Deut 11:13-15; 28:1-4).

81:12 Instead of remaining loyal to the Lord out of gratitude for their redemption and his promise of the future, the people continued to rebel against him—a characteristic typical of their history beginning with the generation in the wilderness (see Pss 78; 95; 106).

81:13 God gives the people over to their sins (see Ps 78:29; Isa 6:9f; 29:10; 63:17; see also Rom 1:24, 26, 28) because of their *stubborn hearts;* but he always reserves the right to "circumcise" their hearts and bring them back to him (see Deut 30:6; 1 Ki 8:58; Jer 31:33; Ezek 11:19; 36:26). *Hearts:* see note on Ps 4:8.

81:14-17 An allusion to the covenant blessings; the era of wars and persecutions will cease (see Lk 21:24), their enemies will be vanquished, and the people will enjoy the best of everything.

81:14 The Lord cannot abandon his people completely. He calls them to return to him and follow his *ways,* i.e., his commandments (see Pss 27:11; 86:11; 128:1; 143:8). For if they listen to God's word, they will respond by faith and repentance, and carry out his will rather than their own.

81:15 If his people return to him, the Lord will quickly come to their aid with his *hand* pressing hard against their enemies.

81:16 If his people return to him, the Lord will mete out to their enemies—*those who hate the LORD*—their just deserts, inflicting on them an everlasting punishment.

81:17 *Finest of wheat:* a staple of life. For Christians, of course, wheat is associated with the Eucharist, and this phrase has given rise to one of the finest modern Eucharistic hymns, *Gift of Finest Wheat,* composed for the 1976 Eucharistic Congress that took place in the United States. *Honey from the rock:* the purest of honey, since it came from places usually not attainable (from a cleft of rock in which bees in Canaan sometimes built their hives). The phrase is reminiscent of God's promise to Moses of a "land flowing with milk and honey" (Ex 3:8).

PSALM 82*

Judgment on Abuse of Authority

1 A psalm of Asaph. *

God takes his place in the divine council; *
in the midst of the gods he pronounces judgment: [d]
2 "How long will you issue unfair judgments
and rule in favor of those who are wicked? * [e] *Selah*
3 * "Grant justice to the weak and the orphan;
defend the rights of the lowly and the poor.
4 Rescue the wretched and the needy;
free them from the hand of the wicked. [f]
5 "They neither know nor understand;
they wander around in darkness
while all the foundations of the earth *
are crumbling.
6 * I declare, 'Although you are gods,
all of you sons of the Most High,
7 you will die as all men do;
like any ruler you will fall.' " *
8 Rise up, O God, and judge the earth,
for all the nations belong to you. *

PSALM 83*

Against a Hostile Alliance

1 A song. A psalm of Asaph. *
2 O God, do not remain silent; *
do not be quiet and inactive, O God. [g]

d Pss 7:9; 58:11; Job 21:22; Isa 3:13-14; 66:16; Joel 4:2.—e Ps 58:3; Deut 1:17; Prov 18:5.—f Pss 35:10; 72:4; 140:13; Deut 1:17; Isa 1:16f; 10:1-3; Zec 7:7-10; Jas 1:27; 2:1.—g Pss 10:1; 44:24; 50:3; 109:1.

Ps 82 The psalmist sets forth a word about just and unjust judges (somewhat similar to Ps 58). He reminds rulers and magistrates that they are earthly members of God's tribunal, associated in the government of the world, and in this respect "gods" (v. 6). Why then does the cause of the poor find such little regard among them? By establishing injustice rather than justice, these powerful people disturb the very order of the world (v. 5). They themselves will therefore be judged by the great King (see Ps 47) and Judge of all the earth (see Ps 94:2; Gen 18:25; 1 Sam 2:10) who "loves justice" (Ps 99:4) and judges the nations in righteousness (see Pss 9:9; 96:13; 98:9). Furthermore, God's justice turns human judgments topsy-turvy; the kingdom of God and his justice will overcome the evildoers and the powers of oppression (see Isa 24:21f).

Even in nations that are not concerned with God or openly deny him, rulers and judges receive their powers from God and are bound to exercise them for justice in accord with his will: "[Civil authorities] are . . . God's representatives for your welfare . . . [and] God's servants to mete out punishment to wrongdoers" (Rom 13:4). This same truth is proclaimed by 1 Pet 2:13f. See also Ps 2:6-11; Isa 44:28; Jer 27:6; Dan 2:21; 4:14, 28f; 5:18; Jn 19:11; Rom 13:1.

82:1a *Asaph:* see notes on Pss 73–89.

82:1b *Divine council:* the psalmist pictures a kind of heavenly assembly (see Ps 89:6; 1 Ki 22:19; Job 1:6; 2:1; Isa 6:1-4) in the Hall of Justice, patterned after the Solomonic one (see 1 Ki 7:7), in which God is dispensing justice. *Gods:* a word applied to rulers and judges who are "godlike" in their function of establishing justice on the earth (see note on Ps 45:7).

82:2 Like other authors of the Old Testament, the psalmist reproaches those in power with the sin of administering justice inequitably and showing partiality toward the wicked (see Ex 23:6; Lev 19:15; Deut 1:17; 2 Chr 19:7; Prov 18:5; Mic 3:1-12).

82:3-4 Rulers and judges are exhorted to protect the powerless against exploiters and oppressors (see Ps 72:2, 4, 12-14; Job 29:11f; Prov 31:8f; Isa 11:4; Jer 22:3, 16; Ezek 22:27, 29; Zec 7:9f). Indeed, to see to it that the weak do not fall into the hands of unscrupulous exploiters is one of the most important functions of government. *Poor:* see note on Ps 34:7.

82:5 When those in authority, instead of sharing in God's wisdom (see 1 Ki 3:9; Prov 8:14-16; Isa 11:2), have no understanding of their most important duty or of the divine norm and standard and do not walk in the light of the revealed will of the eternal Judge (see Job 21:22), then all the supports upon which a well-ordered State rests will crumble (see Pss 11:3; 75:4). *Foundations of the earth:* a metaphor for God's rule on earth (see Pss 11:3; 75:4; 96:10). The Lord has established some order, even in pagan nations, and he condemns the ungodly for undermining that order for their own ends.

82:6-7 These verses can be interpreted to apply to judges or rulers but also to pagan gods. The Lord pronounces sentence and dethrones such gods. Indeed, his judgment is pronounced upon all manifestations of evil, both in the human world and in the angelic world (see Mt 25:41; Rev 20:10, 14f; 21:8). *Gods:* see note on verse 1b. This passage is applied by Christ, in an entirely different context, to Jews instructed by the word of God (see Jn 10:34; see also Acts 17:28; 2 Cor 6:18).

82:7 These corrupt rulers will see death like all other human beings and be judged in the same way. *Like any ruler you will fall:* another possible translation is: "as one man, rulers, you will fall." God will humble the great of the world as he annihilated the false gods likened to personages of the ancient mythology (see Isa 14:12; Ezek 28:11ff).

82:8 The psalmist prays that God's just judgment (see Pss 9:21; 10:12-15; 76:10) will come soon. Whenever we encounter injustice, we can fittingly say our Lord's prayer: "Your kingdom come" (Mt 6:10). This verse can be fittingly applied to Christ, to whom all judgment has been entrusted by the Father (see Jn 5:22).

Ps 83 After the deportation in 587 B.C., Israel ceased to exist as a political entity. The community that has been reestablished in Jerusalem after the return is subjected to the tutelage of great powers and the vexation of their neighbors. The communities that had been scattered among foreign peoples have already experienced more than one persecution. In their struggles with pagan religions and cultures, believers feel threatened in their faith. It seems that all forces have formed a coalition to destroy Israel because it wishes to remain faithful to its vocation as the People of God. As a result, the psalmist directs the following challenge to the Lord: May he let himself be known by crushing the pride of the nations; indeed, may the latter meet the cruel fate of the petty kings who wanted to destroy Israel at the time of the Judges (see notes on Pss 5:11; 35).

Obviously, this is a prayer of vengeance, but even more of salvation. It wishes to provoke Heaven: how could a polytheistic and idolatrous world come to worship the one and all-powerful God if he abandons his people? The chosen people could never resign themselves to such a collapse; that would be tantamount to the defeat of the Lord himself.

Although as Christians we are constantly under threat from the godless, we can ceaselessly implore God the Father (by this psalm) to grant his new People a complete victory over our enemies. We do not desire the eternal death of our foes but ask that God will bring them low and lead them to himself as God and Father.

83:1 *Asaph:* see notes on Pss 73–89.

83:2 *Do not remain silent:* i.e., spring into action (see Pss 35:22; 109:1).

3 * Note how your enemies rage about,
how your foes increase in arrogance. *
4 They formulate shrewd plans against your people,
conspiring against those you love. [h]
5 They say, "Come, let us wipe them out as a nation;
let the name of Israel be totally forgotten."
6 They conspire with a single mind, [i]
forming an alliance * against you:
7 * the tents of Edom and the Ishmaelites,
Moab and the Hagrites, [j]
8 Gebal, Ammon, and Amalek, [k]
Philistia, and the inhabitants of Tyre; [l]
9 Assyria has also joined them as an ally,
offering aid to the descendants of Lot.
Selah
10 * Deal with them as you did with Midian, *
and with Sisera and Jabin at the brook of Kishon, * [m]
11 who were destroyed at Endor
and became manure for the ground. [n]
12 * Make their chieftains like Oreb and Zeeb,
and all their princes like Zebah and Zalmunna,
13 who boasted, "Let us seize for ourselves
the pastures of God."
14 * O my God, treat them like tumbleweed,
like chaff blown before the wind. [o]
15 As a fire rages through a forest,
as a flame sets mountains ablaze, [p]
16 so hound them with your tempests [q]
and terrify them with your stormwinds. *
17 Fill their faces with shame
so that they will seek your name, *
O LORD.
18 * Let them be humiliated and terrified forever;
let them be disgraced and perish.
19 Let them know that you alone,
whose name is the LORD,
are the Most High over all the earth. [r]

h Ps 31:14; Jer 11:9.—i Pss 2:2; 14:4.—j Ps 137:7; Num 20:23; Deut 2:5; 1 Chr 5:10, 19; Am 1:11.—k Gen 19:38; Ex 17:8; Jos 13:5.—l Jos 13:2; Isa 23:3.—m Ex 2:15; Jdg 4:2; Isa 9:3; 10:26.—n 1 Sam 28:7; Jer 8:2.—o Pss 1:4; 35:5; 58:10; Job 27:21; Isa 5:24; 10:17; 17:13; 29:5; Jer 13:24; Ezek 21:3.—p Ps 50:3; Deut 32:22.—q Job 9:17; 27:20; Jer 25:32.—r Pss 46:11; 97:9; Deut 4:39; Dan 3:45.

83:3-5 The words, *Come, let us,* are the very ones used by the leaders of the rebels at the tower of Babel when humanity attempted to usurp the power of the Lord (see Gen 11:3f). They obviously identify the enemies of God and of his people who cunningly plot to show their independence from the Lord and to exterminate Israel as a nation. *Name:* see note on Ps 5:12.

83:3 *Increase in arrogance:* literally, "rear their heads."

83:6 *Alliance:* there is no record of such a vast alliance of nations ever arrayed against Israel at one time. It may be that only some of them were attacking at the moment while passively being supported by the others. Some point to the time when Moab, Ammon, and Edom were invading Judah during the reign of King Jehoshaphat (see 2 Chr 20). *Against you:* the invaders acknowledge openly that the war is intended not only against the people but also against their God.

83:7-9 The members of the hostile alliance are all well-known foes of Israel. The psalmist alludes to the *Edomites,* descendants of Esau, the son of the patriarch Isaac (see Gen 36), and the *Ishmaelites,* who descended from Ishmael, the son of Abraham and Hagar (see Gen 16:15f); he also mentions the *Moabites* (see 2 Chr 20:1) and *Ammonites,* descendants of Lot, the nephew of Abraham (see Gen 19:38); next, he includes the *Hagrites,* an Arabian Bedouin tribe that was encamped on the border of the Syro-Arabian Desert (see 1 Chr 5:10, 19f). Other members were the inhabitants of *Gebal,* in the territory of the Edomites south of the Dead Sea (see Jos 13:5), and the *Amalekites* (see Gen 14:7). The *Philistines,* Israel's foes along the Mediterranean coast of Palestine (see Ex 15:14), were also part of the alliance, as were the inhabitants of *Tyre* (see Isa 23:3). *Assyria* (see Gen 10:11) is mentioned as rendering assistance to the alliance; hence, it must not have become a major power in that area.

83:10-19 These verses are part of the so-called imprecatory (or cursing) psalms that call upon God to mete out justice to enemies (see notes on Pss 5:11; 35). In their thirst for justice, the authors of these psalms use hyperbole (or overstatement) in order to move others to oppose sin and evil.

83:10-13 The psalmist takes heart by recalling two great victories won with God's help against superior forces during the time of the Judges: the victory of Gideon over the Midianites (see Jdg 7) and the defeat of King Jabin (see Jdg 4). He knows that in order for God's kingdom of righteousness and peace to come, his foes must be defeated (see note on Ps 5:11).

83:10 *Midian:* it was at Midian (see Ex 2:15) that Gideon defeated the Midianites and slew the leaders named in verse 12 (see Jdg 7:24-25; 8:5). *Sisera and Jabin:* commander and king, respectively, of the army defeated by Deborah and Barak in the Plain of Esdraelon near Endor at the foot of Mount Tabor (see Jdg 4–5).

83:12-13 The Midianites had despoiled the croplands (v. 13: *Let us seize for ourselves the pastures of God*) and driven fear into the hearts of the Israelites. In their defeat at the hands of the Lord through Gideon, their leaders Oreb, Zeeb, Zebah, and Zalmunna were captured and put to death (see Jdg 7:25; 8:21).

83:14-15 The psalmist likens the fate of the enemies to that of *tumbleweed* and *chaff* carried away by the wind and a *forest* or *mountains* destroyed by fire (common figures of destruction at the hand of the Lord: see Pss 1:4; 35:5; Isa 5:24; 10:17; 17:13; 29:5; Jer 13:24).

83:16 *Tempests . . . stormwinds:* for God in the thunderstorm, see Pss 18:8-16; 68:34; 77:18f; Ex 15:7-10; Jos 10:11; Jdg 5:4, 20f; 1 Sam 2:10; 7:10; Isa 29:5f; 33:3. See also note on Ps 68:5.

83:17 *They will seek your name:* the psalmist prays that God will humiliate the enemies and lead men to seek his name, i.e., realize and accept that the Lord alone is God (see v. 19).

83:18-19 The Chronicler (2 Chr 20:22-29) records the defeat of the alliance and mentions that all the nations were terrified when they learned that the Lord fought on the side of the Israelites. This is precisely what the psalmist asks so that his people will be saved and the Lord will be praised by the whole world.

PSALM 84*

Longing for God's Dwelling

1 For the director. * "Upon the *gittith*." A psalm of the sons of Korah.

2 How lovely is your dwelling place,
O LORD of hosts. * [s]
3 My soul yearns and is filled with longing
for the courts of the LORD.
My heart and my flesh cry out
for the living God. [t]

4 Just as the sparrow searches for a home
and the swallow builds a nest for herself
where she may place her young,
so do I seek your altars, *
O LORD of hosts, my King and my God. [u]

5 Blessed * are those who dwell in your house;
they offer continuous praise to you.
Selah

6 Blessed are those who find strength in you,
who set their hearts upon your ways. *

7 As they pass through the Valley of Baca,
they turn it into a region of springs,
and the early rain covers it with pools. *

8 * They move forward with increasing strength
as they behold the God of gods in Zion.

9 O LORD of hosts, hear my prayer;
listen to my pleas, O God of Jacob.
Selah

10 O God, look upon our shield *
behold the face of your anointed one. [v]

11 It is better to spend one day in your courts
than a thousand elsewhere.
I would rather be a doorkeeper * in God's house
than dwell inside the tents of the wicked.

12 The LORD God serves as our sun * and our shield;
the LORD showers us with grace and glory.
He does not withhold any good thing
from those who walk in integrity.

13 O LORD of hosts,
blessed is the man who puts his trust in you.

PSALM 85*

Prayer for the People's Salvation

1 For the director. * A psalm of the sons of Korah.

2 O LORD, you showed favor to your land;
you restored the good fortune of Jacob. * [w]

---

s Pss 27:4; 43:3; 122:1; 132:5.—t Pss 42:2-3; 63:2-3; 143:6; Jos 3:10; Job 19:27; Isa 26:9.—u Pss 2:6; 5:3; 43:4; 44:5; 68:25; Jer 44:11.—v Pss 2:2; 18:51; 59:12; 89:19; 132:17.—w Pss 14:7; 126:4; Deut 30:3.

Ps 84 During one of the pilgrimages prescribed by the Mosaic Law (see Ex 23:17; 1 Sam 1:3; Lk 2:42), perhaps the one for the harvest, a pilgrim expresses his joy at finding himself near God in the temple. At the last stage, the Lord has already manifested his favor to the faithful pilgrims (vv. 6-7). He reserves even more happiness for those who follow his law. Another opinion holds that this psalm recalls Ps 42 and reflects its circumstances. The psalmist is a Levite who has no access to God's house, possibly at the time when Sennacherib was overrunning Judah (see 2 Ki 18:13-16), and expresses his longing for the closeness in the temple that he experienced in the past.

This pilgrim song, overflowing with the desire for and joy of God, becomes the song of hope and confidence for all Christians en route to the house of the Father where they will sing an Alleluia (or Hallelujah) without end. It also translates the sentiments of all who love Christ's Eucharistic Presence in the tabernacle.

84:1 *For the director:* these words are thought to be a musical or liturgical notation. *"Upon the gittith":* see note on Ps 8:1. *Sons of Korah:* see note on Ps 42:1.

84:2-3 *LORD of hosts:* see note on Ps 24:10. *Soul:* see note on Ps 6:4. *Heart . . . flesh:* i.e., entire being (see Ps 73:26).

84:4 God sees to it that even the "birds of the air have nests" (Mt 8:20); hence, he will welcome his faithful to the shelter of his altars.

84:5, 6, 13 *Blessed:* see note on Ps 1:1.

84:6 *Who set their hearts upon your ways:* literally, "in whose hearts are the open roads."

84:7 Through God's care, even the most fearsome path becomes a path of blessings and praise (see 2 Chr 20:26). *Valley of Baca:* valley of "weeping" or "balsam trees"; in the Vulgate, it is called "the Valley of Tears," which gave rise, in the ascetical and preaching tradition, to the familiar expression, "vale of tears," for our earthly pilgrimage. *Pools:* or "blessings."

84:8-9 *Zion:* see note on Ps 9:12. *LORD of hosts:* see note on Ps 24:10. *Jacob:* i.e., Israel (see Gen 32:28-29).

84:10 *Our shield:* the king (see Ps 89:19). *Anointed one:* either the king (who was God's earthly regent over his people) or the high priest (who led the community of Israel after the disappearance of the royalty).

84:11 *Doorkeeper:* some of the sons of Korah (see v. 1) were doorkeepers or gatekeepers in the temple (see 1 Chr 26:1).

84:12 There is no joy that can outweigh and replace supernatural joys that have their source in God alone, for he denies no grace to his faithful ones. *Sun:* see note on Ps 27:1 on God as "light."

Ps 85 This psalm is a national lament recalling God's goodwill in bringing his people back from the Exile to their homeland (538 B.C.) but also indicates that the repatriates are having difficulty in reestablishing themselves in Judea. The psalmist as much as says: "You have enabled us to come back to our land; now let us come back to our lives." The lament becomes a prayer of hope, for the Prophets had announced a better future (see Isa 58:8; Zec 8:12). The temple of Jerusalem is being rebuilt (520–515 B.C.) and will be a visible sign of the presence of God, of his "glory" (v. 10; see Ezek 43:2). Happiness is promised to those who remain faithful. All these thoughts are similar to those expressed by the post-exilic Prophets (see Hag 1:5-11; 2:6-9; Mal 3:13-21).

In praying this psalm, we can keep in mind that in Jesus, the Son of God, the promise becomes reality (see Jn 14:27; Col 1:20). When love and truth, justice and peace dwell on the earth, a new world is being born, and God is there.

85:1 *For the director:* these words are thought to be a musical or liturgical notation. *Sons of Korah:* see note on Ps 42:1.

85:2 *Restored the good fortune of Jacob:* another translation possible is: "brought Jacob back from exile." *Jacob:* i.e., Israel (see Gen 32:28-29).

3 You forgave the iniquity of your people;
you canceled all their sins. *Selah*
4 You cast aside all your wrath;
you put an end to your great anger. [x]
5 * Restore us once again, O God, our Savior,
and cease your displeasure toward us. [y]
6 Will you remain angry with us forever?
Will you hold onto your wrath for all generations? [z]
7 Will you not once again give us life
so that your people may exult in you?
8 Show us, O LORD, your kindness *
and grant us your salvation.
9 * I will listen for God's response;
surely the LORD will proclaim peace to his people, his saints, *
to those who turn to him with their whole heart.
10 His salvation is indeed near for those who fear him;
his glory * will dwell in our land.
11 * Kindness and faithfulness * will meet;
righteousness and peace will embrace. [a]
12 Faithfulness will spring forth from the earth,
and righteousness * will look down from heaven. [b]
13 * The LORD will grant us prosperity, *
and our land will yield its harvest. [c]
14 Righteousness will go forth in front of him,
and he will set us on the way he treads.

PSALM 86*

Prayer in Suffering and Distress

1 A prayer of David.
Incline your ear, O LORD, and answer me,
for I am poor and needy. *
2 Preserve my life, for I am faithful to you;
save your servant who puts his trust in you.
3 You are my God; * have pity on me, O Lord,
for to you I cry out all day long.
4 Give joy to the soul of your servant,
for to you, O Lord,
I lift up my soul. * [d]
5 O Lord, you are kind and forgiving,
filled with kindness * for all who cry to you. [e]
6 Hear my prayer, O LORD,
and listen to my voice in supplication. [f]
7 In the time of trouble I call to you,
for you will answer me.

x Pss 78:38; 106:23; Ex 32:14; Num 14:20; Isa 48:9; Ezek 20:22; Hos 11:8-9.—y Pss 71:20; 80:4.—z Pss 50:21; 79:5; 89:47.—a Pss 61:8; 89:15; 97:2.—b Ps 72:6; Isa 45:8.—c Pss 67:7; 84:11; Lev 26:4; Ezek 34:27; Hos 2:22-23; Zec 8:12; Jas 1:17.—d Pss 25:1; 143:8.—e Ex 34:6; Joel 2:13.—f Pss 5:3; 17:1; 130:1-2.

85:5-8 The psalmist begs God to favor his penitent people with pardon and peace.

85:8 *Kindness:* see note on Ps 6:5.

85:9-14 God answers the prayer through a reassuring word of a priest or Levite.

85:9 *Saints:* see notes on Pss 4:4; 16:3; 34:10. *To those . . . heart:* other translations possible are: "and to those who turn from folly" and "but let them not return to folly" (the Hebrew word for "folly" includes the connotation of moral deficiency).

85:10-13 Only those who fear God in the spirit of wisdom (in contrast to the spirit of folly, v. 9) will inherit his benefits, which will be their glory. They will experience a renewed spirit since they are the heirs of the new age of restoration, which is described by various terms: salvation and glory (v. 10), kindness, faithfulness, righteousness, and peace (vv. 11-12), good and harvest (v. 13). *Glory:* the Lord's glory—a visible manifestation of his power and divinity—had left the temple and the holy city (see Ezek 11:23); it would return there once the temple was restored (see Ezek 43:2; Hag 2:9). See also Jn 1:14.

85:11-12 People will regulate their lives by the divine norms. The divine attributes, as well as the moral virtues that correspond to them, are here personified (see Pss 89:15; 97:2) as courtiers of the returning king.

85:11 *Kindness and faithfulness:* often found together to express God's loyalty (see Pss 25:10; 40:12f; 57:11; 61:8; Ex 34:6).

85:12 *Righteousness:* personification of God's attribute, which expresses his kingship in and over his people (see Pss 4:2; 22:31, alternative translation).

85:13-14 The goodness and blessings that the psalmist sees in a vision of the future are, for Christians, fulfilled in Christ. Yet the completion of salvation is also for Christians an object of promise and of longing expectation.

85:13 *Prosperity:* the benefits of God's kingdom enjoyed by those who fear him: forgiveness (v. 3), reconciliation, renewal of covenant status (vv. 9-10), and fullness of restoration (vv. 10-14). Thus, faith in God leads to hope in a new age of righteousness (see Gal 5:5; 2 Pet 3:13).

Ps 86 The psalmist passes in turn from supplication to an act of trust and gratitude toward God. This poem, composed most likely after the Exile, is the prayer of devout Israelites who believed in the Lord's goodness as a result of their own experience. After all, he brought Israel back to life in the most somber moment of her history! The Lord seemed so close to them that he could listen, pardon, and save; the psalmist contemplates the mystical experience of Moses encountering God (see Ex 34:6). The conviction of God's goodness overwhelms us by its evidence and its simplicity of expression. It already paves the way for a "missionary" sensitivity. The imprecations against the pagans lose their vehemence, and one foresees the day when, touched by the Lord, they will render glory to the only God.

By means of this psalm, Christians can pray for their well-being in this world and beyond. Prolonging Christ's Passion, the Church and Christians experience the same anguish he did and seek to take refuge in the same heavenly Father.

86:1 *Poor and needy:* see note on Ps 34:7.

86:3 *You are my God:* indeed, God himself has chosen David to be his servant (see 1 Sam 13:14; 15:28; 16:12; 2 Sam 7:8).

86:4 *My soul:* see note on Ps 6:4.

86:5 *Kindness:* see note on Ps 6:5.

8 There is no one among the gods like you,
O Lord,[g]
nor can any deeds compare with yours.
9 All the nations * you have made
will come and bow down before you,
O Lord,
and glorify your name.[h]
10 For you are great and you do marvelous
deeds; *
you alone are God.

11 Teach me your ways, O LORD,
so that I may walk in your truth;[i]
let me worship your name
with an undivided heart. *
12 I will praise you with all my heart, *
O Lord, my God,
and I will glorify your name forever.
13 Your kindness * toward me is great;
you have rescued me from the depths
of the netherworld.[j]

14 Arrogant men are rising up against me,
O God;
a violent mob seeks my life;
they do not keep you before their
eyes. *
15 But you, O Lord, are a merciful and compassionate God,
slow to anger and abounding in kindness and faithfulness. *[k]
16 Turn to me and grant me your gracious
favor;
endow your servant with strength
and rescue the child of your handmaid. *[l]
17 Grant me a sign of your favor, *
so that those who hate me
may see it and be put to shame,
because you, O LORD,
have helped and comforted me.

PSALM 87*

Zion, Home of All Nations

1 A psalm of the sons of Korah. * A song.

The LORD has founded a city *
on the holy mountains.[m]
2 He loves the gates of Zion
more than * any dwelling in Jacob.
3 Glorious things are said of you,
O city of God. *Selah*

4 * "I number Rahab and Babylon
among those who acknowledge the
LORD,
as well as Philistia, Tyre, and Ethiopia;
concerning them it can be said,
'This one was born there.' " * *Selah*

g Pss 35:10; 89:9; Ex 15:11; Deut 3:24; Job 21:22; Jer 10:6.—h Pss 22:28; 66:4; Zec 14:16; Rev 15:4.—i Pss 25:4; 26:3; 27:11; 119:12, 35; 143:8, 10; Jer 24:7; 32:39.—j Pss 30:3; 40:2; 88:6; Jon 2:7.—k Pss 103:8; 111:4; 130:7; 145:8; Ex 34:6.—l Pss 18:3; 25:16; 116:16; Wis 9:5.—m 1-2: Pss 2:6; 48:2; 76:2-3; 78:68-69; Zec 2:16.

86:9 *All the nations:* see note on Ps 46:11. *Your name:* see note on Ps 5:12.

86:10 *Marvelous deeds:* see note on Ps 9:2.

86:11 The psalmist asks God to save him from his enemies and also from himself (see Pss 25:5; 51:9, 12). *Undivided heart:* see 1 Chr 12:33; as well as Ezek 11:19; 1 Cor 7:35.

86:12 The psalmist vows to praise the Lord for his help (see note on Ps 7:18). *Heart:* see note on Ps 4:8.

86:13 The psalmist anticipates being heard. *Kindness:* see note on Ps 6:5. *Depths:* see note on Ps 30:2.

86:14 These haughty foes disregard God—to their ruin (see Ps 54:5; Jer 20:11).

86:15 This verse recalls Ex 34:6.

86:16 *Child of your handmaid:* another translation is: "faithful child." See also Ps 116:16.

86:17 *Favor:* the good things promised in the covenant (see notes on Pss 27:13; 31:20). *Those who hate me . . . put to shame:* the imprecations against enemies that conclude a good number of the psalms are here kept to a minimum.

Ps 87 The psalmist here paints a picture of Jerusalem as the spiritual mother of all peoples and thus prefigures the Church of Christ (see Acts 2:5ff; Gal 4:26). No other canticle has given greater exaltation to the holy city, Zion, the chosen city of God. Not only is she at the heart of Israel, but in her, God lays the basis for the spiritual rebirth of all peoples, even the sworn enemies of Israel, such as Egypt and Chaldea, through their worship of the true God (see Ps 45:15f; Zec 2:15; 8:23). All will be admitted into her bosom, and God will declare her mother of all peoples.

After having encountered the conflicts of peoples and the persecution of Israel in so many psalms, here is a symphony with unforgettable melodies. We are enchanted by this universalist aspect and the perspective of a humanity reunited by God in his presence, in accord with the vision of the Prophets (see Isa 2:2-4; 19:19-25; 25:6; 45:14, 22-24; 56:6-8; 60:3; 66:23; Dan 7:14; Mic 4:1-3; Zec 8:23; 14:16). Such is also the vocation of the Church, the new Jerusalem, to be a leaven for the ingathering of all peoples.

Thus, in praying this psalm, Christians keep in mind not only the earthly Zion with its fulfillment, the Church, but also the heavenly Jerusalem, the heavenly Church, which is our true and definitive home, the source of eternal life and perfect blessedness. At the end of time, this new Jerusalem will come down out of heaven from God, prepared as a bride for her husband (see Rev 21:2, 24).

87:1a *Sons of Korah:* see note on Ps 42:1.

87:1b *LORD has founded a city:* it is the Lord himself who has made Zion his city (see Isa 14:32) and the temple his dwelling. *Mountains:* see note on Ps 2:6.

87:2 *Loves . . . more than:* Zion is more cherished by the Lord than any other Israelite city or town (see Pss 9:12; 78:68; 132:12-14). *The gates of Zion:* a common Hebrew idiom for the city. *Jacob*: i.e., Israel (see Gen 32:28-29).

87:4-5 These verses foresee a wholesale conversion to the Lord on the part of peoples who were longtime enemies of God and his kingdom (see Isa 19:21).

87:4 The Gentiles will be incorporated into the People of God and adopted by Zion, their religious homeland. As the representatives of all the Gentile nations, the psalmist mentions the arrogant Egypt (*Rahab*—the name of an ocean monster used poetically for Egypt) and *Babylon*, the two world kingdoms on the Nile and Euphrates, both of which had fought for centuries for the possession of Palestine. We also hear of the Philistines, archenemy of Israel, wealthy Tyre proud of its independence, and the ambitious Ethiopians.

5 However, of Zion it will be said,
"They were all born there, [n]
for the Most High himself establishes
her." * [o]
6 The LORD records in the register * of the
peoples, [p]
"This one was born there." *Selah*
7 And as they play, they all sing, * [q]
"In you are all my fountains."

PSALM 88*

Prayer in Affliction

1 A song. A psalm of the sons of Korah. * For
the director. According to *Mahalath.* For singing.
A *maskil* of Heman the Ezrahite.
2 * O LORD, the God of my salvation,
day and night I cry out to you. [r]
3 Let my prayer come before you;
give ear to my cry for help. [s]
4 * [t] For my soul * is filled with misery,
and my life draws near to the nether-
world.
5 I am numbered among those who go
down to the pit; *
all strength has failed me.
6 I have been abandoned among the dead,
like the slain who lie in the grave,
like those whom you remember no longer
and whom your hand has abandoned. *
7 * You have lowered me into the depths of
the pit,
into the darkest regions of the abyss.
8 Your wrath lies heavy upon me;
all your waves engulf me. [u] *Selah*
9 You have caused my closest friends to
shun me
and made me hateful in their sight.
I am shut in with no means of escape, * [v]
10 and my eyes grow dim * with my suf-
fering.
* Every day I call out to you, O LORD,
and spread out my hands to you.
11 Do you perform wonders * for the dead?
Do the shades rise up and give you
praise? [w] *Selah*

n Gal 4:26.—o Ps 48:9; Isa 62:4-5.—p Ps 69:29; Ex 32:32; Isa 4:3; Ezek 13:9; Mal 3:16.—q Pss 36:10; 68:25; 149:3.—r Pss 3:5; 77:3.—s Ps 119:170.—t 4-7: Pss 6:3; 25:17; 28:1; 30:4; 40:3; 86:13; 143:7; Num 16:33; Job 17:1; Lam 3:55; Jon 2:6-7.—u Pss 7:12; 18:5; 32:6; 42:8; 69:2; Jon 2:3.—v Pss 31:12; 38:12; 79:4; 80:7; 123:3-4; 142:8; Job 12:4; 19:13; Lam 3:7; Dan 9:16.—w Pss 6:6; 9:2; 30:10; 115:17; Isa 38:18.

87:5 The privileges of the holy city and her spiritual motherhood are divine in origin and hence indefectible. The eschatological community of the faithful is established by the Lord (see Ps 48:9; Isa 14:32; 28:16; 54:11f).

87:6 Here it is a case simply of a list (*register*) of the citizens of Zion (see Isa 4:3; Ezek 13:9) rather than the apocalyptic book of destinies (see Ps 69:28). Each people will thus have two homelands—one material and one spiritual. The basis for the people's security and inclusion in Zion lies in the promise of the Lord and the fact that he is its builder (see Heb 11:10, 16).

87:7 Zion is associated with "the fountain of life" (Ps 36:10), of "salvation" (Isa 12:3), "a river whose streams bring joy to the city of God" (Ps 46:5; see Ezek 47; Rev 22:1-5). *As they play, they all sing:* an alternative translation is: "As they make music, they will sing." Hence, the peoples will be admitted to the official liturgical worship (see Isa 66:21) and will at least be able to participate in the ritual dances (see Pss 149:3; 150:4; 2 Sam 6:5).

Ps 88 The anguish of death has rarely found expression in such touching images as those of the present psalm: prison, shipwreck, solitude, and darkness. The suppliant has experienced the depths of misfortune. Has God abandoned him? Despite the depths of his distress, the believer refuses to admit such a thing; he puts down all thought of rebellion within himself. For although no expressions of hopeful expectation (as in most psalms) are present and the last word speaks of darkness as "my closest friend," the psalmist firmly believes that the Lord is "the God of [his] salvation."

This psalm illustrates the hazy ideas that the ancients harbored about life after death before they arrived at faith in the resurrection: in the netherworld ("Sheol"), in the subterranean pit, the dead have no more communication with God; they are no more than dull shadows of themselves in the land of no recall. It is a prayer of a man who experiences the depths of human misery, a prayer of Israel at the edge of collapse, but also a prayer of everyone on the brink of hopelessness.

This psalm furnishes Christians with a prayer during times of spiritual dryness as well as human calamities of all kinds. We can then express to the heavenly Father our sufferings and distresses in the face of hostility, the weight of our spiritual and human solitude, and our fear in the light of his persistent silence. It will enable us to accept our cup without recrimination and to renew our trust in our God.

88:1 *Sons of Korah:* see note on Ps 42:1. *For the director:* these words are thought to be a musical or liturgical notation. *According to Mahalath:* possibly a tune. *Maskil:* see note on Ps 32:1a. *Heman the Ezrahite:* he is thought to be the son of Zerah (hence, Ezrahite) and member of the tribe of Judah (see 1 Chr 2:6) as well as leader of the Korahite guild (see 1 Chr 6:33, 37).

88:2-3 The psalmist, despite his wretched state, has not lost hope; he believes that the Lord is the God who saves and so he cries out to him for help.

88:4-6 His soul is full of troubles; indeed, he is accounted as one already in the grave and cut off from God (see Ps 143:7; Job 10:15; 17:1).

88:4 *Soul:* see note on Ps 6:4. *Netherworld:* see note on Ps 6:6.

88:5 The psalmist is alive but dead (see Pss 6:6; 107:18) as to his contemporaries (see Pss 22:30; 28:1; 143:7; Prov 1:12). *Pit:* see note on Ps 30:2.

88:6 As far as the psalmist is concerned, he is already in the pit (see note on Ps 6:6), where he cannot call upon God to remember him and come to his aid (see Pss 25:7; 74:2; 106:4).

88:7-10a For some reason God has let a flood of troubles overwhelm the suppliant so that he remains deprived of all human consolation (see Ps 142:7; Lam 3:7).

88:9 Friends interpret the suffering of the suppliant as a punishment from God and remain aloof from him lest they also be struck with it.

88:10a *Eyes grow dim:* see note on Ps 6:8.

88:10b-13 The psalmist prays to be saved in order to continue to praise the Lord for his wondrous deeds, for those in the grave can no longer do so (see notes on Pss 6:6; 9:2).

88:11 *Wonders:* see note on Ps 9:2. *Rise up:* i.e., a simple act of rising to give praise in the kingdom of the dead (see Isa 14:9)—not a bona fide resurrection from the dead.

12 Is your kindness * celebrated in the grave,
or your faithfulness in the tomb?
13 Are your wonders known in the region of darkness,
or your righteous deeds in the land of oblivion? *
14 * But for my part, I cry out to you, O LORD;
in the morning my prayer rises before you.
15 Why do you cast me away, O LORD? *
Why do you hide your face from me?
16 Since infancy I have been wretched and close to death;
I have borne your terrors
and have now reached the point of exhaustion.
17 Your wrath has weighed down upon me;
your terrors have destroyed me. [x]
18 All day long they surround me like a flood;
they encircle me completely.
19 You have caused my friends and neighbors to shun me; [y]
my sole companion now is darkness. *

PSALM 89*

Prayer for the Fulfillment of God's Promise

1 A *maskil* * of Ethan the Ezrahite.
2 * I will sing forever of the LORD's kindness;
with my lips I will proclaim your faithfulness *
throughout the generations. [z]
3 You said, "My kindness lasts forever;
my faithfulness is as firmly established as the heavens.
4 "I have made a covenant with my chosen one;
I have sworn to my servant David:
5 'I will establish your descendants forever
and allow your throne to endure for all generations.' " * [a] *Selah*
6 * Let the heavens * praise your wonders, O LORD,
your faithfulness in the assembly of your holy ones. [b]
7 [c] For who in the skies can be compared to the LORD?
Is there any heavenly being * who is like the LORD,
8 a God who is feared in the council of the holy ones,
greater and more awesome than any who stand in his presence?

x Ps 7:12; Job 6:4; 20:25.—y Ps 38:12; Job 17:13-17; 19:13.—z Pss 30:10; 36:6; 40:11; 57:11; 59:17; 71:19; 100:5; 108:5; 117:2; Isa 63:7.—a Pss 61:7-8; 132:11-12; 2 Sam 7:8-16; 1 Ki 8:16.—b Pss 19:2; 29:1; 82:1; Job 1:6; 5:1.—c 7-9: Pss 35:10; 86:8; 111:1; 113:5; Ex 15:11; Isa 6:3; Jer 10:6.

88:12 The psalmist would be unable to render praise to God if he were to go to the *grave*, also known as the "pit." *Kindness . . . faithfulness:* see notes on Pss 6:5; 36:6f. *The tomb:* literally, "destruction," another name for the grave or the pit; in Hebrew it is *Abaddon* (see Job 26:6; 28:22; Prov 15:11; Rev 9:11).

88:13 The psalmist speaks of death as a place of total darkness, also known as the *land of oblivion*, in contrast with the "land of the living" (Pss 27:13; 52:7; 116:9; 142:6), because those who die are quickly forgotten by the living (see Pss 6:6; 31:13; Eccl 9:5).

88:14-19 Even when human consolation is lacking, suffering can still be bearable if God gives his perceptible consolation; however, the psalmist also feels himself abandoned by God.

88:15 *Why . . . ?:* see note on Ps 6:4. *Hide your face:* see note on Ps 13:2.

88:19 The lamentation ends on a cry of sadness, like Ps 39. However, it is not a cry of despair, for God cannot remain deaf to the prayers of his faithful ones (see Ps 79:9-11; Job 16:18-20).

Ps 89 This psalm constitutes a beautiful hymn to God the Creator and a grand acclamation to the Lord who has given his word and his promise to Israel. And although the facts in Israel's history seem to give the lie to such splendid visions, the believer refuses to rely on appearances. God's word and his promise are solid in spite of a temporary present roadblock, as a long history bears witness. The temporary roadblock may have been the attack on Jerusalem by Nebuchadnezzar and the exile of King Jehoiachin in 597 B.C. (see 2 Ki 24:8-17) or the disappearance of the Davidic dynasty after the Exile (from the sixth century on).

The psalmist sketches a wonderful catalog of God's work: the origins of the world and the election of David; the order of the cosmos and the stability of the royal throne; heaven and earth and the present, past, and future. In time of incertitude, one must make use of this sublime contemplation and continue to believe in the faithfulness of God. Then the Messianic Hope will be renewed; it is the expectation of the coming of the Lord by his anointed, the Messiah.

Through David, it is principally to his Son, Jesus Christ, that God the Father promised love and faithfulness, prosperity and perpetual royal stability upon the new Israel, the Church. Even though catastrophes of all kinds seem to belie God's loving faithfulness, we can pray this psalm with complete confidence.

89:1 *Maskil:* see note on Ps 32:1a. *Ethan the Ezrahite:* he is thought to be the son of Zerah (hence, Ezrahite) and member of the tribe of Judah (see 1 Chr 2:6) as well as founder of one of the three choirs (see 1 Chr 15:19) and identical with the Jeduthun of Ps 39 (see 2 Chr 5:12).

89:2-5 God is true. If anything is certain, it is his kindness and faithfulness. They endure without fail in creation, and they endure in the covenant with David (see 2 Sam 7:8-16; 1 Chr 17:10-15), on which Israel's Messianic Hope is based.

89:2 *Kindness . . . faithfulness:* see notes on Pss 6:5; 36:6f. These words are each repeated eight times in the psalm. *Kindness:* verses 2-3, 15, 18, 25, 29, 34, 50, and *faithfulness:* verses 2-3, 6, 9, 15, 25, 34, 50.

89:5 Despite the fall of the Davidic monarchy, God remains faithful to his covenant, which is an eternal covenant (see 2 Sam 7:16; Isa 54:10; 55:3; 61:8; Jer 31:31-34; Ezek 16:60; 37:26) and the foundation of the Messianic Hope.

89:6-19 The psalmist sings of God's greatness in the secret of heaven where he is surrounded by angels (the *holy ones* and *any heavenly being*, vv. 6-7). He declares the power of the One who created the earth and rules the primitive chaos, symbolized by the mythological monster Rahab. The more deeply the believer divines the mystery of God, the more overwhelmed he becomes with joy.

89:6 *The heavens:* i.e., all beings who are part of God's heavenly kingdom. *Wonders:* see note on Ps 9:2. *Assembly of your holy ones:* the great council in heaven (see Ps 82:1).

89:7 *Heavenly being:* literally, "son of God" (see note on Ps 29:1).

9 O LORD, God of hosts, * who is like you?
Almighty LORD, your faithfulness is never absent.
10 [d] You control the raging sea,
calming its surging waves.
11 You crushed Rahab * with a deadly blow;
you scattered your foes with your mighty arm.
12 Yours are the heavens and yours is the earth;
you founded the world * and all that is in it. [e]
13 You created the north and the south; *
Tabor and Hermon joyously praise your name.
14 Mighty is your arm and strong is your hand;
your right hand is forever raised high.
15 Righteousness and justice are the foundation of your throne;
kindness and faithfulness go before your face. * [f]
16 Blessed * are the people who know how to acclaim you, O LORD,
who walk in the light of your countenance.
17 In your name they rejoice all day long,
and they exult in your righteousness. [g]
18 * You are the strength in which they glory,
and by your kindness our horn * is exalted. [h]
19 For the LORD is our shield,
the Holy One of Israel, our King. [i]
20 * On one occasion you spoke in a vision *
and said to your faithful servants: [j]
"I have appointed as leader one who is mighty;
I have exalted one chosen from the people.
21 I have found David, my servant,
and with my holy oil I have anointed him.
22 [k] "My hand will sustain him;
my arm will make him strong.
23 No enemy will overcome him;
no one who is wicked will oppress him.
24 "I will crush his foes before him
and strike down those who hate him.
25 My faithfulness and my kindness will be with him;
through my name his horn will be exalted.
26 "I will stretch his hand as far as the sea
and his right hand as far as the rivers. *
27 He will cry to me, 'You are my Father, [l]
my God, the Rock of my salvation.'
28 * "I will designate him as my firstborn,
the highest of all earthly kings.
29 [m] Forever I will maintain my kindness for him,
and my covenant with him will never end.
30 I will establish his dynasty forever
and his throne as long as the heavens.

d 10-11: Pss 65:8; 68:2; 74:13-15; 107:29; Job 7:12; Isa 51:9-10.—e Pss 24:1-2; 50:12; Deut 10:14; 1 Chr 29:11; 1 Cor 10:26.—f Pss 85:11-12; 97:2; Ex 34:6-7.—g Pss 30:5; 47:2; 105:3; Zep 3:14.—h Pss 18:2; 75:11; 92:11; 112:9; 148:14.—i Pss 18:3; 47:9; 96:10; 97:1; 99:1; Isa 6:3; 16:5; 33:17, 22.—j 20-21: Pss 78:70; 132:11-12; Ex 29:7; 2 Sam 7:4, 8:16; 1 Ki 1:39; 1 Chr 17:3, 7-14; Isa 42:1; Acts 13:22.—k 22-25: Ps 18:36; 1 Sam 2:9-10.—l 27-28: Pss 2:6; 110:2-3; 2 Sam 7:9, 14; Jer 3:19; Col 1:15; Jn 20:17; Rev 1:15.—m 29-30: Pss 18:51; 61:8; 144:10; 2 Sam 7:11; Isa 55:3.

89:9-10 *LORD, God of hosts:* see note on Ps 59:6. *Sea:* see note on Ps 65:8.

89:11 *Rahab:* a mythical sea monster that may be another name for Leviathan (see Pss 74:14; 104:26) and is used in the Old Testament primarily as a personification of the primeval chaos. Here it is a symbol of God's dominance of the sea and all rebellious creatures. *You scattered . . . arm:* cited in Lk 1:51.

89:12 *Heavens . . . earth . . . world:* the Lord is the almighty Creator of the heavens and the earth as well as everything in them. He is the benign Ruler of these same areas with a love that extends through them to the Messianic Kingdom, symbolized by David (vv. 4, 21). Thus, he not only created but also redeemed them.

89:13 *The north and the south:* some believe that the Hebrew words for these two geographical poles (*saphon* and *yamin*) are the names of two sacred mountains in northern Syria: Mount Zaphon (see Ps 48:3 and note; Jos 13:27; Jdg 12:1; Isa 14:13) and Mount Amana (see Song 4:8), paralleling the mountains Tabor and Hermon (which also stand for east and west). *Tabor:* a low mountain in the Valley of Jezreel in northern Israel. *Hermon:* a tall mountain in Lebanon that marks the southern limit of the Anti-Lebanon range. *Joyously praise:* see note on Ps 65:14.

89:15 The divine attributes are personified (see Pss 85:11-12; 97:2).

89:16 *Blessed:* see note on Ps 1:1. *How to acclaim you:* literally, "the joyful shout."

89:18-19 These verses serve as a transition to the great oracle that follows. The Davidic dynasty and the coming of the Messiah-King depend completely on the Lord.

89:18 *Horn:* symbolizes strong one (see also Ps 18:3, and note, Ps 75:11).

89:20-38 This powerful and faithful God has revealed to his *faithful servants* (the prophets Samuel and Nathan) his plan for David and his posterity. It is a promise that cannot be effaced, a covenant that will never be revoked. It is guaranteed by God's kindness and faithfulness.

89:20 *Vision:* the revelation made to Samuel (see 1 Sam 16:12) or to Nathan (see 2 Sam 7:4-16). *Faithful servants:* those faithful to his covenant.

89:26 *Sea . . . rivers:* David's dominion would extend from the Mediterranean Sea (west) to the Tigris and Euphrates Rivers (east). See Pss 72:8; 80:1.

89:28-30 The only one in whom these promises are fulfilled is Jesus Christ. This is hinted at by the use of *firstborn* and *highest*, which in Hebrew is *elyon*, a divine name (see Ps 83:19) applied to the Messiah, the Son of God (see 2 Sam 7:14; Jn 20:17) and supreme king (see Col 1:18; Rev 1:5).

31 * [n] "If his descendants forsake my law
and refuse to conform to my decrees,
32 if they break my statutes
and do not keep my precepts,
33 I will punish their disobedience with the rod
and their iniquity with scourges.

34 "But I will not deprive him of my kindness
or fail to observe my faithfulness. * [o]
35 * I will not violate my covenant
or alter the promise I have spoken. [p]

36 "By my holiness I have sworn once and for all:
never will I break faith with David. [q]
37 [r] His dynasty will last forever,
and his throne will endure before me like the sun.
38 It will endure forever like the moon,
a faithful witness in the sky." *Selah*

39 * [s] But now you have spurned and rejected him,
you have become filled with wrath against your anointed one. *
40 You have repudiated your covenant with your servant
and dishonored his crown in the dust.

41 [t] You have breached all his walls
and turned his strongholds into ruins.
42 Every passer-by has despoiled him;
he has become a laughingstock to his neighbors.
43 * You have exalted the right hand of his foes
and caused all his enemies to rejoice. [u]
44 You have driven back his drawn sword
and left him to fight without your support.

45 You have put an end to his glory
and toppled his throne to the ground.
46 You have curtailed the time of his youth *
and enveloped him in shame. *Selah*

47 * How long, O LORD? Will you remain hidden forever?
How long * will your wrath blaze like a fire? [v]
48 Remember how brief is my span of life
and how weak you have made all mortals. [w]

49 Who can live and never experience death?
Who can save himself from the power of the netherworld? [x] *Selah*
50 * Where is your kindness of old, O LORD,
which you swore to David in your faithfulness?

51 Remember, O LORD, the insults hurled at your servant;
recall how I have borne in my heart the slanders of all the peoples. [y]
52 Your enemies have leveled insults at us, O LORD;
they have taunted the footsteps of your anointed one.

53 Blessed be the LORD forever.
Amen! Amen! * [z]

n 31-33: Lev 26:14-33; 2 Sam 7:14.—o Ps 40:12; 2 Sam 7:15; Sir 47:22.—p Num 23:19; Jer 33:20-21.—q Ps 110:4; Am 4:2.—r 37-38: Pss 61:8; 72:5; Sir 43:6.—s 39-47: Ps 44:10-25.—t 41-42: Ps 80:13-14; Isa 22:5.—u Pss 13:3; 44:14; 79:4; 123:3-4; Job 12:4; Lam 1:15; Dan 9:16; Zep 2:8.—v Pss 13:2; 44:25; 74:10; 79:5; Deut 4:24.—w Pss 39:5-6; 62:10; 90:9-10; 144:4; Gen 47:9; Job 7:6, 16; 14:1, 5; Wis 2:5; Eccl 6:12; 1 Pet 1:24.—x Pss 22:30; 90:3; Gen 5:24.—y Pss 69:20; 79:12.—z Pss 41:14; 72:18f; 106:48; 150.

89:31-38 God's promises can be said to be partly provisional and partly absolute. As provisional promises, they were not fulfilled in David's descendants who did not carry out the conditions of the covenant (vv. 31-33). As absolute promises, they were fulfilled in the Son of God, who is also the Son of David (vv. 34-38).

89:34 *Fail to observe my faithfulness:* see 2 Sam 7:15.

89:35-36 See Ps 110:4; Isa 31:2; 55:3; Jer 33:20ff; Am 4:2.

89:39-46 Seemingly, God has renounced his covenant. The temple is sacked, the village ruined, the kingship laid open to scorn, contrary to the word given to David. It is of little import as to why such an evil has occurred; the important thing is that God seems inconsistent.

89:39-42 The actions recounted here (repudiating a covenant, casting a crown in the dust, and destroying fortifications) are ordinarily attributed to Israel's enemies. Here, however, they are attributed to the Lord himself, who is seen as repudiating the provisional covenant he had made with his people.

89:43-46 The psalmist asserts that it is the Lord who has enabled Israel's enemies to carry off a victory over his people. As a result, David's throne and his honor have been toppled to the ground and his dynasty is enveloped with shame and disgrace.

89:46 *Curtailed the time of his youth:* the Israelite royalty enjoyed only four and a half centuries of independence: this was the time of its youth (see Ps 129:1) after its birth in the wilderness (see Isa 46:3; Jer 2:2; Hos 11:1).

89:47-52 The psalmist agonizes over the sad state of affairs in his day and puts questions to the Lord. At the same time, he prays to God to remember that his people are weak and ephemeral. If the Lord continues to hide his face, the people may lapse into despair. Hence, the Lord should renew his *kindness* during the psalmist's lifetime. For the people are perishing, the *anointed one* is mocked, and the acts of God's kindness that he promised to David are not forthcoming. The psalmist prays that such acts will return once again.

89:47-49 To give himself hope, the psalmist begs God not to let him die without having assisted at the renewal of the covenant. *How long . . . ?:* see note on Ps 6:4.

89:50-52 May the God who made the promise to David not prove insensitive to the king removed from his throne and the people exiled from their kingdom and forced to experience the taunts of the Gentiles. The believer awaits a new discovery of God, as happened in days gone by at the beginnings of love.

89:53 This doxology is not a part of the psalm but a conclusion to Book III of the Psalter added by a redactor (see note on Ps 41:14).

BOOK IV—PSALMS 90–106*

PSALM 90*

Prayer To Use Time Wisely

1 A prayer of Moses, the man of God. *

LORD, you have been our refuge
from generation to generation.
2 Before the mountains were brought forth
or the earth and the world came into existence,
from everlasting to everlasting you are God. [a]

3 You turn men back to dust,
saying, "Return, * you children of men." [b]
4 For to you a thousand years
are like a yesterday that has passed [c]
or one of the watches of the night. *

5 You snatch them away like a dream; [d]
they are like the grass of the field, *
6 which at dawn flourishes and is green
but by nightfall is withered and dry. [e]

7 *We have been brought low by your anger
and overwhelmed with terror by your wrath.
8 You have not forgotten our iniquities;
our secret sins are clearly visible in your sight. [f]

9 [g] All our days pass away under your wrath;
our years are consumed like a sigh.
10 The span of our life numbers seventy years,
or perhaps eighty, if we have enough strength.
Most of them are marked by toil and emptiness; *
they pass swiftly, and then we fly away.

11 *Who understands the might of your anger
and rightly fears the power of your wrath?
12 Teach us to comprehend how few our days are
so that our hearts may be filled with wisdom.

13 Return, * O LORD. How long must we wait?
Show compassion to your servants.
14 Fill us with your kindness in the morning *[h]
so that we may exult and be glad all our days.

15 Grant us joy for as many days as you have afflicted us
and for as many years as we have known misfortune. [i]

a Pss 48:14f; 55:20; 93:2; 102:13; 135:13; 145:13; Gen 1:1; Ex 15:18; 2 Sam 7:16; Prov 8:25; Isa 55:13; Lam 5:19; Hab 1:12.—b Pss 103:14; 104:29; 146:4; Gen 3:19; 1 Mac 2:63; Job 34:14-15; Eccl 3:20; 12:7; Sir 40:11; 1 Cor 15:47.—c Job 10:5; 2 Pet 3:8.—d Ps 89:48; Gen 19:15.—e Pss 37:2; 102:12; 103:15-16; Job 14:1-2; Isa 40:6-8; Mt 6:30; Jas 1:10.—f Ps 109:14-15; Hos 7:2; Eph 5:12.—g 9-10: Pss 39:5-7; 62:10; 78:33; 102:24-25; 144:4; Gen 6:3; 2 Sam 19:35; Job 7:6, 16; 14:5; Prov 10:27; Wis 2:5; Eccl 6:12; Sir 18:8; Isa 65:20.—h Pss 5:12; 17:15; 31:8; 65:5; 85:7; 103:5.—i Num 14:34; Jer 31:13.

Pss 90–106 Joined to a series of very diverse psalms, many of which lack superscription or indication of origin, is a well-defined group: the psalms of the kingdom of God (Pss 93; 96–99). In this part of the Psalter, praise comes to the fore. The psalmists acclaim the Creator who brought the world into being as well as the Lord who intervenes in history. They await the God who comes to make all things new.

Ps 90 The psalmist (who is well versed in the Scriptures) herein depicts the dismal human condition as contrasted with the majesty and eternity of God. The Lord alone remains. Man passes away, a derisory creature undermined by sin; even if his life is lengthy, it remains precarious. The ancient account of the fall and the malediction of Adam (see Gen 3:19) illustrates the *origin* of our human condition: the ancients accept it with some distress and resignation (see the Book of Ecclesiastes). Man's days are numbered, and it is wisdom to reflect on this fact.

However, such lucidity does not exclude the joy that comes when God's presence illumines the days that he accords to each one and the times that he prepares for his people. This meditation of wisdom becomes a prayer of conversion.

Praying with the expressive formulas of the psalmist will teach us to contemplate the eternity of God and aid us to be detached from the present life, sin, and death, which can prevent us from entering into eternal life.

90:1 *Man of God:* a phrase usually applied to prophets (see 1 Sam 2:27), including Moses (see Deut 33:1; Jos 14:6).

90:3 *Return:* by a word of the Lord, human beings return to the dust from which they were made (see Gen 2:7; 3:19).

90:4 A thousand years are for God like one day or, even less, like a fraction of one night—like one of the three watches into which the night was divided (see Jdg 7:19). This verse is cited in 2 Pet 3:8.

90:5 The life of people is like that of the new grass that appears at dawn and disappears by nightfall under the burning rays of the sun (see Pss 103:16f; 129:6; Job 14:1f; Isa 40:6f). They have no longevity.

90:7-10 Short though it is, human life is filled with trouble because of sin and God's righteous wrath.

90:10 *Most of them are marked by toil and emptiness:* an alternative translation is: "Yet their span is but emptiness and sorrow" (see Gen 6:3; Job 20:8; Prov 10:27; Eccl 12:1ff; Sir 18:8f).

90:11-12 The psalmist prays that God may teach his people to appreciate the number of years given them and to use them in doing God's will. He asks that they may acquire a correct view of life so as not to challenge God's wrath but rather work out their salvation throughout their life. All this is given us in wisdom, which discerns the true values and gives the righteous a realistic attitude in accord with the divine will and adapted to circumstances (see Deut 4:6; 32:29). *Hearts:* see note on Ps 4:8.

90:13 The psalmist now extends to Israel the meditation and prayer that concerned all humanity. *Return:* i.e., "relent." *How long . . . ?:* see note on Ps 6:4.

90:14 The psalmist prays that *in the morning* (the typical time for deliverance and salvation: see note on Ps 49:15) God's love will put an end to the long night of their trial. The fulfillment of this prayer is found in the resurrection (see Rom 5:2-5; 8:18; 2 Cor 4:16-18). *Kindness:* see note on Ps 6:5.

16 Manifest your works to your servants
and your glory to their children.
17 May the favor * of the LORD, our God, rest upon us.
And may the work of our hands prosper—
indeed, may the work of our hands prosper. [j]

PSALM 91*

Security under God's Protection

1 You who abide in the shelter of the Most High, *
who rest in the shadow of the Almighty,
2 say to the LORD, "You are my refuge and my fortress,
my God in whom I place my trust." [k]
3 He will rescue you from the snare of the fowler *
and from virulent pestilence.
4 With his feathers he will shelter you, *
and you will take refuge under his wings;
his faithfulness serves as a protective shield. [l]
5 You will not fear the terror by night *
nor the arrow that flies by day, [m]
6 nor the pestilence that stalks in darkness,
nor the plague * that lays waste at midday. [n]
7 Even though a thousand may fall at your side,
ten thousand at your right hand,
such evils will not afflict you.
8 Rather, your own eyes will behold *
the punishment inflicted on the wicked. [o]
9 You have made the LORD your refuge
and chosen the Most High to be your dwelling.
10 Therefore, no evil will threaten you,
no calamity will come near your dwelling. [p]
11 * For he will command his angels * about you— [q]
to guard you wherever you go. [r]
12 They will lift you up with their hands, [s]
lest you dash your foot against a stone. *
13 You will tread upon the asp and the viper; [t]
you will trample the lion and the dragon. *
14 * "Because he loves me, I will deliver him,

j Ps 33:22; Isa 26:12; Hab 3:2.—k Pss 9:10; 18:3; 31:3-4; 42:10; 142:6; 2 Sam 22:2.—l Pss 17:8; 35:2; 36:8; 57:2; 63:8; Deut 32:10; Ru 2:12; Isa 31:5; Mt 23:37.—m Job 5:21; Prov 3:25; Song 3:8.—n Deut 32:24; Jer 15:8.—o Pss 37:34; 92:12.—p Deut 7:15; Prov 12:21.—q 11-12: Mt 4:6; Lk 4:10f.—r Ps 34:7; Heb 1:14.—s Ps 121:3; Prov 3:23.—t Job 5:22; Isa 11:8; Dan 6:22; Lk 10:19.

90:17 *Favor:* another translation is "beauty," which constitutes the Lord's "goodness" (see Ps 27:4 and note). Thus, the psalmist asks for God's loving help to his people, so that their work may be effective and enduring, even though the workers are apt to disappear quickly. *Indeed, may the work of our hands prosper:* this second occurrence of these words may be an accidental repetition.

Ps 91 This pilgrimage psalm is a glowing testimony to the security that God bestows on those who come to the temple to place themselves under his protection. They will be strengthened by God and his angels all along the path of life in which perils and snares proliferate on every side: the terror by night, the arrow by day, the fowler's snare, pestilence, and plague, as well as the asp and viper, lion and dragon—in a word, every possible threat. Death itself seems to retreat, and one gets a glimpse of the peace and joy of the Messianic Age.

En route toward Jerusalem, or toward God, every believer is a pilgrim. The itinerary is not an idyllic dream; rather, amidst risks and dangers, the Lord delivers us from fear and leads us to salvation, to life in his presence. This peaceful psalm is especially suited to be an evening prayer.

We can regard this psalm as an exhortation of Christ developing the invitation that he addressed to his disciples after the Last Supper: "Do not let your hearts be troubled. You place your trust in God [the Father]. Trust also in me" (Jn 14:1). We are to journey along the path of life with the constant certitude that the divine Persons surround us with a never-ending solicitude.

91:1 *The shelter of the Most High:* a designation in the psalms for the temple (see Pss 27:5; 31:21; 61:5). *The shadow of the Almighty:* literally, "the shadow of the wings of the Almighty" (see Pss 17:8; 36:8; 57:2; 63:8). As indicated by verse 4, the shadow is an image of the safety to be found under the outstretched wings of the cherubim in the Holy of Holies. *Almighty:* literally, "Shaddai," an ancient name for God (see note on Ps 68:15).

91:3 *Snare of the fowler:* a proverbial phrase for danger (see Ps 124:7; Prov 6:5; Hos 9:8).

91:4 *With his feathers he will shelter you:* traditional biblical image (see note on Ps 17:8).

91:5 *Terror by night:* resulting from true or false alerts of enemy attacks; attacks by day were announced by flying *arrows*.

91:6 *Pestilence . . . plague:* dreaded mortal diseases that frequently grew into epidemics (see Deut 32:24; Hos 13:14; Hab 3:5). In place of the *plague that lays waste at midday*, other versions have: "devil at noon" or the "noonday devil" (apparently a mythological expression for a contagious disease presumed to be caused by the noonday sun).

91:8 *Your own eyes will behold:* the righteous will be merely a spectator to the threats mentioned and not be harmed by them.

91:11-12 These words were cited by Satan when tempting Christ to presumption against divine providence (Mt 4:6; Lk 4:10f).

91:11 *His angels:* the teaching on guardian angels is common in the Old Testament (see Ps 34:7; Gen 24:7; Ex 23:20).

91:12 *Against a stone:* along the stony paths of Canaan (see Ps 23:3).

91:13 *Asp . . . viper . . . lion . . . dragon:* these terms correspond to the references found in verses 5-6 and complete the list of deadly threats against God's servants (see Am 5:19).

91:14-16 The psalmist reinforces his message by utilizing the form of a prophetic oracle in which God promises Messianic blessings to all who put their trust in him (see Ps 50:15, 23; Rom 8:30).

I will raise high * the one who acknowledges my name. [u]
15 When he calls to me, I will answer,
and I will be with him in time of distress;
I will rescue him and cause him to be honored. * [v]
16 I will reward him with a long life
and show him my salvation." * [w]

PSALM 92*

Praise of God's Just Rule

1 A psalm. A song. For the Sabbath. *
2 It is good to give thanks to the LORD, [x]
to sing praise to your name, * O Most High,
3 to proclaim your kindness * in the morning
and your faithfulness during the night,
4 with the ten-stringed harp,
to the melody of the lyre. [y]
5 * Your deeds, O LORD, have caused me to exult;
at the works of your hands I shout for joy:
6 [z] How great are your deeds, O LORD!
How profound are your thoughts!
7 * A senseless person cannot grasp this;
a fool * is unable to comprehend it.
8 Even though the wicked may sprout like grass
and all evildoers may prosper, [a]
they are doomed to eternal destruction, *
9 whereas you, O LORD, are exalted forever. *
10 Surely your enemies, O LORD,
surely your enemies will perish,
and all evildoers will be scattered. [b]
11 * You have given me the strength of a wild bull [c]
and anointed me with fresh oil. [d]
12 My eyes have witnessed the downfall of my enemies;
my ears have heard the rout of my wicked foes. [e]
13 * The righteous will flourish like the palm tree;
they will grow like a cedar of Lebanon. [f]
14 They are planted in the house of the LORD *
and will flourish in the courts of our God.
15 They still will bear fruit, in their old age,
and they will remain fresh and green,
16 proclaiming, "The LORD is upright;
he is my Rock, in whom no injustice can be found." [g]

u Pss 9:11; 119:132.—v Isa 43:2; Jer 33:3; Zec 13:9; Jn 12:26.—w Pss 21:5; 50:23; Deut 6:2; Prov 3:2.—x Pss 9:3; 27:6; 33:1; 135:3; 147:1.—y Pss 33:2; 71:22; 144:9.—z 6-7: Pss 111:2; 131:1; 139:6, 17; Wis 13:1; 17:1; Rev 15:3.—a Ps 37:2,35.—b Pss 45:5; 68:2-3; 125:5.—c Pss 75:11; 89:18; Deut 33:17.—d Ps 23:5.—e Pss 54:9; 91:8.—f Pss 1:3; 52:10; Jer 17:8; Hos 14:6.—g Deut 32:4; Job 34:10.

91:14 *Raise high:* i.e., "raise him to a high, safe place." *My name:* see note on Ps 5:12.

91:15 The Lord gives assurance that his faithful will be *honored* for living honestly; they will enjoy themselves as his children in this life (see Pss 73:24; 112:9; 149:5; Isa 43:2; Jer 33:3).

91:16 *With a long life . . . my salvation:* for the sages of Israel, a long life is the reward of the righteous (see Ex 23:26; Deut 4:40; 1 Sam 2:30; Job 5:26; Prov 3:2, 16; 10:27), crowned by salvation (see 1 Tim 4:8f).

Ps 92 This is a didactic psalm, that is, both a praise of the Lord and an instruction for the faithful. The psalmist meditates on God's way of acting. His love and faithfulness are reflected in everything he does, but they must be comprehended. Ultimately the happiness of the wicked will fade like seasonal grass, whereas the lot of the righteous will be like the great trees whose roots are planted in solid ground. For the latter, new seasons are promised in the courts of God. God's joy is like a new spring in the life of believers.

We can make use of this psalm in following Christ's lead to praise the triune God, to sing of the wondrous divine work that delivers us from our spiritual enemies and mysteriously introduces us into eternal life.

92:1 *For the Sabbath:* these words indicate that in the post-exilic temple liturgy this psalm was sung at the time of the morning sacrifice on the Sabbath or seventh day. Psalms sung on the other days were: Ps 24, first day; Ps 48, second day; Ps 82, third day; Ps 94, fourth day; Ps 81, fifth day; and Ps 93, sixth day.

92:2 Human beings have the duty to praise the Lord Most High (see note on Ps 7:18). *Name:* see note on Ps 5:12.

92:3 *Kindness:* see note on Ps 6:5.

92:5-6 God's great deeds (of creating, redeeming, and ruling human beings) bring joy to the psalmist and all who have understanding through his grace.

92:7-10 Evildoers have no knowledge of the Lord's deeds or his dispensing of justice; they are seemingly happy and prosperous now, but they will soon perish under the just judgment of the Lord.

92:7 *Senseless person . . . fool:* enemies of God and his faithful (see notes on Pss 14:1-2; see also Pss 37:33ff; 68:3; 83:4; 94:8-11).

92:8 This verse summarizes the fuller description concerning the wicked in Ps 73. See notes on Ps 90:4, 5.

92:9 *Exalted forever:* since God reigns forever, there is no hope of escape for the senseless.

92:11-12 The psalmist has experienced victory over his enemies thanks to the Lord's doing. He is overjoyed with God's favors (see vv. 5-6). *Strength:* literally, "horn" (see Ps 75:11; Deut 33:17; Lk 1:69). The Lord has enabled him to gain the victory (see Ps 89:23-26) and anointed him with *fresh oil*, i.e., "the oil of gladness" (Ps 45:8; see also Ps 23:5).

92:13-16 In contrast to the lot of the wicked, the righteous are exalted and renewed in their strength and happiness.

92:14 *Planted in the house of the LORD:* the righteous are likened to trees growing in the temple itself, which is a source of life and fertility because of the divine presence (see Ps 36:8-10; Ezek 47:1-12).

PSALM 93*

Glory of the LORD's Kingdom

1 The LORD is King, * adorned in splendor;
the LORD has clothed and girded himself with strength.
* He has made the world firm,
never to be moved. [h]
2 Your throne has stood firm from the beginning;
you have existed throughout eternity, O LORD. [i]
3 The waters * have lifted up, O LORD;
the waters have lifted up their voice;
the waters have lifted up their roar.
4 More powerful than the roar of mighty waters,
more powerful than the crashing waves of the sea, [j]
mighty on high is the LORD. *
5 Your decrees * are firmly established;
holiness adorns your house,
O LORD, throughout the ages.

PSALM 94*

God, Judge, and Avenger

1 O LORD, you are an avenging God; *
shine forth, O God of vengeance. [k]
2 Rise up, O judge of the earth;
repay * the arrogant as they deserve. [l]
3 O LORD, how long will the wicked,
how long will the wicked be triumphant? * [m]
4 * Their mouths pour forth their arrogant words

h Pss 47:8; 75:4; 96:10; 97:1; 99:1; 104:5; Isa 52:7.—i Pss 55:20; 90:2; 102:13; 2 Sam 7:16; Hab 1:12.—j Pss 18:5; 65:8; Jer 6:23; Mk 8:39.—k Deut 32:35, 41; Nah 1:2.—l Num 10:35; Jer 51:56; Lam 3:64.—m Pss 13:3; 75:5; Jer 12:1

Ps 93 This is one of the nine psalms of the kingdom (Pss 47; 93–100), most of which feature the liturgical acclamation "The LORD is King," in which is centered the whole faith of Israel. All these hymns exalt the kingdom of God that extends over the entire universe and dominates the course of time. God reveals his kingship when he brings forth the world; he does so even more when he chooses Israel. Nonetheless, creation and history are still only the beginning and promise; the kingdom of God will be manifested in all its glory at the end of time (see Rev 4:11; 11:15-17): a new heaven, a new earth, and a new Jerusalem—such are the images that allow us to glimpse the joy of a new humanity gathered together in the glory of God (see Rev 21:1—22:5). The acclamation of the psalms of the kingdom already vibrates with this ineffable hope.

Psalm 93 exalts the Lord who reigns, robed in majesty. He affirms his greatness by the forces of creation that he rules, by the law—or "decrees"—that he gives to his people, and by the temple of Jerusalem that he consecrates to his mysterious presence. From his earthly experience, the believer acclaims the splendor of a kingdom that can have no end.

In all truth, we can regard this psalm as applicable to Christ's kingship and sing: "Christ is King." For he vanquishes in himself and in his followers all hostile powers (Satan, death, and sin), delivering believers from the reign of death and transferring them into his kingdom (see Eph 1:2). This is the extraordinary wonder that he continues across the centuries until the full deliverance of his Church and the definitive destruction of his enemies will occur (see Rev 20–22).

93:1a-b *The LORD is King:* a liturgical acclamation that sums up the entire faith of Israel (see Pss 96:10; 97:1; 99:1; see also Zec 14:9).

93:1c-2 The Lord established his kingdom on earth when he created the world and everything in it (see Ps 24:1). Hence, the world will not be moved no matter what pressure is brought to bear on it by hostile forces (see Pss 10:6; 104:5), because the Lord has established his rule over it. Indeed, the Lord is eternal (see Ps 90:2), but his rule was established when his throne was set up at the beginning of history with the creation ("from the beginning"; see Isa 44:8; 45:21; 48:3-8).

93:3 *Waters:* the waters of the primeval chaos that the Lord mastered through his creative word (see Pss 33:7; 104:7-9; Gen 1:6-10; Job 38:8-11; see also note on Ps 65:8). They can also stand for the enemies of God and his people (see Job 7:12; Isa 8:7; 17:12; Jer 46:8; Dan 7:2; Rev 17:15) as well as the ocean currents, whose powers were feared by the pagan nations as indicated in the mythical account of Baal's victory over the sea god Yamm.

93:4 The Lord is the Master of the thundering storms and surging waves by his simple word (see Christ's calming of the storm by a single word in Mk 4:39).

93:5 *Decrees:* these divine judgments constitute revelation in the wide sense insofar as they are the norm of human life (see Ps 119). As stable (see Ps 19:8) as the physical universe and as inviolable (see Ps 95:8-11) as the sanctuary of Jerusalem, this revelation will be the foundation of the Lord's definitive kingdom, inaugurated from the creation and already effective in Israel (see Isa 51:9f, 13; 52:7). *Holiness adorns your house . . . throughout the ages:* the temple, home of the King of Israel, is consecrated forever (1 Ki 8:13; 9:3; Jud 9:1-8; Ezek 42:13f; Rev 21:27). Those who approach the most holy God (see Ps 99) are also consecrated (see Ex 19:6; Lev 10:3; 19:2).

Ps 94 Distressed at God's delays in dispensing justice, the psalmist utters this cry of impatience. Why does God not intervene immediately against the wickedness that crushes the lowly? The reflection of this sage tells him that, despite appearances, the lot of the righteous is in the final analysis the only one that matters. Certainly God's hour will come when the Lord will avenge his "heritage," the true Israel, that is, the poor. He cannot remain indifferent to wrongs and evils that the innocent endure nor suffer the scorn of haughty spirits and wicked hearts. As "an avenging God," he authorizes no one to launch individual reprisals; it is he himself who reestablishes a justice that is troubled by the arrogance of men to the plight of the poor. These comparative tableaus of the arrogant and the innocent have the astonishing power to challenge us: is our life marked by this sense of justice?

Placed in a condition similar to that of the psalmist, we can pray this psalm to implore the divine intervention against those who exploit our brothers and sisters. At the same time, we can use it to proclaim that trials, far from crushing us, instruct us and enable us to discover true joy and happiness in the love of God (see Jn 15:9-11).

94:1 *An avenging God:* i.e., one who redresses wrongs (see Deut 32:35, 41). It is God's prerogative to avenge, as Paul declares in Rom 12:19.

94:2 *Repay:* the central theme of the psalm: God is righteous and repays both the good and the bad as they deserve (see Pss 7:7; 28:4; 62:13; Lam 3:64; Joel 3:4).

94:3 *How long . . . ?:* see note on Ps 6:4.

94:4-7 Not only do the wicked hurl arrogant words, but they also attack God's people, especially those to whom the Lord has promised his protection: the widows, orphans, and aliens (see Ex 22:21; Deut 24:17; Isa 1:17; 10:2; Ezek 22:7). They no longer believe that God is concerned with their activities or demands an accounting from them (see Ps 10:2-11).

as these evildoers never cease to boast. [n]
5 They crush your people, O LORD,
and they oppress your heritage.
6 They slay the widow and the foreigner
and put the orphan to death. [o]
7 They say, "The LORD does not see;
the God of Jacob * pays no attention." [p]
8 * Try to comprehend, you senseless people.
You fools, when will you gain some wisdom? * [q]
9 Does the one who made the ear not hear?
Does the one who fashioned the eye not see? * [r]
10 Does the one who guides the nations * not punish?
Does the one who instructs people lack knowledge?
11 The LORD is well aware of our thoughts *
and how foolish they are. [s]
12 * Blessed * is the man you admonish, O LORD,
the man you teach by means of your law, [t]
13 giving him respite in times of misfortune
until a pit is dug for the wicked.
14 For the LORD will not abandon his people [u]
or forsake his heritage. *
15 Judgment will again be based on righteousness,
and all the upright in heart * will uphold it.
16 * Who will stand up for me against the wicked?
Who will defend me against evildoers?
17 If the LORD had not come to my aid,
I would long ago have been consigned to the kingdom of silence. * [v]
18 When I realized that my foot was slipping,
your kindness, * O LORD, raised me up. [w]
19 When my anxious thoughts multiplied,
your comfort filled my soul with joy. *
20 * Can evil rulers have you as an ally,
those who make use of the law to oppress the helpless? *
21 They conspire against the righteous *
and condemn the innocent to death.
22 But the LORD has been my stronghold, *
my God, the rock in whom I find refuge.
23 He will repay the wicked for their iniquity
and destroy them for their evil deeds; [x]
the LORD, our God, will destroy them. [y]

n Ps 73:7-12; Jer 43:2; Mal 2:17; 3:14.—o Ex 22:21-22; Deut 24:17-22; Isa 1:17.—p Pss 10:11; 64:6; 73:11; Job 22:13-14; Ezek 9:9.—q Deut 32:6; Prov 1:22; 8:5.—r Ex 4:11; Prov 20:12.—s Ps 33:15; Eccl 1:2; 1 Cor 3:20.—t Ps 119:71; Job 5:17; Heb 12:5.—u 1 Sam 12:22; Sir 47:22; Rom 11:1-2.—v Pss 115:17; 124:2.—w Ps 145:14; Deut 32:35f.—x Pss 7:17; 9:17; 35:8; 57:7; Prov 5:22; 26:27; Eccl 10:8; Sir 27:26.—y Pss 107:42; 145:20.

94:7 The psalmist presents an indictment of the wicked. See Pss 10:11; 64:6; 73:11; Ezek 9:9. *Jacob:* i.e., Israel (see Gen 32:29).

94:8-11 The wicked are *senseless* like animals (see Ps 92:7), *fools* (see Ps 49:11) without understanding. The Lord not only hears and sees and knows everything that takes place on earth but also metes out punishment for all wicked deeds.

94:8 This verse recalls Deut 32:6; Prov 1:22; 8:5.

94:9 See Ex 4:11; Prov 20:12; Lam 3:36.

94:10 *Guides the nations:* through chastisement (see Lev 26:18; Jer 31:18). *Instructs people:* about the natural and the supernatural order (see Deut 20:1-17; Isa 28:26).

94:11 This verse was probably added to comment on the preceding verse. It is cited by Paul in 1 Cor 3:20. See also Ps 44:2. *The LORD is well aware of our thoughts:* contrary to what the proud profess to believe.

94:12-15 The psalmist insists that all wisdom comes from God, even the wisdom found among the nations. Yet the Lord has bestowed upon his people a clearer form of instruction. Blessed are those instructed by God, for they know that the Lord sees all and doles out rewards and punishments in his own good time. The righteous receive his protection against all disasters and enjoy the promise of the kingdom, which all the upright in heart seek (see Mt 5:6; 6:33).

94:12 *Blessed:* see note on Ps 1:1. *Law:* in the wide sense, revelation and moral doctrine, as often used in the wisdom writings. This verse recalls Ps 119:71; Job 5:17.

94:14 God guides his people, especially the powerless, through difficult times because they are his possession, and he never rescinds his promises. On the day of the Lord, divine retribution will be meted out and justice will triumph. This verse is cited by Paul in Rom 11:1f.

94:15 The psalmist is certain that God will restore justice for the upright in heart. *Heart:* see note on Ps 4:8.

94:16-19 The faithful psalmist puts his trust only in God. When he was burdened with cares, temptations, difficulties, and trials, God was always there to help, console, and encourage him and bring joy to his soul.

94:17 *Kingdom of silence:* i.e., the silence of the netherworld (see Pss 88:4-6; 115:17).

94:18 The psalmist experienced the Lord's presence (see Ps 24:1) through the support of God's loving *kindness* (see note on Ps 6:5).

94:19 The psalmist was overcome with anxiety and close to despair because of his situation, but the Lord came to his aid and infused him with consolation and joy (see 2 Cor 1:5). *Soul:* see note on Ps 6:4.

94:20-23 The psalmist is confident that the Lord will save his people and call the wicked to account.

94:20 The Lord will never allow evil to be victorious over himself and his faithful ones for long.

94:21 *Righteous:* see note on Ps 1:5.

94:22-23 The Lord is the *stronghold* and *rock* of those who take refuge in him (see Pss 18:2f; 31:3) and the judge and chastiser of those who do evil (see Ps 7:12-17).

PSALM 95*

A Call To Praise and Obey God

1 *Come, let us sing with jubilation to the LORD;
let us cry out to the Rock of our salvation. [z]
2 Let us come before him with thanksgiving
and extol him with our songs.

3 *For the LORD is the great God,
the King who surpasses all other gods. *[a]
4 In his hands are the depths of the earth,
and the peaks of the mountains are his.
5 To him belongs the sea, for he created it, [b]
and also the dry land* that his hands have molded.

6 Come forth! Let us bow down to worship him;
let us kneel before the LORD, our Maker. *
7 For he is our God,
and we are the people he shepherds, *
the flock he protects. [c]
[d] If only you would listen to his voice today:
8 "Harden not your hearts as you did at Meribah, *
as on the day of Massah in the wilderness.
9 It was there that your ancestors sought to tempt me; [e]
they put me to the test
even though they had witnessed my works. *

10 "For forty years* I loathed that generation;
I said, 'They are a people whose hearts go astray,
and they do not know my ways.'[f]
11 Therefore, in my anger I swore,
'They will never enter my rest.' " *

z Ps 5:12; Deut 32:15.—a Pss 47:3; 96:4; 135:5.—b Pss 24:1-2; 146:6.—c Pss 23:1-3; 80:2; 100:3; Ezek 34:11; Mic 7:14.—d 7d-11: Pss 81:8; 106:32; Ex 19:5; Deut 12:9; Heb 3:7-11, 15; 4:3, 5, 7.—e Ex 17:1-7; Num 14:22; 20:2-13; Deut 6:16; 33:8; 1 Cor 10:9.—f Ps 78:8; Ex 16:35; Num 14:34; Deut 32:5f; Job 21:14; Prov 12:26; Isa 53:6.

Ps 95 This psalm calls upon the Israelites assembled in the temple to worship the Lord: "Come, let us sing with jubilation to the LORD." All are invited to give praise, and all acclaim the God of the Covenant. He is the Creator and sovereign Ruler of the world; he is the Shepherd who loves and saves Israel, his flock (see Ezek 34:11, 31; Jn 10).

The Prophets address their oracle to the crowd: "If only you would listen to his voice today. . . ." It is an exhortation to faithfulness, placing them on guard against the sins of yesteryear. The spirit of rebellion has no place in God's land (see Ex 17: 1-7; Num 20:13; Deut 6:16; 33:8).

The people tested God in the wilderness by doubting his power to save and deliver them at that moment despite everything he had done for them in the past. This is not the usual kind of doubt that may be experienced by any honest seeker after God in those times and circumstances when we may question the most fundamental truths of the faith. Rather, it is willful refusal to believe despite the evidence.

We refuse to believe in spite of all that we have seen and known about God. We doubt God's love and goodness despite overwhelming evidence of his care. This second kind of doubt comes from a hardened heart and cuts us off completely from growth in grace. And Scripture likens the sin of the people in the wilderness to this kind of doubt, terming it "refusing to believe" (Heb 4:11).

The Letter to the Hebrews gives a long commentary on this exhortation (3:7—4:11), and this invitation to praise God opens the Church's official prayer, the Liturgy of the Hours. Like Israel in the wilderness, the Church journeys on earth. Christians know God's promises, but they are equally familiar with temptation. If we wish to enter into the new Promised Land, that is, share God's life, we must persevere in the struggle for fidelity. Each day is the "today" in which we must heed the voice of God.

95:1-2 The first duty of the faithful toward God is one of praise and adoration (see Isa 66:18-23; Zec 14:16-21). Thus, the community of God's people is summoned to gather together to worship the Lord because of some act of deliverance that he has wrought. *Rock:* see note on Ps 18:3.

95:3-5 The Lord is *the great God, the King* who deserves to be exalted for he alone rules over all creation. He also rules over the *gods* of the nations. His creative works are the foundation of his kingship.

95:3 As the pagans had different gods for different peoples, regions of the earth and sky, and spheres of life (war, fertility), so, the psalmist indicates, do the Israelites. However, in their case, it is only the Lord who is God of every one of these spheres (*who surpasses all other gods*) (see Pss 47:3; 96:4; Job 36:22; Dan 2:47).

95:4-5 *Depths . . . peaks of the mountains . . . sea . . . dry land:* depths, heights, waters, and dry land—all are God's as well as everything in them.

95:6 Worship is a concrete expression of the people's devotion to their God. The reason for it is made clear by its placement between the Lord's universal kingship (vv. 3-5) and his covenant love for his people (v. 7).

95:7 As the "Maker" of his people (v. 6) because he has brought them into being as his covenant people (see Deut 32:6, 15, 18; Isa 44:2; 54:5), the Lord is also their shepherd, and they are *the people he shepherds* (see Pss 23:1; 79:13; 100:3; Jer 23:1; 25:36; Ezek 34:21; Jn 10:11-14). *If only you would listen to his voice today:* see Ps 81:8, 13; Ex 19:5; beginning with these words, verses 7-11 are cited in Heb 3:7-11.

95:8 *Meribah:* this word means "quarreling" and is the name of the place during the journey in the wilderness where the Israelites "sought to tempt" (v. 9) the Lord; *Massah:* this word means "testing" and is the name of the place where they tested the Lord (see Ex 17:7; Num 20:13). Scholars assign the first episode to a place near and to the southwest of Sinai and the second to a place near Kadesh-barnea in southern Palestine.

95:9 *Had witnessed my works:* God's wonders in Egypt, at the Red Sea, and in the wilderness (see Ex 16; Num 14:11, 22).

95:10 *Forty years:* Israel was condemned to wander forty years in the wilderness when the people refused to advance into Canaan and opted to return to Egypt instead (see Num 14:1-4, 34). *That generation:* the adults who were freed from Egypt and made a covenant with the Lord at Sinai (see Num 32:13). *Hearts:* see note on Ps 4:8. *My ways:* see note on Ps 25:4-7.

95:11 *My rest:* where the Lord had his dwelling (see Ps 132:7, 14) in the land of Canaan (see Deut 12:9; Ezek 20:15). In Heb 3:7ff, this rest is interpreted in the spiritual sense of heavenly beatitude.

PSALM 96*

God, Sovereign and Judge of the Universe

1 Sing to the LORD a new song; *
sing to the LORD, all the earth. [g]
2 Sing to the LORD and bless his name;
proclaim his salvation * day after day.

3 Declare his glory * among the nations,
his wondrous deeds to every people. [h]
4 For great is the LORD and worthy of all praise;
he is more to be feared * than all other gods. [i]

5 The gods of the nations are merely idols, [j]
but it was the LORD who made the heavens. *
6 Majesty and splendor surround him;
power and beauty * are in his sanctuary.

7 Render to the LORD, you families of nations,
render to the LORD glory and power. * [k]
8 Render to the LORD the glory due to his name;
bring an offering and enter his courts. *

9 Worship * the LORD in the splendor of his holiness;
tremble before him, all the earth.
10 Say among the nations, "The LORD is King. *
The world is firmly established, never to be moved.
He will judge the peoples fairly." [l]

11 Let the heavens exult and the earth be glad;
let the sea resound and all that fills it. [m]
12 Let the fields rejoice and all that is in them;
let all the trees * of the forest shout for joy
13 before the LORD, for he is coming,
coming to judge the earth.
He will judge the world with justice
and the nations with equity. * [n]

g Pss 30:4; 33:3; 98:1; Isa 42:10.—h Pss 98:4; 105:1; Rev 15:3.—i Pss 48:2; 89:8; 95:3; 145:3.—j Ps 97:7; Lev 19:4; Isa 40:17; 1 Cor 8:4.—k Pss 22:28; 29:2.—l Pss 67:5; 75:4; 93:1; 97:1.—m Pss 97:1; 98:7; Isa 49:13; Rev 12:12.—n Pss 7:12; 86:11; 98:9; Acts 17:31; Rev 19:11.

Ps 96 Partially cited in 1 Chr 16:23-33, this hymn is comprised of Old Testament reminiscences, especially from the Psalter and Isaiah (e.g., Ps 42:10; Isa 55:12). The peoples and nations of which it speaks were originally the neighbors who attempted to prevent Israel from becoming established in Canaan; later, they were all the peoples of the world who failed to recognize the one true God. Israel, which had been saved at the time of the Judges and brought back from an exile through which she had suffered a kind of annihilation, had experienced the Lord's deliverance more than once. She could well bear witness before the whole world of the power and superiority of the one sole God: the Lord had created the world and had given his people new life.

All peoples are invited to acknowledge him as the sovereign Master; all are summoned to the liturgy, to adoration. Deep emotion will grip the entire universe when God comes as Judge; he who has brought into being an unshakable world will establish all human beings in justice and righteousness.

This song of universal joy is always new with the newness of God himself; the New Testament (see Acts 17:31; Rev 19:11) refers to verse 13 in announcing the final coming of Christ on the day of judgment, when he will make all things new. Thus, by means of it, Christians call upon the whole universe to praise God the Father as well as the risen Jesus, whom the Father has made "Lord and Christ" (Acts 2:36), "leader and Savior" (Acts 5:31), and "ruler of the kings of the earth" (Rev 1:5).

According to the superscription in the Septuagint and Vulgate, this psalm was sung at the dedication of the post-exilic temple. Its Messianic content made it suitable for that occasion.

96:1 *New song:* see note on Ps 33:3. *All the earth:* see note on Ps 9:2; see also Pss 97:1; 100:1.

96:2 *Salvation:* the psalmist does not specify the precise nature of the "salvation" he mentions (see note on Ps 67:3-4). Most likely, it included all God's acts in redemptive history: creation and redemption (vv. 2, 11-12; see Ps 136:4-25). The People of God must assume the lead by praising the Lord (*bless his name*—see note on Ps 5:12) every day.

96:3 *Glory:* see note on Ps 85:10. *Wondrous deeds:* see note on Ps 9:2.

96:4 The Lord is great and worthy to receive praise and reverence (*to be feared*) because he alone is God and there is no other (see Ps 115).

96:5 *Made the heavens:* since the Lord made the heavens, which were supposedly the home of the gods, it follows that he is far greater than all the gods; but he is also greater because they are nothing more than idols.

96:6 The Lord is surrounded by personifications of divine attributes (*majesty and splendor . . . power and beauty*) that extol his universal kingship.

96:7 The psalmist makes use of Ps 29:1f, eliminating any allusion to the theme of "heavenly beings" (i.e., "sons of God") and accentuating the universalist tone (see Ps 47:10; Zec 14:17). All peoples are specifically summoned to pledge their obedience to the Lord.

96:8 *Courts:* i.e., of the temple where the Lord dwells (see Ps 84:3, 11; 2 Ki 21:5; 23:11f). The psalmist may have been thinking of the outermost court of the temple, which was the court of the Gentiles.

96:9 The psalmist calls for the people to *worship* the Lord, i.e., give him their reverence, submission, and awe because of the splendor of his holiness (see Pss 29:2; 99; 110:3; 1 Chr 16:29).

96:10 *The LORD is King:* see note on Ps 93:1a-b. The Lord is not only the Creator of all (as well as the Redeemer of all) but also the Judge of all. Greek and Latin manuscripts have a Christian addition: "from the wood" [of the cross]—a splendid expression of the theology of the cross found in the Gospel of John.

96:11-12 *Heavens . . . sea . . . fields . . . trees:* i.e., the whole world. By being what it is, God's creation gives him glory. However, it will rejoice even more when the fullness of redemption is attained, which it is presently awaiting together with all humanity (see Rom 8:21f).

96:13 The psalmist may have been thinking of the Lord's coming as the one in which he led the exiles back to Jerusalem. But the Lord comes in many ways. In Christ, the Lord came to fulfill the words of this psalm, bringing all peoples back to God, and he will come again at the end of time to judge the living and the dead (Acts 10:42; 17:31). His judgment is righteousness and truth.

PSALM 97*

Divine King and Universal Judge

1 The LORD is King; * let the earth exult;
let the distant isles rejoice. [o]
2 * Clouds and darkness * surround him;
righteousness and justice are the foundation of his throne. [p]
3 Fire * precedes him,
consuming his enemies on every side.
4 His flashes of lightning illumine the world;
the earth sees this and trembles. [q]
5 The mountains melt like wax before the LORD,
before the LORD of all the earth. [r]
6 The heavens proclaim his righteousness, *
and all the nations behold his glory. [s]
7 All who worship images are put to shame,
those who boast of their worthless idols;
bow down before him, all you gods. * [t]
8 Zion hears and rejoices,
and the cities * of Judah exult
because of your judgments, O LORD. [u]
9 For you, O LORD, are the Most High over all the earth;
you are exalted far above all gods. [v]
10 * Let those who love the LORD hate evil,
for he protects the souls of his faithful ones
and rescues them from the hand of the wicked. [w]
11 * Light dawns for the righteous,
and joy for the upright in heart. [x]
12 Rejoice in the LORD, you who are righteous,
and give thanks to his holy name. [y]

PSALM 98*

Praise of the LORD, King and Judge

1 A psalm.
Sing to the LORD a new song, * [z]
for he has accomplished marvelous deeds.
His right hand and his holy arm [a]
have made him victorious.
2 The LORD has made known his salvation;
he has manifested his righteousness for all the nations to see. *

o Pss 75:3; 93:1; 96:11; 99:1; Ex 15:18; Isa 52:7.—p Pss 85:11; 89:15; Ex 19:16; Deut 4:11; 5:22; 1 Ki 8:12; Job 22:14.—q Pss 18:8; 50:3; 77:19; 99:1; 104:32; Jdg 5:4-5.—r Ps 68:3; Jud 16:15; Mic 1:4.—s Pss 50:6; 98:6.—t Ps 96:5; Jer 10:14.—u Pss 9:3; 48:12.—v Pss 7:8; 83:19.—w Ps 121:7; Prov 8:13.—x Pss 4:7f; 112:4.—y Pss 30:5; 104:34.—z Pss 30:4; 96:1; Isa 42:10.—a Ps 44:3; Jos 4:24; Isa 59:16; 63:5; Lk 1:51.

Ps 97 Here is another hymn to King Yahweh, the only Lord and Savior. His coming is described with the grandiose and traditional images of divine manifestations (see Ex 19:16-20). These produce terror among idolaters and joy in Israel. By the time this song was written, all fear of foreign deities had disappeared among the Israelites; the gods themselves, or at least their worshipers, are invited to come and prostrate themselves before the only God. The people's faith in the only Lord is henceforth unshakable.

This majestic Lord is also the God who comes, the one who loves every righteous heart. Furthermore, this God of the universe who is praised is the very same God who is close to us along the paths of life.

The theme of the kingdom of God was dominant in the teaching of Jesus. According to John's Gospel, Jesus was enthroned on the cross and in his Resurrection-Ascension. Hence, as Christians pray this psalm, we can rejoice in Christ's rule.

According to the superscription in the Septuagint and Vulgate, this psalm was sung when David's land was established, hence after the return from the Exile.

97:1 *The LORD is King:* see note on Ps 93:1a-b. *The distant isles:* distant countries accessible only by sea (see 1 Ki 9:26-28; 10:22; Isa 60:9; Jon 1:3).

97:2-6 The psalmist portrays the Lord's appearance by traditional signs of his manifestation at Sinai. These went on to become the signs used to describe the future day of the Lord, when he would come in glory to establish true justice on the earth (see notes on Pss 18:7; 18:8-16).

97:2 *Clouds and darkness:* these served to veil God's ineffable glory from human eyes (see Ex 19:9; 1 Ki 8:12). *Righteousness and justice:* divine attributes personified (see Pss 61:8; 85:12; Prov 16:12; 25:5).

97:3 *Fire:* symbol of God's wrath (see Pss 21:10; 50:3; 83:15; Deut 4:24; 1 Ki 19:12; Isa 10:17).

97:6 *The heavens proclaim his righteousness:* the heavens show forth the glory of their Creator to all peoples (see Ps 19:2-5a).

97:7 Those who trust in false gods are put to shame. For "our God is in heaven; he does whatever he pleases. Their idols are merely silver and gold, the work of human hands" (Ps 115:3f).

97:8 *Cities:* literally, "daughters." *Judgments:* see note on Ps 48:12.

97:10-12 Those who are loyal to the covenant (*the righteous*) live in the light of God's presence, where there is fullness of joy. They glorify his holy name; that is, they honor him by their lives.

97:11-12 *Light:* see notes on Pss 27:1; 36:10. *Name:* see note on Ps 5:12.

Ps 98 Israel has returned from the Exile; God has saved her, and the whole world is a witness of it. Hence, the Lord is pursuing his project of salvation. Let all peoples acclaim him as their sovereign and let joy burst out over the whole face of the earth, for God comes to inaugurate a kingdom of peace and justice for all humanity. The same worldwide perspective is glimpsed in the second part of the Book of Isaiah (Isa 40–55) with which the psalms of the kingdom have much in common.

The previous psalm brought to mind the second coming of Christ. This psalm recalls the first coming of the Lord and the faith of all peoples. Hence, the Christian Liturgy uses it during the Christmas season, since the latter is so filled with joy at the coming of the Lord, the Savior of all human beings.

98:1 God's deliverance of Israel from the Exile, a type of the Messianic redemption, is such a wondrous deed that it deserves to be praised in song. *New song:* see note on Ps 33:3. *Marvelous deeds:* see note on Ps 9:2. *His right hand and his holy arm:* God is portrayed as a champion warrior.

98:2 Reminiscent of his wonders during the Exodus, God has once again revealed his infinite power and greatness (see note on Ps 46:11; see also Isa 52:10).

3 He has remembered his kindness * and his fidelity
to the house of Israel.
The farthest ends of the earth have witnessed
the salvation of our God.
4 Sing joyfully to the LORD, all the earth;
raise your voices in songs of praise.
5 Sing praise to the LORD with the harp,
with the harp and melodious singing.
6 With trumpets and the sound of the horn
sing joyfully to the King, the LORD. * [b]
7 * Let the sea resound and everything in it,
the world * and all its inhabitants. [c]
8 Let the rivers clap their hands
and the mountains shout for joy. [d]
9 Let them sing before the LORD, who is coming,
coming to judge the earth. [e]
He will judge the world with justice
and the nations with fairness. * [f]

PSALM 99*

God, King of Justice and Holiness

1 The LORD is King; *
let the nations tremble.
He sits enthroned on the cherubim;
let the earth quake. [g]
2 The LORD is great in Zion;
he is exalted above all the peoples.
3 Let them praise your great and awesome name: *
holy is he! [h]
4 Mighty King, you love justice,
and you have established fairness;
in Jacob * you have brought about
what is just and right. [i]
5 Exalt the LORD, our God,
and worship at his footstool; [j]
holy is he! *
6 Moses and Aaron were among his priests,
and Samuel was among those who invoked his name; [k]
they cried out to the LORD,
and he answered them. *
7 He spoke to them from the pillar of cloud; *
they obeyed his decrees and the law he gave them. [l]
8 O LORD, our God,
you answered them;
you were a forgiving God to them,
but you punished their wrongdoings. * [m]

b Ps 47:6-7; Ex 19:16.—c Pss 93:3; 96:11.—d Ps 148:9; Isa 44:23; 55:12.—e Pss 75:3; 96:13.—f Pss 7:12; 9:9; 67:5; 96:10.—g Pss 18:8-11; 48:2; 80:2; 93:1; 97:1; Ex 15:18; 25:20, 22; 1 Sam 4:4; 2 Sam 6:2; 1 Chr 16:30f; Isa 52:7.—h Ps 33:21; Isa 6:3.—i Pss 2:6; 72:1; Jer 23:5.—j Ps 132:7; Ex 15:2.—k Ex 28:1; 1 Sam 7:5; Jer 15:1.—l Ps 19:10; Ex 19:18-19; 33:9; Num 12:5.—m Ex 22:26; 32:11; Lev 26:18; Num 14:20; 20:12.

98:3 God has kept the promise he made to the house of Israel, and it is fully visible to all nations. The complete fulfillment of this promise was what God performed in the redemption worked by his Son Jesus Christ—which also was seen by all nations. *Kindness:* see note on Ps 6:5.

98:6 The whole of creation is summoned to acclaim the Lord as King, as Israel acclaimed her kings at their coronation, with trumpets and horns (see 1 Ki 1:34).

98:7-9 All creation is exhorted to honor its King (see note on Ps 96:11-12).

98:7 *Sea . . . world:* the two major areas that contain living things.

98:9 The Lord will come to rule everyone impartially. Jesus announced that the long-awaited coming of the Lord to rule the earth had begun in his ministry (see Mk 1:15: "The kingdom of God is close at hand"). See also note on Ps 96:13.

Ps 99 Each of the two parts of this eschatological hymn is followed by a refrain (vv. 5, 9) that stresses the holiness of the King of Israel (see Isa 6:3-5). In the temple at Jerusalem, the Ark of the Covenant had two winged creatures, the cherubim, which were considered to be the throne of God. It is a weak image of the greatness of the Almighty, for whom Mount Zion is a "footstool." God is so holy that he infinitely transcends all the realities of the universe. However, his holiness is not a far-off greatness, indifferent to human life. In adoring him, we are brought face to face with the demands of justice, rectitude, and faith. The holiness of God is truly astounding. In the final analysis, it constitutes God's intimate presence in our lives.

We can pray this psalm in honor of Christ the King who is all-holy and always obedient to the will of his Father (see Jn 4:34; 14:31). His whole life Jesus carried out what the Father had given him to accomplish, one lengthy self-sacrifice for the salvation of the world (Heb 7:27; 9:28).

99:1 *The LORD is King:* see note on Ps 93:1a-b. *Cherubim:* see note on Ps 18:11.

99:3 *Name:* see note on Ps 5:12. *Holy is he:* God is so holy that he infinitely transcends all the realities of our universe; furthermore, because he is holy himself, God calls upon his people to be holy too (see Lev 11:44). They must consecrate themselves wholly to him (see also Mt 5:48; Rom 12:1).

99:4 God is completely just by nature. He gave the law to his people so that they could live in his ways. Paul characterizes the Gospel as the revelation of the justice ("righteousness") of God (see Rom 1:17). *Jacob:* i.e., Israel (see Gen 32:29).

99:5 God is portrayed seated in heaven with his feet resting on the earth as on a footstool (see Isa 66:1), and more specifically on Mount Zion (see Ps 132:7; 1 Chr 28:2; Lam 2:1). The people are to praise and worship the Lord at his footstool.

99:6 The psalmist wishes to show that the Lord is a gracious King who hears the prayers of all who come to him with the right disposition. To do so, he mentions three great figures who at various stages interceded with the Lord for the nation (see Ex 32:30; Num 17:12f; 1 Sam 7:2-11).

99:7 *Spoke to them from the pillar of cloud:* the pillar of cloud was the symbol of God's presence with his people during the Exodus (see Ex 13:21f), and God spoke to Moses (see Ex 33:9) and to Aaron (see Num 12:5) in the pillar of cloud. But though he spoke to Samuel, we have no record of it being in the pillar of cloud. Hence, the psalmist may here be alluding to the communication itself rather than how God communicated.

99:8 *Punished their wrongdoings:* among those punished for wrongdoings were Moses and Aaron, neither of whom was allowed to enter the Promised Land (see Ps 106:22f; Num 27:14; Deut 3:26).

9 Exalt the LORD, our God,
and worship at his holy mountain,
for the LORD, our God, is holy. *

PSALM 100*

Processional Entrance Hymn

1 A psalm of thanksgiving. *
Acclaim the LORD * with joy, all the earth;
2 serve the LORD* with gladness;
enter his presence with songs of joy.
3 Proclaim that the LORD is God. *
He made us and we are his possession;
we are his people, the flock he shepherds. [n]
4 [o] Offer thanksgiving as you enter his gates, *
sing hymns of praise as you approach his courts;
give thanks to him and bless his name,
5 for the LORD is good.
His kindness endures forever,
and his faithfulness is constant to all generations. *

PSALM 101*

Norm of Life for a Good Ruler

1 A psalm of David.
I will sing of kindness and justice;
to you, O LORD, I will offer praise in song. [p]
2 I will walk in the path of blamelessness;
when will you come to me?*
Within my house * I will act
with integrity of heart. [q]
3 I will not allow any shameful act
to be done before my eyes.
* I will refuse to associate
with people who do evil. [r]
4 Let the perverse of heart remain far from me;
I will not tolerate the wicked.
5 * Anyone who secretly slanders a neighbor [s]
I will reduce to silence.

n Pss 23:1; 95:7; Deut 32:39; Isa 40:10, 13; 64:8; Mic 7:14.—o 4-5: Pss 42:4; 106:1; 107:1; 118:1; 136:1; 138:8; Ezr 3:11; Jer 33:11.—p Pss 33:1; 51:17; 89:2; 145:7.—q Ps 26:11; 1 Ki 3:14; Isa 33:15.—r Prov 11:20; Jer 16:18.—s Ex 20:16; Prov 17:20.

99:9 Refrain similar to that in verse 5.

Ps 100 Although it does not explicitly mention the theme of the Lord as King, this psalm is linked with the group of psalms of the kingdom by its style and ideas and serves as a kind of general conclusion for them. The Lord is King of the world and especially of Israel, his flock. This is the Good News that calls for praise and joy.

The psalmist intimates that in a few brief moments, the sacrifice will be offered by which the people enter into communion with God (see Lev 7:11-15). He invites the throng to celebrate the one God and his providence for the people he has created and chosen for himself. Although this hymn is short, it must have filled the hearts of believers with great wonder since they knew themselves to be in the hand of God. The entire universe is invited to share this endless joy of Israel.

By this hymn, the Church calls Christians to sing to the Lord Jesus with a similar enthusiastic joy, for he too is our Lord and God (see Jn 20:28). In cooperation with his Father he has created and then re-created us (see Jn 1:1-3, 12). Because of this, we belong entirely to him (see 1 Cor 3:22f).

100:1a *Thanksgiving:* this word may indicate that the psalm was to be used in conjunction with a "thank offering" (see Lev 7:12).

100:1b *Acclaim the LORD:* a similar opening phrase occurs in Pss 66; 81; 95. *All the earth:* the entire world is to worship God for all that he is and all that he has done for his people (see Pss 47:2f; 66:1, 4; 97:1; 117:1 for this theme of universalism).

100:2 *Serve the LORD:* the psalmist reminds the people that their first duty is to worship the Lord with mind, heart, and voice in complete gladness.

100:3 *Proclaim . . . God:* acknowledge that the Lord is God and be faithful to him; it is a statement of monotheism (see Deut 4:39; 32:39; Isa 43:10, 13). *Made us . . . his people:* through his choice and the wonders he did for them (see Ps 95:6). *Flock he shepherds:* see note on Ps 95:7. Christians know that God made us his people through Jesus, the Good Shepherd, who gave his life for his sheep (see Jn 10:11).

100:4 *His gates:* of the temple (see note on Ps 24:7, 9). *Courts:* of the temple (see Ps 84:3, 11; 2 Ki 21:5; 23:11f).

100:5 The psalm concludes with the reasons why the Lord is to be praised: he is good (i.e., generous), kind (i.e., merciful), and faithful to his promises from generation to generation (see Pss 106:1; 107:1; 118:1; 136:1; 138:8; 2 Chr 5:13; Ezr 3:11; 1 Mac 4:24; Jer 33:11; Mic 7:18-20; Mt 19:17; 1 Jn 4:7ff).

Ps 101 The Lord's covenant comprises a rule of life for every Israelite, including the king. This psalm constitutes the mirror of the ruler in whom it inculcates essential resolutions: personal integrity, choice of loyal counselors, ferreting out the arrogant, the deceitful, and the slanderous from the royal court, and the battle against injustice. The teaching is classic in the Bible, but its application is rarely carried out. Nonetheless, its main ideas continue to be vitally relevant.

We can pray this psalm in honor of Christ the King, constituted by the Father as supreme Head of the Church and of the world (Eph 1:20-23), who alone has perfectly fulfilled the commitments mentioned herein. He is thus the invisible suzerain from whom all visible leaders (both spiritual and temporal) derive their authority (see Jn 21:15-17; Rev 1:5). Since Christ makes them his representatives, all these leaders must be loving and faithful images before their subjects.

101:2a-b In imitation of the heavenly King, the psalmist himself will lead a blameless life. But to do so he will need God's help, which he prays will be forthcoming (see 1 Ki 3:7-9; see also Ps 72). *When will you come to me?:* some see in these words an allusion to the awaited coming of the Messiah, who was at times called "The one who is to come" (see Mt 11:3; Jn 4:25). Others offer an alternative translation: "I will attend to the wholehearted man / whenever he comes to me."

101:2c-3b *House:* the king promises to make his household free of those who abuse power. *Heart . . . eyes:* in the Old Testament, people were thought to act after inner ("heart") and/or external ("eye") influence (see note on Ps 4:7; see also Ps 119:36f; Num 15:39; Job 31:7; Prov 21:4; Eccl 2:10; Jer 22:17).

101:3c-4 The psalmist will not desire or do evil himself nor condone it in others and will avoid all evildoers.

101:5-6 The norms of the king's private life are also the fundamental principles of his governing. He will bring into his service only the "faithful" and those who follow "the path of integrity." *Reduce to silence:* i.e., destroy (see Pss 54:7; 94:23). *Arrogant:* see note on Ps 31:24.

Anyone with haughty glances and an arrogant heart
I cannot endure. [t]
6 The faithful in the land are the ones
whom I will choose to be my companions.
Only the one who follows the path of integrity
will be allowed to be my servant. [u]
7 No one who practices deceit
will be permitted to remain in my house.
No one who utters lies
will be numbered among my companions. * [v]
8 Morning after morning * I will banish
all the wicked from the land,
removing all evildoers from the city of the LORD.

PSALM 102*

Prayer of an Exile

1 The prayer of one afflicted. When he is wasting away * and pours out his anguish before the LORD.

2 * O LORD, give heed to my prayer;
let my plea for help reach you.
3 Do not conceal your face * from my sight
in the time of my distress.
Incline your ear to me;
on the day when I call out to you,
answer me speedily. [w]
4 [x] For my days are fading away like smoke,
and my bones are burning like live coals.
5 My heart * is stricken, withered like grass;
I am too exhausted to eat my bread.
6 As a result of my incessant groaning,
I am now nothing more than skin and bones.
7 I am like a pelican * of the wilderness,
like an owl among the ruins.
8 I am sleepless * and I moan
like a lone sparrow on a rooftop.
9 All day long my enemies revile me; *
those who rage against me use my name as a curse.
10 * I eat ashes as though they were bread,
and I mingle tears with my drink. [y]
11 Because of your indignation and wrath,
you have raised me up only to cast me down.
12 My days are like a lengthening shadow, [z]
and I am withering away like grass. [a]
13 * But, you, O LORD, are enthroned forever,
and your renown will endure for all generations. [b]

t Prov 21:4.—u Pss 26:11; 119:1; Prov 20:7.—v Ps 5:5; Prov 25:5.—w Pss 22:25; 31:3; 37:2; 69:18; 143:8.—x 4-6: Ps 38:4-9; Lam 1:13.—y Pss 42:4; 80:6; Isa 44:20.—z Pss 109:23; 144:4; 1 Chr 29:15; Job 8:9; 14:2; Eccl 6:12; Wis 2:5.—a Ps 90:5-6; Job 8:12; Jas 1:10.—b Pss 55:20; 90:2; 93:2; 135:13; 145:13; Ex 15:18; Isa 55:13; Lam 5:19; Hab 1:12.

101:7 *Will . . . companions:* another translation is: "will stand in my presence."

101:8 Evildoers will be eradicated from the kingdom. *Morning after morning:* the customary time for administering justice (see 2 Sam 15:2; Jer 21:12) and for receiving God's help (see Pss 59:17; 143:8; Isa 33:2). *City of the LORD:* see Pss 46:5f; 48:2f, 9; 87:3.

Ps 102 Known as the fifth of the seven Penitential Psalms (Pss 6; 32; 38; 51; 102; 130; 143), this psalm combines the lament of an afflicted person overwhelmed with pain and the prayer of the community of poor returned exiles waiting to be able to rebuild the walls of Jerusalem, their holy city. It shows that humanity and the universe pass away, while God remains (vv. 12-13, 26, 28). This is the proof of the Lord's power and the reason for their hopes.

It is also the reason for the hopes of Christians, since we know that in Jesus and in his Church, God has built an imperishable dwelling place for his people, a point emphasized by the Letter to the Hebrews (Heb 1:10-12) when it comments on verses 26-28 of this psalm.

102:1 This superscription is unique, giving neither author nor liturgical or historical note; instead it assigns the prayer to a life situation—when one afflicted is close to giving up, i.e., *wasting away* (see Pss 61:3; 77:4; 142:4; 143:4).

102:2-12 One day, possibly during a grave sickness, the psalmist reaches the bitter conclusion of the inconsistency of human life. And the supreme outrage is that all who see him attribute his sad state to punishment sent by God, for his prayer and repentance receive no answer. The poor man experiences the depths of anguish where everything is falling apart; he can do nothing except cry out to God.

102:3 *Conceal your face:* see note on Ps 13:2.

102:5 *Heart:* see note on Ps 4:8. *Withered like grass:* see note on Ps 90:5.

102:7 *Pelican:* a bird that in Christian times became a symbol of Christ all alone in Gethsemane and of the Eucharist. The word is also translated as "owl." *Owl:* a symbol of desolateness and destruction (see Isa 34:11, 15; Jer 50:39; Zep 2:14).

102:8 *I am sleepless:* some translations omit the words: "and I moan."

102:9 *Enemies revile me:* see note on Ps 5:10; see also Ps 109:25. *Use my name as a curse:* his enemies point him out as an example of divine malediction, saying: "May you become as wretched as so-and-so."

102:10-12 The Israelites indicated their penance externally by covering their heads with ashes and uttering lamentation accompanied by copious tears. To obtain God's pity, the sick psalmist does not hold back. He covers himself with such an abundance of ashes that they are interspersed with his food, and he gives way to so many tears that they mingle with his drink. All the same, he is inexorably on his way toward death.

102:13-23 The people thus experience a time of scorn. Uprooted from their temple and their land, they are too overwhelmed by the loss of what they most cherish for them to think of revenge. They have recourse to God's tender mercies. In their misfortune, they fall back on a single certitude—the goodness of the Lord. At once, hope of restoration begins shining forth, for "the appointed time has come" (v. 14)—so much so that they do not stop at imagining the sole reestablishment of Israel, but their perspective of renewed happiness embraces all humanity.

14 You will arise and show mercy to Zion,
for it is time for you to have pity on her;
the appointed time * has come.
15 For her stones are precious to your servants,
and her dust causes them to weep. *
16 The nations will revere your name, * O LORD,
and all the kings of the earth will sing of your glory. [c]
17 For the LORD will rebuild Zion
and reveal himself in all his glory. *
18 He will answer the prayer of the destitute,
and he will not ignore their petition.
19 Let this be written * for future generations
so that a people yet unborn may praise the LORD: [d]
20 "The LORD looked down from his sanctuary on high
and gazed on the earth from heaven, [e]
21 to hear the sighs of the prisoners
and to set free those under sentence of death." *[f]
22 Then the name of the LORD will be proclaimed in Zion,
and his praise * in Jerusalem
23 when all peoples and kingdoms come together
to worship the LORD. *[g]
24 * He has taken away my strength on my life's journey;
he has cut short my days.
25 So I said: "Do not carry me off, O my God,
before half my days are done, *
for your years endure from age to age. [h]
26 * "Long ago you laid the foundations of the earth,
and the heavens are the work of your hands. [i]
27 They will pass away but you endure;
they will all wear out like a garment.
You will change them like clothing,
and they will perish. *
28 "However, you remain always the same,
and your years will have no end. *
29 The children of your servants will be secure,
and their descendants will dwell in your presence." *[j]

PSALM 103*

Praise of God's Providence

1 Of David.

Bless the LORD, O my soul; *
my entire being, bless his holy name.

c Pss 77:8; 119:126; Deut 32:36; 1 Ki 8:43; Isa 59:19; 66:18.—d Ps 22:31-32; Rom 4:24.—e Pss 11:4; 14:2; 53:2.—f Ps 79:11; Lk 4:18.—g Ps 22:28; Isa 60:3-4; Zec 2:11; 8:22.—h Pss 39:5; 90:10; Job 14:5; 36:26.—i 26-28: Isa 51:6; Heb 1:10-12.—j Pss 25:13; 69:37.

102:14 *Appointed time:* the time established by God for judgment and salvation (see Ps 75:3; Ex 9:5; 2 Sam 24:15; Dan 11:27, 35).

102:15 The psalmist intimates that Zion must be highly cherished by the Lord for she is so dear to his servants.

102:16 See note on Ps 46:11. *Name:* see note on Ps 5:12.

102:17 *And reveal himself in all his glory:* may also be translated as: "and thus appear in his glory" (see v. 16 and note on Ps 46:11; see also Isa 40:1-5). The ultimate fulfillment of this hope will occur in the "new Jerusalem" (see Rev 21).

102:19 *Written:* this is the only place in the Psalter that calls for a written record of God's saving deed. The usual reference is to an oral record (see Pss 22:32; 44:2; 78:1-4).

102:21 *Prisoners . . . those under sentence of death:* see note on Ps 79:11.

102:22 *Name . . . praise:* see notes on Pss 5:12; 9:2.

102:23 See notes on Pss 46:11; 47:10; see also Pss 96; 98; 100; Isa 2:2-4; Mic 4:1-3.

102:24-29 Here the individual lament and the national supplication are combined. Upon meditating on the precariousness of existence before the God who endures forever, a hope arises, the hope of not being abandoned. The Letter to the Hebrews (Heb 13:8) will proclaim: "Jesus Christ is the same yesterday, today, and forever."

102:25 *Before half my days are done:* when the normal life span is only half-completed (see Isa 38:10; Jer 17:11).

102:26-28 This passage is inspired by Isa 51:6-8 and applied to the Messiah (Heb 1:10-12). The restoration of Israel and the coming of the Messiah will be the preface to the eschatological renewal or regeneration that will accompany the end of time (see Isa 65:17; 66:22; Rev 20:11; 21:1).

102:27 Both the "foundations of the earth" and the "heavens" (v. 26, which the ever-living God has made) will *perish* (see Pss 1:6; 90:4; 2 Pet 3:8ff) and be of no use, like discarded clothing (see Isa 51:6).

102:28 By contrast, the Lord remains forever the same (see Heb 13:8); he is the "first and the last" (see Deut 32:39; Isa 41:4; 46:4; 48:12).

102:29 Because God does not change, the children of his people will be secure in the Lord (see Mal 3:6). *Dwell in your presence:* another translation is: "dwell in the [Promised] Land" (see Pss 25:13; 69:37; see also Ps 37:3, 29; Isa 65:9).

Ps 103 In its literary construction and sublime concepts, this psalm is one of the most pure and joyous of the Psalter. Healed of a grave sickness that he considers to have been caused by sin, the psalmist regards this cure doubled by God's pardon as a privileged experience of the love of the Lord. By this favor, God has shown his love for the psalmist in concrete fashion, thus powerfully confirming for him the revelation he made of this love to Israel through the Exodus and to Moses in the meeting on Sinai.

God's love is boundless for the righteous and magnanimous for sinners, disconcerting for the ephemeral creatures that we are and long-suffering to the point of extending to the far-off descendants of his faithful ones. Such is the love of the infinite God whose name is holy, whose throne is in heaven, and whose reign is eternal. He is the Father who will reveal Jesus and whose ineffable goodness Paul will proclaim (see 1 Cor 2:9). We can thus understand how right the psalmist is in calling upon heaven itself to celebrate such a God.

The signal corporal and spiritual cure obtained by the psalmist constitutes only a pale figure of the Resurrection that definitively snatches Jesus from corporal death and the sinful world and shows him his Father's love with incomparable force. By sharing in the Resurrection of Christ through the sacraments, Christians discover that "God is love" in an experience derived from that of Christ and far superior to that of the psalmist. In all truth, every Christian can recite this psalm to praise the God who is love.

103:1 *Soul:* see note on Ps 6:4. *Name:* see note on Ps 5:12.

2 Bless the LORD, O my soul,
and do not forget all his benefits.
3 He forgives all your sins
and heals all your diseases. *
4 He redeems * your life from the pit
and crowns you with kindness and mercy. [k]
5 He satisfies your years with good things
and renews your youth like an eagle's. *
6 The LORD performs acts of righteousness
and administers justice for all who are oppressed. [l]
7 * He made known his ways * to Moses,
his wondrous deeds to the people of Israel.
8 * The LORD is merciful and gracious,
slow to anger and abounding in kindness. [m]
9 He will not always rebuke,
nor will he remain angry forever.
10 He does not treat us as our sins deserve
or repay us according to our offenses.
11 As high as the heavens are above the earth,
so great is his kindness toward those who fear him. * [n]
12 As far as the east is from the west,
so far has he removed our transgressions from us. *
13 * As a father has compassion for his children,
so the LORD has compassion for those who fear him.
14 For he knows how we were formed;
he remembers that we are only dust. * [o]
15 The days of mortal man are like grass;
he flourishes like a flower of the field. [p]
16 The wind sweeps over him, and he is gone,
and his place never sees him again.
17 But from everlasting to everlasting
the kindness * of the LORD is with those who fear him,
and his righteousness with their children's children,
18 with those who keep his covenant
and diligently observe his commandments. *
19 The LORD has established his throne in heaven,
and his kingdom rules over all. *
20 * Bless the LORD, O you his angels, *
you mighty in strength who do his bidding, [q]
who obey his spoken word.
21 Bless the LORD, O you his hosts,
his ministers who do his will.
22 Bless the LORD, all his works,
everywhere in his domain.

Bless the LORD, O my soul. *

k Pss 28:1; 30:4; 34:23; 40:3; 69:16; 88:5; 143:7; Prov 1:12; Jon 2:6.—**l** Pss 9:9; 146:6-7.—**m** Pss 86:15; 145:8; Ex 34:6-7; Num 14:18; Jer 3:12; Joel 2:13; Jon 4:2; Mic 7:18-19; Jas 5:11.—**n** Pss 13:6; 57:11; Isa 55:9; Eph 3:18.—**o** Pss 90:3; 119:73; 139:13-15; Gen 2:7.—**p** Pss 37:2; 90:5-6; 102:12; Job 14:2; Isa 40:6.—**q** Pss 91:11; 148:2; Dan 3:58.

103:3 Following the Old Testament understanding, the psalmist considers sufferings as the punishment for sin (see Ps 41:5; Ex 15:26).

103:4 *Redeems:* i.e., "delivers." *Pit:* i.e., the grave (see note on Ps 30:2).

103:5 *Like an eagle's:* because of its acknowledged long span of life, which at times reaches one hundred years, the eagle was regarded as a symbol of perennial youth and vigor (see Isa 40:31). It was thought that when an eagle became old and its eyes grew dim, it flew toward the sun, so that the film was burned away from its eyes and its plumage was renewed by the sun's scorching rays.

103:7-12 God made known his ways to Moses on Mount Sinai, telling him that his attitude toward human beings and his great works find their inspiration in his loving kindness. Passing mysteriously before Moses, God cried out: "The LORD, the LORD, a compassionate and gracious God, slow to anger and abounding in steadfast love and fidelity, who shows mercy to thousands. He forgives iniquity and transgression and sin, but will by no means forgive the iniquity of the fathers, visiting it upon their sons and their sons' sons, to the third and fourth generation" (Ex 34:6f).

103:7 *His ways:* see note on Ps 25:10.

103:8-10 God pardons sinners who repent, a truth often affirmed (see Pss 86:15; 145:8; Ex 34:6; Neh 9:17; Isa 57:16; Jer 3:12; Joel 2:13; Jon 4:2). *Kindness:* see note on Ps 6:5.

103:11 *Kindness:* see note on 6:5. *Those who fear him:* see note on Ps 15:2-5.

103:12 God places a huge gulf between his faithful and their sins, extending, as it were, from one end of the earth to the other (see Isa 1:18; 43:25; Jer 31:34; 50:20; Mic 7:18f).

103:13-17 What an amazing condescension on the part of God's love. Although he is well aware that we are fragile and ephemeral creatures who, like grass or flowers, are carried off by the slightest breeze, God keeps in his love the whole lives of his servants. He presents a just account of their merits and blesses their descendants who are faithful to his covenant.

103:14 The Lord has compassion on those "who fear him" (v. 13) because he knows their frailty, that they are but *dust* (see Gen 2:7; 3:19; Job 4:19; Eccl 3:20; 12:7).

103:17 *Kindness:* see note on Ps 6:5.

103:18 Keeping the covenant entails obeying the Lord's commandments (see Ex 20:6; Deut 7:9), i.e., doing the will of God (see Mt 6:9-15).

103:19 *His kingdom rules over all:* see Pss 22:29; 145:11-13. The Book of Obadiah concludes with this cry of triumphant eschatology (v. 21: "and dominion will belong to the LORD").

103:20-22 The psalmist calls upon all creatures to join him in praising the heavenly King who rules all things with love (see note on Ps 9:2).

103:20 The angels are God's messengers (see Ps 91:11).

103:22 *Bless the LORD, O my soul:* this last line was probably added by the redactors of the Psalter to show that God's word is efficacious by itself and needs no intermediary.

PSALM 104*

Praise of God the Creator

1 Bless the LORD, O my soul.
O LORD, my God, you are indeed very great.
You are clothed in majesty and splendor,
2 wrapped in light * as in a robe.
You have stretched out the heavens like a tent; [r]
3 you have established your palace * upon the waters.
You make the clouds serve as your chariot;
you ride forth on the wings of the wind.
4 You have appointed the winds as your messengers
and flames of fire * as your ministers. [s]
5 You established the earth on its foundations
so that it will remain unshaken forever. *
6 You covered it with the deep like a cloak;
the waters rose above the mountains.
7 At your rebuke * the waters took to flight;
at the sound of your thunder they fled in terror. [t]
8 They rose up to the mountains
and flowed down to the valleys, *
to the place that you had designated for them.
9 You established a boundary that they were not to cross
so that they would never again cover the earth. [u]
10 * You made springs gush forth in the valleys
and flow between the mountains.
11 [v] They supply water to every beast of the field,
and from them the wild asses quench their thirst.
12 On the banks the birds of the air build nests
and sing among the branches.
13 * From your dwelling you water the mountains,
enriching the earth with the fruit of your labor.
14 You provide grass for the cattle,
and the plants for man to cultivate.
You bring forth food from the earth
15 and wine to gladden the heart * of man,
oil to make his face shine
and bread to strengthen his body.

r Ps 19:2; Gen 1:6-7; Job 9:8; Prov 8:27-28; Isa 40:12; Jer 51:15; Am 9:6.—s Ps 148:8; Gen 3:24; 2 Ki 2:11; Heb 1:7.—t Pss 18:16; 29:3; Ex 9:23; Job 7:12.—u Gen 9:11-15; Job 38:8-11; Jer 5:22.—v 11-14: Pss 135:7; 147:8-9; Gen 1:11-12; Jer 10:13; 51:16.

Ps 104 This hymn calls to mind the majestic poem that opens the Book of Genesis (see Gen 1); perhaps it is even older. The text seems to have undergone the influence of an Egyptian hymn to the sun. It is a rarity at this period for the author to look at the world with the curious eyes of a scientist who is seeking the cause of things and the laws that govern them. The author nevertheless conceives of the universe primarily as a song to God who gives it life. While Ps 103 celebrates the Lord insofar as he shows himself animated by a powerful love in the moral and spiritual order, this psalm—possibly composed by the same poet—invites us to praise him insofar as he reveals himself as a prodigious artist in the initial creation and a benevolent organizer in the governance of the universe.

The power of the creative act brings worlds forth: perfectly mastered, nature and creatures come alive. Divine providence has foreseen everything and organized it all: the seasons, the rhythm of existence, nourishment, and the home of animals and humans. Animated by the Spirit, that is, the divine Breath, creatures sing of the glory of their Creator. The only shadow in this tableau is sin, which risks destroying the beautiful harmony; hence, the author prays that it be eliminated. In the creative Breath (v. 30), the Church sees the Spirit of Pentecost who renews the broken harmony and gives rise to the "new creation," the new human being who is reborn in Christ (see 2 Cor 5:17).

Enlightened by science concerning the unsuspected and amazing wonders of the material universe, all Christians sing to their heavenly Father this psalm of enthusiastic praise. They will also sing it to Christ, intimately associated with the Father both in the creation of these wonders and in their continuance in being (see Col 1:16f). We will praise above all the eminent greatness and power of Father and Son in sending their Spirit to re-create sinful human beings and to renew the spiritual cosmos, the Church (v. 30).

104:2 *Light:* created on the first day (see Gen 1:3-5). In general, the psalmist follows the order of creation found in Gen 1. *Heavens:* created on the second day (see Gen 1:6-8).

104:3 As the ancients represented the world, the rains were stored in reservoirs in the vault of the heavens, which they thought were solid. *Your palace:* God's heavenly dwelling above the upper waters of the sky (see notes on Pss 29:10; 36:9; see also Gen 1:6f). *Clouds . . . your chariot:* see note on Ps 68:5.

104:4 The Letter to the Hebrews cites this verse to show that Christ is superior to the angels. Since God makes use of mere wind and lightning (*flames of fire*) as his messengers and servants, the ministering spirits in heaven that he also uses as his messengers must be infinitely inferior to the eternal Son of God. The cogency of the argument is much greater in Greek (in which the Letter was written) because the word *pneuma* means both "wind" and "spirit" while the word *angelos* means both "messenger" and "angel."

104:5 The ancients regarded the earth as resting upon firm foundations (see note on Ps 24:2).

104:7 *Rebuke:* see Ps 76:7. *Waters took to flight:* poetic description of what took place on the third day of creation (see Gen 1:9f).

104:8 *They rose up to the mountains and flowed down to the valleys:* the sources of the Jordan and the other great rivers of the Near East are in the mountains. Another translation offered is: "The mountains rose high and the valleys went down."

104:10-12 God refreshes the ravines by means of the lower waters.

104:13-15 God refreshes his creatures by means of the reservoir of upper waters (see v. 3; Gen 7:11; Job 38:22; Sir 43:14).

104:15 *Heart:* see note on Ps 4:8.

16 The trees of the LORD have fruit in abundance,
the cedars of Lebanon * that he planted.
17 In them the birds build their nests;
in the fir trees the stork makes its home. [w]
18 The high mountains are inhabited by the wild goats;
in the rocky crags the badgers * find refuge.
19 You created the moon that marks the seasons [x]
and the sun that knows its time for setting. *
20 You bring on darkness, and it is night,
when all the beasts of the forests go on the prowl.
21 The young lions * roar for their prey,
seeking their food from God. [y]
22 When the sun rises, they steal away
and return to their lairs to rest.
23 People go forth to their work
and to their labor until darkness descends.
24 * How countless are your works, O LORD;
by your wisdom you have made them all;
the earth abounds with your creatures. [z]
25 There is the sea, vast and broad,
filled with numberless species,
living creatures both great and small. [a]
26 There the ships sail forth,
and the Leviathan * that you formed to play therein. [b]
27 * All of them look to you
to give them their food at the appropriate time. * [c]
28 * When you provide it for them,
they gather it up;
when you open your hand,
they are filled with good things.
29 When you turn away your face, *
they are dismayed;
when you take away their breath,
they die and return to the dust. [d]
30 When you send forth your Spirit, *
they are created,
and you renew the face of the earth.
31 * May the glory of the LORD abide forever,
and may the LORD rejoice in his works. *
32 When he looks at the earth, it quakes;
when he touches the mountains, they smoke. * [e]
33 I will sing to the LORD as long as I live; *
I will sing praise to my God while I have life. [f]
34 May my meditation be pleasing to him,
for I find my joy in the LORD.

w Ezek 31:6, 13.—x Ps 19:6; Sir 43:6.—y Job 38:39; Am 3:4.—z Pss 8:2; 92:6; Sir 39:16.—a Ps 69:35; Sir 43:26.—b Job 3:8; 40:20; Ezek 27:9.—c Pss 136:25; 145:15-16; Job 36:31.—d Ps 90:3; Gen 3:19; Deut 31:17; Job 34:14-15; Eccl 3:20.—e Pss 97:4; 144:5; Ex 19:18.—f Pss 7:17; 108:2; 146:2; Ex 15:1.

104:16 *Cedars of Lebanon:* see note on Ps 80:11.

104:18 *Badgers:* the hyrax or rock badger, a small, hare-like, ungulate mammal (see Lev 11:5; Deut 14:7; Prov 30:26).

104:19 The ancients governed their lives by the cycles of the sun and moon, which God created on the fourth day for that purpose (see Gen 1:14-19).

104:21-23 The *young lions* and *man* represent the animal and the human kingdom. The psalmist, in accord with the beliefs of his day, postulates that animals come out at night to search for their food, and humans do their working and eating by day. See Jn 9:4, where Jesus uses the inability of humans to work at night (because of the circumstances of his time—absence of light at night) to impart a greater spiritual truth.

104:24-26 The psalmist now takes up God's creation of the sea and everything in it on the fifth day (see Gen 1:20-23). He calls upon the people to worship the Lord's wisdom and creative diversity. Here he emphasizes sea creatures to complement the wild and domesticated animals and humans mentioned in verses 10-18.

104:26 See note on Ps 74:13-14. Here *Leviathan* is a whale or large cetacean. The name is that of a fabled dragon and is already found in Ugaritic poems of the 15th century B.C.

104:27-30 On the sixth day, God enabled everything he had made to fructify (see Gen 1:24-31). All living things on earth and in the sea, whether wild or domesticated, birds, sea creatures, and human beings have some idea of the living Presence by whom they exist (see Pss 145:15f; 147:9). They have their being in God (see Acts 17:24f), and the Lord gives and sustains life by his Spirit. Indeed, God has supreme power over the universe, creating, preserving, and governing all. The lives of all creatures are in his hands.

104:27 All nature depends on its Creator for provisions, and he has arranged for everyone to have enough food.

104:28-29 Creatures are governed by the Lord; they are gladdened by his provisions, terrified by his absence, and encounter death by the withdrawal of his breath.

104:29 *Turn . . . face:* see note on Ps 13:2. *Return to dust:* see note on Ps 90:3.

104:30 *Your Spirit:* the Spirit or "Breath" of God is the divine creative power, source of all natural life (see Gen 1:2; 2:7). So also the Holy Spirit is the source of all supernatural life (see Jn 3:5f). Hence, this verse is applied by the Church to the third Person of the Blessed Trinity.

104:31-34 The psalmist concludes the psalm the way it began—with praise (vv. 1-4). The Lord, who reveals himself in creation in all his splendor (vv. 1-4), has bestowed his glory on it (see Ps 19:2; Isa 6:3), and his handiwork will endure as long as he undergirds it. Hence, his faithful should respond with praise, devotion, and an intention to please the Lord (see Ps 19:15).

104:31 *Rejoice in his works:* as he did at the end of creation (see Gen 1:31).

104:32 The Lord is so much greater than his creation that even a mere look or touch on his part is enough to wreak havoc in it.

104:33 *I will . . . I live:* a perpetual vow to praise the Lord (see note on Ps 7:18).

35 May sinners be banished from the earth,
and may the wicked no longer exist.
Bless the LORD, O my soul. *
Alleluia.

PSALM 105*

God's Faithfulness to the Covenant

1 * Give thanks to the LORD, invoke his name; * [g]
proclaim his deeds among the peoples. [h]
2 Offer him honor with songs of praise;
recount all his marvelous deeds.
3 Glory in his holy name;
let the hearts * of those who seek the LORD exult.
4 Reflect on the LORD and his strength;
seek his face continually. [i]
5 Remember the marvels he has wrought,
his portents, and the judgments * he has set forth.
6 You are the offspring of his servant Abraham,
the children of Jacob, his chosen ones. *
7 He is the LORD, our God;
his judgments prevail all over the earth.
8 He is mindful of his covenant * forever,
the promise he laid down for a thousand generations,
9 the covenant he made with Abraham [j]
and the oath he swore to Isaac. *
10 * He established it as a decree for Jacob,
and as an everlasting covenant for Israel,
11 saying, "To you I will give the land of Canaan
as the portion of your heritage." [k]
12 * [l] When they were few in number,
an insignificant group of strangers in it,
13 they wandered from nation to nation,
from one kingdom to another.
14 He permitted no one to oppress them,
and in their regard he warned kings: *
15 "Do not touch my anointed ones;
do no harm to my prophets." *
16 Then he invoked a famine on the land
and destroyed their supply of bread. [m]
17 But he had sent a man ahead of them,
Joseph, who had been sold as a slave. [n]
18 They shackled his feet with fetters
and clamped an iron collar around his neck, [o]
19 until what he had prophesied was fulfilled
and the word of the LORD proved him true. [p]

g 1-15: 1 Chr 16:8-22.—h Pss 18:50; 96:3; 145:5; Isa 12:4-5; Joel 3:5; Acts 2:21.—i Pss 24:6; 27:8; Deut 4:29.—j Gen 15:1ff; 26:3; Lk 1:73; Gal 3:15-18.—k Gen 12:7; 15:18; Num 34:2.—l 12-13: Deut 4:27; 26:5; Heb 11:9.—m Gen 41:54-57; Lev 26:26; Isa 3:1.—n Gen 37:28, 36; 45:5; Acts 7:9.—o Gen 39:20; 40:15.—p Gen 40:20-22; 41:9-13.

104:35 Before concluding, the psalmist prays that sin may disappear from creation. However, because the hymn cannot end with a malediction (see Ps 139:19), he repeats the words of verse 1 as a refrain: "Bless the LORD, O my soul." *Alleluia:* i.e., "Hallelujah" or "Bless [or praise] the LORD," which most likely belongs to the beginning of Ps 105 (see Pss 105:45; 106:1, 48).

Ps 105 The magnificent hymn in praise of God for creation (see Ps 104) does not suffice for believers. God is he who comes among human beings; hence, they proclaim God's greatness in history by delivering the human race from slavery and leading it to salvation. In order to voice its joy and thanks, Israel loves to recall the events that marked the beginnings of its adventure: the promise made to Abraham and renewed to the patriarchs (vv. 8-15), the adventure of Joseph (vv. 16-23; see Gen 37–50), Moses and the plagues in Egypt (vv. 24-36; see Ex 1–13), the Exodus and the miracles in the wilderness (vv. 37-43; see Ex 14–15), and lastly the entrance into Canaan, the land promised as an inheritance (v. 44).

Contrary to the following psalm (Ps 106), the author is silent about Israel's sins; he wishes to sing of nothing but the action of God. The Lord has always kept his word; he has multiplied wonders for his people, and his providence has guided their steps. Now he has a right to expect them to be faithful to him (v. 45).

This psalm becomes the song of the Church, a people chosen by God in Christ and saved by his Passover (see Eph 1). Since our God is the God of Abraham, Isaac, and Jacob (see Mk 12:26), unchanged and also faithful, we can legitimately base our confidence in him on the promises and proofs he gave to our distant spiritual ancestors. Let us not forget, however, that these promises have received eminent confirmation in the life of Christ, whom God has led—through the dreadful detour of death—from this exile to the true Promised Land. This last proof constitutes the primary foundation of our enthusiasm and confidence.

The first fifteen verses of this psalm are found again in 1 Chr 16:8-22.

105:1-3 These three verses can be regarded as a prelude, and they are counterbalanced by the conclusion comprising verses 44-45.

105:1 *Name:* see note on Ps 5:12. *Proclaim his deeds among the peoples:* see note on Ps 9:2.

105:3 *Hearts:* see note on Ps 4:8.

105:5 *Judgments:* see note on Ps 48:11.

105:6 Here begin the allusions to Genesis (Gen 22:17; see Isa 51:2). *Children of Jacob, his chosen ones:* most manuscripts read instead: "Children of Jacob, his chosen one," which seems to fit better with the previous line.

105:8 *Covenant:* see Gen 15:9-21. This verse (and v. 9) are alluded to in Lk 1:72f.

105:9 *The oath he swore to Isaac:* another possible translation is "the oath concerning Isaac."

105:10-11 These verses recall the promise (see Gen 15:18) on which rest the hopes of Israel (see Pss 47:5; 72:8; Deut 4:31, 40).

105:12-41 The psalmist recapitulates God's saving acts for Israel from the making of the Covenant (see Gen 15:9-21) to its fulfillment (see Jos 21:43). In this connection, see the short summary of salvation prescribed to be said by the individual Israelite reaching the Promised Land (see Deut 26:1-11).

105:14 *He warned kings:* see Gen 12:11ff; 20:7; 26:7ff.

105:15 *My anointed ones . . . my prophets:* the patriarchs, Abraham, Isaac, and Jacob, who were in a sense anointed, that is, consecrated to God, and the recipients of his revelations.

20 The king ordered that he be released;
the ruler of the peoples set him free. [q]
21 He appointed him as master of his household
and as ruler of all his possessions. [r]
22 He was to instruct * his princes as he deemed fit
and to impart wisdom to his elders.

23 Then Israel went down into Egypt; [s]
Jacob lived as an alien in the land of Ham. *
24 God greatly increased the number of his people
and made them too strong for their foes, [t]
25 whose hearts he then turned * to hate his people
and to conspire against his servants. [u]

26 He sent his servant Moses,
and Aaron whom he had chosen. [v]
27 [w] They performed his signs among them
and worked wonders in the land of Ham.

28 * He sent darkness that enveloped the land,
but they rebelled against his warnings.
29 He turned their waters into blood,
and all their fish were destroyed.

30 Their land was saturated with frogs,
even in the royal chambers.
31 At his command there came hordes of flies
and gnats throughout their country.

32 He sent them hail instead of rain,
and flashes of lightning in all their land.
33 He struck down their vines and their fig trees
and demolished the trees of their country.

34 At his word the locusts came,
as well as grasshoppers beyond all count. [x]
35 They gobbled up every green plant in the land
and devoured the produce of the soil.

36 He struck down all the firstborn of the land,
the firstfruits of their manhood.
37 Then he led out his people with silver and gold,
and there was not one among their tribes who stumbled. [y]

38 Egypt was glad when they departed,
for dread of Israel had overwhelmed them.
39 He spread a cloud over his people as a cover *
and a fire to give light by night. [z]

40 At their request he supplied them with quail, [a]
and he filled them with bread from heaven. *
41 He split open a rock and water gushed forth, [b]
flowing through the wilderness like a river. *

42 For he remembered the sacred promise
that he had made to Abraham, his servant.
43 He led forth his people with rejoicing,
his chosen ones with exultation. *

44 He gave them the lands of the nations, [c]
and they inherited the fruit of other people's toil,
45 so that they might keep his decrees [d]
and observe his laws.

Alleluia.

q Gen 41:14.—r Gen 41:41-44.—s Ps 78:51; Gen 46:1—47:12; Acts 7:15.—t Ex 1:7-9; Acts 7:17.—u Ex 1:8-14; Acts 7:19.—v Ex 3:10; 4:27; Num 33:1.—w 27-36: Ps 78:43-51; Ex 7:8—12:51.—x Ex 10:1-20; Joel 1:4.—y Ex 3:21-22; 12:33-36.—z Ps 78:14; Ex 13:21-22; Wis 18:3; 1 Cor 10:1.—a Pss 78:24-28; 114:8; Ex 16:13-15; Num 11:31ff; Deut 8:15; Wis 16:20; Isa 48:21; Jn 6:31.—b Ps 78:15-16; Ex 17:1-7; Num 20:11; 1 Cor 10:4.—c Deut 4:37-40; Jos 11:16-23.—d Ps 78:5-7; Deut 6:20-25; 7:8-11.

105:22 *Instruct:* literally, "bind." The one whose head had been shackled was now empowered to control the *princes* of Pharaoh as he wished and to impart wisdom to the counselors of Pharaoh, who were also delegates of the people. These *elders* most likely had the same function as the elders of Israel: arbitration (see Deut 22:13-19), military commands (see Jos 8:10), and counsel (see 1 Sam 4:3).

105:23 *Land of Ham:* i.e., Egypt.

105:25 *Whose hearts he then turned:* the ancients regarded every happening as coming from God, even evil (see Ex 4:21; 7:3; Jos 11:20; 2 Sam 24:1; Isa 10:5-7; 37:26f; Jer 34:22).

105:28-38 As in Ps 78:43-51, here also the plagues of Egypt are recalled with poetic license so that their order and number are different from Ex 7:14—12:30.

105:39 *As a cover:* the psalmist indicates that the cloud symbolizing God's presence served as a protection for the people against the sun, somewhat like his shading wings (see note on Ps 17:8). Other functions of the cloud given are: to guide the people in the wilderness (see Ps 78:14; Ex 13:21; Num 9:17; Neh 9:12), to protect the people from the Egyptians as a cover of darkness (see Ex 14:19f), and to insulate them from the glorious manifestations of God's overwhelming presence (see Ex 16:10; Num 11:25; Deut 31:15; 1 Ki 8:11).

105:40 *Bread from heaven:* the psalmist names it thusly because it was the immediate gift of the heavenly Father in contrast to the ordinary natural bread. See also note on Ps 78:25 and Christ's use of this phrase in Jn 6:31.

105:41 The psalmist concludes his account of God's saving deeds for Israel with one of the most admired of them: creating a river of water from a rock in the wilderness (see Ps 114:8; Isa 43:19f).

105:43 An allusion to the song of victory of Ex 15.

PSALM 106*

Israel's Confession of Sin and God's Mercy

1 Alleluia.
Give thanks * to the LORD, for he is good;
his kindness endures forever. [e]
2 Who can possibly recount the mighty acts of the LORD
and fully proclaim his praise? *
3 Blessed * are those who do what is right
and practice justice constantly. [f]

4 Remember me, O LORD, out of the love you have for your people; [g]
come to me with your salvation. *
5 Let me delight in the success of your chosen ones,
share in the joy of your nation,
and glory in your heritage.

6 * [h] Like our ancestors, we * have sinned;
we have gone astray and done evil.
7 When our ancestors were in Egypt,
they failed to be mindful of your wonders;
they did not remember your many kindnesses
and rebelled against the Most High at the Red Sea.

8 Yet he saved them for his name's sake * [i]
so that he might make known his mighty power.
9 He rebuked the Red Sea, and it dried up;
he led them through the depths as through a wilderness. [j]
10 He saved them from those who hated them;
from the hand of the enemy he delivered them.

11 The waters closed over their adversaries;
not a single one of them survived.
12 Then they believed his words
and sang his praises. * [k]

13 * But they soon forgot what he had done
and had no confidence in his plan.
14 In the wilderness they yielded to their cravings;
in the wasteland they put God to the test. [l]
15 He gave them everything they wanted
but struck them with a consuming disease. [m]

16 * [n] In the camp they grew envious of Moses
and of Aaron, who was consecrated to the LORD.
17 The earth parted and swallowed Dathan
and closed over the company of Abiram.
18 Fire blazed all through them,
and the wicked were consumed in flames.

19 * [o] They constructed a calf at Horeb
and worshiped this molten image.

---

e Pss 100:5; 103:2; 107:1; 118:1, 29; 136:1-3; 1 Chr 16:34; Jer 33:11; Dan 3:89.—f Ps 15:2; Isa 56:1-2; Hos 12:7.—g Ps 25:7; Neh 5:19; 13:14, 22, 31.—h 6-7: Ps 78:11-17; Ex 14:11; Lev 26:40; Jdg 3:7; 1 Ki 8:47; Neh 1:7; Bar 2:12; Dan 9:5.—i Pss 80:4; 107:13; Ex 9:16; Isa 25:9; Ezek 36:20-22.—j Pss 18:16; 89:10; Ex 14:21-31; Isa 50:2; 63:11-14; Nah 1:4.—k Ps 105:43; Ex 14:31; 15:1-21.—l Ps 78:18; Ex 15:24; 16:3; Num 11:1-6; 1 Cor 10:9.—m Ps 78:26-31; Ex 16:13; 17:2; Num 11:33.—n 16-18: Lev 10:2; Num 16:1-3; Deut 11:6; Isa 26:11.—o 19-20: Ex 32:1-9; Deut 9:8-21; Jer 2:11; Acts 7:41; Rom 1:23.

Ps 106 A beautiful acclamation opens this psalm, but from verse 6 onward the tone changes. We enter into a liturgy of grief and take part in a national confession. It is, especially after the Exile, a psalm for times of distress (see Neh 9:5-37; Isa 63:7—64:11). A repentant Israel evokes the sin of the ancestors, but only to confess its own sin. The people continue the long succession of infidelities of yesteryear. The meditation on Israel's history contrasts with the beautiful hymn of Psalm 105. Taking his inspiration from Numbers and Deuteronomy, the psalmist retains from the past only the concatenation of sins: the ancestors doubted God (v. 7; see Ex 14:12), murmured in the wilderness (v. 14; see Ex 15:24; 16:3; 17:2), adored the golden calf (v. 19; see Ex 32), balked at conquering the Promised Land (v. 24; see Num 14:3f), adopted pagan practices (vv. 28-35; see Num 25; Jdg 2:1-5), and sacrificed to idols (vv. 36-38; see 1 Ki 16:34).

Paul will later evoke how the flood of sin submerges humanity (see Rom 3:23). But the history of sin is opposed to that of the love of God; the Lord always pardons and delivers his people. On recalling such goodness, the community of his people gathered together acknowledges its sins and begs God to save it.

In praying this psalm, Christians recall that the wonders of God's mercy in favor of his chosen people were simple preludes to the works of mercy that he accomplishes in Christ on behalf of sinful but believing humankind (see Rom 5:20). Acknowledgment of sin opens the door to the experience of God's love.

106:1 *Give thanks:* a liturgical call to praise (see Pss 100:5; 103:2; 107:1; 118:1, 29; 136:1-3). *Kindness:* see note on Ps 6:5.

106:2 *His praise:* see note on Ps 9:2.

106:3 The Lord expects his people to persevere in righteousness and justice, because they thus establish his kingdom (see Pss 15:1-5; 99:4; Isa 11:3-5; 33:15-17). *Blessed:* see note on Ps 1:1.

106:4 *With your salvation:* another translation is: "when you save them."

106:6-12 The psalmist sketches the people's lack of faith and their rebellion at the Red Sea (see Ex 14–15).

106:6 This general theme (see Lev 26:40; 1 Ki 8:47; Dan 9:5) is reprised by the Vulgate in Jud 7:29. *We:* the psalmist identifies himself with his sinful people.

106:8 A motive often ascribed to God by Ezekiel (see Ezek 20:9, 14; 36:21f; 39:25). *Name's sake:* see note on Ps 5:12.

106:12 An allusion to Ex 15. Praise is the expression of faith in the divine word (see Pss 119:42, 65, 74, 81; 130:5).

106:13-15 The psalmist recalls the people's forgetfulness of the Lord in their craving for meat in the desert (see Num 11).

106:16-18 The psalmist recounts the challenge to Moses' authority in the camp by Korah, Dathan, and Abiram (see Num 16:1-35).

106:19-23 The psalmist recalls the people's worship of the golden calf at Sinai (see Ex 32; Deut 9:7-29; Hos 4:7; 9:10; 10:5).

20 They exchanged their Glory *
for an image of a bull that eats grass.
21 They forgot the God who had saved them,
who had done great things in Egypt,[p]
22 wonders in the land of Ham, *
and awesome deeds at the Red Sea.
23 He was contemplating their destruction,
but Moses, his chosen one,
stood in the breach * before him
to keep his wrath from destroying them.[q]
24 * [r] Then they derided the land of delights, *
for they had no faith in his word.
25 They grumbled in their tents
and refused to obey the voice of the LORD.
26 Therefore, he swore with uplifted hand
to strike them down in the wilderness
27 and disperse their descendants among the nations,
scattering them in foreign lands.
28 * [s] They joined in worshiping Baal of Peor
and ate food sacrificed to lifeless gods.
29 They provoked the LORD to anger by their evil deeds,
and a plague broke out among them.
30 Then Phinehas stood up and executed judgment,
and the plague came to an end.
31 This was credited to him as righteousness *
for all the generations to come.
32 * [t] At the waters of Meribah * they angered the LORD,
and Moses endured difficulties because of them.
33 For they rebelled against the Spirit of God,
and rash words issued from Moses' lips. *
34 * They did not exterminate the peoples
as the LORD had commanded them to do.[u]
35 Rather, they mingled with the nations
and adopted their practices.[v]
36 [w] They worshiped their idols,
which became a snare to them.
37 They sacrificed to false gods *
their sons and their daughters.
38 They shed innocent blood,
the blood of their sons and daughters,
whom they sacrificed to the idols of Canaan,
polluting the land with their blood.
39 Thus, they defiled themselves by their actions
and prostituted themselves by their conduct. *
40 * Then the anger of the LORD flared up against his people,
and he abhorred his own heritage.
41 He handed them over to the nations,
and their foes became their rulers.[x]
42 Their enemies oppressed them
and kept them in subjection to their power.
43 Time and again he came to their rescue,
but they rebelled against his counsel
and sank low because of their sin.[y]

p Pss 75:2; 78:42-58; Deut 32:18; Jer 2:32.—q Ex 32:11; Num 11:2; Deut 9:25; Ezek 22:30.—r 24-27: Lev 26:33; Num 13:25—14:37; Deut 1:25-36; Ezek 20:15, 23; Heb 3:18-19.—s 28-31: Ps 141:4; Num 25; Deut 26:14; Sir 45:23-24.—t 32-33: Pss 95:8-9; 107:11; Ex 17:1-7; Num 20:1-13; Deut 6:16; 33:8; Isa 63:10.—u Deut 7:1; Jos 9:15; Jdg 2:1-5.—v Lev 18:3; Jdg 1:27-35; 3:5; Ezr 9:1-2.—w 36-38: Ex 22:20; Lev 18:21; Num 35:33; Deut 32:17; Jdg 2:11-13, 17, 19; 2 Ki 16:3; Bar 4:7; Ezek 16:20-21; 1 Cor 10:20.—x Jdg 2:14-23.—y Neh 9:28; Isa 63:7-9.

106:20 *Glory:* none other than their Glorious one (see 1 Sam 15:29; Jer 2:11), their Savior-God (Ps 106: 21).

106:22 *Land of Ham:* see note on Ps 78:51.

106:23 *Stood in the breach:* see Ex 32:11-14, 31f.

106:24-27 The psalmist tells of the people's refusal to capture Canaan via the southern route and their punishment of not entering the Promised Land (see Num 13–14; Deut 1–2).

106:24 *Land of delights:* see the description given in Jer 3:19; 12:10; Zec 7:14.

106:28-31 The psalmist recalls the people's apostasy and rebellion in worshiping Baal of Peor (see Num 25:1-10).

106:31 *Credited to him as righteousness:* reminiscent of Abraham's justification and that of the new People of God (see Gen 15:6; Rom 4:3, 23-25).

106:32-33 The psalmist relives the people's quarreling with the Lord at Meribah, which led Moses to sin (see Num 20:1-13).

106:32 *Meribah:* see note on Ps 95:8. *The LORD:* literally, "him." *Moses endured difficulties:* he was not allowed to enter the Promised Land because of his rash words (see Num 20:12). Deuteronomy 1:37 indicates that Moses was not allowed to do so because of the people's sin, not his own.

106:33 *Spirit of God . . . Moses' lips:* literally, "his Spirit . . . his lips." The Old Testament indicates that the Spirit of God was present and at work in the wilderness (see Ex 31:3; Num 11:17; 24:2; Neh 9:20; Isa 63:10-14).

106:34-39 The psalmist indicts the mingling of the people with the pagan nations and their evil practices (such as idolatry, infant sacrifices, and injustice of all kinds) from the time of the Judges to the Babylonian Exile.

106:37 *False gods:* literally, "demons," i.e., pagan gods.

106:39 The people were made ritually unclean by the evils they practiced, and the land was also defiled by their wickedness (see Num 35:33f; Isa 24:5; Jer 3:1f, 9).

106:40-46 The psalmist recalls God's tempered judgment mingling chastisements and mercies.

44 Even so, he took pity on their distress
when he heard their cries.
45 He called to mind his covenant * with them,
and he relented because of his great mercy. [z]
46 He aroused compassion for them
on the part of all their captors.
47 Save us, O LORD, our God,
and gather us from among the nations,
so that we may give thanks to your holy name
and glory in praising * you. [a]
48 Blessed be the LORD, the God of Israel,
from everlasting to everlasting. *
Let all the people say, "Amen."
Alleluia. * [b]

BOOK V—PSALMS 107–150*

PSALM 107*

God, Savior of Those in Distress

1 "Give thanks to the LORD, for he is good;
his kindness * endures forever." [c]
2 Let this be the prayer of the redeemed of the LORD,
those he redeemed from the hand of the foe [d]
3 and gathered together from the lands, * [e]
from east and west, north and south.
4 * Some wandered in a barren wilderness,
unable to discover a path to an inhabited city. [f]
5 They were hungry and thirsty,
and their life was wasting away. [g]
6 Then they cried out to the LORD in their anguish,
and he saved them from their distress.
7 He led them by a direct route [h]
to a city in which they could dwell. [i]
8 Let them give thanks to the LORD for his kindness *
and for the wonders he does for people.
9 He has satisfied the thirsty
and filled the hungry with good things. [j]

z Lev 26:42; Jer 42:10.—a Ps 28:9; 1 Chr 16:35.—b Pss 41:14; 72:18; 89:53; 1 Chr 16:36; Neh 9:5.—c Pss 100:4-5; 106:1; 1 Chr 16:8; Jer 33:11.—d Ps 106:10; Isa 63:12.—e Neh 1:9; Isa 43:5-6; 49:12; Zec 8:7.—f Deut 8:15; 32:10; Jos 5:6.—g Ex 16:3; Isa 49:10.—h Ezr 8:21; Isa 35:8; 40:3; 43:19.—i Deut 6:10; Jos 24:13.—j Ps 22:27; Isa 49:10; 55:1; 58:11; Mt 5:6; Lk 1:53.

106:45 *Called to mind his covenant:* see Pss 105:8, 42; Ex 2:24; Lev 26:42, 45. *Mercy:* see note on Ps 6:5.

106:47 The psalmist ends on a note of communal prayer for deliverance and restoration from dispersion. The triumph of the Lord results in thanksgiving and praise. *Praising:* see note on Ps 9:2.

106:48a-c This last verse does not belong to the psalm but is the doxology to Book IV (see note on Ps 41:14). The doxology declares the praise of the Lord as the God of Israel (see Lk 1:68). As his "kindness endures forever" (Ps 107: 1), so will his praise from his people be *from everlasting to everlasting.* In hope of deliverance and prosperity (Ps 106: 4-5, 47), the People of God respond with an *Amen* (see 1 Chr 16:35f).

106:48d *Alleluia:* i.e., "Hallelujah" or "Bless [or praise] the LORD," which very likely belongs to the next psalm (see note on Ps 104:35).

Pss 107–150 Book V of the Psalter. Two collections are included in this final part: the pilgrimage chants or "Songs of Ascent" (Pss 120–134) and the Hallel or "Praise" psalms (113–118; 120–136; 146–150). In addition, we see a further group of psalms attributed to David (Pss 138–145). Jewish tradition also groups together Pss 113–118, known as the Egyptian Hallel, for use at the Passover. The "hymn" sung at the Last Supper (see Mk 14:26) was probably part of that Hallel.

Although cries of supplication still form part of the prayer of the psalmist, joy begins to radiate upon the face of the pilgrim who draws near to the Lord; the acclamation voiced in the presence of God will transform the conclusion of the Psalter into a prodigious symphony of happiness.

Ps 107 Even though this psalm is not part of Book IV, many believe that it was originally associated with Pss 105–106 and served as a kind of conclusion to the theme-related Pss 104–107. After the account of God's works in creation (see Ps 104:2-26) and his care for the animal world (see Ps 104:27-30) it recounts "the wonders [God] does for people" (Ps 107:8).

Psalm 107 is a thanksgiving for "God's deliverances." Persons in distress have cried out to him and obtained help: wandering voyagers (vv. 4-9), prisoners (vv. 10-16), the sick (vv. 17-22), and the shipwrecked (vv. 23-32). The Lord reverses situations as he pleases (vv. 33-41), but only the believer can discern the divine action. Beneath the concrete life of the era, evoked at times with humor (vv. 26-27 remind us that the Israelites were not very seaworthy), we see the history of the chosen people: the journeys of the Exodus and the Exile, their temptations and their sins.

Visibly the author takes his inspiration from the Book of Consolation (see Isa 40–55) and the writings of the sages (see Job; Wis 16). Thanksgivings that are at first private, ultimately express the gratitude of an entire people. For the believer, the events become signs: they invite him to discover in his life and that of the community of peoples a secret presence of God.

Christians pray this psalm to praise the Father for redeeming us in Christ. We have been saved by him from the hand of the infernal oppressor, gathered by him into the Church, and delivered by his love from the spiritual death to which we were doomed by the state in which Satan bound us and which was symbolized by the image of the wilderness, captivity, sickness, and the storm.

107:1 A conventional cry of praise in the liturgy of the temple often cited in the Old Testament (see Pss 106:1; 118:1; 136:1; 1 Chr 16:34; 1 Mac 4:24; Jer 33:11; Dan 3:89). *Kindness:* see note on Ps 6:5.

107:3 *From the lands:* e.g., Assyria, Babylonia, Egypt, and Moab, into which the catastrophe of 587 B.C. had dispersed the chosen people (see 2 Ki 17:6; 24:12-16; Isa 11:11f; 43:5f; Jer 52:28-30). *South:* literally, "[the] sea."

107:4-9 The psalmist evokes the Lord's deliverances of his people from the wilderness in which they were lost, hungry, thirsty, and exhausted, especially during the Exodus (see Jos 5:6), which prefigured the just completed return from the Exile (see Neh 1:3). Jesus would later indicate that he delivered people from the same four situations as the Way to the Father (see Jn 14:6), the Bread of Heaven (see Jn 6:41), the Water of Life (see Jn 4:14), and the Giver of Rest (see Mt 11:28).

107:8 This refrain is repeated in verses 15, 21, 31. *Kindness:* see note on Ps 6:5. *Wonders:* see note on Ps 9:2 concerning God's wonders.

10 * Some sat in darkness and the shadow of death, *
bound in misery and in chains,
11 because they had rebelled against the words of God
and spurned the plan of the Most High. [k]
12 He humbled their hearts with hard labor; *
when they stumbled, no one was there to offer help. [l]
13 Then they cried out to the LORD in their need,
and he rescued them from their distress.
14 He brought them forth from darkness and the shadow of death
and tore their chains to pieces. [m]
15 Let them give thanks to the LORD for his kindness
and for the wonders he does for people.
16 He has broken down gates of bronze
and cut through iron bars.
17 * Some were made foolish by their wicked ways
and were afflicted because of their iniquities.
18 All types of food became loathsome to them, [n]
and they were nearing the gates of death. *
19 Then they cried out to the LORD in their anguish,
and he rescued them from their distress.
20 He sent forth his word * and healed them,
saving them from the grave. [o]
21 Let them give thanks to the LORD for his kindness
and for the wonders he does for people.
22 Let them offer sacrifices in thanksgiving
and recount his deeds with jubilation.
23 * Some went down to the sea in ships
and engaged in commerce on the mighty waters. [p]
24 * They beheld the works of the LORD
and his wonders in the deep.
25 He spoke and raised up a storm wind
that stirred up the waves of the sea. [q]
26 They were lifted up to the heavens, then cast down to the depths;
their courage melted away in their plight.
27 They reeled and staggered like drunkards,
and they were at their wits' end. [r]
28 They cried out to the LORD in their anguish,
and he delivered them from their distress.
29 He reduced the storm to a whisper,
and the waves of the sea were hushed. [s]
30 They rejoiced because of the calm,
and he guided them to the port they sought.
31 Let them give thanks to the LORD for his kindness
and for the wonders he does for people.
32 Let them exalt him in the assembly of the people
and praise him in the council of the elders. *
33 * He turns rivers into wasteland,
springs of water into parched ground, * [t]

k Ps 5:11; Job 36:8-9; Prov 1:25; Isa 42:7, 22.—l Ps 106:43; Lev 26:40-41.—m Isa 42:7; 49:9; 51:14; Lk 1:79.—n Job 6:6-7; 17:16; 33:20.—o Ps 147:15; Deut 32:2; Wis 16:12; Isa 55:11; Mt 8:8; Lk 7:7; Jn 1:1.—p Ps 104:26; Sir 43:25; Isa 42:10.—q Ps 93:3; Jon 1:4.—r Isa 19:14; 29:9.—s Pss 65:8; 77:20; 89:10; Isa 43:2; Jon 1:15; Mt 8:26 par.—t Ps 74:15; Isa 35:7; 42:15; 50:2.

107:10-16 The psalmist evokes God's deliverance of his people from foreign bondage, especially in the return from the Exile (see Isa 43:5f; 49:12; Zec 8:7f). In addition, guilt, darkness, grinding toil, and the constriction of chains, gates, and bars are apt figures for the fallen state of human beings.

107:10 See Pss 105:18; 149:8; Isa 42:7; 49:9. The Exile was a chastisement (see Lev 26:41ff; Job 33:19; 36:8ff; Prov 3:12), announced by the Prophets. *Shadow of death:* see note on Ps 23:4.

107:12 *Humbled their hearts with hard labor:* i.e., a labor that broke their spirit. Another translation is: "subjected them to bitter labor."

107:17-22 The psalmist evokes God's deliverance of his people from the chastisement of sickness unto death incurred because of sin.

107:18 *Gates of death:* metaphorical description for death (see Pss 9:14; 88:4) in keeping with the ancient custom of picturing the realm of death as a city in the netherworld with a series of gates that prevented return to the land of the living (see Job 38:17; Mt 16:18).

107:20 The *word* is here personified as God's messenger of healing and deliverance from the *grave* (see Ps 147:15; Job 33:23ff; Wis 16:12; Isa 55:11; Mt 8:8; Jn 1:1).

107:23-32 The psalmist evokes God's deliverance of his people from the perils of the sea.

107:24-29 The merchants who cross the seas in search of wealth witness God's wonderful deeds at sea (see Ps 104:24-26) and his ability to calm a storm on the surging waters (see Pss 65:8; 77:20).

107:32 The merchants are urged to render worship to God by declaring, both in communal worship and in places of leadership, what he has done for them.

107:33-42 The psalmist evokes God's deliverance of his people by a "reversal of fortune."

107:33-35 Imagery like that found in Isa 35:6f; 41:18; 42:15; 43:19f; 50:2.

34 and fertile land into a salt waste, [u]
because of the wickedness of those who live there. *
35 He turns the wasteland into pools of water
and the parched ground into bubbling springs. [v]
36 * There he provides the hungry with a home,
and they build a city where they can settle. [w]
37 They sow fields and plant vineyards
that yield crops for the harvest. [x]
38 He blesses them and they greatly increase in number,
and he does not let their cattle decrease. [y]
39 Eventually their numbers diminish and they are humbled
because of oppression, adversity, and affliction;
40 he who pours forth his contempt on princes
makes them wander in trackless wastes, [z]
41 while he raises the needy from their misery
and increases their families like flocks. [a]
42 The upright see and exult,
while the wicked * are reduced to silence. [b]
43 Let whoever is wise reflect on these things [c]
and understand the merciful love of the LORD. *

PSALM 108*

Prayer for Divine Assistance against Enemies

1 A song. A psalm of David.
2 * [d] My heart * is steadfast, O God,
my heart is steadfast.
I will sing and chant your praise;
awake, my soul!
3 Awake, lyre and harp!
I will awaken the dawn. * [e]
4 * I will give thanks to you among the peoples, O LORD;
I will sing your praises among the nations. [f]
5 For your kindness extends above the heavens;
your faithfulness, to the skies. [g]
6 Be exalted, O God, above the heavens,
and let your glory shine over all the earth.
7 * With your right hand come to our aid
so that those you love may be delivered.
8 * God has promised from his sanctuary, [h]
"In triumph I will apportion Shechem
and measure out the Valley of Succoth.
9 Gilead is mine, and Manasseh is mine;
Ephraim is my helmet, *
Judah is my scepter.

u Gen 13:10; 19:23-28; Deut 29:22; Sir 39:23.—v Ps 114:8; 2 Ki 3:17; Isa 41:18.—w Ezek 36:35.—x 2 Ki 19:29; Isa 65:21; Jer 31:5.—y Deut 7:13-14; Isa 49:21.—z Job 12:21, 23-25.—a Ps 113:7-9; Job 5:16.—b Pss 58:11; 63:12; Rom 3:19.—c Hos 14:9.—d 2-6: Ps 57:8-12.—e Job 21:12; 38:12.—f Pss 9:12; 18:50; 148:13.—g Pss 36:6; 71:19; 106:45; 145:8; Ex 20:6; Num 14:18.—h 7-14: Ps 60:7-14.

107:34 Allusion to Sodom and Gomorrah (see Gen 13:10; 19; Deut 29:22; Sir 39:23). Salt was cast on cities that had been destroyed (see Jdg 9:45).

107:36-41 These verses are written in general terms; however, scholars believe the psalmist is most likely referring here to the settlement and development of the Promised Land (vv. 36ff), the hardships during the Assyrian and Babylonian invasions (v. 39), the humiliation and exile of the last kings of Judah (v. 40), and the restoration of Zion after the Exile (v. 41).

107:42 *Upright . . . wicked:* a comparison often made in the Old Testament (see Prov 2:21f; 11:6f; 12:6; 14:11; 15:8; 21:18; 29:27).

107:43 This conclusion transforms the hymn of thanksgiving and praise into a wisdom psalm. The righteous will become wise by studying the Lord's deliverances of his people.

Ps 108 Two fragments of psalms (with very slight modifications) have been used to make up this song of praise (vv. 2-6 in Ps 57:8-12 and vv. 7-14 in Ps 60:7-14), which Israel proclaims as it awaits liberation. We see the Lord already rallying all his children and taking the lead of their combat, as in the past, to enable them to gain redress against their enemies. This song of martial confidence will become a canticle of hope inculcating joy and praise, for the glory of God will fill all humankind.

Christians can make use of this psalm to thank God for the redemption and for the constant victories that he enables us to obtain over our spiritual enemies by the aid of our Redeemer.

108:2-6 The psalmist offers praise to God's kindness, which gives him steadfast hope.

108:2 The psalmist is at peace because of his trust in the Lord. *Heart:* see note on Ps 4:8. *O God:* after this phrase, some manuscripts lack the words "my heart is steadfast." *Awake, my soul:* another possible translation is: "with all my soul."

108:3 *Dawn:* personified as in Ps 139:9; Job 3:9; 38:12. The psalmist wishes to awaken the dawn, for that is the usual time when deliverance comes from the Lord (see notes on Pss 17:15; 57:8).

108:4-5 A vow to offer ritual praise to the Lord for his kindness (see note on Ps 7:18). *Kindness:* see note on Ps 6:5.

108:7-14 The psalmist prays for God's help against his enemies.

108:8-10 *Shechem* was west of the Jordan, and *the Valley of Succoth* east of it; therefore, they indicate dominion over all Palestine. Next are named four Israelite tribes; hence, there are three regions in all that must be reduced to subjection.

108:9 *Helmet:* a symbol of the strength exhibited by the tribe of Ephraim (see Deut 33:17; Jdg 7:24—8:3). *Scepter:* a symbol of the King-Messiah who had been promised from Judah (see Gen 49:10).

10 Moab is my washbasin; *
upon Edom I will plant my sandal;
over Philistia I will shout in triumph." [i]
11 Who will lead me into the fortified city? *
Who will guide me into Edom?
12 * Is it not you, O God, who have rejected us
and no longer go forth with our armies? [j]
13 Grant us your help against our enemies,
for any human assistance is worthless.
14 With God's help we will be victorious,
for he will overwhelm our foes.

PSALM 109*

Prayer for One Falsely Accused

1 For the director. * A psalm of David.
* O God, whom I praise,
do not remain silent. [k]
2 Wicked and deceitful men
have opened their mouths against me; *
they have spoken against me with lying tongues.
3 They confront me with words of hatred
and assail me without cause.
4 In return for my love they denounce me
even as I offer up prayers for them. *
5 They give me back evil in exchange for good
and hatred in place of my love. * [l]
6 * They say: *
"Choose a wicked man to oppose him,
an accuser to stand on his right.
7 At his judgment, let him be found guilty,
with even his prayers deemed sinful. *
8 "May his remaining days be few,
with someone else appointed to take his office. * [m]
9 May his children become fatherless
and his wife become widowed. [n]
10 "May his children be vagrants and beggars,
driven from the ruins they use for shelter.
11 May the creditor seize all he has,
and strangers abscond with his life savings.
12 * "May no one extend mercy to him
or take pity on his fatherless children.
13 May his posterity be doomed to extinction
and his name be blotted out within a generation. [o]

i Ps 137:7; Gen 19:37; Ru 4:7-8.—j Pss 44:10; 60:12; 68:8; 89:39-52.—k Pss 35:22; 83:1; Ex 15:2; Job 34:29; Jer 17:14.—l Pss 35:12; 38:21; Gen 44:4; Prov 17:13; Jer 18:20.—m Job 15:32; Acts 1:20.—n Ex 22:23; Jer 18:21.—o Pss 9:6; 21:11; Num 14:12; Job 18:19; Prov 10:7.

108:10 *Moab is my washbasin:* i.e., its people will do menial work for the Israelites (see Gen 18:4). *Plant my sandal:* an Eastern way of signifying possession.

108:11 *Fortified city:* doubtless Bozrah in Idumea (see Isa 34:6; 63:1; Am 1:12). It was from this inaccessible refuge that the Edomites sent incursions into Judea.

108:12-14 The psalmist looks to the Lord rather than other human beings for an answer to the people's problems. He calls upon him to end his abandonment and lead his people to victory over their enemies. Indeed, he believes the Lord is still with them and will bring them through this trial with strength, joy, and success (see Pss 44:6; 118:15f).

Ps 109 The Psalter contains other cries of hatred or revenge (Pss 9; 35; 137; 139), but none is harsher than this one (Ps 109: 6-19). It is ordinarily attributed to the psalmist who has been speaking from the beginning of the psalm. However, an attentive examination of the context leads some scholars to attribute these imprecations to another person—most likely, the leader of the psalmist's enemies.

It is a fact, of course, that in the East people enjoy exaggerated expressions, and it is also a fact that it was written before the Christian faith changed the harsh law of revenge or law of talion. But the Gospel itself contains curses (see Mt 23:13-26; Lk 6:24-26), and while it is true that Jesus and the apostles were able to forgive their enemies, they also saw the "ancient serpent" (Rev 12:9) at work against God's will and for their destruction.

In taking up these imprecatory psalms, the Church invites Christians to commence an unceasing struggle against the spirit of evil (see Eph 6:12). Except for a few details, the formulas of this prayer were suitable for Jesus to express his own situation and sentiments and to describe the attitude and machinations of his enemies. In fact, the evangelists record that his enemies fulfilled certain passages to the letter (v. 25; see Mt 27:39; Mk 15:20).

109:1a *For the director:* these words are thought to be a musical or liturgical notation.

109:1b-5 This psalmist has never said and done anything other than good; will betrayal, hatred, and slander be his recompense? Bitter is the calumny that crushes the righteous.

109:2 *Opened their mouths against me:* see note on Ps 5:10.

109:4 *I offer up prayers for them:* the psalmist is not a man of evil and slander; he even prays for his foes, as in Ps 35:13f.

109:5 The psalmist has done nothing but good to his enemies whereas they have repaid him with evil in exchange for goodness and hatred in exchange for friendliness. The psalmist puts this fact before the Lord. Will God the Judge overlook such wicked behavior? This verse recalls Pss 35:12, 22; 38:20-21; 69:5; Jer 18:20.

109:6-15 Pitiless are the words of those who curse the innocent psalmist; he has taken them to heart and remembered every one. See note on Ps 5:11 concerning redress for wrongs.

109:6 *They say:* these words are lacking in the Hebrew, but they are called for by the context. *Wicked man:* or "the evil one." *Accuser:* i.e., a "satan" (see Job 1:6), a name later given to the devil (see 1 Chr 21:1). He stood as an advocate (Ps 109:31) at the right of the accused (see Zec 3:1).

109:7 *With even his prayers deemed sinful:* another possible translation is: "with even his pleas being in vain."

109:8 *With someone else appointed . . . office:* applied to Judas in Acts 1:20.

109:12-13 The Law, the Prophets, and the Gospel all give warnings of what the sins of ancestors can bring down upon the children (see Ex 20:5; 1 Sam 2:31ff; Lk 19:41ff). *Name be blotted out:* see note on Ps 69:29.

14 "May the iniquity of his ancestors be remembered by the LORD,
and the sin of his mother never be wiped out.[p]
15 May their guilt be continually before the LORD,[q]
and may he banish all remembrance of them from the earth.[r]

16 * "For he never thought of showing mercy;
rather, he hounded to death
the poor and the needy and the brokenhearted.
17 He loved to level curses * at others;
may they recoil on him.
He took no pleasure in blessing;
may no blessing be his.

18 * "He clothed himself with cursing as his garment;
it seeped into his body like water
and into his bones like oil.
19 May it be like the robe that envelops him,
like the belt that encircles him every day."

20 May these evils my accusers wish for me
be inflicted upon them by the LORD. *
21 * But you, O LORD, my God,
treat me kindly for your name's sake; *
deliver me because of your overwhelming kindness.

22 For I am poor and needy, *
and my heart is pierced within me.
23 I am fading away * like an evening shadow;
I am shaken off like a locust.

24 [s] My knees are weak from fasting;
my flesh is wasting away.
25 I have become an object of ridicule to my accusers;
upon seeing me, they toss their heads. *

26 Come to my aid, O LORD, my God;
save me because of your kindness. *
27 Let them know that your hand has done this,
that you, O LORD, have accomplished it.

28 When they curse, you will bless;
when they attack, they will be put to shame,
and your servant will rejoice. *
29 My accusers will be clothed in disgrace,
wrapped in their shame as in a cloak.

30 I will thank the LORD with my lips,[t]
and before all the people I will praise him. *
31 For he stands at the right hand of the poor
to save him from his accusers who pass judgment on him. *

---

p Ex 20:5; Isa 65:6-7; Jer 18:23.—q Ps 90:8; Hos 7:2.—r Ps 34:17; Ex 17:14; Deut 32:26.—s 24-25: Pss 22:7-8; 35:13; 69:11-13.—t Pss 35:18; 71:22; 111:1.

109:16-20 No other place expresses with such vivid intensity the terrible logic of judgment whereby what humans choose, they ultimately receive to the full.

109:17 *Curses:* see note on Ps 10:7.

109:18-19 These words, leveled at the psalmist by his enemies, claim that cursing was his clothing as well as his food and drink; he lived, so to speak, by cursing (see Prov 4:17). Cursing was intended to destroy a person, his position, his family, and the remembrance of his name.

109:20 *May these . . . by the LORD:* literally, "May this be the recompense of my accusers from the LORD / and of those who speak evil against me." Accordingly, the preceding curses may be understood as spoken either by the psalmist against his primary foe or by his enemies first and then willed by him to recoil against them. Another translation for the verse is also possible: "This is the work of those / who wish to call down harm upon me from the LORD." In that case, the only imprecations of the psalmist would be the mild ones in verse 29.

109:21-31 The poem seems to begin again at this point. The poor man once again invokes God, reveals his distress, asks for health, cries out his imprecations, and promises to give thanks. It is the rhythm of the prayer of a persecuted person. It testifies to a conviction: in the time of God's judgment, the evil one will return in defeat to the world of darkness where he willed to swallow up everything, but the righteous will obtain access to the glory of the Lord.

109:21 *For your name's sake:* see note on Ps 5:12. The Lord's *kindness* is one of his most defining attributes (see notes on Pss 5:8; 6:5; Ex 34:6; see also Pss 25:10-11; 69:17; 79:8-9; 86:15; 103:8; Num 14:18; Joel 2:13). Kindness is also the love of the covenant between the Lord and his people, and it includes the sentiments that are found in each (grace and love on the part of the Lord and piety on the part of the faithful). It specifically refers to all that God promised to his people (see Deut 7:9,12) through the Davidic dynasty (see Ps 89:25, 29, 34; 2 Sam 7:15; Isa 55:3).

109:22 *Poor and needy:* see note on Ps 22:27. *Heart:* see note on Ps 4:8.

109:23 *I am fading away:* the psalmist's illness draws the scorn of enemies (see note on Ps 5:10). *Like an evening shadow:* similar to Ps 102:12. *Shaken off like a locust:* allusion to the custom of brushing locusts off the plants in order to kill them on the ground. Another translation possible is: "swept away like a locust," an image similar to Job 30:22; in Palestine a strong wind sometimes ends a plague of locusts by blowing them out into the sea (see Ex 10:19; Joel 2:20).

109:25 His accusers seek the psalmist's downfall by casting scorn on him (see Pss 31:12; 79:4; 89:42) and by rejecting him (*[tossing] their heads*: see Ps 22:8; Mt 27:39).

109:26 *Kindness:* see note on Ps 6:5.

109:28 This is a good prayer to turn the edge of an attack (see Rom 8:31ff).

109:30 A vow to praise the Lord for his deliverance (see note on 7:18).

109:31 The final verse puts everything in perspective. At the beginning of this psalm, the enemies of the psalmist are seeking for someone to stand at his right hand in order to accuse him (v. 6) according to the custom of the time. Here we see that the Lord himself is already at the psalmist's right hand—not to accuse but to defend him. The Lord is ever "near to all who call out to him" (Ps 145:18; see also Deut 4:7; Isa 55:6; 58:9; Jer 29:13).

PSALM 110*

The Messiah—King, Prophet, and Conqueror

1 A psalm of David.
The LORD says to my Lord: *
"Sit at my right hand
until I have made your enemies a footstool for you." u
2 The LORD will stretch forth from Zion
your scepter of power. *
The LORD says:
"Rule in the midst of your enemies! *
3 Yours is royal dignity in the day of your birth;
in holy splendor, before the daystar,
like the dew, I have begotten you." * v
4 The LORD has sworn,
and he will not retract his oath:
"You are a priest forever *
according to the order of Melchizedek." w
5 The LORD stands forth at your right hand; *
he will crush kings on the day of his wrath. x
6 He * will judge the nations,
filling their land with corpses
and crushing rulers throughout the earth.
7 He will drink from the stream on his journey,
and then he will lift up his head in triumph. * y

u Jos 10:24; Mt 22:44; Mk 12:36; Lk 20:42f; Acts 2:34-35; 1 Cor 15:25; Heb 1:13; 8:1; 10:12-13; 12:2; 1 Pet 3:22.—v Pss 2:7; 89:28; Ex 15:11; Isa 49:1; Mic 5:7.—w Pss 89:36; 132:11; Gen 14:18; Num 23:19; Heb 5:6; 7:21.—x Pss 2:9; 16:8; Rev 2:27; 12:5; 19:15.—y Pss 3:4; 27:6.

Ps 110 These few surprising verses (which comprise essentially two oracles) became the supreme Messianic psalm in both the Jewish and the Christian traditions. It was so much used and adapted down the centuries before becoming part of the Psalter that it is difficult to reconstruct completely the original text. In its oldest version it certainly goes back to the earliest times of the monarchy.

The psalm was subsequently revised, perhaps on various occasions; the song no longer refers to the kings who are passing away but to the Messiah who is to come at the end of the earthly time and restore everything in the name of God. He will be of royal birth (see 2 Sam 7:16) and will be charged with judging the nations and ruling over the entire world. He will not be counted among the princes of the nations, who have their power from human beings, for God himself will invest him as everlasting King and Priest, as is shown by the parallel with the mysterious Melchizedek, priest and king of Salem, whose earthly ancestry no one knows (see Gen 14:18; Heb 7:3).

Jesus, who claims to be the Christ, that is, the Messiah, and Son of God, fulfills the promise given in this psalm, as he hints to the Pharisees (see Mt 22:42-45; 26:64); the apostles are inspired by this passage to proclaim the glory of the risen Christ, Lord of the universe (see Mk 16:19; Acts 2:33-35; Rom 8:34; 1 Cor 15:25-28; Eph 1:20; Col 3:1; Heb 10:12f; 1 Pet 3:22). The author of the Letter to the Hebrews finds in this psalm the proof that Christ is superior to the priests of the Old Testament and that he alone is the Savior of humankind (Heb 7).

110:1 The first oracle (vv. 1-3) establishes God's anointed as his regent over all (see Ps 2:7-12). *The LORD says to my Lord:* a polite form of address from an inferior to a superior (see 1 Sam 25:25; 2 Sam 1:10). By the word "Lord," the court singer is referring to the king. Jesus, in interpreting this psalm, takes the psalmist to be David, who was acknowledged by all to be referring to the Messiah. Hence, the Messiah must be David's superior and not merely his son or descendant (see Mt 22:41-46 par). *Right hand:* the place of honor beside a king (see Ps 45:10; 1 Ki 2:19), in this case making the Messiah second to God himself (see Mt 26:64; Mk 14:62; 16:19; Lk 22:69; Acts 2:33; 5:31; 7:55f; Rom 8:34; Eph 1:20; Col 3:1; Heb 1:3; 8:1; 10:12; 12:2). *Footstool for you:* there are secular texts and illustrations as well as biblical texts depicting ancient kings placing their feet on those they had conquered (see Jos 10:24; Dan 7:14). The author of 2 Chronicles (2 Chr 9:18) indicates that a footstool was part of the king's throne. Paul made use of this text to show that God has placed everything under Christ's feet (Eph 1:22), including his enemies (1 Cor 15:25; Heb 10:12f).

110:2a-b The Lord will expand the Messiah's reign to the extent that no foe will remain to oppose his rule (see Pss 2:6; 45:7; 72:8).

110:2c-d The Messiah is the Lord's regent over his emerging kingdom.

110:3 *Yours is royal dignity . . . I have begotten you:* this is the usual Catholic translation and comes from the revised Latin Vulgate, which is based on the ancient versions. The current Hebrew is obscure and seems to be corrupt. *Before the daystar:* when the sun had not yet been created, i.e., from all eternity. *Like the dew:* in a secret, mysterious manner. Hence, the Messiah and Son of God existed before the dawn of creation in eternity.

The Hebrew is translated as follows: "Your people will volunteer freely / on your day of battle. / In holy splendor, from the womb of the dawn / the dew of your youth is yours." It refers to numerous royal troops at the Messiah's command. The people come voluntarily on the day of battle, as in the days of Deborah (see Jdg 5:2, 9). They consecrate themselves, are fully prepared, and place themselves at his service. They will be as abundant as the dew at dawn. The image is close to those of Paul about "living sacrifices" (Rom 12:1) or a life poured out like a "libation" (Phil 2:17). It should be noted that, even not considering the linguistic difficulties that argue against this reading and the fact that the Septuagint of pre-Christian times already confirms the text of the Vulgate, the Hebrew reading does not fit the great theme of the psalm as well as the Latin translation does. Every connection with the central thought that speaks of the royal and priestly dignity of Melchizedek is missing.

110:4 The prophet-psalmist pronounces a second divine oracle, guaranteed by an oath. The Lord makes his king his chief priest for life, according to the order and image of Melchizedek. There are three main points of resemblance between Melchizedek and Christ. Both are kings as well as priests, both offer bread and wine to God, and both have their priesthood directly from God (see Gen 14:18; Heb 7). For a prophetic vision of the glorious union of the Messiah-Priest, see Zec 6:13; for the New Testament application, see Heb 5:6-10; 7:22. *Forever:* perhaps alluded to in Jn 12:34.

110:5 *The LORD stands forth at your right hand:* when the king goes out to battle, the Lord, as the Master of the universe, is right with him, and crushing the foes.

110:6 *He:* the Messiah-King. *Filling their land with corpses:* gory imagery symbolizing full victory (see Ps 2:9; Rev 19:11-21) when God's judgment comes to pass.

110:7 Figurative language of uncertain meaning. Some see an allusion to a rite of royal consecration at the spring of Gihon (see 1 Ki 1:33, 38). Others see an image of the Messianic King bowing down in humility to drink of the waters of divine assistance before moving on to more victories (see Isa 8:6; Jer 2:13, 17f).

PSALM 111*

Praise of God for His Wondrous Works

1 Alleluia.
I will give thanks to the LORD with all my heart*
in the council of the upright and in the assembly.[z]
2 Great are the works of the LORD;*
they are pondered by all who delight in them.
3 His deeds* show forth majesty and splendor,
and his righteousness endures forever.
4 He has won renown for his wonders;*
gracious and compassionate is the LORD.[a]
5 He provides food for those who fear him,*
and is forever mindful of his covenant.
6 He has manifested the power of his works to his people
by giving them the lands* of the nations.
7 The works of his hands* are faithful and right,
and all his commandments are trustworthy.
8 They are established forever and ever
to be observed in fidelity and truthfulness.
9 He has granted deliverance to his people
and established his covenant forever;
holy and awe-inspiring is his name.*
10 The fear of the LORD is the beginning of wisdom;*
those who are guided by it will grow in understanding.
His praise will last forever.[b]

PSALM 112*

The Blessings of the Righteous

1 Alleluia.
Blessed* is the man who fears the LORD,
who greatly delights in his precepts.[c]
2 His descendants will be powerful upon the earth;

z Pss 9:2; 27:6; 34:2; 138:1.—a Pss 103:8; 112:4; Deut 4:31.—b Deut 4:6; Prov 1:7; 9:10; Sir 1:16.—c Pss 1:1-2; 13:6; 15:2-5; 103:11; 119:1-2, 14, 16, 47, 92; 128:1; Deut 18:13; Job 1:8; Mt 3:5ff.

Ps 111 A sage sets forth the essence of the religion of Israel: the Lord has delivered his people in order to conclude a covenant with them and to reveal his will to them. The author contemplates the divine "righteousness" (v. 3), i.e., everything the Lord has done in favor of his chosen ones, the wonders that in some way are renewed when they are recalled in the liturgy (v. 4): the miracle of the manna and the quail (v. 5), the gift of the Promised Land (v. 6), and the stability of the laws of the world and the moral order (v. 7). The sages who pursue this meditation and observe the law will be enabled to understand who God is: holy and redoubtable, compassionate and tender, so that they may render thanks to him.

In praying this psalm, we should keep in mind that the wonders to which it alludes are only a pale figure of the wonders that the Father has accomplished through, and in, his Incarnate Son on behalf of his new people, the Church (see Jn 5:20). After various physical cures and raisings from the dead, God works the glorious Resurrection of his Son and our own spiritual resurrection in him (see Eph 2:5f).

111:1 *Heart:* see note on Ps 4:8. *Council of the upright:* probably a circle of friends and advisors, as in Ps 107:32. *In the assembly:* in the temple (see Ps 149:1).

111:2 *Works of the LORD:* sometimes his deeds, as in verse 6, but more often the things he has made (the heavens, Pss 8:4; 19:2; 102:26; and the earth, Ps 104:24). Made "by ... wisdom" (Ps 104:24), these lend themselves to meditation and lead to delight.

111:3 *Deeds:* probably his providential acts as in Deut 32:4. We should keep in mind that, as Isa 45:9-13 indicates, God's creation and providence are of one piece. *Righteousness:* as embodied in his deeds.

111:4 *Won renown for his wonders:* by the celebration of annual feasts (see Ex 23:14), notably the Passover (for Christians, see 1 Cor 11:23-26). See also note on Ps 9:2. *Gracious and compassionate:* classic description of the meaning of God's name (see Ps 103:8; Ex 34:6f).

111:5 *Food for those who fear him:* probably a reference to the manna in the desert (see Ex 16:1ff), which in the New Testament is seen as a type of the Eucharist (see Jn 6:31-33, 49-51). The entire verse may also refer to God's giving of our daily bread (see Mt 6:11) and his daily forbearance. *His covenant:* see Ps 105:8-11.

111:6 *Lands:* literally, "inheritance, heritage."

111:7-8 There is complete harmony between what God does and what he says, between the *works of his hands* and *his commandments.*

111:9 This verse recalls the miracles of the Exodus and the theophany at Sinai. *Name:* see note on Ps 5:12.

111:10 *The fear of the LORD is the beginning of wisdom:* the motto of the Wisdom writings (see Job 28:28; Prov 1:7; 9:10; Eccl 12:13; Sir 1:18, 24; 19:17). Here it refers to God especially as Creator, Redeemer, and Provider.

Ps 112 This psalm provides the same literary characteristics as the preceding one and most likely stems from the same unknown author. By their theme the two chants complete one another. The first celebrates the divine perfections and works, while the second sings of the virtues and deeds of the true righteous person and the happiness he attains.

The ancients believed that the man who faithfully observed the law and was solicitous of his neighbor was assured prosperity, posterity, and renown. In this psalm a sage once again praises the righteous in these terms, but he adds another more mystical religious sentiment. In effect, applying to the righteous the qualities that the preceding psalm attributed to the Lord, he wishes to show that by dint of placing his delight in the will of the Lord, the righteous man ends up resembling him. Hence, the law is not a burden imposed from without, but a power that transforms the heart. To obey is to let oneself be invaded by the sentiments of God: mercy, tenderness, and righteousness. Is there any other source of happiness?

This psalm is also very suitable for describing the Christian ideal, the perfection we must achieve in the steps of the Master and the happiness we will find therein.

112:1 Blessed is the man who follows unswervingly God's will and call. *Blessed:* see note on Ps 1:1. *Fears the LORD:* see note on Ps 15:2-5.

the generation of the upright will be blessed. *

3 His house will be filled with wealth and riches, *
and his righteousness will endure forever.

4 He shines as a light for the upright in the darkness;
kindness, mercy, and justice are his hallmarks. * [d]

5 The future bodes well * for him
who is generous in helping those in need
and who conducts his affairs with justice.

6 * He will never be swayed;
the righteous man will be remembered forever. [e]

7 He has no fear of bad news,
for his heart remains steadfast, trusting in the LORD.

8 Since his heart is tranquil, he will not be afraid,
and he will witness the downfall of his enemies.

9 He bestows gifts lavishly on the poor;
his righteousness will endure forever,
and his horn * will be exalted in glory. [f]

10 The wicked will be furious when he sees this,
gnashing his teeth and pining away;
the desires of the wicked will be fruitless. *

THE EGYPTIAN HALLEL—PSS 113–118*

PSALM 113*

Praise of the LORD for His Care of the Lowly

1 Alleluia.

Praise, you servants of the LORD, *
praise the name of the LORD. [g]

2 * Blessed be the name of the LORD
now and forevermore.

3 From the rising of the sun to its setting
the name of the LORD is to be praised.

d Pss 18:29; 37:6; 97:11; Prov 13:9; Isa 58:10.—e Ps 15:5; Prov 10:7; Wis 8:13.—f Pss 75:11; 86:17; Prov 22:9; Lk 19:8; Acts 9:36; 2 Cor 9:9.—g Pss 22:23; 34:23; 99:3; 103:25; 134:1; 148:13.

112:2 The upright man is blessed in his children and brings blessings on them (see Pss 37:26; 127:3-5; 128:3).

112:3 *Wealth and riches:* see Pss 1:3; 128:2. *His righteousness:* i.e., his happiness, his successes, and his well-being. There is a tacit comparison of the upright person's righteousness to God's (they both *endure forever*: see Ps 111:3b). Some scholars translate the word "righteousness" as "generosity," claiming that the original meaning of the Hebrew word in a later period of the language also acquired the meaning of "liberality, almsgiving" (see Sir 3:30; 7:10; Mt 6:1f).

112:4 The goodness of the righteous man overflows to others. He acts in the same way as God does (see Ps 111:4b). This is brought out more clearly by the older Catholic rendition: "He dawns through the darkness, a light for the upright; / he is gracious and compassionate and righteous."

112:5 *Future bodes well:* i.e., well-being and prosperity await him (see Ps 34:9-15). Good is also the quality of the righteous man. He is good in that he *is generous* (see Pss 34:9-11; 37:21). Just as all the Lord's works are "faithful and right" (see Ps 111:7), so the upright man *conducts his affairs with justice.*

112:6-8 The righteous man observes the commandments of God that are "established forever and ever" (Ps 111:8); hence "he will never be swayed" (Ps 112:6) and *has no fear* (v. 7), for *his heart is tranquil* (v. 8). His trust is in the Lord in spite of *bad news,* reasons to *be afraid,* or problems with others (vv. 7-8).

112:9 As God's name is held in holy awe (see Ps 111:9), so the righteous will be held in honor. Paul uses this verse to support the principle that "if you sow generously, you will reap generously as well" (2 Cor 9:6, 9). *Horn:* here symbolizes dignity.

112:10 The only alternative way of life to that of the righteous is bitter, transient, and futile.

Pss 113–118 The *Hallel* ("praise") psalms are found in three separate collections: the "Egyptian Hallel," also known as the "Little Hallel" (Pss 113–118), the "Great Hallel" (Pss 120–136), and the "Concluding Hallel" (Pss 146–150). The Egyptian Hallel and the Great Hallel (most of which are pilgrimage psalms: Pss 120–134) were sung during the annual feasts (see Lev 23; Num 10:10). The Egyptian Hallel received a special place in the Passover liturgy; by custom Pss 113–114 were recited or sung before the festive meal and Pss 115–118 after it (see Mt 26:30; Mk 14:26). These were probably the last psalms Jesus sang before his Passion. Only the second (Ps 114) speaks directly of the Exodus, but the themes of the others make it an appropriate series to mark the salvation that began in Egypt and would spread to the nations. The concluding Hallel psalms (Pss 146–150) were incorporated into the daily prayers in the synagogue after the destruction of the temple in A.D. 70.

Ps 113 This psalm presents a surprising contrast in the praises of Israel: the acclamation of the glory of the Almighty One attains its summit, and certitude becomes even stronger that God is near to the lowly. His tenderness reaches those whom the powerful of the earth regard as nothing. The God of justice reverses established situations, as both the canticle of Hannah (see 1 Sam 2:4-8) and the Magnificat of Mary (see Lk 1:46-55) attest with equal intensity. In celebrating the salvation of the humiliated poor man and the abandoned woman, Israel keeps alive the hope of a wondrous renewal in the Messianic age (see Pss 76; 87; Isa 49:21; 54:1-8).

In praying this psalm, we are aware that the New Testament provides us with new motives for praising God the Father for the great condescension he manifests toward Zechariah, Mary, and those known as the poor of Yahweh. We can also chant this psalm in honor of the glorified Christ. Exalted by his Father above every earthly power and introduced by him into divine glory (Phil 2:9-11; Heb 2:7-9), Christ shows himself to be incomparable by uniting to his supreme transcendence an astonishing condescension. It was toward the poor and lowly that he stooped during his public ministry, eating and drinking with them (see Mk 2:16), offering them the kingdom of God (see Mt 5:3-12) with its mysteries (see Mk 4:11), and making them the princes of his new people (see Mk 3:13-19). It is on the poor and the weak in the eyes of the world that he continues to confer his spiritual riches and powers (see 1 Cor 1:26-28).

113:1 *Servants of the* LORD*:* the Lord's loyal people, together with the priests and the Levites, come together to worship the Lord. These are all those who know "the name of the LORD" (v. 3; see Ps 50:1; Zep 2:11; Mal 1:11). *Name:* see note on Ps 5:12.

113:2-3 The name of the Lord is to be proclaimed so that every generation may remember what he has done and how he has revealed himself (see Ex 3:16). This praise is to extend in time (*forevermore*) and in space (*from the rising of the sun to its setting,* i.e., from the east to the west; see Mal 1:11).

4 * High is the LORD over all the nations,
and supreme over the heavens is his glory. [h]
5 [i] Who is like the LORD, our God,
the one who is enthroned on high
and who stoops down to look
6 on the heavens and the earth?
7 * He raises the poor from the dust
and lifts the needy from the rubbish heap, [j]
8 seating them with princes,
with the princes of his people.
9 He settles the barren woman * in a home
and makes her the joyful mother of children. [k]

Alleluia.

PSALM 114*

The LORD's Wonders at the Exodus

1 * When Israel came out of Egypt,
the house of Jacob from a people of alien tongue,
2 Judah became God's sanctuary
and Israel his domain. [l]
3 * The sea fled at the sight;
the Jordan turned back. [m]
4 The mountains skipped like rams,
the hills like lambs of the flock. [n]
5 * What causes you to flee, O sea?
Why, O Jordan, do you turn back?
6 Why do you skip like rams, O mountains,
and like lambs of the flock, O hills?
7 * Tremble, O earth, at the presence of the LORD,
at the presence of the God of Jacob, [o]
8 who turns the rock into a pool of water,
and flint into a flowing spring. [p]

PSALM 115*

Hymn to the LORD, the One God

1 * Not to us, * O LORD, not to us,
but to your name give glory

h Pss 99:2; 148:13.—i 5-6: Pss 11:4; 89:7-9.—j Pss 35:10; 68:11; 107:41; 140:13; 1 Sam 2:8.—k 1 Sam 2:5; Isa 54:1; Lk 1:25; Gal 4:27.—l Ps 78:68f; Ex 15:17; 19:6; Jer 2:3.—m Pss 66:6; 74:15; 77:17; Ex 14:21f; 15:8; Jos 3:14-16.—n Ps 29:6; Jdg 5:5; Wis 19:9.—o Ps 68:9; 1 Chr 16:30.—p Ex 17:6; Num 20:11; Deut 8:15; 1 Cor 10:4.

113:4-6 The psalmist calls attention to the contrast: the exalted rule of the Lord and his accommodation to the needs of his people. *Over all the nations:* and by implication over all their gods (see Pss 95:3; 96:4f; 97:9). *Over the heavens:* i.e., above all creation.

113:7-9 The Lord does not ally himself with the high and mighty but takes care of the poor and needy by transforming them from outcasts of society (*the dust*, see Isa 47:1, or *rubbish heap*, see Lam 4:5) into those who have a position of prominence (*with the princes of his people*, v. 8; see 1 Sam 2:8; Job 36:7). The afflicted man will be accorded recognition, and the oppressed woman will be given honor.

113:9 *Barren woman:* a barren wife was considered cursed by God and a social outcast, a disappointment to her husband, to other women, and especially to herself (see Gen 16:2; 20:18; 1 Sam 1:6; 2:5; Lk 1:25). The Lord blesses her with children (see Ps 115:14; Isa 48:19; 54:1-3). *Alleluia:* i.e., "Hallelujah" or "Bless [or praise] the LORD"; it probably was once the first line of Ps 114.

Ps 114 By reason of its literary composition and poetic inspiration, this poem constitutes a little masterpiece. Felicitously, the poet personifies, herein, the elements of nature led in a dance by God during the Exodus, to make them keen-eyed witnesses of the Lord's triumphal march at the head of his people. Israel belongs so strongly to God that it is like his sanctuary and his domain (v. 2). On an epic and triumphal tone, the people underline the time beyond compare when God established this destiny for them: it is the great adventure of their deliverance.

When the Lord passes by with his people, the sea and waters flee (see Ex 14:15-31; Jos 3:7-17), Sinai thunders and smokes (see Ex 19:16-18), the source springs forth in the desert rocks (see Ex 17:1-7; Num 20:1-13). These remembrances of the Exodus are like the prelude to the upheaval of the universe announcing the coming of God at the end of the earthly ages.

We can pray this psalm in union with the Church ceaselessly meditating on and celebrating the privileged hour of her beginnings: the Passover of Christ that opens up for humankind a destiny of salvation in a new Exodus. Nature bows down before the divine Pioneer of this Exodus. The waters become calm and peaceful in the Sea of Galilee at a word from him: "Be still!" (Mk 4:39), while the mountains tremble at the moment of his Death and Resurrection (Mt 27:51; 28:2), as well as at the moment of his great interventions in history (see Rev 11:19; 16:18).

114:1-2 The deliverance from a foreign country was only a preamble to the greater deeds: the election of the chosen people and the making of the covenant on Sinai. Judah, the province of the tribe of that name, became the sanctuary of God and all Israel his kingdom; it was a theocracy, a priestly kingdom (see Ex 19:3-6; Jer 2:3). This was a grand event prefiguring the redemption to come and the birth of the Church.

114:3-4 The wonder of Israel's election as the People of God has its effect on the world of nature. The Red Sea and the Jordan River scurry around to make way for their Creator, and the mountains and hills are all animated and agog at his majestic coming (see Pss 18:8-16; 68:8ff; 77:17-20; Jdg 5:4f; Hab 3:3-10).

114:5-6 The psalmist calls upon the Red Sea, the Jordan, and the mountains to bear witness to the great event when God established his kingdom on earth.

114:7-8 The God of Israel (*Jacob*) is none other than the Lord of the universe (see Ps 97:4-6; Rev 20:11). He is still providing streams of blessings for his people as he did at Kadesh, at the waters of Meribah (see Ps 107:35; Ex 17:6; Num 20:8; Deut 8:15; 1 Cor 10:4) and also at the return from the Exile, prefigured by the Exodus and Conquest (see Isa 41:15ff; 42:15; 43:20). On the symbolism of the waters, see Pss 46:2-7; 110:7.

Ps 115 This psalm was probably used in the course of a celebration of the covenant, with choir and soloists in turn voicing their confidence in the Lord. Ridiculing the jerry-built gods venerated by the pagans, the community professes its attachment to the one true God, from whom it hopes to receive prosperity. The formulas are brief and striking, with a captivating rhythm; the satire against idols has the flavor of a popular caricature. This simple prayer is at the service of a deep and demanding religious thought and turns into praise. After the Exile, such a clear credo was needed for the community of Jerusalem and for the communities of the dispersion who all coexisted with pagan civilizations that welcomed countless gods. Today, it is still necessary for us to depart from idols fashioned according to our tastes and desires and to turn to the one true God.

We can pray this psalm for the Church, the new Israel, who often experiences profound misfortunes and oppressions that seem to proclaim her inferiority and impotence before earthly powers and their satanic idol. We can beg Christ the Lord to intervene to restore the renown of the Church and especially his own in the world.

115:1-3 A song in praise of the living God who is faithful to his people and in derision of the pagan idols who are lifeless.

115:1 *Not to us:* God alone is responsible for Israel's covenant blessings. *Name:* see note on Ps 5:12. *Kindness:* see note on Ps 6:5.

because of your kindness and faithfulness. [q]

2 Why should the nations ask, [r]
"Where is their God?" *

3 Our God is in heaven;
he does whatever he pleases. * [s]

4 [t] Their idols are merely silver and gold,
the work of human hands. * [u]

5 They have mouths but they cannot speak;
they have eyes but they cannot see.

6 They have ears but they cannot hear;
they have noses but they cannot smell.

7 They have hands but they cannot feel;
they have feet but they cannot walk;
their throats can emit no sound.

8 Those who make them end up like them,
as do all who place their trust in them.

9 * The house of Israel trusts in the LORD; [v]
he is their help and their shield. [w]

10 The house of Aaron trusts in the LORD;
he is their help and their shield.

11 Those who fear the LORD trust in the LORD;
he is their help and their shield.

12 * The LORD will be mindful of us and bless us;
he will bless the house of Israel;
he will bless the house of Aaron.

13 He will bless those who fear the LORD,
the small no less than the great. *

14 * May the LORD cause you to increase,
both you and your children.

15 May you be blessed by the LORD,
the Maker of heaven and earth.

16 * The heavens belong to the LORD,
but he has given the earth to humanity. [x]

17 It is not the dead who praise the LORD,
those who sink into silence. * [y]

18 It is we who bless the LORD
from this time forward and forevermore. *

Alleluia.

PSALM 116*

Thanksgiving to God for Help Received

1 I love the LORD because he has heard my voice
and listened to my cry for mercy, *

q Ps 23:3; Ezek 36:22-23.—r Pss 42:4; 79:10.—s Ps 135:6; Jud 9:5.—t 4-10: Pss 29:2; 135:15-20; Wis 15:15-16; Isa 44:9f; Jer 10:1-5; Bar 6:3, 7ff.—u Isa 40:19; Rev 9:20.—v Pss 118:2-4; 135:19-20.—w Pss 28:7; 33:20.—x Pss 8:7-9; 89:12; Gen 1:28.—y Pss 6:6; 30:10; 88:11ff; 94:17; 115:17; Sir 17:22f; Isa 38:18.

115:2 *Where is their God?:* implying that God does not help his people (see Pss 42:4, 11; 79:10; Joel 2:17; Mic 7:10).

115:3 The community expresses the belief that God is supreme and present; everything that happens to Israel, good or bad, is his doing.

115:4 The theme of this verse is one that is often found in the Old Testament: idols, unlike the God of Israel, do not speak, reveal, promise, or utter any spoken word; ultimately, divine revelation is the difference between the religions made by humans and the true religion of the Lord (see Ps 135:15-18; Deut 4:16; Isa 44:9ff; Jer 10:1ff; Bar 6:7ff).

115:9-11 In a litany, the various classes of people express their confidence in the Lord. The threefold division (*house of Israel, house of Aaron, those who fear the LORD*) occurs elsewhere (see Pss 118:2-4; 135:19f, refers to Aaron and Levi). It is unclear whether the phrase "those who fear the LORD" is a synonym for "house of Israel" (see Pss 34:8, 10; 85:10) or all of Israel (laity as well as priests) or whether it identifies a separate class from the house of Israel, namely the "God-fearers" known as the proselytes in the Old Testament (see 1 Ki 8:41; Isa 56:6) and in the New (see Acts 13:16, 26; 16:14).

115:12-15 Utilizing the same group of worshipers as in verses 9-11, the thought moves forward from God's power to save to his power to enrich. The Lord does not discriminate among his people—all will be the recipients of his blessing. Although they may be put to the test by afflictions of various kinds, the Lord remembers those with whom he has made a covenant (see Pss 98:3; 136:23; Isa 49:14f) and delivers them, bringing to fulfillment the promises he has made.

115:13 *The small no less than the great:* the outcasts and the powerful. All will be treated alike by the Lord (see Jer 6:13; 16:6; 31:34; Rev 19:5).

115:14-15 Through these words of blessing, the Lord renews his promise that Abraham's descendants will increase without end (see Ps 127:3-5; Deut 1:11; Isa 54:1-3; Zec 10:8-10).

115:16-18 The psalmist concludes with a short hymn of praise. In so doing, he reminds his people that they have been given the earth to enjoy and care for, while praising the Lord.

115:17 The psalmist stresses that the dead cannot praise the Lord; for, according to the idea of the ancients, in the netherworld the souls of the dead had a kind of shadowy existence with no activity or lofty emotion and could not offer praise to God. *Silence:* a euphemism for the grave (see Ps 94:17; see also notes on Pss 6:6 and 30:2).

115:18 *Forevermore:* some view this as saying that those who serve the living God will themselves live on, unlike the worshipers of lifeless idols (v. 8). This would then add its witness to an afterlife to such passages as Pss 11:7; 16:8-11; 17:15; 23:6; 49:16; 73:23ff; 139:18. *Alleluia:* i.e., "Hallelujah" or "Bless [or praise] the LORD"; the Septuagint and Vulgate add this line as the opening of Ps 116.

Ps 116 Countless are the distresses of human beings and countless too are the deliverances worked by God. This psalm adapts itself to diverse situations; every believer knows the mortal dangers from which the Lord has extricated him in order to bring him to the joy of his presence. In a praying community, all can give thanks. In thanking the divinity it was the custom in the ancient East to pour a cup as a libation, i.e., the "cup of salvation" (that has been granted) (v. 13). The Jews certainly practiced a similar rite during the "peace offerings" (see Lev 7:11ff). By this act of thanksgiving, the Israelites publicly bore witness that God had saved them; this is the loftiest expression of their religion.

It is also the loftiest expression of the Christian religion. It was certainly in this spirit that Jesus recited this psalm with his disciples after having instituted the Eucharist (see Mt 26:30). Who else could have fully relied on God even through the moment of his death? Once this psalm became the prayer of Jesus on the night in which he was betrayed, it proclaimed the hope of a life and a joy that are everlasting. The priest who mystically offers the divine victim anew still says: "We offer to you, God of glory and majesty ... the cup of eternal salvation" (Eucharistic Prayer I) and "We offer you, Father, ... this saving cup" (Eucharistic Prayer II).

In the Hebrew text, this psalm is a single psalm, as the sense requires; in the Septuagint and Vulgate, it is two distinct psalms: Pss 114 (comprising vv. 1-9); 115 (comprising vv. 10-19).

116:1 The psalmist expresses love for God who has heard his prayer. For a similar expression of God's care and people's love of him, see 1 Jn 4:19: "We love because [God] first loved us."

2 because he has inclined his ear to me
on the day when I called out to him. *
3 The bonds of death * encompassed me;
the snares of the netherworld held me tightly.
I was seized by distress and sorrow. [z]
4 Then I cried out in the name * of the LORD:
"O LORD, I entreat you to preserve my life."
5 Gracious is the LORD and righteous;
our God is merciful. [a]
6 The LORD watches over his little ones; *
when I was brought low, he saved me.
7 Be at peace once again, O my soul,
for the LORD has shown mercy to you. [b]
8 He has delivered my soul * from death,
my eyes from tears,
and my feet from stumbling. [c]
9 I will walk in the presence of the LORD
in the land of the living. * [d]
10 I believed; therefore, I said, *
"I am greatly afflicted." [e]
11 In my dismay I cried out,
"All men are liars." * [f]
12 How can I repay the LORD
for all the good he has done for me?
13 I will lift up the cup of salvation *
and call on the name of the LORD.
14 I will fulfill my vows * to the LORD
in the presence of his people.
15 Precious in the eyes of the LORD
is the death * of his faithful ones. [g]
16 O LORD, I am your servant.
I am your servant, the child of your handmaid; * [h]
you have loosed my bonds.
17 I will offer you a sacrifice of thanksgiving
and call on the name of the LORD. [i]
18 I will fulfill my vows to the LORD
in the presence of all his people, [j]
19 in the courts of the house of the LORD,
in your midst, O Jerusalem.
Alleluia. *

PSALM 117*

Universal Praise of God

1 Glorify the LORD, all you nations; *
praise him, all you peoples. [k]
2 For his kindness toward us is constant,
and the faithfulness of the LORD will endure forever.
Alleluia. *

z Ps 18:6-7; 2 Sam 22:6; Jon 2:3.—a Ps 86:15; Ex 34:6; Ezr 9:15.—b Pss 13:6; 62:2; Mt 11:29.—c Pss 56:14; 86:13; Isa 25:8; 35:10; Rev 7:17; 21:4.—d Pss 27:13; 56:14; Isa 38:11; Jer 11:19.—e Ps 9:19; 2 Cor 4:13.—f Pss 5:10f; 12:3; 35:11, 15; 109:2-4.—g Ps 72:14; Num 23:10; Isa 43:4.—h Pss 86:16; 119:125; 143:12; Wis 9:5.—i Lev 7:12ff; Ezr 1:4.—j Jon 2:10.—k Ps 103:1; Rom 15:11.

116:2 *On the day when I called out to him:* see Pss 4:4; 31:23; 34:5; 138:3. Another possible translation is: "I will call on him as long as I live."

116:3 *Bonds of death:* see note on Ps 18:6.

116:4 *Name:* see note on Ps 5:12.

116:6 *Little ones:* just like the "poor," the "little ones" are those who depend on and trust only in the Lord (see Ps 34:7). They have a poverty of spirit, not simply of money. Just as the Spirit of God worked on the primeval darkness to produce all that exists, so the Lord works on his little ones to produce all that is good for them.

116:8 The psalmist here spells out salvation in terms of earthly well-being, but in words that are true at the deepest level (see, e.g., Rom 8:10f; 2 Cor 6:10; Jude 24). *Soul:* see note on Ps 6:4.

116:9 *The land of the living:* reference to this life or to the temple (see Pss 52:7; 116:9; Isa 38:11), where the God of life is present; the psalmist is speaking of the world of the living as opposed to the world of the dead.

116:10 *I believed; therefore, I said:* the psalmist kept faith even in the darkest times (see 2 Cor 4:13 where this text is cited).

116:11 *All men are liars:* the psalmist avers that his enemies are telling falsehoods about him (see Pss 5:10f; 35:11, 15; 109:2-4), because all people are liars. He could also be alluding to the fact that all people offer only a false hope of deliverance. These words are cited in Rom 3:4.

116:13 *The cup of salvation:* probably the libation of wine poured out in gratitude for one's deliverance (see Ex 25:29; Num 15:1-10). These words are used at Mass in Eucharistic Prayer I and II, as indicated in the note on Ps 116. *Name:* see note on Ps 5:12.

116:14 *Vows:* see note on Ps 7:18.

116:15 *Precious . . . is the death:* the psalmist indicates that God consents to the death of his faithful only with difficulty (see Isa 43:4), for death was regarded as taking away their relationship with him (see Pss 6:6; 72:13; 115:17). Some versions interpret this passage according to the dogma of the resurrection: "the death of his faithful ones has worth in the eyes of God." See the analogous expression, "Their blood is precious in his sight" (Ps 72:14).

116:16 *Child of your handmaid:* see note on Ps 86:16.

116:19 *Alleluia:* i.e., "Hallelujah" or "Bless [or praise] the LORD"; the Septuagint and Vulgate add this line as the opening of Ps 117.

Ps 117 This psalm is a short invitatory earnestly exhorting all peoples to praise the Lord, the God of Israel, for the signal kindness and faithfulness that he manifests toward his people. His goodness toward Israel should inspire admiration and enthusiastic praise among foreigners, who are simply witnesses of his wonders (see Sir 36:1-4; Ezek 36).

Since God's kindness and faithfulness are manifested much more forcefully in the life of the Church than in the history of Israel, all people should on that account give more enthusiastic praise to the heavenly Father. Enabling his Son to vanquish his enemies (the devil and death), the Father fills him with divine riches (eternal life in glory, joy, peace, beatitude, royalty). And he has done the same for the Church and her members. Praise of God is to be unanimous (see Rom 15:11).

117:1 All *nations* and *peoples* are called to praise the Lord (see Pss 47:1; 67:4-6; 96:7; 98:4; 100:1-3; see also note on Ps 9:2). This verse is cited in Rom 15:11.

117:2 Universal praise is owed to the Lord because of his fidelity to his people. He has shown them constant kindness and faithfulness, that is, faithful love. Indeed, his love is not only great in depth and height (see Rom 5:20; 1 Tim 1:14) but also lasting (see Ps 89:29); see also note on Ps 6:5. In Christ, the love of God has been even more powerfully shown both to Jews and to Gentiles so that all might praise him for it (see Rom 15:8ff). *Alleluia:* i.e., "Hallelujah" or "Bless [or praise] the LORD"; the Septuagint and Vulgate add this line to open Ps 118.

PSALM 118*

Thanksgiving for Salvation

1 * Give thanks to the LORD, for he is good;
his kindness * endures forever. [l]

2 [m] Let Israel say,
"His kindness endures forever."
3 Let the house of Aaron say,
"His kindness endures forever."
4 Let those who fear the LORD * say,
"His kindness endures forever."

5 * In my distress I called out to the LORD;
he answered by setting me free.
6 With the LORD to protect me I am not afraid.
What can mortals do to me? [n]
7 The LORD is at my side to offer me help;
I will look down upon my enemies.

8 * [o] It is better to take refuge in the LORD
than to place your trust in mortals.
9 It is better to take refuge in the LORD
than to place your trust in princes.

10 * All the nations surrounded me;
in the name of the LORD I overcame them.
11 They surrounded me on every side;
in the name of the LORD I overcame them.
12 They swarmed around me like bees;
they blazed like a fire in the midst of thorns;
in the name of the LORD I overcame them. [p]

13 I was hard pressed and close to falling,
but the LORD came to my aid. [q]
14 The LORD is my strength and my song, [r]
and he has become my salvation. *

15 Joyful shouts of triumph
ring out in the tents of the righteous:
"The right hand of the LORD has done wondrous deeds;
16 the right hand of the LORD is exalted;
the right hand of the LORD has done wondrous deeds."

17 I shall not die; rather I shall live
and recount * the works of the LORD.
18 Even though the LORD punished me harshly,
he did not hand me over to death.

19 * Open to me the gates of righteousness
so that I may enter them and praise the LORD. [s]
20 This is the gate of the LORD
through which the righteous enter.
21 I thank you for having answered me;
you have become my salvation.

---

l Pss 100:5; 105–107; 136:1f; 1 Chr 16:8; 2 Chr 5:13; Ezr 3:11.—m 2-4: Pss 106:1; 115:9-11; 136:1-26.—n Pss 27:1; 56:12; Heb 13:6.—o 8-9: Ps 146:3; Isa 57:13.—p Ps 58:9; Deut 1:44.—q Pss 86:17; 129:1-4.—r Ps 62:3; Ex 15:2; Isa 12:2.—s Ps 24:7; Isa 26:2.

Ps 118 This psalm brings to a close the Egyptian Hallel. As the procession of pilgrims goes up to Jerusalem for the Feast of Tabernacles (vv. 15, 27; see Lev 23:39-43), the celebrants and the crowd conduct a dialogue, the rhythm of which is determined by the stages of the journey. The procession starts out with a familiar refrain (vv. 1-4) and proceeds while singing a hymn of thanksgiving (vv. 5-18); it arrives at the gates of the temple that has been rebuilt (v. 19) and has become the sign of Israel's renewal after the Exile (vv. 22-24) where the priests respond to the acclamations of the people by blessing them (vv. 25-27). Finally, with palms in hand the procession reaches the sanctuary, whose courts are illumined, and the liturgy takes place with the most solemn thanksgiving (vv. 28-29).

Songs of thanksgiving such as this one called to mind the entire history of Israel, from past to present. Israel is ceaselessly put to the test, humbled, and then delivered, and in this very experience, it discovers its calling to be a people that bears witness to God in the midst of the nations and to be the capstone of the world (v. 22).

Jesus makes this calling his own (see Mt 21:42), and the apostles speak of it in their preaching (see Acts 4:11; 1 Pet 2:4-7). For them this psalm expresses in advance the mystery of Christ who is rejected and then exalted and who is the foundation stone of the new People of God (see 1 Cor 3:11; Eph 2:20). This festal song soon became popular; we find the crowd spontaneously singing it on Palm Sunday to greet Jesus as the envoy promised by God (v. 26; see Mt 21:9; Jn 12:13). We find this same acclamation in the *Sanctus* of the Mass; in all the liturgical families, the psalm has become an Easter song.

118:1-4 The liturgical call to praise that begins the procession. All Israel had benefited from God's goodness and kindness, i.e., the congregation of Israel, the priests (*house of Aaron*), and *those who fear the LORD* (see note on Ps 115:9-11). Now the people of God's kingdom (Ps 114:1; Ex 19:5-6) and the priests, the descendants of Aaron, are called to profess that the Lord is King and that he is good and kind in standing behind his covenant.

118:1 A conventional call to praise (see Pss 105–107). *Kindness:* see note on Ps 6:5.

118:2-4 *Israel . . . house of Aaron . . . those who fear the LORD:* see note on Ps 115:9-11.

118:5-18 A song of thanksgiving for deliverance of the whole nation voiced by a single individual. Some believe the speaker is a king, others opt for Israel as a corporate body, and still others for a priest/Levite. In any case, the worshiper does a good job in reciting the deeds God worked in response to the prayers of his people in affliction.

118:8-9 All should be ever mindful of the motto learned through experience that it is better to have confidence in the Lord than to rely on flesh and blood (see Ps 33:16-19; see also Pss 62; 146).

118:10-13 The fury of the assault recalls the attacks experienced by Jesus at his trial (see Lk 22:63—23:25) and even during his public ministry (see Lk 11:53f). *Name:* see note on Ps 5:12.

118:14 This verse is an exact quotation from the song of victory at the Red Sea (see Ex 15:2) and is echoed in verses 15 ("right hand") and 28 ("extol you"). Hence, God's saving acts throughout history bear the stamp of the Exodus events (see 1 Cor 10:6) culminating in the work of Christ (see Lk 9:31: "his departure [literally, 'exodus'], which would come to pass in Jerusalem").

118:17 *Live and recount:* see note on Ps 6:6.

118:19-21 The procession has arrived at the gates of the rebuilt temple; all the righteous may enter and give thanks.

22 * The stone that the builders rejected
has become the cornerstone. [t]
23 This is the LORD's doing,
and it is marvelous in our eyes.
24 This is the day that the LORD has made; *
let us exult and rejoice in it.
25 O LORD, grant us salvation. *
O LORD, grant us success.
26 Blessed is he who comes in the name of the LORD. * [u]
We bless you from the house of the LORD.
27 The LORD is God,
and he has given us light.
Holding leafy branches, join in the festal procession
up to the horns of the altar. *
28 * You are my God, and I will offer thanks to you;
you are my God, and I will extol you.
29 Give thanks to the LORD, for he is good;
his kindness endures forever.

PSALM 119*

Praise of God's Law

Aleph

1 * Blessed are those whose way is blameless,
who walk in accord with the law * of the LORD. [v]
2 Blessed are those who observe his statutes
and seek him with their whole heart. * [w]
3 They do nothing wrong;
they walk in his ways. *
4 * You have ordained
that your commands be diligently observed.
5 May my ways be steadfast
in the observance of your decrees.
6 Then I will never be put to shame
when I take note of all your precepts.
7 I will praise you in sincerity of heart
as I ponder your righteous judgments.
8 I will observe your decrees;
do not forsake me completely.

---

t Isa 28:16; Zec 4:7; Mt 21:42; Lk 20:17; Acts 4:11; Rom 9:33; 1 Cor 3:8; Eph 2:20; 1 Pet 2:7.—u Ps 129:8; Mt 21:9; 23:39; Mk 11:9; Lk 13:35; 19:38; Jn 12:13.—v Pss 1:1-2; 15:2; 112:1; Deut 18:13; Mt 5:3ff.—w Deut 4:29; 2 Chr 31:21.

118:22-23 The community of the righteous join in with thanksgiving. They praise the Lord because he has given prominence to his suffering servant Israel like a *cornerstone*. It was rejected by the worldly powers but has been made the cornerstone for God's salvation of the world in the Messiah. These verses allude to Isa 8:14; 28:16; Jer 51:26; Zec 3:9; 4:7, passages that are interpreted in a Messianic sense. Israel is here a type of Christ, in whom these words have been most eminently fulfilled (see Mt 21:42 par; Acts 4:11; Rom 9:33; 1 Cor 3:11; Eph 2:20; 1 Pet 2:7).

118:24 *This is the day that the LORD has made:* the day given by the Lord in which joy and jubilation are appropriate, the day of thanksgiving and rejoicing because of the wondrous deed of the Lord (vv. 22-23; see Ps 71:17; Jer 32:17, 27), the day of salvation. Used by the Liturgy as an antiphon for the Easter Season, this phrase identifies the "day" as that of Christ's Resurrection.

118:25 *O LORD, grant us salvation:* the Hebrew for this cry has come into English as "Hosanna." The crowd takes it up on Palm Sunday (see Mt 21:9; 23:39; Mk 11:9; Jn 12:13). It has become part of the *Sanctus* at Mass.

118:26 *Blessed is he who comes in the name of the LORD:* words used in the Gospels to welcome Jesus entering the temple on Palm Sunday (see Mk 11:9 par).

118:27 The people respond to the blessing by confessing that the Lord alone is God. He has made his light shine upon them, protecting them from the darkness of great trials (e.g., famine, war, and exile; Ps 43:3). Accordingly, they are here renewing their commitment to the Lord in a formal liturgical celebration. *The horns of the altar:* the four corners of the altar of burnt offerings (see Ex 27:2; 38:2; Lev 4:25, 30, 34).

118:28-29 The psalm concludes with the community's affirmation that the Lord alone is God, similar to the confession of Moses (see Ex 15:2). *Kindness:* see note on Ps 6:5.

Ps 119 This longest of the psalms is a monumental literary piece consisting of twenty-two strophes, each containing eight verses (sixteen lines) and each beginning with a letter of the Hebrew alphabet that is repeated at the beginning of each pair of verses. Each strophe is a unit, but does not have a close connection with the strophe that precedes or follows. The whole is a free-flowing meditation, now sad, now joyous, now peaceful, now passionate. It is a reflection and a prayer in which the author, a sage and a mystic who draws his inspiration from the Prophets and Deuteronomy, converses with God and voices his deepest feelings: love of true wisdom, attachment and fidelity to the word of God in spite of weakness and obstacles; desire to better understand and live the truth; joy of outdoing oneself to follow the will of God manifested in the law.

In practically every verse, there is the word "law" or some equivalent. We can point to eight such terms—four with a more juridic nuance (statutes, precepts, decrees, commands or commandments) and four with a more religious nuance (law, promise, word, laws, or judgments). These terms introduce us into the heart of the psalm, for they signify less an ensemble of laws to observe than the word of God, which sometimes ordains and judges and sometimes reveals and promises. It is a psalm of spiritual intimacy, of love for God (which means doing his will). In meditating on the law, believers contemplate above all the visage of God and let themselves be transformed in the very depths of their hearts. Such observance becomes liberty. Understood in this fashion, the law proclaims to us Jesus Christ, the living revelation of God, given to human beings to lead them to the Father: "I am the way, and the truth, and the life" (Jn 14:6).

119:1-3 Introduction to the entire psalm that stresses the theme: instruction in godly wisdom.

119:1 A beginning analogous to those of Pss 1:1-2; 112:1 (see Ps 101:6; Mt 5:3ff). The word *law* and its synonyms are to be taken in the widest sense of revealed teaching, as transmitted by the Prophets. *Blessed:* see note on Ps 1:1.

119:2 This verse makes explicit what is implicit throughout the psalm: Scripture is revered because it consists in God's statutes; it is God that his servants seek and not the book for its own sake.

119:3 *Ways:* although the Hebrew for this word occurs infrequently in this psalm, it is found often in Deuteronomy and elsewhere. There it refers to the requirements of God's covenant (see note on Ps 25:4-7).

119:4-8 Those who obey God's law have a right to hope that he will come to their assistance.

Beth

9 * How can a young man lead a spotless life?
By living according to your word.
10 I seek you with all my heart; *
do not let me stray from your precepts.
11 I treasure your word in my heart *
for fear that I may sin against you.
12 Blessed are you, O LORD;
teach me your decrees. [x]
13 With my lips I recite
all the judgments you have announced.
14 I rejoice in following your statutes
more than I would rejoice in endless riches.
15 I will meditate on your commands
and respect your ways.
16 I find my delight in your decrees;
I will never forget your word.

Gimel

17 * Be good to your servant
so that I may live * and keep your word.
18 Open my eyes so that I may clearly see
the wonders to be found in your law.
19 I am only a wayfarer on earth, [y]
but do not hide your precepts from me. *
20 My soul is ever consumed
with longing for your judgments.
21 You rebuke the arrogant, * the accursed,
who stray from your precepts.
22 Set me free from scorn and contempt,
for I have observed your statutes.
23 Even though princes assemble and slander me,
your servant meditates on your decrees.
24 Your statutes are my delight,
for they offer me counsel.

Daleth

25 * My soul lies prostrate in the dust; *
revive me in accordance with your word. [z]
26 I proclaim my ways and you answer me;
teach me your decrees.
27 Help me to understand the way of your commandments,
and I will meditate on your wonders.
28 My soul is wasting away in sorrow;
renew my strength in accordance with your word.
29 Keep me from the way of falsehood,
and let me live according to your law.
30 * I have chosen the way of faithfulness;
I have set your judgments before me.
31 I cling to your statutes, O LORD;
do not allow me to be put to shame.
32 I run in the way of your precepts,
for you have set my heart free.

He

33 * Teach me, O LORD, the way of your decrees,
and I will follow it to the end. * [a]
34 Give me understanding, and I will observe your law
and obey it with all my heart. *

x Pss 25:4; 26:3; 27:11; 28:6; 86:11; 143:8, 10; Ex 18:20.—y Ps 39:13; Gen 23:4; Heb 11:13.—z Pss 44:26; 119:50, 107; 143:11.—a Pss 19:12; 119:12.

119:9-16 The love for God's word is love for God, expressed in one's attitude of heart, in actions, and in words. With his entire being the godly person seeks God and delights in his will. Such a sublime teaching can lead *a young man* to keep his way pure.

119:10 The psalmist seeks the God of the law and the promises; he meditates on the latter only because they constitute God's word of life for him. *Heart:* see note on Ps 4:8.

119:11 *Treasure your word in my heart:* Proverbs 2:10-12; Col 3:16 show that those whose hearts are steeped in the word of God are educated by God.

119:17-24 In difficulty and distress, the Lord and his word are a comfort to the godly. God's blessing comes to those who submit to his law, but his curse comes to those who stray deliberately from his revealed will.

119:17 *I may live:* here the psalmist is speaking of living in its fullest sense of happiness, security, prosperity—a frequent theme in Ezekiel (Ezek 3:21; 18; 33; see Ps 133:3)—and, of course, fellowship with God (see Pss 16:11; 36:10; Deut 8:3).

119:19 Though the psalmist is a stranger (or wayfarer) on earth, he is the guest of God to whom the whole universe belongs; he will learn from the Lord how to conduct himself (see notes on Ps 39:13, 13-14).

119:21 *The arrogant:* enemies of God and his faithful who act as though they are a law unto themselves (see notes on Pss 73:4-12 and 86:14; see also Isa 13:11; Mal 3:19). They are *the accursed*, i.e., ready for God's judgment.

119:25-32 Whether in distress or in prosperity, the psalmist is determined to remain close to God's law. In adversities, he becomes more teachable and his spirit is renewed in him, for the word of the Lord has the power to comfort. In prosperity, he enjoys a freedom from anxiety and care that enables him to focus on doing God's will.

119:25 *Lies prostrate in the dust:* see note on Ps 44:26.

119:30-32 Godliness is nicely summed up by the three opening verbs: choosing (see Heb 11:25), clinging (see Acts 11:23), and running (see Phil 3:12-14). *Heart:* see note on Ps 4:8.

119:33-40 Since God alone can interpret his revelation (*teach [it]*, v. 33), the psalmist prays that God will instruct him in his *law* (see Ps 25:4). He asks the Lord to provide spiritual direction and motivation to direct his steps (see Prov 4:11-19) and incline his heart (see Ps 141:4) to do the divine will.

119:33 *And I will follow it to the end:* another possible translation is: "I will keep it as a reward" (see Ps 19:12; Prov 22:4). In both translations the godly person finds his joy in doing the will of God.

119:34 The desire for understanding often voiced in this psalm conforms to the ideal of the sages of Israel. *Heart:* see note on Ps 4:8.

35 Guide me in the way of your precepts,
for in them is my delight. [b]
36 Dispose my heart to follow your statutes
and to flee selfish gain.
37 Turn my eyes away from what is unimportant,
and let me live in your way.
38 Fulfill your word to your servant,
so that you may be feared. *
39 Let me escape the disgrace that I dread,
for your judgments are good.
40 See, I long for your commandments;
in your righteousness preserve my life.

Waw

41 * Let your kindness * descend on me, O LORD,
your salvation in accord with your promise.
42 Then I will respond to those who insult me,
because I trust in your word.
43 Do not remove from my mouth the word of truth, *
for I place my hope in your judgment.
44 I will keep your law continually,
forever and ever.
45 I will walk in complete freedom
because I have sought your commands. *
46 I will speak of your statutes in the presence of kings
and will not be ashamed.
47 Your precepts fill me with delight
because I love them.
48 I lift up my hands * to your precepts, which I love,
and I meditate on your decrees.

Zayin

49 * Remember the word you gave to your servant
by which you have given me hope.
50 This is my consolation in my distress:
your word gives me life.
51 The arrogant * overwhelm me with scorn,
but I refuse to turn away from your law.
52 I recall your judgments of old, O LORD,
and I am greatly comforted.
53 I am filled with fury against the wicked,
those who forsake your law.
54 Your decrees have become my songs
wherever I make my dwelling.
55 Even during the night I remember your name *
and observe your teaching, O LORD.
56 This is my practice:
I obey your commandments.

Heth

57 * My portion, I have said, O LORD,
is to observe your words. *
58 With all my heart * I seek your favor;
fulfill your word and be gracious to me.
59 I have reflected on my ways
and resolved to follow your statutes.
60 I will make haste and not delay
to observe your precepts.
61 Though the nets of the wicked entrap me,
I do not forget your law.
62 At midnight I rise to offer praise to you
for the righteousness of your judgments.
63 I am a friend to all who fear you,
all who observe your commands.
64 The earth overflows with your kindness, * O LORD;
teach me your decrees. [c]

b Pss 1:2; 25:4; 27:11; 86:11; 119:32; 143:8, 10.—c Pss 33:5; 108:5; 119:12, 108.

119:38 *That you may be feared:* as a result of the saving acts that the Lord does in accord with his promises, he is acknowledged as the one true God and feared (see Ps 130:5; 2 Sam 7:25f; 1 Ki 8:39f; Jer 33:8f). Another possible translation is: "Fulfill the word you have spoken / to the servant who fears you."

119:41-48 Here the psalmist, as it were, gives Christians what is needed for them to fulfill their desire to "proclaim [the Lord's] word with all boldness" (Acts 4:29). In order to be spoken, the word must first be appropriated (v. 41), trusted (v. 42f), obeyed (v. 44), sought (v. 45), and loved (v. 47f).

119:41 *Kindness:* see note on Ps 6:5.

119:43 *Do not remove from my mouth the word of truth:* for it will enable the psalmist to respond to the insults and calumnies to which he is subjected (see vv. 61, 85, 95, etc.).

119:45 *Sought your commands:* the psalmist strives to understand the meaning of the Scriptures and make them his rule of life (see vv. 94, 155; see also Ps 111:2; Ezr 7:10; Sir 51:23; Isa 34:16). Such a study is at the origin of the Midrashic literature.

119:48 *I lift up my hands:* as a sign of veneration and praise (see Pss 44:20; 63:4; 134:2; Neh 8:6).

119:49-56 The word of God provides hope and consolation even in suffering. The psalmist observes the commandments of the Lord because in them he finds life, restoration, and consolation.

119:51 *The arrogant:* see note on v. 21.

119:55 *Name:* see note on Ps 5:12.

119:57-64 The Lord is the portion of the psalmist, and it is God's law that fills the earth with joy and security. Hence, far from regarding obedience as a crushing, disagreeable burden, the psalmist considers it a happy lot, a privileged destiny, and a signal favor.

119:57 *My portion . . . your words:* another possible translation is: "You are my portion, O LORD; / I promise to keep your words." A familiar formula of trust (see Pss 16:5; 73:26 and note; 142:5).

119:58 *Heart:* see note on Ps 4:8.

119:64 *The earth overflows with your kindness:* an exclamation of God's cosmic love; the world of creation witnesses to his love (see Pss 104:10-30; 136:1-9). For other glimpses of the world as God's handiwork and kingdom, see Pss 24:1; 33:5; Isa 6:3; Hab 2:14; 3:3.

Teth

65 * You have dealt kindly with your servant
in accord with your word, O LORD.
66 Grant me good judgment and knowledge,
for I place my trust in your precepts.
67 Before I was afflicted * I went astray,
but now I observe your word.
68 You are good, and what you do is good;
teach me your decrees.
69 The arrogant * spread lies about me,
but with all my heart I observe your commands. [d]
70 Their hearts are gross and insensitive, *
but I find my delight in your law.
71 It was a blessing for me to be afflicted,
so that I might learn your decrees.
72 The law from your mouth is more precious to me
than thousands of gold and silver pieces.

Yodh

73 * Your hands have created and formed me; *
grant me understanding so that I may learn your precepts.
74 Those who fear you will rejoice when they see me
because I place my hope in your word.
75 I know, O LORD, that your judgments are righteous
and in your fidelity you have humbled me.
76 May your kindness * bring consolation to me
as you have promised your servant.
77 Grant me your compassion so that I may live,
for your law is my delight.
78 May the arrogant * who oppress me without cause be put to shame;
I will meditate on your commands.
79 May those turn to me who fear you,
those who understand your statutes.
80 May my heart * be without blame toward your decrees
so that I may not be put to shame.

Kaph

81 * My soul * pines for your salvation without ceasing;
I place my hope in your word. [e]
82 My eyes fail, * looking for your word,
and I cry out, "When will you comfort me?" [f]
83 I am shriveled like a smoke-filled wineskin, *
but I do not forget your decrees. [g]
84 How long must your servant wait? *
When will you pass judgment on my persecutors?
85 The arrogant * dig pits to entrap me,
which is not in keeping with your law.
86 All of your precepts are true;
come to my aid, for I am persecuted unjustly.
87 My enemies almost took away my life,
but I have not forsaken your commands.
88 In your kindness * spare my life,
and I will obey the statutes of your mouth.

Lamedh

89 * Your word, O LORD, is everlasting;
it is firmly fixed in the heavens. * [h]

---

d Pss 17:10; 73:8; 109:2; Job 13:4.—e Pss 84:3; 119:20, 43, 123; 130:5.—f Pss 25:15; 119:41, 123; 123:1-2; 141:8; Lam 2:11.—g Ps 119:61; Job 30:30.—h Isa 40:8; 51:6; Mt 5:18; 1 Pet 1:25.

119:65-72 The psalmist ascribes goodness to God in his past and present dealings, to the positive values of the trials God sent him, and to the ultimate value of God's law and divine teaching.

119:67 *Afflicted:* through God's doing (see note on vv. 25-32).

119:69 *The arrogant:* see note on v. 21. *Heart:* see note on Ps 4:8.

119:70 *Gross and insensitive:* literally, "fat as grease," i.e., incapable of understanding divine things (see Pss 17:10; 73:7; Isa 6:10; Jer 5:28).

119:73-80 The psalmist declares his experiential knowledge of God, of his *kindness* and *compassion.* He asks God to give the arrogant their just deserts and so enable the godly to be encouraged and rejoice at God's vindication.

119:73 *Your hands have created and formed me:* see Deut 32:6; Job 10:8; Zec 12:1. *Grant me understanding:* so that the psalmist can carry out what God willed in forming him.

119:76 *Kindness:* see note on Ps 6:5.

119:78 *The arrogant:* see note on v. 21.

119:80 *Heart:* see note on Ps 4:8.

119:81-88 This last strophe of the first part of the psalm brings to a climax the psalmist's need for God. In extreme distress, he looks to the Lord for his salvation as promised in his word, urgently calling upon him to come to his aid and effect justice upon the arrogant who wrong him.

119:81 *Soul:* see note on Ps 6:4.

119:82 *My eyes fail:* see note on Ps 6:8.

119:83 *Like a smoke-filled wineskin:* the psalmist feels as brittle and useless as tanned hides holding wine that are placed near the fireplace.

119:84 *How long . . . wait?:* literally, "How many are the days of your servant?" i.e., the psalmist does not have too much time for God to delay in punishing his persecutors. *Pass judgment on my persecutors:* see note on Ps 5:11.

119:85 *The arrogant:* see note on v. 21.

119:88 *Kindness:* see note on Ps 6:5.

119:89-91 Like the first three verses of the first half of the psalm, these first three verses of the second half teach a general truth: there is constancy and order in all of creation, reflecting the *faithfulness* of the Lord (see Pss 89:3; 104; 147:7-9). Nature serves and abides by the word and the laws of the Lord (see note on Ps 93:5).

119:89 This verse is an echo of Prov 8:22ff where divine wisdom is presented as a living being existing from all eternity (see Wis 7:22—8:1; Isa 40:8).

90 Your faithfulness lasts through all generations;
you established the earth, and it endures.
91 By your judgments all creatures continue to exist,
for they are all your servants.
92 * If your law had not been my delight,
I would have already perished in my misery.
93 Never will I forget your commands,
for through them you have given me life.
94 I am yours; save me,
for I seek your commandments.
95 The wicked lie in wait to destroy me,
but I continue to ponder your decrees.
96 I have seen that every perfection is limited,
but your precept is unlimited. *

Mem

97 * I truly love your law.
It is my meditation throughout the day.
98 * Your precept has given me greater wisdom than my enemies,
for it is mine forever.
99 I am wiser than all my teachers
because I meditate on your commands.
100 I have greater insight than the elders, *
because I keep your commandments. [i]
101 I point my feet away from evil paths
so that I might observe your word.
102 I refuse to ignore your judgments,
for it is you yourself who have taught me.
103 Your words are sweet to my palate,
even sweeter to my tongue than honey. * [j]
104 Through your commandments I achieve wisdom;
therefore, I hate every way that is false.

Nun

105* Your word is a lamp for my feet *
and a light to my path. [k]
106 With a solemn vow I have sworn *
to obey the judgments of your righteousness.
107 I have been afflicted beyond measure;
O LORD, let me live in accord with your word.
108 Receive, O LORD, the homage my lips offer you,
and instruct me about your judgments. [l]
109 Even though I continually take my life in my hands, *
I do not neglect your law.
110 The wicked seek to entrap me,
but I have not strayed from your commands.
111* Your statutes are my everlasting heritage;
they are the very joy of my heart.
112 I have set my heart on keeping your decrees,
even to the end.

Samekh

113* I detest those who are hypocritical, *
but I love your law.

i Deut 6:17; Job 32:6; Wis 4:8-9.—j Ps 19:11; Jer 15:16.—k Ps 18:29; Prov 6:23; 2 Pet 1:19.—l Pss 50:14, 23; 51:17; Heb 13:15.

119:92-96 The psalmist confesses that if through God's law he had not found meaning in the experience of his affliction, he would have perished. Therefore, no matter what his persecutors do, he will not forget God's precepts because they give order and preservation of life. For he knows that just as there are laws for the order in nature, so also are there laws for human conduct.

119:96 Everything on earth is limited; perfection belongs only to God and his commands.

119:97-104 God's law is heavenly wisdom, which is far greater than earthly wisdom. Meditation on it is a form of devotion to the Lord himself, and hence the psalmist regularly cultivates its practice. God's words, likened to honey, are sweet only when God's instruction is received and leads to understanding as well as an obedient life style.

119:98-100 These verses are illuminated by the New Testament, which shows that heavenly wisdom is a gift to "little children," hidden from the worldly wise (see Lk 10:21; 1 Cor 1:18ff; 2:6-10).

119:100 The psalmist speaks in the same vein as Elihu (see Job 32:6ff; Wis 4:9). *Elders:* the aged, taught by experience.

119:103 *Your words are . . . sweeter to my tongue than honey:* see Ps 19:11; Job 23:12; Jer 15:16; Jn 4:32, 34.

119:105-112 The word of the Lord enlightens the psalmist's path of life; therefore, he has accepted the covenant and obeys the Lord. Even in affliction, the psalmist has learned to give God willing praise, for his joy and determination to please the Lord are far greater than the affliction that is constantly with him.

119:105 *Your word is a lamp for my feet:* the word of the Lord is a guide and life-sustaining source (see Pss 18:29; 97:11; 112:4; Prov 6:23; Jn 8:12).

119:106 *With a solemn vow I have sworn:* the psalmist has made a pact to follow God's laws (see Neh 10:29).

119:109 *I continually take my life in my hands:* i.e., my life is constantly exposed to danger, for I am ready to risk it for God (see Jdg 12:3; 1 Sam 19:5; Est C:15=4:16; Job 13:14).

119:111-112 *Heart:* see note on Ps 4:8.

119:113-120 The ways of the righteous and the wicked are completely divergent. The psalmist dissociates himself from the wicked; he hates the double-minded but loves the law of the Lord. He draws near to God, his refuge and his shield. For, unlike the wicked whom the Lord will discard, the godly have hope in and veneration for the Lord.

119:113 *Hypocritical:* those who hesitate between fidelity and infidelity to God (see 1 Ki 18:21); they are "inconsistent in everything [they do]" (Jas 1:8).

114 You are my refuge and my shield;
I put my hope in your word.
115 Depart from my presence, you evildoers,
so that I may observe the precepts of my God. [m]
116 Sustain me according to your promise,
and I will live;
do not delude me in my hope.
117 Uphold me, and I will be saved
and will remain completely focused on your decrees.
118 You cast away all those who swerve from your decrees;
their cunning is futile.
119 You discard all the wicked of the earth like dross; *
therefore, I love your teachings.
120 My flesh trembles * before you in terror;
your judgments fill me with awe.

Ayin

121* Since my conduct has been just and upright,
do not abandon me to those who oppress me.
122 Guarantee the well-being of your servant; *
do not allow the arrogant to oppress me.
123 My eyes fail * as I long for your salvation
and for the promise of your justice.
124 Deal with your servant in accordance with your kindness, *
and teach me your decrees.
125 I am your servant; grant me discernment
so that I may understand your statutes.
126 It is time, O LORD, for you to take action;
your law has been broken.
127 That is why I love your precepts
more than gold, even the purest gold. *
128 That is why I regard all your commandments as right
and despise every way that is false.

Pe

129* Wonderful are your statutes;
therefore, I willingly observe them.
130 The explanation * of your words gives light
and imparts understanding to the simple.
131 I open wide my mouth and sigh, *
longing eagerly for your precepts.
132* Turn and have mercy on me,
as you always do to those who love your name. * [n]
133 Guide my steps in accord with your word
and never let evil triumph over me.
134 Rescue me from the oppression of men
so that I may observe your commandments.
135 Allow your face to shine * upon your servant
and teach me your decrees.
136 Streams of tears flow from my eyes
because your law is disregarded. *

Sadhe

137* You are righteous, O LORD,
and your judgments are right. [o]
138 You have set down your statutes as righteous
and as completely faithful.

m Pss 6:9; 139:19; Job 21:14.—n Pss 6:5; 9:14; 25:16; 86:16; 91:14; 2 Sam 24:14.—o Ex 9:27; Ezr 9:15; Neh 9:13; Tob 3:2.

119:119 *You discard . . . like dross:* the Lord discards evildoers like dross, i.e., the scum that forms in refining precious metals and is discarded (see Jer 6:28-30).

119:120 *My flesh trembles:* a reminiscence of Job 4:15; 23:15 (see Ps 88:16). It denotes the dread of the sacred, the fear of the awesome God.

119:121-128 The psalmist has entrusted himself to God's care and done what is just and upright; now he expects the Lord to keep his promise according to which the godly will be relieved of all adversities. He prays to receive understanding and, while affirming his devotion to the Lord and his commands, calls for God to deal justly with the ungodly, who have broken his law.

119:122 This is the only verse in the psalm that lacks either a direct or an indirect reference to the law of God; some have suggested replacing *servant* by "word" as a remedy. *The arrogant:* see note on v. 21.

119:123 *My eyes fail:* see note on Ps 6:8.

119:124 *Kindness:* see note on Ps 6:5.

119:127 The psalmist compares the Lord's commands favorably with pure *gold* (see Job 22:25; 28:15f; Prov 3:14; 8:10, 19; 16:16).

119:129-136 God's word illumines so that even those not experienced in the realities of life (the *simple*; see Ps 116; Prov 1:4) may gain wisdom (see Ps 19:8). The psalmist longs to receive, understand, and put it into practice. So great is his zeal for God's law that he weeps over the continuance of rebellion and transgression on the part of evildoers.

119:130 The law is a luminous sanctuary that fills souls with its clarity (see Ps 73:16f) when it is explained to them. *Explanation:* literally, "opening."

119:131 *Open wide my mouth and sigh:* same image as in Job 29:23.

119:132-136 The psalmist asks for the Lord's blessing (see Num 6:24-26), which brings down God's grace to enable him to direct his steps in accord with the divine law and away from sin and adversity (Ps 119: 133-134). He also asks for the Lord's face to shine on him (v. 135), i.e., to bring him nothing but good in all circumstances of his life; for when God's face shines on people it brings deliverance and blessings.

119:132 See Pss 5:12; 25:16; 91:15. *Name:* see note on Ps 5:12.

119:135 *Allow your face to shine:* the psalmist asks God to smile on him with favor (see note on Ps 13:2; see also Pss 67:2; 80:4; Num 6:25).

119:136 The godly are saddened in the face of evil (see Ezr 9:3ff; Job 16:20; Ezek 9:4).

119:137-144 The troubles and disgraces of his holy ones reflect upon the Lord and his word. Hence, the psalmist points out his sad state and prays that the Lord will establish righteousness in his world. Though he is still immersed in troubles, he knows the Lord is faithful and so he wholeheartedly puts his trust in him.

139 Zeal has consumed me
because my adversaries ignore your words.
140 Your word has been tested through and through, *
and your servant cherishes it.
141 Although I am despised and unimportant,
I do not forget your commands.
142 Your righteousness is everlasting,
and your law is forever true.
143 I am afflicted by anguish and distress,
but your precepts are my delight.
144 Your statutes are forever righteous;
grant me understanding and I will live.

Qoph

145* I call out to you with my whole heart;
answer me, O LORD, so that I may observe your decrees.
146 I cry out to you;
save me so that I may obey your statutes.
147 I arise before dawn and cry out for help;
I place my hope in your word.
148 My eyes are awake before each watch of the night *
so that I may meditate on your word.[p]
149 In accordance with your kindness * hear my voice, O LORD;
grant me life in accordance with your judgments.
150* Those who plot wickedness draw near me,
but they are far from your law.
151 Yet you, O LORD, are near,
and all your precepts are true.
152 Long have I known your decrees
and that you have established them forever.

Resh

153* See my suffering and deliver me,
for I have not forgotten your law.
154 Defend my cause and redeem me; *[q]
let me live in accord with your word.
155 Salvation is far from the wicked *
because they do not consider your decrees.
156 Great is your compassion, O LORD;
let me live in accord with your judgments.
157 My persecutors and my enemies are many,
but I do not cast aside your statutes.
158 I regard the faithless with indignation *
because they do not observe your word.[r]
159 Consider how I love your precepts, O LORD;
let me live in accord with your kindness. *
160 Every word you utter is true,
and all your righteous judgments * are everlasting.

Shin

161* The powerful persecute me without cause,
but it is your word that awes my heart. *
162 I rejoice in your word
like one who discovers a great treasure.
163 Falsehood I abhor and detest,
but I love your law.

p Pss 63:7; 77:7.—q Pss 35:1; 43:1; 119:25, 41; Jer 50:34; Mic 7:9.—r Pss 119:104, 136; 139:22; Ex 32:19.

119:140 *Tested through and through:* literally, "refined." God's word is fire-tried; it is genuine and reliable.

119:145-152 The psalmist urgently presents his lament before the Lord to be delivered from adversity. So intense is his longing for this salvation that he prays through the night watches. Even though his foes hunt him down, the Lord is near and will rescue him, for the psalmist keeps the law.

119:148 *Each watch of the night:* see note on Ps 63:7.

119:149 *Kindness:* see note on Ps 6:5.

119:150-152 Although the wicked are closing in on the psalmist, he remains serene, for the Lord is also near to protect him (see Pss 69:19; 73:28). The wicked will get nowhere, for they break the statutes of the Lord (v. 150: *are far from your law*), which were meant to last forever.

119:153-160 The lament becomes more intense as the psalmist prays for deliverance, mercy, and life. By protesting his innocence, bringing up his affliction, and mentioning the perfidy of the wicked, he seeks to move God to act, for he alone can preserve the psalmist's full enjoyment of covenant life. The fidelity and righteousness of God's word sustain the psalmist in his belief of total vindication.

119:154 *Redeem me:* or "Be my redeemer" (see Pss 19:15; 69:19; 72:13f).

119:155 The godless haunt the psalmist, for they flaunt the commandments of the Lord. *The wicked:* see note on v. 21 ("the arrogant").

119:158 *I regard the faithless with indignation:* i.e., they are people who have broken the covenant relationship and whose words and acts are unreliable (see Ps 25:3; Isa 48:8; Jer 5:11; Mal 2:10f).

119:159 *Kindness:* see note on Ps 6:5.

119:160 The word (*word . . . righteous judgments*) of the Lord is a source of life that never languishes because it is fed by infinite truth that continues forever. Therefore, it can never be exhausted no matter how many drink from this life-giving fountain.

119:161-168 Despite the continuation of his adversity, the psalmist rejoices in the promise of the Lord, praising him many times a day for his righteous laws. The godly have peace, for they know that the Lord in his righteousness will vindicate them. While waiting for the great day of salvation, the psalmist keeps his hope alive and follows God's commands.

119:161 *Heart:* see note on Ps 4:8.

164 Seven times * a day I praise you
for your righteous judgments.
165 Those who love your law have great peace; *
they encounter no stumbling blocks. [s]
166 I await your salvation, O LORD,
and I carry out your precepts.
167 I obey your statutes,
for I love them dearly.
168 I obey your commands and your statutes;
indeed, all my ways are known to you. *

Taw

169* May my cry come before you, O LORD;
grant me understanding according to your word. * [t]
170 May my supplication come before you;
deliver me according to your word.
171 May my lips proclaim your praise
because you teach me your decrees.
172 May my tongue sing of your word,
for all of your precepts are upright.
173 May your hand * be ready to help me,
for I have chosen your commandments.
174* I long for your salvation, O LORD,
and your law is my delight.
175 Give life to my soul that I may praise you,
and let your judgments sustain me.
176 I have wandered away like a lost sheep; *
seek out your servant,
for I have not forgotten your precepts. [u]

THE SONGS OF ASCENTS AND GREAT HALLEL—PSS 120–136*

PSALM 120*

A Complaint against Treacherous Tongues

1 A song of ascents.
Whenever I am in distress,
I cry out to the LORD and he answers me. [v]
2 Deliver me, O LORD, from lying lips
and from deceitful tongues. * [w]
3 What will he * inflict upon you,
and what more will he add to it,
O deceitful tongue?
4 He has prepared a warrior's sharp arrows
and red-hot coals * of the broom tree. [x]

s Pss 37:11; 72:7; Isa 57:19; 1 Jn 2:10.—t Ps 88:2; Job 16:18.—u Isa 53:6; Jer 50:6; Ezek 34:1ff; Lk 15:1-7.—v Ps 18:7; 2 Sam 22:7; Jon 2:2.—w Pss 12:2-4; 31:19; 52:3-5; Sir 51:3.—x Pss 11:6; 57:5; 140:11; Deut 32:23; Prov 16:27; 25:18; Jas 3:6.

119:164 *Seven times:* a Hebrew idiom for "many times" (see Ps 12:7; Gen 4:24; Prov 24:16; Mt 18:21f; Lk 17:4).

119:165 The godly have peace, for, even surrounded by adversity, they are confident of God's loving care and his promise that they will not stumble (see Prov 4:12; 1 Jn 2:10). *Great peace:* i.e., complete security and well-being (see Ps 37:11; Isa 26:3, 12; 32:17; 54:13; 57:19).

119:168 *All my ways are known to you:* for a similar thought, see Prov 5:21.

119:169-176 In this last strophe, the psalmist offers a prayer for the Lord's salvation. Although his problems have not yet been resolved, he raises the spirit of expectation in those who love God's word. He prays for complete deliverance so that he may praise his faithful God.

119:169-173 The psalmist comes before the Lord with a broken spirit, asking for understanding and deliverance. Looking forward to the moment of redemption, he dwells on the joyful expressions of his thanksgiving.

119:173 *Your hand:* a metaphor for God's powerful deliverance (see Deut 32:39).

119:174-176 These final three verses form the conclusion to the whole. They succinctly restate and summarize the main themes.

119:176 *Lost sheep:* the Prophets' theme of lost sheep is here applied to an individual (see Isa 53:6; Jer 50:6; Ezek 34:16; Zec 11:16; Mt 10:6; Lk 15:4; 1 Pet 2:25). *For I have not forgotten your precepts:* this final line sums up the inner state of the psalmist, who is zealous for the knowledge and practice of the divine law.

Pss 120–136 Human beings are born to be pilgrims in search of the absolute, on a journey to God. We advance by way of stages, from the difficulties of life to the certitudes of hope, from the dispersion of cares to the joyous encounter with God, from daily diversions to inner recollection. The "Songs of Ascents" (Pss 120–134) are prayers for the path we travel as human beings.

This group of psalms, which forms a major part of the Great Hallel (Pss 120–136: see notes on Pss 113–118), served as a kind of handbook for pilgrims as they went up to the holy city for the great annual feasts (see Ex 23:17; Deut 16:16; 1 Ki 12:28; Mt 20:17; Lk 2:41f). Two other explanations are offered but are regarded as less likely: namely, that they were sung by the returning exiles when they "went up" to Jerusalem from Babylon (see Ezr 7:9), or that they were sung by the Levites on the fifteen steps by which they ascended from the Court of the Women to the Court of the Israelites in the temple. The latter would account for the name "Gradual Psalms" or "Psalms of the Steps" by which they also are known. The name "gradual" may also be assigned to them because of their rhythm, in which every other verse continues the thought of the preceding verse.

Ps 120 Ill at ease in a hostile environment, often detested and calumniated because his faith and his law place him apart—such is the pious Jew situated far from Palestine. Sometimes he gets the feeling of living among the savage peoples of the Caucuses and the Syrian Desert (v. 5: "Meshech" and "Kedar"). We can appreciate his desire to return to Jerusalem, the city of his God.

We Christians have the same kind of feeling of nostalgia to be with God (see 2 Cor 5). Without belonging to the world from which Christ's call has taken us (see Jn 15:19), we are sent by him into the world. It is in this hostile environment that we must live while continually journeying toward the Father (see Jn 17:15, 18, 24). Thus, we can in all truth make this psalm our prayer when suffering distress caused by the continuous hostile pressure of this world.

120:2 *Lying lips . . . deceitful tongues:* see note on Ps 5:10.

120:3 *He:* i.e., the Lord. *What more will he add to it:* the full curse formula was: "May the LORD do such and such to you and add still more to it" (see Ru 1:17; 1 Sam 3:17; 14:44; 25:22; 2 Sam 3:35; 1 Ki 2:23).

120:4 *Sharp arrows . . . red-hot coals:* the evil tongue is like a sharp arrow (see Pss 57:4; 64:3; Prov 25:18; Jer 9:8) and a scorching fire (see Prov 16:27; Jas 3:6); but the enemies of the psalmist will be destroyed by the far more potent shafts of God's arrows of truth (see Ps 64:8) and coals of judgment (see Ps 140:11). *Broom tree:* apparently its roots burn well and yield coal that produces intense heat.

5 Why have I been doomed as an exile in Meshech
and forced to dwell among the tents of Kedar? *
6 Far too long have I lived
among people who despise peace. *
7 When I proclaim peace,[y]
they shout for war. *

PSALM 121*

God, Guardian of His People

1 A song of ascents.
I lift up my eyes to the mountains; *
from where will I receive help?[z]
2 My help comes from the LORD,
the Maker of heaven and earth. *[a]
3 He will not permit your foot to stumble;[b]
he who guards you will not fall asleep. *
4 Indeed, the one who guards Israel
never slumbers, never sleeps. *
5 * The LORD serves as your guardian;
he is at your right hand to serve as your shade.[c]
6 The sun will not strike you during the day,[d]
nor the moon during the night.
7 * The LORD will protect you against all evil;
he will watch over your life.[e]
8 The LORD will watch over your coming and your going
both now and forevermore.[f]

PSALM 122*

The Pilgrim's Greeting to the Holy City

1 A song of ascents. Of David.
* I rejoiced when they said to me,
"Let us go to the house of the LORD."[g]

y Pss 35:20; 140:3-4.—z Pss 87:1; 125:2; Jer 3:23.—a Pss 104:5; 124:8; 146:6; Gen 1:1; Hos 13:9.—b Pss 66:9; 91:12; Deut 32:10; 1 Sam 2:9; Prov 3:23.—c Pss 1:6; 16:8; 73:23; Isa 25:4.—d Wis 18:3; Isa 49:10.—e Pss 9:10; 97:10.—f Gen 28:15; Deut 28:6; Job 5:17f.—g Pss 42:4; 43:3-4; 84:2-5; Isa 2:3; Mic 4:2; Zec 8:2.

120:5 *Meshech . . . Kedar:* Meshech is located to the far north in Asia Minor by the Black Sea (see Gen 10:2; Ezek 38:2). Kedar stands for the Arab tribesmen of the south in the Arabian Desert (see Isa 21:16f; Jer 2:10; 49:28; Ezek 27:21). The psalmist feels that he is dwelling among a barbarian and ungodly people.

120:6 The psalmist reminds the Lord that he has been mired for too long among people who despise peace and make war on him (see v. 4: "arrows" and "red-hot coals"). These adversaries have no use for godly persons like himself, so they harass and slander them and make their life unbearable. The psalmist can no longer put up with this unrelenting oppression.

120:7 The godly have nothing in common with the wicked. The godly speak of peace, but the wicked sow discord and adversity (see Gal 5:19-21; Jas 3:14f). God alone can be of help in this situation.

Ps 121 The ground of Palestine is rough, and journeys meant discomforts: rocks, cold, nights in the open; but the pilgrim took courage, for the Lord protects each of his own.

This psalm is a prayer for Christians in a time of uncertainty. We find ourselves engaged, like the patriarchs, in the adventure that will lead us to the "rest" of the Promised Land, across the difficulties and dangers of the wilderness of this world (see Heb 11). We can ask ourselves with distress whence help will come to us that will enable us to complete our pilgrimage. We can be reassured. Sending us into the world on mission and pilgrimage, Jesus guarantees us his almighty assistance together with that of his Father (see Mt 28:19f; Jn 17:15-17). To enable us to overcome the world, its seductions, and its snares, Christ sends us the Holy Spirit, who continues the safeguarding solicitude of the Master toward us (see Jn 14:16f; 16:8).

121:1 *Mountains:* the ridge on which Mount Zion with its temple was situated (see Pss 87:1; 125:2).

121:2 *Maker of heaven and earth:* the psalmist makes what amounts to a credal statement, which has been incorporated into the Apostles' Creed. It affirms the Lord's sovereignty over the whole universe—heaven and earth—and demolishes all claims of sovereignty made for the pagan gods. The source of help can come only from the Lord, whose power is unlimited (see Pss 115:3; 124:8; 134:3; 146:6; Jer 10:11f).

121:3 The pagan gods were said to sleep (as well as eat and drink), but the psalmist points out that the Lord never sleeps. Therefore, he can protect his devoted servants at all times and in all circumstances. The psalmist goes on to specify what this divine guardianship means. The Lord will not permit his faithful to "stumble" (see Pss 55:23; 66:9). He will also be their "shade" (v. 5; see Ps 91:1; Num 14:9; Jer 48:45; Lam 4:20), protecting them during the day or night (v. 6: see Pss 16:8; 91:5-6; 109:31). For the Lord is the Shepherd of his people (see Ps 23), who protects and guides them whether they are awake or sleeping, at home or on a journey, working or resting.

121:4 The Lord also watches over Israel without sleeping. He is a guard who never falls asleep at his post, never goes off duty. He is always watching over his people to protect them from their enemies.

121:5-6 The Lord maintains himself at his faithful's "right hand," the side of favor and trust, to "shade" them from the fierce heat of the sun and the malevolent influence of the moon. The ancients feared the evil spiritual effects of the moon (see Mt 17:15) as well as the bad physical effects of the sun (see Jud 8:3; Isa 49:10). The antiphon used with this psalm during the Easter Season in the Liturgy of the Hours, "The Lord watches over his people, and protects them as the apple of his eye," reminds us that because of Christ's Passion and Resurrection no physical or spiritual force can ever separate us from the love of God that is in Christ Jesus (see Rom 8:31-39).

121:7-8 The Lord is present to deliver his faithful both now and forever. *Your coming and your going:* an idiom signifying all ordinary human activity (see Deut 28:6; 31:2; Jos 14:11; 2 Sam 3:25).

Ps 122 The pilgrims arrive where they can see Jerusalem, and their faces light up with joy, a joy that formed part of the Messianic hope. They come to a halt to admire the holy city restored by Nehemiah, and their remembrances sing in their heart: those of the gathering of the tribes at the Tent of Meeting (see Num 2:2) and of the happy era when David and Solomon ruled in their capital. The latter appeared to them as the symbol of unity and peace—"Shalom" signifies peace. In their desire for happiness, they already dream of the gathering together at some future time (see Isa 33:20; Zec 9:9ff).

One day Paul will speak of Christ present in his Church to reestablish the links of the human family (see Eph 2:19-22), and the visionary of Patmos will celebrate the definitively rediscovered unity in his marvelous description of a heavenly Jerusalem (see Rev 21:2—22:5). Hence, in praying this psalm, we as Christians must go beyond the original sense since we find ourselves drawn along by Christ in a spiritual pilgrimage that causes us to leave the world and enter ever further into the Church. It ultimately leads us from earth to heaven, the heavenly Jerusalem.

122:1-2 The trials of an expatriate (see Ps 120) and the hazards of travel (see Ps 121) are overshadowed now by the joy that had drawn the pilgrim to his journey. The doxology in Jude 24 is the Christian equivalent of this progress and arrival: "To him who is able to keep you from falling [see Ps 121] and to bring you safely to his glorious presence, unblemished and rejoicing [see Ps 122]." *The house of the LORD:* the temple (see 2 Sam 7:5, 13; 1 Ki 5:2, 4).

2 And finally our feet are standing
at your gates, O Jerusalem.
3 Jerusalem is built as a city
that is firmly bound together * in unity. [h]
4 There the tribes go up,
the tribes of the LORD,
as it was decreed for Israel
to celebrate the name of the LORD. * [i]
5 For there the thrones of judgment * were established,
the thrones of the house of David.

6 Pray for the peace * of Jerusalem:
"May those who love you rest secure.
7 May there be peace within your walls
and security in your palaces." [j]

8 * Out of love for my relatives and friends,
I will say, "May peace be within you."
9 Out of love for the house of the LORD, our God,
I will pray for your well-being.

PSALM 123*

Prayer in Time of Spiritual Need

1 A song of ascents.
I lift up my eyes to you, [k]
to you who are enthroned in heaven. *
2 Behold, as the eyes of servants *
are on the hand of their master,
or as the eyes of a maid
focus on the hand of her mistress,
so our eyes are on the LORD, our God,
as we wait for him to show us his mercy.

3 Show us your mercy, O LORD, show us your mercy,
for we have suffered more than our share of contempt. * [l]
4 We have had to suffer far too long
the insults of the haughty *
and the contempt of the arrogant.

PSALM 124*

Thanksgiving for the LORD's Help

1 A song of ascents. Of David.

h Ps 48:13-14; 2 Sam 5:9; Eph 2:19-22.—i Ex 23:17; Deut 16:16.—j Ps 128:5f; Est 10:3; Song 4:4.—k Pss 25:15; 119:82; 121:1; 141:8; Isa 6:1.—l Pss 44:14-15; 123:3-4; Neh 4:4; Job 12:4; 30:1; Dan 9:16.

122:3 *That is firmly bound together:* Jerusalem is the symbol of the unity of the chosen people and the figure of the unity of the Church (see Eph 2:20ff). Some versions have translated this as: "where its community is one."

122:4 This verse presupposes the Deuteronomic law concerning unity of sanctuary (see Deut 12; 16:16; 1 Ki 12:27). *To celebrate the name of the LORD:* because of God's saving acts and blessings for his people.

122:5 Jerusalem was both the religious center, symbolized by the "house of the LORD" (v. 1), and the political center, symbolized by *the thrones of judgment.* The kings of Judah ruled by God's will and upheld his kingship to the extent that they dispensed justice, which was a feature of the Messianic Age (see Isa 9:7; 11:3-5).

122:6ff *Peace:* the customary greeting in Hebrew, *shalom,* which also includes the idea of happiness and prosperity.

122:8-9 Jerusalem is transferred into an ideal, an eschatological expression of what God had planned for his people, and the psalmist prays for the fulfillment of God's plan. What Jerusalem was to the Israelite, the Church is to the Christian.

Ps 123 Upon returning from the Exile, Israel experienced prolonged and harsh humiliations: vexations from nearby nations and from the Persian administration and persecution later on. The pilgrims do not feel the need to recite at length the list of their misfortunes, for these are too well known. The prayer is expressed in a simple attitude: eyes humbly and perseveringly fixed toward the Lord await a sign of hope. Can people be more true before God?

This psalm can serve to show the right attitude we should have toward Christ. John (Jn 10:28f) amply indicates that the inner and outer life of the Church and Christians is sovereignly regulated by the risen Christ together with his Father. Our faith assures us that the almighty hand of Christ will save us when we call for help against our inner and outer enemies. We should keep our eyes fixed continuously on him in the never-ending battle we must wage in this world (see Heb 12:2).

123:1 The psalmist indicates the awesome power of God, the Ruler of the universe enthroned *in heaven,* who "does whatever he pleases" (Ps 115:3), and whose love and wisdom are beyond our calculation (see Ps 36:5; Isa 55:9).

123:2 The fate of male or female slaves was entirely in the hands of their masters or mistresses. Their welfare or their woe depended completely on the will of their overseers, whose hands could bestow benefits or punishments. Hence, the psalmist pictures the slaves as keeping their eyes fixed on their masters and mistresses. In like manner, God's people fix their eyes on their Lord with utter dependence; like *servants* and a *maid,* they look to their Master—for acts of kindness and *mercy.*

For the Lord rules sovereignly. He is on the throne (see Pss 2:4; 11:4; 102:13; 115:3) even when the arrogant assail his people. No matter how exalted this God of Israel may be, he is still the Lord ("Yahweh"), the God who is faithful to the covenant he has made with his people and is ever ready to help them in any adversity.

123:3 The psalmist prays for God's favor (see Pss 6:3; 57:2; 86:3) to right the injustice done to God's children, who have unjustly endured great *contempt* (see Ps 119:22) and ridicule (see Ps 44:13; Neh 2:19; 4:1). It is interesting to recall that in the Sermon on the Mount, contempt ("You fool") ranks as more grievous than anger (see Mt 5:22). Yet, from the Christian point of view, to endure suffering (including contempt) for Christ is a necessity (see Lk 9:23; Col 1:24), as well as an honor (see Acts 5:41), for all his followers as they make their way to glory (see 1 Pet 4:13f).

123:4 As is the case in our day, the People of God are mocked by *the haughty* and *the arrogant* (see Pss 52:3; 73:2ff), who rely on and seek only themselves, giving little thought to God. Although it is entirely permissible to pray to be delivered from this ridicule, another approach is to accept it in union with the suffering Christ. Even the Old Testament has passages recommending the acceptance of such suffering: "Let him offer his cheek to those who strike him and endure their insults. For the rejection by the Lord will not last forever. Even though he punishes, he will be compassionate in the abundance of his unfailing love. For he does not willingly afflict or cause grief to the children of men" (Lam 3:30-33).

Ps 124 This psalm is the thankful cry of the chosen people that God saves because he has made a covenant with them. It contains four classic images—the monster (v. 3: "swallowed"), the water (v. 4: "waters" and "torrent"; v. 5: "waters"), the bull (v. 6: "prey to their teeth"), and the trapped bird (v. 7: "from the snare of the fowlers")—that evoke the trials undergone by Israel as well as the sudden and extreme danger in which each person can find himself.

Christians can pray this psalm with the sentiments suggested by Paul in a similar situation (see 2 Cor 1:8-10). We can direct it to the Father and Christ, through whom God saves the Church. Without Christ, who will be with us till the consummation of the world (see

* If the LORD had not been on our side—
let Israel now proclaim— * [m]
2 if the LORD had not been on our side
when our enemies attacked * us,
3 * then they would have swallowed us alive
as their wrath was kindled against us. [n]
4 * The waters would have washed us away,
the torrent would have swept over us, [o]
5 and we would have drowned
in the raging waters.

6 Blessed be the LORD,
who did not give us as prey to their teeth.
7 We have escaped like a bird
from the snare of the fowlers;
the snare was broken,
and we escaped. *

8 Our help is in the name of the LORD,
the Maker of heaven and earth. * [p]

PSALM 125*

God, Protector of His People

1 A song of ascents.
Those who put their trust in the LORD are like Mount Zion,
which cannot be shaken but stands fast forever. * [q]
2 As the mountains surround Jerusalem, [r]
so the LORD surrounds his people
both now and forevermore. *

3 The scepter of the wicked will not prevail
over the land allotted to the righteous,
so that the righteous will not be tempted
to turn their hands to evil. *

4 * Do good, O LORD, to those who are good,
to those who are upright of heart. * [s]
5 But the LORD will assign to the ranks of the evildoers
those who turn their hearts to wickedness. * [t]

May peace be granted to Israel. [u]

m Pss 118:25ff; 129:1.—n Prov 1:12; Jer 51:34.—o Pss 18:5; 69:2f; 88:18.—p Pss 115:15; 121:2; 134:3; 146:6; Gen 1:1; 2 Sam 17:45.—q Pss 46:5f; 48:3-6; Prov 10:25; Isa 33:20.—r Ps 32:10; Deut 32:11; Mt 28:20.—s Pss 18:26ff; 119:65.—t Ps 92:10; Prov 3:32.—u Pss 128:6; 130:7f.

Mt 28:20), the Church and her members could not hold out against the gates of the netherworld (see Mt 16:18). As the Good Shepherd, Christ gives his life to save his flock from the ravenous wolf who never ceases prowling around her, ready to devour her (see Jn 10:11-15; 1 Pet 5:8). Christ masters the storm that is on the verge of swallowing up the already sinking boat with his disciples (see Mk 4:35-41); he breaks the snare that holds his imprisoned apostles, among others, Peter and Paul (see Acts 5:17-19; 12:1-11; 16:19-26). Truly, we can say with assurance: "Our help is in the name of the LORD, the Maker of heaven and earth" (Ps 124:8).

124:1-2 Because the Lord has been with his people, they have not perished (see Pss 94:17; 119:92) and have hope instead (see Neh 4:14). The ancients had a grateful awareness of God's presence among them.

124:1 *Let Israel now proclaim:* the people are invited to repeat the first phrase like a refrain (see Pss 118:2; 129:1).

124:2 *Enemies attacked:* i.e., the arrogant (see Ps 123:4).

124:3-5 The trials undergone by Israel are described in traditional images (monsters, wild beasts, drowning, and snares) to indicate the totality of the disaster that loomed so near. *Swallowed:* in addition to indicating death at the hands of some beast, it also functions as a metaphor for death itself, which is often portrayed by "the netherworld" that devours its victims (see Ps 55:16; Prov 1:12).

124:4-5 The metaphor of water as a destructive force is common in the Old Testament (see Pss 18:17 and note; 32:6; 42:8; 69:2f, 16; Isa 8:7f; Lam 3:54) because of the destructive torrential rains common to that part of the world (see Jdg 5:21; Mt 7:27).

124:7 A triumphant note underlies this verse: *we escaped* by the Lord's doing; therefore, he is to be praised.

124:8 The psalm culminates in the great confession (see note on Ps 121:2).

Ps 125 In place of the grandeur and freedom to which they aspired during the Exile, Israel, after their return, experiences nothing but difficulties, miseries, and foreign oppressions. Under the weight of this cruel disillusionment, their courage fails and their faith in the Lord wavers. Fortunately, men of strong character like Zephaniah, Ezra, Nehemiah, and the aged prophet, Haggai providentially appear to restore their confidence in the Lord's faithfulness.

The present psalm may date from this period of restoration. It sings of the perfect stability and security assured to his faithful by the Lord, who surrounds them as the mountains surround Jerusalem making it well-nigh impregnable. However, despite threats and against all appearances, God is the only certain power in human existence.

We can pray this psalm mindful of the help the Father granted to Israel of old, but above all, of the far superior aid he accords to the Church, to her Head, as well as to each of her members. It is this same aid that we are to praise with Christ.

125:1 God's people (*those who put their trust in the LORD*) are like Mount Zion, which symbolizes God's help (see Pss 121:1f; 124:8), his presence in helping and protecting his people (see Pss 76:7-10; 132:13-16), and the privileges of the covenant relationship, which cannot be shaken but endures forever (see Pss 16:8; 46:6; 112:6f; Isa 28:16; 54:10).

125:2 In the mountain range around Jerusalem, Mount Zion is surrounded by higher peaks: to the east lies the Mount of Olives, to the north Mount Scopus, to the west and south, other hills. So Mount Zion was regarded as secure because of its natural defensibility. God is around and present to his people (see Ps 34:8; Zec 2:7), *both now and forevermore* (see Pss 113:2; 115:18; 121:8).

125:3 Over the years, the enemies of Israel have invaded and occupied the land of Canaan and even annexed all or part of Israel and Judah (see Ps 124:2-5). However, the psalmist declares that the Lord will never allow such a situation to endure. For foreign rulers often attempted to introduce the worship of their gods to the local population. Such foreign rule (symbolized by the term *scepter*—see Isa 14:5) imposed on Israel cannot coexist with the Lord's protecting presence. For it might be an occasion for some of the godly to be tempted, to lose heart, and to fall away. *Land allotted to the righteous:* i.e., the Promised Land (see Ps 78:55).

125:4-5 Though confident in the Lord's protection, the people pray for his help. For the Lord deals with everyone as that person is and does. In times of trouble, God gives his grace more abundantly; at the same time, he never permits his faithful to be tested beyond their strength. However, he wishes us to pray for that grace. The psalm therefore closes with a petition for grace and judgment. One's own weakness and the malice of the enemy conceal many dangers. May God not refuse his assistance to those who are of goodwill and try to walk the path of virtue, and at the same time may he banish those who follow the path of evil.

125:4 *Heart:* see note on Ps 4:8.

125:5 The *evildoers* are apostates who have turned to *wickedness,* i.e., paths that twist away from the main road (see Jdg 5:6). The psalmist invokes the law of talion against them (see Ps 18:27ff). *Peace be granted to Israel:* perhaps a short form of the priestly blessing (see Num 6:24-26), with Israel designating the group of the poor of the Lord (see Pss 73:1; 102:2; 128:6; 130:7f).

PSALM 126*

God, Our Joy and Our Hope

1 * A song of ascents.

When the LORD brought home the captives to Zion, [v]
we seemed to be dreaming. *
2 Our mouths were filled with laughter
and our tongues with songs of joy. [w]

Then it was said among the nations,
"The LORD has done great things for them." *
3 The LORD has indeed done great deeds for us,
and we are overflowing with joy. *

4 * Once again restore our fortunes, * O LORD,
as you did for the streams in the Negeb.
5 Those who sow in tears *
will reap with songs of joy. [x]
6 Those who go forth weeping,
carrying the seeds to be sown, *
will return with shouts of joy,
carrying their sheaves.

PSALM 127*

Need of Divine Assistance

1 A song of ascents. Of Solomon.

* If the LORD does not build the house, *
those who construct it labor in vain.
If the LORD does not guard the city,
those who keep watch over it do so in vain.

v Pss 14:7; 85:2; Ezr 1:1-3; Hos 6:11.—w Ps 65:9; Job 8:21; Lk 1:49.—x Pss 6:7; 16:11; 20:5; 23:6; 80:6; Isa 35:10; 51:11; 65:19; Jer 50:4; Bar 4:23; Gal 6:9; Rev 21:4.

Ps 126 The Jewish community takes pains to be reestablished. But joy fills the people's hearts. They still resound with the gladness and hope of the caravans returning from the Exile, and every pilgrimage unfolds like a new Exodus (vv. 1-3; see Isa 48:21), a return from the Exile. It is also faith in an even more wondrous future, the gathering together of all by the side of the Messiah. Such happiness is prepared for in the suffering of the present just as the harvest grows out of the grain sown into the earth where it dies (see Jn 12:24; Rom 8:8-25; 1 Cor 15:35-49).

In praying this psalm, we can also be mindful of the wondrous spiritual salvation of sinners worked by Christ in accord with the will of the Father. This salvation constitutes a spiritual Exodus from the sinful world to the divine dwelling of the earthly Church and then of the heavenly Church, a transferral from satanic tyranny to the gentle yoke of Christ and then of the heavenly Father, a conversion from infidelity to fidelity toward Christ and his Father. Such are the wonders that God has worked radically for all in causing Christ to pass from the grave to heaven, from death to glorious life (see Eph 4:8), and that he works effectively for every believer who shares in this mystery through faith (see Jn 5:24).

126:1-3 The edict of the Persian King Cyrus the Great in 538 B.C. that permitted the exiles to return home was totally unexpected despite the oracles issued by Isaiah and Jeremiah. The long period of the captivity had caused many to give up hope. Hence, the joy of their deliverance was indescribable. The Gentiles, too, were impressed by this event; for many nations in the ancient Near East had vanished owing to conquest and exile, and the conventional wisdom was that little Israel would suffer the same fate. When this proved not to be the case, the People of God acknowledged that it was the Lord who had done great things for them.

126:1 The restoration of the captives to Zion took place in 538 B.C., in fulfillment of the prophetic word (see Isa 14:1f; 44:24—45:25; 48:20f; Jer 29:14; 30:3; 33:7, 10f; Am 9:14). However, when the actual moment came, it felt like a mirage. *When the LORD . . . dreaming:* another translation is: "When the LORD restored the fortunes of Zion, / we were like men restored to health."

126:2 So great was the act of restoration and the joy of the people that the nations heard about it too (see Ps 98:2; Isa 52:10; Ezek 36:36) and praised the Lord (see note on Ps 46:10).

126:3 The psalmist affirms that the Lord has done great things for the people, and they are filled with joy. We Christians can use this verse in our own right to declare the manifold blessings bestowed on us in Christ, especially his Resurrection, which turned the disciples' sorrow into joy and brought salvation to the world that had previously been in bondage to the devil.

126:4-6 The reality of life in Canaan soon tempered the joy of the repatriates, for they had to eke out an existence in the land that had remained untended for years. So the people cry out to God for a continuation of the restoration: restoration of their well-being in the land (*fortunes*; see Ps 14:7). And they are assured of God's continued fidelity to his promise.

126:4 The repatriates, disappointed by the limited fulfillment of the prophetic word, turn to the Lord. They beg him to grant them a complete restoration and give them a brighter future even if to do so he has to perform a miracle like creating streams in the Negeb. *Restore our fortunes:* another possible translation is: "Bring back our people from captivity." No matter what the text, the prayer is one for a better future. *Streams in the Negeb:* the wadis of southern Palestine, almost always dry, are suddenly filled by the winter rains and fertilize the earth (see 2 Ki 3:20; Isa 41:18), representing proverbially the sudden coming of God's blessing.

126:5 God will be true to his promise, but the people must also do their part—they must sow the seed in order to have a harvest. God will turn the people's *tears* into *songs of joy* by blessing them in their various endeavors and rewarding their laborious toil.

126:6 The psalm concludes on the expectation of another miracle to take place; the people will return with *shouts of joy* because of the plentiful harvest. The time of exile was like a sowing of tears; it was a time of penance. The time of the harvest has not yet come. But as certainly as in nature the harvest follows upon seeding, so certain is it that a time of joy will follow for God's people. Thus, the psalm attests to the certainty of the Lord's promise. *Seeds to be sown:* "Previously the seed had not sprouted, and the vine and the fig tree, the pomegranate and the olive tree, had borne no fruit. From this day forward I intend to bless you" (Hag 2:19).

Ps 127 Without God, human undertakings are doomed to fail. It is God who is responsible for all of life's blessings (see Deut 28:1-14). There is no need for us to become overly anxious. His providence takes care of us (see Mt 6:25-34; Jn 15:5). This is the constant teaching of the Old and New Testament. Nowadays, we know that natural laws follow a determined course that can be put to use in invention, technology, and the human sciences. But what do we expect to achieve? And if our endless affairs take away from us our time and taste for true joys, e.g., that of breaking bread together and of the fraternal home—what then?

We can and should recite this beautiful psalm in its original sense to praise the Lord who fills us with earthly goods and gifts. We can also transpose it to the spiritual plane to express our radical impotence in this sphere and to proclaim that all success and supernatural fecundity suppose the concurrence of Christ Jesus, acting in the name of the Father, in the Holy Spirit (see Jn 15:4f).

127:1-2 The psalmist wishes to have the people become more God-centered in their everyday lives, for it is the Lord who provides shelter, security, and food.

127:1 The building of a *house* may refer to the construction of a house within the protective walls of the city or to the raising of a "family," for in the Old Testament it is usual to speak of a family

2 It is useless for you to rise earlier
and delay taking your rest at night,
toiling relentlessly for the bread you eat;
for while those he loves sleep,
he provides all of this for them. * [y]

3 * Behold, children are a gift from the LORD,
a reward of the fruit of the womb. [z]

4 Like arrows in the hands of a warrior
are the children born in one's youth. *

5 Blessed is the man
who has filled his quiver with them.
He will never be forced to retreat
when he is confronted by his enemies at the city gate. *

PSALM 128*

Happy Home of the Righteous

1 * A song of ascents.

Blessed * are all those who fear the LORD
and walk in his ways. [a]

2 You will eat the fruit of your labors;
you will enjoy both blessings and prosperity. * [b]

3 Your wife will be like a fruitful vine *
within your house;
your sons will be like shoots of an olive tree
around your table. [c]

4 Such are the blessings that will be bestowed
on the man who fears the LORD.

5 * May the LORD bless you from Zion *
all the days of your life. [d]
May you rejoice in the prosperity of Jerusalem
6 and live to see your children's children. * [e]
Peace be upon Israel. [f]

y Gen 3:17; Num 6:26; Job 11:18; Eccl 2:24-25; Mt 6:11.—z Pss 115:14; 128:3; Gen 1:28; Deut 28:11; Prov 17:6.—a Pss 1:1-2; 37:3-5; 112:1; 119:1-2; 128:1.—b Pss 58:12; 112:3; Isa 3:10.—c Pss 52:10; 144:12; Job 29:5; Jer 11:16; Hos 14:6.—d Pss 20:3; 122:9; 134:3; 135:21.—e Gen 50:23; Job 42:16; Prov 17:6.—f Ps 125:5.

as a house in much the same way as we speak of a prominent family as a dynasty (see Gen 16:2; 30:3; Ex 1:21; Ru 4:11; 1 Sam 2:35; 2 Sam 7:27). Even the best watchmen (see 2 Sam 13:34; 18:24-27; Song 3:3; 5:7) are not enough to protect the city against attack unless the Lord is guarding it (see Pss 121:4; 132).

127:2 The higher way of life is to trust the Lord in one's work. A good harvest results from God's blessing, not endless toil (see Prov 10:22; Mt 6:25-34; 1 Pet 5:7).

127:3-5 It is the Lord, too, who as a sign of his favor gives sons who ensure the perpetuity of the family that is faithful to him and provide protection for the family members.

127:4 Children, especially sons, also provide a sense of security and protection for the family—especially if they are born early in the parents' life (see Prov 17:6; Lam 3:13). As the arrows protect the warrior, so do sons guard the godly man.

127:5 A house full of children is a protection against loneliness and abandonment in society. They will speak on behalf of their aging parents, especially at the *city gate,* where court was held (see Ps 69:13; Deut 17:5; 21:19; 22:15, 24; Prov 31:23; Am 5:12).

Ps 128 A prosperous home, such is the happiness reserved by God for the righteous—so thought the sages of Israel (see Prov 3:33). Although the people soon realized that God's reward is more mysterious, the joy and intimacy of the hearth, delicately invoked in this psalm, and the gathering of all in a Jerusalem radiant with peace remain the most suggestive images of the happiness that God will bestow on the righteous. The psalmist is encouraging the individual to contribute to the building up of the kingdom of God by living a godly life. Through him, his family will be built up, and God's blessing will be extended to all the People of God.

In praying this psalm, we can apply it above all to the spiritual goods that God reserves for Christian families. However, we know that the heavenly Father does not fail to add to his supernatural benefits such natural ones as the blessings and happiness promised by the psalmist: prosperity, professional success, fecundity, longevity, and peace.

128:1-4 The psalmist delineates the blessings of a God-fearing family: the right relationship with God, obedience to his words, fruitful labor, compatible loving parents, godly children, and domestic harmony.

128:1 The wise man was especially concerned with walking in the ways of the Lord (see Pss 1:1; 25:9f; Prov 14:2), ways of love, fidelity, and uprightness. *Blessed:* see note on Ps 1:1. *Fear the LORD:* see note on Ps 15:2-5. *His ways:* i.e., his commandments (see Pss 27:11; 86:11; 143:8).

128:2 In godly living, the judgment of God on humans (see Gen 3:17-19) is alleviated, for labor is truly blessed by God.

128:3 The imagery of vine and olive shoots recalls the times of David and Solomon (see 1 Ki 4:25) and the blessing associated with the Messianic Age (see Mic 4:4; Zec 3:10). To sit under one's vine and fig tree symbolized tranquillity, peace, and prosperity. The metaphor of the *vine* indicates that the wife will be not only fruitful but also everything that a wife should be for the good of the family (see Prov 31:10-31). The children (*shoots of an olive tree*) will be strong and later on continue the father's work (see Ps 52:10; Jer 11:16; Hos 14:6).

128:5-6 The psalmist further summarizes the blessedness of the righteous—unbroken prosperity, true relationship with God, secure national defense, and long life. In doing so, he implicitly calls upon and encourages each one of the faithful to contribute to the building up of the kingdom of God by leading an upright life in the presence of God.

128:5 The presence of God extends to his faithful servant wherever he may live. For the new People of God, it signifies the blessing of God on all who have the Spirit dwelling in them. *From Zion:* see Pss 9:11; 20:3; 135:21.

128:6 *Live to see your children's children:* this prayer for the righteous corresponds to the phrase found in verse 5: "all the days of your life." It calls down upon them God's blessing of longevity, which was one of the greatest favors to be sought in a time when an idea of the afterlife had not yet been fully attained. *Peace be upon Israel:* see note on Ps 125:5. By these words, the psalmist applies God's blessing on the individual to the whole People of God, requesting well-being and prosperity for all. Paul may be echoing this phrase in Gal 6:16: "May peace and mercy be given to all who follow this rule, and to the Israel of God." It sums up Paul's concern that God's people should show themselves true citizens of "the Jerusalem that is above" (Gal 4:26).

PSALM 129*

Prayer in Time of Persecution

1 * A song of ascents.
They have greatly oppressed me from my youth— *
let Israel say— [g]
2 they have greatly oppressed me from my youth,
but never have my enemies prevailed against me. [h]
3 The plowers plowed upon my back, *
making deep furrows. [i]
4 However, the LORD is righteous,
freeing me from the bonds of the wicked.
5 * May all those who hate Zion
be thrown back in shame and confusion. *
6 * May they be like grass on the rooftops
that withers before it can be plucked, [j]
7 so that it can never fill the hands of the reapers
or the arms of the binders of sheaves.
8 May those who pass by never cry out,
"The blessing of the LORD be upon you!
We bless you in the name of the LORD." [k]

g Pss 88:16; 124:1-2.—h Ps 118:13; Mt 16:18; Jn 16:33.—i Isa 51:23.—j Ps 102:12; 2 Ki 19:26; Isa 37:27.—k Ps 118:26; Ru 2:4.—l 1-2: Pss 5:2-3; 55:2-3; 86:6; 142:6f; 2 Chr 6:40; Neh 1:6; Lam 3:55-56; Jon 2:2.—m Ps 143:2; 1 Sam 6:20; Job 9:2; Ezr 9:15; Nah 1:6; Rev 6:17.

Ps 129 The present psalm repeats the theme of Ps 124, concerning the past endurance of Israel, joining to it a prayer for the prompt defeat and eviction of its enemies. Recalling past oppressions and attacked on all sides, the pilgrims besought the Lord to overthrow the post-exilic dominations. From the time of their Egyptian bondage, the chosen people have suffered oppression (vv. 1-2), but the Lord has always delivered them from their enemies. The poet expresses his theme by utilizing rural images. He leaves us a prayer of recourse to God—not of resignation—when we are haunted by the memory of fear or too much distress.

Christians can pray this psalm while evoking the continuous assaults that the Church has suffered from her birth and the future triumph that God will assure her over her enemies. The entire Book of Revelation illustrates this theme.

129:1-4 The enemies of Israel, who are at the same time enemies of the Lord, have much stomped on, oppressed, and tried to snuff out the chosen people from their youth in Egypt and during the Exodus. But they have been unable to do so because the Lord has broken their yoke in time. The psalmist may be thinking of the nomads making incursions at the time of the Judges; the Philistines dangerously invading at the time of Saul and David; the Assyrians conquering and destroying Samaria; and the Babylonians conquering and destroying Jerusalem.

129:1 *From my youth:* from the sojourn in Egypt and the entrance into the Promised Land (see Ps 89:46; Ezek 23:3; Hos 2:15).

PSALM 130*

Prayer for Pardon and Peace

1 A song of ascents.
Out of the depths * I cry to you, O LORD;
2 O Lord, hear my voice. [l]
Let your ears be attentive
to my cries of supplication. *
3 If you, O LORD, kept a record of our sins,
O Lord, who could stand * upright? [m]
4 But with you there is forgiveness
so that you may be revered. *

129:3 *The plowers plowed upon my back:* in Ps 124, the enemies are likened to destructive floods and to a hunter; here, they are likened to a farmer who plows the field with long furrows. The plowers are the warriors, the long furrows are the wounds and adversities, and the field is the back of Israel—a metaphor of Israel's history of suffering (see Isa 21:10; 41:15; Jer 51:33; Am 1:3; Mic 4:13; Hab 3:12).

129:5-8 The psalmist prays that God may humiliate pagan powers to whom Israel remains subject after the Exile (see notes on Pss 5:11; 35).

129:5 Those who hate Zion disregard God and include not only the wicked of the world but also the Israelites, who do not fear the Lord (see Ps 125:5).

129:6-8 May God make the wicked suffer the same fate as the grass that sprouts in the protective coating of clay covering roofs (see 2 Ki 19:26; Isa 37:27), which the dry and burning desert wind brutally withers up or men hastily root out. Just as this grass is taken up neither by the reaper nor by the sower, so may God cause the enemies of Israel, once beaten, to find no one to gather them or lift them up, no ally or reaper to whom others would wish success in his task with the cry, "The LORD be with you," traditionally addressed by passersby to the harvesters who in turn would respond in kind: "The LORD bless you" (see Ru 2:4). May they thus be a wasted growth.

Ps 130 This is the sixth of the seven Penitential Psalms (see Ps 6) and perhaps the psalm that has been most often recited down the centuries since the time when it became an invocation on behalf of the dead. It is both a prayer of sorrow and a hymn of hope. No other psalm reveals in so marvelous a way the mystery of God who forgives, reconciles, and redeems even those who abandon him. While wonderfully suitable for the deceased, it also befits anyone in the depths of sadness (e.g., Israel), for it makes hope rise for them like the dawn.

Because of the lofty plane on which it moves, this psalm does not need a transformation but only a greater profundity to become a Christian prayer. The parable of the Prodigal Son illustrates this perfectly (Lk 15).

130:1 *Depths:* a metaphor of adversity (see Ps 69:2f, 15; Isa 51:10; Ezek 27:34), connoting alienation from God (see Jon 2:2-5) and approaching death.

130:2 In his extremity, the psalmist appeals to the Lord, calling him by his proper name and so obliging him to answer his prayers and intervene. Although the reason for the distress is not indicated here, the petition implies that it is related to sin, and the next verse makes this point explicit.

130:3 The unfortunate psalmist is well aware that the nature of his trouble is different from the depression of illness, homesickness, or persecution seen in some other psalms (e.g., Pss 6; 42; 69). It is guilt for sin, an evil that can cease only if God puts an end to the sins that cause the evil. Unless God granted pardon, no one could *stand,* i.e., pass through his judgment (see Ps 1:5) or enjoy the benefits of his presence (see Ps 24:3).

130:4 God is full of forgiveness (see Dan 9:9; see also Pss 86:5; 103:3; Ex 34:7; 1 Jn 2:1f). And he is feared not only because of his great judgment and chastisement but also because of his great love in forgiving. The righteous respond with love and holy fear (see Deut 5:29; 1 Pet 1:17) as well as the desire not to offend him in the future (see Rom 2:4).

5 I wait for the LORD * in anxious expectation;
I place my hope in his word. [n]
6 My soul waits for the Lord
more than watchmen wait for the dawn. [o]

More than watchmen wait for the dawn *
7 * let Israel wait for the LORD.
For with the LORD there is kindness,
as well as plenteous redemption. [p]
8 He alone will redeem Israel
from all its sins. [q]

PSALM 131*

Childlike Trust in God

1 A song of ascents. Of David.
O LORD, my heart * is not proud,
nor are my eyes raised too high.
I do not concern myself with great affairs
or with things too sublime for me. [r]
2 Rather, I have stilled and calmed my soul, *
hushed it like a weaned child.
Like a weaned child held in its mother's arms,
so is my soul within me. [s]
3 O Israel, put your hope in the LORD
both now and forevermore. *

PSALM 132*

The Divine Promises Made to David

1 A song of ascents.
Remember, O LORD, for David's sake,
all the difficulties he endured. *

n Pss 5:4; 27:14; 40:1; 119:74, 81; Isa 8:17; 26:8; 30:18; 49:23.—o Ps 63:7; 2 Sam 23:4; Isa 21:11; 26:9.—p Pss 25:5; 71:14; 86:15; 100:5; 103:8; 111:9; 1 Chr 21:13; Isa 30:18; Rom 3:24.—q Ps 25:22; Ex 34:7; Mt 1:21; Lk 1:68; Tit 2:14.—r Pss 101:5; 139:6; Job 5:9; Isa 2:12; Jer 45:5; Mic 6:8; Rom 12:16.—s Isa 30:15; 66:12-13; Mt 18:3.

130:5 After noting that God liberally dispenses pardon, the psalmist expresses in splendid phrases his desire (indeed his certitude) of seeing God come close to him soon to grant him pardon. The words *I wait for the LORD* indicate that the psalmist ardently desires God and seeks to draw near to him with all his might. In patient waiting, faith looks up to the Lord to grant his grace (see Lam 3:25f). *In anxious expectation:* literally, "My soul waits": see note on Ps 6:4. *His word:* especially his covenant promises (see Pss 119:25, 28, 37, 42, 49, 65, 74, 81, 107, 114, 147) and his word of pardon.

130:6 The psalmist waits for the Lord with much greater anticipation and certitude than watchmen wait for the dawn when they will be relieved of duty after guarding the city from night attacks (see Ps 127:1). *More than watchmen wait for the dawn:* by this twofold repetition after a fourfold expression of "hope" in the Lord, the psalmist succeeds in inculcating a true sense of longing, dependence, and assurance.

130:7-8 Like the psalmist, crushed by miseries, Israel must also hope and wait for the Lord. Rich in grace (compassionate and saving love) and redemption (pardon), God will redeem Israel from all temporal and spiritual miseries; he will deliver the people from all their misfortunes and sins as he delivered them from Egypt once before. The word *redemption*, at first applied to the deliverance from slavery in Egypt (see Ex 12:27), later designates every type of liberation, every form of salvation (see Pss 25:20; 31:5; 44:27; Isa 43:14); here it signifies the profound liberation effected by the forgiveness of sins. The New Testament uses the word in the same sense—the redemption wrought by Christ (see Lk 2:38; Rom 3:24; Eph 1:7; Col 1:14; Rev 5:9). *Kindness:* see note on Ps 6:5.

Ps 131 Certainly the Prophets dared to state that God was like a mother for his people (see Isa 66:12f; Hos 11:4). But here is a man who has not fled from the experience of life; he lays bare the depth of his heart: the soul of a child before God. This psalm strikes us with great freshness and simplicity, and it is the most moving and evangelical of the psalms. A believer of the Old Testament has discovered the voice of spiritual childhood: "Unless you change and become like little children, you will never enter the kingdom of heaven" (Mt 18:3).

We can pray this psalm with the awareness that after practicing abandonment to God's hands, Jesus offers it as an ideal for us also, for like him we are children of the heavenly Father: "Learn from me, for I am meek and humble of heart" (Mt 11:29). We must flee from all desire to go beyond God and his help (see Mt 23:11; Jas 4:6f; 1 Pet 5:5f). The Father alone can make our labors fruitful through Christ (see Jn 15:1-17; 1 Cor 3:5-8); without Christ we can do nothing (see Jn 15:5).

131:1 *Heart:* see note on Ps 4:8. The psalmist has completely submitted himself to God in all humility (see Mic 6:8). He is not like the proud who rely only on themselves (see note on Ps 31:24). He knows that true holiness begins in a heart bereft of pride (see Prov 18:12), with eyes that do not envy (see Pss 18:28; 101:5; Prov 16:5), and a manner of life that is not presumptuous, not preoccupied with great things (see Jer 45:5) and achievements that are *too sublime*, i.e., too difficult or arduous, beyond one's powers (see Deut 17:8; 30:11).

131:2 *Soul:* see note on Ps 6:4. The psalmist keeps a guard over his desires. He is like a *weaned child*, who no longer frets for what it used to find indispensable and walks trustingly by its mother or lies peacefully in its mother's arms.

131:3 Likewise all Israel, all God's people, must hope only in the Lord. Weaned away from insubstantial ambitions, we must hanker for the sole solid fare: "My food is to do the will of the one who sent me, and to accomplish his work" (Jn 4:34).

Ps 132 By means of this psalm, the pilgrims, assembled for the procession, sing the glory of Zion, the dwelling place of God and the residence of his anointed, i.e., the king descended from David and like him, was consecrated with holy oil. Doubtless, this is a celebration of the anniversary of the bringing of the Ark of the Covenant to Jerusalem at the time of King David (see 2 Sam 6; 1 Chr 13–16). This hymn provides a splendid occasion to remind God of the commitment he made in favor of his people: David had sworn to build a dwelling in which to house the Ark, sign of the divine presence, and it was the Lord who promised him that he would ensure his lineage on the royal throne (see oracle of Nathan: 2 Sam 7; 1 Chr 17) at Jerusalem, where the king had projected to build God's residence.

Each new reign gave birth to a new hope, for every one of David's descendants is "anointed," that is, "Messiah" in Hebrew and "Christ" in Greek. When the fallibility of the monarchy became flagrant, the hope subsisted with more intensity. All Israel awaits a last descendant of David, a true Messiah, who will permanently restore God's reign and his worship forever. It will be the time of God's glory and salvation; it will be the coming of Jesus Christ, Son of David, whom Luke (Lk 1:69) presents to us by citing verse 17 of this psalm. Verses 8-10, 16 are cited by the Chronicler at the end of the prayer of Solomon (see 2 Chr 6:41f).

Therefore, as we pray this psalm, we can remind God of the merits of David as well as those of Christ, asking him to fulfill the oaths made to David as supplementary motives for fulfilling those made to Christ. We can urge him to enthrone his Son fully in the heavenly Zion and establish therein his perfect kingship for the benefit of his faithful and the eternal confusion of his enemies.

132:1 *All the difficulties he endured:* in the conquest of Jerusalem (see 2 Sam 5:6-12) and in bringing the Ark to Jerusalem (2 Sam 6:1-23). Some translate: "and all his anxious care," i.e., to build the temple (see 2 Sam 7:1-17; 1 Ki 8:17).

2 * He swore an oath to the LORD
and vowed to the Mighty One of Jacob:
3 "I will not enter the house I live in
or lie down on the bed where I sleep, [t]
4 neither will I allow myself to fall asleep
or even to close my eyes,
5 until I find a home for the LORD,
a dwelling for the Mighty One of Jacob."
6 We heard of it in Ephrathah;
we came upon it * in the fields of Jaar.
7 * Let us enter his dwelling place,
let us worship at his footstool. [u]
8 [v] Arise, O LORD, and go up to your resting place,
you and the Ark of your might.
9 Let your priests clothe themselves with righteousness, *
and let your saints shout for joy.
10 For the sake of your servant David,
do not reject your anointed one. *
11 The LORD swore this oath * to David, [w]
an oath that he will not renounce: [x]
"One of your own descendants
I will place on your throne.
12 If your sons keep my covenant
and the statutes that I will teach them,
their sons will also rule
on your throne from age to age." *
13 For the LORD has chosen Zion;
he has designated it for his home:
14 "This will be my resting place forever;
here I will reside, for such is my wish.
15 * "I will bless it with abundant provisions
and satisfy its poor with their fill of bread.
16 I will clothe its priests with salvation,
and its saints will shout for joy. [y]
17 "There I will raise up a horn for David *
and prepare a lamp for my anointed one. [z]
18 I will clothe his enemies with shame,
but on his head there will be a resplendent crown." *

PSALM 133*

The Blessings of Brotherly Accord

1 A song of ascents. Of David. *

t 2 Sam 7:1-2,27; 1 Chr 28:2.—u Pss 5:8; 99:5; 122:1; 2 Sam 15:25; 1 Chr 28:2.—v 8-10: Pss 2:2; 68:2; 89:21; 95:11; Num 10:35; 2 Chr 6:41-42; Job 27:6; Sir 24:7; Isa 61:3, 10; Mal 3:3; Eph 6:14.—w Pss 89:4f, 36; 110:4; 2 Sam 7:12; 1 Chr 17:11-14; Mt 1:1; Lk 3:3.—x 11-14: Ps 68:17; 2 Sam 5:9f; 1 Ki 8:13; Sir 24:7.—y Ps 149:5; 2 Chr 6:41; Job 8:21; Isa 61:10; Jer 31:14.—z Pss 18:29; 84:10; 92:11; 1 Sam 2:10; 1 Ki 11:36; Isa 11:1; Jer 33:15; Ezek 29:21; Zec 3:8; Lk 1:69.

132:2-5 Although the oath and vow of David have not been recorded in the Bible, it is clear that when David heard that God had blessed Obed-edom, the guardian of the ark (see 2 Sam 6:12), he immediately made efforts to bring the Ark to Jerusalem. *Mighty One of Jacob:* a title used by Jacob in Gen 49:24 and by Isaiah (49:26; 60:16) that emphasizes God's action in saving and redeeming his people. *Jacob:* a synonym for Israel (see Gen 32:28f).

132:6 *It . . . it:* often regarded as referring to the Ark, but more likely it refers to the call to worship that follows. *Ephrathah:* David's hometown near Bethlehem (see Ru 4:11; Mic 5:1). *Fields of Jaar:* i.e., Kiriath-jearim, where the Ark remained for a few generations (see 1 Sam 7:1f; 2 Sam 6:2; 1 Chr 13:5f).

132:7-8 Together with David and his men, the people wished to worship the Lord in Jerusalem. The Ark had been transported by the priests until it was placed in the tabernacle at Shiloh (see 1 Sam 4:3). With the capture of the Ark by the Philistines, it was taken from city to city (see 1 Sam 4–6) until David brought it to Jerusalem and inaugurated a new era in God's rule over Israel: the Davidic era. The Ark was the footstool of the Lord's throne (see Ps 99:5) and symbolized God's earthly rule (see Ps 99:1f; Num 10:35f; 2 Chr 6:41f). *Arise, O LORD:* the invocation whenever the Ark set out in the days of Moses (see Num 10:35).

132:9 *Righteousness:* here synonymous with salvation (see 2 Chr 6:41), signifying victory, blessing, and deliverance (see Pss 4:2; 22:32; 24:5). *Saints:* the People of God who should be faithful to him (see note on Ps 34:10)

132:10 The Messiah or Christ is the *anointed one* of the Lord (see Ps 2:2; 1 Sam 10:1), the descendant of David awaited by Israel.

132:11 *Swore this oath:* no oath is mentioned in 2 Sam 7. However, elsewhere God's promise to David is called a covenant (see Pss 89:4, 29, 35, 40; 2 Sam 23:5; Isa 55:3), and covenants were made with an oath.

132:12 God's sovereignty decrees that the dynasty of David will rule, but God's holiness and justice stipulate that such will hold only if David and his descendants are loyal to his covenant statutes.

132:15-16 The Lord will bless his people abundantly in his royal presence (see Deut 15:4-6); the poor and the priests will share in this new age.

132:17 *I will raise up a horn for David:* a line close to Ezek 29:21; it has a Messianic sense (see Isa 11:1; Jer 33:15; Zec 3:8). The word "horn" here designates a powerful descendant (see Ps 75:6); God will strengthen the Davidic race from which the Messiah will arise (see Lk 1:69). *Prepare a lamp for my anointed one:* promise recorded in the Books of Kings (see 1 Ki 11:36; 15:4; 2 Ki 8:19). The house in which light no longer dawns is uninhabited (see Job 18:5; Jer 25:10). The Messiah will be the light of the Gentiles (see Isa 42:6; 49:6; Lk 2:32).

132:18 This word of promise contains the Christian hope in the majesty, rule, and dominion of the Lord Jesus, who will put down all God's enemies (see 1 Cor 15:25-28; Rev 19:17-21).

Ps 133 The fragrant oil of anointing and the beneficial dew—such images speak for themselves for a Palestinian; for the poet, they evoke the charm of a living community gathered together around the priests and Levites in the holy city on the occasion of a pilgrimage. The holy city (v. 3), the priesthood (v. 2), and the communion of brothers—all is newness of grace at this moment.

This psalm easily finds an appropriate place on our lips to proclaim the advantages of concord among Christians in the bosom of the house of God, the Church. John the apostle reveals the evils of discord. The person who hates another is a murderer and remains in sin and death. Such a person is not loved by God and can receive no gift from him (see 1 Jn 3:15-17). Fraternal love constitutes the sign of true faith and with it the key to all the divine goods (see Mt 22:34-40; Jn 13:34f; 15:12-17). Only this love manifests that we are true children of God, born of him, and at the same time true disciples of Christ (see Jn 13:35; 1 Jn 4:7).

133:1a *Of David:* these words, omitted from some MSS, refer to the reunion of the tribes of Israel at David's anointing in Hebron (see 2 Sam 5:1ff).

How wonderful and delightful it is
for brothers to live together in unity. *
2 It is like fragrant ointment poured on the head,
running down upon the beard,
running down upon the beard of Aaron, [a]
and flowing on the collar of his robes. *
3 It is like the dew of Hermon
falling upon the mountains of Zion. * [b]
For there the LORD has bestowed his blessing,
life forevermore. [c]

PSALM 134*

Invitation to Night Prayer

1 A song of ascents.
Come forth to bless the LORD,
all you servants of the LORD, *
who minister throughout the night
in the house of the LORD. [d]
2 Lift up your hands toward * the sanctuary
and bless the LORD. [e]
3 May the LORD, the Maker of heaven and earth,
bless you from Zion. * [f]

PSALM 135*

Praise of God, Benefactor of His People

1 * Alleluia.
Praise the name of the LORD;
offer him praise, you servants of the LORD, * [g]
2 you who minister in the house of the LORD,
in the courts of the house of our God. * [h]

a Ex 29:7; 30:25, 30; Job 8:22; 2 Sam 12:30.—b Job 29:19; Isa 26:19; 45:8; Hos 14:6.—c Ps 36:10; Deut 28:8; 30:20.—d Ps 135:1-2; 1 Chr 9:33; Rev 19:5.—e Pss 28:2; 63:4; 141:2.—f Pss 20:3; 118:26; 124:8; 128:5; Lev 25:21; Num 6:24.—g Pss 113:1; 134:1; Neh 7:72.—h Pss 116:19; 134:1; 1 Chr 15:2; Lk 2:37.

133:1b-c The psalmist pronounces a blessing on those who live together in unity, as, for example, those on pilgrimage who included people from many different walks of life, regions, and tribes, coming together for one purpose—to worship the Lord in Jerusalem.

133:2 Brotherly accord is compared with the copious oil running down the head, beard, and robes of the priests who were anointed. Just as the holy oil poured on the priests consecrated them to the Lord's service, so brotherly unity sanctifies God's people. Thus, the fellowship of God's people on earth is an expression of the priesthood of all believers (see Ex 19:6), promised to Israel and renewed for the Church in Christ (see 1 Pet 2:9f).

133:3 *Dew of Hermon . . . mountains of Zion:* because of its height (nearly ten thousand feet above sea level) and the rain, snow, and dew that fell atop it, Mount Hermon was famous for its rich foliage even during the dry summer months (see Ps 89:13; Deut 33:28; Song 5:2; Hos 14:6). Thus, the dew of Mount Hermon would make the mountains of Zion just as fruitful (see Gen 27:28; Hag 1:10; Zec 8:12). The psalmist indicates that no matter how harsh the conditions of the pilgrimage might be, the fellowship of God's people was refreshing. *For there. . . life forevermore:* the divine blessing almost personified (see Lev 25:21; Deut 28:8) will procure happiness and salvation (see Pss 28:9; 36:11) in a definitive manner (see Pss 61:5; 73:26; Deut 30:16, 20).

Ps 134 As the pilgrims leave the temple and invite the priests to keep up their praise during the night, the latter direct to them a blessing that brings to a close the Songs of Ascents, the Pilgrim's Psalter, just as Ps 117 concludes the collection of Alleluia (or Hallelujah) Psalms (Pss 111–117).

This psalm should remind us that Jesus spent whole nights in prayer (see Lk 6:12) and that he urged the disciples to pray always and not lose heart (see Lk 18:1), a point reiterated by Paul in his first Letter: "Pray continually, give thanks in all circumstances" (1 Thes 5:17f). Hence, this dialogued hymn can be exchanged between Christians on earth: those who are often taken away from divine praise by their earthly duties should ask those who are better prepared for this (priests and religious) to assure in their name the work of praise that is so necessary.

134:1 The psalmist calls upon the priests and Levites to lead the people in worship. These are the *servants of the LORD* who *minister* (literally, "stand") in the house of the Lord. The priestly and Levitical ministry is often designated by the verb "stand" (see Ps 135:2; Deut 10:8), and they offered up musical praise to the Lord both day and night (see 1 Chr 9:33; 23:26, 30).

134:2 The priests and Levites also prayed with hands lifted up (see Ps 28:2; 1 Tim 2:8) *toward* the sanctuary (see 1 Ki 8:30).

134:3 The words of this verse recall the words spoken by the priests when blessing (see Num 6:24f). The blessing follows the people wherever they may go or live, because it comes from the Maker of heaven and earth, i.e., the Great King of the universe (see Ps 121:2). Yet, like God's commandments, the blessing is not "beyond reach," not "in heaven," nor "beyond the sea," but "very near" (see Deut 30:11-14; Rom 10:6ff)—*from Zion.* And it is the true Mount Zion, the heavenly Jerusalem, where Jesus the "mediator of a new covenant" reigns in the midst of his people (see Heb 12:22-24).

Ps 135 Composed of fragments taken from other psalms (Pss 113; 115; 134; 136), this hymn sings the praises of the true God. The psalmist acclaims the one who holds the whole universe in his hands; he glorifies the one who chose the people of Israel and guided them to their destiny from the liberation from Egypt up to their establishment in Canaan. The entire people—priests, Levites, faithful, and God-fearers (vv. 19-20)—is convoked to this praise, which celebrates the Creator of the world and the Redeemer of Israel. In the face of such solid faith, all mention of false gods becomes a caricature. Are our hymns to God true enough to cast scorn on all the new idols that we ceaselessly create for ourselves?

We can use this psalm to praise the heavenly Father for his wonders in favor of Israel (with whom we are spiritually united) and in favor of his Son Jesus, King of Israel. We can also use it to praise the Lord Jesus, Master of nature for the service of the new Israel, Savior of his Church, the only true God in the unity of the Father and the Holy Spirit.

135:1-4 An exhortation to praise God, who is good and who has love for his own.

135:1 Taken from Ps 113:1; see Jud 4:14. The praise of God included a recitation of his wonders in creation (Ps 135: 5-7) and in redemptive history (vv. 8-12). *Servants of the LORD:* although the identity of the "servants" is debated, the general consensus, based on the text itself, is that the word denotes the priests and Levites, who praised the Lord day and night (see 1 Chr 9:33; 23:26, 30).

135:2 Taken from Ps 134:1; see Ps 92:14.

3 Praise the LORD, for the LORD is good;
sing to honor his name, for he is gracious. *
4 For the LORD has chosen Jacob for himself,
Israel as his treasured possession. * [i]
5 * I know that the LORD is great,[j]
that our LORD is superior to all gods. *
6 The LORD does whatever he pleases
in heaven and on earth,
in the seas and in all their depths. * [k]
7 He causes clouds to rise
from the ends of the earth;
he sends lightning * with the rain
and brings forth the wind from his storehouses. [l]
8 * [m] He struck down the firstborn of Egypt, *
those of humans as well as of animals.
9 He sent signs and portents into your midst, O Egypt, *
against Pharaoh and all his servants.
10 [n] He struck down many nations
and slew mighty kings:
11 Sihon, king of the Amorites,
Og, king of Bashan,
and all the kings of Canaan. *
12 He then gave their lands as a heritage,
a heritage to his people Israel. *
13 Your name, O LORD, endures forever,
your renown, O LORD, lasts throughout the ages. * [o]
14 For the LORD will vindicate his people
and show compassion to his servants. * [p]
15 * [q] The idols of the nations are silver and gold,
the work of human hands.
16 They have mouths but they cannot speak;
they have eyes but they cannot see.
17 They have ears but they cannot hear,
and there is no breath in their mouths.
18 Those who make them end up like them,
as do all who place their trust in them.
19 * [r] O house of Israel, bless the LORD!
O house of Aaron, bless the LORD!
20 O house of Levi, bless the LORD!
You who fear the LORD, bless the LORD!
21 Blessed from Zion be the LORD,
he who dwells in Jerusalem.

Alleluia. *

i Pss 33:12; 144:15; Ex 19:6; Deut 7:6; Mal 3:17.—j Pss 95:3; 145:3; Ex 18:11.—k Ps 115:3; Mt 6:10.—l Pss 68:9, 11; 148:8; Job 37:9; Isa 30:23; Jer 10:13; 51:16; Joel 2:23; Am 4:13; Zec 10:11.—m 8-9: Pss 78:51; 105:27, 36; 136:10; Ex 4:23; 7:9; 12:29.—n 10-12: Pss 44:3; 136:17-22; Num 21:21-35; Deut 2:24—3:17; Jos 24:8-11.—o Ps 102:13; Ex 3:15; Isa 63:12.—p Deut 32:36; Heb 10:30.—q 15-18: Pss 96:5; 115:4-6, 8.—r 19-20: Pss 115:9-11; 118:2-4.

135:3 Praise is due because the Lord himself is good and gracious (or beautiful; see Ps 27:4). The second part of the verse is close to Ps 147:1. *He is gracious:* another possible translation is: "it is pleasant."

135:4 Although all the nations are the Lord's, he has chosen Israel as his own in a special way. *Treasured possession:* this phrase is found in Ex 19:5; Deut 7:6; 14:2; 26:18; see also Ps 33:12.

135:5-7 The psalmist spells out the greatness of the Creator, who rules over all creation and is above all gods.

135:5 *Our LORD is superior to all gods:* taken from Ex 18:11; see Ps 95:3.

135:6 The Lord does whatever he pleases (see Ps 115:3) in his acts in heaven, on the earth, in the seas, and in the subterranean waters (*all their depths*).

135:7 The Lord's greatness extends to the elements and powers of nature: *lightning* (see Ps 148:8), *rain* (see Ps 29), *wind* (see Ps 104:4), and the *storehouses* from which any of the elements could be brought forth (see Pss 33:7; 65:10f).

135:8-14 The psalmist indicates the greatness of the Lord's redemption of Israel through the Exodus and the Conquest by using climactic strokes. Most of the phrases in these verses reappear in Ps 136:10, 18-22.

135:8 *Struck . . . of Egypt:* the tenth plague (see Pss 78:51; 105:36; Ex 12:29).

135:9 *Into your midst, O Egypt:* similar in form to Ps 116:19, this phrase recalls Ps 136:11 (see Ps 78:43).

135:11 *Sihon . . . Og . . . and all the kings of Canaan:* see Ps 136:19f; Num 21:21-26, 33-35; Deut 2:30-33; 3:1-6; Jos 12:2-24.

135:12 Recalls Ps 136:17-22.

135:13 Extract from Ex 3:15; see Ps 102:12; Isa 63:12. The name God revealed to Moses was to increase in significance as the Lord increased his activities in redemptive history.

135:14 *Show compassion to his servants:* taken from Deut 32:36.

135:15-18 The psalmist reproduces Ps 115:4-6, 8 almost exactly. His point is that idols, unlike the God of Israel, do not speak, reveal, promise, or utter any spoken word. Ultimately, divine revelation is the difference between the religions made by humans and the true religion of the Lord (see Ps 115:4-8; Deut 4:16; Isa 44:9ff; Jer 10:1ff; Bar 6:7ff).

135:19-21 Employing the language of Pss 115:9-11; 118:2-4 (with the addition of "O house of Levi"), the psalmist calls upon all to praise the Lord present in Zion.

135:21 *Alleluia:* i.e., "Hallelujah" or "Bless [or praise] the LORD"; some regard this line as belonging to the beginning of Ps 136.

PSALM 136*

Thanksgiving for the Creation and Redemption

1 * Give thanks to the LORD, for he is good,
for his love endures forever. [s]
2 Give thanks to the God of gods,
for his love endures forever.
3 Give thanks to the LORD of lords,
for his love endures forever.

4 He alone works great wonders, [t]
for his love endures forever.
5 * In his wisdom he made the heavens, [u]
for his love endures forever.
6 He spread out the earth upon the waters, * [v]
for his love endures forever.

7 [w] He made the great lights,
for his love endures forever.
8 He made the sun to rule over the day,
for his love endures forever.
9 He made the moon and stars to rule the night,
for his love endures forever.

10 * [x]He struck down the firstborn of Egypt,
for his love endures forever.
11 He led forth Israel from among them,
for his love endures forever.
12 He did so with a strong hand and outstretched arm, [y]
for his love endures forever.

13 * He divided the Red Sea in two,
for his love endures forever.
14 Then he led Israel through its midst,
for his love endures forever.
15 But he swept Pharaoh and his army into the Red Sea, [z]
for his love endures forever.
16 * Then he led his people through the wilderness, [a]
for his love endures forever.

17 [b] He struck down great kings,
for his love endures forever.
18 He slew powerful kings,
for his love endures forever.
19 Sihon, king of the Amorites,
for his love endures forever.
20 Og, king of Bashan,
for his love endures forever.

21 * He gave their land as a heritage,
for his love endures forever.
22 The heritage was for his servant Israel,
for his love endures forever.

23 The LORD remembered us in our wretched state,
for his love endures forever.
24 He rescued us from our enemies,
for his love endures forever.
25 * He provides food to every creature,
for his love endures forever.

s Pss 100:5; 105:1; 106:1; 118:1; 145:9; 2 Chr 5:13; Ezr 3:11; Jer 33:11; Nah 1:7.—t Ps 72:18; Ex 15:11; Deut 10:17.—u Gen 1:9-19; Prov 3:19; 8:1, 22-31; Jer 51:15.—v Ps 24:2; Gen 1:6; Isa 42:5; Jer 10:12; 33:2.—w 7-9: Gen 1:16; Jer 31:35.—x 10-16: Pss 78:51-52; 105:43; 135:8; Ex 4:23; 12:12, 29, 51; 14:22, 27; 15:22.—y Ex 3:20; 6:1, 6; Deut 4:34.—z Ex 14:21f; 40:38; Num 9:15-22; Deut 1:33; Neh 9:19; Wis 10:17.—a Ps 78:52: Ex 13:18.—b 17-22: Ps 135:10-12; Ex 14:27; Num 21:23-25, 33-35; Deut 29:6ff; Jos 12:1ff; 24:8-11.

Ps 136 This psalm was for Israel the last of the "Great Hallel" psalms or, according to some Jewish authorities, the only Hallel psalm, the supreme song of praise. Associated with the great annual feasts, especially with the Feast of Passover, it is made up of exclamations of gratitude to God (accompanying a list of his wonders) and of enthusiastic assents from the crowd. In this list there are three great wonders that are never separated in Israel. First, the creation and life of the world (vv. 5-9). Next, the deliverances worked by God for Israel: the Exodus from Egypt (vv. 10-12), the passage through the Red Sea (vv. 13-15), the sojourn and victories in the wilderness (vv. 16-20), and the Conquest of the Promised Land (vv. 21-24). Finally, God's solicitude for every living being, the grace of the bread for each day (v. 25). As it goes through this list of favors, Israel sings of God's merciful love.

Such a psalm could not fail to become a favorite of the Church for the Easter Vigil. By his Passion and Resurrection, Christ has given life to a new world; human beings are snatched from slavery to sin and advance in their earthly pilgrimage to become the people reunited around God in the new Promised Land, the kingdom of heaven. In the accents of the Great Hallel, Christians thus sing of the Passover of the world.

136:1-4 The words *give thanks* here mean "confess" or "acknowledge" (see Lev 5:5; Prov 28:13) and therefore, call us to grateful worship indicating what we know of God's glory and his deeds. Since he is *the God of gods* and *the LORD of lords* (see Deut 10:17), he alone is to be thanked for all the acts in creation and redemption (see Ps 72:18; Ex 15:11).

136:5-9 The psalmist here brings together two Old Testament treatments of the creation theme: that of Proverbs, which speaks of the understanding and *wisdom* (v. 5) presupposed by creation (see Prov 3:19f; 8:1, 22-31; see also Ps 104:24; Jer 10:12), and that of Genesis, which gives the account of it (Ps 136: 6-9: see Gen 1:9f, 16-18).

136:6 *Upon the waters:* see Ps 24:2.

136:10-12 Of the many wonders during the Exodus from Egypt, the psalmist mentions the tenth plague (see Pss 78:51; 105:36; 135:8) and the Lord's *strong hand* and *outstretched arm*, a metaphor for God's great and personal strength in favor of his people (see Ex 6:1, 6; Deut 4:34).

136:13-15 At the Red Sea, the Lord discredited Pharaoh and his forces by judging them (see Ex 14:27), while he rescued his people (see Ps 106:7ff; Ex 4:23).

136:16-20 The Lord guided his *people through the wilderness* (see Deut 8:15; Jer 2:6; Am 2:10) and won victories for them. He struck down the great and mighty kings like *Sihon* and *Og* (see Ps 135:11; Deut 2:30ff; 3:1), who are representative of a long number of Canaanite kings. Verses 17-22 are practically identical with Ps 135:10-12.

136:21-24 God was with *his servant Israel* during the Conquest of the Promised Land, which became their heritage (see Ps 135:12), as well as from that time till the present. The Lord's remembrance is based on the covenant and is intended to effectively bring out the complete redemption of his afflicted people (see Ex 6:5).

136:25-26 Finally, it is the Lord who provides daily bread for all his creatures; therefore, all should praise him. *God of heaven:* an expression current during the Persian epoch (see Ezr 1:2; 5:11; 6:9; Neh 1:5; 2:4) that became classic (see Jud 5:8; Dan 2:18).

26 Give thanks to the God of heaven,
for his love endures forever.

PSALM 137*

The Exiles' Remembrance of Zion

1 By the rivers * of Babylon
we sat down and wept
when we remembered Zion. [c]
2 * There on the poplars
we hung up our harps. [d]
3 For it was there that our captors
asked us to sing them a song,
and, tormenting us, demanded a joyful song:
"Sing us one of the songs of Zion." [e]
4 But how could we sing songs of the LORD
while living in a foreign land? *
5 * If I forget you, O Jerusalem,
may my right hand fail me.
6 May my tongue stick to the roof of my mouth
if I do not remember you,
if I do not regard Jerusalem
as the greatest of my joys.
7 * Remember, O LORD, the cruelty of the Edomites
on the day when Jerusalem fell, *
how they shouted, "Tear it down!
Tear it down to its very foundations!" [f]
8 O Daughter * of Babylon, you destroyer,
happy will he be who repays you
for the suffering you inflicted upon us! [g]
9 Happy will he be who seizes your babies
and smashes them against a rock! * [h]

PSALM 138*

Thanksgiving for God's Favor

1 Of David.
I offer you thanks, O LORD, with all my heart; *
before the "gods" I sing your praise. [i]

c Neh 1:4; Lam 3:48; Ezek 3:15.—d Lev 23:40; Job 30:31; Isa 24:8; Jer 25:10; Lam 5:14; Ezek 26:13.—e Pss 79:1-4; 80:6; Jer 51:50; Ezek 16:57.—f Jer 49:7; Lam 4:21-22; Ezek 25:12-14; Ob 11.—g Isa 14:22; 47:1-3; Jer 50–51; Rev 18:6.—h Hos 14:1; Lk 19:44.—i Pss 9:2; 27:6; 95:3; 96:4; 106:2.

Ps 137 Let us imagine the setting in which this psalm was sung for the first time. Some Levites, after returning from the Exile, have gathered for a penitential liturgy. They are unable to suppress the memory of the humiliations they suffered on the banks of the Euphrates, where, to heighten their sadness, they were compelled not to sing the songs they loved, since it would have been a profanation to make these known in a foreign land for the amusement of idolaters. Now their cry of attachment to Jerusalem becomes vehement and their song leads to an outburst of vengeful anger that, though in keeping with the custom of the time, seems to us cruel beyond description (see notes on Pss 5:11; 35).

Events now in the distant past become symbols; the psalm speaks of Edom, but the singers think of all the forces united to destroy the People of God and the righteous; the psalm mentions Babylon, but this suggests the most hateful wickedness. This same wickedness the Book of Revelation will later image forth in the monstrous figure of "Babylon the Great," mother of blasphemers (see Rev 17:5).

We can pray this psalm as citizens of heaven (see Phil 3:20) living in exile on earth (see 2 Cor 5:6f). Strangers to a world that does not acknowledge us as its own, we are hated and persecuted by it for this reason (see Jn 15:18f; 17:14-18). We are cognizant that our exile deprives us of our true home and our Father and dooms us to divers physical and moral miseries including death, and we "groan inwardly as we wait for . . . the redemption of our bodies" (Rom 8:23).

137:1 *Rivers:* the Euphrates and Tigris, as well as the numerous irrigation-canals that branched off from them (see Ezr 8:21; Ezek 1:1; 3:15). *Sat:* the posture of mourning (see Job 2:8, 13; Lam 2:10); it could also refer to the idea of being settled in accord with the word of the prophet Jeremiah who urged the exiles to work for a living, to multiply, and to seek the peace and prosperity of the land (see Jer 29:4-9). *Wept:* see Isa 24:8; Jer 25:10; Lam 3:48; 5:14.

137:2-3 The exiles were tauntingly requested to sing *the songs of Zion* on their harps. The taunts were tantamount to the question "Where is your God?" (Pss 42:4, 11; 79:10; 115:2), and might have concerned the "songs of Zion" that celebrated the Lord's majesty and protection (see Pss 46; 48; 76; 84; 87; 122).

137:4 The exiles could not bring themselves to sing any of the holy songs while they rested on foreign, unclean soil; that would be a profanation (see Hos 9:3; Am 7:17).

137:5-6 The exiles could not forget Jerusalem and what it symbolized: covenant, temple, God's presence and kingship, atonement, forgiveness, and reconciliation. They vowed to wait for the redemption promised by God.

137:7-9 See notes on Pss 5:11; 35.

137:7 *On the day when Jerusalem fell:* literally, "the day of Jerusalem" or "that day at Jerusalem." The "day" in question is either the ninth day of the fourth month (June–July 587 B.C.) when the Babylonians broke through the walls of Jerusalem (see Jer 39:2; 52:7) or the tenth day of the fifth month (July–August 587 B.C.) when the temple was set afire (see Jer 52:12; Zec 7:5; 8:19). The *Edomites* collaborated with the besiegers and did everything they could to disgrace Judah and keep the people from escaping (see Lam 4:21f; Ezek 25:12; 35:12; Ob 11), and their name became a symbol of Israel's enemies, as well as an object of the Lord's judgments (see Isa 63:1-4; Jer 49:7-22; Ezek 25:8, 12-14; 35; Ob 1-21).

137:8 *Daughter:* a personification of Babylon, on whom the Lord had passed judgment (see Isa 13; 21:1-10; 47; Jer 50–51; Hab 2:4-20).

137:9 *Happy will he be who seizes . . . :* in accord with the ruthless practice of ancient warfare, this scene was often played out during the sacking of a city after its fall (see 2 Ki 8:12; 15:16; Isa 13:16, 18; Hos 10:14; 14:1; Am 1:13; Nah 3:10). A beatitude is here transformed into a terrible curse.

Ps 138 This psalm begins a collection of eight Davidic psalms (Pss 138–145). The believer, representing the people of Israel, knows from experience the God who saves the human race from its distress. He does not want to keep this conviction for himself but to share it with all peoples, all human beings. A deep faith in a universal plan of the Lord illumines this beautiful thanksgiving prayer.

We can pray this psalm keeping in mind the various victories that God empowers his Church to achieve against her material and spiritual enemies. These enable us to bless our Savior and to indicate the praise offered to him by earthly powers who witness and suffer under these victories.

138:1 The psalmist stresses that praise belongs to the Lord alone and not to the gods of the nations, whose kings will have to submit to the Lord. After the word "heart" the Greek adds another line: "for you have heard the words of my mouth," which is not in the Hebrew; it seems to have been a variant of verse 4b accidently inserted here. *Heart:* see note on Ps 4:8. *Gods:* the Hebrew is *elohim*, which is the word for "God," "gods," and sometimes "godlike beings," such as the angels. The Septuagint and Vulgate have "angels" (see Ps 8:6); other versions, "kings" or "judges."

2 I bow down toward your holy temple
and I praise your name *
for your kindness and your faithfulness,
for you have exalted above all things
your name and your word.
3 On the day I cried out, you answered me
and granted strength to my spirit.
4 * All the kings of the earth will praise you,
O LORD,
when they hear the words of your
mouth.
5 They will sing of the ways of the LORD:
"How great is the LORD's glory!"
6 For though the LORD is exalted, he cares
for the lowly, *
but he remains far distant from the
proud.[j]
7 Although I walk in the midst of hostility,
you preserve my life.
You stretch out your hand against the
wrath of my enemies,
and with your right hand* you deli-
ver me.
8 The LORD will fulfill his plan for me.
Your kindness, O LORD, endures for-
ever;
do not forsake the work of your hands. *

PSALM 139*

God's Infinite Knowledge and Universal Power

1 For the director. * A psalm of David.
* O LORD, you have examined me
and you know me.
2 You know when I sit and when I stand; *
you perceive my thoughts from a dis-
tance.[k]
3 You mark when I go out and when I lie
down;
all my ways are open to you.
4 A word is not even on my tongue
and you, O LORD, are completely aware
of it.
5 You enfold me from in front and from
behind,
and you place your hand upon me. *
6 Your knowledge is beyond my compre-
hension,
far too sublime for me to attain.[l]
7 * Where can I go to hide from your spirit?
Where can I flee from your presence?
8 If I ascend to the heavens, you are there;
if I take my rest in the netherworld, you
are also there.[m]
9 If I rise on the wings of the dawn *
and settle at the farthest limits of the
sea,
10 even there your hand will guide me,
and your right hand will hold me fast.
11 * If I say, "Surely the darkness will con-
ceal me

j Pss 40:5; 113:7-9; Isa 57:15; Mt 23:12; Lk 1:51-52.—k Ps 44:22; 2 Ki 19:27; Job 12:13; Heb 4:13.—l Ps 131:1; Rom 11:33.—m Job 23:8-9; Jer 23:23-24; Am 9:2-3.

138:2 *Name:* see note on Ps 5:12. *Kindness:* see note on Ps 6:5. *Your word:* i.e., God's promise. By his faithfulness to his promise, God has made his name renowned.

138:4-5 The psalmist prays that the nations, together with their gods and kings, will also pay homage to the Lord (see note on Ps 9:2). For the *words* and *ways* of the Lord reveal how great is his *glory* (see Ps 57:6; Isa 40:5; 60:1).

138:6 The Lord lifts up the *lowly* (see note on Ps 113:7-9; Lk 1:48, 52) and puts down the *proud* (see notes on Pss 31:24; 131:1; see also Ps 101:5).

138:7 The psalmist describes the Lord extending his hand to offer help while passing judgment on those who cause his adversity (see Ps 144:7; Ex 3:20; 9:15). *Right hand:* symbol of strength (see Pss 60:7; 139:10).

138:8 The Lord has loving concern for his people and creation (see Pss 90:16; 92:6; 143:5; Isa 60:21; 64:8) and has a purpose for them (see note on Ps 57:3).

Ps 139 This psalm is one of the pearls of the Psalter in its literary beauty and profound doctrine: the complete knowledge that God has about each person. The human heart is transparent to God's look; he knows the most secret and most unknown movements of our souls. Feeling the hand of God on himself provoked sadness and anxiety in Job (see Job 23–24; Jer 15:6f), but in the psalmist, it instills serenity and abandonment. He no longer asks God to turn away his face but to lead him on the path of fidelity. The psalmist awakens to God; the one whom he thought he had to seek out is already there, present in him as his source of life, more present to him than he is to himself.

We can pray this psalm to remind ourselves of the complete knowledge that Jesus has of us (see Jn 10:14f). For he is our Creator and Savior (see Col 1:16f; Heb 1:1f), who restores the supernatural world and re-creates each of his disciples, making new creatures of them to his own image (see Eph 2:10; Col 3:11).

139:1a *For the director:* these words are thought to be a musical or liturgical notation.

139:1b-6 God is all-seeing and all-knowing. His knowledge is not sterile but personal and active, discriminating in favor of those who are faithful to the Lord.

139:2 *You know when I sit and when I stand:* a Hebrew idiom that, when combined with the parallel "go out and lie down" (or "go out and come in": see Isa 37:28), signifies: "in all that I do."

139:5 *Place your hand upon me:* a gesture performed by the judge or the witness (see Job 9:33). It expresses God's absolute mastery over human beings (see Ex 33:22; Rev 1:17).

139:7-12 God is all-present; he is everywhere to protect his children. He perceives all things in all places and there is no escaping him. The same images and teaching are found in Am 9:2f. See also Job 11:8; 23:8f; Prov 15:11; Isa 7:11; Jer 23:24; Jon 1:3.

139:9 *Rise on the wings of the dawn:* go to the most distant extremities of the east. *Settle at the farthest limits of the sea:* the uttermost bounds of the west.

139:11-12 There is only light with God, and his light brightens up the darkness. *For to you darkness and light are the same:* some consider this line to be a gloss.

and the day around me will turn to night,"
12 even the darkness is not dark to you;
the night is as bright as the day,
for to you darkness and light are the same.
13 * You created my inmost being; [n]
you knit me together in my mother's womb. [o]
14 I praise you because I am wonderfully made;
awesome are your works,
as I know very well.
15 My body was not hidden from you
when I was being made in secret.
When I was woven together in the depths of the earth,
you saw me in the womb. *
16 * The sum total of my days
were all recorded in your book. *
My life was fashioned
before it had come into being. [p]
17 How precious to me are your designs, O God!
How vast in number they are!
18 If I were to attempt to count them,
they would outnumber the grains of sand. [q]
When I awake, *
I am still with you.
19 * If only you would slay the wicked, O God,
and the bloodthirsty would leave me! * [r]
20 They blaspheme your name
and treacherously rise up against you. *
21 Do I not hate those who hate you, O LORD,
and loathe those who rise up against you? [s]
22 My hatred for them is unlimited;
I regard them as my personal enemies.
23 Examine me, O God, and know my heart; *
test me and understand my thoughts. [t]
24 See if I follow an evil way,
and guide me on the way to eternity.

PSALM 140*

Prayer for Deliverance from the Snares of the Wicked

1 For the director. * A psalm of David.
2 * Deliver me, O LORD, from evildoers;
protect me from those who are violent, [u]
3 who plan evil schemes in their hearts *
and stir up strife continually.
4 Their tongues * are as sharp as those of a serpent, [v]
while the venom of vipers is on their lips. *Selah*
5 [w] Guard me, O LORD, from the hands of the wicked;
protect me from those who are violent,

n Ps 119:73; Job 10:11; Dan 2:22.—o Job 1:21; 10:8; Eccl 11:5; Wis 7:1; Jer 1:5.—p Pss 69:29; 90:12; Mal 3:16.—q Ps 40:6; Job 11:7; 29:18; Rom 11:33.—r Pss 5:7; 119:115; Job 21:14; Isa 11:4.—s Pss 26:5; 119:158; 2 Chr 19:2.—t Pss 17:3; 26:2; 1 Sam 16:7; Prov 17:3.—u Pss 17:13; 25:20; 59:2f; 71:4; 142:7.—v Pss 57:5; 58:5; 64:3; Rom 3:13; Jas 3:8.—w 5-6: Pss 28:2, 6; 36:12; 56:7; 57:7; Sir 12:16; Jer 18:22.

139:13-18 God not only sees all and penetrates the inaccessible, but he is completely operative there, creating people and providing a purpose for all.

139:15 God knows all human beings intimately.

139:16-18 The text of these verses is obscure in several places.

139:16 *[They] were all recorded in your book:* an image familiar to the Prophets (see Neh 13:14; Dan 7:10; Mal 3:16) as well as the psalmists (see Pss 69:29; 109:13), which was reprised in the *Dies Irae* (the Sequence formerly used at Masses for the Dead): *Liber scriptus proferetur, in quo totum continetur:* "Lo, the book exactly worded, in which all has been recorded." See note on Ps 56:9.

139:18 *When I awake:* in this context, these words may express a glimpse of the resurrection on the part of the psalmist, as in Ps 17:15 (see note there).

139:19-24 God is all-holy and opposes the wicked, whom he punishes for their wrongdoing. He leads the psalmist and the righteous in the way of God (*the way to eternity:* see Pss 1:6; 5:9; 73:18; 143:10; and note on 16:9-11) and not in the way of idolaters (the *evil way:* see Ps 16:4; Isa 48:5).

139:19-22 See notes on Pss 5:11; 35.

139:20 *And . . . against you:* the Hebrew is uncertain here.

139:23 *Heart:* see note on Ps 4:8.

Ps 140 More than once already we have heard the voice of a suffering, righteous person; he is the persecuted victim of the wicked, thieves, and calumniators. He calls down the vengeance of God on his enemies, while retaining his trust in the Lord. The state of the righteous and the harshness of the wicked are expressed in images often used. The opposition that biblical prayer places between poverty and violence, humility and arrogance, simplicity and falsehood is inescapable. To recite this psalm is to bear human misfortune, to become poor.

We can pray this psalm in the name of the Church who is continuously assailed by treacherous adversaries, both material and spiritual. Knowing the futility of earthly help, the Church takes her heavenly Spouse, Christ, as her sole refuge. He provides spiritual armor that is efficacious against the attacks of the enemy (see Eph 6:13-17; 1 Thes 5:8).

140:1 *For the director:* these words are thought to be a musical or liturgical notation.

140:2-6 The psalmist prays for deliverance from evildoers who sow discord with their speech and devise evil schemes, leading to anarchy and continuous agitation. Instead of following God's way, they have chosen the alternative way of the "father of lies" who was "a murderer from the beginning" (Jn 8:44).

140:3 *Hearts:* see note on Ps 4:8.

140:4 *Tongues:* see note on Ps 5:10.

who are determined to cause my downfall.
6 The arrogant* have set a hidden trap for me;
they have spread out cords as a net,
laying snares for me along the way. *Selah*
7 * I say to the LORD, "You are my God.
Listen, O LORD, to the voice of my supplications." [x]
8 O LORD, my God, my strong deliverer,
you shield my head on the day of battle.
9 Do not grant the desires of the wicked, O LORD;
do not permit their evil plots to succeed,
or they will become proud. *Selah*
10 * Those who surround me raise up their heads;
let them be overwhelmed by the malice they threaten.
11 May burning coals rain down on them;
may they be flung down into the miry depths,
never again to rise. * [y]
12 Do not permit slanderers to find rest in the land;
may evil hunt the violent to their death.
13 * I know that the LORD secures justice for the poor
and upholds the cause of the needy.
14 Then the upright will give thanks to your name,
and the righteous will dwell in your presence. [z]

PSALM 141*

Prayer for Protection against Evildoers

1 * A psalm of David.

O LORD, I call to you; come quickly to my aid;
listen to my plea when I call out to you.
2 May my prayer be like incense* before you,
the lifting up of my hands like the evening sacrifice. [a]
3 * Set a guard over my mouth, O LORD;
keep watch over the door of my lips. [b]
4 Do not permit my heart to be drawn to evil,
or to the pursuit of wicked deeds
in the company of those who do evil;
let me not share in their corruption.
5 * If a righteous man strikes me, I regard it as kindness;
if he rebukes me, it is oil on my head. * [c]
But never let the oil of the wicked anoint my head,
for my prayer is always opposed to their evil deeds.

x Pss 16:2; 31:15.—y Pss 11:6; 21:10; 120:4; Gen 19:24; Num 16:31; Mt 3:10; Lk 12:49; Rev 20:15.—z Pss 11:7; 16:11; 17:15; 138:2.—a Pss 28:2; 63:5; 134:2; Ex 30:8; Lev 2:2; Num 28:4; Lk 1:9; 1 Tim 2:8; Rev 5:8; 8:3.—b Pss 12:3; 34:14; Sir 22:27; Jas 1:26; 3:8.—c Ps 23:5; Ex 29:7; Prov 9:8; 19:25; 25:12; Eccl 7:5.

140:6 The wicked seek to entrap the righteous as a fowler catches animals with a snare, net, or trap (see Pss 31:5; 119:110; 141:10; 142:4; Mt 22:15; Lk 11:54). *Arrogant:* see note on Ps 31:24.

140:7-9 The psalmist seeks protection from the Lord of the covenant, for he alone is God and the Master of the world.

140:10-12 The psalmist's plea now becomes an imprecatory prayer, which is an expression for God's just rule. Using metaphors for the divine judgment (*burning coals* and *miry depths*), he asks for redress (see notes on Pss 5:11; 35).

140:11 Allusion to Sodom (see Gen 19) and Dathan (see Num 16). See also Pss 11:6; 36:13; 55:24; 141:10.

140:13-14 The psalmist is confident that the Lord, the just Judge (see Pss 7:9f; 9:5), will vindicate the righteous poor (see notes on Pss 22:27; 34:7), who will then praise his name (see note on Ps 7:18) and live in his presence (see notes on Pss 23:5-6; 27:4).

Ps 141 Surrounded by the wicked who persecute him in order to drag him with them into impiety, the psalmist offers up an evening prayer, matching the morning prayer referred to in Ps 5:4. The poet begs God to protect him against every defection, to help him refuse all connivance with the wicked, and to enable him ultimately to escape their plots against him.

This psalm is a reminder to us that, impelled by the devil, our greatest enemy, the world hates us because we are not of the world (see Jn 15:19; 17:14). By every available means, it strives to snatch us away from Christ to serve the devil. Aware of our weakness, we should "pray that [we] may not enter into temptation" (Mk 14:38), reciting this psalm when necessary.

141:1-2 The psalmist is in a precarious position, so he hopes his prayer for help will be like a pleasing offering before the Lord.

141:2 *Incense:* literally, "smoke," i.e., the fragrant fumes that wafted from the altar at the daily burning of sacrificial animals or aromatic spices. *The lifting up of my hands:* a symbol of dependence on and praise of the Lord (see Pss 28:2; 63:5; 1 Tim 2:8).

141:3-4 The psalmist, like the sages, carefully watches over his heart so as not to give in to sins of speech or action, for he knows that the wicked use their tongues for destruction (see Ps 140:4) while the righteous express love and fidelity (see Ps 15:2f). He begs the Lord to keep his heart from sin and temptation so that he may do God's will (see Ps 119:10, 36, 133). *Let me not share in their corruption:* literally, "let me not eat of their delicacies."

141:5-7 The psalmist delineates the fate of evil rulers at God's hands, and hopes that the shock may bring their followers to their senses.

141:5 Oil was poured on the head in a gesture of welcome and hospitality (see Lk 7:46).

6 * When their leaders are flung down in stony places,
they will learn that my prayers were heard.
7 As the soil is shattered when the ground is plowed,
so our bones are scattered at the mouth of the netherworld.

8 * But my eyes are turned to you, O Lord GOD;
in you I seek refuge;
do not take my life away. [d]
9 Keep me safe from the traps they have laid for me,
from the snares of evildoers. [e]
10 Let the wicked tumble into their own nets all together
while I pass by unharmed. *

PSALM 142*

Prayer in Time of Abandonment

1 A *maskil* * of David. When he was in the cave. A prayer.

2 * I cry out to the LORD with my plea;
I entreat the LORD to grant me mercy.
3 Before him I pour out my complaint
and tell my troubles in his presence.
4 * No matter how faint my spirit is within me,
you are there to guide my steps. [f]

Along the path on which I travel * [g]
they have hidden a trap for me. [h]
5 I look to my right,
but there is no friend who knows me.
There is no refuge available to me;
no one cares whether I live or perish. * [i]

6 * I cry out to you, O LORD;
I say, "You are my refuge, [j]
my portion in the land of the living." * [k]
7 Listen to my plea for help,
for I am in desperate straits.

Rescue me from those who seek to persecute me,
for they are too strong for me. * [l]
8 Set me free from my prison, *
so that I may praise your name.
Then the righteous will assemble around me
because of your great generosity to me.

d Pss 2:12; 11:1; 25:15; 123:1-2.—e Pss 38:13; 64:6; 140:5; 142:4.—f Pss 6:3; 77:4; 84:3; 88:5; 143:4, 7; Jer 8:18; Lam 1:22.—g Ps 139:24.—h Ps 141:9.—i Pss 16:8; 73:23; 121:5; Jer 30:17.—j Pss 46:2; 91:2, 9.—k Pss 16:5; 27:13; 116:9; Deut 32:9; Isa 38:11.—l Pss 17:1; 25:20; 79:8; Jer 31:11.

141:6-7 The text of these verses is obscure and their meaning uncertain. As it stands here, the meaning of verse 7 may be: "As a farmer breaks up the soil and brings up the rocks, so the bones of the wicked will be scattered without a decent burial" (see Ps 79:2-3).

141:8-10 The psalmist prays for deliverance and for vindication, for he remains with eyes of faith fixed on the Lord (see Ps 25:15).

141:10 God's vindication comes in the form of retribution; the schemes of the wicked will recoil upon them (see notes on Pss 5:11; 35).

Ps 142 The psalmist issues a prayer for deliverance from powerful enemies. Whether he is King David (see 1 Sam 22:10) or someone unknown, he has been trodden upon by everyone and is undergoing the agony and passion of so many others. He is also an image of Christ, isolated and suffering without protest.

Often we too find ourselves exhausted on our journey through life, strewn as it is with many snares. For some, it is social or political oppression that prevents us from leading a fully human and Christian existence. For others, religious persecution itself intervenes to restrain or destroy our goods and freedom. Upon each one, our spiritual enemies (the world and the devil) impose a continuous struggle, both fierce and treacherous, that each must wage practically without human help. In these struggles, we can make use of this psalm to direct to God an ardent and confident appeal.

142:1 *Maskil:* see note on Ps 32; *When he was in the cave:* see Ps 57:1; 1 Sam 22:10; 24:1f.

142:2-3 The psalmist uses the formal third person (customary when addressing kings) to pour out his troubles to God.

142:4-5 The psalmist is at the point of spiritual exhaustion (see Pss 76:13; 77:3; 143:4; Jon 2:8), and only God can help for he knows the faithful's destiny, his present and future life (see Ps 139:24). Yet the Lord is not present to help him along this path of his enemies, which is filled with snares. *My right:* i.e., the place where one's witness or legal counsel stood (see Pss 16:8; 109:31; 110:5; 121:5).

142:4c *Along the path on which I travel:* the present path on which the psalmist is traveling, i.e., the path of his opponents, which is covered with such snares as to fill him with dread, in contrast to the path of the Lord, which leads to such salvation as to fill him with hope (vv. 7-8).

142:5 *No one cares whether I live or perish:* the psalmist is like an outcast for whom no one cares and whom no one comes forward to protect. He is alone and extremely vulnerable.

142:6-8 The psalmist reiterates his distress and his plea for deliverance, confessing that the Lord is his refuge (see Ps 91:2; Jer 17:17) and his hope (*my portion in the land of the living*: see Pss 16:5; 73:26; 119:57; Lam 3:24). In turn, he will give thanks for his deliverance (see note on Ps 7:18), and the righteous will rejoice in the Lord with him (see Pss 22:25; 34:3; 64:10; 107:42).

142:6 Hence, the psalmist cries out to the Lord for help. The Lord is his Covenant God; he most of all should be solicitous for his servant. *In the land of the living:* i.e., here below, during his earthly life (see Ps 27:13).

142:7 The enemies of the psalmist are too strong for him. Unless the Lord comes to his aid, the afflicted man is lost. There is no one else who can save him.

142:8 *Prison:* a word that may denote actual imprisonment or may be a metaphor for the psalmist's desperate plight characterized by adversity and isolation (see Ps 107:10; Isa 42:7). *Assemble around me:* the Greek and Syriac translate this phrase as "hope [or wait] around me" (see Job 36:2). All the friends of God are united in praise and joy (see Pss 22:26; 34:4; 64:11; 107:42).

PSALM 143*

Prayer of a Penitent in Distress

1 * A psalm of David.

O LORD, hear my prayer,
incline your ear to my supplications.
In your faithfulness respond to me
with your righteousness.
2 Do not subject your servant to your judgment,[m]
for no one living is righteous before you. *
3 * An enemy has stalked me unrelentingly
and crushed me into the ground;[n]
he has left me to live in darkness *
like those long dead.[o]
4 My spirit is faint within me,
and my heart * has succumbed to fear.[p]
5 I remember the days of old,
reflecting on all your actions[q]
and meditating on the works of your hands. *
6 I stretch out my hands * to you;
my soul thirsts for you like a parched land.[r] *Selah*
7 * Answer me quickly, O LORD,
for my spirit grows faint.
Do not hide your face from me
or I will be like those who go down to the pit. *[s]
8 At dawn * let me experience your kindness,
for in you I place my trust.
Show me the path I must walk,
for to you I lift up my soul.[t]
9 Deliver me from my enemies, O LORD,
for in you I seek refuge.
10 Teach me to do your will,
for you are my God. *
Let your gracious Spirit lead me
along a level path.
11 For your name's sake, * O LORD, preserve my life;
in your righteousness deliver me from distress.
12 In your kindness, destroy my enemies,
and annihilate all those who oppress me,
for I am your servant. *[u]

PSALM 144*

Prayer for Victory and Peace

1 * Of David.

Blessed be the LORD, * my Rock,

m Ps 14:3; Job 4:17; Eccl 7:20; Rom 3:20.—n Pss 7:6; 130:3; Job 9:2; 14:3f; 15:14; Eccl 7:20.—o Ps 107:10; Lam 3:6; Mic 7:8.—p Pss 30:8; 142:4; Job 17:1.—q Ps 77:6, 12f; Gen 24:63.—r Pss 42:3; 63:2; Ex 9:29.—s Pss 27:9; 28:1; 30:4; 88:5; Prov 1:12.—t Pss 6:4; 17:15; 25:4; 27:11; 86:11; 119:12, 35.—u Pss 8:3; 54:7; 116:16.

Ps 143 This is the seventh and last of the Penitential Psalms (Pss 6; 32; 38; 51; 102; 130; 143), probably because of verse 2, with its admission of universal guilt, the only reference to sin and forgiveness in it. Throughout the Psalter, amid praise and joy, there is the lament of the poor person who is dependent on God for everything. Here is the last pressing supplication of the sufferer who cannot despair of God, of his love and his righteousness. The true Israel, the community of the poor of the Lord, understood it even unto suffering. As Paul indicates (Rom 3:20ff), no one merits to be delivered from evil, not even the person who observes the law; one can only rely on the Lord's unfailing love for human beings. Those who truly pray will experience the Lord's deliverance.

There are many occasions on which we, too, can pray this simple and ardent psalm to implore divine aid. The demons and all those whom they incite never cease to threaten us, either in our material sustenance or in our physical and spiritual life.

143:1-2 The psalmist cries out to God to have mercy because of his faithfulness and righteousness, for he knows that God's judgment could find him guilty of sin and condemn him to remain afflicted (see 130:3).

143:2 *For no one living is righteous before you:* this text is used in Rom 3:20 (see Pss 51:7; 130:3; Job 9:2; 14:3f; 15:14; Eccl 7:20).

143:3-6 The psalmist sketches the distress he suffers and is encouraged by the memory of God's past acts of deliverance.

143:3 The same images are found in Ps 7:6; Lam 3:6; Mic 7:8. *Darkness:* see note on Ps 27:1.

143:4 *Heart:* see note on Ps 4:8.

143:5 See Pss 42:5; 77:6, 12f.

143:6 *Stretch out my hands:* in supplication (see Pss 44:21; 88:10; Ex 9:29). *Soul:* see note on Ps 6:4. *Thirsts for you:* see Ps 63:2.

143:7-12 The psalmist here appends a mosaic of prayers for deliverance, guidance, and commitment to the Lord.

143:7 See similar phrases in Pss 10:1; 28:1; 69:18; 84:3; 88:5; 102:3; 141:1.

143:8 *At dawn:* see notes on Pss 57; 57:9; see also Pss 17:15; 90:14; 101:8; 108:3. *Kindness:* see note on Ps 6:5. *I lift up my soul:* see Pss 25:1; 27:8; 32:6; 33:22; 86:4.

143:10 *Teach me . . . my God:* see Pss 25:4f; 118:28. *Spirit:* the divine Spirit was regarded as a force and not yet as a person (see Ps 51:13; Neh 9:20; Ezek 36:27). *Lead . . . path:* see note on Ps 26:12 (see also Pss 27:11; 139:24).

143:11 *For your name's sake:* see Ps 25:11. *Deliver me from distress:* see Pss 31:5; 119:25, 88; 142:8.

143:12 The psalmist calls upon the Lord to deal righteously with his adversaries, reflecting a hope that is expressed in the imprecatory psalms (see notes on Pss 5:11; 35; see also Ps 54:5). *Kindness:* see note on Ps 6:5.

Ps 144 This psalm combines two compositions that are quite different in rhythm and tone. The first is suited to a royal liturgy and is drawn largely from Ps 18, a canticle of the king's victories. The second part was originally a kind of fine painting to illustrate a time of prosperity. By the time of the final redaction of the psalm, the monarchy had disappeared, and the two compositions were combined into a hymn of the Messianic Hope.

A new David will come, the true Messiah upon whom will rest the blessing of God for the benefit of the whole community. He will inaugurate an era of happiness and peace. The ancient images are nothing more than starting points, giving color and life to this prayer of expectation. The essential point is to preserve the hope of a humanity finally filled with the joy of God. It is in this vein that we can pray it with Christ in mind.

144:1-4 In jubilant language the psalmist praises God as the Redeemer-King who cares for him and watches over him, because he has the inherent weakness of all humans and is in need of help.

144:1 *Blessed be the LORD:* the psalm begins with the prayer of David in 1 Chr 29:10 and the prayers in Tob 3:11; 8:5, 15; 13:1 (see Dan 3:26; Lk 1:68; Eph 1:3). *My Rock . . . for battle:* see Ps 18:35, 47.

who trains my hands for war
and my fingers for battle.
2 You are my safeguard * and my fortress,
my stronghold and my deliverer,
my shield in whom I take refuge,
the one who subdues nations under me.

3 O LORD, what is man that you care for him, [v]
or the son of man that you think of him? *
4 Man is nothing more than a breath;
his days are like a fleeting shadow. * [w]

5 * Part the heavens, O LORD, and descend;
touch the mountains so that they smoke. * [x]
6 Flash forth lightning bolts and scatter my foes;
rout them with your arrows. *

7 Reach forth your hand * from on high;
deliver me and rescue me
from the mighty waters
and from the power of foreign foes
8 whose mouths utter lies *
and whose right hands are raised to swear to untruths.

9 * I will sing a new song to you, my God;
on a ten-stringed lyre I will play music for you. * [y]
10 You grant victory to kings
and deliverance to your servant David
from the cruel sword. * [z]

11 Deliver me and rescue me
from the hands of foreign foes
whose mouths utter lies
and whose right hands are raised to swear to untruths. *

12 * May our sons in their youth
be like carefully nurtured plants,
and may our daughters be like pillars
designed to adorn a palace. * [a]
13 May our barns be filled
with every kind of crop.

May our sheep increase by thousands,
by tens of thousands in our fields, *
14 and may our cattle be well fed. *
May there be no breach in our walls,
no going into exile,
no cries of distress in our streets. [b]

15 Blessed are the people for whom this is true;
blessed * are the people whose God is the LORD. [c]

PSALM 145*

Praise of the Divine Majesty

1 * Praise. Of David.

v Ps 8:5; Job 7:17; Heb 2:6.—w Pss 39:6-7; 62:10; 90:9-10; Job 7:16; 14:2; Eccl 6:12; Wis 2:5.—x Ps 18:10; Isa 64:1.—y Pss 33:2-3; 92:4; 144:9.—z Ps 18:51; 2 Sam 8:14.—a Pss 12:3; 36:4; 106:26; 128:3; Job 42:14-15.—b Lev 26:6; Prov 14:4; Isa 24:11; 65:19; Jer 14:2-3.—c Pss 29:11; 33:12; Deut 28:3.

144:2 This verse reflects Ps 18:3, 48. *My safeguard:* literally, "my unfailing kindness" (see note on Ps 6:5).

144:3 This verse reflects Ps 8:5.

144:4 This verse is close to Ps 39:6-7 (see also Job 14:2).

144:5-8 The psalmist calls upon God to become involved and deliver him, to come as the Divine Warrior as he did at Sinai. There he came accompanied by volcanic eruption, thunder, and lightning to save his people (see Ex 19:11, 18f).

144:5 This verse takes up Pss 18:10; 104:32. It also reveals the anxious expectation of Israel, the prey of persecutors, and the hope of a divine intervention.

144:6 See Ps 18:15. *Arrows:* i.e., the Lord's lightning that serves to rout the enemies and take away their power.

144:7 See Ps 18:17, 46. *Hand:* symbolic of the Lord's power (see Ps 18:17), which is capable of rescuing the psalmist out of the *mighty waters* into which he is sinking, i.e., out of the clutches of foreigners. For the Lord, who has subdued the stormy seas (see Ps 65:8; Gen 1:2), can certainly overpower stormy *foreign foes* (see Isa 56:6; 61:5).

144:8 The enemies are completely opposed to the law of God and filled with lies, deceit, and wickedness. *Mouths utter lies:* see note on Ps 5:10. *Right hands are raised to swear to untruths:* see Ezr 10:19; see also Ps 106:26; Ex 6:8; Deut 32:40.

144:9-10 The psalmist makes a vow to praise the Lord for the expected victory.

144:9 This verse is close to Ps 33:2f (see Pss 40:4; 98:1; 149:1).

144:10 This verse takes up the conclusion of Ps 18. "My servant David" became a Messianic title (see Jer 33:21; Ezek 34:23ff; 37:24); it is found again in Pss 78:70; 89:4, 21.

144:11 The psalmist repeats the prayer in verses 7-8, probably as an introduction to verses 12-15.

144:12-15 The psalmist prays for the people, asking the Lord to bless their children, their lives, and their livelihoods. When the enemies are defeated, the rule of the Lord will reach its height and the Messianic blessings will pour in upon his people and upon the land. The blessings are described in terms that are understandable to a people whose main occupation was agriculture and cattle raising. Even the fortified cities will receive a Messianic blessing, that of invincibility.

144:12 The Hebrew text of this verse is obscure and its meaning uncertain. It may refer to the great strength of the sons and the physical beauty of the daughters.

144:13 Material abundance is a gift of God (see Lev 26:5; Deut 7:13).

144:14 *May our cattle be well fed:* other possible translations are: "may our oxen be heavy with flesh," or "may our oxen be heavy with young," or "may our chieftains be firmly established."

144:15 Blessed are the people who experience the Lord's ability to save, protect, and bless. *Blessed:* see note on Ps 1:1.

Ps 145 This psalm is a hymn to God, the Great King. It is not original, for the psalmist strings together his verses in the order of the alphabet and takes the passages from several other psalms. The cantors of Israel were not reluctant to dip into the common treasury of sacred chant to celebrate God's praise with the same words and phrases. But the repetition of certain terms also enables one to express the ardor of a conviction. By means of the words *kingdom, power, majesty, name, works, mighty deeds, righteousness, faithfulness, compassion, love,* and *truth,* the psalm exalts above all the God of the covenant. It then proclaims his benevolence that is manifested in the help, subsistence, and salvation accorded in some manner to all who invoke him. Thus, the cantor acknowledges God's presence in the world, in history, and in life.

We can pray this psalm to bless, praise, and extol the heavenly Father in his perfections and prodigious works. But we can also recite it in honor of Christ, who shares fully in the perfections (see Col 1:15, 19; Heb 1:3) and works of his Father (see Jn 5:19).

I will extol you, my God and King;
I will bless your name * forever and ever.
2 Every day I will bless you [d]
and praise your name forever and ever. *
3 * Great is the LORD and worthy of the highest praise;
no one can even begin to comprehend his greatness. * [e]
4 Each generation will praise your works * to the next [f]
and proclaim your mighty deeds.
5 People will proclaim the glorious splendor of your majesty,
and I will meditate on your wonderful works. [g]
6 They will speak of the power of your awesome deeds,
and I will relate your greatness. [h]
7 They will celebrate your abundant goodness
and sing joyfully of your saving justice.
8 * The LORD is gracious and merciful,
slow to anger and abounding in kindness. * [i]
9 The LORD is good to all,
showing compassion to every creature. [j]
10 All your creatures praise you, * O LORD,
and all your saints bless you. [k]
11 They relate the glory of your kingdom
and tell of all your power. *
12 They make known to all people your mighty deeds
and the glorious majesty of your kingdom. [l]
13 Your kingdom will last forever,
and your dominion will endure throughout all generations. *
* The LORD is faithful in all his promises
and kind * in all his deeds.
14 The LORD supports all those who are falling
and raises up all who are bowed down. * [m]
15 The eyes of all look hopefully to you,
and you give them their food at the right time. [n]
16 You open your hand
and satisfy the needs of every living creature. *
17 * The LORD is righteous in all his ways
and merciful in everything he does. * [o]
18 The LORD is near to all who call out to him,
to all who call out to him sincerely. * [p]
19 He satisfies the desires of all who fear him;
he hears their cry and saves them. * [q]
20 The LORD watches over all who love him,
but he will completely destroy all the wicked. * [r]
21 May my mouth declare the praise of the LORD,
and may every creature * bless his holy name
forever and ever. [s]

d Pss 34:1; 68:19; 71:8; Isa 25:1; 26:8.—e Pss 48:2; 95:3; 96:4; 2 Sam 22:4; Job 5:9; 36:26.—f Pss 22:31-32; 48:14-15; 71:18; 78:4; Ex 10:2; Deut 4:9; 11:19.—g Pss 96:3; 105:2; 148:13.—h Pss 66:3; 78:4.—i Pss 86:5, 15; 103:8; Ex 34:6f; Num 14:18; Wis 1:13f; Sir 2:11; Isa 63:7.—j Ps 103:13; Wis 1:13-14; 11:24; Mt 19:17.—k Ps 8:7; Dan 3:57.—l Pss 10:16; 102:13; 146:10; Deut 7:9; Tob 13:6ff; Lam 5:19; Dan 3:100; 1 Tim 1:17; Rev 11:15.—m Pss 37:17; 94:18; 146:8.—n Pss 104:27-28; 136:25; Gen 1:30; Mt 6:25-34.—o Deut 32:4; Ezr 9:15.—p Deut 4:7; Isa 55:6; 58:9; Jer 29:13.—q Pss 20:4; 34:18; 85:10.—r Pss 1:6; 34:18; 91:4; 105:35; 139:19; Jdg 5:31.—s Ps 71:8; Sir 39:35.

145:1-2 The psalmist calls for praise of God, the Great King. This praise is to be given unceasingly and forever.

145:1 See Pss 30:2; 44:5; 71:14. *Bless your name:* see note on Ps 5:12.

145:2 See Pss 34:2; 68:20; 71:14; 146:2. This verse has been incorporated into the *Te Deum,* the great prayer of Christian praise to the Trinity.

145:3-7 The psalmist specifies the reason for praising God: his mighty deeds, which reveal his greatness and goodness. The same two themes are combined in Pss 86:10, 17; 135:3, 5.

145:3 See Pss 48:2; 96:3f; Job 36:26.

145:4 See Pss 71:17; 78:4; Isa 38:19. Salvation history is transmitted from generation to generation by the proclamation of God's mighty deeds and wonderful works (see Ps 22:31f). *Your works:* of creation, providence, and redemption.

145:8-13b Now the psalmist moves to praise God because of his divine attributes, e.g., compassion and love. These attributes lead all his works, including the *saints,* to give him thanks for the expressions of his *glory, power,* and *kingdom.*

145:8 See Pss 86:15; 103:8, 13; Ex 34:6f; Num 14:18; Wis 1:13f; Isa 63:7.

145:10 *All your creatures praise you:* see note on Ps 65:14. *Saints:* see notes on Pss 4:4; 34:10.

145:11 See 93:1; 1 Chr 29:11.

145:13 Text cited in Dan 3:100; 4:31, and applied to Christ the King. See Ps 102:13; Tob 13:6ff; Dan 7:14; 1 Tim 1:17; Rev 11:15.

145:13c-16 The psalmist calls for praise of God because of the Lord's faithfulness to the covenant. The first two lines (v. 13c) are not in the Hebrew; they are in the Dead Sea Scrolls and the Septuagint.

145:13d *Kind:* see note on Ps 6:5.

145:14 See Pss 94:18; 146:8.

145:16 See Ps 104:27f; Mt 6:25-34.

145:17-21 The psalmist calls upon all creatures to praise God for his righteous acts—acts of restoration, redemption, and vindication.

145:17 See Deut 32:4.

145:18 See Deut 4:7; Isa 55:6; 58:9; Jer 29:13.

145:19 See Pss 20:4; 34:18; 85:10.

145:20 See Pss 34:18; 91:14; 104:35; 139:19; Jdg 5:31.

145:21 *Every creature:* literally, "all flesh."

THE CONCLUDING HALLEL—PSS 146–150*

PSALM 146*

Trust in God, Creator and Redeemer

1 * Alleluia.

Praise the LORD, O my soul. *
2 I will praise the LORD as long as I live; [t]
I will sing praise to my God throughout my life. *
3 Do not place your trust in princes,
in mortal men who have no power to save. [u]
4 When the spirit departs, they return to the earth;
on that very day all their plans come to naught. * [v]
5 * Blessed is he whose help is the God of Jacob, *
whose hope is in the LORD, his God,
6 the Maker of heaven and earth, *
the sea, and everything in them—
the one who keeps faith forever. [w]
7 He grants justice to the oppressed * [x]
and gives bread to the hungry.
The LORD releases prisoners [y]
8 and opens the eyes of those who cannot see. *
The LORD lifts up those who are bowed down;
the LORD loves the righteous. [z]
9 The LORD watches over the stranger
and sustains the fatherless and the widow, *
but he blocks the way of the wicked. [a]
10 The LORD will reign forever, *
your God, O Zion, for all generations. [b]
Alleluia.

PSALM 147*

Hymn to the City of God

1 * Alleluia.

How good it is to sing praises to our God; [c]

t Pss 7:18; 63:5; 103:1; 104:33; 105:2.—u Pss 60:13; 108:13; 118:8-9; Isa 2:22.—v Pss 90:3; 104:29; Gen 3:19; 1 Mac 2:63; Job 34:14-15; Eccl 3:20; Sir 40:11; Isa 2:22; 1 Cor 2:6.—w Pss 115:15; 121:2; 124:8; Ex 20:11; Deut 7:9; Jer 32:17; Acts 14:15; Rev 14:7.—x Ps 103:6.—y Pss 68:7; 107:9; 145:15; Isa 49:9; 61:1.—z Ps 145:14; Prov 20:12.—a Ps 68:6; Ex 22:22; Deut 10:18.—b Ps 145:13; Ex 15:18; Lam 5:19; Rev 11:15.—c Pss 33:1; 92:2; 135:3.

Pss 146–150 The Concluding Hallel (see notes on Pss 113–118). After all the prayers and praises of the Psalter, we are now at the end; all the instruments of creation and all the voices of human beings enter into a great chorus, a symphony destined never to end. The Psalms are a foretaste of and prelude to the acclamations of eternity.

Ps 146 The long procession of the unhappy and the persecuted has wound its way through the Psalter, endlessly repeating their supplications. This time, their prayer takes the form of a hymn of happiness and security. How uncertain is the help of the mighty! God alone truly frees us of every anxiety.

Inaugurating the third Hallel and composed of reminiscences, this hymn sings of what the Prophets promised (see Isa 29:18f; 49:9; 61:1), promises whose fulfillment Jesus proclaims (see Lk 4:16-21). "The blind receive their sight, the lame walk, those who have leprosy are cured, the deaf hear, the dead are raised to life, and the poor have the good news proclaimed to them" (Mt 11:5)—such is the kingdom that comes; it inaugurates a new time, that of peace. Accordingly, like the next four psalms, it is framed with "Alleluia" or "Hallelujah" ("Praise [or bless] the LORD").

We can pray this psalm in honor of the heavenly Father but also in honor of Christ "[whom] God exalted . . . at his right hand as leader and Savior so that he might grant repentance and forgiveness of sins to Israel" (Acts 5:31).

146:1-4 The psalmist calls upon his people to praise and trust the Lord, for human beings are unable to provide salvation owing to their mortality.

146:1 The Septuagint and Vulgate attribute this psalm to the prophets Haggai and Zechariah. *Soul:* see note on Ps 6:4.

146:2 Life is for the purpose of praising the Lord (see Pss 103:1; 104:33).

146:4 See Pss 90:3; 104:29; Eccl 9:5; 12:7; Isa 2:22.

146:5-10 The psalmist identifies this Lord as the *God of Jacob*, the Covenant God who is Creator and Lord over all, Sustainer and Provider, the Righteous One who dispenses justice to both the godly and the wicked, and the Great King who reigns forever.

146:5 See Ps 2:12; Deut 33:29; Jer 17:7. *God of Jacob:* the God of Zion (see note on v. 10 below), whose kingship is established (see Pss 47:8; 48:2), and who blesses those who trust in him (see Ps 84:13).

146:6 The Lord is faithful, using his power to control creation, including the unruly sea, and to bless his creatures (see Ps 107:8f) with his kindness (see note on Ps 6:5). *Maker of heaven and earth:* see Pss 121:2 and note; 124:8; Ex 20:11; Jer 32:17; Acts 14:15.

146:7 *He grants justice to the oppressed:* see Ps 103:6; Deut 7:9. *The LORD releases prisoners:* see Ps 68:7; Isa 49:9; 61:1.

146:8 *Opens the eyes of those who cannot see:* see Isa 35:5; Bar 6:36; Mt 9:30; Jn 9:1ff; Acts 26:18. *Lifts up those . . . bowed down:* see Ps 145:14; Lk 13:12.

146:9 *Watches over the stranger . . . the fatherless and the widow:* see Ps 68:6; Ex 22:21. *Blocks the way of the wicked:* see Pss 11:6; 147:6; Job 5:12.

146:10 The Lord is the Great King who has promised to dwell with his people and to deliver them (see Pss 29:10; 132:13-15; Ex 15:17). *The LORD will reign forever:* see Ps 145:13; Ex 15:18.

Ps 147 Three times the psalmist sounds the invitation to praise, and three times he acclaims the almighty God. Immense is his power deployed throughout the universe, and without measure is his benevolence for his people. He rebuilds Jerusalem, leads captives back to freedom, and reveals his law. Yet the author of wonders in nature and the liberator of his people is a God who takes pleasure in the lowly. "He will wipe every tear from their eyes" (Rev 21:4)—such will be the grace of the Almighty in the new Jerusalem (see Isa 60; 62).

In the Septuagint and Vulgate, this psalm is divided into two (147:1-11 = Ps 146; 147:12-20 = Ps 147) and attributed to the prophets Haggai and Zechariah. It contains many reminiscences of Isaiah, Job, and Psalms.

We can pray this psalm while keeping in mind that the restoration of Jerusalem and Israel after the disaster of 587 B.C. and the Babylonian Captivity constitutes a wonderful work of God. However, it is only a pale image of a more beautiful work of restoration that the heavenly Father accomplishes through Christ in building his Church.

147:1-6 The psalmist enumerates the reasons why it is good to praise the Lord: the restoration that he has worked for his people in accord with his word by rebuilding Jerusalem and bringing back the exiles; his concern for all creation; and his redemption, i.e., the vindication of his people.

how pleasant it is to give him fitting
praise. *
2 The LORD restores Jerusalem
and gathers together the dispersed
people of Israel. * [d]
3 He heals the brokenhearted
and bandages their wounds. * [e]
4 He fixes the number of the stars
and assigns a name to each. * [f]
5 Great is our LORD and awesome in power;
his wisdom is without limit. * [g]
6 The LORD sustains the poor
but humbles the wicked in the dust. * [h]
7 * Offer songs of thanksgiving to the LORD;
play the lyre in honor of our God. [i]
8 He veils the heavens with clouds,
supplies the earth with rain,
and makes the hills sprout with
grass. * [j]
9 He provides food for the animals
and for the young ravens when they
call. * [k]
10 * He takes no pleasure in the strength of
the horse,
or delight in the fleetness of a runner. [l]
11 The LORD takes pleasure in those who
fear him,
those who place their hope in his kind-
ness.
12 * Praise the LORD, O Jerusalem!
Glorify your God, O Zion!
13 For he strengthens the bars of your gates
and blesses your children within
you. * [m]
14 He brings peace to your borders
and fills you with the finest of wheat. * [n]
15 He sends a command to the earth;
his word runs with utmost speed. [o]
16 [p] He gives the snow like wool
and scatters the frost like ashes. *
17 He hurls down his hail like crumbs;
who can withstand his cold? *
18 He sends his word, and the ice melts;
he stirs up his breezes, and the waters
flow.
19 * [q] He has revealed his word to Jacob,
his decrees and his judgments to Israel.
20 He has not done this for the other nations;
they are not aware of his judgments.

Alleluia.

PSALM 148*

Song of the Universe

1 * Alleluia.
Praise the LORD from the heavens;
offer praise to him in the heights!

---

d Pss 51:20; 106:47; Isa 11:12; 56:8; Jer 31:10.—e Ps 34:18; Num 12:13; Job 5:18; Isa 30:26; 61:1; Jer 33:6; Ezek 34:16.—f Gen 15:5; Isa 40:26; Bar 3:34f.—g Ps 48:2; Jud 16:13; Isa 40:28; Jer 51:15.—h Pss 37:9-10; 146:9; 1 Sam 2:7-8.—i Pss 30:5; 71:22.—j Ps 104:13f; Deut 11:14f; 2 Sam 1:21; Job 5:10; Jer 14:22; Joel 2:23.—k Ps 104:27-28; Job 38:41; Mt 6:26.—l Pss 20:8f; 33:16-18.—m Pss 48:14; 128:5.—n Ps 81:17; Lev 26:6.—o Pss 33:9; 107:20; 148:5; Isa 55:10-11.—p 16-17: Ps 148:8; Job 6:16; 37:10; 38:22.—q 19-20: Ps 78:5; Deut 4:7-8; 33:3-4; Jos 1:8; 2 Ki 22:8; Bar 3:37; Mal 3:23; Rom 3:2; 9:4.

147:1 See Ps 92:2 and note on Ps 135:3.

147:2 See Deut 30:3f; Isa 11:12; 56:8; Jer 31:10; Dan 9:25.

147:3 See Job 5:18; Isa 30:26; 61:1; Jer 33:6; Ezek 34:16. *Brokenhearted:* e.g., those in exile (see Ps 137) and those who returned from exile and attempted to rebuild the walls of Jerusalem (see Neh 2:17-20; 4:1-17).

147:4 See Gen 15:5; Isa 40:26; Bar 3:34f. In this connection, scholars cite the Wisdom of Ahiqar (VIII, 116): "Numerous are the stars of heaven, and no one knows their names."

147:5 See Ps 48:2; Job 36:22, 26; Isa 40:28; Jer 51:15.

147:6 See Pss 37:9-10; 145:20; 146:9; 1 Sam 2:7f; Job 5:11; Lk 1:52.

147:7-11 God is owed praise because he is the Great King over his creation, sustaining all that he has made, both the creatures in the heavens and the creatures on earth. He wants people to trust in him rather than in themselves.

147:8 See Pss 104:10-14, 27f; Job 5:9f; Jer 14:22; Joel 2:23.

147:9 See Job 38:41; Mt 6:26. *When they call:* the Lord feeds the birds, especially the ravens, whose cawing resembles a call for food (see Mt 6:26-30).

147:10-11 Arrogant reliance on one's own natural ability is both futile (see Am 2:14f) and displeasing to God, who comes to the aid of those who trust only in him (see Pss 20:8f; 33:16-18; Eccl 9:11; Mal 3:16f). *Kindness:* see note on Ps 6:5.

147:12-18 The psalmist stresses that God is to be praised because he has brought about restoration, security, peace, and prosperity, for he alone commands the forces of nature.

147:13 See Pss 48:14; 128:5; Isa 65:18f; Jer 33:10f.

147:14 See Ps 81:17 and note; Lev 26:6.

147:16 See Job 37:6, 10.

147:17 See Job 6:16; 37:10; 38:22.

147:19-20 Finally, God is to be praised because he has given his people his word of revelation, making known his saving plan (see Ps 50:16f; Deut 33:3f; Neh 8; Eph 3:10f), which he has done for no other people (see Deut 4:7f; Acts 14:16).

Ps 148 The exiles have returned home, the temple has been rebuilt, and its precincts have been restored. God has reestablished the people he loves. What a testament to his glory (vv. 13-14). Joy invades all hearts and expands to worldwide dimensions. The whole universe and all earthly creatures are invited to praise the Lord, the Creator and Redeemer. This theme also permeates the next two psalms, forming the conclusion and the synthesis of the Psalter.

We can pray this psalm to exhort all creation, both animate and inanimate, to praise the Triune God not only as the Creator but also as the Savior and Sanctifier. For although all creation is presently subject to vanity, it hopes to be freed from corruption so as to enter into the freedom of God's children, when God will transform the universe with a new heaven and a new earth (see Rom 8:19-22; Rev 21:1-5). May the angels and saints of heaven do likewise.

148:1-6 The psalmist calls upon all creatures in the heavens to praise the Lord because of his creative and redeeming acts.

2 Praise him, all his angels;
offer praise to him, all his hosts! * [r]
3 Praise him, sun and moon;
offer praise to him, all you shining stars!
4 Praise him, you highest heavens, *
and you waters above the heavens.
5 Let them praise the name * of the LORD,
for it was at his command that they were created. [s]
6 He established them in place forever and ever;
he issued a law that will never pass away. *
7 * [t] Praise the LORD from the earth,
you sea monsters and ocean depths,
8 fire and hail, snow and clouds,
storm winds that carry out his word, *
9 all mountains and hills,
all fruit trees and cedars, [u]
10 wild animals and all cattle,
creeping creatures and flying birds, * [v]
11 kings of the earth and all nations,
princes and all rulers on the earth,
12 young men and women,
the elderly, as well as children. *
13 * Let them all praise the name of the LORD,
for his name alone is exalted;
his majesty is above the earth and the heavens. * [w]
14 He has raised high a horn * for his people,
to the glory of all his saints,
for the people of Israel who are close to him.
Alleluia.

PSALM 149*

Glorification of God, LORD and Creator

1 * Alleluia.
Sing to the LORD a new song, *
his praise in the assembly of the saints. [x]
2 Let Israel rejoice in its Maker;
let the children of Zion rejoice in their King.
3 Let them praise his name * with dancing
and make music to him with tambourine and lyre. [y]
4 For the LORD takes delight in his people,
and he crowns the humble with salvation. *
5 Let the saints exult in their glory
and sing for joy on their beds. *

r Ps 103:20f; Job 38:7; Dan 3:58-63.—s Ps 33:9; Gen 1:3f; Jud 16:14; Jn 1:3, 10.—t 7-8: Pss 74:13-14; 103:20; 135:6; 147:15-18; Gen 1:21; Ex 9:18; Deut 33:13; Jos 10:11; Job 37:11f.—u Isa 44:23; 49:13; 55:12.—v Gen 1:21, 24f; Isa 43:20.—w Pss 8:2; 30:5; 36:6; 71:19; 108:5; 113:2-4; 138:4; 145:5; 148:13; Deut 4:7.—x Pss 22:23; 26:12; 28:7; 35:18; 40:11; 96:1; 103:1; Jud 16:1; Rev 5:9.—y Pss 68:26; 81:2-3; 87:7; 150:3-4; Ex 15:20; 2 Sam 6:14; Jer 31:4.

148:2 See Ps 103:20f; Job 38:7.

148:4 See Gen 1:6f; 1 Ki 8:27; 2 Cor 12:2; Eph 4:10. *Highest heavens:* literally, "the heavens of the heavens," i.e., the space above the "expanse," which separated the "waters above" from the "waters below" (see Ps 104:3, 13; Gen 1:6f).

148:5 *Name:* see note on Ps 5:12.

148:6 See Jer 31:35f.

148:7-12 The psalmist now calls upon all creatures on earth to praise the Lord: sea creatures, depths, the powers of nature, mountains and hills, fruit trees and the cedars, animals and birds, and finally all human beings, including the powerful as well as the young and old.

148:8 *Carry out his word:* i.e., "do his bidding" (see Ps 147:15).

148:10 See Gen 1:21, 24f; Isa 43:20.

148:12 See Jer 31:13.

148:13-14 The psalmist gives the reasons behind the praise: God is the exalted Ruler, who is not subject to the limitations of the earth or the heavens, and he has unique concern for his people, i.e., those devoted to him, his saints.

148:13 See Pss 108:5; 113:2-4.

148:14 *Horn:* i.e., the Lord's anointed (see note on Ps 18:3; see also Ps 2:2); it may also refer to the strength and power of God's people (see Ps 92:11; 1 Sam 2:1; Jer 48:25; Lam 2:17). *Saints:* see notes on Pss 4:3; 34:10.

Ps 149 The spiritual elite of God's people rebuilt the walls of Jerusalem, weapons at the ready (see Neh 4:11); they put up an unyielding resistance to the persecution of Antiochus IV Epiphanes (see 1 Mac; 2 Mac). They were conscious of defending the rights of God and the right to worship him. This was their glory: Israel was the sword of God against the advance of blasphemous and wicked forces (see Zec 9:13-16). But the images of war foretell victories, those of God's elect over the forces of evil at the time of the Messiah. The seer of the Book of Revelation will also describe great battles in heaven (see Rev 11:14).

We can pray this psalm for the Church, the new People of God, enduring in this world an ever-difficult existence, an ever-renascent war. She scores blows and gains victories against her spiritual enemies, but never decisive ones. Happily, it is Christ who leads her and animates her in battle in order to ensure victory for her and renew her fervor (see Mt 16:18; 28:20).

149:1-5 The psalmist calls on the people to sing a new song in view of the restoration and the eschatological expectation of the Lord's complete victory over evil (see Isa 61:2ff; Rev 14:3). The object of praise is the *Maker* and *King* of his people, and the devout among them are the beneficiaries of his mighty acts.

149:1 *New song:* see note on Ps 33:3. *Saints:* see notes on Pss 4:3; 34:10.

149:3 *Name:* see note on Ps 5:12. *Dancing:* which formed part of the liturgy (see Pss 87:7; 150:4; Ex 15:20; 2 Sam 6:14; Jer 31:4).

149:4 See Ps 73:1; 1 Sam 2:8; Isa 49:13; 61:9; 62:4f.

149:5 *Beds:* the beds, which had before been soaked with tears, share in the Lord's deliverance (see Pss 4:5; 6:7; 63:7; Hos 7:14). Some take "beds" as "couches" used in worship or at banquets.

6 * May the praises of God be on their lips
and a double-edged sword in their hands * [z]
7 to wreak vengeance * on the nations
and punishment on the peoples, [a]
8 to shackle their kings with chains
and their nobles with iron fetters,
9 to execute the judgments decreed against them:
such is the glory for all his saints. *
Alleluia.

PSALM 150*

Harmonious Praise of God

1 Alleluia.
Praise God in his sanctuary;
praise him in the firmament of his power. * [b]
2 Praise him for his awesome acts, *
praise him for his immeasurable greatness. [c]
3 * [d] Praise him with the sound of the trumpet,
praise him with the harp and lyre.
4 Praise him with tambourines and dancing,
praise him with strings and flutes. [e]
5 Praise him with clanging cymbals,
praise him with crashing cymbals.
6 Let everything that breathes
offer praise to the LORD. [f]
Alleluia. *

z Ps 66:17; Neh 4:10-12; 2 Mac 15:27.—a Num 31:3; Wis 3:8; Zec 9:13-16.—b Ps 102:20; Dan 3:53.—c Ex 15:7; Deut 3:24.—d 3ff: Pss 57:9; 81:3-4; 149:3; 2 Sam 6:5; 1 Chr 13:8; 16:5, 42; 2 Chr 5:12-13; 7:6.—e Ps 68:26; Ex 15:20.—f Ps 103:22; Rev 5:13.

149:6-9 The psalmist envisages the eschatological future (see Isa 61:2ff) and presents God's people as the instruments of the divine vindication (see Zec 9:13-16). The Lord will grant victory to his people, as he did to Nehemiah and his men (see Neh 4:10-12), which will be their glory.

149:6 The godly will become the sword of the Lord (see Jdg 3:16; Prov 5:4; Zec 9:13). Some interpret this verse as saying that the praise of God is a fearsome but peaceful weapon in the hands of the godly (see 2 Chr 20:17ff).

149:7 *Vengeance:* see notes on Pss 5:11; 35. The new People of God depends on the "sword of the Spirit" to combat the powers of evil (see 2 Cor 6:7; 10:4; Eph 6:12, 17; Heb 4:12) and will obtain complete victory only at the Last Judgment (see 1 Cor 6:2f).

149:9 Allusion to the prophecies against the nations, announcing their final defeat by Israel (see Ps 139:16 and note; Ezek 25:14; 39:10; Joel 4:2; Mic 4:13; Zec 10:5; 12:6; 14:3, 12ff).

Ps 150 In the same manner in which our "Glory be to the Father" concludes the recitation of our psalms, this doxological psalm concludes the Psalter on an urgent invitation to praise (see the conclusions to the first four Books: Pss 41:14; 72:18f; 89:53; 106:48). May every living creature praise the Lord everywhere, on the part of everyone, and by every means. The word "Alleluia" or "Hallelujah" (translated as "Praise [or bless] the LORD" or "Praise [or bless] him") echoes thirteen times in this psalm. The Psalter could not end on a richer or more powerful note. Everything leads to the immensity of God's glory (see Rev 15:3-4; 19:4-8). "Then I heard every creature in heaven and on earth and under the earth and in the sea, and all that is in them, saying: 'To the One seated on the throne / and to the Lamb / be blessing and honor and glory and might / forever and ever!'. . . Amen!" (Rev 5:13f).

We should heed this recommendation and carry it out, for we Christians are more aware than the psalmist of the work of God and Christ in the world and in us. Christ is enthroned in the highest heavens, his own sanctuary, but he is present and active in the heart of every creature, giving to each existence, motion, and life, as the case may be. He is in the heart of the whole world, directing its march in the material, living, human, and spiritual spheres and realizing his greatest victory in the last—the construction of the Church, his Body, his spiritual Spouse.

150:1 God is to be praised in his sanctuary on earth and his sanctuary in heaven (see Ps 8:3). The Church of the New Covenant has the mission to glorify God in the world, and her members must gather in the house of God in order to carry out this mission. *Firmament of his power:* this is also translated as "mighty heavens," which ensures the well-being of those on earth.

150:2 God is to be praised because of his creating and redeeming *awesome acts* (see Pss 106:2; 145:4, 12), which reveal his greatness (see Pss 145:3; 147:5; 1 Chr 29:11).

150:3-5 God is to be praised with a full orchestra (with *trumpet, harp, lyre,* and *tambourine*) and with dance in a liturgy of praise that will reach as high as the heavens.

150:6 God is to be praised by everyone and everything endowed with life by the Creator (see Pss 103:22; 148:7-12; Rev 5:13). By doing so, Christians will be following the "way" of the Lord, with which the Psalter began (see Ps 1:2), a way that leads to eternal life.

"He who oppresses the poor insults their Creator, but the one who is kind to the needy does him honor" *(Prov 14:31).*

THE BOOK OF PROVERBS

Toward a Way of Life

A proverb is a short, carefully phrased saying that enunciates a truth of experience and wins acceptance because of the perfection of its form and the acuteness of its observation. The Book of Proverbs is rich in such sayings: "He who spares the rod hates his son, but one who loves his son will take care to discipline him" (Prov 13:24) recalls our proverb: "The one who loves well disciplines well." This justifies the title of the Book.

We also find therein fables: *the ant (Prov 6:6-11);* portraits: *the femme fatale (Prov 7:10-27), the inveterate drinker (Prov 23:29-35), and the idler (Prov 26:13-16);* riddles *(Prov 30:15-33);* sermons *meant to advise, encourage, or praise: advice for fools (Prov 1:20-33), praise of the valiant woman (Prov 31:10-31), etc. Yet all these compositions, in quite different literary forms, have but one purpose: to instruct and edify. They are teachings drawn from reality and from life.*

The proverbs were not all composed by a single author, nor do they all belong to the same period. Nine collections can easily be distinguished and given subtitles. If the entire work is attributed to King Solomon, who reigned from 970–931 B.C., it is because this king was regarded as Israel's supreme sage (see 1 Ki 3:2—5:14). The second and fifth of our collections can, in fact, claim his collaboration; they are the oldest sections and preserve popular sayings dating from remote times. The other parts of the Book are recent, especially the first and the last, which may go back to only the fifth century B.C. Therefore, we can spread out the composition of Proverbs, in its essentials, between 950–450 B.C. We have before us not a Book, but different collections, some of which are taken from secular sayings. As the Pentateuch is a "summa" of Israelite legislation and Isaiah a "summa" of prophetism, so Proverbs can be regarded as a "summa" of Israelite wisdom.

At first sight, indeed, the wisdom contained in Proverbs does not seem much different from that of other, non-Jewish peoples. It does not, of course, have the detached and ritual character seen in the eternal wisdom of China; but then, human passions are less restrained in the Near East, and these must always be grasped in concrete particulars. Some of our texts can, however, call to mind Egyptian models (see Prov 22:17f). In any case, the evils denounced here are common to every time and place: perverse women, wine, laziness, corruption, lack of discipline, etc. The values that are highlighted belong to the order of earthly goods: prosperity, consideration, health, long life, and the like. Morality seems to stay on an earthly level: avoid excess, obey the king, respect customs and contracts, be honest. Readers are taught to order their own lives and to control the raging stream of ephemeral passions that debase a person's life. There is a reserve, an interiority, a mastery of self, an honorable uprightness, the sense of impartiality, fidelity, and even generosity, without which life would be nothing but foolishness. But where can we find the supernatural in all of this?

In fact, however, the wisdom of Proverbs is not geared to purely human virtue that is won by reason. In the Book as a whole, the wisdom takes on a rather profound religious and moral meaning, since the way of life it urges is understood as a requirement of fidelity to God, as "fear of God." Furthermore, the human behavior preached here is intended to be, as it were, a reflection of the thought and ways of God or, in other words, of divine wisdom, which is eternal and presides over the creation and the order of the world (Prov 3:19-20; 8:22-36; 16:9; 20:24).

We are thus initiated into a way of seeing and doing with regard to an order of things that surpasses the impatient desire of human beings and their useless vanity. We can compare wisdom to the law (Prov 1:29; 6:23; 15:8-9; 28:7; 29:18). Similar to the latter, it is above all justice before being profitable. At times that recompense must be expected; and one learns to prefer a certain poverty in place of injustice, to esteem the righteous poor more than the unrighteous rich (see Prov 14:20-21, 31; 16:8, 16, 19; 17:5; 19:22; 28:6).

Wisdom thus experiences nights in the faith; let us not forget that at the time of the Proverbs people did not yet envisage retribution after life. This art of living, which often seems so banal to us, demands renunciation and disinterestedness; and without a solid "fear of the LORD" one cannot become an expert at it (Prov 1:7; 9:10; 15:33).

Certainly there are imperfections in this work, but it contains authentic and precious riches. For those who learn to frequent it, this Book keeps alive the question of the true meaning of human existence.

The Book of Proverbs may be divided as follows:

I: Preface of the Redactor (1:1-9)
II: Prologue: Invitation to Wisdom (1:10—9:18)
III: The Proverbs of Solomon (10:1—22:16)
IV: The Sayings of the Wise (22:17—24:22)
V: Other Sayings of the Wise (24:23-34)
VI: Proverbs of Solomon from the Collection of the Men of Hezekiah (25:1—29:27)
VII: The Sayings of Agur (30:1-14)
VIII: Numerical Proverbs (30:15-33)
IX: The Sayings of Lemuel (31:1-9)
X: In Praise of the Valiant Woman or the Perfect Homemaker (31:10-31)

I: PREFACE OF THE REDACTOR*

CHAPTER 1

1 The proverbs of Solomon,* the son of David king of Israel: [a]

2 Designed to enable people to appreciate
wisdom* and discipline
and to comprehend words that foster
insight,
3 to acquire instruction in upright conduct,
righteousness, justice, and honesty, [b]
4 so that prudence* may be imparted to
the simple,
and the young may gain knowledge and
discretion. [c]
5 By listening to them the wise will add to
their learning,
and those gifted with discernment will
increase their ability [d]
6 to perceive the meaning of proverbs and
obscure sayings,
the words of the sages and their riddles. [e]
7 The fear of the LORD* is the beginning of
knowledge;
fools are those who despise wisdom
and instruction. [f]
8 Give heed, my son,* to your father's
instruction,
and do not reject your mother's teaching. [g]
9 They will be a crown of grace for your
head
and a pendant of honor for your
neck. [h]

II: PROLOGUE: INVITATION TO WISDOM*

If Sinners Try To Entice You . . .*

10 My son, if sinners try to entice you,
refuse to join them. [i]

a Prov 10:1; 25:1; Mt 13:3.—b Prov 2:9.—c Prov 8:5, 12.—d Prov 9:9.—e Prov 22:17; Num 12:8; Jdg 14:12; Ps 49:5; Mt 13:10-17.—f Prov 8:33-36; 9:10; Ex 20:20; Deut 4:6; Job 28:28; Pss 103:11; 111:10; 112:1; 128:1; Sir 1:16; Isa 33:6.—g Prov 2:1; 3:1; 6:20; Deut 21:18; Jer 35:8.—h Prov 3:21-22; 4:1-9.—i Prov 16:29; Deut 13:7-8.

1:1-9 The final formulation of the Book of Proverbs—which took place in the fifth or fourth century B.C.—represents the end of a lengthy process. This set of collections in which very diverse maxims and sayings are piled up, often without any order, requires an introduction. This has been composed by a writer whose concern is to emphasize the value of wisdom for the life of the people of his time.

In accordance with an ancient custom in the matter of wisdom, the masters who taught it placed it under the patronage of a sage; our author chooses Solomon and attributes the whole Book of Proverbs to him (see 1 Ki 4:32; Eccl 1:1; Song 1:1). The sapiential reflection of Israel certainly did not cease after this exceptional king, whose prestige was based first and foremost on his balanced and sound discernment. It was perhaps in his time (tenth century B.C.) that the line of these teachers of morality, the sages, began.

Wisdom is an ancient value, and it is handed over only to the person who knows how to listen and study and to become a disciple: "Listen, my son" is a formula that recurs endlessly. This conception of things has been formed in the experience of life, the reflection of schools, and the consciousness of a people. In making use of ancient sayings, one is initiated not into formulas but into an act of doing and thinking, into a way of life that is both human and religious. Wisdom is certainly knowledge but not one that is theoretical; rather, it is a knowledge of how to act, a teaching and understanding of life. It can find its deepest source in the fear of the Lord, i.e., in faith and devotion, in fidelity to the law, in a word, in the certainty that the Lord is present in one's life.

Wisdom is ancient but it is also a treasure! For everyone is invited to learn it, i.e., to experience the values that give true meaning to a person's life.

1:1 *Solomon:* the First Book of Kings (5:12) mentions the wisdom of Solomon as well as his creation of proverbs and songs. He also appears in the headings of Proverbs in 10:1; 25:1 (see also Eccl 1:1, "son of David"; Song 1:1).

1:2 *Wisdom:* i.e., skill in living, in accord with God's plan. The Book of Proverbs advises its readers to obtain wisdom (4:5), for it is more valuable than silver or gold (3:13-14). In the New Testament, Christ is called the wisdom from God (1 Cor 1:30; see Col 2:3). *Discipline:* a way of forming people that eliminates ignorance and leads them away from evil.

1:4 *Prudence:* right judgment and good sense (see Prov 15:5; 19:25). *Simple:* those lacking in maturity and experience and hence easily persuaded for good or evil (see Ps 19:8).

1:7 This verse sets forth the foundation of all religion and the theme of the Book (see Prov 9:10; 31:30) as well as the motto of the Wisdom Books (Job 28:28; Ps 111:10; Eccl 12:13; Sir 1:18, 24; 19:17). *Fear of the LORD:* reverential respect for God that leads to submission to his lordship and obedience to his commands (Eccl 12:13). *Fools:* those who oppose knowledge (Prov 1:22), resent any kind of correction (Prov 12:1), get into quarrels (Prov 20:3), give in to anger (Prov 29:11), are complacent (Prov 1:32), and trust in themselves (Prov 28:26) rather than in God (Ps 14:1).

1:8 *My son:* in the sapiential literature, the relationship of master-disciple is expressed by that of parent-child.

1:10—9:18 The values dear to the heart of our author are uprightness, sincerity, docility, good behavior, and, above all, fear of God, i.e., the believer's upright life in relation to God, to himself or herself, and to others. And the evils opposed to these are also set forth: falsehood, suffering, bad company, and violence. It is the catalogue of virtues and vices that the Book of Proverbs regulates endlessly in the history of Israel. Here, one evil is flogged more particularly: adultery, possibly because it was more prevalent than others at that time.

These first nine chapters are on the whole the work of a fairly recent author, probably in the fifth century B.C. He is not satisfied to string together widely different maxims, but seeks to think about them in a more coherent way. A clear line is drawn between the followers of wisdom and the slaves of folly; by the latter the author means the foolish or senseless persons who let themselves be duped by the appearances of the moment. The author aims, above all, to influence the decisions of the simple and the careless who have not yet made a choice.

In this fine address, Wisdom herself comes on the scene as a person who directs her invitation to men and women in the squares of the city and who calls to each in the depths of their hearts.

1:10-19 The author does not use the demanding or upsetting tone of the Prophets. He excels in counseling and putting on notice, indicative of a moralist attentive to the realism of daily life. He is keenly aware of the temptations that lie in wait for people from the moment they let themselves be drawn into participation in evil. He sets forth an appeal to resist the pressure exerted by entourages of evil.

11 They may say, "Come and join us
as we lie in ambush to shed someone's blood;
let us waylay some innocent man;[j]
12 like the netherworld we can swallow him alive,
in his prime like those who go down to the pit.[k]
13 We will discover riches of every sort *
with which we can fill our houses;
14 so throw in your lot with us
and share in the common purse."[l]
15 My son, do not accompany them!
Do not allow your feet to follow their path![m]
16 For their feet are rushing headlong to evil;
they are hastening to shed blood. *[n]
17 It is useless to spread a net
if the bird is watching. *[o]
18 These men lie in wait for their own blood
and set an ambush against themselves.[p]
19 Such is the fate of all who seek ill-gotten gain;
such greed takes away the life of those who acquire it.[q]

Wisdom Cries Out Her Message in the Street*

20 Wisdom cries out in the street;
she raises her voice in the public squares.[r]
21 She calls out on the crowded street corners;
at the city gates she proclaims her message:[s]
22 "How long will you simple people continue to be fools?
How long will you mockers * delight in your mocking?
How long will you fools continue to hate knowledge?[t]
23 If you would seriously consider my reproof,
I would pour out my thoughts to you
and make my precepts known to you.[u]
24 "However, because you refused to listen to my call,
because no one heeded when I stretched out my hand,[v]
25 and because you rejected all my counsel
and ignored all my warnings,[w]
26 * I in my turn will laugh at your distress
and mock you when panic overwhelms you,[x]
27 when terror suddenly strikes you like a hurricane
and your doom approaches like a whirlwind,
when distress and anguish come upon you.[y]
28 "Then they will cry out to me but I will not answer;
they will search for me, but not find me. *[z]
29 For they hated knowledge
and chose not to fear the LORD. *[a]
30 They refused to accept my advice
and spurned all my warnings.[b]
31 "Now they must eat the fruits of their conduct
and be glutted with the results of their schemes. *[c]

j Prov 1:18; 12:6; Ps 10:8-10.—k Ps 28:1, 35:25.—l Prov 1:19.—m Prov 4:14; Ps 119:101.—n Prov 6:18; Isa 59:7.—o Job 35:11.—p Prov 1:11.—q Prov 15:27.—r Prov 8:1-3; 9:3.—s Mt 10:27.—t Prov 7:7; 8:5.—u Acts 2:17.—v Isa 65:2, 12; 66:4; Jer 7:13.—w Lk 7:30.—x Deut 28:63; Ps 2:4.—y Rom 2:9.—z Prov 8:17; 1 Sam 8:18; Jer 11:11.—a Job 21:14.—b Ps 81:11.—c Prov 14:14; Jer 6:19; 14:16.

1:13 *Riches of every sort:* Proverbs teaches that, contrary to the belief of sinners, it is wisdom that gives people the greatest riches they could ever have (see Prov 3:14-16; 16:16; see also Job 28:12-19).

1:16 This verse is the same as the first two lines of Isa 59:7, and part of it is cited in Rom 3:15. See Prov 6:17-18.

1:17 When birds see a hunter spread out his net, they do not fall into it. In the same way, the young person who understands the dangers facing those who follow sinners will be able to avoid them.

1:20-33 Here and in three other places in Proverbs (3:15-18; 8:1-36; 9:1-12), Wisdom is personified. People think of Wisdom as confined to palaces and schools, but she is present in public squares. Like the Prophets, she has a strong voice to preach, threaten, and encourage. Indeed, it is right in the middle of the daily affairs that one must listen to the call to conversion. We are called to state our views clearly; if we fail to do so, our days will slip away into meaninglessness. False securities cannot bring about the changes necessary in an existence devoid of deep attention.

1:22 *Mockers:* i.e., those who are haughty (Prov 21:24), filled with insults, hatred, and strife (Prov 9:7-8; 22:10; 29:8), and reject correction (Prov 13:1; 15:12) that is due them (Prov 19:25; 21:11). Another name for them is "scoffers."

1:26-27 Wisdom laughs in reaction to the foolishness of the mockers who have rejected her warnings and brought ruin on themselves. They suffer the same fate as the scoundrel (Prov 6:12-15).

1:28 When they are in trouble, the foolish will search for wisdom—but without success (e.g., see Jn 7:34; 8:21).

1:29 *Fear the LORD:* see note on verse 7.

1:31 Sinners reap the consequences of their actions (see Wis 11:16), and those who do find wisdom find life and blessing (see Prov 1:32; 3:13; 8:17, 35; 14:14). "A person will reap only what he sows" (Gal 6:7).

32 For the stubbornness of the simple kills them;
fools come to final ruin by their own complacency. [d]
33 But whoever listens to me will be secure
and live in peace, without fear of disaster." [e]

CHAPTER 2

Wisdom Will Enter into Your Heart*

1 My son, if you take my words to heart
and look upon my instructions as a treasure, [f]
2 attuning your ear to wisdom
and inclining your heart to understanding, [g]
3 if you cry out for the gift of discernment *
and plead for understanding, [h]
4 if you seek for it as for silver
and search for it as for buried treasure, [i]
5 then you will understand the fear of the LORD *
and discover the knowledge of God. [j]

6 For the LORD himself is the one who bestows wisdom;
from his mouth come forth knowledge and understanding. [k]
7 He reserves his wisdom for the upright
and is a shield to those who lead blameless lives, [l]
8 for he guards the paths of justice
and keeps watch over the way of his faithful ones. [m]

9 Then you will understand equity and justice
as well as righteousness—every good path. [n]
10 For wisdom will enter your heart
and knowledge will delight your soul. * [o]
11 Prudence will protect you,
and understanding will watch over you. [p]

12 Thus, you will be preserved from the ways of evil
and from those whose speech is perverse, * [q]
13 who stray far from the straight paths *
to walk along roads of darkness, [r]
14 who take pleasure in doing evil
and delight in leading perverse lives, [s]
15 whose paths are crooked
and whose ways are devious. [t]

16 You will be saved from the wife of another,
from the adulteress * with her seductive words, [u]
17 who forsakes the partner of her youth
and forgets her sacred covenant with God. [v]
18 For her house leads downward to death *
and her paths descend to the shades. [w]
19 Anyone who goes to her never returns
or regains the paths of life. [x]

20 Take care, then, that you follow the way of the good
and keep to the paths of the righteous.
21 For the upright will live in the land, *
and those who are innocent will remain there. [y]

d Prov 5:22; Isa 66:4.—e Prov 3:23; Ps 112:8.—f Prov 3:1.—g Prov 22:17.—h 1 Ki 3:9.—i Job 3:21; Mt 13:44.—j 2 Chr 1:10-12.—k Job 22:22; Ps 51:6; Jas 1:5.—l Prov 30:5-6; Ps 84:10.—m 1 Sam 2:9.—n Prov 8:20.—o Prov 14:33.—p Prov 4:6.—q Prov 10:32.—r Prov 4:19; 9:6; Job 24:15-16.—s Prov 10:23.—t Prov 21:8; Ps 125:5.—u Prov 5:20; 6:3, 24; 7:5; 22:14.—v Mal 2:14.—w Prov 5:5f; 7:27.—x Eccl 7:26.—y Ps 37:22-28.

2:1-22 Coming from God, wisdom serves to enlighten our lives and is indeed the best of the inspirations that guide us. Her ideal far surpasses the human passions. For the ancients, there are two modes of life, two components, and two ways. On the one side are those whose conduct is marked by respect for God and uprightness and who are destined for the Promised Land, the covenant, i.e., true success. On the other side are people full of rebellion, thievery, and injustice. To which side do we belong, and what convictions mark our daily projects and attitude? This text remains capable of posing such a question to us. (Here we also find the theme of the adulterous woman on which the author will often dwell, notably in chs. 5–7.)

2:2-3 *Wisdom . . . understanding . . . discernment:* these are names for the same gift.

2:5 *Fear of the LORD:* see note on Prov 1:7.

2:10 *Knowledge will delight your soul:* in the same way that the words of a wise man are "sweet to the soul" (Prov 16:24; see Prov 3:17).

2:12 *Speech is perverse:* deceitful speech is also mentioned in Prov 6:12; 8:13; 10:31-32; 17:20; 19:1, 28; see also Eph 4:29; Jas 3:6.

2:13 *Straight paths:* see Prov 3:6; 9:15-16. *Roads of darkness:* humans love darkness rather than light (see Jn 3:19-21; see also Job 24:15-16; Isa 29:15; Rom 13:12).

2:16 *Wife of another . . . adulteress:* literally, "stranger" and "foreigner" (see Prov 5:20; 7:5). The "immoral woman" (Prov 6:24) and "prostitute" (Prov 23:27) correspond to "wife of another." The Prophets made use of the metaphor of adultery to indicate that the people had abandoned the true God to run after false gods—an apostasy that leads to the netherworld (see v. 18; 5:5-6; 7:26-27).

2:18 *Leads downward to death:* see Prov 7:27: "Her house is the pathway to the netherworld." Immorality leads to death (see Prov 5:5; 9:18).

2:21 *The upright will live in the land:* i.e., in the land of Canaan that had been promised to the people by their God (see Gen 17:8; Deut 4:1). The psalmist (Ps 37:9, 11, 29) says that the upright will possess the land (see also Mt 5:5: "The meek . . . will inherit the earth").

22 However, the wicked will be cut off from the land,
and those who are faithless will be uprooted from it. [z]

CHAPTER 3

Blessed Is the Person Who Has Found Wisdom*

1 My son, do not forget my teaching,
but cherish my commandments in your heart, [a]
2 for they will bring you length of days,
more years of life, * and an abundance of prosperity. [b]
3 Do not let kindness and fidelity leave you;
fasten them around your neck
and inscribe them on the tablet of your heart. [c]
4 Then you will gain favor and a good name
in the sight of God and man. [d]
5 Trust wholeheartedly in the LORD
rather than relying on your own intelligence.
6 In everything you do, acknowledge him,
and he will see that your paths are straight. [e]
7 Do not pride yourself on your own wisdom;
fear the LORD and turn your back on evil. [f]
8 This will provide healing for your flesh
and restore strength to your body. [g]
9 Honor the LORD with your wealth
and with the firstfruits of all your crops. * [h]
10 Then your barns will be filled with plenty, *
and your vats will overflow with new wine. [i]
11 * My son, do not ignore the LORD's discipline
or refuse to accept his rebuke. [j]
12 For the LORD disciplines those whom he loves,
just as a father chastises a beloved son. [k]
13 Blessed * is the person who has found wisdom,
the one who has gained understanding. [l]
14 For she is far more valuable than silver,
and her revenue is greater than that of gold. [m]
15 She is more precious than pearls, *
and nothing that you desire can compare with her. [n]
16 In her right hand is length of days;
in her left hand, riches and honor. [o]
17 Her ways are pleasant to follow,
and all her paths lead to peace. [p]
18 She is a tree of life to all who embrace her,
and blessed are all who hold her fast. [q]

By His Wisdom the LORD Laid the Earth's Foundations*

19 By his wisdom the LORD laid the earth's foundations;

z Prov 10:30; Deut 28:63; 29:28; Job 18:17.—a Prov 1:8.—b Prov 4:10; 9:10-11; 10:27; 1 Ki 3:13, 14.—c Prov 7:3; Deut 6:8; Ps 85:11; 2 Cor 3:3.—d 1 Sam 2:26; Lk 2:52.—e Prov 16:3; Jer 42:3.—f Prov 26:5, 12; Ex 20:20; Isa 5:21; Rom 11:25; 12:16.—g Prov 4:22; Job 21:24.—h Ex 22:29; Deut 26:2.—i Ps 144:13; Joel 2:24.—j Job 5:17; Heb 12:5f.—k Prov 13:24; Deut 8:5; Rev 3:19.—l Prov 8:34f.—m Prov 8:19; 16:16; Job 28:15.—n Prov 8:11; Job 28:17-19.—o 1 Ki 3:13-14.—p Mt 11:28-30.—q Prov 4:13; 11:30; Gen 2:9; Rev 2:7.

3:1-18 Wisdom is religious fidelity, attentiveness to God. Those who observe this are under the eye of the Lord like a child. The author has no doubt, that even in the present, the best of rewards are coming to him. In fact, true happiness is much more than our desires to possess things and to put on appearances, and the author already experiences it. In verses 14-18, he suggests something of this profound secret of life, which Christ will call the hidden treasure or pearl of great price (Mt 13:44-46). Wisdom is a tree of life, not the fruit prohibited to human beings that sprouted on the tree in paradise (see Gen 3).

3:2 *Bring you length of days, more years of life:* the "fear of the LORD" brings health to the body (v. 8) and "prolongs life" (Prov 10:27; see also Prov 9:10-11). *Abundance of prosperity:* generally speaking, the righteous are prosperous and happy while the wicked are overwhelmed with misfortune and miserable (see Prov 12:21). However, sometimes the wicked prosper and lead a carefree life (see Ps 73:3, 12)—at least for a time (see Ps 73:17-19)—while the righteous suffer (see Job 1–2).

3:9 *Firstfruits of all your crops:* the people of God were commanded to give to the priests the first part of the crops of olive oil, wine, and grains well as other products they grew each year (see Lev 23:10; Num 18:12-13).

3:10 *Filled with plenty:* those who bring their offerings to God will receive still greater blessings from him (see Mal 3:10; see also Deut 28:8-12; 2 Cor 9:8).

3:11-12 As already seen (v. 2 and note), the righteous are not always prosperous. They suffer affliction as a way of learning how to live (see Prov 12:1; Job 5:17; 36:22; Ps 119:71). The author of Hebrews quotes these two verses (Heb 12:5-6) and then adds: "[God disciplines us] for our benefit" (Heb 12:10).

3:13 *Blessed:* see note on Prov 31:28.

3:15 *[Wisdom] is more precious than pearls:* similar to Job 28:18. A worthy wife is also "more precious than pearls" (Prov 31:10).

3:19-20 The author has a lofty idea of the knowledge of life proposed to humans. Is it not the reflection of the thought that presides in the very projects of God (see Prov 8:22-31) and about which Job (chs. 38–40) never ceased being astounded?

by his understanding he established the heavens. [r]
20 Through his knowledge the depths broke open
and the clouds dropped down dew. [s]

You Will Proceed on Your Way Securely*

21 My son, without letting them slip out of your sight
safeguard sound wisdom and prudence. [t]
22 They will give life to your soul
and provide adornment for your neck. [u]
23 Then you will proceed on your way securely,
and your feet will avoid stumbling. [v]
24 When you lie down, you will not be afraid, *
and on your bed your sleep will be sweet. [w]
25 Have no fear of sudden terror
or of the destruction * that overtakes the wicked. [x]
26 For the LORD will be your assurance
and will keep your feet from the trap. [y]
27 Do not withhold kindness from anyone to whom it is due
when it is in your power to grant it. [z]
28 Do not say to your neighbor,
"Go away and come back again; I will repay you tomorrow,"
when you can give him what is owed right then. [a]
29 Do not plot any evil against your neighbor
who is living in peace beside you. [b]
30 Do not quarrel with someone without cause
when that person has done you no harm. [c]
31 Do not envy a violent man
or choose to emulate any of his ways. [d]
32 For the perverse man is an abomination to the LORD
whose friendship is bestowed only upon the upright. [e]
33 The curse of the LORD falls on the house of the wicked, *
but he blesses the abode of the righteous. [f]
34 He shows only disdain to those who are scornful,
but he showers his kindness on the humble. [g]
35 Glory is the crown given to the wise;
fools inherit nothing but disgrace.

CHAPTER 4

Acquire Wisdom*

1 Listen, my children, to a father's instruction;
pay attention and gain understanding. [h]
2 What I am offering to you is sound advice;
do not forsake my teaching. [i]
3 When I was a young boy in my father's house,
tender in years and my mother's only child, [j]
4 he taught me and said:
"Let your heart hold fast to my words;
follow my instructions and you will live. [k]
5 "Acquire wisdom and gain understanding;

r Prov 8:27-29; Ps 136:5-9.—s Gen 7:11; Job 36:28; 38:8.—t Prov 1:8-9; 4:20-22; 6:20.—u Prov 1:-8-9; 4:13; Deut 30:20.—v Prov 1:33; 4:12; Ps 37:24.—w Lev 26:6; Job 11:18; Ps 112:8; Jer 31:26.—x Job 5:21; 1 Pet 3:14.—y 1 Sam 2:9; Job 4:6.—z Gal 6:10.—a Lev 19:13; Deut 24:15.—b Zec 8:17.—c Rom 12:18.—d Prov 23:17; 24:1-2, 19; Ps 37:1.—e Job 29:4; Ps 101:4.—f Prov 14:11; Job 5:3; Ps 37:22; Zec 5:4.—g Prov 1:26; Ps 18:28; Jas 4:6; 1 Pet 5:5.—h Prov 1:8; 19:20; Job 8:10.—i Prov 1:8; 3:1.—j 1 Chr 22:5; 29:1.—k Prov 7:2.

3:21-35 There is a serenity that one sometimes discovers in a person whose life is above all profound fidelity. True wisdom is found neither in beautiful ideas nor in fine sentiments but in the practice of peace, trust, self-offering, and true human relationships. Opposed to it are wickedness, vain mockery, foolishness, and the like. To call down God's maledictions upon this folly is, for the ancients, a way of breaking away from it.

3:24 *When you lie down, you will not be afraid:* this is one of the blessings of the covenant (see Lev 26:6; Job 11:18-19; Mic 4:4; Zep 3:13; see also Prov 1:33). *Your sleep will be sweet:* see Prov 6:22; Ps 4:9.

3:25 *Sudden terror . . . destruction:* the Lord shields the righteous from harm of any kind (see Prov 10:25; Job 5:21; Ps 91:3-16). *The wicked:* see Prov 1:26-27.

3:33 The contrasting fate of the wicked and the righteous at God's hands indicated in this verse is also set forth in Deut 11:26-28. *Curse of the LORD falls on the house of the wicked:* see Jos 7:24-25; Zec 5:3-4. *Blesses the abode of the righteous:* see Job 42:12-14.

4:1-27 We already know the essence that this warm (though overly loquacious) exhortation preaches. In the name of Deuteronomy, it insists on vigilance and fidelity. For in this world of traditions, wisdom is transmitted like an education, from parents to children, from masters to disciples. Nonetheless, all must experience the cost for themselves: vigilance and the guarding of one's heart constitute, as it were, the necessary inner freedom that allows people to make progress along the way. Mastery of self merits reward even now. By contrast, in verses 16-19, a fine psychological analysis paints the picture of the wicked, the person haunted repeatedly by deadly personal projects.

never forget or turn aside from my
words. [l]
6 Do not forsake wisdom, and she will preserve you;
love her, and she will watch over you. [m]
7 "The beginning of wisdom is: acquire wisdom,
and no matter what the cost, acquire understanding. * [n]
8 Extol wisdom, and she will exalt you; [o]
if you embrace her, she will honor you.
9 She will place on your head a lovely garland
and bestow on you a crown of beauty." [p]
10 Listen, my son, and take my words to heart,
and the years of your life will be multiplied. [q]
11 I have instructed you in the ways of wisdom
and led you along the paths of righteousness. [r]
12 When you walk, your steps will be unimpeded,
and when you run, you will not stumble. * [s]
13 Hold fast to instruction and never let her go;
guard her carefully, for she is your life. [t]
14 Do not set foot on the path of the wicked
or walk on the road that evildoers follow. [u]
15 Avoid it; do not go by it;
turn aside from it and go on your way.
16 For they cannot rest until they have first done wrong; *
they cannot sleep unless they have made someone stumble. [v]
17 The bread of wickedness is their food,
and the wine of violence is their drink. * [w]
18 The path of the righteous is like the light of dawn,
which increases in brightness to the fullness of day. [x]
19 But the way of the wicked is like deep darkness, *
and they cannot even see what they have stumbled over. [y]
20 My son, concentrate attentively on my words;
pay heed to the instructions I pass on to you. [z]
21 Do not let them slip from your mind;
keep them forever in your heart. [a]
22 For they are life to those who find them
and provide health to their entire being. [b]
23 Guard your heart with all possible vigilance,
for from it flow the wellsprings of life. * [c]
24 Turn away from the mouth that deceives
and keep your distance from lips that mislead. * [d]
25 Let your eyes look straight ahead;
fix your gaze on what lies before you. [e]
26 Ensure that the path you tread is level,
and then your ways will be sure. [f]
27 Do not swerve either to the right or to the left;
keep your foot far from evil. [g]

CHAPTER 5

Keep Far Away from an Adulteress*

1 My son, pay close attention to my wisdom,

l Prov 2:12; 3:13-18.—m Prov 2:11.—n Prov 23:23; Mt 13:44-46.—o Prov 3:18; 8:18.—p Prov 1:8-9; Wis 5:16.—q Prov 1:8-9; 3:2; Deut 11:21.—r 1 Sam 12:23; 2 Sam 22:37; Ps 5:9.—s Prov 3:23; Job 18:7.—t Prov 3:22.—u Prov 1:15; Ps 1:1.—v Ps 36:5; Mic 7:3.—w Prov 13:2; Ps 80:6; Jer 22:3.—x 2 Sam 23:4; Job 17:9; Phil 2:15.—y Prov 2:13; Deut 32:35; Job 3:23; Isa 8:15.—z Prov 1:8-9; 5:1; Ps 34:12-17.—a Prov 3:21.—b Prov 3:8; 8:35.—c Prov 10:11; 2 Ki 10:31; Lk 6:45.—d Prov 6:12; 8:13.—e Job 31:1.—f Heb 12:13.—g Deut 5:32.

4:7 It is the beginning of wisdom to strive to acquire wisdom—and to do so no matter what the cost (see note on Prov 3:1-18).

4:12 In the path of life, wisdom is the best companion and guide; she will remove the obstacles that we can encounter.

4:16 *They cannot rest until they have first done wrong:* the same trait is alluded to in Ps 36:5; Mic 2:1. King David, on the other hand, refused to rest until he had first done right, i.e., found a house for the Lord (see Ps 132:3-5).

4:17 Evildoers are totally committed to wickedness and violence (see Prov 13:2; Job 15:16).

4:19 *Deep darkness:* a path that leads to destruction (see note on Prov 2:13; see also Isa 59:9-10; Jer 23:12; Jn 11:10; 12:35).

4:23 *Guard your heart . . . wellsprings of life:* those who store up good things in their hearts ensure that their words and actions will be good. Jesus said, "The mouth speaks from the abundance of the heart" (Mt 12:34).

4:24 See note on Prov 2:12.

5:1-14 The tone becomes lyrical in order to restrain the man who is captivated by the charms of women other than his wife. The seductresses are enticing, but woe to the man who lets himself become entangled with them! This first part of the Book of Proverbs insists on the temptation of other women but barely speaks of prostitutes. Could it be that morals had been relaxed to the point of favoring adultery, which was so severely condemned by the law, or was it the presence of foreign women coming from other religions and nations that had become a risk to purity of faith?

and listen carefully to my discernment, [h]
2 so that you may always act prudently
and your lips may safeguard knowledge.
3 The lips of an adulteress * drip with honey
and her mouth is smoother than oil, [i]
4 but in the end she is as bitter as wormwood *
and as sharp as a two-edged sword. [j]
5 Her feet go down to death; *
her steps lead directly to the netherworld. [k]
6 Far from following the path of life,
she unknowingly wanders off in different directions. [l]

7 So now, my son, listen to me,
and do not stray from the advice that I offer. [m]
8 Keep far away from her
and do not go anywhere near the door of her house, [n]
9 lest you turn over your life to others
and your years to one without mercy,
10 lest strangers grow prosperous on your wealth *
and your arduous toil enrich another man's house. [o]

11 Then, at the end of your life, you will groan
when your flesh and your body are consumed. [p]
12 You will say, "Why did I despise discipline
and allow my heart to spurn correction? [q]
13 Why did I fail to heed the voice of my teachers
and refuse to listen to my instructors?
14 Now I am at the brink of utter ruin
in the midst of the public assembly." * [r]

Rejoice in the Wife of Your Youth*

15 Drink the water from your own cistern,
fresh water from your own well. * [s]
16 Do not allow your springs * to overflow,
gushing forth water into the streets.
17 Let them be for you alone
and not be shared by strangers.
18 May your fountain be blessed,
and may you rejoice in the wife of your youth: [t]
19 a lovely deer, a graceful fawn—
let her affection fill you with delight
and ever hold you captive. * [u]
20 Why then be seduced by another man's wife, my son,
and succumb to the embraces of an adulteress? [v]
21 For each man's ways are observed by the LORD,
and he examines each man's paths. [w]
22 The wicked man will be ensnared by his own iniquities
and held fast in the bonds of his sins. [x]
23 He will perish for lack of discipline,
condemned by his own excessive folly. [y]

A: Four Recommendations*

CHAPTER 6

Do Not Take On Impossible Tasks*

1 My son, if you have guaranteed the debt of your neighbor
or the bond of a stranger, [z]

h Prov 1:8; 4:20.—i Prov 7:5; Ps 55:22.—j Eccl 7:26.—k Prov 2:18; 7:26-27.—l Prov 9:13; 30:20.—m Prov 1:8-9.—n Prov 2:16-19; 6:20-29; 7:1-27.—o Prov 3:16-18; 29:3.—p Ezek 24:23.—q Prov 12:1.—r Prov 1:24-27; 6:33; 31:3.—s Prov 5:18; 9:17.—t Eccl 9:9; Mal 2:14.—u Song 4:5; 8:14.—v Prov 2:16.—w Prov 15:3; Job 14:16; 31:4; 34:21; Ps 119:168; Jer 29:23; Heb 4:13.—x Prov 1:31-32; Num 32:23.—y Prov 10:21; 11:5; Job 4:21; 34:21-25.—z Prov 1:8; 11:15; 22:26; Job 17:3.

5:3 *Adulteress:* see note on Prov 2:16. The words of an adulteress are "soothing" (Ps 55:22) but laden with flattery (Prov 29:5) and treachery (Ps 5:10).

5:4 *Wormwood:* a bitter herb (see Deut 29:17; Lam 3:15, 19; Am 6:12). *Two-edged sword:* a fearful weapon (see Jdg 3:16; see also Pss 55:22; 149:6; Heb 4:12; Rev 1:16).

5:5 *Her feet go down to death:* her immorality hastens the end of the adulteress (see note on Prov 2:18).

5:10 *Strangers grow prosperous on your wealth:* the man who has consort with an adulteress loses all (see Prov 29:3) while the man who adheres to wisdom is enriched in every way (see Prov 3:16-18).

5:14 The man who gave in to an adulteress was wont to suffer financial as well as physical ruin; his action brought him "beatings and contempt" (Prov 6:33) and possibly a condemnation to death (see Deut 22:22).

5:15-23 True fidelity knows how to rediscover the happiness of first love. Proverbs has a beautiful idea of marriage.

5:15 *Your own cistern . . . your own well:* a reference to the wife. Wells and cisterns were privately owned and had great value (see 2 Ki 18:31; Jer 38:6).

5:16 *Springs:* these also refer to the wife as does "fountain" in verse 18 (see Song 4:12, 15).

5:19 The author alludes to the joys of marital love (which in Song 4:10 is described as better than wine).

6:1-19 Every civilization has maxims based on observation of life. Here are some of them—very ancient morsels mislaid in this prologue that they interrupt.

6:1-5 People are to preserve with prudence the fruit of their work and not undertake impossible tasks. This is a popular and cautious wisdom that is found under all skies. For example, a guarantor is exhorted to urge the debtor to make payment, since otherwise he, the guarantor, will have to pay.

2 you have been trapped by the utterance
of your lips,
ensnared by the words of your
mouth. [a]
3 To extricate yourself from this situation,
this is what you must do, my son.
Since you have fallen into his power,
go directly to your neighbor and plead
with him. [b]
4 Give your eyes no sleep,
your eyelids no slumber. [c]
5 Break free like a gazelle from a trap
or like a bird from the grasp of a
fowler. [d]

Contemplate the Ant, You Sluggard*

6 Contemplate the ant, you sluggard; *
observe its ways and gain wisdom. [e]
7 Even though it has no chief,
no governor or ruler, [f]
8 it stores its provisions throughout the
summer
and gathers its food at the time of har-
vest. [g]
9 How long do you intend to lie there, you
sluggard?
When will you rise from your sleep? [h]
10 A little sleep, a little slumber,
a little folding of the arms to rest, [i]
11 and poverty will overtake you like a
robber,
and scarcity like an armed man. [j]

Portrait of a Scoundrel*

12 A scoundrel, * a villainous man, is he
who specializes in crooked talk. [k]
13 He winks with his eyes,
gives signals with his feet,
and makes gestures with his fingers. [l]
14 His perverted heart is ever bent toward
devising evil
as he constantly sows discord. [m]
15 Therefore, disaster will strike him sud-
denly;
in an instant he will be crushed beyond
recovery. [n]

Six Things That the LORD Hates*

16 There are six things that the LORD
hates,
seven that are abhorrent to him: [o]
17 haughty eyes, * a lying tongue,
hands that shed innocent blood, [p]
18 a heart that devises wicked schemes, *
feet that are quick to rush into evil, [q]
19 a false witness * who spews out lies,
and one who sows dissension among
brothers. [r]

The Wiles of a Seductress*

20 Observe your father's command, my
son,
and do not reject your mother's teach-
ing. [s]
21 Bind them forever in your heart;
tie them around your neck. [t]
22 When you walk, they will guide you;
when you lie down, they will watch over
you;
when you awaken, they will instruct
you. [u]

a Prov 5:22.—b Lk 11:8.—c Prov 20:13; Ps 132:4.—d Ps 91:3; Isa 13:14.—e Prov 6:6-11; 20:4.—f Prov 30:27.—g Prov 10:4; 30:24-25.—h Prov 24:30-34; 26:13-16.—i Prov 24:33; Eccl 4:5.—j Prov 20:13; 24:30-34.—k Prov 10:31-32.—l Prov 16:30; Ps 35:19.—m Prov 6:16-19; Ps 140:3.—n Prov 14:32; 29:1; Ps 55:16.—o Prov 3:32; 8:13; 15:8-9.—p Prov 12:22; Deut 19:10; Isa 1:21.—q Prov 1:16, 31; 24:2; Gen 6:5; Job 15:31.—r Prov 19:5; Ps 12:3; Zec 8:17.—s Prov 1:8; 3:21.—t Prov 3:3; 7:1-3; Deut 6:8.—u Prov 2:11; 3:23.

6:6-11 Before the French writer La Fontaine, Job too was entranced by the life of animals. Here the ant becomes a teacher of virtue.

6:6 *Sluggard:* an idler who refuses to work (see Prov 10:26; 13:4; 15:19; 19:24; 20:4; 22:13; 24:30; 26:13-16).

6:12-15 Moralists readily cultivate the art of portrait-making so that they may better fashion the sentiments of their hearers or readers.

6:12 *Scoundrel:* a wicked man of little worth (see Jdg 19:22; 1 Sam 25:25; Job 34:18). *Crooked talk:* see Prov 2:12 and note; 19:28.

6:16-19 This is the first "numerical proverb"; it reflects a popular way of coining incisive maxims that are easy to remember and imitate, being a kind of conundrum. Here the description of the deceitful and liars is rendered more realistic by the enumeration that evokes the different parts of the human body.

6:17 *Haughty eyes:* they are usually the outward sign of a proud heart, and both will incur the judgment of God (see Prov 21:4; 30:13; Pss 18:28; 101:5). *Lying tongue:* see Prov 2:12 (and note); 12:19; 17:7; 21:6. *Hands that shed innocent blood:* see Prov 1:11, 16; 28:17.

6:18 *A heart that devises wicked schemes:* see Prov 1:31; 24:2; Gen 6:5. *Feet that are quick to rush into evil:* see Prov 1:16.

6:19 *False witness:* Proverbs sets forth the harm caused by the false witness (see Prov 12:17-18; 25:18); see also note on Ps 5:10. It also indicates the punishment that awaits him (see Prov 6:15; 19:5, 9; 21:28). *Spews out lies:* see Prov 14:5, 25. *Sows dissension:* by false accusations he foments distrust, which leads to alienation and strife (see Prov 18:6).

6:20—7:27 The exhortation resumes and we soon rediscover the theme of the perverse woman whose frequentation is more dangerous than commerce with prostitutes. The author knows how to describe the behavior of a seductress. Like a magician, she weaves a spell over the naive man so as to catch him in her nets. In order to escape her clutches, it is not enough for a man to see clearly. He needs to be modest and humble, not presume on his strength, and take to flight rather than confronting the seductress and becoming lost in situations from which no one can emerge unscathed. It is at least good psychology in the context of the morals of that time. Nonetheless, in the background of this picture sketched by the moralist with its warnings and threats, we see the lofty idea that our author has of conjugal fidelity.

23 For this command is a lamp, this teaching is a light, *
and the corrections of discipline point the way to life, [v]
24 to preserve you from an immoral woman,
from the seductive tongue of an adulteress. [w]
25 Do not lust after her beauty in your heart
or allow her to entice you with her eyes. [x]
26 For if a prostitute seeks a loaf of bread,
the adulteress endangers your very life. *[y]
27 Can a man kindle a fire in his bosom
without burning his clothes? [z]
28 Or can a man walk on red-hot coals
without scorching his feet? [a]
29 So it is with the man
who consorts with his neighbor's wife;
no one who touches her will escape punishment. [b]
30 People attach little blame to a thief
if he steals only to satisfy his hunger. [c]
31 However, once caught, he must pay back sevenfold *
and hand over all his household possessions. [d]
32 But the one who commits adultery lacks sense;
only someone who wants to destroy himself does so. [e]
33 He will get nothing but beatings and contempt,
and his disgrace will never be wiped away. [f]
34 For jealousy inflames a husband's anger,
and he will be merciless in taking revenge. [g]
35 He will not consider any compensation,
and he will reject even the most lavish gifts. [h]

CHAPTER 7

1 My son, keep my words
and make my commands your treasure. [i]
2 Follow my precepts, and you will live;
keep my teachings as the apple of your eye. [j]
3 Bind them to your fingers;
inscribe them on the tablet of your heart. [k]
4 Say to wisdom, * "You are my sister,"
and regard understanding as your friend,
5 so that they may keep you from another's wife,
from the adulteress with her seductive words. [l]
6 While standing at the window of my house
I looked out through my lattice, [m]
7 and as I glanced at the immature youths,
I observed among the simple ones *
a lad with no sense. [n]
8 He walked along the street near her corner
and then turned in the direction near her house, [o]
9 at twilight, as the day was fading,
at dusk when the night grows dark. [p]
10 Then a woman came forth to meet him,
dressed like a prostitute with a scheming heart. [q]
11 She was loud-mouthed and brazen,
one who is never content to rest at home, [r]
12 always on the streets or the public squares,
lying in wait at every corner. [s]
13 She caught him and kissed him,
and brazenly said to him: [t]
14 "I had to make sacrificial peace offerings, *
and I have fulfilled my vows today. [u]

v Prov 10:17; Ps 119:105.—w Prov 2:16; 7:5; Gen 39:8; Ps 55:22.—x Sir 9:8; 25:21; Mt 5:28.—y Prov 7:22-23.—z Job 31:12.—a Isa 43:2.—b Ex 20:14, 17; Sir 9:9.—c Job 38:39.—d Ex 22:1-14.—e Prov 7:7; 9:4, 16; Ex 20:14.—f Prov 5:9-14.—g Gen 34:7; Num 5:14.—h Job 31:9-11; Song 8:7.—i Prov 1:8.—j Prov 4:4.—k Prov 3:3; Deut 6:8.—l Prov 2:16; 6:24; 7:4; Job 31:9.—m Jdg 5:28.—n Prov 1:22; 6:32.—o Prov 7:12.—p Job 24:15.—q Gen 38:15; Ezek 16:15.—r Prov 9:13.—s Prov 23: 27-28.—t Prov 1:20; Gen 39:12.—u Lev 7:11-18.

6:23 *Lamp . . . light:* similar to the theme of the psalmist: "[The word of God] is a lamp for my feet and a light to my path" (Ps 119:105; see also Ps 19:9).

6:26 Both a prostitute and an adulteress hold no good for a man. However, the adulteress is more dangerous, for she can cost him his whole life (see Deut 22:22-24) while a prostitute demands only a wage.

6:31 *Pay back sevenfold:* Exodus (Ex 22:8) provides for a double payment in restitution. The number *seven* is an indefinite number, signifying "much more."

7:4 *Wisdom:* i.e., the body of knowledge of life handed down by the sages.

7:7 *The simple ones:* see note on Prov 1:4.

7:14 *Sacrificial peace offerings:* in this type of offering, part of the meat was eaten by the one who brought it and by his friends or family (see Lev 7:11-18). *I have fulfilled my vows today:* a fellowship offering was offered as the result of a vow, and it had to be eaten on the first or second day (see Lev 7:15-16).

15 And so I came out to meet you,
to look for you, and now I have found you.
16 I have spread coverlets over my bed,
covered sheets of Egyptian linen. * [v]
17 "I have perfumed my bed
with myrrh, aloes, and cinnamon. [w]
18 Come, let us take our fill of love till morning,
abandoning ourselves to a feast of love. [x]
19 For my husband is not at home;
he is away on a long journey.
20 He took a bag of money with him
and will not be back until the moon is full."
21 With her persistent urging she persuaded him,
luring him astray with her seductive words. * [y]
22 Bemused, he followed her,
like an ox being led to the slaughter,
like a stag stepping into a noose, [z]
23 until an arrow pierces its liver,
like a bird rushing into a snare,
not realizing its life is at stake. [a]
24 So now, my son, listen to me
and be attentive to what I have to say. [b]
25 Do not let your heart stray into her ways
or wander into her paths. [c]
26 For many are those she has led to death;
her victims are beyond number. [d]
27 Her house is the pathway to the netherworld, *
the descent to the chambers of death. [e]

CHAPTER 8

Wisdom Reenters the Scene*

1 Does Wisdom not call?
Does Understanding not lift up her voice? [f]
2 On the heights, by the wayside,
at the crossroads—she takes her stand; [g]
3 by the gates leading into the city,
at the roads of access she cries out: [h]
4 "I call out to you, O men;
my appeal is to the sons of men. [i]
5 You who are simple, acquire prudence;
you who are foolish, acquire understanding. [j]
6 Listen, for I speak of important matters;
what I proclaim is honest and right. [k]
7 For my mouth proclaims the truth;
wickedness is abhorrent to my lips. [l]
8 "All the words of my mouth are upright;
not a single word is false or crooked. [m]
9 All of them are clear to those who are intelligent *
and right to those who have acquired knowledge. [n]
10 Choose my instruction rather than silver
and knowledge instead of pure gold. [o]
11 For Wisdom is better than pearls,
and no object of desire can compare with her. [p]
12 "I, Wisdom, dwell with prudence,
and I possess knowledge and discretion. * [q]
13 The fear of the LORD implies hatred of evil; *
I hate pride and arrogance,
evil ways and perverse speech. [r]
14 From me issue forth counsel and prudence;
insight and strength * are mine. [s]

v Isa 19:9; Ezek 27:7.—w Ps 45:9; Am 6:4.—x Gen 39:7.—y Prov 5:3; 6:24; 7:5.—z Job 18:10.—a Prov 6:26; Eccl 7:26.—b Prov 1:8-9; 8:32.—c Prov 5:7-8.—d Sir 19:2.—e Prov 2:18ff; 5:5; Rev 22:15.—f Prov 1:20f; 9:3; Job 28:12.—g Prov 9:3, 14.—h Prov 8:34.—i Isa 42:2.—j Prov 1:4, 22.—k Prov 23:16.—l Jn 8:14.—m Deut 32:5.—n Prov 14:6.—o Job 28:17; Ps 19:11.—p Prov 3:15; Job 28:17-19; Wis 7:8.—q Prov 1:4.—r Prov 6:16f; 16:5; Ex 20:20; Jer 44:4.—s Prov 21:22; Job 9:4; Eccl 7:19.

7:16 *Covered sheets of Egyptian linen:* in Prov 31:22, linen is associated with wealth, and Egyptian linen was very highly regarded.

7:21 *Persistent urging . . . seductive words:* see notes on Prov 2:16; 5:3; see also v. 5; 6:24.

7:27 *Pathway to the netherworld:* see notes on Prov 2:18; 5:5; see also Prov 14:12; 16:25; Mt 7:13; 1 Cor 6:9-10.

8:1-21 Once more, Wisdom challenges human beings everywhere. The art of living and the values that she proposes constitute the treasure spoken of in the Gospels. It is this true wealth that must be preferred to everything else; one must sacrifice all things to acquire this wisdom. While the Prophets (except for Jonah) were sent only to Israel, Wisdom claims to address everyone. She is not abstract speculation because she knows how to become political virtue like Greek philosophy. Those who wield authority have need, more than others, of lucidity and good judgment so as not to govern arbitrarily. For them especially, but also for all human beings, Wisdom is a force leading to a way of uprightness.

8:9 *Those who are intelligent:* i.e., those who are wise. *Those who have acquired knowledge:* especially the knowledge of God (see note on Prov 2:5).

8:12 *Prudence . . . knowledge and discretion:* see notes on Prov 1:4; 2:2-3.

8:13 *The fear of the LORD implies hatred of evil:* see Prov 1:7 and note; 3:7; 9:10; 16:6. *I hate pride and arrogance:* see Prov 16:18; 1 Sam 2:3; Ps 10:2-11; Isa 13:11. *Evil ways and perverse speech:* see Prov 2:12 and note; 6:12, 16-19.

8:14 *Counsel and prudence; insight and strength:* these are all qualities of the Lord (see Prov 2:6-7; Job 12:13, 16; Isa 40:13-14; Rom 16:27) and the Spirit of the Lord (see Isa 11:2).

15 Through me kings reign,
and rulers decree what is just. [t]
16 By me princes and nobles rule,
all those who govern rightly. [u]

17 "I love those who love me,
and those who diligently seek me will find me. [v]
18 With me are riches and honor,
enduring wealth and prosperity. [w]
19 My fruit is better than the finest gold,
and what I yield surpasses pure silver. [x]
20 I walk on the way of righteousness,
along the paths of justice, [y]
21 bestowing wealth on those who love me
and heaping up their treasures. [z]

By the Side of the God of the Origins*

22 "The LORD created me as the firstborn of his ways,
before the oldest of his works. [a]
23 I was established in the earliest times,
at the beginning, before the earth. [b]
24 I was brought forth when there were no ocean depths,
when there were no springs overflowing with water. [c]
25 Before the mountains had been shaped,
before the hills, I was brought forth, [d]
26 when he had not yet made the earth and the fields
or the mass of the world's soil.

27 "When he set the heavens in place, I was there,
when he designated where the ocean and the horizon * meet, [e]
28 when he fixed the canopy of the clouds above
and limited the fountains of the deep, [f]
29 when he assigned the boundaries of the sea
so that the waters would not transgress his command,
and when he established the foundations of the earth, [g]
30 then I was beside him as a master craftsman, *
and I was his delight day after day,
exulting in his presence continually, [h]
31 rejoicing in his inhabited world
and delighting in the children of men. * [i]

32 "So now, my sons, listen to me;
blessed * are those who keep my ways. [j]
33 Listen to instruction and gain wisdom;
do not reject it. [k]
34 Blessed is the one who listens to me,
who keeps watch daily at my gates,
waiting at my doorway. [l]
35 For whoever finds me finds life
and receives favor from the LORD. [m]
36 But whoever sins against me harms himself,
and all who hate me love death." [n]

B: Wisdom and Folly

CHAPTER 9

At God's Banquet*

1 Wisdom has built her house;
she has hewn her seven pillars. [o]

t Prov 16:12; Ps 2:10; Rom 13:1.—u Prov 29:4; 2 Chr 1:10.—v Prov 1:28; 1 Sam 2:30; Jn 14:21-24.—w Prov 3:16.—x Prov 3:14; Job 28:17-19.—y Ps 5:9; Mt 21:32.—z Prov 15:6; 24:4.—a Wis 9:9; Sir 1:1; 24:9.—b Sir 1:4.—c Gen 7:11.—d Job 15:7; 38:6.—e Prov 3:19; Job 26:7.—f Gen 1:7; Job 9:8; 26:10; 36:28.—g Gen 1:9; Job 38:8; Ps 16:6.—h Prov 3:19; Wis 9:9; Rev 3:14.—i Prov 30:4; Job 28:25-27; Ps 104:1-30; Jn 1:1-4; Col 1:15-20.—j Prov 3:13; 7:24; Pss 119:1-2; 128:1; Lk 11:28.—k Prov 4:1; 15:32.—l 1 Ki 10:8.—m Prov 3:13-18; 4:22; 9:6.—n Prov 15:32; Isa 3:9.—o Eph 2:19-22; 1 Pet 2:5.

8:22-36 Wisdom is a *craftsman* (v. 30)—or "daughter of God," according to an old translation—in God's plan of creation. How can we fail to listen to her who is the very echo of God's inspiration? This passage represents a high point in the thought of the wisdom teachers: in their eyes wisdom is too sublime and too ancient to be a merely human discovery. The inspiration that gives the world its order and beauty becomes a kind of "quality" of God. Here it becomes a person, as it were, created by God after the manner of a father who gives life to his child. She lives in close intimacy with the Lord, "with God," like the Word of whom the Gospel of John speaks at the beginning of the Prologue. She was created before anything else existed; in God's presence, and filled with the joy she had from the beginning, she inspired the picture of the world. Is it not she who, in the name of God, joyously associates with human beings and brings them the joy of his presence?

In this song of wisdom and creation Christians may see an anticipation, as it were, of what will become a certitude of faith for John (1:1-5) and Paul (1 Cor 1:24-30; Col 1:15-17), i.e., that there exists in God the eternal Word, inseparable from him. The Catholic Liturgy has readily made use of this passage. In that context, Wisdom personified becomes an image calling to mind the mystery of the Virgin Mary, whom God had in mind from all eternity and who is the masterpiece of his creation.

8:27 *Horizon:* the vault of heaven.

8:30 *Craftsman:* the term "wise" was sometimes applied to a craftsman, e.g., Bezalel, who designed and constructed the tabernacle (see Ex 31:3-4). In this verse, it highlights the skill required for creating the world and everything in it.

8:31 *Delighting in the children of men:* made in God's image, human beings constituted the culminating point of creation (see Gen 1:26-28).

8:32, 34 *Blessed:* the blessings that flow from gaining wisdom are also indicated in Prov 3:13-18; see note on Prov 31:28.

9:1-6 This beautiful poem once again presents Wisdom as a person. She invites men and women to a feast in her house, the seven pillars of which symbolize perfection. The theme of the feast at which the wise are gathered was dear to antiquity; Christ, too, will speak to us of guests invited to the royal feast (see Mt 22:2; Lk 14:16). Reading this fascinating invitation, Christians will be reminded of the Eucharistic Supper where Christ offers them the word and the bread. It is the sign and foreshadowing of the royal feast to which are called all human beings, and where all will experience the joy of God.

2 She has slain her animals and mixed her wine,
and she has spread her table. [p]
3 She has sent forth her maidservants
and proclaimed from the heights of the city, [q]
4 "Let those who are simple * turn in here."
To the person without understanding she says, [r]
5 "Come and partake of my food,
and taste the wine that I have prepared! [s]
6 Abandon foolishness so that you may live;
walk in the way of understanding. [t]

A Parenthesis about the Arrogant*

7 "If you correct an arrogant man, you invite insults;
if you rebuke a wicked man, you incur abuse. [u]
8 If you reprove an insolent man, he will hate you;
if you reprove a wise man, he will love you. [v]
9 Instruct a wise man, and he will become wiser still;
teach a righteous man, and he will advance in learning. [w]
10 * "The fear of the LORD is the beginning of wisdom, *
and knowledge of the Holy One is understanding. [x]
11 For by me your days will be multiplied,
and years will be added to your life. [y]
12 If you are wise, it is to your advantage;
if you are arrogant, you alone will bear the blame." [z]

Folly Sits at the Door of Her House*

13 The woman Folly * acts impulsively; [a]
she is undisciplined and lacking in knowledge. [b]
14 She sits at the door of her house,
upon a seat commanding the city, [c]
15 calling out to the passers-by
who are hurrying on their straight way, [d]
16 "You who are simple, turn in here."
To the fool she says, [e]
17 "Stolen water is sweet,
and bread eaten in secret tastes good." [f]
18 But little does he know that the dead are there
and that her guests are headed for the netherworld. [g]

III: THE PROVERBS OF SOLOMON*

CHAPTER 10

The One Who Leads an Honest Life . . .*

1 The Proverbs of Solomon:

A wise son brings joy to his father,
but a foolish son gives grief to his mother. [h]

p Isa 25:6; 62:8; Lk 14:16-23.—q Prov 1:20; 8:1-3; 9:14.—r Prov 1:22; 6:32; 9:16.—s Isa 44:3; 55:1; Jn 7:37-38.—t Prov 3:1-2; 8:35.—u Prov 23:9; Mt 7:6.—v Prov 15:12; Ps 141:5; Sir 19:8.—w Prov 1:5, 7; 12:15; 13:10; 14:6.—x Prov 1:7; 30:3; Job 28:28; Ps 111:10; Sir 1:16.—y Prov 3:2, 16; 10:27; Deut 11:21.—z Job 22:2.—a 13-18: Prov 7:7-27.—b Prov 5:6; 7:11.—c Prov 9:3; Ezek 16:25.—d Prov 1:20.—e Prov 1:22.—f Prov 20:17.—g Prov 2:18; 7:26-27.—h Prov 1:1; 15:20; 17:25; 19:13; 25:1; 29:3, 15.

9:4 *Simple:* see note on Prov 1:4.

9:7-12 This parenthesis about the arrogant continues the reflections already set forth in the preceding chapters. In the manner of certain psalms, the author attacks scoffers and abandons them to their lot. For they are those who eschew the meaning of their lives, the respect for others, and the consideration of God as if they were fleeing from their true destiny, their value as human beings. This is folly.

9:10-12 These three verses summarize the message that is found in the first nine chapters.

9:10 *The fear of the LORD is the beginning of wisdom:* see note on Prov 1:7.

9:13-18 In contrast with Wisdom, who is God's hostess, here is a picture full of irony. Folly holds her banquet too, but she can offer only *stolen water, bread eaten in secret,* and, in the end, death, the sojourn in the land of oblivion and hopelessness (i.e., the netherworld). This comparison of Wisdom and Folly, this contrast of the two banquets, recalls the opposition of the two ways: here we are called to make our choice.

9:13 The description of *Folly* in this verse links her to the adulteress of Prov 2:16; 7:10ff.

10:1—22:16 This section makes up the oldest part of the Book of Proverbs, and there is a probability that some of its sayings go back to Solomon or even earlier. They represent an ancient fund of rural, familial, social, or human wisdom. The collection unrolls a long series of isolated maxims; they are rarely brought together around a single theme, but they resemble one another by their brief, rhythmic, and thought-provoking form. It is difficult to remain attentive while attempting a continuous reading; it is better to concentrate on random phrases here and there. Some sayings stand out by their picturesqueness: concerning laziness (Prov 10:26) or concerning an insupportable woman (Prov 11:22; 12:4; 21:9). Others are characterized by their teaching about the spirit of justice (Prov 11:26), by their humanity (Prov 10:12), and by their religious sense: about the poor (Prov 14:31, 34; 17:5); about God who sees everything (Prov 15:3, 11); and about sincere offering (Prov 15:8; 21:3, 27).

Any attempt to systematize the sayings is likely to be artificial. To stimulate the imagination, we highlight simply one or another theme.

10:1-32 In these scattered elements, we might note the idea that one has of justice in his human relations, the aversion to laziness, the cost of the true word, the horror of lying (vv. 19-21), and finally the certitude that God takes in hand the cause of the righteous.

2 Treasures obtained by wicked means profit nothing,
but a righteous life brings delivery from death. [i]

3 The LORD will not allow the righteous to go hungry,
but he foils the craving of the wicked. [j]

4 Idle hands ensure poverty,
but the hands of the diligent bring riches. * [k]

5 A son who gathers the crops during the summer is wise,
but a son who sleeps at harvest-time * is shameful. [l]

6 Blessings are showered on the head of the righteous,
but sorrow will cover the face of the wicked. [m]

7 The righteous is remembered with blessings,
but the name of the wicked fades away. [n]

8 A wise man will heed commandments,
but a babbling fool will come to grief. [o]

9 Anyone who leads an honorable life walks in safety,
but whoever pursues wicked ways will be found out. [p]

10 Anyone who winks with the eye causes trouble,
but the one who rebukes promotes peace. [q]

11 The mouth of the righteous is a fountain of life,
but the mouth of the wicked is filled with violence. [r]

12 Hatred stirs up strife,
but love overlooks all offenses. [s]

13 Wisdom is found on the lips of one who has understanding,
but a rod is in store for the back of a fool. [t]

14 Wise men store up knowledge,
but the mouth of a fool precipitates ruin. [u]

15 The wealth of the rich man is his stronghold;
the poverty of the lowly is his undoing. * [v]

16 The reward of the righteous leads to life;
the gains of the wicked lead to sin. * [w]

17 Whoever heeds admonition is on the path to life,
but anyone who rejects correction goes astray. [x]

18 Lying lips conceal hatred,
and anyone who slanders another is a fool.

19 Where many words are spoken, sin is not absent,
but whoever restrains his tongue is prudent. [y]

20 The tongue of the just man is like pure silver;
the heart of the wicked is without worth. [z]

21 The lips of the righteous nourish many,
but fools die for lack of sense. [a]

22 The blessing of the LORD is what brings wealth,
and our toil adds nothing to it. * [b]

23 Doing wrong affords pleasure to the fool,
but wisdom is a delight to an intelligent man. [c]

24 What the wicked man fears * catches up with him,
but what the righteous man desires is granted. [d]

---

i Prov 10:16; 11:4, 6; 13:11; 21:6.—j Prov 13:25; Mt 6:25-34.—k Prov 6:6-8, 11; 12:24; 13:4; 21:5.—l Prov 6:9-11; 19:15; 20:13; 24:30-34.—m Prov 10:8.—n Job 18:17; Pss 9:6; 109:13; 112:6.—o Prov 10:14; Mt 7:24-27.—p Prov 28:18; Ps 37:24.—q Prov 6:13; Ps 35:19.—r Prov 10:21.—s Prov 17:9; 1 Cor 13:4-7; 1 Pet 4:8.—t Prov 10:31; 14:3; 15:7; Deut 25:2; Ps 37:30.—u Prov 11:13; 12:23; Mt 12:37.—v Prov 18:11; 19:7.—w Prov 11:18f; Deut 30:15; Mt 7:17-18.—x Prov 6:23; 15:10.—y Prov 17:27; 20:25; 21:23; Job 1:22; Sir 20:17; Jas 1:19.—z Prov 8:19; 16:16.—a Prov 5:22-23; Jer 5:4; Hos 4:1, 6, 14.—b Gen 13:2; Deut 8:18; 2 Chr 25:9; Sir 11:22.—c Prov 2:14.—d Ps 37:4; Isa 65:7; 66:4; Ezek 11:8.

10:4 This is a theme that runs throughout the Book: diligence is good and brings prosperity while laziness is bad and leads to unhappy consequences (see Prov 6:6; 12:11, 24, 27; 13:4; 14:23; 15:19; 18:9; 19:15; 27:23-27; 28:19).

10:5 *Sleeps at harvest-time:* the same condemnation is found in Prov 6:9-11; 19:15; 20:13.

10:15 This verse states an obvious fact of human life: money is power and poverty is powerlessness; but the author does not approve of this fact. It is true that wealth brings friends (Prov 14:20; 19:4) and power (Prov 18:23; 22:7), while poverty has no influence (Prov 18:23), no friends (Prov 19:4, 7), and no security. However, the only real security is found in God (Ps 52:7-10).

10:16 *The gains of the wicked lead to sin:* and the corollary to this is Paul's dictum: "The wages of sin is death" (Rom 6:23).

10:22 Labor without God's blessing leads nowhere.

10:24 *What the wicked man fears:* e.g., distress and anguish (see Prov 1:27; 3:25; Job 15:21; Isa 66:4). *What the righteous man desires:* e.g., happiness in the Lord's presence, serving God in holiness, and an answer to prayers (Pss 27:4; 37:4; 145:19; Mt 5:6; 1 Jn 5:14-15).

25 When the storm ends, the wicked man is no more,
but the righteous man stands firm forever. [e]

26 Like vinegar to the teeth and smoke to the eyes,
so is the sluggard * to those he serves. [f]

27 The fear of the LORD prolongs life,
but the years of the wicked are cut short. [g]

28 The hope of the righteous brings them joy,
but the expectations of the wicked are frustrated. [h]

29 The way of the LORD * is a stronghold for the upright,
but destruction for evildoers. [i]

30 The righteous man will never be destroyed,
but the wicked will not remain in the land. [j]

31 The mouth of the righteous dispenses wisdom,
but the perverse tongue will be cut off. [k]

32 The lips of the righteous utter words of kindness,
but the mouth of the wicked knows only how to pervert. [l]

CHAPTER 11

The Fruit of the Righteous . . .*

1 False scales are an abomination to the LORD,
but a true weight is pleasing to him. [m]

2 When pride is nurtured, disgrace soon follows,
but wisdom is the hallmark of the humble. [n]

3 The upright are guarded by their integrity;
the treacherous are destroyed by their own duplicity. [o]

4 Riches will be of no avail on the day of wrath, *
but righteousness delivers from death. [p]

5 The virtue of the honest man keeps his way straight,
whereas the evil man falls as a result of his wickedness. [q]

6 The righteousness of the upright saves them,
but the treacherous are trapped by their own schemes. [r]

7 When a wicked man dies, all his expectations die with him,
and the hope he placed in his riches comes to nought. [s]

8 The righteous man escapes affliction,
and the wicked man incurs it instead. [t]

9 With his mouth the godless man seeks to ruin his neighbor,
but knowledge enables the righteous to be delivered. [u]

10 The city rejoices when the upright prosper,
and when the wicked are ruined, there is exultation. [v]

11 Through the blessing of the righteous a city is raised,
but it is destroyed by the mouth of the wicked. [w]

12 A man who lacks sense belittles a neighbor,
but an intelligent man remains silent. [x]

13 One who gossips reveals secrets,
but a trustworthy man keeps things hidden. [y]

14 For lack of leadership a nation collapses;
safety is assured with a multitude of advisers. [z]

e Prov 12:3, 7; Ps 20:9; Mt 7:24-27.—f Prov 13:17; 25:13; 26:6.—g Prov 3:2; 9:11; 14:27; Deut 11:9; Job 15:32.—h Prov 11:7; Ps 112:10; Job 8:13.—i Prov 21:15; Hos 14:9.—j Prov 2:20-22; Ps 37:9.—k Prov 10:13; 15:2; 31:26.—l Ps 59:8; Eccl 10:12.—m Prov 16:11; 20:10; Lev 19:35; Deut 25:13-16; Ezek 45:10.—n Prov 16:18; 18:12; 29:23.—o Prov 11:5; 13:6.—p Prov 10:2; Job 20:20; Ezek 7:19; 27:27.—q Prov 11:3; 13:6; 28:18; 1 Ki 8:36.—r Est 7:9.—s Prov 10:28; Job 8:13.—t Prov 21:18.—u Prov 12:6; 29:5.—v Prov 28:12; 29:2; 2 Ki 11:20.—w Prov 14:34; 29:8.—x Prov 14:3; Job 6:24.—y Prov 10:14; 20:19.—z Prov 15:22; 20:18; 24:6.

10:26 *Sluggard:* see note on Prov 6:6.

10:29 *Way of the LORD:* i.e., the way that God desires for us, the life of wisdom (see Pss 27:11; 143:8; Mt 22:16; Acts 18:25).

11:1-31 Once again we see the opposition between the righ-teous and the wicked. For there are two ways of life, and no person escapes choosing one of them. The reward of the righteous is already inscribed in the heart in some manner in his life, whereas the wicked has no valid perspective before him. The themes of kindness and mercy are joined to those of truth, uprightness, and good.

11:4 *Day of wrath:* i.e., the day of judgment (see Isa 10:3; Zep 1:18).

15 Whoever puts up bail for a stranger will suffer loss,
but the one who refuses to do so will be safe. [a]

16 A gracious woman acquires honor,
while the woman who hates virtue is covered with shame.
Those who are lazy become destitute,
but those who are diligent gain wealth. * [b]

17 A kind man benefits himself,
whereas a cruel man hurts himself. [c]

18 The labors of the wicked man produce little profit,
but the one who sows righteousness reaps a sure reward. [d]

19 Whoever is steadfast in righteousness finds life,
but the one who pursues evil is on the road to death. [e]

20 Those with perverse hearts are abhorrent to the LORD,
but those whose ways are blameless are dear to him. [f]

21 You need have no fear that the wicked will not be punished,
but those who are righteous will escape harm. [g]

22 Like a ring of gold * in a pig's snout
is a beautiful woman without good sense. [h]

23 The righteous desire only what is good;
the expectation of the wicked ends in wrath. [i]

24 One man gives lavishly and increases his wealth,
while another is tight-fisted and ends up impoverished. * [j]

25 A generous person will be enriched;
he who refreshes others will also be refreshed. [k]

26 The people curse those who hoard grain,
but the one who sells it earns their blessing. [l]

27 Whoever strives for good earns great acclaim,
but the one who pursues evil will be afflicted by it. [m]

28 Whoever places his trust in riches will fall,
but the righteous will flourish like sprouting leaves. [n]

29 Whoever causes trouble for his family inherits the wind,
and a fool will become a servant to the wise man. [o]

30 The fruit of the righteous is a tree of life,
and the wise man wins souls. * [p]

31 If the just man receives his deserts on earth,
how much more will the wicked and the sinner! [q]

CHAPTER 12

On the Way of Righteousness*

1 Whoever loves discipline loves knowledge,
but the one who hates correction is stupid. [r]

2 The good man wins the favor of the LORD,
but the malicious man incurs his condemnation. [s]

3 No one earns security by wickedness,
but the roots of the righteous will not be shaken. [t]

4 A good wife is her husband's crown,
but one who disgraces him is like decay in his bones. [u]

---

a Prov 6:1f; 17:18; 22:26-27.—b Prov 31:31.—c Mt 5:7; 25:34-40.—d Prov 10:16; Ex 1:20; Hos 10:12-13.—e Prov 10:2; Deut 30:15; 1 Sam 2:6; Ps 89:49; Jer 43:11.—f Prov 3:32; Num 14:8; 1 Chr 29:17; Pss 5:2; 119:1.—g Prov 16:5.—h Gen 24:47; Ezek 16:15.—i Rom 2:8-9.—j Prov 13:7; 28:27; Ps 112:9; Mt 19:29; 2 Cor 9:6.—k Prov 22:9; Isa 32:8; 2 Cor 9:6-9.—l Prov 24:24; Gen 42:6.—m Prov 5:22; Ps 7:16-17.—n Job 31:24-28; Pss 49:7; 52:9f; 92:12-14.—o Prov 14:19.—p Prov 10:11; Gen 2:9.—q Jer 25:29; 49:12; 1 Pet 4:18.—r Prov 5:11-14; 9:7-9; 29:1.—s Prov 11:20; 2 Sam 15:6; Job 33:26-28; Ps 84:12.—t Prov 10:25.—u Prov 18:22; Ru 3:11; Sir 26:1, 16.

11:16 This verse follows the Greek. The Hebrew reads: "A kindhearted woman gains respect,/ but ruthless men acquire wealth."

11:22 *Ring of gold:* usually worn by women on their nose (see Gen 24:47; Ezek 16:20).

11:24 Generosity brings greater blessings and prosperity (see Prov 3:9-10; Ps 112:9; Eccl 11:1-2; 2 Cor 6:9), while the one who is tight-fisted makes no friends and harms himself (see Prov 21:13).

11:30 *And the wise man wins souls:* the Greek reads: "but violence takes lives away."

12:1-28 In this endless and already known variation on the theme of the righteous and the wicked and the sage and the fool, one could perhaps note a more marked insistence on truth in human relationships and on dislike of the foolish word. However, each maxim brings its own observation or its own teaching from popular good sense and sometimes from its religious certitude. From time to time, opposing portraits of women are evoked.

5 The aims of the righteous are honorable,
but the schemes of the wicked are full of deceit. [v]

6 The words of the wicked are snares to shed blood,
but those of the upright keep them safe. [w]

7 Once the wicked are overthrown, they are no more,
but the house of the righteous remains firm. [x]

8 A man will be praised if he exhibits good sense,
but one with a perverse mind is despised. [y]

9 It is better to be a laborer and have food to eat
than to put on airs and have an empty stomach. [z]

10 A righteous person supplies the needs of his animals, *
but the heart of the wicked is without mercy. [a]

11 One who tills his land has an abundance of food,
but he who chases fantasies * is a fool. [b]

12 The wicked desire the prey of evil men,
but the root of the righteous bears fruit.

13 The wicked man is ensnared by the sin of his lips,
but the righteous frees himself from misfortune. [c]

14 An abundance of good things flow from the fruit of one's lips,
and a man's labor will give him a suitable reward. * [d]

15 The fool is convinced of the rightness of his ways,
but the man who listens to advice shows wisdom. [e]

16 A fool is quick to show his anger,
but a prudent man ignores an insult. [f]

17 A truthful witness is honest in his testimony,
but a false witness testifies deceitfully. [g]

18 Thoughtless words wound like a sword thrust,
but the tongue of the wise produces healing. [h]

19 Truthful speech endures forever,
but deceitful lies last only for a moment. * [i]

20 Deceit is in the heart of those who plot evil,
but those who counsel peace have joy. [j]

21 No harm befalls the righteous,
but endless are the misfortunes of the wicked. [k]

22 The LORD abhors lying lips,
but he delights in those who are truthful. [l]

23 A prudent man does not flaunt his knowledge,
but the heart of fools proclaims their folly. [m]

24 Authority will be granted to the diligent,
but the lazy will be enslaved. [n]

25 Anxiety in the human heart weighs it down,
but a kind word makes it glad. [o]

26 A righteous man gives good advice to his neighbor,
but the way of the wicked leads them astray.

27 A lazy man never reaps a rich harvest,
but the diligent man acquires precious wealth.

28 The way of righteousness leads to life,
but the way of vengeance leads to death. [p]

---

v Mt 12:35.—w Prov 11:9; 14:3.—x Prov 10:25; 14:11; 15:25.—y Isa 19:14; 29:24.—z Sir 10:26.—a Prov 27:23; Num 22:29; Deut 25:4.—b Prov 28:19; Sir 20:27.—c Prov 18:7; 21:23; Ps 59:13.—d Prov 13:2; 14:14; 15:23; 18:20.—e Prov 9:7-9; 14:12; 16:2.—f Prov 29:11; Job 5:2.—g Prov 14:5, 25; Ps 12:3.—h Prov 15:4; 25:18; Ps 55:22.—i Prov 19:19.—j Rom 14:19.—k Job 4:7.—l Prov 6:17; 11:20; 1 Ki 13:18.—m Prov 10:14; 18:2; Pss 38:6; 59:8.—n Prov 10:4; 13:4.—o Prov 15:13; 17:22.—p Prov 10:2; Deut 30:15.

12:10a A person who is good is kind even to animals (see Prov 27:23; Deut 25:4).

12:11 This text is repeated almost verbatim in Prov 28:19. *Chases fantasies:* schemes to acquire ill-gotten goods.

12:14 A man's words of wisdom will yield a good harvest in the same way that his physical labor will bring him an abundant crop (see note on Prov 1:31; see also Job 34:11).

12:19 A person who has spoken the truth has said it once and for all and need not open the mouth again; a liar must fall back on ever-new lies.

CHAPTER 13

The Light of the Righteous Shines Brightly*

1 A wise son listens to his father's correction,
but a mocker will not accept any rebuke. * [q]

2 A good man derives nourishment from the fruit of his words,
but one who is treacherous craves violence. [r]

3 He who guards his mouth makes his life secure,
but one who talks excessively ensures his own downfall. * [s]

4 The idler * craves for food and remains unsatisfied,
but the appetite of the diligent is fully sated. [t]

5 The righteous man hates words that are deceitful,
but the evildoer slanders and defames.

6 Righteousness stands guard over one who is honest,
but sin brings about the ruin of the wicked. [u]

7 One man pretends to be rich, yet has nothing;
another pretends to be poor, * yet has great wealth. [v]

8 A wealthy man pays a ransom to save his life; *
a poor man never has to worry about such threats. [w]

9 The light of the righteous shines brightly,
but the lamp * of the wicked is extinguished. [x]

10 An ignorant man causes strife by his insolence,
but wisdom is found with those who take advice. [y]

11 Wealth hastily acquired will dwindle away,
but when amassed little by little, it will increase. [z]

12 Hope deferred sickens the heart,
but a desire fulfilled is a tree of life. [a]

13 One who refuses to accept advice is headed for destruction,
but he who respects a command will be rewarded. * [b]

14 The teaching of the wise is a fountain of life
enabling one to avoid the snares of death. * [c]

15 Good sense wins favor,
but the way of the faithless leads to their destruction. [d]

16 Every prudent man acts out of knowledge,
but a fool proudly parades his folly. [e]

17 An unreliable messenger engenders trouble,
but a trustworthy envoy brings healing. [f]

18 Poverty and disgrace befall one who ignores discipline,
but one who takes correction is honored. [g]

19 A desire fulfilled is sweet to the soul,
while fools regard turning from evil as an abomination. [h]

---

q Prov 12:1; 15:5.—r Prov 12:14; 18:20.—s Prov 10:19; 18:7; 21:23; Job 1:22; Ps 34:14.—t Prov 21:25.—u Prov 11:3, 5f; Jer 44:5.—v 2 Cor 6:10; Rev 3:17.—w Prov 15:16.—x Prov 4:18-19; 24:20; Job 18:5.—y Prov 9:9.—z Prov 10:2; 28:20, 22.—a Prov 3:18; 13:19.—b Prov 19:16; Ex 9:20; Num 15:31.—c Prov 10:11; 14:27.—d Prov 3:4; Lk 2:52.—e Ps 38:6; Eccl 10:1.—f Prov 10:26; 25:13.—g Prov 1:7; 12:1; 25:12; Eccl 7:5.—h Prov 13:12.

13:1-25 In this uninterrupted accumulation of ancient proverbs, we find words about education and good sense; if one proverb highlights the burden of wealth, another presents it as a reward. However, in these diverse aphorisms the idea of a righteous life is always there, even though the author allows strongly opposed conceptions to be expressed. In all countries, each proverb finds its counter-maxim; but from the whole a vision of things comes through that is proper to a civilization or a religion.

Rather than giving direct teaching, the Book of Proverbs provides us with an atmosphere in which to reflect; we are to learn to appreciate the mood and the felicitous formulation, without taking each maxim literally. We must bear in mind the penchant of Semitic poetry for strong expressions and its use of parallelism (either repetition or contrast).

13:1 *A mocker will not accept any rebuke:* see notes on Prov 1:22; 9:7-12.

13:3 The tongue has the power over life and death (see Prov 10:19; 18:21; 21:23; Jas 3:6).

13:4 *Idler:* see note on Prov 6:6.

13:7 *Pretends to be rich . . . pretends to be poor:* both pretenses are foolish and lead to folly (see Prov 11:28; 12:9; 14:8).

13:8 *Pays a ransom to save his life:* the wealthy have the means to ward off enemies (see note on Prov 10:15). The poor are never held for ransom.

13:9 *Light . . . lamp:* symbols of life (see Job 3:20). *Lamp of the wicked is extinguished:* see Prov 20:20; 24:20; Job 18:5; 21:17.

13:13 The reward indicated is to receive the benefits of wisdom (see note on Prov 3:2; see also v. 21; 3:16-18).

13:14 *Life . . . death:* in this and other similar proverbs, these two words indicate "a long and happy life" and a "premature death" respectively.

20 Whoever walks with the wise becomes wise,
but he who mingles with fools will suffer harm. * [i]

21 Misfortune afflicts the sinful,
but good fortune is the reward of the upright. [j]

22 A good man leaves an inheritance to his children's children,
but the wealth of the sinner is stored up for the righteous. [k]

23 The fields of the poor may yield much food,
but it is stolen from them through injustice.

24 He who spares the rod * hates his son,
but one who loves his son will take care to discipline him. [l]

25 The righteous man has enough food to appease his hunger,
but the belly of the wicked man is empty. [m]

CHAPTER 14

Righteousness Is a Sign of a Nation's Greatness*

1 Wisdom builds herself a house,
but Folly tears down hers with her own hands. [n]

2 One whose conduct is upright fears the LORD, *
but one whose paths are crooked despises him. [o]

3 The words of a fool ensure a rod for his back, *
but the lips of the wise keep them safe. [p]

4 Where there are no oxen, the barn is empty of grain,
but abundant crops come through the strength of the ox. [q]

5 A truthful witness does not lie,
but a false witness lies incessantly. * [r]

6 In vain does a scoffer * seek wisdom,
but knowledge comes easily to the man of discernment. [s]

7 Do not remain in the presence of a fool,
for you will not gain any wisdom there.

8 The prudent possess the wisdom to follow the right way,
but the folly of fools misleads them. [t]

9 Fools see no need to atone for guilt,
but the upright do so and enjoy God's favor. [u]

10 The heart knows its own grief best,
and no one else can share its joy. [v]

11 The house of the wicked will be destroyed,
but the tent of the upright will stand firm. [w]

12 There is a way that seems right to a man,
but the end of it leads to death. [x]

13 Even at times of laughter the heart may be sad,
and joy may end in grief. [y]

14 The perverse man suffers the consequences of his ways,
while a good man reaps what his deeds deserve. [z]

15 A simple man believes everything he hears,
but a prudent man carefully considers every step. [a]

16 A wise man is cautious and turns away from evil,
but the fool is reckless and shows no restraint. [b]

17 A quick-tempered man acts foolishly,
but a prudent man is long-suffering. [c]

i 2 Chr 10:8; Sir 6:34; 8:8, 17.—j Gen 4:7; Ezek 14:13; 18:4.—k Est 8:2; Job 27:17; Eccl 2:26.—l Prov 19:18; 22:15; 23:13f; 29:15; Eph 6:4; Heb 12:7.—m Prov 10:3.—n Prov 24:3.—o Prov 19:1; Job 12:4.—p Prov 12:6; Eccl 10:12.—q Ps 144:14.—r Prov 12:17; Ps 12:3.—s Prov 9:9.—t Prov 14:15, 24; 21:29.—u Prov 8:35; 9:8.—v 1 Ki 1:10.—w Prov 3:33; 12:7; 15:25; 21:12.—x Prov 12:15; 16:25.—y Eccl 2:2; 7:3, 6.—z Prov 1:31; 12:14; 2 Chr 15:7.—a Prov 14:8.—b Prov 22:3; 1 Sam 25:25.—c Prov 15:18; 2 Ki 5:12.

13:20 This verse stresses the need to choose friends and associates wisely (see Prov 2:20; 12:26) and to steer clear of the wicked (see Prov 1:10, 18; 2:12; 16:29; 22:24-25).

13:24 *Rod:* most likely a symbol for any kind of discipline, which protects one's children from folly and leads them away from evil paths (see Prov 19:18; 23:13-14). A "rod" of correction is really a "rod" of love—even God makes use of it for the good of his faithful (see note on Prov 3:11-12).

14:1-35 Fear of God, wisdom, common sense, understanding, and honesty build up one's life. Folly tarnishes all that it touches; it destroys the values of humans and society, for it is falsehood, vanity, and injustice. The upright take the side of the poor and the lowly, whereas the evildoer is the person without pity and without feelings. In passing, we will pause at the fine psychological notation about human suffering (vv. 10, 13). Readers will take up again the phrase that entices or offends them; the essential thing is to find some points of departure to achieve a more just idea of life.

14:2 *Fears the LORD:* see note on Prov 1:7.

14:3 *Rod for his back:* see note on Prov 13:24.

14:5 See note on Prov 6:19.

14:6 *Scoffer:* see note on Prov 1:22.

18 The simple are adorned with folly,
but the prudent have knowledge as their crown.

19 Evil men will bow down before the good,
and the wicked will do so at the gates of the righteous. [d]

20 The poor man is disliked even by his neighbor,
but one who is wealthy never lacks for friends. [e]

21 Anyone who despises his neighbor is a sinner,*
but blessed is he who is kind to the poor. [f]

22 Do not those who hatch evil go astray?
But those who plan good are loyal and faithful. [g]

23 Diligent labor always yields profit,
but idle conversation only leads to poverty. [h]

24 The crown of the wise is their riches;
the garland of fools is their folly. [i]

25 A truthful witness saves lives;
anyone who utters lies is an impostor. [j]

26 He who fears the LORD * provides strong security,
and in him one's children will find a refuge. [k]

27 The fear of the LORD * is a fountain of life
enabling a man to avoid the snares of death. [l]

28 Many subjects ensure the glory of a king,
but if his subjects are few, he is of no importance. [m]

29 A patient man shows good sense,
but a quick-tempered man displays the height of folly. [n]

30 A tranquil heart gives life to the body,
but envy causes the bones to rot. [o]

31 He who oppresses the poor insults their Creator,
but the one who is kind to the needy *
does him honor. [p]

32 The evildoer is undone by his malice,
but the upright finds refuge in his integrity. [q]

33 Wisdom finds a home in an understanding heart, *
but she is not found in the heart of fools. [r]

34 Righteousness is a sign of a nation's greatness,
but sin degrades any people. [s]

35 A king favors a prudent servant
but is angry with a shameful servant. [t]

CHAPTER 15

The LORD Loves Anyone Whose Goal Is Righteousness*

1 A gentle reply turns away wrath,
but a harsh word arouses anger. [u]

2 The tongue of the wise distills knowledge,
but the mouth of a fool utters nothing except folly. * [v]

3 The eyes of the LORD are everywhere, *
keeping a close watch on the evil and the good. [w]

---

d Prov 11:29.—e Prov 19:4, 7; Sir 6:8, 12.—f Prov 11:12; 19:17.—g Prov 4:16-17.—h Prov 10:4.—i Prov 14:8.—j Prov 12:17.—k Prov 18:10; Ps 9:10.—l Prov 10:11; 13:14.—m 2 Sam 19:7.—n Prov 14:17; 16:32; 19:11; Eccl 7:8-9; Jas 1:19.—o Prov 17:22.—p Prov 17:5; Deut 24:14; Mt 25:40.—q Prov 6:15; Job 13:15; Ps 34:22.—r Prov 2:6-10.—s Prov 11:11.—t Est 8:2; Mt 24:45-51; 25:21-23.—u Prov 25:15; 1 Ki 12:7; 2 Chr 10:7.—v Prov 15:7; Ps 59:8; Eccl 10:12.—w 2 Chr 16:9; Jer 16:17; Heb 4:13.

14:21 *Anyone who despises his neighbor is a sinner:* for the Lord had said: "You shall love your neighbor as yourself" (Lev 19:18). *Blessed is he who is kind to the poor:* such a person "does . . . honor" to God (v. 31) and will "suffer [no] want" (Prov 28:27; see also Prov 21:13; Ps 41:2). Proverbs indicates some of the ways one can be kind to the poor: sharing one's food with them (Prov 22:9), giving them money (Prov 28:8), and defending their rights (Prov 31:9).

14:26 *Fears the LORD:* see note on Prov 1:7.

14:27 *The fear of the LORD:* see note on Prov 1:7.

14:31 Since God created both the rich and the poor in his image (see Prov 22:2; Job 31:15; Jas 3:9), whoever oppresses the poor insults their Creator. *Kind to the needy:* see note on verse 21. *Does him honor:* i.e., carries out his will and also "lends to the LORD" (Prov 19:17; see Mt 25:40).

14:33 *Heart:* for the Semites the heart was the seat of knowledge and understanding (see note on Ps 4:8).

15:1—16:9 An honest, reflexive, and sober life—such seems to be the ideal of the sages whose maxims are collected in this part of the Book of Proverbs. It is a conviction that must be reflected everywhere in thought and word, in sentiments and relationships—a wisdom that is very human and well grounded, like all these recommendations. Yet, is it so banal as to be true and righteous in one's heart and in one's behavior? It is like a reflection of the very sentiments of God. Hence, we will not be surprised to find here maxims in which human behavior becomes religion, devotion, and fear of God. In those distant times, people did not yet imagine a life with God beyond their years on earth. God's blessing consisted above all in material, familial, and social success. Nonetheless, they did already realize that the contemplation of God, even during the short earthly sojourn, is worth more than success and fortune.

15:2 *The mouth of a fool utters nothing except folly:* see vv. 7, 28; 12:23; 13:16.

15:3 *The eyes of the LORD are everywhere:* see Prov 5:21; 2 Chr 16:9; see also notes on Ps 139:1b-6; 139:2; 139:7-12; 139:13-18; Jer 16:17.

4 A wholesome tongue is a tree of life,
but an undisciplined tongue crushes the spirit. [x]

5 A fool spurns his father's correction,
but whoever heeds admonition is prudent. [y]

6 In the house of the righteous there is no lack of treasures,
but the earnings of the wicked are never secure. [z]

7 The lips of the wise spread knowledge;
such is not true of the heart of a fool. [a]

8 The sacrifice of the wicked is an abomination to the LORD, *
but he delights in the prayer of the upright. [b]

9 The way of the wicked is an abomination to the LORD,
but he loves anyone whose goal is righteousness. [c]

10 Severe punishment awaits the one who strays from the right path;
whoever hates a rebuke will die. [d]

11 The netherworld and the abyss lie open to the LORD;
how much more is this true of the human heart. * [e]

12 A scoffer * does not like to be reproved,
and he refuses to consult the wise. [f]

13 A glad heart makes the face cheerful,
but anguish of heart breaks one's spirit. [g]

14 The mind of one who is wise seeks further knowledge,
but the mouth of a fool feeds on folly. [h]

15 Every day is wretched for those who are sorrowing,
but to one who is cheerful, every day is a perpetual feast. * [i]

16 It is better to have a little and fear the LORD *
than to possess immense wealth and suffer anguish. [j]

17 Better a dish of herbs served with love
than a fattened ox accompanied by hatred. [k]

18 An ill-tempered man provokes quarrels,
but a patient man quiets dissension. [l]

19 The path of the idler * is covered with thorns,
but the path of the upright is a broad highway. [m]

20 A wise son is a joy to his father,
but a foolish son has no respect for his mother. [n]

21 Folly delights the one without sense,
but a man of understanding follows a straight path. [o]

22 Plans miscarry when counsel is lacking,
but they succeed when there are many counselors. [p]

23 A man is joyful when he utters apt answers,
and even more satisfying is a word in season. [q]

24 The path of life leads upward for the prudent man
so that he may escape going down to the netherworld. * [r]

25 The LORD tears down the proud man's house, *
but he preserves the widow's boundaries. [s]

26 The LORD abhors the thoughts of the wicked,
but he is pleased with the words of the pure. [t]

---

x Prov 10:11; 12:18; Ps 5:10.—y Prov 10:17; 12:1; 13:1, 18.—z Prov 8:21; 10:16.—a Prov 10:13; 15:3.—b Prov 21:27; Eccl 4:17; Sir 34:18ff; Isa 1:11-15.—c Prov 6:16; 11:20; 21:21; Deut 7:13.—d Prov 1:31-32; 12:1.—e 2 Chr 6:30; Job 26:6; Ps 44:22; Rev 2:23.—f Prov 9:8; 12:1.—g Prov 12:25; 17:22; 18:14; Sir 30:22.—h Prov 18:15.—i Prov 15:13.—j Prov 15:17; 16:8; Ps 37:16-17.—k Prov 15:16; 17:1; Eccl 4:6.—l Prov 14:17; 26:21; 29:22; Gen 13:8; Sir 28:11.—m Prov 22:5.—n Prov 10:1; 29:3.—o Prov 2:14.—p Prov 11:14; 24:6; Ps 16:7; 1 Ki 1:12.—q Prov 12:14; 25:11; Sir 20:6.—r Prov 2:19; Col 3:1-2.—s Prov 12:7; 23:10-11; Deut 19:14.—t Prov 6:16, 18; Ps 94:11.

15:8 *The sacrifice of the wicked is an abomination to the LORD:* the sacrifices of the wicked are without value in God's eyes (see Prov 21:3 and note; 21:27; Eccl 4:17; Isa 1:11-15; Jer 6:20). *He delights in the prayer of the upright:* see Prov 3:32.

15:11 Nothing remains inaccessible to God, whether it be the netherworld and the abyss (see Job 26:6; Ps 139:8) or the human heart (see 1 Sam 16:7).

15:12 *Scoffer:* see note on Prov 1:22.

15:15 *To one who is cheerful, every day is a perpetual feast:* see Prov 14:30; see also Lev 23:39-41.

15:16 *Fear the LORD:* see note on Prov 1:7.

15:19 *Idler:* see note on Prov 6:6.

15:24 The wise man will prolong his life and thus delay for a long time his descent to the region of the dead; he will enjoy happiness in this world for years to come.

15:25 *Tears down the proud man's house:* see Prov 2:22; 10:25; 14:11. *Preserves the widow's boundaries:* by keeping intact the boundary stones that acted as landmarks for a person's property (see Prov 22:28; Deut 19:14; Job 24:2; Ps 68:5).

27 He who is greedy for dishonest gain
brings disaster on a house,
but he who refuses to accept bribes will
have life. [u]

28 The righteous man reflects before
answering,
but the mouth of the wicked pours out
evil. [v]

29 The LORD keeps his distance from the
wicked,
but he listens to the prayer of the righ-
teous. [w]

30 A kindly glance gives joy to the heart,
and good news refreshes the bones. [x]

31 He who accepts saving reproof has life
and will enjoy the company of the
wise. [y]

32 He who rejects correction despises him-
self,
but whoever accepts admonition will
gain understanding. [z]

33 The fear of the LORD* provides instruc-
tion in wisdom,
and to be humble is the way to honor. [a]

CHAPTER 16

1 A man may make plans in his heart,
but the LORD provides the words that
his tongue utters. * [b]

2 A man's ways may seem honorable to
him,
but the LORD weighs his motives. [c]

3 Entrust everything that you do to the
LORD,
and your plans will turn out to be suc-
cessful. [d]

4 The LORD has made everything for his
own purposes,
even the wicked for the day of disas-
ter. * [e]

5 The LORD abhors the proud man;
be assured that such a man will not go
unpunished. [f]

6 Iniquity is expiated by kindness and
faithfulness,
and by fear of the LORD* man turns
away from evil. [g]

7 When the LORD is pleased with some-
one's conduct.
he makes even that man's enemies
friends with him. * [h]

8 It is better to have little and be righteous
than to acquire great riches with injus-
tice. [i]

9 A man may plan his own course,
but the LORD makes his steps se-
cure. * [j]

The Justice of Kings*

10 The lips of a king utter inspired oracles;
he does not err when he pronounces
judgment. [k]

11 Accurate scales and balances belong to
the LORD;
all the weights in the bag* are his con-
cern. [l]

12 Kings regard wrongdoing as abhorrent,
for their throne's foundation depends
upon righteousness. [m]

13 Honest speech is the delight of a king,
and he loves a man who speaks truth-
fully. [n]

14 A king's wrath is like a messenger of
death,
but one who is wise will appease it. [o]

u Ex 23:8; Isa 1:23; 33:15.—v Prov 15:2.—w Prov 15:8; Ps 145:18-19; Jn 9:31.—x Prov 25:25.—y Prov 9:7-9; 12:1; 25:12.—z Prov 1:7; 12:1; Eccl 7:5.—a Prov 1:7; 16:18; Sir 1:24; Isa 66:2.—b Prov 16:9; 19:21.—c Prov 21:2; 1 Sam 2:3; 2 Chr 6:30; Lk 16:15.—d Prov 3:5-6; Ps 37:5-6.—e Ex 9:16; 2 Chr 34:24; Rom 9:22.—f Prov 6:16f; 8:13; 11:20-21.—g Gen 20:11; Ex 1:17; 20:20.—h Jer 39:12; 42:12.—i Prov 15:16; Ps 37:16; Eccl 4:6.—j Prov 16:1; 19:21; 20:24.—k Prov 17:7.—l Prov 11:1; Ezek 45:10.—m Prov 20:28; 25:5; 29:14.—n Prov 14:35; 22:11.—o Prov 19:12; 20:2; Gen 40:2.

15:33 *Fear of the LORD:* see note on Prov 1:7.

16:1 People make plans, but it is God's grace that enables them to accomplish them (see Prov 19:21).

16:4 God's providence works in every life and in all history (see Eccl 7:14; Rom 8:28). Even the wicked, in their punishment, glorify God and his justice (see Ex 9:16).

16:6 When God's people repent of sin and obey his will, God offers forgiveness and withholds his chastisement (see Isa 1:18-19; 55:7; Jer 3:22; Ezek 18:23, 30-32; 33:11-16; Hos 14:1-4). Hence, iniquity can be said to be expiated by kindness and faithfulness—inasmuch as the latter ward off God's wrath against it. *Fear of the LORD:* see note on Prov 1:7.

16:7 By his grace God turns the enemies of his faithful into their friends (see Rom 8:28).

16:9 When making plans for our future, we must always remember that they depend on God's will: "If it is the Lord's will, we shall live to do this or that" (Jas 4:15).

16:10-15 A ruler's true greatness lies in making use of his power to dispense justice inspired by the sentiments of God. Were there any kings even in Israel who were completely faithful to such an ideal?

16:11 The Lord desires that all scales be accurate (see Prov 11:1; 20:23; Ezek 45:10). *All the weights in the bag:* in their bags merchants carried various sizes of stones for weighing money; money was paid by weight, since coins were unknown. God condemns fraud.

15 When a king's face brightens it spells life,
and his favor is like a rain shower* in spring. [p]

The Path of the Upright*

16 It is better to acquire wisdom rather than gold,
and more desirable to acquire understanding rather than silver. [q]

17 The path of the upright avoids evil;
he who treads carefully preserves his life. [r]

18 Pride goes before disaster,
and a haughty spirit goes before a fall. [s]

19 It is better to live humbly among the lowly
than to share plunder with the proud. [t]

20 The one who pays heed to instruction prospers,
and blessed* is he who trusts in the LORD. [u]

21 A wise man is esteemed for being pleasant,
and his friendly words increase his influence. [v]

22 Wisdom is a fountain of life to one who possesses it,
but folly is the punishment of fools. [w]

23 A wise man's heart guides his mouth,
and his lips increase learning. [x]

24 Pleasing words are like a honeycomb,
sweet to the soul and affording health to the body. * [y]

25 Sometimes a path may seem to be right,
but in the end it leads to death. [z]

26 The laborer's appetite works on his behalf,
as hunger spurs him on. * [a]

27 A scoundrel* concocts evil,
and his lips are like a scorching fire. [b]

28 A perverse man sows strife,
and a tale-bearer destroys close friendships. [c]

29 One who indulges in violence entices his neighbor
and leads him into evil ways. [d]

30 One who winks his eye is plotting perverse deeds;
one who purses his lips is bent on mischief. [e]

31 Gray hair is a crown of glory;
it is gained by a righteous life. [f]

32 It is better to be a patient man rather than a warrior,
one who controls his temper rather than one who captures a city. [g]

33 The lot* is cast into the lap,
but the decision comes from the LORD. [h]

CHAPTER 17

1 It is better to have a dry crust to eat in peace
than to feast in a house that is filled with strife. [i]

2 A wise servant will rule over an unworthy son
and will share the inheritance as one of the brothers. [j]

3 The crucible is for silver and the furnace is for gold,
but it is the LORD who tests the heart. [k]

4 An evildoer listens eagerly to wicked lips,
and a liar pays heed to a slanderous tongue.

5 Anyone who mocks the poor insults their Creator; *
whoever gloats at another's distress will not go unpunished. [l]

p Prov 19:12; 25:2-7.—q Prov 8:13-14; Job 28:15.—r Prov 19:16.—s Prov 11:2; 1 Sam 17:42; Isa 13:11; Jer 48:29.—t Prov 29:23; Ex 15:9.—u Prov 19:8; Ps 32:10; Jer 17:7.—v Prov 16:23.—w Prov 10:11.—x Prov 16:21; Job 15:2.—y Prov 24:13-14; 1 Sam 14:27.—z Prov 12:15; 14:12; Est 3:6.—a Prov 10:3.—b Prov 2:10; Ps 140:3; Jas 3:6.—c Prov 6:14, 19; 17:9; Sir 28:15.—d Prov 1:10; 12:26.—e Prov 6:13.—f Prov 20:29.—g Prov 14:29.—h Prov 18:18; Lev 16:8; Jos 7:14.—i Prov 15:16-17; 16:8.—j Prov 3:1, 2.—k Prov 27:21; 1 Chr 29:17; Ps 26:2; 1 Pet 1:7.—l Prov 14:31; Ezek 25:3; Ob 12.

16:15 *Rain shower:* bringing the awaited rain for the growth of the vegetation.

16:16—17:28 The maxims follow one another, in no real order, to oppose the righteous and the wicked, the wise and the foolish. Under different formulas, the same virtues are always set forth. In this group, we will see above all the recommendations to be attentive to what one says and to hold in the cry of anger, which is reputed as wisdom (Prov 16:32). We will have discerned little by little that the Book of Proverbs contains a complete morality of the human word. Humility is placed in value (notably in Prov 17:19), and at times we divine better the meaning of poverty (Prov 17:5), pardon (Prov 7:9), and understanding (Prov 16:16, 22, 27).

16:20 *Blessed:* see note on Prov 31:28.

16:24 See note on Prov 2:10.

16:26 See 2 Thes 3:10.

16:27 *Scoundrel:* see note on Prov 6:12.

16:33 *Lot:* an allusion to the high priest's pectoral and to the Urim and Thummim that it contained, which were used for casting lots. However, the lot is controlled by God's providence (see Eph 1:11).

17:5 *Anyone who mocks the poor insults their Creator:* see note on Prov 14:31.

6 Grandchildren are the crown of the aged,
and the glory of children is their parents. [m]

7 Fine words are not becoming to a fool,
and much less are false words to a noble. [n]

8 A bribe is like a magic stone to one who offers it;
wherever he turns, he meets with success. * [o]

9 One who forgives a misdeed fosters friendship,
but he who divulges it separates good friends. [p]

10 A reproof makes a far greater impression upon a discerning person
than a hundred blows will upon a fool.

11 A wicked man is only interested in fomenting rebellion;
hence a cruel messenger will be sent against him.

12 It is better to come upon a bear robbed of her cubs
rather than confronting a fool in his folly. [q]

13 One who returns evil for good
will forever have misfortune in his house. [r]

14 To begin a quarrel is like unleashing a flood;
so desist before the quarreling begins. [s]

15 Absolving the wicked and condemning the innocent
are both equally abominable to the LORD. [t]

16 Of what advantage is money in the hands of a fool?
Can he purchase wisdom if he has no desire to learn? [u]

17 A true friend is one at all times,
and a brother is born to render help in time of need. [v]

18 A man without sense gives a pledge
to become surety for a neighbor. * [w]

19 One who sows discord enjoys strife,
and one who constructs a high threshold invites disaster. [x]

20 One whose heart is perverse will never prosper,
and one whose tongue is evil will come to trouble.

21 The father of a fool endures endless sorrow
and receives no joy from having begotten him. [y]

22 A cheerful heart * is excellent medicine,
but a crushed spirit dries up the bones. [z]

23 A wicked man conceals a bribe * under his cloak
to divert the course of justice. [a]

24 A discerning man sets his face toward wisdom,
but the eyes of a fool range to the ends of the earth. * [b]

25 A foolish son causes grief to his father
and brings sorrow to the mother who bore him. [c]

26 It is not right to fine the innocent
or to flog princes for their integrity. [d]

27 One who uses words sparingly is truly wise;
a man of discernment keeps his tongue under control. [e]

28 Even a fool who keeps silent is considered wise;
if he closes his lips, he is regarded as intelligent. [f]

CHAPTER 18

The Words of the Mouth*

1 Someone who lives alone seeks only to fulfill his desires
and ignores the advice of others. [g]

---

m Prov 16:31; Job 42:16.—n Prov 16:10.—o Prov 19:6.—p Prov 10:12; 16:28.—q 1 Sam 25:25.—r Gen 44:4; 1 Sam 19:4; Ps 35:12; Mt 5:39; 1 Thes 5:15; 1 Pet 3:9.—s Mt 5:25-26.—t Prov 24:24; Ex 23:6-7; Isa 5:23; Lam 3:34-36.—u Prov 23:23.—v Prov 18:24; 27:10; 2 Sam 15:21.—w Prov 6:1f; 11:15; 22:26-27.—x Prov 15:18.—y Prov 10:1.—z Prov 12:25; 14:30; 15:13.—a Ex 23:8; 1 Sam 8:3.—b Job 31:1; Eccl 8:1.—c Prov 10:1; 29:15.—d Prov 17:15; Ps 94:21.—e Prov 10:19; 14:29; Jas 1:19.—f Prov 10:19; Job 2:13; 13:5.—g Jude 19.

17:8 Such is human behavior that bribes open doors (see v. 23; 18:16; 21:14), but both bribe-giving and bribe-taking are evil acts that corrupt the human heart and are abhorrent to the Lord (see Deut 10:17) who condemns them (see Prov 15:27; Deut 16:19; 1 Sam 12:3; Ps 26:10; Eccl 7:7; Isa 1:23; 33:15; Am 5:12; 1 Tim 6:10).

17:18 See note on Prov 6:1-5.

17:22 *Cheerful heart:* see Prov 14:30; 15:13, 30; 16:15.

17:23 *Bribe:* see note on v. 8.

17:24 The prudent look directly in front of them; fools go astray.

18:1-24 In this sparse series of sayings, whose themes are now familiar to the reader, a few reflections stand out, e.g., concerning the danger of the human word and the difficulty of the righteous during a trial. Once again we note the unfavorable state of the poor (v. 23).

2 A fool takes no pleasure in understanding
but only delights in expressing his own opinions. [h]

3 When wickedness comes, it is accompanied by contempt,
and with dishonor comes disgrace. [i]

4 The words of the mouth are turbulent waters,
but the fountain of wisdom is a flowing brook. [j]

5 It is not right to show partiality* to the guilty
or to deprive the innocent of a just judgment. [k]

6 The lips of a fool cause strife,
and his mouth provokes a flogging. [l]

7 The mouth of a fool leads to his ruin,
and his lips are a snare to his very life. * [m]

8 The whispers of a gossiper are tasty morsels
that corrode one's inner being. [n]

9 Anyone who is lazy in his work
is a brother to the man who wages destruction. [o]

10* The name of the LORD is a tower of strength;
the upright man runs to it and finds refuge. [p]

11 The wealth of a rich man is his stronghold;
he regards it as a high wall that cannot be scaled. [q]

12 A man is haughty until disaster overtakes him,
but humility comes before honors. [r]

13 One who answers before listening
exposes his folly and incurs shame. [s]

14 A man's spirit can manage to endure sickness,
but when the spirit is crushed, who can bear it? [t]

15 A discerning mind gains knowledge,
and the ears of the wise eagerly seek knowledge. [u]

16 A gift opens doors for the giver
and wins him access to the powerful. [v]

17 The one who pleads his case first will seem right
until his opponent comes forth to interrogate him. *

18 Casting lots* can settle disputes
and avoid contention between powerful rivals. [w]

19 An offended brother is stronger than a fortress,
and quarrels are more difficult to overcome than castle gates. [x]

20 From the fruit of the mouth one's stomach is filled;
contentment is gained from the yield of one's lips. [y]

21 The tongue has the power over life and death; *
those who cherish it will enjoy its fruits. [z]

22 One who finds a wife finds happiness
and receives favor from the LORD. * [a]

23 A poor man uses language of entreaty,
but the rich man replies with insults. [b]

24 Some friends can lead us to ruin,
but a true friend is closer than a brother. [c]

h Prov 12:23.—i Prov 15:9.—j Prov 20:5; Ps 18:17; Jn 7:38.—k Prov 17:15; 24:23; 28:21; Ps 82:2.—l Prov 10:14.—m Prov 10:14; 12:13; 13:3; Ps 64:9; Eccl 10:12.—n Prov 26:22.—o Prov 28:24.—p Prov 14:26; Pss 20:2; 61:4.—q Prov 10:15.—r Prov 11:2; 15:33; 16:18; Sir 10:15.—s Prov 20:25; Sir 11:8.—t Prov 15:13; 17:22.—u Prov 15:14.—v Prov 19:6; 21:14; Gen 32:19.—w Prov 16:33.—x 1 Sam 17:28.—y Prov 12:14; 13:2.—z Prov 13:2-3; Ps 12:5; Mt 12:37.—a Prov 12:4; 19:14; 31:10; Job 33:26; Sir 7:26.—b Prov 22:7.—c Prov 17:17; Jn 15:13-15.

18:5 *Partiality* toward anyone was condemned in the law (see Lev 19:15; Deut 1:17; 16:19).

18:7 One who cannot curb his tongue is a fool (see Jas 3), for it is through our words that we are justified or condemned (see Mt 12:37). Our speech should always be seasoned with salt so that we may know how to respond to each person (see Col 4:6).

18:10-11 In the struggle of life the faithful find support and refuge in the Lord, while the foolish put their trust in their wealth. *Name of the LORD:* the name stands for the person since it expresses his nature and qualities (see note on Ex 3:13-15). *Tower:* towers were the only safe places against robbers and enemies. *The wealth . . . stronghold:* same as Prov 10:15 (see note there). *Cannot be scaled:* unscalable for humans but not for God (see Isa 25:12).

18:17 This verse can apply to many situations, but it can also be interpreted as being directed toward judges to persuade them to hear both sides of a case (see Deut 1:16).

18:18 *Casting lots:* see note on Prov 16:33.

18:21 *The tongue has the power over life and death:* see note on Prov 13:3.

18:22 *Receives favor from the LORD:* identical to Prov 8:35, where the favor results from finding wisdom.

CHAPTER 19

Better Poor and Honest than Wealthy and Perverse*

1 It is better to be poor and lead an honest life
than to be wealthy and perverse in one's ways. [d]

2 Zeal is useless when not accompanied by knowledge,
and acting hastily causes one to stumble. [e]

3 A man's own folly leads to his ruin,
yet it is against the LORD that his heart rages. *[f]

4 Wealth attracts many friends,
but a poor man's only friend will desert him. [g]

5 A false witness will not escape punishment,
neither will the one who tells lies. [h]

6 Many court the favor of the great,
and everyone is a friend to a man who bestows gifts. [i]

7 The poor man is despised by all his brothers;
how much more do his friends desert him!
He pursues them with entreaties
but all in vain. [j]

8 Whoever gains wisdom loves his own soul;
one who cherishes understanding will prosper. [k]

9 A false witness will not escape punishment,
and the one who tells lies will perish. [l]

10 It is not fitting for a fool to live in luxury,
much less for a slave to rule over princes. [m]

11 A man with good sense is slow to anger,
and he earns glory for overlooking an offense. [n]

12 A king's anger is like the roaring of a lion,
but his favor is like dew on the grass. [o]

13 A foolish son * is a calamity to his father,
and a nagging wife is like an endless dripping of water. [p]

14 A house and wealth are inherited from parents,
but a prudent wife is a gift from the LORD. [q]

15 Laziness results in excessive sleep,
and an idle man suffers hunger. * [r]

16 Whoever observes the commandments will live,
but the one who scorns them will die. [s]

17 Whoever is kind to the poor lends to the LORD *
who will recompense him for his kindness. [t]

18 Chastise your son while there is still hope for him,
but do not allow your anger to cause his death. [u]

19 One with a violent temper must bear the consequences;
if you spare him, you make his evil worse. *

20 Heed advice and accept instruction
so that your wisdom may increase in the future. [v]

21 Many are the plans in a human mind,
but it is the purpose of the LORD that will prevail. * [w]

22 A man's attraction is his kindness;
it is far better to be poor than to be a liar.

---

d Prov 28:6.—e Prov 29:20.—f Prov 11:3; Isa 32:6; Jas 1:13-15.—g Prov 14:20; 19:7; Sir 13:20ff.—h Prov 19:9; 21:28; Deut 19:16-20; Ex 23:1.—i Prov 17:8; 18:16; 29:26.—j Prov 10:15; 19:4.—k Prov 16:20.—l Prov 19:5; Deut 19:19.—m Prov 26:1; 30:21-23; Eccl 10:5-7.—n 2 Ki 5:12.—o Prov 16:14-15; 20:2; Ps 133:3; Est 1:12.—p Prov 10:1; 17:25; 21:9; Est 1:18.—q Prov 12:4; 18:22; 2 Cor 12:14.—r Prov 6:9ff; 10:4; 20:13.—s Prov 13:13; 16:17.—t Prov 14:21; 22:9; 28:27; Deut 24:14, 19; Mt 10:42.—u Prov 13:24; 23:13f.—v Prov 4:1; 12:15.—w Prov 16:9; Ps 33:11.

19:1-29 In the proverbs found in this chapter, we will pay special attention to those that describe the condition of the poor (vv. 1, 4-7, 17, 22) or those who care about the difficulty of obtaining justice (vv. 5, 9, 28); we will also note the theme of charity (the one who gives to the poor lends to God—v. 17) and mercy (v. 22). Once more, a warning is issued to idlers (vv. 15, 24), and reflections on the family and education are set forth (vv. 13-14, 18, 26). Our maxim "Man proposes but God disposes" is foreshadowed by the words in verse 21: *Many are the plans in a human mind, but it is the purpose of the LORD that will prevail.*

19:3 *It is against the LORD that his heart rages:* i.e., he blames the Lord for all his troubles (see Gen 4:5; Isa 8:21; Lam 3:39).

19:13 *Foolish son:* see Prov 17:21, 25. *Nagging wife:* she is also upbraided in Prov 21:9, 19; 25:24; 27:15.

19:15 See note on Prov 10:4.

19:17 *Lends to the LORD:* the Lord regards kindness to the poor as kindness done to him (see Mt 25:40).

19:19 *If you spare him, you make his evil worse:* another possible translation: "If you rescue him, you will have to do it again."

19:21 See Prov 16:1; 16:9 and notes.

23 The fear of the LORD * leads to life,
enabling one to eat and sleep without fear of harm. [x]

24 The idler * will dip his hand into the dish,
but he will not so much as lift it to his mouth. [y]

25 If you strike a scoffer, * the simple will learn prudence;
if you reprove an intelligent man, he will gain understanding. [z]

26 Anyone who maltreats his father and casts out his mother *
is a shameful and despicable son. [a]

27 If a son ceases to accept correction,
he strays from the words of knowledge. [b]

28 A lying witness makes a mockery of justice,
and the mouth of the wicked feasts on iniquity. [c]

29 Punishments were meant for scoffers
and flogging for the backs of fools. [d]

CHAPTER 20

Who Can Find Someone Truly Faithful?*

1 Wine encourages recklessness and strong drink leads to brawls;
anyone who allows them to seduce him is not wise. * [e]

2 The anger of a king is like the roar of a lion;
he who provokes him places his life in jeopardy. [f]

3 It is honorable to avoid strife,
but every fool is quarrelsome. [g]

4 The idler * does not plow in season;
so at harvest-time he looks for a crop in vain. [h]

5 The purpose of a man's heart is like deep water,
but a discerning person will draw it out. [i]

6 Many declare their loyalty,
but who can find someone truly faithful? [j]

7 When a man leads a blameless and upright life,
blessed are the children who succeed him. [k]

8 A king who is seated on the throne of judgment
will eradicate all evil with a mere glance. [l]

9 Who can truly say, "I have cleansed my heart
and I am purified of all sin"? * [m]

10 Weights and measures that are not consistent
are an abomination to the LORD. [n]

11 By his very actions a child reveals
whether his conduct is innocent and upright. [o]

12 The ear that hears and the eye that sees—
the LORD has made both of them. [p]

13 Do not love sleep if you wish to avoid poverty;
remain awake and you will never lack food. [q]

14 "No good, no good," says the buyer,
but then he goes forth to boast about his bargain. *

x Prov 10:27.—y Prov 26:15.—z Prov 9:9; 17:10; 21:11; Ps 141:5.—a Prov 28:24; Sir 3:16.—b Prov 1:8.—c Job 15:16.—d Prov 26:3; Deut 25:2.—e Prov 23:29-35; 1 Sam 25:36.—f Prov 16:14; 19:12; Est 7:7.—g Gen 13:3; 1 Sam 25:25.—h Prov 6:6; Eccl 10:18.—i Prov 18:4; Ps 18:17.—j Ps 12:2; Mt 6:2; Lk 18:11.—k Prov 19:1; Pss 26:1; 37:25-28; 112:2.—l Prov 20:26; 25:4-5; 1 Ki 7:7.—m Job 14:4; 15:14; Ps 130:3-4; Eccl 7:20; 1 Jn 1:8.—n Prov 11:1; 20:23.—o Prov 22:6; Mt 7:16.—p Ex 4:11; Ps 94:9.—q Prov 6:11; 19:15.

19:23 *Fear of the LORD:* see note on Prov 1:7.

19:24 Almost identical to Prov 26:15. *Idler*: see note on Prov 6:6.

19:25 *Strike a scoffer:* see note on Prov 1:22; see also v. 29; 14:3. *Simple:* see note on Prov 1:4.

19:26 *Maltreats his father and casts out his mother:* children were forbidden to maltreat their parents physically or verbally (see Ex 21:15, 17).

20:1-30 In the midst of these stand-alone proverbs, a few present the ideal figure of a king who dispenses justice (vv. 8, 26, 28); others delicately note commercial customs (v. 14), flog idlers again (vv. 4, 13), and return to trickery used in weights and measures (v. 23) or in fraud of any kind (vv. 17, 21). If one saying justifies corporal punishment (v. 30), others inveigh against the desire for vengeance (vv. 3, 22). Then amidst these sayings for familial, social, and even economic life, there appears a more profound reflection on the mystery of life in which God is at work (vv. 24, 27). A witness of a deep moral and religious sense, verse 9 recognizes the ineradicable tendency of human beings toward evil, from which they cannot free themselves by their own powers.

20:1 Those who drink too much wine or hard liquor become scoffers and brawlers (see Hos 7:5). Drunkenness leads to poverty (Prov 23:20-21), strife and brawling (Prov 23:29-30), and perversion of justice (Prov 31:4-5).

20:4 *Idler:* see note on Prov 6:6.

20:9 No humans can claim to be sinless (see Job 14:4; Rom 3:23), except those whose sins are forgiven through the power of God (see 1 Ki 8:46ff; Job 4:17; 14:4; Pss 51:2ff; 130:3-4; Rom 3:23-24; 1 Jn 1:8).

20:14 In Old Testament times, people arrived at the price of things through bargaining. The buyers would devalue things in order to buy them at bargain prices and then boast about their purchase.

15 There is gold or an abundance of costly pearls,
but the lips that reveal knowledge are a rare jewel. [r]

16 Take the garment of anyone who becomes surety for a stranger;
demand a pledge as security for persons unknown to you. * [s]

17 Bread obtained by deceit may taste sweet to a man,
but afterward his mouth is filled with grit. [t]

18 Plans will succeed when good advice is accepted;
follow wise guidance when waging war. [u]

19 A tale-bearer will reveal secrets;
so do not associate with a gossip. [v]

20 If anyone curses his father or mother, *
his lamp will go out in utter darkness. [w]

21 Possessions that are quickly acquired in the beginning
will not be blessed in the end. [x]

22 Do not say, "I will repay evil," *
but trust in the LORD, who will help you. [y]

23 Differing weights are an abomination to the LORD,
and dishonest scales are not acceptable to him. [z]

24 A man's steps are directed by the LORD;
how then can anyone understand his own way? [a]

25 It is rash to pledge a sacred gift,
or to make a vow and then have second thoughts. * [b]

26 A wise king winnows the wicked
and requites them for their guilt. * [c]

27 The human spirit is the lamp of the LORD
that searches out the innermost self. [d]

28 Loyalty and faithfulness preserve the king,
and his throne is founded on saving justice. [e]

29 The glory of youths is their strength,
but the splendor of the aged is their gray hair. [f]

30 Evil is cleansed away by blows that wound,
and beatings chasten the innermost being. * [g]

CHAPTER 21

The LORD Weighs the Heart*

1 A king's heart is like a stream of water in the hand of the LORD;
he directs it wherever he pleases. [h]

2 A man's ways may seem right to him,
but the LORD weighs the heart. [i]

3 To do what is right and just
is more acceptable to the LORD than sacrifice. * [j]

4 Haughty eyes * and a proud heart—
the lamp of the wicked—are nothing but sin. [k]

r Prov 3:14-15.—s Prov 27:13; Ex 22:26.—t Prov 9:17; Lam 3:16.—u Prov 11:14; 24:6.—v Prov 11:13.—w Prov 30:11, 17; Ex 21:17; Lev 20:9; Job 18:5; Mt 15:4.—x Prov 23:5.—y Prov 24:29; Mt 5:39; Rom 12:17, 19; 1 Thes 5:15; 1 Pet 3:9.—z Prov 11:1; 20:10; Deut 25:13.—a Prov 16:9; 19:21; Jer 10:23.—b Eccl 5:1; Jer 44:25.—c Prov 20:8.—d Prov 16:2; Ps 119:105.—e Prov 16:12; Ps 40:12; Isa 16:5.—f Prov 16:31.—g Prov 22:15; Isa 53:5.—h Jer 39:11-12.—i Prov 16:2.—j 1 Sam 15:22; Isa 1:11; Hos 6:6; Mic 6:6-8; Mal 1:12.—k Prov 6:17.

20:16 The words are like those of a judge against one who has imprudently made himself a guarantor (see Prov 6:1-5). A garment could be taken as security for a debt (see Deut 24:10-13).

20:20 *Curses his father or mother:* such an action (see also Prov 30:11, 17) was punishable by death (see Ex 21:17; Lev 20:9).

20:22 *I will repay evil:* vengeance is the province of the Lord, not of his faithful people. He will repay the wicked for their actions (see Deut 32:35; Ps 94:1). *Trust in the LORD:* see Pss 27:14; 37:34.

20:25 Vows should be made without haste and should always be carried out (see also Eccl 5:1; Jer 44:25).

20:26 *Winnows the wicked and requites them for their guilt:* literally, "winnows the wicked and causes the wheel to pass over them," an example taken from the carts used in threshing at that time. The wheel of the cart separated the grain from the husk (see Isa 28:27-28); in the same way, the wicked will be separated from the righteous and punished.

20:30 Once again (see Prov 10:13; 13:24, and note; 14:3; 19:29; 22:15) the idea is put forth that some type of punishment is needed to restrain evil.

21:1-31 There is nothing unexpected in these reflections that oppose the lot of the righteous and that of the wicked, or in these comparative illustrations of wisdom and folly. The traditional teaching then in vogue about the earthly recompense of the righteous and the conviction that the wicked hasten to their ruin even on earth remain in full force. We will read two apt words about the quarrelsome woman, but this is not the first time this caricature appears in the Book. Verse 18 seems to stem from a pessimistic realism: wickedness will forever play its part in the universe! But we will meditate above all on the affirmation that the entire destiny of human beings is found in the hands of God (vv. 2, 30-31).

21:3 *More acceptable to the LORD than sacrifice:* internal goodness is more acceptable to the Lord than external sacrifice (see v. 27; 15:8; 1 Sam 15:22; Isa 1:11-15; Am 5:22; Hos 6:6; Mic 6:7-8; Mal 1:12).

21:4 *Haughty eyes:* see note on Prov 6:17; see also Prov 16:5, 18.

5 The plans of the diligent will ensure profit,
but rash haste will surely lead to poverty. [l]

6 One who amasses a fortune by means of a lying tongue
is pursuing a fleeting vapor that leads to death. [m]

7 The violence of the wicked will sweep them away
because they refuse to do what is right. [n]

8 The way of the guilty is crooked,
but the conduct of the innocent is straightforward. [o]

9 It is better to live on the corner of a roof
than to share a spacious house with a nagging wife. * [p]

10 The soul of the wicked man is intent on evil;
his neighbor beholds no pity in his countenance.

11 When the scoffer * is punished, the simple become wiser;
when the wise man is instructed, he increases in knowledge. [q]

12 The Righteous One watches the house of the evildoer
and brings the evildoer to destruction. [r]

13 One who shuts his ears to the cries of the poor
will himself also cry out and not be heard. [s]

14 A gift given secretly appeases anger,
and a gift concealed in the cloak will avert violent wrath. [t]

15 When justice is done, the upright rejoice,
but evildoers are filled with terror. [u]

16 Anyone who strays from the way of prudence
will rest in the company of the shades. * [v]

17 Whoever craves pleasure will end up in want;
whoever loves wine and oil will never grow rich. [w]

18 The wicked man serves as a ransom for the righteous, *
as does the faithless man for the upright. [x]

19 It is better to live alone in the wilderness
than with a nagging and irritable wife. [y]

20 The house of the wise man is filled with precious treasure and oil,
but the fool squanders all he has. [z]

21 Whoever pursues righteousness * and kindness
will find life and honor too. [a]

22 A wise man can storm a city of warriors
and overthrow the stronghold * upon which they relied. [b]

23 One who guards his mouth and his tongue
will preserve himself from trouble. [c]

24 A scoffer * is a proud and insolent man
who is haughty in everything he does. [d]

25 The cravings of the idler * will prove fatal,
since his hands will do no work. [e]

26 All day long the godless man continues to covet,
whereas the righteous man gives unsparingly. [f]

27 The sacrifice of the wicked is abhorrent,
and more so when it is offered for evil motives. * [g]

28 A false witness will perish,
but a truthful witness will never be silenced. [h]

---

l Prov 10:4.—m Prov 10:2.—n Prov 11:5.—o Prov 2:15.—p Prov 19:13; 21:19; 25:24; 27:15; Sir 25:22.—q Prov 19:25.—r Prov 14:11.—s Job 29:12.—t Gen 32:20-21.—u Prov 10:29.—v Ezek 18:24.—w Prov 23:20-21, 29-35.—x Prov 11:8; Isa 43:3.—y Prov 21:9.—z Job 20:15, 18.—a Ps 25:13; Mt 5:6.—b Prov 8:14.—c Prov 10:19; 12:13; 13:3; Ps 34:14.—d Jer 43:2.—e Prov 13:4.—f Lev 25:35; 2 Sam 17:27.—g Prov 15:8; 1 Ki 14:24; Sir 34:18ff.—h Prov 19:5, 9; Isa 29:21.

21:9 *Nagging wife:* see note on Prov 19:13.

21:11 *Scoffer:* see note on Prov 1:22; see also Prov 14:3; 19:29. *Simple:* see note on Prov 1:4.

21:16 *Company of the shades:* i.e., the dead in the netherworld.

21:18 *The wicked man serves as a ransom for the righteous:* this thought is exemplified in the history of Israel; e.g., God ransomed the exiles of Judah from the Persian conqueror Cyrus by giving him three nations (Egypt, Ethiopia, and Seba) in ransom (see Isa 43:1ff).

21:21 *Pursues righteousness:* see Prov 15:9. *Life and honor:* these are the same benefits received by those who seek wisdom (see note on Prov 3:2; see also Prov 3:16; 8:18; 22:4).

21:22 *A wise man can . . . overthrow the stronghold:* i.e., "wisdom is better than power" (Eccl 9:16). See also Prov 24:5; 2 Cor 10:14, both of which indicate that spiritual weapons have divine power to overthrow strongholds.

21:24 *Scoffer:* see note on Prov 1:22. Such a person is punished because of his pride (see v. 11; 3:34; 19:25, 29).

21:25 *Idler:* see note on Prov 6:6.

21:27 See note on Prov 21:3.

29 A wicked man puts up a bold front,
but an upright man amends his ways. [i]

30 Neither wisdom nor understanding nor counsel
can be of avail against the LORD. [j]

31 The horse is prepared for the day of battle,
but victory rests with the LORD. * [k]

CHAPTER 22

Reflections on the Human Condition*

1 An honorable name* is more to be desired than great riches,
and high esteem is preferable to silver and gold. [l]

2 The rich and the poor have this in common:
all of them were made by the LORD. * [m]

3 A prudent man perceives danger and seeks shelter,
while the simple* continue forward and pay for it. [n]

4 The reward of humility and fear of the LORD*
is wealth, honor, and life. [o]

5 Thorns and snares cover the path of the perverse;
whoever values his life will steer clear of them. [p]

6 Train a child in the way he should go,
and he will not deviate from it, even in old age. [q]

7 The wealthy man lords it over the poor,*
and the borrower becomes the slave of the lender. [r]

8 Whoever sows injustice will reap calamity,
and the rod of his wrath will disappear. [s]

9 One who is kindly will be blessed,*
for he shares his food with the poor. [t]

10 Banish the scoffer* and strife will cease;
discord and abuse will come to an end. [u]

11 The LORD loves the pure of heart;
the man of gracious speech will have the king as a friend. [v]

12 The eyes of the LORD* preserve knowledge,
but he ruins the plans of the unfaithful.

13 The idler cries out, "There is a lion outside;
I will be killed if I go out on the street." * [w]

14 The mouth of an adulteress* is a deep pit;
the man with whom the LORD is angry will fall into it. [x]

15 Folly is rooted deep in the heart of a child,
but the rod of correction* will remove it far from him. [y]

16 A man becomes rich by crushing the poor,
but presents to the rich will only impoverish him. * [z]

i Prov 14:8.—j Job 12:13; 15:25; Isa 8:10.—k Ps 33:12-19; Isa 31:1.—l Eccl 7:1.—m Prov 29:13; Job 31:15.—n Prov 14:16; 27:12.—o Prov 10:27; 15:33.—p Prov 15:19.—q Deut 6:7; Eph 6:4.—r Deut 15:6; Mt 18:25, 34.—s Job 4:8; Sir 7:3; Hos 8:7; Gal 6:7-8.—t Prov 11:25; 19:17; Deut 14:28.—u Prov 26:20.—v Prov 18:13; Mt 5:8.—w Prov 26:13.—x Prov 5:3-5; 23:27; Eccl 7:26.—y Prov 13:24; 20:30.—z Jer 30:16.

21:31 Neither horses nor chariots nor any other means of fighting a battle can ensure victory (see Ps 20:8; Hos 1:7; see Deut 7:16), since it is the Lord alone who ensures victory (see 1 Sam 17:47; Pss 3:9; 27:1; 28:9; 33:12-19; Isa 31:1; 43:3; Rev 7:10).

22:1-16 Like the preceding chapters, this last chapter of the second part of Proverbs collects—in no particular order—observations on the life of human beings, reflections of moralists, and affirmations of believers. Thus, for better or worse and in spite of contradictions, we are presented with a certain image of the life and behavior of those who cling to true values, i.e., to the wisdom that God inspires in human beings.

22:1 *Honorable name:* see also Prov 3:4; 10:7; Eccl 7:1. *Preferable to silver and gold:* the same is true of the possession of wisdom (see Prov 3:14; 16:16).

22:2 See note on Prov 14:31.

22:3 *Simple:* see note on Prov 1:4.

22:4 *Fear of the LORD:* see note on Prov 1:7; see also Prov 15:33.

22:7 *The wealthy man lords it over the poor:* see note on Prov 10:15.

22:9 *One who is kindly will be blessed:* see note on Prov 11:24. *Shares his food:* see note on Prov 14:21.

22:10 *Scoffer:* see note on Prov 1:22.

22:12 *The eyes of the LORD:* see Prov 5:21; 15:3; Job 31:4; 34:21; Jer 16:17; Heb 4:13. *Preserve knowledge:* i.e., God watches over those who possess knowledge (see Pss 1:6; 34:16). *Ruins the plans of the unfaithful:* see Prov 16:19; and there is no defense against God (Prov 21:30).

22:13 The idler overstates difficulties in order to escape putting forth effort (see also note on Prov 6:6).

22:14 *Mouth of an adulteress:* i.e., her seductive words (see notes on Prov 2:16 and 5:3; see also Prov 7:5). *Deep pit:* this may refer to a well or to the trap laid by a hunter (see Prov 5:22; 7:22-23).

22:15 *Rod of correction:* see note on Prov 13:24.

22:16 The man who gains money by crushing the poor will inevitably lose it by paying tribute to those who are richer.

IV: THE SAYINGS OF THE WISE*

Lend Your Ear*

17 These are the sayings of the wise:

Incline your ear and listen to my words,
and apply your mind to the knowledge I impart. [a]
18 They will afford pleasure if you keep them in your heart
and have all of them ready on your lips. [b]
19 In order that your trust may be in the LORD,
I will make them known to you today. [c]
20 Have I not written for you thirty sayings *
of admonition and knowledge
21 to show you what is right and true
so that you can offer sound answers to the one who sent you? [d]

Practical Counsels*

22 Do not rob the poor because they are helpless
or oppress the needy at the gate. [e]
23 For the LORD will take up their cause *
and rob of life those who despoiled them. [f]
24 Never make friends with a man prone to anger,
and do not associate with anyone who is wrathful.
25 Otherwise you may learn his ways *
and find yourself entangled in a snare. [g]
26 Do not be one of those who give pledges
and become surety for another's debts. [h]
27 For if you have no means of paying,
your bed will be taken from under you. [i]
28 Never remove the ancient boundary stone
that your ancestors set up. [j]
29 If you see a man who is skilled in his work, *
remember that he will serve kings;
he will not stand before common people. [k]

CHAPTER 23

When You Sit Down To Dine with a Ruler . . .*

1 When you sit down to dine with a ruler,
take careful note of what is before you. [l]
2 Control yourself*
if you are given to overindulgence.
3 Do not yearn for the ruler's delicacies,
for they are deceptive food. [m]

Wealth Passes Away*

4 Do not wear yourself out in the pursuit of wealth,
and cease even to think about it. [n]
5 When you fix your gaze upon it,
it is gone before you realize it.
For it suddenly sprouts wings
and flies up to the sky like an eagle. [o]

Do Not Dine with a Stingy Man*

6 Do not dine with a stingy man
or hanker for his delicacies. [p]
7 For, like a hair,
they will stick in your throat.
"Eat and drink," he will say to you,
but he does not mean it in his heart.
8 You will vomit up the little you have eaten

a Prov 1:8; 2:2; 5:1.—b Mt 12:37.—c Prov 3:5; Jer 17:7.—d Eccl 12:10.—e Ex 23:6; Job 5:15.—f Prov 23:11; Job 29:16; Ps 140:13.—g 1 Cor 15:33.—h Prov 6:1f; 11:15; 17:18.—i Prov 11:15; 17:18.—j Prov 23:10; Deut 19:14; 27:17.—k Gen 39:3; 41:46; 1 Ki 11:28.—l Lk 14:8-11.—m Prov 23:6-8.—n Prov 28:20; Mt 6:19.—o Prov 27:24; Mt 6:19.—p Prov 23:1-3; Ps 141:4.

22:17—24:22 This collection of sayings may have been intended for the training and reflection of persons in positions of responsibility. Critics find in it some analogies with an Egyptian book containing the wisdom of a certain Amenemope (tenth century B.C.). But unlike the latter, which could only have served as a model, our collection teaches trust in God, under whose gaze the actions of human beings, especially of the mighty, are done. This collection sought to group its proverbs into some kind of order, although it never really reached that goal. It readily dispenses its counsels and loves warning formulas: *Do not rob the poor. . . . Never make friends . . .* (Prov 22:22, 24).

22:17-21 This warm invitation greatly resembles the preface to chapter 1. The sage is a happy person who places trust in God.

22:20 *Thirty sayings:* there are thirty units in this section, most of them two or three verses long. *The Wisdom of Amenemope* also contains thirty sections.

22:22-29 These are practical counsels inspired by respect for the poor, by prudence, and by the sense of justice. These virtues are essential for a responsible society. The ending remains obscure: one notes that the capable person quickly reaches the level of success, a simple fact about which no judgment is made.

22:23 *Will take up their cause:* i.e., the cause of the poor (see Prov 23:11; Pss 12:6; 140:13; Isa 3:14-16; Mal 3:5).

22:25 *May learn his ways:* i.e., the ways of the wicked, a theme repeated by Paul: "Bad company corrupts good morals" (1 Cor 15:33).

22:29 *Who is skilled in his work:* see note on Prov 8:30.

23:1-3 When people are in society, they must know how to conduct themselves. Proverbs claims to impart an art of how to live.

23:2 *Control yourself:* literally, "put a knife to your throat"—a proverbial metaphor for restraining one's appetites.

23:4-5 This is an excellent warning: power exposes one to the temptation to amass a fortune with ill-gotten goods: "The love of money is the root of all evils" (1 Tim 6:10; see Prov 15:27; 28:20; Heb 13:5). We must place our trust in God not money (see Jer 17:11; Lk 12:21; 1 Tim 6:17).

23:6-9 What good is accepting an invitation that is given out of envy rather than friendship!

and find that your compliments have been wasted.
9 Do not waste your words on a fool
who will only despise the wisdom of your comments. * [q]

God Vindicates the Defenseless*

10 Do not move an ancient boundary stone
or encroach on the lands of orphans. [r]
11 For their redeemer is powerful,
and he will take up their cause against you. [s]

Direct Your Heart along the Right Path*

12 Apply your heart to instruction
and your ears to words of knowledge. [t]
13 Do not withhold discipline from a child;
if you beat him with a rod, he will not die. [u]
14 Rather, if you beat him with a rod,
you will save him from the netherworld. * [v]
15 My son, if your heart is wise,
then my heart will be glad. [w]
16 Also my innermost being will rejoice
when your lips utter what is right. [x]
17 Do not allow your heart to envy sinners,
but always be zealous for the fear of the LORD; * [y]
18 there truly is a future for you,
and your hope will not be cut short. [z]
19 Listen, my son, and be wise
as you direct your heart along the right path. [a]
20 Do not consort with drunkards *
or be one of those who gorge themselves with meat. [b]
21 For the drunkard and the glutton will become impoverished,
and stupor will clothe them in rags. [c]
22 Listen to your father who begot you,
and do not despise your mother * when she is old. [d]
23 Buy truth and do not sell it;
this is wisdom, instruction, and understanding. [e]
24 The father of a good man will rejoice;
he who begets a wise son will delight in him. [f]
25 May your father and mother be glad;
may the one who bore you exult. [g]

The Prostitute Is a Deep Well*

26 My son, pay attention to me
and let your eyes delight in my ways. [h]
27 For a prostitute is a deep well,
and an adulteress is a narrow pit. [i]
28 Such a woman lies in wait like a robber,
and many are the men she deludes. [j]

The Joys and Dangers of Wine*

29 Who endures misery? Who endures remorse?
Who has strife? Who has anxiety?
Who becomes bruised without knowing the reason?
Who has blackened eyes? [k]
30 Those who linger over their wine too long,
those who sample blended wines. [l]
31 Do not note how red the wine is,
how it sparkles in the cup,
and how smoothly it goes down. [m]
32 For in the end its bite is like that of a serpent
or that of a poisonous viper. [n]

q Prov 9:7.—r Prov 22:28; Deut 19:14.—s Prov 22:23; Ex 22:22.—t Prov 2:2.—u Prov 13:24; 19:18; Sir 30:1.—v Prov 13:24; 19:18; 29:15, 17.—w Prov 29:3.—x Prov 23:24; 27:11; 29:3.—y Prov 3:31; 24:1, 19; Pss 37:1; 73:3.—z Prov 24:14, 19-20; Pss 9:19; 37:1-4.—a Prov 28:7; Deut 4:9.—b Isa 5:11, 22; Hab 2:15.—c Prov 21:17.—d Lev 19:32.—e Prov 4:7; 17:16.—f Prov 10:1; 23:15-16.—g Prov 10:1.—h Prov 5:1-6; Ps 18:21.—i Prov 22:14.—j Prov 7:10-27.—k Prov 23:20-21; Isa 5:1.—l Prov 20:1; 23:20-21; Sir 19:2; Isa 5:11.—m Hab 2:5.—n Job 20:16; Isa 11:8.

23:9 *Despise the wisdom of your comments:* fools despise wisdom (Prov 1:7), hate knowledge and correction (Prov 1:22; 12:11), and hurl abuse on those who correct them (Prov 9:7).

23:10-11 God comes to the aid of those who do not have anyone to defend them, especially orphans and widows, for he is "the Father of orphans and the defender of widows" (Ps 68:6; see also Jer 50:34). *Will take up their cause:* see Pss 12:6; 140:13; Isa 3:14-16; Mal 3:5.

23:12-25 A father here speaks to his son in order to counsel him, for wisdom is tradition, an apprenticeship in how to behave, the acceptance of an ideal that has shown its value. The conceptions of education set forth undoubtedly deserve to be reviewed and adapted in accordance with the evolution of cultures. But doesn't the joy of parents consist in knowing that they are understood when they bear witness from the best of themselves!

23:14 The ancients thought that in order to give instruction one has to be severe (see Prov 19:18). In this ancient conception, a good education was the guarantee of good behavior. Hence, it was a buffer against the punishment of God reserved for the wicked and against the punishment of the netherworld, i.e., death.

23:17-18 *Fear of the LORD:* see note on Prov 1:7. *Future . . . hope:* see Prov 24:14; Pss 9:19; 37:37; 73:24; Jer 29:11.

23:20 *Do not consort with drunkards:* see notes on verses 29-35; 20:1. Drunkenness is also condemned in Deut 21:20; Mt 24:49; Lk 21:34; Rom 13:13; 1 Cor 6:10; Gal 5:21; Eph 5:18; 1 Tim 3:3; 1 Pet 4:3.

23:22 *Do not despise your mother:* see Prov 15:20; 30:17.

23:26-28 The danger of letting oneself be led astray by a woman who prostitutes herself is described more at length in Prov 5:2; see also note on Prov 2:16.

23:29-35 This portrait of a drunkard is lacking in no detail. The last verse indicates the most damaging effect of drunkenness on the drunkard: the desire to drink again and total unconcern for bodily or spiritual harm.

33 Then your eyes will behold strange sights,
and your heart will utter distorted words. [o]
34 You will become like one sleeping at sea
or clinging to the top of the mast.
35 You will say, "They struck me, but I was not hurt.
They beat me, but I did not feel it.
When will I awaken,
so that I can seek another drink?" [p]

CHAPTER 24

Do Not Be Envious of the Wicked*

1 Do not be envious of the wicked
or desire to be in their company. [q]
2 For their hearts scheme of violence,
and their lips speak only of mischief. [r]
3 By wisdom a house is built;
by understanding it is made secure. [s]
4 By knowledge its rooms are filled
with rare and desirable riches of all kinds. [t]
5 A wise man is mightier than a strong man,
and a man of knowledge prevails over one who has strength. [u]
6 For you wage war by wise guidance,
and victory depends on a host of counselors. [v]
7 Wisdom is too lofty for a fool;
at the city gate he does not open his mouth. * [w]
8 Anyone who plans to do evil
earns a reputation for intrigue. [x]
9 The intrigues of fools are sinful, *
and men find the scoffer abhorrent.
10 If you lose heart in time of adversity,
your strength will indeed be limited. [y]
11 * Rescue those who are being led away to death
and save those who are on their way to execution.
12 If you say, "I do not know this man,"
will he who tests the heart not perceive it?
He who is the guardian of your soul knows it,
and he will repay you as your deeds deserve. [z]
13 Eat honey, * my son, for it is good,
and the drippings of the honeycomb are sweet to the taste. [a]
14 In much the same manner
will wisdom be sweet to your soul.
If you find it, you will have a future,
and your hope * will not be cut off. [b]
15 Do not lie in wait at the home of a righteous man;
do not raid his dwelling.
16 For a righteous man falls seven times *
and rises again,
but the wicked stumble into calamity. [c]
17 Do not be glad when your enemy falls;
when he stumbles, do not let your heart exult, [d]
18 for fear that the LORD will be displeased at the sight
and withdraw his wrath from your enemy. [e]
19 Do not become outraged about evildoers
or be envious of the wicked. * [f]
20 For they will have no tomorrow;
the lamp of the wicked will be extinguished. [g]
21 My son, fear the LORD and fear the king; *
avoid those who rebel against them. [h]

o Prov 2:12; 20:1.—p Prov 20:1; Jer 5:3.—q Prov 3:31; 23:17-18.—r Ps 10:7; Isa 30:12; Hos 4:1.—s Prov 14:1.—t Prov 8:21.—u Prov 21:22.—v Prov 11:14; 20:18; Lk 14:31.—w Sir 6:21.—x Rom 1:30-31.—y Job 4:5.—z 1 Sam 2:3; Job 34:11; Pss 62:13; 139:2; Mt 16:27; Rom 2:6.—a Isa 7:15.—b Prov 16:24; 23:18; Ps 119:104.—c Job 5:19; Ps 34:22.—d 2 Sam 3:32; Ob 12; Mic 7:8.—e Job 31:29.—f Prov 24:1; Ps 37:1; Jer 12:1.—g Prov 13:9; 23:17-18; Job 18:5.—h Rom 13:1-5.

24:1-22 Evildoers make others envious; every moral teacher must show that, in one way or another, evil does not pay, that it is a pathway to death. Faced with the lure of desires that are easily available but dishonest, they must show the human and spiritual value of good behavior—it is the sole way of approach. The teacher of wisdom devotes himself to this difficult task.

24:7 Public business was conducted at the gate of the city.

24:9 *The intrigues of fools are sinful:* see Prov 1:11-16; 9:13-18. *Men find the scoffer abhorrent:* because he is arrogant and abusive (Prov 9:7), and a fomenter of strife (Prov 22:10). See also note on Prov 1:22.

24:11-12 One who can prove that a condemned man is innocent must try to save him (see Prov 17:15; Isa 58:6-7). *[God] knows it:* God knows us through and through (see Prov 16:2; 21:2; Ps 94:9-11).

24:13 *Honey:* i.e., wisdom, which is the honey of the soul.

24:14 Wisdom is sweet to the soul by bringing nourishment and healing to it (see Prov 16:24). *Future . . . hope:* see Prov 23:18; Pss 9:19; 37:37; 73:24; Jer 29:11.

24:16 *Seven times:* i.e., many times (see Prov 6:16; Job 5:19 and note). *Rises again:* the Lord has promised to come to the aid of the righteous (see Pss 34:20; 37:24; Mic 7:8). *The wicked stumble into calamity:* see Prov 24:22; 4:19; 6:15; 11:3, 5; Pss 1:6; 37:13, 20; 119:155; 146:9.

24:19 This verse is very close to Ps 37:1; see Prov 23:17; 24:1.

24:21 *Fear the LORD and fear the king:* the faithful are to render obedience to the Lord and to civil authority (see Eccl 8:2-5; Mt 18:21-22; Lk 17:4; Rom 13:1ff; 1 Pet 2:13-17). Scripture regards the king as the punisher of the wicked (see Prov 20:8, 26).

22 For disaster will strike them suddenly,
and who knows what ruin will afflict them and their friends? *

V: OTHER SAYINGS OF THE WISE*

23 * These also are sayings of the wise:
To show partiality in judgment
is an invidious act. [i]
24 Whoever says to the wicked, "You are innocent,"
will be cursed by peoples and denounced by nations. [j]
25 But those who convict the evildoer will fare well,
and they will be blessed with prosperity.
26 Anyone who offers an honest answer
gives a kiss on the lips. [k]
27 Plan what you want outside
and make everything ready on the land;
once you have done this,
you can go forth and build your house. [l]
28 Never be a witness against your neighbor without good reason
or deceive with your lips. [m]
29 Never say, "I will do to him as he has done to me;
I will pay him back for what he has done." [n]

I Passed by the Field of a Lazy Idler . . .*

30 I passed by the field of a lazy idler, *
by the vineyard of a man without sense. [o]
31 I saw that it was completely overgrown with thorns;
the ground was covered with weeds,
and its stone wall was broken down. [p]
32 And as I gazed at it and reflected,
I drew this lesson from the sight: [q]
33 a little sleep, a little slumber,
a little folding of the arms to rest, [r]
34 and poverty will come upon you like a thief,
and want will assail you like an armed warrior. [s]

VI: PROVERBS OF SOLOMON FROM THE COLLECTION OF THE MEN OF HEZEKIAH*

CHAPTER 25

1 These are some other proverbs of Solomon that were transcribed by the men of King Hezekiah of Judah: [t]

God, the King, and the People*

2 To keep something secret is the glory of God,
but to have it searched out is the glory of kings. [u]
3 Like the heavens in height and the earth in depth,
the heart of a king is unfathomable. *
4 If you remove the dross from silver,
it emerges completely purified. [v]

i Prov 18:5; 28:21; Ex 18:16; Lev 19:15; Deut 1:17; 16:19; Ps 72:2; Jer 22:16.—j Prov 17:15.—k Prov 11:3.—l Prov 14:1; 28:19.—m Prov 19:5; 25:18; Ps 7:5.—n Prov 20:22; Mt 5:38-41.—o Prov 6:6-11; 26:13-16.—p Isa 5:5.—q Prov 22:17.—r Prov 6:10f.—s Prov 10:4; Eccl 10:18.—t Prov 1:1; 1 Ki 4:1.—u Prov 16:10-15.—v Prov 8:19; Ezek 22:18.

24:22 After this verse, the Greek text adds five verses as follows:

22a A son who keeps the commandment will escape destruction,
for he embraced it willingly.
22b Let no falsehood be spoken by the tongue of the king,
yes, let no falsehood proceed from his tongue.
22c The king's tongue is a sword, not some fleshly thing,
and whoever is handed up to him will be crushed.
22d For if his wrath is provoked,
he destroys men with all their sinews.
22e He devours men's bones
and like a flame burns them up,
so that they are not even fit to be eaten by young eagles.

The Greek text then appends here chapter 30:1-14.

24:23-34 This is a brief appendix written in the same style and spirit as the preceding collection.

24:23-29 To the ancient counsels on respect for justice in trials and on prudence, a new one is added: evil must not be done (see Mt 16:12, 14-15).

24:30-34 A splendid lesson about things that would also be a fine popular song.

24:30 *Idler:* see note on Prov 6:6.

25:1—29:27 The kingdom of the North disappeared in 721 B.C. with the fall of Samaria; only the southern kingdom, the Kingdom of Judah remained. Hezekiah was the first to preside over the latter's destiny after the great catastrophe in the North. He left behind him the memory of a founder and organizer (2 Ki 18–20; 2 Chr 29–32). One of his undertakings was to assemble at Jerusalem the writings that Israel already possessed, those of the North as well as those of the South. With the help of the scribes, who were the educated people of the time, he organized a kind of national library. At that time some proverbs were collected as they stood; these, no doubt, form the main block in this part of the Book. Later on, scribes transcribing and commenting on this collection must have added further sayings. Together with chapters 10–22, to which it is related by content and style, this collection is the oldest part of the present Book of Proverbs. In general, the sayings remain without order; once or twice, however, the authors have tried to group together some proverbs that are concerned with the same theme. Accordingly, we will suggest simply a few points that merit attention.

25:2-7 Since the prince is held in great esteem by his subjects, above all he is expected to be just.

25:3 *The heart of a king is unfathomable:* i.e., it cannot be understood—like the four things in Prov 30:18-19—yet God has control over a king's heart (see Prov 21:1).

5 If you remove the wicked from the king's presence,
his throne will be founded on righteousness. [w]

6 * Do not push yourself forward in the king's presence
or take a place where the great assemble.
7 For it is better to be told, "Come up closer,"
than to be humiliated in the presence of the prince. [x]

Observations and Recommendations*

8 What your eyes have witnessed,
do not hastily testify to at the trial;
for what will you do at the end
when your neighbor puts you to shame? [y]
9 Argue your case with your neighbor
but do not disclose another's secret, [z]
10 for fear your listener will reproach you
and your reputation will be irretrievably damaged. *
11 Like apples of gold inlaid with silver
are words that are aptly spoken. [a]
12 Like a gold ring or a necklace of fine gold
is a wise man's rebuke to an attentive ear. [b]
13 Like the coolness of snow at the time of harvest
is a faithful messenger to those who dispatch him;
he revives the spirit of his masters. [c]
14 Like clouds and wind that bring no rain *
is the one who boasts of gifts that are never given. [d]
15 A ruler may be won over by patience,
and a gentle tongue can break bones. [e]
16 If you find honey, eat only enough to satisfy you,
for if you consume too much, you will vomit it up. [f]
17 Do not enter too frequently into your neighbor's house
lest he become tired of you and begin to hate you.
18 Like a club or a sword or a keen arrow
is one who bears false witness against a neighbor. [g]
19 Like a decaying tooth or a lame foot
is trust in a faithless man on the day of trouble. [h]
20 Like one who takes away clothing on a cold day,
like one who dresses a wound with vinegar,
is one who sings songs to a grieving heart. * [i]
21 * If your enemy is hungry, give him something to eat;
if he is thirsty, offer him something to drink. [j]
22 By doing so you will heap fiery coals upon his head,
and the LORD will reward you. [k]
23 The north wind produces rain,
and a backbiting tongue causes angry looks.
24 It is better to live on the corner of a roof
than to share a spacious house with a nagging wife. * [l]
25 Like cold water to a thirsty throat
is good news from a distant land. [m]
26 Like a muddy spring or a polluted well
is a righteous man who trembles before the wicked. [n]
27 It is not good to eat too much honey,
neither is it honorable to seek one's own honor. [o]
28 Like a city that has been breached and made defenseless
is the man devoid of self-control.

w Prov 16:12; 20:8; 2 Sam 7:13.—x Lk 14:7-10.—y Mt 5:25-26.—z Mt 18:15.—a Prov 15:23; 25:12.—b Prov 13:18; 25:11; Ps 141:5.—c Prov 10:26; 13:17.—d 2 Pet 2:17; Jude 12.—e Prov 15:1, 4; Eccl 10:4.—f Prov 25:27.—g Prov 12:18.—h Prov 16:29.—i Sir 30:24.—j Rom 12:20.—k 2 Chr 28:15; Ps 18:9; Mt 5:44; Rom 12:20.—l Prov 21:9.—m Prov 15:30.—n Ezek 32:2.—o Prov 25:16; 27:2; Mt 23:12.

25:6-7 Jesus spoke of a similar situation and called for humility (see Lk 14:10).

25:8-28 In these varied sayings, one will find many considerations about human relations: trials, the true word, fidelity. There is also a less current idea that recommends going to the aid of enemies (vv. 21-22), which is cited by Paul in Rom 12:20 to inculcate love of enemies; the coals may signify the remorse that leads to repentance.

25:10 *Your reputation will be irretrievably damaged:* an honorable name is more precious than great wealth (see note on Prov 22:1).

25:14 *Clouds . . . that bring no rain:* this image is applied by the New Testament to those who bear no fruit (see Jude 12).

25:20 The bitterness of suffering is increased because of a neighbor's insensitivity.

25:21-22 These two verses are quoted by Paul (see Rom 12:20) as expressing a way to overcome evil with good (see also Prov 20:22).

25:24 We have already seen this pessimistic saying in Prov 21:9.

CHAPTER 26

How To Deal with the Foolish*

1 Like snow in the summer or rain during the harvest, *
honor does not befit a fool. [p]
2 Like a fluttering sparrow or a swallow in flight,
an undeserved curse will never reach home. [q]
3 Use a whip for a horse, a bridle for a donkey,
and a stick for the back of fools. * [r]
4 * Do not reply to a fool in the terms of his folly
or you yourself may become a fool like him. [s]
5 Reply to a fool in the terms of his folly
or he will consider himself wise. [t]
6 Like cutting off one's foot or submitting to violence
is sending a message by a fool. [u]
7 Like the legs of a lame man dangling helplessly
is a proverb in the mouth of a fool. [v]
8 Like tying a stone into a sling
is the giving of honor to a fool. [w]
9 Like a thorn branch brandished by a drunkard
is a proverb in the mouth of a fool. [x]
10 Like an archer who wounds all who pass by
is one who hires a fool or a drunkard.
11 As a dog returns to its vomit, *
so a fool reverts to his folly. [y]
12 Do you know someone who regards himself as wise? *
There is more hope for a fool than for him. [z]

A Portrait of Idlers*

13 The idler says, "There is a lion in the road,
a lion in the middle of the street." * [a]
14 As a door turns on its hinges,
so does the idler on his bed. [b]
15 One who is lazy will dip his hand into the dish,
but he is too lazy to lift it to his mouth. * [c]
16 The idler considers himself to be more wise
than seven men who can offer a sensible reply. [d]

How Human Relations Are Perverted*

17 Like one who lifts up a stray dog by the ears
is he who meddles in another person's quarrel.
18 Like a madman shooting at random
his deadly firebrands and arrows, [e]
19 so is the one who deceives his neighbor
and then says, "I was only joking."
20 When there is no wood, the fire goes out,
and when there is no talebearer, quarreling ceases. [f]
21 Like coal for burning embers and wood for fire,
so is a quarrelsome man for kindling strife. [g]
22 The whispers of a gossiper are tasty morsels
that corrode one's inner being. [h]
23 Like glaze that is spread on earthenware
are smooth lips and a spiteful heart. [i]

p Prov 19:10; 26:8; 1 Sam 12:17.—q Deut 23:5.—r Prov 19:29; Ps 32:9; Sir 33:25.—s Prov 26:5; Isa 36:21.—t Prov 3:7; 26:4.—u Prov 10:26.—v Prov 26:9.—w Prov 26:1.—x Prov 26:7.—y 2 Pet 2:22.—z Prov 3:7; 29:20.—a Prov 6:6-11; 22:13; 24:30-34.—b Prov 6:9.—c Prov 19:24.—d Prov 26:5, 12.—e Isa 50:11.—f Prov 22:10.—g Prov 14:17; 15:18; 29:22.—h Prov 18:8.—i Mt 23:27; Lk 11:39.

26:1-12 Opposed to wisdom is folly, which is not mere thoughtlessness but rather stupidity that is synonymous with wickedness, vicious fickleness or instability, and the refusal to consider God, humans, and the order of things. Such folly is, in the eyes of the ancients, congenital and without remedy. Hence, the Book of Proverbs never seeks to convert the foolish or senseless; its purpose is to caution the naive and the simple against such behavior. This is a point of pride, however, for the greatest folly is to believe oneself to be a sage (Prov 3:7).

26:1 *Rain during the harvest:* rain rarely occurs in Palestine during the harvest, i.e., June through September.

26:3 *A stick for the back of fools:* see Prov 14:3; 19:29.

26:4-5 These are two deliberately contradictory sayings, signifying: do not pay attention to the words of a fool or else make him realize his folly, depending on the case.

26:11 *As a dog returns to its vomit:* cited in 2 Pet 2:22 in regard to false teachers.

26:12 *Someone who regards himself as wise:* this description is applied to the idler in verses 5, 16 and to the rich in Prov 28:11.

26:13-16 The popular proverbs use sarcasm in their biting caricatures of idlers. The Book of Proverbs has collected numerous sayings about this subject (see note on Prov 6:6) and here others have been appended.

26:13 See note on Prov 22:13.

26:15 This verse is almost identical to Prov 19:24.

26:17-28 Once anger has allowed it to come to the fore, when will the demon of divisiveness, falsehood, and calumny come to a halt? As fine psychologists, the ancients had noticed how such tendencies deaden the human heart in the manner of a bad ineradicable herb.

24 With his lips an enemy may speak fair words,
but deep within he harbors treachery.
25 When he speaks graciously, do not believe him,
for seven abominations* lurk in his heart.[j]
26 A man may cloak his hatred with guile,
but his wickedness will be exposed later in the assembly.
27 Whoever digs a pit will fall into it,*
and the stone comes back on the one who rolls it.[k]
28 A lying tongue hates its victims,
and a flattering mouth causes devastation.[l]

CHAPTER 27

Dictums about Every Circumstance*

1 Do not boast about tomorrow,
for you can never be certain what today may bring.*[m]
2 Let another praise you, and not your own mouth;
let it come from the lips of someone else and not your own.[n]
3 Stone is heavy and sand is a dead weight,
but heavier than both is a fool's provocation.[o]
4 Wrath is cruel and anger is overwhelming,
but who can withstand jealousy?[p]
5 Better is an open rebuke
than concealed love.*[q]
6 The blows given by a friend* are well meant,
but the kisses of an enemy are filled with deceit.[r]
7 One whose appetite is sated refuses honey,
but to the man who is hungry even bitter food tastes sweet.[s]
8 Like a bird that strays from its nest
is anyone who is far away from home.[t]
9 Perfume and incense gladden the heart,
and friendship's sweetness comforts the soul.*[u]
10 Do not forsake your friend or the friend of your father,
and do not run to your brother's house when troubles befall you;
far better is a friend nearby
than a brother who is far away.[v]
11 Acquire wisdom, my son, and gladden my heart,
so that I may rebut anyone who insults me.[w]
12 The prudent man perceives danger and seeks shelter,
while the simple* continue forward and pay the penalty.[x]
13 Take the garment of anyone who becomes surety for a stranger;
demand a pledge for persons unknown* to you.[y]
14 If someone blesses his neighbor at dawn with a loud voice,
it will be reckoned to him as a curse.*
15 A constant dripping on a rainy day
is much like a nagging wife;*[z]
16 one might as well try to restrain the wind
as to control her,
or to pick up oil with one's fingers.
17 As iron sharpens iron,
so a man sharpens the wits of his neighbor.
18 Whoever tends a fig tree eats its fruit,
and whoever looks after his master will be honored.[a]

j Ps 28:3; Sir 12:10; 27:23; Jer 9:4.—k Prov 28:10; Est 7:10; Ps 7:16; Eccl 10:8-9.—l Prov 29:5; Ps 12:4.—m Mt 6:34; Jas 4:13-16.—n Prov 25:27.—o Job 6:3; Sir 22:14f.—p Num 5:14.—q Prov 28:23.—r Prov 26:24; Ps 141:5.—s Prov 25:16; Job 6:7; Lk 15:17.—t Isa 16:2.—u Prov 16:21, 24; Est 2:12; Ps 45:9.—v Prov 17:17.—w Prov 10:1; 23:15-16.—x Prov 22:3.—y Prov 20:16.—z Prov 21:9; 25:24; Est 1:18.—a Lk 19:12-27; 1 Cor 9:7.

26:25 *Seven abominations:* i.e., "many."

26:27 *Whoever digs a pit will fall into it:* see Pss 7:16-17; 35:8; 141:10; see also Prov 1:18; 28:10; 29:6; Est 2:23; 7:10; Eccl 10:8-9; Sir 27:25f.

27:1-22 Among these simple but striking proverbs, several evoke the cost of friendship (vv. 6-10), one in verse 13 places people on guard against surety for foreigners (see Prov 6:1-5; 20:16), and one in verse 15 brings together the pessimistic proposal about a nagging wife (see Prov 19:13).

27:1 See Prov 16:9; Mt 6:34; Jas 4:13-16; see also Isa 56:12 and the words of the rich fool in Lk 12:19-20.

27:5 A true friend brings out not only his friend's virtues but also his vices, thus rendering a great service to his friend.

27:6 *The blows given by a friend:* these are termed a "kindness" in Ps 141:5. *Kisses of an enemy:* see Mt 26:49.

27:9 *Friendship's sweetness comforts the soul:* see Prov 16:21, 24.

27:12 *The simple:* see note on Prov 1:4.

27:13 See Prov 20:16 and note. *Persons unknown:* Vulgate reading; the Hebrew has: "a foreign woman."

27:14 Premature praise can become an affliction (see Ps 12:3).

27:15 See note on Prov 19:13.

19 Just as water reflects one's face,
so does one human heart reflect another. * [b]

20 The netherworld and the abyss * are never satisfied;
the same is true of human eyes. [c]

21 As silver is tested by a crucible and gold by a furnace,
so too is a man tested by the praise he is given. [d]

22 You may use a pestle to pound a fool into a mortar,
but his folly will never be driven out of him. [e]

Take Good Care of Your Herds*

23 Be aware at all times of the condition of your flocks
and take good care of your herds. [f]

24 For riches do not last forever,
nor will a crown endure from age to age. [g]

25 When the grass is gone and the aftergrowth appears
and the green growth of the mountains is gathered,

26 the lambs will provide for your clothing,
and the goats will give you the price of a field;

27 there will be enough goats' milk *
to feed you and your household
and to provide sustenance for your servant girls.

CHAPTER 28

Two Types of Men*

1 The wicked flee even though no one is pursuing them,
but the righteous are as confident as young lions. [h]

2 When a land is in revolt, it has many leaders, *
but it will enjoy security under a prudent leader.

3 A needy man * who oppresses the poor
is like a drenching rain that destroys the crops. [i]

4 Those who forsake the law * praise the wicked man,
but those who observe the law are in constant opposition to him. [j]

5 Evildoers simply cannot comprehend justice,
but those who seek the LORD * understand it completely. [k]

6 It is far better to be poor and beyond reproach
than to become rich through dishonest means. [l]

7 A wise son obeys the law,
but a companion of gluttons shames his father. [m]

8 Whoever increases his wealth by charging exorbitant interest *
amasses it for another who will be generous to the poor. [n]

b Prov 20:5.—c Prov 30:16; Eccl 4:8; Hab 2:5.—d Prov 17:3.—e Jer 2:30.—f Prov 12:10.—g Prov 23:5.—h Lev 26:17; Ps 138:3.—i Prov 14:31; Mt 18:28.—j Rom 1:32.—k Jn 12: 39-40; 1 Cor 2:15; 1 Jn 2:20.—l Prov 19:1.—m Prov 23:19-21. —n Job 27:17; Ezek 18:8.

27:19 The Greek has: "As no two faces are ever alike, / unlike also are the hearts of men."

27:20 *The netherworld and the abyss:* see note on Job 26:6; see also Prov 15:11. *Are never satisfied:* see Isa 5:14. *The same is true of human eyes:* see Eccl 4:8.

27:23-27 For the wisdom of the countryside, it is an art and a duty, both of prudence and humanity, to make one's goods bear fruit.

27:27 *Goats' milk:* the milk of both goats and cows was drunk (see Deut 32:13-14; Isa 7:21-22).

28:1—29:27 The proverbs succeed each other without any connection among them. There is little new in these chapters for those who have already perused the great collection of Solomon, i.e., chapters 1–22. Perhaps the continuous reading of these disparate verses brings out more clearly the opposition between wisdom and folly, justice and evil. There is no middle ground between these two lines of life, these two modes of thought, these two ways of feeling. Whether pauper or prince, everyone belongs to one or the other. Indeed, human beings make their choice each day in their private and in their social behavior, in their education and in their duties. Wisdom is an option for authenticity, a profound comprehension of life. Since the remote time when these proverbs were fashioned, the cultural climate has changed. Yet it is still true that our age of conflict and self-indulgent desires has need of a wisdom, a rectitude, a supplement for one's soul without which there is no respect for self, for others, and for God! These ancient texts do not give us a letter to be observed; rather they invite us to discover for ourselves a meaning to life and put it into practice.

28:2 When a nation is corrupt, its *leaders* have no permanency, revolts spring up, and various personages appear who scheme to win the crown at any cost.

28:3 *A needy man:* another translation is "a ruler" (or "tyrant"). *Who oppresses the poor:* see Prov 14:31. *Drenching rain:* a similar phrase is used to indicate a destructive army (Isa 28:2), while a gentler rain is used to indicate a righteous king (Ps 72:6-7).

28:4 *The law:* it can refer to the teachings of wisdom (Prov 3:1; 7:2) or the law of Moses (Ps 119:53).

28:5 *Those who seek the LORD:* i.e., those who fear him (see note on Prov 1:7). *Understand it completely:* they "understand equity and justice / as well as righteousness—every good path" (Prov 2:9).

28:8 *Exorbitant interest:* was forbidden (see Ex 22:24; Lev 25:35-37; Deut 23:20-21; Ezek 22:12). *Amasses it for another:* see Prov 13:22. *Generous to the poor:* see Prov 14:31.

9 When anyone turns a deaf ear to the law,
even his prayer is detestable. * [o]
10 Whoever tempts the upright into following evil ways
will fall into his own pit,
but the blameless will have a good inheritance. [p]
11 The rich man may believe he is wise,
but the poor man with discernment will see through him. [q]
12 When the righteous triumph, there is a great celebration,
but when the wicked prevail, the people go into hiding. [r]
13 No one who conceals his transgressions will prosper,
but one who confesses and renounces them will obtain mercy. * [s]
14 Blessed is the man who guards himself against temptation, *
but anyone who hardens his heart will be overtaken by evil. [t]
15 Like a roaring lion or a bear on the prowl
is a wicked man who governs a powerless people. [u]
16 A ruler who lacks sense will oppress his subjects,
but one who detests ill-gotten gain will have a long life. [v]
17 Someone guilty of murder will be a fugitive till death;
no one should attempt to stop him. [w]
18 Anyone who leads a blameless life will be safe,
but whoever follows a crooked path will fall into the pit. [x]
19 One who tills his land will not lack for food,
but he who chases fantasies * will live in poverty. [y]
20 One who is trustworthy will abound with blessings, *
but no one who seeks to get rich quickly will go unpunished. [z]
21 To show partiality * is never good;
a man may do wrong even for a morsel of bread. [a]
22 The miser is in a hurry to get rich,
never considering that want may eventually afflict him. * [b]
23 Whoever rebukes another * will in the end win more thanks
than one who flatters with his tongue. [c]
24 Anyone who robs his father or mother
and denies that he has sinned
is no better than a marauding bandit. [d]
25 A greedy person provokes quarrels,
but whoever trusts in the LORD will have success. [e]
26 Anyone who trusts in his own wits is a fool,
but he whose guide is wisdom * will come through safely. [f]
27 No one who gives to the poor will suffer want,
but one who closes his eyes to them will get many a curse. * [g]
28 When the wicked gain power, people go into hiding,
but when the wicked perish, the righteous increase in number. [h]

CHAPTER 29

1 One who remains stubborn despite frequent reproof
will suddenly be crushed beyond hope of repair. [i]
2 When the righteous are in authority, the people rejoice,

o Prov 15:8; 21:27; Isa 1:13.—p Prov 26:27; Ps 57:7.—q Prov 20:5; 26:5, 16.—r Prov 29:2; Eccl 10:6.—s Lev 5:5; 2 Sam 12:13; Job 31:33; Ps 32:1-5; 1 Jn 1:9.—t Prov 23:17.—u Prov 19:12; 20:2.—v Prov 1:19.—w 1 Ki 20:20; Jer 41:15.—x Prov 10:9; Jer 19:18.—y Prov 12:11.—z Prov 13:11; 28:22.—a Prov 18:5; 24:23; Lev 19:15; Ezek 13:19.—b Prov 28:20.—c Prov 27:5-6.—d Prov 19:26; Mk 7:11ff.—e Prov 14:17; 29:25.—f 1 Cor 3:18.—g Prov 19:17; 22:9.—h Prov 28:12.—i 2 Chr 36:16; Jer 17:23.

28:9 Prayers offered without good faith are detestable—like the sacrifice of the wicked (see Prov 15:8; see also Prov 3:32; Ps 66:18; Isa 1:15; 59:1-2).

28:13 Sin weighs heavily on those who do not own up to it (see Prov 3:7-8; Ps 32:3), but those who acknowledge their sin find mercy, forgiveness, and joy (see Ps 32:5, 10-11).

28:14 *Guards himself against temptation:* i.e., fears the Lord (see note on Prov 1:7; see also Prov 23:17).

28:19 *Chases fantasies:* hatches plots to gain ill-gotten goods (see also Prov 12:11).

28:20 *Will abound with blessings:* i.e., God's blessings (see Prov 3:13-18; 10:6; Gen 49:25-26; Deut 33:13-16).

28:21 *Partiality:* see note on Prov 18:5. *May do wrong . . . bread:* may refer to taking a bribe in the form of bread (see Ezek 13:19).

28:22 Get-rich-quick schemes often lead to ruin; only the man who is generous will prosper (see note on Prov 11:24).

28:23 *Rebukes another:* see Prov 15:31; 25:12. *Flatters with his tongue:* see Prov 16:13; 26:28; 29:5.

28:26 *He whose guide is wisdom:* i.e., he who trusts in the Lord (see Prov 3:5; 29:25).

28:27 Generosity to the poor brings blessings (see Prov 11:24 and note; 14:21; 19:17).

but they groan when the wicked ascend
to power.[j]
3 A man who loves wisdom makes his
father glad,
but a patron of prostitutes squanders
his wealth.[k]
4 By ruling justly a king gives stability to his
country,
but one who takes bribes causes its
downfall.[l]
5 Anyone who flatters his neighbor
is spreading a net to trip him up.[m]
6 An evildoer is ensnared by his own sin,
but an upright man goes forward hap-
pily.[n]
7 A righteous man has concern for the con-
dition of the poor,
but an evildoer shows no interest in this
matter.[o]
8 Scoffers can set a city aflame, *
but wise men turn away wrath.[p]
9 If a wise man argues with a fool,
he will get nowhere whether he rages or
laughs.[q]
10 Bloodthirsty men hate one who is blame-
less, *
but the upright show concern for
him.[r]
11 A fool gives free rein to his anger,
but a wise man bides his time and
calms it.[s]
12 If a ruler listens to the testimony of liars,
all of his officials will adopt evil ways.[t]
13 A poor man and an oppressor have this in
common:
the LORD gives light to the eyes of
both. *[u]
14 If a king zealously defends the rights of
the poor,
his throne will stand firm forever.[v]
15 The rod of correction * bestows wisdom,
but an unreprimanded youth will bring
shame on his mother.[w]
16 When the wicked are in power, sins
increase,
but the righteous will witness their
downfall.[x]
17 If you correct your son, * he will give you
peace of mind
and bring delight to your soul.[y]
18 Without prophecy the people become
uncontrollable,
but blessed are those who keep the
law. *[z]
19 Mere words do not suffice to control a
servant;
even though he understands, he will
not obey you.[a]
20 Do you see someone who is too eager to
speak?
There is more hope for a fool than for
him.[b]
21 If you pamper a slave from his childhood,
in the end he will prove ungrateful. *
22 A bad-tempered man provokes quarrels,
and a hothead commits a host of
offenses.[c]
23 A man's pride will bring him low,
but lowly souls will rise to honor.[d]
24 The accomplice of a thief is his own
enemy,
for he hears the curse * but refuses to
answer.[e]
25 The fear of others will prove to be a snare,
but whoever trusts in the LORD is
secure.[f]
26 Many seek the favor of a ruler,
but it is the LORD who administers jus-
tice.[g]

j Prov 11:10; 28:12; 2 Ki 11:20.—k Prov 5:10; 6:26; 10:1; 23:15-16; Lk 15:11-32.—l Prov 8:15-16; 29:14.—m Prov 26:28; Job 32:21.—n Prov 26:27; Eccl 9:12.—o Prov 31:8-9.—p Prov 11:11; 16:14.—q Mt 11:16-19.—r Prov 29:27; 1 Jn 3:12.—s Prov 12:16; Sir 21:26.—t 2 Ki 21:9.—u Prov 22:2; Mt 5:45.—v Prov 16:12; 29:4; Ps 72:1-5.—w Prov 13:24; 22:15; 23:13f.—x Pss 91:8; 92:12.—y Prov 29:15.—z Pss 1:1-2; 18:12; 119:1-2.—a Sir 33:25f.—b Prov 19:2; 26:12; Eccl 5:1.—c Prov 15:18; 26:21.—d Prov 11:2; 15:33; 16:18; 18:12; Job 22:29.—e Lev 5:1.—f Prov 16:20; 28:25.—g Prov 16:33; 19:6.

29:8 *Scoffers can set a city aflame:* see note on Prov 1:22; see also Prov 6:14; 11:11; 26:21.

29:10 *Bloodthirsty men hate one who is blameless:* and they hatch plots against him (see Prov 1:11-16).

29:13 *The LORD gives light to the eyes of both:* i.e., gives life, just as he makes the sun to shine on the just and the unjust (see Mt 5:45).

29:15 *Rod of correction:* see note on Prov 13:24.

29:17 *Correct your son:* teach him and train him (see Prov 13:24; 22:6).

29:18 The Prophet was not only God's spokesperson but also the people's teacher and guide, leading them to keep the divine law. *Blessed are those who keep the law:* see note on Prov 31:28.

29:21 Vulgate reading; the meaning of the Hebrew is uncertain.

29:24 The meaning of the Hebrew is uncertain. *Curse:* i.e., the curse leveled at an unidentified criminal or at a witness who fails to come forward (see Lev 5:1; Jdg 17:2).

27 A sinful man is abhorrent to the upright,
and one who leads a holy life is hated by the wicked. [h]

VII: THE SAYINGS OF AGUR*

CHAPTER 30

1 The sayings of Agur, son of Jakeh, from Massa: *

This is my statement: I am weary, O God;
I am weary, O God, and worn out. [i]

Like Job*

2 I count myself among the most stupid of men,
and I am bereft of human understanding.
3 I have not learned wisdom,
nor do I have any knowledge of the Most Holy One. [j]
4 Who has ever gone up to heaven and come down again?
Who has cupped the wind in the hollow of his hands?
Who has wrapped the waters in the fold of his garment?
Who has established all the boundaries of the earth?
What is his name or the name of his son?
Do you know it? * [k]
5 Every word of God has proved to be true;
he is a shield to those who trust in him. * [l]
6 Add nothing to his words,
lest he reprove you and expose you as a fraud. [m]

Like Solomon*

7 Two things * I ask of you;
do not deny them to me before I die: [n]
8 Keep falsehood and lying far from me;
give me neither poverty nor riches,
but simply provide me with the food that I need. [o]
9 For if I have too much, I may deny you
and say, "Who is the LORD?"
And if I am destitute, I may begin to steal
and profane the name of my God. [p]

People with Neither Faith Nor Law*

10 Do not slander a servant to his master,
lest he curse you and you will be held guilty
11 There are those who curse their fathers
and do not bless their mothers. * [q]
12 They regard themselves as pure
and yet have not been cleansed of their filth. [r]
13 They have eyes that are haughty * [s]
and glances that reveal their disdain.
14 They have teeth that are swords
and jaws that are knives.
They devour the poor of the earth
and the needy from among men. [t]

VIII: NUMERICAL PROVERBS*

Insatiable Things*

15 The leech has two daughters,
each of whom demands, "Give! Give!"
There are three things that are never satisfied,
four that never say "Enough!": [u]

h Prov 29:10.—i Prov 22:17.—j Prov 9:10.—k Deut 30:12; Ps 24:1-2; Jn 3:13; Eph 4:7-10.—l Gen 15:1; Pss 12:7; 18:31.—m Deut 4:2.—n Gen 45:28.—o Mt 6:11.—p Deut 6:12; Jos 24:27; Hos 13:6.—q Prov 20:20.—r Prov 16:2; Jer 2:23, 35.—s 2 Sam 22:28.—t Job 4:10; Pss 3:8; 57:5; Am 8:4.—u Prov 27:20.

30:1-14 This is a short collection of the sayings of a foreigner, one of the "sons of the East" whose wisdom was greatly esteemed (1 Ki 5:10; Jer 49:7), men such as Lemuel (see Prov 31:1-9) or Job and his friends. Agur may be an imaginary personage, but bringing him on the scene is evidence that wisdom transcends the borders of the chosen people. Wisdom is universal and must welcome the truth wherever it is found. Agur is a simple man, amazed by the mystery of nature, who humbly prays for perseverance.

30:1 The second part of this verse presents translation difficulties. Both the Vulgate and the Septuagint have different interpretations. *Massa:* an Ishmaelite tribe north of Arabia, in the eastern part of Palestine (see Gen 25:14).

30:2-6 In this dialogue with God, the sage loses all his assurance; he is no longer the man who knows everything. The mystery of God is divined in creation, but who could attain such knowledge! Can human beings do anything else but respectfully embrace his word, i.e., the Law and the Prophets and perhaps the teachings of the sages?

30:4 See the similar use of rhetorical questions to express God's greatness in Job 38:4-11; Isa 40:12. *Do you know it?:* see Job 38:4.

30:5 This verse is very close to Ps 18:31.

30:7-9 In a humble prayer, human beings can ask for a good heart and, for the rest, their share of bread: what is necessary suffices (see Mt 6:11). Indeed, if wretchedness leads to the edge of revolt, wealth easily leads to contempt for God.

30:7 *Two things:* these sayings are fond of using lists (see vv. 15, 18, 21, 24, 29). See note on Prov 6:16-19.

30:10-14 After verse 10, there is a diatribe against falsehood and violence, i.e., the crime of those who wish to dominate by despising others.

30:11 See note on Prov 20:20.

30:13 *Eyes that are haughty:* see note on Prov 6:17.

30:15-33 These are termed "numerical proverbs" because they use numbers: *There are three things . . . four . . .*; these figures stand for a quantity that cannot be exactly counted. They propose a truth in a witty way that constitutes their charm (see also note on Prov 6:16-19). Some proverbs of another kind (vv. 17-20, 32-33) have slipped in like intruders in this short collection.

30:15-16 Here we see presented the leech, model of the parasite. Then the proverb evokes the power of a desire that is never fulfilled. The netherworld is the abyss of death that ceaselessly swallows up human generations.

16 The netherworld and the barren womb,
the earth that is thirsty for water,
and fire that never says "Enough!" [v]

Woe to the Wicked Son

17 The eye that mocks a father
or shows scorn to an aged mother
will be plucked out by the ravens of the valley
and eaten by the vultures.* [w]

The Astounding Mystery of Generation

18 There are three things too wonderful for me to comprehend,
four that are beyond my understanding: [x]
19 the way of an eagle in the sky,
the way of a snake over a rock,
the way of a ship on the high seas,
and the way of a man with a maiden. *

"I Have Done Nothing Wrong"*

20 This is the way of an adulteress:
she eats, then wipes her mouth
and says, "I have done nothing wrong." [y]

The Insolence of the Newly Successful

21 There are three things that cause the earth to tremble,
indeed four things that it cannot endure: [z]
22 a slave crowned as a king,
a fool gorged with food, [a]
23 a hateful woman when she snares a husband,
and a servant girl when she supplants her mistress. [b]

The Resourceful Little Ones*

24 There are four creatures among the tiniest on the earth
who are nevertheless exceedingly wise:
25 the ants, a species without strength,
yet they gather their food in the summer; [c]
26 the rock-badgers, a species without power,
yet they make their home in the rocks; [d]
27 the locusts, a species without a king,
yet they all march forth in formation; [e]
28 the lizards, a species you can catch in your hands,
yet they are found in the palaces of kings. [f]

The King, Majestic among Other Animals*

29 There are three creatures that are stately in their stride,
four that are stately as they walk: [g]
30 the lion, the mightiest of wild animals,
who retreats from nothing;
31 the strutting rooster, the he-goat, *
and a king at the head of his army.

Silence Is Golden, Especially in Time of Anger

32 If you have been foolish enough to exalt yourself *
or if you have devised evil,
put your hand over your mouth. [h]
33 For as churning the milk produces curds
and twisting the nose produces blood,
so stirring up anger produces strife.

IX: THE SAYINGS OF LEMUEL*

CHAPTER 31

A Splendid Program for a King

1 These are the words of Lemuel, king of Massa, which were taught to him by his mother: * [i]

v Prov 27:20; Isa 5:14; 14:9, 11; Hab 2:5.—w Deut 21:18-21; Job 15:23.—x Prov 30:15.—y Prov 5:3.—z Joel 2:10; Am 8:8.—a Prov 19:10; 29:2; Eccl 10:6f.—b Gen 16:3; Deut 21:15-17; Isa 54:1.—c Prov 6:6-8.—d Lev 11:5; Ps 104:18.—e Ex 10:4.—f Lev 11:20, 27.—g Prov 6:16; 30:15, 18, 21.—h Job 29:9.—i Prov 22:17.

30:17 See verse 11 and note on Prov 20:20.

30:19 *The way of a man with a maiden:* an obscure saying that may mean how a man is born of a young woman (see Ps 139:13-18), or how the affection that draws a man to a young woman is awakened in him.

30:20 A reader who has misunderstood the poetry in the preceding verses has added this reflection, which is closer to his moralizing preoccupations: the adulteress is cunning enough to camouflage her offense.

30:24-28 The labor of the ant has already been cited, e.g., in Prov 6:6-8. The rock-badger, a small mammiferous savage, shows how to find shelter even if one is not among the powerful. In evoking the lizard, one is undoubtedly thinking of the courtesan of modest state who comes to sneak into the palace where she does nothing but gild herself in the king's sunshine.

30:29-31 Here we have a bit of popular irony before a ceremonial parade. True majesty is something else.

30:31 *He-goat:* goats were used to lead flocks of sheep (see Jer 50:8; Dan 8:5).

30:32 *Exalt yourself:* see condemnation of pride in Prov 8:13; 11:2; 16:18. *Devised evil:* see Prov 6:14; 16:27. *Put your hand over your mouth:* i.e., cease your plotting (see Job 21:5; 40:4).

31:1-9 Lemuel is the unknown (and possibly legendary and imaginary) leader of a foreign tribe. The fact that words of wisdom are attributed to him proves that wisdom is found everywhere.

More than other people, kings are exposed to the danger of loose women and drunkenness. A prince who is sober and vigilant, humane and just, is the ideal of the desert chiefs. He is set against the fake refinement of overly civil princes.

31:1 *His mother:* the queen mother had great influence (see 1 Ki 1:11-13; 15:13). The whole chapter brings out the huge role played by wise women in society.

2 O my son, O son of my womb,
O son of my vows![j]
3 Do not surrender your vigor to women
or consort with those who cause the ruin of kings. *[k]
4 It is not for kings, O Lemuel,
not for kings to drink wine,
not for princes to crave strong liquor, *[l]
5 lest in their stupor they forget what has been decreed
and pervert the rights of those who are in distress.[m]
6 Give strong drink to someone about to die,
wine to someone in anguish.[n]
7 Let him drink and forget his misfortune
and no longer remember his misery.[o]
8* Speak out for those who cannot speak for themselves,
and defend the rights of the destitute.[p]
9 Speak out and pronounce righteous judgments;
defend the rights of the wretched and the poor.[q]

X: IN PRAISE OF THE VALIANT WOMAN OR THE PERFECT HOMEMAKER*[r]

10 Who can find a worthy wife?
She is far more precious than pearls.[s]
11 Her husband entrusts his heart to her,
for in her he has an unfailing blessing.[t]
12 She works to give him good and not evil
all the days of her life.
13 She selects wool and flax
and works with skillful hands.[u]
14 She is like merchant ships,
accumulating a store of food from far off.
15 She rises while it is still dark *
and apportions food for her household
while assigning tasks to her servant girls.[v]
16 She carefully chooses a field to purchase,
and out of her earnings she plants a vineyard. *
17 She girds herself to work
and plies her arms with vigor.[w]
18 She ensures that her dealings are profitable; *
her lamp remains undimmed throughout the night.[x]
19 She sets her hands to the distaff,
and her fingers grasp the spindle. *[y]
20 She holds out her hands to the poor *
and opens her arms to the needy.[z]
21 When snow arrives, she has no fear for her household,
for all of her servants are warmly clothed.[a]
22 She makes her own bed quilts
and wears fine clothes of linen * and purple.[b]
23 Her husband is well respected at the city gates
as he takes his seat with the elders of the land.[c]

j Jdg 11:30.—k Prov 5:1-14; Deut 17:17; 1 Ki 11:3.—l Prov 20:1; Eccl 10:16-17; Isa 5:22.—m Prov 16:12; 1 Ki 16:9.—n Gen 14:18.—o Est 1:10.—p 1 Sam 19:4.—q Prov 24:23; 29:7.—r 10-31: Sir 26:1ff, 13-18.—s Prov 8:35; 18:23; Ru 3:13.—t Prov 12:4; Gen 2:18.—u 1 Tim 2:9-10.—v Prov 20:13; Lk 12:42.—w Prov 31:25.—x Prov 20:20.—y Eph 4:28.—z Prov 31:9; Deut 15:11.—a Prov 31:13.—b Prov 7:16; Gen 41:42.—c Ex 3:16.

31:3 A warning against sexual misconduct (see Prov 5:9-11; 1 Ki 11:1; Neh 13:26).

31:4 A warning against drunkenness (see note on Prov 20:16; see also Eccl 10:16-17; Hos 7:5).

31:8-9 As the defender of the poor, the king is a representative of God (see Prov 16:10; Job 29:12-17; Ps 82:3; Isa 1:17).

31:10-31 The entire family gathers together to heap praise on the mistress of the home. The husband, a considerate man, devotes himself to his public life. Without fear he can leave to his wife the care of directing the household, providing for domesticity, taking care of the marketing, the fields, and the vine. This golden woman joins to her practical qualities and her sense of work a discreet and communicative piety, the gift of education, the efficacious foresight for all, and attentiveness to the poor. These are natural (but nonetheless attractive) qualities for her. She deserves to be celebrated.

This short poem is better known under the title "Praise of a Strong Woman." Each verse has two parallel members and begins with a letter of the Hebrew alphabet; there are as many verses as there are letters in that alphabet. The passage has therefore been carefully and artfully composed; there is nothing improvised about it. But in the person of the virtuous woman it is ultimately Wisdom herself that is extolled. Wisdom, a profound force in a people, was presented to us at the beginning of the Book as a person who actively intervenes in the human world; the end of the Book harks back to the beginning. The picture drawn is meant to leave us with an attractive ideal of life.

31:15 *She rises while it is still dark:* in this respect, she is the exact opposite of the idler (see Prov 6:9-10; 20:13).

31:16 *She carefully chooses a field to purchase, and . . . she plants a vineyard:* she shows good judgment.

31:18 *Her dealings are profitable:* like wisdom, she is "far more precious than pearls" (v. 10; see Prov 3:15; 8:11). *Her lamp remains undimmed:* a lighted lamp in a family is a sign of prosperity and life; an unlighted lamp is a sign of calamity and death (see Prov 13:9 and note; 20:20; 24:20; 1 Sam 3:3; Job 18:5; 21:17).

31:19 *Distaff . . . spindle:* she takes care of work that was assigned to women at the time.

31:20 *She holds out her hands to the poor:* see Prov 14:21; 22:9; Job 31:16-20.

31:22 *Fine clothes of linen:* a sign of nobility (see Prov 7:16; Gen 41:42). *Purple:* a sign of royalty (see Jdg 8:26; Song 3:10) or wealth (see Lk 16:19; Rev 18:16).

24 She weaves linen garments and sells them,
and she supplies the merchants with sashes. [d]
25 She is clothed with strength and dignity,
and she can afford to laugh at the days to come. * [e]

26 When she opens her mouth, wisdom issues forth,
and on her tongue is kindly advice. * [f]
27 She keeps close watch on the conduct of her household,
and she does not eat the bread of idleness. [g]

28 Her children stand up and proclaim her blessed, *
and her husband joins them in praising her:
29 "Many are the women who have done admirable things, *
but you outdo them all."

30 Charm is deceptive * and beauty is fleeting,
but the woman who fears the LORD is to be praised. [h]
31 Give her a share in what her hands have accomplished, *
and let her works bring her praise at the city gates. [i]

d Jdg 14:12; Isa 3:22.—e Prov 31:17; Job 29:14; Isa 61:10.—f Prov 10:31.—g 2 Thes 3:9-10.—h Prov 11:22; 1 Tim 2:9.—i Prov 11:16; 1 Tim 2:10.

31:25 *She can afford to laugh at the days to come:* i.e., she is without anxiety or worry (see Job 39:7).

31:26 She dispenses wisdom and good advice (see Prov 1:8; 6:20).

31:28 *Blessed:* the happy state of life in fellowship with God, revering him and obeying his laws (see Prov 3:13; 8:34; 28:20; 29:18; Pss 72:17; 94:12; 112:1; 119:1f; 128:1).

31:29 *Many . . . have done admirable things:* see Isa 32:20.

31:30 *Charm is deceptive:* see Prov 5:3. *Beauty is fleeting:* see Job 14:2; 1 Pet 3:3-5. *Who fears the LORD:* see note on Prov 1:7.

31:31 *Share in what her hands have accomplished:* see Prov 12:14. *Bring her praise:* because of her "humility and fear of the LORD" (Prov 22:4).

THE BOOK OF ECCLESIASTES

A Meditation on the Human Condition

This incisive little work is offered to us over the signature of Solomon. His patronage is undoubtedly fictitious, since vocabulary, style, and content make it clear that the work dates back barely to the middle of the third century B.C., when Palestine, now subject to the Ptolemies, was beginning to feel Hellenistic influences.

The author's origin seems rather modest. We may imagine him as residing in an area of traders. In this land with numerous relations to foreign places, Qoheleth has acquired a notably universal culture.

What he says is so simple as to confound the official wisdom. Here is a man who has the courage to put received ideas, and even his own faith, to the test of facts. If Qoheleth curses illusions, he does so with a certain humor and with a certain feeling of tenderness toward people.

It is impossible not to be surprised at finding such a document in the Bible, and in fact it is an exception. It criticizes current wisdom and never mentions the great events of the history of salvation. It is difficult to determine the precise meaning of individual passages, and yet clear lines of thought emerge that bear the mark of the particular motifs of each part.

In fact, the speaker does not offer a doctrine or even a body of ideas. We would say rather that he makes us reflect first and foremost on the human condition, on the interpretations given of it, and on the reality that facts impose. He leads us to reflect in the midst of events without rebelling against them.

In the theology of the Bible this is a transitional book. The old ideas on earthly rewards, whether those of the chosen people or those of the individual righteous person, have been too often contradicted by the facts, and Job had been scandalized by this. Qoheleth does not yet know of eternal rewards. He represents an anxious moment of transition between yesterday's religion and tomorrow's faith.

The author teaches only not to regard earthly success as the ultimate human goal; that is not the form God's reward takes. This criticism of traditional values was needed in order that one day people would be ready to listen to him who will cause scandal by saying: "Blessed are the poor . . . Blessed are the meek," and who will speak, as of something obvious, of a life that does not end when earthly ties are broken—i.e., the astounding announcement of Jesus.

This is a book of transition for us too and hence a book of actuality. In the trial of civilization, in the crisis and uncertainty of religion, in the disorder of culture, Qoheleth suggests to each of us to entrust ourselves serenely to God and God alone. He identifies the human frontiers with their ridiculous pretensions for profit, power, and glory. In a world of conflicts, he points out to us how to cope with the reality of daily living.

Our lives must be centered on God or they will be without meaning and totally unsatisfying (Eccl 2:25). On the contrary, if we "fear God" (Eccl 12:13), we will accept life and its gifts gratefully, use them diligently, and enjoy them fully (Eccl 2:26; 11:8). In the end, we will leave the future to God in the firm hope that he will take care of us, bringing "to judgment all of our deeds" (Eccl 12:14).

The Book of Ecclesiastes may be divided as follows:

I: EDITOR'S NOTE*

CHAPTER 1

1 The words of Qoheleth son of David, king in Jerusalem. [a]

2 Vanity * of vanities, says Qoheleth,
vanity of vanities! Everything is vanity. [b]

3 What profit does anyone gain from all his labor
at which he toils under the sun? * [c]

II: INTRODUCTORY POEM*

There Is Nothing New under the Sun

4 One generation passes away and another generation succeeds it,
but the earth stands firm forever. [d]

a Eccl 1:12; 7:27; 12:8f.—b Eccl 12:8; Pss 39:6-7; 62:10.—c Eccl 2:11, 22; 3:9; 5:15-16.—d Job 8:19; 14:2; Pss 104:5; 119:90.

1:1-3 The author is introduced under the name of Ecclesiastes or Qoheleth, i.e., a person whose function is to speak in the assembly (*ekklesia* in Greek, *qahal* in Hebrew). His editor has come up with a happy formula to sum up the author's thinking (*Vanity of vanities . . .*); it is so good that he will repeat it as a conclusion. And, since the Book represents a new line of thought, he puts it on the lips of Solomon—without naming him but using the phrase *son of David*.

1:2 *Vanity:* Hebrew word meaning "mist," "breath," or "puff of wind" (see Pss 39:6, 12; 62:10; 144:4). The author uses it in the sense of the illusory nature of things. *Vanity of vanities:* an expression that indicates the greatest degree of uselessness and emptiness.

1:3 Jesus expands on this same theme in Mk 8:36-38. *Under the sun:* i.e., the present world and its limits. A synonym is "under heaven" (see v. 13; 2:3; 3:1).

1:4-11 The author takes the opposite tack to the wonder and adoration excited by the universe in Job (chs. 38–40); for him, no event can change the course of things: nothing deserves to occupy our memories to this point: there is no history!

5 The sun rises and the sun sets;
then it returns to the place where it rises.
6 The wind blows southward and then veers to the north,
constantly turning as it repeats its course.
7 All the rivers go to the sea,
and yet the sea never overflows,
for the rivers continue to return
to their place of origin.
8 All things * are wearisome
and very difficult to express.
The eyes are not satisfied with seeing
and the ears do not have their fill of hearing. [e]
9 What has been will be so again,
and what has been done will be done again;
there is nothing new under the sun. [f]
10 Whatever is perceived to be new
has already existed in the ages before us. [g]
11 Those people who died in ages past
are no longer remembered,
and the people yet to be born
will not be remembered by those who come after them. [h]

III: THE IMPOSSIBLE HAPPINESS*

Much Wisdom, Much Anguish.* 12 When I,
Qoheleth, ruled as king over Israel in
Jerusalem, 13 I applied the wisdom I pos-
sessed to study and explore everything that is
done under the sun, a thankless task that
God has given to men to keep us occupied. [i]
14 I have seen everything that has been done
under the sun, and behold, all is vanity and a
chase after the wind. * [j]

15 What is crooked cannot be made straight,
and what is lacking cannot be counted.

16 I thought to myself, "I have acquired
great wisdom, far surpassing all those who
preceded me in Jerusalem. My mind has
mastered every facet of wisdom and knowl-
edge." [k] 17 However, as I applied my mind to
gain a complete understanding of wisdom
and knowledge, madness and folly, I came to
realize that this too is a chase after the wind.

18 For much wisdom can result in much sorrow,
and those who increase their knowledge also increase their grief. * [l]

CHAPTER 2

What Good Is It To Be Successful?* 1 Then I
said to myself, "All right, I will pursue plea-
sure and the enjoyment of good things."
However, this also proved to be vanity. [m] 2 I
regarded laughter as madness and pleasure
as vanity. 3 Then, while my mind was guiding
me with wisdom, I sought to cheer my body
with wine and the pursuit of folly, for I was
determined to discover what was the best
way for men to spend the few days of their life
under the heavens. * [n]

4 I undertook grandiose projects. I built
houses for myself and planted vineyards. 5 I
made for myself gardens and parks and filled
them with every kind of fruit tree. 6 I devel-
oped pools that would enable me to water my
grove of growing trees.

7 I purchased male and female slaves, and
slaves were also born in my house. In addi-
tion, I had large herds and flocks, far more
than any who had preceded me in Jerusalem.
8 I amassed for myself silver and gold and the
treasures of kings and provinces. I acquired
singers, both male and female, and every
possible human luxury. * 9 In this way I

e Eccl 8:17; Prov 27:20.—f Eccl 2:12; 3:15; 6:10.—g Eccl 3:15.—h Eccl 2:16; 9:5.—i Eccl 8:9.—j Eccl 2:11, 17.—k Eccl 2:9.—l Eccl 2:23; 12:12.—m Eccl 2:24; Prov 14:13; Lk 12:19-20.—n Eccl 2:24-25; 3:12-13; Jdg 9:13.

1:8 *All things:* or "words," i.e., everything mentioned in verses 4-7.

1:12—6:12 Here is a very unusual interpretation of the success of the great King Solomon. It shows that the current wisdom has been surpassed, namely the wisdom that appeases the torment of people while they await success as a reward for virtue. The ancient ideas about recompense no longer hold, which was a dramatic discovery for Job.

1:12-18 Using the first person and speaking as Solomon (use of the third person returns only in the conclusion: Eccl 12:9-14), the author shows that both human endeavor (vv. 12-15; see 2:1-11) and the quest for human wisdom (vv. 16-18; see 2:12-17) are vanity.

1:14 *A chase after the wind:* an image of futility, useless effort, and waste of time (see Hos 12:2). The author uses the phrase eight more times in the first half of the Book: v. 17; 2:11, 17, 26; 4:4, 6, 16; 6:9.

1:18 The author has found that what is wisdom in theory is not so in practice and vice versa.

2:1-11 Here is a complete experience of life. Nothing is lacking to Qoheleth, neither free spontaneity, nor the rapture of joys and pleasures, nor wisdom itself. He enjoys the best of relationships, and his goods superabound.

2:3 Under the guidance of wisdom, the author tries all manner of things to discover what is good and worthwhile for himself—i.e., what leads to happiness.

2:8 *And every possible human luxury:* the meaning of the Hebrew here is uncertain. Other possible translations are: "and delights of the heart, and many concubines." All this is in keeping with the reputation of Solomon, who is said to have acquired seven hundred wives and three hundred concubines (1 Ki 11:3).

became great, and I surpassed all my predecessors in Jerusalem, while my wisdom continued to strengthen me. [o]

10 I did not deny my eyes anything that they coveted,
nor did I deprive my heart of any pleasure.
For I found delight in all my labors,
and this was the reward I had for all my efforts.
11 However, once I began to reflect on all that my hands had accomplished
and the effort I had exerted in achieving it,
I again came to the realization that everything was vanity and a chase after the wind,
and that there was nothing to be gained under the sun.

The Wise Man Must Die No Less than the Fool

12 Then my reflections focused on wisdom
as well as madness and folly,
and I came to the realization that whoever succeeds a king can do nothing,
since everything has already been done.
13 I also came to understand that more is to be gained from wisdom than from folly, *
just as light is more profitable than darkness.
14 The wise keep their eyes open,
whereas fools walk in darkness.
And yet at the same time I realized
that the same fate befalls them both. [p]

15 Then I thought to myself,
"If the fate of the fool will also be my fate,
then why have I been wise?
In what way do I profit?"
And I came to the conclusion
that this too is vanity. [q]
16 The wise man is remembered no longer than the fool,
because in the days to come both will have been forgotten.
The wise man must die no less than the fool. [r]
17 As a result, I came to hate life,
since I loathe the work that is done under the sun;
for all is vanity and a chase after the wind.

A: A Chase after the Wind

So Many Labors with the Profit Going to Others.* 18 Therefore, I have come to hate all
my labor and toil under the sun because I
now must bequeath its fruits to my successor. * [s] 19 And I have no way of knowing in
advance whether he will be wise or a fool.
Either way, he will be the master of all the
fruits of my work for which I toiled and
employed my wisdom under the sun. This too
is vanity.
20 As a result, I surrendered to feelings of
despair concerning all of my labor and toil
here under the sun. 21 For even though a man
may labor with wisdom and knowledge and
skill, he must leave everything he has to be
enjoyed by another who has not toiled for it
in any way. This also is vanity and a great
misfortune.
22 For what does a man gain from all the
toil and effort that he has expended under
the sun? [t] 23 His days are filled with pain and
his labors are filled with stress. Even at night
he has no peace of mind. This also is vanity.

The Happiness of Simple Things.* 24 There is
nothing better for a man than to eat and
drink and to experience pleasure in his
achievements. And I also came to realize that
this too comes from God's hand. 25 For without him who could eat or drink?
26 God gives wisdom and knowledge and
joy to those who please him, but to sinners he
gives the task of gathering and amassing
wealth that is to be given to someone who
pleases him. This also is vanity and a chase
after the wind. * [u]

o Eccl 1:12.—p Eccl 9:2f; Ps 49:11.—q Eccl 6:8, 11.—r Eccl 1:11; Wis 2:4.—s Eccl 1:3; Ps 39:7.—t Eccl 1:3.—u Job 27:16-17; Prov 13:22.

2:13 *More is to be gained from wisdom than from folly:* it is better to be wise, just as to walk in light is better than walking in darkness. However, as far as death is concerned, both the wise believer and the foolish unbeliever meet the same fate (see Ps 49:11).

2:18-23 One day the best of our efforts will slip out of our hands, and we will lose all control over and use of them. Hence, a radical insecurity and disquietude weigh upon our human condition.

2:18 *Bequeath its fruits to my successor:* see verse 21; Ps 39:7; Lk 12:20.

2:24-26 The acknowledgment that life is a gift frees us from the deception of time that flies, and this happiness suffices for the ancient sages; Qoheleth is appreciative of this simple happiness, for he knows that true happiness is found only in acknowledging and revering God (Eccl 12:13).

2:26 Qoheleth finds fault with the teaching of the sages concerning the problem of the wicked who prosper (see Job 27:16-17; Prov 11:8; 13:22). For him, this teaching about divine justice does not seem to be borne out by facts.

CHAPTER 3

A Time for Everything*

1 For everything there is a season,
and a time* for every activity under heaven.
2 A time to be born, and a time to die;
a time to plant, and a time to uproot what is planted.[v]
3 A time to kill, and a time to heal;
a time to tear down, and a time to build up.
4 A time to weep, and a time to laugh;
a time to mourn, and a time to dance.
5 A time to scatter stones, and a time to gather them;
a time to embrace, and a time to refrain from embracing.
6 A time to seek, and a time to lose;
a time to keep, and a time to discard.
7 A time to tear, and a time to mend;
a time to be silent, and a time to speak.
8 A time to love, and a time to hate:
a time for war, and a time for peace.[w]

9 What gain does the worker have from his
toil?[x] 10 I have observed the tasks that God
has designated to keep men occupied. 11 He
has made everything suitable for its time, and he has given men a sense of past and future,* but they never have the slightest comprehension of what God has wrought from beginning to end.[y]

12 I understand that man's greatest happiness is to be glad and do well throughout his
life. 13 And when we eat and drink and find satisfaction in all our labors, this is a gift of God.

14 I know that whatever God does endures forever; nothing can be added to it or subtracted from it. God has done this so that everyone will be in awe standing in his presence.

15 Whatever is now has already been,
that which is to come already is,
and God will restore whatever might be displaced.[z]

The Problem of Retribution.* 16 Moreover, I
observed something else under the sun:

Where justice should be, there was wickedness,
and iniquity was in the place of righteousness.[a]
17 But I remained confident in my belief
that God will judge both the righteous and the wicked,
for he has appointed a time for every matter
and he will issue a judgment on every work.[b]

18 I said to myself that in dealing with men it is God's purpose to test them in order to
show them that they are animals. 19 For the
fate of men and beasts is identical: as the one dies, so does the other. They all have the same life-breath, and man has no advantage over the beast in this regard. For everything is vanity.
20 All go to the same place: all were made from the dust, and to the dust all will return.[c]

21 Who knows whether the human spirit goes upward and the spirit of an animal goes
downward to the earth?* 22 And so I came to
realize that there is nothing better for man than to enjoy his work, since that is his lot. No one has the power to let him see what will happen after he is gone.

CHAPTER 4

The Victor and the Tyrant. 1 Then I contem-
plated all the acts of oppression that are committed under the sun:

I saw the tears of the oppressed,
with no one present to comfort them.
Power was wielded by their oppressors,
and no one was there to comfort them.[d]
2 As a result, I regarded the dead as fortunate,
because they had already died
and thus were happier than the living
who were still alive.[e]

v Job 14:5.—w Mt 10:34; Lk 14:26.—x Eccl 1:3.—y Eccl 8:17; 11:5; Gen 1:31; Job 11:7; Rom 11:33.—z Eccl 1:9; 6:10.—a Eccl 4:1.—b Eccl 11:9; 12:14; Ps 96:13.—c Eccl 12:7; Gen 3:19; Wis 2:3; Sir 17:1.—d Eccl 5:7; Ps 12:6; Lam 1:16.—e Eccl 7:2; Job 3:17.

3:1-15 Our mortality is neither chastisement nor recompense but only the mystery of the human condition. We participate better in God's creation when we accept each moment as a gift.

3:1 *Time:* which is appointed by God (see Ps 31:16; Prov 16:1-9).

3:11 *Given . . . a sense of past and future:* or "has set eternity in their heart."

3:16-22 By themselves human beings cannot decide anything about the last fate of the just and the unjust except that all must entrust themselves to God. Once again, only the present is accessible to human vision, and all the rest is a mystery.

3:21 Qoheleth expresses doubt about the final state of the human spirit, but by the end of the Book it is resolved: "the spirit returns to God who gave it" (Eccl 12:7). The answer was revealed gradually (see Pss 16:9-11; 49:16; 73:23-26; Isa 26:19; Dan 12:2-3) and fully revealed by Jesus who "abolished death and brought life and immortality to light through the gospel" (2 Tim 1:10).

3 But happier than both of these
is the one yet unborn
who has not witnessed the evil deeds
that are done under the sun.

Concurrence of Toil and Envy.* 4 Then I came to realize that all toil and skill in work derive from one person's envy of another. This also is vanity and a chase after the wind.

5 The fool folds his arms
and consumes his own flesh. *
6 Better is one handful with peace of mind
than two handfuls with toil
and a chase after the wind.

Union Builds Strength. 7 Again I observed vanity under the sun:

8 There was a solitary individual,
without a friend, with neither a son nor a brother.
Yet there was no end to his toil,
and wealth did not satisfy his greed.
"For whom am I toiling," he asked,
"and depriving myself of pleasures?"
This also is vanity
and a worthless task.
9 Two are better than one:
they earn a far greater reward for their toil.
10 And if one should fall,
his companion will help him up.
How pathetic is the man who is alone and falls
and has no one to assist him to his feet.
11 In the same way, if two sleep together,
they keep warm,
but how can one who sleeps by himself keep warm?
12 And where a single man can be overcome,
two together will be able to resist.
A cord with three strands is not easily broken.

Deception of Political Regimes.* 13 Better is a poor but wise youth than an old and foolish king who will no longer take advice. 14 One can emerge from prison to be crowned as a king, even though he was born in poverty in that kingdom.[f]

15 And I observed all those who live and move under the sun willingly give their support to that young man who succeeded the king. * 16 There was a mass of people beyond counting over whom he reigned. And yet those who succeed him will not venerate his memory. This also is vanity and a chase after the wind.

The Religious Illusion. 17 Be circumspect when you visit the house of God. Drawing near to listen is far better than the offering of a sacrifice by fools, for fools do not know how to avoid doing wrong.[g]

CHAPTER 5

1 Never be in a hurry to speak
or hastily make a promise to God,
for God is in heaven
and you are on earth;
therefore, let your words be few.[h]
2 As dreams come when there are many cares,
so does the speech of a fool when there are many words. *

3 When you make a vow * to God, do not delay in fulfilling it, for God has no pleasure in fools. Fulfill the vow you have made. 4 It is preferable not to make a vow than to make it and fail to fulfill it.[i]

5 Do not allow your mouth to lead you into sin and then plead before God's messenger * that it was all a mistake. Otherwise God will become angered at your words and destroy the work of your hands. 6 A profusion of dreams leads to excessive vanity. Therefore, fear God.[j]

Under the Pretext of General Interests. 7 If in some part of the realm you witness the oppression of the poor and the violation of rights and justice, do not be surprised; for every high official is supervised by one who is higher in rank, and the one who has the highest rank keeps watch over them all.[k]

f Gen 41:14.—g 1 Sam 15:22; Prov 15:8; Hos 6:6.—h Ps 115:3; Mt 6:7.—i Num 30:3; Deut 23:24; Prov 20:25.—j Eccl 12:13; Deut 10:12.—k Eccl 3:16; 4:1; Ps 12:6.

4:4-6 Certainly labor and success would merit our praise if the desire to possess would not introduce the poison of jealousy therein. Observe how the two sayings in verses 5-6 are contradictory; the first was undoubtedly inserted later on by a scrupulous scribe.

4:5 *Consumes his own flesh:* i.e., refuses to work, thus going hungry and bringing on ill health (see Eccl 10:18; Prov 6:6-11; 24:30-34).

4:13-16 A government becomes entrenched in solitude, and it must be stripped of power through sedition. The history of Israel gives us nothing but too many examples of the terrible temptations of power.

4:15 Even a ruler is scarcely remembered after he has died.

5:2 *Many words:* probably refers to the offering of rash vows to God (see v. 6).

5:3 *Vow:* see Deut 23:21-23; 1 Sam 1:11, 24-28. *Fools:* persons who refuse to learn (see Prov 1:20-27).

5:5 *Messenger:* i.e., the priest. An allusion to sins committed or vows uttered inadvertently (see Lev 4:2, 22, 27; Num 15:22, 29).

[8] A country is best served when a king is in charge of the fertile fields. *

Money: An Insatiable Desire

9 One who is covetous will never be satisfied with money,
nor will the lover of wealth be content with gain.
This too is vanity. *l*

10 When riches increase,
so do those who are eager to accumulate them,
and those who have accumulated them must remain content
simply to feast their eyes on them.

11 Sleep is sweet to the laborer,
whether he has much or little to eat,
but the vast riches of a wealthy man
do not allow him to sleep.

[12] There is a grievous evil that I have seen under the sun:

Riches are hoarded by their owner to his disadvantage,
13 or riches are lost by some misfortune,
so that he has nothing remaining to leave to his son.
14 Just as he came forth naked from his mother's womb,
so shall he depart, naked as he came,
with nothing remaining from his labor
that he can carry away in his hands. *m*

[15] This too is a grievous evil:

Just as he came, so must he go,
and what profit can he have after toiling for the wind?
16 All of his days are spent in darkness
with great anxiety, sickness, and resentment.

The Happiness Suitable for Humans. [17] This is the conclusion I have reached: it is fitting for a man to eat and drink and find satisfaction in the results of his labors under the sun during the brief span of life that God has allotted him. *n* [18] Moreover, the one to whom God grants wealth and possessions and the ability to enjoy them and to find contentment in his toil receives a gift from God. [19] For it is unlikely that he will brood about the passing years inasmuch as God keeps his heart filled with joy. *

CHAPTER 6

The Impossible Profit.* [1] There is another evil that I have seen under the sun, and it weighs heavily on the human race. [2] God may grant a man wealth, prosperity, and honor so that he lacks none of the things he desires. However, if God does not enable him to enjoy these gifts but rather allows someone else to revel in their benefits, this is vanity and a grievous ill. *o*

[3] A man may father a hundred children and live for many years, but no matter how many his days may be, if he does not have the opportunity to enjoy the good things of life and in the end receives no burial, I maintain that a stillborn child is more fortunate than he. *

[4] For that child came in vain and departed in darkness, and in darkness will his name be enveloped. [5] Moreover, it has never seen the sun or known anything, yet its state is better than his. [6] It could live a thousand years twice over and experience no enjoyment, yet both will go to the same place. * *p*

7 All man's toil is for the mouth,
yet his appetite is never satisfied.
8 For what advantage does the wise man have
over the fool,
or what advantage do the poor have
in knowing how to conduct themselves in life?
9 What the eye sees is better
than what desire craves.
This also is vanity
and a chase after the wind.

B: What a Human Being Is: Conclusion to Part I

10 Whatever exists was given its name long ago,
and the nature of man is known,
as well as the fact that he cannot contend
with one who is stronger than he. *

l Prov 28:22.—m Job 1:21; Ps 49:18; 1 Tim 6:7.—n Eccl 2:3, 24; 3:12-13.—o Eccl 2:18f.—p Eccl 2:14.

5:8 The translation and meaning of this verse are much debated.

5:19 See note on Eccl 2:24-26.

6:1-9 The desire to possess does away with any chance of really living, for no one is certain of hanging on to his goods, as is illustrated by three portraits. Not even sages possess security.

6:3 Many children, a long life, and a proper burial were what constituted true riches. To be without any of these was a disgrace.

6:6 *Same place:* i.e., the grave. Qoheleth is still speaking about what humans can observe; they see both the good and the evil die, but they do not see what happens to each of them (see v. 12; 3:21).

6:10 *One who is stronger than he:* i.e., God.

11 The more words we speak,
the more our vanity increases,
so what advantage do we gain?

12 For who knows what is good for a man while he lives the few days of his vain life, through which he passes like a shadow? Who can tell him what will happen here afterward under the sun? [q]

IV: SEARCH FOR HUMAN EQUILIBRIUM

A: How To Discover?

CHAPTER 7

Laughter and Anguish*

1 A good name is better than precious ointment,
and the day of death than the day of birth. *[r]

2 It is better to go to the house of mourning
than to the house of feasting.
For that is the end of every man;
let the living take it to heart. [s]

3 Sorrow is better than laughter,
because a sad countenance may conceal a joyful heart.

4 The heart of the wise is in the house of mourning,
but the heart of fools is in the house of gaiety.

5 It is better to pay heed to the rebuke of the wise
than to listen to the songs of fools.

6 For like the crackling of thorns under a pot,
so is the laughter of fools.
This also is vanity.

7 Oppression can make a wise man foolish
and a bribe corrupts the heart.

The Refuge of Wisdom*

8 Better is the end of anything than its beginning;
better are the patient in spirit than the proud in spirit.

9 Do not become easily angered,
for anger lodges in the heart of fools.

10 Do not assert that the past was better than the present,
for such a statement is not a sign of wisdom.

11 Wisdom is as good as an inheritance
and an advantage to those who see the sun.

12 Safeguard wisdom as you would a legacy,
and the advantage of knowledge is this:
it bestows life on the one who possesses it. [t]

13 Consider the work of God.

Who can make straight
what God has made crooked? [u]

14 When things are going well, be grateful for your blessings,
and in times of adversity consider this:
God has made both of them,
so that we cannot predict with confidence
what the future holds. [v]

Whoever Wants To Be an Angel Ends Up as a Beast*

15 During my span of life I have seen everything:

Righteous people who perish in their uprightness,
and wicked people who grow old in their wickedness.

16 Do not be excessively righteous
or show yourself to be unduly wise. *
Why should you destroy yourself?

17 Do not be excessively wicked
or act like a fool.
Why should you die before your time? *

q 1 Chr 29:15; Job 8:9; 10:20; 14:2; Pss 39:7; 102:12; Jas 4:14.—r Eccl 4:2; Prov 22:1; Sir 41:13.—s Eccl 2:14; 4:2.—t Prov 3:18.—u Eccl 1:15.—v Job 1:21.

7:1-7 We must realize that there is no equality between life and death; death will always have the last word. It is useless for us to try to evade this point; a proper equilibrium lies in accepting the human condition such as it is.

7:1 *The day of death [is better] than the day of birth:* see 2 Cor 5:1-10; Phil 1:21-23. In verses 2-6, Qoheleth shows how we learn more from times of trial than from times of happiness.

7:8-14 Wisdom is a refuge for human beings. The present moment is God's gift to humans; by living it correctly we get closer to God (see Rom 8:28-29).

7:15-24 We should not imagine that by dint of our performance in justice, i.e., in virtue, we could guarantee our future and rejoice at the fall of the wicked. Such a pretense would ordinarily become perverted into pride and severity. Wisdom is the power of life, but no one can possess it; we can only try to live wisely and humbly.

7:16 *Excessively righteous . . . unduly wise:* these attitudes are to be avoided, for they lead to self-righteousness and pride.

7:17 In Old Testament times, the wicked were regarded as certain to undergo an untimely end at the hand of God (see 1 Sam 2:31-34; Ps 55:24; Prov 10:27; Jer 17:11).

18 It would be best for you to hold on to one
and not let go of the other. *
For the one who fears God will eventually succeed.

19 Wisdom gives greater strength to the wise man
than ten rulers in a city.

20 There is no one on earth who is so righteous
that he does nothing but good and never sins. * [w]

21 If you do not pay attention to all that people say,
you will never hear your servant speaking ill of you.

22 For you know in your heart
that you have often spoken ill of others.

23 All this I have put to the test of wisdom:
I said, "I am determined to be wise,"
but such wisdom was beyond my reach.

24 This state of wisdom is far off and buried very deep.
Who can discover it?

Man and Woman*

25 I then turned my thoughts
in the direction of knowledge.
My mind sought to search out and seek wisdom
and the reason why things are as they are,
only to realize that it is foolish to be wicked
and madness to act like a fool. [x]

26 I find more bitter than death
the woman who is a snare: *
her heart is a net
and her arms are chains.
One who pleases God escapes her clutches,
but the sinner is captured by her.

27 Behold, this is what I have discovered, says Qoheleth:
As I have added one thing to another in order to draw some conclusion,
28 which my mind has sought repeatedly
but has not yet discovered,
I have found one man out of a thousand,
but a woman among them all I have not found.

29 This alone have I found out:
God made human beings straightforward,
but they often follow devious paths.

CHAPTER 8

The Smile of a Wise Man*

1 Who is like the wise man?
Who else knows how to interpret things?
A man's wisdom lights up his face,
softening the hardness of his countenance.

When Man Dominates Man.* 2 Obey the command of the king because of your sacred oath, 3 and do not be hasty to ignore it. Do not support him in some evil scheme, for he does whatever he pleases. 4 Since his word is sovereign, who can say to him, "What are you doing?"

5 Whoever obeys a command will come to no harm,
and the wise mind will know the time and the way. [y]

6 For there is a time and a way for everything,
although a man's troubles are a great affliction. [z]

7 For he is ignorant of what the future holds,
inasmuch as no one will make known to him what is in store.

w 1 Ki 8:46; Ps 14:3; Prov 20:9; Rom 3:12, 23.—x Eccl 3:4.—y Prov 12:21.—z Eccl 3:1, 17.

7:18 *Hold on to one and not let go of the other:* i.e., the words in verses 16-17.

7:20 For more on the truth set forth in this verse, see Rom 3:9-20 and note; 5:12-21 and note.

7:25-29 The wisdom of the time easily set forth its warnings about the seductress in the belief that every woman is by nature a trap for men. Qoheleth recalls these clichés, but one has the impression that he regards them as caricatures; for he knows that man is more complicated, or, better, that he makes things more complicated.

7:26 *The woman who is a snare:* this is the seductress about whom men are warned (see Prov 2:16-19; 5:1-14; 6:24-29; 7:1-27), but elsewhere Scripture exalts the virtues of man's lifetime companion (see Eccl 9:9; Prov 5:15-23; 31:10-31).

8:1 With a bit of meditation and a serene judgment, even the distresses of life mentioned in Eccl 7:1-7 become less dramatic.

8:2-9 The kingship is recognized as being of divine institution (see 2 Sam 8; Ps 89); it is part of this sacred world to which human beings must be submissive. In any case, it is better to keep account of the pretense of power that holds humans at its mercy and before which they remain without recourse. But no matter how great it is, power does not have the last word in the events of the world.

8 No one has it in his power
to restrain the wind from blowing
or to forestall the day of death.
No one can escape the perils of war,
nor can wickedness preserve those who
engage in it.

9 All this I have observed as I carefully con-
centrated my mind on everything that is
done under the sun, while one person tyran-
nizes another and causes suffering.

The Desire To Do Evil. 10 Meanwhile I have
observed the wicked being carried to their
graves. They used to approach and enter
the holy place, and they were praised in the
city for having done such things. This also is
vanity. *

11 Because the sentence for committing an
evil act is not carried out quickly, people's
hearts are prone to act wickedly. 12 Even
though the sinner does wrong a hundred
times and continues to live, I am confident
that things will go well for those who fear
God because of their fear of him. [a]
13 However, things will not go well with the
wicked, and their days will not lengthen like a
shadow, because they do not stand in fear
before God.

What Constitutes Happiness.* 14 Another
vanity that takes place on earth is that
sometimes righteous people are treated as
though they had acted in an evil way, and
wicked people are treated as though they
had lived righteous lives. This too, I say, is
vanity. 15 Therefore, I commend enjoyment,
since there is nothing better for a man
under the sun than to eat and drink and be
glad. This is his reward for his toil during
the days of life that God grants him under
the sun. [b]

B: How To Know?

The Claims of a Wise Man. 16 Having pur-
sued my goal to acquire wisdom and to
observe the tasks undertaken on earth by
man, whose eyes do not find rest either by
day or by night, 17 I came to the realization
that man is unable to discover all God's
work* that is done under the sun. However
great an effort a man exerts in this search,
he will never succeed. A wise man may
claim to know, but he is in no way able to
do so. [c]

CHAPTER 9

Love, Hatred, and Death.* 1 To all this I have
applied my mind, and I came to this conclu-
sion: the righteous and the wise and their
deeds are in the hand of God. As to whether
they will earn love or hatred, we have no way
of knowing. 2 Everything that confronts them
is futile, inasmuch as the same fate comes to
all, to the upright, and the wicked, to the good
and the bad, to the clean and the unclean, to
those who offer sacrifice and those who do
not.

As it is with the good person,
so is it with the sinner;
as it is with the one who takes an oath,
so is it with the one who is fearful of
doing so. [d]

3 The worst evil of all the things that hap-
pen under the sun is this: that the same fate
befalls everyone. Moreover, the hearts of
men are filled with evil; madness is in their
hearts throughout their lives, and afterward
they descend to the dead. 4 However, the one
who is counted among the living still has
hope. It is preferable to be a living dog rather
than a dead lion.

5 The living realize that they will die,
whereas the dead know nothing what-
ever.
They will have no further reward,
and even the memory of them will be
obliterated. [e]

6 For them all love and hatred and jealousy
have already perished.
Never again will they have any share
in anything that is done under the
sun.

Eat, Drink, and Love.* 7 Go forth, then. Eat
your bread with joy and drink your wine with

a Eccl 3:14; Deut 12:28; Ps 37:11, 18-19.—b Eccl 2:1, 3, 24; 9:7.—c Eccl 3:11; Ps 73:16; Rom 11:33.—d Eccl 2:14; Job 9:22; Ps 73:3.—e Eccl 1:11; Ps 9:7.

8:10 The text of this verse is badly transmitted and is difficult to translate.

8:14-15 Since things are the way they are and situations are such as we have just understood them, we must accept the modest joy of each day rather than becoming weary in trying to investigate the merits and demerits of human beings. See also note on Eccl 2:24-26.

8:17 *Unable to discover all God's work:* see Deut 29:28 for what humans can and cannot know.

9:1-6 Qoheleth does not yet foresee the hope of a resurrection, and the pious teachings concerning prosperity of the righteous and the ruin of the wicked have for him a taste of useless opium. But he clings to the idea that it is good to live!

9:7-10 In the modest trilogy (eat, drink, and love) of happiness, love, which endures for a lifetime, replaces the joy of labor. Even if Qoheleth hasn't the slightest presentiment of an eternal life, he has learned to accept the present as a gift of God.

a cheerful heart, for God long ago approved what you do.[f] 8 At all times dress in white garments and always anoint your head with oil.

9 Enjoy life with the wife whom you love throughout all the days of your allotted span of life that have been given to you under the sun, because that is your lot while you live and labor here under the sun. 10 Whatever task your hand finds to do, expend all your efforts on it, for you will find no work or planning or knowledge or wisdom in the netherworld to which you are going.[g]

Destiny and Life. 11 Another thing I have observed here under the sun:

The race is not won by the swift,
nor the battle by the brave.
Food does not belong to the wise,
nor wealth to the intelligent,
nor success to the skillful.
Rather, time and chance govern all alike.

12 For no one is able to anticipate the time of disaster:

Like fish caught in a treacherous net,
and like birds caught in a snare,
so people are trapped
when misfortune suddenly falls upon them.

War and Peace.* 13 I have also seen the following example of wisdom under the sun, and I find it of great significance.

14 There was a small town with very few inhabitants. A great king advanced against it and surrounded it while building great siegeworks. 15 In the town there lived a man who, though poor, was wise, and by his wisdom he delivered the town. Yet no one remembered this poor man afterward. 16 Therefore, I said, "Wisdom is better than power." Yet the poor man's wisdom is despised, and his words go unheeded.[h]

A Wise Man in the City of Fools*

17 The quiet words of the wise are more to be heeded
than the shouts of a ruler of fools.
18 Wisdom is better than weapons of war,
but one mistake can undo a great deal of good.

CHAPTER 10

1 Just as dead flies give perfumes a foul smell,
so a little folly can outweigh wisdom and honor.
2 The heart of a wise man inclines to the right;
the heart of a fool inclines to the left.
3 Even when a fool walks down the road,
he lacks sense
and indicates to everyone how stupid he is.
4 If the anger of a ruler rises against you,
do not leave your post,
for calmness will mitigate grave offenses.
5 There is an evil that I have seen under the sun,
a great error to which rulers are prone:
6 Fools are ensconced in a lofty position,
while the rich sit in a lowly place.
7 I have seen slaves on horseback
while princes walked on foot like slaves.
8 Whoever digs a pit will fall into it,
and whoever breaks through a wall
will be bitten by a snake.[i]
9 Whoever quarries stones will be hurt by them,
and whoever chops wood places himself at risk.
10 If an ax becomes dull from lack of sharpening,
then one must exert greater strength,
but skill helps one to succeed.
11 If a snake bites because it has not been charmed,
there is no profit for the charmer.
12 The words of a wise man win favor,
but a fool's tongue is his undoing.[j]
13 The words a fool utters are grounded in stupidity,
and they end in total madness.
14 A fool talks at great length,
but no one knows what direction his words will take,
and who can foretell what the future holds?[k]

f Eccl 2:1, 24; 8:15; 11:9.—g Eccl 11:6; Ps 6:6; Isa 38:18.—h Prov 24:5.—i Pss 7:16; 9:16; 57:7; Prov 26:27; Am 5:19.—j Prov 10:32; 14:3; Sir 21:19.—k Eccl 5:2; 8:7; 9:1.

9:13-16 Wisdom is more important than arms to save nations, but humankind seems unable to understand this. In all the eras of history, it prefers to keep the memory of its war leaders.

9:17—10:20 Qoheleth inserts some sayings and illustrations on the subject of chance. Merit means nothing in the face of chance (Eccl 9:11-12), and many things succeed or fail because of trivial causes (Eccl 9:13—10:20); hence risk is an essential part of life (Eccl 11:1-6).

15 A fool quickly gets worn out by his labor,
and he cannot even find his own way into town. *

16 Woe to you, O country, when your king is a servant
and your princes start feasting in the morning.

17 Blessed are you, O land,
when your king is a nobleman
and your princes feast at the proper time
for strength and not for drunkenness.

18 Because of your negligence the roof begins to collapse,
and when hands remain idle, the house leaks.

19 Feasts are designed for merriment,
wine makes us cheerful,
and money solves every need. *

20 Even in your thoughts,
do not curse the king,
nor revile the rich even in your bedroom;
for a bird of the air may carry your voice,
or a winged creature may repeat what you have said.

CHAPTER 11

The Splendid Adventure of Life*

1 Cast your bread upon the waters, *
and eventually you will get it back. [l]

2 Share with seven or with eight, *
for you never can predict what disasters will come.

3 * When clouds are full of rain,
they will pour it out upon the earth.
Whether a tree falls to the south or to the north,
wherever it falls, there will it lie.

4 One who continues to watch the wind will never sow,
and one who keeps staring at the clouds will never reap.

5 Just as you do not know the path of the wind
or how the body is formed in a woman's womb,
so you do not know the work of God,
the Creator of all. [m]

6 In the morning sow your seed,
and do not cease your labor until evening.
For you do not know which of the sowings will succeed
or whether all alike will turn out well.

V: POEM ON YOUTH AND OLD AGE*

A: In the Evening of Life

God and Light

7 Light is sweet,
and it is pleasant for the eyes to see the sun.

8 No matter how many years you may live,
you should enjoy all of them,
for remember that the days of darkness will be many.
Everything that is to come is vanity.

Rejoice in Your Youth

9 Rejoice, young man, while you are young,
and make the most of the days of your youth.
Follow the inclinations of your heart
and the desires of your eyes.
Yet remember that for all these things
God will demand an account. * [n]

10 Banish grief from your heart
and ignore the sufferings of your body,

---

l Eccl 11:6; Isa 32:20; Hos 10:12.—m Eccl 8:17; Ps 139: 14-16.—n Eccl 2:10; 3:17.

10:15 *And he cannot even find his own way into town:* probably a proverbial expression for extreme stupidity.

10:19 *Money solves every need:* this may be taken in various ways: (1) as a simple statement about the very versatile character of money, (2) as good advice to earn a living rather than seeking a great time, or (3) as an ironic comment about human values (see Lk 16:9).

11:1-6 Qoheleth calls upon us to take risks. This alone depends on us, while everything else remains in the mystery of God. Qoheleth has called upon us to trust in God without having recourse to pathetic discourses and taught us the true hope, one based on the proof of facts.

11:1 *Cast your bread upon the waters:* a summons to be adventurous like those who braved the rigors of seagoing trade and achieved wealth (see Prov 11:24).

11:2 *Share with seven or with eight:* this may refer to sharing our resources with others or to avoiding putting all our eggs in one basket.

11:3-6 *Clouds . . . tree . . . wind . . . seed:* we must keep in mind that nothing is ever really certain to occur in life. Our task is to make an educated guess about future projects and act on them as best we can.

11:7—12:7 This section is one of the most beautiful poetic compositions of the Bible. It sings of the sun and the joy of youth with a touch of melancholy. This is followed by a moving portrait of old age that is very fair and very true (Eccl 12:3-5).

The writer speaks of an eternal home, although this means a survival of which he knows nothing. As the dust returns to the earth, the breath, i.e., the life, returns to God who, as it were, stores it up. Our author, who sees the world as an eternal return of all things (see ch. 1), can also speak of a return to God.

11:9 *God will demand an account:* hence, every detail of life is in no way meaningless or vanity but of great importance.

for youth and the prime of life are fleeting.

CHAPTER 12

Remember Your Creator . . .

1 Remember your Creator in the days of your youth
before the bad times come
and the years draw near when you will say,
"I take no pleasure in them";
2 before the sun and the light of day
give way to darkness,
before the moon and the stars grow dim
and the clouds return after the rain;
3 * when the guardians of the house tremble
and the strong men are bent over,
and the women who grind the meal
cease working because they are few in number,
and those who look through the windows
realize that their eyesight is failing;
4 when the doors to the street are shut
and the sound of grinding begins to fade,
when one waits to hear the chirping of a bird,
but all the songbirds are silent;
5 when one is afraid of heights
and is concerned about dangers on the streets.

And You Return to Your Eternal Home

Remember him—when the almond tree blossoms
and the grasshopper is sluggish
and desire is no longer stirred,
and you return to your eternal home
while the mourners assemble in the streets.
6 Remember him—before the silver cord is snapped
or the golden bowl is broken
or the pitcher is shattered at the spring
or the wheel is broken at the well
7 and the dust returns to the earth from which it came
and the spirit returns to God * who gave it.

B: Final Editor's Note

8 Vanity of vanities, says Qoheleth;
all things are vanity. [o]

9 In addition to his wisdom, Qoheleth taught the people knowledge, having weighed, studied, and arranged many proverbs. 10 Qoheleth sought to express his thoughts in a pleasing way and to convey truths with precision.

11 The sayings of the wise are as sharp as goads; like spikes firmly positioned are the lessons offered by a single shepherd. 12 In regard to anything beyond these, my child, beware. There is no end to the writing of many books, and extensive study results in a weariness of the flesh. [p]

13 This is the end of my teaching.
All has been heard.
Fear God * and keep his commandments,
for that is the responsibility of everyone.
14 For God will bring to judgment all of our deeds *
and reveal all of our secrets,
whether good or bad. [q]

o Eccl 1:1-2.—p Eccl 1:18.—q Eccl 3:17; 11:9; Ps 90:8.

12:3-6 The usual interpretation is this: *the guardians*: the hands; *the strong men*: the legs; *the grind[ers] . . . and those who look through the windows*: the teeth and eyes; *the doors*: the lips; *grinding*: the mouth. Next there is reference to the failure of hearing; the blossoming of the almond tree: white hair; the grasshopper: sexual vigor.

12:7 *The dust returns to the earth . . . and the spirit returns to God:* the part of human beings that is earthly *(dust)* returns to earth, but the part that comes from God *(spirit)* returns to God who gave it—which foreshadows the continuation of life with God.

12:13 *Fear God:* reverence for God is the basis of wisdom (see Ps 111:10; Prov 1:7; 9:10) as well as its content (see Job 28:28) and the responsibility of everyone.

12:14 *God will bring to judgment all of our deeds:* see Eccl 3:17; 8:12-13; 11:9 and note; Mt 12:36; 1 Cor 3:12-15; 2 Cor 5:9-10; Heb 4:12-13.

Thus, at the end of this search, human beings are, as it were, liberated from false religious efforts as well as all pessimism. They discover that they are worth more than what they can possess and more than the situations that they wish to dominate. In the end, conscious of their limits, they do not rebel but learn to accept a true joy without any illusions. Abandoning all thoughts of vindication or fear, they adore the mystery of God with human freedom. The path to hope becomes possible.

"You are all-beautiful, my love, without the slightest blemish" *(Song 4:7)*.

THE SONG OF SONGS

The Most Beautiful Song of Love

The expression "Song of Songs" meant, to a Hebrew, "the song par excellence," "the most beautiful song." This Book is so rich in the turbulent sentiments of the heart, of the passion of love, that it could shock some readers but also render mystical souls enthusiastic.

Experts find that this Song is, in fact, made up of six or seven songs. In them the calls of the young man and the young woman to one another alternate, and the chorus intervenes expressing the thoughts of the public, somewhat like the choral voice of fate in ancient tragedies. These verses exude an atmosphere of youthful freshness and ardent desires, of anxious searching and passionate encounters. The author evokes flowers, the beloved landscape of the Holy Land, and the thousand perfumes of the East. The poetic inspiration that animates these songs is difficult to resist.

It is also difficult to interpret the songs. Of what love are they speaking? Of the love between God and Israel or simply of the love between a man and a woman?

We may take it as almost certain that the Song of Songs was accepted among the inspired Books because Jews and, later on, Christians read in it the story of the relationship between God and his people. Hosea and other prophets after him used nuptial images to signify this relationship (Hos 2; Jer 2:2; 3:1-12; and especially Ezek 16; 23; Isa 50:1; 54:6-7, for example, the restoration of Israel is represented by the image of a conjugal reconciliation).

However, the Song mentions the Lord only once (8:6, alternative translation in note). In addition, the style of these songs is very close to that of the love poems of the East. As we read the Song, we have the impression of dealing with a collection of love songs.

It is probable that the original inspiration for these songs was the desire to write a book about human love. Later on, it was given a religious interpretation as a symbol of the love between God and his people. We shall, therefore, read each text in both perspectives. First of all, we shall allow ourselves to be captivated by the song of love between man and woman, and then meditate on the riches of the covenant between God and his people.

By singing of unconditional love, based on a free choice, and, therefore, of the unity of the couple, the Song throws new light on the people of that time, when marriage was first and foremost a decision of the clan and the families, while monogamy remained the lot of the poor. In this love that is beyond our imagining, the Spirit gives us the most beautiful and truest image of God's tender love for his people.

We might better say that the mutual love of man and woman is a gift by which God enables them to attain to the wellspring of life that is his own heart. God is love (1 Jn 4:8), and all love has its birth in God and in his Son, Jesus Christ: this is what Christians believe. For this reason Paul could write: "Husbands, love your wives, just as Christ loved the Church" (Eph 5:25). "Church" can also mean each individual member of it. The mystics realized this, and the discovery was decisive for their lives.

The arrangement of these different poems composes, in some way, a little drama about love; however, it is difficult to discover a real progression in the series of these songs. By the end of the first poem, the union of the lovers has been realized. There then develops a theme of seeking—which signifies that once love is found it is continuously seeking to achieve a greater depth.

The Song of Songs received its definitive form in the fifth or fourth century B.C., but the short poems that are used in it may go back to a fairly early time, perhaps even to Solomon. Written in poetry that is apparently popular, these songs reveal a deep understanding of sentiments of love. That is why they reach the very source of the love that the Song of Songs expresses concerning the covenant between God and his people and the union between man and woman.

The Song of Songs may be divided as follows:

I: Title and Prologue (1:1-4)
II: First Poem (1:5—2:7)
III: Second Poem (2:8-17)
IV: Third Poem (3:1—5:1)
V: Fourth Poem (5:2—6:3)
VI: Fifth Poem (6:4—8:4)
VII: Epilogue (8:5-14)

CHAPTER 1

I: TITLE AND PROLOGUE*

1 The Song of Songs by Solomon. *[a]

Longing for Love

BRIDE:

2 Let him kiss me with the kisses of his
mouth.
Your * love is more delightful than wine; [b]
3 fragrant is the scent of your anointing
oils. *
Your name is a perfume poured out,
and that is why the maidens love you. [c]
4 Take me with you, and let us make haste;
bring me into your chamber, O king.

COMPANIONS:

We will exult and rejoice in you; *
we will praise your love more than
wine;
how right it is to love you. [d]

II: FIRST POEM

Tell Me, You Whom My Heart Loves

Let Me Not Be Found Wandering . . .*

BRIDE:

5 I am dark * but lovely,
O daughters of Jerusalem,
like the tents of Kedar,
like the curtains of Salma. [e]
6 Do not stare at me because I am dark,
for I was scorched by the sun.
My mother's sons vented their rage
against me;
they forced me to look after the vine-
yards,
but my own vineyard * I could not
watch over. [f]
7 Tell me, you whom my heart loves,
where you pasture your flocks,
and where you rest them at midday, *
so that I may not be found wandering
beside the flocks of your compan-
ions. [g]

COMPANIONS:

8 If you do not know,
O fairest among women,
follow the tracks of the flocks
and pasture your young goats
close to the tents of the shepherds. [h]

To Sit in His Shadow Is My Delight*

BRIDEGROOM:

9 I compare you, my beloved,
to a mare * harnessed to Pharaoh's
chariot. [i]

a 1 Ki 5:12.—b Song 1:4; 4:10.—c Ps 45:8; Jn 12:3.—d Song 1:2; 2:3; 4:10; Ps 45:16.—e Song 5:16.—f Song 8:12.—g Gen 37:16.—h Song 5:9; 6:1.—i 1 Chr 1:15.

1:1-4 Solomon composed poems and songs, and tradition decided to place this Book under his patronage. But let us go on to the text itself.

The bride is seized with the desire to rejoin her bridegroom in a perfect and joyous union. She issues a call for him to be with her and musters up her hope. In uninterrupted variations, the Song will take up again the same call and the same hope.

Is it not equally true that the people of God in the solitude of the Exile wait impatiently for the day on which God, their King, will manifest himself anew and lead them back to the Holy Land and Jerusalem. Today, the Church—and every believer with her—remains in wait for the coming of her Lord.

1:1 The speakers are indicated by the captions BRIDE, BRIDEGROOM, and COMPANIONS respectively. In some cases, the divisions are open to question. *By Solomon:* Solomon is said to have authored one thousand and five songs (1 Ki 5:12).

1:2 *Him . . . his . . . Your:* these all refer to the bridegroom. *Love:* i.e., expressions of love (see v. 4; 4:10; 7:12; see also Prov 7:18; Ezek 16:8; 23:17). *More delightful than wine:* words used by the bridegroom in Song 4:10.

1:3 *Fragrant . . . your anointing oils:* an image of the charms that attract the heart. *Maidens*: perhaps members of the royal court (see Song 6:8-9). They may also stand for the nations (see Isa 23:12; 37:22; 47:1; Jer 14:17).

1:4 *We will exult and rejoice in you:* joy is one of the greatest blessings of the Messianic prophecies of salvation (see Pss 14:7; 16:9; 21:1; Isa 9:2; 66:10; Joel 2:21, 23; Zep 3:17).

1:5-8 A bride separated from her bridegroom shows signs of the trial. Her entourage may no doubt give her grief concerning some weaknesses, but she rediscovers her self-esteem and decides to set out in search of her lover. Her companions form the chorus that will continuously intervene in the unfolding of these poems that are more or less arranged in the form of a drama. Hearing the calls of the bride, they jest with her and suggest that she follow the other shepherds!

Thus, far from the land from which it has been exiled as a result of too many infidelities, Israel seeks God; but how can the temptation for its people to turn toward foreign gods be rooted out? No matter what defeats may be incurred, the community of believers must unceasingly rediscover its hope on its pilgrimage to the Lord.

1:5 *Dark:* burnt by the sun from laboring in the vineyard of her brothers. *Daughters of Jerusalem:* the chorus (COMPANIONS) with whom the bride and the bridegroom interact (see Song 5:9; 6:1). *Kedar:* name of a Bedouin tribe descended from Ishmael (Gen 25:13) that lived in the Desert of Arabia and was famous for its flocks (see Isa 60:7; Ezek 27:21).

1:6 *My own vineyard:* i.e., her body (see Song 2:15; 8:12). She has given her heart to the bridegroom.

1:7 The bride is now seeking the bridegroom because they are apart. This theme runs throughout the Book (Song 3:1-4; 4:8; 5:2-8; 6:1), and the resolution occurs at the end of the Book with the mutual possession of the couple (see Song 8:5). *Midday:* a time for rest in hot climates. It also stands for supreme happiness (see Job 11:17; Ps 37:6; Isa 58:10).

1:9—2:7 The bridegroom has heard the call of his beloved and soon appears. They have a feast, each one singing the charms and the presence of the other as well as evoking the plants and flowers of Israel. The lovers withdraw to a corner brimming with greenery. The beloved falls into the arms of her lover and rests in the dream of love fulfilled.

In somewhat the same way, God responds to his people's call. If Israel returns to him with love, she will remain his beloved among the nations. The Lord, her King, will be for her joy and favor. The last Book of the New Testament, the Book of Revelation, foresees the day when believers will be filled with the refound joy of God.

1:9 *Mare:* allusion to the splendid mounts of the Pharaoh. The comparison was a classic one in the East.

10 Your cheeks are beautiful with pendants
and your neck with its jeweled neck-
laces. [j]
11 We will make ornaments of gold for you
that are studded with silver. [k]

BRIDE:

12 While the king reclines on his couch,
my nard * yields its fragrance. [l]
13 My beloved is for me a sachet of myrrh *
that lies between my breasts. [m]
14 My beloved is for me a cluster of henna *
blossoms
in the vineyards of En-gedi. [n]

BRIDEGROOM:

15 How beautiful you are, my beloved,
how beautiful you are;
your eyes are doves. * [o]

BRIDE:

16 How handsome you are, my love,
and how you delight me.
Our couch is verdant. * [p]

BRIDEGROOM:

17 The beams of our house are cedar;
our rafters are all of pine. [q]

CHAPTER 2

BRIDE:

1 I am a rose of Sharon, *
a lily of the valley. [r]

BRIDEGROOM:

2 As a lily growing among thorns,
so is my beloved among maidens. * [s]

BRIDE:

3 Like an apple tree among the trees of the
forest,
so is my beloved among young men.
To sit in his shadow is my delight,
and his fruit is sweet to my taste. [t]
4 He escorts me into his banquet hall
and his banner * over me is love. [u]
5 Strengthen me with raisins,
restore me with apples, *
for I am sick with love. [v]
6 His left arm is under my head
and his right arm embraces me. [w]

BRIDEGROOM:

7 I charge you, daughters of Jerusalem, *
by the gazelles and the wild does:
Do not stir up or awaken love
before its time has come. [x]

III: SECOND POEM*

Let Me See You

BRIDE:

8 Hark! I hear the voice of my beloved.
Look, here he comes,
leaping across the mountains *
bounding over the hills. [y]
9 My beloved is like a gazelle
or a young stag.
Look where he stands
behind our wall,
peering in through the windows,
gazing through the lattice. [z]
10 My beloved speaks,
and he says to me:
"Arise, my beloved,
my fair one, and come! [a]

j Song 5:13; Isa 61:10.—k Song 1:10.—l Song 4:11-14.—m Ps 45:9.—n Song 4:13.—o Song 4:1, 7; 7:7.—p Song 2:3.—q 1 Ki 6:9.—r Hos 14:6.—s Song 1:14.—t Song 4:16.—u Song 1:4.—v Song 5:8.—w Song 8:3.—x Song 3:5; 8:4.—y Song 2:17; 8:14.—z 2 Sam 2:18; Prov 9:6.—a Song 2:13; 5:2.

1:12 *Nard*: a precious perfume (see Song 4:13-14; Mk 14:3; Jn 12:3), which symbolizes the bride (see Song 4:14).

1:13 *Myrrh:* a feminine perfume (see Est 2:12; Prov 17:7). The *sachet of myrrh,* which women carried in their bosom, was a sign of love for their husbands. Myrrh was also used on royal nuptial robes (see Ps 45:8).

1:14 The *henna* plant had highly perfumed blossoms. *En-gedi:* an oasis on the western shore of the Dead Sea, to which David retreated when hunted by Saul (see 1 Sam 24:1).

1:15 *Your eyes are doves:* symbolic of an innocent and personable individual.

1:16 The lovers embrace in the field under the trees.

2:1 *Sharon:* a plain on the seacoast, extending from Joppa to Mount Carmel, which was proverbial for its beauty, fertility, and pasturage (see 1 Chr 27:29; Isa 35:2). *Lily of the valley:* a symbol of loveliness (see also Song 2:16; 4:5; 6:3).

2:2 *Maidens:* see note on Song 1:3.

2:4 *Banner:* i.e., a military flag; just as such a flag is used to show location or possession, her bridegroom's love does the same in her case (see Num 1:52; Ps 20:6).

2:5 *Raisins . . . apples:* probably a reference to the affection and embraces of love.

2:7 This refrain also occurs in Song 3:5; 8:4. *Daughters of Jerusalem:* see note on Song 1:5.

2:8-17 In her home, the bride longs for the return of her bridegroom; he appears in the window and invites her to take a walk in the freshness of springtime. How each of them wishes to reach the heart of the other. But their time together turns short. The young woman's companions appear and liken the lovers to the marauding little foxes that people distrust (v. 15)—in spring the foxes set their cubs down amid the flowering vines. The bride responds sharply and protests her love; she invites the bridegroom to return that evening.

God too searches for his people; obstacles ceaselessly appear and prevent the rediscoveries even when Israel is in her own land. More than once God seems to disappear. Rediscovering the new strength of its love, the community pleads for the return of the Lord, who offers his people a covenant, a union capable of fulfilling all the aspirations of human beings.

2:8 *Mountains:* i.e., of Judah (see Isa 40:3-5, 9-11; 52:7; 62:10-12).

11 * For see, the winter is past,
the rains are over and gone. [b]
12 The flowers appear in the countryside;
the season of joyful songs has arrived,
and the voice of the turtledove
is heard in our land.
13 The fig tree puts forth its figs
and the blossoms on the vine give forth
their fragrance.
Arise, my beloved,
my fair one, and come!" [c]

BRIDEGROOM:

14 O my dove, hiding in the clefts of the rock,
in the sheltered recesses of the cliff,
let me see you,
let me hear your voice.
For your voice is sweet,
and your face is lovely. [d]

COMPANIONS:

15 Catch the foxes for us,
the little foxes
that ruin our vineyards,
for our vineyards are blossoming. [e]

BRIDE:

16 My beloved belongs to me, and I am his; *
he pastures his flock among the lilies. [f]
17 Before the dawn * comes,
and the shadows flee,
return, my beloved,
like a gazelle or a young stag
upon the mountains of the covenant. [g]

IV: THIRD POEM

CHAPTER 3

I Found the One My Heart Loves*

BRIDE:

1 Night * after night upon my bed
I sought the one my heart loves.
I sought him, but I could not find him. [h]
2 I said, "I will rise and go through the city,
along the streets and in the squares.
I will seek the one my heart loves."
I sought him, but I could not find him. [i]
3 The watchmen * came upon me
as they made their rounds of the city,
and I asked them,
"Have you seen the one my heart loves?" [j]

4 I had hardly gone past them
when I found the one my heart loves.
I held him and would not let him go
until I had brought him to my mother's house, *
to the very room where she had conceived me. [k]

BRIDEGROOM:

5 I charge you, daughters of Jerusalem,
by the gazelles and the wild does:
Do not stir up or awaken love
before its time has come. * [l]

Solomon on the Day of His Wedding*

COMPANIONS:

6 What is this coming up from the desert
like a column of smoke,

b Joel 2:23.—c Song 7:12.—d Song 1:5; 8:13.—e Song 7:13; Jdg 15:4.—f Song 6:3; 7:11.—g Song 2:8-9; 4:6; 8:14.—h Song 5:6.—i Jer 5:1.—j Song 5:7.—k Song 8:2.—l Song 2:7; 8:4.

2:11-13 Spring in bloom is the time of love as well as the symbol of salvation (see Hos 14:6-8).

2:16a This verse is patterned after the covenant formula of the Prophets: "They . . . will be my people, and I will be their God" (Jer 32:38; see also Hos 2:25; Jer 31:33).

2:17 *Dawn:* the image of the dawn symbolizes the hour of deliverance (see Ps 17:15). *Covenant:* literally, "Bether," whose meaning is uncertain.

3:1-5 Night has come, but in vain has the bride awaited the bridegroom. Driven by the ardor of her love, she hastens through the village to find him. Her love guides her to him so that she will take him home and he will embrace her. Already she seems to hear her husband wish that his weary beloved should be left to take her rest.

Human love remains a symbol of divine love. God hides from those who fail to seek him with all their heart. He lets himself be found by those who love him and render glory to him in the temple of Jerusalem where he is, as it were, the spouse of the chosen nation. It is from there that he watches over his people.

Is the life of the Church anything else but the passionate quest for persons who one day heard the Lord's call?

3:1 *Night:* a symbol of anxious waiting (see Ps 130:6; Isa 5:30; 8:22; 9:1; 21:11; 26:9; 59:9). *I sought the one my heart loves . . . but I could not find him:* this is symptomatic of the people's search for God. He can be found only by a true conversion (see Hos 3:5; 5:6, 15; Jer 29:13).

3:3 *Watchmen:* they stood on the walls (see 2 Sam 13:34; Ps 127:1; Isa 52:8) or at the gates of the city (see Neh 3:29) and patrolled the streets as well (Song 5:7).

3:4 *Mother's house:* mothers are referred to frequently in this Book, though fathers are completely ignored.

3:5 See note on Song 2:7.

3:6-11 A dream gives various forms to desire. Like a fairy tale, a love song takes delight in images of splendor. The bride sees the bridegroom come to her in the sumptuous garb of the most pompous of kings accompanied by heroes of his guard; he takes possession of his throne on the day of his espousals! For those in love, the betrothal surpasses all the splendors of the world.

Solomon, whose name signifies "peace," is one of the figures of the Messiah. Thus, this scene may evoke also the triumphal appearance of a savior before the People of God to effect a definitive restoration for them. The Book of Revelation abounds with sumptuous images to announce the meeting of God and those who love him in the heavenly Jerusalem, that is to say, at the supreme fulfillment of all hopes.

perfumed with myrrh and frankincense
and with all the fragrant spices of the merchant? [m]
7 Look, it is Solomon being carried in his litter,
and escorted by sixty valiant guards,
the bravest of the mighty warriors of Israel, [n]
8 all of them expert swordsmen
and experienced in warfare,
each with his sword ready at his side
to guard against the terrors by night. * [o]
9 King Solomon had made himself a carriage
from the wood of Lebanon.
10 He made its posts of silver,
its base of gold,
its seat of purple cloth,
and its framework inlaid with ivory. [p]
11 Daughters of Zion, * come forth
and welcome King Solomon
as he wears the crown
that his mother had placed upon his head
on the day of his wedding,
on the day of his heart's joy. [q]

CHAPTER 4

How Beautiful You Are, My Beloved*

BRIDEGROOM:

1 How beautiful you are, my beloved;
your beauty has achieved perfection.
Your eyes are doves *
behind your veil.
Your hair is like a flock of goats
streaming down the slopes of Mount Gilead. [r]
2 Your teeth are like a flock of shorn ewes
that have come up from the washing.
Each one of them has a twin;
not a single one is unpaired with the other. [s]
3 Your lips are like a scarlet thread,
and your mouth is lovely.
Your cheeks behind your veil
are like halves of a pomegranate. [t]
4 Your neck is like the tower of David
built layer upon layer;
a thousand bucklers hang upon it,
all of them shields of valiant warriors. [u]
5 Your two breasts are like two fawns,
young twins of a gazelle
that graze among the lilies. [v]
6 Before the dawn comes,
and the shadows flee,
I will hasten to the mountain of myrrh
and the hill of frankincense. [w]

7 You are all-beautiful, my love,
without the slightest blemish. * [x]
8 Come with me from Lebanon, my promised bride; *
come with me from Lebanon.
Descend quickly from the heights of Amana,
from the peaks of Senir and Hermon,
from the dens of lions,
from the mountains of leopards. [y]

9 You have stolen my heart,
my sister, * my bride.
You have stolen my heart with a single glance,
with one jewel of your necklace. [z]
10 How beautiful is your love,
my sister, my bride!
How much more delightful is your love than wine,
and the fragrance of your perfumes than any spices. [a]

---

m Song 4:6, 14; 6:10; 8:5.—n 1 Sam 8:11.—o Ps 91:5.—p Song 1:5.—q Isa 3:16.—r Song 1:15; 6:5ff; Mic 7:14.—s Song 6:6.—t Song 5:16; 6:7.—u Song 7:5; Ezek 27;10.—v Song 2:16; 7:4.—w Song 2:17; 3:6.—x Song 1:15.—y Song 4:12; 5:1; Deut 3:9.—z Song 6:5.—a Song 1:2f; 7:7.

3:8 *The terrors by night:* see Ps 91:5.

3:11 *Daughters of Zion:* elsewhere "daughters of Jerusalem" (see note on Song 1:5). *Crown:* a wedding decoration (see Isa 61:10).

4:1—5:1 The bridegroom takes delight in detailing the charms of his bride. He compares her to flowers, to fruits, and to all the perfumes of the East. He ardently desires to be united with the one who has reserved herself for him. The bride, too, calls on the breath of the passion that comes to complete the loving embrace.

The comparison is a daring one but it must be made: God, too, contemplates the beauty of his people enriched with the many calls and favors that they have received on earth. Israel is the exclusive property of the Lord, and he invites her to come and encounter him on the hill of incense, i.e., at the temple of Jerusalem. Humankind is precious in the Lord's eyes: it is still the Church called to partake in the Lord's love, the unfailing joy of the new times, the feast of God.

4:1 *Doves:* see note on Song 1:15. *Gilead:* a region across the Jordan, with extensive stock farms, whose goats were usually black.

4:7 See the description of the Church in Eph 5:27. The Liturgy applies this verse to our Lady in the celebration of the Immaculate Conception on December 8.

4:8 *Promised bride:* i.e., the betrothed. *Amana . . . Senir . . . Hermon:* names of peaks in the Anti-Lebanon. The Lebanon and Anti-Lebanon are two mountain chains on the borders of Palestine. These far-off mountains symbolize the distance that separates the two lovers.

4:9 *Sister:* a word of endearment that was common in the language of love of the ancient East.

11 Your lips drip with honey, * my promised bride,
milk and honey are under your tongue,
and the fragrance of your garments
is like the fragrance of Lebanon. [b]

12 You are an enclosed garden,
my sister, my promised bride;
you are a garden that is locked,
a fountain that is sealed. * [c]

13 You are like an orchard that brings forth pomegranates,
an orchard with the choicest fruits: * [d]

14 nard * and saffron, calamus and cinnamon,
with all the incense-bearing trees,
myrrh and aloes
with all the finest spices. [e]

15 You are a garden fountain,
a well of living water,
streams flowing down from Lebanon. [f]

BRIDE:

16 Awake, north wind,
and come, south wind.
Blow upon my garden
so that its fragrance may spread abroad.
Let my beloved come to his garden
and eat its choicest fruits. * [g]

CHAPTER 5

BRIDEGROOM:

1 I have come to my garden, my sister, my bride;
I gather my myrrh and my spices,
I eat my honeycomb and my honey,
I drink my wine and my milk.

COMPANIONS:

Eat, friends, and drink deeply,
until you are drunk with love. * [h]

V: FOURTH POEM

I Sought Him, but I Could Not Find Him

Open to Me*

BRIDE:

2 I was sleeping, but my heart was awake.
Listen! My beloved is knocking:
"Open to me, my sister, my beloved,
my dove, my perfect one.
For my head is drenched with dew, *
my hair with the wetness of the night." [i]

3 I have taken off my robe;
must I put it on again?
I have bathed my feet;
must I soil them again? * [j]

4 My beloved thrust his hand through the opening in the door, *
and my heart began to tremble. [k]

5 I arose to open to my beloved
with myrrh dripping from my hands;
the liquid myrrh from my fingers
ran onto the handle of the bolt. [l]

6 I opened to my beloved,
but he had turned away and was gone;
my heart sank at his disappearance.
I sought him, but I could not find him;
I called out to him, but he did not answer. * [m]

---

b Song 5:1.—c Song 4:16; 6:2, 11; Prov 5:15-18.—d Song 7:13.—e Song 1:12; 3:6; Ex 30:23; Num 24:6.—f Prov 5:18; Isa 58:11.—g Song 2:3; 4:10, 12; 7:14.—h Song 4:8, 11-12; 6:2; Isa 55:1.—i Song 1:15; 3:1f; 4:7; 6:9.—j Lk 11:7.—k Jer 31:20.—l Song 5:13.—m Song 3:1; 6:1-2.

4:11 *Your lips drip with honey:* the bridegroom speaks of love (see Prov 5:3; 16:24). *Milk and honey:* possibly a reference to the fruitfulness of the Promised Land (see Ex 3:8).

4:12 *Enclosed . . . locked . . . sealed:* words that indicate the bride is the bridegroom's and faithful to him (see Prov 5:15-19).

4:13 The bridegroom sings of the bride's features that delight him, likening them to sweet-smelling plants.

4:14 *Nard:* see note on Song 1:12. *Saffron:* a purple-flowered crocus used as a cooking spice. *Calamus:* an aromatic spice cane used in the anointing oil (see Ex 30:23-24) and in incense (see Isa 43:23-24). *Cinnamon:* an aromatic spice used in the anointing oil (see Ex 30:23, 25). *Myrrh:* see note on Song 1:13. *Aloes:* a fragrant resin used in perfuming nuptial robes (see Ps 48:8).

4:16 The beloved invites the bridegroom to come to her.

5:1 The lovers are urged to share their love, which is an image of the love between Christ and his Church (see Eph 5:29-32).

5:2-6 The bride is sleeping, and the thought of the bridegroom is with her even in her dreams. Suddenly, he knocks on the door. Happiness and fear meld together; how can she receive him in the middle of the night? She hesitates and makes believe that she cannot open the door, even though she is already trembling with joy at the coming encounter. However, when she finally dares to open the door, the bridegroom has disappeared into the night and she is alone.

For Israel, too, God remains hidden when the people are tardy in answering his call. The time is near—this is the message of John the Baptist. "Behold, I am standing at the door, knocking": such is the seductive but demanding image of Christ in the Book of Revelation (Rev 3:20).

5:2 *Dew:* a symbol of divine blessings (see Ps 133:3; Hos 14:6).

5:3 Silly reasons for not opening the door, which will be overcome by the bride's love.

5:4 *Opening in the door:* through it a wooden key was inserted from the outside to remove the bolt.

5:6 This is the same prophetic formula used previously (see Song 3:1, 3 and notes). Here it is combined with another traditional formula indicating the Lord's withdrawal from an unfaithful Israel (see Prov 1:28; Isa 50:2; 65:12; 66:4; Jer 7:27).

I Am Sick with Love*

7 The watchmen * came upon me
as they made their rounds of the city.
They beat me and wounded me
and took my cloak from me,
those guardians of the walls. [n]

8 I charge you, daughters of Jerusalem,
if you should find my beloved,
please tell him this:
that I am sick with love. [o]

COMPANIONS:

9 In what way is your beloved better than any other,
O fairest of women?
In what way is your beloved better than any other
that you lay this charge upon us? [p]

BRIDE:

10 * My beloved is radiant and ruddy,
one who would stand out in a group of ten thousand. [q]
11 His head is golden, of the purest gold;
his hair is like palm branches,
black as the raven. [r]
12 His eyes are like doves *
by water streams,
bathed in milk,
and mounted like jewels. [s]
13 His cheeks are like beds of spices
pouring forth fragrant scents.
His lips are like lilies, *
distilling choice myrrh. [t]
14 His arms are rods of gold
adorned with jewels.
His body is a block of ivory
covered with sapphires. [u]
15 His legs are pillars of marble
set in sockets of pure gold.
His appearance is like Lebanon,
as imposing as the cedars. [v]
16 His mouth is most sweet,
and he is totally desirable.
Such is my beloved and such is my friend,
O daughters of Jerusalem. [w]

CHAPTER 6

I Belong to My Beloved*

COMPANIONS:

1 Where has your beloved gone,
O loveliest of women?
In what direction has your beloved turned
so that we may join you in searching for him? [x]

BRIDE:

2 My beloved has gone down to his garden,
to the beds of spices,
to browse in his garden
and to gather lilies. [y]
3 I belong to my beloved, and my beloved is mine; *
he browses among the lilies. [z]

VI: FIFTH POEM

One Alone Is My Dove, My Perfect One

You Are Beautiful, My Beloved*

BRIDEGROOM:

4 You are as beautiful as Tirzah, * my beloved,
as lovely as Jerusalem,
as majestic as an army with banners. [a]

n Song 3:3.—o Song 2:5, 7.—p Song 1:8; 5:16.—q Song 1:15; Ps 45:3.—r Song 5:2.—s Song 1:15; Gen 49:12.—t Song 1:10; 2:1; 5:5.—u Dan 10:6.—v Ps 9:13.—w Song 1:5; 4:3; 7:10.—x Song 1:8; 5:6.—y Song 5:1.—z Song 2:16; 7:11.—a Jos 12:24.

5:7-16 Distraught at having missed the rendezvous, the bride runs to seek out the bridegroom. What an adventure this journey into the night becomes! She runs into the guardians of the walls who maltreat her; then a group of young women joke at her: What do you see in your beloved? Her reply comes from the heart, for she bears the portrait of her beloved within her—what a treasure!

In Israel, after so many losses, there is reborn a new ardor to seek God when trials and mockeries mount up, at the return from the Exile or in the pagan dispersion. There is no clearer witness than a sincere conversion. But is not God the first to awaken the human heart in which he is secretly present? In St. Augustine's words, "You would not be seeking me if you had not already found me." The more we understand God, the more ardently do we seek his countenance.

5:7 *Watchmen:* see note on Song 3:3.

5:10-16 The bride describes the great physical qualities of the bridegroom.

5:12 *Doves:* see note on Song 1:15.

5:13 *Lilies:* see note on Song 2:1.

6:1-3 Enchanted now by the fresh passion of the bride, the young women become her accomplices and seek to help her in her search. Their services are superfluous, for the bridegroom has appeared.

God, too, in an unexpected way, is near to those who truly seek him. And suddenly we will be called to see God as he is.

6:3 *I . . . mine:* see note on Song 2:16a.

6:4-12 The bridegroom allows himself to be led to his rendezvous and praises his beloved: he stresses above all her undivided love, which is much different from that of Solomon, which was comprised of numerous and imperfect loves. For this young man, all his delight is in his unique beloved. This is the song of true love.

Israel can no longer forget that God prefers his people among all nations. And finally, the Lord's love is unique for everyone, as St. Paul so boldly declares: "The Son of God . . . loved me and gave himself up for me" (Gal 2:20).

6:4 *Tirzah:* i.e., "the charming," "the desired," was the capital of the northern kingdom before Samaria was built (see 1 Ki 14:17). *As majestic as an army with banners:* the bridegroom is as struck by his beloved's beauty as he is by watching an army majestically moving forward with its banners unfurled.

5 Turn away your eyes from me,
for they leave me defenseless.
Your hair is like a flock of goats
streaming down the slopes of Gilead. [b]
6 Your teeth are like a flock of sheep
as they come up from the washing;
each of them has a twin,
and not one is alone. [c]
7 Your cheeks are like halves of a pomegranate
behind your veil. [d]
8 There are sixty queens and eighty concubines,
and maidens * beyond numbering. [e]
9 One alone is my dove, my perfect one,
the darling of her mother,
the favorite of the one who bore her.
The maidens saw her and proclaimed her blessed;
the queens and concubines sang her praises. [f]

COMPANIONS:

10 Who is this that comes forth like the dawn,
beautiful as the moon, bright as the sun,
formidable as an army with banners? [g]

BRIDE:

11 I went down to the orchard of nut trees
to look at the green shoots in the valley, *
to see whether the vines had budded
and whether the pomegranates were in bloom. [h]
12 Before I realized it, my desire had placed me
in a chariot beside my prince. * [i]

CHAPTER 7

How Beautiful You Are and How Charming*

COMPANIONS:

1* Come back, come back, O Shulammite; *
come back so that we may gaze upon you.

BRIDEGROOM:

Why are you looking at the Shulammite
as at a dance of Mahanaim? [j]

COMPANIONS:

2 How beautiful are your feet in sandals,
O prince's daughter.
Your rounded thighs are like jewels,
the handiwork of a master hand. [k]
3 Your navel is a well-rounded bowl
that never lacks mixed wine.
Your belly is a mound of wheat *
surrounded by lilies. [l]
4 Your two breasts are like two fawns,
twins of a gazelle. [m]
5 Your neck is like an ivory tower;
your eyes are like the pools in Heshbon *
by the gate of Bath-rabbim.
Your nose is like the Tower of Lebanon [n]
that faces toward Damascus.
6 Your head is held high like Carmel; *
your flowing locks are as dark as purple,
and a king is held captive in your tresses. [o]

BRIDEGROOM:

7 How beautiful you are and how charming,
my beloved, my delight. [p]
8 You are as stately as a palm tree, *
and your breasts are like clusters of fruit. [q]
9* I have decided to climb the palm tree
and take hold of its fruit.

b Song 4:1.—c Song 4:1-2.—d Song 4:3.—e Est 2:14; Ps 45:10.—f Song 1:15; 5:2.—g Song 3:6; 8:5.—h Song 4:12ff; 7:13.—i Ps 113:8.—j Gen 32:2.—k Ezek 16:10.—l Song 4:5.—m Song 4:5.—n Song 4:4.—o Isa 35:2.—p Song 4:7.—q Song 7:4.

6:8 *Queens . . . concubines . . . maidens:* either all the women of Solomon's harem or all the beautiful women in the land.

6:11 *Look . . . in the valley:* for the early signs of spring (see note on Song 2:11-13).

6:12 The meaning of the entire verse is uncertain. The Vulgate reads: "I did not know, and I was disturbed because of the chariots of Amminadab."

7:1-10a The chorus sees the bride as resembling Abishag the Shunammite, the exceptionally beautiful girl of whom 1 Ki 1:1-4 speaks. The passionate praise is received by the bride while she dances with joy.

In the poetic comparison, the terms are taken from the geography of Israel; this is a way of also singing the happiness of the people who rediscover their land. Thus, our chants will exult in the joy of the kingdom of God and the happiness that radiates from the holy city where all will be gathered together.

7:1-6 The comparisons have to be understood in the light of Eastern esthetics, and even then they are not always easy to understand.

7:1 *Shulammite:* usually interpreted as referring to a woman from Shunem, specifically Abishag the Shunammite (1 Ki 1:1-4).

7:3 *Wine . . . wheat:* symbols of fertility.

7:5 *Heshbon:* a city in the Transjordan blessed with a great supply of spring water. *Bath-rabbim:* "Daughter of many," so named perhaps because at that gate people went in crowds for water. *Tower of Lebanon:* probably the beautiful and towering mountains of Lebanon.

7:6 *Carmel:* a region on the west coast of the kingdom famous for its majesty and beauty.

7:8 *Palm tree:* a tree known for its stateliness.

7:9-10a The bride's beauty is an irresistible draw for her husband.

May your breasts be like clusters of the vine,
the scent of your breath as sweet as apples, [r]
10 and your mouth like fragrant wine.

Come, My Beloved, I Will Give You My Love*

BRIDE:

* May the wine go straight to my beloved,
gliding over the lips and teeth. [s]
11 I belong to my beloved,
and his desire is for me. * [t]
12 Come, my beloved,
let us go forth into the fields
and spend the night in the villages. [u]
13 Let us go to the vineyards early
and see if the vines are budding,
if their blossoms have opened
and the pomegranates are in bloom;
there I will give you my love. [v]
14 The mandrakes * emit their fragrance,
and at our doors are the rarest of fruits,
fresh as well as ripened,
which I have kept in store for you, my beloved.

CHAPTER 8

1 Oh, if only you were to me like a brother,
nursed at my mother's breast.
Then if I met you out of doors,
I could kiss you
without people regarding me with scorn. *
2 I would lead you
and bring you into the home of my mother.
There you would teach me to give you spiced wine to drink
and the juice of my pomegranates. [w]
3 His left hand is under my head
and his right arm embraces me. [x]

BRIDEGROOM:

4 I charge you, daughters of Jerusalem:
Do not stir up or awaken love
before its time has come. * [y]

VII: EPILOGUE

Love Is as Strong as Death*

COMPANIONS:

5 Who is this coming up from the wilderness
leaning on her beloved?

BRIDEGROOM:

Under the apple tree * I awakened you;
it was there that your mother conceived you,
and there where she who conceived you bore you. [z]

BRIDE:

6 * Set me as a seal on your heart,
as a seal upon your arm.
For love is as strong as death, *
and ardor is as relentless as the netherworld.
Its flames are flashes of fire,
an unending blaze. * [a]
7 Flood waters cannot quench love,
nor can torrents drown it.
If one were to offer all his wealth for love,
he would be regarded with contempt. [b]

r Song 2:5; 7:4.—s Song 1:2; 4:3.—t Song 2:16; 6:3.—u Song 2:10; 4:8.—v Song 4:16; 6:11.—w Song 3:4; Prov 9:2.—x Song 2:6.—y Song 2:7; 3:5.—z Song 3:6; 6:10.—a Num 5:14.—b Prov 6:31, 35.

7:10b—8:4 In her turn, the bride lets the cry of her heart come forth; she invites the bridegroom to a promenade in the exuberant countryside of the new spring. Everything reminds them of the joy of union. However, there is a bit of regret: how she would like to bear witness before everyone that she and her lover belong to one another, and how she would like to take him home to her mother for their marriage! The poem concludes with a refrain that evokes the bride asleep, filled with tenderness and love.

Again, the destiny of Israel seems to us to be very close to this adventure. Overwhelmed by God's love, the people will one day respond perfectly to the invitations of the one who is their spouse. And for more than one mystic there is no better image for the spiritual encounter with God than the new joy of a betrothal.

7:10b-c The bride offers the wine of her love to the bridegroom.

7:11 See notes on Song 2:16a; 6:3.

7:14 *Mandrakes:* herbs thought to inspire love and increase fertility (see Gen 30:14).

8:1 *Without people regarding me with scorn:* the bride could show her affection openly and incur no scorn.

8:4 See note on Song 2:7.

8:5-7 The chorus no longer recognizes the bride; love has awakened her to a new life. Quite violent is the passion that makes the lovers into one single being. Love seizes them as a force that cannot be resisted. They can no more escape it than they can escape death and the subterranean pit that, in the words of the ancients, one day will snatch all the living, the netherworld. God, who created love, willed this unity that nothing can divide. "And the two shall become one flesh," declares Paul the Apostle (Eph 5:31) with the Gospel (Mt 19:5) and the Book of Genesis (Gen 2:24). Such a love cannot be acquired at the price of silver.

It is something unheard of that between God and his people there is established a definitive link that holds despite all kinds of trials and dramas. And how can one hide forever from the Lord's ardor?

8:5 *Under the apple tree:* fruit trees were regarded as conducive to lovers' embraces.

8:6-7 *Love is as strong as death:* starting with these words, the author gives three climactic wisdom sayings about the awesome power of true love. Love stands its ground against the greatest powers on earth: death, fire, and water, and conquers even great wealth. *An unending blaze:* another translation may be: "Like the very flame of the LORD," showing that love is enkindled by God.

One Who Brings Peace*

COMPANIONS:

8 "Our sister is little,
and her breasts are not yet formed.
What shall we do for our sister
on the day she is spoken for?
9 If she is a wall,
we will build a silver battlement upon it;
if she is a door,
we will board her up with planks of cedar."

BRIDE:

10 I am a wall,
and my breasts are like towers.
So now in his eyes
I have become one who brings peace.

My Vineyard Is under My Control*

11* Solomon had a vineyard at Baal-hamon, *
and he entrusted that vineyard to tenants.
For its fruit each one would have to pay him
a thousand pieces of silver. [c]
12 My vineyard * is under my control.
You, O Solomon, may have the thousand silver pieces,
and those who tend the fruit may have two hundred. [d]

BRIDEGROOM:

13 O you who dwell in the gardens,
my companions are listening for your voice;
let me hear it. [e]

BRIDE:

14 Make haste, my beloved,
and be like a gazelle or a young stag
upon the spice-filled mountains. [f]

c Eccl 2:4; Isa 7:23.—d Prov 27:18.—e Song 2:14.—f Song 2:8-9, 17; 4:6.

8:8-10 Suddenly a life that is still young finds itself mature with passion; already love has decided the future of the bride even though her brothers are still thinking of the men to whom they could contract her in marriage. They did not notice their little sister becoming a woman. Elders always have trouble admitting that their siblings have already entered into life, that love has already brought new freedom to them.

Israel, apparently always adolescent and indecisive, the most insignificant of nations in any case, is fulfilled more than one could believe by faith in God. And the believer, so fragile in his own eyes, finds an inconceivable freedom in the Lord's presence.

8:11-14 The great monarch Solomon had a large harem, which had to be guarded by officers of the palace. The bridegroom, a poor shepherd, has his beloved all to himself. She awaits his call and will then flee her tactless companions: the two of them alone! Love is an ever renewed quest.

In this final song of love, the community of Christ can also express its expectation. It is above all a call: "Come, Lord Jesus, come"; and it is also and above all a certitude: I am coming soon. *Maranatha.* It is with this Hebrew word, *maranatha,* that the last Book of the Bible comes to a close (Rev 22:17-20). Human love is most suitable to be a symbol of divine love.

8:11-12 These verses are capable of various interpretations. In addition to the one given in the previous note, they may be interpreted as the bride saying to an imaginary Solomon that his vineyard has only monetary value while she is making a free gift of her vineyard (which is herself) to her bridegroom—in keeping with the text of verse 7b that insists that there is no price great enough to buy love.

8:11 *Baal-hamon:* an unidentified place, which is said to have a vineyard worth a thousand pieces of silver. Since it means "Lord of multitudes," it may be intended to contrast the single beloved of the Song with the many wives of Solomon.

8:12 *My vineyard:* i.e., the bride herself as in Song 1:6. It is contrasted with the vineyard of Solomon in 8:11. In what may be a satirical note, she offers Solomon the owners' portion for her vineyard and two hundred pieces of silver to the tenants.

"I [Solomon] prayed, and understanding was given to me; I pleaded, and the spirit of Wisdom came to me" *(Wis 7:7)*.

THE BOOK OF WISDOM

The Jewish Faith Is Confronted by Greek Culture

Toward the middle of the first century B.C., the great city of Alexandria in Egypt included an important Jewish community, faithful to the religious traditions of its ancestors. Throughout the land, Hellenism was flourishing in the form of a curious mixture of philosophical systems and arcane religions, in which the worship of the stars was united with that of animals. Remaining faithful in such a pagan environment was most difficult.

The Book of Wisdom sought to come to grips with this situation, but it also harbored the desire to avoid antagonizing the pagans who might be led to read it.

The author writes in Greek, which is unique in the case of the Old Testament. A Jew of Alexandria, he appears to have been formed in Greek culture and, at the same time, no less nourished on the Sacred Scriptures. He is a sage but prefers to let Solomon speak, because the tradition of Israel considered that king to be wise beyond compare.

The Book intends to teach true Wisdom, that which is necessary to lead an upright life. This does not mean the science that can be acquired by living and thinking but a Wisdom that comes from God. Indeed, this divine Wisdom has revealed that true happiness belongs to the friends of God. In other words, human beings cannot discover the meaning of life unless it is revealed to them by the Lord.

Among other things, the author of Wisdom provides the first clear and detailed affirmation of individual immortality. In doing so, he develops a theme found in Ps 73:23-28—union with the Lord continues on into the hereafter.

He also personifies Wisdom in the style of two previous Sapiential Books (Prov 8; Sir 24). The Prologue in John's Gospel makes use of the description of Wisdom (ch. 7) in setting forth its teaching on the word of God.

The literary genre used by the author of Wisdom is usually described as exhortatory discourse, i.e., an exhortation to persuade people to follow some course of speech or action by showing that what one urges is just, lawful, fitting, honorable, gratifying, and practicable.

The Book of Wisdom may be divided as follows:

I: Invitation To Seek Wisdom (1:1-15)
II: Wisdom or the Meaning of Our Destiny as Human Beings (1:16—5:23)
III: At the Source of Wisdom (6:1—9:18)
IV: The Destiny of Israel or Wisdom at Work in History (10:1—19:22)

I: INVITATION TO SEEK WISDOM*

CHAPTER 1

Seek God, Not Death

1 Love justice, * you who govern the earth,
turn your minds to the LORD in a righteous way,
and seek him with an upright heart. [a]
2 For he will be found by those who do not put him to the test,
and he will reveal himself to those who do not cease to have confidence in him.
3 Perverse thoughts separate a man from God,
and when his power is put to the test,
it reproaches the foolish. [b]
4 Wisdom refuses to enter a soul devoted to evil
or to dwell in a body indebted to sin. [c]
5 For the holy spirit of discipline * shuns deceit,
shrinks away from foolish discourse,
and is ashamed at the approach of injustice. [d]
6 [e] Wisdom is a spirit filled with kindness,
but it will not excuse the guilt incurred by the blasphemer for his words,
since God is the witness of his innermost self, *
accurately observing his heart
and listening to every word of his mouth.
7 For the spirit of the LORD fills the world,
and that which holds all things together is well aware of everything that is said. * [f]
8 Therefore, no one who utters wicked thoughts will escape detection,
nor will justice, in its chastisement, pass him by. [g]
9 For the schemes of the wicked man will be investigated,
and the sound of his words will reach the LORD
to convict him of his transgressions,
10 [h] because a jealous ear listens to everything,

a 1 Sam 3:9; 1 Chr 29:17; Ps 2:10; Isa 26:9; 56:1.—b Isa 59:2.—c Sir 15:7-8; Rom 7:14, 24.—d Ps 51:13; Isa 63:10.—e 6f: Pss 7:10; 139:4; Jer 23:24-25.—f Wis 12:1; Ps 139:7-12.—g Prov 19:5; 22:12.—h 10f: Ex 20:15; Num 14:27-28.

1:1-15 Inasmuch as he wishes to place this Book under the authority of Solomon, the author directs the first discourse to those who govern the earth (v. 1), the powerful of this world. In fact, however, the invitation is addressed to every believer exposed to the seduction of the gods and doctrines proper to the culture of that age. Each is presented with a choice (and no one is exempt from it): God or death.

1:1 The state of *justice* or *righteous[ness]* was defined as being in accord with the will of God as indicated in the law and the demands of conscience. *Seek him:* a recurring invitation in both the sages and the Prophets (see Pss 34:11; 45:7-8; 105:4; Prov 8:17; Isa 55:6; Jer 29:13). Jesus also taught that we should "seek the kingdom of God and his righteousness" (Mt 6:33).

1:5 *Holy spirit of discipline:* Wisdom (called "discipline" here) was regarded as dispensed by a "holy spirit" (see Ps 51:13; Isa 63:10-11); the whole phrase seems to indicate the power of God that directs the life of human beings and of the universe. The reference is ultimately to the work of the Holy Spirit (see Jn 14:26).

1:6 *Innermost self:* literally, "kidneys," which were regarded as the center of human emotions and impulses (see Job 19:27; Pss 16:7; 73:21; Prov 23:16), while the "heart" was the center of intellect and will. These two words were often used together (translated as "mind and heart") to indicate all of the inner forces of human beings (see Pss 7:10; 26:2; Jer 11:20; 17:10; 20:12; Rev 2:23).

1:7 The Liturgy for Pentecost applies this verse to the Holy Spirit.

thing,

and no sound of grumbling remains
secret.
11 Therefore, beware of futile grumbling
and restrain your tongue from calumny, *
for even something said in secret has repercussions,
and a lying mouth destroys the soul.
12 Do not invite death by a life prone to error,
nor incur destruction by the works of your hands.
13 [i] For God did not make death,
nor does he delight in the death of the living.
14 He created all things so that they might have existence,
and the creatures of the world engender life.
There is no deadly poison in any of them,
and the domain of the netherworld * is not on the earth,
15 for righteousness is immortal. * [j]

II: WISDOM OR THE MEANING OF OUR DESTINY AS HUMAN BEINGS*

A: The Covenant with Death

Born by Chance and Destined for Oblivion?*

16 But the godless by their words and deeds summoned death,
regarded it as a friend, and longed for it.
They made a covenant with it
since they deserve to be in its company. * [k]

CHAPTER 2

1 These people said to themselves with deluded reasoning:
"Brief and burdensome is our life,
and there is no remedy when death summons,
nor has anyone been known to have returned * from the netherworld. [l]
2 For we were born as the result of happenstance,
and afterward we shall be as though we had never existed.
The breath in our nostrils is merely a puff of smoke,
and our reason is a spark enkindled by the beating of our hearts.
3 Once it is extinguished, our body will turn to ashes,
and our spirit will melt away like empty air. [m]
4 Our name will be forgotten with the passing of time,
and no one will remember our deeds.
Our life will pass away like the wisps of a cloud
and be scattered like mist
pursued by the rays of the sun
and overwhelmed by its heat.
5 For our lifetime is but a passing shadow,
and there is no way to recall our end
because it is sealed, and no one can bring it back. [n]

A Challenge To Rejoice

6 "Come, therefore, let us enjoy the good things of life,
and use creation fully, with youthful ardor. [o]
7 Let us take our fill of expensive wine and perfumes
and allow no flower of spring to escape our notice;

i 13f: Ezek 18:32; 33:11; 2 Pet 3:9.—j Wis 3:4; 15:3; Isa 51:6-8.—k Prov 8:36; Isa 28:15, 18.—l Job 7:9; 14:1-2; Pss 39:5-7; 89:49.—m Job 7:9; Ps 104:29; Jas 4:14.—n Pss 39:6; 144:4; Eccl 6:12.—o Eccl 11:9; Isa 22:13; 56:12; 1 Cor 15:32.

1:11 *Calumny*: used here in the sense of criticism of God and his providence.

1:13-14 *Netherworld:* this word signifies here more than simply the place where the dead are shut up without hope or future. Rather, it constitutes the hostile power of death, which seeks to disfigure the work of God. It represents the whole hideous weight of evil that fights against what God wills for the world and for human beings.

1:15 The one who is righteous is assured of immortality. The Latin version adds: "but injustice acquires death."

1:16—5:23 In the terminology of the ancients, to speak of Wisdom is to seek to individualize the real destiny of human beings. Everyone desires to live and be happy; life and civilization offer possibilities and attractions, but so do illusion, error, and perversion. This first part of the Book (1:16—5:23) enables the Old Testament to advance in the reflection on the human condition, opening perspectives on eternity.

1:16—2:5 The stage is now given to the blasphemer who sings the praises of nothingness. In order to avoid the responsibility of being a human being, he strives to prove the absurd, to destroy the value of life and sully the mystery of existence so that he will no longer have to be astounded and perhaps have to acknowledge a God who takes an interest in the destiny of human beings.

1:16 *Deserve to be in its company:* literally, "deserve to belong to its portion." In other words, the godless belong to death as Israel belongs to God (see Deut 32:9; 2 Mac 1:26; Zec 2:16) and as God belongs to those who are faithful to him (see Pss 16:5; 73:26; 142:6).

2:1 *Known to have returned:* another translation is: "known to have been delivered." The author places on the lips of fools an entire philosophy of life: the little time allotted to humans on earth must be used in enjoyment because there is no hereafter. This theme is also found in Job 7:1-10; Ps 39:5-14; Lk 12:16-21; 1 Cor 15:32.

8 let us crown ourselves with rosebuds
before they wither. *
9 Let none of us fail to share in our wanton doings;
let us leave traces of our revelry everywhere,
since this is our portion, this our lot. [p]

Let Us Wait in Hiding for the Righteous Man*

10 "Let us oppress the righteous man who is in need; *
let us not spare the widow
or show respect for the venerable gray head of the aged. [q]
11 Rather, let our might serve as the yardstick of justice,
for what is feeble has proved itself useless.
12 Let us wait in hiding for the righteous man,
for he inconveniences us and opposes our deeds.
He reproaches us for our sins against the law
and accuses us of failures in what we have been taught. [r]
13 He claims to have knowledge of God
and refers to himself as a child of the LORD. [s]
14 He has become for us a reproof to our manner of thinking,
and the very sight of him is a source of pain to us. [t]
15 For his life is unlike that of others,
and his ways are just as different. *
16 He considers us to be counterfeit,
and he steers clear of our ways as unclean.
He proclaims the final end of the righteous as blessed,
and he boasts that God is his Father. [u]
17 Let us see if what he says is true,
and let us probe what will happen at the conclusion of his life. [v]
18 For if the righteous man is a child of God, * he will defend him
and deliver him from the power of his enemies. [w]
19 Let us test him with insults and torments
so that we may be able to measure his gentleness
and ascertain the depths of his forbearance of evil.
20 Let us condemn him * to a shameful death,
since, according to his words, he will be protected." [x]

The Horrible Face of Death*

21 Such was their reasoning, but they were wrong,
for their own malice blinded them. [y]
22 They did not discern the hidden plans of God,
or hope for the recompense of holiness
or recognize the reward destined for innocent souls. [z]
23 For God created us to be immortal
and formed us in the image of his own nature. * [a]
24 But as a result of the devil's envy, death entered the world,
and those who follow him experience it. [b]

p Isa 57:6; Jer 13:25.—q Ex 22:22ff; Lev 19:32; 25:35-37.—r Jer 11:19; Hos 8:1.—s Mt 11:27; 27:43; Lk 22:70.—t Isa 53:3; Mt 9:4.—u Sir 23:1, 4; Isa 3:10; 63:16; 64:7; Mt 5:10.—v Gen 37:20; Mt 29:49.—w Ps 22:9; Isa 42:1; Mt 27:43; Jn 5:18.—x Jer 11:19; Jas 5:6.—y Jn 3:19; Rom 1:21.—z Ps 18:23; Prov 11:18; Mt 11:25; 13:11.—a Gen 1:26-27; 2:7; Isa 54:16 LXX.—b Gen 3:1-24; Jn 8:44; Rom 5:12.

2:8 Most Latin versions add: "let no meadow be free of our excesses."

2:10-20 The violence of those without a conscience crushes the righteous who entrust themselves to God. Already one seems to envisage the leader who hunts down Christ and all the poor that he represents. Yet, who is really the free person? Many even regard these verses as directly prophetic of Christ's Passion (see Mt 27:41-44).

2:10 *The righteous man who is in need:* the godless jeer that the righteous man is in need despite the promises of Scripture (see Tob 4:21; Pss 37:25; 112:3; Prov 3:9-10; 12:21).

2:15 The author is here reproducing the opinion current in the world of his day that the Jewish people were set apart from all others by their belief and way of life.

2:18 The righteous and the poor (vv. 10-12) bear the name of *child of God*, a title applied to the whole people of Israel (Ex 4:22-23; Hos 11:1), to the king and Messiah (2 Sam 7:14; Ps 2:7), and finally, to Christ (Heb 1:3-4; 12:3) and, by extension, to all Christians who live in him.

2:20 *Him:* i.e., the faithful Jew who was mocked and persecuted for his faith. Christian tradition sees in this verse a foreshadowing of Christ's Passion, the innocent One hated by his enemies (see Heb 12:3; see also Mt 27:43).

2:21-24 A mysterious adversary (in the juridic sense: "accuser") for human beings—called here the *devil* (*diabolos*: the word that, in the Septuagint, translates the Hebrew for Satan; see Job 1:6)—is at work; for the first time, he is presented as the tempter of human beings.

2:23 *Nature:* other translations: "eternity" or "likeness."

B: For the Righteous—Life Eternal*

CHAPTER 3

Their Hope Is Full of Immortality*

1 * But the souls of the righteous are in the hand of God,
and no torment can overtake them. [c]
2 From the viewpoint of the foolish, they seemed to be dead,
and their passing away was reckoned as a misfortune,
3 and their departure from us as their ruin.
But they are at peace. * [d]
4 Although in the eyes of others they were chastised,
their hope is full of immortality.
5 Having endured a slight chastisement, they will receive great blessings,
because God tested them
and found them worthy to be with him. * [e]
6 He put them to the proof like gold in a furnace,
and he accepted them as a sacrificial burnt offering. * [f]
7 In the time of their visitation* they will shine brightly
and spread like sparks among the stubble. [g]
8 They will judge nations and have dominion over peoples,
and the LORD will be their King forever. [h]
9 Those who trust in him will understand truth,
and the faithful will dwell with him in love,
because grace and mercy are reserved for his holy ones,
and he shows concern for his elect. [i]
10 However, the godless will receive a punishment in accord with their reasoning,
for they had no concern for the righteous
and rebelled against the LORD.
11 Those who despise wisdom and discipline are wretched:
vain is their hope, unprofitable are their labors,
and worthless are their achievements. [j]
12 Their wives are foolish and their children depraved;
their lineage is accursed. [k]

Better Is Virtue than Offspring*

13 Blessed is the barren woman who is undefiled,
who has not experienced a sinful union;
she will bear fruit at the visitation of souls.
14 Blessed also is the eunuch whose hands have committed no iniquity
and who has never harbored any wicked thoughts against the LORD;
he shall receive a special grace for his faithfulness
and a more illustrious share in the temple of the LORD.
15 For the fruit of good works is glorious,
and the root of understanding is ever fruitful. [l]
16 But the children of adulterers will never see maturity,
and the offspring of an unlawful union will disappear.

c Job 5:19; 12:10; Jn 10:28.—d Isa 57:2.—e Tob 12:13-14; Rom 8:18; 2 Cor 4:17; 1 Pet 1:6-7.—f Job 23:10; Ps 51:17-19; Prov 17:3; Sir 2:5; Isa 48:10.—g Dan 12:3; Ob 18; Mal 3:3; Mt 13:43.—h Wis 8:14; Ps 149:6-8; Prov 8:16; Dan 7:22, 27; Mt 19:28; Rev 20:4.—i Wis 4:15; Job 10:12; Prov 28:5; Eccl 2:26; Jn 15:10.—j Prov 1:7; 10:16; 11:18; Sir 41:8.—k Deut 28:18ff.—l Wis 1:15; 2:23; Prov 10:16; Sir 1:20.

3:1—5:23 Longevity, posterity, and success—those grand realities in which the ancients strove to decipher the signs of divine recompense—are found to be valueless. The scale of values is reversed: true happiness is life with God, starting from the present and moving into an unimaginable eternity. The destiny of human beings is enlightened by a new day.

3:1-12 Influenced by Greek thought, the author speaks of immortality, though still not arriving at the idea of a resurrection of the body.

3:1-8 The Liturgy applies these verses to martyrs.

3:3 *Peace:* this word here refers to a state without evil (see Job 3:17f; Isa 57:2) where there is security or happiness under God's protection and in intimacy with him (see vv. 1, 9).

3:5 Trials and sufferings purify the righteous (Tob 12:13; 2 Mac 6:12-17; 7:32-33; Pss 66:10; 119:75; Prov 3:11-12; 1 Cor 11:32; Heb 12:11).

3:6 *Sacrificial burnt offering:* the allusion is to the sacrifice in which the victim was offered to God and completely consumed by fire to show total dedication to him (Lev 1:1ff).

3:7 *Visitation:* a biblical term for an intervention of God (see Isa 10:3) that is used here to designate God's judgment of the righteous (probably immediately after death). In Wis 14:11, it is used to designate the judgment of the wicked. See also verse 13.

3:13—4:6 Up to this time, the entire hope of human beings lay in their children, who could perpetuate one's name and memory; apart from this, death appeared as the inexorable abyss that swallowed up everything. Hence, sterility was regarded as a curse, and eunuchs were excluded from the community (Deut 23:2). The Book of Wisdom overturns principles that were profoundly anchored, as Jesus will also do by affirming the new and exceptional value of those who are celibate for the kingdom of God (Mt 19:11f). The prize of a good life is no longer a posterity, but a future life.

17 Even should they achieve a long life, they will be regarded as of no account,
and in the end their old age will be without honor.
18 But if they die young, they will have no hope,
nor any consolation on the day of judgment,
19 for the fate of a wicked generation is harsh. [m]

CHAPTER 4

1 Far better than this is childlessness accompanied by virtue, *
for immortality is gained by a remembrance of virtue,
since it is acknowledged both by God and by men. [n]
2 When it is present, men imitate it,
and they long for it in its absence.
And throughout eternity it marches crowned in triumph,
victorious in the struggle for prizes that are undefiled. *
3 However, the prolific progeny of the wicked will avail nothing;
none of their illegitimate stock will put forth deep roots
or lay a firm foundation. [o]
4 For even if they put forth branches for a time,
without a firm foundation they will be shaken by the wind
and torn up by the violence of the storms.
5 Their immature branches will be broken off
and their fruit will be useless,
not ripe enough to eat and fit for no purpose.
6 For children born of unlawful unions
bear witness to the wickedness of their parents
when God brings them to judgment. *

Better To Die Young than To Die in Wickedness*

7 But the righteous man, even if he dies prematurely, will be at rest. * [p]
8 For the honor that comes with age is not due to the length of life
or determined by the number of years. [q]
9 Gray hairs for anyone consists in understanding,
and ripe old age consists in a blameless life.
10 * He has sought to please God, so God has loved him;
while living among sinners, he has been taken up. [r]
11 He has been snatched away so that evil would not pervert his understanding
or guile deceive his soul.
12 For the spell of wickedness beclouds what is good,
and the swirl of desire corrupts the simple heart. [s]
13 Having achieved perfection in a short time,
he attained a lengthy span of years.
14 Since his soul was pleasing to the LORD,
he quickly removed him from the midst of wickedness.

People observed this yet failed to comprehend,
nor did they reflect on this fact, [t]
15 that grace and mercy are reserved for God's holy ones
and he shows concern for his elect. * [u]
16 The righteous man who dies condemns the godless who are still alive,
and youth that has quickly achieved perfection
condemns the prolonged age of the wicked.
17 For they observe the death of the wise man
but understand neither the designs of the LORD for him
nor why he has kept him safe.

m Pss 34:22; 37:38.—n Wis 3:13; Ps 112:6; Prov 3:3-4; Sir 16:1ff.—o Sir 23:25; 40:15; Mt 15:13.—p Wis 3:3; Isa 57:1-2.—q Job 12:12; 32:9; Sir 25:4ff.—r Gen 5:24; Sir 44:16; Heb 11:5.—s Wis 2:21; Ps 4:3; Dan 13:9.—t Gen 19:22, 29; Isa 57:1-2; 2 Pet 2:7.—u Wis 3:9; Sir 4:12.

4:1 The Liturgy applies this verse in its Latin translation to the glory of virginity: "Oh, how beautiful is the chaste generation in its glory."

4:2 Paul uses the image of sporting competition in 1 Cor 9:24-27.

4:6 Here it is a case of the *judgment* of God (see Wis 3:18).

4:7-19 The premature death of the righteous person was a shock to the ancients who were convinced that God had to reward him by a long life. The Book of Wisdom overturns this principle that was so solidly entrenched. Since death was henceforth regarded as the threshold of eternity, the old religious ideas of recompense were evolving. It must have been scandalous, at this time, to affirm that death can be a mark of favor given by the Lord to someone that he wishes thereby to keep out of sin.

4:7 This *rest* is peace; i.e., for the author of Wisdom, not an eternal sleep but a fullness of life (see Wis 3:3).

4:10-11 These verses contain allusions to Enoch, who was young in terms of the life-span of the Patriarchs (Gen 5:21-24) and Lot (Gen 19:10-11; 2 Pet 2:7-8). *Taken up:* the righteous are "taken up" like Enoch (Gen 5:24), Elijah (2 Ki 2:1, 11), and Christ at the Ascension (Acts 1:11, 22).

4:15 These two lines repeat the last two lines of Wis 3:9.

18 They look on and sneer contemptuously at him,
but the LORD will laugh them to scorn. [v]
19 Afterward they will become dishonored corpses
and objects of contempt among the dead forever.
For he will cast them speechless to the ground
and shake them to their very foundations.
They will be completely laid waste,
overwhelmed with grief,
and their memory will perish. [w]

The Final Judgment of the Wicked*

20 The godless will cringe with terror when their sins are reckoned,
and their lawless deeds will convict them to their face.

CHAPTER 5

1 Then will the righteous man stand with great confidence
in the presence of his oppressors
and those who derided his sufferings. [x]
2 On beholding him, his oppressors will be seized with terrible dread
and will be amazed at his unexpected deliverance.
3 With remorse they will speak to one another,
and groaning in distress of spirit they will say:
4 "This is the one whom we once mocked
and made a target of our insults, fools that we were.
We regarded his way of life as madness
and his end as dishonorable.
5 Why is he now reckoned among the children of God,
sharing the lot of the saints? [y]
6 Clearly we have been the ones who have strayed from the way of truth,
and the light of justice has not shone for us
or the sun risen upon us. [z]
7 We had our fill of traversing the paths of lawlessness and ruin
and wandered across trackless deserts,
but of the way of the LORD we have been ignorant.
8 Of what avail has arrogance been to us?
What advantage have we received from our vaunted wealth? [a]
9 "All these things have passed like a shadow,
much like a fleeting notice;
10 * like a ship that sails through the surging waters
of whose passage—once it has passed by—no trace can be found,
no wake from its keel in the waves;
11 or like a bird that flies through the air
and no sign of its passage is left,
for the light air, whipped by the beat of its pinions
and cleft by the force of its speed,
is traversed by the flapping wings,
and afterward there is no sign of its passage;
12 or as when an arrow is shot at a target,
the air is parted but immediately comes together again,
and no evidence remains of its passage;
13 so we also, as soon as we were born, ceased to be
and had not a trace of virtue to exhibit
but were consumed in our wickedness." * [b]
14 The hope of the godless is like chaff carried on the wind,
and like sea spray swept before a storm;
it is dissipated like smoke confronted by the wind,
and it passes away like the memory of a guest who stays but a single day. [c]
15 But the righteous live forever,
and their recompense is with the LORD; *
the Most High provides for them. [d]
16 Therefore, they will receive a glorious crown

v Pss 2:4; 37:13; 59:9; Prov 1:26.—w Neh 1:10 LXX; 2 Mac 3:29; Pss 18:26-28; 109:15; Jer 23:39-40.—x Mt 13:43; Col 2:15; 2 Thes 1:6-7.—y Acts 26:18; Col 1:12.—z Ps 119:105; Prov 2:13; 4:18-19; 21:16.—a Ps 49:6-7; Prov 10:2.—b Sir 44:9; Ezek 33:10.—c Wis 16:29; Job 20:8; 21:18; Pss 1:4; 37:20; 68:3; Prov 11:7.—d Gen 15:1; Isa 62:11; Jer 1:12; Rev 22:12.

4:20—5:23 The author gives us a poem of the precariousness and the brevity of earthly life; completely unfortunate is one who makes it the be-all and end-all of existence (Wis 5:8-13)!

5:10-12 Some of the same images used here are found in Job 9:25-26; Prov 30:19.

5:13 After this verse the Vulgate adds the words: "This is what the sinners say in hell" as verse 14, necessitating a change in the enumeration of the rest of the verses in the chapter.

5:15 *Their recompense is with the LORD:* for he is their portion (see Pss 16:5-6; 73:26; see also Wis 3:14).

and a splendid diadem from the hand of the LORD.
For he will shelter them with his right hand
and shield them with his arm.

17 He will take zeal as his armor
and arm all creation to repulse his foes.*
18 He will put on justice as a breastplate,
and wear an infallible judgment as a helmet.
19 [e] He will take invincible holiness as a shield
20 and sharpen unrelenting wrath for a sword,*
and the whole world will unite with him to fight against the reckless.
21 Shafts of his lightning, accurately aimed, will fly forth,
hurtling from the clouds as from a well-drawn bow toward their target,
22 while the hailstones of his wrath will be hurled as from a sling.
The waters of the sea will rage against them,
and the rivers will relentlessly engulf them.
23 A mighty wind will rise against them
and will winnow them like a tempest.
Lawlessness will make the whole earth a wasteland,
and evildoing will overthrow the thrones of the mighty.[f]

III: AT THE SOURCE OF WISDOM*

A: Seek and You Will Find

CHAPTER 6

A Rigorous Judgment Awaits the Mighty*

1 Listen, then, O kings, and try to comprehend;
learn, O judges of the whole earth.*
2 Pay attention, you who govern multitudes,
and take pride in the huge number of your peoples.
3 Your sovereignty was bestowed on you by the LORD
and your power by the Most High,
who will probe your deeds and scrutinize your intentions.* [g]
4 Since as servants of his kingdom you neither ruled justly,
nor kept his law,
nor walked in the paths designated by the will of God,
5 he will move against you terribly and swiftly,
for stern is the judgment decreed against the high and the mighty.* [h]
6 The lowly will be pardoned through mercy,
but the mighty will be tested with rigor.
7 For the Lord of all is not in awe of anyone,
nor does he show any deference to worldly rank,
since he himself made small and great alike,
and he provides for all equally.[i]
8 But a strict examination awaits those in positions of power.

9 To you, then, O monarchs, are these words of mine directed
so that you may learn wisdom and not go astray.
10 For those who observe holy precepts with holiness will be accounted holy,
and those who have become learned in them will have a defense* to offer.
11 Therefore, be zealous in heeding my words;
long for them, and you will receive instruction.

e 19f: Wis 16:17; Deut 32:40ff.—f Wis 11:20: Sir 10:13-14.—g 1 Chr 29:12; 2 Chr 36:23; Prov 8:15-16; Jn 19:11.—h Lk 12:48; 1 Thes 5:3; Heb 10:30-31; Jas 2:13.—i Wis 8:3; Deut 10:17; Ps 145:9; Prov 22:2; Rom 2:11; Gal 2:6.

5:17 God's offensive and defensive weapons are a classic theme in the imagery of the judgment (see Ps 17:14-15; Isa 59:17). Paul applies them to the Christian's battle against the devil (Eph 6:13-17).

5:20 *Sword [of God]:* see Isa 49:2; Ezek 21:8-10; Heb 4:12; Rev 1:16; 19:15.

6:1—9:18 A mysterious force animates the conduct of the righteous and opens to them the hope of immortality: this is Wisdom. It cannot come simply from this earth and result solely from human effort; it finds its origins beyond these horizons—and comes from heaven. To make it accepted, the author ably presents his own experience and reflection (chs. 6–9) as sentiments of Solomon, the wise man beyond compare.

6:1-11 This text places all on guard against the abuse of their power, their prestige, and their state. Who in their own way are not tempted to be high and mighty? Let them learn to serve and to live under the judgment of God who is righteous.

6:1 The Vulgate adds these words as verse 1 of this chapter: "Wisdom is better than strength, / and the prudent man is better than the mighty." This necessitates a change in the enumeration of all the verses of the chapter.

6:3 The ancient East regarded the person and authority of the king to be of divine origin. All authority is delegated (see Dan 5:18-20; Jn 19:11).

6:5 God's punishment of wrongdoing was felt by Moses (Num 20:12), David (2 Sam 24:10-17), and Hezekiah (2 Ki 20:16-19), among others.

6:10 *Defense:* see Job 31:14; Prov 22:21; Sir 8:9; Hab 2:1.

Wisdom Is Seated at the Door of Those Who Love Her*

12 Radiant and never-fading is Wisdom;
she is easily discerned by those who love her
and is found by those who search for her. [j]
13 [k] She hastens to make herself known
to those who desire her. *
14 He who rises early to seek her will not have to toil,
for he will discover her seated at his door.
15 To meditate on her is to achieve perfection in understanding,
and he who is vigilant in seeking after her will soon be free from care.
16 For she herself goes about seeking those who are worthy of her,
and she graciously appears to them as they tread life's paths,
meeting them with all benevolence. [l]
17 [m] The beginning of Wisdom is a sincere desire for instruction,
and concern for learning is evidence of love for her;
18 but love for her is shown by keeping her laws,
and observing her laws brings the assurance of incorruptibility.
19 Now incorruptibility brings people close to God;
20 thus the desire for Wisdom leads to a kingdom.
21 Therefore, if you take delight in thrones and scepters, you rulers of the peoples,
honor Wisdom so that you may reign as kings forever. *

Wisdom Is Not the Exclusive Possession of the Initiated*

22 Now I will explain what Wisdom is and how she came to be;
I will not hide her secrets from you.
I will trace her steps from the beginning of creation
and bring knowledge of her to full light
without swerving from the truth. [n]
23 Nor will I allow corrosive envy to accompany me,
for it has nothing in common with Wisdom.
24 The abundance of the wise is the salvation of the world,
and a prudent king is the stability of his people. [o]
25 Therefore, learn what I have to teach you,
and you will profit.

CHAPTER 7

1 I too am mortal, like everyone else,
descended from the first being formed out of the earth. *
I was molded into flesh inside the womb of my mother,
2 solidified in blood within a period of ten months *
from the seed of a man and the pleasure that accompanies marriage.
3 And I too, when I was born, began to breathe the common air
and fell upon an earth equal for everyone;
the first sound I uttered was a cry, as is true of all.
4 I was nurtured in swaddling clothes
and surrounded with care.
5 No king has begun life in any other way,
6 for there is only one way of entering life, and only one way of leaving it.

j Wis 7:10; Prov 8:17; 14:6; Sir 6:27-28; Jn 14:21.—k 13ff: Prov 8:3, 17, 34; Sir 15:2.—l Prov 1:20-21; 8:2-3, 20-21; Sir 15:1-2.—m 17-21: Wis 5:16; Ps 2:10ff; Prov 4:4-9; 7:1-4; Dan 7:27; Jn 14:15, 21.—n Tob 12:7, 11; Mt 13:11; Jn 15:15.—o Prov 24:6; 29:4; Sir 10:1ff.

6:12-21 When we truly desire the force of life that is Wisdom, she comes before us. For our author, it is the intimate invitation that reaches all human beings in the secret of the heart. It is neither a legalism nor an annoying moralism imposed from outside, but an inner transformation, which becomes the hope of immortality.

6:13 Wisdom, like God himself, always takes the initiative. In this way, she foreshadows God's prevenient grace (see Jn 6:44-46; 10:25-27; Phil 2:13; 1 Jn 4:19).

6:21 The Vulgate adds here: "Love the light of Wisdom, all you who govern nations," which in its numbering scheme becomes verse 23.

6:22—7:6 Not even Solomon, despite all his renown, had a monopoly on the gift from heaven that is Wisdom. All who share the human condition have need of her; she is a conviction that becomes contagious to transform the world, and no one has the right to make her his own preserve.

7:1 The author consistently fails to name the persons of sacred history to whom he refers. See, for example, chapter 10. The author here notes that a king is only a mere mortal—a Jewish conception that was foreign to the ancient East and, in part, also to the Greek world, which divinized its sovereigns. The purity of the Jewish monotheism imposed this view, which is counterbalanced by the certitude that Wisdom—which is a divine gift—is necessary in order to rule well.

7:2 *Ten months:* this refers to "lunar" months, the common method of calculation among the ancients.

Wisdom Is Worth More than Any Riches

7 Therefore, I prayed, and understanding was given to me;
I pleaded, and the spirit of Wisdom came to me.[p]
8 [q] I preferred her to scepters and thrones,
and I accounted riches as nothing compared with her. *
9 Neither did I reckon any precious stone to be her equal,
because, compared with her, all gold is but a few grains of sand,
and beside her, silver is accounted as clay.
10 I loved her more than health and beauty
and preferred her to the light
because her radiance is unceasing.
11 Together with her, all good things came to me,
and in her hands are countless riches.[r]
12 And I delighted in them all, since Wisdom was their source,
although I did not realize at the time that she was their mother.
13 I pass on ungrudgingly what I learned about her with an open mind;
her riches I do not conceal.
14 For she is an inexhaustible treasure for all;
those who acquire her achieve friendship with God,
commended to him by the gifts that derive from her instruction. *[s]

B: Wisdom Is Divine

Maker of All Things*

15 May God grant me the ability to speak according to understanding
and to express thoughts worthy of the gifts I have received,
since it is he that guides Wisdom
and directs the wise.[t]
16 For in his hand are both we and our words,
as are also all understanding and skill in crafts.
17 It was he who granted me accurate knowledge of what exists,
so that I might understand the constitution of the world and the operation of its elements:
18 the beginning and the end and the midpoint of times,
the alternation of the solstices and the changes of the seasons,
19 the cycles of the year and the positions of the stars,
20 the natures of animals and the dispositions of wild beasts,
the powers of spirits and the thoughts of men,
the varieties of plants and the properties of roots.
21 All that was hidden and all that was manifest I learned,
22 [u] for Wisdom, who fashioned all things, instructed me.

Reflection of God's Light*

* Within Wisdom is a spirit that is intelligent, holy,
unique, manifold, subtle,
mobile, clear, unstained,
certain, invulnerable, benevolent, shrewd,
irresistible, beneficent, 23 kindly,
steadfast, secure, tranquil,
all-powerful, all-surveying,
and penetrating all spirits
that are intelligent, pure, and very subtle.
24 For Wisdom has more mobility than any motion;
she is so pure that she pervades and penetrates all things.

p 1 Ki 3:5-15; 5:9-14; Prov 2:3-11; Sir 47:12-17.—q 8f: Wis 8:5; 1 Ki 10:21; Job 28:15-19; Pss 19:11; 119:72; Prov 3:14ff; 8:10, 18-19.—r 1 Ki 3:13; Prov 8:21; Sir 47:18.—s Wis 7:27; Sir 6:19; Lk 12:33.—t Sir 51:30; Eph 6:20.—u 22f: Heb 4: 12-13; Jas 3:17.

7:8 Nothing can be compared with Wisdom, and she is acquired only at a very great price. It is the same for the kingdom of heaven, the pearl of great price, the hidden treasure (see Mt 13:44-46).

7:14 *Instruction:* the same as "discipline" (see note on Wis 1:5).

7:15-22a Wisdom is not merely conduct of life but also awe before the secrets of the visible and invisible universe. Here the author attributes to Solomon—famous for his knowledge (see 1 Ki 5:9-14)—the most recent acquisitions of Hellenistic thought about the universe.

7:22b—8:1 Scholars will recognize herein the questions and the vocabulary of Greek philosophers, astounded by the inexhaustible mystery of the human conscience. But our author goes so far as to admire the source that gives rise to the spiritual condition of human beings—which is divine.

In this description of Wisdom, the reflection is oriented toward a new understanding of the divine mystery: the New Testament would eventually reveal the existence in God of the personality and action of the Holy Spirit, and above all, of the Son, image of the Father and creative Word (Jn 1; Rom 8; Col 1:15). Subsequently, Christian tradition has almost always recognized in Wisdom (Greek, *sophia*) the second Person of the Trinity.

7:22b-23 The attributes given for Wisdom are twenty-one in all, which constitutes a most perfect number (three times seven).

25 She is the breath of the might of God
and a pure emanation of the glory of the Almighty;
therefore, nothing that is defiled can enter into her.
26 For she is the reflection of eternal light,
the spotless mirror of the active power of God
and the image of his goodness. [v]
27 Although she is only one, she can do all things;
while unchanging herself, she makes all things new.
Generation after generation she enters into holy souls,
and turns them into friends of God*
and prophets. [w]
28 For God loves nothing more
than one who dwells with Wisdom.
29 [x] She is more beautiful than the sun
and outshines every constellation of the stars.
In comparison with the light she is far superior,
30 for light is supplanted by the night,
but evil cannot overpower Wisdom.

CHAPTER 8

1 She reaches mightily from one end of the earth to the other,
and she governs all things exceedingly well.

A Companion in Life*

2 I loved Wisdom and searched for her from my youth;
I resolved to have her for my spouse
and was in love with her beauty. [y]
3 She manifests her noble birth by union of life with God,
for the LORD of all has loved her.
4 She is privy to the secrets of the knowledge of God
and chooses his works.
5 If riches are deemed a desirable possession in life,
what offers greater wealth than Wisdom who fashions everything that exists? [z]
6 [a] If understanding is at work,
who is a more effective fashioner of whatever exists than she?
7 And if one prizes righteousness,
the fruits of her labors are virtues.
For she teaches temperance and prudence,
justice and fortitude,*
and nothing in life is of more value for men than these.
8 Or again, if one yearns for great experience,
she knows the things of the past and foresees those of the future.
She understands the subtleties of speech and the solutions of riddles;
she has advance knowledge of signs and wonders
and can predict the outcome of times and ages. [b]
9 And so I determined to take her as my life companion,
confident that she would counsel me in times of prosperity
and comfort me in times of anxiety and sorrow.
10 [c] Because of her presence I will receive glory among the multitudes
and honor among the elders, even though I am young.
11 I will be considered wise when I sit in judgment,
and I will win the admiration of rulers.
12 When I remain silent, they will await my utterances;
when I do speak, they will listen carefully.
And should I speak at great length,
they will put their hands over their mouths.*
13 Through her I will achieve immortality
and leave an everlasting memory to my successors. [d]

---

v Jn 1:9; 14:9; 2 Cor 4:4; Col 1:15; Heb 1:3.—w Ex 33:11; Job 42:2; Pss 102:28; 104:29; Joel 3:1; Jas 1:17.—x 29f: Song 6:3, 9; Jn 1:5; 16:33.—y Ps 45:11; Prov 5:18; 8:17; Sir 15:2.—z Wis 7:21; Prov 8:18-19.—a 6f: Prov 8:14-15; Sir 37:30.—b Prov 1:6; Sir 39:1ff.—c 10ff: 1 Ki 3:28; Job 29:8ff, 21-22.—d Wis 8:17; Ps 112:6; Sir 15:6; 39:9; 41:12-13; Isa 56:5.

7:27 *Friends of God:* like Abraham (see 2 Chr 20:7; Isa 41:8; Jas 2:23; see also Jn 15:14-15).

8:2-16 Wisdom is, for our author, a word and a symbol that evokes the supreme goods of private and public life. Certainly, his mentality and his vocabulary appear to us to be poetic speculations very far from our way of saying things, yet these pages are precious to us. They guard us from shutting ourselves up within the limits of what we know, what we can do, and what we have. There is for human beings a greater horizon that breaches the threshold of the divine. Those who claim to master science are well advised to reflect on this.

8:7 The four cardinal virtues. They are already found in Plato and Aristotle.

8:12 Onlookers will put their hands over their mouths as a sign that there is nothing to refute and nothing to add (see Job 21:5; 29:9; 40:4; Prov 30:32; Sir 5:14; Mic 7:16).

14 I will govern peoples, and nations will become subject to me;
15 fierce monarchs will be in dread when they hear my name,
but among the people I will be regarded as good and as valiant in battle.
16 When I return to my home I will rest beside her,
for to be in her company involves no bitterness,
and life with her entails no pain,
but only gladness and joy.

LORD, Send Forth Your Wisdom*

17 Reflecting upon these things within myself
and having concluded in my heart
that there is immortality in kinship with Wisdom
18 and pure delight in friendship with her,
inexhaustible wealth in the works of her hands
and understanding in frequenting her company
as well as great renown in conversing with her,
I began to search in all directions,
seeking to win her for myself. [e]
19 As a child I was blessed with natural gifts,
and a good soul was my heritage,
20 or rather, being good, I had entered into an undefiled body. *
21 But realizing that I could not possess Wisdom* unless God gave her to me—
and this itself was an indication of understanding, to know the source of that gift—
I turned to the LORD and implored him
and with all my heart I said: [f]

CHAPTER 9

1 "God of my ancestors and LORD of mercy,
by your word* you have created all things,
2 and in your wisdom you have fashioned man
to have power over all the creatures you have made, [g]
3 to govern the world in holiness and righteousness,
and to mete out justice with an upright heart.
4 Grant me Wisdom, who sits beside your throne, *
and do not exclude me from the number of your children. [h]
5 "For I am your servant and the son of your handmaid,
a weak man with but a short time to live
and with meager comprehension of justice and law.
6 Indeed, even one who is perfect among the sons of men
will be of no account
if he lacks the Wisdom that comes from you. [i]
7 You have chosen me to be king of your people
and to sit in judgment over your sons and daughters.
8 You have commanded me to build a temple on your holy mountain,
and an altar in the city that is your dwelling,
a replica of the sacred tabernacle that you prepared from the beginning. *[j]
9 With you is Wisdom, who knows your works
and was present when you created the world.
She understands what is pleasing in your eyes
and what is in conformity with your commandments.
10 "Send her forth from your holy heavens,
and dispatch her from the throne of your glory,

e Wis 8:2, 9.—f 1 Ki 3:9; 4:29; Prov 2:6; Sir 1:1; Jas 1:5.—g Gen 1:26, 28; Ps 8:7; Sir 17:2ff.—h 2 Chr 1:10; Sir 1:1; Bar 3:29.—i 1 Ki 11:4; 1 Cor 3:18ff.—j Ex 25:8-9; 2 Sam 7:13; 1 Ki 5:19; 2 Chr 6:1-2; 7:7; Tob 1:4; Pss 2:6; 15:1; 48:2-3.

8:17—9:18 The author attributes to the young Solomon this fervent and wonderful prayer (see 1 Ki 3:6-9; 2 Chr 1:8-10), which takes up again, with the charm of a humble petition to God, themes already repeatedly developed. The sage is free to read the "signs of the times," to seek out in all events and circumstances what God expects from humans.

8:20 The author does not intend to affirm that the soul exists first; rather, he corrects the impression given by the preceding verse that the body has preeminence.

8:21 *I could not possess Wisdom:* this is the preferred reading; the Vulgate translated it as: "I could not be chaste."

9:1 *Your word:* i.e., God's creative Word (see Gen 1), a concept that is like a prelude for the revelation of the Word of God, Jesus Christ (Jn 1:1-14).

9:4 *Wisdom, who sits beside your throne:* it is from there that the word of judgment will be launched against Egypt (see Wis 18:15). God is conceived as a sovereign who, from his throne, creates the universe, governs and judges it; his Wisdom conceives and executes.

9:8 The temple was built according to the model of the tabernacle that God had Moses construct in the image that he showed him at Sinai (Ex 25:9, 40; 26:30), which—according to a Jewish tradition—had existed from the beginning of creation.

so that she may labor at my side
and I may learn what is pleasing to you.[k]
11 For she knows and understands all things,
and with prudence she will guide me in my deeds
and guard me with her splendor.
12 Then will my works be acceptable to you,
and I will judge your people uprightly
and be worthy of the throne of my father.
13 "What person can have knowledge of the counsel of God,
or who can discern what the will of the LORD is?[l]
14 The reasonings of mortals are faulty
and our reflections are unstable.
15 For a perishable body burdens the soul,
and its earthly tent* weighs down the mind filled with many cares.
16 With difficulty do we assess what is on earth,
and that which is within our reach we discover only after arduous labor;
who then can seek out the things of heaven?
17 Who could ever have known your counsel
if you had not given Wisdom
and sent your Holy Spirit from on high?[m]
18 And thus the paths of those on earth were straightened,
and men were taught what pleases you
and were saved by Wisdom."

IV: THE DESTINY OF ISRAEL OR WISDOM AT WORK IN HISTORY*

CHAPTER 10

A: The History of the Patriarchs*

Adam, Cain, Noah

1[n] Wisdom preserved the first-formed father of the world*
when he alone had been created.
She delivered him from his transgression
2 and gave him the power to rule over all things.
3 But when the wicked man* forsook her in his wrath,
he perished because of his fratricidal fury.
4 When a flood overwhelmed the earth because of him, Wisdom again saved it,
steering the righteous man* to safety on a fragile piece of wood.[o]

Abraham and Lot

5 And when the nations were thrown into confusion after indulging in wicked conspiracy,
Wisdom singled out the righteous man* and kept him blameless in God's sight
and steeled him in the face of his compassion for his son.[p]
6 Wisdom rescued the righteous man* from the midst of the godless who were being destroyed,
and he escaped the fire that rained down on the Five Cities.
7 As evidence of their wickedness,
there still remains a smoldering waste,
together with plants whose fruit never ripens;
and a pillar of salt stands
as a memorial of an unbelieving soul.*
8 For by forsaking Wisdom
they not only lost the ability to recognize what is good,
but also bequeathed to humanity a reminder of their folly

k Wis 9:4-5; 18:15; Mt 5:34; Jn 3:17; 20:21.—l Job 38:4-37; Isa 40:13; Bar 3:31; Rom 11:34.—m Ps 51:12-13; Mt 11:27; Lk 10:22; Jn 14:26; Acts 2:33; 1 Cor 2:10-11.—n 1-16: Heb 11: 17-27.—o Wis 9:18; 14:5-6; Gen 6:5-9; 7:21-23.—p Gen 22: 7-10; Sir 44:21.

9:15 *Earthly tent:* our spirit, because it is incarnated, is limited in the knowledge of things. The images of the "body subject to corruption" and the "earthly tent" are dear to Paul (see 2 Cor 4:7; 5:1-4). The fact that the body constitutes a burden for human beings does not mean that the flesh is evil.

10:1—19:22 From here on, the author considers the entire unfolding of sacred history, and especially the Exodus, from the viewpoint of Wisdom. The protagonists will receive the name of "righteous" or "wicked" according to whether they have followed the path of Wisdom or have gone astray, for it is Wisdom that steers history.

10:1-14 In the style of the rabbinic commentaries of the time, the author now sets forth sketches of seven exemplary Israelite ancestors, whose destiny God guided and whose courage he rewarded (Adam, Cain, Noah, Abraham, Lot, Jacob, and Joseph).

Adam knew how to expiate his faults and preserve for human beings their mastery over creation. And from the beginning, injustice, like that of Cain, led to perdition.

10:1 *Father of the world:* i.e., Adam (Gen 1:26—5:5).

10:3 *Wicked man:* i.e., Cain (Gen 4:8-12).

10:4 *Righteous man:* i.e., Noah; he alone emerged from a humankind submerged by its fatal hatred (Gen 5:28—9:29).

10:5 *Righteous man:* i.e., Abraham, who was obedient even to the extent of being ready to offer his only son to God (see Gen 12; 22).

10:6 *Righteous man:* i.e., Lot (see Gen 14:2; 19:1-26). *Five Cities:* i.e., the Pentapolis, a group of cities close to the Dead Sea: Sodom, Gomorrah, Admah, Zeboiim, and Zoar.

10:7 *Unbelieving soul:* i.e., Lot's wife (see Gen 19:26).

so that their offenses might never be forgotten.

Jacob and Joseph*

9 But Wisdom rescued from tribulations those who served her.
10 When the righteous man was fleeing from the anger of his brother,
she steered him to straight paths.
She showed him the kingdom of God
and bestowed upon him a knowledge of holy things.
She gave success to his labors
and multiplied the fruit of his work. [q]
11 She aided him against the greed of his oppressors
and made him a wealthy man.
12 She protected him from his enemies
and saved him from ambushers.
In his arduous struggle she brought him victory
so that he might realize that piety* is more powerful than anything else. [r]
13 [s] When the righteous man* was sold, Wisdom did not desert him,
but she delivered him from sin.
14 She descended with him into the dungeon,
and she did not forsake him in his chains
until she had brought him a royal scepter
and power over his adversaries.
She exposed the falsity of his accusers
and bestowed on him everlasting glory.

B: The Wonders of the Exodus*

15 It was Wisdom who delivered a holy people and blameless race
from a nation of oppressors.
16 She entered the soul of a servant of the Lord*
and withstood dread kings with signs and wonders.
17 [t] She gave the holy ones the recompense of their labors;*
she guided them on a wondrous way,
becoming a shelter for them by day
and a starry light throughout the night.
18 She brought them across the Red Sea
and led them through the deep waters.
19 But she submerged their enemies
and cast them up from the bottom of the deep.
20 Therefore, the righteous despoiled the wicked;*
they extolled your holy name, O Lord,
and with one voice praised your protecting hand; [u]
21 for Wisdom opened the mouths of the dumb
and loosened the tongues of infants.*

CHAPTER 11

1 Through the holy prophet, Wisdom* gave them success in everything.
2 [v] They journeyed through an inhospitable wilderness
and pitched their tents in untrodden wastes;
3 they stood firm against their enemies
and turned back their foes.
4 When they were thirsty they cried out to you,
and water was given to them out of unyielding rock,
a refreshment for their thirst out of hard stone.*

---

q Gen 27:43ff; 28:12-15.—r Gen 32:24-29; 33:1-4; Sir 11:14; Hos 12:4-5; 1 Tim 4:8.—s 13f: Gen 37—45.—t 17ff: Wis 14:3; 19:7; Ex 13:21-22; 14–15; Pss 77:19-20; 78:13, 53.—u Ex 12:35-36; 15:1-21.—v 2ff: Ex 16:1; 17:2-6; Num 20:1-13; Pss 63:2; 107:4-7; Jer 2:6.

10:9-14 Jacob, in exile and hunted by his brother (see Gen 27:41-45), puts his trust in God (see Gen 28–30). The innocent Joseph, sold into slavery, resists sin; tribulation prepares him for the highest of destinies (Gen 37ff).

10:12 *Piety:* i.e., "fear of the LORD" (see Prov 1:7). In Jacob's spiritual struggle with God, it was Wisdom that aided him to realize that the only help for human beings is in fear of the Lord.

10:13-14 *Righteous man:* i.e., Joseph (see Gen 37ff).

10:15—11:14 To provide the most powerful demonstration of the superiority of Israel, the author begins his use of antitheses, to which he will return in chapter 16. This first antithesis deals with the theme of the waters, which turned into the plague of blood for the Egyptians (Ex 7:14-24) but into refreshment for the Israelites (Ex 17:3-6).

10:16 *Servant of the Lord:* i.e., Moses (see Ex 3:12; 4:12; 7:1). *Dread kings:* the author may be alluding generally to various kings who afflicted the Israelites, but he is thinking specifically of the Egyptian Pharaoh. A good deal of the saving activity, here attributed to Wisdom, had been assigned to God by Isaiah (Isa 63:11-14).

10:17 *Recompense of their labors:* i.e., the riches and precious articles that the Hebrews carried off at the time of the Exodus (Ex 12:35-36).

10:20a The author seems to be alluding to a tradition that the Israelites took away the weapons of the dead Egyptians.

10:21 The Lord loosened the mouth of the victorious Israelites (*infants*) so that they might utter his praises (see Ex 15:1ff) just as he had loosened the mouth of Moses so that he could speak to Pharaoh (see Ex 4:10; 6:12-30).

11:1 *Wisdom:* From this point on, the author mentions Wisdom only in Wis 14:2, 5. In her place, he brings before his readers God himself by means of the references he makes to God's "Spirit" (v. 20; 12:1), his "word" (Wis 12:9; 16:12; 18:15), his "hand" (v. 17; 14:6; 16:15; 19:8), and his "arm" (v. 21; 16:16).

11:4 The author fails to mention that it was either Moses or Aaron who called upon the Lord for their people.

5 The very means that had served to punish their enemies
became a benefit for them in their need. *
6 [w] Instead of the spring of an ever-flowing river *
befouled by blood mingled with water
7 as a rebuke for the decree to slaughter infants,
you gave them abundant water unexpectedly,
8 showing them by their thirst at that time
how you punished their enemies.
9 [x] For when they themselves were tested,
although they were only chastised in mercy,
they comprehended the torments of the godless who had been judged in anger.
10 You tested the former, admonishing them like a father,
but the latter you sifted as a stern king does in condemnation.
11 Whether far off or close by, * they were afflicted alike, [y]
12 for a twofold grief seized them,
and a groaning over the remembrances of the past.
13 When they heard that through their punishment the righteous had received benefits,
they perceived the presence of the Lord. *
14 For the one whom long before they had cast out, exposed, and rejected * with scorn,
they regarded with admiration at the end of the events,
when they experienced thirst vastly different from that of the righteous. [z]

C: God's Kindness toward the Peoples*

A Dose of Chastisement for Egypt*

15 In return for the foolish reasonings of their wickedness,
which misled them into worshiping serpents bereft of reason and insects devoid of worth,
you sent as punishment upon them hordes of irrational creatures, *
16 so that they might learn that the agents of one's sin are the instruments of one's punishment. *
17 [a] For your all-powerful hand,
which created the world out of formless matter, *
had the wherewithal to send upon them a host of bears or savage lions,
18 or newly created, ferocious, unknown beasts
either breathing fiery blasts
or belching forth thick smoke
or flashing frightful sparks from their eyes.
19 These could not only destroy people by the harm they did
but also strike them dead by their terrifying appearance alone.
20 Even without these, a single breath would have sufficed to overcome them
when pursued by justice
and dispersed by your powerful spirit.

w 6ff: Wis 18:5; Ex 1:22; 7:17-24.—x 9ff: Deut 8:2-5; Ps 6:2; Prov 3:12; 2 Mac 6:12-16.—y Ps 6:2.—z Wis 18:5; Ex 2:3.—a 17ff: Wis 12:8f; 16:1, 5; Gen 1:1f; Deut 32:24; 2 Ki 17:25f; Hos 13:4-8.

11:5 *The very means . . . their need:* the theme of this part of the Book (which can be better understood by reviewing the texts indicated by the cross-references) as well as the principle of interpretation for all that follows: God utilizes the same elements (water, fire, etc.) as a blessing for his people and as a malediction for his enemies. Each element, and even its natural properties, can be transformed at the will of God to save or to judge.

11:6 *Ever-flowing river:* i.e., the Nile (see Ex 7:14f). The author contrasts the first plague of Egypt (see Ex 7:17-24) with the water drawn from a rock at Horeb (see Ex 17:5-7; Num 20:8-11).

11:11 *Whether far off or close by:* both after and before the departure of the Hebrews, the Egyptians were overwhelmed with grief.

11:13 The Vulgate adds: "and marveled at the outcome of these events."

11:14 *One . . . cast out, exposed, and rejected:* i.e., Moses, exposed on the waters (see Ex 1:22; 2:3) and rejected by Pharaoh (see Ex 5:2-5; 7:13, 22).

11:15—12:27 In its history, each people amasses accounts of its glorious deeds and victories over enemies. In doing this, Israel also wanted to proclaim the greatness of God and to assure its own destiny. The idea was a just and remarkable one, but its expression was rather barbaric. In time, the people could no longer be content with very rudimentary accounts in the wake of their refined consciences, their experience of setbacks, and their encounter with other cultures that had their own past. Nonetheless, faith in God's grandeur remained with them and increased.

11:15-20 In this collection of the past, the author is concerned with forewarning his compatriots against the allure of the cults of animals, which were flourishing in Alexandria at that time.

11:15 *Hordes of irrational creatures:* i.e., frogs (Ex 8:1-2), gnats (Ex 8:13-14), flies (Ex 8:20), and locusts (Ex 10:12-15).

11:16 This adage expresses one of the rules of the divine pedagogy, which makes use of the fault to bring about repentance (see Ps 7:15-17). This "law of talion" (or "tit for tat") is found in Ex 21:23ff; Lev 24:18ff; Deut 19:21; 2 Mac 4:38; 5:10; 13:8; 15:32ff; Mt 5:38ff; 7:2.

11:17 *Formless matter:* the author uses this concept derived from Greek philosophy (see note on v. 15) to describe the chaos of Gen 1:2.

But you have ordered all things by measure, number, and weight. [b]

You Have Compassion on All Because You Can Do All Things

21 For you always have the option to exert great strength,
and who can withstand the might of your arm?
22 Indeed, before you, the whole world is like a speck that tips the scales,
or like a drop of morning dew that falls on the ground.
23 Yet you are merciful to all, for you can do all things,
and you overlook men's sins so that they may repent. [c]
24 For you love everything that exists
and abhor nothing that you have created,
since you would not have fashioned anything that you hated. *
25 How could anything have continued to exist unless you had willed it,
or be preserved if it had not been called forth by you?
26 You spare all things,
for they are yours, O Lord, you who love souls. [d]

CHAPTER 12

1 Your imperishable spirit permeates all things;
2 that is why, bit by bit, you correct those who err,
and you admonish them and call to mind the very things in which they go wrong,
so that they may renounce their wickedness and believe in you, O Lord.

God Cares Even for the Canaanites*

3 [e] The ancient inhabitants of your holy land
4 you despised for their loathsome practices:
their acts of sorcery and sacrilegious rites,
5 their merciless slaughter of children,
and their cannibalistic feasting on human flesh and blood. *
Those initiates of secret rituals,
6 those parents who slaughtered defenseless children,
you willed to destroy by the hands of our ancestors,
7 so that the land cherished by you above all others
might receive a worthy colony of children of God.
8 * But even these, since they were men, you spared,
and you sent wasps as forerunners of your army
to exterminate them little by little.
9 It was well within your power to have the godless vanquished in battle by the righteous
or to destroy them in an instant by savage beasts or by one stern word.
10 But by carrying out your sentence in stages,
you gave them the chance to repent.
You were well aware that they came from an evil stock,
and that their wickedness was innate,
and that their way of thinking would never change, [f]
11 for they were an accursed race from the beginning.

God's Power and Goodness

Again, it was not because of fear of anyone
that you allowed their sins to go unpunished.
12 For who can say to you: "What have you done?"
or who can challenge your judgment?
Who can bring accusation against you
when the nations you have created are destroyed?
Or who can come into your presence
as the defender of the wicked? [g]
13 For there is no other god besides you, who show concern for the wellbeing of all people,

b Wis 1:7; Job 4:8-9; Ps 18:16; Isa 11:4; 30:33; Acts 28:4.—c Wis 12:2, 10; Deut 9:27; Pss 62:12-13; 145:9; Acts 17:30; Rom 2:4; 3:25; 11:32; 2 Pet 3:9.—d Wis 12:16; Gen 2:7; Isa 63:9; Ezek 18:23; 33:11.—e 3ff: Wis 14:23; Deut 18:9-12; Pss 5:5; 106:28, 34-39; Jer 19:4-5; Ezek 16:3, 20-21, 36.—f Wis 11:23; 12:2; Sir 16:9; Am 4:6; Rom 2:4.—g 2 Sam 16:10; Job 9:12; Eccl 8:4; Sir 46:19; Isa 45:9; Dan 4:32; Rom 9:19ff.

11:24 This verse is simply the explanation of the refrain found in Genesis (Gen 1:10): "And God saw that it was good." The existence of the world proves God's goodness.

12:3-11a The Canaanites were regarded as accursed forever (Gen 9:25). Our author gives a repugnant description of their customs; for him, Canaan is the symbol of the most odious perversion, expressed in the practice of sacrificing infants.

12:5 *And their cannibalistic feasting on human flesh and blood:* there is no consensus about the translation of this line, which is obscure in the Greek text and in all other translations of it. In any case, crimes of this kind were not unheard of in the ancient pagan world.

12:8-10 By judging the Canaanites *little by little* (see also Ex 23:29-30), God gave them *the chance to repent* (see Heb 12:17).

to whom you must prove that you have not been unjust in your judgments. [h]
14 Nor can any king or ruler confront you in defense of those you have punished.
15 You are righteous, and you govern all things with righteousness,
considering it not in keeping with your power
to condemn anyone not deserving of punishment.
16 For your strength is the source of righteousness,
and your universal dominion makes you gracious to all. * [i]
17 You display your strength when people doubt the absolute degree of your power,
and you rebuke any insolence shown by those who are aware of your might.
18 But even though your strength is unsurpassed, you show mercy in your judgment,
and you govern us with great leniency,
for you possess the power to act whenever you so choose. [j]

The Righteous Must Be Kind to Others*

19 [k] By acting in this way you have taught your people
that the righteous man must be kind to others,
and you have gifted your children with blessed hope
because you grant them repentance for their sins. *
20 For if you have shown such great solicitude and indulgence
in punishing the enemies of your children who deserved to die
and have granted them time and opportunity to repudiate their wickedness,
21 with what attentiveness have you judged your children
to whose ancestors you made such wonderful promises through oaths and covenants! [l]
22 Hence, while you chastise us, you scourge our enemies ten thousand times more,
so that we may recall your goodness when we judge,
and when we are judged, we may hope for mercy.

The Judgment of God*

23 This is why against those who lived wicked lives of folly
you used their own abominations to torment them.
24 For they went far astray along the paths of error,
accepting as gods the vilest and most despicable animals,
being deluded like foolish infants.
25 Therefore, as though they were children unable to reason,
you imposed a sentence upon them to mock them.
26 However, those who have paid no heed to the warning of mild rebukes
will experience the full weight of God's judgment.
27 They were angered at their suffering,
finding themselves punished because of those creatures they had regarded as gods.
But then they saw and recognized as the true God
the one whom previously they had refused to know,
and with this the very height of condemnation fell upon them. * [m]

---

h Wis 6:7; Deut 3:24; 32:39; Isa 44:6, 8; 1 Pet 5:7.—i Wis 2:11; 11:26; Ps 103:19.—j Pss 115:3; 135:6; Dan 4:32.—k 19f: Wis 11:23; Sir 17:29; Rom 9:22-24.—l Wis 18:22; Gen 50:24; Deut 7:6-14; Ps 105:8ff.—m Wis 16:16; Ex 14:4, 28.

12:16 The wicked use power to defeat justice (see Wis 2:11), but God uses his strength to temper justice.

12:19-22 God's moderation in the midst of the harsh actions of peoples also constitutes a discovery of the values of humankind. May his people henceforth show respect and consideration for every person, across frontiers of race and religion. This is a new affirmation, doubtless fostered by frequent contacts with foreign worlds and their ideas. In the next century, Christ will affirm with unforgettable clarity the primacy of love for every human being in all circumstances (see Mt 5:43-48; 1 Jn 4:20-21), and on reading verse 22, one is already reminded of that other word of Christ: "Do not judge, so that you in turn may not be judged. For you will be judged in the same way that you judge others" (Mt 7:1-2; see also Lk 6:37-42).

12:19 Sacred history, which reveals the way God behaves, is the source of the moral life. If God and his Wisdom have manifested love in history (see Wis 1:6), the righteous must in their turn be the friends of human beings. In the New Testament, Jesus will give the conduct of the Father toward human beings as the criterion for the whole of moral life; see, e.g., Mt 20:15: "Are you envious because I am generous?" See also Tit 3:4-5.

12:23-27 In the eyes of the author, the chastisements in Egypt were intended to lay bare idolatry and its vanity. The Letter to the Romans (Rom 1:20-21) will later give the verdict on such conduct: "The conduct of these people is inexcusable. Despite knowing God, they refused to honor him as God or give thanks to him." We must grasp the measure of this sin in order to understand the extraordinary salvation in Jesus.

12:27 At first, Pharaoh was obstinate (see Ex 7–11), but in the end, he acknowledged the power of God (Ex 12:31-32), though he did not repent.

D: The Folly of Idolatry*

CHAPTER 13

Dazzled by the World's Beauty*

1 For all men were inherently foolish * who
remained in ignorance of God,
and did not come to know him who is,
even while observing the good
things around them,
nor recognize the artisan while study-
ing his works. [n]
2 To their way of thinking, either fire or
wind or the swift air,
or the periphery of the stars, or tem-
pestuous water,
or the luminaries of heaven * were the
gods that govern the world.
3 If they have been deluded by the beauty of
these things into believing that
these were gods,
let them come to understand how far
superior to these is their Lord,
since he was the source of beauty that
fashioned them. [o]
4 And if they were astonished at their
power and energy,
let them realize from observing these
things how much more powerful is
he who made them.
5 For from the grandeur and the beauty of
created things
is derived a corresponding perception
of the Creator. [p]
6 Yet these people incur minimal blame, *
for they may have gone astray
while seeking God and eagerly desiring
to find him.
7 For while diligently searching among his
works,
they are distracted by the beauty of
these things.
8 But even so, they cannot be completely
absolved of guilt.
9 For if they achieved a sufficient degree of
knowledge to investigate the world,
how did they fail to find its Lord more
quickly?

Dead Gods

10 But the truly wretched ones are those who
place their hopes in dead things, *
and give the title of gods to the work of
human hands:
gold and silver skillfully fashioned,
likenesses of animals,
or useless stone sculpted by some
ancient artisan. [q]
11 * [r] Consider, for example, a skilled wood-
worker who cuts down a suitable
tree,
carefully strips it of all its bark,
and then, with admirable artistry,
produces some article suitable for daily
use.
12 The small pieces of wood left over from
his work
he burns so that he may cook his food
and eat his fill.
13 However, left over among these remnants
is a useless piece of wood,
crooked and full of knots,
which he puts aside to whittle at his
leisure.
He carves it skillfully during his spare
time,
forming it into the likeness of a man,
or makes it resemble some worthless
animal,
14 giving it a coat of vermilion and covering
its surface with red paint
while smearing over every blemish in it.

---

n Wis 13:5; Acts 14:17; Rom 1:18-20; Eph 4:17ff.—o Ps 8:3-4.—p Wis 13:1.—q Wis 3:11; 15:5, 17; Deut 4:25-28; 7:25; 27:15; 2 Ki 19:18; Ps 115:4; Isa 40:18-20; Hos 14:4; Acts 17:29; Rom 1:23.—r 11-19: Isa 44:9-20.

13:1—15:19 For Jews in the first century B.C., the collision between faith in God and the paganism of Egypt was verified in their own conscience. The author sets before them a systematic criticism of the pagan cults, a criticism that is at times simplistic and takes no account of the religious sentiment that animated those who practiced them (see Ps 115; Isa 44:9-20). He does not act as an historian but as a defender of the faith.

13:1-9 This path that leads to the discovery of God through the beauty of nature, reprised by Paul the Apostle (Rom 1:19-23) and so many contemplatives, remains one of the human and Christian ways to reflect on the existence of God. However, to stop at the creature in the search for God is inexcusable (Wis 13:8), although understandable (v. 6).

13:1 *Inherently foolish:* literally, "vain." The same word is often applied to false gods. Those who ignore God and follow idols are as "vain" as such gods (see Jer 2:5; Rom 1:21). *Him who is:* the sacred Name of God (see Ex 3:14).

13:2 *Luminaries of heaven:* the Vulgate makes this phrase more specific by replacing it with "sun and moon" (see Gen 1:16). *Gods that govern:* see Deut 4:19.

13:6 *Minimal blame:* the blame assigned to those mentioned here is much less than the blame of the wicked dealt with in verses 10; 15:14ff.

13:10 *Dead things:* the author finds it hard to see why idols are worshiped, for they are without life or power. The forces of nature are at least active and fruitful and so might more readily be mistaken for gods. Above all, however, is the fact that only God is to be worshiped, for he is the "living God" (Jos 3:10; Pss 42:3, 9; 84:3; Mt 16:16).

13:11-19 In the manner of the Psalmists and the Prophets, the author adopts a tone of irony that heaps scorn on idols (see Ps 135:15-18; Isa 40:19-20; Jer 10:3-5; Bar 6).

15 Then he provides for it a suitable shrine
and places it on the wall, fastening it there with nails.
16 In this way, he takes precautions so that it will not fall,
since he realizes that it cannot help itself,
for, being merely an image, it requires help. [s]
17 But when he prays regarding his possessions or his marriage or his children,
he feels no shame in addressing this lifeless object.
18 In asking for health he petitions something that is weak,
and for life he entreats the dead;
for aid he prays to something totally inept,
and for a prosperous journey he beseeches something that is unable to walk.
19 And for profits, work, and success in affairs,
he asks the assistance of something whose hands are completely immobile.

CHAPTER 14

1 Again, someone preparing to embark on a voyage through turbulent waves
invokes a piece of wood more frail than the ship that carries him.
2 It was desire for profit that devised that vessel,
and Wisdom was the shipwright that built it. *
3 However, O Father, your providence * guides it,
since you have provided it with a pathway through the sea
and with a safe passage through the waves, [t]
4 indicating that you can save from every danger,
so that even an inexperienced person can put out to sea.
5 It is your will that the works of your Wisdom should not be sterile;
thus men entrust their lives even to the most fragile wood,
and they safely reach land even after sailing through the waves on a raft.
6 For in the beginning, when arrogant giants were being destroyed,
the hope of the world took refuge on a raft *
and, guided by your hand, bequeathed to the world the seed of a new generation.
7 For blessed is the wood through which a righteous work is accomplished, *
8 but the idol made with hands is accursed, as is its maker—
he for having made it, and it because, even though perishable, it was called a god. [u]
9 Equally hateful to God are the godless man and his ungodliness;
10 the work and the artificer will both be punished.
11 Therefore, a visitation will overtake even the idols of the nations
because among the creatures of God they have become an abomination,
a scandal for human souls,
and a pitfall for the feet of the foolish. [v]

Idols Make Their Entry into the World*

12 The invention of idols marked the origin of immorality;
their discovery corrupted human life. [w]
13 They did not exist at the beginning,
and they will not last forever.
14 They entered the world as a result of human vanity,
and therefore a speedy demise has been planned for them.
15 A father overcome with grief at an untimely death
had an image made of the child so quickly taken from him.
And he honored as a god what was formerly a corpse

s 1 Sam 5:3ff; Bar 6:57.—t Pss 77:20; 107:23-30; Isa 43:16.—u Deut 27:15; Ps 115:4; Rom 1:23.—v Wis 3:7; 14:14; Ex 23:33; Num 33:4; Jos 23:13; Ps 115:4; Jer 6:15; 10:15; 46:25; Hos 9:15.—w Deut 31:16; Rom 1:23ff.

14:2 *Wisdom . . . built it:* i.e., the technical skill of the artisan that built it is a fruit of Wisdom (see Wis 8:6; Ex 31:3; 35:31).

14:3 *Providence:* a term borrowed from Greek philosophy to express an idea that is biblical (see Pss 145:8-9, 15-16; 147:9).

14:6 *Raft:* i.e., Noah's ark.

14:7 *Blessed is the wood . . . accomplished:* often applied to the cross of Christ.

14:12-31 The cult of idols perverts human beings. The *immorality* spoken about in verse 12 is undoubtedly infidelity toward God and his covenant (see Hos 1–2), and the incommunicable name (Wis 14:21) is that of God, with the supreme sacrilege being to have it borne by a creature.

and handed on to his household the observance of sacrifices and ceremonies.

16 With the passing of time this impious custom became established and was observed as a law,
and at the command of rulers graven images were worshiped. [x]

17 When the subjects of a monarch lived at such a distance that they could not honor him in person,
they would have a likeness made of their far-off ruler,
thereby possessing a visible image of the king they desired to honor,
zealously in this way flattering the absent ruler as though he were present. *

18 Even those who did not know the king
were aroused to promote his worship by the ambition of the artisan

19 who, perhaps in his eagerness to please his ruler,
used all his skill to depict him in the most favorable way;

20 and the people, attracted by the beauty of his artistry,
began to worship as a god someone whom they had previously honored as a man.

21 Thus, this became a snare for humankind,
since people, whether victimized by misfortune or by tyranny,
assigned to objects of stone and wood the name that belongs to no other.

22 [y] Then it was not sufficient for them to have mistaken notions in their knowledge of God;
for, even though they live in the midst of a great war of ignorance,
they term such horrible evils peace.

23 They engage in the ritual murders of children and in occult rites,
and they hold frenzied orgies replete with unnatural ceremonies.

24 They no longer cherish the purity of their lives and marriages,
either treacherously murdering their neighbor or aggrieving him by committing adultery with his spouse.

25 [z] Chaos reigns supreme—blood and murder, theft and fraud,
corruption, treachery, riot, perjury,

26 destruction of the tranquillity of decent men, ingratitude,
defilement of souls, sexual perversion,
disorder in marriages, adultery, and debauchery.

27 For the worship of nameless idols
is the beginning, the source, and the end of every evil.

28 Idolaters either become frenzied in their exultation or prophesy what is untrue,
or live wicked lives or do not hesitate to commit perjury. [a]

29 Since they place their trust in lifeless idols,
they have no fear of punishment in swearing false oaths.

30 * But justice will overtake them on two counts:
because in their devotion to idols they ignored God,
and because in their contempt for holiness they deliberately committed perjury. [b]

31 For it is not the power of the things by which men swear
but the just punishment reserved for those who sin
that always overtakes the transgression of the wicked.

CHAPTER 15

The Israelites, a People That Does Not Worship Idols*

1 But you, our God, are good and faithful,
slow to anger, and showing mercy in governing the universe. [c]

2 Even if we sin, we are yours, for we acknowledge your power;
but we will not sin, for we know that we are yours.

3 To know you constitutes complete righteousness,

x Dan 3:4-6; 1 Mac 1:43, 47-50.—y 22-31: Jer 2:20; 3:1-25; Hos 4:1-2, 9-19; Rom 1:26-31; Gal 5:19ff; 1 Tim 1:9-10.—z 25f: Jer 7:8-9; 22:17; Mt 15:19; Mk 7:21-22; Rom 1:29-31; 1 Tim 1:9-10.—a Wis 14:23; Jer 5:3-4, 31; 29:26.—b Wis 1:1, 8; 11:20; Jer 5:2, 7.—c Ex 34:6-7; Num 14:18; Pss 86:5, 15; 145:8-9, 14.

14:17 An allusion to the pagan cult in honor of kings who were divinized. This custom, besides being a true idolatry, is contrary to the law, which prohibited all images of God and human beings (see Ex 20:4).

14:30-31 Perjury deserves to be punished even when it is practiced in the name of dead gods.

15:1-6 The author emphasizes that whatever their faults might be, the originality of the Jewish people lay in their acknowledgment of the true God, the God of goodness who lifts up and pardons. The contrast is striking in a world swarming with dead gods.

and to know your power constitutes the
root of immortality. *
4 We have not been led astray by the evil
creations of human skill
or by the barren toil of painters,
figures covered over with varied colors,
5 the sight of which arouses in fools
a yearning for the lifeless form of a
dead image.
6 Lovers of evil and deserving of similar
yearnings
are those who make such figures,
those who desire them, and those
who worship them.

The Folly of Idol-Makers*

7 A potter laboriously kneads the soft
earth,
molding each object for our use,
fashioning out of the same clay
both the vessels that will serve noble
purposes
and those designed for a contrary use.
But what shall be the purpose of each
object
is determined by the potter. * [d]
8 With misspent effort he will mold a false
god from the same clay;
although he himself was made out of
earth a short time before,
after a brief interval, he will return to
that earth from which he was
taken,
when he is required to return on
demand the life that was lent to
him. [e]
9 However, he is not concerned about
death
or that his span of life is brief;
rather he competes with artisans in gold
and silver
and emulates workers in bronze,
and he takes pride in making models of
false gods.
10 His heart is ashes, his hopes of less value
than common dirt,
and his life less worthy than clay,
11 because he failed to recognize the one who
fashioned him
and breathed into him an active soul
and infused into him a living spirit.[f]
12 Indeed, he considered this life of ours as
an idle game,
and our span of years as a market that
will be a source of profit.
"No matter how wicked the means," he
says, "one must make a living."
13 For this man, more than all others, knows
that he is committing sin,
when from the same earthy materials
he makes both fragile pots and
idols.

The Grotesque Character of Idolatry

14 But the most foolish of all, and infantile in
their acts,
are the enemies who enslaved your
people.
15 For they regarded as gods all their hea-
then idols,
although these cannot use their eyes
to see
or their nostrils to breathe the air.
Neither can they use their ears to hear
or the fingers on their hands to touch;
and their feet are useless for walking. [g]
16 [h] For it was a man who made them;
they were fashioned by one whose very
breath is on loan.
For no artisan can form a god to resemble
himself;
17 since he is mortal, what he is able to
form with his impious hands is
dead.
Thus, he is superior to the objects of his
worship,
since he has the life that his idols never
had.
18 * And besides, they worship even the most
loathsome animals,
worse than all the others in their lack of
intelligence,
19 and without the slightest hint of beauty
that might make them seem desir-
able;

---

d Wis 13:11; Sir 38:31-33; Isa 29:16; 45:9; Jer 18:3-4; Rom 9:21; 2 Tim 2:20-21.—**e** Gen 2:7; 3:19; Eccl 12:7; Lk 12:10.—**f** Gen 2:7; Zec 12:1.—**g** Wis 14:11; Deut 4:28; Pss 115:4-7; 135:15ff.—**h** 16f: Wis 13:10; Gen 2:7; Ps 104:29-30; 1 Cor 8:4.

15:3 Jesus will say: "Eternal life is this: to know you, the only true God" (Jn 17:3). This knowledge implies an intimate and personal union made up of knowledge and love.

15:7-13 Among those who fashion idols, the ceramists are, in the author's eyes, the most ridiculous. This type of craftsmanship was widespread in the Greek world, and Paul had a bone to pick with the organization of silversmiths of Ephesus, whose very profitable commerce he had put in jeopardy (see Acts 19:23-40).

15:7 An image of the potter who alone judges the destination of his vases. The Letter to the Romans (Rom 9:19-24), following the Prophets (see Isa 64:7), employs this symbol to explain the freedom of the divine election and the gratuity of the Christian vocation.

15:18ff The author now picks up again the main theme of chapters 11–19 that had been interrupted by material found in Wis 13:1—15:17.

they have been excluded both from the
approval of God and from his blessing. *

E: Nature at the Service of God's Wisdom*

CHAPTER 16

Frogs and Quail*

1 Therefore, these idolaters were deservedly punished by creatures like these
and tormented by swarms of vermin.
2 But in contrast to this punishment, you treated your people with kindness,
sending them quail to eat,
a rare delicacy to satisfy their hunger. [i]
3 Thus, the idolaters, repulsed by the sight of loathsome creatures * sent to plague them,
lost their appetite even though suffering from hunger,
while your own people, after a short period of privation,
partook with pleasure of rare delicacies.
4 For these idolaters necessarily had to be afflicted with inexorable want,
sufficient to indicate to your people how their enemies were being tormented.

Locusts and the Bronze Serpent

5 [j] Even when the venomous rage of wild animals terrorized your people
and they were perishing from the bites of wriggling serpents,
your anger did not continue to the uttermost.
6 They were afflicted for a short time as a warning,
and they were then given a symbol of salvation to remind them of the precepts of your law. *
7 For he who turned toward it was saved,
not by what he beheld,
but by you, the Savior of all.
8 And by such means also you convinced our enemies
that it is you who deliver from every evil.
9 For they were slain from the bites of locusts and flies,
and no remedy was devised to save their lives
because their punishment by such creatures was well deserved. [k]
10 However, not even the fangs of venomous snakes could overwhelm your people,
for your mercy intervened to heal them.
11 They were bitten so that they would be reminded of your decrees,
and then they were quickly healed
so that they would not fall into profound forgetfulness
and fail to respond to your kindness.
12 For it was neither herb nor poultice that cured them
but your all-healing word, O LORD.
13 [l] For you have power over life and death,
bringing people down to the gates of the netherworld and then back again; *
14 whereas, man may slay in malice,
but he has no power to restore the breath of life
or to set free the soul imprisoned by death.

Hailstones and Manna

15 However, from your hand it is impossible to escape.
16 For the godless who refused to acknowledge you
were scourged by the might of your arm,

i Wis 11:13; 19:11-12; Ex 16:13; Num 11:31-32; Ps 105:40.—j 5f: Wis 11:19-20; Num 21:4-9; Deut 32:24; Jer 8:17 LXX.—k Wis 11:15-16; Ex 8:16-28; 10:4-19; Pss 78:45-46; 105:31, 34; Rev 9:1-11.—l 13ff: Deut 32:39; 1 Sam 2:6; Tob 13:2; 2 Mac 6:26; 7:23; Pss 30:4; 78:39; 86:13; 107:18.

15:19 At the Creation, God had blessed the living creatures (Gen 1:22, 28; 2:3). After the Fall, the serpent was cursed (Gen 3:14-15); the same condemnation is reserved for the animal-gods of the Egyptians.

16:1—19:22 The author takes up anew the parallelism between Egypt and Israel that he began in 11:5-14: the Wisdom of God has recourse to the same forces of nature both to punish oppressor Egyptians and to save the Israelites. The order of the events is of little concern to him; in the desire to encourage his compatriots, he exalts Israel to the point of forgetting its rebellions and its errors.

16:1-4 Little animals surged forth to provoke disgust and famine among the Egyptians while birds came to satisfy Israel (Ex 7:26—8:11; 16:1-36). Here is a way to give believers a lesson in trust.

16:3 *Loathsome creatures:* i.e., frogs (see Ex 7:28).

16:6 According to the Book of Numbers (Num 21:8-9), it was sufficient to look upon the symbol of the bronze serpent to remain alive. Here the author seems to want to eliminate every purely magical interpretation: God alone saves. The New Testament indicates that it is the Father who gives life to all those who turn toward the sign of the serpent, toward the Son of Man raised up on the cross (Jn 3:14-16).

16:13 The author teaches that God has absolute power over life and death. He can save from imminent death (see Pss 9:13; 107:18-19; Isa 38:10-17). He can also bring someone in the netherworld back to life (see 1 Sam 2:6; 1 Ki 17:17-23; 2 Ki 4:33-35; 13:21).

pursued by unusual rains and hailstorms
and unrelenting downpours
and devoured by fire.
17 And, defying all logic, in water, which quenches all things,
the fire raged more fiercely than ever,
for creation itself defends the righteous. [m]
18 [n] At one time the flames would die down
so that they would not consume the creatures inflicted upon the wicked,
but that, seeing this, the latter might know
that they were being pursued by the judgment of God.
19 At yet another time the flames would burn with far greater intensity, even in the water,
to destroy the products of a sinful land.
20 In contrast, you nourished your people with the food of angels, *
and with no labor on their part, you supplied them with bread from heaven that was ready to eat,
filled with every delight and pleasing to every taste. [o]
21 The sustenance you offered manifested your kindly mercy to your children,
for the bread that conformed to the desire of those who ate it
was transformed to appeal to each one's preference.
22 Snow and ice * withstood the fire and did not melt,
so that they would realize that the harvesters of their enemies
were destroyed by a fire that blazed in the hail
and flashed through the falling rain;
23 whereas, that same fire even forgot its own strength
so that the righteous might be fed.
24 For creation, at the service of you, its maker,
strains mightily to effect the punishment of the wicked,
but relaxes for the benefit of those who trust in you.
25 Therefore, at that time too, it was transformed in endless ways
to serve your all-nourishing bounty,
according to the desires of those in need, [p]
26 so that your beloved children, O LORD, might learn
that it is not the various crops of the earth that nourish them,
but it is your word that sustains those who trust in you. * [q]
27 For whatever was not destroyed by fire *
melted when merely warmed by a passing sunbeam,
28 to instruct us that we must rise before the sun to offer thanks to you
and must pray to you at the dawning of the day.
29 For the hope of an ungrateful person will melt like the frost of winter
and flow away like water no longer of any use. [r]

CHAPTER 17

Darkness and the Luminous Cloud*

1 Great are your judgments and difficult to expound;
for this reason obtuse souls were led into error.
2 For when the wicked believed that they held your holy nation in their power,
they themselves became prisoners of darkness, shackled by the endless night,
confined under their own roofs, banished from eternal providence.

---

m Wis 10:20; 19:20; Ex 9:23-28; 2 Mac 8:36; 14:34; Ps 78:47-49.—n 18f: Wis 16:22; 19:20-21.—o Ex 16:4; Num 11:8; Pss 78:24-25; 105:40; Jn 6:31.—p Wis 19:18; Pss 104:27-28; 136:125; 145:16.—q Deut 8:3; Jer 15:16; Mt 4:4.—r 2 Sam 14:14; Ps 58:8.

16:20 *Food of angels:* i.e., the manna (Ps 78:23-25), which tasted like a honey cake (Ex 16:31) and was a sign of God's mercy (v. 21; Pss 34:8; 119:103). As the text shows, Jewish tradition had embellished the more sober text of Exodus (Ex 16:13-21). The Liturgy uses these texts with regard to the Eucharist.

16:22 *Snow and ice:* i.e., the manna (v. 27; Wis 19:21). It is compared to dew (Ex 16:14) and to ice (Num 11:7 LXX).

16:26 This shows the last stage of the spiritual interpretation of the manna: food for the body in the wilderness (Ex 16), sent by God in order to test the people and reveal to them the primacy of the word of God as food for human beings (Deut 8:3, cited by Jesus at the time of the temptation, Mt 4:4), and here the food of true life. Jesus took inspiration from these texts to say: "My food is to do the will of the one who sent me" (Jn 4:34).

16:27 *Whatever was not destroyed by fire:* i.e., what remained of the manna.

17:1—18:4 The author embellishes the data of the biblical account (Ex 10:20-23), utilizing legends and rabbinic speculations to evoke the anguish of those without hope in the face of a hostile nature. In this way, the ninth plague of Egypt becomes a symbol signifying everything that arouses consternation and terror in the human heart, above all, the inner night and the prison of a bad conscience in which the slightest things bring fear. Those who are steeped in darkness oppose themselves to the Wisdom of God that lit up Israel's journey by a luminous cloud (Ex 13:21-22; 14:24) and by a spiritual light.

3 [s] For those who believed that their secret sins were unnoticed
behind a dark veil of forgetfulness
were scattered in fright and trembling,
terrified by apparitions.
4 Not even the dark corners that sheltered them could offer them refuge from fear,
for terrifying sounds echoed around them,
and frightening, grim-faced apparitions appeared before their eyes.
5 No fire had sufficient intensity to provide them with light,
nor was the blazing brilliance of the stars sufficient
to illumine the somber night. [t]
6 The only light their eyes perceived
came from a terrifying, spontaneous blaze. *
And, when no longer seen, in their fright they regarded the darkness
as preferable to that sight.
7 The illusions of their magic art were held up to ridicule,
and their vaunted wisdom was laughed to scorn,
8 for they who had boasted of their power to drive out fears and disorders from sick souls
were now themselves sick with dread that was ludicrous.
9 Even if there was nothing disturbing to frighten them,
they were panic-stricken because of the crawling vermin and the hissing of snakes,
10 and, convulsed with terror, they perished,
even refusing to look upon the air whose presence cannot be avoided.
11 For wickedness is a cowardly trait that is condemned by its own testimony,
and when confronted by conscience, * it tends to magnify difficulties. [u]
12 For fear is nothing but the rejection of the aids that are provided by reason;
13 and the less one expects from them,
the more one prefers to remain ignorant of what is causing the torment.
14 And so, throughout that night, which was powerless over them, *
and which descended upon them from the depths of the powerless netherworld,
they all experienced the same sleep—
15 now tormented by monstrous apparitions,
now incapacitated by their souls' surrender—
for sudden and unlooked-for fear had overcome them.
16 And so, whoever was there fell down
and was confined in a prison that lacked bars. [v]
17 For whether he was a farmer or a shepherd
or a laborer toiling in the wilderness,
he was overtaken to suffer the inescapable fate,
18 * for a single chain of darkness bound all.
And whether it was merely the whistling wind,
or the melodious sound of birds in the spreading branches,
or the steady rhythm of rushing water,
19 or the violent crash of cascading rocks,
or the unseen gallop of leaping animals,
or the roaring of savage wild beasts,
or an echo reverberating from the hollow of the mountains,
it immobilized them with fear.
20 [w] For the whole world was bathed in brilliant light
and was at work without any hindrance.
21 But over them alone an oppressive darkness spread,
a replica of the darkness that next awaited them;
yet heavier than the darkness was the burden that they were to each other.

CHAPTER 18

1 But for your holy ones there shone a very great light.
Their enemies who heard their voices but did not see their forms
considered them blessed because they had not also suffered.

---

s 3f: Wis 1:7-8; 10:8; 18:17; Job 15:21-24; 24:15-17.—t Wis 10:17; Ex 32:7-8; Jer 23:24 LXX.—u Wis 4:6; 10:7; Sir 40:1ff; Rom 2:15.—v Wis 18:4; Ex 10:23.—w 20f: Ex 10:23; Job 18:18; Isa 9:1; 60:1ff; 2 Pet 2:17.

17:6 *Blaze:* i.e., lightning bolts.

17:11 *Conscience:* a technical term in Stoicism that manifests the Hellenistic culture of the author.

17:14 *Powerless over them:* the netherworld has no power against God or those who do not submit to its darkness (see Wis 1:14ff). It is a place of the silent and meek (Pss 88:12; 115:17; Isa 14:9; 38:18-19).

17:18-19 The author uses seven events to indicate the fear of the Egyptians.

2 They were grateful that your holy ones
had not done them any injury
despite being previously wronged,
and they asked forgiveness for having
been their enemies. [x]
3 Instead of darkness, you provided for your
people a pillar of fire
to guide them on their unfamiliar
journey,
and a gentle sun for their glorious pil-
grimage.
4 But their enemies deserved to be denied
light and to be incarcerated in dark-
ness,
for they had made prisoners of your
children
through whom the incorruptible light
of your law was to be given to the
world. * [y]

The Exterminator

5 After they had decided to slay the infants
of your holy ones,
and just a single boy * had been aban-
doned and rescued,
you in retribution carried off a multitude
of their sons
and destroyed them all in the raging
waters. [z]
6 That night had been made known before-
hand * to our ancestors,
so that, with accurate knowledge of the
promises in which they had put
their confidence,
they could be of good heart. [a]
7 Your people thus awaited
the salvation of the righteous and the
destruction of their enemies.
8 For you employed the same means to
punish our adversaries
as you did to glorify us when you called
us to yourself.
9 For the holy children of good people were
offering sacrifices in secret,
and with one accord they agreed to
keep the divine law,
so that your holy ones would share alike
both blessings and dangers,
after first chanting the praises of the
ancestors. * [b]
10 In response came the dissonant cry of
their enemies,
and the piteous lamentation for their
children spread abroad.
11 The slave received the same punishment
as the master,
and now commoner and king had to
endure identical sufferings.
12 And all alike, afflicted by the same form
of death,
had corpses too many to count.
For there were not enough who were left
alive to bury the dead,
since in a single instant their most
precious offspring had been de-
stroyed.
13 Formerly they had disbelieved everything
as a result of their sorceries,
but at the destruction of their firstborn
they acknowledged this people to be
the offspring of God. [c]
14 * For when profound silence encompassed
all things
and the night was at midpoint in its
swift course,
15 your all-powerful Word leapt from your
royal throne in heaven
like a relentless warrior into the midst
of a land doomed to destruction.
16 Carrying the sharp sword of your inex-
orable decree,
and touching the heavens while stand-
ing on earth,
he filled the universe with death. [d]
17 Immediately the godless were terrified by
apparitions in terrible dreams,
and unexpected fears attacked them.
18 Cast down to the ground half-dead, some
here, others there,
they revealed clearly why they were
dying.
19 For the dreams that disturbed them had
forewarned them of this

---

x Ex 11:8; 12:33, 36; Ps 105:38.—y Wis 11:16; 17:2; Ps 119:105; Isa 2:3, 5; 42:1-6.—z Wis 11:7, 14; Ex 1:16, 22; 2:3, 6-10; 15:10; Neh 9:11.—a Wis 12:21; Ex 6:8; 13:5.—b Ex 12:21-28; 2 Chr 30:21; Sir 44–50.—c Wis 17:7; Ex 4:22-23; 7:11; 12:12, 29; 13:2, 13, 15; Hos 11:1.—d 1 Chr 21:16; Heb 4:12; Rev 1:16; 10:2, 5.

18:4 The Prophets had declared that the Jews would be the light of the nations (see Isa 42:1; 60:9-11; Jn 4:22).

18:5 *Single boy:* i.e., Moses.

18:6 *Made known beforehand:* by Moses, who transmitted to the people the orders and promises he received from God (Ex 11–12), and perhaps also by the Patriarchs (Gen 15:13-14).

18:9 *Praises of the ancestors:* see Wis 10; Sir 44–50.

18:14-15 God intervenes by his word in the middle of the night. A Jewish tradition assigned to the night of the Passover the great events of the history of the chosen people: Creation, appearance of Abraham, the Exodus, and the coming of the Messiah. The Liturgy has applied this text in the accommodated sense to the birth of Jesus ("Word" of God) that took place precisely by night.

Concerning the *Word*, a double-edged sword that executes God's judgments, see Isa 49:2; Heb 4:12; Rev 1:16; 2:12.

so that they would not perish without
knowing the reason for their suffering.
20 Even the righteous were touched by the experience of death
when large numbers of them were struck down by a plague in the wilderness.
But the wrath did not endure for long.
21 For a blameless man* hastened to be their champion,
bearing the weapons of his ministry,
prayer and propitiating incense;
and he withstood the wrath and put an end to the plague,
thereby showing that he was indeed your servant.
22 He overcame the wrath
neither by physical strength nor by force of arms;
rather, by his word he subdued the avenger,*
calling to mind the oaths and the covenants given to our ancestors.[e]
23 For when the corpses were already piled up in heaps,
he intervened and held back the wrath
and cut off its way to the living.
24 For the entire world was depicted on his full-length robe,*
and the glorious names of our ancestors were carved on the four rows of stones,
and your majesty was seen on the diadem upon his head.[f]
25 To these the destroyer yielded, for these he feared;
a mere sampling of wrath was sufficient.

CHAPTER 19

The Transformation of the Red Sea and of Nature*

1 But the godless were assailed to the very end by merciless anger,
for God knew beforehand what they would do—
2 that although they had agreed to let his people go
and had hastened to send them forth,
they would have a change of heart and pursue them.
3 For while they were still conducting their funeral rites
and mourning at the tombs of their dead,
they made another rash decision
and pursued as fugitives
those whom they had entreated to leave and had sent away.
4 For the fate they deserved urged them on to this decision
and made them forget what had already befallen them,
so that they might experience the full range of torments required to complete their punishment,
5 and so that your people might experience a glorious* journey
while their enemies would meet an unusual death.[g]
6 For the whole creation with its varied elements was fashioned anew*
in compliance with your commands
so that your children might be preserved safe and sound.[h]
7 The cloud was seen to overshadow the camp,
and dry land emerged where previously water had flowed.
In the midst of the Red Sea an unobstructed road appeared,
a grassy plain arising out of the raging waves,
8 over which crossed the entire nation protected by your hand
after beholding marvelous wonders.
9 For they frolicked about like horses
and bounded about like lambs,
praising you, O LORD, who delivered them.[i]
10 For they still recalled the events of their exile,

e Wis 12:21; Ex 32:12-13; Ps 20:7.—f Ex 28:6, 15-21, 31-38; Sir 45:8-12; 50:11.—g 2 Mac 6:14.—h Wis 5:17; 16:24; Job 37:12; Ps 148:8.—i Wis 10:20; 16:8; Ex 15:1-18; Pss 77:21; 78:52; 114:4-6; Isa 63:11.

18:21 *Blameless man:* i.e., Aaron, carrying out the duties of his office as high priest and intercessor.

18:22 *Avenger:* i.e., the destroying angel; see Wis 18:25.

18:24 *Robe:* according to a tradition, symbols of the whole world adorned the vestment of the high priest.

19:1-12 The author embellishes history in order to better awaken confidence in God; it becomes the poetic symbol of the unimaginable happiness that God reserves for those who have embraced his love, a happiness that never stopped astonishing Paul the Apostle (see 1 Cor 2:9).

19:5 *Glorious:* it can also be translated as "wondrous" (see v. 22; 18:8).

19:6 *Fashioned anew:* a principle of interpretation of sacred history: creation and its various elements are at the service of the divine plan for the salvation of Israel and the defeat of the wicked.

how instead of producing animals the land brought forth gnats,
and instead of fish the river disgorged swarms of frogs.[j]
11 [k] Later they were introduced to a new kind of bird
when, moved by appetite, they demanded savory food,
12 and quail came up from the sea to satisfy them.

Egypt More Guilty than Sodom*

13 The punishments did not rain down on the sinners
without previous warnings in the form of violent thunder. *
And they justly suffered for their wicked deeds,
since they had exhibited such bitter hatred to strangers.
14 [l] There had been others * who had refused to receive strangers who had come to them,
but these had made slaves of their guests who were their benefactors.
15 There will indeed be punishment inflicted upon the former
since they had offered a hostile reception to strangers.
16 But the latter, after first welcoming them with festive celebrations,
afterward oppressed with terrible sufferings
those who had already shared with them the same rights.
17 Therefore, they were also struck with blindness, *
like the sinners at the door of the righteous man,
when, surrounded by yawning darkness,
all of them had to grope their way to their own doorways.

Nature Transformed during the Exodus

18 A new arrangement of the elements occurred,
just as the strings of a harp can produce varied rhythms
while each note remains the same.
This can be clearly perceived
from an observation of what took place.
19 Land animals * became water creatures,
while creatures that swim migrated to dry land.
20 [m] Even in water, fire maintained its normal strength,
and water forgot its fire-quenching nature.
21 Flames, by contrast, failed to consume the flesh
of perishable animals that walked in their midst,
nor did they melt the icelike composition of heavenly food so prone to liquefy.

Conclusion*

22 In every way, O LORD, you have exalted and glorified your people;
you have never failed to help them at any time and in every circumstance.[n]

j Ex 7:27ff; 8:12-15; Ps 105:30-31.—k 11f: Wis 16:2; Ex 16:13; Num 11:31; Ps 78:18-19.—l 14f: Gen 15:13; Ex 2:22.—m 20f: Wis 16:17ff, 22-23, 27; Ex 16:14.—n Wis 18:8; Lev 26:44; Ps 126:3; Isa 45:17, 25.

19:13-17 For the author, the events of history must unfold in accord with the law of talion ("an eye for an eye,"Ex 21:23ff). His explanation seems to play fast and loose with the facts and especially after the announcement of God's mercy for all nations, an announcement made by Christ (see Mt 5:38-48). Nonetheless, human beings and nations must again be called to order when injustice sweeps them along.

19:13a Allusion to the storm that preceded the passage through the Red Sea (see Ex 14:21-24).

19:14 *Others:* the inhabitants of Sodom (Gen 19). *Benefactors:* Joseph had rendered great services to the Egyptians in his day, but the Israelites were reduced to slavery by the Egyptians who came later.

19:17 *Blindness:* allusion to the plague of darkness (Ex 10:21-23).

19:19 *Land animals:* i.e., the Israelites together with their cattle who passed across the Red Sea. *Creatures that swim:* i.e., frogs (Ex 7:26ff).

19:22 Other concluding doxologies are found in Tob 14:15; Ps 150; Sir 51:30.

"All wisdom derives from the Lord and remains with him forever" *(Sir 1:1)*.

THE WISDOM OF BEN SIRA

The Mirror of Jewish Fidelity

The cultural atmosphere in which this writing originated, in the beginning of the second century B.C., the Battle of Panion in 198 B.C. had transferred Palestine from the dominion of the Ptolemies (Egypt) to that of the Seleucids (Syria). With the aim of unifying their part of the Empire, exposed to too many internal conflicts, the new kings develop a policy of assimilation and seek to impose the Greek way of life introduced into the East by Alexander the Great.

Among the Jews, one group accepts it as a good thing to open themselves to the new Greek culture so as to adapt Judaism—which they regard as too closed in upon itself—to a more universal civilization. However, a strong traditionalist group opposes this novelty in order to safeguard the faith and vocation of Israel, the witness of the one God before all the nations. This is the same frame provided by the beginning of the Second Book of Maccabees.

The test of might between the pagan rulers and the Jewish faithful will become inevitable. But at the time of this writing, it has not yet occurred. At this very moment, a certain Jesus, son of Sira (see 50:27—hence from the Greek form we obtain Sirach), composes a lengthy meditation on Jewish fidelity as an appeal to his contemporaries. If there is any wisdom and any richness for the believing community, they find their source in worship and in the law. The author is convinced of this and seeks his inspiration both in the great events of the past and in the teachings of the wise, which he reports in great detail in order to better emphasize their relevancy.

Written in Hebrew, this work was not admitted into the Palestinian collection of the sacred books, and indeed was forgotten by the Jews. However, St. Jerome succeeded in seeing it, and it was cited by medieval Jewish writers. But then its text was lost. Ample parts of it were found in the 19th century (amounting to about two-thirds), but they were in an unsatisfactory state.

The Greek text that has come down to us was translated by the author's nephew, about 130 B.C., for his numerous compatriots living in Alexandria, Egypt. This text, which was favored by the first generations of Christians, may be regarded as the true canonical text. Passages from it were frequently read in liturgical assemblies—which possibly accounts for its name up to modern times: Ecclesiasticus.

This translation is based on a critically established text using both the Hebrew and other ancient witnesses to the original, and following the numbering of the critical Greek text edited by J. Ziegler. When there are gaps in the verse numbering, they are filled from ancient manuscripts and placed in brackets. In this present case, the brackets are not used to denote glosses but to indicate material that might well have been part of the original Hebrew text and been in some way lost in the translation. This explains the diversity of numeration of verses with respect to other editions.

The Wisdom of Ben Sira may be divided as follows:

I: Prologue (1-35)
II: Counsels of a Teacher of Wisdom (1:1—33:18)
III: The Testament of a Teacher of Wisdom (33:19—42:14)
IV: Praise to the Lord of Nature and of Israel (42:15—50:29)
V: Additions (51:1-30)

I: PROLOGUE*

[1]Many important teachings [2]have come down to us through the Law and the Prophets and the other writers who succeeded them, [3]and, as a result, praise is due to Israel for its traditions of learning and wisdom.

[4]It devolves upon those who read the Scriptures not only to understand them thoroughly [5]but as lovers of learning to use their skill [6]in writing and speaking to increase the knowledge of others. [7]My grandfather Jesus, having devoted himself to the intensive reading [8]of the Law [9]and the Prophets [10]and the other Writings of our ancestors, [11]and having gained considerable proficiency in them, [12]was inspired himself to compose some writings on the subject of learning and wisdom, [13]in order that, by becoming familiar with what he had written, those who love learning [14]might achieve even greater progress in living in conformity with the Law.

[15]Therefore, you are [16]invited to read this [17]attentively and with an open mind [18]and to exhibit a spirit of understanding forgiveness [19]when, despite the most diligent efforts in translation, [20]I may seem to have rendered some passages inadequately. [21]For words originally expressed in Hebrew [22]do not have the same sense when translated into another language. [23]Not only this present Book [24]but even the Law itself, the Prophets, [25]and the rest of the Books [26]differ quite a bit when they are read in the original.

[27]When in the thirty-eighth year of the reign of King Euergetes [28]I arrived in Egypt and set up my residence there, [29]I discovered that the Book has great educational value,* [30]and I considered it essential to devote some energy and labor to its translation. [31]During this period of time I have applied my skill day and night [32]in working toward the completion of this Book [33]and supervising its publication [34]for the benefit of those living abroad who wish to acquire learning [35]and are disposed to live their lives according to the Law.

P 1-35 After completing his work, the translator adds a prologue that provides interesting information. First of all the Book was written in Hebrew by his grandfather. And at that era, the sacred books were already grouped into three titles that have become traditional: the Law (or Torah), the Prophets, and the Writings (among which were the Psalms, Job, and the Sapiential texts). It was the author's purpose to give a commentary or a meditation on these sacred texts. This prologue is generally regarded as noncanonical.

P 29 *I discovered . . . great educational value:* some early MSS; Greek reads: "I found opportunity for no little instruction."

II: COUNSELS OF A TEACHER OF WISDOM*

A: The Roots of Wisdom

CHAPTER 1

All Wisdom Derives from the Lord*

1 All wisdom* derives from the Lord
and remains with him forever. [a]
2 The sands of the sea, the drops of rain,
and the days of eternity—who can count them?
3 The height of the sky, the breadth of the earth,
the depth of the abyss*—who can explore them?
4 Wisdom was created before all other things;
and prudent understanding has existed from eternity.
[5 The fount of wisdom is God's word in the highest heaven,
and her ways are the eternal laws.]*

6 To whom has the root of wisdom been revealed?
Who understands her subtleties? [b]
[7 To whom has an understanding of wisdom been disclosed?
And who has known her resourcefulness?]*
8 Only one is wise and greatly to be feared,
seated upon his throne—the Lord.
9 [c] He is the one who created her,*
observed her, and recognized her value,
and so poured her forth upon all his works,
10 upon all flesh as he chose,
lavishing her upon those who love him.
* [The love of the Lord is glorious wisdom;
he apportions her to those to whom he appears, that they may see him.]

The Beginning of Wisdom Is Fear of the Lord*

11 The fear of the Lord is glory and exultation,
happiness and a crown of joy. [d]
12 The fear of the Lord gladdens the heart,
bestowing happiness and joy and a long life.
* [The fear of the Lord is a gift from the Lord;
also for love he makes firm paths.]
13 The one who fears the Lord will experience a happy end;
he will be blessed on the day of his death.
14 The beginning of wisdom is the fear of the Lord;
she is created with the faithful in their mothers' wombs. [e]
15 She has made her home among men an age-old foundation,
and among their descendants she will show her beneficence.
16 The fear of the Lord is the full measure of wisdom;
she intoxicates people with her fruits. [f]
17 She fills their homes with desirable goods
and their storehouses with her fruits.
18 The crown of wisdom is the fear of the Lord
as she bestows peace and perfect health.
* [Both are gifts of the Lord for peace;
glory opens out for those who love him.

a Prov 2:6; Wis 9:4.—b Job 28:12-23; Bar 3:15, 20-22.—c 9f: Job 28:27; Eccl 2:26.—d Sir 9:16.—e Job 28:28; Ps 111:10; Prov 1:7; 9:10.—f Prov 8:18-19; 11:30; Eccl 12:13.

1:1—33:18 There follow, in no precise plan, thoughts about disparate topics, interspersed from time to time with poetic pieces in praise of Wisdom or the Creator.

1:1-10 The mystery of creation seems inaccessible, and still more sublime, is the wisdom that it manifests. Thus, in the Book of Proverbs (Prov 8:22f), she is presented to us as the thought and the plan of God, his coworker in all that he has made. She is given to human beings as a grace, as the most profound treasure of their life. Every Christian is marked by the Holy Spirit with the seal of wisdom (Acts 2:17-33).

1:1 *Wisdom:* the author uses this word in various senses. Sometimes he speaks of wisdom as divine, at other times as human, and at still others as a synonym for God's law. All three types derive from God. In this and the following seven verses, he is alluding to true wisdom, God's external revelation of himself. *Lord*: used by the translator of Sirach for "Yahweh" and even for other divine names.

1:3 *Depth of the abyss:* some early MSS read simply: "the abyss."

1:5 Added by some early MSS.

1:7 Added by some early MSS.

1:9 *Created her:* the Vulgate adds "in the Holy Spirit."

1:10c-d Added by some early MSS.

1:11-20 The beginning of wisdom is fear of the Lord. But this fear is no longer the terror in the face of Yahweh's terrifying power that appears in the Historical Books. It is close to love, reverence, admiration, and the freedom of children who entrust themselves to their father and are showered with wondrous gifts. In short, it is the true religious sense, the happiness of believing. Indeed, fear of the Lord is an important ingredient of faith (see Deut 4:9f; 8:5f; 10:12; 2 Chr 19:7; 26:5; Job 28:28; Ps 111:10; Prov 1:7; 9:10). And the expression, or its equivalent, occurs twelve times in this Book, since twelve was a sacred number for the ancients (e.g., twelve tribes of Israel, twelve months of the year).

1:12c-d Added by some early MSS.

1:18c-d-e Added by some early MSS.

He saw her and recognized her value.]
19 The Lord has seen and appraised her,
showering down knowledge and discerning understanding
and heightening the glory of those who possess her.
20 The root of wisdom is fear of the Lord,
and her branches bring forth long life. [g]
[21 The fear of the Lord takes away sin,
and he who perseveres turns away all anger.] *

Wisdom Teaches Patience*

22 Unjustified anger can never be excused;
anger will be the cause of a man's downfall.
23 A patient man endures difficulties for a time,
and then he regains his sense of contentment.
24 Until the appropriate moment he keeps his thoughts to himself,
and then the lips of many affirm his wisdom.

If You Desire Wisdom, Keep the Commandments*

25 The treasuries of wisdom contain wise maxims,
but the fear of God is an abomination to the sinner.
26 If you desire wisdom, keep the commandments,
and the Lord will lavish her upon you. *
27 For the fear of the Lord is wisdom and discipline,
fidelity and humility are his delight. [h]
28 Do not disregard the fear of the Lord,
or approach him with a divided heart.
29 Do not act out a role before others;
keep careful watch over your lips.
30 Do not exalt yourself, lest you fall
and bring dishonor upon yourself.
For then the Lord will reveal your secrets
and overthrow you before the whole community,
since you did not practice the fear of the Lord
and your heart was full of deceit.

B: At the School of Wisdom

CHAPTER 2

When You Come To Serve the Lord, Be Prepared To Endure Trials*

1 My child, when you come to serve the Lord,
prepare yourself to endure trials. [i]
2 Be sincere of heart and steadfast,
and do not be alarmed when confronted with adversity.
3 Cling to him and do not forsake him,
so that your final days will be blessed.
4 Accept whatever befalls you,
and be patient whenever you suffer humiliation.
5 For gold is tested in the fire,
and worthy men in the furnace of humiliation. [j]
[In sickness and poverty, place your trust in him.] *
6 Trust him, and he will help you;
follow a straight path and hope in him. *
7 You who fear the Lord, wait for his mercy;
do not stray, for otherwise you will fall.
8 You who fear the Lord, trust in him,
and you will not forfeit your reward.
9 You who fear the Lord, hope for good things,
for everlasting joy and mercy.
[For his reward is an everlasting gift of joy.] *

g Sir 1:12.—h Sir 3:17; 4:8; 10:28; 45:4; Prov 15:33.—i 2 Tim 3:12; Jas 1:2-4; 1 Pet 4:12; Rev 2:10.—j Rom 5:3; Jas 1:2-4.

1:21 Added by some early MSS.

1:22-24 Here is the first of many good recommendations that the author will make throughout his Book: he is dispensing a practical wisdom, i.e., a mastery of life.

1:25-30 The conduct that pleases God is to keep the law that he has given. It initiates us into a life marked by truth and justice. Keeping the law will be the first thing Jesus asks of the rich young man who comes to him seeking to gain eternal life (Mt 19:17).

1:26 Wisdom and keeping the law go hand in hand (see Sir 19:20). Indeed, wisdom is the reward for keeping the law (see Eccl 12:13).

2:1-18 For believers, nothing, including suffering, is futile about God's plan, which guides all things with wisdom. Humans need courage to entrust themselves to him, for he never abandons those who remain faithful, as the past bears witness: "Though he hoped against hope, [Abraham] believed," according to Paul (Rom 4:18).

2:5c Added by some early MSS.

2:6 *Follow . . . hope in him:* some early MSS read: "hope in him, and he will make straight your ways."

2:9c Added by some early MSS.

10 Recall the former generations and reflect:
has anyone who trusted in the Lord ever been disappointed?
Has anyone who persevered in fear of the Lord ever been forsaken,
or has anyone who called upon him been ignored? [k]
11 For the Lord is compassionate and merciful;
he forgives sins and saves in the time of distress.
12 Woe to faint hearts and unwilling hands,
and to the sinner who treads a double path.
13 Woe to those with timid hearts who have no faith
and who therefore will be unprotected.
14 Woe to you who have forsaken patience;
what will you do at the coming of the Lord?
15 Those who fear the Lord do not disobey his words,
and those who love him keep his ways. [l]
16 Those who fear the Lord seek to please him,
and those who love him are steeped in his law.
17 Those who fear the Lord keep their heart prepared
and humble themselves before him.
18 Let us fall into the hands of the Lord
and not into the hands of men.
For equal to his majesty
is the mercy that he exhibits.
[And his works are in keeping with his name.]* [m]

CHAPTER 3

Honor Your Father and Mother*

1 My children, listen to me, for I am your father;
do this to be saved.
2 For the Lord desires that a father be honored by his children,
and he confirms a mother's rights over her children.
3 He who honors his father atones for sins,
4 and he who respects his mother stores up riches.
5 He who honors his father will rejoice in his own children,
and when he prays he will be heard.
6 He who respects his father will be blessed with a long life,
and he who gives comfort to his mother obeys the Lord.
7 He who fears the Lord honors his father
and submits to his parents as his masters.
8 Honor your father by word and deed,
so that his blessing may come upon you; [n]
9 for a father's blessing strengthens the houses of his children,
but a mother's curse uproots their foundations. [o]
10 Do not revel in any disgrace that may affect your father,
for your father's dishonor will not be a source of honor to you.
11 The honor of a father is one's own honor as well,
and the dishonor of a mother is a disgrace to her children.*
12 My child, look after your father when he is old;
do nothing to cause him grief as long as he lives. [p]
13 Even if his mind fails, be sympathetic toward him;
do not despise him simply because you yourself are healthy and strong.
14 Kindness* shown to a father will never be forgotten,
and it will be credited to you as reparation for your sins.
15 In the time of your tribulation it will not be forgotten
and like frost in warm weather your sins will melt away.
16 If you forsake your father, you are no better than one who blasphemes,
and if you anger your mother, you will be accursed by the Lord.

k Job 4:7; Pss 22:5-6; 31:2; 37:25; 145:18-19.—l Sir 1:28; 4:15, 21, 23; Pss 105:28; 107:11; Jn 14:23.—m Sir 3:18; 7:17; 18:4-6, 21; Wis 11:23; 12:16.—n Ex 20:12; Deut 5:16; Mt 15:4; Mk 7:10; Eph 6:2.—o Gen 27:29; 49:2-27; Deut 33:1-25.—p Prov 23:22; Mt 15:4-6.

2:18e Added by some early MSS.

3:1-16 Filial piety is the sign of a generous heart and a source of blessing. The author seems to allude (vv. 8-10) to the accounts of the sons of Noah and those of Jacob, which nicely illustrate the importance of the paternal blessing in the Old Testament.

3:11 *And the dishonor . . . to her children:* an alternative reading is: "and you multiply sin when you demean your mother."

3:14-15 *Kindness:* literally, "righteousness" or "almsgiving." One of the greatest signs of righteousness was considered to be almsgiving (see Tob 1:3; 2:10; 4:7-11; 14:9-11). It obtained God's forgiveness for sins.

Do Not Seek To Learn What Is Too Sublime for You*

17 My child, carry out your duties with humility,
and you will be loved more than a benefactor.
18 The greater you are, the greater should be your humility;
in this way, you will find favor with the Lord. [q]
[19 Many are the lofty and the renowned,
but it is to the humble that he makes known his secrets.] *
20 For great is the power of the Lord,
yet he is glorified by the humble.
21 Do not seek to learn what is too sublime for you;
investigate not those things that are beyond your scope. [r]
22 Concentrate on what you have been commanded,
for what is hidden is not your concern.
23 Do not meddle in matters that are beyond you,
for much has been revealed to you that is beyond your comprehension.
24 Many have been led astray by their own presumptions,
and false deductions have impaired their judgments.
25 Where there are no eyes, there is no light,
and where there is no knowledge, there is no wisdom.

26 A stubborn person will come to a bad end,
and the one who loves danger will perish in it.
27 A stubborn man will be burdened by troubles;
a sinner heaps sin upon sin.
28 When calamity befalls the proud, there is no cure,
for an evil growth has taken root there. [s]
29 The mind of the intelligent meditates on proverbs,
and an attentive ear is the desire of the wise. *

Do Not Avert Your Eyes from the Needy*

30 As water extinguishes a blazing fire,
so almsgiving atones for sins. [t]
31 He who repays a favor is mindful of the future;
when he falls, he will find support.

CHAPTER 4

1 My child, do not cheat the poor man of his livelihood,
or turn your back on one who is in need. [u]
2 Do not grieve one who is hungry
or exasperate someone in distress.
3 Do not add to the problems of those who are desperate,
or keep them waiting for your charity.
4 Do not neglect a suppliant in distress,
or turn your face away from the poor.
5 Do not avert your eyes from the needy,
and give no one any reason to curse you.
6 For if in bitterness of soul someone should curse you,
the one who made him will hear his prayer.

7 Endear yourself to the community,
and bow your head in the presence of authority.
8 Pay attention to the entreaties of a poor man,
and return his greeting courteously.
9 Rescue the oppressed from the power of the oppressor,
and deliver your judgments with justice.
10 Be like a father to the fatherless,
and be like a husband to their mother.
You will then be like a son of the Most High,
and his love for you will surpass that of your own mother. * [v]

q Mt 20:26-28; 23:12; Phil 2:5-8.—r Ps 131:1; Eccl 1:13.—s Deut 32:32; Prov 3:34; 9:7f; 14:8; 19:25, 29; Wis 12:10.—t Deut 24:13; Tob 4:7-11; 12:9; Prov 16:6; Dan 4:24.—u Sir 29:8; Tob 4:7-11; Prov 17:5; 30:17; Jer 20:7.—v Ex 22:22; Ps 41:1-3; Isa 49:15; Lk 6:35; Jn 14:21, 23.

3:17-29 Hellenistic culture could salve one's spirit. What good are all the refinements of civilization if pride corrupts them. Wisdom consists above all in meditating on the law and the teachings of the past.

3:19 Added by some early MSS.

3:29 *And an attentive ear is the desire of the wise:* or "and to an attentive ear, wisdom is a joy."

3:30—4:10 Those who are attentive to the misery of others draw down upon themselves the Lord's benevolence, for they regard all human beings as brothers and sisters born of the same Father—God.

4:10 The author uses the biblical imagery of father and mother to set forth God's concern for the faithful. His language is metaphorical and does not imply that there is gender (male and female) in God. The Lord transcends all human categories, including sex. Furthermore, his relationship to creatures goes far beyond a father and mother to them.

Wisdom—Instructor of Human Beings*

11 Wisdom exalts her children
and helps those who seek her.
12 Whoever loves her loves life,
and those who seek her out diligently
will be filled with joy. [w]
13 Whoever regards her as of great value
will inherit glory;
the LORD will bestow his blessings
wherever she enters.
14 Those who serve her minister to the Holy
One,
and the Lord loves those who love her. [x]
15 Whoever obeys her will judge nations;
whoever listens to her will dwell se-
curely. [y]
16 Whoever entrusts himself to her will pos-
sess her,
and his descendants will also inherit
her.
17 At first she will lead him along tortuous
paths,
putting him to the test,
filling him with fear and dread
and trying him with her discipline
until he comes to fully trust her.
18 Then she returns to lead him along the
straight path,
bring him happiness,
and reveal her secrets to him.
19 However, if he goes astray, she will aban-
don him
and hand him over to his own destruc-
tion.

C: Knowing How To Discern the True Values

Do Nothing That Will Make You Ashamed*

20 Take account of circumstances and
beware of evil
so that you will have no cause to be
ashamed.
21 There is a shame that leads to sin,
and a shame that is honorable and
gracious.
22 Do not be the cause of your own down-
fall by showing favoritism,
or incur ruin by your deference to
others.
23 Do not refrain from speaking at an
opportune time,*
and do not conceal your wisdom.
24 For wisdom becomes known through the
spoken word,
and learning through the words of the
tongue.
25 Never attempt to speak what is contrary
to the truth
but rather feel ashamed at your own
ignorance.
26 Do not be ashamed to confess your
sins,
and do not attempt to struggle against
a river's currents. *
27 Do not subject yourself to the foolish,
or show partiality to the powerful.
28 Fight to the death for truth,
and the LORD God will ally himself on
your side. [z]
29 Do not be impudent in your speech,
or careless and slack in your deeds.
30 Do not be like a lion* in your home,
or be suspicious of your servants.
31 Do not keep your hand outstretched to
receive
but closed when it is time to repay.

CHAPTER 5

Do Not Be Overconfident*

1 Do not rely on your wealth
or say, "Now I am self-sufficient." [a]
2 Do not follow your inclinations and
energy
in pursuing the desires of your heart.
3 Do not say, "Who can prevail against
me?"*
for the LORD will certainly punish your
arrogance.
4 Do not say, "Even though I have sinned,
nothing has befallen me,"*
for the LORD is patient.

w Prov 3:16-18; Wis 6:14; 8:17f.—x Ps 146:8; Wis 7:28.—y Wis 3:8; 1 Cor 6:2.—z Ex 14:14; 2 Mac 14:15; Prov 18:10; Jn 18:37.—a Sir 11:24; Ps 62:11f; Lk 12:19.

4:11-19 Wisdom is here personified (see Prov 1:23-25; 8:12-21; 9:1-6) as a good teacher. She leads those who seek her to happiness for she knows how to temper the overzealous. By the word wisdom, the author evokes an idea and practice of life; it is by the quality and the effort of life that people render true worship to the *Holy One* (v. 14), that is, to God.

4:20-31 People must be true in their language, and their lives, ways of acting, and speech must be in accord.

4:23 *Opportune time:* or "time of salvation."

4:26 *Do not attempt to struggle against a river's currents:* it is as futile to attempt to conceal our sins from God as it is for us to try to prevent a river from flowing.

4:30 *Do not be like a lion:* i.e., do not be wild, relentless, and destructive.

5:1-8 The temptation to be proud of one's riches and to flee from inner demands is stronger when success seems within easy reach. Riches and presumption usually go hand in hand.

5:3 *Do not say, "Who can prevail against me?":* i.e., like a fool who does not believe in God's providence (see Ps 53:2).

5:4 *Do not say, "Even though I have sinned, nothing has befallen me,":* i.e., like the skeptic who is defiant of God's justice when it is delayed.

5 Do not be so confident of pardon*
that you add sin upon sin.
6 Do not say, "His mercy is great;
he will forgive* my many sins."
For from him will come both mercy and retribution,
and upon sinners his anger will fall. [b]
7 Do not delay your return to the LORD,
and do not put it off from one day to the next.
For suddenly the wrath of the LORD will descend upon you,
and on the day of punishment you will be destroyed.
8 Do not rely upon ill-gotten gains,
for they will avail you nothing on the day of disaster. [c]

Be Resolute and in Control of Yourself*

9 Do not winnow in every wind,
or walk along every road. *
10 Be steadfast in your convictions
and consistent in your speech.
11 Be quick to listen
but deliberate in offering your answer.
12 If you have understanding, reply to your neighbor,
but if not, put your hand over your mouth.*
13 Both honor and dishonor can result from speaking;
the tongue* can be the cause of a person's downfall. [d]
14 Do not gain a reputation for spreading scandal,
or set traps with your tongue.
For shame lies in store for the thief,
and severe condemnation for the double-tongued.
15 Do not be the cause* of harm in either great or small matters,
and do not become an enemy instead of a friend.

CHAPTER 6

1 For a bad name will result in shame and reproach,
as is the case of the double-tongued sinner.
2 [e] Do not fall into the grip of passions,
for these can tear you apart as if by a bull.*
3 They will devour your foliage and destroy your fruit,
and you will be left standing like a withered tree.
4 For evil passions destroy the one who harbors them
and make him the laughingstock of his enemies.

A Faithful Friend Is beyond Price*

5 Kindness in speech multiplies friends,
and a gracious tongue leads to friendly responses.
6 Be at peace with many people,
but allow only one in a thousand to be your adviser.
7 [f] When you wish to acquire a new friend,
first test him,
and do not be too hasty to trust him.
8 One type of person is only a friend when it suits him,
but at the first sign of trouble he will desert you.
9 Another type of friend will eventually become your enemy
and shame you by making public your quarrel.
10 And still another will be your guest at table
but will not stand by you in time of trouble.
11 When you are prospering, he is your second self
and lords it over your servants;
12 however, if you are brought low, he will turn against you
and avoid any contact with you.

---

b Sir 16:11; Ex 20:5f; Isa 1:18-20.—c Prov 10:2; 11:4, 28; Ezek 7:19; Mt 13:22.—d Prov 18:21; Jas 3:6.—e 2-4: Sir 9:8; 18:30—19:3; 23:17; Job 31:12; Isa 56:3.—f 7ff: Sir 12:8f; 37:1-6; Prov 17:17; 19:4.

5:5 *Pardon:* or "atonement."

5:6 *Forgive:* or "atone for."

5:9—6:4 Those who have few words are appreciated by all. This wisdom is suspicious of the dynamism of human beings and leads, above all, to condemnation of opportunism and instability. People must "be" rather than "seem to be."

5:9 *Do not winnow in every wind, or walk along every road:* this is the author's way of condemning duplicity. Some early MSS add: "as is the way of the double-tongued sinner," which appears to be a doublet of verse 1.

5:12 *Put your hand over your mouth:* a graphic expression to indicate one should keep silent inasmuch as one has no competency to speak.

5:13 *The tongue:* The author will return frequently to the theme of the use and abuse of the tongue (Sir 19:6-17; 20:17-20; 22:27—23:15; 28:13-26).

5:15 *Be the cause:* Hebrew; Greek reads: "be ignorant."

6:2 *Bull:* some translate as "fire."

6:5-17 One's true friends are known only on the day of distress. People usually get the friends they deserve. According to the author's view, true friendship establishes a profound and almost religious bond between beings.

13 Keep clear of your enemies
and be wary of your friends.
14 A faithful friend is a sure shelter;
anyone who finds one possesses a treasure. [g]
15 A faithful friend is beyond price;
there is no possible way to measure his worth.
16 A faithful friend is the elixir of life,
and he who fears the Lord will find him.
17 He who fears the Lord directs his friendship aright,
for as he is, so also will his neighbor be.

D: The Apprenticeship of Wisdom

With All Your Soul Approach Her*

18 [h] My child, choose instruction from your youth,
and you will still possess wisdom when your hair turns to gray.
19 Approach her like one who plows and sows,
and wait for her bountiful fruit.
For in cultivating her you will labor but little,
and very soon you will enjoy her harvest.
20 How harsh she seems to the undisciplined;
the fool cannot abide her.
21 She will serve as a heavy stone to test him,
and he will lose no time in casting her aside.
22 For wisdom* is true to her name;
she is not accessible to many.
23 Listen, my child, and take my advice;
do not reject my counsel.
24 Put your feet into wisdom's fetters
and your neck into her collar.
25 Stoop to carry her on your shoulders,
and do not complain about her bonds.
26 With all your soul approach her,
and keep her ways with all your might.
27 If you search her out and follow her trail, she will make herself known,
and once you have found her, do not let her go.
28 For in the end you will find your rest in her,
and she will be turned into your joy.
29 Her fetters will serve as a strong defense for you
and her collar as a magnificent robe.
30 Her yoke* is a golden ornament,
and her bonds a purple cord.
31 You will wear her like a robe of glory
and bear her as your splendid crown.* [i]
32 *If it is your wish, my child, you can be taught;
if you apply yourself, you will become clever.
33 If you are willing to listen, you will learn,
and if you pay attention, you will become wise.
34 When you frequent the company of the elders,
if there is anyone who is wise, attach yourself to him.
35 Listen eagerly to every godly conversation;
allow no expression of wisdom to escape you. [j]
36 If you see a man of understanding, rise early to visit him;
let your feet wear out his doorstep.
37 Reflect on the decrees of the Lord
and constantly meditate on his commandments.
He will enlighten* your mind,
and the wisdom you desire will be granted to you. [k]

g Prov 18:19; Eccl 4:9-12.—h 18f: Prov 8:18f; Wis 7:14; Lam 3:27.—i Prov 4:9; Isa 62:3.—j Sir 8:9.—k Ps 1:2.

6:18-37 For the ancients, wisdom is tradition, transmission of a conception and practice of life (see Prov 4); she is acquired at the cost of harsh discipline. She is, therefore, learned at the school of the ancients and by meditating on the word of God. But she is not content to repeat principles and customs; she wishes to come to life again in the persevering experience of whoever seeks to acquire her.

6:22 *Wisdom:* the Greek word for "discipline," in the sense of wisdom, is *musar*, which is a homonym for, *musar*, meaning "removed" or "withdrawn." Hence, wisdom is *not accessible to many.*

6:30 *Her yoke:* Hebrew; Greek reads: "upon her."

6:31 *Splendid crown:* Greek reads: "crown of gladness."

6:32-37 These last three stanzas have as their theme to seek wisdom in the following ways: (1) by desire and a willingness to listen (vv. 32-33), (2) by associating with those who are wise (vv. 34-36), and (3) by reflecting on the Lord's decrees and commandments, i.e., keeping the law (v. 37).

6:37 *Enlighten:* Greek reads: "confirm."

E: The Conduct of the Wise in Public Life*

CHAPTER 7

Do No Evil, and No Evil Will Befall You*

1 Do no evil, and no evil will befall you;
2 avoid wickedness, and it will turn away from you.
3 My child, do not sow in the furrows of injustice
so that you will not reap a sevenfold crop. [l]
4 Do not ask the LORD for a position of authority
or the king for a seat of honor.
5 Do not flaunt your righteousness before the LORD,
or assert your wisdom in the presence of the king. [m]
6 Do not seek to become a judge,
for you may not be strong enough to root out injustice,
or you may show favoritism to the powerful
and thereby compromise your integrity.
7 Commit no offense against the people of the city,
thereby disgracing yourself before everyone.
8 Never fall into the trap of repeating a sin,
for not even for one will you go unpunished.
9 Do not say, "He will take into consideration the great number of my gifts,
and when I make an offering to God Most High he will accept it." [n]
10 Do not grow tired of praying,
or neglect to give alms.
11 Do not deride anyone whose heart has become embittered,
for there is One who both humbles and exalts. *
12 Do not make up lies about your brother,
or do the same to a friend.
13 Refuse to ever tell a lie,
for it is a habit that never has a positive result.
14 Do not babble on* in the assembly of the elders,
and in your prayers do not repeat yourself. [o]
15 Do not shun laborious tasks
or farming, an occupation ordained by the Most High. [p]
16 Do not attach yourself to the ranks of sinners;
remember that retribution will not tarry.
17 Humble yourself to the greatest possible degree,
for the godless will suffer the punishment of fire and worms. * [q]
18 Do not exchange a friend for the sake of money,
or a true brother for the gold of Ophir. *
19 Do not turn against a wise and good wife;
her gracious demeanor is worth more than gold.
20 Refrain from the ill-treatment of a servant who performs his duties faithfully, [r]
or of a hired laborer who devotes himself to his task.
21 Love a diligent slave with deep affection,
and do not refuse to grant him freedom. *

---

l Job 4:8; Prov 22:8; Gal 6:7f.—m Job 9:2; Ps 143:2; Prov 25:6; Lk 18:9-14; 1 Cor 4:4.—n Sir 34:21; 35:15; Ps 50:7-15; Prov 15:18; 21:27.—o Sir 32:7ff; Eccl 5:2; Mt 6:7.—p Gen 2:15; 3:17; Prov 24:27.—q Sir 3:17-24; Jud 16:17; Isa 66:24; Mk 9:48.—r Sir 33:25-33; Lev 19:13; Deut 24:14f; Jas 5:4.

7:1—15:10 Many of the formulas in this Book seem to characterize a right way of acting rather than a right way of thinking, and for the most part, it is concerned with customs and conceptions of an age gone by. But the author seeks to preserve the values of Jewish life against the encroachment of what is easy. Beyond the difference of conditions of life, as well as the diversity of our options, we must continually verify our courage as humans and as believers.

7:1-21 *Do No Evil, and No Evil Will Befall You:* in these varied counsels, which place us on guard against ambition, intrigues, pretense, and the like, we rediscover the fundamental attitude: know your limitations, and do not believe anyone, yet do not let yourself despise others in social life. This Book that often announces the mercy of God does not want it to be dishonored by stressing the ease of its attainment: Christ thus issued a threat to those who mock God and their brothers and sisters (see v. 6; Mk 9:48). We should note the respect given to manual labor (v. 15). Placed in the context of the time, the last verses concerning wives and servants bear witness to much humanity.

7:11 It is God who humbles and exalts, for he is sovereign in judgment and in redemption (see 1 Sam 2:7; Ps 75:8; Lk 1:32).

7:14 *Babble on:* brevity of words was regarded as a sign of respect (see Eccl 5:1; Mt 6:7).

7:17 *For . . . worms:* Hebrew reads: "for the expectation of men is worms."

7:18 *Gold of Ophir:* i.e., gold of first quality (see 1 Ki 9:28; 10:11; Job 22:24). Ophir is not identified with certainty; it may have been in central Arabia.

7:21 Freedom had to be granted after six years (see Ex 21:2-6).

Family Duties

22 *Do you have cattle? Look after them,
and if they prove profitable, keep them.
23 Do you have sons? Discipline them,
and insist on their obedience* from their childhood. [s]
24 Do you have daughters? Be concerned for their chastity,
and do not allow yourself to be over-indulgent toward them. [t]
25 When you give your daughter in marriage, you have completed a great task,
but give her to a sensible man.
26 If you have a wife who pleases you, do not divorce her,
but do not trust yourself to one whom you are unable to love.*
27* Honor your father with all your heart,
and never forget the birth pangs suffered by your mother. [u]
28 Remember that you were born of these parents;
how can you repay them for all that they have done for you?

Fear God and Revere His Priests*

29 With all your soul fear God,
and revere his priests.*
30 With all your strength love your Maker,
and do not abandon his ministers.
31 Fear God and honor the priest,
and give him his portion* as you have been commanded:
the firstfruits, the guilt offering, and the shoulder of the sacrificial victim,
the sacrifice of sanctification and the firstfruits of holy things. [v]

Let Your Generosity Extend to All*

32 Be generous in your gifts to the poor
so that your blessing may be complete.
33 Let your generosity also extend to all the living,
and do not let your kindness be withheld even from the dead.
34 Do not turn your back on those who weep,
but mourn with those who mourn. [w]
35 Do not neglect to visit the sick,
for as a result of such deeds you will be loved. [x]
36 In everything you do, remember your end,*
and you will never sin.

F: Circumspection and Reflection: Various Cases

CHAPTER 8

Prudence in Dealing with Others

1* Do not oppose one who is powerful,
lest you fall into his hands.
2 Do not quarrel with a rich man,
for he may use his resources to prevail over you.
For gold has been the cause of the downfall of many
and has perverted the hearts of kings. [y]
3* Do not engage in a dispute with an argumentative man
and thereby heap wood upon his fire. [z]

s Sir 30:8-13; Prov 13:24.—t Sir 42:9ff.—u Ex 20:12; Tob 4:4.—v Ex 29:27f; Lev 2:1-10; 7:31-36; Num 18:9-20.—w Job 30:25; Rom 12:15.—x Job 2:11-13; Mt 25:36.—y Sir 31:6; Deut 16:19.—z Sir 28:10; Prov 26:20.

7:22-25 This text comes to us from a civilization that had a far different approach to education than we do. However, its main principle is completely apropos—a sense of responsibility and the refusal to flee from the pedagogical task.

7:23 *Insist on their obedience:* Greek, "bend their necks."

7:26 For the sage, finding the woman of one's heart and knowing how to keep her (see v. 17) is a joy. We recall the praise of the valiant woman (Prov 31:10-31). For that day and age, it was a veritable acknowledgment of women. However, it had not yet reached reflection on the mutual support of spouses in the journey of the couple to eliminate misunderstandings and mistrust.

7:27-28 The author holds a sublime idea of fatherhood and motherhood; parents share in the creative power of God.

7:29-31 To revere priests means to cling to the cult at Jerusalem of which the priests are the depositaries, to help maintain—in the liturgical structure of that time—the sign of faith in one God. The offerings enumerated in verse 31 are prescribed by the laws of worship that are found in the Books of Exodus, Leviticus, Numbers, and Deuteronomy.

7:29 The author has much reverence for the liturgy and its priests (see ch. 50).

7:31 *His portion:* the different gifts mentioned here are: *the firstfruits* (Num 18:11-18); *the guilt offering* (Lev 5:6); *the shoulder of the sacrificial victim* (Ex 29:27; Lev 7:32-33; Deut 18:3); and *the sacrifice of sanctification* (Lev 2:1-16).

7:32-36 The objects of generosity are the poor, the afflicted, the sick, and the dead: concern for burial (see Tob 1:17f; 2:1-7; 12:12) as well as prayers and sacrifices on their behalf (see 2 Mac 12:38-46).

7:36 *Remember your end:* the Hebrew reads: "remember *the* end," i.e., "pay attention to the consequences of your acts." The Greek substitutes *your* for *the* thus giving this maxim an eschatological sense. The realization that the end of a sinner is bound to be a sad one should serve as a powerful deterrent against sin.

8:1-2 The author advises his readers not to go up against the rich or powerful either physically (Deut 33:7), or verbally by quarreling (Gen 26:20), or juridically, i.e., by a lawsuit (Isa 3:13; 57:16)—for they have no chance of winning. In the second verse, there is a hint of offering a bribe to a judge in order to influence his verdict, something that was condemned (Sir 20:29; Ex 23:8; Deut 16:19).

8:3-4 The author urges the wise to avoid disputes with those who are loudmouths or senseless, for such persons will become even more boisterous when someone responds to them.

4 Do not ridicule one who is ill-bred,
lest he proceed to insult your ancestors.
5* Avoid reproaching a repentant sinner;
remember that we are all guilty. [a]
6 Do not despise an elderly man,
for some of us will also become aged.
7 Do not rejoice over anyone's death;
remember that we all must die.

8 Ignore not the discourse of the wise,
but familiarize yourself with their maxims,
since from these you will gain instruction
and learn the art of serving the great.
9 Do not reject the opinions of the aged,
for they themselves were taught by their parents.
From them you will learn how to reason
and how to reply when the need arises. [b]

10* Do not kindle the coals of a sinner,
lest you be burned in his flaming fire.
11 Refuse to be provoked by an insolent man,
for he may seek to trap you in your own words.
12 Do not lend to someone who is more powerful than you are;
but if you do lend anything, write it off as a loss. [c]
13 Do not stand surety beyond your resources,
but should you do so, be prepared to pay.
14 Do not oppose a judge in a lawsuit,
for he will win the judgment because of his rank.
15 Do not set out on a journey with one who is reckless,
lest he become a burden to you.
For he will do whatever he pleases,
and his folly will result also in your ruin.

16 Do not provoke an argument with one who is quick-tempered,
or journey with him through sparsely inhabited regions.
For bloodshed is an inconsequential matter to him,
and where no help is at hand, he will strike you down.

17 Never discuss your plans with a fool,
since he is unable to keep a confidence.
18 In the presence of a stranger do nothing that should be kept secret,
for you cannot be certain what use he will make of it. * [d]
19 Do not reveal your thoughts to anyone,
or he may take away your happiness.

CHAPTER 9

Advice Concerning Women*

1 Do not be jealous of your beloved wife,
or you may thereby encourage her to cause you harm. *
2 Let no woman gain power over you
and thereby trample underfoot your strength. [e]
3 Do not approach a loose woman,
lest you become entangled in her snares.
4 Do not dally with a singer,
lest you be trapped by her wiles.
5 Do not harbor lustful thoughts against a virgin,
or you may incur punishment on account of her.
6 Do not give yourself to prostitutes,
lest you suffer the loss of your inheritance.
7 Do not let your gaze stray through the streets of a city,
or wander around its deserted areas.
8 Turn away your eyes from a comely woman,
and do not stare at the beauty of another's wife.
Many have been destroyed as a result of a woman's beauty,
which causes passion to flare up like a fire. [f]

a 1 Ki 8:46; 1 Jn 1:8.—b Sir 5:11; 11:8; Prov 22:21; 24:26; Col 4:6.—c Sir 29:4-7; Prov 17:18.—d Prov 25:9f.—e Prov 31:3.—f Sir 25:21; 41:21.

8:5-7 The author counsels not to reproach a repentant sinner, for *we are all guilty* (see 1 Ki 8:46; 2 Chr 6:36; Eccl 7:20; Rom 3:9-10; 1 Jn 1:8). He urges respect for the elderly for *some of us will also become aged.* Lastly, we should *not rejoice over anyone's death*, for *we all must die.*

8:10-19 The author intermingles a little mistrust into his counsel as well as much experience, alas, concerning passion, injustice, and the fickleness of human beings.

8:18 *What use he will make of it:* or "what it will engender."

9:1-9 The tradition of the sages of the East seems unanimous in placing naive souls on guard against feminine charms. Strongly marked by the society and mentality of that time, these counsels have not lost all value today; indeed, human relations are not simply a futile game, and sexuality should not be treated as something banal. Moreover, the fidelity of those who love one another cannot be achieved without some vigilance to guard one's eyes and heart from easy and dangerous desires.

9:1 A husband's jealousy may poison the marital relationship and lead the wife to do the very thing he was worried about in the first place.

9 Never dine with a married woman,
or join her to drink some wine,
lest you allow your heart to succumb to her
and in your passion plunge to your destruction.

Watch Your Relationships with Others*

10 Do not abandon an old friend,
for a new one will not adequately replace him.
A new friend is like new wine;
only when it has sufficiently aged can you drink it with pleasure.

11 Do not envy the success of a sinner,
for you can never be sure what his end will be.
12 Take no delight in the pleasures of an ungodly man;
remember that before his death he will endure some retribution.
13 Keep far removed from anyone who has the power to kill,
and you will not be haunted by the fear of death.
However, should you approach him, make no false step,
or he may take your life.
Realize that you are treading among snares
and walking on the battlements of the city.

14 To the best of your ability, become knowledgeable about your neighbors,
and consult with those who are wise.[g]
15 Engage in conversation with one who is sensible,
and devote all of your discussions to the law of the Most High.
16 Choose honorable men for your dinner companions,
and let your glory be in the fear of God.
17 Artisans are praised for the skill of their hands,
but a leader of the people is esteemed for his words of wisdom.
18 One who speaks incessantly is feared in his city,
and one who is rash in his speech is despised.

CHAPTER 10

An Able Leader Is a Gift of Providence*

1 A wise magistrate educates his people,
and the government of a prudent man is well regulated.[h]
2 [i] As is the people's magistrate, so are his officials;
as is the ruler of a city, so are its inhabitants.
3 An undisciplined king causes the ruin of his people,
whereas a city will prosper through the prudence of its rulers.
4 The governance of the earth is in the hand of God;
he will raise up the right leader over it at the proper time.[j]
5 All human success is also in the hand of God;
it is he who confers honor upon the lawgiver.*

The Sin of Pride*

6 Do not become angry at every offense committed by your neighbor,
and do not resort to acts of violence.[k]
7 Arrogance is hateful in the sight of both the Lord and man,
and injustice is abhorrent to both.
8 Sovereignty passes from nation to nation
as the result of injustice, arrogance, and wealth.
[Nothing is more evil than one who loves money,
for such a person places his soul on sale.]

g Sir 6:34; 8:8; 37:7ff.—h Wis 6:24.—i 2f: Prov 29:12.—j Ps 113:4-8; Prov 8:15f; Wis 6:1-11; Lk 1:52.—k Lev 19:16-18; Mt 5:21-24; 18:21f.

9:10-18 It is wise not to run to judgment and to choose well those with whom one consorts. The climate of intrigues that surrounds all ambition for power and success had so scandalized the author that he is unable to refrain from evincing a serious pessimism.

10:1-5 It is not enough for a ruler to receive or to acquire power. He must know how to wield authority with knowledge and integrity.

10:5 *Lawgiver:* Hebrew; Greek reads: "scribe."

10:6-18 The author repeats this time after time: the supreme sin is to want to put oneself above the Creator and to despise human solidarity. Nothing is more intolerable, and it is to reestablish the order of things that God punishes the proud. The sage is evidently thinking of the examples from the political life of his day, which was filled with the succession of rival dynasties (v. 8) and the collapse of more than one pretentious regime (vv. 16-20). This passage reminds us of the canticle of Hannah (1 Sam 2:4-8), which inspired the Magnificat (Lk 1:46-52).

9* For what reason are dust and ashes proud?
Even in life the body is subject to decay.
10 A lengthy illness baffles the doctor;
the king of today will be a corpse tomorrow.
11 One who dies receives only an inheritance
of maggots and wild animals* and worms. [l]
12 The beginning of human pride is the forsaking of the Lord,
the withdrawal of one's heart from its Maker.
13 For pride is the beginning of sin,
and those who cling to it pour forth filth.
For this reason God afflicts them with unheard-of calamities
and destroys them completely. [m]
14 The Lord overthrows the throne of rulers
and seats the humble in their place.
15 The Lord plucks up the roots of the nations*
and plants the lowly in their place.
16 The Lord lays waste the territory of the nations
and destroys them to the very foundations of the earth.
17 He sweeps away every trace of some of the nations
and blots out the memory of them from the earth.
18 Pride was not created for men,
nor violent anger for one born of woman.

True Glory Is To Fear God*

19 Whose offspring are worthy of honor?
Human offspring.
Whose offspring are worthy of honor?
Those who fear the LORD.
Whose offspring deserve contempt?
Human offspring.
Whose offspring deserve contempt?
Those who break the commandments. [n]
20 The members of a family hold their leader in honor,
but he who fears the LORD is worthy of honor in his eyes.
[21 The fear of the LORD is the beginning of acceptance,
while stubbornness and pride are the beginning of rejection.]*
22 The wealthy, the noble, and the poor
achieve their glory in the fear of the LORD.
23 It is not right to despise someone who is intelligent but poor,
nor is it proper to honor anyone who is sinful. [o]
24 The prince, the judge, and the ruler are held in honor,
but none is as great as the one who fears the LORD.
25 When those who are free serve a wise servant,
an intelligent man will not complain. [p]

Value Yourself at Your True Worth*

26 Do not flaunt your wisdom in doing your work,
and do not put on airs when you are in need.
27 Better the diligent worker who has plenty of everything
than one who boasts on an empty stomach. [q]
28 My child, in the practice of humility do not neglect your self-respect;
value yourself at your true worth.
29 Who will acquit one who condemns himself?
Who will honor one who holds himself in low esteem?
30 The poor man is honored for his skill,*
the rich man for his wealth.
31 One who is honored in poverty, how much more so in wealth!
And one who is dishonored in wealth, how much more so in poverty!

---

l Sir 7:17; Job 17:14; Isa 14:11.—m Prov 18:12.—n Jer 9:23f; 1 Cor 1:26-31; 2 Cor 10:17.—o Jas 2:1-4.—p Prov 17:2; 19:10; 30:22; Eccl 10:6f.—q Prov 12:9.

10:9-10 Life is so uncertain that no one has reason to be proud. One may be a king today but gone tomorrow!

10:11 *Wild animals:* Hebrew reads: "vermin."

10:15 *Nations:* some early MSS read: "proud nations."

10:19-25 The teaching of the sage agrees with the teaching of the Prophets (Jer 9:22f): human beings are honorable not by the dignity of their function nor by their social rank but by the authenticity of their religious life.

10:21 Added by some early MSS.

10:26-31 To be true and humble does not consist in cultivating sentiments of inferiority but in accepting what one really is.

10:30 *Skill:* some early MSS read: "wisdom."

CHAPTER 11

Do Not Trust in Appearances*

1 Wisdom enables the poor man to hold his head high
and to take his seat among the great. [r]
2 Do not praise anyone for his good looks,
or despise any on the basis of his appearance. [s]
3 Among the winged creatures the bee is small,
but its produce is the choicest of sweet harvests.
4 Do not boast about your elegant clothes,
or become proud when you receive honors.
For the works of the LORD are marvelous,
but his works are hidden from humans.
5 Many kings have been forced to sit on the ground,
while others who were never considered worthy of respect have worn a crown.
6 Many rulers have fallen into complete disgrace,
and those who have received honors have fallen into the power of others.

Think before Acting, and Act Calmly

7 Do not find fault before checking out the evidence;
examine first, and then criticize.
8 Do not answer without first listening,
and do not interrupt while someone else is speaking. [t]
9 Do not engage in arguing about something that does not concern you,
or become involved in the disputes of sinners.

10 My child, do not become involved in too many matters;
if you attempt too much, you will suffer the consequences.
No matter how much you pursue, you will never overtake,
nor will you escape by attempting to flee.
11 Some people toil away and struggle and press on,
and yet fall farther behind. [u]

Trust in the Lord and Remain at Your Task*

12 There is also the slow kind of person in need of help,
lacking in strength and abounding in poverty.
Yet the eyes of the LORD look favorably upon him;
he lifts him out of his wretched condition
13 and raises up his head,
to the amazement of many.
14 Good fortune and bad, life and death,
poverty and wealth—all come from the LORD.* [v]
[15* Wisdom, understanding, and knowledge of the law come from the LORD;
love and the performance of good works are the gift of the Lord.
16 Error and darkness were created with sinners from their birth,
and evil grows old with those who take delight in it.]
17 To the devout the Lord's gift remains constant,
and his favor brings unending success.
18 A man may become rich through caution and self-denial,
and this is the reward he receives for it:
19 although he says, "Now I have found rest and I can live on my possessions,"
he does not know how long it will be before he must die and leave his possessions to others. [w]
20 Know your obligations and fulfill them;
grow old at your work.
21 Do not admire the achievements of the wicked,
but trust in the LORD and remain at your task.

r 1 Sam 2:8; Ps 113:8.—s 1 Sam 16:7; 2 Cor 10:10f.—t Sir 5:11f; Prov 18:13.—u Ps 127:1f; Eccl 4:8; 9:11.—v Job 1:21; 2:10; Isa 45:7.—w Ps 49:17f; Eccl 4:8; 6:2; Lk 12:19.

11:1-6 People should be judged on their true worth rather than on appearances; it is wisdom that enables one to do this.

11:12-28 Trust in God, even if it can sometimes be called the "duty of the unforeseeable," is a more profound security than the precarious possessions and honor of humans. Jesus may have been inspired by this passage in proposing the parable of the rich fool (Lk 12:16-21): "You fool! This very night your life will be required of you. And who then will get to enjoy the fruit of your labors?"

11:14 God's providence governs the lives of all, and he can bring good out of evil (see Rom 8:28).

11:15-16 Added by some early MSS.

For it is no problem for the LORD
suddenly, in an instant, to make a poor person rich.
22 The blessing of the LORD is the reward of the righteous,
and he quickly causes his blessing to multiply.
23 Do not say, "What do I need,
and what further benefits can be mine?"
24 Do not say, "I am self-sufficient;
what harm can come to me now?"
25 In prosperous times disasters are forgotten,
and in times of hardship prosperity is not remembered. [x]
26* For on the day of death it is easy for the Lord
to reward individuals according to what they deserve.
27 A moment's affliction causes former pleasures to be forgotten,
and at the close of one's life, one's deeds are revealed.
28 Call no one happy before his death,
for it is by his end that a person becomes known for what he is.

Beware of Scoundrels and Their Evil Schemes*

29 Do not invite everyone into your home,
for many are the snares of the devious man.
30 Like a decoy partridge in a cage is the mind of the proud man,
and like a spy he looks for your downfall. *
31 For he lies in wait for an opportunity to turn good into evil,
and to characterize praiseworthy deeds as blameworthy.
32 A single spark can set many coals afire,
and a sinner lies in wait to spill blood.
33 Beware of a scoundrel and his evil schemes,
for he may smear your reputation forever.
34 If you invite a stranger into your home,
he will stir up trouble for you
and will estrange you from your own family.

CHAPTER 12

If You Do Good, Know for Whom You Are Doing It*

1 If you do good, know for whom you are doing it,
and your good deeds will have their desired effect.
2 Good deeds performed for the righteous man will be repaid—
if not by him, then by the Most High.
3 [y] No good comes to the one who persists in evil,
or to one who refuses to give alms.
4 Give to the devout man,
but never aid the sinner.
5 Give aid to the humble man,
but give nothing to a godless man.
Do not even offer him bread,
for that might enable him to subdue you.
For every good deed you do for him
you will be repaid twofold with evil.
6 For the Most High himself also hates sinners
and inflicts on the godless the punishment they deserve.
[And he is keeping them for the day of their punishment.] *
7 Give to one who is deserving,
but never offer help to a sinner.

If You Get Bitten, It Is Your Fault*

8 When you are enjoying prosperity it is not easy to know who your friends are,
but in times of adversity there is no problem in discerning your enemies. [z]
9 When you prosper even your enemies are grieved, *

x Sir 18:25; Jn 16:21.—y 3ff: Prov 25:21f; Mt 5:43-47; Rom 12:20f.—z Prov 17:17.

11:26-28 Writing before the revelation brought by Christ, the author expected divine retribution to be meted out on the day of one's death. *By his end:* Greek reads: "through his children."

11:29-34 Hospitality is a virtue of the East. Guests are more than occasional visitors. This is not without consequence for the welcoming home. At an age when Greek families embraced all cults easily, the entrance of a non-Jew into a believing family was bound to present problems.

11:30 *Downfall:* Greek reads: "weak spots."

12:1-7 Here the morality of the sage is a little narrow. Even the Mosaic Law invites people to be more generous (Ex 23:4f; Lev 19:17f), and the new law of Christ preaches a charity without limits (Mt 5:43-48).

12:6c Added by some early MSS.

12:8-18 Nothing but misfortune can overtake those who keep bad company. Flatterers in good times await only bad times to supplant the one whom in the past they touted as their friend.

12:9 *Grieved:* Greek; Hebrew reads: "friendly."

but in adversity even your friends will shun you. [a]
10 Never trust your enemy;
just as bronze tarnishes, so does his wickedness.
11 Even if he acts humbly and in a subservient manner,
take care to be on your guard against him.
Behave toward him as if you were polishing a mirror,
and you will see that his tarnish does not last.
12 Do not allow him to stand near you,
lest he overthrow you and take your place.
Do not let him sit on your right hand
or he may oust you and take your seat,
and in the end you will realize the truth of my warning
and recall my admonition with regret.
13 Who has sympathy for a snake charmer when he is bitten,
or for those who go near wild animals?
14 In the same way, no one pities a person who associates with sinners
and becomes involved in their evil deeds. [b]
15 He may stand by you for a while,
but if you falter, he will not stay around.
16 An enemy utters honeyed words,
but his heart is scheming to cast you into a pit.
The eyes of an enemy may be filled with tears,
but if an opportunity arises, he will never have enough of your blood. [c]
17 If misfortune overtakes you, you will find him there ahead of you,
and, pretending to help, he will trip you up.
18 Then he will shake his head* and clap his hands,
go about whispering, and change his countenance.

CHAPTER 13

How Can the Clay Pot Be Used with the Iron Cauldron?*

1 Whoever touches pitch will have blackened hands,
and anyone who associates with a proud man will become like him.
2 Do not bear a burden too heavy for you,
or associate with someone who is greater or wealthier than you.
How can the clay pot be used with the iron cauldron?
When they collide, the pot will be smashed.
3 The rich man does wrong and boasts about it;
the poor man is wronged and has to beg for forgiveness.
4 The rich man will exploit you if you can be useful to him,
but if you are in need, he will abandon you.
5 As long as you are well-off, he will be constantly at your side;
he will drain your resources without a qualm.
6 When he needs you he will deceive you
and will smile at you and raise your hopes.
He will speak kindly to you
and ask, "Is there anything you need?"
7 He will embarrass you with his hospitality,
but after he has drained your resources two or three times
he will end up by laughing at you.
Afterward, when he sees you, he will pass you by
and shake his head about you.
8 Take care not to be led astray
and humiliated as a result of your own stupidity.
9 When an influential man issues you an invitation, be slow to accept,
and he will be all the more insistent in his request.
10 Do not be too forward or you may be rebuffed,
but neither should you keep aloof lest you be forgotten.
11 Do not try to converse with him as an equal,
or trust his effusive words.
The more he speaks, the more he is testing you,

a Prov 19:4-7.—b Sir 3:26.—c Prov 26:24-26; Jer 9:8.

12:18 *He will shake his head:* a sign of derision (see Job 16:4; Pss 22:8; 109:25).
13:1-26 Those who frequent the circles of the rich and powerful only risk being hurt. This chapter should be read as a satire about the "sharks" of society, as a bloody critique of the disproportionate condition between the rich and the poor, between the "wolf" and the "lamb" (v. 17).

and while he smiles he is evaluating you.
12 Those who do not keep your secrets are cruel,
and they will not spare you injury or imprisonment.
13 Confide in no one and be on your guard,
for you are walking to your own downfall.[d]
[14 When you hear these things, awake from your sleep;
as long as you live, love the Lord and pray to him for your salvation.] *
15 Every living thing loves its own kind,
and every man loves someone like himself.
16 All creatures associate with their own kind,
and every man sticks close to those like himself.
17 What does a wolf have in common with a lamb?
The same applies to a sinner with a devout man.[e]
18 What peaceful state can exist between a hyena and a dog?
What peaceful condition can there be between the rich and the poor? *
19 Just as the wild asses of the wilderness are the prey of lions,
so are the poor the pasture of the rich.
20 Humility is abhorrent to the proud,
and so also is the poor man abhorrent to the rich.
21 When the rich man stumbles, he is supported by friends;
when the poor man trips, even his friends ignore his plight.[f]
22 When the rich man slips, many rush to his rescue;
even if he says something nonsensical, people justify him.
When the poor man slips, he is criticized,
and no attention is paid when his words are filled with wisdom.
23 When the rich man speaks, all listen in silence
and praise his wisdom to the skies.
When the poor man speaks, others say "Who is that?"
and even push him to the ground if he stumbles.
24 Wealth is good when it has been acquired honestly,
but poverty is regarded as evil by the mouth of the godless. *
25 The heart changes one's countenance
either for good or for evil.
[And a glad heart effects a cheerful countenance.][g]
26 The proof of a happy heart is a cheerful expression,
but to devise wise maxims involves wearisome work.

CHAPTER 14

Blessed Is the Man Whose Conscience Does Not Reproach Him*

1[h] Blessed is the man who has not come to grief through careless speech
and who has no need to feel remorse for sin.
2 Blessed is the man whose conscience does not reproach him
and who has never lost hope.

Treat Yourself Well, and Be Generous*

3 Wealth serves no purpose for the stingy man;
of what use are riches to the covetous?
4 He deprives himself only to amass wealth for others,
and others will live luxuriously on his possessions.
5 To whom will a person be generous when he is stingy with himself?
He does not even enjoy his own riches.
6 There is nobody worse than the man who is grudging to himself;
in this way, he receives just recompense for his miserliness.[i]

d Sir 15:12; Prov 1:10-15; 3:31; 16:29.—e 2 Cor 6:14ff.—f Prov 19:4, 7.—g Prov 15:13.—h 1f: Sir 19:16; 25:8; Pss 17:3; 39:4; 141:3f; Jas 3:2.—i Sir 11:18f; Prov 11:17; Eccl 5:9-12.

13:14 Added by some early MSS.

13:18 In Palestine, the hostility between the dogs that guarded the flocks by night and the hyenas was taken for granted.

13:24 The author is indicating that poverty that does not stem from a person's sin or laziness is not evil even though the arrogant regard it as such.

14:1-2 True happiness may be found in the purity and truth of life; this is a teaching that the Bible repeats more than once. The Beatitudes of the Gospel will make more precise the completely unexpected conditions of this human happiness (Mt 5:1-12).

14:3-19 The thought of death should detach people from riches, for these do not follow them into the grave. It is far better for them to use their wealth profitably for themselves and their friends. The author was not yet aware of the promises of eternity; for him, the pact with the netherworld (v. 16)—i.e., with the place without hope where the dead sojourn—signals the end one day of all the pain that people give themselves.

7 If he does any good, he does so by mistake,
and in the end his greed will be revealed.
8 Wicked is the eye of the miser,
looking the other way and despising the lives of others.
9 The eyes of a greedy man are not content with his share;
greed shrivels his soul.

10 The miser begrudges bread
and sets a table with scanty provisions.
11 My child, treat yourself as well as you can in accord with your means,
and present worthy offerings to the LORD.[j]
12 Remember that death does not tarry
and that the decree of the netherworld*
has not been revealed to you.
13 Be kind to your friend before you die
and give him a generous portion according to your ability.
14 Do not deprive yourself of the good things of today;
do not forgo your share of good things.
15 Will you not have to leave your riches to others,
with the fruit of your labors to be divided by lot?
16 Give and receive; enjoy life,
because no pleasures will be found in the netherworld.
17 As is true of a garment, all flesh wears away;
the age-old decree is: all must die.[k]
18* Like thick foliage on a spreading tree,
with some leaves falling and others sprouting,
so with the generations of flesh and blood:
one dies and another is born.
19 All work decays and ceases to exist,
and its author will pass away with it.*

Blessed Is the Man Who Meditates on Wisdom*

20 Blessed is the man who meditates on* Wisdom
and reasons with intelligence,[l]
21* who reflects on her ways in his heart
and ponders her secrets,
22 who pursues her like a hunter
and lies in watch by her paths,
23 who peers through her windows
and listens at her doors,
24 who lodges near her house
and drives his tent-peg into her walls,
25 who pitches his tent near her,
having found there an excellent lodging,
26 who places his children under her shade
and camps beneath her branches,
27 who is sheltered by her from the heat
and makes his home in her glory.*

CHAPTER 15

1 The one who fears the LORD will do this,
and he who follows the law will obtain wisdom.[m]
2 She will come forth to meet him like a mother;
like a young bride she will receive him,
3 nourish him with the bread of understanding,
and give him the water of wisdom to imbibe.[n]
4 He will lean on her and not fall,
rely on her and not be put to shame.
5 She will exalt him above his neighbors
and provide him with eloquence in the midst of the assembly.
6 He will experience happiness and a crown of joy
and inherit an everlasting name.
7 The foolish will never obtain her,
nor will sinners behold her.
8 She keeps herself distant from the arrogant,
and liars never call her to mind.
9 Praise is unseemly on the lips of a sinner,
for its source has not been God.

j Prov 3:9.—k Ps 103:14ff; Isa 40:6; Jas 1:10; 1 Pet 1:24.—l Ps 1:2; 119:15, 23, 148; Prov 8:32-35.—m Sir 1:11-30; 6:32-37.—n Prov 9:5; Isa 55:1; Jn 4:10; 6:31ff.

14:12 *Decree of the netherworld:* most likely a reference to a decree that assigned the day of death (see Isa 28:15, 18).

14:18-19 These verses touch upon the precarious character of human existence (see also Sir 30:17; 41:1-4; Pss 39:5, 7, 12; 62:10; Eccl 6:12).

14:19 The Book of Revelation (Rev 14:13) modifies the notion that all human works will perish, indicating that a person's works will follow after him into the glory of a new life: "They will find rest from their labors, for their deeds go with them."

14:20—15:10 Wisdom, which teaches the real reasons for living, is not easy to attain. People must seek assiduously, scrutinizing the law and the sayings of the sages. But to those who pursue their quest unceasingly, she offers herself like a young bride and brings them happiness and renown.

14:20 *Meditates on:* some early MSS read: "dies in."

14:21-27 The structure of these verses follows the Hebrew.

14:27 *Glory:* this may refer to the cloud that used to manifest the presence of Yahweh (see Ex 16:10; 24:16).

10 Praise is uttered only by the tongue of the wise,
and the LORD himself prompts it.

G: God's Providence and Human Freedom*

God Created Man and Left Him Free*

11 Do not say, "God is responsible for my falling away,"
for you ought not do * what he hates.
12 Do not say, "It was he who led me astray,"
for he has no need of a sinner. [o]
13 The LORD hates everything that is abominable,
and those who fear him love it not.
14 In the beginning, when God created man,
he left him free to make his own decisions. [p]
15 If you choose, you can keep the commandments,
and to act faithfully is within your power.
16 He has set before you fire and water;
stretch out your hand for whichever you choose.
17 Before each man are life and death,
and whichever one he chooses will be given.
18 For great is the wisdom of the LORD;
he is mighty in power and all-seeing.
19 His eyes are on those who fear him,
and he is aware of every human action.
20 He has not commanded anyone to be wicked,
and he has given no one permission to sin.

CHAPTER 16

God Judges an Individual According to His Deeds*

1 Do not desire a brood of unprofitable * children,
and take no joy in offspring who are godless.
2 No matter how many your children, do not rejoice in them
unless the fear of the LORD is in them.
3 [q] Do not count on their growing old
or rely on their numbers.
[For you will grieve in untimely mourning
and know of their unexpected end.] *
For one can be better than a thousand,
and to die childless is better than to have godless children.
4 Through one wise man an entire city can be populated,
but a tribe of lawless people can bring about its destruction.

5 Many such things my eyes have seen,
and my ears have heard things even more impressive.
6 Against an assembly of sinners a fire is kindled,
and retribution blazes upon a godless nation.
7 God did not forgive the leaders of old
who rebelled in their strength. [r]
8 He did not spare the neighbors of Lot
whom he abhorred for their arrogance. *
9 He showed no pity toward the doomed people
who were dispossessed because of their sins. *
[He did all these things to the obstinate nations,
and he was not appeased by the multitude of his holy ones.] *
10 Neither did he show pity toward those six hundred thousand foot soldiers *
who perished because of their stubborn defiance.
* [Chastising and sparing, striking and healing,

o Gen 3:13; Jas 1:13.—p Gen 1:27.—q 3f: Deut 28:15-19; Ps 55:24; Wis 4:1f.—r Gen 6:4; Wis 14:6; Bar 3:26ff.

15:11—18:14 Sin infests life; it seems ineradicable. This is a mystery of the human condition.

15:11-20 The Lord is horrified by sin and cannot be the origin of evil. Even though human beings are created by God and none of their acts escapes God, they remain completely masters of their destiny (Gen 2:16f; Deut 30:15). Life and death, i.e., fidelity and impiety, are offered each day to the dramatic choice of humans.

15:11 *You ought not do:* some early MSS read: "he does not do."

16:1-16 The number of one's children is no longer regarded as a sign of God's blessing of a father. It is much better to be concerned with their faithfulness, for each lives under the eye of God. God treats all persons according to their merits (Gen 9:1-29; Num 14:20-35; Jos 6:21). Human beings are responsible for their actions.

16:1 *Unprofitable:* Hebrew reads: "worthless."

16:3c-d Added by some early MSS.

16:8 The people of Sodom and Gomorrah (see Gen 19:24-25; Ezek 16:49-50).

16:9 The people who lived in Canaan.

16:9c-d Added by some early MSS.

16:10 *Six hundred thousand foot soldiers:* See Ex 12:37; Num 11:21. These men perished in the wilderness and never reached Canaan, the Promised Land (see Num 14:20-33).

the LORD persisted in showing mercy
and dispensing discipline.]*
11 Even if there had been only one stiff-necked man,
it would have been a miracle if he had escaped retribution.
For mercy and anger alike belong to the LORD;
he shows his might in his forgiveness
and also as he pours out his wrath.[s]
12 As great as his mercy is his chastisement;
he judges an individual according to his deeds.
13 The sinner will not escape with plunder,
nor will the patience of the godly be forgotten.
14 He does not forget any act of mercy;
everyone will be treated in accordance with his deeds.
[15*The LORD hardened Pharaoh's heart so that he did not recognize him
whose works were manifest under the heavens;
16 his mercy was seen by all creation,
and he separated the light from the darkness among the sons of Adam.]

Foolish Are Those Who Think God Does Not See Them*

17 Do not say, "I am hidden from the LORD;
who above gives any thought to me?
Among so many people I will not be noticed;
for what am I in the immensity of creation?
18 Behold, heaven itself, the highest heaven,
the abyss, and the earth tremble at his visitation.
[The entire world, past and present, is in his will.]*
19 The mountains and the foundations of the earth
quiver and quake when he looks upon them.[t]
20 What human mind can grasp this
or comprehend his ways?
21 Like a storm wind that is invisible,
so his works for the most part are concealed.[u]
22 Who will report about his acts of justice?
Or who can wait for them, since the covenant* is far in the future
[and a scrutiny for all comes at the end]?"*
23 Such are the thoughts of the one who lacks understanding,
senseless and misguided in his foolish reasoning.

God the Creator and Lawgiver*

24 Listen to me, my child, and acquire knowledge;
pay close attention to what I have to say.
25 I will impart discipline precisely
and proclaim knowledge accurately.
26 When God created his works in the beginning,
in doing so he determined their boundaries.[v]
27 He defined their functions for all time
and their domains for all generations.
They never hunger or grow weary,
nor do they ever abandon their tasks.
28 Never do they crowd one another,
nor do they ever disobey his word.
29 Then the Lord looked upon the earth
and filled it with his good things.[w]
30 With every kind of living creature he covered its surface,
and into it they must return.

CHAPTER 17

1 The Lord fashioned man from the earth
and causes him to return to it again.[x]

---

s Sir 5:6; Ex 34:6f.—t Job 37:1-7; Ps 18:8.—u Sir 23:18; Ps 10:4, 11, 13.—v Gen 1:4ff.—w Gen 1:20ff.—x Gen 2:7; 3:19; Ps 146:4; Eccl 3:20.

16:10c-d Added by some early MSS.

16:15-16 Added by some early MSS. *Among the sons of Adam:* or "with a plumb line."

16:17-23 The author shows that God is concerned with each person. To stress this intervention of God in creation, he evokes natural phenomena with their unforeseeable and inexplicable aspects.

16:18c Added by some early MSS.

16:22 *Covenant:* Hebrew reads: "decree."

16:22c Added by some early MSS.

16:24—17:24 In his demonstration, the author introduces a hymn to God the Creator that is also a chant for human beings. Sacred history is linked with the work of creation: God has revealed his law to his chosen people and concluded a covenant with his own. The song of praise concludes with a moral lesson; the past shows that all human beings, especially those who belong to the chosen people, will answer to God for their actions. But the Lord is a judge who is ever ready to pardon those who implore him and to reward those who uphold their brothers and sisters (Sir 17:22).

2 [y] He granted him a fixed span of days
and gave him dominion over everything on earth.
3 He endowed him with strength like his own
and made him in his own image.
4 He put the fear of him into all living things
and made him the master over beasts and birds.
[5 He received the use of the five faculties from the Lord;
as a sixth he gave him the gift of mind,
and as a seventh the gift of reason, the interpreter of one's faculties.]*
6 He fashioned men's tongues, eyes, and ears
and gave them minds with which to think.
7 He filled them with wisdom and understanding
and a knowledge of good and evil.
8 He placed the fear of him into their hearts
to display to them the majesty of his works [z]
[9 and to enable them to proclaim his marvelous deeds]*
10 so that they may give praise to his holy name.
11 He granted knowledge to them,
endowing them with the law of life.
[Thus, they might know that those who are living are mortal.]*
12 An everlasting covenant he established with them,
and his decrees* he revealed to them.
13 Their eyes beheld his glorious majesty,
and their ears heard the glory of his voice.* [a]
14 He said to them, "Refrain from all wrongdoing,"
and he gave them a commandment concerning duties toward one's neighbor.
15 Their ways are always known to him;
they cannot be hidden from his sight.
[16 Their ways from childhood tend toward evil,
and they cannot transform their stony hearts into hearts of flesh.]*
17 He appointed a ruler* over every nation,
but Israel is the Lord's own portion. [b]
[18 Since Israel is his firstborn,
he rears him with discipline,
bestowing on him the light of his love
and not neglecting him.]*
19 All their deeds are as clear as the sun to him,
and his eyes are ever upon their ways.
20 Their iniquities are not hidden from him;
all their sins are before the Lord.
[21 Yet the Lord, who is compassionate
and knows how they are formed,
has neither left nor abandoned them
but spared them.]*
22 Almsgiving is like a signet ring to him,
and he cherishes kindness like the apple of his eye.
[He apportions repentance to his sons and daughters.]*
23 In the end, he will rise up and repay the wicked,
bringing down retribution on their heads. [c]
24 But to those who repent he allows a return,
and he encourages those who have lost hope.

Return to the Lord*

25 Therefore, return to the Lord and renounce your wicked ways;
pray in his presence and lessen your offense.
26 Return to the Most High, turn away from iniquity,

y 2ff: Gen 1:26ff; Job 14:1f; Pss 8:4-8; 90:10; Wis 9:2f.—z Wis 13:1; Rom 1:19f.—a Ex 19:16-19; 24:15-17; 34:10ff; Deut 4:11f; Isa 30:30.—b Ex 19:5; Deut 4:19f; 7:6; 32:8f; Dan 10:13-21; 12:1; Rom 13:1.—c Job 19:25; Joel 4:4.

17:5 Added by some early MSS.

17:9 Added by some early MSS.

17:11c Added by some early MSS.

17:12 *An everlasting covenant . . . his decrees:* a reference to the covenants that God made with human beings (e.g., Gen 2:15ff; 17:1-22, and especially the covenant of Mount Sinai when God gave the Mosaic Law, Ex 19:16ff).

17:13 The author evokes the Lord's manifestation at Sinai (Ex 19:16-25).

17:16 Added by some early MSS.

17:17 *Ruler:* this term can be taken as referring to a civil ruler or to angels who are placed over nations as their guardians (see Deut 32:8). *The Lord's own portion:* an allusion to Israel's special position with God (see Deut 32:8f).

17:18 Added by some early MSS.

17:21 Added by some early MSS.

17:22c Added by some early MSS.

17:25-32 It is the Lord who gives life and allows people to live on earth. The author still regards the sojourn of the dead as a place in which there is no hope and from which there is no return. Other believers affirm that this life of humans cannot be definitively destroyed by death (Wis 3; 2 Mac 7; 12:44; Dan 12:2-3). Christ will say: "I have come / that they may have life, / and have it in abundance" (Jn 10:10).

[for he will guide you out of darkness
and into the light of health,] *
and hate intensely what he abhors.
27* [d] Who will glorify the Most High in the netherworld
in place of the living who give praise?
28 The dead cannot offer praise anymore
than those who have never lived;
only those who are alive and well sing the Lord's praises.
29 How great is the mercy of the Lord
and the forgiveness he offers to those who return to him!
30 Many things are beyond the human capacity to achieve,
since the son of man is not immortal.
31 Is anything brighter than the sun? Yet it is subject to eclipse.
Thus, flesh and blood devise evil plans. *
32 God watches over the hosts of the highest heavens,
but all men are merely dust and ashes.

CHAPTER 18

The Wonders of the Lord Are Unfathomable*

1 He who lives forever is the Creator of the entire universe;
2 the LORD alone is righteous.
[2b * And there are no others beside him.
3 He guides the world with a turn of his hand,
and all things obey his will;
for he is king of all things by his power,
separating the holy things among them from the profane.]
4 [e] To no one has he given the power to adequately proclaim his works,
and who can fathom his mighty deeds?
5 Who can assess his majestic power
or fully recount all of his mercies?
6 The wonders of the Lord can be neither diminished nor increased,
nor are they possible to fathom.
7 When a man finishes, he is still only beginning,
and when he stops, he is still confused.

What Is a Man?*

8 What is a man? What purpose does he serve?
What about him is good, and what is evil? [f]
9 [g] The span of his life is great
if he attains one hundred years.
[But the death of each one is beyond the calculation of all.] *
10 Like a drop of water from the sea or a grain of sand,
such are these few years compared with eternity.
11 That is why the Lord is patient with men
and pours out his mercy on them.
12 He sees and recognizes how wretched their end will be,
and thus he is even more lavish with his compassion.
13 Man's compassion is for his neighbor,
but the compassion of the Lord extends to everyone.
He rebukes, trains, and teaches them,
and he brings them back into the fold
as a shepherd does his flock. [h]
14 He has compassion on those who accept his teaching
and are diligent in obeying his precepts.

H: Excesses of the Tongue and Greed Are the Enemies of Wisdom*

The Manner of Giving Is Worth More than the Gift*

15 My child, do not temper your good deeds with reproach,
or spoil your gifts with harsh words.

---

d 27f: Pss 6:6; 30:10; 88:11-13; 115:17f; Isa 38:18f.—e 4f: Sir 1:3, 6; 42:17; Job 9:10; Ps 145:3.—f Job 7:17; Pss 8:5; 144:3.—g 9f: Sir 1:2; 17:2; Ps 90:3-6, 10.—h Pss 23:1-4; 80:2; Isa 40:11; Ezek 34:11-16; Jn 10:11.

17:26b Added by some early MSS.

17:27-28 One reason for repentance is that in the netherworld there is no loving contact with God (see Pss 6:5; 30:9; 115:17f; Isa 38:18f; Bar 2:17). By repentance human beings come *alive* and *sing the Lord's praises.*

17:31 The author seems to be saying that human beings are unable to understand God's plans and are bent toward evil.

18:1-7 Even though their dignity is great, human beings remain weak and doomed to death in contrast to the Sovereign Master of the world, the Almighty One who knows no end and whom they can never understand (vv. 5-6).

18:2b-3 Added by some early MSS.

18:8-14 Believers share the questions of all human beings. God's universal mercy and its pedagogical character constitute a new aspect of the Old Testament.

18:9c Added by some early MSS.

18:15—23:28 After a lengthy debate about the human condition entrusted to God's mercy, the author sets forth anew a succession of practical counsels whose main themes we highlight.

18:15-18 The author stresses that in doing a charitable act the giver must be careful not to humiliate the receiver (v. 16).

16 Does not dew give relief from the heat?
In the same way, a word can do more than a gift.[i]
17 Sometimes a word is better than an expensive gift;
both are the hallmark of a gracious person.
18 A fool offers nothing but insult,
and a gift given begrudgingly dims the expectant eyes.

Know How To Reflect and Foresee*

19 Be fully informed before you speak;
before you fall sick, take care of your health.
20 Before judgment comes, examine yourself,
and at your hour of scrutiny you will find forgiveness.*
21 Before you fall ill, humble yourself,
and repent as soon as you have sinned.
[Do not delay in giving up sinning,
or neglect to do so until you are in distress.
Do not set a time for giving up sinning;
be mindful that death will not delay its coming.]*
22 Let nothing hinder you from promptly discharging your vows;
do not wait until the moment of death to fulfill them.[j]
23 Before making a vow, give it careful consideration,
do not imitate one who puts the Lord to the test.
24 Think of his wrath on the day of death,
and of the moment of vengeance when he turns away his face.
25[k] Remember the time of famine in the time of plenty;
think of poverty and need in the days of wealth.
26 Between morning and evening changes occur;
all things are fleeting in the sight of the Lord.
27 The wise man is cautious in every respect;
during sinful times he is on his guard against wrongdoing.
28 Every person of intelligence recognizes wisdom
and praises anyone who finds her.
29 Those who are trained in her words must proclaim her wisdom
and pour forth sound proverbs.
[It is better to trust in the one Lord
than to cling with a deadened heart to dead idols.]*

Do Not Be Governed by Your Passions*

30 Do not be governed by your passions,
but keep your desires in check.[l]
31 If you succumb to the enticements of base desires,
you will become the laughingstock of your enemies.
32 Do not revel in luxurious living,
or the expense involved may cause your impoverishment.
33 Do not become a beggar by feasting on credit
when you have nothing in your money bag.
[For you will be plotting against your own life.]*

CHAPTER 19

1 A drunken workman* will never grow rich,
and carelessness in small matters will lead to one's ruin.
2 Wine and women lead intelligent men astray,
and the man who consorts with prostitutes becomes ever more reckless.
3 Decay and worms will take possession of him,
and because of his recklessness he will lose his life.

Discretion in Believing and Repeating Gossip*

4 One who too readily trusts others displays a shallow intelligence,

---

i Sir 43:22; Hos 13:15; Jon 4:8.—j Num 30:3; Deut 23:22; Ps 50:14; Prov 20:25; Eccl 5:4.—k 25f: Sir 11:25; Job 4:17-21; Ps 90:4-6; Lk 12:16-21.—l Rom 6:12; 13:14.

18:19-29 The ancients regarded sickness as a punishment for sin. Living a good life gave some assurance of escaping sickness and of avoiding the threat of a premature death. In this and in other things, the sage is concerned with a prudent way of acting.

18:20 One way of obtaining forgiveness mentioned often in Scripture is by giving alms (see Sir 3:30-31; 29:1; Tob 12:12-13; Dan 4:24; Lk 16:9; Acts 10:31).

18:21c-d-e-f Added in some early MSS.

18:29c-d Added in some early MSS.

18:30—19:3 Wine, women, excess, and passion pervert sensible people. Wisdom is to maintain control over one's passions.

18:33c Added in some early MSS.

19:1 *A drunken workman:* Hebrew reads: "The one who does this."

19:4-12 Those who babble are prone to slander. Under every sky, the wise have stressed the misdeeds of the tongue. The author seems to have made a special effort not to dishonor the human word.

and one who sins does serious harm to himself.
5 One who rejoices in wickedness will suffer condemnation,
[5b * but one who resists pleasures crowns his life.
6a One who curbs the tongue lives without strife],
6 but by hating gossip he avoids evil.
7 Never repeat gossip,
and you will come to no harm. [m]
8 Report nothing accusatory to friend or foe;
do not reveal anything unless it would be sinful for you not to do so.
9 For one may hear it and mistrust you
and in time come to hate you.
10 Have you heard a rumor? Let it die with you;
be assured, if you hold it in, it will not cause you to burst asunder.
11 A fool who has heard something suffers birth pangs
like a woman in labor with a child.
12 Like an arrow lodged in a person's thigh
is gossip in the heart of a fool.

You Cannot Believe Everything You Hear*

13 Question your friend—perhaps he may not have done what he is accused of,
and if he has, your action may ensure that he will not do it again. [n]
14 Question your neighbor—perhaps he may not have said what he is accused of,
and if he has, your action may ensure that he will not say it again.
15 Question your friend—often he may be the victim of slander;
you cannot believe everything you hear.
16 And of course a man may let something slip without intending to do so;
is anyone's tongue free of guilt? [o]
17 Question your neighbor before you break with him,
and thereby you will give due place to the law * of the Most High.
[17c * Do not give in to anger.
18 The fear of the Lord is the beginning of his clemency,
and wisdom wins his love.
19 The knowledge of the Lord's commandments is life-giving instruction,
and those who do what pleases him exult in the fruit of the tree of immortality.]

Do Not Confuse Wisdom with Cleverness*

20 All wisdom is the fear of the LORD,
and it derives from the fulfillment of the law. [p]
* [It also derives from the knowledge of his universal sovereignty.
21 If a servant says to his master,
"I will not do what you want,"
even if later he does it,
he angers the man who has him in his care.]
22 The knowledge of wickedness is not wisdom,
nor is there prudence in the advice of sinners.
23 There is a cleverness that is foul;
however, he who does not have wisdom is a fool.
24 It is better to be short of sense and God-fearing
than to be highly intelligent and violate the law.
25 There is a cleverness that is scrupulous but dishonest,
and there are those who abuse favors to win a favorable decision.
26 There is a wicked man who bows his head in mourning
but is filled with guile within.
27 He hides his face and pretends not to hear,
but when no one is paying attention, he will take advantage of you.
28 And if lack of strength prevents him from sinning,
he will nevertheless do evil deeds at the first opportunity.
29 You can learn a great deal about a man simply by observing his appearance;

m Prov 17:9; 25:10.—n Lev 19:17; Mt 18:15; Lk 17:3.—o Sir 14:1; 28:26; Jas 3:2.—p Sir 1:1, 12, 14; Job 28:28; Ps 111:10; Prov 1:7; 9:10.

19:5b-6a Added by some early MSS.

19:13-19 These verses deal with the charitable concern we owe friends after hearing gossip about them. Above all, if the gossip turns out to be true, we should admonish them so that they will avoid making the same mistake in the future.

19:17 *You will give due place to the law:* a reference to Lev 19:17-18.

19:17c-19 Added by some early MSS.

19:20-30 Not all clever people are wise, neither are all sinners fools. But guile has nothing in common with humility except habit; there are certain airs that do not deceive.

19:20c-21 Added by some early MSS.

a sensible man is recognized as such
when he is first encountered.
30 A man's attire and his hearty laughter,
as well as the way he walks, reveal his
character.

CHAPTER 20

The Wise Remain Silent until the Right Moment*

1 A rebuke on occasion can be untimely,
and a man may show wisdom by keeping silent.
2 But how much better it is to rebuke than
to fume,
3 for the one who admits his faults will
be preserved from disgrace.
4 Like a eunuch lusting to ravage a
maiden
is the person who does what is right
out of obligation.*
5 One man is silent and considered to be
wise,
while another incurs hatred for talking
too much.[q]
6[r] One man keeps silent because he has
nothing to say,
while another keeps quiet because he
knows when to speak.
7 A wise man remains silent until the
right moment,
but a boasting fool never seems aware
of the proper time.
8 The one who talks too much is detested,
and the one who pretends to be an
authority is hated.
[How good it is to show repentance when
you are rebuked,
for you will thereby avoid deliberate
sin.]*

Disconcerting Contrasts*

9 There is the man who finds good fortune in adversity,
and the good fortune that may result
in a loss.
10 There is the gift that profits you nothing,
and the gift that must be paid back
double.
11 The search for glory may lead one man
to humiliation,
while another man may rise from
humble circumstances to a position of eminence.[s]
12 A man may buy much for little
but pay for it seven times over.

The Courtesies and Discourses of Fools*

13 A wise man can become beloved by
means of his* words,
but the courtesies of fools are futile.
14 The gift of a fool will profit you nothing,
[neither will that of a miser who gives
solely out of obligation]*
for he covets to receive more than he
gave.
15 He gives little and criticizes much,
opening his mouth like a town crier.
He lends today and demands payment
tomorrow;
such a man is detestable.
16 The fool will say, "I have no friends,
and I get no thanks for my good deeds;
17 those who eat my bread have malicious
tongues."
He will be laughed at frequently by
many.
[For he did not receive honestly what he
possesses,
and what he lacks is not important to
him.]*
18 A slip on the pavement is better than a
slip of the tongue;
the downfall of the wicked will come
just as quickly.
19 A coarse person is like an indiscreet
story
that is continually on the lips of the
ignorant.
20 A proverb is rejected when it comes
from the lips of a fool
since he does not utter it at the proper
time.

---

q Prov 17:28.—r 6f: Ps 12:4f; Prov 10:19; 15:23; 17:28; 25:11; Eccl 3:7.—s 1 Sam 2:4-9; Pss 75:8; 113:7-9; Lk 1:52.

20:1-8 The wise know how to be silent. But there is also a time to respond, to explain oneself, and to excuse oneself.

20:4 An "outward" act of wrongdoing can be prevented, even if by force, but not an internal act of wrongdoing (see v. 21).

20:8c-d Added by some early MSS.

20:9-12 Circumstances lead to success or failure, and the wise know how to profit from everything.

20:13-23 Rather than being a gift, certain presents are acts of guile and wickedness.

20:13 *His:* Hebrew reads: "few."

20:14b Added by some early MSS.

20:17c-d Added by some early MSS.

21 Poverty may prevent one from sinning;
so when he takes his rest, his conscience does not disturb him.
22 One may lose his life through false shame
or perish from fear of the opinion of a fool.
[For the latter has a foolish look.] *
23 Another, out of shame, makes promises to a friend
and needlessly turns that friend into an enemy.

A Lie Is an Ugly Blot on Anyone*

24 A lie is an ugly blot on anyone
and is ever on the lips of the ignorant. [t]
25 A thief is preferable to a habitual liar,
yet both will suffer disaster.
26 The path of a liar leads to disgrace;
his shame lasts forever.

Hidden Wisdom and Treasure Are Valueless*

27 A wise man advances himself by his words;
a prudent man is pleasing to the great.
28 He who tills his soil has an abundant harvest;
he who pleases the great will secure pardon for offenses.
29 Favors and gifts blind the eyes of the wise;
like a muzzle over the mouth they silence criticism. [u]
30 *Hidden wisdom and unseen treasure—
of what value is either?
31 Better is the man who hides his folly
than one who conceals his wisdom.
[32 It is better to serve the Lord while awaiting the inevitable
than to be an ignorant helmsman of one's own life.] *

CHAPTER 21

Sin and Sinners*

1 My child, have you sinned? Do not sin anymore,
and ask forgiveness for your past sins.
2 Flee from sin as from a snake,
for it will bite you if you approach it.
Its teeth are like a lion's teeth
and can take away human lives.
3 All law-breaking is like a two-edged sword;
the wound it inflicts cannot be healed. [v]
4 Panic and violence will wipe out riches;
similarly the house of the proud man will be laid waste. *
5 The prayer of the poor man goes from his lips straight to the ear of God,
and justice is speedily granted him.
6 One who hates reproof walks in the sinner's path,
but the man who fears the Lord repents in his heart. [w]
7 A skillful speaker is widely known,
but the wise man is well aware of his own faults.

8 To build a house with other people's money
is like gathering stones for one's own tomb.
9 A band of the wicked is like a bundle of fibers;
it will end in a blazing fire. [x]
10 The path of sinners is smoothly paved,
but it ends in the depths of the netherworld. *

Portraits of the Wise and the Foolish*

11 He who keeps the law controls his thoughts;
the fear of the Lord results in wisdom.
12 The one who is not clever cannot be taught,
but there is a cleverness that is a source of bitterness.

t Prov 13:5.—u Ex 23:8; Deut 16:19; Prov 18:16; 21:14.—v Jdg 3:16; Prov 5:4; Ps 149:6f; Heb 4:12; Rev 1:16.—w Sir 32:17; Prov 12:1.—x Sir 16:6; Ps 21:10.

20:22c Added by some early MSS.

20:24-26 Lies lead only to dishonor and to eternal shame. The author also discusses the evils of lying in Sir 7:13 and 25:2. See Ps 5:7; Prov 6:6-19.

20:27-32 In order to teach others, the wise must in some way have access to the powerful; it is then, above all, that they must guard against being bought.

20:30-31 The author stresses that wisdom must be shared with others so that it will redound to the good of all (see Mt 25:14-30).

20:32 Added by some early MSS.

21:1-10 The way of sinners leads to perdition (whose symbol is *the netherworld*), the place without hope (v. 10). But God takes into consideration the prayer and repentance of the poor, i.e., the lowly.

21:4 *Laid waste:* some early MSS read: "uprooted."

21:10 *The path of sinners . . . the depths of the netherworld:* the author urges people to repent, for in the netherworld, there is no loving contact with God (see Pss 6:6; 30:10; 88:5-11; 115:17-18; Isa 38:18-19; Bar 2:17). It remained for Christ to reveal an eternal retribution (see Mt 7:13f; 25:41-46; Lk 16:19-31).

21:11-28 Reverence toward the Lord, observance of the law, and mastery of one's existence, thoughts, and words are the qualities that are lacking to the foolish and distinguish the wise.

13 The knowledge of a wise man increases like a flood,
and his counsel is like a life-giving spring. [y]
14 The mind of a fool is like a broken jar;
it cannot retain any knowledge.
15 When an intelligent man hears words of wisdom,
he praises them and adds to them.
When a fool hears them, he is scornful
and casts them aside behind his back.
16 The chatter of a fool is like traveling with a heavy load,
but delight is to be found upon the lips of a wise man.
17 The views of a wise man are sought in the assembly,
and his words are pondered carefully.
18 Like a house in ruins is wisdom to a fool;
the ignorant man regards knowledge only as incoherent talk.
19 Instruction is like fetters on the feet to the fool,
and like a manacle on his right hand.
20 A fool laughs at the top of his voice,
but a prudent man smiles quietly. [z]
21 Like an ornament of gold is instruction to a sensible man,
like a bracelet on his right arm.
22 A fool steps boldly into a house,
whereas the well-bred person waits outside respectfully.
23 A boor peers into a house through the doorway,
but a cultured man remains outside.
24 It is bad manners for someone to listen at a door;
a cultured man would regard this as disgraceful, things that are not his business.
25 The lips of gossipers repeat the words of others,
but the prudent carefully weigh their words.
26 The heart of fools is in their mouth,
but the mouth of the wise is in their heart.
27 When a godless man curses an adversary, *
he is cursing himself.
28 A scandal-monger degrades himself
and earns the hatred of his neighbors. [a]

CHAPTER 22

Idlers Are Despised

1 * An idler is like a filthy stone;
everyone hisses at his disgrace.
2 An idler is like a lump of dung;
anyone who picks it up will shake it off his hand.

Parents and Children

3 It is a disgrace to be the father of an unruly son,
but the birth of a daughter is a loss. [b]
4 A sensible daughter will find a husband,
but one who acts shamefully is the source of grief to her father.
5 A brazen daughter brings shame upon her father and her husband
and is despised by both.
6 Inopportune conversation is like music in a time of mourning,
but thrashings and correction are wisdom at all times.
[7 * Children whose upbringing leads to a good life
make one forget the humble origin of their parents.
8 Children who are puffed up with disdain and haughtiness
blemish the nobility of their family.]

Working with Fools Is a Lost Cause*

9 c Teaching a fool is like gluing together pieces of pottery,
or like rousing a sleeper from deep slumber.
10 You might as well talk to someone who is sound asleep as to a fool,
for when you have finished, the fool will say, "What was that?"

y Prov 13:14; 16:22.—z Eccl 7:6.—a Sir 5:14—6:1; 28:13; Jas 3:8.—b Sir 16:1-5; Prov 17:21; 19:13.—c 9-12: Prov 23:9.

21:27 *Adversary:* three senses have been attributed to this term: (1) when godless persons curse an adversary for leading them into sin, they are really cursing themselves for having succumbed; (2) the adversary they curse is the sinful nature of human beings; or (3) the adversary they curse is the devil, for the Hebrew word used is *satan* (see 1 Chr 21:1; Zec 3:2; 2 Pet 2:12f; Jude 9).

22:1-8 For the author, idlers, as well as unruly children, are a disgrace. The sages of all antiquity believed that in education it was better to be severe toward the guilty than to condone. To encourage the parents, the author stresses that their reputation is at stake.

22:7-8 Added by some early MSS.

22:9-18 Once more, the author paints one of his lively portraits of the foolish. Is it just, as he says, to discourage any commerce with them, or rather to inspire someone to make the effort necessary, so that one will not be counted among those culpable for the degeneration of heart and spirit? For it is about this foolishness that the Bible speaks.

11 Weep for the dead man, for he has taken leave of the light;
weep for the fool, for he has taken leave of his wits.
Weep fewer tears for the dead man, for he is at rest,
but the life of a fool is sadder than death.
12 Mourning for the dead lasts seven days,
but for the foolish and the ungodly it lasts all the days of their life.
13 Do not speak often with a fool,
or visit a stupid person.
[For since he is without sense,
he will despise everything about you.] *
Beware of him or you may find yourself in trouble
and be splattered by contact with him.
Avoid him and you will have peace of mind
and not be exasperated by his lack of sense.
14 What is heavier than lead,
and what is its name but "Fool"?
15 Sand, salt, and a lump of iron
are easier to bear than a stupid man. [d]
16 A wooden beam firmly bonded into a building
is not dislodged by an earthquake.
So, too, a mind firmly resolved after due reflection
will not be shaken in a moment of crisis.
17 A mind based on intelligent reflection
is like fine decoration on a smooth wall.
18 Fences * lying on a high place
will not stand firm against the wind.
Neither can a mind made timid by foolish plans
withstand any kind of fear.

Friendship Does Not Dispense with Tact*

19 Jab an eye and you will bring tears;
jab a heart and you will lay bare its feelings.
20 If you throw a stone at birds, you frighten them away;
if you revile a friend, you destroy a friendship.
21 If you draw a sword against a friend,
do not despair, for it can still be undone.
22 If you have quarreled with a friend,
do not fear, for you can still be reconciled.
But as for taunts, arrogance, betrayal of secrets, and stabs in the back—
these will drive away any friend. [e]
23 Be faithful to your neighbor while he is poor
so that you may later rejoice with him in his good fortune.
Stand by him in times of distress
so that you may share with him in his inheritance.
[For no one should ever despise someone's appearance
or marvel at a stupid man who is rich.] *
24 Just as the fumes and smoke of a furnace precede the flames,
so do insults precede bloodshed.
25 I will not be ashamed to shelter a friend,
nor will I hide myself from him.
26 But if harm should come to me because of him,
everyone who hears about it will beware of him.

Prayer for a Good Life*

27 Who will set a guard over my mouth,
and a seal of prudence on my lips,
to prevent them from becoming my downfall
and to keep my tongue from causing my ruin? [f]

CHAPTER 23

1 O Lord, Father and Master of my life,
do not abandon me to their control,
and do not permit me to fall because of them.
2 Who will administer whips to my thoughts
and the discipline of wisdom to my mind,

d Deut 28:48; Job 6:3; Prov 27:3; Jer 28:13f.—e Prov 11:13; 20:19; 25:9.—f Sir 28:24-26; Pss 39:2; 141:3; Prov 13:3; 18:7, 21.

22:13c-d Added by some early MSS.

22:18 *Fences:* some early MSS read: "Pebbles."

22:19-26 Friendship does not dispense from tact. True, it may surmount misunderstandings and obstacles, but behaviors can kill it. Verses 23-24 deal with a more general manner of relations in society.

22:23e-f Added by some early MSS.

22:27—23:6 The wise know their weakness, the power of passions, and the difficulties that must daily be confronted. Thus, they implore God's help so that truth and purity may be fixed more and more firmly in their hearts. The author inserts here a beautiful prayer witnessing to the fact that true education—of the heart—is a grace of God.

lest my failings may be spared
or any sins of mine be overlooked,
3 lest my failings be multiplied
and my sins abound,
lest I succumb to my adversaries
and my enemy gloat over me?
[For hope of receiving mercy from them is remote.] *
4 O Lord, Father and God of my life,
do not allow haughtiness to mark my gaze,[g]
5 and remove evil desire from my heart.
6 Let neither gluttony nor lust gain power over me,
and do not give me over to shameless passions.[h]

Do Not Swear Oaths Lightly*

7 Listen, my children, to the instruction of my mouth;
anyone who does so will never be shamed.
8 The sinner is ensnared by his own lips;
both the abusive and the arrogant man are tripped up by them.
9 Do not let your mouth fall into the habit of swearing oaths,
or become accustomed to uttering the name of the Holy One.[i]
10 For just as a servant who is constantly observed
is never without bruises,
so also the person who swears continuously by the Name
will never be cleansed from sin.
11 The one who swears many oaths is filled with iniquity,
and the scourge will never be far from his home.
If he swears in error, he still incurs guilt,
and if he disregards his oath, he sins twice.
If he swears a false oath, he will not be treated as innocent,
and his house will be filled with calamities.* [j]

The Wise Watch Their Words*

12 There are words that are fraught with death;
may they never be heard among Jacob's descendants.
For such conduct will be avoided by the devout;
they will not wallow in sin.
13 Do not use your mouth for coarse and foul language,
since that involves sinful speech.
14 Remember your father and mother
when you are sitting among the mighty,
or you may forget yourself in their presence
and by such habits make a fool of yourself.
Then you will wish you had never been born
and curse the day of your birth.
15 A man who gets into the habit of using shameful language
will never be reformed as long as he lives.

The Blindness of the Immodest*

16 Two types of people multiply sins,
and a third * incurs wrath.
For burning passion that blazes like a fire
cannot be quenched until it burns itself out:
One who becomes sexually involved with close relatives
will never cease until the fire consumes him.
17 A fornicator finds every cake is sweet *
and he will not desist until he dies.[k]
18 One who dishonors his marriage bed
says to himself: "Who can see me?
Darkness surrounds me, walls conceal me,
and no one can see me; why should I worry?
The Most High will not remember my sins."

g Gen 39:7; Ps 131:1; Prov 6:25; Mt 5:28.—h Rom 13:13.—i Ex 20:7; Lev 19:12; Deut 5:11; Jas 5:12.—j Lev 5:4ff.—k Prov 9:17.

23:3e Added by some early MSS.

23:7-11 To call God to witness, without first reflecting on it, is to give him no respect.

23:11 The author seems to set forth three cases of swearing oaths ranging from light to heavy sinfulness: (1) a sincere oath that is not fulfilled; (2) an oath that is undertaken lightly; and (3) an oath that is undertaken in bad faith.

23:12-15 Using abusive, coarse, and foul speech is habit-forming. The wise watch their every word to avoid such a habit.

23:16-21 The immodest reassure themselves that they sin in secret, but God sees everything: no thought, word, or deed escapes his notice.

23:16 *Two types of people . . . and a third:* this numerical proverb, a common literary form (see Sir 25:1-2, 7-11; 26:5f, 28; Prov 6:16-19), singles out three kinds of lechers: the dissolute (v. 16), the incestuous (v. 17), and the adulterous (vv. 18-21).

23:17 *Every cake is sweet:* to emphasize his point, the author makes use of a euphemism for the adulterer's unending quest for new liaisons.

19 He fears only human eyes
and does not realize that the eyes of the Lord
are ten thousand times brighter than the sun,
observing every aspect of human behavior
and gazing into the most secret corners. [l]
20 All things were known to him before they were created, *
and they still are, now that they are finished.
21 [m] This man will be punished in the streets of the city;
when he least expects it, he will be seized. *

The Trial of an Adulteress*

22 The same is true of a woman who is unfaithful to her husband
and presents him with an heir by another man.
23 For first of all she has disobeyed the law of the Most High;
second, she has been false to her husband;
third, by her fornication she has committed adultery
and conceived children by another man.
24 *She will be presented before the assembly for judgment,
and her punishment will extend to her children.
25 Her children will not strike root,
nor will her branches bear fruit.
26 She will leave behind an accursed memory,
and her disgrace will never be effaced.
27 Thus, those who survive her will recognize
that nothing is better than fear of the Lord
and that nothing is sweeter than to adhere to his commandments. [n]
[28 To follow God is a great honor,
and to be acceptable to him is to lengthen one's days.] *

I: The Praise of Wisdom*

CHAPTER 24

Wisdom Sings Her Own Praises*

1 [o] Wisdom sings her own praises
and proclaims her glory in the midst of her people.
2 In the assembly of the Most High she opens her mouth,
and in the presence of the heavenly host she declares her glory:
3 [p] "I came forth from the mouth of the Most High
and covered the earth like a mist. *
4 I dwelt in the highest heavens,
and my throne was in a pillar of cloud. [q]
5 Alone I encircled the vault of heaven
and traversed the depths of the abyss.
6 Over the waves of the sea, over the whole earth,
and over every people and nation I have held sway.
7 Among all these I sought a place of rest;
in whose territory should I abide?
8 "Then the Creator of all things gave me his command;

l Sir 17:19f; Ps 33:13-15; Prov 15:3, 11; 17:3; 24:12.—m 21f: Lev 20:10; Deut 22:21.—n Sir 1:11-20, 26; Prov 3:1f.—o 1f: Job 28:1-28; Ps 82:1; Prov 1:20-33; 8:6-8; 9:1-6; 31:8f, 26; Isa 34:4; Bar 3:9—4:4.—p 3ff: Prov 8:22-36.—q Ex 13:21f; 40:38; Prov 8:2, 12; Wis 9:10; 10:17; Jn 1:1.

23:20 *Known to him before they were created:* God's antecedent knowledge of creation is divine wisdom itself (Prov 8:22f). *And they still are, now:* after creating the world, God continues to watch over it. Indeed, the Lord knows all things, both past and future (see Sir 42:18; Ps 139:1-16).

23:21 Capital punishment for the adulterer is not mentioned. Hence, it appears that the death penalty decreed in Lev 20:10; Deut 22:22-24 had been replaced in the author's time, possibly by scourging (see Prov 5:11-14; 6:32f).

23:22-27 A society that regards women as inferior to men will not pardon the misconduct of an unfaithful spouse, and her children will bear the punishment. Our moralist dramatizes the situation to discourage, beforehand, a type of dangerous envy.

23:24-25 It was the *assembly* that passed judgment on the illegitimacy of children born of adultery or incest and excluded them from the "assembly of the LORD" (Deut 23:3). See also Wis 3:16-19; 4:3-6.

23:28 Added by some early MSS.

24:1-34 In imitation of the sages who preceded him (Job 8; Prov 1:20-33; see also Bar 3:9—4:4), while deepening their thought, the author sings the praises of wisdom and introduces us truly into the heart of his work.

24:1-22 In a lyrical mode, Wisdom, presented once again as a person, recounts her origin and history. She comes from God, of whom she is the word and Spirit (v. 3). She collaborates in creation; then leaving heaven, she has traversed the earth to live with human beings. She has finally established herself in the midst of the chosen people; in the temple of Jerusalem. She invites all to the infinite quest for the true life. We immediately think of Christ, whom John will present to us as the way, the truth, and the life, as the bread of heaven and the living water.

Such a discovery of Wisdom, revelation of God to human beings and divine inspiration of their conduct, already prefigures the Word (the Speech and Revelation of God) and the Holy Spirit. Christians are fond of reading in this beautiful text a sketch of their thought concerning the mystery of the Divine Persons (Jn 1:1-18; Acts 2:1-4).

24:3 Allusion to the "Spirit of God hover[ing] over the waters" (Gen 1:2).

he who created me decreed where I should dwell,
saying, 'Make your dwelling in Jacob,
and in Israel receive your inheritance.'
9 Before all ages, in the beginning, he created me,
and I shall not cease to be for all eternity.
10 In the holy tent I ministered before him,
and then I became established in Zion.
11 Thus, in the beloved city he gave me a resting place,
in Jerusalem I wield my power.
12 I have taken root in an honored people,
in the portion of the Lord, his heritage.
13 "There I grew tall like a cedar on Lebanon,
like a cypress on Mount Hermon.
14 I grew tall like a palm tree in En-gedi,
like a rosebush in Jericho,
like a fair olive tree in the field,
or like a plane tree beside the water.
15 Like cinnamon or camel-thorn I gave forth perfume,
and like choice myrrh I spread my fragrance,
like galbanum, onycha, and spices
and like the odor of incense in the tent. [r]
16 I spread out my branches like a terebinth, *
and my branches are glorious and graceful.
17 Like the vine I bud forth delights,
and my blossoms become fruit fair and abundant. [s]
[18 I am the mother of fair love,
of fear, of knowledge, and of holy hope;
being eternal, I am given to all my children,
to those who are appointed by him.] *
19 "Come to me, all of you who desire me,
and eat your fill of my fruits. [t]
20 For the memory of me is sweeter than honey;
to possess me is sweeter than the honeycomb.
21 Whoever feeds on me will hunger for more; [u]
whoever drinks of me will thirst for more.
22 Whoever obeys me will never be put to shame;
whoever follows my instructions will never sin."

The Law, Source of Wisdom*

23 All this is the book of the covenant of the Most High God,
the law that Moses enjoined on us
as an inheritance for the assemblies of Jacob. [v]
[24 Do not cease to be strong in the Lord,
and cling to him that he may strengthen you.
The Lord Almighty alone is God,
and there is no savior apart from him.] *
25*[w] It overflows, like the Pishon, with wisdom,
like the Tigris at the time of the firstfruits.
26 It runs over, like the Euphrates, with understanding,
like the Jordan at the time of the harvest.
27 It pours forth instruction like the Nile, *
like the Gihon at the time of vintage.
28 The first man never fully comprehended wisdom,
nor will the last succeed in understanding her.
29 For her thoughts are more vast than the sea
and her counsel more profound than the great abyss.
30 As for me, I was like a conduit from a river,
like a stream into a garden.
31 I said to myself, "I will water my garden
and drench its flower beds."

---

r Ex 30:22-25.—s Sir 4:21; Prov 3:16; 8:18f, 21; Jn 15:1.—t Sir 6:18-38; Prov 8:4-10, 32-36; 9:4; Mt 11:28-30.—u Isa 55:1; Jn 6:35.—v Sir 1:11-30; 6:32-37; 15:1; 19:20; Ex 24:7; Deut 33:4.—w 25ff: Gen 2:11-14.

24:16 *Terebinth:* a type of oak.

24:18 Added by some early MSS. In place of verse 18c-d the Vulgate reads (as vv. 24-25): "In me is all grace of the way and of the truth; / in me is all hope of life and strength." These words clearly manifest themselves as a Christian gloss (with allusion to Jn 14:6 where Wisdom is identified with Christ). The Liturgy has taken delight in applying these words to the Blessed Mother.

24:23-34 For the Israelites, the law is a summary of faith, history, and tradition. It resembles the current of living water that irrigated the earthly paradise (Gen 2:11-13) like the rivers that fertilize the East. An inexhaustible source, it irrigates abundantly the heart of human beings. As for the wise, they become prophets and canals through whom the waves of wisdom overflow on all coming generations.

24:24 Added by some early MSS.

24:25-27 The *Tigris* and the *Gihon* were rivers of the earthly paradise (see Gen 2:11-13).

24:27 *It pours forth instruction like the Nile:* Greek reads: "It causes instruction to radiate like the light."

And suddenly my conduit became a river,
and my river expanded into a sea. [x]
32 I will again make learning shine forth like the dawn,
so that its light may be seen far and wide.
33 I will again pour out my teaching like prophecy
and leave it as a legacy to future generations.
34 And understand that I have not labored for myself alone
but for all who seek wisdom. [y]

J: Reflections for Daily Life

CHAPTER 25

Desirable Things and Undesirable Things

1 There are three things in which I delight,
and they are beautiful in the sight of the Lord and of men: *
concord among brethren, friendship among neighbors,
and a husband and wife who live in perfect harmony.
2 There are three kinds of men I hate,
for their manner of life I consider loathsome:
a pride-filled poor man, a lying rich man,
and a lecherous old fool.

The Glory of the Aged*

3 If you have gathered nothing in your youth,
how can you discover anything in your old age?
4 What a pleasure is sound judgment in those with gray hair,
and wise counsel with those advanced in years.
5 How admirable is wisdom in the aged,
and understanding and counsel in the venerable. [z]
6 The crown of the aged is their wealth of experience,
and their glory is the fear of the Lord.

Beatitudes*

7 I can think of nine whom I would call blessed,
and a tenth whom my tongue proclaims:
blessed is the man who delights in his children,
and the one who lives to see the downfall of his enemies;
8 blessed is the one who lives with a sensible wife
and the one who does not plow with ox and ass together; *
blessed is the one who does not sin with the tongue
and the one who does not serve an inferior;
9 blessed is the one who finds a friend
and the one who speaks to an attentive audience.
10 How great is the one who finds wisdom,
but without equal is the one who fears the Lord.
11 The fear of the Lord surpasses everything;
to whom can we compare the one who possesses it? [a]
[12 The fear of the Lord is the beginning of loving him,
and faith is the beginning of clinging to him.] *

Wicked and Virtuous Women*

13 Any wound is preferable to a wound of the heart;
any wickedness is better than the wickedness of a woman.
14 Any suffering is preferable to that inflicted by those who hate;
any vengeance is better than that devised by a foe.

x Isa 11:9; Ezek 47:1-12; Jn 7:38.—y Sir 33:18.—z Wis 4:8f.—a Sir 1:11-21, 25-27.

25:1 *I delight . . . and of men:* Greek reads: "I was beautified in three things and I stood in beauty before both the LORD and men."

25:3-6 The author holds up as a model the aged who have acquired wisdom: their glory is the fear of the Lord.

25:7-12 Under the agreeable form of a numerical proverb, the author enumerates some aspects of happiness; the list of these human successes gives value to the true happiness that is wisdom, the fear of God. Pleasure at the fall of an enemy (v. 7) is indeed human; we are not yet at the level of the Sermon on the Mount where we will find the Beatitudes of Christ (Mt 5:12).

25:8 *And ass together:* lacking in Greek. *The tongue:* some early MSS read: "a friend."

25:12 Added by some early MSS.

25:13—26:27 The author seems to be partial and pessimistic in his diatribe against wicked women. Nonetheless, twice in the present text the trial of the wicked woman is followed by the praise of the wife endowed with charm and virtue. The image of the detestable woman is probably painted in more somber colors to make us better appreciate how great a treasure is the gracious and sensible wife.

15 No poison is worse than that of a snake;
no fury is worse than that of an enemy.
16 I would rather dwell with a lion or a dragon
than live with an evil woman. [b]
17 Wickedness changes a woman's appearance
and makes her visage as surly as that of a bear.
18 When her husband sits with his neighbors,
he cannot refrain from sighing bitterly.
19 Any iniquity fades in comparison with that of a woman;
may the fate of the sinner befall her.
20 Like a sandy ascent for aged feet
is a garrulous wife to a quiet husband.
21 Do not be tempted by a woman's beauty,
nor desire her for her possessions.
22 Wrath, insolence, and disgrace hold sway
when a wife supports the husband.
23 Dejected spirits, downcast face, and a broken heart:
these are the results brought on by an evil wife.
24 Feeble hands and weak knees afflict the husband
whose wife does not bring him happiness.
25 Sin began with a woman,
and because of her we must all die. [c]
26 Allow water no outlet,
nor a wife free reign to speak.
27 If she does not do as you direct,
put her away from you. *

CHAPTER 26

1 Blessed is the husband of a good wife;
because of her his life span will be doubled. [d]
2 A loyal wife brings joy to her husband;
he will live out his years in peace.
3 A good wife is an incalculable blessing,
and she is bestowed on the man who fears the Lord. [e]
4 Whether rich or poor, his heart is content,
and his face is always wreathed in smiles.
5 There are three things that cause my heart to quake,
and a fourth that terrifies me:
slanderous charges in the city, the gathering of a mob,
and false accusations—all these are worse than death.
6 But when a wife is jealous of a rival, it causes heartache and sorrow,
and everyone suffers the scourge inflicted by her tongue.
7 A bad wife is like a yoke that does not fit; *
trying to control her is more difficult than handling a scorpion.
8 A drunken wife arouses great anger,
for she is unable to conceal her shame.
9 An unchaste wife can be discerned by her haughty stare;
her sidelong glances reveal the truth.
10 Keep a strict watch over a headstrong wife, *
or else, when she senses an opportunity, she will seize her chance.
11 Be on the lookout for her imprudent glance,
and do not be surprised if she disgraces you.
12 As a thirsty traveler will open his mouth
and drink from any water source that he comes across,
so she will settle down in front of every tent-peg
and open her quiver to any arrow.
13 A gracious wife delights her husband,
and her thoughtfulness puts flesh on his bones.
14 A silent wife is a gift from the Lord;
her disciplined virtue is of surpassing value.
15 A modest wife is the choicest of blessings;
no scales can weigh the worth of her chastity. [f]
16 Like the sun rising in the heavens of the Lord
is the beauty of a virtuous wife in a well-managed home.
17 Like the light shining on the sacred lampstand
is a beautiful face on a stately figure.

---

b Prov 21:9, 19; 25:24; 27:15.—c Gen 3:1-6; Rom 5:12; 1 Cor 15:32; 1 Tim 2:14.—d Sir 25:8; Prov 18:22; 31:10ff.—e Sir 36:29.—f Sir 6:15; 7:19; Prov 31:10f.

25:27 *Put her away from you:* literally, "separate her from your flesh." The Mosaic Law allowed divorce (see Deut 24:1-4).
26:7 *A yoke that does not fit:* it hurts the animal that bears it.
26:10 *Wife:* literally, "daughter."

18 Like golden pillars on silver bases
are shapely legs and steadfast feet. *
[19 * My child, take care of your health in the bloom of your youth,
and do not waste your strength on strangers. [g]
20 Search out the entire plain for a fertile field,
and there sow your own seed, trusting in your fine stock.
21 In this way, your children will prosper around you,
growing up confident in their breeding.
22 A prostitute is looked upon as no better than spittle,
but a married woman is a deadly snare for those who embrace her.
23 A godless woman is a suitable partner for a lawless husband,
but a pious woman is granted to the man who fears the Lord.
24 A brazen woman constantly acts in a disgraceful manner,
but a virtuous daughter is modest even in the presence of her husband.
25 A headstrong woman is looked upon as no better than a dog,
but one who is modest fears the Lord.
26 A woman who honors her husband is thought of as wise by all,
but if she dishonors him, others will regard her as proud and ungodly.
Blessed is the husband of a good wife,
for she doubles the length of his life.
27 A loud-mouthed, garrulous wife can be regarded
as a battle trumpet sounding the charge.
Any husband who responds to that summons
will live a life marked by the turbulence of war.]

Things That Cause Grief*

28 Two things cause grief to my heart,
and a third arouses my anger:
a warrior suffering distress because of poverty,
wise individuals treated with contempt,
and a man who turns from justice to sin,
for whom the Lord will get ready the sword. [h]

Moral Dangers in the Business World*

29 It is a rare occurrence when a merchant avoids wrongdoing
or when a shopkeeper is innocent of dishonest practice.

CHAPTER 27

1 Many have sinned for the sake of monetary gain;
he who seeks riches must turn a blind eye.
2 As a peg is driven firmly into the joint between stones,
so the sin of dishonesty will wedge itself in between selling and buying.
3 Unless a man holds firmly to the fear of the Lord,
his house will be quickly overthrown. [i]

The Test of a Man Is in His Conversation*

4 When a sieve is shaken, the rubbish appears;
so too do the defects of a man after he speaks.
5 As the work of a potter is tested in a furnace,
so the test of a man is in his conversation. [j]
6 The fruit of a tree reveals the care with which it was cultivated;
in the same way, a man's speech reveals his mindset. [k]
7 Do not praise anyone who has not yet spoken,
since this is the way men are tested.

The Righteous Are Known by Their Deeds*

8 If you pursue righteousness, you will attain it
and put it on like a festal robe. [l]

---

g Sir 9:6; Prov 5:7-14; 7:24-27; 31:3.—h Ezek 18:24ff.—i Sir 13:16; Prov 3:33; 12:7; 14:11; 15:25.—j Sir 13:11; 1 Pet 1:7.—k Mt 7:20.—l Sir 6:31; Job 29:14; Isa 61:10; Zep 2:3; Rev 1:13.

26:18 Once the imagination takes over, the theme is inexhaustible.

26:19-27 Added by some early MSS.

26:28 It is doubtless the mediocrity of his contemporaries that the sage deplores.

26:29—27:3 The world of business often resembles a robbers' fair, and particular interests take precedence over just weights and the sense of the common good.

27:4-7 The reflection on people's speech holds a large place in this Book, as it does in every reflection of the sages of antiquity.

27:8-15 The righteous become such by practicing justice and honesty and refraining from evil deeds. The foolish, i.e., those who do not master their thoughts and their lives, speak and act irrelevantly.

9 Birds associate with their own kind,
and honesty comes home to those who practice it.
10 As a lion lies in wait for its prey,
so does sin for those who do evil deeds.
11 The conversation of the devout is always wise,*
but the fool is as changeable as the moon.
12 Limit the time when you are in the presence of fools,
but linger as much as possible among those who are thoughtful.
13 The conversation of fools is offensive,
and their raucous laughter centers around their wanton sinfulness.
14 Their oath-filled chatter can make your hair stand on end,
and their quarrels cause others to shut their ears.
15 The arguments among the arrogant lead to bloodshed;
their abuse is painful to listen to.[m]

Indiscretion Destroys Friendship*

16 Anyone who betrays secrets forfeits any right to trust,
and he will never find a close friend.[n]
17 Love your friend and keep faith with him,
but if you betray his secrets, do not attempt to remain by his side.
18 For as one destroys an enemy,
so you will have destroyed your neighbor's friendship.
19 Like a bird that you have let escape from your hand,
so have you let your neighbor go with no chance of being caught again.
20 Do not pursue him, for he will be far away,
having escaped like a gazelle from a trap.
21 A wound can be bandaged, and an insult forgiven,
but the betrayer of secrets has lost all hope.[o]

Whoever Digs a Pit Will Fall into It*

22 Anyone who winks slyly is plotting mischief,
and no one can dissuade him from it.
23 He speaks sweetly while in your presence,
and admires your every word,
but later he will change his tune,
and with your own words he will trip you up.
24 I have found many things to hate, but nothing so much as this man,
and the Lord despises him too.
25 Whoever throws a stone straight up into the air will see it descend on his own head,
and a treacherous blow will cut both ways.
26 Whoever digs a pit will fall into it,
and whoever sets a snare will be caught in it.
27 Whoever does evil deeds will have that evil recoil upon him
without having the slightest idea where it came from.
28 Mockery and abuse issue from an arrogant man,
but vengeance lies in wait for him like a lion.
29 Those who rejoice at the downfall of the godly will be ensnared,
and they will be consumed with pain before their death.*

Forgive, and You Will Be Forgiven*

30 Wrath and anger are also habits to abhor,
yet sinners will have both of them.

CHAPTER 28

1 Everyone who acts vengefully will have to face the vengeance of the Lord,
for he keeps a strict account of his sins.[p]
2 Forgive your neighbor for any wrongs he has done to you;
then, when you pray, your sins will be forgiven.[q]

---

m Sir 23:7-15.—n Sir 22:22; Prov 11:13; 20:19; 25:8-10.—o Sir 22:20; Pss 16:9f; 22:5f, 9; 76:7f; Rom 4:18.—p Deut 32:35; Job 14:16f; Ps 13:3; Rom 12:19.—q Mt 6:14.

27:11 *The conversation . . . always wise:* the Vulgate reads: "The holy man remains fixed in wisdom like the sun."

27:16-21 More than once the author stresses the sacred value of a secret entrusted to someone.

27:22-29 If popular sentiment has ever wished anyone to fall into a pit, it is the hypocrite who combines, in an odious way, looseness and wickedness.

27:29 The author follows the traditional Old Testament teaching that divine retribution would take place in time (see Job 21:20-21).

27:30—28:7 *Forgive, and You Will Be Forgiven:* Jesus makes the same recommendation to his disciples when he teaches them the Our Father (Mt 6:12, 14f).

3 Anyone who harbors anger against another
can hardly expect healing from the LORD. [r]
4 Anyone who refuses mercy to his peers
cannot rightfully seek pardon for his own sins.
5 If a mere creature cherishes wrath,
who will forgive his sins?
6 Keep in your thoughts the end of your own life and set enmity aside;
remember corruption and death, and be faithful to the commandments. [s]
7 Remember the commandments and do not bear ill-will toward your neighbor;
keep in mind the covenant of the Most High, and overlook faults.

Strife Disturbs Peace*

8 If you refrain from quarreling, your sins will be fewer,
for a hot-tempered man provokes strife.
9 A sinner disrupts friendships
and sows discord among those who are peacefully disposed. [t]
10 [u] The more fuel there is, the fiercer the fire will burn;
the greater the obstinacy shown, the fiercer will be the strife.
The greater is the power of a man, the greater will be his anger;
the greater his wealth, the greater his wrath will be.
11 A sudden quarrel kindles a fire,
and a hasty dispute leads to bloodshed.
12 If you blow on a spark, it will flare into a flame;
if you spit on it, it will die out;
yet you achieve both results with your mouth.

The Greatest Scourge Is the Tongue*

13 Cursed be the gossipers and the double-tongued,
for they destroy many who live in harmony.
14* An intrusive tongue has disrupted the peace of many
and driven them from country to country.
It has resulted in the destruction of strong cities
and overthrown the houses of the great.
15 An intrusive tongue can drive out virtuous women
and deprive them of the fruit of their labors.
16 Anyone who pays heed to it will never find rest
or achieve peace of mind.
17 A blow from a whip raises a welt,
but a blow from the tongue breaks bones.
18 Many have fallen by the edge of the sword,
but not as many as have fallen by the tongue. [v]
19 Blessed is the one who has been sheltered from it,
who has not been exposed to its fury,
who has not borne its yoke
or been bound with its chains.
20 For its yoke is a yoke of iron,
and its chains are chains of bronze.
21 The death it inflicts is a horrible death;
the netherworld is preferable to it.
22 It has no power over the righteous;
they will not be burned in its flames.
23 However, those who forsake the Lord will fall victim to it;
it will blaze among them and will never be extinguished.
It will be launched forth against them like a lion;
like a leopard it will tear them to pieces.
24 Just as you enclose your property with a hedge of thorns
and lock up your silver and gold, [w]
25 set a bolted door over your mouth
and weigh and measure your every word.
26 Take care not to err with your tongue
and thereby fall victim to your enemy who lies in wait.

---

r Sir 28:5; Gen 20:17; Ex 15:26; Hos 6:1; Mt 18:23ff.—s Sir 7:36; 38:20.—t Prov 15:18.—u 10ff: Prov 26:20f.—v Jas 3:5ff.—w Sir 22:27; 2 Ki 5:23; Tob 9:5; Pss 39:2; 141:3.

28:8-12 The author has observed how from time to time a whole group of people can be brought down by a conflict.

28:13-26 The evil tongue inflames conflicts and destroys reputations; it is evil personified. The just preserve themselves from its blows and refrain from lending a willing ear to it. James was surely thinking of this advice when he wrote his Letter (Jas 3:1-12).

28:14-15 *Intrusive tongue:* literally, "third tongue." The phrase "third tongue" may refer to a tongue that inserts itself into a quarrel or a tongue that makes three victims: the one who utters slander, the one who listens to the slander, and the one who is slandered.

[For your case will then become incurable, leading to death.] *

CHAPTER 29

Lending to Others Is Full of Risks*

1 He who is compassionate lends to his neighbor;
by offering a helping hand, he fulfills the commandments. [x]
2 Lend to your neighbor in his hour of need,
and repay him when a loan to you falls due. [y]
3 Keep your promise and be honest with him,
and you will find that your needs will always be met.
4 Many treat a loan as a windfall
and cause problems for those who helped them out.
5 Until he gets a loan, a man will kiss his neighbor's hand
and speak with respect of his benefactor's wealth.
However, when the repayment of the loan is due, he delays,
repays with empty words, and asserts that the times are hard.
6 If the borrower can be forced to pay, the creditor will get back barely half,
and will regard that as an unexpected windfall.
But otherwise such a creditor will be cheated of his money
and will gain an enemy in the bargain.
The borrower will repay him with curses and insults,
and with abuse instead of honor.
7 Hence, many refuse to lend, not out of malice,
but out of fear of being needlessly defrauded.

Spend Your Money on Others*

8 Nevertheless, be patient with someone in humble circumstances,
and do not keep him waiting for his alms.
9 In obedience to the commandment, help the poor,
and in their need do not send them away empty-handed. [z]
10 Spend your money on your brother or your friend;
do not hide it under a stone where it will rust away.
11 Dispose of your treasure according to the commandment of the Most High,
and it will profit you more than gold. [a]
12 Store up almsgiving in your treasury,
and it will deliver you from every misfortune.
13 Better than a stout shield and a weighty spear,
it will fight for you against the enemy.

Standing Surety for Others Can Lead to Ruin*

14 A good man will stand surety for his neighbor;
only a shameless wretch would let him down.
15 Do not forget the kindness of your benefactor
for he has staked his very life for you. [b]
16 A sinner wastes the property of his benefactor;
17 an ungrateful schemer abandons his rescuer.
18 Going surety has ruined many who were prosperous
and tossed them about like waves of the ocean.
It has driven influential people into exile
and caused them to wander through foreign lands.
19 A sinner comes to grief through surety;
his headlong pursuit of profit will result in lawsuits.
20 Therefore, assist your neighbor according to your means,
but be careful not to fall yourself.

x Ex 22:24-26; Lev 25:25-37; Deut 15:8; Ps 112:5; Prov 19:17; Ezek 18:8.—y Ex 22:24ff; Lev 25:36; Mt 5:42.—z Sir 4:1ff; Lev 19:9f; 23:22; Deut 15:8.—a Sir 17:22; Tob 4:7ff; Mt 6:19-21.—b Prov 22:26f.

28:26c Added by some early MSS.

29:1-7 The author respects the law that prescribes lending without interest in order to help those who are in need (Ex 22:24; Lev 25:35-37). Nonetheless, persons of experience know also that lending often leads to severing the best of relationships.

29:8-13 The law prescribes the necessity of aiding the poor (Deut 15:7-11). In the final analysis, human beings are the stewards rather than the owners of riches that they have.

29:14-20 The author issues a rather obvious requirement—to be loyal to those who stand surety for one. Alas, the moralist must often recall what he had given, and on this subject, the Book of Proverbs (Prov 6:1-5) was even more mistrustful.

Rather Be Poor at Home than a Guest-Servant*

21 The basic necessities of life are water, bread, and clothing,
as well as a house to ensure privacy.[c]
22 Preferable is the life of a poor man in a crude hut
than sumptuous banquets in someone else's home.
23 Be content with what you have, whether much or little,
and you will not be scorned as a guest.
24 It is a miserable life to go from house to house,
realizing that as a guest you dare not open your mouth.
25 You receive no gratitude for serving the drinks,
and in addition you must listen to bitter words like these:
26 "Come here, stranger, and set the table;
let me eat the food you have there."
27 "Leave now, stranger, for someone more important has arrived;
my brother has come for a visit, and I need the guest room."
28 A sensitive man finds two things difficult to bear:
criticism from members of his household and the insults of his creditors.

CHAPTER 30

The Training of Children*

1 A man who loves his son chastises him often
so that in his old age the son may be his joy.[d]
2 The man who disciplines his son will reap the benefits
and boast of him to his acquaintances.
3 The man who educates his son will make his enemy envious
and will show his delight in him among his friends.
4 When the father dies, it will be as though he were not dead,
for he has left behind him a duplicate of himself,
5 whom he looked upon with joy during his life,
and about whom he felt no anxiety on his deathbed.
6 He has left behind him someone to exact vengeance from his enemies
and to repay his friends for their acts of kindness.
7 A man who coddles his son will bandage his wounds
and suffer heartbreak at every cry he unleashes.
8 An unbroken colt turns out stubborn,
and an unchecked son grows up headstrong.
9 Pamper your son, and he will terrorize you;
indulge him, and he will cause you grief.
10 Do not share in his laughter or you will share also in his sorrow,
and in the end you will gnash your teeth.[e]
11 When he is young, do not give him any freedom,
and do not close your eyes to his errors.
12 Bend his neck in his youth,
and chastise him soundly while he is still a child,
or he may become stubborn and disobedient,
and you will experience deep sorrow.[f]
13 Discipline your son and take pains with him,*
so that you may not have reason to be humiliated by some disgraceful act of his.

Health and Fitness Are Better than Gold*

14 You are better off to be poor and healthy and fit
than to be rich and tormented in one's body.
15 Health and fitness are better than gold,
and a strong body* is better than countless riches.

---

c Sir 39:26.—d Prov 13:24; 22:6; 23:13; 29:15; Heb 12:7.—e Jer 31:29; Ezek 18:2; Mt 8:12; 24:51; Lk 13:28.—f Sir 7:23.

29:21-28 The author does not like the obsequiousness of spongers and gives a lively critique of them.

30:1-13 In the eyes of the ancients, a man who loves his son chastises him often; well-reared children are the joy and honor of their parents, who are thus assured of living on in a progeny that is worthy of them. The development and formation of the person from infancy always entails a responsibility that is full of requirements.

30:13 *Take pains with him:* Hebrew reads: "make his yoke heavy."

30:14-20 Sickness is often regarded as a punishment from God (v. 19).

30:15 *Strong body:* Hebrew reads: "good spirit."

16 There is no treasure to compare with health of body
and no happiness to surpass a joyful heart.
17 Death is better than a life of misery,
and eternal rest* is preferable to chronic illness.[g]
18 Gourmet foods set before one who cannot eat
are like delicacies placed on a grave.[h]
19 Of what use is a sacrifice to an idol
that can neither taste nor smell?
So it is with the man afflicted by the Lord;
20 he gazes and groans,
as a eunuch groans when embracing a maiden.
[So it is with the one who does right under obligation.]*

Avoid Sorrow and Brooding

21 Do not abandon yourself to sorrow,
or torment yourself by brooding.*[i]
22* A joyful heart is a source of life,
and a cheerful disposition lengthens one's life span.
23 Indulge yourself and take comfort,
and banish sorrow far from your heart.
For grief has brought about the death of many,
and no advantage has ever been gained as a result of it.
24 Envy and anger shorten one's life,
and anxiety brings on premature old age.
25* The man who is lighthearted and merry while dining
benefits from what he eats.[j]

CHAPTER 31

The Right Attitude toward Riches*

1 Sleeplessness over wealth causes a man to lose weight,
and the resultant anxiety drives away sleep.
2 Apprehension prevents slumber
just as a serious illness banishes sleep.
3 The rich man toils to amass a fortune,
and when he relaxes he enjoys every kind of luxury.
4 The poor man toils to eke out a meager living,
and if he ever rests he finds himself in want.

5 The man who loves gold will not be free from sin;
the man who pursues wealth will be led astray by it.[k]
6 Many have come to their downfall as the result of gold,
finding themselves face to face with ruin.
7 It is a stumbling block to those who are avid for it,
and every fool is trapped by it.

8 Blessed is the rich man who is found to be blameless
and who does not chase after gold.
9 Who is he, that we may praise him?
For he has done wonders among his people.
10 Who has been tested by it and escaped unscathed?
This should be a cause of pride for him.
He could have sinned, but he refrained from doing so;
he could have done evil and did not do it.
11 His prosperity will be established,
and the assembly will proclaim his charitable acts.[l]

K: Social Conventions and Correctness*

Table Etiquette

12 When you are seated at a lavish table,*
do not display your greed
or exclaim: "Look at all this!"

g Sir 41:2; Tob 3:6, 10, 13; Job 3:11, 13, 17; Eccl 4:1f.—h Tob 4:17.—i Sir 38:20; Prov 12:25; 15:13; 17:22.—j Prov 15:15.—k Sir 14:3; Prov 28:20; Eccl 15:9; 1 Tim 1:9f.—l Prov 29:14.

30:17 The author was not aware of the huge value placed on suffering that was only fully revealed in the New Testament by Christ's Passion and Death. *Eternal rest:* lacking in some early MSS.

30:20c Added by some early MSS.

30:21 This sound advice reminds us of the words of Christ: "Do not worry about tomorrow, for tomorrow will take care of itself. Each day has enough troubles of its own" (Mt 6:34).

30:22-24 These words have been validated by modern psychology and medicine, which have found that, for the most part, cheerfulness and joyfulness lengthen life while grief and resentment, as well as envy and anger, shorten it.

30:25—33:16 All the Greek MSS place 33:16—36:13 *before* 30:25—33:16, but the Syriac and Latin versions, as well as the Hebrew fragments, maintain the original order.

31:1-11 If gold seduces by its prestige, it undermines the health of its devotees and exposes them to sin, as Jesus will also indicate later: "It is easier for a camel to pass through the eye of a needle than for someone who is rich to enter the kingdom of God" (Lk 18:25).

31:12—32:13 The author is a practical educator; he has left us an agreeable code of table etiquette. He does not denigrate either good meals or gaiety; as a well-educated person, he finds pleasure in social conventions and correctness.

31:12 *At a lavish table:* Greek reads: "at the table of the great."

13 Remember that a greedy eye is a bad thing.
Is any creature more greedy than the eye?
Therefore, it sheds tears at the slightest provocation. [m]
14 Do not reach out for anything your host is eyeing,
or dip in the dish together with him.
15 Judge your neighbor's feelings by your own,
and be thoughtful in every respect.
16 Eat what is set before you like a well-bred person;
do not gulp down your food and make yourself objectionable.
17 Be the first to stop eating, as befits good manners,
and do not be a glutton, lest you give offense. [n]
18 If you are dining with a large group,
do not reach out your hand before the others.
19 A small portion is sufficient for someone of good upbringing;
when he lies down, he experiences no discomfort.
20 Moderate eating ensures sound sleep;
such a man rises early and feels refreshed.
However, sleeplessness, nausea, and colic are the lot of the glutton. [o]
21 If perchance you have eaten too much,
get up and empty your stomach, and you will find relief.
22 Listen to me, my child, and do not disregard me;
eventually you will find that my advice is on the mark.
Be moderate * in everything you do,
and no illness will befall you.

Praise for Munificent Hosts

23 Much praise is given to the man who is liberal in serving food,
and the testimony to his generosity is fulsome. [p]
24 The man who is miserly with food is denounced universally,
and the testimony to his stingy nature is substantial.

The Right Attitude toward Wine*

25 Do not try to prove your strength with wine,
for wine has been the ruin of many.
26 As the furnace tests the tempering of steel,
so wine tests the hearts in the disputes of the insolent.
27 Wine is a source of life
if taken in moderation.
What is life to someone who has been deprived of wine?
It was created to make men happy. [q]
28 Wine is the cause of a joyful heart and cheerful spirits
when consumed at the right time and in the proper amount. [r]
29 However, wine drunk to excess causes bitter feelings
and leads to quarrels and retaliation.
30 Drunkenness increases the anger of a fool to his own harm,
sapping his strength and exposing him to injury.
31 Do not rebuke your neighbor when wine is served,
or ridicule him when he is enjoying himself.
Speak no words of reproach to him,
or distress him by making demands of him.

CHAPTER 32

The Proper Behavior at Banquets*

1 If you are chosen to preside at a banquet, do not become puffed up with your own importance;
mingle with the guests as one of them.
Do not sit down yourself until you have first taken care of them;
2 then, when you have discharged all of your duties, you may take your place,
so that you may share in their joy

m Sir 37:28ff; Prov 23:1f.—n Sir 37:29.—o Sir 37:29-31.—p Prov 22:9.—q Ps 104:15; 1 Tim 5:23.—r Jdg 9:13; 1 Tim 5:23.

31:22 *Be moderate:* Greek reads: "Be industrious."

31:25-31 Wine is one of God's good creations (see Ps 104:15). It is a joy when taken in moderation (see Sir 40:20), but if drunk to excess, it can lead to ruin (see Prov 20:1; 23:29-35; Am 6:6). Misuse of wine violates the divine order and brings its own recompense (vv. 29-30). The author is reminded of an allied concept on the proper use of words and applies it to wine: one should use words carefully to those who are "merry," that is, lighthearted but not drunk (v. 31).

32:1-13 Under the influence of the Greeks or the Romans, the custom took hold in Palestine of holding elaborate banquets with an organizing chairman or steward chosen by lot or by vote, who was responsible for preparing the menu, choosing the wine, seating the guests, and the like (see 2 Mac 2:27; Jn 2:8). Later, the rabbis warned against these customs. Here, the author is laying down the rules of good manners at such events.

and win praise for your service as an excellent host.
3 As you grow older, you may speak, for you are entitled to do so,
but do not flaunt your knowledge and do not interrupt the music.
4 When there is entertainment, do not pour out a stream of talk;
such is the wrong time to display your wisdom.
5 [s] Like a jewel in a setting of gold
is a concert of music at which wine is served.
6 Like an emerald in a setting of gold
are the strains of music with superb wine.
7 [t] You who are young, speak only if you are obliged to do so,
and no more than twice, and then only if asked.
8 Be brief, but say much in a few words;
convey the impression of knowledge but preferring to hold your tongue.
9 Among eminent people do not act as if you were their equal,
and do not continue to babble on when someone else is speaking.
10 As lightning flashes before thunder strikes,
so does esteem go ahead of a modest man.
11 Leave at an appropriate time, and do not be the last to depart;
go home quickly, without lingering.
12 There amuse yourself as you wish,
but do not sin by arrogant talk.
13 Above all, give praise to the one who made you
and has bestowed his favors on you so abundantly.

L: Trust in the LORD*

A Safe Way*

14 Whoever fears the LORD * will accept his discipline,
and whoever searches for him will gain his favor. [u]
15 The man who seeks the law will be nourished by it,
but the hypocrite will regard it as a stumbling block.
16 The man who fears the LORD will win his approval,
and his righteous deeds will shine like a beacon. [v]
17 However, the sinner pays no attention to reproof,
and he will devise specious arguments to justify his desires. [w]
18 A man who is sensible will never ignore reasonable counsel,
whereas an arrogant and godless man will not be deterred by anything.
19 Never do anything without careful deliberation,
but once you have acted, do not regret your decision. [x]
20 Do not choose to travel on a way beset with hazards,
and do not stumble on stony ground. *
21 Be cautious even when traversing a smooth way,
22 and beware also of your children. *
23 Trust yourself * in everything you do,
for in this way you will keep the commandments.
24 The man who keeps the law preserves himself,
and the man who trusts the LORD will never suffer loss.

CHAPTER 33

1 No evil will befall the one who fears the LORD;
during times of trial such a one will always be rescued. [y]
2 The man who is wise does not hate the law,
but the one who is a hypocrite about it ends up being tossed around like a boat in a storm.

s 5f: 2 Sam 19:26; Eccl 2:8; Isa 5:12; 24:7-9.—t 7ff: Sir 7:14; Job 29:7-10.—u Sir 4:13; 18:14.—v Pss 37:6; 119:105; Prov 6:23; 28:5.—w Sir 21:6; Prov 12:1.—x Sir 37:16; Tob 4:18; Prov 12:15.—y Job 5:19; Ps 91:10; Prov 12:21; 24:16.

32:14—33:18 As a good moralist, the author reassures the faithful, too easily at times: but he inculcates a deep trust in God. This will maintain the faithful in the difficult times that the author fails to mention.

32:14—33:6 People of the Old Testament find their essential directives in the practice and understanding of the law. It is a charter of life that guards them from preferring the changeable passions to true values. Those who regulate their life by it fear God (see Mt 5:19).

32:14 *Whoever fears the LORD:* Greek reads: "Whoever seeks God."

32:20 *On stony ground:* Hebrew reads: "over its obstacles twice."

32:22 *And beware also of your children:* Hebrew reads: "and watch carefully where you step."

32:23 *Trust yourself:* Hebrew reads: "guard yourself."

3 A sensible man will trust in the law,
regarding it as dependable as an oracle.
4 Carefully prepare what you have to say,
and you will be listened to;
draw upon your learning, and then give your answer. [z]
5 The mind of a fool is like the wheel of a cart,
and his thoughts spin like an axle.
6 A sarcastic friend is like a stallion
that neighs no matter who is on its back.

Concerning Inequalities in Conditions*

7 Why is one day more important than another,
although every day in the year receives its light from the sun?
8 It is because of the knowledge of the LORD that they differ;
he was the one who designated the various seasons and feasts. [a]
9 Some days he exalted and sanctified,
and others he made ordinary days.
10 All men originate from the ground,
for humankind itself* was created out of the earth.
11 Yet in the fullness of his knowledge the Lord has distinguished men
and caused them to walk along different ways.
12 Some he has blessed and exalted,
sanctifying them and drawing them near to himself;
others he has cursed and humbled,
and removed from their position.
13 Like clay in the hands of a potter,
to be molded just as he pleases,
so are men in the hands of their Maker,
to be dealt with according to his justice. [b]
14 Just as good is the opposite of evil, and life is the opposite of death,
so the sinner is the opposite of the godly. [c]
15 Contemplate all the works of the Most High—
they come in pairs, one the opposite of the other.
16 Now I was the last to keep vigil;
I was like a gleaner following the grape pickers,
17 and by the blessing of the Lord I arrived early enough
to fill my winepress as completely as any of them.
18 And please note that I have not labored for myself alone
but for all who seek instruction.

III: THE TESTAMENT OF A TEACHER OF WISDOM*

A: The Heritage of the Teacher

Remain Master in All Things*

19 Listen to me, you who hold high positions among the people!
You leaders of the assembly, pay heed to what I have to say! [d]
20 Neither to son or wife, nor to brother or friend,
give power over yourself as long as you live.
And do not give your property to another,
in case you change your mind and want it back.
21 As long as you are alive and have breath within you,
do not yield authority over yourself to anyone.
22 It is far better for your children to beg for your help
than for you to have recourse to their handouts.
23 Be in control in everything that you do,
and allow no stain to tarnish your reputation.
24 Only on the day that your life draws to a close,
at the hour of death, should you distribute your inheritance.

z Sir 32:19; 37:16; Prov 3:3; 6:21.—a Gen 1:14.—b Wis 15:7; Isa 29:16; 45:9; Jer 18:1-6; Rom 9:20-23.—c Sir 42:25. —d Wis 6:1f.

33:7-18 Why are there holy days and secular days? Why also is the condition of humans so diverse and the world full of contrasts? There is no response at the reach of human beings except to entrust themselves to God; the wise maintain a sentiment of modesty in fulfilling their vocation. The conclusion of verses 16-18 is like a signature of the author.

33:10 *Humankind itself:* Hebrew; Greek reads: "Adam himself."

33:19—42:14 More than simply dispensing instruction, the sage is concerned with teaching his disciples to live by wisdom. Thus, he will present, at the end of his work, the great personages of Israel: they are models of fidelity to the covenant, the great figures of the tradition of the People of God.

33:19-24 These recommendations flow from simple common sense. However, to erect them into a final and absolute rule of human conduct would be to do harm to other pages of the Bible that go further.

How To Treat Slaves*

25 To a donkey belong fodder, the stick, and burdens;
to slaves belong bread, discipline, and work.
26 If you work your slave hard, you will have rest for yourself;
if you allow his hands to be idle, he will seek his freedom.
27 Yoke and harness will bow the neck of an ox;
for a wicked slave, apply the rack and torture.
28 Put him to work so that he will not be idle,
29 for idleness is a superb teacher of mischief.[e]
30 Put him to work, for that is his purpose in life;
and if he does not obey, burden him with fetters.
However, do not be overbearing toward anyone,
and do nothing contrary to justice.
31 If you have only one slave, treat him like yourself,
for you have acquired him with blood.
If you have only one slave, treat him as a brother,
since you will need him as much as you need yourself.[f]
32 If you ill-treat him and he runs away,
33 where will you go to look for him?

CHAPTER 34

How To Judge Dreams*

1 Vain and false are the hopes of the senseless,
and dreams offer wings to a fool.
2 Like one who clutches at shadows or chases the wind
is someone who pays heed to dreams.
3 What you see in dreams is simply an image,
the reflection of a face in a mirror.
4 From something unclean what can be clean?
From something false what can be true?[g]
5 Divinations, omens, and dreams are all unreal;
the mind portrays what you already expect.
6 Unless they are sent through the intervention of the Most High,
pay no attention to them.
7 For dreams have led many astray,
and those who have placed their hopes in them have been greatly disappointed.[h]
8 Without such deceptions the law is fulfilled,
and wisdom is perfected in the mouth of the faithful.*

Travel Is Instructive

9 Someone who is well traveled* knows many things,
and someone who is experienced understands what he is talking about.
10 Someone who is inexperienced knows few things,
11 whereas one who has traveled extensively acquires cleverness.
12 I have seen many things during my travels
and have come to understand more than I can put into words.
13 I have often been in danger of death,
but I have been saved because of these things.

Blessed Is the Soul That Fears the Lord*

14 The spirit of those who fear the Lord will live,[i]
15 for their hope is in him who is their Savior.

e 2 Thes 3:11f.—f Sir 7:21.—g Job 14:4.—h Jer 23:25-27; 29:8f.—i Isa 38:16f.

33:25-33 This text reflects the situation of one epoch and the harsh ideas that ruled all education in antiquity. In this environment, the author tempers the harshness of the customs, for he recognizes a justice toward slaves to save them from the arbitrariness of the master (Ex 21:1-6, 26-27; Lev 25:46), and the last verse expresses a discreet note of humanity.

For the attitude toward slavery in the New Testament, see Eph 6:9; Col 4:1; Philem 16.

34:1-8 The ancients regarded dreams as a means by which God could communicate with human beings. The author does not exclude this possibility of which the Bible gives many examples (Gen 28:10-17; 35:5-11; 2 Ki 3:4-14; Mt 1:20f). But he maintains a healthy mistrust, for one cannot, in practice, verify the origin of dreams.

34:8 The author stresses that dreams are deceptive but the law and wisdom are ever true.

34:9 *Someone who is well traveled:* some early MSS read: "Someone who is educated."

34:14-20 This passage praises the virtues and blessings of the wise, those who *fear the Lord*, of which the author is himself an excellent example. With the Lord at their side they can courageously face all of life's dangers and difficulties. The last word in the passage (*blessing*) synthesizes all the material and spiritual gifts the Lord has allotted to his people.

16 The man who fears the Lord is never fearful of anything else,
never cowardly, for he is his hope.[j]
17 Blessed is the soul that fears the Lord.
18 To whom does he look? Who is his support?
19 The eyes of the Lord watch over those who love him;
he is their powerful shield and firm support,
a shelter from the scorching wind and a shade from the noonday sun,
a guard against stumbling and a help against falling.[k]
20 He revives the soul and brightens the eyes;
he gives health, life, and blessing.

True Worship*

21 A sacrifice of ill-gotten goods is tainted;
22 the gifts of the wicked are not acceptable.
23 The Most High takes no pleasure in the offerings of the godless,
nor do their many sacrifices gain his pardon for their sins.
24 Like the man who slays a son in his father's presence
is the one who offers a sacrifice taken from the possessions of the poor.
25 [l] The bread of charity is life itself to the poor;
whoever deprives them of it is a murderer.
26 To take away a neighbor's livelihood is to commit murder;
27 to deny a laborer his wages is to shed blood.

28 When one builds up and another tears down,
what have they gotten out of it but hard work?
29 When one prays and another curses,
to whose voice will the Lord listen?
30 If someone bathes after touching a corpse and then touches it again,
what has been gained by washing?[m]
31 So it is with the one who fasts for his sins
and then goes out and commits them again.
Who will listen to his prayer?
And what has he gained by his penance?

CHAPTER 35

1 [n] The one who observes the law multiplies his offerings;
2 one who keeps the commandments sacrifices a peace offering.
3 The one who returns a kindness offers choice flour,*
4 and one who gives alms presents a sacrifice of praise.
5 If you wish to please the Lord, abandon wickedness;
to forsake wrongdoing is a sacrifice of atonement.

6 [o] Do not appear before the Lord empty-handed,
7 for all that you offer is in fulfillment of the commandments.
8 The offering of the righteous enriches the altar,
and its pleasing odor rises before the Most High.
9 The sacrifice of the righteous is acceptable,
nor will it ever be forgotten.
10 Have a spirit of generosity when you honor the Lord;
do not begrudge the firstfruits of your labor.
11 With every gift show a cheerful countenance,
and dedicate your tithes in a spirit of joy.[p]
12 Give to the Most High as he has given to you,
as generously as your means allow.
13 For the Lord never neglects to repay,
and he will reward you sevenfold.
[The man who gives to the poor makes God his debtor;
who will make recompense if not God?]*

j Sir 15:19; Pss 23:4; 33:18; 112:7f; Prov 3:23ff; 28:1.—k Pss 22:20; 33:18; 34:18; 61:3f; 91:11f; 121:3, 5f; Prov 2:7; 30:5; Isa 4:6; 25:4f.—l 25f: Lev 19:13; Deut 24:14f; Tob 4:14.—m Num 19:11f; Prov 26:11; 2 Pet 2:22.—n 1ff: 1 Sam 15:22; Ps 51:20f; Isa 1:11-18; Hos 6:6; Am 5:21-24.—o 6f: Ex 23:15; 34:20; Deut 16:16.—p Sir 7:31; 45:20f; Tob 1:6-8; 2 Cor 9:7.

34:21—35:13 The author loves the liturgy, but he holds that the cult and law, religion and morality, always go together. Above all, worship must be true and not a rite of falsehood and injustice—the Prophets said it much more vehemently (Isa 1:11; Jer 7:21-23; Am 5:22-25; Hos 8:13). Love, justice, and fidelity are part of the true sacrifice imposed by the law (Lev 2; 3; 7:11; 16).

35:3 *Choice flour:* an offering to God prescribed by Lev 2:1ff.

35:13c-d Added by some early MSS.

God Judges According to the Heart*

14 Do not offer God a bribe, for he will not accept it,
15 and do not place your hope in a dishonest sacrifice.
For the Lord is a judge,
and he is completely impartial. [q]
16 He will not show favoritism to the detriment of the poor,
and he listens to the cries of the oppressed.
17 [r] He does not ignore the supplication of the orphan,
or that of the widow when she pours out her complaint.
18 Do not the tears of the widow stream down her cheeks
19 as she cries out against the one who has been their cause?
20 The one who serves God wholeheartedly will be heard;
his petition will reach the heavens.
21 The prayer of the lowly pierces the clouds;
it does not rest until it reaches its goal.
Nor will it desist until the Most High responds,
22 relieves the sufferings of the righteous,
and reestablishes equity.

Indeed God will not delay,
nor will he cease to act on their behalf, *
until he has crushed the bones of the merciless [s]
23 and wreaked vengeance on the nations,
until he has destroyed the insolent multitude
and shattered the scepters of the wicked,
24 until he has requited each one according to his deeds
and repaid his works as his intentions deserve,
25 until he has rendered justice to his people
and disposed them to rejoice in his mercy.
26 His mercy is as welcome in a time of affliction
as rain clouds in a time of drought.

CHAPTER 36

Show Mercy, Lord, to the People Called by Your Name*

1 Have pity on us, Master, Lord of the universe,
2 and put the nations in dread of you.
3 Lift up your hand against the foreign nations,
and let them behold your mighty deeds.
4 As you have used us to display your holiness to them,
so now use them to show your glory to us. [t]
5 Let them acknowledge * you, as we ourselves have acknowledged
that there is no God but you, O Lord.
6 Give new signs and work other wonders;
7 show forth the glorious splendor of your right hand and arm.
8 Rouse your anger and pour forth your wrath;
9 destroy the adversary and wipe out the foe. [u]
10 Hasten the day and remember your oath; *
give people cause to recount your mighty deeds.
11 Let your burning wrath consume the survivors,
and let destruction be the fate of those who oppress your people.
12 Crush the heads of hostile rulers
who proclaim, "There is no one else but us."
13 Gather all the tribes of Jacob,* [v]
16 and grant them their inheritance as you did in earlier times.
17 Show mercy, Lord, to the people called by your name,

---

q Sir 34:21f; Deut 10:17; 2 Chr 19:7; Job 34:19; Prov 21:27; Wis 6:7; Acts 10:34; Rom 2:11; Gal 2:6; 1 Pet 1:17.—r 17f: Ex 22:22.—s Isa 42:13ff; 2 Pet 3:9.—t Deut 28:7-13, 36f; Ezek 20:41; 28:22, 25; 38:16, 21-23.—u Ps 79:6.—v Isa 11:11f; Jer 3:18; Ezek 36:8-11; Am 9:14.

35:14-26 God cannot be bought by offerings, but he hears the cry of the poor, those whom society despises and sacrifices. Is not this the situation of those who are oppressed and marginalized because of their religion? God's mercy is for them.

35:22 *Nor . . . behalf:* Hebrew reads: "and like a warrior he will not be patient."

36:1-22 This prayer, formulated some twenty years before the persecution of Antiochus IV Epiphanes and the revolt of the Maccabees, is a moving one. It expresses the suffering of a people threatened in its national and religious traditions, in its deepest convictions. It vibrates with the hope—which until then had been absent from the writings of the sages—that the salvation announced by the Prophets and attained by Israel will come.

36:5 *Let them acknowledge:* Hebrew reads: "Then they will know."

36:10 *Your oath:* Hebrew reads: "the appointed time."

36:13 This chapter in the Greek lacks verse numbers 14 and 15 although there is no text missing.

Israel, whom you treated as* your firstborn. [w]
18 Have compassion on the holy city,
Jerusalem, your dwelling place. [x]
19 Fill Zion with your majesty*
and your people with your glory.
20 Vindicate those whom you created in the beginning,*
and fulfill the prophecies spoken in your name.
21 Reward those who hope in you,
and let your prophets be proved true.
22 Hear, O Lord, the prayer of your servants,
according to the blessing of Aaron for* your people.
Thus, all who live on the earth will acknowledge
that you are the LORD, the God of the ages.

Giving Proof of Discernment*

23 The stomach takes in all kinds of food,
yet some foods are better than others.
24 As the palate discerns the types of meat,
so a discerning mind can recognize lying words.
25 A perverse mind causes grief,
but a man of experience knows how to pay such a one back.

Knowing How To Choose a Good Wife*

26 A woman will accept any man as a husband,
yet one daughter will be preferable to another.
27 A woman's beauty causes a man's face to light up,
and there is nothing a man desires more.
28 And if, perchance, her speech is kind and gentle,
her husband is the most fortunate of men.
29 A wife is her husband's greatest treasure,
a suitable helper for him and a pillar to provide support. [y]
30 Where there is no fence, the property will be plundered;
when a man has no wife, he wanders about aimlessly and in misery.
31 Who will trust an armed thief
who shifts quickly from city to city?
32 So it is with the man who has no nest
but lodges wherever night overtakes him.

CHAPTER 37

True and False Friends*

1 Every friend can say, "I too am your friend,"
but some are friends in name only. [z]
2 Is it not a sorrow comparable to that of death
when a dear friend turns into an enemy?
3 O inclination to evil, why were you created
to blanket the earth with deceit?
4 A false friend will rejoice in your prosperity
but turn against you when misfortune strikes. [a]
5 A good friend will help you for his stomach's sake
but will serve as your shield-bearer against your enemies.
6 Do not forget your friend in your heart,
and remember him in your prosperity.

Be Wary of One Who Offers Advice*

7 All counselors praise the advice they offer,
but some provide counsel with their own interests in mind.
8 Be wary of one who offers advice;
find out first what his interest is.
For he may be thinking only of his own best interests,
and his advice may not be to your advantage.

w Ex 4:22; Deut 28:10; Isa 63:19; Jer 14:9.—x 2 Chr 6:41; Ps 132:8, 14; Isa 2:1ff; Mic 4:1ff.—y Sir 26:1-4; Gen 2:18; Prov 18:22.—z Sir 6:7ff; Prov 20:6.—a Pss 41:10; 55:13-15.

36:17 *You treated as:* some early MSS read: "you have named."

36:19 *Your majesty:* Greek reads: "with the celebration of your marvelous deeds." *People:* Hebrew reads: "temple."

36:20 *Those whom you created in the beginning:* i.e., the Patriarchs; the author may also be thinking of wisdom created "in the beginning" (see Sir 24:9).

36:22 *According to the blessing of Aaron for:* Hebrew reads: "according to your goodwill toward."

36:23-25 After the moment of emotion, we rediscover the current teaching of the master who loves well-rhymed and beautiful images.

36:26-32 Certainly, the situation between men and women at this epoch is far from one of equality. Therefore, the elevated idea that the author—so distrustful at times—has of the good wife is most relevant (see Sir 26:1-4, 15-18).

37:1-6 The touchstone of friendship is fidelity in difficult times. So strongly does the author believe this that he here proposes it for the third time (see Sir 12:8-18; 22:19-26).

37:7-15 It is better to address oneself to a sage, i.e., a just and disinterested person. However, in the final analysis, it is in fidelity to themselves and in reflection before God that people must make their decision.

9 He may tell you how good your way will be
and then stand aside to see what happens to you.
10 Do not consult anyone who regards you with suspicion
or reveal your plans to those who are jealous of you.
11 Never consult with a woman about her rival
or with a coward about war,
with a merchant about business
or with a buyer about selling,
with a miser about generosity
or with a cruel person about goodness of heart,
with an idler about any kind of work
or with a casual worker about completing the job,
with a lazy servant about a large undertaking:
do not depend on these for any counsel. [b]
12 Rather, associate with a devout person
whom you know to be a keeper of the commandments,
who is of one mind with you
and who will sympathize with you if you fall.
13 In addition, trust your own judgment,
for you have no counselor more reliable for you.
14 Your own conscience will sometimes give you a more accurate warning
than seven watchmen stationed on a high tower.
15 But above all, pray to the Most High,
asking that he direct your steps on the path of truth.

Those Who Are Truly Wise*

16 Reason should precede every work,
and deliberation should come before every undertaking. [c]
17 Thoughts are rooted in the heart,
which sprouts forth four branches:
18 good and evil, life and death,
and their mistress is always the tongue.
19 One man may be clever enough to teach many
and yet be useless to himself.
20 Another may be a brilliant speaker and be detested,
then end up by starving to death,
21 if the LORD has withheld grace and charm
by depriving him of wisdom.
22 [d] When one is wise to his own advantage,
the fruits of his knowledge are seen in his own person.
23 When one is wise to his people's advantage,
the fruits of his knowledge will be enduring.
24 One who is truly wise has praise heaped upon him,
and all who see him will call him blessed.
25 The days of a man's life are numbered,
but the days of Israel are without number.
26 One who is truly wise will gain the confidence * of his people,
and his name will endure forever. [e]

Be Vigilant over Your Life*

27 [f] My child, test yourself throughout your life;
determine what is bad for you and do not indulge in it.
28 For not everything is good for everyone,
nor do we all enjoy the same things.
29 [g] Do not go to excess with any enjoyment,
and do not be greedy for food.
30 For overeating leads to illness,
and gluttony brings on nausea.
31 Many have died as a result of gluttony,
but one who guards against it prolongs his life.

CHAPTER 38

A Physician and Health Are Gifts of God*

1 Honor the physician, for he is essential to you;

b Sir 14:5-10; Deut 20:8; Jdg 7:3; Prov 20:14.—c Sir 32:19.—d 22-24: Sir 15:1ff; 37:19; Job 29:11; Prov 12:14; 18:20.—e Sir 39:9, 11; 41:11-13; 44:13-15; Ps 112:6, 9; Eccl 2:16.—f 27f: Sir 36:23; 37:28; 1 Cor 6:12; 10:23.—g 29f: Sir 31:13, 16ff; Num 11:18-20.

37:16-26 True wisdom does not lie in the art of beautiful speech; it is a gift of God given to the people of Israel.

37:26 *Will gain the confidence:* some early MSS read: "will inherit the honor."

37:27-31 Being vigilant over one's life is also part of the art of living, with which the sage is concerned (see Sir 31:19-22).

38:1-15 Since, according to the mentality of the time, sickness was regarded primarily as punishment for sin, one had to have recourse to God before all else; yet the service of the physician should not be disdained. His science and his art also come from the Creator. This may be a first step in the recognition of a scientific competence for medicine without opposing it to the faith.

for that profession was established by the LORD.
2 The gift of healing comes from the Most High,
and the king provides for the physician's sustenance.
3 His knowledge gives the physician high standing
and earns him the admiration of those who are great.
4 The LORD has created medicines from the earth,
and no one who is sensible will despise them.
5 Was not water once sweetened by a tree*
so that his power might be revealed? [h]
6 He has endowed human beings with skill
so that he might be glorified in his marvelous works.
7 Through them the physician heals and relieves pain,
8 and the pharmacist prepares suitable medicines.
Thus, there is no end to the works of God,
from whom well-being continues to spread throughout the entire world.

9 My child, when you are ill, do not delay,
but pray to God and he will heal you. [i]
10 Purify yourself, keep your hands unsoiled,
and cleanse your heart from all sin.
11 Offer your sweet-smelling oblation and a memorial sacrifice of flour,
and a rich sacrifice according to your means. [j]
12 Then summon the physician—the LORD created him too—
and do not let him leave you, for you need him at your side.
13 There are times when your recovery will be in the hands of a physician,
14 for he too prays to the LORD
to grant him success in relieving the sickness
and in finding a cure to preserve a patient's life.
15 One who sins against his Maker
will fall into the hands of the physician.*

Prolonging One's Mourning Serves No Purpose*

16 My child, shed tears for one who has died,
and as one in great sorrow, begin the lament.
Bury the body with proper ceremony,
and do not neglect to honor the grave.
17 Let your weeping be bitter and your wailing passionate;
make your mourning worthy of the departed.
Mourn for a day or two to avoid criticism;
then be comforted in your sorrow.
18 For grief can lead to death,
and a grieving heart can sap one's strength.
19 After the burial, grief should cease,
for a life of misery weighs down the heart. [k]
20 Do not abandon yourself to grief;
banish it, and think rather of your own end.
21 Do not forget: there is no coming back;
you cannot help the dead person, and you will only harm yourself.
22 Remember that his fate will also be yours;
for him it was yesterday; for you it will be today. [l]
23 When the dead have been laid to rest, let their memory cease;
be comforted for them once their spirits have departed.

h Ex 15:25.—i Ex 15:26; Job 5:18; Isa 38:2f; Hos 6:1.—j Lev 2:1ff; Ps 20:2-6.—k Prov 12:25; 15:13; 17:22.—l Jas 4:13ff.

38:5 This verse gives a natural explanation of the miracle of Moses at Marah described in Ex 15:23-25.

38:15 *Will fall into the hands of the physician:* some early MSS read: "will be defiant toward the physician."

38:16-23 Not knowing the lot reserved for the dead, the author finds comfort in arguments from common sense. Likewise in the matter of affliction, he has no use for excesses and submits himself to the reality of life that God has made. In the first Christian writing, Paul the Apostle will proclaim another hope: we will rise again with Christ (1 Thes 4:13-14).

B: The Splendid Vocation of the Scribe*

No Craft Is Useless*

24 Leisure affords the scribe the opportunity to increase in wisdom;
only the one who is burdened by few tasks can become wise. [m]

25 How can anyone become wise who handles a plow
and who takes great pride in wielding the goad,
who drives oxen, engrossed in that task,
and whose main topic of conversation centers around cattle?
26 His major concern is for plowing furrows,
and he loses sleep in order to give the heifers their fodder.

27 The same is true for every artisan and craftsman
who labors both night and day,
intent on engraving seals
and diligently fashioning a variety of designs;
he concentrates on producing an exact likeness
and stays up late to finish the task. [n]

28 So too with the smith who sits by his anvil,
intent on forging iron.
The intensity of the fire scorches his flesh
as he toils amid the searing heat of the furnace.
The noise of the hammer deafens his ears,
and his eyes are focused on the model of the object.
He concentrates on completing his task
and stays up late to finish it perfectly.

29 So too with the potter sitting at his work
and turning the wheel with his feet.
He is always concerned about his products,
and he turns them out in quantity.
30 He molds the clay with his hands
and softens it with his feet.
He concentrates on doing the glazing correctly
and stays up late to clean the furnace.
31 All of these workers rely on their hands,
and all are experts in their craft.
32 Without them no city would be constructed,
neither could people live or walk in one.*
33 Yet they are not sought out for public discussions,
nor do they attain prominent positions in the assembly.
They do not sit on the judge's bench,
nor do they comprehend the decisions of the courts.
They do not expound on culture or law,
nor are they counted among the authors of proverbs.
34 However, they maintain the fabric of this world,
and their concern is for the experience of their craft.

The Noble Vocation of the Sage*

How different a situation it is with the man who devotes himself to the fear of God
and to the study of the law of the Most High.

CHAPTER 39

1 He researches the wisdom of all the ancients
and occupies himself with the study of the prophecies.
2 He preserves the sayings of famous men
and penetrates the subtleties of parables.
3 He seeks out the hidden meanings of proverbs
and ponders the obscure sense of parables. [o]

4 He enters the service of the great
and appears in the presence of rulers.
He travels in foreign countries,
experiencing a wide spectrum of human good and evil.

---

m 1 Cor 1:20.—n Sir 45:11; Ex 28:11; Wis 14:19.—o Prov 1:6; Wis 8:8.

38:24—39:11 With a notable artistic talent and acute observations the author describes the crafts commonly practiced in Palestine. All activities are depicted in a negative fashion so as to highlight the most sublime profession of the scribe. He alone, master of Scripture and wisdom, finds the freedom to understand life and the law and teach others.

38:24-34 Very artfully, the author evokes the skillful actions and the concerns of peasants and artisans. He acknowledges the need of their work for the life of human beings. But, in his opinion, work completely occupies those who give themselves to it and takes away the leisure to reflect and study.

38:32 *Neither . . . one:* some early MSS read: "and wherever they stay, they will not go hungry."

38:34c—39:11 This text gives witness of a deep love of the task of teaching and animation amid the community and the synagogue. At this epoch, scribes take the lead in the intellectual and spiritual domain. The author may be forgiven for including a bit of vanity in his description. He is not simply presenting one craft among other human ones; he is expressing the sublime idea he has of a vocation.

5 He makes sure to rise early
to seek the Lord, his Maker;
he petitions the Most High
as he opens his mouth in prayer
and asks pardon for his sins.
6 If such is the will of the Lord Almighty,
he will be filled with the spirit of understanding.
He will pour forth words of wisdom of his own devising
and give thanks to the LORD in prayer.
7 The Lord will direct his counsel and his knowledge
as he meditates upon the mysteries of God.
8 He will show the wisdom of what he has learned
and will glory in the law of the Lord's covenant.
9 Many will praise his intelligence,
and his fame will never be forgotten.
The memory of him will never die,
and his name will live through all generations.
10 Nations will speak of his wisdom,
and the assembly will proclaim his praise.
11 If his life span is great, his name will be more glorious
than those of a thousand other people;
and if he dies, that will be all right with him.

C: God's Greatness and Human Weakness

Praise to the Creator*

12 I have still further thoughts on which I wish to expound;
I am as full as the moon at midmonth.
13 Listen to me, my faithful children, and blossom,
like a rose planted by a stream of water. [p]
14 Send out your fragrance like incense,
and bring forth blossoms like a lily;
scatter your fragrance and sing a hymn of praise,
blessing the Lord for everything he has done.
15 Proclaim the greatness of his name,
and offer your praise and gratitude to him;
with songs accompanied by harps and stringed instruments,
this is what you must say in thanksgiving: [q]
16 "All the works of God are marvelous,
and everything that he commands will occur at the designated time.
Let no one ask 'What is this?' or 'Why is that?'
In due time all such questions will be answered.* [r]
17 At his command the waters piled up,
and the word of his mouth created reservoirs to encompass them. * [s]
18 When he commands, his will is done;
no one can thwart his saving power. [t]
19 The deeds of all people are before him,
and nothing can be hidden from his eyes.
20 His gaze stretches from the beginning to the end of time,
and nothing is too marvelous for him.
21 Thus, let no one ask 'What is this?' or 'Why is that?'
for all things have been created for a purpose.
22 "His blessing overflows like a river,
and like the flood it enriches the surface of the earth.
23 Thus, the nations experience his wrath,
just as he transformed the waters into a salt desert. [u]
24 For the devout his paths are smooth,
but for the wicked they are full of obstacles. [v]

p Num 24:6; Ps 1:3; Ezek 31:3-9.—q 1 Chr 13:8; Pss 33:2f; 43:4; 57:8; 150:3f.—r Sir 39:34; Gen 1:31; Pss 33:9f; 104:24; Eccl 3:11.—s Gen 1:6-10; Ex 14:21f; Jos 3:16.—t 1 Sam 14:6; Wis 11:22-26; Isa 40:12-31.—u Gen 13:10; 19:24-28; Deut 29:22; Ps 107:33-35.—v Ps 18:26f; Hos 14:10.

39:12-35 Human beings cannot always understand what they see nor what happens to them. However, in everything the sage divines a plan of God, and the day will come, he firmly hopes, when the harmony of the world will be evident to the eyes of all. How many goods placed by God at the disposition of humans for their use; how many elements in this world that he utilizes to exercise his mercy and chastisement! And is it not the wicked use of these realities by humans that brings on the punishment that is theirs? *Sooner or later everything will prove its worth* (v. 34).

39:16 *Let no one ask . . . will be answered:* these two lines are found only in the Greek MSS, and they are in part a doublet of verse 21.

39:17 This verse recalls God's mighty deeds connected with water: creation (Gen 1:9), the flood (Gen 7:11), the crossing of the Red Sea (Ex 14:21-22) and the Jordan River (Jos 3:16), and the mystery of the clouds as reservoirs of water (Ps 104:6-13).

25 From the beginning good things were created for the upright,
but also bad things for sinners.
26 The basic necessities of human life
are water, fire, iron, salt,
wheat flour, milk, and honey,
the juice of the grape, oil, and clothing. [w]
27 All these are good for those who are good,
but for the wicked they turn out to be bad.
28 "Some winds have been created as means of punishment,
and in their fury they can scourge mightily.*
On the day of reckoning they will unleash their violence
and appease the anger of their Maker.
29 Fire and hail, famine and pestilence—
all these have been created for retribution.
30 Ravenous beasts, scorpions, and vipers,
and the avenging sword to destroy the ungodly—
31 all of them delight in his commandment,
always prepared for his service on the earth,
and when their time comes, they never disobey his commands.
32 I have been convinced of all this from the beginning;
that is why I have thought it all over and have written:
33 All the works of God are good,
and he supplies every need as it arises. [x]
34 There is therefore no reason to say: "This is worse than that,"
for sooner or later everything will prove its worth.
35 So now, sing with all your heart and voice,
and bless the name of God." [y]

CHAPTER 40

The Painful Destiny Given to Human Beings*

1 Strenuous labor is the lot of everyone,
and a heavy yoke has been laid on the children of Adam,
from the day when one emerges from his mother's womb
until the day when he returns to the earth, the mother of all the living.* [z]
2 Matter for his reflection and anxiety for his heart
are offered by the thought of what awaits him and the day of death.
3 Whether he sits in splendor on a throne
or grovels in dust and ashes,
4 whether he wears the purple and a crown
or is clothed in burlap,
5 his life is filled with anger and envy, trouble and unrest,
fear of death, fury and strife.
Even when he goes to bed at night,
his sleep is disturbed by confusion and worry.
6 He receives little if any rest,
struggling while he dreams as he does when he is awake.
Terrified by nightmares,
he is like someone who has fled from the battlefield.
7 Just as he reaches safety, he wakes up,
astonished to realize that his fears were groundless.
8 To all flesh, human and animal—
but to sinners seven times more—
9 come death and bloodshed, strife and sword,
disasters and famine, affliction and plague. [a]
10 All these calamities were created for the wicked,
and the flood came because of them.
11 All that is of the earth returns to the earth,
and all that is from the waters returns to the sea.*

w Sir 29:21; Gen 49:11; Ex 3:8; Lev 20:24; Num 13:27; Deut 6:3; 2 Chr 32:28; Neh 10:38; Jer 31:12; Hos 2:10.—x Sir 39:16; Gen 1:31; Eccl 3:11.—y Ps 145:21.—z Sir 16:29f; 51:5; Gen 3:17; Job 7:1; 14:1; Ps 90:10; Eccl 2:23; Mt 6:34.—a Sir 39:28ff; Deut 28:22; Isa 51:19; 60:18; Ezek 5:16f.

39:28 *Scourge mightily:* Hebrew reads: "dislodge mountains."

40:1-11 The author is a decided optimist, but he bows down before reality: the shadow of death stretches out over creation, and human sin has destroyed the beautiful harmony of the origins. And since he has hardly an inkling of redemption and even less of everlasting life, the author finds in the common lot of human beings a lesson of realism and humility (see Sir 10:6-18).

40:1 *Mother of all the living:* i.e., the earth (see Gen 2:7; 3:19-20; Job 1:21; Ps 139:15).

40:11 *And all that is from the waters returns to the sea:* Hebrew reads: "and what comes from above returns above" (see Eccl 12:7).

What Passes Away and What Remains*

12 All bribery and injustice will be blotted out,
but good faith will stand forever.[b]
13 That wealth whose source is wickedness will dry up like a river
and vanish as quickly as a clap of thunder during a storm.
14 [c] As the righteous man rejoices in opening his hands,
so transgressors will come to ruin.
15 The children of the godless put forth very few branches,
for tainted roots are planted only on sheer rock.
16 They are like reeds along the riverbank
that are plucked before any other plants.
17 However, goodness is a paradise of blessings.

Better Still Is the Fear of God*

18 Wealth and wages make life sweet,
but better than either is finding a treasure.
19 Children and the founding of a city will preserve one's name,
but better than either is finding wisdom.
Cattle and orchards make a man well known,*
but better than either is a perfect wife.
20 Wine and music gladden the heart,
but better than either is the love of wisdom.[d]
21 The flute and the harp make sweet melody,
but better than either is a pleasant voice.
22 The eye delights to gaze upon grace and beauty,
but better than either are the green shoots in a cornfield.
23 A friend and a companion are encountered in good time,
but better than either is a sensible wife.*
24 A brother and a helper are cherished in times of stress,
but better than either is the aid provided by almsgiving.[e]
25 Gold and silver make one's way secure,
but better than either is sound advice.
26 Riches and vigor build up self-confidence,
but better than either is fear of God.
With the fear of the Lord, nothing is lacking;
whoever has it does not need to seek any further help.
27 The fear of God is a paradise of blessings
and offers greater protection than any possible glory able to be achieved.[f]

It Is Better To Die than To Beg*

28 My child, do not lead the life of a beggar;
it is better to die than to beg.
29 When you start to eye someone else's table,
your life truly is not worth calling a life.
The gullet is defiled with the food of strangers;
anyone who is wise and well-instructed will guard against doing that.
30 In the mouth of the shameless, begging is sweet,
but inside him the fires of resentment burn.

CHAPTER 41

Do Not Fear Death's Sentence*

1 O death, how bitter is the thought of you
to someone who lives at ease among his possessions,
who is free from worries and prosperous in all things
and still healthy enough to enjoy food.
2 O death, how welcome is your sentence
to someone in want whose strength is failing,

b Sir 35:14; Ex 23:8; Ps 15:5; Prov 17:23.—c 14f: Sir 23:24f; Wis 4:3ff.—d Ps 104:15.—e Prov 17:17.—f Isa 4:5.

40:12-17 Side by side with so much crying injustice, there is good faith, charity, and grace. One day, order will be reestablished in everything once again, and then only authentic values will remain.

40:18-27 In diverse ways, freedom, progeny, wisdom, love, music, fortune, beauty, and other advantages endow existence with a certain charm. Ultimately, only filial respect toward God can fulfill the aspirations of human beings.

40:19 *But better than either is finding wisdom . . . make a man well known:* lacking in Greek.

40:23 *A sensible wife:* Greek reads: "a wife with her husband."

40:28-30 The author attaches too much importance to work and reputation not to regard begging as an insupportable disgrace.

41:1-4 Willingly or unwillingly, sooner or later, everybody is subject to the law of death. The author, who does not yet have any clear experience of eternal life, humbly accepts this reality of the human condition.

worn out with age and burdened by endless anxiety,
resentful and no longer blessed with patience.[g]

3 Do not fear death's sentence;
remember it embraces those who preceded you and those who will come after.

4 This is God's sentence on all flesh,
so why do you reject the pleasure of the Most High?
Whether one's life lasts ten years, or a hundred, or a thousand,
no questions will be asked about it in the netherworld.[h]

Malediction Follows the Wicked*

5[i] The children of sinners are a loathsome lot,
and they frequent the homes of the ungodly.

6 The inheritance of the children of sinners is doomed to perish,
and their descendants will live in perpetual disgrace.

7 Children will blame a godless father
for the reproach they endure because of him.

8 Woe to you who are godless,
who have forsaken the law of God Most High.

9 If you have children, they will endure calamity;
you will beget them solely for groaning.
When you stumble, lasting joy prevails;
and when you die, a curse is your lot.

10 All that comes from the earth returns to the earth;
so too the wicked go from malediction to destruction.

11 Men grieve over their bodies,
but the bad name of sinners will be blotted out. *

A Good Name Lasts Forever*

12 Have regard for your name, for it will outlive you
far longer than a thousand hoards of gold.[j]

13 The days of a good life are numbered,
but a good name lasts forever.

D: Final Instructions*

14 My children, keep my instructions,
and live in peace.
Concealed wisdom and buried treasure—
of what value is either?

15 Better is one who hides his folly
than one who hides his wisdom.

Things That Require a Sense of Shame*

16 Therefore, provide a sense of shame in the following matters,
for shame is not always appropriate in every instance,
nor is it to be approved in every situation.

17 Be ashamed to be caught by your father or mother in an act of sexual immorality,
or by a ruler or a prince in lies,

18 or before a judge or a magistrate in a crime,
or by the assembly of the people in a violation of the law,
or by a friend or a partner in dishonesty,[k]

19 or by an act of thievery in the place where you live.
Be ashamed of violating the truth of God and his covenant
and of putting your elbows on the table,
of being ungracious when giving or receiving

20 and of ignoring those who greet you,
of gazing at a prostitute

21 and of rejecting an appeal for help from a relative,
of misappropriating someone's rightful share
and of eyeing another man's wife,

22 of making advances toward his servant girl,
or of approaching her bed,

g Sir 14:12; 30:17; Eccl 12:1-6.—h Sir 14:16; 17:28; Gen 3:19; 6:3; Eccl 6:6; 9:10.—i 5ff: Sir 3:9ff; Wis 3:16-19.—j Prov 22:1; Eccl 7:1.—k Job 21:34.

41:5-11 In order to frighten those who turn away from God and his law, the author reiterates old conceptions: dishonor is transmitted from one generation to another as an ineradicable evil.

41:11 *Men grieve . . . blotted out:* Hebrew reads: "The human body is a fleeting thing, / but a virtuous man will never be annihilated."

41:12-13 For the author who has many questions about reputation and honor, the survival of a name is not something indifferent.

41:14—42:14 The idea that one has of shame or the concerns of human beings still reveals—as in the maxims that follow—a certain conception of life.

41:16-22 What is it that you find dishonest or inconvenient in your opinion? Your response contains your philosophy of life. In this passage we will discover—as in a negative resume—the essence of the author's practical teaching.

of using abusive words to friends,
or of giving an insulting lecture after an act of charity. [l]

CHAPTER 42

1 Be ashamed of repeating everything you hear
and of betraying a confidence.
Then you will show a proper sense of shame
and find favor with everyone.

Things That Do Not Require a Sense of Shame

But of the following things do not be ashamed,
and do not sin in fear of the opinions of others.
2 Do not be ashamed of the law of the Most High and of his covenant,
or of acting justly even if it results in the acquittal of the ungodly; [m]
3 of reckoning expenses with a partner or a traveling companion,
or of sharing an inheritance with friends;
4 of ensuring the accuracy of scales and measures,
or of acquiring possessions, whether few or many; [n]
5 of earning a profit in dealing with merchants,
or of frequent disciplining of children,
or of drawing blood from the back of a wicked servant;
6 of employing a seal on your door if you have an erring wife,
or of using a key to make things secure where there are many hands;
7 of numbering every deposit,
or of recording all that is taken in or given out;
8 of correcting an ignorant or a foolish man,
or a dotard who bickers with the young;
in this way, you will exhibit your sound training
and win universal approval.

May Your Daughter Not Make You Ashamed*

9 A daughter is a treasure that makes her father anxious,
and in his worry about her he loses sleep:
when she is young, for fear she may never marry,
and when she is married, for fear her husband may hate her; [o]
10 when she is a virgin, for fear she may be seduced
and become pregnant in her father's house;
when she has a husband, for fear she may prove unfaithful,
and after marriage, for fear she may prove to be barren.
11 Keep a close watch on a headstrong daughter,
lest she make you an object of ridicule to your enemies,
causing you to be the talk of the town, the subject of gossip,
and an object of derision in public gatherings.
Make sure that her room has no lattice,
no spot that overlooks the approaches to the house. [p]
12 Do not allow her to parade her beauty before any man [q]
or spend her time with married women;
13 for just as out of clothes comes the moth
so from a woman comes woman's wickedness.
14 Better is the wickedness of a man than a woman's goodness,
but better is a religious daughter than a son without shame.

IV: PRAISE TO THE LORD OF NATURE AND OF ISRAEL*

A: The Canticle of Creatures*

The Works of the LORD Are Full of His Glory

15 Now I will recall the works of the LORD
and declare what I have seen.

---

l Sir 18:15-18; 2 Sam 11:1-4.—m Deut 1:17; 16:18-20.—n Lev 19:35f; Prov 11:1; 16:11; Hos 12:8; Am 8:5; Mic 6:11.—o Sir 7:24f.—p Sir 26:10; Prov 7:6.—q 12f: Sir 9:1-9.

42:9-14 Women constituted a mystery in the eyes of the ancients. Their virtue seemed threatened, and moreover, they seemed to be a plague along the path of men (see vv. 12-14). We find this mistrust and this paradox among many ancient Jewish authors. But we would do the author an injustice if we did not recall how beautifully he sang the praises of the good wife (see Sir 26:1-4, 15-18; 36:21-27).

42:15—50:29 The inaccessible thought of God and his wondrous work are nothing else but the sign of supreme wisdom. It is wisdom that the sage, filled with admiration, contemplates in such a well-ordered universe, and it is wisdom that he discerns even more clearly in the destiny of human beings. In these lengthy pages of contemplation and praise, the author thus invites the Jews, his brothers and sisters, to revive in themselves a deeper sense of God and better discern the vocation of their people in the face of the Greek paganism threatening to overcome them.

42:15—43:33 The chant of creation springs forth more than once in the Bible. These chapters form part of such a group of texts. Paul the Apostle will later affirm that the glory of God is

By the word of the LORD his works came into existence
and all his creatures do his will. [r]
16 As the sun illumines everything with its brilliant rays,
so the works of the LORD are full of his glory.
17 Yet the LORD has not empowered even his holy ones*
to tell of all his marvelous works,
which the LORD Almighty has accomplished
so that the universe may stand firm in his glory.
18 He fathoms both the abyss and the human heart
and comprehends their innermost secrets.
For the Most High possesses all knowledge
and observes the signs of the times.*
19 He makes known the past and the future
and reveals the evidence of hidden things.
20 No thought escapes his notice,
and not a single thing is hidden from him. [s]
21 He has set in order the splendors of his wisdom,
for he is from everlasting to everlasting.
Nothing can be added to him or taken away;
he needs no one to give him counsel. [t]
22 How beautiful are all his works,
and how dazzling they are to the eye.
23 All of his works endure and will abide forever for every need,
and all are obedient in any circumstance.
24 All things come in pairs, one the counterpart of the other;
he has made none of them imperfect.
25 Each complements the good qualities of the other.
Who could ever grow weary of gazing at their splendor?

CHAPTER 43

The Sun, God's Herald*

1 [u]The pride of the higher realms is the clear vault of the sky,
a vision of glory like the sight of the heavens.
2 As the sun comes into view, it proclaims as it rises,
"What a marvelous creation it is, the work of the Most High."
3 At noontime it parches the surface of the earth,
and who can endure its blazing heat?
4 A man stokes a furnace in burning heat,
but three times as hot is the sun that scorches the mountains.
It breathes out fiery vapors,
and the eyes are blinded by the intensity of its rays.
5 Great indeed is the LORD who made it,
and whose command speeds it on its course.

The Moon, Queen of Feasts and Seasons*

6 He also created the moon that marks the changing seasons,
governing the divisions of time, their everlasting sign. [v]
7 From the moon we are able to calculate when feast days are to be observed;
its light wanes when its course has been completed.*
8 "Month" derives its name from the moon;*
it waxes wondrously as its phases change.
It is a beacon to the hosts on high,
shining in the vault of the heavens.

r Gen 1:3ff; Jud 16:14; Job 15:17; Pss 33:6; 77:12f; Wis 9:1; Jn 1:1-3.—s Sir 39:19; Ps 139:1-4; Wis 1:6-10.—t Sir 18:6; Eccl 3:14; Isa 40:13; Rom 11:34.—u 1ff: Sir 14:27; Pss 8:3; 19:2f, 7.—v Lev 23:5; Num 28:11-14; Pss 81:4; 89:38.

visible in the universe that he offers for our contemplation (Rom 1:20): e.g., God's creation and preservation of the universe (Sir 42:15ff, 23, 25; 43:1-26); his omniscience (v. 18ff); his perfect wisdom (vv. 21-22); and his eternity (v. 23). The author concludes the passage with a hymn of praise (Sir 43:27-33). See also Sir 16:24—18:14.

42:17 *Holy ones:* i.e., the angels.

42:18 It was believed by the ancients that the destiny of human beings was written in the stars, which regulated the course of time. *And observes the signs of the times:* Hebrew reads: "and from the beginning he has seen the things that are to come."

43:1-5 In the metaphorical language of Scripture, the sun is symbolic of the law (Ps 19:7), of God's cheering presence (Ps 84:11), of the person of the Savior (Jn 1:9; Mal 3:20), and of the purity of heavenly creatures (Rev 1:16; 10:1; 12:1).

43:6-8 The Israelites established their calendar starting from the observation of the lunar system. The unfolding of the days and the years flows from the regularity that the moon seems to possess in their eyes.

43:7 The full moon marked the beginning of the two greatest Jewish feasts (Passover and Tabernacles) and lasted eight days.

43:8 *"Month" derives its name from the moon:* Hebrew reads: "As its name suggests, each month the moon renews itself."

The Stars, Heavenly Sentinels

9 The brilliance of the stars enhances the beauty of the heavens,
a glittering array in the heights of the LORD. [w]
10 At the command of the Holy One they remain in their appointed places,
and they never relax in their vigils.

The Rainbow, Aureole of Glory*

11 Look at the rainbow and praise its Maker,
for it glows with a surpassing beauty. [x]
12 It spans the heavens with its glorious ark,
a bow stretched out by the hands of the Most High.

Natural Phenomena

13 By his command he sends the snowstorm
and speeds the lightning to execute his judgment.
14 In the same manner, the storehouses are opened,
and the clouds fly out like vultures.
15 In his majesty he gives the clouds their strength
and breaks the hailstones into smaller pieces.
16a At the sight of him the mountains quake,
17a the thunder of his voice makes the earth writhe.
16b At his will the south wind blows,
17b [y] as do the storm from the north and the whirlwind.
He scatters the snowflakes like birds alighting;
they descend like a swarm of locusts.
18 The eye is dazzled by the beauty of their whiteness,
and the mind is entranced with its steady fall.
19 He scatters frost over the earth like salt,
and icicles form like pointed thorns.
20 At a blast from the frigid north wind,
water freezes to ice on the ponds,
settling on every pool of water
and covering it like a breastplate.
21 He consumes the hills and burns up the wilderness,
and withers the vegetation like fire,
22 but a mist restores them all,
and the dew brings refreshment after the intense heat.

The Sea

23 By his design he calmed the deep
and planted islands there.
24 [z] Those who sail the sea recount its perils,
and we are astonished at what we hear.
25 In it are strange and wondrous creatures,
all kinds of living things and huge sea monsters.
26 Because of him, each of his messengers succeeds,
and by his word all things are accomplished. [a]

Where Can We Find the Skill To Glorify God?*

27 No matter how much we say, our words will never prove adequate;
to sum it all up: "He is the all!" *
28 Where can we find the skill to glorify him,
for he is greater than all his works.
29 The LORD is awe-inspiring in his majesty,
and marvelous is his power.
30 Glorify and exalt the LORD to the extent of your ability,
and yet even that will prove inadequate.
Summon all your strength to exalt him,
and do not grow weary, for you can never finish.
31 For who has seen him and can describe him,
or who can praise him as he truly is?
32 Many mysteries even greater than these remain,
for we have seen only a few of his works.
33 The LORD has created all things,
and to those who are devout he has granted wisdom. [b]

---

w Ps 8:4; Bar 3:33-35.—x Sir 50:7; Gen 9:13; Ezek 1:28.—y 17b-e: Ps 147:16; Prov 30:27; Isa 29:6; Jer 23:19; Ezek 13:11, 13.—z 24f: Ps 104:25-30.—a Ps 33:6.—b Sir 1:11f; 42:17; Gen 1:1—2:4; Job 28:28.

43:11-12 The Jews regarded the rainbow as a sign of the covenant that God made with the human race after the great catastrophe of the flood (Gen 9:13).

43:27-33 The astonishment that human beings feel in the midst of such a varied universe is a direct result of their contemplation of it.

43:27 *He is the all!:* i.e., all creatures manifest the divine presence.

B: The Heroes of Sacred History*

CHAPTER 44

Let Us Praise Illustrious Men*

1 Let us now praise illustrious men,
our ancestors in their successive generations.
2 The Most High apportioned to them an abundance of glory
and displayed his greatness from of old.[c]
3 Some ruled over kingdoms
and were renowned for their valor.
Others were prudent counselors
and spoke with prophetic power.
4 Some guided the people by their counsel,
by their knowledge of the popular mind,
and by the wise words of their instruction.
5 Some were composers of music
or authors of poetry.
6 Others were rich and powerful,
living peacefully in their homes.
7 All these were honored in their own generation
and were illustrious in their day.

8 Some of them have left behind a name,
so that their praiseworthy deeds are recounted.
9 But of others no memory remains;
they have perished as though they had never existed.
They have become as though they had never been born,
they and their children after them.

10 Yet these also were godly men
whose virtuous deeds have not been forgotten.
11 Their wealth has been handed on to their descendants,
and their inheritance to future generations.
12 Their descendants have remained faithful to the covenants,
and, so have their children for their sake.
13 Their offspring will endure for all time,
and their glory will never fade.
14 [d]Their bodies are buried in peace,
but their name lives on for all generations.
15 The peoples proclaim their wisdom,
and the assembly sings their praise.

Enoch, the Privileged One*

16 ENOCH pleased the LORD and was taken up
as an example of repentance for future generations.[e]

Noah the Just, Second Father of Humankind

17 NOAH was found to be perfect and righteous,
and in the time of God's wrath he kept the race alive.
Because of him a remnant survived on the earth,
and with a pledge to him the flood came to an end.[f]
18 Everlasting covenants were established with him,
that never again would all life be blotted out by a flood.

Abraham, Father of the People of God

19 ABRAHAM was the great father of a multitude of nations;
no one has been found to be his equal in glory.[g]
20 He observed the law of the Most High
and entered into a covenant with him.
He confirmed the covenant in his flesh,*
and when he was tested he proved faithful.[h]
21 Therefore, God assured him with an oath

c Deut 32:8f.—d 14f: Sir 38:16; 41:11; Tob 14:1, 12f; Prov 10:7; Wis 3:3.—e Sir 49:14; Gen 5:18-24; Heb 11:5.—f Gen 6:8—9:29; Heb 11:7.—g Gen 12:1—25:10; Gal 3:6; Heb 11: 8-19.—h Gen 17:10; 22:1; Heb 11:17.

44:1—50:29 The work of divine wisdom in the universe is admirable, and even more so is God's initiative in the history of human beings, of the sublime figures chosen to lead the destiny of the holy people. An unconditional admirer of the cult where God is present, he is especially interested in priests and devotes himself to evoking the different covenants concluded between God and his people in the course of history; by contrast, he judges with severity the faults of kings. If he celebrates the glories of the past, it is first of all to condemn the laxity of his contemporaries and to inspire fidelity.

For similar historical surveys, see Neh 9:6-37; Jud 5:5-21; 1 Mac 2:51-64; Pss 78; 105; 135; 136; Wis 10:1—12:27; Ezek 20:4-44; Acts 7:2-53; Heb 11:2-39; Jas 5:10-11.

44:1-15 Kings, sages, prophets, and chanters—whether celebrated or ignored, men of God abound in Israel. They are too numerous for one to evoke the remembrance of every one. Some of them found a family among the people, and their remembrance remains alive and exciting.

44:16 The patriarch Enoch, made popular by ancient traditions, ended his life in a mysterious manner (Gen 5:24; see Heb 11:5; Jude 14-15).

44:20 *In his flesh:* allusion to circumcision (see Gen 17:10, 23). *And . . . faithful:* allusion to the sacrifice of Isaac, rewarded by the promise of numerous progeny (see Gen 22:16-18).

that the nations would be blessed
through his descendants,
that he would make his offspring as
numerous as the dust of the earth,
and that they would be exalted like the
stars,
and that he would give them an inheri-
tance extending from sea to sea,
and from the river to the ends of the
earth.*

Isaac and Jacob or the Birth of the Twelve Tribes*

22 To ISAAC also, God gave the same assur-
ance
for the sake of Abraham his father.[i]
23 He caused the blessing of all people and
the covenant
to rest on the head of JACOB.
He acknowledged him with his blessings
and gave him the land as his inheri-
tance.
He divided the land into portions
and distributed them to the twelve
tribes.

CHAPTER 45

Moses, Lawgiver and Servant of God*

1 From Jacob's stock God raised up a
devout man
who found favor in the eyes of all,
beloved by God and the people,
MOSES, of blessed memory.[j]
2 [k] God made him equal in glory to the holy
ones,*
and strengthened him, to the fright-
ened consternation of his enemies.
3 At his word God caused signs* to cease
and raised him high in the regard of
kings.
He gave him commandments for his
people
and revealed to him a portion of his
glory.[l]
4 As a result of his loyalty and meekness,
God consecrated him,
choosing him from all humankind.[m]
5 He permitted him to hear his voice
and led him into the dark cloud,
where, face to face,* he gave him the
commandments,
the law of life and knowledge,
so that he might teach his covenant to
Jacob,
and to Israel, his decrees.

The Glory of Aaron the High Priest*

6 [n] He also raised up AARON, a holy man like
Moses,
who was his brother, of the tribe of
Levi.
7 He made an everlasting covenant with
him
and conferred on him the priesthood*
of his people.
He adorned him with splendid vestments
and gave him a robe of glory.
8 He clothed him in magnificent apparel
and invested him with rich ornaments:
the linen undergarments, the long
robe, and the ephod.
9 To encircle the hem of his robe he gave
him pomegranates,
with many golden bells all around,
to sound melodiously as he walked,
ringing aloud throughout the temple
as a reminder to his people;
10 with the sacred vestment of gold and
violet,
and purple, the work of an embroi-
derer;
with the oracle of judgment, the sacred
lots;
11 with scarlet thread, the product of an
artisan;
with precious stones engraved like seals,
mounted in gold, the work of a
jeweler,
to commemorate with inscriptions
each of the tribes of Israel;

---

i Gen 26:3, 5, 24; 27:28f; 28:14.—j Ex 2:2; 11:3; 33:11; Num 12:7.—k 2-5: Ex 7; Deut 34.—l Ex 4:17; 7:1; 33:18-23; 34: 5-8.—m Num 12:3, 7; Heb 3:2, 5.—n 6ff: Ex 28–29; Wis 18:24.

44:21 *From the river to the ends of the earth:* i.e., from the Euphrates to the southern end of Palestine, marked by the Nile of Egypt (see Gen 15:18).

44:22-23 It is the remembrance of Isaac and Jacob that will be evoked to explain the ideal structure of the people of Israel.

45:1-5 Moses, who spoke with God and was liberator of his people, incarnates the law, i.e., the rule of life given by God to a people, the first five Books of the Bible that are the basic charter. He is the man of the Sinaitic Covenant (Ex 19).

45:2 *Holy ones:* i.e., the angels.

45:3 *Signs:* i.e., the plagues by which the Egyptians were stricken (Ex 8–10).

45:5 *Face to face:* concerning the relationship Moses had with God (see Ex 33:11; Num 12:8; 1 Cor 13:12).

45:6-22 The author here gives more importance to the figure of the first high priest than do all the other Books of the Bible. He wishes to describe the origin of the liturgy in Israel and to express the happiness of the cultic life. In his view, God has a predilection for priests, who fulfill an irreplaceable role in the relations of humans with God and in the transmission of the law.

45:7 *Priesthood:* this priesthood of Aaron gave way to the priesthood of Christ (see Heb 7:18-28).

12 with a gold diadem upon his turban,
inscribed with the seal of consecration,
majestic ornamentation, stupendous work,
a delight of rich adornment to the eyes.
13 Before him such beautiful things had never existed,
nor has anyone ever worn them
except for his sons
and his descendants throughout the ages.
14 Twice every day, without exception,
they present his sacrifice, to be wholly consumed.

15 Moses ordained him
and anointed him with the holy oil.
This was an everlasting covenant for him
and for his descendants, as long as the heavens endure,
that he should be God's minister by means of his priesthood
and bless his people in his name. [o]
16 God chose him out of all the living
to offer sacrifices to him,
incense and sweet-smelling oblations for a memorial,
to make expiation for his people.
17 He entrusted him with his commandments
and gave him the authority to enact laws and make judgments,
to teach Jacob his decrees
and to enlighten Israel in regard to his law.

18 [p] Others became envious of Aaron
and conspired against him in the wilderness:
Dathan and Abiram and their followers,
and the band of Korah in defiant wrath.
19 The LORD saw this and was angered;
in his burning wrath he destroyed them.
He worked miracles against them,
as they were consumed in his blazing fire.
20 [q] Then he increased the glory of Aaron
and gave him a heritage;
he allotted to him the choicest offerings of the firstfruits,
thus ensuring that they would have bread in abundance.
21 For they eat the sacrifices of the LORD
that he gave to Aaron and his descendants.
22 However, he has no inheritance in the land of the people;
he has no portion among them;
for the LORD himself is his portion and inheritance
in the midst of the Israelites.

Phinehas, Champion of God's Rights*

23 PHINEHAS, the son of Eleazar, ranks third in glory
because of his zeal in the fear of the LORD,
and for standing firm with noble courage of soul
when the people refused to obey;
and by so doing he made expiation for Israel. [r]
24 Therefore, a covenant of friendship was established with him,
conferring on him the right to be in charge of the sanctuary and of the people,
so that he and his descendants should have
the dignity of the high priesthood forever.
25 Just as a covenant was established with David,
the son of Jesse, of the tribe of Judah,
that the royal succession was always to pass from father to son,
so the priestly succession was to pass from Aaron to his descendants. [s]

26 And now bless the LORD
who has crowned you with glory.
May God grant you* a mind endowed with wisdom
to rule his people with justice,
so that the virtues of your ancestors may never vanish
and their glory may be passed on to all their descendants.

---

o Lev 8:1-13, 22; Num 25:13; Ps 89:30; Mal 2:4f.—p 18f: Num 16:1—17:15; 18:8-19; Deut 18:1; Ps 106:16-18.—q 20f: Ex 29:28, 31; Num 18:11-21; Deut 10:9; Ps 16:5.—r Num 25:7-13; 1 Mac 2:26, 54; Ps 106:30f.—s 2 Sam 7:12-16; 2 Chr 13:5; Pss 8:6; 89:3-5, 29f.

45:23-26 Phinehas, grandson of Aaron, is a secondary figure in the most ancient accounts (Num 25). Here, his role is highlighted to show the superiority of the priesthood over the royalty (v. 25) and to give a better understanding of the legitimacy of the priesthood of Jerusalem in a time when usurpers are no longer far removed.

45:26 *May God grant you . . . :* exhortation that the author directs to his contemporary priests.

CHAPTER 46

Joshua and Caleb, Heroes of the Conquest*

1 JOSHUA, son of Nun, was a valiant warrior
and the successor of Moses in the prophetic office,
destined to become, as his name implies,*
the great savior of God's chosen people,
to wreak vengeance on the enemies who attacked them
and thus bring Israel into its inheritance. [t]
2 How glorious he was when with uplifted hands
he brandished his sword against cities! [u]
3 Who could withstand him
when he fought the battles of the LORD?
4 Was it not through him that the sun stood still
so that one day was lengthened into two? [v]
5 He called upon the Most High God
when his enemies pressed him on every side,
and the great LORD answered him
with hailstones of mighty power.
6 He overwhelmed that hostile nation in battle
and destroyed his assailants as they fled down the slope,
so that all the nations might know his power
and that he was fighting before the LORD.
For he was a devoted follower of God,
7 in the lifetime of Moses proving his loyalty.

Joshua and CALEB, son of Jephunneh,
stood their ground against the rebellious assembly,
restrained the people from sin,*
and silenced their wicked grumbling. [w]
8 As a result, out of the six hundred thousand infantry,
these two alone were spared
to lead the people into their inheritance,
a land flowing with milk and honey. [x]
9 And the strength that the LORD gave to Caleb
remained with him even in his old age;
thus, he was able to invade the hill country
and win possession of it for an inheritance,
10 so that every Israelite might see
how good it is to follow the LORD.

The Judges, Defenders of an Oppressed Israel

11 The JUDGES too, every one of them by name,
whose hearts did not succumb to idolatry
and who did not turn their backs on the LORD—
may their memory be blessed. [y]
12 May their bones send forth new life from the grave,
and may the names of those illustrious men
live again in their children.

Samuel, a Prophet for the People*

13 Honored among his people and beloved by his Creator,
pledged in a vow from his mother's womb,
and consecrated to the LORD in the prophetic office
was SAMUEL, the judge who offered sacrifice.
At God's word, he established the monarchy
and anointed rulers of his people. [z]
14 He judged the community according to the law of the LORD,
and the LORD watched over the people of Jacob.
15 By his faithfulness he was proved to be a prophet,
and his words substantiated his trustworthy role as a seer.
16 When his enemies pressed him on every side,

t Ex 17:9; Num 27:18; Deut 3:28; 34:9; Jos 1:1-4.—u Jos 8:18.—v Jos 10:13.—w Num 13:30; 14:6.—x Ex 3:8, 17; Lev 20:24; Deut 6:3; Num 14:22-38; Jer 11:5.—y Jdg 1:1—16:31.—z 1 Sam 1:10ff; 8:4ff; 10:1; 16:13.

46:1-10 The names of Joshua and Caleb are synonymous with bravery and trust in the word of God.

46:1 *As his name implies:* in Hebrew, Joshua means "God is savior."

46:7 *Restrained the people from sin:* some early MSS read: "averted God's wrath from the people."

46:13-20 Hero of the holy war (1 Sam 7) before becoming the founder of the royalty and anointing the first two kings of Israel, Samuel remains a great figure. He was the conscience of the fallen monarch Saul (1 Sam 13:10-14; 28:12-19), and he remains the man of God calling out constantly for integrity.

he called upon the LORD, the Mighty One,
offering him a suckling lamb. [a]
17 Then the LORD thundered from heaven,
and made his voice heard with a mighty roar. [b]
18 He routed the leaders of the enemy
and all the rulers of the Philistines.
19 When the time drew near for his eternal sleep,
Samuel bore witness to the LORD and his anointed:
"I have never taken from anyone any property,
not even a pair of shoes."
And no one could contradict his statement. [c]
20 Even after he had fallen asleep, he prophesied once again,
warning the king of his approaching death.
He raised his voice in prophecy from the depths of the earth
to put an end to the wickedness of the people. [d]

CHAPTER 47

Nathan, the King's Prophet*

1 After him arose NATHAN
to prophesy in the days of David. [e]

David, the Lord's Warrior and Psalmist*

2 Just as the fat of the sacred offerings is set apart,
so DAVID was chosen out of all Israel. [f]
3 He frolicked with lions as though they were young goats,
and with bears as though they were lambs of the flock.
4 While still a young boy he killed a giant
and eradicated the shame of his people.
By hurling a stone from his sling
he put an end to the boastful arrogance of Goliath. [g]
5 For he called on the Most High God,
who gave strength to his right arm
to strike down that mighty warrior
and demonstrate the power of his people.
6 Therefore, they exalted him as the conqueror of tens of thousands,
praised him while they blessed the LORD,
and offered him a crown of glory. [h]
7 For he destroyed his enemies on every side,
annihilating the hostile Philistines
whose power remains crushed to the present day. [i]
8 In everything he did he offered thanks to the Holy One,
proclaiming the glory of the Most High.
He sang hymns of praise with all his heart
to demonstrate his love for his Maker.
9 He assigned singers to stand before the altar
and to provide sweet melody with their voices.
[And they sang his praise daily.] * [j]
10 He invested the festivals with splendor
and designated their times throughout the year,
when the LORD's holy name is praised
and the sanctuary resounds from the moment of dawn.
11 The LORD took away his sins
and endowed him forever with great power.
By a covenant he gave him the kingship
and a glorious throne in Israel.

Solomon: From a Wise Youth to a Sad End*

12 He was succeeded by a wise son,
who, thanks to him, ruled a vast domain. * [k]
13 SOLOMON reigned in an age of peace,
for God gave tranquillity to all his borders,

---

a 1 Sam 7:9.—b Ps 18:14.—c 1 Sam 12:3.—d 1 Sam 28:14-19.—e 2 Sam 7:2.—f Lev 4:8; 1 Sam 16:11.—g 1 Sam 17:49.—h 1 Sam 18:7.—i 2 Sam 5:6-25.—j 1 Chr 16:4ff; 23:2ff; 25:1-7.—k 1 Ki 2:12.

47:1 By mentioning Nathan at the beginning of this part of his Book, the author calls attention to a conviction dear to the hearts of the chosen people: that there had been a succession of prophets from the time of Moses (see Sir 46:1, 13, 20; 48:1-4, 12, 22; 49:6, 8, 10; Jer 7:25; Hos 12:14; Am 2:11; 3:7f).

47:2-11 By his exploits and his political shrewdness, David has made his people a prosperous and united nation (see the Books of Samuel). In addition, as musician and poet, this king composed numerous psalms and organized the cult at Jerusalem (1 Chr 16; 22–26). One cannot forget his adultery (2 Sam 11–12) or his pardon by God, together with the promise made to his lineage that it would retain the throne of the people of Israel (2 Sam 7).

47:9c Added by some early MSS.

47:12-22 The author of Sirach is more concerned with truth than the Chronicler (2 Chr 1–9), who is the inspiration for this historical fresco, and he does not hesitate to denounce the excesses that marred the end of a splendid reign (1 Ki 11).

47:12 *Ruled a vast domain:* Hebrew reads: "lived in security."

so that he might build a house to his name
and prepare an everlasting sanctuary. [l]
14 [m] How wise you were in your youth, Solomon,
filled with intelligence like an overflowing river! *
15 Your understanding covered the earth,
and you filled it with difficult sayings.
16 Your reputation spread to far-distant islands,
and you were loved for your peaceful reign.
17 Your songs, your proverbs, your sayings,
and the answers you provided astounded the nations.
18 In the name of the LORD God
who is called the God of Israel, *
you amassed gold like so much tin
and accumulated silver like lead.
19 However, you summoned women to be at your side
and became subject to them as a result of your bodily appetites.
20 You soiled your reputation
and sullied your family line,
bringing wrath upon your children
and grief at your folly,
21 because the empire was split in two,
and in Ephraim a rebel kingdom arose. [n]
22 But the LORD never ceases his mercy
or allows any of his works to perish.
He will never wipe out the posterity of his chosen one
or destroy the line of the one who loved him.
And so he gave a remnant to Jacob
and let one root of David survive. [o]

Rehoboam and Jeroboam*

23 Solomon finally rested with his ancestors
and left behind to succeed him one of his sons,
prone to folly and lacking in sense,
REHOBOAM, whose policies caused the people to revolt.
Then JEROBOAM, the son of Nebat, led Israel into sin
and provided Ephraim with its wicked course. [p]
24 Their sins increased more and more
until they were driven into exile from their native land.
25 For they attempted every kind of wickedness
until punishment overtook them.

CHAPTER 48

In the Northern Kingdom: Elijah and Elisha*

1 Then arose like a fire the prophet ELIJAH,
whose words were like a flaming torch. [q]
2 He brought a famine on the people,
and by his zeal he decimated their number.
3 By the word of the LORD he shut up the heavens
and three times he called down fire from the skies. [r]
4 How glorious you were, Elijah, in your miracles!
Whose glory is equal to yours?
5 You raised a corpse from death
and from the netherworld, by the word of the Most High. [s]
6 You dragged down kings to their destruction,
and also nobles from their sickbeds. [t]
7 You heard a rebuke at Sinai
and avenging judgments at Horeb. [u]
8 You anointed kings to effect retribution
and prophets to succeed you. [v]
9 You were taken up to the heavens in a whirlwind of fire,
in a chariot drawn by fiery horses. [w]
10 It is written that you are destined at the appointed time
to allay the wrath of God before it erupts in fury,

l 1 Ki 5:1-5.—m 14-18: 1 Ki 3:1-28; 5:9-14; 10:14-28.—n 1 Ki 12:1ff.—o 2 Sam 7:15; Ps 89:34ff.—p 1 Ki 11:43; 12:13, 21; 13:34; 2 Ki 17:6ff.—q 1 Ki 17:1.—r 1 Ki 17:1; 18:38; 2 Ki 1:9-14.—s 1 Ki 17:22.—t 1 Ki 21:19; 2 Ki 1:17.—u 1 Ki 19:8ff.—v 1 Ki 19:15ff.—w 2 Ki 2:11.

47:14 *Like an overflowing river!:* Hebrew reads: "like the Nile."

47:18 *In the name of the LORD God who is called the God of Israel:* the reference is to the name "Jedidiah," which means "beloved of the LORD" and is used of Israel in Jer 11:15.

47:23-25 Solomon's son and his rival Jeroboam consummated the division facilitated by the despotic needs of Solomon (1 Ki 12). Moreover, because of David, the Lord keeps his promise to his descendants. The impiety of Jeroboam and his successors led to the ruin of the northern kingdom in 721 B.C.

48:1-15 In accord with a belief widely held in Israel, Elijah was to come at the time of the Messiah; verse 11 seems to refer to it (see Mal 3:23; Mt 17:10-13). The word of the Prophets was not enough to maintain the fidelity of the northern kingdom, which will fall in 721 B.C. Only the little kingdom of Judah will subsist while waiting to experience exile.

to turn the hearts of parents back to their children
and to restore the tribes of Jacob. [x]
11 Blessed is he who will see you
and those who have fallen asleep in love,
for we also shall certainly live. *
12 After Elijah had been enveloped in a whirlwind,
ELISHA was filled with his spirit.
[He wrought twice as many signs,
and marvels by the utterance of his mouth.] *
Throughout his lifetime no ruler ever caused him to tremble,
nor was anyone able to intimidate him in the slightest. [y]
13 No task was too difficult for him, [z]
and even after his death his body continued to prophesy from beyond the grave.
14 In his life he accomplished wonders,
and in death also his deeds were marvelous.
15 Despite all this, the people did not repent,
nor did they give up their sins
until they were carried off as captives from their land
and scattered over all the earth. [a]
16 The people who were left were few in number,
under a ruler from the house of David.
Some of them did what was right,
but others continued to sin, and to a far greater extent.

Hezekiah, the Faithful King, and Isaiah, the Great Prophet*

17 HEZEKIAH fortified his city
and brought water into it;
with iron tools he cut through the rock
and built cisterns to hold the water. [b]
18 During his reign Sennacherib invaded the country
and sent Rabshakeh, * his commander.
He shook his fist against Zion,
and in his arrogance he boasted loudly. [c]
19 As a result, the people's hearts were unnerved and their hands trembled;
they were in anguish, like that of women in labor.
20 But they called upon the merciful LORD,
stretching out their hands toward him.
In heaven the Holy One swiftly heard their cries,
and he delivered them through ISAIAH. [d]
21 God struck the camp of the Assyrians,
and his angel annihilated them. [e]
22 For Hezekiah did what was pleasing to the LORD
and held firmly steadfast to the ways of David, his ancestor,
as was commanded by the prophet Isaiah,
whose visions were true and trustworthy.
23 During his lifetime he caused the sun to go backward
and he prolonged the life of the king. [f]
24 [g] In the power of his spirit he saw the end of times,
and he comforted the mourners in Zion.
25 He revealed the future to the end of the ages
and hidden things long before they occurred.

CHAPTER 49

Josiah, Last of the Good Kings*

1 The memory of JOSIAH is like blended incense
made lasting by the skill of a perfumer.
It is as sweet as honey to every mouth
or like music at a banquet. [h]
2 He followed the right course by reforming the people

x Mal 3:23-24; Lk 1:17.—y 2 Ki 2:9; 3:13; 6:13-16; 6:31—7:2.—z 13f: 2 Ki 13:21.—a 2 Ki 15:29; 18:11f.—b 2 Ki 20:20; 2 Chr 32:3ff, 30.—c 2 Ki 18:13ff; Isa 36:1ff.—d 2 Ki 19:20; Isa 37:21ff.—e 2 Ki 19:35; Isa 37:36.—f 2 Ki 20:11; Isa 38:8.—g 24f: 2 Ki 20:17; Isa 40:1ff; 42:9; 46:10; 48:6; 61:2.—h Sir 32:5f; 2 Ki 22:1; 2 Chr 34:1; Prov 24:13.

48:11 Text is uncertain. In our arrangement, the author states that those who will see Elijah when he returns, as well as those who have fallen asleep in love, will live forever. The defective Hebrew text alludes only to Elijah's disappearance (2 Ki 2:10).

48:12c-d Hebrew; lacking in Greek.

48:17-25 All seems lost when in 701 B.C., Sennacherib besieges Jerusalem. But the prophet Isaiah adjures the king not to weaken and to trust in God. The Assyrian army suddenly lifts the siege, doubtless because of being decimated by an epidemic (2 Ki 18:17—19:37; Isa 36–37). At the end of this passage, allusion is made to the second part of Isaiah, the Book of Consolation (Isa 40).

48:18 *Rabshakeh:* this is not a proper name but the title of the epic song.

49:1-3 Josiah became famous for the religious reform that he undertook when the Book of Deuteronomy was found in the temple (2 Ki 22f).

and eliminating loathsome and abominable practices.
3 He kept his heart fixed on God,
and in lawless times he made godliness prevail.

The Fate of Judah and the Word of the Prophets

4* Except for David, Hezekiah, and Josiah,
they were all great sinners,
for they abandoned the law of the Most High;
so the kings of Judah came to an end.
5 They handed over their power to others
and their glory to a foreign nation.
6 The chosen city, the city of the sanctuary, was set on fire,
and its streets were left desolate,
7 as JEREMIAH had predicted.
For they had mistreated him,
even though while still in the womb he had been consecrated a prophet
to uproot, pull down, and destroy,
but also to build and plant. [i]

In the Exile and the Restoration

8 EZEKIEL was privileged to behold a vision of glory,
which God showed to him above the chariot of the cherubim. [j]
9 He also referred to JOB,
who always persevered in the path of justice. [k]
10 May the bones of the TWELVE PROPHETS
send forth new life from where they lie,
for they gave new strength to the people of Jacob
and saved them with confident hope. [l]

The Pioneers of the Jewish Restoration*

11[m] How can we find suitable words to praise ZERUBBABEL,
who was like a signet ring on the right hand?
12 So too was JESHUA, the son of Jozadak;
in their days they rebuilt the house
and raised a temple holy to the LORD,
destined for everlasting glory.
13 Great too is the memory of NEHEMIAH,
who reconstructed our fallen walls,
restored our defensive structures,
and rebuilt our ruined houses. [n]

Above Every Other Living Creature Was Adam*

14 No one has been * created on earth equal to ENOCH,
for he was taken up from the earth in bodily form.
15 Nor has anyone ever been born who was like JOSEPH,
the ruler of his brothers and the foundation of his people; *
even his bones were cared for. [o]
16 SHEM and SETH * were the recipients of great honor,
but above every other living creature was ADAM. [p]

CHAPTER 50

Praise of the High Priest Simon*

1 It was the high priest SIMON, son of Onias,
in whose lifetime the house was repaired
and in whose days the temple was fortified.
2 He also laid the foundations for the high double walls
that enclosed the temple precincts.
3 In his time a water cistern was constructed,
a pool with the vastness of the sea.
4 His concern was to ward off disaster from his people,
and he fortified the city against siege.
5 How glorious he was, with the people thronging around him,

---

i Jer 1:5, 10.—j Ezek 1:4ff.—k Ezek 14:14, 20.—l Sir 46:12.—m 11f: Ezr 3:2; Hag 1:12; Zec 3:1.—n Neh 1:1; 3:1.—o Gen 37–50; Ex 13:19; Jos 24:32.—p Gen 1:27; 4:25f; Wis 10:1f.

49:4-10 The author casts a severe judgment on the heads of Judah and excepts only three of the more remarkable kings. They were unable to maintain their faith above everything. But from the collapse to the restoration, the Prophets make the word of God resound, condemning sin and offering consolation in trials. Indeed, this word is relevant to the author's contemporaries.

49:11-13 We are at the morrow of the Exile; the restoration was long and difficult. In these times when Judaism was born, a few names emerge.

49:14-16 The praise of the ancients concludes with a brief return to the age of the patriarchs and the origins; in a word, one glorifies the father of human beings. Luke will also trace Jesus' lineage back to Adam, the father of humanity (Lk 3:28).

49:14 *No one has been:* Hebrew reads: "Few have been."

49:15 *The ruler . . . people:* lacking in Greek.

49:16 *SHEM and SETH:* Hebrew adds: "and Enosh."

50:1-24 To the review of the glories of the past, the author has added—possibly at a later date—a long compliment in honor of the high priest Simon II (220–195 B.C.), whom he seems to have known. The discourse evokes the works realized by the pontiff but above all, in the exercise of his religious functions.

as he emerged from behind the veil of the sanctuary.
6 He was like the morning star shining among the clouds,
like the full moon at the festal season,
7 like the sun shining on the temple of the Most High,
like the rainbow appearing in a cloudy sky, [q]
8 like a rose in springtime,
like a lily by a spring of water,
like a green shoot on Lebanon on a summer's day,
9 like incense set afire in the censer,
like a vessel of beaten gold
embellished with every kind of precious stone,
10 like an olive tree laden with fruit,
like a cypress reaching to the clouds.
11 When he put on his magnificent robes
and clothed himself in his garments of splendor,
as he went up to the holy altar,
he brought majestic glory to the court of the sanctuary. [r]

12 When he received the portions from the hands of the priests
while he stood by the hearth of the altar,
with his brethren encircling him like a garland,
he was like a young cedar of Lebanon
surrounded by the trunks of palm trees.
13 All the sons of Aaron in their splendor
held the LORD's offerings in their hands
as they stood in the presence of the whole assembly of Israel.
14 When he had completed the rites at the altar
and arranged the sacrificial offerings
to the Almighty, the Most High,
15 he stretched forth his hand for the cup
and poured out a libation from the juice of the grape,
pouring it out at the foot of the altar,
a sweet-smelling fragrance to the Most High, the king of all.
16 Then the sons of Aaron would shout
and blow their trumpets of beaten metal,
sounding a mighty fanfare
as a reminder before the Most High. [s]
17 Then all together the people
would quickly fall prostrate to the ground
in adoration of their LORD,
the Almighty, God Most High.

18 Then the choir would chant hymns of praise
that were sweet, melodious, and full-toned,
19 while the people were pleading with the LORD Most High
and praying before the Merciful One,
until the service of the LORD was finished
and the liturgical ceremony was completed.
20 Then Simon would come down and raise his hands
over the whole assembly of the Israelites
to pronounce the blessing of the LORD with his lips
and to glory in his name. [t]
21 And once again the people would bow down in worship
to receive the blessing of the Most High.

22 And now, bless the God of all
who works great wonders everywhere on the earth,
who has raised us up from our birth
and who deals with us according to his mercy.
23 May he grant us joy in our hearts,
and may there be peace in our days
in Israel, for all time to come.
24 May his mercy toward us be confirmed,
and may he deliver us in our times.

Hereditary Foes of Israel*

25 My whole being detests two nations,
while a third is not a nation at all:
26 those who live on the mountains of Samaria, the Philistines,
and the foolish people who dwell in Shechem. [u]

The Author's Signature and Farewell*

27 Instruction in understanding and knowledge
I have written in this book,

q Pss 44:4; 74:12; 98:6; 145:1; Isa 6:5; Jer 46:8.—r Sir 45:8-12; Ex 28:2-5; 39:1-36.—s Num 15:5.—t Num 6:23-26.—u 2 Ki 17:24; Ps 137:7; Ezek 25:12-14; Jn 4:9.

50:25-26 It is a question here of the Edomites, Philistines, and Samaritans, whose quarrels with the Jews are indicated, notably in the Books of Kings, Ezra, and Nehemiah. *Shechem:* a city of Samaria.

50:27-29 The author can give only good wishes to his eventual readers.

I, Jesus, son of Sirach, son of Eleazar, of Jerusalem,
whose heart has poured forth a fountain of wisdom.
28 Blessed is the one who devotes himself to these things;
if he takes them to heart, wisdom will be his.
29 And if he puts them into practice, he will be able to cope with anything,
for the light of the LORD is their path.
[He gives wisdom to devout men.
Blessed be the LORD forever. Amen. Amen.] *

V: ADDITIONS*

CHAPTER 51

A: Prayer of Thanksgiving

1 I give thanks to you, O LORD and King,
and praise you, O God my Savior.
I give thanks to your name, [v]
2 for you have been my protector and my support.
You have rescued me from destruction,
from the snare laid by a slanderous tongue,
and from lips that fabricate falsehood.
In the face of my adversaries you came to my aid; [w]
3 in the greatness of your mercy and of your name you rescued me:
from the gnashing teeth waiting to devour me,
from the hands of those who sought my life,
and from the many ordeals I endured, [x]
4 from the choking fire that enveloped me,
and from the fire that I had not kindled, [y]
5 from the deep recesses of the netherworld,
from deceiving lips and lying words [z]
6 and a treacherous slander delivered to the king.
I was at the point of death,
and my soul was hovering near the depths of the netherworld. [a]
7 I was surrounded on every side
and there was no one to help me.
I looked for human assistance
but there was none.
8 Then I remembered your mercy, O LORD,
and your kind deeds from the ages.
For you deliver those who put their trust in you
and rescue them from the power of their enemies.
9 Therefore, from the earth I sent up my plea,
begging to be rescued from death.
10 I cried out: "LORD, you are my Father,
and the champion of my salvation;
do not abandon me in my days of ordeal,
for I am helpless when confronted by the arrogant.
I will praise your name continually
and sing hymns of thanksgiving." [b]
11 Thereupon my prayer was heard,
for you saved me from destruction
and delivered me from my desperate plight.
12 For this reason, I thank you and I praise you;
I bless the name of the LORD. *

v Ps 138:1.—w Deut 32:10; Pss 3:2; 56:10; 91:3; 124:2.—x Pss 5:8; 40:5f; 141:9; Prov 18:7; 22:25.—y Ps 66:12; Dan 3:24-94.—z Job 13:4, 7; Ps 71:20; Jon 2:3.—a Pss 88:4; 94:17.—b Job 30:3; 38:27; Pss 89:27; 145:1f.

50:29c-d Added by some early MSS.

51:1-30 Two passages are added to the original work, a prayer of thanksgiving and a poem about wisdom. They exhibit a tone of trust and a manner of composition that set them off from the style of the original author.

51:12 After verse 12, the Hebrew adds the following psalm of praise:

Give thanks to the LORD, for he is good,
for his mercy endures forever.
Give thanks to the God of praises,
for his mercy endures forever.
Give thanks to the Guardian of Israel,
for his mercy endures forever.
Give thanks to the Creator of all things,
for his mercy endures forever.
Give thanks to the Redeemer of Israel,
for his mercy endures forever.
Give thanks to him who gathers the dispersed of Israel,
for his mercy endures forever.
Give thanks to him who rebuilt his city and his sanctuary,
for his mercy endures forever.
Give thanks to him who causes a horn to sprout for the house of David,
for his mercy endures forever.
Give thanks to him who has chosen the sons of Zadok to serve as priests,
for his mercy endures forever.
Give thanks to the Shield of Abraham,
for his mercy endures forever.
Give thanks to the Rock of Isaac,
for his mercy endures forever.
Give thanks to the Mighty One of Jacob,
for his mercy endures forever.
Give thanks to him who has chosen Zion,
for his mercy endures forever.
Give thanks to the King of the kings of kings,
for his mercy endures forever.
He has raised up a horn for his people,
praise for all his faithful ones.
For the children of Israel, the people close to him,
praise the LORD!

B: Invitation to Wisdom*

13 While I was still young, before I set off on my travels,
I openly sought wisdom in my prayers.[c]
14 Outside the temple I prayed for her,
and I will seek her until my death.
15 From the first blossoming to the ripening of her grape,
she has been my heart's delight.
My foot has continued unswervingly on a level path;
I have sought her since my youth.
16 I inclined my ear slightly and received her,
and I profited thereby with much instruction.
17 Thanks to her I have advanced,
and I will give glory to him who has granted me wisdom.
18 I resolved to put into practice what I had learned;
I earnestly pursued goodness, and I will never be put to shame.
19 With all my strength I strove to possess wisdom,
and I was scrupulous in keeping the law.

I stretched out my hands on high
and lamented how little I really knew of her.
20 I set my heart on possessing wisdom,
and by keeping myself pure I found her.
With her I gained understanding immediately;
therefore, I will never be forsaken.[d]
21 I yearned to discover her from the very core of my being;
therefore, I have gained a prize possession.
22 As my reward the LORD has granted me eloquence,
which I will use to sing his praises.
23 Come close to me, you who are unlearned,
and take up your lodging in my school.[e]
24 Why do you complain that you still lack these things,
and why do you continue to endure such great thirst?
25 I have opened my mouth and spoken:
Acquire wisdom for yourselves without cost.[f]
26 Put your neck under her yoke,
and allow your souls to receive instruction;
it is close by if you wish to find it.[g]
27 See for yourselves that my labors were minimal,
but my reward of serenity has been great.
28 You may expend a great deal of silver to acquire instruction,
but, as a result, you will gain much gold.*
29 May your soul rejoice in the mercy of the LORD,
and may you never be ashamed to praise him.
30 Do your work in the appointed time,
and in his own time God will give you your reward.[h]

c Sir 6:18; 34:10; Prov 8:17; Wis 8:2.—d Prov 4:6.—e Prov 8:5.—f Sir 6:19; Prov 4:5-7; Isa 55:1.—g Sir 6:24.—h Sir 1:1–10:26; 2:8; Job 34:11; Jn 9:4.

51:13-30 At the end of the wisdom literature, it is good to reread this last text. The search for a good life and right thinking is a work that demands one's whole existence. The road seems long and arduous, but it is a road to happiness. Thus, the author invites his readers to become his companions in wisdom.

51:28 *You . . . gold:* Hebrew reads: "Hear but a little of my instruction, / and through me you will acquire silver and gold."

THE PROPHETIC BOOKS

The prophets were chosen by God to speak in his name to the chosen people, rebuking and threatening them when they moved away from the Lord and encouraging them with visions of a happy future when they were being tried.

The Bible speaks of prophets as early as the time of Samuel (11th century B.C.). But the prophets who were most influential as spiritual leaders of the people were those who lived between the ninth and the fifth centuries B.C. No writing has come down to us from some of these men, for example, Elijah and Elisha. There are, however, sixteen whose oracles and prophecies have been preserved. Among these sixteen, four are known as "major prophets": Isaiah, Jeremiah, Ezekiel, and Daniel. The other twelve are called "minor," only because of the shortness of the Books bearing their names: Hosea, Joel, Amos, Obadiah, Jonah, Micah, Nahum, Habakkuk, Zephaniah, Haggai, Zechariah, and Malachi.

Old Testament Prophetism

The word "prophet" is derived from the Greek *prophêtês*, which signifies not so much someone who foretells the future as someone who "speaks in the name of God." It corresponds to the Hebrew word *nabi*, which means a herald, mouthpiece, or messenger (of the divinity). Everything can be the subject of their words, since the word of God has no limits.

From its beginnings Israel knew persons endowed with the prophetic spirit. One such was the great Moses, to whom God spoke "mouth to mouth" (Num 12:8). The prophetic period in the full and proper sense begins, however, with Samuel. For almost six centuries (ca. 1050–540 B.C.) prophets succeed one another with striking frequency. We are now in the period of the monarchy, which Samuel inaugurated against his will and judgment (1 Sam 8f). At David's side was Nathan, a kind of court prophet, who had the courage to make the king admit his sin (2 Sam 12) and who, above all, had for his mission to foretell the future of David's dynasty, in a passage which the believing people would repeatedly reread (2 Sam 7). At this time the monarchy was regarded as a gift from God.

At the death of Solomon (ca. 931 B.C.), when the northern kingdom went into schism, we meet Ahijah of Shiloh (1 Ki 11:29; 14:1f), who predicts the division of the people and even dares curse, in God's name, the king whom he himself had acknowledged a few years before. But no one can be compared with the great figure of Elijah, the prophet of God who accepts no compromises and whose motto is: "By the life of the Lord, in whose presence I stand." His protest against the mingling of the various pagan religions has unparalleled power: it rouses the people, it demands that the people really choose and live out the covenant. Elijah confronts the mighty, but he also knows discouragement. He experiences a mystical meeting with God, the Absolute, who calls for justice, brotherhood, righteousness, and respect (1 Ki 17; 2 Ki 2).

Of no less importance in the development of Israel was Elijah's successor, Elisha, who is regarded as a teacher and father by the group of inspired persons to which he seems to belong (see 2 Ki 2:12; 4:8-38; 6:1f, 12, 21). This man of God, whom the people visited and consulted (2 Ki 4:22), left behind him an exceptional reputation as a miracle worker. He also played a dominant role in the political development of the northern kingdom.

The Prophetic Books

Around 750 B.C., a new period began that saw writing prophets, the men who authored the prophetic books of the Bible. The first testimonies to this phenomenon go back to the period of Amos, Hosea, Micah, and Isaiah, a generation of prophets who lived a hundred years after Elisha. Not only the record of their activities, but above all, their message is contained in collections of oracles.

The oracles are transmitted in the form of poetry that is rich in images and fine rhythms; the stories about the life and activities of the prophets are in prose. Initially there may have been, on the one hand, collections of oracles and, on the other, collections of stories, which editors gradually combined to form books. We have, then, and this is the important thing, both word and witness.

They communicated their message through preaching (see Jer 7:1-15) or through symbolic actions (see Isa 20; Jer 13; 19; Ezek 4–5). Sometimes the message was immediately written down (see Jer 36). The poetic form helped people remember it; perhaps it was sung.

A prophet was someone called. He did not choose but was chosen (Am 7:10-17). The prophets were seized by God and his message, and they sacrificed themselves to their word, their faith, their inspiration. Jeremiah, a solitary, carried his calling like a terrible weight (Jer 15:17; 20:7). We have the impression that the hearts of these men were shaken by what they saw and understood: the perverseness of human beings, the greatness and love of God.

We do not have their message in verbatim form; it has reached us as interpreted by disciples and through the patchwork of later editors. Prophecy continued after the great representatives of it; the word entrusted to them is always a word to be studied and assimilated, a word to be interpreted for the present time.

Historical Outline

Prophecy is a widespread phenomenon in the history of Israel, and we shall never know the names of all those who spoke in God's name. The prophetism shown in the biblical books can, however, be located within four phases.

a) *Assyrian domination.* Toward the middle of the eighth century, Judah and Israel thought themselves secure and looked to their political and economic future with assurance. But internal decadence was undermining the people. Then, suddenly, the Assyrian conqueror appeared. The northern kingdom went under. Samaria fell in 721 B.C., and the enemy besieged Jerusalem, while imposing its domination on the kingdom of Judah. Amos and Hosea, Micah and Isaiah rose up to denounce false securities, the deceptiveness of policies based on human alliances, and the idolatry and injustice that were hiding behind the law and tradition. Amos called for justice; Hosea defended God's love; Micah demanded righteousness; Isaiah proclaimed faith. The covenant consisted primarily in being true to these essential things.

b) *Babylonian threat.* The pressure from Assyria lessened in the second half of the seventh century, and in the land of Judah, King Josiah was able to undertake a reform that was perhaps initiated by the prophet Zephaniah. Then a new power arose: Babylon, which annihilated the Assyrians and demolished the city of Carchemish in 605 B.C. Liberation seemed to have come to the Middle East, an expectation reflected in the song of Nahum. But the new overlord soon imposed his own law on the many small states. Habakkuk felt all the injustice of this, even though he knew that his people deserved punishment.

The most fascinating prophet of this period is Jeremiah, who attacked a religion from which the heart was absent. He raised the alarm and endured the great suffering to which his "confessions" bear witness, but, like a living prefiguration of Christ, he also announced a new covenant based not on institutions but on the hearts of people. A contemporary of Jeremiah but living in exile, Ezekiel suffered because of his people's sins and lamented them. Other voices, those of Obadiah and the Lamentations, also preserve the memory of that season of bitterness and of hope.

c) *Exile.* This was a time for meditation, purification, and deeper understanding. The prophetic writings circulated among scattered groups and gradually became books. Isaiah, Jeremiah, and Ezekiel asked the reasons for the destruction but also offered motives for renewed hope.

Other prophets spoke to the scattered communities; these men were perhaps less brilliant, but what faith we see in the author of the second part of Isaiah! What hope in the singer of the return from Exile! God's plan remained unchanged despite all the failures! In addition, another prophet would come, a mysterious servant, who is humble and suffers, but as a victim of love.

d) *Return from Exile.* The little groups of survivors who returned to Jerusalem, lacking everything and having no political pretensions, would not be helped by issuing loud denunciations of their enemies. The important thing was to help find the daily courage to believe, to understand the law more fully, and to recreate the institutions essential to a living religion. The third part of Isaiah sings of the new temple; Haggai and Zechariah instill courage for building the future; Joel urges a collective conversion; Malachi criticizes mediocrity and inertia; Jonah proclaims the freedom of God, who wants all human beings to be saved.

After this, prophecy ceases, and the silence is felt as a source of suffering. For two centuries the little community in Judah lives in quiet seclusion. It is at this time that the collection of prophetic books took on its definitive form. Followers of the prophets added supplements; later writings were brought together under the name of Baruch, Jeremiah's secretary. Soon, however, believers found both their lives and their faith threatened. The Maccabees revolted (1 Mac—2 Mac) and circulated stories of hope (Tobit, Judith, Esther). The resistance of minds and hearts found expression in the impassioned Book of Daniel.

The Prophets and Christ

Above all else, the prophets asserted monotheism against tendencies to idolatry. They fought against moral corruption and social injustices and defended the weak, the poor, and the oppressed. They foretold divine punishments, but they also proclaimed a radiant hope. The sublime figure of a descendant of David would bring the fulfillment of the greatest promises. The Savior of Israel, and even of all humanity, would come—and his presence is already described. The prophets give him various names: Immanuel, Servant of Yahweh, Shoot of David, Messiah.

In the prophets, then, the Old Testament becomes, in the fullest sense, an announcement of and preparation for the New. John the Baptist is a prophet like the ancient prophets of Israelite history, and he displays all the characteristic marks. But he is also a living symbol, a guarantee that the awaited Messiah has finally come and is present (Lk 7:24-27; Jn 1:19-27, 35-36). The Old Testament has come to an end. Jesus of Nazareth is the one whom the prophets foretold; in him their prophecies of hope and expectation are fulfilled, but so are their prophecies of suffering and martyrdom. Jesus will say to the disciples on the road to Emmaus: "Everything written about me in the law of Moses, the Prophets, and the Psalms must be fulfilled" (Lk 24:44).

"The Law and the Prophets": the inseparable pair that stand for the entire Old Testament in its expectation of Jesus, the Son of God, the Word who "became flesh and dwelt among us" (Jn 1:14; see 2 Mac 15:9; Mt 11:13; Lk 24:27).

"Then one of the seraphim flew to me, holding in his hand a burning coal. . . . He touched my mouth with it and said: . . . 'your guilt has been removed' " *(Isa 6:6-7).*

THE BOOK OF ISAIAH

Faith and Events

Born into the Jerusalem nobility, Isaiah received God's call in the very temple of the Lord, at the end of the reign of Uzziah, that is, around 740 B.C.

His Book has preserved for us a moving account of this call (ch. 6). The prophet then immediately proclaims his message with its strikingly fresh and incisive tone, its noble poetic expression, and its brilliant images.

Isaiah exercised his prophetic ministry for about fifty years. A sad period! He saw the growing threat from the Assyrians, as well as the fall of Samaria and the northern kingdom in 721 B.C. He would go down in history as the man who kept up the hopes of the people during the siege of Jerusalem in 701 B.C. These were the difficult years in which Judah lost its temporary prosperity, and the independence of the nation was diminished day by day.

Amid all these events Isaiah proclaimed what was, for him, a dazzling certainty: the greatness and holiness of God. Even while involved in the feverish labors of human beings, he returned continually to his practical conviction that God alone matters. That is faith! It, and it alone, suffices. Strengthened by this assurance, Isaiah confronted the mighty, since they were primarily responsible for the political and religious disintegration.

This man of faith saw only too clearly that Judah could not find its salvation in alliances that were made and canceled at the whim of circumstance. It was in themselves and in their faith and fidelity that the people had to find the moral strength to face the impending dangers; nothing could be counted on except the Covenant of the Lord when put into practice.

As an ardent patriot, Isaiah believed in the perpetuity of Jerusalem and in the dynastic line established by David. Whatever might happen, the posterity of David and the people could not perish for good. The Covenant remained, and a "remnant" would survive to carry the promise of the Lord to all the nations. Inspired by this conviction, Isaiah became the singer of the Messiah, who would be God's authentic representative and on whom the Spirit would rest.

Threats and promises sum up the conflictual relationship of a people with its own age. Those pronounced by Isaiah were collected by his disciples and form the basic theme of the first part of the Book (chs. 1–39). Indeed, not everything in these thirty-nine chapters is from the prophet himself, but it is impossible to be deceived in some passages; Isaiah can be recognized by the torrent of language, the new and expressive images, and the tone that both provokes the readers and wins them over. Due to his way of reproaching and convincing and to his farsighted announcement of the Messiah, he is the greatest of the prophets. His message continued after him in Judah.

For several decades his disciples repeated his message and adapted it to new situations, while also accepting the influence of other prophets such as Jeremiah and while themselves in their turn being tested by what history was teaching them. The mysterious prophet of the Exile, who is known as "Second Isaiah," is faithful to the ideas of his distant predecessor and, over a century later, sings of the radiant and triumphal reign of God (chs. 40–55, part II). He is not full of terrifying threats, but his tone is more melancholy. He speaks words of consolation in a time of despair. In these chapters, known as the "Book of Consolation," his oracles, exhortations, and hymns are gathered together, but not in any particular order. At the climax of a testing that gives no sign of ending, he, or one of his successors, will discover the unforgettable face of the suffering just man, the authentic servant of God who takes upon himself the failures and sins of humanity, to the point of being crushed by them. No one can any longer ignore the passages known as the "Servant Songs," which seem at times like anticipations of the Gospel.

Chapters 56–66 (part III) bring together scattered fragments. The setting which they suggest is post-Exilic. We feel the disappointment of the repatriates as they clash with the people who had remained behind and who have been contaminated by pagan cults. The repatriates manage with difficulty to regain their place, thanks to the concern of a foreign protector. The anonymous prophets who speak in these chapters address the repatriates, encouraging the more fervent and struggling against the religious negligence of the others; they proclaim the demands of interior religion and describe the glories of the new Jerusalem that is being prepared.

The Jewish tradition (see Sir 48:23f) and later, the Christian, have always considered Isaiah to form a single whole.

The Book of Isaiah may be divided as follows:

- *A: The Book of Judgment (1:1—39:8)*
  - *I: Indictment of Israel and Judah (1:1—5:30)*
  - *II: The Book of Immanuel (6:1—12:6)*
  - *III: Oracles among the Pagan Nations (13:1—23:18)*
  - *IV: Apocalypse of Isaiah (24:1—27:13)*
  - *V: The Lord Saves Israel and Judah (28:1—33:24)*
  - *VI: The Lord, Zion's Defender (34:1—35:10)*
  - *VII: Historical Appendix (36:1—39:8)*
- *B: The Book of Consolation (40:1—66:24)*
  - *I: The Lord's Majesty in Israel's Liberation (40:1—48:22)*
  - *II: Expiation of Sin, Redemption of Israel (49:1—55:13)*
  - *III: Return of the First Captives (56:1—66:24)*

A: The Book of Judgment*

I: INDICTMENT OF ISRAEL AND JUDAH*

CHAPTER 1

The Sins of Israel. 1 The vision of Isaiah, the son of Amoz, concerning Judah and Jerusalem which he received during the reigns of Uzziah, Jotham, Ahaz, and Hezekiah, kings of Judah. [a]

2 * Listen, O heavens, and pay close attention, O earth,
for the LORD is speaking.
I reared children and brought them up,
but they have rebelled against me. [b]
3 An ox knows its owner
and the donkey its master's stall,
but Israel does not know,
my people do not understand.

4 You are a sinful nation,
a people weighed down with iniquity,
a race of evildoers
whose children are corrupt;
you have forsaken the LORD,
despised the Holy One of Israel,
and turned your backs on him.

5 * Why do you continue to seek further beatings?
Why do you persist in your rebellion?
Your entire head is sick
and your whole heart is faint. [c]
6 From the sole of your foot to your head
there is not a single healthy area
nothing but bruises and welts and open sores
that have not been drained or bandaged
or soothed with ointment.
7 Your country is a desolate waste,
and fire has destroyed your cities.
Before your very eyes
foreigners have devoured your land
and left it as desolate
as Sodom after it had been overthrown.

8 Daughter Zion* is left
like a shack in a vineyard,
like a shed in a field of cucumbers,
like a besieged city.
9 If the LORD of hosts*
had not left us a few survivors,
we would have become like Sodom
and been like Gomorrah. [d]

10 * Hear the word of the LORD,
you rulers of Sodom.
Listen to the teaching of our God,
you people of Gomorrah.
11 What do I care about your unceasing sacrifices?
says the LORD.

---

a Isa 2:1.—b Deut 32:1, 5f; Mic 1:2.—c Isa 31:6.—d Gen 45:7; Rom 9:29.

1:1—39:8 This first part of the Book presents Isaiah himself and his message, although some sections are clearly from a later date, such as chapters 24–27; 34–35, which are often called "the Isaiah apocalypses." But the oracles in the collection do not follow a strict chronological order.

In the midst of political upheaval, Isaiah proclaimed the greatness of God, the "Holy One of Israel," who governs the world. He opposed King Ahaz, who nonetheless called on Assyria for help and came under its control; he opposed Hezekiah, who wanted to defy Assyria by allying himself with Egypt. Such insecure and shifting alliances could do nothing to change the fate of the people of God; the nation would, however, be safe if it learned to emphasize above all else its covenant with God, in which justice was a supreme value. Judah should have found within itself the courage for a moral renewal. Yet the people of the covenant remain strong thanks above all to their faith.

1:1—12:6 *The vision of Isaiah:* thus begins the book; Isaiah in fact remains an unparalleled seer in the history of humanity. The title, "Vision," applies above all to the first twelve chapters. Nothing, whether the powers of this world, or external events, or domestic intrigues, can turn the prophet's gaze from the holiness of God, before whom everything else disappears. In this entire body of oracles, we can distinguish several collections: oracles uttered in the most diverse circumstances during fifty years of prophetic ministry from the last days of Uzziah (740 B.C.) to the death of Hezekiah (687 B.C.).

The first five chapters perhaps correspond most closely to the beginning of Isaiah's activity; the remainder belong to the course of the Syro-Ephraimite war against Judah in 732 B.C. It is true that some of the verses look more to the northern kingdom (9:7) and to Assyria (10:5), but on the whole, the oracles are addressed to the people of Judah. The "Book of Immanuel" that begins in chapter 6 is doubtless the jewel of Isaiah's work and has won him the title of supreme prophetic foreteller of the coming of Jesus. The Advent liturgy draws upon these chapters.

1:2-31 Isaiah must denounce decadence and open the eyes of those who no longer want to see. He first takes on himself the suffering involved in the fate of his country by remaining in solidarity with the very people whom he accuses and even severely indicts.

1:5-9 The enemy, perhaps Sennacherib (in 701 B.C.), has ravaged the realm and taken many inhabitants captive. The country has suffered a deadly blow. Only Jerusalem, the *Daughter Zion*, has been spared.

1:8 *Daughter Zion:* a personification of Jerusalem. *Shack:* huts for keeping the grapes were built among the vines during the grape harvest.

1:9 *LORD of hosts:* literally, "Lord of armies (Hebrew, *sabaoth*)," indicates that the God of Israel is master of everything, from the armed hosts of Israel to the stars and every celestial power. *Sodom* and *Gomorrah* are cities constantly recalled (even in Mt 10:15) as an example of moral depravity that calls down punishment from God (see Gen 18:16—19:29).

1:10-20 Right in the temple of Jerusalem, young Isaiah raises his voice in denunciation of hypocrisy in worship. He compares the leaders and people to the most dissolute sinners of Sodom and Gomorrah (Gen 18:16—19:29). The diatribe against hypocritical worship occurs frequently in the Bible (Pss 40:6-8; 50:5-15; Jer 6:20; Am 5:21-27; Hos 6:6; Mic 6:5-8). We already think of the scathing words of Jesus against Pharisaism (Mt 7:21) and of his forceful action against the sellers in the temple (Lk 19:45-46; Jn 2:13-22).

I am weary of burnt offerings of rams
and the fat of well-fed animals.
I derive no delight in the blood
of bulls and lambs and goats. [e]

12 When you come into my presence,
who has asked you to present such offerings?
Never again trample my courts!
13 To bring me offerings is futile;
I regard your incense as loathsome.
New moons and Sabbaths and sacred assemblies—
I cannot tolerate your iniquity that accompanies them. [f]
14 I loathe your new moons and your festivals;
they have become a burden to me
and I can no longer endure bearing them.
15 When you stretch out your hands,*
I will turn away my eyes from you.
Even if you pray endlessly,
I will not listen,
for your hands are covered with blood. [g]
16 Wash yourselves and become clean;
remove your evil deeds
far from my sight.
Cease to do evil
17 and learn to do good.
Pursue justice and rescue the oppressed;
listen to the plea of the orphan*
and defend the widow.

18 Come now and let us discuss this,
says the LORD.
Though your sins are like scarlet,
they shall be like snow.
Though they are as red as crimson,
they shall become as white as wool. [h]
19 If you are willing to obey,
you will eat the best food
that the land has to offer.
20 However, if you refuse and rebel,
the sword will devour you,
for the mouth of the LORD has spoken.

21 How the faithful city
has become an adulteress,*
she who used to be a symbol of justice.
Righteousness used to dwell in her,
but now she is the abode of murderers.
22 Your silver has turned to dross,
and your wine is mixed with water. [i]
23 Your princes are rebels
and companions of thieves.
All of them love bribes
and are eager to receive gifts.
They do not treat the orphan with justice,
and they refuse to listen to the pleas of widows.

24 Therefore, the LORD of hosts,
the Mighty One of Israel, says this:
I am determined to vent my anger upon my enemies
and wreak vengeance on my foes. [j]
25 I will turn my hand against you
and refine your dross in the furnace,
purging all of your impurities.
26 And I will restore your judges
as in the days of old
and your counselors as at the beginning.
Then you will be called the city of righteousness,
the faithful city. [k]

27 Zion will be redeemed by judgment
and those who are repentant by righteousness.
28 But rebels and sinners alike will be destroyed,
and those who forsake the LORD will perish.

29 You will be ashamed of the sacred oaks*
which offered you such delight,
and you will blush when you behold the gardens
which you chose in their stead.
30 You will be like a tree whose leaves are withered,
like a garden without water. [l]
31 The strong man will become like straw
and his work like a spark.

---

e Ps 50:8-13; Mic 6:7.—f Isa 66:3; Jer 6:20.—g Prov 1:28; Sir 34:21-23.—h Isa 41:1; Ps 51:9; Rev 7:14.—i Lam 44:1; Ezek 22:18.—j Gen 49:24; Deut 32:41.—k Isa 32:16; Jer 33:7ff; Zec 8:3.—l Jer 8:13.

1:15 *Hands:* the habitual manner of praying was to extend the hands with the palms open upwards.

1:17 *Orphan, widow:* these were the people most defenseless and most exposed to injustice in the social order of the time. This is why they are constantly mentioned in ethical passages of the Bible.

1:21 *Adulteress:* the term signifies infidelity to God, inasmuch as the covenant between God and his people had its most appropriate image in the bond of conjugal love. This allegory recurs constantly.

1:29 *Sacred oaks:* a reference to places of idolatrous worship, which was practiced for the most part in sacred groves on high places.

Both will burn together,
and no one will be able to quench the flames.

THE INTERNAL DECADENCE OF A PEOPLE

CHAPTER 2

Jerusalem, the Religious Center.* 1 This is the vision seen by Isaiah, the son of Amoz, concerning Judah and Jerusalem.

2 In days to come
the mountain of the LORD's house
will be established as the highest mountain
and raised high above the hills.
Then all the nations will stream toward it;[m]
3 many peoples will come to it and say,
"Come, let us ascend the mountain of the LORD,
to the house of the God of Jacob,
so that he may teach us his ways
and we may walk in his paths."
For from Zion will go forth instruction,
and the word of the LORD from Jerusalem.
4 He will judge between the nations
and serve as an arbiter for many peoples.
They will beat their swords into plowshares
and their spears into pruning hooks.
One nation will not lift up a sword against another,
nor will they ever again be trained for war.[n]

The LORD's Triumph Will Come*

5 Come, O house of Jacob,
let us walk in the light of the LORD.
6 For you, O LORD, have abandoned your people,
the house of Jacob.
They are surrounded by fortune tellers
and by soothsayers like the Philistines,
and they are allying themselves with foreigners.*
7 Their land is full of silver and gold,
and their treasures are without limit.
Their land is filled with horses,
and there is no end to their chariots.*
8 Their land is full of idols;
they bow down before the work of their hands,
before what their own fingers have fashioned.[o]
9 Therefore human nature has been humbled
and mankind has been brought low;
do not forgive them.
10 Let them conceal themselves among the rocks
and hide in the dust
in their terror of the LORD
and from the splendor of his majesty.
11 The haughty looks of men will be brought low
and human arrogance will be humbled;
the LORD alone will be exalted
on that day.[p]
12 For the LORD of hosts has ordained a day
against all those who are proud and haughty,
against all those who have been exalted and raised high,
13 against all the lofty and proud cedars of Lebanon
and against all the oaks of Bashan,
14 against all the soaring mountains
and all the towering hills,
15 against every high tower
and every fortified wall,
16 against all the ships of Tarshish*[q]
and every stately vessel.
17 Human pride will be humbled
and human arrogance will be brought low.
On that day,
the LORD alone will be exalted.
18 The idols will completely disappear;
19 they will crawl into the caves of the rocks
and the holes of the ground,

m Isa 11:9; 56:7; Mic 4:1ff.—n Isa 11:4; Ps 72:3f.—o Isa 2:18.—p Isa 2:9; Ezek 31:10.—q Isa 23:1, 14.

2:1-4 This theme, which returns often in the third part of the Book (Isa 56:6-8; 60:11-14) and in the Psalms of Zion, especially Ps 48, prepares the way for the expectation of a Messianic city in which all human beings are invited to share the joy of Christ (Heb 12:22; Rev 14:1; 21:10-26).

2:5-22 Isaiah is probably referring here to the northern kingdom and its capital, Samaria, which were boasting of their prosperity at the very time when Assyrian invaders were already on the move (722 B.C.).

2:6 Despite Israelite law and the preaching of the prophets, divination was widely practiced even in Palestine, as in the whole of the East.

2:7 *Chariots:* war chariots, the use of which in Palestine went back to Solomon.

2:16 *Ships of Tarshish:* Tarshish was perhaps Tartessos in Spain; the name was used for ships capable of lengthy voyages.

fleeing from the terror of the LORD
and the splendor of his majesty
when he arises to strike the world with terror.[r]

20 On that day people will throw away
to the moles and to the bats
their idols of silver and gold
that they had made for themselves to worship.
21 They will crawl into the crevices of the rocks
and the clefts in the cliffs
to hide from the terror of the LORD
and the splendor of his majesty
when he arises to terrify the earth.

22 Have nothing more to do with men
who have only the breath in their nostrils.
Of what value are they?

CHAPTER 3

Ruling against Judah and Jerusalem

1 Now the Lord, the LORD of hosts,
is about to deprive Jerusalem and Judah
of resources and provisions—
all supplies of bread and water—[s]
2 warriors and soldiers,
judges and prophets,
fortune tellers and elders,
3 captains and dignitaries,
counselors, skilled magicians,
and expert enchanters.
4 I will appoint young boys as their princes,
mere lads to rule over them.

5 People will oppress one another,
each one ill-treated by his neighbor.
The young will be arrogant toward their elders,
as will the lowly toward the honorable.

6 A man will take hold of his brother
in their father's house, saying,
"You have a cloak;
you will be our leader,
and this heap of ruins
will be under your rule."
7 But on that day
the other will cry out, saying,
"I am not qualified to undertake this;
in my house there is neither bread nor clothing.
You will not make me leader of the people."[t]

8 Jerusalem has been brought low
and Judah has fallen
because by their words and their deeds
they turned against the LORD
and defied his glorious presence.
9 The look on their faces bears witness against them;
they proclaim their sins like Sodom
without any effort to conceal them.
Woe to them!
For they have brought disaster upon themselves.

10 Happy are the righteous,
for they will eat the fruit of their labors.
11 Woe to the wicked.
All will go ill with them.
They will be repaid
as their actions deserve.
12 O my people, children are oppressing you
and women have become your rulers.
O my people, your rulers are leading you astray
and putting you on the road to ruin.[u]

13 The LORD has risen to argue his case;
he stands up to judge his people.
14 The LORD enters into judgment
against the elders and the princes of his people:
It is you who have ravaged the vineyard;
the spoils you have taken from the poor
are in your houses.
15 What right do you have to crush my people
and grind the faces of the poor?
says the Lord GOD of hosts.[v]

16 The LORD said:
Because the daughters of Zion are haughty,
walking with their heads held high,
glancing wantonly with their eyes,
moving provocatively with mincing steps
and with their anklets tinkling,
17 the LORD will cover with scabs
the scalps of the daughters of Zion,
and he will lay bare their foreheads.

r Jdg 6:2; Job 30:6.—s Isa 5:13; 65:13; Lev 26:26; Ezek 4:16.—t Jer 8:22; Ezek 34:4; Hos 5:13.—u Jer 23:13.—v Isa 10:1-2.

18 * On that day the LORD will take away
their finery: anklets, headbands, and cres-
cents; [w] 19 pendants, bracelets, and shawls;
20 headdresses, bangles, necklaces, perfume
boxes, and amulets; 21 signet rings and nose
rings; 22 fine dresses, wraps, cloaks, and
purses; 23 mirrors, linen garments, turbans,
and veils.

24 Then instead of perfume there will be a stench,
and instead of a sash, a rope;
instead of a lovely hair setting, baldness,
instead of a rich gown, a sackcloth* dress,
and instead of beauty, branding marks.
25 O Zion, your men will fall by the sword
and your warriors will perish in battle.
26 Your gates will lament and mourn;
ravaged, you will sit desolate on the ground. [x]

CHAPTER 4

1 On that day,
seven women will take hold of one man, saying,
"We will eat our own food
and provide for our own clothing.
Just let us bear your name.
Take away our disgrace."

The Seed of the LORD*

2 On that day the branch of the LORD
will be beautiful and glorious,
and the fruit of the land
will be the pride and splendor
of the survivors of Israel. [y]
3 Whoever is left in Zion
and whoever remains in Jerusalem
will be called holy,
everyone whose survival in Jerusalem was decreed.
4 When the Lord has washed away
the filth of the daughters of Zion
and cleansed the bloodstains of Jerusalem from its midst
by a spirit of judgment and of cleansing,
5 then the LORD will create
over every house on Mount Zion,
and over those who assemble there,
a cloud of smoke by day
and a bright flame of fire by night. [z]
The glory of the LORD will be a canopy over all,
6 serving as a shade by day from the heat
and a refuge and a shelter from the storm and the rain.

CHAPTER 5

The Song of the Vineyard*

1 Now let me sing for my beloved
the song of my friend concerning his vineyard.
My beloved had a vineyard
on a fertile hillside. [a]
2 He dug it, cleared it of stones,
and planted it with choice red vines.
In its midst he built a watchtower
and also hewed out a winepress.
He expected it to yield a rich crop of grapes,
but the only thing it brought forth was wild grapes.

3 And now, inhabitants of Jerusalem and people of Judah,
I ask you to judge between me and my vineyard.
4 What more could I have done for my vineyard
that I did not do?
When I expected it to yield choice grapes,
why did it bring forth wild grapes? [b]

5 Now listen to me as I tell you
what I am planning to do to my vineyard.
I will take away its hedge
and use it for grazing.
I will knock down its wall
and let it be trampled upon.

---

w Jdg 8:21.—x Isa 14:31; Lev 26:31.—y Isa 11:1; Jer 23:5-6; 33:15; Zec 3:8.—z Ex 13:21.—a Isa 27:2; Jn 15:1.—b 2 Chr 36:15; Jer 2:5-7; Mic 6:3-4.

3:18-23 Of these various garments and jewels some would have had a magical or idolatrous significance.

3:24 *Sackcloth:* a coarse cloth of which sacks were made.

4:2-6 The name *branch* will be given to the future Messiah because he will be the true Son of David, and from him will spring a new people (Jer 23:5; Zec 3:8; 6:12). The promise will stir and direct the hope of the faithful amid the conflicts and failures of coming centuries. John, the seer of Patmos, will see the new Jerusalem in which the promise will find its complete fulfillment (Rev 21).

5:1-7 The image of the beloved vineyard that is ravaged is often used by the prophets (Jer 2:21; Ezek 15:1-8; etc.). Jesus, too, will like this comparison (Mt 21:33-34) and will describe himself as the true vine whose branches will be tended by the vinedresser, his Father (Jn 15).

6 I will let it go to waste;
it will be neither pruned nor hoed,
but left overgrown with briars and thorns.
I will also command the clouds
not to allow any rain to fall upon it.
7 The vineyard of the LORD of hosts
is the house of Israel,
and the people of Judah
are the plant he cherished.
He expected justice but found bloodshed;
he expected righteousness but heard cries of distress. [c]

The Doom of Sinners

8 Woe to you who add house to house
and join field to field
until there is no further space remaining
and you are left to dwell alone
in the midst of the land. [d]
9 The LORD of hosts in my hearing
has sworn this solemn oath:
Many houses will be left desolate,
large and fine mansions
with no one to inhabit them. [e]
10 For ten acres of vineyard
will yield only one barrel,
and ten bushels of seed
will yield only a single bushel.
11 Woe to those who rise early in the morning
to imbibe strong drink,
and who linger far into the night
inflamed with wine.
12 Their feasts are marked with harps and lyres,
tambourines and flutes and wine.
But they never give thought to the deeds of the LORD,
or note what his hands have accomplished. [f]
13 Therefore, my people shall end up in exile
because they have no knowledge of my deeds.
Their nobles are dying of hunger
and their masses are parched with thirst.

14 As a result, the netherworld has increased its appetite
and opened its jaws to an immeasurable extent,
swallowing the nobility of Jerusalem and her masses,
her throngs and all who exult in her. [g]
15 People are bowed down, everyone is brought low,
and the eyes of the haughty are humbled.
16 But the LORD of hosts is exalted by his judgment,
and by righteousness the holy God has displayed his holiness.
17 Lambs will graze there as in their pasture,
and yearlings will feed among the ruins.

18 Woe to those who drag iniquity along
with the cords of perversity,
and who drag sin along
as though with cart ropes;
19 woe to those who say, "Let the LORD make haste
and speed up his work that we may see it;
let the Holy One of Israel
be brought to fulfillment
so that we may know it." [h]

20 Woe to those who call good what is evil
and call evil what is good,
who classify as darkness what is light
and designate as light what is darkness,
who make sweet what is bitter
and make bitter what is sweet.

21 Woe to those who are wise in their own eyes
and consider themselves to be prudent.[i]
22 Woe to those who are unmatched in their consumption of wine
and unsurpassed in mixing drinks,
23 who accept bribes to acquit the guilty
and deny justice to the innocent. [j]

24 As tongues of fire devour the stubble,
and as dry grass shrivels in the flames,
so their root will decay
and their blossoms will be scattered like dust;
for they have rejected the law of the LORD of hosts
and scorned the word of the Holy One of Israel.

25 Therefore, the anger of the LORD
blazed forth against his people;

c Isa 10:2; Ezek 9:9.—d Mic 2:2.—e Isa 6:12; Mt 23:38.—f Isa 24:8; Job 21:12; Am 6:5f.—g Num 16:30; Prov 30:16; Hab 2:5.—h Isa 1:4; Ezek 12:22; 2 Pet 3:4.—i Isa 47:10; Prov 3:7; Rom 12:16; 1 Cor 3:18-20.—j Isa 1:17; Ex 23:8; Prov 17:15; Ezek 22:12.

he raised his hand against them
and struck them down.
The mountains quaked,
and their corpses lay like refuse in the streets.
But despite all this
his anger has not been sated,
and his hand is still stretched out.

Deliverance*

26 He will deliver a signal to a far-distant nation
and summon them from the ends of the earth;
they will respond swiftly without any delay.* [k]
27 None of them are weary, none of them stumble,
no one slumbers or sleeps.
None of them have their belts unfastened
or sandals with a broken strap.
28 Their arrows are sharpened
and all their bows are bent.
The hoofs of their horses seem like flint,
and their chariot wheels are like a whirlwind.
29 Their roar is like that of a lion;
they growl like young lions.
They roar as they seize their prey,
and no one can prevent them from carrying it off.
30 They will roar over it on that day,
similar to the roaring of the sea.
And if anyone looks at the land,
he will behold only darkness and distress,
with the light fading at the approaching clouds. [l]

II: THE BOOK OF IMMANUEL

CHAPTER 6

Isaiah's Call.* 1 In the year that King Uz-
ziah died, I saw the LORD sitting on a high
and lofty throne, and the train of his robe
filled the temple. 2 In attendance above him
were seraphim.* Each of them had six
wings: with two they covered their faces,
with two they covered their feet, and with
the third pair they flew. [m] 3 And they called
out to one another,

"Holy, holy, holy is the LORD of hosts.
The entire earth is filled with his glory." [n]

4 The voices of those who called out shook
the thresholds, and the temple was filled
with smoke. 5 Then I said,

"Woe is me! I am doomed.
For I am a man of unclean lips,
and I live among a people of unclean lips,
yet my eyes have seen the King, the LORD of hosts." [o]

6 Then one of the seraphim flew to me,
holding in his hand a burning coal that he
had removed from the altar with a pair of
tongs. 7 He touched my mouth with it and
said,

"Now that this has touched your lips,
your guilt has been removed
and your sin has been blotted out." [p]

8 I then heard the voice of the LORD say-
ing, "Whom shall I send? Who will go for
us?" I said, "Here I am. Send me!" [q] 9 Then
he replied: Go forth and tell this people:

No matter how carefully you listen,
you will not understand.
You will continue to look,
but you will not comprehend. [r]

k Isa 7:18; Deut 28:49; Zec 10:8.—l Isa 8:22; Jer 50:42; Lk 21:25.—m Ezek 1:5; 10:15; Rev 4:8.—n Ex 15:11; Rev 4:8.—o Ex 20:19; 33:20; Deut 5:26; Jdg 6:22; 13:22.—p Jer 1:9; Dan 10:16; 1 Jn 1:7.—q Acts 9:4.—r Jer 5:21; Mt 13:14f; Mk 4:12; Lk 8:10.

5:26-30 The Assyrian invaders arrive; the forces assembled under the banner of the lion, the emblem of Assyria (see v. 29), are irresistible.

5:26 To summon warriors, a banner was raised on the top of a hill and a horn was sounded.

6:1-13 In around 740 B.C., in the midst of the temple ceremonial, the prophet was seized by the glory of God, who is beyond every creature. The "seraphs," beings of fire, seem to surround God but are unable to endure the splendor of his mystery. Heaven resounds with the great acclamation of the Lord of hosts, that is, the Lord of all the creatures of the universe; God's "glory," his mysterious, active presence fills the worlds.

In the moment in which Isaiah experiences the greatness and holiness of God, he is pierced by a sense that he is nothing but sin. But it is not possible to discover God without also opening oneself to some demand; in the Bible, there is no call without a mission. God wills that he should need human beings in order to carry out his plan. His call purifies the one whom he chooses. From now on, Isaiah will be another person, one charged with the mission of censuring his fellow Israelites who are blinding themselves and closing their ears. Only when the people, greatly reduced in numbers, will have lost every illusion and every human support, will salvation from God arise out of the little group of survivors. This vocation story introduces the "Book of Immanuel" (Isa 7–12), which conveys the essentials of his message.

6:2 *Seraphim:* the word means "burning, blazing." Here, they are heavenly beings in human form. Isaiah is the first in the Bible to connect them with Yahweh.

10 Make the minds of this people dull;
stop up their ears
and close their eyes.
Otherwise their eyes will see,
their ears will hear,
their hearts will understand,
and they will change their ways
and be healed. [s]

11 Then I asked, "How long, O LORD?" He
replied:

Until the cities lie in ruins
and become deserted,
until the houses are unoccupied
and the land lies completely desolate,
12 until the LORD drives the people far away
and the country will be totally abandoned.
13 Even if a tenth of the people remain there,
that area too will be destroyed,
like a terebinth or an oak
whose stump remains when it is felled;
the holy seed is its stump. [t]

CHAPTER 7*

The Coming of Immanuel. 1 * During the
period when Ahaz, the son of Jotham and the
grandson of Uzziah, was king of Judah, King
Rezin of Aram and King Pekah of Israel, the
son of Remaliah, went forth to conquer
Jerusalem, but they were unable to mount an
attack against it. [u] 2 When the house of David
was informed that Aram had pitched camp
in Ephraim, the heart of King Ahaz and the
hearts of his people began to tremble just as
trees of the forest shake in the wind.

3 Then the LORD said to Isaiah: Go forth
with your son Shear-jashub* to meet Ahaz
at the end of the conduit of the upper pool,
on the road to the Fuller's Field, [v] 4 and say
to him, Pay close attention to me. Remain
calm and be unafraid. Do not let your
courage fail because of these two smoldering
stumps of firewood. Do not yield to the
fierce anger of Rezin and Aram and the son
of Remaliah, 5 or become fearful because
Aram, Ephraim, and the son of Remaliah
have been plotting against you and saying,
6 "Let us go forth and attack Judah. Let us
tear it apart, force it to surrender to us, and
appoint the son of Tabeel * there as king."

7 Therefore, thus says the Lord GOD:

This will not happen,
either now or ever.
8 For the head of Aram is Damascus
and the head of Damascus is Rezin.
The head of Ephraim is Samaria,
and the head of Samaria is the son of Remaliah.
9 Within sixty-five years
Ephraim will no longer be a people.
If you do not stand firm in your faith
you will not stand firm at all. [w]

10 * Again the LORD spoke to Ahaz, saying:

11 Ask the LORD, your God for a sign;
let it be as deep as the netherworld
or as high as the heavens.

12 But Ahaz replied, "I will not ask. I will
not put the LORD to the test." [x] 13 Then
Isaiah said:

Listen, O house of David!
Are you not satisfied to try the patience of men?
Must you also try the patience of my God? [y]

s Deut 32:15; Jer 5:21; Mk 8:18; Jn 12:40.—t Isa 1:9; 10:22; Job 14:7.—u 2 Ki 15:37; 16:5; 2 Chr 28:5-15.—v Isa 10:21-22; 36:2; 2 Ki 18:17.—w Isa 8:6ff; 2 Chr 20:20.—x Deut 4:34; Mt 4:7.—y Isa 1:14; 7:2.

7:1—12:6 The "Book of Immanuel" records the major interventions of Isaiah in the politics of the kingdom of Judah, especially from 734–732 B.C., that is, at the time of the Syro-Ephraimite war which was on the point of dragging the throne of David down to destruction (see 2 Ki 16:5). In this period of uncertainty, a promise kindles a light: a boy child will be born and named Immanuel, that is, "God with us." For Christians, this promise finds its complete fulfillment in the coming of Jesus. Some later oracles have been inserted into the Book of Immanuel.

7:1-9 Assyrian expansion roused concern throughout the Near East, while the kingdom of Israel plotted to free themselves from the Assyrian yoke. Their intention was to bring the king of Jerusalem into this affair, by force if necessary. The undertaking was a dangerous one and could cost this king his throne and put an end to the house of David. The king of Judah, in order to escape from the pressure of his neighbors, was going to put himself under the protection of mighty Assyria and was ready to become its vassal. But Isaiah stood up to him: the king must trust in God alone.

7:3 *Shear-jashub:* a symbolic name, signifying "a remnant will return" (see Isa 10:20-22). The *pool* was south of Jerusalem.

7:6 *Tabeel:* a region across the Jordan. The two kings want to put someone not of Davidic descent on the throne of Judah.

7:10-17 King Ahaz hesitates and does not know what to do with a sign from heaven. In God's name Isaiah announces a solemn promise: a virgin will bear a son; his name, "God with us," signifies salvation. The child's nourishment recalls the great days of nomadic life and of the Exodus, the ideal period when Israel was poor and close to God. It foretells, along with a hereditary ruler, a different age, and a different Messiah, expectation of whom will never be erased from the Hebrew heart. Later on, the Greek tradition will specify that the "young woman" who is to give birth is a *virgin* (v. 14). Matthew and the Christian tradition will see this prediction as completely fulfilled in the coming of Jesus, the true Immanuel, born of the Virgin Mary by a supernatural intervention (Mt 1:23).

14 Therefore, you will be given this sign
by the LORD himself:
The virgin will be with child,
and she will give birth to a son,
and she will name him Immanuel. [z]
15 He will feed on curds and honey
by the time he learns to reject the bad
and choose the good.
16 Before that child has learned
to reject the bad and choose the good,
deserted will be the lands
of those two kings whom you dread.
17 The LORD will inflict on you,
and on your people and your father's house,
days far worse than any that have been seen
since Ephraim* broke away from Judah—
you will become subjects of the king of Assyria. [a]
18 When that day arrives,
the LORD will summon flies from the distant streams of Egypt
and bees from the land of Assyria.
19 They will all come forth and settle
in the steep ravines and in the clefts of the rocks,
on all the thornbushes and in all the pastures.
20 On that day the LORD will shave
with a razor hired from across the river *
(with the king of Assyria)
the head and the hair between the legs
as well as the beard.
21 When that day comes,
each man will keep a young cow and two sheep,
22 and because of the abundant milk they give
he will subsist on curds.
For all those who are left in the land
will eat curds and honey. [b]
23 On that day,
wherever there used to be a thousand vines
worth a thousand pieces of silver,
that area will then be covered
with brambles and thornbushes.
24 Men will go there with bows and arrows,
for the entire country will be covered
by briers and thorns.
25 For fear of briers and thorns [c]
you will not venture upon any hills
that used to be hoed with a hoe.
They will become a place for cattle to graze
and where sheep may tread. [d]

CHAPTER 8

Isaiah's Son. 1 * The LORD said to me: Take
a large scroll and write on it in ordinary
letters: "Maher-shalal-hash-baz." 2 I had
it attested for me by reliable witnesses,
Uriah, the priest, and Zechariah, son of
Jeberechiah.

3 Then I went to the prophetess, and she
conceived and bore a son. The LORD said to
me: Name him Maher-shalal-hash-baz, 4 for,
before the child knows how to say "father"
or "mother," the wealth of Damascus and
the spoils of Samaria will be carried off by
the king of Assyria.

5 * Once again the LORD spoke to me and
said:

6 Because this people has rejected
the waters of Shiloah that flow gently
and trembled in fear
before Rezin and the son of Remaliah, [e]
7 the LORD will therefore raise against it
the mighty flood waters of the river
(the king of Assyria and all his glory).
The river will rise above all its channels
and overflow all its banks;
8 it will sweep on into Judah like a flood
reaching up to the neck,
and its wings, spreading out,
will cover the breadth of your land,
Immanuel.

z Gen 24:43; Ex 3:12; Lk 2:12.—a Isa 7:20; 1 Ki 12:16; 2 Chr 28:20.—b Isa 7:15; 14:30; Gen 18:8.—c Isa 5:6.—d Isa 5:17; 7:19; Hag 1:11.—e Isa 7:1, 2, 6; Jn 9:7, 11.

7:17 *Ephraim:* though but one region, it stands here for the entire northern kingdom. The division of the two kingdoms went back to 931 B.C.

7:20 The *river* is the Euphrates. Prisoners were shaved to disfigure and shame them.

8:1-4 The prophet performs an action rich in symbolism: he sires a boy child whose name has been determined in advance; the name means "Quick to the plunder, swift to the spoil." In this way, the prophet foretells the punishment in store for those who have formed a coalition against the kingdom of Judah. And in fact, Damascus and the provinces of northern Israel will fall into the hands of the Assyrians in 732 B.C.

8:5-8 Jerusalem had but a single reservoir, the spring of Shiloah. Was this not perhaps a sign of the invisible protection of God? But when faced with the threat from Syria, the king and people sought a more obvious form of security. As a result, the flood waters of the Euphrates (*the river*, v. 7), that is, the hordes of the Assyrian invaders, will overwhelm Judah.

9 Realize this, you peoples, and be afraid.
Listen, all you far-distant nations.
Arm yourselves, but be frightened;
arm yourselves, but be frightened.
10 No matter what plans you devise,
they will come to naught,
for God is with us.

Isaiah's Followers. 11 This is what the LORD
said to me when he held me firmly with his
hand and warned me not to follow the ways
of this people:[f]

12 * Do not call conspiracy what this people calls conspiracy,
and do not fear what they fear
or stand in awe of them.
13 The LORD is the one whom you should proclaim holy;
he must be the object of your fear and awe.[g]
14 He will become a snare, an obstacle,
a rock over which the two houses of Israel * will stumble,
a trap and a snare to the inhabitants of Jerusalem.[h]
15 And many of them will stumble;
they will fall and be broken;
they will be snared and taken captive.
16 Bind up the testimony and seal the teaching
so that my disciples can keep it in their hearts.
17 I will wait eagerly for the LORD
who has hidden his face from the house of Jacob;
I will place my hope in him.
18 I stand here with the children
whom the LORD has given me
to be signs and portents in Israel
sent by the LORD of hosts
who dwells on Mount Zion.
19 People may say to you,
"Seek guidance from ghosts and mediums
who whisper and mutter.
Should not a people consult its gods
and the dead on behalf of the living[i]
20 while seeking instruction or a message?"
Those who offer suggestions like this
will experience no dawn.
21 They will wander through the land
greatly distressed and starving.
Once their hunger becomes acute,
they will be enraged
and curse their king and their gods.
They will turn their gaze upward,
22 or downward to the earth,
but they will behold only distress and anguish,
confusion and the gloom of darkness.

23 As the land of Zebulun* and the land of
Naphtali were humbled in the past by the
LORD, so in the future he will make glorious
the way of the sea, the land beyond the
Jordan, the district of the Gentiles.

CHAPTER 9

The Prince of Peace*

1 The people who walked in darkness
have seen a great light;
upon those who dwelt in the shadow of death
a light has dawned.[j]
2 You have enlarged the nation
and given them great joy;
they rejoice before you
as those who rejoice at the harvest,
as they exult when dividing spoils.
3 For the yoke that burdened them,
the bar across their shoulders,
and the rod of their oppressor
you have broken as on the day of Midian.*
4 For every boot of a warrior that tramped in battle
and every garment soaked in blood
will be burned as fuel for the fire.[k]
5 For a child has been born to us,
a son has been given to us.

f Ezek 3:14.—g Isa 5:16; Num 20:12.—h Ezek 11:16; Rom 9:33; 1 Pet 2:8.—i Isa 29:4; Lev 19:31; Deut 18:10ff.—j 2 Ki 15:29; Mt 4:15f.—k Isa 37:36-38; Jdg 7:25.

8:12-13 The *conspiracy* is the league between Ahaz and Assyria; the conspiracy which the people fear is the Syro-Ephraimite coalition.

8:14 *Two houses of Israel:* that is, the kingdoms of Judah and of Israel.

8:23 *Zebulun . . . Naphtali:* Galilee.

9:1-6 After the threats and predictions of sorrow, the prophet bursts into a song of hope and deliverance. He consoles the Galileans who have been deported by the king of Assyria in 732 B.C. (2 Ki 15:29). Another vision is given to the seer, and hope springs up in the hearts of believers: The Lord will set free the oppressed and will establish his people in peace. All power will be given to the mysterious child who is to be born of royal blood, the Immanuel who has already been foretold (Isa 7:14). This is an ideal passage for the Christmas liturgy and in fact, is prominent there.

9:3 See the description of Gideon's victory over the Midianites in Jdg 7:16-25.

Upon his shoulders dominion rests,
and this is the name he has been given:
Wonderful Counselor, Mighty God,
Eternal Father, Prince of Peace.
6 His dominion will grow continually,
and there will be endless peace
bestowed on David's throne
and over his kingdom.
He will establish and sustain it
with justice and integrity
from this time onward and forevermore;
the zeal of the LORD of hosts will accomplish this. [l]

Fall of the Northern Kingdom

7 The LORD has sent forth his word against Jacob,
and it has fallen on Israel.
8 * All the people were aware of this,
Ephraim and the inhabitants of Samaria,
but they said in their arrogance and pride of heart, [m]
9 "The bricks have fallen down,
but we will rebuild with dressed stones.
The sycamores have been cut down,
but we will replace them with cedars." [n]

10 In response the LORD raised up foes against them
and spurred on their enemies,
11 the Arameans on the east and the Philistines on the west,
and they devoured Israel with gaping jaws.
Yet after all this his anger has not abated
and his hand is still outstretched.

12 But the people did not turn to him who struck them,
nor did they seek the LORD of hosts. [o]
13 Therefore, the LORD cut off from Israel
head and tail, palm branch and reed,
in a single day.
14 [The elders and the nobles are the head;
the prophets who teach lies are the tail.]
15 For those who were leaders of the people led them astray,
and those who were led by them were swallowed up. [p]
16 For this reason
the LORD did not show pity to their young people
or have compassion on their orphans and widows,
since all of them were godless evildoers
and every word they spoke was impious.
Yet after all this, his anger has not abated
and his hand is still outstretched.

17 For wickedness continued to burn like a fire,
consuming briers and thorns,
and setting ablaze the thickets of the forest
which rose upward in a column of smoke.
18 The land was set ablaze
by the wrath of the LORD of hosts,
and the people became like fuel for the fire;
no one spared his brother.
19 They gorged on the right but were still hungry;
they devoured on the left but were not satisfied;
many ate the flesh of their own offspring.
20 Manasseh devoured Ephraim,
and Ephraim devoured Manasseh;
together they turned against Judah.
21 Yet after all this, his anger has not abated
and his hand is still outstretched. [q]

CHAPTER 10

Social Injustice

1 Woe to those who enact unjust laws
and enforce oppressive statutes, [r]
2 thereby depriving the needy of justice,
and making it impossible for the poorest of my people
to have their rights upheld,
as they plunder the widow
and make the orphans their prey. [s]

3 What will you do on the day of punishment
when disaster befalls you from afar?
To whom will you flee for help,
and where will you leave your riches,

l Jer 23:5; Mt 28:18; Lk 1:32f; Jn 3:16.—m Prov 16:18.—n Isa 7:2, 9; Ezek 2:4; Zec 7:11.—o 2 Ki 16:6; 2 Chr 28:18.—p Jer 2:8; 5:31; 20:6; 23:13f; 29:30ff; Ezek 13:1-7; 22:28; Mic 3:11; Mt 24:24.—q Isa 5:25; 9:12; Deut 5:15.—r Jer 8:8.—s Isa 1:23; 5:23.

9:8—10:4 In all likelihood, this song goes back to about 739 B.C.; at that time Israel, now subject to the Assyrians, was assailed by its neighbors (2 Ki 15:19).

4 so that you can avoid cowering among the captives
or falling among the slain?
Yet after all this, his wrath has not abated;
his hand is still outstretched.

The LORD Punishes the King of Assyria

5 * Woe to Assyria, the rod of my anger;
the club in their hands is my fury. [t]
6 Against a godless people I send him forth,
against a nation who aroused my wrath,
commanding him to pillage and plunder
and to trample on them like mud in the street.
7 But this is not his intention,
nor does he have this in mind.
His only thought is complete destruction
and to liquidate as many nations as possible.
8 For he says,
"Are not my commanders all kings?
9 Is not Calno like Carchemish?
Is not Hamath like Arpad?
Is not Samaria like Damascus? *
10 My hand has overcome idolatrous kingdoms
that had more images than Jerusalem and Samaria.
11 As I did to Samaria and her idols,
shall I not also do to Jerusalem and her images?" [u]

12 When the LORD has completed all his
work on Mount Zion and on Jerusalem, he
will punish the king of Assyria for his arro-
gant boasts and his haughty demeanor,
13 because that king had said,

"By my own power I have accomplished all this,
and also by my wisdom, for I have great intelligence.
I have wiped out the boundaries of nations
and have plundered their treasures;
like a giant I have subjugated their inhabitants. [v]
14 My hand has discovered a nest
in which the riches of the nation have been stored.
And as one gathers eggs that have been abandoned,
so I have collected the entire world;
not one fluttered a wing
or opened a beak to chirp."
15 Does the ax consider itself more important
than the man who swings it,
or does the saw claim greater credit
than the man who uses it?
No sword can control the man who yields it,
nor can a club have power over the one who raises it. [w]
16 Therefore, the Lord, the LORD of hosts,
will afflict a debilitating illness on his sturdy warriors,
and beneath his glory a fever will be kindled
like the burning of fire.
17 The Light of Israel will become a fire
and its Holy One a flame
that in a single day
will burn up and consume
his thorns and his briers.
18 His splendid forests and orchards
will be totally destroyed, both body and soul,
as when an invalid wastes away.
19 What remains of the trees of the forest
will be so few
that any young child
will be able to record their number.
20 * When that day arrives,
the remnant of Israel
and the survivors of the house of Jacob
will cease to rely upon the one who struck them *
and will rather place their trust in the LORD,
the Holy One of Israel. [x]
21 A remnant will return, the remnant of Jacob,
to the mighty God.
22 Although your people, O Israel,

t Jer 50:23; Zep 2:13.—u Isa 2:8; 36:18-20; 2 Ki 19:12-13.—v Isa 47:7; Deut 8:17.—w Isa 7:20; 45:9; Rom 9:20-21.—x Isa 11:10-11; 12:1, 4; Zec 9:16.

10:5-19 We are now in a different period, perhaps 701 B.C. It is already twenty years since the northern kingdom was destroyed. Judah in turn is about to succumb (Isa 36–39).

10:9 Some fortified cities of Syria are listed that have already been subdued by the Assyrians in earlier wars.

10:20-23 The trial is a hard one, but the promise remains (see Isa 7:3 and the symbolic name of Isaiah's elder son: Shear-jashub, which means "a remnant will return").

10:20 *Who struck them:* in 734 B.C., Ahaz had imprudently asked the Assyrians for help.

may be as numerous as the sands of the sea,
only a remnant of them will return.
Destruction has been decreed
as righteousness and justice demand. [y]
23 For throughout the entire land
the Lord GOD of hosts will enforce
the final destruction that has been decreed. [z]

24 Therefore, the Lord GOD of hosts says this:

O my people who dwell in Zion,
do not be afraid of the Assyrians,
even when they beat you with a rod
and raise their staff against you
as the Egyptians did.
25 For it will be only a short time
until my wrath will subside
and I will direct my anger to their destruction.
26 Then the LORD of hosts will inflict his retribution
as he did when he struck Midian at the rock of Oreb,
and he will raise his staff over the sea
as he did against Egypt. [a]
27 On that day
his burden will be removed from your shoulder
and his yoke will be broken
and fall from your neck.

Sennacherib's Assault*

Sennacherib and his army have come up from Rimmon,
28 and they have come to Aiath.
They have passed through Migron
and stored their supplies at Michmash.
29 Once they crossed the ravine,
they camped for the night at Geba.
Ramah is terrified,
Gibeah of Saul has fled.
30 Cry out loudly, Bath-gallim!
Listen carefully, Laishah!
Answer her, Anathoth!
31 Madmenah is in flight;
the inhabitants of Gebim have sought cover.
32 This day Sennacherib will halt at Nob
and shake his fist
at the mount of daughter Zion,
the hill of Jerusalem. [b]
33 Behold, the Lord GOD of hosts
will sever the boughs with frightening power.
The tallest trees will be cut down
and the lofty ones will be laid low.
34 The thickets of the forest he will demolish with an ax,
and Lebanon will fall at the onslaught of the Mighty One.

CHAPTER 11

A Reign of Justice and Peace*

1 A shoot will spring forth from the stump of Jesse,
and a branch will grow from his roots. [c]
2 The Spirit of the LORD will rest upon him:
a Spirit of wisdom and understanding,
a Spirit of counsel and power,
a Spirit of knowledge and fear of the LORD,
3 and his delight will be the fear of the LORD.

He will not judge by outward appearances
or reach a verdict based on hearsay.
4 Rather, he will judge the poor with justice
and render fair decisions for the weak and the poor. [d]
He will strike the ruthless with the rod of his mouth,
and with the breath of his lips he will slay the wicked.
5 Righteousness will be the belt around his waist

y Isa 48:19; Rom 9:27f.—z Isa 6:12; 28:22; Rom 9:27-28. —a Isa 37:36-38; Ex 14:16; Jdg 7:25.—b 1 Sam 21:1.—c Zec 6:12; Lk 3:32; Rev 5:5.—d Isa 14:30; Pss 72:2, 4; 98:9; 2 Thes 2:8.

10:28-34 The places listed were all north of Jerusalem.

11:1-9 For the third time the prophet promises the people a king descended from David, the son of Jesse. In contrast to corrupt leaders, he will introduce justice; in contrast to rulers who brought war and destruction, he will inaugurate an era of peace. Filled with every gift (all the gifts which have become the gifts of the Holy Spirit in the Christian tradition), he will be the perfect king, a new Solomon, a new David, and a new Moses. His reign will restore a golden age, as at the beginning of the world. Christians will immediately recognize Christ in this majestic figure, who represents an ideal in whom each individual can see realized the best aspirations of human beings.

and faithfulness the belt around his loins.
6 Then the wolf will live alongside the lamb,
and the leopard will lie down with the kid;
the calf and the young lion will browse together,
with a little child to guide them. [e]
7 The cow and the bear will graze side by side;
their young will lie down together,
and the lion will eat hay like the ox.
8 The infant will play by the cobra's den,
and the young child will lay his hand
on the viper's nest.
9 No injury or harm will occur
on all my holy mountain;
for the earth will be filled with knowledge of the LORD
just as water covers the sea. [f]

Ephraim and Judah United

10 On that day the root of Jesse
will be established as a signal to the nations.
They will come forth to unite under him,
and his dwelling will be glorious. [g]
11 When that day comes,
the LORD will reach out his hand a second time
to recover the remnant of his people
from Assyria and Egypt,
from Patmos,* Ethiopia, and Elam,
from Shinar, Hamath, and the islands of the sea.
12 He will raise a signal to the nations
and assemble the outcasts of Israel.
He will also gather the dispersed of Judah
from the four corners of the earth.
13 The jealousy of Ephraim will cease
and the hostility of Judah will end.
Ephraim will not be jealous of Judah,
nor will Judah have any hostility toward Ephraim. [h]
14 Together they will swoop down
on the foothills of the Philistines to the west
and plunder the people of the east.
Edom and Moab will become subject to their rule,
and the Ammonites will obey them.*
15 The LORD will dry up a pathway
through the Sea of Egypt,
and he will wave his hand over the Euphrates
in his fierce anger,
splitting it into seven streams [i]
so that it can be crossed on foot.
16 Thus there will be a highway
for the remnant of his people from Assyria,
as there was for the Israelites
when they came up from the land of Egypt.

CHAPTER 12

Thanksgiving for Salvation

1 On that day you will say:

I will give you thanks, O LORD.
Even though you were angry with me,
your anger has abated
and you have consoled me.
2 God truly is my salvation;
I will trust in him and be unafraid.
For the LORD is my strength and my source of courage;
he has been my salvation. [j]

3 With joy you will draw water
from the fountain of salvation,
4 and you will say on that day:

Give thanks to the LORD,
invoke his name;
make known his deeds among the nations;
proclaim that his name is exalted.
5 Sing praise to the LORD for his mighty deeds;
let this be known throughout the entire world. [k]
6 Cry out and shout for joy,
all of you who dwell on Zion,
for great in your midst
is the Holy One of Israel. [l]

---

e Isa 65:25.—f Isa 65:11; 66:19-20; Hab 2:14.—g Isa 49:22; Lk 2:32; Jn 12:32; Rom 15:12.—h Jer 3:18; Ezek 37:16.—i Isa 37:25; Ex 14:29.—j Isa 17:10; 25:9; Ex 15:2; Ps 118:14.—k Ex 15:1; Ps 98:1.—l Isa 54:1; Jer 20:13; Ezek 39:7; Zep 3:14; Zec 2:10.

11:11 *Patmos:* the Hebrew has Pathros, which was in Upper Egypt. *Ethiopia:* Cush. *Elam:* Persia. Babylonia: Hebrew, *Shinar. Hamath:* in Syria.

11:14 The peoples listed were Israel's neighbors and traditional enemies.

III: ORACLES AMONG THE PAGAN NATIONS*

CHAPTER 13

Babylon.* 1 An oracle concerning Babylon that Isaiah, the son of Amoz, received in a vision:

2 Upon a barren hill raise a banner;
cry aloud to them.
Wave your hand to them
to enter the gates of the nobles.
3 I have commanded my consecrated soldiers
and summoned my dedicated warriors
to carry out my vengeance. [m]
4 Listen to the great tumult on the mountains
like that of an immense gathering.
Listen to the uproar of the kingdoms,
of nations assembling;
the LORD of hosts is mustering
an army for battle. [n]
5 From a distant land,
from the end of the heavens,
the LORD and the instruments of his wrath
are coming to destroy the entire earth.
6 Cry out in anguish,
for the day of the LORD is near;
it will come like devastation from the Almighty. [o]
7 Therefore, every hand will hang limp
and every man's courage will fade;
8 they will all be panic-stricken,
overcome with pangs and agony
and writhing like a woman in labor.
They will look aghast at each other,
with their faces aflame with fear. [p]
9 Behold, the day of the LORD is coming,
a cruel day of wrath and burning anger,
to reduce the land to a desert waste
and to destroy all the sinners within it.
10 The stars of the heavens and their constellations
will no longer give forth their light.
The sun will be dark when it rises,
and the moon will not provide its light. [q]
11 By taking this course
I will punish the world for its wickedness
and those who are evil for their iniquity.
I will put an end to the pride of the arrogant
and humble the insolence of tyrants. [r]
12 I will make human beings more scarce than pure gold,
far more rare than the gold of Ophir.
13 Therefore, I am determined to make the heavens tremble
and the earth will be shaken to its very foundations,
at the wrath of the LORD of hosts,
on the day of his blazing anger.
14 Like a gazelle fleeing from a hunter,
or like a flock of sheep that no one gathers,
everyone will return to his own people
and flee to his native land. [s]
15 Any who are found will be slaughtered;
without exception they will be slain by the sword.
16 Their infants will be smashed to pieces before their eyes;
their houses will be plundered
and their wives will be ravished. [t]
17 Behold, I am stirring up against them the Medes
who have no interest in silver
and are not tempted by gold.* [u]
18 With their bows they will slaughter the young men,
and they will show no pity for young children.

m Jer 51:11; Joel 3:11.—n Jer 50:9; Joel 3:14.—o Jer 46:10; Ezek 30:2; Joel 1:15.—p Isa 21:3; Gen 3:16; Ps 48:7.—q Isa 24:23; Rev 8:12.—r Isa 2:17; 3:11; Ezek 28:2.—s 1 Ki 22:17; Jer 50:16; Mt 9:36.—t Nah 3:10.—u Isa 21:2; 2 Ki 18:14-16; Jer 51:11, 28.

13:1—23:18 The oracles grouped together in chapters 13–23 arose in historical situations that were very diverse and often remote from one another in time. Some of the oracles were composed by Isaiah, others by some of his later disciples. These inspired men saw in the development of events and the collisions of peoples a fulfillment of the judgment of God, who offers salvation to every people that turns to him. Discreetly but firmly, the national boundaries of Israel are ignored, and the theme of the call of the nations makes its appearance.

13:1-22 The editor of the Book attributes this lament to Isaiah himself. This lament describes the fall of Babylon after the manner of the fall of Nineveh. In fact, the city conquered by Cyrus in 539 B.C., was not destroyed, but the disappearance of the Assyrian capital, like that of Sodom and Gomorrah, always remained a paradigm for the prophets.

13:17 The Medes were originally warlike tribes from the mountains east of Babylonia; once gathered as a kingdom, they were first allied with Babylon against the Assyrians; later, joined with the Persians, they would contribute to the fall of Babylon.

19 And Babylon, the most glorious of kingdoms,
the splendor and jewel of the Chaldeans,
will be like Sodom and Gomorrah
when they were overthrown by God. [v]
20 It will never be inhabited;
no future generations will ever reside there.
No Arab will ever again pitch his tent there,
nor will shepherds rest their flocks in that land. [w]
21 However, wild animals of the desert will dwell there,
and its houses will be filled with jackals.
There ostriches will reside,
and there wild goats* will dance.
22 Hyenas will howl in her castles
and jackals in her luxurious palaces.
Her time draws near,
and her days will not be prolonged.

CHAPTER 14

Taunting the King of Babylon. 1 The LORD
will have compassion on Jacob, and he will
once again choose Israel. He will resettle
them on their native soil, where foreigners
will join them and attach themselves to the
house of Jacob. [x] 2 Nations will take them
and escort them to their homeland, and the
house of Israel will accept them as male and
female slaves in the LORD's land. The house
of Israel will also enslave those who had
enslaved them and will rule her oppressors.
3 * When that day arrives that the LORD
affords you relief from your suffering and
trouble and from the cruel servitude that
had been imposed upon you, [y] 4 you will take
up this taunt-song against the king of
Babylon:

Behold how the oppressor has come to an end!
Behold how his arrogance has ceased!
5 The LORD has broken the rod of the wicked,
the scepter of rulers,
6 that struck down the peoples in wrath,
inflicting continuous blows,
and that furiously crushed the nations
with relentless persecution.
7 The entire world is at rest and peaceful;
shouts of joy resound.
8 The cypresses exult over you,
as do the cedars of Lebanon, saying,
"Now that you have been laid low,
no one approaches to cut us down." * [z]

9 The netherworld below is all astir
to greet you upon your arrival.
To welcome you it aroused the departed spirits,
all the rulers of the earth.
It raised from their thrones
all those who were kings of the nations.
10 All of them will speak out
and greet you with these words,
"You too have become as weak as we are.
You have become like us." [a]
11 Your pomp has descended to the netherworld
along with the music of your harps.
Maggots compose the mattress upon which you lie,
and worms serve as your blanket.

12 To what depths have you fallen from the heavens,
O morning star, son of the dawn!
How you have been cut down to the ground,
you who laid the nations low!
13 You used to say in your heart,
"I will scale the heavens.
I will raise my throne
above the stars of God.
I will sit on the Mountain of Assembly,
in the far recesses of the north.
14 I will ascend above the highest clouds;
I will be like the Most High." [b]
15 Instead you have been hurled down to the netherworld,
to the depths of the abyss.

---

v Isa 47:5; Gen 19:25; Rev 14:8.—w Isa 14:23; Jer 51:62.—x Isa 56:3; 60:4; Ps 102:14; Jer 24:6; 33:26; Zec 1:17; 10:6.—y Isa 11:10; Jer 30:10.—z Isa 37:24; 2 Ki 19:23; Ezek 31:16.—a Ezek 26:20; 32:21.—b Gen 3:5; Ezek 28:2.

13:21 *Wild goats:* or "satyrs," popular personifications of the demons who dwelt in ruins.

14:3-21 The passage refers perhaps to Sargon II, king of Assyria, or, more probably, to Nebuchadnezzar, king of Babylonia. The Fathers of the Church saw in the Lucifer of verse 12 the leader of the angels, who had become the prince of demons in punishment for his boundless pride.

14:8 The kings of Assyria and Babylon had had a great many of the cedars of Lebanon cut down for their building projects.

16 Those who see you will stare at you,
and as they do so they will wonder,
"Is this the man who made the earth tremble
and overthrew kingdoms,
17 who turned the world into a desert,
laid its cities in ruins,
and refused to let his prisoners return home?"
18 All the kings of the nations lie in honor,
each one in his own tomb.
19 But you have been cast out without burial,
like some loathsome piece of flesh;
you are covered with the dead,
with those pierced by the sword
who descend to the rocks of the abyss.
20 You will never be buried with those kings
because you have destroyed your land
and brought death to your people.
The offspring of the wicked
will never again be mentioned. [c]
21 Make ready to slaughter his sons
because of the guilt of their father.
Let them never again rise to possess the earth
and cover the face of the earth with their cities.

22 I will rise up against them, says the LORD
of hosts, and I will deprive Babylon of her
name and remnant, her offspring and pos-
terity, says the LORD. [d] 23 I will cause it to
become a haunt of the hedgehogs and a
marshland; I will sweep it with the broom of
destruction, says the LORD of hosts.

Assyria*

24 The LORD of hosts has sworn:
As I have resolved, so will it be;
as I have planned, so will it come to pass.
25 I will break the Assyrian in my land
and trample him underfoot on my mountains;
his yoke will be lifted from my people,
and his burden will be removed from their shoulders.
26 This is the plan that the LORD has prepared
for the entire world,
and this is the hand that he has outstretched
over all the nations. [e]
27 For the LORD of hosts has devised this plan;
who can thwart it?
His hand is outstretched;
who can turn it back?

Philistia. 28 In the year that King Ahaz died, this oracle was proclaimed:

29 Let not a single one of you rejoice, O Philistia,
that the rod that struck you is broken.
For from the root of a snake will be born a viper,
and its fruit will be a flying serpent.
30 The poor of my people will eat in my pasture,
and the destitute will lie down in safety.
But I will make your offspring die of hunger,
and I will then slay the remnant.
31 Howl, O gate! Cry out, O city!
Let all Philistia be stricken with fear!
For a mighty foe is coming from the north,
without a single straggler in its ranks.
32 What reply will then be given
to the envoys of that nation?
"The LORD has established Zion,
and the afflicted of his people
will find refuge in her." [f]

CHAPTER 15

Moab*

1 * An oracle concerning Moab:

Having been laid waste in a single night,
Ar of Moab is destroyed.
Having been laid waste in a single night,
Kir of Moab is destroyed. [g]
2 The daughter of Dibon goes up
to the high places to weep.
Moab wails unceasingly
over Nebo and Medeba.
Every head has been shaved,
every beard has been cut off.
3 In the streets they wear sackcloth;
on the roofs and in the public squares
everyone wails and collapses in tears. [h]

c Job 18:19.—d 2 Sam 18:18; Job 18:17; Jer 51:62.—e Isa 23:9; Ex 15:12.—f Isa 2:2; 37:9; Pss 87:5; 102:17f; Zep 3:12.—g Isa 13:1; 16:7; Jer 48:24, 41.—h Isa 3:24; Lam 2:1.

14:24-27 In 701 B.C., Sennacherib invaded the kingdom of Judah and surrounded Jerusalem. He had to lift the siege, however: an epidemic was destroying his army. This was the beginning of the decline of this empire.

15:1—16:14 Moab, ancient rival and enemy of Israel, was devastated during the Assyrian war of 701 B.C.

15:1-5 The names are those of places belonging at that time to the kingdom of Moab.

4 Hesbon and Elealeh cry out in distress;
their voices are heard as far away as Jahaz.
As a result, the bravest of Moab's warriors cry out
and their hearts grow faint.

5 My heart cries out for Moab;
her fugitives have arrived close to Zoar,
at Eglath-shelishiyah.
They climb the slope of Luhith,
weeping as they make their ascent;
on the road to Horonaim
they emit heart-rending cries. [i]

6 The waters of Nimrim
have become a desolate waste.
The grass is parched,
the plants have withered away,
and nothing green can be seen.
7 Therefore, the people carry away
across the Ravine of the Willows
whatever possessions they can manage
and the savings they have accumulated.

8 Their cry of distress has echoed
around the land of Moab.
Their wailing reaches as far as Eglaim;
it can be heard even to the land of Beer-elim.
9 The waters of Dimon are filled with blood,
but I have far worse in store for Dimon:
a lion for those who are fleeing from Moab,
as well as for those who are left on its soil. [j]

CHAPTER 16

1 * Send forth lambs to the ruler of the land,
from Sela across the desert
to the mount of daughter Zion.
2 Like fluttering birds,
like scattered nestlings,
are the women of Moab
at the fords of the Arnon.

3 Offer your counsel,
grant us your justice.
At high noon
let your shadow be like night.
Hide those who are outcasts
and do not betray the fugitives. [k]
4 Allow the outcasts of Moab
to settle among you,
and be their refuge from the destroyer.
When the oppression has ceased
and the devastation is at an end,
and the marauders who have trampled the land
have finally departed,
5 a throne established in faithful love
will be established in the tent of David,
and on it will sit in fidelity [l]
a judge who offers fair judgment
and is prompt to ensure justice.

6 We have heard about the pride of Moab,
about how truly intense that pride is,
with its arrogance, its pride, and its insolence,
as well as its boasts which have little basis. [m]
7 Therefore, let Moab wail,
every one of its inhabitants.
In their grief they will long
for the raisin cakes of Kir-hareseth.
8 The vineyards of Heshbon have withered,
the vines of Sibmah.
The lords of the nations
have destroyed the choicest vines
that once reached as far as Jazer
and spread out toward the desert,
and whose shoots with their spreading branches
spread across the sea.

9 Therefore, I weep with Jazer
for the vines of Sibmah.
I drench you with tears,
Heshbon and Elealeh,
for the cries of battle have fallen
over your harvest and vintage. [n]
10 Joy and gladness
have been taken away from the fields.
In the vineyards no songs are sung,
no joyful shouts are raised.
No one treads out wine in the winepresses
no cheers of happiness are heard.

11 That is the reason why
my heart throbs like a harp for Moab
and my soul for Kir-hareseth.

i Isa 16:9; Gen 13:10; Jer 48:3, 31.—j Isa 15:2; 2 Ki 17:25; Ezek 25:8-11.—k 1 Ki 18:4.—l Isa 32:1; Mic 4:7.—m Jer 48:29; Zep 2:8.—n Isa 15:4; Jer 48:32; Ezek 27:31.

16:1-4 The text is uncertain— verse 2 belongs before verse 1, as a continuation of 15:9. Then, it seems, the ruler of Moab is urged to send a messenger to ask for asylum in Jerusalem, to which verses 3-4 refer.

12 When the Moabites approach
and exhaust themselves on the high places,
they will flock to their sanctuaries to pray,
but it will avail them nothing. [o]

13 This was the word that the LORD spoke
about Moab in the past. 14 But now the LORD
says: In three years, as a hired worker reckons them, the glory of Moab will be regarded with contempt, despite its vast multitude. The remnant that survive will be few in number and very feeble.

CHAPTER 17

Damascus

1 An oracle concerning Damascus:

Before long Damascus will cease to be a city,
and she will be reduced to a heap of ruins. [p]
2 Her towns will be abandoned forever;
they will serve as pastures for flocks
who will lie there undisturbed.
3 No longer will Ephraim have a fortress
or Damascus a kingdom.
The glory of the remnant of Aram
will be like that of the children of Israel,
says the LORD of hosts.
4 On that day
the glory of Jacob will grow dim
and the flesh of his body will grow lean, [q]
5 as when the reaper gathers the standing grain,
harvesting the ears with his arms,
or as when one gleans the ears of grain
in the Valley of Rephaim.*
6 Nothing will remain except the scattered remnant,
as when an olive tree is beaten:
two or three olives on the highest bough,
four or five on each of its fruitful branches,
says the LORD, the God of Israel.
7 On that day,
men will look to their Creator,
and they will turn their eyes
to the Holy One of Israel. [r]
8 They will not gaze upon the altars, their handiwork,
nor shall they regard what their fingers have made
the sacred poles and the altars of incense.
9 On that day their strong cities will be
like those abandoned by the Hivites and the Amorites
which they deserted because of the Israelites' advance;
their cities will be left desolate. [s]
10 You have forgotten the God of your salvation
and have not kept in mind the Rock, your refuge.
Therefore, you plant your pagan gardens
and sow exotic seeds for a foreign god. [t]
11 Even though you cause them to sprout
on the day that you plant them,
and make them sprout blossoms
on the following morning,
yet the harvest will disappear
when struck by a wasting disease and incurable blight.
12 Listen to the thunder of vast hordes,
its volume like that of the roaring sea.
Listen to the roar of nations,
its volume like that of mighty waves.
13 But when God rebukes them
they flee far away,
driven like chaff on the mountains before the wind
and like whirling dust before the storm. [u]
14 In the evening terror has spread,
but by the morning it has disappeared.
Such is the fate of those who plunder us,
the lot of those who despoil us.

CHAPTER 18

Ethiopia

1 Woe to the land of buzzing locusts
beyond the rivers of Ethiopia,*
2 sending ambassadors by sea
in papyrus vessels across the waters.
Go forth, you swift messengers,
to a nation tall and bronzed,

o Isa 15:2; Jer 48:13.—p Isa 13:1; Gen 14:15; Jer 49:23.—q Isa 10:16; 17:3.—r Isa 2:11; 10:20; Mic 5:12.—s Isa 27:10; Ezek 35:4.—t Isa 51:13; Jer 2:32; Ezek 22:12; Hos 8:14.—u Isa 13:14; Job 21:18.

17:5 *Valley of Rephaim:* west of Jerusalem.

18:1 *Rivers of Ethiopia:* the reference is to the Upper Nile and its tributaries.

to a people dreaded near and far,
a mighty and conquering nation
whose land is crossed by many rivers. [v]
3 All you who inhabit the world,
you who dwell on the earth,
you will see when the signal is raised on the mountains
and hear when the trumpet is sounded.
4 For this is what the LORD said to me:
I will quietly look down from my dwelling
like the shimmering heat of the summer sun,
like a cloud of dew during the harvest heat.
5 For prior to the harvest, when the flowering is over
and the blooms become ripening grapes
the shoots will be cut off with pruning hooks,
and the branches will be cut away and discarded.
6 They will all be left
to the birds of prey on the mountains
and to the wild beasts of the earth.
In summer the birds of prey will dwell there,
while the wild animals will winter on them.

7 At that time offerings will be brought to
the LORD of hosts from a tall and bronzed
people dreaded near and far, a mighty and
conquering nation whose land is crisscrossed
by rivers, to Mount Zion, the place where the
name of the LORD of hosts dwells. [w]

CHAPTER 19

Egypt

1 An oracle concerning Egypt:

Behold, the LORD is riding on a swift cloud,
and he is coming to Egypt.
The idols of Egypt will tremble before him,
and the hearts of the Egyptians will melt within them. [x]
2 I will stir up Egyptians against Egyptians,
and they will fight against one another,
brother against brother, neighbor against neighbor,
city against city, kingdom against kingdom.
3 The spirit of the Egyptians will ebb away within them,
and I will throw their deliberations into disarray.
They will then resort to consulting idols
and the spirits of the dead,
as well as ghosts and sorcerers. [y]
4 I will deliver the Egyptians
into the power of a harsh master,
a cruel king who will rule over them—
says the Lord, the LORD of hosts.
5 The waters of the Nile will ebb away,
and the river will become parched and dry. [z]
6 Its canals will emit a terrible stench,
and its branches will diminish and dry up;
reeds and rushes will wither away.
7 All the plants on the banks of the Nile
and all the vegetation of the Nile
will dry up, blow away, and vanish.
8 The fishermen will groan and mourn,
all those who cast their hooks into the Nile,
while those who spread their nets on the water
will lose heart.
9 The linen-workers will despair,
as will the combers and weavers. [a]
10 The spinners will be dismayed,
and all who work for wages will be crushed.
11 The princes of Zoan* are utter fools;
the wisest of Pharaoh's counselors offer stupid advice.
How can you dare to say to Pharaoh,
"I am descended from sages;
I spring from ancient kings"?
12 Where then are your sages?
Let them tell you,
so that all may know
what the LORD of hosts has planned against Egypt. [b]

---

v Isa 18:7; Ex 2:3; Job 9:26.—w Isa 45:14; 60:7; 2 Chr 9:24; Zep 3:10.—x Isa 13:1; Ex 12:12; Joel 3:19.—y Isa 44:25; Lev 19:31; 1 Chr 10:13.—z Isa 44:27; Jer 50:38; Ezek 30:12.—a Prov 7:16; Ezek 16:10; 27:7.—b Isa 14:24; Rom 9:17; 1 Cor 1:20.

19:11 *Zoan:* the Tanis of the Greeks, a city in the Nile Delta. Egyptian wise men enjoyed a high reputation in the ancient East.

13 The princes of Zoan have become fools.
and the princes of Memphis have been deceived.
The chiefs of her tribes
have led Egypt astray.
14 The LORD has infused them
with a spirit of confusion;
they have made Egypt stagger in everything she does,
just as a drunkard staggers around in his vomit. [c]
15 Neither head nor tail,
neither palm branch nor reed,
will be able to do anything for Egypt.

16 On that day the Egyptians will be like
women, trembling with fear because the
LORD of hosts has raised his hand against
them. [d] 17 And the land of Judah will
become a source of terror to the Egyptians. Every time they remember Judah,
they will tremble with fear because of the
plan that the LORD of hosts has devised
against them.

18 On that day there will be five cities in
the land of Egypt speaking the language of
Canaan and swearing allegiance to the
LORD of hosts. One of these will be called
the City of the Sun.

19 On that day there will be an altar to
the LORD in the land of Egypt, and a sacred
pillar to the LORD at its border. 20 It will
serve as a sign and a witness to the LORD of
hosts in the land of Egypt. When they cry
out to the LORD for his help against their
oppressors, he will send them a savior to
defend and deliver them. 21 The LORD will
make himself known to the Egyptians, and
the Egyptians will acknowledge the LORD
on that day. They will offer sacrifices and
oblations, and they will make vows to the
LORD and fulfill them. [e] 22 The LORD will
strike Egypt severely, but he will then bring
them healing. After that they will return to
the LORD, and he will listen to their prayers
and heal them.

23 On that day there will be a highway
from Egypt to Assyria. The Assyrians will
enter Egypt, and the Egyptians will enter
Assyria, and Egyptians and Assyrians will
worship together.

24 On that day Israel will be a member of
a triumvirate with Egypt and Assyria, a
blessing at the center of the world, [f] 25 and
the LORD of hosts will bless them with
these words: "Blessed be my people Egypt,
and Assyria the work of my hands, and
Israel my heritage."

CHAPTER 20

The Fate of Egypt and Ethiopia.* 1 In the
year that the commander-in-chief, who
had been sent by King Sargon of Assyria,
came to Ashdod, he fought against it and
captured it. 2 At that time the LORD spoke
to Isaiah, the son of Amoz, and issued this
warning, "Go forth, take off the sackcloth
from your waist, and remove the sandals
from your feet." Isaiah did as he had been
instructed, walking naked and barefoot. [g]

3 Then the LORD said, "Just as my servant Isaiah has gone naked and barefoot
for three years as a sign and portent
against Egypt and Ethiopia, 4 so shall the
king of Assyria lead away the captives of
Egypt and the exiles from Ethiopia, both
the young and the aged, naked and barefoot, with their buttocks exposed, to the
shame of Egypt. 5 Then they will be dismayed and ashamed of Ethiopia their
hope and of Egypt their boast. [h] 6 On that
day the inhabitants of the coastland will
say, 'Observe what has happened to those
in whom we hoped and to whom we fled
for help and deliverance from the king of
Assyria. How will we now be able to
escape?' " [i]

CHAPTER 21

The Defeat of Babylon*

1 An oracle concerning the wilderness of
the sea:

c Prov 12:8; Mt 17:17.—d Isa 2:17; Deut 2:25; Jer 50:37.—e Gen 27:29; Zec 14:16.—f Isa 11:11; 19:23.—g Isa 13:1; Zec 13:4.—h Isa 30:3, 5; 2 Ki 18:21; Ezek 29:16.—i Isa 31:3; 36:6; 2 Ki 18:21; Mt 23:33.

20:1-6 Because it had incited an anti-Assyrian coalition, the Philistine city of Ashdod was captured in 711 B.C. by the supreme commander of Sargon II. Isaiah performs a prophetic gesture; his incongruous behavior illustrates the fate reserved for prisoners from the contingent, which Egypt and Ethiopia had sent to serve under the Philistines.

21:1-10 Proud Babylon has fallen. The reference is either to 710 B.C., when Babylon was attacked by the Assyrian, Sargon, who put down the rebellion of Merodach-baladan (see 2 Ki 20:10; Jer 39:1-8), or to its fall in 539 B.C. under the attack of Cyrus. Tradition has it that the city was taken by the allied Medes and Persians during the night, while the ruler and his men were feasting in the assurance that the walls were impregnable (v. 5; see Dan 5).

Like whirlwinds sweeping over the Negeb,*
there comes from the desert,
from a land that inspires terror,
2 a harsh vision that is shown to me:
the traitor betrays
and the despoiler despoils.
Go forth, O Elam;*
lay siege, O Media.
I will bring to an end
all the pain she has inflicted.[j]

3 Therefore, my loins are filled with anguish;
pangs have seized me
like those of a woman in labor.
I am so distraught that I cannot hear;
I am too frightened even to look.[k]
4 My mind reels,
and I am overcome with dread;
the twilight I yearned for
has become horrifying to me.

5 They set the table;
they spread out the rugs;
they eat and they drink.
Rise up, O princes;
oil your shields.[l]
6 For this is what the LORD has said to me:
Go forth and post a lookout;
let him report what he sees.
7 If he should see cavalry,
horsemen riding in pairs,
men mounted on donkeys,
men mounted on camels,
instruct him to watch closely
and to listen diligently.

8 Then the lookout shouted,
"I stand on the watchtower, O Lord,
all day long,
and I remain stationed at my post
throughout the night.[m]
9 Behold, here come the cavalry now,
horsemen riding in pairs."

Then the LORD responded:
Fallen, fallen is Babylon,
and all the images of her gods
have been smashed to the ground.[n]

10 O my people,
you who have been trodden
upon the threshing floor,
what I have heard from the LORD of hosts,
from the God of Israel,
I have proclaimed to you.[o]

Edom

11 An oracle concerning Edom:

Someone is calling to me from Seir,
"Watchman, when will the night end?
Watchman, when will it end?"
12 The watchman replies,
"Morning will come, and so will the night.
If you wish to ask, do so;
come back again."[p]

Arabia

13 An oracle concerning Arabia:

In the thickets of the desert you will encamp,
you caravans of Dedanites.
14 Bring water to the thirsty
and greet the fugitives with bread,
you inhabitants of the land of Tema.*[q]
15 For they have fled from the sword,
from the sharp edge of the drawn sword,
from the bent bow,
and from the stress of battles.

16 For these are the words spoken to me by
the LORD: Within a year, as a hired worker
reckons time, all the glory of Kedar* will
come to an end. 17 Hardly any of Kedar's
valiant warriors will be left, for the LORD, the
God of Israel, has spoken.

CHAPTER 22

Jerusalem*

1 An oracle concerning the Valley of Vision:*

What possible reason can there be
for all of you to have gone up on the housetops,
2 dwellers in a city full of commotion,
a city exultant and filled with tumult.

j Isa 13:17; 24:16; Gen 10:22; Jer 25:25.—k Isa 26:17; Gen 3:16; Ps 38:8.—l 2 Sam 1:21.—m Hab 2:1.—n Isa 21:7; 46:1; Lev 26:30; Jer 50:2; 51:8; Rev 14:8.—o Isa 51:23; Jer 51:33; Mt 3:12.—p Job 36:20.—q Gen 25:15; Job 6:19.

21:1 *The desert:* the plain of Babylonia. *The Negeb:* the vast southern wilderness of Palestine.

21:2 *Elam:* an ancient people dwelling in the area from which the Persians would come. For the Medes, see 13:17.

21:14 *Tema:* an oasis in the northeastern Arabian peninsula.

21:16 *Kedar:* a powerful tribe in southern Arabia.

22:1-14 Delighted by a passing military success, or by the defeat of Sennacherib in 701 B.C. (Isa 36–37), the city celebrates. The inhabitants are proud of their preparations for war, their strengthened defenses, and the subterranean channel which King Hezekiah had had dug in order to provide the city with drinking water.

22:1 *Valley of Vision:* the valley around southeastern Jerusalem.

Your slain did not fall by the sword,
nor did they perish in battle. [r]
3 All your leaders fled away together,
only to be captured
without a weapon to defend themselves.
All of them who were found were captured
even though they had fled in all directions.

4 That is the reason why I said:
Turn your eyes away from me;
let me weep bitterly.
Do not try to console me
about the destruction of my people. [s]
5 For this is a day ordained by the LORD of hosts,
a day of rout, tumult, and confusion
in the Valley of Vision,
a day on which walls will be battered down
and cries for help echo through the mountains. [t]
6 Elam has taken up his quiver,
the chariots of Aram have their horses prepared,
and Kir has bared his shield.
7 Your fairest valleys are filled with chariots,
and the cavalry stands ready at the gates;
8 the LORD has removed his sheltering hand from Judah.

On that day you checked out the supply of
weapons in the House of the Forest.* [u] 9 You
observed that there were many breaches in
the City of David, and you collected the
waters of the lower pool. 10 You counted the
buildings in Jerusalem, and you tore down
some to strengthen the wall. 11 Between the
two walls you constructed a reservoir for the
water of the old pool. But you did not look to
the city's Maker or give a thought to him
who built it long ago. [v]
12 On that day the Lord,
the LORD of hosts,
called on you to eat and mourn,
to shave your head and put on sackcloth. [w]
13 But instead you indulged in joy and merriment,
the killing of oxen and the slaughtering of sheep,
the eating of meat and the drinking of wine,
saying, "Let us eat and drink,
for tomorrow we die." [x]

14 Then the LORD of hosts revealed this to
me:

This wickedness will not be forgiven you
until you die,
says the Lord GOD of hosts.

Shebna and Eliakim

15 Thus says the Lord GOD of hosts:

Go forth and find that official,
Shebna, the master of the palace, and say:
16 What are you doing here,
and who gave you permission
to hew a tomb for yourself here?
By what right have you hewn your grave on a height
and chiseled out your tomb in the rock? [y]

17 The LORD is about to hurl you away violently;
he will grasp you firmly
18 and roll you up and throw you like a ball
into a vast expanse.
There you will die,
and there your splendid chariots will lie;
you are a disgrace to your master's household. [z]
19 I will remove you from your office,
and you will be pulled down from your post.

20 On that day I will summon
my servant Eliakim, the son of Hilkiah. [a]
21 I will clothe him with your robe
and place your sash around his waist,
and I will bestow upon him your authority.
He will be a father to the inhabitants of Jerusalem
and to the house of Judah.

r Isa 5:14; 32:13; 2 Ki 25:3; Ezek 22:5.—s Isa 15:3; Jer 6:26; 9:1; 14:17; Lam 1:16.—t Isa 2:12; 37:3.—u Isa 2:12; 1 Ki 7:2; 2 Chr 32:5.—v 2 Ki 25:4; 2 Chr 32:5; Jer 39:4.—w Joel 2:17; Mic 1:16.—x Isa 56:12; 1 Cor 15:32.—y Gen 50:5; Mt 27:60.—z Isa 14:19; Job 15:15.—a Isa 36:3; 2 Ki 18:18, 37.

22:8 *House of the Forest:* a hall supported by cedar columns and serving as an armory; see 1 Ki 7:2-5; 10:17.

22 I will place on his shoulder
the key of the house of David.
When he opens,
no one will close;
when he closes,
no one will open.* [b]
23 I will fasten him like a peg in a secure place,
and he will become a throne of honor for his family.
24 Upon him will depend all the glory of his family,
his descendants, and his offspring,
and even the smallest vessels, from cups to pitchers. [c]
25 On that day, says the LORD of hosts,
the peg that was securely fastened
will give way, break loose, and fall,
and whatever had been hanging on it will be lost.
For the LORD has spoken.

CHAPTER 23

Tyre and Sidon*

1 An oracle concerning Tyre:
Wail, O ships of Tarshish,
for your harbor has been destroyed.
From the land of Cyprus
the news has reached them.
2 Be silent, you who dwell along the coast,
you merchants of Sidon,
whose messengers crossed over the sea
3 to the vast ocean.
The grain of Shihor, the harvest of the Nile
provided your revenue;
you were the merchant for the nations. [d]
4 Be ashamed, O Sidon, the fortress of the sea,
for the sea has declared:
"I have not endured the anguish of labor,
nor have I given birth;
I have not reared young men
or brought up young women." [e]
5 When the news reaches Egypt,
they will writhe in anguish
upon hearing the fate of Tyre.
6 Cross over to Tarshish;
wail, you inhabitants of the coast.
7 Is this your vibrant city
founded in the days of old,
and whose feet have led her away
to settle in distant lands? [f]
8 Who has devised this plan
against Tyre, the bestower of crowns,
whose merchants were princes
and whose traders were held in the highest esteem
throughout the earth?
9 The LORD of hosts has devised this plan
to deflate the glory of the proud
and to humiliate the honored men of the earth. [g]
10 Cross over to your own land,
you ships of Tarshish,
for your harbors no longer exist.*
11 The LORD has stretched out his hand over the sea
and brought kingdoms to their knees;
he has commanded the destruction
of the fortresses of Canaan.
12 He has said:
You will exult no more,
O greatly oppressed virgin daughter of Sidon.
Arise and cross over to Cyprus,
but even there you will find no rest. [h]
13 Look at the land of the Chaldeans;
it was this people, not Assyria,
who erected siege-towers,
tore down its palaces,
and left it in ruins.
14 Cry out in anguish, O ships of Tarshish,
for your fortress has been destroyed.

15 From that day, Tyre will be forgotten for
seventy years, the span of one king's life. At
the end of those seventy years, the plight of
Tyre will be identical to that of the prostitute
in the song: [i]

16 Take your harp
and walk throughout the city,
you long-forgotten prostitute.

b Isa 9:6; Mt 16:19; Rev 3:7.—c Ezek 15:3.—d Isa 19:7.—e Gen 10:15, 19.—f Ezek 26:13.—g Isa 14:24; Job 40:11; Ezek 27:3; 28:7.—h Isa 37:22; Jer 14:17; Ezek 28:21f; Rev 18:22.—i Jer 25:11, 22; 29:10.

22:22 *Key . . . close . . . open:* symbolizes the power to govern.

23:1-18 Two songs oddly combined, one by Isaiah (vv. 1-4, 12-14), the other of much more recent date (vv. 5-11); the two describe the fall of Tyre and Sidon, the capitals of maritime trade. Sennacherib destroyed Sidon around 701 B.C. In the sixth century, Nebuchadnezzar, and later on (in 332 B.C.) Alexander, would besiege the impregnably fortified island of Tyre.

23:10 Once Tyre fell, trade with Spain and Tarshish was left to its own resources.

Pluck your strings sweetly
and sing many songs
so that they may remember you.

17 At the end of the seventy years the LORD will visit Tyre. She will once again ply her trade and prostitute herself with all the kingdoms of the world on the face of the earth. [j]
18 But her merchandise and her profits will be dedicated to the LORD; they will not be stored up or hoarded, but they will provide abundant food and clothing to those who live in the presence of the LORD. [k]

IV: APOCALYPSE OF ISAIAH*

CHAPTER 24

Universal Judgment: A Grateful Remnant

1 Behold how the LORD is preparing
to lay waste the earth;
he will turn it into a desert
and scatter its inhabitants, [l]
2 with the same fate afflicting both priest and people,
slave and master,
maid and mistress,
seller and buyer,
lender and borrower,
creditor and debtor.
3 The earth will be totally ravaged
and completely despoiled;
this has the LORD decreed.

4 The earth mourns and fades away;
the world languishes and withers;
the exalted of the earth are brought low. [m]
5 The earth is defiled
by those who dwell in it;
for they have transgressed laws,
violated statutes,
and broken the everlasting covenant.*
6 Therefore, a curse has consumed the earth,
and its inhabitants pay the penalty of their guilt;
as a result, the number of its inhabitants dwindles,
and only a few survive.
7 The new wine dries up
and the vine withers away
as the revelers groan in their sorrow. [n]
8 The cheerful sound of tambourines is stilled;
the shouts of the revelers fade away;
the lyre's joyful melodies are no longer heard. [o]
9 The people drink wine but without any singing;
strong liquor tastes bitter to those who consume it.

10 The city is shattered and in a state of chaos;
every house has its entrance barred.* [p]
11 In the streets the people cry out for wine;
no joy can be observed;
happiness seems to have been banished from the land. [q]

12 Only desolation remains in the city;
its gates have been smashed so badly
that they are beyond hope of repair.
13 This condition will hold true
among all the nations throughout the world;
as happens to an olive tree after it is beaten
or to the gleanings that remain
after the grape harvest. [r]
14 The people raise their voices in joyful praise,
proclaiming from the west the majesty of the LORD,
15 "Let the LORD be glorified in the east;
in the coastlands of the sea
glorify the name of the LORD,
the God of Israel." [s]

16 From the ends of the earth we hear songs

j Ezek 27:12.—k Isa 18:7; Ex 28:36; Mic 4:13.—l Isa 2:19-21; 13:9; Jer 25:29.—m Isa 15:6; Jer 12:11; Joel 1:10.—n Isa 15:6; Joel 1:5, 10.—o Isa 5:12; Jer 7:34; Hos 2:13; Rev 18:22.—p Isa 6:11; 25:2.—q Jer 14:3; 48:33.—r Isa 17:6; Ob 5; Mic 7:1.—s Isa 42:10, 12; Zep 2:11; Mal 1:11.

24:1—27:13 It was probably a political disaster that inspired this striking picture, which celebrates the coming of a new world as predicted by Isaiah and later by Ezekiel. The inspired prophet sees the final judgment of the universe coming. He announces the reign of God who is victorious over all hostile forces on earth and in heaven. The city of God, which is promised a glorious future, arises before our eyes on the ruins of the city of evil. This kind of transposition of events in prophecies of judgment, this kind of intermingling of cataclysm and renewal, is characteristic of the literary genre known as apocalypse, that is, revelation of the hidden destiny of the world, with images of terror and light providing a key to understanding it.

24:5 *Everlasting covenant:* the covenant entered into with the entire human race in the person of Noah (Gen 9:16).

24:10 A city in complete disorder and symbolically contrasted with the city of God.

that praise the glory of the Righteous One.
But I said, "I am wasting away.
I am wasting away. Woe is me!
For the traitors continue to betray;
the traitors have acted with great treachery. [t]
17 Terror and the pit and the snare
threaten all of you inhabitants of the earth.
18 Anyone who flees from the sound of terror
will fall into the pit,
and whoever climbs out of the pit
will be caught in the snare.
For the windows of heaven will be opened
and the foundations of the earth will shake.
19 The earth will be totally shattered,
the earth will be torn apart
the earth will be violently convulsed.
20 The earth will stagger like a drunkard
and sway like a fragile hut;
its transgressions will weigh heavily upon it,
and it will fall, never to rise again." [u]
21 On that day the LORD will punish
in the heavens the host of the heavens,*
and on the earth the kings of the earth.
22 They will be herded together,
jammed in like prisoners in a dungeon.
They will be shut up in a pit
and punished after many years.
23 Then the moon will seem to fade away
and the sun will hide in shame.
For the LORD of hosts will reign
on Mount Zion and in Jerusalem,
and he will manifest his glory
to the elders of his people. [v]

CHAPTER 25

1 O LORD, you are my God.
I will exalt you and praise your name,
for you have accomplished wonderful things,
formulated in ages past, faithful and sure. [w]
2 You have made the city a heap of ruins,
the fortified city a mass of rubble.
The citadel of foreigners is a city no more,
and it will never be rebuilt. [x]
3 Therefore, mighty peoples will honor you,
and the cities of ruthless nations
will regard you with awe.
4 For you have been a refuge for the poor,
a refuge to the needy in their distress,
a shelter from the storm
and a shade from the heat. [y]
5 The blast of the ruthless
is like a winter storm or a scorching drought,
but you subdue the roar of the foe,
and the song of the ruthless fades away.
6 On this mountain* the LORD of hosts
will prepare for all peoples
a feast of rich food and vintage wines,
of succulent foods and well-aged wines. [z]
7 On this mountain the LORD will destroy
the veil that shrouds* all the peoples,
the path spread over all the nations; [a]
8 he will destroy death forever.
Then the Lord GOD will wipe away
the tears from every face,
and from the entire earth he will remove
the shame of all his people;
for the LORD has spoken.
9 It will be said on that day,
"Behold, this is our God;
in him we place our hope for deliverance.
This is the LORD for whom we have waited;
let us rejoice and be glad that he has saved us." [b]
10 For the hand of the LORD will not rest on this mountain,

t Isa 28:5; Lev 26:39; Ezr 9:15.—u Isa 1:28; 43:27; Job 12:25.—v Isa 13:10; Ezek 48:35; Heb 12:22.—w Isa 7:13; Ex 15:2.—x Isa 17:1; Jer 9:11.—y Isa 14:32; 2 Sam 22:3; Nah 1:7.—z Isa 2:2; Mt 8:11.—a Isa 60:1, 3; Eph 4:18; Rev 7:17; 21:4.—b Isa 2:11; 30:18f.

24:21 *The host of the heavens:* the stars, often adored as divinities by the ancients.

25:6 Among the Semites a sacred banquet was an important act of worship. Beginning with this passage, the idea of a Messianic banquet becomes customary in Judaism and on into the New Testament. The *mountain* is Zion.

25:7 *Shrouds:* signifies the inability to recognize truth; therefore, religious ignorance.

but Moab will be trodden under his feet
as straw is trodden into the dung-heap.
11 The LORD will stretch forth his hands in Moab
as a swimmer stretches out his hands to swim,
and he will humble their pride
as his hands sweep over them. [c]
12 He will overthrow the high fortifications of their walls,
casting them down to the ground
and making them level with the dust. [d]

CHAPTER 26

A Song of Victory. 1 On that day this song will be sung in the land of Judah:

We have a strongly fortified city,
with walls and ramparts established to protect us.
2 Open the gates
to allow the upright nation to enter,
the nation that keeps faith. [e]
3 O LORD, you grant peace to those who are steadfast
because of their trust in you.
4 Trust in the LORD forever,
for the LORD is an eternal rock. [f]
5 He has brought low those in high places
and leveled their citadel,
casting it down to the ground
and flinging it down to the dust, [g]
6 to be trampled underfoot
by the feet of the poor and the oppressed.
7 The path of the righteous is smooth,
for you make level the way of the just. [h]
8 As we proceed in the path of your judgments,
we wait for you, O LORD;
your name and your renown
are all that our heart desires.
9 My soul longs for you throughout the night,
and my spirit within me seeks your presence.
For when your judgments are revealed to the earth,
the inhabitants of the world learn to practice justice. [i]
10 If favor is granted to the wicked,
they will never learn justice.
In the presence of the upright they will act perversely
and fail to behold the majesty of the LORD. [j]
11 O LORD, your hand is raised high
but they fail to see it.
Let them be ashamed
when they behold your zeal for your people;
let the fire reserved for your enemies consume them.
12 O LORD, you will grant us peace;
everything we have accomplished you have done for us. [k]
13 O LORD, our God,
other lords besides you have ruled us,
but we acknowledge only your name.
14 The dead will not come back to life;
their departed spirits will not rise again.
For you have punished and destroyed them
and eradicated all memory of them.
15 O LORD, you have enlarged the nation,
and in enlarging it you have been glorified;
you have extended all the frontiers of the country. [l]
16 O LORD, in our distress we cried out to you,
pouring forth our prayers
as we suffered your chastisement. [m]
17 As a woman who is pregnant
writhes and cries out in her agony
when her time of delivery is near,
so were we because of you, O LORD. [n]
18 We were with child and writhed with pain,
but we gave birth only to wind.
We have achieved no salvation for the earth,
and no one has been born to inhabit the world.
19 But your dead will live
and their bodies will rise again.
Awake and sing for joy,
you who sleep in the dust.

c Isa 5:25; 16:6f, 14.—d Isa 2:15; 26:5; Jer 51:44.—e Isa 1:26; 4:3; Ps 118:19f.—f Isa 12:2; 30:29; Gen 49:24; Ps 62:8.—g Isa 25:2, 12; 32:19; Ezek 26:11.—h Isa 40:4; 42:16; Ps 23:3f; Prov 11:5.—i Isa 55:6; Ps 94:15; Mt 6:33.—j Isa 5:12; 32:6; Mt 5:45.—k Isa 9:6; Jer 29:11; Mic 5:4a.—l Isa 14:2; 54:2f; Neh 9:22-23.—m Isa 29:4; Hos 6:1.—n Isa 21:3; Mic 4:10; Jn 16:21.

For your dew will be radiant,
and the earth will give birth again
to those who have long been dead. [o]

The LORD's Vindication

20 Go forth, my people, enter your chambers,
and shut your doors behind you.
Withdraw for a short while
until the wrath has subsided.
21 For the LORD emerges from his dwelling place
to punish the inhabitants of the earth
for their wickedness.
The earth will reveal the blood shed upon it
and will no longer hide its slain. [p]

CHAPTER 27

1 On that day,
the LORD will use his sword
that is cruel and great and strong
to punish Leviathan* the fleeing serpent,
Leviathan the writhing serpent,
and he will slay that dragon
that resides in the sea. [q]

2* On that day,
sing of the pleasant vineyard. [r]
3 I, the LORD, am its keeper,
and I water it frequently
lest any harm come to it;
I guard it night and day. [s]

4 I do not quickly succumb to anger,
but if I were to find briars and thorns,
I would march against them in battle
and consume them in fire. [t]
5 However, if they decide to ask for my protection,
let them make their peace with me;
otherwise I cannot protect them. [u]

6 In days to come,
Jacob will take root,
Israel will bud and blossom,
and the entire world will be covered with fruit.
7 Has the LORD struck them down
as he struck down those who struck him?
Has he slaughtered them
as their attackers were slaughtered?
8 By expelling and exiling them
he has taken action against them,
removing them with a breath
as fierce as the east wind. [v]
9 In this way will the guilt of Jacob be expiated
and the full fruit of renouncing his sin will occur,
when he crushes all the altar stones to pieces
like lumps of chalk,
and no sacred poles and incense altars
will remain standing. [w]

10 For the fortified city will be abandoned,
a deserted pasture, a forsaken wilderness;
the calves will graze and lie down there,
destroying its branches.
11 When its boughs grow dry and snap off,
women will come and use them for firewood.
For this is a people that lacks understanding;
therefore their Maker will not have compassion for them;
he who formed them will not show mercy toward them. [x]

12 On that day,
the LORD will thresh the grain
from the streams of the Euphrates
to the Wadi of Egypt,
and you will be gathered one by one,
O people of Egypt.
13 On that day,
a great trumpet will be sounded,
and those who were lost in the land of Assyria
and those who were outcasts in the land of Egypt
will come to worship the LORD
on the holy mountain in Jerusalem. [y]

---

o Isa 25:8; Ezek 37:5f; Dan 12:2; Hos 6:2.—p Isa 29:6; Mic 1:3; Lk 11:50-51.—q Job 40:25-32; Ezek 32:2.—r Isa 5:1; Jer 2:21.—s Isa 5:2ff; 58:11; Ps 121:4f; Jn 6:39.—t Isa 10:17; 27:11; Mt 3:12; Heb 6:8.—u Isa 25:4; Job 22:21; Rom 5:1.—v Isa 50:1; Gen 41:6; Jer 18:17.—w Ex 23:24; Lev 26:30; Rom 11:27.—x Isa 10:33; Deut 32:28; Jer 11:16.—y Lev 25:9; Jdg 3:27; Mt 24:31.

27:1 *Leviathan:* a sea monster in Semitic mythology, a symbol of the forces of evil.

27:2-5 This impressive passage has come down to us in a rather defective textual form.

V: THE LORD SAVES ISRAEL AND JUDAH*

CHAPTER 28

Against Samaria

1 Woe to the proud garlands of Ephraim's drunkards
and to the fading flowers of its glorious beauty,
the crowning glory of a nation of men
overcome with wine and lying in the streets. [z]
2 But behold, the LORD has one in his service
who is mighty and strong,
and who, like a storm of hail,
like a destroying tempest,
like a torrent of rain and raging flood waters,
will hurl them violently to the ground. [a]
3 The majestic garlands of Ephraim's drunkards
will be trampled underfoot.
4 And the fading blooms of its glorious beauty,
at the head of the lush valley,
will be like early figs before the summer;
whoever sees them will pluck them
and immediately consume them. [b]
5 On that day the LORD of hosts
will be a crown of glory
and a beautiful diadem
to the remnant of his people,
6 a spirit of justice
to the one who sits in judgment,
and a spirit of strength to those
who repel the enemy at the city gates. [c]

Against Judah

7 These also stagger from wine
and stumble due to strong drink.
Priests and prophets are confused because of liquor;
alcohol leaves them unable to think clearly
or to pronounce fair judgments. [d]
8 Every table is covered with filthy vomit;
no place is clean.
9 "To whom will the prophet impart knowledge?
To whom will he explain his message?
To babies who are newly weaned,
to those just taken from the breast?
10 With him we are given
command after command, command after command,
rule after rule, rule after rule,
here a little, there a little."*

11 Now, with stammering lips
and in an alien tongue,
he will speak to this people, [e]
12 to whom he has said,
"This is the place for rest;
give rest to the weary.
This is the place for repose."
However, they would not listen.
13 Therefore, to them the word of the LORD will be,
"Command after command, command after command,
rule after rule, rule after rule,
here a little, there a little." [f]

14 Therefore, listen to the word of the LORD,
you arrogant rulers of this people in Jerusalem.
15 Proudly you have boasted,
"We have made a covenant with death
and entered into a pact with the netherworld.
And so, when the overwhelming scourge occurs,
it will not afflict us.
For we have made lies our refuge
and taken shelter in falsehood." [g]

16 Therefore, the Lord GOD
has this to say to you in response:
Behold, I am laying a stone in Zion,
a stone that has been tested,
a precious cornerstone as a firm foundation;
those who place their trust in it will not falter. [h]

---

z Lev 10:9.—a Isa 29:6; 30:30; 40:10; Jos 10:11.—b Song 2:13; Hos 9:10; Nah 3:12.—c Isa 11:2-4; 2 Sam 14:20; Jn 5:30.—d Isa 56:10, 12; Lev 10:9; Eph 5:18.—e Isa 33:19; Gen 11:7; Deut 28:49; Jer 5:15; Bar 4:15.—f Isa 8:15; 28:10; Mt 21:44.—g Isa 8:19; Wis 1:16; Jer 5:12.—h Isa 14:32; Ps 118:22; Mt 21:42; Acts 4:11; Rom 9:33; 2 Tim 2:19; 1 Pet 2:6.

28:1—33:24 The following oracles mark, as it were, the advance of the troops which, toward the end of the eighth century, extended Assyrian dominion toward the western edge of the Fertile Crescent and as far as Egypt. The Hebrew people involved themselves in a dangerous game of alliances. When invasion threatens, Isaiah reminds them that it is in faith that they will find true courage and that amid the whirlwind of events, there is no security except in God. Some parts of this collection are from a later period.

28:10 In Hebrew, this verse (and v. 13) is a series of monosyllables that imitate the babbling of a drunkard: *sau lasau, sau lasau, kau lakau, kau lakau,* etc.

17 And I will make justice the measuring line,
with righteousness as the plumb line.
Hail will sweep away the refuge of lies,
and flood waters will submerge your hiding place.
18 Then your covenant with death will be annulled
and your pact with Sheol will not survive.
When the raging waters roar forth,
you will be overwhelmed by them. [i]
19 As often as the flood sweeps through,
it will engulf you,
sweeping over you day and night,
as terror conveys the message clearly.
20 For your bed will be too short
to enable you to stretch out,
and the blanket will be too narrow
to cover you sufficiently.
21 Then the LORD will rise up as on Mount Perazim,
and he will rage as he did in the Valley of Gibeon,
to accomplish his work, his mysterious work,
and to perform his deed, his strange deed.* [j]
22 Therefore, cease your arrogance,
or your bonds will be further tightened.
For the Lord GOD of hosts has revealed to me
the destruction he has decreed for the entire earth. [k]
23 Listen carefully to my words;
pay close attention to what I have to say.
24 Does the plowman spend his entire time plowing,
breaking up and harrowing his land?
25 Once he has leveled its surface,
does he not scatter the fennel and sow cummin,
and plant wheat and barley,
with spelt around the borders?
26 God has instructed him in this
and trained him correctly. [l]
27 Fennel must not be threshed with a sledge,
nor is a cartwheel rolled over cummin.
28 Grain must be crushed for bread,
but it cannot be done so to excess;
one maneuvers the cartwheels and the horses
but is careful not to grind it too fine.
29 All this knowledge comes from the LORD of hosts
whose counsel is wonderful
and whose wisdom is great. [m]

CHAPTER 29

The Siege of Jerusalem

1* Woe to Ariel, Ariel,*
the city where David encamped.
Year after year will pass,
and the festivals will be celebrated annually. [n]
2 Yet I will inflict distress upon Ariel,
and there will be endless mourning and lamentation
as she becomes like an altar of fire.
3 I will encamp against you like David,
completely surround you with my forces
and erect siege-works against you. [o]
4 Then, as you lie prostrate, you will speak,
and from the dust of the earth
your words will come forth.
Your voice will rise from the ground
like that of a ghost,
and your words will whisper out of the dust.
5 But the vast throng of your enemies
will be like fine dust,
and the horde of your ruthless foes
will be like flying chaff.
Then suddenly, in an instant, [p]
6 you will be visited by the LORD of hosts,
accompanied by thunder and earthquake and intense din,
by whirlwind and tempest
and the flame of devouring fire.
7 Then the horde of all the nations
that fight against Ariel,

i Isa 5:5; 7:7; 28:15.—j Isa 10:12; Jos 10:10; 2 Sam 5:20; 1 Chr 14:11.—k Isa 10:23; 2 Chr 36:16; Jer 29:18.—l Ps 94:10.—m Isa 9:6; Jer 32:19; Rom 11:33.—n Isa 1:14; 22:12-13; 28:1; 2 Sam 5:9.—o 2 Ki 25:1; Ezek 4:2; Lk 19:43-44.—p Isa 17:13; Deut 9:21; Ps 18:43; Job 21:18.

28:21 Recalls David's victory over the Philistines (2 Sam 5:17-25).

29:1-12 The visitation of God is a dramatic moment because it brings both punishment and salvation. Jerusalem will soon experience it.

29:1 *Ariel:* "lion of God," a symbolic name of Jerusalem.

all who fight against her,
besieging her and causing her great anguish,
will fade away like a dream,
like a vision in the night. [q]
8 Just as when a hungry man dreams of eating
and then awakens with an empty stomach,
or as when a thirsty man dreams of drinking
and then awakens to find his throat still parched,
so will it be with the horde of all the nations
that make war against Mount Zion.

Hypocrisy and Deception

9 If you stupefy yourselves,
you will remain in a stupor.
If you blind yourselves,
you will remain blind.
Be drunk, but not on wine;
stagger, but not from strong drink. [r]
10 For the LORD has poured out on you
a spirit of deep sleep;
he has closed your eyes, you prophets,
and covered your heads, you seers. [s]

11 The prophetic vision of all this has
become like the words of a sealed scroll. If
you hand it to someone who is able to read
and you say to him, "Please read this," he
will answer, "I cannot, because it is sealed." [t]
12 And if you hand it to someone who cannot
read and say to him, "Please read this," he
will reply, "I cannot read."

13* Then the LORD said:
Because this people draws near to me
only with their words
and honors me only with their lips
while their hearts are far from me,
and their reverence for me has become
nothing but a human commandment
that has been memorized, [u]
14 therefore, I will continue to deal with this people
in shocking and amazing ways.
The wisdom of their wise men will perish,
and the understanding of their discerning men will cease. [v]

15 Woe to those who go to extreme measures
to conceal their plans from the LORD,
who perpetrate their evil deeds in the dark,
saying, "Who sees us? Who knows where we are?" [w]
16 Such people are truly perverse.
Is the potter no better than the clay?
Can what is made say of its maker,
"He did not make me"?
Can a pot say of the potter,
"He really has no particular skill"? [x]

Deliverance

17 It will be but a very short time
before Lebanon will become a fertile field
and its orchards will be regarded as forests.
18 On that day the deaf will hear
the words of a book being read,
and the eyes of the blind will see,
delivered from gloom and darkness. [y]
19 The lowly will once again rejoice in the LORD,
and those who are poor will exult
in the Holy One of Israel. [z]
20 For the tyrants will be no more
and the arrogant will cease to exist;
all those who revel in evil deeds will be destroyed: [a]
21 those whose lies cause a man to be judged guilty,
those who set traps to capture just arbiters
and thereby deprive the innocent
from being granted justice. [b]

22 Therefore, thus says the LORD,
the deliverer of Abraham,
in regard to the house of Jacob:
No longer will the house of Jacob be ashamed,
nor will their faces grow pale. [c]
23 For when they see in their midst
their children, the work of my hands,
they will acknowledge my name as holy.

q Job 20:8; Mic 4:11; Zec 12:9.—r Isa 19:14; 28:7f; Jer 4:9.—s Isa 6:10; Mic 3:6; Rom 11:8.—t Isa 28:7; Dan 12:4; Mt 13:11.—u Isa 58:2; Ezek 33:31; Mt 15:8f; Mk 7:6f.—v Isa 6:9-10; Jer 8:9; 49:7; 1 Cor 1:19.—w Isa 30:1; Gen 3:8; Ezek 8:12; Jn 3:19f.—x Isa 10:15; 45:9; Gen 2:7; Jer 18:6; Rom 9:20.—y Isa 35:5; 42:6f; Mt 11:5; Mk 7:37.—z Isa 3:15; 61:1; Mt 5:5.—a Isa 28:22; 2 Chr 36:16; Ezek 11:2.—b Isa 5:23; 32:7; Am 5:10, 12.—c Isa 45:17; Gen 17:16; Zep 3:11.

29:13-14 Jesus will remind the Pharisees of this passage of Isaiah (Mt 15:7). "Not everyone who says to me, 'Lord, Lord,' will enter the kingdom of heaven" (Mt 7:21).

They will reverence the Holy One of Jacob
and stand in awe of the God of Israel.
24 Those who err in spirit will gain understanding,
and those who are obstinate will receive instruction. [d]

CHAPTER 30

Doomed Alliance with Egypt

1 Woe to the rebellious children, says the LORD,
who devise plans that were not in accord with my will,
who make alliances that were not inspired by me,
thereby adding sin upon sin.
2 They depart for Egypt
without seeking my counsel,
to take refuge in Pharaoh's protection
and to take shelter in Egypt's shadow. [e]
3 Therefore, Pharaoh's protection will be your shame,
and the shelter of Egypt's shadow
will be your humiliation. [f]
4 For though his princes are at Zoan
and his envoys have reached Hanes,*
5 everyone has been put to shame
by a people who cannot be of any use,
who afford them neither help nor profit
but only shame and disgrace. [g]

6 An oracle on the beasts of the Negeb:

Through a land of hardship and distress,
of the lioness and the roaring lion,
of the viper and the flying serpent,
they carry their wealth on the backs of donkeys
and their treasures on the humps of camels
to a nation that cannot be of help to them.
7 For Egypt's help is vain and futile;
therefore I have called her
"Rahab * the Worthless."
8 * And so go forth and in their presence
write it on a scroll,
inscribe it on a tablet,
so that it may serve hereafter
as an eternal witness. [h]
9 They are a rebellious people,
deceitful children,
children who refuse to listen
to the instruction of the LORD. [i]
10 To the seers they say,
"Cease to have visions!"
To the prophets they demand,
"Do not prophesy to us what is right;
reveal to us pleasant things; prophesy illusions. [j]
11 Cease with your warnings;
turn aside from the straight path.
We wish to hear nothing further
about the Holy One of Israel." [k]

12 Therefore, thus says the Holy One of
Israel:

Because you have rejected this warning,
placing your trust in fraud and deceit
and relying on them,
13 this guilt of yours will become for you
like a crack appearing in a high wall
that bulges out and continues to widen
until suddenly, in an instant,
that wall will come hurtling to the ground. [l]
14 It will crash and break like an earthenware pot,
shattered so completely
that among its fragments not a single shard can be found
to remove an ember from the hearth
or to scoop out water from a cistern. [m]

15 For thus says the Lord GOD,
the Holy One of Israel:
Your salvation depends upon repentance and tranquility
and your strength upon quiet trust.
But you would have none of it. [n]
16 "No," you said. "We will flee upon horses."
Therefore, you will flee.
"We will ride on swift horses," you added.
But your pursuers will be even more swift. [o]

---

d Jer 31:34; Heb 8:11.—e Isa 31:1; 36:6; 2 Ki 25:26; Jer 2:18, 36.—f Isa 20:5; 36:6; Jer 2:36f.—g Isa 36:6; 2 Ki 18:21; Jer 37:3-5; Ezek 17:15.—h Isa 8:1, 16; Ex 17:14; Jer 36:2; Hab 2:2.—i Isa 1:4; 28:15; Jer 7:28; Ezek 2:6.—j 1 Sam 9:9; 1 Ki 22:8; Jer 5:31.—k Isa 29:10; Job 21:14f.—l 1 Ki 20:30; Prov 6:15; Ezek 13:14.—m Jer 19:11.—n Isa 7:4; Mic 7:7.—o Isa 31:3; Jer 46:6.

30:4 *Hanes:* like Tunis, a city in the Nile Delta and a residence of the pharaoh.

30:7 *Rahab:* a monster in Eastern mythologies, often used in the Bible as a symbol for Egypt.

30:8-17 These verses show that Isaiah made use of writing.

17 A thousand will tremble at the threat of one;
if five threaten you, you will flee,
until you are left
like a flagstaff on the top of a mountain
or like a banner on a hill.
18 But even so the LORD is waiting to be gracious to you,
and he will rise up to grant you his compassion.
For the LORD is a God of justice;
blessed are all those who wait for him. [p]
19 O people of Zion who dwell in Jerusalem,
you will weep no more.
The LORD will be gracious to you
when you cry out to him for help;
when he hears your call,
he will answer you. [q]
20 Although the LORD may give you the bread of adversity
and the water of affliction,
he who is your Teacher will no longer hide himself,
but with your own eyes you will see your Teacher. [r]
21 And when you stray from your path,
whether to the right or to the left,
you will hear his voice behind you,
sounding in your ears and saying,
"This is the way; continue to follow it." [s]
22 Then you will realize how unclean
are your silver-plated idols
and your gold-plated images.
You will cast them away like polluted rags
and shout at them, "Away with you!" [t]

God's Promise of Prosperity

23 God will send rain
for the seed you sow in the ground,
and the crops that the soil brings forth
will be rich and abundant.
When that day comes,
your cattle will graze in broad pastures. [u]
24 The oxen and the donkeys that plow the land
will be fed with fodder
that has been winnowed with shovel and pitchfork.
25 On every lofty mountain and on every high hill
there will be streams of water
on the day of the great slaughter
when the strongholds fall. [v]
26 The light of the moon will match that of the sun,
and the light of the sun itself
will be seven times brighter than before,
like the light of seven days compressed into one,
when the LORD binds up the wounds of his people
and heals the injuries inflicted by his blows. [w]

Divine Punishment of Assyria

27 See, the name of the LORD approaches from afar,
with burning anger and dense clouds of smoke.
His lips are brimming over with anger,
and his tongue is like a devouring fire.
28 His breath is like a rushing flood
that reaches up to the neck;
it will winnow the nations with the sieve of destruction
and place on the jaws of the people
a bridle that will lead them astray. [x]
29 But as for you, your songs will be
like those on the night of a holy festival,
and you will experience joy in your hearts
such as occurs when, to the sound of a flute,
people make a pilgrimage to the mountain of the LORD,
to the Rock of Israel. [y]
30 Then the LORD will make his majestic voice heard
and allow his arm to be seen
as it descends in furious anger
and a flame of devouring fire
amid cloudbursts and thunderstorms and hail.
31 Assyria will be shattered at the voice of the LORD
as he strikes with his rod. [z]
32 Every stroke that the LORD inflicts upon Assyria
with his punishing rod

p Isa 42:14; Ps 34:9; Jer 17:7.—q Isa 25:8; 58:9.—r Isa 28:9; 1 Ki 22:27; Am 8:11.—s Isa 29:24; Jer 31:33f.—t Isa 31:7; Ex 32:4.—u Isa 65:21-22; Lev 26:4-5; Job 36:31.—v Ex 17:6; Joel 4:18.—w Isa 24:23; Jer 30:17; Rev 21:23.—x Isa 11:4; 2 Ki 19:28; Am 9:9.—y Isa 25:6; Mt 26:30.—z Isa 10:5, 12; 11:4.

will be accompanied by the sound
of timbrels and lyres
as he engages in battle
with his uplifted hand.
33 The pyre has been ready for a long time,
prepared for the king.
His pyre is deep and broad,
with fire and wood in abundance.
And the breath of the LORD, like a steam of sulfur,
will set it ablaze.* [a]

CHAPTER 31

Forbidden Alliance with Egypt

1 Woe to those who go down to Egypt for help
and who rely on horses,
who place their trust in a large number of chariots
and in the great strength of their horsemen,
but do not look to the Holy One of Israel
or seek the LORD's guidance. [b]
2 Yet he, too, is wise and can bring disaster,
and he does not take back his threats.
He will rise up against the house of the wicked
and against those who come to the support of evildoers.
3 The Egyptians are mortal, not divine;
their horses are flesh, not spirit.
When the LORD stretches out his hand,
the helper will stumble and the one helped will fall;
all of them will perish together. [c]

4 This is what the LORD said to me:

As a lion or a lion cub
growls over its prey,
and when a band of shepherds
gather together to drive it off,
it is not frightened by their shouting
or daunted by their clamor,
so the LORD of hosts will come down
to do battle on the heights of Mount Zion. [d]
5 Like a hovering bird
the LORD of hosts will protect Jerusalem;
he will protect and deliver it,
he will spare and rescue it. [e]
6 Come back to the one
whom you have completely deserted,
O children of Israel. [f]
7 For on that day
all of you will cast away
your idols of silver and your false gods of gold
which your own sinful hands have made.

Destruction of Assyria

8 Then Assyria will fall by a sword not brandished by a man
and be devoured by a sword that no human yields;
he will flee before the sword,
and his young warriors will endure forced labor. [g]
9 His stronghold will be abandoned in terror,
and his commanders will panic and desert him.
Thus says the LORD whose fire is in Zion
and whose furnace burns in Jerusalem.

CHAPTER 32

A Righteous King

1 Behold, a king will reign with righteousness
and princes will rule with justice. [h]
2 Each of them will be like a shelter from the wind
and a refuge from the storm,
like streams of water in arid land,
like the shade of a great rock in a desolate area. [i]
3 Then the eyes of those who see will not be closed,
and the ears of those who hear will listen attentively.
4 The minds of the rash will show good judgment,
and those who stutter will speak promptly and clearly.
5 No longer will a fool be called noble,
nor will a villain be considered to be honorable.
6 For the fool speaks foolishly
while his heart is planning evil.

a Gen 19:24; 2 Ki 23:10.—b Isa 30:2; 36:6; Ps 20:8; Prov 21:31; Jer 37:5.—c Isa 20:5; Ps 146:3ff; Ezek 28:9.—d Num 24:9; 1 Sam 17:34; Hos 11:10.—e Gen 1:2; Ps 91:4; Zec 9:15.—f Isa 1:5, 27; Job 22:23; Jer 3:12.—g Isa 37:36; Ex 12:12.—h Isa 16:5; 55:4; Ps 72:2ff; Jer 23:5.—i Isa 4:6; 25:4; Jer 31:9.

30:33 A place for human sacrifices to the god Baal in the Valley of Ben-hinnom, outside Jerusalem.

He practices ungodliness
and spreads malicious untruths about the LORD.
He starves the hungry by withholding their food
and deprives the thirsty of anything to drink. [j]
7 The methods of the scoundrel are wicked,
and he devises infamous schemes
to destroy the poor with his lies
even when the pleas of the needy are just.
8 But the man who is noble plans noble deeds,
and in that respect he stands firm. [k]

The Restoration of Jerusalem

9 Listen carefully to what I have to say,
you women who are so complacent.
Pay attention to my words,
you who feel so secure.
10 In little more than a year from now
you complacent ones will be shaken.
For the vintage will fail
and there will be no harvest. [l]
11 Tremble, you complacent women;
shudder, you who feel secure.
Strip yourselves bare,
with only a loincloth to cover you. [m]
12 Beat your breasts in mourning
for the pleasant fields and the fruitful vines,
13 for the soil of my people
overgrown with thorns and briars,
and for all the joyful houses
in this city of revelry. [n]
14 The citadel * will be abandoned
and the crowded streets will be deserted;
the hill and the watchtower will become wasteland forever,
in which wild asses may frolic and flocks may pasture,
15 until a spirit from on high
is poured out upon us,
and the wilderness becomes an orchard
and the fruitful field becomes a forest. [o]
16 Then justice will dwell in the wilderness,
and righteousness will abide in the orchard.
17 The effect of righteousness will be peace,
and its result will be quiet and security forever. [p]
18 My people will abide in a peaceful land,
in secure dwellings and peaceful resting places. [q]
19 Even if the forest were to be totally destroyed
and the city were to be completely leveled,
20 how blessed you will be
to sow your seed beside every stream
and to have your cattle and your donkeys roam freely. [r]

CHAPTER 33

Overthrow of Assyria

1 Woe to you, O destroyer,
who yourself have not been destroyed!
Woe to you, O traitor,
who yourself have not been betrayed!
When you have finished destroying,
you yourself will be destroyed;
when you have ceased betraying,
you yourself will be betrayed.
2 O LORD, be merciful to us,
for we have placed our hope in you.
Be our strength every morning,
our salvation in times of trouble. [s]
3 At the sound of tumult, peoples flee;
nations scatter when they behold your majesty.
4 Your spoil is gathered as if by caterpillars;
like a swarm of locusts men descend upon it. [t]
5 The LORD is exalted, for he dwells on high;
he has filled Zion with justice and righteousness.
6 Her strength will derive from the LORD's unchanging stability;
her deliverance will result from wisdom and knowledge;
her treasure is the fear of the LORD. [u]

---

j Isa 26:10; Prov 10:32; 19:3; 24:2; Eccl 10:12f.—k 1 Chr 29:9; Prov 11:25.—l Isa 5:5-6; 24:7; Zep 1:13.—m Isa 33:14; Jer 4:8; Mic 1:8.—n Isa 16:9; 24:7; Nah 2:7.—o Isa 11:2; 29:17; 35:1; 44:3; Ezek 37:9.—p Isa 54:13f; Ps 72:7; Rom 14:17; Jas 3:18.—q Isa 2:4; Am 9:14; Mic 4:4.—r Isa 30:23; Deut 28:12; Eccl 11:1.—s Isa 25:9; 40:10; Ezek 9:8.—t 2 Ki 7:16; 2 Chr 20:25.—u Isa 12:2; Mt 6:33.

32:14 *Citadel:* Hebrew, *Ophel*, the southern part of the hill of Zion.

7 Listen to the valiant cry aloud in the streets for help;
the ambassadors who seek peace weep bitterly.
8 The highways are deserted;
no longer are there any travelers on the road.
Treaties are broken and their terms are ignored;
no one is deemed worthy of respect. [v]
9 The land languishes in mourning;
Lebanon withers in its shame.
Sharon has become a desert;
Bashan and Carmel are stripped bare.* [w]

10 Now I will rise up, says the LORD.
Now I will be exalted,
now I will be lifted up.
11 You conceive chaff and give birth to stubble;
like fire my Spirit will devour you.
12 The peoples will be burned as though by lime,
like thorns that have been cut
and consumed in the fire.

13 You who are far away,
listen to what I have done,
and you who are near,
acknowledge my strength. [x]
14 The sinners in Zion are filled with terror;
trembling has seized the godless.
"Can any of us survive the devouring fire?
Can any of us survive the everlasting flames?" [y]
15 Those who walk righteously and speak honestly,
who refuse to enrich themselves by extortion,
who reject any bribes offered to them
and stop their ears from listening to plans for murder
and shut their eyes from looking on evil— [z]
16 these people will dwell on the heights;
their refuge will be rocky cliffs,
where they will have an abundance of food and water.

Peace and Prosperity in Zion

17 Your eyes will behold the king in his splendor
and gaze upon a land that stretches far and wide. [a]
18 Your mind will then meditate on the terror.
"Where is the man who did the counting?
Where is the man who weighed the tribute?
Where is the man who counted the towers?"

19 No longer will you encounter the insolent people,
those who employ an obscure speech
that you cannot understand
and who stammer in a language
that you are unable to comprehend. [b]
20 Gaze upon Zion,
the city of our sacred feasts.
Your eyes will behold Jerusalem as a quiet abode,
as a tent that will not be moved,
whose stakes will never be pulled up
and none of whose ropes will be broken.

21 There we will behold the LORD in all his majesty,
in a place of rivers and broad streams,
upon which no enemy galleys with oars can go
or a majestic ship can sail. [c]
22 For the LORD is our judge,
the LORD is our lawgiver.
The LORD is our king;
he is the one who will save us. [d]

23 If the rigging of an enemy ship is loose,
unable to hold the mast in place
or to keep the sails spread out,
then abundant spoils will be divided;
even the lame will carry off the plunder.
24 No inhabitant will say, "I am sick,"
for the people who live there
will be forgiven for their sins. [e]

---

v Isa 60:15; Jdg 5:6.—w Isa 3:26; 2 Ki 19:23; Jer 22:6.—x Isa 34:1; 48:16; 49:1.—y Isa 1:28; Nah 1:6; Zec 13:9.—z Isa 58:8; Pss 15:2-6; 24:4f; Ezek 22:13.—a Isa 4:2; 6:5; 26:15.—b Isa 28:11; Gen 11:7; Deut 28:49.—c Isa 32:2; Ex 17:6.—d Isa 2:3; 11:4; Jas 4:12.—e Num 23:21; 2 Chr 6:21; 1 Jn 1:7-9.

33:9 The places listed were the most fertile parts of the land of Israel. *Sharon* is a plain; *Bashan* and *Carmel*, wooded mountains.

VI: THE LORD, ZION'S DEFENDER*

CHAPTER 34

The End of Edom

1 Draw near, you nations, and listen;
pay attention, you peoples.
Let the earth and everything in it listen,
the world and all that issues forth from it. [f]
2 For the LORD is angry with all the nations
and enraged against all their armies;
he has decreed their doom
and given them over to slaughter.
3 Their slain will be cast out,
and their corpses will emit a stench;
the mountains will flow with their blood. [g]
4 All the host of heaven will crumble into nothing,
and the heavens will be rolled up like a scroll.
All their host will wither away
as the leaves wither on a vine
or as the fruit withers on a fig tree. [h]
5 When my sword has drunk its fill in the heavens,
lo, it will descend upon Edom,
upon a people I have doomed to destruction. [i]
6 The LORD has a sword sated with blood;
it is greasy with fat,
with the blood of lambs and goats,
with the fat of the kidneys of rams.
For the LORD has a sacrifice in Bozrah
and a great slaughter in the land of Edom.
7 Wild oxen will also be struck down alongside them
as will the bullocks with the bulls.
Their land will be drenched with blood
and their soil will be greasy with fat.
8 For the LORD has a day of vengeance,
a year of reprisal by Zion's defenders. [j]
9 The streams of Edom will be turned into pitch
and her soil into sulfur;
her land will become burning pitch.*
10 Night or day it will never be quenched;
its smoke will rise forever.
From generation to generation it will lie waste;
never again will anyone pass through it. [k]
11 But the hawk and the hedgehog will possess it;
the owl and the raven will dwell in it.
The LORD will stretch out over it
the measuring line of chaos
and the plumb line of desolation.
12 There will be no more nobles there
to proclaim the king;
all of its princes will have vanished. [l]
13 Its citadels will be overgrown with thorns,
and nettles and briars will cover its fortresses.
It will become an abode for jackals
and a haunt for ostriches. [m]
14 Desert creatures will frolic with hyenas,
and wild goats will call out to each other;
there, too, the nightjar will return to rest
and find a place for repose.
15 There will the owl nest and lay eggs,
and hatch and gather its young under her wings;
there, too, the buzzards will gather,
each one with its mate.
16 Consult the book* of the LORD and read it.
Not one of these will be missing,
not one will be without its mate.
For the mouth of the LORD has commanded this,
and his Spirit has gathered them together. [n]
17 He has allotted the portion for each;
his hand has measured out their shares.
They will possess it forever
and dwell there from generation to generation. [o]

---

f Isa 33:13; 41:1; 32:1.—g Isa 5:25; Ezek 32:4, 6; Joel 2:20.—h Isa 13:10; Job 9:7; Ezek 32:7f; 2 Pet 3:10.—i Deut 32:41-42; Jer 46:10; Ezek 21:5; Zec 13:7.—j Isa 2:12; 13:9; 63:4; Ezek 25:12-14.—k Jer 49:18; Mal 1:3; Rev 14:10-11.—l Jer 21:7; Ob 18.—m Isa 5:6; 13:21; Jer 9:11; Hos 9:6.—n Isa 30:8; 40:26.—o Isa 17:14; Jer 13:25.

34:1—35:10 This section, often called "The Little Apocalypse of Isaiah," in order to distinguish it from the "Great Apocalypse" in chapters 24–27, was redacted after the Exile. In imaginative and symbolic language, it describes the vengeance and anger of God in the terrible combats that are imagined as occurring at the end of time and as prelude to the judgment in which the Lord will restore Jerusalem, itself a sign of salvation in a new and peaceful land.

34:9 The language recalls the punishment of Sodom and Gomorrah.

34:16 *Book:* perhaps a collect of Isaiah's oracles.

CHAPTER 35

God's Judgment and Promise*

1 The desert and the parched land will be glad.
The wilderness will rejoice and blossom. [p]
2 Like the crocus it will bloom with abundant flowers
and rejoice with songs of joy.
The glory of Lebanon will be given to it,
the splendor of Carmel and Sharon.
They will behold the glory of the LORD,
the splendor of our God. [q]

3 Strengthen the hands that are weak,
and make firm the knees that give way. [r]
4 Say to those who are faint-hearted,
"Be strong! Do not be afraid!
Here is your God;
he will come with vengeance.
With divine retribution
he is coming to save you." [s]
5 Then the eyes of the blind will be opened
and the ears of the deaf will no longer be sealed. [t]
6 Then the lame will leap like a stag
and the tongue of the dumb will shout joyfully.
For waters will spring up in the wilderness
and rivers in the desert. [u]
7 The burning sand will evolve into a pool,
and the thirsty ground will become springs of water.
The haunts where jackals used to live
will bring forth grass and reeds and papyrus.
8 A highway will be there
that will be called the Way of Holiness.
No one who is unclean may pass over it;
it will serve as a path for pilgrims
and no fool will be able to use it. [v]
9 No lion will be there;
no ravenous beast will be encountered along it.
Such animals will not be seen there;
only the redeemed will be allowed to use it. [w]
10 Those whom the LORD has ransomed will return
and come to Zion with songs of happiness,
their heads crowned with everlasting joy.
Gladness and joy will accompany them,
while sorrow and mourning will flee away. [x]

VII: HISTORICAL APPENDIX*

CHAPTER 36

Sennacherib's Challenge.* 1 In the four-
teenth year of Hezekiah's reign, King Sen-
nacherib of Assyria attacked all the fortified
towns of Judah and captured them. [y] 2 From
Lachish the king of Assyria sent his chief
officer to King Hezekiah at Jerusalem with a
great army. When the chief officer took up
his position near the conduit of the upper
pool on the highway to the Fuller's Field
3 there came out to meet him Eliakim son of
Hilkiah, who was master of the palace, as
well as Shebna the secretary, and the
recorder Joah, son of Asaph. [z]
4 The chief officer said to them, "Tell
King Hezekiah: This is the message of the
great king, the king of Assyria. On what do
you base this great confidence of yours?
5 Do you think that mere words can over-
come strategy and military strength? On
whom are you relying for help that you
dare to rebel against me? 6 This Egypt, the
staff on whom you rely, is a broken reed
that will pierce the hand of anyone who
leans on it. Such is Pharaoh king of Egypt
to all who rely upon him. [a] 7 And if you say
to me that you are relying on the LORD,
your God, is he not the one whose high

p Isa 27:10; 32:15; 55:12f; Song 2:1.—q Isa 60:13; Ps 96:12; Song 7:5.—r Job 4:3f; Heb 12:12.—s Isa 41:10; 2 Chr 32:6-8; Zec 8:13; Rev 22:12.—t Isa 29:18; 32:3; 42:18; Jn 9:6-7.—u Isa 41:18; 43:19; Mt 15:30; Jn 5:8-9.—v Isa 11:16; Mt 7:13-14.—w Isa 30:6; 62:10; Lev 26:6.—x Isa 1:27; 51:11; Rev 7:17.—y 2 Ki 18:9, 13; 2 Chr 32:1.—z Isa 22:20; Gen 41:40; 2 Sam 8:17.—a Isa 30:2; 2 Ki 17:4; Ezek 17:17.

35:1-10 The promises are inspired by the second part of the Book (see Isa 41:19). Jesus intends by his activity to inaugurate this period of deliverance for the poor (Mt 11:5), citing verses 5-6 of the present passage; in John 4:7, 38, he takes up the theme of the gushing waters.

36:1—39:8 Some disciples of Isaiah took and adapted a part of the Second Book of Kings (18:13—20:19), in order to show that in two or three dramatic instances Isaiah had spoken truly. During the same period, there were other less favorable developments: the independence of Judah became increasingly precarious; pagan divinities continued to make their way even into the temple in Jerusalem. But the editors passed over these facts of general history.

36:1—37:20 This event, to which Isaiah often refers, occurred in 701 B.C. Sennacherib spread his armies across Palestine, invaded Judah, and besieged Jerusalem.

places and altars Hezekiah removed, com-
manding Judah and Jerusalem to worship
at this altar? [b]
8 "Now I challenge you to make a wager
with my master, the king of Assyria. I will
give you two thousand horses if you can find
riders for them. 9 But how could you repulse
even a single one of my master's soldiers,
even though you are depending upon Egypt
for chariots and horsemen? 10 Moreover, do
you believe that I have come to attack this
land and destroy it without the consent of
the LORD? The LORD himself said to me, 'Go
forth against this land and destroy it.' " [c]
11 Then Eliakim, Shebna, and Joah said to
the chief officer, "Please speak to your ser-
vants in Aramaic,* for we understand it. Do
not speak to us in Judean within earshot of
the people on the ramparts." [d] 12 The chief
officer replied, "Has my master sent me
here to speak these words only to your mas-
ter and to you, and not also to the people sit-
ting on the wall who along with you will be
doomed to eat their own dung and drink
their own urine?"
13 Then the chief officer stood up and
shouted loudly in the Judean language,
"Hear the words of the great king, the king
of Assyria. [e] 14 Thus says the king: Do not let
Hezekiah deceive you, for he will not be able
to deliver you. 15 Do not let Hezekiah per-
suade you to rely on the LORD by saying,
'The LORD will surely deliver us. This city
will not fall into the power of the king of
Assyria.' 16 Do not listen to Hezekiah, for
thus says the king of Assyria, 'Make peace
with me and surrender. Then each of you
will be free to eat the fruit of his own vine
and drink the water of his own cistern [f]
17 until I come to take you to a land like your
own, a land of grain and wine, a land of
bread and vineyards. 18 Do not let Hezekiah
mislead you by saying that the LORD will
save you. Have any of the gods of the nations
saved their lands from the power of the king
of Assyria? [g] 19 Where are the gods of Ha-
math and Arpad? Where are the gods of
Sepharvaim? Have they delivered Samaria
from my clutches? * [h] 20 Which of all the
gods of these countries has saved his coun-
try from my hand? Will the LORD then save
Jerusalem from my power?' "
21 However, the people remained silent
and did not respond with even a single word,
for the king had ordered them not to reply to
him. [i] 22 Then Eliakim son of Hilkiah, who
was the master of the palace, and Shebna
the secretary, and the recorder Joah son of
Asaph, came to Hezekiah with their clothes
torn and reported the words of the chief
officer.

CHAPTER 37

1 When King Hezekiah heard their report,
he tore his clothes, wrapped himself in sack-
cloth, and went into the temple of the
LORD. [j] 2 He sent Eliakim, who was in charge
of the palace, and Shebna the secretary, and
the elders of the priests, covered with sack-
cloth, to the prophet Isaiah son of Amoz
3 and gave him this message:

"Thus says Hezekiah, 'Today is a day of
distress, of rebuke, and of disgrace. Children
come to the moment of birth, but there is no
strength to bring them forth. 4 It may be that
the LORD, your God heard the words of the
chief officer, whom his master, the king of
Assyria, sent to taunt the living God, and
that he will be rebuked for the words which
the LORD, your God has heard. Offer your
prayer for the remnant that still survive.' "
5 When the ministers of King Hezekiah
came to Isaiah, 6 he said to them, "Say to
your master, 'Do not be alarmed because of
the words that you have heard with which
the servants of the king of Assyria have blas-
phemed me. [k] 7 I will put a spirit in him so
that when he hears a certain rumor he will
go back to his own country, and there I will
cause him to fall by the sword.' "
8 Meanwhile, the chief officer returned
and discovered that the king of Assyria had
departed from Lachish and was fighting
against Libnah,* 9 since he had heard that
King Tirhakah of Ethiopia was on his way
to attack him. On learning this, he sent
envoys to Hezekiah with this message:
10 "Thus shall you say to King Hezekiah of
Judah: 'Do not let your God upon whom you

b Deut 12:2-5; 2 Ki 18:4.—c Isa 10:5f; 1 Ki 13:18.—d Isa 36:13; Ezr 4:7.—e Isa 37:4; 2 Chr 32:18.—f 1 Ki 4:25; Zec 3:10.—g Isa 37:11.—h Isa 10:9; 37:13; 2 Ki 15:29; 17:24; 18:34.—i Prov 9:7-8; 26:4.—j Gen 37:29; 1 Ki 8:33; 2 Chr 34:19.—k Isa 7:4; 41:10-14; 51:7; Num 15:30; Jos 1:9.

36:11 *Aramaic:* a Semitic language that spread throughout the entire Near East; after the Exile it became, even in Palestine, the language of the people, replacing Hebrew.

36:19 People from Arpad and Sepharvaim were introduced into Samaria, which had been occupied by Sargon; the two places were, like Hamath, cities of Syria (see 10:9).

37:8 *Libnah:* north of Lachish. Sennacherib moved a little further south in order to attack Pharaoh Tirhakah, who belonged to a dynasty of Ethiopian origin.

rely deceive you with the promise that Jerusalem will not be handed over to the king of Assyria. [l] 11 You yourself must have learned by now what the kings of Assyria have done to all the other countries, subjecting them to complete destruction. Will you then be delivered? 12 Did the gods of the nations whom my ancestors destroyed deliver them: Gozan, Haran, Rezeph, and the people of Eden who were living in Telassar? 13 Where is the king of Hamath, the king of Arpad, the king of Lair, Sepharvaim, Hena, or Ivvah?' "

14 Hezekiah took the letter from the hand of the messengers and read it. 15 Then he went up to the temple of the LORD and, spreading it out before him, he prayed to the LORD: 16 "O LORD of hosts, God of Israel, enthroned upon the cherubim, you alone are God of all the kingdoms of the world. You have created the heavens and the earth. [m] 17 Incline your ear, O LORD, and listen; open your eyes, O LORD, and see. Hear all the words of Sennacherib whose purpose is to taunt the living God. 18 Truly, O LORD, the kings of Assyria have laid waste all the nations and their lands. 19 They have cast their gods into the fire because they were not truly gods but the work of human hands, fashioned from wood and stone—and so they were destroyed. [n] 20 Therefore, O LORD, our God, save us from his hands so that all the kingdoms of the earth will know that you alone, O LORD, are God."

Sennacherib's Punishment. 21 Then Isaiah, the son of Amoz, sent the following message to Hezekiah: "Thus says the LORD, the God of Israel: In answer to your prayer to me requesting help against King Sennacherib of Assyria, 22 this is the pronouncement that the LORD has made in regard to him:

"The virgin daughter of Zion
despises you and scorns you.
While you retreat the daughter of Jerusalem
tosses her head at you. [o]
23 Whom have you insulted and blasphemed?
Against whom have you raised your voice,
and haughtily lifted up your eyes?
Against the Holy One of Israel! [p]
24 Through your servants you have insulted the LORD
and boasted: 'With my many chariots
I have ascended the mountain heights,
the farthest peaks of Lebanon.
I have felled its tallest cedars,
its finest cypresses.
I have reached its highest peak
and its most luxuriant forest.
25 I have dug wells in foreign lands
and drunk the water there,
and with the soles of my feet
I have dried up all the rivers of Egypt.'
26 "Have you not heard
that I devised this plan long ago?
I planned it from days of old,
and now I have brought this to fruition:
you have reduced your fortified cities
into heaps of rubble, [q]
27 while their inhabitants, shorn of strength,
are dismayed and frustrated;
they have become like plants of the field,
like tender green herbs,
like grass on housetops and fields
scorched by the east wind.
28 "I know when you stand or sit,
I know when you come in or go out,
and I am aware how you rage against me.
29 Because you have raged against me
and your arrogance has reached my ears,
I will put my hook in your nose
and my bit in your mouth
and force you to return
by the way you came. [r]
30 This will be the sign for you:
This year you will eat what grows by itself,
and in the second year what springs forth from that.
However, in the third year sow and reap,
plant vineyards and eat their fruit.
31 The surviving remnant of the house of Judah
will again take root below
and bear fruit above.
32 For out of Jerusalem will come forth a remnant,
and from Mount Zion a band of survivors.

l Isa 36:14; 2 Chr 32:11, 15.—m Gen 3:24; Deut 10:17; Acts 4:24.—n Isa 26:14; Jer 16:20; Gal 4:8.—o Isa 10:32; 23:12; 2 Ki 19:21; Job 16:4.—p Num 15:30; Job 15:25; Ezek 36:20.—q Acts 2:23; 1 Pet 2:8.—r Isa 10:12; 2 Chr 33:11.

The zeal of the LORD of hosts will do
this. [s]

33 "Therefore, this is the word of the LORD
in regard to the king of Assyria:
He will not come into this city
or shoot an arrow at it;
he will not advance against it with a
shield
or build a siege-ramp against it.
34 By the way that he came,
by that same way he will return;
he will not enter this city, says the
LORD. [t]
35 I will protect this city and save it
for my own sake
and for the sake of my servant David." [u]

36 Then the angel of the LORD went forth
and struck down one hundred and eighty-
five thousand men in the Assyrian camp. [v]
When morning dawned, the ground was
covered with corpses.* 37 Then King Se-
nnacherib of Assyria broke camp and re-
turned home to Nineveh. [w]
38 One day, as he was worshiping in the
temple of his god Nisroch, his sons Adram-
melech and Sharezer slew him with the
sword and then fled to the land of Ararat.
His son Esarhaddon succeeded him.

CHAPTER 38

Hezekiah's Sickness and Recovery. 1 During
that period, Hezekiah fell ill and was at the
point of death. The prophet Isaiah, son of
Amoz, came to him and said, "Thus says the
LORD: Put your affairs in order, for you are
about to die; you will not recover." [x]
2 Then Hezekiah turned his face to the wall
and prayed to the LORD, 3 "I beg you, O
LORD, to remember how I have conducted
myself faithfully in your presence and have
always done what was pleasing to you." And
Hezekiah wept bitterly. [y]
4 Then the word of the LORD came to
Isaiah, 5 "Go and say to Hezekiah: Thus says
the LORD, the God of your ancestor David. I
have heard your prayer and I have seen your
tears. Therefore, I have decided to heal you.
In three days you will go up to the temple of
the LORD, and I will add fifteen years to your
life. 6 I will deliver you and this city from the
hand of the king of Assyria and defend this
city." [z]
[21 Isaiah thereupon ordered a poultice of
figs to be prepared and applied to the boil so
that Hezekiah might recover. 22 Then Heze-
kiah asked, "What is the sign to confirm that
I will go up to the temple of the LORD?"]
7 Isaiah replied, "This will be the sign to
you from the LORD that he will do as he has
promised. 8 I will make the shadow cast by
the declining sun on the stairway of Ahaz to
turn back ten steps." And the sun then
retreated the ten steps it had previously
advanced. [a]

Hezekiah's Hymn of Thanksgiving.* 9 A canti-
cle written by King Hezekiah of Judah after
his recovery from his illness:

10 Once I said,
"In the noontime of my life
I must depart.
I will be consigned to the gates of Sheol
for the rest of my years." [b]
11 I said, "I will no longer see the LORD
in the land of the living.
I will no longer see any of my fellow men
as I did when I dwelled in the world.

12 "My dwelling has been torn down and
thrown away
like a shepherd's tent;
like a weaver I have rolled up my life
and the last thread has been severed.
Day and night I am subject to torment; [c]
13 I cry out for help until the dawn.
All my bones are crushed, as if by a lion;
day and night I suffer in torment.

14 "Like a swallow I twitter;
I moan like a dove.
My eyes have grown dim looking up to
heaven;
O LORD, come to my aid in my suffer-
ing.
15 Yet how can I complain? What should I
say?
He himself has done this.
I will wander aimlessly for the rest of my
years
because of the bitterness of my soul. [d]

16 "However, you, O LORD, are always pres-
ent to protect me,
and you grant life to my spirit;

s Isa 1:9; 9:7; 11:11.—t Isa 37:29.—u Isa 31:5; 1 Ki 15:4f; 1 Chr 17:19; Ezek 36:21-22.—v Isa 10:12; 17:14; Ex 12:12, 23.—w Gen 10:11; 2 Ki 19:35f; 2 Chr 32:21; Nah 1:1.—x Isa 37:2; 2 Sam 17:23; 2 Ki 8:10; 20:1.—y Deut 6:18; 1 Ki 8:61; 2 Ki 18:5f.—z Isa 31:5; 37:35.—a Jos 10:13; 2 Ki 20:9, 11.—b Job 17:11, 16; Ps 102:25; 2 Cor 1:9.—c Job 7:6; 2 Cor 5:1, 4; Heb 1:12; 2 Pet 1:13-14.—d 2 Sam 7:20; 1 Ki 21:27; Job 7:11.

37:36 In the effort to emphasize the breadth of God's triumph, the writer is not afraid to exaggerate numbers.

38:9-20 This prayer, which is lacking in 2 Kings, seems to be post-Exilic.

you will restore me to health
and enable me to live.
17 Clearly it was for my benefit
that I suffered such anguish,
but you have preserved my life
from the pit of destruction,
for you have cast all my sins
behind your back. [e]
18 For Sheol cannot give you thanks,
nor can death praise you.
Those who go down into the pit
cannot hope for your kindness. [f]
19 It is the living, only the living, who can thank you
as I am doing today,
just as fathers make known to their sons
your faithfulness, O God. [g]
20 "The LORD is my savior,
and we will sing to stringed instruments
all the days of our lives
in the house of the LORD."

CHAPTER 39

Hezekiah's Foolishness.* 1 At that time the
king of Babylon, Merodach-baladan, the son
of Baladan, sent envoys with letters and a gift
to Hezekiah, for he heard that Hezekiah had
been ill but had recovered. 2 Hezekiah was
delighted at this, and therefore he showed the
envoys his entire treasury: the silver, the gold,
the spices, the precious oil, his entire armory,
and all that was in his storerooms. There was
nothing in his palace or in his entire realm
that Hezekiah did not show them. [h]
3 Then the prophet Isaiah came to King
Hezekiah and said to him, "What did these
men say to you? Where did they come from?"
Hezekiah replied, "They came to me from a
distant country, from Babylon." 4 Isaiah then
asked him, "What did they see in your
palace?" Hezekiah said, "They have seen
everything in my palace. There is nothing in
my storerooms that I did not show them." [i]
5 Thereupon Isaiah said to Hezekiah,
"Hear the word of the LORD of hosts.
6 Behold, the days are coming, says the LORD,
when everything in your palace, and everything that your ancestors have stored up
until this day, will be carried off to Babylon.
Nothing will be left. [j] 7 Some of your own sons
who were fathered by you will be taken away
and forced to serve as eunuchs in the palace
of the king of Babylon." [k] 8 Hezekiah replied
to Isaiah, "The word of the LORD that you
have spoken is comforting." For he thought
to himself, "There will be peace and security
during my lifetime." [l]

B: The Book of Consolation*

I: THE LORD'S MAJESTY IN ISRAEL'S LIBERATION*

CHAPTER 40

Salvation of the LORD*

1 Comfort my people and console them,
says your God. [m]

e Jer 31:34; Rom 8:28; Heb 12:11.—f Num 16:30; Pss 6:6; 88:11-13; Eccl 9:10.—g Deut 4:9; 6:7; 11:19.—h 2 Ki 20:13; 2 Chr 32:31.—i Deut 28:49; Jer 17:3.—j 2 Ki 24:13; 25:13ff.—k 2 Ki 24:15; 2 Chr 33:11; Dan 1:2f.—l Jdg 10:15; 2 Chr 32:26.—m Isa 12:1; Jer 31:13; Zep 3:14-17.

39:1-8 The deportation of Jews to Babylonia over a century later, in 587 B.C., will be the tragic result of this policy; at least this is the view of the editor, who takes advantage of the episode to place a prophecy of exile on the lips of Isaiah himself.

40:1—55:13 Over a century had passed since the death of Isaiah. The Jewish people had lost their independence. The process of decline seemed irreversible. Jerusalem fell in 587 B.C., and then came the Exile. Beginning in 550 B.C., a new people entered the scene in the Near East. They were not Semitic but Aryan; they were the Persians and were led by a man who would make history: Cyrus. Within ten years, he made the East subject to him; to the peoples who had been oppressed, crushed, and deported by the Babylonians, he appeared as a liberator. From that point on, stories, oracles, and songs began to appear among the exiled Hebrews that extolled God's work in the history of the world. The time was now past in which idols held sway; they saw the true God, the only God, in control of events that were leading to the salvation and liberation of his people. This noble idea of God and this new hope of deliverance burst forth in the "Book of Consolation," which is also known as Second Isaiah or Deutero-Isaiah (chs. 40–55). In 539 B.C. Babylon fell. Cyrus gave the Israelites leave to return to their homeland and practice their own religion. The most religious among the Jews began to think that the time of the "new covenant" or "new testament" announced by the prophets (Jer 31:33; Ezek 36:26) had arrived. Should they perhaps see in Cyrus the Lord's messenger, a "messiah?" But God's Messenger, who would complete his work, was not Cyrus, although Cyrus was a glorious figure in human history. It would be necessary to wait for this Messenger to come in a humbler form, that of a just man who expiates by his own suffering for the sins of all humanity. Thus, amid the cries of hope for a new Exodus, there is already present a purer expectation: the expectation of God's authentic Messenger, whose portrait is sketched in the four "Servant Songs."

40:1—49:7 A minority among the deportees has reflected on Israel's extraordinary history: Is it possible that God formerly delivered his people by so many miracles only to see the whole process end in exile? In light of Cyrus' dazzling military sweep, the idea was born that a new Exodus was on the way, an exodus even more marvelous than the liberation from Egypt and the journey to the Promised Land.

40:1-11 From the very outset, this second part of the Book of Isaiah has a new tone: that of consolation. An unknown prophet arises in the night of exile. He realizes that God now speaks of love and forgiveness and will never again change his language. The prophet's most obvious call is to speak to his people about the strength and tenderness of God's love for them. The day will come when the voice will be that of John the Precursor, who will lead his fellow countrymen on the path of conversion and open the way for Christ.

2 Speak tenderly to Jerusalem
and proclaim to her
that her time of servitude is over
and that her guilt has been expiated.
Indeed she has received from the LORD's hand
double punishment for all her sins. [n]

3 A voice cries out:
In the wilderness prepare the way of the LORD;
make a straight path in the desert for our God. [o]
4 Let every valley be filled in
and every mountain and hill be made low.
Uneven ground will be made smooth
and the rugged places will become a plain.
5 Then the glory of the LORD will be revealed,
and all mankind will see it together,
for the mouth of the LORD has spoken.

6 A voice says, "Cry out!"
I reply, "What shall I cry out?"
"All mortals are grass;
they last no longer than the flowers of the field. [p]
7 The grass withers, the flower fades,
when the breath of the LORD falls upon them.
Surely the people are grass.
8 The grass may wither and the flower may fade,
but the word of our God will endure forever."

9 Climb to the top of a high mountain,
O Zion, herald of good tidings.
Cry out as loudly as you can,
O Jerusalem, herald of good news.
Lift up your voice without fear
and proclaim to the cities of Judah,
"Here is your God!" [q]
10 See the Lord GOD approaching with power,
he who rules with his powerful arm.
His reward is with him
and his recompense* is before him.
11 He will feed his flock like a shepherd,
and in his arms he will gather the lambs,
carrying them in his bosom
and gently leading the pregnant ewes to water. [r]

The Creator's Power To Save His People

12 Who has measured the waters of the sea
in the hollow of his hand,
or marked off the heavens
with the breadth of his hand?
Who has held the dust of the earth in a measure
and weighed the mountains in scales
and the hills in a balance? [s]

13 Who has directed the Spirit of the LORD?
What counselor dared to instruct him? [t]
14 Whom did he consult to gain enlightenment?
Who taught him the path of justice?
Who taught him knowledge
or showed him the way of understanding?

15 In his eyes the nations are
like a drop in a bucket,
like dust on the scales.
To him coasts and islands*
weigh no more than fine dust, [u]
16 Lebanon would not supply enough wood for fuel,
nor are its animals sufficient for a burnt offering.
17 All the nations are as naught in his sight;
he reckons them as nothing and void.

18 To whom then will you compare God?
To what image can you liken him? [v]
19 Perhaps an idol that a craftsman casts
and a goldsmith overlays with gold
and for which he fashions silver chains? [w]
20 Or should mulberry wood be chosen,
a wood that will not rot,
and then a skilled artisan be designated
to fashion an idol that will not fall over? [x]

21 Do you not know?
Have you not heard?

n Gen 34:3; Lev 26:41.—o Prov 3:5-6; Mal 3:1; Mt 3:3; Mk 1:3; Jn 1:23.—p Gen 6:3; Job 8:12; 14:2; Ps 37:2; Sir 14:18; Jas 1:10; 1 Pet 1:24.—q Isa 41:27; Nah 1:15; Acts 13:32.—r Isa 49:9f; 63:11; Ezek 34:23; 37:24; Mic 5:4; Jn 10:11.—s Job 39:4-11; Prov 30:4; Heb 1:10.—t Isa 11:2; Job 38:1ff; Wis 9:13; Rom 11:34; 1 Cor 2:16.—u Isa 2:22; 29:5.—v Ex 8:10; Deut 4:15; 1 Sam 2:2; Acts 17:29.—w Ex 20:4; Ps 115:4-7; Jer 2:8, 28; Hab 2:18.—x Isa 44:13, 19; 1 Sam 5:3; 12:21.

40:10 *Recompense:* the liberation of the people.

40:15 *Islands:* the Mediterranean archipelagoes and, in general, the distant lands.

Were you not told from the beginning?
Have you not understood from the foundation of the earth? [y]
22 God sits enthroned above the vault of the earth,
and its inhabitants are like grasshoppers.
He stretches out the heavens like a canopy
and spreads them out like a tent to dwell in. [z]
23 He brings princes to naught
and reduces the rulers of the earth to nothing.
24 Scarcely have crops been planted or sown,
scarcely have their stems taken root in the ground,
before he breathes on them and they wither,
and storm winds carry them off like chaff. [a]
25 To whom then can you compare me,
or who is my equal? says the Holy One.
26 Lift up your eyes to the heavens.
Who created these things?
He leads forth their host and numbers them,
summoning them all by name.* [b]
Because of his mighty power and great strength,
not one of them is missing.
27 Why do you say, O Jacob,
and complain, O Israel,
"My way is hidden from the LORD,
and my cause is disregarded by my God"?
28 Do you not know?
Have you not heard?
The LORD is the eternal God,
the Creator of the earth's farthest boundaries.
He does not faint or grow weary;
his understanding cannot be scrutinized. [c]
29 He gives strength to the weary
and new vigor to those who are powerless.
30 Even though young men faint and grow weary
and youths stumble and fall,
31 those who place their hope in the LORD
will regain their strength.
They will soar as with eagles' wings,
they will run and not grow weary,
they will walk and not become faint. [d]

CHAPTER 41

The LORD Redeems Israel

1 Be silent and listen to me, O coastlands;
let the peoples renew their strength.
Let them draw near and speak;
let us meet together at the place of judgment.
2 Who has raised up a victor from the east
and summoned him to his service?
He delivers up nations to him
and overthrows their kings.
With his sword he scatters them like dust,
and with his bow he reduces them to stubble. [e]
3 He pursues them and advances unscathed,
scarcely touching the path with his feet.
4 Who has performed these deeds and accomplished this?
Who has summoned the nations from the beginning?
I, the LORD, am the first,
and I will be there with the last. [f]
5 The coastlands have seen and become frightened;
the ends of the earth tremble.
These things are fast approaching;
they will come to pass. [g]
6 Each worker helps another;
they encourage each other to take heart.
7 The craftsman encourages the goldsmith,
and the polisher the one who strikes the anvil;
he declares the soldering to be good,
and he fastens the image with nails
so that it will be secure.
8 But you, Israel, my servant,
Jacob, whom I have chosen,
the descendants of my friend Abraham, [h]

y 2 Ki 19:25; Acts 14:17.—z Gen 1:1; Num 13:33; 2 Chr 6:18; Ps 104:2.—a Isa 11:4; 2 Sam 22:16.—b Isa 51:6; Ps 147:4f; Neh 9:6.—c Isa 37:16; Deut 33:27; Rom 11:33.—d 1 Sam 2:4; 2 Ki 6:33; Lk 18:1.—e 2 Sam 22:43; Ezr 1:2; Jer 50:3.—f Isa 44:7; 46:10; Gen 1:1; Deut 32:39; Rev 1:8.—g Isa 11:11; Deut 30:4; Ezek 26:17-18.—h Isa 44:1f, 21; 45:4; 2 Chr 20:7; Jas 2:23.

40:26 To call by name is a sign of mastery.

9 you whom I have taken to myself
from the ends of the earth
and summoned from its farthest corners,
to whom I have said, "You are my servant;
I have chosen you and will not cast you off.
10 Do not fear, for I am with you;
do not be afraid, for I am your God.
I will strengthen you and give you help,
I will uphold you with my victorious right hand." [i]
11 All those who rage against you
will be put to shame and disgraced;
those who oppose you
will be reduced to nothing and perish.
12 You will search for those who oppose you
but you will not find them.
Those who take up arms against you
will be reduced to nothing.
13 For I, the LORD, am your God
and I grasp your right hand.
It is I who say to you,
Do not fear; I will help you.
14 Do not fear, you worm, Jacob,
you maggot, Israel.
I will help you, says the LORD;
your redeemer* is the Holy One of Israel. [j]
15 Now I will make of you a threshing sledge,
sharp, new, with numerous teeth.
You will thresh the mountains and crush them,
and you will reduce the hills to chaff.
16 You will winnow them,
the wind will carry them away,
and the gale will scatter them.
Then you will rejoice in the LORD
and glory in the Holy One of Israel.
17 When the poor and needy search for water
and there is none,
and their tongues are parched with thirst,
I the LORD will come to their aid;
I, the God of Israel, will not forsake them. [k]
18 I will open up rivers on the barren heights
and fountains in the midst of valleys.
I will turn the wilderness into a lake
and the dry land into springs of water.
19 In the wilderness I will plant cedars,
acacias, myrtles, and olive trees;
in the wasteland I will place cypress trees
to grow side by side with plane trees and pine trees,
20 so that all may see and know,
observe and understand,
that the hand of the LORD has done this,
that the Holy One of Israel has created it.
21 Present your case, says the LORD.
Produce your arguments, says the king of Jacob. [l]
22 Let them bring forth their idols
and reveal to us what is going to happen.
What happened in the past?
Inform us so that we may reflect on it
and that we may know what the outcome will be
or declare to us the things to come. [m]
23 Reveal to us what is yet to come
so that we may know that you are gods.
Do something, whether good or bad,
that will cause us to be alarmed and terrified.
24 But you cannot do so, for you are nothing,
and your works are truly worthless.
To choose you is an abomination. [n]
25 I have stirred up one from the north,
and he has come forth;
from the east he has been summoned by name.
He will trample on rulers as if they were mud,
like a potter treading clay. [o]
26 Who revealed this to us from the beginning
so that we might know it,
or advised us beforehand
so that we might say, "He is right"?
No one foretold it, no one proclaimed it,
no one has heard you say anything in this regard. [p]

i Gen 15:1; Deut 3:22; Jos 1:9; Rom 8:31.—j Gen 15:1; Ex 15:13.—k Isa 35:7; 43:20; Deut 31:6.—l Isa 41:1; 44:6.—m Isa 43:9; 44:7; Jn 13:19.—n 1 Sam 12:21; Jer 8:19; 1 Cor 8:4.—o 2 Sam 22:43; Ezr 1:2; Jer 50:9, 41.—p Isa 52:6; 1 Ki 18:26; Hab 2:18-19.

41:14 A *redeemer* (Hebrew, *goel*) in the Old Testament is a relative whose duty it is to protect the interests and rights of the family (Lev 25:24-25; Num 35:19; Ru 2:20; 4:4).

27 I was the first to declare it to Zion,
and I sent a bearer of glad tidings to Jerusalem.
28 But when I look around, I see no one;
there is not a single one of them to offer counsel
or to give an answer when I question them.
29 No, they are a delusion.
Nothing they do amounts to anything;
their idols are empty wind. [q]

CHAPTER 42

The Mission of the Servant*

1 Here is my servant whom I uphold,
my chosen one in whom my soul delights.
I have put my Spirit upon him;
he will establish justice among the nations. [r]
2 He will not cry out or shout
or make his voice heard in the street.
3 He will not break a bruised reed,
nor will he snuff out a smoldering wick;
faithfully he will establish justice. [s]
4 He will not falter or become discouraged
until he has established justice upon the earth;
and the coastlands wait for his teaching.

5 Thus says God, the LORD,
who created the heavens and stretched them out,
who fashioned the earth and all that grows in it,
who gives breath to the people who dwell on it
and spirit to those who walk upon it: [t]
6 I, the LORD, have called you for a righteous purpose;
I have taken you by the hand.
I have formed you and established you
to be a covenant to the people
and a light to the nations, [u]
7 to open the eyes of the blind,
and to lead captives out of prison,
and to release from the dungeon
those who live in darkness. [v]

8 I am the LORD; that is my name.
My glory I do not grant to another,
nor my praise to idols.
9 Behold, the earlier prophecies have come to pass,
and now I will reveal new things.
Before they actually occur,
I will announce them to you.

Israel Saved despite Its Sins

10 Sing to the LORD a new song,
his praise from the ends of the earth.
Let the sea resound and all that fills it,
the coastlands and all its inhabitants. [w]
11 Let the desert and its towns rejoice,
the villages where Kedar* dwells.
Let the inhabitants of Sela sing for joy;
let them shout from the top of the mountains.
12 Let them all give glory to God
and sing his praise in the coastlands.
13 The LORD marches forth like a hero;
like a warrior he stirs up his fury.
He shouts forth his battle cry
and triumphs against his foes.* [x]
14 For a long time I have restrained myself;
I have maintained my silence and held my peace.
Now I will cry out like a woman in labor,
gasping and panting.
15 I will lay waste mountains and hills
and dry up all their vegetation.
I will convert rivers into islands
and dry up the pools. [y]

q Isa 37:19; 1 Sam 12:21; Jer 5:13.—r Isa 49:6; Mt 20:28; Lk 9:35; 1 Pet 2:4, 6.—s Job 13:25; Mt 12:20.—t Isa 48:13; Gen 1:6; Acts 17:24.—u Isa 45:13; Ex 31:2; Jer 23:6; Mal 3:1.—v Isa 32:3; Mt 11:5; Lk 4:18.—w Ex 15:1; Pss 96:1; 117;1.—x Ex 14:3, 14; Jos 6:5; Jer 25:30.—y Isa 11:15; Ex 9:25; 10:15; 14:21; Ps 105:33ff; Ezek 38:20; Nah 1:4-6.

42:1-9 The repatriated Jews have toned down their enthusiasm, for they had not passed through a flowering wilderness; they were not many in number, and their return had not converted anyone. An unknown poet reawakens their hope while also giving a more spiritual cast to their dreams of glory. Beyond Cyrus, a temporary servant, God is preparing for himself a humble agent of salvation, filled with the spirit of the prophets. He will renew the covenant, make love shine forth in the midst of the people, and without violence will establish true justice. As a result, a very lofty idea of the liberator and of salvation is henceforth part of the Jewish consciousness. Jesus will accomplish the mission of this servant; Matthew cites verses 1-4 of this song (Mt 12:17-21); verse 1 echoes in the words of the Father as he presents Christ to the human race at the Jordan (Mt 3:17; Mk 1:11; Lk 3:23) and later on Tabor (Mt 17:5; Mk 9:7; Lk 9:35).

42:11 *Kedar* and *Sela* stand for Arabia.

42:13 The depiction of God as a warrior in order to indicate his intervention in history is common in Old Testament epic and lyrical poetry beginning with the Canticle of Deborah (Jdg 5:4).

16 I will lead the blind*
and guide them along paths they do not know.
I will turn darkness into light before them
and make straight their winding roads.
These are the things I will do for them,
and I will not forsake them. [z]
17 But those who place their trust in idols
and who say to carved images,
"You are our gods,"
will be turned back in bitter shame.

18 You who are deaf, listen!
You who are blind, look and see!
19 Who is so blind as my servant,
or so deaf as the messenger I send?
Who is so blind as the one dedicated to my service,
or so deaf as the servant of the LORD? [a]
20 You have seen many things without comprehending them;
your ears are open but you do not hear.
21 For the sake of his justice the LORD was pleased
to make his law great and glorious.
22 But this is a people despoiled and plundered,
all of them trapped in holes
and hidden away in dungeons.
They have been pillaged with no one to rescue them;
they are plundered with no one to demand their release. [b]

23 Who among you will pay heed to this?
Who will pay attention and listen in the future?
24 Who handed over Jacob to be plundered,
who gave up Israel to be despoiled?
Was it not the LORD,
against whom we have sinned?
They refused to walk in his ways,
and they would not obey his laws.
25 Therefore, he poured out upon them
his blazing anger and the fury of battle.
It enveloped them in flames,
but they did not understand,
it burned them,
but they did not take it to heart. [c]

CHAPTER 43

Redemption and Restoration Promised

1 But now this is the word of the LORD,
he who created you, O Jacob,
and formed you, O Israel.
Have no fear, for I have redeemed you.
I have called you by name; you are mine.
2 When you pass through the waters,
I will be with you;
nor will the waters engulf you.
When you walk through fire,
you will not be burned;
the flames will not consume you. [d]

3 For I am the LORD, your God,
the Holy One of Israel, your savior.
I give Egypt as your ransom,
Ethiopia and Seba* in exchange for you. [e]
4 Because in my eyes you are precious,
because you are honored and I love you,
I will give people in exchange for you
and nations in return for your life. [f]

5 Do not be afraid, for I am with you.
I will bring your offspring from the east,
and from the west I will gather you.
6 I will say to the north, "Give them up,"
and to the south, "Do not hold them back."
Bring back my sons from afar
and my daughters from the ends of the earth— [g]
7 everyone who bears my name,
whom I created for my glory,
whom I formed and made.

8 Bring forth my people,
those who have eyes yet are blind,
those who have ears yet are deaf. [h]
9 Let all the nations gather together
and let the peoples assemble.
Who among them foretold this
and proclaimed to us former events?
Let them produce witnesses to prove themselves right;

z Ex 13:21; Jer 31:8-9; Lk 1:78-79; Acts 26:18.—a Isa 43:8; Ezek 12:2.—b Isa 24:18; Jdg 6:4; 2 Ki 24:13.—c 2 Ki 22:13; Job 40:11; Ezek 7:19; Lam 2:3.—d Isa 8:7; Ex 14:22.—e Ex 20:2.—f Isa 49:5; Ex 19:5; Deut 4:37; Hos 11:1; Rev 3:9.—g Isa 49:22; Deut 30:4; 2 Cor 6:18.—h Isa 6:9-10; 42:20; Ezek 12:2.

42:16 *The blind:* these are the Israelites who have not been willing to recognize the Lord.

43:3 *Seba:* Nubia. God grants Cyrus this territory as a reward for having freed Israel. In fact, it was Cambyses, Cyrus's successor, who conquered Egypt.

let those who hear them say, "It is true!"

10 You are my witnesses, says the LORD,
and my servants whom I have chosen,
so that you may know and believe in me
and understand that it is I. [i]
No god was formed before me,
nor will there be any after me.

11 I am the LORD,
and there is no other savior but me.
12 I have revealed and saved and proclaimed,
and not some strange god among you;
you are my witnesses to this, says the LORD.
13 I am God, and from eternity I am he;
no one can deliver from my hand;
no one can overrule or alter what I do. [j]

14 Thus says the LORD, your redeemer,
the Holy One of Israel:
For your sake I will send an army to Babylon
to uproot all the prison bars,
and the triumphant shouts of the Chaldeans
will turn to cries of lamentation.
15 I am the LORD, your Holy One,
the Creator of Israel, your king.

16 Thus says the LORD,
who opened a way through the sea,
a path through raging waters, [k]
17 who led out chariots and horsemen
and an army of formidable strength,
until the enemy lay prostrate, unable to rise,
extinguished and snuffed out like a wick. [l]

18 Do not linger thinking about events of the past;
consider not the things of old.
19 I am about to do something new.
Now it comes to fruition;
can you not perceive it?
I will make a path through the wilderness
and rivers in the desert.

20 The wild beasts will honor me,
the jackals and the ostriches,
because I will provide water in the desert
and rivers in the wasteland
where my chosen people may drink,
21 the people whom I formed for myself
so that they may proclaim my praise. [m]

22 Yet you did not call upon me, O Jacob;
you grew weary of me, O Israel.
23 You have not brought me sheep for burnt offerings
or honored me with your sacrifices.
I have not exacted grain offerings from you
or wearied you with demands for incense. [n]
24 You have not purchased aromatic cane for me
or sated me with the fat of your sacrifices.
Rather, you have burdened me with your sins;
you have wearied me with your crimes.

25 I, I alone, am the one
who blots out your transgressions for my own sake,
and I will remember your sins no more. [o]
26 If you choose to review the past,
let us go to trial;
state your defense and prove your innocence. [p]

27 Your first ancestor sinned,
and your spokesmen rebelled against me.
28 Therefore, I expelled the leaders of the sanctuary,
placing Jacob under the curse of destruction
and subjecting Israel to scorn.

CHAPTER 44

1 Now listen to me, O Jacob, my servant,
Israel whom I have chosen.
2 Thus says the LORD who made you,
who formed you in the womb
and will continue to help you: [q]

Do not fear, O Jacob, my servant,
Jeshurun* whom I have chosen.
3 For I will pour down rain on the thirsty land

i Isa 41:1; 45:20; 48:14.—j Isa 41:4; Deut 32:39; Job 9:12.—k Isa 11:15; 51:10f; Ex 14:21, 29; 15:8.—l Ex 15:4; Jer 51:21; Ezek 38:4.—m Isa 43:7; Gen 2:7; Mal 3:17.—n Ex 29:41; Jer 6:20; Am 5:25; Zec 7:5-6.—o 2 Sam 12:13; 2 Chr 6:21; Mk 2:7; Lk 5:21.—p Isa 1:18; 41:1.—q Isa 14:1; 44:21.

44:2 *Jeshurun:* a poetic endearment of uncertain meaning. See Deut 33:5, 26, where it is put on the lips of Moses.

and open up streams on the dry ground.
I will pour out my Spirit upon your offspring
and my blessing upon your descendants.
4 They will spring up amid the grass
like willows besides flowing waters. [r]
5 One person will say, "I am the LORD's,"
while another will call himself a son of Jacob.
And on his hand still another will write "The LORD's,"
and adopt Israel as a surname. [s]

The One True God and False Gods

6 Thus says the LORD, the LORD Almighty,
Israel's king and redeemer:
I am the first and I am the last;
there is no god but me. [t]
7 Who is like me? Let him stand up and speak.
Let him declare it and set forth his evidence.
Who in the past has foretold future events?
Let him foretell to us what is yet to occur.
8 Do not fear or be afraid.
Did I not proclaim all this
and foretell it long ago?
You are my witnesses in this regard.
Is there any god besides me?
There is no other Rock;
I am aware of none. [u]

9 All those who make idols amount to
nothing, and the images in which they take
such pride profit no one. Their witnesses are
blind and ignorant, and therefore they
become objects of scorn. [v] 10 Who would
waste his time in fashioning a god or casting
an image that will serve no purpose? 11 All
who believe in their power will be put to
shame, as will the craftsmen who fashioned
them. Let them all assemble and approach
me with terror and with shame.
12 The blacksmith fashions an ax over the
coals, shaping it with hammers and forging
it with his strong arm. Then he becomes
hungry and his strength fails, and he
becomes exhausted because he has not consumed any water. [w]
13 The woodworker measures with a line
and marks out an outline with a stylus. He
shapes it with a plane and marks it with a
compass. Then he carves it into the shape of
a man, comely in appearance and dignity, to
be placed in a shrine.
14 He also cuts down cedars or chooses a
cypress or an oak that he has allowed to grow
strong among the other trees of the forest,
and a pine tree that he had planted and the
rain has nourished. 15 When such trees are
suitable to burn, he can use some of them to
keep warm or to bake bread, but with others
he fashions a god and worships it, shaping it
into an idol and bowing down before it. [x]
16 Half of the trees he uses to burn in the
fire to roast meat which he eats and is satisfied, while at the same time he warms himself and says, "Ah, how warm I am from the
heat of the fire." 17 With the remainder he
fashions a god, an idol before which he bows
down and offers worship. He prays to it and
says, "Save me, for you are my god." [y]
18 Such idols possess neither knowledge
nor understanding, for their eyes are shut so
that they cannot see, and their minds are
incapable of reasoning. [z] 19 Yet such a workman does not have the wisdom or the discernment to reflect, "Half of the wood I have
burned in the fire, and I also used its embers
to bake bread and to roast meat which I ate.
Does it make sense to fashion an abomination with the remainder? Am I right to worship a block of wood?" 20 He feeds on ashes.
His deluded mind has led him astray, and he
cannot save himself. He will not admit to
himself, "What I have in my hand is a fraud."

21 Remember these things, O LORD,
and you also, O Israel,
for you are my servant.
I fashioned you to be my servant;
O Israel, I will never forget you.
22 I have swept away your transgressions like a cloud
and your sins like a mist.
Return to me,
for I have redeemed you. [a]
23 Shout in triumphant joy, O heavens,
for the LORD has done this;
shout aloud, O depths of the earth.
Break forth into song, you mountains,
you forests, with all your trees.

r Isa 54:1ff; Lev 23:40.—s Isa 43:7; 45:14; Ex 13:9; Jer 50:5; Zec 8:20-22.—t Isa 41:4; 43:15; 45:21; 48:12; 54:5; Deut 6:4; Rev 1:8, 17.—u Isa 40:21; 42:9; 43:10; Gen 49:24; Deut 32:4.—v Isa 48:5; Ex 20:4; Lev 19:4.—w Isa 40:19; 41:6-7; Wis 13:11f; Acts 17:29.—x Ex 20:5; 2 Chr 25:14; Rev 9:20.—y Ex 20:5; Jdg 10:14; 1 Ki 18:26.—z Isa 1:3; Jer 10:8.—a 2 Sam 12:13; 2 Chr 6:21; Acts 3:19.

For the LORD has redeemed Jacob
and displayed his glory in Israel.

24 Thus says the LORD, your redeemer,
who formed you in the womb:
I am the LORD who made all things;
by myself I stretched out the heavens
by myself I spread out the earth. [b]
25 I frustrate the omens of false prophets
and make fools of diviners.
I confound wise men
and reveal the foolishness of their thoughts.
26 I confirm the words of my servants
and carry out the plans revealed by my messengers.
I say to Jerusalem, You will be inhabited,
and to the cities of Judah, You will be rebuilt.
I will raise up their ruins.
27 I say to the deep waters, Become dry;
I will dry up your rivers. [c]
28 I say to Cyrus, You will be my shepherd,
and he will carry out my every wish,
so that Jerusalem will be rebuilt
and the foundations of the temple will be laid. [d]

CHAPTER 45

1 * Thus says the LORD to his anointed,
to Cyrus whose right hand I have grasped,
to subdue nations before him
and to remove the armor of kings,
opening doors before him
and leaving no gates barred:
2 I myself will advance before you
and level the mountains;
I will tear down bronze gates*
and cut through bars of iron. [e]

3 I will give you treasures concealed in darkness
and riches hidden away in secret places,
so that you may know that I am the LORD,
the God of Israel who calls you by your name.
4 For the sake of my servant Jacob
and of Israel my chosen one,
I have called you by your name,
and I have given you a title,
even though you do not know me. [f]
5 I am the LORD and there is no other;
there is no god besides me.
I am the LORD who armed you
even though you did not know me,
6 so that it may be acknowledged from east to west
that there is no god besides me.
I am the LORD, and there is no other. [g]
7 I form the light and create the darkness;
prosperity and disaster depend upon my will;
I, the LORD, do all these things.

8 Rain down righteousness, you heavens;
let the skies pour it down from above.
Let the earth open up
so that salvation may blossom forth,
and let justice also spring up;
I, the LORD, have created it. [h]

9 Woe to anyone who rises up against his Maker,
or to the pot that is displeased with the potter.
Does the clay say to the one who molds it,
"What are you doing?
Your work makes no sense." [i]
10 Woe to anyone who asks a father,
"What are you begetting?"
or who says to a mother,
"To what have you given birth?"

11 Thus says the LORD,
the Holy One of Israel and its Maker:
How dare you question me about my children
or command me regarding the work of my hands?
12 I was the one who made the earth
and created mankind upon it.
It was my hands that stretched out the heavens
and commanded all their host. [j]

b Isa 40:22; 43:14; Gen 2:1; Job 9:8; 19:25.—c Isa 11:15; 19:5; 42:15; 51:10; Rev 16:12.—d Isa 41:2; 2 Chr 36:22; Ezr 1:2-4.—e Ps 107:16; Nah 3:13.—f Isa 14:1; 41:8-9; Acts 17:23.—g Isa 11:9; 43:10; Zec 2:15.—h Pss 72:6; 85:11; Hos 10:12; Joel 3:18; Am 5:24.—i Isa 29:16; Jer 18:6; Rom 9:20; 1 Cor 10:22.—j Gen 1:1; Job 38:32; Neh 9:6.

45:1-13 Around 540 B.C., Cyrus's victories perturbed many Israelites. In the eyes of the religious minority, among whom was the prophet, Cyrus was a messiah, that is, a man charged from on high with accomplishing the major deeds of God in his century. Our expectations of heaven are that justice would come and that "the just one," that is, the final Messiah, Jesus Christ, would also come. This is how the Vulgate (Latin translation of the Bible) reads verse 8.

45:2 *Bronze gates:* Babylon had a hundred of these.

13 I have raised this man for the triumph of justice,
and I will smooth all his paths.
He will rebuild my city
and set my exiles free
without price or ransom,
says the LORD of hosts.

14 Thus says the LORD:
The wealth of Egypt, the commerce of Ethiopia,
and the Sabeans, tall of stature,
will come over to you and belong to you;
they will follow you, wearing chains.
They will bow down before you
and pray to you, saying,
"God is with you alone, and there is no other;
there is no god aside from him." * [k]

15 Truly you are a God who is hidden,
O God of Israel, the Savior. [l]
16 All the makers of idols are disgraced and humbled;
they perish in their shame.
17 But Israel is saved by the LORD,
a salvation that is everlasting.
You will never be put to shame or humiliated
forever and ever. [m]

18 For thus says the LORD,
the Creator of the heavens,
he who is God,
the one who formed the earth and created it
and established it;
he did not create it to be a wasteland,
but a place to be lived in.
I am the LORD,
and there is no other.

19 I did not speak in secret,
in realms of darkness.
I did not say to the offspring of Jacob,
"Search for me in an empty waste."
I the LORD proclaim the truth;
I declare what is right.

20 Gather together and come forth;
assemble, all you survivors of the nations.
Bereft of knowledge are those
who parade with their wooden idols
and pray to gods who are unable to save them. [n]
21 Come forward and present your case
once you have examined the evidence.
Who foretold this in ages past?
Who revealed it long ago?
Was it not I, the LORD?
There is no god aside from me,
I alone am the righteous God and Savior.

22 If you turn to me, you will be saved,
all you ends of the earth,
for I am God, and there is no other. [o]

23 By myself I have sworn
that the word that issues forth from my mouth
is righteous and irrevocable.
To me every knee will bow,
every tongue will swear, [p]
24 saying, "In the LORD alone
are righteousness and strength;
all those who formerly defied him
and vented their rage against him
will come before him in shame.
25 Then all the descendants of Israel
will be triumphant and glory in the LORD."

CHAPTER 46

The Idols of Babylon*

1 Bel* bows down, Nebo stoops low;
their idols are borne by beasts and cattle.
The images you used to carry on your shoulders
are now a burden for weary animals. [q]
2 They stoop and bow down together
but are unable to transport their burden safely,
and they too move forth into captivity.

3 Listen to me, O house of Jacob,
all who remain of the house of Israel,
you who have been carried by me since your birth
and borne by me from the womb. [r]

k Isa 43:3; Gen 27:29; Zec 8:20-22.—l Isa 1:15; 25:9; Deut 31:17; Prov 25:2.—m Jer 23:6; Rom 11:26.—n Isa 43:9; Deut 32:37; Jer 10:5.—o Num 21:8-9; 2 Chr 20:12; Zec 12:10.—p Gen 22:16; Rom 14:11; Phil 2:10.—q Isa 21:19; 1 Sam 5:2-3; Jer 50:2.—r Isa 44:2; 51:1; Deut 1:31.

45:14 The prophet sees Egypt, and especially Ethiopia and Nubia, being conquered by the Persians; the prisoners taken captive pass through Palestine and acknowledge the true God.

46:1-13 The Chaldeans fleeing before Cyrus carry away their idols, marking the end of an empire and a religion. Israel, on the contrary, is always led by its God. The legions of Cyrus with their eagle banner (the *bird of prey* in v. 11) cause chaos among the peoples; Israel is to see in the event an action of God for their salvation.

46:1 *Bel:* the title of the principal Babylonian divinity; *Nebo,* his son, was the god of wisdom.

4 Even when you reach old age
I will still be the same.
Even when your hair is gray,
I will still carry you.
I have made you and I will uphold you;
I will carry you and save you.
5 Whom can you regard as my equal?
To whom can you compare me as identical?
6 Some pour out gold from a purse
and weigh out silver on the scales.
Then they hire a goldsmith
who fashions it into a god
before which they prostrate themselves in adoration. [s]
7 They lift it to their shoulders and carry it;
when they return it to its place, it stands there,
unable to budge from the spot.
If you cry out to it, it cannot reply,
nor can it save anyone from trouble.
8 Remember this and stand firm in your resolve;
keep it foremost in your mind, you rebels.
9 Remember the things that happened long ago;
for I am God, and there is no other;
I am God, and there is no one like me. [t]
10 From the beginning I reveal the end;
in advance I foretell what has not yet occurred.
I proclaim that my plan will be fulfilled
and that I will accomplish my intention.
11 I summon a bird of prey from the east,
a man from a distant country to fulfill my purpose.
I have spoken, and I will bring it to pass;
what I have planned, I will accomplish. [u]
12 Listen to me, you whose hearts are stubborn
and who are far removed from deliverance. [v]
13 I will bring near my justice;
it is not far distant,
and my salvation will not be delayed.
I will grant my salvation to Zion
and my glory to Israel.

CHAPTER 47

The Fall of Babylon

1 Come down and sit in the dust,
O virgin daughter of Babylon.
Sit on the ground without a throne,
O daughter of the Chaldeans.
Never again will you be called
tender and delicate.*
2 Take the millstone and grind meal;
remove your veil,
strip off your skirt, bare your legs,
and wade through the rivers.
3 Your nakedness will be exposed
and your shame will be seen.
I will take vengeance,
and I will show clemency to no one. [w]
4 Thus says our redeemer,
the Holy One of Israel,
whose name is the LORD of hosts.
5 Sit in silence and conceal yourself in darkness,
O daughter of the Chaldeans.
For never again will you be called
the mistress of kingdoms. [x]
6 Because I was angry with my people
I profaned my inheritance
and gave them over into your power.
You showed them no mercy,
and you laid a very heavy yoke on the aged.
7 You said, "I will be a queen forever."
Thus you did not reflect carefully on your actions
or give any consideration to their outcome. [y]
8 Now listen to this, you voluptuous woman,
as you sit securely on your throne,
thinking to yourself,
"I am the only one who matters.
I will never be a widow
or experience the loss of children." [z]
9 However, both of these things will befall you,
suddenly, in a single day;
both the loss of children and widowhood
will come upon you in full measure

s Isa 40:19; Ex 20:5; Hos 13:2.—t Ex 8:10; Deut 32:7; Mk 12:32.—u Gen 41:25; Ezr 1:2.—v Isa 9:9; Ex 32:9; Jer 2:5.—w Gen 3:10; Ezek 16:37; Nah 3:5.—x Job 2:13; Lam 1:1; Rev 18:7.—y Isa 10:13; 14:13f; Deut 32:29; Rev 18:7.—z Isa 32:9; 45:6; Lam 1:1; Rev 18:7.

47:1 The splendor of a young woman (a virgin) is the customary image in Hebrew poetry for the splendor of a city.

despite all your sorceries
and all your potent spells. [a]
10 You felt secure in your wickedness
as you thought, "No one can see me."
But your wisdom and your knowledge
led you astray,
and you said to yourself,
"I am the only one who matters."
11 As a result, evil will come upon you,
and you will not know how to conjure
it away,
disaster will befall you
that you will not be able to avert;
complete ruin which you did not foresee
will suddenly afflict you. [b]
12 * But continue to persist in your spells
and your many sorceries
in which you have placed your confidence
throughout your life.
Perhaps you can succeed with them;
perhaps you can inspire terror.
13 You have exhausted yourself with consultations
ever since your youth.
Let the astrologers now come forth to
save you,
those who seek the future in the stars
and who predict at each new moon
what will befall you next. [c]
14 But they are like stubble;
the fire consumes them.
They cannot even deliver themselves
from the heat of the flames.
These flames are not meant to sit
beside;
these glowing embers are not meant
for keeping warm.
15 Of absolutely no use to you are your
astrologers
upon whom you have depended from
your youth.
Each of them follows his own path;
not one of them can save you. [d]

CHAPTER 48

A Plea to the Captives

1 Hear this, O house of Jacob,
you who are called by the name of
Israel,
and who came forth from the stock of
Judah,
who swear by the name of the LORD
and invoke the God of Israel
but not with righteousness or good
faith,
2 even though you call yourselves citizens
of the holy city
and rely on the God of Israel
whose name is the LORD of hosts. [e]
3 Things that happened in the past
I foretold long before they occurred.
These predictions issued forth from my
mouth,
and I made them known to you;
then suddenly I acted and they came
to pass. [f]
4 Because I know full well that you are
obstinate,
with your neck an iron sinew
and your forehead firm as bronze,
5 I foretold these events to you long ago
and declared them to you before they
happened
so that you could not assert, "My idols
did them;
my carved statue and my molten
image ordained them."
6 You have heard what I said; now consider it
and admit the truth of what I have
stated.
From now on I will reveal new things,
hidden things of which you have not
been aware. [g]
7 They have just been brought into existence, and not long ago;
before today you have never heard of
them,
so that you cannot claim to have
already known them.
8 You neither heard nor knew;
knowledge of them never reached your
ears before now.
For I knew how treacherous you are
and that from your birth you were
rebellious. [h]
9 For the sake of my name I will restrain
my anger;
for the sake of my honor I will be
patient with you
lest I should be tempted to destroy
you.

a Jer 15:8; 1 Thes 5:3; Rev 18:8-10.—b Isa 10:3; 1 Thes 5:3; Lk 17:27.—c Isa 57:10; Jer 51:58; Hab 2:13.—d Isa 47:13; Rev 18:11.—e Neh 11:1; Mt 4:5; Rom 2:17.—f Isa 40:21; 41:22; 45:21.—g Isa 42:9; Rom 16:25.—h Isa 1:3; 43:22ff; Deut 9:24; Mal 2:11, 14.

47:12-13 Babylon was famous for its astronomers and astrologers.

10 See, I have tested you,
but not in the manner that silver is tested;
I have tested you in the furnace of affliction. [i]
11 For my sake, for my own sake, I do this,
for why should my name be profaned?
I will not yield my glory to another.
12 Listen to me, O Jacob,
and Israel, whom I have called.
I am he; I am the first
and I am the last. [j]
13 My hand laid the foundations of the earth,
and my right hand spread out the heavens;
when I summon them,
they all present themselves immediately. [k]
14 Assemble, all of you, and listen!
Who among the idols has revealed what will happen—
that he whom I love* will do my will
against Babylon and the Chaldeans?
15 I myself have spoken and summoned him;
I have brought him,
and his mission will succeed.
16 Draw near to me and hear this:
From the very beginning
I have not spoken in secret.
From the time it came to be, I have been there.
Now the Lord GOD has sent me and his Spirit. [l]
17 Thus says the Lord GOD,
your redeemer, the Holy One of Israel:
I am the LORD, your God
who teaches you what is for your own good
and who leads you in the way you should go.
18 If only you had listened to my commandments,
your prosperity would have been like a river
and your success like the waves of the sea. [m]
19 Your descendants would have been as numerous as the sand
and your offspring like its countless grains.
Their name would never be erased
or blotted out from my sight. [n]
20 Go forth from Babylon! Flee from Chaldea!
Proclaim this with shouts of joy
and make it known.
Send the message to the ends of the earth and say,
"The LORD has redeemed his servant Jacob."
21 Those whom he led through desert lands
never endured thirst.
He caused water to flow from the rock for them;
he split open the rock and waters streamed forth. [o]
22 Thus says the LORD:
There is no peace for the wicked.

II: EXPIATION OF SIN, REDEMPTION OF ISRAEL

CHAPTER 49

Message to Israel*

1 Listen to me, O coastlands.
Pay attention, you distant peoples.
The LORD called me before I was born;
while I was still in my mother's womb
he gave me my name. [p]
2 He made my tongue like a sharp sword
and hid me in the shadow of his hand.
He formed me into a polished arrow,
and he concealed me in his quiver.
3 He said to me, "You are my servant,
Israel, through whom I will manifest my glory."
4 I formerly believed that I had labored in vain
and had exhausted my strength for nothing
and for no discernible purpose. [q]

i Isa 1:25; 1 Ki 8:51; Jer 6:29f; Zec 13:9; Mal 3:2.—j Lev 18:21; Deut 32:27; 1 Sam 12:22.—k Isa 40:22, 26; 45:12, 18; Gen 2:1; Ex 20:11.—l Isa 33:13; 41:1; Zec 2:9, 11.—m Isa 42:23; 54:13; Deut 5:29.—n Gen 12:2; Job 5:25; Jer 35:19.—o Isa 30:25; 35:6; Ex 17:6; Num 20:11.—p Isa 41:9; 43:1; 44:2, 24; 46:3; Jer 1:5; Mt 1:20; Gal 1:15.—q Isa 40:27; 55:2; Lev 26:20; Job 27:2.

48:14 *He whom I love:* Cyrus. The false gods have not been able to prevail.

49:1-7 The mysterious unknown personage will be called by God and come to revive the hopes of the disappointed repatriates; he is depicted as a prophet whose words have divine power (Jer 1:9); through him God will renew the covenant with his people.

5 Yet now the LORD has spoken;
he formed me in the womb to be his servant
so that I could bring back Jacob to him
and enable Israel to be gathered to him.
For I am honored in the sight of the LORD,
and my God is the source of my strength.
6 It is not enough for you to be my servant, he says,
to raise up the tribes of Jacob
and to bring back the survivors of Israel.
I will make you a light to the nations
so that my salvation may reach
to the ends of the earth. [r]

7 Thus says the LORD,
the redeemer, the Holy One of Israel,
to the one who is despised
and whom the people abhor,
the slave of tyrants:
Kings will rise up when they see you,
and princes will prostrate themselves in homage,
because of the LORD who is faithful,
the Holy One of Israel who has chosen you. [s]

The Deliverance and Restoration of Zion

8* Thus says the LORD:
In a time of my favor I have answered you;
on the day of salvation I have helped you.
I have formed you and have destined you
to be a covenant to the people,
to restore the land
and to allot the desolate heritages, [t]
9 to say to the prisoners, "Come out,"
and to those who are in darkness, "Show yourselves."
They will find sustenance along the way,
and any bare height will serve as their pasture. [u]
10 They will not hunger or thirst,
and neither scorching wind nor sun will weaken them,
for he who pities them will lead them,
and he will guide them beside springs of water. [v]
11 I will blaze a path through all my mountains,
and my roads will be level. [w]
12 Behold, some will come from far away,
others from the north and the west,
and still others from the land of Syene.*

13 Sing for joy, O heavens, and rejoice, O earth;
break forth into song, O mountains.
For the LORD has comforted his people,
and he will show mercy to his afflicted ones.

14 But Zion cried out, "The LORD has forsaken me;
my LORD has forgotten me." [x]
15 Can a woman forget the infant at her breast;
or feel no compassion for the child of her womb?
Even should she forget,
I will never forget you. [y]
16 Behold, I have inscribed your name
on the palms of my hands;
your walls are continually before my eyes. [z]
17 Those who rebuild you do so far more swiftly
than those who destroyed you.
18 Lift up your eyes and look around you;
they are all gathering to come to you.
As I live, says the LORD,
you will put all of them on like jewels;
you will adorn yourself with them like a bride.

19 You had lived in a desolate wasteland,
amid devastated ruins.
Now the land is too tiny for its inhabitants,
while those who destroyed you will be far away. [a]

r Isa 9:1; 42:1-6; Zec 8:22; Lk 2:32; Jn 1:9; Acts 13:46f.—s Isa 49:23; 55:5; Gen 27:29.—t Isa 60:10; Ezek 36:10; 2 Cor 6:2.—u Isa 41:18; 42:7, 18ff; 61:1; Lk 4:18.—v Isa 14:1; 33:16; 48:17; 51:14; Rev 7:16.—w Isa 11:16; 40:3f; Jer 31:9.—x Isa 27:8; 40:27; 54:6.—y Isa 43:4; 44:21; 46:3f; 66:13; 1 Ki 3:26.—z Isa 62:6; Ex 28:9.—a Lev 26:33; Ezek 36:10-11; Zec 10:10.

49:8—55:13 The following chapters no longer speak either of Cyrus or of Babylon; their attention is focused entirely on the restoration of Jerusalem and the joy of the people as they return to the Promised Land. A new age is beginning, and the holy city will be seen rising from ruins and becoming the capital in which the glory of the Lord is manifested. But amid those hymns to the future, the figure of the Servant insistently reappears, as though to give a deeper foundation for the hope.

49:12 *Syene:* the Elephantine of the Greeks; the modern Aswan near the first cataract of the Nile, on the border of Upper Egypt. A Jewish community existed there from the sixth century B.C.

20 The children born during your bereavement
will say in your hearing,
"This place is too cramped for me;
make room for me to live in."
21 Then you will say to yourself,
"Who bore these children for me?
I was bereaved and barren,
I was exiled and repudiated;
who has reared them?
I was left all alone;
where then have these come from?" [b]
22 Thus says the Lord GOD:
Behold, I will beckon to the nations
and raise my signal to the peoples.
Then they will bring your sons in their arms,
and they will carry your daughters on their shoulders. [c]
23 Kings will be your foster-fathers,
and their princesses will serve as your nursing mothers.
They will bow down to you
with their faces to the ground
and lick the dust from your feet.
Then you will know that I am the LORD;
those who hope in me will not be disappointed. [d]
24 Can spoil be taken from a warrior,
or can the tyrant's captives be set free?
25 Thus says the LORD:
Even a warrior's captives can be rescued,
and booty can be retrieved from a tyrant.
I myself will contend with those who oppose you,
and I will deliver your children.
26 I will force your oppressors to eat their own flesh,
and they will become drunk on their own blood
as if with wine.
Then all mankind will know
that I, the LORD, am your Savior
and your Redeemer, the Mighty One of Jacob. [e]

CHAPTER 50

God's Offer of Salvation Remains

1 * Thus says the LORD:
Where is your mother's bill of divorce
by which I repudiated her?
Or which creditor of mine was it
to whom I sold you?
No, you were sold because of your sins,
and your mother was repudiated,
because of your rebellious acts. [f]
2 Why was no one there when I came?
Why did no one answer when I called?
Is my hand too short to redeem?
Have I no power to deliver?
By my rebuke I can dry up the sea
and turn the rivers into a desert.
Their fish rot for lack of water
and die of thirst. [g]
3 Did I not clothe the heavens in black
and cover them with sackcloth?
4 * The Lord GOD has given me
the tongue of one who has been well taught
so that I am able to console the weary
with a message of encouragement.
Morning after morning he opens my ears
so that I may listen to their concerns. [h]
5 And I have not rebelled,
I have not turned away.
6 I offered my back to those who struck me,
my cheeks to those who plucked my beard.
I did not shield my face
from insults and spitting. [i]
7 The Lord GOD is my help;
therefore I have not been disgraced.
Rather, I have set my face like flint,
knowing that I will not be put to shame. [j]

b Isa 29:23; 54:1ff; 66:7-8; Jer 10:20.—c Isa 5:26; 11:10; 13:2.—d Gen 27:29; Ex 6:7; Rev 3:9.—e Isa 19:2; Ex 6:7; Ezek 38:21; Zec 14:13.—f Isa 54:6ff; Deut 24:1-4; Jdg 3:8; Neh 5:5; Hos 2:2; Mt 19:3; Mk 10:2ff.—g Gen 18:14; Ex 7:18; Num 11:23; Ps 105:29.—h Isa 61:1; Ex 4:12; Mt 11:28.—i 2 Sam 10:4ff; Mt 26:67; 27:30; Mk 14:65; Lk 22:63; Jn 19:1.—j Isa 41:10; Ezek 3:9; Jer 1:18.

50:1-3 This incomplete song attests to the fidelity of God despite the sins of human beings. He has never publicly separated himself from them, but he has broken the bonds linking him to his people.

50:4-11 We cannot imagine a more profound docility and self-surrender than that of this mysterious Servant. He is filled with the sense of God to the point that nothing can make him waver. Sent as he is to strengthen his discouraged brothers and sisters, he does not weaken but endures persecution, for he is sure of God's power within him. His lot makes us think of the treatment inflicted on Jesus. Instructed by his example, pious Jews and pagans (v. 10) can acknowledge God as Savior.

8 He who upholds me is near;
thus, if anyone wishes to oppose me,
let us confront each other.
Is there anyone who has a case against me?
Let him come forward.
9 The Lord GOD is my defender;
who then will dare to condemn me?
All of them will wear out like a garment
the moth will devour them. [k]

10 Who among you fears the LORD
and obeys his servant's voice?
Who among you walks in darkness
without any light?
Let him trust in the name of the LORD
and rely on his God. [l]
11 But all of you kindle a fire
and arm yourselves with firebrands.
Walk by the light of your fire
and the firebrands that you have set ablaze.
This is what you will receive from my hand:
you will lie down in torment.

CHAPTER 51

Exhortation To Trust in the LORD*

1 Listen to me, you who pursue justice,
you who seek the LORD.
Look to the rock from which you were hewn,
and to the quarry from which you were dug. [m]
2 Look to Abraham, your father,
and to Sarah who gave birth to you.
When I called him, he was but one,
but I blessed him and made him many. [n]

3 The LORD will comfort Zion
and have pity on all her ruins.
He will make her deserts like Eden
and her wastelands into the garden of the LORD.
Joy and gladness will resound in her,
thanksgiving and the sound of music.
4 Listen attentively to me, my people,
and pay heed to me, my nation.
For the law will issue forth from me,
and my justice will serve as a light to the nations. [o]
5 My justice will issue forth swiftly,
my salvation will appear,
and I will judge the nations with my arm.
The coastlands and the islands
will place their hope in me
and trust in my protection.
6 Raise your eyes to the heavens
and gaze down on the earth below.
For the heavens will vanish like smoke,
and the earth will wear out like a garment
as its inhabitants die like flies.
But my salvation will be everlasting
and my justice will never cease. [p]

7 Listen to me,
you who truly comprehend the meaning of justice
and who have my teaching in your hearts.
Do not fear the reproach of others
or allow their reviling to dismay you.
8 For they will be like a garment eaten away by moths,
like wool devoured by grubs.
But my saving justice will be everlasting
and my deliverance for all generations. [q]
9 Awake, awake, O arm of the LORD!
Clothe yourself in strength.
Awake as in the days of old,
in ages long past.
Was it not you who hacked Rahab* to pieces
and pierced the dragon through? [r]
10 Was it not you who dried up the sea,
the waters of the great deep,
and turned the depths of the sea into a path
for the redeemed to pass over? [s]
11 Therefore, those whom the LORD has redeemed will return
and enter Zion singing,
their heads crowned with everlasting joy.
They shall experience joy and gladness,
while sorrow and mourning will disappear.

k Isa 51:6-8; Job 13:28; Ps 102:27; Rom 8:1, 34.—l Isa 43:11; 44:1f; Prov 1:7; Hag 1:12; Acts 26:18.—m Isa 46:3; Deut 16:20; Rom 9:30f.—n Isa 29:22; Gen 12:2ff; 22:17; Ezek 33:24.—o Isa 2:3; 3:15; Ex 6:7; Deut 18:18.—p Mt 24:35; Lk 21:33; 2 Pet 3:10.—q Isa 14:11; 50:9; Job 13:28; Jas 5:2.—r Ex 6:6; 15:16; Jdg 5:12; Job 9:13; 26:12; Pss 74:13; 89:11.—s Ex 14:22; Zec 10:11; Rev 16:12.

51:1—52:12 Forgetting henceforth Cyrus and his victories and passing over the destruction of Babylon, the prophet focuses his attention on a restored Jerusalem and on the new era of justice and of God's favor.

51:9 *Rahab* is a personification of Egypt (see Isa 30:7; Pss 87:4; 89:10). The *dragon* is the crocodile, the emblem of Egypt—allusion to the ten plagues.

12 I, I alone, am the one who comforts you.
Why then do you fear mortal men who must die,
human beings who must perish like grass? [t]
13 You have forgotten the LORD, your maker,
who stretched out the heavens
and laid the foundations of the earth.
You are in constant fear every moment of the day,
dreading the fury of the oppressor
who is bent on your destruction.
But where now is the oppressor's fury? [u]
14 The oppressed will soon be set free;
they will not die in the dungeon,
nor will they be without food.

15 For I am the LORD, your God
who stirs up the sea and makes its waves roar;
the LORD of hosts is my name. [v]
16 I have put my words into your mouth
and sheltered you in the shadow of my hand,
I who stretched out the heavens
and laid the foundations of the earth,
and who say to Zion,
You are my people.

The Cup of Salvation

17 Awake, awake!
Rise up, O Jerusalem!
You have drunk from the LORD's hand
the cup of his wrath;
and have drained to the dregs
the goblet that causes men to become inebriated. [w]
18 Of all the sons you have brought forth,
there is no one to guide you;
of all the sons you have reared,
there is no one to take you by the hand.

19 Who is there to grieve with you
about the twofold disaster you have suffered?
Devastation and destruction, famine and sword:
who can comfort you?
20 Your children are lying helpless
at the corner of every street
like antelopes trapped in a net.
They are filled with the wrath of the LORD,
with the rebuke of your God.

21 Therefore, hear this, you who are afflicted,
you who are drunk although not with wine. [x]
22 Thus says your sovereign LORD,
your God who defends his people:
I have taken from your hand
the cup of inebriation;
you will never again drink
from the bowl of my wrath. [y]
23 I will hand it over to your tormentors,
those who said to you,
"Lie on the ground
so that we may walk over you."
And you flattened your back
like ground beneath their feet,
like a road for them to walk on.* [z]

CHAPTER 52

The Joy of Zion

1 Awake, awake!
Clothe yourself in strength, O Zion.
Put on your glorious garments,
O Jerusalem, the holy city.
For the uncircumcised and the unclean
will no longer enter you. [a]
2 Shake off the dust from yourself and rise up
O captive Jerusalem.
Remove the chains from your neck,
O captive daughter of Zion.

3 For thus says the LORD:
You were sold for nothing
and you will be redeemed without money.
4 Then the Lord GOD continues:
Long ago my people went down to Egypt
and settled there as aliens;
the Assyrians also oppressed them without cause. [b]

5 Therefore, says the LORD,
what should now be done?
My people have been carried off without cause;
their rulers boast triumphantly,
and my name is constantly reviled
throughout the day, declares the LORD. [c]

---

t 2 Ki 1:15; 2 Cor 1:4; 1 Pet 1:24.—u Isa 17:10; Gen 1:1; Job 8:13.—v Ex 14:21; Jer 31:35.—w Jdg 5:12; Job 21:20; Jer 25:15ff.—x Isa 14:32; 29:9; 51:17; 54:11.—y Jer 25:15; Mt 20:22.—z Isa 14:4; Jos 10:24; Zec 12:2.—a Isa 51:17; Ex 28:2; 1 Sam 2:4.—b Isa 10:24; Gen 46:6.—c Isa 37:23; Ezek 36:20, 23; Rom 2:24.

51:23 Conquerors signified their victory by putting their foot on the neck of the conquered.

6 Therefore, on that day,
my people will know my name
and understand that it is I who say:
Here I am!

7 How beautiful upon the mountains
are the feet of the messenger who announces peace,
who bears good news and proclaims glad tidings,
announcing salvation and saying to Zion,
"Your God is king." [d]

8 Listen! Your watchmen raise a cry
and together they shout for joy,
for with their own eyes they clearly behold
the return of the LORD to Zion. [e]

9 Burst forth together with songs of joy,
you ruins of Jerusalem.
For the LORD has comforted his people;
he has redeemed Jerusalem.

10 The LORD has bared his holy arm
in the sight of all the nations.
All the ends of the earth will see
the salvation of our God.

11 Depart, depart! Leave that place behind!
Touch nothing that is unclean.
Go forth from its midst and purify yourselves,
you who carry the vessels of the LORD.* [f]

12 But you need not rush forth in haste,
nor should you take flight like fugitives.
For the LORD will go before you,
and your rear guard will be the God of Israel. [g]

Humiliation and Triumph of the LORD's Servant*

13 Behold, my servant will prosper;
he will be exalted and raised to great heights.

14 Just as many people recoiled at the sight of him—
he was so disfigured
that he no longer appeared to be human— [h]

15 so will he startle many nations,
and kings will be speechless before him.
For they will see what they had not been told,
and they will contemplate
what they had not previously heard. [i]

CHAPTER 53

1 Who has believed what we have heard?
And to whom has the arm of the LORD been revealed? [j]

2 He grew up before him like a sapling,
like a shoot in arid ground.
He had no beauty or majesty
that would cause us to look at him;
nothing in his appearance would attract us to him. [k]

3 He was despised and shunned by others,
a man of sorrows who was no stranger to suffering.
We loathed him and regarded him as of no account,
as one from whom men avert their gaze. [l]

4 Although it was our afflictions that he bore,
our sufferings that he endured,
we thought of him as stricken,
as struck down by God and afflicted. [m]

5 But he was pierced for our offenses
and crushed for our iniquity;

d Isa 40:9; 2 Sam 18:26; Nah 1:15; Lk 2:14; Rom 10:15.—e Isa 62:6; Num 10:36; Jer 6:17; Ezek 3:17.—f Num 8:6; 2 Cor 6:17.—g Ex 12:11; 14:19; Mic 2:13; Jn 10:4.—h Job 18:20; 2 Sam 10:4; Ps 69:8.—i Lev 14:7; Jdg 18:19; Mic 7:16.—j Isa 28:9; 30:30; 52:10; Jn 12:38; Rom 10:16.—k Isa 4:2; 11:1; Job 14:7.—l Job 19:18; Ps 31:11ff; Mt 16:21; Mk 9:12.—m Jer 10:19; Mt 8:17.

52:11 Cyrus restored the sacred vessels of the temple, "the vessels of the house of the LORD" (Ezr 1:7-11).

52:13—53:12 The song turns into a kind of dialogue in which two divine oracles frame the reflections of people astounded by what happens to the Servant.

But who is this suffering Servant? We have already seen his mysterious face in three other poetic compositions (Isa 42:1-7; 49:19a; 50:4-11). We think spontaneously of a wise man or a prophet, a man of God who disagrees with his compatriots on their very ideas of God's plan. For the Servant, the success of God's plan means something quite different from political success. But the people could not tolerate this criticism of their all too human hopes. The prophet was mistreated and condemned to death (Isa 53:7-8).

But the Servant is also Israel, whose destiny the prophet embodies. The chosen people, contaminated by pagan forms of worship, was almost eradicated by the Exile. But it carries out its mission as a people that bears witness to God who chose it and is bringing it back to life; in the radiance of its resurrection, pagans will be able to recognize that the Lord of Israel is the living God who loves his people without ever changing his mind, the Savior of the human race.

The experience of the suffering Just One, whether prophet or people of God, highlights the fundamental law governing the history of salvation and every spiritual life: the power of God is manifested in human weakness. What a paradox: the Servant succeeds where Cyrus failed, because salvation comes not from battles but from martyrdom!

the punishment that made us whole fell upon him,
and by his bruises we have been healed. [n]
6 We had all gone astray like sheep,
each of us following his own way,
but the LORD laid upon him
the guilt of us all. [o]

7 Although harshly treated and afflicted,
he did not open his mouth.
Like a lamb led to the slaughter
and like a sheep that keeps silent before its shearers,
he did not open his mouth. [p]
8 Unjustly condemned, he was taken away,
and who gave any thought to his future?
For he was cut off from the land of the living
and stricken for the sins of his people. [q]
9 They assigned him a grave with the wicked
and a burial place with evildoers,
even though he had done no act of violence
nor had he ever spoken deceitfully. [r]
10 Yet it was the will of the LORD
to crush him with pain.
For if he gives his life as a sacrifice for sin,
he will see his offspring and prolong his life,
and through him the will of the LORD will be accomplished.
11 As a result of his anguish
my servant will behold the light and be content.
Through his humiliation he will justify many,
and their guilt he will bear.

12 Therefore, I will allot him a portion among the great,
and he will divide the spoils with the mighty,
because he exposed himself to death
and was counted among the transgressors,
even though he bore the sins of many
and interceded for the transgressors. [s]

CHAPTER 54*

The New Zion*

1 Sing with happiness,
you barren woman who never bore a child.
Burst forth in shouts of joy,
you who never have been in labor.
For more numerous are the children of the deserted wife
than are the children of the wedded wife,
says the LORD. [t]
2 Enlarge the site for your dwelling
and stretch out your tent curtains
to the greatest possible extent.
Lengthen your ropes
and strengthen your tent stakes. [u]
3 For you will spread out
to the right and to the left;
your descendants will dispossess the nations
and settle in the desolate cities.

4 Have no fear, for you will not be put to shame;
do not be discouraged, for you will not be humiliated.
You will forget the shame of your youth,
and you will no longer remember
the reproach of your widowhood.
5 For your Creator has now become your husband;
his name is the LORD of hosts.
The Holy One of Israel is your redeemer;
he is called the God of the entire world. [v]

6 The LORD has called you back
like a forsaken wife grieved in spirit,
like the repudiated wife of a man's youth,
says your God. [w]
7 For a brief moment I did forsake you,
but with great compassion I will take you back.
8 In an outburst of anger
I hid my face from you for a moment,
but with everlasting love
I will have compassion on you,
says the LORD, your Redeemer.

n Ex 28:38; Jn 3:17; Rom 4:25; 1 Cor 15:3; 1 Pet 2:24.—o Lev 16:21ff; 1 Pet 2:24-25.—p Mt 26:63; Mk 14:61; Jn 1:29; Acts 8:32.—q Isa 53:12; Mk 14:49; Acts 8:32-33.—r Mt 27:38; Mk 15:27; Lk 23:32; Jn 19:18; 1 Pet 2:22f.—s Ex 15:9; Mt 26:28, 38, 39, 42; Mk 15:28; Lk 22:37.—t Isa 66:7; Gen 30:1; 1 Sam 2:5; Gal 4:27.— u Isa 26:15; 49:20; Gen 26:22; Ex 35:18.—v Isa 51:13; Jer 3:14.—w Isa 49:14-21; Mal 2:14f.

54:1—55:13 The Book of Consolation ends with a song about trust and love regained.

54:1-17 The holy city is as it were a spouse of the Lord.

9 This for me is like the days of Noah.
Just as I swore that the waters of Noah
would never again flood the earth,
so I have sworn that I never will be angry with you
and that I will never rebuke you. [x]
10 Although the mountains may be shaken
and the hills may totter,
my steadfast love will not depart from you,
and my covenant of peace will never be shaken,
says the LORD who has compassion on you. [y]

11 O afflicted city, storm-battered and not comforted,
I will build you with precious stones
and lay your foundations with sapphires. [z]
12 I will use rubies to make your battlements,
jewels for your gates,
and precious stones for all your walls.
13 All of your sons will be taught by the LORD,
and great will be their prosperity. [a]

14 With justice you will be established;
you will be free from the fear of oppression,
and no terror will afflict you.
15 Should anyone attack you,
it will not be my doing,
and anyone who does stir up strife
will fall before you.

16 It was I who created the blacksmith
to blow on the coals in the fire
and produce a weapon suitable for its purpose.
I also created the ravager
to destroy and wreak havoc.
17 No weapon used against you will prevail,
and you will refute every accusation
that is raised in court against you.
This is the heritage of the servants of the LORD,
their vindication from me, says the LORD. [b]

x Gen 9:15; Jer 3:5; Ezek 39:29.—y Gen 9:16; Ex 34:10; Ps 46:3; Heb 12:27.—z Isa 14:32; Ex 24:10; 1 Chr 29:2; Rev 21:18-21.—a Mic 4:2; Jn 6:45; Heb 8:11.—b Isa 29:8; 41:11.—c Jer 2:13; Jn 4:10ff; 6:35; 7:37ff; Rev 21:6; 22:17.—d Eccl 6:2; Hos 4:10; Mic 6:14.—e 2 Sam 7:12-16; Rom 10:5.—f Isa 2:3; 49:6.—g Deut 4:29; 2 Chr 15:2; Acts 17:27.—h Isa 40:13-14; Num 23:19; Job 11:8.

CHAPTER 55

An Everlasting Covenant

1 All you who are thirsty,
come to the water;
all you who have no money,
come forward, buy, and eat.
Come, buy wine and milk,
without money and without cost. [c]

2 Why spend money for that which is not bread,
your wages for that which fails to satisfy.
Listen carefully to me, and you will eat well
and delight in rich food. [d]
3 Come to me and pay close attention;
listen so that you may have life.
I will make an everlasting covenant with you
to love you with the faithful love promised to David. [e]

4 I appointed him to be a witness to the peoples,
a leader and commander of nations.
5 You in turn will summon nations unknown to you,
and nations that do not know you will hasten to you,
because of the LORD, your God,
the Holy One of Israel,
for he has glorified you. [f]

6 Seek the LORD while he still may be found;
call to him when he is close at hand. [g]
7 Let the wicked abandon their ways
and those who are evil their thoughts.
Let them return to the LORD
so that he may have mercy upon them;
and to our God,
for he is rich in forgiveness.

8 For my thoughts are not your thoughts,
nor are your ways my ways, says the LORD.
9 As the heavens are higher than the earth,
so are my ways higher than your ways
and my thoughts above your thoughts. [h]

10 For just as the rain and the snow
come down from the heavens
and do not return there
until they have watered the earth,

making it fertile and fruitful,
giving seed for the one who sows
and bread for those who eat, [i]
11 so shall my word be
that issues forth from my mouth.
It will not return to me unfulfilled,
but it will accomplish my purpose
and achieve what I sent it forth to do.
12 Yes, you will go forth in joy,
and you will be led back in peace.
The mountains and hills before you
will burst forth into song,
and all the trees in the countryside
will clap their hands. [j]
13 A cypress will grow in place of the thornbush,
and myrtles will come up instead of briars.
All this will increase the LORD's renown,
an everlasting sign that will not be cut off.

III: RETURN OF THE FIRST CAPTIVES*

CHAPTER 56

The LORD Welcomes All People

1 Thus says the LORD:
Maintain justice
and do what is right.
For my salvation is close at hand,
and my righteousness will soon be revealed.
2 Happy is the man who does this,
the one who holds fast to my instructions,
who observes the Sabbath without profaning it
and refrains from every evil deed. [k]
3 Let no foreigner who has joined himself to the LORD say,
"The LORD will surely exclude me from his people."
Permit no eunuch* to believe,
"I am nothing but a dried-up tree."
4 For thus says the LORD:
To the eunuchs who observe my Sabbaths,
who choose to do my will
and hold fast to my covenant, [l]
5 I will give in my house
and within my walls
a monument and a name
better than sons and daughters.
I will give them an everlasting name
that will never be effaced. [m]
6 The foreigners who pledge their allegiance to the LORD,
who minister to him,
who love the name of the LORD
and become his servants,
who keep the Sabbath and do not profane
and who hold fast to my covenant:
7 all these I will bring to my holy mountain
and make them joyful in my house of prayer;
their burnt offerings and their sacrifices
will be accepted on my altar,
for my house will be called
a house of prayer for all peoples. [n]
8 Thus says the Lord GOD
who gathers the exiles of Israel:
There are others whom I will call forth
besides those who have already been gathered.

Wicked Rulers

9 All you wild beasts of the fields and of the forest,
come forth and gorge yourselves. [o]
10 Israel's watchmen are all blind;
they perceive absolutely nothing.
They are all dumb watchdogs
that are unable to bark,
dreaming as they lie there,
loving the opportunity to sleep. [p]
11 The dogs have a ravenous appetite;
meanwhile the shepherds are never satisfied.
They comprehend nothing;
each of them goes his own way,
all of them interested solely in their own gain.
12 "Come," says each one, "I will fetch some wine,
and we will fill ourselves with strong drink.

i Gen 47:23; Lev 25:19; Job 14:9.—j Isa 35:2; 54:10, 13; 1 Chr 16:33.—k Isa 56:4; 58:13; Ex 20:8, 10.—l Ex 31:13; Wis 3:14f; Jer 38:7.—m Isa 26:1; 1 Sam 15:12.—n 1 Ki 8:29f; Ezek 20:40; Mt 21:13; Rom 12:1.—o Isa 18:6; Jer 12:9; Ezek 34:5, 8.—p Isa 52:8; Jer 6:17; Ezek 3:17.

56:1—66:24 The oracles of the third part of the Book of Isaiah give us a glimpse chiefly of the difficulties faced by Judaism, which was born during the Exile. Most of the passages seem to come from the most difficult years, those following upon the return (530–510 B.C.). All are not the work of one and the same author. The oracles endeavor to lead believers to a surer, but also purer and more spiritual hope.

56:3 *Eunuch*[s] were to be equal in every respect to the other members of the community of Israel (see Deut 23:2).

And tomorrow will be like today,
or perhaps even better." [q]

CHAPTER 57

1 Those who are righteous perish,
but no one takes it to heart.
Those who are devout are taken away,
and no one understands
that the righteous are taken away
to be spared from evil.
2 Those who have walked uprightly
enter into peace;
they find rest as they lie in death.

The Unrighteous

3 But as for you, come here,
you children of a sorceress,
you offspring of an adulterer and a harlot! [r]
4 Whom are you mocking?
At whom do you open your mouths
and stick out your tongues?
Are you not a rebellious brood,
the offspring of liars?
5 You burn with lust among the oaks
and under every spreading tree,
sacrificing your children in the ravines
and under the clefts in the rocks.* [s]
6 The smooth stones of the ravines will be your portion;
these are your lot.
To them you poured out libations
and brought forth your cereal offerings.
Should such acts appease me?
7 Upon a high and lofty mountain
you have placed your bed,
and there you went up to offer sacrifice. [t]
8 Behind the door and the doorpost
you have displayed your pagan symbols.
Forsaking me, you have uncovered your bed;
you climbed into it and opened it wide.
You struck a profitable bargain
with those whose beds you love,
and you gazed endlessly at their nakedness. [u]
9 You approached the king with oil,
having lavished your body with perfumes.
You sent forth your procurers far and wide,
even to the depths of Sheol.*
10 Although exhausted by your endless travels,
you never said, "It is useless."
You realized that your desire had been rekindled,
and so you never gave up. [v]
11 Whom did you so greatly dread and fear
that you betrayed me
and no longer remembered me
or gave me any thought?
Is it because I was silent for so long a time
that you do not fear me?
12 Now I will expose your conduct
that you regard as so righteous.
13 When you cry out for help,
your collection of idols will not save you.
The wind will carry off all of them;
a gentle breeze will bear them away.
But whoever makes me his refuge
will possess the land
and inherit my holy mountain. [w]

Compassion for the Afflicted

14 Then the LORD will say:
Build up, build up! Prepare the way!
Remove every obstruction from my people's path. [x]
15 For thus says the One who is high and exalted,
who lives eternally
and whose name is holy:
I dwell in a high and holy place
but I am with the contrite and the humble,
to revive the spirit of the humble
and to revive the heart of the contrite. [y]
16 I will not accuse forever,
nor will I always be angry.
For then the spirits of the souls that I have made
would grow faint because of me.

q Isa 28:7ff; Lev 10:9; Prov 23:20; Wis 2:7; Lk 12:18.—r Ex 22:17; Mal 3:5; Mt 16:4.—s Lev 18:21; 2 Ki 16:4; Jer 7:31; 19:5; Ezek 20:28, 31.—t Isa 65:7; Jer 2:20; 3:6; Ezek 6:13; 16:16; Hos 4:13.—u Ezek 16:26; 23:7, 18.—v Isa 47:13; Mal 3:14.—w Isa 40:7, 24; Jdg 10:14; Jer 22:20.—x Isa 11:16; 40:3f; 62:10; Jer 18:15.—y Isa 61:2f; Deut 33:27; Job 16:19; Mic 6:8.

57:5 The reference is to fertility cults.
57:9 If there is a play on the Hebrew word *melek*, Molech is perhaps the king (see 2 Ki 23:10); the second part of the verse alludes to the worship of underworld divinities or of the dead.

17 Because of their wicked avarice I was angry,
and I struck them, keeping myself hidden,
but they continued on their rebellious path. [z]
18 I saw how they behaved, but I will heal them;
I will lead them and fill them with consolation,
both them and those who mourn for them.
19 Peace, peace to all, both far and near,
and I will heal them, says the LORD. [a]
20 But the wicked are like the restless sea that cannot be still;
its waters cast up mud and dirt.
21 There is no peace for the wicked,
says my God. [b]

CHAPTER 58

Proper Fasting

1 Shout loudly, without holding back.
Lift up your voice like a trumpet.
Proclaim to my people their wicked deeds,
to the house of Jacob their sins.
2 Yet they search for me day after day
in their desire to know my ways,
as if they are a nation that adheres to righteousness
and has not abandoned the law of their God. [c]
They request that I make righteous judgments,
and they long to be near God.
3 They ask, "Why should we fast
when you do not even notice?
Why should we mortify ourselves
when you pay no heed?"

The truth is that on your fast days
you serve your own interests
and oppress all your workers.
4 Your fasting only leads to quarrels and fights
and lashing out with vicious blows.
Such fasting as you currently practice
will not make your voice heard on high. [d]
5 Is this the type of fast that pleases me,
a day for a man to humble himself,
to bow his head like a reed
and lie in sackcloth and ashes?
Is this what you call a fast,
a day acceptable to the LORD? [e]
6 This rather is the type of fast that I wish:
to loosen the fetters of injustice,
to undo the thongs of the yoke,
to set free those who are oppressed
and to break every yoke,
7 to share your bread with the hungry
and to offer shelter to the homeless poor,
to clothe the naked when you behold them
and not turn your back on your own kin. [f]
8 Then your light will break forth like the dawn,
and your wound will quickly be healed;
your righteousness will go before you,
and the glory of the LORD will be your rear guard. [g]
9 Then, when you call, the LORD will answer;
you will cry out for help,
and he will say, "Here I am."

If you cease to tolerate the yoke of oppression,
the pointing of fingers* and malicious words,
10 if you offer your food to the hungry
and satisfy the needs of the afflicted,
then your light will rise in the darkness,
and your night will become like midday.
11 The LORD will guide you continually
and satisfy your needs in the barren desert.
He will strengthen your limbs,
and you will be like a watered garden,
like a spring whose waters never run dry. [h]
12 Your ancient ruins will be rebuilt,
constructed on foundations from generations past.
You will be called the rebuilder of broken walls
and the restorer of ruined streets and dwellings. [i]

z Isa 1:15; 30:15; 56:11; Jer 8:10.—a Lk 2:14; Acts 2:39; Heb 13:15.—b Isa 26:3; 48:22; 59:8; Ezek 13:16.—c Deut 32:15; Tit 1:16; Jas 4:8.—d Isa 1:15; 59:2; 1 Ki 21:9-13.—e 1 Ki 21:27; Job 2:8; Zec 7:5; Mt 6:16.—f Job 22:7; Ezek 18:7, 16; Mt 25:35; Lk 3:11.—g Ex 14:19; Job 11:17.—h Isa 42:16; 51:3; Ps 23; Song 4:15; Jn 4:14.—i Isa 44:28; 49:8; 61:4; Neh 2:17.

58:9 *Pointing of fingers:* as a sign of scorn or a curse.

13 If you refrain from traveling on the Sabbath
and from engaging in your own interests on my holy day,
if you call the Sabbath a day of joy
and regard the LORD's holy day as honorable,
if you honor it by not going your own way,
serving your own interests,
or attending to your own affairs;
14 then you will find true happiness in the LORD,
and I will enable you to ride
upon the heights of the earth.
I will nourish you with the heritage of your father Jacob,
for the mouth of the LORD has spoken. [j]

CHAPTER 59

Sin and Repentance

1 Truly the arm of the LORD is not too short to save,
nor is his ear too dull to hear. [k]
2 Rather, it is your iniquities that have been barriers
between you and your God.
Your sins have caused him to hide his face
so that he does not hear you.
3 For your hands are stained with blood
and your fingers with guilt.
Your lips utter lies
and your tongue mutters wicked things. [l]
4 No one brings a suit justly
or pleads honestly in court.
They all rely on empty words and utter lies;
they conceive mischief and bring forth evil.
5 They hatch adders' eggs
and weave the spider's web;
whoever eats their eggs will die;
crush one and a viper emerges. [m]
6 Their webs are useless for clothing;
what they make cannot serve to cover them.
Their works are deeds of evil,
and acts of violence flow from their hands.
7 Their feet rush headlong to do evil,
and they do not hesitate to shed innocent blood.
Their thoughts are those of iniquity;
their paths are marked by havoc and ruin. [n]
8 They do not know the way of peace,
and justice is not seen along their paths.
The roads they follow are crooked,
and no one who travels on them knows any peace.
9 Therefore, justice is far removed from us,
and righteousness is far beyond our reach.
We look for light but behold only darkness,
for brightness but we walk in gloom.
10 Like blind men we grope along a wall,
feeling our way like those bereft of eyes.
We stumble at noon as if it were twilight;
in the midst of the strong we are like the dead. [o]
11 All of us growl like bears;
like doves we continue to moan mournfully.
We wait for justice but receive none,
for deliverance but it is far from us. [p]
12 For our transgressions against you are numerous,
and our sins bear witness against us.
We are unable to forget our offenses,
and we are well aware of our iniquities:
13 our rebellion and our denial of the LORD
and our turning away from following him,
threatening acts of oppression and revolt,
and uttering lies conceived in our hearts. [q]
14 Justice has been rebuffed
and righteousness stands at a distance.
For truth stumbles in the public square
and uprightness cannot enter.
15 Truth has disappeared,
and those who turn from evil are terrorized.

j Isa 1:20; Deut 32:13; Job 22:26.—k Isa 30:19; 41:20; 50:2; 58:9; Num 11:23.—l Isa 1:15; 3:8; 2 Ki 21:16; Ezek 22:9.—m Job 20:12-16; Mt 3:7.—n 2 Ki 21:16; Prov 6:17; Mic 3:10; Rom 3:15.—o Deut 28:29; Lam 4:14; Zep 1:17.—p Isa 38:14; Ezek 7:16.—q Num 11:20; Prov 30:9; Mt 10:33.

Zion's Redeemer Comes

When the LORD witnessed this, he was displeased
that justice had ceased to exist.
16 He saw that no help was in sight,
and he was outraged that no one sought to intervene.
Therefore, his own arm effected the victory,
with his righteousness as his support. [r]
17 He put on justice like a breastplate
and a helmet of salvation on his head.
He clothed himself with garments of vengeance
and wrapped himself in a cloak of zeal. [s]
18 He will repay his enemies
according to their deeds:
wrath to his adversaries,
retribution to his enemies;
he will render requital
to the islands and the coastlands.
19 And so those in the west will fear the name of the LORD,
and those in the east his glory.
He will come like a pent-up stream
that is driven by the breath of the LORD.
20 He will come as a redeemer to Zion,
and to those in Jacob who cease to rebel.
This is the word of the LORD. [t]
21 As for me, says the LORD,
this is my covenant with them:
my Spirit which rests upon you
and my words that I have put into your mouth
will not depart from your mouth
or out of the mouths of your children,
or out of the mouths of your children's children,
says the LORD, from now on and forevermore. [u]

CHAPTER 60

Zion's Glory Dawns

1* Arise and shine forth, for your light has come
and the glory of the LORD has dawned upon you. [v]
2 Even though darkness covers the earth
and thick darkness enshrouds the peoples,
upon you the LORD will shine,
and over you his glory will appear.
3 Nations will be guided by your light
and kings by the brightness of your radiance. [w]
4 Raise your eyes and look around;
they are all assembling and returning to you.
Your sons are coming from far away,
and your daughters will be carried
in the arms of their nurses. [x]
5* Then you will be radiant at what you behold,
and your hearts will throb and rejoice.
For the riches of the sea will be brought to you,
and the wealth of the nations will come to you.
6 Droves of camels will cover your land,
the young camels from Midian and Ephah;
all from Sheba will come,
laden with gold and frankincense,
while the people proclaim the praises of the LORD. [y]
7 All the flocks of Kedar will be gathered to you;
the rams of Nebaioth will serve your needs.
They will be acceptable offerings on my altar,
and I will enhance the splendor of my house. [z]
8 Who are these that fly along like clouds
and like doves to their dovecotes?
9 All the vessels are assembled
from the seacoasts and the islands,

---

r Isa 41:28; 51:5; 53:12.—s Isa 63:3; Wis 5:17ff; Ezek 5:13; Eph 6:14; 1 Thes 5:8.—t Job 19:25; Rom 11:26f.—u Gen 9:16; Ex 4:15; Deut 29:13-14.—v Isa 52:2; Jn 8:12; Eph 5:14.—w Isa 42:6; 44:5; 45:14; 49:6; Mt 2:1-11; Rev 21:24.—x Isa 2:3; 11:12; 49:18: Jer 30:10.—y Gen 25:2; Jdg 6:5; Jer 6:20.—z Gen 25:13; Ezek 20:40; Zep 3:10.

60:1—62:12 Neither the walls nor the temple of the holy city have yet been rebuilt. The repatriates are tired of waiting for the renewal whose coming is delayed. To encourage them, the poet repeats the promises made during the Exile (Isa 54) and expounds his grandiose vision of a Jerusalem restored and renewed by the Lord. For human beings who grope along, questing in darkness, this vision awaits a fulfillment that is beyond time; the Book of Revelation will repeat it (Rev 21).

60:5-9 The sea symbolizes the maritime powers, among them Phoenicia and Greece. *Midian*, *Ephah*, and *Sheba* (see 1 Ki 10:1-13) are peoples of Arabia. *Kedar* and the Nabateans (*Nebaioth*) are nomadic tribes. The islands evoke distant lands. *Tarshish* was a trading center set up in Spain by the Phoenicians, whose ships were therefore equipped for lengthy journeys and used for trading with the western Mediterranean.

with the ships of Tarshish in the lead;
they are bringing your children from far away,
along with their silver and gold,
to pay honor to the name of the LORD, your God,
the Holy One of Israel,
for he has glorified you. [a]
10 Foreigners will rebuild your walls,
and their kings will be your servants.
Although I struck you down in my wrath,
now in my mercy I will show you my favor.
11 Your gates will always be open;
day and night they will never be shut,
so that the wealth of the nations may be brought to you,
led by their kings in triumphal procession. [b]
12 For the nation or the kingdom that refuses to serve you
will be totally destroyed
and suffer widespread devastation.
13 The glory of Lebanon will come to you,
the cypress, the plane tree, and the pine,
one and all,
to adorn my holy sanctuary
and to honor the place where I stand.* [c]
14 The sons of those who oppressed you
will come forward and bend low before you,
and all those who despised you
will bow down at your feet;
they will call you "City of the LORD,"
"Zion of the Holy One of Israel." [d]
15 Whereas you have been forsaken and hated,
with no one traveling through you,
I will make you an object of everlasting pride
and a source of never-ending joy. [e]
16 You will suck the milk of nations
and be nursed at royal breasts.
Then you will know
that I, the LORD, am your Savior
and your Redeemer, the Holy One of Israel.
17 Instead of bronze I will bring you gold,
instead of iron I will bring you silver;
instead of wood, bronze,
and instead of stone, iron.
I will ensure that you will be governed in peace
and be ruled with righteousness.
18 No longer will violence appear in your land,
nor will devastation and ruin occur within your borders.
You will call your walls "Salvation"
and your gates "Praise."
19 The sun will no longer serve
as the source of your light by day,
nor will the brightness of the moon
afford light to you during the night.
Rather, the LORD will be your everlasting light,
and your God will be your splendor. [f]
20 Never again will your sun go down,
nor will your moon withdraw its light.
For the LORD will be your everlasting light,
and your days of mourning will be ended.
21 Your people will all be righteous
and possess the land forever.
They are the shoot that I have planted,
my handiwork to exhibit my glory.
22 The least of you will become a thousand,
and the weakest will become a mighty nation.
I am the LORD, and I will accomplish all this
at the appointed time. [g]

CHAPTER 61

A Message of Consolation

1* The Spirit of the Lord GOD is upon me
because the LORD has anointed me.
He has sent me to announce good news to the oppressed,
to strengthen the brokenhearted,
to proclaim freedom to those held in captivity

a Isa 2:16; 11:11; Gen 10:4; 1 Ki 10:22.—b Isa 61:6; 62:10; Mic 2:13; Rev 21:25.—c Isa 35:2; 41:19; 1 Chr 28:2; Ezr 3:7.—d Gen 27:29; Heb 12:22; Rev 3:9.—e Isa 1:7-9; 6:12; 54:6; Ezek 16:1-13.—f Isa 24:23; Rev 21:23; 22:5.—g Isa 5:19; Gen 12:2; 17:6; Deut 1:10.

60:13 The trees of Lebanon will serve in the rebuilding of Jerusalem as they did long ago for Solomon's temple.

61:1-9 The Spirit of the Lord rests on human beings who are destined to bear witness to true salvation: for example, on the infant Messiah (Isa 11:2) and on the Servant (Isa 42:1). He also energizes a prophet who is witness to the difficult years of the return. In the synagogue of Nazareth, Jesus will read this passage and declare that it is fulfilled in him (Lk 4:18-19).

and release to those who have been imprisoned, [h]
2 to proclaim a year of the LORD's favor
and a day of vengeance for our God,
to comfort all who mourn, [i]
3 to give to all those who mourn in Zion
a garland instead of ashes,
the oil of gladness instead of mourning,
a glorious mantle instead of a spirit of despair.
And they will be called oaks of righteousness
planted by the LORD to show forth his glory.

Israel's Reward

4 They will rebuild the ancient ruins
and raise up sites that have long been desolate.
They will restore the ruined cities
that for generations have been merely ravaged wastes. [j]
5 Strangers will come forth to shepherd your flocks;
foreigners will farm your land and dress your vines.
6 But you will be called priests of the LORD;
and you will be named ministers of our God.
You will enjoy the wealth of the nations,
and their former glory will be yours. [k]
7 Because you endured a double measure of shame
and were regarded as deserving of dishonor and disgrace,
you will receive a double portion,
and everlasting joy will be yours. [l]
8 For I, the LORD, love justice,
and I hate robbery and wrongdoing.
I will be faithful in rewarding such victims,
and I will make an everlasting covenant with them. [m]
9 Their descendants will be renowned among the nations
and their offspring among the peoples.
All who behold them will acknowledge
that they are a people whom the LORD has blessed.
10 I rejoice in the LORD with all my heart;
my soul exults in my God.
For he has clothed me in garments of salvation
and wrapped me in a robe of saving justice,
like a bridegroom adorned with a garland
or a bride bedecked with her jewels.
11 As the earth puts forth its shoots
and a garden causes its seeds to sprout,
so the Lord GOD will cause his justice and praise
to spring up in the sight of all the nations. [n]

CHAPTER 62

Jerusalem, the LORD's Spouse

1 For Zion's sake I will not keep silent,
and for Jerusalem's sake I will not be quiet,
until her vindication shines forth like the dawn
and her salvation like a burning torch.
2 The nations will see your vindication
and all the kings your glory.
You will be called by a new name
that the mouth of the LORD will reveal. [o]
3 You will be a glorious crown in the hand of the LORD,
a royal diadem held by your God.
4 No longer will you be called "Forsaken,"
nor will your land be known by the name "Desolate."
Rather you will be called "My Delight Is in Her,"
and your land will be known as "Married."
For the LORD will take delight in you,
and your land will be his spouse. [p]
5 As a young man marries a virgin,
so will your builder marry you,
and as a bridegroom rejoices in his bride,
so will your God rejoice over you.

Zion Restored and Glorified

6 Upon your walls, O Jerusalem,
I have stationed sentinels.
Neither by day nor by night
will they be silent.

h Isa 42:1; 48:16; Job 5:16; Mt 11:5; Lk 4:18f; 2 Cor 3:17.—i Isa 49:8; Job 5:11; Mt 5:4; Lk 6:21.—j Isa 58:12; Ezek 36:33; Am 9:14; Zec 1:16-17.—k Ex 19:6; Deut 33:19; 1 Pet 2:5.—l Isa 29:22; 40:2; Deut 21:17.—m Isa 1:17; 55:3; 59:21; Gen 9:16; Heb 13:20.—n Isa 45:8; 58:11.—o Isa 40:5; 45:14; Gen 32:29; Rev 2:17; 3:12.—p Isa 49:15f; 54:1ff; Lev 26:43; 2 Ki 21:1; Zep 3:17.

You whose responsibility is to call upon the LORD,
give yourselves no rest,
7 and also give no rest to him
until he restores Jerusalem
and makes her renowned throughout the earth.
8 The LORD has sworn by his right hand
and by his mighty arm:
Never again will I give your grain
to serve as food for your enemies,
nor shall foreigners drink the wine
for which you have toiled. [q]
9 However, those who harvest the grain will eat it
and give praise to the LORD,
while those who gather the grapes will drink the wine
within my sacred courts. [r]
10 Pass through, pass through the gates,
and clear a path for my people.
Build up, build up the highway;
clear it of stones
and lift up a standard over the nations. [s]
11 The LORD has made this proclamation
to the farthest bounds of the earth:
Say to the daughter of Zion,
"See, your Savior comes!
His reward is with him
and his recompense precedes him."* [t]
12 They will be called "The Holy People,"
"The Redeemed of the LORD."
And you will be called "Sought After,"
"A City No Longer Forsaken." [u]

CHAPTER 63

God's Judgment of Edom

1* Who is this that comes from Edom,
from Bozrah in crimson garments?
Who is this so magnificently attired,
marching with his mighty strength?
"It is I, proclaiming victory,
I who possess the power to save."
2 Why are your robes red,
like the garments of those
who tread the winepress? [v]
3 "I have trodden the winepress alone;
not one of the nations came to my aid.
I trod the nations in my anger
and trampled them in my wrath.
Their blood spurted out all over my garments
and stained all my robes.
4 I resolved in my heart on a day of vengeance,
and my year for redeeming was at hand. [w]
5 I looked all around, but there was no one to help;
I was outraged that no one offered any assistance.
Even so, my own arm brought me victory
and my wrath sustained me. [x]
6 I trampled down the peoples in my anger;
I crushed them in my wrath
and sent their blood streaming forth over the ground."

A Plea for Deliverance*

7 I will recount the favors of the LORD,
the glorious deeds of the LORD,
because of all that the LORD has done for us
and the great kindness he has shown
to the house of Israel.
He has favored us with his mercy
and the abundance of his steadfast love. [y]
8 For he said, "These are indeed my people,
children who will not betray me,"
and he became their Savior.
9 In all their difficulties
it was no messenger or an angel
but he himself who saved them.
In his love and his pity he redeemed them;
he lifted them up and carried them
through all the days of old. [z]
10 However, they rebelled
and grieved his Holy Spirit.

q Isa 14:24; 52:10; Gen 22:16; Deut 28:30-33.—r Lev 23:39; Deut 12:7f; 14:23; Joel 2:26; Am 9:14.—s Isa 11:16; 57:14; 60:11.—t Isa 40:10; Deut 30:4; Zec 9:9; Mt 21:5.—u Isa 62:4; Ex 19:6; 1 Pet 2:9.—v Gen 49:11; Lam 1:15; Rev 19:13.—w Isa 1:24; 34:8; 61:2; Jer 50:15.—x Isa 33:2; 41:28; 59:16; 2 Ki 14:26.—y Isa 26:15; 54:8; Ex 18:9; Eph 2:4.—z Ex 14:19; Deut 4:37f; Ezr 9:9; Job 37:23.

62:11 God buys his people and pays the price for it. This is the meaning of the image of "reward."

63:1—66:24 After songs of profound joy, a tragic theme returns. Once again, judgment looms on the horizon like an apocalypse; it brings out the dramatic aspect of human history. These oracles sing, in sometimes fierce language, a hymn to the greatness of God who, in the final analysis, decides the destinies of the human race.

63:7—64:12 This moving prayer, a psalm of desolation, was uttered on the morrow of the collapse of 587 B.C. or, in any case, at the beginning of the Exile.

Therefore, he became their enemy
and he himself fought against them.
11 Then they remembered the days of old
and Moses his servant.
Where is he who brought up from the water
the shepherd of his flock?
Where is he who put his Holy Spirit
in their midst, [a]
12 whose glorious arm led them
to march at the right hand of Moses,
who divided the waters before them
to win for himself everlasting renown,
13 and who led them through the depths?
Like horses in open country,
they did not stumble.
14 Like cattle descending into a valley,
the Spirit of the LORD afforded them rest.
15 Look down from heaven and see,
from your holy and glorious dwelling.
Where are your zeal and your might,
your compassion and your tender mercy?
Do not withhold them from me. [b]
16 For you are our Father.
Although Abraham does not know us
and Israel * does not acknowledge us,
you, O LORD, are our Father;
forever you have been called our Redeemer.
17 Why, O LORD, do you allow us
to wander from your ways,
and harden our hearts
so that we do not fear you?
Return for the sake of your servants,
for the tribes that are your heritage. [c]
18 For a brief period of time
your people possessed your holy place,
but now your enemies have trampled
down your sanctuary.
19 For far too long we have been
like those whom you do not rule,
like those who do not bear your name.

CHAPTER 64

1 Oh that you would tear open the heavens and come down
so that the mountains would quake in your presence,
2 as when fire sets brushwood ablaze
or causes water to boil.
Thus your name would be known to your adversaries
and the nations would tremble at your presence. [d]
3 When you descended to perform awesome deeds
that we did not anticipate,
the mountains quaked when you appeared.
4 Throughout the ages no ear has ever heard,
nor has any eye ever seen,
any other god except you
performing such deeds for those who trust him. [e]
5 You welcome those who lead an upright life
and rejoice to imitate your ways.
When we sin, you become angry,
but when we follow your ways,
we know that we will be saved.
6 All of us have become unclean,
and all of our righteous deeds are like filthy rags
We all become withered like leaves,
and our iniquities carry us away like the wind. [f]
7 There is no one who invokes your name
or attempts to hold fast to you.
For you have hidden your face from us
and have delivered us up because of our sins.
8 Yet, O LORD, you are our Father;
we are the clay and you are our potter;
all of us are the work of your hands.
9 Do not let your anger go to extremes, O LORD,
and do not remember our sinfulness forever.
Look upon us all,
for we are all your people.
10 Your holy cities have become a desert;
Zion has become a wilderness,
Jerusalem a desolate waste. [g]
11 Our holy and glorious temple
in which our ancestors praised you
has been burned to the ground,
and all that we treasured lies in ruins.

---

a Ex 14:22, 30; Num 11:17.—b Isa 9:7; Deut 26:15; 1 Ki 22:19; Lam 3:50; Bar 2:16.—c Gen 20:13; Ex 4:21; Num 10:36.—d Isa 30:27; Jer 5:22.—e Isa 30:18; 43:10-11; 1 Cor 2:9.—f Isa 46:12; Lev 5:2; Jer 4:12.—g Isa 54:8; 57:17; Ps 79:1; Lam 5:22.

63:16 *Israel:* that is, Jacob. Descent from the patriarchs did not provide the needed protection.

12 After all this, will you restrain yourself,
O LORD?
Will you remain silent
and punish us beyond our endurance?

CHAPTER 65

Punishment of the Idolaters

1 I was eager to respond
to those who did not consult me.
I was anxious to be approached
by those who did not seek me.
I said, "Here I am! Here I am!"
to a nation that did not summon me. [h]
2 Throughout each day I held out my hands
and appealed to a rebellious people
who walk along evil paths
in pursuit of their own desires. [i]
3 * These people provoke me to anger
continually, to my face,
offering sacrifices in gardens
and burning incense on bricks.
4 They live in the midst of tombs
and spend the night in secret places,
eating the flesh of pigs
and filling their plates with unclean food,
5 as they cry out, "Keep away!
Do not touch me,
for I am too sacred for you."
Such people to me are like choking smoke,
a fire that smolders throughout the day. [j]
6 Their deeds have been inscribed in my memory;
I will not remain silent until I have repaid in full
7 your iniquities and those of your ancestors,
says the LORD.
Since they burned incense on the mountains
and shamed me on the hills,
I will measure into their laps
the full payment that their deeds deserve. [k]

Fate of Israel's Righteous and Unfaithful

8 Thus says the LORD:
As in the harvest of grapes
juice is often still found in the cluster,
and people say, "Do not discard them,
for some good still remains in them,"
so I will act for the sake of my servants
and not destroy them all.
9 From Jacob I will bring forth descendants,
and from Judah those who will inherit my mountains.
My chosen ones will take possession of the land,
and my servants will settle there.
10 Sharon will serve as a pasture for flocks
and the Valley of Achor will be
a resting place for cattle. [l]
11 However, those of you who forsake the LORD
and forget my holy mountain,
who spread a table for Fortune*
and fill cups of mixed wine for Fate,
12 I will destine you for the sword,
and all of you will submit to the slaughter,
because, when I called, you did not respond,
and when I spoke, you refused to listen. [m]
Rather, you did what was evil in my sight
and chose to do what displeases me.
13 Therefore, this is what I have decreed,
says the Lord GOD:
My servants will eat,
but you will go hungry;
my servants will drink,
but you will be thirsty;
my servants will rejoice,
but you will be put to shame;
14 with gladness in their hearts
my servants will sing for joy,
but you will cry out in heartfelt grief
and wail in your anguish of spirit. [n]
15 The Lord GOD will strike you dead
and his chosen ones will use your name as a curse,
but he will call his servants by a different name. [o]

h Hos 1:10; Rom 10:20; Eph 2:12.—i Isa 1:2, 23; 66:18; Prov 24:2; Rom 10:21.—j Prov 10:26; Mt 9:11; Lk 7:39.—k Isa 22:14; Ex 20:5; Jer 32:18.—l Jos 7:26; 1 Chr 27:29; Acts 9:35.—m Isa 1:20; 66:4; 2 Chr 36:15-16; Prov 1:24; Jer 7:13; Mic 5:15.—n Zep 3:14-20; Mt 8:12; Jas 5:13.

65:3-4 Allusions to idolatrous practices. The night spent in secret places refers perhaps to the rite of incubation, during which people awaited revelations through dreams.

65:11 *Fortune:* literally, "Gad," the Aramean god of fortune. *Fate:* literally, "Meni," another divinity.

16 Then anyone in the land who blesses himself
will bless himself by the God of truth,
and anyone who takes an oath in the land
will swear by the God of truth,
because the troubles of the past will be forgotten
and hidden from my sight.

A Renewed World*

17 For behold, I am about to create
new heavens and a new earth.
The past will not be remembered
or ever again called to mind. [p]
18 Rather, rejoice and be filled with delight forever
at what I am creating;
for I am about to create Jerusalem as a delight
and her people as a cause of joy. [q]
19 I will take delight in Jerusalem
and rejoice in my people.
No more will be heard there
the sound of weeping or the cries of distress. [r]
20 Never again will an infant be there
who dies after a few days of life
or an old man who fails to live his allotted days.
For one who dies at the age of one hundred
will be regarded as a youth,
while one who fails to achieve a hundred years
will be considered accursed.*
21 They will live in the houses they have built;
they will plant vineyards and eat their fruit. [s]
22 They will not build houses for others to dwell in
or plant for others to eat.
For the days of my people will be
like the days of a tree,
and my chosen ones will enjoy
the work of their hands.
23 They will not labor in vain
or bear children destined for calamity.
For they will be offspring blessed by the LORD,
as will their descendants after them. [t]
24 Even before they call out to me,
I will answer;
while they are still speaking,
I will respond.
25 The wolf and the lamb will feed together,
and the lion will eat straw like the ox,
but as for the serpent,
its food will be dust.
No harm or destruction will be done
on all my holy mountain,
says the LORD. [u]

CHAPTER 66

True and False Worship

1 Thus says the LORD:
The heavens are my throne
and the earth is my footstool.
What house could you build for me?
What is to be my resting place? [v]
2 All these things were made by me,
and so all these things are mine,
says the LORD.
The one for whom I have regard
is humble and contrite in spirit
and trembles at my word. [w]
3 Whoever slaughters an ox
is like one who kills a man;
whoever sacrifices a lamb
is like one who breaks a dog's neck;
whoever presents an offering of grain
is like one who offers a swine's blood;
whoever burns incense as a memorial
is like one who blesses an idol.
These people have chosen their own ways,
and they delight in their loathsome abominations. [x]
4 I in turn will choose to punish them harshly
and bring upon them what they fear

o Deut 29:19; Job 11:16.—p Isa 66:22; Jer 3:16; 2 Cor 5:17; 2 Pet 3:13; Rev 21:1.—q Isa 25:9; Deut 32:43; Rev 21:2.—r Isa 35:10; Deut 30:9; Rev 7:17.—s 2 Ki 19:29; Ezek 28:26; Am 9:14.—t Deut 28:32, 41; Jer 16:3-4; 1 Cor 15:58.—u Isa 11:6-9; Gen 3:14; Mic 7:17.—v 2 Sam 7:4ff; 1 Ki 8:27; Jn 4:20-21; Acts 7:49; 17:24.—w Isa 40:26; Lk 18:13-14; Acts 7:50.—x Isa 1:11; Lev 11:7; Deut 27:15; Ezek 8:9-13.

65:17-25 The oracle looks beyond a restored Jerusalem to a future time when the prosperity and harmony that marked the beginnings of humankind are to be restored; this prosperity and harmony are expressed in images of paradisal life that were familiar to the ancients. Amid oracles that strike terror, here is a song of indestructible hope: a renewed world is coming in which sin will no longer exist (see also Isa 11:6-9). The Church awaits this new world for all of humanity; the dawn of this world breaks on Easter morning (2 Pet 3:13; Rev 21).

65:20 Since the prospect of resurrection is still unknown, longevity is seen as a special sign of divine protection.

because, when I called, no one answered,
and when I spoke, they refused to listen.
Rather, they did what was evil in my sight
and chose what displeased me. [y]
5 Hear the word of the LORD,
you who tremble at his word.
Your brethren who hate you
and reject you because of my name, have said,
"Let the LORD be glorified
so that we may witness your joy";
however, they themselves will be put to shame.
6 Listen! There is an uproar from the city,
a voice from the temple.
Such is the sound of the LORD
bringing retribution to his enemies. [z]

Mother Zion

7 Before she entered into labor,
she gave birth.
Before she experienced the birth pains,
she delivered a son. [a]
8 Who ever heard of such a thing?
Who has ever seen anything like this?
Can a country be born in a single day?
Can a nation be delivered in a single moment?
Yet Zion was scarcely in labor
when she brought forth her children. [b]
9 Shall I open the womb and not deliver?
says the LORD.
Shall I close the womb at the moment of delivery?
says your God.

10 Rejoice with Jerusalem and be glad for her,
all you who love her.
Be joyful as you rejoice with her,
all you who mourned over her, [c]
11 so that you may suck fully and be satisfied
from her consoling breast,
as you drink deeply with delight
at her abundant bosom.

12 For thus says the LORD:
I will make prosperity flow over her like a river,
and the wealth of the nations
like a turbulent overflowing stream.
You will be nursed and carried in her arms
and fondled in her lap.
13 As a mother comforts her child,
so will I comfort you;
in Jerusalem you will find your comfort. [d]
14 When you behold this, your heart will rejoice,
and your bodies will flourish like grass in spring.
The LORD will make his power known to his servants
but reveal his wrath to his enemies.

15 Behold the LORD as he comes in fire,
his chariots like the whirlwind,
to enact retribution with his furious anger
and his rebukes with fiery flames. [e]
16 For the LORD will execute his judgment
on all mankind with fire and sword,
and many will be those slain by the LORD.

17 Those who sanctify and purify themselves to enter the groves and follow the one in the center, consuming the flesh of pigs, vermin, and rats—they will all perish together, says the LORD, along with their deeds and their thoughts.* [f]

Glory among the Nations. 18 I am coming to gather every nation and every language. They will come forth to behold my glory. 19 I will set a sign among them, and I will send some of their survivors to the nations: to Tarshish,* Put and Lud, Mosoch, Tubal, and Javan, to the distant coasts and islands that have never heard of me or seen my glory.

They will proclaim my glory among the nations, 20 and from all the nations they will bring all your kindred as an offering to the LORD, on horses and in chariots, in carts and on mules and camels, to my holy mountain Jerusalem, says the LORD, just as the Israelites themselves bring their grain offerings in clean vessels to the house of the LORD. [g] 21 Some of these I will appoint as priests and Levites, says the LORD.

Eternal Reward and Punishment

22 As the new heavens and the new earth
that I am making

y Isa 10:12; 65:12; Prov 1:24; Jer 7:13.—z Lev 26:28; 1 Sam 2:10; Joel 3:7; 4:16; Am 1:2.—a 7-9: Isa 49:18-21; 54:1.—b Isa 49:20-22; 64:4; Jer 18:13.—c Isa 25:9; Deut 32:43; Rom 15:10.—d Isa 49:15; 2 Cor 1:4; 1 Thes 2:7.—e Isa 1:31; Deut 28:20; 2 Ki 2:11.—f Isa 1:28-29; 65:3-5; Lev 11:7, 29.—g Deut 33:19; Ezek 34:13.

66:17 A condemnation of pagan mystery cults.

66:19 *Tarshish:* a large island in the western Mediterranean or simply a faraway place.

will endure before me, says the LORD,
so will your descendants and your name endure. [h]
23 From new moon to new moon
and from one Sabbath to another,
all mankind will come to worship before me,
says the LORD.
24 And as they go out,
they will see the corpses
of those who rebelled against me.
For their worm will never die,
nor will their fire be quenched,
and they will be abhorrent to all humanity.* [i]

h Isa 65:17; Jn 10:27-29; Heb 12:26-27; 2 Pet 3:13; Rev 21:1.—i Isa 1:2; 14:11; 34:10; Mk 9:44, 46, 48.

66:24 A reference to the Valley of Ben-hinnom (Gehenna) outside the walls of ancient Jerusalem. In Mk 9:48, the images of the worm and the fire are used to signify an eternal punishment.

"Then the LORD stretched forth his hand and touched my mouth, and he said to me: Behold, I have placed my words into your mouth" *(Jer 1:9).*

THE BOOK OF JEREMIAH

To Uproot and To Plant

Jeremiah, a native of Anathoth, a Levitical town, was undoubtedly a descendant of the priest Abiathar, whom Solomon banished to that little village a few kilometers north of Jerusalem (1 Ki 2:26). Jeremiah's activity, which lasted some forty years (626–587 B.C.), was carried on during the darkest period of his people's history. He bore the marks of it in his flesh day after day. A century ago (in 721 B.C.), Israel, the northern kingdom, had been forever swept away by the Assyrians, and the tiny state of Judah had barely survived. But what could this people do without resources and while being squeezed by the great powers? The reform of Josiah (in 622 B.C.) was able to halt the decline for only a little while. In 605 B.C., at the decisive battle of Carchemish, Assyria made way for Babylon, and Nebuchadnezzar became the undisputed master of the Near East. In 598 B.C., Jerusalem was captured a first time and a first wave of refugees departed. In addition, the state of Judah was threatened by a religious and social breakdown that was ceaselessly denounced by the prophets, and it led to the disaster of 587 B.C., when the holy city was razed to the ground and the population was decimated and deported. This was the blackest moment in the history of the people of God (for the entire period, see 2 Ki 18–25 and 2 Chr 29–36).

All of Jeremiah's preaching is focused on the crisis into which his people had entered. "To uproot and to pull down, . . . to build and to plant." Contradiction is implicit in his very calling (Jer 1:10); the prophet will be a man torn by intolerable conflicts that are at bottom an opposition between an attitude of violence and an attitude of mercy.

"To uproot and to pull down." Jeremiah's invectives are violent, his sermons gloomy. He is aware of the evil that is eating away at his people and threatening the very reason for its existence, namely, the covenant. Corruption by the ancient Canaanite cults reigns everywhere; there are even sacrifices of children; the gods of the Assyrian masters find faithful servants even in the forecourts of the temple. This contempt for God mirrors a contempt for human beings: killings, adulteries, injustices. Society is degenerating because evil is sinking its ineradicable roots in the heart of society.

Though misunderstood, persecuted, even threatened with death, Jeremiah, a timid man but a friend of God, ceaselessly launches anguished appeals for conversion; he does not hesitate to point the finger at the authorities who have led the people astray: king, political leaders, priests, and prophets who have no mandate from God. He is angered by the false consciousness of the orthodox, who think they are in the right when they observe religious practices but do not live them in their souls. What good are temples, sumptuous sacrifices, pilgrimages, and other external observances if religion does not transform the concrete life of the community and the individual?

Jeremiah will, therefore, be at the side of the devout King Josiah when, starting in 622 B.C., he begins to cleanse the country of the high places with their pagan practices, to undertake a serious renewal of the covenant, and to restore the unity of Israel as it had been in the time of David. But with the advent of Jehoiakim, in 609 B.C., the doors are opened once again to all the excesses of immorality, injustice, and idolatry. Jeremiah strives with all his authority to stem this flood of wickedness. He pleads, threatens, and lays consciences bare, but he can accomplish nothing. The capture and sack of Jerusalem and the mass deportation of the people sadly fulfill the prophet's threats.

"To build and to plant" was an even more difficult task in these times of anarchy and discouragement. And yet, even in the midst of the agony, when everything is collapsing, Jeremiah dares proclaim the most radiant visions of the future. In his own suffering and in his tender love for his people, he has learned to know the very heart of God. He knows that the Lord has no second thoughts when it comes to his love and his plan. Sin may seem beyond healing, but there is still forgiveness and resurrection, which are the work of divine grace. Jeremiah sees already rising on the ruins of the old covenant a new covenant that is more beautiful and more lasting. To know God will no longer mean simply observing an exterior law; it will mean obeying the interior movement of the Spirit and discovering a deep communion with the Lord. Chapter 31 (vv. 4, 31-33) offers a first statement of the new covenant that Jesus Christ will seal with his blood on the eve of Passover.

In the form in which it has come down to us, the Book of Jeremiah is one of the most muddled of the Old Testament: sermons, threats, exhortations, and intimate musings are mixed in with biographical narratives and historical fragments, all without any concern for chronology. The Book is clearly a composite work, and we must give up on trying to determine the precise point at which each part of the Book should come. However, there is good reason for thinking that it took shape on the basis of oracles recorded at the dictation of Jeremiah himself; later on, his disciples added others which they had heard from his mouth (36:4, 32). Baruch, an educated man and Jeremiah's faithful secretary, must have added a good many references to the mission and the tormented life of the prophet.

Finally, the present text seems to have emerged in the period of the Exile; the deportees undoubtedly circulated and meditated closely on the writings of Jeremiah in order to nourish their faith in a time of bewilderment; they inserted into the Book their own reflections, their own awareness of their situation, their hopes. As a result, Jeremiah, prophet of suffering and of mercy, who prefigures more than any other the person of Jesus, remains for his people and for all Christians a witness to hope. He is also a model of incorruptible fidelity to his vocation despite all difficulties. His close relationship with God, and the religion of the heart which he lived out and preached, make of him the prophet par excellence of the interior life.

The Book of Jeremiah may be divided as follows:

- *I: Prophecies in the Days of Josiah (1:1—6:30)*
- *II: Prophecies Mainly in the Days of Jehoiakim (7:1—20:18)*
- *III: Prophecies in the Last Years of Jerusalem (21:1—33:26)*
- *IV: The Fall of Jerusalem (34:1—45:5)*
- *V: Prophecies against the Nations (46:1—51:64)*
- *VI: Historical Appendix (52:1-34)*

I: PROPHECIES IN THE DAYS OF JOSIAH*

CHAPTER 1

[1] The words of Jeremiah, the son of Hilkiah, a member of the priestly family in Anathoth in the territory of Benjamin. [2] The word of the LORD came to him during the thirteenth year of the reign of King Josiah, son of Amon, king of Judah. [a] [3] Then it continued through the reign of Jehoiakim, son of Josiah, king of Judah, until the eleventh year of Zedekiah, son of Josiah, king of Judah, when in the fifth month the inhabitants of Jerusalem were carried off into exile.

Jeremiah's Call from God. [4] The word of the LORD came to me, saying:

5 Before I formed you in the womb I knew you,
and before you were born I consecrated you.
I appointed you as a prophet to the nations. [b]

[6] Then I replied, "Ah, Lord GOD! You must be aware that I am not skilled in the art of speaking. I am only a young boy." [7] But the LORD said:

Do not say, "I am only a young boy."
You will go to whomever I send you,
and you will speak whatever I command you.
8 Do not be afraid of them,
for I am with you to deliver you,
says the LORD. [c]

[9] Then the LORD stretched forth his hand and touched my mouth, and he said to me:

Behold, I have placed my words into your mouth. [d]
10 This day I have established you
over nations and kingdoms,
to uproot and to pull down,
to destroy and to demolish,
to build and to plant.

[11] * The word of the LORD came to me, inquiring, "What do you see, Jeremiah?" I replied, "I see a branch of an almond tree."

a 2 Ki 21:18-24; 22:1.—b Gal 1:15f.—c Ezek 2:6.—d Isa 6:7.

1:1—25:38 This lengthy section, which occupies half of the Book and begins with the call of Jeremiah, contains mainly prophecies addressed to the kingdom of Judah. They occur throughout the career of the prophet, although it is not possible to show a clear reductional plan.

1:11-19 In Hebrew, the word for *almond tree* means "watchful." Because of its early blooming, the tree seems, as it were, to be waiting for spring in order to proclaim its presence. The *boiling cauldron* of verse 13 refers to misfortune, which, for Palestine, usually came from the north. Hard trials await Jeremiah (v. 17ff), but God will be with him.

12 Then the LORD said to me, "You have
answered well, for I am watching to ensure
that my word is fulfilled."
13 The word of the LORD came to me a sec-
ond time, asking, "What do you see?" I
replied, "I see a boiling cauldron that is tilt-
ing away from the north." 14 Then the LORD
said: [e]

From the north disaster will boil over
upon all the inhabitants of the land.
15 For now I am summoning all the tribes
of the kingdoms of the north, says the
LORD.
Their kings will advance,
and each will establish his throne
in front of the gates of Jerusalem,
against all its surrounding walls
and against all the cities of Judah.[f]
16 I will issue my judgments against them
for all their wickedness in abandon-
ing me,
in offering sacrifices to other gods
and worshiping what their hands have
fashioned.

17 As for you, be prepared for action;
stand up and tell them
everything that I command you.
Do not have any fear of them
or I will make you cringe in terror be-
fore them.
18 For this very day
I have made you into a fortified city,
a pillar of iron, a wall of bronze,
to overcome the entire country—
the kings and the princes of Judah,
its priests and its people.[g]
19 They will fight against you
but they will not be victorious,
for I will be at your side to deliver you,
says the LORD.

CHAPTER 2*

Israel's Unfaithfulness. 1 * The word of the
LORD came to me, saying: 2 Go forth and
proclaim this message in the hearing of
Jerusalem: Thus says the LORD:

I remember the devotion you displayed
in your youth,
your love like that of a bride,
when you followed me through the
desert,
through a land that was unsown.[h]
3 Israel was sacred to the LORD,
the firstfruits of his harvest.
Any people who partook of them were
deemed guilty,
and disaster afflicted them, says the
LORD.

4 Listen to the word of the LORD, O house
of Jacob and all the families of the house of
Israel. 5 Thus says the LORD:

What fault did your ancestors find in me
that causes them to stray so far from
my side,
pursuing worthless idols*
and thereby becoming worthless
themselves?[i]
6 They never thought to ask, "Where is the
LORD
who brought us up from the land of
Egypt
and led us through the wilderness,
through a land of deserts and ravines,
a land of drought and intense darkness,
a land through which no one travels,
and a land in which no one dwells?"[j]

7 I brought you into a fertile land
bursting forth with fruit and rich pro-
duce.
But when you entered, you defiled my
land
and made my heritage loathsome.
8 The priests did not ask,
"Where is the LORD?"
Those who dealt with the law did not
know me,
and even the shepherds rebelled
against me.
The prophets prophesied by Baal
and worshiped gods who were power-
less.[k]
9 Therefore, says the LORD,
I will once again accuse you,
and I will further accuse
even your children's children.
10 Cross over to the coast of the Kittim*
and inquire;
send to Kedar and observe carefully.

e Ezek 11:3, 7; 24:3.—f Jer 4:16; 6:22.—g Jer 6:27; 15:20.—h Deut 2:7.—i Jer 13:15; Mic 6:3.—j Ex 20:2f; Deut 8:15.—k Jer 8:8ff.

2:1-37 In speaking of the covenant, which is an essential structure in the life of the Israelite people, Jeremiah uses the bold conjugal imagery of the prophet Hosea.

2:1-19 Foreign divinities are like poisoned wells. The image is a powerful one in a country in which water was rare and precious.

2:5 *Worthless idols:* they are incapable of saving their worshipers.

2:10 *Kittim:* Cyprus. *Kedar:* a nomad tribe of the Arabian Desert (see Jer 49:28).

See if anything similar to this
has ever previously occurred.
11 Has a nation ever changed its gods,
even though they are not gods at all?
Yet my people have exchanged their glory
for something that cannot help them in any way,[l]
12 Be incredulous at this, O heavens;
shudder in your horror, says the LORD.
13 For my people are guilty of two evils:
they have forsaken me,
the fountain of living water,
and they have dug cisterns for themselves,
cracked cisterns that hold no water.[m]

14 Is Israel a slave?
Was he born to be a servant?
Why then has he become plunder?
15 His enemies roar loudly at him like lions;*
they have made his country a wasteland;
his cities are burned to the ground and deserted.
16 The people of Memphis* and Tahpanhes
have shaved the crown of your head.

17 Have you not brought all this upon yourself
by forsaking the LORD, your God,
when he guided you along the way?[n]
18 What advantage would you now achieve
by traveling to Egypt
to drink the waters of the Nile?
What would you gain by traveling to Assyria
to drink the waters of the Euphrates?
19 Your wickedness will bring about your punishment,
and your infidelities will condemn you.
Therefore, concentrate your thoughts
and see how bitter it is
to forsake the LORD, your God,
and to have no fear of me,
says the LORD, the God of hosts.

20 A long time ago you broke your yoke
and burst your bonds,
saying, "I will not serve."
On every high hill
and under every green tree
you have sprawled and given yourself
to harlotry.[o]
21 I had planted you as a choice vine
from the purest stock.
How then did you degenerate
into a wild and corrupt vine?[p]
22 Even if you would scrub yourself with lye
and use soap in great abundance,
the stain of your guilt
would still be clearly visible to me,
says the Lord GOD.

23 How can you say, "I am not defiled;
I have not gone after the Baals"?
Recall your conduct in the valley;
realize what you have done:
you have been like a restless she-camel
24 sniffing the wind in her lust;
who can restrain her ardor?
No males should exhaust themselves seeking her;
in her month they will find her.
25 You should stop before you wear out your shoes
and your throat becomes parched.
But you said, "It is hopeless.
I love these strangers,
and I must go after them."[q]

26 As a thief is ashamed when he is caught,
so the house of Israel will be ashamed:
they, their kings, their officials,
their priests, and their prophets,
27 those who say to a piece of wood, "You are my father,"
and to a stone, "You gave birth to me."
They have turned their backs to me,
not their faces;
yet, in their time of trouble, they cry out,
"Rise up and save us!"
28 Where are the gods you have made for yourself?
Let them come to save you
in your time of trouble.
For you have as many towns
as you have gods, O Judah.[r]

29 Why do you dare to plead with me?
You have all rebelled against me, says the LORD.
30 In vain I struck down your children,
but they refused to accept my correction.
Your own sword has devoured your prophets
like a ravening lion.

l Ps 106:20; Rom 1:23.—m Jer 17:13; Ps 36:9; Isa 1:4.—n Jer 4:18; Dan 3:28.—o Jer 3:6, 13.—p Ps 80:9; Isa 5:4.—q Jer 18:12; Mal 3:14.—r Jer 11:13; Deut 32:37; Isa 57:13.

2:15 *Lions:* the Assyrians, whose arms bore the emblem of the lion.

2:16 *Memphis:* capital of Lower Egypt. *Tahpanhes:* in the eastern part of the Nile Delta. The shaving is a sign of the victor's contempt.

31 You of this generation,
behold the word of the LORD!
Have I been a desert for Israel
or a land of darkness?
Why then do my people say,
"We have broken away;
we will come to you no more"?
32 Does a girl forget her jewelry
or a bride her sash?
Yet for days beyond number
my people have forgotten me. [s]
33 How well you direct your course
in the pursuit of love.
Even wanton women have profited
from their observance of your ways.
34 On your clothing can be found
the life-blood of the innocent poor,
whom you never caught breaking into a house.
Despite all this,*
35 you continue to proclaim, "I am innocent;
obviously, he has no cause to be angry with me."
But behold, I will bring judgment upon you
for claiming that you have not sinned.
36 How nonchalant you are
as you change your course.
Just as you were shamed by Assyria,
you will be put to shame by Egypt.
37 From there also you will depart
with your hands upon your head.
For the LORD has rejected those upon whom you rely,
and with them you will not prosper. [t]

CHAPTER 3

1* If a man divorces his wife,
and she leaves him
and marries another man,
does he have the right to return to her?
Would not that land be completely defiled?
But, says the LORD,
you have been unfaithful with many lovers,
and yet you would return to me?
2 Lift up your eyes to the barren heights
and recall whether there is any place
that you have not offered your body to another.
By the waysides you waited for lovers
like an Arab in the desert.
You defiled the land
with your harlotry and wickedness. [u]
3 Therefore, the rain showers were withheld
and the spring rains have not fallen.
Yet you have the brazen boldness of a prostitute,
and you refuse to blush with shame.
4 Not so long ago you addressed me,
"My Father, the beloved friend of my youth,
5 will you be angry with me forever
and continue your wrath toward me to the end?"
This is how you speak,
but you continue to be obstinate
and to do every evil you can.

Judah and Israel. 6 During the reign of King
Josiah, the LORD said to me: Have you seen
what that faithless Israel has done, how she
went to the top of every high hill and under
every green tree and there played the harlot? [v]
7 But I truly believed that after she had done
all this, she would return to me. However, she
did not return, and her faithless sister Judah
saw this. 8 She also saw that I had sent that
faithless Israel away with a decree of divorce
because of all of her acts of adultery.

However that faithless sister Judah was not
frightened; she too went off and played the
harlot. 9 In her eagerness to sin, she polluted
the land, committing adultery with stones
and pieces of wood. [w] 10 Despite all this, her
faithless sister Judah did not return to me
with sincerity of heart but only as a show of
pretense, says the LORD.

Promises of Restoration. 11 Then the LORD
said to me: Compared with the traitorous
Judah, faithless Israel has proved to be less
guilty. 12 Go forth and proclaim these words
toward the north, saying:

Return, rebel Israel, says the LORD.
I will not look upon you in anger.
For I am merciful, says the LORD;
my wrath will not continue forever.
13 Simply acknowledge your guilt
and your rebellion against the LORD, your God,

s Deut 32:18.—t Jer 17:5.—u Ezek 16:24f.—v Jer 2:20; Deut 12:2.—w Jer 2:27.

2:34 An allusion to sacrifices of children: see Jer 7:31. It was permissible to kill thieves caught in the act (see Ex 22:1).

3:1—4:4 "Return" is the key word in the following oracles, which have to do with both the return from exile and the return to God. Jeremiah is a pitiless censor of his people's sins, but he will not give up the hope of conversion.

how you prostituted yourself with strangers
under every green tree
and refused to listen to my voice,
says the LORD. [x]

14 * Return, rebellious children, says the
LORD, for I am your Master. I will take you,
one from a city and two from a family, and I
will bring you to Zion. 15 Over you I will
appoint shepherds after my own heart, and
they will direct you with knowledge and
understanding. [y] 16 And when you have multi-
plied and grown numerous in the land, says
the LORD, they will no longer say in those
days, "The Ark of the Covenant of the LORD."
They will no longer think of it, or remember
it, or realize that it is gone, or make another.
17 When that time comes, Jerusalem will be
called the throne of the LORD, and all the
nations will gather in Jerusalem to honor the
name of the LORD. No longer will they stub-
bornly follow their own evil inclinations. [z]
18 In those days the house of Judah will unite
with the house of Israel, and together they
will come from the land of the north to the
land that I gave to your fathers as a heritage.

Call for Conversion

19 * I then gave consideration
as to how I would treat you as sons
and give you a pleasant land,
the most beautiful heritage of all the nations.
Further, I thought that you would call me
"Father" and never cease to follow me. [a]

20 But like a woman who is unfaithful to her husband,
so you have been unfaithful to me,
O house of Israel, says the LORD.

21 A cry on the bare heights is heard,
the plaintive weeping of Israel's children,
because they have perverted their ways
and forgotten the LORD, their God. [b]

22 Return, you rebellious children,
and I will forgive your faithlessness.

Here we are! We are returning to you,
for you are the LORD, our God.

23 The hills are truly a delusion,
as is the tumult on the mountains.
Truly in the LORD, our God alone
is the salvation of Israel.

24 Ever since we were young,
Baal has devoured everything
for which our fathers toiled:
their flocks and their herds,
their sons and their daughters.

25 Let us lie down in our shame
and let our dishonor cover us.
For we have sinned against the LORD, our God,
we and our ancestors,
from our youth even to this very day,
and we failed to obey the voice of the
LORD, our God. [c]

CHAPTER 4

1 If you return, O Israel, says the LORD,
if you return to me,
if you banish your loathsome idols from my sight
and do not go astray,

2 and if you swear, "As the LORD lives!"
in truth, in justice, and in uprightness,
then the nations will bless themselves by him
and will glory in him. [d]

3 For these are the words of the LORD to the
people of Judah and Jerusalem:

Break up your unplowed ground
and do not sow among thorns. [e]

4 For the sake of the LORD be circumcised
and remove the foreskin of your hearts,
O men of Judah and inhabitants of Jerusalem,
or my wrath will leap forth like fire
and burn with no one to quench it
because of your evil deeds.

Invasion from the North*

5 Announce it in Judah;
proclaim it in Jerusalem.
Blow the trumpet throughout the land;
shout aloud the command,
"Gather together!
Let us flee to the fortified cities!"

6 Raise the signal to proceed toward Zion!
Flee for safety! Do not delay!

---

x Jer 2:20, 25.—y Jer 23:4; Ezek 34:23.—z Ps 86:9; Isa 2:2.—a Ps 89:27; Isa 63:16.—b Ezek 23:35.—c Jer 16:11f; 22:21.—d Deut 10:20.—e Hos 10:12; Mt 13:7, 22.

3:14-18 To the promise of a return of the exiles from the north, a redactor has added this later oracle, which looks to the entire people.

3:19ff The song of conversion, which began in verses 1-15, continues here.

4:5-31 The nation has grown stubborn in its degradation; now the symbol of the boiling pot (Jer 1:13) is about to be made real. Punishment is at hand. It is impossible to determine whether the prophet is speaking of the Assyrians, the Chaldeans, the Scythians, or even some other army.

For I am bringing disaster from the north
as well as immense destruction.
7 A lion has come forth from its lair
the destroyer of nations has set forth.
He has left his lair
to make your towns a wasteland;
they will be in ruins and uninhabited.[f]
8 Therefore, wrap yourselves in sackcloth,
beat your breasts and wail,
because the blazing anger of the LORD
has not turned away from us.
9 On that day, says the LORD,
the courage of the kings and the princes
will fail;
the priests will be horrified
and the prophets will be astounded.
10 Then I said, "Alas, Lord GOD,
you completely deceived the people and
Jerusalem
when you promised that we would have
peace,
for now the sword is held at our
throats."[g]

11 At that time it will be said to this people
and to Jerusalem:

A scorching wind comes forth from the
desert heights
and sweeps down on my people,
although not to winnow or to cleanse.
12 A wind far too strong for that
will come forth at my bidding,
and I myself will pass judgment on
them.
13 Behold, he advances
like storm clouds;
like a whirlwind are his chariots.
His horses are swifter than eagles.
Disaster threatens us. We are lost.
14 Cleanse your heart of all wickedness
so that you may be saved.
How long will you allow evil thoughts to
lodge within you?[h]
15 A voice from Dan* declares the news
proclaiming disaster from Mount
Ephraim.
16 Announce this to the nations,
make it known to Jerusalem:
Besiegers are coming from a distant
land,
shouting their war cry against the cities
of Judah.
17 They surround her like watchmen guard-
ing a field
because she has rebelled against me,
says the LORD.[i]
18 Your conduct and your evil deeds
have brought this upon you.
How bitter is your punishment!
It has pierced the depths of your heart.
19 How great is my anguish
that causes me to writhe in pain!
I cannot keep silent in my agony
as my heart beats wildly.
For I have heard the sound of the trumpet
and that of the battle cry.
20 One disaster follows upon another;
the entire land lies in ruins.
My tents are suddenly destroyed,
everything that offered me shelter.
21 How long must I see the standard raised
and hear the sound of the trumpet?
22 My people are fools;
they do not know me.
They are senseless children
who have no semblance of under-
standing.
They are skilled in the practice of evil
but they do not know how to do good.[j]
23 I looked at the earth,
and it was a formless wasteland;
I gazed at the heavens,
but I could not discern any light.[k]
24 I looked at the mountains,
and they were quaking,
while all the hills moved back and
forth.
25 I looked, but I could not see anyone;
even the birds of the air had flown
away.
26 I looked, and the fertile land had become
a desert;
all of its towns lay in ruins
before the LORD, before his blazing
anger.

27 Thus says the LORD:

The entire land will be a desolate waste,
but I will not destroy it completely.[l]
28 Because of this the earth will mourn
and the heavens above will grow dark.
For I have spoken and made clear my
intention,
and I will not relent or turn back.

f Jer 2:15; 5:6.—g Jer 6:14.—h Isa 1:16.—i Jer 6:3.—j Deut 32:5f, 28.—k Gen 1:2; Isa 5:30.—l Jer 5:18.

4:15 *Dan:* the northernmost city of Palestine.

29 At the shouts of horsemen and archers
every city takes to flight.
Some people crawl into the thickets
while others scale the rocks.
All the cities are abandoned,
with no one to live in them.

30 What are you doing, you who are doomed,
by clothing yourself in purple,
adorning yourself with ornaments of gold
and shading your eyes with cosmetics?
You are beautifying yourself in vain,
for your lovers despise you,
and they only seek your life.

31 I hear cries like those of a woman in labor,
the anguished groans of one bearing her first child.
They are the screams of daughter Zion gasping for breath
as she stretches forth her hands and cries out,
"Woe is me; I am dying.
I sink exhausted before my murderers." [m]

CHAPTER 5*

Evil Everywhere

1 Roam through the streets of Jerusalem,
look around and take careful note;
search through the public squares.
If you can find even one person
who acts justly and seeks the truth,
I will pardon this city. [n]

2 Even though they say, "As the LORD lives,"
they are in fact swearing falsely.

3 Do your eyes not search for truth, O LORD?
When you struck them, they felt no anguish;
when you brought them down, they refused correction.
They have made their faces harder than stone
and refused to repent.

4 Then I thought, "These are only the poor;
they tend to act foolishly.
For they do not know the way of the LORD
or the ordinances of their God.

5 Therefore, I will go to their leaders
and speak to them.
Surely they will know the way of the LORD
and their responsibilities to their God."
But those, too, had broken the yoke
and torn away from their bonds. [o]

6 Therefore, lions from the forest will tear them to pieces,
and wolves from the desert will ravage them.
Leopards will be on the prowl around their cities;
all those who depart from them
will be torn to pieces
because of their many crimes
and their apostasies
without number.

7 Why should I forgive you?
Your children have forsaken me to swear by gods
that are not gods in any way.
When I gave them everything they needed,
they committed adultery
and hastened to the houses of prostitutes.

8 They are well-fed and lusty stallions,
each one neighing for his neighbor's wife. [p]

9 Shall I not punish them for these things?
asks the LORD.
Shall I not take vengeance on a nation such as this?

10 Ascend to her vineyards and ravage them
but do not totally destroy them.
Strip off her branches,
for these people no longer belong to the LORD.

11 Both the house of Israel and the house of Judah
have been completely unfaithful to me,
says the LORD.

12 They have denied the LORD,
boldly asserting, "He will do nothing.
No harm will come to us;
we will not endure either sword or famine. [q]

13 The prophets are nothing but wind;
the word is not in them.
Their dire predictions will redound upon them."

14 Therefore, the LORD, the God of hosts,
has this to say:

m Jer 6:24.—n Gen 18:32; Ezek 22:30; Mic 7:2.—o Jer 6:13; Mic 3:1.—p Jer 13:27; 29:23.—q Jer 23:17; 2 Chr 36:13.

5:1-31 No one is as sensitive as Jeremiah to the sin that is spreading like a canker. God has been hunted from the life of his people, without hope of a return.

Because you have said these things,
my words will become a fire in your mouth,
and I will make this people like wood
that the fire will consume.
15 Be forewarned that I will bring against you
a nation from a great distance,
O house of Israel, says the LORD—
a long-existent nation,
a nation founded long ago,
a people whose language you do not know
and whose speech you cannot understand.[r]
16 The quivers of these people are like open graves;
all of them are mighty warriors.
17 They will devour your harvest and your food,
they will devour your sons and your daughters;
they will devour your flocks and your herds,[s]
they will devour your vines and your fig trees;
with their swords they will destroy
your fortified towns in which you place your trust.

18 * Yet even in those days, declares the
LORD, I will not completely destroy you.
19 And when the people ask, "Why has the
LORD, our God, done all this to us?" reply to
them, "As you have forsaken the LORD and
served alien gods in your own land, so you will
serve strangers in a land that is not yours."[t]

20 Announce this in the house of Jacob,
proclaim it in Judah:
21 Pay attention to this,
you foolish and senseless people,
who have eyes but do not see,
who have ears but do not hear.
22 Do you have no fear of me? asks the LORD.
Do you not tremble before me?
I was the one who established the sand
as the boundary for the sea,
a perpetual barrier that it can never pass.
Its waves may rise up but cannot prevail;
they may roar but cannot cross the limits.[u]
23 But this people has a rebellious and stubborn heart;
they have risen up in defiance and gone away.
24 Nor do they say to themselves,
"Let us fear the LORD, our God,
who gives us in their proper season
the autumn and spring rains
and unfailingly provides for us
the weeks designated for the harvest."
25 Your iniquities have upset the order of nature,
and your sins have deprived you of its bounty.
26 For there are wicked scoundrels among my people
who, like fowlers, set traps,
but with men as their quarry.
27 Like a cage full of birds,[v]
their houses are full of treachery.
As a result, they have grown rich and powerful,
28 well fed and well groomed.
Their wickedness knows no bounds,
and they do not practice justice in their dealings.
They do not uphold the rights of the orphan
or defend the cause of the needy.
29 How can I fail to punish such things?
says the LORD.
How can I refuse to exact vengeance on a nation such as this?
30 An appalling and outrageous situation
has occurred in the land.
31 The prophets prophesy falsely,
the priests are in league with them,
and the people are delighted with this situation.
But when the end comes, what will you do?[w]

CHAPTER 6*

Invasion and Destruction

1 O people of Jerusalem, flee for safety!
Depart immediately from Jerusalem!
Sound the trumpet in Tekoa! *
Raise a signal over Beth-haccherem!

r Deut 28:49; Isa 5:26.—**s** Jer 30:11.—**t** Jer 16:13.—**u** Job 38:10f; Ps 104:9.—**v** Ps 10:9; Prov 1:11.—**w** Jer 14:14; Mic 2:11.

5:18-19 These two verses were added by a later editor in order to soften the harshness of the preceding passage.

6:1-30 The nation has not heeded the word of God. God is about to strike without pity.

6:1 *Tekoa,* a little south of Bethlehem, and *Beth-haccherem,* west of Jerusalem, were places near the capital. The poetic style allowed the use of varied concrete names instead of repeating "Jerusalem."

For disaster looms from the north,
immense destruction will ensue.[x]
2 The beautiful and delicate daughter Zion
faces imminent destruction.
3 Shepherds will advance against her with their flocks;
they will pitch their tents all around her,
each one grazing his own portion of the pasture.[y]

4 "Prepare for war against her!
Arise! We will attack at noon."
"It is now too late.
The daylight is fading,
and the evening shadows have begun to lengthen."
5 "On your feet! Let us attack by night
and destroy her palaces."

6 These are the words of the LORD of hosts:
Cut down her trees
and raise up siege-ramps against Jerusalem.[z]
This city must be punished,
for oppression is rampant within her.
7 As a well keeps its water fresh,
so she keeps fresh her wickedness.
Sounds of violence and destruction resound within her;
sickness and wounds are never out of my sight.[a]
8 Heed my warning, O Jerusalem,
or I will turn away from you in revulsion
and reduce you to a desert,
a desolate land where no man dwells.

9 These are the words of the LORD of hosts:
Glean thoroughly like a vine
the remnant of Israel.
Like one who picks the grapes,
pass your hand once again over its branches.

10 To whom should I speak and issue warning
so that they may hear?
See, their ears are closed,
and so they cannot pay heed
They regard the word of the LORD as offensive
and they take no pleasure in it.[b]
11 However, I am filled with the wrath of the LORD,
and I am weary of holding it in.
I will pour it out on the children in the street
as well as on the gatherings of young men.
Both husband and wife will be taken,
the elderly and those far advanced in years.
12 Their houses will be turned over to others,
together with their fields and their wives,
when I stretch out my hand
against those who dwell in the land,
says the LORD.[c]

13 For from the least to the greatest,
all are greedy for gain.
All of them practice fraud,
prophets and priests alike.
14 They treat the wound of my people
as though it were a minor bruise,
saying, "All is well,"
when in reality, disaster looms on the horizon.
15 They should be ashamed
because of their abominable deeds.
Yet they are never ashamed
they do not know how to blush.
Therefore, they will fall along with the others;
they will be cast down when I punish them,
says the LORD.[d]

16 These are the words of the LORD of hosts:
Stand at the crossroads and look around;
ask for the ancient paths.
When you are shown where the good way lies,
walk along it and your souls will find rest.
However, they said, "We will not take it."
17 I also posted sentinels for you and said,
"Listen to the sound of the trumpet!"
But they said, "We will not give it any heed."

18 Therefore, hear, you nations,
and come to understand, you people,
the fate that will befall them.
19 Let all on earth come to understand
the extent of the disaster I will inflict on this people,
the inescapable fruit of their schemes,

x Jer 1:14f; Ps 140:12.—y Jer 4:17; Lk 19:43.—z Jer 32:24; Ezek 4:2.—a Isa 57:20; 59:6.—b Jer 7:26; Acts 7:51.—c Jer 8:10; Deut 28:30ff.—d Jer 3:3; 8:12.

because they have not given heed to my words
and have rejected my law. [e]
20 What use do I have for incense imported from Sheba
or fragrant cane from a distant land?
I do not regard your burnt offerings as acceptable,
nor are your sacrifices pleasing to me.
21 Therefore, thus says the LORD:
Behold, I will now place obstacles before this people
that will cause them to stumble.
Fathers and sons, friends and neighbors,
will all perish together.

22 These are the words of the LORD of hosts:
Behold, a people is approaching
from the land of the north;
a great nation is coming forth
from the ends of the earth. [f]
23 Armed with bow and javelin,
they are cruel and lack any semblance of mercy.
Their sound is like the thunder of the sea
as they ride forth on their horses;
they approach in battle formation
to fight against you, O daughter of Zion.

24 As news about them reaches us,
our hands become limp.
Anguish has gripped us,
pain like that of a woman in labor. [g]
25 Do not venture forth into the countryside
or walk along the roads.
Terror lurks on every side
from the swords of the enemy.

26 O daughter of my people,
wrap yourselves in sackcloth
and roll in the ashes.
Mourn as you would for an only child
with bitter lamentation.
For suddenly approaching us,
we will behold the destroyer.

27 * I have designated you as a tester of my people
so that you may learn and test their ways. [h]
28 All of then are unrepentant rebels,
comfortable in slander and corrupt without exception,
hard as bronze and iron.
29 The bellows roar
and the lead is consumed by the fire.
In vain does the smelter do his work,
for the wicked are not purged out. *
30 They are called "rejected silver,"
for the LORD has indeed rejected them. [i]

II: PROPHECIES MAINLY IN THE DAYS OF JEHOIAKIM

CHAPTER 7

True Worship. 1 * This is the word of the
LORD that was delivered to Jeremiah: 2 Stand
at the gate of the house of the LORD, and pro-
claim there this message: Hear the word of
the LORD, all you people of Judah who enter
through these gates to worship the LORD. [j]
3 This is the message that the LORD of hosts,
the God of Israel, proclaims to you: Amend
your ways and your deeds so that I may
remain with you in this place. 4 Do not place
your trust in these deceptive words: This is
the temple of the LORD, the temple of the
LORD, the temple of the LORD.
5 However, if you truly amend your ways
and your deeds, if you are upright in your
dealings with your neighbor; 6 if you do not
oppress the alien, the orphan, and the
widow; if you do not shed innocent blood in
this place; and if you do not follow other gods
and thereby cause your own destruction, [k]
7 then I will allow you to live in this place, in
the land that I gave as a permanent gift to
your fathers long ago.
8 You have been placing your trust in
deceitful words that are completely worth-
less. 9 Will you steal, murder, commit adul-
tery, engage in perjury, burn incense to Baal,
and follow other gods about whom you know
nothing, 10 and then come and stand before
me in this house which bears my name and
say, "We are safe," all the while intending to
continue doing these abominable deeds? [l]
11 Has this house which bears my name

e Prov 1:31; Isa 1:2.—f Jer 1:15; 5:15; 50:41.—g Jer 4:31; Isa 21:3.—h Jer 1:18.—i Jer 7:29.—j Jer 26:2.—k Ex 22:21-24; Lk 6:35.—l Jer 32:34.

6:27-30 The prophet's work is useless: Israel refuses purification.

6:29 Smelters of silver used lead because when this melted and oxidized on contact with air it drew to itself the dross from the precious metal.

7:1—8:3 We are here in the period of Jehoiakim, and there has been a revival of idolatry. But there is another and even more serious danger: the temple and its sacrifices have become a barrier between God and his people. If the people persist in their impious behavior, even offering libations to the goddess of fecundity (v. 18), nothing will be able to save them, and the temple itself will not escape the ruin! The example of another temple, the one in Shiloh, in which even the Ark had rested (see 1 Sam 4:12-18) and the ruin of the entire northern kingdom in 721 B.C. (v. 15) are precedents which ought to make people think.

become in your eyes a den of thieves? Be
assured that I am fully aware of what you are
doing, says the LORD.
12 Go now to my shrine of Shiloh which I
originally designated as the dwelling place of
my name. There you can observe what I did
to it as the result of the wickedness of my
people Israel.* 13 And now, because you have
done all these things, says the LORD, and
refused to listen when I spoke to you contin-
uously, and would not answer when I called
you, 14 I therefore will do to the house that
bears my name, to this house in which you
trust, and to this place which I gave to you
and your fathers, just what I did to Shiloh. [m]
15 And I will cast you out of my sight, just as
I cast out all your kinsfolk, all the offspring of
Ephraim.

Abuses in Worship. 16 For your part, Jere-
miah, do not intercede for this people, do not
raise a plea or a prayer on their behalf, and
do not intercede with me, for I will not listen
to you. 17 Do you not observe what they are
doing in the towns of Judah and in the streets
of Jerusalem? 18 The children gather up
the wood, their fathers light the fire, and the
women knead dough to make cakes for the
queen of heaven. And to arouse my anger,
they pour out drink offerings to other gods. [n]
19 But am I the one whom they hurt? asks
the LORD. Is it not rather themselves, to their
own shame? 20 Therefore, says the Lord GOD,
my anger and wrath will pour forth on this
place, on man and beast, on the trees of the
field and the fruits of the earth, and burn
without being quenched.
21 Thus says the LORD of hosts, the God of
Israel: Add your burnt offerings to your sac-
rifices and consume all the flesh yourselves.
22 For when I brought forth your ancestors
out of the land of Egypt, I gave them no com-
mands in regard to burnt offerings and sac-
rifices. 23 What I commanded them was this:
Listen to my voice, and I will be your God,
and you will be my people. If you follow all
the ways that I command you, then you will
prosper. [o]
24 However, they did not obey or pay heed
to my words. Rather, they persisted in follow-
ing their own evil inclinations with stubborn
hearts and turned their backs to me, not
their faces. 25 From the day your ancestors
left Egypt until today, I unfailingly sent all my
servants the prophets to them. 26 Yet they
have not listened to me or paid attention;
instead they stiffened their necks and proved
to be worse than their ancestors. [p]
27 When you speak all these words to them,
they will not listen to you. When you call out
to them, they will not answer you. 28 Then you
are to say to them: This is the nation that did
not obey the LORD, their God, or accept cor-
rection. Truth has perished. It no longer
issues forth from their mouths.

29 * Cut off your hair and cast it away;
raise a lamentation on the barren heights.
For the LORD has rejected and abandoned
the generation that has provoked his wrath.

30 The people of Judah have perpetrated
deeds that are evil in my sight, says the LORD.
They have defiled the house that bears my
name by setting up within it their loathsome
idols. [q] 31 Furthermore, they have built the
high places of Topheth* in the Valley of Ben-
hinnom to burn their sons and daughters in
the fire—a deed that I never ordered and
that never even entered my mind.
32 Therefore, beware, for the days are com-
ing, says the LORD, when the names of
Topheth and the Valley of Ben-hinnom will
no longer be used. They will rather be
referred to as the Valley of Slaughter. Be-
cause of a scarcity of space, Topheth will
become a burial ground. 33 The corpses of
this people will serve as food for the birds of
the sky and the animals of the earth, and no
one will frighten them away. 34 In the towns of
Judah and the streets of Jerusalem I will ban-
ish all sounds of joy and gladness and the
voices of the bridegroom and bride, for the
entire land will have become a desert. [r]

CHAPTER 8

1 At that time, says the LORD, the bones of
the kings and officials of Judah, the bones of
its priests and prophets, and the bones of the
inhabitants of Jerusalem will be exhumed
from their graves. [s] 2 They will be spread out

m Jer 19:12; 26:9.—n Jer 19:13; 44:17.—o Jer 11:4; Isa 3:10.—p Jer 25:3-4.—q Jer 32:34.—r Jer 16:9; Isa 24:7.—s Ezek 6:5.

7:12 It is from this verse (and see Jer 26:6) and from Ps 78:60 that we know the end of the sanctuary at Shiloh.

7:29—8:3 The Valley of Ben-hinnom, where sacrifices of children were offered, would become an open-air charnel house. And in the neighborhood of the city, the desecrated bones of worshipers of the stars (see Jer 8:2) would remain exposed before the gaze of their helpless divinities. The privation of burial and the desecration of graves were curses.

7:31 *Topheth* probably means "furnace, pyre."

before the sun and the moon and all the host of heaven which they loved and served, and which they followed, consulted, and worshiped. Their bones will not be gathered up and buried but will be left upon the ground like dung.
3 And death will be preferred to life by the survivors of the wicked race in any of the places to which I have banished them, says the LORD of hosts.

Israel's Infidelity

4* Then you are to say to them,
Thus says the LORD:
When someone falls, does he not stand up again?
If people go astray, do they not turn back? [t]
5 Why then do these people continue to rebel
and persist in their obstinate infidelity?
Why do they continue in their treachery
and refuse to turn back?
6 I have listened to them attentively
but they never utter a truthful word.
Not a single one repents of his wickedness,
saying, "What have I done?"
All of them continue to follow the same course
like a horse charging into battle. [u]
7 Even the stork in the sky
knows its appointed seasons;
turtledoves, swallows, and cranes
are aware when it is time to migrate.
But my people do not know
the ordinances of the LORD.
8 How can you say, "We are wise, [v]
for we have the law of the LORD,"
when that law has been falsified
by the lying pen of the scribes?
9 The wise will be put to shame;
they will be dismayed and caught in errors.
Since they have rejected the word of the LORD,
of what value is their wisdom?

Unrepentant for Their Sins

10 Therefore, I will give their wives to other men
and their fields to new owners.
From the least to the greatest,
everyone is greedy for ill-gotten gain.
All of them practice fraud,
including prophets and priests. [w]
11 They bandage the wound of my people
as though it were a minor injury.
"Peace! Peace!" they say,
when there is no peace.
12 They should be embarrassed at their loathsome deeds,
yet they are not the least bit ashamed;
they do not even know how to blush.
Therefore, they will join the others who have fallen;
when the day of punishment arrives,
they will be thrown down, says the LORD.

A Prophet's Lament

13 I will gather them all in,
the LORD has promised;
there will be no grapes on the vine,
no figs on the fig trees.
Even the leaves will be withered;
what I have given them
will be taken away from them. [x]
14 Why are we just sitting idly here?
It is time to mobilize.
Let us march into the fortified cities
and perish there.
For the LORD, our God, has doomed us for destruction
and given us poisoned water to drink
because we have sinned against him.
15 We are praying for peace, but to no avail;
for a time of healing,
only to be confronted with terror.
16 The snorting of horses is heard from Dan;
the neighing of his stallions
causes the entire land to quake.
The enemy is advancing to devour the land
and all that it contains,
the city and those who dwell there.
17 Behold, I will send against you
venomous snakes that cannot be charmed,
and they will bite you, says the LORD. [y]
18 There is no cure for my grief,
and my heart is faint within me.
19 Listen to the cry of distress
from my people in a distant land.
"Is the LORD no longer in Zion?
Is her king no longer in their midst?"

t Prov 24:16; Mic 7:8.—u Job 33:27-28; Ps 14:2.—v Jer 4:22; Rom 1:22.—w Deut 28:30; Isa 56:11.—x Jer 7:24; Lev 26:20.—y Num 21:6.

8:4—10:25 Among the rebukes and threats in this part of the Book is inserted a sorrowful lament: the people do not know the Lord! To know God and heed his word is true wisdom. Because it has preferred its own wisdom, the nation is plunging into ruin.

(Why do they provoke me with their idols
and with their foreign gods?)
20 "The time of harvest is past,
the summer is at an end,
and we are not saved."

21 The suffering of my people causes me to suffer too.
I mourn, overcome with terror.
22 Is there no more balm in Gilead?*
Can no physician be found there?
Why has there not been any progress
to restore the health of my people? [z]

CHAPTER 9

A Faithless People

1 Oh, if only my head were a spring of water
and my eyes a fountain of tears
so that I might weep day and night
for the slain of the daughter of my people.
2 Would that I could find in the desert
a wayside shelter for travelers
so that I might depart from my people
and leave them far behind.
For all of them are adulterers,
a faithless mob of traitors.
3 Their tongues are like devious weapons,
bent like a drawn bow.
With falsehood rather than truth
they have gained power in the land.
They commit one crime after another,
but they do not acknowledge me, says the LORD. [a]

4 Each of you should be on guard against your neighbor
and place no trust in a brother.
For everyone seeks to supplant his brother, as Jacob did,
and every friend is a slanderer.
5 They all deceive each other;
no one speaks the truth.
They have trained their tongues in the art of lying;
immersed in iniquity, they cannot repent.
6 With their repeated acts of oppression and deceit,
they refuse to acknowledge me, says the LORD.

7 Therefore, thus says the LORD of hosts:
Now I will refine and test them.
How else should I deal with this people?
8 Their tongue is a deadly arrow;
their mouth utters words of deceit.
They speak cordially with their neighbors,
but inwardly, they are plotting to ambush them. [b]
9 For such deceitful dealings
shall I not punish them, says the LORD,
and shall I not exact vengeance
on such a nation?

Dirge over Zion

10 Raise up cries of weeping and lamentation for the mountains
and chant a dirge for the pasture lands,
because they have been so scorched
that no one passes there,
and the lowing of cattle is not heard.
Birds of the air and the animals:
all have fled and are gone.
11 I will turn Jerusalem into a heap of ruins,
a lair for jackals,
and I will lay waste the towns of Judah
so that no one can live there. [c]

12 Who is wise enough to understand this?
Who has been commanded by the LORD to
make it known? Why has the land been rav-
aged and laid waste like a desert through
which no one is able to pass? 13 The LORD
says, "This was permitted to happen be-
cause they have rejected my law which I set
before them, and they have not followed it or
listened to my voice. 14 Rather, they have
stubbornly obeyed the wishes of their own
hearts and followed the Baals, as their
ancestors had taught them."

15 Therefore, thus says the LORD of hosts,
the God of Israel, "Now I will give this peo-
ple wormwood to eat and poisoned water to
drink. 16 I will scatter them among nations
that neither they nor their ancestors have
known, and I will pursue them with the
sword until I have completely annihilated
them." [d]

17 Thus says the LORD of hosts:
Listen to my command! Summon the mourning women;
send for those who are most skilled in this regard.
18 Let them come quickly
and raise a dirge for us

z Jer 14:19; 46:11.—a Jer 9:8; Ps 64:4.—b Jer 5:26.—c Jer 10:22; Ezek 35:4.—d Lev 26:33; Deut 28:64.

8:22 *Gilead:* in the Transjordan area, famous for its medicinal spices.

so that our eyes may overflow with tears
and our cheeks may be wet with weeping.
19 May a sound of lamenting be heard in Zion,
"Great is our ruin;
intense is our shame.
We must leave our land;
our homes have been destroyed." * [e]

20 Listen, you women, to the word of the LORD;
let your ears receive the message he imparts.
21 Death has climbed through our windows
and has entered our palaces.
It has cut down the children in the streets
and the young people in the public squares.
22 The corpses of the slain will be strewn
like dung on an open field,
like sheaves left behind by the reaper
with no one to gather them.

True Wisdom

23 Thus says the LORD:
Let not the wise man boast of his wisdom,
or the strong man boast of his strength,
or the rich man boast of his wealth.[f]
24 But if any wish to boast,
let them boast of this:
that they understand and know me.
For I am the LORD who governs the earth
with unfailing love, justice, and righteousness.
In these things I delight,
says the LORD.

25 "Behold, the days are coming," says the
LORD, "when I will demand an account of all
those who are circumcised only in the flesh:[g]
26 Egypt, Judah, Edom, the Ammonites, Moab,
and all those with shaved temples who dwell
in the desert.* For all those nations, and the
entire house of Israel as well, are uncircumcised in heart."

CHAPTER 10

The True God.
1 Listen to the word that the
LORD addresses to you, O house of Israel.
2 Thus says the LORD:

Do not adopt the ways of the nations
or become frightened at the signs in the heavens,*
even though the nations are terrified of them.
3 For the carved images of the nations are powerless;
they are nothing more than wood cut from a forest,
fashioned with a knife by craftsmen
4 and embellished with silver and gold.
Then they are fastened with hammers and nails
to prevent them from toppling.[h]

5 Like scarecrows in a cucumber field
they are unable to speak,
and they must be carried from place to place
since they cannot walk.
Do not be afraid of them,
for they can do no harm,
nor do they have any power to do good.

6 O LORD, there is no one like you;
you are great,
and great is the might of your name.[i]
7 Who would not fear you,
O King of the nations?
This is your due.
Of all the wisest men in the nations
and throughout all their kingdoms,
there is no one like you.

8 They are all senseless and foolish,
and the idols they venerate are nothing but wood,
9 adorned with beaten silver from Tarshish
and gold from Ophir.
Their idols are the work of craftsmen and goldsmiths
and clothed with violet and purple;
all of them are the product of skilled workers.
10 But the LORD is the true God;
he is the living God and the everlasting King.
When confronted with his wrath the earth quakes,
and no nation can endure his fury.[j]

11 Convey this message to them: The gods
who did not make the heavens and the earth
will perish from the earth and from under
the heavens.

---

e Jer 4:13; 15:1.—f Ps 49:7; Prov 21:30.—g Jer 4:4; Rom 2:28f.—h Isa 41:7.—i Deut 33:26; Ps 86:8ff.—j Ps 10:16; Isa 40:15.

9:19 Probably an allusion to a campaign of Nebuchadnezzar in Palestine in 602 or 598 B.C. (see 2 Ki 24:1-10).

9:26 *Desert:* or "desert and who clip the hair by their foreheads," which would refer to an idolatrous practice.

10:2 *Signs in the heavens:* the allusion is to horoscopes based on the stars.

12 The LORD made the earth by his power,
established the world by his wisdom
and spread out the heavens by his understanding. [k]
13 When his voice thunders forth,
the waters in the heavens are in tumult,
and he brings forth clouds
from the most remote areas of the earth.
He causes lightning to flash during the rainfall
and brings forth the wind from his storehouses. [l]
14 Everyone is ignorant and devoid of knowledge;
every goldsmith is put to shame by his idols,
for the figures he molds are fraudulent,
lacking even a semblance of breath.
15 They are worthless, worthy only of mockery;
when the time of judgment comes
they will no longer exist.
16 But not like these is the portion of Jacob,
for he is the Maker of all things,
and Israel is the tribe of his heritage;
the LORD of hosts is his name. [m]

Destruction of Judah*

17 Gather up your belongings and depart from the land,
you who are living under siege. [n]
18 For thus says the LORD:
This time I am determined to cast out
the inhabitants of this land,
and I will inflict such distress on them
that they will find it difficult to bear.
19 I face disaster because of my injuries.
My wounds are incurable.
However, I thought, "This is my punishment,
and somehow I must endure it."
20 My tent has been destroyed,
and all of its ropes are severed.
My children have left me,
and they are no more.
No one remains to help me pitch my tent again
or to put up its curtains. [o]
21 The shepherds have proved to be stupid;
they failed to search for the LORD.
As a result, they have not prospered,
and their entire flock is scattered.
22 Listen! There is a tremendous noise,
and it comes ever closer;
a great uproar from the land of the north;
the towns of Judah will be reduced to a desert
and become a lair for jackals.

Jeremiah's Prayer

23 I am finally aware, O LORD,
that man is not in control of his destiny
and that it is not in his power
to determine the course of his life.
24 Correct me, O LORD,
but do so with moderation,
and not in your anger,
or you will reduce me to nothing.
25 Pour forth your wrath on the nations
that refuse to acknowledge you,
as well as on the tribes
that refuse to invoke your name.
For they have devoured Jacob;
they have devoured and made an end of him
and laid waste his homeland. [p]

CHAPTER 11

Plea to Observe the Covenant.* 1 *This is the
word that came to Jeremiah from the LORD:
2 Listen to the terms of this covenant, and
then relate them to the people of Judah and
to the inhabitants of Jerusalem. 3 Say to
them: Thus says the LORD, the God of Israel:
Cursed be anyone who does not observe the
terms of this covenant 4 which I enjoined
upon your ancestors when I brought them
forth from the land of Egypt, from that iron
foundry, saying: If you listen to my voice and
do everything I command you, then you will
be my people, and I will be your God. [q] 5 I will
thus fulfill the oath that I swore to your
ancestors, when I pledged to give them a
land flowing with milk and honey, the land

k Ps 104:5, 24.—l Pss 29:3; 135:7.—m Jer 31:35; Pss 16:5, 119:57.—n Ezek 12:3ff.—o Jer 4:20.—p Ps 79:6f.—q Deut 4:20; 1 Ki 8:51.

10:17-22 This lament is a continuation of chapter 9.

11:1—25:38 In 622 B.C., a "Book of the Law" was discovered in a cupboard in the temple wall during repairs (see 2 Ki 22–23). This codex, which became the nucleus of Deuteronomy (see 2 Chr 34:14f), aided in the national and religious renewal which Josiah promoted after its discovery, for it preached love of God and unity among the Israelites. This renewal meant a genuine restoration of the covenant and would be wholeheartedly pursued by Jeremiah.

11:1-14 The editor played an important part in the formulation of these two oracles. The first passage proclaims the discovery of the law (vv. 1-8), but already added to it is a reflection on the failure of this attempt to renew the covenant (vv. 9-14). In fact, the reform was not continued after the death of Josiah.

you now possess. Then I answered, "So be it,
LORD."
[6] Then the LORD said to me: Proclaim all
these words in the cities of Judah and in the
streets of Jerusalem: Hear the words of this
covenant and follow them. [7] When I brought
your ancestors up out of the land of Egypt, I
solemnly warned them, and continued even
to this day to do so persistently, urging them
to obey my commands. [r] [8] But they refused to
listen and did not pay attention to what I
said. Rather, each one followed the inclina-
tions of his stubborn and wicked heart. As a
result, I inflicted upon them all the curses I
had threatened if they did not obey the
covenant in accordance with my commands.
[9] Then the LORD said to me: There is clear-
ly a conspiracy that exists among the people
of Judah and the inhabitants of Jerusalem.
[10] They have reverted back to the sins of their
ancestors who refused to heed my words.
They are following strange gods and serving
them. The house of Israel and the house of
Judah have broken the covenant that I made
with their ancestors.
[11] Therefore, thus says the LORD, I will
inflict upon them a disaster that they will not
be able to escape. Even should they cry out
to me, I will refuse to listen to them. [s] [12] Then
the cities of Judah and the citizens of Je-
rusalem will go forth and cry out for help to
the gods to whom they make offerings, but
these gods will be of absolutely no help to
them when disaster strikes.

13 For you have as many gods
as you have towns, O Judah.
And you have as many altars to offer sac-
rifice to Baal
as there are streets in Jerusalem.

[14] Do not intercede for this people or offer
a prayer on their behalf, for I will not listen
to their cries for help that they will raise dur-
ing the time of their misfortune. [t]

The LORD Rebukes Judah

15 What right does my beloved have to be in
my house
when she perpetrates such vile deeds?
Can vows and sacrificial meat
turn away the disaster that threatens
you
and allow you to exult?
16 The LORD once called you a green olive
tree
that was filled with leaves and fruit.
But now, with the roar of a mighty storm,
he will set it ablaze,
and its branches will be consumed.

[17] The LORD of hosts who planted you has
decreed that misfortune will befall you
because of the evil done by the house of
Israel and the house of Judah, having pro-
voked me to anger by offering sacrifices to
Baal. [u]

Jeremiah's Persecution*

18 I was aware of this, O LORD,
because you had made it known to me
then you revealed to me their evil
deeds.
19 I had been like a trusting lamb
that was being led to the slaughter.
And I was not aware about the schemes
that they were plotting against me,
saying,
"Let us destroy the tree and its fruit;
let us cut him off from the land of the
living
so that his name will no longer be
remembered." [v]
20 O LORD of hosts, you who judge righ-
teously
and test the heart and the mind,
allow me to behold your vengeance on
them,
for to you I have committed my cause.

[21] Therefore, in regard to the people of
Anathoth who are determined to end my life
and who say, "Do not prophesy in the name
of the LORD or we will kill you," [w] [22] this is
what the LORD has to say, "I am about to
punish them. Their young men will die by
the sword, and their sons and daughters will
perish by famine. [23] Not a single one of them
will survive. For in the year of reckoning for
them, I will bring disaster upon the people of
Anathoth."

---

r Jer 7:25; Ex 15:26.—s Jer 14:12; Mic 3:4.—t Jer 7:16; Ex 32:10.—u Jer 44:8; Isa 5:2.—v Ps 109:13; Isa 53:7.—w Am 2:12.

11:18—12:6 Threatened with death, Jeremiah raises the thorny problem of the just who suffer and the wicked who prosper; this was a scandal to which traditional teaching on retribution had no valid answer. And in fact, it is not possible to rise above the scandal without a very radical act of faith. God himself promises Jeremiah ever harder trials in which he must be bold enough to trust solely in the Lord. Modern readers may perhaps be put off by the vindictive sentiments of the prophet, but these must be seen in the setting of the times. There was still no idea of retribution in a future life or even of a resurrection; therefore, the call for revenge seemed the only way of expressing faith in the justice of God. The image of the lamb led to slaughter (Jer 11:19) will later be applied by Second Isaiah (Isa 53:7) to the suffering Servant and, in the New Testament, to Jesus.

CHAPTER 12

1 You are always in the right, O LORD,
whenever I take a position that conflicts with yours;
nevertheless, let me plead my case before you.
Why does it happen that the wicked prosper
and that treacherous people thrive? [x]
2 When you planted them, they took root,
flourished, and brought forth fruit.
Your name is always on their lips,
but you are far from their hearts.
3 You know me, O LORD, and you see me;
you are aware that my heart is devoted to you.
Drag off the wicked like
sheep for a sacrifice;
set them apart for the day of slaughter.
4 For how long a period must the land be in mourning
and the green grass wither throughout the countryside?
The animals and the birds are perishing
because of the wickedness of those who dwell there
and assert that God is not concerned about them. [y]

God's Response

5 If you become exhausted in a footrace with men,
how will you compete with horses?
And if you fall headlong in a peaceful land,
how will you fare in the thickets of the Jordan?
6 Even your brothers and your own family
continue to deal treacherously with you
as they pursue you while shouting threats.
Do not trust them
even when they speak gentle words to you. [z]

The LORD's Lament*

7 I have abandoned my house
and forsaken my heritage.
I have given the beloved of my heart
into the hands of her enemies.
8 My own people have become to me
like a lion in the forest;
they have threatened me incessantly,
and therefore, I despise them.
9 Why has my land become a lair for hyenas,
with birds of prey hovering on every side?
Go forth and gather all the wild beasts
so that they may assemble for the feast. [a]
10 My shepherds have ravaged my vineyard
and trampled my heritage underfoot.
They have made the plot of land that is my delight
into a desolate wilderness.
11 They have made it into a wasteland,
the sight of which causes me to mourn.
The entire land has become desolate,
and no one shows the slightest bit of concern.
12 Upon all the barren heights of the desert
those who wreak destruction have arrived.
For the LORD will wield a devouring sword
from one end of the land to the other;
no living thing will remain unscathed. [b]
13 Men have sown wheat only to reap thorns;
they have worked to the point of exhaustion
but have profited nothing.
Their harvests are a source of disappointment
because of the fierce anger of the LORD.

Judah's Evil Neighbors. 14 Thus says the
LORD, "As for all my evil neighbors who have
seized the inheritance I gave to my people
Israel, I will uproot them from their land, and
from among them I will uproot the house of
Judah. 15 But after I uproot them, I will again
take pity on them and bring them back, each
one to his own heritage and his own land. [c]
16 "Then, if they carefully adhere to the
ways of my people and swear by my name,
saying, 'As the LORD lives,' just as previously
they taught my people to swear by Baal, then
they will be reestablished among my people.

x Job 21:7; Mal 3:15.—y Hos 4:3.—z Jer 9:4f.—a 2 Ki 24:2; Isa 56:9.—b Jer 16:5; Isa 42:25; 57:21.—c Jer 29:14; Am 9:14.

12:7-13 An editor has linked to the prophet's call for vengeance (v. 3) the following two oracles, both of which speak of the judgment of God. The passage is probably an echo of the repression that was followed by the rebellion of Jehoiakim against his sovereign (Nebuchadnezzar). With the approval of the king of Babylon, some neighboring peoples engaged in a series of raids against Judah in about 599 B.C. (see 2 Ki 24:13). An accounting for their cruelty will be demanded of them, as well as the possibility of entering into the saving covenant, provided they renounce their false god, Baal, and follow the Lord. This marks the beginning of the call to universal salvation.

17 But if any nation refuses to listen, I will
uproot that nation and destroy it complete-
ly," says the LORD. [d]

CHAPTER 13*

Warnings to Judah. 1 The LORD said to me:
Go forth and purchase for yourself a loin-
cloth. Wrap it around your loins, but do not
dip it in water. 2 I purchased the loincloth as
instructed by the LORD and wrapped it
around my loins.

3 Then the LORD spoke to me a second
time, saying: 4 Take the loincloth that you
purchased and are wearing, and go now to
the Euphrates and conceal it there in a cleft
of the rock. [e] 5 So I went to the Euphrates and
hid it as the LORD had commanded me.

6 After a long period of time, the LORD
said to me: Go now to the Euphrates and
retrieve the loincloth that I instructed you
to hide there. 7 And so I returned to the
Euphrates and searched for the cleft, and I
then retrieved the loincloth from the place
where I had hidden it. But the loincloth had
now rotted and was good for nothing.

8 Then the word of the LORD came to me:
9 Thus says the LORD: In the same way I will
ruin the pride of Judah and the enormous
pride of Jerusalem. [f] 10 Because these wick-
ed people refuse to listen to my words and
stubbornly follow their own inclinations as
they run after other gods to serve them and
worship them, they will become like this
loincloth, which is good for nothing. 11 For
just as a loincloth clings to a man's loins, so
I made the whole house of Israel and the
whole house of Judah cling to me, says the
LORD, in the hope that they would become
my people, my praise, and my pride. But
they refused to listen. [g]

The Shattered Wineflask. 12 Therefore, pro-
claim this message to them: Thus says the
LORD, the God of Israel: Every wineflask
should be filled with wine. If they reply, "Do
you think we do not know that every wine-
flask is meant to be filled with wine?" 13 say
to them in reply: Thus says the LORD: I will
fill all the inhabitants of this land with wine
until they are drunk—the kings who sit on
David's throne, the priests, the prophets,
and all the inhabitants of Jerusalem. [h]
14 Then I will smash them one against the
other, parents and children together, says
the LORD. I will show no pity, I will not
spare or show compassion, when I destroy
them.

A Vision of Exile

15 Listen carefully and suppress your pride,
   for it is the LORD who speaks.
16 Give glory to the LORD, your God,
   before the darkness descends,
before your feet stumble
   on the mountains at twilight,
before the light you hope for
   will gradually turn to gloom
   and then into thick darkness. [i]
17 If your pride does not allow you to listen,
   I will weep in secret for you.
My eyes will be filled with tears
   because the LORD's flock is being led
      into captivity.

18* Say to the king and the queen mother,
   "Descend from your thrones,
since your glorious crowns
   have fallen from your heads."
19 The cities in the Negeb are besieged,
   and no one will be able to offer them
      relief.
All Judah has been taken into exile;
   every inhabitant has been led away.

Jerusalem's Shame

20 Lift up your eyes and behold
   those who are coming from the north.
Where is the flock that was entrusted to
      you,
   the sheep that were your pride? [j]
21 What will you say when they appoint as
      your rulers
   those whom you chose as your allies?
Will not pangs seize you
   like those of a woman in labor?

22 And if you should ask yourself,
   "Why has all this happened to me?"
it is because of your many grievous sins
   that your skirts have been stripped
      away
   and you have been violated. [k]

d Isa 60:12.—e Jer 51:63.—f Prov 16:18.—g Ex 19:5.—h Jer 25:15-18; Isa 51:17.—i Isa 5:30; Am 8:9.—j Jer 6:22f.—k Jer 5:19.

13:1-27 Judah, which should be a source of renown and glory for the Lord (v. 11), has become intoxicated by its title of chosen people. The oracles collected here by the editor denounce this pride; the prophecies are filled with threats to be carried out in the very near future. The oracles certainly preceded the first deportation in 598 B.C.

13:18-19 The king is certainly Jehoiachin, son of Jehoiakim; he was a young man of 18 and would ascend the throne only to be led away a prisoner (see 2 Ki 24:8).

23 Can an Ethiopian change the color of his skin
or a leopard change its spots?
Neither are you able to do good
when you are schooled in evil.

24 I will scatter you like chaff
that is driven by the desert wind.
25 This is your lot, says the LORD,
the portion I have measured out to you,
because you have forgotten me
and placed your trust in false gods.

26 I myself will tear off your skirts
so that your shame will be seen. [l]
27 Your adulteries, your cries of lustful pleasure,
your shameless acts of prostitution:
all these abominable deeds of yours
I have observed on the hills of the countryside.
Woe to you, Jerusalem!
How long will it be
before you are made clean?

CHAPTER 14

The Great Drought.* 1 This is the word of the LORD that was given to Jeremiah during the drought:

2 Judah is in mourning,
and her towns languish.
Her people lie on the ground in mourning;
a cry of anguish goes up from Jerusalem. [m]

3 The nobles send their servants for water,
but when they come to the cisterns
they find no water,
and they return with their jars empty.
Ashamed and in despair
they cover their heads.*
4 Because the ground is cracked
due to a total lack of rainfall,
the farmers are desperate,
and they too cover their heads.

5 Even the doe in the open country
abandons her newborn fawn
because there is no grass.
6 Wild donkeys stand on the bare heights
and pant for air like jackals,
while their eyes grow dim
because of a lack of pasture.

7 Even though our sins bear witness against us,
take action, O LORD, for your name's sake;
forgive us for our many acts of infidelity,
our countless sins against you. [n]
8 O LORD, you are the hope of Israel
and its savior in time of need.
Why are you like a stranger in the land,
like a traveler who only stays for a single night?
9 Why should you be taken unawares,
like a warrior who is powerless to help us?
You are in our midst, O LORD,
and we bear your name.
Do not forsake us!

10 Thus says the LORD about this people:
Truly they have loved to stray
and have not restrained their feet.
Therefore, the LORD no longer takes pleasure in them;
he will now remember their iniquity
and punish their sins. [o]

11 Then the LORD said to me: Do not intercede for this people or pray for their welfare.
12 If they fast, I will not listen to their cry. If they offer holocausts or grain offerings, I will not accept them. Rather, I will destroy them by the sword, famine, and plague.

13 In response I said, "Ah, Lord GOD, the prophets continue to say to them that they will suffer neither sword nor famine, since you will give them lasting peace in this place."

14 Then the LORD said to me: The prophets are prophesying lies in my name. I did not send them or give them any orders or speak to them. They are prophesying to you lying visions, worthless divinations, and delusions of their own minds. [p]

15 Therefore, thus says the LORD about the prophets who are prophesying in his name: Although I did not send them, they continue to assert that neither sword nor famine will afflict this land. By sword and famine those same prophets will perish.
16 Furthermore, the people to whom they are prophesying will be thrown out into the streets of Jerusalem, victims of famine and the sword. No one will bury them or their wives, their sons or their

l Ezek 16:37.—m Isa 3:26.—n Ps 79:8-9; Isa 59:12.—o Jer 2:25; Hos 8:13.—p Jer 5:31; 23:16; Deut 18:20.

14:1—15:9 In some memorable circumstances, Moses had become the advocate for his people (Ex 32:11; Num 14:13). In the hour of catastrophe, Jeremiah does the same, but the Lord refuses to be softened.

14:3 *Cover their heads:* a sign of mourning.

daughters. I will pour down on them their
own wickedness.

17 This is the message you are to deliver to them:
Let my eyes stream with tears
day and night without ceasing,
for my virgin daughter—my people—
has suffered a crushing blow
and is grievously injured.[q]
18 If I go out into the open fields,
I see those slain by the sword.
If I go into the city,
I behold those who have perished through famine.
Even prophets and priests roam in confusion
in a land they do not know.
19 Have you rejected Judah completely?
Has Zion become loathsome to you?
Why have you afflicted us
to a point where we cannot be healed?
We hope for peace, but to no avail,
for a time of healing, only to encounter terror.
20 O LORD, we acknowledge our wickedness
and the guilt of our fathers;
we have indeed sinned against you.[r]
21 For your name's sake do not reject us;
do not dishonor your glorious throne.
Remember your covenant with us
and do not break it.
22 Can any worthless idols of the nations bring rain?
Do the heavens send down rain showers on their own?
No, it is you who accomplish all this,
O LORD, our God,
and therefore, we place our hope in you.

CHAPTER 15

1 The LORD then said to me: Even if Moses
and Samuel stood before me, my heart
would not have pity on this people. Send
them away from my presence! Let them
go! 2 And if they should ask you where they
should go, say to them: Thus says the LORD:

Those destined for the plague, to plague;
those destined for the sword, to the sword;
those destined for famine, to famine;
those destined for captivity, to captivity.[s]

3 Furthermore, four kinds of destroyers I
will send against them, says the LORD: the
sword to kill, dogs to drag away, birds of the
sky and beasts of the earth to devour and
destroy. 4 I will make them an object of hor-
ror to all the kingdoms of the earth because
of what King Manasseh of Judah, the son of
Hezekiah, did in Jerusalem.

5* Who will there be to pity you, O Jerusalem?
Who will mourn for you?
Who will have the slightest concern
to inquire how you are?[t]
6 You have rejected me, says the LORD,
and you have turned your back on me.
Therefore, I have stretched out my hand over you
in order to destroy you;
I am weary of having compassion for you.[u]
7 I have winnowed them with a winnowing fork
at every city gate in the land.
I have brought bereavement and destruction on my people
because they would not abandon their evil ways.
8 I have made their widows more numerous
than the sands of the sea.
I brought a destroyer at noonday
against the mothers of young men.
Without warning, I afflicted them
with anguish and terror.
9 The mother of seven sons will grow faint
and gasp for breath.
Her sun went down while it was still day;
she has been shamed and disgraced.
As for the rest, I will give them to the sword
to perish at the hands of assassins, says the LORD.

Jeremiah's Call Renewed*

10 "O my mother, how I wish
that you had never given birth to me,

q Jer 9:18.—r Dan 9:8.—s Jer 14:12; Ezek 5:12.—t Isa 51:19.—u Am 7:8.

15:5-9 This oracle may date from a little after the events of 598 B.C.

15:10-21 The prophet has spent himself without reservation to maintain the covenant and be a witness of the Lord. He has gotten in return only misunderstanding, hostility, and isolation. The words he speaks in the depths of his suffering sound blasphemous. For this reason, the Lord has not given him even a single word of approval. The prophet has departed from the right way: he must return to it! Verses 12-14 were very clumsily inserted into this passage by a copyist.

a man of strife and contention for the
entire land.
I have never borrowed from anyone,
nor have I lent to anyone,
yet everyone curses me. [v]
11 Have I not truly done my best
to serve you, O LORD?
Have I not interceded with you
in times of disaster and times of distress? [w]
12 "Can iron and bronze
break iron from the north?
13 Your wealth and your treasures
I will hand over as plunder, without
repayment,
because of all your sins
throughout your territory.
14 I will force you to serve your enemies
in a land you do not know,
for my anger will kindle a fire
that will blaze against you.
15 O LORD, you know me well.
Remember me and visit me
and avenge me on my persecutors.
Continue to be patient with me
and do not cast me aside;
remember the insults I suffer for your
sake. [x]
16 "When I discovered your words, I devoured them;
they became a source of joy to me
and the delight of my heart,
because I bore your name,
O LORD, God of hosts.
17 "I have never associated with revelers
or rejoiced in their company;
I sat alone because I felt your hand
on me,
and you had filled me with indignation.
18 Why then is my suffering continuous
and my wound incurable, refusing to
be healed?
You have indeed become for me a
treacherous brook
whose waters cannot be relied upon." [y]
19 In reply the LORD said to me:
If you repent, I will restore you,
and you will stand in my presence.
If you utter precious words
and not what is worthless,
you will be my spokesman.
This people may turn to you,
but you must not turn to them.
20 I will make you appear in the eyes of this
people
to be a fortified wall of bronze.
They will fight against you
but they will not prevail,
for I am with you [z]
to save and deliver you, says the LORD.
21 I will rescue you from the clutches of the
wicked
and redeem you from the grasp of the
violent.

CHAPTER 16*

Warning to Jeremiah. 1 The following word
of the LORD then came to me: 2 You shall not
take to yourself a wife or have sons and
daughters in this place. 3 For thus says the
LORD concerning the sons and daughters
who are born in this place, and about the
mothers who give birth to them and the
fathers who beget them in this land: 4 They
shall perish from deadly diseases. Unlamented and unburied, they will be like
dung spread over the ground. They will perish by sword and by famine, and their
corpses will serve as food for the birds of the
sky and the beasts of the earth. [a]

5 The LORD then continued: Do not enter a
house of mourning; do not go there to lament
or offer words of comfort. For I have withdrawn my blessing from this people, says the
LORD, as well as my love and my mercy.
6 Both the powerful and the lowly will perish
in this land, without burial or lamentation.
There will be no gashing or shaving of the
head for them. 7 * No one is to break bread
with the mourners to comfort them in their
bereavement or offer them the cup of consolation to drink for their father or mother. [b]

8 Nor are you to enter a house where people are feasting and sit with them to eat and
drink. 9 For thus says the LORD of hosts, the

v Jer 20:14.—w Jer 39:11-14.—x Jer 12:3; Ps 69:7-9.—y Jer 14:19; 30:15.—z Jer 1:18-19.—a Jer 7:33.—b Ezek 24:17.

16:1-21 Like Hosea's marriage (see Hos 1:3), Jeremiah's celi-bacy had fed the public's curiosity. The prophet lived alone and took part in neither funerals nor festivities. He wanted to make it understood that this was no longer a time for establishing families or for gathering for feasts. In order to temper the severity of this oracle, an editor has introduced a more comforting passage regarding the return of those who would be scattered (v. 14f); these verses have their more appropriate setting in Jer 23:7-8. And in order to end on an optimistic note, three verses have been added (vv. 19-21) that foretell the conversion of the nations and are inspired by Isa 45:14.

16:7-8 The practices described here were connected with mourning.

God of Israel: In your lifetime, and before
your very eyes, I will banish from this place
the cries of joy and gladness, the voices of
bridegroom and bride.
10 When you relate all these words to the
people, they will ask you, "Why has the LORD
decreed that all these evils are to befall us?
What evil have we done? What sin have we
committed against the LORD, our God?" [c]
11 Then you will give them this answer: This
will occur because your ancestors aban-
doned me, says the LORD, and followed other
gods and served and worshiped them. They
forsook me and did not keep my law. 12 And
you have behaved even more wickedly than
your ancestors. For each one of you stub-
bornly follows his own wicked inclinations
and refuses to listen to me. 13 Therefore, I will
cast you out of this land into a land that is
completely unknown to you or your ances-
tors. There you can serve other gods day and
night, for I will show you no further favor.

The Israelites Return. 14 However, the days
are surely coming, says the LORD, when it
will no longer be said, "As the LORD lives
who brought the Israelites up out of the land
of Egypt," [d] 15 but rather, "As the LORD lives
who brought the Israelites up out of the land
of the north and out of all the countries
where he had driven them." For I will bring
them back to the land that I gave to their
ancestors.

Twice the Punishment. 16 Now I will send for
many fishermen, says the LORD, and they
will catch them. After that, I will send for
many hunters, and they will hunt them
down from every mountain and every hill,
and from the crevices of the rocks. [e] 17 For
my eyes are focused on all their ways: they
are not hidden from my sight, nor does their
iniquity escape my gaze. 18 And I will doubly
repay them for their iniquity and their sin,
since they have polluted my land with their
detestable idols and filled my heritage with
their abominations.

The People's Conversion

19 O LORD, my strength and my stronghold,
my refuge in times of distress,
the nations will come to you
from the ends of the earth and say,
"Our fathers inherited nothing but false gods,
idols that are worthless and without power."
20 Can men make their own gods?
These are not gods in any way. [f]
21 Therefore, I intend to give my people knowledge;
this time I will teach them
about my power and my might,
and then they will know
that my name is the LORD.

CHAPTER 17

Judah Punished for Its Idolatry

1* The sin of Judah is written
with an iron stylus,
engraved with a diamond point
on the tablet of their hearts
and on the horns of their altars, [g]
2 while their children remember
their altars and their sacred poles
beside every green tree
and on the high hills,
3 the mountains in the open country.

Your wealth and all your treasures
I will hand over as spoil
in repayment for all your sins
throughout your territory.
4 You will be forced to surrender your heritage
which I gave to you.
I will require you to serve your enemies
in a land you do not know,
for my fiery anger has been kindled by you,
and it will burn forever.

Wisdom Sayings

5 Thus says the LORD:
Cursed is anyone who places his trust
in human beings
and relies on human strength
while his heart turns away from the LORD. [h]
6 Such a person is like a shrub in the desert;
when relief comes, he will not be aware of it.
He will continue to live
in the parched areas of the desert,
in an uninhabited salt land.

7 Blessed are those who trust in the LORD
and whose hope is the LORD.

c Jer 5:19; 13:22.—d Jer 23:7-8.—e Lam 4:19; Hab 1:14-15.—f Jer 2:11.—g Job 19:24; Prov 3:3.—h Ps 146:3.

17:1-18 According to Jeremiah, a prophet of the interior life, relations with God are formed in the human heart; so too the source of sin is in the heart.

8 They will be like a tree planted by the water
that spreads out its roots to the stream.
When the heat comes, it does not fear;
its leaves stay green.
It is not concerned in a year of drought,
and it never fails to bear fruit. [i]

9 The heart is more deceitful than any other thing,
and it is also perverse.
Who can uncover its secrets?
10 I, the LORD, search the heart
and probe the mind
to reward all according to their conduct
and as their deeds deserve.

11 Like a partridge* hatching eggs that it has not laid,
so is the man who amasses riches unjustly.
When his life is half completed,
they will desert him;
and when his life is at an end,
he will prove to have been a fool.

Israel's True Hope

12 A glorious throne, exalted from the beginning:
such is the shrine of our sanctuary. [j]
13 O LORD, you are the hope of Israel;
all those who abandon you will be put to shame.
Those who turn away from you
will have their names inscribed in the netherworld
because they have forsaken the LORD,
the source of living water.

Prayer for Vengeance

14 Heal me, O LORD, and I will be healed;
save me, and I will be saved;
you are the one whom I praise.
15 People continue to say to me,
"Where is the word of the LORD?
Let it come to pass." [k]
16 I have never tried to avoid
being a shepherd in your service,
nor have I desired the clay of despair.
Every word that passed my lips
has always been known to you.

17 Do not become a source of terror to me;
you will be my refuge on the day of disaster. [l]
18 Let my persecutors be confounded, and not me;
let them, not me, be terrified.
Bring upon them the day of disaster;
crush them with unending destruction.

The Sabbath Observed.* 19 Thus said the
LORD to me: Go forth and stand at the Gate
of Benjamin* through which the kings of
Judah enter and depart, and stand also at all
the other gates of Jerusalem. 20 There you are
to say to them: Hear the word of the LORD,
you kings of Judah, all you people of Judah as
well, and all you inhabitants of Jerusalem
who pass through these gates.

21 Thus says the LORD: If you value your
lives, take care that you do not carry a burden on the Sabbath day or bring it through
the gates of Jerusalem. [m] 22 Bring no burden
out of your houses on the Sabbath day, and
do no work. You are to keep the Sabbath
day holy, as I commanded your ancestors.
23 However, they did not listen or pay attention; rather, they stiffened their necks and
would not heed my warnings or accept
instruction.

24 But if you listen carefully to me, says the
LORD, and carry no burden through the
gates of this city on the Sabbath day, keeping the Sabbath holy and doing no work on
that day, 25 then kings will come through the
gates of this city, kings who will sit on the
throne of David. They will come riding in
chariots or on horseback, escorted by their
officials, the people of Judah, and the citizens of Jerusalem. This city will be inhabited forever. [n]

26 People will come from the towns of
Judah and the villages around Jerusalem,
from the territory of Benjamin and the
foothills, from the hill country and the
Negeb, to bring holocausts and sacrifices,
grain offerings and incense and thank offerings, to the house of the LORD. 27 However, if
you do not listen to my commands to keep
the Sabbath day holy and to carry no burden
through the gates of Jerusalem on the
Sabbath day, then I will set fire to the gates,

i Ps 1:3; Ezek 47:12.—j Jer 3:17.—k Isa 5:19.—l Jer 16:19.—m Deut 4:9; Neh 13:15-21.—n Jer 22:4; Isa 58:14.

17:11 The *partridge* that hatches the eggs of another bird will see itself abandoned by these chicks.

17:19-27 This vehement defense of the law concerning the Sabbath rest is not in Jeremiah's style. The passage must therefore have been introduced after the Exile. The same idea is found in Neh 13:15-22: the happy or unhappy future of the nation depends on fidelity to this observance.

17:19 *Gate of Benjamin:* (Jer 37:13; 38:7), this was the most used gate; it faced north toward the lands of the tribe of Benjamin. One gate of the temple had the same name (Jer 20:2).

an unquenchable fire that will consume the
palaces of Jerusalem.[o]

CHAPTER 18

The Potter's House. 1 *This is the message
delivered by the LORD to Jeremiah. 2 "Arise
and go forth to the potter's house, and then I
will tell you what I have to say." 3 Therefore,
I proceeded to the potter's house, where I
found him working at his wheel. 4 Whenever
the vessel he was making of clay turned out
badly in his hands, he would use that clay to
remold it into another vessel as he saw fit.

5 Then the word of the LORD came to me:
6 Can I not do to you what this potter does, O
house of Israel? Like the clay in the hand of
the potter, so are you in my hand, O house of
Israel.[p] 7 On occasion I may threaten to
uproot, tear down, and destroy a particular
nation or kingdom. 8 However, should that
nation which I have threatened turn away
from its evil ways, I will then relent and not
inflict the disaster I had devised. 9 On anoth-
er occasion I may promise to build up and
plant a nation or kingdom. 10 However, if that
nation follows an evil path and refuses to
obey me, then I will cease to bestow upon it
the blessings that I had promised.

11 Therefore, now deliver this message to
the people of Judah and the inhabitants of
Jerusalem: Thus says the LORD: Be fore-
warned! I am preparing a disaster for you
and designing a plan against you. So now,
each one of you, turn away from your evil
pursuits and amend your conduct and your
actions. 12 However, they will reply, "It is no
use. We intend to continue our ways and fol-
low the wicked inclinations of our heart."[q]

Judah's Apostasy

13 Therefore, thus says the LORD:
Ask among the nations:
Who has ever heard anything like this?
The virgin Israel has done
a truly horrible thing.
14 Does the snow of Lebanon
ever disappear from its rocky slopes?
Do the torrents of gushing waters
ever cease to flow?
15 Yet my people have forgotten me;
they burn incense to worthless idols,
causing them to stumble
as they forsake ancient roads
to travel along unfamiliar paths.[r]
16 Their land will be laid waste,
an object of unending scorn.
Those who pass by will be appalled on beholding it
and shake their heads.
17 Like the east wind,
I will scatter them before their enemies.
On the day of their downfall
I will show them my back, not my face.

Another Prayer for Vengeance. 18 They then
raised a cry, "Let us devise a plot against
Jeremiah. We will still receive instruction
from the priests. Wise men will still offer us
counsel, and prophets will still proclaim the
word. Therefore, let us bring charges against
him and refuse to pay attention to anything
he says."[s]

19 Pay heed to me, O LORD,
and listen to what my adversaries are saying.
20 Should good be repaid with evil?
Now they are digging a pit for me.
Remember how I stood before you,
interceding on their behalf
and begging you to turn away your wrath from them.
21 Therefore, give their children over to famine
and abandon them to the power of the sword.[t]
Let their wives become childless and widowed;
let their men die of pestilence
and their young men be slain by the sword in battle.
22 May screams be heard from their houses
when you bring marauders upon them suddenly.
For they have dug a pit to catch me
and laid snares for my feet.
23 Yet you, O LORD, are fully aware
of all their murderous plots to slay me.
Do not pardon their guilt
or blot out their sin from your sight.
Let them be thrown down before you;
deal with them at the height of your anger.[u]

---

o Jer 22:5; Am 2:5.—p Isa 45:9; Mt 20:15.—q Jer 2:25; 7:24.—r Jer 2:32.—s Jer 11:19; Mal 2:7.—t Ps 109:9f; Isa 13:18.—u Ps 35:4; Neh 4:5.

18:1—20:6 A visit to a potter suggests to the prophet Jeremiah the idea that God manipulates history as a potter does the clay: he softens and shapes it with the motion of the wheel, and he casts aside the waste.

CHAPTER 19

Symbol of the Broken Jug. 1 Thus said the
LORD: Go forth and purchase a potter's
earthenware jug. Then take along with you
some of the elders of the people and some of
the priests, 2 and go forth to the Valley of
Ben-hinnom,* close to the entrance of the
Potsherd Gate. 3 There proclaim the words I
tell you: Hear the word of the LORD, O kings
of Judah and inhabitants of Jerusalem. This
is the message of the LORD of hosts, the God
of Israel: I am prepared to bring such disas-
ter upon this place that the ears of everyone
who hears of it will tingle.

4 For these people have forsaken me and
have profaned this place by offering sacri-
fices in it to foreign gods whom neither they
nor their ancestors nor the kings of Judah
ever knew. They have filled this place with
the blood of the innocent,[v] 5 building the
high places of Baal to sacrifice their sons as
burnt offerings to Baal. I never commanded
or mentioned such a thing, nor did it ever
enter my mind.

6 Therefore, the days are surely coming,
says the LORD, when this place will no longer
be called Topheth, or the Valley of Ben-
hinnom, but the Valley of Slaughter. 7 In this
place, I will make void the plans of Judah and
Jerusalem, and I will make them fall by the
sword before their enemies and by the hands
of those who are determined to slaughter
them. Their corpses I will give as food to the
birds of the sky and the beasts of the earth.

8 Moreover, I will make this city an object
of horror and a source of derision. Every
passerby will be horrified at the sight and be
amazed at the disaster it has incurred. 9 I
will make them eat the flesh of their sons
and daughters, and all will devour one
another's flesh during the siege because of
the incredible distress with which they have
been afflicted by their enemies and those
who seek their lives.[w]

10 Then you are to break the jug in the
presence of the men who have accompanied
you 11 and say to them: Thus says the LORD
of hosts: In the same way I will smash this
people and this city, as one smashes a pot-
ter's earthenware jug so that it can never be
repaired, and the dead will be buried in
Topheth until no further space for burial
remains.

12 This is what I am determined to do with
this place and its inhabitants, says the LORD.
I will make this city like Topheth.[x] 13 And the
houses of Jerusalem and those of the kings of
Judah will be defiled like this place, Topheth,
all of the houses upon whose roofs they
burned incense to all the host of heaven and
poured out libations to other gods.

14 When Jeremiah returned from Topheth,
where the LORD had sent him to prophesy,
he stood in the court of the LORD's house and
proclaimed to all the people, 15 "Thus says
the LORD of hosts, the God of Israel: I am
now prepared to inflict upon this city and
upon all its towns the total disaster with
which I threatened it, because they have
remained steadfast in their stubbornness
and refused to listen to my words."[y]

CHAPTER 20

1 When the priest Pashhur, the son of
Immer, who was the chief officer in the
house of the LORD, heard Jeremiah pro-
claiming this prophecy, 2 he ordered him to
be scourged, and then placed him in the
stocks at the Upper Gate of Benjamin in the
house of the LORD.

3 The next morning, after Pashhur had
released Jeremiah from the stocks, Jeremiah
said to him, "The LORD's name for you is not
Pashhur but 'Terror-on-Every-Side.' 4 For
thus says the LORD, 'I will make you a terror
to yourself and to all your friends. They will
fall by the sword of their enemies before
your very eyes. And I will deliver all Judah to
the king of Babylon, and he will take the peo-
ple captive and carry them off to Babylon or
put them to the sword.

5 " 'All the wealth of this city, all of its cher-
ished possessions, and all of the treasures of
the kings of Judah I will hand over as plun-
der to their enemies who will seize it and
carry it off to Babylon.[z] 6 Furthermore, you,
Pashhur, and all the members of your
household will be taken into captivity and
led off to Babylon. There you will die, and
there you will be buried, you and all your
friends, because you have prophesied falsely
to them.' "

---

v Deut 28:20; 2 Ki 21:16.—w Deut 28:53; Lam 4:10.—x 2 Ki 23:10.—y Jer 7:26.—z Jer 3:24; 2 Ki 20:17.

19:2 *The Valley of Ben-hinnom:* the scene of the prophet's symbolic action (see Jer 7:32—8:2) had been declared unholy by King Josiah and had begun to be the rubbish dump for the city. It would later be known as the Valley of Gehenna.

Jeremiah's Confession*

7 O LORD, you deceived me,
and I allowed myself to be deceived.
You were too powerful for me,
and you have prevailed.
All day long I am an object of ridicule;
everyone mocks me. [a]
8 Whenever I speak, I must cry out;
my message is violence and destruction.
For the word of the LORD has caused me to endure
reproach and derision all day long.
9 If I say, "I will not mention him
or speak any longer in his name,"
within me I experience a fire burning in my heart
and imprisoned in my bones.
I am weary holding it in,
and I can no longer do so. [b]
10 For I hear many whispering,
"Terror surrounds us.
Denounce him! Let us denounce him!"
All those who were my close friends
are waiting for me to stumble, saying,
"Perhaps we can trick him,
and we will be able to prevail
and take our revenge against him." [c]
11 But the LORD is at my side
like a mighty warrior.
Therefore, my persecutors will stumble,
and they will not prevail.
Because of their failure,
they will be greatly shamed,
and the disgrace that they will endure
will be everlasting and unforgettable.
12 O LORD of hosts, you test the righteous
and probe the mind and the heart.
Let me behold your retribution on them,
for to you I have committed my cause. [d]
13 Sing to the LORD;
praise the LORD.
For he has rescued the life of the poor
from the power of the wicked.
14 Cursed be the day
on which I was born!
May the day when my mother bore me
be forever unblessed.
15 Cursed be the man
who brought the news to my father.
"A child, a son, has been born to you,"
thereby bringing great joy to his heart.
16 Let that man be like the cities
that the LORD overthrew without mercy.
Let him hear the cry of warning in the morning
and shouts of battle at noon [e]
17 because he did not kill me in the womb.
Then my mother would have been my grave,
with her womb confining me forever.
18 Why did I come forth from the womb
to see toil and sorrow
and spend my days in shame? [f]

III: PROPHECIES IN THE LAST YEARS OF JERUSALEM*

CHAPTER 21

God's Response to Zedekiah's Prayer. 1 This
is the word that came to Jeremiah from the
LORD when King Zedekiah sent to him
Pashhur, the son of Malchiah, and the priest
Zephaniah, the son of Maaseiah, with this
request, 2 "Please inquire of the LORD on our
behalf, because Nebuchadnezzar, the king of
Babylon, is making war against us. Perhaps
the LORD will perform one of his wonderful
works for us as he has done in the past and
force him to withdraw."
3 However, Jeremiah replied to them, "This
is what you are to say to Zedekiah: 4 Thus
says the LORD, the God of Israel: I will turn
against you the weapons of war with which
you are fighting against the king of Babylon
and against the Chaldeans who are besieging
you outside the walls, and I will gather them
together in the center of the city. 5 I myself will
fight against you with outstretched hand and
mighty arm, in anger, fury, and great rage. [g]
6 "I will strike down the inhabitants of this
city, both man and beast. They will die as the

a Ps 22:8; Mic 3:8.—b Jer 6:11; Job 32:18-20.—c Ps 31:13; Lk 11:53.—d Jer 11:20; Ps 54:7.—e Jer 18:22; Gen 19:25; Isa 13:19.—f Jer 3:25; Job 14:1.—g Isa 63:10; Lam 2:3.

20:7-18 These pages from the prophet's personal diary were scrupulously preserved by his disciples and slipped, here and there, in his book. We have already met these "confessions" of the prophet (Jer 11:18—12:6; 15:10-21; 17:12-18; 18:18-23); here, three of the most direct and effective passages are introduced.

21:1—23:8 While the star of Nebuchadnezzar is rising on the horizon, the death of Josiah in 609 B.C. sounds the death knell for the kingdom of Judah and the monarchy. The corruption, inexperience, or weakness of Josiah's successors only exacerbate the political and religious crisis. Jeremiah passes a blunt judgment on the successive kings as unfaithful pastors who have allowed their flock to perish (Ezek 34). The only thing left to do is to wait with trust for the day when the Lord takes pity on his flock and installs on the throne the true Son of David, who will see to right and justice in the land.

result of a terrible plague. 7 After that, says
the LORD, I will deliver King Zedekiah of
Judah and his servants and the people, all
those in this city who have managed to survive pestilence, war, and famine, into the
hands of King Nebuchadnezzar of Babylon,
and into the hands of their enemies and
those who are determined to slay them. He
will put them to the sword and show them
no pity or mercy or compassion.

8 "You are to say further to this people:
Thus says the LORD: Behold, I am offering
you a choice between the way of life and the
way of death. [h] 9 Whoever remains in this city
will die by the sword, by famine, or by pestilence, but those who leave and surrender to
the Chaldeans who are now besieging you
will survive and escape with their lives. 10 For
I am determined that this city must endure
disaster and not revel in prosperity, says the
LORD. It will be handed over to the king of
Babylon, and he will burn it to the ground."

Prophecies Concerning the Kings

11 To the royal houses of Judah, say:
Listen to the word of the LORD.
12 O house of David,
thus says the LORD:
Dispense justice each morning
and deliver the victim from his oppressor,
lest my wrath burst forth like fire
that burns and cannot be quenched
because of your evil deeds.
13* Beware! I am against you,
O residents of the valley,
O rock of the plain, says the LORD,
you who say, "Who can possibly attack us
and penetrate our places of refuge?"
14 I will punish you, says the LORD,
as your deeds deserve.
I will kindle a fire in your forests,
and it will devour everything around it. [i]

CHAPTER 22

1 Thus said the LORD to me: Go down to
the palace of the king of Judah and there
deliver this message: 2 Listen to the word of
the LORD, O king of Judah, as you sit on the
throne of David—you, your officials, and
your people who enter through these gates.
3 Thus says the LORD: Act justly and with
righteousness, and rescue the victim from
the hand of his oppressor. Do not ill-treat
aliens, orphans, and widows, or show violence toward them, or shed innocent blood
in this place. [j]

4 If you will indeed be faithful in carrying
out these commands, then the kings who
succeed to the throne of David will continue
to enter through the gates of this palace, riding in chariots or on horseback—they, their
officials, and their people. 5 But if you do not
obey these commands, then I swear by
myself, says the LORD, that this palace will
become a ruin.

6 For thus says the LORD concerning the
palace of the king of Judah:

Although you are like Gilead to me,
like a peak of Lebanon,
I swear that I will turn you into a desert,
an uninhabited city.
7 I will send forth destroyers to annihilate
you,
each man equipped with his weapons.
They will cut down your finest cedars
and cast them into the fire. [k]

8 People from many nations will pass by
this city, and they will ask one another, "Why
has the LORD dealt in this manner with this
great city?" [l] 9 And the answer will be given,
"Because they abandoned their covenant
with the LORD, their God, in order to worship other gods and serve them."

Jehoahaz

10 Do not weep for the man who is dead;
mourn not for him.
Weep rather for him who has gone into
exile,
for he will never return again
to see the land of his birth. [m]

11 For thus says the LORD about Shallum,
the son of King Josiah of Judah, who succeeded his father Josiah as king and was
forced to leave this place, "He will never
return. 12 Rather, he will die in the place
where he was sent into exile, and he will
never see this land again."

Jehoiakim

13 Woe to the man who builds his house
without righteousness
and his upper room with injustice,

h Deut 30:15, 19.—i 2 Chr 36:19; Isa 3:11.—j Jer 21:12; Ezek 45:9.—k Jer 21:14; Isa 10:3.—l Deut 29:24.—m Jer 44:14.

21:13-14 Jerusalem is built on a seemingly impregnable hill. *Forests* is a picturesque name for a great gallery of cedar columns in the royal palace; the gallery was known as the "Forest of Lebanon" (see 1 Ki 7:2).

who forces his neighbors to work for nothing
and gives them no recompense for their labor, [n]
14 who says, "I will build myself a spacious home
with large upper rooms,"
and who inserts windows in it,
panels it with cedar,
and paints it with vermilion.

15 Are you any better a king
because your cedar is so splendid?
Did not your father have enough to eat and drink?
But because he did what was right and just,
all went well with him. [o]
16 Because he dispensed justice to the poor and needy
things continued to go well for him.
Is this not what it means to know me?
asks the LORD.
17 But your eyes and your heart
are concerned only with your own interests;
you do not hesitate to shed innocent blood
and to perpetrate oppression and violence.

18 Therefore, thus says the LORD concerning King Jehoiakim of Judah, the son of Josiah:

They will not lament for him, saying,
"Alas, my brother!" or "Alas, sister!"
They will not mourn for him.
"Alas, my master!" "Alas, his splendor!" [p]
19 He will be buried like a dead donkey
dragged forth and cast out
beyond the gates of Jerusalem. [q]

Jeconiah

20 Go up to Lebanon and cry out;
lift up your voice in Bashan.
Cry out from Abarim,
for all your lovers have been crushed.*
21 I spoke to you when you enjoyed prosperity,
but you replied, "I will not listen."
You have behaved this way from your youth,
refusing to listen to my voice.
22 The wind will carry away all your shepherds,
and your lovers will go off into captivity.
Then you will be ashamed and blush
because of all your wickedness.
23 You who live in Lebanon
and make your nest among the cedars,
how you will groan when anguish overcomes you,
pangs like those of a woman in labor. [r]

24 As I live, says the LORD, even if you, King
Coniah of Judah, the son of Jehoiakim, were
the signet ring on my right hand, I would still
tear you off 25 and deliver you into the hands
of those who seek your life, into the hands of
those whom you fear, into the hands of
Nebuchadnezzar, king of Babylon, and into
the hands of the Chaldeans. 26 I will fling you
and the mother who bore you into another
country, where neither of you were born, and
there you both will die. [s] 27 You will never
return to the country to which you so desperately long to return.

28 Is this man Coniah a despised damaged pot,
a vessel in which no one is interested?
Why are he and his offspring cast out
and thrown into a land
that they know nothing about?
29 O land, land, land,
hear the word of the LORD!
30 Thus says the LORD:
Designate this man as childless,
a man who will not prosper during his lifetime.
No descendant of his will succeed;
none will sit on the throne of David
or rule again over Judah. [t]

CHAPTER 23

Messianic Oracles. 1 Woe to the shepherds who lead astray and scatter the sheep of my pasture, says the LORD. 2 Therefore, this is what the LORD, the God of Israel, has to say in regard to the shepherds who shepherd my people: You have scattered my flock and driven them away, and you showed not the slightest concern about taking care of them. Therefore, I will not hesitate to punish you for your evil deeds, says the LORD. [u]

n Mic 3:10; Hab 2:9, 12.—o Jer 7:5; 2 Ki 23:25.—p Jer 34:5; 1 Ki 13:30.—q Jer 36:30.—r Jer 4:31; 6:24.—s 2 Ki 24:15.—t 1 Chr 3:16f; Mt 1:12.—u Ezek 34:4ff.

22:20 The mountainous regions named dominate the Palestinian landscape and are places from which the proclamation may spread everywhere.

3 I myself will gather the remnant of my flock from all the lands where I have driven them, and I will bring them back to their meadows where they will be fruitful and multiply. 4 I will appoint shepherds for them who will treat them kindly, so that they will no longer fear or experience terror, nor will any be discovered missing, says the LORD.

5 Behold, the days are coming, says the LORD,
when I will raise up a righteous branch
from the line of David.
He will reign as king and rule wisely
and ensure justice and righteousness in the land. [v]
6 In his days Judah will live in safety,
and Israel will dwell in security.
And this is the name that will be given to him:
"The LORD Our Righteousness."

7 Therefore, the days are coming, says the LORD, when people will no longer say, "As the LORD lives who brought the Israelites out of the land of Egypt," 8 but rather, "As the LORD lives who brought forth the offspring of the house of Israel up from the land of the north and out of all the lands where he had dispersed them." Then they will again inhabit their own land.

The False Prophets*

9 As for the prophets,
my heart is broken within me,
and all my bones never cease to tremble.
I have become like a drunken man,
like someone overcome with wine,
because of the LORD
and because of his holy words.
10 For the land swarms with adulterers;
because of them the country mourns
and the pastures in the desert have withered. [w]
11 Both the prophets and the priests are godless;
even in my own house have I observed their wickedness,
says the LORD.
12 Therefore, they will find that the paths they travel
will be slippery beneath their feet;
in the darkness where they are driven,
they will fall headlong.
For I will inflict disaster upon them
in the year of their punishment,
says the LORD. [x]
13 Among the prophets of Samaria
I beheld this repulsive deed:
they prophesied in the name of Baal
and led my people astray.
14 But among the prophets of Jerusalem
I have seen deeds that are even more shocking:
they commit adultery and persist in lying
and uphold those who are evil
so that no one turns away from wickedness.
To me they have all become like Sodom,
and its inhabitants are like Gomorrah.

15 Therefore, thus says the LORD of hosts in regard to the prophets:

I intend to give them wormwood to eat
and force them to drink poisoned water.
For from the prophets of Jerusalem
ungodliness has spread throughout the land. [y]

16 Thus says the LORD of hosts:
Do not listen to the words of the prophets;
their prophecies are designed to delude you.
They concoct visions from their own minds
and not from the mouth of the LORD.
17 To those who despise the word of the LORD
they say, "Peace will be yours."
To those who follow their own stubborn inclinations
they say, "No harm will befall you." [z]

18 Yet which of them has stood in the council of the LORD
to see or to hear his word?
Which of them has heeded his word
and proclaimed it?
19 Behold the storm of the LORD!
His wrath bursts forth

v Jer 33:14-16; Isa 4:2; 11:1-5.—w Jer 5:7f; 9:2.—x Ps 35:6.—y Jer 8:14; 9:15.—z Jer 5:12; Mic 3:11.

23:9-40 Jeremiah is heartsick at these professional prophets who flatter the people instead of shaking them up, and who take their dreams as the word of God or accommodate their message to the tastes of the day.

like a frightening tempest
that whirls around the heads of the
wicked.[a]
20 The anger of the LORD will not subside
until he has fully accomplished
the purposes he has in mind.
When the time comes,
you will understand this clearly.
21 I did not send these prophets,
yet they went forth in haste.
I did not speak to them,
yet they prophesied.
22 But if they had stood in my council,
they would have then proclaimed my
words to my people
and caused them to turn back from their
evil ways
and from the wickedness of their
deeds.
23 The LORD asks:
Am I a God only when I am near at
hand,
but not when I am far away?[b]
24 Can someone hide in a secret place
so that I cannot see him?
Do I not fill heaven and earth?

25 I have heard what the prophets say who
prophesy lies in my name. "I have had a
dream," they cry out. "I have had a dream."
26 How much longer must we endure
prophets who prophesy lies and proclaim
their own delusions? 27 By means of the
dreams that they relate to one another, they
believe that they will make my people forget
my name, just as their fathers forgot my
name and replaced it with Baal.[c] 28 Let the
prophet who has a dream relate his dream,
but let the one who receives my word deliv-
er it truthfully.

What does straw have in common with
wheat?
asks the LORD.
29 Is not my word like fire, says the LORD,
like a hammer shattering a rock?

30 Therefore, says the LORD, I have set
myself in opposition to the prophets who
steal my words from one another.[d] 31 I am
against those prophets who concoct their
own prophecies and then assert, "Thus says
the LORD." 32 I am against those prophets
who prophesy lying dreams, says the LORD,
and then recount them, thereby leading my
people astray with their lies and reckless
bragging. They have not received any com-
mission from me, and so they are of no ben-
efit to this people in any way, says the LORD.

33 And when this people or a prophet or a
priest asks you, "What is the burden of the
LORD?" you are to reply, "You are the bur-
den, and I will cast you off," says the LORD.
34 If a prophet or a priest or anyone else
speaks of "the burden of the LORD," I will
punish that man and his household.

35 Therefore, when speaking to one anoth-
er, you are to ask, "What answer did the
LORD give?" or "What did the LORD say?"
36 But you must never again speak of "the
burden of the LORD," because each man's
word becomes his own burden, and you
therefore pervert the words of the living
God, the LORD of hosts, our God.[e]

37 Therefore, you are to ask a prophet,
"What answer has the LORD given?" or "What
has the LORD said?" 38 But if you say "the bur-
den of the LORD," the LORD will reply,
"Because you have used the words 'the bur-
den of the LORD' when I forbade you to use
that expression, 39 therefore, I will lift you up
and cast you away from my presence, both
you and the city that I gave to you and your
ancestors. 40 And I will inflict upon you ever-
lasting disgrace and eternal and unforget-
table shame."[f]

CHAPTER 24*

The Good and Bad Figs. 1 The LORD showed
me two baskets of figs placed in front of the
temple of the LORD.[g] This occurred after
King Nebuchadnezzar of Babylon had exiled
from Jerusalem Jeconiah, the son of Jehoi-
akim, the king of Judah, and the princes of
Judah, the artisans, and the skilled workers,
and brought them to Babylon. 2 One basket
contained excellent figs that tend to ripen
early; the other basket had figs of an
extremely poor quality, so bad that they
could not be eaten. 3 The LORD said to me,
"What do you see, Jeremiah?"[h] "Figs," I
answered. "The good figs are superb, but the
poor ones are so bad that they are not fit to
eat."

4 Then the word of the LORD came to me:
5 Thus says the LORD, the God of Israel: Just
as these figs are good, so I will regard as

a Jer 25:32; 30:23.—b Ps 139:1-10.—c Jdg 3:7; 8:33.—d Deut 18:20; Ezek 13:8.—e Jer 10:10.—f Jer 52:3.—g Am 8:1.—h Jer 1:11, 13.

24:1-10 After the first deportation (598 B.C.), Jeremiah intervenes against those who want to get revenge: all hopes for the future now rest not on such people but on the exiles.

good the exiles from Judah whom I have sent
away from this place to the land of the
Chaldeans. 6 I will watch over them carefully
to ensure their welfare, and I will bring them
back to this land. I will build them up and
not tear them down. I will plant them and
not uproot them.[i] 7 I will give them a heart
that will enable them to know that I am the
LORD. They will be my people and I will be
their God, for they will return to me with
their whole heart.

8 As for the bad figs that are so dreadful that
they cannot be eaten, thus says the LORD: In
the same way I will treat King Zedekiah of
Judah and his princes, the remnant of Je-
rusalem remaining in this land, and those
who live in the land of Egypt.[j] 9 I will make
them an object of horror to all the kingdoms
of the earth, a reproach and a byword, a taunt
and a curse, in all the places where I will drive
them. 10 And I will send against them the
sword, famine, and pestilence, until they have
completely vanished from the land that I gave
to them and their ancestors.[k]

CHAPTER 25*

Seventy Years of Captivity.* 1 This is the word
that came to Jeremiah concerning all the
people of Judah, in the fourth year of King
Jehoiakim of Judah, the son of Josiah, which
was the first year of King Nebuchadnezzar of
Babylon. 2 The prophet Jeremiah thus spoke
as follows to all the people of Judah and all
the inhabitants of Jerusalem:

3 For twenty-three years—from the thir-
teenth year of King Josiah of Judah, the son
of Amon, until this very day—the word of the
LORD has come to me, and I have spoken to
you unceasingly, but you have not listened.[l]
4 And though the LORD continued to send all
his servants the prophets to you again and
again, you refused to listen or to pay any
heed to their message when they warned,
5 "If you turn back, each of you, from your
evil ways and your wicked deeds, says the
LORD, you can remain in the land that I have
given to you and to your fathers forever. 6 If
you do not follow other gods to serve and
worship them, and you do not provoke me
with what your hands have made, then I will
not harm you. 7 But you have not listened to
me, says the LORD, and thus you have pro-
voked me to anger with your handiwork to
your own harm."[m]

8 Therefore, thus says the LORD of hosts:
Because you have not listened to my words,
9 I intend to summon all the tribes of the
north, says the LORD, as well as my servant
Nebuchadnezzar, the king of Babylon, and I
will bring them against this land and its
inhabitants and against all the surrounding
nations. I will totally destroy them and make
them an object of horror and scorn and
everlasting disgrace. 10 No longer will there
emerge from them the sounds of rejoicing
and gladness, the voices of bride and bride-
groom, the sound of the millstones and the
light of the lamp.[n] 11 This entire country will
become a wasteland of desolation, and these
nations will be enslaved to the king of
Babylon for seventy years.

12 However, at the end of those seventy
years, says the LORD, I will punish the king of
Babylon and that nation, the land of the
Chaldeans, for their guilt, and I will turn it
into a desolate wasteland. 13 * I will inflict
upon that land all the scourges that I threat-
ened against it, everything written in this
book and prophesied by Jeremiah against all
the nations. 14 Mighty nations and powerful
kings will reduce them to a life of slavery,
and thus I will requite them as their deeds
and their handiwork deserve.[o]

The Cup of Wrath on the Nations. 15 For these
are the words that the LORD, the God of
Israel, proclaimed to me, "Take this cup of
the wine of wrath from my hand and com-
mand all the nations to whom I send you to
drink from it. 16 After they drink, they will
stagger and become mad because of the
sword that I am inflicting upon them."[p]

17 Therefore, I took the cup from the hand
of the LORD and ordered all the nations to
whom the LORD had sent me to drink from
it: 18 Jerusalem and the towns of Judah, its
kings and officials, to transform them into a
desolate ruin and a desert, an object of
ridicule and cursing, as they are today;

---

i Jer 12:15.—j Jer 29:17.—k Jer 21:9; 27:8; Isa 51:19.—l Jer 1:2; 2 Chr 34:1-3.—m Jer 7:17ff.—n Ezek 26:13; Rev 18:22f.—o Jer 50:9, 41f; 51:6, 24.—p Jer 51:7.

25:1-38 The end of the seventh century B.C. saw the clash of great empires. Assyria and Egypt made way for Babylon. The year 605 B.C. was one of the most important in the history of the ancient East: Nebuchadnezzar defeated Egypt at Carchemish.

25:1-14 An exile is announced that will last for seventy years. The number is not intended as strictly arithmetical but represents a period longer than the average duration of human life.

25:13-29 This passage probably served as a conclusion to the oracles against the nations, which have been removed from their proper place and put at the end of the Book (chs. 46–51).

[19] Pharaoh, the king of Egypt, his servants,
his officials, and all his people, [20] with the
various groupings of people: all the kings of
the land of Uz; all the kings of the land of the
Philistines—Ashkelon, Gaza, Ekron, and the
remnant of Ashdod;[q] [21] Edom, Moab, and
the Ammonites; [22] all the kings of Tyre, all
the kings of Sidon, and all the kings of the
coastland across the sea; [23] Dedan, Tema,
Buz, and all who have shaven temples; [24] all
the kings of Arabia and all the kings of the
mixed peoples that dwell in the desert; [25] all
the kings of Zimri, all the kings of Elam, and
all the kings of Media; [26] all the kings of the
north, both close neighbors and those who
are distant from each other—in other words,
all the kingdoms on the face of the earth.
And, last of all, the king of Sheshach* shall
drink.

[27] Then say to them: Thus says the LORD of
hosts, the God of Israel: Drink! Get drunk
and vomit! Fall down, never to rise again,
because of the sword that I am sending
against you. [28] Should they refuse to accept
the cup from your hand and drink, then you
are to say to them: Thus says the LORD of
hosts: You must drink![r] [29] Behold, I am
beginning to bring disaster on the city that is
called by my name. Do you believe that you
can possibly avoid punishment? You will not
go unpunished, for I am summoning a sword
against all the inhabitants of the earth, says
the LORD of hosts.

[30] Therefore, prophesy against them all
these words and proclaim to them:

The LORD roars from on high;
he thunders from his holy dwelling place.
He will roar mightily against his fold;
like those who tread the grapes, she shouts aloud
against all the inhabitants of the earth.[s]

[31] The uproar will resound to the ends of the earth,
for the LORD has an indictment against the nations,
he will pass judgment upon all mankind
and put the wicked to the sword.
This the LORD has sworn.

[32] Thus says the LORD of hosts:
Behold, disaster is spreading
from nation to nation,
and a mighty storm has been unleashed
from the farthest corners of the earth.

[33] Those whom the LORD has slain on that
day will be scattered from one end of the
earth to the other. No one will mourn for
them. Nor will they be gathered up for buri-
al. Rather, they will become like dung spread
over the surface of the ground.[t]

[34] Wail, you shepherds, and weep aloud;
roll in the dust, you leaders of the flock.
The time for you to be slaughtered has arrived;
you will fall and be shattered
like a valuable vase.

[35] The shepherds have no place to seek refuge;
the leaders of the flock have no way of escape.[u]

[36] Listen to the cry of the shepherds
and the wails from the lords of the flock.
For the LORD has ravaged their pasture,
[37] and their peaceful sheepfolds lie in ruins
because of the fierce anger of the LORD.

[38] Like a lion he has abandoned his lair,
for their land has become a desolate waste
because of the sword of the oppressor
and the fierce anger of the LORD.[v]

CHAPTER 26

Jeremiah's Arrest and Conviction.* [1] *At
the beginning of the reign of King Jehoiakim
of Judah, the son of Josiah, this word came
from the LORD to Jeremiah: [2] Thus says the
LORD: Stand in the court of the LORD's house
and speak to all the people from the towns of
Judah who come to worship in the house
of the LORD. Tell them everything I order you
to say, without omitting a single word.[w]
[3] Perhaps they will listen and all of them will

q Jer 47:1-7; Job 1:1.—r Jer 49:12.—s Isa 42:13; Am 1:2.—t Jer 16:4, 6; Isa 66:16.—u Jer 32:4.—v Jer 4:7.—w Jer 7:1ff.

25:26 *Sheshach:* a cabalistic transcription of the name "Babylon."

26:1—35:19 This second section of the Book is made up of discourses and oracles from different periods that are inserted into biographical narratives from the pen of Baruch, Jeremiah's secretary. Out of present trials, a new destiny for the nation will slowly emerge.

26:1-19 This account gives a concrete example of Jeremiah's preaching, as he attacks the false security that relies on the temple and the holy city as if these were God's inviolable dwelling place despite all the sins of Israel. The prophet's sacrilegious words are scandalous! People want to lynch him.

turn from their evil ways, causing me to
relent in my determination to inflict disaster
upon them because of their evil deeds.

4 Say to them: Thus says the LORD: If you
refuse to listen to me and to live according to
my law that I have set before you, 5 and if you
fail to heed the words of my servants the
prophets, whom I send to you time and again
even though you do not listen to them, 6 then
I will treat this house like Shiloh, and I will
make this city an object of cursing for all the
nations of the earth. [x]

7 The priests, the prophets, and all the peo-
ple heard Jeremiah speak these words in the
house of the LORD. 8 But when Jeremiah had
finished saying everything that the LORD had
commanded him to proclaim to all the peo-
ple, then the priests, the prophets, and all the
people seized him and cried out, "You will be
put to death for this. 9 Why have you prophe-
sied in the LORD's name that this house will
be like Shiloh and that this city will be deso-
late and deserted?" And all the people
crowded around Jeremiah in the house of the
LORD.

10 When the high officials of Judah heard
what was happening, they came up from the
king's palace to the house of the LORD and
took their places there at the entry of the
New Gate* of the house of the LORD. 11 The
priests and the prophets then addressed
the officials and all the people, saying, "This
man deserves to be condemned to death
because he has prophesied against this city
all the things that you heard with your own
ears."

12 Then Jeremiah replied to all the officials
and all the people, saying, "The LORD himself
sent me to prophesy against this house and
this city all the things you have heard. 13 Now,
therefore, if you amend your ways and your
actions and listen to the word of the LORD,
your God, the LORD will relent in his deter-
mination to inflict the disaster that he has
decreed for you. [y] 14 As for me, I am in your
hands. Do with me whatever seems right and
proper to you. 15 However, you can be certain
that if you put me to death, you will bring the
guilt of innocent blood upon yourselves and
upon this city and its inhabitants. For truly
the LORD sent me to speak all these things for
you to hear."

16 Then the officials and all the people said
to the priests and the prophets, "This man
does not deserve to be sentenced to death, for
he has spoken to us in the name of the LORD,
our God." 17 And some of the elders of the
land came forward and said to all the assem-
bled people, 18 "Micah of Moresheth, who
prophesied during the days of King Hezekiah
of Judah, proclaimed this to all the people of
Judah: Thus says the LORD of hosts:

Zion will become a plowed field,
  Jerusalem will become a heap of ruins,
  and the temple mount a wooded
    height. [z]

19 "Did King Hezekiah of Judah and the
people of Judah put him to death for this?
Rather, did they not fear the LORD and
entreat his favor, and did the LORD then not
revoke the disaster with which he had threat-
ened them? Are we not on the verge of inflict-
ing a terrible disaster upon ourselves?"

The Prophet Uriah's Fate. 20 There was also
another man who used to prophesy in the
name of the LORD, Uriah, the son of She-
maiah, from Kiriath-jearim. He prophesied
exactly the same things against this city and
this land just as Jeremiah had done. 21 When
King Jehoiakim, with all his warriors and
officials, heard his words, the king was deter-
mined to put Uriah to death. However, Uriah
learned of this plot and fled in fear to Egypt.

22 Then King Jehoiakim sent Elnathan, the
son of Achbor, to Egypt with some other
men. 23 They brought back Uriah from Egypt
and took him to King Jehoiakim, who had
him put to the sword and consigned his dead
body into the burial place used for common
people.

24 However Ahikam, the son of Shaphan,
gave his support to Jeremiah, and as a result,
Jeremiah was not handed over to the people
to be put to death. [a]

CHAPTER 27

Jeremiah's Message. 1 *At the beginning of
the reign of King Zedekiah of Judah, the son

x Jer 25:3-4.—y Jer 7:3; 18:11.—z Mic 1:1; 3:12.—a Jer 39:14.

26:10 The *New Gate* is mentioned only here and in Jer 36:10.

27:1—29:32 After the first disaster of 598 B.C., national self-respect was humbled. In this troubled atmosphere, short-sighted politicians cooked up their intrigues and found willing ears. Soon a spirit of revenge swept through Judah and its neighbors; plans and plots were made with Egypt. Jeremiah saw things more clearly, and he advised a loyal submission to the Chaldeans.

Jeremiah rested his hopes on the community in exile. The center of gravity of the future Israel was no longer Jerusalem but Babylon, where another prophet, Ezekiel, was already at work. Out of trials a new people will arise.

of Josiah, this word came to Jeremiah from
the LORD: 2 Thus said the LORD to me:
Collect for yourself some straps and cross-
bars and put them on your neck as a yoke.
3 Then send word to the kings of Edom, of
Moab, of the Ammonites, of Tyre, and of
Sidon, through the envoys who have come to
Jerusalem to visit Zedekiah, the king of
Judah.

4 Give them the following message for their
masters: Thus says the LORD of hosts, the
God of Israel: This is what you are to say to
your masters: 5 It was I who, by my great
power and my outstretched arm, made the
earth as well as the people and the animals
that inhabit the earth, and I can give it to
whomever I wish.

6 Now, at the present time, I have given all
these lands to my servant King Nebuchad-
nezzar of Babylon, and I have even made the
wild animals subject to him.[b] 7 All nations
will serve him and his son and his grandson,
until the time of his land will also come, and
mighty nations and great kings will make
him their slave. 8 But in the meantime, if any
nation or kingdom will not serve King
Nebuchadnezzar of Babylon or submit its
neck under the yoke of the king of Babylon,
then I will punish that nation with the sword,
with famine, and with pestilence, says the
LORD, until I have ensured their destruction
by his hand.

9 You, therefore, must not listen to your
prophets, your diviners, your dreamers, your
soothsayers, and your sorcerers when they
say to you that you are not to serve the king
of Babylon.[c] 10 For they are prophesying a lie
to you, as a result of which you will be
removed far away from your land. I will drive
you out, and you will perish. 11 However, if a
nation is prepared to submit its neck to the
yoke of the king of Babylon and serve him, I
will leave it in peace on its own land, says the
LORD, to till it and live there.

12 I addressed the identical message to
King Zedekiah of Judah: Submit your necks
to the yoke of the king of Babylon. Serve him
and his people, and you will live. 13 Why
should you and your people die by the sword,
by famine, and by pestilence, as the LORD has
promised to any nation that will not serve the
king of Babylon? 14 Do not listen to the words
of those prophets who are urging you not to
serve the king of Babylon, for they are proph-
esying lies to you.[d] 15 I have not sent them,
says the LORD, but they are prophesying
falsely in my name. As a result, I will drive
you out, and you will perish, as will all the
prophets who are prophesying to you.

16 [e] Then I spoke to the priests and all the
prophets as follows: Thus says the LORD: Do
not listen to the words of your prophets who
say, "In a very short time, the vessels of the
house of the LORD will be brought back from
Babylon." They are prophesying lies to you.
17 Refuse to listen to them. Serve the king of
Babylon, and you will save your lives. Why
should this city become a pile of ruins?

18 If they are truly prophets and the word
of the LORD is really with them, then they
should be pleading with the LORD of hosts
that the vessels that remain in the house of
the LORD, in the house of the king of Judah,
and in Jerusalem will not be carried away to
Babylon.

19 For thus says the LORD of hosts con-
cerning the pillars, the sea,* the stands,
and the rest of the vessels that remain in
this city, 20 which King Nebuchadnezzar of
Babylon did not carry away when he took
into exile from Jerusalem to Babylon King
Jeconiah of Judah, the son of Jehoiakim,
along with all the nobles of Judah and
Jerusalem. 21 Thus says the LORD of hosts,
the God of Israel, in regard to the vessels
that still remain in the house of the LORD,
in the house of the king of Judah, and in
Jerusalem: 22 [f] They will be carried off to
Babylon, and there they will remain, until
the day when I turn my attention to them,
says the LORD. Then I will bring them back
and restore them to this place.

CHAPTER 28

Breaking the Yokes. 1 During that same
year, at the beginning of the reign of King
Zedekiah of Judah, in the fifth month of the
fourth year, the prophet Hananiah, the son
of Azzur, from Gibeon, said to the prophet
Jeremiah in the house of the LORD in the
presence of the priests and all the people,
2 "Thus says the LORD of hosts, the God of
Israel: I will break the yoke of the king of
Babylon. 3 Within two years I will bring back
to this place all the vessels of the house of the
LORD that King Nebuchadnezzar of Babylon

b Jer 25:9; 28:14; Ezek 29:18-20.—c Deut 18:10; Isa 8:19.—d Jer 14:14; Ezek 13:22.—e Jer 28:3; 2 Chr 36:7, 10.—f 2 Ki 25:13; 2 Chr 36:18.

27:19 *The sea:* the great vessel of water in the temple (see 1 Ki 7:23-25).

took away from this place and carried off to Babylon. 4 I will also bring back to this place King Jeconiah of Judah, the son of Jehoiakim, and all the exiles of Judah who went to Babylon, says the LORD, for I will break the yoke of the king of Babylon."[g]

5 Then the prophet Jeremiah replied to the prophet Hananiah in the presence of the priests and all the people who were standing in the house of the LORD. 6 He said, "Amen. May the LORD do so. May the LORD fulfill the words that you have prophesied by bringing the vessels of the house of the LORD and all the exiles back from Babylon to this place. 7 But now, listen carefully to what I am going to say for you and all the people to hear. 8 The prophets who preceded you and me in ancient times prophesied war, famine, and pestilence for many countries and for great kingdoms. 9 However, the prophet who prophesies peace can be recognized as one who has been truly sent by God only when his word comes true.[h]

10 Then the prophet Hananiah took the yoke from the neck of the prophet Jeremiah and broke it, 11 as he announced in the presence of all the people, "Thus says the LORD: This is how I will break the yoke of King Nebuchadnezzar of Babylon from the neck of the nations within two years." On hearing this, the prophet Jeremiah departed.

12 A short time after the prophet Hananiah had removed the yoke from the neck of the prophet Jeremiah and broken it, the word of the LORD came to Jeremiah, 13 "Go to Hananiah and tell him this: Thus says the LORD: You have broken a wooden yoke, only to have it replaced with a yoke of iron.[i] 14 For thus says the LORD of hosts, the God of Israel: I will place a yoke of iron on the neck of all these nations and force them to serve King Nebuchadnezzar of Babylon. They will become his slaves. I have even given him the wild animals."

15 Then the prophet Jeremiah further said to the prophet Hananiah, "Listen carefully, Hananiah! The LORD has not sent you, and you have led this people to trust in false prophecies. 16 Therefore, thus says the LORD, 'I intend to remove you from the face of the earth. Before this year comes to a close, you will be dead, because you have preached rebellion against the LORD.'"[j]

17 During that same year, in the seventh month, the prophet Hananiah died.

CHAPTER 29

The Letter to the Exiles. 1 This is the letter that the prophet Jeremiah sent from Jerusalem to the surviving elders among the exiles and to the priests, the prophets, and all the people whom Nebuchadnezzar had taken into exile from Jerusalem to Babylon. 2 This was after King Jeconiah and the queen mother, the court officials, the leaders of Judah and Jerusalem, the artisans, and the skilled workmen had gone into exile from Jerusalem.[k] 3 He entrusted the letter to Elasah, the son of Shaphan, and to Gemariah, the son of Hilkiah, whom Zedekiah, the king of Judah, had sent to Babylon, to King Nebuchadnezzar of Babylon. The letter stated:

4 Thus says the LORD of hosts, the God of Israel, to all the exiles whom I deported from Jerusalem to Babylon: 5 Build houses and dwell in them; plant gardens and eat what they produce. 6 Marry and beget sons and daughters; choose wives for your sons and husbands for your daughters, so that they may bring forth sons and daughters. While you are there, you must increase in number, not decrease.

7 In addition, seek to promote the prosperity of the city to which I have exiled you. Pray to the LORD on its behalf, for on its welfare will depend your welfare.[l] 8 For thus says the LORD of hosts, the God of Israel: Do not be deceived by the prophets and the diviners who are in your midst or listen to the dreams they relate, 9 for they are prophesying lies to you in my name. I did not send them, says the LORD.

10 For thus says the LORD: When the seventy years that I have granted to Babylon have been completed, I will visit you and fulfill my promise to you and bring you back to this place. 11 For I know full well the plans I have for you, plans for your welfare and not for your misfortune, plans that will offer you a future filled with hope.

12 When you call out to me and come forth and pray to me, I will listen to you.[m] 13 When you search for me, you will find me. When you seek me with all your heart, 14 I will allow you to discover me, says the LORD. I will restore your fortunes and gather you from all the nations and from all the places where

g Jer 22:24, 26; 27:8.—h Deut 18:22.—i Isa 45:2.—j Deut 6:15; 13:6.—k 2 Ki 24:15.—l Ps 122:6; 1 Tim 2:1-2.—m Jer 33:3; Ps 50:15.

I have driven you, says the LORD, and I will bring you back to the place from which I sent you into exile.[n]

[15] You have said that the LORD has raised up prophets for you in Babylon. [16] This is what the LORD has to say concerning the king who sits on the throne of David and concerning all the people who live in this city, your countrymen who did not go forth with you into exile: [17] Thus says the LORD of hosts: I will afflict them with sword, famine, and pestilence; I will make them like rotten figs that are so repulsive they cannot be eaten.

[18] I will pursue them with sword, famine, and pestilence, and I will make them abhorrent to all the kingdoms of the earth. They will be an object of cursing and horror, of scorn and derision, to all the nations among whom I have driven them. [19] For they refused to listen to my words, says the LORD, despite the fact that I persisted in sending them my servants the prophets. They continued in their stubbornness and refused to listen, says the LORD.[o]

[20] But now, all you exiles whom I sent away from Jerusalem to Babylon, hear the voice of the LORD. [21] Thus says the LORD of hosts, the God of Israel, concerning Ahab, the son of Kolaiah, and Zedekiah, the son of Maaseiah, who prophesy lies to you in my name: I intend to hand them over to King Nebuchadnezzar of Babylon, and he will put them to death before your very eyes.

[22] Because of them, all the exiles from Judah who were sent to Babylon will use this curse. "May the LORD make you like Zedekiah and Ahab, whom the king of Babylon roasted to death in a blazing fire." [23] For they have perpetrated outrageous crimes in Israel; not only did they commit adultery with their neighbors' wives, but in my name they have spoken lies that I never commanded them to utter. I know these things and bear witness to them, says the LORD.[p]

Prophecy of Shemaiah. [24] Address these words to Shemaiah the Nehelamite. [25] "Thus says the LORD of hosts, the God of Israel: Acting on your own authority, you have sent a letter to all the people in Jerusalem, to the priest Zephaniah, the son of Maaseiah, and to all the other priests [26] asserting that the LORD has appointed you as priest in place of Jehoiada, and that you are to appoint officers to be in charge of the LORD's house and place any madman into the stocks or the pillory who poses as a prophet. [27] Why then have you not rebuked Jeremiah of Anathoth who poses as a prophet among you? [28] He has even sent us a message in Babylon, saying, 'It will be a long time. Build houses and dwell in them; plant gardens and eat what they produce.' "

[29] When the priest Zephaniah read this letter to the prophet Jeremiah, [30] the word of the LORD came to Jeremiah. [31] "Send this message to all of the exiles. 'Thus says the LORD in regard to Shemaiah of Nehelam, "Because Shemaiah has prophesied to you even though I did not send him to do so, and has led you to place your trust in false prophecies, [32] therefore, says the LORD, I intend to punish Shemaiah of Nehelam and his descendants. None of them will survive among this people to witness the happiness that I will bestow on my people, says the LORD, because he has preached rebellion against the LORD." ' "[q]

CHAPTER 30

Israel Restored. [1] * This is the word that came to Jeremiah from the LORD: [2] Thus says the LORD, the God of Israel: Write in a book all the words that I have spoken to you. [3] For the days are surely coming, says the LORD, when I will restore the fortunes of my people Israel and Judah, and I will bring them back to take possession of the land that I gave to their ancestors.[r]

[4] These are the words that the LORD spoke in regard to Israel and Judah:

5 Thus says the LORD:
We have heard a cry of panic,
of terror, not of peace.
6 Inquire now and see:
Can a man bear a child?
Why then do I see every man grasping his loins
like a woman in labor?
Why has every face turned pale?[s]
7 How frightening that day will be!
There will be none like it.
It will be a time of anguish for Jacob,
although he will be saved from it.

n Jer 3:3-8; Isa 55:6-9.—o Jer 25:4; 26:5.—p Jer 23:14; Prov 5:21.—q Jer 36:31.—r Jer 29:14; 32:37.—s Jer 4:31; 6:24.

30:1—33:26 Though Jeremiah prophesies misfortune, he also sings of hope. In his view, as in that of the prophets who preceded him, the Lord committed himself to the covenant once and for all and without second thoughts; if he punishes his faithless people, it is in order to cleanse them of their sins and persuade them to yield unconditionally to his love. The prophet is so convinced of this that he already celebrates the return of the scattered brothers and sisters of the former northern kingdom.

8 On that day, says the LORD of hosts, I will
break off the yoke from your necks, and I will
snap your bonds. Strangers will no longer
enslave you. [t] 9 Instead, Israel and Judah will
serve the LORD, their God, and David, their
king, whom I will raise up for them.

10 Therefore, do not be afraid, Jacob my servant,
and do not despair, O Israel, says the LORD.
Behold, I will rescue you from distant countries
and your descendants from the land of their captivity.
Jacob will return and live in peace,
tranquil, with no one to trouble him.
11 For I am with you, and I will save you,
says the LORD.
I will totally destroy the nations
among whom I have scattered you,
but I will not make an end of you.
However, I will chastise you as you deserve;
I will not allow you to go unpunished. [u]

12 For thus says the LORD:
Your wound is incurable,
your injury is serious.
13 There is no one to plead your cause,
no remedy for your wound,
no healing available for you.
14 All of your friends have forgotten you;
they have ceased to think of you.
I have struck you as an enemy strikes
and punished you cruelly. [v]

15 Why do you cry out over your wound?
Your pain is incurable.
I have treated you in this way
because of your great guilt
and your numerous sins.
16 But all those who devour you will be devoured;
all your enemies will go into exile.
All those who plunder you will be plundered,
and all those who pillage you will be pillaged. [w]
17 For I will restore you to health
and heal your wounds, says the LORD,
because you were called an outcast,
with no one to avenge you.

18 Thus says the LORD:
I will restore the tents of Jacob
and have compassion for his dwellings.
The city will be rebuilt on its hill
and the citadel restored on its traditional site.
19 From them will come forth songs of thanksgiving
and the sounds of rejoicing.
I will increase their number;
they will not diminish.
I will make them honored;
no longer will they be disdained. [x]

20 Their sons will be as they formerly were,
and their community will be firmly established;
any who try to oppress them, I will punish.
21 Their leader will be one of their own,
and their ruler will emerge from their midst.
I myself will bring him near
and allow him to approach me.
For who otherwise would dare to risk his life
by approaching me? says the LORD.
22 You will be my people,
and I will be your God.

23 Observe the storm of the LORD
that will burst forth in wrath,
with a roaring wind that bursts upon
the heads of the wicked. [y]
24 The fierce anger of the LORD will not subside
until he has fully completed the purposes
he has set out to accomplish.
In days to come,
you will fully understand this.

CHAPTER 31

Restoration of Israel

1 At that time, says the LORD:
I will be the God of all the families of Israel,
and they will be my people.
2 Thus says the LORD:
The people who survived the sword
found favor in the wilderness.
When the people of Israel sought for rest,
3 the LORD appeared to them from afar, saying,
"I have loved you with an everlasting love;
therefore, I have continued to be merciful to you. [z]

t Isa 9:4; Ezek 34:27.—u Jer 46:28; Am 9:8f.—v Lam 1:2; 2:4.—w Isa 33:1.—x Isa 35:10; 51:11.—y Jer 23:19.—z Deut 7:8; Hos 11:4.

4 I will build you up again,
and you will be rebuilt,
O virgin Israel.
You will once again carry your tambourines
and go forth to dance with the merry throng.
5 You will once again plant vineyards
on the mountains of Samaria,
and those who plant them will enjoy their fruit. [a]
6 Yes, a day will come when the watchmen
will cry out on the hills of Ephraim,
'Come, let us go up to Zion,
to the LORD, our God.'"

The Glorious Return

7 For thus says the LORD:
Raise shouts of joy for Jacob;
sing your praises for the chief of the nations.
Proclaim your praises as you say,
"The LORD has delivered his people,
the remnant of Israel."
8 Behold, I will bring them back
from the land of the north,
and I will gather them together
from the ends of the earth.
Among them will be the blind and the lame,
expectant mothers and women in labor;
they will return as a vast throng. [b]
9 They will return, weeping uncontrollably,
but I will console them as I lead them back.
I will lead them beside streams of water
along a level path where they will not stumble.
For I am a father to Israel,
and Ephraim is my firstborn son.
10 Pay heed, you nations, to the word of the LORD;
proclaim it even on the distant coastlands and say:
He who scattered Israel will now gather them together
and watch over his flock like a shepherd.
11 For the LORD has ransomed Jacob
and redeemed him from the hands of a foe
far too strong for him. [c]
12 The people will come forth
and shout for joy on the heights of Zion
as they behold the bounty of the LORD:
the grain, the new wine, and the oil,
the young of the flocks and herds.
They themselves will be like a well-watered garden,
and never again will sorrow afflict them.
13 Then the young girls will dance in their happiness,
and the old and the young men will rejoice.
I will turn their mourning into gladness;
I will comfort them
and replace their sorrow with joy.
14 I will strengthen my priests with choice food,
and my people will be overwhelmed with my lavish gifts,
says the LORD.

No More Mourning

15 Thus says the LORD:
A voice is heard in Ramah
marked by lamentation and bitter weeping.
Rachel is mourning for her children,
and she refuses to be consoled
because they are no more.* [d]
16 Thus says the LORD to her:
Cease your cries of lamentation
and wipe the tears from your eyes.
For your labors will be rewarded, says the LORD,
and your children will return from the land of mercy.
17 Thus there is hope for your future, says the LORD;
your children will return to their homeland.
18 I have indeed heard Ephraim pleading,
"You chastised me, and I accepted your discipline,
I was like an untamed calf.
Bring me back! Allow me to return,
for you are the LORD, my God. [e]
19 After I turned away, I repented;
once I began to understand, I beat my breast.

a Isa 65:21; Am 9:14.—b Jer 3:18; 23:8.—c Isa 44:23; 48:20.—d Ps 77:2; Mt 2:17-18.—e Job 5:17; Ps 80:3.

31:15 In Ramah, which lay between Benjamin and Ephraim, that is, in the land of the descendants of Rachel, Jacob's wife (Gen 35:24; 41:51), a caravan of deportees to Babylon will be formed (Jer 40:1), a moving image of the common mother who mourns for the children snatched from her. Matthew the evangelist would later use it in reference to the children slain at Bethlehem (Mt 2:17-18).

I was ashamed and humiliated,
and I reproach myself for the sins of my youth."

20 Thus says the LORD:
Is not Ephraim still my dear son,
the child in whom I delight?
No matter how often I speak against him,
I still remember him lovingly.
Therefore, my heart yearns for him,
and I have great compassion for him.[f]

Blessing and Restoration

21 Set up road markers for yourself;
make yourself guideposts.
Concentrate your thoughts on the road,
the route along which you traveled.
Return, O virgin Israel;
come back to these towns of yours.

22 How long will you wander aimlessly,
O rebellious daughter?
For the LORD has created something new on the earth:
a woman must strengthen a man.*

23 Thus says the LORD of hosts, the God of
Israel: In the land of Judah and in its towns,
they will once again use these words when I
restore their fortunes,

"May the LORD bless you,
O holy mountain,
abode of righteousness."[g]

24 And in the land of Judah and all its
towns, the farmers and those who care for
the flocks will dwell together. 25 For I will pro-
vide the weary with all they need, and I will
restore the strength of all those who have
grown faint with hunger.
26 At this moment I awakened and looked
around, and I realized that my sleep had
been pleasant.*
27 The days are coming, says the LORD,
when I will sow the house of Israel and the
house of Judah with the seed of men and the
seed of animals. 28 And as I once watched
over them to uproot and pull down, to
demolish, destroy, and inflict disaster, so now
I will watch over them to build and to plant,
says the LORD.[h] 29 In those days they will no
longer say,

"The fathers have eaten sour grapes,
and the children's teeth are set on edge."

30 For each one will die for his own sins. The
teeth of everyone who eats sour grapes will
be set on edge.

The New Covenant. 31 The days are coming,
says the LORD, when I will make a new
covenant with the house of Israel and the
house of Judah.* 32 However, it will not be like
the covenant I made with their ancestors
when I took them by the hand and brought
them out of the land of Egypt, a covenant that
they broke even though I was their master.
33 However, this is the covenant that I will
make with the house of Israel after those
days, says the LORD. I will establish my law in
their minds and inscribe it in their hearts. I
will be their God, and they will be my peo-
ple.[i] 34 No longer will there be any need for
them to teach one another, or to say to one
another, "Know the LORD," because they will
all know me, says the LORD, from the least of
them to the greatest. For I will forgive their
iniquity and no longer remember their sin.

Assurance of God's Promise

35 Thus says the LORD:
who provides us with the sun to light our day
and the moon and the stars to shine at night,
who stirs up the sea so that its waves roar,
and whose name is the LORD of hosts:

36 If this established order were ever to cease
in my presence, says the LORD,
then the race of Israel would cease forever
to be a nation before me.[j]

37 Thus says the LORD:
Only if the heavens above can be measured
and the foundations of the earth below
can be fathomed
will I reject the entire race of Israel
because of all they have done, says the LORD.

f Isa 63:15; Hos 11:8-9.—g Jer 30:18; Isa 1:26.—h Jer 1:10; 18:7.—i Jer 32:40; Heb 10:16.—j Jer 33:20; Am 9:8-9.

31:22 The verse is obscure. The same Hebrew verb is used in Deut 32:10 and Ps 32:10 of God's solicitous care for humanity. The usual interpretation of the present verse is that Israel, formerly so faithless, will show the greatest love and attachment to her husband.

31:26 "During this vision, I seemed to be dreaming."

31:31 Like a sudden gush of water comes this beautiful insight of Jeremiah, one of the high points of Old Testament thought; it is a verse that should be committed to memory and constantly meditated on. The former law with its exterior demands will become God's gift and an interior impulse, because God will awaken in souls a love for him and the strength to be faithful. Jesus will bring the gift of it in the Gospel when he announces "the new covenant in my blood which is poured out for you" (Lk 22:20; see Heb 8:7-13).

Jerusalem Rebuilt. 38 The days are coming, says the LORD, when this city will be rebuilt for the LORD, [k] from the Tower of Hananel to the Corner Gate. 39 * The measuring line will then be stretched from there straight to the hill of Gareb and then turn to Goah. 40 The entire valley, with its corpses and ashes, and all the fields sloping toward the Kidron Valley on the east as far as the corner of the Horse Gate, will be sacred to the LORD. Never again will that city be uprooted or destroyed.

CHAPTER 32

Promise of Restoration. 1 This is the word that came to Jeremiah from the LORD in the tenth year of the reign of King Zedekiah of Judah, which was the eighteenth year of Nebuchadnezzar. 2 At that time the army of the king of Babylon was besieging Jerusalem, and the prophet Jeremiah had been imprisoned in the courtyard of the guard that was attached to the royal palace. [l]

3 King Zedekiah had ordered Jeremiah to be confined there, saying, "Why do you continue to prophesy in this manner? According to you, this is what the LORD says, 'I intend to hand over this city to the king of Babylon, and he will capture it. 4 Nor will King Zedekiah of Judah escape the clutches of the Chaldeans; rather, he will be handed over to the king of Babylon, and he will speak with him face to face and behold him with his own eyes. 5 Then Zedekiah will be taken to Babylon, where he will remain until I am ready to deal with him. If you fight against the Chaldeans, you will experience no success.' "

6 Jeremiah replied: This word of the LORD was delivered to me: 7 Hanamel, the son of your uncle Shallum, will come to you and say, "Purchase for yourself my field at Anathoth in the territory of Benjamin. As my closest relative, you have the first right of redemption." [m] 8 Then, just as the LORD had foretold, my cousin Hanamel came to me in the courtyard of the guard and said, "Buy my field at Anathoth in the land of Benjamin, for the right of redemption and possession is yours as next of kin. Therefore, purchase it for yourself." I then knew that this was the word of the LORD.

9 Therefore, I bought the field at Anathoth from my cousin Hanamel and weighed out the money to him—seventeen shekels of silver. 10 I signed the deed, sealed it, had it witnessed, and weighed the money on the scales. 11 Then I took the deed of purchase, * both the sealed copy containing the terms and conditions and the unsealed one, 12 and handed them over to Baruch, the son of Neriah, son of Mahseiah, in the presence of my cousin Hanamel and of the witnesses who had signed the deed of purchase and of all the Judeans who then happened to be sitting in the courtyard of the guard. [n]

13 In their presence I gave the following instructions to Baruch: 14 Thus says the LORD of hosts, the God of Israel: Take the documents of the deed of purchase, both the sealed and the unsealed copies, and place them in an earthenware jar so that they may be preserved for a long period of time. 15 For thus says the LORD of hosts, the God of Israel: Houses and fields and vineyards will again be bought in this land.

16 After I had given the deed of purchase to Baruch, the son of Neriah, I offered this prayer to the LORD, 17 "Ah, Lord GOD, you made the heavens and the earth by your great power and your outstretched arm. Nothing is impossible for you. [o] 18 You show your steadfast love to thousands, but you permit children to be punished for the guilt of their parents, O great and mighty God whose name is the LORD of hosts. 19 Great in counsel and mighty in deed, your eyes observe closely all the ways of men, rewarding each one according to his conduct and as his deeds deserve.

20 "You performed marvelous signs and wonders in the land of Egypt, and you have continued to do so in Israel and among all mankind, gaining renown that continues to this very day. [p] 21 With a mighty hand and outstretched arm you led your people out of Egypt amid signs and wonders and great terror.

22 "You gave them this land which you had promised with an oath to their ancestors, a land flowing with milk and honey. 23 They

k Neh 3:1; Zec 14:10f.—l Jer 33:1; 37:21; 39:14.—m Lev 25:25; Ru 4:4.—n Jer 36:4.—o Jer 1:6; 2 Ki 19:15.—p Deut 4:34; Dan 9:15.

31:39-40 *Gareb* and *Goah* are places unknown to us. The boundaries of the new city will include even places formerly unholy: the valley of dead bodies and ashes, that is, the Valley of Gehenna and of the Kidron, which were formerly places of idolatrous practices (see Jer 2:23; 7:31). For the Tower of Hananel and the Horse Gate, see Neh 3:1, 28.

32:11 *The deed of purchase* was written out twice on a single page; one copy was then rolled up and sealed, the other was left hanging open so that everyone could consult it.

entered and took possession of it, but they
did not obey you or live in accordance with
your law. And since they refused to do what
you had commanded, you permitted all
these disasters to befall them.
24 “Behold, the siege-works are already in
position to force your people into submis-
sion, and the city, a victim of sword, famine,
and pestilence, will be handed over to the
Chaldeans who are attacking it. What you
threatened has come to pass, as you yourself
can see. [q] 25 And yet, Lord GOD, you yourself
told me, ‘Purchase the field with money and
summon witnesses.’ However, the city has
already succumbed to the power of the
Chaldeans.”
26 Then this word of the LORD came to
Jeremiah: 27 I am the LORD, the God of all
mankind. Is anything impossible for me to
accomplish? 28 Therefore, thus says the
LORD: I intend to hand over this city to the
Chaldeans and to Nebuchadnezzar, the king
of Babylon, and he will take it. 29 While
attacking this city, the Chaldeans will enter
it, set it on fire, and burn it to the ground,
along with the houses on whose roofs the
people provoked me to anger by burning
incense to Baal and by pouring out libations
to other gods. [r]
30 From their youth the people of Israel
and the people of Judah have done nothing
but evil in my sight. Indeed the people of
Israel have done nothing but provoke me
with the works of their hands, says the LORD.
31 From the day this city was built until
today, it has so aroused my anger and my
wrath that I intend to remove it from my
sight, 32 because of all the evil that the people
of Israel and the people of Judah have per-
petrated to provoke me. 33 They have turned
their backs to me, not their faces, and
although I continued to teach them, they
would not listen or accept correction. [s]
34 They defiled the house that bears my
name by setting up within it their loathsome
idols. 35 They built high places for Baal in the
Valley of Ben-hinnom to immolate their
sons and daughters to Molech. I gave them
no command to do so, nor did the thought
ever enter my mind that they would do such
an abominable deed and thereby cause
Judah to sin.
36 Now, therefore, thus says the LORD, the
God of Israel, in regard to this city about
which you say, “It has been handed over into
the power of the king of Babylon by the sword,
by famine, and by pestilence:” 37 Behold, I
am determined to gather them together
from all the lands to which I banished them
in my furious anger and intense wrath. I will
bring them back to this place and allow
them to live there in peace. [t] 38 They will be
my people, and I will be their God. 39 I will
grant them unity of heart and unity of con-
duct so that they will fear me always, for
their own good as well as for the good of
their children after them.
40 I will make an everlasting covenant with
them never to cease ensuring their welfare,
and I will put the fear of me into their hearts
so that they will never turn away from me.
41 I will delight in doing good to them, and I
will plant them firmly in this land with all
my heart and soul.
42 For thus says the LORD: Just as I afflicted
this people with such great calamity, so I will
grant them all the good things I have
promised them. 43 Once again fields will be
purchased in this land about which you are
saying, “It is a desolate waste, without peo-
ple or animals, for it has been handed over to
the Chaldeans.” [u] 44 Fields will be purchased
with money; deeds will be signed, sealed, and
witnessed in the land of Benjamin, in the dis-
tricts around Jerusalem, and in the towns of
Judah, of the hill country, of the foothills, and
of the Negeb. For I will restore their fortunes,
says the LORD.

CHAPTER 33

Jerusalem Restored. 1 While Jeremiah was
still imprisoned in the courtyard of the
guard, the word of the LORD came to him a
second time: 2 Thus says the LORD who made
the earth, who formed and established it—
the LORD is his name: 3 Call to me and I will
answer you and reveal to you great and mys-
terious secrets about which you are unaware. [v]
4 For thus says the LORD, the God of Israel,
about the houses of this city and the palaces
of the kings of Judah which are in the process
of being destroyed by siege-works and the
sword 5 in the battle against the Chaldeans:
The houses will be filled with the corpses of
those whom I will strike down in my anger
and rage, those whose wickedness has
caused me to hide my face from this city.
6 Nevertheless, I intend to treat and as-
suage the wounds of this city. I will heal the

q Jer 33:4; Ezek 14:21.—r Jer 21:10; 37:8ff.—s Jer 2:27; 7:13.—t Jer 23:3; Deut 30:3.—u Jer 33:10.—v Ps 50:15; Isa 48:6.

people and grant them an abundance of
peace and prosperity. 7 I will restore the for-
tunes of Judah and Israel and rebuild them
as they were formerly.[w] 8 I will cleanse them
of all the guilt they incurred by their sins
against me, and I will forgive them for their
offenses by which they sinned and rebelled
against me.[x] 9 Then Jerusalem will become
for me a name of joy and praise and pride
for all the nations of the earth to behold.
When they learn of all the good that I will do
for her, they will be overcome with fear and
trembling because of all the peace and pros-
perity I have provided.

10 Thus says the LORD: In this place about
which you say, "It is a wasteland, without
men or animals," and in the cities of Judah
and the streets of Jerusalem that are now
deserted, inhabited by neither men nor ani-
mals, there will once again be heard 11 the
cries of joy and the cries of gladness, the voice
of the bridegroom and the voice of the bride,
and the joyful sounds of those who bring
thank offerings to the LORD, saying,

> "Give thanks to the LORD of hosts,
> for the LORD is good;
> his love endures forever."

For I will restore the fortunes of the land as
they were once before, says the LORD.[y]

12 Thus says the LORD of hosts: In this
place that is now a wasteland, without men
or animals, and in all its towns, there will
again be pastures in which shepherds can
rest their flocks. 13 In the towns of the hill
country, of the foothills, and of the Negeb, in
the land of Benjamin, in the districts around
Jerusalem, and in the towns of Judah, flocks
will again pass under the hands of the one
who counts them, says the LORD.

14 * The days are coming, says the LORD,
when I will fulfill the promise of blessings I
made to the house of Israel and to the house
of Judah:

> 15 In those days and at that time
> I will cause a righteous branch
> to spring up from the line of David
> he will do what is just and upright in
> the land,[z]
> 16 In those days Judah will be saved
> and Jerusalem will live in safety.
> This is the name by which the city will be
> called:
> "The LORD Our Righteousness."

17 For thus says the LORD: Never will David
lack a male descendant to succeed to the
throne of the house of Israel, 18 nor will the
Levitical priests ever fail to have available
one of their number to stand before me to
present burnt offerings, to burn cereal offer-
ings, and to offer sacrifices each day.

19 The word of the LORD came to Jeremiah:
20 Thus says the LORD: If you could break my
covenant with the day and my covenant with
the night so that day and night would no
longer occur at their appointed time,[a] 21 then
my covenant with my servant David could
also be broken so that he would not have a
son to reign on his throne, and my covenant
with the Levites who minister as priests to
me could also be broken. 22 Just as the host of
heaven cannot be numbered and the sands
of the sea cannot be counted, so I will in-
crease the descendants of my servant David
and of the Levites who minister to me.

23 This word of the LORD came to Jere-
miah: 24 Have you not noticed what these
people say, "The two families that were cho-
sen by the LORD have been rejected by him"?
As a result, they look upon my people with
such contempt that they no longer regard
them as a nation.

25 [b] Thus says the LORD: If I had not estab-
lished my covenant with day and night and
fixed the laws governing heaven and earth,
26 then I would reject the descendants of
Jacob and of my servant David and not
choose any of David's descendants to serve
as rulers over the descendants of Abraham,
Isaac, and Jacob. For I will restore their for-
tunes and have mercy upon them.

IV: THE FALL OF JERUSALEM

CHAPTER 34

Zedekiah Condemned. 1 While Nebuchad-
nezzar, the king of Babylon, and his entire
army and all the kingdoms of the earth
under his dominion and all the people in the
empire he ruled were waging war against
Jerusalem and all its towns, this word came
to Jeremiah from the LORD: 2 Go forth to
Zedekiah, the king of Judah, and say to him:
Thus says the LORD: I intend to hand over
this city to the king of Babylon, and he will
order that it be burned to the ground.[c] 3 And
you yourself will not escape his clutches, for

w Jer 32:44; Am 9:14.—x Ezek 36:25.—y 1 Chr 16:34; Ezr 3:11; Ps 100:5.—z Jer 23:5-6; Ps 72:1-5; Isa 4:2; 11:1.—a Jer 31:36f; Ps 89:37.—b Jer 31:36f; Isa 14:1.—c Jer 22:1-2; 32:29.

33:14-26 At this point, we change periods: we are now in the time of the return from exile (538 B.C.).

there is no doubt that you will be captured and delivered into his hands. With your own eyes you will see the king of Babylon, and he will speak with you face to face. Then you will go to Babylon.

4 But even so, listen to the promise of the LORD to you, Zedekiah, king of Judah. This is what the LORD promises in your regard: You will not die by the sword. 5 Rather, you will die a peaceful death. And just as the people burned spices in honor of your ancestors, the kings who preceded you, so they will mourn your passing and burn spices for you, as they lament, "Alas, O king." I myself have made this promise, says the LORD.

6 The prophet Jeremiah revealed all these things to Zedekiah, the king of Judah, in Jerusalem 7 while the army of the king of Babylon was attacking Jerusalem and the remaining cities of Judah that were left, Lachish and Azekah,* for these were the only fortified cities of Judah that were still standing.

The Broken Promise. 8 This word came to Jeremiah from the LORD after King Zedekiah had made a covenant with all the people in Jerusalem to issue a proclamation of freedom for their slaves.[d] 9 Everyone who had Hebrew slaves, whether male or female, was to grant them freedom, and no one would be allowed to keep a fellow Jew in the state of slavery.

10 All of the officials and the people who entered into this agreement, swearing that they would set free their male and female slaves so that they would not again be enslaved, obeyed and granted them their freedom. 11 Afterward, however, they changed their minds and once again forced back into slavery those to whom they had granted their freedom.

12 Then this word of the LORD came to Jeremiah: 13 Thus says the LORD, the God of Israel: I made a covenant with your fathers when I brought them out of the land of Egypt, out of the place of slavery, saying, 14 "Every seventh year each one of you must set free any Hebrew who has sold himself to you as a slave and has served you for six years."

Your fathers, however, did not listen to me or obey me. 15 Recently you repented and did what is right in my sight by proclaiming that freedom was to be given to your brethren and even making a covenant with me in the house that bears my name. 16 Now, however, you have renounced that agreement and profaned my name when each of you took back the male and female slaves to whom you had granted freedom and forced them once again to be your slaves.[e]

17 Therefore, thus says the LORD: Inasmuch as you have not obeyed me and refused to grant deliverance to your neighbors and kinsmen, now I will proclaim deliverance for you—deliverance to the sword, to plague, and to famine. I will make you an object of horror to all the kingdoms of the earth. 18 As for those who have violated my covenant and refused to observe the terms of the covenant to which they agreed in my presence, I will treat them like the calf which they cut in two and then passed between its pieces.* 19 The leaders of Judah and Jerusalem, the eunuchs, the priests, and all the people of the land who walked between the pieces of the calf 20 will be handed over to their enemies who seek their lives. Their corpses will become food for the birds of the air and the animals of the earth.[f]

21 As for Zedekiah, the king of Judah, and his officials, I will hand them over to their enemies who seek their lives and to the army of the king of Babylon which has withdrawn from you. 22 I will issue the command, says the LORD, and I will bring them back to this city. They will attack it and capture it and burn it to the ground. And I will turn the towns of Judah into a desolate wasteland where no one dwells.[g]

CHAPTER 35

Faithfulness of the Rechabites. 1 This is the word that came to Jeremiah from the LORD in the days of King Jehoiakim of Judah, the son of Josiah: 2 Go forth to the clan of the Rechabites* and speak to them. Have them accompany you into one of the rooms of the house of the LORD and offer them wine to drink.

3 Therefore, I took Jaazaniah, the son of Jeremiah, the son of Habazziniah, his brothers and all his sons, the entire clan of the

d Lev 25:10.—e Lev 19:12.—f Jer 7:33; 19:7.—g Jer 37: 8-10; 44:22.

34:7 *Lachish and Azekah:* two cities southwest of Jerusalem, on the coastal plain.

34:18 *The calf. . . :* the reference is to an ancient rite for ratifying an agreement (see Gen 15:9).

35:2 *Rechabites:* a Kenite tribe (1 Chr 2:55) of nomads, allied with Israel. Jonadab (v. 6) had helped Jehu in his struggle against the worshipers of Baal (2 Ki 10:15-27). The Rechabites were now in Jerusalem as refugees from the invasion.

Rechabites, 4 and I brought them into the
house of the LORD, to the room of the sons of
Hanan, son of Igdaliah, the man of God. This
room adjoins the chamber of the princes and
is above the room of Maaserah, the son of
Shallum, the guardian of the threshold.
5 Then I set pitchers full of wine and some
cups before the Rechabites, and I said to
them, "Have some wine to drink." 6 However,
they replied, "We never drink wine. Our
ancestor Jonadab, the son of Rechab, gave us
this command, 'Neither you nor your chil-
dren will ever drink wine.[h] 7 Nor will you
build houses or sow seed or plant vineyards
or even own them. Rather, you will dwell in
tents all the days of your life, so that you may
live for a long time on the land where you are
sojourners.'
8 "We have carefully followed all the com-
mands given to us by our ancestor Jonadab,
the son of Rechab. Throughout our lives we
have never consumed wine, nor have our
wives, our sons, or our daughters. 9 We have
not built houses to live in, and we have no
vineyards or fields or seed. 10 On the con-
trary, we have lived in tents and scrupulous-
ly obeyed everything commanded by our
father Jonadab. 11 But when Nebuchadnez-
zar, the king of Babylon, invaded this land,
we said, 'Let us go to Jerusalem so that we
may escape the armies of the Chaldeans and
the Arameans.' That is the reason why we
are living in Jerusalem."
12 Then the word of the LORD came to
Jeremiah: 13 Thus says the LORD of hosts, the
God of Israel: Go forth and say to the people
of Judah and the inhabitants of Jerusalem:
Will you never come to your senses and obey
my words? says the LORD.[i] 14 The command
of Jonadab, the son of Rechab, to his descen-
dants never to drink wine has been observed
to this very day; in obedience to their ances-
tor, they have drunk no wine. But despite the
fact that I have repeated this command to
you countless times, you have not obeyed me.
15 I have continued to send to you all my
servants the prophets who warned you
repeatedly, "Turn back, every one of you,
from your evil conduct, and cease to follow
other gods to serve them. Then you will con-
tinue to live in the land that I gave to you and
your ancestors." But you did not pay atten-
tion and you refused to listen to me.[j] 16 The
descendants of Jonadab, the son of Rechab,
have honored the command that their
ancestors gave them. You, however, have not
heeded my warnings.
17 Therefore, thus says the LORD, the God
of hosts, the God of Israel: I am determined
to bring upon Judah and upon all the inhab-
itants of Jerusalem every disaster with which
I threatened them because they would not
listen when I spoke to them and did not
answer when I called to them.
18 However, to the clan of the Rechabites
Jeremiah said, "Thus says the LORD of hosts,
the God of Israel: Because you have obeyed
the command of your father Jonadab, fol-
lowed all of his instructions, and did every-
thing that he ordered you to do, 19 therefore,
thus says the LORD of hosts, the God of
Israel: There will never fail to be a descen-
dant of Jonadab, the son of Rechab, to stand
before me forever."[k]

CHAPTER 36*

Baruch Writes the Prophecies on a Scroll.

1 *In the fourth year of King Jehoiakim of
Judah, the son of Josiah, this word came to
Jeremiah from the LORD: 2 Take a scroll and
write on it all the words I have spoken to you
against Israel, Judah, and all the nations,
from the day when I first spoke to you, dur-
ing the reign of Josiah, until today. 3 Perhaps
when the house of Judah hears about all the
disasters that I intend to inflict upon them,
they will all turn back from their evil ways.
Then I will forgive their wickedness and
their sins.[l]
4 Then Jeremiah summoned Baruch, the
son of Neriah, and dictated everything that
the LORD had spoken to him so that Baruch
might write it all on a scroll. 5 He also gave
Baruch the following instruction. "Inasmuch
as I am prevented from entering the house
of the LORD, 6 you yourself must go there,
and on a fast day, in the hearing of all the
people in the LORD's house, you shall read
from the scroll the words of the LORD that
you wrote at my dictation.

"You shall read them also in the hearing of
all the people of Judah who travel there from

h 2 Ki 10:15; 1 Chr 2:55.—i Jer 32:33.—j Jer 25:4f.—k Jer 33:17.—l Jer 26:3; Isa 55:7.

36:1—45:5 This third part of the Book is drawn from the memoirs of Baruch and reveals the suffering of Jeremiah in the last years of his life (605–587 B.C.). Nowhere else in the Book does the prophet appear more human, more "Christian." His painful life joins him with the suffering Servant of Second Isaiah (Isa 53). The suffering he endured for almost twenty years made the poor and humiliated Jeremiah one of the purest anticipations of Christ.

36:1-32 When Nebuchadnezzar, scourge of God, came on the scene in 605 B.C., he brought a turning point in history.

their towns. 7 Perhaps they will then plead before the LORD, and all of them will turn from their evil ways. For great is the anger and wrath that the LORD has threatened against this people."[m] 8 Then Baruch, the son of Neriah, prepared to do everything that the prophet Jeremiah had ordered him about reading from the scroll the words of the LORD in the LORD's house.

9 In the ninth month of the fifth year of the reign of King Jehoiakim of Judah, the son of Josiah, a fast before the LORD was proclaimed for all the people of Jerusalem and all those who came from the towns of Judah to Jerusalem. 10 Then Baruch read the words of Jeremiah from the scroll, in the room of Gemariah, the son of Shaphan the scribe, which was in the upper court, at the entrance of the New Gate of the LORD's house, in the hearing of all the people.[n]

11 When Micaiah, the son of Gemariah, the son of Shaphan, heard all the words of the LORD that had been read from the scroll, 12 he went down to the king's palace and entered the scribe's chamber, where all the officials were in session: Elishama the scribe, Delaiah, the son of Shemaiah, Elnathan, the son of Achbor, Gemariah, the son of Shaphan, Zedekiah, the son of Hananiah, and all the other officials.

13 After Micaiah had reported to them all that he had heard when Baruch read from the scroll to the people, 14 the officials then sent Jehudi, the son of Nethaniah, the son of Shemaliah, the son of Cushi, to say to Baruch, "Come to us and bring with you the scroll that you read publicly to the people." Holding the scroll in his hand, Baruch, the son of Neriah, came into their presence.

15 "Sit down," they said to him, "and read it to us." Baruch read it to them, 16 and when they had heard all the words, they turned to one another in alarm and said to Baruch, "We must certainly report this to the king."

17 They then asked Baruch, "Please tell us how you came to write all these words. Were they dictated to you by Jeremiah?" 18 Baruch replied, "Jeremiah dictated all these words, and I wrote them down in ink on the scroll." 19 Then the officials said to Baruch, "You and Jeremiah must go into hiding, and be extremely careful not to let anyone know where you are."

20 Leaving the scroll in the room of Elishama the scribe, the officials then went to the court of the king, and they reported all that had occurred. 21 The king sent Jehudi for the scroll, and he brought it from the room of Elishama the scribe and read it to the king and all the officials standing beside him.

22 Since it was the ninth month of the year, the king was sitting in his winter residence, and there was a fire burning in a brazier in front of him. 23 Each time Jehudi had read three or four columns of the scroll, the king would cut them off with a scribe's knife and throw them into the fire in the brazier until the entire scroll was finally consumed in the brazier's flames.

24 However, despite hearing all these words, neither the king nor any of his officials showed the slightest alarm, nor did they tear their garments.[o] 25 And although Elnathan and Delaiah and Gemariah pleaded with the king not to burn the scroll, he refused to listen to them. 26 Then the king ordered his son Jerahmeel, and Seraiah, the son of Azriel, and Shelemiah, the son of Abdeel, to arrest the scribe Baruch and the prophet Jeremiah. However, the LORD had hidden them.

27 After the king had burned the scroll with all the words that Baruch had written at Jeremiah's dictation, this word of the LORD came to Jeremiah: 28 Take another scroll and inscribe on it everything that was written on the first scroll which King Jehoiakim of Judah has burned. 29 Also state clearly to Jehoiakim, the king of Judah: Thus says the LORD: You have dared to burn that scroll, saying: Why did you write in it that the king of Babylon without question will come and destroy this land and leave it devoid of men and animals?

30 Therefore, thus says the LORD about King Jehoiakim of Judah: He will have no descendant to succeed him on the throne of David, and his dead body will be exposed to the blazing heat of the day and icy frost at night.[p] 31 I will punish him and his offspring and his attendants for their wickedness, and I will bring down on them and on the citizens of Jerusalem and on the people of Judah all the disasters with which I threatened them, because they paid no heed to my warnings.

32 Then Jeremiah took another scroll and gave it to the scribe Baruch, the son of Neriah, who wrote on it at Jeremiah's dictation all the words of the scroll that King Jehoiakim of Judah had burned in the fire, in addition to many more words than there had been previously.

m Deut 31:17; 2 Ki 22:13.—n Jer 26:10.—o 2 Ki 19:1f.—p Jer 22:19; 2 Ki 24:12ff.

CHAPTER 37*

Jeremiah's Arrest. 1 Zedekiah, the son of
Josiah, was appointed by King Nebuchad-
nezzar of Babylon to be king in the land of
Judah, succeeding Coniah, the son of Jehoi-
akim.[q] 2 However, neither he nor his officials
nor the people of the land paid any heed to
the words of the LORD that he spoke through
the prophet Jeremiah.

3 Even so, King Zedekiah sent Jehucal, the
son of Shelamiah, and the priest Zephaniah,
the son of Maaseiah, to the prophet Jeremiah
with this message, "Please pray to the LORD,
our God, for us." 4 At that time Jeremiah had
not been imprisoned, and he was still able to
move freely among the people. 5 Meanwhile,
Pharaoh's army had set forth from Egypt,
and when the Chaldeans who were besieging
Jerusalem learned of this, they withdrew
from there.

6 Then the word of the LORD came to the
prophet Jeremiah: 7 Thus says the LORD, the
God of Israel: Give this reply to the king of
Judah who sent you to consult me: Pharaoh's
army which has set out to help you will with-
draw to its own country of Egypt,[r] 8 and the
Chaldeans will then resume their attack
upon this city. They will capture it and burn
it to the ground.

9 Thus says the LORD: Do not deceive your-
selves with the belief that the Chaldeans will
cease their attack on you, for they will not
disappear. 10 Even if you managed to defeat
the entire force of the Chaldeans who are
fighting against you, and only those who
were wounded were still left, they would rise
up and burn this city to the ground.

11 When the Chaldean army had with-
drawn from their attack on Jerusalem after
they learned of the approach of Pharaoh's
army, 12 Jeremiah set out from Jerusalem for
the territory of Benjamin to take possession
of his share of a piece of property that he had
inherited. 13 However, when he reached the
Benjamin Gate, he encountered there the
captain of the guard whose name was Irijah,
the son of Shemaliah, the son of Hananiah.
Irijah arrested the prophet Jeremiah, saying,
"You are deserting to the Chaldeans." 14 Jere-
miah answered him, "That is a lie. I am not
deserting to the Chaldeans." But Irijah
refused to listen to him, and he arrested
Jeremiah and brought him to the officials.

15 The officials were enraged at Jeremiah.
After having him beaten, they ordered him
to be confined in the house of Jonathan the
scribe, which had been converted into a jail.
16 Jeremiah was placed in a cell in the dun-
geon where he remained for a lengthy peri-
od of time.[s]

17 Later, King Zedekiah had Jeremiah
brought to him, and he questioned him pri-
vately in his palace, asking him, "Is there any
word from the LORD?" "There is," Jeremiah
replied. "You will be handed over to the king
of Babylon." 18 Jeremiah then asked King
Zedekiah, "In what way have I wronged you
or your ministers or this people that caused
you to order me to be thrown into prison?
19 Where are your prophets now who proph-
esied to you that the king of Babylon would
not attack you or this land?

20 "Therefore, I beg you, my lord king, to
grant my petition. Do not send me back to
the house of Jonathan the scribe. If you do, I
will die there." 21 Therefore, King Zedekiah
issued an order that Jeremiah was to be con-
fined to the court of the guard, and that a
loaf of bread was to be given to him each day
from the Street of the Bakers until there was
no more bread remaining in the city. And so
Jeremiah remained in the court of the
guard.[t]

CHAPTER 38

Jeremiah in the Muddy Cistern. 1 Shephatiah,
the son of Mattan, Gedaliah, the son of
Pashhur, Jucal, the son of Shemaliah, and
Pashhur, the son of Malchiah, heard
Jeremiah speaking these words to all the peo-
ple, 2 "Thus says the LORD: Whoever remains
in this city will die by the sword, or famine, or
pestilence. However, anyone who leaves it
and surrenders to the Chaldeans will live; his
life will be spared and he will live. 3 Thus says
the LORD: Without any doubt this city will be
handed over to the army of the king of
Babylon who will capture it.

4 Then the officials said to the king, "This
man should be put to death. There is no
question that he is discouraging the soldiers
who are left in this city as well as all the peo-
ple by saying such things to them. For this
man is not interested in the welfare of these
people but rather is seeking their ruin."

q 2 Ki 24:17; 2 Chr 36:10.—r Ezek 17:17.—s Jer 38:6, 26.—t Jer 32:2f; 38:13, 28.

37:1—40:6 We leap ahead here to the dark years, 588–587 B.C., that would see Jerusalem besieged and sacked by the Babylonian army. Jeremiah did not cease his denunciation of the policy that led Judah to destruction. The nationalist party was enraged and sought to rid itself at any cost of this troublesome man, but neither prison nor blows silenced the prophet.

5 King Zedekiah replied, "He is in your power." For the king was powerless to oppose them. 6 Therefore, they took Jeremiah and threw him into the cistern of Malchiah, the king's son, which was in the court of the guard, letting him down with ropes. There was no water in the cistern, but only mud, and Jeremiah sank into the mud. [u]

7 However, it so happened that an Ethiopian, Ebed-melech,* who was a eunuch in the king's palace, heard that Jeremiah had been put into the cistern. Therefore, he decided to report this to the king, 8 and he left the palace to speak to the king who at that moment was seated at the Benjamin Gate. 9 "My lord king," he said, "these men have acted wickedly in their treatment of the prophet Jeremiah. They threw him into a cistern and left him there to die of hunger, for there is no more bread left in the city." [v]

10 The king instructed Ebed-melech the Ethiopian, to take three men along with him and lift the prophet Jeremiah out of the cistern before he perished. 11 Ebed-melech went to the palace with the men after first taking from a storage closet in the palace some old tattered rags and worn-out clothes which he lowered with ropes to Jeremiah in the cistern. 12 Then Ebed-melech the Ethiopian called down to Jeremiah, "Put those old rags and clothes under your armpits to pad the ropes." Jeremiah did so, 13 and then they pulled him up with the ropes out of the cistern. But Jeremiah continued to remain in the court of the guard.

14 King Zedekiah summoned the prophet Jeremiah and received him at the third entrance to the temple of the LORD. "I have something to ask you," the king said to Jeremiah. "Do not conceal anything from me." 15 Jeremiah replied to Zedekiah, "If I speak in a straightforward manner, you will have me put to death, won't you? And if I give you advice, you will not listen to me." [w] 16 But King Zedekiah then swore this oath secretly to Jeremiah, "As the LORD lives who gave us the breath of life, I will not put you to death, nor will I hand you over to those who seek your life."

17 Then Jeremiah said to Zedekiah, "Thus says the LORD, the God of hosts, the God of Israel: If you surrender to the officials of the king of Babylon, your life will be spared, and this city will not be burned to the ground, and you and your family will live. 18 However, if you do not surrender to the officials of the king of Babylon, this city will fall into the hands of the Chaldeans, who will destroy it with fire, and you yourself will not be able to escape their clutches."

19 King Zedekiah then said to Jeremiah, "I am afraid of the Judeans who have deserted to the Chaldeans. It very well might be that I will be handed over to them and they will be ruthless in their treatment of me." [x] 20 Jeremiah replied, "You will not be handed over to them. If you obey the LORD by doing everything I tell you, all will go well with you, and your life will be spared. 21 But if you refuse to surrender, this is what the LORD has shown me. 22 He has given me a vision of all the women left in the palace of the king of Judah being led off to the officials of the king of Babylon and saying,

'They have misled you and triumphed
over you,
your trusted friends.
Now that your feet are stuck in the mud,
they have deserted you.'

23 "All your wives and your children will be led off to the Chaldeans, and you yourself will not escape their clutches. Rather, you will be handed over to the king of Babylon, and this city will be burned to the ground." [y]

24 Then Zedekiah said to Jeremiah, "Do not let anyone know of this conversation, or you will die. 25 If the officials learn that I have spoken with you, and they say to you, 'Tell us what you said to the king and what he said to you; do not hold anything back from us or we will put you to death,' 26 give them this answer, 'I was simply pleading with the king not to send me back to the house of Jonathan to die there.' "

27 All the officials did come to Jeremiah to interrogate him, and he replied to them in the very same words that the king had commanded. Therefore, they ceased to question him, for no one had heard their conversation. 28 And Jeremiah remained in the court of the guard until the day that Jerusalem was captured. [z]

CHAPTER 39

Jeremiah and Gedaliah. 1 In the tenth month of the ninth year of King Zedekiah of Judah, Nebuchadnezzar, the king of Bab-

u Jer 37:16.—v Jer 37:21; 52:6.—w Lk 22:67f.—x 2 Chr 30:10; Isa 51:12f.—y Jer 41:10.—z Jer 39:14.

38:7 *Ebed-melech* was guardian of the royal harem and a very influential person.

ylon, marched into battle against Jerusalem
with his entire army and laid siege to it.[a]
2 Then, in the eleventh year of Zedekiah, on
the ninth day of the fourth month, a breach
was made in the wall of the city. 3 Thereupon,
all of the officials of the king of Babylon
came forward and took their seats at the
middle gate: Nergal-sharezer, Samgar-nebo,
Sarsechim, who was a high dignitary, anoth-
er Nergal-sharezer, who was the chief astrol-
oger, and all of the other dignitaries in the
king's service.

4 When King Zedekiah of Judah beheld
them, he and all of his soldiers fled, depart-
ing from the city during the night by way of
the king's garden through the gate between
the two walls, and they set off in the direction
of the Arabah. 5 However, the army of the
Chaldeans set off in pursuit of them and
overtook Zedekiah in the plains of Jericho.
After they had captured him, they took him
to Nebuchadnezzar, the king of Babylon, at
Riblah in the land of Hamath, who passed
sentence on him.

6 The king of Babylon ordered the sons of
Zedekiah to be slaughtered at Riblah before
their father's eyes, and he also sentenced all
the nobles of Judah to be put to death. 7 Then
he put out the eyes of Zedekiah and ordered
him to be taken to Babylon bound in
chains.[b]

8 The Chaldeans burned to the ground the
royal palace and the houses of the people, and
they demolished the walls of Jerusalem.[c]
9 Then Nebuzaradan, the commander of the
guard, deported to Babylon the rest of the
people who were left in the city, those who had
deserted to him, and the remaining work-
men. 10 However Nebuzaradan, the comman-
der of the guard, left behind in the land of
Judah some of the poor people who owned
nothing, and at the same time, he gave them
vineyards and fields.[d]

11 Concerning Jeremiah, King Nebuchad-
nezzar of Babylon gave the following orders
to Nebuzaradan, the commander of the
guard, 12 "Take him and look after him. Do
him no harm, but grant him whatever he
requests." 13 Then Nebuzaradan, the com-
mander, the commander of the guard, and
Nebushazban, a high-ranking dignitary, and
Nergal-sharezer, an important official, and all
the chief officers of the king of Babylon
14 ordered Jeremiah to be taken from the
court of the guard and entrusted to Gedaliah,
the son of Ahikam, the son of Shaphan, to be
brought safely home. Thus he remained
among his own people.[e]

A Blessing for Ebed-melech. 15 While
Jeremiah was confined in the court of the
guard, the word of the LORD came to him.
16 "Go and tell Ebed-melech the Ethiopian:
Thus says the LORD of hosts, the God of
Israel: Behold, I am now going to fulfill the
words I have spoken against this city for its
ruin and not for its prosperity, and those
promises will be fulfilled before your very
eyes.

17 "However, I will rescue you on that day,
says the LORD. You will not be handed over to
those whom you so greatly fear. 18 For I will
save you. You will not fall by the sword, but
you will escape with your life because you
have placed your trust in me, says the LORD."[f]

CHAPTER 40

Jeremiah Remains in Judah. 1 This word
came to Jeremiah from the LORD after
Nebuzaradan, the commander of the guard,
had released him at Ramah, where he had
found him imprisoned in chains with all the
other captives from Jerusalem and Judah
who were being deported to Babylon.[g]

2 The commander of the guard took
Jeremiah aside and said to him, "The LORD,
your God, foretold the disaster that would
overwhelm this place. 3 Now he has brought
about what he threatened to do to your peo-
ple because they sinned against the LORD
and refused to obey him. 4 But today I am
removing the chains from your hands. If you
so wish, you can come with me to Babylon,
and I will take good care of you. However,
if you do not wish to come with me to
Babylon, you need not do so. Endless
stretches of land lie before you. Go wherever
you think it is best for you."

5 Then, before Jeremiah could reply,
Nebuzaradan added, "You can also go back
to Gedaliah, the son of Ahikam, the son of
Shaphan, whom the king of Babylon has
appointed governor of the towns of Judah,
and stay with him among your people, or go
anywhere else you please." Then the com-
mander of the guard gave him food and gifts
and let him go.[h] 6 Jeremiah thereupon went
to Gedaliah, the son of Ahikam, in Mizpah,

a Jer 52:4-7; 2 Ki 25:1-4.—b Jer 32:4f; Ezek 12:13.—c Jer 52:13f; 2 Ki 25:9f.—d Jer 52:16; 2 Ki 25:12.—e Jer 38:28.—f Jer 45:5; Ps 37:40.—g Jer 39:9, 14.—h Jer 39:14; 2 Ki 25:22.

and he stayed with him among the people who were left in the land.

7 * When all the military leaders of the forces still in the open country heard that the king of Babylon had appointed Gedaliah, the son of Ahikam, as governor over the land and had placed in his care the men, women, and children who were the most destitute of all the people there who had not been carried off into exile to Babylon, 8 they went with their forces to Gedaliah in Mizpah: Ishmael, the son of Nethaniah; Johanan and Jonathan, the sons of Kareah; Seraiah, the son of Tanhumeth; the sons of Ephai of Netophah; Jezaniah, the son of Beth-maacah.

9 Gedaliah, the son of Ahikam, the son of Shaphan, swore an oath to reassure them and their men, saying, "Do not be afraid to serve the Chaldeans. Settle down in the land, serve the king of Babylon, and all will go well with you.[i] 10 I myself will remain in Mizpah to represent you before the Chaldeans who come to us. As for you, harvest the wine, the summer fruits, and the oil. Store them in your vessels and settle in the towns that you have seized."

11 When all the Judeans who were living in Moab with the Ammonites, in Edom, and elsewhere heard that the king of Babylon had left a remnant in Judah and had appointed Gedaliah, the son of Ahikam, the son of Shaphan, as governor over them, 12 they all returned to Judah from the places to which they had been driven. They presented themselves to Gedaliah at Mizpah and gathered a rich harvest of wine and summer fruits.

Gedaliah's Murder. 13 Now Johanan, the son of Kareah, and all the leaders of the forces still stationed in the open country came to Gedaliah at Mizpah 14 and said to him, "Are you at all aware that Baalis, the king of the Ammonites, has sent Ishmael, the son of Nethaniah, to assassinate you?" But Gedaliah, the son of Ahikam, refused to believe them.[j]

15 Then Johanan, the son of Kareah, spoke privately to Gedaliah at Mizpah, saying, "Please authorize me to go and kill Ishmael, the son of Nethaniah. No one will be the wiser. Why should he be allowed to assassinate you, thus causing all the Jews who have rallied around you to be scattered and the remnant of Judah to perish?" 16 But Gedaliah, the son of Ahikam, replied to Johanan, the son of Kareah, "Do not even think of doing such a thing. What you are saying about Ishmael is untrue."

CHAPTER 41

1 In the seventh month, Ishmael, the son of Nethaniah, the son of Elishama, who was a member of the royal family and one of the chief officers of the king, came with ten men to Gedaliah, the son of Ahikam, at Mizpah.[k] While they were eating together there at Mizpah, 2 Ishmael, the son of Nethaniah, and the ten men who had accompanied him rose up and struck Gedaliah, the son of Ahikam, the son of Shaphan, with their swords and assassinated him because the king of Babylon had appointed him to be the governor of the land. 3 Ishmael also killed all the Judeans who were with Gedaliah in Mizpah as well as the Chaldean soldiers who were present.

4 On the day after Gedaliah had been slain, before news of the assassination had spread, 5 eighty men arrived from Shechem, Shiloh, and Samaria, with their beards shaved and their clothes torn and their bodies covered with self-inflicted gashes. They were carrying grain offerings and incense to present at the temple of the LORD.[l]

6 Ishmael, the son of Nethaniah, went out from Mizpah to meet them, weeping as he proceeded, and as he met them, he said, 7 "Come to Gedaliah, the son of Ahikam." But when they had proceeded a good distance into the city, Ishmael, the son of Nethaniah, and his men slaughtered them and threw them into a cistern.

8 However, there were ten men among them who cried out to Ishmael, "Do not kill us. We have large stores of wheat and barley, oil and honey, buried in the fields." Therefore, he spared them and did not kill them, as he had done with their companions. 9 The cistern into which Ishmael threw the corpses of all the men he had killed was the large cistern that King Asa had built as a defensive measure against Baasha, the king of Israel. Ishmael, the son of Nethaniah, filled this cistern with the slain.[m]

10 Ishmael, the son of Nethaniah, then led

i Jer 27:12f; 2 Ki 25:24.—j Jer 41:10.—k Jer 40:6, 8, 14; 2 Ki 25:25.—l Jer 16:6; 1 Ki 16:24, 29.—m 1 Ki 15:16; 2 Chr 16:6.

40:7—44:30 It was not in the interests of the Chaldeans to allow anarchy, and therefore, they appointed a governor, Gedaliah, a Jew. A civil war broke out, and the governor was its first victim. Fearing the reaction of the Chaldeans, the people of Judah fled to Egypt. Jeremiah refused to take part in this exodus but was drawn against his will into this painful business.

away as prisoners the remaining people who
were in Mizpah—the king's daughters as
well as all the others who were left there, and
over whom Nebuzaradan, the captain of the
guard, had appointed Gedaliah, the son of
Ahikam. With these captives, Ishmael, the
son of Nethaniah, set out to cross over to the
Ammonites.

Flight to Egypt. 11 When Johanan, the son of
Kareah, and all of the army officers who
were with him learned of the crimes that
Ishmael, the son of Nethaniah, had commit-
ted, 12 they took all their men and set forth to
attack Ishmael, the son of Nethaniah, finally
catching up with him by the great pool in
Gibeon.
13 At the sight of Johanan, the son of
Kareah, and the other army leaders, the
people who were Ishmael's captives were de-
lighted. 14 All the people whom Ishmael had
taken as prisoners from Mizpah went over to
Johanan, the son of Kareah. 15 However,
Ishmael, the son of Nethaniah, escaped from
the clutches of Johanan and fled to the
Ammonites with eight men.
16 Then Johanan, the son of Kareah, and all
the military leaders who were with him, led
away all of the remaining people whom
Ishmael, the son of Nethaniah, had carried
away as prisoners from Mizpah after he had
slain Gedaliah—soldiers, women, children,
and eunuchs, whom he had brought from
Gibeon. 17 After they started out, they
stopped at Chinham, near Bethlehem, in-
tending to flee into Egypt.[n] 18 They had no
wish to engage in a confrontation with the
Chaldeans, since Ishmael, the son of Neth-
aniah, had slain Gedaliah, the son of
Ahikam, whom the king of Babylon had
appointed as governor over the country.

CHAPTER 42

1 *Then all the military commanders,
including Johanan, the son of Kareah, and
Azariah, the son of Hoshaiah, and all the
people, from the lowest to the highest rank,
approached 2 the prophet Jeremiah and said,
"Please grant our petition and intercede for
us and for this meager remnant. For where
we once were great in number, now there are
very few of us that remain, as your eyes can
discern. 3 Please petition the LORD, your
God, to show us the path we should follow
and what we must do."
4 The prophet Jeremiah said to them in
reply, "I will grant your request and pray to
the LORD, your God. Whatever answer the
LORD has for you, I will tell you and not with-
hold anything from you."[o] 5 They in their
turn said to Jeremiah, "May the LORD be a
true and faithful witness against us if we do
not follow all the instructions that the LORD,
your God, will send us. 6 Whether or not
what he has to say is to our liking, we will
obey the voice of the LORD, our God, to
whom we are sending you, so that all may go
well with us when we heed his instructions."
7 After ten days had passed, the word of
the LORD came to Jeremiah. 8 Then he sum-
moned Johanan, the son of Kareah, and all of
the military commanders who were with
him, as well as all the people, from the least
to the greatest, 9 and he said to them, "Thus
says the LORD, the God of Israel, to whom
you sent me to present your petition:
10 " 'If you resolve to remain in this land, I
will build you up and not tear you down; I will
plant you and not uproot you. For I deeply
regret the disaster that I have inflicted upon
you.[p] 11 Do not be afraid of the king of
Babylon whom at this moment you so great-
ly fear. You have no reason to be frightened of
him, says the LORD, for I am with you to
ensure your safety and to rescue you from his
power. 12 I will have compassion on you, and
he will then treat you mercifully and allow
you to return to your land.[q]
13 " 'However, if you persist in your stub-
born refusal to stay in this land, thereby dis-
obeying the voice of the LORD, your God,
14 and you say, "We are determined to go to
Egypt, where we will not be forced to endure
further war or hear the trumpet's call to bat-
tle or be hungry for bread; it is there that we
will stay," 15 then hear the word of the LORD,
O remnant of Judah: Thus says the LORD of
hosts, the God of Israel: If you are deter-
mined to go to Egypt, and if you actually do
make that journey and settle there, 16 then
the sword you fear so greatly will overtake
you there in the land of Egypt, the famine
you dread will continue to afflict you to the
same degree in Egypt, and it is there that
you will perish.[r]
17 " 'All those people who are determined
to go to Egypt and settle there will die by the

n Jer 42:14; 2 Sam 19:37f.—o Jer 23:28; 1 Sam 3:17-18.—
p Jer 31:28; Ezek 36:36.—q Ps 106:45f.—r Jer 44:13f, 27.

42:1—43:13 The order of the narrative seems to have been disturbed somewhat by the displacement of some verses.

sword, famine, or plague. Not a single person
will survive or escape the disaster that I will
inflict upon them. 18 For thus says the LORD
of hosts, the God of Israel: Just as my anger
and my fury were poured out on the inhabi-
tants of Jerusalem, so will my wrath be
poured out on you when you go to Egypt. You
will become an object of execration and hor-
ror, of cursing and ridicule, and you will
never again see this place.'
19 "The LORD has spoken clearly to you in
regard to this matter, O remnant of Judah.
Do not go to Egypt. You can never make the
claim that I did not give you a solemn
warning. 20 You were not speaking sincerely
when you yourselves sent me to the LORD,
your God, saying, 'Intercede for us with the
LORD, our God. Make known to us exactly
what the LORD, our God, says, and we will
do it.'
21 "Today I have told you what you wanted
to know, but you have refused to obey the
voice of the LORD, your God, in anything that
he sent me to tell you. 22 Therefore, do not
nurture any doubt that you will die by the
sword, by famine, and by pestilence in the
place where you wish to go and settle." [s]

CHAPTER 43

1 When Jeremiah had finished relating to
the people all these words that the LORD,
their God, had sent him to reveal to them,
2 Azariah, the son of Hoshaiah, Johanan, the
son of Kareah, and all the rest of the insolent
men said to Jeremiah, "You are telling bla-
tant lies. The LORD, our God, did not send
you to say, 'Do not go to Egypt and settle
there.' 3 Rather it is Baruch, the son of
Neriah, who continues to incite you against
us and keeps urging you to hand us over to
the Chaldeans so that they can put us to
death or deport us into exile in Babylon." [t]
4 Therefore, Johanan, the son of Kareah,
and all the military leaders and all the peo-
ple refused to obey the LORD's command to
remain in the land of Judah. 5 Instead
Johanan, the son of Kareah, and all the mili-
tary leaders led away the entire remnant of
Judah who had been scattered among all the
nations and who then had returned to settle
in the land of Judah: 6 men, women, and chil-
dren, the daughters of the king, and every-
one whom Nebuzaradan, the captain of the
guard, had entrusted to Gedaliah, the son of
Ahikam, the son of Shaphan, including the
prophet Jeremiah and Baruch, the son of
Neriah. [u] 7 In disobedience to the LORD's
command, they traveled to the land of Egypt
and arrived at Tahpanhes.

Invasion of Egypt. 8 Then the word of the
LORD came to Jeremiah at Tahpanhes. 9 "Take
some large stones and bury them in the
cement in the terrace at the entrance to
Pharaoh's palace in Tahpanhes, while the
men of Judah can see you. 10 Then say to
them, 'Thus says the LORD of hosts, the God
of Israel: I intend to send for my servant
Nebuchadnezzar, the king of Babylon, and he
will set his throne upon these stones that I
have buried, and he will spread his canopy
over them. [v] 11 He will come and ravage the
land of Egypt:

> "'Those destined for the plague, to plague,
> those for captivity, to captivity,
> and those for the sword, to the sword.

12 "'He will set fire to the temple of the
gods of Egypt, burning their gods and carry-
ing them off. He will scour the land of Egypt
as a shepherd scrubs off the vermin from his
cloak, and he will depart from there safely. [w]
13 He will smash the obelisks of the temple of
the sun in the land of Egypt, and he will
destroy the temples of the Egyptian gods
with fire.'"

CHAPTER 44

1 This is the word that came to Jeremiah
for all the Judeans who were living in the land
of Egypt, at Migdol, at Tahpanhes, at Mem-
phis, and in the district of Pathros. 2 Thus
says the LORD of hosts, the God of Israel: You
have seen the immense disaster that I have
inflicted on Jerusalem and all the towns of
Judah. Today they lie in ruins and are left
uninhabited. [x] 3 This was the result of all the
wicked deeds your ancestors committed that
provoked me to anger, as they went forth to
serve other gods and offer sacrifices to them
whom neither they, nor you, nor your ances-
tors ever had known before.
4 Even though I continued to send to them
all my servants the prophets with this plea,
"Do not do this abominable thing that I
hate," 5 they would not listen or pay any heed
to my warning to refrain from their wicked
deeds and cease to offer sacrifices to other
gods. [y] 6 Therefore, my fury and my wrath

s Jer 43:11; Hos 9:6.—t Jer 38:4.—u Jer 41:10.—v Jer 25:9, 11; 27:6.—w Jer 46:25; Ezek 30:13.—x Jer 34:22; Mic 3:12.—y Jer 7:24; 11:10.

poured forth, burning to ashes the towns of
Judah and the streets of Jerusalem and
reducing them to the desolate wasteland they
are today.
7 And now this is what the LORD God of
hosts, the God of Israel, has to say: Why are
you inflicting such a total disaster upon your-
selves? Why are you uprooting men and
women, children and babies, from Judah,
thus leaving yourselves without a remnant?
8 Will you continue to provoke me to anger by
the works of your hands as you make sacri-
fices to strange gods in Egypt where you have
come to settle, cutting yourselves off and
becoming an object of cursing and ridicule
among all the nations of the earth?
9 Have you forgotten the wicked crimes
committed by your ancestors and by the
kings of Judah and their wives, and also your
own crimes and those of your wives, all of
them committed in the land of Judah and in
the streets of Jerusalem? 10 To this very day
they have shown no remorse or fear, nor have
they observed my law and my statutes which
I prescribed for you and for your ancestors. [z]
11 Therefore, thus says the LORD of hosts,
the God of Israel: I am determined to inflict
disaster upon you and to destroy Judah com-
pletely. 12 I will take the remnant of Judah
who were determined to come to the land of
Egypt and settle there, and in Egypt, they will
all perish. They will fall by the sword and by
famine. From the least to the greatest they
will die by the sword and by famine, and they
will become an object of execration and hor-
ror, a curse and a reproach. [a]
13 I will punish those who live in the land of
Egypt as I punished Jerusalem, with the
sword, with famine, and with pestilence.
14 None of the remnant of Judah who have
come to settle in the land of Egypt will
escape or survive to return to the land of
Judah, even though they may long to return
and live there. None will be allowed to
return, except for a few refugees.
15 Then all the men who were aware that
their wives had been burning incense to other
gods, and all the women who were standing
there in a great assemblage, and all the peo-
ple who lived in Pathros in the land of Egypt
replied to Jeremiah, 16 "We have no intention
of giving credence to the word that you have
spoken to us in the name of the LORD. [b]
17 Rather, we will continue to do everything
we have vowed to do. We will make offerings
to the queen of heaven and pour out libations
to her, as we and our ancestors, our kings and
our officials, used to do in the towns of Judah
and in the streets of Jerusalem. In those days
we used to have an abundance of food; we
prospered and endured no misfortune. 18 But
from the time we ceased to make offerings to
the queen of heaven and to pour out libations
to her, we have been in great need, and we
have perished by the sword and by famine."
19 The women added, "When we made
offerings to the queen of heaven and poured
out libations to her, do you think that our
husbands were not aware that we made
cakes depicting her image and that we
poured out libations to her?" * [c]
20 Then to all the people, both men and
women, who had given him this answer,
Jeremiah said, 21 "In regard to the incense
offerings that you and your ancestors, your
kings and your officials, and the people of the
land burned in the cities of Judah and the
streets of Jerusalem, the LORD certainly
remembered them and kept them in mind.
22 When the LORD could no longer endure
your wicked deeds and your loathsome prac-
tices, your land became a desolate waste, an
accursed object of horror without inhabi-
tants, as it is to this day. [d] 23 The disaster you
are now enduring has befallen you because
you burned incense and sinned against the
LORD, refusing to obey the voice of the LORD
and failing to live in accordance with his law,
his statutes, and his decrees."
24 Jeremiah then said further to all the peo-
ple, and in particular to all the women,
"Listen to the word of the LORD, all you
Judeans in the land of Egypt. 25 Thus says the
LORD of hosts, the God of Israel: You and your
wives have accomplished with your hands
what you promised with your mouths when
you said, 'We are determined to fulfill the
vows we have made to burn incense to the
queen of heaven and to pour out libations to
her.' Very well, keep your vows and do what
you promised.
26 "However, listen attentively to the word
of the LORD, all you people of Judah who are
living in the land of Egypt. I swear by my
great name, says the LORD, that my name
will never issue forth from the lips of any of

z Jer 26:4.—a Jer 42:15, 18, 22.—b Jer 6:16f.—c Jer 7:18; Num 30:6-7.—d Jer 15:6.

44:19 See the note on Jer 7:1—8:3.

the people of Judah throughout the land of
Egypt. No one of them will ever say, 'As the
Lord GOD lives.'[e]
27 "I intend to watch over them to ensure
their harm rather than their well-being. All
the people of Judah who have settled in the
land of Egypt will perish either by the sword
or by famine, until not a single one remains.
28 Those who escape the sword and return
from the land of Egypt to Judah will be few in
number. Then the entire remnant of Judah
who were determined to settle in Egypt will
come to the realization that it has been my
word that prevailed, and not theirs.[f]
29 * "This is the sign from me to you that I
will punish you in this place, says the LORD,
in order that you may realize that my
promise to you will be carried out. 30 Thus
says the LORD: Behold, I will hand over
Pharaoh Hophra, the king of Egypt, to his
enemies, to those who seek his life, just as I
handed over Zedekiah, the king of Judah, to
his enemy who sought his life, Nebuchad-
nezzar, the king of Babylon."[g]

CHAPTER 45*

Encouraging Message to Baruch. 1 This is the
message that the prophet Jeremiah ad-
dressed to Baruch, the son of Neriah, when
Baruch inscribed these words on a scroll at
Jeremiah's dictation in the fourth year of King
Jehoiakim of Judah, the son of Josiah:
2 Thus says the LORD, the God of Israel, to
you, Baruch: 3 You said, "Woe is me, for the
LORD has added further grief to my pain. I
am exhausted from groaning, and I can find
no respite."
4 Say this to him, "Thus says the LORD: I
intend to tear down what I have built, and to
uproot what I have planted throughout the
entire land.[h] 5 Should you therefore seek
great things for yourself? Do not seek them,
for I intend to inflict evil upon all mankind,
says the LORD. However, I will allow you to
escape with your life wherever you may go."

V: PROPHECIES AGAINST THE NATIONS*

CHAPTER 46

1 This is the word of the LORD that came to
the prophet Jeremiah in regard to the nations.

Against Egypt.* 2 Concerning Egypt and
the army of Pharaoh Neco, the king of
Egypt, which was stationed at Carchemish
on the Euphrates River, and which Nebu-
chadnezzar, the king of Babylon, defeated in
the fourth year of King Jehoiakim of Judah,
the son of Josiah:

3 Prepare your bucklers and
shields and march forth for battle.
4 Harness the horses;
let the riders mount.
Don your helmets
and take your stations.
Sharpen your spears
and put on your breastplates.
5 What is this shameful spectacle I behold?
They fall back in terror.
Their warriors are routed
and are in headlong flight
without glancing back.
There is terror on every side,
says the LORD.[i]
6 The swift cannot flee,
nor can the brave warriors escape.
In the north, by the River Euphrates,
they have stumbled and fallen.
7 Who is this that rises like the Nile,
like rivers of torrential waters?
8 Egypt rises up like the Nile,
like rivers of torrential waters.
I will rise up, Egypt says, and cover the
earth;
I will destroy cities and their inhabi-
tants.[j]
9 Advance, O horses,
and drive madly, O chariots.
Let the warriors advance:
men from Ethiopia and Put bearing
shields,
and men from Lud who draw their
bows.

---

e Jer 5:2; Gen 22:16.—f Deut 28:62; Isa 10:19, 22.—g Jer 39:5; 46:25f; Ezek 29:2f.—h Jer 18:7-10; Isa 5:5f.—i Jer 6:25; 49:29.—j Isa 37:24; Ezek 32:2.

44:29-30 According to Herodotus, Pharaoh Hophra was murdered by the people in 568 B.C.

45:1-5 The faithful secretary concludes his memoirs by citing a short oracle addressed to him personally.

46:1—51:64 These threats to the nations are not in their proper place here at the end of the Book. It is thought that they were originally located between verses 1-13 and verses 14-19 of chapter 25, these two sections being respectively an appeal of the prophet to his fellow countrymen and a vision of the cup of the Lord's wrath. And, in fact, it is at that point that the ancient Greek translation usually inserts the present chapters.

46:2-28 When the Assyrian empire broke up, two powers entered the lists to win control of the Mediterranean East: the kingdoms of Babylon and of Egypt. Shortly before being enthroned as king, Nebuchadnezzar II (605–561 B.C.) defeated the army of Pharaoh Neco (609–593 B.C.) at Carchemish (today Jerablus), an ancient Hittite metropolis on the upper Euphrates. The battle was a historical turning point.

10 This day belongs to the Lord GOD of hosts,
a day of retribution
and vengeance on his enemies.
The sword will devour and be sated
until drunk with their blood.
For the Lord GOD of hosts
is holding a sacrificial feast
in the land of the north
by the River Euphrates.[k]
11 Go up to Gilead and obtain balm,
O virgin daughter Egypt.
The many medicines you have used
have afforded you no healing.
12 The nations have heard of your shame;
the earth is filled with your cries.
Warrior stumbles against warrior,
and both fall down together.

13 [l]The word that the LORD spoke to the
prophet Jeremiah in regard to the advance
of Nebuchadnezzar, the king of Babylon, to
attack the land of Egypt:

14 Announce it in Egypt and proclaim it in Migdol;
proclaim it also in Noph and Tahpanhes.
Say, "Take your stations and be prepared,
for the sword will devour those around you."
15 Why have your warriors been laid low?
They were unable to stand
because the LORD has thrust them down.
16 They stumbled and fell,
and then they said to one another,
"Come, let us return to our own people
and to the land of our birth,
far from the swords of our oppressors."[m]
17 They gave this nickname to Pharaoh, the king of Egypt:
"One who boasts but never succeeds."
18 As I live, says the King,
whose name is the LORD of hosts,
one is coming like Tabor* among the mountains,
like Carmel by the sea.
19 Prepare your baggage to go into exile,
you inhabitants of Egypt.
Memphis will become a desert waste,
a desolate, uninhabited ruin.
20 Egypt is a beautiful heifer,*
but a gadfly from the north
is preparing to move against her.
21 Even the mercenaries in her midst
are like fatted calves,
but they have turned and fled together
rather than stand their ground.
For the day of disaster has overtaken them,
the time of their punishment.
22 Egypt is hissing like a retreating snake,
for her enemies are advancing in force.
They move against her with axes,
like men who fell her trees.
23 They will cut down her forest,* says the LORD,
even though it appears impenetrable,
because they are more numerous than locusts;
they are beyond counting.[n]
24 Daughter Egypt will be disgraced,
handed over to a people from the north.

25 The LORD of hosts, the God of Israel, has
said: Behold, I will punish Amon* of Thebes,
and Egypt, her gods and her kings, Pharaoh
and those who trust in him. 26 I will hand
them over to those who seek their lives, to
Nebuchadnezzar, the king of Babylon, and
his officials. At a later time, Egypt will be
inhabited again as in times past, says the
LORD.[o]

27 But as for you, my servant Jacob, fear not;
Israel, do not be dismayed.
Behold, I will rescue you from afar
and your descendants from the land of their exile.
Jacob will return and be at peace again,
tranquil, with no one to trouble him.
28 Have no fear, my servant Jacob,
for I am with you, says the LORD.
I will make an end of all the nations
where I have dispersed you,
but I will not make an end of you.
I will discipline you only as you deserve;
I will not allow you to escape totally unpunished.[p]

k Deut 32:42; Isa 13:6.—l Jer 43:10f; Isa 19:1.—m Lev 26:36f.—n Jer 21:14; Jdg 6:5; Joel 2:25.—o Jer 44:30; Ezek 29:11-14.—p Jer 30:11.

46:18 *Like Tabor:* the reference is to Nebuchadnezzar. Tabor dominates the plain of Galilee.

46:20 *Heifer:* an allusion to the worship of Hathor, the cow-headed goddess.

46:23 The *forest* symbolizes the especially dense population of the Nile Delta.

46:25 *Amon:* the national god of Egypt.

CHAPTER 47*

Against the Philistines. 1 This is the word of
the LORD that came to the prophet
Jeremiah concerning the Philistines before
Pharaoh attacked Gaza.[q] 2 Thus says the
LORD:

Behold how the waters are rising from the north;
they will become an everlasting torrent.
They shall flood the land and all that is in it,
the towns and those who live in them.
People will cry out for help,
and all the inhabitants of the land will wail.

3 On hearing the thundering hooves of the stallions,
the noise of the chariots and their rumbling wheels,
fathers do not turn to help their children;
their hands fall limp,[r]
4* because the day has come
to destroy all the Philistines,
and to cut off Tyre and Sidon
from any allies who could support them.
The LORD is destroying the Philistines,
the remnant from the coasts of Caphtor.
5 Baldness has afflicted Gaza;
Ashkelon has been silenced.
O remnant of the Philistine strength,
how long will you continue to gash yourselves?

6 Ah, sword of the LORD,
how long will it be before you rest?
Return back to your scabbard.
Cease and be still.
7 But how can you be at rest
when the LORD has given you an order,
when he has commanded you to subdue
Ashkelon and the seacoast?[s]

CHAPTER 48*

Against Moab. 1 In regard to Moab, thus
says the LORD of hosts, the God of Israel:

How sad it is that Nebo has been laid waste;
Kiriathaim has been captured and put to shame.
The fortress has been disgraced and overthrown;
2 the glory of Moab no longer exists.
In Heshbon, they plot her downfall:
"Come, let us put an end to her as a nation."
And you too, inhabitants of Madmen,
will be reduced to silence,
slain by the sword.
3 Cries of anguish rise up from Horonaim,[t]
speaking of devastation and complete destruction.
4 Moab has been crushed;
the agonized cries of her little ones
can be heard as far away as Zoar.
5 On the ascent to Luhith
they climb weeping bitterly.
On the descent to Horonaim
the anguished cry of destruction is heard:
6 "Flee! Save your lives!
Survive like a wild ass in the desert!"

7 Because you placed your trust
in your strongholds and your treasures,
you also will be captured.
Chemosh will go into exile,
along with all his priests and attendants.[u]
8 The destroyer will move against every town;
not a single town will escape.
The valley will be laid waste,
and the plain will be destroyed,
as the LORD has said.

9 Set aside salt for Moab,
for she will be laid waste;
her towns will be left in ruins,
without a single inhabitant.
10 Accursed are those who are negligent
in doing the work of the LORD,
and accursed also is the one
who withholds his sword from bloodshed.

11 From its earliest days
Moab has been undisturbed
and never has gone into exile.

---

q Ezek 25:15f; Am 1:6; Zep 2:4.—r Jer 8:16.—s Ezek 14:17.—t 3ff: Isa 15:5.—u Jer 9:23; Num 21:29.

47:1-7 The king of Babylon was God's sword in punishing Judah and all the people. Here he was, at work against the Philistines, the terrible enemies of former times. The song is undoubtedly later than 605 B.C.

47:4-5 *Caphtor:* Crete, from which, it seems, the Philistines came. The cuts (v. 5) were signs of mourning.

48:1-47 This lengthy composition, marked by bitterness and irony, on the lot in store for Moab shows that Israel had long pondered its resentment against this neighbor, which had thrown itself on Israel like dogs unleashed against the game by the hunter (see 2 Ki 24:2).

It has been like wine settled on its lees
that has never been transferred
from one decanter to another.
Thus its flavor has remained unaltered,
and its aroma has stayed unchanged. [v]
12 Therefore, the days are coming, says the LORD,
when I will send men to him
to tilt the jars.
They will empty the vessels
and smash the jars.
13 Moab will then be ashamed of Chemosh,
as the house of Israel was ashamed of Bethel*
in which they placed their trust. [w]
14 How can you say, "We are heroes,
men who are valiant in battle"?
15 The destroyer of Moab and its towns
has launched an attack,
and the flower of its youth has been slaughtered,
says the King, whose name is the LORD of hosts.
16 The destruction of Moab is near at hand,
and its doom will come shortly.
17 Grieve, all you neighbors of Moab
and all who were familiar with its name.
Say, "How the mighty staff is broken,
the glorious scepter!"
18 Descend from your seat of glory
and sit on the parched ground,
you who dwell in Dibon.
For the ravager of Moab has advanced against you
and destroyed your strongholds. [x]
19 Stand by the roadside and watch,
you who dwell in Aroer.
Question the man fleeing and the woman escaping;
ask them, "What has happened?"
20 Moab has been destroyed and reduced to shame.
Wail and cry out, proclaim by the Arnon,
that Moab has been laid waste. [y]

21 Judgment has come upon the plateau:
upon Holon, Jahzah, and Mephaath, 22 upon
Dibon, Nebo, and Beth-diblathaim, 23 upon
Kiriathaim, Beth-gamul, and Beth-meon,
24 upon Kiriath, and Bozrah, and all the
towns of the land of Moab, far and near.

25 The horn of Moab has been cut off,
and her arm has been broken, says the LORD.

26 Make Moab drunk, because she has
placed herself on an equal level with the
LORD. Let Moab wallow in her vomit and
become a laughingstock. 27 Israel was once a
laughingstock for you, although she was
never caught in the company of thieves. Yet
each time you spoke about her, you would
shake your head. [z]

28 Leave your towns, O inhabitants of Moab,
and make your home among the rocks.
Be like a dove that makes its nest
along the edge of a gorge.
29 * We have heard about the pride of Moab,
pride that exceeds all bounds:
her pride and her arrogance
and the haughtiness of her heart.
30 I am fully aware of her arrogance, says the LORD;
her boasts are false, her deeds are false.
31 Therefore, I wail over Moab;
I cry out in anguish for all of Moab;
I mourn for the men of Kir-heres. [a]
32 More than for Jazer I weep for you,
O vineyard of Sibmah.
Your branches stretched beyond the sea,
reaching all the way to Jazer.
Upon your harvest and your vintage,
the despoiler has descended. [b]
33 Gladness and joy have been removed
from the orchards of Moab.
I have stanched the flow of wine from the vats;
the joyful shouts of the treader of grapes
can no longer be heard.

34 Heshbon and Elealeh utter cries of
anguish that can be heard as far away as
Jahaz. The shrieks echo from Zoar to Horo-
naim and Eglath-shelishiyah. For even the
waters of Nimrim have become a desert
waste. 35 In Moab, I will bring to an end the
practice of those who offer holocausts on the
high places or burn incense to their gods,
says the LORD.

---

v Jer 22:21; Zep 1:12.—**w** Isa 16:12.—**x** Jer 46:19; Num 21:30.—**y** Isa 16:7.—**z** Jer 2:26; Zep 2:8ff.—**a** Isa 16:7, 11.—**b** Isa 16:8f.

48:13 *Bethel:* the sanctuary in the northern kingdom, erected in opposition to the temple in Jerusalem.

48:29-39 Moab, a pleasant and prosperous region, has now been devastated and weeps over its ruins. In this passage may be seen some parallels with chapters 15–16 of the Book of Isaiah.

36 That is the reason why my heart wails
like a flute for Moab and laments like a flute
for the men of Kir-heres. The wealth that
they accumulated has been lost. [c]
37 Every
head has been shaved, and every beard has
been cut off. There are gashes on every
hand, and every waist is covered with sack-
cloth.
38 On all the housetops of Moab and in all
its squares nothing is heard but cries of
lamentation, for I have broken Moab like a
piece of pottery that no one wants, says the
LORD.
39 How terrified Moab is, and how
loudly does it wail as it retreats in shame.
Moab has become a laughingstock and a
source of horror to all of its neighbors.

40 For thus says the LORD:
Behold, like an eagle I will swoop down
and spread my wings over Moab. [d]
41 The towns will be captured
and the strongholds will be seized.
On that day, the hearts of Moab's warriors
will be like the heart of a woman in labor.
42 Moab will be destroyed as a nation,
for it established itself in opposition to the LORD. [e]

43 Terror, the pit, and the snare await you,
O inhabitants of Moab, says the LORD.
44 Everyone who flees from the terror
will fall into the pit,
and everyone who climbs out of the pit
will be caught in the snare.
For I will bring all this upon Moab
in the year of her punishment, says the LORD.

45 In the shadow of Heshbon,
the fugitives stop in exhaustion.
For a fire has blazed forth from Heshbon,
and flames from the house of Sihon,
consuming the brow of Moab
and the skulls of the noisy revelers.* [f]

46 Woe to you, O Moab!
You have been destroyed, O people of Chemosh.
For your sons have been led forth in exile
and your daughters into captivity.
47 Even so, I will restore the fortunes of Moab
in the days to come, says the LORD. [g]

Thus far is the judgment on Moab.

CHAPTER 49

Against the Ammonites.* 1 In regard to the Ammonites, thus says the LORD:

Has Israel no sons?
Has he no heir?
Why then has Milcom inherited Gad,
and why have his people settled in its towns?
2 Therefore, the days are coming,
says the LORD,
when I will sound the battle cry
against Rabbah of the Ammonites.
It will become a desolate mound,
and its villages will be burned to the ground.
Then Israel will dispossess
those who dispossessed her, says the LORD.

3 Wail, O Heshbon, for Ai has been laid waste.
Cry out, O daughters of Rabbah.
Wrap yourselves in sackcloth and mourn;
run to and fro and gash your bodies.
For Milcom will go into exile
together with his priests and his attendants. [h]
4 Why do you glory in your strength
that is now beginning to ebb?
O rebellious daughter,
you place your trust in your treasures,
saying, "Who will dare to attack me?"

5 I will bring terror upon you from every side,
says the Lord GOD of hosts.
Every one of you will be driven away and scattered,
with no one to rally the fugitives. [i]
6 But afterward, says the LORD,
I will restore the fortunes of the Ammonites.

Against Edom.* 7 In regard to Edom, thus says the LORD of hosts:

c Isa 15:5, 7; 16:11.—d Jer 49:22.—e Isa 37:23; Zep 2:9f.—f Num 21:28f.—g Jer 49:6, 39.—h Jer 48:2; Isa 15:2ff.—i Jer 46:5.

48:45 The oracle recalls Sihon, the Amorite king defeated by Egypt in Moses' time (Num 21:23-29); Heshbon had been his capital (Num 21:26).

49:1-6 Ammon, a racial brother of Israel, was also a hostile brother (Gen 19:38; 2 Ki 24:2). But his chief crime was to have attacked the sacred domain of the Lord by occupying the territory of the tribe of Gad, his neighbor (see Jos 13:24-28). His god was Molech; Rabbah is the present-day Amman, capital of Jordan.

49:7-22 Entrenched as it was on rocky summits, the land of Edom, with its two districts, Teman and Dedan, may have thought itself sheltered. It was also a country of wise men (see Job 15:17-19). The people were descended from Esau, brother of

Can wisdom no longer be found in Teman?
Has counsel ceased to exist in the prudent?
Has their wisdom become a thing of the past?
8 Turn away and flee, O inhabitants of Dedan;
seek refuge in remote locales.
For I will inflict retribution on Esau
when I decide upon the time to punish him.
9 If those who gather grapes were to come upon you,
would they not leave behind some gleanings?
If thieves came during the night,
would they not steal only what they wanted?[j]
10 But I for my part will strip Esau bare;
I will discover his hiding places,
and he will have nowhere to conceal himself.
His children will perish,
as will his relatives and neighbors,
and he will be no more.[k]
11 Leave behind your orphans;
I will support them,
and your widows will place their trust in me.

12 For thus says the LORD: If those who were
not doomed to drink the cup still must drink
it, should you alone be the one to go unpun-
ished? You will not go unpunished. You will be
required to drink it. 13 For by my own self I
have sworn, says the LORD, that Bozrah will
become an object of horror and reproach, a
desolate wasteland, and a curse, and all her
towns will be ruins forevermore.[l]

14 I have received a message from the LORD,
a herald has been sent to all the nations,
"Gather together and prepare to attack her;
rise up for battle."
15 I will make you the least among the nations,
the most despised of people, O Edom.[m]
16 You have been deceived by your proud heart
and by the terror you inspire,
you who dwell in rocky crags
and look down from the heights of the hill.
Even though you build your nest as high as the eagle's,
I will drag you down from there, says the LORD.

17 Edom will become an object of horror.
Everyone who passes by will be appalled and
astounded at the sight of all her wounds. 18 As
when Sodom and Gomorrah and their neigh-
bors were overthrown, no one will live there,
nor will anyone ever again settle there.[n]

19 As when a lion comes up to rich pastures
from the dense thickets of the Jordan,
so will I in an instant drive away Edom from its land
and designate those whom I wish to settle there.
For who is like me?
Who can bring charges against me?
What shepherd can stand his ground against me?[o]
20 Therefore, hear the plan
that the LORD has devised against Edom
and the schemes that he has in mind
to forestall the inhabitants of Teman.
They will be dragged away
like the smallest of the flock,
and their pastures will be completely destroyed.
21 At the sound of their downfall,
the earth will tremble,
and their anguished cries will be heard
as far away as the Red Sea.
22 Like an eagle he will soar and swoop down
and spread his wings against Bozrah,
and the hearts of Edom's warriors on that day
will be like the heart of a woman in labor.[p]

Against Damascus.* 23 Concerning Damas-
cus:

Hamath and Arpad are deeply troubled,
for they have heard distressing news.

---

j Ob 5.—k Ob 6; Mal 1:3.—l Jer 44:26; Isa 34:6.—m Ob 2.—n Jer 50:40; Deut 29:23.—o Jer 12:5; 50:44; Isa 46:9.—p Jer 4:13.

Jacob (see Gen 26), and had engaged in continual quarrels and conflicts with the Hebrews; this hostile brother had struck Israel in the back and had shown itself especially hateful at the time when Jerusalem was in ruins (see Ezek 25:12-14; 35:15).

49:23-27 Damascus and the other Syrian cities had often seen invaders passing through their land. Damascus was the capital of an Aramean state that was a stubborn rival of Israel. This magnificent oasis was at the center of the great communication routes. Some of its princes bore the name Ben-hadad.

In their concern, they are filled with anxiety,
tossed about like the sea
that cannot be calmed.
24 Damascus has been weakened;
gripped with panic, she prepares to flee.
Anguish and sorrow have overwhelmed her;
her pain is like that of a woman in labor.
25 How can this renowned city be forsaken
in which I take such delight? [q]
26 Her young men will fall in her squares,
and all her warriors will perish on that day,
says the LORD of hosts.
27 Then I will set fire to the walls of Damascus
that will devour the palaces of Ben-hadad.

Against Arabia.* 28 In regard to Kedar and the kingdoms of Hazor that were conquered by Nebuchadnezzar, the king of Babylon, thus says the LORD:

Rise up and attack Kedar.
Destroy the desert dwellers of the east.
29 Carry away their tents and their flocks,
their tent curtains and all their goods.
Seize their camels for yourselves
and let the shout be raised,
"There is terror on every side." [r]
30 Flee quickly to distant areas,
and take refuge in remote places,
inhabitants of Hazor, says the LORD.
For King Nebuchadnezzar of Babylon
is determined to eradicate you
and has formulated a plan against you.
31 Thus says the LORD:
Rise up against a nation
that never bothers to strengthen its security,
that has no gates or bars
and is located in a remote area.
32 Their camels will become your booty,
and their herds of cattle will be your spoil.
I will scatter to the winds
those who shave their temples,
and I will bring ruin on them
from every side, says the LORD. [s]
33 Hazor will become the lair of jackals,
an everlasting place of desolation,
where no one will live anymore,
nor will anyone stay there again.

Against Elam.* 34 This word of the LORD came to the prophet Jeremiah in regard to Elam, at the beginning of the reign of Zedekiah, the king of Judah. 35 Thus says the LORD of hosts:

Behold, I will break the bow of Elam,
the mainstay of their might.
36 I will bring upon Elam the four winds
from the four quarters of the heavens.
I will scatter them to all these winds,
and there will not be a single nation
to which the exiles of Elam will not go. [t]
37 I will cause the people of Elam
to tremble before their foes
and before those who are determined to kill them.
I will bring disaster upon them,
my burning anger, says the LORD.
I will pursue them with the sword
until I have completely destroyed them.
38 Then I will establish my throne in Elam
and destroy their king and his officials,
says the LORD.
39 However, in the days to come
I will restore the fortunes of Elam,
says the LORD.

CHAPTER 50

A Prophecy against Babylon. 1 *This is the word which the LORD spoke against Babylon and the land of the Chaldeans, through the prophet Jeremiah: [u]

2 Declare this among the nations and proclaim it;
lift up a banner and proclaim it;
keep nothing back, but announce,

q Jer 33:9.—r Jer 4:20.—s Jer 9:26; Ezek 12:14.—t Ezek 5:10.—u Isa 13:1.

49:28-33 The king of Babylon is urged to deal ferociously with these people who were the distant descendants of Ishmael. We may think of the elusive Bedouin, whose caravans cross the desert, and of the sheik-led seminomadic or semisedentary tribes installed with their immense flocks in villages of tents and of straw mixed with clay on the edge of the steppes.

49:34-39 Elam, in the region northeast of the Persian Gulf, was famous for its archers (see v. 35; Isa 22:6). This people was not strictly an enemy of Israel.

50:1—51:57 In Jeremiah's eyes, Babylon was only an instrument in God's hands, and he knew that sooner or later its control of the East would be taken from it. The prophet had predicted that Israel would be reprieved. Made confident by these reflections of Jeremiah, his disciples here proclaim the judgment of the Lord against the Chaldeans, at a time when, toward the middle of the sixth century B.C., their power was beginning to decline and the deportees were hoping for deliverance. We are in the atmosphere that reigned before 538 B.C. and which we know from Second Isaiah.

"Babylon will be captured;
Bel* will be put to shame;
Marduk will be dismayed.
Her images are disgraced;
her idols are shattered."
3 A nation from the north is marching against her
that will turn her land into a desolate waste,
so that no one will be able to live there anymore;
both men and beasts have fled and are gone. [v]

4 In those days and at that time,
says the LORD,
the people of Israel and of Judah will come,
weeping as they seek the LORD, their God.
5 They will ask the way to Zion
and turn their faces toward it, saying,
"Come, let us bind ourselves to the LORD
in an everlasting covenant
that will never be forgotten."

6 My people were lost sheep;
their shepherds led them astray
and caused them to roam on the mountains.
They wandered over mountains and hills
and lost the way to their fold. [w]
7 Whoever came upon them devoured them,
and their enemies insisted,
"We incur no guilt,
because they have sinned
against the LORD, their true pasture,
against the LORD, the hope of their fathers."

8 Flee from Babylon and the land of the Chaldeans;
be like male goats leading the flock.
9 Behold, I will stir up against Babylon
a host of mighty nations from the land of the north.
They will advance against her,
and there she will be conquered.
Their arrows are like those of a skilled warrior
that are never shot unsuccessfully. [x]
10 Chaldea will be plundered,
and all who plunder her will be sated,
says the LORD.

11 O you who plundered my heritage,
although you rejoice and exult,
although you playfully frolic
like heifers on the grass
and neigh like stallions,
12 your mother* will be cruelly put to shame;
she who bore you will be completely disgraced.
She is now the least of the nations,
a desert, a parched land, a wilderness. [y]
13 Because of the wrath of the LORD
she will not be inhabited
but will be totally desolate.
Everyone who passes by Babylon will be appalled
and stunned at the enormity of her wounds. [z]

14 Take up your positions and surround Babylon,
all you who draw the bow.
Shoot at her, and do not spare your arrows,
for she has sinned against the LORD.* [a]
15 Raise your war cries against her on all sides;
shout in triumph,
"She has surrendered,
her bastions have fallen,
her walls have been demolished."
This is the vengeance of the LORD.
Avenge yourselves on her;
as she has done, so do to her. [b]

16 Drive out from Babylon the sowers
and those who wield the sickle at harvest time.
To escape the destroying sword,
all of them will return to their own people;
all of them will flee to their own land.
17 Israel is a scattered flock
that was pursued by lions.
First the king of Assyria devoured her,
and now her bones have been crushed
by Nebuchadnezzar, the king of Babylon.

18 Therefore, thus says the LORD of hosts, the God of Israel:

v Jer 51:48; Isa 13:17.—w Isa 53:6; Ezek 34:5.—x Jer 51:27.—y Jer 51:43.—z Jer 19:8.—a Jer 51:11; Isa 21:2.—b Jer 51:24.

50:2 *Bel* was an ancient Sumerian deity; his name was then taken over by the Babylonian national god, Marduk.
50:12 *Mother:* the Babylonian nation.
50:14 The archers here are the Elamites.

I intend to punish the king of Babylon
and his land,
as I formerly punished the king of Assyria.[c]
19 I will restore Israel to her pastures,
and she will graze on Carmel and in Bashan;
on the hills of Ephraim and in Gilead
her hunger will be satisfied.

20 In those days, and at that time,
says the LORD,
you will search for evidence of the iniquity of Israel,
but there will be none,
and for the sins of Judah,
but these will no longer be found,
for I will pardon the remnant
of those that I have preserved.[d]

21 Attack the land of Merathaim*
and the inhabitants of Pekod.
Put them to the sword and destroy them;
do all I have commanded you, says the LORD.
22 The noise of battle amid great destruction
is heard throughout the land.
23 See how the hammer of the whole world
has been broken and shattered,
how Babylon has become
an object of horror among the nations.

24 I set a snare for you, O Babylon,
and you were caught before you realized it.
You were discovered and seized
because you challenged the LORD.[e]
25 The LORD has opened his armory
and brought forth the weapons of his wrath.
For the Lord GOD has work to do
in the land of the Chaldeans.

26 Come against her from every side;
open her granaries,
pile up her goods in heaps,
and completely destroy her
until nothing of her is left.
27 Slay all her bulls;
lead them down to the slaughterhouse.
Woe to them, for their time has come,
their day of punishment.

28 Listen! Fugitives and refugees
from the land of Babylon
have arrived in Zion to proclaim
the vengeance of the LORD, our God,
the vengeance he inflicts for his temple.[f]

29 Summon against Babylon the archers,
all those who are skilled with the bow.
Surround her on all sides;
allow no one to escape.
Repay her in full for her misdeeds;
treat her as she has treated others.[g]
30 Therefore, her young men will fall in the streets,
and all her soldiers will be destroyed on that day,
says the LORD.[h]

31 I am against you, O arrogant city,
says the LORD of hosts.
For your day has come,
the time for me to punish you.
32 You will stumble and fall, O arrogant city,
and no one will offer to raise you up.
I will kindle a fire in your cities
that will devour everything within it.[i]

33 Thus says the LORD of hosts:
The people of Israel are oppressed,
as are the people of Judah.
All their captors hold them fast
and refuse to let them go.

34 But their redeemer* is strong;
his name is the LORD of hosts.
He will successfully take up their cause,
thereby affording rest to the earth
while leaving the inhabitants of Babylon in turmoil.[j]

35 A sword against the Chaldeans, says the LORD,
against the inhabitants of Babylon,
and against her officials and her wise men.
36 A sword against her false prophets;
they will become fools.
A sword against her warriors;
they will succumb to panic.
37 A sword against her horses and her chariots
and all the foreign troops in her midst;
they will become like women.
A sword against her treasures;
they will be plundered.
38 A drought against her waters;
they will be dried up.

c Isa 10:12; Ezek 31:3.—d Jer 31:34; Isa 1:9; Mic 7:19.—e Jer 51:57.—f Jer 51:10-11; Isa 48:20.—g Jer 51:56.—h Jer 49:26; 51:4.—i Jer 21:14; Isa 10:12-15.—j Jer 51:19, 36.

50:21 *Merathaim* and *Pekod:* regions of Babylonia, the Hebrew names of which ("twofold rebellion" and "visit, punish") lend themselves to a play on words.

50:34 *Redeemer:* Hebrew, *goel*; see Lev 25:25.

For it is a land of idols,
and they will be overcome with terror
when confronted by them. [k]

39 Therefore, wildcats and jackals will dwell there,
and there ostriches will make their home.
Never again will it be inhabited;
no people ever again will dwell there.
40 As when God overthrew Sodom and Gomorrah
and all their neighboring towns, says the LORD,
no one will live there anymore
or attempt to settle there. [l]

41 Look! A people is coming from the north,
a mighty nation.
Many kings are rousing themselves
from the ends of the earth.
42 They wield bows and spears,
and their cruelty allows no mercy.
As they ride forth on their horses,
their sound resembles that of the roaring sea.
All of them are arrayed for battle
to fight against you, daughter of Babylon.

43 News of their approach has reached the king of Babylon,
and his hands fall limp at his side.
Anguish has seized him,
pangs like those of a woman in labor. [m]
44 Behold, like a lion coming up
from the thickets of the Jordan
to the perennial feeding grounds,
I will in a single instant drive them away
and appoint over her whomever I choose.
For who is there like me?
Who can challenge me?
What shepherd can stand up to me?

45 Therefore, hear the plan
that the LORD has devised against Babylon,
and what he proposes to do
against the land of the Chaldeans:
The young of the flock will be dragged away,
and he will completely destroy their pastures. [n]

46 The earth will tremble at the news,
and the shouting will be heard among the nations.

CHAPTER 51

Another Prophecy against Babylon

1 Thus says the LORD:
Against Babylon and the inhabitants of Chaldea
I will rouse a destructive wind.
2 I will send foreigners to Babylon
to winnow her and lay waste her land.
They will besiege her from all sides
on the day of disaster. [o]

3 Let no archer draw his bow
or array himself in his coat of armor.
Do not spare her young men;
completely destroy her entire army.
4 Let them be slain in the land of the Chaldeans,
lying mortally wounded in her streets.

5 For Israel and Judah have not been forsaken
by their God, the LORD of hosts,
although their land is full of guilt
that will not be ignored by the Holy One of Israel.
6 Flee from Babylon!
Save your lives, each one of you!
Do not perish for her guilt.
This is the time of vengeance for the LORD;
he will exact full recompense for their deeds. [p]

7 Babylon was a golden cup
in the hand of the LORD,
and she made the entire earth drunk.
The nations drank her wine,
and now they have gone mad.
8 Suddenly Babylon has fallen and is shattered.
Wail for her.
Fetch balm for her wounds;
perhaps she can be cured.

9 We tried to heal Babylon,
but she cannot be healed.
Leave her and let us depart,
each one to his own land.
For her judgment reaches up to heaven
and touches the clouds. [q]
10 The LORD has made clear our vindication.
Come, let us proclaim in Zion
what the LORD, our God, has done.

k Jer 51:32, 36.—l Jer 49:18; Gen 19:24-25.—m Jer 51:31; Isa 13:7.—n Jer 51:12; Isa 14:24.—o Jer 15:7; Isa 41:16.—p Jer 50:8, 15.—q Jer 50:16; Rev 18:5; Isa 13:14.

11 Sharpen the arrows;
fill the quivers.
The LORD has stirred up
the spirit of the kings of the Medes
because he is determined to destroy Babylon.
This will be the vengeance of the LORD,
vengeance for his temple. [r]
12 Raise the standard against the walls of Babylon.
Strengthen the watch.
Post sentinels and prepare ambushes,
for the LORD has both planned and will carry out
his threat against the inhabitants of Babylon.
13 You lands that lie on the shores of abundant waters
and are rich in treasures,
your end has now come,
the cessation of your power.
14 The LORD of hosts has sworn by himself,
"I will fill you with enemies
as numerous as a swarm of locusts,
and they will raise a shout of victory over you."

15 By his power, he made the earth;
by his wisdom, he established the world;
by his discernment, he stretched out the heavens. [s]
16 When he thunders,
there is a tumult of waters in the heavens,
and he causes the clouds to rise
from the farthest ends of the earth.
He sends forth lightning with the rain,
and he brings out the wind from his storehouses.

17 Everyone is stupid and lacking in knowledge;
goldsmiths are put to shame by their idols,
for the images they cast are a sham,
with no breath of life in them.
18 They devise worthless objects of mockery;
at the time of judgment, they will perish.
19 Not like these is the portion of Jacob,
for he is the Creator of all things,
and Israel is the tribe of his inheritance;
the LORD of hosts is his name.

20 You are my war club,
my weapon in battle.
With you I shatter nations,
with you I destroy kingdoms.
21 With you I crush horse and rider,
with you I crush chariot and charioteer. [t]
22 With you I crush man and woman,
with you I crush old and young,
with you I crush youth and maiden.
23 With you I crush shepherd and flock,
with you I crush the plowman and his team,
with you I crush governors and magistrates.
24 Thus will I repay Babylon
and all the inhabitants of Chaldea
for all the wrongs that they have done in Zion
before your very eyes, says the LORD.

25 I am against you, O mountain of destruction,
destroyer of the entire earth, says the LORD. [u]
I will stretch forth my hand against you,
send you tumbling down from the cliffs,
and make you a burned-out mountain.
26 No rock will be taken from you
to be used for a cornerstone,
nor any stone for a foundation,
for you will be forever desolate,
says the LORD.

27 Raise a standard throughout the earth.
Blow the trumpet among the nations.
Consecrate nations for war against her.
Summon against her these kingdoms:
Ararat,* Minni, and Ashkenaz.
Appoint a commander against her.
Bring forward horses bristling like locusts. [v]
28 Consecrate nations for war against her:
the kings of Media,
its governors and magistrates,
and all the lands under their rule.
29 The earth trembles and writhes
as the LORD's plan against Babylon is carried out,
turning the land of Babylon into a desert waste.
30 The warriors of Babylon have ceased to fight;
they remain in their strongholds.

---

r Jer 46:4; Isa 13:17.—s Jer 10:12-16; Prov 3:9.—t Ex 15:4; Dan 7:7, 19, 23.—u Jer 50:31; Rev 8:8.—v Jer 50:2; Isa 13:2.

51:27 *Ararat* and *Minni* are regions of Armenia. *Ashkenaz* refers to the Scythians.

Their courage has failed;
they are now like women.
Their buildings have been set on fire,
and their gates are shattered.
31 One courier appears after another,
and one messenger follows another,
to inform the king of Babylon
that his entire city has been taken. [w]
32 The river crossings have been seized,
the marshes have been set afire,
and the soldiers are overcome with terror.

33 For thus says the LORD of hosts, the God of Israel:

The daughter of Babylon is like a threshing floor
at the time it is being trodden.
Yet it will only be a short while
before the time of her harvest will come. [x]
34 "King Nebuchadnezzar has devoured us;
he has routed us
and set us aside like an empty dish.
Like a serpent he has swallowed us,
filled his stomach with our delicacies,
and then spewed us out.
35 May our torn flesh be avenged on Babylon,"
the inhabitants of Zion say.
"May my blood be avenged
on the inhabitants of Chaldea,"
Jerusalem says.
36 Therefore, thus says the LORD:
I will take up your cause
and ensure that you will be avenged.
I will dry up her sea*
and cause her springs to run dry.
37 Babylon will become a heap of ruins,
a haunt of jackals,
an object of horror and scorn,
where no one lives. [y]
38 Like lions they roar together
and growl like lion cubs.
39 But when they are afflicted with fever,
I will set a drink before them
and cause them to become drunk
so that they will sink into an unending sleep,
never to awaken again, says the LORD.
40 I will bring them down like lambs to the slaughter,
like rams and goats.
41 Babylon has been seized and conquered,
she who was the pride of the entire world.
What an object of horror
has Babylon become among the nations. [z]
42 The sea has surged over Babylon,
covering her with its roaring waves.
43 Her cities have become desert wastelands,
nothing more than parched and arid land,
an area in which no one lives
and through which no one passes.
44 I will punish Bel in Babylon
and compel him to spew out what he has swallowed.
The nations will no longer stream to him;
the wall of Babylon has fallen.
45 Leave her, my people.
Save your lives, each one of you,
from the fierce anger of the LORD.
46 Do not become faint-hearted or fearful
at various rumors that are heard in the land.
One year a certain rumor will spread,
the next year another one,
with rumors of possible violence in the land
and of conflicts between rulers. [a]
47 But behold, the days are coming
when I will punish the idols of Babylon;
her entire territory will be put to shame,
and all her slain warriors
will lie fallen within her borders.
48 The heavens and the earth
and all that are in them
will shout for joy in regard to Babylon,
for marauders will descend from the north
and attack her, says the LORD. [b]
49 Babylon, too, must fall
because of the slain of Israel,
just as the slain of all the earth
have fallen at the hands of Babylon.
50 You who have escaped the sword,
leave and do not linger.
Remember the LORD from afar,
and let Jerusalem remain in your thoughts.

---

w 2 Chr 30:6.—x Rev 14:15; Isa 21:10.—y Jer 50:39; Isa 13:20.—z Isa 13:19.—a Mt 24:6f.—b Rev 18:20.

51:36 The *sea* and the *springs* are the Euphrates and its branches.

51 We have been put to shame
because of the insults we have endured.
Our faces were covered in confusion
because foreigners have dared to enter
the holy places of the LORD's house. [c]

52 However, the days are surely coming,
says the LORD,
when I will punish her idols,
and the wounded will groan
throughout all her land.

53 Even if Babylon were to scale the heavens
and reinforce her inaccessible citadel,
I would send forth destroyers,
and they would come to her.

54 Agonized cries can be heard from Babylon,
and sounds of great destruction
from the land of the Chaldeans.

55 For the LORD is laying waste to Babylon
and stilling her loud cries of anguish.
Massive waves of enemies will roar like
mighty waters,
and their clamor will be heard from
afar.

56 A destroying force is moving against Babylon;
her warriors are captured,
and their bows are broken.
For the LORD is a God of retribution,
and he never fails to repay in full. [d]

57 I will make her princes and her wise men
drunk,
as well as her governors,
her prefects and her warriors.
They will sink into an unending sleep,
never to awaken again,
says the King whose name is the LORD
of hosts.

58 * Thus says the LORD of hosts:
The thick walls of Babylon will be leveled
to the ground,
and her lofty gates will be destroyed by
fire.
Thus the peoples exhaust themselves for
nothing,
and the nations weary themselves only
for the flames. [e]

Destruction of Babylon Foretold. 59 This is
the message that the prophet Jeremiah gave
to the quartermaster Seraiah,* the son of
Neriah, the son of Mahseiah, when he went
to Babylon with King Zedekiah of Judah in
the fourth year of his reign.
60 Jeremiah had enumerated on a scroll all
of the disasters that would befall Babylon—
everything that had been recorded in regard
to Babylon. 61 He said to Seraiah, "When you
reach Babylon, make sure that you read all
these words aloud. 62 Then say, 'O LORD, you
yourself declared your firm resolve to
destroy this place so that neither man nor
beast will ever live here again; it will be a
desolate waste forever.'
63 "When you have finished reading this
scroll, tie a stone to it and cast it into the
middle of the Euphrates. [f] 64 Then say, 'In the
same way will Babylon sink, never again to
rise because of the disaster I intend to inflict
upon her.' "

Thus far are the words of Jeremiah.

VI: HISTORICAL APPENDIX

CHAPTER 52*

The Siege of Jerusalem. 1 Zedekiah was
twenty-one years old when he became king,
and he reigned for eleven years in Jerusalem.
His mother's name was Hamutal, the
daughter of Jeremiah of Libnah. 2 He did
what was evil in the eyes of the LORD, just as
Jehoiakim had done. 3 Indeed Jerusalem and
Judah so aroused the anger of the LORD that
he cast them away from his presence.

Zedekiah rebelled against the king of
Babylon. 4 [g] Therefore, in the ninth year of
his reign, on the tenth day of the month,
Nebuchadnezzar, the king of Babylon,
advanced against Jerusalem with his entire
army. They encamped around the city and
constructed siege-works against it on every
side. 5 The city remained under siege until
the eleventh year of King Zedekiah.
6 On the ninth day of the fourth month
there was such a severe famine in the city
that there was no food available for the people
to eat. 7 Then a breach was made in the

c Ps 74:18.—d Ps 94:1-2; Nah 1:2.—e Jer 50:15; Hab 2:13.—f Rev 18:21.—g 4-16: Jer 39:1-10; 2 Ki 25:1-7.

51:58-64 Although the preceding collection of oracles cannot be attributed directly to Jeremiah, there is no serious reason for not attributing to him this symbolic action which is very much in his style. The editor decided to place this story after the lengthy prophecy that precedes.

51:59 *Seraiah:* brother of Baruch; see Bar 1:1.

52:1-34 This final chapter, which is found almost identically in Jer 39:1-7; 2 Ki 24:18-20; 25:1-21, 27-30, is not from Jeremiah. It seems that toward the end of the Exile, the editor introduced it as a conclusion in which to render homage and justice to a prophet who had been so assailed and questioned during his lifetime.

city wall, and all of the soldiers fled, departing from the city under the cover of darkness by the gate between the two walls near the king's garden, and they set off in the direction of the Arabah, even though the Chaldeans were surrounding the city. 8 The army of the Chaldeans set off in pursuit of the king, and they overtook Zedekiah in the plains of Jericho, while his army deserted him and scattered in all directions.

9 After Zedekiah was captured, he was taken to Riblah in the land of Hamath, where the king of Babylon passed sentence on him. 10 He had the sons of Zedekiah slaughtered before their father's eyes, and he also put to death the princes of Judah at Riblah. 11 Then the king of Babylon put out the eyes of Zedekiah, bound him in fetters, and took him to Babylon, confining him in prison until the day of his death.

The Fall of Jerusalem. 12 On the tenth day of the fifth month—this was in the nineteenth year of Nebuchadnezzar, king of Babylon—Nebuzaradan, the captain of the guard, arrived at Jerusalem as the representative of the king of Babylon. 13 He burned to the ground the house of the LORD, the royal palace, and all the houses of Jerusalem. Every large house he ordered to be set afire. 14 Meanwhile, all the Chaldean troops who had accompanied the captain of the guard demolished the walls that surrounded Jerusalem.

15 Then Nebuzaradan, the captain of the guard, led into exile some of the poorest people and those who remained in the city, those deserters who had defected to the king of Babylon, and the remaining artisans. 16 However, Nebuzaradan, the captain of the guard, left behind some of the poorest people of the land to serve as vinedressers and farmers.

17 The Chaldeans broke up into pieces the pillars of bronze that were in the house of the LORD, and the wheeled stand and the bronze sea that were in the house of the LORD, and they carried away all the bronze to Babylon. 18 They removed the pots, the shovels, the snuffers, the basins, the ladles, and all the bronze vessels used in worship.

19 The captain of the guard also took away the small bowls, the censers, the sprinkling bowls, the ash containers, the lampstands, the goblets, and the saucers—everything that was made of gold or of silver.

20 The bronze of the two pillars, of the one sea, and of the twelve oxen under the sea, and the wheeled stands that King Solomon had ordered to be made for the house of the LORD, encompassed more than could be weighed. 21 Each of the pillars was eighteen cubits high, and the circumference of each was twelve cubits; although it was hollow inside, its thickness was four fingers. 22 Upon it was a capital of bronze. The height of each capital was five cubits, encircled at the top of the capital with latticework and bronze pomegranates. 23 There were ninety-six pomegranates on the sides, with one hundred pomegranates encircling the latticework.

24 The captain of the guard took as prisoners the chief priest Seraiah, Zephaniah, who was the next highest in rank, and the three guardians of the threshold. 25 He also took from the city an officer who had been in command of the soldiers, seven members of the king's council who were discovered in the city, the secretary of the army commander who mustered the people of the land, and sixty of the common people who had not departed from the city.

26 Then Nebuzaradan, the captain of the guard, arrested these men and brought them to the king of Babylon at Riblah. 27 There at Riblah, in the land of Hamath, the king of Babylon ordered them to be executed. Thus Judah went into captivity after being deported from its own land.

28 * This is the number of people whom Nebuchadnezzar led away into exile: in the seventh year, three thousand and twenty-three Judeans; 29 in the eighteenth year of Nebuchadnezzar, eight hundred and thirty-two people were deported from Jerusalem; 30 in the twenty-third year of Nebuchadnezzar, Nebuzaradan, the captain of the guard, took into exile seven hundred and forty-five Judeans. Thus there was a total of four thousand six hundred persons.

Honor Bestowed on Jehoiachin. 31 [h] In the thirty-seventh year of the exile of Jehoiachin, the king of Judah, in the twelfth month, on the twenty-fifth day of the month, Evil-merodach, the king of Babylon, in the year

h 31-34: Gen 40:13; 2 Ki 25:27-30.

52:28-30 This piece of information, which is dated according to the Babylonian calendar, shows that a third deportation was added to those of 599 and 587 B.C. The figures, which are doubtless incomplete, do not correspond to those in 2 Ki 24:14-16 and do not agree given the total number of deportees.

he ascended the throne, pardoned Jehoiachin, the king of Judah and ordered him to be released from prison. [32] He spoke kindly to him and gave him a seat of honor above the seats of the other kings who were with him in Babylon.

[33] Jehoiachin laid aside his prison clothes, and for the rest of his life, he always dined at the king's table. [34] In addition, the king of Babylon granted him a regular daily allowance for as long as he lived, up to the day of his death.

THE BOOK OF LAMENTATIONS

A Humiliated People

Each of the five lamentations uses striking images to describe a national tragedy and the anguish of a humiliated people.

The fall of Jerusalem under the battering of Nebuchadnezzar was the darkest day in the entire biblical history and has already been frequently called to mind in the preceding books of the Bible. The population had been deported, the city razed to the ground, the temple destroyed. Jerusalem is nothing but a heap of ruins in which a few believers live on like ghosts. Crushed by events, they have time to think.

Their eyes are opened to the preceding moral and spiritual decadence of the people. Is not their present lot to be seen, as perhaps, the well-deserved punishment for betraying the covenant? Their funeral lament becomes an examination of conscience, a cry of repentance, a cry for mercy, a plea for forgiveness.

In the present confusion, a memory, only one, persists: the Lord is always there, his power remains unaffected despite the wrongs done by his people. He does not bear grudges forever. Now that his justice has been seen, the people must learn to discover his mercy; he will allow his mercy to take over. Out of discouragement a confident prayer already arises, a prayer marked by invincible trust.

These sorrowful songs have consoled and strengthened many who are afflicted. The Church used to use them in the liturgy of the last three days of Holy Week, in celebrating the passion of Christ, who carries the hope of the world.

Jeremiah was a devastated witness of the destruction of Jerusalem. An ancient tradition attributes these songs of mourning and unobtrusive hope to him, but many signs contradict the attribution.

Songs so carefully developed are not in keeping with the spontaneous genius of the great prophet; in fact, each lamentation is an acrostic poem, that is, each verse begins with a letter of the Hebrew alphabet in alphabetical order. We will rather have to say that these songs of mourning were composed by Jews who remained on the scene after the fall and during the years following the destruction.

CHAPTER 1

Jerusalem Deserted and Forsaken*

1 How deserted now is the city
that was formerly overflowing with people!
Once she was the greatest of the nations;
now she is like a widow.
Once she was a princess among the provinces;
now she is subjected to forced labor. [a]

a Jer 42:2.

1:1-22 This poet describes the sad state of Jerusalem after the destruction by the Chaldeans. Pleading for God's help, the city joins in the prophet's laments (v. 12) with the terrible realization that it was God's wrath that Jerusalem suffered be-

2 She weeps bitterly throughout the night,
with tears running down her cheeks.
Not a single one of those who loved her
remains to offer her comfort.
All of her friends * have betrayed her
and have become her enemies. [b]

3 After enduring intense suffering and endless servitude,
Judah has gone into exile.
She lives among the nations
but finds no resting place.
In the midst of her distress
her persecutors have overtaken her.

4 The roads to Zion mourn,
for no pilgrims now come to her festivals.
All of her gateways are deserted;
her priests groan,
her young maidens are grief-stricken
and their fate is bitter. [c]

5 Her foes have become her masters,
and her enemies prosper,
for the LORD has made her suffer
for her endless transgressions.
Her children are no longer there,
having been taken captive by their oppressor.

6 Every vestige of splendor
has departed from the daughter of Zion. *
Her princes have become like stags
that can find no pasture;
with their strength exhausted
they flee before their pursuers.

7 In the days of her misery and distress
Jerusalem will remember those times
when her people were overcome by the enemy,
and she had no one to help her.
Her foes mocked her unceasingly
and laughed over her downfall.

8 Because Jerusalem had sinned so grievously,
she was regarded as an object of defilement.
All those who honored her now despise her
after having beheld her nakedness.
She herself groans in anguish
and turns her face away. [d]

9 Her filthiness befouled her skirts;
she gave no thought to her future.
Her downfall was incredible,
and there was no one to comfort her.
"O LORD, look at my affliction,
for the enemy has triumphed."

10 The enemy stretched out their hands
to seize all her treasures.
She beheld the nations
invade her sanctuary,
those whom you had forbidden
to come into your assembly. [e]

11 All her people groan
as they desperately search for bread.
They trade their treasures for food
to keep themselves alive.
Look, O LORD, and see
how worthless I have become.

12 All of you who pass this way,
look and see.
Is there any sorrow like the sorrow
that has been inflicted upon me
which the LORD forced me to suffer
on the day of his fierce anger?

13 From on high he sent down fire
that lodged deep in my bones.
He spread a net for my feet
and turned me back.
He left me desolate
and in a state of weakness all day long.

14 My sins have been bound into a yoke,
woven together by his hand.
They weigh down my neck
and sap my strength.
The LORD has handed me over
to those whom I cannot withstand.

15 The LORD has totally rejected
all the warriors in my midst,
and he has summoned an army against me
to crush my young warriors. [f]
The LORD has trodden in the winepress
the virgin daughter of Judah.

16 This is why I weep
and my eyes flow with tears.
Anyone who could comfort and strengthen me
is far from my presence.
My children are desolate,
for the enemy has prevailed. [g]

---

b Jer 9:17; 30:14; Ps 69:20-21.—c Jer 14:2.—d Isa 47:2f.—e Deut 23:3; Ps 74:4-8; Jer 51:51.—f Isa 63:6; Ps 69:4; Jer 8:16.—g Ps 69:21; Jer 13:17.

---

cause of its infidelity. Verse 22 implores God to deal as harshly with the enemies of Jerusalem as he had with them.

1:2 *Friends:* the military allies of the Israelites.

1:6 *Daughter of Zion:* the city of Jerusalem and its people.

17 Zion stretches out her hands
but there is no one to comfort her
The LORD has commanded the neighbors of Jacob
to become his enemies.
In their midst Jerusalem has become
an unclean thing to be avoided.

18 The LORD has acted justly,
for I rebelled against his command.
Listen, all you peoples,
and behold my suffering.
My maidens and my youths
have been taken into captivity. [h]

19 I called out to my allies
but they failed me.
My priests and my elders
perished in the city
where they searched for food
to keep themselves alive. [i]

20 Behold, O LORD, how great is my distress.
My inner being is in turmoil.
My heart recoils within me
because I have been so rebellious.
In the streets the sword causes bereavement;
in the houses death reigns. [j]

21 People have heard my groans,
but no one has offered to comfort me.
All my enemies have learned of my troubles,
and they are pleased at what you have done.
Hasten the day* you have proclaimed
so that they may become like me.

22 Let all their wicked deeds come before you,
and deal with them
as you have dealt with me
because of all my sins.
My groans never cease,
and I am sick at heart.

CHAPTER 2

The Judgment of the LORD

1 Behold how the LORD in his anger
has enveloped in darkness the daughter of Zion.
He has hurled down from heaven to earth
the glory of Israel,
without any sign of regard for his footstool
on the day of his anger.

2 Without mercy, the LORD has destroyed
all the dwellings of Jacob.
In his wrath he has torn down
the fortresses of the daughter of Judah.
He has thrown to the ground in dishonor
the kingdom and its rulers.

3 In his fierce anger he broke off
all the strength of Israel.
He withdrew the protection of his right hand
at the approach of the enemy.
He blazed against Jacob like a flaming fire
that consumes everything in its path.

4 Like an enemy he bent his bow,
with his right hand prepared for action.
Like a foe he slew all those
in whom he once took great pride.
He poured forth his fury like fire
over the tent of the daughter of Zion.

5 The LORD has become an enemy;*
he has annihilated Israel.
He has destroyed all its palaces
and left all its strongholds in ruins.
For the daughter of Judah
he has multiplied mourning and lamentation. [k]

6 He has laid waste his dwelling like a garden
and destroyed his tabernacle.
The LORD has erased in Zion
every memory of festivals and Sabbaths.
In his fierce anger he has treated with contempt
king and priest alike. [l]

7 The LORD has rejected his altar
and abandoned his sanctuary.
He has delivered the walls of her palaces
into the power of the enemy
who raised a clamor in the house of the LORD
as on a festival day.

8 The LORD was determined to destroy
the walls of the daughter of Zion.
He marked off its boundaries with a measuring line
and did not relent in his purpose.
He caused both wall and rampart to lament;
together they crumbled to the ground. [m]

---

h Deut 28:32, 41.—i Jer 30:14.—j Lam 2:11; Jer 4:19.—k Lam 2:2; Jer 30:14.—l Lam 1:4; Isa 1:13.—m Jer 5:10.

1:21 *The day:* of God's intervention and punishment.

2:5 *The LORD has become an enemy:* the one who had been their best friend had turned against them and left them powerless against their foes.

9 The bars of her gates have been shattered,
and the gates themselves have sunk into the ground.
Her king and her princes are in exile among the Gentiles;
there is no instruction any longer from priests,
and her prophets have not received
any vision from the LORD.* [n]

10 The elders of the daughter of Zion
sit on the ground in silence.
They have strewn dust on their heads
and wrapped themselves in sackcloth.
The maidens of Jerusalem
bow their heads to the ground.

11 My eyes are exhausted from weeping,
and torment afflicts my innermost being.
My gall is poured out on the earth
because of the destruction of my people,
as children and infants faint
in the streets of the city.

12 They keep crying out to their mothers,
"Where is there bread and something to drink?"
as they faint like the wounded
in the streets of the city,
and breathe their last
in their mothers' arms. [o]

13 To what can I liken you or compare you,
O daughter of Jerusalem?
What can I do to rescue and comfort you,
O virgin daughter of Zion?
Your ruin is as vast as the sea.
Who can heal you?

14 The visions that your prophets revealed to you
were false and worthless.
They did not lay bare your guilt
so that you might reverse your fortunes.
The visions they proclaimed to you
were erroneous and deceptive.* [p]

15 All those who pass by
clap their hands at you.
They hiss and wag their heads
at the daughter of Jerusalem,
"Is this the city once described as perfect in beauty,
the joy of the whole world?"

16 All your enemies do not hesitate
to open their mouths against you.
They hiss and gnash their teeth;
they cry out, "We have devoured her!
This is the day we longed for;
at last we have seen it."

17 The LORD has done what he planned;
he has carried out his threat.
As he decreed from days of old,
he has destroyed without pity.
He has permitted the enemy to rejoice over you [q]
and exalted the strength of your foes.

18 Cry out to the LORD,
O wall of the daughter of Zion.
Let your tears flow like a torrent
both day and night.
Allow yourself no respite;
give your eyes no rest.

19 Arise and cry out during the night
at the beginning of every watch.*
Pour out your heart like water
in the presence of the LORD.
Lift up your hands to him
for the lives of your children
who are fainting from hunger
at the corner of every street.

20 Look, O LORD, and consider:
whom have you ever treated in this fashion?
Should women eat their little ones,
the children to whom they gave birth?
Should priest and prophet be killed
in the sanctuary of the LORD? [r]

21 The young and the old are lying dead
on the ground in the streets.
My young women and my young men
have fallen by the sword.
On the day of your anger you have slain them,
slaughtering them without pity. [s]

22 As if it were for a day of festival,
you summoned my enemies from every side.
On the day of the LORD's anger
no one escaped and no one survived.

---

n Deut 28:36; Neh 1:3.—o Lam 1:11.—p Isa 58:1; Jer 23:32.—q Deut 28:15.—r Lam 4:10; Deut 28:53.—s 2 Chr 36:17; Jer 6:11.

2:9 God had blessed his people with priests and prophets, but because they had persecuted them and denounced their visions, the people would be without prophets and visions.

2:14 How to distinguish between true and false prophets is necessary to grow in the spiritual life (see 1 Jn 4:1-6). It's easy to listen to those who say what we want to hear, but much better to gain the wisdom of true prophets who challenge and question our actions and motives.

2:19 *Watch:* there were three each night.

All those whom I bore and reared
my enemy has completely annihilated.

CHAPTER 3

The Enduring Love of the LORD

1* I am a man who has known affliction
under the rod of God's wrath.
2 He has led me and forced me to walk
in darkness, not in the light.
3 Against me alone he has turned his hand
again and again, throughout the day.
4 He has caused my flesh and my skin to waste away;
he has broken my bones. [t]
5 He has besieged me and enveloped me
with bitterness and hardship.
6 He has forced me to dwell in darkness
like those long dead.
7 He has walled me in so that I cannot escape,
and he weighed me down with heavy chains.
8 Even when I cry out and plead for help,
he shuts out my prayer. [u]
9 He has barred my way with blocks of stones
and obstructed my paths.
10 He has been for me a bear lying in wait
or a lion hiding in ambush. [v]
11 He has led me away and torn me to pieces,
leaving me helpless.
12 He has bent his bow and used me
as the target for his arrows.
13 He has pierced deep within me
with the shafts from his quiver. [w]
14 I have become a laughingstock to my people;
they taunt me in song throughout the day.
15 He has given me my fill of bitter herbs
and sated me with wormwood. [x]
16 He has broken my teeth* with gravel
and trampled my face into the dust.
17 My soul is deprived of peace;
I no longer remember what happiness is.
18 Thus I cry out that my glory is gone
as well as everything that I had hoped for from the LORD.
19 The realization of my poverty and homelessness
is wormwood and gall to me.
20 My soul continually reflects on this
and is left downcast within me.
21 However, I will call this to mind
as the reason for my hope:
22* The love of the LORD is never exhausted,
nor do his deeds of mercy ever come to an end.
23 They are renewed every morning;
his faithfulness never ceases.
24 The LORD is my portion, I say to myself;
therefore, I will place my hope in him. [y]
25 The LORD is good to those who wait for him,
to the soul that seeks him.
26 It is good to wait in silence
for the salvation of the LORD.
27 It is good for a man to bear
the yoke from his youth.
28 Let that man sit alone and in silence
when the yoke is laid upon him.
29 Let him bury his head in the dust;
there may still be hope.
30 Let him offer his cheek to those who strike him
and endure their insults. [z]
31 For the rejection by the LORD
will not last forever.
32 Even though he punishes, he will be compassionate
in the abundance of his unfailing love. [a]
33 For he does not willingly afflict
or cause grief to the children of men.
34 When all the prisoners in a country
are trampled underfoot,
35 when human rights are perverted
in defiance of the Most High,
36 when someone is deprived of justice in the courts—
is the LORD not aware of such evils?
37 Who has only to command and it is done
if the LORD has not given his approval?

---

t Job 30:30; Isa 38:13.—u Job 3:23; Ps 22:2.—v Job 10:16; Hos 13:8.—w Job 6:4; Ps 38:3.—x Job 9:18; Jer 9:14; 23:15.—y Pss 16:5; 73:26.—z Isa 50:6; Mt 5:39.—a Lam 3:22; Isa 54:8-9.

3:1-16 The repeated use of the word *he* in ascribing the many ways that God has inflicted punishment on his wayward people emphasizes their repeated indiscretions that wore down his divine patience resulting in his divine retribution.

3:16 *Broken my teeth:* the metaphor expresses extreme prostration.

3:22-23 In the midst of the seemingly endless recital of destruction and loss suffered because of their sinfulness, a note of hope is interjected. God's mercy and abiding faithfulness will never cease. In this day, we turn to this glorious hope in the midst of our intense suffering.

38 Is it not from the mouth of the Most High
that evil and good proceed? [b]
39 Why then should any people complain
about being punished for their sins?

40 Let us examine and test our ways
and return to the LORD.
41 Let us lift up our hearts and our hands
to God in heaven. [c]
42 We have sinned and rebelled,
and you have not forgiven us.

43 You have veiled yourself in anger and pursued us,
slaying us without pity.
44 You have wrapped yourself in a cloud
that no prayer can pierce.
45 You have reduced us to filth
and rubbish among the nations. [d]

46 All of our enemies have opened their mouths
in a chorus of jeers against us.
47 Terror and pitfall, devastation and ruin,
have been our lot.
48 My eyes flow with a torrent of tears
because of the destruction of my people.

49 My eyes will flow with unceasing tears,
and there will be no respite
50 until the LORD from heaven
looks down and sees.
51 My eyes are swollen with grief
at the fate of all the daughters of my city.

52 Those who were my enemies without justification
have hunted me down like a bird.
53 They thrust me alive into a pit
and hurled down stones at me. [e]
54 The waters rose above my head,
and I said, "I am lost."

55 I called upon your name, O LORD,
from the depths of the pit.
56 You heard me plead,
"Do not close your ear to my cry for help!"
57 You came near when I called out to you,
and you said, "Do not fear."

58 O LORD, you have taken up my cause,
and you have redeemed my life.
59 You have seen the unjust treatment I endure;
grant me justice. [f]
60 You have seen all their vindictiveness,
all their plots against me.

61 You have heard their insults, O LORD;
all their plots against me,
62 the whispers and murmuring of my foes
against me all day long.
63 Whether they sit or stand,
see how I am the object of their taunts.

64 Pay them back for their deeds, O LORD;
punish them as they deserve.
65 Give them hardness of heart
as your curse upon them. [g]
66 Pursue them in anger and destroy them
from under your heavens, O LORD.

CHAPTER 4

The Punishment of the Prophet and People

1 How the gold has become tarnished,
how the pure gold has lost its luster!
The sacred stones lie scattered
at every street corner.

2 The precious sons of Zion
were formerly worth their weight in gold.
Now they are reckoned as no more valuable
than clay jars fashioned by a potter.

3 Even jackals bare their breasts
and nurse their young.
But the daughters of my people have become
as cruel as ostriches* in the desert. [h]

4 The tongue of an infant
sticks to the roof of its mouth in thirst.
Little children beg for bread,
but no one offers them a crumb.

5 Those who once feasted on delicacies
now lie dying in the streets.
Those who once wore purple garments
now grovel in rubbish heaps.

6 The punishment inflicted on my people
has been greater than that of Sodom,
which was overthrown in an instant
without a hand being lifted to help her. [i]

7 Her princes were once brighter than snow
and whiter than milk.

b Isa 45:7.—c Ps 143:6; Isa 55:7.—d 1 Cor 4:13.—e Jer 37:16; 38:6-9.—f Ps 35:23; Jer 18:19-20.—g Jer 11:20; 2 Tim 4:14.—h Job 39:13-16.—i Gen 19:23-29; Jude 7.

4:3 *Ostriches:* it was thought that ostriches did not take care of their young.

Their bodies were more ruddy than coral,
more precious than sapphire.

8 Now their faces are blacker than soot,
and no one recognizes them in the streets.
Their skin has shriveled tightly over their bones,
as dry as a stick.

9 More blessed were those who died by the sword
than those who died of hunger,
with their limbs wasting away,
deprived of the produce of the field.

10 With their own hands, compassionate women
have boiled their own children;
those offspring became their food
when my people were on the verge of extinction.[j]

11 The LORD let his blazing anger pour forth
and gave full vent to his wrath
as he kindled a fire in Zion
that devoured her foundations.

12 The kings of the earth never believed,
nor did any of the inhabitants of the world,
that any adversary or enemy
could ever penetrate the gates of Jerusalem.

13 That occurred because of the sins of her prophets
and the crimes of her priests
who had shed within her walls
the blood of the righteous.*[k]

14 They staggered blindly in the streets,
so defiled with blood
that not one of the people dared
to touch their garments.

15 "Go away! You are unclean!" the people shouted.
"Keep away! Do not touch us!"
Wherever they fled, the people would cry out,
"You cannot stay here any longer!"

16 The LORD himself scattered them;
he no longer watches over them.
He showed no favor to the priests
or kindness to the elders.

17 Continually we strained our eyes,
looking in vain for help.
From our towers we watched endlessly
for a nation that could not save us.[l]

18 Men dogged our steps
so that we were unable to walk in our streets.
Our end drew near; our days were numbered;
our time had come.

19 Our pursuers were swifter
than eagles in the heavens.
They hounded us over the mountains
and lay in ambush for us in the wilderness.[m]

20 The LORD's anointed,* our breath of life,
was caught in their traps,
he in whose shadow we thought
that we could live in safety among the nations.

21 Rejoice and be glad, O daughter of Edom,
you who live in the land of Uz.
But to you also the cup will be passed;
you will become drunk and strip yourself naked.[n]

22 O daughter of Zion, your punishment is now complete;
he will not prolong your exile.
But, daughter of Edom, he will punish your iniquity,
and he will lay bare your sins.[o]

CHAPTER 5

The Prophet's Plea for Mercy

1 Remember, O LORD, what has befallen us
look, and see our disgrace.
2 Our inherited lands have been given to strangers,
our homes to foreigners.[p]
3 We have become orphans and fatherless;
our mothers are like widows.
4 We must purchase the water we drink;
we must pay for our own wood.
5 On our necks is the yoke of those who persecute us;
although we are exhausted, we are afforded no rest.

6 We have submitted to Egypt and Assyria
to get enough bread to sustain us.

j Lam 2:20; Deut 28:57.—k Jer 5:31; 6:13.—l Jer 37:7.—m Jer 4:13; Hab 1:8.—n Jer 25:15.—o Isa 40:2.—p Ps 79:1.

4:13 The sins of the priests and prophets were cause for great hurt and destruction for the people. This is true in our day as well, and a cause for deep repentance and renewal in the church.

4:20 *The LORD's anointed:* King Zedekiah, *the LORD's anointed,* was taken prisoner (see 2 Ki 25:4-7).

7 Our ancestors who sinned are no longer alive,
but we bear the burden of their guilt.
8 Slaves have become our rulers;
there is no one to deliver us from their hands.
9 We earn our bread at the peril of our lives
because of the sword in the wilderness.*
10 Our skin is blackened as in a furnace
from the scorching heat of famine.[q]
11 Women have been raped in Zion
and virgins in the towns of Judah.[r]
12 Princes have been hung up by their hands;
elders are shown no respect.
13 Young men toil, carrying the millstones;
boys stagger under their loads of wood.
14 The old men no longer assemble at the city gate;*
the young men have given up their music.
15 Joy has vanished from our hearts;
our dancing has turned to mourning.[s]
16 The garlands have fallen from our heads;
woe to us, for we have sinned.
17 This is why we are sick at heart;
because of this our eyes have grown dim.
18 Mount Zion lies desolate,
overrun with jackals.
19 But you, O LORD, reign forever;
your throne endures from age to age.[t]
20 Why have you ceased to remember us?
Why have you abandoned us for so long a time?[u]
21 Restore us back to you, O LORD, and we will return.*
Renew our days as we had of old,
22 unless you have utterly rejected us
with an anger that is beyond measure.[v]

q Lam 4:8.—r Isa 13:16; Zec 14:2.—s Jer 25:10; Am 8:10.—t Pss 9:8; 102:13, 27.—u Ps 13:2.—v Jer 14:19.

5:9 *Sword in the wilderness:* they could get bread only by exposing themselves to the dangers of the wilderness.

5:14 *Gate:* public life and political activity were carried on at the gates of the city.

5:21 The first part of this verse is more familiar to us in the Vulgate translation: "Convert us, O LORD, and we shall be converted!"

THE BOOK OF BARUCH

Prayer and Hope

The prestige that became associated with the name of Jeremiah, the prophet, after the Exile, also touched his faithful secretary Baruch. Thus, in accord with a procedure of that day, Baruch was made the author of a whole series of writings posterior to him by a few centuries, of which the Bible has preserved at least one.

This work lacks literary unity. Most of it is made up of parts taken from, or dependent on, other biblical passages (Dan 9; Job 28; Isa 40–66). It comprises four very different parts: an introductory account, a psalm of repentance, a hymn of instruction, and a message of consolation. It is difficult to propose a date; however, scholars believe that the whole was not anterior to the second century B.C. The so-called Letter of Jeremiah, which has been appended to this Book, may be from the same time, if not more recent.

The Book of Baruch has the honor of revealing the profoundly religious soul of the Jews dispersed throughout the world who, quite surprisingly, still remained united with their people. Their faith testifies to a very vivid sense of national sin; in their eyes, Israel's past has been nothing but one long infidelity. Defeat and captivity are the aftermath and the just chastisement of this constant rebellion.

However, this Book contains, above all, a message of hope: in the face of Israel's infidelity rests God's immutable faithfulness. The Lord will bring about conversion and bestow pardon, and the covenant will be revived to be more beautiful than before. It will be an eternal covenant that will gather the dispersed children into a radiant Jerusalem, city of God forever.

The Book of Baruch may be divided as follows:

- *I: Introduction (1:1-15a)*
- *II: Prayer for the Exiles in Babylon (1:15b—3:8)*
- *III: Praise of Wisdom (3:9—4:4)*
- *IV: Prophetic Discourse of Exhortation and Consolation for Jerusalem (4:5—5:9)*
- *V: The Letter of Jeremiah (6:1-72)*

I: INTRODUCTION*

CHAPTER 1

Meeting in Babylon. 1 Following are the
words of the book composed by Baruch, son
of Neriah, son of Mahseiah, son of Zedekiah,
son of Hasadiah, son of Hilkiah, in Babylon, [a]
2 on the seventh day of the month, during the
fifth year after the Chaldeans had captured
Jerusalem and destroyed it by fire. [b] 3 [c] Baruch
read aloud the text of this book to Jeconiah,
son of Jehoiakim, king of Judah, and to all
those who came to hear his words: [d] 4 to the
nobles, the princes, the elders, and the entire
populace of both exalted and lowly rank—
that is, all the people who lived in Babylon by
the River Sud.*
5 Then they wept and fasted and raised
their voices in prayer before the LORD. 6 A
collection was made, with all contributing as
much money as they could. [e] 7 They sent the
proceeds of this collection to Jerusalem, to
the high priest Jehoiakim, son of Hilkiah, son
of Shallum, and to the priests and all the
people who were with him in Jerusalem. 8 At
the same time, on the tenth day of the month
Sivan,* Baruch took the vessels of the house
of the LORD that had been stolen from the
temple and returned them to the land of
Judah. These were the silver vessels that
Zedekiah, the son of Josiah, king of Judah,
had ordered to be made, 9 after King
Nebuchadnezzar of Babylon had deported
Jeconiah from Jerusalem together with the
princes, artisans, nobles, and the people, and
brought them to Babylon as captives. [f]

A Message to Jerusalem. 10 This is the mes-
sage they sent: "Use this money we are send-
ing you to purchase burnt offerings, sin
offerings, and frankincense, and to prepare
grain offerings. Offer these on the altar of the
LORD, our God, [g] 11 along with prayers for
Nebuchadnezzar, king of Babylon, and his
son Belshazzar,* that their lifetimes may
continue as long as the heavens are above
the earth. [h] 12 May the LORD give us strength
and wisdom as we live under the protection
of Nebuchadnezzar, king of Babylon, and
that of his son Belshazzar, and serve them
for many years and enjoy their favor.
13 "Pray also to the LORD, our God, for us,
for we have sinned against the LORD, our
God, and his anger and wrath that we have
incurred have not yet been withdrawn from
us even to the present day. 14 Finally, we
exhort you to read publicly this book we are
sending you in the house of the LORD on the
festival days and the days of assembly, [i]
15 and to proclaim:

II: PRAYER FOR THE EXILES IN BABYLON*

Confession of Guilt. "Justice is the hall-
mark of the LORD, our God, and we, the peo-
ple of Judah and the citizens of Jerusalem,
are filled with shame this day, [j] 16 that we,
together with our kings and rulers, our
priests and prophets, and our ancestors,
17 have sinned against the LORD 18 by refus-
ing to obey him. We have not heeded the

a Jer 32:12; 36:4; 45:1-5.—b 2 Ki 25:8ff.—c 2 Ki 24:8-17; Jer 22:24-30; 51:59-64.—d 3-4: 2 Ki 23:1-2.—e Deut 16:17.—f Jer 24:1; 2 Ki 24:10-16.—g Jer 17:26.—h Deut 11:21; Jer 29:7; Dan 5:1-2; 1 Tim 2:1f.—i Ex 23:14ff; Lev 23:35f; Sir 50:6; Hos 9:5.—j Bar 2:6; 3:8; Ezr 9:6-15; Neh 9:6-37; Dan 9:4-19.

1:1-15a This scenario, which explains the origin of the Book, may have been inspired by the episode of Baruch reading the prophecies before the court at Jerusalem (see Jer 36). However, it is an artificial composition and confuses the dates of known chronology. According to Jer 43:6f, Baruch was taken into Egypt with his master. A later Jewish tradition, however, placed him in Babylonia. This Book imagines him to be in Babylonia at the modest court of King Jeconiah (or Jehoiachin), who was freed from prison in 561 B.C. (see 2 Ki 25:27; Jer 52:31-34), thirty-five years after his deportation. Verse 11 recalls a prince Belshazzar at the time of Nebuchadnezzar; we know of a prince by that name, but he lived at the time of the fall of Babylon in 539 B.C.

1:4 *Sud* refers to one of the canals that irrigated Babylon.

1:8 *Sivan*: the date corresponds to May-June.

1:11 *Belshazzar:* see note on 1:1-15a above.

1:15b—3:8 This psalm of collective supplication, which may reprise the prayer of Daniel (Dan 9:4-19), seems to have been part of a penitential liturgy of the time. It testifies to a keen sense of sin.

commands of the LORD, our God, or obeyed the laws that the LORD enjoined on us.

[19] "From the day the LORD brought our forefathers out of Egypt until the present time, we have disobeyed the LORD, our God, and paid no heed to his voice. [20] Even today we continue to be afflicted with the evils and the curse pronounced by the LORD through his servant Moses when he led forth our ancestors out of Egypt to bestow upon us a land flowing with milk and honey. [k] [21] We did not listen to the voice of the LORD, our God, as he spoke to us in the admonitions of the prophets whom he sent to us, [22] but instead followed our own wicked inclinations, choosing to serve other gods and to do what is evil in the sight of the LORD, our God.

CHAPTER 2

Punishment of Sin. [1] "Therefore, the LORD carried out the penalty that he threatened to inflict upon us: upon our judges who governed Israel, upon our kings and rulers, and upon the people of Israel and Judah. [2] [l] The evils he permitted to afflict Jerusalem have been of such intensity that they have never been paralleled anywhere under the heavens, as was foretold in the law of Moses: [3] that we would sink to the depravity of eating the flesh of our young sons and daughters. [4] The LORD made us subject to all the kingdoms that surround us. All the nations among which he has scattered us regard us as an object of scorn, and our land is regarded as a wilderness. [m] [5] Instead of being raised up, we have been brought low, because in ignoring his precepts, we have sinned against the LORD, our God. [n]

[6] "Justice is the hallmark of the LORD, our God, but we, like our fathers, are the object of shame even today. [o] [7] All of the evils that the LORD threatened to inflict upon us we have experienced, [8] [p] yet we did not entreat the LORD for relief and pledge to renounce the desires of our evil hearts. [9] The LORD did not ignore our misdeeds but inflicted evils upon us in recompense, for the LORD is just in all the works he has commanded us to do. [q] [10] Yet we did not heed the voice of the LORD or obey the precepts that he enjoined upon us.

Prayer for Deliverance. [11] "And now, LORD, God of Israel, who delivered your people out of the land of Egypt with a mighty hand, with signs and wonders, and with great power and outstretched arm, winning for yourself a great name that is revered even today, [r] [12] we admit that we have sinned by our godless actions and our violation of all your precepts, O LORD, our God. [s] [13] Avert your wrath from us, for only a scant portion of us still remains among the nations where you have scattered us. [t] [14] Pay heed, O LORD, to our prayers and requests. For your own sake deliver us, and enable us to gain the approbation of those who have led us into exile, [15] so that the entire world may acknowledge that you are the LORD, our God, and that Israel and his descendants bear your name. [u]

[16] "Look down, O LORD, from your holy dwelling, and keep us in your thoughts. Turn your ear toward us, O LORD, and listen to us. [v] [17] Look upon us, LORD, and see. It is not the dead in Hades, whose spirit no longer dwells in their bodies, who can render praise and vindication to you, O LORD. [w] [18] Rather, it is those who are living and deeply grieved, bent over and frail in their movements, with failing eyesight and hungering soul, who will praise your glory and justice, O LORD. [x]

[19] "It is not because of the righteous deeds of our ancestors and our kings that we make bold to approach you with our plea for mercy, O LORD, our God. [20] You have rained down your wrath and anger upon us, as you had announced through your servants the prophets, saying: [21] 'Thus says the LORD: Bow your shoulders in the service of the king of Babylon, so that you can remain in the land that I gave to your fathers. [y] [22] But if you refuse to heed the LORD's command to serve the king of Babylon, [23] I will banish from the cities of Judah and from the streets of Jerusalem the shouts of joy and the sounds of gladness, the voice of the bridegroom and the voice of the bride, and the whole land will be a desolate waste, without a single inhabitant.' [z]

[24] "However, we disobeyed your command to serve the king of Babylon, and therefore you carried out the warning you had issued

k Lev 26:14-39; Deut 28:15-68.—l 2f: 2 Ki 6:28f; Jer 19:9; Lam 2:20; 4:10; Ezek 5:10.—m Jer 29:18.—n Dan 28:13.—o Bar 1:15.—p 8-9: Dan 9:13f.—q Jer 1:12; 31:28; 44:27.—r Deut 6:21-22.—s Ps 106:6.—t Deut 4:27; Jer 42:2.—u Sir 36:11; Jer 14:9.—v Deut 26:15.—w Ps 6:6; Isa 38:18.—x Zep 2:3.—y Jer 27:12.—z Jer 7:34.

through your servants the prophets, that the
bones of our kings and the bones of our
ancestors would be uprooted from their
burial sites.[a] 25 And indeed, those bones have
been exposed to the daytime heat and the
nighttime frost.[b] They died in dreadful
anguish, as a result of famine and sword and
pestilence. 26 Therefore, because of the
wickedness of the kingdom of Israel and the
kingdom of Judah, the house that bears your
name you have reduced to its present state.[c]

God's Promises Recalled. 27 "Yet, O LORD,
our God, you have treated us with all your
goodness and all your mercy, 28 [d] exactly as
you promised through your servant Moses,
on the day you commanded him to write
down your law in the presence of the
Israelites when you said: 29 'If you do not lis-
ten to my voice, this huge and multitudinous
people will be reduced to a tiny remnant
among the nations where I will scatter them.
30 [e] I well realize that they will not heed me,
because they are a stiff-necked people. But
in the land of their exile, they will return to
themselves 31 and come to realize that I am
the LORD, their God. I will give them an obe-
dient heart and attentive ears,[f] 32 and they
will praise me in the land of their exile as
they invoke my name.[g] 33 [h] Remembering
the fate of their ancestors who sinned
against the LORD, they will forsake their
stubborn obstinacy and their evil deeds.

34 " 'Then I will again lead them back to the
land that I promised under oath to give to
their fathers, to Abraham, Isaac, and Jacob,
and they will rule over it. Their numbers will
increase as I ordain; they will not diminish.[i]
35 And I will enter with them into an eternal
covenant, that I will be their God and they
will be my people. Never again will I banish
my people Israel from the land I have given
them.'[j]

CHAPTER 3

1 "LORD Almighty, God of Israel, the
anguished soul and the troubled spirit cry
out to you. 2 Listen to us, O LORD, and have
mercy, for we have sinned against you.
3 While we are perishing forever, you are
enthroned forever.[k] 4 LORD Almighty, God of
Israel, listen to the prayer of the people of
Israel, the children of those who have sinned
against you. They have not heeded the voice
of the LORD, their God, and therefore, evils
continue to befall us. 5 Do not call to mind the
iniquity of our fathers, but during this time of
calamity, remember instead your power and
your name. 6 For you are the LORD, our God,
and it is you, O LORD, whom we will praise.
7 To effect this, you have put the fear of you
into our hearts so that we will invoke your
name. We now praise you in exile, for we have
cast away from our hearts all the iniquity of
our fathers who sinned against you.[l] 8 Look
upon us today in our exile, where you scat-
tered us. We have become a reproach and a
curse, to be condemned for all the iniquities
of our fathers who turned away from the
LORD, our God."

III: PRAISE OF WISDOM*

9 Pay heed, O Israel, to the command-
ments that offer life;
lend an ear to obtain prudence.[m]
10 Why is it, O Israel, that you dwell in the
land of your enemies,
growing ever older in a foreign coun-
try?
Why do you defile yourself with the dead,
11 numbered among those who descend
to the netherworld?[n]
12 You have forsaken the fountain of wis-
dom![o]
13 If you had walked in the way of God,
you would have dwelt in peace for-
ever.[p]
14 Learn where there is prudence,
where there is strength,
where there is wisdom,
so that you may also know
where may be found length of days, and
life,
where there is light for the eyes, and
peace.[q]
15 Who has discovered where wisdom
dwells;[r]
who has entered her treasure house?
16 Where now are those who ruled nations,
those who had dominion over the ani-
mals of the earth[s]

a Jer 8:1f.—b Jer 7:34; 14:12; 31:30.—c Jer 7:10-15.—d 28f: Deut 28:58, 62.—e Deut 30:1f; 31:27.—f Ps 40:7; Jer 24:7; Ezek 36:26.—g Tob 13:7.—h 33f: Deut 30:1-10.—i Lev 26:42; Deut 6:10; Jer 32:37.—j Jer 31:31; Lam 4:22; Ezek 36:26-29; Am 9:15.—k Pss 29:10; 102:12f.—l Jer 31:33.—m Prov 4:20ff.—n Ps 88:5.—o Jer 2:13; Jn 4:10, 14.—p Isa 48:18.—q Prov 3:2; 8:14.—r 15ff: Job 28:1-28.—s Jer 27:6.

3:9—4:4 In this beautiful hymn, a wise prophet wishes to teach his people—like all his ancient colleagues—the secret of happiness: to find anew the wisdom that God had given with the law.

17 and made sport of the birds of the heavens?
Where are those who amassed hoards of silver and gold
in which people place their trust,
those whose greed knew no limit?
18 Where are those silversmiths expert in their craft
of whose work not a trace remains?
19 They have all vanished, descending into the netherworld,
and others have risen up to take their place.
20 Succeeding generations have seen the light of day
and have come to dwell in the land,
but the way to knowledge they have not learned;
21 they have not discerned her paths or embraced her.
Not even their children have reached her;
indeed, they have strayed far from her way.
22 Wisdom has not been heard of in Canaan,
nor has she been seen in Teman. [t]
23 The descendants of Hagar who seek after worldly wisdom,
the merchants of Midian and Teman,
the storytellers and the searchers for understanding—
these have not discovered the way to wisdom
or even remembered her paths.*
24 O Israel, how great is the house of God,
how vast the region of his dominion.
25 It is immense and without bounds,
lofty and immeasurable.
26 There were born the giants,* renowned of old,
mighty in stature, skilled in war. [u]
27 Yet these were not the ones chosen by God,
nor did he teach them the way of understanding. [v]
28 They perished because of their lack of prudence;
they perished through their own folly. [w]
29 Who has ever gone up to heaven to get her
and bring her down from the clouds? [x]
30 Who has ever traversed the oceans and found her,
and will exchange the finest gold for her?
31 No one knows the way to her,
nor is anyone concerned with the path to her.
32 [y] However, he who knows all things knows her;
by his understanding he has discovered her.
He it is who established the earth for all time
and filled it with four-footed creatures.
33 He who sends forth the light and it takes flight,
summons it and, trembling, it obeys.
34 Before him the stars in their designated places shine and rejoice;
35 he summons them, and they reply, "Here we are,"
and shine with delight for the one who made them. [z]
36 This is our God;
no other can compare to him.
37 He has discerned the entire path to wisdom
and revealed her to Jacob, his servant,
and to Israel, whom he loved. [a]
38 After that, she appeared on earth
and lived with humankind. [b]

CHAPTER 4

1 She is the book of God's commandments,
the law that endures forever.
All who adhere to her will live,
but those who forsake her will die. [c]
2 Return, O Jacob, and lay hold of her;
approach the radiance of her light. [d]
3 Do not yield your glory to another
or your privileges to a foreign people.
4 Blessed are we, O Israel,
for what is pleasing to God has been revealed to us. [e]

t Jer 49:7; Ezek 28:4-5; Zec 9:2.—u Gen 6:4; Wis 14:6.—v 1 Sam 16:7-10.—w Sir 10:8.—x Deut 30:12f; Sir 24:4; Rom 10:6f.—y 32-34: Job 28:23-26; Prov 8:22-31.—z Job 38:7; Ps 147:4; Isa 40:26.—a Ps 147:19; Sir 24:8-12.—b Wis 9:18; Jn 1:14.—c Deut 4:6-8; Prov 8:35f; Sir 24:22.—d Prov 4:13,19.—e Deut 4:32-37; 33:29.

3:23 The wisdom of the Phoenicians and Arabians was proverbial.

3:26 *Giants:* this is doubtless a reference to the legendary giants of antediluvian times (Gen 6:4). According to later Jewish speculations, they had communicated to human beings wondrous knowledge—which had brought about the flood.

IV: PROPHETIC DISCOURSE OF EXHORTATION AND CONSOLATION FOR JERUSALEM

The Exile

5 Rouse your courage, my people,
you who keep alive the memory of Israel.
6 You were sold to the nations
but not for the purpose of your destruction.
You were handed over to your enemies
because you provoked God's indignation.[f]
7 [g] You offended the one who made you
by offering sacrifices to demons and not to God.
8 You turned your back on the Everlasting * who nourished you,
and caused sorrow for Jerusalem who reared you.
9 She saw the wrath of God descending upon you,
and she exclaimed:

"Listen, you neighbors of Zion.
God has afflicted me with great sorrow.
10 For I have beheld the exile of my sons and daughters
that the Everlasting has brought upon them.
11 Joyfully I raised them,
but with tears and lamenting I had to watch them depart.
12 Let not one of you rejoice over my fate,
a widow who has lost so many of her own;
I have been left desolate because of the sins of my children
who deviated from the law of God.[h]
13 They refused to obey his statutes,
and did not walk in the ways of God's commandments
or follow the paths of discipline that his justice required.
14 Let Zion's neighbors come
to observe the captivity of my sons and daughters
that the Everlasting has inflicted upon them.
15 He caused a faraway nation to war against them,
a ruthless nation speaking a foreign tongue,
that showed neither respect for the aged
nor pity for the young.[i]
16 They have led into exile the widow's beloved sons
and left her alone, without a solitary surviving daughter.

The Deliverance

17 "How can I possibly be of help to you?
18 The one who afflicted you with these disasters
will deliver you from the power of your enemies.[j]
19 Go, my children, go,
for I have been left desolate.
20 I have removed my robes of peace
and donned sackcloth for prayers of supplication;
throughout my life I will cry out to the Everlasting.[k]
21 "Take courage, my children; call out to God,
and he will deliver you from oppression
and from the hands of your enemies.[l]
22 I place my trust in the Everlasting for your deliverance,
and joy has come to me from the Holy One,
because of the mercy that will soon come to you
from the Everlasting, your Savior.
23 With mourning and laments I watched you depart,
but God will give you back to me with everlasting joy and gladness.[m]
24 For as the neighbors of Zion have witnessed your captivity,
they will soon behold your deliverance by your God,
which will come to you with the great glory and splendor of the Everlasting.[n]

---

f Jdg 2:14; Isa 50:1; 52:3.—g 7-8: Deut 32:13-18; 1 Cor 10:20.—h Lam 1:1-2, 7.—i Deut 28:49f; Jer 5:15; 6:22f.—j Jer 32:42.—k Jud 9:1; Est 4:16.—l Jer 51:5.—m Ps 126:6; Jer 31:12f.—n Isa 60:1ff.

4:8 *The Everlasting:* the Greek translator of chapter 4 (see vv. 8, 10, 14, 20, 22, 24, 35) has, with felicitous intuition, rendered by the word "Everlasting," the Hebraic name, *Yahweh* (Ex 3:14-15).

25 "My children, endure with patience the wrath
that has come upon you from God.
Your enemy has persecuted you,
but shortly you will witness his destruction
and trample upon his neck with your foot. [o]
26 My delicate children have had to traverse rocky paths,
taken away like sheep carried off by the enemy. [p]
27 Have courage, my children, and cry out to God;
he who has thus afflicted you will not forget you. [q]
28 As the thought once came to you to go astray from God,
now you must increase your efforts tenfold to seek him.
29 He who afflicted you with these disasters
will bring you everlasting joy with your deliverance." [r]

Jerusalem Assured of Help

30 Take courage, Jerusalem!
The one who gave you your name will comfort you. [s]
31 Great will be the terror of those who harmed you
and rejoiced over your ill-fortune.
32 Disaster awaits those cities where your children were slaves,
wretched the city that received your offspring. [t]
33 [u] Just as that city rejoiced at your downfall
and was exultant to witness your ruin,
so shall she grieve over her own devastation.
34 I shall despoil her of the multitudes in which she took such joy,
and her insolent pride shall be turned to mourning.
35 Fire from the Everlasting will besiege her for many days,
and demons will inhabit her for a lengthy period of time. [v]

Invitation to Hope

36 Gaze toward the east, Jerusalem,
and behold the joy that is coming to you from God. [w]
37 The children whom you saw depart are returning;
they are returning, gathered together from the east and the west,
at the command of the Holy One,
rejoicing in the glory of God. [x]

CHAPTER 5

1 Remove your robe of mourning and affliction, O Jerusalem, [y]
and adorn yourself forever with the splendor of the glory of God.
2 Wrap yourself with the cloak of God's justice,
and place on your head the diadem of the glory of the Everlasting. [z]
3 For God will reveal your splendor to every nation under the heavens;
4 and you will forever be called by God:
"The Peace of Justice and The Glory of Piety." [a]
5 Arise, O Jerusalem, stand upon the heights
and look toward the east;
behold your children gathered from the west and the east
at the command of the Holy One,
rejoicing that God has remembered them.
6 They departed from you on foot,
led away by their enemies.
But God will bring them back to you,
borne aloft in glory as though on a royal throne. [b]
7 For God has decreed
that every high mountain and the everlasting hills be leveled
and that the valleys be filled to make level ground,
so that Israel may walk securely in the glory of God. [c]
8 The woods and every type of fragrant tree
have provided shade for Israel at God's command. [d]
9 For God will lead Israel with joy,
by the light of his glory,
with the mercy and uprightness that come from him.

---

o Isa 51:23.—**p** Lam 2:22.—**q** Isa 40:1.—**r** Isa 35:10.—**s** Ps 46:5; Isa 60:14.—**t** Jer 51:43.—**u** 33f: Isa 13:20ff; 47:1-11; Jer 50:13.—**v** Isa 34:9-14.—**w** Isa 60:4f.—**x** Isa 43:5.—**y** Isa 52:1.—**z** Ex 39:30; Wis 18:24; Isa 61:10; 62:3.—**a** Isa 1:26; 32:17; Jer 33:16.—**b** Isa 49:22.—**c** Isa 40:3f.—**d** Isa 41:19.

V: THE LETTER OF JEREMIAH*

CHAPTER 6

1 This is the text of a letter sent by Jeremiah[e] to those who were to be taken as captives to Babylon by the king of the Babylonians, in order to deliver to them a message at God's command:

Duration of the Exile. Because of the sins you have committed before God, you are being deported to Babylon as captives by Nebuchadnezzar, king of the Babylonians. 2 Once you have arrived in Babylon, your period of exile will last for many years, up to seven generations. After that I will bring you home from that place in peace. 3 In Babylon you will see people carrying upon their shoulders gods of silver and gold and wood, which inspire fear in the pagans.[f] 4 Be careful not to imitate these pagans or to allow fear of these gods to overwhelm you 5 when you see the heathen crowds before and behind them, worshiping them. Rather, say in your hearts, "Only you, O LORD, are worthy of worship." 6 For my angel is with you, and he cares for your lives.[g]

Origin of Idols. 7 The tongues of these gods are polished to a smooth finish by artisans, and the idols, themselves, are overlaid with gold and silver. However, they are fraudulent and are unable to utter a word.[h] 8 People take gold as they would for a maiden obsessed with how she adorns herself, 9 and they use it to fashion crowns for the heads of their gods. Yet at times the priests will surreptitiously take the silver and gold from these gods and spend it on themselves; 10 they will even use some of it in payment for services to the temple prostitutes.

They elegantly robe these idols of silver and gold and wood as if they were human; 11 however, even though these gods are arrayed in purple attire, they are unable to protect themselves from the damage caused by corrosion and insects. 12 Their faces must be wiped clean of the thick dust of the temple that settles upon them. 13 * Like a ruler of a country, each god holds a scepter, yet none has the power to destroy anyone who offends it. 14 Each has in its right hand a sword and an ax, but none is able to defend itself from war or thievery. Thus it is evident beyond question that these are not gods; so have no fear of them.

Impotence of Idols. 15 Just as a pot is of no further use once it is broken, 16 so are these gods enshrined in their temples. Dust raised up from the feet of those who enter fills their eyes. 17 Their courtyards are walled in like those of someone in prison and awaiting execution for an act against the king, so the priests attempt to make the temples secure, reinforcing them with doors and bars and bolts to guard against thievery. 18 The priests light more lamps for the gods than they do for themselves, yet not even one of these can the idols see.

19 The gods are like one of the temple beams, but, it is said, their hearts are eaten away, as insects crawl out of the ground to consume them and their garments without their even being aware of it. 20 Their faces are blackened by the smoke that rises in the temple. 21 Bats and swallows and birds of every species perch on their bodies and heads, and so do cats. 22 All this makes it abundantly clear that they are not gods. Therefore, have no fear of them.

23 Although they are adorned with a layer of gold, these idols will not gleam unless someone wipes off the tarnish. Even when they were being molded they did not feel anything. 24 They were purchased no matter what the cost, yet the breath of life is not in them. 25 Because of their lack of feet, they are borne on the shoulders of others, an indication to all of their true lack of worth. And those who serve them feel a sense of shame,[i] 26 inasmuch as if one of them should fall to the ground, it cannot get up by itself. If anyone sets an idol upright, it cannot move by its own devices, and if it is tipped, it cannot straighten itself on its own.

A gift offered to such idols might as well be offered to the dead. 27 Any sacrifices made to these idols are sold by the priests, who then pocket the proceeds. Likewise, their wives

e Jer 29:1.—f Isa 46:7; Jer 10:1-16.—g Ex 23:20.—h Ps 135:16.—i Wis 13:16.

6:1-72 After the first deportation of 598 B.C., Jeremiah had sent a message to the exiles (Jer 29:6-32), to encourage them to establish themselves, for the moment, in exile. We have here another letter from the same prophet, addressed to those deported to Babylon, to place them on guard against idolatry. In reality, this document is very late; though inspired by texts of the sixth or fifth century (Isa 44:9-20; Jer 10:1-16), it probably dates from the Greek period and seems to be speaking of Babylonian cults that flourished in the third century under the domination of the Seleucids.

6:13-14 In representations of the Babylonian deities, the scepter symbolizes authority, while the sword and the ax reflect power over nature.

salt and preserve parts of the meat that is offered, but they refuse to offer any share whatsoever to the poor or the helpless.[j] 28 Even women who are menstruating or who have just given birth are permitted to touch these sacrifices. Thus there should not be the slightest doubt that these are not gods; therefore, have no fear of them.[k]

29 How can they be called gods, these idols of silver and gold and wood, when women serve meals to them?* 30 And in their temples, the priests sit wearing torn garments, their hair and beards shaved, and their heads uncovered.[l] 31 They shout and shriek in the presence of their gods as others do at a funeral banquet. 32 The priests remove some of the idols' clothing and use it to clothe their own wives and children.

33 Whether these gods are treated well or badly by someone, they are unable to repay that person in like manner. They can neither enthrone nor depose a king.[m] 34 Similarly they are incapable of bestowing wealth or money. If anyone fails to fulfill a vow made to them, they will never exact it. 35 They will never save anyone from death or deliver the weak from the strong.[n] 36 They cannot restore the sight of the blind nor rescue anyone in trouble. 37 They cannot have pity for the widow nor show concern for the orphan.[o] 38 These wooden statues overlaid with gold and silver are like stones quarried from the mountains, and those who worship them will be put to shame.[p] 39 How then can anyone consider them to be gods or call them gods?[q]

40 Even the Chaldeans* themselves betray their lack of respect for them, for when they see someone who is incapable of speech, they lead the mute into the temple and ask Bel to give that person the power of speech, as though Bel were able to understand. 41 However, they are unable to reflect on their foolish practice and abandon these gods, for they lack all sense of perception. 42 [r] Meanwhile women, with cords around their waists, burn bran for incense. 43 And whenever one of these has been solicited by a passer-by and lain with him, she taunts her neighbor who was not chosen because of a lesser degree of attractiveness and who has not had her cord broken. 44 Everything that has to do with these gods is fraudulent. How then can anyone consider them to be gods or call them so?

Nature of Idols. 45 Idols are fashioned by carpenters and goldsmiths, and they can be nothing more than what their artisans wish them to be.[s] 46 Even those who produce them cannot last long. 47 How, then, can the things made by them be gods? They have bequeathed nothing but frauds and dishonor to their descendants. 48 When war or a disaster befalls them, the priests consult among themselves where they can hide with their gods. 49 How, then, can anyone fail to realize that these are not gods when they are unable to save themselves from war or disaster?

50 Since they are composed of nothing but wood that has been overlaid with gold and silver, they eventually will be recognized for the frauds that they are. It will be crystal-clear to every nation and king that they are not gods but have been created by human hands, and that they do not possess the slightest degree of divine power.

51 Who can fail to realize that they are not gods? 52 They cannot appoint a king to rule over a country or supply people with rain. 53 They cannot regulate their own affairs or remedy an injustice, because they have no power. 54 They are like crows fluttering between heaven and earth. When fire breaks out in a temple that houses these wooden gods overlaid with gold and silver, the priests will dash for safety, but they themselves will be consumed in the flames like timbers. 55 They cannot offer any resistance to a king or enemy forces. 56 How, then, can anyone assert or still believe that they are gods?

Absolute Uselessness of Idols. These idols of wood overlaid with gold and silver are not able to prevent being plundered by thieves and bandits. 57 Anyone of a mind to do so will strip them of their gold and silver and run off, also, with the robes in which they were garbed, and they are powerless to help themselves. 58 It is far better to be a king who displays his courage or a household utensil of use to its owner than these false gods; better even the door of a house that safeguards whatever is within than these false gods; better even a wooden pillar in a palace than these false gods.[t]

59 The sun and the moon and the stars shine brightly in obedience to the purpose they are assigned. 60 Flashes of lightning are seen over a large area, and the wind likewise

j Lev 12:4; 15:19f; Deut 14:28f.—k Lev 12:1-8.—l Lev 10:6; 21:5, 10.—m Job 12:18; Dan 2:21.—n Pss 68:6; 146:7ff.—o Ps 146:9.—p Hab 2:19.—q Jer 2:28; 1 Cor 8:5.—r 42-43: Jer 3:2.—s Ps 115:4; Isa 40:19; Jer 10:9.—t Wis 13:10-15; 15:7ff.

6:29 Jewish women had no official roles in the public worship.
6:40 *Chaldeans:* Babylonian priests.

blows throughout the land. 61 When God
issues a command to the clouds to pass over
the whole earth, they obey, 62 and fire that is
sent from above to consume mountains and
forests does what it has been ordered.
However, these idols cannot be compared
with these forces of nature, either in beauty
or in power. 63 Therefore, you cannot consid-
er them to be gods or call them such, since
they are powerless to pronounce judgment or
to be of help to anyone. 64 Therefore, realizing
that they are not gods, do not fear them.
65 These idols cannot curse or bless kings,
66 nor can they offer the nations any signs in
the heavens or shine like the sun or provide
light like the moon. 67 Wild beasts are more
blessed, for they can save themselves by flee-
ing to a place of safety. 68 In no respect is
there the slightest evidence that they are
gods; therefore, do not fear them. 69 These
wooden idols, overlaid with silver and gold,
provide no greater protection than does a
scarecrow in a field of cucumbers. 70 Like a
thornbush in a garden upon which every
species of bird perches, or like a corpse
thrown out into the darkness, are these
wooden gods overlaid with gold and silver.
71 The purple and the linen rotting on their
backs give clear evidence that they are not
gods. In the end they will be eaten away and
bring dishonor to their country. 72 Far more
fortunate, then, is the upright person who
has no idols, for such a one will never incur
dishonor.

"Thus says the Lord GOD to these [dry] bones: I am going to cause breath to enter you, and you will come to life" *(Ezek 37:5)*.

THE BOOK OF EZEKIEL

Witnesses to Hope

Just as Nebuchadnezzar found himself at the crossroads (Ezek 21:26), so also, the beginning of the sixth century B.C. marked a period of profound crisis for the people of God. It was in this moment that the prophet Ezekiel delivered his clear, penetrating diagnosis of the situation. He was a priest who had been deported from Israel at the end of the first Babylonian campaign against Judah in 598 B.C. It was there in Babylon, where he lived among his fellow countrymen who had been exiled so far away from their homeland, that Ezekiel pronounced the sentence of God upon his people. (This fact made it difficult for the Jewish scholars to accept this Book, for it was written outside of the boundaries of Israel.) With words and symbolic actions, he waited for, proclaimed, and commented upon a new invasion that would end with the total destruction of Jerusalem in 587 B.C. Those living in exile clung to their false hopes for deliverance, but Ezekiel did not. Through his insight, which came from his gift of inspiration, he was able to see that his world as he knew it was coming to an end. His visions all but crushed him. He speaks of how the message was sweet to proclaim, but how difficult it was to digest (2:1ff). He was not even able to mourn the death of his beloved wife (24:15ff), an indication of how the people in exile were to respond to the news that the temple in Jerusalem had been destroyed (for its destruction was a fulfillment of God's judgment that the people were to accept obediently).

He speaks of Jerusalem as being an unfaithful wife, mocked by those around her (16:57; 23:12-17). God had cared for her and protected her from all of her enemies, but she had turned her back on him. She would be shamed and wounded (16:39-40). Her end was at hand (7:6). Her "watchman" (3:17) never rested, for the prophet condemned her day by day without rest. Slowly, bit by bit, her agony was to be fulfilled. Some would understand her fate, but most would not, for she possessed a rebellious spirit (2:5). Her evil choices had corrupted the children of Israel for far too long. She could be healed only by a powerful intervention on the part of God (16:3, 33f; 20:8; 23:3). She was concerned only with her own riches, her adornments (7:2). She had forgotten and rejected God, turning to idols (14:1-11; 22:12; 23:35). Prideful, idolatrous, forgetful of and disrespectful to God: these were the evils that the people had continuously committed. The prophet knew that he had to confront Israel with her sinfulness, for he was responsible for this warning (33:1ff). Yet, ultimately, they were responsible for their own fate, for each person is responsible for his own sins (14:12ff; 18:1ff).

When the crisis came, the exiles were thrown into despair. They had been cast out from the city where they had hoped to find refuge. They were sent off into a foreign land. They found themselves crying by the waters of Babylon as they remembered Zion (see Ps 136:1).

Suddenly, unexpectedly, a prophet appeared in their midst (2:5). He had judged their past and censured their present. Eventually, he would speak of their future. The ferocious beasts who had brought God's judgment down upon Israel were about to pay for their monstrous pride (chs. 25–32). These condemnations are painful for us to listen to, for we have been spoiled by the merciful message of the Gospels. But the revenge that Ezekiel seeks is not a question of an eye for an eye. What the prophet was trying to emphasize is the overwhelming might of God, his holiness.

The future would be a time of renewal. The children of Israel would have a new heart in which a new spirit lived (36:26f). They would bear the word of God upon their foreheads, giving witness to their faith in thought and action (9:4ff). They would worship in a new temple. All of Jerusalem would be rebuilt as the center of a new and faithful Israel (chs. 40–48). The condemnations of the past would be over, and the people would live in hope for the future.

Ezekiel is a prophet who proclaims a radical renewal of Israel. He speaks of a new covenant which, unlike the previous covenant that had been written upon stone, would be written upon the hearts of the people of Israel (36:26). His message is the same that was preached by Jesus, especially as it is recorded in the Gospel of John. One would come who would heal, not only the disgrace of the nations (36:7), but also the sin of the house of Judah (4:6). The one to come would take away the sins of the world (Jn 1:29; 1 Jn 2:2).

Both the fourth Gospel and the Book of Revelation frequently borrow images and phrases from the Book of Ezekiel. They use them to proclaim that God is willing to live in the midst of his people (37:27), especially in the person of Jesus Christ (Jn 1:14; Rev 21:3). He is the new temple, the site of a sincere and universal worship of God (Jn 2:21; 4:21, 24). He gives new birth in water and spirit (36:25, 27; Jn 3:5). He is the Good Shepherd who leads and gathers his people (37:24; Jn 10:16) and fills them with life (Jn 11:17-44), thus fulfilling the prophecy of the dry bones found in Ezekiel 37.

Much of the imagery of the Book of Revelation is taken from the Book of Ezekiel: the four living creatures (1:5; Rev 4:6-8); the throne from which springs a stream of water (47:1-12; Rev 22:1f); Jerusalem, the Lord's bride (Rev 21:9); the Lord, temple of his people (11:16; Rev 21:22); the heavenly Jerusalem (Rev 21). These images come from a deep symbolism through which Ezekiel communicates his somewhat challenging message of condemnation, but it is a punishment that leads to hope and renewal (the same message as that proclaimed in the Book of Revelation).

The Book of Ezekiel may be divided as follows:

- *I: Call of the Prophet (1:1—3:27)*
- *II: Before the Siege of Jerusalem (4:1—24:27)*
- *III: Prophecies against Foreign Nations (25:1—32:32)*
- *IV: Israel's Restoration (33:1—39:29)*
- *V: The New Israel (40:1—48:35)*

I: CALL OF THE PROPHET*

CHAPTER 1

The Vision of Four Living Creatures. 1 * * In the thirtieth year, on the fifth day of the fourth month, while I was among the exiles by the River Chebar, the heavens opened, and I saw divine visions.[a] 2 On the fifth day of the month—it was the fifth year of the exile of King Jehoiachin—3 the word of the LORD came to the priest Ezekiel, the son of Buzi, in the land of the Chaldeans by the River Chebar. There the hand of the LORD was upon him.[b]

4 * As I looked, I beheld a stormy wind coming from the north: an immense cloud with flashing fire and a brilliant light surrounding it. In the middle of the fire there was something that looked like gleaming amber.* 5 Within it, there seemed to be four living creatures with human forms.* 6 Each had four faces; each had four wings. 7 Their legs were straight, and they had hooves like those of a calf, sparkling with a gleam like that of burnished bronze.

8 Below their wings, they had human hands on their four sides. All four of them had faces and wings. 9 They touched one another with their wings. They did not turn as they moved; each of them moved straight ahead.

10 As for their faces, each of the four had the face of a man, the face of a lion on the right side, the face of an ox on the left side, and the face of an eagle.[c] 11 Their wings were spread upward. Each creature had one wing touching the wing of another creature on

a Ezek 43:3.—b 1 Ki 18:46.—c Rev 4:7.

1:1—24:27 Ezekiel, a priest of Jerusalem, is torn away from the temple and the worship that he loves, and joins the caravan of deportees whom Nebuchadnezzar drags off to Babylon after the first capitulation of Jerusalem in 598 B.C. At this time, Ezekiel is a contemporary of Jeremiah and has insight into the evils that are coming. The prophet denounces the infidelity of the people. Moreover, he cannot accept any longer the ancient idea of collective responsibility. He seeks rather to point out the personal responsibility of each individual.

1:1—3:27 During a vision that reminds us of the prophet Isaiah's vision (Isa 6:1-13), Ezekiel, the poor "son of man," is abruptly placed in the presence of the glory of the Lord. He suddenly understands the holiness of the God who seeks his people, even in exile, there on the banks of the Kebar. He understands, too, the tragic fate of this people whose sin can be removed only by being burned in fire (Deut 4:24; Isa 33:14; Heb 12:29).

1:1-3 We are introduced to an amazing narrative that is difficult to read because numerous additions have been made to the original version, either by the prophet himself or by one of his disciples. This can be seen even in these first three verses. Kebar is a wide, navigable canal of water leading from the Euphrates in Babylonia.

1:4-28 The prophet Isaiah had had the same vision, but his took place in the temple of Jerusalem (Isa 6). Ezekiel's comes to him in the midst of pagan Babylonia. The vision comes from the north. It was from the north that the refugees had come: they left Palestine, skirted the Desert of Syria, and followed the Fertile Crescent. The "glory" of the Lord is no longer in the Jerusalem temple—and it is a priest who says so! Surrounding this glory of God as he comes are fantastic beings, represented in images taken from Babylonian art. The text adds details without restraint in order to show that God is present everywhere; the wheels, which are decorated with motifs using eyes, symbolize the Lord who sees and knows everything. These beings form a throne, as it were, for the glory of God. So great is the distance between God and human beings that the prophet does not have words to suggest the ineffable divine reality, but he nonetheless asserts its presence.

1:4 *Amber:* a naturally occurring alloy of four-fifths gold and one-fifth silver, and amber in color; it is from amber that the Greek name is derived.

1:5 The four living beings are imagined as Assyro-Babylonian cherubim, who are regarded as servants of the various divinities and placed as guardians before temples and palaces.

either side, and two wings covering its body. 12 Each one went straight ahead. Wherever the Spirit wished them to go, they would do so; they never turned as they moved.

13 In the middle of the living creatures was what appeared to be burning coals of fire, like torches darting to and fro between the living creatures. The fire was bright, and lightning issued forth from the fire. 14 The living creatures kept disappearing and reappearing like flashes of lightning.

15 As I looked at the living creatures, I saw a wheel on the ground beside each of the four living creatures. 16 As for the appearance and the structure of the wheels, they all held the appearance of sparkling chrysolites, and all four of them looked alike; they were so constructed that each wheel appeared to have another wheel inside it. 17 They could move in any of the four directions they faced, without veering as they moved.

18 The four of them had rims that were awesome in their size, and those rims were filled with eyes all around.[d] 19 When the living creatures moved, the wheels moved beside them, and when the living creatures rose from the ground, the wheels also rose with them. 20 They moved in whatever direction the Spirit wished to go, and the wheels rose with them, for the Spirit of the living creatures was in the wheels. 21 When the creatures moved, the wheels also moved. When the creatures stood still, the wheels also stood still. When the creatures left the ground, the wheels also left the ground, for the Spirit of the living creatures was in the wheels.[e]

22 Over the heads of the living creatures, there was what appeared to be a firmament, glittering like crystal and spread out over their heads. 23 Beneath the firmament, their wings were stretched out straight, one toward another, and each of the creatures had two wings covering its body. 24 I also heard the sound of their wings, like the roar of mighty waters, like the thunder of the Almighty. When they moved, the sound was like the noise emanating from an armed camp. And when they stood still, they lowered their wings.*

25 And there came a voice from above the dome over their heads as they stood with lowered wings. 26 Above the dome over their heads there was something like a sapphire in the form of a throne, and seated high above the likeness of a throne there was a form with the appearance of a man.[f]

27 Upward from what resembled his waist I beheld what looked like fire that gave forth a brilliant light all around. 28 The radiance of the encircling light was like a rainbow in the clouds on a rainy day.

Such was the appearance of the likeness of the glory of the LORD. When I beheld it, I prostrated myself on the ground, and I heard a voice speaking to me.[g]

CHAPTER 2

The Vison of the Scroll. 1 He said to me: Stand up, son of man.* I wish to speak with you. 2 As he spoke to me, a Spirit entered into me and stood me on my feet, and I listened to him speaking.[h]

3 He said to me: Son of man, I am sending you to the Israelites, a rebellious nation that has rebelled against me. They and their ancestors have been in revolt against me to this very day. 4 Because they are obstinate and stubborn, I am sending you to them. You shall say to them, "Thus says the Lord GOD." 5 Whether they listen to you or whether in their rebelliousness they refuse to listen, they will know that there is a prophet among them.

6 But as for you, son of man, do not be afraid of them or of what they say, even though they resist and reject you and you find yourself sitting on scorpions. Do not be afraid of their words or be alarmed by their looks, for they are a rebellious tribe. 7 You will deliver my words to them whether they listen or whether in their rebelliousness, they refuse to listen. 8 But as for you, son of man, listen to what I say to you and do not be rebellious like that rebellious tribe. Open your mouth and eat what I am about to give you.

9 I saw a hand stretched out to me, and in it was a written scroll. 10 He unrolled it in front of me. It had writing on the front and on the back, and written on it were words, of lamentation and dirges and woe.[i]

---

d Ezek 10:12; Rev 4:6, 8.—e Ezek 10:17.—f Ezek 10:1; Ex 24:10.—g Dan 8:17; Rev 1:17.—h Ezek 3:24.—i Rev 5:1.

1:24 The picture which Ezekiel paints fits in with the way in which the throne of God appears to Moses (Ex 24:10). The same images will be used in the Apocalypse (Ezek 4:2f).

2:1ff *Son of man:* the phrase is repeated about a hundred times in Ezekiel and is intended to say that the creature is nothing before God.

CHAPTER 3

1 He said to me: Son of man, eat what is in front of you. Eat this scroll, and then go forth to speak to the house of Israel. 2 Therefore, I opened my mouth, and he gave me the scroll to eat. 3 He said to me: Son of man, eat this scroll that I have given you, and eat your fill. Then I consumed it, and in my mouth it was as sweet as honey.[j]

4 He then said to me: Son of man, go now to the house of Israel and deliver my message to them. 5 For you are not being sent to a people that speaks a difficult and barbaric language, but to the house of Israel. 6 I am not sending you to great nations, whose speech you would not be able to comprehend, although they would listen to what you had to say.

7 However, the house of Israel will not listen to you because it would not listen to me. The whole house of Israel is defiant and obstinate in heart. 8 But I will make you as defiant and obstinate as they are. 9 I will make your resolve as hard as a diamond. I have made your forehead like the hardest stone, harder than flint. Do not fear them, or be concerned about their appearance, for they are a rebellious house.[k]

10 He went on: Listen carefully, son of man, to all my words. Receive them into your heart and hear them with your ears. 11 Then go to your countrymen in exile and say to them, "Thus says the LORD," whether they listen or refuse to listen.

12 Then a Spirit lifted me up, and I heard behind me the sound of loud rumbling as the glory of the LORD rose from its place:[l] 13 the sound of the wings of the living creatures brushing against one another, and the sound of the wheels beside them, a fierce rumbling sound. 14 The Spirit lifted me up and carried me away, and I departed in bitterness and anger, as the hand of the LORD rested heavily upon me. 15 I came to the exiles at Tel-abib* who lived by the River Chebar, and for seven days I sat among them in a state of consternation.

The Prophet as Sentry. 16 At the end of seven days the word of the LORD came to me: 17 Son of man, I have appointed you as a watchman for the house of Israel. Whenever you hear a word from my mouth, you shall give them my warning.[m] 18 If I say to a wicked man, "You will surely die," and you fail to warn him about this or do not advise him to cease his wicked conduct and thereby save his life, the wicked man will die because of his iniquity, but I will hold you responsible for his death. 19 But if you have warned him and he continues to persist in his evil ways, he will die for his sin, but you will have saved your life.

20 Again, if a virtuous man ceases to be virtuous and does wrong, and I set a trap for him, he will die because you failed to warn him. He will die for his sin, and his virtuous deeds will no longer be remembered. However, I will hold you responsible for his death because you did not warn him. 21 However, if you have warned an upright man not to sin and he does not sin, then he will have saved his life because he heeded your warning, and you will have saved your life.

Ezekiel Struck Dumb. 22 * While I was there, the hand of the LORD was upon me, and he said to me: Rise up, go out into the valley, and there I will speak to you.[n] 23 I arose, and then went out to the valley, the glory of the LORD was there, like the glory I had seen by the River Chebar, and I fell prostrate on the ground.

24 Then a Spirit entered into me and raised me to my feet, and he spoke with me and said: Go forth and shut yourself up in your house.[o] 25 You will be tied and bound with ropes, O son of man, so that you cannot go out among the people. 26 I will make your tongue stick to your palate so that you will become dumb and be unable to reprove them, for they are a rebellious people. 27 But when I have spoken to you, I will open your mouth, and you will say to them, "This is what the LORD God said." If anyone wishes to listen, he may listen. If anyone refuses to listen, he may refuse. For they are a rebellious house.

II: BEFORE THE SIEGE OF JERUSALEM

CHAPTER 4

Symbols of Siege and Exile. 1 As for you, son of man, take a clay tablet and lay it in front

j Rev 10:9-10.—k Isa 50:7.—l Ezek 8:3; Acts 8:39.—m Ezek 33:7-9; Jer 6:17.—n Ezek 8:4.—o Ezek 2:2.

3:15 *Tel-abib:* an unidentified place in Babylonia; the name means "hill of the ear of grain."

3:22—5:17 In words all the more impressive because preceded by mimed scenes, Ezekiel foretells the siege and destruction of Jerusalem. A first series of such scenes (Ezek 4:1-3, 9-17; 5:1-17) must date from the very year of the prophet's call. A second must be closer to the moment of the fall of Jerusalem in 587 B.C.

of you. Draw on it a city, Jerusalem.*
2 Portray it under siege, erect towers against
it, pitch camps, and set up battering rams all
around it.[p] 3 Then take an iron griddle and
place it as though it were an iron wall
between you and the city. Keep your gaze
fixed upon the city; it will be in a state of
siege, and you will be the besieger. This will
be a sign for the house of Israel.*

4 * Then lie on your left side while I place
the guilt of the house of Israel upon you. You
will bear their guilt for the number of days
that you lie on your side. 5 Allowing one day
for every year of their guilt, I ordain that you
bear Israel's punishment for three hundred
and ninety days.

6 When you have completed these days,
you shall lie down again, this time on your
right side, and bear the punishment of the
house of Judah for forty days: one day for
each year I have allotted you. 7 Then fix your
gaze on the siege of Jerusalem, and with
bared arm you shall prophesy against it. 8 I
will tie you with ropes so that you cannot
turn from one side to the other until you
have completed the days of your siege.

9 * Then take wheat and barley, beans and
lentils, millet, and spelt. Put them all into the
same pot and make bread for yourself. You
are to eat it for as many days as you lie upon
your side—three hundred and ninety days.
10 The food that you shall eat shall weigh
twenty shekels a day, and you are to eat it at
fixed times. 11 You are also to measure out
and drink the same amount of water each
day at fixed times—one-sixth of a hin. 12 The
food that you eat shall be in the form of a
barley cake. Bake it in the sight of the people
with human dung as fuel.

13 The LORD then said: Thus will the
Israelites be forced to eat defiled food
among the nations to which I will banish
them. 14 "Lord GOD," I protested, "from my
youth until this very day I have never defiled
myself. I have never eaten an animal that
died a natural death or was torn to pieces by
wild beasts. No unclean meat has ever
entered my mouth."[q] 15 He replied: Very
well. I will permit you to use cow dung
instead of human dung to prepare your
bread.*

16 Then he said to me: Son of man, I in-
tend to reduce greatly the supply of food in
Jerusalem. The people will ration anxiously
the bread they eat and sip carefully the mea-
sure of water they are allotted each day.
17 Because of the scarcity of bread and water,
they will be overwhelmed with fear and
waste away because of their iniquity.

CHAPTER 5

1 Son of man, take a sharp sword and use
it as a barber's razor to shave your head and
your beard. Then take scales and divide the
hair you have cut off. 2 When the days of
the siege come to an end, burn one-third of
the hair inside the city. Take another third
and cut it up with the sword throughout the
city. Scatter the last third to the wind while I
pursue it with the sword. 3 In addition, take a
few of these hairs and conceal them in a fold
of your robe. 4 From these, however, take
some and cast them into the fire and burn
them completely. A fire will spread from
there against the entire house of Israel.

5 Thus says the Lord GOD: This is Jeru-
salem, which I have established in the midst
of the nations and surrounded with foreign
countries. 6 But she has rebelled against my
ordinances and my statutes more wickedly
than all the nations and the countries
around her, rejecting my ordinances and
refusing to obey my laws.[r]

7 Therefore, thus says the Lord GOD:
Because you have been more rebellious than
the nations that surround you and have not
followed my statutes or respected my ordi-
nances and have not even observed the laws
of the nations that surround you, 8 therefore,
thus says the Lord GOD: I too am coming
against you, and I will execute my judgments
on you for all the nations to see. 9 And
because of all your abominable offenses, I
will inflict punishment on you that I have
never done before and the like of which I will
never do again. 10 Those of you who are par-
ents will eat your children, and children will

---

p Ezek 21:22.—q Ex 22:30; Lev 17:15; Deut 14:3.—r Ezek 16:47; Jer 11:10.

4:1 For writing and drawing, the Babylonians used thin tablets of clay that had not yet dried, on which they wrote with a suitable stylus.

4:3 Verse 3 should be followed directly by verse 7.

4:4-6 The length of the atonement, which is given in round figures, is taken from the length of the period of exile for Israel and Judah respectively (721–538 B.C. and 587–538 B.C.).

4:9-17 A day will come when Jerusalem, a city being starved out, will have to ration food: about 250 grams of dry bread and a liter of water.

4:15 Dried manure is still used as fuel in some parts of the East.

eat their parents. I will execute judgments on you, and any of you who survive I will scatter to the winds.

11 Therefore, as I live, says the Lord GOD, because you have defiled my sanctuary with all of your detestable and vile abominations, I will destroy you. I will not take pity on you or spare you. 12 One-third of you will die of pestilence or perish because of famine, one-third will fall by the sword outside your walls, and one-third I will scatter to the four winds and pursue them with the sword.

13 Then, once my anger has abated and I have vented my wrath against them, they will know that I, the LORD, have spoken in my jealousy. 14 I will make you a desolate waste and the object of mockery among the nations that surround you, a fate clearly evident to all those who pass by. 15 You will be an object of mockery and abuse, a frightening warning to the nations that surround you, when I execute my judgment on you in anger and fury and dreadful punishments. I, the LORD, have spoken.

16 [s] When I loose my deadly arrows of famine against you, arrows of destruction which I will send forth to destroy you, and when I afflict you with one famine after another and cut off your supply of food, 17 I will afflict you with even more intense famine and wild beasts, and you will be left childless. Plague and bloodshed will sweep through you, and I will bring the sword against you. I, the LORD, have spoken.

CHAPTER 6

Against the Mountains of Israel. 1 This word of the LORD came to me: 2 Son of man, turn your face toward the mountains of Israel and prophesy against them. 3 Say: Mountains of Israel, hear the word of the Lord GOD. Thus says the Lord GOD to the mountains and the hills, to the ravines and the valleys: Behold, I am going to bring a sword against you, and I will destroy your high places. 4 Your altars will be demolished and your incense stands will be shattered, and I will throw down your slain in front of your idols. [t]

5 I will lay the corpses of the people of Israel in front of their idols, and I will scatter their bones all around your altars. 6 Wherever you live, your towns will be destroyed and your high places will be laid waste, your idols will be shattered and destroyed, your incense stands will be smashed, and all of the idols you have made will be obliterated. 7 As the slain will fall in your midst, you will know that I am the LORD.

8 However, among the nations I will spare some of you who will manage to escape the sword and be scattered throughout foreign lands. 9 Those of you who escape will remember me among the nations where you were carried away as captives—how I crushed their adulterous hearts for having deserted me and by their wanton eyes for lusting after idols. Then they will loathe themselves for all the evils that they have done with their abominable practices. 10 And they will know that I, the LORD, was not uttering a vain warning when I threatened to inflict this disaster upon them.

11 Thus says the Lord GOD: Clap your hands, stamp your feet, and cry, "Alas!" because of all the loathsome abominations of the house of Israel, for which the people will fall by the sword, famine, and pestilence. 12 Those who are far off will die of pestilence; those who are near will fall by the sword; any who survive and are spared will die of famine. Thus, I will exhaust my wrath upon them.

13 Then you will know that I am the LORD, when their slain lie among the idols around their altars, on every high hill, on every mountaintop, under every green tree, and under every leafy oak, wherever they offered sweet-smelling sacrifices to any of their idols. 14 I will stretch out my hand against them and reduce every place where they have settled to a desolate waste, from the desert to Riblah.* Then they will know that I am the LORD. [u]

CHAPTER 7

The End Is Near. 1 This word of the LORD came to me: 2 Son of man, thus says the Lord GOD to the land of Israel:

It is finished. The end is coming
upon the four corners of the land.
3 Now the end is upon you.
I will unleash my anger against you.
I will judge you according to your conduct
and punish you for all your loathsome deeds.

s :16f Ezek 4:16; Deut 32:23.—t Lev 26:30.—u Ezek 14:13; Isa 5:25.

6:14 *From the desert to Riblah:* the southern and northern boundaries of Palestine.

4 I will not look upon you with pity
or be merciful to you.
I will punish you for your evil conduct
and for your abominable practices.[v]
Then you will know
that I am the LORD.

5 Thus says the Lord GOD:

Disasters are coming, one after another.
6 The end is coming; it is coming upon you.
Behold its approach!
7 Your doom is coming upon you,
O inhabitant of the land.
The time is coming, the day is near—
a time of panic and not of rejoicing.

8 Soon I will pour out my wrath upon you
and vent my anger against you.
I will judge you according to your conduct
and punish you for your abominable deeds.
9 I will not look upon you with mercy,
nor will I have pity on you.
I will repay you for your conduct
and for the abominations in your midst.
Then you will know
that it is I, the LORD, who strike.

10 Now is the day of the LORD.
Behold, the end is at hand.
The scepter has blossomed;
insolence is at its peak.
11 Violence has now become the means
to punish wickedness.
None of the people will be left,
nor their wealth nor anything of value.
12 The time has come; the day is near.
Let not the buyer rejoice nor the seller mourn,
for fury engulfs the entire populace.

13 The seller will not be able to recover what he has sold as long as he lives. Neither party will be willing to cancel out the transaction.

14 They have sounded the trumpet
and made everything ready,
but no one goes to battle;
my wrath falls upon all alike.
15 The sword is outside;
pestilence and famine are within.
Those in the country will die by the sword;
those in the city will be devoured
by famine and pestilence.[w]
16 If any manage to survive,
they will escape to the mountains
like doves of the valleys.
There I will slaughter them all,
each one for his iniquity.

17 All their hands will be limp,
and all their knees will turn to water.
18 They will put on sackcloth,
their entire body trembling.
Shame shall be on all their faces,
and their heads will be shaved.[x]

19 They shall fling their silver into the streets,
and their gold shall be considered as refuse.[y]
Their silver and gold will not be able to save them
on the day of the LORD's wrath.
They will not be able to satisfy their hunger
or to fill their bellies,
for wealth was the reason for their iniquity.

20 They used to take pride
in their beautiful jewelry
from which they would fashion
vile, abominable images.
Therefore, I will regard their jewelry
as nothing more than filth.
21 I will hand it all over to foreigners as plunder
and as booty to the wicked of the earth,
and they will defile it.
22 I will turn my face away from them
while they profane my treasured land;
the violent shall enter and defile it.

23 Prepare chains,
because the land is full of bloodshed
and the city is filled with violence.
24 I will bring in the cruelest of the nations
to seize their houses.
I will put an end to the arrogance of the strong,
and their sanctuaries will be profaned.
25 When terror comes, they will seek peace,
but there will be none.

26 There will be disaster after disaster
and rumor upon rumor.
Prophets will be pestered endlessly for a vision;

v Ezek 5:11.—w Ezek 5:12; Deut 32:25.—x Isa 15:2; Am 8:10.—y Prov 11:4; Zep 1:18.

priests will fail to offer guidance,
and the elders will provide no counsel.[z]

27 The king will go into mourning;
the prince will be enveloped in despair;
the hands of the common people will tremble.
I will deal with them as their conduct deserves,
and I will judge them in accordance with their judgments.
Thus they will know that I am the LORD.

CHAPTER 8

Idolatry in the Temple. 1 * In the sixth year, on
the fifth day of the sixth month, as I was sit-
ting in my house, with the elders of Judah sit-
ting beside me, suddenly the hand of the
LORD fell upon me there.

2 As I looked, I beheld a figure that had the
form of a man. From the area of his waist
downward, he appeared to be like fire, and
upward from his waist, he seemed to have
a brilliance like gleaming amber. 3 He
stretched forth what appeared to be a hand
and grasped me by a lock of my hair. A Spirit
then lifted me up between earth and heaven,
and in divine visions he brought me to Jeru-
salem,[a] to the entrance of the inner north
gate, where stood the idol that arouses one to
jealousy.* 4 The glory of the God of Israel
was present before me, like the vision I had
seen in the valley.

5 Then the LORD said to me, "Son of man,
look toward the north." I raised my eyes
toward the north, and there, north of the
temple gate, a statue of jealousy stood at the
entrance. 6 He asked, "Son of man, do you
see what they are doing? Behold the loath-
some abominations that the house of Israel
is engaging in here in their determination to
drive me out of my sanctuary. And you will
see still greater abominations."

7 Then he brought me to the entrance of
the court, where I perceived a hole in the
wall. 8 He then ordered, "Son of man, dig
through the wall." After I dug through the
wall, I beheld a door. 9 He said to me, "Enter
and behold the vile abominations in which
they are engaged there."

10 I entered and looked around. Upon the
wall were depicted the carved figures of
every kind of creeping thing and loathsome
animals and all the idols of the house of
Israel.* 11 Before them stood seventy of the
elders of the house of Israel, including
Jaazaniah, the son of Shaphan. Each of them
held a censer in his hand, and all the fra-
grance of the incense ascended upward.

12 Then he said to me, "Son of man, have
you seen what the elders of the house of
Israel are doing in the dark, each one at the
shrine of his own idol? They think that the
LORD has forsaken the land and that he does
not see them."[b] 13 He also said to me, "You
will see even greater abominations practiced
by them."

14 Next he took me to the entrance of the
north gate of the house of the LORD, where
women were sitting, weeping for Tammuz.
15 Then he said to me, "Son of man, do you
see this? You will see even greater abomina-
tions than these."

16 He then brought me into the inner court
of the house of the LORD. There, at the
entrance of the temple of the LORD, between
the portico and the altar, were about twenty-
five men, with their backs to the temple of
the LORD and their faces toward the east,
prostrating themselves toward the east
before the rising sun.[c]

17 Then he said to me, "Do you see this, son
of man? Is it not bad enough for the house of
Judah to do the loathsome things they have
done here? They have filled the land with
violence and provoked me to anger time
after time. Observe how they put the branch
to their nose.* 18 Therefore, I will turn
against them in fury. I will not pity them or
spare them. No matter how loudly they may
cry out to me, I will not listen to them."

CHAPTER 9*

Punishment of the Idolaters. 1 Then he
shouted loudly for me to hear: "The scourges

z Ezek 21:7; Ps 74:9.—a 2 Cor 12:2.—b Ezek 9:9.—c Deut 4:19.

8:1—11:25 When some elders of Judah, fellow deportees, come to consult Ezekiel, the prophet falls unexpectedly into an ecstasy. He sees himself transported to the temple in Jerusalem.

8:3 *The idol that arouses one to jealousy:* a mysterious object that excites the wrath of God, whose love for Israel has been betrayed. Tammuz (v. 14), the Adonis of the Greeks, was the god of the first flowering and the spring vegetation in Mesopotamia.

8:10 The creeping things and the animals seem to refer to cults of Egyptian origin.

8:17 The end of the verse probably refers to a practice in the worship of the sun. It consisted in covering the nostrils with sacred twigs in order not to contaminate the air at sunrise.

9:1-11 The Apocalypse (Ezek 7:2) will use similar imagery in describing the end of the world.

of the city are drawing near, each brandish-
ing his weapon of destruction." 2 Thereupon,
I saw six men approaching from the direc-
tion of the upper gate which faces north,
each one with a weapon for slaughter in his
hand. Among them was a man clothed in
linen,* with the necessary paraphernalia for
writing in his hand. They went in and stood
beside the bronze altar.

3 The glory of the God of Israel had risen
above the cherubim upon which it rested to
the threshold of the temple. Then he called
to the man clothed in linen who had the
writing case at his side, 4 and he said to him:
"Go throughout the city, throughout Jeru-
salem, and mark* with a cross the foreheads
of all those who grieve and lament over all
the abominable practices that run rampant
throughout its boundaries." [d]

5 To the others I heard him say: "Follow
him throughout the city and kill, without
looking upon them with pity or showing
them any mercy. 6 Cut down old men, young
men and maidens, small children and
women, but touch no one who is marked on
the forehead with a cross. Begin at my sanc-
tuary." And so they began with the elders
who were in front of the temple. 7 Then he
said to them: "Defile the temple and fill the
courtyards with the slain." Then they went
forth and killed their way through the city.

8 While they continued with their mission
of slaying, I was left alone. Throwing myself
on the ground, I cried out, "Ah, Lord GOD,
will you annihilate all that is left of Israel by
pouring out your wrath on Jerusalem?" [e]
9 He answered: "The guilt of the house of
Israel and Judah is exceedingly great. The
land is filled with bloodshed and the city is
filled with perversity. They believe that the
LORD has forsaken the land and that he
does not see. 10 However, I will not look
upon them with pity or show them any
mercy. I will bring down their deeds upon
their heads."

11 Then the man clothed in linen and car-
rying the writing case reported, "I have done
as you commanded me."

CHAPTER 10

God's Glory Leaves the Temple. 1 Then I
looked and observed that above the vault
that was over the heads of the cherubim
there was what appeared to be a sapphire in
the shape of a throne. [f] 2 The LORD said to the
man clothed in linen, "Go within the wheels
beneath the cherubim. Fill both of your
hands with burning coals from among the
cherubim and scatter them over the city." As
I looked on, the man entered.

3 The cherubim were standing on the right
side of the temple as the man went in, and
the cloud filled the inner court. 4 Then the
glory of the LORD rose from above the cheru-
bim to the threshold of the temple. The tem-
ple was filled with the cloud, and the entire
court was filled with the brightness of the
glory of the LORD. [g] 5 The sound of the wings
of the cherubim could be heard as far away
as the outer court, like the voice of God when
he speaks.

6 When the LORD had commanded the
man dressed in linen to take fire from
between the wheels, from between the
cherubim, the man entered and stood by
one of the wheels. 7 Then one of the cheru-
bim stretched out his hand to the fire in their
midst, took up some of it, and put it into the
hands of the man clothed in linen, who took
it and then went outside. 8 The cherubim
seemed to have under their wings what
appeared to be a human hand.

9 As I looked on, I saw that there were four
wheels beside the cherubim, one wheel be-
side each cherub, and the wheels had the
appearance of sparkling chrysolite. 10 As for
their appearance, all four seemed to be iden-
tical, something like a wheel within a wheel.

11 When the cherubim moved, they went in
any of the four directions without veering
from their course. In whatever direction the
front wheel faced, the others followed with-
out swerving as they moved. 12 Their entire
bodies—their backs, their hands, and their
wings—were filled with eyes, as were their
wheels. [h]

13 As for the wheels, I heard them called
"the wheelworks." 14 Each one had four faces.
The first face was that of a cherub, the sec-
ond was that of a human, the third was that
of a lion, and the fourth was that of an eagle.

15 The cherubim rose up—the identical liv-
ing creatures that I had seen by the River
Chebar. 16 When the cherubim moved, the

d Ex 12:7; Rev 7:3.—e Ezek 11:13; Jos 7:6.—f Ezek 1:22; Rev 4:2.—g Ezek 1:28; Ex 40:34-35; 1 Ki 8:10-11.—h Rev 4:6, 8.

9:2 *Linen:* was used for priestly vestments.

9:4 The *mark* was a *tau*, that is, the last letter of the Hebrew alphabet; in ancient writing, *tau* was in the form of a cross.

wheels moved beside them, and when the
cherubim lifted up their wings and rose from
the ground, the wheels at their side did not
veer.[i] 17 When they stopped, the others
stopped, and when they rose up, the others
rose with them, for the Spirit of the living
creatures was in them.

18 * Then the glory of the LORD came forth
from the threshold of the temple and paused
above the cherubim. 19 The cherubim lifted
up their wings, and I beheld them as they
rose from the ground, with the wheels beside
them. They halted at the entrance of the east
gate of the house of the LORD, and the glory
of the God of Israel was with them.

20 These were the living creatures that I
had seen beneath the God of Israel by the
River Chebar, and I knew that they were
cherubim. 21 Each had four faces and four
wings, and underneath their wings were what
appeared to be human hands. 22 Their faces
were identical to those I had seen by the River
Chebar. Each one moved straight ahead.

CHAPTER 11

Punishment of the Rulers. 1 The Spirit lifted
me up and brought me to the gate of the
temple of the LORD that faces eastward.
There at the entrance to the gate twenty-five
men were standing. Among them I saw
Jaazaniah, the son of Azzur, and Pelatiah,
the son of Benaiah, princes of the people.

2 The LORD said to me, "Son of man, these
are the men who are plotting evil deeds and
offering wicked counsel in this city. 3 They
say, 'The time has not yet come to build
houses. This city is the cooking pot and we
are the meat.'[j] 4 Therefore, prophesy against
them, son of man, prophesy!"

5 Then the Spirit of the LORD fell upon me,
and he instructed me to say: Thus says the
LORD. This is what you are saying to your-
selves, house of Israel, and I am well aware of
what you are plotting. 6 You have killed many
in this city and filled its streets with the slain.

7 Therefore, thus says the Lord GOD: Those
in the city whom you have slain are the
meat, and the city is the pot, but I shall
remove you from it.* 8 You are in dread of
the sword, and I fully intend to bring the
sword upon you, says the Lord GOD.

9 I will drive you from the city and hand
you over to foreigners, and inflict punish-
ments upon you. 10 You will fall by the sword,
and I will pass judgment upon you at the
border of Israel. You will know that I am the
LORD.

11 This city shall not be a cooking pot for
you, nor shall you be the meat inside it. I will
judge you at the border of Israel. 12 Then you
will know that I am the LORD whose statutes
you have not obeyed and whose judgments
you have not followed. Rather you have con-
formed to the ordinances of the nations
around you.

13 * While I was prophesying, Pelatiah, the
son of Benaiah, fell dead. I threw myself on
the ground and cried out in a loud voice,
"Lord GOD, do you intend to wipe out com-
pletely the remnant of Israel?"[k]

Restoration of the People in Exile. 14 Then the
word of the LORD was addressed to me:
15 Son of man, it is about your brothers and
your kinsmen and the entire house of Israel
that the inhabitants of Israel have said,
"They have strayed far from the LORD. This
land has been given to us as our possession."

16 Therefore say: Thus says the Lord GOD:
Although I removed them far away among
the nations and scattered them over the
earth, I have nevertheless been a sanctuary
to them for a time in the countries where
they settled.

17 Therefore say: Thus says the Lord GOD: I
will gather you from the nations and bring
you together from the countries where you
have been scattered, and I will give you the
land of Israel.

18 When they return there, they will purge
it of all its vile and abominable practices. 19 I
will give them a new heart and put a new
spirit within them. I will remove the heart of
stone from their bodies and give them a
heart of flesh.[l]

20 Thus, they will live according to my
statutes and observe and obey my ordi-
nances. Then they shall be my people, and I
will be their God. 21 However, those whose
hearts are determined to continue their vile
and abominable practices I will force to

i Ezek 1:19.—j Ezek 24:3, 6.—k Ezek 9:8.—l Ezek 36:26; Jer 31:33.

10:18-22 Ezekiel's discourse must have seemed scandalous. The continuation of this passage is in Ezek 11:22-25.

11:7ff The image of the pot is developed further in Ezek 24:1-5.

11:13-21 On the horizon can be seen the gathering of the dispersed and the new covenant that God will establish in the very hearts of human beings; Ezekiel develops this theme in Ezek 34:11-31; 36:13-38; 37.

answer for all they have done. Thus says the
Lord GOD.
22 Then the cherubim lifted their wings,
with the wheels beside them and the glory of
the God of Israel above them, and the glory
of the God of Israel was above them. 23 The
glory of the LORD rose from the center of the
city and halted on the mountain to the east
of it. 24 The Spirit lifted me up and brought
me in a vision by the Spirit of God to the
exiles in Chaldea. After the vision I had seen
faded, 25 I told the exiles everything that the
LORD had revealed to me.[m]

CHAPTER 12

Acts Symbolic of the Exile.* 1 This word of
the LORD came to me: 2 Son of man, you are
living among a rebellious people. They have
eyes with which to see, but they do not see,
and they have ears with which to hear, but
they do not hear, for they are rebellious by
their very nature.[n]
3 Therefore, son of man, while they observe
you, pack up your belongings and set off
from your home into exile during the day.
Perhaps this will cause them to understand
that they are a rebellious people. 4 Bring out
your belongings during the day as they are
watching, and in the evening, again as they
watch, go forth like one who has been driven
into exile.
5 Then, as they continue to observe you,
dig a hole in the wall and make your way
through it. 6 In their presence, lift your pack
onto your shoulder and set out into the dark-
ness. Cover your face so that you may not
see the land, for I have established you as a
sign for the house of Israel.[o]
7 I did exactly what I had been command-
ed. In the daytime I brought out my belong-
ings that had been packed for exile, and in
the evening I dug through the wall with my
own hands. While they looked on, I set out in
the darkness, shouldering my burden.
8 On the following morning, this word of
the LORD was addressed to me: 9 Son of man,
did the house of Israel, that rebellious people,
not even ask you what you were doing? 10 Say
to them: Thus says the Lord GOD: This oracle
concerns the prince in Jerusalem and the
entire house of Israel living within its territo-
ry. 11 Tell them: I am a sign for you. As I have
done, so will it be done to them. As captives
they will go into exile. 12 Their prince who is
among them will shoulder his pack in the
darkness and go out through a hole that he
has dug in the wall. He will cover his face so
that he cannot see the land.
13 However, I will spread my net over him,
and he will be caught in my snare. I will take
him to Babylon, into the land of the
Chaldeans, where he will die without ever
seeing it.[p] 14 As for his retinue, his atten-
dants, and all his troops, I will scatter them
to the four winds and pursue them with the
sword.
15 Then they will know that I am the LORD
when I disperse them among the nations
and scatter them throughout foreign coun-
tries. 16 However, I will allow a few of them to
escape the sword, famine, and pestilence so
that they may relate all of their abominable
practices to the nations where they have
been exiled. Thus they will know that I am
the LORD.
17 Then the word of the LORD came to me:
18 Son of man, tremble as you eat your bread,
and shake with anxiety as you drink your
water, 19 and you are to say to the people of
that land: Thus says the LORD about those
who live in Jerusalem and in the land of
Israel: They will eat their bread in fearfulness
and drink their water in despair, for their
land will be stripped of everything within it
because of the violence of all those who live
there. 20 The inhabited cities will lie in ruins,
and the land will be a desolate waste. Thus
you will know that I am the LORD.

Fulfillment of Visions. 21 This word of the
LORD then came to me: 22 Son of man, there
is a saying that has become fashionable
in regard to the land of Israel: "The days
drag by, and no visions are ever fulfilled."
23 Therefore, tell the people: Thus says the
Lord GOD: I will put an end to this proverb,
and it will never again be spoken in the land
of Israel.
Rather, say to them: The days are close at
hand when every vision will be fulfilled.
24 There will no longer be any false visions or
deceptive divinations within the house of
Israel. 25 For I, the LORD, will speak, and what
I say will come true without the slightest
delay. In your lifetime, O rebellious house,
whatever I speak will be fulfilled, says the
Lord GOD.

m Ezek 2:7.—n Ezek 2:6-8; Jer 5:21.—o Isa 8:18.—p Ezek 17:20.

12:1-20 Israel will go into exile; her king, after trying to escape, will leave Palestine, blinded and in chains (see 2 Ki 25:4-7).

26 This word of the LORD then came to me:
27 Son of man, the house of Israel is saying,
"The vision that this man relates is meant to
be fulfilled in the far distant future."[q]
28 Therefore say to them, "Thus says the
Lord GOD: The fulfillment of my words will
not be delayed any longer. What I have said
will be done now. This is the word of the
Lord GOD."

CHAPTER 13

Prophecy against False Prophets. 1 This
word of the LORD came to me: 2 Son of man,
prophesy against the prophets of Israel who
are now prophesying. Say to those whose
prophesies are formulated in their own
minds: Hear the word of the LORD.

3 Thus says the Lord GOD: Disaster will
engulf those foolish prophets who follow
thoughts that are fabricated in their own
imaginations and have received no visions.[r]
4 Your prophets, O Israel, are like jackals for-
aging among ruins. 5 They have not bothered
to reinforce the breaches in the walls of the
house of Israel so that it may stand firm in
battle on the day of the LORD.

6 The visions they saw were false, and their
divinations were baseless. They assert:
"Thus says the LORD," despite the fact that
the LORD did not send them, and then they
expect their words to be proved true. 7 Have
you not seen false visions or uttered lying
divinations when you have asserted, "Thus
says the LORD," even though I have not said
any such thing?

8 Therefore, thus says the Lord GOD:
Because you have spoken untruths and pro-
claimed false predictions, I have now set
myself in opposition to you, says the Lord
GOD. 9 My hand will be raised against those
prophets whose visions are baseless and
whose divinations are clearly false. They will
not be granted any position in the council of
my people, nor will their names be enrolled
in the register of the house of Israel, nor will
they be permitted to set foot in the land of
Israel. Then you will know that I am the
LORD.

10 Because they lead my people astray, cry-
ing aloud, "Peace!" when there is no peace,
and because, when the people were repair-
ing a flimsy wall, these prophets concealed
its flaws by smearing whitewash on it, 11 say
to those who covered it with whitewash that
it will collapse, for I will cause rain to fall in
torrents, and I will send hailstones hurtling
down and unleash a wind of gale force.
12 When the wall collapses that you have
smeared with whitewash and it falls to the
ground so that its foundations will be laid
bare, you will be destroyed along with it, and
thus you will know that I am the LORD.

13 Therefore, thus says the Lord GOD: I
intend to unleash a violent stormwind in my
rage, torrential rain in my anger, and hail-
stones in my fury,[s] 14 and I will shatter the
wall that you smeared with whitewash and
knock it to the ground and lay bare its foun-
dations. It will fall, and you will perish
beneath it. Then you will know that I am the
LORD.

15 When I have vented my fury upon the
wall and upon those who smeared it with
whitewash, I will say to you, "The wall is
gone, and so are those who smeared it—16 the
prophets of Israel who prophesied about
Jerusalem and envisioned peace for it when
there was no peace," says the Lord GOD.

Prophecy against False Prophetesses. 17 As
for you, son of man, set your face against the
daughters of your people whose prophecies
emerge from their own imaginations.
Prophesy against them 18 and say: Thus says
the Lord GOD: Woe to those women who sew
magic bands on their wrists and make veils
for the heads of persons of every height as
they strive to ensnare their souls. Will you
seek to ensnare the souls of my people and
still preserve your own?

19 You have dishonored me in the eyes of
my people for a few handfuls of barley and a
few scraps of bread. By lying to my people
who listen to lies, you have caused the death
of persons who should not die and kept alive
those who should not live.[t]

20 Therefore, thus says the Lord GOD:
Behold, I am now determined to move
against your magic bands with which you
entrap men's lives. I will rip them from your
arms and set free those people whom you
have ensnared like birds. 21 I will tear off your
veils and rescue my people from your clutch-
es, and they will no longer fall prey to your
power. Then you will know that I am the
LORD.

22 Because you have intimidated the righ-
teous with your lies and disheartened them
when I had done nothing to cause them to be

q Dan 10:14.—r Jer 23:28-32; Lam 2:14.—s Isa 30:30; Rev 11:19.—t Ezek 20:39; Jer 23:14, 17.

alarmed, and because you have encouraged
the wicked not to abandon their wicked ways
and save their lives, 23 therefore, you will
never again see false visions or practice div-
inations. I will rescue my people from your
clutches, and then you will know that I am
the LORD.

CHAPTER 14

Idolatry of the Elders. 1 Some of the elders
came into my presence and sat down before
me.* 2 Then the word of the LORD came to
me: 3 Son of man, these men have reserved a
special place in their hearts for their idols
and have continued to revere the occasions
of sin that led to their downfall. Why should
I allow myself to be consulted by them?

4 Therefore, speak to them and declare
this: Thus says the Lord GOD: To all those
belonging to the house of Israel who contin-
ue to revere their idols in their hearts and
fail to remove the stumbling block of their
iniquity and then approach a prophet, I, the
LORD, will deliver my answer to those who
approach me with their multitude of idols.
5 In this way, I will recapture the hearts of the
house of Israel, all of those who have been
estranged from me through their idols. [u]

6 Therefore, say to the house of Israel: Thus
says the Lord GOD: Repent and turn away
from your idols, and turn away your faces
from all your abominations. 7 For if any
members of the house of Israel or any aliens
who reside in Israel separate themselves
from me, holding the memory of their idols
in their hearts and keeping the cause of their
iniquity before their eyes, and then approach
a prophet to consult me, I, the LORD, will
answer them myself. 8 I will set my face
against them, and I will make them an
example and a byword. I will cut them off
from the midst of my people, and thus you
will know that I am the LORD.

9 If a prophet is led astray into making a
prophecy, I, the LORD, shall have been the
one who deceived that prophet. I will stretch
out my hand against him and eradicate him
from the presence of my people Israel. [v]
10 The punishments received by the inquirer
and the prophet shall be identical, 11 so that
the house of Israel will never again stray from
me or defile themselves any longer with all
their sins. Thus, they shall be my people, and
I will be their God, says the Lord GOD.

Individual Responsibility.* 12 This word of the
LORD came to me: 13 Son of man, if a country
sins against me by being unfaithful, and I
stretch out my hand against it and cut off its
supply of food, inflicting famine on it and
removing from its midst all of its inhabitants
and its animals, 14 even if the three men,
Noah, Daniel,* and Job were there, they
could save no one but themselves by their
own righteousness, says the Lord GOD. [w]

15 If I were to unleash wild animals
throughout the land to ravage it, so that it
would become a desolate wasteland through
which no one could traverse because of the
savage beasts, 16 even if those three men
were in it, as I live, says the Lord GOD, they
would save neither sons nor daughters; they
alone would survive.

17 Or if I were to bring the sword down on
that country, commanding the sword to pass
through the land, isolating it from man and
beast, 18 even if those three men were in it,
says the Lord GOD, they would be unable to
save either their sons or their daughters;
they alone would be saved.

19 Or if I were to inflict a pestilence upon
that land and pour out my wrath upon it
with blood, destroying all people and ani-
mals with it, 20 even if Noah, Daniel, and Job
were in it, as I live, says the Lord GOD, they
would save neither son nor daughter; they
would only save themselves by their righ-
teousness.

21 Thus says the Lord GOD: Even if I were
to inflict upon Jerusalem my four dreadful
scourges—sword, famine, wild animals, and
pestilence—to cut off from it both men and
animals, [x] 22 even so some survivors will be
left in it, both men and women. When they
come to you and you observe their conduct
and their actions, you will be consoled
despite the disaster I have inflicted upon

u Isa 1:4; Jer 2:11.—v 1 Ki 22:23.—w Gen 6:8; Job 1:1.—
x Ezek 5:17; Rev 6:8.

14:1 The elders are the heads of the communities of exiles.

14:12-23 This passage states a basic idea in Ezekiel's teaching and will be repeated at greater length in other passages (Ezek 18; 33:10-20). The prophet Jeremiah has already said that the Lord will no longer yield to the prayers of the great intercessors unless the people are converted. Ezekiel is even more explicit: the salvation or ruin of individuals depends not on their forebears, or on solidarity with the people, or even on their own past; they are each responsible for themselves individually and according to their dispositions at any moment; they will be repaid each according to their conduct.

14:14 *Daniel:* a famous sage of the ancient East; a Phoenician poem speaks of him. He will also be the chief character of the biblical Book of the same name.

Jerusalem.* [23] They will be a source of consolation when you reflect upon their conduct and their deeds, and you will come to realize that it was not without good reason that I have done to it what I did.

CHAPTER 15*

The Useless Vine. [1] This word of the LORD came to me:

2 Son of man, how is the wood of the vine
better than any other wood,
the vine branch from a tree in the forest? [y]
3 Is its wood used to make anything?
Are pegs fashioned from it to hang anything?
4 If it is thrown on the fire for fuel,
and the fire consumes both ends and chars the middle,
is it useful for anything?
5 When it was whole,
it served no purpose.
How much less, when the fire has consumed it
and it is charred,
can it be used for anything?

[6] Therefore, thus says the Lord GOD:

Like the wood of the vine among the trees of the forest
that I have thrown on the fire for fuel,
so will I treat the inhabitants of Jerusalem.
7 I have set my face against them.
Although they escape from the fire,
that fire will still devour them.
And you will know that I am the LORD
when I turn my face against them. [z]
8 I will reduce the entire land into a desolate waste
because they have been unfaithful,
says the Lord GOD.

CHAPTER 16*

The Unfaithful Wife. [1] This word of the LORD was addressed to me: [2] Son of man, make known to Jerusalem her abominable practices. [3] Say to her: Thus says the Lord GOD to Jerusalem: By origin and birth, you belong to Canaan. Your father was an Amorite and your mother was a Hittite. [a]

[4] As for your birth, on the day you were born your navel cord was not cut. You were neither bathed in water, nor rubbed with salt, nor wrapped in swaddling clothes. [5] No one took pity on you or did any of these deeds out of compassion for you. Rather, you were thrown out into an open field, for you were regarded as something loathsome on the day you were born.

[6] Then I passed by and saw you kicking helplessly in your blood. I said to you as you lay there in your blood, "Live, [7] and grow like a plant of the field." You grew up and developed and reached the stage of full womanhood. Your breasts had formed and your hair had grown, but you were still naked and exposed.

[8] I passed by you again and saw that you were old enough for love. I spread the edge of my cloak over you and covered your nakedness. I swore an oath to you and made a covenant with you, says the Lord GOD, and you became mine. [b] [9] Then I bathed you in water, washed away the blood from your body, and anointed you with oil.

[10] After this, I clothed you with embroidered gowns and sandals of fine leather, as well as with a linen headband and a silk cloak. [11] I adorned you with jewels: bracelets for your arms, a chain around your neck, [12] a ring in your nose, pendants for your ears, and a beautiful crown for your head.

[13] Thus, you were adorned with gold and silver, and your garments were of fine linen, silk, and embroidered cloth. Fine flour, honey, and oil were your food. You grew exceedingly beautiful, fit to be a queen. [c] [14] You were renowned among the nations because of your beauty, since it was perfect because of the splendor I had bestowed upon you, says the Lord GOD.

[15] But you became infatuated with your own beauty, and you exploited your renown as you freely offered to play the harlot to every passerby. [16] You used some of your garments to decorate colorful shrines for yourself where you played the harlot. [d] [17] You also took the beautiful gold and silver jewelry that

y Isa 5:1-7; Hos 10:1.—z Ezek 14:8; Isa 24:18.—a Hos 1:2-3.—b Ex 19:5; Rev 3:9.—c Deut 32:13-14.—d Hos 2:7.

14:22 The behavior of these survivors will show how depraved Jerusalem was, and the exiles will recognize that the destruction of the city was a just punishment.

15:1-8 Ezekiel likes allegories and parables (Ezek 17:2). We have already met in Isaiah, the song of the disappointed vineyard owner (Isa 5:7). A vineyard was valuable for its fruit, not for its wood.

16:1-63 The great depictions of the history of Israel are stories of infidelity; we need only read the Books of Kings to sense the full tragedy. In three pictures, Ezekiel paints a great fresco of the history of his people: verses 1, 20, 23.

I had given you and made for yourself male images, with which you committed fornication.

18 Furthermore, you took your embroidered clothes to cover these images and set my oil and my incense before them. 19 You also took the food that I had given you—the fine flour, the oil, and the honey with which I fed you—and set it before them as a pleasant odor, says the Lord GOD.

20 You took the sons and daughters you had borne to me and offered them as sacrifices. Was it not enough that you had become a harlot?[e] 21 You slaughtered my children and immolated them as an offering to your idols. 22 And throughout all your abominations and your harlotries you never gave a thought to your youth when you were naked and bare and kicking helplessly in your own blood.[f]

23 Then, after all your wicked deeds—woe, woe to you! says the Lord GOD—24 you built for yourself a platform and erected for yourself a lofty place in every square. 25 At the head of every street, you built your dais and degraded your beauty, offering your body to every passerby in countless acts of harlotry. 26 You also played the whore with the Egyptians, your lustful neighbors, and provoked me to anger with your repeated acts of fornication.

27 Therefore, I stretched out my hand against you, reduced your supply of food, and delivered you into the hands of your enemies, the Philistine women, who were horrified by your lewd behavior. 28 You also played the whore with the Assyrians in your insatiable lust, and even then you were not satisfied. 29 Again and again you continued to play the harlot in Chaldea, the land of merchants, and still you remained unsatisfied.

30 How truly sick you are, says the Lord GOD, for engaging in the deeds of a brazen prostitute, 31 building your platform at every street corner and erecting your lofty dais in every square. Yet you do not truly fulfill the role of a prostitute because you scorn any payment.

32 An adulterous wife welcomes strangers instead of her husband. 33 All prostitutes receive gifts, but you gave gifts to all your lovers, bribing them to come from everywhere to receive your favors. 34 Thus in your harlotry, you were different from other such women. No one sought you out for prostitution, and you gave payment instead of receiving it. You are the complete opposite of all other whores.

35 Therefore, you harlot, listen to the word of the LORD. 36 Thus says the Lord GOD: Because you poured forth your lust and revealed your nakedness in your promiscuous dealings with your lovers, and because you surrendered to them the blood of your children,[g] 37 therefore, I will gather together all your lovers in whom you took pleasure, all those whom you loved and all those whom you disliked. I will gather them from all sides and expose you naked for them to see.

38 I will inflict on you the sentence that is imposed on adulteresses and murderesses and bring down upon you the bloody vengeance of my wrath and jealousy. 39 I will deliver you into their hands, and they will destroy your platforms and tear down your lofty places. They will strip off your clothes, take away your jewels, and leave you stark naked. 40 They will assemble a mob to punish you, stoning you and cutting you to pieces with their swords. 41 They will burn down your houses and execute judgments against you while many women look on. Thus, I shall put an end to your harlotry, and never again will you make payments to your lovers.[h]

42 Once my fury against you has been exhausted, then my jealousy will turn away from you. I will be calm and will no longer be provoked to anger. 43 Because you have never called to mind the days of your youth but enraged me with all of your wicked deeds, I have brought your conduct down upon your head, says the Lord GOD. For did you not add lewd behavior to all of your other abominable deeds?

44 Everyone who quotes proverbs will use this one in regard to you: "Like mother, like daughter." 45 You are a true daughter of your mother who loathed her husband and her children, and you are a true sister of your sisters who loathed their husbands and their children. Your mother was a Hittite, and your father was an Amorite. 46 Your elder sister is Samaria, who lives to the north of you with her daughters, and your younger sister is Sodom, who lives to the south of you with her daughters. 47 You not only followed their ways and imitated their loathsome practices, but

e Ezek 20:26, 31; Lev 18:21.—f 2 Ki 16:3.—g Ezek 23:10.—h Deut 13:16; 2 Ki 25:9.

within a brief period of time you were more
corrupt than they in all of your ways.
48 As I live, says the Lord GOD, your sister
Sodom and her daughters have not done as
you and your daughters have done. 49 The
crimes of your sister Sodom were pride,
gluttony, and lack of concern for the poor
and needy.[i] 50 They were haughty and com-
mitted abominable deeds in my presence.
Therefore, I swept them from my sight, as
you have seen.
51 Samaria did not commit half of the sins
of which you have been guilty. You have done
far more abominable crimes than they did,
and you have made your sisters appear to be
innocent because of all the abominations
that you have committed. 52 Bear the shame
of your disgrace, as a result of which you
have made possible a more favorable judg-
ment for your sisters. Because your conduct
was far more abominable than theirs, they
appear to be more upright in comparison
with you. Therefore, blush for shame, and
bear the disgrace of having made your sis-
ters appear to be righteous.
53 I intend to restore the fortunes of
Sodom and her daughters and the fortunes
of Samaria and her daughters, and your own
fortunes along with theirs, 54 so that you may
bear your own disgrace and be ashamed of
all you have done as you offer consolation to
them.
55 As for your sisters, when Sodom and her
daughters will be restored to their former
state and Samaria and her daughters will be
restored to their former state, then you and
your daughters will return to your former
state. 56 Did you not regard with contempt
your sister Sodom in the days of your pride,
57 before your wickedness was revealed? Now
you are regarded with contempt by the
daughters of Edom and all her neighbors
and by the daughters of the Philistines—all
these people despise you. 58 You must suffer
the consequences of your lewdness and your
loathsome abominations, says the LORD.
59 For thus says the Lord GOD: I will deal
with you as you have deserved, you who
despised your oath and broke the covenant.
60 However, I will remember the covenant I
made with you in the days of your youth, and
I shall establish with you an everlasting
covenant.[j] 61 Then you will recall your for-
mer conduct and be ashamed when I take
your sisters, both those who are older than
you and those who are younger, and give
them to you as daughters, even though I am
not bound to do so by my covenant with
you.
62 Thus I will reestablish my covenant with
you, and you will know that I am the LORD,
63 and thus remember and be ashamed and
be reduced to silence when I forgive you for
everything that you have done, says the
Lord GOD.

CHAPTER 17*

Allegory of the Eagles and Vine. 1 This word
of the LORD was addressed to me: 2 Son of
man, propose a riddle and expound this
parable to the house of Israel. 3 Say: Thus
says the Lord GOD:

A great eagle with large wings and long pinions,
rich with multi-colored plumage,
came to Lebanon.
He took the top of the cedar tree
4 and plucked off its topmost shoot.
He carried it off to a land of tradesmen
and planted it in a city filled with merchants.

5 Then he took some of the seed of the land
and placed it in fertile soil.
Close to a source of abundant water
he set it like a willow tree.[k]
6 It sprouted and became a vine,
low-lying and spreading forth.
Its branches turned toward him,
but its roots remained firmly in place.
Thus it became a vine, produced branches,
and put forth lofty shoots.

7 But there was another great eagle
with large wings and thick plumage.
From the plot where it had been planted
this vine stretched forth its roots toward him
so that he might water it.

---

i Gen 19:24.—j Ezek 37:26; Jer 32:40; Hos 52:14-15.—k Deut 8:7-9; Isa 44:4.

17:1-24 The *great eagle* is evidently Nebuchadnezzar; he exiles Jehoiachin (v. 12), who is "the top of the cedar tree," and replaces him with Zedekiah, the *seed* of verse 5 (see 2 Ki 24:15). The latter is at first a docile vassal (see 2 Chr 36:13), but he soon negotiates with the pharaoh, the second great eagle (vv. 7, 15), who is already weakened and unable to save anyone. The pessimistic description ends with a ray of hope: someday the ruined Davidic dynasty will be restored. The coming of the future shoot (v. 22), the Messiah, will show once again how the Lord acts on behalf of his people (see Ezek 21:26).

It turned away from the bed where it was
planted.
8 In a fertile field by abundant waters,
it was planted so that it might branch
forth,
bear fruit, and become a noble vine.
[9] Therefore, thus says the Lord GOD:

Will such a vine flourish?
Will it not be uprooted
with its fruit stripped off
and its freshly sprouted leaves becom-
ing withered?
No great strength or a mighty army is
needed
to pull it up by its roots.
10 If it is transplanted, will it flourish?
Will it not totally shrivel up
as though destroyed by the east wind
on the bed where it was growing?

[11] Then the word of the LORD came to me:
[12] Say now to this rebellious people: Do you
not understand what all this means? Say to
them: The king of Babylon came to
Jerusalem, took its king and its princes, and
brought them back to Babylon with him.
[13] Then he selected a prince of the royal fam-
ily and made a covenant with him, binding
him under oath, and he deported the leading
men of the land [14] so that the kingdom would
be humble and submissive and be able to
survive only by keeping his covenant and
obeying him.

[15] However, the prince rebelled against him
and sent envoys to Egypt with a request for
horses and a large army. Will he succeed?
Can one escape who does such things? Can
he break the covenant and remain un-
scathed? [l]

[16] As I live, says the Lord GOD, I swear that
that man will die in Babylon, in the country
of the king who appointed him to rule, whose
oath he forsook and whose covenant he
broke. [17] Despite Pharaoh's mighty army and
hordes of troops, he will not be able to save
him in war, no matter how many ramps are
raised up and siege-towers are built to
destroy many lives. [18] He has violated the
treaty and disregarded the oath by breaking
the treaty he had pledged to observe. Since he
has done all this, he will not go unpunished.

[19] Therefore, thus says the Lord GOD: As I
live, I will bring down upon his head my oath
that he despised and my covenant that he
broke. [20] I will spread my net over him, and
he will be trapped in my snare. I will take him
to Babylon and bring him to judgment there
for the treasonous acts he has committed
against me. [21] All of his most valiant troops
will fall by the sword, and those who survive
will be scattered to the winds. Then you will
know that I, the LORD, have spoken.

[22] Thus says the LORD:

I myself will break off a tender shoot
from the highest branch of a tall
cedar
and plant it on a high and lofty moun-
tain.
23 On the highest mountain in Israel I will
plant it
so that it may put forth branches and
bear fruit
and become a majestic cedar.
Birds of every kind will live beneath it;
in the shelter of its branches
winged creatures of every kind will
dwell.
24 All the trees of the countryside will
know
that I am the LORD.
I will bring low the tall tree
and raise high the lowly tree.
I cause the green tree to wither
and make the shriveled tree bear
fruit.
I, the LORD, have spoken;
so will I do. [m]

CHAPTER 18*

Individual Responsibility. [1] This word of the
LORD came to me: [2] Why do you insist on
repeating this proverb in the land of Israel:

The parents have eaten sour grapes,
and their children's teeth are set on
edge? [n]

[3] As I live, says the Lord GOD, you will no
longer repeat this proverb in Israel. [4] Do not
forget that all lives are mine. The life of the
father and the life of the son are both mine.
Only the person who sins shall die.

l 2 Ki 24:20.—m Ezek 21:26; Ps 96:12.—n Jer 31:29.

18:1-32 The life and thought of Israel were controlled by a clan morality. Ezekiel, however, sets down a revolutionary principle: retribution is individual, each person receiving what he or she deserves. It is authentic righteousness that is spoken of here, the point of departure for an examination of conscience by the people as a whole and by the individual (vv. 5-9). In Ezek 14:12, the new basis of moral judgment has already made its explicit entrance into the Bible. It is not only a reminder to everyone; it is first of all an exhortation to a personal conversion (see Ezek 14:12-23; 33:10-20).

5 Reflect upon a virtuous man
who does what is lawful and right.
6 He does not eat* on the mountains
or lift up his eyes
to the idols of the house of Israel.
He does not defile his neighbor's wife
or have relations with a woman
during her menstrual period.
7 He does not oppress anyone
but returns his pledge to a debtor.
He does not commit robbery
but gives his food to the hungry
and his clothes to those who are naked.[o]
8 He does not lend money for profit
or charge interest.
He refrains from evildoing
and judges fairly between a man and his opponent.
9 He obeys my laws
and is careful to observe my ordinances.
Such a man is righteous;
he shall surely live,
says the Lord GOD.

10 But this man may have a son who is vio-
lent and sheds blood, 11 or does any of these
other deeds, even though his father has done
none of them:

He eats at the mountain shrines
and defiles his neighbor's wife.
12 He oppresses the poor and the needy,
commits robbery,
and does not return pledges.
He lifts his eyes to idols,
does abominable things,
13 and lends for profit or charges interest.

Will such a man live? He will not. Since he has done all of these detestable acts, he shall surely be put to death, and his blood will be on his own head.

14 But suppose this man has a son who observes all the sins his father has committed, and even though he sees them, he refuses to follow in his footsteps:

15 He does not eat on the mountains
or lift up his eyes
to the idols of the house of Israel.
He does not defile his neighbor's wife;
16 he does not oppress anyone
or exact a pledge for a loan.
He does not commit robbery
but gives his food to the hungry
and his clothes to those who are naked.
17 He refrains from evildoing
and accepts no usury or excessive profit.
He obeys my laws
and is careful to observe my ordinances.

This man will not die for his father's sin; he
will surely live. 18 But his father will die for
his iniquity because he practiced extortion, robbed his brothers, and never did what was good for his people.

19 You may ask, "Why should not the son
share the guilt of his father?" If the son has done what is lawful and just, and he has been careful to observe all my laws, he will surely
live. 20 The person who sins is the one who
will die. A son shall not bear the responsibility for his father's guilt, nor shall a father be charged with the guilt of his son. The righteousness of the righteous man shall be credited to him, and the wickedness of the wicked man shall be charged against him.[p]

21 However, if the wicked renounce all of
the sins that they have committed and keep all my statutes and do what is right and just, they shall surely live; they shall not die.
22 None of the crimes that they have commit-
ted shall be remembered against them; they shall live because of the righteous deeds that
they have done 23 Do I derive any pleasure
from the death of the wicked? asks the Lord GOD. Would I not rather rejoice to see them turn away from their wickedness and live?[q]

24 But if the righteous turn away from their
virtuous ways to follow the path of evil and do the same kind of abominable deeds that the wicked do, can they do this and live? None of their virtuous deeds will be remembered. Because of their infidelity and the sins they have committed, they shall die.

25 Yet you say, "The way of the LORD is
unjust." Now listen, O house of Israel! Is my way unfair? Or, rather, is it not your ways
that are unfair?[r] 26 When those who are righ-
teous turn away from their righteousness and turn to evil pursuits, they shall die as a result of the iniquity that they have committed.

27 Similarly, when those who are wicked
turn away from the wickedness that they have committed and do what is right and

o Lev 25:36-37; Mt 25:35.—p Deut 24:16; Rom 2:9-10.—q Ezek 33:11; 2 Pet 3:9.—r Ezek 33:17, 20.

18:6 *Eat:* some idolatrous rites involved meals.

just, they shall save their life. 28 Since they
have chosen to renounce all of the evil ways
that they have followed, they shall surely live;
they shall not die.

29 Yet the house of Israel says, "The way of
the LORD is unfair." O house of Israel, are my
ways unfair? Is it not your ways that are
unfair?

30 Therefore, I will judge you, O house of
Israel, each one of you according to his ways,
says the Lord GOD. Repent and renounce all
your transgressions. Otherwise your iniquity
will prove to be your downfall.[s] 31 Cast away
from you all the transgressions you have
committed, and strengthen yourself with a
new heart and a new spirit. Why should you
die, O house of Israel? 32 I take no pleasure in
the death of anyone, says the Lord GOD.
Repent and live![t]

CHAPTER 19*

Allegory of the Lions*

1 Raise a lamentation for the princes of
Israel, 2 and say:

What a lioness was your mother
among the lions!
She lay down among the young lions,
rearing her cubs.
3 She raised up one of her cubs;
he grew into a young lion,
and he learned to tear apart his prey;
he devoured men.
4 Then the nations sounded an alarm against him,
and he was caught in their pit.
They dragged him off with hooks
to the land of Egypt.

5 When his mother saw that her hopes were thwarted
and her expectations would not be fulfilled,
she took another of her cubs
and made a young lion of him.[u]

6 He prowled among the lions
and grew into a young lion.
He learned to seize his prey;
he devoured men.
7 He ravaged their strongholds
and laid waste their cities.
The land and all of its inhabitants were terrified
at the sound of his roars.

8 The nations came forth against him
from the surrounding regions.
They spread their net over him,
and he was trapped in their pit.
9 With hooks they dragged him into a cage
and took him away to the king of Babylon.
He was imprisoned, and his roars were no longer heard
on the mountains of Israel.

Allegory of the Vine Branch

10 Your mother was like a vine
planted by the water.
It was fruitful and full of branches
because of the abundant water.
11 Its branches were strong,
suitable for a ruler's scepter.
It towered in stately height
among the dense foliage.
It was conspicuous for its height
and its many branches.

12 However, it was uprooted in fury
and thrown to the ground.
Its strong branches became withered
and were consumed by fire.[v]
13 Now it has been transplanted to the desert,
to a dry and thirsty land.
14 Fire burst forth from its stem,
devouring its branches and fruit.
It no longer has any strong branch
that could serve as a ruler's scepter.

This is a lamentation, and it is used for
this purpose.

CHAPTER 20

History of Israel's Infidelity. 1 In the seventh
year, on the tenth day of the fifth month,
some of the elders of Israel came to consult
the LORD and were sitting with me.

2 Then this word of the LORD came to me:
3 Son of man, speak to the elders of Israel
and say to them: Thus says the Lord GOD:
Have you come to consult me? As I live, I will

s Ezek 33:20; Mt 3:2.—t Ezek 18:23; 33:11; 2 Pet 3:9.—u 2 Ki 23:33-34.—v Hos 13:15.

19:1-14 Israel had fallen far, but it had never divinized its kings. Ezekiel's lament here refers to Zedekiah, last king of Jerusalem.

19:1-9 The *lioness* represents the nations, and the *cubs* its kings. Two sadly exemplary destinies are set forth: that of Jehoahaz and that of Jehoiachin. The first was deposed by Pharaoh Neco and taken to Egypt (2 Ki 23:34); the second reigned only three months and was exiled to Babylon (2 Ki 24:8-17; 25:27-30). King Jehoiakim, whose reign was less fleeting and who died a natural death, is not mentioned; his lot did not lend itself to a practical lesson!

refuse to be consulted by you, says the Lord GOD.

4 Will you judge them, son of man, will you judge them? Then make clear to them the abominations of their ancestors, 5 and say to them: The LORD says: On the day when I chose Israel, I swore to the offspring of the house of Jacob and revealed myself to the land of Egypt, declaring: I am the LORD, your God.[w]

6 On that day I swore that I would bring them out of the land of Egypt into a land that I had personally chosen for them, a land flowing with milk and honey, the fairest of all lands. 7 And I said to them, "Each one of you must cast away the loathsome things upon which your eyes have feasted and refuse to defile yourselves with the idols of Egypt. I am the LORD, your God."

8 However, they rebelled against me and refused to listen to me. Not a single one of them cast aside the loathsome things that seemed so desirable, nor did any of them forsake the idols of Egypt. Then I resolved to pour out my wrath on them and to vent my anger against them in the land of Egypt. 9 However, for the sake of my name I acted in such a way that it would not be profaned in the sight of the nations among whom they lived, and I promised to bring them out of the land of Egypt.

10 Therefore, I led them out of the land of Egypt and brought them into the desert. 11 I gave them my laws and made known to them my ordinances according to the observance of which they would live.[x] 12 And I also gave them my Sabbaths as a sign between me and them so that they would know that I, the LORD, made them holy.

13 However, the house of Israel rebelled against me in the desert. They refused to obey my statutes, and they rejected my ordinances whose observance is necessary for life. Furthermore, they profaned my Sabbaths. I then resolved to pour out my fury on them in the desert and destroy them. 14 But I acted for the sake of my name so that it would not be profaned in the sight of the nations, in whose presence I had brought them out.

15 Furthermore, I swore to them in the desert that I would not bring them into the land I had given them, a land flowing with milk and honey, the fairest of all lands, 16 because they rejected my ordinances, they did not observe my statutes, and they desecrated my Sabbaths, for their hearts were devoted to their idols.[y] 17 Nevertheless, I pitied them too much to destroy them, and I did not make an end of them in the wilderness.

18 Then I gave this warning to their children in the desert: Do not follow the statutes of your parents or observe their ordinances or defile yourselves with their idols. 19 I, the LORD, am your God. You must obey my laws and be careful to observe my ordinances. 20 Keep holy my Sabbaths as a sign between me and you so that you will know that I am the LORD, your God.

21 However, the children rebelled against me. They did not observe my statutes or keep my ordinances, even though observance of them would lead to life. Moreover, they profaned my Sabbaths. Then I again resolved to pour forth my wrath against them and vent my anger on them in the wilderness. 22 But I restrained my hand and acted for the sake of my name, so that it would not be profaned in the sight of the nations in whose presence I had brought them out.

23 Nevertheless, I swore to them in the wilderness that I would disperse them among the nations and scatter them over the earth,[z] 24 because they had rejected my laws and profaned my Sabbaths and had regard only for the idols of their ancestors. 25 Furthermore, I imposed on them statutes that were not good and ordinances by which they could never live. 26 I also defiled them through their offerings, making them sacrifice their firstborn son, in order to fill them with revulsion. Thus they would know that I am the LORD.

27 Therefore, son of man, speak to the house of Israel and say to them: Thus says the Lord GOD: In this way also your ancestors blasphemed me by dealing treacherously with me. 28 For when I had brought them into the land I had sworn to give them and they saw any high hill or leafy tree, there they offered their sacrifices and made offerings that aroused my anger; there they sent up offerings of pleasing odors, and there they poured out their drink offerings. 29 I then said to them, "What is this high place to which you go?" And ever since it has been called Bamah.

w Deut 7:6.—x Lev 18:5; Rom 10:5.—y Num 15:39.—z Deut 28:64; Lev 26:33.

30 Therefore, say to the house of Israel:
Thus says the Lord GOD: Will you defile
yourselves the way your fathers did and lust
after their loathsome gods? 31 When you
offer your gifts and burn your children as
sacrifices, you defile yourselves with all your
idols even to this day. Shall I allow myself to
be consulted by you, O house of Israel? As I
live, says the Lord GOD, I swear that I will
not allow myself to be consulted by you.

32 When you say to yourselves, "We shall
become like the nations and peoples of for-
eign lands, worshiping wood and stone," you
are making plans for something that will
never occur. 33 As I live, says the Lord GOD,
with a mighty hand and an outstretched
arm, and with my wrath poured out, I shall
reign over you. 34 I will bring you out from
the peoples and gather you from the lands
where you have been dispersed with a
mighty hand and an outstretched arm and
with my wrath poured out.

35 Then I will lead you into the wilderness
of the peoples, and there I will bring you to
judgment face to face. 36 As I judged your
ancestors in the Desert* of Egypt, so will I
judge you, says the Lord GOD. 37 I will make
you pass under the staff and bring you into
the bond of the covenant. 38 I will purge out
those of you who revolt and rebel against
me. I will bring them out of the land where
they reside as aliens, but they will not set foot
on the soil of Israel. Thus, you will know that
I am the LORD.

39 As for you, O house of Israel, thus says
the Lord GOD: Continue, each one of you, to
serve your idols, now and hereafter, if you
will not listen to me. But later on you will lis-
ten to me and never again profane my name
with your gifts and your idols. 40 For on my
holy mountain, on the mountain heights of
Israel, there in the land the entire house of
Israel will serve me, and there I will accept
them. There I will require your presents and
your choicest offerings and all your conse-
crated gifts. [a] 41 I will accept you as a pleasing
odor when I bring you back from the peoples
and gather you out of the countries to which
you have been scattered. Through you I will
manifest my holiness in the sight of all the
nations.

42 You shall know that I am the LORD when
I bring you back to the land of Israel, to the
country that I swore to give to your ances-
tors. 43 There you will remember your past
conduct and all the deeds by which you have
defiled yourselves. Then you will loathe your-
selves for all the wickedness you have com-
mitted. 44 You will know that I am the LORD
when I deal with you thus for your name's
sake, and not as your wicked behavior and
corrupt deeds deserve, O house of Israel,
says the Lord GOD.

45 The word of the LORD came to me:
46 Son of man, turn your face to the south.
Preach against the south and prophesy
against the forest land of the Negeb. 47 Say
to the forest of the Negeb: Hear the word of
the LORD. Thus says the Lord GOD: I am
about to kindle a fire in you, and it will
burn up every green tree in you and every
dry tree. The blazing flame will not be
quenched, and from south to north every
face shall be scorched by it. 48 All flesh shall
see that I, the LORD, have kindled it, and it
will not be extinguished. [b] 49 Then I said,
"Ah, Lord GOD, they are always saying of
me, 'He only speaks in riddles.' "

CHAPTER 21*

The Unsheathed Sword. 1 Then the word of
the LORD was addressed to me: 2 Son of man,
turn your face in the direction of Jerusalem;
preach against the sanctuaries and prophesy
against the land of Israel. 3 Say to the land of
Israel: Thus says the LORD: Behold, I am
coming against you. I will draw my sword
from its sheath and cut off from you both the
upright and the wicked. [c]

4 Because I will cut off from you both the
upright and the wicked, my sword shall be
unsheathed against everyone from south to
north, 5 and all people will know that I, the
LORD, have drawn my sword from its sheath,
and it will never again be sheathed.

Symbols of the City's Fall. 6 As for you, son of
man, groan. With a breaking heart grieve
bitterly as they look on. 7 And when they ask
you why you are groaning, you shall reply:
Because of the news that is about to come.
Every heart will melt and every hand will
become feeble; every spirit will grow faint
and all knees will turn to water. Behold, it is

a Ezek 17:23; Mic 4:1.—b Jer 7:20; 17:27.—c Jer 21:13.

20:36 *Desert:* the Syro-Arabian Desert between Palestine and Babylonia.

21:1-32 *Sword* is the word that links the following passages, which differ widely in their subject. It might be thought that the prophet is being excessively cruel as he announces the punishment and destruction of all; but exaggeration is part of the literary genre and of Ezekiel's style.

coming now. It will surely take place, says the
Lord GOD.

Song of the Sword. 8 Then the word of the
LORD came to me: 9 Prophesy, son of man,
and say: Thus says the LORD:

A sword, a sword has been sharpened;
it has also been burnished.
10 It is sharpened for slaughter,
burnished to flash like lightning.
11 The sword has been polished to be wielded
and to be placed in the slayer's hand.
12 Cry out and wail, son of man,
for it will be wielded against my people.
All of Israel's princes
will fall by the sword.
And so slap your thigh, my people, [d]
13 for the sword has been tested.
And why should it not be so,
says the Lord GOD,
since you have spurned the rod?

14 As for you, son of man, prophesy,
and strike your hands together.
Let the sword strike twice,
even three times.
It is a sword for killing,
a sword for great slaughter,
that threatens their enemies on every side.

15 Therefore, make their hearts melt
and cause many to fall.
I have posted at the gates
the sword for slaughter.
The great sword of slaughter
will flash like lightning.
16 Be prepared on the right,
be ready on the left—
wherever your sword is needed.
17 I, too, will strike my hands together
and satisfy my fury.
I, the LORD, have spoken.

The King of Babylon at the Crossroads.
18 The following word of the LORD was
addressed to me: 19 Son of man, mark out
two roads for the sword of the king of Bab-
ylon to take. Both roads shall begin from the
same land. Then put up a signpost for the
place where the roads diverge. 20 Indicate the
route which the sword should take for Rabbah
of the Ammonites, and the one for Judah and
the fortress of Jerusalem.

21 For the king of Babylon will stand at the
fork where the two roads divide to seek an
omen. He will shake the arrows, consult the
household gods, and inspect the liver. 22 Into
his right hand the arrow marked Jerusalem
will fall. Here, then, he will issue the com-
mand for slaughter, sound the battle cry,
post battering rams at the gates, cast up
siege-ramps, and build siege-towers. 23 The
inhabitants who have sworn allegiance* to
him will believe that this is a false omen, but
he will remind them of their guilt and take
them captive.

24 Therefore, thus says the Lord GOD: Be-
cause your open rebellion has caused us to
remember your guilt, in that you have parad-
ed your misdeeds and flaunted your sins in all
your deeds, you shall be taken into captivity.

25 As for you,
O vile and wicked ruler of Israel,
the day of your doom is approaching,
the time of your final punishment.

26 Thus says the LORD:

Remove your diadem; take off your crown;
everything is destined to be changed.
The lowly will be exalted
and the exalted will be brought low. [e]
27 A ruin! A ruin!
I will make it all a ruin
until the rightful ruler comes.

The Ammonites' Punishment. 28 As for you,
son of man, prophesy and say: Thus says the
LORD in regard to the Ammonites and their
insults:

A sword, a sword, drawn for slaughter,
burnished to consume and to flash like lightning.
29 In spite of false visions about you
as well as lying divinations,
that sword will be laid on the necks
of the wicked who are to be slain—
those whose day has come,
the hour of final punishment.
30 Return it to its sheath.
I will judge you
in the place where you were created,
in the land of your origin.

31 I will pour forth my wrath upon you
with the fire of my blazing anger.
I will hand you over to barbarous men
who are skilled in the art of destruction.

d Jer 31:19.—e Ezek 16:12; Jer 13:18.

21:23 *Sworn allegiance:* probably that binding Zedekiah to the Babylonians. See 2 Ki 24:17.

32 You will serve as fuel for the fire,
and your blood shall flow throughout
the land.
You shall remember no more,
for I, the LORD, have spoken.[f]

CHAPTER 22

The Sins of Jerusalem. 1 This word of the
LORD came to me: 2 Son of man, are you
ready to judge? Will you judge this city
renowned for its bloodshed and confront
her with all of her abominable deeds?[g]

3 Say to her: Thus says the LORD: Woe to
the city that sheds blood within itself. You
thus hasten your doom, having made idols
and thereby defiling yourself. 4 You have
incurred guilt by the blood that you have
shed, and you have become defiled by the
gods that you have fashioned. Thus, you have
shortened your lifespan; the end of your
years are at hand. This is why you are now
regarded by the nations as a disgrace. You
have become a laughingstock to all foreign
lands. 5 Those who are near you and those
who are far off shall mock you because you
have become infamous for your great per-
versity.

6 The princes of Israel who dwell in your
land are there only for the purpose of shed-
ding blood. 7 The fathers and the mothers
within your borders are treated with con-
tempt. The resident aliens are forced to
endure extortion. Orphans and widows are
oppressed. 8 You have spurned what is holy
to me, and you have profaned my Sabbaths.

9 In you are those whose slander incites to
bloodshed; in you are those who eat* on the
mountains and revel in their lewdness. 10 In
you are men who have exposed the naked-
ness of their fathers and who violate women
during their menstrual periods. 11 In you are
men who engage in abominable practices
with their neighbors' wives and lewdly defile
their daughters-in-law. Still others among
you ravish their sisters, the daughters of
their fathers.[h] 12 In you are those who take
bribes to shed blood. Others lend for profit
and charge interest. Still others profit from
extortion against their neighbors. You have
forgotten about me, says the Lord GOD.

13 I will strike my hands together because
of the unjust profits you have made and the
unending bloodshed in your midst. 14 Will
your courage endure and your hands remain
strong in the days when I will deal with you?
I, the LORD, have spoken, and I intend to act.
15 I will scatter you among the nations and
disperse you throughout foreign countries,
and I will thereby purge you of your filthi-
ness. 16 When I shall be profaned through
you in the sight of the nations, you will know
that I am the LORD.

17 Then the word of the LORD came to me:
18 Son of man, the house of Israel has be-
come dross in my eyes; all of them are noth-
ing more than copper and tin, iron and lead,
that have become dross in the midst of a fur-
nace.[i]

19 Therefore, thus says the Lord GOD:
Because all of you have become dross, I will
gather you together inside Jerusalem. 20 As
one gathers silver, bronze, iron, lead, and tin
and smelts it in a blazing furnace, so I will
gather you in my furious wrath and cause
you to be melted down. 21 When I have
assembled you, I will blow upon you with the
fire of my wrath, and you shall be melted
down within the city. 22 As silver is smelted in
a furnace, so shall you be melted down with-
in the city, and you will know that I, the
LORD, have poured forth my wrath upon
you.

23 This word of the LORD came to me:
24 Son of man, say to the land: You are a land
that has not been cleansed or rained upon in
the day of my anger. 25 Your princes have
been like a roaring lion tearing apart its
prey. They have devoured people, absconded
with their wealth and precious treasures,
and caused many women within it to be-
come widows.

26 Your priests have violated my law and
made profane my holy things. They have
failed to make any distinction between the
sacred and the profane, nor have they taught
the difference between the clean and the
unclean. They have completely ignored my
Sabbaths, and I have been profaned in their
midst. 27 Your priests are like wolves tearing
apart their prey, shedding blood, and killing
people in the pursuit of dishonest gain.[j]
28 Your prophets whitewash their deeds by
revealing false visions and offering lying
prophecies asserting that the Lord GOD has
spoken when the LORD has not spoken.
29 Meanwhile the people of the land practice
extortion and commit robbery. They have

f Ezek 25:10; Mal 1:4.—g Ezek 20:4.—h Ezek 18:11; Lev 18:15.—i Isa 1:22; Jer 6:28.—j Mic 3:11; Zep 3:3.

22:9 *Eat:* the banquets celebrated in idolatrous worship.

oppressed the poor and needy and forced resident aliens to submit to injustice.

30 I searched among my people for someone who could build a barricade and stand before me in the breach to keep me from destroying the land, but I found no one. 31 Therefore, I poured forth my fury upon them and consumed them with my fiery wrath. I have brought down their conduct upon their heads, says the Lord GOD.

CHAPTER 23*

The Sins of Two Sisters. 1 This word of the LORD came to me: 2 Son of man, there once were two women, the daughters of the same mother. 3 Even as young girls they became prostitutes in Egypt. There the Egyptians caressed their bosoms and fondled their virginal breasts.[k] 4 The older was named Oholah,* and her sister was Oholibah. They were mine, and they bore sons and daughters. As for their names, Oholah is Samaria, and Oholibah is Jerusalem.

5 Oholah became a whore even though she belonged to me. She lusted after her lovers, the Assyrians—6 warriors dressed in purple, governors and commanders, all of them handsome young men and skilled horsemen. 7 She offered herself as a prostitute to all the elite of the Assyrians, and she defiled herself with the idols of all those for whom she lusted. 8 Nor did she discontinue the harlotry she had begun in Egypt, where men had slept with her as a young girl, fondling her virginal breasts and pouring out their lust upon her.

9 Therefore, I abandoned her to her lovers, the Assyrians, for whom she had lusted. 10 They stripped her naked, and after they took away her sons and her daughters, they slew her with the sword. She became a byword among women for the justice that was inflicted upon her.[l]

11 Her sister Oholibah saw all this, but she was even more depraved in her lust than her sister, and she surpassed her in harlotry. 12 She too lusted after the Assyrians—governors and commanders, warriors arrayed in full armor, skilled horsemen, all of them handsome young men. 13 Then I realized that she, too, had been defiled. Both she and her sister had traveled the same path.

14 However, this younger sister went even further in her harlotry. When she saw male figures carved on the wall, images of the Chaldeans portrayed in vermilion, 15 with belts around their waists and flowing turbans on their heads, all of them looking like Babylonian officers, natives of Chaldea; 16 as soon as she saw them, she lusted after them and sent messengers* to them in Chaldea. 17 Then the Babylonians came to her, shared her bed of love, and defiled her with their lust. And after she had defiled herself with them, she turned away from them in disgust.

18 After she had flaunted her harlotry so openly and her nakedness was revealed, I turned from her in disgust as I had withdrawn from her sister. 19 Yet she became even more promiscuous, remembering the days of her youth when she had played the whore in Egypt 20 and lusted for her lecherous paramours there, whose members were like those of donkeys and whose ejaculations were like those of stallions.

21 You longed for the lewdness of your youth when the Egyptians fondled your bosom and caressed your breasts. 22 Therefore, Oholibah, thus says the Lord GOD: I will now stir up against you your lovers from whom you turned away in disgust, and I will bring them against you from every side: 23 the Babylonians and all the Chaldeans, the men of Pekod and Shoa and Koa, and all the Assyrians with them, handsome young men, all of them governors and commanders, officers and warriors, and all of them mounted on horses. 24 They shall come against you from the north with chariots and wagons and a host of people, and they will position themselves against you on every side with bucklers, shields, and helmets. I shall authorize them to pass judgment upon you, and they will judge you according to their own ordinances.

25 I will direct my jealous wrath against you so that they will vent their fury against you. They will cut off your nose and your ears, and

k Ezek 20:8; Jos 24:14.—l Ezek 16:37.

23:1-49 Ezekiel more than once speaks of the terrible weight of sin on the history of Israel (Ezek 16; 20; 22). He has already made use of the allegory of marriage in speaking of this history. Calling here again on the idea of marriage, the prophet tells the story of two cities, Samaria and Jerusalem, that is, of the two parts into which the Hebrew nation broke after the death of Solomon: the kingdom of Israel and the kingdom of Judah. The course taken by the two cities is once more illustrated by the history of the faithless wife.

23:4 *Oholah:* "his tent," a reference to the two illegitimate sanctuaries established by Jeroboam, as opposed to *Oholibah,* "My tent [is] in her," i.e., the true temple of the Lord in Jerusalem.

23:16 *Sent messengers:* the mission was perhaps sent in the time of Hezekiah, when the Assyrian threat was imminent.

your survivors will perish by the sword. They
will seize your sons and your daughters, and
what remains of your family will be con-
sumed by fire.* 26 They shall also strip off
your clothes and rob you of your jewels.
27 Thus, I will put an end to the debauchery
and lewdness you instituted in Egypt. You will
not look back in fond remembrance on the
wicked acts you committed or think of Egypt
ever again.

28 For thus says the Lord GOD: I intend to
hand you over to those whom you hate, to
those whom you regard with disgust. 29 They
shall treat you with hatred and seize all the
fruit of your labors and leave you stark
naked. Your lewdness and your promiscuity
30 have brought this upon you because you
played the whore with the nations and defiled
yourself with their idols.

31 Because you have followed in the path of
your sister, I will place her cup into your
hand. 32 Thus says the Lord GOD: *m*

You shall drink your sister's cup,
a cup both wide and deep.
You shall be scorned and mocked
since it holds so much.
33 You shall be filled with drunkenness and
sorrow
from this cup of ruin and devastation,
the cup of your sister Samaria.
34 You shall drink from it and completely
drain it;
then you shall dash it to pieces
and tear out your breasts.

Thus I have spoken, says the Lord GOD.

35 Therefore, thus says the Lord GOD:
Because you have forgotten me and cast me
behind your back, you must bear the conse-
quences of your lewdness and your harlotry.

36 Then the LORD said to me: Son of man,
are you willing to pass judgment on Oholah
and Oholibah? Then confront them with
their abominable deeds. *n* 37 For they have
committed adultery, and their hands are
stained with blood. They have committed
adultery with their idols and offered to them
as food the children whom they bore to me.

38 Furthermore, they have also done this to
me: At that same time, they defiled my sanc-
tuary and profaned my Sabbaths. 39 For
when they had slaughtered my children for
their idols, they entered my sanctuary on the
same day to desecrate it. That is what they
did in my house.

40 They even sent messengers to invite
men to come from distant lands. And when
they arrived, you bathed yourself for them,
painted your eyes, and adorned yourself
with jewels. 41 Then you reclined on an ele-
gant couch, with a table spread before it
upon which you had placed my incense and
my oil. 42 Meanwhile, the shouts of a raucous
mob were heard in the city, and they were
brought in together with many of the rabble
who had arrived from the wilderness in a
drunken stupor. They put bracelets on the
arms of the women and beautiful crowns on
their heads.

43 Then I thought: This woman is worn out
with endless acts of adultery, but neverthe-
less they carry on relentlessly their sexual
acts with her. 44 For they came to her as men
come to a prostitute. Thus, they came to
Oholah and Oholibah, those wanton women.
45 However, righteous judges will declare
them guilty of adultery and of bloodshed,
because they are adulteresses and blood is
on their hands. *o*

46 Thus says the Lord GOD: Convoke an
assembly against them and deliver them
over to terror and plunder. 47 The assembly
shall stone them and slay them with their
swords. They shall kill their sons and daugh-
ters and set their houses afire. 48 Thus will I
put an end to lewdness in the land, so that all
women will be solemnly warned not to com-
mit any lewd acts as you have done. 49 They
will inflict upon you the penalty for your
lewdness, and you will suffer the conse-
quences for your sins of idolatry. Thus, you
will know that I am the Lord GOD.

CHAPTER 24*

Allegory of the Boiling Pot. 1 In the ninth
year, on the tenth day of the tenth month,
this word of the LORD came to me: 2 Son of
man, write down the date of this day. For the
king of Babylon has laid siege to Jerusalem
this very day. 3 Therefore, propose this para-
ble to this tribe of rebels and say to them:
Thus says the Lord GOD:

Set up the cooking pot on the fire
and pour in some water.

m Isa 51:17; Jer 25:15.—n Ezek 20:4; 22:2.—o Ezek 16:38; Lev 20:10.

23:25 Adulteresses had their noses cut off.

24:1-27 Ezekiel reports this misfortune to the exiles around him: he notes the date of the disaster, describes the scene with the pot, does not mourn his wife, and receives the first fugitive.

4 Put pieces of meat into it,
all the choice pieces, the leg and the shoulder;
fill it with choice bones.
5 Take the choicest animal from the flock,
and pile the wood beneath it.
Cook it thoroughly
and boil the bones in it.

6 Therefore, thus says the Lord GOD:

Woe to the bloody city,[p]
the pot whose rust is in it,
the rust that cannot be removed.
Empty it piece by piece,
and do not bother casting lots.
7 For the blood she shed is in her midst;
she has poured it on a bare rock.
She did not pour it on the ground
where the soil would cover it.*
8 To stir up anger and take revenge,
I placed her blood on the bare rock
so that it would not be covered.

9 Therefore, thus says the Lord GOD:

Woe to the city running with blood.
I plan to build a great fire.
10 Heap on the wood,
and kindle the fire.
Mix in the spices,
and let the bones be thoroughly burned.
11 Stand the empty pot on the coals
so that it may become red-hot,
until the copper glows
and the filth inside it melts,
and its rust is consumed.
12 Yet not even with fire
will its rust disappear.
13 And when I expended my efforts
to cleanse you of your filthy lewdness,
you did not allow yourself
to be purged of your filth.
Now you shall not again be cleansed
until I have exhausted my anger upon you.

14 I, the LORD, have spoken. The time is coming, and I will take action. I will not refrain, nor will I spare, nor will I relent. You will be judged by your conduct and by what you have done, says the Lord GOD.

Death of Ezekiel's Wife. 15 This word of the LORD was addressed to me: 16 Son of man, with a single blow I am about to take away from you the delight of your eyes. However, you are not to lament or weep or shed any tears. 17 Groan in silence, and do not mourn for the dead. Wrap your turban around your head, and put sandals on your feet. Do not cover your beard or eat the bread of mourners.

18 Therefore, I spoke to the people in the morning; in the evening my wife died. And on the following morning I did as I had been commanded. 19 Thereupon, the people said to me, "Will you not explain to us what all these things you are doing mean for us?"

20 Then I said to them: This is what the Lord GOD said to me, 21 "Say to the house of Israel: Thus says the Lord GOD: I am prepared to desecrate my sanctuary, the stronghold in which you take such pride, the delight of your eyes, and the desire of your heart. Your sons and your daughters whom you have left behind will fall by the sword.[q]

22 "Then you shall do as I have done. You shall not cover your upper lip or eat the bread of mourners. 23 Your turbans shall remain on your heads and your sandals on your feet. You shall not mourn or weep. Further, you will waste away because of your iniquities and groan to one another.[r]
24 Thus, Ezekiel will be a sign for you; you shall do just as he has done. When this occurs, then you will know that I am the Lord GOD."

End of Ezekiel's Muteness.* 25 As for you, son of man, on the day when I take from them their stronghold, their crowning joy, the delight of their eyes, the joy of their hearts, as well as their sons and daughters, 26 on that day, a fugitive will come and report this news to you. 27 On that day, your mouth will be opened and you shall no longer be mute. Thus, you shall be a sign for them, and they shall know that I am the LORD.[s]

p Nah 3:1; Hab 2:12.—q Jer 7:14.—r Ezek 33:10; Job 27:15.—s Ezek 3:26; 33:22.

24:7 Blood was regarded as the seat of life; therefore the prohibition against eating flesh with blood still in it, since this would have been like making one's own the life, of which, the divinity alone could dispose (Gen 9:4; Lev 17:10-12; Deut 12:16, 23-25). For the same reason, blood spilled was not to be left uncovered, since it might contain some inauspicious power (Gen 4:10; Job 16:18).

24:25-27 We learn here that Ezekiel ceases to be mute when a refugee arrives who has seen Jerusalem fall into the hands of the enemy. The passage corresponds to the symbolic gesture described in Ezek 3:26.

III: PROPHECIES AGAINST FOREIGN NATIONS*

CHAPTER 25

Against Ammon. 1 The following word of the
LORD was addressed to me: 2 Son of man,
turn toward the Ammonites and prophesy
against them. [t] 3 Say to the Ammonites: Hear
the word of the Lord GOD. Thus says the
Lord GOD: Because you raised shouts of joy
over my sanctuary when it was profaned, and
over the land of Israel when it suffered dev-
astation, and over the house of Judah when it
went into exile, 4 therefore I am handing you
over to the people of the East* to be their
possession. They will establish their camps
among you and pitch their tents in your
midst. They will eat your fruit and drink your
milk. 5 I will turn Rabbah into a pasture for
camels and the towns of Ammon into a rest-
ing place for sheep. Then you will know that I
am the LORD.

6 For thus says the LORD: Because you
have clapped your hands and stamped your
feet and taken malicious delight in the fall of
the land of Israel, 7 I therefore have stretched
out my hand against you, and I will hand you
over as plunder to the nations. I will cut you
off from other peoples and obliterate you as
a country. I intend to completely destroy
you. Then you shall know that I am the
LORD.

Against Moab. 8 [u] Thus says the Lord GOD:
Because Moab said that the house of Judah
is like all other nations, 9 therefore, I will lay
open the flank of Moab, beginning with the
towns on its frontier—Beth-jesimoth, Baal-
meon, and Kiriathaim—the jewels of the
country. 10 I will give both Moab and
Ammon to the people of the East as their
possession. As a result, Ammon will not be
remembered among the nations. 11 More-
over, I will render judgment upon Moab, so
that they will know that I am the LORD.

Against Edom. 12 [v] Thus says the Lord GOD:
Since Edom has acted with vengeance
against the house of Judah and has commit-
ted a grievous offense in taking vengeance
upon them, 13 the Lord GOD has made this
decision: I will stretch forth my hand against
Edom and remove from it both people and
animals. I will lay it waste from Teman as far
as Dedan, and they will all fall by the sword.
14 I will wreak my vengeance on Edom by the
hand of my people Israel, and they will treat
Edom according to my anger and my fury.
Thus they will know my vengeance, declares
the Lord GOD.

Against Philistia. 15 [w] Thus says the Lord
GOD: Inasmuch as the Philistines have
engaged in endless hostilities with ven-
geance, and with malice in their hearts took
revenge in destruction, 16 therefore, thus says
the Lord GOD: I will stretch forth my hand
against the Philistines, cut off the Cher-
ethites, and destroy those remaining along
the seacoast. 17 I will execute great ven-
geance on them and punish them in my
wrath. Therefore, they will know that I am the
LORD when I exact my vengeance on them.

CHAPTER 26

Against Tyre.* 1 * In the eleventh year, on the
first day of the month, the word of the LORD
came to me: 2 [x] Son of man, Tyre has said in
regard to Jerusalem:

Aha! The gateway to the nations has been
shattered;
she has opened her doors to me.
Now that she lies in ruins,
her wealth will be mine.

3 Therefore, thus says the Lord GOD:

Behold, I am against you, O Tyre,
and as the sea raises up its waves,
I will raise up many nations against
you.
4 They will destroy your walls, O Tyre,
and demolish your towers.
I will scrape away your soil
and reduce you to a bare rock.

---

t Am 1:13ff; Zep 2:8ff.—u 8-11: Isa 15:1-9; 16:1-14; Jer 48:1-47; Am 2:1.—v 12-14: Am 1:11; Ob 10-16.—w 15-17: Jer 47:1-7; Zep 2:4-7.—x 2-4: Isa 23-1.

25:1—32:32 *The day of the LORD* (Ezek 30:3) is approaching, the day of the judgment on the nations. These are punished for having scorned the people who are God's servants; the house of Israel will be gathered together again. The people are, therefore, to realize during their afflictions that these are not final; God transcends them. "They will know that I am the LORD" (Ezek 28:24-26): this is the fundamental motif of this section.

25:4 *People of the East:* the Bedouin of the Syro-Arabian Desert.

26:1—28:26 The fate of Tyre seems to set a pattern, and Ezekiel lingers over it, mingling gloomy laments of great poetic power with prophecies of destruction. At the beginning of the sixth century B.C., this fortified island enjoyed an exceptional status, being as it was at the forefront of commercial activity and in possession of immense wealth.

26:1-21 The siege of Tyre proved difficult; it was begun by Nebuchadnezzar in 585 B.C. and lasted thirteen years, ending with the surrender of the city.

5 You shall become a drying ground for nets
in the midst of the sea.
Thus I have decreed, says the Lord GOD,
you will become the prey of the nations,
6 and your towns on the mainland will be destroyed.
Thus, everyone will know that I am the LORD.

7 For thus says the Lord GOD: From the north I will bring against Tyre King Nebuchadnezzar of Babylon, the king of kings, with horses, chariots, cavalry, and a large and powerful army.[y]

8 He will put to the sword
the inhabitants of your neighboring towns.
He will construct siege-works against you,
surround you with a siege-ramp,
and raise his shields against you.
9 He will direct the power of his battering rams
against your walls
and demolish your towers with his axes.
10 His horses shall be so great in number
that you will be covered with their dust.
Your very walls will shake
from the noise of cavalry, wheels, and chariots
when he enters your gates,
like those entering a city
whose walls have been breached.
11 All of your streets will be trampled
by the hoofs of his horses.
He will put your people to the sword
and throw your massive pillars to the ground.
12 Your riches will be plundered,
and your merchandise will be looted.
They will tear down your walls,
and your fine houses will be destroyed.
Your stones and timber and even your rubble,
they will cast into the sea.
13 I will silence the music of your songs;
the sound of your lyres will no longer be heard.[z]
14 I will make Tyre a bare rock,
a place where nets are spread to dry.
You shall never again be rebuilt,
for I, the LORD, have spoken,
says the Lord GOD.

15 Thus says the Lord GOD to Tyre: Will not
the islands quake at the noise of your fall,
amid the groaning of your wounded and the
slaughter taking place in your midst? 16 Then
all the princes of the sea will step down from
their thrones, remove their robes, and take
off their embroidered garments. Their bodies having been overcome with incessant
trembling, they will sit on the ground, totally appalled at you. 17 Then they will raise a
lament over you:

How you have perished, swept from the sea,
O greatly renowned city!
You were once mighty on the sea,
you and your inhabitants,
who used to spread terror
on all the mainland.
18 Now the coastlands tremble
on the day of your fall;
the islands of the sea
are appalled at your passing.

19 For thus says the Lord GOD: When I
make you a ruined city, like other deserted
cities, when I raise the deep over you and its
mighty waters cover you, 20 then I will thrust
you down with those who have descended
into the pit, to the people of past ages, and I
will force you to live in the netherworld, in
the ruins of primeval times, with those who
have gone down into the pit, so that you will
never again be inhabited or take your place
in the land of the living.[a] 21 I will bring you to
a horrible end, and you will be no more.
People will search for you, but you will never
be found again.

CHAPTER 27

Lamentation over Tyre. 1 This word of the
LORD came to me: 2 Son of man, raise
lament over Tyre, 3 and say to Tyre which is
enthroned at the entrance to the sea and
serves as the center of trade between the
nations and many coastlands: Thus says the
Lord GOD:

O Tyre, you often used to declare,
"I am a ship perfect in beauty."
4 Your frontiers bordered the high seas,
and your builders perfected your beauty.

y Ezek 23:24; Jer 27:3-6.—z Isa 23:16; Rev 18:22.—a Ezek 32:18.

5 They used cypress from Senir*
to construct all your planks;
they took cedar of Lebanon
to make a mast above you.

6 From oaks of Bashan,
they made your oars;
they constructed your deck with cypress*
from the coasts of Kittim. [b]

7 Fine embroidered linen from Egypt
was used for your sail
and also for your flag.
Purple and scarlet from the coasts of Elishah*
served as your awnings.

8 The inhabitants of Sidon and Arvad
served as your oarsmen.
Skilled men of Zemer were aboard
to act as your sailors.

9 The elders and craftsmen were available
to caulk your seams.
All the ships of the sea with their sailors
came to you to trade for your wares.

10 Men from Persia and Lud and Put*
served as warriors in your army.
They proudly displayed on your walls
their shields and helmets to bring you splendor.

11 Men of Arvad and Helech
guarded your walls on every side,
while the men of Gamad manned your towers.
They hung their shields all around your walls,
thereby perfecting your beauty.

12 * Tarshish* traded with you because of
the vast abundance of your wealth, exchang-
ing silver, iron, tin, and lead for your wares.
13 * Javan, Tubal, and Meshech also traded
with you, exchanging slaves and articles of
bronze for your merchandise. [c]

14 Beth-togarmah exchanged horses,
steeds, and mules for your wares. 15 The
Rhodians dealt with you; many islands
engaged in trade with you and paid you with
ivory tusks and ebony. 16 Edom traded with
you because of the large variety of your prod-
ucts; for your wares they exchanged tur-
quoise, purple, embroidered work, fine linen,
coral, and rubies. 17 Judah and the land of
Israel also traded with you, exchanging for
your goods wheat, figs, honey, oil, and balm.

18 Damascus traded with you because of
your great wealth, offering to you wine from
Helbon and wool from Zahar. 19 * Danites
and Javanites traded wrought iron, cassia,
and aromatic cane from Uzal for your wares,
20 while Dedan traded with you for saddle
blankets.

21 Arabia and all the sheikhs of Kedar were
your customers, paying you with lambs,
rams, and goats. 22 Merchants from Sheba
and Raamah traded with you, offering in
exchange the finest spices, every kind of pre-
cious stones, and gold. [d]

23 Haran, Canneh, and Eden, the mer-
chants of Sheba, Asshur, and Chilmad traded
with you, * 24 offering in return rich garments,
embroidered purple cloaks, and materials of
many colors bound with cords that were
firmly woven.

25 The ships of Tarshish were employed
as carriers for your wares.
Therefore, you were filled and heavily laden
as you sailed the high seas.

26 Your oarsmen rowed through deep waters
on their journey home.
But the east wind* wrecked you
when you were far out at sea.

27 Your riches, your goods, your cargo,
your sailors and your crew,
your caulkers, your dealers in merchandise,
and all their warriors and passengers
sank into the depths of the sea
on the day of your shipwreck.

28 The coasts will begin to quake
upon hearing the cries of your sailors.

b Isa 2:13; Jer 2:10.—c Ezek 38:2.—d Gen 10:7; 1 Ki 10:1-2.

27:5 *Senir:* the massif of Mount Hermon.

27:6 *Cypress:* in Hebrew, *Kittim.* The name is used here in a broad sense to include the islands and coasts of the Mediterranean.

27:7 *Coasts of Elishah:* identification uncertain; elsewhere described as near places on the Mediterranean.

27:10 *Put:* in Africa, near the Indian Ocean.

27:12-25 A section in prose is introduced into the middle of the lament; it provides valuable information on international trade in the sixth century B.C., especially in the Palestinian area.

27:12 *Tarshish:* a city founded on the Spanish coast by people from Tyre; it symbolizes the far-off places of the then known world.

27:13-18 *Tubal, and Meshech:* south of the Caucasus. *Beth-togarmah:* in Armenia. *Rhod*[*es*]: the Hebrew has "Dedan" (v. 20), which was in Arabia. *Helbon:* an Assyrian city.

27:19-21 References are to tribes in southern Arabia.

27:23 Mesopotamian cities.

27:26 *East wind:* the Babylonians, who, like the wind, destroy every country and people.

29 Then those who handle the oars
will begin to desert their ships.
The sailors and all the seafaring people
will remain ashore.
30 They will mourn aloud over you
and weep bitterly.
They will throw dust on their heads
and roll in ashes. [e]
31 They will shave their heads for you
and put on sackcloth.
For you, they will weep in anguish
and with heartfelt bitterness.
32 In their mourning, they will raise a dirge
and lament over you:

Who was ever destroyed like Tyre
in the midst of the sea?
33 When your goods were unloaded,
you satisfied a multitude of peoples.
You enriched the kings of the earth
with your abundant wealth and merchandise.
34 Now you have been demolished by the sea
in the watery depths.
Your merchandise and all your crew
have gone down with you.

35 All who dwell on the coastlands
are aghast at your fate.
Their kings are horrified;
their faces are convulsed.
36 The merchants among the nations
now hiss at you.
Destruction has overwhelmed you,
and you will be no more. [f]

CHAPTER 28

The Prince of Tyre. 1 This word of the LORD came to me: 2 Son of man, say to the prince of Tyre: Thus says the Lord GOD:

Your heart has grown proud,
and thus you say, "I am a god;
I sit on a godly throne
in the heart of the seas."
But in reality you are a man, and not a god,
even though you compare your mind
with that of a god.

3 Are you as wise as Daniel?
Is no secret hidden from you?
4 By your wisdom and your intelligence,
you have amassed great wealth for yourself.
You have deposited gold and silver
into your treasuries.
5 Because of your skill in trading,
your wealth has greatly increased;
and as a result of your riches,
your heart is filled with arrogant pride. [g]

6 Therefore, thus says the Lord GOD:

Because you consider your wisdom
to be equal to that of God,
7 I will bring foreigners against you,
the most barbarous of all the nations.
They will draw their swords
against the beauty of your wisdom
and defile your splendor.
8 They will hurl you down to the pit,
and you will die a violent death
in the heart of the seas.
9 Will you then still say, "I am a god,"
when your murderers confront you?
No, you are a man, not a god,
in the hands of those about to slay you.
10 You will die the death of the uncircumcised
at the hands of foreigners.

I have spoken, declares the Lord GOD.

11 This word of the LORD was then addressed to me: 12 Son of man, raise a lament for the king of Tyre and say to him: Thus says the Lord GOD:

At one time, you were a model of perfection,
full of wisdom and perfect in beauty.
13 You were in Eden, the garden of God,
and adorned with every precious stone:
ruby, topaz, and emerald,
chrysolite, onyx, and jasper,
sapphire, turquoise, and jade.
Your settings and mountings were made of gold;
on the day you were created, they were made.
14 I appointed a cherub as your guardian;
you were on the holy mountain of God,
walking amid the fiery stones. [h]
15 You were blameless in your behavior
from the day you were created,
until iniquity first appeared in you. [i]

16 As a result of your abundant trade,
you became filled with violence, and you sinned.

e Job 2:12; Rev 18:19.—f Jer 18:16; Zep 2:15.—g Zec 9:3.—h Ezek 20:40; Rev 18:16.—i Ezek 27:3-4; Isa 14:12.

Therefore, I cast you down in disgrace
from the mountain of God,
and the guardian cherub drove you out
from among the fiery stones.
17 Your heart had grown proud
because of your beauty,
and for the sake of your splendor,
you corrupted your wisdom.
I flung you to the earth,
so great was your guilt,
and I made you a spectacle to behold
in the sight of kings.
18 Because of the immense number of your crimes
and your dishonesty in business,
you profaned our sanctuaries.
Therefore, I have brought forth fire from your midst,
and I allowed it to devour you.
I have reduced you to ashes on the ground
for everyone to behold.
19 All of the nations who knew you
were aghast at your fate.
You have come to a hideous end,
and you will be no more.

Against Sidon. 20 This word of the LORD
came to me:[j] 21 Son of man, turn toward
Sidon* and prophesy against her, and say:
22 Thus says the Lord GOD:

I am against you, O Sidon,
and I will show my glory in your midst.
Then people will know that I am the LORD
when I inflict punishments on her
and manifest my holiness in her.
23 For I will send a plague upon her,
and there will be bloodshed in her streets.
And the dead shall fall in her midst
by the sword raised against her from all sides;
then they will know that I am the LORD.

24 No longer will the people of Israel have
to endure thorns that wound, or briars that
tear from hostile neighbors who treat them
with contempt. Then they will know that I
am the LORD.

25 Thus says the Lord GOD:[k] When I gath-
er the house of Israel from the people among
whom they are scattered and manifest my
holiness in them in the sight of all the
nations, then they will live on the land that I
gave to my servant Jacob. 26 They will live
there in safety, building houses and planting
vineyards. They will live there in security
while I inflict punishments upon all their
neighbors who have despised them. Thus
they will know that I am the LORD, their
God.

CHAPTER 29

Against Egypt. 1 * In the tenth year, on the
twelfth day of the tenth month, this word of
the LORD came to me: 2 Son of man set your
face against Pharaoh, king of Egypt, and
prophesy against him and against the whole
of Egypt. 3 Speak to him and say: Thus says
the LORD:

Behold, I am against you, Pharaoh,
king of Egypt,
you great crocodile
lurking in the streams of the Nile,
you who claimed, "The Nile is mine;
it is I who made it."
4 I will put hooks through your jaws
and cause the fish of your Nile
to stick to your scales.
Then I will draw you up
from the midst of its tributaries,
with all the fish of those channels
clinging to your scales.
5 I will fling you into the desert,
you and all the fish of your tributaries.
You will fall upon the open field
and not be taken up or buried.
I will give you as food
to the animals of the earth
and the birds of the air.
6 Then all the inhabitants of Egypt shall know
that I am the LORD.
The support they gave the Israelites
was no greater than a staff of reed.[l]

j Isa 23:1-18.—k 25-26: Ezek 37:25-26; Isa 11:12; Jer 32:37.—l Isa 36:6.

28:21 *Sidon* had been the capital of Phoenicia before Tyre.
29:1—32:32 After being defeated at Carchemish in 605 B.C., Egypt was no longer able to support the small Syro-Palestinian states in an effective way against the growing power of Babylon (see 2 Ki 24:7). Despite this, and despite the repeated warnings of the prophet Jeremiah, the kings of Judah did not stop flirting with the pharaoh and calling on his army for help (see Jer 37:1-10). A bad choice, since Egypt had lost its rank as a great power, and the kings only draw down upon themselves the harsh vengeance of the king of Babylon (see 2 Ki 25:1f). Jeremiah (Jer 44:26f; 46) and Ezekiel (Ezek 16:26; 17:7; 23:3; 27:7; and the chapters that follow here) were keenly critical of this policy of alliance with Egypt. In these oracles, the irony is often bitter, but the poetry is splendid.

7 When they grasped you,
you splintered in their hands.
Whenever they leaned on you, you broke,
causing all their limbs to give way.

8 Therefore, thus says the Lord GOD: I will
bring a sword against you and cut off from
your presence both man and animal. 9 The
land of Egypt will become a desolate waste,
and the inhabitants will know that I am the
LORD.

Because you said, "The Nile is mine; I was
the one who made it," 10 therefore I am
against you and your tributaries. I will make
the land of Egypt a ruin and a desolate
waste, from Migdol* to Syene, and even
beyond to the frontiers of Ethiopia. 11 No
human foot shall pass through it, nor shall
any animal foot do so. It shall remain unin-
habited for forty years. 12 I shall make Egypt
the most desolate of countries, and its cities
will be the most deserted of all those that
have been laid waste for forty years.
Moreover, I intend to scatter the Egyptians
among the nations and disperse them over
foreign lands.

13 However, thus says the Lord GOD: After
forty years have passed, I will gather the
Egyptians back from the peoples among
whom they were scattered. 14 I shall restore
the fortunes of Egypt and resettle her people
in the land of Pathros, the land of their ori-
gin, and there they will become a lowly king-
dom.[m]

15 Egypt will be the most insignificant of
kingdoms and never again will exalt itself
above the nations. I will make them few in
number so that it will never again rule over
the nations. 16 Egypt will no longer be a
nation for the house of Israel to trust in, but
will rather be for Israel a reminder of its
guilt when they turned to Egypt for help.
Thus they will know that I am the Lord GOD.

Nebuchadnezzar's Payment. 17 In the twenty-
seventh year, on the first day of the first
month, this word of the LORD came to me:
18 Son of man, Nebuchadnezzar, the king of
Babylon, has led his army in an exhausting
campaign against Tyre. Everyone's head was
rubbed bare and the skin of every shoulder
was raw, yet neither he nor his army derived
any profit from the campaign he led against
Tyre.

19 Therefore, thus says the Lord GOD: I
now intend to hand over the land of Egypt to
Nebuchadnezzar, the king of Babylon. He
shall carry off its wealth, despoil and plunder
it, and amass the wages for his army.[n] 20 As
regards payment for his toil, I have given
him the land of Egypt because he and his
army did it for me, says the Lord GOD.

21 On that day, I will make a horn sprout
up for the house of Israel, and I will empow-
er you to speak out in their midst. Then they
will know that I am the LORD.

CHAPTER 30

The LORD's Vengeance on Egypt. 1 This word
of the LORD came to me: 2 Son of man,
prophesy, and say: Thus says the Lord GOD:

Cry out, "Alas for the day!"[o]
3 For near is the day.
The day of the LORD is near.
It will be a day of clouds,
a day of reckoning for the nations.

4 The sword will fall on Egypt,
and there will be anguish in Ethiopia
when the slain fall in Egypt,
when her riches are seized
and her foundations are destroyed.
5 Ethiopia and Put and Lud,
and all Arabia and Lybia,
and the people of the covenant land
will fall with them by the sword.

6 Thus says the LORD:

Those who support Egypt shall fall,
and her proud strength will be brought low.
From Migdol to Syene,
they shall fall by the sword,
says the Lord GOD.
7 They will be the most desolate of desolate lands,
and their cities will lie
in the midst of ruined cities.
8 Then they will know that I am the LORD
when I set fire to Egypt
and all her helpers are crushed.

9 On that day, I will commission messen-
gers to hasten forth by ship at my command
to strike terror into the hearts of the com-
placent Ethiopians, and anguish will afflict
them on the day of Egypt's destruction,
which is near at hand.

m Ezek 30:14.—n Jer 46:2.—o Isa 13:6.

29:10 *Migdol:* a northern Egyptian city; *Syene* was in the far south.

10 Thus says the Lord GOD:
I will put an end to the hordes of Egypt
by the hand of Nebuchadnezzar, king of Babylon.
11 He and his armed forces,
the most ruthless of the nations,
will be brought in to ravage the land.
They shall draw their swords against Egypt,
and the land will be covered with corpses.
12 I will dry up the channels of the Nile
and sell the land to wicked men.
By the hand of foreigners
the entire land and everything in it
will be laid waste.
I, the LORD, have spoken.

13 Thus says the Lord GOD:[p]
I will destroy the idols
and put an end to the false gods in Memphis.
There will no longer be a prince in Egypt,
and I will instill terror in that land.
14 I will make Pathros a place of desolation;
I will set fire to Zoan
and inflict my punishments on Thebes.
15 I will pour forth my wrath upon Pelusium,*
the stronghold of Egypt,
and destroy the hordes of Thebes.
16 I will set fire to Egypt;
Syene shall writhe in agony.
Thebes shall be breached,
and its walls shall be demolished.
17 The young men of On and Pi-beseth
shall fall by the sword,
and the cities themselves
shall be taken into captivity.

18 At Tahpanhes, the day will turn into darkness
when I shatter the scepter of Egypt there,
and its proud might shall come to an end.
Egypt will be covered with a cloud,
and her villages will go into captivity.
19 These will be the punishments I inflict upon Egypt.
Then they will know that I am the LORD.

Pharaoh's Broken Arm. 20 In the eleventh
year, on the seventh day of the first month,
this word of the LORD came to me: 21 Son of
man, I have broken the arm of Pharaoh, the
king of Egypt. As you can see, it has not been
bound up for healing or wrapped with a bandage to make it strong enough to wield a
sword.

22 Therefore, thus says the Lord GOD: I am
prepared to move against Pharaoh, the king
of Egypt. I will break his arms, both the uninjured one and the one that was broken, and
make the sword fall from his hand. 23 I will
disperse the Egyptians among the nations
and scatter them throughout the lands. 24 I
will strengthen the arms of the king of
Babylon and put my sword in his hand.
However, I will break the arms of Pharaoh,
and he will lie wounded and groaning before
him like a dying man.[q]

25 I will strengthen even more the arms of
the king of Babylon, but the arms of
Pharaoh will fall. Then they shall know that I
am the LORD, when I put my sword into the
hand of the king of Babylon for him to wield
against the land of Egypt. 26 I will scatter the
Egyptians among the nations and disperse
them in foreign countries. Then they will
know that I am the LORD.

CHAPTER 31

Allegory of the Great Cypress. 1 In the
eleventh year, on the first day of the third
month, this word of the LORD was addressed
to me: 2 Son of man, say to Pharaoh, the king
of Egypt, and to his hordes:

What can compare in greatness with you?
3 Consider Assyria, formerly a cypress in Lebanon,
with beautiful branches and lofty in stature,
and its top above the thick foliage.
4 The waters nourished it;
deep springs caused it to grow tall;
those springs also made its rivers flow
around the place it was planted,
sending forth streams of water
to all the trees of the field.*

5 Therefore, it towered in height
above all other trees of the field.
Its branches grew long
because of the abundant water.

p Isa 19:1; Zec 13:2.—q Zec 10:12.

30:15 *Pelusium:* Hebrew, "Sin," a fortress on the northeastern border of Egypt.

31:4 It was thought that the rivers were fed by the great ocean, on which the land was imagined as sitting.

6 All the birds of the air
rested in its boughs.
Under its branches, all the wild animals
of the field
gave birth to their young,
and numerous people of every race
dwelt in its shade.
7 It was beautiful and stately
in the length of its branches,
for its roots sank down
to a source of abundant water.

8 The cedars in the garden of God
could not compare with it,
nor could the fir trees equal its
boughs.
No plane tree had such branches;
no tree in the garden of God
could equal its beauty. [r]
9 I made it beautiful
with its mass of foliage;
it was the envy of all the trees in Eden
that were in the garden of God.

10 Therefore, thus says the Lord GOD:
Because it grew to a towering stature, with
its top reaching the clouds, and then became
arrogant with pride about its height, 11 I
handed it over to the prince of the nations.*
I empowered him to deal with it as its
wickedness deserves. I have rejected it.

12 Foreigners from the most barbarous
nations cut it down and abandoned it. Its
branches have fallen on the mountains and
in all the valleys, and its boughs lie broken in
every ravine throughout the land. All the
peoples of the land fled from its shade and
abandoned it.

13 On its fallen trunk
all the birds of the air rested,
and all the wild animals
sought shelter among its branches.

14 Thus, never again will any tree by the
waters grow to a lofty height and stretch its
top to the clouds, nor will any well-watered
tree ever attain such a height.

For all of them are destined for death,
for the depths below,
along with all mortal beings
who go down to the abyss.

15 Thus says the Lord GOD: On the day it
went down to Sheol, I closed the deep over it.
I stopped its streams, and its mighty waters
were held back. I cast gloom over Lebanon
because of it, and all the trees of the coun-
tryside began to wither. 16 I made the nations
quake at the sound of its fall when I hurled it
down to Sheol with those who go down to the
abyss. All the trees of Eden, the loveliest and
the best of Lebanon, were consoled, all that
were well watered. 17 Those who dwelt in its
shade, its allies among the nations, went
down with it to Sheol, to those killed by the
sword.

18 Which among the trees of Eden was your
equal in glory and greatness? Yet you have
been hurled down with the trees of Eden to
the world below. You shall lie in the company
of the uncircumcised who have been slain by
the sword. Thus, it will be for Pharaoh and all
his hordes, says the Lord GOD.

CHAPTER 32

Lamentation over Pharaoh.* 1 In the twelfth
year, on the first day of the twelfth month,
this word of the LORD came to me: 2 Son of
man, raise a lament for Pharaoh, the king of
Egypt:

Lion of the nations, your end has come.
You are like a monster in the seas,
thrashing about in your streams,
churning up the water with your feet
and fouling the streams.

3 Thus says the Lord GOD:

When many nations are assembled,
I will throw my net over you
and haul you up in my seine. [s]
4 I will throw you on the ground
and fling you onto an open field.
I will let all the birds of the air settle on
you,
and I will urge all the beasts of the
earth
to eat their fill of you.

5 I will strew your flesh on the mountains
and fill the valleys with your carcass.
6 I will drench the land with your flowing
blood
all the way to the mountains,
and the riverbeds will be filled with
your blood.

7 * When I blot you out,
I will cover the heavens,
and all their stars I will darken.

r Gen 2:8.—s Ezek 12:13; 17:20.

31:11 *Prince of the nations:* Nebuchadnezzar.

32:1-16 The pharaoh is first depicted as a lion, but then suddenly becomes a marine monster of fabulous size.

32:7-8 Apocalyptic language, used to indicate divine punishment. The pharaohs regarded themselves as sons of the sun god.

I will cover the sun with clouds,
and the moon shall not give its light.[t]
8 All the shining lights in the heavens
I will dim because of you,
and I will spread darkness over your land,
says the Lord GOD.
9 I will grieve the hearts of many peoples
when I lead you as captives among the nations,
into countries unknown to you.
10 I will cause many peoples to be appalled at you,
and their kings will shudder in horror at your fate
when I brandish my sword in their presence.
On the day of your downfall,
each one will tremble for his life.

11 For thus says the Lord GOD:

The sword of the king of Babylon
will come against you.
12 I will demolish your hordes
with the swords of my warriors,
the most ruthless among the nations.
They shall cause the pride of Egypt to be shattered,
and all its hordes will be destroyed.
13 I will destroy all its livestock
on the shores of abundant waters.
No human foot will cause them further trouble,
nor shall the hooves of cattle disturb them.
14 Then I will make their waters crystal clear
and cause her streams to flow like oil,
says the Lord GOD.
15 When I have turned the land of Egypt
into a wasteland,
and when the land is stripped
of everything that was in it,
and when I strike down all its inhabitants,
then they shall know that I am the LORD.
16 This is a lamentation and it will be chanted;
the daughters of the nations* will chant it.
They shall raise the lamentation
over Egypt and all its hordes,
says the Lord GOD.

Lamentation over Egypt. 17 On the fifteenth day of the first month in the twelfth year, this word of the LORD came to me:

18 Son of man, raise a cry of lament
over the hordes of Egypt
and the daughters of mighty nations
and consign them to the world below
with those who go down to the pit.[u]
19 Say to them, "Whom do you surpass in beauty?
Go down and lie with the uncircumcised."

20 They shall fall in the midst of those slain
by the sword, and room will be made to
accommodate them and their hordes.
21 From the depths of Sheol, the mighty lead-
ers will say of Egypt and its allies, "They
have come down, they and their allies; they
lie there, the uncircumcised dead, slain by
the sword."
22 Assyria is there with all her hordes.
Their graves surround her on all sides, all of
them slaughtered, victims of the sword.
23 Their graves are located in the farthest
depths of the pit, and her army lies around
Egypt's grave, all of them slain by the sword,
after spreading terror in the land of the
living.
24 Elam is there with all her hordes around
Egypt's grave, all of them slain by the sword.
Having spread terror in the land of the liv-
ing, they descended uncircumcised into the
world below. They bear their shame with
those who go down to the pit. 25 A bed has
been made for Elam among the slain with
all her hordes' graves surrounding it. All of
them were uncircumcised, and they were
slain by the sword for having spread terror in
the land of the living. They bear their shame
with those who go down to the pit, and they
have been placed among the slain.
26 Meshech and Tubal* are there with the
graves of their followers all around them. All
of them are uncircumcised, slain by the
sword, for they spread terror in the land of
the living.[v] 27 They do not lie with the fallen
warriors of ages past who went down to the
netherworld with their weapons of war,
whose swords were laid under their heads
and whose shields were placed over their
bones, since they filled the land of the living
with terror. 28 Therefore, you will lie broken

t Isa 13:10; Joel 3:15; Mt 24:29.—u Mic 1:8.—v Ezek 27:13; Gen 10:2.

32:16 *Daughters of the nations:* the pagan peoples.
32:26 *Meshech and Tubal:* places near the Black Sea.

among the uncircumcised, with those who
are slain by the sword.

29 Edom is there, with her kings and all her
princes; who, despite their might, have been
placed with those slain by the sword. They lie
with the uncircumcised, with those who go
down to the pit.

30 All of the princes of the north and all the
Sidonians are there. They descended in
shame with the slain because of all the terror
that they caused by their might. They lie
uncircumcised with those who were killed by
the sword, and they bear their shame with
those who descend into the pit.

31 When Pharaoh sees them, he will be
comforted for all his hordes slain by the
sword—Pharaoh and all his army, says the
Lord GOD. 32 Since he spread terror through-
out the land of the living, he will be laid
among the uncircumcised, with those who
are slain by the sword—Pharaoh and all his
multitude, says the Lord GOD.

IV: ISRAEL'S RESTORATION*

CHAPTER 33

Ezekiel as Sentry. 1 This word of the LORD
came to me: 2 Son of man, speak to your fel-
low countrymen and say to them: When I
bring the sword upon a country, and the peo-
ple of that country designate one of their
number to be their watchman, 3 and if he
sees the sword coming against that country
and blows his trumpet to warn the people,
4 then if any who hear the sound of the trum-
pet pay no attention to the warning, and the
sword comes against them and destroys
them, they shall bear the responsibility for
their own death.

5 Since they had heard the sound of the
trumpet and nevertheless ignored the warn-
ing, their blood will be on their own heads.
But if they had heeded the warning, they
would have saved their lives. 6 However, if the
watchman sees the sword coming and fails
to blow the trumpet to warn the people, and
the sword then comes and slays anyone, I
will hold the watchman responsible for that
person's death.

7 I have appointed you, son of man, as a
watchman for the house of Israel. Therefore,
whenever you hear a word from my mouth,
you must pass along my warning to them.[w]
8 If I say to the wicked person, "You shall
surely die," and you do not speak up to warn
that person to renounce his evil ways, he will
die because of his guilt, but I will hold you
responsible for his death. 9 However, if you
warn a wicked person to renounce his ways
and repent, and he fails to do so, then he will
die for his guilt, but you will have saved your
life.

Message of Conversion.* 10 Son of man, say
to the house of Israel: You continually com-
plain, "Our crimes and our sins weigh heavi-
ly upon us, and we are wasting away because
of them. How are we to go on living?" 11 Say
to them: As I live, says the Lord GOD, I take
no pleasure in the death of the wicked, but
rather in their decision to turn from their
evil ways and live. Repent and turn from
your evil ways. Why should you die, O house
of Israel?[x]

12 As for you, son of man, say to your coun-
trymen: The virtue of a righteous man will
not save him when he transgresses. Nor will
the evil deeds of a wicked man cause his
downfall once he renounces his wickedness,
any more than the righteous will be able to
live by their righteousness when they sin.

13 If I say to the righteous that they will
surely live, but then they presume on their
righteousness and commit iniquity, none of
their righteous deeds will be remembered.
Because of the wrong they have done, they
will die.

14 Again, if I say to the wicked that they will
surely die, and then they turn away from sin
and do what is lawful and upright, 15 give
back what they took in pledge for a loan,
return what they have stolen, adhere to the
practices that ensure life, and commit no
wrongful acts, they shall surely live; they
shall not die. 16 None of the previous sins they
committed will be remembered against
them. Because they have done what is law-
ful and upright, they shall surely live.

17 Yet your countrymen say, "The way of
the LORD is not just," when it is their own
way that is not just. 18 When a virtuous man
turns away from his righteous ways and does
wrong, he shall die for it. 19 And when a

w Ezek 3:17-21.—x Ezek 18:23-32; 2 Pet 3:9.

33:1—39:29 "I will make a covenant of peace with them..., and establish my sanctuary among them forever" (Ezek 37:26). This promise is the basic motif of this section of the Book.

33:10-20 We find here, in fuller form and as an invitation to a fullness of life, the great idea of personal retribution that has already been stated in Ezek 18:1-32 and will be repeated in chapter 36.

wicked man turns from his wicked ways and does what is lawful and right, he shall live. 20 Yet you say, "The way of the LORD is not just." I will judge each one of you according to your ways, O house of Israel.[y]

The Fugitive from Jerusalem.* 21 In the twelfth year of our exile, on the fifth day of the tenth month, a fugitive arrived from Jerusalem and said to me, "The city has fallen." 22 The evening before the fugitive had arrived, the hand of the LORD had come on me, but he had opened my mouth by the time the fugitive had come to me in the morning. Therefore, my mouth was opened, and I was no longer unable to speak.

Desolation in Judah. 23 This word of the LORD then came to me: 24 Son of man, those people who live in the ruins of the land of Israel say repeatedly, "Even though he was merely one person, Abraham received possession of this country. But we are many in number. Surely the land has been given to us as our possession."

25 Tell them this in response: Thus says the Lord GOD: You consume meat with the blood still in it, you raise your eyes to worship idols, and you shed blood. Should you then be permitted to possess the land? 26 You rely on your swords, you engage in abominable practices, and each of you defiles his neighbor's wife. Should you then be permitted to possess the land?

27 Give them this message: Thus says the Lord GOD: As I live, I swear that those who dwell in the ruins shall fall by the sword, those who live in the countryside I will give to the wild animals to be devoured, and those who inhabit dens and caves will die of the plague. 28 I will make the land a desolate waste, and its proud strength will come to an end. Furthermore, the mountains of Israel will be so desolate that no one will cross them. 29 Then they will know that I am the LORD when I have made the land a desolate waste because of all the abominable deeds that they have committed.

Ezekiel's False Popularity. 30 As for you, son of man, your fellow countrymen gossip incessantly about you along the walls and in the doorways of houses, saying to one another, "Let us go to hear what message the LORD has to give us." 31 My people come to you, as they are accustomed to do. They sit down in front of you and listen to your words, but they refuse to obey them. They flatter you with their lips, but their hearts are only interested in dishonest gain.[z]

32 To them you are like a singer of lovely songs with a beautiful voice and skill in playing a musical instrument. They listen to your words, but they refuse to obey them. 33 But when all this comes to pass—and that moment is soon approaching—they will know that a prophet has been in their midst.

CHAPTER 34*

The Shepherds of Israel.* 1 This word of the LORD came to me: 2 Son of man, prophesy against the shepherds of Israel. Prophesy and say to them: Thus says the Lord GOD: Woe to you shepherds of Israel. Prophesy and say to them: Thus says the Lord GOD: Woe to the shepherds of Israel who have been feeding themselves. Should not shepherds rather feed their flock?[a]

3 You have fed on their milk, you have clothed yourselves with their wool, and you have slaughtered the fatlings, but you have not fed the sheep. 4 You have not strengthened the weak, you have not healed the sick, and you have not bandaged those who were injured. Nor have you bothered to bring back those who strayed or searched for the lost. On the contrary, you have ruled them with cruelty and harshness.

5 Therefore, they were scattered for lack of a shepherd, and thus they became the prey of all the wild beasts.[b] 6 My sheep were scattered, wandering aimlessly over all the mountains and on every high hill. My flock has been scattered over the entire world, with no one to inquire about them or search for them.

7 Therefore, you shepherds, hear the word of the LORD: 8 As I live, says the Lord GOD, because my sheep are without a shepherd and thus have been ravaged and have become food for all the wild animals, and

y Ezek 18:25.—z Ezek 14:1; Isa 29:13; Mt 13:22.—a Jer 23:1.—b Jer 10:21; 23:1-6; Mt 9:36.

33:21-22 The fugitive who brings news of the disaster has already been mentioned in Ezek 3:22-27; 24:26.

34:1-31 Ezekiel takes over from Jeremiah (Ezek 23) the theme of the shepherd and the flock, but he develops other aspects of it. He censures the kings and other leaders of Israel, showing them that in the end the destiny of the people is in the hands of God.

34:1-16 The image of the shepherd was a traditional one for kings in the ancient East. The prophets frequently use it, speaking of unworthy leaders as wicked shepherds (Jer 2:8; 10:21; Zec 11:4-17).

because my shepherds have not gone forth
in search of my sheep, but have fed them-
selves and not been concerned about feeding
my sheep, 9 therefore, you shepherds, hear
the word of the LORD.

10 Thus says the Lord GOD: I intend to pun-
ish the shepherds. I will remove the sheep
from their charge and not allow them to feed
the flock. As a result, the shepherds will no
longer be able to feed themselves. I will res-
cue my sheep from their mouths so that they
will no longer use them for their food.

11 * For thus says the Lord GOD: I myself
will search for my sheep and look after them.
12 As a shepherd goes forth in search of his
flocks when they are scattered from him in
every direction, so I will go forth in search of
my sheep. I will retrieve them from all the
places to which they have been scattered on
a day of clouds and darkness.

13 I will bring them back from among the
peoples and gather them from foreign lands,
I will lead them back to their own land and
pasture them on the mountains of Israel, in
the ravines, and in all the inhabited areas of
the country. 14 I will feed them in fertile pas-
tures, and the mountain heights of Israel will
be their grazing grounds. There they will lie
down on good grazing land and feed in rich
pastures on the mountains of Israel.

15 I, myself, will pasture my sheep, and I,
myself, will give them rest, says the Lord
GOD. 16 I will search for those who are lost; I
will bring back those who have strayed away.
I will bind up the injured and strengthen the
weak, but the fat and the strong, I will
destroy. I will shepherd my flock with jus-
tice. [c]

Judgment of the Sheep. 17 * As for you, my
flock, the Lord GOD says this: I will judge
between one sheep and another, between
rams and goats. 18 Is it not sufficient for you
to graze on the best pasture land? Must you
also trample with your feet on the rest of the
pastures? Is it not enough for you to drink
clear water? Must you also foul the rest with
your feet? 19 As a result, my sheep must
graze on what you have trampled underfoot
and drink what you have befouled with your
feet.

20 Therefore, thus says the Lord GOD to
them: I myself will judge between the fat
sheep and the lean sheep. 21 Because you
have shoved with flank and shoulder and
butted all the weak sheep with your horns
until you have scattered them in every direc-
tion, 22 I will save my flock, and they will
never again be treated unfairly. I will judge
between one sheep and another.

23 * I will raise up one shepherd, my ser-
vant David, to care for them. He shall feed
them and be their shepherd. [d] 24 I, the LORD,
will be their God, and my servant David will
be a prince in their midst. I, the LORD, have
spoken.

25 I will make a covenant of peace with
them and rid the land of wild animals so that
they may live in the desert and sleep in the
woods free from danger. 26 I will make them
and the region surrounding my hill a bless-
ing, and I will send them rain in due season
that will be showers of blessing.

27 The trees of the field shall bear their
fruit, and the soil will yield its crops. My
people will be secure on their own soil and
they will know that I am the LORD when I
break the bars of their yoke and rescue them
from the power of those who enslaved them.

28 They will no longer be plundered by the
nations or devoured by the wild animals of
the land. They will live in safety, and no one
ever again will terrify them. 29 I will make
their land bring forth abundant crops so
that they will never again be the victims of
famine or have to suffer the insults of the
nations.

30 Thus, they will be assured that I, the
LORD, their God, am with them, and that
they, the house of Israel, are my people, says
the Lord GOD. 31 You are my sheep, the sheep
of my pasture, and I am your God, says the
Lord GOD. [e]

c Isa 49:26; Mt 18:11.—d Isa 40:11; Hos 3:5; Jn 10:11.—e Ps 100:3; Jn 10:11.

34:11-16 The true shepherd of Israel is the Lord (Gen 49:24; Ps 80:1). Since there are no real leaders, he himself will restore his people (see Pss 23; 77:20; Isa 40:11; Jer 23:3). Jesus will use the image of the shepherd looking for the lost sheep, in order to show how great is God's concern for lost human beings (Mt 18:12; Lk 15:4) and will describe himself as the only Good Shepherd (Jn 10).

34:17-22 God's visitation of his flock will be first and foremost for judgment, for separating the good and the bad. He will establish the social justice often proclaimed in Ezekiel's preaching (see Ezek 18:5-9, 12-13; 33:14f; 45:9-12). When the only true shepherd comes, the leaders will take their place in the flock and will be judged according to their injustice. We may think here of the judgment scene that Jesus will one day describe (Mt 25:1-46).

34:23-31 In the midst of ruin, Ezekiel foretells an age of fidelity, peace, and prosperity. A new shepherd will be in charge, a true successor to David, who was portrayed as the ideal king in the service of his people (see 1 Sam 16:19; 2 Sam 7:7; Ps 78:70-72).

CHAPTER 35*

Against Edom. 1 This word of the LORD
came to me: 2 Son of man, set your face
against Mount Seir and prophesy against it.
3 Say to it: Thus says the Lord GOD:

Behold, I am against you, Mount Seir
I will stretch out my hand against you
and reduce you to a desolate waste.[f]
4 I will lay your towns in ruins,
and you will become a wasteland.
Then you will know that I am the LORD.
5 Because you refused to cease an ancient feud,
you handed over the people of Israel
to the power of the sword
on the day of their distress,
the hour of their final punishment.
6 Therefore, as I live, says the Lord GOD,
blood shall be your destiny,
and it will pursue you.
Since by shedding blood you incurred guilt,
bloodshed will pursue you.
7 I will make Mount Seir a desolate waste
and prevent anyone from going there or departing.
8 I will fill its mountains with the slain;
those slain by the sword will fall
on your hills and in your valleys and ravines.
9 I will make you desolate forever,
and your towns will never again be inhabited.
Thus, you shall know that I am the LORD.

10 Because you said, "These two nations
and the two lands will be mine, and we will
take possession of them," even though I, the
LORD, was there, 11 therefore, as I live, says
the Lord GOD, I will act with the same anger
and jealousy that you showed in your hatred
for them, and I will make myself known
among you when I judge you.[g]

12 You will know that I, the LORD, have
heard of all the contemptible things you have
uttered against the mountains of Israel, saying, "They have been laid waste and have
been given to us to devour." 13 You made
insolent remarks about me and showed no
restraint in your insults, and I have heard
them.

14 Thus says the Lord GOD: I will make you
a desolate wasteland, and the entire earth
will rejoice. 15 As you were unable to conceal
your joy over the devastation of the heritage
of the house of Israel, so will I treat you. You
will be desolate, Mount Seir, you and all of
Edom. Thus, they shall know that I am the
LORD.

CHAPTER 36

Restoration of the Land. 1 *Son of man,
prophesy to the mountains of Israel and say:
Mountains of Israel, hear the word of the
LORD.[h] 2 Thus says the Lord GOD, The
enemy has gloated over you, saying: "Aha!
These ancient heights have become our possession."

3 In reply, prophesy and say: Thus says the
Lord GOD: Since you have been ravaged and
hounded from all sides, and thus have
become the possession of the rest of the
nations and the object of people's gossip and
slander, 4 therefore, mountains of Israel,
hear the word of the Lord GOD and what the
Lord GOD says to the mountains and hills, to
the ravines and valleys, to the desolate ruins
and the deserted towns which have been
plundered and have become a source of
ridicule to the surrounding nations.

5 Therefore, thus says the Lord GOD: With
seething jealousy I am speaking against the
rest of the nations, and against the whole of
Edom, who, with wholehearted joy and utter
contempt, took my country as their possession so that they might plunder its pastures.[i]

6 Therefore, prophesy concerning the land
of Israel, and say to the mountains and hills,
the ravines and valleys: Thus says the Lord
GOD: I am speaking with jealous fury
because you have been forced to endure the
insults of the nations. 7 Therefore, thus says
the Lord GOD: I raise my hand and swear
that the nations all around you will have to
endure insults.

---

f Ezek 25:13; Jer 6:12.—g Am 1:11; Mt 7:2.—h Ezek 6:3.—i Ezek 38:19; Jer 50:11; Mic 7:8.

35:1-15 The prophecy against the mountains of Egypt is an announcement of punishment; the prophecy on the mountains of Israel in chapter 36 is a promise of salvation. The parallel is deliberate, chosen in order to highlight the second prophecy. Here the prophecy is against Mount Seir, which is south of the Dead Sea and represents the entire population of Edom. Israel has many complaints against Edom as a deceitful brother.

36:1—37:28 These two chapters, which at first sight are like what we have already read, convey the very heart of the Book of Ezekiel, for they give his vision of reality and sum up his theology, that is, his idea of God, of the Lord's relationship with human beings and with his people, of the vocation of Israel, and of the destiny of the nations.

8 As for you, mountains of Israel, you shall
grow branches and bear fruit for my people
Israel, for they will soon return home.
9 Behold, I am coming to you. It is to you
that I shall turn. You will be tilled and
sown, 10 and I will multiply your popula-
tion, that of the whole house of Israel. The
towns will again be inhabited, and the ruins
will be rebuilt.

11 Furthermore, I will settle large numbers
of human beings and animals upon you.
They will multiply and be fruitful, and I will
make you as populous as in your former
times. Moreover, I will make you more pros-
perous than ever before. Thus you will know
that I am the LORD. 12 I will cause my people
Israel to tread your soil once again. They will
possess you, and you will be their heritage.
Never again will they be left childless.

13 Thus says the Lord GOD: Because it has
been said of you, "You are a land that
devours people, and you bereave your nation
of children," 14 therefore, you will no longer
devour people or make your nation childless,
says the Lord GOD. 15 I will never again let
you hear the taunts of the nations; no longer
will you be forced to endure the insults of the
peoples; no longer will your people be
deprived of their children, says the Lord
GOD.

Restoration of the People. 16 * This word of
the LORD was addressed to me: 17 Son of
man, when the people of the house of Israel
lived in their own land, they defiled it with
their conduct and their deeds. In my eyes,
their conduct was like the uncleanness of a
woman during her menstrual period.

18 Therefore, I poured out my wrath upon
them because of the blood that they had
shed upon the land, and because of their
idols with which they had defiled it. 19 I scat-
tered them throughout the nations, and they
were dispersed in many lands. I passed sen-
tence on them in accordance with their con-
duct and their deeds.

20 But whenever they came to the nations,
they profaned my holy name, so that the
people there would say about them, "These
are the people of the LORD, yet they have
been banished from his land."[j] 21 However, I
have relented because of my concern about
my holy name which the house of Israel has
profaned among the nations where they
have gone.

22 Therefore, say to the house of Israel:
Thus says the Lord GOD: It is not for your
sake, O house of Israel, that I am acting, but
for the sake of my holy name which you have
profaned among the nations where you have
gone. 23 I intend to prove the holiness of my
great name which has been profaned among
the nations, and which you have profaned
among them. Thus, the nations will know
that I am the LORD, says the Lord GOD, when
through you I will display my holiness in
their sight.

24 I will take you from among the nations
and gather you from all the foreign lands,
and I will bring you back to your own land.
25 I will sprinkle clean water upon you to
cleanse you from everything that defiles you.
I will cleanse you from all your impurities
and from all your idols.[k]

26 I will give you a new heart and place a
new spirit within you. I will remove from
your body a heart of stone and give you a
heart of flesh in its place. 27 I will put my
Spirit in you and make you follow my
statutes and my ordinances.[l]

28 Then you will live in the land that I gave
to your ancestors. You will be my people, but
I shall be your God. 29 I will save you from
everything that defiles you. I will command
the grain to be abundant and not allow any
famine to afflict you. 30 I will make abundant
the fruit of the trees and the crops in your
fields, so that you will never have to suffer
the disgrace of famine among the nations.

31 Then you will remember your evil con-
duct and your wicked deeds, and you will
loathe yourselves for your sins and your
abominable deeds. 32 I assure you that it is
not for your sake that I am doing all this,
says the Lord GOD. Let that be clearly under-
stood. Be ashamed and feel intense disgrace
for your conduct, O house of Israel.

---

j Isa 52:5; Rom 2:24.—k Ps 51:4; Zec 13:1; Heb 10:22.—l Ezek 37:14; Isa 42:1; 44:3; 59:21.

36:16-32 We reach here the high point of the revelation given through Ezekiel. God's work consists in removing humanity from sin and making it one with himself as the center. This is truly grace, such that this work of God is essentially unmerited. It completely renews the links between God and his people or, better, between God and humanity (see Ezek 16:60; 37:26; Jer 31:31-34; Isa 54:10). The prophet sees the renewal taking the form of a grandiose liturgy in which cleansing water pours from the temple, which is God's house and the center of worship (see Ezek 47:1-13). Humanity will then emerge from this liturgy with a new heart, a feeling heart; it will have a new spirit and share in the very Spirit of God. There could not be a more attractive prefiguration of Christian baptism.

33 Thus says the Lord GOD: On the day when I cleanse you from all your sins, I will repopulate your towns, and your ruins will be rebuilt. 34 The wasteland will be cultivated instead of being a desolate sight to all who walk past it.

35 People will say, "The land that was desolate is now like the Garden of Eden, and the towns that were once in ruins, desolate wastelands, are now inhabited once again and fortified."[m] 36 Then the neighboring nations that are still left around you will know that I, the LORD, have rebuilt what was destroyed and replanted what was desolate. I, the LORD, have spoken, and I will do it.

37 Thus says the Lord GOD: I also will allow the house of Israel to persuade me to do this for them: I shall increase their numbers like a flock. 38 Like the flocks of sacrificial sheep in Jerusalem on its appointed feasts, so shall the formerly ruined cities be filled with flocks of people. Then they shall know that I am the LORD.

CHAPTER 37

Vision of the Dry Bones.* 1 The hand of the LORD came upon me, and he carried me away by the Spirit of the LORD and set me down in the middle of a valley that was full of bones. 2 He made me walk among them in every direction so that I would be aware how great was the number of these bones on the floor of the valley, and they were exceedingly dry.

3 He said to me, "Son of man, can these bones live?" I replied, "Lord GOD, only you can know that." 4 Then he said to me, "Prophesy over these bones and say to them: Dry bones, hear the word of the LORD. 5 Thus says the Lord GOD to these bones: I am going to cause breath to enter you, and you will come to life. 6 I will put sinews on you and cause flesh to grow over you and cover you with skin. I will put breath within you, and you will live, and you will know that I am the LORD."

7 Therefore, I prophesied as I had been commanded to do, and as I was prophesying, I heard a noise, a sound of rattling, as the bones came together, bone uniting with bone. 8 As I watched, sinews and flesh grew upon the bones, and skin covered them, but there was no breath in them.

9 Then he said to me, "Prophesy to the Spirit. Prophesy, son of man, and say to the Spirit: Thus says the Lord GOD: Come from the four winds, O Spirit, and breathe into these slain so that they may live." 10 I prophesied as he had commanded me, and the Spirit entered into them. They came to life and stood on their feet, an immense army.[n]

11 Then he said to me, "Son of man, these bones are the whole house of Israel. They continue to say, 'Our bones are dried up, our hope has vanished, and we are cut off completely.' 12 Therefore, prophesy and say to them, 'Thus says the Lord GOD: My people, I am going to open your graves and raise you up from them and bring you back to the land of Israel. 13 Then you will know that I am the LORD, when I open your graves and raise you up from them, O my people. 14 When I put my Spirit within you, you will live, and I will resettle you on your own soil. Then you will know that I, the LORD, have spoken and I have done this, says the LORD.' "[o]

Union of the Two Sticks.* 15 This word of the LORD came to me: 16 Son of man, take a stick and write on it: "Judah and those Israelites associated with him." Then take another stick and write on it: "Joseph (the stick of Ephraim) and all the house of Israel associated with him." 17 Then join the two sticks together so that they form one stick in your hand.

18 When your countrymen say to you, "Will you not tell us what you mean by this?" 19 say to them: Thus says the Lord GOD: I will take the stick of Joseph, which is in Ephraim's hand, and of the tribes of Israel loyal to him, and I will join it to the stick of Judah. I will make them a single stick instead of two, and they shall be one in my hand.[p]

20 When the sticks upon which you have written are held up in your hand for everyone to see, 21 say to them: Thus says the Lord GOD: I will take the Israelites from the nations among which they have been exiled.

m Ezek 31:9; Isa 51:3; Joel 2:3.—n Rev 11:11.—o Ezek 39:29.—p Zec 10:6.

37:1-14 In this macabre picture of lifeless bodies being suddenly brought to life by the Spirit of the Lord, Ezekiel's intention is not to proclaim a resurrection of the dead but to inspire hope in the dejected exiles.

37:15-28 To keep the attention of his hearers, the prophet follows his usual tack and makes a very simple symbolic gesture. This becomes the starting point for a proclamation that applies to the entire world. All the old divisions will be overcome and all the schisms suppressed. This is the renewed covenant with God! Jesus will bring out the full meaning of this prophesied unity when he speaks of a single flock and a single shepherd (Jn 10:1-18; 11:52; Eph 2:11-22); he is Ezekiel's new David.

I will gather them from every side and bring
them back to their land.
22 I will unify them into one nation in the
land, on the mountains of Israel, and one
king will rule over them all. Never again will
they be two separate nations, nor will they be
divided into two kingdoms. 23 They will no
longer defile themselves with their idols and
their loathsome images or with any of their
transgressions. I will save them from all of
their sins of apostasy that they have com-
mitted, and I will cleanse them. Thus, they
will be my people, and I will be their God.
24 My servant David will be their king, and
they all will have one shepherd. They will fol-
low my laws and be scrupulous in obeying
my statutes. [q] 25 They will live in the land that
I gave to my servant Jacob, the land in which
your ancestors lived. They and their children
and their children's children will live there
forever, and my servant David will be their
prince forever.
26 I will make a covenant of peace with
them, and I will bless and multiply them and
establish my sanctuary among them forev-
er. [r] 27 I will make my dwelling with them; I
will be their God, and they will be my people.
28 Then the nations will know that I, the
LORD, sanctify Israel when I establish my
sanctuary among them forevermore.

CHAPTER 38

First Prophecy against Gog. 1 *This word of
the LORD came to me: 2 Son of man, turn
your face toward Gog, in the land of Magog,
the chief prince of Meshech and Tubal, and
prophesy against him.
3 Say: Thus says the Lord GOD: I am
against you, Gog, chief prince of Meshech
and Tubal. 4 I will turn you around and affix
hooks in your jaws, and I will lead you forth
with your entire army—your horses and
your horsemen, all of them fully equipped,
and a huge horde with bucklers and shields,
all of them brandishing their swords. [s]
5 Accompanying them will be the forces of
Persia, Ethiopia, and Put, all with shields and
helmets; 6 Gomer* and all its troops; Beth-
togarmah from the far north with all its
troops—a huge assemblage gathered in sup-
port of you. 7 Get ready and be prepared, you
and all your troops and all your allies that
have come together to support you. Keep
yourselves at my disposal.
8 After a long period of time, you will be
given orders, and sometime thereafter you
will invade a land that has emerged from
ruin. Its people have been assembled from
many nations on the mountains of Israel
which had long been desolate, and all of
them are living in safety. 9 You will advance,
coming forth like a storm. You will cover the
land like a cloud, you and all your troops and
the many nations who have come to support
you.
10 Thus says the Lord GOD: On that day
thoughts will arise in your mind, and you
will devise an evil scheme. 11 You will say, "I
will attack this country that has no means of
defense and march against this peaceful
nation which dwells with a sense of security,
even though it has no walls or bars or gates.
12 I will plunder and loot and strip bare the
settlements which once lay in ruins but are
now inhabited by a people gathered from the
nations who dwell at the very center of the
world, a people engaged in trade and breed-
ing cattle."
13 Sheba and Dedan, and the merchants of
Tarshish and all her villages, will say to you,
"Is it for plunder that you have come? Have
you assembled your horde to carry off silver
and gold, to take away cattle and goods, and
to seize a great amount of booty?"

Second Prophecy against Gog. 14 Therefore,
prophesy, son of man, and say to Gog: Thus
says the Lord GOD: On that day when my
people Israel are living securely, will you not
rouse yourself 15 and come forth from your
home in the far recesses of the north, you
and many nations with you, a mighty army
of soldiers beyond counting, all of them rid-
ing on horses? 16 You will come forth against

q Ezek 34:23.—r Ps 110:4.—s 2 Ki 19:28.

38:1—39:29 It would be useless to try to identify persons and countries in this fanciful description. The poet uses apocalyptic ideas and mythology in order to teach us how to read the main guiding lines of the history of salvation as seen through the tragic experience of the exiles. Israel has been uprooted and mistreated by the pagans whom God has used in punishing his people; the forces of the world seem to have formed a coalition which serves God as a weapon against the rebellious nation. But this time of suffering leads to peace and prosperity, and then all of Israel's enemies will be under its feet. These pictures with their vivid colors are made up of numerous fragments; they make use of elements—plague, earthquakes, floods, fire and brimstone—that gradually become characteristic of the way in which the Jewish tradition represents the critical moment, the final conflict between good and evil, God and sin. The name of Gog, with its reputation for savagery, stands for all the nations that have oppressed Israel and that always come from the north. The battle will take place in a distant future which cannot be specified and in which the unlikely is imagined as happening.

38:6 *Gomer* represents the Cimmerians, north of the Black Sea. *Beth-togarmah* is Armenia.

my people Israel like a cloud covering the
earth. In the final days, I will bring you
against my land so that the nations will know
me when through you, O Gog, I display my
holiness before their eyes.[t]

17 Thus says the Lord GOD: It was you of
whom I spoke in former days through my
servants, the prophets of Israel, who proph-
esied for many years that I would bring you
against them. 18 On that day, when Gog
attacks the land of Israel, says the Lord GOD,
my fury will be aroused.

19 In my jealousy and in my blazing wrath,
I swear that there will be a tremendous
earthquake in the land of Israel. 20 The fish of
the sea, and the birds of the air, and the
beasts of the field, and all the reptiles that
crawl on the ground, and every human being
on the face of the earth will tremble at my
presence. Mountains will be thrown down,
cliffs will crumble, and every wall will tum-
ble to the ground.

21 I will summon the sword against Gog on
all my mountains, says the Lord GOD, and
the swords of all will be turned against their
comrades.[u] 22 With pestilence and blood-
shed, I will bring judgment upon him, and I
will pour down torrential rain, hailstones,
fire and brimstone upon him and his troops
and the many nations that are supporting
him. 23 I will, thereby, display my greatness
and my holiness and make myself known to
many nations. Then they will know that I am
the LORD.

CHAPTER 39

Third Prophecy against Gog. 1 Son of man,
prophesy against Gog and say: Thus says the
Lord GOD: Behold, I am coming against you,
Gog, chief prince of Meshech and Tubal. 2 I
will turn you around and drive you forward.
I will lead you from the most remote recess-
es of the north and bring you to the moun-
tains of Israel.

3 Then I will strike the bow from your left
hand and cause your arrows to drop from
your right hand. 4 You will fall upon the
mountains of Israel, you and all your troops
as well as the nations that are with you. I will
give you as food to birds of prey of every kind
and to the wild beasts.

5 You will fall in the open field, for I have
spoken, declares the Lord GOD. 6 I will send
fire on Magog and upon those who live
undisturbed in the coastlands. Then they will
know that I am the LORD.[v]

7 I will make my holy name known among
my people Israel, and I will not allow my
holy name to be profaned. Thus the nations
will know that I am the LORD, the Holy One
in Israel. 8 All this will happen. All this will
take place, says the Lord GOD. This is the day
about which I have spoken.

9 Then those who dwell in the towns of
Israel will go forth and set fire to the weapons
to provide themselves with fuel—bucklers
and shields, bows and arrows, clubs and
spears—and they will make fires of them for
seven years. 10 They will have no need to
bring in wood from the fields or cut down
any trees in the forests, inasmuch as they
will use their weapons to make fires. They
will despoil those who despoiled them and
plunder those who plundered them, says the
Lord GOD.

11 On that day I will give to Gog a well-
known place in Israel for his grave, the Valley
of Abarim east of the sea, a valley that is
inaccessible to travelers. There Gog and all
his horde will be buried. It will be called the
Valley of Hamon-gog. 12 The house of Israel
will spend seven months burying them in
order to purify the land.

13 All the people of the land will bury them,
thus gaining renown for doing so on the day
that I reveal my glory, says the Lord GOD.
14 Some men will be designated for the
assignment to pass through the land and
bury any travelers who remain lying on the
ground, so as to purify it. They will begin
their search at the end of seven months.

15 As these searchers go through the coun-
try, if anyone sees a human bone, he must
put up a marker beside it until the gravedig-
gers have buried it in the Valley of Hamon-
gog. 16 (A city named Hamonah is there
also.) Thus the land will be purified.

17 As for you, son of man, the Lord GOD
says this: Say to the wild birds of every kind
and to all the wild animals: Assemble and
come together. Gather from all sides for the
sacrificial feast I am preparing for you, a
magnificent sacrificial feast on the moun-
tains of Israel.[w] 18 You will consume the flesh
of the mighty, and you will drink the blood of
the princes of the earth—of rams, lambs,
goats, and bulls, all of them fatlings of
Bashan.

t Ezek 36:23.—**u** Ezek 14:17; 2 Chr 20:23.—**v** Ezek 38:22; Am 1:4.—**w** Isa 34:6-7; Rev 19:17.

19 At the sacrificial feast I am preparing for you, you will eat fat until you are filled and drink blood until you are drunk. 20 At my table you will be filled with horses and riders, with warriors and soldiers of every kind, says the Lord GOD.

Israel's Reunion.* 21 I will display my glory among the nations, and all the nations will see the punishment that I inflict and the hand that I lay upon them. 22 From that day forward, the house of Israel will know that I am the LORD, their God.

23 Furthermore, the nations will know that the people of the house of Israel were exiled because of their iniquity, inasmuch as they dealt treacherously with me. Therefore, I hid my face from them and handed them over to their enemies, so that they all fell by the sword. 24 I dealt with them according to their uncleanness and their offenses, and I hid my face from them.

25 Therefore, thus says the Lord GOD: Now I will restore the fortunes of Jacob and have mercy on the whole house of Israel, and I will be jealous for my holy name. 26 They will forget their disgrace and all the acts of infidelity they committed against me when they will live in security in their land, with no one to make them afraid.

27 When I have brought them back from the peoples and gathered them from the lands of their enemies, I will display through them my holiness in the sight of many nations. 28 Then they will know that I am the LORD, their God, because, having sent them into exile among the nations, I then reunited them into their own land and left none of them behind.[x] 29 Never again will I hide my face from them, for I will pour out my Spirit upon the house of Israel, says the Lord GOD.

V: THE NEW ISRAEL*

A: The Future Temple

CHAPTER 40

The Man with a Measuring Rod. 1 During the twenty-fifth year of our exile, at the beginning of the year, on the tenth day of the month, fourteen years after the fall of the city, on that very day the hand of the LORD came upon me, and he brought me there. 2 In divine visions, he brought me to the land of Israel and set me down on a very high mountain, to the south of which a city seemed to have been built.

3 When he had brought me there, I beheld a man whose appearance was like that of bronze. He had a linen cord* and a measuring rod in his hand, and he was standing in the gateway.[y] 4 The man said to me, "Son of man, look carefully and listen attentively, and pay close attention to all that I will show you. That is the reason why you were brought here. Report to the house of Israel everything that you see."

5 Then I beheld an outer wall that surrounded the temple on all sides. The length of the measuring rod that the man was holding was six cubits long, each cubit* being a cubit and a handbreadth in length. He measured the thickness and the height of the wall; each was one rod.

The East Gate. 6 Then he went to the gate which faced eastward, mounted its steps, and measured the gate's threshold; it was one rod deep. 7 Each cell was one rod long and one rod wide, and the walls between the cells measured five cubits. The threshold of the gate adjoining the vestibule of the gate at the inner end measured one rod.

x Ezek 34:30.—y Ezek 1:7; Rev 11:1; 21:15.

39:21-29 This is, in a way, the conclusion of all the preceding chapters. After punishing them, God will lead his people back to their country, since he is the God of Israel; his name will be made known to all through the covenant. These few verses summarize the teaching of Ezekiel: he is the prophet who in the midst of the passing events of history makes known, above all else, the glory of God.

40:1—48:35 Exactly forty years after the fall of Jerusalem in 587 B.C., Ezekiel unexpectedly resumes his prophetic activity.

He sees a city, the future city, in which the people of tomorrow, of the last times, will dwell. He sees and touches this city, which is reduced in size to the limited dimensions of the temple and its accessory buildings; he traverses it in every direction, he examines all its details and wants to show all of them to us. The story of this walk through the future city occupies chapters 40–48. It is difficult to understand the text of these final chapters of Ezekiel. In substance, they contain the account of what the prophet has seen in one or more visions. At a later date, however, Ezekiel and his disciples must have completed and extended the account with clarifications and details that now overload it to the point of making it at times incomprehensible. They express a burning faith in God, the holy God, who is present on earth, in his land, and in the temple of Jerusalem. This section has been called "the law of Ezekiel," as if it stated anew the ancient law of the covenant that had been given to Moses.

St. John's description, in his Apocalypse, of the heavenly Jerusalem, the definitive dwelling of God in humanity, is influenced by Ezekiel (see Rev 21:1—22:5).

40:3 The *linen cord* was used for taking longer measurements, the *measuring rod* for short ones.

40:5 The *measuring rod* was about 340 cm. The *cubit* was about 58 cm.

8 Then he measured the vestibule of the gateway, 9 which was eight cubits, and its pilasters, which were two cubits. The vestibule of the gate was at the inner end. 10 Inside the east gate were three cells on each side. All of them were identical in size, and the pilasters on either side were also of equal size.

11 After this, he measured the width of the entrance of the gateway, which was ten cubits, while its length was thirteen cubits. 12 There was a wall, one cubit high, in front of each cell, and the cells were six cubits square. 13 He then measured the width of the gate from the back wall of one cell to the back of the cell on the opposite side. The width was twenty-five cubits from wall to wall. 14 After this, he measured the vestibule, which was twenty cubits, and also the pilasters adjoining the court on either side, which were six cubits.

15 From the front of the entrance gate to the far end of its portico, the distance was fifty cubits. 16 Both the guardrooms and their pilasters had windows on the inside of the gateway, and the vestibules also had windows all around; the pilasters were decorated with palm trees.

The Outer Court. 17 Then he brought me to the outer court, where there were rooms and a paved terrace all around the court. There was a total of thirty rooms.[z] 18 The pavement was laid along the side of the gates, its width equaling the length of the gates. This was the lower pavement. 19 Then he measured the width of the court, from the front of the lower gateway to the outside of the inner court; there were one hundred cubits between them.

The North Gate. 20 Then he measured the length and breadth of the gate leading into the outer court that faced north. 21 Its cells, three on either side, and its pilasters and its vestibules were of the same size as those of the first gate. Its depth was fifty cubits, and its width was twenty-five cubits.

22 Its windows, its vestibule, and its palm trees were identical in size to those of the gate that faced toward the east. Seven steps led up to it, and its vestibule was at the inner end. 23 Opposite the north gate there was a gate that led to the inner court, exactly like the one opposite the east gate. He measured one hundred cubits from one gate to the other.

The South Gate. 24 Then he led me to the south side, and I saw a gate facing south. He measured its cells, its pilasters, and its vestibule; they all had the same dimensions as the others. 25 The gate and its vestibule had windows all around. Each window was fifty cubits in depth and twenty-five cubits in width.

26 There were seven steps leading up to it. Its vestibule was on the inside, and palm trees decorated its pilasters, one on either side. 27 The inner court had a gate facing south. He measured the distance from this gate to the outer gate on the south—one hundred cubits.

The Inner Court Gates. 28 Then he brought me into the inner court by the south gate. He measured the south gate, which had the same dimensions as the others. 29 Its cells, its pilasters, and its vestibule were the same size as those of the others. The gate and its vestibule had windows all around; it was fifty cubits long and twenty-five cubits wide.

30 The vestibules of the gateways around the inner court were twenty-five cubits wide and five cubits deep. 31 However, the major vestibule faced the outer court. Palm trees were carved on its pilasters, and it had a stairway of eight steps.

32 Then he brought me to the inner court on the east side and measured the gate, its dimensions were identical to those of the others. 33 Its cells, its pilasters, and its vestibule were the same size as those of the others. The gate and its vestibule had windows all around; it was fifty cubits long and twenty-five cubits wide. 34 Its vestibule opened onto the outer court. There were palm trees carved on its pilasters, and there were eight steps leading up to it.

35 Then he brought me to the north gate, and he measured it. Its dimensions were identical to those of the others. 36 Its cells, its pilasters, and its vestibule were of the same size as those of the others, and it had windows all around. It was fifty cubits long and twenty-five cubits wide. 37 Its portico faced the outer court; it had a palm tree carved on its pilasters on either side, and its stairway had eight steps.

The Side Chambers. 38 * There was a room that was entered through a door in the

z Ezek 10:5; 41:6.

40:38-39 Ezekiel's vision seems interrupted here by later additions, the style of which is different.

vestibule of the gateway. That was where
the burnt offerings were to be washed. [39] In
the vestibule of the gate, there were two
tables on either side, on which the burnt
offerings, sin offerings, and guilt offerings
were slaughtered.

[40] On the outside of the vestibule, near the
entrance of the north gate, were two tables,
and on the other side of the vestibule of the
gate were two tables. [41] Thus, four tables
were inside the gate and four tables were
outside the gate—eight tables upon which
the sacrifices were slaughtered.

[42] There were also four slabs of cut stone
that were used for holocausts—one and a
half cubits long, one and a half cubits wide,
and a cubit high—on which were placed the
instruments for slaughtering the burnt offer-
ings and the other sacrifices. [43] Double-
pronged hooks, a handbreadth wide, were
attached to the nearby wall, and on the
tables the flesh of the offering was laid.

[44] Then he led me into the inner court,
where there were two rooms—one on the
side of the north gate, facing south; the other
on the side of the south gate, facing north.
[45] He said to me, "This room that faces south
is for the priests who are in charge of the
temple. [46] The room that faces north is for
the priests who have charge of the altar.
These are the descendants of Zadok, who
alone among the descendants of Levi are
allowed to come near to minister to the
LORD." [a] [47] Thereupon, he measured the
court. It was a perfect square, one hundred
cubits long and one hundred cubits wide,
with the altar standing in front of the temple.

The Temple. [48] Then he brought me into the
vestibule of the temple and measured the
pilasters of the vestibule; it was five cubits on
either side. The width of the gate was four-
teen cubits, and the side walls of the gate
were three cubits on either side. [49] The
vestibule was twenty cubits long and twelve
cubits wide. There were ten steps leading up
to it, and there were pillars beside the
pilasters, one on either side.

CHAPTER 41

[1] Then he brought me into the sanctuary
and measured the pilasters. They were six
cubits wide on each side. [2] The width of the
entrance was ten cubits, and the walls on
either side of the entrance were five cubits
each. Then he measured the length of the
nave, which was fifty cubits, while its width
was twenty cubits.

[3] Then he went into the inner room and
measured the pilasters at the entrance; they
were two cubits. The width of the entrance
was six cubits, and the walls at either side of
the entrance were seven cubits. [4] Beyond the
nave, he measured the length of the inner
sanctuary, which was twenty cubits, and its
width, which was also twenty cubits, after
which he said to me, "This is the Holy of
Holies." [b]

[5] Then he measured the wall of the temple,
which was six cubits thick. The width of the
side chambers was four cubits all around the
temple. [6] The side chambers were on three
levels, one above the other, with thirty cham-
bers on each level. There were ledges all
around the wall of the temple that were
designed to serve as supports for the side
chambers, but there were no supports in the
wall of the temple itself.

[7] The passageway leading upward to the
side chambers became broader from story
to story, for the structure surrounding the
temple was constructed in successive stages,
so that the width of the cells increased from
one story to the next. One ascended from
the lowest story to the highest story by
means of the middle one.

[8] I also noted that there was a raised pave-
ment encircling the temple all around. This
formed the foundation of the side chambers,
measuring a full rod, six cubits high. [9] The
thickness of the outer wall of the side cham-
bers was five cubits. Between the cells of the
temple [10] and the chambers of the court,
there was an open space, twenty cubits wide,
surrounding the temple on every side.

[11] The side chambers had entrances to the
open space, one entrance on the north side
and one on the south side. The width of the
free space was five cubits all around. [12] On
the western side, the building that faced the
temple yard was seventy cubits wide. The
wall of the building was five cubits thick all
around, and its length was ninety cubits.

[13] Then, he measured the temple, whose
length was one hundred cubits. [14] The tem-
ple courtyard and the buildings with its walls
were also one hundred cubits. [15] Next, he
measured the length of the building facing
the courtyard, and together with its walls on
either side, it came to one hundred cubits.

a 1 Ki 2:35.—b 1 Ki 6:20; 2 Chr 3:8.

The Temple Interior. The inner nave of the temple and the inner room and outer vestibule [16] were paneled with precious wood from the floor up to the windows and thresholds, and the windows were covered with latticework. [17] The wood extended up to the lintel of the door, even to the outer sanctuary. And on all the walls throughout the inner room and the nave there was a pattern [18] that depicted cherubim and palm trees, with one palm tree between every pair of cherubim.[c]

Each cherub had two faces: [19] a human face turned toward the palm tree on one side, and the face of a young lion turned toward the palm tree on the other side. [20] From the floor to the lintel above the door, the cherubim and the palm trees were carved on the wall. [21] The doorposts of the temple were square.

In front of the sanctuary, there was something that resembled [22] an altar of wood, three cubits high and two cubits long. Its corners, its base, and its sides were of wood. He said to me, "This is the table of the LORD."[d] [23] The nave and the holy place each had a double door. [24] The double doors each had two hinged leaves, two leaves for each door.

[25] Carved upon the doors of the nave were cherubim and palm trees, like those carved in the walls. Also, there was a wooden lattice over the vestibule. [26] On both sides of the vestibule were recessed windows and palm trees.

CHAPTER 42

Other Structures. [1] Then he led me toward the north into the outer court and brought me to the rooms that were opposite the temple courtyard and facing the building on the north. [2] The length of the building on the north side was one hundred cubits, and its width was fifty cubits.

[3] Facing the twenty cubits of the inner court and the pavement of the outer court, there were three parallel rows of chambers on each level facing each other. [4] In front of the chambers, there was a passageway, ten cubits wide and one hundred cubits long, and the entrances to the rooms faced north.

[5] The chambers on the upper level were narrower than those on the two levels below because the galleries took up more of the width on the upper level. [6] For they were divided into three stories and they had no pillars as the courts had. Thus, the upper chambers were more narrow than those on the lower and middle levels.

[7] There was an outer wall parallel to the chambers that extended out toward the outer court; it was fifty cubits long. [8] The chambers facing the outer court were fifty cubits long, while those facing the temple were one hundred cubits long.

[9] Below these chambers there was a passage that one entered from the east so that one could enter them from the outer court. [10] On the south side that faced the open area and the building, there were chambers.

[11] There was a passage that ran in front of these chambers. They were identical in design to those on the north, with the same length and width, and with the same exits and entrances and doorways. [12] Before the chambers on the south side, there was an entrance from the east at the end of each passage, by means of which one could enter from the east.

[13] Then he said to me, "The north and the south chambers which open out onto the courtyard are the chambers of the sanctuary. It is there that the priests approach the LORD and eat the most sacred offerings. There they deposit these most sacred offerings—the grain offerings, the sin offerings, and the guilt offerings—for this is a holy place. [14] When the priests have entered the holy place, they must not depart from the holy place and enter the outer court without first leaving there the vestments they have worn while performing their duties, since these vestments are holy. They shall first clothe themselves in other garments before they go near the area designated for the people."[e]

Measurements of the Outer Court. [15] When he had completed his measurements of the interior of the temple area, he brought me out through the gateway that faces east, and he measured the temple area all around.

[16] He measured the east side with his measuring rod, and it was five hundred cubits. [17] He then turned and measured the north side, and it was five hundred cubits. [18] He next turned and measured the south side, and it was five hundred cubits. [19] Then he turned and measured the west side, and it was five hundred cubits.

c 1 Ki 6:29; 2 Chr 3:5.—d Ex 30:1; Rev 8:3.—e Ex 29:4-9; Zec 3:4.

[20] Thus, he measured the area on all four
sides. The wall around it was five hundred
cubits long and five hundred cubits wide, to
separate the sacred from the profane.

B: Restoration of the Temple

CHAPTER 43

The LORD's Return. [1] * Then the man
brought me to the gate that faces the east,
[2] and there I beheld the glory of the God of
Israel coming from the east. The sound of his
coming was like the sound of a mighty tor-
rent of waters, and the earth shone with his
glory.

[3] The vision I beheld was like the man I
had seen when he had come to destroy the
city, and like the vision I had seen by the
River Chebar, and I fell prostrate.[f]

[4] As the glory of the LORD entered the tem-
ple by way of the east gate, [5] the Spirit lifted
me up and brought me to the inner court,
and I beheld the glory of the LORD fill the
temple.

[6] While the man stood beside me, I heard
someone speaking to me from the temple.
[7] He said to me: Son of man, this is the place
of my throne and the place for the soles of
my feet. This is where I will dwell forever
among the Israelites. Never again will the
house of Israel defile my holy name, neither
they nor their kings, by their whoring and by
the corpses of their kings.

[8] When they placed their threshold next to
my threshold and their doorposts beside my
doorposts, with only a wall separating me
and them, they were defiling my holy name
by the loathsome practices in which they
engaged. Therefore, I will destroy them in
my anger.* [9] From now on, they must cease
their harlotry and remove the corpses of
their kings from my presence. Then I will
dwell among them forever.

The Temple Law. [10] As for you, son of man,
describe this temple to the house of Israel, so
that they will be truly ashamed of their iniq-
uities. [11] And if they are ashamed of all that
they have done, make known to them the
design and arrangement of the temple, its
exits and entrances, its shape, and all its
ordinances. [12] This is the law of the temple:
all the surrounding area on the top of the
mountain shall be most holy. Such is the law
of the temple.

Measurements of the Altar. [13] * These were
the dimensions of the altar in cubits of one
cubit and a handbreadth. Its base was one
cubit high and one cubit wide, with a rim of
one span around its edge. This was the height
of the altar. [14] From its base on the ground
up to the lower ledge, it was two cubits high
and one cubit wide, and from the lower ledge
to the upper ledge, it was four cubits high
and again one cubit wide.

[15] The altar hearth was four cubits high,
and from the hearth, four horns projected
upward. [16] The hearth was a square, twelve
cubits long by twelve cubits wide. [17] The
upper ledge was also a square, fourteen
cubits long by fourteen cubits wide, with a
rim around it a half cubit wide and a sur-
rounding base of one cubit. The steps of the
altar face the east.

[18] Then he said to me: Son of man, thus
says the Lord GOD: These are the regulations
for the altar when it has been erected for the
offering of holocausts upon it and for the
sprinkling of blood upon it. [19] You are to pre-
sent a young bull as a sin offering to the
Levitical priests of the family of Zadok who
are authorized to draw near me in order to
minister to me, says the Lord GOD.[g]

[20] You are to take some of its blood and put
it on the four horns of the altar and on the
four corners of the ledge and upon the sur-
rounding rim. Thus, you will purify it and
make atonement for it. [21] Then take the bull

f Ezek 1:1; Dan 8:17.—g Ezek 44:15; 1 Ki 2:35.

43:1-7 The departure of the glory of God (Ezek 10:18-22; 11:22-25) had signified a break between God and his people, because idolatry was rife among them. Now God returns, because he has purified and renewed his people. A new worship begins. The Lord dwells among his own. This is the mystery of God's dwelling among human beings, the God who becomes present in a sanctuary, even though he has no need of any place or any sign, and even though nothing can contain him, since heaven is his throne and the earth his footstool (see Isa 66:1; Acts 7:49). The whole universe is too little for God, but he nonetheless wills that there be a sign manifesting his presence.

43:8 Before the Exile, the royal palace abutted the temple.

43:13—48:35 This second part of chapters 40–48 is more complicated than the first. Into the continuation of the vision or, perhaps, into the description of a new episode in this vision of Ezekiel, the prophet and his successors have inserted texts that differ greatly from each other: prophetic predictions, documents on the status of persons (priests, Levites, the prince), and liturgical details or rubrics.

This last part of the Book of Ezekiel pays a great deal of attention to the office of priesthood. But alongside such passages are others containing quite contrary ideas; these doubtless reflect the discussions and conflicts which arose, beginning with the Exile, concerning the role of the priests.

Two series of passages reflecting opposed tendencies can also be seen in what is said about the office and place of the prince. Note that the text no longer speaks of a king but only of a prince.

designated for the sin offering and immolate
it in the designated part of the temple area
outside the sanctuary.

[22] On the second day, you are to present an
unblemished male goat as a sin offering, and
the altar must be purified again, as was done
with the bull. [23] When you have finished puri-
fying it, choose an unblemished young bull
and an unblemished ram from the flock.
[24] After you present them before the LORD,
the priests will throw salt on them and offer
them to the LORD as burnt offerings.

[25] For seven days you are to offer a male
goat for a sin offering, as well as a young bull
and an unblemished ram from the flock.
[26] In this way, they will make atonement for
the altar and cleanse it, and thereby conse-
crate it.

[27] Once these days have been completed,
from the eighth day onward the priests will
offer your burnt offerings and your peace
offerings on the altar. Then I will accept you,
says the LORD.

CHAPTER 44

The Shut Gate. [1] Then he brought me back
to the outer gate of the sanctuary that faces
east, but it was shut. [2] The LORD said to me:
This gate will remain closed. It shall not be
opened, and no one may enter through it.
[3] Only the prince himself may sit inside the
gate to eat his meal in the presence of the
LORD. He must enter by way of the vestibule
of the gate, and he must depart by the same
way.

C: The New Law

Admittance to the Temple. [4] Then he brought
me by way of the north gate to the front of
the temple. And when I looked, I beheld the
glory of the LORD filling the LORD's temple,
and I fell upon my face. [5] Then he said to me:
Son of man, pay attention, look carefully,
and listen closely to everything that I will tell
you in regard to all the ordinances of the
temple of the LORD and all its laws. Also,
mark carefully those who are admitted to
the temple and those who are to be excluded
from the sanctuary.

[6] Say to the rebels of the house of Israel:
Thus says the Lord GOD: I have endured
enough of these abominable practices in
which you engage, O house of Israel. [7] You
have allowed foreigners, uncircumcised in
heart and body, to enter my sanctuary and
profane it when you offer to me my food, the
fat and the blood. Thus, you have broken my
covenant with all of your loathsome prac-
tices. [h]

[8] Instead of taking charge of my sacred
offerings, you have assigned foreigners to
serve me in my sanctuary in your place.
[9] Thus says the Lord GOD: No foreigner,
uncircumcised in heart and flesh, shall be
permitted to enter my sanctuary, not even
those foreigners who dwell among the
Israelites.

Levites. [10] But as for the Levites who aban-
doned me when Israel strayed far from me
by following its idols, they must suffer the
consequences for their iniquity. [11] They may
be permitted to serve as ministers in my
sanctuary, with the responsibility of guard-
ing the gates of the temple and serving in the
temple. They may be allowed to slaughter
the burnt offerings and the sacrifices for the
people as well as attending to the needs of
the people and serving them.

[12] However, because they used to minister
to them in front of their idols and thereby
caused the house of Israel to fall into a state
of sin, therefore, I have sworn an oath
against them, says the Lord GOD, that they
shall be punished for their iniquity. [13] They
may never again be permitted to approach
me in order to serve as priests, nor will they
be allowed to come near any of my holy
things or my most sacred offerings. Rather,
they must bear the shame of their abom-
inable deeds. [14] However, I will assign them
the responsibility of service to the temple
and for all the work that has to be done in it.

Priests. [15] As for the Levitical priests, the
descendants of Zadok, who continued to ful-
fill faithfully their responsibility for caring
for my sanctuary when the Israelites strayed
far from me, they shall draw near me in
order to minister to me, and they will stand
in my presence to offer me the fat and the
blood, says the Lord GOD. [i] [16] They are the
ones who will enter my sanctuary, the ones
who will approach my table to minister to
me and serve me.

[17] Whenever they approach the gates of the
inner court, the priests are to wear linen
vestments. They must not wear any garment
of wool when they minister at the gates of
the inner court or inside the temple. [18] They

h Gen 17:14; Ex 12:43-49.—i Ezek 40:46; 48:11; Deut 10:8.

are to have linen turbans on their heads and linen undergarments on their loins, and they may not wear anything that might cause them to perspire.

[19] Before they go out to the people in the outer court, they are to remove the clothes in which they have been performing their ministry, and they are then to put on other garments so that they will not communicate holiness to the people with their garments.

[20] Priests are not permitted to shave their heads or to let their hair grow long. Rather, they must keep their hair carefully trimmed, [21] nor are they allowed to drink wine on the day they are to enter the inner court.

[22] Priests may not marry either widows or divorced women, but only virgins of the race of Israel. However, they may marry women who are the widows of priests. [23] They shall teach my people to distinguish between the sacred and the profane, and they shall make known to them the difference between what is clean and what is unclean.

[24] In any dispute, the priests are to serve as judges, and they shall render their decisions according to my decrees. They must observe my laws and my statutes for all of my appointed feasts, and they shall keep my Sabbaths holy.

[25] Priests may not make themselves unclean by coming near a dead person. However, if the deceased is a father or mother, son or daughter, brother or unmarried sister, then they are permitted to defile themselves. [26] After such a priest has been purified, he must wait a further seven days. [27] On the day that he enters the inner court of the sanctuary to minister in the sanctuary, he shall offer a sin offering for himself, says the Lord GOD.

[28] Priests will have no inheritance. I, myself, will be their inheritance. You will not give them any possession in Israel. I, myself, am their possession.[j] [29] They will eat the grain offering, the sin offering, and the guilt offering. Everything in Israel that is dedicated by vow to God will be theirs.

[30] The best of all the firstfruits of every kind and the best of all your offerings of every kind shall belong to the priests. Likewise, you shall give to the priests the best of your dough so that a blessing may rest upon your house.[k] [31] In addition, the priests must not eat the flesh of a bird or animal that has died a natural death or been killed by a wild animal.

CHAPTER 45

The Sacred Plot. [1] When you draw lots to divide the country as an inheritance, you shall set aside a sacred portion of the land for the LORD, twenty-five thousand cubits long and twenty thousand cubits wide. Its entire area will be regarded as sacred. [2] Of this land, a plot, five hundred cubits square, shall be set aside for the sanctuary, and that plot will be surrounded by an open space of fifty cubits.

[3] Out of this area you must also set aside a section twenty-five thousand cubits long and ten thousand cubits wide, within which will be the sanctuary, the Holy of Holies. [4] This will be the sacred portion of the land belonging to the priests who minister in the sanctuary and approach the LORD to serve him. It will be both a place for their houses as well as a holy place for the sanctuary.

[5] Another section, twenty-five thousand cubits long and ten thousand cubits wide, will be set apart for the Levites who minister at the temple, so that they will have towns in which to live. [6] Near the land belonging to the sanctuary, you are to grant the city possession of an area five thousand cubits wide and twenty-five thousand cubits long. This shall belong to the whole house of Israel.

[7] To the prince will belong the land that borders on both sides of the sacred district and the property of the city, extending westward from the west and eastward from the east, corresponding in length to one of the tribal portions and extending from the western to the eastern borders [8] of the land. This will be his property in Israel. Therefore, the princes of Israel will no longer oppress my people, but they will grant the land to the house of Israel according to their tribes.[l]

Weights and Measures. [9] Thus says the Lord GOD: Enough, you princes of Israel! Cease your violence and oppression and do what is right and just. Stop evicting my people from their land, says the Lord GOD.

[10] * You must use scales that are accurate, and have an honest ephah and an accurate

j Num 18:20; Deut 18:1.—k Ex 34:26; Deut 18:4.—l Jer 22:3.

45:10-12 The *ephah* (measure of grain) and the *liquid measure* were about 45 liters. *Homer:* About four and a half hectoliters. *Gerah:* A little more than a half gram.

liquid measure.[m] 11 The ephah and the liquid measure must be of equal size. The liquid measure must contain one-tenth of a homer, and the ephah must contain one-tenth of a homer. The homer will be the standard measure for both. 12 The shekel must consist of twenty gerahs. Twenty shekels, twenty-five shekels, and fifteen shekels will constitute one mina.

Grain Offerings. 13 This is the special offering you shall make: one-sixth of an ephah from each homer of wheat, and one-sixth of an ephah from each homer of barley. 14 The prescribed portion of oil: one-tenth of a measure for every measure of oil, consisting of ten liquid measures to a kor (or a homer, since ten liquid measures equal one homer).

15 In addition, you must take from the pastures of Israel one sheep from every flock of two hundred. These will be used for sacrifice—burnt offerings and peace offerings and fellowship offerings—to make atonement for the people, says the Lord GOD.

16 All the people of the land will be required to contribute to this offering for the prince of Israel. 17 The prince himself has the obligation to provide the holocausts, the cereal offerings, and the libations for all of the feasts, new moons, Sabbaths, and appointed festivals of the house of Israel. He, himself, must provide the sin offerings, the grain offerings, the burnt offerings, and the fellowship offerings to make atonement for the house of Israel.

The Feast of Passover. 18 Thus says the Lord GOD: On the first day of the first month you shall sacrifice an unblemished young bull to purify the sanctuary. 19 The priest must take some of the blood of the sin offering and put it on the doorposts of the temple, on the four corners of the ledge of the altar, and on the doorposts of the gates of the inner court. 20 You are to do the same on the seventh day of the month for anyone who has sinned inadvertently or because of ignorance. In this way, you will make atonement for the temple.

21 On the fourteenth day of the first month, you must celebrate the Feast of the Passover, and for seven days, everyone must eat unleavened bread.[n] 22 On that day the prince must provide a bull as a sin offering for himself and for all the people of the land.

23 On each of the seven days of the feast, the prince must offer as a holocaust to the LORD seven bulls and seven rams without blemish, and as a sin offering, he must offer one male goat each day. 24 He also is to provide as a grain offering one ephah for each bull and one ephah for each ram, as well as a hin* of oil for each ephah.

The Feast of Booths. 25 On the fifteenth day of the seventh month, and for the entire seven days of the festival, he shall provide the same sin offerings, burnt offerings, grain offerings, and oil.

CHAPTER 46

Sabbath Offerings. 1 Thus says the Lord GOD: The east gate of the inner court must remain closed during the six working days. However, it shall be opened on the Sabbath and on the day of the new moon. 2 The prince is to enter from the outside through the vestibule of the gate and stand by the doorposts of the gate. Then the priest must offer his burnt offerings and his peace offerings, and he shall bow down at the threshold of the gate. After this, he will go out, but the gate is not to be closed until evening. 3 The people of the land shall worship before the LORD at the entrance of the gate on the Sabbaths and the days of the new moon.

4 The burnt offering that the prince offers to the LORD on the Sabbath shall consist of six lambs without blemish and one unblemished ram.[o] 5 The grain offering presented with the ram shall be an ephah, and the grain offering with the lambs shall be whatever he chooses to present; also, a hin of oil must be included for every ephah.

6 On the day of the new moon, the prince must offer an unblemished young bull, six unblemished lambs, and one unblemished ram.[p] 7 As a grain offering, he shall provide an ephah with the bull and an ephah with the ram. With the lambs, he shall provide as much as he wishes to give, adding a hin of oil for every ephah.

Ritual Regulations. 8 Whenever the prince comes in, he must enter by the porch of the gate, and he must depart by the same way. 9 When the people of the land come to worship before the LORD on designated festival days, anyone who enters by the north gate to

m Lev 19:15; Deut 25:13-16; Am 8:5.—n Ex 12:6; Lev 23:5; Num 28:16.—o Num 28:9f.—p Num 28:11-15.

45:24 *Hin:* a sixth of an ephah.

worship must depart by the south gate, and anyone who enters by the south gate must leave by the north gate. No one may return through the gate by which he entered but must depart by the opposite gate.[q] 10 The prince will be in their midst, coming in when they enter and also departing with them as they leave.

11 On feast days and solemn festivities, the grain offering shall be one ephah for every bull, one ephah for every ram, and as much as he wishes to give for the lambs, together with a hin of oil for every ephah. 12 When the prince makes a free-will offering to the LORD, whether a burnt offering or a peace offering, the east gate will be opened for him. After presenting his burnt offering or peace offering as he does on the Sabbath, then he will leave, and the gate will be closed after his departure.

13 The prince will offer as a daily sacrifice to the LORD, a yearling without blemish for a burnt offering. He must offer this every morning.[r] 14 With it in addition, he must regularly provide as a grain offering, morning after morning, one-sixth of an ephah and one-third of a hin of oil to moisten the fine flour. The presentation of this grain offering to the LORD is a mandatory decree, prescribed for all time. 15 The lamb, the grain offering, and the oil must be offered every morning as an established holocaust.

The Prince's Inheritance. 16 Thus says the Lord GOD: If the prince makes a gift of a portion of his inheritance to any of his sons, it will belong to his sons. That gift becomes their property by inheritance. 17 However, if he makes a gift of a portion of his inheritance to one of his servants, it will belong to that servant until the year of liberation; then it must revert to the prince. Only the sons of the prince may rightfully keep their inheritance.*

18 On the other hand, the prince may not seize any of the inheritance of the people by evicting them from their property. He must provide an inheritance for his sons out of his own property, so that none of my people will be deprived of holdings that are rightfully theirs.

The Temple Kitchens. 19 Then he led me through the entrance on the side of the gate to the rooms facing north that were reserved for the priests. There before us, at the western end, he pointed to a space, 20 and he said to me, "This is the place where the priests must boil the guilt offering and the sin offering, and where they bake the cereal offering, so that they may avoid bringing them into the outer court and thereby run the risk of transmitting holiness to the people."

21 Then he brought me to the outer court and led me around to its four corners. In each of the corners, I saw that there was another court. 22 In each of the four corners of the court, there were four small courts, forty cubits long and thirty cubits wide, all four being the same size.

23 On the inside, around each of the four courts, there was a ledge of stone, with a hearth all around at the bottom of the wall. 24 Then he said to me, "These are the kitchens where the temple servants boil the sacrifices offered by the people."

CHAPTER 47*

The Temple Stream. 1 Then he brought me back to the entrance of the temple, and I beheld water flowing out eastward from under the threshold of the temple, for the temple faced east. The water was flowing down from the southern end of the temple, south of the altar.[s] 2 He took me out through the north gate and led me around on the outside to the outer gate that faces the east, where I saw that the water was trickling forth from the south side.

3 The man walked off to the east with a measuring line in his hand, and he measured off a thousand cubits. Then he led me through the water, which was ankle-deep. 4 Again, he measured off a thousand cubits and made me wade across the stream again. This time the water reached my knees. Again, he measured off a thousand cubits and made me wade across the stream again. This time the water reached my waist.

q Ex 23:17.—r Num 28:3-8.—s Zec 13:1; Rev 22:1.

46:17 This regulation was meant to hinder the dispersal of the nation's patrimony.

47:1-12 In the new land of the new people water will gush forth more abundantly than it did from the rock which Moses struck (Ex 17:1-7) and will provide copious irrigation for a Palestine that will have been changed into a new earthly paradise, as in the first days of humanity's existence (Gen 2:10-14). This stream will more than ever show itself to be a gift of God, who is present in the temple and from there pours out his favors on his purified people. St. John considers this promise to be fulfilled when, on the cross, water flows from the open side of Christ, the new temple, like streams of water leaping up for everlasting life (see Jn 2:21; 4:14; 7:37; 19:34). In the Apocalypse, he will speak of the great river of life that springs from the throne of the Lamb (Rev 22:1).

5 Once again, he measured off a thousand cubits, but now I beheld a river that I could not cross, for the water had risen, and it was deep enough to swim in, a river that could not be crossed except by swimming. 6 He asked me, "Have you seen this, son of man?" Then he brought me back to the bank of the river.

7 When I arrived there, I saw a great number of trees on each side of the river. 8 He said to me, "This water flows east and goes down into the Arabah and empties into the sea, whose salt waters it makes fresh.

9 "Wherever the river flows, swarms of living creatures will live there and multiply. There will be an abundance of fish, for this water flows there and makes the salt water fresh. [t] 10 Also, fishermen will gather along its banks from En-gedi to Englaim, spreading their nets. All kinds of fish will be found there, like the fish of the Great Sea.

11 "However, its swamps and marshes will not become fresh; they will be left for salt. 12 Along the river, on both banks, fruit trees of every kind will grow, with leaves that never wither and with fruit that never fails. They will bear fresh fruit every month, because they will be watered by the flow from the sanctuary. Their fruit will serve as food, and their leaves will serve for healing."

D: The New Israel

Boundaries of the Land. 13 Thus says the Lord GOD: These are the boundaries by which you are to divide the land as an inheritance for the twelve tribes of Israel, with two portions allotted to Joseph. 14 You are to divide it equally among them. Because I swore to your fathers that I would give it to your forefathers, this land will be given to you as your inheritance.

15 These will be the boundaries of the land: On the north side, from the Great Sea by the road from Hethlon, past Lebo-hamath, and on to Zedad, 16 Berothah, and Sibraim, between the border of Damascus and the border of Hamath, as far as Hazar-enon, which is on the border of Hauran. 17 Thus, the border will extend from the sea to Hazar-enon, with the frontier of Hamath and Damascus to the north. This was the northern boundary. [u]

18 On the east side, between Hauran and Damascus, along the Jordan between Gilead and the land of Israel, to the eastern sea and as far as Tamar. This is the eastern boundary.

19 On the south side, from Tamar to the waters of Meribath-kadesh, and from there along the Wadi of Egypt to the Great Sea. This is the southern boundary.

20 On the west side is the Great Sea, which forms the boundary as far as a point parallel to and opposite Lebo-hamath. This is the western boundary.

The Northern Allotment. 21 You are to distribute this land yourselves among the tribes of Israel 22 and allot it as an inheritance for yourselves and for the aliens who reside in your midst and have begotten children among you. You are to treat them as children of Israel. With you, they shall be allotted as an inheritance among the tribes of Israel.* 23 In whatever tribe an alien settles, there you shall assign him his inheritance. This is the word of the Lord GOD.

CHAPTER 48

1 What follows is the list of the tribes: [v]

At the northernmost border, Dan will have one portion, in the direction of Hethlon, through Lebo of Hamath to Hazar-enon, on the border of Damascus to the north, next to Hamath, his portion extending from the eastern to the western boundary.

2 Asher will have one portion, bordering Dan, from the eastern to the western boundary.

3 Naphtali will have one portion, bordering Asher, from the eastern to the western boundary.

4 Manasseh will have one portion, bordering Naphtali, from the eastern to the western boundary.

5 Ephraim will have one portion, bordering Manasseh, from the eastern to the western boundary.

6 Reuben will have one portion, bordering Ephraim, from the eastern to the western boundary.

7 Judah will have one portion, bordering Reuben, from the eastern to the western boundary.

t Rev 21:6.—u Num 34:9.—v Ezek 47:15ff.

47:22 The old law (Deut 23:2-9) denied aliens the right to inherit property.

The Sacred Allotment. 8 Adjoining the territory of Judah from the eastern to the western boundary shall be the portion that you are to set apart—twenty-five thousand cubits wide, and its length the same as each of the other tribal portions from the eastern to the western boundary. The sanctuary of the LORD shall be located in the center of it.

9 The portion that you set aside for the LORD shall be twenty-five thousand cubits long and ten thousand cubits wide. 10 This will be the sacred portion for the priests. It will measure twenty-five thousand cubits on the north, ten thousand cubits on the east, ten thousand cubits on the west, and twenty-five thousand cubits on the south. The sanctuary of the LORD will be placed in the center of it.

11 This will be for the consecrated priests, the descendants of the tribe of Zadok, who remained faithful in their service to me and did not follow the Israelites in going astray, as the Levites did, 12 it will belong to them as a special gift set aside from the sacred portion of the land, adjoining the territory of the Levites.

13 The territory of the Levites shall correspond to that of the priests, twenty-five thousand cubits long and ten thousand cubits wide. Its total length will be twenty-five thousand cubits, and its total width will be ten thousand cubits. 14 They will not be allowed to sell or exchange any part of it. This is the choice portion of the land, and it cannot be transferred, because it is holy to the LORD.

15 The remaining area, five thousand cubits in width and twenty-five thousand cubits in length, shall be used at the discretion of the city for dwellings and pasture lands. The city shall be located in the middle of it, 16 and these shall be its dimensions: on the north side, four thousand five hundred cubits; on the south side, four thousand five hundred cubits; on the east side, four thousand five hundred cubits; on the west side, four thousand five hundred cubits.

17 The pasture land of the city will be two hundred and fifty cubits to the north, two hundred and fifty cubits to the south, two hundred and fifty cubits to the east, and two hundred and fifty cubits to the west. 18 The remainder of the area, along the sacred tract, will be ten thousand cubits to the east and ten thousand cubits to the west. Its produce will provide food for the workers of the city.

19 The workers of the city who farm this land will come from all the tribes of Israel. 20 The entire tract that you set apart will be a square, twenty-five thousand cubits by twenty-five thousand cubits. As a sacred gift, you must set apart the sacred tract together with the property of the city.

21 What remains on both sides of the sacred portion and of the property of the city shall belong to the prince. Extending eastward along the twenty-five thousand cubits to the eastern border, and extending westward along the twenty-five thousand cubits to the western border, parallel to the tribal portions, it will belong to the prince. The sacred portion and the sanctuary of the temple will be in the center. 22 Therefore, aside from the property of the Levites and the property of the city, which lie in the midst of the prince's property, everything between the borders of Judah and the borders of Benjamin shall belong to the prince.

The Southern Allotment. 23 These are the remaining tribes:

Benjamin will have one portion, from the eastern boundary to the western boundary.

24 Simeon will have one portion, bordering the territory of Benjamin from east to west.

25 Issachar will have one portion, bordering the territory of Simeon from east to west.

26 Zebulun will have one portion, bordering the territory of Issachar from east to west.

27 Gad will have one portion, bordering the territory of Zebulun from east to west.

28 The southern boundary of Gad will extend from Tamar to the waters of Meribath-kadesh, and from there along the Wadi of Egypt to the Great Sea.

29 This is the land that you are to allot as inheritances among the tribes of Israel, and these are their portions, says the Lord GOD.

The City Gates. 30 These are the exits from the city, the gates of which are named after the tribes of Israel.

On the north side, which will measure four thousand five hundred cubits in length, 31 there will be three gates: the gate of Reuben, the gate of Judah, and the gate of Levi.

32 On the east side, which will measure four thousand five hundred cubits in

length, there will be three gates: the gate of Joseph, the gate of Benjamin, and the gate of Dan.
33 On the south side, which will measure four thousand five hundred cubits in length, there will be three gates: the gate of Simeon, the gate of Issachar, and the gate of Zebulun.
34 On the west side, which will measure four thousand five hundred cubits in length, there will be three gates: the gate of Gad, the gate of Asher, and the gate of Naphtali.
35 The perimeter of the city will measure eighteen thousand cubits. And the name of the city from that time on will be: "The LORD Is There."

"The words inscribed are *MENE, TEKEL,* and *PERES.* This is what the words mean: . . . God has numbered the days of your kingdom and brought it to an end" *(Dan 5:25f).*

THE BOOK OF DANIEL

The Kingdom of the World and the Kingdom of God

This Book was probably written during the dramatic period when Judaism was in danger of being wiped out, namely, during the persecution by Antiochus IV Epiphanes, of which the Books of the Maccabees tell us.

In 175 B.C., Antiochus IV Epiphanes, an unscrupulous politician, came to power in Syria. The empire he had to govern was too disparate in character and too big; the vassal peoples grew restless from time to time. In order to keep the empire united, Antiochus undertook a policy of systematic Hellenization. All the nations were to have a single administration, a single way of life, and the same customs; all were to accept the religion of the Greek state, since religion was part of public life, and, in addition, they were to venerate the sovereign as a god.

A number of peoples, those that had no special difficulty in accepting a variety of gods into their pantheon, could accept this policy without running any great risks to their own religion. The same was not true of the Jews; for them, to participate in this kind of public life with its state-imposed worship meant turning to idolatry and renouncing their faith in the one God, the faith of their fathers. Conflict was therefore unavoidable. The monarch did indeed find accomplices among some of the more influential Jews, but when he went so far as to set up a pagan statue in the temple, the famous "abomination that causes desolation" (1 Mac 1:54; Dan 9:27; 11:31), a revolt broke out among the lower priesthood, who were joined by intellectuals and common folk who remained faithful to the covenant. For three and a half years Antiochus attempted to suppress resistance with weapons.

After the events, the Books of Maccabees provided a passionate account of those tragic times, but a different literature, of which the Book of Daniel is a part, came into existence and was circulated at the very time of the persecution, its purpose being to support the persecuted in their trials.

The author of the Book of Daniel has a primarily theological view of history; in his mind, all the events that have occurred since the Exile are part of God's plan. Addressing a people who are continually persecuted, he speaks to them in a coded language that will mislead the police forces of the oppressor but will, at the same time, set forth his own religious ideas of current history. He pretends to have lived in an earlier time and to be seeing as future that which, in reality, is contemporaneous with him. In fact, it can easily be shown that he is very well informed about the beginning of the second century before our era; on the other hand, the information he provides about the past, in which he pretends to have lived, is very confused and inaccurate; he is also vague on events that would take place after the persecutions. We must therefore conclude that he was writing during the persecution itself.

If he nonetheless makes Daniel speak as though he were a prophet living during the Exile in the sixth century (just as the later sapiential books put their sayings in the mouth of Solomon), he does so in order to connect all events, even those contemporary with him, with the word of God; but there are no more prophets in this second century. There is, instead, a fervent cult of the past. The struggles going on are, in the author's eyes, the symbol of powers hostile to God and of the coming victory of the reign of God; such is the central idea of the Book. The author also attempts to describe this still uncertain future. All of these traits taken together characterize the apocalypses, of which this Book provides a complete model.

The hero of the Book is righteous and wise; he has a name well known in the Jewish tradition (Ezek 14:14f; 28:3) and made famous throughout the East by many stories. The first part of the Book (chs. 1–6) takes the form of a series of edifying stories, which at times are based on historical facts, although in a very free way. Such could be the case, for example, with Belshazzar's feast. The second part of the Book (chs. 7–12), which is an apocalypse in the proper sense, attributes to Daniel a series of visions in which the author makes use of primitive Babylonian traditions and other historical and biblical texts (see Joel 4; Zec 14).

The various elements used in composing the Book make it a complicated one. Moreover, some of its chapters are written in Hebrew, others in Aramaic, the current language, and still others, added later, in Greek. But the author, an intellectual who belongs to the group in rebellion, has succeeded in putting together an original work that does not lack unity and inspiration and that retains a lasting value. It bears witness that the kingdom of God is built up slowly in the course of world history, as the Lord always ends by triumphing over hostile forces that are opposed to his plans. Above and beyond passing earthly regimes, there is an everlasting kingdom, whose meaning the "son of man" (7:13) is coming to reveal, and in which all realities acquire their true nature. The new order associated with the resurrection can already be glimpsed: the martyrs will live with God (12:2). While it is useless to seek in Daniel for a means of calculating the coming of the end of time, the Book, by reason of its special literary genre, does offer a message of hope for those who struggle and suffer for justice, for the true reign of God. It has had a strong influence on later apocalyptic writings and especially on Christian apocalypses.

The Book of Daniel may be divided as follows:

I: Edifying Accounts: The Acts of Daniel and His Companions (1:1—6:29)
II: Apocalypse: Visions of Daniel concerning the Future (7:1—12:13)
III: Appendix (13:1—14:42)

I: EDIFYING ACCOUNTS: THE ACTS OF DANIEL AND HIS COMPANIONS*

A: Daniel and His Companions Trained for the King's Service

CHAPTER 1

The Food Test.* [1] In the third year of the reign of King Jehoiakim of Judah, Nebuchadnezzar, the king of Babylon, marched into Jerusalem and laid siege to it.* [a] [2] The Lord allowed King Jehoiakim of Judah to fall into his power, as well as some of the vessels of the temple of God, which he carried off to the land of Shinar and placed in the temple treasury of his own god. [b]

[3] Then the king commanded Ashpenaz, his chief eunuch, to bring into the palace some Israelites from the royal family and from the nobility; [4] young men who were handsome and without physical defects of any kind, possessing an aptitude for every branch of knowledge and with great insight, clearly showing the necessary competence to serve in the king's palace. Those so chosen were to be instructed in the language and the literature of the Chaldeans.

[5] The king designated a daily allotment of food and wine from the royal table for them. After having been educated for three years, they would enter the king's service. [6] Among these were Daniel, Hananiah, Mishael, and Azariah from the tribe of Judah. [7] The chief eunuch assigned them different names: Daniel would be called Belteshazzar, Hananiah would be called Shadrach, Mishael would be called Meshach, and Azariah would be called Abednego.

[8] However, Daniel was determined not to defile himself by partaking of food and wine from the royal table, and he pleaded with the chief eunuch to spare him this defilement. [c] [9] God influenced the eunuch to grant this favor and to treat Daniel with compassion. [d] [10] However, the eunuch said to Daniel, "I am afraid of my lord the king. He has specifically designated what food and drink are to be supplied to you. If he should notice that you appear to be notably thinner than the other young men of your age, he would probably issue a command that I be beheaded."

[11] Then Daniel said to the guard whom the eunuch had assigned to supervise Daniel, Hananiah, Mishael, and Azariah, [12] "Please test your servants for a period of ten days, during which we will be given only vegetables to eat and water to drink. [13] You can then compare our appearance with that of the young men who eat only the food designated by the king. Then deal with your servants and treat us in accordance with what you observe."

[14] The guard agreed to this proposal and tested them for a period of ten days. [15] At the end of the ten days they looked better nourished and healthier than any of the young men who had subsisted solely on the food provided by the king. [16] Therefore, the guard continued to withdraw the food and the wine they were to drink, and he provided them with vegetables. [17] To these four young men God gave knowledge and skill in every aspect of literature and learning. In addition, Daniel was given the gift of interpreting visions and dreams of every kind. [e]

[18] When the time arrived that the king had designated for their presentation to him, the eunuch brought all the young men into the

a 2 Ki 24:1; 2 Chr 36:6; Jer 25:1.—b Dan 5:2; Gen 10:10; 2 Ki 24:1; 2 Chr 36:7.—c 1 Mac 1:62.—d Gen 39:4, 21; Est 2:9.—e Gen 41:12.

1:1—6:29 Instead of simply asserting truths, the sacred author illustrates these with stories that contain lessons. On the basis of his rather inaccurate knowledge of history, he imagines some young Jewish men at a pagan court, in the setting of the Babylonian and Persian regimes; these young men *do not lack physical gifts, education, courage, and, above all, faith.* Among these a certain Daniel stands out.

1:1-21 A well-told little incident that encourages Jews to remain faithful to the law of Moses: let them refuse to adopt the pagan customs that Antiochus wants to impose on them. God will reward their fidelity (see 2 Mac 6:18; 7:42).

1:1 The verse combines two expeditions of Nebuchadnezzar against Jerusalem, one in the third year of his reign (605 B.C.), the other in 598–597 B.C., when he captured the city and took away its sacred vessels. He also took away King Jehoiachin, who had very recently succeeded Jehoiakim; it was against the latter, who had rebelled, that the king of Babylon had been moving (see 2 Ki 24:1, 10-16; 2 Chr 36:5-10).

presence of Nebuchadnezzar. 19 After the king had spoken with all of them, no one was found to compare with Daniel, Hananiah, Mishael, and Azariah. Therefore, all four of them were appointed to the king's court. 20 In regard to whatever point of wisdom or understanding the king would question them, he found them ten times better than all the magicians and enchanters throughout his entire kingdom. 21 Daniel remained there until the first year of the reign of King Cyrus.*[f]

B: Nebuchadnezzar's Dream of the Shattered Statue*

CHAPTER 2

The King's Dream. 1 During the second year of his reign, King Nebuchadnezzar had a dream that troubled him deeply and made sleep impossible. 2 Therefore, the king commanded that the magicians, the sorcerers, and the Chaldeans* were to be summoned to interpret his dream. When they arrived and stood in his presence, 3 he said to them, "I have had a dream, and my mind is troubled because I have been unable to interpret it." 4 The Chaldeans replied to the king in Aramaic,* "May you live forever, O king. Relate your dream to us, your servants, and we will reveal its meaning to you."

5 The king answered the Chaldeans, "This is what I have decided to do. If you are unable to tell me both the dream I had and its meaning, I will command that you be torn limb from limb, and your houses will be totally destroyed. 6 However, if you are able to tell me what I dreamed and its meaning, I will present you with gifts, rewards, and great honors. Therefore, tell me the content of the dream and its meaning."

7 They replied a second time, "Let the king first reveal his dream to his servants, and we shall interpret its meaning for you." 8 But the king responded, "It is clear to me that you are stalling for time, since you know what I have already resolved to do. 9 If you are unable to interpret my dream for me, there will only be one verdict for you. You have obviously decided to stall for time in the hope that some compromise may be reached. Therefore, relate the content of my dream to me so that I will be able to determine whether you can interpret it correctly."

10 The Chaldeans answered the king, "There is not a man on earth who can do what you request, O king. Never has there been a king, no matter how great or powerful, who has asked such a thing of any magician or enchanter or Chaldean. 11 What you are requiring of us is much too difficult, and no one can satisfy the king's demand except for the gods, whose dwelling is not among mortals."

12 On hearing this, the king flew into a violent rage and ordered that all the wise men of Babylon were to be put to death. 13 Therefore, the decree was issued for their execution, and a search was also made for Daniel and his companions so that they also might be executed.

14 As Arioch, the commander of the king's guard, prepared to execute the wise men of Babylon, Daniel approached him, and with prudent words and discretion 15 he said to him, "May I ask you why the king has issued such a harsh decree?" When Arioch explained what had occurred, 16 Daniel went off and asked the king to decree a stay of execution so that he might have the opportunity to offer his interpretation to the king.

The Prayer of Daniel. 17 Then Daniel went home and informed his companions, Hananiah, Mishael, and Azariah, what had happened. 18 He also asked them to implore the God of heaven* for his mercy in regard to the mystery so that he and his companions might not perish along with the rest of the wise men of Babylon. 19 Then the mystery was revealed to Daniel in a vision during the night, and Daniel blessed the God of heaven. 20 This is what Daniel said,

f Dan 6:28.

1:21 *The first year of the reign of King Cyrus:* that is, 539 B.C., the year of Cyrus's conquest of Babylon.

2:1-49 How was the author to circulate subversive writings on the coming end of the reign of Antiochus IV, without naming the king? How was he to proclaim the coming of God's reign, when a pagan prince was in control? Here is one of the stories that, doubtless, circulated behind the king's back. To a small extent it makes use of the story of Joseph at the pharaoh's court (Gen 41), but draws more direct and important conclusions. In this allegory, dreams, which the ancients considered a means used by divinities to communicate with human beings, play an important part. Dreams serve chiefly as a literary device for writers of apocalypses, such as the Book of Daniel.

2:2 *Chaldeans:* some Chaldeans studied astrology.

2:4 *Aramaic:* from this verse to the end of chapter 7, the original is written in Aramaic, the current language of the period.

2:18 *God of heaven:* a title frequently used in the Persian period for the true God, Yahweh; Daniel and his companions ask mercy from this God.

"Blessed be the name of God forever and
ever,
for wisdom and power are his.[g]
21 He directs the changes of the times and
seasons;
he controls the appointment and the
removal of kings.
He endows the wise with wisdom
and confers knowledge on those who
have understanding.[h]
22 He reveals deep and hidden mysteries
and knows what lies in the darkness,
for light dwells with him.[i]
23 To you, O God of my fathers,
I offer thanks and praise
because you have given me wisdom
and power.
Now you have made known to me
what we asked of you;
you have revealed to us the king's
dream."

The Statue Turned Upside Down. 24 * Then
Daniel went to Arioch, whom the king had
designated to execute the wise men of
Babylon, and he said to him, "Do not put
the wise men of Babylon to death. Bring
me into the presence of the king, and I will
reveal to him the interpretation of the
dream."
25 Arioch immediately brought Daniel to
the king and said to him, "Among the exiles
from Judah I have located a man who can
reveal the meaning of the dream to the
king." 26 The king said to Daniel, "Are you
able to tell me the dream that I experienced
and to reveal its meaning to me?"
27 Daniel stood in the king's presence and
replied, "None of the wise men, the en-
chanters, the sorcerers, or the astrologers
has been able to explain to the king the
dream about which you have been so dis-
turbed. 28 However, there is a God in heaven
who reveals mysteries, and he has disclosed
to King Nebuchadnezzar what is to take
place at the end of this age. These were the
dreams and the visions that passed through
your head as you lay in your bed.[j]
29 "While you were lying there, O king,
thoughts came to you about what would
happen in the future, and the revealer of
mysteries showed you what will take place.
30 This mystery has been revealed to me, not
because I have greater wisdom than any liv-
ing person, but for the sole purpose that the
interpretation may be made known to you
and also that you may understand the
thoughts that have entered your mind.
31 "In the vision that you had, Your
Majesty, you beheld a huge statue that was
dazzling in its brightness. It stood before
you, frightening in its appearance. 32 The
head of the statue was of fine gold, its chest
and its arms were of silver, its belly and its
thighs were of bronze, 33 its legs were of iron,
and its feet were partly of iron and partly of
clay.
34 "While you were gazing at the statue, a
stone broke away, untouched by any human
hand, and struck the statue on its feet of iron
and clay, shattering them to pieces. 35 Then
the iron, the clay, the bronze, the silver, and
the gold were all shattered into pieces as fine
as the chaff on the threshing floor during the
summer.[k] The wind carried them away
without leaving a trace. However, the stone
that struck the statue became a great moun-
tain and filled the entire earth.
36 "That was the dream. Now we shall offer
to the king its interpretation. 37 Your Maj-
esty, you are the king of kings to whom the
God of heaven has given the kingdom with
its power, its might, and its glory. 38 He has
entrusted to your care men, wild beasts, and
birds of the air, wherever they may dwell.
You are the head of gold.[l]
39 "After you another kingdom will arise,
inferior to yours, followed by a third king-
dom of bronze, which shall rule over the
whole earth. 40 There will then be a fourth
kingdom, as strong as iron. Just as iron
crushes and smashes everything to pieces, it
will crush and pulverize all the other king-
doms.[m]
41 "Like the feet and the toes that you saw,
composed partly of potter's clay and partly
of iron, it shall be a divided kingdom, but it
will have some of the strength of iron just as
you saw the iron mixed with the clay tile.
42 And as the toes of the feet were partly iron
and partly potter's clay, the kingdom will be

g Neh 9:5; Job 12:13; Ps 41:14; Rev 5:12.—h Prov 2:6; Acts 1:7; Rom 13:1.—i Ps 139:11f; Jn 1:9; 8:12; 1 Cor 4:5; 1 Jn 1:6-7.—j 1 Cor 2:10f; Rev 1:1, 19; 4:1.—k Ps 1:4.—l Jer 27:6.—m Dan 7:7; 8:5, 21; 11:3.

2:24-25 This odd statue, the parts of which are listed in order of decreasing value, may simply illustrate the sequence of the ages of the world. The present story describes the succession of human empires from Nebuchadnezzar to Antiochus IV. The last of these regimes is the weakest, and the linking by marriage of the Greek sovereigns of Egypt (the Ptolemies) and those of Antioch (the Seleucids) is unable to restore a balance among the successors of Alexander. God will finally destroy these regimes and establish another kingdom, his own, which will be everlasting.

partly strong and partly brittle. 43 And just as
you saw the iron mixed with the clay, so will
the people mix together in marriage, but
they will not remain united, just as iron does
not mix with clay.
44 "In the times of those kings, the God of
heaven shall establish a kingdom that will
never be destroyed, nor shall this kingdom
fall under the power of another people. It
shall crush all these kingdoms and bring
them to an end, and it shall endure forever.[n]
45 This is the meaning of your vision of the
stone untouched by human hands being
hewn from the mountain and crushing the
iron, the bronze, the clay, the silver, and the
gold. The great God has shown the king what
will take place in the future. The dream is
true, and its interpretation is trustworthy."

**Nebuchadnezzar Prostrates Himself before
God.** 46 Then King Nebuchadnezzar fell pros-
trate and paid homage to Daniel, and he
gave orders that a grain offering and incense
be presented to him. 47 The king said to
Daniel, "Truly your God is the God of gods,
the Lord of kings, and the revealer of mys-
teries. That is why you were able to reveal
this mystery."
48 Then the king conferred a high rank on
Daniel and gave him many handsome gifts.
He also appointed him ruler over the whole
province of Babylon and chief prefect over
all the wise men of Babylon. 49 Furthermore,
at Daniel's request, the king appointed
Shadrach, Meshach, and Abednego as admin-
istrators of the province of Babylon. However,
Daniel remained at the king's court.

CHAPTER 3

C: The Three Young Men in the Fiery Furnace*

The Trial of Daniel's Companions.* 1 King
Nebuchadnezzar ordered a golden statue*
to be made, sixty cubits high and six cubits
wide, and he decreed that it be placed on the
plain of Dura in the province of Babylon.
2 King Nebuchadnezzar then commanded
the satraps, the prefects, the governors,
the counselors, the treasurers, the judges, the
magistrates, and all the officials of the
provinces to assemble for the dedication of
the statue that he had set up. 3 Therefore, the
satraps, the prefects, the governors, the coun-
selors, the treasurers, the judges, the magis-
trates, and all the officials of the provinces
assembled for the dedication of the statue
that King Nebuchadnezzar had set up.
4 Then a herald proclaimed in a loud
voice, "Peoples and nations of every lan-
guage: when you hear the sound of the horn,
flute, lyre, zither, harp, bagpipe, and every
other musical instrument, 5 you are com-
manded to prostrate yourselves and worship
the golden statue set up by King Nebu-
chadnezzar. 6 Anyone who refuses to pros-
trate himself and worship shall immediately
be thrown into a blazing furnace."
7 Therefore, as soon as they heard the
sound of the horn, flute, lyre, zither, harp,
bagpipe, and every other musical instru-
ment, all the peoples and nations of every
language prostrated themselves and wor-
shiped the golden statue that King Nebu-
chadnezzar had set up.
8 Immediately some Chaldeans came for-
ward before the king and made a malicious
accusation against the Jews. 9 They said to
King Nebuchadnezzar, "O king, may you live
forever! 10 You have issued a decree, Your
Majesty, that when the people hear the
sound of the horn, flute, lyre, zither, harp,
bagpipe, and every other musical instru-
ment, they are to prostrate themselves and
worship the golden statue, 11 and that who-
ever fails to do so is to be cast into a furnace
of blazing fire.
12 "Now there are certain Jews whom you
have put in charge of the affairs of the
province of Babylon. These men, Shadrach,
Meshach, and Abednego, have ignored your
command, O king. They do not serve your
God, and they refuse to worship the golden
statue that you have set up."
13 On hearing this, Nebuchadnezzar be-
came infuriated and was filled with rage,
and he sent for Shadrach, Meshach, and

n 2 Sam 7:16; Mt 21:44; Lk 1:33; 20:18.

3:1-97 Another story of resistance that was very likely clandestine. Is the story a legend? Perhaps, but it was written at a dramatic moment. The purpose of the story is primarily to encourage an absolute rejection of idolatry, at the cost, if necessary, of martyrdom.

The prayer of Azariah and the canticle of the three young men, which make up these verses, are inspired additions to the Aramaic text of Daniel, translated from the Greek form of the Book. Their original (in Hebrew or Aramaic) is not extant. The Church regards them as part of the canonical Scriptures.

3:1-23 The author plays with history: he speaks of Nebuchadnezzar but he is thinking of Antiochus, the king diseased by his greatness and pride.

3:1 *Golden statue:* the colossus was about ninety feet tall and nine feet wide.

Abednego. When the three men were brought
into his presence, 14 King Nebuchadnezzar
said to them, "Is it true, Shadrach, Meshach,
and Abednego, that you do not serve my god
or worship the golden statue that I have set
up? 15 When you hear the sound of the horn,
flute, lyre, zither, harp, bagpipe, and every
other musical instrument, are you ready to
fall down and worship the statue that I have
made? If you refuse to worship it, you shall be
immediately thrown into a furnace of blazing
fire. What god is there that can deliver you
from my power?"

16 Shadrach, Meshach, and Abednego
replied to King Nebuchadnezzar, "There is
no need for us to defend ourselves to you in
this regard. 17 If our God, whom we serve, is
able to deliver us from the white-hot blazing
furnace and from your power, O king, let
him deliver us. [o] 18 But even if he does not do
so, Your Majesty, be assured that we will not
serve your god or worship the golden statue
you have set up."

19 This reply so infuriated Nebuchadnez-
zar against Shadrach, Meshach, and Abed-
nego that his countenance became distorted.
He ordered that the furnace was to be heat-
ed seven times more than customary, 20 and
he commanded some of the strongest sol-
diers in his army to bind Shadrach, Meshach,
and Abednego and hurl them into the fiery
furnace.

21 The three young men were then bound
while still wearing their cloaks, their
trousers, their head coverings, and their
other garments and thrown into the fiery
furnace. 22 Because the king's command was
so urgent and the heat of the furnace was so
intense, the raging flames killed the men
who were carrying Shadrach, Meshach, and
Abednego. 23 However, the three young men,
Shadrach, Meshach, and Abednego, fell,
bound, into the fiery furnace.

D: Two Inspired Additions of Prayer Texts

The Prayer of Azariah.* 24 [p] They walked
amidst the flames, all the while singing
hymns to God and blessing the Lord.
25 Azariah then stood up, surrounded by
flames, and said this prayer:

26 "Blessed are you and deserving of all
praise,
O Lord, the God of our fathers,
and glorious is your name forever. [q]
27 For you have shown justice in all you
have done for us;
all your deeds are true, all your ways
are right,
and all your judgments are correct. [r]
28 You have made proper judgments
in all that you have brought upon us
and upon Jerusalem, the holy city of
our ancestors.
By a judgment, you have done all this
because of our sins.
29 "For we have sinned and broken your law
in our rebellion against you;
we have fallen short in every way. [s]
30 We have neglected to obey your com-
mandments
and have failed to do what you com-
manded for our own good.
31 [t] Therefore, in all the misfortunes you
have inflicted upon us,
in all you have done to us,
you have executed proper judg-
ments.
32 You have handed us over to our ene-
mies,
lawless and godless rebels,
and to a wicked king, the most evil in
the entire world.
33 "Now we cannot open our mouths;
we, your servants who worship you,
have become a cause of shame and
dishonor.
34 For your name's sake, do not abandon us
forever
or renounce your covenant. [u]
35 Do not withdraw your mercy from us
for the love of Abraham, your friend,
Isaac, your servant, and Israel, your
holy one, [v]
36 to whom you spoke, promising to make
their descendants
as numerous as the stars in the heavens
and the grains of sand on the sea-
shore. [w]

o Ps 37:39f.—p Dan 9:3-19; Ezr 9:6-15.—q Dan 4:34; 1 Chr 29:10, 20.—r Neh 9:33; Tob 3:2-6; Rev 16:7; 19:2.—s Dan 9:5-8; Neh 1:7; Isa 59:12ff; Bar 1:17ff.—t 31-33: Lev 26:14-38; Deut 28:15, 63ff.—u Ex 32:11-13.—v 2 Chr 20:7; Isa 41:8; Jas 2:23.—w Gen 15:5; 22:17.

3:24-50 The condemned men are kept safe from the flames by an angel, through a special intervention of God who does not abandon his own to the madness of the wicked. The canticle, which is found only in Greek manuscripts, is a collective lament, filled with biblical echoes and well adapted to times of persecution.

37 "For we, O Lord, have become the least of all nations,
humiliated throughout the world in our day
because of our sins. [x]
38 We now have no ruler, no prophet, no leader,
no burnt offering or sacrifice or oblation of incense,
no place to make an offering before you and to find mercy. [y]
39 But may we be accepted by you
as we approach you with a contrite heart
and with a submissive spirit. [z]
40 As though we were presenting burnt offerings of rams and bulls
or thousands of fat lambs,
so may our sacrifice be in your presence today
as we follow you unreservedly,
for those who trust in you will never be put to shame. [a]
41 "And now with all our heart we shall follow you;
even though we fear you, we seek your face.
42 Do not let us be put to shame,
but deal with us in your patience
and in your great mercy.
43 Deliver us by your wonderful deeds,
and let your name be glorified, O Lord.
44 Let those who harm your servants be brought low;
let them be put to shame and rendered powerless,
and may their strength be crushed. [b]
45 Let them know that you alone are the Lord God,
glorious throughout the whole world." [c]

46 Now the king's servants who had thrown
the three young men into the furnace con-
tinued to stoke it with brimstone, pitch, tow,
and brushwood 47 until the flames rose forty-
nine cubits above the furnace 48 and spread
out, burning to death those Chaldeans who
were standing nearby. 49 But the angel of the
Lord came down into the furnace where
Azariah and his companions had been cast.
He drove the fiery flames out of the furnace
50 and made the inside of the furnace as
though a dewy breeze was wafting through
it. The fire did not touch them in the least
way and caused them no pain or harm.

The Canticle of the Three Young Men.*
51 Then those three men in the furnace began to sing in unison, glorifying and blessing God:

52 "Blessed are you, Lord, the God of our ancestors,
worthy of praise and glory forever.
Blessed is your holy and glorious name,
worthy of praise and glory forever. [d]
53 Blessed are you in the temple of your holy glory,
worthy of praise and glory forever. [e]
54 Blessed are you on the throne of your kingdom,
worthy of praise and glory forever.
55 Blessed are you who behold the depths
from your throne upon the cherubim,
worthy of praise and glory forever. [f]
56 Blessed are you in the firmament of heaven,
worthy of praise and glory forever.

57 "Bless the Lord, all you works of the Lord;
praise and exalt him forever. [g]
58 Angels of the Lord, bless the Lord;
praise and exalt him forever. [h]
59 You heavens, bless the Lord;
praise and exalt him forever. [i]
60 All you waters above the heavens, bless the Lord;
praise and exalt him forever.
61 All you powers of the Lord, bless the Lord;
praise and exalt him forever. [j]
62 Sun and moon, bless the Lord;
praise and exalt him forever. [k]
63 Stars of heaven, bless the Lord;
praise and exalt him forever.

64 "All rain and dew, bless the Lord;
praise and exalt him forever.
65 All you winds, bless the Lord;
praise and exalt him forever. [l]

---

x Deut 28:62; Jer 42:2.—y Lam 2:9; Hos 3:4.—z Ps 51:19; Hos 6:6; Mic 6:7f.—a Ps 25:3.—b Pss 35:26; 40:15.—c Ps 83:18.—d Dan 3:26.—e Ps 150:1; Isa 6:1.—f Ex 25:18; 2 Sam 6:2.—g Pss 103:22; 145:10.—h Pss 103:20; 148:2.—i Ps 148:4.—j Ps 145:1.—k Ps 148:3.—l Ps 148:8.

3:51-90 This second canticle, which is likewise found only in Greek manuscripts, is a lengthy canticle of praise. It brings together some of the most magnificent verses from the Psalms (Pss 103; 148; 150). The whole of creation is urged to take part in this great symphony.

66 Fire and heat, bless the Lord;
praise and exalt him forever.
67 Cold and chill, bless the Lord;
praise and exalt him forever.
68 Dew and rain, bless the Lord;
praise and exalt him forever.
69 Frost and chill, bless the Lord;
praise and exalt him forever.
70 Ice and snow, bless the Lord;
praise and exalt him forever.
71 Nights and days, bless the Lord;
praise and exalt him forever.
72 Light and darkness, bless the Lord;
praise and exalt him forever.
73 Lightning and clouds, bless the Lord;
praise and exalt him forever. [m]
74 "Let the earth bless the Lord;
praise and exalt him forever.
75 Mountains and hills, bless the Lord;
praise and exalt him forever.
76 Every plant that grows, bless the Lord;
praise and exalt him forever.
77 Springs of water, bless the Lord;
praise and exalt him forever.
78 Seas and rivers, bless the Lord;
praise and exalt him forever.
79 Dolphins and all creatures that live in water, bless the Lord;
praise and exalt him forever.
80 Every kind of bird, bless the Lord;
praise and exalt him forever.
81 All animals, wild and tame, bless the Lord;
praise and exalt him forever. [n]

82 "All the human race, bless the Lord;
praise and exalt him forever.
83 O Israel, bless the Lord;
praise and exalt him forever. [o]
84 You priests of the Lord, bless the Lord;
praise and exalt him forever.
85 You servants of the Lord, bless the Lord;
praise and exalt him forever. [p]
86 Spirits and souls of the upright, bless the Lord;
praise and exalt him forever.
87 You who are holy and humble in heart, bless the Lord;
praise and exalt him forever.

88 "Hananiah, Azariah, and Mishael, bless the Lord;
praise and exalt him forever.
For he has rescued us from the netherworld
and saved us from the power of death.
He has liberated us from the fiery furnace,
and from the fire he has delivered us.
89 Give thanks to the Lord, for he is good,
for his mercy endures forever. [q]
90 Bless the God of gods, all you who fear the Lord;
praise him and give thanks to him,
for his mercy endures forever."

The Miracle Is Accomplished.* 91 Then King
Nebuchadnezzar leaped to his feet in amazement and asked his advisors, "Weren't there three men that we tied up and threw into the fire?"

They replied, "Certainly, O king."
92 He said, "Look! I see four men walking around in the fire, unbound and unharmed, and the fourth looks like a son of God." *
93 Nebuchadnezzar then approached the opening of the blazing furnace and shouted, "Shadrach, Meshach, and Abednego, servants of the Most High God, come out! Come here!"

So Shadrach, Meshach, and Abednego came out of the fire,
94 and the satraps, prefects, governors, and royal advisors crowded around them. They saw that the fire had not harmed their bodies, nor was a hair of their heads singed; their robes were not scorched, and there was no smell of fire on them.
95 Then Nebuchadnezzar said, "Praise be to the God of Shadrach, Meshach, and Abednego, who has sent his angel and rescued his servants! They trusted in him and defied the king's command and were willing to give up their lives rather than serve or worship any god except their own God.
96 Therefore, I decree that the people of any nation or language who say anything against the God of Shadrach, Meshach, and Abednego be cut into pieces and their houses be turned into piles of rubble, for no other God can save in this way." [r]

m Ps 148:8.—n Ps 148:10.—o Ps 135:19.—p Ps 134:1.—q Pss 106:1; 136:1.—r Dan 6:27.

3:91-97 Nebuchadnezzar, who is really Antiochus IV, is compelled to acknowledge the true God. The miracle seems to reward appeals inspired by limitless faith, such as we find in the psalter (Ps 70:1) and in Isaiah (Isa 43:2). Mentions of this story in the Letter to the Hebrews (Heb 11:34) and in the Quran (85) attest to its popularity.

3:92 *A son of God:* other versions have "a son of the gods."

97 Then the king promoted Shadrach,
Meshach, and Abednego in the province of
Babylon.

E: King Nebuchadnezzar's Madness

Vision of the Great Tree. 98 King Nebuchad-
nezzar, to the nations and peoples of every
language dwelling throughout the entire
world: May you prosper abundantly. 99 I am
pleased to make known the signs and won-
ders with which I have been favored by the
Most High God.

100 How great are his signs,
how mighty are his wonders.
His kingdom is an everlasting kingdom,
and his sovereignty endures through all generations.[s]

CHAPTER 4*

1 * I, Nebuchadnezzar, was living in con-
tentment at home and enjoying the luxury of
my palaces. 2 However, as I lay in my bed, I
had a dream that frightened me, and the
visions that I experienced in my mind were
a source of torment.

3 Therefore, I issued a decree that all the
wise men of Babylon were to be brought
before me and offer me their interpretation
of the dream. 4 When the magicians, the
soothsayers, the Chaldeans, and the diviners
arrived, I related to them the content of the
dream, but they were unable to explain its
meaning.

5 Finally Daniel, whom I had renamed
Belteshazzar, after the name of my god and
in whom resides the Spirit of the holy God,
came into my presence, and I related to him
my dream.[t] 6 "O Belteshazzar, chief of the
magicians, I know that the Spirit of the holy
God resides in you and that no mystery is
too difficult for you to resolve. Listen to the
dream that I experienced, and tell me its
interpretation.

7 "These were the visions that came to me
as I lay in my bed:

"I beheld a tree at the center of the earth,
and its height was great.[u]

8 The tree became ever taller and stronger
until its top reached the heavens,
and it was visible to the ends of the earth.

9 Its foliage was beautiful,
and its fruit was abundant,
providing fruit for all.
The wild beasts found shade under it,
the birds of the air rested in its branches,
and from it all living creatures were nourished.[v]

10 "In the vision I saw as I lay in my bed, I
next beheld a holy sentinel coming down
from heaven. 11 He shouted loudly:

"'Hew down the tree and lop off its branches;
strip off its foliage and scatter its fruit.

12 However, leave the stump and its roots in the ground,
bound with iron and bronze
in the grass of the field.
Let him be bathed by the dew of heaven,
and let his lot be to eat, among wild beasts,
the grass of the earth.

13 Let his mind be changed from that of a human,
and let the mind of a beast be given to him,
until seven years pass over him.

14 'Such is the sentence decreed by the sentinel,
the verdict announced by the holy ones,
so that all who live may learn
that the Most High rules over the kingdom of mortals.
He confers it on whomever he wishes
and appoints over it the lowliest of men.'[w]

15 "This is the dream that I, King Nebu-
chadnezzar, had. Now I am depending upon
you, Belteshazzar, to interpret its meaning,
although none of the wise men in my king-

s Dan 2:44; 4:31; 7:14.—t Dan 5:11, 14; 13:45; Gen 41:38.—u Ezek 31:3-14.—v Ezek 17:23; Mt 13:31f.—w 1 Sam 2:8; 16:11-13; Job 36:7; Jer 27:5.

4:1-34 There do exist, in fact, some documents about a king who withdrew for some years to an oasis and who consulted a Jewish seer. This would be Nabonidus, who reigned a half-century after Nebuchadnezzar (556–539 B.C.). Everyone knows of the immense pride of Nebuchadnezzar, who turned his city into one of the wonders of the world. In our story, the author has drawn on recollections and information that were not accurate, while reserving the right to attribute everything to the person with whom he is concerned, Nebuchadnezzar.

4:1-18 The king is tormented by the way in which a tree, the symbol par excellence of life and immortality (see Gen 3:9), is treated in his dream. In the Bible, a tree serves also to describe the destiny of a person, of a sovereign (Pss 1:3; 37:35; Ezek 31). By reserving to Daniel the responsibility for interpreting the king's nightmare, the author shows the superiority of Jewish wisdom in explaining the difficult mysteries of human existence.

dom can interpret its meaning, you can do
so because the Spirit of the holy God resides
in you."

Daniel Interprets the Dream.* 16 Then Daniel,
who was called Belteshazzar, was greatly
upset and confused. The king said, "Bel-
teshazzar, do not allow the dream and its
meaning to terrify you." Belteshazzar re-
plied, "My lord, may the dream be meant for
those who hurt you, and its interpretation
for your enemies. 17 The tree that you saw,
which grew great and strong, with its top
reaching the sky so that it could be seen
throughout the entire earth, 18 a tree with
beautiful foliage and abundant fruit, provid-
ing food for all and affording shade for the
wild beasts, with the birds of heaven dwelling
in its branches—19 that tree is you, O king.
You have grown great and strong. Your power
has increased and now reaches the sky; your
sovereignty extends to the ends of the earth.

20 "In regard to the king's vision of a holy
sentinel descending from heaven and saying:
'Cut down the tree and destroy it, but leave
the stump and its roots in the ground, bound
with iron and bronze, in the grass of the
field; let him be bathed by the dew of heav-
en, and let his lot be with the wild beasts
until seven years pass over him,' 21 this is
the interpretation, O king. It is a decree that
the Most High has issued upon my lord the
king:

22 "You will be banished from human so-
ciety,
and you will dwell among the wild ani-
mals.
You will be forced to eat grass like oxen,
and you will be drenched with the dew
of heaven.
Seven years will pass over you
until you have learned
that the Most High rules over the king-
dom of men
and gives it to whomever he wishes. [x]

23 "As for the command to leave un-
touched the stump and the roots of the tree,
this means that your kingdom will once
again be subject to your rule once you come
to acknowledge the sovereignty of Heaven.*
24 May the king be willing to take my advice.
Atone for your sins with deeds of righteous-
ness, and for your iniquities with mercy to
the oppressed. If you do so, you will enjoy a
long and peaceful life."* [y]

The Dream Is Fulfilled. 25 All this happened
to King Nebuchadnezzar. 26 At the end of
twelve months, as he was walking on the roof
of the royal palace, 27 the king said, "How
magnificent Babylon is! Was it not built as a
royal residence by my mighty strength and
for my majestic glory?"*

28 These words were not completely out of
his mouth when a voice came from heaven:

"To you, King Nebuchadnezzar, it is de-
creed:
your kingdom has been taken from
you.
29 You shall be banished from human so-
ciety
as you are forced to dwell with wild
beasts
and feed on grass as the oxen do.
Seven years shall pass over you
until you have learned
that the Most High rules over the king-
dom of men
and gives it to whomever he wishes."

30 This sentence was immediately ful-
filled. Nebuchadnezzar was cast out from
human society, and he ate grass as oxen do.
His body was drenched with the dew of
heaven until his hair grew like the feathers
of an eagle and his nails became like a bird's
talons.

31 When the period was over, I, Nebu-
chadnezzar, raised my eyes to heaven and
my power of reasoning was restored to me.

I blessed the Most High,
and I praised and glorified him
who lives forever. [z]
32 All who dwell on earth count for noth-
ing;
he does as he pleases with the powers
of heaven*
and the inhabitants on earth.

x Dan 5:21.—y Sir 3:30; 4:8.—z Dan 3:100; 7:14.

4:16-24 This is a kind of prophecy that announces the lot reserved for Nebuchadnezzar: this most prestigious and most acclaimed of kings will undergo a trial before being converted unless he changes his present ways.

4:23 God is called *Heaven* in order not to profane God's name by uttering it; to him alone, dominion belongs.

4:24 A classic locus for the doctrine of the efficacy of good works.

4:27 The words of the king are similar to those found in royal inscriptions of the Mesopotamian kings.

4:32 *The powers of heaven* are the heavenly creatures.

No one can stay his hand
or say to him, "What are you doing?" [a]

33 At that very moment my power of rea-
son returned to me, and my glory and
splendor were restored to me. My coun-
selors and my lords sought my counsel. I
was reestablished in my kingdom, and my
power was greatly increased.

34 Therefore, now I, Nebuchadnezzar,
praise and exalt and glorify
the King of heaven.
For all of his works are right,
and all of his ways are just.
Also, he is able to humble
all those who follow the path of pride. [b]

F: Belshazzar's Banquet*

CHAPTER 5

The Writing on the Wall. 1 King Belshazzar
hosted a magnificent banquet for a thousand
of his nobles, and he was drinking wine in
their presence. 2 Under the influence of the
wine, he gave orders that the gold and silver
vessels that his father Nebuchadnezzar had
taken out of the temple in Jerusalem were to
be brought in so that the king, his nobles, his
wives, and his concubines might drink from
them.

3 Therefore, the gold and silver vessels that
had been removed from the temple, the
house of God in Jerusalem, were brought in,
and the king, his nobles, his wives, and his
concubines drank from them. 4 They drank
their wine and praised their gods of gold and
silver, of bronze and iron, of wood and stone.

5 Suddenly, the fingers of a human hand
appeared and began to write on the plaster
of the wall of the royal palace next to the
lampstand, and the king watched the hand
as it wrote. [c] 6 Then the king turned pale, and
his thoughts terrified him. His legs grew
limp, and his knees began to knock.

7 Then the king shouted aloud, ordering
the enchanters, the Chaldeans, and the
astrologers to be brought in. When they
entered, he addressed the wise men of
Babylon and said, "Whoever can read this
writing and tell me its interpretation shall be
clothed in purple, wear a gold chain around
his neck, and rank third in the government
of the kingdom."

8 However, none of the king's wise men
could either read the writing or explain to
the king what it meant. 9 Then King
Belshazzar became greatly terrified. His
face grew even more pale, and his lords were
in a state of confusion.

10 When the queen heard the commotion
made by the king and his lords, she came
into the banqueting hall and said, "May Your
Majesty live forever. Do not let your thoughts
terrify you. Why should you look so pale? 11 In
your kingdom there is a man who has with-
in him the Spirit of the holy God. During
your father's lifetime this man was re-
nowned for his enlightenment, insight, and
godlike wisdom, and to such. a degree that
King Nebuchadnezzar, your father, appoint-
ed him as chief of the magicians, enchanters,
Chaldeans, and diviners. [d]

12 "Therefore, since this Daniel, whom the
king named Belteshazzar, has a keen mind,
and is endowed with knowledge and under-
standing and the ability to interpret dreams,
explain riddles, and solve difficult problems,
summon him. He will be able to give you the
interpretation you seek."

13 Then Daniel was brought into the king's
presence. The king said to him, "Are you the
Daniel who was one of the Jewish exiles that
my father the king brought from Judah? 14 I
have been told that the Spirit of God is in
you, and that you are renowned for your
knowledge, understanding, and exceptional
wisdom.

15 "Now the wise men and the enchanters
have been brought in to me to read this writ-
ing and reveal its meaning to me, but they
have been unable to interpret it. 16 Yet I have
been told that you can give interpretations
and solve problems. If you are able to read
this writing and make known its interpreta-

a Job 9:12; Eccl 8:4; Isa 40:22-24; 45:9; Rom 9:20.—b Dan 3:27; Deut 32:4.—c Dan 5:24-28.—d Dan 4:5.

5:1-30 If there was a historical Belshazzar, he was the son of Nabonidus, not of Nebuchadnezzar; in any case, he was not given an opportunity to ascend the throne, but simply substituted for his father until Babylon fell in 539 B.C. under the blows of Cyrus the Persian, who had first subdued the Medes. The text speaks of Darius the Mede (6:1), but the only Dariuses known to history were all Persians. It is not a matter of concern that the author mixes up overly vague historical memories. His purpose is a different one: to denounce once more the human pride that claims the right to laugh at God. On the figure of Belshazzar are imposed the characteristics of Antiochus IV, who sacked temples, profaned things holy, and had himself worshiped as a god, while haughtily controlling the destiny of human beings (see 1 Mac 1:16-64; 6:1-5; 2 Mac 3:1-40; 5:11-20; 9:2).

tion, you shall be clothed in purple, have a
chain of gold around your neck, and rank
third in the government of the kingdom."

Daniel Explains the Writing. 17 Then Daniel
replied to the king, "Your Majesty, keep the
gifts for yourself or give them to someone
else. However, I will read the writing to Your
Majesty and make known to you its inter-
pretation.

18 "O king, the Most High God gave your
father Nebuchadnezzar a kingdom with
power, glory, and majesty. 19 He made him so
powerful that the nations and peoples of
every language trembled with fear before
him. He killed those whom he wished to kill;
he spared those whom he wished to spare; he
honored those whom he wished to honor,
and he degraded those whom he wished to
degrade.

20 "However, when his heart became filled
with pride and his spirit became hardened
with arrogance, he was deposed from his
kingly throne and stripped of his glory. 21 He
was banished from human society, and his
mind became like that of an animal. He was
forced to live with the wild asses, he fed on
grass like oxen, and his body was drenched
with the dew of heaven, until he learned that
the Most High God has sovereignty over the
kingdom of men and appoints whomever he
wishes to rule it. [e]

22 "Even though you, Belshazzar, his son,
were aware of all this, you did not humble
your heart. 23 You have exalted yourself
against the Lord of heaven. You ordered the
vessels of his temple to be brought to you,
and you, your nobles, your wives, and your
concubines have drunk your wine from
them. You have praised the gods of silver and
gold, of bronze and iron, of wood and stone,
that neither see, nor hear, nor have intelli-
gence. But you have not glorified the God in
whose hands are your breath of life and the
entire course of your life. [f]

24 "That is why he sent the hand that wrote
the inscription. 25 The words inscribed are
MENE, TEKEL, and *PERES.** This is what the
words mean:

26 "*MENE:* God has numbered the days of
your kingdom and brought it to an end.

27 "*TEKEL:* you have been weighed on the
scales and been found wanting.

28 "*PERES:* your kingdom has been divided
and given to the Medes and Persians."

29 Then, at Belshazzar's command, Daniel
was clothed in purple, with a gold chain
around his neck, and a proclamation was
made declaring that Daniel would rank third
in the government of the kingdom.

30 On that very night Belshazzar, the king
of the Chaldeans, was slain.

G: Daniel in the Lions' Den*

CHAPTER 6

The Plot against Daniel. 1 Darius the Mede
succeeded Belshazzar as king, at the age of
sixty-two. 2 It pleased Darius to appoint one
hundred and twenty satraps to rule through-
out his kingdom.* 3 Over them he designat-
ed three administrators, including Daniel, to
whom the satraps were to be accountable. In
this way the king's interests were to be safe-
guarded.

4 Daniel quickly became recognized as
superior to the other administrators and
satraps because of his exceptional qualities,
and the king decided to place him in charge
of the entire kingdom. 5 Therefore, the ad-
ministrators and the satraps tried to find
some grounds upon which they could bring
charges against Daniel. But they could find
no basis for complaint or the slightest evi-
dence of corruption on his part, because he
was so faithful in performing his duties that
there was no possibility of charging him with
negligence or corruption. 6 Therefore, they
concluded, "We shall never find any basis to
lodge a complaint against Daniel unless it is
in connection with his God."

7 As a result, these administrators and
satraps conspired together, and then they
came in a group to the king, saying, "May
King Darius live forever! 8 All of us, the min-
isters of the kingdom, the prefects and the
satraps, the counselors and the governors,

e Dan 4:22.—f Job 12:10.

5:25 The words of the inscription are names of weights or monies, allowing the play on words in the interpretation.

6:1-29 The Babylonian kings are followed by a Persian monarch. Because he has been advanced to high offices in the empire, Daniel has aroused the jealousy of other officials. His manner of praying becomes the basis for an accusation, and he is condemned. But the trust and fidelity of the righteous will be rewarded: Daniel will be saved. Moreover—and this is the apologetic purpose of the story—the astonished king will make a public profession of faith in *the living God* who *delivers, rescues*, and will, himself, proclaim the unending reign of God (vv. 27-28).

6:2 The division of the empire into satraps was effected by Darius I of Persia in 521 B.C.

are unanimous in our belief that the king should issue an edict and enforce a decree that whoever presents a petition to anyone, whether divine or human, during the next thirty days, other than to you, O king, shall be thrown into a den of lions.[g] 9 We ask that Your Majesty ratify this edict immediately and sign the document, thereby making it unalterable, for the law of the Medes and the Persians cannot be revoked." 10 Therefore, King Darius signed the document, thereby establishing its contents as a law.

Daniel Continues To Pray. 11 Even after Daniel learned that the document had been signed, he continued his custom of retiring to his house, in which the windows in the upper room opened toward Jerusalem. Three times a day he fell to his knees, praying to God and giving him thanks, as he had always done.* 12 The conspirators, who were ever on the watch, broke into his room and found Daniel praying and pleading with God.[h]

13 The conspirators were then granted an audience with the king during which they reminded him of the royal edict. "Your Majesty," they said, "did you not sign a decree forbidding anyone for the next thirty days to present a petition to anyone, divine or human, except to you, O king, under the penalty of being thrown into the lions' den?" The king replied, "The decree stands, according to the law of the Medes and the Persians, which cannot be revoked." 14 Then they said to the king, "Daniel, one of the exiles from Judah, has totally disregarded both you, O king, and the decree you signed. He continues to offer his prayer three times a day."

15 When the king heard this, he was greatly distressed, and he became determined to save Daniel. Until sunset he made every effort possible to rescue him. 16 Meanwhile, the conspirators continued to press the king in this matter, saying, "Your Majesty surely must know that it is a law of the Medes and Persians that no edict or decree can be changed once it has been issued by the king."

Daniel Thrown into the Lions' Den. 17 Finally the king ordered Daniel to be brought forth and thrown into the den of lions, after first having said to Daniel, "May your God, whom you faithfully serve, deliver you." 18 A stone was then brought forward and placed over the mouth of the pit. The king sealed it with his own signet ring and with the rings of his nobles to forestall any tampering in an attempt to rescue Daniel.

19 Then the king returned to his palace and spent the night in fasting. He refused to receive any concubines into his chamber and found himself unable to sleep. 20 At the first light of dawn he stood up and hurried to the lions' den. 21 As he drew near, he cried out sorrowfully to Daniel, "O Daniel, servant of the living God, has your God, whom you serve so faithfully, been able to deliver you from the lions?"

22 Daniel answered the king, "May Your Majesty live forever![i] 23 My God sent his angel to seal the lions' jaws, and they were not able to harm me, because I was judged blameless before him. Nor have I done any harm to you, O king."[j]

24 The king was overcome with great joy, and he ordered that Daniel be taken up out of the lions' den. Therefore, Daniel was released from the den, and he was completely unhurt, because he had trusted in his God. 25 The king then commanded that the men who had accused Daniel were to be thrown into the lions' den, together with their wives and their children. Before they reached the bottom of the pit, the lions overpowered them and crushed all their bones.

The King's Profession of Faith. 26 Then King Darius wrote to the nations and peoples of every language throughout the entire world, "May your property increase. 27 I decree that throughout my royal domain everyone is to tremble and fear before the God of Daniel:

"For he is the living God,
enduring forever.
His kingdom will never be destroyed,
and his dominion shall be without end.[k]
28 He delivers, rescues,
and works signs and wonders
in heaven and on earth.
For he has delivered Daniel
from the power of the lions."

29 Therefore, Daniel flourished during the reign of Darius and the reign of Cyrus the Persian.[l]

g Est 3:8-9.—h Pss 5:7; 28:2; 55:17; 138:2.—i 1 Mac 2:60.—j Dan 3:49.—k Dan 4:31.—l Dan 1:21.

6:11 The verse tells us how a fervent Jew prayed: *three times a day,* facing *toward Jerusalem.*

II: APOCALYPSE: VISIONS OF DANIEL CONCERNING THE FUTURE*

A: The Visions of the Beasts and the Son of Man*

CHAPTER 7

Four Great Beasts Come Up from the Sea.*
1 In the first year that Belshazzar was king of
Babylon, Daniel had a dream and experienced visions in his mind as he lay in bed. Then he wrote down his account of the dream as follows:

2 In the vision I saw during the night, I,
Daniel, beheld the four winds of heaven
churning up the great sea. 3 Four huge beasts
then emerged from the sea, each one differ-
ent from the others. 4 The first was like a
lion, but with the wings of an eagle. As I watched, its wings were plucked off, and it was lifted up from the ground and made to stand on two feet as if it were a human being. It was also given a human heart.

5 Then a second beast appeared that looked like a bear. It was raised up on one of its sides, and it had three ribs in its mouth between its teeth. The order was given to it: "Arise and gorge yourself with bodies."

6 After this, as I watched, another beast appeared, like a leopard. On its back it had four wings like those of a bird, and it had four heads. This beast was given dominion.

7 After this, in my night visions, I beheld a fourth beast terrifying, fearsome, and exceedingly strong. With its great iron teeth it devoured and crushed its victims, and it trampled their remains with its feet. It was different from all of the preceding beasts, and it had ten horns.

8 While I was gazing up at these horns, I beheld another horn, a small one, sprouting in their midst. Three of the other horns were uprooted to make room for it. This horn had eyes like human eyes, and a mouth that spoke with arrogance. [m]

One Like the Son of Man*

9 While I was watching,
thrones were set in place,
and the Ancient One sat on his throne.
His robe was as white as snow,
and the hair on his head was as pure as wool.
His throne was ablaze with fiery flames,
and its wheels were a burning fire. [n]
10 A stream of fire surged forth
and flowed out from his presence.
Thousands upon thousands served him,
and myriads upon myriads stood before him.
The court was in session,
and the books lay open. [o]

11 Then I continued to watch because of the arrogant words that the horn was speaking. And as I watched the beast was put to death. Its body was destroyed and thrown into the fire to be consumed. 12 As for the other beasts, they lost their dominion, but their lives were prolonged for a season and a time.

m Rev 13:1-2.—n Mk 9:3.—o Ps 50:3; Rev 5:11.

7:1—12:13 Up to this point we have been edified by events in the life of a hero. Now he, himself, speaks in the chiaroscuro language of the apocalypses. The narrative transports the reader beyond the passing scene: the great empires that come and are swallowed up are simply preparations for the events that will mark the end of time. The prophet will also proclaim the mysterious coming of a "son of man" and the resurrection of the righteous.

7:1-28 This is the most important eschatological passage in the Book of Daniel. The immediate explanation is concerned with the time of Antiochus IV. But there are other Antiochuses in the course of human history.

7:1-8 These fabulous animals, close relatives of the forces of disorder which are often mentioned in the Bible (Ps 74; Isa 51:9) or in the primitive traditions of the peoples, stand here for the empires that controlled the East from the seventh to the second century before our era. If we may judge by the images he uses, the author sees the order of regimes as follows: Babylon, the Medes, the Persians, and then the Greeks, who have recently astonished the world by the conquests of Alexander the Great, who died in 323 B.C. Alexander's successors have divided his empire among themselves, and it is this that is presently sowing terror. Horns are always a sign of power; here they symbolize the kings of the Greek dynasty of the Seleucids, who control Syria. The little, destructive horn is Antiochus IV Epiphanes (175–163 B.C.), who has rid himself of more than one of his rivals. This entire scenario, then, is intended to fill out the portrait of this persecuting ruler. But Antiochus IV has passed away, and other haughty regimes have arisen that must be identified with the same critical clarity. The Book of Revelation (Rev 13) takes over the image of the horned beast to signify evil in all the forms in which it is directed against the community of those whom Christ has brought together.

7:9-14 At this point, a mysterious personage is enthroned: the Man par excellence, who calls to mind the figure of the Servant in Isaiah (Isa 52:13-15) and represents the group of spiritual believers to whom God entrusts his kingdom forever (Dan 7:18, 22, 27). He stands at the head of the kingdom of God announced by the Prophets. In this way the coming fall of Antiochus and of the persecuting regimes is prefigured; it will be possible once again to profess the faith freely. In addition, the vision promises a new era in which the whole of humanity will be gathered into the one kingdom of God. Also included here is the title *son of man*, which Jesus will apply to himself and which, once freed from nationalistic interpretations, will suggest the newness of God's work in the world, namely, the gospel message. In the Christian Apocalypse, the title designates Christ as judge at the end of time (Mt 24:30; Rev 1:13; 14:14).

13 As the night visions continued,
I beheld approaching on the clouds of heaven
one like a son of man.
He came before the Ancient One
and was presented to him.
14 Dominion and glory and kingship
were conferred upon him
so that all peoples and nations of every language
would become his servants.
His dominion is an everlasting dominion
that will never pass away,
and his kingdom is one
that will never be destroyed.[p]

The Kingdom of the Holy Ones of the Most High. [15] I, Daniel, experienced great anguish of spirit, and the visions that flashed through my mind truly terrified me. [16] Therefore, I approached one of those who were standing there and asked him what all this truly signified. He in turn revealed to me what all these things meant, [17] "These four great beasts represent four kingdoms that will arise from the earth. [18] But the holy ones of the Most High shall receive kingly power and possess it forever and ever."

[19] Then I expressed my desire to know about the fourth beast, since it was different from all the rest, and terrifying to behold with its iron teeth and bronze claws, and trampling underfoot and devouring its victims. [20] I also wanted to know about the ten horns on its head, and why the other horn sprouted, before which three of them fell, the horn that had eyes and an arrogant mouth, and whose appearance was more imposing than that of the others.

[21] As I watched, this horn was waging war against the holy ones and prevailing over them, [22] until the Ancient One came and pronounced judgment in favor of the holy ones of the Most High, and the time came when the holy ones gained possession of the kingdom. [23] This is the explanation he offered:

"As for the fourth beast,
it signifies a fourth kingdom on earth
that will differ from all other kingdoms.
It shall devour the earth,
trample it underfoot, and crush it to pieces.
24 As for the ten horns,
from this kingdom ten kings shall rise,
and another shall arise after them.
This last king will be different from the earlier ones,
and he will overcome three kings.
25 He will insult the Most High
and oppress the holy ones of the Most High
in his stubborn determination
to change the sacred seasons and the law.
They shall be given into his power
for a time, two times, and half a time.
26 Finally the court will sit in judgment,
and his power will be taken away,
with his sovereignty completely destroyed forever.
27 Then kingship and dominion and the splendor
of all the kingdoms under the heavens
will be given to the holy people of the Most High,
whose kingdom will be everlasting,
and all dominions will serve and obey him."[q]

[28] Here the account ends. I, Daniel, was greatly disturbed by my thoughts, and I turned pale, but I kept these things to myself.

B: Daniel's Vision of a Ram and a Goat*

CHAPTER 8

Vision of the Ram and He-Goat. [1] In the third year of the reign of King Belshazzar, I, Daniel, had another vision subsequent to the first vision that I had previously experienced. [2] In my vision I saw myself in the citadel of Susa* in the province of Elam, standing by the Ulai canal.

p Dan 3:100; 4:31; Ps 110:1f; Mic 4:7; Lk 1:32.—q 2 Sam 7:16.

8:1-27 Daniel has a new vision. First, there is a ram with two horns of unequal length (that is, of unequal power): the Medes and the Persians. Then a goat comes from the West, a king of Greece, to snatch them from their place: Alexander the Great. When the latter dies, in 323 B.C., his successors, or Diadochi, will argue over the empire: the Lagids, the Seleucids, the Antigonids, and later the Attalids. Finally, *the beautiful land*, Jerusalem, falls into the power of Antiochus (v. 9), who attempts to subdue the soul of Israel by violence (v. 10). He identifies himself with God, suppresses the daily sacrifice (in 167 B.C.), and erects an altar for Zeus over the altar in the temple. But the days of the persecutor are numbered.

8:2 *Susa*, the capital of Elam, was the summer residence of the Persian kings.

3 When I looked up, I saw a ram standing
beside the river. It had two horns. Both of
the horns were tall, but one was taller than
the other, although the other had appeared
first. 4 I observed the ram butting toward the
west, the north, and the south. No beast
could withstand it or escape from its power.
It did as it pleased and became very strong.

5 As I was pondering this, a he-goat ap-
peared from the west, skimming over the
entire surface of the world without touching
the ground, and between its eyes it had one
prominent horn. 6 It approached the two-
horned ram, which I had seen standing by
the river, and charged it with savage fury.

7 I saw it charge the ram in a fit of rage and
attack it with the full force of its fury, break-
ing both of its horns and leaving the ram
powerless to withstand the attack. Having
thrown the ram to the ground, it trampled it
underfoot, and there was no one there to res-
cue the ram. 8 The he-goat then grew even
more powerful but at the height of its
strength the great horn shattered, and in its
place there came forth four majestic horns
pointing toward the four winds of heaven.

9 Out of one of these horns sprang forth a
small horn which grew ever larger and
poured forth its strength toward the south
and the east and toward the beautiful land. [r]
10 It grew until it reached the host of heaven,
after which it flung down to the earth some
of the host as well as some of the stars and
trampled on them.

11 It even challenged arrogantly the power
of the prince of the host. It abolished his
right to offer the daily sacrifice and
destroyed his sanctuary. 12 The army, too,
was abolished, while the daily sacrifice was
replaced by sin. It cast truth to the ground
and succeeded in everything it did.

13 Then I heard a holy one speaking, and
another holy one said to the speaker, "How
long will it be before this vision is fulfilled—
the vision of sacrifice, the desolation of
transgressions, and daily trampling of the
sanctuary and the host?" [s] 14 The first one
replied, "Until two thousand three hundred
evenings and mornings have passed. Then
the sanctuary will be purified."

Interpretation of the Vision. 15 While I,
Daniel, tried to understand the vision that I
had seen, I saw someone standing before me
who had the appearance of a man. 16 Then I
heard a human voice from the Ulai cry out,
"Gabriel, explain to him the meaning of the
vision." 17 As he then approached the place
where I was standing, I fell prostrate in ter-
ror. However, he said to me, "Understand
this, son of man. The vision refers to the end
time." [t]

18 As he spoke to me, I fell to the ground in
a trance, face downward. However, he
touched me and raised me to my feet. 19 "I
will show you," he said, "what will take place
later in the period of wrath, for at the
appointed time there will be an end.

20 "The two-horned ram that you saw rep-
resents the kings of Media and Persia. 21 The
male goat is the king of Greece, and the large
horn between its eyes represents the first
king. 22 As for the horn that was broken and
replaced by four other horns, four kingdoms
shall rise from his nation but be lacking his
power.

23 "At the end of their reign,
when their sins have reached their zenith,
a king will arise,
bold in countenance and skilled in intrigue.

24 His strength will continually increase,
but not by any power of his own.
He will wreak untold havoc
and succeed in whatever he does.
He will destroy mighty nations
as well as the holy ones, God's people. [u]

25 "By cunning and deceit,
he will succeed in his treacherous plans.
He will devise great schemes
and wreak havoc on unsuspecting people.
He will finally challenge the power
of the Prince of princes,
but he will be broken
without any human intervention.

26 The vision of the evenings and the mornings
that has been revealed is true.
However, you must keep this vision secret,
because it points to times far ahead."

27 Then I, Daniel, was overcome by ex-
haustion, and I lay sick for several days. After
that I arose and attended to the king's busi-

r Dan 11:16, 41; Zec 7:14.—s Dan 12:6.—t Ezek 2:1.—u Dan 11:36.

ness. But I was perplexed by the vision, which I was unable to understand.

C: The Prophecy of the Seventy Weeks*

CHAPTER 9

According to the Word Revealed to Jeremiah . . . 1 In the first year of Darius, son of Ahasuerus, a Mede by birth, who became ruler of the kingdom of the Chaldeans—2 in the first year of his reign, I, Daniel, was studying the Scriptures and reflecting on the seventy years that, according to the word of the LORD to the prophet Jeremiah,[v] had to pass before the desolation of Jerusalem would come to an end.

3 Then I turned to the Lord God and pleaded with him in earnest prayer, with fasting, sackcloth, and ashes. 4 I prayed to the LORD, my God, and made this confession, saying:

Lord, Have Mercy.* "O Lord, great and awesome God, you who keep your covenant and show your steadfast love to those who love you and observe your commandments:[w] 5 we have sinned and done what is wrong, we have acted wickedly and rebelled, we have rejected your commandments and your laws.[x] 6 We have not listened to your servants the Prophets, who spoke in your name to our kings, our princes, and our fathers, and to all the people of the land.

7 "Righteousness is on your side, O Lord. As for us, we are filled with shame even to this day—we, the people of Judah, the inhabitants of Jerusalem, and all Israel, those who are near and those who are far away, in all the countries to which you have dispersed us because of the treachery that we have committed against you.

8 "O LORD, we are filled with shame—our kings, our princes, and our fathers—for having sinned against you. 9 But you, O Lord, our God, are always prepared to show compassion and forgiveness. Yet we rebelled against you 10 and have not obeyed the voice of the LORD, our God, by following your laws that you have given to us through your servants the Prophets.

11 "All Israel has transgressed your law and turned away from you, refusing to obey your commands.[y] Therefore, the curse and the oath written in the law of Moses, the servant of God, have been poured down upon us because we have sinned against you. 12 You confirmed your threats, which you made against us and our rulers by bringing upon us in Jerusalem the greatest calamity that the world has ever experienced.

13 "Just as it is written* in the law of Moses, all this disaster has come upon us. We failed to entreat the favor of the LORD, our God, by renouncing our wickedness and reflecting upon his fidelity. 14 Therefore, the LORD has watched us carefully, and now he has brought this disaster upon us. The LORD is just in all of his dealings with us, but we have not listened to his voice.

15 "And now, O Lord, our God, who led your people out of the land of Egypt with your mighty hand and caused your name to be renowned, even to this very day: we have sinned, we have acted wickedly.[z] 16 Lord, in keeping with your saving deeds, we beg you to allow your anger and wrath to turn away from your city Jerusalem, your holy mountain. As a result of our sins and the crimes of our fathers, Jerusalem and your people have become an object of scorn to all those who surround us.[a]

17 "Now therefore, our God, listen to the prayers and supplications of your servant, and for your own sake, O Lord, let your face shine upon your desolate sanctuary. 18 Incline your ear, O my God, and listen. Open your eyes and look upon our desolation and upon the city that bears your name. We present our petition to you, relying not upon our upright deeds but rather upon your great mercy.[b]

19 "Listen to us, O Lord! Forgive us, O Lord! Do not delay, O my God, for your own sake, because your city and your people bear your name."

Seventy Weeks Are Decreed.* 20 While I was still speaking, still occupied with my prayer

v 2f: Jer 25:11; 29:10.—w Neh 1:5.—x Bar 1:17.—y Deut 27:15.—z Ex 14:22; Bar 2:11.—a Ps 44:13.—b Jer 25:29.

9:1-27 By means of this prediction, the author, who is writing for the contemporaries of Antiochus IV Epiphanes, seeks to shore up the courage of the persecuted until the end of the oppression, which will not be long in coming. But the deeper insight goes beyond the immediate circumstances of the passage, for it is a call to persevere in faith while awaiting the coming of the Lord.

9:4b-19 This prayer recalls the canticle of Azariah (included in the Septuagint as Dan 3:26-45) and the liturgies of repentance after the Exile (Ezr 9; Neh 9).

9:13 *Just as it is written:* first usage of this formula of Scripture citation in the Bible.

9:20-27 This prophecy is one of the best known and most difficult of the Old Testament. In this coded and therefore obscure passage some think they discover figures that correspond to the coming of the Messiah and provide a means of calculating the end and confessing my sins and the sins of my people Israel and presenting my supplication to the LORD, my God, on behalf of his holy mountain—21 while I was still speaking in prayer, the man Gabriel, whom I had seen previously in a vision, swooped down on me in rapid flight at the time of the evening sacrifice.[c]

22 He then spoke these words to me: "Daniel, I have now come down to you to give you understanding. 23 As you began your supplications, an answer was given, and I have come to make it known to you, for you are greatly beloved. Therefore, consider carefully the answer and comprehend the vision.

24[d] "Seventy weeks are decreed
for your people and your holy city:
for bringing an end to transgression,
for putting an end to sin,
for expiating iniquity,
for introducing everlasting righteousness,
for ratifying vision and prophecy,
and for anointing the Holy of Holies.

25[e] "Know therefore, and understand this:
From the time that the message was sent:
'Return and rebuild Jerusalem,'
until the coming of an anointed prince,
there shall be seven weeks.
During sixty-two weeks
it shall be rebuilt and restored
with streets and trenches
in a troubled time.

26 "After the sixty-two weeks
an anointed one will be cut off
and have nothing.
And the troops of a leader who is to come
will destroy the city and the sanctuary.
Then the end will come like a torrent,
and until the end there will be war,
the devastation that has been decreed.

27[f] "During the space of one week
he will make a firm alliance with many people,
and for the space of half a week
he will put a stop to sacrifice and oblation.
And on the temple wing
will be the terrible abomination
until the end that has been decreed
is poured out upon the desolate city."

D: Israel's Suffering and Deliverance*

CHAPTER 10

Vision of the Hellenistic Wars. 1 In the third year of Cyrus, king of Persia, a revelation was given to Daniel, who had been given the name Belteshazzar. The revelation, which dealt with a great conflict, was valid, and its meaning was disclosed to him in a vision.

2 At that time I, Daniel, had been mourning for three weeks.

3 I refrained from eating any choice food, abstaining from consuming meat or wine, and I did not anoint myself until those three weeks had passed.

4 On the twenty-fourth day of the first month, as I stood on the bank of the great river, the Tigris, 5 I looked up and saw a man dressed in linen, with a belt of pure gold around his waist.[g] 6 His body was like beryl, his face shone like lightning, and his eyes were like fiery torches. His arms and his feet gleamed like burnished bronze, and the sound of his voice was like the roar of a multitude.

c Dan 8:16.—d Isa 53:11; Rom 3:24-26.—e Ezr 3:1-3.—f 2 Mac 6:2; Mt 24:15.—g Mt 28:3; Rev 1:13-15.

of the world. But the author, who is a contemporary of Antiochus IV and caught up in the daily tragedy of persecution, has other concerns than to offer hidden calculations. His purpose is to proclaim the proximate end of the oppression. His counting, like that of Jeremiah, starts with the beginning of the Exile in 587 B.C.; but the years become weeks of years, that is, periods of seven years. Thus, what was originally thought of in relation to the return from exile and the rebuilding of the temple is now shifted to apply to the age of Antiochus IV. The first seven weeks, or forty-nine years, cover rather well the duration of the Exile, since it was in 538 B.C. that the priest Joshua presided over the reestablishment of the Jewish community in Palestine; but the rebuilding of the temple came in 515 B.C. (see Ezr 3–6) and the rebuilding of the city walls in 445 B.C. (Neh 1–7). And the following sixty-two weeks no longer correspond to his-tory; in fact, from the edict of Cyrus in 538 B.C., to the assassination of Onias III the high priest in 170 B.C. (he is the anointed one of v. 26), sixty-seven years are lacking for the figures to match. Did the author perhaps make a mistake in counting? For the final week, however, and this is the one that interests the author (v. 27), the prediction turns out well. The alliance of the intriguers and apostates around the tyrant, and the disorders introduced into Jewish life by the complicity of the upper clergy after the death of Onias, lasted a week, or about seven years, from 171–164 B.C. In 167 B.C., the daily sacrifice in the temple was suppressed and replaced by the worship of Zeus; this was *the abomination that causes desolation* or supreme horror (1 Mac 1:54). Three and a half years, or a half-week, later, Jewish worship will be restored by Judas Maccabeus, while Antiochus dies.

10:1—12:13 Another coded presentation of contemporary history; the puzzle solves itself if we compare what is said here with what we know from other sources about the events and personages that mattered in Palestine at the beginning of the second century. If Daniel is artificially located in the time of Cyrus, it is to facilitate the spread of his coded message. Observe that in this final vision, a very important place is still given to the angels and the assertion of a resurrection.

7 I, Daniel, was the only one who saw this
vision. Those who were with me did not see
the vision, but they were seized with such
great fear that they fled and hid themselves.[h]
8 Thus I was left alone to behold this great
vision. My strength drained away, and I was
powerless, as my face turned deathly pale.
9 Then I heard the sound of his voice and as
I did so I fell into a trance with my face to the
ground.

The Mission of the Angel Gabriel. 10 But then
I felt a hand touch me, and as I trembled I
was raised to my hands and knees. 11 He said,
"Daniel, you are greatly loved. Pay close
attention to the words that I am about to
speak to you. Stand up now, for I have been
sent to you." And when he said this to me, I
stood up trembling.

12 Then he continued, "Do not be afraid,
Daniel, for from the first day that you
resolved to gain understanding and to hum-
ble yourself before God, your prayer was
heard. It is because of your resolve that I have
come to you. 13 The prince of the kingdom of
Persia thwarted me for twenty-one days, but
finally Michael,* one of the chief princes,
came to help me. I left him there to confront
the prince of the kingdom of Persia, 14 and I
have come to explain to you what will happen
to your people in the final days. For there is
yet a further vision for those days."

15 While he was speaking these words to
me, I prostrated myself on the ground and
was speechless. 16 Then someone who looked
like a man touched my lips. I opened my
mouth and said to the person standing
before me, "My lord, anguish has overcome
me at this vision, and I no longer have any
further strength. 17 How can I, my lord's ser-
vant, speak to you now that I have no
strength left in me and my breath fails me?"

18 The one who looked like a man touched
me again and strengthened me, saying,
19 "Do not be afraid, greatly beloved. You
have been specially chosen. Peace be with
you. Have courage and be strong." 20 As he
spoke to me, I once again felt strong, and I
said, "Speak, my lord, for you have strength-
ened me."

Then he asked, "Do you know why I have
come to you? I must first return to fight
against the king of Persia, and when I have
overcome him, the prince of Greece will
appear. 21 But I have been delegated to tell
you what is inscribed in the book of truth.
There is no one to lend me support except
Michael, your prince.[i]

CHAPTER 11

1 "As for me, in the first year of Darius the
Mede, I came forth to support and strength-
en him.

**Early Struggles between Seleucids and
Ptolemies.** 2 * "Now I shall tell you the truth
about these things. Three more kings shall
arise in Persia. Then a fourth will appear
who will be far richer than all of them, and
when he has enhanced his power through his
wealth, he will mobilize the entire empire
against the kingdom of Greece.*

3 "Then a powerful king* shall arise who
will govern a vast empire and do whatever he
pleases. 4 But as his power continues to
increase, his kingdom will be broken up and
parceled out to the four winds of heaven.
However, it will not be inherited by his
descendants, nor will it be ruled in the same
fashion, for his kingdom will be uprooted and
pass to others rather than to his descendants.

5 "The king of the south shall grow strong,
but one of his princes shall grow even
stronger and rule an empire greater than
his. 6 After some years the two will enter into
an alliance, and the daughter of the king of
the south shall come to the king of the north.
However, she will not be able to retain her
power, and his offspring will not endure. She
will be handed over, along with her atten-
dants and her child and her husband.*

7 "Later on, a descendant* from her line
will arise to take her place. He shall pene-

---

h Acts 9:7.—i Rev 12:7.

10:13 *Michael* is the angel who protects Daniel.

11:2-39 A clear passage gives the succession of kings from Cyrus to Antiochus IV Epiphanes. The historian can easily construct a detailed account. The author's interest is mainly in the struggle, now overt, now covert, between the Lagids of Egypt, in the south, and the Seleucids of Syria, in the north, both of them being heirs to Alexander's empire. Due to his excesses, Antiochus IV Epiphanes would come to be regarded as the Antichrist who opposes the reign of God.

11:2 The three successors of Cyrus II (558–530 B.C.) were, in order: Cambyses (530–522 B.C.), Darius I (521–486 B.C.), and Xerxes I (485–465 B.C.). It was under Xerxes that the battles of Salamis and Thermopylae took place during the war against Greece. The greatest political and economic pressure, however, was exerted by Artaxerxes I (465–424 B.C.), who roused himself to hurl all the might of Persia against Greece; other kings would later continue to war against the Greeks.

11:3 *A powerful king:* Alexander the Great.

11:6 Antiochus II (261–246 B.C.) married Berenice, daughter of Ptolemy II.

11:7 *A descendant:* Ptolemy III avenged his sister Berenice by conquering Antioch, the capital of Syria.

trate the defenses of the king of the north,
enter his stronghold, and succeed in con-
quering them. 8 He will even carry away into
Egypt, as spoils of war, their gods, with their
molten images and precious vessels of silver
and gold. For several years he will refrain
from attacking the king of the north.

9 "After that, the latter will invade the
kingdom of the king of the south but then
return to his own country. 10 However, his
sons will prepare for war and assemble a
great army that will sweep forth like a flood
and advance as far as the enemy's fortress.*

11 "The king of the south will then become
enraged and set out to engage in battle with
the king of the north. The latter will muster
an immense army that will suffer a crushing
defeat and be carried off.* 12 The heart of
the king of the south shall be exalted, and he
shall slaughter tens of thousands, but he
shall not prevail.* 13 For the king of the north
will once again raise another army, even
larger than before, and finally, after some
years, he will advance with a huge force and
a great abundance of supplies.

14 "During those times many will take up
arms against the king of the south. However,
those among your own people who are law-
less will rebel in fulfillment of the vision, but
they will fail.[j] 15 Then the king of the north
will come and erect siege-works and capture
the well-fortified city. The army of the south
will not be able to withstand him, and not even
the elite forces will be strong enough to resist.

16 "The invader will do as he pleases, and
no one will be able to withstand him. He will
establish a stronghold in the glorious land,
and it shall fall completely into his power.
17 He will set his mind on conquering the
entire kingdom and will make a treaty with
the king of the south. Further, he will give
him a daughter in marriage in order to over-
throw the kingdom, but this will not succeed
or be to his advantage.*

18 "Next he will focus his attention on the
coastlands and capture many of them, but a
commander will put a stop to his outrageous
conduct and turn his insolence back upon
him.* 19 He shall then turn back to the strong-
holds of his own land, but he will stumble and
fall, never to be seen again. 20 His successor*
shall send forth a tax collector throughout the
glorious kingdom, but within a short time this
king will also be overthrown and meet his
end, although not in anger or in battle.

Antiochus IV Epiphanes. 21 "His place shall
be taken by a despicable creature upon whom
the royal insignia shall not be conferred.
Rather, he will come forth without any warn-
ing and seize the kingdom through stealth and
fraud. 22 A powerful army shall be completely
routed and crushed by him. Both it and the
prince of the covenant* will be destroyed.

23 "After he enters into an alliance, he will
act deceitfully, and by treacherous means he
will rise to power with only a few supporters.
24 Without advance warning he will invade
the most prosperous provinces and do what
his fathers or his grandfathers had never
done, lavishing plunder, spoil, and riches
among them, yet all the while devising plans
against their strongholds, but only for a time.

25 "He shall arouse his strength and
courage to lead a great army against the
kingdom of the south. Meanwhile the king of
the south will wage war with a much greater
and more powerful army, but he will not suc-
ceed because of the plots devised against
him. 26 Even those who shared his food will
seek to destroy him. His army will be swept
away, and many will be slain in battle.*

27 "The two kings, their hearts bent on evil
though seated at the same table, will
exchange lies, but they will not succeed,
because the end will not take place until the
appointed time. 28 Then the king of the north
will return to his land with great riches, but
his heart will be set against the holy
covenant. He will devise his future plans and
return to his own land.

29 "At the appointed time he shall return
again to the south, but this time the outcome
will not be as it was before. 30 For ships of the
Kittim shall come against him, and he will
lose heart and withdraw. As he retreats he

---

j Ps 2:1.

11:10 Antiochus III the Great attacked Egypt.

11:11 Beneath the fortress of Raphia, on the border between Egypt and Palestine, Antiochus was defeated by Ptolemy IV.

11:12 Ptolemy conquered Palestine and Syria.

11:17 Antiochus made a treaty with Ptolemy and married the latter's daughter.

11:18 After conquering some coastal cities, Antiochus suffered a great defeat by the Romans at Magnesia in 179 B.C.

11:20 *His successor:* Heliodorus, sent by Seleucus IV, sacked the Jerusalem temple (see 2 Mac 3:7-13).

11:22 The *prince of the covenant* was the high priest Onias III, who was deposed by Antiochus IV and then assassinated in 170 B.C.

11:26 Antiochus attacked Egypt and captured Ptolemy VI.

will vent his fury and direct his energy against the holy covenant, and he will once again show his favor to those who forsake that holy covenant.

31 “Armed forces of his shall obey his command to desecrate the sanctuary, abolish the daily sacrifice, and install the abomination that causes desolation.* 32 He will seduce by his deceit those who break the covenant, but those people who are loyal to their God will stand firm and take action.

33 “Wise leaders of the nation shall instruct many, although for a time they will fall by the sword and fire or suffer captivity and exile. 34 When they fall, they will receive a little help, but many will have ulterior motives in offering support. 35 Some of the wise leaders will stumble so that they may be tested, refined, and purified, until the end time, which is still appointed to come.

36 “The king will do as he pleases, exalting himself and considering himself to be greater than any god. He will utter monstrous blasphemies against the God of gods, and he will prosper until the period of divine wrath is completed, for what has been determined must be fulfilled. 37 He shall have no regard for the gods of his ancestors or for the god beloved by women* or for any other god, for he shall consider himself greater than all.

38 “Instead of these, he will honor the god of fortresses, a god unknown to his ancestors. This god he shall honor with gold and silver, precious stones and costly gifts. 39 He will assign the people of a foreign god to defend the fortresses, and he will confer great honors on those whom he favors by appointing them as rulers over many people and distributing land to them as a reward.*

The End Time.* 40 “When the time comes for the end, the king of the south will prepare to attack the king of the north, but the latter will overwhelm him with chariots and cavalry and a large fleet. He will invade countries and sweep over them like a flood. 41 He will invade the beautiful land, and many countries will fall, but Edom and Moab and the leaders of the Ammonites will escape from his power.

42 “He will extend his power over many countries, and the land of Egypt will not escape. 43 He will seize control of the treasures of gold and silver and all the riches of Egypt, and the Libyans and Ethiopians will be subject to him.

44 “However, reports from the east and the north shall be a cause of alarm to him, and he will set out in great fury to bring ruin and total destruction to many. 45 He will pitch the tents of the royal pavilion between the sea and the beautiful holy mountain. Yet he shall come to his end, with no one to help him.

CHAPTER 12

1 “At that time there shall arise
Michael, the great prince,
the guardian of your people.
Then there will be a period
that will be unsurpassed in distress
since nations first came into existence.
At that time your own people will be spared,
everyone whose names are found written in the book.[k]

2 “Many of those shall awake
who sleep in the dust of the earth.
Some shall gain everlasting life;
others will earn shame and everlasting disgrace.[l]

3 However, the wise will shine
like the brightness of the heavens,
and those who lead many to righteousness
will be as bright as the stars forever and ever.[m]

4 As for you, Daniel,
keep these words secret,
and seal the book until the time of the end.
Many shall fall away,
and evils shall increase.”

---

k Rev 12:7.—l Mt 25:46; Jn 5:29.—m Wis 3:7.

11:31 *Abomination that causes desolation:* see Dan 9:27; 12:11; this is the characterization of the altar to the pagan god Zeus Olympios set up in 168 B.C. by Antiochus IV Epiphanes, which prefigured a similar abomination that Jesus predicted would be erected (see Mt 24:15; Lk 21:10).

11:37 *The god beloved by women* is the god Tammuz (see Dan 8:14).

11:39 The reference is to Jupiter Capitolinus, whom Antiochus had come to know in Rome, where he had been taken after his defeat at Magnesia. He built a temple in honor of the god in Antioch.

11:40—12:4 The martyrs and sages who resisted will be glorified even in their bodies. This is one of the great passages that, toward the end of the Old Testament, announce the resurrection of the flesh (see Isa 26:19; 2 Mac 7:9-14, 23-26; 12:43-45); the Book of Wisdom had highlighted mainly the immortality of the soul (Wis 2:23-24; 3:1-9).

Daniel's Final Revelation.* 5 I, Daniel, then looked and saw two others standing, one on the bank of the river and one on the opposite bank. 6 One of them said to the man clothed in linen, who was upstream, "How long shall it be until these incredible events take place?"

7 The man robed in linen who was upstream raised both his right hand and his left hand toward heaven, and I heard him swear by him who lives forever, "It will be for a year, for two years, and half a year, and then all these things will cease when the power of the destroyer of the holy people will come to an end." [n]

8 I heard what was said but I did not understand, so I asked, "My lord, what will be the outcome of all these things?" 9 He replied, "Go on your way, Daniel, for these words are to be kept secret and remain sealed until the end time.

10 "Many shall be purified, cleansed, and refined, but the wicked will persist in their evil ways. 11 From the time that the daily sacrifice is abolished and the appalling abomination is set up, one thousand two hundred and ninety days will elapse.

12 "Blessed is the man who perseveres and attains one thousand three hundred and thirty-five days. 13 But you, go on your way and rest. Then you will rise for your reward at the end of the ages."

III: APPENDIX*

A: The Chaste Susanna

CHAPTER 13

Attempted Seduction of the Virtuous Susanna. 1 Dwelling in Babylon was a man whose name was Joakim. 2 He had married the daughter of Hilkiah, named Susanna, a God-fearing woman of remarkable beauty. 3 Her parents were devout Jews who had raised their daughter according to the law of Moses. 4 Joakim was a wealthy individual, and adjoining his home was a lovely garden. He was visited frequently by the Jews because they greatly respected him above everyone else.

5 During that year there were appointed two elders of the people to serve as judges. In their regard the Lord had said, "Wickedness has arisen in Babylon through the elders designated to govern the people in the role of judges." 6 Those two elders were often present at Joakim's house, and people would come to them there for a hearing of their legal cases.

7 The people would depart at midday, and then Susanna would stroll through her husband's garden. 8 Each day the two elders would see her as she was entering the garden, and walking around, and they began to lust for her. 9 They ignored the light of reason, averting their eyes from heaven and forsaking their duty to act justly. 10 Although overcome with passion for her, they did not admit this failing to each other, 11 for they were ashamed to reveal the lust they harbored to seduce her. 12 Day by day they waited eagerly to catch a glimpse of her.

13 One day they said to each other, "Let us return to our homes. It is time for lunch." So they parted and headed off, 14 but both then returned. When they encountered each other and asked the reason, they admitted their lustful desires. From that time they plotted to find an opportunity to surprise her when she was alone.

15 While they were waiting for a favorable opportunity, Susanna entered the garden for her usual stroll, accompanied by two maids; and inasmuch as it was quite warm, she decided to bathe there. 16 No one else was present, aside from the two elders who were watching her from their concealed hiding place. 17 She instructed the maids, "Bring me some oil and soap and then shut the garden doors so that I may bathe." 18 The maids followed her instructions: they closed the doors and left the garden by a side entrance to obtain what she had requested them to bring, unaware of the presence of the elders who remained in hiding.

19 No sooner had the maids departed than the two elders sprang up and ran over to Susanna. 20 "Look," they pleaded with her, "the garden doors are shut, and no one can

n Rev 10:5f.

12:5-13 The author predicts that the trial will last three and a half years. This approximate time corresponds to the half week of the great prophecy (Dan 9:27); it will subsequently become the symbolic duration of all persecution. The image of the sealed book hints that they will not be understood until the events are fulfilled. In the Book of Revelation (Rev 6) the seals are opened by the Lamb, that is, the risen Jesus, in whom history gets its meaning. Destined to comfort martyrs, the final numbers (vv. 11-12) are possibly witnesses of a hope that is disappointed several times before it is finally fulfilled: the recompense is near.

13:1—14:42 As a legendary hero in the East, who also became a national glory of the Jewish people, Daniel drew the attention of many writers. Attributed to him here are three popular stories that had long been in circulation before the Alexandrian Jews told them in Greek.

see us. We are burning with desire for you;
consent and give yourself to us. 21 Should
you refuse, we shall swear under oath that
you were here with a young man in the gar-
den, and that this was the reason why you
sent the maids away."

22 Susanna then cried out in anguish, "No
matter what I decide, I am trapped. If I yield,
it means death for me. If I refuse, I cannot
evade your hands.[o] 23 But I choose not to suc-
cumb to your evil desire. I much prefer to
remain innocent and fall into your power
than to commit a sin against God's law."

24 Then Susanna began to scream, and the
two elders shouted against her, 25 as one of
them ran to open the garden doors. 26 On
hearing the noisy uproar in the garden, the
people in the house rushed in through the
side entrance to see what was happening.
27 When the elders told their story, the ser-
vants were stunned, for no such allegation
had ever been raised against Susanna.

**Susanna Falsely Accused and Condemned to
Death.** 28 The next day the townspeople
assembled at the home of Susanna's hus-
band Joakim. The two elders also were pres-
ent, determined to pursue their wicked plot
to have Susanna condemned to death. 29 In
the presence of the people they ordered,
"Bring before us Susanna, the daughter of
Hilkiah, the wife of Joakim." When she was
summoned, 30 she came, accompanied by
her parents and children and all her rela-
tives. 31 Possessed of a delicate grace and
beauty, 32 Susanna was veiled; the wicked
elders ordered her veil to be removed so that
they could further sate themselves with her
loveliness. 33 All of her relatives and the
onlookers were weeping.

34 The two elders stood up in the midst of
all present and placed their hands on her
head,[p] 35 while the tearful Susanna looked up
to heaven, for she placed her complete trust
in the Lord. 36 The elders then testified, "We
were walking by ourselves in the garden
when this woman entered with two maids.
After shutting the garden doors, she sent the
maids away. 37 Then a young man who had
been hiding in the garden went over to her,
and they lay together. 38 From the corner of
the garden where we were, we observed the
crime taking place, and we ran toward them.
39 We surprised them lying together, but we
were unable to subdue the man because he
was much too strong for us. He flung open
the doors and escaped. 40 However, we did
seize this woman, but when we demanded
that she reveal the identity of the young man,
41 she refused to tell us. We testify to this."
Since they were elders and judges of the peo-
ple, those who were assembled there accept-
ed their testimony and condemned her to
death.

42 However, Susanna cried out in a loud
voice, "O eternal God, no secret is hidden
from you, and you are aware in advance of
everything that will happen.[q] 43 You know
that these elders have perjured themselves in
their testimony against me. And now I am
condemned to die, even though I bear no
guilt in regard to any of their wicked charges
against me." 44 And the Lord heard her cry.

Susanna Rescued and Acquitted. 45 As Su-
sanna was being led off to the place of execu-
tion, God stirred up the holy spirit of a young
man named Daniel, 46 inspiring him to shout
out in protest, "I will bear no responsibility
for the death of this woman."

47 On hearing this, all the people turned
toward him and asked, "What do you mean
by that?" 48 Standing in their midst, he re-
plied: "Are you complete fools, O Israelites,
in condemning a daughter of Israel without
making a thorough investigation to deter-
mine the truth? 49 Reopen the inquiry, for
they have testified falsely in her regard."

50 All the people hurried back, and the
remaining elders said to Daniel, "Come and
sit with us and explain your thoughts, since
God has given you the wisdom of an elder."
51 He replied, "Separate these two men and
keep them far apart from one another while
I question them."

52 After they had been separated, Daniel
summoned one of them and said, "You have
grown ever more wicked with age. Behold,
the sins you committed in the past are com-
ing to the light: 53 pronouncing unjust sen-
tences, condemning innocent people, and
acquitting those who were guilty, although
the Lord has said, 'You must not put an
innocent and righteous person to death.'[r]
54 *Now, then, if you really saw this woman,
tell me under what tree you observed her
and the young man lying together." He

o Lev 20:10; Deut 22:22; Jn 8:4f.—p Lev 24:14.—q Pss 33:13-15; Heb 4:13.—r Ex 23:7.

13:54-55 *Under what tree:* in Greek there is a play on the words for the tree ("mastic tree") and the sentence passed ("will cut you in two").

replied, 55 “Under a mastic tree.” Daniel re-
plied, “Excellent. That lie will cost you your
head, for the angel of God has already re-
ceived the sentence from God and will cut
you in two.”

56 Placing that elder off to the side, Daniel
then commanded the other one to be
brought forward. “Offspring of Canaan, not
of Judah,” Daniel said to him, “beauty has
seduced you and lust has perverted your
heart. 57 This is the manner in which you
have been treating the daughters of Israel,
and because of their terror they gave in to
you. However, here is a daughter of Judah
who would not put up with your iniquity.
58 * Now, then, tell me under what tree you
discovered them lying with each other.”
59 He replied, “Under an oak tree.”
“Indeed,” said Daniel. “That lie will also
cost you your life. The angel of God is wait-
ing with a sword to split you in two and to
destroy both of you.”

60 Then the entire assembly gave forth a
great shout of thanksgiving and blessed God,
who saves those who hope in him. 61[s] And
they rose up against the two elders whom
Daniel had convicted on the basis of their
own perjured testimony and inflicted on
them the identical penalty that they in their
wickedness had intended to inflict on their
neighbor. 62 In accordance with the law of
Moses, they put them to death. Thus an
innocent life was spared that day.

63 Hilkiah and his wife praised God for
their daughter Susanna, as did her husband
Joakim and all her relatives, inasmuch as she
had been declared innocent of a shameful
deed. 64 And from that day forward Daniel
was held in the highest esteem among the
people.

B: Bel and the Dragon*

CHAPTER 14

A God without Life. 1 After King Astyages
was laid to rest with his ancestors, Cyrus the
Persian succeeded him as king. 2 Daniel was
a close associate of the king and the most
highly respected of all his friends. *

3 The Babylonians had an idol called Bel, *
and every day they provided it with an offer-
ing of twelve bushels of the finest flour, forty
sheep, and six measures of wine. 4 Even the
king revered this idol and went each day to
worship it. But Daniel adored only his own
God.

5 So the king asked him, “Why do you
refuse to adore Bel?” Daniel replied: “Be-
cause I do not worship idols that were fash-
ioned by human hands. I worship only the
living God who created heaven and earth
and has dominion over all living creatures.”

6 The king persisted: “Do you not believe
that Bel is a living god? Can you not see
how much he eats and drinks every day?”
7 Laughing, Daniel said, “Do not be de-
ceived, O king. This idol of yours is com-
posed of nothing but clay inside and bronze
outside. It has never eaten or drunk any-
thing.”

8 On hearing these words the king became
infuriated. He summoned the priests of Bel
and said to them, “If you do not tell me who
is consuming these provisions, you shall die.
9 However, if you can prove that it is Bel who
is eating and drinking them, then Daniel
shall be put to death for his blasphemy
against Bel.” Daniel said to the king, “Let it
be as you say.”

10 Now there were seventy priests of Bel,
in addition to their wives and children. The
king, accompanied by Daniel, entered the
temple of Bel, 11 and the priests of Bel said
to him, “We will now take our leave. We ask
you, O king, to set out the food yourself and
the wine you have prepared. Then lock the
door and seal it with your signet ring.
12 When you return in the morning, if you do
not discover that Bel has consumed all of it,
order us to be put to death. If such is not the
case, then Daniel must die for his blasphe-
my in making false charges against us.”
13 They were not worried about the outcome
because beneath the table they had con-
structed a secret entrance through which
they always used to come in and consume
all the provisions.

s 61f: Deut 19:16-21.

13:58-59 Again, a play on the words for the tree (“an oak”) and the sentence (“split [or, sawn] in two”).

14:1-42 Written to combat idolatry, these two accounts caricature the pagan cults. They prove that the false gods do not eat and that the divinized animals can break apart from indigestible food. The hero ends up—as in the episode in chapter 3—in the lions' den. Onto the account of the dragon, the author has grafted an edifying portrait of the prophet Habakkuk carried away by the angel, possibly based on Ezekiel (Ezek 8:3). In the face of so many present deeds, one can only glorify the God of the Jews!

14:2 The Septuagint reads: “There was once a priest by the name of Daniel, the son of Abal, and a favorite of the king of Babylon.”

14:3 *Bel:* Marduk, the Babylonian god corresponding to Baal, which was a name common to many Semitic divinities.

14 After the priests had departed and the
king had set out the food for Bel, Daniel
ordered his servants to bring some ashes
and to scatter them throughout the temple,
in the presence of the king. They then all
went outside, sealed the locked door with the
royal signet ring, and departed. 15 The
priests, as was their custom, came by night
with their wives and children, and they ate
and drank everything.

16 Early the next morning the king rose
and came with Daniel. 17 The king asked,
"Are the seals unbroken Daniel?" "They are
unbroken, O king," he replied. 18 As soon as
the door was opened, the king looked at the
table and cried out, "Great are you, O Bel.
There is no deceit in you." 19 But Daniel
laughed as he restrained the king from
entering.

"Look at the floor," he said, "and take note
whose footprints these are." 20 The king
replied, "I see the footprints of men, women,
and children."

21 Enraged, the king ordered the priests to
be arrested together with their wives and
children. They showed him the secret door
through which they used to enter to con-
sume the provisions on the table. 22 The king
ordered them to be put to death, and he
handed over Bel to Daniel, who destroyed
both the idol and its temple.

Again among the Lions. 23 The Babylo-
nians also worshiped a huge dragon.*
24 The king said to Daniel, "You surely can-
not deny that this is a living god. Therefore,
I command you to adore it." 25 Daniel re-
plied, "I adore only the Lord, my God, for
he is the living God. 26 If you give me per-
mission, O king, I shall kill this dragon
without using either sword or club." "I
grant you permission," said the king.

27 Then Daniel gathered some pitch, fat,
and hair. He boiled them together and
formed the mixture into cakes, which he
placed into the mouth of the dragon. When
the dragon swallowed them, he burst open.
Daniel said, "Behold what you have been
worshiping."

28 When the Babylonians learned about
this, they became enraged and turned their
anger against the king. "The king has be-
come a Jew," they said. "He has destroyed
Bel, slain the dragon, and put the priests to
death." 29 Therefore, they went to the king
and demanded, "Hand Daniel over to us,
or else we shall slay you and your family."
30 Faced with this violent threat, the king
was compelled to turn over Daniel to them.

31 They threw Daniel into the den of lions,
and, he was left there for six days. 32 In that
den there were seven lions, and each day
two human carcasses and two sheep had
usually been fed to them. Now, however,
they were given nothing, to ensure that they
would devour Daniel.

33 In Judea at that time, there was the
prophet Habakkuk. Having prepared a stew
and mixed it in a bowl with some bread, he
was on his way to take it to the reapers in the
field. 34 The angel of the Lord instructed him,
"Take the meal you have prepared to Daniel
who is in Babylon in the lions' den.
35 Habakkuk replied, "Sir, I have never been
to Babylon, and I do not have any idea where
the den is." 36 Thereupon the angel of the
Lord grasped him by the crown of his head
and, carrying him by his hair, with the speed
of the wind, set him down in Babylon above
the den. [t]

37 Habakkuk shouted, "Daniel, Daniel,
take the food that God has sent to you."
38 Daniel said, "You have remembered me,
O God. You have not abandoned those who
love you." 39 He then got up and began to eat.
Meanwhile the angel of the Lord immedi-
ately carried Habakkuk back to his own
country.

40 On the seventh day the king came to
weep for Daniel. When he arrived at the den
and looked in, he saw Daniel sitting there.
41 The king cried aloud, "You are great, O
Lord, the God of Daniel, and there is no
other god but you." 42 He then had Daniel
lifted out of the den and ordered those who
had plotted Daniel's destruction to be
thrown into it. Those individuals were
devoured before his eyes in an instant.

---

t Ezek 8:3.

14:23 The Greek historian Herodotus (fifth century B.C.) attests to the worship of a living serpent in Babylon!

"Finally she will say, 'I will return to my first husband, since I was far better off then than I am now' " *(Hos 2:9)*.

THE BOOK OF HOSEA

Bonds of Love

From 931 B.C. on, the people of Israel were divided into two kingdoms (see 1 Ki 12). The northern kingdom, often called Israel or Ephraim, chose Samaria as its capital and celebrated the worship of the true God especially at Dan and Bethel. The southern kingdom, that of Judah, had its center in Jerusalem. There were conflicts between the two fraternal kingdoms; in addition, the northern kingdom had to win back territories from its Syrian neighbor; it also lived through many palace revolts. But in the middle of the eighth century all this seemed to belong to the distant past, while on another front, Assyria had been in eclipse for about thirty years. As a result, peace and prosperity seemed to be a reality toward the end of the long reign of Jeroboam II.

Around 750 B.C., a new prophet appeared. His name was Hosea, and he had undoubtedly felt the influence of the priests who maintained the ancient sanctuaries and preserved the traditions. Hosea spoke on behalf of the covenant and made it clear that this no longer really inspired the life of the people. He stated that the security that people felt at this time was a false security; and, in fact after Jeroboam II, the successive regimes in Samaria proved to be short-lived. Assyria, though momentarily occupied elsewhere, would fulfill its dream of dominating the Near East.

In 733 B.C. Samaria and Damascus hoped to gain release from Assyrian tutelage and sought to draw Judah into their conspiracy. A hopeless undertaking! It would, however, lead to the Syro-Ephraimite War, and the politics of alliances would poison the life of the two kingdoms. In 732 B.C. the northern kingdom came under Assyrian domination and in 728 B.C. it finally collapsed with the fall of Samaria. Hosea sensed the danger lurking behind the facade of peace and prosperity. He roused his people, who were ready to betray the ideal of the covenant and were giving themselves to the superstitious and erotic practices of the worship of Baal, the god of fertility. God was being forgotten, and the law governing the life of the people was being mocked.

The task of the prophets was to maintain and continually renew the covenant in the hearts of the people, and Hosea did this in an original fashion, as he pleaded the cause of God with the unfaithful people. In Hosea's view, the Lord is bound to his people with ties that are not simply those of possession and belonging, but of love. His relationship with them unfolds like that of a father's or a spouse's love; the prophet summons up all the degrees of feeling: lasting affection, restless passion, profound tenderness, and inexorable fierceness.

The Book that brings us the words of the prophet was, in all probability, written by a disciple and weighed down by numerous commentaries. In speaking of relations between God and Israel, between God and humanity, the prophet has achieved a new delicacy and a new sensitivity. He uses the image of marriage, which is common in the biblical tradition and will be taken over into the New Testament especially by St. John (Jn 3:29; Rev 19:7; 21:2; etc.) and St. Paul (Eph 5:22f; 2 Cor 11:2f), who apply it to Jesus and to the Church, the new Israel, in which every baptized person enters into a special relationship with the Lord.

The Book of Hosea may be divided as follows:

- *I: Prologue: The Word of the LORD (1:1)*
- *II: The Marriage of Hosea is a Symbol (1:2—3:5)*
- *III: God Puts an Adulterous People on Trial (4:1—9:9)*
- *IV: At the Roots of the Evil of Israel (9:10—14:10)*

I: PROLOGUE

The Word of the LORD

CHAPTER 1

[1] This is the word of the LORD* that came to Hosea, the son of Beeri, during the reigns of Uzziah, Jotham, Ahaz, and Hezekiah, kings of Judah, and during the reign of Jeroboam, son of Joash, king of Israel. [a]

II: THE MARRIAGE OF HOSEA IS A SYMBOL*

A: The Harlot and Her Children*

[2] When the LORD began to speak through Hosea, the LORD said to Hosea:

"Go forth and take a harlot for a wife,
and father children of harlotry,
for the people have devoted themselves
to adultery
and turned away from the LORD."

[3] Therefore, Hosea went forth and took Gomer, the daughter of Diblaim, and she conceived and bore him a son. [4] Then the LORD said to him:

a Jer 25:1; Am 1:1.

1:1 *The word of the LORD:* refers to the entire revelation received by the prophet over the course of a ministry that began around 750 B.C. The indications of the period of the prophet's activity are somewhat vague; indeed, the list of kings is incomplete as far as the kingdom of Israel is concerned.

1:2—3:5 A prophet proclaims his message not only by what he says but also by what he does and by the way he lives. Hosea becomes a sign by reason of his strange and painful marital history and also by reason of the provocative names that he gives to his children. We are given two accounts of his marriage; these repeat and complete each other. His married life is a kind of parable of the history of Israel. God is attached to his people with a passion that resembles that of a husband; as time passes, Israel increasingly betrays the covenant by seeking to find its happiness in the many Canaanite fertility cults. Degradation leads to a complete break, but God cannot forever abandon his own; one day they will return and enjoy a new life. The Lord remains faithful, despite the continuing infidelity of the people.

1:2—2:3 Gomer was perhaps a sacral prostitute at some high place, or perhaps simply a young girl who vowed herself to the god Baal in order to become fertile. She represents here the situation of the country and its children, who have been contaminated by the worship of false gods. Even the name given to the children symbolizes the threat that hangs over Israel and the royal house. At Jezreel, royal residence of the northern kingdom, Jehu had ordered the massacre, in 841 B.C., of all the descendants of the wicked King Ahab (see 2 Ki 9–10). The new dynasty has likewise become unfaithful, and King Zechariah will pay for his misdeeds with his life after only a six months' rule. The bow (v. 5), that is, the military power, will be broken in 732 B.C., by Tiglath-pileser III, who turns the Transjordan area and Galilee into Assyrian provinces. Contrary to all custom, the name of Hosea's second child is a negative one, signifying the end, at least provisionally, of God's mercy. The name of the third child signifies the complete break.

"Name the boy Jezreel,
for in a short time
I will punish the house of Jehu
for the blood shed at Jezreel, [b]
and I will bring an end to the kingdom
of the house of Israel.
5 On that day I will demolish the bow of
Israel
in the Valley of Jezreel." [c]

6 When Gomer conceived again and bore him a daughter, the LORD said to him:

"Give her the name Lo-ruhama,
for I no longer have compassion for the
house of Israel,
nor do I wish to forgive them. [d]
7 However, I do have pity on the house of
Judah,
and I will save them by the LORD, their
God. [e]
But I will not deliver them by war,
nor by sword or bow,
nor by horses or horsemen." *

8 After Gomer had weaned Lo-ruhama, she conceived and bore him a son. 9 Then the LORD said:

"Give him the name Lo-ammi,
for you are not my people,
and I am not your God." [f]

CHAPTER 2

To Conjure Up One's Destiny

1 The Israelites will be as numerous [g]
as the sands of the sea,
which can be neither measured nor
numbered.
And in the very place where it was said to
them,
"You are not my people,"
they will be called, "Children of the
Living God."
2 The people of Judah and of Israel
shall be gathered together.
They will choose one person to be their
leader,
and they shall enlarge their bound-
aries,
for great will be the day of Jezreel.
3 Say to your brothers, "You are my peo-
ple,"
and to your sisters, "You are beloved."

B: Repudiation and Return to First Love*

I Shall Strip Her Bare*

4 Insist that your mother repent, *
for she is no longer my wife,
and I am not her husband.
If she does not cease her harlotry
and the use of her breasts in adulter-
ous acts,
5 I shall strip her bare, * [h]
leaving her as naked as the day she was
born.
I shall make her as barren as the wilder-
ness
and as parched as the desert,
leaving her to die of thirst. [i]
6 Nor will I feel any pity for her children,
since they are the offspring of adul-
tery. [j]
7 Yes, their mother has been a whore;
she who conceived them has acted
shamefully.
For she said, "I will go after my lovers;
they will supply me with my bread and
my water,
my wool and my flax, my oil and my
drink."
8 That is why I will block her path with
thornbushes
and erect a wall to hinder her,
so that she cannot proceed on her
journey.
9 Although she pursues her lovers, *
she will not be able to overtake them.
If she looks for them,
she will not find them.

b 2 Ki 10:11.—c Jer 49:35.—d Gen 29:33.—e Isa 37:35.—f Gen 4:17.—g 1-3: Rom 9:26.—h 2 Mac 4:38; Jn 8:11.—i Isa 50:2; Ezek 16:39.—j 2 Sam 12:6; Lam 2:17.

1:7 This verse was probably added by a Judean editor in order to exclude Jerusalem from the threat; Jerusalem was, in fact, spared from the Assyrian peril in 701 B.C.

2:4-25 This passage gives the religious meaning of the history of Hosea. The prophet attributes to God the language of love, passion, jealousy, threats, but also tender love and forgiveness.

2:4-15 Rich and harsh images are presented here, showing the trial of unfaithful Israel, for whom God had done everything and had drawn her out of wretchedness like an abandoned daughter (see Ezek 16:8). He is now going to bar the way and prevent her from falling back into this wretchedness, because with the false gods, her lovers, she has messed up the country received as a marriage gift. The land will be sacked. Then perhaps the hearts of the ungrateful ones will return, for God cannot bring himself to apply to them what the law calls for—the punishment of death (see Lev 20:1-27).

2:4 *Your mother repent:* the reference seems to be to amulets or other signs representing Baal.

2:5 *I shall strip her bare:* this seems to have been a customary punishment for adultery.

2:9 *Lovers:* the Canaanite divinities of fertility (the Baal of v. 8).

Finally she will say,
"I will return to my first husband,
since I was far better off then than I am now."
10 She has never realized
that I was the one who gave her
the grain, the wine, and the oil,
and who lavished upon her the silver and gold
that they used for Baal.
11 For this reason I intend to take back
my grain when it is ready for the harvest
and my new wine during the time of vintage.
And I will retrieve the wool and the flax
with which her nakedness was to be covered.
12 Now I will reveal her lewdness
before the eyes of her lovers,
and no one shall rescue her from my hands.
13 I will put an end to all her merrymaking,
her festivals, her new moons, and her sabbaths,
and all of her solemn festivals. [k]
14 I will lay waste her vines and her fig trees,
about which she said,
"These are the payment
I have received from my lovers."
I shall allow them to grow wild,
and ferocious beasts will devour them.
15 I will inflict punishment on her
for the festival days of the Baals,
when she burned incense to them,
and adorned herself with her rings and jewels
and ran after her lovers
while she forgot me, says the LORD.

I Intend To Allure Her . . . and Speak Tenderly to Her*

16 As a result, now I intend to allure her,
lead her into the wilderness,
and speak tenderly to her. [l]
17 From there I will restore her vineyards to her
and make the Valley of Achor * a gateway of hope.
There she will respond as she did in the days of her youth,
when she came up from the land of Egypt.
18 On that day, says the LORD,
she will call me "My husband,"
and never again call me "My Baal."
19 I will remove the names of the Baals from her mouth;
never again shall their names be invoked.
20 On that day I will make for you
a covenant with the wild animals,
with the birds of the air,
and the things that creep on the ground. [m]
I will destroy bows and swords and warfare
and banish them from the land
so that you may lie down in security.
21 I will betroth you to myself forever;
I will espouse you in righteousness and in justice,
in steadfast love and in mercy.
22 I will take you for my wife in fidelity,
and you will know the LORD.

23 On that day I will respond,
says the LORD.
I will respond to the heavens,
and they will respond to the earth,
24 and the earth will respond to the grain,
the wine, and the oil,
and they will respond to Jezreel.
25 I will sow her for myself in the land,
and I will have pity on Lo-ruhama.
I will say to Lo-ammi, "You are my people,"
and he will say, "You are my God." [n]

C: The Triumph of Love*

CHAPTER 3

1 The LORD said to me:

k Am 8:10.—l Isa 54:5.—m Job 5:23.—n Ru 1:16; Rom 9:25; 1 Pet 2:10.

2:16-25 The prophet announces that God's love does not accept being checked. To better reconquer his people, he brings them back to the time of Sinai, the place where he showed his initial tenderness and the first covenant.

2:17 *Valley of Achor:* this served as a passageway from the area of Jericho to the plateaus of the interior. The Israelites took possession of it when they conquered Canaan: the name means "Valley of Misfortune" (see the sad end of Achan in Jos 7:24-26).

3:1-5 Before belonging to Hosea, Gomer had to be redeemed and submit to the conditions which, according to ancient views, would free her from her sacral tie to a pagan cult and allow her to return to an orderly life. There was, so to speak, a period of quarantine, and this became a symbol of the Exile, which Israel must accept in order to withdraw from its promiscuous behavior with false gods. At that time the people will be deprived of every political and religious institution. The sacred stone and the ephod were elements of a worship more or less connected with pagan rites.

"Go forth and offer your love to a woman
who has a lover and is an adulteress,
just as I, the LORD, love the people of Israel [o]
even though they turn to other gods
and love raisin cakes." *

2 Therefore, I purchased her for fifteen
shekels of silver, a homer of barley, and a
measure of wine, 3 and I said to her:

"You must remain in my house for a long time,
and you shall not continue to play the harlot.
You shall not have relations with anyone else,
nor even with me."

4 For the Israelites shall spend a long time
without a king or leader,
without sacrifice or sacred pillar,
without ephod or household idols.

5 Afterward the Israelites shall return
and seek the LORD, their God,
and David, their king. *
They will come trembling to the LORD
to beg for his bounty in the final days. [p]

III: GOD PUTS AN ADULTEROUS PEOPLE ON TRIAL

CHAPTER 4

A Deep Corruption of Morals

1 Hear the word of the LORD,
people of Israel,
for the LORD has decreed an indictment
against the inhabitants of the land.
There is no faithfulness or loyalty,
nor any knowledge of God in the land. [q]

2 Instead, people swear oaths and break them;
they lie, murder, steal, and commit adultery,
with never-ceasing bloodshed. [r]

3 Therefore, the land is in mourning,
and all who dwell in it languish,
including the wild beasts and the birds of the air;
even the fish of the sea are perishing.

My Quarrel Is with You, O Priests

4 But let no one protest
or make accusations;
my quarrel is with you, O priests.

5 You shall stumble in the daylight,
while the prophets will stumble with you at night,
and I will destroy your mother.

6 My people are perishing
for want of knowledge.
Because you have rejected knowledge,
I will reject you as my priests.
And since you have forsaken the law of your God,
I will also reject your children.

7 The more the number of priests increased,
the more they sinned against me,
turning their glory into shame.

8 They feed on the sins of my people;
they are insatiable in their hunger for iniquity.

9 The priests and the people will share the same fate;
I shall punish them for their conduct
and repay them for their deeds. [s]

10 They will eat but never be satisfied;
they will engage in prostitution but never have children,
because they have abandoned the LORD

11 to devote themselves to immorality.

Idolatry and Debauchery

Wine, both old and new,
deprives my people of understanding.

12 They consult a piece of wood for advice,
and their divining rod* provides the answers they seek.
For a spirit of promiscuity has led them astray,
and their immorality causes them to forsake their God.

13 They offer sacrifice on the mountaintops
and burn incense on the hills,
beneath oak and poplar and terebinth
because the shade they afford is pleasant.

---

o Deut 23:6.—p Ezek 34:23; Hos 11:11.—q 1 Cor 15:34.—r Ex 20:13-17; Mk 10:19.—s Isa 24:2; 47:6; Jer 25:14.

3:1 The *raisin cakes* were offered at pagan ritual feasts.

3:5 *David, their king:* i.e., the Messianic King of the line of David who will restore the Kingdom of the People of God (see Isa 4:2; 9:5f; 11:1-5; Jer 23:5; 33:14ff; Ezek 34:23f). *The final days:* i.e., the Messianic Age.

4:12 *Piece of wood . . . divining rod:* i.e., an idol used to foretell the future.

14 I shall not punish your daughters for becoming prostitutes
or your daughters-in-law for committing adultery.
For your men themselves consort with harlots
and offer sacrifice with temple prostitutes;
a people thus devoid of understanding is doomed.

15 Though you, O Israel, play the whore,
do not allow Judah to incur such guilt.
Do not come to Gilgal
or go up to Beth-aven,[t]
and do not swear, "As the LORD lives!" *

16 For Israel is as stubborn as a heifer;
will the LORD now feed them
like lambs in a broad meadow?

17 Ephraim has associated with idols;
let them alone.

18 When their drinking binge has ended,
they indulge in sexual orgies,
preferring lewdness to their glory.

19 The wind has carried them off in its wings,
and their sacrifices will only bring them shame.

CHAPTER 5

I Shall Punish Them All

1 Hear this, O priests!
Listen closely, O house of Israel!
Give heed, O house of the king,
for you will be called to judgment!
For you have been a snare at Mizpah,*
and a net spread out upon Tabor,[u]

2 and a deep pit at Shittim;
I shall punish all of them.

3 I know Ephraim,
and Israel is not hidden from me.
Despite this, O Ephraim, you have played the harlot,
and Israel is defiled.

4 Their deeds do not allow them
to return to their God.
For the spirit of immorality has possessed them,
and they no longer know the LORD.[v]

5 Israel's arrogance testifies against them;
Ephraim stumbles in their guilt,
and Judah stumbles with them.[w]

6 With their sheep and their cattle,
they shall go forth to seek the LORD.
However, they will not find him,
for he has withdrawn from them.

7 They have betrayed the LORD,
for they have borne illegitimate children.*
Now the new moon shall devour them
along with their fields.

War between Israel and Judah*

8 Blow the horn in Gibeah,*
the trumpet in Ramah.
Sound the alarm at Beth-aven:
"Look behind you, O Benjamin!"

9 Ephraim shall become a wasteland
on the day of punishment.
Against the tribes of Israel
I have decreed certain doom.

10 The rulers of Judah act like men
who move their neighbor's boundary line.
On them I will pour out
my wrath like a flood.[x]

11 Ephraim is oppressed, crushed in judgment,
being intent on pursuing idols.

12 Therefore, I am like an infectious sore for Ephraim,
like maggots for the house of Judah.

13 When Ephraim realized that he was ill
and Judah noted that he was covered with sores,
Ephraim went to Assyria,
and Judah sent envoys to the great king.

---

t Jer 3:6.—u Jdg 2:3; Mic 3:1.—v Tit 1:16.—w Jud 11:11; Hos 7:10.—x Deut 19:14; 27:17; Jud 2:7; Ezek 20:8.

4:15 A scribe from the land of Judah inserted verse 15 at this point in order to put his fellow citizens, likewise, on guard. Gilgal was in fact a place of worship near Jericho (see 1 Sam 11:15), where sacrifice was undoubtedly still being offered. Beth-aven ("House of wickedness") is a sarcastic deformation of Bethel ("House of God"), indicating that the worship offered at this sanctuary was corrupt. In the eyes of the editor, who writes after Josiah's reform of 622 B.C., all the high places apart from Jerusalem were already corrupt. In fact, Hosea is addressing Ephraim, that is, the principal tribe of the northern kingdom, and therefore the entire kingdom.

5:1-2 *Mizpah ... Tabor:* places of idolatrous worship.

5:7 *Illegitimate children:* the description continues the image of marital infidelity: the mother of these children had given herself to Baal.

5:8-15 In 734 B.C., the northern kingdom endeavored, with the help of Syria, to take possession of Judah. Judah called on Assyria, and the threat was removed, so much so that the Judeans pursued the armies of Israel and annexed territories not belonging to them. Both countries had entered into alliances with pagans, making pacts with nothingness instead of relying on God.

5:8 *Gibeah* and *Ramah* were in Judah; *Beth-aven* was in Israel. All three were on the border between the two kingdoms.

However, he has no power to cure you
or to heal your sores.
14 For I will be like a lion to Ephraim,
like a young lion to the house of Judah.
I myself will maul them and depart;
I will carry them off,
and no one will be able to rescue them.
15 I shall go back to my dwelling place
until they acknowledge their guilt
and seek my presence.*

In their affliction,
they will beseech my favor.

CHAPTER 6

Steadfast Love Rather than Sacrifice Is What Pleases Me

1* "Come, let us return to the LORD;
he has wounded us, but he will heal us;
he has struck us down, but he will bind up our wounds.
2 After two days he will revive us;
on the third day* he will raise us up[y]
to live in his presence.
3 Let us know the LORD;
let us strive to know him.
His coming is as sure as the dawn;
he will come to us like a shower,
like the spring rains that water the earth."[z]

4 What can I do with you, Ephraim?
What can I do with you, Judah?
Your love is like a morning mist,
like the dew that quickly evaporates.
5 That is the reason why I cut them to pieces
by means of the prophets.
I have slaughtered them by the word of my mouth,
and my judgment goes forth like the dawn.
6 For steadfast love rather than sacrifice
is what pleases me,
and knowledge of God rather than burnt offerings.[a]

Their Wicked Deeds Are Constantly before My Eyes

7 But in their land* they broke the covenant;
it was there that they were unfaithful to me.
8 Gilead* is a city of evildoers,
stained with bloody footprints.
9 Like robbers waiting in ambush,
priests are banded together.
They commit murder on the road to Shechem,
perpetrating monstrous crimes.
10 I have witnessed a horrible thing
in the house of Israel.
There Ephraim engages in prostitution
and Israel is defiled.[b]
11 And for you also, O Judah,
a harvest of reprisal has been designated.*

CHAPTER 7

1 Whenever I decide to restore the fortunes of my people
and prepare to heal Israel,
the guilt of Ephraim confronts me
as well as the wicked deeds of Samaria.
They practice deceit;
thieves break into houses
while bandits plunder in the streets.*
2 But they somehow fail to remind themselves
that I remember all their wickedness.
I will not forget their wicked deeds;
they are constantly before my eyes.

The Conspirators

3 They delight the king with their wickedness
and the princes with their treachery.
4 All of them are adulterers;
they are like an oven all ablaze
whose fire the baker does not need to stoke
from the kneading of the dough until it has risen.

---

y Mk 9:31; Jn 6:54; 1 Cor 15:4.—z 1 Jn 4:16.—a 1 Sam 15:22; Eccl 4:17; Mt 9:13; 12:7; 1 Cor 13:2; 2 Pet 1:2.—b Jer 3:2; Am 7:17.

5:15a Seeking to lead his people to repent, the Lord withdraws his presence from them.

6:1—7:2 The passage refers to some crime greater than others and paints a picture of general wickedness. The heart of Israel is irremediably turned in on itself and can no longer be converted.

6:2 *Two days . . . third day:* that is, soon. God is merciful.

6:7 *Their land:* some think that Adam, a place on the right bank of the Jordan, is meant.

6:8 *Gilead:* across the Jordan.

6:11 The verse is outside its proper context.

7:1 In healing the sick, physicians would have the sick person strip.

5 On the festal day of their king,
the princes become inflamed with wine
while the king extends his hand
to those who mock him.* [c]
6 For they are heated like ovens
while their heart burns within them.
All through the night their passion slumbers;
in the morning it blazes forth like a flaming fire.
7 All of them are as hot as ovens,
and they consume their rulers.
All their kings have fallen;
not one of them calls out to me.

They Call upon Egypt, They Turn to Assyria

8 Ephraim mixes with the nations;
Ephraim is a half-baked cake.*
9 Foreigners have sapped his strength,
but he is unaware of it.
His hair is beginning to turn gray,
but he does not realize it.
10 Israel's arrogance testifies against them,
but despite all this,
they do not return to the LORD, their God,
nor do they seek him. [d]
11 Ephraim has become like a dove,
silly and without any sense.
They call upon Egypt;
they turn to Assyria.
12 Wherever they turn,
I will cast my net over them.
I will bring them down
like birds of the sky.
I will discipline them
because of their evil deeds. [e]
13 Woe to them,
for they have strayed from me!
Destruction to them,
for they have rebelled against me!
I longed to redeem them,
but they continued to tell lies about me. [f]
14 They have not cried out to me from their hearts
while they wailed upon their beds.
When they gash themselves to obtain grain and new wine,*
they are still rebelling against me.
15 Even though I supported and strengthened them,
they devise evil plots against me.
16 Everything they devise is of no avail;
they are like a defective bow.
Their leaders will fall by the sword
because of their insolent words.
As a result, they will be ridiculed
in the land of Egypt. [g]

CHAPTER 8

When Israel Sows the Wind, It Will Reap the Whirlwind

1 Put the trumpet to your lips!
An eagle is circling over the sanctuary of the LORD.
The people have broken my covenant
and been unfaithful to my law.
2 Israel cries out to me,
"We acknowledge you to be our God." [h]
3 However, Israel has rejected what is good;
the enemy will pursue them.
4* They anointed kings, but not by my authority;
they appointed princes, but without my knowledge.
With their silver and gold they made idols for themselves, [i]
idols for their own destruction.
5 I reject your calf-idol, O Samaria!
My anger burns against them.
How long will it be
before they regain their innocence?
6 The calf was made in Israel;
it is no god at all,
for it was fashioned by a craftsman.
The calf of Samaria
will be broken to pieces.
7 When Israel sows the wind,
it will reap the whirlwind.
When the standing grain has no heads,
it will yield no flour.
And if it were to yield flour,
foreigners would devour it.

c Isa 28:7.—d Hos 5:5; Jn 5:44.—e Jer 6:21.—f 2 Ki 17:7; Am 9:10.—g Wis 15:15; Jer 42:17.—h Jer 2:27.—i Jos 9:14.

7:5 Probably an allusion to the assassination of Elah (see 1 Ki 16:8-14).

7:8 *Ephraim is a half-baked cake:* Ephraim (Israel) has suffered a decrease in power as a result of interfering in the politics of the surrounding peoples.

7:14 *When they gash themselves to obtain grain and new wine:* a practice that was prevalent in the Near East during prayers of supplication (see 1 Ki 18:28) but that was prohibited by the Israelite religion (see Lev 19:28; Deut 14:1).

8:4-6 *Idols . . . calf-idol:* another reference to the condemnation of idolatrous cults. The prophet is here concerned to rebuke political schism as well as religious.

8 Israel is swallowed up;
now they are among the nations
like something of no value.[j]
9 For they have gone up to Assyria
like a wild ass wandering on its own;
Ephraim has bargained for lovers.
10 Because they have bargained with the nations,
I will now gather them up.
They will soon begin to suffer
under the weight of kings and princes.
11 Although Ephraim built many altars for sin offerings,
those altars became occasions for sin.[k]
12 I provided Ephraim with many written laws,
but they regarded such laws as irrelevant.
13 Although they offer sacrifices to me
and eat the meat,
the LORD does not accept them.
On the contrary, he will remember their iniquity
and punish their sins;
they will be forced to return to Egypt.
14 Israel has forgotten his Maker
and built palaces;
Judah also has fortified many cities.
However, I will send fire upon his cities
that will devour their citadels.[l]

CHAPTER 9

Such Sacrifice Will Be Like Mourners' Bread

1 Do not rejoice, O Israel!
Do not exult like the other nations!
For you have been unfaithful to your God;
you have loved the wages of a prostitute
upon every threshing floor.*
2 Threshing floors and winepresses will not feed them,
and the new wine will fail them.[m]
3 They will not remain in the land of the LORD;
Ephraim will return to Egypt*
and eat unclean food in Assyria.
4 No longer will they pour libations of wine to the LORD,
nor will their sacrifices please him.
To them such sacrifice will be like mourners' bread
that defiles all who eat of it.
Whatever food they have will be for them alone;
it cannot enter the house of the LORD.
5 What will you do on the solemn feasts,
on the festival day of the LORD?*[n]
6 Even if the people escape destruction,
Egypt will gather them
and Memphis* will bury them.
Weeds will swallow up their treasures of silver,
and thorns will overrun their tents.

The Prophet Is Ridiculed

7 The days of punishment have come;[o]
the days of retribution are here.
Israel cries out,
"The prophet is a fool,
the inspired man is a maniac."
Because your iniquity is great,
all the greater is your hostility.
8 The prophet has been appointed by God
to serve as a watchman over Ephraim.
Yet snares await him on all his paths
and he incurs hostility in the house of his God.
9 They have immersed themselves in corruption
as in the days of Gibeah.*
God will remember their iniquity
and punish their sins.[p]

IV: AT THE ROOTS OF THE EVIL OF ISRAEL*

The Crimes of Baal-peor and Gilgal

10 It was like finding grapes in the desert
when I found Israel.
When I saw your fathers,
it was like seeing the early frost on a fig tree.

j Deut 11:6.—k Ezek 44:12.—l Ezek 39:6; Am 1:10; 2:5.—m Zec 9:17.—n Lev 23:4f.—o Jer 50:27; Lk 21:22.—p Jer 14:10.

9:1f *Upon every threshing floor:* a reference to harvest feasts in honor of the god Baal, to whom the Israelites had ascribed the fertility of the land (see Hos 2:7).

9:3 *Ephraim . . . Egypt:* Ephraim will be enslaved in Assyria as it once was in Egypt. In exile, in a country controlled by idols, everything is unclean; thus it is not possible even to offer sacrifices to the Lord.

9:5 *The festival day of the Lord:* most likely the autumnal Feast of Booths (or Tabernacles), which was the most important Israelite public celebration (see Lev 23:34).

9:6 *Memphis:* in Lower Egypt.

9:9 *The days of Gibeah:* a reference to the evil committed at Gibeah in the time of the Judges (see Jdg 19:22-30).

9:10—14:10 In this last part of the Book of Hosea there are more warnings and threats occasioned by contemporary sins, but the root of the evil is looked for in the historical errors of Israel.

However, when they came to Baal-peor,
they consecrated themselves to a shameful idol,
and they became as loathsome as the thing they loved.
11 Ephraim's glory will fly away like a bird—
no birth, no pregnancy, no conception.
12 Even if they were to bear children,
I will take away from them every single one.
Woe to them
when I turn away from them! [q]
13 Ephraim once seemed to me like Tyre,
planted in a beautiful meadow.
But now Ephraim will be required
to lead out his children for slaughter.
14 Give them, O LORD—
what will you give?
Give them wombs that miscarry*
and dried-up breasts.
15 All of their wickedness had its root in Gilgal;*
it was there that I came to hate them.
Because of their evil deeds,
I will drive them out of my house.
I will no longer love them;
all of their rulers are rebels. [r]
16 Ephraim is stricken;
their root is withered,
and they yield no fruit.
Even if they bring forth children,
I will slay the cherished offspring of their womb.
17 My God will cast them off
because they have not listened to him;
they will become wanderers among the nations. [s]

CHAPTER 10

Duplicity of Heart

1 Israel is a luxuriant vine
bringing forth a great bounty of fruit.
The more his fruit increased,
the more altars he built.
The more prosperous his land became,
the richer he made the sacred pillars.
2 Their heart is false;
now they must pay the penalty for the guilt.
God himself will destroy their altars
and demolish their sacred pillars. [t]
3 Then they will say,
"We have no king
because we did not serve the LORD.
But even if we had a king,
what could he do for us?"
4 They make many empty promises,
swear false oaths and draw up treaties.
Thus litigation spreads like poisonous weeds
in the furrows of the fields.
5 The inhabitants of Samaria tremble
for the calf of Beth-aven.
The people mourn for it,
and its idolatrous priests mourn over it,
over its glory that has departed from it. [u]
6 It will be carried to Assyria
as an offering to the great king.
Ephraim will be disgraced,
and Israel will be shamed by his schemes.
7 The king of Samaria will float away
like a flimsy twig drifting on the water.
8 The high places of Aven will be destroyed,
the shrines where Israel sinned.
Thorns and thistles shall flourish
and cover their altars.
Then they will say to the mountains, "Cover us!"
and to the hills, "Fall on us!" [v]
9 Since the days of Gibeah,
you have sinned, O Israel,
and there you have remained.
Did not war overtake
the evildoers in Gibeah? [w]
10 I have come to confront the rebels
and to chastise them.
Nations shall mass against them
to punish them for their two crimes. [x]
11 Ephraim was a trained heifer
that loved to thresh grain.
I myself laid a yoke
upon her fair neck.
However, I will harness Ephraim;
Judah will be forced to plow,
and Jacob will harrow the land.

q Isa 3:9.—r 1 Sam 8:5; Ezek 21:29.—s Am 8:12.—t Mic 5:12-13.—u Am 3:14.—v Isa 34:13; Lk 23:30; Rev 6:16.—w Hos 9:9.—x 2 Mac 10:24; Wis 11:9.

9:14 *Wombs that miscarry:* probably a reversal of the ancient blessing of Joseph (see Gen 49:25f) wherein the fruitfulness of the Patriarch is dignified by his son Ephraim's name; now Hosea calls down the scourge of extinction upon the descendants of Ephraim.

9:15 *Gilgal:* the people had gathered in Gilgal to establish the monarchy (see 1 Sam 11:4ff).

12 Sow righteousness for yourselves,
and reap a harvest of steadfast love.
Break up your fallow ground;
it is time to seek the LORD
so that he may come and rain down righteousness upon you.[y]
13 However, you have plowed wickedness
and reaped depravity;
you have eaten the fruit of falsehood.
Because you have trusted in your chariots
and in your multitude of warriors,
14 the tumult of war will engulf your people,
and all your fortresses will be destroyed,
as Salman* devastated Beth-arbel on the day of battle
when mothers were dashed to pieces with their children.[z]
15 Thus shall it be done to you, O Bethel,
because of your great wickedness.
At dawn the king of Israel
will be utterly destroyed.

CHAPTER 11

With Human Attachments and with Bonds of Love

1 When Israel was a child, I loved him,
and out of Egypt I called my son.*[a]
2 But the more I called them,
the further they went from me.
They offered sacrifice to the Baals
and burning incense to idols.
3 Yet it was I who taught Ephraim to walk,
I who took them up in my arms.
However, they did not know
that I was the one caring for them.
4 I led them with cords of human kindness,
with bonds of love.
I lifted them to my cheek as I would an infant,
and I bent down to feed them.
5 They shall return to the land of Egypt,
and Assyria will be their king
because they refused to return to me.
6 The sword shall be brandished in their cities;
it will destroy the bars of their gates
and devour them because of their evil schemes.
7 My people are determined to ignore me;
if they are summoned to approach me,
not one of them makes any attempt to do so.
8 How can I give you up, O Ephraim?
How can I hand you over, O Israel?
How can I treat you like Admah?*
How can I make you like Zeboiim?
My heart is overwhelmed within me;
tender compassion is enkindled in my heart.[b]
9 I will not give rein to my fierce anger;
I will not destroy Ephraim again.
For I am God and not a mortal.
I am the Holy One in your midst;
I will not come to you in wrath.
10 * They will follow the LORD
who roars like a lion.
And when he roars,
his children will come trembling from the west.
11 They will come trembling like sparrows from Egypt,
like doves from Assyria.
I will resettle them in their homes,
says the LORD.

CHAPTER 12

Israel Ever Deceitful

1 Ephraim has surrounded me with lies,
and the house of Israel with deceit.
But Judah still remains aligned with God
and is faithful to the Holy One.
2 Ephraim chases the wind,
ever pursuing the east wind throughout the day.
Numerous are his lies and treachery;
he makes a treaty with Assyria
while sending oil to Egypt.
3 The LORD has a charge to bring against Judah;

---

y Isa 37:30; 45:8.—z Jer 4:20; Ezek 13:11.—a Gen 37:3; Mt 2:15.—b Gen 19:24f; Jer 31:20.

10:14 *Salman:* a Moabite king who led a raid into Gilead. *Beth-arbel* was in the Transjordan region.

11:1 *Out of Egypt I called my son:* like most of the Prophets, Hosea dates the beginning of Israel from the time of Moses and the Exodus. In the New Testament, this text is applied to the return of the infant Jesus from Egypt (Mt 2:15).

11:8 *Admah* and *Zeboiim:* two cities destroyed along with Sodom and Gomorrah, according to Deut 29:22.

11:10-11 These two verses on the restoration of Israel were certainly added after the Exile. The Lord roars like a lion in order to frighten his enemies and call his children back from the dispersion. To Palestinians, Egypt represented the West.

he will punish Jacob as his conduct deserves;
he will requite him according to his deeds.
4 While still in the womb he supplanted his brother,
and as a man he struggled with God.[c]
5 He contended with the angel and prevailed;
he wept and entreated his favor.
He met God at Bethel
and spoke with him there.
6 The LORD, the God of hosts,
the LORD is his name.
7 Turn back with God's help;
remain loyal and act justly,
and always put your trust in him.

8 Merchants use dishonest scales,
for they love to defraud.
9 Ephraim says,
"I have become very rich;
I have made a fortune."
But all his wealth will avail him nothing
because of the guilt incurred by his sin.

10 I am the LORD, your God
who brought you out of the land of Egypt.
I will make you live in tents yet again
as in the days of the appointed festival.
11 I spoke to the prophets,
to whom I granted many visions
and through whom I will speak in parables.

12 Gilead is a hotbed of iniquity;
the people there are worthless.
In Gilgal they sacrifice bulls;
their altars are like piles of stones
on a plowed field.
13 Jacob fled to the country of Aram;
Israel did service to obtain a wife,
paying for her by tending sheep.[d]
14 By a prophet* the LORD brought Israel out of Egypt,
and by a prophet they were protected.[e]
15 Ephraim gave bitter provocation to the LORD;
therefore he will suffer for the blood he has shed,
and the LORD will punish him for his insults.

CHAPTER 13

The Cult of Calves

1 When Ephraim spoke, the people trembled;
he was exalted in Israel,
but he incurred guilt by worshiping Baal, and died.
2 And now the people continue to sin even more
by casting images for themselves,
idols of silver fashioned after their own concept,
all of them the work of artisans.
They say, "Offer sacrifices to these,"
and people kiss the calf-idols.
3 Therefore, they will be like the morning mist
or like the dew that quickly fades away,
like chaff that a storm drives from the threshing floor,
or like smoke escaping through a window.

You Know No God but Me, Nor Any Savior Other than Me

4 I am the LORD, your God,
who brought you out of the land of Egypt.
You know no God but me,
nor any savior other than me.[f]
5 I cared for you in the desert,
in the land of burning heat.
6 When I fed them, they were satisfied;
when they were satisfied, they became proud of heart
and quickly forgot me.
7 So now I will be like a lion to them;
like a leopard I will lurk beside the road.
8 Like a bear robbed of her cubs, I will attack them
and rip their hearts from their breasts.
Like a lion I will devour them;
like a wild beast I will tear them apart.

9 You are destroyed, O Israel;
who is there to help you?
10 Where now is your king
that he may save you?

c Gen 25:26; 32:25.—d Gen 28:5; 29:20.—e Ex 14:21f; Jdg 6:8.—f 1 Chr 17:20; Isa 43:11; Ezek 20:19.

12:14 *A prophet:* i.e., Moses.

Where in all your cities are your rulers,
about whom you said,
"Give me a king and rulers"? [g]
11 I gave you a king in my anger,
and in my wrath I took him away.*

O Death, Where Are Your Plagues?

12 The guilt of Ephraim is stored up;
his sins are kept on record.
13 He experiences the pangs of childbirth,
but he is a child lacking in wisdom.
When his time for birth arrives,
he does not leave the womb.
14 Shall I deliver them from the power of the netherworld?*
Shall I redeem them from death?
O death, where are your plagues?
O netherworld, where is your sting?
Compassion will be banished from my sight. [h]
15 Although Ephraim may be more fruitful than his brothers,
an east wind* from the LORD will come,
rising from the desert,
causing his springs to be arid
and his fountain to dry up.
His treasury will be plundered
of every precious thing. [i]

CHAPTER 14

1 Samaria will be severely punished[j]
because she has rebelled against her God.
Her people will fall by the sword;
her little ones will be dashed to pieces,
and her pregnant women will be ripped open.*

Come Back, O Israel, and I Will Love You*

2 Return, O Israel, to the LORD, your God;
your iniquity has been the cause of your downfall.
3 Prepare in advance what you want to say,
and return to the LORD.
Say to him, "Take away all guilt
and give us what is good,
so that we may present as offerings
the bullocks from our stalls.
4 Assyria will not save us,
nor shall we mount horses of war.
We shall never again say 'Our god'
to the work of our hands,
for in you the fatherless find compassion."
5 I will forgive them for their apostasy,
and I will love them freely,
for my wrath is turned away from them. [k]
6 I will be like the dew to Israel;
they will blossom like a lily;
they will strike root like the cedars of Lebanon.
7 They will put out fresh shoots;
their splendor shall be like that of the olive tree
and their fragrance like the Lebanon cedar.
8 They shall again dwell in my shade
and once again flourish like grain.
They shall blossom like the vine,
and their fame will be like that of the wine of Lebanon. [l]
9 What further dealings does Ephraim have with idols?
I hear you and look out for your welfare.
I am like an evergreen cypress;
your prosperity derives from me. [m]

Final Notice

10 Let those who are wise understand these words,
and let the prudent acknowledge them.
For straight are the ways of the LORD;
the upright walk in them,
but sinners stumble.*

g 1 Sam 8:5.—h Mic 4:10; Zec 11:6; 1 Cor 15:54—i Ezek 19:12.—j Dan 9:9; Am 9:10.—k Isa 57:18.—l Isa 11:1; Lk 13:19.—m Dan 4:34; Jn 15:5.

13:11 *I gave you a king in my anger, and in my wrath I took him away:* the Lord chastises the people of the northern kingdom by sending them inept kings.

13:14a This verse affirms the Lord's idea to destroy Israel. It is cited by St. Paul in a different sense (1 Cor 15:4f)—i.e., the sense of the final victory of life over death at the resurrection of the body on the last day achieved through the Passion and Resurrection of Christ.

13:15 *East wind:* an image of the Assyrian armies.

14:1 Symbolize human means of winning safety.

14:2-9 No matter how somber this tableau appears to be, the threats cannot be the last word of humans to God since they are not the last words of God himself. Hosea wishes to prepare his people for conversion. Now he announces a kind of liturgy of repentance. God responds with a grand promise of grace. He desires the profound return of his people, ties of true and loyal love. He wants people to uproot sin, idolatry, and self-sufficiency; the last word will remain about salvation. After such sadness, what a moving promise!

14:10 An editor has added this note urging the reader to understand properly how God's providence seeks to lead human beings to salvation.

"Blow the trumpet in Zion; . . . for the day of the LORD is coming" *(Joel 2:1).*

THE BOOK OF JOEL

The Day of the LORD Is Near

Over a century and a half has passed since the return from exile. The temple and city of Jerusalem have been rebuilt, and the small group of Jews, who have little interest in politics, are leading a relatively tranquil life. Then there is an unexpected calamity: a swarm of locusts destroys the crops. Everyone runs to the temple to lament. A prophet, otherwise unknown to us, arises and exhorts the people to true repentance and conversion of heart. In the scourge of the moment he sees a summons from God: the Lord is asking his people to turn to him.

In the first part of the Book, we are in the presence of a liturgy of true repentance. Then the horizons expand; from the present disaster and present hopes, the prophet passes on to the judgment and salvation that the last times will bring. The day of God is near; all are called to judgment. The face of the world will be renewed by the Spirit of the Lord, who must conquer the hearts of his children, regardless of age, sex, and social class. Joel speaks in this community that has come together again in Jerusalem after the Exile; his outlook is still nationalistic, but a Christian reading of his work will give it a universal dimension.

Although Joel cites or repeats the older prophets, he is a poet who is able to cry out his own message in clear language and in lyrical tomes. He is the prophet of Lent and Pentecost. During the weeks before Easter, passages from Joel exhort us to a serious conversion. The story of Pentecost tells that the gifts of the Spirit, which this prophet promises, are poured out on the entire world (Acts 2:17-21).

The Book of Joel may be divided as follows:

I: Mourning and Repentance in Judea (1:1—2:27)

II: The Advent of New Times (3:1—4:21)

I: MOURNING AND REPENTANCE IN JUDEA

CHAPTER 1

The Countryside Is Ravaged.* 1 This is the
word of the LORD that came to Joel, the son
of Pethuel:

2 Hear this, you elders!
Listen to me, all you inhabitants of the land!
Has anything like this ever happened in your days
or in the days of your ancestors? [a]
3 Tell your children about it,
and let them relate it to their children,
and their children to the next generation. [b]

4 What the cutting locust left,
the swarming locust has eaten.
What the swarming locust left,
the hopping locust has eaten.
And what the hopping locust left,
the destroying locust has eaten. [c]

5 Wake up, you drunkards, and weep!
Lament, all you winedrinkers!
For the juice of the grape
will be snatched from your mouth. [d]
6 For a nation has invaded my land,
powerful and too vast to count,
possessing teeth like those of a lion,
and the fangs of a lioness. [e]
7 It has laid waste my vines
and destroyed my fig trees,
stripping off their bark
and leaving their branches white. [f]

8 Lament like a virgin garbed in sackcloth
grieving for the betrothed of her youth. [g]
9 Grain offerings and drink offerings are cut off
from the house of the LORD.
The priests, the ministers of the LORD,
are in mourning. [h]
10 The fields are destroyed;
the earth mourns.
The grain has been ruined;
the wine has dried up;
the oil has failed.

11 Despair, you farmers,
and wail, you vinedressers,
over the wheat and the barley;
the harvest of the fields is lost.
12 The vine has withered;
the fig tree droops.
The pomegranate, the palm, and the apple tree—
all the trees of the field have dried up.
And the joy of the people
has also withered away.

Announce a Holy Fast; Proclaim a Solemn Assembly*

13 Put on sackcloth and lament, you priests!
Wail, you ministers of the altar!
Come, pass the entire night in sackcloth,
you ministers of my God!
For the house of your God is deprived
of grain offerings and libations. [i]
14 Announce a holy fast;
proclaim a solemn assembly.
Summon the elders
and all the inhabitants of the land
to the house of the LORD, your God,
and cry out to the LORD. [j]

15 Woe to us on that day!
For the day of the LORD* is near,
coming as destruction from the Almighty.
16 Has not the food been cut off
before our very eyes?
Have not joy and gladness disappeared
from the house of our God?
17 The seed has shriveled under the clods;
the storehouses are empty,
and the granaries are deserted
because the grain has dried up.
18 How loudly the cattle groan!
The herds of oxen are bewildered
because they have no pasture;
even the flocks of sheep are wasting away.
19 To you, O LORD, I cry,
for fire has consumed the open pastures

a Jer 2:10.—b Ex 10:2.—c Ex 10:12; Am 4:9.—d Lk 22:18; Jas 5:1.—e 2 Chr 24:23.—f Jer 8:13.—g Jon 3:6.—h Deut 34:8; 1 Mac 3:51.—i 2 Sam 12:16; Jas 5:1.—j Joel 2:15; Deut 31:28; Lam 2:18.

1:1-12 The prophet convokes the ancients, the chiefs of the villages. In some harrowing images, he evokes the disaster without compare: an invasion of locusts, which wreaks more devastation than an invasion by an army.

1:13-20 In the midst of stupor and distress, one turns toward God; for in the eyes of the prophet and his contemporaries, suffering a calamity was a sign of heaven's wrath. May everyone take part in a grand liturgy: mourning, fasting, and praying must prepare hearts for a true conversion.

1:15 *The day of the LORD* is that of a judgment: which one often imagines under the form of a general catastrophe preceding the reestablishment of the reign of God. *Almighty:* i.e., an ancient biblical name for God (*El-shaddai*) used here because of its play on words in Hebrew.

and flames have destroyed every tree
in the countryside.
20 Even the beasts of the field
cry out to you.
For the streams of water have dried up,
and fire has devoured the open pastures. [k]

CHAPTER 2

The Day of the LORD Is Coming*

1 Blow the trumpet in Zion;
sound the alarm on my holy mountain.
Let all the inhabitants of the land tremble,
for the day of the LORD is coming. [l]
2 A day of darkness and gloom is near,
a day of clouds and blackness.
Like the dawn spreading over the mountains,
a vast and powerful army approaches.
Their like has never been seen,
nor will it ever be seen again
in the ages to come.
3 Their vanguard is a devouring fire,
while behind them is a consuming flame.
Ahead of them the land is like the Garden of Eden,
but behind them lies a desert waste,
and from that army there is no escape. [m]
4 They have the appearance of horses;
like cavalry they charge.
5 They leap over the mountaintops
with a deafening din like that of chariots,
like the crackling of a blazing fire
devouring stubble,
like a mighty army
drawn up for battle.
6 At the sight of them
people shrink back in anguish,
their faces without color.
7 Like warriors they press forward;
like soldiers they scale the walls.
They advance, marching straight ahead,
without swerving from their paths. [n]
8 They do not jostle one another;
each marches straight ahead.
They surge through defenses
without breaking ranks.
9 They burst ahead to assault the city,
leaping onto the walls.
They climb into the houses,
entering like thieves through the windows.
10 As they move forward,
the earth quakes before them
and the heavens tremble.
The sun and the moon are darkened,
and the stars withhold their light. [o]
11 The LORD's voice thunders
at the head of his army.
Mighty and numerous are his forces,
and they enforce his orders.
Great is the day of the LORD
and exceedingly terrible;
who can endure it? [p]

Rend Your Hearts and Not Your Garments*

12 Yet even now, says the LORD,
return to me with all your heart,
with fasting, with weeping, and with mourning.
13 Rend your hearts and not your garments,
and turn back to the LORD, your God.
For he is gracious and merciful,
slow to anger, rich in kindness,
and always prepared to relent from punishing. [q]
14 Perhaps he will turn back and relent,
and leave a blessing behind him,
cereal offerings and libations
to be presented to the LORD, your God. [r]
15 Blow the trumpet in Zion!
Proclaim a fast!
Announce a solemn assembly! [s]
16 Gather the people together;
summon the community;
assemble the elders;
gather the children,
even infants at the breast.
Call forth the bridegroom from his bedroom

k Jer 48:34; Am 7:4.—l Hos 5:8.—m Isa 51:3; Rev 11:5.—n 2 Sam 20:15; Jud 2:19-20.—o Joel 4:15; Isa 13:10; Ezek 32:7f; Mt 24:29; Mk 13:24; Lk 21:25f; Acts 2:20; Rev 9:2.—p Jer 25:30; 30:7; Am 5:18; Zep 1:15; Mal 3:23.—q Neh 9:31; Ps 86:5; Dan 9:4; Jon 4:2.—r Ezr 7:17; Jon 3:9.—s Joel 1:14; Lev 23:24.

2:1-11 The *day of the LORD* refers to the judgment. The text is from those who express fear before the greatness of the God who comes. The cloud of insects that is advancing like an invading army in battle array destroys everything in its path, and nothing can stop it. It announces the judgment of God.

2:12-17 The moment has come to cry out to God; however, the collective liturgy must not be an external rite but rather must signify a collective movement of conversion. The Lord regards the inner part of humans rather than their outward appearances.

and the bride from her wedding chamber.
17 Let the priests, the ministers of the LORD,
stand weeping, between the temple porch and the altar,
as they say, "Spare your people, O LORD,
and do not allow your heritage* to be mocked
and subjected to the contempt of the nations.
Why should the peoples say
'Where is their God?' "

Rejoice in the LORD Your God.* 18 Thereupon,
the LORD was stirred to feel concern for his
land, and he took pity on his people. 19 In
response to their request, the LORD said to
his people:

I will send you
grain and wine and oil,
and you will have all you need.
Never again will I expose you
to the contempt of the nations. [t]
20 I shall drive the northern army far from you
and banish them to an arid and desolate land,
with their vanguard toward the eastern sea,*
and their rearguard toward the western sea.
They will give off a stench,
and a foul stench will rise up.
21 Fear not, O land;
be glad and rejoice,
for the LORD has done great things. [u]
22 Be not afraid, you beasts of the field,
for the open pastures are green once again.
The trees will bear fruit;
the fig tree and the vine will yield a full harvest.
23 O children of Zion, be glad,
and rejoice in the LORD, your God.
For he has given you food in good measure
by sending you rain,
the autumn and spring rains as before. [v]
24 The threshing floors will be full of grain,
and the vats will overflow with wine and oil.
25 I will repay you for the years
that the swarming locust has eaten,
the hopping, the destroying, and the cutting locust,
my great army which I sent against you.
26 You will eat until you are satisfied,
and you will praise the name of the LORD, your God,
for he has dealt wondrously with you,
and my people will never again be put to shame.
27 And you shall know
that I am in the midst of Israel.
I am the LORD, your God, and there is no other;
my people shall never again be put to shame. [w]

II: THE ADVENT OF NEW TIMES

CHAPTER 3

I Will Pour Out My Spirit on All Mankind*

1 [x] After this,
I will pour out my Spirit on all mankind.
Your sons and your daughters will prophesy;
your old men shall dream dreams,
and your young men shall see visions.
2 Even on the male and female slaves
I will pour out my Spirit in those days.
3 I will show portents
in the heavens and on the earth,
blood and fire and columns of smoke.
4 The sun will be turned to darkness
and the moon to blood
before the coming of the day of the LORD,
that great and terrible day. [y]
5 Then everyone will be saved
who calls on the name of the LORD.
For on Mount Zion
there will be a remnant,
as the LORD has said,
and in Jerusalem there will be survivors
whom the LORD will call. [z]

---

t Prov 3:10; Ezek 36:30.—u 2 Chr 7:10; Ps 126:3.—v Hos 10:12; Zec 10:7.—w Ex 8:18; Isa 45:18.—x 1-5: Ps 55:17; Isa 44:3; Zec 12:10; Acts 2:17-21.—y Joel 2:10; Acts 2:20; Rev 6:12.—z 1 Ki 18:24; Ps 55:17; Rom 10:13.

2:17 *Your heritage:* can refer to the people of Israel or to the land of Palestine.

2:18-27 In events that take place, the people of the Old Testament recognize the wrath of God; but it is not the last word.

2:20 It was from the north that invading armies usually entered Palestine. The *eastern sea* and the *western sea* are, respectively, the Dead Sea and the Mediterranean.

3:1-5 On Pentecost, Peter will tell the Jews that the gift of tongues received by the Apostles is the complete fulfillment of this prophecy (Acts 2:17-21).

CHAPTER 4

I Shall Bring All the Nations to Judgment

1 In those days, and at that time,
when I restore the fortunes of Judah and Jerusalem,
2 I will gather all the nations together
and bring them down to the Valley of Jehoshaphat.
There I shall bring them to judgment
on account of my people
and my inheritance Israel,
because they have scattered them among the nations
and divided my land among themselves. [a]
3 They cast lots for my people,
trading boys for prostitutes
and girls for wine to drink.

4 What are you to me, Tyre and Sidon and
all the regions of Philistia? Are you deter-
mined to take vengeance against me? If you
seek revenge on me, I will swiftly and speedi-
ly have your deeds recoil upon your own
hands. 5 You took my silver and gold and car-
ried off my valuable treasures into your tem-
ples. 6 You sold the people of Judah and
Jerusalem to the Greeks, thus removing
them far away from their own borders.

7 But I will rouse them to leave the places
to which you have sold them, and I will make
your deeds recoil upon your own heads. 8 I
will sell your sons and your daughters to the
people of Judah, and they will sell them to
the Sabeans,* a nation far distant. Thus has
the LORD spoken.

The Combat of the Last Judgment

9 Proclaim this among the nations:
Prepare for war!
Summon all the soldiers
to advance for the attack. [b]
10 Beat your plowshares into swords,
and your pruning hooks into spears;
let the weakling say, "I am a warrior."
11 Hasten and come, all you nations,
and gather together there;
send us your warriors, O LORD.
12 Let the nations rouse themselves
and come up to the Valley of Jehoshaphat.*
For there I will sit in judgment
upon all the neighboring nations.
13 Wield the sickles,
for the harvest is ripe.
Come and trample the grapes,
for the winepress is full.
The vats are overflowing,
for great is their wickedness. [c]
14 Multitudes, multitudes,
in the Valley of Decision.*
For the day of the LORD is near
in the Valley of Decision. [d]
15 The sun and the moon are darkened,
and the stars withhold their light. [e]
16 The LORD roars from Zion
and thunders from Jerusalem,
so that the heavens and the earth shake.
However, the LORD is a refuge for his people,
a stronghold for the people of Israel. [f]
17 Then you will know
that I, the LORD, am your God,
dwelling on Zion, my holy mountain.
Then Jerusalem will be holy,
and foreigners shall never again pass through it.

You Will Know That the LORD Is Your God, Dwelling in Zion

18 When that day comes,
the mountains will run with new wine.
The hills will flow with milk,
and all the channels of Judah
will flow with water.
A fountain will spring from the house of the LORD
to water the Valley of Shittim. [g]
19 Egypt will become a desolation
and Edom a desert waste
because of the violence done to the people of Judah
as well as the innocent blood shed in their land. [h]
20 But Judah will be inhabited forever,
and Jerusalem from generation to generation.
21 I will avenge their blood
and not allow it to go unpunished.
The LORD dwells in Zion.

a Bar 2:4; Ezek 17:20.—b 1 Chr 16:24; Mic 3:5.—c Mk 4:29; Rev 14:15.—d Ezek 12:23; Ob 15.—e Joel 2:10; 3:4; Am 5:20; Rev 8:12.—f Sir 46:17; Jer 25:30; Am 1:2.—g Ezek 47:1-12; Am 9:13.—h Lev 26:43; Jer 49:13.

4:8 *Sabeans:* Arab traders.
4:12 *Valley of Jehoshaphat:* a symbolic place is determined for the meeting with God; *Jehoshaphat* means "God is judge."
4:14 *Valley of Decision:* another symbolic name.

"On that day . . . I will make the sun go down at noon" *(Am 8:9).*

THE BOOK OF AMOS

Against Social Injustices

Amos was a shepherd of Tekoa, in southern Judah. Around 760 B.C., the call to be a prophet seized him at his work. He went to the northern kingdom and to Bethel, its religious center, where he denounced injustice, the pride of the wealthy, and the illusion created by an outward practice of religion. In an era of peace and prosperity rarely known before, this troublesome man already saw the threat from Assyria on the horizon and foretold the almost complete destruction of the people. But his message scandalized his hearers, and he was expelled. He returned to his own country, where he must certainly have continued his preaching. (On this period of history, see the introduction to Hosea.)

There were evidently prophets before Amos, but he is the first for whom we have a collection of fragmentary sermons and accounts of personal details. Other elements were added later to this collection.

Amos's personality impresses us from the very outset: this simple and upright man has a very deep sense of the justice of God and the value of the covenant; he is therefore unable to accept the immorality and injustice that were poisoning human relationships and even religion. People looked on the covenant as an easy form of security, and religion as a diversion; they made a display of their wealth with disregard for the poor; injustice reigned, and with it the corruption of the influential and land-owning classes. This kind of social hypocrisy filled Amos with indignation, because it was an insult to God. According to him, punishment could not be far off, since human history, and especially the journey of the people of the covenant, could not continue indefinitely amid forgetfulness of God and the injustice of human beings to one another.

Amos's mission was a difficult one, for it disturbed those who considered that they had peaceful consciences; but the prophet did not lack courage. His message is simple, clear, and resolute.

The Book of Amos may be divided as follows:

I: The Judgment Is Near (1:1—2:16)
II: Charges against Israel (3:1—6:14)
III: Visions: Amos, Confidant of God (7:1—9:8a)
IV: The Time of Renewal (9:8b-15)

I: THE JUDGMENT IS NEAR

A: Judgment of the Nations

CHAPTER 1

Title and Introduction.* 1 These are the words of Amos, a shepherd of Tekoa, concerning visions in regard to Israel during the reigns of Uzziah, king of Judah, and Jeroboam, son of Joash, king of Israel, two years prior to the earthquake. [a] 2 He said:

"The LORD roars from Zion,
and his name thunders forth from Jerusalem.
The pastures of the shepherds will wither
and the summit of Carmel will be arid." [b]

For Three Crimes of Damascus

3 * These are the words of the LORD:

For three crimes of Damascus, and for four,
I will not revoke my decree.
Because they threshed Gilead
with threshing-sledges of iron, [c]
4 I will send fire on the house of Hazael,
and it will devour the palaces of Ben-hadad.* [d]
5 I will demolish the gate bars of Damascus
and destroy the inhabitants in the Valley of Aven,
as well as the sceptered ruler of Beth-eden;*
the people of Aram will be exiled to Kir,
says the LORD. [e]

For Three Crimes of Gaza

6 Thus says the LORD:

For three crimes of Gaza, and for four,
I will not revoke my decree.
Because they deported entire communities
and sent them in exile to Edom,
7 I will send fire down on the walls of Gaza
to devour its palaces.
8 I will destroy the inhabitants of Ashdod
and the sceptered ruler at Ashkelon.
I will turn my hand against Ekron,
and the remnant of the Philistines will perish,
says the Lord GOD. [f]

For Three Crimes of Tyre

9 Thus says the LORD:

For three crimes of Tyre, and for four,
I will not revoke my decree.
Because they delivered entire communities to slavery in Edom
and ignored the covenant of brotherhood, [g]
10 I will send fire down on the walls of Tyre
to devour its palaces. [h]

For Three Crimes of Edom

11 Thus says the LORD:

For three crimes of Edom, and for four,
I will not revoke my decree.
Because he pursued his brother with the sword
and stifled any semblance of pity,

a Hos 1:1; Zec 14:5.—b Sir 46:17; Jer 25:30.—c Joel 4:16.—d Ezek 30:16; Hos 8:14.—e Hos 10:8.—f Ezek 25:16.—g Isa 23:1; Mt 11:21-22.—h Lk 17:29.

1:1-2 Amos's message comes in the middle of a peaceful century, the eighth century B.C. According to the editor, the message applies to the whole Israelite people; this is why he mentions the king of the south (Uzziah: 781–740 B.C.) as well as the king of the north (Jeroboam II: 783–743 B.C.). We have no other information regarding the time of the great earthquake, which must have shaken Amos's contemporaries, since they would have seen it as fulfilling the prophet's threats.

1:3—2:5 In the course of liturgical celebrations, the prophets often cursed the enemies of Israel. In the curses uttered by Amos, God judges the peoples, not on the basis of Israel's interests, but in the name of a morality that obliges all human groups. Amos's ethical sense is exemplary.

1:4 *Hazael . . . Ben-hadad:* Kings of Damascus (see 2 Ki 8:7-15; 13:3).

1:5 *Beth-eden:* "Valley of delights," a sarcastic name for Damascus. *Kir:* the place of origin of the Arameans (see Amos 9:7).

because he was unceasing in his anger
and constantly nurtured his wrath, [i]
12 I will send down fire on Teman
to devour the palaces of Bozrah.

For Three Crimes of Ammon

13 Thus says the LORD:
For three crimes of the Ammonites, and for four,
I will not revoke my decree.
Because they ripped open the pregnant women in Gilead
in their determination to enlarge their territory,
14 I will send down fire upon the walls of Rabbah*
to devour its palaces
amid war cries on the day of battle
and violent storms on the day of the whirlwind.
15 Then their king will go into exile,
accompanied by his chief advisors,
says the LORD. [j]

CHAPTER 2

For Three Crimes of Moab

1 Thus says the LORD:
For three crimes of Moab, and for four,
I will not revoke my decree.
Because they incinerated to ashes
the bones of the king of Edom,*
2 I will send down fire on Moab
to devour the palaces of Kerioth.
Moab will perish amid the uproar,
amid war cries and the sound of trumpets.
3 I will destroy its rulers
and slaughter all of his officials with him.

For Three Crimes of Judah

4 Thus says the LORD:
For three crimes of Judah, and for four,
I will not revoke my decree.
Because they have spurned the law of the LORD
and have not observed his statutes,
having been led astray
by the lies which their fathers followed,
5 I will send fire down on Judah
to devour the palaces of Jerusalem.

B: The Trial of Israel

For Three Crimes of Israel

6 Thus says the LORD:
For three crimes of Israel, and for four,
I will not revoke my decree.
They sell righteous people for silver
and the poor for a pair of sandals.
7 They have trampled the heads of the poor
into the dust of the earth
and thrust the lowly out of their way.
Father and son lie with the same prostitute,
profaning my holy name. [k]
8 They lie down beside every altar
upon garments acquired as surety,*
while drinking in the house of their God
the wine purchased with the fines they impose. [l]
9 Yet I was the one
who destroyed the Amorites* before them;
they were as tall as the cedars
and as strong as the oaks.
I was the one
who destroyed their fruit above
and their roots below. [m]
10 I was the one
who brought you up from the land of Egypt
and for forty years led you through the desert
to take possession of the land of the Amorites. [n]
11 I was the one
who raised up some of your sons to be prophets
and some of your young men to be Nazirites.
Is this not indeed true, O Israelites?
says the LORD.
12 But you forced the Nazirites to drink wine
and commanded the prophets, "Do not prophesy!"

i 2 Chr 28:17; Ezek 25:12.—j Lam 1:18; Hos 10:6.—k Lev 18:21; Mt 7:6.—l Ex 22:26; Am 4:1.—m Num 21:24; Deut 2:24-37; Jos 24:8.—n Ex 14:21; Deut 8:2, 14; Dan 9:15.

1:14 *Rabbah:* capital of the Ammonites.

2:1 In the view of the ancients, the refusal of proper burial meant leaving the dead person in an unhappy situation; this was regarded as the height of immorality.

2:8 *Surety:* according to the law (Ex 22:25; Deut 24:12), a garment taken as a pledge must be restored before nightfall.

2:9 The *Amorites* represent the Canaanites, the inhabitants of Palestine.

13 Therefore, I will crush you
just as a cart crushes when it is fully laden.[o]
14 The swift will be unable to take flight;
the strong man will not retain his strength,
and the warrior will be unable to save his life.
15 The archer will not stand his ground;
the swift of foot will not escape,
nor will the horseman save his life.
16 Even the bravest of warriors
will flee away naked on that day,
says the LORD.

II: CHARGES AGAINST ISRAEL

CHAPTER 3

The First Word. 1 O men of Israel, hear this word that the LORD has spoken against you, against the whole family that I brought up out of the land of Egypt:

2 Of all the families of the earth,
you alone have I favored.
That is why I will punish you
for all your iniquities.[p]

The LORD Speaks: Who Would Not Prophesy?

3 Do two people travel together
unless they have first agreed to do so?
4 Does a lion roar in the forest
when it has no prey?
Does a young lion cry out from its den
unless it has caught something?
5 Does a bird fall into a snare on the earth
unless a trap has been set for it?
Does a snare spring up from the ground
unless something has been caught in it?
6 Are people not alarmed
if a trumpet sounds in the city?
If disaster strikes a city,
can that occur without the approval of the LORD? *
7 Indeed, the Lord GOD does nothing
without revealing his plan
to his servants, the prophets.
8 The lion roars;
who will not be frightened?
The Lord GOD has spoken;
who will not prophesy?[q]

Violence and Pillage in Their Palace

9 Proclaim this from the
palaces of Ashdod
and from the palaces of the land of Egypt:
"Assemble on the hills of Samaria
and observe the great disorders there,
as well as the oppression in her midst."
10 For they do not know how to do what is right,
says the LORD,
as they store up in their palaces
their ill-gotten gains from violence and robbery.

11 Therefore, this is what the Lord GOD has to say:

An enemy shall surround your land;
he will tear down your strongholds
and pillage your palaces.

12 The LORD says further:

As the shepherd rescues from the jaws of a lion
two legs or the tip of an ear,
so will the Israelites who live in Samaria be rescued
with the corner of a couch or the edge of a cot.

I Will Deal with the Altars of Bethel

13 Listen and testify against the house of Jacob, says the Lord GOD, the God of hosts:[r]

14 On the day when I punish Israel for its crimes,
I will also deal with the altars of Bethel:
the horns of the altar shall be hacked off
and fall to the ground.
15 I shall destroy the winter house
as well as the summer house.
The houses of ivory will perish,
and many mansions will be no more,
says the LORD.

CHAPTER 4

The Second Word

1 Listen to this warning, you cows of Bashan,
you women who dwell on the mount of Samaria,
you who oppress the weak and crush the needy,

o Ps 89:24.—p Jer 21:14.—q Acts 4:20; Jer 20:9.—r Am 3:13.

3:6 The sufferings experienced by sinners through the permissive will of God are, according to the Old Testament understanding, attributed to the Lord.

who command your husbands, "Bring
us something to drink!"
2 The Lord GOD has sworn by his holiness:
The time is surely coming upon you
when you will be dragged away with hooks,
and the last of you with fishhooks.[s]
3 Through breaches in the wall you will leave
each one straight ahead,
and you shall be flung out atop a dungheap,
says the LORD.

Run to Your Sanctuary

4 Come to Bethel and sin!
Come to Gilgal and sin even more!
Bring your sacrifices every morning,
your tithes every third day.[t]
5 Burn your thank offering of leavened bread,
and brag publicly about your free-will offerings.
For this is what you love to do,
O children of Israel, says the Lord GOD.

You Have Not Come to Me

6 Although I made your teeth
clean of food in all your cities
and spread famine in all your villages,
you still would not return to me, says the LORD.
7 I even withheld the rain from you
when there were still three months before the harvest.
I would allow rain to fall upon one town
but not upon another.
One field would be watered by rain,
while another would receive none and dry up.[u]
8 People from two or three towns
would stagger to a neighboring town to drink water,
yet their thirst remained unquenched.
Yet even then you would not return to me,
says the LORD.
9 I struck you with mildew and blight,
I laid waste your gardens and vineyards;
the locust devoured your fig trees and your olive trees,
but still you would not return to me,
says the LORD.[v]
10 I sent among you a plague like that of Egypt,
and I slaughtered your young men with the sword.
I allowed your horses to be captured;
I filled your nostrils with the stench of your camps.
And still you would not return to me,
says the LORD.[w]
11 I brought destruction among you
like that which devastated Sodom and Gomorrah.
You were like a brand snatched from the fire,
and still you would not come back to me,
says the LORD.[x]
12 Therefore, O Israel,
this is what I plan to do with you.
And because I intend to do this,
prepare to meet your God, O Israel.

Homage to the LORD

13 He is the one who formed the mountains
and created the wind,
and who reveals to men his thoughts,
who changes the dawn into darkness
and strides upon the heights of the earth:
the LORD, the God of hosts, is his name.[y]

CHAPTER 5

Funereal Chant

1 Listen to these words that I utter against
you in lamentation, O house of Israel:[z]
2 She has fallen, to rise no more,
the virgin Israel.
She lies forsaken on her own soil,
with no one to raise her up.
3 For thus says the Lord GOD:
The city that marched out to war with a thousand
will be left with a hundred;
and the one that marched out with a hundred
will have only ten left.

Seek the LORD and Live.
4 For thus says the
LORD to the house of Israel:

s Ps 89:35.—t Deut 12:11; 2 Ki 16:15.—u Ex 9:33; 2 Chr 7:3; Jer 3:3.—v Ps 78:46-47; Hag 2:17.—w 2 Sam 24:15; Lev 26:25.—x Gen 19:24; 2 Pet 2:6.—y Isa 45:8; 2 Cor 4:6.—z Jer 9:19.

If you seek me, you will survive,
5 but do not go to Bethel.
Do not journey to Gilgal,
and do not cross over to Beer-sheba.
For Gilgal will surely be led into exile,
and Bethel shall come to nothing.
6 Seek the LORD and you will live,
or else, like a fire,
he will sweep through the house of Joseph,
with no one able to quench the flames.[a]

Hymn to God the Creator

8 He who made the Pleiades and Orion,
who turns heavy darkness into dawn
and darkens day into night,
who summons the waters of the sea
and pours them out over the surface of the earth,[b]
9 who brings destruction on the strong
and ruin upon the fortress:
the LORD is his name.

7 Woe to those who turn justice to wormwood
and thrust righteousness to the ground.

Because You Crush the Weak

10 They hate the one who preaches justice at the city gate
and abhor the one who speaks the truth.
11 Therefore, because you have trampled upon the poor
and extorted levies on their wheat,
even though you have built houses of hewn stone,
you will never live in them;
although you have planted pleasant vineyards,
you will never drink their wine.[c]

12 For I know how many are your crimes
and how monstrous are your sins.
You oppress the innocent, accept bribes,
and push aside the destitute at the gates.
13 Therefore, the prudent man keeps silent in such a situation,
for it is an evil period.

Seek the Good So That You Will Live

14 Seek good and not evil,
so that you may live.
Then the LORD, the God of hosts, will be with you
as you claim he is.[d]
15 Hate evil and love good,
and let justice prevail at the city gate.
Then it is possible that the LORD, the God of hosts,
will show mercy to the remnant of Joseph.*[e]

The Countryside Is Devastated. 16 Therefore,
this is what the LORD, the God of hosts, the
Almighty, has to say:

In every public square there will be lamentation;
in every street they will cry out, "Alas! Alas!"
They will summon the farmers to wail,
and the professional mourners to lament.
17 There will be wailing in every vineyard,
for I will pass through your midst,
says the LORD.
18 Woe to those who long for the day of the LORD.
What will this day of the LORD mean to you?
It will mean darkness, not light,[f]
19 as if someone fled from a lion
and was met by a bear,
or entered his house
and rested his hand against the wall
and was bitten by a snake.
20 Will not the day of the LORD
be darkness, not light,
day of gloom without any brightness?[g]

I Despise Your Feasts

21 I loathe, I despise your festivals,
and I take no delight in your solemn assemblies.[h]
22 Even though you bring me
your burnt offerings and your grain offerings,
I will not accept them.
Nor will I look favorably
upon your stall-fed peace offerings.
23 Spare me the noise of your chanting;
I will not listen to the melodies of your harps.
24 Rather, let justice flow like a river,
and righteousness like an ever-flowing stream.

---

a Deut 4:1; Jer 27:17.—b Am 4:13; 9:6; Gen 6:17.—c Deut 4:26; Zep 1:13.—d Ps 34:15; 1 Thes 5:15.—e Ps 97:10; Prov 14:22; Rom 12:9; 1 Pet 3:11.—f Jer 30:7; Ezek 7:19; Joel 2:11; Zep 1:15.—g Isa 8:22; Mt 24:29.—h Am 8:10; Isa 1:11; Jer 6:20.

5:15 *The remnant of Joseph:* the northern kingdom in its already decimated state.

25 Did you bring me sacrifices and offerings
during those forty years in the desert,
O house of Israel? [i]
26 You have lifted up Sakuth, your king,
and Kaiwan, your star god,
the images that you have made for yourselves.
27 Therefore, I will drive you into exile beyond Damascus,
says the LORD, whose name is the God of hosts.

CHAPTER 6

Bloody Description of the Orgy of the Head of Israel

1 Alas for those who are at ease in Zion,
and for those who feel secure on the mount of Samaria,
the leaders of the most important of the nations
to whom the people of Israel have recourse. [j]
2 Cross over to Calneh* and see;
travel on from there to Hamath the great,
and then go down to Gath of the Philistines.
Are you better than these kingdoms?
Is your territory greater than theirs?
3 You put aside all thoughts of the evil day
and thereby hasten the reign of violence.
4 Alas for those who lie on beds of ivory
and lounge on their couches.
They feast on lambs from the flock
and stall-fattened calves. [k]
5 They improvise on the music of the harp,
and, like David, they invent musical instruments.
6 They drink wine by the bowlful
and anoint themselves with the finest oils,
but they feel no grief over the ruin of Joseph. [l]
7 Therefore, they will now be the first to go into exile,
and their wanton revelry will come to an end.

There Will Be Nothing Left of Israel

8 The Lord GOD has sworn by himself.
Thus say I, the LORD, the God of hosts:
I abhor the pride of Jacob
and hate his palaces,
I shall deliver up the city
and all that is in it. [m]
9 If ten men are left in a single house,
they will die.
10 Only a few will be left
to carry out the dead from the house.
If someone calls to a man inside the house,
"Are there any more there?"
and he answers, "No,"
then he will say, "Hush,"
for the name of the LORD must not be mentioned.
11 At the LORD's command,
the great house will be shattered to bits,
and the small houses will be reduced to rubble. [n]
12 Can horses gallop over rocks?
Can one plow the sea with oxen?
Yet you have turned justice into poison
and the fruit of justice into venom—
13 you who rejoice in Lodebar,*
who say, "Have we not, by our own strength,
seized Karnaim for ourselves?"
14 Beware, O house of Israel,
for I am raising up against you a nation,
says the LORD, the God of hosts,
and that nation shall oppress you
from Lebo of Hamath even to the Wadi Arabah.

III: VISIONS: AMOS, CONFIDANT OF GOD

CHAPTER 7

The Vision of Locusts. 1 This is what the Lord GOD showed me: he was forming a swarm of locusts after the king's share* had been harvested and the second growth was beginning to sprout. 2 When the locusts had finished eating all the grass in the land, I said:

---

i Deut 12:6; Isa 43:23; Acts 7:42.—j Ezek 34:2; Lk 6:24.—k Tob 7:9.—l Jer 35:5; Dan 5:2.—m Jer 51:14; Heb 7:21.—n Ezr 6:11.

6:2 *Calneh*, near Aleppo, and *Hamath* were two principalities of Syria.

6:13 *Lodebar* and *Karnaim* had been conquered by the Israelites (see 2 Ki 13:25; 14:25).

7:1 *The king's share:* part of the first mowing was reserved for the king as a kind of tax.

Lord GOD, forgive, I beg you.
Jacob is so small;
how can he survive?

[3] Thereupon the LORD relented. "This shall
not happen," said the Lord GOD. [o]

The Vision of Fire. [4] This is what the Lord
GOD then showed me: the Lord GOD was
summoning a fire of judgment to devour the
great abyss and to consume the land. [p] [5] I
said:

Lord GOD, cease, I beg you.
Jacob is so small;
how can he survive?

[6] Thereupon the LORD relented. "This also
shall not happen," said the Lord GOD.

The Vision of the Plumb Line. [7] Then the
LORD showed me this: he was standing by a
wall, with a plumb line in his hand. [8] The
LORD asked me, "What do you see, Amos?" I
replied, "A plumb line." Then the LORD said:

Behold, I am setting a plumb line
in the midst of my people Israel;
never again will I forgive their offenses.
9 The high places of Isaac shall be laid waste,
and the sanctuaries of Israel will be left desolate;
with sword in hand
I will rise against the house of Jeroboam.

Amos Expelled by the Priests of Bethel.
[10] Then Amaziah, the priest of Bethel, sent
the following message to Jeroboam, the king
of Israel: "Amos has conspired against you
here in the heart of the house of Israel, and
the country cannot tolerate his message. [q]
[11] For this is what Amos is saying:

" 'Jeroboam will die by the sword,
and the Israelites will be taken into captivity,
far away from their native land.' "

[12] To Amos himself Amaziah said, "Go, O
seer, and flee to the land of Judah. There you
can prophesy and earn your living. [13] But
never again prophesy at Bethel, for this is
the king's sanctuary and a royal shrine."

[14] Amos replied to Amaziah, "I am not a
prophet, nor a prophet's son. I was a shepherd and a dresser of sycamore-fig trees.
[15] But the LORD took me away from tending
the flock and said to me, 'Go forth and
prophesy to my people Israel.' [16] So now, listen to the word of the LORD. You tell me that
I am not to prophesy against Israel or to
preach against the house of Isaac. [17] Therefore, thus says the LORD:

" 'Your wife will become a prostitute in the city,
and your sons and daughters will fall by the sword.
Your land will be parceled out by a measuring line;
you yourself will die in a pagan country,
and Israel will be deported in captivity
far from its native land.' " [r]

CHAPTER 8

The Vision of the Fruit Basket. [1] * This is what
the Lord GOD showed me: a basket of ripe
fruit. [s] [2] He asked, "What do you see, Amos?"
I replied, "A basket of ripe fruit." Then the
LORD said to me:

The time is ripe for my people Israel;
I will never again pardon their offenses.
3 The songs of the temple shall become wailings on that day;
there will be corpses strewn everywhere.
Be silent! Thus says the Lord GOD. [t]

Listen, You Who Crush the Poor

4 Hear this, you who crush the needy
and trample upon the poor of the land. [u]
5 "When will the new moon be over," you ask,
"so that we may sell our grain,
and the Sabbath,
so that we may market our wheat?
Then we can make the bushel measure smaller
and increase the shekel-weight
by adjusting the scales fraudulently.
6 We can buy the poor man for silver
and the needy for a pair of sandals;
we can even sell the refuse of the wheat."
7 The LORD has sworn by the pride of Jacob:
Never will I forget any of their deeds.

o Isa 7:7.—p Wis 16:19; Mt 3:12.—q 1 Ki 13:33; Jer 38:4.—r Ezek 24:21.—s Deut 26:4.—t Ezek 24:17; Nah 3:3.—u Hos 5:1.

8:1-2 In Hebrew there is a play on words between *ripe fruit* and "ripe time."

8 Will not the land tremble because of this?
Will not everyone mourn who dwells in it?
The whole earth will rise like the Nile,
swelling and then subsiding
like the River of Egypt.

I Will Turn Your Feasts into Mourning

9 On that day, says the Lord GOD,
I will make the sun go down at noon
and darken the earth in broad daylight.[v]
10 I will turn your feasts into mourning,
and all your songs into lamentation.
I will make you cover your loins with sackcloth
and shave your heads.
I will make it like mourning for an only son
and the end of it like a bitter day.*[w]
11 The days are surely coming, says the Lord GOD,
when I will send a famine upon the land,
not a hunger for bread or a thirst for water,
but for hearing the word of the LORD.[x]
12 People will stagger from sea to sea
and wander from north to east,
in search of the word of the LORD,
but they will not find it.
13 On that day, fair maidens and young men
will faint from thirst.
14 Those who swear by the shameful idol of Samaria
and say, "As your god lives, O Dan,"
and, "By the sacred path to Beersheba,"
will all fall and never rise again.*

CHAPTER 9

The Vision of the Destroyed Sanctuary. 1 I saw the LORD standing beside the altar, and he said:

Strike the tops of the pillars until the thresholds shake,
and bring them down on the heads of all the people.
Should any survive,
I will slay them with the sword.
Not one will be able to flee;
not one will escape.
2 Even should they dig down to the netherworld,
from there my hand will take them.
Even though they climb up to heaven,
I will bring them down.[y]
3 Should they hide themselves on the summit of Carmel,
there I will track them down and take them.
Should they hide from my sight at the bottom of the sea,
I will command the serpent there to bite them.
4 If they are led by their enemies into captivity,
there I shall command the sword to slay them.
I will fix my eyes on them
for evil, and not for good.[z]

Psalm of Praise

5 The LORD, the God of hosts,
touches the earth and it melts
so that all who live on it mourn,
while the entire earth rises up like the Nile*
and then subsides like the River of Egypt.
6 He builds his upper chambers in the heavens
and establishes his vault of the sky over the earth—
the LORD is his name.[a]

7 The LORD says:

Are you not like the Ethiopians to me,
O people of Israel?
Did I not bring Israel up from the land of Egypt,
and the Philistines from Caphtor,
and the Arameans from Kir?[b]
8 Behold, I, the Lord GOD,
have my eyes upon this sinful kingdom,
and I will destroy it from the face of the earth.[c]

v Isa 8:22; Mic 5:9.—w Gen 37:34; Tob 2:6; Jer 48:37.—x Ps 74:9; Ezek 5:17.—y Job 34:22; Ps 139:8; Jer 51:40.—z 2 Ki 11:15; Jer 39:16; 44:11.—a Am 5:8; Pss 78:69; 103:19.—b Deut 2:23; 2 Sam 5:25; Jer 47:4.—c Deut 11:12; Zep 1:3.

8:10 The wearing of sackcloth and the shaving of the head were rites of mourning; mourning was especially solemn at the death of an only son, since this meant the end of the family line.

8:14 A reference to illegitimate or pagan practices, an oath, being also a profession of religious faith.

9:5 *The Nile* was famous for its periodic flooding.

IV: THE TIME OF RENEWAL

I Will Raise Up the Hut of David

However, I will not completely destroy
the house of Jacob,
says the LORD.
9 For I will give the command
and shake out the house of Israel
from among all the nations,
as one sifts with a sieve
without one pebble falling to the ground.
10 All the sinners among my people shall die by the sword,
those who say, "Evil will not approach or overtake us." [d]
11 On that day I shall raise up
the fallen hut of David.
I will repair the gaps in its walls,
restore its ruins,
and rebuild it as in the days of old, [e]
12 so that Israel may possess the remnant of Edom
and of all the nations that bear my name;
I, the LORD, will accomplish this.

I Will Reestablish My People Israel

13 The days are surely coming,
says the LORD,
when the plowman shall overtake
the one who reaps,
and the treader of grapes will overtake
the one who sows the seed.
New wine will drip from the mountains,
and every hill will flow with it. [f]
14 I will restore the fortunes of my people Israel;
they will rebuild the ruined cities and inhabit them.
They will plant vineyards and drink their wine,
cultivate gardens and eat their fruit. [g]
15 I will plant them in their own soil,
and they shall never again be uprooted
from the land I have given them.
This is the word of the LORD, your God.

d Jer 11:22; Ezek 3:19.—e Isa 61:4; Acts 15:16.—f Jer 31:27; Joel 4:18.—g Isa 61:4; Jer 31:5.

THE BOOK OF OBADIAH

Against Those Who Profit from the Misfortune of Others

In 587 B.C., Judah and the city of Jerusalem fell under the assault of the Chaldeans. Some poor unfortunates lived on amid the ruins. The small neighboring kingdom of Edom took the opportunity to loot what remained and to strengthen its position at the expense of the ruined population. The prophet Obadiah lets us hear an echo of those hopeless times. His message is first and foremost that the Edomites' nasty blow against a people who were their brothers will unleash the wrath of the Lord and that in the end Israel will have its revenge. In Obadiah's view, God is not the God of a single people only but judges the human race; there is a justice, a moral standard, that must be observed among groups and people, and he will not allow it to be violated.

Rise Up! Let Us Attack Edom

1 The vision of Obadiah about Edom:
I heard a message from the LORD,
and a herald has been sent to advise the nations:
"Rise up! Let us attack Edom!" [a]
2 The LORD says to Edom:
I will make you the least of all the nations;
you are the object of utter contempt. [b]
3 The pride in your heart has led you astray,
you who live in the crannies of the rock,
whose dwelling is on the heights.
You think to yourself,
"Who can bring me down to the ground?"
4 Even though you soar like an eagle
and your nest is set among the stars,
from there I will bring you down
says the LORD.
5 If thieves approached you,
or robbers during the night,

a Isa 34:5; Jer 49:14.—b 2ff: Num 24:18; Jer 49:15f.

you would not be destroyed,
for wouldn't they steal only what they wanted?
If grape-pickers were to come to you,
wouldn't they leave gleanings? [c]
6 But note how they will ransack Esau
and steal his hidden treasures. [d]
7 All your former allies
will drive you to your borders.
Your confederates will overpower you,
those who eat your bread will set a trap for you,
but you will not realize it.*
8 On that day, says the LORD,
I will destroy all the wise men of Edom,
and wisdom will disappear from the mountains of Esau. [e]
9 Your warriors will be so terrified, O Teman,*
that there will be no survivors on the mountains of Esau.
10 Because of the slaughter and the violence
inflicted on your brother Jacob,
shame will cover you
and you will be cut off forever. [f]
11 On the day when you stood aside
while strangers carried off his wealth,
and foreigners passed through his gates
and cast lots for Jerusalem,
you were as evil as they were.

Do Not Gloat over Your Brother on the Day of His Misfortune

12 Do not gloat over your brother
on the day of his misfortune.
Do not rejoice over the children of Judah
on the day of their ruin,
nor boast unfeelingly
on the day of their distress. [g]
13 Do not enter the gate of my people
on the day of their calamity.
Do not join in the gloating
on the day of their calamity.
Do not lay your hands on their possessions
on the day of their calamity.
14 Do not wait at the crossroads
to slaughter their fugitives.
Do not hand over the survivors
on the day of their distress.
15 For the day of the LORD is near
for all the nations.
As you have done,
so will it be done to you;
your deeds will recoil upon your own head. [h]

Dominion Will Belong to the LORD

16 Just as you have drunk on my holy mountain,
so shall all the nations drink continually;
they shall drink and gulp it down
and be as though they had never been.
17 But on Mount Zion a remnant will be saved;
it will be holy,
and the house of Jacob will take possession
of those who dispossessed them.
18 Then the house of Jacob will be a fire,
and the house of Joseph a flame.
The house of Esau will be stubble;
it will be set afire and consumed,
and no one of the house of Esau will survive,
for the LORD has spoken. [i]
19 My people from the Negeb*
will occupy the mount of Esau,
and people from the lowlands
will occupy the foothills
of the land of the Philistines.
They will occupy the fields of Ephraim and Samaria,
and Benjamin will possess Gilead.
20 The exiles of the Israelites
will possess Phoenicia as far as Zarephath,*
and the exiles of Jerusalem who are in Sepharad
will possess the towns of the Negeb.
21 Those who have been saved
will ascend Mount Zion
to rule over the mountains of Esau,
and dominion will belong to the LORD. [j]

---

c Jer 49:9.—d Jer 49:10.—e Ps 37:20; Isa 29:14; 1 Cor 1:19.—f Gen 27:41f; Ps 83:18; Jer 49:13.—g Ps 35:15; Prov 24:17.—h Ps 137:7ff; Joel 1:15.—i Zec 12:6; Am 5:6.—j Ps 22:29; Dan 7:27.

7 The Edomites, a not very numerous people, supposedly descended from Esau (Gen 36), the grandson of Abraham, had settled to the southeast of the Dead Sea; their capital was the city of Petra. Entrenched in their precipitous terrain, they were able to remain safe while the armies of Nebuchadnezzar were on the loose. But their enemies would find them out and make a clean sweep of their land.

9 *Teman* was south of Edom.

19 *Negeb:* the extreme south of Palestine. *Foothills:* the Shephelah or coastal plain. *Gilead:* across the Jordan.

20 *Zarephath:* in Phoenicia. *Sepharad:* unidentified.

THE BOOK OF JONAH

A Religion without Borders

This Book is full of improbabilities.

Was Jonah a real person? The Bible does know of a prophet by that name, the son of Amittai (see 2 Ki 14:25), who lived around the middle of the eighth century. Here, however, the impression is given that "Jonah" is simply a straw man.

Jonah did exist, but in a different sense: in the same sense that the murderous vinedressers existed (Mt 21:33-41), or the rich man and the impoverished Lazarus (Lk 16:19-21), or the prodigal son and his father (Lk 15:11-32). In the author's intention, we are to see in Jonah those religious Jews of the postexilic period who huddled around the Jerusalem temple, whose hopes were limited by a narrow nationalism, and who had nothing but scorn for the great mass of human beings astray in the world.

The story told in this Book is, then, a parable, and it has a rightful place among the Prophets. In fact, it gives the real meaning of the countless threats against the pagans that occupy so much space in the Prophets (Am 1:3—2:3; Isa 13–27; Jer 48–51; Ezek 25–32; etc.): God desires not the destruction of the nations but their conversion (Jer 12:15-16; 16:19; Isa 45:22; 49:6; Jon 3:10; 4:2, 11; etc.). The author ridicules a narrow-minded and jealous nationalism and asserts that God's forgiveness knows no limits. Even the pagans are called, and Jesus goes beyond Jonah when he says that the Ninevites will be the Pharisees' accusers at the judgment (see Mt 12:41-42; Lk 11:21-32). In speaking to his contemporaries, Jesus will use the image of Jonah to announce his own resurrection (Mt 12:39-40).

This Book, written in a late form of Hebrew and drawing its inspiration from the prophets Jeremiah and Ezekiel, was composed in the postexilic period and is one of the most interesting testimonies to the missionary ideal of the People of God and to the universal scope of the message of salvation.

This Book may be divided as follows:

I: Recalcitrant Prophet (1:1—2:1)
II: Prayer of Deliverance (2:2-11)
III: An Unforeseen Success (3:1—4:5)
IV: The Last Lesson (4:6-11)

I: RECALCITRANT PROPHET*

CHAPTER 1

1 The word of the LORD came to Jonah, son
of Amittai: [a] 2 "Go immediately to the great
city of Nineveh and denounce it, for their
wickedness has revealed itself to me." [b] 3 But
Jonah decided to run away from the LORD
and flee to Tarshish.* He went down to
Joppa, where he found a ship that was about

a 2 Ki 14:25.—b Jon 3:3; Sir 4:11; 17:16; Zep 2:13.

1:1—2:1 The story of the whale resembles stories told among all the coastal peoples of the Mediterranean basin. It serves simply to end the whole episode, in the atmosphere of the marvelous, that pervades the entire account. Jesus will use Jonah's experience with the whale as an image of his own burial and resurrection (see Mt 12:39-40; Lk 11:29-30).

1:3 *Tarshish:* perhaps Tartessos in Spain, a seaport that marked the outer limits of communication. *Joppa:* the Mediterranean port for Jerusalem.

to sail to Tarshish. He paid his fare and
boarded the ship to journey with the sailors
to Tarshish, and away from the presence of
the LORD.

4 However, the LORD caused a violent wind
to stir up the sea, and such a furious storm
arose that the ship seemed to be on the verge
of breaking up. 5 The sailors were terror-
stricken, and each of them cried out to his
god. They also lightened the weight of the
ship by throwing the cargo overboard.

Meanwhile, Jonah had gone down into the
hold of the ship and was lying there fast
asleep. 6 The captain found him there and
said, "What are you doing there, sound
asleep? Get up and call upon your God.
Perhaps he will take pity on us and not allow
us to perish."

7 The sailors then said to each other, "Let
us cast lots so that we can discover who is to
blame for bringing us this bad luck."
Therefore, they cast lots, and the lot fell on
Jonah.[c] 8 Then they said to him, "Tell us why
this calamity has come upon us. What is your
occupation? Where do you come from? What
is your country? What is your nationality?"
9 Jonah replied, "I am a Hebrew. I worship
the LORD, the God of heaven, who made the
sea and the dry land."[d]

10 On hearing this, the sailors were even
more terrified, and they said to him, "How
could you have done this to us?" For they
knew that he was fleeing from the LORD
because he had told them so. 11 Then they
said, "What shall we do with you to make the
sea calm down for us?" For the sea was
becoming increasingly more turbulent.
12 Jonah replied, "Pick me up and throw me
overboard. Then the sea will calm down for
you. I know it is my fault that this great
storm has struck you."

13 Even so, the sailors rowed with all their
might to reach the shore, but they were
unable to do so inasmuch as the sea was
becoming increasingly turbulent. 14 Finally
they cried out to the LORD, "Do not allow
us to perish, LORD, for taking this man's
life. Do not hold us responsible for causing
the death of an innocent man. For you
yourself, O LORD, have brought this all
about."[e] 15 Then they picked up Jonah and
threw him into the sea, and the raging of
the sea subsided. 16 On witnessing this, the
men were seized by a great fear of the
LORD, and they offered a sacrifice to the
LORD and made vows to him.

CHAPTER 2

1 Then the LORD ordained that a large fish
would swallow Jonah and he remained in the
belly of the fish for three days and three
nights.[f]

II: PRAYER OF DELIVERANCE *

2 Then from the belly of the fish Jonah
offered this prayer to the LORD, his God:

3 In my distress I called to the LORD,
and he answered me.
From the belly of the netherworld I cried out for help,
and you heard my voice.[g]

4 For you cast me into the deep,
into the heart of the sea,
and the flood enveloped me;
all your waves and your billows swept over me.[h]

5 Then I thought, "I have been banished from your sight.
Will I ever be allowed again
to look upon your holy temple?"[i]

6 The waters around me rose to my neck,
and the deep was closing around me;
seaweed was twined around my head.[j]

7 Down I plunged to the roots of the mountains,
sinking to the netherworld
whose bars would imprison me forever.
But you brought me up alive from the pit,
O LORD, my God.[k]

8 As my life was ebbing away,
I remembered the LORD,
and my prayer reached you
in your holy temple.[l]

9 Those who worship false gods
abandon the source of their mercy.[m]

10 But I with hymns of praise
will offer sacrifice to you.
What I have vowed I will fulfill.
Salvation comes from the LORD.[n]

c Ps 22:19; Jn 19:24.—d Ps 95:5.—e Mt 14:30.—f Jon 2:2; Mt 12:40; 16:4; Lk 11:30; 1 Cor 15:4; Rev 12:16.—g 2 Sam 22:7; Pss 18:7; 34:7; 120:1; Sir 51:10.—h Job 30:19; Pss 42:8; 88:18.—i 2 Ki 23:27; Ps 31:23; Isa 38:11; Jer 13:19.—j Gen 1:2; Pss 18:5; 69:2.—k Num 16:33; Pss 16:10; 30:4; Sir 48:5; Isa 38:17.—l 2 Chr 30:27; Pss 5:8; 18:7; 88:3; Sir 51:8.—m Deut 32:21; Ps 31:7; Wis 14:27.—n Gen 9:11; Ps 50:14.

2:2-11 The author inserts, here, an appeal whose images give a vivid description of every kind of distress (see Ps 69:1-2, 15).

11 Then, in response to a command from
the LORD, the fish spewed Jonah out upon
the land.

III: AN UNFORESEEN SUCCESS

CHAPTER 3

1 The word of the LORD then came to
Jonah for a second time:[o] 2 "Set out for the
great city of Nineveh and proclaim to it the
message that I give you."* 3 Therefore,
Jonah set out and journeyed to Nineveh in
obedience to the command of the LORD.

Now Nineveh was an exceedingly large
city; it required three days simply to walk
across it. 4 Jonah began his journey into the
city, walking for an entire day. Then he pro-
claimed, "After forty days, Nineveh will be
overthrown."[p] 5 The people of Nineveh be-
lieved this message from God. They pro-
claimed a fast, and everyone, from the
greatest to the least, put on sackcloth.[q]

6 When the news reached the king of
Nineveh, he rose from his throne, laid aside
his robe, covered himself with sackcloth, and
sat down in ashes. 7 Then he had this procla-
mation delivered throughout Nineveh:
"Neither man nor beast, neither herd nor
flock, is to eat anything. Do not allow them
to eat or drink. 8 Every man and beast is to
be covered with sackcloth. Let all cry out
with fervor to God, and let them turn from
their evil ways and their violent behavior.
9 Who knows? Perhaps God may change his
mind and relent, and his fierce anger may
abate, so that we will not perish."[r]

10 When God saw by their actions that
they had turned from their evil ways, he
relented and did not inflict upon them the
punishment that he had threatened.

CHAPTER 4

Jonah's Anger; God's Reproof. 1 This deci-
sion greatly displeased Jonah, and he became
very angry. 2 Praying to the LORD, he said,
"LORD, isn't this exactly what I predicted
when I was still in my own country? That is
why in the beginning I fled to Tarshish. I knew
that you are a gracious and compassionate
God, who is slow to anger, abounding in
mercy, and ready to relent from inflicting
punishment.[s] 3 Therefore, LORD, please take
my life from me, for it is better for me to die
than to live."[t] 4 The LORD replied, "Do you
have any right to be angry?"

5 Then Jonah left Nineveh and walked to
the east of the city. After making a booth for
himself there, he sat under it in the shade
while he waited to see what would happen to
the city.

IV: THE LAST LESSON

6 The LORD God then ordained that a
gourd plant should grow up above Jonah to
cast shade over his head and relieve his dis-
comfort. Jonah was very happy about this
plant.

7 But at dawn the next day, God ordained
that a worm should infest the gourd plant,
and it withered.[u] 8 Then, when the sun rose,
God ordained that a scorching wind should
blow from the east. The sun beat down on the
head of Jonah to such an extent that he grew
faint. Then he begged that he might die, say-
ing, "I would be better off dead than alive."

9 God said to Jonah, "Is it right for you to be
angry about the plant?" Jonah replied, "I
have every reason to be angry, angry enough
to die."[v]

10 The LORD then said, "You are concerned
about the plant, for which you did not labor
and which you did not grow. It came into
being in one night, and it perished in one
night. 11 Therefore, why should I not be con-
cerned about Nineveh, that great city in
which there are more than one hundred and
twenty thousand persons who cannot tell
their right hand from their left, as well as
innumerable cattle?"

---

o Jon 1:1.—p Jer 48:42.—q 1 Ki 21:12; Mt 12:41; Lk 11:32.—r Ex 32:12; Joel 2:14.—s Num 14:18; Ps 86:5; Joel 2:13.—t 1 Ki 19:4; Tob 3:6.—u Joel 2:25; Am 7:1.—v 1 Ki 21:5.

3:2ff Nineveh is described as a city of very unlikely size. The story required that this very pagan city be immense.

"But from you, O Bethlehem . . . will come forth for me one who is to be a ruler in Israel" *(Mic 5:1).*

THE BOOK OF MICAH

The Rights of the Poor

By the end of the eighth century, the People of God had, in large measure, lost that great sense of all being brothers and sisters within the one covenant, that had marked them in the beginning. As in other countries, a social hierarchy had formed and prevailed: the wealthy classes claimed power and honors, and thought only of extending their domain. Whereas Isaiah, an aristocrat, voiced his anger at the official classes in Jerusalem, the prophet Micah, a humble peasant of southern Palestine, raised his voice in protest on behalf of the poor, who were exploited by exacting masters and brought to ruin by the Assyrian invader. The latter destroyed the northern kingdom in 721 B.C., and subsequently put down the repeated rebellions of the kings of Jerusalem, who were overconfident of being safe behind the walls of the capital.

With strong words and simple images, Micah denounces the abuses and injustices that are undermining faith in the one God and the fraternal unity of the chosen people. These are harsh pages that are as powerful today as they were then.

Jeremiah's testimony (Jer 26:18), a century later, shows that Micah had made a strong impression.

Micah's work, as we have it, is made up chiefly of a collection of threats and reproaches that are only brief testimonies to a lengthy activity in the service of God's word. But the prophet also brings the hope of a "remnant" that is preserved by God to be the nucleus of a renewed kingdom. After the Exile, with the intention of mitigating the prophet's terrible threats, some men of letters extensively expanded these glimmers of hope.

But just as Micah in his day had been unable to see the conversion of Israel as occurring apart from punishment by the Lord, so these later writers could not imagine a restoration of the people that was not accompanied by the annihilation of their enemies. These cries for vengeance, which so irk us, are not the most profound element in the message; this element is rather the affirmation of the greatness of God and the conviction that salvation will come. Once we have read the two splendid passages on true religion (6:6-8) and divine forgiveness (7:18-20), we will find Micah unforgettable.

The Book of Micah may be divided as follows:

I: A Trial of God against Israel (1:1—3:12)
II: The Expectation of Renewal (4:1—5:14)
III: A New Trial against Israel (6:1—7:7)
IV: Poems of Hope (7:8–20)

I: A TRIAL OF GOD AGAINST ISRAEL

CHAPTER 1

1 This is the word of the LORD that came to Micah of Moresheth* during the reigns of Jotham, Ahaz, and Hezekiah, kings of Judah, and which he received in visions concerning Samaria and Jerusalem.

I Will Reduce Samaria to a Ruin

2 Listen, all you peoples!
Give heed, O earth, and all who dwell in it.
Let the Lord GOD be a witness against you,
the LORD from his holy temple. [a]
3 Take note that the LORD is leaving his dwelling place;
he comes down and treads upon the heights of the earth. [b]
4 The mountains melt at his touch,
and the valleys are torn open,
like wax near a fire,
like water pouring down a hillside.

5 All this is the result
of the crime of Jacob
and the sins of Israel.
What is the crime of Jacob?
Is it not Samaria?
And what is the sin of the house of Judah?
Is it not Jerusalem?
6 Therefore, I will reduce Samaria
to a ruin in the open country,
a place for planting vineyards.
I will hurl down her stones into the valley
and lay bare her foundations. [c]
7 All of her idols will be shattered,
all of her earnings will be consumed by fire,
and all of her statues I will lay waste.
For she amassed her gifts
from the wages of prostitution,*
and the earnings of a prostitute
they once more will become. [d]

I Will Lament and Wail*

8 This is the reason why I will lament and wail,
why I will go barefoot and naked.
I will howl like a jackal
and mourn like a desert owl. [e]
9 There is no remedy for the wounds
that the LORD inflicts;
now the blow has fallen on Judah.
It has reached the very gate of my people,
even to Jerusalem.

10 Do not announce it in Gath,
nor shed any tears.
In Beth-leaphrah
roll yourselves in the dust.
11 Begin your journey,
you inhabitants of Shaphir.

---

a Deut 32:1; Jos 24:27; Ps 49:2; Isa 1:2.—b 3f: Sir 16:17; Ps 97:5; Isa 26:21; Ezek 26:18; Nah 1:5; Hab 3:10.—c Gen 19:26; Ezek 13:14.—d Ps 146:4; Ezek 6:6; Hos 9:1.—e 1 Mac 9:41; Job 30:29; Hos 6:5.

1:1 We are in the period after 740 B.C., the time of the great threats to Samaria and Jerusalem. *Moresheth* was southwest of Jerusalem. *Jotham* reigned 738–736 B.C.; *Ahaz:* 736–721 B.C.; *Hezekiah:* 721–693 B.C.

1:7 *Wages of prostitution:* the gifts left for the idols, according to custom, in Canaanite sanctuaries; the invaders will take these and use them, in the same way, in their own rituals.

1:8-16 Micah weeps over his little homeland that has been ravaged by an Assyrian raid; the year is probably 701 B.C., and Sennacherib's armies are on the march.

Those who dwell in Zaanan
have not left their city.
Beth-ezel is filled with lamentation
and no longer can offer you support.
12 The inhabitants of Maroth
are filled with despair.
For disaster has come down from the LORD
to the very gate of Jerusalem.

13 Harness the steeds to the chariots
you inhabitants of Lachish.
You first led the daughter of Zion into sin;
the crimes of Israel can be traced to you.
14 Therefore, you shall offer parting gifts
to Moresheth-gath.
Beth-achzib will prove to be deceptive
to the kings of Israel.
15 I will again send a conqueror against you,
O inhabitants of Mareshah.
And the glory of Israel
shall be transferred to Adullam.

16 Shave your heads in mourning
for the children who were your delight.
Make yourselves as bald as the eagle,
for they have gone from you into exile.

CHAPTER 2

Those Who Covet Fields and Homes

1 Woe to those who plot evil,
who lie in their beds planning iniquity.
When morning dawns they perform their wicked deeds
since they have the power to do so.[f]
2 They seize the fields that they covet;
they confiscate houses as well.
They lay hands on the owner of a house,
and take his inheritance as well.

3 Therefore, thus says the LORD:

Behold, I am planning against this people an evil
from which you will not be able to save your necks.
Nor will you walk proudly,
for it will be a time of disaster.[g]
4 On that day they will ridicule you,
and your mournful dirge will be heard:
"We are utterly ruined;
our land has been appropriated by our captors.
Our fields have been awarded to renegades,
and no one can retrieve them."
5 Therefore, you will have no one
to divide the land by lot
in the assembly of the LORD.

Against Prophets of Ease

6 "Do not preach," they advise;
"one should not expound on such matters;
disgrace will not overtake us."
7 O house of Jacob, should it be said:
"Has the LORD's patience been exhausted?
Does he do such things?
His words only prophesy good
to those who are upright."[h]

8 But now you have risen up
as an enemy to my people.
You strip the cloaks from travelers
who pass by peacefully,
or from soldiers returning from battle.
9 The women of my people you drive forth
from their pleasant homes
and deprive their children
of my glory forever,
10 commanding them, "Get up and depart,
for you cannot stay here."
To obtain something worthless for yourselves,
you do not hesitate to practice extortion.[i]

I Will Assemble the Remnant of Israel

11 If someone were to go about
uttering falsehoods and lies, and saying,
"I prophesy that you will have your fill
of wine and strong drink,"
such a man would be the perfect prophet
for a people like this.

12 I will gather all of you together, O Jacob;
I will assemble the remnant of Israel.
I will gather them together
like sheep into a fold,
like a flock in a pasture;
no longer will they be filled with panic.

f Eccl 10:16; Isa 5:20.—g Jer 36:31; Am 5:13.—h Jer 32:42; 2 Pet 3:15.—i Lam 1:3.

13 With their leader proceeding before them,
they shall break through the gate and go out.
Their king will go forth before them,
the LORD at their head.[j]

CHAPTER 3

The Leader Devours the Chair of My People

1 Then I said:

Listen, you leaders of the house of Jacob,
you rulers of the house of Israel.
Should you not be responsible
to know what is right?
2 And yet you hate what is good
and love what is evil.[k]
3 You eat the flesh of my people
and strip off their skin;
you break their bones into pieces
like flesh for the pot,
like meat in a cauldron.
4 Then they will cry out to the LORD,
but he will not answer them.
He will conceal his face from them at that time
because of the evil they have done.

Against Prophets Who Lead the People Astray

5 Thus says the LORD about the prophets
who lead my people astray,
who promise prosperity
when they have something to eat,
but who declare war against those
who put no food into their mouths.[l]
6 Therefore, you will have night without vision
and darkness without divination.
The sun will go down on the prophets;
for them the daytime will be black.[m]
7 Then the seers will be disgraced
and the diviners will be put to shame.
They will all cover their lips,
for there is no answer from God.[n]
8 But as for me, I am filled with strength,
with the Spirit of the LORD,
with justice and might
to declare to Jacob his crime
and to Israel his sin.

A Civilization Built on Injustice

9 Listen to this,
you leaders of the house of Jacob,
you rulers of the house of Israel,
who despise justice
and pervert what is right,
10 who build Zion through bloodshed
and Jerusalem through wickedness.
11 Her leaders accept bribes for favorable judgments,
her priests render judgments for a fee,
her prophets practice divination for money.
And yet they rely upon the LORD, saying,
"Isn't the LORD in our midst?
No harm can come upon us."[o]
12 Therefore, because of you,
Zion will be plowed like a field.
Jerusalem will be reduced to a heap of rubble,
and the temple mount to a height
overgrown with thickets.[p]

II: THE EXPECTATION OF RENEWAL*

CHAPTER 4

We Shall Go to the Mountain of God

1 In days to come,
the mountain of the LORD's house
will be established as the highest of the mountains,
towering above other hills.
Peoples will stream toward it;[q]
2 many nations will come and say,
"Come, let us go up to the mountain of the LORD,
to the house of the God of Jacob,
so that he may teach us his ways
and we may walk in his paths."
For out of Zion will instruction go forth,
and from Jerusalem the word of the LORD.
3 He will judge between many peoples
and serve as an arbiter,
between mighty and distant nations.
They will beat their swords into plowshares
and their spears into pruning hooks.
Nation will not take up the sword against nation,
nor will they ever again be trained for war.

j Isa 45:2; Lk 1:17.—k Am 2:7; Zec 11:16.—l Jer 23:32; Ezek 13:10.—m Ps 139:12; Isa 60:19; Jer 15:9; Am 8:9.—n Pss 18:42; 53:6.—o Jer 5:12; Zep 3:3.—p Jer 7:34; 26:18.—q 1ff: Isa 2:2ff; 66:16; Jer 48:47.

4:1—5:14 In this section it is difficult to determine what is from Micah and what is postexilic.

4 Each man will sit under his own vine
or under his own fig tree
with no cause for alarm,
for the mouth of the LORD of hosts has spoken.
5 For all the peoples go forth,
each in the name of its god,
but we will walk in the name of the LORD, our God,
forever and ever. [r]

Gathering Up the Dispersed Flock

6 On that day, says the LORD,
I will gather the lame;
I will assemble those who have been driven away
and those whom I have afflicted.
7 I will make the lame into a remnant,
and turn into a strong nation those who were cast off.
The LORD will reign over them on Mount Zion
now and forevermore. [s]
8 As for you, O tower of the flock,*
hill of daughter Zion,
the promises made to you
will be fulfilled,
and your former security will be restored,
the sovereignty of daughter Jerusalem.

A Sorrowful Childbirth

9 Why are you now crying out?
Have you no king any longer,
or has your counselor perished,
that you are afflicted with pains
like a woman in labor?
10 Writhe in pain and cry aloud,
O daughter Zion,
like a woman in labor.
For now you must go forth from the city
and camp in the open country.
You will go to Babylon
where you will be saved.
There the LORD will deliver you
from the hands of your enemies.

The Nations Crush the Land of God

11 But now many nations
are gathered against you.
They say, "Let her be profaned;
let us gloat over Zion."
12 However, they do not know
the thoughts of the LORD
or comprehend his plan.
For he has gathered them
like sheaves on the threshing floor.
13 Arise and thresh,
O daughter of Zion,
for I will make your horn like iron
and your hooves like bronze
so that you may crush many peoples.
You shall devote their ill-gotten gains to the LORD,
their wealth to the LORD of the whole earth. [t]

From You Bethlehem There Will Be Born the One Who Will Rule*

14 Now withdraw behind your walls,
for they have laid siege against you.
With a rod they will strike on the cheek
the ruler of Israel.

CHAPTER 5

1 But from you, O Bethlehem Ephrathah,*
among the tiniest of the clans of Judah,
from you will come forth for me
one who is to be a ruler in Israel,
one whose origins are from the distant past,
from ancient times. [u]
2 Therefore, the LORD will abandon them
only until she who is in labor has given birth.
Then those of the people who survive
will be reunited with the Israelites. [v]
3 He will rise up to shepherd his flock
by the strength of the LORD,
in the majesty of the name
of the LORD his God.

r Jer 23:16; Hos 14:10.—s Ps 29:10; Wis 3:8; Isa 6:13; Dan 7:14; Zep 3:19; Lk 1:32-33.—t Lev 26:19; 2 Chr 14:12; Isa 41:15; Hos 10:11.—u Ru 1:2; 1 Sam 17:12; Isa 23:7; Mt 2:6; Jn 1:27; 7:42.—v 2f: Isa 7:14; 11:1f; 49:6.

4:8 *Tower of the flock:* a symbolic name for Jerusalem.

4:14—5:5 As had already happened in the past, the new leader, the new David, is to come from a modest rural family (see 1 Sam 16:1-13; 17:12), and the prophet sings of his glory. As we read in St. Matthew (Mt 2:5-6) and St. John (Jn 7:42), in the time of Jesus this oracle was interpreted as predicting the birthplace of the Messiah. It is a fine example of how God chooses someone unexpected and weak in order to confound the mighty and the strong (see Jdg 6:15; 1 Sam 9:21; 1 Cor 1:27). Speaking of the woman who is to give birth (Mic 5:2), the prophet alludes to the promise given by Isaiah (Isa 7:14) some years before, in which the Christian tradition, following the lead of the first Gospel (Mt 1:23), sees a veiled announcement of the birth of Jesus.

5:1 *Bethlehem Ephrathah:* the second name distinguishes this Bethlehem from a Bethlehem in Galilee. Ephrathah was the name of the family group that settled there; it then came to signify the city.

And they will live in security,
for then his greatness will be renowned
to the ends of the earth.
4 He will ensure their peace.

If Assyria Invades Our Country...

If the Assyrians invade our country
and set foot upon our land,
we shall raise against them seven shepherds
and appoint eight* men to serve as rulers.
5 They will rule the land of Assyria with the sword,
and the land of Nimrod with drawn swords.
And we will be delivered from Assyria
if it invades our country
or treads upon our borders.

The Remnant of Jacob

6 Then the remnant of Jacob,
surrounded by many peoples,
will be like dew from the LORD,
like showers on the grass,
which do not depend upon man
or wait for any man's bidding.
7 And among the nations the remnant of Jacob
will be surrounded by many peoples,
like a lion among the beasts of the forest,
like a young lion among the flocks of sheep,
trampling and tearing to pieces as it goes,
with no one able to stop the carnage.
8 Your hand will be lifted up over your foes,
and all your adversaries will be destroyed. [w]
9 On that day, says the LORD,
I will slaughter your horses
and destroy your chariots.
10 I will demolish the cities of your land
and raze all your fortresses to the ground.
11 I will eliminate your sorcerers,
and there will be no more soothsayers among you.
12 I will cut down your images
and the sacred pillars in your midst;
you will no longer worship
the work of your hands. [x]
13 I will uproot your sacred poles*
and destroy your cities.
14 In anger and fury, I will wreak vengeance
on the nations that have disobeyed me.

III: A NEW TRIAL AGAINST ISRAEL

CHAPTER 6

My People, What Have I Done to You?

1 Listen to what the LORD has to say:
Arise and state your case before the mountains,
and let the hills hear your voice. [y]
2 Hearken, you mountains, to the LORD's accusations;
listen, you foundations that support the earth.
For the LORD has a case against his people;
he intends to present it to Israel.
3 O my people, what, have I done to you?
How have I wearied you? Answer me! [z]
4 For I brought you up from the land of Egypt,
I redeemed you from the place of slavery,
and I sent as your leaders
Moses, Aaron, and Miriam. [a]
5 My people, remember the plan
that Balak, the king of Moab, devised,
and what Balaam, the son of Beor, answered him.
Recall also your journey from Shittim* to Gilgal
so that you may know the saving justice of the LORD. [b]

True Religion

6 With what will I come before the LORD
when I bow down before God on high?
Will I come before him with burnt offerings,
with calves a year old? [c]
7 Will the LORD be pleased with thousands of rams,
with ten thousand rivers of oil?

w 2 Sam 22:41; Ps 18:38.—x Tob 14:6; Hos 3:4; 10:1f; Nah 1:14.—y Deut 5:27; Ob 1-21; Rom 10:18.—z Jer 2:5; Rom 9:19.—a Ex 15:20; Ps 81:11.—b Num 22:23; Jos 5:9.—c 6f: 2 Sam 24:22; Ezr 3:6; Hos 6:6; 8:13; Am 5:21.

5:4 *Seven . . . eight:* a way of signifying a sizeable number; here it indicates the superiority of Israel.

5:13 *Sacred poles:* sacred poles symbolizing the female Canaanite divinity of the vegetation.

6:5 Balak wanted Balaam to curse the Israelites, but God made Balaam change the curse into a blessing (see Num 22–24). *Shittim* and *Gilgal* recall the entrance into the Promised Land (see Jos 3–4).

Should I offer my firstborn son for my transgressions,
the fruit of my body for the sin of my soul? *
8 The LORD has told you, O man, what is good.
And what does the LORD require of you?
Only this: to do what is right, to show mercy,
and to walk humbly with your God. * [d]

Those Who Commit Fraud Will Themselves Be Frustrated

9 Consider carefully what the LORD cries out to the city,
for to fear his name is a mark of wisdom:
10 "Listen, you tribe of assembled citizens!
How can I ignore the false measure
and the accursed short bushel?
11 Can I overlook rigged scales
or a bag of fraudulent weights?
12 The wealthy men of the city are steeped in violence;
its inhabitants are liars
and their tongues speak deceitfully.
13 Therefore, I intend to strike you with devastation
because of your sins. [e]
14 You will eat but not be satisfied,
for your stomach will continue to experience hunger.
You will acquire but be unable to save,
and what you do save,
I will deliver up to the sword. [f]
15 You will sow
but you will not reap;
you will press the olives
but you will not anoint yourself with oil;
you will tread the grapes
but you will not drink the wine. [g]
16 For you have kept the statutes of Omri
and all the practices of the house of Ahab;
you have adopted all their policies.
Therefore, I will make your land desolate
and your citizens an object of scorn.
From this time on
you will endure the scorn of other nations."

CHAPTER 7

More than One Righteous Person among the People

1 How great is my misery!
I have become like one who,
when the summer fruit has been gathered
and the vines have been gleaned,
finds not a single cluster of grapes to eat,
nor any of those early figs for which I long.
2 The faithful have vanished from the land;
there is no honest person to be found.
They all lie in wait to shed blood;
each one hunts his brother with a net. [h]
3 Their hands are skilled in performing evil deeds;
the ruler demands gifts,
the judge asks for a bribe,
the powerful man follows his own desires. [i]
4 The best of them is like a briar,
the most upright like a thorn hedge.
The day of their punishment now approaches;
now they will be seized by confusion.

5 Put no trust in a friend:
have no confidence in a loved one.
Guard the portals of your mouth
against her who lies in your embrace. [j]
6 For a son maligns his father,
a daughter rebels against her mother,
a daughter-in-law rises up against her mother-in-law;
your enemies are to be found in your own household. [k]
7 But as for me, I will look to the LORD.
I place my hope in God my savior;
my God will hear me. [l]

d Deut 26:16; Ps 119:3; Wis 1:1; Zec 7:9; Mt 23:23.—e 1 Sam 17:46.—f Sir 25:3; Ezek 24:23; Hos 4:10.—g Deut 28:38; Eccl 11:4; Am 5:11; Hag 1:6.—h Wis 14:25; Isa 1:21; Hos 4:2.—i Isa 1:23.—j Ps 146:3; Jer 9:3.—k Deut 27:16; Mt 10:35f; Mk 13:12; Jas 4:11.—l Pss 52:10; 77:2; Isa 8:17.

6:7 Sacrifice of the firstborn seems to have been frequently practiced at this time, the idea being to obtain the divine favor by offering the firstfruits of human life. The Prophets protested strongly against this aberration of the religious sense (see 2 Ki 16:3; Jer 7:31; Ezek 20:26).

6:8 Even if this magnificent verse were the only memorable passage in the Book of Micah, the Book would be worth reading and rereading; the verse is one of the richest summations of prophetic preaching (Isa 19:19; Hos 6:6; Am 5:21-22).

IV: POEMS OF HOPE*

I Shall Rise Up

8 Do not gloat over me, O my enemy.
Although I have fallen, I will arise.
Although I sit in darkness,
the LORD is my light. [m]
9 I must endure the anger of the LORD
because I have sinned against him,
until he takes up my cause
and forgives my wrongs,
until he brings me into the light
and I will behold his saving justice.
10 When my enemies see this,
they will be filled with shame,
those who said to me,
"Where is the LORD, your God?"
My eyes will see their downfall
as they are trampled underfoot
like mud in the streets.
11 That will be the day for rebuilding your walls,
the day for extending your boundaries.
12 On that day a people will come to you,
all the way from Assyria and from Egypt,
from Tyre to the Euphrates,
from sea to sea and from mountain to mountain. [n]
13 And the earth will be a wasteland
because of its inhabitants,
as a suitable punishment for their deeds.* [o]

Make Us See Wonders

14 Shepherd your people with your staff,
the flock that is your heritage,
that lives by itself in a forest
with meadows surrounding it.
Let them graze in Bashan* and Gilead,
as in the days of old.
15 Show us wondrous signs
as in the days when you came out
from the land of Egypt.
16 The nations will see and be confounded
despite all their power.
They will put their hands over their mouths;
their ears will become deaf. [p]
17 They will lick the dust like snakes,
like reptiles that crawl on the ground.
They will come trembling out of their strongholds
and turn in dread to behold the LORD, our God,
as they approach him in awe and terror.

The God Who Forgives

18 What god can compare with you,
the God who takes away guilt
and forgives the transgressions
of the remnant of your people?
You will not allow your anger to fester forever,
for your delight is in bestowing mercy. [q]
19 You will again show us compassion
and wash away our guilt;
you will cast all our sins
into the depths of the sea.
20 You will show faithfulness to Jacob
and unswerving mercy to Abraham
as you swore to our ancestors
from the days of old. [r]

m Pss 18:29; 30:2.—n Isa 27:13; Zec 14:16.—o Ps 107:34; Jer 44:22.—p 1 Mac 1:28; Jer 50:2.—q Ex 15:11; Ps 103:3; Jer 10:6; Acts 10:43.—r Jos 21:43; Pss 89:4; 105:6; Isa 41:8; 63:16.

7:8-20 Because of their subjects and the events they recall, these canticles, which are liturgical in tone, seem not to date from Micah's time; they are suited, rather, to the situation of the Jews who have returned from exile after the second half of the sixth century.

7:13 The threat is due to the neighboring enemies of Israel and their behavior toward those who have returned from exile.

7:14 *Bashan* and *Gilead*, beyond the Jordan, were regions of fertile pasture and forests.

THE BOOK OF NAHUM

The Fall of an Empire

The prophecy of Nahum is connected with an important historical event: the fall of Nineveh in 612 B.C. These oracles were delivered over the fifteen-year period preceding that date, and they coincide with the beginning of the career of the great prophet Jeremiah. They echo the exultant joy of the little states of the East, Judah among them, as they saw themselves being delivered from the control of the Assyrians. A century earlier, this great empire had gained control as far as the borders of Egypt; it had destroyed Samaria in 721 B.C. and had besieged Jerusalem in 701 B.C. Beginning in 625 B.C. the Babylonians regained their independence and, together with the Medes, definitively gained the upper hand over the impressive power of Assyria in 612 B.C.

The Book of Nahum is a literary masterpiece but it is also not lacking in religious value. There is, doubtless, a breath of nationalism and revenge that runs through all its verses, from beginning to end, but the Book is quite different from a savage-hymn of victory; it celebrates not only the satisfaction of Judah's desire for revenge by the sight of proud and terrifying Nineveh being punished, but also the Lord's revenge on human tyrants, represented at this time by Assyria. Woe to those who dare to oppose God and make themselves the masters of the world!

The judgment upon Nineveh, which is described with an excessively cruel rejoicing, is an element in the conception of history that runs through the entire Bible: no human being can permanently usurp the dominion that belongs to God; times of restoration come to shed light on the times of enslavement, until the day when God's plan is fully accomplished, when the heavenly city arrives in which the Christian Apocalypse sees all believers permanently united in the joy of God (see Rev 21).

The Book of Nahum may be divided as follows:

I: The Fury of God (1:2—2:3)

II: The Agony of Nineveh (2:4—3:19)

CHAPTER 1

Title. 1 This is an oracle about Nineveh, the book of the vision of Nahum of Elkosh. *

I: THE FURY OF GOD*

In the Face of His Ardent Anger, Who Could Resist Him?*

2 The LORD is a jealous God
who does not hesitate to wreak vengeance
or to show his anger.
The LORD takes vengeance on his adversaries
and stores up wrath against his enemies.
3 The LORD is slow to anger but great in power,
and he will never allow the guilty
to escape punishment.
He makes his way in whirlwind and storm,
and the clouds are the dust beneath his feet. [a]
4 He rebukes the sea and leaves it dry,
and he dries up all the rivers.
Bashan and Carmel wither,
and the greenery of Lebanon fades. * [b]

a Ex 19:16ff; Deut 23:22; Ps 145:8.—b Isa 33:9; Hos 13:15; Jas 1:11.

1:1 *Elkosh* was probably a place in Judea. This verse tells us what the subject of the Book is to be.

1:2—2:3 The faith of Israel judges these events differently from the way secular historians do through the sudden leaps of history; it is the project of salvation of God that is accomplished: it is he who destroys Nineveh. Thus, before describing the unfolding of facts, the Book raises this drama to the level of a great manifestation of God, who brings back order and justice into the universe of men.

1:2-8 One must let himself be carried away by the force of this triumphal psalm, which proclaims the victory of the All-Powerful whom no one can resist. Nevertheless, this terrible God leans toward the wicked.

1:4 The places named were places of classic opulence.

5 The mountains quake before him,
and the hills dissolve;
the earth collapses before him,
the world and all who live in it. [c]
6 When confronted by his anger,
who can stand firm?
Who can endure his burning wrath?
His fury is poured out like fire,
and the rocks are shattered before him. [d]
7 The LORD is good,
an unfailing refuge in a time of distress.
He takes care of those who place their trust in him,
8 even if they are in peril from a raging flood.
He will make an end of those who oppose him,
and he will pursue his enemies into darkness.

They Will Be Wasted Like Dry Straw*

9 Why do you devise plots against the LORD?
He will make an end of you.
None of his adversaries rise up to confront him
for a second time.
10 Like a thicket of thornbushes, they are entangled;
like dry straw they will be utterly consumed.
11 From your number, one has emerged
who plots evil against the LORD
and counsels wickedness.

12 Thus says the LORD:

No matter how numerous they are,
no matter how great their strength,
they will be cut down and pass away.
Even though I have afflicted you,
I will make you suffer no more. [e]
13 Now I will break off their yoke from your neck
and snap the shackles that bind you. [f]
14 In regard to you, Nineveh,
the LORD has decreed
that no more descendants will be born
to perpetuate your name.
I will remove carved images and sculpted idols
from the temple of your gods.
And I will prepare your grave,
for you are worthless.

CHAPTER 2

The Message of Liberation

1 Behold on the mountains the feet of the herald
who proclaims good news and announces peace.
Celebrate your festivals, O Judah,
and fulfill your vows.
For never again will the wicked invade you;
they will be completely destroyed. [g]
2 The LORD will restore the majesty of Jacob
as well as that of Israel,*
even though the plunderers have ravaged them
and destroyed their vines.
3 A destroying enemy is advancing against you;
guard the ramparts.
Keep watch on the road,
gird your loins,
and prepare to exert
every last ounce of courage.

II: THE AGONY OF NINEVEH*

Devastation, Plunder, and Destruction*

4 The shields of his warriors are red with blood;
their garments are scarlet in color.
The metal on the chariots flashes
as he summons them for battle;
the horses are frenzied in anticipation.
5 The chariots charge madly through the streets,
rushing back and forth through the squares.

c Sir 16:17; Isa 24:3.—d Mic 1:4; Zep 1:15; 2:3; Rev 6:17.—e Ps 37:20; Isa 13:11.—f Ps 107:14; Isa 9:4; 10:27; Jer 28:4.—g Ps 147:1; Isa 52:7; Rom 10:15.

1:9-14 Master of the world, the Lord is also Master of history. He acts as the arbitrator of his oppressed people and Assyria, which incarnates the powers of evil: the first shall be liberated and the second shall be destroyed. Belial ("is worth nothing"), a term of scorn often assigned to an infernal power, fits very well upon Sennacherib, of sinister memory (see 2 Ki 18:19). If the God of the Bible appears to us often as one of chastisement, he is first of all the God of liberation.

2:2 *Restore the majesty of Jacob as well as that of Israel:* Assyria had destroyed the northern kingdom and its people (2 Ki 17:3-6) and attacked the southern kingdom. Now is the time for all Israel to be renewed and restored!

2:4—3:19 Described by types of fire, the chastisement is at the doors of Nineveh. In these oracles there is the explosion of joy for the world which is awakening from a nightmare after a century of Assyrian domination.

2:4-11 This tableau of extraordinary power reaches fine art: it describes a decisive assault against a powerful village.

They have the appearance of a blazing fire;
they dash about like lightning bolts.
6 His finest troops are summoned
and rush forward to the attack.
They hasten toward the wall
and set up the mantelet.
7 The river gates are opened
and the palace trembles.
8 The captives are taken into exile
and its slave girls are carried away,
moaning like doves
and beating their breasts.
9 Nineveh is like a lake
whose waters are ebbing away.
"Stop! Stop!" goes up the cry,
but no one turns back. [h]
10 "Plunder the silver!
Plunder the gold!
There is no end to the treasure,
an abundance of wealth
from precious things of every kind."
11 Devastation, desolation, and ruin
confront faint hearts and trembling knees.
The loins of all are filled with anguish;
every face is drained of color. [i]

Where Is the Lions' Den?*

12 Where now is the lions' den,
the cave where they fed their whelps,
where the lion and lioness cared for their cubs,
with no one to disturb them?
13 There the lion stored up
sufficient food for his whelps
and strangled prey for his mate.
He filled his dens with prey
and his caves with torn flesh.
14 "I come against you,"
says the LORD of hosts.
"I will set your chariots aflame,
and the sword will devour your young lions.
I will cut off your prey from the earth,
and the threats of your messengers
will no longer be heard." [j]

CHAPTER 3

Woe to the Bloodstained City*

1 Woe to the bloodstained city,
festering with lies,
full of booty,
never ceasing in its plunder. [k]
2 Endless are the crack of the whip
and the rumbling of wheels,
galloping horses
and jolting chariots,
3 charging cavalry,
flashing swords,
shimmering spears,
endless piles of the slain,
heaps of corpses,
endless bodies to stumble over.
4 Because of the persistent debaucheries of the harlot,
with her alluring facade as a mistress of sorcery,
who enslaved nations by her harlotries
and peoples by her witchcraft. [l]
5 "I am against you,"
says the LORD of hosts.
"I will lift up your skirts over your face
and exhibit your nakedness to the nations,
your shame to the kingdoms. [m]
6 I will pelt you with filth,
and treat you with contempt,
and make a spectacle of you.
7 Then all those who see you
will shrink from you and say,
'Nineveh is destroyed.'
Who will console her?
Where can anyone be found to comfort you?"

Are You Better than No-amon?*

8* Are you better than No-amon,
a city situated among streams
and surrounded by water,
with the seas serving as her rampart
and water as her wall? [n]
9 Ethiopia and Egypt were her strength,
and that strength was boundless;
Put and the Lybians were her allies.

h 1 Mac 9:45.—i Wis 17:10; Joel 2:6.—j Isa 14:31; Jer 21:14.—k Ezek 24:6; Hab 2:12; Zep 3:1.—l Wis 15:14; Mic 1:7; Rev 17:1f.—m Isa 20:4; 47:3; Jer 13:26; Ezek 16:39; Hos 2:12; Rev 17:16.—n Lam 2:8; Am 6:2.

2:12-14 The princes and the armies of Assyria carry lions as their emblem. Nineveh is the den crowded with fruit of the plunder.

3:1-7 Hallucinating description of the last days of Nineveh: the seductive gluttony of the peoples undergoes the pain of adulterous women.

3:8-11 Nineveh will know the fate that she herself inflicted, at the time of her splendor, at Thebes, the opulent city of Egypt plundered, in 767 B.C., by Ashurbanipal. This tragic change of situation underlies the fragility of empires built by men.

3:8-9 *No-amon:* called Thebes by the Greeks, was the capital of Upper Egypt; it, too, fell despite the power of Pharaoh Tirhakah (an Ethiopian by origin; see v. 9). *Put:* a non-Semitic population in southern Egypt.

10 Nevertheless, even she became an exile
and went into captivity.
Even her infants were dashed to pieces
at every street corner.
Lots were cast for her nobles,
and all her leaders were put in chains.
11 You, too, will become drunk
and go into hiding.
You, too, will flee,
seeking a refuge from the enemy. [o]

The Situation of Nineveh Is Desperate*

12 All your fortresses are fig trees
that bear early fruit.
As soon as they are shaken,
they fall into the mouth of the eater.
13 Look at your troops.
You are a nation of women.
The gates of your country
lie open to your enemies;
fire has consumed the bars of your gates. [p]
14 Draw yourselves water for the siege!
Strengthen your fortifications!
Trample the clay,
tread the mortar,
repair the brickwork!
15 Then the fire will consume you
and the sword will cut you off.
Multiply yourselves like the locusts,
make yourselves as numerous as the grasshoppers.

Like the Locusts, Strip the Land and Fly Away*

16 You have increased the number of your merchants
until they now outnumber the stars of the heavens,
but like the locusts, they strip the land
and then fly away.
17 Your guards are like locusts,
and your scribes are like swarms of grasshoppers
that settle in the walls
on a cold day.
However, when the sun rises, they fly away,
and no one knows where they have gone.

Incurable Is Your Sickness*

18 Alas, your shepherds are asleep,
O king of Assyria;
your neighbors lie down to rest.
Your people are scattered on the mountains
with no one to gather them.
19 There is no way to relieve your wound;
your injury is mortal.
All who hear this news about your fate
clap their hands over your downfall.
For who has not suffered
as a result of your relentless cruelty? [q]

o Ps 61:4.—p Ps 78:63; Jer 51:30.—q Jer 30:13.

3:12-15 What good, then, is it to work to repair the gaps with clay and intrigues.

3:16-17 Like a swarm of insects, a crowd of businessmen and functionaries had battered the Orient. The wind turns and goes, and takes away the evil-doing swarm.

3:18-19 This funereal chant, full of irony, reveals to what point the Assyrian tyranny had reached.

THE BOOK OF HABAKKUK

In the Face of Oppression

A prophet here questions God: Why the misfortune that oppresses the people? Habakkuk lived around 600 B.C. After the disappearance of Assyria, another empire controlled the Near East and settled its people in Syria and Palestine. Nebuchadnezzar II, king of Babylon, had shortly before defeated Pharaoh Neco, at Carchemish, in 605 B.C., and nothing could then stop him. Harassed by armies of occupation and tormented by their neighbors, Judah found itself in a trap, and the Jewish people were almost destroyed.

In the chorus of prophets who, at the time when threats are growing in number, indict the people and predict punishment for them, one voice rises in protest: Habakkuk, otherwise unknown, cries out his outrage. A degenerate Israel has certainly merited punishment, but why should it see this inflicted by a nation that is prouder and more cruel than itself? How can the holy and just God permit pagans, who are even more corrupt than his own people, to abuse their superiority by crushing the oppressed, namely, Judah and its neighbors? Why should the strong have a privilege or right over the weak, the conqueror over the conquered? Habakkuk rises above his sense of outrage in a cry of faith: despite his anguish, he retains an unfailing trust; he is convinced that the wrath of God will break out and restore a just order. In anticipation, the prophet sings in wonder to the mighty Lord who will destroy all the forces ranged against him. The prophet, thereby, offers Christians a moving lesson: it is to God that we must look for life, even if we do not yet know the way to it.

The Hebrew text of the Book of Habakkuk is often poorly preserved. Readers will, therefore, not be surprised to find that translations differ somewhat; the general sense of the message, however, is clear.

The Book of Habakkuk may be divided as follows:

- *I: Habakkuk's Discussion with God (1:2—2:4)*
- *II: Warning to the Arrogant (2:5-20)*
- *III: Habakkuk's Prayer (3:1-19)*

CHAPTER 1

1 * This is the oracle that the prophet Habakkuk received in a vision.

I: HABAKKUK'S DISCUSSION WITH GOD

2 How long, O LORD, must I cry for help
while you do not listen?
I cry out to you, "Violence!"
but you refuse to intervene. [a]
3 Why do you make me witness wrongdoing
and confront me with wickedness?
Destruction and violence confront me;
strife is everywhere, and discord abounds.
4 As a result, the law becomes ineffective
and justice never prevails.
The wicked hem in the righteous,
and judgment becomes perverted.
5 "Gaze upon the nations and see.
You will be amazed, even astounded.
You will not believe it when you are told
what I am doing in your days. [b]
6 For I am stirring up the Chaldeans,
that savage and unruly people,
who march across the whole earth
to seize dwellings of other people. [c]
7 They inspire fear and terror,
and they impose justice and judgment
according to their own standards.

a Jud 7:25; Ps 70:6.—b Jn 20:29; Acts 13:41.—c Deut 28:49; Am 6:14.

1:1—2:4 Habakkuk encounters the great problem of evil: among peoples and individuals, the strong always oppress the weak, unless God intervenes. The prophets explain the situation by seeing oppressors as the instruments of God's anger who punish the sin of the people. Like Job, Habakkuk rejects such an explanation as overly simplistic.

8 Their horses are swifter than leopards
and more frightening than wolves at dusk.
Their horses gallop on,
with riders advancing from far away,
swooping like eagles to devour their prey.
9 They are all bent on violence,
a horde moving steadily forward like an east wind;
they scoop up captives like sand.
10 They scoff at kings,
they despise rulers.
They regard every fortress with contempt,
as they build earthen ramps to conquer it.
11 Then they sweep past like the wind and are gone,
as they ascribe their strength to their god."

12 "O LORD, are you not from everlasting,
my holy God, you who are immortal?
You have marked them for judgment, O LORD;
you, O Rock, have designated them for punishment.
13 Your eyes are too pure to gaze upon evil,
and you cannot countenance wrongdoing.
Why then do you remain silent
as you gaze on the treachery of the wicked,
watching them while they devour
those who are more righteous?
14 You have made men like the fish of the sea,
like crawling creatures without a ruler.
15 The wicked haul all of them up with a hook
or catch them in a net.
They gather them up in a seine,
and then rejoice and exult. [d]
16 Therefore, the wicked offer sacrifice to their net
and burn incense to their seine,
for, thanks to them, they live sumptuously
and enjoy elegant food.
17 Shall they then be allowed
to draw their sword unceasingly,
and to slaughter nations without mercy?

CHAPTER 2

1 I will stand at my post
and take up my position on the rampart,
and keep watch to see what he will say to me
and what answer he will offer to my complaints." [e]

2 Then the LORD answered me and said:

Write down the vision,
inscribe it clearly on tablets
so that it can be read easily.
3 For the vision is for the appointed time;
it will speak of the end,
and it will not lie.
If it delays in coming, wait for it,
for it will surely come before too long.
4 The proud man's heart is not upright,
but the righteous man will live
because of his faith. *[f]

II: WARNING TO THE ARROGANT

5 Moreover, wealth is treacherous;
those who are arrogant do not endure.
They open their throats as wide as Sheol
and are as unstable as death.
They gather to themselves all the nations
and make a harvest of all the peoples.
6 Everyone should taunt such people
and turn on them with mockery and say,
"Woe to you who store up
what is not your own.
Woe to you who enrich yourself
with goods taken in pledge.
7 Will not your creditors rise up suddenly?
Will not those who make you tremble wake up?
Will you not become a victim to them?
8 Since you have plundered many nations,
all the nations that survive will plunder you
because of the bloodshed and the violence
you have inflicted on cities
and all their inhabitants.

9 "Woe to the one who amasses
ill-gotten gains for his household

d Ezek 32:3.—e Ps 85:9; Jer 48:19.—f Mk 5:34; Rom 1:17; Gal 3:11; 1 Tim 6:17; Heb 10:38.

2:4 St. Paul takes this promise and gives it a new application: it is faith that "justifies," that is, saves human beings from sin and gives them the life of God (Gal 3:11; Rom 1:17).

so as to set his nest on high
and thereby evade the reach of misfortune.[g]
10 You have managed to bring shame upon your house
by cutting off many peoples;
you have placed your own life in jeopardy.
11 The very stones will cry out from the wall,
and the beam will respond from the woodwork.
12 "Woe to the man who builds a city
by means of bloodshed
and founds a town on the basis of iniquity.[h]
13 Is it not in the eternal design
of the LORD of hosts
that what the people labor for
is destined for the flames,
and that everything the nations
exhaust themselves to achieve
will come to naught.[i]
14 However, the earth will be filled
with the knowledge of the LORD's glory
just as the waters cover the sea.[j]
15 * "Woe to you who encourage your neighbors to drink,
pouring it abundantly until they are drunk,
so that you can gaze upon their nakedness.
16 You will be filled with shame instead of glory
as you stagger in your drunkenness.
The cup in the LORD's right hand
will be passed on to you,
and shame will overshadow your glory.
17 For the violence done to Lebanon will overwhelm you,
and the massacre of the animals will terrify you,
all as a result of the bloodshed and violence you inflicted
on cities and all who dwell in them.
18 "Of what use is an idol
after its maker has shaped it?
It is only a presentation, a source of lies.
And why should its sculptor place his faith in it,
a dumb idol that he has made?
19 Woe to anyone who says,
'Wake up!' to a block of wood,
'Rouse yourself!' to a lifeless stone.
Can such a thing offer guidance?
It may be overlaid with gold and silver,
but there is no breath of life within it.
20 However, the LORD is in his holy temple.
Let all the earth be silent before him."[k]

III: HABAKKUK'S PRAYER

CHAPTER 3

Canticle

1 What follows is a prayer of the prophet Habakkuk, accompanied by a plaintive tune.

2 O LORD, I have heard of your renown;
your work, O LORD, fills me with awe.
Make it live once again in our own time;
in the course of the years make it known,
and in your wrath remember to have compassion on us.
3 God comes from Teman,
the Holy One from Mount Paran.
His radiance covers the heavens,
and with his glory the earth is filled.[l]
4 His splendor is like that of the sunrise;
rays shine forth from his hand
where his power lies hidden.
5 Pestilence goes before him,
and plague follows close behind.
6 When he stands up, the earth trembles;
at his glance the nations panic.
The eternal mountains are shattered;
along his ancient pathways,
the age-old hills bow down.
7 The tents of the Ethiopians are in distress;
the dwellings of the land of Midian are trembling.[m]
8 Are you angry with the rivers, O LORD?
Or is your wrath directed against the streams,
or your rage against the sea,
that your horses are mounted
and you drive your chariots to victory?

g Isa 5:20; Jer 11:11.—h Jer 22:13; Ezek 24:9; Nah 3:1.—i Isa 16:12; Jer 51:58.—j Sir 47:15; Isa 11:9; Rom 15:14.—k Ps 11:4; Am 8:3; Zec 2:17.—l Deut 33:2; Ps 47:8.—m Ezr 10:9; Isa 19:1.

2:15-17 The armies of Nebuchadnezzar have devastated the cedars of Lebanon and slaughtered the flocks of the conquered. In the Bible, cedars and flocks also symbolize leaders and their subjects. Lebanon was often ravaged, because it was a place of passage for invading armies.

9 You uncover your bow
and fill your quiver with arrows;
into rivers you split the earth.
10 At the sight of you the mountains tremble;
a torrent of water rushes by
and the ocean thunders aloud.
11 At the glint of your flying arrows
and the gleam of your flashing spear,
the sun forgets to rise
and the moon remains motionless in the heavens. [n]

12 In fury you stride across the earth;
in anger you trample the nations.
13 You go forth to deliver your people,
to save your anointed one.
You shatter the house of the wicked,
laying bare its foundations to the bedrock. [o]
14 You pierced with your arrows
the leader of those warriors
who stormed toward us like a whirlwind,
ready to devour the wretched who were in hiding.
15 You trampled the sea with your horses,
churning the mighty abyss.

16 I hear, and my body trembles;
my lips quiver at the sound.
Decay afflicts my bones,
and my legs tremble beneath me.
I wait calmly for the day of disaster
that will dawn on the people who attack us.
17 Even though the fig tree does not blossom
and there is no fruit on the vines,
even though the olive crop will fail
and the orchards will yield no food,
even though the flock is cut off from the fold
and there is no herd in the stalls,
18 I will continue to rejoice in the LORD,
and exult in the God of my salvation.
19 The Lord GOD is my strength;
he makes my feet as swift as those of a deer
and enables me to tread on the heights. [p]

n Jos 10:12; Pss 18:15; 144:6.—o 2 Mac 15:16; Ps 20:7; Isa 51:9ff.—p 18f: Ex 15:2; 1 Chr 16:10; Ps 18:32f; Mic 7:7.

THE BOOK OF ZEPHANIAH

The Restoration of Judah

Zephaniah was active in the years around 640 B.C., shortly before Jeremiah. King Josiah, the great reformer, was still a minor. The little state of Judah was in the midst of a crisis: there was a growing reaction against the policy of alliance with Assyria, which the wicked King Manasseh (687–642 B.C.) had inaugurated a little earlier, for it was a servile policy that was humiliating to the national sense of honor and a deadly blow to religious integrity. In addition, Assyria was now experiencing a decline that allowed a rebirth of patriotic hopes and of projects for religious reform.

The recovery project, which Josiah was to pursue very tenaciously, had its pioneers, and Zephaniah was one of them. In the name of the Lord, this prophet proclaims and describes a terrible judgment upon his corrupt fellow countrymen. He is not satisfied to denounce idolatry, religious formalism, and social injustices; he also points out the hidden sources of these evils, these sources being, in his view, a lack of faith and, above all, pride. He sees sin as the breaking of a personal relationship with God, as an offense against his greatness, patience, and love. Violent language and threats were necessary in order to shake up circles that had settled down in mediocrity.

But this prophet of misfortune is also a man of hope. He focuses his attention especially on the "remnant" that will escape condemnation and for which the promises of salvation are meant. This remnant will be a select group of poor but faithful persons who rely, above all else, on the love of the God who saves, and in complete trust place themselves at his disposal. Zephaniah is already directing the religious spirit of the people toward the religion "in Spirit and truth" (Jn 4:23-24), which Jesus, "meek and humble of heart" (Mt 11:29), will establish.

The Book of Zephaniah may be divided as follows:

I: I Extend My Hand over Judah (1:2-18)
II: Anger Will Strike at the Four Corners of the World (2:1-15)
III: Woe to Jerusalem, the Rebel (3:1-8)
IV: Toward a Tomorrow of Exultance (3:9-20)

CHAPTER 1

1 This is the word of the LORD that came
to Zephaniah, the son of Cushi, the son
of Gedaliah, the son of Amariah, the son of
Hezekiah, in the days when Josiah, the son of
Amon, was king of Judah.

I: I EXTEND MY HAND OVER JUDAH

2 I will completely sweep away everything
from the face of the earth,
says the LORD. [a]
3 I will sweep away both men and animals,
the birds of the air and the fish of the sea.
I will force the wicked to their knees
and wipe out all people from the face of the earth,
says the LORD. [b]
4 I will stretch out my hand against Judah
and against all the inhabitants of Jerusalem.
I will wipe out from this place every remnant of Baal,
the very name of his idolatrous priests:
5 those who bow down on the roofs
to worship the host of the heavens,
and those who prostrate themselves before the LORD [c]
but swear by Milcom,
6 and those who have turned their backs on the LORD,
and those who do not seek him.
7 Keep silent in the presence of the Lord GOD,
for the day of the LORD is near.
The LORD has prepared a sacrifice;
he has consecrated his guests. [d]
8 On the day of the LORD's sacrifice,
I will punish the officials and the king's sons,
and all those who clothe themselves in foreign apparel.
9 On that day I will punish
all who leap over the threshold*
and fill the house of their master
with violence and deceit.
10 * On that day, says the LORD,
crying will be heard from the Fish Gate,
wailing from the New Quarter,
a loud crash from the hills.
11 Wail, O inhabitants of the Mortar,
for all the merchants will perish,
and all those who weigh out silver will be ruined.
12 At that time
I will search Jerusalem by lantern-light
and punish all those people
who have become complacent,
like wine thickening in its sediment,
and who say in their hearts,
"The LORD will do nothing,
either good or bad." [e]
13 As a result, their wealth will be plundered
and their houses will lie in ruins.
Though they build houses,
they will not dwell in them;
though they plant vineyards,
they will not drink their wine. [f]
14 The great day of the LORD is near,
near and coming quickly.
The sound of the day of the LORD is bitter
when the warrior shouts his cry of war.
15 That day is a day of wrath, [g]
a day of anguish and distress,
a day of ruin and devastation,
a day of darkness and gloom,
a day of clouds and heavy darkness,
16 a day of trumpet blasts and battle cries [h]
against the fortified cities
and against lofty battlements.

a Job 20:28; Isa 28:17.—b Ps 145:20; Hos 4:3; Rev 12:15.—c Jer 8:2; 19:13; Dan 14:24-25.—d Jer 46:10; Zec 2:17.—e Ps 89:33; Isa 13:11.—f Deut 28:39; Ps 49:11; Am 5:11.—g Sir 18:24; Jer 30:7; Ezek 30:3; Joel 2:11; Am 5:18.—h Jer 49:2; Am 2:2.

1:9 *Over the threshold:* the avoidance of stepping on the threshold is probably connected with the "rite of the threshold": that is, of entering and leaving the temple without setting one's foot on the threshold.

1:10-11 *Fish Gate:* this gate led to the new sections of Jerusalem. *Mortar:* in all probability, a quarter in the lower part of the city. Coins were not in use at this time, and money was calculated by weight. But the alternative was always there: God or money (see Mt 6:24).

17 I will bring such dire distress on the people
that they will walk like the blind
because they have sinned against the LORD.
Their blood will be poured out like dust
and their entrails like dung.
18 Neither their silver nor their gold
will be able to save them [i]
on the day of the LORD's wrath,
when by the fire of his jealousy
the entire earth will be consumed.
For he will make a sudden and terrible end
of all who dwell on the earth.

II: ANGER WILL STRIKE AT THE FOUR CORNERS OF THE WORLD

CHAPTER 2

1 Gather together, gather yourselves together,
O shameless nation,
2 before you are driven away
and disappear like chaff,
before you are forced to confront
the fierce anger of the LORD,
before you are overtaken
by the day of the LORD's anger.
3 Seek the LORD,
all you humble of the land*
who obey his commands.
Seek righteousness, seek humility;
then perhaps you may find shelter
on the day of the LORD's anger.
4* For Gaza will be deserted
and Ashkelon will be reduced to ruins.
The people of Ashdod will be driven out at midday,
and Ekron will be uprooted.* [j]

5 Woe to you inhabitants of the seacoast,
you nation of the Cherethites.
This is the word of the LORD against you:
"I will destroy you, land of the Philistines,
until not a single inhabitant remains." [k]
6 The coastland of the Cretans
will be reduced to pastures,
to grazing grounds for shepherds
and folds for flocks.
7 And the coastland will become the possession
of the remnant of the house of Judah.
They will pasture their flocks there,
and when evening arrives
they will lie down in the houses at Ashkelon.
For the LORD, their God, will be mindful of them
and restore their fortunes.

8* "I have heard the insults of Moab
and the taunts of the Ammonites
when they reviled my people
and threatened their frontiers.
9 Therefore, as I live," says the LORD of hosts,
the God of Israel,
"Moab will become like Sodom
and the Ammonites like Gomorrah:
a land filled with nettles and salt pits,
a wasteland forevermore.
The remnant of my people will plunder them,
and the survivors of my nation will dispossess them."

10 This will be the price they pay for their pride,
inasmuch as they insulted and mocked
the people of the LORD of hosts.
11 The LORD will fill them with fear
when he causes all the gods of the earth
to waste away.
Then all the coasts and the islands of the nations*
shall worship him,
each from its own territory.

12 You also, O Ethiopians,
will be killed by the sword of the LORD.
13 And he will stretch out his hand against the north
and destroy Assyria.

i Zep 3:8; Job 20:20; Ezek 7:19; Rev 20:9.—j Wis 4:4; Ezek 12:20; Am 1:6ff; Zec 9:5.—k Isa 13:11.

2:3 *Humble of the land:* those called, in Hebrew, the *anawim*, who have such an important place in the Bible.

2:4-15 In the style of the time, all these harsh oracles are assertions of the greatness of God as compared with any human power; they are also an assurance that the chosen people still have a mission, despite all their moral degradation.

2:4 The cities named were Philistine cities, to the west of Judah. Along with Gath, which is not mentioned, they formed a confederation of coastal cities.

2:8-9 Moab and Ammon, east of Israel, were its enemies. According to Gen 19:30-38, these peoples were descendants of Lot, who survived the disastrous fate of Sodom.

2:11 *The islands of the nations:* the lands and people of the eastern Mediterranean, which the Palestinians never knew well. The idea is: "even the most distant lands."

He will make Nineveh a wasteland,
as arid as the desert.
14 Flocks and herds will lie down there,
creatures of every kind.
The desert owl and the screech owl [l]
will roost on her columns;
will hoot at the window
while the raven croaks at the doorway.
15 Is this the exultant city
that once took pride in its security,
that said to itself,
"I am supreme, without an equal"?
And what now has it come to?
It is nothing but a desolate waste,
a lair for wild animals,
at which every passer-by
will hiss and shake his fist.

III: WOE TO JERUSALEM, THE REBEL

CHAPTER 3

1 Woe to the city of tyrants,
rebellious and defiled.
2 It has not heeded any warning voice,
it has not accepted any correction. [m]
It has not placed its trust in the LORD;
it has not drawn near to its God.

3 The officials within it
are roaring lions;
its judges are wolves of the wasteland
that leave nothing in reserve for the morning. [n]
4 Its prophets are arrogant;
they are treacherous men.
Its priests have profaned what is holy
and done violence to the law. [o]
5 The LORD within this city is just;
he does no wrong.
Morning after morning he renders judgment
unfailingly at dawn.

6 I have cut off nations;
their strongholds lie in ruins.
I have laid waste their streets
so that no one walks along them.
Their cities have been laid waste,
and now they are deserted,
without inhabitants. [p]
7 I thought, "Surely you will now fear me
and be willing to accept correction.
You will not fail to realize
how I have inflicted punishments on you."
However, they only seemed more eager
to make all their deeds corrupt.

8 Therefore, wait for me, says the LORD;
wait for the day when I stand up to accuse you.
For I am determined to gather nations
and assemble kingdoms
in order to pour forth my wrath upon them,
all the heat of my anger.
The entire earth will be consumed
by the fire of my jealousy. [q]

IV: TOWARD A TOMORROW OF EXULTANCE*

9 Then I will purify
the lips of my people,
so that all may call on
the name of the LORD
and serve him with one accord.
10 From beyond the rivers of Ethiopia
my suppliants, my scattered ones,
will bring offerings to me. [r]

11 On that day you will not be put to shame
as a result of all the deeds
by which you have rebelled against me.
For then I will remove from your midst
those who are proud and arrogant,
and then you will never again flaunt your pride
on my holy mountain.
12 For I will leave in your midst
those who are meek and humble;
they will seek refuge in the name of the LORD. [s]
13 This remnant of Israel will do no wrong
and utter no lies.
Nor will a deceitful tongue
be found in their mouths.
They will eat and lie down,
and no one will cause them to be afraid. [t]

14 Cry out with joy, daughter of Zion;
shout aloud, O Israel.

l Isa 34:11.—m Ps 78:22; Jer 7:28.—n Ezek 22:27; Mic 3:11.—o Jer 23:32; Ezek 22:26; Rom 1:30.—p Jos 24:8; 1 Mac 15:29; Jer 2:15.—q Zep 1:18; Deut 32:22; Hos 13:11.—r Ex 20:24; Ezek 44:15.—s Ps 11:1; Hos 14:4; Mt 11:29.—t Ps 119:3; Ezek 32:13; Mic 4:4.

3:9-20 Despite the dark perspectives connected with the day of the Lord, Zephaniah follows the practice of the other prophets, in looking, now, to a future in which God will save his people, who will be renewed and gathered around him once again. Whatever may happen, it is certain that God's plan intends life and not death.

Rejoice and exult with all your heart,
O daughter, Jerusalem. [u]
15 The LORD has canceled the punishments against you;
he has turned away your enemies.
The king of Israel, the LORD, is in your midst;
you need never again fear any harm.
16 On that day it will be said to Jerusalem:
Fear not, O Zion;
do not let your hands grow weak. [v]
17 The LORD, your God, is in your midst,
a warrior and a savior.
He will rejoice over you with gladness
and renew you through his love. [w]
He will exult over you with shouts of joy
18 as on a day of festival.
I will remove your misfortune
so that you no longer will need to endure reproach.
19 At that time I will deal
with all those who oppress you.
I will rescue the lame
and gather the dispersed.
I will win for them praise and renown
throughout the whole world. [x]
20 At that time I will gather you together
and bring you home.
For I will make you renowned and praised
among all the peoples of the earth,
when I restore your fortunes
before your eyes, says the LORD.

u Ps 35:27; Zec 9:9.—v Ps 91:5; Joel 2:21; Mt 14:27.—w Ps 68:4; Isa 60:16.—x Ezek 36:29; Am 9:14; Mic 4:6.

THE BOOK OF HAGGAI

Rebuilding of the Temple and the Community

The time is the period after the return from Exile. In 538 B.C., many Jews who had been deported to Babylon returned to Palestine; Cyrus, king of the Persians and their liberator, authorized them to rebuild the temple in Jerusalem. But in order to have the food they needed in a region of ruins and devastation, they settled in the countryside around Jerusalem rather than in the city itself. Their first concern was to defend themselves; some managed to settle down and achieve a certain prosperity.

It seems that these people had not yet acquired the strength of mind or the imagination or even the capacity to set in motion a plan for national unity. Zerubbabel, a descendant of David, and Joshua, the high priest at this time, presided over the destinies of the group of returnees at this difficult time. These two men represented the two forces capable of bringing a restoration: the Davidic line, that is, the Messianic dynasty, and the priesthood.

Quite soon, the high priest would take over the leadership, and the successor of the royal dynasty would disappear, but we have not reached that point as yet. The restoration is difficult. It runs up against the inertia and even the hostility of those who had remained behind in the country and had become half-pagan. To this difficulty was added a period of scanty harvests.

It is understandable that in these circumstances the Jews hesitated to undertake the rebuilding of the temple. The community was so demoralized that in 520 B.C., eighteen years after the return of the first group, the task of reconstruction had hardly begun.

It was at this point that the prophet Haggai, a man undoubtedly devoted to worship and animated by the Spirit of God, sought to give a strong boost to the work and to encourage his brethren. He had returned with the first repatriates, and perhaps had been among the deportees of 587 B.C.

His short discourses of encouragement all develop the same theme: you must rebuild the temple, and all will go well.

For the Jews, the temple was in fact the sign of God's presence, of a life under the guidance of the covenant; it was also the symbol of a united community. The four oracles of Haggai, all of which are precisely dated, convey the message of restoration. The temple had to be the most important symbol in the initial plans of the reestablished people; we today would say that the house of God should have its place right in the midst of the dwellings of humanity, and this not so much materially as spiritually.

On this period see the early chapters of Ezra. The prophet Zechariah will do his preaching in the same setting.

The Book of Haggai may be divided as follows:

I: Consider Your Situation (1:1-15)
II: Courage, I Am with You (2:1-9)
III: What They Offer Me Is Unclean (2:10-19)
IV: Promise to the Descendants of David (2:20-23)

I: CONSIDER YOUR SITUATION*

CHAPTER 1

1 In the second year of King Darius, on the
first day of the sixth month, the word of the
LORD was communicated by the prophet
Haggai to the governor of Judah, Zerub-
babel, the son of Shealtiel, and to the high
priest Joshua, the son of Jehozadak: [a] 2 "Thus
says the LORD of hosts: 'This people says that
the time has not yet come to rebuild the
house of the LORD.'" 3 Then the word of the
LORD came through the prophet Haggai: 4 "Is
this a time for you to live in your paneled
houses while this house lies in ruins?" [b]

5 Now the LORD of hosts has this to say:
Reflect on your way of life.
6 You have sown much but harvested little;
you have eaten, but never enough to satisfy you.
You drink, but never enough to cheer you;
you are clothed, but never experience warmth.
And the one who earns wages
puts them into a bag with a hole in it. [c]

7 Therefore, thus says the LORD of hosts:
Consider carefully how you have fared.
8 Go up into the hill country,
collect timber, and build the house
so that I may take pleasure in it
and manifest my glory,
says the LORD.
9 You expected much,
but it proved to be little.
When you brought in the harvest,
I blew it away.
And why did I do this?
asks the LORD of hosts.
Because my house lies in ruins,
while each of you is concerned
only about your own house. [d]
10 Therefore, the heavens have withheld their rain
and the earth has withheld its crops. [e]
11 And I have called for a drought
to afflict the land and the mountains,
the grain, the new wine, and the oil,
and everything that the soil produces,
and to afflict, as well, men and animals,
and all the products of their labor.

12 Zerubbabel, the son of Shealtiel, and the
high priest Joshua, the son of Jehozadak, and
the entire remnant of the people listened to
the voice of the LORD, their God, and to the
words of the prophet Haggai that the LORD,
their God, had sent him to deliver. As a
result, the people were filled with fear
because of the LORD.

13 Thereupon Haggai, the messenger of the
LORD, proclaimed to the people the LORD's
message: "I am with you," declares the
LORD. [f] 14 Then the LORD stirred up the spir-
it of the governor of Judah, Zerubbabel, the
son of Shealtiel, and the spirit of the high
priest Joshua, the son of Jehozadak, and the
spirit of all the remnant of the people. They

a Ezr 4:24; 5:1; 6:14; Neh 12:1; Jer 50:1.—b 2 Sam 7:2; Jer 35:7.—c Deut 28:38ff; Mic 6:15.—d 1 Ki 2:15; 2 Ki 25:9; Job 30:26; Sir 21:18.—e Gen 27:28; Job 22:7; Joel 1:5; Am 4:6-9.—f Mt 28:20.

1:1-15 The oracle dates from August of 520 B.C., and should logically end with a passage to be found further on in Hag 2:15-19.

came and began to work on the house of the
LORD of hosts, their God, 15 on the twenty-
fourth day of the sixth month.

II: COURAGE, I AM WITH YOU*

CHAPTER 2

In the second year of King Darius, 1 on the
twenty-first day of the seventh month, the
word of the LORD came through the prophet
Haggai: 2 Speak to the governor of Judah,
Zerubbabel, the son of Shealtiel, and to the
high priest Joshua, the son of Jehozadak, and
to the remnant of the people, and say:

3 Is there anyone left among you
who beheld this house in its former glory?
How does it appear to you now?
Does it not seem to you
as though it were not even there?
4 But now take courage, Zerubbabel,
says the LORD.
Take courage, Joshua, the high priest,
son of Jehozadak.
Take courage, all you people of the land,
says the LORD.
Begin the work,
for I am with you,
says the Lord of hosts. [g]
5 This is the promise that I made to you
when you came out of Egypt.
My Spirit is present among you.
Do not be afraid. [h]

6 For thus says the LORD of hosts:

In a little while from now
I will shake the heavens and the earth,
the sea and the dry land. [i]
7 I will shake all the nations,
and the treasures of all the nations will flow in.
And I will fill this house with glory,
says the LORD of hosts. [j]
8 Mine is the silver, mine is the gold,
says the Lord of hosts.
9 The glory of this new house
will surpass that of the former,
says the LORD of hosts.
And in this place I will grant peace,
says the LORD of hosts. [k]

III: WHAT THEY OFFER ME IS UNCLEAN*

10 On the twenty-fourth day of the ninth
month, in the second year of King Darius, the
word of the LORD came to the prophet
Haggai. 11 Thus says the LORD of hosts: Ask
the priests to give a ruling on this. [l] 12 If a man
is carrying consecrated meat in the fold of his
garment and he allows the fold to come in
contact with bread or broth or wine or oil or
food of any kind, will that also become conse-
crated? The priests answered, "No."

13 Haggai then asked, "If anyone who has
been defiled by contact with a corpse touch-
es any of those, does that become unclean?"
The priests replied, "It will become un-
clean." [m] 14 Then Haggai continued,

So it is with this people and this nation
in my view, says the LORD.
So also are all the works of their hands;
whatever they offer here is unclean.

15 But now, think back to recent times as
you ponder the future. Before one stone was
laid upon another in the temple of the LORD,
how did you fare?

16 When you came to a heap
of twenty measures of grain,
you would find only ten.
When you came to a wine vat
to draw fifty measures,
you would find only twenty. [n]
17 I struck you and all the products of your toil
with blight and mildew and hail.
Even so, you would not return to me,
says the LORD.

18 Now consider from this day forward,
from the twenty-fourth day of the ninth
month. From the day on which the founda-
tions of the temple of the LORD was laid, con-
sider:

19 Previously the seed had not sprouted,
and the vine and the fig tree,
the pomegranate and the olive tree,
had borne no fruit.
From this day forward
I intend to bless you. [o]

---

g Jer 1:8; Zec 8:9; Acts 23:11.—h Ex 29:45; Lev 26:45; Jdg 6:23.—i Sir 16:18; Joel 2:10; Heb 12:26.—j Gen 49:10; Jos 6:19; 2 Chr 36:18; Isa 60:5, 9, 11; Mal 3:1; Rev 21:26.—k 2 Sam 12:11; Isa 2:2ff; Zec 6:13.—l Deut 17:8-13; Jer 25:32; Zec 7:3.—m Lev 7:21; Num 19:11, 13, 22; Isa 52:11.—n Lev 19:35; Isa 5:10.—o Gen 12:2; Hab 3:17.

2:1-9 The second, and rather modest temple, finished in 515 B.C., will later be replaced by a much more grandiose structure, due to the initiative of King Herod. Christ himself will admire its magnificence (Mk 13:1), but he will also proclaim that he himself is the true temple in which all human beings will be brought together in unity (Jn 4:20-21). Haggai foretells the new order which Jesus will then bring to pass.

2:10-19 This oracle dates from December of 520 B.C.; verses 15-19 should be placed after Hag 1:15a.

IV: PROMISE TO THE DESCENDANTS OF DAVID*

20 On the twenty-fourth day of the month, the word of the LORD came a second time to Haggai: 21 Tell this to Zerubbabel, the governor of Judah:

I will shake the heavens and the earth;
22 I will overthrow the thrones of kingdoms
and destroy the power of the kings of the nations.
I will overthrow the chariots and their riders;
both the horses and their riders will fall,
every one of them by the sword of a comrade. [p]
23 On that day,
says the LORD of hosts,
I will take you, Zerubbabel,
my servant, son of Shealtiel, says the LORD,
and I will make you like a signet ring,
for I have chosen you,
says the LORD of hosts. [q]

p Jer 14:12; Ezek 38:21; Dan 2:44; Zep 1:3; Zec 14:13; Lk 1:52.—q Song 8:6; Sir 49:11; Isa 42:1; 44:1f; Jer 22:24; Zec 13:2; Jn 15:19.

2:20-23 Zerubbabel, who rebuilds the temple, is celebrated as a savior of the people: the Lord is with him as he had been with David, his ancestor (2 Sam 7:12-16). For a moment, the entire Messianic expectation connected with the Davidic dynasty is here summed up; but in fact, the dynastic successor will disappear from the scene, to the advantage of the priesthood. Christ will be presented by the Gospels, though in a much different context, as the Son of David (Mt 9:27; 21:9; Lk 1:27; Mk 12:35;...).

On a *signet ring*, which was used to seal documents, there was a likeness of the owner, who kept it very carefully on a cord around his neck (Gen 38:18). In the eyes of Haggai and Zechariah (see Zec 6:12), then, the descendant of David is God's representative.

THE BOOK OF ZECHARIAH

The Last Times

The Book of Zechariah is one of the most bewildering in the Bible. All the prophetic books contain visions, as well as symbolic signs and actions, but, when they bring up essential points, these men of God turn directly to the hearers to enjoin conversion on them, strengthen them, and give them a great hope. Here, however, we find ourselves faced with striking visions that are composed of descriptions of scenes in heaven, and we are always left with some uncertainty about their interpretation. For this reason, instead of trying to understand every detail, it is preferable to get an overall impression of the picture being painted.

The Book is not certainly the work of a single author. The first part (chs. 1–8) can be readily dated: it has to do with the rebuilding of the temple and the restoration of the holy city toward the end of the sixth century B.C., that is, about twenty years after the return from Exile. These first chapters, therefore, are indeed the work of Zechariah. In the remainder of the Book, on the other hand, daily life and its concerns have been forgotten, as have specific events of a given period; instead, rich, and perhaps even grandiose, but rather enigmatic images are projected to depict the last times of the world.

These visions and proclamations can only belong to the fourth and third centuries. They assert a truth: the Lord will someday take direct control of the entire world and, after having mounted the final attacks on evil, will consecrate all human beings to his worship.

However, despite the different dates of the various parts, the Book of Zechariah does have a certain unity. After the Exile, Israel no longer enjoyed political autonomy and saw no immediate possibility that the throne of David would be restored. It was a small nation in the midst of great empires that disposed of Israel rather as they wished. Until this point, God's plan had seemed bound up with the success of Israel; what would become of that plan from now on? What is said in the Book of Zechariah conveys an essential truth: despite all that has happened, God's plan has not been frustrated; the true God is mightier than all human empires, however powerful; humanity is not destined to disappear amid the conflicts between nations.

We ought not be surprised that the several authors say all this in a quite obscure way and that they imagine the restoration of humanity in the form of military revenge taken by Israel. Such was the mentality of the time, the inheritance with which these writers were working.

But there is a profound intuition at work: the disasters that devastate the human race and of which the authors give no details, do not yet represent the end. The end is God present in the midst of humanity.

The Book of Zechariah may be divided as follows:

- *I: Rebuilding a People for God (1:1-6)*
- *II: Renewal of the Holy City (1:7—2:17)*
- *III: The Leaders of the Holy City (3:1—4:14)*
- *IV: The People of the Holy City (5:1—6:8)*
- *V: The Present, a Promise for the Future (6:9—8:23)*
- *VI: The New People of God (9:1—11:3)*
- *VII: The New Shepherd of Israel (11:4—13:9)*
- *VIII: The Final Combat and the New Jerusalem (14:1-21)*

I: REBUILDING A PEOPLE FOR GOD*

CHAPTER 1

Be Converted to Me.* [a] 1 In the second year
of Darius, in the eighth month, this word of
the LORD came to the prophet Zechariah,
the son of Berechiah, the son of Iddo:

2 The LORD was greatly angered at your
ancestors. [b] 3 Therefore, say to the people:
Thus says the LORD of hosts: Return to me,
says the LORD of hosts, and I will return to
you, says the LORD of hosts. 4 Do not be like
your ancestors, to whom the prophets of that
time proclaimed. Thus says the LORD of
hosts: Forsake your evil ways and your evil
deeds. But they refused to listen or to pay
attention to me, says the LORD. [c]

5 Where are your ancestors now? And the
prophets, do they live forever? 6 As for my
words and my decrees which I entrusted to
my servants the prophets, did they not over-
take your ancestors? As a result, they repent-
ed and said, "The LORD of hosts has treated
us as he had determined to do, according to
what our lives and our deeds deserve." [d]

II: RENEWAL OF THE HOLY CITY*

The Four Horsemen.* 7 On the twenty-
fourth day of the eleventh month, the month
of Shebat, in the second year of Darius, the
word of the LORD came to the prophet
Zechariah, the son of Berechiah, the son of
Iddo.

Zechariah related: 8 During the night I had
a vision in which a man was riding a red
horse among the myrtle trees in a glen.
Behind him were red, sorrel, and white hors-
es. [e] 9 "What are these, sir?" I asked, and the

a Ezr 4:24; 5:1; 6:14.—b Deut 9:20; Ezek 8:18.—c Ex 7:13; Jer 25:5; 35:15; Ezek 33:11; Mal 3:7.—d Lev 26:14ff; Deut 28:15; 1 Ki 14:8; Lam 2:17; 2 Jn 6.—e Rev 6:4; 9:17.

1:1—8:23 During the Exile in Babylon and even after returning, some Jews undoubtedly cherished the hope of avenging the devastation of their homeland and restoring its past grandeur. But twenty years after the deportation had ended (538–519 B.C.) their enthusiasm had cooled. They had to resign themselves to an impoverished existence in a ravaged land. Judea remained under Persian control and in ruined Jerusalem everything had to be reconstructed and rebuilt, beginning with the temple, the new foundations of which had recently been laid. Along with Haggai, the prophet Zechariah became the guiding spirit of the restoration, which was being directed by the high commissioner, Zerubbabel, of the royal house of David, and by the high priest Joshua, who took precedence, even over Zerubbabel.

1:1-6 The messages of the prophets might be occasioned by quite different situations: they also passed quite different judgments on events at hand. Fundamentally, however, they were calls to conversion. When men of God pray, they see this conversion as a gift from heaven, a grace (Ps 51:10-12; Ezek 36:25-27). When they speak, they must remind the people that they themselves must make the effort to change. The dialectic of grace and freedom is always at work.

Zechariah began to preach in 520 B.C., only a few months after the first message of Haggai; he reminds his hearers that past defeat was the result of infidelity. He criticizes a religion still marked by fear and self-interest, and predicts a more radical return to God, a more solid faith in his covenant.

1:7—2:17 Twenty years have passed since the authorization was given to return, but not all have made the journey to Jerusalem, nor are they anxious to do so. On the other hand, those who did make the journey are now asking whether it had not been a mistake. The building of the temple seems at last to be progressing, but all do not have the same enthusiasm for it. In order to raise morale, the prophet presents a first series of visions: God is on the point of restoring his people, and he asks the doubtful to return to Judah and take part in the work of reconstruction.

1:7-17 The scene takes place in God's dwelling, as the evergreen myrtle trees symbolically indicate.

angel who was conversing with me said, "I
will show you what they are."
10 The man standing among the myrtle
trees said, "They are the ones whom the
LORD has sent to patrol the earth." 11 Then
they in turn spoke to the angel of the LORD
who was standing among the myrtle trees,
"We have been patrolling the earth, and the
entire earth is tranquil and at peace." [f]
12 Then the angel of the LORD asked, "O
LORD of hosts, how long will you withhold
your mercy from Jerusalem and the cities of
Judah who have been the object of your
wrath for the last seventy years?" [g] 13 There-
upon, the LORD replied with kind and com-
forting words to the angel who had talked
with me. [h]
14 The angel who was talking with me then
said to me: Proclaim this message. Thus says
the LORD of hosts: I feel very protective
toward Jerusalem and Zion, [i] 15 but I am
deeply angry with the nations that feel com-
placent and secure. Previously I was angry
only to a certain extent, but they added to
the disaster. [j]
16 Therefore, says the LORD, I will return to
Jerusalem with compassion, and there is
where my house will be rebuilt, says the
LORD of hosts, and the measuring line will be
stretched out over Jerusalem. [k] 17 Proclaim
in addition: Thus says the LORD of hosts: My
cities will once again overflow with prosper-
ity. The LORD will again comfort Zion and
again choose Jerusalem. [l]

CHAPTER 2

Vision of the Four Horns and the Workers.* 1 I
looked up and beheld four horns. 2 I in-
quired of the angel who was conversing with
me what these were. He answered me,
"These are the horns that scattered Judah,
Israel, and Jerusalem." [m]
3 Then the LORD showed me four black-
smiths. And I said, "What are these coming
to do?" 4 He replied, "Those horns scattered
Judah so completely that no one dared to
raise his head. However, those blacksmiths
have come to terrify them and to strike
down the horns of the nations that raised
their horns against the land of Judah in
order to scatter its people."

The New Jerusalem.* 5 Following this, I
raised my eyes and observed a man with a
measuring line in his hand. [n] 6 When I asked
him, "Where are you going?" he replied, "To
measure Jerusalem, to discover what is its
width and what is its length." [o]
7 When the angel who was talking to me
walked away, another angel came out to
meet him 8 and said to him, "Run and tell
that young man: Jerusalem will remain
without walls because of the great multitude
of men and animals dwelling there. [p] 9 But I
will be a wall of fire all around it, says the
LORD. And I will be the glory within it."

10 Up, up! Flee from the land of the north,
says the LORD.
For I have scattered you to the four
winds of heaven,
says the LORD. [q]
11 Away, away! Escape to Zion,
you who presently live in daughter
Babylon.
12 For thus said the LORD of hosts
after he sent me forth,
in regard to the nations that plundered
you:
Whoever touches you
touches the apple of my eye. [r]
13 Behold, I will wave my hand over them,
and they will be plunder
for those they have enslaved.
Thus you will know
that the LORD of hosts has sent me.
14 Sing and rejoice, O daughter Zion.
For I am coming to dwell in your
midst,
says the LORD. [s]

15 On that day
many nations will be converted to the
LORD.
Yes, they will become his people,
and he will dwell among you.
Then you will know that the LORD of
hosts
has sent me to you.
16 The LORD will claim Judah
as his portion in the holy land,
and once again he will choose Jeru-
salem.

---

f Zec 6:7; 1 Mac 15:41.—g Zec 7:5; Jer 25:11; Dan 9:2.—h Ru 2:13; Jer 29:10.—i Zec 8:2; Joel 2:18; Lk 2:10.—j Isa 47:6; 62:1; Ob 10-14.—k Zec 8:3; Ezr 6:14; Tob 13:16; Jer 31: 38-39.—l Isa 51:3; Jer 33:13; Ezek 36:35.—m Zec 6:4.—n Ezek 47:3; Rev 11:1.—o Rev 21:15.—p Ezek 36:11.—q Isa 13:14; Jer 49:36.—r Deut 32:10; Ps 17:8; Jer 35:18; Ezek 36:6.—s Isa 49:13; Ezek 37:26-27; Zep 3:14.

2:1-4 Measuring the city signifies that it will be rebuilt.

2:5-17 The prophet urges the exiles to rejoin their brothers and sisters in Palestine, because God has for the first time returned to his temple (see Ezek 43:1-12).

17 Let all people be silent
in the presence of the LORD.
For he has roused himself
from his holy dwelling. [t]

III: THE LEADERS OF THE HOLY CITY*

CHAPTER 3*

Joshua the High Priest. 1 Then he showed me Joshua, the high priest, standing before the angel of the LORD, with Satan standing at his right to accuse him. [u] 2 And the angel of the LORD said to Satan, "May God rebuke you, Satan! May the LORD who has chosen Jerusalem rebuke you! Is not this man a brand snatched from the fire?" [v]

3 Now Joshua was dressed in filthy clothes as he stood before the angel. 4 The angel then said to those who were standing before him, "Remove his filthy garments and clothe him in fine vestments." [w] 5 He also said, "Place a clean miter on his head." Therefore, they put a clean miter on his head and clothed him in clean garments, while the angel of the LORD stood by and said, "Behold, I have removed your guilt."

6 The angel of the LORD then declared to Joshua: 7 "Thus says the LORD of hosts: If you walk in my ways and observe my ordinances, you will rule over my house and be in charge of my courts, and I will give you the right of access to all those who are standing here.

8 "Therefore listen, Joshua, high priest, you and your colleagues who are seated here in attendance before you. For they are an omen of things to come. I will now bring in my servant, the Branch. [x] 9 Gaze upon the stone that I have set before Joshua, a single stone with seven facets. I will engrave its inscription, says the LORD of hosts, and I will remove the guilt of this land in a single day. [y] 10 On that day, says the LORD of hosts, you will invite each other to come under your vines and your fig trees." [z]

CHAPTER 4*

Vision of the Lampstand and Olives. 1 Then the angel who had talked with me returned and roused me, as though awakening someone who was asleep. 2 He asked me, "What do you see?" I replied, "I see a lampstand of solid gold, with a bowl at the top. There are seven lamps on it, with seven openings to hold the lamps. [a] 3 Alongside it are two olive trees, one to the right and the other to the left." [b]

4 I then said to the angel who was speaking to me, "What are these things, my lord?" 5 The angel who was speaking to me replied, "Do you not know what they are?" "No, my lord," I answered. 6 Then he said to me, "This is the LORD's message to Zerubbabel: Not by force, nor by strength, but by my Spirit, says the LORD of hosts. 7 What are you, O great mountain? Compared with Zerubbabel, you are nothing more than a plain. He will bring out the capstone amid shouts of acclamation." [c]

8 This word of the LORD was then addressed to me as follows: 9 "The hands of Zerubbabel have laid the foundation of the house, and his hands will complete the work. Then you will know that the LORD of hosts has sent me to you. [d] 10 For those who spoke disparagingly on that day of small beginnings will rejoice to see the chosen stone in the hands of Zerubbabel. These seven facets are the eyes of the LORD that range throughout the entire earth." [e]

11 Then I asked the angel, "What is the significance of those two olive trees to the left

t Zep 1:7.—u Num 22:31; 1 Chr 21:1; Tob 5:4; Hag 1:1; Lk 4:5; Rev 21:10.—v Job 2:2; Rom 8:33; Jude 9.—w Lk 15:22.—x 2 Mac 5:4; Isa 4:2; 11:1; Jer 23:5; 33:15.—y Zec 4:10; 1 Chr 21:8.—z Mic 4:4.—a Rev 1:12.—b Rev 11:4.—c Zec 14:10; Ps 118:22.—d Num 16:28; Ezr 3:11ff; 6:14ff; Isa 48:13.—e Zec 3:9; Prov 15:3.

3:1—4:14 Although they have been set free, the Jews do not enjoy political independence. Zerubbabel, a descendant of David, is only the high commissioner of the king of Persia. The Jews still hope to see him invested with the royal dignity and seated on the throne of David; this is a dream that will soon fade. The high priest Joshua, who had been repatriated with the others, occupies a position of the first importance. Since the people have no real political autonomy, they attach themselves to the high priest, the one leader who can do something about their religious destiny. He is the one who will inherit the royal power, and under his influence the religious aspect of Israel's life will take precedence over the political. The two visions that follow shed light on this situation.

3:1-10 The new garments in which Joshua is robed signify that, after the Exile, he has to be reinstated in his office as high priest of the new temple; at the same time, the garments convey the idea that in his person the entire forgiven people will experience prosperity, each individual (according to the traditional image) under his own vine and his own fig tree. The mysterious rock with seven eyes (v. 9) doubtless symbolizes the coming Messiah, whose knowledge will be complete and who is foretold under the name *Branch* because he must come from the royal line of David.

4:1-14 The golden seven-branched lampstand (see Ex 25:31-38) represents divine providence, which concerns itself with human beings. The two olive trees are Joshua, who is dedicated to worship, and Zerubbabel, whom the Jews hope to see anointed king, since he is a descendant of David. The vision is, then, a promise that the two powers, the religious and the civil, will be linked together to restore the prestige of the chosen but now impoverished people (see Jer 33:14-18). The words: *This is the LORD's message to Zerubbabel* (v. 6a) and *in the hands of Zerubbabel* (v. 10a), should be placed at the end of the chapter.

and the right of the lampstand?" 12 And I asked him further, "What is the meaning of the two olive branches that pour forth the oil through the two golden channels?"

13 "Do you not know what these are?" he said to me. "No, my lord," I replied. 14 He answered, "These are the two anointed ones who stand in attendance on the LORD of the entire earth."

IV: THE PEOPLE OF THE HOLY CITY*

CHAPTER 5

Vision of the Scroll that Flies.* 1 Again I looked up, and I beheld a flying scroll.[f] 2 The angel said to me, "What do you see?" I answered, "I see a flying scroll. It is twenty cubits in length and ten cubits in width."

3 Then he said to me, "This is the curse that goes forth over the entire earth. According to the writing on one side, every thief will be swept away, and according to the writing on the other side, everyone who commits perjury in my name will be banished. 4 I have sent it forth, says the LORD of hosts, and it will enter the house of the thief and the house of anyone who commits perjury in my name. It will lodge inside such a house and consume it, both timber and stones."[g]

Vision of the Bushel Coming Forth.* 5 Then the angel who was speaking to me came forward and said, "Raise your eyes and see what this is that is coming forth." 6 I asked, "What is it?" The angel replied, "This is a bushel basket coming forth." And he added, "This is their guilt throughout the land."

7 Then a leaden cover was lifted up, and there was a woman sitting inside the bushel basket. 8 "This is Wickedness," the angel said. He immediately pushed her back into the basket and pressed the leaden cover into the opening.

9 Then I raised my eyes and beheld two women coming forward, with the wind in their wings which were like those of a stork. As they lifted up the bushel basket into the air, 10 I asked the angel who had been conversing with me, "Where are they taking the bushel basket?" 11 He replied, "To the land of Shinar, to build a house for it. When the house is completed, they will set down the bushel basket on a pedestal designed for it."[h]

CHAPTER 6

Vision of the Four Chariots. 1 Again I raised my eyes and beheld four chariots coming out between two mountains—and the mountains were mountains of bronze. 2 The first chariot had red horses, the second chariot had black horses,[i] 3 the third chariot had white horses, and the fourth chariot had spotted horses.

4 I asked the angel who was conversing with me, "What are these, my lord?" 5 The angel replied, "These are the four winds of heaven which are now ready to depart after presenting themselves for review by the LORD of all the earth.[j] 6 The chariot with the black horses is departing for the land of the north, the red and the white horses will follow after them, and the chariot with the spotted horses will leave for the land of the south."

7 As these horses emerged, eager to set off and patrol the earth, he said to them, "Go forth and patrol the earth," and they did so. 8 Then he called to me and said, "Those who are going forth to the land of the north have allowed my Spirit to rest on the land of the north."

V: THE PRESENT, A PROMISE FOR THE FUTURE*

The Coronation.* 9 The word of the LORD came to me: 10 Collect silver and gold from the exiles, from Heldai, Tobijah, and Jedaiah, and go on the very same day to the house of Josiah, the son of Zephaniah. 11 Take the sil-

f Ezek 2:9.—g Lev 19:12; Isa 22:25.—h Gen 11:2ff; Dan 1:2.—i Zec 1:8; Sir 48:9; Rev 6:4; 9:17.—j Ps 104:4; Mt 24:31.

5:1—6:8 It is not enough to restore political and religious buildings and structures; the essential thing is to implement the moral and spiritual conditions that are needed for a new community. These final three visions proclaim that the Lord intends to sanctify his people and make them truly faithful to their mission of salvation.

5:1-4 A scroll was a strip of parchment that was written on and then rolled up. The ancients thought that a prediction written on a scroll would certainly be fulfilled.

5:5-11 The woman seen in a dream personifies the evil which God will remove from his people when he comes to save them.

6:9—8:23 This part of the Book, the last that really belongs to the prophet Zechariah, focuses on the theme of the rebuilding of the temple and the national restoration that has already begun. It begins, however, with a promise of a more universal, but also more distant salvation. It is already foreseen, but for a time that remains still undetermined, that the Lord will save his people once and for all and that he will reign from Jerusalem over the entire earth. This is a perspective that the second part of the Book will broaden considerably.

6:9-15 This prophecy retains its value, to the extent that it looks beyond the immediate moment. It foretells the work of salvation to be accomplished by Jesus the Messiah, an authentic descendant of David by way of Zerubbabel (see Mt 1:12-13; Lk 3:27) and a True Priest, even the One High Priest.

ver and the gold and make a crown, and set
it upon the head of the high priest Joshua,
the son of Jehozadak, [k] 12 and say this to him:
Thus says the LORD of hosts: Here is a man
whose name is Branch. He will branch out
from where he is, and he will build the tem-
ple of the LORD. [l]

13 Yes, he will build the temple of the LORD,
and, wearing the royal insignia, he will sit on
his throne and govern. There will be a priest
at his right hand, and peaceful harmony will
exist between the two of them. [m] 14 The
crown will serve as a memorial in the tem-
ple of the LORD for Heldai, Tobijah, Jedaiah,
and Josiah, the son of Zephaniah. 15 And
those who are now far off will come and
work on the building of the temple of the
LORD. Then you will realize that the LORD of
hosts has sent me to you. All this will happen
if you diligently obey the voice of the LORD,
your God. [n]

CHAPTER 7*

Must I Continue to Do Penance? 1 In the
fourth year of King Darius, the word of the
LORD came to Zechariah on the fourth day
of the ninth month, the month of Kislev.
2 *Bethel-sarezer sent Regem-melech and
his men to entreat the favor of the LORD
3 * and to ask the priests in the house of the
LORD, and the prophets, "Should I continue
to mourn and to fast in the fifth month, as I
have been doing for these many years?" [o]

4 Then the word of the LORD of hosts came
to me: 5 Say to all the people of the country
and to the priests: When you fasted and
mourned in the fifth month and the seventh
month during these seventy years, was it
truly for my sake that you fasted? [p] 6 And
when you were eating and drinking, were
you not eating and drinking for yourselves?
7 Were not these the words that the LORD
proclaimed through the prophets in the past,
when Jerusalem was inhabited and enjoying
peace, as were her surrounding towns, and
when the Negeb and the foothills were
inhabited? [q]

8 This word of the LORD came to Zech-
ariah: 9 Thus says the LORD of hosts: Render
fair judgments, and show kindness and com-
passion to one another. [r] 10 Do not oppress
the widow, the orphan, the alien, or the poor.
Do not plot evil in your heart against one
another. [s] 11 But they refused to listen; they
defiantly turned their backs and stopped
their ears so that they would not hear. [t]
12 They were adamant in their refusal to
accept the teaching and the law that the
LORD of hosts had transmitted by his Spirit
through the former prophets. [u]

Therefore, the wrath of the LORD of hosts
was aroused. 13 Since they refused to listen
when he called to them, he in turn would not
listen when they cried out to the LORD of
hosts. [v] 14 Rather, he scattered them with a
whirlwind among all the nations where they
were strangers. Therefore, the land they left
was desolate after their departure, and no
one came or went. They had turned their
pleasant land into a desert. [w]

CHAPTER 8

Behold, I Will Save My People. 1 This word of
the LORD of hosts came to me:

2 Thus says the LORD of hosts:

I am intensely jealous for Zion,
and I am filled with jealous wrath for
her. [x]

3 Thus says the LORD:
I will return to Zion,
and I will dwell in the heart of Jeru-
salem.
Jerusalem will be called the faithful city,
and the mountain of the LORD of
hosts
will be called the holy mountain. [y]

4 The LORD of hosts says this:
Old men and old women once again
will sit
in the squares of Jerusalem,
each one leaning on a stick
because of old age.

5 And her streets will be filled
with boys and girls at play.

6 The LORD of hosts says this:
Even if this seems impossible

k 2 Sam 12:30.—l Zec 3:8; 1 Ki 8:19; Wis 9:8; Eph 2:20; Heb 3:3.—m Ps 110:4; Wis 3:8; Heb 3:1.—n Deut 13:5; 2 Chr 6:7; Eph 2:19f.—o Zec 8:19.—p Isa 58:5; Rom 14:6.—q Deut 5:22; Jer 17:26.—r Isa 58:6; Col 3:12.—s Ex 22:21-24; Deut 24:17; Sir 7:8; Isa 1:17; Jer 5:28.—t Neh 9:29; Ezek 3:7; Hos 4:16.—u Neh 9:29; Ezek 11:19; 36:26; Mk 8:18; 1 Pet 1:12.—v Isa 1:15; Ezek 20:8; Mic 3:4.—w Deut 4:27; 8:2.—x Nah 1:2; 2 Cor 11:2.—y Isa 2:2; 51:11; Jer 31:23.

7:1-14 The time is November, 518 B.C. Twenty years have passed since the first group of Jews made the return.

7:2-3 *Bethel-sarezer:* a city about twenty km north of Jerusalem. *The prophets:* Haggai and Zechariah.

7:3-5 The fast of the fifth month was for the anniversary of the destruction of Jerusalem; the fast of the seventh month was for the assassination of Gedaliah (see Jer 41:1-2).

to the remnant of this people in those
days,
will it also seem impossible to me?
says the LORD.

7 The LORD of hosts says this:

I will rescue my people
from the countries of the east
and from the countries of the west. [z]
8 I will bring them back
to dwell in Jerusalem.
They will be my people,
and I will be their God,
a God of faithfulness and justice. [a]

9 Thus says the LORD of hosts: Take heart, all you who today hear the promises from the words spoken by the prophets who were present when the foundation of the house of the LORD of hosts was laid for the rebuilding of the temple. [b] 10 Before that time, men were not paid their wages, nor was any recompense offered for the work of the animals. In addition, those who went out or came in were provided with no protection from the enemy, for I had set every man against his neighbor.

11 However, now I will not deal with the remnant of this people as I did in former days, says the LORD of hosts. 12 Now they will sow in peace. The vine will bring forth its fruit, the soil will yield its produce, and the heavens will provide their moisture. All these things I will endow to the remnant of this people. 13 Just as you once were a curse among the nations, O house of Judah and house of Israel, so now I will save you, and you will be regarded as a blessing. Do not be afraid. Do not lose heart. [c]

14 Thus says the LORD of hosts: Whereas I resolved to bring disaster upon you when your ancestors provoked me to wrath, says the LORD of hosts, and I did not relent, [d] 15 so now I have resolved in these days to show favor to Jerusalem and the house of Judah. Do not be afraid.

16 These are the things I require you to do: speak truthfully to one another, render judgments at your gates that reflect honesty and peace, [e] 17 and do not plot evil against another in your heart, or love perjury. For all these are practices that I hate, says the LORD. [f]

The Saving Fast. 18 The word of the LORD came to me: 19 Thus says the LORD of hosts: The fast of the fourth month, and the fasts of the fifth, the seventh, and the tenth months, shall be periods of joy and gladness and of cheerful festivals for the house of Judah. Therefore, love truth and peace. *

20 Thus says the LORD of hosts: In the future, peoples will come, the inhabitants of many cities. 21 Those who dwell in one city will approach those of another and say, "Come, let us go to entreat the favor of the LORD and to seek the LORD of hosts; I myself will go." [g] 22 Many peoples and strong nations will come to seek the LORD of hosts in Jerusalem and to entreat the favor of the LORD. [h]

23 Thus says the LORD of hosts: In those days, ten men from nations of every language will grasp a Jew by the edge of his garment and say, "Permit us to go with you, for we have heard that God is with you." [i]

VI: THE NEW PEOPLE OF GOD**

CHAPTER 9

The New Land*

1 * An oracle:

The word of the LORD
is against the land of Hadrach,
and it will come to rest upon Damascus.
For the cities of Aaron belong to the
LORD,
as do all the tribes of Israel,

z Isa 11:11; Jer 30:18; Ezek 13:21.—a Ezek 36:28; 2 Cor 6:16.—b Ezr 5:1-2; Hag 2:18.—c Isa 19:24; Jer 42:18; Zep 3:20.—d Jer 31:28; Lam 2:8.—e Zec 7:9; Eph 4:25.—f Zec 7:10; Prov 3:29.—g 1 Chr 16:10; Isa 2:3.—h Isa 60:3.—i Isa 45:14; 66:23.

8:19 The added fasts of the fourth and tenth months were for the opening of the breach in the walls of Jerusalem and for the beginning of the siege (see 2 Ki 25:1-4).

9:1—14:21 In the second part of the Book, concrete situations and their difficulties are forgotten; the perspectives are vaguer and more distant, the visions more grandiose. The tiny populace of Judah remains the chosen people and becomes the agent of a universal conquest in which God exerts his power and makes his presence felt in the midst of people of every nation; after having conquered the last terrible assaults of evil, he dedicates all of these people to his worship. The only connection these chapters have with the first eight is that they proclaim a promise of salvation. They contain ideas that are at times difficult to understand. They are broken up into a number of short passages, composed of bits from other sources or from writings that date from two or three centuries after the initial restoration. Their basic concern is with the new era that the Messiah will inaugurate and that involves the entire people. This second part of the Book of Zechariah is like a repository of Messianic texts; two rather different portraits of the Messiah himself are sketched. The hope that is roused projects into a still inscrutable future a number of experiences that will, in fact, come together in the person and life of Jesus.

9:1—11:3 The following oracles depict essentially an ideal restoration of Israel and, therefore, a new image of the earth, the king, freedom, fidelity, and so on.

9:1-6 The references are to Syria, Phoenicia, and Philistia. *Hadrach* was the capital of a small Syrian state. *Damascus:* literally, "the pearl of Aram." The cities in verses 5-6 are in Philistia.

2 as well as Hamath also,
which borders on it,
and on Tyre and Sidon,
even though they are very wise. [j]
3 Tyre has built a stronghold for itself
and heaped up silver like dust
and gold like the dirt of the streets.
4 But the Lord will strip it of its possessions
and destroy its power on the sea,
and the city itself will be consumed by fire. [k]

5 Ashkelon will witness this and be terrified,
as will Gaza who will writhe in anguish;
the same will be true of Ekron
whose hopes will come to naught.
The king will vanish from Gaza,
and Ashkelon will be uninhabited.
6 Foreigners will settle in Ashdod,
and I will demolish the pride of the Philistines. [l]
7 I will snatch the bloody meat from their mouths
and their abominations from between their teeth.
They, too, will be a remnant belonging to our God;
they will be like a clan in Judah,
and Ekron will become like the Jebusites.*
8 I will stand guard at my house
so that no one may pass by unchallenged.
No oppressor will ever again overrun them,
for now I am determined to protect them.

Behold, Your King Comes to You*

9 Rejoice with all your heart, O daughter Zion.
Shout for joy, O daughter Jerusalem.
See, your king is coming to you,
triumphant and victorious,
humble and riding on a donkey,
on a colt, the foal of a donkey. [m]
10 He will banish the chariot from Ephraim
and the horses of war from Jerusalem.
The warrior's bow will be banished,
and he will proclaim peace to the nations.
His dominion will be from sea to sea,
and from the river to the ends of the earth. [n]

The Reestablishment of Israel

11 As for you,
because of the blood of my covenant with you,
I will set free your prisoners
from the waterless dungeon. [o]
12 Return to the fortress,
you prisoners who have waited in hope.
This very day I promise
that I will reward you twofold. [p]
13 For I have strung Judah as my bow
and made Ephraim its arrow.
I have roused your sons, O Zion,
and have made you like a warrior's sword
against your sons, O Javan.

14 Then the LORD will appear over them,
and his arrow will flash forth like lightning.
The Lord GOD will sound the trumpet
and march forth in the stormwinds of the south.
15 The LORD of hosts will protect them,
and they will overcome
as they trample underfoot the slingstones.
They will drink blood like wine,
filled to the brim like a bowl,
drenched like the corners of the altar.

16 The LORD, their God, will save them on that day,
for they are his flock, his own people.
Like the precious stones of a crown
they will sparkle throughout his land. [q]
17 What wealth and what beauty will be theirs,
with grain to make the young men flourish
and with new wine for the maidens!

j Jer 49:23; Mt 11:22.—k Isa 23:1-18; Ezek 26:1–28:26; Joel 1:20.—l Isa 13:11; Am 1:8.—m Ps 98:4; Isa 62:11; Jer 23:5; Zep 3:14; Mt 21:5; Jn 12:15.—n 2 Chr 14:4; Hos 1:7.—o Gen 41:14; Ex 24:8; Isa 42:7.—p Isa 61:7; Jer 16:18.—q Jdg 10:15; Isa 62:3.

9:7 The reference is to the custom of eating meat with blood in it, contrary to the practice in Israel. The Jebusites were the former inhabitants of Jerusalem, before it was captured by David.

9:9-10 The plan of God will be brought to fulfillment not amid military and political greatness but in humility and peace. When Jesus enters Jerusalem on Palm Sunday, he will fulfill this prediction to the letter (see Mt 21:4f). *Ephraim* stands for the entire kingdom of Israel, of which it was the principal tribe. The prophet is thinking, therefore, of a gathering of all the nations. *From sea to sea:* from the Mediterranean to the Persian Gulf. *The river* is the Euphrates.

CHAPTER 10

Be Faithful to the LORD

1 Ask the LORD for rain in the springtime.
It is the LORD who makes the storm clouds.
He will send forth the showers of rain
and grass in the fields for everyone. [r]
2 For the household gods utter nonsense,
and diviners are misled by false signs.
The dreams they relate are deceitful,
offering empty consolation.
That is why the people
wander about like sheep;
they are in distress
for lack of a shepherd. [s]

I Will Reunite and Save

3 My anger has been set ablaze by the shepherds,
and I will punish the leaders of the flock.
For the LORD of hosts cares for his flock,
the house of Judah,
and will make it his royal warhorse.
4 From Judah will emerge the cornerstone,
from it the tent peg,
from it the bow ready for battle,
from it all the commanders.
5 Together they will be like warriors
trampling the mud of the streets in battle.
They will fight because the LORD is with them,
and they will rout even those on horseback.

6 I will strengthen the house of Judah,
and I will save the house of Joseph.
I will bring them back
because I have taken pity on them,
and they will be
as though I had never cast them off;
for I am the LORD, their God,
and I will answer them.
7 Then the people of Ephraim will be like warriors,
and their hearts will be cheered as if by wine.
Their children will see it and rejoice;
their hearts will rejoice in the LORD.
8 I will signal them to gather together,
for I have redeemed them;
they will be as numerous
as they were before. [t]
9 I scattered them among the nations,
yet in far-off countries they will remember me;
they will rear their children and return.
10 I will bring them home from the land of Egypt
and gather them from Assyria.
I will lead them into Gilead and into Lebanon,
until there is no more room to accommodate them. [u]
11 They will pass through the Sea of Egypt,
and the waves of the sea will be subdued,
while the depths of the Nile will be dried up.
The pride of Assyria will be cast down,
and the scepter of Egypt will be taken away. [v]
12 I will make them strong in the LORD,
and they will march in my name,
says the LORD. [w]

CHAPTER 11

1 Open your doors, O Lebanon,
so that the fire may devour your cedars.
2 Wail, you cypress trees,
for the cedars have fallen,
the majestic trees have been ravaged.
Wail, you oaks of Bashan,
for the impenetrable forest has been felled.
3 Listen to the wailing of the shepherds,
for their majesty has been destroyed.
Listen to the roar of the lions,
for the dense thickets of the Jordan
have been ravaged.

VII: THE NEW SHEPHERD OF ISRAEL

The Two Shepherds.* 4 Thus says the LORD, my God: Be a shepherd to the flock destined for slaughter. 5 Those who buy them kill them and go unpunished, while those who sell them say, "Blessed be the LORD, for I have become rich." Even their own shepherds feel no pity for them. [x]

---

r Deut 11:14; Ps 135:7; Jer 14:22.—s 2 Chr 18:16; Jer 10:8; Ezek 34:8.—t Gen 1:22; Ezek 36:37.—u Isa 11:11; 49:20; Jer 23:3; Hos 11:11.—v 2 Ki 19:24; Isa 11:15; Ezek 30:13.—w Ps 128:1; Mic 4:5.—x Jer 50:7; Mal 3:15.

11:4-17 The separation of the Samaritans became final around 328 B.C., and foreign invasions will occur from the fourth to the second century. At the end, an editor has added a curse against a wicked leader. Matthew 27:9-10 quite rightly applies to Jesus what is said (Zec 11:12-13) about the derisive wage of thirty pieces of silver: the one who came to save humankind was repaid with hatred and betrayal.

6 I will no longer have any pity for the
inhabitants of the earth, says the LORD.
Rather, I will deliver each one of them into
the power of his neighbor or into the clutch-
es of the king. They will devastate the earth,
and I will not deliver anyone from their
hands.

7 And so I became a shepherd of the flock
that was destined to be slaughtered by the
sheep dealers. I took two staffs, one of which I
named Favor and the other one of which I
named Unity, and I pastured the sheep
myself.[y] 8 In a single month I got rid of the
three shepherds. However, I soon lost pa-
tience with the flock, and they detested me.

9 Finally I said. "I will not be your shepherd
any longer. What is to die, let it die. What is to
be destroyed, let it be destroyed. Those who
are left can devour one another."[z]

10 Then I took my staff "Favor" and
snapped it in two, thereby annulling the
covenant I had made with all the peoples.
11 Therefore, it was annulled on that day, and
the dealers who were watching me realized
that this was the word of the LORD. 12 I said to
them, "If it seems right to you, give me my
wages; if not, then forget about it." Then they
weighed out my wages, thirty pieces of
silver.[a]

13 However, the LORD said to me, "Throw it
into the treasury—the princely sum at which
they valued my efforts." Therefore, I took the
thirty pieces of silver and threw them into
the treasury of the house of the LORD.[b]
14 Then I broke my second staff, "Unity," in
half, annulling the ties of brotherhood
between Judah and Israel.

15 The LORD thereupon said to me: Take
once again the equipment of a worthless
shepherd. 16 For I am now going to raise up a
shepherd in the land who will have no con-
cern for those who are perishing, nor go off
in search of the strays, nor heal the injured,
nor nourish those who survive, but who will
eat the meat of the fat animals, tearing off
even their hoofs.[c]

17 Woe to the worthless shepherd
who abandons his flock.
May the sword fall upon his arm
and upon his right eye.
Let his arm be completely withered
and his right eye be totally blinded.[d]

CHAPTER 12

The LORD Undertakes Defense of Jerusalem.
1 An oracle: the word of the LORD concerning
Israel. Thus says the LORD, who spread out
the heavens and founded the earth and
formed the human spirit within:[e]

2 Behold, I will make Jerusalem a cup that
will intoxicate all the surrounding nations,
and Judah will be besieged as well as
Jerusalem.[f] 3 On that day, when all the
nations of the world are gathered against
her, I will make Jerusalem a heavy stone for
all the peoples. All those who try to lift it will
hurt themselves seriously, even though all
the nations of the earth will be massed
against her.[g]

4 On that day, says the LORD, I will strike
all the horses with panic and their riders
with madness. Further, I will strike blind all
the horses of the peoples, but I will keep a
watchful eye on the house of Judah. 5 Then
the people of Judah will say to themselves,
"The inhabitants of Jerusalem derive their
strength from the LORD of hosts, their God."

6 On that day, I will make the families of
Judah like a brazier burning in a woodland,
like a torch aflame among sheaves, and they
will consume all the surrounding nations on
their right and on their left, while the people
of Jerusalem will reside peacefully in their
city.[h] 7 The LORD will save the tents of Judah
first, so that the glory of the house of David
and the glory of the inhabitants of Jerusalem
will not surpass that of Judah. 8 On that day,
the LORD will shield the inhabitants of
Jerusalem. The weakest of them will be like
David when that day comes, and the house
of David will be godlike, with the angel of the
LORD at their head.[i]

9 On that day I will set out to destroy all
the nations that attack Jerusalem.

**They Will Cry over Him Whom They Have
Pierced.*** 10 Further, I will pour out a spirit of
grace and supplication on the house of
David and on the inhabitants of Jerusalem

y Ezek 37:16; Hos 5:6.—z Jer 15:2; Rev 13:10.—a Gen 30:28; Ex 21:32; Mt 26:15.—b 2 Sam 24:24; Mt 27:9f.—c Jer 23:2; Ezek 34:2ff.—d Mt 23:16; Jn 10:12.—e Isa 42:5; Mal 1:1.—f Isa 51:17, 22; Jer 51:7.—g Ezek 29:21; Mt 21:44.—h Ob 8; Zep 1:18.—i Ex 32:34; Isa 37:35.

12:10-14 The passage repeats thoughts expressed in the Servant Song in the Book of Isaiah (Isa 52:13—53:12): suffering rather than victory is the source of salvation, and those who were preparing the Servant's downfall were in fact preparing the triumph of God. St. John (Jn 19:37) cites Zec 12:10 in connection with the piercing of the dead Jesus' side with a lance.

so that they will look on me, the one whom
they have pierced, and mourn for him as one
mourns for an only son, and they will grieve
over him as one grieves over a firstborn.[j]

11 On that day the mourning in Jerusalem
will be as great as the mourning over Hadad-
rimmon in the plain of Megiddo.*[k] 12 And
the land will mourn, each family individually:

The family of the house of David by itself,
and their women by themselves;
the family of the house of Nathan by itself,
and their women by themselves;
13 the family of the house of Levi by itself,
and their women by themselves;
the family of the house of Shimei by itself,
and all their women by themselves;
14 all the remaining families by themselves,
and their women by themselves.

CHAPTER 13

The Country Will Be Purified. 1 On that day a
fountain will be opened for the house of
David and the inhabitants of Jerusalem to
cleanse them from sin and impurity.[l]

2 On that day, says the LORD of hosts: I will
banish the names of the idols from the land,
so that they will be remembered no more. I
will also rid the land of the prophets and the
spirit of impurity.[m] 3 If a man continues to
prophesy, his parents, his own father and
mother, will say to him, "You will not live, for
you have uttered lies in the name of the
LORD." And while he is prophesying, his par-
ents, his own father and mother, will pierce
him through.[n]

4 On that day, every prophet will be
ashamed to relate his own prophetic vision,
and he will not wear a hairy mantle in order
to deceive. 5 Rather, he will say, "I am no
prophet. I am a tiller of soil, for the land has
been my possession since my youth."[o] 6 And
if anyone asks him, "What are these wounds
on your chest?" he will reply, "I received
them in the house of my friends."[p]

The Song of the Sword

7 Awake, O sword, against my shepherd,
against the man who is my associate,
says the LORD of hosts.
Strike the shepherd,
so that the sheep may be scattered,
and I will turn my hand against their young.*[q]
8 Throughout the land, says the LORD,
two-thirds in it will be cut off and perish,
and one-third will be left.
9 I will put that one-third through fire,
and I will refine them as silver is refined,
and I will test them as gold is tested.
They will call on my name
and I will hear them.
I will say, "These are my people,"
and they will say, "The LORD is our God."[r]

VIII: THE FINAL COMBAT AND THE NEW JERUSALEM*

CHAPTER 14

1 Behold, a day is coming for the LORD,
when the plunder taken from you will be
divided in your midst. 2 For I will gather all
the nations against Jerusalem for battle. The
city will be taken, the houses plundered, and
the women raped. Half of the city will go into
exile, but the rest of the people will not be
taken away from the city.

3 Then the LORD will go forth and fight
against those nations, fighting as on a day of

j Tob 13:14; Jer 6:26; Lam 2:19; Jn 19:34; Rev 1:7.—k 2 Chr 35:22-25; 1 Mac 12:52.—l Heb 9:14; 1 Pet 1:18f; Rev 1:5.—m Hos 2:20; Mic 5:12; 2 Pet 2:1.—n Deut 18:20; 2 Ki 10:19; Mic 3:5ff.—o Gen 4:2; Am 7:14.—p Isa 1:25.—q Mt 26:31.—r Ps 66:10; Jer 30:22; Hos 2:25.

12:11 Probably a reference to the disaster that caused the death of Josiah, the reformer, near Megiddo (2 Ki 23:29). Others think the reference is to the celebration of a Canaanite rite in honor of the god Hadad-rimmon.

13:7 Jesus cites this verse in foretelling his passion and the flight of the apostles (Mt 26:31).

14:1-21 After the chosen people had passed through so many struggles, an editor pulled together details for a picture of a final battle. The account tests the imagination and brings the conflict between God and the forces of evil to an end with a victory of God. The style is that of the apocalypses, as seen in the discourse of Jesus on the ruins of Jerusalem and the end of the world (Mk 13; Lk 21; Mt 24). These details were perhaps imagined or gathered at the time of the Maccabean resistance in the second century B.C. At that time, Jerusalem had fallen into the hands of persecuting pagan rulers, and it was possible for the Jews to think that the end of time was at hand: the age of salvation would now begin and the outcome of the struggle would be different. The battle is followed by a great liturgy in which the Feast of Tabernacles acquires a basic importance, since this is the Feast of God as King (see the Books of the Maccabees).

It is on this history-inspired development that the priests based their theology of Jerusalem as the center of a world in which everything is sacred. This grandiose vision of the future is close to that of John's Apocalypse (Rev 21:3-4). The literary display in the depiction of the scene is overwhelming, but at bottom the passage is a proclamation of God in the face of all seemingly dominant forces; it expresses expectation of a salvation that can only be a gift.

battle. 4 On that day his feet will stand on the Mount of Olives, which lies to the east of Jerusalem. The Mount of Olives will be split in two from east to west by an immense valley, so that half of the mountain will move north and the other half will move south. 5 You will flee by the valley of the LORD's mountain, for the valley between the hills will be blocked, and the new valley between them will reach as far as Azal. It will be filled in, as it was by the earthquake, in the days of King Uzziah of Judah. Then the LORD, my God, will come, and all his holy ones with him. *

6 On that day there will be neither cold nor frost. 7 And it will be one continuous day, known only to the LORD, and there will be no more day and night, for there will be light even during the evening. [s] 8 And when that day comes, living waters will flow out from Jerusalem, half flowing toward the eastern sea * and half toward the western sea, and they will continue to flow in both summer and winter. [t] 9 The LORD will become king over the whole earth. When that day comes, he will be the only LORD, and his name will be the only name. [u]

10 The entire land will be transformed into a plain, from Geba to Rimmon in the Negeb, but Jerusalem will remain exalted in its place and be filled with people, from the Gate of Benjamin to the site of the former gate, to the Corner Gate, and from the Tower of Hananel to the king's winepresses. [v] 11 It will be inhabited, and never again will it be doomed to destruction. Jerusalem will abide in security. [w]

12 This will be the plague with which the LORD will strike all the nations that have fought against Jerusalem: their flesh will rot while they are still standing on their feet, their eyes will rot in their sockets, and their tongues will rot in their mouths. 13 On that day men will be stricken by the LORD with great panic. Every man will seize his neighbor's hand, and they will begin to beat each other. 14 Even Judah will fight at Jerusalem. The wealth of all the surrounding nations will be gathered up: gold, silver, and garments in great quantities. 15 In addition, a plague similar to this one will afflict the horses, mules, camels, donkeys, and all other animals in those camps. [x]

16 The survivors of all the nations that attacked Jerusalem will come up year after year to worship the King, the LORD of hosts, and to celebrate the Feast of Booths. * [y] 17 If any of the families of the earth do not go up to Jerusalem to worship the King, the LORD of hosts, no rain shall fall upon them. 18 And should any family of Egypt fail to come up and present themselves, then upon them will fall the plague that the LORD will inflict upon those nations that fail to go up to celebrate the Feast of Booths. 19 Such will be the punishment that befalls Egypt and any other nations that do not come up to celebrate the Feast of Booths.

20 On that day, the words, "Holy to the LORD," will be inscribed upon the bells of the horses, and the cooking pots in the house of the LORD will be as holy as the sacred bowls in front of the altar. 21 Every cooking pot in Jerusalem and Judah will be holy to the LORD of hosts, and all who come to offer sacrifice will take them and cook in them. And there will no longer be any traders in the house of the LORD of hosts. [z]

---

s Isa 60:20; Rev 21:23.—t Zec 13:1; Ezek 47:1-8; Joel 4:18.—u Deut 6:4; Wis 3:8; 1 Cor 8:6; Eph 4:5f; Rev 11:15.—v Zec 12:6; Neh 3:6; 12:38-39.—w Gen 9:11; Jer 31:40; Rev 22:3.—x 2 Chr 21:14.—y Lev 23:34, 43; Neh 8:14; Isa 60:6, 9.—z Ezek 12:24; Mt 21:12; Jn 2:13-16.

14:5 The earthquake must have been a very violent one if it made history and can serve as a parallel for the catastrophe in the Pentapolis. The historical books make no reference to this earthquake (see Am 1:1; 4:11).

14:8 *Eastern sea:* the Dead Sea.

14:16 The Feast of Tabernacles recalled the sojourn of Israel in the wilderness after the deliverance from Egypt (Lev 23:33-42).

THE BOOK OF MALACHI

Sincere Worship

Urged on by the prophets Haggai and Zechariah, the Jewish community that had been repatriated from Babylon had rebuilt the temple in Jerusalem and had returned to a quasi-normal existence toward the end of the sixth century. But by about fifty years later, the burden of daily life had made itself felt once again: the great summons of Haggai and Zechariah were now in the distant past, and carelessness soon crept in: people skimped on the offerings and tithes, they married foreign women, they divorced. Religion seemed to have become a more or less respected formality; it was no longer a vital force.

A new prophet arose; perhaps he remains anonymous, since the name Malachi can also mean simply, "My messenger."

Malachi attacks abuses rather sternly, and, in the spirit of Deuteronomy, calls for fidelity to the covenant. Mere submission to a cold set of laws is meaningless; instead, people must respond to a God who loves them and demands of them an attitude of respect and love. The Lord has no use for a hurried worship in which the heart is not engaged; he takes the side, instead, of all who are the victims of selfishness and violence.

In a few years' time, the reformers Ezra and Nehemiah will try to translate into institutional form the very energetic message of Malachi.

Malachi's tone recalls that of the pre-Exilic prophets: no visions, just direct language. In his Book we have six segments, all constructed on the same pattern: the prophet makes a statement; the hearers wonder at it and question him; he answers by developing his thought and especially by emphasizing its practical consequences. This was a wonderful way of making the listeners share in the lively preaching of a prophet in Jerusalem, perhaps in the temple, after the Exile. In all likelihood, it was an editor who added the title, the final exhortation (3:22), and the subsequent statement about the return of Elijah (3:23-24).

Malachi's rebukes and appeals are still a stimulus for today's readers to overcome the temptation of Pharisaism, that is, of a religion cut off from everyday life, or, in the case of priests, to reflect on the seriousness of their ministry.

Malachi goes even further: new perspectives and new demands lead directly toward the new covenant. There is the announcement of a mysterious precursor of God (3:1) and, above all, of a perfect offering; Christian readers see this last already fulfilled.

The emphasis on marriage as indissoluble, in accordance with the original intention of God, likewise, anticipates the demands made by Jesus (see Mk 10:1-12).

The Book of Malachi may be divided as follows:

- *I: The LORD'S Love for Israel (1:2-5)*
- *II: The Blemished Offerings and Other Faults of Priests (1:6-14)*
- *III: You Have Made Many People Stumble (2:1-9)*
- *IV: Profaned Marriage (2:10-16)*
- *V: God Will Come and Do Justice (2:17—3:5)*
- *VI: Make the Tithe Offering to the LORD (3:6-12)*
- *VII: The Just Will Have Their Revenge (3:13-21)*
- *VIII: Final Exhortation and Promise (3:22-24)*

CHAPTER 1

1 This is an oracle relating the word of the LORD to Israel through Malachi.

I: THE LORD'S LOVE FOR ISRAEL

2 I have loved you, says the LORD,
but you ask, "How have you shown your love?" [a]
3 Was not Esau Jacob's brother? asks the LORD.
Even so, I loved Jacob but I hated Esau.
I reduced his hill country into a wasteland
and made his heritage into a desert for jackals. [b]
4 When Edom says, "We have been crushed,
but we will rebuild the ruins,"
thus says the LORD of hosts:
They may build, but I will demolish.
They will be called a country of wickedness,
the people with whom the LORD is angry forever. [c]
5 Your own eyes will see this, and you will say,
"Great is the LORD,
even beyond the borders of Israel." [d]

II: THE BLEMISHED OFFERINGS AND OTHER FAULTS OF PRIESTS*

6 A son honors his father,
and a servant fears his master.
If then I am a father,
where is the honor due to me?
So says the LORD of hosts
to you priests who despise my name.
You ask, "How have we despised your name?"
7 By offering polluted food on my altar.
Then you ask, "How have we polluted it?"
By thinking that the table of the LORD may be despised. [e]
8 When you offer blind animals in sacrifice,
is this not evil?
And when you offer in sacrifice
those who are lame or sick,
is this not evil?
If you offer such sacrifices to your governor,
will he be pleased with them,
or show you special favor,
asks the LORD of hosts. [f]
9 In the same way,
if you implore God to show mercy toward you
when you have presented such offerings,
do you think he will grant your request?
Thus says the LORD of hosts.
10 Oh, if only one of you would close the temple gates
and thus bring to an end
the pointless lighting of fires on my altar!
I derive no pleasure from you,
says the LORD of hosts,
and I will not accept
any sacrifice from your hands.
11 For from the rising of the sun to its setting
my name is great among the nations.
Everywhere incense and a pure sacrifice
are offered to my name.
For my name is great among the nations,
says the LORD of hosts.* [g]
12 However, you profane my name
when you claim that the table of the LORD is polluted,
and that therefore the food offered on it
is not worthy of respect.
13 You also assert, "How tiresome all this is!"
and you sniff scornfully at me,
says the LORD of hosts.
You bring an animal
that is stolen, lame, or diseased,
and you present it to me as a sacrifice.
Shall I accept this from your hands,
asks the LORD.
14 Accursed is the deceiver
who has a male in his flock
and vows to give it,
but then sacrifices a blemished animal to me.

a Deut 7:6ff; Jer 31:3; Ezek 16:1-63.—b Gen 25:23; Isa 9:18; Rom 9:13.—c Isa 34:5f; 63:1-6; Jer 49:7-22; Ezek 13:14; Ob 21.—d 1 Chr 16:25; Isa 60:1-22.—e Isa 24:5.—f Lev 22:19-25; Num 15:20; Deut 15:21.—g Ps 113:3; Isa 59:19; Heb 13:15.

1:6-14 This passage foretells a different and perfect sacrifice, which Christians identify with the Eucharistic sacrifice.

1:11 The Hebrew verbs are in the present tense, which, in the prophetic style, stands for the future. It is part of Christian tradition, confirmed by the Council of Trent (Session XXII), that this pure sacrifice foretells the bloodless sacrifice of the Mass. This passage is echoed today in the Third Eucharistic Prayer: "You never cease to gather a people to yourself, so that from the rising of the sun to its setting a pure sacrifice may be offered to your name."

For I am a great king,
says the LORD of hosts,
and my name is held in awe among the nations.

III: YOU HAVE MADE MANY PEOPLE STUMBLE

CHAPTER 2

1 And now, O priests,
this commandment is for you.
2 If you refuse to listen to me
and do not sincerely resolve
to give glory to my name,
says the LORD of hosts,
I will send a curse on you,
and I will turn your blessings into a curse.
Indeed, I have already done so
because you have not heeded my warning. [h]
3 I will deprive you of the shoulder
and spread dung on your faces,
the dung of your offerings,
and I will banish you from my presence.
4 Then you will know
that I sent you this commandment
because I wish to maintain
my covenant with Levi,
says the LORD of hosts. [i]
5 My covenant with him
was one of life and peace,
which I bestowed on him.
He revered me
and held my name in awe. [j]
6 The instruction he offered was true,
and no dishonesty issued from his mouth.
He walked with me in integrity and uprightness,
and he turned many away from a sinful life. [k]
7 The lips of a priest should safeguard knowledge,
and people should seek instruction from his mouth
because he is the messenger of the LORD of hosts. [l]
8 But you have turned aside from the way
and caused many to stumble
as the result of your instruction.
You have destroyed the covenant of Levi,
says the LORD of hosts.
9 Therefore, I have made you despised and vile
in the eyes of all the people,
inasmuch as you have disregarded my ways
and have not been impartial
in your interpretation of the law.

IV: PROFANED MARRIAGE*

10 Do we all not have the one Father?
Has not one God created us?
Why then do we break faith with one another,
profaning the covenant of our ancestors? [m]
11 Judah * has broken faith,
and an abominable thing has been done
in Israel and in Jerusalem.
By marrying the daughter of a foreign god,
Judah has profaned the LORD's beloved sanctuary. [n]
12 May the LORD banish from the tents of Jacob
any who do this,
and also deprive them of any witness or advocate
or someone to present offerings to the LORD of hosts.

You Betray the Woman of Your Youth*

13 And this you are to do as well:
you must cover the altar of the LORD
with tears, with weeping and moaning,
because at present he refuses to consider your offering
or to accept it with satisfaction from your hand.

h Lev 26:14-45; Deut 28:5-68; Mt 6:15.—i Lev 26:9; Num 25:12f.—j Num 25:12; Deut 28:10; Ezek 37:26ff.—k Deut 33:8-11; Prov 20:7.—l Lev 10:10f; Deut 17:9f; Sir 1:26; Jer 18:18; Hag 2:12.—m Jud 16:14; Job 31:15; Mt 23:9; Eph 4:6.—n Ezr 9:2; Neh 13:25; 2 Mac 8:2; Ezek 15:8.

2:10-16 What importance does marriage any longer have in the setting of the covenant if it becomes the accepted thing to take an idolatrous wife or have ready recourse to divorce? The prophet is angered by these practices.

2:11 *Judah:* signifies here all who belong to the people of God. Centuries-long experience (beginning with Solomon: 1 Ki 11:4) had shown how dangerous marriages with foreign women were: these women, holding tightly to their various forms of worship, drew their husbands into them.

2:13-16 Like all the peoples of the time, Israel allowed a husband to repudiate his wife (Mt 24:1-4). The prophet is more demanding: in his eyes, marriage is a sacred bond that cannot be broken without going against the intention of the Creator (Gen 2:24). This passage leads toward the ideal that Jesus will propose (Mt 19:1-9).

14 If you ask the reason why,
it is because the LORD stands as witness
between you and the wife of your youth
with whom you have broken faith,
even though she is your partner
and your wife by a solemn covenant. [o]
15 Did not the one God make her,
both flesh and spirit?
And what does the one God require
but God-given offspring?
Therefore, you must safeguard your own life,
and let none of you be unfaithful
to the wife of your youth. [p]
16 For I hate divorce,
says the LORD, the God of Israel,
as well as covering one's garment with injustice,
says the LORD of hosts.
Therefore, have respect for your own life,
and do not be unfaithful.

V: GOD WILL COME AND DO JUSTICE

17 You have wearied the LORD with your words.
Yet you ask, "How have we wearied him?"
By asserting, "All who do evil
are good in the eyes of the LORD;
indeed, he delights in them."
Or by asking,
"Where is the God of justice?"

CHAPTER 3

1 Behold, I am sending my messenger *
to prepare the way before me.
And suddenly the Lord whom you seek
will come to the temple,
as well as the messenger of the covenant
in whom you delight.
Indeed he is coming,
says the LORD of hosts. [q]
2 But who will be able to endure
the day of his coming,
and who can stand when he appears?
For he is like a refiner's fire
or like a fuller's soap.
3 He will sit refining and purifying;
he will purify the descendants of Levi
and refine them like gold or silver
so that they may in righteousness
offer due sacrifice to the LORD. [r]
4 Thus the offerings of Judah and Jerusalem
will be pleasing to the LORD
as in the days of old,
as in the years long past.
5 Then I will draw near to you for judgment,
and I will be swift to bear witness
against the sorcerers, adulterers, and perjurers,
against those who defraud the hired laborer of his wages,
against those who wrong widows and orphans,
against those who thrust aside the foreigner,
and against those who do not fear me,
says the LORD of hosts.

VI: MAKE THE TITHE OFFERING TO THE LORD*

6 For I, the LORD, do not change,
and you have not ceased to be sons of Jacob.
7 Since the days of your fathers
you have turned aside from my statutes
and have not kept them.
Return to me,
and I will return to you,
says the LORD of hosts.
Yet you ask,
"How can we return?" [s]
8 Can a man rob God?
Yet you are robbing me.
You ask, "How do we rob you?"
In your tithes and offerings. [t]
9 There is a curse on you all,
for your entire nation has defrauded me.

o Gen 31:49f; 1 Sam 12:5; Prov 5:18ff.—p Gen 2:7, 22ff; Ps 25:3.—q Isa 40:3; Ezek 39:8; Mt 11:10; Mk 1:2; Lk 1:17; 3:4; 7:27.—r Ex 5:3; Isa 1:25; Zec 13:9.—s Jer 4:1; Zec 1:3f; Acts 7:51.—t Neh 13:10-14.

3:1 The mysterious *messenger* of whom this verse speaks was probably a figure familiar to those who, at this period, attempted to imagine the final times: according to a passage added later (vv. 23-24), the reference was to Elijah, whose return was expected among the Jews. Jesus will apply the text to John the Baptist (see Mt 11:10; Mk 1:1; Lk 1:17). *The messenger of the covenant* is God himself; in Mt 11:10, it is Christ.

3:6-12 To take the tithe for the Lord up front was a way of acknowledging him as master of the land, rendering him homage, and drawing down his blessing on crops threatened by drought or by insect invasions. The produce thus brought served the needs of the temple and of the priests who saw to the performance of worship (see Num 18:21-32).

10 Bring the tithes in full into the treasury
so that there may be food in my house.
Put me thus to the test,
says the LORD of hosts,
and see if I will not open
the windows of heaven for you
and pour down blessings upon you
without measure. [u]
11 For your sake I will forbid the locusts
to destroy the produce of your soil,
and the vines in your fields will not be barren,
says the LORD of hosts.
12 Then all nations will call you blessed,
for yours will be a land of delight,
says the LORD of hosts.

VII: THE JUST WILL HAVE THEIR REVENGE

13 * You have spoken harsh words against me,
says the LORD.
Yet you ask,
"What have we said against you?"
14 You have said,
"It is useless to serve God.
What do we profit by keeping his commands
or by going about in penitential garb
before the LORD of hosts? [v]
15 For our part,
we regard the arrogant as happy.
Evildoers not only prosper,
but when they put God to the test,
they come to no harm." [w]

16 Then those who feared the LORD
spoke with one another.
The LORD listened attentively,
and a book of remembrance was written before him
of those who feared him
and trusted in his name. [x]

17 They shall be mine,
says the LORD of hosts,
my own special possession
on the day when I act,
and I will have compassion on them
as a father has compassion
on the son who serves him. [y]
18 Then you will once again see the difference
between the just and the wicked,
between the one who serves God
and the one who refuses to serve him.

19 For look, the day that is coming
will blaze like a furnace,
and all the proud and all the evildoers
will be stubble.
And the day that is coming
will set them ablaze,
leaving them neither root nor branch,
says the LORD of hosts. [z]
20 But for you who fear my name
the sun of justice will arise
with its healing rays.
You will emerge leaping
like calves released from the stall [a]
21 and tread down the wicked.
They will be ashes
under the soles of your feet
on the day when I act,
says the LORD of hosts.

VIII: FINAL EXHORTATION AND PROMISE

22 Remember the law of Moses my servant,
which I enjoined upon him at Horeb,
the statutes and ordinances
for all Israel. [b]
23 Lo, I will send you the prophet Elijah
before the day of the LORD comes,
that great and terrible day.
24 He will reconcile parents to their children
and children to their parents,
so that I will not come
and strike the land with a curse. [c]

---

u Gen 30:30; 2 Chr 31:10f; Neh 10:38; 13:12; Prov 3:9f.—v Job 21:14f; 22:17; Ps 73:11f; Jn 12:26.—w Ps 53:5.—x Ps 116:1; Rev 20:12.—y Ex 19:5; Num 8:14; Deut 7:6; Pss 103:13; 135:4; Mic 7:19.—z Lev 10:6; Isa 13:9; 34:8; Ezek 7:10; Joel 3:3; Zep 1:18; 2 Pet 3:7.—a Lk 1:78f; Acts 10:38; Eph 4:32.—b Ex 20:1-26; Lev 26:1-46; Num 15:40; Deut 4:1, 5f; Eccl 12:13.—c Mal 3:2; Mt 11:14; 17:10; Mk 9:11ff; Lk 1:17; Rev 6:8.

3:13-24 The rather harsh images at the end of this passage must be understood according to the mentality of the time. They express, in an excessive way, the hope which the just had of seeing evil someday disappear.

THE
NEW TESTAMENT

GENERAL INTRODUCTION TO THE NEW TESTAMENT

During the second century A.D. there were many writings in circulation that bore the name of Gospel, Acts, or Letter and claimed to be from the pen of an apostle, but only a few of these gained a place in the liturgy, catechesis, and preaching. Toward the end of that same century, it became customary to give the name "New Testament" to the collection of writings that had acquired authority everywhere in the Church as an important point of reference for the faith and that carried the guarantee of apostolic origin.

The first Christians did not immediately get the idea of connecting their writings with the Bible, Israel's book of revelation, which Christians were using in their liturgy and teaching. Gradually, however, the new writings acquired equal importance. To distinguish them from the Law and the Prophets or, in other words, the Bible, Christians spoke of a "New Testament," so that the other became in fact the "Old Testament."

The word "testament," in this context, is a translation of the Greek word used to convey the idea of a pact, that is, in this case, the Covenant that God had made with the people he had chosen. To speak of a "new covenant" was a bold step. It meant that the Covenant of Sinai, which was the foundation of the Jewish faith, had been completed and transcended by the coming of Christ. In the "passing over" of Jesus, God had established a new and definitive relationship with all human beings.

Henceforth, the Christian Bible had two parts: the Old and New Testaments. The Old was not rejected, but was interpreted as a prediction of the New and a way toward it. In reading the ancient texts, people now thought of the coming of Christ, which, for Christians, was the historical fulfillment of the hope of Israel.

The *twenty-seven Books* of the New Testament constitute the literature that is closest to Christian origins. Close in date, to be sure, but close, above all, by reason of the experience and faith to which they bear witness.

I. THE FACE OF THE NEW TESTAMENT

A Collection of Varied Writings

The New Testament writings are, then, close to Christ both in their date and in the experience they communicate. At the same time, however, even the writings that speak directly of him—the Gospels and Acts—are not in any sense a direct "news report"; they are testimonies and not reports. It is true that in one way or another all the New Testament writings communicate the essentials of a great event, but above all they are concerned with the meaning of that event. The Christ-event continues in the life of the community, and these writings are an expression of this continuity.

Texts Written at Various Periods

It must also be emphasized that the New Testament writings are not all from the same period. The earliest texts date from about twenty years after the death of

Jesus. The earliest text is not one of the Gospels but the First Letter of Paul to the Christians of Thessalonica.

If we go through the Letters of the Apostle in their chronological order, we can discover evidence of a development of his thinking and see the series of problems that the communities of that particular period encountered.

The definitive form of the Synoptic Gospels points to a different period of writing, from about A.D. 65 to 80, the time when the need was felt to have available works covering the entire message and life of Christ.

The Church, which was widely scattered throughout the known world of the time, was gradually being separated from the period of her foundation, and no one wanted to lose the inspiration that came from it. The Church needed some essential points of reference, so that the person, message, and mystery of Christ would not be diluted or lost due to time, the movement away from the original geographical center, new currents of thought, and the problems raised by a different age. The idea was not that the Church should be fixated on the past but that she should preserve the memory of the living, concrete face of Jesus and the fervor of Pentecost.

We are, then, in the presence of a *new generation of believers*. The mother Church disappeared after the destruction of Jerusalem in A.D. 70.

The communities strengthened their bonds of union within the same region, since they had to face the same problems there. Given the ferment of new currents of religious thought, there was the need to know the essentials of the faith and catechesis, the true tradition. Christians were set apart, were regarded as suspect, and therefore needed to be encouraged. Some were overcome by nostalgia and mourned for the Jewish religion with its prestigious past, its highly developed body of law, its grandiose ceremonies, and its temple. Others looked with interest on new pagan religious trends.

Amid this jumble of cultures and religions it was necessary to determine the criteria of Christian authenticity and to organize the communities. The Catholic Letters, the Letter to the Hebrews, and the Pastoral Letters attributed to Paul, as well as the collection of works that go under the name of St. John, reflected comparable situations that had developed especially in Asia Minor.

When, subsequently, open persecution broke out and aimed to destroy Christianity in a systematic way, the Book of Revelation by its tone and its words encouraged Christians.

II. THE PERIOD

The Roman Empire

The Mediterranean was Roman. In all the lands that were in contact with its shores the Empire had established its legates, its procurators, its troops, and even its revenue agents. The great cities experienced notable growth. The most important ports, those in which Paul founded Christian communities, contained several hundred thousand inhabitants. Slaves made up about two-thirds of the population.

In philosophy, Epicureanism and Stoicism were the dominant schools. The latter managed to make its teaching popular because of its grand vision of the universe and of the human person and the earnestness of its moral demands.

Religions swarmed. Local divinities welcomed imported gods without showing any jealousy. During this period of uncertainty, more emotional kinds of cults were introduced from Asia: mystery cults with their secret initiations and ecstatic excitements. In their symbols and myths they succeeded in grasping the suffering and desire for rebirth that are innate in every soul.

In the more distant past Hellenistic rulers had imposed worship of the king, and the Jews had paid dearly for their rejection of this form of civic life and of submission. Rome had developed within a more republican tradition and was not quick to divinize its emperors, except verbally. But this cult seemed a means of more quickly unifying so many and such disparate peoples. Venerating the reigning emperor and bowing before his statue that had been turned into an idol—these became civic gestures, and Asia Minor was the soil most ready to spread this imperial cult.

However, for Christians Jesus alone is "Lord," that is, God; to proclaim the "emperor as lord," as they were asked to do, seemed an act of blasphemy and apostasy. Their refusal made them suspect and soon the object of persecution as well, as the Book of Revelation attests.

The Jews of the Diaspora enjoyed a special status that allowed them to remain faithful to their own religion and their own law; they were excused from worship of the emperor, on condition that they pray for him. For a long time the Christian communities, even though they admitted pagans into their midst, profited by that privilege. But soon the Jews, like the public authorities, could no longer tolerate this blurring of lines.

Judaism

The diversity within Judaism was a sign of a broad pluralism. In Judea, people were rather conservative and obsessed with the country's past; the temple, the Law, and the many observances derived from the Law were the focus of religious attention. The Bible was read in Hebrew, but there was freedom to paraphrase and interpret it in Aramaic, the then current language of the people.

In *Samaria,* the Law of Moses was observed, but a temple was built there to compete with the one in Jerusalem.

In *Galilee,* which was more distant, the populace seemed dangerously mixed. The temple was far off, and for ordinary religious services Jews gathered in synagogues, which played a decisive role.

The Jews of the *Diaspora* were educated to a quite different mentality. In general, they were loyal to their faith and the Law, but they read the Bible in Greek, the usual language in the Mediterranean countries. These Jews, who were scattered almost everywhere and were called "Hellenists," often went on pilgrimage to Jerusalem. They were present in the city on Pentecost and some of them were baptized.

We must bear in mind that for internal affairs the Jews had their own tribunal, the *Great Sanhedrin,* composed of 71 members.

These included representatives of the lay aristocracy (the elders) and the principal priestly families (the chief priests, all of them Saddeucees), as well as the scribes or interpreters of the Law, who were predominantly Pharisaic in outlook. The high priest currently in office presided over the Sanhedrin.

With the entry of Pompey into Jerusalem in 63 B.C. the country was subjected to Roman rule, which put an end to the last period of freedom that had been won by hard struggles in the time of the Maccabean wars.

The Herodian Rulers

At this time, then, the Jews were living in subjection to rulers imposed on them by the occupier. The *Herodians* were a dynasty of mixed blood; they earned the dislike of all by their cruelty, intrigues, and immorality. Herod the Great, who was married to a descendant of the Maccabees, reigned from 37 to 4 B.C.; this extraordinary builder began to rebuild a sumptuous temple, but he did not hesitate to rid himself without scruple of anyone who inconvenienced him, even his wives and his sons. The story of the slaughter of the innocents has kept alive over the centuries the impression of cruelty that he left behind him.

At his death, three of his sons divided the kingdom. *Antipas* governed Galilee and Perea from the city of Tiberias, which he built on the shore of Lake Gennesaret. He killed John the Baptist, who had become bothersome to him, and he hoped to meet Jesus. His half-brother, *Philip,* reigned over Ituraea and Trachonitis until A.D. 34. He beautified Panion and gave it the name Caesarea (known therefore as Caesarea Philippi, "Philip's Caesarea"). Finally, *Archelaus,* Antipas's brother, governed Judea, Samaria, and Idumea; but the Romans deposed him shortly afterward because of his arbitrary and unmeasured cruelty.

After the removal of Archelaus, Judea was united to the Province of Syria, and its government was entrusted to a procurator who was appointed directly by Rome and resided in Caesarea of Palestine. More than one of these men came to be hated by the populace for their detestable provocations; this was true especially of Pontius Pilate.

For a short period (A.D. 41–44), thanks to his friendship with the Emperor Claudius, *Agrippa I,* a nephew of Herod, was able to rule over a part of the Palestinian states, including Judea. In his desire to please the Jews, he launched the first persecution of Christians and had the Apostle James the Less executed. Agrippa was struck down by a sudden death.

His son, *Agrippa II,* did not receive the whole of his father's inheritance; he did have jurisdiction over the temple and obtained the government of the regions on the borders of Palestine. Like his sister Drusilla, he was pleased to listen to Paul, then a prisoner; this was on the occasion of a visit that he, along with his sister Berenice, paid to Festus, the procurator in Caesarea.

Jewish Uprisings

The period of Jesus' life and of the Church's beginnings was marked by serious upheavals. Repeated insurrections gave vent to the anger of many at the abuses of arbitrary and arrogant power, but they also expressed a refusal to accept with resignation the disappearance of Israel. The Jewish War, from A.D. 66 to 70, is one of the most tragic pages in the history of the Jewish people. The heroism of the rebels contrasted with the depth of their despair and the horror of the battle. The temple was destroyed in A.D. 70 and has remained in that condition to our day. Judaism, however, was reborn under the leadership of the Pharisees, with its center in the life of the synagogues, and, amid surprising ups and downs, it has survived until today. A second revolt in Palestine, from A.D. 132 to 135, was put down in a bloodbath.

The Pharisees

The *Pharisees* constituted the most important of the religious groups. They were not closed to new religious ideas, such as the resurrection, but they did have a scrupulous respect for the Law and were endlessly interpreting its details. They were "the pure"; they kept themselves free from political entanglements, detested the conceited power of the Sadducees and the arrogant intrigues of the Herodians, and accepted the Roman occupation.

Like Paul, who came from their ranks, they worked with their hands to earn their living. Despite their attitude of superiority, they became masters at teaching the people their religion and even domineered over consciences. They regarded it as inconceivable, however, that anyone should keep company with known sinners, and beyond imagining that tax collectors could be privileged recipients of God's mercy.

Jesus made some friends among them; one of them would provide him with a tomb. But he scandalized them deeply by his special attention to the poor and the outcasts of the Jewish religion and by his freedom in regard to legalistic and alienating observances. They were unable to share his joyous sense of God's mercy toward human beings and of the divine fatherhood that is so receptive of everyone.

According to the Gospels, Jesus regarded the Pharisees as hypocrites and faced up to them from the very beginning. They were the representatives of the traditional religion in the time of Jesus and were therefore, in the eyes of Christians, representatives of the synagogue's rejection of the Gospel. But we ought not generalize unduly: the Pharisees were often close to the Gospel. After the breakup of A.D. 70, they laid the moral and doctrinal foundations of future Judaism.

The Sadducees

The *Sadducees* were men of the temple. They linked themselves with the priestly line of Zadok. They represented official religious authority, the rich class, and the aristocracy of the rural areas. They were intriguers who collaborated with the occupying power and had nothing but contempt for the common people; in return, people hated them deeply. In religion they were conservatives and even ridiculed the resurrection so as to deny it more conspicuously. They were at home in Jerusalem; from the moment Jesus entered the city, he had to face this ruling class, which would decide on his death.

The Priests

What has been said of the Sadducees did not apply to the *priests*, who were divided into twenty-four classes and took turns officiating in the temple. Many of them were humble, devout, and faithful men, like Zechariah, father of John the Baptist. Some of them were among the first converts. The latter may have retained a nostalgia for the beautiful ceremonies of Jewish worship.

The Zealots

The *Zealots*, who arose at the beginning of the first century, were the sworn enemies of the Sadducees, the Herodians, and the occupying authorities. They were also called *sicarii*, from the Roman name for their weapon, a short dagger (*sica*) which they could easily hide and which they used in order to settle accounts secretly.

They were the leaders of the armed rebellions; they would be the great heroes but also, unfortunately, the victims of the Jewish War of A.D. 66–70 and later of the revolt of 135. Christ never tried to justify their actions, even though some of his disciples came from their circles.

The Herodians

The *Herodians* sided with the reigning dynasty and were quick to engage in denunciations and intrigues. For this reason they were distrusted.

The Essenes

The *Essenes*, finally, broke with the official religious institutions in order to recreate an Israel that awaited God. They lived in monastic austerity, without wives, without money, without violence, but they also seemed distrustful of joy. Christian religious circles shared several religious ideas with them. The monastery of Qumran, the life of which has become known to us through the famous Dead Sea Scrolls, may represent Essene spirituality.

The Scribes

The Gospels often speak of the *scribes* or *teachers* of the Law. Their official function was to interpret the Scriptures and religious teaching. We find them in the streets and synagogues; on the whole, they tended to be Pharisees.

III. JESUS OF NAZARETH

The Life of Jesus

This man, who was ignored by the age in which he lived, is unquestionably the most important figure in the history of humanity, due to the effect his name and his ideas have had down the centuries. Yet he is mentioned only on a couple of occasions, and then in vague terms, by historians of his time, specifically Tacitus and Suetonius at the beginning of the 2nd century.

He was sentenced and condemned to death by the Roman governor, Pontius Pilate, but the records of this trial have not been preserved. Nevertheless, of all the religious movements of that age, that of Jesus is the only one that has not disappeared.

The life of Jesus can be dated with some accuracy. We need only refer to the passages in which the Gospels mention personages and events that can be identified from other sources. Thus, we know that the first year of the Christian era was not accurately calculated: Jesus was born in the year 7 or 6 before the beginning of that era. He died on a Friday, the eve of Passover, between A.D. 28 and 33, perhaps on April 7, 30.

The Stages of Jesus' Preaching

The Galilean period began in a very promising way. There was a springtime atmosphere about it, a kind of explosion of joy at the proclamation that salvation had come. But the proclamation was not unambiguous. Jesus Christ spoke of the Kingdom of God; that is, in order to make himself understood, he used a word that was heavy with the hopes and expectations of the Jewish people. Consequently, the titles that others gave him—Son of David, Messiah, Son of God, or the title he gave himself: Son of Man—all had overtones of grandeur, but they also carried with them all too human hopes.

In fact, he was to carry out his vocation as Savior, the one who takes responsibility for the religious destiny of the world, in the form of the Suffering Servant, the unexpected figure described long before in the Book of Isaiah (42; 49; 50; 52:13—53:12). People refused to hear this, and understandably so. They were looking forward to a radical upheaval of the political situation, a glorious rehabilitation of Israel, and revenge on the pagan nations, for it was these that the Scriptures seemed to suggest.

Jesus, however, did not speak of this brutal turnaround, but of a new beginning, a change, a conversion, a new life. The lack of understanding between him and the crowd continued to grow. It reached its high point after the multiplication of the loaves, when he had to flee because some wanted to seize him and make him king.

When the misunderstanding reached the point of no return, Jesus changed his way of acting. He knew he would experience nothing but rejection, and he therefore devoted himself to the training of his disciples, the formation of the core group of individuals who would proclaim the kingdom once he was no longer there. He met with misunderstanding even among these men, but, more importantly, he won their unshakable affection. Through the experiences they shared with him, they learned his way of thinking and responding, and they would be able to pass this on later. The Kingdom of God was entrusted to a community, the Church.

The point came when the prospect of death became imminent; it was written in the foreseeable course of events. But Jesus did not change his program, even though he had to struggle with the instinctive horror of atrocious torment. Henceforth he clashed openly with entrenched positions, whether political or religious or social. The Gospel has preserved for us the tragic encounter of Jesus with the leaders of Judaism. He had to learn from experience that he would change the wills of human beings only by willingly making the supreme gift of his life.

IV. THE YOUTHFUL YEARS OF THE CHURCH

After the unforgettable experience of Pentecost, the group of disciples grew rapidly, as the disciples realized they were the agent of God's plan for the whole human race. The Spirit and events had given them this formidable mission. In the very beginning, indeed, the Church seemed desirous of falling back into the way of life and thinking of Judaism, but her destiny was to be one of continual and often difficult expansion, out to the ends of the then known world.

Believers of Palestinian origin were joined by others from the Diaspora: the Hellenists or Greek-speaking Jews. This was the first occasion for somewhat serious internal tensions and for the first efforts at organization; above all, however, it was the seed of development in new cultural areas. Various personages came to the fore in those early days: the Apostles Peter and John; the deacons Stephen and Philip, the former as the first martyr, the latter as one who overcame all difficulties in order to proclaim the Gospel. The first persecution, in 44—which claimed the Apostle James as a victim and would have claimed Peter, were it not for a miraculous deliverance—led to the dispersal of the community. From that point on, we know almost nothing about the majority of the Apostles.

Outside of Palestine, on the other hand, a dynamic enterprise, initially hidden, was brought fully into the open. Such men as Barnabas, John, Mark, and soon Paul, the converted persecutor who was aided by Timothy, began to establish one missionary center after another on the shores of the Mediterranean, moving finally into Europe; the Book of Acts creates for us a map of this expansion. Yet these men were certainly not the only missionaries.

We can only hint at the immense effort that the communities needed to set forth in order to give form to their experience and to express it. The Palestinian Jewish world was enmeshed in internal tensions, while the Christians affirmed that Jesus was the Christ, that is, the Messiah. They venerated him as the Son of God and celebrated him in the Liturgy, declaring his presence among them.

To affirm that Jesus was alive it was necessary to reinterpret his life and his work, the whole Old Testament and all the ideas of humanity concerning the meaning of life. These affirmations were not made in specialized schools but amid the demands of life, with its problems and its unforeseen questions, while seeking greater depth of understanding, which at times entailed tentative gropings.

The organization of the inner equilibrium of communities was also necessary. Jews and non-Jews, Greeks and barbarians, those privileged by culture or fortune and poor people, slaves and freemen had to acknowledge one another and express themselves as believers equally and entirely.

In a few years an unequaled transformation was worked in the name of a certitude: Jesus and his Spirit, and the salvation of all humanity. In a world turned upside down, a new seed was introduced. The little group had become a great community of believers, the Church; the first announcement had given rise to a magnificent Gospel. Without the Easter faith, which was at the origin of the movement and remained its core, none of this would have taken place. There would have been no Christianity, and the name of Jesus would forever be effaced from human memory.

BOOKS OF THE NEW TESTAMENT

ST. MATTHEW
1942
ST. MARK

ST. LUKE
ST. JOHN

THE GOSPELS

The Bible's table of contents (the "canon" of the Scriptures) gives the Gospels in the following order: Matthew, Mark, Luke, and John.

As a matter of fact, only the Book of Mark calls itself a "Gospel"; the others were given this title during the second century.

Alongside these officially recognized writings, a number of other gospels (known as the "apocrypha," that is, "secret" writings) circulated, but they were never accepted by the Church as inspired.

The Differences

The differences among the four Gospels are such that it is very difficult to combine their varied and often contrasting bits of information into a complete and solidly based biography of Jesus.

All four Gospels are very similar in their accounts of the Passion. But apart from that particular sequence, the difference between John and the other three is radical. When we read John, we are told that during his public life Jesus went up to Jerusalem three or four times for Passover and other feasts (Jn 2:13; 5:1; 7:10; 12:12); the other three Gospels report only one journey to the holy city, the one that ended in his arrest and death. According to the fourth Gospel, Jesus carried on a baptismal ministry at the same time as that of John the Baptist; the three Synoptic Gospels locate John's entire activity prior to that of Jesus (see Mt 4:12; Mk 1:14; Lk 3:1—4:15; and Jn 3:24).

Most importantly, the material in the majority of John's chapters is unknown to Matthew, Mark, and Luke, who nonetheless abound in sayings and stories; this cannot be explained as forgetfulness on either side. Finally, John's style has nothing in common with that of the other three. In the Synoptics, Jesus speaks in short, carefully wrought sentences that were easy to remember and to pass on orally; the Gospel of John, on the other hand, always starts with a solemn gesture of Jesus and follows with lengthy discourses that are marked by a careful and complex progression.

The Synoptic Problem

In contrast to John, the first three Gospels have much in common. They report the Christ-event according to the same pattern. In addition, the texts are similar, and each frequently follows the other two even in the details of images and sayings. This similarity makes it possible to read these three Gospels together, in parallel columns; we can read them "synoptically," that is, "seeing them together or at the same time" (Greek: *synopsis*), whence the name "Synoptic Gospels" or "Synoptics." In fact, of the 661 verses in Mark, 600 are found in Matthew and 350 in Luke.

At the same time, however, there are major differences. Matthew and Luke have many passages in common that are completely unknown to Mark. In addition, each Gospel has a sizable group of texts that are found only in it.

How are we to explain these surprising similarities and differences? This is the "Synoptic problem." The similarities are to be explained mainly by the development in the communities of a well-structured oral tradition and by the formation of written collections organized according to genres or forms (parables, miracle stories, controversies, and so on). The kind of research known as the "study of forms" or literary genres endeavors to understand passages that had taken shape in the development of preaching.

But we have to go farther, because among the three Gospels there exist not only affinities due to tradition but also obvious editorial connections, so that it is also necessary to look into what is known as "redaction history." Different explanations of this history have been proposed, but scholars are generally in agreement on a hypothesis that includes the following points:

—The Synoptics use as their first source either the present Gospel of Mark (in the case of Matthew and Luke) or this same text but in an earlier editorial stage (all three evangelists).

—Matthew and Luke also use another source that had preserved chiefly the sayings of Jesus. This source could have been a single document or a family of similar documents.

—It can be presumed that prior to the composition of the Gospels there were contacts between the different sources at the various stages of their formation.

—Each Gospel also draws on sources of its own.

—Finally, each Gospel has its own point of view, its own way of proceeding, and its own visions of things, and all these are explained by the purpose the author set for himself, the setting in which he was living, and the readership he was addressing. We shall speak of these in the introduction to each Gospel.

The Purpose of the Gospels

These differences make clear the freedom that the communities and the authors had in adapting the Gospel story to the mentalities and problems of the communities. The purpose of the authors was not to present a detailed, structured story but rather a vision of what Jesus was and of what he presently is for the Church. A document that lacks all biographical detail is not a Gospel; on the other hand, a Gospel is always a theological discourse, a faith-inspired presentation, and not a simple historical description. The starting point of the Gospels is the Easter faith.

Consequently, before being a historical document and while having all the value of a historical document, a Gospel is an event. The Gospels preserve for us many biographical details about Jesus, but they are not primarily biographies, lives of Jesus. Their purpose is to bear witness to the Gospel, that is, the Good News of God's coming into the midst of humanity. In Jesus and by means of Jesus, God speaks the final word about himself and about the destiny of humanity and the world.

"From now on you will see the Son of Man seated at the right hand of the Power and coming on the clouds of heaven" *(Mt 26:64).*

THE GOSPEL ACCORDING TO MATTHEW

The Teaching of Jesus for the Life of the Communities

The form of the Our Father that we use in prayer and the formulation of the Beatitudes that we customarily follow are those that we read in the Gospel of Matthew; we also use this Gospel for most of the actions and words of Jesus. Since the very early centuries, Matthew's Gospel has stood at the head of the New Testament writings, thus earning it the name "the first Gospel."

Why has this Gospel enjoyed such success? It is pleasing for its literary qualities—its distinctive tone, its short, clear narratives, its well-organized text—but it is striking, above all, because the teaching of Jesus occupies such a very large place in it. Matthew's Gospel is par excellence the book of the Church and has rightly been called the "ecclesial Gospel," because as he reports what Jesus said, he has the life of the community constantly in mind.

What was the origin of this Gospel? The earliest tradition attributes it to the Apostle Matthew, also known as Levi, son of Alphaeus. Once this tax collector made the acquaintance of Jesus he was struck by his personality and immediately left his trade (a profitable one, even if at that time regarded as quite a reprehensible one) to join the group of disciples (Mt 9:9; Mk 2:14). Later on, according to this tradition, he gathered up his recollections in a book. Careful research has led to less simple conclusions. In its present form our first Gospel was written in Greek and completed in A.D. 70 or perhaps a little later. Other less fully developed collections preceded it. The first texts, written in Hebrew or Aramaic (the languages of Palestine at that time), date perhaps from the forties or fifties, a period still close to the death of Jesus.

The Book as we have it has drawn upon the Gospel of Mark and on another source on which Luke, too, draws. Despite these influences, Matthew reflects, better than the others, the early preaching to Christians of Jewish origin, and is perhaps the Book used for Christian preaching in Palestine. Rather than a simple biography, it is meant as God's word regarding our life and the world.

Each Gospel has its own way of highlighting the important moments in the activity of Jesus, culminating in the story of the Passion and Resurrection. Matthew has, then, his own characteristic traits. The "Good News" is proclaimed principally in Galilee: it is a joyous event, and Jesus immediately calls some disciples. But the drama of rejection soon begins; from that moment on, the tempo quickens, as Jesus remains apart from the crowds and trains his disciples, thus preparing for the coming Church. The clash with official Judaism at last becomes open and unrelenting. This tragic development ends in the Passion. Along the line of this general movement Matthew locates some key points: the discourses that are so characteristic of his Book. Each gathers together the sayings of Jesus about a theme, because Matthew is thinking primarily of forming the community, of "catechizing" it, as we might say today.

As a result, the five great discourses of Matthew's Gospel, separated from each other by sections of narrative, sum up the principal elements of a code of Christian life. The five are: the Sermon on the Mount, including the Beatitudes; the missionary discourse; the parables; the teaching on life in community; and perspectives on the end of the world. None of these discourses is developed like a fine lecture. Rather, the tradition Matthew follows gradually gathered sayings of Jesus on some central themes (the same sayings are often cited by the other evangelists in different contexts). In fact, as compositions, these discourses are quite unsuccessful. And yet what power flows from them to guide us in living a life worthy of the Christian name!

A Gospel is first and foremost the proclamation of Jesus as Savior of the human race. Matthew expresses this essential faith in words, ideas, and images that were accessible to the people of that time who were of Jewish origin. Therefore, he presents Jesus as the Messiah who had been promised and was long awaited, but then was rejected. And to give greater force to his arguments he heaps up citations from the Old Testament. More than once, this "proof" from Scripture seems artificial in its details, but the author is nonetheless able to explain the fate of Jesus in the light of the Bible as a whole.

Matthew's Gospel is the Gospel of the Church. And indeed it sets forth, for the community called together by Jesus, the main lines of a Christian life, and presents the life of the disciples as a model for all those who accept the mindset of the kingdom of God.

The Gospel of Matthew may be divided as follows:

Prologue: The Birth of the Messiah, Jesus of Nazareth (1:1—2:23)

- *I: Jesus Inaugurates His Ministry as Savior (3:1—7:29)*
- *II: The Signs of the Kingdom of God (8:1—10:42)*
- *III: Jesus Is the Expected Messiah (11:1—13:52)*
- *IV: The Authentic Faith of Those Converted (13:53—18:35)*
- *V: The Coming of the Son of Man (19:1—25:46)*
- *VI: The Passion and Resurrection (26:1—28:20)*

PROLOGUE: THE BIRTH OF THE MESSIAH, JESUS OF NAZARETH*

CHAPTER 1

The Genealogy of Jesus.* 1 The account of the genealogy of Jesus Christ,* the son of David, the son of Abraham.[a]

2 b Abraham was the father of Isaac,
Isaac the father of Jacob,
Jacob the father of Judah and his brothers.[c]
3 Judah was the father of Perez and Zerah, with Tamar * being their mother.
Perez was the father of Hezron,
Hezron the father of Ram,[d]
4 Ram the father of Amminadab.
Amminadab was the father of Nahshon,
Nahshon the father of Salmon,[e]
5 Salmon the father of Boaz, with Rahab being his mother.
Boaz was the father of Obed, whose mother was Ruth.
Obed was the father of Jesse,[f]
6 and Jesse was the father of King David.
David was the father of Solomon, whose mother had been the wife of Uriah.[g]

a Gen 2:4; 5:1; 22:18; 1 Chr 17:11; Gal 3:16.—b 2-17: Lk 3: 23-38.—c Gen 21:3; 25:26; 29:35; 1 Chr 2:1.—d Gen 38:29-30; Ru 4:18; 1 Chr 2:4-9.—e Ru 4:19-20; 1 Chr 2:10-11.—f Ru 4:21-22; 1 Chr 2:11-12; Heb 11:31.—g 1 Sam 16:1; 2 Sam 12:24; 1 Chr 2:15; 3:5.—h 7-11: 2 Ki 25:1-21; 1 Chr 3:10-15; Jer 27:20; Dan 1:1.—i 12-16: 1 Chr 3:16-19; Ezr 3:2.

1:1—2:23 Who was Jesus? Where did he come from? The prologue of Matthew's Gospel immediately confronts us with this question. The author has not simply gathered up some scattered recollections to complete his album on the life of Christ; rather, from the very first moment he is transmitting the Church's testimony of faith.

1:1-17 To the ancients a genealogical tree was not only a set of data on one's civil status but also a manifestation of one's membership in a community and the importance of ancestry (Gen 5:1-11; Ex 6:14-24; 1 Chr 1—9; Ezr 2:59-63). The genealogy of Jesus is drawn up with special care; it is perhaps somewhat artificial, but it is quite solemn. In bringing Jesus on the scene, the entire history of the nation is recapitulated. He is the son of Abraham, in whom all the nations shall be blessed (Gen 18:18); he is the son of David, to whom the future of the people was entrusted (2 Sam 7:13-14); in other words, he is the one who will carry out God's plan for Israel and the entire human race; he is the One Sent, the consecrated of God (Messiah, Christ).

The opening sentences of the Gospel are thus a "Book of Genesis," an account of the new beginning of humanity and the world (Gen 2:4; 5:1). Luke will carry the genealogy of Jesus back to Adam himself (Lk 3:23-38). In Matthew's list Joseph plays a well-defined part: it is by means of him that Jesus is given a *de jure* place in history. But at this point the Gospel unexpectedly avoids the phrase "the father of" ("begot"), and Joseph is simply the husband of Mary. The entire mystery of Jesus' origin is already stated in these few words.

7 h Solomon was the father of Rehoboam,
Rehoboam the father of Abijah,
Abijah the father of Asa.
8 Asa was the father of Jehoshaphat,
Jehoshaphat the father of Joram,
Joram the father of Uzziah.
9 Uzziah was the father of Jotham,
Jotham the father of Ahaz,
Ahaz the father of Hezekiah.
10 Hezekiah was the father of Manasseh,
Manasseh the father of Amos,
Amos the father of Josiah.
11 Josiah was the father of Jechoniah and his brothers at the time of the deportation to Babylon.

12 i After the deportation to Babylon,
Jechoniah was the father of Shealtiel,
Shealtiel the father of Zerubbabel,
13 Zerubabbel the father of Abiud.
Abiud was the father of Eliakim,
Eliakim the father of Azor,
14 Azor the father of Zadok.
Zadok was the father of Achim,
Achim the father of Eliud,
15 Eliud the father of Eleazar.
Eleazar was the father of Matthan,
Matthan the father of Jacob.
16 Jacob was the father of Joseph, the husband of Mary, who gave birth to Jesus who is called the Christ. *

17 Therefore, in total there were fourteen generations from Abraham to David, another fourteen generations from David to the deportation to Babylon, and another fourteen generations from the deportation to Babylon to the Christ.

1:1 *Christ:* is the Greek translation of the Hebrew "Messiah," which means "anointed," that is, consecrated. Priests were anointed (Lev 4:3, 5; 16:15); so were kings (1 Sam 10:1 [Saul]; 16:11 [David], etc.), so much so that the reigning monarch was sometimes given the title of "Messiah," or "Anointed One" (see Pss 2:2; 89:38; etc.). The name "Jesus Christ," which at this point was still an alternative for or associated with "Jesus of Nazareth," is already to be found in the initial preaching of the apostles (see Acts 3:6).

1:3 The genealogy names four women: Tamar (see Gen 38; 1 Chr 2:4), Rahab (see Jos 2; 6:17), the wife of Uriah, i.e., Bathsheba (see 2 Sam 11; 12:24), and Ruth (see Book of Ruth). These four women were foreigners who in some way became part of the history of Israel. They symbolize the salvation that God intends for all peoples.

1:16 It is important to note that in the case of Christ's birth, the text uses a formula that is far different from the one used for the other persons in the genealogy. In doing so, the evangelist is paving the way for the teaching of Christ's virginal conception, which took place without the intervention of any man.

The Birth of Jesus.* 18 The birth of Jesus Christ occurred in this way. When his mother Mary was engaged to Joseph, but before they came to live together, she was found to be with child through the Holy Spirit. 19 Her husband Joseph was a just man and did not wish to expose her to the ordeal of public disgrace; therefore, he resolved to divorce her quietly.

20 After he had decided to follow this course of action, an angel of the Lord appeared to him in a dream and said, "Joseph, son of David, do not be afraid to receive Mary into your home as your wife. For this child has been conceived in her womb through the Holy Spirit.[j] 21 She will give birth to a son, and you shall name him Jesus, * for he will save his people from their sins."

22 All this took place in order to fulfill what the Lord had announced through the prophet:

23 "Behold, the virgin shall conceive and
give birth to a son,
and they shall name him Emmanuel,"[k]

a name that means "God is with us." *

24 When Joseph rose from sleep, he did what the angel of the Lord had commanded him. He took Mary into his home as his wife,[l] 25 but he engaged in no marital relations* with her until she gave birth to a son, whom he named Jesus.[m]

CHAPTER 2

The Wise Men Render Homage to the Messiah.* 1 After Jesus had been born in Bethlehem * of Judea during the reign of King Herod, wise men traveled from the east and arrived in Jerusalem,[n] 2 inquiring, "Where is the newborn king of the Jews? We saw the rising of his star, and we have come to pay him homage."[o]

3 On hearing about their inquiry, King Herod was greatly troubled, as was true of the whole of Jerusalem. 4 Therefore, he summoned all the chief priests * and the scribes and questioned them about where the Christ was to be born.[p] 5[q] They replied, "In Bethlehem of Judea, for thus has the prophet written:

6 'And you, Bethlehem, in the land of
Judah,
are by no means least among the
rulers of Judah,
for from you shall come a ruler
who will shepherd my people
Israel.' " *

7 Then Herod secretly summoned the wise men, and he ascertained from them the exact time of the star's appearance, 8 after which he sent them on to Bethlehem, saying: "Go forth and search diligently for the child. When you have found him, bring me word, so that I can go and pay him homage."

9 After receiving these instructions from the king, the wise men set out. And behold, the star that they had seen at its rising proceeded ahead of them until it stopped over

j Mt 2:13-19; Gen 16:7; Lk 1:35; Acts 7:38.—k Isa 7:14 LXX.—l Acts 5:19.—m Lk 2:7.—n Lk 2:4-7.—o Num 24:17.—p Jn 7:42.—q 5-6: 2 Sam 5:2; Mic 5:1.

1:18-25 At the beginning of creation the Spirit made the waters fruitful (Gen 1:2; Ps 33:6-7); the Spirit restored life to a people who had been destroyed and were in exile (Ezek 37:1-14; Isa 44:2-4). Now the Spirit creates the new human being, the new Israel, in the womb of the Virgin. How mysterious the interventions of God that turn upside down the course of events and the ways of human beings! Joseph, who is irrevocably bound to Mary because at that time an espousal was a definitive act, is witness to the incomprehensible; he has too much trust in his wife to abandon her to the sentence imposed by the Law if she were to be thought an adulteress. But who will show him the way out of this impossible situation? A revelation of heaven makes his mission known to him in a dream, as the announcement of angels and messengers had to the patriarchs. Joseph obeys, and through him Jesus finds a place publicly in the dynasty of David.

What will this son become, whose name "Jesus" is already a program, since it means "God saves"? The prophecy of Isaiah, which had remained mysterious to the minds of believers, is now fulfilled. Such is the main message of this text that was originally addressed to Jews, namely, that God is in our midst to give us victory and to live the covenant to the full. "Emmanuel" means "God is with us" (Lk 1:31; Jn 1:14). That is the ultimate message.

1:21 *Jesus:* is a transcription of the Greek *Iêsous*, which in turn is a transcription of the Hebrew *Jehoshuah* ("Joshua" in translations) or *Jeshua* in its later form. It means "God saves."

1:23 See Isa 7:14. God's promise of salvation to Judah in the time of Isaiah is seen to be fulfilled in the birth of Jesus. This is the first of some 60 citations, most of them Messianic, that Matthew takes from the Old Testament.

1:25 *Engaged in no marital relations:* literally, "did not know," "know" being the usual word for conjugal relations (see Gen 4:1). The meaning of "he engaged in no marital relations with her . . . " is: "without his knowing her, she bore a son." The Hebrew word "until" neither implies nor excludes marital conduct after Jesus' birth.

2:1-12 We shall never be able to identify with certainty these men of study and prayer, who may also have been astrologers (called by a Persian name, "Magi"). Orientals thought that a new star appeared at the birth of great persons (Num 24:17). In any case, the hour has come for pagans to share in the joy of encounter with God. This Gospel also confirms the expectation of Israel and cites the Prophets (Mic 5:1; 2 Sam 5:1-3): the new future of the People of God originates in the dynasty of David and in his native place, Bethlehem (1 Sam 16), but the mission of the Messiah goes beyond religious and national frontiers. The Messianic age is beginning (see Ps 72:10-11; Isa 9:1, 5; 49:23; 60:1-5; Lk 2:30-34).

2:1 *Bethlehem:* about five miles south of Jerusalem.

2:4 *Chief priests:* in the plural signifies the high priest now in office and his predecessors and members of their respective families. Herod's act of consulting with the chief priests and teachers of the Law has some affinity with a Jewish legend about the child Moses in which Pharaoh is warned by sacred scribes about the coming birth of a deliverer of Israel from Egypt and plots to destroy the deliverer.

2:6 This prophecy of Micah (5:1) had been pronounced seven centuries earlier.

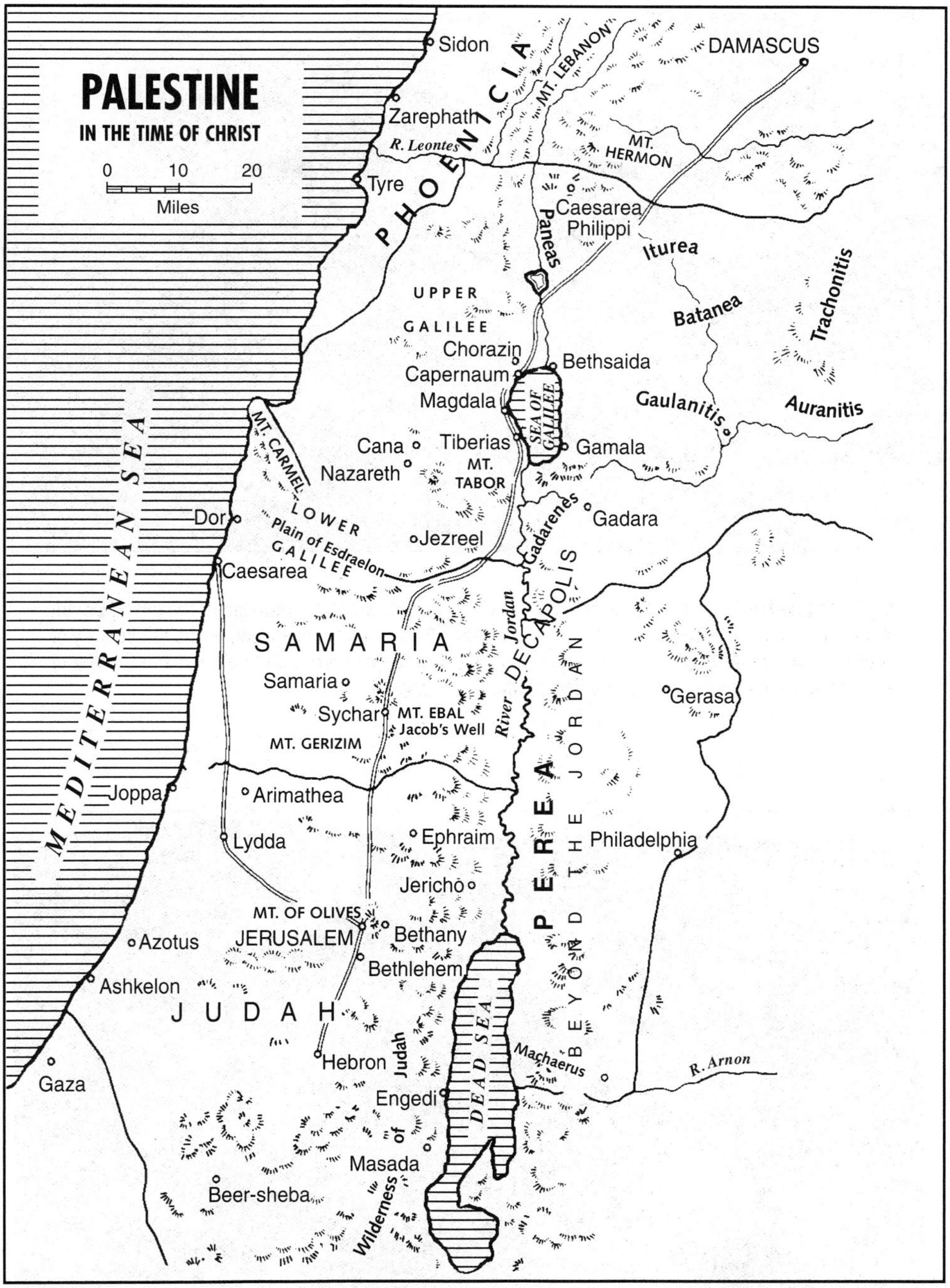

PALESTINE IN THE TIME OF CHRIST (37 B.C.—A.D. 36) — **(a)** Herod the Great becomes king under the Romans in 37 (and is kept by Caesar Augustus in 29). Herod's reign is one of continual fear of plots and he does not hesitate to execute his own relatives and children, while erecting magnificent edifices. **(b)** Jesus is born sometime before Herod's death (7–6 B.C.?). **(c)** In 4 B.C. Herod's kingdom is divided among his sons. Archelaus becomes tetrarch of Judea but is deposed in A.D. 6 and **Judea** and **Samaria** become part of the Roman province of Syria. Antipas becomes tetrarch of **Galilee** and **Perea** until A.D. 39 Philip becomes tetrarch of **Trachonitis** until his death in A.D. 34. **(d)** In A.D. 7 Annas is made high priest. **(e)** In A.D. 15 Tiberius Caesar becomes Roman Emperor. **(f)** In A.D. 26 Joseph Caiaphas is made high priest. **(g)** In A.D.26 Pontius Pilate is sent as governor of Judea and outrages the Jews by letting the Romans bring ensigns into the temple.

Matson Photo Service

BETHLEHEM: TOWN OF CHRIST'S BIRTH — A view from the south of Bethlehem, the city of David, a town five miles southwest of Jerusalem. It rises 2550 feet above sea level, in the hill country of Judea, on the main highway to Hebron and Egypt. In the distance is the belfry of the Church of the Nativity built on the site where Christ was born. (See Mt 2:1)

Matson Photo Service

NAZARETH: SCENE OF CHRIST'S EARLY LIFE — A view of Nazareth (from the east, taken from the ancient bridal-path to Tiberias), a town in lower Galilee located in a geographical basin blocking off the surrounding countryside. However, from the edge of the basin a distance of 30 miles can be seen in each direction. This was the home of the Holy Family after the flight into Egypt. (See Mt 2:19-23)

the place where the child was. [10] The sight of
the star filled them with great joy, [11] and
when they entered the house they beheld the
child with Mary his mother. Falling to their
knees, they paid him homage. Then they
opened their treasure chests and offered
him gifts of gold, frankincense, and myrrh. *
[12] [r] And since they had been warned in a
dream not to return to Herod, they depart-
ed for their own country by another route. [s]

The Flight into Egypt. [13] After the wise men
had left, an angel of the Lord appeared to
Joseph in a dream and instructed him,
"Arise, take the child and his mother, and
flee to Egypt. Remain there until I tell you.
Herod seeks the child to kill him." [t]
[14] Therefore, he got up, took the child and his
mother, and departed that night for Egypt,
[15] where they remained until the death of
Herod. This was to fulfill what the Lord had
spoken through the prophet: "Out of Egypt I
called my son." * [u]

The Slaughter of the Innocents at Bethlehem.
[16] When Herod realized that the wise men
had deceived him, he flew into a rage and
issued an order to kill all the boys in
Bethlehem and the surrounding area who
were two years old or less, in accordance
with the information that he had obtained
from the wise men. [17] * Thus were fulfilled
the words that had been spoken through the
prophet Jeremiah:

[18] "A voice was heard in Ramah,
lamenting and sobbing bitterly:
Rachel weeping for her children,
and refusing to be consoled,
because they were no more." [v]

The Return to the Land of Israel.* [19] After the
death of Herod, an angel of the Lord
appeared in a dream to Joseph in Egypt
[20] and said, "Arise, take the child and his
mother, and go to the land of Israel, for those
who sought to kill the child are dead." * [w]
[21] He got up, took the child and his mother,
and returned to the land of Israel.

[22] But when Joseph learned that Ar-
chelaus * had succeeded his father Herod in
Judea, he was afraid to go there. After he had
been warned in a dream concerning this, he
withdrew to the region of Galilee. [23] He set-
tled in a town called Nazareth, * so that what
had been spoken through the Prophets
might be fulfilled: "He shall be called a
Nazorean." [x]

I: JESUS INAUGURATES HIS MINISTRY AS SAVIOR

CHAPTER 3

John the Baptist Preaches and Baptizes. [1] * In
those days, John the Baptist * appeared in
the desert of Judea, preaching: [y] [2] "Repent, *
for the kingdom of heaven is close at hand." [z]
This was the man of whom the prophet
Isaiah spoke when he said: [a]

r Ps 72:10-11, 15; Isa 60:3.—s 1 Ki 13:9.—t Mt 2:19; Jer 26:21.—u Hos 11:1.—v Jer 31:15.—w Ex 4:19.—x Mt 13:54; Mk 1:9; Lk 2:39; 4:34; Jn 19:19.—y 1-12: Mk 1:3-8; Lk 3:2-17.—z Mt 4:17; 10:7; Acts 2:38.—a Isa 40:3; Jn 1:23.

2:11 Because of the Old Testament texts of Ps 72:11, 16; Isa 60:6, the wise men were thought to be kings. *House:* indicates that the wise men did not visit Jesus on the night of his birth as did the shepherds. Although there are three gifts, this does not mean there were three wise men.

2:15 The citation from Hos 11:1, which originally referred to God's calling Israel (God's son) out of Egypt, is here applied to Jesus. Just as Israel was called out of Egypt at the time of the Exodus, so Jesus, the Son of God, will be called out of Egypt at the New Exodus.

2:17-18 The citation of Jer 31:15 originally referred to Rachel, the wife of Jacob, weeping for her children taken into exile in 721 B.C. Matthew applies it to the mourning for the Holy Innocents.

2:19-23 Herod died in 4 B.C. We do not know for sure to which prophecies (note the plural "Prophets") v. 23 is alluding. Some believe Matthew is here thinking of the Old Testament declarations that the Messiah would be despised (e.g., Ps 22:6; Isa 53:3), for "Nazorean" was a synonym for "despised" (see Jn 1:45f). Or he may be saying that according to the plan of God Jesus was to live his childhood and youth in Nazareth and begin his ministry there. Some think "Nazorean" fulfills the prophecy of Isaiah (11:1): Jesus is the "shoot" (*nezer* in Hebrew) of the race of Abraham and David.

2:20 *For those who sought to kill the child are dead:* another subtle reference to the Moses-Christ parallel. After fleeing from Egypt because the Pharaoh sought to kill him, Moses was told to return in similar words: "for all the men who wanted to kill you are dead" (Ex 4:19).

2:22 *Archelaus:* son of Herod who ruled Judea and Samaria for ten years (4 B.C. to A.D. 6) and was deposed because of his cruelty. After him Judea became a Roman province administered by "procurators" appointed by the Emperor. *Galilee:* the northern part of Palestine, whose principal cities were: Capernaum, Cana, Nazareth, and Tiberias. Its people were not very highly esteemed by the Jews of Jerusalem and Judea (see Jn 1:46; 7:52) probably because of the strong Hellenization of the region and the mixed (Jew-Gentile) population there. It was the primary region of Jesus' public ministry and is viewed as a providential indicator of his Messianic mission to the Gentiles (see Isa 66:18f; Am 9:11f).

2:23 *Nazareth:* a town that stands on the last spurs of the Galilean hills, some 87 miles north of Jerusalem.

3:1-17 This account is concerned with the person and prophetic message of John (vv. 1-6), his baptism (v. 6), his criticism of the Pharisees and Sadducees (vv. 7-10), his teaching about Jesus (vv. 11-12), and his baptism of Jesus (vv. 15-17).

3:1 *John the Baptist:* the cousin and precursor of Jesus (see Lk 1:5-80). *Desert of Judea:* a twenty-mile barren region from the Jerusalem-Bethlehem plateau to the Jordan River and the Dead Sea.

3:2 *Repent:* a change of heart and conduct—a return to keeping the Mosaic Law. *Kingdom of heaven:* a phrase found only in Matthew (33 times); in Mark and Luke it is "kingdom of God." The kingdom of heaven is the rule of God, both as present reality and as future hope. The kingdom is a central part of Jesus' message.

3 "The voice of one crying out in the
wilderness:
'Prepare the way of the Lord,
make his paths straight.' " *
4 John's clothing was made of camel's
hair,[b] with a leather loincloth around his
waist, and his food consisted of locusts and
wild honey. * 5 The people of Jerusalem and
the whole of Judea and the entire region
along the Jordan went out to him, 6 and as
they confessed their sins they were baptized
by him in the Jordan River.
7 * But when he observed many of the
Pharisees and Sadducees coming for bap-
tism, he said to them, "You brood of vipers!
Who warned you to flee from the wrath to
come?[c] 8 Produce good fruit as proof of your
repentance. 9 Do not presume to say to your-
selves: 'We have Abraham as our father.' For
I tell you that God is able to raise up children
for Abraham from these stones.[d] 10 Even
now the ax is laid to the root of the trees.
Therefore, every tree that does not bear
good fruit will be cut down and thrown into
the fire.[e]
11 * "I baptize you with water for repen-
tance, but the one who is coming after me is
more powerful than I am. I am not worthy
to carry his sandals. He will baptize you with
the Holy Spirit and fire.[f] 12 His winnowing
fan is in his hand. He will clear his threshing
floor and gather his wheat into his barn, but
the chaff he will burn with unquenchable
fire." *[g]

Jesus Is Baptized.* 13 Then Jesus arrived
from Galilee and came to John at the Jordan
to be baptized by him.[h] 14 John tried to dis-
suade him, saying, "Why do you come to
me? I am the one who needs to be baptized
by you." 15 But Jesus said to him in reply,
"For the present, let it be thus. It is proper
for us to do this to fulfill all that righteous-
ness demands." * Then he acquiesced.
16 After Jesus had been baptized, as he
came up from the water, suddenly the heav-
ens were opened and he beheld the Spirit of
God descending like a dove and alighting on
him.[i] 17 And a voice came from heaven, say-
ing, "This is my beloved Son, in whom I am
well pleased." *[j]

CHAPTER 4

Jesus Is Tempted by the Devil.* 1 [k] Then Jesus
was led by the Spirit into the desert to be
tempted by the devil. 2 He fasted for forty
days and forty nights, after which he was
famished.[l]
3 Then the tempter approached him and
said, "If you are the Son of God, * command
these stones to be transformed into loaves of

b Mt 11:7-8; 2 Ki 1:8; Zec 13:4.—c Mt 12:34; 23:33; Isa 59:5; Jn 5:35.—d Jn 8:33, 39; Rom 9:7-8; Gal 4:21-31.—e Jn 15:2, 6.—f Jn 1:26-27, 33; Acts 1:5; 2:3-4.—g Mt 13:30; Wis 5:14, 23; Isa 41:16; Jer 15:7.—h 13-17: 2 Ki 5:1-14; Mk 1:9-11; Lk 3:21-22; Jn 1:31-34.—i Isa 11:2; 42:1.—j Mt 12:18; 17:5; Gen 22:2; Deut 4:12; Ps 2:7; Isa 42:1; Acts 13:33.—k 1-11: Mk 1:12-13; Lk 4:1-13; Heb 2:18.—l Ex 24:18; Deut 8:2; 1 Ki 19:8.

3:3 All four Gospels quote Isa 40:3 and apply it to John the Baptist. *Make his paths straight:* a phrase that is equivalent to "Prepare the way for the Lord" in Lk 3:4. In ancient times, when the king was to travel to a distant land, the roads were improved. Similarly, the spiritual preparation for the coming of the Messiah was made by John in calling for repentance and the remission of sins and announcing the need for a Savior.

3:4 John's simple food, clothing, and lifestyle were reminiscent of Elijah (see 2 Ki 17), and Jesus later declares that John was the Elijah who had already come (see Mt 17:10ff; see also Mal 4:5).

3:7-10 John heavily criticizes members of two religious sects of the Jews who come to receive his baptism. The Pharisees were a legalistic and separatist group who strictly kept the Law of Moses as well as the unwritten "tradition of the elders" (Mt 15:2). The Sadducees were more worldly and politically minded, closely connected with the high priests, and they accepted only the first five Books of the Old Testament as their Scriptures. They also rejected belief in the resurrection after death.

3:11-12 *I am not worthy to carry his sandals:* bearing sandals was one of the duties of a slave. The baptism of John prepares for the purifying action *with the Holy Spirit and fire* that Jesus will effect (see Isa 1:25; Zec 13:9; Mal 3:2) and that was seen very dramatically at Pentecost (Acts 1:5, 8; 2:1-16). Refusal of this Baptism instituted by Christ leads to final condemnation in imperishable fire (see Isa 34:8ff; Jer 7:20).

3:12 The separation of the good and the bad that will take place at Christ's Second Coming is compared to the way farmers separated *wheat* from *chaff.* After trampling out the grain, they used a large fork to pitch the grain and the chaff into the air. The kernels of wheat fell to the ground while the light chaff was borne away by the wind, then gathered up and burned.

3:13-17 The theophanies of the Old Testament were meant to convey something of the ineffable transcendence of God (Ex 3); the theophany that here begins the New Testament reveals something of the inner life of God: God is three persons. The dove perhaps suggests the Creator Spirit (Gen 1:2), but may also symbolize the divine goodwill that was restored after the flood (Gen 8:8-12), or the very People of God (Hos 7:11; 11:11; Isa 60:8), the formation of which is the work of the Spirit.

3:15 *All that righteousness demands:* i.e., all observances, everything that is part of God's plan. Jesus obeys the Father's will in everything (Phil 2:8).

3:17 This heavenly pronouncement intermingles language from Ps 2:7 and Isa 42:1, prophetic terminology that was well known to those with Messianic expectations (see Mt 17:5; Mk 1:11; 9:7; Lk 3:22; 9:35).

4:1-11 This important passage is again filled with echoes and citations of the Old Testament. The intention is to show the experience and struggles of the Messiah, the new head of the People of God. Just as Moses remained forty days on Sinai, so the Messiah remains forty days in the wilderness (Ex 34:28), forty days being symbolic of a time of preparation for divinely planned activities. Jesus refuses to make use of his miraculous power simply to relieve human need (v. 3f), or to satisfy requests of unbelievers (v. 5ff), or to embrace a Messianic role that would be purely political. The basic theme is the obedience of Jesus to God as he is known through the Old Testament. He rebuffs all three temptations with Scriptural truth from Deuteronomy.

4:3 *If you are the Son of God:* in the sense of the Messianic King of Ps 2.

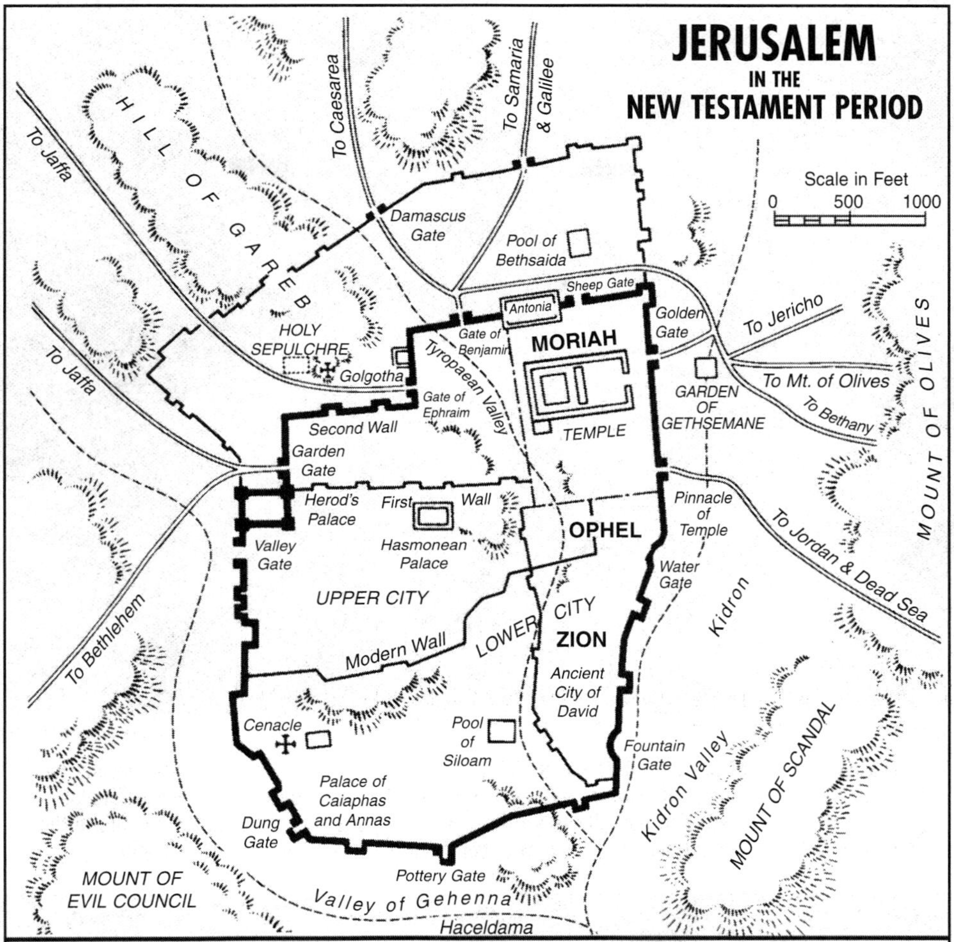

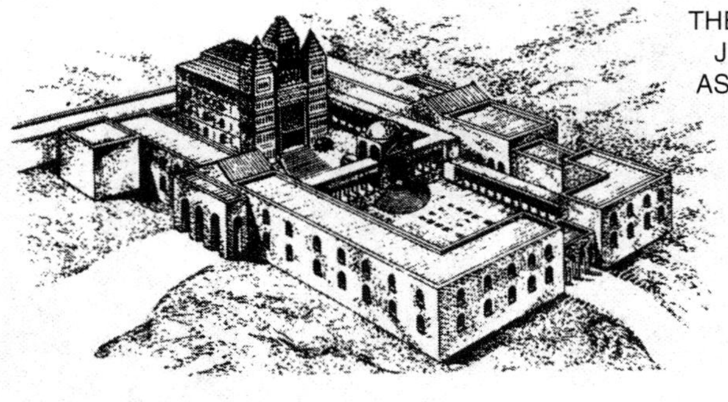

THE TEMPLE OF JERUSALEM AS REBUILT BY HEROD

JERUSALEM IN THE NEW TESTAMENT PERIOD — (a) This period in the history of Jerusalem rivals the Solomonic period in the external glories added to it by Herod the Great. There is the great fortress **Antonia** of the temple enclosure, three great towers, Phasael, Hippicus, and Mariamne, as well as the magnificent **palace**—all at the north corner. The most splendid addition is the rebuilt **temple** (started in 19 B.C. and finally completed in A.D. 62). **(b)** It is to this city that Jesus is brought as an infant (Lk 2:22-38) and as a youth (Lk 2:41-52). It is here that during his public ministry Jesus cleanses the **temple** (Jn 2:13-25), heals a man at the pool of **Bethsaida** (Jn 5:1-47), attends the feast of Tabernacles (Jn 7:2; 10:21), and the Dedication (Jn 10:22-39). **(c)** Jesus spends the final week of his life in and around the city (Mt 27; Jn 12:12—19:42). **(d)** After his resurrection Jesus appears to various people (Lk 24) and his disciples (Jn 20:26-29; Lk 24:49) in Jerusalem and ascends from the **Mount of Olives** nearby (Lk 24:50-53).

Matson Photo Service

JERUSALEM: SCENE OF THE FINDING IN THE TEMPLE — An air view of Jerusalem showing the temple area from the north with the village of Siloam in the distance and the Golden Gate leading to the Kidron Valley on the left. As a twelve-year-old Jesus was taken by his parents to the temple in Jerusalem and found by them after being lost for three days. (See Lk 2:41-50)

Ewing Galloway

MARY'S SPRING IN NAZARETH — View of the only spring located in Nazareth. It has always been considered certain that Jesus and Mary visited this well many times both before and after the finding in the temple. (See Lk 2:51-52)

bread." 4 Jesus answered, "As it is written: [m]
'Man does not live by bread alone,
but by every word that comes forth
from the mouth of God.' " *
5 Next the devil took him to the holy city
and had him stand on the summit of the
temple. * 6 * Then he said to him, "If you are
the Son of God, throw yourself down. For it
is written: [n]
'He will command his angels concerning
you,
and with their hands they will raise
you up
lest you dash your foot against a
stone.' "
7 Jesus said to him, "It is also written: [o]
'You shall not put the Lord your God to
the test.' "
8 Finally, the devil took him to an exceed-
ingly high mountain and showed him all the
kingdoms of the world in their splendor.
9 Then he said to him, "All these will I give
you if you kneel down and worship me."
10 Jesus said to him in reply, "Depart from
me, Satan! It is written: [p]
'You shall worship the Lord your God,
and him alone shall you serve.' " *
11 Then the devil departed from him, and
suddenly angels came and ministered to
him.

Jesus Begins His Ministry in Galilee. 12 [q] * When
Jesus learned that John had been arrested, * he
withdrew to Galilee. 13 Departing from
Nazareth, he settled in Capernaum * by the
sea, in the region of Zebulun and Naphtali, [r]
14 in order that what had been spoken through
the prophet Isaiah might be fulfilled:
15 [s] "Land of Zebulun and land of Naphtali,
the passageway to the sea, beyond
the Jordan,
Galilee of the Gentiles:
16 The people who lived in darkness
have seen a great light,
and for those who dwell in a land
darkened by the shadow of death
light has dawned." [t]
17 From that day forward Jesus began to pro-
claim the message: "Repent, for the king-
dom of heaven is close at hand." [u]

Jesus Calls the First Disciples.* 18 [v] As Jesus
was walking by the Sea of Galilee, he saw
two brothers, Simon who is called Peter, and
his brother Andrew, casting a net into the
water, for they were fishermen. 19 He said to
them, "Come, follow me, and I will make
you fishers of men." [w] 20 Immediately, they
abandoned their nets and followed him.
21 As he proceeded farther, he saw two
more brothers, James the son of Zebedee,
and his brother John. They were in a boat
with their father Zebedee, mending their
nets, and he called them. [x] 22 Immediately,
they left their boat and their father and fol-
lowed him.

**Jesus Proclaims the Message and Heals the
Sick.*** 23 Jesus traveled all throughout Galilee,
teaching in their synagogues, proclaiming
the good news of the kingdom, and curing
every type of disease and illness among the

m Deut 8:3.—n Ps 91:11-12.—o Deut 6:16.—p Mt 16:23; Deut 6:13; 1 Chr 21:1.—q 12-13: Mk 1:14-15; Lk 4:14, 31.—r Mk 1:21; Jn 2:12.—s 15-16: Isa 8:23 LXX; 9:1.—t Lk 1:79; Jn 8:12b.—u Mt 3:2.—v 18-22: Mk 1:16-20; Lk 5:1-11; Jn 1:35-42.—w Jn 21:3.—x Mt 13:47-50.

4:4 A citation of Deut 8:3, indicating that the miracles of the Exodus were signs of God's religious care for Israel.

4:5 *Summit of the temple:* the southeast corner of the wall of the Jerusalem temple, projecting over a ravine.

4:6-7 The devil applies Ps 91:11-12 to the Messiah since it deals with God's protection of the righteous. Jesus declares (through the words of Deut 6:16) that we should not demand miracles from God as evidence of his care for us.

4:10 The citation (Deut 6:13) used by Jesus calls for the basic attitude of worship that everyone should have toward God.

4:12-25 By action and word Jesus inaugurates the kingdom of heaven. The phrase means the kingdom of God, but, like the Jews of his time, Matthew avoids naming God and says, instead, "heaven." This kingdom or reign is a power that will continue to make its way into the world from now on. Jesus begins his activity in Galilee, a northern province, which some, thinking of Isa 8:23 and 9:1, regarded as the Messiah's land. It was a region in which different populations and religions lived side by side. The faithful followers of Yahweh, who were pretty much cut off from Jerusalem and its temple, gathered in the synagogues. Different populations, even in the pagan Decapolis (a confederation of ten independent Greek cities, beyond the Jordan), acknowledge the Messiah.

4:12-17 *John had been arrested:* after John's arrest (v. 12), Jesus makes Capernaum the center of his activity (v. 13) and preaching (v. 17). The citation from Isa 9:1-2 identifies the ministry of Jesus as fulfilling the prophecy of the restoration of the northern kingdom defeated by the Assyrians in 721 B.C. See notes on Mk 1:14 and Lk 3:20.

4:13 *Capernaum:* on the shore of the Lake (in Hebrew: Sea) of Galilee (v. 18), also known as the Lake of Tiberias or Gennesaret, in territory that had belonged to the tribes of Zebulun and Naphtali.

4:18-22 We see the first Church being born; disciples follow the Lord not only to share intimacy with him but to be *fishers of men*, to be witnesses to him and gather together people in his name—for he is the Messiah. Three of the four (Simon, James, and John) will go on to hold a closer relationship with Jesus (see Mt 17:1; 26:37; Lk 8:51).

4:23-25 As a conclusion to the first part of his Gospel, Matthew gives a summary of Jesus' ministry, which consisted in teaching, preaching, and healing (v. 23; see also Mt 9:35).

people.[y] 24 His reputation spread through-
out Syria,* and they brought to him all
those who were sick, afflicted with various
diseases, racked with pain, or possessed by
demons, as well as those who were stricken
with epilepsy or paralyzed, and he healed
them.[z] 25 Great throngs from Galilee, the
Decapolis,* Jerusalem, and Judea, and from
beyond the Jordan, followed him.[a]

CHAPTER 5

A: The Sermon on the Mount—Magna Carta of the Christian Life*

The Beatitudes.* 1 When Jesus saw the
crowds, he went up on the mountain. After he
was seated, his disciples gathered around
him. 2 Then he began to teach them as follows:

3 [b] "Blessed are the poor in spirit,
for theirs is the kingdom of heaven.
4 Blessed are those who mourn,
for they will be comforted.[c]
5 Blessed are the meek,
for they will inherit the earth.[d]
6 Blessed are those who hunger and thirst
for justice,
for they will have their fill.[e]
7 Blessed are the merciful,
for they will obtain mercy.[f]
8 Blessed are the pure of heart,
for they will see God.[g]
9 Blessed are the peacemakers,
for they will be called children of
God.[h]
10 Blessed are those who are persecuted
in the cause of justice,
for theirs is the kingdom of heaven.[i]

11 "Blessed are you when people insult you
and persecute you and utter all kinds of
calumnies against you for my sake.[j]
12 Rejoice and be glad, for your reward will be
great in heaven. In the same manner, they
persecuted the prophets who preceded you.[k]

Salt of the Earth and Light of the World.*
13 "You are the salt of the earth. But if salt
loses its taste, what can be done to make it
salty once again? It is no longer good for
anything, and thus it is cast out and tram-
pled underfoot.[l]

14 "You are the light of the world. A city
built upon a mountain cannot be hidden.[m]
15 Nor would someone light a lamp and then
put it under a basket; rather, it is placed
upon a lampstand so that it may afford light
to all in the house.[n] 16 In the same way, your
light must shine so that it can be seen by
others; this will enable them to observe your
good works and give praise to your Father in
heaven.[o]

B: The New Law*

The Fulfillment of the Law. 17 "Do not think
that I have come to abolish the Law or the
Prophets. I have come not to abolish but to
fulfill them.[p] 18 Amen, I say to you, until heav-
en and earth pass away, not a single letter,*

y Mt 9:35; Mk 1:39; Lk 4:15, 44—z Mt 8:16, 28.—a Mk 3:7-8; Lk 6:17-19.—b 3-12: Lk 6:20-23.—c Isa 61:2-3; Rev 7:17; 21:4.—d Gen 13:15; Ps 37:11; Rom 4:13.—e Isa 51:1.—f Mt 18:33; Lk 6:36; Jas 2:13.—g Ex 33:20; Pss 24:4-5; 73:1.—h Prov 12:20.—i 1 Pet 2:20; 3:14; 4:14.—j Mt 10:22; Acts 5:41; Phil 1:29.—k 2 Chr 36:16; Col 1:24; Heb 11:32-38; Jas 5:10.—l Lev 2:13; Num 18:19; Mk 9:50; Lk 14:34-35.—m Jn 8:12.—n Mk 4:21; Lk 8:16; 11:33.—o Jn 3:21; 1 Cor 10:31.—p Rom 3:31.

4:24 *Syria:* the area north of Galilee, between Damascus and the Mediterranean Sea.

4:25 *Decapolis* (i.e., the Ten Cities): a league of Greek cities; all were east of the Sea of Galilee and the Jordan River except Sythcopolis (Beth Shan).

5:1—7:28 The Sermon on the Mount is the first of five great discourses in this Gospel (chs. 5—7; 10; 13; 18; 24—25). The Lucan parallel is the "Sermon on the Plain" (Lk 6:20-49), although some of the sayings in the "Sermon on the Mount" have parallels in other parts of Luke. Matthew's Sermon contains beatitudes or declarations of blessedness (5:1-12), admonitions (5:13-20; 6:1-7, 23), and contrasts between Jesus' moral teaching and Jewish legislative traditions (5:21-48).

Matthew here presents a catechism of Christian initiation and opposes it to the Jewish religious ideal. The ensemble of moral, social, religious, cultural, general, and collective requirements that holds good for the whole People of God was received by Moses on Mount Sinai. Jesus presents a new charter that he gives "on the Mount" (5:1) as if on a new Sinai. It does not take anything away from the Law but goes to the root of human conduct. Good intentions are not to replace act and obedience, but all that takes place in the heart and spirit of persons, their plans and their intentions, are already acts.

5:1-12 The Beatitudes have been rightly termed "Eight Words for Eternity." If we read them carefully, we will realize that the happiness proclaimed by Jesus is poles apart from what we habitually think, say, and do. In the first three Beatitudes are listed the faults that must be corrected if human beings are to be perfect—spiritual arrogance, pride, and desire for pleasure. In the next three Beatitudes are found the virtues that must regulate our relations with God, our neighbor, and ourselves—justice, mercy, and purity. In the last two Beatitudes, Christ urges his followers to be zealous in spreading the Gospel and peace, and he promises that they will be rewarded with honor and power in the kingdom of God for all that they have had to suffer for him.

5:13-16 Only the certitude that God comes into our very midst can open up a horizon to our human condition. But where can we read the testimony of such a coming if not in the experience of the disciples? We cannot receive Jesus or discern the Father unless we strive to lead better lives.

5:17-48 The Gospel of Matthew wants to stress the point that Jesus has no contempt for "the Law or the Prophets" (= the Old Testament); on the contrary, he takes them very seriously. But throughout his life he felt free to proclaim the true meaning of the Law by placing himself above even Moses. In his view, the Law is good, and there is nothing to discuss. In contrast to the commonly accepted rules, Jesus does not deal with secondary details; the essentials, on the other hand, cause no problem; therefore he does not discuss the Law. Instead, he goes farther and deeper, down into the human heart.

5:18 *Single letter:* literally, *iota* (Greek) = Hebrew *yod,* the smallest letter of the Hebrew alphabet. *Tiny portion of a letter:* literally, the *apex* or tip of a letter, the bit that distinguishes similar letters.

not even a tiny portion of a letter, will disappear from the Law until all things have been accomplished.[q] [19] Therefore, whoever breaks even one of the least of these commandments and teaches others to do the same will be considered least in the kingdom of heaven. But whoever observes these commandments and teaches them will be called great in the kingdom of heaven.[r] [20] I tell you, if your righteousness does not exceed that of the scribes and Pharisees, you will never enter the kingdom of heaven.[s]

Anger.* [21] "You have heard that your ancestors were told: 'You shall not kill,[t] and anyone who kills will be subject to judgment.' [22] But I say this to you: Anyone who is angry with his brother will be subject to judgment, and whoever addresses his brother in an insulting way will answer for it before the Sanhedrin, and whoever calls his brother a fool will be liable to the fires of Gehenna.[u] *

[23] "Therefore, when offering your gift at the altar, if you should remember that your brother has something against you,[v] [24] leave your gift there at the altar and first go to be reconciled with your brother. Then return and offer your gift.

[25] [w] "Come to terms quickly with your opponent while you are on the way to court with him. If you fail to do so, he may hand you over to the judge, and the judge will put you in the custody of the guard, and you will be thrown into prison. [26] Believe the truth of what I tell you: you will not be given your freedom until you have paid your debt down to the last penny. *

Adultery. [27] * "You have heard that it was said of old: 'You shall not commit adultery.'[x] [28] But I say to you that anyone who looks with lust at a woman has already committed adultery with her in his heart. [29] [y] If your right eye causes you to sin, tear it out and throw it away. It is preferable for you to lose one part of your body than to have your whole body thrown into Gehenna. [30] And if your right hand causes you to sin, cut it off and throw it away. It is preferable for you to lose one of your limbs than to have your whole body thrown into Gehenna.

Divorce. [31] "It has also been said: 'Whoever divorces his wife shall give her a certificate of dismissal.'[z] [32] But I say to you that anyone who divorces his wife, except if the marriage was unlawful, causes her to commit adultery, and whoever marries a divorced woman commits adultery.[a]

Oaths.* [33] "Again, you have heard that our ancestors were told: 'Do not swear falsely, but fulfill the vows you have made to the Lord.'[b] [34] [c] But what I tell you is this: Do not swear at all, either by heaven, since it is God's throne, [35] or by earth, since that is his footstool, or by Jerusalem, since that is the city of the great King. [36] Nor should you swear by your head, for you cannot turn one hair of it white or black. [37] All you need to do is to say 'Yes' if you mean 'Yes' and 'No' if you mean 'No.' Anything beyond this comes from the evil one.

Retaliation.* [38] "You have heard that it was said: 'An eye for an eye and a tooth for a tooth.'[d] [39] [e] But I say to you: Offer no resistance to someone who is wicked. If someone strikes you on your right cheek, turn and

q Lk 16:17.—r Jas 2:10.—s Rom 10:3; Phil 3:9.—t Ex 20:13; Deut 5:17.—u Eccl 7:9; Eph 4:26; Jas 1:19-20.—v Mk 11:25.—w 25-26: Mt 18:34-35; Lk 12:58-59.—x Ex 20:14; Deut 5:18.—y 29-30: Mt 18:8-9; Mk 9:43-47; Rom 14:21; 1 Cor 8:13.—z Mt 19:3-9; Deut 24:1.—a Lk 16:18; 1 Cor 7:10-11.—b Mt 23:16-22; Lev 19:12; Num 30:3; Deut 23:21.—c 34-37: Ps 48:2; Sir 23:9; Isa 66:1; 2 Cor 1:17-19; Jas 5:12.—d Ex 21:24; Lev 24:19-20.—e 39-42: Lk 6:29-30; Rom 12:19, 21.

5:21-26 Murderers must appear before the highest Jewish judicial body, the Sanhedrin, and they deserve death and the fire, symbolized by Gehenna, the valley southwest of Jerusalem that was the center for an idolatrous cult during the monarchy in which children were offered in sacrifice (see 2 Ki 23:10; Jer 7:31). To embrace the kingdom of God is to become a person of reconciliation, to free oneself of all murderous desires. Indeed, even when they suffer offenses but are innocent, the disciples of Jesus must have the courage to take the first step toward establishing peace.

5:22 *Gehenna:* a little valley southwest of Jerusalem and a popular image of hell because of the refuse that burned there continually.

5:26 *Penny:* the smallest Roman copper coin.

5:27-32 At this period, the laws on divorce were tolerant for husbands, intransigent for wives. Jesus rejects this inequality and confronts husbands with their responsibilities by radically condemning divorce. Matthew's text contains the clause, "except if the marriage was unlawful," which is lacking in the parallel passages of Luke and Mark, but occurs again in Mt 19:9. The Greek word *porneia*, "unchastity," is generic and so has given rise to much discussion. The widely accepted opinion among scholars today is that it was a technical term used by the Jewish Christian community to signify a degree of relationship that constituted an impediment to marriage according to the Law (Lev 18:6-18; Acts 15:29).

5:33-37 What good is multiplying oaths between God and human beings? Is this not a sign that lying and unbelief have perverted human realities? In the kingdom of God, the dialogue between persons will rediscover its truth and its loyalty.

5:38-42 The Old Testament commandment of an eye for an eye (see Lev 24:20) was intended to moderate vengeance—seeking to ensure that the punishment not exceed the injury done. Jesus calls for further moderation and liberality by giving suggestions for breaking the infernal circle of hatred and disputation.

offer him the other cheek as well.[f] 40 If anyone wishes to sue you to gain possession of your tunic, give him your cloak as well. 41 If someone forces you to go one mile, go with him for a second mile. 42 Give to anyone who begs from you, and do not turn your back on anyone who wishes to borrow from you.[g]

Love for Enemies.* 43 [h] "You have heard that it was said: 'You shall love your neighbor and hate your enemy.'[i] 44 But I say to you: Love your enemies and pray for those who persecute you.[j] 45 This will make you children of your heavenly Father. For he causes his sun to rise on evil people as well as on those who are good, and his rain falls on both the righteous and the wicked.[k] 46 If you love only those who love you, what reward will you receive? Do not even tax collectors * do the same? 47 And if you greet only your brethren, what about that is so extraordinary? Even the pagans do as much.

Perfection.* 48 "Therefore, strive to be perfect, just as your heavenly Father is perfect.[l]

C: The True Practice of Religion*

CHAPTER 6

Giving Alms in Secret. 1 "Beware of performing righteous deeds before others in order to impress them. If you do so, you will receive no reward from your Father in heaven.[m] 2 Therefore, whenever you give alms, do not trumpet your generosity, as the hypocrites do in the synagogues and in the streets in order to win the praise of others. Amen, I say to you, they have already received their reward.[n] 3 But when you give alms, do not let your left hand know what your right hand is doing. 4 Your almsgiving must be done in secret. And your Father who sees everything that is done in secret will reward you.[o]

Praying in Secret. 5 "Whenever you pray, do not be like the hypocrites, who love to stand and pray in the synagogues and on street corners so that others may observe them doing so. Amen, I say to you, they have already received their reward. 6 But when you pray, go into your room, close the door, and pray to your Father in secret. And your Father who sees everything that is done in secret will reward you.[p]

The Lord's Prayer.* 7 "When you pray do not go on babbling endlessly as the pagans do, for they believe that they are more likely to be heard because of their many words.[q] 8 Do not imitate them. Your Father knows what you need before you ask him.

9 [r] "This is how you should pray:

'Our Father in heaven,
hallowed be your name.[s]
10 Your kingdom come.
Your will be done
on earth as it is in heaven.[t]
11 Give us this day our daily bread.[u]
12 And forgive us our debts
as we forgive our debtors.[v]
13 And do not lead us into temptation, *
but deliver us from the evil one.'[w]

14 If you forgive others for the wrongs they have done, your heavenly Father will also forgive you.[x] 15 But if you do not forgive others, then your Father will not forgive your transgressions.[y]

---

f Lam 3:30.—g Deut 15:7-8.—h 43-48: Lk 6:27, 32-36.—i Lev 19:18; Gal 5:14.—j Acts 7:60; Rom 12:20.—k Lk 6:35.—l Lev 11:44; 19:2; Deut 18:13; Jas 1:4; 1 Pet 1:16; 1 Jn 3:3.—m Mt 5:16; 23:5.—n Am 4:5; Jn 5:44; 12:43.—o Ps 139:1-3.—p 2 Ki 4:33; Isa 26:20; Dan 6:11.—q Eccl 5:2; Sir 7:14.—r 9-13: Lk 11:2-4.—s Ezek 36:23.—t Mt 26:42; Dan 4:32.—u Prov 30:8-9.—v Mt 18:21-22; Sir 28:2; Eph 4:32.—w Jn 17:15; 2 Thes 3:3.—x Mt 18:35; Sir 28:1-5; Mk 11:25; Col 3:13.—y Jas 2:13.

5:43-47 Just as God invites the unrighteous to respond to him through the evidence of his love, so the disciples of Jesus must bear the same love toward their enemies.

5:46 *Tax collectors:* those who collected taxes on behalf of the occupying authorities; for this reason, and also because they engaged in fraud, they were regarded as public sinners.

5:48 The life of the kingdom is that of children of God; therein lies its secret and its demands (see Lev 11:43; Deut 18:13).

6:1—7:29 Almsgiving (vv. 2-4), prayer (vv. 5-15), and fasting (vv. 16-18) are characteristics of the Jewish religion, or of the "righteous." Jesus does not teach other practices but is concerned with the spirit of our religious acts so that they may lead to God's presence and bring the joy of being children of God. Believers do not vaunt themselves or make a show of their religion; they listen to God. True religion is authentic spiritual life rather than spectacle and confusion or human respect.

6:7-15 In response to a request from his disciples to teach them to pray (see Lk 11:1), Jesus entrusts them with the fundamental Christian prayer, the Our Father. It is also called the Lord's Prayer because it comes to us from the Lord Jesus, the master and model of prayer. The Lord's Prayer constitutes the summary of the whole Gospel, lies at the center of the Scriptures, and is the most perfect of prayers. The object of the first three petitions is the glory of the Father: the sanctification of his name, the coming of the kingdom, and the fulfillment of his will. The four others present our wants to him: they ask that our lives be nourished, healed of sin, and made victorious in the struggle of good over evil.

6:13 *Temptation:* in the New Testament, temptation is a test in which Satan tries to destroy the believer. Consequently, it cannot be attributed to God. God, however, can give the strength and means of overcoming it: this is the meaning of the petition. The Semitic expression "do not lead us into" is therefore to be understood as meaning "do not allow us to enter into or succumb to temptation" (see Mt 26:41; 1 Tim 6:9).

Fasting in Secret.* [16] "Whenever you fast, do not assume a gloomy expression like the hypocrites who contort their faces so that others may realize that they are fasting. Amen, I say to you, they have received their reward. [z] [17] But when you fast, put oil on your head and wash your face, [a] [18] so that the fact that you are fasting will not be obvious to others but only to your Father who is hidden. And your Father who sees everything that is done in secret will reward you.

Treasures in Heaven.* [19] "Do not store up treasures for yourselves on earth, where they will be destroyed by moth and rust and where thieves break in and steal. [b] [20] [c] Rather, store up treasure for yourselves in heaven, where neither moth nor rust destroys and where thieves cannot break in and steal. [21] For where your treasure is, there will your heart also be.

The Lamp of the Body.* [22] "The eyes are the lamp of the body. If your eyes are sound, your whole body will be filled with light. [d] [23] However, if your eyes are diseased, your whole body will be in darkness. If then the light within you is darkness, how great will that darkness be!

God and Money. [24] [e] "No one can serve two masters. For you will either hate the one and love the other or be devoted to the one and despise the other. You cannot serve both God and money. *

Seek First the Kingdom of God.* [25] [f] "Therefore, heed my words. Do not be concerned about your life and what you will have to eat or drink, or about your body and what you will wear. Surely life is more than food, and the body is more than clothing.

[26] "Gaze upon the birds in the sky. They do not sow or reap or store in barns, and yet your heavenly Father feeds them. Are you not of far greater value than they? [g] [27] Can any of you through worrying add a single moment to your span of life?

[28] "And why are you concerned about what you are to wear? Consider the lilies of the field and how they grow. They neither labor nor spin. [29] Yet I tell you that not even Solomon in all his royal splendor was clothed like one of these. [h] [30] If God so clothes the grass of the field, which grows today and tomorrow is thrown into the furnace, will he not all the more clothe you, O you of little faith?

[31] "Therefore, stop being anxious about such things. Do not say: 'What shall we eat?' or 'What shall we drink?' or 'What shall we wear?' [32] These are things that are of concern to the Gentiles. Your heavenly Father is fully aware of all your needs. [33] Rather, seek the kingdom of God and his righteousness, and all these things will be given to you as well. [i]

[34] "So do not worry about tomorrow, for tomorrow will take care of itself. Each day has enough troubles of its own. [j]

CHAPTER 7

Do Not Judge.* [1] [k] "Do not judge, so that you in turn may not be judged. [l] [2] For you will be judged in the same way that you judge others, and the measure that you use for others will be used to measure you. [m]

[3] "Why do you take note of the splinter in your brother's eye but do not notice the wooden plank in your own eye? [4] How can you say to your brother, 'Let me remove that splinter from your eye,' while all the time the wooden plank remains in your own? [n] [5] You hypocrite! First remove the wooden plank from your own eye, and then you will be able to see clearly enough to remove the splinter from your brother's eye.

z Isa 58:5.—a Jud 10:3.—b Jas 5:2-3.—c 20-21: Job 22: 24-26; Lk 12:33-34.—d Lk 11:34-36.—e Lk 16:13.—f 25-33: Ps 127; Lk 12:22-31.—g Pss 145:15-16; 147:9.—h 1 Ki 10: 1-29.—i Isa 51:1.—j Jas 4:13-14.—k 1-5: Lk 6:37-38, 41-42.—l Rom 2:1-2; 1 Cor 4:5.—m Wis 12:22; Ezek 35:11; Mk 4:24.—n Jn 8:7.

6:16-18 Fasting is an action that evinces a desire to live more closely in the disinterested service of God; this produces profound joy. The sole fast prescribed by the Mosaic Law was that of the Day of Atonement (see Lev 16:31), but in later Judaism fasting became a regular practice (see *Didache* 9:1).

6:19-21 In this and the two following texts Jesus is responding to the faulty side of our way of thinking and acting. In order to affirm the primacy of God so simply and surely, we must live unceasingly in the presence of the Father. Those who guard their inner freedom, the desire for light, understand Jesus. But it is impossible to be open to God when desire for possessions has become the motivating force of one's life.

6:22-23 Those with good vision can readily direct their bodily movements. Similarly, those who utilize the prophetic vision of Christ can direct their way to God.

6:24 *Money:* literally, "Mammon" (an Aramaic word), a personification of wealth.

6:25-34 Jesus warns us against making real human needs the object of overly anxious cares and thus becoming enslaved by them. The remedy for such an attitude is to seek first God's kingdom and to show confidence in God's providence.

7:1-5 Those who judge others separate themselves from their neighbors; those who love them are completely present to their neighbors. God has not given us consciences to judge others but to judge ourselves.

Do Not Profane Sacred Things.* 6 “Do not give to dogs anything that is holy. And do not cast your pearls before swine, lest they trample them under their feet and then proceed to tear you to pieces. [o]

Ask, Seek, Knock.* 7 [p] “Ask, and it will be given to you; seek, and you will find; knock, and the door will be opened to you. [q] 8 For everyone who asks will receive, and those who seek will find, and to those who knock the door will be opened. [r]

9 “Is there anyone among you who would give a stone to his son if he asks for bread, 10 or hand him a snake if he asks for a fish? 11 If you then, despite your evil nature, know how to give good gifts to your children, how much more will your Father in heaven give good things to those who ask him! [s]

The Golden Rule of Love.* 12 “In everything, deal with others as you would like them to deal with you. [t] This is the Law and the Prophets.

The Two Ways.* 13 “Enter through the narrow gate, for the gate is wide and the road broad that leads to destruction, and those who enter through it are many. [u] 14 But small is the gate and narrow the road that leads to life, and those who find it are few in number. [v]

False Prophets and True Disciples.* 15 “Be on guard against false prophets who come to you disguised in sheep’s clothing, but who inwardly are ravenous wolves. [w] 16 By their fruits you will know them. Does one pick grapes from thornbushes or figs from thistles? [x] 17 In the same way, every good tree bears good fruit, but a rotten tree produces bad fruit. 18 A good tree cannot bear bad fruit, nor can a bad tree bear good fruit. 19 Every tree that does not bear good fruit is cut down and thrown into the fire. [y] 20 Thus, by their fruits you will know them.

21 “Not everyone who says to me, ‘Lord, Lord,’ will enter the kingdom of heaven, but only the one who does the will of my heavenly Father. [z] 22 [a] Many will say to me on that day, * ‘Lord, Lord, did we not prophesy in your name? Did we not drive out demons in your name? Did we not perform many miracles in your name?’ [b] 23 Then I will tell them plainly, ‘I never knew you. Depart from me, you evildoers!’ [c]

The Wise and Foolish Builders.* 24 [d] “Everyone who hears these words of mine and acts in accordance with them will be like a wise man who constructed his house on a rock foundation. 25 The rain came down, the flood waters rose, and fierce winds battered that house. However, it did not collapse, because it had its foundations on rock. [e]

26 “In contrast, everyone who hears these words of mine and does not act in accordance with them will be like a fool who constructed his house on a foundation of sand. 27 The rain came down, the flood waters rose, and the winds blew and buffeted that house. And it collapsed with a great crash.” [f]

The Authority of Jesus.* 28 When Jesus had finished this discourse, the crowds were astounded at his teaching, 29 because he taught them as one who had authority, and not as their scribes. [g]

---

o Prov 23:9; Sir 22:9-10.—p 7-11: Mk 11:24; Lk 11:9-13.—q Mt 18:19; Deut 4:29.—r Lk 18:1-8; Jn 14:13.—s Jas 1:5,17; 1 Jn 5:14-15.—t Tob 4:15; Lk 6:31; Rom 13:8-10.—u Deut 30:15; Lk 13:24.—v Jn 10:9-10.—w Deut 13:2-6; 2 Pet 2:1.—x 16-17: Mt 12:33; Lk 6:43-44; Jas 3:12.—y Mt 3:10; Jn 15:6.—z Isa 29:13; Lk 6:46.—a 22-23: Lk 13:26-27.—b Mk 9:38; 1 Cor 13:2.—c Pss 5:5; 6:9.—d 24-27: Lk 6:47-49; Rom 2:13; 1 Jn 2:17.—e Prov 10:25.—f Job 8:15.—g Mk 1:22; Lk 4:32.

7:6 Jesus stresses the point that teaching should be given in accordance with the spiritual capacity of the learners. *Dogs:* unclean dogs of the street were held in low esteem.

7:7-11 To acknowledge God as Father one must have the audacity to pray and the certitude that this appeal is not in vain, for the disciple seeks the One whom he knows as Love.

7:12 Here in a word is what one must retain of the Law and the Prophets, i.e., the Old Testament: to have for others the same concern one has for oneself, out of love for God. This so-called Golden Rule is found in negative form in rabbinic Judaism as well as Hinduism, Buddhism, and Confucianism.

7:13-14 In Jewish literature, we often encounter this doctrine of the “two ways”; it is also found in the *Didache* and the *Epistle to Barnabas*. It is a way of enabling the reader to choose for God. It means that one does not enter the kingdom except by a conversion of life—the choice to follow Jesus.

7:15-23 There will always be impostors to exploit religious sentiments and the Gospel itself for advancement of their own ideas, their own persons, and their own circle. Jesus offers a criterion to discern true disciples: do their lives, attitudes, and comportment bear witness to the spirit of Jesus?

7:22 *On that day:* i.e., on the day of judgment; Jesus speaks of himself as the final judge of human beings (see Mt 25:32-46).

7:24-27 Jesus calls for obedience to his Word: those who build their lives on the Gospel are united with Christ, and nothing else can provide meaning and force to a human life in the always unforeseen elaboration of problems and events.

7:28-29 These two verses constitute the formula with which the evangelist concludes each of the five great discourses of Jesus. Verse 29 expresses the newness of the Gospel teaching. The scribes based their teaching on the Scriptures and on the instructions of their teachers. Jesus, on the other hand, speaks as a supreme legislator who has power to modify even the Scriptures.

Jesus’ astounding authority is not that of religious tradition; it radiates from his person. He himself incarnates this “new justice,” this new mode of living and thinking that he teaches and establishes among human beings. Jesus’ listeners could easily see the great difference between the kind of teaching of the scribes and Pharisees and that of Jesus with its total confidence and power.

II: THE SIGNS OF THE KINGDOM OF GOD*

A: Ten Miracles*

CHAPTER 8

Jesus Heals a Man with Leprosy.* 1 [h] When he had come down from the mountain, large crowds followed him. 2 Suddenly, a man with leprosy approached, knelt before him, and said, "Lord, if you choose to do so, you can make me clean." 3 He stretched out his hand and touched him, saying, "I do choose. Be made clean." Immediately, his leprosy was cured. 4 Then Jesus said to him, "See that you tell no one, but go and show yourself to the priest and offer the gift that Moses prescribed. That will be proof for them." [i]

Jesus Heals the Centurion's Servant.* 5 [j] When Jesus entered Capernaum, a centurion approached him and pleaded for his help. 6 "Lord," he said, "my servant is lying at home paralyzed and enduring agonizing sufferings." 7 Jesus said to him, "I will come and cure him." 8 The centurion replied, "Lord, I am not worthy to have you come under my roof. But simply say the word and my servant will be healed. * 9 For I myself am a man subject to authority, with soldiers who are subject to me. I say to one 'Go,' and he goes, and to another, 'Come here,' and he comes, and to my servant, 'Do this,' and he does it." [k]

10 When Jesus heard this, he was amazed, and he said to those who were following him, "Amen, I say to you, in no one throughout Israel have I found faith as great as this. 11 [l] Many, I tell you, will come from the east and the west to sit with Abraham and Isaac and Jacob at the banquet in the kingdom of heaven. 12 But the heirs of the kingdom will be thrown into the outer darkness, where there will be weeping and gnashing of teeth."

13 Jesus then said to the centurion, "Return home. Your petition has been granted because of your faith." And at that very hour the servant was healed.

Jesus Heals Peter's Mother-in-Law. 14 [m] Jesus then entered the house of Peter and found Peter's mother-in-law lying in bed with a fever. 15 He touched her hand and the fever left her, and she got up and began to serve him. [n]

Jesus Drives Out the Evil Spirits.* 16 That evening they brought to him many who were possessed by demons. He cast out the spirits with a command and cured all who were sick. 17 This was to fulfill the words of the prophet Isaiah:

> "He took away our infirmities
> and bore our diseases." [o]

The Cost of Following Jesus.* 18 When Jesus saw the great crowds around him, he gave orders to cross to the other side of the lake. [p] 19 A scribe approached him and said, "Teacher, I will follow you wherever you

---

h 1-4: Mk 1:40-44; Lk 5:12-14.—i Lev 14:2-32; Mk 1:34; Lk 17:14.—j 5-13: Lk 7:1-10; Jn 4:46-53.—k Ps 33:9; Bar 3:33-35.—l 11-12: Mt 13:42, 50; 22:13; 24:51; 25:30; Ps 107:3; Lk 13:28-29.—m 14-16: Mk 1:29-34; Lk 4:38-41; Acts 3:7.—n Mt 9:25.—o Isa 53:4.—p Mk 4:35.

8:1—10:42 This section gathers together ten accounts of miracles of Jesus. Interspersed among them are sayings of Jesus about discipleship. This has led some authors to speak of a portrayal of Jesus as "Messiah of the Word" in chs. 5—7 and "Messiah of the Deed" in 8—9. By his sayings and actions Jesus bears witness that evil and sickness are no longer the last word for people, for human beings are not slaves of fate since the goodness of God is manifested in the goodness of Jesus.

8:1—9:34 The ten miracle stories found herein are a third of the miracle stories that are told in detail in all the Gospels together. But the New Testament contains repeated references to a thaumaturgic activity that was continual (see Mt 4:23; Lk 4:41; Acts 2:22).

8:1-4 Leprosy made a person ceremonially unclean as well as physically afflicted. The man with leprosy in this passage technically breaks the Law as he comes to prostrate himself at the feet of Jesus. The Master also breaks the Law when he touches the man and sovereignly decides to heal him. The sick man welcomes Christ's word, and the kingdom is opened to him. He becomes a model and sign of the Christian made clean by Christ.

8:5-13 Jesus commends a Roman centurion (leader of a hundred soldiers) for having greater faith than any Israelite and prophesies the ingathering of the Gentiles before healing his servant from afar. This passage shows that the great pilgrimage of peoples toward the kingdom has begun and evokes the beautiful image of the feast wherein all believers are definitively gathered together. Outside of this communion and joy there is only darkness; the "weeping and gnashing of teeth" (a phrase found outside Matthew only in Lk 13:28) describes the anguish of those who have remained insensitive to the call that has been welcomed by the very people they have denigrated.

8:8 *Lord, I am not worthy . . . will be healed:* these words of the centurion have become those of believers who go to encounter the Lord in Holy Communion.

8:16-17 Jesus is the Servant announced by Isa 53:4 who will expiate the sins of humankind. By the power of his Word he triumphs over the evil that keeps human beings in bondage symbolized by sickness.

8:18-22 Jesus has subordinated family ties to the needs of his mission of salvation and requires the same sacrifice of those called to share that mission, while other members of the family can perform the deeds of filial piety. These are "dead" only in the sense that they have not received the same call to separate themselves from family responsibility in order to preach the Gospel of the kingdom. They can nonetheless be his disciples in another sense.

Hence, following Jesus means Christians should be ready to make whatever sacrifice he asks of them. In the final analysis, they are followers of Christ, people who believe in him. They received faith in Christ at Baptism and are bound to serve him. By recourse to frequent prayer and true friendship with the Lord, they should strive to discover what Jesus asks of them in their service of him.

go." [q] 20 Jesus told him, "Foxes have holes and
birds of the air have nests, but the Son of
Man* has nowhere to lay his head." [r]
21 Another man, one of the disciples, said,
"Lord, allow me to go first and bury my
father." 22 Jesus answered him, "Follow me,
and let the dead bury their own dead."

Jesus Calms the Storm.* 23 [s] He then got
into the boat, followed by his disciples.
24 Suddenly, a great storm came up on the
lake, so that the boat was being swamped by
the waves. But he was asleep. 25 [t] And so they
went to him and awakened him, saying,
"Lord, save us! We are going to die!" 26 He
said to them in reply, "Why are you so fright-
ened, O you of little faith?"

Then he stood up and rebuked the winds
and the sea, and there was a great calm.
27 They were amazed and asked, "What sort
of man is this, whom even the winds and the
sea obey?"

Jesus Heals Two Demon-Possessed Men.*
28 [u] When he reached the region of the
Gadarenes* on the other side of the lake,
two men who were possessed by demons
came out of the tombs and approached him.
They were so fiercely violent that no one
dared to pass that way. 29 Suddenly, they
shouted, "What do you want with us, Son of
God?* Have you come here to torment us
before the appointed time?" [v]

30 Some distance away a large herd of pigs
was feeding. 31 The demons pleaded with
him, "If you cast us out, send us into the
herd of pigs." [w] 32 He said to them, "Go,
then!" They came out and entered the pigs.
The entire herd rushed down the steep bank
into the lake, and they perished in the water.
33 Those tending the pigs ran off, and when
they reached the town, they related the
whole story including what had happened to
the men who had been possessed. 34 Then
the whole town came out to meet Jesus, and
when they saw him they begged him to leave
their region.

CHAPTER 9

The Healing of a Paralyzed Man.* 1 [x] There-
fore, Jesus got into a boat and, crossing over
the lake, arrived at his hometown.* 2 Some
people then approached him, carrying a
paralyzed man lying on a bed. On perceiving
their faith, Jesus said to the man, "Take
heart, son. Your sins are forgiven." [y]

3 [z] On hearing this, some of the scribes
said to themselves, "This man is blasphem-
ing."* 4 Jesus perceived what they were
thinking, and he said, "Why do you harbor
evil thoughts in your hearts? [a] 5* Which is
easier, to say: 'Your sins are forgiven,' or to
say: 'Stand up and walk'? 6 But so that you

q 19-22: Lk 9:57-60.—r Ps 84:4; 2 Cor 8:9.—s 23-27: Jon 1:4ff; Mk 4:35-40; Lk 8:22-25.—t 25-26: Pss 65:8; 107:28-29.—u 28-34: Mk 5:1-17; Lk 8:26-37.—v 2 Pet 2:4.—w Lk 4:34, 41.—x 1-8: Mk 2:3-12; Lk 5:18-26.—y Lk 7:48.—z Jn 10:33-36.—a Lk 6:8.

8:20 *Son of Man:* the most common and enigmatic title of Christ used in the Gospels (81 times) and in Acts 7:56—frequently by Christ himself. It was well suited to his purpose of both veiling and revealing his person and mission. On the one hand, it meant simply "man" (see Ezek 2:1) and emphasized the lowliness of the human condition (Mt 8:20; 11:19; 20:28), especially in Christ's humiliation and death (Mt 17:22). On the other hand, it expressed the triumph of Christ's Resurrection (Mt 17:9), his return to glory (Mt 24:30; Dan 7:13), and his Second Coming as judge of the world (Mt 25:31).

Christ made use of this title at his trial before the Sanhedrin (Mt 26:64) when he prophesied that he would be vindicated and be seated in future glory at the right hand of God not merely as man but as Lord (see Dan 7:13; Mk 14:62).

This title was employed by Jewish apocalyptic literature (1 Enoch, 2 Ezra, 2 Baruch) to describe a unique religious personage endowed with extraordinary spiritual power who would receive the kingdom from God at the end of the ages. Early Christians revered this title as a reminder of Christ's twofold destiny of humiliation and joy, which was also their own (Mt 24:30f).

8:23-27 This passage attests to Jesus' power over nature and its frightful forces. This fact is preserved as a sign, for the Church resembles a boat buffeted by so many storms. She is invited to place herself in Christ's hands with great trust.

8:28-34 The sense of the anecdote about the pigs who serve as refuge for the demons and perish by drowning is that the Messiah has come; he triumphs over the evil powers that keep human beings in bondage and oppose the kingdom of God. The deliverance of the mentally ill signified that the "time" of the devil had come to an end. Thus, this is another account calling for confidence and courage in the struggle against evil. It must have especially delighted the Jews for whom pigs were unclean animals according to the Law (Lev 11:7) and who saw the pagan owners of the accursed flock suffering a loss.

8:28 *Gadarenes:* the city of Gadara was eight miles south of the lake.

8:29 *Son of God:* on the lips of the demons, this phrase is tantamount to "Messiah," for they would scarcely set themselves in opposition to him if they knew his full divinity. The same title is given to Jesus in Mk 3:12. *To torment us before the appointed time:* to confine us to hell (see Lk 8:31) before the Last Judgment. Until then, the demons have a certain freedom to roam about the world (see 2 Pet 2:4 with 1 Pet 5:8).

9:1-8 The two preceding accounts have attested Jesus' power over the frightful forces of nature and the unchained powers of hell. Here Christ delivers human beings from sin itself. For the first time he proclaims the forgiveness of sins—which is an act of God.

9:1 *His hometown:* Capernaum, which Jesus had made his headquarters.

9:3 *Blaspheming:* i.e., usurping God's prerogative to forgive sins.

9:5-6 Christ indicates that it is easier to heal a person physically than to heal him spiritually. It is easier to heal a broken leg than a broken heart. As Son of Man, in his human nature, Christ has the power to forgive sins. Therefore, he could also bestow it on his apostles (see Mt 18:18; Jn 20:22); and just as they worked miracles only in his name (see Acts 3:6), they and their successors can forgive sins only in his name and by his authority.

may come to realize that the Son of Man has authority on earth to forgive sins"—he said to the paralyzed man—"Stand up, take your bed, and go to your home."[b] 7 The man got up and returned to his home. 8 When the crowd saw this, they were filled with awe, and they glorified God for having given such authority to men.[c]

Jesus Calls Matthew. 9 *[d] As Jesus walked on from there, he noticed a man named Matthew sitting at the tax collector's booth. Jesus said to him, "Follow me," and he got up and followed him.

Jesus Dines with Sinners. 10 When he was sitting at dinner in the house, many tax collectors * and sinners were seated with Jesus and his disciples.[e] 11 On seeing this, the Pharisees said to his disciples, "Why does your teacher eat with tax collectors and sinners?" 12 When Jesus heard this, he said, "It is not the healthy who need a physician, but rather those who are sick. 13 Go and learn what this text means: 'I desire mercy, not sacrifice.' I have come to call not the righteous but sinners."[f]

A Time of Joy and Grace.* 14 [g] Then the disciples of John came to him and asked, "Why do we and the Pharisees fast but your disciples do not do so?" 15 Jesus answered, "How can the wedding guests mourn while the bridegroom is still with them? But the time will come when the bridegroom is taken away from them, and then they will fast.[h]

16 "No one sews a piece of unshrunken cloth on an old cloak, because the patch eventually pulls away from the cloak and a worse tear results. 17 Nor do people pour new wine into old wineskins, for if they do, the wineskins burst, the wine spills forth, and the skins are ruined. Rather, they pour new wine into fresh wineskins. In this way both are preserved."

Jesus Heals a Sick Woman and Raises a Dead Girl.* 18 [i] While he was saying these things to them, an official * came forward. He knelt before him and said, "My daughter has just died. But if you come and lay your hand on her, she will live." 19 Jesus then rose and followed him, together with his disciples.

20 Suddenly, a woman who had suffered from bleeding for twelve years came up behind him and touched the fringe of his cloak. 21 For she thought to herself, "If only I touch his cloak, I shall be healed."[j] 22 Jesus turned and saw her, and he said, "Take heart, daughter! Your faith has healed you." And from that moment the woman was cured.

23 When Jesus arrived at the official's house and saw the flute players * and the crowd making a commotion, 24 he said, "Go away! The girl is not dead; she is asleep," * but they laughed at him.[k] 25 When the people had been sent outside, he went in and took her by the hand, and the little girl stood up. 26 And the news of this spread throughout the entire district.

Jesus Heals Two Blind Men. 27 [l] As Jesus proceeded from there, two blind men followed him, crying out loudly, "Son of David, * have pity on us."[m] 28 When he had gone indoors, the blind men approached him. Jesus said to them, "Do you believe that I can do this?" They replied, "Yes, Lord, we do." 29 Then Jesus touched their eyes, saying, "Let it be done for you according to your faith." 30 And their sight was restored. Then Jesus sternly warned them, "See to it that no one learns about this."[n] 31 But as soon as they had

b Jn 5:27.—c Acts 4:21.—d 9-13: Mk 2:14-17; Lk 5:27-32.—e Mt 11:19; Lk 15:1-2; 19:1-10.—f Mt 12:7; Hos 6:6; 1 Tim 1:15.—g 14-17: Mk 2:18-22; Lk 5:33-39.—h Jn 3:29.—i 18-26: Mk 5:22-43; Lk 8:41-56.—j Mt 14:36; Num 15:37-38; Acts 19:12.—k Jn 11:11-13.—l 27-31: Mt 20:29-34.—m Mt 15:22.—n Mk 1:34.

9:9-13 Jesus calls Matthew the tax collector to follow him, then eats at Matthew's house together with "many tax collectors" and "sinners." The Jews are shocked, but Jesus reminds them that it is the sick who need a doctor and God desires mercy rather than sacrifice.

9:10 *Tax collectors:* see note on Mt 5:46.

9:14-17 The time when Jesus lived on earth was one of joy and grace. Later there would be a time for Jesus' disciples to fast, for the Bridegroom would be taken from them. In ancient times, goatskins were used to hold wine. As the wine fermented, it would expand and the new wineskins would stretch. But a used wineskin could not expand any more and would break. In the same way, the teaching that Jesus brings cannot be kept in the old forms.

9:18-26 Jesus rewards the faith of a father in distress and the trust of a sick and timid woman. He does not deceive those who believe him to be Master of the impossible. Human beings organize ceremonies of sorrow that are important in the East (v. 23); Jesus brings life, for this twofold gesture announces that in the kingdom of God sickness and death no longer have a place (see Jn 5:26-29): this is the message that the Church must proclaim.

9:18 *Official:* literally, "ruler" or "leader." See note on Mk 5:22.

9:23 *Flute players:* musicians who were hired to play at mourning ceremonies. *Crowd:* mourners who were hired to wail and lament.

9:24 *Asleep:* sleep is a metaphor for death (see Ps 87:6 LXX; Dan 12:2; 1 Thes 5:10). Jesus does not deny the child's death but indicates that she will arise from it as from a sleep.

9:27 *Son of David:* a popular Jewish title for the Messiah who was to come (e.g., Mt 12:23; 20:30; 21:9; 22:41-45; see note on Mt 1:1).

departed, they spread the news about him throughout that entire district.

Jesus Heals a Mute Demoniac. 32 [o] As they left, a man who was possessed and unable to speak was brought to him. 33 When the demon had been driven out, the man who had been mute was able to speak. The crowds were amazed, and they said, "Nothing like this has ever been seen in Israel." [p] 34 But the Pharisees responded, "He casts out demons by the prince of demons." * [q]

The Harvest Is Abundant.* 35 Jesus traveled through all the towns and villages, teaching in their synagogues, proclaiming the good news of the kingdom, and curing every kind of illness and disease. [r] 36 When he saw the crowds, he had compassion on them because they were distressed and helpless like sheep without a shepherd. [s] 37 [t] Then he said to his disciples, "The harvest is abundant, but the laborers are few. 38 Therefore, ask the Lord of the harvest to send forth laborers for his harvest."

B: Instructions to the Apostles: The Charter of the Apostolate*

CHAPTER 10

Jesus Sends Out the Twelve Apostles.* 1 [u] Calling his twelve disciples together, he gave them authority over unclean spirits, with the power to drive them out and to cure every kind of disease and illness. [v]

2 These are the names of the twelve apostles: first, Simon, also called Peter, and his brother Andrew; James the son of Zebedee, and his brother John; 3 Philip and Bartholomew; Thomas and Matthew the tax collector; James the son of Alphaeus, and Thaddaeus; 4 Simon the Zealot, and Judas Iscariot, * the one who betrayed him. [w]

5 [x] These twelve Jesus sent forth after giving them the following instructions: "Do not travel* to the territory of the Gentiles, and enter no Samaritan town. [y] 6 Go rather to the lost sheep of Israel. [z] 7 And as you go, proclaim: 'The kingdom of heaven is near.' [a] 8 Cure the sick, raise the dead, cleanse those who have leprosy, drive out demons. You received without payment; give in the same way. [b] 9 [c] Take along no gold or silver or copper in your purses, 10 no sack for your journey, or an extra tunic, or sandals, or a staff. For the laborer deserves his keep. [d]

11 [e] "Whatever town or village you enter, look for some honorable person who lives there, and stay with him until you leave. 12 As you enter a house, extend your blessing upon it. 13 If the house is worthy, let your peace come upon it, but if it is not worthy, let your peace return to you. 14 If anyone will not welcome you or listen to your message, shake the dust from your feet * as you leave that house or town. [f] 15 Amen, I say to you, it will be more bearable for the land of Sodom and Gomorrah * on the day of judgment than for that town. [g]

No Servant Is above His Master.* 16 "I am sending you out like sheep among wolves. Therefore, be as cunning as serpents and yet

---

o 32-34: Mt 12:22-24; Lk 11:14-15.—p Mk 2:12; 7:37.—q Mt 10:25; 12:24; Mk 3:22.—r Mt 4:23; Lk 8:1.—s Mt 14:14; Num 27:17; 1 Ki 22:17; Jer 30:6; Ezek 34:5; Mk 6:34; 8:2; Zec 10:2.—t 37-38: Lk 10:2; Jn 4:35-38.—u 1-4: Mk 3:14-19; 6:7; Lk 6:13-16; Acts 1:13.—v Lk 9:1.—w Acts 1:16.—x 5-15: Mk 6:7-13; Lk 9:1-6.—y Lk 9:52-53; Jn 4:9, 40.—z Mt 15:24; Jer 50:6.—a Mt 3:2; 4:17.—b Acts 8:20.—c 9-10: Isa 55:1 Mk 6:8-9; Lk 9:3; 10:4; 22:35.—d Lk 10:7; 1 Cor 9:14; 1 Tim 5:18.—e 11-15: Mk 6:10-11; Lk 9:4-5; 10:5-12.—f Acts 13:51; 18:6.—g Mt 11:24; Gen 13:13; 19:1-29; Jude 7.

9:34 The debate with the Pharisees on this claim will continue in Mt 12:25ff.

9:35-38 As in Mt 4:23-25, the evangelist concludes this part of his book with an action of Christ that shows compassion for the distress of the crowds and inculcates confidence in his followers. Jesus insistently works to impart the mercy of God upon all who come to him. He calls upon all who have the privilege of believing in him and benefiting from his salvation to share his concern for the misery of their neighbors. He seeks people who, like him and after him, will apply themselves to this task.

10:1-42 This section of Matthew is called the Instructions to the Apostles; collected in it are the texts describing the mission of the disciples, applicable to the early Church and for all future time. The disciples begin the great enterprise; through them Christ's authority and power continue among human beings—so long as they act truly in his Spirit and share his lot. Thus is born a new People of God.

10:1-15 Israel was made up of twelve tribes; the kingdom of Jesus was to have twelve founders (see Mt 19:28; Rev 21:12-14): the "Twelve" or the "apostles." The latter is a Greek word (plural) meaning "those who are sent"; Jesus himself chose the term (Lk 6:13).

10:4 *Iscariot:* i.e., "Man from Kerioth," a place in the southernmost part of Palestine.

10:5 *Do not travel:* the Good News about the kingdom was to be proclaimed first to Jews alone. After his Death and Resurrection, Jesus commanded the disciples to take the message to all nations (Mt 28:19; see Mt 21:43). *Samaritans:* a race of mixed blood resulting from the intermarriage of Israelites left behind when the people of the northern kingdom were exiled and Gentiles were brought into the land by the Assyrians (2 Ki 17:24). In the time of Jesus, Jews and Samari-tans were bitterly opposed to one another (see Jn 4:9).

10:14 *Shake the dust from your feet:* a symbolic act practiced by the Pharisees when they left an unclean Gentile area. Here it represents a solemn warning to those who reject God's message.

10:15 *Sodom and Gomorrah:* see Gen 19:23-29.

10:16-25 The disciples are prolongations of Christ, so to speak. Whatever happened to him will also happen to them. But if they persevere they will be saved.

as innocent as doves.[h] 17 [i]Be on your guard,
for people will hand you over to courts* and
scourge you in their synagogues,[j] 18 and you
will be brought before governors and kings
because of me to testify before them and the
Gentiles.[k]

19 "When they hand you over, do not be
concerned about how you are to speak or
what you are to say. When the time comes,
you will be given what you are to say.[l] 20 For
it will not be you who speak but the Spirit of
your Father speaking through you.[m]

21 [n]"Brother will betray brother to death,
and a father his child. Children will rise up
against their parents and have them put to
death. 22 You will be hated by all because of
my name, but he who stands firm to the end
will be saved. 23 When you are persecuted in
one town, flee to another. Amen, I say to you,
you will not have finished traveling through
all the towns of Israel before the Son of Man
comes.*

24 [o]"No student is greater than his teacher,
nor a servant greater than his master. 25 It is
enough for the student to be like his teacher
and the servant like his master. If they have
called the master of the house Beelzebul,*
how much more those of his household?

The Conditions of Discipleship.* 26 [p]"There-
fore, do not be afraid of them. There is noth-
ing hidden that will not be disclosed, and
nothing secret that will not become known.[q]
27 What I say to you in the dark, proclaim in
the daylight, and what you hear whispered,
shout from the housetops.

28 "Have no fear of those who kill the body
but cannot kill the soul. Rather, fear the one
who can destroy both soul and body in
Gehenna.*[r]

29 "Are not two sparrows sold for a penny?
Yet not one of them can fall to the ground
without your Father's knowledge. 30 Even the
hairs on your head have all been counted.[s]
31 So do not be afraid; you are worth far
more than any number of sparrows.

32 "Whoever acknowledges me before
men, I will also acknowledge before my
Father in heaven. 33 But whoever denies me
before men, I also will deny before my heav-
enly Father.[t]

34 [u]"Do not think that I have come to
bring peace to the earth. I have not come to
bring peace but a sword.*

35 For I have come to set a man against his
father,
a daughter against her mother,
and a daughter-in-law against her
mother-in-law;
36 and one's enemies will be the mem-
bers of his own household.[v]

Whoever Receives You Receives Me.
37 [w]"Anyone who loves his father or mother
more than me is not worthy of me, and any-
one who loves his son or daughter more than
me is not worthy of me, 38 and anyone who
does not take up his cross* and follow me is
not worthy of me. 39 Whoever finds his life
will lose it, and whoever loses his life for my
sake will find it.*[x]

40 "Whoever receives you receives me; and
whoever receives me receives the one who
sent me.[y] 41 Whoever receives a prophet*
because he is a prophet will receive a
prophet's reward, and whoever welcomes a
righteous man because he is righteous will
receive a righteous man's reward. 42 And
whoever gives even a cup of cold water to
one of these little ones because he is a disci-
ple, amen, I say to you, he will not go unre-
warded."[z]

h Lk 10:3; 1 Cor 14:20.—i 17-22: Mk 13:9-13; Lk 21:12-19; Jn 16:1-4.—j Acts 5:40.—k Jn 15:27.—l Ex 4:11-12; Jer 1:6-10; Lk 12:11-12.—m Acts 4:8, 31.—n 21-22: Mt 24:9, 13; Jn 15:21.—o 24-25: Lk 6:40; Jn 13:16; 15:20.—p 26-33: Lk 12:2-9.—q Mk 4:22; Lk 8:17; 1 Tim 5:25.—r Isa 8:12, 13; Jas 4:12; 1 Pet 3:14; Rev 2:10.—s Lk 21:18; Acts 27:34.—t Mk 8:38; Lk 9:26; 2 Tim 2:12; Rev 3:5.—u 34-35: Lk 12:51-53.—v Mic 7:6.—w 37-39: Mt 16:24-25; Deut 33:9; Lk 14:26-27.—x Mk 8:35; Lk 9:24; Jn 12:25.—y Lk 9:48; 10:16; Jn 12:44; 13:20; Gal 4:14.—z Mt 25:40; Prov 14:31; Mk 9:41.

10:17 *Courts:* the lower courts, connected with local synagogues, that tried less serious cases and scourged those found guilty.

10:23 *You will not have finished . . . before the Son of Man comes:* this may be interpreted in two ways: (1) the disciples will not have converted all of Israel before the Second Coming of Christ; (2) the disciples will not have preached the Gospel in all the towns of Palestine before the destruction of Jerusalem occurs in A.D. 70, which is a portent of the end of the world.

10:25 *Beelzebul:* "Baal the Prince," or Beelzebub, "Lord of the Flies." The former is the name of an ancient pagan divinity (see 2 Ki 1:1-14), the latter a contemptuous distortion of the name.

10:26-36 In the face of fierce opposition and trials of all kinds, the apostles must not lose heart, for they will be given the courage to bear true witness to Jesus and his message.

10:28 *Gehenna:* see note on Mt 5:22.

10:34 As Simeon predicted (Lk 2:34), Jesus will be a sign of contradiction even within families. Those who accept the Gospel will be at peace with God, but they will have to bear persecution at the hands of those who do not.

10:38 *Take up his cross:* this is the first time Matthew mentions the cross, which was an instrument of death. The picture is of a man, already condemned, required to carry the beam of his own cross to the place of execution (see Jn 19:17). Here it symbolizes the necessity of total commitment—even unto death—on the part of Jesus' disciples.

10:39 Those who renounce their earthly life in order to confess Jesus will obtain the happiness of eternal life.

10:41 *Prophet:* the last prophet of the old covenant was John the Baptist.

III: JESUS IS THE EXPECTED MESSIAH*

A: Jesus and John the Baptist*

CHAPTER 11

Report to John What You Hear and See.*
1 When Jesus had finished giving these in-
structions to his twelve disciples, he moved
on from there to teach and preach in their
towns.
2 [a]When John who was in prison heard
what Christ was doing, he sent his disciples
3 to ask him, “Are you the one who is to
come,* or are we to wait for another?” [b]
4 Jesus answered them, “Go back and tell
John what you hear and see: 5 the blind
receive their sight, the lame walk, those who
have leprosy are cured, the deaf hear, the
dead are raised to life, and the poor have the
good news proclaimed to them. [c] 6 And
blessed is anyone who takes no offense at
me.” * [d]

**John Is the Elijah Who Was Destined To
Return.*** 7 As John’s disciples were departing,
Jesus spoke to the crowds about John: “What
did you go out into the desert to see? A reed
swaying in the wind? [e] 8 Then what did you
go out to see? Someone robed in fine cloth-
ing? Those who wear fine clothing are found
in royal palaces. 9 What then did you go out
to see? A prophet? Yes, I tell you, and far
more than a prophet. [f] 10 This is the one
about whom it is written:

‘Behold, I am sending my messenger
ahead of you,
who will prepare your way before
you.’ [g]

11 “Amen, I say to you, among those born
of women, no one has been greater than
John the Baptist, and yet the least in the
kingdom of heaven is greater than he. *
12 From the days of John the Baptist until
now the kingdom of heaven has been sub-
jected to violence, and the violent are taking
it by force. 13 For all the Prophets and the
Law prophesied until the arrival of John. [h]
14 And if you are willing to accept it, John is
the Elijah who was destined to return. [i] 15 He
who has ears to hear, let him hear!

Indecisive Children.* 16 [j]“To what shall I
compare this generation? It is like children
who sit in the marketplace and call to one
another:

17 ‘We played the flute for you,
but you would not dance;
we sang a dirge,
and you refused to mourn.’

18 For John came neither eating nor drink-
ing, and they said, ‘He is possessed.’ [k] 19 The
Son of Man came eating and drinking, and
they say, ‘Look at him! He is a glutton and a
drunkard, a friend of tax collectors and sin-
ners.’ Yet wisdom is proved right by her
actions.” [l]

---

a 2-11: Lk 7:18-28.—b Deut 18:15; Jn 1:21.—c Isa 26:19; 29:18-19; 35:5-6; 61:1.—d Jn 6:61.—e Mt 3:3, 5.—f Lk 1:76-79.—g Ex 23:20; Mal 3:1; Mk 1:2; Lk 1:76; Acts 13:24.—h Lk 16:16.—i Mt 17:10-13; Mal 3:23; Lk 1:17.—j 16-19: Lk 7:31-35.—k Mt 3:4; Lk 1:15.—l Mt 9:10-11.

11:1—13:52 To be committed to Christ means to acknowledge him as the expected Messiah. By his words and his actions, he takes a clear position toward John and toward the Pharisees. To decide for Christ means to discover the inner life of Jesus. It is not right to proclaim the coming of the kingdom; we are invited to experience it, to experience the power of God. The following passages enable us to question ourselves about our faith.

11:1-30 In striking images John had proclaimed the time of wrath and the purification by God. Jesus himself had joined in this movement of renewal. Now the prophet is in prison, the victim of his mission. All around Jesus the enthusiasm of the crowds concerning John begins to falter. How then can they be made to acknowledge the awaited Messianic revolution consisting in the decisive judgment of the wicked and the liberation of the righteous (Mt 3:12)? But then who is the Messiah and what is the kingdom of God? One must pass from questioning to decision, to the act of faith in Jesus.

11:1-6 By letting John know that the announcement of the Prophets is being fulfilled (Isa 26:19; 29:18; 35:5f; 61:1), Jesus reassures him and places him on guard against an overly human idea of the Messiah; he encourages the Baptist to persevere in faith until the end. The kingdom of God is not to be confused with the accomplishment of our projects and our human victories; it is a gift of God.

11:3 *The one who is to come:* i.e., the Messiah. *Wait for another:* it is not clear whether John is uncertain about Jesus or is simply sending his disciples to Jesus.

11:6 *Takes no offense at me:* literally, “is not scandalized,” that is, for whom I am not a hindrance or stumbling block (Greek: *skandalon*). It is from the idea of a stumbling block on the way of goodness that “scandal” derives its moral meaning, in both the active sense of giving scandal and the passive sense of taking scandal. In current idiom, a bad example is called “scandalous” when it causes a stir.

11:7-15 Jesus eulogizes the strength of John the Baptist’s religious convictions, the austerity of his life (v. 7f), and his unique prophetic role as precursor of the kingdom of God, which for Jesus is the salvation of human beings (vv. 4-5), not political revolution or the acquisition of power.

11:11 John’s greatness consists primarily in his task of announcing the imminence of the kingdom of God (Mt 3:1). Yet to be a member of the kingdom is so sublime a privilege that even the least member is greater than the Baptist!

11:16-19 Indecisive children do not want to play either at a wedding when a flute is sounded or at a funeral when a dirge is sung; such are the Jews who reject the salvation that God offers them: the severity of John frightens them and the goodness of Jesus shocks them. People often hesitate as much before joy as before repentance! But the kingdom of God does not wait; God realizes here below his plan—his “Wisdom”—as the acts of John and Jesus bear witness.

Woe to the Cities of Galilee.* 20 [m] Then he began to reproach the cities in which most of his mighty deeds had been performed because they had refused to repent. 21 "Woe to you, Chorazin! Woe to you, Bethsaida! If the mighty deeds performed in your midst had been done in Tyre and Sidon, they would have repented long ago in sackcloth and ashes. [n] 22 But I tell you, on the day of judgment it will be more tolerable for Tyre and Sidon than for you. 23 And as for you, Capernaum:

'Will you be exalted to heaven?
You will be cast down to the netherworld.' [o]

For if the mighty deeds performed in your midst had been done in Sodom, it would be standing to this day. 24 But I tell you, on the day of judgment it will be more tolerable for the land of Sodom than for you." [p]

The Self-Revelation of Jesus.* 25 [q] At that time, Jesus said, "I thank you, Father, Lord of heaven and earth, because you have hidden these things from the wise and the learned and have revealed them to children. [r] 26 Yes, Father, such has been your gracious will.

27 "All things have been entrusted to me by my Father. No one knows the Son except the Father, and no one knows the Father except the Son and those to whom the Son wishes to reveal him. [s]

The Gentle Mastery of Christ.* 28 "Come to me, all you who are weary and overburdened, and I will give you rest. [t] 29 Take my yoke upon you and learn from me, for I am meek and humble of heart, and you will find rest for your souls. [u] 30 For my yoke is easy and my burden is light." [v]

B: Jesus Is the True Servant of God*

CHAPTER 12

Picking Grain on the Sabbath. 1 * [w] At that time, Jesus was walking through a field of grain on the Sabbath. His disciples were hungry, and they began to pick some heads of grain and eat them. [x] 2 When the Pharisees saw this, they said to him, "Look at your disciples. They are doing what is forbidden on the Sabbath." * [y]

3 * [z] He answered, "Have you not read what David did when he and his companions were hungry? 4 He entered the house of God and they ate the consecrated bread, which neither he nor his companions but only the priests were permitted to eat. [a] 5 * Or have you not read in the Law that on the Sabbath the priests in the temple violate the

m 20-24: Lk 10:12-15.—n Dan 9:3; Joel 4:4; Jon 3:6.—o Isa 14:13-15.—p Mt 10:15.—q 25-27: Lk 10:21-22.—r 1 Cor 1:26-29.—s Wis 2:13; Jn 3:35; 6:46; 7:28; 10:15.—t Ps 34:19.—u Prov 3:17; Sir 51:26; Jer 6:16.—v Acts 15:10.—w 1-8: Mk 2:23-28; Lk 6:1-5.—x Deut 23:25.—y Ex 20:10.—z 3-4: 1 Sam 21:2-7.—a Lev 24:5-9.

11:20-24 The fate of the privileged cities of Chorazin (about two miles from Capernaum) and Bethsaida (on the northeast shore of the Sea of Galilee) will be worse than that of cities traditionally regarded as godless (Tyre and Sidon: Am 1:9f; 1 Sam 23; Ezek 26—28; Zec 9:2-4) or wicked (Sodom: Gen 18:16-19; Ezek 16:46-56), which did not have the opportunity to witness Jesus' miracles and hear his preaching as had the people in most of Galilee. The people of Chorazin and Bethsaida have failed to recognize the presence of God in Jesus because they wanted to avoid penance. The same is true for the people of Capernaum, Jesus' headquarters on the north shore of Galilee (see Mt 4:13).

11:25-27 The self-revelation of Jesus reached one of its high points in this moving prayer. It enables us to enter into the most hidden core of his life, into his innermost experiences. Between him and the Father there is an exchange of life, a profound and unique bond, a mutual commitment of their entire being—in short, an inexpressibly mysterious oneness. In the Bible, all this is summed up in the verb "know." This is why Jesus alone can reveal to other human beings who the Father is for them.

11:28-30 *Yoke* and *burden* evoke the Mosaic Law. The law of Christ is sweet, for it is not a list of customs, obligations, and conventions but primarily the sharing of a life, an apprenticeship of love.

12:1-50 The Good News of the kingdom spreads from town to town; a new law of salvation is announced and runs up against the refusal of those in authority. The conflict between Jesus and Judaism now appears inevitable. The newness of the Gospel totally upsets recognized habits of thinking and ways of acting. The more Jesus bypasses the Law for the service and salvation of human beings, the more he enters into conflict with his religious environment. Those who are close to Jesus are those who believe in him.

12:1-14 Jesus reminds the Pharisees, who are attached to the letter of the Law, that a religion without love is worthless (Hos 6:6), and in order to make them face up to their blindness he cites an incident of the Old Testament (David and his companions: 1 Sam 21:2-7), a practical aspect of worship (the priests do not abstain from work in the temple on the Sabbath: Lev 24:8; Num 28:9), and a requirement of good sense (the sheep in the pit). Jesus utters his decision with authority: he claims to be Lord of the Sabbath, and he is more than the Sabbath, that is, the very place of God's presence.

12:2 The Pharisees had set down 39 categories of actions forbidden on the Sabbath, based on interpretations of the Law and Jewish customs. One of these was harvesting. By picking wheat and rubbing it in their hands, the disciples were technically harvesting according to the religious leaders. But the disciples were picking grain because they were hungry, not because they wanted to harvest the grain for profit. Hence, they were not working on the Sabbath.

12:3-4 Each Sabbath 12 fresh loaves of bread (the bread of the Presence) were to be set on a table in the Holy Place (Ex 25:30; Lev 24:5-9). The old loaves were eaten by priests. The loaves given to David (1 Sam 21:1-6) were the old loaves that had just been replaced by fresh ones. Although the priests were the only ones allowed to eat this bread, David and his men were allowed to eat it because of their need for food, showing that laws should be enforced with discernment and compassion.

12:5-6 The Sabbath-work is related to worshiping God, changing the shewbread (Lev 24:8), and doubling the usual daily burnt offerings (Num 28:9f). Hence, the Law itself requires works that break the Sabbath rest (*violate the Sabbath*) because of the higher duty of God's service. If temple duties outweigh the Law, how much more does the presence of Jesus with his proclamation of the kingdom (*one greater than the temple*) justify the conduct of his disciples. If people become more concerned with the means of worship than with the God they worship, they will miss God even while they think they are worshiping him.

Sabbath, but they are considered to be with-
out guilt? [b] 6 I tell you, one greater than the
temple is here. 7 If you had truly understood
what is meant by the words, 'I desire mercy
and not sacrifice,' you would not have con-
demned these men who are without guilt. [c] 8
For the Son of Man is Lord of the Sabbath." * [d]

The Man with a Withered Hand.* 9 [e] Moving on
from that place, Jesus entered their
synagogue. 10 A man was there who had a
withered hand, and hoping to find some
reason to accuse Jesus they asked him, "Is it
lawful to heal on the Sabbath?" [f]

11 He said to them, "Suppose you had only
one sheep and it fell into a pit on the
Sabbath. Would you not lay hold of it and lift
it out? [g] 12 How much more valuable a man
is than a sheep! Therefore, it is lawful to do
good on the Sabbath." [h] 13 Then he said to
the man, "Stretch out your hand." He
stretched it out, and it was restored, so that
it was as sound as the other one. 14 But the
Pharisees went out and began to plot how
they might put him to death. * [i]

The Servant of the Lord.* 15 When Jesus
became aware of this, he departed from that
place. Many people followed him, and he
healed all who were ill, 16 but he warned
them not to make him known. 17 This was to
fulfill what had been spoken through the
prophet Isaiah:

18 [j] "Behold, my servant, whom I have chosen,
my beloved in whom I delight.
I will place my spirit upon him,
and he will proclaim justice to the Gentiles.
19 He will not cry out or shout,
nor will anyone hear his voice in the streets.
20 A bruised reed he will not break,
nor will he snuff out a smoldering wick,
until he establishes justice as victorious;
21 and in his name the Gentiles will place their hope."

Whoever Is Not with Me Is against Me.*
22 [k] Then they brought to him a man who was
unable to either see or speak and who was
possessed by a demon. He cured him, so that
the man who was mute both spoke and saw.
23 All the people were astonished, and they
said, "Is this not the Son of David?" * [l] 24 But
when the Pharisees heard this, they said, "It
is only by Beelzebul, * the prince of demons,
that this man casts out demons." [m]

25 He knew what they were thinking, and
he said to them, "Every kingdom divided
against itself is laid waste, and every city or
household divided against itself cannot
survive. [n] 26 If Satan drives out Satan, he is
divided against himself. How then can his
kingdom survive? [o] 27 If it is by Beelzebul
that I cast out demons, by whom do your
own children cast them out? Therefore,
they will be your judges. 28 But if it is by the
Spirit of God that I cast out demons, then
the kingdom of God has come to you. [p]

29 "Or again, how can anyone break into a
strong man's house and steal his possessions
unless he first ties up the strong man? Then
indeed he can ransack the house.

30 "Whoever is not with me is against me,
and whoever does not gather with me scat-
ters. [q] 31 [r] Therefore, I tell you that every sin

b Lev 24:8; Num 28:9-10; Jn 7:22, 23.—c Hos 6:6; Mic 6:6-8.—d Jn 5:16-17.—e 9-15: Mk 3:1-6; Lk 6:6-11.—f Lk 20:20.—g Lk 14:5.—h Ex 20:8f; Eccl 3:19.—i Jn 5:18.—j 18-21: Isa 42:1-4.—k 22-24: Mt 8:29; 9:32-34; Lk 11:14-15.—l Mt 9:27.—m Mt 10:25; Mk 3:22.—n 25-29: Job 8:3; Mk 3:23-27; Lk 11:17-22.—o Job 1:6.—p Mt 3:2; Lk 11:20.—q Mk 9:40; Lk 11:23.—r 31-32: Mk 3:28-30; Lk 12:10; 1 Jn 5:16.

12:8 *Lord of the Sabbath:* the ultimate justification for the disciples' violation of the Sabbath rest is that Jesus is the Son of Man, the Messiah, who has supreme authority over the Law.

12:9-14 By healing the man with a withered hand, Jesus corroborates his teaching: it is licit to do good on the Sabbath; no law can oppose the doing of good. He thus rejects the false interpretation put forth by the Pharisees who are attached to the letter of the Law to the detriment of the glory of God and the good of human beings. The very persons who are scandalized by Christ's miracle are in no way held back from plotting his death even though it is the Sabbath.

12:14 *Pharisees . . . began to plot how they might put him to death:* even though Matthew does not mention them here, the Herodians were also involved in the plot (see Mk 3:6).

12:15-21 Evidently, at least for a while, Jesus gave up preaching in the synagogues (*he departed*). The prohibition against making known his miracles was in this case probably due to the wish to avoid conflict with the Pharisees. If we want to understand Jesus' purpose and way of life, we will find the appropriate images in the Servant Songs of Isaiah; here the second of these (Isa 42:1-4) is cited. Jesus recalled these passages, which are the most profound in the Old Testament, when he thought about and spoke of his mission.

12:22-32 On certain days, Jesus confronts physically, so to speak, the forces of evil that keep human beings enslaved, as in the case of a possessed man rendered deaf and mute. By healing him Jesus shows that he frees people from every type of alienation and possession; he sets back the incursion of evil. How could the Pharisees suspect that Jesus belongs to this world of darkness? Moreover, they admit that their own "children," i.e., disciples, also fight to free human beings from the powers of evil! When Jesus acts, the Spirit is at work, the kingdom of God is at hand, and everyone must take part in it. The *blasphemy against the Spirit* consists in ascribing to the devil the work of the Holy Spirit and is the result of becoming hardened in an attitude of refusal, which may one day be irremediable. This warning is given to the Pharisees and, through them, to every reader.

12:23 *Son of David:* see note on Mt 9:27.

12:24 *Beelzebul:* see note on Mt 10:25.

and blasphemy will be forgiven but blasphe-
my against the Spirit will not be forgiven.
32 Whoever speaks a word against the Son of
Man will be forgiven, but whoever speaks
against the Holy Spirit will not be forgiven,
either in this age or in the age to come. *

A Tree and Its Fruits.* 33 [s] "Make a tree good
and its fruit will be good, or make a tree bad
and its fruit will be bad. For a tree is known
by its fruit. 34 You brood of vipers! How can
your speech be virtuous when you your-
selves are evil? For the mouth speaks from
the abundance of the heart. [t] 35 A good man
brings forth good things from the good
stored up within him, but an evil man brings
forth evil things from his store of evil. 36 [u] I
tell you that on the day of judgment people
will have to render an account for every
careless word they utter. 37 For by your
words you will be justified, and by your
words you will be condemned."

The Sign of Jonah.* 38 [v] Then some of the
scribes and Pharisees said to him, "Teacher,
we would like you to show us a sign." [w] 39 He
replied, "An evil and adulterous * genera-
tion asks for a sign, but the only sign it will
be given is the sign of the prophet Jonah.
40 For just as Jonah spent three days and
three nights in the belly of the whale, so will
the Son of Man be in the heart of the earth
for three days and three nights. *
41 * "On the day of judgment the inhabi-
tants of Nineveh will rise up with this gener-
ation and condemn it, for they repented at
the preaching of Jonah, and now one greater
than Jonah is here. [x] 42 On the day of judg-
ment the queen of the south will rise up with
this generation and condemn it, because she
came from the farthest reaches of the earth
to hear the wisdom of Solomon, and now
one greater than Solomon is here. [y]

New Offensive from the Evil Spirit.* 43 [z] "When
an unclean spirit goes out of a person, it
wanders through waterless regions seeking a
place to rest, but it finds none. 44 Then it
says, 'I will return to the home from which I
departed.' And when it returns, it finds that
home empty, swept clean, and put in order.
45 Then it goes off and brings back with it
seven other spirits more wicked than itself,
and they enter and settle there. As a result,
the plight of that person is worse than
before. So it will also be with this evil gener-
ation." [a]

The True Family of Jesus.* 46 While he was
still speaking to the crowds, his mother
and his brethren * appeared. They were
standing outside, wishing to speak with
him. [b] [47 Someone told him, "Behold, your

s 33-35: Mt 7:16-20; Lk 6:43-45.—t Mt 3:7; 15:11-12; 23:33; Sir 27:6; Lk 3:7.—u 36-37: Prov 10:14; Jas 3:1-2.—v 38-42: Mt 16:1-4; Jon 2:1; 3:1-10; Mk 8:11-12; Lk 11:29-32.—w 1 Cor 1:22.—x Rom 2:27.—y 1 Ki 10:1-10; 2 Chr 9:1.—z 43-45: Lk 11:24-26.—a 2 Pet 2:20.—b 46-50: Mk 3:31-35; Lk 8:19-21.

12:32 God desires the salvation of all human beings (1 Tim 2:4) and calls everyone to repentance (2 Pet 3:9). Christ's Redemption is superabundant satisfaction for all sin and reaches every person (Rom 5:12-21). Christ gave his Church the power to forgive sins through the Sacraments of Baptism and Penance. This power is unlimited; she can forgive every sin of the baptized as often as they confess with the necessary dispositions.

12:33-37 Jesus denounces hypocrites whose words are vanity and calumny. Every spoken word reflects the heart's overflow and is known to God. Hence words are critically important (see Eph 5:3f, 12; Col 3:17; Jas 1:19; 3:1-12).

12:38-42 An opinion current among circles of apocalyptic thought at the time looked for the Messiah to perform a unique sign. Jesus offers only the sign of his Death and Resurrection typified by the story of Jonah in the belly of the whale (Jon 2:1).

12:39 *Adulterous:* i.e., in the spiritual sense of being unfaithful to the generation's spiritual husband (God).

12:40 *Three days and three nights:* this manner of speaking denotes a common Jewish way of reckoning time and includes at least part of the first and part of the third day. Any part of the whole was counted as if it were the whole. Thus, even the time from Jesus' Death till sunset on Good Friday is counted as a day. (The Old Testament depicted the Messiah as one who would suffer [Ps 22; Isa 53] and rise from the dead on the third day [Ps 16:9-11; Isa 53:10f].)

12:41-42 The people of Nineveh who repented (see Jon 3:1-10) and the queen of the south (i.e., of Sheba—see 1 Ki 10:1-3—a country in southwest Arabia now called Yemen) were pagans who responded to lesser opportunities than the one that had been presented to Israel in the person of Jesus, *one greater* than Jonah or Solomon.

12:43-45 A person's religious history is a repeated exchange of good and evil. The option for evil can reach the point of taking full possession of the person. The same is true for the religious leaders of Israel. Just cleaning up one's life without filling it with God leaves plenty of room for Satan to return.

12:46-50 Belonging to Jesus has nothing to do with the bonds of blood relations. The Church is never based on attachments of race, class, or culture. She is the family of God. Only one who does the will of Jesus' *heavenly Father* belongs to his true family.

12:46 *His mother and his brethren:* "brethren" here is used in the sense of "cousins" or "relatives." If they were true brothers of Jesus, sons of Mary, the Gospel would say: "his mother and the sons of his mother," which was the normal manner of speaking in Israel of that time. The Church has never wavered in her teaching that Mary was a Virgin and that Jesus was her *only* son, just as he is the *only* Son of the Father (Lk 1:26).

In the ancient tongues of Hebrew, Arabic, and Aramaic, there were no concrete words to indicate the different types of relatives that exist in modern languages. In general, all who belonged to the same family clan, including tribes, were called "brethren" or "sisters." (See, for example, Jn 19:25, which mentions a certain Mary, sister of Mary the Mother of Jesus. If they were really sisters, they would not bear the same name. Also note that in Mt 27:56, the second Mary is called "the mother of James and Joses" [i.e., Joseph], two personages who are called "brethren" of the Lord in Mt 13:55.)

In addition, in the first Christian community when the Gospels were written, there existed a very influential group composed of Jesus' relatives and his countrymen of Nazareth, called the "brethren of the Lord." The leader seemed to be James, who became bishop of the Judean community. This group was late in believing in Jesus even though they had lived with him for several years (Mk 3:21; Jn 7:3-5). When speaking of them, the evangelists use the name the community gave them: "brethren of the Lord" or "N. brother of Jesus."

mother and your brothers are standing outside. They want to speak with you."] * 48 But Jesus replied to that man, "Who is my mother? Who are my brethren?" [c] 49 Then, pointing to his disciples, he said, "Behold, my mother and my brethren. 50 Whoever does the will of my heavenly Father is my brother and sister and mother."

CHAPTER 13

C: Jesus Teaches in Parables*

The Day of Parables. 1 [d] That same day Jesus went out of the house and sat by the side of the lake. 2 However, such large crowds gathered around him that he got into a boat and sat down while all the people stood on the shore. 3 Then he told them many things in parables. *

The Parable of the Sower.* He said: "A sower went out to sow. 4 As he sowed, some seeds fell on the path, and the birds came and ate them up. 5 Other seeds fell on rocky ground, where there was little soil. They sprouted quickly, since the soil had very little depth, 6 but when the sun rose they were scorched, and since they lacked roots, they withered away. 7 Other seeds fell among thorns, and the thorns grew up and choked them. 8 But some seeds fell on rich soil and produced a crop—some a hundred, some sixty, and some thirty times what was sown. [e] 9 He who has ears, let him hear!"

The Reason for Parables.* 10 Then his disciples approached and asked him, "Why do you speak to them in parables?" 11 He replied, "To you has been granted knowledge of the mysteries * of the kingdom of heaven, but to them it has not been granted. [f] 12 To the one who has, more will be given, and he will have an abundance. As for the one who does not have, even what little he has will be taken away. [g] 13 The reason I speak to them in parables is that they see but do not perceive and they listen but do not hear or understand. [h] 14 [i] In them is fulfilled the prophecy of Isaiah that says:

'You will indeed hear but not understand,
you will indeed look but never see. [j]
15 For this people's heart has become hardened;
they have stopped up their ears
and they have shut their eyes,
so that they might not see with their eyes
and hear with their ears
and understand with their heart
and then turn to me,
and I would heal them.'

The Privilege of Discipleship.* 16 [k] "But blessed are your eyes because they see, and your ears because they hear. 17 Amen, I say to you, many prophets and righteous people longed to see what you see but did not see it, and to hear what you hear but did not hear it. [l]

The Explanation of the Parable of the Sower.* 18 [m] "Therefore listen to the parable of the sower. 19 When anyone hears the word of

c Deut 33:9.—d 1-15: Mk 4:1-12; Lk 8:4-10.—e Gen 26:12; Jn 15:8.—f Mt 11:25; Rom 16:25.—g Mt 25:29; Mk 4:25; Lk 8:18; 19:26.—h Deut 29:4; Jer 5:21; Ezek 12:2; Jn 9:39.—i 14-15: Isa 6:9-10; Jn 12:40; Acts 28:26-27; Rom 11:8.—j Mk 4:12; Lk 8 8:10.—k 16-17: Lk 10:23-24; 1 Pet 1:10-12.—l Jn 8:56; Heb 11:13.—m 18-23: Mk 4:13-20; Lk 8:11-15.

12:47 This verse is omitted in some mss.

13:1-52 This is the beginning of the Third Discourse in Matthew's Gospel, which includes seven parables of Jesus about the kingdom of heaven, a plan hidden in God and only incompletely manifested to us (13:10-17, 34f; see Eph 3:4ff). Each parable presents a different aspect of the kingdom and helps us to perceive the multifaceted reality that is growing among us throughout history. However, there is no point in looking for a meaning in every detail of a parable; it is more profitable to look for the essential message.

13:3a *Parables:* stories that are illustrative comparisons between religious truths and events of everyday life. Those told by Jesus are so living, direct, and natural as to be unforgettable. They bear witness to a true poetic and pedagogical genius. The Synoptic Gospels contain some 30 parables. John's Gospel contains no parables but makes good use of other figures of speech.

13:3b-9 At this period, seed was scattered everywhere on as yet uncultivated ground, before any plowing was done and without the sower having a clear idea of whether it would take root. Some seed was wasted, but the sower was not discouraged, knowing that the harvest would come and this was all that counted. In the Old Testament, the harvest was a symbol of the Messianic age (see Ps 126:5-6; Am 9:13).

13:10-15 The parables make use of a language that is clear and rich for those whose heart is open but obscure and deceptive for those whose heart is closed. Already Jesus sees the new community, where his message is richness of life, separating itself from official Judaism, which will lose even that which it has, i.e., its role as custodian of God's Covenant. The Word of Christ always works in a twofold way; it fills those who accept it but leads to the hardening up of those who refuse it.

13:11 *Mysteries:* also translated as "secrets." The word is used in Dan 2:18, 19, 27 and in the Dead Sea Scrolls to designate a divine plan or decree affecting the course of history that can be known only when revealed. In this case, the secret or mystery is that the kingdom is already present in the ministry of Jesus.

13:16-17 The disciples, unlike the unbelieving crowds, have seen and heard what *many prophets and righteous people* of the Old Testament *longed to see . . . and to hear* without having their longing filled.

13:18-23 It is not enough for us to hear the word; we must accept it with all its demands so that it may transform our existence. The four types of persons described in the parable are: (1) those who never accept the *word of the kingdom* (v. 19); (2) those who believe for a while but fall away because of *persecution* (vv. 20-21); (3) those who believe, but in whom the word is choked by *worldly cares* and *the lure of riches* (22); and (4) those who hear *the word* and produce an abundant crop (v. 23).

the kingdom and does not understand it, the evil one comes and snatches away what has been sown in his heart; that is the seed sown on the path.[n] 20 As for the seed sown on rocky ground, this is the one who hears the word and immediately receives it with joy.[o] 21 But such a person has no deep root, and he endures for only a short time. When some trouble or persecution arises on account of the word, he immediately falls away.

22 "The seed sown among thorns is the one who hears the word, but worldly cares and the lure of riches choke the word and it bears no fruit.[p] 23 However, the seed sown in rich soil is the one who hears the word and understands it; he indeed bears fruit and yields a hundred or sixty or thirty times what was sown."[q]

The Parable of the Weeds.* 24 He then proposed another parable to them: "The kingdom of heaven may be compared to a man who sowed good seed in his field. 25 While everyone was asleep, his enemy came, sowed weeds * among the wheat, and then went away. 26 When the wheat sprouted and ripened, the weeds also appeared.

27 "The owner's servants came to him and asked, 'Master, did you not sow good seed in your field? Where then did these weeds come from?' 28 He answered, 'One of my enemies has done this.' The servants then asked him, 'Do you want us to go and pull up the weeds?'

29 "He replied, 'No, because in gathering the weeds you might uproot the wheat along with them. 30 Let them both grow together until the harvest. At harvest time, I will tell the reapers, "Collect the weeds first and tie them in bundles to be burned. Then gather the wheat into my barn." ' "[r]

The Parable of the Mustard Seed.* 31 [s] He proposed still another parable: "The kingdom of heaven is like a mustard seed that a man took and sowed in his field. 32 It is the smallest of all the seeds, but when it has grown it is the greatest of plants and becomes a tree large enough for the birds to come and make nests in its branches." *[t]

The Parable of the Yeast.* 33 And he offered them yet another parable: "The kingdom of heaven is like yeast that a woman took and mixed with three measures of flour until it was completely leavened."[u]

The Use of Parables.* 34 [v] Jesus told the crowds all these things in parables. Indeed he never spoke to them except in parables. 35 This was to fulfill what had been spoken through the prophet:

> "I will open my mouth to speak in parables;
> I will proclaim what has been hidden since the foundation of the world."[w]

Explanation of the Parable of the Weeds.* 36 Then he dismissed the crowds and went into the house. His disciples approached him and said, "Explain to us the parable of the weeds in the field." 37 He answered, "The one who sows good seed is the Son of Man. 38 The field is the world, and the good seed stands for the children of the kingdom. The weeds are the children of the evil one,[x] 39 and the enemy who sowed them is the devil. The harvest is the end of the world, and the reapers are angels.[y]

40 "Just as the weeds are collected and burned in the fire, so will it be at the end of the world. 41 The Son of Man will send forth his angels, and they will gather out of his kingdom all who cause sin and all whose deeds are evil. 42 They will throw them into

n Deut 30:14.—o 1 Thes 1:6.—p Jer 4:3.—q Gal 5:22; Jn 15:8, 16.—r Mt 3:12; Jn 15:6.—s 31-32: Mk 4:30-32; Lk 13:18-19.—t Ps 104:12; Ezek 17:23; 31:6; Dan 4:7-9, 17-19.—u Gen 18:6; Lk 13:20-21.—v 34-35: Mk 4:33-34.—w Ps 78:2; Rom 16:25, 26.—x 1 Jn 3:10.—y Joel 4:13; Rev 14:15.

13:24-30 The parable of the weeds is proper to Matthew. Through it Jesus teaches that the Last Judgment (of which the "harvest" is a common metaphor), i.e., the separation of the good from the wicked, is to be awaited with patience. The explanation is given in Mt 13:37-43.

13:25 *Weeds:* probably darnel, which looks very much like wheat while it is young, but can later be distinguished.

13:31-32 The mustard seed is the smallest one used by the Palestinian farmers and gardeners of that day, but it could reach a height of some ten or twelve feet. Thus, the kingdom of heaven, notwithstanding the humble ministry of Jesus, is already dawning and in the end will be shown in all its magnificence.

13:32 *Tree . . . its branches:* an allusion to Dan 4:21, indicating that the kingdom of heaven will become worldwide and people from all nations will find refuge therein (see also Ezek 17:23; 31:6; Dan 2:35, 44f; 7:27; Rev 11:15).

13:33 The parable of the yeast is an invitation to faith in the efficacy of the ministry of Jesus. Despite its modest and unspectacular character, it constitutes a stage in the eschatological coming of the kingdom of God. The greatness of the kingdom is shown by the enormous amount of flour, enough to feed well over a hundred people.

13:34-35 Matthew stresses that Jesus speaks in parables to reveal God and his kingdom; in this way he shows that the Messiah fulfills the Scriptures. The "prophet" is, in this case, the psalmist (see Ps 78:2).

13:36-43 The explanation of the parable of the weeds stresses the Last Judgment in which Christ and those who have believed in him will triumph over the forces of evil. It thus teaches one to be converted without delay and to remain steadfast in faith till the end.

the fiery furnace, where there will be weep-
ing and gnashing of teeth. [z] 43 Then the righ-
teous will shine like the sun in the kingdom
of their Father. He who has ears to hear, let
him hear! [a]

**The Parables of the Hidden Treasure and the
Pearl.*** 44 [b] "The kingdom of heaven is like
treasure buried in a field, which a man
found and buried again. Then in his joy he
went off and sold everything he had and
bought that field.

45 "Again, the kingdom of heaven is like a
merchant searching for fine pearls. 46 When
he found one of great value, he went off and
sold everything he had and bought it.

The Parable of the Net.* 47 "Again, the king-
dom of heaven is like a net cast into the sea
where it caught fish of every kind. 48 When it
was full, they hauled it ashore. Then they sat
down and collected the good fish into baskets
but discarded those that were worthless.
49 Thus will it be at the end of the world. The
angels will go forth and separate the wicked
from the righteous [c] 50 and throw them into
the fiery furnace, where there will be weep-
ing and gnashing of teeth. [d]

Conclusion.* 51 "Have you understood all
this?" he asked. They answered, "Yes."
52 Then he said to them, "Therefore, every
teacher of the law who has been instructed
about the kingdom of heaven is like the
owner of a house who brings forth from his
storeroom new treasures as well as old."

IV: THE AUTHENTIC FAITH OF THOSE CONVERTED*

A: Jesus Encounters Mixed Receptions*

Jesus Is Rejected at Nazareth.* 53 When Jesus
had finished these parables, he departed
from that district.

54 [e] He came to his hometown, and he
began to teach the people in the synagogue.
They were astonished and wondered,
"Where did this man get such wisdom and
these mighty deeds? [f] 55 Is this not the car-
penter's son? Is not his mother called Mary?
Are not James and Joseph and Simon and
Judas his brethren? [g] 56 And are not all his
sisters here with us? Where then did this
man get all this?" 57 And so they took offense
at him.

But Jesus said to them, "A prophet is
always treated with honor except in his
hometown and in his own house." [h] 58 And he
did not work many mighty deeds there
because of their lack of faith. [i]

CHAPTER 14

John the Baptist, Herod, and Jesus.* 1 [j] At that
time Herod the tetrarch* heard reports

z Mt 8:12; Rev 21:8.—a Dan 12:3.—b 44-45: Mt 19:21; Prov 2:4; 4:7.—c Mt 25:32.—d Mt 8:12.—e 54-58: Mk 6:1-6; Lk 4:16-30.—f Mt 2:23; Jn 1:46; 7:15.—g Mt 12:46; 27:56; Lk 3:23; Jn 6:42.—h Mk 6:5.—i Mt 8:10.—j 1-12: Mk 6:14-29.

13:44-46 The parables of the hidden treasure and the pearl reveal the hidden character of the kingdom of heaven and its great worth. It represents the supreme value to which human beings must aspire.

13:47-50 The parable of the net repeats the teaching of the parable of the weeds, with its emphasis upon the final exclusion of the wicked from the kingdom. It thus calls for an authentic conversion on the part of the listeners.

13:51-52 To those who believe, the parables reveal God's mysterious plan for human beings. Thus, the teacher of the law, the scribe, once he has become a disciple, knows how to see the link between the Old and the New Testaments and is enriched by their basic harmony.

13:53—18:35 A new and tragic phase in the life of Jesus, and therefore also in the life of the kingdom, begins here and illustrates the accounts and words of this fourth part of the Gospel. The drama is infused with a growing intensity. Christ hides himself from the enthusiasm of the crowds who want him to embrace their hope for national freedom. This stirs up hostility and leads to defection. The kingdom that he proclaims is suspect in the eyes of the defenders of legalism and traditions; not even his disciples have a good understanding of the life that he teaches. Powerless, they live under this tension, which prepares for the Passion, and their incredulity will even contribute to it; but they still remain the core of the new community of believers.

13:53—17:27 The main purpose of this section is to place the Person of Jesus at the center of the mystery of the kingdom of God. The evangelist shows Jesus receiving a mixed reception, beginning with his rejection at Nazareth and the execution of the Baptist (Mt 13:53—14:12). He then alludes to the Eucharistic mystery in the accounts of the multiplication of the loaves (Mt 14:19; 15:36), and the walking on the water (Mt 14:22-33). Finally, he reports the doctrinal conflict between Jesus and the religious authorities (Mt 15:1-20) and raises anew the question of the sign of Jonah (Mt 16:1-4; see note on Mt 12:38ff). This sign will later be explained as referring to the Passion, Death, and Resurrection of Jesus (Mt 16:21ff), which must occur before the kingdom of God reaches a new stage (Mt 16:28). This is the message of the Scriptures (Mt 17:5).

13:53-58 At Nazareth, everyone knows the mother of Jesus and his brothers and sisters, i.e., his closest relatives, as it was customary to say in those days (see note on Mt 12:46). He thus has his place in this little village. But how can the villagers be expected to acknowledge the Messiah in one of their compatriots? God's action and word manifested among men is the mystery of the Incarnation; this seems too human. Even the believer might hesitate in believing in the Lord present among us, in the places and times in which daily life unfolds.

14:1-12 At the ominous banquet in the fortress of Machaerus we find various members of the family of Herod. Antipas was the second-born of Herod the Great and ruled over Galilee and Perea. We come upon him several times in the New Testament (Lk 9:7; 23:7; Acts 4:27); Caligula will exile him to Gaul in A.D. 39. His half-brother Philip died in Rome without ever attaining political power. Herodias, niece of both men and wife of Philip, was ambitious and desired to be the wife of a ruler.

14:1 *Tetrarch:* ruler of one quarter of the kingdom of his father, Herod the Great.

about Jesus,[k] 2 and he said to his servants,
"This man is John the Baptist. He has risen
from the dead. That is why such powers are
at work in him."

3 [l]Now Herod had ordered the arrest of
John, put him in chains, and imprisoned
him on account of Herodias, his brother
Philip's wife. 4 For John had told him, "It is
against the law for you to have her."[m]

5 Herod wanted to put John to death, but
he was afraid of the people because they
regarded John as a prophet.[n] 6 But at a
birthday celebration for Herod, the daugh-
ter of Herodias * danced in front of the
guests, and she pleased Herod so much
7 that he promised with an oath to give her
anything she asked for. 8 Prompted by her
mother, she said, "Give me here the head of
John the Baptist on a platter."

9 The king was distressed, but because of
his oaths and the guests present there, he
ordered that her request be granted. 10 He
had John beheaded in the prison. *[o] 11 The
head was brought in on a platter and given
to the girl, who took it to her mother.
12 John's disciples came and removed the
body and buried it. Then they went and told
Jesus.[p]

Jesus Feeds Five Thousand Men. 13 *[q] When
Jesus received this news, he withdrew from
there in a boat by himself to a deserted
place, but when the people learned of it,
they followed him on foot from the towns. *
14 When he came ashore and saw the vast
crowd, he had compassion on them and
healed those who were sick.

15 When evening approached, the disciples
came up to him and said, "This is a desert-
ed place and the hour is now late. Send the
people away now so that they can go to the
villages to buy some food for themselves."
16 Jesus replied, "There is no need for them
to depart. Give them something to eat your-
selves." 17 But they answered, "All we have
here are five loaves of bread and two fish."
18 Jesus said, "Bring them here to me."

19 Then he ordered the people to sit down
on the grass. Taking the five loaves and the
two fish, he looked up to heaven, blessed and
broke the loaves, and gave them to the disci-
ples, and the disciples gave them to the
crowds. *[r] 20 They all ate and were satisfied.
Then they gathered up the fragments that
were left over—twelve full baskets. 21 Those
who had eaten numbered about five thou-
sand men, in addition to women and chil-
dren. *

Jesus Walks on the Water.* 22 [s]Then Jesus
instructed the disciples to get into the boat
and go on ahead to the other side while he
dismissed the crowds. 23 After he sent them
away, he went by himself up on the moun-
tain to pray. When evening came, he was
there alone.[t] 24 Meanwhile, the boat was
already some distance from the shore, bat-
tered by waves and a strong wind.

k Mk 8:15; Lk 3:1.—l 3-4: Mt 4:12; Lk 3:19-20.—m Lev 18:16; 20:21.—n Mt 11:9; 21:26.—o Mt 17:12.—p Acts 8:2.—q 13-21: Mt 15:32-38; Mk 6:32-44; Lk 9:10-17; Jn 6:1-13.—r 2 Ki 4:42-44.—s 22-33: Mk 6:45-51; Jn 6:15-21.—t Mk 1:35; Lk 3:21; 5:16; 6:12.

14:6 *The daughter of Herodias:* her name was Salome, as we are told by the Jewish historian Flavius Josephus.

14:10 The beheading of the Baptist probably occurred in A.D. 29 in the fortress of Machaerus, east of the Dead Sea, as is attested by Flavius Josephus.

14:13—16:12 Exegetes have named this the "Section of the Loaves" because of the frequency with which the word "bread" is used therein. It seems to symbolize the teaching and salvific acts of Jesus, with a particular reference to the founding of the Church.

14:13-21 At the time of the temptation in the desert, Jesus had refused to renew the miracle of the manna either for himself or to attain his own success. Moreover, six times in the Gospels (two of which are in Matthew) we read an account like this one. Thus, the first generation of Christians attached a particular importance to the deed. It is first of all an act of mercy, a sign of the goodness of God, who satisfies material and spiritual hunger at the last days. It is also the manifestation of Jesus as the new Moses, as the new founder of the people—he too feeds the crowd in the desert (Ex 16); he acts like the great men of God such as Elisha (2 Ki 4:42-44). In addition, something even more mysterious is part of this extraordinary moment. How can one not discern in this account a climate of Liturgy? For Christians the giving of bread announces the joy of the Eucharist: the Lord present in the assembly, satisfying every hunger with the Bread of Life that is himself (see Jn 6).

14:19 Note the resemblance of this verse to that of the institution of the Eucharist (Mt 26:26). Obviously in the eyes of the primitive Church this meal was a prelude and prefiguration of the Eucharistic banquet, which in its turn recalls the Messianic banquet. Particularly allusive are the breaking of the bread and the action of the disciples in distributing the bread.

14:21 *In addition to women and children:* women and children were not permitted to eat with men in public. Hence they were in a place by themselves and would greatly increase the number given for the men: 5000!

14:22-33 For people of the Bible, raging waves and the dead of night evoke the forces hostile to God and his faithful. In calming the storm, Jesus has manifested himself as the master of the powers of evil. To follow him means to escape from their clutches. This is a dangerous path at times in which we must risk everything for him because it is he. "It is I," he says, and in these words any Christian, after the Ascension and Resurrection, would detect echoes of "I am," the decisive self-disclosure of God (Ex 3:14; Isa 43:10; 51:12). In Peter himself, the first among the disciples, we discern the drama of every believer: strong when he entrusts himself totally to the Lord, yet threatened and uncertain when he does not take refuge in him alone.

25 During the fourth watch * of the night, Jesus came toward them, walking on the water. 26 When the disciples saw him walking on the water they were terrified, and they cried out in their fright, "It is a ghost!" 27 But Jesus immediately spoke to them, saying, "Have courage! It is I. Do not be afraid." [u]

28 Peter answered, "Lord, if it is you, command me to come to you across the water." 29 He said, "Come!" Then Peter got out of the boat and started walking on the water toward Jesus. 30 [v] But when he realized the force of the wind, he became frightened. As he began to sink, he cried out, "Lord, save me!" 31 Jesus immediately reached out his hand and caught hold of him, saying, "O you of little faith, why did you doubt?" 32 After they got into the boat, the wind died down. 33 Those in the boat fell to their knees in worship, saying, "Truly you are the Son of God." * [w]

Jesus Heals the Sick at Gennesaret. 34 [x] After they had completed the crossing, they landed at Gennesaret. * 35 When the people there recognized him, they sent word of his presence throughout the region. They also brought him all those who were sick 36 and begged him to let them touch only the edge of his cloak. All who touched it were completely healed. [y]

CHAPTER 15

Traditions That Falsify the Law of God. 1 [z] Then Pharisees and scribes came to Jesus from Jerusalem and asked, 2 * "Why do your disciples ignore the tradition of the elders? They do not wash their hands before eating." [a] 3 He answered them, "And why do you break the commandment of God for the sake of your tradition? 4 For God said, 'Honor your father and your mother,' and 'Whoever curses his father or mother shall be put to death.' [b] 5 But you say, 'If anyone says to his father or mother, "Anything I might have used for your support is dedicated to God," 6 then he is excused from his duty to honor his father or mother.' To uphold your tradition you have made God's word null and void. 7 You hypocrites! How rightly did Isaiah prophesy about you when he said:

8 'This people honors me with their lips,
but their hearts are far from me; [c]
9 in vain do they worship me,
teaching as doctrines the commandments of men.' " [d]

Clean and Unclean.* 10 Then he called the people to him and said to them, "Listen and understand. [e] 11 It is not what goes into one's mouth that defiles a person; what comes out of the mouth is what defiles him." [f]

12 The disciples approached and said to him, "Do you realize that the Pharisees were greatly offended when they heard what you said?" 13 He answered, "Every plant that my Father has not planted will be uprooted. [g] 14 Leave them alone. They are blind guides. And if one blind person guides another, they will both fall into a pit." [h]

15 Peter said to him, "Explain that parable to us." [i] 16 Jesus replied, "Are even you still without understanding? 17 Do you not realize that whatever goes into the mouth passes through the stomach and is discharged into the sewer? 18 But what comes out of the mouth originates in the heart, and this is

u Mt 9:2; Acts 23:11.—v 30-31: Mt 6:30; 8:25-26.—w Mt 16:16; Ps 2:7.—x 34-36: Mk 6:53-56.—y Mt 9:20-22.—z 1-20: Mk 7:1-23.—a Lk 11:38; Gal 1:14; Col 2:8.—b Ex 20:12; 21:17; Lev 20:9; Deut 5:16; Prov 20:20; Lk 18:20.—c Ps 78:37; Isa 29:13 LXX.—d Mal 2:2; Col 2:23.—e Mk 7:14.—f Mt 12:34; Acts 10:14.—g Jn 15:2; Acts 5:38.—h Mt 23:16, 19, 24; Lk 6:39; Jn 9:40; Rom 2:19.—i Mk 4:13.

14:25 *Fourth watch:* 3:00–6:00 A.M. The Romans divided the night into four watches: (1) 6:00–9:00 P.M., (2) 9:00–midnight, (3) midnight–3:00 A.M., (4) 3:00–6:00 A.M. The Jews divided the night into three watches: (1) sunset–10:00 P.M., (2) 10:00 P.M–2:00 A.M., (3) 2:00–sunrise. Apparently, the apostles labored for several hours against the storm waves. Their enthusiasm of the previous evening for an overly earthly Messianism had greatly evaporated in the face of hard labor and the fear of being shipwrecked.

14:33 *Son of God:* the apostles probably used this title in a Messianic way (see Mt 3:17; 11:25-30) but with superficial understanding. Since Jesus' divine nature was hidden during his life on earth, the disciples did not yet grasp his divinity at this time (Phil 2:5-8). But they were beginning to realize that he was the Messiah.

14:34 *Gennesaret:* the plain northwest of the lake of the same name.

15:2ff The "oral" tradition consisted of practices and regulations meant to fill out the written Law of Moses; many Pharisaic Jews did not hesitate to claim that this tradition, like the Torah, had been revealed on Sinai. The oral tradition allowed for a vow by which a man could free himself from his obligations to his own parents: the material goods meant for them were promised to God and thus declared "sacred offerings."

15:10-20 Every ancient religion attempted to distinguish clearly the two notions of clean and unclean as regards objects and affairs of life. The Book of Leviticus proposes a developed code of ritual purity, which was above all a way of expressing the grandeur of God and of establishing laws of respect in the behavior of human beings. However, as time went on, this great inspiration was lost in a soulless formalism. In the tightly regulated life of the Jews of the first century A.D., the dispositions of the heart held such a small place that even the apostles have trouble understanding the teaching of Jesus. He unmasks hypocrisy. How can one not be shocked by his words, which overturn even the religious assurance of humans!

what defiles a person.[j] 19 For from the heart come evil thoughts, murder, adultery, fornication, theft, perjury, slander.[k] 20 These are the things that defile a person, but to eat with unwashed hands does not make anyone unclean."

The Faith of a Pagan Woman.* 21 [l]Jesus then left that place and withdrew to the region of Tyre and Sidon. * 22 And behold, a Canaanite woman from that region came out to meet him and cried out, "Have pity on me, Lord, Son of David. My daughter is sorely tormented by a demon."[m] 23 But he did not say a word to her in reply.

So his disciples came and urged him, "Send her away, for she keeps shouting after us."[n] 24 He answered, "I was sent only to the lost sheep of the house of Israel."[o] 25 But she came and knelt at his feet, saying, "Lord, help me!" 26 He answered, "It is not right to take the children's bread and throw it to the dogs." 27 She replied, "Yes, Lord, but even the dogs eat the scraps that fall from their masters' table." 28 Then Jesus answered her, "Woman, you have great faith. Let it be done for you as you wish." And from that moment her daughter was healed.[p]

Jesus Heals Many People. 29 * After leaving that region, Jesus walked along the shores of the Sea of Galilee, and going up onto the mountain, he sat down.[q] 30 Large crowds flocked to him, bringing with them the lame, the blind, the deformed, the mute, and many others. They placed them at his feet, and he cured them.[r] 31 The crowds were amazed when they observed the mute speaking, the crippled made whole, the lame walking, and the blind with their sight restored, and they gave praise to the God of Israel.[s]

Jesus Feeds Four Thousand Men. 32 [t]Jesus called his disciples to him and said, "I am moved with compassion for these people, because they have been with me now for three days and have nothing to eat. I do not want to send them away hungry, or they may collapse on the way."

33 The disciples said to him, "Where can we ever get enough bread in this deserted place to feed such a great crowd?"[u] 34 Jesus asked them, "How many loaves do you have?" "Seven," they replied, "and a few small fish."

35 He ordered the crowd to sit down on the ground. 36 Then he took the seven loaves and the fish, and after giving thanks he broke them and gave them to the disciples, and the disciples gave them to the people. 37 They all ate and were satisfied. Afterward, they picked up seven baskets full of what remained.[v] 38 Those who had eaten numbered four thousand men, not counting women and children. 39 And when he had sent away the crowds, he got into the boat and went to the region of Magadan.

CHAPTER 16

The Demand for a Sign.* 1 [w]The Pharisees and Sadducees came, and to put him to the test they asked him to show them a sign from heaven.[x] 2 He answered them, "When it is evening, you say, 'Tomorrow there will be fair weather, for the sky is red,' 3 and in the morning you say, 'It will be stormy today, for the sky is red and threatening.' You know how to interpret the appearance of the sky, but you cannot interpret the signs of the times.[y] 4 An evil and adulterous * generation asks for a sign, but no sign will be given to it except the sign of Jonah." Then he left them and went away.[z]

The Yeast of the Pharisees and Sadducees.* 5 [a]In crossing to the other side of the lake, the disciples had forgotten to bring bread.

j Mt 12:34; Jas 3:6.—k Gal 5:19-21.—l 21-28: Mk 7:24-30.—m Mt 9:27.—n Lk 11:8.—o Mt 10:6; Rom 15:8.—p Mt 8:10.—q Mk 7:31.—r Isa 35:5-6.—s Mk 7:37.—t 32-39: Mk 8:1-10.—u 2 Ki 4:43.—v Mt 16:10; Ps 78:29.—w 1-10: Mk 8:11-21.—x Mt 12:38; Jn 6:30.—y Lk 12:54-56.—z Mt 12:39; Jon 2:1.—a 5-12: Mk 8:14-21.

15:21-28 The Israelites regarded themselves as *children* of God because they were heirs of the promises made to the patriarchs and depositaries of the divine revelation. On the contrary, they called the Gentiles *dogs* out of contempt for their idolatrous and immoral practices. Jesus makes use of these two terms but softens the second, which in the Greek is "little dogs," i.e., pet dogs in the home. His point was that the Gospel was to be offered first to the Jews. The woman understood his implication and was willing to settle for the "crumbs." Jesus rewarded her faith.

15:21-22 *Tyre* and *Sidon:* these were Phoenician cities; *Canaanite* was the ancient name of their populations.

15:29-39 This second miracle of the loaves has many analogies with the first multiplication of the loaves. Therefore, some exegetes speak of a duplication, i.e., a different reporting of the same episode. However, there are so many diverse circumstances in the two episodes that Matthew and Mark believe in two distinct miracles.

16:1-4 The preaching, works, and extraordinary miracles of Jesus constituted a convincing proof of his Messiahship. The Pharisees and Sadducees demand *a sign from heaven,* like the stopping of the sun. Jesus flatly refuses to do so. He offers only *the sign of Jonah,* which foreshadows the mystery of his Death and Resurrection (see Mt 12:38-42).

16:4 *Adulterous:* i.e., unfaithful to the Lord.

16:5-12 The disciples at first misunderstand their Master, for whom the nourishment of humans is not reduced to bread alone. Jesus wishes to preserve his own from legalism. The yeast of the Pharisees and Sadducees is the rigid teaching of specialists of religion who snuff out freedom, joy, spontaneity, and commitment.

[6]Jesus said to them, "Be careful, and beware
of the yeast of the Pharisees and Sad-
ducees."[b] [7]They talked about this among
themselves and concluded: "It is because we
brought no bread."

[8]Aware of what they were saying, Jesus
said, "O you of little faith, why are you talk-
ing about having no bread? [9]Do you still not
understand? Do you not remember the five
loaves for the five thousand and the number
of baskets you collected? [c] [10]Or the seven
loaves for the four thousand and how many
baskets you gathered? [d] [11]How could you fail
to see that I was not speaking about bread
when I said, 'Beware of the yeast of the
Pharisees and Sadducees'?" [12]Then they
understood that he had not told them to
beware of the yeast used in bread but of the
teaching of the Pharisees and Sadducees.

Peter's Confession of Christ's Divinity.
[13]* [e]When Jesus came to the region of
Caesarea Philippi, * he asked his disciples,
"Who do people say that the Son of Man is?"
[14]They replied, "Some say John the Baptist;
others, Elijah; and still others, Jeremiah or
one of the Prophets."[f] [15]"But you," he said
to them, "who do you say that I am?"
[16]Simon Peter replied, "You are the Christ,
the Son of the living God." *[g]

[17]Then Jesus said to him in reply,
"Blessed are you, Simon son of Jonah. For
flesh and blood * has not revealed this to
you but my heavenly Father. [h] [18]And I say
to you: You are Peter, and on this rock I will
build my Church,* and the gates of the
netherworld will not prevail against it. [i] [19]I
will give you the keys of the kingdom of
heaven. Whatever you bind on earth shall
be bound in heaven, and whatever you
loose on earth shall be loosed in heav-
en." *[j] [20]Then he gave the disciples strict
orders not to tell * anyone that he was the
Christ. [k]

Jesus Predicts His Passion. [21] [l]From then
onward Jesus made it clear to his disciples
that he must go to Jerusalem and endure
great suffering at the hands of the elders,
the chief priests, and the scribes, and be
put to death, and be raised on the third
day. * [m]

[22]* Peter took him aside and began to
rebuke him, saying, "God forbid, Lord.
Such a fate must never happen to you."
[23]He turned and said to Peter, "Get behind
me, Satan! You are an obstacle to me. You
are thinking not as God does, but as men
do." [n]

The Conditions of Discipleship. [24]Jesus then
said to his disciples, "Anyone who wishes to
follow me must deny himself, take up his

b Lk 12:1.—c Mt 14:17-21; Mk 4:13; Jn 6:9.—d Mt 15:34-38.—e 13-16: Mk 8:27-29; Lk 9:18-20.—f Mt 14:2; Mk 6:15; Jn 1:21.—g Mt 4:3; Jn 6:69; Ps 42:3.—h 1 Cor 15:50.—i Job 38:17; Jn 1:42.—j Jn 20:23; Isa 22:22; Rev 3:7.—k Mk 8:30; Lk 9:21.—l 21-28: Mk 8:31—9:1; Lk 9:22-27.—m Mt 17:22-23; 20:17-19; Lk 9:51; 13:33; Acts 10:40.—n Mt 4:10.

16:13ff Following the section of the bread (Mt 14:13—16:12), the evangelist appends a series of episodes that have to do with the revelation of the mystery of Christ. In addition to the text taken from Mark, which sets forth the theology of the Messianic secret and the suffering Servant, he presents the passages that speak of the primacy of Peter (Mt 16:17-19) and the payment of the temple tax (Mt 17:24-27), thus highlighting the theme of the foundation of the Church. The new People of God will then rise not from a Messianic triumphalism but from the mysterious drama of the Messiah's Passion and Resurrection.

16:13 *Caesarea Philippi* had been built by Herod Philip near the springs of the Jordan, at the foot of Mount Hermon. The name "Caesarea" was given as an act of homage to the Roman Emperor; since so many cities had the name, some further qualifier had to be added ("Philip's Caesarea"). "Caesarea in Palestine," to take one example, was the ordinary residence of the governor (see Acts 23).

16:16 *The Son of the living God:* in addition to the Messiahship of Jesus found in the other Synoptics at this point, Matthew also has an acknowledgment by Peter of Jesus' divinity. Many exegetes believe this is an addition based on Peter's later understanding of the mystery of Christ after the risen Lord appeared to him (see 1 Cor 15:5; Lk 24:34). In any case, Matthew has already mentioned that all the disciples had recognized the divinity of Christ (Mt 14:33).

16:17 *Flesh and blood:* a Scriptural expression that designates human beings in their weak and fragile condition. *Has not revealed this to you but my heavenly Father:* the source of Peter's confession of Christ's divinity is the heavenly Father.

16:18 *You are Peter, and on this rock I will build my Church:* the Aramaic word for "rock" (*kepa*) is transliterated into Greek as *Cephas*, the name used for Peter in the Pauline letters (1 Cor 1:12; Gal 1:18), and is translated as "Peter" in Jn 1:42. *Church:* a word that occurs only here and in Mt 18:17 (twice) in the New Testament. The Church will have Peter as her foundation stone. But of course her real foundation is faith in Jesus, the Son of God. Peter will have the primacy among all the apostles and be the visible head of the Church, as will his successors, the Popes. *The gates of the netherworld* designate the powers of death. The Church will resist all the vicissitudes of time because of her foundation on a rock.

16:19 Receiving the power of the *keys*, symbol of authority, Peter becomes Christ's representative on earth. He is given the power to *bind* and *loose*, i.e., to condemn or absolve, to prohibit or allow. Peter is the *doorkeeper* (Mk 13:34) but not the *Teacher* or the *Father* (Mt 23:9-10).

16:20 *Not to tell:* since the Jews were looking for a national and political Messiah, Jesus urged his disciples not to tell anyone that he was the Messiah.

16:21 The apostles now knew that Jesus was the Messiah, but their idea of it was inexact. They thought of a political Messiah, the glorious dominator of peoples. Jesus offers a triple prediction that spells out the last stages of his ministry. He thus prepares them for the scandal of the cross (see Mt 17:22f; 20:17f) and enlightens them concerning the true Messianism, which is spiritual, humble, and suffering.

16:22-23 Peter unknowingly offers Jesus the facile and worldly Messianism that would put him in opposition to the will of the Father. He unwittingly repeats the temptation of Satan at the beginning of Christ's ministry (Mt 4:1-11).

cross, and follow me. [o] [25] For whoever wishes to save his life will lose it, but whoever loses his life for my sake will find it. * [p] [26] What will it profit a man if he gains the whole world and forfeits his very life? Or what can he give in exchange for his life?

[27] "For the Son of Man will come with his angels in the glory of his Father, and then he will repay everyone according to what has been done. [q] [28] Amen, I say to you, there are some standing here who will not taste death before they see the Son of Man coming in his kingdom." *

CHAPTER 17

Jesus Is Transfigured.* [1] [r] Six days later, Jesus took Peter and James and his brother John and led them up a high mountain * by themselves. [2] And in their presence he was transfigured; his face shone like the sun, and his clothes became dazzling white. [s] [3] Suddenly, there appeared to them Moses and Elijah, conversing with him. [4] [t] Then Peter said to Jesus, "Lord, it is good for us to be here. If you wish, I will make three tents here—one for you, one for Moses, and one for Elijah."

[5] While he was still speaking, suddenly a bright cloud cast a shadow over them. Then a voice from the cloud said, "This is my beloved Son, with whom I am well pleased. Listen to him." [6] When the disciples heard this, they fell on their faces and were greatly frightened. [7] But Jesus came and touched them, saying, "Stand up, and do not be frightened." [8] And when they raised their eyes, they saw no one, but only Jesus.

Elijah Has Already Come.* [9] [u] As they were coming down from the mountain, Jesus commanded them, "Tell no one about this vision until the Son of Man has been raised from the dead." [10] And the disciples asked him, "Why then do the scribes say that Elijah must come first?" [11] He said in reply, "Elijah will indeed come, and he will set everything right again. [v] [12] [w] However, I tell you that Elijah has already come, and they did not recognize him, but they did to him whatever they pleased. In the same way, the Son of Man will suffer at their hands." [13] Then the disciples understood that he was speaking to them about John the Baptist.

Jesus Heals a Boy with a Demon.* [14] [x] When they returned to the crowd, a man came up to Jesus, fell to his knees before him, [15] and pleaded, "Lord, have pity on my son, for he is subject to epileptic seizures and endures great suffering. He falls often into fire and often into water. [16] I brought him to your disciples, but they could not cure him."

[17] Jesus said in reply, "O unbelieving and perverse generation, how much longer shall I remain with you? How much longer must I put up with you? Bring the boy here to me." [y] [18] Then Jesus rebuked the demon, and it came out of the boy, and he was cured from that very moment.

[19] Then the disciples came to Jesus and asked him privately, "Why were we not able to cast it out?" [20] He answered, "Because you have such little faith. Amen, I say to you, if you have faith as tiny as a mustard seed, you will be able to say to this mountain: 'Move from here to there,' and it will move. Nothing will be impossible for you. [z] [[21] But this kind of demon does not come out except by prayer and fasting.]" *

Jesus Predicts His Passion a Second Time.* [22] When they were together in Galilee, Jesus

o Mt 10:38; Lk 14:27; 2 Cor 4:10-11.—p Lk 17:33; Jn 12:25.—q Mt 25:31-33; Job 34:11; Ps 62:13; Jer 17:10; Ezek 18:20; Jn 14:3; Rom 2:6; 2 Thes 1:7-8.—r 1-8: Mk 9:2-8; Lk 9:28-36; 2 Pet 1:16-18.—s Mt 28:3; Dan 7:9; 10:6; Rev 4:4; 7:9; 19:14.—t 4-5: Mt 3:17; Ex 13:22; 19:16; Deut 18:15; Isa 42:1; 2 Pet 1:17.—u 9-13: Mk 1:34; 9:9-13.—v Lk 1:17; Mal 4:23-24.—w 12-13: Mt 3:1; 11:14.—x 14-21: Mk 9:14-29; Lk 9:37-43.—y Deut 32:5 LXX; Acts 2:40; Phil 2:15.—z Mt 21:21; Mk 11:22-23; Lk 17:6; 1 Cor 13:2.

16:25 In order to receive eternal life, one must be ready to bear any sacrifice—even the renunciation of earthly life. The Greek word for "life" means either "life" or "soul;" also in v. 26.

16:28 Coming after v. 27, which alludes to the Second Coming of Christ, i.e., as Judge at the end of the world, this verse may refer to the destruction of Jerusalem in A.D. 70, which came to be regarded as a punishment from God for the refusal of the Jews to accept Jesus as the Messiah. The verse may also refer to Christ's Resurrection and his appearances thereafter as well as to the Transfiguration, which is a manifestation of his glory.

17:1-8 At the Transfiguration, the same voice that at the moment of his Baptism had indicated to Jesus the way of a suffering Messianism now manifests him as the true Messiah to the three apostles who would witness his agony in the garden. For a few seconds Jesus' humanity is resplendent with the divine glory of which he had divested himself during his earthly life.

17:1 *A high mountain:* since the 4th century, this has been identified with Tabor (1843 feet high) on the Plain of Esdraelon.

17:9-13 According to an ancient story, Elijah was assumed into heaven, while a prophecy claimed that he would return to prepare the people for the Messianic Age (see Mal 3:23-24; Sir 48:1-11).

17:14-21 This miracle has the purpose of highlighting the power of Jesus against the power of Satan, thus erasing all doubts that Jesus is the Messiah. Jesus states with some disappointment that not even his disciples have attained true faith.

17:21 This verse is missing in the most important manuscripts and seems to be taken from Mk 9:29.

17:22-23 This is the second of Christ's three predictions of his Passion (see Mt 16:21-23) and the least detailed. The disciples are *overwhelmed with grief.*

said to them, "The Son of Man is going to be
handed over into the power of men. [a] 23 They
will kill him, and on the third day he will be
raised." And they were overwhelmed with
grief.

Jesus Pays the Temple Tax.* 24 When they
arrived at Capernaum, the collectors of the
temple tax came up to Peter and asked,
"Doesn't your teacher pay the temple tax?" [b]
25 "Yes, he does," he replied.

When Peter went into the house, but
before he had a chance to speak, Jesus asked
him, "Simon, what is your opinion? From
whom do the kings of the earth exact tolls
and taxes—from their own sons or from
others?" [c] 26 And when he said, "From
others," Jesus replied, "Then their sons are
exempt. 27 However, lest we give offense to
them, go to the lake and cast a hook. Take
the first fish that you catch and open its
mouth. There you will find a silver coin. Take
it and give it to them for me and for your-
self." [d]

B: Instructions to the Disciples: The Charter of the Community*

CHAPTER 18

Become Like Little Children.* 1 [e] At that time,
the disciples came to Jesus and asked, "Who
is the greatest in the kingdom of heaven?" [f]
2 Then Jesus beckoned a child to come to
him, placed it in their midst, 3 and said,
"Amen, I say to you, unless you change and
become like little children, you will never
enter the kingdom of heaven. [g] 4 Whoever
humbles himself and becomes like this child
is the greatest in the kingdom of heaven. [h]

Woe to the World because of Scandals.*
5 "And whoever receives one such child in
my name receives me. 6 [i] But if anyone caus-
es one of these little ones who believe in me
to sin, it would be better for him to have a
millstone fastened around his neck and to be
drowned in the depths of the sea. 7 Woe to
the world because of scandals. Such things
are bound to occur, but woe to the one
through whom they come.

8 * [j] "If your hand or your foot is an occa-
sion of sin for you, cut it off and throw it
away. It is preferable for you to enter into life
maimed or crippled than to have two hands
or two feet and be cast into the eternal fire.
9 And if your eye causes you to sin, tear it out
and throw it away. It is preferable for you to
enter into life with one eye than to have two
eyes and be cast into the fires of Gehenna.

10 [k] "Take care that you do not despise one
of these little ones, for I tell you that their
angels in heaven gaze continually on the face
of my heavenly Father. [l] [11 For the Son of
Man has come to save what was lost.] *

The Parable of the Lost Sheep.* 12 "Tell me
your opinion. If a man owns a hundred
sheep and one of them wanders away, will he
not leave the other ninety-nine on the hill-
side and go off in search of the one who went
astray? [m] 13 And if he finds it, amen, I say to
you, he is more filled with joy over it than
over the ninety-nine who did not wander off.
14 In the same way, it is not the will of your
Father in heaven that a single one of these
little ones should be lost. [n]

a 22-23: Mt 16:21; 20:18-19; Acts 10:40.—b Ex 30:11-16; Neh 10:33.—c Rom 13:7.—d Jn 6:61.—e 1-5: Mk 9:33-37; Lk 9:46-48.—f Lk 22:24.—g Mt 19:14; Mk 10:15; Lk 18:17; 1 Pet 2:2.—h Mt 23:12.—i 6-7: Mk 9:37, 42; Lk 17:1-2.—j 8-9: Mt 5:29-30; Mk 9:43-47.—k 10-14: Lk 15:3-7; Ezek 34:1-3, 16.—l Gen 48:16; Ps 34:8.—m Lk 19:10; Ezek 34:4, 16.—n Jn 6:39.

17:24-27 On reaching the age of twenty, every Jew had to pay two drachmas each year (Ex 30:13; 2 Chr 24:9; Neh 10:32). It was approximately two days' wages and was used for the upkeep of the temple. The two drachmas had to be paid in Jewish money; this explains the presence of money changers in the entrance halls of the temple (Mt 21:12; Jn 2:15). *Silver coin:* literally, a "stater," which was worth four drachmas, or twice the amount of the tax.

Jesus submits to the law out of respect for others, but he affirms that as Son of Man he is not bound by it. Christians who obey the law remain free with respect to all authority and are subject to God alone.

18:1-35 In this fourth collection of the sayings of Jesus, there are a good number that we have already met, and we recognize here, at times, the tone of the "Sermon on the Mount" (chs. 5—7). Everything is focused on the coming of the kingdom, but the words of Jesus now apply to the community life of the disciples. Chapter 18 is known as the "ecclesiastical discourse" because it describes the demands made by brotherhood in the Church of Jesus, which is a community of love, prayer, and forgiveness.

18:1-4 The true disciple of Jesus must renounce all ambition and become as simple and humble as a child.

18:5-11 Woe to those who give scandal to the *little ones*, i.e., the disciples of the Gospel, so as to make them fall. The Lord identifies himself with them and issues severe threats for those who wish to pervert them. Indeed, they have angels who always see the face of the Father in heaven—the guardian angels—thus showing their great worth in God's eyes.

18:8-9 These verses are already to be found substantially in Mt 5:29-30; the evangelist repeats them because they have to do with "scandal." The point is that no one can be saved who does not break completely with evil.

18:11 This verse is missing from the most important manuscripts and seems to have been transferred to this point from Lk 19:10.

18:12-14 In this parable, Jesus suggests what price the Father attaches to the salvation of sinners. The evangelist uses it as an appeal to the community that it may never become inhospitable to the least of believers, no matter how lost they may appear.

The Church: Community of Love, Prayer, and Pardon.* 15 "If your brother wrongs you, go and take up the matter with him when the two of you are alone. If he listens to you, you have won your brother over. [o] 16 But if he will not listen, take one or two others along with you, so that every detail may be confirmed by the testimony of two or three witnesses. [p] 17 If he refuses to listen to them, report it to the Church. And if he refuses to listen to the Church, treat him as you would a Gentile or a tax collector. [q]

18 "Amen, I say to you, whatever you bind on earth shall be bound in heaven, and whatever you loose on earth shall be loosed in heaven. [r] 19 [Amen,] I say to you, further, if two of you on earth agree about anything you ask for, it will be granted to you by my Father in heaven. [s] 20 For where two or three are gathered together in my name, I am there in their midst." [t]

21 [u] Then Peter came up to him and asked, "Lord, if my brother sins against me, how often must I forgive him? As many as seven times?" 22 Jesus answered, "I say to you, not seven times but seventy times seven. * [v]

The Parable of the Unmerciful Servant.* 23 "For this reason, the kingdom of heaven may be compared to a king who decided to settle accounts with his servants. [w] 24 When he began the accounting, a man was brought to him who owed him ten thousand talents. * 25 Since he had no possible way to repay what he owed, his master ordered him to be sold, together with his wife, his children, and all his property, to satisfy the debt. [x] 26 At this, the servant fell to his knees, saying, 'Be patient with me, and I will repay you in full.' 27 Moved with compassion, the master of that servant let him go and canceled the debt.

28 "However, when that servant left, he encountered one of his fellow servants who owed him one hundred denarii, * and, choking him, he demanded, 'Pay me back what you owe.' 29 His fellow servant fell to his knees and pleaded with him, saying, 'Be patient with me and I will repay you.' 30 But he turned a deaf ear and had him thrown into prison until he had repaid the debt.

31 "When his fellow servants observed what had happened, they were greatly upset, and, going to their master, they reported everything that had taken place. 32 Then his master sent for the man and said to him, 'You wicked servant! I forgave you for your complete debt because you begged me. 33 Should you not have had mercy on your fellow servant as I had mercy on you?' [y] 34 And in his anger his master handed him over to be tortured until he repaid the entire debt. 35 In the same way, my heavenly Father will also deal with you unless each of you forgives his brother from the heart." [z]

V: THE COMING OF THE SON OF MAN*

A: The Ministry in Judea and Jerusalem

CHAPTER 19

Marriage and Celibacy.* 1 [a] When Jesus had finished this discourse, he left Galilee and came into the region of Judea beyond the

o Lev 19:17; Sir 19:13; Lk 17:3; Gal 6:1.—p Deut 19:15; Jn 8:17; 2 Cor 13:1; 1 Tim 5:19; Heb 10:28.—q Rom 16:17; 1 Cor 5:11.—r Mt 16:19; Jn 20:23.—s Mt 7:7-8; Jn 15:7, 16.—t Mt 28:20; 1 Cor 5:4.—u 21-22: Mt 6:12; Lk 17:4.—v Gen 4:24; Lk 23:34.—w Mt 25:19.—x Lev 25:29; Lk 7:42.—y Sir 28:4.—z Mt 6:15; Lk 23:34; Jas 2:13.—a 1-9: Mk 10:1-12.

18:15-22 When believers live with trust in God and in communion with one another, Christ is in their midst. Doubtless, judgment is to be passed upon those who "sin," i.e., who gravely and publicly injure the unity; but all must remain ready to forgive without measure.

18:22 *Seventy times seven:* the Greek word may also be translated "seventy-seven times."

18:23-35 The law of pardon must ceaselessly renew the fraternal relationships in the Church. It is founded on the goodness of God who gratuitously forgives the immense sin of human beings.

18:24 *Ten thousand talents:* an enormous sum, equivalent to about 250,000 kg of silver. The Attic talent in circulation at that time was worth 6000 drachmas, and a drachma weighed about 4 gr.

18:28 *One hundred denarii:* the denarius was a Roman silver coin with the image and name of the emperor on it; it weighed about 4 gr and was the salary for a day's work. A hundred denarii were therefore a sum 600,000 times less than the ten thousand talents.

19:1—25:46 A new series of incidents, followed by a great discourse on the end of the world, make up the fifth part of the Gospel of Matthew. Jesus now goes to Judea, location of the official religion.

19:1-12 The interpreters of the Law thought up many subtle ways of making divorce easy; they lacked understanding of the essential point. Jesus' purpose is to recover the purity of the original state and the will of the Creator himself for the human race. He could not allow the unity of the couple to be at the mercy of circumstances, since this unity had been asserted by God as a call inherent in the very condition of man and woman (see Gen 2:24).

Did the rule admit exceptions? The phrase in v. 9: "except if the marriage was unlawful," has been the subject of much debate (on this point see what was said at Mt 5:32). In the Judaism of that age, not to marry seemed something repugnant and almost a crime; not to have a posterity seemed a punishment; however, some religious sects did practice voluntary continence. John and Jesus had renounced marriage in order to live solely for their mission of proclaiming the kingdom of God.

Jordan. [b] 2 Large crowds followed him, and
he healed them there.

3 Some Pharisees came forward and test-
ed him by asking, "Is it lawful for a man to
divorce his wife for any reason whatsoev-
er?" [c] 4 He replied, "Have you not read that
from the beginning the Creator 'made them
male and female' [d] 5 and said: 'That is why a
man leaves his father and mother and is
joined to his wife, and the two become one
flesh'? [e] 6 And so they are no longer two but
one flesh. Therefore, what God has joined
together, let no one separate."

7 They said to him, "Why then did Moses
command that a man give his wife a certifi-
cate of divorce and send her away?" [f] 8 He
replied, "It was because you were so hard-
hearted that Moses allowed you to divorce
your wives, but it was not like this from the
beginning. 9 Now I say to you: if a man
divorces his wife for any reason except if the
marriage was unlawful and marries anoth-
er, he commits adultery." [g]

10 His disciples said to him, "If that is the
situation between a husband and wife, it is
better not to marry." 11 He replied, "Not
everyone can accept this teaching, but only
those to whom it has been given. [h] 12 For
there are eunuchs who have been made so
from birth and eunuchs who were made so
by others, and there are eunuchs who have
made themselves eunuchs for the sake of the
kingdom of heaven. Let those accept this
who can do so." *

Jesus Receives Little Children.* 13 [i] Then peo-
ple brought children to him so that he might
lay his hands on them and pray. The disci-
ples rebuked them, 14 but Jesus said, "Let the
little children come to me, and do not hin-
der them. For it is to such as these that the
kingdom of heaven belongs." [j] 15 And after he
had laid his hands on them he proceeded on
his way.

The Rich Young Man.* 16 [k] Then a man came
forward and asked him, "Teacher, what good
thing must I do to achieve eternal life?" [l]
17 He said to him, "Why do you ask me about
what is good? There is only one who is good.
But if you wish to enter into life, keep the
commandments." [m] 18 [n] He said, "Which
ones?" And Jesus answered, "You shall not
kill. You shall not commit adultery. You shall
not steal. You shall not bear false witness. [o]
19 Honor your father and your mother. Love
your neighbor as yourself."

20 The young man said to him, "I have
observed all these. Is there anything more I
must do?" 21 Jesus replied, "If you wish to be
perfect, go, sell your possessions, and give the
money to the poor, and you will have trea-
sure in heaven. Then come, follow me." [p]
22 When the young man heard this, he went
away grieving, for he possessed great wealth.

23 Then Jesus said to his disciples, "Amen,
I say to you, it will be difficult for a rich man
to enter the kingdom of heaven. [q] 24 Again I
tell you, it is easier for a camel to pass
through the eye of a needle than for some-
one who is rich to enter the kingdom of
heaven." [r] 25 When the disciples heard this,
they were astonished, and they asked, "Who
then can be saved?" 26 Jesus looked at them
and said, "For men this is impossible, but for
God all things are possible." [s]

Reward for Following Jesus.* 27 Then Peter
said in reply, "We have given up everything
to follow you. What then will there be for
us?" [t] 28 Jesus replied, "Amen, I say to you, at
the renewal of all things, when the Son of
Man is seated on his glorious throne, you
who have followed me will yourselves sit on
twelve thrones, judging the twelve tribes of
Israel. [u] 29 And everyone who has left houses
or brothers or sisters or father or mother or
children or lands for the sake of my name
will receive a hundred times more and will
inherit eternal life. 30 But many who are first
will be last, and the last will be first. [v]

b Lk 9:51.—c Lk 11:54; Jn 8:6.—d Gen 1:27.—e Gen 2:24; 1 Cor 6:16; Eph 5:31.—f Mt 5:31; Deut 24:1-4.—g Mt 5:32; Lk 16:18; 1 Cor 7:10-11.—h 1 Cor 7:7-9, 17.—i 13-15: Mk 10:13-16; Lk 18:15-17; 1 Tim 4:14.—j Mt 18:3; 25:34; 1 Pet 2:1-2.—k 16-30: Mk 10:17-30; Lk 18:18-30.—l Lk 10:25.—m Lev 18:5.—n 18-19: Ex 20:12-16; Lev 19:18; Deut 5:16-20; Rom 13:9.—o Jas 2:11.—p Mt 5:48; 6:20; Acts 2:45.—q Mt 13:22; 1 Tim 6:9, 10.—r Mt 7:14.—s Gen 18:14; Job 42:2; Jer 32:17, 27; Lk 1:37.—t Mt 4:20, 22.—u Mt 20:21; 25:31; Dan 7:9, 22; Lk 22:30; Rev 3:21; 20:4.—v Mt 20:16; Lk 13:30.

19:12 The virginity recommended by Jesus manifests the new creation of the New Covenant and is the prelude to the kingdom (see Mt 22:30). However, the renunciation of marriage out of love for the kingdom is possible only through the medium of a charism, a special gift of God (see 1 Cor 7:7).

19:13-15 The Gospel has retained this spontaneous and true gesture because it is also a sign. To enter into the kingdom, i.e., into intimacy with God, one must be free of all pretense and become poor and little for humans are always weak and needy before God.

19:16-26 To follow Jesus means to be as poor and free as he is. But how can people detach themselves from what they are? Nothing would seem more impossible. Yet to be a Christian is to believe in the impossible things that God can accomplish in human beings.

19:27-30 Communion of life with Jesus is worth far more than all the things of the earth abandoned by the disciples, for they will reign with him in his eschatological kingdom.

CHAPTER 20

The Parable of the Workers in the Vineyard.*
1 "The kingdom of heaven is like a landown-
er who went out early in the morning to hire
laborers for his vineyard. [w] 2 After agreeing
with the laborers for a denarius * a day, he
sent them into his vineyard. 3 Going out
about nine o'clock, * he saw some others
standing idle in the marketplace. 4 He said to
them, 'You also go into my vineyard and I
will give you what is just.' 5 When he went out
again around noon and at three in the after-
noon, * he did the same. 6 Then, about five
o'clock, * he went out and found others
standing around, and he said to them, 'Why
have you been standing here idle all day?'
7 They answered, 'Because no one has hired
us.' He said to them, 'You too go into my
vineyard.'

8 "When evening came, the owner of the
vineyard said to his foreman, 'Summon the
workers and give them their pay, beginning
with those who came last and ending with
the first.' [x] 9 When those who had started to
labor at five o'clock came, each of them
received a denarius. 10 Therefore, those who
had come first thought that they would
receive more, but they were paid a denarius,
the same as the others. 11 And when they
received it, they began to grumble against
the landowner, [y] 12 saying, 'These men who
were hired last worked only one hour, and yet
you have rewarded them on the same level
with us who have borne the greatest portion
of the work and the heat of the day.' [z]

13 "The owner replied to one of them,
'Friend, I am not treating you unfairly. Did
you not agree with me to work for a
denarius? 14 Take your pay and leave. I have
chosen to pay the latecomers the same as I
pay you. 15 Am I not free to do as I wish with
my own money? Or are you envious because
I am generous?' [a] 16 Thus, the last will be first
and the first will be last." [b]

Jesus Predicts His Passion a Third Time.*
17 [c] As Jesus was going up to Jerusalem, he
took the twelve disciples aside by themselves
and said to them, 18 "Behold, we are now
going up to Jerusalem, and the Son of Man
will be handed over to the chief priests and
the scribes, and they will condemn him to
death. 19 Then they will hand him over to
the Gentiles to be mocked and scourged
and crucified, and on the third day he will
be raised to life." [d]

The Son of Man Has Come To Serve.* 20 [e] Then
the mother of the sons of Zebedee came to
Jesus with her sons and made a request of
him after kneeling before him. 21 "What do
you wish?" he asked her. She said to him,
"Promise that these two sons of mine may
sit, one at your right hand and the other at
your left, in your kingdom." [f] 22 Jesus said in
reply, "You do not know what you are asking.
Can you drink the cup * I am going to
drink?" They said to him, "We can." [g]

23 He then said to them, "You shall indeed
drink my cup, but to sit at my right hand and
at my left is not in my power to grant. Those
places belong to those for whom they have
been prepared by my Father." [h]

24 [i] When the other ten disciples heard this,
they were indignant at the two brothers.
25 But Jesus called them over and said, "You
know that the rulers of the Gentiles lord it
over them, and their great ones make their
authority over them felt. 26 This must not be
so with you. Instead, whoever wishes to be
great among you must be your servant,
27 and whoever wishes to be first among you
must be your servant. [j] 28 In the same way,
the Son of Man did not come to be served
but rather to serve and to give his life as a
ransom for many." * [k]

---

w Mt 21:28, 33.—x Lev 19:13; Deut 24:15.—y Jon 4:1.—z Lk 12:55.—a Deut 15:9; Rom 9:19-21.—b Mt 19:30; Lk 13:30.—c 17-19: Mt 16:21; 17:22-23; Mk 10:32-34; Lk 18:31-33.—d Acts 10:40.—e 20-28: Mk 10:35-45.—f Mt 19:28.—g Mt 26:39; Jn 18:11.—h Rom 8:17; Phil 3:10.—i 24-27: Mk 10:41-45; Lk 22:25-27.—j Mk 9:35.—k Mt 8:20; 26:28; Isa 53:10; Rom 5:6; 2 Cor 4:5; Phil 2:7; 1 Tim 2:6.

20:1-16 The parable of the workers in the vineyard teaches that the promised kingdom is a gift of grace and not a wage. For salvation is not the fruit of a commercial contract but consists in a communion of love, a filial response on the part of humans to the initiative of God, who offers them his friendship. Christians who do good cannot boast of rights before God. They should merely do all they can to correspond with God's call and render themselves ever less unworthy of his friendship.

20:2 *Denarius:* a Roman coin that was the normal daily wage at the time—what a Roman soldier also received.

20:3 *Nine o'clock:* literally, "the third hour."

20:5 *Noon . . . three in the afternoon:* literally, "the sixth hour . . . the ninth hour."

20:6 *Five o'clock:* literally, "the eleventh hour."

20:17-19 At the moment when he starts out for Jerusalem, Jesus clearly confronts the drama of his sacrifice. This third prediction of the Passion is much more detailed than the first two.

20:20-28 The apostles were still dreaming of an earthly Messianic kingdom and seeking an important role in it. However, their recompense would be a gift from the heavenly Father, not a right of their own. Jesus' mission in the world was to save human beings and not to assign them their prize.

20:22 *Drink the cup:* in the idiom of the Bible, this meant to meet suffering (see Isa 51:17; Jer 25:15; Ps 75:9).

20:28 As the suffering Servant (Isa 53), Jesus has come to expiate the sins of all, offering the Father his own life as the price of the ransom, i.e., as the supreme expression of love.

Two Blind Men Receive Sight.* 29 [l] As they
were leaving Jericho, a large crowd followed
Jesus. 30 Two blind men were sitting by the
roadside, and when they learned that Jesus
was passing by, they shouted, "Lord, Son of
David, take pity on us." [m] 31 The crowd
rebuked them and told them to be silent, but
they only shouted even more loudly, "Lord,
Son of David, take pity on us."

32 Jesus stopped and called them, saying,
"What do you want me to do for you?"
33 They said to him, "Lord, grant that our
eyes may be opened." 34 Jesus, moved with
compassion, touched their eyes. Immediate-
ly, they received their sight and followed
him. [n]

B: Encounters at Jerusalem

CHAPTER 21

The Entry into Jerusalem.* 1 [o] When they
drew near Jerusalem and had reached
Bethphage on the Mount of Olives, Jesus
sent off two disciples, [p] 2 saying to them, "Go
to the village directly ahead of you, and as
soon as you enter you will find a tethered
donkey and a colt with her. Untie them and
bring them to me. 3 If anyone says anything
to you, tell them, 'The Lord needs them.'
Then he will let you have them at once."
4 This was to fulfill what had been spoken by
the prophet:

5 "Say to the daughter of Zion: *
'Behold, your king is coming to you,
humble and riding on a donkey,
and on a colt, the foal of a donkey.' " [q]

6 The disciples went off and did as Jesus
had instructed them. 7 They brought the
donkey and the colt, and laid their cloaks on
their backs, and he sat on them. * [r] 8 A very
large crowd spread their cloaks on the road,
while others cut branches from the trees and
spread them on the road. [s] 9 The crowds that
preceded him and those that followed kept
shouting:

"Hosanna to the Son of David!
Blessed is he who comes in the name
of the Lord! *
Hosanna in the highest!" [t]

10 And when he entered Jerusalem, the
whole city was filled with excitement. "Who
is this?" the people asked, 11 and the crowds
replied, "This is the prophet Jesus from
Nazareth in Galilee." [u]

Jesus Cleanses the Temple.* 12 [v] Then Jesus
entered the temple and drove out all those
whom he found buying and selling there. He
overturned the tables of the money chang-
ers and the seats of those who were selling
doves. [w] 13 He said to them, "It is written:

'My house shall be called a house of
prayer,'
but you are making it a den of
thieves." * [x]

14 The blind and the crippled came to him
in the temple, and he cured them. [y] 15 But
when the chief priests and the scribes wit-
nessed the wonderful things he was per-
forming and heard the children crying out
in the temple area, "Hosanna to the Son of
David," they became infuriated [z] 16 and said
to him, "Do you hear what they are saying?"

l 29:34: Mk 10:46-52; Lk 18:35-43.—m Mt 9:27.—n Mt 8:3.—o 1-11: Mk 11:1-11; Lk 19:28-38; Jn 12:12-15.—p Mk 14:26; Lk 19:37.—q Mt 11:29; Gen 49:11; Isa 62:11; Zec 9:9.—r 1 Ki 1:33.—s 2 Ki 9:13.—t Mt 9:27; Ps 118:25-26; Lk 2:14.—u Deut 18:15; Jn 1:21, 25.—v 12-17: Mk 11:15-19; Lk 19:45-48; Jn 2:14-22.—w Lev 1:14; 5:7; Neh 13:7.—x Isa 56:7; Jer 7:11.—y Mt 4:23; 2 Sam 5:8 LXX.—z Mt 9:27; Lk 19:39.

20:29-34 Until the very end Jesus is the one who hears the cry of the distressed, the one who gives human beings light and calls them to follow him.

21:1-11 One of the key events in the life of Jesus. He seemed to be fulfilling what was most attractive in the Old Testament prophecies: here is the Messiah in the midst of his people, God's messenger in the midst of the human race, and joyous shouts of acclamation arise on every side. *Hosanna* means "Grant salvation!" but it is above all a shout of applause. Jesus allows himself to be acclaimed as the "Son of David," the Savior from the royal line, the figure that the believing people had, generation after generation, tried to picture for themselves in light of the promise made to David (2 Sam 7). But the sumptuous display in the courts of princes was of quite a different nature. Once again, Jesus rejects all dreams of prestige; here he is, in the midst of the people, riding the beast of the poor, the donkey, and linking himself in this manner with the Davidic tradition.

21:5 *Daughter of Zion:* i.e., Jerusalem, which rises on Mount Zion; the citation is from Isa 62:11. There follows the prophecy of Zec 9:9, which describes the Messiah, a humble and meek king taking peaceful possession of his kingdom.

21:7 *He sat on them* [the cloaks]: from Mark (11:2) and Luke (19:30), we know that Jesus rode on the colt. It was customary for a mother donkey to follow her offspring closely. Hence Matthew mentions two animals.

21:9 *Blessed is he who comes in the name of the Lord:* taken from Ps 118:26f, this phrase does not express the customary greeting directed at the pilgrim who had reached the Holy City. Like the *Hosanna* mentioned above, it is an acclamation to the Messiah who is taking possession of his kingdom.

21:12-17 As if to stress the authority of the Messiah, the evangelist follows up the entry into Jerusalem with Jesus' cleansing of the temple. He then adds the acclamation of the children, in whom he sees the fulfillment of another prophecy. John, on the other hand, places the cleansing of the temple at the beginning of Christ's public ministry. While not ruling out two distinct cleansings, scholars usually prefer the chronology of John, since the Synoptics have chosen to assign the whole of Christ's activity in Judea to the last period of his life.

21:13 Jesus combines two Old Testament prophecies: Isa 56:7 ("My house shall be called a house of prayer") and Jer 7:11 ("Has this house, which bears my name become in your eyes a den of thieves?").

Jesus replied, "Yes. Have you never read the text:

'Out of the mouths of infants and babies
who are nursing
you have received fitting praise'?" [a]

17 Then he left them and went out of the city to Bethany, where he spent the night. [b]

The Lesson of the Withered Fig Tree.* 18 [c] Early the next morning, as he was returning to the city, he was hungry. 19 Noticing a fig tree by the side of the road, he went over to it but found nothing on its branches except leaves. Then he said to it, "May you never give forth fruit again!" And instantly the fig tree withered away. [d]

20 When the disciples witnessed this, they were stunned, and they asked, "How could that fig tree wither away in an instant?" 21 Jesus answered them, "Amen, I say to you, if you have faith and do not doubt, not only will you do what has been done to this fig tree, but even if you say to this mountain, 'Be lifted up and thrown into the sea,' it will be accomplished. [e] 22 Whatever you ask for in faith-filled prayer, you will receive." [f]

The Authority of Jesus Questioned.* 23 [g] When he entered the temple and began to teach, the chief priests and the elders of the people approached him and asked, "By what authority are you doing these things? And who gave you this authority?" [h] 24 Jesus said to them in reply, "I will also ask you one question. If you give me an answer, then I will tell you by what authority I do these things. 25 Where did John's baptism originate? From heaven or from men?" [i]

They argued among themselves, "If we say: 'From heaven,' he will say to us, 'Then why did you not believe him?' 26 But if we say, 'From men,' we are afraid of the people, for they all regard John as a prophet." [j]

27 Therefore, they answered Jesus, "We do not know." And Jesus said to them, "Then neither shall I tell you by what authority I do these things. *

The Parable of the Two Sons.* 28 "What is your opinion about this? A man had two sons. He went to the first and said, 'My son, go and work in the vineyard today.' [k] 29 He answered, 'I will not,' but later he had a change of heart and went. 30 The father then gave the same instruction to the second son, who answered, 'Of course I will,' but then did not go. 31 Which of the two complied with his father's instruction?" They responded, "The first."

Then Jesus said to them, "Amen, I say to you, tax collectors and prostitutes are entering the kingdom of God ahead of you. [l] 32 For John came to show you the path of righteousness, but you did not believe him, whereas the tax collectors and the prostitutes did. Yet even after you realized that, you still refused to change your minds and believe in him. [m]

The Parable of the Tenants.* 33 [n] "Listen to another parable. There was a landowner who planted a vineyard, fenced it in on all sides, dug a winepress in it, and built a watchtower. Then he leased it to tenants and went off on a journey. [o]

34 "When the time for harvest approached, he sent his servants to the tenants to collect his share of the produce. [p] 35 But the tenants seized his servants and beat one of them, killed another, and stoned a third. [q] 36 Again, he sent more servants, but they treated them in the same manner.

---

a Ps 8:3 LXX; Wis 10:21.—b Mk 11:11; Lk 21:37.—c 18-22: Mk 11:12-14, 20-24.—d Isa 34:4; Jer 8:13; Lk 13:6-9.—e Mt 17:20; Lk 17:6; 1 Cor 13:2; Jas 1:6.—f Mt 7:7; 1 Jn 3:22.—g 23-27: Mk 11:27-33; Lk 20:1-8.—h Jn 2:18; Acts 4:7.—i Jn 3:27.—j Mt 11:9; 14:5; 16:14.—k Mt 20:1.—l Lk 7:50.—m Lk 7:29-30.—n 33-46: Mk 12:1-12; Lk 20:9-19.—o Ps 80:9; Isa 5:1-2, 7.—p Mt 22:3.—q Mt 22:6; Heb 11:36-37.

21:18-22 The cursing of the fig tree is a symbolic act, a kind of parable in action. It signifies the condemnation of Israel, which has now become a sterile plant. The ancient Prophets often had recourse to this type of teaching.

21:23-27 This is the first of five controversies between Jesus and the religious authorities of Judaism in Mt 21:23—22:46. They are in a question-and-answer form and are interrupted after the first by three parables on the judgment of Israel (Mt 21:28-32; 21:33-46; 22:1-14).

21:27 The religious authorities claim ignorance of the origin of John's baptism and thereby demonstrate that they cannot speak with authority. Therefore, Jesus refuses to tell them by what authority he acts.

21:28-32 The parable of the two sons denounces a religion that is content with words and appearances. The facile "Yes" on the lips is a poor disguise for the refusal of the heart. To the hypocrisy of the recognized teachers, Jesus opposes the true faith of the poor. The evangelist utilizes this parable to indicate the end of Israel's privileges and the entrance of Gentiles into the growing Church.

21:33-46 The parable repeats, almost word for word, passages from the beautiful, sad song of the vineyard in Isa 5; Jesus is speaking of God and his people. How can we forget the tragic history of the Prophets, who were rejected, tormented, and stoned to death (2 Chr 24:21; Heb 11:37; Lk 13:34)? Is not the son here Jesus himself?

Scholars believe that some allegorical elements have been added herein to a basic parable originally spoken by Christ. One reason for their belief is the newly found apocryphal Gospel of Thomas, which contains (#65) a more primitive form of the parable.

37 "Finally, he sent his son to them, think-
ing, 'They will respect my son.' 38 But when
the tenants saw the son, they said to one
another, 'This is the heir. Come, let us kill
him and get his inheritance.'[r] 39 And so they
seized him, threw him out of the vineyard,
and killed him.[s]

40 "Now what do you think the owner of
the vineyard will do to those tenants when
he comes?" 41 They said to him, "He will kill
those evil men, and then he will lease his
vineyard to other tenants who will give him
the produce at the harvest."

42 Jesus then said to them, "Have you
never read in the Scriptures:

'The stone that the builders rejected
has become the cornerstone;
by the Lord has this been done,
and it is wonderful in our eyes'?[t]

43 Therefore, I tell you, the kingdom of God
will be taken away from you and given to a
people that will produce fruit in abun-
dance.[u] [44 The one who falls on this stone
will be broken into pieces, and the one on
whom it falls will be crushed.]" *

45 When the chief priests and the
Pharisees heard his parables, they realized
that he was speaking about them. 46 They
wanted to arrest him, but they were afraid of
the crowds, who regarded him as a prophet.[v]

CHAPTER 22

The Parable of the Wedding Banquet.* 1 [w] Jesus
spoke to them again in parables, saying,
2 "The kingdom of heaven may be compared
to a king who gave a wedding banquet for his
son.[x] 3 He sent forth his servants to sum-
mon those who had been invited to the ban-
quet, but they refused to come.[y] 4 Then he
sent other servants, saying, 'Tell those who
have been invited, "Behold, my banquet has
been prepared, my oxen and my fattened
cattle have been slaughtered, and everything
is ready. Come to the wedding banquet." '

5 "But they ignored his invitation. One
went off to his farm, another to his business,
6 while the rest seized his servants, mistreat-
ed them, and killed them.[z]

7 "The king was enraged, and he sent forth
his troops who destroyed those murderers
and burned their city to the ground.[a] 8 Then
he said to his servants, 'The wedding
banquet is ready, but those who were invited
were not worthy of that honor.[b] 9 Go forth,
therefore, to the main roads and invite every-
one you can find to the wedding banquet.'
10 The servants went forth into the streets
and gathered together everyone they could
find, good and bad alike. And so the wedding
hall was filled with guests.

11 * "But when the king came in to greet
the guests, he noticed one man who was not
properly dressed for a wedding.[c] 12 'My
friend,' he said to him, 'how did you gain
entrance here without a wedding garment?'
The man was speechless. 13 Then the king
said to the attendants, 'Bind his hands and
feet and cast him outside into the darkness,
where there will be weeping and gnashing of
teeth.'[d] 14 For many are called, but few are
chosen." * [e]

God or Caesar.* 15 [f] Then the Pharisees went
off and made plans to trap him in what he
said.[g] 16 They sent some of their disciples to
him, along with the Herodians, * and said,
"Teacher, we know that you are truthful and
that you teach the way of God in accordance
with the truth. Nor are you concerned with
anyone's opinion for you do not care about

---

r Ps 2:8; Jn 3:16-17; Heb 1:2.—s Heb 13:12.—t Ps 118:22-23; Isa 28:16; Acts 4:11; Eph 2:20; 1 Pet 2:7.—u Rom 11:11.—v Mt 16:14.—w 1-14: Prov 9:1-6; Lk 14:15-24.—x Mt 8:11.—y Mt 21:34.—z Mt 21:35.—a Lk 19:27.—b Rev 19:7.—c Rev 19:8.—d Mt 8:12; 25:30.—e Rev 17:14.—f 15-22: Mk 12:13-17; Lk 20:20-26.—g Lk 11:54.

21:44 Some manuscripts do not have this verse, which indicates that both hostility and apathy are wrong responses to Christ. It may be an early addition to this Gospel based on Lk 20:18.

22:1-14 The meaning of this parable is similar to that of the preceding one. The Messianic Kingdom is likened to a nuptial banquet. The king is God; the servants are the Prophets; the invited guests are the Israelites; the punishment of the city refers to the destruction of Jerusalem in A.D. 70; the new invitees are the Gentiles. Some retouches have made the parable a warning to the Church of Matthew as well as a statement of God's judgment on Israel.

22:11-13 Scholars speak of these verses almost as another parable, that of the wedding garment. In this world the good and the wicked are mixed together, for it is the time of patience and mercy. During this time Christians must cooperate with God's grace, which is tantamount to wearing the wedding garment.

22:14 *Many . . . chosen:* this does not seem to allude to the number of the elect, since that is a secret that the Father had reserved to himself. It means that all the Israelites have been invited, but only a few of them have accepted the Gospel.

22:15-22 Here the series of controversies between Jesus and the religious authorities is resumed, beginning with the question of paying taxes to the Roman emperor. For over twenty years, the Roman emperor had been levying a tax on Palestine; the Jewish people regarded it as a sign of unjust oppression. To pay it was regarded as a denial of Jewish hopes; to challenge it meant taking the side of revolutionary agitators. Only the elderly and children were exempt; the Zealots forbade their members to pay it.

22:16 *Herodians:* partisans and courtiers of the reigning dynasty of the Herods. Though they were Jews in religion, their spirit was Gentile. They conspired with their enemies the Pharisees against Christ.

people's opinions. [h] 17 Tell us then what you
think about this: Is it lawful or not for us to
pay taxes to Caesar?" [i]

18 Jesus was aware of their malicious
intent, and he said, "You hypocrites! Why are
you trying to trap me? 19 Show me the coin
that is used for paying the tax." When they
brought him a denarius, * 20 he asked them,
"Whose image is this, and whose inscrip-
tion?" 21 They replied, "Caesar's." On hear-
ing this, he said to them, "Give to Caesar
what is due to Caesar, and to God what is
due to God." *[j] 22 Stunned on hearing this
reply, they went away and left him alone.

Marriage and the Resurrection.* 23 [k] On that
same day, the Sadducees, who assert that
there is no resurrection, approached him
and posed this question, [l] 24 "Teacher, Moses
said that if a man dies without having chil-
dren, his brother * is to marry his brother's
wife and raise up children for his brother. [m]
25 Now there were seven brothers who
belonged to our group. The first one married
and died without issue, and therefore left his
wife to his brother. 26 The same result
occurred with the second brother and the
third, right down to the seventh. 27 Finally,
the woman herself died. 28 Now at the resur-
rection, whose wife of the seven will she be,
inasmuch as all of them had her?"

29 Jesus answered them, "You are in error,
for you do not understand the Scriptures or
the power of God. 30 At the resurrection they
will neither marry nor be given in marriage.
They are like the angels in heaven. [n]

31 "And in regard to the resurrection of the
dead, have you not read what God himself
said to you: 32 'I am the God of Abraham, the
God of Isaac, and the God of Jacob'? He is
not the God of the dead but of the living." [o]

33 When the crowds heard this, they were
astonished at his teaching.

The Greatest Commandment.* 34 [p] When the
Pharisees learned that he had silenced the
Sadducees, they gathered together, 35 and, to
test him, one of them, a lawyer, asked this
question, [q] 36 "Teacher, which is the greatest
commandment in the Law?"

37 Jesus said to him, " 'You shall love the
Lord your God with all your heart, and with
all your soul, and with all your mind.' [r]
38 This is the greatest and the first com-
mandment. 39 The second is like it: 'You
shall love your neighbor as yourself.' [s]
40 Everything in the Law and the Prophets
depends on these two commandments." [t]

Jesus Is Lord.* 41 [u] While the Pharisees were
assembled together, Jesus asked them this
question, 42 "What is your opinion about the
Christ? Whose son is he?" They replied, [v]
"He is the son of David." 43 He responded,
"How is it then that David, under the inspi-
ration of the Spirit, calls him 'Lord,' saying:

44 'The Lord said to my Lord,
"Sit at my right hand
until I put your enemies under your
feet" '? [w]

45 If David calls him 'Lord,' how can he be his
son?" 46 No one was able to give him an
answer, and from that day onward no one
dared to ask him any further questions. [x]

CHAPTER 23

Portrait of the Scribes and Pharisees.* 1 [y] Then
Jesus addressed the crowds and his disci-
ples: 2 "The scribes and the Pharisees sit on
Moses' seat. 3 Therefore, be careful to do
whatever they tell you, but do not follow
their example, for they do not practice what

h Mk 3:6.—i Mt 17:25.—j Rom 13:7.—k 23-33: Mk 12:18-27; Lk 20:27-40.—l Acts 23:8; 1 Cor 15:12.—m Gen 38:8; Deut 25:5-6.—n Wis 5:5.—o Ex 3:6; Col 1:12.—p 34-40: Mk 12:28-33; Lk 10:25-28.—q Lk 7:30.—r Deut 6:5.—s Mt 5:43; Lev 19:18; Jas 2:8.—t Mt 7:12; Rom 13:8-10; Gal 5:14.—u 41-46: Mk 12:35-37; Lk 20:41-44.—v Mt 9:27; 2 Sam 7:1.—w Mt 26:64; Ps 110:1; Acts 2:35; 1 Cor 15:25; Heb 1:13.—x Mk 12:34; Lk 20:40.—y 1-39: Mk 12:38-39; Lk 11:37-52; 13:34-35; 20:45, 46.

22:19 *Denarius:* the daily wage of a laborer.

22:21 Jesus emphasizes that it is not enough to give to Caesar what is due to Caesar; people must also give to God what is due to God, i.e., worship and good works (see Mt 21:41, 43).

22:23-33 Faith in a resurrection became common only toward the end of the Old Testament period. Not all shared the certainty; the Sadducees, the aristocrats of the priestly class and men concerned more with politics than with religion, considered it a rather debatable theological novelty. They debate it with Jesus, using arguments that emerge as caricature and prevent access to the heart of the question. Jesus answers in the name of the Jewish faith in God: God stands on the side of life.

22:24 *If a man dies . . . his brother:* this custom is known as the "law of the levirate," from the Latin word for brother-in-law (*levir*). It was intended to continue the family line of the deceased brother (see Deut 25:6).

22:34-40 Instead of dividing the Law into a string of precepts (the Rabbis counted 248) and prohibitions (365), Jesus unifies it in two essential commandments: love of God (Deut 6:5) and neighbor (Lev 19:18). These form the basis of every precept.

22:41-46 For centuries people had been awaiting a Christ, or Messiah, who would be a son of David; they saw him pictured in an ancient royal psalm that became a song of Messianic expectation (Ps 110). But Christ is more than the heir to David's throne; he possesses the authority of God. Only during his Passion will Jesus expressly claim to be the Messiah (Mt 26:63-64).

23:1-7 It was considered a fine thing to show off Jewish piety even in the way one dressed: men wore phylacteries (see note on v. 5, below), and made extra long the tassels with which, according to the Law, their prayer shawls should be adorned.

they preach.[z] 4 They tie up heavy burdens that are difficult to bear and lay them on the shoulders of others, but they will not lift a finger to be of assistance.[a]

5 "Everything they do is meant to attract the attention of others. They widen their phylacteries * and lengthen their tassels.[b] 6 [c] They love to have places of honor at banquets and the best seats in synagogues, 7 and to be greeted with respect in the marketplaces and to be addressed as 'Rabbi.'

Do Not Be Called Teacher.* 8 "But do not allow yourselves to be called 'Rabbi,' for you have only one Master, and you are all brethren.[d] 9 Call no one on earth your father, for you have but one Father, and he is in heaven.[e] 10 You must not be called 'teacher,' for you have only one Teacher, the Christ. 11 The greatest among you must be your servant.[f] 12 All those who exalt themselves will be humbled, and all those who humble themselves will be exalted.[g]

Woe to You, Teachers of the Law.* 13 "Woe to you, scribes and Pharisees, you hypocrites! You shut the entrance to the kingdom of heaven in people's faces. You yourselves do not enter, nor do you allow others to enter.[h]

[14 "Woe to you, scribes and Pharisees, you hypocrites! For you devour the houses of widows, while for the sake of appearance you recite lengthy prayers. As a result, you will receive the severest possible condemnation.] *

15 "Woe to you, scribes and Pharisees, you hypocrites! You journey over sea and land to make a single convert, * and then you make that convert twice as worthy of Gehenna as you are.

16 * "Woe to you, blind guides! You say, 'If someone swears by the temple, that is not binding, but if someone swears by the gold of the temple, he is bound by his oath.'[i] 17 You blind fools! Which is greater: the gold, or the temple that makes the gold sacred?

18 "And you say, 'If someone swears by the altar, that is not binding, but if someone swears by the offering that lies on the altar, he is bound by his oath.' 19 You blind fools! Which is of greater value—the offering, or the altar that makes the offering sacred?[j]

20 [k] "The one who swears by the altar swears both by it and by everything that lies upon it. 21 The one who swears by the temple swears both by it and by the one who dwells within it.[l] 22 And the one who swears by heaven swears both by the throne of God and by the One who is seated upon it.[m]

23 * "Woe to you, scribes and Pharisees, you hypocrites! You pay tithes of mint and dill and cumin, but you have neglected the more important aspects of the Law: justice, mercy, and faithfulness. You should have practiced these without neglecting the others.[n] 24 You blind guides! You strain out a gnat and then swallow a camel![o]

25 [p] "Woe to you, scribes and Pharisees, you hypocrites! You cleanse the outside of a cup and dish, but you leave the inside full of greed and self-indulgence. 26 Blind Pharisee! First cleanse the inside of the cup and dish so that the outside may also be clean.

27 "Woe to you, scribes and Pharisees, you hypocrites! You are like whitewashed tombs *

z Deut 17:10.—a Lk 11:46; Rom 2:17-24.—b Mt 6:1-6; Ex 13:9, 16; Num 15:38-39; Deut 6:8; 11:18; Am 4:5.—c 6-7: Mk 12:38-39; Lk 11:43; 14:7; 20:46; Jn 1:38.—d Jn 13:13.—e Mal 1:6.—f Mt 20:26; Mk 9:35.—g 1 Sam 2:8; Ps 18:27; Lk 1:52; 14:11; 18:14.—h Lk 11:52; Isa 5:8.—i Mt 15:14; Rom 2:19.—j Ex 29:37.—k 20-22: Mt 5:34-35.—l 1 Ki 8:13.—m Ps 11:4.—n Lev 27:30; Deut 14:22; Am 5:21; Lk 11:42.—o Lev 11:41-45.—p 25-26: Mk 7:4; Lk 11:39.

23:5 *Phylacteries:* little boxes containing tiny parchment scrolls that had texts of Scripture on them (Ex 13:1-10; 13:11-16; Deut 6:4-9; 11:13-21) and were placed in little tubes; the boxes were attached to the forehead and the left forearm, in keeping with a literal interpretation of Deut 6:8; 11:18. The tassels had a blue thread running through them as a symbol of heaven; they were to remind the wearer of the commandments of God (Num 15:38).

23:8-12 Here Jesus obviously does not abolish the words "Rabbi," "father," and "teacher." He condemns ambition and despotism on the one hand and blind servility on the other. The true Father of Christians is God, and the true Master is Christ, the Son of God. In others, paternal and magistral authority is never absolute, but relative and subordinate to the divine authority.

23:13-28 At that period, Jews tried to win Gentiles over to their religion; those who came were called proselytes. There were also Gentiles who sympathized with Jewish ways and were called "God-fearers." There must have been rivalries between Jews and Christians in this area.

23:14 This verse is identical with Mk 12:40 and seems to have been interpolated from that text.

23:15 *Convert:* a proselyte, that is, a Gentile who had accepted the faith of Israel. *Worthy of Gehenna:* worthy of damnation.

23:16-22 Jesus shows that the Pharisees were wrong in saying that swearing by the gold of the temple and by the offering that lies on the altar is more binding than swearing by the temple or by the altar.

23:23-24 The Law prescribed a tithe on the most important products. However, the Pharisees had extended it to even the most insignificant herbs, and yet they neglected the duties toward one's neighbor, such as justice, compassion, and fidelity. Thus, they strained their liquids so as not to involuntarily swallow an insect and render themselves unclean yet gave no thought to observing the more grave commandments of the moral law.

23:27 *You are like whitewashed tombs:* an allusion to the custom of whitewashing tombs so that no one might inadvertently touch them and contract a legal uncleanness (see Num 19:16).

that look beautiful on the outside, but inside they are full of the bones of the dead and of all kinds of decay.[q] 28 In the same way, on the outside you appear to be righteous, but inside you are full of hypocrisy and wickedness.[r]

The Judgment of God Has Already Come on This Generation.* 29 "Woe to you, scribes and Pharisees, you hypocrites! You build the tombs of the Prophets and adorn the graves of the righteous, 30 and you say, 'If we had lived in the time of our ancestors, we never would have collaborated with them in shedding the blood of the Prophets.'[s] 31 Thus, you acknowledge that you are the descendants of those who murdered the Prophets.[t] 32 Go and complete the work that your ancestors began.[u]

33 "You snakes! You brood of vipers! How can you escape being condemned to Gehenna?[v] 34 [w] Behold, therefore, I am sending you prophets and wise men and teachers. Some of them you will kill and crucify, and some of them you will scourge in your synagogues and pursue from town to town.[x] 35 As a result, upon you will fall the guilt of all the innocent blood that has been shed upon the earth, from the blood of the righteous Abel to the blood of Zechariah son of Barachiah, whom you murdered between the sanctuary and the altar.[y] 36 Amen, I say to you, the guilt for all this will fall upon this generation.

The Lament over Jerusalem.* 37 [z] "Jerusalem, Jerusalem, you murder the Prophets and stone the messengers sent to you! How often have I longed to gather your children together as a hen gathers her chicks under her wings, but you would not allow it![a] 38 Behold, your house has been abandoned and left desolate.[b] 39 I tell you, you will not see me again until you say: 'Blessed is he who comes in the name of the Lord.' "[c]

C: Instructions for the Coming of the Kingdom*

CHAPTER 24

The Time of the End*

Jesus Announces the Destruction of the Temple.* 1 [d] As Jesus left the temple and was walking away, his disciples came up to him to call his attention to the buildings of the temple. 2 He thereupon said to them, "Do you see all these? Amen, I say to you, not one stone here will be left upon another; every one will be thrown down."[e]

The End Has Not Yet Come.* 3 As he was sitting on the Mount of Olives, the disciples approached and spoke to him when they were alone. "Tell us," they said, "when will this happen, and what will be the sign of your coming and of the end of the age?"[f]

4 Jesus answered them, "Take care that no one deceives you. 5 For many will come in my name, saying, 'I am the Christ,' and they will lead many astray.[g] 6 You will hear of wars and rumors of wars. Do not be alarmed, for those things are bound to happen, but the end is still to come.[h] 7 For nation will rise against nation and kingdom against kingdom, and there will be famines and earth-

q Lk 11:44; Acts 23:3.—r Lk 16:15; 18:9.—s Lk 11:47.—t Acts 7:52.—u Ezek 20:4; 1 Thes 2:15-16.—v Mt 3:7; 12:34.—w 34-36: Mt 5:12; Gen 4:8; 2 Chr 24:20-22; Zec 1:1; Lk 11:49-51; Rev 16:16; 18:24.—x Acts 22:19.—y Heb 11:4.—z 37-39: Lk 13:34-35; 19:41-44.—a Mt 21:35; 22:6; Ps 57:2; Isa 31:5.—b Jer 7:14; 12:7.—c Ps 118:26; Acts 2:33.—d 1-44: Mk 13:1-37; Lk 21:5-36.—e Lk 19:44.—f Mt 13:39; Lk 17:30.—g 1 Jn 2:18.—h Dan 2:28 LXX.

23:29-36 The final curse becomes a prophecy of judgment. It sketches the long history of the opposition between the Israel of human beings and the Israel of God, from the first murder of which the Bible speaks to the last (in the order in which the books of the Bible were placed at that period), that is, from Abel (Gen 4:8) to Zechariah (2 Chr 24:20-22).

23:37-39 Jesus offers a lament over Jerusalem, which by failing to accept him opened herself to catastrophe. However, at the end time the Israelites will be converted and acclaim Jesus in his Second Coming (Ps 118:26; see Rom 11:25-33).

24:1—25:46 Five discourses give the Gospel of Matthew its characteristic structure. Here is the last discourse, which brings together prophecies and parables that speak of the last times of humanity and distinguish its phases. At the center of the scenario is the return of Christ. This great passage is known as the "eschatological discourse," because it deals with the end, the last times (Greek: *eschaton*).

24:1-31 The prophetic sayings about the last "days" abound in descriptions of panic, wars, earthquakes, and cosmic upheavals; these descriptions are called "apocalypses," that is, "revelations." They defy the imagination in order better to bring out the greatness of God's manifestation in the history of humanity (see Isa 13:10-13; Jer 21:9; Ezek 5:12; Am 8:8-9; Joel 2:10; 3:3; 4:17-21). Jesus makes use of this entire scenario in order to warn believers about the trials and conflicts in which their fidelity will be tested, and in order to encourage the missionaries of the Gospel.

24:1-2 Jesus announces the destruction of the temple, which is the sign of God's presence among his people. Hence, one must envisage a radical change in the religious life.

24:3-14 There are many indications of Christ's coming at the end of the world. However, no one should be mistaken. Neither the explosion of religious movements, nor the confusion of human societies, nor the catastrophes that pervade human history are signs of the end. The believer must stand fast under trials, which may appear to be excessive at times.

quakes in various places.[i] 8 All these are only the beginning of the labor pains.[j]

9 "Then you will be handed over to be tortured and put to death, and you will be hated by all nations because of my name.[k] 10 At that time, many will fall away from the faith; they will betray and hate one another. 11 Many false prophets will appear and lead many astray,[l] 12 and with the increase of lawlessness, the love of many will grow cold. 13 But whoever endures to the end will be saved.[m] 14 And the good news of the kingdom will be proclaimed throughout the entire world as a testimony offered to all the nations. And then the end will come.[n]

The Great Trial.* 15 "Therefore, when you see the abomination of desolation, about which the prophet Daniel spoke, standing in the Holy Place (let the reader understand),[o] 16 then those who are in Judea must flee to the mountains, 17 the one who is standing on the roof must not come down to collect what is in his house,[p] 18 and someone who is in the field must not turn back to retrieve his coat.

19 "Woe to those who are pregnant and to those who are nursing infants in those days! 20 Pray that you will not have to take flight in the winter or on a Sabbath. 21 For at that time there will be great suffering that has not been equaled since the beginning of the world until now, and will never again be duplicated.[q] 22 And if those days had not been cut short, no one would be saved; but for the sake of the elect they will be shortened.[r]

False Messiahs and False Prophets. 23 "Therefore, if anyone says to you, 'Look, here is the Christ,' or 'There he is,' do not believe it.[s] 24 For false christs and false prophets will arise, and they will perform great signs and wonders that are impressive enough to deceive even the elect, if that were possible.[t]

25 "Remember, I have forewarned you about this. 26 So if anyone says to you, 'Behold, he is in the wilderness,' do not go out there. If they say, 'Behold, he is in the inner rooms,' do not believe it. 27 [u] For just as lightning comes from the east and is visible even in the west, so will the coming of the Son of Man be. 28 Wherever the corpse is, there the vultures will gather.* [v]

The Coming of the Son of Man.* 29 "Immediately after the distress of those days,

'the sun will be darkened
and the moon will not give forth its light;
the stars will fall from the sky
and the powers of the heavens will be shaken.'[w]

30 "Then the sign of the Son of Man will appear in heaven, and all the peoples of the earth will mourn, and they will see the Son of Man coming on the clouds of heaven with power and great glory.[x] 31 And he will send forth his angels with a trumpet blast, and they will gather his elect from the four winds, from one end of the heavens to the other.[y]

D: Be Vigilant in Expectation of the End*

The Parable of the Fig Tree.* 32 "Learn this lesson from the fig tree. As soon as its twigs become tender and its leaves begin to sprout, you know that summer is near. 33 In the same way, when you see all these things take place, know that he is near, at the very gates. 34 Amen, I say to you, this generation will not pass away until all these things have taken place.[z] 35 Heaven and earth will pass away, but my words will never pass away.[a]

i Isa 19:2; Acts 11:28.—j Jn 16:21; Rom 8:22.—k Mt 10:17; Jn 16:2.—l 2 Thes 2:3.—m Mt 10:22.—n Mt 4:23; 28:19; Acts 11:28; Rom 10:18.—o Dan 9:27; 11:31; 12:11; Mk 13:14.—p 1 Sam 9:25; Lk 17:31—q Dan 12:1.—r Rev 7:14.—s Lk 17:23.—t Deut 13:2-3; 2 Thes 2:3.—u 27-28: Lk 17:24, 37.—v Job 39:30.—w Isa 13:10, 13; Ezek 32:7; Joel 2:10; 3:4; Am 8:9.—x Mt 8:20; 26:64; Dan 7:13; Zec 12:12-14; Rev 1:7.—y Mt 13:41; Isa 27:13; 1 Cor 15:52; 1 Thes 4:16; Heb 12:19.—z Mt 10:23; 16:28.—a Ps 119:89; Isa 40:8; 51:6.

24:15-22 *The abomination of desolation:* was a pagan idol placed in the midst of the Jerusalem temple (see Dan 9:27; 11:31; 12:11; 1 Mac 1:54). The destruction of Jerusalem in A.D. 70 is described here in order to convey a lesson about the future.

24:28 A popular proverb cited also in Lk 17:37. In this context it signifies both the uncertain time of the Lord's coming and his universal presence.

24:29-31 The coming of the Son of Man is described in the words of the Old Testament (see Isa 13:9-10; 34:4; Am 5:18; Zec 12:10) in order to express the glory and power of God and the confusion of humanity. Christ dead and risen: this is the sign that converts human beings.

24:32—25:46 The perspective of the end of the world must keep the community on its guard. But it also concerns each disciple, for it has an effect on the end of each individual too. Let everyone be vigilant and active so as not to find oneself barred from the kingdom.

24:32-35 This parable is intended to revive the hope of the first Christians, who are under persecution, with the perspective of the proximity of the glorious kingdom, in accord with the schema of the apocalyptic tradition. Indeed, every Christian lives in this expectation, for with Christ the last period of history has begun.

The Day and Hour Unknown.* 36 "As for the
exact day and hour, no one knows, neither
the angels in heaven, nor the Son, but only
the Father.[b] 37 [c] For as it was in the days of
Noah, so will it be at the coming of the Son
of Man. 38 In the days before the flood, peo-
ple were eating and drinking, marrying and
being given in marriage, up to the day that
Noah entered the ark. 39 They knew nothing
about what would happen until the flood
came and swept them all away.

"That is how it will be at the coming of the
Son of Man. 40 [d] Two men will be out in the
field; one will be taken and the other will be
left. 41 Two women will be grinding at the
mill; one will be taken and the other will be
left. 42 [e] Therefore, keep watch, for you do not
know the day when your Lord is coming.

The Parable of the Owner of the House.*
43 "But keep this in mind: if the owner of the
house had known at what time of night the
thief was coming, he would have stayed
awake and not allowed his house to be
broken into.[f] 44 Therefore, you must also be
prepared, because the Son of Man will come
at an hour when you do not expect him.

The Parable of the Faithful Servant.*
45 [g] "Who, then, is the faithful and wise ser-
vant whom his master has put in charge of
his household to give its members their food
at the proper time? 46 Blessed is that servant
if his master finds him doing so when he
returns home. 47 Amen, I say to you, he will
put him in charge of all his property.

48 "But if that servant is wicked and says
to himself, 'My master is detained,' 49 and he
proceeds to beat his fellow servants and eats
and drinks with drunkards, 50 the master of
that servant will return on a day when he
does not expect him and at an hour he does
not know. 51 He will punish him and assign
him a place with the hypocrites, where there
will be weeping and gnashing of teeth.[h]

CHAPTER 25

The Parable of the Ten Virgins.* 1 "Then * the
kingdom of heaven will be like ten virgins
who took their lamps and went forth to meet
the bridegroom.[i] 2 Five of them were foolish
and five were wise. 3 When the foolish ones
took their lamps, they neglected to take any
oil with them, 4 whereas those who were wise
took flasks of oil with their lamps. 5 Since the
bridegroom was delayed in coming, they all
became drowsy and fell asleep.[j]

6 "At midnight, a shout was raised: 'Be-
hold, the bridegroom! Come out to meet
him!' 7 Then all the virgins got up and
trimmed their lamps. 8 The foolish ones
said to the wise, 'Give us some of your oil,
for our lamps are going out.' 9 The wise
ones replied, 'No, for there may not be
enough for both us and you. You had better
go to the merchants and buy some.'

10 "While they went off to purchase it, the
bridegroom arrived, and those who were
ready went in with him to the wedding
banquet. Then the door was locked.[k]
11 [l] Afterward, the other virgins returned, and
they cried out, 'Lord! Lord! Open the door
for us!' 12 But he replied, 'Amen, I say to you,
I do not know you.' 13 Therefore, stay awake,
for you know neither the day nor the hour.[m]

The Parable of the Talents.* 14 [n] "Again, the
kingdom of heaven will be like a man going
on a journey who summoned his servants
and entrusted his property to them.[o] 15 To
one he gave five talents, * to another two

b Mk 13:32; Acts 1:7.—c 37-39: Mt 24:3,30; Gen 6:5—7:23; Lk 17:26-27; 2 Pet 3:6.—d 40-41: Lk 17:34-35.—e 42-44: Mt 25:13; Lk 12:39-40.—f 1 Thes 5:2.—g 45-51: Lk 12:42-46.—h Mt 13:42; 25:30.—i Lk 12:35-38.—j 1 Thes 5:6.—k Rev 19:9.—l 11-12: Mt 7:21, 23; Lk 13:25-27.—m Mt 24:42; Mk 13:33; Lk 12:40.—n 14-30: Lk 19:12-27.—o Mk 13:34.

24:36-42 The early Church is exhorted not to fall into indifference because judgment comes less quickly than expected. The life of humans cannot be exhausted in the gloomy flow of hours and days; it has another horizon: the coming of God, which is unforeseeable but completely certain. It hovers like a threat over the uncaring who seclude themselves in their securities. But it is a power and a source of strength for believers.

24:43-44 This very brief parable of the owner of the house and the thief reinforces the theme of vigilance, for one does not know when the Son of Man will come.

24:45-51 Jesus addresses the religious leaders of his time to place them on guard: the time to render accounts has arrived. But the coming of God is still to take place, and the disciples will be tempted to no longer believe in it. The parable of the faithful servant remains a wake-up call for them. The religious leaders and Christians must not neglect to work for the kingdom as if the Master were always present—God is in their midst.

25:1-13 The parable of the ten virgins illustrates a fundamental thought: we must wait with watchful perseverance for the coming of Christ glorified, likened to the arrival of a bridegroom. In the dazzling nuptial ceremony of Palestine, the bride awaited the bridegroom while merrymaking with friends. Around midnight the bridegroom would come accompanied by lamps. After an initial explosion of joy, the cortège would return to the house of the bridegroom, where the banquet would be celebrated.

25:1 *Then:* at the time of the Second Coming.

25:14-30 The parable of the talents completes the preceding one. The Christian religion is not a simple passive expectation. It demands a complete commitment. One must make fruitful the gifts given by God while awaiting the Lord's glorious return.

25:15 *Talents:* a talent was equivalent to 6000 denarii, that is, to the salary for 6000 days of work.

talents, to a third one talent—to each
according to his ability. Then he set forth on
his journey.[p]

16 "The servant who had received the five
talents promptly went to invest them and
gained five more. 17 In the same manner, the
servant who had received the two talents
gained two more. 18 But the servant who had
received the one talent went off and dug a
hole in the ground and hid his master's
money.

19 "After a long period of time, the master
of those servants returned and settled
accounts with them. 20 The one who had
received the five talents came forward,
bringing an additional five. 'Master,' he said,
'you gave me five talents. Behold, I have
gained five more.' 21 His master said to him,
'Well done, good and faithful servant. Since
you have been faithful in small matters, I
will give you much greater responsibilities.
Come and share your master's joy.'[q]

22 "Next, the one who had received the two
talents also came forward and said, 'Master,
you gave me two talents. Behold, I have
gained two more.' 23 His master said to
him, 'Well done, good and faithful servant.
Since you have been faithful in small
matters, I will give you much greater respon-
sibilities. Come and share your master's joy.'

24 "Then the one who had received the one
talent came forward and said, 'Master, I
knew that you were a hard man, reaping
where you did not sow, and gathering where
you did not scatter seed. 25 Therefore, out of
fear I went off and hid your talent in the
ground. Behold, I give it back to you.'

26 "His master replied, 'You wicked and
lazy servant. So you knew that I reap where
I have not sown and gather where I have not
scattered! 27 Then you should have deposited
my money with the bankers, and on my
return I would have gotten back my money
with interest.

28 " 'Therefore, take the talent from him
and give it to the one with the ten talents.
29 For to everyone who has, more will be
given, and he will have an abundance. But
from the one who has not, even what he
does have will be taken away.[r] 30 As for this
worthless servant, cast him outside into the
darkness, where there will be weeping and
gnashing of teeth.'[s]

The Solemn Judgment at the End of Time.*

31 "When the Son of Man comes in his glory,
and all the angels with him, then he will sit
on the throne of his glory.[t] 32 All the nations
will be gathered before him, and he will sep-
arate people one from another as a shep-
herd separates the sheep from the goats.[u]
33 He will place the sheep on his right and the
goats on his left.

34 "Then the King will say to those on his
right, 'Come, you who are blessed by my
Father, inherit the kingdom prepared for
you from the foundation of the world.[v]
35 [w] For I was hungry and you gave me some-
thing to eat; I was thirsty and you gave me
something to drink; I was a stranger and you
welcomed me;[x] 36 I was naked and you
clothed me; I was ill and you took care of me;
I was in prison and you came to visit me.'

37 "Then the righteous will say to him,
'Lord, when did we see you hungry and give
you something to eat, or thirsty and give you
something to drink? 38 When did we see you
a stranger and welcome you, or naked and
clothe you? 39 When did we see you ill or in
prison and come to visit you?' 40 And the
King will answer, 'Amen, I say to you, what-
ever you did for one of the least of these
brethren of mine, you did for me.'[y]

41 "Then he will say to those on his left,
'Depart from me, you accursed, into the
eternal fire prepared for the devil and his
angels.[z] 42 [a] For I was hungry and you did
not give me anything to eat; I was thirsty
and you did not give me anything to drink;
43 I was a stranger and you did not welcome
me; I was naked and you did not give me any
clothing; I was ill and in prison and you did
not visit me.'

44 "Then they will ask him, 'Lord, when did
we see you hungry or thirsty or a stranger or
naked or ill or in prison and not minister to
you?' 45 He will answer them, 'Amen, I say to
you, whatever you failed to do for one of the
least of these brethren of mine, you failed to
do for me.' 46 And they will go away to eter-

p Mt 18:24.—q Mt 24:47; Lk 16:10.—r Mt 13:12; Mk 4:25; Lk 8:18; 19:26.—s Mt 8:12.—t Mt 16:27; 19:28; Deut 33:2 LXX.—u Ezek 34:17; Mal 3:18.—v Rom 8:17; Eph 1:4.—w 35-36: Isa 58:7; Ezek 18:7.—x Tob 4:16; Job 31:32.—y Mt 10:40, 42; Heb 13:2.—z Mt 7:23; Isa 66:24; Lk 13:27.—a 42-43: Job 22:7; Jas 2:15-16.

25:31-46 This passage constitutes the conclusion of the eschatological discourse with the description of the Last Judgment. In the second part of the great discourse (Mt 24:37), the individual judgment was repeatedly indicated. Now there comes before us the supreme Judge, Jesus Christ in glory, who at the end of time will judge all peoples, without distinction between Jew and Gentile, and will separate the good from the wicked in accord with everyone's works.

nal punishment, but the righteous will enter eternal life." [b]

VI: THE PASSION AND RESURRECTION*

CHAPTER 26

The Plot against Jesus.* 1 When Jesus had finished discoursing on all these subjects, he said to his disciples, 2 [c] "In two days it will be Passover, at which time the Son of Man will be handed over to be crucified."

3 Meanwhile, the chief priests and the elders of the people assembled together in the palace of the high priest, [d] whose name was Caiaphas, * 4 and they made plans to arrest Jesus by deceit and have him put to death. 5 However, they said, "It must not occur during the feast, or the people may begin to riot."

A Woman of Bethany Anoints Jesus.* 6 [e] Now when Jesus was in Bethany at the house of Simon the leper, 7 a woman came up to him with an alabaster jar of very expensive ointment and poured it over his head as he reclined at table. 8 When the disciples saw this, they became indignant, and they remarked, "Why this waste? 9 This ointment could have been sold for a considerable sum, with the money given to the poor."

10 Jesus was aware of their attitude, and he said to them, "Why are you bothering this woman? She has performed a good deed for me. 11 The poor you will always have with you, * but you will not always have me. [f] 12 In pouring this ointment on my body, she has prepared me for burial. [g] 13 Amen, I say to you, wherever in the whole world this gospel is proclaimed, what she has done will be told in remembrance of her."

Judas Betrays Jesus.* [h] 14 Then one of the Twelve, the man called Judas Iscariot, went to the chief priests 15 and asked, "What are you willing to give me if I hand him over to you?" They paid him thirty pieces of silver, [i] 16 and from that moment he began to look for an opportunity to betray him.

The Preparations for the Passover Supper.* 17 [j] On the first day of the feast of Unleavened Bread, * the disciples came to Jesus and asked, "Where do you want us to make the preparations for you to eat the Passover?" [k] 18 He said: "Go to a certain man in the city and say to him, 'The Teacher says, "My appointed time is near. I intend to celebrate the Passover at your house with my disciples." ' " [l] 19 The disciples thereupon followed Jesus' instructions, and they prepared the Passover.

The Treachery of Judas Foretold.* 20 When evening came, he reclined at table with the Twelve. 21 And while they were eating, he said, "Amen, I say to you, one of you will betray me." 22 Greatly distressed on hearing this, they began to ask him, one after another, "Is it I, Lord?"

23 He answered, "The one who has dipped his hand into the bowl with me is the one

b Mt 19:29; Dan 12:2; Jn 5:29.—c 2-5: Mk 14:1-2; Lk 22:1-2.—d Ps 2:2; Jn 11:47-53; Acts 4:25-27.—e 6-13: Mk 14:3-9; Lk 7:37, 38; Jn 12:1-8.—f Deut 15:11.—g Jn 19:40.—h 14-16: Mk 14:10-11; Lk 22:3-6.—i Gen 37:28; Ex 21:32; Zec 11:12.—j 17-25: Mk 14:12-21; Lk 22:7-23.—k Ex 12:14-20; Deut 16:5-8.—l Jn 2:4; 12:23.

26:1—28:20 One person dominates this account: Jesus. He submits to the death that hangs over sinful humanity, but he comes forth from the tomb as conqueror of death and evil. Matthew constantly cites Scripture in order to convince the intended readers of his work, Christians converted from Judaism, that the seeming failure of Jesus was in reality the fulfillment of God's plan.

26:1-5 Matthew emphasizes Jesus' awareness to carry out his Father's saving plan. Probably the plot was hatched on Wednesday.

26:3 Joseph, surnamed Caiaphas, son-in-law of Annas, was high priest, that is, supreme head of the Jewish priesthood and president of the Sanhedrin, from A.D. 18 to 36.

26:6-13 The anointing at Bethany anticipates the burial rites for the Savior after his death. Providing for burial was in the eyes of the Jews a more important good work than almsgiving itself. In Jn 12:1-8, the woman is called Mary, and Judas is the apostle who becomes indignant. Luke (7:36-50) reports another anointing.

26:11 *The poor you will always have with you:* with these words Jesus does not intend to sanction poverty as if to condemn efforts to eradicate misery. He makes a simple observation: his disciples will have many occasions to aid the poor who, as Deut 15:11 states, will never be wanting in Israel.

26:14-16 For the early Christians, if there is a dark deed it is the ever incomprehensible deed of Judas, who comes to the fore here. Matthew is thinking of the prophecy of the righteous man sold for thirty pieces of silver (see Zec 11:12). That amount is also the compensation paid to one whose slave has been gored by an ox (see Ex 21:32).

26:17-19 In the history of Israel one event dominates all others, the Passover (Ex 12—13), and in the worship of Israel one feast summarizes the whole faith, the Passover. It celebrates the passage of God in the midst of his people and is the hour of liberation, salvation, and the covenant. Jesus' Death and Resurrection constitute the true Passover, definitive for all humankind. The Last Supper of Jesus will be its inauguration.

26:17 *The first day of the feast of Unleavened Bread:* this date corresponds with Thursday, the 14th of Nisan. The feast really began on the 15th of Nisan and lasted until the 21st. However, since the leavened bread was eliminated from all the houses before midday on the 14th, the morning of this date was improperly regarded as the first day of the feast, which in reality began only with the setting of the sun, when according to Jewish custom the 15th began. Passover here refers to the paschal lamb, which was immolated around three o'clock on the 14th of Nisan.

26:20-25 The Passover supper began around six o'clock on Thursday. This passage focuses on the divine foreknowledge of Jesus, who is not overcome by the course of events and regards them as ordinary. He sees them as the putting in motion of the will of his Father.

who will betray me.[m] 24 The Son of Man
indeed goes, as it is written of him, but woe
to that man by whom the Son of Man is
betrayed. It would be better for that man if
he had never been born."[n]

25 Then Judas, the one who would betray
him, said: "Is it I, Rabbi?" Jesus replied, "You
have said so."

The Last Supper.* 26 [o] While they were
eating, Jesus took bread, and after he had
pronounced the blessing, he broke it and
gave it to his disciples, saying, "Take this and
eat; this is my body."[p] 27 Then he took a cup,
and after offering thanks he gave it to them,
saying, "Drink from this, all of you. 28 For
this is my blood of the covenant, which will
be shed on behalf of many for the forgive-
ness of sins.[q] 29 And I tell you, from now on I
shall not drink this fruit of the vine until the
day when I shall drink it anew with you in
the kingdom of my Father."[r]

30 And after singing a hymn, they went out
to the Mount of Olives.

Jesus Predicts Peter's Denial.* 31 [s] Then Jesus
said to them, "This very night you
will all be scandalized because of me, for it is
written:

'I will strike the shepherd,
and the sheep of the flock will be
scattered.'[t]

32 But after I have been raised up, I shall go
ahead of you to Galilee."

33 Peter said to him, "Even if all the others
will be scandalized because of you, I will
never be." 34 [u] Jesus replied, "Amen, I say to
you, this very night, before the cock crows,
you will deny me three times."*[v] 35 Peter
said to him, "Even if I have to die with you,
I will not deny you." And all the other disci-
ples said the same thing.

The Agony in the Garden.* 36 [w] Then Jesus
went with his disciples to a place called
Gethsemane, and he said to them, "Sit here
while I go over there to pray."[x] 37 [y] He took
Peter and the two sons of Zebedee, and he
began to suffer grief and anguish.[z]

38 Then he said to them, "My soul is sor-
rowful, even to the point of death. Remain
here and keep watch with me."[a] 39 Moving
on a little farther, he threw himself prostrate
on the ground in prayer, saying, "My Father,
if it is possible, allow this cup to be taken
from me. Yet let your will, not mine, be
done."[b]

40 Returning to the disciples, he found
them sleeping. He said to Peter, "Could you
not keep watch with me for just one hour?
41 Stay awake and pray that you may not
enter into temptation. The spirit is indeed
willing, but the flesh is weak."[c]

42 He went apart for a second time and
prayed, "My Father, if it is not possible for
this cup to be taken away unless I drink it,
your will be done."[d] 43 Then he came back
again and found them sleeping, for their
eyes were heavy.

44 He left them there and went away again,
praying for the third time in the same words
as before. 45 Then he returned to the disci-
ples and said to them, "Are you still sleeping
and taking your rest? Behold, the hour has
come for the Son of Man to be betrayed into
the hands of sinners.[e] 46 Get up! Let us be
going! Look, my betrayer is approaching."

m Ps 41:10; Jn 13:18.—n Isa 53:8-10; Dan 9:26.—o 26-30: Mk 14:22-26; Lk 22:14-23; 1 Cor 11:23-25.—p 26-27: 1 Cor 10:16.—q Ex 24:8; Isa 53:12; Zec 9:11; Mal 2:5.—r Acts 10:41.—s 31-35: Mk 14:27-31.—t Mt 11:6; Zec 13:7; Jn 16:32.—u 34-35: Lk 22:33-34; Jn 13:37-38.—v Mt 26:69-75.—w 36-46: Mk 14:32-42; Lk 22:39-46.—x Jn 18:1.—y 37-39: Heb 5:7.—z Mt 4:21.—a Ps 42:6, 12; Jon 4:9.—b Ps 40:7-9; Jn 4:34; 6:38; Rom 5:19; Phil 2:8.—c Mt 6:13.—d Mt 6:10; Heb 10:9.—e Jn 12:23; 13:1; 17:1.

26:26-30 This is the beginning of the new Covenant promised in Jer 31:31-33, the new sacrifice. For Jesus this meal is more than a final farewell; his entire work is summed up in this sign. He shares his life and love with sinners; he acts as the Servant of God whose sacrifice of himself ransoms his fellow human beings from sin and reconciles them with the Father (see Isa 42:6; 49:6; 53:11-12). Jesus anticipates his sacrifice; he anticipates his gift of himself. By offering his body and blood on the cross he saves humankind. A Covenant is established in which all the saved will share in the same love (see Jer 31:31-34). The Eucharist replaces Sinai (see Ex 24:6-8).

26:31-35 During the Passover meal, some psalms were sung, i.e., the so-called Hallel (113—118). Two followed the account of the origin of Passover. The others were recited after the meal. On the way to the Mount of Olives, Jesus predicts to the disciples their crisis of faith. They have indeed acknowledged him as Messiah and have a deep love for him, as shown by Peter's words. However, they have not yet understood the scandal of the cross, and so their fidelity will be shaken, at least momentarily.

26:34 The cock would begin crowing at 3:00 A.M. (see Mk 13:35).

26:36-46 The first Christian community never succumbed to the temptation to make Jesus into a hero. Never did he appear more human and more pitiable than in this passage. His inner turmoil in the face of his approaching suffering and death could not be more profound than in this hour of the agony. Three times the prayer of the Our Father rises on the lips of Christ; it is a prayer of complete abandonment into God's hand. And Jesus bears this "temptation," this trial, alone as perhaps no other human could have done. He utters no word of resentment or pride at the moment when he accepts and confronts the ultimate and sorrowful stage of his mission.

Jesus Is Arrested.* 47 *[f] While he was still speaking, Judas, one of the Twelve, arrived. With him there was a large crowd of men, armed with swords and clubs, who had been sent by the chief priests and the elders of the people. 48 Now his betrayer had agreed with them on a signal, saying, "The one I shall kiss is the man. Arrest him." 49 Proceeding directly to Jesus, he said, "Greetings, Rabbi!" and kissed him.[g] 50 Jesus said to him, "Friend, do what you are here to do." Then they came forward, seized Jesus, and placed him under arrest.

51 Suddenly, one of those who were accompanying Jesus reached for his sword, drew it, and struck a servant of the high priest, slicing off his ear. 52 Then Jesus said to him, "Put back your sword into its place. For all who take the sword shall die by the sword. 53 Do you suppose that I cannot appeal to my Father for help * and he will not immediately send me more than twelve legions of angels?[h] 54 But then how would the Scriptures be fulfilled that say it must happen in this way?"

55 At that hour, Jesus said to the crowd, "Why are you coming forth with swords and clubs to arrest me, as though I were a bandit? Day after day I sat teaching in the temple, and you did not arrest me.[i] 56 But all this has taken place so that the writings of the Prophets might be fulfilled." Then all the disciples deserted him and fled.[j]

Jesus Is Condemned by the Sanhedrin.* 57 [k] Those who had arrested Jesus led him away to Caiaphas the high priest where the scribes and the elders had gathered. 58 Meanwhile, Peter followed him at a distance up to the courtyard of the high priest. Then, going inside, he sat down with the attendants to see what the outcome would be.[l]

59 The chief priests and the whole Sanhedrin tried to elicit some false testimony against Jesus so they could put him to death, 60 [m] but they failed in their efforts, even though many witnesses came forward with perjured testimony. Finally, two men came forward 61 who stated, "This man said, 'I can destroy the temple of God and rebuild it within three days.' "

62 The high priest then rose and said to him, "Have you no reply to counter the testimony that these witnesses have given?" 63 But Jesus remained silent. Then the high priest said to him, "I command you to tell us before the living God whether you are the Christ, the Son of God."[n] 64 Jesus replied, "You have said it. But I tell you:

> From now on you will see the Son of Man
> seated at the right hand of the Power
> and coming on the clouds of heaven."[o]

65 Then the high priest tore his robes and exclaimed, "He has blasphemed! What need do we have for any further witnesses? Behold, you have just heard the blasphemy. 66 What do you think?" They shouted in reply, "He deserves to die." 67 Then they spat in his face and struck him with their fists. Some taunted him as they beat him,[p] 68 "Prophesy to us, Christ! Who hit you?"

Peter Denies Jesus.* 69 [q] Meanwhile, Peter was sitting outside in the courtyard. One of the servant girls came over to him and said, "You too were with Jesus the Galilean." 70 But he denied it before all of them, saying, "I do not know what you are talking about." 71 When he walked out to the entrance gate, another servant girl caught sight of him and said to the people around her, "This man was with Jesus of Nazareth."[r] 72 And again

f 47-56: Mk 14:43-50; Lk 22:47-53; Jn 18:3-11.—g Mt 26:23.—h Dan 7:10; Jn 18:36.—i Mk 12:35; Jn 18:20.—j Mt 1:22; 26:31.—k 57-68: Mk 14:53-65; Lk 22:54-55, 63-71; Jn 18:12-14, 19-24.—l Jn 18:15.—m 60-61: Deut 19:15; Ps 35:11; Jn 2:19; Acts 6:14.—n Mt 4:3; Isa 53:7.—o Mt 27:11; Ps 110:1; Dan 7:13.—p Mt 16:21; Wis 2:19; Isa 50:6.—q 69-75: Mk 14:66-72; Lk 22:56-62; Jn 18:17-18, 25-27.—r Mt 2:23.

26:47-56 Jesus practices what he had taught (Mt 5:39). He regards himself as the suffering Servant (see Isa 53) who accepts his sacrifice in silence so as to accomplish his mission. It is love that reestablishes order, for in the face of hypocritical force violence remains powerless.

26:47-48 Judas was well aware of the customs of his Master, and that he was wont to retire to the garden of Gethsemane. A kiss was the customary greeting of a disciple for his teacher.

26:53 *Do you suppose that I cannot appeal to my Father for help . . .?:* by these words Jesus emphasizes the voluntary character of his Passion. Jesus freely accepts the will of God, expressed in Scripture. The same reason is repeated in v. 56. *Twelve legions:* a Roman legion consisted of 6000 men.

26:57-68 According to Matthew and Mark, immediately after his arrest Jesus was led before the Sanhedrin for a session that very night. Another session was held in the morning; then Jesus was consigned to Pilate. The religious trial has two phases: the first centers upon the false testimony of the witnesses, the second upon the question put to Jesus by the high priest. The Law (Deut 17:6) required that two witnesses agree in their testimony against an accused person. Jesus supposedly had said that he had power over the temple, which was the house of God. But had he not said that his body was the true dwelling of the Father (Jn 2:21)? Now that every political and nationalist interpretation of his words seems excluded, since he is alone, rejected, helpless, he dares to say that he is the Messiah and not only the son but the lord of David (Ps 110:1; Dan 7:13).

26:69-75 At the very moment when the Master openly proclaims himself to be the Messiah, no one acknowledges it. In the opinion of all, he is lost. Even Peter, the leader of Jesus' followers, denies any link with him.

he denied it, this time with an oath: "I do not
know the man."
73 Shortly afterward, some bystanders
came up to Peter and said to him, "You
unquestionably are one of them. Even your
accent gives you away." [s] 74 Then Peter began
to shout curses, and he swore an oath: "I do
not know the man." At that very moment, a
cock crowed, 75 and Peter remembered what
Jesus had said: "Before the cock crows, you
will deny me three times." And he went out-
side and began to weep uncontrollably. [t]

CHAPTER 27

Jesus Is Handed Over to Pilate.* 1 [u] When
morning came, all the chief priests and the
elders of the people met together in council
to decide how to put him to death. 2 They
bound him and led him away, and handed
him over to Pilate, the governor. [v]

Judas Hangs Himself.* 3 [w] When Judas dis-
covered that Jesus, whom he betrayed, had
been condemned he was seized with a sense
of remorse, and he brought back the thirty
pieces of silver to the chief priests and the
elders. [x] 4 "I have sinned," he said, "for I have
betrayed innocent blood." They replied, "Of
what importance is that to us? That is your
responsibility." 5 Flinging the silver pieces
into the temple, he departed. Then he went
off and hanged himself. [y]
6 The chief priests retrieved the silver
coins and said, "It is not lawful for us to
deposit this into the temple treasury, for it is
blood money." 7 They conferred together,
and then used it to purchase the potter's
field as a burial place for foreigners. 8 This is
the reason why that field to this very day is
called the Field of Blood.
9 Thus was fulfilled what had been spoken
through the prophet Jeremiah: *

"And they took the thirty pieces of silver,
the price set on his head by the peo-
ple of Israel,
10 and they used them to purchase the
potter's field
as the Lord had commanded me." [z]

Jesus Is Questioned by Pilate. * 11 [a] Mean-
while, Jesus was brought into the presence
of the governor, who asked him, "Are you
the king of the Jews?" Jesus replied, "You
have said so." * 12 And when he was accused
by the chief priests and the elders, he
offered no reply. [b] 13 Pilate then said to him,
"Have you not heard how many charges
they have brought against you?" 14 But he
did not offer a single word in response,
much to the governor's amazement. *

Jesus Is Sentenced to Death. 15 [c] Now on the
occasion of the feast, the governor's custom
was to release to the people one prisoner
whom they had designated. 16 At that
particular time, they had in custody a noto-
rious prisoner named Barabbas. 17 There-
fore, after the people had gathered, Pilate
asked them, "Which man do you want me to
release to you: Barabbas, or Jesus who is
called the Christ?" 18 For he knew that it was
out of envy that they had handed him over.
19 [d] While he was still seated on the judge's
bench, his wife sent him a message: "Have
nothing to do with that innocent man. I have
been greatly troubled today by a dream that
I had about him." *

s Lk 22:59.—t Mt 26:34; Jn 13:38.—u 1-2: Mk 15:1; Lk 23:1; Jn 18:28.—v Acts 3:13.—w 3-10: Acts 1:18-19.—x Mt 10:4; 26:15.—y Acts 2:18.—z Zec 11:12-13.—a 11-14: Mk 15:2-5; Lk 23:2-3; Jn 18:29-38.—b Isa 53:7; Mk 14:61.—c 15-26: Mk 15:6-15; Lk 23:17-25; Jn 18:39—19:16.—d Gen 20:6; Jn 19:13.

27:1-2 According to Matthew and Mark, the members of the Sanhedrin came together officially for a second time in the morning to pronounce the sentence of condemnation. In the light of a different scenario found in Luke and John, scholars believe it is more probable that during the night Jesus appeared before Annas for a private interrogation and then was brought to Caiaphas. In the morning he appeared before the Sanhedrin, where he was declared deserving of death. The Jewish tribunal did not have the power over life and death. Therefore, Jesus was led before Pontius Pilate, who from A.D. 26 to 36 was the governor (procurator) in Judea, which passed into the direct dominion of Rome in A.D. 6.

27:3-10 This story is typical of Matthew's style; the sad incident suggests to him various references to the Scriptures (Zec 11:12-13; Jer 18:2-3; 32:6-15). The memory of Judas was a burden to the early Christians (see Acts 1:16-20).

27:9 *Spoken through the prophet Jeremiah:* the statement actually comes from Zec 11:12, 13. However, the Hebrew canon of Scripture was divided into three sections: The Law, The Writings, and The Prophets (see Lk 24:44). Since Jeremiah came first in the order of the Prophetic Books, the Prophets were at times collectively referred to by his name.

27:11-26 For a second time (the wise men were the first to use the title, Mt 2:1-12), Jesus is called "King of the Jews," and once again it is a pagan who gives him the title. The governor says he is convinced of the innocence of Jesus (see Deut 21:6), but he yields to the insistence of the Jewish authorities.

27:11 The members of the Sanhedrin had condemned Jesus because of his claim to be a transcendent and superhuman Messiah. Now before Pilate, they cleverly laicize the accusation, portraying Jesus as a dangerous political instigator opposed to the Roman domination. The whole trial is begun on the alleged kingship of Jesus.

27:14 The silence of Jesus recalls the attitude of the Servant of the Lord, who like a lamb does not open his mouth in the face of those who shear him (Isa 53:7).

27:19 A Gentile woman declares Jesus' innocence. *By a dream:* for Matthew, dreams are the means of communication from God (1:20; 2:12, 13, 19, 22).

20 Meanwhile, the chief priests and the elders had persuaded the crowd to ask for the release of Barabbas and to have Jesus executed.[e] 21 Therefore, when the governor asked them, "Which of the two men do you want me to release to you?" they shouted, "Barabbas!" 22 Pilate asked them, "Then what shall I do with Jesus who is called the Messiah?" All of them shouted, "Let him be crucified!" 23 He asked, "Why? What evil has he done?" But they only screamed all the louder, "Let him be crucified!"

24 When Pilate saw that he was getting nowhere and that a riot was about to occur, he took some water and washed his hands * in full view of the crowd, saying, "I am innocent of this man's blood. It is your responsibility."[f] 25 With one voice the entire crowd cried out, "Let his blood be on us and on our children!" *[g] 26 He then released Barabbas to them, and after Jesus had been scourged, he handed him over to be crucified.

Jesus Is Crowned with Thorns.* 27 [h] Then the governor's soldiers took Jesus inside the praetorium and gathered the whole cohort around him. 28 They stripped him and put a scarlet robe on him, 29 and after twisting some thorns into a crown, they placed it on his head and put a reed in his right hand. Then, bending the knee before him, they mocked him, saying, "Hail, King of the Jews!"[i] 30 They also spat upon him and, taking the reed, used it to strike him on the head.[j] 31 And when they had finished mocking him, they stripped him of the robe, dressed him in his own clothes, and led him away to crucify him.

The Way of the Cross. 32 As they went out, they encountered a man from Cyrene * named Simon, and they forced him to carry the cross.[k]

Jesus Is Crucified on Calvary. 33 [l] When they came to a place called Golgotha, which means the Place of the Skull, * 34 they offered him some wine to drink that had been mixed with gall; but after tasting it, he refused to drink the mixture. *[m] 35 And after they had crucified him, * they divided his garments among them by casting lots.[n] 36 Then they sat down there to keep guard over him. 37 Above his head was inscribed the charge against him: "This is Jesus, the King of the Jews." 38 Two thieves were crucified with him, one on his right and the other on his left. *[o]

39 Those people who passed by jeered at him, shaking their heads[p] 40 and saying, "You who claimed you could destroy the temple and rebuild it within three days, save yourself! If you truly are the Son of God, come down from the cross!"[q]

41 In much the same way, the chief priests, together with the scribes and the elders, joined in the mockery, saying, 42 "He saved others, but he cannot save himself. If he is the king of Israel, let him come down from the cross right now, and we will believe in him. 43 He trusted in God; now let God deliver him if he wants him, for he said, 'I am the Son of God.' "[r] 44 The thieves who were crucified with him also taunted him in the same way.

e Acts 3:14.—f Deut 21:1-8; Ps 26:6.—g Jer 26:15; Acts 5:28.—h 27-31: Mk 15:16-20; Jn 19:2-3.—i Mt 27:11; Isa 53:3.—j Isa 50:6.—k Mk 15:21; Lk 23:26; Heb 13:12.—l 33-44: Mk 15:22-32; Lk 23:32-38; Jn 19:17-19, 23-24.—m Ps 69:22.—n Ps 22:19.—o Isa 53:12.—p Ps 22:7; Jer 18:16.—q Mt 4:3, 6; 26:61.—r Ps 22:9; Wis 2:12-20.

27:24 *Washed his hands:* this gesture of Pilate was in use among the Jews (see Deut 21:6) and among other peoples. However, this symbolic action does not exempt the Roman procurator of his responsibility. He has acknowledged the innocence of the accused yet has condemned him.

27:25 The nation accepts the responsibility for Jesus' death. The Second Vatican Council has declared that the guilt for Jesus' death is not attributable to all the Jews of his day or to any Jews of later times. We are responsible for Jesus' death. He died for our sins.

27:27-31 Jesus is delivered up to suffering, misunderstanding, ridicule. "He was despised and shunned by others, a man of sorrows, who was no stranger to suffering"; "I did not shield my face from insults and spitting" (Isa 53:3; 50:6). The praetorium was the residence of the Roman governor.

27:32 *Cyrene:* a Greek colony on the Libyan coast; a large Jewish community lived there. See note on Mk 15:21.

27:33 *Skull* (Latin: *calvaria*): a rounded, rocky elevation, about fifteen feet high. It was a former quarry that functioned as a garbage dump.

27:34 The wine mixed with gall was meant to alleviate suffering.

27:35 *Crucified him:* crucifixion was an excruciating means of execution that the Romans had borrowed from Persians, Phoenicians, and Carthaginians. The victims were nailed to a cross by means of heavy wrought-iron nails driven through their wrists and heels. Most hung on the cross for days before dying of suffocation (when the legs were no longer able to support the body, the diaphragm was constricted and breathing became impossible). Although the pain would be unbearable as the hours dragged on, some did linger and had to have their legs broken to hasten death (see Jn 19:33). The recent discovery of the bones of a crucified man, near Jerusalem, dating between A.D. 7 and 66, sheds light on the position of those nailed to the cross. A few late manuscripts add here: "lots," so that the word spoken by the Prophet might be fulfilled: 'They divide my garments among them, and for my clothing they cast lots' " (Ps 22:19).

27:38 The crucifixion between two thieves recalls the prophecy of Isa 53:12: "He was counted among the transgressors."

Jesus Dies on the Cross.* 45 [s] Beginning at
midday, there was darkness over the whole
land until three in the afternoon. [t] 46 And
about three o'clock* Jesus cried out in a
loud voice, "*Eli, Eli, lema sabachthani?*"—
that is, "My God, my God, why have you for-
saken me?" [u]

47 On hearing this, some of the bystanders
said, "This man is calling for Elijah." 48 One
of them immediately ran off to get a sponge,
which he soaked in vinegar, put on a stick,
and gave to him to drink. [v] 49 But the others
said, "Wait! Let us see whether Elijah will
come to save him." 50 Then Jesus again cried
out in a loud voice and gave up his spirit.

51 And behold, the veil of the sanctuary
was torn in two from top to bottom. The
earth quaked and rocks were split apart. [w]
52 The tombs were opened, and the bodies of
many saints who had fallen asleep were
raised. [x] 53 And coming forth from their
tombs after his resurrection, they entered
the holy city and appeared to many. * 54 Now
when the centurion and those who were
keeping watch over Jesus with him wit-
nessed the earthquake and all that was hap-
pening, they were terrified, and they said,
"Truly, this man was the Son of God."

55 Many women were also present, looking
on from a distance.They had followed Jesus
from Galilee and ministered to him. [y]
56 Among these were Mary Magdalene,*
Mary the mother of James and Joseph, and
the mother of the sons of Zebedee.

Jesus Is Placed in the Tomb.* 57 [z] When
evening came, there arrived a rich man
from Arimathea named Joseph, who had
himself become a disciple of Jesus. [a] 58 He
went to Pilate and requested the body of
Jesus. So Pilate ordered that it be handed
over to him.

59 Joseph took the body, wrapped it in a
clean linen shroud, 60 and laid it in his own
new tomb that he had hewn out of the
rock. He then rolled an immense stone
against the entrance of the tomb and
departed. [b] 61 Mary Magdalene and the
other Mary were there, sitting opposite the
sepulcher.

The Guard at the Tomb. 62 The next day, on
the morning after the preparation day,* the
chief priests and the Pharisees came to
Pilate in a group 63 and said to him, "Your
Excellency, we recall that while he was still
alive, this impostor said, 'After three days I
will be raised up.' [c] 64 Therefore, issue orders
that the tomb be kept under surveillance
until the third day. Otherwise, his disciples
may go there and steal his body, and then
tell the people, 'He has been raised from the
dead.' This final deception would be worse
than the first."

65 Pilate said to them, "You have a guard.
Go and make the grave as secure as you
can." 66 And so they went forth and made the
tomb secure by sealing the stone and post-
ing a guard. [d]

CHAPTER 28

Jesus Is Raised from the Dead.* 1 [e] After the
Sabbath, at dawn on the first day of the week,
Mary Magdalene and the other Mary went
to visit the sepulcher. 2 And behold, there was
a violent earthquake, for an angel of the
Lord, descended from heaven, came and
rolled back the stone and sat upon it. [f] 3 His
face shone like lightning, and his garments
were as white as snow. [g] 4 The guards were so
paralyzed with fear of him that they became
like dead men.

---

s 45-56: Mk 15:33-41; Lk 23:44-49; Jn 19:28-30.—t Am 8:9.—u Ps 22:2.—v Ps 69:22.—w Ex 26:31-36; Pss 68:9; 77:19.—x Dan 12:1-3; 1 Pet 3:19.—y Lk 8:2, 3.—z 57-61: Mk 15:42-47; Lk 23:50-56; Jn 19:38-42.—a Isa 53:9.—b Acts 13:29.—c Mt 12:40; 16:21; 17:23; 20:19.—d Dan 6:18.—e 1-10: Mk 16:1-8; Lk 24:1-12; Jn 20:1-10.—f Mt 27:51; Acts 5:19.—g Mt 17:2; Dan 7:9; 10:6.

27:45-56 Everything proclaims that the Son of God, dying on the cross, is triumphant over the forces of the world and of death; the old covenant is finished, and the time is coming when the kingdom will be open to all human beings (see Heb 9:12; 10:20; Ezek 37; Dan 12:2; Rev 21).

27:45-46 *Midday . . . three o'clock:* literally, "the sixth hour" . . . "the ninth hour." Psalm 22, whose first verse is here invoked by Jesus, recapitulates all the sufferings of the just people in the Old Testament. It clearly expresses their extreme anguish but also their certainty of final vindication.

27:53 The phenomena that accompany the death of Jesus evoke the apocalyptic literary genre of the Day of the Lord. In fact, according to the evangelists, that day corresponds with the day of the death of Jesus, which signals the beginning of the new era. Because of the obscurity of this language it is difficult to determine the historicity of the resurrection of some dead people mentioned here. Some Fathers of the Church and exegetes believe this passage refers to the liberation from limbo of the just of the Old Testament, who then enter with Jesus into the glory of the heavenly Jerusalem.

27:56 *Magdalene:* "Of Magdala," a place on the west side of Lake Tiberias, near Capernaum.

27:57-61 The story of the burial provided by a rich man certainly recalls Isaiah's prophecy of the Servant (53:9 LXX). See also note on Mk 15:42-47.

27:62 *Preparation day:* this was Friday, the day on which the meal was prepared for the Sabbath, which was a day of complete rest.

28:1-10 The Resurrection of Christ is a mystery of faith; it was not accessible to the senses, as other events are. Our faith in it is based on the word of those who witnessed the risen Christ.

5 But the angel said to the women, "Do not
be afraid! I know that you are looking for
Jesus who was crucified. [h] 6 He is not here, for
he has been raised, as he promised he would
be. Come and see the place where he lay.
7 Then go quickly and tell his disciples: 'He
has been raised from the dead and now he is
going ahead of you to Galilee. There you will
see him.' Behold, I have told you." [i]

8 They were filled with fear and great joy,
and they ran from the tomb to inform his
disciples. 9 [j] And behold, Jesus came to meet
them, saying, "Greetings." They approached
him, embraced his feet, and worshiped him.
10 Then Jesus said to them, "Do not be fear-
ful. Go and tell my brethren to go to Galilee.
There they will see me." *

The Report of the Guard.* 11 While the
women were on their way, some of the
guards went into the city and reported to
the chief priests everything that had hap-
pened. [k] 12 After the chief priests had con-
ferred with the elders, they presented a large
sum of money to the soldiers 13 and gave
them this order: "Say, 'His disciples came by
night and stole the body while we were
asleep.' 14 And should the governor hear any-
thing in this regard, we will explain the
situation to him and you will be safe." 15 The
soldiers took the money and did as they had
been instructed. And this story is still circu-
lated among the Jews to this very day.

Jesus Gives the Great Commission.* 16 [l] Then
the eleven disciples set out for Galilee, to the
mountain where Jesus had told them to
meet him. [m] 17 When they saw him, they
prostrated themselves before him, although
some doubted. 18 Then Jesus approached
them and said, "All authority in heaven
and on earth has been given to me. [n]
19 [o] Go, therefore, and make disciples of all
nations, baptizing them in the name of the
Father and of the Son and of the Holy
Spirit, * 20 and teaching them to observe all
that I have commanded you. And behold, I
am with you always, to the end of the
world." [p]

---

h Mt 14:27.—i Mt 26:32.—j 9-10: Jn 20:14-18; Rom 8:29.—k Mt 27:65.—l 16-20: Mk 16:14-16; Lk 24:36-49; Jn 20:19-23.—m Mt 26:32.—n Dan 7:14 LXX; 1 Cor 15:27.—o Isa 49:6; Acts 1:8; 2:38.—p Mt 1:23; 13:39; 24:3; Deut 31:6; Jn 14:18-21; Acts 2:42.

28:10 It is difficult to harmonize the accounts of the appearances of the risen Jesus set forth by the four evangelists and St. Paul (1 Cor 15:3-7). There are no authentic divergences, only independent narratives. Every sacred author gives one episode or other and stresses one phrase or other of the Lord in accord with some unknown criteria or particular theology.

Scripture describes at least ten appearances of Jesus to his apostles and disciples between his Resurrection and his Ascension forty days later. He appeared to: (1) Mary Magdalene at the tomb (Mk 16:9; Jn 20:11-18); (2) the women on the road (Mt 28:9, 10); (3) the two disciples on the road to Emmaus (Lk 24:13-35); (4) Peter (Lk 24:34; 1 Cor 15:5); (5) ten of the eleven apostles, with Thomas absent (Lk 24:36-43; Mk 16:14; Jn 20:19-25); (6) all eleven apostles, with Thomas present (eight days later) (Jn 20:26-31); (7) seven disciples by the shore of the Sea of Galilee (Jn 21:1-25); (8) more than 500 disciples, most likely on a mountain in Galilee (1 Cor 15:6); (9) James (1 Cor 15:7); and (10) the apostles at his Ascension (Acts 1:3-11). After his Ascension he also appeared to Paul (1 Cor 15:8).

28:11-15 Matthew is here combating the fables that were circulated in Jewish circles to ridicule the testimony of the early Church.

28:16-20 The last passage of the Gospel is not a conclusion but a new beginning, a new departure. From a mountain whose vantage point embraces the ends of the earth and the limits of history, we see the destiny of humankind. Now Jesus is established in his lordship in dazzling glory, and his hands hold the fate of the world. Now his faithful spread his message and his mystery; now there is one Baptism for all humanity and one communion with God for all persons. It is the time of the universal mission: God is with us; such is the very name of Jesus: "Emmanuel" (Mt 1:23; see Isa 7:14). On the face of Christ we read the mystery of the Church.

28:19 The evangelist places on the Lord's lips the trinitarian formula that was in use in the baptismal Liturgy of the time (A.D. 70–80).

"Jesus said to the paralyzed man, 'Son, your sins are forgiven. . . . Stand up, take your bed, and go to your home' " *(Mk 2:5, 11).*

THE GOSPEL ACCORDING TO MARK

Who Is Jesus?

Who is the author of this book? Ever since the 2nd century the tradition has held that the author was Mark, a personage known to us from the New Testament under the name of John, who was also called Mark (Acts 12:25). He accompanied his cousin Barnabas on a mission (Acts 13:5, 13; 15:39). He also became a companion of Paul for a time, but later separated from the latter, taking with him his cousin due to disagreement with Paul (Acts 13:13; 15:37-39). Toward the end, however, we find him once again a valuable helper of Paul (Col 4:10; Philem 24; 2 Tim 4:11). He must have had connections with Peter (Acts 12:12; 1 Pet 5:13), and it is thought that his Gospel reflects chiefly the preaching of the first apostle.

According to the majority of present-day scholars, this Gospel was written shortly before the destruction of Jerusalem in A.D. 70. It was written in Greek, perhaps at Rome, and is addressed to Christians of non-Jewish origin. By reason of its date, Mark's is the first Gospel known to history, the one that inaugurates this genre of writings that put us in touch with the actions and words of Jesus and with the mystery of his Death and Resurrection. And, in fact, both Matthew and Luke were familiar with the text of Mark when they wrote their own works; they complete or correct his Gospel in light of the information available to them and according to the needs of their readers. This explains why Mark was neglected by the Fathers and, until the recent reform, by the Liturgy. And yet what an extraordinary picture of Jesus he gives us!

Mark's language and talent are those of a popular storyteller. His work follows no particular order; its grammar is rudimentary, its vocabulary limited. In its expression it is often monotonous and schematic, but it can suddenly become animated, varied, and impressive; at such moments, its style is lively and picturesque.

Mark does not intend to paint a portrait or write a biography of Jesus, but rather to draw his readers' attention to the mystery of Christ's person. He also puts readers in the presence of the events, and forces them to participate in the action.

Unlike the other Gospels, Mark's begins abruptly with the preaching of John the Baptist and places us in the midst of the ongoing action.

This Gospel reports few of Jesus' discourses, but does like to tell the stories in detail. Rather than any teaching, it is the fate and work of Jesus that are meant to elicit the readers' response.

The Gospel of Mark may be divided as follows:

I: Preparation for the Mission of Jesus (1:1-13)
II: Is Jesus the Messiah? (1:14—8:30)
III: The Mystery of Jesus Is Revealed (8:31—16:8)
Appendix: The Longer Ending (16:9-20)

I: PREPARATION FOR THE MISSION OF JESUS*

CHAPTER 1

Beginning of the Good News.* 1 The beginning of the gospel of Jesus Christ, the Son of God.

2 [a] It is written in the prophet Isaiah: *

"Behold, I am sending my messenger
ahead of you;
he will prepare your way. [b]
3 The voice of one crying out in the
wilderness:
'Prepare the way of the Lord,
make his paths straight.' " [c]

4 Hence, John the Baptist appeared in the desert, proclaiming a baptism of repentance for the forgiveness of sins. [d] 5 People from the entire Judean countryside and all the inhabitants of Jerusalem went out to him, and as they confessed their sins they were baptized by him in the Jordan River.

6 John was clothed in a garment of camel's hair, with a leather belt around his waist, and his food consisted of locusts and wild honey. [e] 7 And this was the message he proclaimed: "One who is far more powerful than I am is coming after me. I am not worthy even to stoop down and loosen the straps of his sandals. [f] 8 I have baptized you with water, but he will baptize you with the Holy Spirit."* [g]

Jesus Is Baptized by John.* 9 At that time,* Jesus came from Nazareth in Galilee and was baptized by John in the Jordan. [h] 10 * And as he was coming up out of the water, he beheld the heavens break open and the Spirit descending upon him like a dove. 11 And a voice came from heaven: "You are my beloved Son; in you I am well pleased." [i]

Jesus Is Tempted in the Desert.* 12 [j] The Spirit immediately drove him out into the desert. 13 He remained there for forty days, during which time he was tempted by Satan. He lived there among the wild beasts, while the angels ministered to him.

a 2-8: Mt 3:1-11; Lk 3:2-16.—b Mal 3:1; Mt 11:10.—c Isa 40:3; Jn 1:23.—d Mt 3:1.—e 2 Ki 1:8.—f Jn 1:27.—g Isa 44:3; Acts 1:5; 11:16.—h 9-11: Mt 3:13-17; Lk 3:21-22; Jn 1:32-33.—i Mk 9:7; Ps 2:7; Isa 42:1.—j 12-13: Job 1:6; Mt 4:1-11; Lk 4:1-13.

1:1-13 Around the year 30, after centuries of silence, a prophet named John appears and unsettles his contemporaries. They are captivated by the force of his personality and the vehemence of his message. Then Jesus comes on the scene. Mark uses this story as a kind of prologue for his book, a kind of key for understanding the pages that follow: the Gospel, the "good news," is here bursting out in the midst of humanity; the action of Jesus inaugurates the kingdom of God, the time of salvation.

1:1-8 The Gospel is not primarily a book but rather God's action for the salvation of humankind. The entire Book of Mark depicts Jesus as the promised and awaited one (the Messiah) and as the Son of God (see Mk 8:35; 10:29).

1:2 *The prophet Isaiah:* the quotation that follows is a combination of Malachi (3:1) and Isaiah (40:3). See note on Mt 27:9.

1:8 *Baptize you with the Holy Spirit:* see note on Mt 3:11.

1:9-11 Mark retains only the essential elements of the divine manifestation, which here is given only to Jesus, whose mission is announced.

1:9 *At that time:* Jesus probably began his public ministry about A.D. 27 at approximately 30 years of age (see Lk 3:23). *Nazareth:* see note on Mt 2:23. *Baptized by John:* see note on Mt 3:15 for the meaning of Jesus' baptism.

1:10-11 This passage has the involvement of all three persons of the Trinity: (1) the Father speaks; (2) the Son is baptized; and (3) the Holy Spirit descends on the Son.

1:12-13 Jesus is already committed to his mission of combating Satan, the representative of all the forces of evil that batter humanity.

II: IS JESUS THE MESSIAH?*

A: First Testimonies of the Messiah's Mission

Jesus Inaugurates His Mission. 14 [k] After John had been arrested,* Jesus came to Galilee proclaiming the gospel of God, and saying, 15 "The time of fulfillment has arrived, and the kingdom of God is close at hand. Repent, and believe in the gospel." [l]

The First Disciples.* 16 [m] As Jesus was walking along by the Sea of Galilee, he saw Simon and his brother Andrew casting their nets into the sea, for they were fishermen. 17 Jesus said to them, "Come, follow me, and I will make you fishers of men." 18 Immediately, they abandoned their nets and followed him.

19 As he proceeded farther, he saw James, the son of Zebedee, and his brother John. They also were in a boat mending their nets. 20 Immediately, he called them, and they left their father Zebedee in the boat with the hired workers and followed him.

Jesus Heals a Man with a Demon.* 21 [n] They journeyed to Capernaum, and on the Sabbath Jesus immediately entered the synagogue and began to instruct the people. 22 They were astounded at his teaching, for he taught them as one who had authority, and not as the scribes. [o]

23 In that synagogue there was a man with an unclean spirit, and he shrieked, 24 "What do you want with us, Jesus of Nazareth? Have you come to destroy us? I know who you are—the Holy One of God." * [p] 25 But Jesus rebuked him, saying, "Be silent, and come out of him!"

26 The unclean spirit threw the man into convulsions and with a loud cry emerged from him. [q] 27 The people were all amazed, and they began to ask one another, "What is this? It must be a new kind of teaching! With authority he gives commands even to unclean spirits, and they obey him!" 28 His reputation quickly began to spread everywhere throughout the entire region of Galilee. [r]

Jesus Heals Peter's Mother-in-Law. 29 [s] Immediately on leaving the synagogue, he went with James and John into the house of Simon and Andrew. 30 Simon's mother-in-law * was lying in bed, sick with a fever, and they informed Jesus at once about her. 31 Jesus approached her, grasped her by the hand, and helped her up. Then the fever left her, and she began to serve them. [t]

Other Healings. 32 That evening, after sunset, they brought to him all those who were sick or possessed by demons. * 33 The whole town was present, crowded around the door. 34 He cured many who were afflicted with various diseases, and he drove out many demons, although he would not permit them to speak because they knew who he was. [u]

Jesus Proclaims the Message and Heals the Sick. 35 Early the next morning, long before dawn, he arose and went off to a secluded place, where he prayed. 36 Simon and his companions set forth in search of him, 37 and when they found him they said, "Everybody is looking for you." 38 He replied, "Let us move on to the neighboring towns so that I may proclaim the message there as well. For this is the reason why I came." [v] 39 Then he traveled all throughout Galilee, preaching in their synagogues and driving out demons.

Jesus Heals a Man with Leprosy. 40 [w] A man with leprosy* approached and, kneeling before him, begged him, "If you choose to do so, you can make me clean." 41 Moved

---

k 14-15: Mt 4:12-17; Lk 4:14-15.—l Dan 7:22; Mt 3:2; Rom 1:1.—m 16-20: Mt 4:18-22; Lk 5:2-11.—n 21-28: Lk 4:31-37.—o Mt 7:28-29.—p Jdg 13:5; Acts 4:10.—q Mk 9:20.—r Mt 9:26.—s 29-34: Mt 8:14-16; Lk 4:38-41.—t Mk 5:41.—u Mk 3:12.—v Isa 61:1; Jn 18:37.—w 40-44: Mt 8:2-4; Lk 5:12-14.

1:14—8:30 People had a simple idea of the Messiah as a glorious figure: they were expecting a national hero, a political liberator, a restorer of their independence and their public worship, a leader who would bring Israel to world domination. But the reason why Jesus comes before the nation is quite different. This first part of Mark's Gospel describes three periods. Three times the author gives a general summary of the activity of Jesus and describes a mission of the disciples; each period ends with a scene of hostility and lack of understanding. At the end of this first half of the book, the confession of Peter at Caesarea recognizes the Messiah without any misunderstanding. From that point on, the road will lead to the Passion; that development occupies the second half of the Gospel.

1:14 *After John had been arrested:* the ministry of Jesus begins under the sign of his precursor's martyrdom. This simple chronological marker is a veiled prefiguration of the suffering and death that await the Messiah. See note on Lk 3:20.

1:16-20 See note on Mt 4:18-22.

1:21-28 See note on Lk 4:31-41.

1:24 *The Holy One of God:* this title is used only here and in Lk 4:34 and Jn 6:69. It refers more to Jesus' divinity than to his Messiahship (see Lk 1:35).

1:30 *Simon's mother-in-law:* Paul (in 1 Cor 9:5) speaks of Peter being married.

1:32 At sunset, the strictly enjoined Sabbath rest came to an end.

1:40 *Leprosy:* see Lev 13—14.

with pity, he stretched out his hand and touched him,* saying, "I do choose. Be made clean!"[x] [42] Immediately, the leprosy left him and he was cured.[y]

[43] Jesus then sent him away at once, after first sternly warning him, [44] "See that you tell no one anything about this. Just go and show yourself to the priest and offer for your cleansing what Moses prescribed. That will be proof for them."*[z] [45] How-ever, he went forth and began to proclaim the entire story, spreading the word far and wide. As a result, Jesus could no longer go openly into any town. Rather, he stayed outside in deserted places, and people continued to come to him from every quarter.[a]

B: First Oppositions*

CHAPTER 2

Jesus Heals a Paralyzed Man.[b] [1] When Jesus returned some days later to Capernaum, the word quickly spread that he was at home. [2] Such large multitudes gathered there that no longer was any space available, even in front of the door, and he was preaching the word to them.

[3] Some people arrived, bringing to him a man who was paralyzed, carried by four men. [4] Since they were unable to bring him near Jesus because of the crowd, they made an opening in the roof above him and then lowered the bed on which the paralyzed man was lying.

[5] On perceiving their faith, Jesus said to the paralyzed man, "Son, your sins are forgiven."[c] [6] Now some scribes* were sitting there, thinking to themselves: [7] "How can this man say such things? He is blaspheming! Who can forgive sins but God alone?"[d]

[8] Jesus was able immediately to discern in his spirit what they were thinking, and he asked, "Why do you entertain such thoughts in your hearts? [9] Which is easier: to say to the paralyzed man, 'Your sins are forgiven,' or to say: 'Stand up, take your mat, and walk'? [10] But that you may come to realize that the Son of Man* has authority on earth to forgive sins"—he said to the paralyzed man—[11] "I say to you, stand up, take your bed, and go to your home." [12] The man stood up, immediately picked up his bed, and went off in full view of all of them. The onlookers were all astonished and they glorified God, saying, "We have never before witnessed anything like this."[e]

Jesus Calls Levi (Matthew). [13] Once again Jesus went out to the shore of the lake,* and as a large crowd came to him, he taught them.[f] [14][g] As he was walking along, he saw Levi* the son of Alphaeus sitting at the tax collector's booth. Jesus said to him, "Follow me," and he got up and followed him.

Jesus Eats with Sinners. [15] When he was sitting at dinner in his* house, many tax collectors and sinners were seated with him and his disciples, for there were many who followed Jesus. [16] Some scribes who were Pharisees noticed that Jesus was eating with sinners and tax collectors, and they asked his disciples, "Why does he eat with tax collectors and sinners?"[h] [17] When Jesus overheard this remark, he said, "It is not the healthy who need a physician, but rather those who are sick. I have come to call not the righteous but sinners."[i]

A Time of Joy and Grace.* [18][j] John's disciples and the Pharisees were observing a fast. Some people came to Jesus and asked, "Why do John's disciples and those of the Pharisees fast but your disciples do not do so?"[k] [19] Jesus answered, "How can the wedding guests fast while the bridegroom is still with them? As long as they have the bridegroom with them, they cannot fast. [20] But the time

x Mk 5:30.—y Lk 17:14.—z Lev 14:2-32.—a Lk 5:15; Jn 6:2.—b 1-12: Mt 9:2-8; Lk 5:18-26.—c Mt 8:10; Lk 7:48.—d Ps 32:5; Isa 43:25.—e Mt 9:33.—f Mk 4:1.—g 14-17: Mt 9:9-13; Lk 5:27-32.—h Acts 23:9.—i Lk 19:10.—j 18-22: Mt 9:14-17; Lk 5:33-39.—k Acts 13:2.

1:41 *Touched him:* an act that caused defilement according to the Law (see Lev 13:45-46). Jesus' compassion superseded any consideration of defilement.

1:44 For this ritual cleansing, see Lev 14:1-32.

2:1—3:6 In the five controversy stories that are combined here, the plot to put Jesus to death, which is the key to Mark's Gospel, is already made clear.

2:6 *Scribes:* men trained in the oral traditions that flowed from the written Law. In this Gospel, they are adversaries of Jesus except in one incident (Mk 12:28-34).

2:10 *Son of Man:* see note on Mt 8:20.

2:13 *Lake:* Tiberias.

2:14 *Levi:* another name of Matthew (Jews often had two names). The taxes in question were collected on goods that entered or left the city. The system was established by the Romans, but the collection of taxes and duties was handed over to private organizations whose employees were not infrequently corrupt. See also note on Mt 5:46.

2:15 *His:* i.e., Levi's (see Lk 5:29). *Sinners:* those who were ostentatiously wicked and those who did not follow the Law as interpreted by the scribes. The term was customarily applied to collaborators, robbers, adulterers, and the like.

2:18-22 See notes on Mt 9:14-17 and Lk 5:33-39.

will come when the bridegroom is taken away from them, and then on that day they will fast. *[l]

21 “No one sews a piece of unshrunken cloth on an old cloak. If he does, the patch tears away from it, the new from the old, and a worse tear results. 22 Nor does anyone pour new wine * into old wineskins. If he does, the wine will burst the skins, and then the wine and the skins are both lost. Rather, new wine is poured into fresh wineskins.”

Picking Grain on the Sabbath.* 23 [m] One day, as Jesus was passing through a field of grain on the Sabbath, his disciples began to pick some heads of grain as they walked along. 24 The Pharisees said to him, “Behold, why are your disciples doing what is forbidden on the Sabbath?” [n]

25 He answered, “Have you never read what David did when he and his companions were hungry and in need of food? 26 He entered the house of God when Abiathar * was high priest and ate the sacred bread that only the priests were permitted to eat, and he shared it with his companions.” [o] 27 Then he said to them, “The Sabbath was made for man, not man for the Sabbath. *[p] 28 That is why the Son of Man is Lord even of the Sabbath.”

CHAPTER 3

A Man with a Withered Hand.* 1 [q] Again, Jesus entered the synagogue, and a man was there who had a withered hand. 2 They watched him closely to see whether he would cure him on the Sabbath so that they might accuse him. [r] 3 He said to the man with the withered hand, “Come here.” 4 Then he said to the onlookers, “Is it lawful to do good or to do evil on the Sabbath, to save life or to kill?” But they offered no reply. 5 Looking at them with anger, he was saddened at the hardness of their hearts, and he said to the man, “Stretch out your hand.” He stretched it out, and his hand was restored. [s] 6 Then the Pharisees went out and immediately began to plot with the Herodians how they might put him to death. [t]

C: The Disciples Bear Witness to the Kingdom of God*

Summary of the Activity of Jesus.* 7 [u] Thereupon Jesus withdrew with his disciples to the lakeshore, and a great multitude of people from Galilee followed him. 8 In addition, having heard of all he was doing, large numbers also came to him from Judea, Jerusalem, Idumea, beyond the Jordan, and the region of Tyre and Sidon. *

9 He instructed his disciples to have a small boat ready for him so that he would not be crushed by the crowds. 10 For he had healed so many that all who were afflicted in any way came crowding around to touch him. [v] 11 And whenever unclean spirits saw him, they would fall at his feet and shout, “You are the Son of God.” [w] 12 But he strictly ordered them not to make him known. [x]

Jesus Establishes the Group of the Disciples.* 13 [y] Jesus then went up onto the mountain and summoned those whom he wanted, and they came to him. 14 * He

---

l Lk 17:22.—m 23-28: Mt 12:1-8; Lk 6:1-5.—n Deut 23:25.—o Lev 24:5-9; 1 Sam 21:1-6.—p Deut 5:14; 2 Mac 5:19.—q 1-6: Mt 12:9-14; Lk 6:6-11.—r Lk 14:1.—s Lk 14:4; Eph 4:18.—t Mt 22:16.—u 7-12: Mt 4:23-25; 12:15; Lk 6:17-19.—v Mk 5:30.—w Mk 1:34; Mt 8:29; Lk 4:41.—x Acts 16:17, 18.—y 13-19: Mt 10:1-4; Lk 6:12-16.

2:20 The Jews were obliged to fast only on the Day of Atonement. However, devout persons fasted two times a week (on Monday and Thursday). Jesus does not disapprove of such acts. He merely points out that his coming has inaugurated the time of joy foretold by the Prophets, in which it was legitimate for his disciples to benefit from the presence of the Bridegroom, i.e., the Messiah. He then alludes to his violent death after which his disciples would fast while awaiting the glorious and definitive coming of the heavenly Bridegroom.

2:22 *New wine:* the Gospel; the old wine is the practices of Judaism.

2:23-28 See notes on Mt 12:2; 12:3-4; 12:5-6; and 12:8.

2:26 *Abiathar:* high priest in the time of David. In 1 Sam 21:2-3 his father, Ahimelech, is named.

2:27 Mark alone has preserved this saying of Jesus.

3:1-6 See note on Mt 12:9-14.

3:7-35 This is the second period in the first half of the Gospel. A group of disciples has been formed; to these men who are really listening to him Jesus explains his message of the coming kingdom.

3:7-12 Mark begins this second section with a summary of the activity of Jesus.

3:8 This verse demonstrates Jesus' great popularity with people from all of Israel as well as its surrounding neighbors. Mark recounts Jesus' work in all the regions mentioned except Idumea: Galilee (1:14), the region beyond the Jordan (5:1; 10:1), Tyre and Sidon (7:24, 31), Judea (10:1), and Jerusalem (11:11). *Idumea:* the Greek form of the Hebrew “Edom”; but here it refers to an area in western Palestine south of Judea rather than the earlier Edomite territory.

3:13-19 Among those who listened to Jesus there was a group that included women and 72 men who were later sent on mission (see Lk 10:17). Following the Ascension, the group had swelled to 120 believers who waited in Jerusalem (Acts 1:15). From such followers, Jesus here chooses 12 to be apostles (those given a special commission).

3:14-16 Lists of the apostles are also found in Mt 1:2-4; Lk 6:12-16; and Acts 1:13. The order in which the names are given varies, but Peter always comes first and Judas is always placed at the end.

appointed twelve—whom he also named apostles—* that they might be his companions and that he might send them out to proclaim the message,[z] [15] with the authority to drive out demons. [16] The twelve he appointed were: Simon, to whom he gave the name Peter; [17] [a] James the son of Zebedee and John the brother of James, to whom he gave the name Boanerges, that is, "Sons of Thunder";* [18] Andrew, Philip, Bartholomew, Matthew, Thomas, James the son of Alphaeus; Thaddaeus, Simon the Zealot, [19] and Judas Iscariot, who betrayed him.

D: Contrasting Reactions to the Person of Jesus*

The Concern of Jesus' Relatives.* [20] Jesus then returned home, * and once again such a great crowd collected around them that they did not even find it possible to eat.[b] [21] When his relatives heard about this, they went out to take charge of him, saying, "He has gone out of his mind."[c]

The Blasphemy of the Scribes.* [22] [d] Meanwhile, the scribes who had come down from Jerusalem said, "He is possessed by Beelzebul," and "He casts out demons by the prince of demons."[e] [23] Summoning them to him, he spoke to them in parables, "How can Satan drive out Satan? [24] If a kingdom is divided against itself, that kingdom cannot survive. [25] And if a household is divided against itself, that household will not be able to survive. [26] If Satan has risen up against himself and is divided, he cannot survive; he is doomed.

[27] "But no one can break into a strong man's house and steal his possessions unless he first ties up the strong man; then he can ransack the house.[f]

[28] "Amen, I say to you, all sins that people commit and whatever blasphemies they utter will be forgiven.[g] [29] But whoever blasphemes against the Holy Spirit will not be forgiven; he is guilty of an eternal sin." [30] He said this because they had claimed he was possessed by an unclean spirit.

The True Family of Jesus.* [31] [h] Then his mother and his brethren arrived, and, standing outside, they sent someone in to call him. [32] A crowd was sitting around him, and they said, "Behold, your mother and your brethren are outside asking for you." [33] He replied, "Who are my mother and my brethren?" [34] Then, looking around at those who were near him, he said: "Behold, my mother and my brethren. [35] Whoever does the will of God is my brother and sister and mother."

CHAPTER 4

E: The Parables—A Veiled Language*

The Parable of the Sower. [1] [i] On another occasion he began to teach by the side of the lake. However, such a large crowd gathered that he got into a boat and sat in it out on the lake, while the whole crowd gathered on the shore facing the lake.[j] [2] Then he taught them many things in parables.

In the course of his teaching, he said to them: [3] "Listen! A sower went out to sow. [4] As he sowed, some seed fell on the path, and the birds came and ate it up. [5] Other seed fell on rocky ground, where there was little soil. It sprouted quickly, since the soil had no depth, [6] but when the sun rose, it was scorched, and since it lacked roots, it withered away. [7] Other seed fell among thorns, and the thorns grew up and choked it, and it produced no crop. [8] But some seed fell onto rich soil and brought forth grain, increasing and yielding thirty, sixty, and a hundred times what was sown."[k] [9] He then added, "He who has ears to hear, let him hear!"

---

z Mk 6:7.—a Mt 16:18; Lk 9:54; Jn 1:42.—b Mk 2:2.—c Jn 7:5; 10:20.—d 22-30: Mt 12:24-32; Lk 11:15-22; 12:10.—e Mt 15:1.—f Isa 49:24, 25.—g Lk 12:10.—h 31-35: Mt 12:46-50; Lk 8:19-21.—i 1-12: Mt 13:1-13; Lk 8:4-10.—j Mk 2:13; 3:7; Lk 5:1.—k Jn 15:5; Col 1:6.

3:14 *Whom he also named apostles:* missing in some manuscripts.

3:17 *Sons of Thunder:* the Aramaic nickname emphasizes the fiery character of the two brothers.

3:20-35 In these verses, which are peculiar to Mark's Gospel, the author highlights contrasting reactions to the person of Jesus. The crowds search him out. His relatives think he is out of his mind and understand nothing about his mission; they want to take him by force and bring him back to his own town.

3:20-21 The foundation of the eschatological community is followed by this passage, which recounts the failure to comprehend even on the part of relatives and above all the hostile refusal of the leaders of Judaism to accept him.

3:20 *Home:* i.e., Matthew's house (see Mt 2:15).

3:22-30 See notes on Mt 12:22-32 and 12:32.

3:31-35 See notes on Mt 12:46-50 and 12:47.

4:1-34 Mark has, so to speak, his own "theory of parables," which he here places on the lips of Jesus. In his view, parables were and remained enigmatic: their meaning was clear only to the disciples, those who really "heard" Jesus ("hear" is the key word in these texts) and believed in him. See notes on Mt 13:1-51; 13:3a; 13:3b-9; 13:10-15.

The Reason for Parables. 10 When he was
alone, the Twelve and his other companions
asked him about the parables. 11 He told
them, "To you has been granted knowledge
of the mysteries * of the kingdom of God,
but to those outside, everything comes in
parables, [l] 12 so that

'they may look and see but not perceive,
and hear and listen but fail to understand,
lest they be converted and be forgiven.' " * [m]

The Explanation of the Parable of the Sower.*
13 [n] He went on to say to them, "Do you not
understand this parable? How then are you
to understand any of the parables? 14 What
the sower is sowing is the word. [o]

15 "Some people are like seed that falls
along the path where the word is sown. As
soon as they hear it, Satan immediately
comes and carries off the word that has
been sown in them.

16 "Others are like the seed sown on
rocky ground. As soon as they hear the
word they immediately receive it with joy.
17 But they have no deep root and they
endure for only a short time. When some
trial or tribulation arises on account of the
word, they immediately fall away.

18 "Those sown among thorns are the
ones who hear the word, [p] 19 but worldly
cares, the lure of riches, and the desire for
other things come in and choke the word,
and it bears no fruit. [q]

20 "But those sown in rich soil are those
who hear the word and accept it and bear
fruit and yield thirty or sixty or a hundred
times what was sown."

The Parable of the Lamp.* 21 [r] He said to
them, "Is a lamp brought in to be put under
a basket or under a bed? To the contrary, it is
placed on a lampstand. [s] 22 For nothing is
hidden that will not be disclosed, and nothing is secret that will not be brought to light. [t]
23 If anyone has ears to hear, let him hear!" [u]

The Parable of the Measure.* 24 He also told
them, "Pay careful attention to what you
hear. The measure you give will be the
measure you will receive, and you will
receive more in addition. [v] 25 To the one
who has, more will be given; from the one
who does not have, even what little he has
will be taken away." * [w]

The Parable of the Secretly Growing Seed.*
26 [x] He went on to say, "The kingdom of God
is like this. A man scatters seed on the
ground. 27 Night and day, while he sleeps and
while he is awake, the seed sprouts and
grows, though he does not understand how.
28 The ground produces fruit of its own
accord—first the shoot, then the ear, then the
full grain in the ear. 29 And when the crop is
ripe, he immediately stretches out the sickle,
because the time for harvest has come."

The Parable of the Mustard Seed.* 30 [y] He
then said, "With what shall we compare the
kingdom of God, or what parable can we
use to explain it? 31 It is like a mustard seed
that, when it is sown in the ground, is the
smallest of all the seeds on the earth. 32 But
once it is sown, it springs up and becomes
the greatest of all plants, and it puts forth
large branches so that the birds of the air
can make nests in its shade." [z]

The Usefulness of Parables.* 33 [a] With many
such parables as these he spoke the word
to them so far as they were able to comprehend it. [b] 34 He never spoke to them
except in parables, but he explained everything to his disciples when they were by
themselves.

l Rom 16:25, 1 Cor 5:12; Col 4:5.—m Isa 6:9; Jn 12:40; Acts 28:26; Rom 11:8.—n 13-20: Mt 13:18-23; Lk 8:11-15.—o Acts 4:31.—p Jer 4:3-4.—q Mt 19:23.—r 21-25: Lk 8:16-18.—s Mt 5:15; Lk 11:33.—t Mt 10:26; Lk 8:17; 12:2; Jer 16:17.—u Mt 11:15.—v Mt 7:2; Lk 6:38.—w Mt 13:12; 25:29; Lk 19:26.—x 26-29: Mt 13:24; Jas 5:7; Rev 14:15-16.—y 30-32: Mt 13:31-32; Lk 13:18-19.—z Dan 4:12.—a 33-34: Mt 13:34.—b Jn 16:12.

4:11 *Mysteries:* see note on Mt 13:11.

4:12 The citation is from Isa 6:9-10. Acts (28:26-27) and Romans (11:7-16, 29-32) cite the same passage of Isaiah to show that the rejection by the people of the Covenant had been foretold and that God's plan cannot be checkmated by the defection of human beings. It is not that God wants them to reject the word. They do that on their own because they do not want to receive God's forgiveness.

4:13-20 See note on Mt 13:18-23.

4:21-23 Just as a lamp is placed to provide light, not to hide it, so Jesus, the light of the world, is destined to be revealed.

4:24-25 As an example of the way in which the sayings of Jesus were handed on, we may observe that the parable about measure is applied here to the reception of the "word," but is used in Matthew (7:2) and Luke (6:38) with reference to judgment of one's brother or sister.

4:25 *To the one who has, more will be given . . . :* one of the meanings of this text is that those who appropriate the truth more will receive more truth in the future; however, those who do not respond to what little truth they may know already will not profit even from that amount.

4:26-29 This parable, the only one peculiar to Mark, illustrates his idea of the power of the Gospel. The term *harvest* is an image of the judgment (see Joel 4:13; Rev 14:15).

4:30-32 See notes on Mt 13:31-32 and 13:32.

4:33-34 These words mitigate and partly explain the warning in v. 12. Jesus with his parables adapted himself to the imaginative eastern mentality, without running afoul of the susceptibility of that people who were still stubbornly attached to the idea of a triumphal Messiah. He offered the possibility of reflections and further elucidations.

F: Jesus Overcomes Evil and Effects Salvation*

Jesus Calms the Storm.* 35 [c] On that day, as evening approached, he said to them, "Let us cross over to the other side." 36 And so, leaving the crowd behind, they took him with them in the boat just as he was. Some other boats joined them. [d]

37 Suddenly, a great storm came up, and the waves were crashing over the boat so that it was almost swamped. 38 Jesus was in the stern, asleep on a cushion. They awakened him and said, "Teacher do you not care that we are perishing?"

39 Then he stood up and rebuked the wind, and he said to the sea, "Quiet! Be still!" The wind ceased, and there was a great calm. 40 He said to them, "Why are you so frightened? Are you still without faith?" [e] 41 They were filled with awe and said to one another, "Who can this be? Even the wind and the sea obey him." [f]

CHAPTER 5

Jesus Heals the Gerasene Demoniac.* 1 [g] They reached the region of the Gerasenes * on the other side of the lake. 2 No sooner had he stepped out of the boat than a man with an unclean spirit came up to him from the tombs. * [h] 3 The man had been living in the tombs, and no one could restrain him any longer, not even with chains. 4 For he had frequently been bound with shackles and chains, but he had snapped the chains and smashed the shackles to pieces, and no one had sufficient strength to subdue him. 5 Day and night among the tombs and on the mountains, he would howl and gash himself with stones.

6 When the man caught sight of Jesus from a distance, he ran up and prostrated himself before him, 7 as he shouted at the top of his voice, "What do you want with me, Jesus, Son of the Most High God? I implore you in God's name: do not torment me!" [i] 8 For Jesus had said to him, "Unclean spirit, come out of the man!" 9 Then he asked him, "What is your name?" He replied, "My name is Legion, for there are many of us." * [j] 10 And he begged him earnestly not to send them out of the country.

11 Now on the mountainside a great herd of pigs was feeding. 12 And they pleaded with him, "Send us into the pigs. Let us enter them." 13 He allowed this. With that, the unclean spirits came out and entered the pigs, and the herd, numbering about two thousand, charged down the steep bank into the lake and were drowned in the waters.

14 Those tending the pigs ran off and reported the incident in the town and throughout the countryside. As a result, people came out to see what had happened. 15 When they came near Jesus, they saw the man who had been possessed by Legion sitting there fully clothed and in his right mind, and they were frightened. 16 Those who had been eyewitnesses to the incident confirmed what had happened to the demoniac and what had happened to the pigs. 17 Then they began to implore Jesus to leave their region.

18 As Jesus was getting into the boat, the man who had been possessed with demons pleaded to be allowed to go with him. 19 However, Jesus would not permit him to do so, and instead told him, "Go home to your own people and tell them what the Lord has done for you, and how he has had mercy on you." 20 The man then departed and began to make known throughout the Decapolis what Jesus had done for him. And everyone was amazed. * [k]

c 35-40: Mt 8:18, 23-27; Lk 8:22-25.—d Mk 3:9; 5:2.—e Mt 14:31.—f Mk 1:27.—g 1-20: Mt 8:28-34; Lk 8:26-39.—h Mk 4:1.—*i* Acts 16:17; Heb 7:1.—j Mt 12:45; Lk 8:2; 11:26.—k Mk 1:34; Mt 4:25.

4:35—5:43 The so-called "Parables of the Lake" are followed by a characteristic grouping of four miracles, which demonstrate the evangelist's Christological intention. With his merciful power, Jesus appears as the Master of natural elements, demons, sickness, and death itself. The section gives a very accurate selection of prodigies worked by the Savior. The accounts are possibly pre-Marcan, and they have been endowed by the evangelist with a particularly vivid narrative taken from the preaching of Peter. These are the so-called "Miracles of the Lake."

4:35-40 See note on Mt 8:23-27.

5:1-20 The scene shifts to the Decapolis, a group of ten more or less autonomous cities east of the Jordan; it is as if in a pagan land the forces of evil could enslave and destroy human beings. The demons are condemned to take refuge in the pigs, impure animals par excellence in Jewish eyes. See also note on Mt 8:28-34.

5:1 *The region of the Gerasenes:* the area was southeast of Lake Tiberias.

5:2 Caves were used for tombs.

5:9 *My name is Legion . . . there are many of us:* a Roman legion was made up of 6000 men. The word "legion" gives the idea that the man was possessed by many demons and also provides an inkling of the numerous powers opposed to Jesus, who incorporates the divine power.

5:20 See note on Mt 4:25.

Jesus Heals a Woman and Raises a Child.* 21 When Jesus had crossed again in the boat to the other side, a large crowd gathered around him, and he stayed by the lake.[l] 22 [m] Then one of the leaders of the synagogue,* named Jairus, came forward, and when he saw Jesus he threw himself down at his feet[n] 23 and pleaded with him, saying, "My little daughter is at the point of death. I beg you to come and lay your hands on her so that she may recover and live."[o] 24 Jesus went with him, and a large number accompanied him and crowded around him.

25 There was a woman who had suffered from bleeding for twelve years.[p] 26 In spite of long and painful treatment at the hands of many doctors, her condition not only had failed to improve but had actually become worse, and she had spent everything she had.[q] 27 Having heard about Jesus, she came up behind him in the crowd and touched his cloak, 28 for she thought, "If I simply touch his clothing, I shall be made well." 29 And immediately her bleeding dried up, and she felt in her body that she was healed of her affliction.

30 Instantly aware that power had gone forth from him, Jesus turned around in the crowd and asked, "Who touched my clothing?"[r] 31 His disciples said in reply, "You see this vast throng pressing upon you. How can you ask, 'Who touched me?' " 32 However, he continued to look around to determine who had done it. 33 Then the woman, knowing what had happened to her, approached in fear and trembling. She knelt before him and revealed to him the whole truth. 34 He said to her, "Daughter, your faith has healed you. Go in peace and be freed from your affliction."[s]

35 While he was still speaking, some people from the house of the synagogue leader arrived and said, "Your daughter has died. Why bother the Teacher any further?" 36 Jesus heard the message they had delivered, but he said to the leader of the synagogue, "Do not be afraid. Just have faith." 37 He allowed no one to accompany him except Peter, James, and John,* the brother of James.

38 When they arrived at the house of the synagogue leader, he observed a great deal of commotion, with people weeping and wailing loudly. 39 [t] When he entered, he said to them, "Why this commotion and weeping? The child is not dead; she is asleep." 40 In response, they laughed at him.

After sending them all outside, he took with him the child's father and mother and his own companions and entered the room where the child was. 41 He took the child by the hand and said to her, "*Talitha koum!*" which means: "Little girl, I say to you, arise!"[u] 42 And immediately the girl, a child of twelve, got up and began to walk around.

On witnessing this, they were all overcome with amazement, 43 but he gave them strict instructions that no one should be told anything about this. Then he told them to give her something to eat.

CHAPTER 6

Jesus Is Rejected at Nazareth.* 1 [v] Departing from that district, Jesus went to his hometown accompanied by his disciples. 2 On the Sabbath, he began to teach in the synagogue, and many of those who heard him asked in amazement, "Where did this man get all this? What is this wisdom that he has been granted? What mighty deeds he performs![w] 3 Is this not the carpenter, the son of Mary, and the brother* of James and Joses and Judas and Simon? Are not his sisters here with us?" And so they took offense at him.[x]

l Mk 2:13.—m 22-43: Mt 9:18-26; Lk 8:41-56.—n Acts 13:15.—o Mt 19:13; Lk 4:40.—p Lev 15:25-30.—q Tob 2:10.—r Lk 5:17.—s Mt 8:10; Lk 7:50.—t 39-40: Acts 9:40.—u Mk 9:27.—v 1-6a: Mt 13:54-58; Lk 4:16-30.—w Mk 1:21.—x Mk 15:40; Mt 12:46; Jn 6:42.

5:21-43 A woman, who according to the ideas of the time was unclean and would contaminate by her touch, touches Jesus in a hidden gesture of hope; he frees her from her disease with kind words.

When Jesus restores the girl to life, he does it privately, because he does not want the Messiah to be thought of as a magician; only three witnesses are there, those present at the transfiguration (Mk 9:2) and the agony (Mk 14:33). These men would bear witness to the mystery of Jesus who dies and rises in order to save humanity from evil and death, and thus to Jesus as the authentic Messiah. See note on Mt 9:18-26.

5:22 *Leaders of the synagogue:* laymen who held administrative responsibilities such as taking care of the building and supervising the worship. Most synagogues had only one ruler, but there were exceptions (see Acts 13:15). There were also cases of honorary leaders.

5:37 *Peter, James, and John:* while Matthew focuses his attention mainly on Peter, Mark stresses this privileged group of three disciples. They will be witnesses of the raising of Jairus's daughter (Mk 5:37-43), the transfiguration of Jesus (Mk 9:2-13), and the agony in the garden (Mk 14:32-42). Obviously Mark depends on the preaching of Peter, yet Peter rarely emphasized his privilege.

6:1-6a This story of a breach completes the second section of the first part. See note on Mt 13:53-58.

6:3 *Brother:* see note on Mt 12:46.

4 Then Jesus said to them, "A prophet is always treated with honor except in his hometown, and among relatives, and in his own house."[y] 5 And he was unable to perform any mighty works there, aside from curing a few sick people by laying his hands on them.[z] 6 He was amazed at their lack of faith.

G: Who Is Jesus?*

Jesus Sends Out the Twelve on Mission.* Jesus traveled through the villages teaching.[a] 7 Calling the Twelve together, he began to send them out two by two, with authority over unclean spirits.[b] 8 He instructed them to take nothing for their journey except a walking staff—no bread, no sack, no money in their purses. 9 They were to wear sandals but not to take along a second tunic.

10 He said to them, "Whenever you enter a house, you are to stay there until you leave the area. 11 And if any will not welcome you and refuse to listen to you, leave them immediately and shake off the dust that is on your feet in testimony against them." 12 Then they set off and preached the need for repentance.[c] 13 They cast out many demons, and they anointed with oil many people who were sick and cured them.* [d]

The Name of Jesus Becomes Renowned.* 14 [e] King Herod heard of it, for Jesus' name had become renowned, and some people were saying, "John the Baptist has been raised from the dead. That is why such powers are at work in him."[f] 15 But others said, "He is Elijah," while still others proclaimed, "He is a prophet, like one of the prophets of old."[g] 16 But when Herod heard of it, he said, "John, whom I beheaded, has been raised from the dead."

The Death of John the Baptist.* 17 It was this same Herod who had ordered John to be arrested and put in chains in prison on account of Herodias, his brother Philip's wife, because Herod had married her.[h] 18 For John had told Herod, "It is unlawful for you to have your brother's wife."[i]

19 As for Herodias, she was filled with resentment against John and wanted to have him killed, but she was unable to do so, 20 because Herod was afraid of John, knowing him to be a holy and righteous man. Therefore, he protected him from harm. When he heard John speak, he was greatly perplexed by his words, but even so he liked to listen to him.

21 Her opportunity came when Herod on his birthday gave a banquet for his court officials and military officers and the leaders of Galilee.[j] 22 When the daughter of Herodias came in, she performed a dance that delighted Herod and his guests. The king said to the girl, "Ask me for whatever you wish, and I will give it to you." 23 And he solemnly swore to her, "Whatever you ask I will give you, even half of my kingdom."[k]

24 The girl went out and said to her mother, "What shall I ask for?" She replied, "The head of John the Baptist." 25 The girl then hurried back to the king and made her request, "I want you to give me at once the head of John the Baptist on a platter."

26 The king was greatly distressed, but because of the oath he had sworn and the presence of the guests, he was unwilling to break his word to her. 27 [l] Therefore, he immediately ordered an executioner to bring him John's head. The man went off and beheaded him in the prison. 28 Then he brought in the head on a platter and gave it to the girl, and the girl in turn gave it to her mother. 29 When John's disciples heard about this, they came and removed his body and laid it in a tomb.

y Lk 4:24; Jn 4:44.—z Mk 7:32; 1 Tim 4:14.—a 6b-11: Mt 10:1, 9-14; Lk 9:1-5; 10:4-11.—b Mk 3:13-15.—c Lk 9:6.—d Jas 5:14.—e 14-29: Mt 14:1-12.—f 14-16: Lk 9:7-8.—g Mt 16:14; Mal 3:23.—h Mt 4:12; Lk 3:19-20.—i Lev 18:16.—j Est 1:3.—k Est 5:3, 6.—l 27-28: Lk 9:9.

6:6b—8:30 The very term "Messiah" is charged with too many facile hopes and misunderstandings, and Jesus avoids using it. If he reveals himself, it is through words and actions in the midst of events and encounters. The tragic end of John the Baptist prefigures his own destiny. Jesus bears witness to the goodness of God, shepherd of his people, and nourishes human beings with his word and his bread. His relationship with the disciples becomes closer and closer. Despite their failure to attain a full understanding of who he is, they are given the grace to recognize him as the Messiah.

6:6b-13 Jesus impresses on the disciples that the preaching of the Gospel demands a genuine and unconditional detachment from earthly things.

6:13 At the time of Jesus, *oil* was frequently used to heal sickness. The anointing by the apostles set forth the healing power conferred on them by Jesus and prefigured the Sacrament of the Anointing of the Sick.

6:14-16 Jesus' name is known even in the palace of the tetrarch of Galilee: Antipas, a son of Herod the Great; out of habit, the people continue to call this Herod "king."

6:17-29 See note on Mt 14:1-12.

The Return of the Twelve. 30 The apostles * returned to Jesus and reported to him all that they had done and taught. [m] 31 He said to them, "Come away with me, by yourselves, to a deserted place and rest for a while." For people continued to come and go in great numbers, and they had no time even to eat. [n]

32 [o] And so they went off by themselves in a boat to a deserted place. 33 Now many people saw them departing and recognized them, and they hurried there on foot from all the towns and arrived ahead of them. 34 As Jesus went ashore and beheld the vast crowd, he had compassion on them, for they were like sheep without a shepherd; and he began to teach them many things. [p]

Jesus Feeds Five Thousand Men.* 35 When it began to be late in the day, his disciples came up to him and said, "This is a deserted place, and it is getting very late. 36 Send the people away now so that they can go to the farms and villages in the area and buy something for themselves to eat." 37 He replied, "Give them something to eat yourselves." They said to him, "Are we to go and spend two hundred denarii * on bread for them to eat?" [q] 38 He asked, "How many loaves do you have? Go and see." When they found out, they reported: "Five loaves, and two fish." [r]

39 Then he ordered them to have all the people sit down on the green grass in groups. 40 They sat down in groups of hundreds and fifties. 41 Taking the five loaves and the two fish, he looked up to heaven, blessed and broke the loaves, and gave them to the disciples to distribute among the people. He also divided the two fish among them. 42 They all ate and were satisfied. 43 Then they gathered up the fragments of the bread and fish—twelve full baskets. * 44 Those who had eaten the loaves numbered five thousand men.

Jesus Walks on the Water.* 45 [s] Immediately afterward, Jesus instructed his disciples to get into the boat and to go on ahead to Bethsaida on the other side of the lake while he dismissed the crowd. 46 And when he had taken leave of them, he went up on the mountain to pray.

47 When evening came, the boat was far out on the water while he was alone on the shore. 48 He could see that the disciples were having difficulty in rowing the boat in the face of a headwind. Around the fourth watch of the night he came toward them, walking on the water. He was going to pass by them, 49 but when the disciples saw him walking on the water they thought it was a ghost and they cried out, [t] 50 for they all had seen him and were terrified. But immediately he spoke to them, saying, "Have courage! It is I! * Do not be afraid!" 51 Then he got into the boat with them, and the wind died down. They were utterly astounded, [u] 52 for they had not understood about the loaves. Their minds were closed. [v]

Jesus Heals the Sick at Gennesaret.* 53 [w] After they had completed the crossing, they landed at Gennesaret and moored the boat. [x] 54 When they disembarked, the people recognized Jesus immediately. 55 They rushed throughout the entire countryside, and began to bring the sick to him on pallets wherever they heard he was. 56 Everywhere he went, whether to village or town or countryside, they laid the sick in the marketplaces and begged him to let them touch even the edge of his cloak. And all who touched it were completely healed. [y]

CHAPTER 7

Traditions That Falsify the Law of God.* 1 [z] When the Pharisees, along with some

m Lk 9:10; Acts 1:2, 26.—n Mk 3:20; Mt 14:13; Lk 9:10.—o 32-44: Mt 14:13-21; Lk 9:10-17; Jn 6:1-13.—p Mt 9:36.—q 2 Ki 4:42-44.—r Mt 15:34.—s 45-51: Mt 14:22-32; Jn 6:15-21.—t Lk 24:37.—u Mk 4:39.—v Mk 4:13; 8:17-21.—w 53-56: Mt 14:34-36.—x Jn 6:24-25.—y Mk 5:27-28; Acts 5:15.—z 1-23: Mt 15:1-20.

6:30 *Apostles:* this word occurs in Mark only here; it is also found in some manuscripts in Mk 3:14. The apostles were authorized representatives of Jesus, and in this sense it is used in the New Testament of the Twelve (Mk 3:14) and also of Paul (Rom 1:1). In a broader sense it is applied to a larger group including Barnabas (Acts 14:14), James, "brother of the Lord" (Gal 1:19), and possibly Andronicus and Junia (Rom 16:7). See also note on Mk 3:13-19.

6:35-44 See notes on Mt 14:13-21; 14:19; and 14:21.

6:37 *Two hundred denarii:* two hundred days' wages, for a day's wage was one denarius (see Mt 20:2).

6:43 The Jews regarded bread as a gift of God. Accordingly, the scraps that fell during a meal were to be picked up and placed in small wicker baskets that people carried about. The disciples each filled a basket.

6:45-52 See notes on Mt 14:22-33 and 14:25.

6:50 *It is I:* literally, "I am," the formula that reveals the name of the Lord in the Old Testament (see Ex 3:14; Isa 41:4, 10, 14; 43:1-3, 10, 13). Hence, the evangelist is alluding to Jesus as the Son of God.

6:53-56 The verses describe the responses of Jesus to the crowd's interest in him; they believe in his power to alleviate their sufferings.

7:1-13 Jesus reproaches the teachers, who insist upon "traditions" that they themselves have sometimes invented, with a legalism that allows them to have a good conscience, even as they disregard the essential demands of the Law (Ex 20:12; 21:17; Lev 20:9; Isa 29:13). See also note on Mt 15:2ff.

scribes who had come from Jerusalem, gathered around Jesus, 2 they noted that some of his disciples were eating with defiled hands, that is, without washing them.[a] 3 For the Pharisees, and in fact all Jews, do not eat without thoroughly washing their hands, thereby observing the tradition of the elders.[b] 4 And on coming from the marketplace they do not eat without first washing. In addition, there are many other traditions that they observe, such as the washing of cups and jugs and bronze kettles and tables.*[c]

5 Therefore, the Pharisees and the scribes asked him, "Why do your disciples not follow the tradition of the elders but eat with unclean hands?"[d] 6 He answered, "How rightly Isaiah prophesied about you hypocrites, as it is written:[e]

'This people honors me with their lips,
  but their hearts are far from me;
7 in vain do they worship me,
  teaching as doctrines the commandments of men.'

8 You thrust aside the commandment of God in order to preserve the traditions of men."*

9 Then he said to them, "How cleverly you have set aside the commandment of God to preserve your own tradition! 10 For Moses said, 'Honor your father and your mother,' and 'Whoever curses father or mother will be put to death.'[f] 11 But you say, 'If anyone tells his father or mother: "Anything I might have used for your support is *Corban*"'* (that is, dedicated to God),[g] 12 then he is forbidden by you from that very moment to do anything for his father or mother. 13 You nullify the word of God for the sake of your tradition that you have handed down. And you do many other things just like that."[h]

Clean and Unclean.* 14 [i] Then he called the people to him and said to them: "Listen to me, all of you, and understand. 15 There is nothing that goes into a person from outside that can defile him. The things that come out of a person are what defile him. [16 If anyone has ears to hear, let him hear!]"*

17 When he had gone into the house, away from the crowds, his disciples questioned him about the parable.[j] 18 He said to them, "Then are you also without understanding? Do you not realize that whatever goes into a person from outside cannot defile him, 19 since it enters not into the heart but into the stomach and is discharged into the sewer?" Thus, he pronounced all foods clean.[k]

20 Then he went on, "It is what comes out of a person that defiles. 21 For from within, from the human heart, come evil thoughts, unchastity, theft, murder,[l] 22 adultery, avarice, malice, deceit, indecency, envy, slander, arrogance, and folly.[m] 23 All these evils come from within, and they defile a person."

The Faith of a Gentile Woman.* 24 [n] He moved on from that place to the region of Tyre. He went into a house and did not want anyone to know he was there, but he was not able to avoid being recognized. 25 Almost immediately, a woman whose daughter was possessed by an unclean spirit heard about him and hastened to fall down at his feet. 26 The woman was a Gentile of Syrophoenician origin, and she begged him to drive the demon out of her daughter.[o]

27 Jesus said to her, "Let the children be fed first. For it is not right to take the children's bread and throw it to the dogs." 28 She replied, "Yes, Lord; but even the dogs under the table eat the scraps from the children." 29 Then Jesus said to her, "For saying this, you may go. The demon

a Acts 10:14; Rom 14:14.—b Lk 11:38.—c Mt 23:25.—d Gal 1:14; Col 2:8.—e Isa 29:13.—f Ex 20:12; 21:17; Lev 20:9; Deut 5:16; Eph 6:2.—g Mt 23:16.—h Heb 4:12.—i 14-23: Mt 15:10-20.—j Mk 4:10, 13; 9:28.—k Acts 10:15; Rom 14:1-12; Col 2:16.—l Jer 17:9.—m Mt 20:15.—n 24-30: Mt 15:21-28.—o Mt 8:29.

7:4 Moses had prescribed a few ablutions for priests when they prepared for service at the altar (Ex 30:17-21). However, Rabbinic tradition had gone beyond the spirit of this prescription and arbitrarily extended it. Jesus condemns this Pharisaic formalism and censures his opponents who out of love for their traditions had nullified the more important commandments of the Law. His disciples—like the great majority of the common people—paid little attention to these prescriptions of the Pharisees. *And tables:* found only in some early manuscripts.

7:8 *The commandment of God . . . the traditions of men:* Jesus makes a clear contrast between the two. The commandment of God is found in Scripture and is binding; the traditions of men (also known as the tradition of the elders: v. 3) are not found in Scripture and are not binding.

7:11 *Corban:* an Aramaic word meaning "offered to God."

7:14-23 Jesus settles the question of clean and unclean foods that was erecting a barrier between Jews and pagans and was troubling Jews who had converted to Christianity (see Acts 10:11, 15; Rom 14:14-23; 1 Tim 4:3-4; Tit 1:15). See also note on Mt 15:10-20.

7:16 This verse is lacking in some of the most ancient manuscripts; it was probably added here from Mk 4:9 or 4:23.

7:24-30 See notes on Mt 15:21-28 and 15:21-22.

has gone out of your daughter." 30 And
when she returned home, she found the
child lying in bed and the demon gone.

Jesus Heals a Deaf Man.* 31 [p] Returning
from the region of Tyre, Jesus traveled by
way of Sidon to the Sea of Galilee, and into
the region of the Decapolis. 32 Thereupon
people brought to him a deaf man who had a
speech impediment and begged him to lay
his hand on him. [q] 33 He took him aside, away
from the crowd, and put his fingers into the
man's ears and, spitting, touched his
tongue. [r] 34 Then, looking up to heaven, he
sighed and said to him, *"Ephphatha!"* which
means, "Be opened!" [s] 35 At once, the man's
ears were opened, his tongue was loosened,
and he spoke properly. [t]

36 Then he ordered them not to tell any-
one, but the more he ordered them not to
do so, the more widely they proclaimed it.
37 Their astonishment was beyond mea-
sure. "He has done all things well," they
said. "He even makes the deaf able to hear
and the mute able to speak." [u]

CHAPTER 8

Jesus Feeds Four Thousand.* 1 [v] In those
days, a great crowd had again assembled,
and they had nothing to eat. Jesus called his
disciples to him and said to them, 2 "I am
moved with compassion for these people,
because they have been with me now for
three days and have nothing to eat. [w] 3 If I
send them away hungry to their homes,
they will collapse on the way—and some of
them have come from far off."

4 His disciples replied, "How can anyone
find enough bread here in this deserted
place to feed these men?" 5 He asked them,
"How many loaves do you have?" They
replied, "Seven."

6 Jesus ordered the crowd to sit down on
the ground. Then he took the seven loaves,
and after giving thanks he broke them and
gave them to his disciples to distribute,
and they distributed them to the people.
7 There were also a few small fish, and after
blessing them he commanded that these
too should be distributed. [x] 8 They ate and
were satisfied. Afterward, the disciples
picked up the fragments left over—seven
full baskets. 9 The people there numbered
about four thousand. And when he had
sent them away, 10 he immediately got into
the boat with his disciples and went to the
district of Dalmanutha.*

The Demand for a Sign.* 11 [y] The Pharisees
came forward and began to argue with
him. To put him to the test they asked him
to show them a sign from heaven. [z]
12 Sighing from the depths of his spirit, he
said, "Why does this generation ask for a
sign? Amen, I say to you, no sign will be
given to this generation." [a] 13 Then he left
them, got into the boat again, and sailed
across to the other side.

The Yeast of the Pharisees.* 14 [b] They had
forgotten to bring any bread with them,
and they had only one loaf in the boat.
15 Jesus then gave them this warning, "Be
careful, and beware of the yeast of the
Pharisees and the yeast of Herod." [c] 16 They
talked about this to one another and con-
cluded: "It is because we have no bread."

17 Becoming aware of what they were dis-
cussing, he said to them, "Why are you talk-
ing about having no bread? Do you still not
understand or comprehend? Are your
hearts hardened? [d] 18 Do you have eyes and
fail to see? Do you have ears and fail to hear?

"And do you not remember? [e] 19 When I
broke the five loaves for the five thousand,
how many baskets filled with fragments did
you collect?" They answered, "Twelve." [f]
20 "When I broke the seven loaves for the
four thousand, how many baskets filled with
fragments did you collect?" They answered,
"Seven." [g] 21 He said to them, "Do you still
not understand?"

Jesus Heals a Blind Man.* 22 They arrived at
Bethsaida, and some people brought a blind

p 31-37: Mt 15:29-31.—q Lk 11:14.—r Mk 8:23.—s Jn 11:41.—t Isa 35:5, 6.—u Mt 15:31.—v 1-10: Mk 6:34-44; Mt 15:32-39.—w Mt 9:36.—x Mt 14:19.—y 11-13: Mt 12:38-39; 16:1-4.—z Lk 11:16.—a Mk 7:34.—b 14-21: Mt 16:5-12; Lk 12:1.—c Mk 12:13; 1 Cor 5:6-8.—d Mk 4:13; Isa 6:9, 10.—e Jer 5:21; Ezek 12:2.—f Mt 14:20; Jn 6:13.—g Mt 15:37.

7:31-37 The miracle of the deaf mute is omitted by the other evangelists. This man may also have been a pagan, for the population of the Decapolis was mostly pagan. The various gestures that Jesus performs on the man had the sole purpose of strengthening his faith. Mark might have recounted them in detail to foreshadow the future Christian Sacraments.

8:1-10 See note on Mt 15:29-39.

8:10 *Dalmanutha:* location unknown.

8:11-13 See note on Mt 16:1-4.

8:14-21 See note on Mt 16:5-12.

8:22-26 Jesus' actions and the healing of the blind man seem to have the same purpose as his actions and the healing of the deaf mute (see Mk 7:3-37). Some scholars regard both healings as a means of expressing the gradual enlightenment of the disciples about Jesus' Messiahship.

man to Jesus and begged that he touch him. 23 He took the blind man by the hand and led him outside the village. Then, putting saliva on his eyes, he laid his hands on him and asked, "Can you see anything?" [h] 24 Looking up, the man responded, "I can see people, but they look like trees walking around." 25 Jesus placed his hands on the man's eyes again, and the man looked around intently. His sight was restored, and he was able to see everything clearly. 26 Then he sent him away to his home, saying, "Do not even go into the village."

Peter's Confession That Jesus Is the Messiah.* 27 [i] Then Jesus and his disciples set out for the villages of Caesarea Philippi. Along the way he asked his disciples, "Who do people say that I am?" 28 They responded, "[Some say] John the Baptist; others say Elijah; and still others, one of the prophets." [j] 29 "But you," he asked, "who do you say that I am?" Peter answered him, "You are the Christ." [k] 30 Then he gave them strict orders not to tell anyone about him.

III: THE MYSTERY OF JESUS IS REVEALED*

A: The Way of the Son of Man*

Jesus Predicts His Passion.* 31 [l] After that, he began to teach them that the Son of Man must endure great suffering, be rejected by the elders, the chief priests, and the scribes, * and be put to death, and rise again after three days. 32 He told them these facts in plain words. [m]

Then Peter took him aside and began to rebuke him. 33 At this, Jesus turned and, looking at his disciples, rebuked Peter and said, "Get behind me, Satan! You are thinking not as God does, but as men do."

The Conditions of Discipleship.* 34 He then called the people and his disciples to him and said to them, "Anyone who wishes to follow me must deny himself, take up his cross, and follow me. [n] 35 * For whoever wishes to save his life will lose it, but whoever loses his life for my sake and the sake of the gospel will save it. [o] 36 What does it profit a man to gain the whole world and forfeit his very life? 37 Indeed, what can he give in exchange for his life?

38 "If anyone in this adulterous and sinful generation is ashamed of me and of my words, the Son of Man will also be ashamed of him when he comes in the glory of his Father with the holy angels." [p]

CHAPTER 9

1 Then he said to them, "Amen, I say to you, there are some standing here who will not taste death before they see that the kingdom of God has come with power." * [q]

Jesus Is Transfigured.* 2 [r] Six days later, Jesus took Peter, James, and John and led them up a high mountain apart by themselves. And in their presence he was transfigured; 3 his clothes became dazzling white—whiter than anyone on earth could bleach them. [s] 4 And Elijah with Moses appeared, conversing with Jesus.

5 Then Peter said to Jesus, "Rabbi, it is good for us to be here. Let us make three tents—one for you, one for Moses, and one for Elijah." 6 He did not know what to say, for they were so frightened. 7 Then a cloud cast a shadow over them, and a voice came out of the cloud: "This is my beloved Son. Listen to him." [t] 8 Suddenly, when they looked around, they saw no one with them anymore, but only Jesus.

h Mk 7:33; Jn 9:6.—i 27-30: Mt 16:13-20; Lk 9:18-21.—j Mal 3:23.—k Jn 6:69.—l 31-38: Mt 16:21-27; Lk 9:22-26.—m Jn 18:20.—n Mt 10:38-39; 16:24-27; Lk 14:26-27.—o Jn 12:25.—p Mt 10:33; Lk 12:8.—q Mt 16:28; Lk 9:27; Rom 1:4.—r 2-13: Mt 17:1-13; Lk 9:28-36.—s Dan 7:9.—t Ex 24:16.

8:27-30 Many scholars believe that Peter's confession of Jesus' Messiahship constitutes the central point of this Gospel. It is the decisive doctrinal turning point in which we have the end of the Messianic Secret. Up to this point Jesus demanded the greatest secrecy about the mystery of his person. Henceforth, Jesus utters repeated exhortations concerning the following of the Messiah.

The apostles had recognized the Messiah through Peter's confession in spite of the humble and insignificant appearances of their Master's public activity. Now they must cling with faith to the suffering Messiah and accept the scandal of the cross.

8:31—16:8 Where are we to find the revelation that God wants to communicate to humanity? We must look to the cross, understand and share the condition of Jesus, and answer the call that he gives us to follow him. It is a suffering and humiliated Christ who saves the human race. Of this Mark is certain.

8:31—10:52 It is with full awareness and deliberation that Jesus sets out toward the fulfillment of his mission. He speaks on three occasions of the way of suffering and humiliation that he sees opening before him, and on all three occasions he encounters closed minds.

8:31-33 See notes on Mt 16:21 and 16:22-23.

8:31 *The elders, the chief priests, and the scribes:* the members of the Sanhedrin.

8:34—9:1 See note on Mt 16:25.

8:35-37 The Greek word for "life" can also mean "soul." "Life" is used in a double sense—earthly life and eternal life.

9:1 *Come with power:* the reference is to the new age of humanity that begins with the death of Jesus.

9:2-8 See notes on Mt 17:1-8 and 17:1.

Elijah Has Already Come.* 9 As they were coming down from the mountain, Jesus ordered them to tell no one what they had seen until the Son of Man had risen from the dead.[u] 10 Therefore, they kept the matter to themselves, although they did argue about what rising from the dead could possibly mean.

11 [v] And they asked him, "Why do the scribes say that Elijah must come first?" 12 He said to them, "Elijah will indeed come first and restore all things. Yet how is it written about the Son of Man?—that he must endure great suffering and be treated with contempt! 13 However, I tell you that Elijah has come, and they did to him whatever they pleased, as it is written about him."[w]

Jesus Heals a Boy Possessed by a Spirit.* 14 [x] When they returned to the disciples, they saw a large crowd surrounding them, and some scribes were engaged in an argument with them. 15 As soon as the people saw Jesus, they were overcome with awe and ran forward to greet him. 16 He asked them, "What are you arguing about with them?"

17 A man in the crowd answered him, "Teacher, I have brought you my son who is possessed by a spirit that makes him unable to speak. 18 Wherever it seizes him, it flings him to the ground, and he foams at the mouth, grinds his teeth, and becomes rigid. I asked your disciples to drive it out, but they were unable to do so."

19 Jesus said to them in reply, "O unbelieving generation, how much longer shall I remain with you? How much longer must I put up with you? Bring the boy to me." 20 When they brought the boy to him, the spirit saw him and immediately threw the child into convulsions. He fell to the ground and rolled around, foaming at the mouth.[y]

21 Jesus asked the father, "How long has the boy been in this condition?" "From childhood," he replied. 22 "It has often tried to kill him by throwing him into a fire or into water. If it is possible for you to do anything, have pity on us and help us." 23 Jesus answered, "If it is possible! All things are possible for one who has faith."[z] 24 Immediately, the father of the child cried out, "I do believe. Help my unbelief."[a]

25 When Jesus saw that a crowd was rapidly gathering around them, he rebuked the unclean spirit, saying to it, "Deaf and mute spirit, I command you: come out of him and never enter him again!"[b] 26 Shrieking and throwing the boy into convulsions, it came out of him. He lay there like a corpse, so that many remarked, "He is dead." 27 But Jesus, taking him by the hand, raised him, and he stood up.[c]

28 When he went indoors, his disciples asked him privately, "Why were we not able to cast it out?"[d] 29 He answered, "This kind cannot be driven out except by prayer [and by fasting]." *

Jesus Predicts His Passion a Second Time.* 30 [e] They proceeded from there and began to journey through Galilee, but Jesus did not want anyone to know about it[f] 31 because he was teaching his disciples. He told them, "The Son of Man * will be handed over into the power of men. They will kill him, and three days after being killed he will rise."[g] 32 But they did not understand what he was saying, and they were afraid to ask him about it.[h]

The Greatest in the Kingdom.* 33 [i] They came to Capernaum, and once they were in the house he asked them, "What were you arguing about during the journey?" 34 But they remained silent, for on the way they had been arguing about which one of them was the greatest.

35 Then he sat down, summoned the Twelve, and said to them, "If anyone wishes to be first, he must become the last of all and the servant of all."[j] 36 He then took a child, placed it in their midst, and put his arms around it as he said, 37 "Whoever receives one such child in my name re-

u Mk 8:31.—v 11-12: Isa 53:3; Mal 3:23.—w 1 Ki 19:2-10.—x 14-29: Mt 17:14-21; Lk 9:37-43.—y Mk 1:26.—z Jn 11:40.—a Mt 8:10.—b Mk 7:37.—c Mt 8:15.—d Mk 7:17.—e 30-32: Mk 8:31; Mt 17:22-23; Lk 9:43-45.—f Jn 7:1.—g Acts 2:23.—h Jn 12:16.—i 33-37: Mt 18:1-5; Lk 9:46-48.—j Mt 20:27; Lk 22:26.

9:9-13 See note on Mt 17:9-13.

9:14-29 See note on Mt 17:14-21.

9:29 Other ancient manuscripts omit: "and by fasting."

9:30-32 Mark very effectively alternates the glorious and suffering aspects of the Messiah, following up the most spectacular exorcism in the Gospel with Jesus' second prediction of his Passion. He also implies that the initiative for the death of the Servant (see Isa 53) belongs to God.

9:31 *Son of Man:* see note on Mt 8:20.

9:33-37 This incident and the sayings that follow it are most likely intended to be a commentary on the lack of understanding exhibited by the disciples. They are to serve the poor and lowly. Jesus used children as the symbol for the *anawim,* the poor in spirit, i.e., the lowly in the Christian community.

ceives me; and whoever receives me receives not me but the one who sent me." [k]

Whoever Is Not against Us Is for Us. 38 [l]John said to him, "Teacher, we observed someone expelling demons in your name, and we forbade him because he was not one of us." * 39 Jesus replied, "Do not hinder him, for no one who performs a miracle in my name will be able soon afterward to speak evil of me. [m] 40 Whoever is not against us is for us. [n] 41 Amen, I say to you, whoever gives you a cup of water to drink because you bear the name of Christ will certainly not go unrewarded. [o]

Woe to the World because of Scandals.* 42 [p]"If anyone causes one of these little ones who believe in me to sin, it would be better for him if a great millstone were hung around his neck and he were thrown into the sea.

43 "If your hand causes you to sin, cut it off. * It is preferable for you to enter life maimed than to have two hands and go into the unquenchable fire of Gehenna [44 where the devouring worm never dies and the fire is never quenched]. * 45 And if your foot causes you to sin, cut it off. It is better for you to enter life crippled than to have two feet and be thrown into Gehenna [46 where the devouring worm never dies and the fire is never quenched]. 47 And if your eye causes you to sin, tear it out. It is preferable for you to enter into the kingdom of God with one eye than to have two eyes and be cast into Gehenna, 48 where the devouring worm never dies and the fire is never quenched. [q]

The Simile of Salt. 49 "For everyone will be salted with fire. * 50 Salt is good, but if salt loses its saltiness, how can you revive its flavor? Have salt in yourselves, and be at peace with one another." [r]

CHAPTER 10

Marriage and Divorce.* 1 After departing from there, Jesus came into the region of Judea beyond the Jordan. * Again the crowds gathered around him, and, as was his custom, he began to teach them. [s]

2 [t]Some Pharisees came forward and in order to test him asked, "Is it lawful for a man to divorce his wife?" [u] 3 He replied, "What did Moses command you?" 4 They said, "Moses allowed a man to write a certificate of divorce and dismiss her." [v] 5 But Jesus said to them, "It was because of the hardness of your hearts that he wrote this commandment for you. [w] 6 But from the very beginning of creation, 'God made them male and female.' [x] 7 [y]'That is why a man leaves his father and mother and is joined to his wife, 8 and the two become one flesh.' And so they are no longer two but one flesh. 9 Therefore, what God has joined together, let no one separate."

10 When they were again in the house, the disciples once more questioned Jesus about this. 11 [z]He said to them, "If a man divorces his wife and marries another, he commits adultery against her. 12 In the same way, if a wife divorces her husband and marries another, she commits adultery." [a]

Jesus Receives Little Children.* 13 [b]People were bringing little children to him so that he might touch them, and the disciples sternly rebuked them. [c] 14 But when Jesus became aware of this, he was indignant

k Mt 10:40; 18:5; Jn 13:20.—l 38-41: Num 11:28; Lk 9:49-50; 1 Cor 12:3.—m Acts 3:16.—n Mt 12:30; Lk 11:23.—o Mt 10:42; 1 Cor 3:23.—p 42-47: Mt 5:29-30; 18:6-9; Lk 17:1-2.—q Isa 66:24.—r Lev 2:13; Mt 5:13; Lk 14:34-35; Rom 12:18; 2 Cor 13:11; Col 4:6.—s Mk 1:5; Jn 10:40.—t 2-12: Mt 19:3-9.—u Mk 2:16.—v Mt 5:31; Deut 24:1-4.—w Ps 95:8; Heb 3:15.—x Gen 1:27; 5:2.—y 7-8: Gen 2:24; 1 Cor 6:16; Eph 5:31.—z 11-12: Mt 5:32; Lk 16:18; 1 Cor 7:10-11.—a Rom 7:3.—b 13-16: Mt 19:13-15; Lk 18:15-17.—c Lk 9:47.

9:38-41 *Not one of us:* though the man was not one of the Twelve, he was a believer in Jesus and acted in his name. Therefore, Jesus counsels the Twelve that they should not oppose him.

9:42-47 See note on Mt 18:5-11.

9:43 *Cut it off:* Jesus is here using hyperbole, a figure of speech that exaggerates to make a point. He means that sometimes sin can be overcome only by taking drastic action. *Gehenna:* the name, from the Hebrew *Ge Hinnon,* of a small valley southwest of Jerusalem; it was a popular image for hell because of the refuse that was continually burned there.

9:44, 46 These verses are omitted in the best manuscripts; they are repetitions of v. 48 (see Isa 66:24).

9:49 This somewhat obscure verse was perhaps introduced because of the reference to fire in v. 48. Fire signifies the testing that precedes God's judgment (see 1 Cor 3:13-15). Salt, a symbol of fidelity, was sprinkled on sacrificial victims so that they might be pleasing to God (Lev 2:13). When the testing is endured with fidelity, it makes the believer acceptable to God.

10:1-12 Divorce was practiced by permission of the Mosaic Law (Deut 24:1). But a permission supposes a weakness; it does not represent the law that gives life. From the beginning, God willed the unity of the couple in marriage (see Gen 1:27 and 2:24). Jesus recalls this requirement and shows, too, that the Scriptures ought to be interpreted in light of the fundamental perspectives of God's plan and not on the basis of the changeable desires and needs of human beings.

10:1 *Region of Judea beyond the Jordan:* Judea was the southern part of Palestine, which had formerly been the southern kingdom. Jesus went south from Capernaum over the mountains of Samaria into Judea and then east across the Jordan to Perea, the territory of Herod Antipas.

10:13-16 This episode is common to the Synoptics, but Mark alone recounts the human traits of the divine Master, such as his indignation at the disciples' hindering action and his affectionate attitude in embracing the children.

and said to them, "Let the little children
come to me; do not hinder them. For it is
to such as these that the kingdom of God
belongs. 15 Amen, I say to you, whoever
does not receive the kingdom of God like a
little child will never enter it."[d] 16 And he
took them up into his arms, laid his hands
on them, and blessed them.[e]

The Rich Young Man.* 17 [f] As Jesus was start-
ing out on a journey, a man came running up
to him, knelt down, and asked him, "Good
teacher, what must I do to inherit eternal
life?"[g] 18 Jesus said to him, "Why do you call
me good? No one is good but God alone.
19 You know the commandments: 'Do not
kill. Do not commit adultery. Do not steal.
Do not bear false witness. Do not defraud.
Honor your father and your mother.' "[h]

20 The man said to him, "Teacher, I have
observed all these since I was a child."
21 Looking at him, Jesus was moved with
love and said, "You need to do one further
thing. Go and sell what you own, and give
to the poor, and you will have treasure in
heaven. Then come, follow me."[i] 22 When
he heard these words, the man's face fell
and he went away grieving, for he pos-
sessed great wealth.

23 Then Jesus looked around and said to
his disciples, "How difficult it will be for
those who are rich to enter the kingdom of
God!"[j] 24 The disciples were astounded on
hearing his words, but Jesus insisted:
"Children, how difficult it is to enter the
kingdom of God![k] 25 It is easier for a camel
to pass through the eye of a needle than for
someone who is rich to enter the kingdom
of God."[l] 26 The disciples were even more
greatly astonished, and they said to one
another, "Then who can be saved?" 27 Jesus
looked at them and said, "For men it is
impossible, but not for God. For God all
things are possible."

Reward for Following Jesus.* 28 Peter said to
him, "We have given up everything to fol-
low you." 29 Jesus answered, "Amen, I say to
you, there is no one who has given up
house or brothers or sisters or mother or
father or children or lands for my sake and
for the sake of the gospel 30 who will not
receive in this age a hundred times more
houses, brothers and sisters, mothers and
children, and lands—as well as persecu-
tions—and in the age to come, eternal
life.[m] 31 But many who are first will be last,
and the last will be first."[n]

Jesus Predicts His Passion a Third Time.*
32 [o] As they were on the road going up to
Jerusalem, Jesus walked ahead of them.
The disciples were amazed, and those who
followed were apprehensive. Once again,
he took the Twelve aside and began to tell
them what would happen to him.
33 "Behold, we are now going up to
Jerusalem," he said, "and the Son of Man
will be handed over to the chief priests and
the scribes, and they will condemn him to
death. Then they will hand him over to the
Gentiles,[p] 34 who will mock him, and spit
upon him, and scourge him, and put him
to death. And after three days he will rise
again."[q]

The Son of Man Has Come To Serve.*
35 [r] Then James and John, the sons of
Zebedee, came forward and said to him,
"Teacher, we want you to do for us whatev-
er we request." 36 He asked them, "What is
it that you want me to do for you?" 37 They
said to him, "Allow us to sit, one at your
right hand and the other at your left, in
your glory." 38 Jesus said to them, "You do
not know what you are asking. Can you
drink the cup that I drink, * or be baptized
with the baptism with which I am bap-
tized?"[s] 39 They said to him, "We can."

d Mt 18:3.—e Mk 9:36.—f 17-31: Mt 19:16-30; Lk 18:18-30.—g Mk 1:40.—h Ex 20:12-16; Deut 5:16-21.—i Lk 12:33.—j Pss 52:9; 62:10; Prov 11:28.—k Mt 7:13, 14.—l Lk 12:16-20.—m Mt 6:33.—n Mt 19:30; Lk 13:30.—o 32-34: Mk 8:31; Mt 20:17-19; Lk 18:31-33.—p Mt 27:1-2.—q Acts 2:23.—r 35-45: Mt 20:20-28.—s Job 38:2; Lk 12:50.

10:17-27 See note on Mt 19:16-26.

10:28-31 See note on Mt 19:27-30.

10:32-34 See note on Mt 20:17-19. *Gentiles, who will . . . put him to death:* the predictions of the Passion in Mark's Gospel do not mention the word "crucified." However, crucifixion is implied by the fact that he was to be handed over to the Gentiles to be killed, since this was the customary Roman means of executing non-Romans.

10:35-45 What was Christ's own understanding of his life, of the kingdom, of what it meant to be a disciple? An answer is given in this decisive passage (see vv. 42-45). So important are these verses that Luke points up their essential context by placing them in the account of the Supper (Lk 22:24-27) and John in the explanation of the washing of the feet (Jn 13:12-17). The kingdom of God has nothing to do with ambitions for political or social power; true greatness is found not in prestige or rule but only in service.

10:38 *Drink the cup that I drink:* a Hebraism for sharing someone's fate. In the Old Testament, the "cup of wine" was a metaphor for God's wrath against sin and rebellion (Ps 75:9; Isa 51:17-23; Jer 25:15-28; 49:12; 51:7). Thus, the cup Jesus had to drink refers to the punishment of sins that he bore in place of all human beings (see Mk 10:45; 14:36). *Baptism:* an image of Jesus' suffering and death.

Matson Photo Service

THE GOLDEN GATE — A city gate was very important in the lives of the ancients. Markets were held there and the main item sold gave its name to the gate ("Sheep Gate," etc.); important announcements were made at the city gate; there the law was read, legal business was transacted, and public gatherings were held.

The above is a view of "the beautiful gate." This gate in the present wall built by the Turks in the 17th century A.D. overlooks the Kidron Valley and Gethsemane. Christians have traditionally venerated this gate as the place of Jesus' triumphal entry into Jerusalem. It is quite probable that Jesus did enter the city through a gate in the ancient wall located approximately where this Golden Gate (now walled up) stands. (See Mk 11:11)

Arab Information Center

PALM SUNDAY IN JERUSALEM — A modern Procession on Palm Sunday from Bethphage, via the Mount of Olives and Gethsemane through St. Stephen's Gate to St. Anne's Convent—in commemoration of Christ's triumphal entry into Jerusalem. In the background is the Church of All Nations directly opposite the Golden Gate through which Christ passed. (See Mk 11:11)

VILLAGE OF BETHANY — View of Bethany, the home of Mary, Martha, and Lazarus, situated about two miles southeast of Jerusalem and sometimes referred to as the "Judean home of Jesus." The tower in the center marks the tomb of Lazarus. The ruins at the upper right are the remains of a medieval abbey. It was to this village that Jesus returned after the triumphal entry into Jerusalem. (See Mk 11:11)

Then Jesus said to them, "The cup that I
drink you shall indeed drink, and with the
baptism with which I am baptized you
shall be baptized. [t] 40 But to sit at my right
hand or at my left is not in my power to
grant. Those places belong to those for
whom they have been prepared."

41 When the other ten heard this, they
began to be indignant at James and John.
42 [u] Therefore, Jesus called them over and
said, "You know that those considered to
be rulers among the Gentiles lord it over
them, and their great ones make their
authority over them felt. 43 But this must
not be so with you. Instead, whoever wish-
es to become great among you must be
your servant, 44 and whoever wishes to be
first among you must be the servant of all.
45 For even the Son of Man did not come to
be served but to serve and to give his life as
a ransom for many."

Jesus Heals a Blind Man.* 46 [v] Then they
came to Jericho. And as Jesus, his disciples,
and a huge crowd were leaving Jericho, a
blind man, Bartimaeus, the son of Ti-
maeus, * was sitting by the roadside asking
for alms. 47 When he heard that it was Jesus
of Nazareth, he began to shout, "Jesus, Son
of David, have pity on me!" 48 Many
rebuked him and told him to be silent, but
he only shouted all the louder, "Son of
David, have pity on me!"

49 Jesus stopped and said, "Call him." So
they called the blind man, saying to him,
"Take heart! Stand up! He is calling you!"
50 Casting aside his cloak, he jumped up
and went to Jesus. 51 Then Jesus said to
him, "What do you want me to do for you?"
The blind man said to him, "Rabbi, * let me
receive my sight." [w] 52 Jesus said to him,
"Go on your way! Your faith has made you
well." Immediately, he received his sight
and followed him along the road. [x]

B: Jesus at Jerusalem—The Break with Judaism*

CHAPTER 11

The Entry into Jerusalem.* 1 [y] When they
drew near Jerusalem, to Bethphage and
Bethany, near the Mount of Olives, he sent
off two of his disciples, 2 saying to them,
"Go into the village directly ahead of you,
and as soon as you enter it you will find
tied there a colt on which no one has ever
ridden. Untie it and bring it here. [z] 3 If any-
one says to you, 'Why are you doing this?'
say: 'The Lord needs it and will send it
back immediately.' "

4 The two went off and found a colt tied
beside a door outside on the street. As they
were untying it, [a] 5 some of them said to
them, "What are you doing, untying that
colt?" 6 They answered as Jesus had
instructed them, and they allowed them to
take it. 7 Then they brought the colt to
Jesus and spread their cloaks on its back.
And he sat on it. 8 Many people spread
their cloaks on the road, and others spread
leafy branches that they had cut in the
fields. 9 Those who went ahead and those
who followed kept crying out: [b]

"Hosanna! *
Blessed is he who comes in the
name of the Lord!
10 Blessed is the coming kingdom of our
father David.
Hosanna in the highest heavens!" [c]

11 He entered Jerusalem and went into
the temple, where he looked around at
everything. Then, since the hour was
already late, he went out to Bethany with
the Twelve. [d]

Jesus Curses a Sterile Fig Tree.* 12 [e] On the
next day, as they were leaving Bethany, he
felt hungry. 13 Noticing in the distance a fig

t Acts 12:2; Rev 1:9.—u 42-45: Lk 22:25-27.—v 46-52: Mt 20:29-34; Lk 18:35-43.—w Jn 20:16.—x Mt 8:10.—y 1-10: Mt 21:1-9; Lk 19:29-38; Jn 12:12-15.—z Num 19:2.—a Mk 14:16.—b 9-10: 2 Sam 7:16; Ps 118:26.—c Lk 2:14.—d Mt 21:10, 17.—e 12-14: Mt 21:18-20; Lk 13:6-9.

10:46-52 This healing is the last miracle of Jesus in Mark's Gospel.

10:46 *Son of Timaeus* is the meaning of *Bartimaeus* in Aramaic.

10:51 *Rabbi:* means "master" (see Jn 20:16; Mt 23:7).

11:1—12:16 We are at Jerusalem, where the decisive action takes place. Jesus' confrontation with the established religion takes on an irremediable character. Mark groups together in three days the events that consummate the break and thus open the way of faith in Christ to the whole world. The time of Israel is ended. The presence of Jesus in the Holy City and in the temple is like a visit from God, a fulfillment, and a judgment.

11:1-11 The simplicity of the event and the modest mount ridden by Jesus (see Zec 9:9) suggest that "the coming kingdom" (v. 10) will not bring a political restoration and that the Messiah was not to be a national hero. See also note on Mt 21:1-11.

11:9 *Hosanna:* an acclamation meaning "Grant salvation!" The citation is from Ps 118:25.

11:12-14 The Prophets used the image of a fig tree with respect to Israel (see Jer 8:13; 29:17; Joel 1:7; Hos 9:10, 16). Jesus' cursing of the fig tree is regarded as a parable in action representing a judgment on Israel's barrenness and Jerusalem's rejection of Jesus' teaching (see Isa 34:4; Hos 2:14; Lk 13:6-9).

tree in leaf, he went to see if he could find any fruit on it. When he reached it, he found nothing except leaves, since it was not the season for figs. 14 Then he said to it, "May no one ever again eat fruit from your branches." And his disciples heard him say this.

Jesus Cleanses the Temple.* 15 [f] Then they came to Jerusalem. He entered the temple and began to drive out those who were engaged there in buying and selling. He overturned the tables of the money changers and the seats of those who were selling doves. 16 Nor would he allow anyone to carry anything through the temple. 17 Then he taught them, saying: "Is it not written: * [g]

'My house shall be called a house of
prayer for all the nations'?
But you have made it a den of
thieves."

18 When the chief priests and the scribes heard about this, they plotted to do away with him. For they were afraid of him because the whole crowd was spellbound by his teaching. [h] 19 And when evening came, they left the city. [i]

The Lesson of the Withered Fig Tree.* 20 [j] Early the next morning, as they passed by, they saw the fig tree withered away to its roots. 21 Then Peter, recalling what had happened, said to Jesus: "Rabbi, look! The fig tree that you cursed has withered away." [k]

22 Jesus said to them, "Have faith in God. 23 Amen, I say to you, whoever says to this mountain, 'Be lifted up and thrown into the sea,' and does not doubt in his heart but believes that what he says will happen, it will be accomplished for him. [l] 24 So I tell you, whatever you ask for in prayer, believe that you have received it, and it will be yours. [m]

25 "And whenever you stand in prayer, forgive whatever grievance you have against anybody, so that your Father in heaven may forgive your wrongs too. [n] [26 But if you do not forgive others, then your Father in heaven will not forgive you your transgressions.]" *

The Authority of Jesus Questioned.* 27 [o] They returned once again to Jerusalem. As Jesus was walking in the temple, the chief priests, the scribes, and the elders approached him 28 and asked, "By what authority are you doing these things? Or who gave you the authority to do them?" 29 Jesus said to them, "I will ask you one question. Give me an answer, and I will tell you by what authority I do these things. 30 Did John's baptism originate from heaven or from men? Tell me!"

31 They argued among themselves, "If we say: 'From heaven,' he will say, 'Then why did you not believe him?' 32 But how can we say, 'From men'?"—for they were afraid of the people, who all regarded John as a true prophet. [p]

33 Therefore, they answered Jesus, "We do not know." And Jesus said to them, "Then neither shall I tell you by what authority I do these things."

CHAPTER 12

The Parable of the Tenants.* 1 [q] Then Jesus began to speak to them in parables: "A man planted a vineyard, put a fence around it, dug a pit for the winepress, and built a watchtower. [r] Then he leased it to tenants and went off on a journey.

2 "When the time arrived, he sent a servant to the tenants to collect from them his share of the produce of the vineyard. 3 But they seized the servant, beat him, and sent him away empty-handed. 4 Again, he sent them another servant, but they beat him

f 15-18: Mt 21:12-13; Lk 19:45-46; Jn 2:14-16.—g Isa 56:7; Jer 7:11.—h Mk 12:12; Mt 21:46.—i Lk 21:37.—j 20-24: Mt 21:20-22.—k Mt 23:7.—l Mt 17:20-21; Lk 17:6; 1 Cor 13:2.—m Mt 7:7; Jn 11:22; 14:13.—n Mt 6:14; 18:35.—o 27-33: Mt 21:23-27; Lk 20:1-8.—p Mt 11:9.—q 1-12: Mt 21:33-46; Lk 20:9-19.—r Isa 5:1-7; Jer 2:21.

11:15-19 During his trial Jesus will be accused of having tried to set up a new temple (Mk 14:58; 15:29).

11:17 The first part of the citation is from Isa 56:7. Only Mark has reported to us the expression *for all the nations*. Thus, the gesture of Jesus takes on a Messianic meaning, alluding to the conversion of the Gentiles. *Den of thieves:* see Jer 7:11.

11:20-26 See note on Mt 21:18-22.

11:26 This verse is found only in some manuscripts; it was probably added from Mt 6:15.

11:27-33 The increasing hostility toward Jesus arose from the chief priests, scribes, and elders (v. 27) as well as the Herodians and Pharisees (Mk 12:13) and the Sadducees (Mk 12:18). They rejected the messengers sent by God—John the Baptist and Jesus—and so incurred the judgment alluded to in these verses and confirmed by the parable of the tenants (Mk 12:1-12).

12:1-12 This parable was probably inspired by the peasant rebellions of the period. The parable would have an immediate impact on Jewish hearers, who were well acquainted with the "Song of the Vineyard" in Isa 5:1ff. See also note on Mt 21:33-46.

over the head and treated him shamefully.
5 Then he sent another, and that one they
killed. He also sent many others, some of
whom they beat, and others of whom they
killed.

6 "Finally, he had only one other to
send—his beloved son. And so he sent him
to them, thinking: 'They will respect my
son.'[s] 7 But those tenants said to one
another, 'This is the heir. Come, let us kill
him, and the inheritance will be ours!'
8 And so they seized him, killed him, and
threw him out of the vineyard.

9 "What then will the owner of the vine-
yard do? He will come and put those
tenants to death and give the vineyard
to others. 10 Have you not read this Scrip-
ture:[t]

'The stone that the builders rejected
has become the cornerstone;[u]
11 by the Lord this has been done,
and it is wonderful in our eyes'?"

12 They wanted to arrest him because
they realized that this parable was directed
at them, but they were afraid of the crowd.
Therefore, they left him and went away.[v]

C: Controversies*

God or Caesar.* 13 [w] Then they sent some
Pharisees and Herodians to trap him in
what he said.[x] 14 They came and said to
him, "Teacher, we know that you are truth-
ful and are not concerned with anyone's
opinion no matter what his station in life.
Rather, you teach the way of God in accor-
dance with the truth. Is it lawful or not for
us to pay taxes to Caesar? Should we pay
them or not?"

15 He was aware of their hypocrisy and
said to them, "Why are you trying to trap
me? Bring me a denarius* and let me
examine it." 16 When they brought one, he
asked them, "Whose image is this, and
whose inscription?" They replied and said
to him, "Caesar's." 17 Jesus said to them,
"Give to Caesar what is due to Caesar, and
to God what is due to God." His reply left
them completely amazed at him.[y]

Marriage and the Resurrection.* 18 Then
some Sadducees, who assert that there is
no resurrection, approached him and
posed this question,[z] 19 "Teacher, Moses
wrote down for us that if a man's brother
dies, leaving a wife but no child, the man
shall take his brother's wife and raise up
children for his brother.[a] 20 Now there were
seven brothers. The first brother took a wife
and died, leaving no children. 21 The second
brother married the widow and died, leav-
ing no children. The same was true of the
third brother. 22 None of the seven left any
children. Last of all, the woman herself
died. 23 Now at the resurrection, when they
rise up, whose wife will she be, inasmuch as
all seven had her?"

24 Jesus said to them, "Is not this the
reason you are in error—namely, that you
do not understand the Scriptures or the
power of God?[b] 25 For when they rise from
the dead, they will neither marry nor be
given in marriage. They are like angels in
heaven.[c]

26 "And in regard to the dead being
raised, have you not read in the book of
Moses, in the account about the bush, how
God said to him: 'I am the God of
Abraham, the God of Isaac, and the God of
Jacob'?[d] 27 He is not the God of the dead
but of the living. You are very badly mis-
taken."

The Greatest Commandment.* 28 [e] Then one
of the scribes who had listened to these dis-
cussions, and who had observed how well
Jesus answered them, asked Jesus, "Which is
the first of all the commandments?"*

29 Jesus answered, "The first is: 'Hear, O
Israel: the Lord our God, the Lord is one!
30 You shall love the Lord your God with all

s Heb 1:1-3.—t 10-11: Ps 118:22-23; Isa 28:16.—u Acts 4:11.—v Mk 11:18.—w 13-27: Mt 22:15-33; Lk 20:20-39.—x Mk 3:6.—y Rom 13:7.—z Acts 23:8; 1 Cor 15:12.—a Deut 25:5.—b 2 Tim 3:15-17.—c 1 Cor 15:42.—d Ex 3:6.—e 28-34: Mt 22:34-40; Lk 10:25-28.

12:13-44 The discussions continue. His opponents seek to have Jesus contradict himself so as to accede to their demands. But the questioners are caught in their own trap. And the masks of their false religion fall away. Who among us has not in some way acted like these scribes, Pharisees, and Sadducees when a decision of faith had to be made!

12:13-17 See note on Mt 22:15-22.

12:15 *Denarius:* the daily wage of a laborer.

12:18-27 To the conservative Sadducees, the resurrection of the dead—asserted toward the end of the Old Testament (see Isa 26:19; 2 Mac 7:9-14, 23-26; 12:43-46; Wis 2:23-24; 3:1-9; Dan 12:2-3)—was an idea to be eliminated by ridicule. They postulate an unlikely application of the law of the levirate, according to which a man must provide a posterity for the widow of his brother, if the latter has died childless. See also note on Mt 22:23-33.

12:28-34 This friendly dialogue between Jesus and a scribe is unique in the Synoptic Gospels. See also note on Mt 22:34-40.

12:28 *First of all the commandments:* among the 613 precepts listed by the teachers of the Law; of these, 365 (as many as the days of the year) were negative, that is, contained prohibitions, and 248 (as many as the parts of the human body were thought to be) were positive.

your heart, and with all your soul, and with
all your mind, and with all your strength.'[f]
31 The second is this: 'You shall love your
neighbor as yourself.'[g] There is no other
commandment greater than these."
32 Then the scribe said to him, "Well said,
Teacher. You have truly said, 'He is one,
and there is no other besides him.'[h] 33 And
'to love him with all your heart, and with
all your understanding, and with all your
strength, and to love your neighbor as
yourself,' is worth more than any burnt
offerings and sacrifices."[i] 34 And when
Jesus saw with what great understanding
he had spoken, he said to him, "You are not
far from the kingdom of God." And after
that no one dared to ask him any ques-
tion.[j]

Jesus Is Lord.* 35 [k] While Jesus was teach-
ing in the temple area, he said, "How can
the scribes say that the Christ is the Son of
David? * 36 David himself, inspired by the
Holy Spirit, declared:

> 'The Lord said to my Lord:
> "Sit at my right hand
> until I put your enemies under your
> feet." '[l]

37 David himself calls him 'Lord'; so how
can he be his son?" And the large crowd lis-
tened to him with delight.[m]

Denunciation of the Scribes.* 38 [n] In his
teaching, he said, "Beware of the scribes,
who like to walk around in long robes, to be
greeted respectfully in the marketplace,
39 and to have the best seats in the syna-
gogues and the places of honor at banquets.
40 They devour the houses of widows, while
for the sake of appearance they recite
lengthy prayers. They will receive the sever-
est possible condemnation."

The Poor Widow's Offering.* 41 [o] As Jesus was
sitting opposite the treasury,* he watched
the crowd putting money into the treasury.
Many wealthy people put in large sums.[p]
42 A poor widow also came and put in two
copper coins, that is, about a penny. * 43 Then
he called his disciples to him and said,
"Amen, I say to you, this poor widow has
given more than all the other contributors to
the treasury. 44 For the others have all con-
tributed out of their abundance, but she out
of her poverty has given everything she pos-
sessed, all that she had to live on."[q]

D: When Will the End Come?*

CHAPTER 13

Jesus Announces the Destruction of the Temple.* 1 [r] As Jesus was making his depar-
ture from the temple, one of his disciples
said to him, "Teacher, look at the size of
these stones and buildings!" 2 Jesus said to
him, "Do you see these great buildings? Not
a single stone will be left upon another;
every one will be thrown down."[s]

The End Has Not Yet Come.* 3 [t] As he was sit-
ting on the Mount of Olives directly across
from the temple, Peter,* James, John, and

f Deut 6:4-5.—g Lev 19:18; Rom 13:9; Gal 5:14; Jas 2:8.—h Deut 4:35; Isa 45:6.—i Deut 6:4; Ps 40:7-9; Am 5:22.—j Mt 22:46; Lk 20:40.—k 35-37: Mt 22:41-45; Lk 20:41-44.—l 2 Sam 23:2; Ps 110:1.—m Jn 12:9.—n 38-40: Mt 23:1-7; Lk 11:43; 20:45-47.—o 41-44: Lk 21:1-4.—p 2 Ki 12:9; Jn 8:20.—q 2 Cor 8:12.—r 1-2: Mt 24:1-2; Lk 21:5-6.—s Lk 19:44.—t 3-8: Mt 24:3-8; Lk 21:7-11.

12:35-37 Every king was an "Anointed" (Messiah or Christ), and Ps 110, which is cited here, is an acclamation addressed to a king. The Israelite tradition was utterly convinced that the Anointed One par excellence would belong to the dynasty of David (2 Sam 7:1-17). Then, too, many psalms, including 110, were attributed to David. Against this background Jesus asks a question based on this psalm, with the intention of carrying the thought a step further: he suggests that the Messiah's origin is mysterious and that his kingship differs from that which his contemporaries await. The early Church will use the same psalm to show that the Resurrection of Jesus is his authentic enthronement as Messiah (see Heb 1:3; 5:6; 6:20; 7:11, 21; 10:12-13).

12:35 The audience of Jesus is not specified here; in Matthew he is speaking to the Pharisees, and in Luke to the scribes.

12:38-40 See notes on Mt 23:1-39.

12:41-44 Jesus praises the offering of the poor widow because she gave more than all the others, although her gift was by far the smallest. She willingly gave out of her poverty (*all that she had to live on*), while the others gave *out of their abundance*. Therefore, she provides a striking contrast to the pride and pretentiousness of the scribes, who were denounced in the previous section.

12:41 *Treasury:* a room with thirteen boxes, near the inner court of the temple, into which women could enter.

12:42 *[She] put in two copper coins, that is, about a penny:* literally, "She put in two *lepta*, which is a fourth of an *as*." The fact that the poor widow gives two *lepta* shows that she could have given less. A *lepton* was the smallest Greek coin. For his readers' sake, Mark explains the amount in Roman terms ("fourth of an *as*," a penny).

13:1-37 For over two centuries the Jewish world had been familiar with these strange visions that were meant to explain in advance the events that would occur at the end of the world. The series of pictures describes the unfolding of a catastrophe. These literary pieces were known as "apocalypses," that is, revelations (see Isa 24—27; Ezek 34—36; Dan 7—12; Zec 14:1-20; etc.).

In the present discourse, the longest in Mark's Gospel, Jesus, too, speaks of the final destiny of the human race and borrows from the Jewish apocalypses the somewhat terrifying images that became part of the literary genre of apocalypse as found in the first three Gospels. The discourse is therefore known as "the Synoptic apocalypse." And because it bids us reflect on the ultimate lot of humankind and the world, it is also known as the "eschatological discourse," that is, a discourse about the end.

13:1-2 See note on Mt 24:1-2.

13:3-8 See note on Mt 24:3-14.

13:3 *Peter:* the disciples named were the first to be called (see Mk 1:16-20). In Mark, all of Jesus' teaching is given privately to these four disciples.

Andrew questioned him when they were
alone.[u] 4 "Tell us," they said, "when will this
happen, and what will be the sign that all
those things are about to be accomplished?"

5 Jesus began to say to them, "Take care
that no one deceives you.[v] 6 Many will
come in my name, saying, 'I am he,' and
they will lead many astray. 7 And when you
hear of wars and rumors of wars, do not be
alarmed, for those things are bound to
happen, but the end is still to come. 8 For
nation will rise against nation and king-
dom against kingdom. There will be earth-
quakes in various places, and there will be
famine. These are only the beginning of the
labor pangs.

The Coming Persecution. 9 *[w] "Be on your
guard. For they will hand you over to courts
and beat you in synagogues. You will stand
before governors and kings because of me
to testify before them.[x] 10 But first the
gospel must be preached to all nations.

11 [y] "When they arrest you and bring you to
trial, do not be concerned beforehand about
what you are to say. Simply say whatever is
given to you when that time comes, for it will
not be you who speak but the Holy Spirit.

12 "Brother will betray brother to death,
and a father his child. Children will rebel
against their parents and have them put to
death.[z] 13 You will be hated by all because
of my name, but whoever stands firm to the
end will be saved.

The Great Trial. 14 [a] "Therefore, when you
see the abomination of desolation * stand-
ing where it does not belong (let the reader
understand), then those who are in Judea
must flee to the mountains,[b] 15 the one who
is standing on the roof must not come down
or go inside to take anything out of the
house,[c] 16 and someone who is in the field
must not turn back to retrieve his coat.

17 "Woe to those who are pregnant and
those who are nursing infants in those days.[d]
18 Pray that all this may not occur in winter.
19 For in those days there will be such suffer-
ing as has not been since the beginning of the
creation that God made until now and will
never be again.[e] 20 And if the Lord had not
cut short those days, no one would be saved;
but for the sake of the elect whom he chose,
he did cut short those days.

False Messiahs and False Prophets.*
21 "Therefore, if anyone says to you, 'Look,
here is the Christ!' or 'Look, there he is!' do
not believe it.[f] 22 For false christs and false
prophets will arise, and they will perform
signs and wonders to lead astray God's
chosen ones, if that were possible.[g] 23 Be on
your guard! I have forewarned you about
everything.[h]

The Coming of the Son of Man.* 24 [i] "But in
those days, following that distress,

> the sun will be darkened[j]
> and the moon will not give forth its light,
> 25 and the stars will be falling from the sky,
> and the heavenly powers will be shaken.

26 Then they will see 'the Son of Man coming
in the clouds' with great power and glory.[k]
27 And he will send forth his angels and
gather his elect from the four winds, from
the ends of the earth to the ends of the
heavens.[l]

The Parable of the Fig Tree.* 28 [m] "Learn
this lesson from the fig tree. As soon as its
twigs become tender and its leaves begin to
sprout, you know that summer is near. 29 In
the same way, when you see these things
come to pass, know that he is near, at the
very gates. 30 Amen, I say to you, this gen-
eration will not pass away before all these
things have taken place. *[n] 31 Heaven and

u Mk 5:37.—v Jer 29:8; Eph 5:6; 2 Thes 2:3.—w 9-13: Mt 24:9-14; Lk 21:12-19.—x Mt 10:17.—y 11-12: Mt 10:19-22; Lk 12:11-12.—z Mic 7:6.—a 14-23: Mt 24:15-22; Lk 21:20-24.—b Dan 9:27; Mt 24:15.—c Lk 17:31.—d Lk 23:29.—e Mk 10:6; Dan 12:1; Joel 2:2.—f Lk 17:23.—g 2 Thes 2:9, 10.—h 2 Pet 3:17.—i 24-27: Mt 24:29-31; Lk 21:25-27.—j 24-25: Isa 13:10; Ezek 32:7; Joel 2:10.—k Mk 14:62; Dan 7:13-14.—l Deut 30:3-4; Zec 2:6.—m 28-32: Mt 24:32-36; Lk 21:29-33.—n Mk 9:1.

13:9-20 See note on Mt 24:15-22.

13:14 *The abomination of desolation* refers, in Dan 11:31; 12:11, and 1 Mac 1:54; 6:7, to the statue of the pagan emperor that was set up in the temple as a symbol of his divinity. Jesus is thus foretelling that this scandalous event will be repeated.

13:21-23 False messiahs who try to lead Christians astray can be resisted by clinging to revealed Truth taught by Christ's Church.

13:24-27 The discourse now takes on clearly cosmic proportions. The upheaval in the elements is described in the customary expressions derived from apocalyptic language. However, the whole passage is centered upon the glorious appearance of the Messiah in his Second Coming. The emphasis is on the joy of the elect at the coming of the Son of Man rather than on their terror over the destruction of the world. See note on Mt 24:29-31.

13:28-31 See note on Mt 23:32-35.

13:30 It was typical of apocalypses that they announced events as if they had to do with the present generation. It was a way of involving the reader, of saying: "This passage has to do with you."

earth will pass away, but my words will never pass away.

The Day and Hour Unknown.* 32 "But as for that day or that hour, no one knows, neither the angels in heaven, nor the Son, but only the Father. [o] 33 [p] Be on your guard and keep alert, because you do not know when the time will come.

34 "It is like a man going on a journey. He leaves his house and puts his servants in charge, each with his own duties to perform, and he commands the doorkeeper to remain alert. [q] 35 Therefore, keep watch, for you do not know when the master of the house will return, whether in the evening, or at midnight, or at cockcrow, or at dawn, 36 lest he arrive unexpectedly and find you asleep. 37 What I say to you, I say to all: Keep awake!"

E: The Mystery Is Fully Manifested in the Passion and Resurrection*

CHAPTER 14

The Plot against Jesus.* 1 [r] It was now two days before the Passover and the feast of Unleavened Bread, and the chief priests and the scribes were seeking to arrest Jesus by deceit and put him to death. [s] 2 They said, "It must not occur during the feast, or the people may begin to riot."

A Woman of Bethany Anoints Jesus.* 3 [t] When Jesus was in Bethany reclining at table in the house of Simon the leper, a woman came in with an alabaster jar of very costly ointment, made of pure nard. She broke open the jar and poured the ointment over his head. [u] 4 Some of those present said to one another indignantly, "Why was this ointment wasted in such a manner? 5 It could have been sold for more than three hundred denarii,* with the money given to the poor." And they began to rebuke her sharply.

6 However, Jesus said, "Let her alone! Why are you bothering her? She has performed a good action toward me. 7 The poor you will always have with you, and you can show kindness to them whenever you wish, but you will not always have me. [v] 8 She has done what she could. She has anointed my body to prepare for my burial. [w] 9 Amen, I say to you, wherever in the whole world this gospel is proclaimed, what she has done will be told in remembrance of her." [x]

Judas Betrays Jesus.* 10 [y] Then Judas Iscariot, who was one of the Twelve, went to the chief priests and offered to hand him over to them. [z] 11 They were delighted when they heard his proposal, and they promised to give him money. Then he began to look for an opportunity to betray him.

The Preparations for the Passover.* 12 [a] On the first day of the feast of Unleavened Bread, when it was customary to sacrifice the Passover lamb, the disciples said to Jesus, "Where do you want us to go and make the preparations for you to eat the Passover?" [b]

13 [c] He sent forth two of his disciples, instructing them: "Go into the city, and a man carrying a jug of water will meet you. Follow him! 14 Wherever he enters, say to the master of the house, 'The Teacher asks: "Where is the room where I can eat the Passover with my disciples?" ' 15 Then he will show you a large upper room furnished and ready. Make the preparations for us there." [d] 16 The disciples went forth, entered the city, and found everything just as he had told them, and they prepared the Passover.

---

o Acts 1:7; 1 Thes 5:1-2.—p 33-37: Mt 24:42; 25; 13-15.—q Mt 25:14-30; Lk 19:12-27.—r 1-2: Mt 26:2-5; Lk 22:1-2; Jn 11:45-53.—s Mt 26:17.—t 3-9: Mt 26:6-13; Jn 12:1-8.—u Lk 7:37-39.—v Deut 15:11.—w Jn 19:40.—x Mk 16:15.—y 10-11: Mt 26:14-16; Lk 22:3-6.—z Mk 3:16-19.—a 12-16: Mt 26:17-19; Lk 22:7-13.—b 1 Cor 5:7.—c 13-15: 1 Sam 10:2-5.—d Acts 1:13.

13:32-37 See note on Mt 24:36-42.

14:1—16:8 The Passion Narrative that makes the deepest impression is perhaps that of Mark's Gospel. The writer does not aim to move the reader, still less to satisfy our curiosity with edifying anecdotes and points of information. The description is vivid, unpolished, clear-cut. Mark piles up concrete, detailed incidents in order to highlight the tragic character of the struggle that Jesus is carrying on alone, isolated in his silence and humiliation. It is precisely in his abasement that Jesus shows himself to be the Messiah, the King of Israel, Son of God, and Savior of the world.

14:1-2 We are at the religious high point of the year, the time of Passover, which is followed by the feast of Unleavened Bread, that is, an eight-day celebration during which only unleavened bread was eaten (see Deut 16:1-8; Ex 12:5-20).

14:3-9 At this period the burial of the dead was regarded as an indispensable work of charity and of greater merit than almsgiving. In the present circumstances of Jesus, the woman's gesture of respect becomes a sign of his imminent death. In addition, in Mark's Gospel the ointment is poured on the head of Jesus, suggesting an act of consecration.

14:5 *Three hundred denarii:* a year's wages, a denarius being a day's wages for a laborer.

14:10-11 See note on Mt 26:14-16.

14:12-16 See notes on Mt 26:17-19 and 26:17.

Matson Photo Service

THE UPPER ROOM — In Jerusalem an "upper room" was frequently built on the roof of houses and used in summer because it was cooler than the regular living quarters. (See Mk 14:15; Lk 22:12; Acts 1:13; 20:8)

The room above is a medieval structure marking the traditional site in the southern corner of the Upper City of Jerusalem where the Last Supper took place as well as the descent of the Holy Spirit on the disciples. (See Mk 14:14-17; Acts 2:1-11)

Wide World

MOUNT OF OLIVES — A range of hills with three peaks rising east of Jerusalem beyond the Kidron Valley. In the foreground is the Church of All Nations built in the Garden of Gethsemane; above and to the right of the Church of the Agony and in the center on the summit is the tower of the Church of the Ascension. This Mount was closely connected with the closing years of our Lord's life and it was here that he retired after the Last Supper. (See Mk 14:26)

Matson Photo Service

GARDEN OF GETHSEMANE — Close-up of the Garden across the Kidron Valley from Jerusalem; showing the Church of All Nations on the left and the city wall with the Golden Gate on the hill beyond. It was in this general area of the Mount of Olives that Christ's Passion began with his agony and arrest. (See Mk 14:32-52)

The Treachery of Judas Foretold.* 17 [e]Now when evening came, he arrived with the Twelve. 18 And as they reclined at table and were eating, Jesus said, "Amen, I say to you, one of you will betray me, one who is eating with me." 19 On hearing this they began to be distressed and to say to him, one after another, "Is it I?"

20 He said to them, "It is one of the Twelve, one who is dipping bread into the bowl with me. 21 For the Son of Man goes as it is written of him, but woe to that man by whom the Son of Man is betrayed! It would be better for that man if he had never been born."

The Last Supper.* 22 [f]While they were eating he took bread, and after he had pronounced the blessing, he broke it and gave it to them, saying, "Take it; this is my body." [g] 23 Then he took a cup, and after offering thanks he gave it to them. After they all drank from it, [h] 24 he said to them, "This is my blood of the covenant, which will be shed on behalf of many. 25 Amen, I say to you, from now on I shall not drink this fruit of the vine until the day when I shall drink it anew in the kingdom of God."

26 [i]And after singing a hymn, they went out to the Mount of Olives.

Jesus Predicts Peter's Denial.* 27 Then Jesus said to them, "You will all be scandalized, for it is written:

'I will strike the shepherd,
and the sheep will be scattered.' [j]

28 But after I have been raised up, I shall go ahead of you to Galilee." [k] 29 Peter said to him, "Even if all the others will be scandalized, I will never be." 30 Jesus replied, "Amen, I say to you, this very night, before the cock crows twice, you will deny me three times." [l] 31 But Peter insisted, "If I have to die with you, I will not deny you." And they all said the same thing.

The Agony in the Garden.* 32 [m]Then they went to a place that was called Gethsemane, and Jesus said to his disciples, "Sit here while I pray." [n] 33 He took with him Peter and James and John, and he began to suffer distress and anguish. [o] 34 And he said to them, "My soul is sorrowful, even to the point of death. Remain here and keep watch." [p]

35 Moving on a little farther, he threw himself on the ground and prayed that, if it were possible, the hour might pass him by, 36 saying, "Abba, Father, for you all things are possible. Take this cup from me. Yet not my will but yours be done." [q]

37 Returning to the disciples, he found them sleeping. He said to Peter, "Simon, are you asleep? Could you not keep watch for one hour? 38 Stay awake and pray that you may not enter into temptation. The spirit is indeed willing but the flesh is weak." [r]

39 Again, he went apart and prayed, saying the same words. 40 Then he came again and found them sleeping, for their eyes were very heavy, and they did not know what to say to him. 41 When he returned a third time, he said to them, "Are you still sleeping and taking your rest? Enough! The hour has come when the Son of Man is to be betrayed into the hands of sinners. 42 Get up! Let us go! Look, my betrayer is approaching."

Jesus Is Arrested.* 43 [s]At once, while he was still speaking, Judas, one of the Twelve, arrived. With him there was a crowd of men, armed with swords and clubs, who had been sent by the chief priests, the scribes, and the elders. 44 Now his betrayer had agreed with them on a signal, saying, "The one I shall kiss is the man. Arrest

e 17-21: Mt 26:20-24; Lk 22:21-23; Jn 13:21-26.—f 22-25: Mt 26:26-30; Lk 22:19-20; 1 Cor 11:23-25.—g Mt 14:19.—h 1 Cor 10:16.—i 26-31: Mt 26:30-35; Lk 22:34, 39; Jn 13:36-38.—j Zec 13:7; Jn 16:32.—k Mk 16:7.—l Jn 13:38.—m 32-42: Mt 26:36-46; Lk 22:40-46.—n Jn 18:1.—o Mk 5:37.—p Jn 12:27.—q Rom 8:15.—r Rom 7:5, 22-23.—s 43-50: Mt 26:47-56; Lk 22:47-53; Jn 18:3-11.

14:17-21 See note on Mt 26:20-25.

14:22-25 Four accounts of the Lord's Supper are found in the New Testament (Mt 26:26-28; Mk 14:22-24; Lk 22:19-20; and 1 Cor 11:23-25). Matthew and Mark are similar to one another while Luke and Paul are also similar to each other. All four accounts include (1) the taking of the bread; (2) the thanksgiving or blessing; (3) the breaking of the bread; (4) the saying, "This is my body"; (5) the taking of the cup; and (6) the explanation of the relation of blood to the Covenant. Only Luke and Paul record the command to continue to celebrate the Supper, "Do this in memory of me" (Lk 22:19; 1 Cor 11:24).

In giving his body and blood Jesus anticipates the action of his enemies, and his death becomes an offering to God, the sacrifice of the Servant who expiates the sin of the entire people (Isa 53). By this act he establishes the New Covenant; it inaugurates a new relationship between God and humanity.

14:27-31 Despite the protestations of the Twelve that they will never abandon him, Jesus predicts that they will do so. But he also reassures them that after his Resurrection he will see them again in Galilee (Mk 16:7; see Mt 26:32; 28:7, 10, 16; Jn 21) where he first called them (Mk 1:14-20).

14:32-42 See note on Mt 26:36-46.

14:43-52 See notes on Mt 26:47-56 and 26:47-48.

him, and lead him away under guard!" 45 And so, when he came, he proceeded directly to Jesus and said "Rabbi!" and kissed him. 46 Then they seized him and placed him under arrest. 47 Meanwhile, one of the bystanders drew his sword and struck a servant of the high priest, slicing off his ear.

48 Then Jesus said to them, "Why are you coming forth with swords and clubs to arrest me, as though I were a bandit? 49 Day after day I was with you in the temple teaching, and you did not arrest me. But in this way the Scriptures must be fulfilled." [t] 50 Then everyone deserted him and fled. 51 * Among those who had followed Jesus was a young man wearing nothing but a linen cloth. They caught hold of him, 52 but he slipped out of the linen cloth and ran off naked. [u]

Jesus Is Condemned by the Sanhedrin.* 53 [v] They led Jesus away to the high priest, where the chief priests, the elders, and the scribes were gathering. 54 Meanwhile, Peter had followed him at a distance, right into the courtyard of the high priest, and he was sitting there with the attendants, warming himself at the fire. [w]

55 The chief priests and the entire Sanhedrin * tried to elicit testimony against Jesus so that they could put him to death, but they failed in their efforts. 56 Many witnesses offered perjured testimony against him, but their statements did not agree. 57 Then some stood up and gave this false witness against him: 58 "We heard this man say, 'I will destroy this temple made with human hands, and in three days I will build another not made with hands.' " [x] 59 But even on this point their statements did not agree.

60 The high priest then rose among them and asked Jesus, "Have you no reply to counter the testimony that these witnesses have given?" 61 * But he remained silent and offered no response. Again, the high priest questioned him, asking, "Are you the Christ, the Son of the Blessed One?" * [y] 62 Jesus replied, "I am.

And you will see the Son of Man
seated at the right hand of the Power
and coming with the clouds of heaven." [z]

63 Thereupon the high priest tore his garments and exclaimed, "What need do we have of any further witnesses! [a] 64 You have heard his blasphemy. What is your decision?" They all condemned him as guilty and deserving of death. [b] 65 Some of them began to spit at him. They blindfolded him and struck him, taunting him as they said, "Prophesy!" And the guards also slapped him. [c]

Peter Denies Jesus.* 66 [d] While Peter was below in the courtyard, one of the high priest's servant girls came by. 67 When she noticed Peter warming himself, she stared at him and said, "You also were with Jesus, the man from Nazareth." [e] 68 But he denied it, saying, "I neither know nor understand what you are talking about." Thereupon he went forth into the outer courtyard. Then the cock crowed. * 69 The servant girl saw him and again began to say to the bystanders: "This man is one of them." 70 But again he denied it.

Shortly afterward, some bystanders said to Peter, "You are unquestionably one of them, for you are a Galilean." [f] 71 Then he began to shout curses, and he swore an oath: "I do not know this man you are talking about." 72 At that very moment, a cock crowed for a second time, and Peter remembered that Jesus had said to him, "Before the cock crows twice, you will deny me three times." And he broke down and wept. [g]

t Isa 53:7-12.—u Am 2:16.—v 53-65: Mt 26:57-68; Lk 22:54-55, 63-65, 67-71; Jn 18:12-13.—w Jn 18:18.—x Mk 15:29; Jn 2:19; 2 Cor 5:1.—y Isa 53:7; Mt 27:12.—z Mk 13:26; Ps 110:1; Dan 7:13; Mt 24:30; Rev 1:7.—a Lev 10:6.—b Lev 24:16.—c Lk 22:63-65.—d 66-72: Mt 26:69-75; Lk 22:56-62; Jn 18:16-18, 25-27.—e Mt 2:23.—f Acts 2:7.—g Jn 13:38.

14:51-52 This detail is only in Mark. Many commentators have considered the young man to be Mark himself.

14:53-65 See note on Mt 26:57-68.

14:55 *Sanhedrin:* the highest tribunal of the Jews. In New Testament times, it numbered 71 members: chief priests, elders, and scribes, plus the high priest who presided over the proceedings. The Romans gave the tribunal much authority but not over capital punishment (see Jn 18:31). See also note on Mt 27:1-2.

14:61-65 Just when he is being judged and abased, Jesus for the first time openly declares himself to be the Messiah, of royal descent and divine rank (Ps 110:1; Dan 7:13).

The Jewish authorities are scandalized and condemn him. He then suffers the harsh lot of the Servant prophet.

14:61 *Son of the Blessed One:* in late Judaism people avoided uttering the name of God, as a sign of respect; they preferred other expressions such as "the Blessed One" or "the Power" (v. 62).

14:66-72 See note on Mt 26:69-75.

14:68 *Then the cock crowed:* these words are found in most manuscripts but omitted in some.

CHAPTER 15

Jesus before Pilate.* 1 [h] As soon as it was morning, the chief priests held a council with the elders and the scribes and the whole Sanhedrin. They bound Jesus and led him away, and handed him over to Pilate. [i]

2 Pilate asked him, "Are you the king of the Jews?" Jesus replied, "You have said so." [j] 3 Then the chief priests brought many charges against him. 4 Again, Pilate questioned him, "Have you no answer to offer? Just consider how many charges they are leveling against you." 5 But Jesus offered no further reply, so that Pilate was amazed. [k]

Jesus Is Sentenced to Death. 6 [l] Now on the occasion of the feast, he released a prisoner to them, anyone for whom they asked. * 7 At the time, a man named Barabbas was in prison along with some rebels who had committed murder during an uprising. 8 When the crowd came forward and began to ask him to do the customary favor for them, 9 Pilate asked them, "Do you want me to release for you the king of the Jews?" * 10 For he realized that it was out of envy that the chief priests had handed him over.

11 However, the chief priests incited the crowd to have him release Barabbas for them instead. [m] 12 Pilate then asked, "And what shall I do with the man you call the king of the Jews?" 13 They shouted back, "Crucify him!" 14 Pilate asked them, "Why? What evil has he done?" But they only screamed all the louder, "Crucify him!" 15 And so Pilate, anxious to appease the crowd, released Barabbas to them, and after ordering Jesus to be scourged, he handed him over to be crucified. [n]

Jesus Is Crowned with Thorns.* 16 [o] Then the soldiers led Jesus away inside the palace, that is, the Praetorium, and they called the whole cohort together. 17 They dressed him in a purple robe and after twisting some thorns into a crown, they placed it on him. 18 Then they began to salute him with the words, "Hail, King of the Jews!" 19 They repeatedly struck his head with a reed, spat upon him, and knelt down before him in homage. 20 And when they had finished mocking him, they stripped him of his purple robe and dressed him in his own clothes. [p] Then they led him out to crucify him.

The Way of the Cross.* 21 They compelled a passer-by who was returning from the country to carry his cross. The man was Simon of Cyrene, the father of Alexander and Rufus. [q]

Jesus Is Crucified. 22 [r] They brought him to the place called Golgotha, which means the place of the skull. 23 They offered him some wine that had been mixed with myrrh, but he refused to take it. [s] 24 Then they crucified him and divided his garments among them, casting lots for them to see what each should take. * [t]

25 It was around nine o'clock in the morning when they crucified him. * 26 The inscription giving the charge against him read, "The King of the Jews." 27 Along with him they crucified two thieves, one on his right and the other on his left. [u] [28 Thus was the Scripture fulfilled that says, "And he was counted among the wicked."] *

29 Those people who passed by jeered at him, shaking their heads and saying, "Aha! You who claimed you could destroy the tem-

h 1-5: Mt 27:1-2, 11-14; Lk 23:1-3.—i Lk 22:66; Jn 18:28.—j Mt 2:2.—k Mk 14:61.—l 6-15: Mt 27:15-26; Lk 23:17-25; Jn 18:39-40.—m Acts 3:14.—n Isa 53:6.—o 16-20: Mt 27:27-31; Jn 19:2-3.—p Jn 19:17: Heb 13:12.—q Mt 27:32; Lk 23:26; Rom 16:13.—r 22-38: Mt 27:33-51; Lk 23:32-46; Jn 19:17-30.—s Ps 69:22; Prov 31:6.—t Ps 22:19.—u Isa 53:12; Lk 23:33.

15:1-5 See notes on Mt 27:11-26 and 27:11.

15:6 Outside the Gospels no such Passover privilege is explicitly found in other sources. However, this does not mean it didn't exist.

15:9 According to Mark, Barabbas had been arrested in a rebellion, possibly in a political rebellion against the Romans. Thus, he was a hero with the people and fed their national pride. When Herod brings forth Jesus as the King of the Jews, the same people will have none of it—a Messiah reduced to a pitiful state, chained, and despised!

15:16-20 See note on Mt 27:27-31.

15:21 Those condemned to death were usually forced to carry the crossbeam of the cross, often 30 to 40 pounds, to the place of crucifixion. Jesus starts out by doing the same (see Jn 19:7), but he is so weak as a result of his scourging and overall ill-treatment that the soldiers decide to have someone else take over that task. The man chosen is Simon, a man from Cyrene, an important city of Libya, North Africa, with a large Jewish population, who is probably in Jerusalem for the Passover celebration. *Alexander and Rufus:* the sons are named probably because they were known to the early Christians to whom Mark's Gospel is addressed.

15:24 See note on Mt 27:35.

15:25 Mark sketches the Passion in a quasi-liturgical fashion and as it were in thirds: the coming together of the Sanhedrin at the first hour (6 A.M.); crucifixion at the third hour (9 A.M.); darkness at the sixth hour (12 P.M.); and death at the ninth hour (3 P.M.). The "third hour," however, must be taken in a wide sense, between 9 A.M. and 12 P.M., for Jesus was crucified at 12 P.M. (see Jn 19:14). See also note on Mt 27:35.

15:28 This verse is omitted by the best manuscripts.

ple and rebuild it within three days,[v] 30 save yourself and come down from the cross."

31 In much the same way, the chief priests and the scribes joined in the mockery among themselves, saying, "He saved others, but he cannot save himself. 32 Let the Christ, the King of Israel, come down from the cross right now so that we may see it and come to believe." Those who were crucified with him also taunted him.[w]

Jesus Dies on the Cross.* 33 Beginning at midday, there was darkness over the whole land until three in the afternoon. 34 At three o'clock, Jesus cried out in a loud voice, "*Eloi, Eloi, lema sabachthani?*" which means, "My God, my God, why have you forsaken me?"[x]

35 On hearing this, some of the bystanders said, "Listen! He is calling Elijah." 36 Someone ran off, soaked a sponge with sour wine, put it on a stick, and gave it to him to drink, saying, "Wait! Let us see whether Elijah will come to take him down."[y]

37 Then Jesus cried out in a loud voice and breathed his last.[z] 38 And the veil of the sanctuary was torn in two, from top to bottom.[a] 39 [b] When the centurion who was standing facing him saw how Jesus had breathed his last, he said, "Truly this man was the Son of God."[c]

40 A number of women were also present, looking on from a distance. Among them were Mary Magdalene, Mary the mother of James the younger* and of Joses, and Salome.[d] 41 These women used to follow Jesus when he was in Galilee and minister to his needs. And there were many other women there who had come up with him to Jerusalem.

Jesus Is Placed in the Tomb.* 42 [e] It was the Day of Preparation, that is, the day before the Sabbath. So when evening came,[f] 43 Joseph of Arimathea, a respected member of the council, who was also awaiting the kingdom of God, boldly went to Pilate and requested the body of Jesus.[g] 44 Pilate was surprised to hear that Jesus was already dead, and he summoned the centurion to ascertain that Jesus had indeed died. 45 When he learned from the centurion that such was the case, he turned over the body to Joseph.

46 Having purchased a linen shroud, he lowered Jesus from the cross, wrapped him in the shroud, and laid him in a tomb that had been hewn out of rock. He then rolled a stone against the entrance of the tomb.[h] 47 Mary Magdalene and Mary the mother of Joses saw where the body was buried.

CHAPTER 16

Jesus Is Raised from the Dead.* 1 [i] When the Sabbath was over,* Mary Magdalene, Mary the mother of James, and Salome purchased aromatic spices so that they might go and anoint Jesus.[j] 2 And very early on the first day of the week, just after sunrise, they went to the tomb.

3 They had been asking each other, "Who will roll back the stone for us from the entrance to the tomb?"[k] 4 But when they looked up, they observed that the stone, which was extremely large, had already been rolled back. 5 On entering the tomb, they saw a young man arrayed in a white robe sitting on the right hand side, and they were stunned.[l]

6 He said to them, "Do not be alarmed. You are looking for Jesus of Nazareth, who was crucified. He has been raised. He is not here. See the place where they laid

v Ps 22:8; Jn 2:19.—w Lk 23:39.—x Ps 22:2.—y Ps 69:22.—z Jn 19:30.—a Heb 10:19-20.—b 39-41: Mt 27:54-56; Lk 23:47-49.—c Mk 1:1, 11.—d Mk 6:3; Lk 8:2-3.—e 42-47: Mt 27:57-61; Lk 23:50-56; Jn 19:38-42.—f Mt 27:62.—g Lk 2:25.—h Mk 16:3.—i 1-8: Mt 28:1-8; Lk 24:1-10; Jn 20:1-10.—j 1-2: Mt 28:1; Lk 23:56.—k Mk 15:46.—l Jn 20:12.

15:33-41 After hours on the cross, there comes a final humiliation (v. 36). While God remains silent, the crucified Jesus cries out his aloneness in the words of Ps 22:2, and breathes his last. But the work of Jesus has been completed. The end of Judaism has come, signified by the tearing of the curtain of the temple. Even now a pagan recognizes Jesus as the Son of God; this is the first time in Mark's Gospel that a human being is allowed to give him this title.

15:40 *James the younger:* this James is known as "the Lesser," to distinguish him from the other apostle of the same name, the son of Zebedee and brother of John. From Mt 27:56 we know that Salome was the wife of Zebedee.

15:42-47 The burial of Jesus is arranged by Joseph of Arimathea, a respected member of the Sanhedrin who had not consented to the decision of that body concerning Jesus (see Lk 23:51). Matthew calls Joseph a "rich man" (Mt 27:57), which recalls the text of Isaiah's prophecy about the Suffering Servant (53:9: "They assigned him a grave with the wicked and a burial place with evildoers").

16:1-8 What has happened so surprises the women that they do not take the trouble to spread the message of joy. The Gospel of Mark ends on this fascinating note of mystery.

The scene at the tomb is not meant as a proof of the resurrection but as a proclamation of it; we are told that Jesus' destiny has been accomplished; the reality of his person is now fully revealed, and the order is given to announce that the crucified one is risen. See also the note on Mt 28:1-10.

16:1 *The Sabbath was over:* the time therefore is after sunset. The duty of the Sabbath rest ended at sunset.

him.[m] [7] But go forth and tell his disciples and Peter: 'He is going ahead of you to Galilee. There you will see him just as he told you.'"[n] [8] Then the women emerged from the tomb and fled, overcome with trembling and amazement. They said nothing to anyone, for they were afraid.

APPENDIX

The Longer Ending*

Jesus Appears to Mary Magdalene. [9] [o] After he had risen from the dead early on the first day of the week, Jesus appeared first to Mary Magdalene, from whom he had driven out seven demons.[p] [10] [q] She then went forth and related the story of his appearance to his mourning and weeping companions. [11] However, when they heard that he was alive and that she had seen him, they refused to believe it.

Jesus Appears to Two Disciples. [12] [r] After this, Jesus appeared in a different form to two of them as they were on their way into the country. [13] They then returned and reported the news to the others, but they did not believe them either.

Jesus Appears to and Commissions the Eleven. [14] Still later, he appeared to the eleven while they were at table. He reproached them for their lack of faith and their hardness of heart because they refused to believe the witness of those who had seen him after he had risen.[s]

[15] [t] Then he said to them, "Go forth into the whole world and proclaim the gospel to all creation.[u] [16] Whoever believes and is baptized will be saved; whoever does not believe will be condemned.[v] [17] These are the signs that will mark those who believe: In my name they will cast out demons. They will be granted the gift of speaking in new languages.[w] [18] If they pick up serpents in their hands or drink any deadly poison, they will remain unharmed. The sick on whom they lay their hands will recover."[x]

Jesus Ascends to Heaven. [19] Then, after he had spoken to them, the Lord Jesus was taken up into heaven, and there he took his place at the right hand of God.[y] [20] And they went forth to proclaim the gospel everywhere, while the Lord worked with them and confirmed the word by means of the signs that accompanied their preaching.[z]

Noncanonical Endings

The Shorter Ending.* And they reported all the instructions briefly to Peter and his companions. Afterward, through them Jesus sent forth from east to west the sacred and perpetual proclamation of eternal salvation.

The Freer Logion.* And they excused themselves, saying, "This age of lawlessness and unbelief is under Satan, who does not allow the truth and power of God to prevail over the unclean things of the spirit. Therefore, reveal your righteousness now"—thus they spoke to Christ. And Christ replied to them, "The limit of the years of Satan's power has been reached, but other terrible things draw near. And for those who sinned I was handed over to death, that they might return to the truth and no longer sin, in order that they might inherit the spiritual and incorruptible glory of righteousness, which is in heaven."

m Mt 2:23.—n Mk 14:28; Jn 21:1-23.—o 9-20: Mt 28:1-10; Jn 20:11-18.—p Mk 15:47.—q 10-11: Lk 24:10-11; Jn 20:18.—r 12-14: Lk 24:13-35.—s Lk 24:36-49; 1 Cor 15:5.—t 15-16: Mk 13:10; Mt 28:18-20; Lk 24:47; Jn 20:21; Col 1:23.—u Acts 1:8.—v Jn 3:16.—w Mk 9:38; Acts 5:16.—x Mt 10:1; Lk 10:19; Acts 28:3-6.—y Lk 24:50-53; Acts 1:9-11.—z Jn 4:48; 1 Tim 3:16.

16:9-20 *The Longer Ending:* this passage is found in the great majority of manuscripts. It has traditionally been accepted as a canonical part of the Gospel and was defined as such by the Council of Trent. Although it is cited by the Fathers of the Church as early as the 2nd century, its vocabulary and style point to someone other than Mark as the author. It is a summary of the material concerning the appearances of the risen Lord and reflects traditions found in Luke (ch. 24) and John (ch. 20). It is probable that first-generation Christians wanted to complete Mark's work with a summary of the Resurrection stories and a summary view of the Church's mission. The Lord, who has been restored to his divine glory with the Father, is present and at work in the missionary activity of his disciples; this fact is highlighted in a wonderful sentence that is found only here in the New Testament.

The Shorter Ending: this passage is found in four late Greek manuscripts after v. 8 before the Longer Ending. It is thought to have originated to provide an ending in itself or to give a smoother transition between v. 8 and v. 9.

The Freer Logion: this passage is found in one manuscript, preserved in the Freer Gallery of Art in Washington, D.C., and was known to St. Jerome in the 4th century. It is regarded as an interpolation to soften the condemnation of the disciples in v. 14.

"She . . . began to bathe his feet with her tears and to dry them with her hair. Then she kissed his feet and anointed them with the ointment" *(Lk 7:38).*

THE GOSPEL ACCORDING TO LUKE

The Good News

Christian tradition has always identified Luke as the companion of Paul and his "beloved physician" (Col 4:14; Philem 24). In any case, the author of the third Gospel, who also wrote the Book of Acts, seems to be a conscientious historian.

As he himself says at the beginning of his work, he was very diligent in collecting testimonies and traditions, both oral and written, concerning the life of Jesus. He certainly knew the Gospel of Mark and, in addition, drew upon a source that Matthew likewise used. On the whole, the episodes and words found in the other Gospels are found also in Luke and in almost the same order. But many stories have reached us only through his Gospel. The book has its own style, its own way of presenting the material; from a literary point of view, it is more carefully written.

The work shows us, first and foremost, the author's deep faith in Jesus and his concern for the life of the Gospel. He contemplates the Lord with a special degree of sympathy, and an interiority and mysticism shine through his writing that make it far different from Mark's rough style. Jesus is Luke's savior and redeemer, his joy.

While writing at almost the same period as Matthew, Luke addresses his work to converts from the pagan world, men and women who must live in that world. He is therefore realistic in his teaching.

In addition, this Gospel will be continued in the Acts of the Apostles. In the latter work, Luke describes the beginnings of the young Christian Church, which had been charged by its Lord with proclaiming to all human beings that they have been saved, no matter what the culture was to which they belonged.

The Gospel is a personal and original work by a witness to the faith of the Church. Luke's primary desire is to present the mystery of Christ to us. Christ has brought to fulfillment the plan of God and therefore all the Old Testament promises.

The author does not multiply citations from the Bible, as Matthew does, but his continual, though unobtrusive, allusions to the Scriptures enable us to see in Jesus the new Moses and therefore the new head of the People of God, the new David, the new Solomon, the new Elijah, or, in short, the one who brings to fruition God's plan for the human race. It is to be observed that Luke calls Jesus "Lord" 16 times. This is the title that the Church immediately gave to the risen and glorified Christ, and it is the name given to God in the Old Testament.

More clearly than the other evangelists, Luke portrays the kindness of Jesus to sinners, showing him as the image of the limitless kindness of God. Jesus comes through as the Savior of sinners who seeks out the lost, the despised, and the outcasts and comforts them with the message of forgiveness. The motto of his ministry is found in the words of Jesus that occur only in Luke (19:10): "The Son of Man has come to seek out and to save what was lost." Luke's Book is the Gospel of mercy.

The evangelist emphasizes the universality of the message of Jesus (2:14; 2:32). In the genealogy, Jesus appears as the son of Adam, the father of all mankind (3:38); and the final command of the risen Lord is to proclaim the remission of sins to all nations (24:47).

Love of neighbor is another essential theme of Luke's Gospel. It is at the core of the Sermon on the Plain (6:20-49) and the teaching of the Parable of the Good Samaritan (10:29-37).

Luke is also the evangelist of the Holy Spirit. The latter breaks through from on high as a gift of God and acts with his divine power both in the life of Jesus and in his Messianic community (1:15; 3:22; 4:1; 10:21; 11:13; 12:12).

Another feature of this Gospel is its emphasis on prayer, which is connected with the action of the Holy Spirit. All the Gospels speak of the prayer of Jesus, but Luke alone shows Jesus praying at the most important stages of his ministry (3:21; 6:12; 9:18; 9:28; 11:1; 22:41; 23:46). The evangelist then goes on to stress the duty to pray on the part of all who follow Jesus. They must pray always, without ceasing (18:1ff).

This work has also been termed the Gospel of Women because of its domestic scenes (2:41-51; 10:38-42; 11:5-8) as well as other scenes in which women are mentioned (7:11-17; 8:2f; 23:17-31). From the account of Christ's birth in which Mary, Elizabeth, and Anna are prominent (1—2) to the events of the day of the Resurrection in which women have a large role (24:1-10), Luke brings out the major role that women played in the life and ministry of our Lord.

Finally, Luke calls for unconditional attachment to the things that can be truly good and the renunciation of material things (12:16-21; 16:19-31). Moreover, throughout his Gospel Luke stresses and exalts poverty (5:11; 5:28; 18:22). The evangelist also issues a series of warnings against the danger of riches (6:24; 12:13-21; 14:33, etc.).

The Gospel of Luke may be divided as follows:

Prologue (1:1-4)

- *I: The Infancy Narrative (1:5—2:52)*
- *II: The Beginning of Jesus' Ministry (3:1—4:13)*
- *III: The Ministry of Jesus in Galilee (4:14—9:50)*
- *IV: The Journey to Jerusalem (9:51—19:27)*
- *V: The Activity of Jesus at Jerusalem (19:28—21:38)*
- *VI: The Passion and Resurrection (22:1—24:53)*

CHAPTER 1

PROLOGUE*

1 [a] Since many different individuals have undertaken the task to set down an account of the events that have been fulfilled among us, 2 in accordance with their transmission to us by those who were eyewitnesses and ministers of the word from the beginning, [b] 3 I too, after researching all the evidence anew with great care, have decided to write an orderly account for you, Theophilus, who are so greatly revered, 4 so that you may learn the unquestioned authenticity of the teachings you have received. [c]

I: THE INFANCY NARRATIVE*

Announcement of the Birth of John.* 5 At the time of the reign of King Herod of Judea,* there was a priest named Zechariah, a member of the priestly order of Abijah. His wife Elizabeth was a descendant of Aaron. [d] 6 Both of them were righteous in the eyes of God, observing blamelessly all the commandments and ordinances of the Lord. [e] 7 But they had no children, because Elizabeth was barren and both were advanced in years. [f]

8 On one occasion, when his division was on duty and he was exercising his priestly office before God, 9 he was designated by lot to enter the sanctuary of the Lord and offer incense.* [g] 10 At the hour of the offering of incense, all the people were outside, praying. [h] 11 Then there appeared to him the angel of the Lord, standing to the right of the altar of incense.

12 When Zechariah beheld him, he was terrified and overcome with fear. 13 But the angel said to him, "Do not be afraid, Zechariah, for your prayer has been heard. Your wife Elizabeth will bear for you a son, and you shall name him John. [i] 14 He will be a source of joy and delight to you, and many will rejoice at his birth, 15 for he will be great in the sight of the Lord.

"He will never imbibe wine or any strong drink. Even when he is still in his mother's womb, he will be filled with the Holy Spirit, [j] 16 and he will bring back many of the people of Israel to the Lord their God. [k] 17 With the spirit and power of Elijah he will go before him, to reconcile fathers with their children and to convert the disobedient to the ways of the righteous, so that a prepared people might be made ready for the Lord." [l]

18 Zechariah said to the angel, "How can I be assured of this? For I am an old man and my wife is well past the stage of giving birth." [m] 19 The angel replied, "I am Gabriel. I stand in the presence of God, and I have been sent to speak to you and to convey to you this good news. [n] 20 But now, because you did not believe my words, which will be fulfilled at their appointed time, you will lose your power of speech and will become mute until the day that these things take place." [o]

21 Meanwhile, the people were waiting for Zechariah and were surprised that he was

a 1-4: Acts 1:1; 1 Cor 15:3.—b Jn 15:27; Eph 3:7.—c Jn 20:31.—d 1 Chr 24:10.—e Gen 6:9.—f Gen 18:11; Jdg 13:2-5; 1 Sam 1:5f.—g Ex 30:7; Acts 1:26.—h Lev 16:17.—i Lk 1:57, 60, 63; Mt 1:20.—j Lev 10:9; Num 6:2f; Jer 1:5.—k Lk 1:76.—l Sir 48:10; Mal 3:23f; Mt 17:10-13.—m Gen 15:8.—n Dan 8:16; 9:21.—o Ex 4:11.

1:1-4 Like the Greek historians of his time, Luke begins his book with a prologue. He dedicates the work to a distinguished person, Theophilus (otherwise unknown to us), who has already been taught the good news. Some scholars believe that the name is symbolic for it means "lover of God," hence all Christians.

1:5—2:52 The Gospel is first and foremost a proclamation of what Jesus did and taught and, above all, of his Death and Resurrection for the salvation of humankind; everything that the preachers of the mission and message of Jesus proclaimed led toward the mystery of Easter. But, like Matthew, Luke decided to preface all that with a description of the period preceding the public appearance of Jesus, because the Church wanted to know the mystery of Jesus back to its very beginnings.

The events described by Matthew, however, are not focused on the birth, which is recounted for us through the experiences of Joseph; Luke speaks directly of the birth through the experience of Mary. Regarding Mary, the opening pages of the third Gospel have provided the Church down the centuries with an abundant, and still flowing, wellspring for its faith (Marian teachings), its devotion (the "Hail, Mary"), and its art.

Some points emerge with utter clarity: Mary is the Mother of Jesus; the birth took place at Bethlehem; and the newborn child was placed in a manger. The primary statement made is undoubtedly this: that Jesus was born not by the will of human beings but by the initiative of God, and that he was born of a virgin mother.

1:5-25 The time is toward the end of the reign of Herod the Great (37–4 B.C.). A faithful and devout couple have been praying for the salvation of the people (v. 13). The husband belonged to the eighth class of priests (1 Chr 24:10) and had the joy of entering every so often into the sanctuary. In the midst of the service, an angel—Gabriel, the messenger of the time of salvation (Dan 9:21-27)—appears to him and tells him of an unexpected birth. Like Isaac (Gen 21:2), Samson (Jdg 13:3-7), and Samuel (1 Sam 1), this child will be the result of a miracle, and, even before his birth, he is destined for the service of God; he will live as an ascetic, a "Nazirite" (see Num 6:3-4; Jdg 13:4-5); he will be the mysterious forerunner of the last times, the new Elijah whom the people expected in accordance with an old tradition (Mal 3:23-24). His name will be John, which means: "The Lord is gracious."

1:5 *Judea:* meant here is the entire territory of Palestine.

1:9 Incense was offered in the Holy Place, the room in front of the Holy of Holies or innermost part of the temple. The rite of incense was performed morning and evening at the time of sacrifice.

Philip Gendreau

THE WAILING WALL OF THE TEMPLE — The gigantic blocks of stone formed part of Herod's temple. It was customary for Jews to insert therein parchments containing their prayers and pleas. This was the temple in which Zechariah was perfoming his priestly function when he received word he would be the father of the forerunner of the Messiah, John the Baptist. (See Lk 1:5-19)

Wide World

ANCIENT SYNAGOGUE OF CAPERNAUM — Capernaum was a town on the northwest shore of the Sea of Galilee used by Jesus as his headquarters during his Galilean ministry. Extensive ruins have been unearthed there, including those of the 3rd century synagogue which probably stood on the very site of the one Jesus attended and in which he preached. (See Lk 4:31-32)

VILLAGE OF NAIN— View of the village of Nain, below Mount Tabor. It is located six miles southeast of Nazareth and commands a beautiful view over the hills of lower Galilee and the great plain of Mount Carmel by the sea. This is where Jesus raised a widow's son from the dead. (See Lk 7:11-17)

delaying so long in the sanctuary. 22 When he
did emerge, he could not speak to them, and
they realized that he had seen a vision while
he was in the sanctuary. He was only able to
make signs to them, but he remained unable
to speak.

23 When his term of service was complet-
ed, he returned home. 24 Shortly thereafter
his wife Elizabeth conceived, and she
remained in seclusion for five months,
saying, 25 "The Lord has granted me this
blessing, looking favorably upon me and
removing from me the humiliation I have
endured among my people." * [p]

Announcement of the Birth of Jesus.* 26 In
the sixth month, * the angel Gabriel was sent
by God to a town in Galilee called Nazareth,
27 to a virgin * betrothed to a man named
Joseph, of the house of David. The virgin's
name was Mary. [q]

28 The angel came to her and said, "Hail,
full of grace! * The Lord is with you." [r] 29 But
she was greatly troubled by his words and
wondered in her heart what this salutation
could mean.

30 Then the angel said to her, "Do not be
afraid, Mary, for you have found favor with
God. 31 Behold, you will conceive in your
womb and bear a son, and you will name
him Jesus. 32 He will be great and will be
called Son of the Most High. The Lord God
will give him the throne of his ancestor
David. [s] 33 He will rule over the house of
Jacob forever, and of his kingdom there will
be no end." [t]

34 Mary said to the angel, "How will this
be, since I am a virgin?" * 35 The angel an-
swered, "The Holy Spirit will come upon
you, and the power of the Most High will
overshadow you. Therefore, the child to be
born will be holy, and he will be called the
Son of God. [u] 36 * And behold, your cousin
Elizabeth in her old age has also conceived a
son, and she who was called barren is now in
her sixth month, 37 for nothing will be
impossible for God." [v]

38 Then Mary said, "Behold, I am the ser-
vant of the Lord. Let it be done to me
according to your word." After this, the
angel departed from her.

Mary Visits Elizabeth.* 39 In those days,
Mary set out and journeyed in haste into the
hill country to a town of Judah * 40 where she
entered the house of Zechariah and greeted
Elizabeth. 41 When Elizabeth heard Mary's
greeting, the baby leaped in her womb.

Then Elizabeth was filled with the Holy
Spirit, 42 and she exclaimed with a loud cry,
"Blessed are you among women, and
blessed is the fruit of your womb. [w] 43 And
why am I so greatly favored that the mother
of my Lord should visit me? 44 For behold,
the moment that the sound of your greeting
reached my ears, the child in my womb

p Gen 30:23.—q Mt 1:18.—r Jdg 6:12; Ru 2:4.—s 2 Sam 7:1; Isa 9:6; Mic 4:7.—t Ps 89:4; Dan 2:44; 7:14; Mt 28:18.—u Mt 1:20.—v Gen 18:14; Jer 32:27; Mt 19:26; Rom 4:21.—w Jdg 5:24; Jud 13:18.

1:25 *The humiliation I have endured among my people:* lack of children deprived the parents of personal happiness but also brought about social reproach (see Gen 16:2—Sarai; 25:21—Rebekah; 30:23—Rachel; 1 Sam 1:1-18—Hannah; see also Lev 20:20-21; Ps 128:3; Jer 22:30).

1:26-38 Mary, a young girl, is betrothed, despite the fact that she has the unusual intention of remaining a virgin; "betrothed": that is, according to the custom of the time, she was legally married but did not yet live with her husband. Confronted with this surprising message, she gives no sign of fear or doubt: she reflects, meditates, believes. This woman has the "grace," that is, the favor of God; she is greeted as if Messianic joy were being proclaimed to the Daughter of Zion, the new Jerusalem (see Zep 3:14; Zec 9:9).

The Bible has often spoken of promised sons; but this Jesus is the very Messiah of Israel, according to the mysterious prophecy of Isaiah on which Israel constantly and hopefully meditated (vv. 32-33; see Isa 7:14; 9:6); he is even far more: the Son of God (v. 35). The body of Jesus was to take form in the flesh of Mary, and this was to come about not through human planning but through the presence and action of God himself (see Ex 40:34-35; Num 9:15; 10:34), of the Spirit who creates and gives life (Gen 1:2; Ps 104:30; Isa 11:1-6).

1:26 *In the sixth month:* i.e., after the time of John's conception.

1:27 *Virgin:* i.e., one who had not yet had sexual relations. Mary's question in v. 34 and the reference in v. 27 that she was "betrothed" (pledged to be married) clearly make this point. Mary had just entered her teens, for betrothal usually took place after puberty, but intercourse was not allowed until marriage. The betrothal could be severed only by divorce or death.

1:28 *Hail, full of grace:* this phrase may also be translated as "Hail, O highly favored one." *The Lord is with you:* other ancient manuscripts add: "Blessed are you among women" (as in Lk 1:42).

1:34 *I am a virgin:* literally, "I do not know man," "know" referring to the conjugal relationship.

1:36-37 In confirmation of what the angel has said to her, Mary is given word of the pregnancy of her aged relative Elizabeth. God has effected a pregnancy for a woman past childbearing years. Thus, he can effect a pregnancy for Mary also, because nothing is impossible for him.

1:39-45 By the account of the Visitation, Luke establishes the connection between the traditions about John and those about Jesus. At first commonplace, this meeting of two expectant mothers goes beyond the ordinary. As conscious believers, enlightened by the Holy Spirit, they understand that the time of salvation is inaugurated by the young lives they bear within themselves. We are already made aware that John bears witness to Jesus. And the first Christian generations place on the lips of Elizabeth the praise of Mary the believer.

1:39 *A town of Judah:* according to tradition, this was Ain Karim, 100 miles south of Nazareth and four miles west of Jerusalem.

leaped for joy. [45] And blessed is she who
believed that what the Lord has said to her
will be fulfilled." [x]

The Canticle of Mary.* [46] And Mary said:

"My soul proclaims the greatness of the Lord [y]
47 and my spirit rejoices in God my Savior. [z]
48 For he has looked with favor on the lowliness of his servant;
henceforth all generations will call me blessed. [a]
49 The Mighty One has done great things for me,
and holy is his name. [b]
50 His mercy is shown from age to age
to those who fear him. [c]
51 He has shown the strength of his arm,
he has routed those who are arrogant in the desires of their hearts. [d]
52 He has brought down the mighty from their thrones
and lifted up the lowly. [e]
53 He has filled the hungry with good things
and sent the rich away empty. [f]
54 He has come to the aid of Israel his servant,
ever mindful of his merciful love, [g]
55 according to the promises he made to our ancestors,
to Abraham and to his descendants forever." [h]

[56] Mary remained with Elizabeth for about
three months and then returned to her home.

The Birth of John. [57] When the time came
for Elizabeth to give birth, she bore a son.
[58] Her neighbors and relatives heard that the
Lord had shown his great mercy to her, and
they shared in her rejoicing.

[59] On the eighth day, when they came to
circumcise the child, they were going to
name him Zechariah after his father. [i]
[60] However, his mother objected. "No," she
said. "He is to be called John." [61] They said to
her, "There is no one in your family who has
this name." [62] They then made signs to his
father to ask what name he wanted to be
given to the child. [63] He asked for a writing
tablet, and he wrote: "His name is John." [j]
They were all filled with wonder.

[64] Immediately, his mouth was opened
and his tongue was freed, and he began to
speak, giving praise to God. [k] [65] All their
neighbors were overcome with awe, and all
these things were related throughout the
entire hill country of Judea. [66] All who heard
them were deeply impressed, and they wondered,
"What then is this child going to be?"
For the hand of the Lord was with him.

The Canticle of Zechariah.* [67] Then the
child's father Zechariah was filled with the
Holy Spirit and prophesied:

68 "Blessed be the Lord, the God of Israel,
for he has visited his people and redeemed them. [l]
69 He has raised up a horn of salvation for us
from the house of his servant David, [m]
70 just as he proclaimed through the mouth of his holy prophets from age to age: [n]
71 salvation from our enemies and from the hands of all who hate us, [o]
72 [p] to show the mercy promised to our fathers
and to remain mindful of his holy covenant,
73 the oath that he swore to our father Abraham,
and to grant us that, [74] delivered from the power of our enemies, [q]
without fear we might worship him [75] in holiness and righteousness
in his presence all our days.

76 [r] "And you, my child, will be called prophet of the Most High,

x Jn 20:29.—y 1 Sam 2:1; Isa 61:10.—z Ps 18:47; Hab 3:18; 1 Tim 1:1.—a Lk 11:27; Gen 30:13; Ps 113:7.—b Ps 111:9.—c Ex 20:6; Ps 103:17.—d Job 5:12; Ps 138:6; 1 Pet 5:5.—e Ps 75:8.—f Ps 107:9.—g Ps 98:3; Isa 41:9.—h Gen 13:15; 22:18.—i Gen 17:10; Lev 12:3.—j Lk 1:13.—k Lk 1:20; Ezek 24:27.—l Gen 24:27; Pss 41:14; 74:12; 111:9.—m 1 Sam 2:1, 10.—n Jer 30:10.—o Ps 106:10.—p 72f: Lev 26:42; Ps 105:9-10; Jer 11:5; Mic 7:20.—q Gen 22:16-18.

1:46-55 Mary's splendid canticle, the *Magnificat,* proclaims a new course for history, the end of injustice, and the birth of a new world, that of the kingdom, in which everything is different from our habitual experience. Every people gives thanks to God; the joy of the poor bursts forth; hope is born for the salvation of the despised of this world.

The *Magnificat,* which is very similar to the canticle of Hannah (see 1 Sam 2:1-10) and has become the Christian song of thanksgiving, lends itself to be the prayer of those who have suffered but have never lost their hope in God. The entire prayer of the Old Testament converges upon this one, but with a wholly renewed power; it is easy to see why the Church never tires of reciting it. It is one of the gems of the Church's daily office of Evening Prayer (Vespers).

1:67-79 The hour of light has come, and the Messiah is the star that rises (v. 78; see Num 24:17; Isa 60:1; Mal 3:20) or, again, the branch that springs from David (Jer 23:5; 33:15; Zec 3:8; 6:12). The Canticle of Zechariah, the Benedictus, rings out daily in the liturgical office of Morning Prayer (Lauds). The whole faith of the Old Testament is woven into its proclamation of peace, that is, fulfillment and joy for humanity, as a gift from God.

for you will go before the Lord to
prepare his ways,
77 to give his people knowledge of
salvation
through the forgiveness of their sins,
78 [s] because of the tender mercy of our God
by which the dawn from on high will
break upon us
79 to shine on those who sit in darkness
and in the shadow of death,
to guide our feet along the path of
peace." [t]

The Son of the Wilderness. 80 The child grew
and became strong in spirit. He lived in the
wilderness until the day he appeared pub-
licly to Israel.

CHAPTER 2

The Birth of Jesus. 1 * In those days, a
decree was issued by Caesar Augustus that a
census should be taken throughout the
entire world. [u] 2 This was the first such regis-
tration, and it took place when Quirinius *
was governor of Syria. [v]
3 Everyone traveled to his own town to be
enrolled. 4 Joseph therefore went from the
town of Nazareth in Galilee to Judea, to the
city of David called Bethlehem, because he
was of the house and family of David. [w] 5 He
went to be registered together with Mary,
his betrothed, who was expecting a child. [x]
6 While they were there, the time came for
her to have her child, 7 and she gave birth to
her firstborn son. She wrapped him in swad-
dling clothes and laid him in a manger, *
because there was no room for them in the
inn.
8 In the nearby countryside there were
shepherds living in the fields and keeping
watch over their flock throughout the night.
9 Suddenly, an angel of the Lord appeared to
them, and the glory of the Lord shone
around them. They were terror-stricken, [y]
10 but the angel said to them, "Do not be
afraid, for I bring you good news of great joy
for all the people. 11 For this day in the city of
David there has been born to you a Savior
who is Christ, the Lord. [z]
12 "This will be a sign for you: you will find
an infant wrapped in swaddling clothes and
lying in a manger." [a] 13 And suddenly there
was with the angel a multitude of the heav-
enly host, praising God and saying,

14 "Glory to God in the highest heaven,
and on earth peace to all those on
whom his favor rests." * [b]

The Visit of the Shepherds. 15 After the
angels had departed from them to heaven,
the shepherds said to one another, "Come,
let us go to Bethlehem to see this thing that
has taken place, which the Lord has made
known to us." 16 And so they set off in haste
and found Mary and Joseph, and the baby
lying in a manger.
17 When they saw the child, they recount-
ed the message that had been told them
about him. 18 All who heard it were amazed
at what the shepherds said to them. 19 As for
Mary, she treasured all these words and

r 76f: Lk 1:16; Isa 40:3; Mal 3:1; Mt 11:10.—s 78f: Isa 42:7; Mal 3:1; Jn 8:12; 2 Pet 1:19.—t Isa 11:6; Jer 6:1.—u Mt 22:17.—v Mt 4:24.—w 1 Sam 16:1-13; Mic 5:1; Mt 2:6; Jn 7:42.—x Mt 1:18.—y Ex 24:16; Tob 5:4.—z Mt 1:21; Acts 5:31.—a 1 Sam 2:34; Isa 9:5f.—b Lk 19:38; Isa 9:6; Ezek 3:12.

2:1-21 The Gospel of Jesus' birth is perhaps the best known passage of the Bible.

The birth of Jesus is described both as parallel to and in contrast with the birth of John. For lack of room in the inn, the young mother looks to a stable for an unobtrusive retreat in which to give birth to her son. Beginning in the 2nd century, the place was said to be a cave close to Bethlehem. She had a manger in which to lay the child.

Apart from Mary and Joseph, there were no relatives or friends present to welcome this child: only a few shepherds, people who lived on the margins of society and whose trade was at that time severely criticized and despised by the teachers of the Law.

The passage is full of grand ideas about faith; we may say also that it is rich in theology. The birth is described as the coming of the Messianic child. We are in Bethlehem, the native city of David who founded a royal and Messianic dynasty and who marked, as it were, a new beginning (1 Sam 16:1f; Mic 5:1). God bursts into the midst of the poor, proclaiming joy and peace for the whole world.

The event went unnoticed by the chroniclers of the age, and yet it changed the destiny of the human race. In order to bring out its universal significance, Luke locates it in relation to the history of the world: Herod the Great (37–4 B.C.) is still in power; Augustus (29 B.C.—A.D. 14) has imposed Roman rule on the entire Mediterranean world, "the entire world" (Greek: *oikumenê*) known at the time (v. 1). But the general census that Augustus has ordered is the instrument of providence for fulfilling the prophecies, since it leads to Mary's journey from Nazareth to Bethlehem (v. 4).

A 6th-century monk, Dionysius Exiguus ("Little Denis"), wanted to mark the beginning of the Christian year, but he miscalculated and dated the birth of Jesus as occurring in the year 754 from the foundation of Rome (instead of 6–7 years earlier). But the mistake is of little importance, for Dionysius' insight was correct: this event, more than any other, deserves to date the history of humanity, for it is the hinge on which all of history turns.

2:2 *Quirinius:* Publius Quirinius, legate of Syria, conducted a census of Palestine in A.D. 6, ten years after the death of Herod the Great. The information we have does not allow us to decide whether Luke is referring to this census or to another.

2:7 *Manger:* the legend of the ass and the cattle at the manger was perhaps suggested by Isa 1:3.

2:14 *On whom his favor rests:* some read "to men of goodwill," but it seems better not to contrast God's peace and human goodwill.

pondered them in her heart.[c] 20 And the shepherds went back, glorifying and praising God for all they had heard and seen, just as they had been told.[d]

The Circumcision and Naming of Jesus. 21 * On the eighth day, when the time for the child's circumcision had arrived, he was given the name Jesus, the name the angel had given him before he had been conceived in the womb.[e]

Jesus Is Presented in the Temple. 22 When the days for their purification were completed according to the Law of Moses, they brought the child up to Jerusalem to present him to the Lord,[f] 23 [g] as it is prescribed in the Law of the Lord: "Every firstborn male shall be consecrated to the Lord," 24 and to offer a sacrifice in accordance with what is stated in the Law of the Lord, "a pair of turtledoves or two young pigeons."

The Prophecy of Simeon. 25 At that time, there was a man in Jerusalem whose name was Simeon. This upright and devout man was awaiting the consolation of Israel, and the Holy Spirit rested on him.[h] 26 It had been revealed to him by the Holy Spirit that he would not experience death before he had seen the Christ of the Lord.

27 Prompted by the Spirit, Simeon came into the temple. When the parents brought in the child Jesus to do for him what was required by the Law, 28 he took him in his arms and praised God, saying:

29 "Now, Lord, you may dismiss your servant in peace,
according to your word;[i]
30 for my eyes have seen your salvation,[j]
31 which you have prepared in the sight of all the peoples,
32 a light of revelation to the Gentiles
and glory for your people Israel."[k]

33 The child's father and mother marveled at what was being said about him. 34 Then Simeon blessed them and said to Mary his mother: "This child is destined for the fall and rise of many in Israel, and to be a sign that will be opposed,[l] 35 so that the secret thoughts of many will be revealed, and you yourself a sword will pierce."[m]

The Witness of Anna. 36 [n] There was also present a prophetess, Anna, the daughter of Phanuel, of the tribe of Asher. She was very advanced in years, having lived with her husband for seven years after their marriage, 37 and then as a widow to the age of eighty-four. She never left the temple, but worshiped with fasting and prayer night and day.[o] 38 At that moment, she came forward and began to praise God, while she spoke about the child to all who were looking forward to the deliverance of Jerusalem.

The Return to Nazareth. 39 When they had fulfilled everything required by the Law of the Lord, they returned to Galilee, to their own town of Nazareth.[p] 40 The child grew and became strong, filled with wisdom, and God's favor was upon him.[q]

The Boy Jesus in the Temple.* 41 Every year his parents used to go to Jerusalem for the feast of Passover.[r] 42 And when Jesus was twelve years old, they made the journey as

c Lk 2:51.—d Lk 5:26; 7:16.—e Lk 1:31; Gen 17:12; Mt 1:21.—f Lev 12:2-6.—g 23f: Ex 13:2; Lev 12:8; Num 3:13.—h Isa 42:1; 52:9.—i Acts 2:24.—j 30ff: Isa 46:13; 49:6; 52:10; Jn 8:12.—k Acts 13:47.—l Lk 12:51ff; 1 Cor 1:23.—m Jn 9:39; 19:35f; Rom 9:33; 1 Pet 2:7.—n 36f: Jud 8:4-6.—o 1 Tim 5:9.—p Mt 2:23.—q Lk 1:80.—r Ex 23:15; Deut 16:1-8.

2:21-40 This section describes the Jewish rites associated with a birth. In addition to circumcision, forty days after the birth Jewish parents celebrated the rites of purification and ransoming, which in the context of the ancient religion represented a respect for life and a sense of the sacred (see Ex 13:2; Lev 12:2-8; Num 18:15-16). This child, who is bought back with the offering of the poor, is the Messiah and has come to carry out the mission entrusted to the Servant as foretold in the great prophetic songs of Isaiah (42:6; 49:6; 52:10): to save all of humankind, to bring light to all peoples.

Some hearts are already drawn by the joyous conviction that the prophecies are fulfilled, and the hymn of the elderly prophet Simeon is, despite its brevity, among the richest of Christian canticles. But who can recognize the mission of the Messiah unless they accept the light of God? That mission elicits hostility; and Mary will experience the repercussions of the Savior's painful lot, because faith in the Savior will bring to light the deep religion of hearts and put an end to the legalism of Judaism.

2:41-50 In the village where Jesus spends his apprenticeship as a human being and grows "in wisdom and in age and in grace with God and men (v. 52)," this favor of God did not prevent him from sharing the life lived by everyone else. Then a significant event interrupted the course of everyday life.

Jesus had reached the age when a Jewish boy had completed his religious instruction and was beginning to observe the precepts of the Law; he was recognized as religiously mature. Therefore, he joined his parents in the pilgrimage to Jerusalem.

In this passage we find him in the temple in open discussion with those charged with teaching the Law. What he has to say reveals an extraordinary religious vision. In acting as he does, he claims a freedom that surprises his parents.

Thus, at his first encounter with Judaism and its religious center, at the moment when he speaks for the first time, Jesus declares himself Son of God and is aware of his own mystery and of his mission. That is what Luke wants to bring out in this story.

Mary and Joseph are now informed of the boy's uncommon destiny, but the unexpected thunderbolt of Jesus' statement confuses them; it utters a mystery that is beyond them.

The Lord is not done with surprising even believers, indeed believers first of all! There are days when we must draw inspiration from the attitude of Mary as she meditates on what God has done.

usual for the feast. 43 When the days of the feast were over and they set off for home, the boy Jesus stayed behind in Jerusalem. His parents were not aware of this. 44 Assuming that he was somewhere in the group of travelers, they journeyed for a day. Then they started to look for him among their relatives and friends, 45 but when they failed to find him, they returned to Jerusalem to search for him.

46 After three days they found him in the temple, where he was sitting among the teachers, listening to them and asking them questions. 47 And all who heard him were amazed at his intelligence and his answers. [s] 48 When they saw him, they were astonished, and his mother said to him: "Son, why have you done this to us? Your father and I have been searching for you with great anxiety." 49 Jesus said to them, "Why were you searching for me? Did you not know that I must be in my Father's house?" [t] 50 But they did not comprehend what he said to them.

Jesus Grows in Wisdom and Grace. 51 [u] Then he went down with them and came to Nazareth, and he was obedient to them. His mother pondered all these things in her heart. 52 And Jesus increased in wisdom and in age and in grace with God and men.

s Lk 4:22; Jn 7:15-16.—t Jn 2:16.—u 51f: Lk 2:19; 1 Sam 2:26; Prov 3:4.—v Jer 1:2; Hos 1:1.—w 3-10: Mt 3:1-10; Mk 1:2-6.—x Isa 40:3ff; Jn 1:23.—y Ps 98:2.—z Lk 19:9; Isa 51:2; Jn 8:39.—a 10f: Acts 2:37; Jas 2:15; 1 Jn 3:17.—b Isa 58:7; Ezek 18:7.—c Lk 7:29.—d Ex 23:1.

3:1—4:13 The word of God finds expression in the history of humankind. By listing the many temporal rulers and religious authorities, Luke enables us to date John's activity as occurring between the fall of A.D. 27 and Passover of 28. But he also wants to contrast these earthly rulers and religious authorities with the sovereignty and authority of Jesus. The deeper movement of history does not take place at the level of official appearances; in fact, it is Jesus who is fulfilling the destiny of the world by giving history its true meaning.

Luke sums up in a single passage all the information that he intends to offer on the work of John. More than the other evangelists, he stresses the point that salvation is offered to everyone; in his citation of Isaiah he highlights the final verse, thereby underscoring the thought that the new age is meant for the authentic children of Abraham and not solely for the chosen people. At the end of the passage he immediately jumps ahead to the imprisonment of John, of which Mark and Matthew speak at a later point and at greater length (Mt 14:1-12; Mk 6:14-29). His intention is to make a clear distinction between the Jesus movement and the Johannine movement: when the time of Christ begins, that of John, the forerunner, is finished.

3:1 *Lysanias:* an unknown governor. *Abilene:* a region northeast of Damascus.

3:2 *Caiaphas* was the current high priest (A.D. 18–36). Annas, that is, Ananiah, had preceded him from 5 B.C. to A.D. 15. He is named here because he still exercised considerable influence.

II: THE BEGINNING OF JESUS' MINISTRY*

CHAPTER 3

The Ministry of John the Baptist. 1 In the fifteenth year of the reign of Tiberius Caesar, when Pontius Pilate was governor of Judea, and Herod was tetrarch of Galilee, and his brother Philip was tetrarch of the region of Ituraea and Trachonitis, and Lysanias * was tetrarch of Abilene, 2 during the high priesthood of Annas and Caiaphas, * the word of God came to John the son of Zechariah in the desert. [v] 3 [w] He journeyed throughout the entire region of the Jordan valley, proclaiming a baptism of repentance for the forgiveness of sins, 4 as it is written in the book of the words of the prophet Isaiah:

"The voice of one crying out in the
wilderness:
'Prepare the way of the Lord,
make straight his paths. [x]
5 Every valley shall be filled in,
and every mountain and hill shall be
leveled;
the winding roads shall be straightened
and the rough paths made smooth,
6 and all mankind shall see the salvation
of God.' " [y]

7 He admonished the crowds who came out to be baptized by him: "You brood of vipers! Who warned you to flee from the wrath to come? 8 Produce good fruits as proof of your repentance. Do not begin to say to yourselves, 'We have Abraham as our father.' For I tell you, God is able to raise up children for Abraham from these stones. [z] 9 Even now the ax is laid to the root of the trees. Therefore, every tree that does not bear good fruit will be cut down and thrown into the fire."

10 [a] When the crowds asked him, "What then should we do?" 11 he said to them in reply, "Anyone who has two coats must share with the person who has none, and whoever has food must do likewise." [b] 12 Even tax collectors were coming to him to be baptized, and they asked him, "Teacher, what should we do?" [c] 13 He answered them, "Cease collecting more than the amount prescribed." 14 Some soldiers also asked him, "What about us? What should we do?" He replied, "Do not extort money from anyone, do not falsely accuse or threaten anyone, and be satisfied with your wages." [d]

15 [e]As the people began to experience a
feeling of expectancy, they all wondered in
their hearts whether John might be the
Christ. 16 John answered, telling them all: "I
baptize you with water, but there is one
coming who is more powerful than I am. I
am not worthy to loosen the straps of his
sandals. He will baptize you with the Holy
Spirit and fire.[f] 17 His winnowing fan is in his
hand to clear his threshing floor and to gath-
er the wheat into his barn, but the chaff he
will burn with unquenchable fire."[g] 18 And
with many other exhortations, he pro-
claimed the good news to the people.

19 [h]But Herod the tetrarch, after having
been rebuked by John because of his affair
with Herodias, his brother's wife, in addition
to all the other evil deeds he had done,
20 added still this, that he put John in
prison.*

The Baptism of Jesus.* 21 [i]After John had
baptized all the people, and while Jesus was
engaged in prayer after also having been bap-
tized, heaven opened 22 and the Holy Spirit
descended on him in bodily form like a dove.
And a voice came from heaven: "You are my
beloved Son; in you I am well pleased."[j]

The Genealogy of Jesus.* 23 [k]When Jesus
began his ministry, he was about thirty years
old. He was the son, as it was thought, of
Joseph,* [l]

the son of Heli, 24 the son of Matthat,
the son of Levi, the son of Melchi,
the son of Jannai, the son of Joseph,

25 the son of Mattathias, the son of Amos,
the son of Nahum, the son of Esli,
the son of Naggai, 26 the son of Maath,
the son of Mattathias,
the son of Semein, the son of Josech,
the son of Joda, 27 the son of Joanan,
the son of Rhesa, the son of Zerubbabel,
the son of Shealtiel,

the son of Neri,[m] 28 the son of Melchi,
the son of Addi, the son of Cosam,
the son of Elmadam, the son of Er,
29 the son of Joshua,

the son of Eliezer, the son of Jorim,
the son of Matthat, the son of Levi,
30 the son of Simeon, the son of Judah,
the son of Joseph,

the son of Jonam, the son of Eliakim,
31 the son of Melea, the son of Menna,
the son of Mattatha, the son of Nathan,
the son of David,[n]

32 the son of Jesse, the son of Obed,
the son of Boaz, the son of Sala,
the son of Nahshon, 33 the son of Am-
minadab,
the son of Admin,

the son of Arni, the son of Hezron,
the son of Perez, the son of Judah,[o]
34 the son of Jacob, the son of Isaac,
the son of Abraham,

the son of Terah, the son of Nahor,[p]
35 the son of Serug, the son of Reu,
the son of Peleg, the son of Eber,
the son of Shelah,

36 the son of Cainan, the son of Arphaxad,
the son of Shem, the son of Noah,
the son of Lamech,[q] 37 the son of
Methuselah, the son of Enoch,

the son of Jared, the son of Mahalaleel,
the son of Cainan, 38 the son of Enos,
the son of Seth, the son of Adam,
the son of God.[r]

e 15-18: Mt 3:11f; Mk 1:7f; Acts 13:25.—f Jn 1:27; Acts 1:5; 11:16.—g Isa 30:24; Mt 3:12.—h 19f: Mt 14:3; Mk 6:17f.—i 21f: Mt 3:13-17; Jn 1:32f.—j Isa 42:1; 2 Pet 1:17.—k 23-38: Mt 1:1-17.—l Lk 1:27; Mt 4:17; 13:55.—m 1 Chr 3:17; Mt 1:12.—n 2 Sam 5:14.—o Gen 38:29; Ru 4:18; 1 Chr 2:10-12.—p Gen 11:24, 26.—q Gen 11:12.—r Gen 5:1, 2.

3:20 John's imprisonment occurred sometime after the beginning of Jesus' ministry (see Jn 3:22-24). Luke mentions it here to bring his section on John's ministry to a conclusion before starting his account of that of Jesus (see also Mt 4:12; Mk 1:14). Later he alludes to John's death (Lk 9:7-9). See also note on Mk 1:14.

3:21-22 Jesus here shows himself to be in solidarity with sinners by receiving the bath of repentance. But a unique event also takes place: The Messiah receives his investiture from heaven. The Holy Spirit will be present in him (see Isa 11:2); over him are pronounced the words used in consecrating kings (Ps 2:7), but here they attest that he is the Son of God in a sense hitherto unsuspected (see Lk 1:35).

3:23-38 Luke gives a genealogy that is meant not as a historical document but as the assertion of a legal status. Jesus is linked to Joseph, even though it was known that the link was not one of blood; the reason for doing so is that at that time only men and not women had rights. The genealogy then moves back to David, without following the line of kings. From that point it continues again, not only as far as Abraham, but—and this is the chief novelty of the passage—as far as Adam, who comes from the hand of God. Luke's intention is to stress the point that Jesus belongs not only to the chosen people but to the entire human race, which he has come to save.

Whereas Matthew specifically mentions three groups of 14 generations, Luke lists 77 names, according to a scheme of sevens. From the beginning of the human race until Jesus there are eleven series of seven (11 x 7). Jesus comes as Messiah in the eschatological stage of history (see 4 Esdras 14:11).

3:23ff It may be helpful to record another interpretation of the difference between this genealogy and that of Matthew: in virtue of the law of the levirate, Joseph (it is said) had two fathers, one biological (Jacob), the other legal (Heli); thus two different lists are used as far back as Shealtiel.

CHAPTER 4

Jesus Is Tempted by the Devil.* 1 [s] Filled with
the Holy Spirit, Jesus returned from the
Jordan and was led by the Spirit into the
desert [t] 2 for forty days, where he was tempt-
ed by the devil. During that time he ate
nothing, and at the end of it he was fam-
ished. [u]

3 The devil said to him, "If you are the Son
of God, command this stone to be trans-
formed into bread." 4 Jesus answered him:
"As it states in Scripture:

'Man does not live by bread alone.' " [v]

5 Then the devil led him up and showed
him in a single instant all the kingdoms of
the world, 6 saying to him, "To you will I give
all this dominion with its accompanying
glory, for it has been delivered into my
power, and I can bestow it on whomever I
choose. [w] 7 All this will be yours if you wor-
ship me." 8 Jesus answered him: "Scripture
says:

'You shall worship the Lord your God,
and him alone shall you serve.' " [x]

9 Next the devil led him to Jerusalem and
had him stand on the summit of the temple.
Then he said to him, "If you are the Son of
God, throw yourself down from here, 10 for
according to Scripture:

'He will command his angels concern-
ing you,
to protect you,'

11 and:

'With their hands they will raise you up
lest you dash your foot against a
stone.' " [y]

12 Jesus answered him, "Scripture says:

'You shall not put the Lord your God to
the test.' " [z]

13 When the devil had ended all his tempt-
ing, he departed from him until an oppor-
tune time. [a]

III: THE MINISTRY OF JESUS IN GALILEE*

Jesus Is Accepted throughout Galilee.
14 Then Jesus, filled with the power of the
Spirit, returned to Galilee, and reports
about him began to spread throughout the
surrounding region. [b] 15 He taught in their
synagogues and was praised by everyone.

Jesus at Nazareth. 16 * [c] When he came to
Nazareth, where he had been brought up, he
went to the synagogue on the Sabbath day,
as was his custom. He stood up to read,
17 and they handed him the scroll of the
prophet Isaiah. Unrolling the scroll, he
found the passage where it is written:

18 "The Spirit of the Lord is upon me,
because he has anointed me
to bring the good news to the poor.
He has sent me to proclaim release to
prisoners
and recovery of sight to the blind,
to let the oppressed go free, [d]
19 and to proclaim the year of the Lord's
favor." [e]

20 Then he rolled up the scroll, returned it to
the attendant, and sat down. The eyes of all in
the synagogue were fixed intently on him. [f]

21 Then he began by saying to them,
"Today this Scripture has been fulfilled in
your hearing." 22 All present spoke highly of
him and were amazed at the gracious words
that flowed from his lips. They also asked, "Is
this not the son of Joseph?" [g]

23 He said to them, "Undoubtedly you will
quote to me the proverb: 'Physician, heal
yourself,' and say: 'Do here in your home-

s 1-13: Mt 4:1-11; Mk 1:12f.—t Ezek 37:1.—u Ex 34:28.—v Deut 8:3.—w Jer 27:5; Jn 12:31; Rev 13:2ff.—x Deut 6:13.—y Ps 91:11f.—z Deut 6:16.—a Jn 13:2, 27; Heb 4:15.—b Lk 5:15; Mt 3:16; 4:12.—c 16-30: Mt 13:53-58; Mk 6:1-6.—d Isa 61:1f; Zep 2:3; Mt 3:16.—e Lev 25:10; Ps 102:21.—f Acts 6:15.—g Lk 3:23; Jn 6:42; 7:46.

4:1-13 By means of images, we are shown the drama Jesus experienced in his conscience, his struggle to follow with determination the great options of his existence. He knows the temptations for immediate success, domination, and prestige, the temptations to which Israel succumbed during its sojourn in the desert and that remain the lot of the Church, every believer, and every person. Jesus refuses to use his powers for his own benefit but accepts poverty and destitution; he does not seek the glory of a political Messiah and does not yield to the idols of power. He turns away from the seduction of prestige; when he goes to Jerusalem it will not be to mount the pinnacle of the temple but to carry the supreme trial of the cross. There is, in this choice without compromise, a radical recognition of God and the true values he is forever giving us to reflect upon. The victory of Christ over the forces of evil foreshadows the power of his mission (see Lk 10:18; 11:22; 12:16), which is achieved through patience on the cross and the triumph of the Resurrection after the final attacks of the spirit of evil (see Lk 22:3, 53). To live with Christ is to accept this struggle humbly and resolutely.

4:14—9:50 The Gospel does not try to reconstitute an exact chronology and geography of the life of Christ. Its intention is to present to us the sayings and actions of the Lord, to arouse and renew our faith in him, and to make us grasp the essential requirements of our existence. As in Matthew and Mark, the first stage of Jesus' mission, which takes place in Galilee, leads to the recognition of Jesus as it moves from the first question about him to the profession of faith.

4:16-21 By reading his own vocation and mission in the great passage from Isaiah (61:1), Jesus will direct the thinking of the Church and every apostle: God's work is to proclaim salvation to the poor and the oppressed.

town* the deeds we have heard that you performed in Capernaum.' [h] 24 Amen, I say to you," he went on, "no prophet is accepted in his own country.

25 * "I tell you in truth, there were many widows in Israel in the days of Elijah when the skies remained closed for three and a half years and there was a severe famine throughout the land. [i] 26 Yet it was to none of them that Elijah was sent, but to a widow at Zarephath in the land of Sidon. [j] 27 There were also many people with leprosy in Israel in the time of the prophet Elisha, but not one of these was cleansed except for Naaman the Syrian." [k]

28 When they heard these words, all the people in the synagogue were roused to fury.* 29 They leapt up, drove him out of the town, and led him to the top of the hill upon which their town was built, intending to hurl him off the cliff. [l] 30 However, he passed through the midst of the crowd and went on his way. [m]

Jesus Heals a Man with a Demon. 31 * [n] Jesus then went to Capernaum, a town in Galilee, and began to teach the people on the Sabbath. 32 They were astounded at his teaching because his message had authority. [o]

33 In the synagogue there was a man possessed by the spirit of an unclean demon, and he shrieked loudly, 34 "Leave us alone! What do you want with us, Jesus of Nazareth? Have you come to destroy us? I know who you are—the Holy One of God."* 35 [p] But Jesus rebuked him, saying, "Be silent and come out of him!" Then the demon threw the man down in front of them and emerged from him without doing him any harm. [q] 36 The people were all amazed, and they said to one another: "What is this teaching? For with authority and power he gives commands to unclean spirits, and they come forth." [r] 37 And reports about him began to spread throughout the entire region.

Jesus Heals Peter's Mother-in-Law. 38 [s] On leaving the synagogue, he entered Simon's house. Simon's mother-in-law was suffering from a high fever, and they begged him to help her. 39 Jesus stood over her and rebuked the fever, and it left her. She got up immediately and began to serve them.

Jesus Ministers throughout Galilee. 40 [t] At sunset they brought to him all those who were sick with various diseases. He laid his hands on each of them and healed them. 41 Demons also emerged from many people, shouting, "You are the Son of God!" But he rebuked them and would not allow them to speak because they knew that he was the Christ.

Jesus Is the Envoy of God for All Israel.* 42 At daybreak he departed and made his way to a secluded place. [u] But the crowds went forth in search of him, and when they located him, they tried to prevent him from leaving there. 43 However, he said to them, "I must preach the kingdom of God to the other towns as well, because this was the purpose for which I was sent." 44 Thus, he continued to preach in the synagogues of Judea.

CHAPTER 5

Jesus Calls the First Disciples.* 1 [v] One day, as Jesus was standing by the Lake of Gen-

h Mk 1:21-28.—i 1 Ki 17:1-7; Jas 5:17.—j 1 Ki 17:9.—k 2 Ki 5:14.—l Num 15:35; Jn 7:30; Acts 7:58.—m Jn 8:59.—n 31-37: Mt 4:13; Mk 1:21-28.—o Mt 7:28f.—p Mt 8:29; Mk 1:24; Acts 3:14.—q Mt 8:26.—r Lk 1:12.—s 38f: Mt 8:14ff; Mk 1:29ff.—t 40f: Mt 8:16; Mk 1:32ff.—u Mk 1:35-38.

4:23 *Hometown:* i.e., Nazareth, where Jesus was brought up. *Capernaum:* see notes on Mt 4:12-17; 4:12; and 4:13.

4:25-27 These verses illustrate the theme of universal salvation, so dear to Luke, with allusions to the miracles of Elijah and Elisha (1 Ki 17; 2 Ki 5).

4:28 The words of Jesus hinted at the rejection of the people of Israel and the election of the Gentiles. The people of Nazareth become infuriated, but Jesus escapes their fury in a mysterious manner.

4:31-41 In the Gospel, the accounts of miracles are intended to attest, first of all, that God the Savior is present for people in Jesus Christ. There is a sensible and visible evil in the sickness, wherein we see hostile forces at work. Christ brings healing; he changes the condition of human beings and saves them from alienation. Demons are sharper than humans in penetrating the divine powers of him who frees humans from the grip of death. However, Jesus reduces them to silence, because he does not want people to regard him as a triumphant liberator but to discover, in his words and actions as man amidst his human brothers and sisters, the true visage of the Messiah, Son of God.

4:34 See note on Mk 1:24.

4:42-44 The good news of the kingdom, this announcement of the coming of God (Lk 4:18; 6:20-28), must reach all human beings.

5:1-11 This passage demonstrates the art of the writer. Luke inserts the call of the first disciples into a context of preaching and performing mighty deeds. He slightly weakens the abrupt character that the event retains in Mark (1:16-18) and gives a greater human plausibility to the response of these men. But he stresses just as much the demands of the apostolic task. Trying to draw people away from the evils that assail them entails many difficulties. God requires humans to participate in this endeavor and to carry out their missionary work as a team in which all must share the pain. In this passage, Peter already occupies a representative place. Nonetheless, upon meeting Christ he discovers how much he himself is the victim of evil and sin. Jesus expects those who are his to be totally committed to the Word and, if necessary, to renounce their profession, their situation, and their security.

nesaret, with people crowding around him
to hear the word of God, 2 he caught sight of
two boats at the water's edge. The fishermen
had gotten out of the boats and were wash-
ing their nets. 3 Getting into one of the boats,
the one belonging to Simon, he asked him to
put out a little way from the shore. Then he
sat down and taught the crowds from the
boat. [w]

4 When he had finished speaking, he said
to Simon, "Put out into deep water and let
down your nets for a catch." [x] 5 Simon
answered, "Master, we worked hard
throughout the night and caught nothing;
but if you say so, I will let down the nets." [y]
6 When they had done this, they caught such
a great number of fish that their nets were
beginning to tear. [z] 7 Therefore, they signaled
to their companions in the other boat to
come and help them. They came and filled
both boats to the point that they were in
danger of sinking.

8 When Simon Peter saw what had hap-
pened, he fell at the knees of Jesus, saying,
"Depart from me, Lord, for I am a sinful
man." [a] 9 For he and all of his companions
were amazed at the catch they had made.
10 So too were Simon's partners James and
John, the sons of Zebedee. Then Jesus said to
Simon, "Do not be afraid. From now on you
will be catching men." [b] 11 When they
brought their boats to the shore, they left
everything and followed him. [c]

Jesus Heals a Man with Leprosy.* 12 [d] In one
of the towns that he visited, a man appeared
whose body was covered with leprosy. When
he saw Jesus, he fell prostrate before him
and pleaded for his help, saying, "Lord, if
you choose to do so, you can make me
clean." 13 He stretched out his hand and
touched him, saying, "I do choose. Be made
clean." Immediately, the leprosy left him.

14 He then instructed him to tell no one.
"Just go," he said, "and show yourself to the
priest, and make an offering for your cleans-
ing, as prescribed by Moses. That will be
proof for them." [e] 15 However, the reports
about him continued to spread, so that large
crowds assembled to listen to him and to be
healed of their diseases. [f] 16 But he would
withdraw to deserted places to pray. [g]

Jesus Pardons and Heals a Paralyzed Man.*
17 [h] One day, as he was teaching, Pharisees
and teachers of the law were sitting there.
They had come from every village of Galilee
and Judea, and from Jerusalem. And he pos-
sessed the power of the Lord to heal. [i]

18 Then some men appeared, carrying a
paralyzed man on a bed. They tried to bring
him in and set him down in front of Jesus.
19 However, finding no way to bring him in
because of the crowd, they went up onto the
roof and lowered him on the bed through
the tiles into the middle of the crowd sur-
rounding Jesus.

20 On perceiving their faith, Jesus said,
"Friend, your sins are forgiven you." 21 Then
the scribes and the Pharisees began to ask
each other, "Who is this man uttering
blasphemies? Who can forgive sins but God
alone?" [j]

22 Jesus discerned what they were think-
ing, and he said in reply, "Why do you enter-
tain such thoughts in your hearts? [k] 23 Which
is easier—to say: 'Your sins are forgiven you,'
or to say: 'Stand up and walk'? 24 But that
you may come to realize that the Son of
Man has authority on earth to forgive
sins"—he said to the paralyzed man—"I say
to you, stand up, and take your bed, and go
to your home." 25 Immediately, the man
stood up before them, picked up his bed, and
went home glorifying God. 26 They were all
overcome with amazement, and they
praised God as, awestruck, they said, "We
have witnessed unbelievable things today."

Jesus Calls Levi (Matthew).* 27 * [l] After
this, he went out and noticed a tax collec-
tor named Levi sitting at his customs post.

v 1-11: Mt 4:18-22; Mk 1:16-20; Jn 1:40-42.—w Mt 13:2.—x Jn 21:6.—y Lk 8:24, 45; 9:33.—z Jn 21:11.—a Gen 18:27; Ex 33:20.—b Jn 21:15-17.—c Lk 12:33.—d 12ff: Mt 8:2ff; Mk 1:40-44.—e Lev 14:2-32.—f Lk 4:14.—g Lk 3:21.—h 17-26: Mt 9:1-8; Mk 2:1-12.—i Lk 2:46; Mt 15:1.—j Isa 43:25.—k Jn 2:25.—l 27-38: Mt 9:9-17; Mk 2:14-22.

5:12-16 When duly confirmed as the Law requires (see Lev 14:2-3), the cure of a leper will attest to the priests the power of Jesus over an evil that destroys humans.

5:17-26 The description of the miracle worked for the paralyzed man is vivid, as in Matthew and Mark, even if, in order to make it more intelligible to his readers, Luke speaks simply of a roof instead of a Palestinian roof-terrace.

5:27-32 No one could be regarded as more of a sinner in the time of Jesus than the tax collectors (also translated as "publicans") sitting at their customs post. Christ, more than once, created a scandal in the eyes of right-thinking people, who were quick to distinguish between the righteous and sinners. The Church recalls these occasions to keep herself from becoming a closed sect. The lesson is still valid today: to refuse to associate with others because we have catalogued them as sinners and because we consider ourselves to be in the ranks of the righteous is opposed to the Gospel. We must all regard ourselves as sinners and rejoice over the salvation that Jesus offers everyone. Moreover, only those receive salvation who loyally acknowledge the need of being saved.

5:27-28 See notes on Mt 5:46 and Mk 2:14.

Jesus said to him, "Follow me," 28 and, leaving everything behind, he got up and followed him.

Jesus Dines with Sinners. 29 [m] Then Levi gave a great banquet in his house for him, and a large crowd of tax collectors and others were at table with them. [n] 30 The Pharisees and their scribes complained to his disciples, saying, "Why do you eat and drink with tax collectors and sinners?" * [o] 31 Jesus said to them in reply, "It is not the healthy who need a physician, but rather those who are sick. 32 I have not come to call the righteous but sinners to repentance."

A Time of Joy and Grace.* 33 [p] Then they said to him, "John's disciples fast frequently and pray often, and the disciples of the Pharisees do likewise, but your disciples eat and drink." 34 Jesus said to them, "How can the wedding guests fast while the bridegroom is still with them? [q] 35 But the time will come when the bridegroom is taken away from them, and then, in those days, they will fast." [r]

36 He also told them this parable: "No one tears a piece from a new cloak and sews it on an old cloak. If he does, the new cloak will be torn, and the piece from it will not match that of the old. 37 Nor does anyone pour new wine into old wineskins. If he does, the new wine will burst the skins and spill out, and the skins will be destroyed. 38 Rather new wine must be put into fresh wineskins. 39 And no one who has been drinking old wine will wish for new wine, for he says, 'The old is better.' "

CHAPTER 6

Picking Grain on the Sabbath. 1 * [s] On one Sabbath, when Jesus was going through a field of grain, his disciples picked some heads of grain, rubbed them in their hands, and ate them. 2 Some of the Pharisees said, "Why are you doing what is forbidden on the Sabbath?"

3 Jesus answered them, "Have you not read what David did when he and his companions were hungry? 4 He entered the house of God and took and ate the sacred bread that only the priests were permitted to eat, and he shared it with his companions." [t] 5 Then he said to them, "The Son of Man * is lord of the Sabbath."

A Man with a Withered Hand. 6 [u] On another Sabbath, Jesus entered the synagogue and began to teach. A man was there whose right hand was withered. [v] 7 The scribes and the Pharisees watched him closely to see whether he would cure him on the Sabbath so that they would have a charge to bring against him.

8 But Jesus was fully aware of their thoughts, and he said to the man with the withered hand, "Come here and stand before us." The man got up and stood there. 9 Then Jesus said to them, "I put this question to you: Is it lawful to do good or to do evil on the Sabbath, to save life or to destroy it?" 10 After looking around at all of them, he said to the man, "Stretch out your hand." He did so, and his hand was restored. 11 But they were filled with fury and discussed among themselves what they might do with Jesus.

Jesus Chooses the Twelve Apostles.* 12 [w] It was in those days that he went onto the mountain to pray, and he spent the entire night in prayer to God. [x] 13 Then, when it was daylight, he summoned his disciples and chose twelve of them, whom he designated as apostles: 14 Simon, to whom he gave the name Peter, and his brother Andrew, James, John, Philip, Bartholomew, 15 Matthew, Thomas, James the son of Alphaeus, Simon called the Zealot, [y] 16 Judas the son of James, and Judas Iscariot, who became a traitor.

m 29-32: Mt 9:10-13; Mk 2:15ff.—n Lk 15:1.—o Acts 23:9.—p 33-39: Mt 9:14-17; Mk 2:18-22.—q Jn 3:29.—r Lk 9:22.—s 1-5: Mt 12:1-8; Mk 2:23-28.—t Ex 25:30; Lev 24:5, 9; 1 Sam 21:7.—u 6-11: Lk 13:10-17; 14:1-6; Mt 12:9-14; Mk 3:1-6.—v Lk 11:53; Jn 5:18.—w 12-16: Mt 10:1-4; Mk 3:13-19.—x Acts 1:13.—y Mt 9:9.

5:30 *Sinners:* see note on Mk 2:15.

5:33-39 For the moment, Jesus refuses to impose on his disciples the ascetic and devout practices of Judaism. (See note on Mk 2:20.) The Messiah is here—it is a time of joy. God, so to speak, becomes the Spouse of all people. The three Synoptic Gospels add other sentences, which underline the newness of the Gospel. It is not a rearrangement of ancient law and doctrines; the New Covenant requires a new mentality and a new openness.

The last verse, proper to Luke, alludes to the refusal to accept the Gospel on the part of the teachers of the law. They rejected the wonderful newness of the Gospel and were content with the teachings to which they were accustomed.

6:1-11 In resisting servitude to traditions, Jesus gives the example of the freedom David showed in face of the Law (see 1 Sam 21:2-7); in his act of healing Jesus recalls the true meaning of the Sabbath. See notes on Mt 12:1-14; 12:2; 12:3-4; 12:5-6; 12:8; 12:9-14.

6:5 *Son of Man:* see note on Mt 8:20.

6:12-16 This is an important moment in Luke's eyes, as shown by the fact that Jesus prepares himself through prayer. The apostles are twelve in number in order to make clear their future work, which is comparable to that of the twelve tribes of Israel: that is, they are the builders of the new People of God (see Acts 1:25). The word "apostle" is derived from a Greek word meaning "sent," "missionary."

The Crowds Seek Out Jesus.* [17] [z] He then came down with them and stood on a spot of level ground, where there was a large crowd of his disciples and a great multitude of people from all sections of Judea and Jerusalem and the coastal region of Tyre and Sidon. [18] They had come there to listen to him and to be healed of their diseases. Those who were afflicted by unclean spirits were cured. [19] And everyone in the crowd was trying to touch him, because power came forth from him and healed them all.

A: The Sermon on the Plain*

The Beatitudes.* [20] [a] Then, turning to his disciples, he began to speak:

"Blessed are you who are poor,
for the kingdom of God is yours.
21 Blessed are you who hunger now,
for you will have your fill.
Blessed are you who weep now,
for you will laugh. [b]

[22] "Blessed are you when people hate you and ostracize you, when they insult you and denounce your name as evil on account of the Son of Man. [c] [23] Rejoice on that day and dance for joy, for your reward will be great in heaven. This was the way their ancestors treated the Prophets.

24 "But woe to you who are rich,
for you have received your consolation. [d]
25 Woe to you who are well fed now,
for you will go hungry.
Woe to you who laugh now,
for you will mourn and weep. [e]
26 Woe to you when all speak well of you,
for their ancestors treated the false prophets in the same fashion.

Love of Enemies.* [27] "But to those of you who are listening to me, I say: Love your enemies, do good to those who hate you, [f] [28] bless those who curse you, pray for those who mistreat you. [g] [29] [h] If anyone strikes you on one cheek, offer him the other cheek as well, and should someone take your cloak, let him have your tunic as well. [30] Give to everyone who begs from you, and do not demand the return of what is yours from the one who has taken it. [i]

[31] "Deal with others as you would like them to deal with you. [j] [32] If you love only those who love you, what credit is that to you? Even sinners love those who love them. [k] [33] And if you do good to those who do good to you, what credit is that to you? Even sinners do as much. [34] And if you lend only to those from whom you expect to be repaid, what credit is that to you? Even sinners lend to sinners, expecting to be repaid in full. [l]

[35] "Rather, you must love your enemies and do good to them, and lend without expecting any repayment. In this way, you will receive a great reward. You will be sons of the Most High, for he himself is kind to the ungrateful and the wicked. [36] Be merciful, just as your Father is merciful. [m]

z 17ff: Mt 4:24f; Mk 3:7-12.—a 20-23: Mt 5:1-12.—b Isa 55:1-2; Rev 7:17.—c Jn 9:22.—d Lk 16:25; Isa 5:8-12; Am 6:1.—e Prov 14:13; Isa 65:13f; Jas 5:1.—f Mt 5:44; Rom 12:20.—g 1 Pet 3:9.—h 29f: Mt 5:39-42.—i Deut 15:7-8.—j Tob 4:15; Mt 7:12.—k Mt 5:46.—l Deut 15:8; Mt 5:42.—m Lk 11:2; Ex 34:6-7; Rom 8:15.

6:17-19 The picture of the crowds pressing upon Jesus shows the hope raised by Jesus from the very beginning of his public ministry. People came to him from everywhere, even from the nearby pagan towns, to obtain healing. Jesus came among us as the sign of salvation and the act by which God delivered it to us. When giving the Beatitudes in the Sermon on the Plain, he will announce the true salvation.

6:20-49 The remainder of ch. 6 corresponds to the "Sermon on the Mount," which the Gospel of Matthew places at the beginning of Jesus' activity (Mt 5—7). Luke offers a more concise and less solemn text. His readers have little knowledge of Jewish life; it was therefore pointless to contrast the old Law with the demands of the Gospel. The latter are stated in a more absolute manner. Matthew describes the interior attitude, the disposition of heart, without which no one can enter the kingdom of God. Luke prefers to evoke a more concrete and living tone. He underlines with special insistence the deportment in regard to riches; this is the test of entrance into the kingdom.

6:20-26 The Beatitudes of the Gospel of Matthew bring forth an unexpected message (Mt 5:3-12). The short sentences in which Luke opposes the blessedness and woe of people reach us in an even more powerful manner. The Old Testament loved such contrasting formulas, but here the reader is directly challenged: "you." In announcing the kingdom Jesus overturns the system of values on which we base our lives, relations, judgments, and actions. He denounces as false our more recurrent ideas. More than once, Luke underlines God's predilection for the most deprived, who do not let themselves be deceived by pretension or by riches. Here we touch upon an essential point of a Christian conception of existence.

6:27-36 *Love your enemies*—here is one of the most revolutionary slogans of the Gospel for each age and each existence. It is quite common to recommend solidarity with those who are near to us through family, religion, homeland, or political affiliation. Judaism, for example, insisted on love of neighbor inside the community. Jesus shatters all limits and sweeps away all objections that restrict charity. For him, the call to love others is not guided by our preferences but by the need and distress of others. The correlation of conflicts and hatred must be broken. A love that is gratuitous and without boundaries—like the love of God taught to us by Jesus—is the mark of a true disciple. The Lord himself gave us an example of such love on the cross (see Lk 23:34).

Relations with Others. 37 * "Do not judge, and you will not be judged. Do not condemn, and you will not be condemned. Forgive, and you will be forgiven. [n] 38 Give, and it will be given to you. A good measure, pressed down, shaken together, and running over, will be poured into your lap. The measure that you use for others will be used to measure you." [o]

Parable of the Blind Leading the Blind. 39 He also told them a parable: "Can one blind man guide another who is also blind? Will not both of them fall into a pit? [p] 40 No student is greater than his teacher, but a fully trained student will be like his teacher. [q]

41 [r] "Why do you take note of the splinter in your brother's eye but do not notice the wooden plank in your own eye? 42 How can you say to your brother, 'Brother, let me remove the splinter that is in your eye,' while all the time you do not notice the wooden plank that is in your own eye? You hypocrite! First remove the wooden plank from your own eye, and then you will be able to see clearly enough to remove the splinter that is in your brother's eye.

A Tree Is Known by Its Fruit. 43 * [s] "No healthy tree can bear rotten fruit, nor does a rotting tree bear healthy fruit. 44 Every tree is known by its own fruit. For people do not pick figs from thornbushes or grapes from brambles. 45 A good man produces good from the store of goodness in his heart, whereas an evil man produces evil from the store of evil within him. For the mouth speaks from the abundance of the heart. [t]

Parable of the Two Foundations. 46 "Why do you call me, 'Lord, Lord,' but fail to do what I tell you? [u] 47 [v] I will show you what everyone is like who comes to me and hears my words and acts in accordance with them. 48 He is like a man who in building a house dug deeply and laid its foundations on rock. When the flood rose, it burst against that house but could not shake it because it had been solidly constructed. 49 In contrast, the one who hears and does not act in accordance with my words is like a man who built a house on the ground without a foundation. As soon as the river burst against it, the house collapsed and was completely destroyed."

B: From the Beatitudes to the Parables*

CHAPTER 7

Jesus Heals the Centurion's Servant.* 1 [w] After Jesus had finished speaking to the people, he entered Capernaum. [x] 2 A centurion who dwelt there had a servant whom he regarded highly and who was ill and near death. 3 When he heard about Jesus, he sent some Jewish elders to ask him if he would come and heal his servant.

4 When they came to Jesus, they pleaded earnestly with him, saying, "He deserves this favor from you, 5 for he loves our people, and he was the one who built our synagogue for us."

6 Jesus went with them. When he drew near the house, the centurion sent friends to say to him, "Lord, do not trouble yourself, for I am not worthy to have you come under my roof. 7 That is the reason why I did not presume to approach you personally. But say the word and let my servant be healed. [y] 8 For I also am a man subject to authority, with soldiers who are subject to me. I say to one: 'Go,' and he goes, and to another: 'Come here,' and he comes, and to my servant: 'Do this,' and he does it."

n Mt 7:1; Jas 2:13.—o Ps 79:12; Mk 4:24.—p Mt 15:14.—q Mt 10:24; Jn 13:16.—r 41f: Mt 7:3ff.—s 43ff: Mt 7:16ff; 12:33ff.—t Prov 4:23; Mk 7:20.—u Mt 7:21; Rom 2:13; Jas 1:22.—v 47ff: Lk 8:21; Mt 7:24-27.—w 1-10: Mt 8:5-13; Jn 4:43-54.—x Mt 7:28.—y Ps 107:20.

6:37-42 These varied sentences have to do with the relations of people to one another. Developed is the meaning of mercy (v. 37)—a characteristic trait of Luke's work—generosity (v. 38), and clear-sightedness regarding self that prevents one from judging others (v. 37). In Matthew's Gospel, the parable of the blind leading the blind is used to denounce the false teachers of Judaism (Mt 15:13-14). In Luke, it has become a recommendation of clear-sightedness addressed to the disciples. This varied usage of the same theme demonstrates the liberty of the evangelists—or of tradition—in the working out of a theme.

6:43-49 An authentic life does not deceive; it is by someone's acts that we discern what truly fills the heart. True disciples are not satisfied with talk and appearances. For them, listening to the Word of God means transforming their whole existence.

7:1-50 The first 17 verses in this section recount two miracles of Christ, which highlight his mission both to the Jews and to the Gentiles. The next 33 verses then have to do with Jesus and the Baptist. The first Christian generations no doubt encountered groups who were followers of John the Baptist. Hence, it was most necessary to comprehend well the destiny of this prophet. Several times Luke sketches a parallel between John and Jesus (see Lk 1:5-56; 3:1-20; 9:7-9). Each time the Baptist impresses us by his courage, and each time Christ's mission seems so different from his. Between these two destinies there is a kind of rupture, the difference of the two Testaments.

7:1-10 Every miracle testifies to Christ's power to save people. But this miracle is reported above all to teach the cost of faith in Jesus and to astound us with the faith of a pagan. Luke describes the deep religious attitude of this man. At that time, it was only at great cost that a Roman official would invite a Jew or show consideration for the one God worshiped by a conquered people. This miracle, granted to a pagan who trusted solely in the power of Jesus, discreetly announces the call of non-Jews to salvation (see Acts 10:34-35).

9 When Jesus heard these words, he was
amazed, and, turning to the crowd that
was following him, he said, "I tell you, in no
one throughout Israel have I found faith as
great as this." [z] 10 When the messengers
returned to the house, they found the ser-
vant completely healthy.

Jesus Raises the Son of a Widow.* 11 [a] Soon
afterward, Jesus went to a town called Nain,
accompanied by his disciples and a large
crowd. 12 As he drew near to the gate of the
town, a man who had died was being carried
out, the only son of his widowed mother. A
large group of people from the town accom-
panied her.

13 When the Lord saw her, he was filled
with compassion, and he said to her, "Do not
weep." [b] 14 After this, he came forward and
touched the bier, and the bearers halted.
Then he said, "Young man, I say to you,
arise!" [c] 15 The dead man sat up and began
to speak, and Jesus gave him to his mother.

16 Fear seized all who were present, and
they glorified God, saying, "A great prophet
has risen among us," and "God has visited
his people." [d] 17 The news of what he had
done spread throughout Judea and the sur-
rounding region. [e]

Jesus Answers the Baptist's Question.*
18 [f] When the disciples of John brought him
reports about all these things, 19 John desig-
nated two of his disciples and sent them to
the Lord to ask, "Are you the one who is to
come, or are we to wait for another?"
20 When they came to him, they said, "John
the Baptist has sent us to you to ask: 'Are
you the one who is to come, or are we to wait
for another?' "

21 At that time, Jesus had just cured many
people of diseases and afflictions and evil
spirits, and had restored the sight of many
who were blind. 22 And he gave them this
reply: "Go back and tell John what you have
seen and heard: the blind receive their sight,
the lame walk, those who have leprosy are
cleansed, the deaf hear, the dead are raised
to life, the poor have the good news pro-
claimed to them. [g] 23 And blessed is anyone
who takes no offense at me."

Jesus Praises John the Baptist. 24 * When
John's messengers had departed, Jesus
spoke to the crowds about John: "What did
you go out into the desert to see? A reed
swaying in the wind? 25 What did you go out
to see? Someone robed in fine clothing?
Those who are robed in gorgeous clothing
and live luxuriously are to be found in royal
palaces. 26 Then what did you go out to see?
A prophet? Yes, I tell you, and far more than
a prophet. 27 This is the one about whom it is
written:

'Behold, I am sending my messenger
ahead of you,
who will prepare your way before
you.' [h]

28 "I tell you, among those born of women,
no one is greater than John, and yet the least
in the kingdom of God is greater than he."

29 (All the people who heard him, includ-
ing the tax collectors, acknowledged the sav-
ing justice of God, for they had received
John's baptism. [i] 30 However, the Pharisees
and the teachers of the Law who had refused
his baptism rejected God's plan for them.)

Indecisive Children. 31 [j] "Then to what shall
I compare the people of this generation?
What are they like? 32 They are like children
sitting in the marketplace and calling to
each other:

'We played the flute for you,
but you would not dance;
we sang a dirge,
and you refused to mourn.'

33 "For John the Baptist has come, eating
no bread and drinking no wine, and you say:
'He is possessed.' 34 The Son of Man has
come eating and drinking, and you say:
'Look at him! He is a glutton and a drunk-
ard, a friend of tax collectors and sinners.' [k]

z Mt 8:10.—a 11-16: 1 Ki 17:17-24; Mk 5:21-24.—b Lk 10:1; 13:15.—c Acts 9:40.—d Lk 1:65; 1 Ki 17:23; Mt 16:14.—e Lk 4:14.—f 18-27: Mt 11:2-11.—g Isa 29:18; 35:5f.—h Isa 40:3; Mal 3:1.—i Lk 3:12; Mt 21:32.—j 31-35: Mt 11:16-19.—k Jn 6:35.

7:11-17 Luke is the only one who reports this incident, which takes place in a village in the area of Nazareth. God manifests himself once again as he did in the time of the prophets Elijah and Elisha (see 1 Ki 17:17-24; 2 Ki 4:18-37).

7:18-23 Jesus answers John by telling him of the signs which he, Jesus, is performing: those foreseen by the Prophets (Ps 72:2, 12-13; Isa 61:1-2). He is not the liberator of a nation but someone who takes the side of the wretched and marginalized of this world (see Lk 4:16-19).

7:24-35 John the Baptist, messenger of the Savior, surpasses the Prophets because he precedes and announces the coming of the Lord (Lk 1:17, 76; Mal 3:1), but Jesus alone inaugurates this new time of the kingdom. The austere preaching of John moved the people and the tax collectors, those who were despised, whereas the officials of the religion rejected him in the same way they disdained the call to joy addressed to them by Jesus. This shows the narrow-mindedness of those who believe themselves wise in the face of the unexpected accomplished by God. But the true believers welcome the plan of the Lord who saves, i.e., his "wisdom."

35 Yet wisdom is proved right by all her chil-
dren."

Jesus Pardons a Sinful Woman.* 36 One of
the Pharisees invited Jesus to dine with him.
When he arrived at the Pharisee's house, he
took his place at table. [l] 37 [m] A woman of that
town, who was leading a sinful life, learned
that Jesus was a dinner guest in the
Pharisee's house. Carrying with her an
alabaster jar of ointment, [n]* 38 she stood
behind him at his feet, weeping, and began
to bathe his feet with her tears and to dry
them with her hair. Then she kissed his feet
and anointed them with the ointment.

39 When the Pharisee who had invited him
saw this, he said to himself, "If this man
were really a prophet, he would have known
who and what kind of woman this is who is
touching him—that she is a sinner." 40 Jesus
then said to the Pharisee, "Simon, I have
something to say to you." He replied, "What
is it, Teacher?"

41 "There were two men who were in debt
to a certain creditor. One owed him five hun-
dred denarii, and the other owed fifty.
42 When they were unable to repay him, he
canceled both debts. Now which one of them
will love him more?" 43 Simon answered, "I
would imagine that it would be the one who
was forgiven the larger amount." Jesus
replied, "You have judged rightly."

44 Then, turning toward the woman, he
said to Simon, "Do you see this woman? I
entered your home, and you provided no
water for my feet, but she has bathed them
with her tears and wiped them with her
hair. [o] 45 You gave me no kiss, but she has not
ceased to kiss my feet from the time I came
in. [p] 46 You did not anoint my head with oil,
but she has anointed my feet with oint-
ment. [q] 47 Therefore, I tell you: her many sins
have been forgiven her because she has
shown great love. But the one who has been
forgiven little has little love."

48 Then Jesus said to her, "Your sins are
forgiven." [r] 49 Those who were at table began
to say to themselves, "Who is this man who
even forgives sins?" 50 But Jesus said to the
woman, "Your faith has saved you. Go in
peace." [s]

CHAPTER 8

C: Hearing the Word

The Women Who Minister to Jesus. 1 After
that, Jesus journeyed through towns and vil-
lages preaching and proclaiming the king-
dom of God. Traveling with him were the
Twelve, [t] 2 * as well as some women who had
been cured of evil spirits and infirmities:
Mary, called Magdalene, from whom seven
demons had gone out; [u] 3 Joanna, the wife of
Herod's steward Chuza; Susanna; and many
others. These women provided for them out
of their own resources.

The Parable of the Sower.* 4 When a large
crowd gathered together as people from
every town flocked to him, he said in a para-
ble: 5 "A sower went out to sow his seed. And
as he sowed, some of the seed fell along the
path and was trampled upon, and the birds
of the sky ate it up. 6 Some fell on rock, and
when it came up, it withered for lack of
moisture. 7 Some seed fell among thorns,
and the thorns grew with it and choked it. [v]
8 And some fell onto good soil, and when
it grew it produced a crop of a hundred-
fold."

After saying this, he cried out, "He who
has ears to hear, let him hear."

The Purpose of Parables.* 9 [w] Then his disci-
ples asked him what the parable meant.
10 He said, "To you has been granted knowl-

l Lk 11:37; 14:1.—m 37ff: Mt 26:6-13; Mk 14:3-9; Jn 12: 1-8.—n Mt 21:32.—o Gen 18:4; 1 Tim 5:10.—p Lk 22:47-48.—q Ps 23:5; Eccl 9:8.—r Mt 9:2.—s Acts 15:33.—t Lk 4:43; Mt 4:23; Mk 1:39.—u Lk 24:10; Mt 27:55f; Mk 15:40f; 16:9; Jn 19:25.—v Jer 4:3-4.—w 9-15: Mt 13:10-23; Mk 4:10-20.

7:36-50 The other three evangelists place this incident just before the Passion. Luke, however, keeps it here to show that his primary concern is with the mercy and forgiveness of God. He is the only evangelist to hand down the memory of good relations between Jesus and the Pharisees who invite him to dine (see also Lk 11:37; 14:1): these men, too, are children of Israel and will be given the instruction that they really need.

7:37 The woman is certainly not Mary Magdalene (see Lk 8:2) nor Mary the sister of Lazarus (Lk 10:39; Jn 11:5). The immense popularity of Mary Magdalene was due to a confusion, which occurred as far back as Christian antiquity, between the sinful woman who is forgiven here and the real Mary Magdalene, who was one of the main figures on Calvary and at the tomb.

8:2-3 Some women belong to the group of disciples; this was an occurrence quite rare at that period. As for Mary of Magdala (Mary Magdalene), the expression "seven demons" suggests some violent illness with symptoms that were disconcerting for a woman.

8:4-8 Since the time of the Prophets, harvesting was a current image of the Judgment (Joel 4:13). Sowing evokes the activity of Jesus. Jesus knows from experience that preaching the Gospel converts only hearts that are well disposed. Nevertheless, he underlines with optimism the growth of the seed: despite all risks and obstacles, the Word of God will make progress among human beings.

8:9-10 At the moment, only the disciples are sensitive to the riches of the Gospel; the others do not yet have a free heart. See also note on Mt 13:11.

edge of the mysteries of the kingdom of God, but for others they are made known in parables, so that

'looking they may not see,
and hearing they may not understand.'[x]

The Explanation of the Parable of the Sower.* 11 "The meaning of the parable is this. The seed is the word of God. 12 The seed on the path represents those who hear, but then the devil comes and carries off the word from their hearts so that they may not come to believe and be saved. 13 Those on rock are the ones who, when they hear the word, receive it with joy. But these have no root; they believe for a short while, but in time of trial they fall away.[y]

14 "That which has fallen among thorns are the ones who have heard, but as they go along, they are choked by the concerns and riches and pleasures of life, and they fail to produce mature fruit.[z] 15 But that which is on rich soil are the ones who, when they have heard the word with a good and upright heart, keep it and yield a harvest through their perseverance.

The Parable of the Lamp.* 16 [a] "No one after lighting a lamp covers it with a pot or places it under a bed. Rather he places it on a lampstand so that those who enter may see the light.[b] 17 For nothing is hidden that will not be disclosed, and nothing is concealed that will not be made known and brought to light.[c] 18 Take great care, therefore, about how you listen. For to the one who has, more will be given; from the one who does not have, even what he thinks he has will be taken away."[d]

The True Family of Jesus.* 19 [e] Then his mother and his brethren arrived, looking for him, but they could not get near him because of the crowd. 20 He was told, "Your mother and your brethren* are standing outside, and they want to see you."[f] 21 But he replied, "My mother and my brethren are those who hear the word of God and put it into practice."[g]

D: The Progressive Revelation of the Mystery of Jesus

Jesus Calms the Storm.* 22 [h] One day, Jesus got into a boat with his disciples and said to them, "Let us cross over to the other side of the lake." And so they set forth, 23 and as they sailed he fell asleep. Then a windstorm swept down on the lake. As a result, the boat was becoming filled with water, and they were in danger. 24 So they went to him and awakened him, saying, "Master! Master! We are perishing!"[i]

Then he awakened and rebuked the wind and the turbulent waves. They subsided and there was calm. 25 He said to them, "Where is your faith?" They were filled with fear and a sense of awe, and they said to one another, "Who can this be? He gives orders to the winds and the water, and they obey him."

Jesus Casts Out a Legion of Demons.* 26 [j] Then they sailed to the region of the Gerasenes, which is opposite Galilee. 27 As he stepped ashore, he was approached by a man from the town who was possessed by demons. For a long time he had worn no clothes. Moreover, he did not live in a house but among the tombs.

28 When the man caught sight of Jesus, he cried out and fell at his feet, shouting at the top of his voice, "What do you want with me, Jesus, Son of the Most High God? I implore you, do not torment me!"[k] 29 For he had ordered the unclean spirit to come out of the man. Many times in the past it had seized

---

x Isa 6:9; Jn 12:40; Acts 28:26.—y Mt 11:6.—z Lk 21:34; 1 Tim 6:9-10.—a 16ff: Mk 4:21-25.—b Lk 11:33; Mt 5:15.—c Lk 12:2; Mt 10:26.—d Lk 19:26; Mt 13:12; 25:29.—e 19ff: Mt 12:46-50; Mk 3:31-35.—f Jn 7:5.—g Lk 11:27f; Jn 14:21.—h 22-25: Mt 8:23-27; Mk 4:35-41.—i Lk 4:35; Ps 107:28-29.—j 26-39: Mt 8:28-34; Mk 5:1-20.—k Lk 4:34; Mt 4:3.

8:11-15 In the meditation of the early communities, the parable of the sower becomes a lesson for the believer. In daily life, in trials, in the pleasures of life, the work of the demon is an obstacle to the Gospel. Jesus knows this. He also knows the generosity of which humans are capable. He puts us on guard but also calls us to make a persevering effort to let our life be transformed by his teachings.

8:16-18 Are the mysteries of the kingdom definitively denied to others (v. 10)? No. The secret is not forever. Soon the disciples will bring the message to all people (see Lk 12:1-12). How will they receive it? We will be judged on the yield of the Word in our life (see Lk 19:25-26).

8:19-21 The true family of Jesus is made up of those who hearken to the Word. Luke places this episode as a conclusion to the texts on receiving the Gospel. Belonging to Jesus is the joy of the believer.

8:20 *Brethren:* i.e., according to Hebrew idiom, close relatives. See note on Mt 12:46.

8:22-25 God alone is master of the sea (see Pss 65:7; 89:10; 107:25-28). The authority of Jesus over the unleashed elements shows his power divine.

8:26-39 The incident is meant to show that Jesus is stronger than all the forces of evil lumped together, the forces of Satan himself. Jesus goes to face these forces in a pagan region east of the Lake of Tiberias, where, it was thought, Satan must be reigning supreme. There is a herd of pigs there, animals unclean in Jewish eyes; the herd dashes over the cliff, signifying the return of the demons to their hell.

him, and on such occasions they used to
restrain him with chains and shackles, but
he would manage to break loose and be
driven by the demon into the wilds.

30 Then Jesus asked him, "What is your
name?" "Legion," he replied, for many
demons had entered him. 31 And they begged
him not to order them to go back into the
abyss.[l]

32 Now on the mountainside a large herd of
pigs was feeding, and they pleaded with him
to let them go into the pigs. He allowed this.
33 The demons then came out of the man and
entered the pigs. Thereupon the herd
charged down the steep bank into the lake
and drowned.

34 When those tending the herd saw what
had occurred, they ran off and reported the
incident in the town and throughout the
countryside. 35 As a result, people came out
to see what had happened. When they came
near Jesus, they found the man from whom
the demons had gone out sitting at Jesus'
feet, fully clothed and in his right mind, and
they were frightened.[m]

36 Those who had been eyewitnesses to
the incident told how the one who had
been possessed by demons had been
healed. 37 Then all the people of the region
of the Gerasenes asked Jesus to depart
from them, for they were seized with great
fear. So he got into the boat and went
away.[n]

38 The man from whom the demons had
gone out pleaded that he be allowed to go
with him, but Jesus sent him away, saying,
39 "Return to your home and give witness to
what God has done for you." He then
departed, proclaiming throughout the town
what Jesus had done for him.

Jesus Heals a Woman and Raises a Child.*

40 [o] When Jesus returned, the crowd wel-
comed him, for they had all been waiting
for him. 41 Then a man named Jairus, a
leader of the synagogue, came forward.
Throwing himself at the feet of Jesus, he
pleaded with him to come to his house,
42 because he had an only daughter, about
twelve years old, who was dying. And as
Jesus went forth, the crowds were pressing
in on him.

43 There was a woman who had been suf-
fering from bleeding for twelve years, but no
one had been able to cure her affliction.[p]
44 Coming up behind him, she touched the
fringe of his cloak, and her bleeding stopped
immediately.

45 Jesus then asked, "Who was it who
touched me?" When everyone denied doing
so, Peter said, "Master, the crowds are sur-
rounding you and pressing closely upon
you." 46 But Jesus said, "Someone touched
me, for I could sense power going out from
me."[q]

47 When the woman realized that she had
not escaped notice, she came forward, trem-
bling, and knelt down before him. In the
presence of all the people, she related why
she had touched him and how she had been
healed immediately. 48 Then Jesus said to
her, "Daughter, your faith has healed you.
Go in peace."[r]

49 While he was still speaking, someone
came from the house of the synagogue
leader and said, "Your daughter has died.
Do not bother the Teacher any further."
50 When Jesus heard this, he said, "Do not
be afraid. Just have faith, and she will be
saved."

51 When he arrived at the house, he per-
mitted no one to go in with him except
Peter, John, and James, and the child's
father and mother. 52 Everyone was weep-
ing and mourning for her, but he said,
"Stop your weeping! She is not dead; she is
asleep."[s] 53 They laughed at him because
they knew that she had died.

54 However, Jesus took her by the hand
and called out to her, "Little child, arise."
55 Her spirit returned, and she stood up
at once. Then Jesus directed that she be
given something to eat. 56 Her parents were
stunned, but he gave them strict instruc-
tions to tell no one what had happened.[t]

---

l Rev 9:1-2; 11:7.—m Lk 10:39.—n Acts 16:39.—o 40-56: Mt 9:18-26; Mk 5:21-43.—p Lev 15:25-30.—q Lk 6:19; Mt 14:36.—r Mt 8:10.—s Lk 23:27.—t Lk 1:12.

8:40-56 This episode places before us two distressed people. The first is a father on the verge of losing his young daughter, with the rites of mourning under the specter of death already organized. The second is a woman humiliated by a sickness that carries the stigma of legal impurity, preventing her from participating in religious services and from approaching the Prophet (see Lev 15:19-27). Jesus intervenes in their distress and manifests his power and goodness, both of which are those of God. Nevertheless, he refuses to give his intervention a dramatic character; the only witnesses of the girl's raising from the dead—described in the same way as the action of Elijah (see 1 Ki 17:17, 22)—will be apostles, who are no longer seeking miracles. Here then is the portrait of Jesus: he brings life to those who approach him with faith.

CHAPTER 9

Jesus Sends Out the Twelve on Mission.* 1 [u]Calling the Twelve together, Jesus gave them power and authority to cast out all demons and to cure diseases, 2 and he sent them forth to proclaim the kingdom of God and to heal the sick.

3 He said to them, "Take nothing for the journey, neither walking staff, nor sack, nor bread, nor money. Nor are you to have a second tunic. [v] 4 Whatever house you enter, stay there until you depart from that area. [w] 5 As for those who do not welcome you, when you leave that town shake the dust from your feet in testimony against them." [x] 6 Then they set forth and traveled from village to village, preaching the gospel and curing diseases everywhere.

John the Baptist, Herod, and Jesus.* 7 [y]Now Herod the tetrarch heard about all that was taking place, and he was perplexed because some people were saying that John had been raised from the dead, 8 others that Elijah had appeared, and still others that one of the ancient prophets had come back to life. [z] 9 But Herod said, "John I beheaded. Then who is this about whom I hear such things?" And he was anxious to see him. [a]

Jesus Feeds Five Thousand Men.* 10 [b]On their return, the apostles reported to Jesus what they had done. Then he took them along and withdrew privately to a town named Bethsaida. 11 When the people learned of this, they followed him. Jesus welcomed them and spoke to them about the kingdom of God. He also cured those who were in need of healing.

12 When evening was approaching, the Twelve came to Jesus and said, "Send the people away now so that they can go to the villages and farms in the area and obtain food and lodging, for we are in a deserted place." 13 He replied, "Give them something to eat yourselves." They said, "All we have are five loaves and two fish—unless we go and buy food for all these people." 14 For there were present about five thousand men.

Then he instructed his disciples, "Make them sit down in groups of about fifty." 15 They did so and made them sit down. 16 Taking the five loaves and the two fish, he looked up to heaven and blessed and broke them and gave them to the disciples to distribute among the people. [c] 17 They all ate and were satisfied. Then they gathered up what was left over—twelve baskets of fragments.

Peter's Confession That Jesus Is the Christ. 18 * [d]Once while Jesus was praying by himself, he asked his disciples who were standing close by, "Who do the people say that I am?" 19 They answered, "Some say John the Baptist; others say Elijah; and still others, that one of the ancient prophets has arisen." 20 "But you," he said to them, "who do you say that I am?" Peter answered him: "The Christ of God." [e] 21 Thereupon he gave them strict orders and commanded them not to tell this to anyone.

Jesus Predicts His Passion. 22 He then went on to say, "The Son of Man must endure great suffering, be rejected by the elders, the chief priests, and the scribes, and be put to death, and on the third day be raised." [f]

The Conditions of Discipleship.* 23 [g]Then he said to all who were with him, "Anyone who

u 1-6: Mt 10:1, 8-14; Mk 3:13-15; 6:7-13.—v Lk 10:4.—w Lk 10:7; Acts 9:43.—x Acts 13:51.—y 7ff: Mt 14:1f; Mk 6:14ff.—z Jn 1:21.—a Lk 23:8.—b 10-17: Mt 14:13-21; Mk 6:30-44; Jn 6:1-13.—c Mk 7:34; Jn 17:1.—d 18-21: Mt 16:13-20; Mk 8:27-30; Jn 6:67-69.—e Lk 2:26; Jn 1:49.—f Lk 24:7, 26; Mt 16:21; Mk 8:31; Acts 2:23.—g 23-26: Mt 16:24-28; Mk 8:34-38; 9:1.

9:1-6 The Twelve are to share the mission of Jesus, to announce and attest the coming of salvation. Like their Lord, the apostles of the kingdom must be disinterested and conscious of the grave importance of the Gospel. They will accept hospitality simply and without consideration of personal interest. It is by clearly dissociating themselves from incredulity that they will announce the judgment that is coming (see Acts 13:51; 18:5).

9:7-9 People speak of the return of Elijah as a precursor of the day of the Lord (Mal 3:23). They have known John. Now Jesus' renown reaches the palace of the prince whom he will encounter in the course of his Passion (see Lk 23:7-12). The murderer of John evinces an idle curiosity. The action of Jesus compels each of us to ask ourselves: What do we say of Jesus?

9:10-17 The preaching of Jesus so excites the crowd that they go so far as to disturb him in his retreat. He receives them and speaks to them about the kingdom of God. The miracle of the loaves is like a renewal of the prodigy of the manna expected at the time of the Messiah. In this account, Christians already discern the signs of the Eucharist: God nourishes his people. See also notes on Mt 14:13-21; 14:19; and 14:21; and Mk 6:43.

9:18-36 At the opening of this passage, Jesus is found in prayer—thus Luke underlines the importance of the moment. Christ invites the Twelve to declare themselves concerning who he is. Peter precedes the others—in the Gospel, Peter's faith has a large role (see Lk 22:31-33)—in acknowledging Christ as God, that is, as the expected Messiah whose unity with God is astonishing. In order to avoid all ambiguity about himself, Jesus recommends secrecy and for the first time announces his Passion. Contrary to what people expect, the Messiah will not save his people by a popular or political uprising but by his Death and Resurrection. The title "Son of Man" suggests the Passion and announces a glorious coming on the last day.

9:23-27 To believe in Christ is to strive to share the mystery of his Death and Resurrection. To do so it is necessary for each of us to go beyond ourselves and our egoism in the ordinary conditions of life. *See the kingdom of God:* this expression evokes the appearances of the risen Lord or the work of the Spirit in the primitive Church.

wishes to follow me must deny himself, take up his cross daily, and follow me.[h] [24] For whoever wishes to save his life will lose it, but whoever loses his life for my sake will save it.[i] [25] What does it profit a man if he gains the whole world and loses or forfeits himself?

[26] "If anyone is ashamed of me and of my words, the Son of Man will be ashamed of him when he comes in his glory and in the glory of the Father and of the holy angels.[j] [27] Truly I say to you, there are some standing here who will not taste death before they see the kingdom of God."

Jesus Is Transfigured.* [28] [k] About eight days after he had said this, Jesus took Peter, John, and James and went up on a mountain to pray. [29] [l] And while he was praying, the appearance of his face underwent a change, and his clothing became dazzling white. [30] Suddenly, there were two men talking with him, Moses and Elijah, [31] who appeared in glory and spoke of his departure, which would come to pass in Jerusalem.[m] [32] Peter and his companions were very sleepy, but when they became fully awake they beheld his glory and the two men standing beside him.[n]

[33] When they were ready to leave, Peter said to Jesus, "Master, it is good for us to be here. Let us make three tents—one for you, one for Moses, and one for Elijah." But he did not truly know what he was saying. [34] While he was speaking, a cloud came and cast its shadow over them, and the three disciples became frightened as they entered the cloud. [35] Then a voice came out of the cloud, saying, "This is my Son, my Chosen One.* Listen to him."[o] [36] After the voice had spoken, they beheld only Jesus. They kept silent and at that time they did not tell anyone about what they had witnessed.[p]

E: End of the Galilean Ministry

Jesus Heals a Boy with a Demon.* [37] [q] On the following day, when they descended from the mountain, a large crowd came forth to meet him. [38] Then, suddenly, a man in the crowd cried out, "Teacher, I implore you to look at my son. He is my only child. [39] A spirit seizes him and with a shriek suddenly throws him into convulsions until he begins to foam at the mouth. It hardly ever leaves him, continuously torturing him. [40] I begged your disciples to drive it out, but they were unable to do so."

[41] Jesus said in reply, "O unbelieving and perverse generation! How much longer shall I remain with you and have to endure you? Bring your son here!"[r] [42] As the boy was approaching him, the demon threw him into convulsions. But Jesus rebuked the unclean spirit, cured the boy, and gave him back to his father.[s] [43] And all those present were awestruck at the greatness of God.

Jesus Predicts His Passion a Second Time.* Amid the astonishment of the crowds at everything he was doing, Jesus said to his disciples, [44] [t] "Listen carefully to these words. The Son of Man is going to be handed over into the power of men." [45] But they did not understand what he was saying. Its meaning was hidden from them so that they could not comprehend his message, and they were afraid to ask him what he meant.[u]

True Greatness.* [46] [v] The disciples then began to argue about which of them was the greatest.[w] [47] Jesus, aware of their inner thoughts, took a child, placed him by his side, [48] and said to them, "Whoever receives this child in my name receives me; and whoever receives me receives the one who sent me. For the one who is least among all of you is the one who is the greatest."[x]

---

h Lk 14:27; Mt 10:38.—i Lk 17:33: Mt 10:39; Jn 12:25.—j Lk 12:9; Mt 10:33; 2 Tim 2:12.—k Mt 16:28; Mk 9:2.—l 29-36: Mt 17:2-9; Mk 9:2-10.—m 2 Pet 1:15.—n Mt 26:43.—o Isa 42:1; 2 Pet 1:17.—p Mt 17:9.—q 37-43: Mt 17:14-18; Mk 9:14-27.—r Deut 32:5; Acts 2:40.—s Lk 7:15.—t 44f: Mt 17:22f; Mk 9:31ff.—u Mk 4:13.—v 46ff: Mt 18:1-5; Mk 9:33-37.—w Lk 22:24.—x Lk 10:16; Mt 10:40; 18:5; Jn 13:20.

9:28-36 In a vision on a mountain, three disciples behold, for one instant, the divine splendor of Jesus. Moses and Elijah, who announced God's plan in the Law and the Prophets, attest that it will now be accomplished by the Passion, that "passage" of Jesus, which is the new "Exodus." As formerly in the Exodus God manifested himself in the cloud, now through the one he designates as his Son, his Chosen One (see Isa 42:1; 49:7), he will give to all people the definitive liberation. The evangelist hardly explains the unfolding of this mysterious event. He gives us the shattering experience of Jesus' inner life to prompt our faith in Christ: to hear this man is to hear God.

9:35 *My Chosen One:* this is similar to a Palestinian Jewish title found in the literature of the Dead Sea Scrolls and to Isa 42:1.

9:37-43a Returning to the people, Jesus resumes the struggle. In contrast with the lapse of the disciples, the Messiah manifests his sovereign power against all the forces that enchain us, of which the person afflicted with a demon is a striking example.

9:43b-45 Amid popular success, Jesus keeps his eyes fixed on his Passion, the decisive act of salvation. For the believers, as for the disciples, it remains difficult to accept the necessity of the cross.

9:46-48 As a result of their lack of pretense, children are the beloved of God and become models for the believer (see Lk 18:15-17). We must share this regard of Christ for the little ones, even in the way of thinking and living.

Whoever Is Not against You Is with You.* [49]John then said, "Master, we saw someone expelling demons in your name, and we forbade him because he is not with us." [50]Jesus replied, "Do not hinder him! For whoever is not against you is with you."[y]

IV: THE JOURNEY TO JERUSALEM*

A: The Departure

Passing through Samaria.* [51]As the time drew near for him to be taken up, Jesus resolutely set his sights on Jerusalem,[z] [52]and he sent messengers ahead of him. They entered a Samaritan village to make arrangements for his arrival, [53]but the people there would not receive him because his destination was Jerusalem. [54][a]When the disciples James and John saw this, they asked, "Lord, do you want us to call down fire from heaven to consume them?"* [55]But Jesus turned and rebuked them. [56]Then they journeyed forth to another village.

The Cost of Following Jesus.* [57][b]As they traveled along the road, a man said to him, "I will follow you wherever you go." [58]Jesus told him, "Foxes have holes, and birds of the air have nests, but the Son of Man has nowhere to lay his head."

[59]To another he said, "Follow me." The man replied, "Lord, allow me to go first and bury my father." [60]Jesus said to him, "Let the dead bury their own dead. You are to go and proclaim the kingdom of God."

[61]Another man said, "I will follow you, Lord, but allow me first to say farewell to my family at home."[c] [62]Jesus said to him, "No one who puts his hand to the plow and then looks back is fit for the kingdom of God."[d]

B: The Mission of All the Disciples

CHAPTER 10

The Mission of the Seventy-Two. [1]* After this, the Lord appointed seventy-two others and sent them on ahead of him in pairs to every town and place he intended to visit.[e] [2]He said to them: "The harvest is abundant, but the laborers are few. Therefore, ask the Lord of the harvest to send forth laborers for his harvest.[f]

[3]"Go on your way. Behold, I am sending you out like lambs among wolves.[g] [4][h]Carry no money bag or sack and wear no sandals. Greet no one on the road. [5]Whatever house you enter, let your first words be, 'Peace to this house!' [6]If a man of peace lives there, your peace will rest on him; if not, it will return to you.

[7]"Remain in the same house, and eat and drink whatever is offered to you, for the laborer deserves his wages. Do not move around from house to house.[i] [8]Whenever you enter a town and its people welcome you, eat whatever is set before you.[j] [9]Cure the sick who are there, and say, 'The kingdom of God has come unto you.'[k]

[10]"But whenever you enter a town and the people do not welcome you, go out into the streets and say,[l] [11]'Even the dust of your town that clings to us we wipe off our feet as a sign against you. Yet know this: the kingdom of God is at hand.'[m] [12]I tell you, on that day* it will be more bearable for Sodom than for that town.

Woe to the Cities of Galilee. [13]* "Woe to you, Chorazin! Woe to you, Bethsaida! If the mighty deeds performed in your midst had been done in Tyre and Sidon, they would have come to repentance long ago, sitting in sackcloth and ashes.[n] [14]But at the judgment

y Lk 11:23.—z Lk 13:22; 17:11; 18:31; 19:28; 24:51; Mt 19:1; Mk 10:1.—a 2 Ki 1:10.—b 57-60: Mt 8:19-22.—c 1 Ki 19:19ff.—d Phil 3:13.—e Ex 24:1; Mt 10:1.—f Mt 9:37; Jn 4:35.—g Mt 10:16.—h 4-7: Lk 9:3ff.—i Mt 10:10; 1 Tim 5:18.—j 1 Cor 10:27.—k Mt 3:2; 4:17.—l Mt 10:7.—m Acts 13:51.—n Lk 6:24-26; Mt 11:21-24.

9:49-50 It is necessary to accept the initiative of all those who make use of the name of Christ.

9:51—19:27 We are at a crossroads in the life of Christ: Jesus begins to go to Jerusalem where his mystery is to be accomplished. This journey will take him from Galilee to the Holy City. In this section, Luke brings together a part of the teaching of Jesus that the other evangelists do not have or that they give in very different contexts. In these ten chapters, we find some of the most moving words of Christ about the mercy of God.

9:51-56 The Samaritans refused passage to Jewish pilgrims on their way to the temple in Jerusalem, because they did not give recognition to that sanctuary. The critical text says simply that Jesus "rebuked" the disciples (v. 55); some manuscripts have: "And he said, 'You do not know what kind of spirit you are of, for the Son of Man did not come to destroy lives, but to save them.' "

9:54 An allusion to 2 Ki 1:10-12.

9:57-62 Jesus demands an unconditional commitment from those who hesitate. The preaching of the kingdom is of primary urgency. On its account, we are to renounce every possession and free ourselves from even the most sacred human attachments.

10:1-16 The number of those sent suggests universality, since the ancient leaders of Israel traditionally numbered seventy-two (see Num 11:24-29), and seventy-two pagan nations were listed (see Gen 10). In this passage, Luke brings together various recommendations of Jesus in order to draw up a program for the missionaries.

10:12 *That day:* the day of judgment.

10:13-15 See note on Mt 11:20-24.

it will be more tolerable for Tyre and Sidon than for you. 15 And as for you, Capernaum:

> Will you be exalted to heaven?
> You will be brought down to the netherworld. *[o]

16 "Whoever listens to you listens to me, and whoever rejects you rejects me. And whoever rejects me rejects the one who sent me."[p]

Joy of the Missionaries.* 17 The seventy-two returned rejoicing, and they said, "Lord, in your name even the demons are subject to us." 18 He said to them, "I watched Satan fall from heaven like lightning.[q] 19 Behold, I have given you the power to tread upon snakes and scorpions and all the forces of the enemy, and nothing will ever harm you.[r] 20 Nevertheless, do not rejoice in the knowledge that the spirits are subject to you. Rejoice rather that your names are inscribed in heaven."[s]

Joy of Jesus. 21 *[t] At that very hour, Jesus rejoiced in the Holy Spirit and said, "I thank you, Father, Lord of heaven and earth, because you have hidden these things from the wise and the learned and have revealed them to children. Yes, Father, such has been your gracious will.

22 "All things have been entrusted to me by my Father. No one knows who the Son is except the Father, or who the Father is except the Son and those to whom the Son wishes to reveal him."[u]

The Privilege of Discipleship. 23 [v] Then he turned to his disciples and said privately, "Blessed are the eyes that see what you see. 24 I tell you, many prophets and kings desired to see what you see but did not see it, and to hear what you hear but did not hear it."[w]

The Greatest Commandment. 25 * And behold, a lawyer came forward to test Jesus by asking, "Teacher, what must I do to gain eternal life?"[x] 26 Jesus said to him, "What is written in the Law? How do you read it?" 27 He answered, "You shall love the Lord your God with all your heart, and with all your soul, and with all your strength, and with all your mind, and your neighbor as yourself."[y] 28 Jesus then said to him, "You have answered correctly. Do this and you will live."[z]

The Parable of the Good Samaritan. 29 But because the man wished to justify himself, he asked, "And who is my neighbor?"[a] 30 Jesus replied, "A man was going down* from Jerusalem to Jericho, when he was attacked by robbers. They stripped him and beat him, and then went off leaving him half-dead. 31 A priest happened to be traveling along that same road, but when he saw him he passed by on the other side.[b] 32 A Levite* likewise came to that spot and saw him, but he too passed by on the other side.

33 "But a Samaritan who was traveling along that road came upon him, and when he saw him he was moved with compassion. 34 He went up to him and bandaged his wounds after having poured oil and wine on them. Then he brought him upon his own animal to an inn and looked after him.[c]

35 "The next day, he took out two denarii* and gave them to the innkeeper, saying, 'Look after him, and when I return I will repay you for anything more you might spend.'

36 "Which of those three, do you think, was a neighbor to the man who fell into the hands of the robbers?" 37 He answered, "The one who showed him mercy." Jesus said to him, "Go and do likewise." *

---

o Isa 14:13ff.—p Lk 9:48; Mt 10:40; Mk 9:37; Jn 13:20.—q Isa 14:12; Rev 9:1.—r Ps 91:13; Mk 16:18; Acts 28:5; Rev 12:9.—s Rev 20:12.—t 21f: Mt 11:25ff; 1 Cor 1:26-29.—u Jn 1:18.—v 23f: Mt 13:16f.—w 1 Pet 1:10-12.—x Lk 18:18; Mt 19:16.—y Lev 19:18; Deut 6:5.—z Lev 18:5; Prov 19:16; Rom 7:10.—a Lk 16:15.—b Lev 21:1-3.—c 2 Chr 28:15.

10:15 *The netherworld:* the place of the dead, i.e., the underworld (as in Acts 2:27, 31).

10:17-20 In the joy of the disciples, Jesus sees the beginning of the defeat of the forces of evil inflamed against human beings, and of their leader Satan (see Lk 11:20). Jesus shares their joy; but he invites them to rejoice most of all that they are the elect of the Father, a happiness that radically surpasses all missionary success.

10:21-24 In this inspired prayer, Jesus lays bare the profound movement of his heart and the very mystery of his person. He is gripped by the revelation made to the poor (i.e., *children*); he lives, in an inexpressible fashion, in unity with the Father in the Spirit. The expectation of kings and prophets, i.e., of the Old Testament, is now accomplished, for Jesus is here and shares with human beings God's mysterious presence. The Church knows that by herself she is nothing in this world, but she is astounded to bring forth for all people this great revelation of God. This text constantly brings her back home to the heart of the Gospel.

10:25-37 Jesus gives pride of place in his teaching to the commandment of love, which sums up the entire Law (see Mt 22:40); but love of God and love of neighbor are henceforth joined inseparably.

10:30 *Going down:* Jericho lies in the deepest depression on earth, at 800 feet below sea level.

10:32 *Levite:* a minister of the temple.

10:35 *Denarii:* plural for *denarius,* a laborer's daily wage.

10:37 The scribe had asked who was his neighbor. Jesus responds with the example of the Samaritan who, without regard for national rancors and religious disputes, recognizes the neighbor in an unknown person who is in need of help. Hence, the person who loves will know immediately how to individualize who his neighbor is. It is not necessarily—as the Jews thought—a person of the same nation, race, or religion.

Martha and Mary.* [38] In the course of their journey, he came to a village where a woman named Martha welcomed him into her home. [d] [39] She had a sister named Mary who sat at the Lord's feet and listened to what he was saying. [e]

[40] But Martha was distracted by her many tasks. So she came to him and said, "Lord, do you not care that my sister has left me to do all the work by myself? Tell her to come and help me." [41] The Lord answered her: "Martha, Martha, you are anxious and upset about many things, [f] [42] when only one thing is necessary. Mary has chosen the better part, and it will not be taken away from her." [g]

CHAPTER 11

C: Prayer

The Lord's Prayer.* [1] One day, Jesus was praying in a certain place. When he finished, one of his disciples said to him, "Lord, teach us to pray, as John taught his disciples." [h] [2] [i] He said to them, "When you pray, say:

Father,
  hallowed be your name.
Your kingdom come.
3 Give us each day our daily bread.
4 And forgive us our sins,
  for we ourselves forgive everyone
    who is in debt to us.
And do not lead us into temptation." [j]

The Parable of the Persistent Friend. [5] * He also said to them, "Suppose one of you has a friend, and he goes to him at midnight and says: 'My friend, lend me three loaves of bread, [6] for a friend of mine has arrived at my house from a journey, and I have nothing to offer him,' [7] and the friend answers from inside: 'Do not bother me. The door is already locked, and my children and I are in bed; I cannot get up now to give you anything.' [8] I tell you: even though he will not get up and give it to him because of their friendship, he will get up and give him whatever he needs because of his persistence. [k]

Ask, Seek, Knock. [9] [l] "Therefore, I say to you: ask, and it will be given you; seek, and you will find; knock, and the door will be opened to you. [m] [10] For everyone who asks will receive, and those who seek will find, and to those who knock the door will be opened.

The Parable of the Good Father. [11] "Is there any father among you who would hand his son a snake when he asks for a fish, [12] or hand him a scorpion when he asks for an egg? [13] If you, then, despite your evil nature, know how to give good gifts to your children, how much more will the heavenly Father give the Holy Spirit to those who ask him!"

D: For or against Jesus*

Jesus and Beelzebul.* [14] [n] Jesus was driving out a demon that was mute, and when the demon had gone out, the man who was mute spoke, and the crowd was amazed. [15] But some of them said, "He casts out demons by Beelzebul, the prince of demons." [o] [16] Others, to test him, demanded a sign from heaven. [p]

[17] However, he knew what they were thinking, and he said to them, "Every king-

d Jn 11:1f; 12:2.—e Lk 8:35.—f Mt 6:25-34; 1 Cor 7:35.—g Ps 27:4.—h Lk 3:21.—i 2ff: Mt 6:9-13.—j Mt 18:35; Jas 1:13.—k Lk 18:1-6.—l 9-13: Mt 7:7-11.—m Mk 11:24.—n 14-22: Mt 12:22-29; Mk 3:22-27.—o Mt 9:34.—p Lk 11:29; Mt 16:1; Mk 8:11.

10:38-42 The incident is intended to teach that the disciples of Jesus must not allow secondary things to take precedence over essentials, namely, the hearing of the Word of God in order to feed on it and put it into practice (see Lk 6:47; 8:21; 11:28; Acts 6:2). The village in which the two sisters lived was Bethany. Like the preceding parable, this thoughtful incident is told only in Luke.

11:1-4 In the eyes of Luke, the prayer of the disciples is connected to the prayer of Jesus himself. It is a profession of faith in which the community says the essence of what it requests: the kingdom of God, daily sustenance, forgiveness, and strength in time of trial. The form of the Our Father given here is shorter than the one handed down in the Gospel of Matthew.

11:5-13 In the Palestine of that time, people went to bed early; moreover, the entire family slept in a single room, and the door was secured from inside with a heavy bar. Thus, awakening a neighbor caused a great deal of inconvenience, but the latter would be ashamed to remain insensitive. And since God is mercy itself, could he refuse the request of believers when it concerns essentials (see Lk 18:1-8; 22:44)?

11:14—12:12 The suspicion with which his adversaries regard Jesus becomes accusation and snare; they treat him as an agent of Satan and demand signs of him. In this confrontation that is more and more manifest, Jesus does not soften his message in any way; rather he demands that one choose for or against him. The time of waiting is over; the time of decision is at hand.

11:14-22 There are groups who claim to cast out demons—the word "children" designates the members or disciples of a group. Why then should his opponents be suspicious of Jesus, especially since he actually heals sicknesses? The miracles that he works manifest the power of God, for in order to conquer Satan who is reputedly at work in sicknesses one must be stronger than he is.

dom divided against itself is laid waste, and a house divided against itself will collapse. 18 If Satan is divided against himself, how can his kingdom stand?

"For you say that I cast out demons by Beelzebul. 19 Now, if it is by Beelzebul that I cast out demons, by whom do your own children cast them out? Therefore, they will be your judges. 20 But if it is by the finger of God that I cast out demons, then the kingdom of God has come to you. [q]

21 "When a strong man is fully armed and guards his palace, his possessions are safe. 22 But when someone who is stronger than he is attacks and overpowers him, he carries off all the weapons upon which the owner relied and distributes the plunder. [r]

No Compromise. 23 "Whoever is not with me is against me, and whoever does not gather with me scatters. [s]

New Offensive from the Evil Spirit. 24 [t] "When an unclean spirit goes out of a person, it wanders through waterless regions seeking a place to rest, and if it finds none it says, 'I will return to the home from which I departed.' 25 However, when it returns, it finds that home swept and put in order. 26 Then it goes off and brings back seven other spirits more wicked than itself, and they enter and settle there. As a result, the plight of that person is worse than before." [u]

True Blessedness.* 27 While he was speaking, a woman in the crowd called out to him and said, "Blessed is the womb that bore you and the breasts that nursed you!" [v] 28 Jesus replied, "Blessed, rather, are those who hear the word of God and obey it!" [w]

The Sign of Jonah.* 29 [x] As the crowd continued to increase in number, Jesus said to them, "This is an evil generation. It asks for a sign, but the only sign it will be given is the sign of Jonah. [y] 30 For just as Jonah became a sign to the inhabitants of Nineveh, so will the Son of Man be to this generation.

31 "On the day of judgment the queen of the south will rise up with the men of this generation and condemn them, because she came from the farthest reaches of the earth to hear the wisdom of Solomon, and now one greater than Solomon is here. [z] 32 On the day of judgment, the men of Nineveh will rise up with this generation and condemn it, because they repented at the preaching of Jonah, and now one greater than Jonah is here. [a]

The Parable of the Lighted Lamp. 33 * "No one lights a lamp and then puts it in a cellar or under a basket; rather, he places it upon a lampstand so that people may see the light when they come in. [b]

The Lamp of the Body. 34 "Your eyes are the lamp of your body. If your eyes are sound, your whole body will be filled with light. However, if your eyes are diseased, your whole body will be in darkness. 35 See to it then that the light inside you is not darkness. 36 Therefore, if your whole body is full of light, with no part of it in darkness, it will be as full of light as when a lamp illuminates you with its rays."

Woe to the Scribes and Pharisees.* 37 When he had finished speaking, a Pharisee invited him to dine at his house. He went in and took his place at table. [c] 38 The Pharisee was surprised to see that he had not first washed* before the meal. [d] 39 But the Lord said to him, "You Pharisees cleanse the outside of a cup and dish, but you leave the inside full of greed and wickedness. [e] 40 You fools! Did not the one who made the outside also make the inside? [f] 41 Let what is inside be given as alms to the poor, and everything will be clean for you. [g]

---

q Ex 8:15; Mt 12:28.—r Isa 49:25.—s Lk 9:50; Mt 12:30; Mk 9:40.—t 24ff: Mt 12:43ff.—u 2 Pet 2:20.—v Lk 23:29.—w Deut 30:14; Prov 8:32; Rev 1:3.—x 29-32: Mt 12:38-42.—y Mt 16:1; Mk 9:11f; Jn 6:30f.—z 1 Ki 10:1-10; 2 Chr 9:1.—a Jon 3:5.—b Lk 8:16; Mt 5:15; Mk 4:21.—c Lk 7:36; 14:1.—d Mt 15:2; Mk 7:2, 5.—e Mt 23:25f; Mk 7:20-23.—f Lk 12:20; 1 Cor 15:36.—g Lk 12:33.

11:27-28 The happiness of the kingdom of God is open to those who accept the Word of Jesus. This is a warning to adversaries who reject it. Thus, the true grandeur of Mary is not in having given Jesus his body but in having welcomed the message (see Lk 1:38; 8:21).

11:29-32 Many long for prodigies that would forcibly remove the need for faith. Their desire is vain. The true sign that attests the mission of Jesus is the totality of his work and the force of his person as well as his call to conversion. Thus, past generations had seen messages for them in the wisdom of Solomon (see 1 Ki 10:1-11) and the word of Jonah (Jon 3).

11:33-36 Luke here brings together two sentences that have a theme of the lamp. It is a call to throw off blindness and be open to the light that is Jesus (see Lk 8:16). The light of faith transforms one's life.

11:37-54 In Luke these strong rebukes seem to have been given by Jesus in private conversations with Pharisees and scribes, whereas in Matthew (23:13ff) the charges are uttered publicly in the presence of outsiders. This is a further aspect of the "gentleness of Christ," which Luke means to communicate.

11:38 *Had not first washed:* this referred to the ceremonial washing, which was part of the "oral" traditions of the Pharisees, i.e., practices and regulations meant to fill out the written Law of Moses (see Mt 15:9; Mk 7:3, and note on Mk 7:4).

42 “Woe to you Pharisees! You pay tithes *
of mint and rue and every garden herb, but
you neglect justice and the love of God. You
should have practiced these without neglect-
ing the others. [h]
43 “Woe to you Pharisees! You love to have
the best seats in synagogues and to be greet-
ed with respect in the marketplaces. [i]
44 “Woe to you! For you are like unmarked
graves * upon which people tread without
realizing it.” [j]
45 On hearing this, one of the lawyers said,
“Teacher when you say such things you are
insulting us too.” 46 He replied, “Woe also to
you lawyers! For you impose burdens on
people that are difficult to bear, but you
yourselves do not lift a finger to be of assis-
tance. [k]
47 [l] “Woe to you! For you build the tombs
of the Prophets whom your ancestors mur-
dered. 48 By acting in this way you bear wit-
ness to and approve of what your ancestors
did. They killed the Prophets, and you
build their tombs. [m]
49 [n] “That is why the Wisdom of God said,
‘I will send them Prophets and apostles,
some of whom they will kill and persecute,’
50 so that this generation may be charged
with the responsibility for the blood of all the
Prophets shed since the foundation of the
world, 51 from the blood of Abel to the blood
of Zechariah * who perished between the
altar and the sanctuary. Yes, I tell you, this
generation will have to answer for it all. [o]
52 “Woe to you lawyers! For you have taken
away the key of knowledge. You yourselves
did not enter, and you blocked those from
entering who were trying to go in.” [p]
53 When he left the house, the scribes and
the Pharisees were extremely hostile and
they began to interrogate him about many
things, [q] 54 hoping to trap him in something
he might say in reply. [r]

CHAPTER 12

The Yeast of the Pharisees. 1 * Meanwhile a
crowd of many thousands of people had
gathered, and they were so tightly packed
together that they were trampling on each
other. Then Jesus began to speak, saying
first to his disciples: “Beware of the yeast of
the Pharisees—which is their hypocrisy. [s]
2 [t] There is nothing hidden that will not be
disclosed, and nothing secret that will not
become known. [u] 3 Therefore, whatever you
have said in the dark will be heard in the
daylight, and what you have whispered
behind closed doors will be shouted from
the housetops. [v]

Courage in Time of Persecution. 4 “I tell you,
my friends, have no fear of those who kill the
body and after that can do nothing further. [w]
5 But I will tell you whom to fear. Be afraid
of the one who, after he has killed, has the
authority to cast into Gehenna. I tell you,
fear him! [x]
6 “Are not five sparrows sold for two pen-
nies? And yet not one of them is forgotten in
God’s sight. 7 Even the hairs on your head
have all been counted. Do not be afraid. You
are worth far more than any number of
sparrows. [y]
8 “I tell you this: whoever acknowledges
me before men, the Son of Man will also
acknowledge before the angels of God. [z]
9 But whoever denies me before men, he will
be denied before the angels of God. [a]

Sayings about the Holy Spirit. 10 [b] “Every-
one who speaks a word against the Son of
Man will be forgiven, but the person who
blasphemes against the Holy Spirit will not
be forgiven. * 11 [c] When you are brought

h Lk 18:12; Deut 6:5; Mt 23:23.—i Lk 20:46; Mt 23:6f; Mk 12:38f.—j Mt 23:27.—k Mt 23:4.—l 47f: Mt 23:29ff.—m Acts 7:51-53.—n 49ff: Mt 23:34ff; 1 Cor 1:24.—o Gen 4:8; 2 Chr 24:20ff.—p Mt 23:13.—q Lk 6:11; Mt 22:15f.—r Mk 12:13.—s Mt 16:6, 12; Mk 8:15.—t 2-9: Mt 10:26-33.—u Lk 8:17.—v Mk 4:22.—w Mt 10:28-31; Jn 15:15.—x Heb 10:31; Jas 4:12.—y Lk 21:18; Mt 12:12.—z Lk 15:10; Mt 10:32.—a Lk 9:26; Mk 8:38; 2 Tim 2:12.—b Mt 12:31f; Mk 3:28f.—c 11f: Lk 21:12-15; Mt 10:17-20; Mk 13:11.

11:42 *Tithes:* see note on Mt 23:23-24.

11:44 *Like unmarked graves:* as Passover drew near, Jews used to whitewash tombs in order to avoid touching them inadvertently, which would have caused a legal uncleanness (see Num 19:16).

11:51 *Abel . . . Zechariah:* these two names recall the first and the last slayings recounted in the Hebrew Bible (see Gen 4:1-16; 2 Chr 24:17-22). What is being recalled is therefore the entire history of murders committed against men of God in the course of the Old Testament.

12:1-12 True disciples do not let the message become altered and are not afraid to bear clear witness to the Gospel, to confess their faith in Jesus. Persecutions should not intimidate them; indeed, it is better to be condemned by opinion than to lose God. Believers are certain that the Lord will never abandon them; they rely on the help of the Spirit to proclaim simply and without alteration the essence of the message (see Acts 4:8; 5:12; 7:55).

12:10 *Everyone who speaks . . . against the Holy Spirit will not be forgiven:* the meaning of this verse is obscure. Perhaps the meaning is that when Jesus was alive, people could be excused from failing to recognize him as the Savior, but such an excuse will no longer be possible once his mission has been confirmed by the power of the Spirit at Pentecost.

before synagogues and rulers and authori-
ties, do not be concerned about how or what
you are to answer or what you are to say.
12 When the time comes, the Holy Spirit will
teach you what you are to say." [d]

E: Be Poor in Order To Be Free

A Saying about Greed. 13 * Someone in the
crowd said to him, "Teacher, tell my broth-
er to share the family inheritance with
me." 14 Jesus answered him, "Friend, who
appointed me to be a judge and arbitrator
in your regard?"

15 * After this, he said to the crowd, "Take
care to be on your guard against all kinds
of greed. Life does not depend upon an
abundance of one's possessions." [e]

The Parable of the Rich Fool. 16 Then he told
them a parable: "There was a wealthy man
whose land yielded an abundant harvest. [f]
17 He thought to himself, 'What shall I do, for
I do not have sufficient space to store my
crops?' 18 Then he said, 'This is what I will
do. I will pull down my barns and build
larger ones, where I will store my grain and
other produce, 19 and I shall say to myself,
"Now you have an abundance of goods
stored up for many years to come. Relax,
eat, drink, and be merry." ' [g]

20 "But God said to him, 'You fool! This
very night your life will be required of you.
And who then will get to enjoy the fruit of
your labors?' [h] 21 That is how it will be for
the one who stores up treasure for himself
yet fails to become rich in the sight of
God." [i]

Trust in God.* 22 [j] Then he said to his disci-
ples, "Therefore, heed my words. Do not be
concerned about your life and what you will
have to eat, or about your body and what
you will wear. [k] 23 For life is more than food,
and the body is more than clothing.

24 "Consider the ravens. They do not sow
or reap, they have no storehouse or barn,
and yet God feeds them. You are of far
greater importance than birds. [l] 25 Can any
of you through worrying add a single
moment to your span of life? 26 If then such
a small thing is beyond your power, why
should you be concerned about the rest?

27 "Consider the lilies and how they grow.
They neither labor nor spin. Yet I tell you
that not even Solomon in all his royal splen-
dor was clothed like one of these. [m] 28 If God
so clothes the grass that grows today in the
field and is thrown into the furnace tomor-
row, how much more will he clothe you, O
you of little faith!

29 "Hence, do not be greatly concerned
about what you are to eat and what you are
to drink. Do not worry. 30 The nations of the
world are concerned for all these things.
Your Father is aware of your needs. [n]
31 Rather, seek his kingdom, and these things
will be given to you as well.

Treasure in Heaven.* 32 "Fear not, little
flock, for your Father has chosen to give you
the kingdom. [o] 33 Sell your possessions and
give to those in need. Provide money bags
for yourselves that do not wear out, an inex-
haustible treasure in heaven that no thief
can come near and no moth can destroy. [p]
34 For where your treasure is, there will your
heart also be.

F: Parables about Watchfulness*

The Parable of the Vigilant Steward.*
35 "Fasten your belts for service and have
your lamps lit. [q] 36 [r] Be like servants who are
waiting for their master to return from a

d Ex 4:12; Jn 14:26.—e Job 20:20; Ps 62:11.—f Lk 15:11.—g Prov 27:1; Sir 11:24; 1 Tim 6:17; Jas 4:13-15.—h Ps 39:7; Rev 3:17-18.—i Mt 6:19ff.—j 22-31: Mt 6:25-33.—k Ps 55:23; 1 Pet 5:7.—l Job 38:41; Ps 147:9.—m 1 Ki 10:4-7.—n Mt 6:8.—o Lk 22:29; Mt 14:27; 25:34; Rev 1:6.—p Prov 13:7; Mt 6:20f; Acts 4:34.—q Eph 6:14; 1 Pet 1:13.—r 36ff: Mk 13:34f.

12:13-14 The Law of Moses dealt with temporal questions (see Ex 2:14; Acts 7:27), and the rabbis willingly offered their opinions. Jesus has not come to sustain us in our personal interests but to save us. The Gospel does not foster greed in any form; it demands detachment from earthly goods. This episode serves as an introduction to a series of teachings concerning money, an important theme for the Gospel of Luke.

12:15-21 The desire for and the satisfaction in accumulating riches closes one to God and deprives one of lucidity. The goods of earth do not have a vocation for eternity. The spiritual future of human beings is more important. The Word and Life of Jesus are sustained by this conviction.

12:22-31 When the concern for earthly goods rules one's whole life, and even one's prayer, we have become enslaved to them. Christ's disciples remain free: they trust in God. Jesus does not preach unconcern but concern for what is essential: to accept the kingdom and to live the Gospel.

12:32-34 This recommendation to be detached from one's goods and to give them to those in need is more pressing in Luke. The true treasure of the kingdom is to be detached from money.

12:35-48 The Jews were wont to ask: "When will the kingdom come?" Christians asked: "When will the Lord return?" When forced to be vigilant, attention inevitably wanes. But the Lord is near, and our life is with him; we must not be sleeping when he returns.

12:35-38 Vigilant servants are bound to work and to be ready even into the night. The disciples are to be focused on meeting their Lord, who will be their joy.

wedding banquet, so that they may open the door as soon as he comes and knocks.[s] 37 Blessed are those servants whom the master finds awake when he arrives. Amen, I say to you, he will fasten his belt, have them recline to eat, and proceed to wait on them himself.[t] 38 If he comes in the second watch* or in the third and finds them still awake, blessed are those servants.

The Hour of the Son of Man.* 39 [u] "But keep this in mind: if the owner of the house had known at what hour the thief was coming, he would not have left his house to be broken into.[v] 40 So you must also be prepared, because the Son of Man will come at an hour when you do not expect him."[w]

The Parable of the Faithful Servant.* 41 Then Peter asked, "Lord, are you directing this parable to us or do you mean it for everyone?" 42 [x] The Lord replied, "Who then is the faithful and wise steward whom his master will put in charge of his household to give its members their allotment of food at the proper time? 43 Blessed is that servant if his master finds him doing so when he arrives home. 44 Truly I tell you, he will put him in charge of all his property.

45 "But if that servant says to himself, 'My master is detained in arriving,' and he proceeds to beat the menservants and the maids, and to eat and drink and get drunk, 46 the master of that servant will return on a day when he does not expect him and at an hour he does not know. He will punish him and assign him a place with the unfaithful.

47 "The servant who knew his master's wishes but did not get ready or do what his master wanted will receive a severe beating.[y] 48 But the one who did not know those wishes, and who acted in such a manner as to deserve a beating, will be beaten less severely. Much will be demanded of a person to whom much has been given, and even more will be asked of a person to whom more has been entrusted.[z]

G: The Urgency of Making the Decision

Jesus and His Passion.* 49 "I have come to spread fire on the earth, and how I wish it were already blazing! 50 I have a baptism with which to be baptized, and how great is my anguish until it has been completed![a]

Jesus, Cause of Dissensions.* 51 [b] "Do you think that I have come to bring peace to the earth? No, I tell you, but rather division.[c]

52 "From now on a household of five will be divided, three against two and two against three; 53 they will be divided, father against son and son against father, mother against daughter and daughter against mother, mother-in-law against daughter-in-law and daughter-in-law against mother-in-law."[d]

Discerning the Signs of the Times.* 54 He also said to the crowds, "When you see a cloud rising in the west, you immediately say, 'It is going to rain,' and so it happens.[e] 55 And when you see the wind blowing from the south, you say, 'It is going to be hot,' and so it happens. 56 You hypocrites! You know how to interpret the appearance of earth and sky. Why then do you not know how to interpret the present time?

Reconciling with Others before the Judgment.* 57 "And why do you not judge for yourselves what is right? 58 Thus, when you are going to court with your opponent, make an effort to settle the matter with him on the way. If you fail to do so, he may drag you before the judge, and the judge will hand you over to the officer, and the officer will throw you into prison.[f] 59 I tell you, you will not be given your freedom until you have paid your debt down to the very last penny."[g]

---

s Mt 25:1-13.—t Lk 22:27; Mt 24:42; Jn 13:4-5.—u 39f: Mt 24:43f.—v 1 Thes 5:2; 2 Pet 3:10.—w Lk 21:36; Mk 13:33.—x 42-46: Mt 24:45-51; 1 Cor 4:1ff.—y Deut 25:2.—z Lev 5:17; Num 15:27-30.—a Lk 9:22; Mk 10:38.—b 51ff: Mt 10:34ff.—c Lk 2:34.—d Mt 10:21; Mic 7:6.—e Mt 16:2f.—f Mt 5:25.—g Mk 12:42.

12:38 *Second watch:* i.e., between 9:00 P.M. and midnight. *Third:* i.e., between midnight and 3:00 A.M. See note on Mt 14:25.

12:39-40 See note on Mt 24:45-51.

12:41-48 When Peter poses this question, he is answered by a parable summoning all leaders of the community to faithful vigilance.

12:49-50 The allusion is to the baptism in fire and the Spirit that begins on Pentecost (see Lk 3:16; Acts 2:3, 19) and also to the Passion that is to cleanse the people of their sins (see Mk 10:38).

12:51-53 The Gospel brings not security but the division (see Lk 2:34-35) that, according to Micah (7:6), is a prelude to the last times.

12:54-56 Understanding the signs of the times means recognizing the time of salvation, the time of Jesus. No concern is more important than this, for one's very salvation is in question.

12:57-59 One must put one's life in order before the judgment, for afterward it will be too late. We are urged to settle disputes quickly in accord with Gospel values. Matthew will turn this text into an inducement to fraternal charity (Mt 5:25-26).

CHAPTER 13

Jesus Calls for Repentance.* 1 At that time, some people who were present told Jesus about the Galileans whose blood Pilate had mingled with the blood of their sacrifices.[h] 2 He asked them, "Do you think that because the Galileans suffered in this way they were worse sinners than all other Galileans?[i] 3 No, I tell you. But unless you repent, you will all perish as they did. 4 Or those eighteen people who were killed when the tower fell on them at Siloam—do you think that they were more guilty than all the others living in Jerusalem?[j] 5 No, I tell you—but unless you repent, you will all perish as they did."[k]

The Parable of the Barren Fig Tree.* 6 Then he told them this parable: "A man had a fig tree planted in his vineyard, but whenever he came looking for fruit on it, he found none.[l] 7 Therefore, he said to his vinedresser, 'For three years I have come looking for fruit on this fig tree and have never found any. Cut it down! Why should it continue to use up the soil?' 8 But the vinedresser replied, 'Sir, let it alone for one more year while I dig around it and fertilize it. 9 Perhaps it will bear fruit next year. If so, well and good. If not, then you can cut it down.' "[m]

Jesus Heals a Woman on the Sabbath.* 10 [n] On one Sabbath as Jesus was teaching in the synagogue,[o] 11 a woman was present, possessed by a spirit that had crippled her for eighteen years. She was bent over and completely unable to stand up straight. 12 When Jesus saw her, he called her forward and said, "Woman, you are freed from your infirmity." 13 Then he laid his hands on her, and immediately she stood up straight and began praising God.[p]

14 But the leader of the synagogue was indignant because Jesus had effected a cure on the Sabbath, and he said to the assembled people, "There are six days when work is permitted. Come on those days and be cured, and not on the Sabbath."[q] 15 The Lord said to him in reply, "You hypocrites! Is there a single one of you who does not untie his ox or his donkey and lead it from its stall to give it water on the Sabbath?[r] 16 Should not this woman, a daughter of Abraham, whom Satan has held bound for eighteen long years, be set free from this bondage on the Sabbath?"

17 At these words, all his adversaries were put to shame, and the people rejoiced at all the wonderful things he was doing.[s]

The Parable of the Mustard Seed. 18 * [t] He went on to say, "What is the kingdom of God like? To what shall I compare it? 19 It is like a mustard seed that a man took and sowed in his garden. It grew and became a tree, and the birds of the air made nests in its branches."[u]

The Parable of the Yeast. 20 [v] Again he said, "To what shall I compare the kingdom of God? 21 It is like yeast that a woman took and mixed with three measures of flour until it was completely leavened."[w]

H: The Destiny of Israel

Who Will Enter into the Kingdom of God?* 22 Jesus continued journeying through towns and villages, teaching as he made his way to Jerusalem.[x] 23 Someone asked him, "Lord, will only a few be saved?" He answered, 24 "Strive to enter through the narrow door, for many, I tell you, will try to enter but will not succeed in doing so.[y]

25 "When once the master of the house has gotten up and shut the door, you may find yourself standing outside knocking on the door and begging, 'Lord, open the door for

h Mt 27:2.—i Jn 9:2.—j Jn 9:7, 11.—k Jn 8:24; Acts 2:38.—l Isa 5:2; Jer 8:13; Mt 21:19.—m Jn 15:2.—n 10-17: Lk 14:1-6.—o Mt 4:23.—p Mk 5:23.—q Ex 20:9.—r Lk 14:5; Mt 12:11.—s Isa 66:5.—t 18f: Ezek 17:23; Mt 13:31f; Mk 4:30ff.—u Lk 17:6.—v 20f: Mt 13:33.—w 1 Cor 5:6.—x Lk 9:51.—y Mt 7:13f.

13:1-5 Jesus is told of a bloody repression that had just occurred in Galilee. He indicates that it is useless to fix the blame upon its victims (see Jn 9:3). Such events remind us that the judgment is only suspended and that death can surprise us at any time. Hence, they are a call to repent.

13:6-9 In the other Synoptic Gospels (Mt 21:18-22; Mk 11:12-14, 20-25) the incident of the barren fig tree stresses the strictness of the judgment. In Luke's parable, the threat of judgment is replaced by a lesson on God's patience.

13:10-17 The cure of a crippled woman on the Sabbath is in the eyes of the ancients a direct victory over Satan; it is an act of God who sets human beings free. The religious leaders are prevented by their conformist attitude from recognizing the cure as an obvious sign from God. In the face of such absurd legalism Jesus calls for simple common sense.

13:18-21 The work of Jesus will have a future of infinite proportions although it had such seemingly insignificant beginnings. See notes on Mt 13:31-32; 13:32; and 13:33.

13:22-30 This passage brings together scattered quotations of Jesus. After recalling that salvation demands effort and is not given by acquired privilege, the words open up frightful perspectives on the refusal of Israel while showing the Gentiles abounding in the kingdom. The religious conception is reversed here. People must not presume upon the certainty of their salvation. Salvation is a grace that needs their cooperation.

us.' He will say in reply, 'I do not know where you come from.'[z] 26 Then you will protest, 'We ate and drank with you, and you taught in our streets.' 27 But he will say, 'I do not know where you come from. Depart from me, all you evildoers!'[a]

28 "There will be weeping and gnashing of teeth when you see Abraham and Isaac and Jacob and all the Prophets in the kingdom of God as you yourselves are being thrown out.[b] 29 Then from the east and the west, and from the north and the south, people will come and take their places at the banquet in the kingdom of God. 30 Indeed some are last who will be first, and some are first who will be last."[c]

Herod's Desire To Kill Jesus.* 31 At that time, some Pharisees came and said to him, "Leave this place and go somewhere else, for Herod wants to kill you." 32 He answered them, "Go and tell that fox: 'Behold, today and tomorrow I will be casting out demons and healing people, and on the third day I will finish my work. 33 Yet I must continue to go on today and tomorrow and the next day, since it would not be right for a prophet to be killed outside Jerusalem.

The Lament over Jerusalem.* 34 [d] "Jerusalem, Jerusalem, you murder the Prophets and stone the messengers sent to you! How often have I longed to gather your children together as a hen gathers her chicks under her wings, but you would not allow it! 35 Behold, your house has been abandoned. I tell you, you will not see me until you say: 'Blessed is he who comes in the name of the Lord.' "[e]

CHAPTER 14

I: A Dinner Given by a Pharisee*

Jesus Heals a Man with Dropsy on the Sabbath.* 1 [f] On one Sabbath, Jesus went to dine at the home of a prominent Pharisee, and the people were watching him closely.[g] 2 In front of him there was a man suffering from dropsy, 3 and Jesus asked the lawyers and the Pharisees, "Is it lawful to heal on the Sabbath or not?"[h] 4 When they offered no reply, he took the man, healed him, and sent him on his way. 5 Then he said to them, "If one of you has a son or an ox that has fallen into a well, will you not immediately pull him out on the Sabbath day?"[i] 6 And they were unable to give him any answer.

The Parable of the Ambitious Guest.* 7 When he noticed how the guests were securing places of honor, he told them a parable: 8 [j] "When you have been invited by someone to attend a wedding banquet, do not sit down in the place of honor in case someone who is more distinguished than you may have been invited, 9 and then the host who invited both of you may approach you and say, 'Give this man your place.' Then you will be embarrassed as you proceed to sit in the lowest place.

10 "Rather, when you are invited, proceed to sit in the lowest place, so that when your host arrives, he will say to you, 'My friend, move up to a higher place.' Then you will be honored in the presence of all your fellow guests. 11 For everyone who exalts himself will be humbled, and the one who humbles himself will be exalted."[k]

Invite the Needy.* 12 Then he said to the one who had invited him, "When you host a luncheon or a dinner, do not invite your friends or your brothers or your relatives or your

z Mt 25:10-12.—a Ps 6:9; Mt 7:23; 25:41.—b Mt 8:11f.—c Mt 19:30; 20:16; Mk 10:31.—d 34f: Lk 19:41-44; Mt 23:37ff.—e Lk 19:38; Ps 118:26; Jer 12:17.—f 1-6: Lk 6:6-11; 13:10-17.—g Lk 7:36.—h Mk 3:4.—i Lk 13:15; Mt 12:11.—j 8f: Lk 11:43; Prov 25:6f; Mt 23:6.—k Lk 18:14; Mt 23:12.

13:31-33 Some Pharisees who are friends of Jesus alert him to the danger, but he does not fear the ruler of Galilee. In his eyes, Herod is nothing more than a sly fox, and no longer the lion, symbol of mortal danger. Despite any threats, Christ is resolved to pursue his mission till the very end with its tragic result in Jerusalem.

13:34-35 Like the Prophets, Jesus foretells the destruction of the Holy City, but he also evokes a day when all peoples will acknowledge the Lord (see Lk 21:24; Rom 11:25-27). See also note on Mt 23:37-39.

14:1-24 Luke is an artful composer of Gospel scenes. Here he brings together different themes in the unfolding of a repast. The Jews thought of the kingdom of God as a gathering of people at a banquet in heaven. And, for Luke, this repast doubtless has the value of an announcement and a symbol. Jesus has the honor of being invited on the Sabbath to dine with a group of Pharisees, the representatives of Jewish thought. His hosts follow solid principles of thought and congratulate themselves on their good education. They closely watch Jesus' behavior out of curiosity mingled with apprehension. And one might say that Jesus goes out of his way to shock them.

14:1-6 Jesus does not lose himself in compliments and conversation but posits an act, a sign of the salvation that he brings to human beings. This is a new miracle, again performed on a Sabbath. Religion is for the liberation of persons, not their enslavement. To keep the Sabbath is to bear witness to it (see Lk 6:6-11; 13:10-17). See note on Mt 12:9-14.

14:7-11 These reflections on the choice of places at a banquet could be nothing more than simple counsels of worldly wisdom. But Jesus wishes to stress that humility holds first place in the values of the kingdom, contrary to the values of the world (see Lk 1:51-52; 18:14).

14:12-14 A repast should not be a worldly affair. Luke calls for humility (see Lk 1:53; 6:20; 7:22) and disinterest.

wealthy neighbors, lest they invite you back and thus repay you.[l] 13 Rather, when you hold a banquet, invite the poor, the crippled, the lame, and the blind. 14 Then indeed will you be blessed because they have no way to repay you. But you will be repaid at the resurrection of the righteous." [m]

The Parable of the Great Supper.* 15 On hearing this, one of the dinner guests said to him, "Blessed is the man who will dine in the kingdom of God." [n] 16 [o] Jesus said in reply, "A man gave a sumptuous banquet, to which he invited many. 17 When the hour for the banquet drew near, he sent his servant to say to those who had been invited: 'Come, for everything is now ready.'

18 "But one after another they all began to make excuses. The first said, 'I have bought a parcel of land, and I must go out to inspect it. Please accept my apologies.' 19 Another said, 'I have purchased five yoke of oxen, and I am on my way to try them out. Please accept my regrets.' 20 Still another said, 'I have just gotten married, and therefore I am unable to come.' [p]

21 "When the servant returned, he reported all this to his master. Then the owner of the house became enraged, and he said to his servant, 'Go out quickly into the streets and alleys of the town and bring in here the poor, the crippled, the blind, and the lame.' 22 Shortly afterward, the servant told him, 'Sir, your orders have been carried out, and some room is still available.' 23 Then the master said to the servant, 'Go out to the open roads and along the hedgerows and compel people to come,* so that my house may be filled. 24 For I tell you, not one of those who were invited shall taste my banquet.' " [q]

J: Conditions To Be a Disciple*

Renunciation of Everything for Jesus.* 25 Great crowds were accompanying Jesus on his journey, and he turned to them and said, 26 "If anyone comes to me and does not hate his father and mother,* wife and children, brothers and sisters, yes, and even his own life, he cannot be my disciple.[r] 27 Whoever does not carry his own cross and follow me cannot be my disciple.[s]

28 * "Which one of you, intending to build a tower, would not first sit down and estimate the cost, to see whether he has sufficient funds for its completion? 29 Otherwise, if he has laid the foundation and then finds himself unable to finish the work, all who see it will ridicule him, saying, 30 'There goes the man who started to build but was unable to complete the work.'

31 "Or what king marching into battle against another king will not first sit down and consider whether with ten thousand soldiers he can defeat the enemy coming to oppose him with twenty thousand? 32 If he cannot, then, while the enemy is still a long distance away, he will send a delegation to ask for terms of peace. 33 In the same way, any one of you who does not renounce all of his possessions cannot be my disciple.[t]

The Simile of Salt.* 34 "Salt is good. But if salt loses its taste, what can be done to make it salty once again?[u] 35 It is fit neither for the soil nor for the dungheap. Thus, it can only be thrown away. He who has ears to hear, let him hear!"

---

l Lk 6:32-35.—m Acts 24:15.—n Isa 25:6; Rev 19:19.—o 16-23: Mt 22:2-10.—p Deut 24:5.—q Mt 21:43; Acts 13:46.—r Mt 10:37.—s Lk 9:23; Mt 10:38; 16:24; Mk 8:34; Jn 12:26.—t Phil 3:7-8.—u Mt 5:13; Mk 9:50.

14:15-24 The kingdom of God is portrayed as a banquet in which God gathers together the Elect. People can refuse the call, but one day the gathering of joy will take place—this is one of Jesus' principal certitudes. The parable goes farther; the officials, the habitués of religion, cheat themselves. Their affairs come before the joy of the kingdom, which opens itself to those who are regarded as ordinary and are often excluded: the marginalized of society or of religion. This proposal is shocking for official Judaism. And it should also be for any society that is closed in upon itself, and especially if it calls itself the Church of Jesus. See note on Mt 22:1-14.

14:23 *Compel people to come:* they must be emphatic on the need to enter, but the Gospel excludes any coercion.

14:25-35 This section is tantamount to a short catechism on discipleship. The phrase "cannot be my disciple" runs through it like a refrain (vv. 26, 27, 33).

14:25-33 This passage indicates that one must renounce everything to follow Jesus, even the most legitimate values and attachments, for the Gospel relegates all other considerations to a secondary level. That is the point of the word "hate" in the Old Testament (see Lk 16:13; Gen 29:31, 33; Deut 21:15-16; Isa 60:15). This renunciation is not some passing fancy but a radical demand: the two parables of the builder and the warrior could have been nothing more than simple invitations to reflect before deciding anything; Luke turns them into a call to make a serious commitment.

14:26 *Hate his father and mother:* Jesus does not intend to abolish the fourth commandment about honoring and taking care of one's parents. He simply sets forth the supreme conditions to be his disciple. In order to follow him, one must be disposed to sacrifice the most tender affections and even to renounce one's life (see Jn 12:25). The expression is softened and explained in Mt 10:37.

14:28-30 Whoever wishes to follow Jesus must weigh his own strengths so as not to launch out into a spiritual adventure thoughtlessly and rashly. Jesus illustrates this thought with two comparisons.

14:34-35 If the energy and conviction of disciples who have made a commitment begin to weaken, they become like salt that has lost its taste or its value.

K: Salvation—Joy and Torment of God*

CHAPTER 15

This Man Receives Sinners.* 1 Now the tax collectors and sinners were all crowding around to listen to Jesus, [v] 2 [w] and the Pharisees and the scribes began to complain, saying, "This man welcomes sinners and eats with them." [x]

The Parable of the Lost Sheep.* 3 [y] Therefore, he told them this parable: 4 [z] "Which one of you, if you have a hundred sheep and lose one of them, will not leave the ninety-nine in the wilderness and go after the one that is lost until he finds it? 5 And when he does find it, he lays it on his shoulders joyfully. 6 Then, when he returns home, he calls together his friends and neighbors and says to them, 'Rejoice with me, because I have found my sheep that was lost.' [a] 7 In the same way, I tell you, there will be more rejoicing in heaven over one sinner who repents than over ninety-nine righteous people who have no need of repentance. [b]

The Parable of the Lost Coin.* 8 "Or again, what woman who has ten silver coins * and loses one will not light a lamp and sweep the house, searching thoroughly until she finds it? 9 And when she has found it, she calls together her friends and neighbors and says to them, 'Rejoice with me, for I have found the coin that I lost.' 10 In the same way, I tell you, there is rejoicing among the angels of God over one sinner who repents."

The Parable of the Lost (or Prodigal) Son.* 11 Then he said: "There was a man who had two sons. [c] 12 The younger of them said to his father, 'Father, give me the share of your estate that I will inherit.' And so the father divided the property between them.

13 "A few days later the younger son gathered together everything he had and traveled to a distant country, where he squandered his inheritance on a life of dissolute living. [d] 14 When he had spent it all, a severe famine afflicted that country, and he began to be in need. 15 [e] So he went and hired himself out to one of the local inhabitants who sent him to his farm to feed the pigs. * 16 He would have willingly filled his stomach with the pods that the pigs were eating, but no one gave him anything.

17 "Then he came to his senses and said, 'How many of my father's hired workers have more food than they can consume, while here I am, dying of hunger. 18 I will depart from this place and go to my father, and I will say to him, "Father, I have sinned against heaven and against you. [f] 19 I am no longer worthy to be called your son. Treat me like one of your hired workers." '

20 "So he set out for his father's house. But while he was still a long way off, his father saw him and was filled with compassion. He ran to him, threw his arms around him, and kissed him. [g] 21 Then the son said to him, 'Father, I have sinned against heaven and against you. I am no longer worthy to be called your son.' [h]

22 "But the father said to his servants, 'Quickly bring out the finest robe we have and put it on him. Place a ring on his finger and sandals on his feet. [i] 23 Then bring the fatted calf and kill it, and let us celebrate with a feast. 24 For this son of mine was dead and has come back to life. He was lost, and now he has been found.' And they began to celebrate. [j]

---

v Lk 5:29; Ex 34:6; Hos 11:8-9.—w 2-7: Mt 9:10-13.—x Lk 5:30; 19:7.—y Mt 13:3.—z 4f: Ezek 34:11-16; Ps 23; Mt 18:12ff.—a Lk 19:10.—b Ezek 18:23; 33:11.—c Mt 21:28.—d Lk 16:1; Prov 29:3.—e Lev 11:7.—f Lev 26:40; Mt 3:2.—g Gen 45:14; Isa 55:7.—h Ps 51:6.—i Zec 3:4; Rev 6:11.—j Eph 2:1, 5.

15:1-32 These three joyous parables of Luke's Gospel disclose the sentiments that the Father and Jesus have toward human beings. God is untiringly concerned for those who are far off, the sinners or unbelievers. His joy is to seek out and find those who are lost. This desire and this joy of God are revealed to us in the comportment of Christ himself toward sinners. In turn, the Church must trust in the mercy of God and must seek out and welcome those who seem far away. May she always bear witness to the value that human beings have in the eyes of God.

15:1-2 In the name of God's love for sinners, Jesus overthrows several customs of his day. He refuses to accept the attitudes held by well-regarded religious figures: scorn toward others and smugness in their own self-sufficiency.

15:3-7 The parable of the lost sheep pushes antithesis to the extreme so that persons may never doubt God's tenderness for them.

15:8-10 The parable of the lost coin demonstrates what a great contrast there is between the joy of heaven and the disdain of the Pharisees and the so-called clean!

15:8 *Coins:* literally, "drachmas," a drachma being the Greek coin corresponding to the Roman denarius, a laborer's daily wage.

15:11-32 The parable of the prodigal son, one of the most enchanting stories of Jesus, completes the two preceding parables. It is God who awaits sinners, and it is humanity that is encouraged to seek God. We recognize in it all the misery of sin: abandonment, solitude, and distress. The parable describes the path to conversion and finally the great certitude of the believer: beyond all human hope, God harbors for every person the unfailing affection of a father for his child. He awaits the child and welcomes it joyously. It is easy to see in the discontent of the elder son the anger of the Pharisees at the welcome Jesus gives to sinners.

15:15 *Pigs:* unclean animals for the Jews.

25 "Now the elder son had been out in the
fields, and as he returned and drew near the
house, he could hear the sounds of music
and dancing. 26 He summoned one of the
servants and inquired what all this meant.
27 The servant replied, 'Your brother has
come home, and your father has killed the
fatted calf because he has him back safe and
sound.' 28 The elder son then became angry
and refused to go in. His father came out
and began to plead with him, [k] 29 but he said
to his father in reply, 'All these years I have
worked like a slave for you, and I never once
disobeyed your orders. Even so, you have
never even given me a young goat so that I
might celebrate with my friends. 30 But
when this son of yours returns after wasting
his inheritance from you on prostitutes, you
kill the fatted calf for him.' [l]

31 "Then the father said to him, 'Son, you
are with me always, and everything I have is
yours. [m] 32 But it was only right that we
should celebrate and rejoice, because this
brother of yours was dead and has come to
life; he was lost and now he has been
found.' " [n]

CHAPTER 16

L: Riches and Poverty*

The Parable of the Crafty Steward.* 1 Jesus
also said to his disciples: "There was a rich
man who had a steward, and he was
informed that this steward was squandering
his property. [o] 2 Therefore, he summoned
him and said, 'What are these reports that I
hear about you? Give me an accounting of
your stewardship, because you can no longer
be my steward.'

3 "Then the steward said to himself, 'What
am I going to do, now that my master is dis-
missing me from being steward? I am not
strong enough to dig, and I am too ashamed
to beg. 4 What I must do is to make sure that
people will welcome me into their homes
once I am removed from being steward.'

5 "Then he summoned his master's
debtors one by one. He asked the first, 'How
much do you owe my master?' 6 When he
was told, 'One hundred jars of olive oil,' he
said to the man, 'Take your bill, sit down
quickly, and change the number to fifty.'
7 Then he asked another, 'And you, how much
do you owe?' When he was told, 'One hundred
measures of wheat,' he said to him, 'Take your
bill and make it eighty.' 8 The master com-
mended the crafty steward because he had
acted shrewdly. For the children of this world
are more shrewd in dealing with their own
kind than are the children of light. * [p]

Application of the Parable.* 9 "And I tell you:
use your worldly wealth to make friends for
yourselves so that, when it has been exhaust-
ed, they will welcome you into eternal
dwellings. [q]

10 "Whoever can be trusted in small mat-
ters can also be trusted in great ones, but
whoever is dishonest in small matters will
also be dishonest in great ones. [r] 11 There-
fore, if you have not been trustworthy in
handling worldly wealth, who will entrust
you with true riches? 12 And if you have not
shown yourself to be trustworthy with what
belongs to another, who will give you any-
thing of your own?

13 "No servant can serve two masters. For
you will either hate the one and love the
other or be devoted to the one and despise
the other. You cannot serve both God and
money." [s]

M: Teachings concerning Justice and the Judaic Law

A Saying against the Pharisees.* 14 The
Pharisees, who loved money, heard all this
and they ridiculed him. [t] 15 He said to them,
"You people pretend to be upright when you
wish to impress others, but God knows what
is in your hearts. That which is highly

k Jon 4:1.—l Prov 29:3.—m Jn 17:10.—n Mal 3:17.—o Lk 15:11.—p Ps 17:14; Jn 8:12; Eph 5:8.—q Lk 12:33; Tob 4:9-10; Sir 29:12.—r Lk 19:17; Mt 25:21.—s Mt 6:24.—t Lk 23:35.

16:1-13 From the very origins of the Gospel tradition, the parable of the crafty steward has created difficulty. People could evolve abusive applications from it: e.g., does it promote fraud? In order to avoid any false interpretation, different sentences of Jesus concerning money have been joined to the parable.

16:1-8 It is a fact that people bring a great deal of initiative and intelligence to their affairs even when these are worthy of criticism or unjust. Alas, believers put forth little effort for the kingdom! This is the lesson to be retained from the parable. It is a call for lucidity and creative intelligence. Jesus is suggesting the *skill* of a swindler, not fraud or theft.

16:8 *Children of light:* a Hebrew expression signifying those enlightened by a superterrestrial faith as opposed to the *children of this world,* who are focused solely on their earthly interests.

16:9-13 Money dominates all of life and society. The attitude toward money is a test of the fidelity of Christians. Those who seek imperishable goods are detached from perishable ones. They know how to give alms (v. 9), and they earn and manage their goods with honesty (vv. 10-11). Yet money means little in reality; the true good is the gift of God (v. 12). Hence, the quest for gain and fortune must not be first in the life of Christians, for then money would become a false god for them (v. 13).

16:14-15 More than once Jesus denounces the pretense of those who pass themselves off as religious people (see Lk 11:39-40; 18:9; 20:47).

esteemed in the eyes of men is detestable in the sight of God. [u]

Sayings about the Law. [16] [v] "The Law and the Prophets were in effect until John. From that time the kingdom of God has been proclaimed, and everyone is trying to force his way in. * [17] It is easier for heaven and earth to pass away than for one letter of the Law to be discarded. * [w]

Sayings about Divorce.* [18] "Anyone who divorces his wife and marries another commits adultery, and anyone who marries a woman divorced from her husband commits adultery. [x]

N: The Rich Man and Lazarus: A Warning

The Parable of the Rich Man and Lazarus.* [19] "There was a rich man who used to dress in purple garments and the finest linen and who feasted sumptuously every day. [y] [20] And at his gate lay a poor man named Lazarus, covered with sores, [z] [21] who would have been grateful to be fed with the scraps that fell from the rich man's table. Even the dogs would come and lick his sores. [a]

[22] "Now the poor man died, and he was carried away by the angels to Abraham's side. The rich man also died and was buried. [23] In the netherworld, * where he was in torment, he looked up and saw Abraham, far off, and Lazarus by his side. [24] And he called out, 'Father Abraham, have pity on me. Send Lazarus to dip the tip of his finger in water and cool my tongue, for I am in agony in these flames.'

[25] "But Abraham replied, 'My child, remember that during your lifetime you received many good things, while Lazarus suffered greatly. Now he is being comforted while you are in agony. [b] [26] Moreover, between us and you a great chasm has been established, so that no one who wishes to do so can pass from our side to yours, nor can anyone pass from your side to ours.'

[27] " 'Then I beg you, father,' he said, 'to send him to my father's house, [28] to warn my five brothers, lest they too end up in this place of torment.' [c] [29] But Abraham responded, 'They have Moses and the Prophets. Let them listen to them.' [d]

[30] "He said, 'No, father Abraham, but if someone from the dead goes to them, they will repent.' [31] Abraham answered, 'If they will not listen to Moses and the Prophets, they will not be persuaded even if someone should rise from the dead.' " [e]

O: Various Episodes and Instructions

CHAPTER 17

Warning against Giving Scandal.* [1] [f] Jesus said to his disciples, "Scandals are bound to occur, but woe to the man through whom they come! [2] It would be better for him if a millstone were fastened around his neck and he were thrown into the sea than for him to cause one of these little ones to sin. [g] [3] Be on your guard!

The Need To Forgive.* "If your brother should sin, rebuke him, and if he repents, forgive him. [h] [4] Even if he wrongs you seven times a day, and comes back to you seven times to say, 'I am sorry,' you must forgive him." [i]

Faith Knows How To Make Miracles.* [5] The apostles said to the Lord, "Increase our faith." [6] The Lord replied, "If you had faith as tiny as a mustard seed, you could say to this mulberry tree, 'Be uprooted and planted in the sea,' and it would obey you. [j]

Unprofitable Servants.* [7] [k] "Which of you, when your servant returns from plowing or

u Lk 18:9-14; Jer 11:20.—v Mt 11:12.—w Mt 5:18.—x Mt 5:32; 19:9; Mk 10:11f; 1 Cor 7:10f.—y Ezek 16:49.—z Acts 3:2.—a Mt 15:27.—b Lk 6:24f; Ps 17:14.—c Acts 2:40.—d Lk 24:44; Jn 1:45; Acts 15:21.—e Jn 5:46f.—f 1f: Mt 18:6f; Mk 9:42.—g Mt 5:29.—h Eph 4:32; Col 3:13.—i Mt 18:21f.—j Lk 13:19; Mt 21:21; Mk 11:23.—k 7ff: Jn 13:4-5.

16:16 The Law and the Prophets designates the Old Testament as it was read in the synagogues. We must make an effort in order to enter the kingdom of God.

16:17 The Law will not pass away, for it includes the whole revelation given to the chosen people, with its prophetic character (see Lk 24:27, 44).

16:18 Divorce was allowed and regulated by Old Testament law (see Deut 24:1-4). The position of Jesus is a radical one, as numerous New Testament passages attest (see Mt 5:31-32; 19:1-12; Mk 10:1-12; 1 Cor 7:10-11).

16:19-31 The rich man cannot avoid the message of this passage; indeed, this is for him a sufficient sign and a more persuasive one than the most amazing miracle. *Abraham's side:* literally, "Abraham's bosom"; in the language of the day this suggested the post of honor at the heavenly banquet (see Mt 8:11).

16:23 *Netherworld:* see note on Lk 10:15.

17:1-3a Scandal is the snare that one extends to others in order to lead them into evil. It is especially grave when it is placed along the way of the "little ones."

17:3b-4 Fraternal pardon is one of the best signs of the presence of the Gospel. Faults among brothers and sisters are continual; hence, openness to reconciliation must be constant.

17:5-6 See note on Mt 21:18-22.

17:7-10 The Pharisees and many religious people are more concerned about their reward than about what they can do for God. The disciple is subservient to his master in a work that is far greater than himself. That is his happiness and his recompense even here below.

tending sheep in the fields, would say to him, 'Come right away and sit down to eat'? 8 Would you not rather say, 'Prepare my dinner, put on your apron, and wait on me while I eat and drink, and then afterward you yourself may eat and drink'? [l] 9 Would you be grateful to that servant for doing what he was commanded? 10 So should it be with you. When you have done all that you were ordered to do, say, 'We are unprofitable servants; we have only done our duty.' " [m]

Jesus Heals Ten Men with Leprosy.* 11 As he continued on his journey to Jerusalem, he traveled along the border between Samaria and Galilee. [n] 12 When he entered a village, ten lepers approached him. Standing some distance away, [o] 13 they called out to him, "Jesus, Master, have pity on us." 14 When he saw them, he said, "Go and show yourselves to the priests." And as they went, they were cleansed. [p]

15 One of them, when he realized that he had been cured, came back, praising God in a loud voice. 16 He prostrated himself at the feet of Jesus and thanked him. This man was a Samaritan. [q]

17 Jesus asked, "Were not all ten made clean? Where are the other nine? 18 Has no one except this foreigner returned to give thanks to God?" 19 Then he said to him, "Stand up and go on your way. Your faith has made you well." [r]

The Coming of the Kingdom of God.* 20 Once, the Pharisees asked him when the kingdom of God was coming. He answered, "The coming of the kingdom of God will not occur with signs that can be observed. 21 Nor will people say, 'Here it is,' or 'There it is.' For the kingdom of God is in your midst."

The Day of the Son of Man.* 22 Then he said to his disciples, "The time will come when you will long to see one of the days of the Son of Man, and you will not see it. [s] 23 [t] People will say to you, 'Look, there he is,' or 'Look, here he is.' Do not go running after them. 24 For just as lightning flashes and lights up the sky from one end to the other, so will the Son of Man be in his day. [u] 25 But first he must endure great suffering and be rejected by this generation. [v]

26 [w] "Just as it was in the days of Noah, so will it also be in the days of the Son of Man. 27 People were eating and drinking, marrying and being given in marriage, up to the day that Noah entered the ark. Then the flood came and destroyed all of them.

28 [x] "The same thing happened in the days of Lot. People were eating and drinking, buying and selling, planting and building. 29 But on the day that Lot left Sodom, fire and brimstone rained down from heaven and destroyed all of them.

30 "It will be like that on the day that the Son of Man is revealed. [y] 31 On that day, the one who is standing on the roof, with his possessions inside, must not come down to collect them, and someone who is in the field must not turn back. [z] 32 Remember Lot's wife. [a] 33 Whoever tries to preserve his life will lose it, and whoever loses his life will save it. [b]

34 "I tell you, on that night two people will be in one bed. One will be taken and the other will be left. 35 And there will be two women grinding grain together. One will be taken and the other will be left. [c] [36 Two men will be out in the field. One will be taken and the other will be left.]" *

37 They asked him, "Where, Lord?" He said in reply, "Where the corpse is, there the vultures will gather." [d]

CHAPTER 18

The Parable of the Importunate Widow.* 1 Then Jesus told them a parable about the

l Lk 12:37.—m Job 35:7; 1 Cor 9:16.—n Lk 9:51; Jn 4:3-4.—o Lev 13:45-46.—p Lk 5:14; Lev 13:9-34; Mt 8:4; Mk 1:44.—q Mt 10:5.—r Mt 9:22.—s Mt 8:20; Jn 8:56.—t 23f: Lk 21:8; Mt 24:23, 26; Mk 13:21.—u Mt 24:27.—v Lk 9:22; Mk 13:30.—w 26f: Gen 6—8; Mt 24:37ff.—x 28f: Gen 19:1-29.—y Mt 10:23; 2 Pet 3:4.—z Lk 21:21; Mt 24:17f; Mk 13:15f.—a Gen 19:26.—b Lk 9:24; Mt 10:39; Mk 8:35; Jn 12:25.—c Mt 24:40.—d Mt 24:28.

17:11-19 The episode of the ten people afflicted with leprosy illustrates first of all the ingratitude of Israel—which believes that the gifts of God are owed to it—and the faith of the Gentiles. For a Jewish author, it is odious to give an example containing a Samaritan, a heretic regarded as more disgraceful than a pagan. However, a stranger more open to the Lord's call than the average believer would provide an example capable of inculcating admiration forever.

17:20-21 As for when the kingdom will come, it is useless to wait for mysterious signs. The kingdom is already at work in the personal action of Jesus.

17:22-37 This description of events must be read in light of the particular literary genre being used, but this does not lessen its urgency. The other two Synoptic Gospels place these exhortations in the "eschatological discourse."

17:36 Some manuscripts add this verse, probably taken from Mt 24:40.

18:1-8 We might ask whether prayer is useless or whether it is unfitting to remain insistent in God's presence. This parable recommends a tenacious persistence. If the Lord is tardy in coming or in responding, it is to allow time for conversion and for faith. But the prayer of believers is not a cry in the wind. It is especially necessary during the end times, which will be a great trial for the faith and for trust in the Lord.

need for them to pray always and never to lose heart.[e] [2]He said, "In a certain town there was a judge who neither feared God nor had any respect for people. [3]In that same town there was a widow who kept coming to him and pleading, 'Grant me justice against my adversary.'[f]

[4]"For a long time he refused her request, but finally he said to himself, 'Even though I neither fear God nor have any respect for people, [5]yet because this widow keeps pestering me, I will see to it that she gets justice. Otherwise, she will keep coming and wear me out.' "[g]

[6]Then the Lord said, "You have heard what the unjust judge says. [7]Will not God, therefore, grant justice to his elect who cry out to him day and night? Will he delay in answering their pleas?[h] [8]I tell you, he will grant them justice quickly. But when the Son of Man comes, will he find faith on the earth?"

The Parable of the Pharisee and the Tax Collector.* [9]He also told the following parable to some people who prided themselves about their own righteousness and regarded others with contempt:[i] [10]"Two men went up to the temple to pray. One was a Pharisee and the other was a tax collector.[j] [11]The Pharisee stood up and said this prayer to himself: 'I thank you, God, that I am not like other people—greedy, dishonest, adulterous—or even like this tax collector.[k] [12]I fast twice a week and pay tithes on all my income.'[l]

[13]"The tax collector, however, stood some distance away and would not even raise his eyes to heaven. Rather, he kept beating his breast as he said, 'God, be merciful to me, a sinner.'[m] [14]This man, I tell you, returned to his home justified, whereas the other did not. For everyone who exalts himself will be humbled, but the one who humbles himself will be exalted."[n]

Jesus Blesses the Children.* [15][o]People were bringing even infants to Jesus so that he might touch them. When the disciples observed this, they rebuked them. [16]However, Jesus called the children to him and said, "Let the little children come to me, and do not hinder them. For it is to such as these that the kingdom of God belongs. [17]Amen, I say to you, whoever does not receive the kingdom of God like a little child will never enter it."[p]

The Rich Young Man. [18]*[q]A certain ruler asked him, "Good Teacher, what must I do to inherit eternal life?"[r] [19]Jesus said to him, "Why do you call me good? No one is good but God alone. [20]You know the commandments: 'Do not commit adultery. Do not kill. Do not steal. Do not bear false witness. Honor your father and your mother.' "[s]

[21]The man replied, "I have kept all these since I was a child." [22]On hearing this, Jesus said to him, "You need to do one further thing. Sell everything you own and distribute the money to the poor, and you will have treasure in heaven. Then come, follow me."[t] [23]But when he heard this, he became sad, because he was very rich.

Danger of Riches. [24]Jesus looked at him and said, "How difficult it is for those who are rich to enter the kingdom of God![u] [25]Indeed, it is easier for a camel to pass through the eye of a needle than for someone who is rich to enter the kingdom of God." [26]Those who heard this asked, "Then who can be saved?" [27]He replied, "What is impossible for men is possible for God."

The Reward of Renunciation. [28]Peter said to him, "We have given up our homes to follow you." [29]Jesus replied, "Amen, I say to you, there is no one who has given up house

---

e Lk 11:9ff; Isa 40:31; Rom 12:12; Col 4:2.—f Prov 25:15; Isa 1:17.—g Lk 11:8.—h Ex 22:22; Ps 88:2; Sir 35:19.—i Lk 16:15; Isa 65:5; Mt 23:28.—j Acts 3:1.—k Mt 6:5.—l Isa 58:3; Mal 3:8.—m Lk 23:48; Isa 66:2; Jer 31:19.—n Lk 14:11; Mt 23:12.—o 15ff: Mt 19:13ff; Mk 10:13-16.—p Mt 11:25.—q 18-30: Mt 19:16-29; Mk 10:17-30.—r Lk 10:25.—s Ex 20:12-16; Deut 5:16-20; Rom 13:9.—t Lk 12:33.—u Prov 11:28.

18:9-14 What Jesus criticizes is not the Pharisee's ascetical effort but his sense of self-sufficiency before God, himself, and other human beings, and his harshness toward others. On the other hand, Jesus does not approve of the everyday behavior of the tax collector, but offers his sincerity, humility, and repentance as an example. God's goodness bewilders us: from it sinners can expect compassion and grace; salvation is an unmerited and unexpected gift.

18:15-17 One must receive the kingdom as a little child, that is, as a poor person who is regarded as insignificant in society and who awaits everything from its father. One can never stop being struck by this insistence of Jesus concerning the spirit of childhood. It is a reversal of the daily norms of our lives (see Lk 9:46-48).

18:18-30 A rich young man is animated by the desire for a more personal commitment, going beyond the simple observance of the ten commandments. However, he cannot resolve himself to the first radical gesture—giving up his possessions. The Christian community retained this example as a warning. Riches, as Luke often stresses, are an obstacle to salvation. In a life encumbered by riches, there is no place for the Lord. Yet the Lord fills to the brim whoever has the courage to prefer him to everything else. Such courage is the gift of God (see Lk 12:33).

or wife or brothers or parents or children for
the sake of the kingdom of God[v] 30 who will
not receive many times as much in this age,
and eternal life in the age to come."

Jesus Predicts His Passion a Third Time.*
31 [w] Then Jesus took the Twelve aside and
said to them, "Behold, we are now going up
to Jerusalem, and everything that has been
written by the Prophets about the Son of
Man will be fulfilled. 32 He will be handed
over to the Gentiles, and he will be mocked
and insulted and spat upon.[x] 33 After they
have scourged him, they will put him to
death, and on the third day he will rise
again."[y]

34 But they understood nothing of this. Its
meaning remained obscure to them, and
they failed to comprehend what he was
telling them.

Jesus Heals a Blind Man.* 35 [z] As Jesus ap-
proached Jericho, a blind man was sitting by
the roadside begging.[a] 36 When he heard the
crowd going past, he inquired what was hap-
pening. 37 They told him, "Jesus of Nazareth
is passing by." 38 He shouted, "Jesus, Son of
David, have pity on me!"[b] 39 The people in
front rebuked him and ordered him to be
silent, but he only shouted all the louder,
"Son of David, have pity on me!"[c]

40 Jesus stopped and ordered that the man
be brought to him. And when he had come
near, Jesus asked him, 41 "What do you want
me to do for you?" He answered, "Lord, let
me receive my sight." 42 Jesus said to him,
"Receive your sight. Your faith has made you
well."[d] 43 Immediately, he received his sight
and followed Jesus, praising God. And all the
people who witnessed this also gave praise
to God.[e]

CHAPTER 19

Jesus and Zacchaeus, the Rich Tax Collector.*
1 Jesus entered Jericho and was passing
through it.[f] 2 A man there, named
Zacchaeus, was a chief tax collector and a
rich man.[g] 3 He wanted to see who Jesus
was, but since he was short in stature, he
could not see him because of the crowd.
4 Therefore, he ran ahead and climbed a
sycamore tree in order to catch a glimpse of
him for he was going to pass that way.[h]

5 When he reached that spot, Jesus looked
up and said to him, "Zacchaeus, hurry and
come down, for I must stay at your house
today."[6] Zacchaeus came down quickly and
welcomed him joyfully.

7 When the people observed this, they
began to complain, saying, "He has gone to
be the guest of a man who is a sinner."[i] 8 But
Zacchaeus stood there and said to the Lord,
"Behold, Lord, I intend to give half of every-
thing I possess to the poor, and if I have
defrauded someone of anything, I will repay
that amount four times over."[j]

9 Then Jesus said to him, "Today salvation
has come to this house, because this man
too is a son of Abraham.[k] 10 For the Son of
Man has come to seek out and to save what
was lost."[l]

The Parable of the Ten Gold Coins.*
11 [m] While the people were listening to him
speak, Jesus went on to tell them a parable,
because now he was near Jerusalem and
because they thought that the kingdom of
God might appear immediately.[n] 12 He said,
"A man of noble birth was preparing to go
to a distant country to receive a kingdom
and then return. 13 So he summoned ten of
his servants and gave them ten gold coins, *
instructing them, 'Trade with the money I
have given you until I return.'[o] 14 But the
citizens of his country hated him and sent a
delegation after him to give this message,
'We do not want this man to be our king.'

15 "When he returned after having been
made king, he sent for the servants to whom

v Lk 14:26.—w 31ff: Lk 9:22; Ps 2:2; Mt 20:17ff; Mk 10:32ff.—x Lk 23:1.—y Acts 3:18.—z 35-43: Mt 20:29-34; Mk 10:46-52.—a Lk 19:1.—b Lk 18:13.—c Mt 9:27.—d Mt 9:22.—e Lk 13:17.—f Lk 18:35.—g Mt 5:46.—h 1 Ki 10:27; 1 Chr 27:28.—i Lk 5:30.—j Lk 3:12, 13; Ex 21:37; 2 Sam 12:6.—k Mt 21:31.—l Lk 15:6, 9; Ezek 34:12, 16; Mt 18:11.—m 11-27: Mt 25:14-30.—n Lk 17:20.—o Mk 13:34.

18:31-34 Six times in Luke's Gospel Jesus refers to his tragic end, so deeply does this affect his entire work. The Prophets had borne witness to it beforehand.

18:35-43 The community retains this episode as an example of faith and witness to Jesus, Son of David, that is, the people's Messiah and Savior.

19:1-10 The lesson is obvious: it is God who saves the rich (see Lk 18:27), because he alone can change the human heart. Zacchaeus's generosity in atoning for the wrongs he has done goes beyond anything the Jewish or the Roman law could require of a judged and condemned thief.

19:11-27 This parable is unusual in that its chief personage is an aspirant to the throne, for it seems to be inspired by the story of Archelaus, who went to Rome in 4 B.C. to obtain the succession to Herod the Great in Judea, and whose return was marked by a slaughter not yet forgotten in the memory of the people.

19:13 *Gold coins:* literally, *minas;* a *mina,* was a Greek coin equal to a hundred drachmas or Roman denarii, that is, a hundred times the daily wage of a laborer. In the time of Jesus, it weighed about 350 grams of silver.

he had given the money to ascertain what
profit they had made through their trading.
16 The first came forward and said, 'Sir, your
money has increased tenfold in value.' 17 He
said to him, 'Well done, my good servant.
Because you have proved trustworthy in this
very small matter, you shall be in charge of
ten cities.' [p]

18 "Next, the second servant came forward
and said, 'Sir, your money has increased
fivefold in value.' 19 He said to him, 'You shall
be in charge of five cities.'

20 "Then the third one came forward, say-
ing, 'Sir, here is your money. I kept it
wrapped up in a handkerchief. 21 For I was
afraid of you, because you are a hard man.
You take out what you did not put down, and
you reap what you did not sow.' [q]

22 "The master said to him, 'I will con-
demn you by your own words, you wicked
servant. You knew I was a hard man, taking
out what I did not put down, and reaping
what I did not sow. [r] 23 Why then did you
not deposit my money into a bank so that
on my return I could have drawn it out
with interest?'

24 "Then he said to those standing by,
'Take the money from him and give it to the
one with the ten gold coins.' [s] 25 They said to
him, 'But sir, he already has ten gold coins.'
26 He replied, 'I tell you, to everyone who has,
more will be given, but from the one who
has not, even what he does have will be taken
away. [t] 27 But as for those enemies of mine
who did not want me for their king, bring
them here and put them to death in my
presence.' "

V: THE ACTIVITY OF JESUS AT JERUSALEM*

Jesus Enters Jerusalem as the Messiah.*
28 [u] After he had said this, Jesus proceeded
on his journey up to Jerusalem. 29 As he drew
near to Bethphage and Bethany at the place
called the Mount of Olives, he sent off two of
the disciples, saying, 30 "Go into the village
directly ahead, and upon entering it, you will
find tied there a colt on which no one has
ever ridden. Untie it and bring it here. 31 If
anyone asks you, 'Why are you untying it?'
simply say, 'The Lord needs it.' "

32 The two disciples who had been sent
went off and found everything just as he had
told them. [v] 33 As they were untying the colt,
its owners asked them, "Why are you unty-
ing the colt?" 34 They answered, "The Lord
needs it."

35 Then they brought the colt to Jesus, and
after spreading their cloaks over the colt,
they helped Jesus to mount it. 36 As he rode
along, people kept spreading their cloaks on
the road. [w] 37 And when he approached the
downward path of the Mount of Olives, the
entire multitude of his disciples began to
praise God joyfully with a loud voice for all
the mighty works they had seen him per-
form, [x] 38 proclaiming:

"Blessed is the king
who comes in the name of the Lord.
Peace in heaven
and glory in the highest heavens." [y]

39 [z] Some of the Pharisees in the crowd
said to him, "Teacher, rebuke your disci-
ples." 40 He answered, "I tell you, if they keep
silent, the stones will cry out." [a]

The Lament over Jerusalem.* 41 [b] As Jesus
drew near and beheld the city, he wept over
it, [c] 42 saying, "If only you had recognized on
this day what would bring you peace! But
now it is hidden from your sight. 43 Indeed,
the days will come upon you when your ene-
mies will raise up fortifications all around
you and hem you in on every side. [d] 44 They
will smash you to the ground, you and your
children with you, and they will not leave one
stone upon another in you, because you did
not recognize the time of your visitation." [e]

p Lk 16:10; Prov 27:18.—q Mt 25:24.—r 2 Sam 1:16; Job 15:6.—s Lk 20:16.—t Lk 8:18; Mt 13:12; Mk 4:25.—u 28-38: Mt 21:1-9; Mk 11:1-10; Jn 12:12-15.—v Lk 22:13.—w 2 Ki 9:13.—x Jn 12:18.—y Lk 13:35; Ps 118:26.—z 39f: Mt 21:15f.—a Hab 2:11.—b 41-44: Lk 12:54-56; 13:34f.—c Isa 22:4.—d Isa 29:3; Jer 6:6.—e Lk 21:6; Ps 137:9; Mt 24:2; Mk 13:2.

19:28—21:38 The Messiah reaches Jerusalem, where he is to complete God's plan. His encounter with the city is a powerful one, but will end in his rejection. The plan of God will nonetheless be carried out in a way different from human expectations: in suffering, Death, and Resurrection, in the Paschal Mystery.

19:28-40 By accepting the acclamations of his many disciples, Jesus proclaims himself to be the Messiah, the king, the son of David, whom Israel has awaited. The scene seems to be a repetition of the ceremony of Solomon's proclamation and consecration (see 1 Ki 1:33-40). The surprising thing is the modest circumstances: the colt is the mount of the poor, the mount of the ancient period of nomadism. The Old Testament imagined various scenarios for the coming of the Messiah; they were all glorious, except for one, that of Zechariah (9:9).

19:41-44 Luke alone records the incident of Jesus weeping over Jerusalem—here and in Lk 13:34, although Mt 23:21 does show Jesus grieving over it. The method mentioned by which Israel's enemies will conquer and level Jerusalem is precisely the one used by the Romans in A.D. 70.

Jesus Cleanses the Temple.* 45 [f]Then he entered the temple and began to drive out those who were engaging in selling, 46 saying to them, "It is written,

'My house shall be a house of prayer,'
but you have made it a den of thieves." [g]

47 Every day he was teaching in the temple. But the chief priests, the scribes, and the leaders of the people plotted to kill him. [h] 48 However, they were unable to do so because all the people hung on his every word.

A: Verbal Clashes*

CHAPTER 20

The Authority of Jesus Questioned.* 1 [i]One day as Jesus was teaching in the temple and proclaiming the good news, [j] the chief priests and scribes, accompanied by the elders, approached and 2 said to him, "Tell us by what authority you are doing these things. Or who is it that gave you this authority?" [k] 3 He said to them in reply, "I will also ask you one question. Tell me: 4 Did John's baptism originate from heaven or from men?" [l]

5 The question caused them to discuss it among themselves, saying, "If we say: 'From heaven,' he will say, 'Why did you not believe him?' 6 But if we say: 'From men,' all the people will stone us, for they are convinced that John was a prophet." [m]

7 Therefore, they answered that they did not know where it came from. 8 And Jesus said to them, "Then neither shall I tell you by what authority I do these things."

The Parable of the Tenants.* 9 [n]Then Jesus began to tell the people this parable: "A man planted a vineyard, leased it to tenants, and went off on a journey for a long period. [o]

10 "When the time arrived, he sent a servant to the tenants to receive his share of the produce of the vineyard. But the tenants beat the servant and sent him away empty-handed. 11 Again, he sent another servant, but him they also beat and treated shamefully and sent away empty-handed. 12 Then he sent a third servant, but him too they wounded and cast out.

13 "Then the owner of the vineyard said, 'What shall I do? I will send my beloved son. Perhaps they will respect him.' 14 But when the tenants saw him, they said to one another, 'This is the heir. Let us kill him so that the inheritance will be ours.' 15 And so they threw him out of the vineyard and killed him.

"What then will the owner of the vineyard do to them? 16 He will come and put those tenants to death and give the vineyard to others."

When the people heard this, they said, "God forbid!" [p] 17 But Jesus looked directly at them and said, "Then what is the meaning of that which is written:

'The stone that the builders rejected
has become the cornerstone'? [q]

18 Everyone who falls on that stone will be broken into pieces, and the one on whom it falls will be crushed." [r]

19 The scribes and the chief priests realized that this parable was directed at them, and they wanted to seize him at that very hour, but they feared the people. [s]

God or Caesar.* 20 [t]So they watched him closely and sent spies who pretended to be honorable men. They intended to trap Jesus in something he might say so that they could hand him over to the authority and jurisdiction of the governor. [u]

21 They posed this question to him: "Teacher, we know that you say and teach what is right. Moreover, you show no partiality to anyone but teach the way of God in accordance with the truth. [v] 22 Is it lawful or not for us to pay taxes to Caesar?"

f 45f: Mt 21:12f; Mk 11:15ff; Jn 2:14ff.—g Isa 56:7; Jer 7:11.—h Mk 11:18; Jn 18:20.—i 1-8: Mt 21:23-27; Mk 11:27-33.—j Lk 8:1.—k Jn 2:18; Acts 4:7.—l Mk 1:4.—m Lk 7:29.—n 9-19: Mt 21:33-46; Mk 12:1-12.—o Isa 5:1-7; Mt 25:14.—p Lk 19:27.—q Ps 118:22; Isa 28:16.—r Isa 8:14-15.—s Lk 11:53; 19:47.—t 20-26: Mt 22:15-22; Mk 12:13-17.—u Mt 27:2.—v Jn 3:2.

19:45-48 Jesus demands respect for the temple and installs himself in it to proclaim the message of God. It is thus that he conceives and exercises the royal authority of the Messiah. Like the Prophets, he refuses to allow religion to deteriorate into a business affair.

20:1—21:4 "Who gave you this authority?" Sooner or later, such a question was bound to be asked of Jesus. However, coming from the members of the Jewish high tribunal, it is nothing more than a snare. Jesus places himself in solidarity with John the Baptist, the envoy of God. If they do not have the courage to speak about the dead prophet, how can they be ready to loyally confront the response of Christ? He reduces them to silence, debate being useless.

20:1-8 See note on Mk 11:27-33.

20:9-19 When we read ch. 5 of Isaiah, we understand that it is God who puts the authorities of this people on trial. The parable sums up in a few words the entire history of conflict between the leaders and God's messengers; is not the last messenger, that is, the heir, Jesus himself? See also note on Mt 21:33-46.

20:20-26 The tribute was a tax collected by the Roman occupiers. To justify its payment meant collaborating with the enemy of the people; to disallow its payment meant labeling oneself as rebellious in the eyes of the Romans. The snare seems to be inescapable, but Jesus foils the plan by loudly proclaiming the absolute primacy of God (see Lk 12:31). See also note on Mt 22:15-22.

23 Jesus saw through their duplicity and said to them, 24 "Show me a coin. * Whose image is this, and whose inscription?" They replied, "Caesar's." 25 He said to them, "Give to Caesar what is due to Caesar, and to God what is due to God."[w] 26 They found they could not trap him by anything he said in the presence of the people, and, stunned at his reply, they fell silent.

Marriage and the Resurrection.* 27 [x] Then some Sadducees, who assert that there is no resurrection, approached him and posed this question:[y] 28 "Teacher, Moses wrote down for us that if a man's brother dies, having a wife but no children, the man must marry his brother's wife and raise up children for his brother.[z] 29 Now there were seven brothers. The first married a woman but died childless. 30 Then the second 31 and the third married the widow, and it was the same with all seven: they all died leaving no children. 32 Last of all, the woman also died. 33 Now at the resurrection, whose wife will the woman be, inasmuch as all seven had her?"

34 Jesus said to them, "The children of this age marry and are given in marriage, 35 but those who are judged worthy of taking part in the age to come and in the resurrection of the dead will neither marry nor be given in marriage.[a] 36 They are no longer subject to death, for they are like angels; and they are the children of God because they are children of the resurrection.

37 "That the dead are raised Moses himself showed in the account about the bush where he calls the Lord the God of Abraham, the God of Isaac, and the God of Jacob.[b] 38 He is not the God of the dead, but of the living, for in his sight all are alive."

39 Some of the scribes then said, "Teacher, you have answered well." 40 And they no longer dared to ask him anything.[c]

Jesus Is Lord.* 41 [d] Then Jesus said to them, "How can they say that the Christ is the Son of David? 42 For David himself says in the Book of Psalms:

'The LORD said to my Lord:
"Sit at my right hand
43 until I make your enemies your footstool." '[e]

44 David thus calls him 'Lord'; so how can he be his son?"

Denunciation of the Scribes.* 45 While all the people were listening, Jesus said to his disciples, 46 "Beware of the scribes who like to walk around in long robes and who love to be greeted respectfully in the marketplaces, and to have the best seats in the synagogues and the places of honor at banquets.[f] 47 They devour the houses of widows, while for the sake of appearance they recite lengthy prayers. They will receive the severest possible condemnation."

CHAPTER 21

The Poor Widow's Offering.* 1 [g] Looking up, Jesus saw wealthy people putting their offerings into the treasury,[h] 2 and he also noticed a poor widow putting in two copper coins. 3 He said: "Truly I tell you, this poor widow has given more than all the rest. 4 For the others have all contributed out of their abundance, but she out of her poverty has given all that she had to live on."[i]

B: The Destruction of the Temple and the Return of Christ*

Jesus Announces the Destruction of the Temple.* 5 [j] When some people were talking

w Lk 23:2; Rom 13:7.—x 27-38: Mt 22:23-33; Mk 12:18-27.—y Acts 23:8; 1 Cor 15:12.—z Deut 25:5.—a Phil 3:11.—b Ex 3:6.—c Mt 22:46; Mk 12:34.—d 41-44: Mt 22:41-45; Mk 12:35ff.—e Ps 110:1.—f Lk 11:43; Mt 23:6f; Mk 12:38ff.—g 1-4: Mk 12:41-44.—h Jn 8:20.—i 2 Cor 8:12.—j 5-19: Mt 24:1-14; Mk 13:1-13.

20:24 *Coin:* i.e., a *denarius,* the normal day's wage for a laborer at that time.

20:27-40 The party of the Jewish high priests had not yet accepted the belief in the resurrection that had been proclaimed for two or three centuries (Dan 12:2-3) and that the Pharisees had accepted (see Acts 23:8). When the present life is taken as a model of the future life, the reality of the resurrection is misunderstood, since the resurrection radically transforms the human condition.

20:41-44 Most Jews expected the Messiah to be simply an heir of God's chosen king (see 2 Sam 7:1-17). Citing an ancient royal psalm, Jesus conveys that the Messiah is of divine origin and that he will bring a kingdom that transcends anything we might ordinarily imagine.

20:45-47 Jesus reproaches the teachers of religious thought for their vanity (Lk 11:43), greed (Lk 16:14), and artificial and ostentatious piety (Lk 18:11-12).

21:1-4 See note on Mk 12:41-44.

21:5-38 Scenes of terror and visions of hope alternate in this great discourse. If we are to understand its tone and vocabulary, we must put ourselves in the atmosphere created by various terrifying and magnificent pages of the Old Testament. On the eve of the catastrophe that destroyed both Jerusalem, for the first time, and the state of Israel in 587 B.C., some prophets had a presentiment of the spiritual ruin of the people and had warned them, with harsh invectives, of future punishments. Later on, people began to ask about the ultimate destiny of the world and humanity; this created a restlessness that was eschatological, that is, concerned with the ultimate end, the last times.

In the "apocalypses" or "revelations," some authors imagined awe-inspiring scenes of wars, disasters, and judgment, which would usher in the coming of God and the salvation of the people. These accounts, which are to be read in accordance with their particular literary genre, always remain bewildering.

21:5-6 Around the year 19 B.C., Herod the Great undertook a splendid reconstruction of the temple. The very magnificence of the restored temple caused a sense of self-reliance and presumption (see Lk 13:34-35; 19:46; Jer 7:1-15; 26; Ezek 8:11; Mic 3:9-12).

about how the temple was adorned with
beautiful stones and votive offerings, Jesus
remarked, 6 “As for all these things that you
are gazing at now, the time will come when
not one stone here will be left upon another;
everything will be thrown down.” [k]

The Signs of the End. 7 * They then asked
him, “Teacher, when will this happen? And
what will be the sign that it is about to take
place?” 8 He answered, “Take care not to be
deceived. For many will come in my name,
saying, ‘I am he,’ and ‘The time is near.’ Do
not follow them. [l] 9 And when you hear of
wars and insurrections, do not be terrified,
for those things are bound to take place first,
but the end will not follow immediately.”

10 Then he added, “Nation will rise against
nation and kingdom against kingdom. [m]
11 There will be tremendous earthquakes,
famines, and plagues in various places, as
well as dreadful portents and great signs
from heaven. [n]

The Coming Persecution. 12 [o] “But before all
this happens, they will seize you and
persecute you. You will be handed over to
synagogues and imprisoned, and you will
be brought before kings and governors
because of my name. 13 This will give you
an opportunity to bear witness to me. [p]
14 But do not even consider preparing your
defense beforehand, 15 for I myself will give
you a depth of wisdom and eloquence that
none of your adversaries will be able to
resist or contradict. [q]

16 “You will be betrayed even by parents
and brothers, relatives and friends, and
some of you will be put to death. [r] 17 You will
be hated by all because of my name, 18 but
not a hair of your head will be lost. [s] 19 By
standing firm you will gain life. [t]

The Great Trial.* 20 [u] “When you see
Jerusalem surrounded by armies, you may
be certain that her desolation is near. 21 Then
those who are in Judea must flee to the
mountains, and those who are within the city
must escape from its boundaries, and those
who are in country areas must not return. [v]
22 For those will be days of retribution when
all that is written will come to pass. [w]

23 “Woe to those who are pregnant and
those who are nursing infants in those days.
For there will be great distress on the earth,
and terrible wrath shall afflict this people.
24 They will fall by the sword and be carried
away as captives among all the nations, and
Jerusalem will be trampled underfoot by the
Gentiles until the times of the Gentiles have
been fulfilled. [x]

The Coming of the Son of Man. 25 * [y] “There
will be signs in the sun, the moon, and the
stars, and on earth nations will be in great
distress, bewildered at the roaring of the sea
and its waves. [z] 26 Men will grow faint with
terror and apprehension at what is coming
upon the earth, for the powers of the heav-
ens will be shaken. 27 And then they will see
the Son of Man coming in a cloud with
power and great glory. [a] 28 When these things
begin to take place, look up and hold your
heads high, because the time of your
redemption is drawing near.” [b]

The Parable of the Fig Tree. 29 [c] Then he told
them this parable: “Look at the fig tree or
indeed at any other tree. 30 As soon as it
begins to bud, you know that summer is
already near. 31 In the same way, when you
see these things come to pass, know that the
kingdom of God is near. 32 Amen, I say to
you, this generation will not pass away until
all these things have taken place. * [d]
33 Heaven and earth will pass away, but my
words will never pass away. [e]

k Lk 19:44.—l Lk 17:23.—m 2 Chr 15:6; Isa 19:2.—n Isa 29:6; Joel 3:3.—o 12-15: Lk 12:11f; Mt 10:17-20; Jn 15:20.—p Phil 1:12.—q Acts 6:10.—r Lk 12:52, 53.—s Mt 10:30.—t Heb 10:36, 39.—u 20-23: Mt 24:15-20; Mk 13:14-18.—v Lk 17:31.—w Isa 63:4; Dan 9:24-27; Hos 9:7.—x Isa 5:5; Dan 8:13; Rev 11:2.—y 25ff: Ps 65:8ff; Mt 24:29f; Mk 13:24ff.—z Isa 13:10; Ezek 32:7; Joel 4:15; 2 Pet 3:10, 12.—a Dan 7:13.—b Lk 18:7.—c 29-33: Mt 24:32-35; Mk 13:28-31.—d Lk 9:27; 11:50; Mt 16:28.—e Isa 40:8.

21:7-19 For a Jew, the destruction of the temple inaugurates the great tribulation of the end times. We understand that the disciples are worried. Jesus gives them signs: those more distant (vv. 10-11) will be taken up again even later on (vv. 25-26); those closer describe the events of the troubled years 66-70: appearances of false messiahs, civil wars and struggles, persecution of Christians. This persecution is a privileged sign of the coming of the kingdom of God, and it is seen to be severe. But let those who bear witness to Christ take courage, for they will not be abandoned. The Passion is the way to glory for the Christian community as it is for the Lord. Courage will be given to them to announce the essence of the message: Jesus Christ dead, risen, and to come.

21:20-24 The evils that overtake the holy city are like a judgment of God upon it. But the tragic fate of Jerusalem and its temple inaugurates the laborious period in which is born the new world until all the pagans have heard the Good News of salvation and Israel itself is converted (see Rom 11:25-27).

21:25-33 At the end of the final crisis, which is described in the violent images dear to the Prophets and the authors of the apocalypses (see Isa 13:10; 24:23; 34:4; Ezek 32:7-8; Joel 4:15), Jesus, the victorious Christ, will come to judge the world and deliver those who have remained faithful and are ready to welcome him (see Dan 7:13). The signs, especially persecutions, are pledges of hope and deliverance (see Rom 8:23; Eph 1:14; 4:30).

21:32 In the apocalyptic genre, a “generation” signifies an age of the world, a stage in God’s plan.

Exhortation To Be Vigilant.* 34 “Be on your guard lest your hearts be weighed down by carousing and drunkenness and the anxieties of this life and that day will catch you unawares,[f] 35 like a trap. For that day will come upon everyone in the world. 36 Be vigilant at all times, praying for the strength to survive all those things that will take place and to stand in the presence of the Son of Man.”[g]

Jesus’ Last Days in Jerusalem.* 37 Each day Jesus was teaching in the temple, but every evening he would go forth and spend the night on the hill called the Mount of Olives.[h] 38 And all the people would rise early every morning to listen to him in the temple.[i]

VI: THE PASSION AND RESURRECTION*

CHAPTER 22

The Conspiracy against Jesus.* 1 [j] Now the feast of Unleavened Bread, known as the Passover, was drawing near, 2 and the chief priests and the scribes were looking for some way to put Jesus to death, for they were afraid of the people.

Judas Betrays Jesus.* 3 Then Satan entered into Judas, called Iscariot, who was one of the Twelve.[k] 4 [l] And he went to the chief priests and temple guards to discuss how he might betray Jesus to them.[m] 5 They were delighted and agreed to give him money.[n] 6 He accepted their offer and began to look for an opportunity to betray him to them when no crowd was present.

A: The Last Supper*

The Preparations for the Passover.* 7 [o] When the day of the feast of Unleavened Bread arrived, on which the Passover lamb had to be sacrificed,[p] 8 Jesus sent Peter and John, saying, “Go and make the preparations for us to eat the Passover.”[q] 9 They asked him, “Where do you want us to make the preparations?”

10 He replied, “When you enter the city, a man will meet you carrying a jug of water. Follow him into the house that he enters 11 and say to the master of the house, ‘The Teacher says this to you: “Where is the room where I can eat the Passover with my disciples?” ’ 12 Then he will show you a large upper room that is furnished. Make the preparations there.” 13 They went forth and found everything just as he had told them, and they prepared the Passover.[r]

The Last Supper.* 14 When the hour came, Jesus took his place at table along with the apostles.[s] 15 He said to them, “I have eagerly desired to eat this Passover with you before I suffer. 16 For I tell you that from this moment on I shall never eat it again until it is fulfilled in the kingdom of God.”

17 Then he took a cup, and after giving thanks he said, “Take this and share it among yourselves. 18 For I tell you that from this moment I will not drink of the fruit of the vine until the kingdom of God comes.”[t]

---

f Lk 12:40; Mk 4:19; 1 Thes 5:3.—g Mt 26:41; Eph 6:18.—h Lk 19:47; Mk 11:19.—i Jn 8:2.—j 1f: Mt 26:2-5; Mk 14:1f; Jn 11:47-53.—k Jn 13:2, 27.—l 4f: Mt 26:14ff; Mk 14:10f.—m Acts 4:1.—n Zec 11:12.—o 7-13: Mt 26:17-19; Mk 14:12-16.—p Ex 12:18-20; Deut 16:5-8.—q Acts 3:1, 11.—r Lk 19:32.—s Mk 14:17-18.—t Mt 26:29; Mk 14:25.

21:34-36 Since in Luke’s perspective the end of the world is not considered to be imminent, the exhortation to be vigilant voiced here is more pressing so that the delay may not numb the heart of the Christian. At the same time, there is an invitation to pray that the day of the Lord may not come unexpectedly and find us unprepared to appear before the divine Judge.

21:37-38 During the final week of his life (Sunday to Thurs-day), Jesus taught in the temple in the morning, and all the people came to hear him.

22:1—24:53 The salvation of human beings is accomplished in a unique event: Christ’s Death and Resurrection. This is the Paschal mystery. The account that follows is fashioned by this principal testimony; hence it must be read as a unified whole. From the beginnings of the Church, this is the Gospel, the essence of the Christian announcement.

22:1-2 Before the episodes of the Passion unfold, the plot thickens with the adversaries of Jesus. The leaders of the people take the initiative in the plot, and the traitor serves them as an instrument, but it is the spirit of evil who initiates the last combat.

22:3-6 See note on Mt 26:14-16.

22:7-38 Now we see the initiative of Jesus, which appears so clearly in this last supper. The account is an integral part of the Passion, i.e., the Death and Resurrection of Jesus, for the Church that announces the Gospel of Christ the Savior is also the Christian community that celebrates the Eucharist, the memorial of salvation. Jesus enters the decisive event; this last act is, as it were, the summary of his every act and word: sharing, offering, gift, presence, and covenant of God in the midst of his followers.

Luke has placed actions and words of Jesus here that the other evangelists report in other contexts. This is so the community can meditate on them each time it assembles to break the bread of the Lord. He thus leaves us a liturgical rule (the text of the Eucharistic institution) and, connected with it, communitary and missionary directives.

22:7-13 Jesus takes the initiative, freely and fully, for this last Passover of the old covenant, this repast that inaugurates a new covenant.

22:14-18 For the Jews, the Passover is the memorial of the liberation of the people (see Ex 12); for Jesus, it prefigures the Messianic Banquet in which all human beings are reunited in the presence of God. All his hope for happiness becomes a promise for believers.

Jesus Gives His Body and His Blood.*
19 [u] Then he took bread, and after giving
thanks he broke it and gave it to them,
saying, "This is my body, which will be
given for you. Do this in memory of me."
20 And he did the same with the cup after
supper, saying, "This cup is the new
covenant in my blood, which will be
poured out for you. [v]

The Betrayer Foretold.* 21 [w] "But behold,
the hand of the one who will betray me is
here with me on the table. [x] 22 The Son of
Man goes on his appointed path, but woe
to that man by whom he is betrayed." [y]
23 Then they began to question among
themselves as to which one of them might
do this.

The Disciples Are To Serve on Earth.* 24 Then
a dispute also broke out among them as to
which one of them should be considered the
greatest. [z] 25 [a] Jesus said to them, "The kings
of the Gentiles lord it over them, and those
who exercise authority over them are given
the title of 'Benefactor.' *

26 "But it must not be so with you. Rather,
the greatest among you should be like the
youngest, and the leader must be like the one
who serves. [b] 27 For who is greater—the
one seated at table or the one who serves?
Surely, the one who sits at table. And yet I
am in your midst as one who serves. [c]

Judges of the Twelve Tribes.* 28 "You are the
ones who have stood by my side in my tri-
als, [d] 29 and now I confer on you a kingdom
just as my Father has conferred one on me. [e]
30 In my kingdom, you will eat and drink at
my table, and you will sit on thrones, judging
the twelve tribes of Israel. * [f]

Peter's Denial Foretold.* 31 "Simon, Simon,
behold, Satan has desired to sift all of you
like wheat. [g] 32 But I have prayed that your
own faith may not fail. And once you have
turned back, you must strengthen your
brethren." [h] 33 Simon said to him, "Lord, I
am ready to go with you to prison and to
death." [i] 34 Jesus replied, "I tell you, Peter,
before the cock crows today, you will deny
three times that you know me." [j]

Instructions for the Time of Crisis.* 35 Then
Jesus said to them, "When I sent you forth
without a money bag or sack or sandals,
were you ever in need of anything?" They
answered, "No, not a thing." [k] 36 He then
remarked, "But now, the one who has a
money bag should take it with him, as well
as a sack. And if you do not have a sword, sell
your cloak and purchase one.

37 "For I tell you that this Scripture must
be fulfilled in me: 'He was numbered with
the wicked.' Indeed, everything written
about me is being fulfilled." [l] 38 They said,
"See, Lord, here are two swords." He said to
them, "That is enough."

B: The Passion

The Agony in the Garden.* 39 [m] Jesus then
went forth and made his way, as was his
custom, to the Mount of Olives, and the
disciples followed him. [n] 40 When he reached
the place, he said to them, "Pray that you
may not enter into temptation." [o] 41 After
withdrawing from them about a stone's
throw, he knelt down and prayed, [p] 42 saying,

u 19f: Mt 26:26ff; Mk 14:22ff; 1 Cor 11:23ff.—v Ex 24:8; Isa 42:6.—w 21ff: Mt 26:20-25; Mk 14:17-21; Jn 13:21-30.—x Ps 41:10.—y Acts 2:23.—z Lk 9:46; Mk 9:34.—a 25ff: Mt 20:25-28; Mk 10:42ff.—b 1 Pet 5:5.—c Jn 13:4-15.—d Jn 15:27.—e 2 Tim 2:12.—f Mt 19:28; Rev 3:21.—g Job 1:6-12; Am 9:9.—h Jn 17:9, 15.—i Acts 21:13.—j Lk 22:61; Mt 26:33ff; Mk 14:29ff; Jn 13:36ff.—k Lk 10:4; Mt 10:9.—l Lk 23:32; Isa 53:12.—m 39-46: Mt 26:30, 36-46; Mk 14:26, 32-42.—n Jn 18:2.—o Mt 6:13.—p Lk 18:11.

22:19-20 In a prophetic gesture Jesus proclaims and establishes the new covenant between God and humanity (see Ex 24:8; Jer 31:31), which he is preparing to seal by his freely accepted sacrifice. In this action, by changing the bread and wine into his body and blood (see 1 Cor 10:6; 11:23-27), he institutes the Eucharist, which calls to mind and renders present to the gathered community his act of love for humanity (see Acts 2:42,46). Along with Paul, Luke has preserved for us what is perhaps one of the earliest texts of the first Christian Eucharists.

22:21-23 The announcement of Judas's plan stresses the initiative of Jesus, who does not deviate from his sacrifice. Celebrating the Eucharist, believers and the leaders of the community must question themselves concerning their loyalty toward the Lord.

22:24-27 To celebrate the Eucharist means to abandon one's search for honor and to discover that all authority in the Christian community has no other title except that of service.

22:25 *Benefactor:* a term often used for leaders of pagan nations.

22:28-30 See note on Mt 19:27-30.

22:30 The image, drawn from the Jewish tradition, signifies a privileged share in the glory of the Messiah.

22:31-34 It is not in the quality of her human leaders but in the prayer of Jesus that the Church finds the assurance of perseverance in the faith.

22:35-38 A time of happiness is ending. Henceforth, the Church must confront trials. And she must not think of defending herself with the weapons employed by societies to achieve their freedom or ensure their interests.

22:39-46 Tempted to refuse the terrible and humiliating trial of the cross, Jesus struggles in prayer to accept the will of the Father. The divine aid that he receives, as once Elijah did (see 1 Ki 19:7-8), does not mitigate the tragedy of the moment. This passage remains one of the great texts on the distress of human beings in the face of their death. It is intended to be a lesson, as is emphasized, from its beginning to its end, by the repeated invitation to pray so as not to be the prey of a temptation that seems to be all-consuming.

"Father, if you are willing, take this cup from me. Yet not my will but yours be done."[q]

43 * Then an angel from heaven appeared to him and gave him strength.[r] 44 In his anguish, he prayed so fervently that his sweat became like great drops of blood falling on the ground.

45 When he rose from prayer and returned to the disciples, he found them sleeping, exhausted by grief. 46 He said to them, "Why are you sleeping? Get up and pray that you may not enter into temptation."

Jesus Is Betrayed and Arrested.* 47 [s] While he was still speaking, a crowd of men suddenly approached, and the one called Judas, one of the Twelve, was leading them. He came up to Jesus to kiss him, 48 but Jesus said, "Judas, would you betray the Son of Man with a kiss?"

49 When Jesus' disciples realized what was about to happen, they asked, "Lord, should we strike with our swords?" 50 And one of them struck a servant of the high priest, slicing off his right ear. 51 But Jesus said, "Stop! No more of this!" He then touched the servant's ear and healed him.

52 Then Jesus said to the chief priests, the officers of the temple guard, and the elders who had come for him, "Why are you coming forth with swords and clubs as though I were a bandit? 53 [t] When I was with you day after day in the temple, you did not raise a hand against me. But this is the hour for you and the power of darkness." *

Peter Denies Jesus.* 54 [u] Then they arrested Jesus and led him away. They brought him into the house of the high priest, and Peter followed at a distance.[v] 55 Lighting a fire in the middle of the courtyard, they sat around it, and Peter sat with them.

56 A servant girl saw him sitting by the fire, looked closely at him, and said, "This man also was with him." 57 But he denied it, saying, "Woman, I do not know him." 58 A short time later, someone else saw him and said, "You too are one of them," but Peter replied, "No, I am not."

59 About an hour later, another person strongly insisted, "This man was unquestionably with him, for he is a Galilean."[w] 60 Peter said, "My friend, I do not know what you are talking about." At that very moment, while he was still speaking, a cock crowed, 61 and the Lord turned and looked at Peter. Then Peter recalled the word that the Lord had spoken to him: "Before the cock crows today, you will deny me three times."[x] 62 And he went out and wept uncontrollably.

63 [y] The men who were guarding Jesus began to mock him and to beat him. 64 They also blindfolded him and kept asking him, "Prophesy! Who hit you?" 65 And they continued to taunt him with insult after insult.

Jesus before the Sanhedrin.* 66 [z] When the dawn came, the council of the elders of the people, both the chief priests and the scribes, assembled, and they brought him before their Sanhedrin. *[a] 67 Then they said, "If you are the Christ, tell us!" He replied, "If I tell you, you will not believe; 68 and if I question you, you will not answer.[b] 69 But from now on, the Son of Man will be seated at the right hand of the power of God."[c]

70 All of them asked, "Are you then the Son of God?" He replied, "It is you who say that I am."[d] 71 Then they said, "What need

q Acts 21:14.—r Mt 4:11.—s 47-53: Mt 26:47-56; Mk 14:43-50; Jn 18:3-11.—t Mt 8:12; Jn 12:27.—u 54-62: Mt 26:58, 69-75; Mk 14:54, 66-72; Jn 18:15-18, 25ff.—v Mt 26:57.—w Lk 23:6.—x Lk 22:34; Mt 26:34; Mk 14:30; Jn 13:38.—y 63f: Mt 26:67ff; Mk 14:65; Jn 18:22-23.—z 66-71: Mt 26:59-66; Mk 14:55-64; Jn 10:24-25.—a Mt 27:1; Mk 15:1.—b Lk 20:3-8.—c Ps 110:1.—d Lk 23:3; Wis 2:13; Mt 27:11; Jn 10:30, 36.

22:43-44 These two verses are not found in some early mss.

22:47-53 Immediately cutting short any resistance on the part of his disciples, Jesus heals the servant wounded by one of them—this is the single miracle in the account of the Passion. It is typical of Luke that the servant be healed (for tradition holds that Luke was a physician).

22:53 All the events happen under the sign of Satan, who has stirred up the powers of darkness against Jesus.

22:54-65 Luke seems to report the true chronology of the events more exactly than Matthew and Mark. After his arrest, Jesus is quickly brought to the house of the high priest, where Annas his predecessor most likely also dwelled. Annas interrogates him but in a private manner (Jn 18:12-24). While Jesus is waiting for the trial, which according to Luke took place only in the morning, the guards pass time by insulting him and making fun of him.

Peter finds himself in the same courtyard and, recognized by the bystanders, denies his Master. Jesus, who has probably heard everything from where he stood, looks at him (a point mentioned only by Luke), strengthening him in his faith that had been profoundly shaken (v. 61). Note how Luke does not emphasize the crescendo of the denials. Rather, he attenuates them, and moreover does not speak of curses and oaths.

22:66-71 In contrast to Matthew and Mark, Luke does not mention the false testimonies brought against Jesus. In any case, the authorities have resolved to put him to death and seek only to have their decision confirmed. Jesus speaks solemnly about his mission and his person. He is the Envoy of God, united with him in a very particular way, and his kingdom will be inaugurated henceforth, from his Resurrection (v. 69; Ps 110:1; Dan 7:13).

22:66 *Sanhedrin:* see note on Mk 14:55.

do we have for any further testimony? We have heard it ourselves from his own lips."

CHAPTER 23

Jesus before Pilate.* 1 Then the entire assembly rose and brought Jesus before Pilate. [e] 2 [f] They began to accuse him, saying, "We charge this man with subverting our nation, opposing the payment of taxes to Caesar, and claiming that he is the Christ, a king." [g] 3 Pilate asked him, "Are you the king of the Jews?" He replied, "You have said so." [h]

4 Pilate then said to the chief priests and the crowds, "I find no evidence of a crime in this man." [i] 5 But they continued to insist, saying, "He is stirring up the people by his teaching throughout all Judea, from Galilee, where he started, all the way to here." [j]

6 When Pilate heard this, he asked if the man was a Galilean, [k] 7 and upon learning that he came under Herod's jurisdiction, he sent him to Herod who was also in Jerusalem at that time.

Jesus before Herod.* 8 Herod was delighted when he saw Jesus, for he had heard about him and had been hoping for some time to see him and perhaps to witness him perform some sign. [l] 9 He questioned him at length, but Jesus gave him no reply.

10 The chief priests and the scribes meanwhile were present, and they vehemently made accusations against him. 11 Herod and his soldiers treated him with contempt and mocked him. Then Herod had him clothed in an elegant robe and sent him back to Pilate. [m] 12 That very day Herod and Pilate became friends, although previously they had been enemies. [n]

Jesus before Pilate Again. 13 * Pilate then summoned the chief priests and the rulers and the people, 14 and said to them, "You brought this man before me and accused him of inciting the people to rebellion. I have examined him here in your presence and have not found him guilty of any of the charges you have brought against him. [o] 15 Nor did Herod, for he has sent him back to us. It is clear that he has done nothing deserving of death. 16 Therefore, I will have him scourged and then release him." [p]

Jesus Is Condemned to Death. [17 Now Pilate was obliged to release one man to them at the time of the festival.] * 18 [q] And then the crowd all shouted in unison, "Away with this man! Release Barabbas to us!" [r] 19 (He had been imprisoned for an insurrection that had occurred in the city as well as for murder.)

20 In his desire to release Jesus, Pilate again pleaded with them, 21 but, they continued to shout, "Crucify him! Crucify him!" 22 A third time he addressed them: "Why? What evil has he done? I have not found in him any crime that deserves death. Therefore, I will have him scourged and let him go."

23 However, with loud shouts they continued to insist that he should be crucified, and their voices prevailed. 24 Pilate ordered that what they wanted was to be granted. [s] 25 He released the man they asked for, who had been thrown into prison for insurrection and murder, and he handed over Jesus to them to deal with as they wished.

The Way of the Cross.* 26 As they led him away, they seized a man from Cyrene named Simon, who was returning from the country. They put the cross on his back and forced him to carry it behind Jesus. [t] 27 A large number of people followed Jesus,

---

e Mt 27:1f; Jn 18:28.—f 2-6: Lk 20:20-26; Mt 27:11-14; Mk 15:2-5; Jn 18:29-38.—g Lk 20:22-25; Jn 19:12; Acts 17:7; 24:5.—h Mt 27:11; Mk 15:2; Jn 18:33.—i Mt 27:23; 2 Cor 5:21; 1 Tim 6:13.—j Mk 1:14.—k Lk 22:59.—l Lk 9:9.—m Mk 15:17-19.—n Acts 4:27.—o Jn 19:4.—p Jn 19:1; 2 Cor 11:23.—q 18-25: Mt 27:15-26; Mk 15:7-15; Jn 18:39—19:16.—r Acts 21:35.—s Acts 3:14f.—t Lk 14:27; Mt 27:31f; Mk 15:20f; Jn 19:17.

23:1-7 The Roman governor, who usually resided at Caesarea in Palestine, was in the religious capital at the time when the Passover was being celebrated. The religious leaders accuse Jesus before him as the civil power. Twisting the reality (see Lk 21:20-26), they invent political wrongs so as to have Jesus put to death. From the beginning the Roman governor is convinced of Jesus' innocence, and he would prefer to extricate himself from this case and give it to others, for it could create nothing but trouble for him with the people and the leaders.

23:8-12 Also present in Jerusalem was Herod Antipas, ruler of Galilee, a man interested in extraordinary phenomena, ready to be scornful of them, and unwilling to accept any responsibility (see Lk 9:9; Acts 4:27).

23:13-25 Pilate is convinced that the accused is innocent. But he proposes to punish him so that the authorities might have the impression of having been heard. Finally, he yields to violence. Luke emphasizes above all the decisive responsibility of the leaders of the people. See notes on Mt 27:11-26; 27:11; 27:14; 27:24; 27:25.

23:17 Many manuscripts add this verse, probably taken from Mt 27:15 or Mk 15:6.

23:26-31 In place of solitude, Luke speaks of numerous people who take pity on Jesus; the people are already distancing themselves from the ignoble decision of their leaders. This recalls the conversion announced by the prophet Zechariah (Zec 12:10-14). But Jesus is haunted by a sorrowful vision: the ruin of Jerusalem and the official religion in which the Word of God has no effect. See also note on Mk 15:21.

among them many women who were
mourning and lamenting over him. [u]
[28] But he turned to them and said,
"Daughters of Jerusalem, do not weep for
me. Weep rather for yourselves and for your
children. [v] [29] For behold, the days are coming
when people will say, 'Blessed are the bar-
ren, the wombs that never bore children and
the breasts that never nursed.' [w] [30] Then they
will begin to say to the mountains, 'Fall on
us!' and to the hills, 'Cover us!' [x] [31] For if they
do these things when the wood is green,
what will happen when it is dry?" [y]

Jesus Is Crucified.* [32] There were also two
others, both criminals, who were led away
to be executed with him. [z] [33] [a] When they
came to the place called The Skull, they
crucified * Jesus there along with the two
criminals, one on his right and the other on
his left. [34] Then Jesus said, "Father, forgive
them, for they do not know what they are
doing." * And they cast lots to divide his
garments. [b]
[35] [c] The people stood there watching. *
Meanwhile, the rulers jeered at him and
said, "He saved others. Let him save him-
self if he is the Christ of God, the Chosen
One." [d] [36] Even the soldiers mocked him.
As they came forward to offer him sour
wine, [e] [37] they said, "If you are the King of
the Jews, save yourself!" [38] There was also
an inscription above his head that said,
"This is the King of the Jews." [f]
[39] One of the criminals hanging there
taunted Jesus, saying, "Are you not the
Christ? Save yourself and us!" [g] [40] But the
other rebuked him, "Have you no fear of
God, since you are under the same sen-
tence? [41] In our case, we have been con-
demned justly, for we are getting what we
deserve for our deeds. But this man has
committed no wrong." [42] Then he said,
"Jesus, remember me when you come into
your kingdom." [43] Jesus said to him, "Amen,
I say to you, today you will be with me in
Paradise." * [h]

Jesus Dies on the Cross.* [44] [i] It was now
about noon, and darkness came over the
whole land until three in the afternoon, [j]
[45] for the sun was darkened. Then the veil of
the temple was torn in two. [k] [46] He cried out,
"Father, into your hands I commend my
spirit." [l] And with these words he breathed
his last. *
[47] On seeing what had taken place, the cen-
turion praised God and said, "Surely, this
man was innocent." [m] [48] When all the people
who had gathered there to witness the spec-
tacle saw what had happened, they returned
home beating their breasts. * [n] [49] However, all
his acquaintances, including the women who
had followed him from Galilee, stood at a
distance and watched all these events. [o]

Jesus Is Buried.* [50] [p] Now there was a good
and upright man named Joseph * who was a

u Lk 8:52.—v Lk 19:41-44.—w Lk 11:27.—x Isa 2:19; Hos 10:8; Rev 6:16.—y Ezek 21:3.—z Lk 22:37; Isa 53:12.—a 33f: Mt 27:33; Mk 15:22-24; Jn 19:17.—b Ps 22:19; Acts 7:60.—c 35-38: Mt 27:39-43; Mk 15:29-32.—d Ps 22:18; Isa 42:1.—e Pss 22:8; 69:22; Mt 27:48.—f Jn 19:19.—g Mt 27:44; Mk 15:32.—h 2 Cor 12:3-4; Rev 2:7.—i 44-46: Mt 27:45-50; Mk 15:33-37.—j Am 8:9.—k Ex 26:31-33; Heb 9:3, 8.—l Ps 31:6; Jn 19:30; Acts 7:60.—m Mt 27:54; Mk 15:39.—n Lk 18:13.—o Lk 24:10; Ps 38:12.—p 50-55: Mt 27:57-61; Mk 15:42-47: Jn 19:38-41.

23:32-43 Jesus is placed in the ranks of evildoers. He is stripped of his clothes and vinegar is presented to him, fulfilling Psalms 22:19 and 69:22 before our very eyes. The people are silent. The leaders make fun of a Messiah who wishes to save human beings. The soldiers deride his royal title, the reason for his condemnation well affixed to the wood of the cross. This apparently humiliated king testifies to a true royalty by the unheard-of love that he gives: he asks for pardon of his killers and welcomes into his kingdom the thief who repents. See also note on Mt 27:35.

23:33 *Crucified:* see note on Mt 27:35.

23:34 This is the first word uttered by Jesus from the cross, reported only by Luke, the evangelist of mercy and meekness. Its authenticity is seemingly not open to doubt even though it is omitted in numerous codices written in an anti-Semitic age.

23:35 *Stood there watching:* Luke, the friend of the crowds, does not include the people with those leaders who insulted the Crucified. They are there to watch.

23:43 This is the second word of the crucified Jesus, also reported only by Luke, and it concludes with the pardon of the good thief. Thus, salvation flows from the cross.

23:44-49 The crucified Just One expires and everything bears testimony in his behalf: a prayer of complete trust rises to his lips, a pagan acknowledges his innocence, the people already manifest their repentance (see Zec 12:10), and his dear ones are nearby. Is this a tableau of desolation? Yet a mysterious expectation grips us.

23:46 Luke omits the word of abandonment found in Matthew and Mark. Instead, Jesus dies as the prototypical good person, who at the end of his life commends his spirit into the hands of the Father. Luke leaves aside the citation from Psalm 22 and reports verse 6 of Psalm 31, the prayer that the rabbis were wont to recite in the evening and that is still recited today at Night Prayer in the Liturgy of the Hours.

23:48 To the confession of the centurion, Luke adds that of the crowds, who had assisted in silence at the drama of the crucifixion. The centurion symbolizes the Roman world that recognizes the innocence and transcendental dignity of Christ, while the crowds indicate the rejection on the part of the chosen people.

23:50-56 The burial of Jesus, a human gesture, must be accomplished before the rise of the evening star or before the lights are lit for the evening, for then the Sabbath will have arrived—when all work is prohibited.

23:50 *Man named Joseph:* Luke shows the goodness of Joseph of Arimathea. At the same time, he shows that not every member of the Sanhedrin voted to condemn Jesus.

member of the council. [51] However, he had not agreed to their plan and the action they had taken. He came from the Jewish town of Arimathea, and he was awaiting the kingdom of God. [q] [52] This man went to Pilate and requested the body of Jesus. [53] Then he took it down, wrapped it in a linen shroud, and laid him in a tomb that had been hewn out of rock in which no one had ever been interred. [54] It was the Day of Preparation, and the Sabbath was about to begin. [r]

[55] The women who had accompanied Jesus from Galilee followed Joseph. They saw the tomb and how his body was laid in it. [56] Then they returned and prepared spices and ointments. But on the Sabbath they rested in obedience to the commandment. [s]

C: The Resurrection

CHAPTER 24

Jesus Rises from the Dead.* [1] [t] At daybreak on the first day of the week, the women came to the tomb with the spices they had prepared. [u] [2] They found the stone rolled away from the tomb, [3] but when they went inside, they did not find the body of the Lord Jesus.

[4] While they stood there wondering about this, suddenly two men in dazzling clothes appeared at their side. [v] [5] They were terrified and bowed their faces to the ground, but the men said to them, "Why do you look among the dead for one who is alive? [6] He is not here. He has been raised. Remember what he told you while he was still in Galilee: [w] [7] that the Son of Man must be handed over to sinners and be crucified and rise again on the third day." [x] [8] Then they recalled his words. [y]

[9] [z] When they returned from the tomb, they reported all these things to the Eleven and to all the others. [10] It was Mary Magdalene, Joanna, Mary the mother of James, and the other women with them who told this to the apostles. [a] [11] However, this story of theirs seemed to be nonsense, and the apostles did not believe them. [12] Nonetheless, Peter got up and ran to the tomb. Bending over, he looked inside and saw only the linen cloths. Then he returned home, wondering what had occurred. [b]

Jesus Appears to Two Disciples at Emmaus.* [13] Now that same day two of them were on their way to a village called Emmaus, about seven miles from Jerusalem, [c] [14] and they were talking with each other about all these things that had occurred. [15] While they were conversing and discussing these events, Jesus himself drew near and walked along with them, [16] but their eyes were prevented from recognizing him. [d]

[17] He asked them, "What are you discussing with each other as you walk along?" They stood still, their faces filled with sadness. [18] Then one of them, whose name was Cleopas, answered him, "Are you the only stranger in Jerusalem who is not aware of all the things that have taken place there in these days?" [e] [19] When he asked, "What things?" they replied, "The things that happened to Jesus of Nazareth, who was a prophet powerful in word and deed before God and all the people, [f] [20] and how our chief priests and rulers handed him over to be sentenced to death and had him crucified. [g]

[21] "We had been hoping that he would be the one who would redeem Israel. And what is more, this is the third day since all of this took place. [h] [22] Some women from our group have now given us astounding news. They went to the tomb early this morning,

---

q Lk 2:25.—r Mt 27:62.—s Lk 24:1; Ex 12:16; Mk 16:1.—t 1-8: Mt 28:1-8; Mk 16:1-8.—u 1ff: Jn 20:1ff.—v Jn 20:12.—w Mt 17:22.—x Lk 9:22; Mt 16:21; 17:22f; Mk 9:31.—y Jn 2:22.—z 9ff: Mk 16:10f.—a Lk 8:2f; Mk 6:30.—b Lk 24:24; Jn 20:3-7.—c Mk 16:12f.—d Jn 20:14; 21:4.—e Jn 19:25.—f Mt 2:23; 16:14; Acts 2:22.—g Lk 23:13.—h Lk 1:54; 2:38.

24:1-12 The man who was thought to have been buried forever receives the important title "the Living One," a title that the Old Testament reserves to the Lord (see Jos 3:10; Jdg 8:19; Rev 1:18), and the hearts of the witnesses are opened to the Word of God. This is the first Christian Sunday, the Lord's Day, the new day (v. 1). Luke does not mention the order given to the disciples to wait for Jesus in Galilee; in his view, the mystery finds its completion in Jerusalem, and it is from Jerusalem that the Christian mission will make its way throughout the entire world.

24:13-35 Since Friday nothing has taken place; God has not intervened. These two followers of Jesus are overwhelmed by the catastrophe and wounded in their hopes. A stranger overtakes them and seems indifferent to what has taken place. Indeed, he even knows how to explain its meaning. But a shared meal suffices for them to recognize Jesus in the breaking of the bread.

This is an astonishing lesson about the design of God and the meaning of the cross. The entire history of the people of God teaches us that suffering is a source of life and death is a passage to a resurrection. Christ, in whom the whole history of humanity is recapitulated, could follow no other road in order to open the entrance to the kingdom of his Father. This wonderful account of the disciples at Emmaus always teaches us the paths of faith and how everything is decided in the encounter with Christ, in the acceptance of his Word, in the acknowledgment of his presence. He no longer sojourns among us under earthly conditions: the essential thing is to live his Word and partake in his Eucharist.

23 but they failed to find his body. When they returned, they told us that they had seen a vision of angels who reported that he was alive. 24 Some of our companions went to the tomb and found everything exactly as the women had said, but they did not see him."

25 [i] Then he said to them, "How foolish you are, and how slow to believe all that the Prophets have spoken! 26 Was it not necessary that the Christ should suffer these things and enter into his glory?" [j] 27 Then, beginning with Moses and going through all the Prophets, he interpreted for them all the passages from the Scriptures that pertained to him. [k]

28 As they approached the village to which they were going, he acted as though he would be going further. 29 However, they urged him strongly, "Stay with us, for it is nearly evening and the day is almost over." And so he went in to stay with them.

30 When he was at table with them, he took bread, blessed and broke it, and gave it to them. 31 Then their eyes were opened and they recognized him, but he vanished from their sight. 32 They said to each other, "Were not our hearts burning within us while he spoke to us on the road and opened the Scriptures to us?" [l]

33 They set out immediately and returned to Jerusalem, where they found gathered together the Eleven and their companions 34 who were saying, "The Lord has truly been raised, and he has appeared to Simon!" * [m] 35 Then the two described what had happened on their journey and how he had made himself known to them in the breaking of the bread.

Jesus Appears to the Disciples in Jerusalem.* 36 While they were still conversing about this, Jesus himself stood in their midst and said to them, "Peace be with you." [n] 37 Startled and terrified, they thought that they were seeing a ghost. [o]

38 He said to them, "Why are you troubled, and why are doubts arising in your hearts? 39 Look at my hands and my feet. It is I myself. Touch me and see. For a ghost does not have flesh and bones as you can see that I have." [p] 40 [q] And when he had said this, he showed them his hands and his feet.

41 In spite of their joy and amazement, they were still incredulous. So he said to them, "Do you have anything here to eat?" 42 They gave him a piece of fish, 43 and he took it and ate it in their presence. [r]

44 Then he said to them, "This is what I meant when I told you while I was still with you: Everything written about me in the Law of Moses, the Prophets, and the Psalms must be fulfilled." [s] 45 Thereupon, he opened their minds to understand the Scriptures.

46 And he said to them, "Thus it is written that the Christ would suffer and on the third day rise from the dead, [t] 47 and that in his name repentance and forgiveness of sins are to be proclaimed to all nations, beginning from Jerusalem. [u] 48 You are witnesses to all these things. [v]

49 "And behold, I am sending upon you the gift promised by my Father. Therefore, stay here in the city until you have been clothed with power from on high." [w]

Jesus Ascends to Heaven.* 50 [x] Then he led them out as far as Bethany, and lifting up his hands he blessed them. 51 While he was blessing them, he departed from them and was taken up to heaven. [y] 52 They worshiped him and then returned to Jerusalem filled with great joy, 53 and they were continually in the temple praising God. [z]

---

i 25f: Lk 18:31; Acts 3:24.—j Heb 2:10; 1 Pet 1:11.—k Lk 24:44; Gen 3:15: Num 21:9; Deut 18:15; Ps 22:1-19; Isa 53; 1 Pet 1:10f.—l Ps 39:4.—m 1 Cor 15:5.—n Jn 20:19f.—o Mk 6:49.—p Jn 20:27; 1 Jn 1:1.—q 40f: Jn 21:9f, 13.—r Acts 10:41.—s Lk 9:45; Pss 2; 22; 69; 72; 110; 118.—t Lk 9:22; Hos 6:2.—u Mt 3:2; 28:19; Mk 16:15f; Acts 10:42.—v Acts 1:8; 1 Pet 5:1.—w Jn 14:26; Acts 1:4; 2:3f.—x 50f: Lev 9:22; Sir 50:20; Mk 16:19.—y Lk 9:51; 2 Ki 2:11.—z Acts 2:46.

24:34 In this verse Luke has included one of the earliest testimonies to the appearance of the Risen Lord to Peter (see Lk 22:21-32; 1 Cor 15:5).

24:36-49 It is truly the Lord who is present, the one whom they have known and seen die. He therefore has truly risen! But nothing is as it was before: his presence is not explained; it merely attests, by its reality, that salvation is given, that death and sin are vanquished. Now the disciples realize that the salvation announced in a mysterious fashion by the Old Testament is accomplished in Jesus. And the Risen Lord charges them to proclaim it everywhere, to teach people about it by their testimony and by the power of the Spirit of Pentecost. This passage contains, in summary form, an entire model for Christian preaching: the fulfillment of the Scriptures and of God's plan, the proclamation of forgiveness and conversion, the call to faith and holiness. The Book of Acts will tell how the Church carried out this mission.

24:50-53 Recognized and worshiped as Lord by his disciples, Jesus is taken away from our world. The Gospel of Luke ends with this vision, which the Acts of the Apostles situates forty days later (Acts 1:2-3, 9-11). Regardless of the date and the unfolding, the event surpasses history and time; after his resurrection, Jesus is established in his dignity of the Son of God. Henceforth, we live on earth in the time of praise and bearing witness.

"I give you a new commandment: love one another. . . .
This is how everyone will know that you are my disciples:
if you love one another" *(Jn 13:34f)*.

THE GOSPEL ACCORDING TO JOHN

The Way, the Truth, and the Life

Who had the ability to compose a Gospel so different from the others? It took a remarkable personality to tackle such a work. On two occasions the Book itself specifically offers a guarantee provided by an eyewitness (Jn 1:14; 19:35). A disciple appears several times whose name is persistently omitted and who is called simply "the disciple whom Jesus loved" (Jn 13:23; 19:26; 21:7, 20). There is nothing to prevent his being identified with the "other disciple" (Jn 18:15-16; see Jn 1:35-39), who appears with Peter but whose name is not given.

We have reason, then, to be somewhat puzzled. But think a bit. This Gospel cites the names of apostles (although it never gives a complete list); but it is a surprising fact that it never names John, although, according to all the other New Testament writings, he had a prominent place, alongside Peter, in the group of the Twelve. It is, then, a short, though not strictly demonstrable, step to identify the anonymous disciple of the fourth Gospel with John the apostle. And, in fact, since its early days, the Christian tradition has attributed the Gospel to John.

The fourth Gospel is written in Greek, in unaffected language and a style that is often solemn, sometimes monotonous. The work matured over a lengthy period, in a setting and an age in which many religious currents could have exerted an influence on it. Examples of such influences are an unusual vocabulary, distinctive symbols, and the very content of the themes developed. It is possible to identify Jewish and Christian motifs, an echo of the professions of faith and the Liturgy, perhaps a homiletic style, and even words that were in common usage at that time.

As we have it today, the fourth Gospel was, in all likelihood, published around the nineties of our era for the Christians of Asia Minor.

The fourth Gospel is rather different from the Synoptic Gospels. The latter pile up stories, miracles, and sayings of Jesus until they have made us familiar with that world which we all know. In the fourth Gospel, on the other hand, the selection of incidents is limited, and lengthy discourses are connected with them; almost everything takes place in Jerusalem and on the occasion of a feast; finally, the language is rather different. All this cannot be a matter of chance.

In fact, John seeks to express the message through especially significant incidents; these he calls "signs." These signs, seven in number, give the book its structure: seven sections, the last of which is in turn divided into seven parts. The discourses bring to light, and deepen our understanding of, the ideas that the signs suggest.

As a matter of fact, the incidents chosen by John do not follow in chronological order. Rather, they all contribute to highlighting the fundamental aspects of the mystery of Jesus. Despite this, the method of presentation chosen by the author does not detract from the historical truth of the facts reported. These incidents, which seem to be constructed with the same freedom as is shown in the discourses, have preserved many accurate details, and excavations in Palestine have confirmed some that are reported only in this Gospel.

John reaches his great insights into the life of Jesus in the light of Easter or, more accurately, in the light of the cross. It is in this perspective that he interprets the events and develops the discourses.

The life of Jesus is presented as an epiphany, the manifestation of the Word of God. The flesh is unable to hide the glory of the Son of God. This glory, almost in spite of itself, pierces through the veil of Christ's humanity. Thus when, during the Passion, Jesus presents himself to those who have come to arrest him, the latter draw back and fall on the ground. What is the reason if not that they have encountered the Lord in the person of Jesus.

In spite of this glorious aspect, John's Gospel is intensely dramatic. The life of Jesus is portrayed as a ruthless contest of cosmic proportions, a merciless duel between Light and Darkness, between Life and Death, between the Son of God and the Prince of this world. The conflict grows in intensity and culminates in the condemnation of Jesus. At that moment, darkness seems to have swallowed the Light. But it is precisely at that moment, at that "hour," that the perspectives are suddenly reversed. Paradoxically, the Condemned reveals himself as the Judge of the world, the Crucified as the Victor. The hour of death is precisely that of glory.

The Gospel according to John may be divided as follows:

I: A New Creation (1:1—2:12)
II: Worship of the Father in Spirit and Truth (2:13—4:54)
III: Jesus Restores the Work of God (5:1-47)
IV: The Bread of Life (6:1-71)
V: The Light of the World (7:1—9:41)
VI: The Shepherd Who Gives Up His Life (10:1—11:54)
VII: The True Passover That Brings About the Salvation of Humankind (11:55—20:31)

Epilogue (21:1-25)

I: A NEW CREATION*

CHAPTER 1

A: In the Beginning Was the Word*

The Word of God, Source of Life*

1 In the beginning was the Word,
and the Word was with God,
and the Word was God. [a]
2 He was with God in the very beginning. [b]
3 Through him all things came into existence,
and without him there was nothing.
That which came to be [c]
4 found life in him,
and the life was the light of the human race. [d]
5 The light shines in the darkness,
and the darkness has been unable to overcome it. [e]

Faith Means Welcoming the Word of God Made Man.* 6 A man appeared, sent by God,
whose name was John. *[f] 7 He came as a wit-
ness to give testimony to the light, so that
through him all might come to believe. [g] 8 He
himself was not the light; his role was to bear
witness to the light. [h]

9 The true light that enlightens everyone
was coming into the world. [i]
10 He was in the world,
the world had come into existence through him,
yet the world did not recognize him.
11 He came to his own,
but his own did not accept him. [j]

12 However, to those who did accept him
and who believed in his name
he granted the power to become children of God, [k]
13 who were born not from blood
or human desire or human will,
but from God. [l]

14 And the Word became flesh
and dwelt among us.
And we saw his glory,
the glory as of the Father's only Son,
full of grace and truth. [m]

Jesus Christ, Fullness of Truth.* 15 John testi-
fied to him, proclaiming, "This is the one of
whom I said, 'The one who comes after me
ranks ahead of me because he existed before
me.' " [n]

16 From his fullness we have all received,
grace upon grace. [o]
17 For the Law was given through Moses,
but grace and truth came through Jesus Christ. [p]

---

a Jn 8:24; 10:30; Gen 1:1-5; Job 28:12-27; Prov 8:22-25; Wis 9:1-2; Phil 2:6; Col 1:1, 15; 1 Jn 1:1-2; Rev 3:14; 19:13.—b Jn 8:58; Rev 1:8.—c Ps 33:10; Wis 9:1; Sir 42:15; 1 Cor 8:6; Col 1:16; Heb 1:2; Rev 3:14.—d Jn 5:26; 8:12; Ps 36:9; Acts 3:15; 1 Jn 1:2.—e Jn 3:19; 8:12; 9:5; 12:35, 46; Ps 18:29; Wis 7:29-30; 1 Thes 5:4; 1 Jn 2:8.—f Mt 3:1; Mk 1:4; Lk 3:2-3.—g Jn 1:19-34; 3:26; 5:33.—h Jn 5:35.—i Jn 3:19; 8:12; 9:39; 12:46; Wis 7:26; Isa 49:6.—j Isa 53:3.—k Jn 3:11-12; 5:43-44; 12:46-50; Deut 14:1; Hos 2:1; Gal 3:26; 4:6-7; Eph 1:5; 1 Jn 3:2.—l Jn 3:5-6; Jas 1:18.—m Jn 14:6; Ex 33:18; 40:34; Lev 26:11-12; Sir 24:4, 8; Isa 40:5; 60:1; Ezek 43:7; Joel 4:17; Hab 2:14; 1 Jn 1:2; 4:2; 2 Jn 7.—n Jn 1:30; 3:27-30; Mt 3:11.—o Eph 1:23; Col 1:19.—p Jn 7:19; Ex 34:28.

1:1—2:12 As believers contemplate Christ, they cannot but reflect on the fate of the universe and the destiny of the human race. They believe that creation is the work of God. In Jesus they see the Word who is of God and has come to renew creation. In the view of the evangelist, both the testimony of John the Baptist and the changing of water into wine at the wedding feast of Cana attest to this renewal.

These first texts seem to comprise a week in the life of Jesus, as if the author wanted to establish a parallel between the first week of creation and the new work of God in Jesus.

1:1-18 Rather than being an introduction, this well-known "Prologue of John" resembles an "overture." The entire Gospel is summed up in a few lines and all its essential themes are brought together. The great conviction of faith is immediately proclaimed: Jesus is God who has entered into the world and history to save us. With this key in hand, it is possible to understand all that Jesus says and does. This majestic prelude, written in rhythmic prose, unfolds in three stages (1:1-5; 1:6-14; 1:15-18).

1:1-5 In the first stage of the Prologue, we wonder at Jesus, the Word, whose person and existence infinitely transcend the world and history. We also call to mind creation, which is from the very outset an action of the Word, that is, of the creative Word of God, the divine Wisdom and source of life that makes the world exist (see Gen 1:1; Prov 8:22f.). At the same time, we proclaim the new creation, for the Word offers human beings a new life that comes from God and illumines their entire existence.

This Prologue is a hymn to the *Word* (in Latin, *Verbum;* in Greek, *Logos*). The term "Word" sums up and goes beyond everything that the Old Testament had glimpsed of the presence of God amid humanity by means of his Word; it includes and is superior to everything that the philosophy of the age could imagine regarding God's reflection in the universe.

1:6-14 The second stage of the Prologue calls to mind the struggle of human beings against the light. John came, a man sent to announce the coming of the light to God's own, that is, the people of Israel. But he was not the Messiah! In Jesus, and in Jesus alone, the very Word of God became flesh, in order that the gift of the Lord might be present among us, in our human existence.

1:6 *John,* i.e., the Baptist.

1:15-18 The third stage of the Prologue expresses our conviction. Human beings may await various messiahs and various revelations, but Jesus is the only true Christ foretold by the Law, that is, by the Old Testament. He is more than a new Moses, because in him the former covenant yields place to the new and definitive covenant. He is not only the extraordinary and only One Sent, but he is the Son, equal in every way to the Father (John gives us here the perfect formulation of the mystery of the incarnation).

18 No one has ever seen God.
It is the only Son, God,
who is at the Father's side,
who has made him known. [q]

B: Jesus Is the Expected Messiah*

John the Baptist Is Not the Messiah.* 19 This
is the testimony offered by John when the
Jews * sent priests and Levites from
Jerusalem to ask him, "Who are you?" [r] 20 He
confessed, he did not deny, but confessed, "I
am not the Christ." * [s] 21 Then they asked
him, "Who then are you? Are you Elijah?" *
He said, "I am not." "Are you the Prophet?"
He answered, "No." [t] 22 Therefore, they said
to him, "Who are you, so we may have an
answer to give to those who sent us? What
do you have to say about yourself?" 23 He
replied, in the words of the prophet Isaiah,

"I am the voice of one crying out in the
wilderness,
'Make straight the way of the
Lord.' " [u]

24 Some Pharisees were present in this
group, 25 and they asked him, "Why then are
you baptizing if you are neither the Christ,
nor Elijah, nor the Prophet?" [v] 26 John
answered them, "I baptize with water; but
among you there is one whom you do not
know, [w] 27 the one who is coming after me. I
am not worthy to loosen the strap of his san-
dal." 28 This took place in Bethany, beyond
the Jordan, where John was baptizing. [x]

**Behold, the Lamb of God, Who Takes Away
the Sin of the World.*** 29 The next day John saw
Jesus coming toward him, and he said,

"Behold, the Lamb of God,
who takes away the sin of the world. [y]
30 This is the one of whom I said,
'After me is coming one
who ranks ahead of me
because he existed before me.' [z]
31 I myself did not know him, *
but the reason I came to baptize with
water
was so that he might be revealed to
Israel."

32 John also gave this testimony, saying,

"I saw the Spirit
descending from heaven like a dove,
and it came to rest on him. * [a]
33 I myself did not know him,
but the one who sent me to baptize with
water told me,
'The one on whom you see the Spirit
descend and rest
is the one who is to baptize with the
Holy Spirit.' * [b]
34 And I myself have seen and have testified
that this is the Son of God." [c]

q Jn 3:11; 5:37; 6:46; Ex 33:20; Jdg 13:21-22; Col 1:15; 1 Tim 6:16; 1 Jn 4:12.—r Jn 2:18.—s Jn 3:28; Lk 3:15; Acts 13:25.—t Deut 18:15, 18; 2 Ki 2:11; Sir 48:10; Mal 3:1; Mt 11:14; 17:11-13; Mk 9:13; Acts 3:22.—u Isa 40:3; Mt 3:1, 3; Mk 1:2; Lk 3:4.—v Ezek 36:25; Zec 13:1; Mt 16:14.—w Mt 3:11; Mk 1:7-8; Lk 3:16; Acts 13:25.—x Jn 3:26; 10:40.—y Jn 1:36; Gen 22:8; Isa 53:7; 1 Pet 1:19; Rev 5:6; 17:14.—z Jn 1:15; Mt 3:11; Mk 1:7; Lk 3:16.—a Song 5:2; Isa 11:2; 61:1; Hos 11:11; Mt 3:16; Mk 1:10; Lk 3:21-22.—b Isa 42:1; Mt 3:11; Mk 1:8; Lk 3:16.—c Isa 42:1; Mt 3:17; Mk 1:11; Lk 9:35; 23:35.

1:19-51 Right from the Prologue, Jesus Christ is present in this Gospel as the Word and the only-begotten Son of God. Jesus communicates his life to us and makes known to us his glory. We are present at a great trial. In this trial, Jesus appears as witness of the truth, he alone. John's whole Gospel draws the reader, page after page, into this drama.

1:19-28 At that time, there was lively expectation in Israel that the great personages of the past would reappear in order to prepare for the coming of the Messiah (in Greek: Christ) (see Deut 18:15; Sir 48:10-11; Mal 3:23).

The sudden popularity of John the Baptist alarms "the Jews," i.e., all those who have authority. In the political circles of the priesthood, there is fear of uprisings; among the "pure," i.e., the Pharisees, there is concern for the good observance of the practices of the Law. The response comes—public and confirmed by the prophet Isaiah (40:3): John is not the Messiah, but the Precursor who announces him. By contrast, here is a testimony to the unique role of Jesus.

1:19 *The Jews:* this phrase occurs more than 70 times in the fourth Gospel—sometimes in a favorable sense (Jn 4:20), others in a neutral sense, but most often in a pejorative sense referring to the leaders of the Jews who were hostile to Jesus (Jn 8:48, etc.). Here it means the delegation sent by the Sanhedrin to assess the activities of an unauthorized teacher.

1:20 *Christ:* the Messiah, the anointed vicegerent of the Lord, usually regarded as the heir of David.

1:21 *Elijah:* this prophet who had been carried away to heaven in a fiery chariot was expected to return to earth to announce the end time. *The Prophet:* i.e., the Prophet mentioned in Deut 18:15, 18, the one like Moses (see Acts 3:22), who was expected to be the Messiah and repeat the prodigies of the Exodus.

1:29-34 John knows that he acts as a prophet gripped by the mission of God. And at the threshold of the Gospel, he presents the image of the lamb who will be evoked again at the end of the Passion. It is connected with the Jewish Passover and symbolizes the deliverance from Egypt (Ex 12:1-28); it also fits in with the portrait of the mysterious Servant of God, foretold by a prophet as an innocent victim led like a lamb to the slaughter, who was not only to atone for the sins of humanity but also to justify sinners (Isa 53:7, 11-12). It further recalls the great apocalyptic Lamb who would destroy evil in the world (Rev 5—7; 17:14).

1:31 *I myself did not know him:* this may refer to the fact that John lived in the desert until he appeared publicly to Israel (see Lk 1:80) and thus did not know Jesus very well. It may also indicate that John did not know that Jesus was the Messiah until he saw the sign mentioned in vv. 32-33.

1:32 For Jesus' Baptism, see notes on Mt 3:13-17; 3:15; 3:17.

1:33 *The one who is to baptize with the Holy Spirit:* John baptized with water, but Jesus would baptize with the Holy Spirit. We can see in this a reference to the sending of the Holy Spirit. In this Gospel that occurs on Easter Sunday (Jn 20:22).

We Have Found the Messiah.* 35 [d]The next day John was standing there with two of his disciples, 36 and as he watched Jesus pass by, he said, "Behold, the Lamb of God." 37 On hearing him say this, the two disciples began to follow Jesus. 38 When Jesus turned and saw them following him, he asked them, "What are you looking for?" They said to him, "Rabbi" (which, translated, is "Teacher"), "where are you staying?" [e] 39 He answered them, "Come and see." So they went and saw where he was staying, and they remained with him for the rest of that day. It was about four o'clock in the afternoon. *

40 One of the two who had heard John speak and had followed Jesus was Andrew, the brother of Simon Peter. 41 The first thing Andrew did was to seek out his brother Simon and say to him, "We have found the Messiah" * (which, translated, is "Christ"), [f] 42 and he took him to Jesus. Jesus gazed at him and said, "You are Simon son of John. You will be called Cephas" * (which, translated, is "Peter"). [g]

43 The next day Jesus * decided to go to Galilee. Encountering Philip, he said to him, "Follow me." [h] 44 Philip came from the same town, Bethsaida, * as Andrew and Peter. 45 Philip found Nathanael * and said to him, "We have found the one about whom Moses in the Law and also the Prophets wrote—Jesus the son of Joseph, from Nazareth." [i] 46 Nathanael said to him, "Can anything good come from Nazareth?" Philip replied, "Come and see." [j]

47 When Jesus saw Nathanael coming toward him, he said of him, "Behold, a true Israelite, in whom there is no deception." * [k] 48 Nathanael asked him, "How do you know me?" Jesus answered him, "Before Philip summoned you, when you were under the fig tree, * I saw you." [l] 49 Nathanael said to him, "Rabbi, you are the Son of God. You are the King of Israel." [m] 50 Jesus responded, "Do you believe because I told you that I saw you under the fig tree? You will see greater things than that." 51 Then he added, "Amen, amen, I say to you, you will see the heavens opened and the angels of God ascending and descending upon the Son of Man." * [n]

CHAPTER 2

C: The First Sign Worked by Jesus

The Wedding Feast at Cana.* 1 On the third day, there was a wedding at Cana * in Galilee. The mother of Jesus was there, [o] 2 and Jesus and his disciples had also been invited. 3 When the wine was exhausted, the mother of Jesus said to him, "They have no wine." 4 Jesus responded,

d 35-51: Mt 4:18-22; Mk 1:16-20; Lk 5:1-11.—e Mt 23:7.—f Jn 4:25.—g Gen 17:5, 15; Mt 16:18; Mk 3:16.—h Jn 6:5-7; Mt 10:3.—i Jn 21:2; Lk 3:23.—j Jn 7:41, 42.—k Ps 32:2; Rom 9:4, 6.—l Mic 4:4; Zec 3:10.—m Jn 12:13; Ex 4:22; Deut 14:1; 2 Sam 7:14; Job 1:6; 2:1; 38:7; Pss 2:7; 89:27; Wis 2:18; Sir 4:10; Dan 3:25; Hos 11:1; Mt 14:33; 16:16; Mk 13:32.—n Gen 28:10-17; Dan 7:13.—o Jn 4:46; 21:2; Jdg 14:12; Tob 11:8.

1:35-51 The movement of Jesus is separated from the movement of the Baptist. In the very first encounter, Jesus wins over Andrew, and perhaps the disciple who is not named was the beloved disciple, sufficiently interested in Andrew's call to still remember the hour (v. 39). Jesus gives Simon a new name indicative of his future mission (see Mt 16:18); with authority he calls Philip, and he reads the heart of Nathanael.

In this man so unexpected because of his lowly origin (v. 46), the disciples recognize the Messiah Israel expected. And Jesus unveils to them his mystery: Messiah of Israel, he is also the Son of Man who reunites heaven and earth in his kingdom. He is the sole mediator who gives access to the Father, as indicated in v. 51, an allusion to the dream of Jacob (see Gen 28:12).

The Gospel then offers us a meditation on the free gift and the happiness of being called by Jesus, a charter of the spiritual life. The dialogue with the first disciples lets us understand where Jesus leads those who follow him: there where he dwells at the side of the Father (see Jn 1:18). Intimacy with Christ, shared knowledge, and faith are the principal traits that describe the life of disciples. The Church must be the community where people share the certainty and the joy of having encountered Christ.

1:39 *Four o'clock in the afternoon:* literally, "the tenth hour" (from sunrise: 6:00 A.M.) in the Roman method of telling time.

1:41 *Messiah:* Greek transliteration of the Hebrew word for "Anointed One," which is used only here and in Jn 4:25 in this Gospel. The Greek translation *Christos* ("Christ") appears everywhere else.

1:42 *Cephas* in Aramaic signifies "stone, rock" (see Mt 16:18). It was not used at that time as a personal name. *Peter:* i.e., *Petros,* the Greek equivalent of *Cephas.*

1:43 *Jesus:* literally, "he," which could also refer to Peter.

1:44 *Bethsaida:* on the northern shore of Lake Tiberias.

1:45 *Nathanael* was certainly the apostle Bartholomew; see Mt 10:3.

1:47 *A true Israelite, in whom there is no deception:* this phrase recalls the fact that Jacob was the first to bear the name "Israel" (Gen 32:29), but he was an "Israelite" in whom there *was* deception (Gen 27:35-36).

1:48 *Under the fig tree:* a phrase signifying Messianic peace (see Mic 4:4; Zec 3:10).

1:51 *Son of Man:* see note on Mt 8:20 for the use of this term in the New Testament. In John, it occurs 13 times and is commonly associated with themes of crucifixion and suffering (Jn 3:14; 8:28) and revelation (Jn 6:27, 53) as well as eschatological authority (Jn 5:27; 9:39).

2:1-12 The evangelist calls special attention to the presence of the Mother of Jesus. Her role is to call Jesus to the cross and then stand by him in his Passion (Jn 19:25-26).

2:1 *Cana* was five miles northeast of Nazareth.

Matson Photo Service

CANA OF GALILEE — View of the town of Cana in the highlands of Galilee (showing the Nazareth-Tiberias road) about five miles northeast of Nazareth. Here Jesus attended a marriage feast with his mother and disciples and worked his first miracle. (See Jn 2:1-11)

Matson Photo Service

THE RIVER JORDAN— The most important river in Palestine measures 135 miles in a straight line, but because of its numerous windings covers a distance of about 250 miles. Its width varies from 80 to 180 feet and its depth from 5 to 12 feet. It was at the Jordan that Jesus was pointed out by John the Baptist and eventually baptized by him. (See Jn 1:19-37 and Mt 3:13)

TRADITIONAL SITE OF JACOB'S WELL — Both Samaritans and Jews have always believed this to be the well referred to as Jacob's well in John (4:6). The ground mentioned by John had been purchased by Jacob (Gn 33:19) and the area was later forcibly taken away from the Amorites (Gn 48:22). A narrow opening four feet long led from the floor of the vault into the well which was dug through limestone. The depth has not been determined. The well is near Mount Gerizim, which might have prompted our Lord to use the words "this mountain" in his conversation with the Samaritan woman. (See Jn 4, especially verse 21)

Matson Photo Service

Matson Photo Service

CHURCH OF ST. ANNE IN JERUSALEM — Located in the northeast part of the city, this church dating back to the Crusades commemorates the miracle of the cure effected by Jesus at the Pool of Bethesda. In 1888, while it was being repaired, a reservoir was discovered which is thought to be the ancient pool. (See Jn 5:2)

Matson Photo Service

THE POOL OF BETHESDA — Reservoir discovered in northeast Jerusalem in 1888, about 55 feet in length and 12 feet in width. It is approached by a steep and winding flight of steps. A fresco on the wall depicts an angel troubling the waters in remembrance of the cure effected by Jesus. (See Jn 9:1-16)

"Woman,* what concern is this to us? My
hour has not yet come."[p] 5 His mother said
to the servants, "Do whatever he tells you."[q]

6 Now standing nearby there were six
stone water jars, of the type used for Jewish
rites of purification, each holding twenty to
thirty gallons.[r] 7 Jesus instructed the ser-
vants, "Fill the jars with water." When they
had filled them to the brim, 8 he ordered
them, "Now draw some out and take it to
the chief steward," and they did so.

9 When the chief steward tasted the water
that had become wine, he did not know
where it came from, although the servants
who had drawn the water knew. The chief
steward called over the bridegroom[s] 10 and
said, "Everyone serves the choice wine first,
and then an inferior vintage when the guests
have been drinking for a while. However, you
have saved the best wine until now."*

11 Jesus performed this, the first of his
signs,* at Cana in Galilee, thereby revealing
his glory, and his disciples believed in him.[t]
12 After this, he went down to Capernaum
with his mother, his brethren,* and his disci-
ples, and they remained there for a few days.[u]

II: WORSHIP OF THE FATHER IN SPIRIT AND TRUTH*

A: The Mystery of the New Temple

Jesus Casts the Merchants Out of the Temple.* 13 [v] When the time of the Passover of
the Jews was near, Jesus went up to
Jerusalem.[w] 14 In the temple he found people
selling cattle, sheep, and doves, as well as
money changers seated at their tables.[x]
15 Making a whip of cords, he drove them all
out of the temple, including the sheep and
the cattle. He also overturned the tables of
the money changers, scattering their coins,
16 and to those who were selling the doves he
ordered, "Take them out of here! Stop turn-
ing my Father's house into a marketplace!"[y]
17 His disciples recalled the words of
Scripture, "Zeal for your house will consume
me."[z]

18 The Jews then challenged him, "What
sign can you show us to justify your doing
this?"[a] 19 Jesus answered, "Destroy this tem-
ple, and in three days I will raise it up."[b]
20 The Jews responded, "This temple has
taken forty-six years to build, and you are
going to raise it up in three days!" 21 But the
temple he was talking about was the temple
of his body.[c] 22 After he had risen from the
dead, his disciples remembered that he had
said this, and they believed the Scripture
and the words that Jesus had spoken.[d]

B: The Mystery of the New Covenant

Jesus in Jerusalem. 23 * While Jesus was in
Jerusalem for the feast of Passover, many
people saw the signs he was performing and

p Jn 7:30; 8:20; 12:23; 13:1; 19:26; Jdg 11:12; 1 Ki 17:18; 2 Ki 3:13; 2 Chr 35:21; Hos 14:9; Mt 8:29; 26:18; Mk 1:24; 5:7; 7:30; 12:23; 13:1.—q Gen 41:55.—r Jn 3:25; Lev 11:33; Am 9:13-14; Mt 15:2; 23:25-26; Mk 7:2-4; Lk 11:38.—s Jn 4:46.—t Jn 3:2; 4:54; Ex 14:31.—u Mt 12:46; Acts 1:15.—v 13-22: Mt 21:12-13; Mk 11:15-17; Lk 19:45-46.—w Deut 16:1-6; Lk 2:41.—x Lev 1:14; 5:7; Deut 14:25.—y Lk 2:49.—z Ps 69:10.—a Jn 4:48; 6:30.—b Mt 24:2; 26:61; 27:40; Mk 13:2; 14:58; 15:29; Lk 21:6; Acts 6:14.—c 1 Cor 6:19.—d Jn 5:39; 12:16; 14:26; 20:9; Ps 16:10; Mt 12:6; Lk 24:6-8; Rev 21:22.

2:4 *Woman:* a universal address from son to mother; it is used again in Jn 19:26, where its meaning becomes evident: Mary is the new Eve, mother of the living (Gen 3:15, 20). *My hour has not yet come:* the hour is that of Jesus' glorification and return to the Father (see Jn 7:30; 8:20; 12:23, 27; 13:1; 17:1; 19:27). It is determined by the Father and cannot be anticipated. The miracle worked at Mary's intercession is a prophetic symbol of it.

2:10 The first wine represents the first Covenant, the second better wine represents the New Covenant. Jesus is prefiguring the Messianic banquet.

2:11 *Signs:* a term used by John to indicate Jesus' miracles, emphasizing the significance rather than the marvelous character of the event (see Jn 4:54; 6:14; 9:16; 11:47). These signs reveal Jesus' glory (Jn 1:14, Isa 35:1-2; Joel 3:18; Am 9:13).

2:12 *Brethren:* that is, his close relatives. See notes on Mt 12:46-50 and 12:47.

2:13—4:54 The author of the fourth Gospel brings us from one Jewish feast to another; he seems to want to make them the points of reference with which to link the discourses of Jesus.

The incidents that follow are therefore connected with the feast of Passover. They attest that Jesus has come to establish a new and spiritual worship that is no longer reserved to a single people or to a place.

2:13-22 Passover is the feast of Unleavened Bread, a sign of renewal (see Ex 12:15). Jesus knows, better than the Prophets (Isa 1:11; Jer 7:4; Am 5:21), that his Father has nothing to do with this traffic in sacrifices and offerings, if the interior gift of the heart is lacking.

In fact, in the evangelist's view, this temple of stone has already lost its function, and the true dwelling of the Father among human beings will be the humanity of the risen Jesus, who is the focal point of all worship. The construction of the new temple in Jerusalem had been begun by Herod the Great in 20–19 B.C. According to v. 20, then, we are in the year A.D. 27–28.

2:23—3:12 To be filled with wonder at what Jesus can do, as was Nicodemus, is not yet faith. Faith is acceptance of the testimony of Jesus about God and about the plan of Jesus. Faith is another life, a transformed existence. The flesh—i.e., we with our material and intellectual possibilities—does not have the power to transform our life.

This transformation comes like the wind—mysterious and surprising—the same word in Hebrew and Greek expressing spirit and wind. The idea here is to bring to mind an event (rebirth) in which God alone has the initiative. Only those who open themselves to the Spirit, those who want to be reborn in Baptism and transformed as children of God, can believe in the new life that Jesus reveals and whose source is the Spirit—for they live it as by a gift.

came to believe in his name.[e] 24 However,
Jesus would not entrust himself to them
because he fully understood them all. 25 He
did not need evidence from others about
man, for he clearly understood men.[f]

CHAPTER 3

Nicodemus Goes To Visit Jesus. 1 There was
a man from the Pharisees named
Nicodemus,* a member of the Jewish ruling
council,[g] 2 who came to Jesus at night.
"Rabbi," he said, "we know that you are a
teacher who has come from God, for no one
would be able to perform the signs that you
do unless God were with him."[h] 3 Jesus
replied,

"Amen, amen, I say to you,
no one can see the kingdom of God*
without being born from above."[i]

4 Nicodemus asked, "How can a man be
born again once he is old? Is it possible for
him to enter a second time into his mother's
womb and be born?"[j] 5 Jesus said,

"Amen, amen, I say to you,
no one can enter the kingdom of God
unless he is born of water and the Spirit.*[k]
6 What is born of the flesh is flesh,
and what is born of the Spirit is spirit.[l]
7 "You should not be astonished when I say,
'You must be born from above.'
8 The wind blows where it chooses,
and you hear the sound of it,
but you do not know where it comes from
or where it goes.
So it is with everyone who is born of the Spirit."[m]

9 "How is this possible?" asked Nico-
demus.[n] 10 Jesus responded, "You are a
teacher of Israel and you do not know these
things?[o]

11 "Amen, amen, I say to you,
we speak of what we know
and we testify to what we have seen,
and yet you do not accept our testimony.[p]
12 If I tell you about earthly things
and you do not believe,
how will you believe
when I speak to you about heavenly things?[q]

Jesus Christ, Savior and Judge*

13 "No one has gone up to heaven
except the one who descended from heaven,
the Son of Man.[r]
14 And just as Moses lifted up the serpent in the desert,
so must the Son of Man be lifted up,*[s]
15 in order that everyone who believes in him
may have eternal life.[t]
16 "For God so loved the world
that he gave his only Son,
so that everyone who believes in him
may not perish
but may attain eternal life.[u]
17 "For God did not send his Son into the world
to condemn the world
but in order that the world might be saved through him.[v]

e Jn 4:45.—f Jn 6:61, 64; 1 Ki 8:39; Pss 33:15; 94:11; Sir 42:18; Isa 11:3; Jer 17:10; 20:12.—g Jn 7:50-51; 19:39; Lk 23:13.—h Jn 9:4, 16, 33; 10:21; 11:10; 13:30; Mt 22:16; Mk 12:14; Lk 20:21; Acts 2:22.—i Mt 18:3; Jas 1:18.—j Jn 1:13.—k Jn 1:32; 7:39; 19:30, 34-35; Isa 32:15; 44:3; Ezek 36:25-27; Joel 3:1-2; Mt 3:5; Tit 3:5.—l Jn 6:63; Gen 6:3; 1 Cor 15:44-50.—m Eccl 11:4-5; Acts 2:2-4; 1 Cor 2:14-16.—n Jn 6:52, 60.—o Lk 2:46.—p Jn 3:32, 34; 8:14; Mt 11:27.—q Jn 6:62-65; Wis 9:16-17; 1 Cor 15:40; 2 Cor 5:1; Phil 2:10; 3:19-20.—r Jn 1:18; 6:62; Prov 30:4; Dan 7:13; Rom 10:6; Eph 4:9; Heb 4:14.—s Jn 8:28; 12:32-34; Num 21:4-9; Wis 16:5-7.—t Gen 15:6; Num 14:11; Acts 13:39.—u Rom 5:8; Eph 2:4; 1 Jn 4:9.—v Jn 5:22, 30; 8:15-18; 12:47; Isa 53:11; 2 Cor 5:19; 1 Tim 1:15.

3:1 *Nicodemus:* a member of the Sanhedrin or ruling council in virtue of his being a teacher of the Law.

3:3 *Kingdom of God:* this is the basic theme of the preaching of Jesus in the Synoptic Gospels. In John, it appears explicitly only in this verse. However, in the Synoptics it almost disappears in the Passion Narrative, whereas in John it is given particular emphasis there. John identifies the kingdom of God with the very person of Jesus. During the public ministry, the splendor of Jesus' kingship was somewhat veiled by his fragile humanity, but in the Passion it comes shining through in his exaltation on the cross, which, for John, is intrinsically connected with Jesus' glorification in heaven. *From above:* the Greek word *anothen* could be translated "from above" or "again." Jesus means "from above," but Nicodemus understands "again."

3:5 *Born of water and the Spirit:* this phrase refers to Christian Baptism, the necessary vehicle for our spiritual rebirth, wrought by the Holy Spirit. It may be that here the evangelist is clarifying the words of the Lord according to a later and more mature understanding of Christian teaching, as lived in the primitive community.

3:13-21 The evangelist prolongs the conversation with Nicodemus in meditation on Jesus. What, then, is the mystery of Jesus and what does he bring to the human condition? The evangelist meditates on the Son of God, the divine messenger now glorified at his Father's side.

From Jesus, life came through the cross—as is suggested by the allusion to the bronze serpent intended to cure dying Hebrews (see Num 21:9). The cross was a testimony of God's love for the world and for each one of us. The cross was also the light given to us. This light enables us to recognize our conduct in truth and compels us to make a decisive choice: either to submit to Jesus and be saved, or to flee and be condemned.

3:14 *So must the Son of Man be lifted up:* the reference is to the lifting up on the cross, which in John's view is identical with the glorification of Jesus.

18 Whoever believes in him is not condemned,
but whoever does not believe in him
already stands condemned,
because he has not believed in the name
of the only-begotten Son of God. [w]
19 "And the judgment is this:
the light has come into the world,
but people preferred darkness to light
because their deeds were evil. [x]
20 Everyone who does evil hates the light
and avoids coming near the light
so that his misdeeds may not be exposed. [y]
21 However, whoever lives by the truth
comes to the light
so that it may be clearly seen
that his deeds have been done
in God." [z]

Final Witness of John the Baptist.* 22 [a] After
this, Jesus went with his disciples into the
Judean countryside, where he spent some
time with them and baptized. 23 John was
also baptizing at Aenon* near Salem,
because there was an abundance of water
there, and people were coming to be bap-
tized. 24 At that time, John had not yet been
imprisoned. [b]

25 Now a dispute about ceremonial wash-
ings arose between a certain Jew and the
disciples of John. [c] 26 Therefore, they came to
John and said to him, "Rabbi, the one who
was with you beyond the Jordan, to whom
you bore witness, is baptizing, and everyone
is flocking to him." [d] 27 John replied,

"No one can receive anything
except what has been given to him from heaven. [e]
28 You yourselves can testify that I said,
'I am not the Christ.
I have been sent before him.' [f]
29 "It is the bridegroom who has the bride,
but the friend of the bridegroom
who stands by and listens for him
rejoices greatly when he hears the bridegroom's voice.
This joy of mine
is complete. [g]
30 He must increase;
I must decrease. [h]

He Who Comes from Above*

31 "The one who comes from above is above all.
The one who is of the earth is earthly
and speaks of earthly things.
The one who comes from heaven is above all. [i]
32 He bears witness to the things he has seen and heard,
yet no one accepts his testimony. [j]
33 "Whoever accepts his testimony [k]
attests that God speaks the truth.
34 For the one whom God has sent
speaks the words of God,
for God gives him the Spirit without measure. * [l]
35 The Father loves the Son,
and he has entrusted everything into his hand. [m]
36 Whoever believes in the Son has eternal life;
whoever does not believe in the Son will not see life,
but the wrath of God rests upon him." [n]

C: The Savior of the World and the New Worship

CHAPTER 4

Journeying to Galilee through Samaria.*
1 Now when the Lord learned that the

w Jn 5:24; Mk 16:16.—**x** Jn 1:5, 9-11; 8:12; 9:5; Ps 52:5.—**y** Job 24:13-17; Eph 5:11, 13.—**z** Gen 47:29 LXX; Jos 2:14 LXX; 2 Sam 2:6 LXX; 15:20 LXX; Tob 4:6 LXX; 13:6; Isa 26:10 LXX; Mt 5:14-16.—**a** 22-23: Jn 4:12.—**b** Mt 4:12; 14:3; Mk 1:14; 6:17; Lk 3:20.—**c** Jn 2:6.—**d** Jn 1:26, 32-34, 36; Mt 23:7.—**e** Jn 19:11; 1 Cor 4:7; 2 Cor 3:5; Heb 5:4; Jas 1:17.—**f** Jn 1:20-23; Mt 3:1; Lk 3:15.—**g** Jn 15:11; 17:13; Mt 9:15; Phil 2:2.—**h** 2 Sam 3:1.—**i** Jn 8:23; 1 Jn 4:5.—**j** Jn 3:11; 8:26.—**k** 33-34: Jn 8:26; 12:44-50; 1 Jn 5:10.—**l** Isa 42:1; Acts 10:38.—**m** Jn 13:3; Mt 11:27; 28:18; Lk 10:22.—**n** Jn 3:16; Mt 3:7; 1 Jn 5:13.

3:22-30 Using an image familiar to the Jews (see Deut 31:16; Jer 2:2; Hos 2:18f; Mt 9:15), John attests that Jesus is the true Bridegroom, that is, the one in whose person God enters into the new and definitive covenant with his own.

The witness, moreover, sets himself aside: he is only the friend of the Bridegroom, whose role is to ask for the hand of the bride and, when the wedding feast is prepared, to introduce her to the Bridegroom.

3:23 *Aenon:* the place has not been identified with certainty.

3:31-36 The evangelist continues his reflection on the mystery of Christ. Jesus is the Son who receives from his Father the fullness of life. He has the mission to reveal it and communicate it to those who believe in him, by giving them the Spirit with whom he himself is filled (v. 34). In rich and symbolic words, he is to show how much the believer's life is a gift of God and a newness of existence beyond anything that is in the earthly power of people.

3:34 *For God gives him the Spirit without measure:* another translation is: "And he gives the Spirit without measure."

4:1-3 Jesus is forced to leave Judea in order to distance himself from the hostility of the Pharisees who are jealous of his growing popularity. The journey through Samaria affords him an opportunity to proclaim the Gospel in a mission land, so to speak, for the Samaritans were tantamount to Gentiles in the eyes of the Jews.

Pharisees had been informed that he had
more disciples and was baptizing more peo-
ple than John [o] 2 (although actually it was not
Jesus himself but his disciples who were bap-
tizing), 3 he left Judea and set forth for
Galilee.

Jesus and the Samaritan Woman.* 4 He had
to pass through Samaria. * [p] 5 So he came to
a Samaritan town called Sychar, * near the
plot of land that Jacob had given to his son
Joseph. [q] 6 Jacob's well was there, and Jesus,
tired from his journey, sat down at the well.
It was about noon. *

7 When a Samaritan woman came to
draw water, Jesus said to her, "Give me
some water to drink." [r] 8 His disciples had
gone into the town to purchase food. 9 The
Samaritan woman said to him, "You are a
Jew. How can you ask me, a Samaritan
woman, * for some water to drink?" (Jews
do not share anything in common with
Samaritans.) [s] 10 Jesus replied,

"If you recognized the gift of God
and who it is that is asking you for
something to drink,
you would have asked him
and he would have given you living
water." [t]

11 "Sir," the woman said, "you do not have
a bucket, and the well is deep. * Where can
you get this living water? 12 Are you greater
than our ancestor Jacob who gave us this
well and drank from it himself along with his
sons and his cattle?" [u] 13 Jesus said to her,

"Everyone who drinks this water
will be thirsty again.
14 But whoever drinks the water that I will
give him
will never be thirsty.
The water that I will give him
will become a spring of water within him
welling up to eternal life." [v]

15 The woman said to him, "Sir, give me
this water so that I may not be thirsty and
have to come here to draw water." [w]

16 Jesus told her, "Go, call your husband
and come back here." 17 The woman
answered him, "I have no husband." Jesus
said to her, "You are right in saying, 'I have
no husband'; 18 for you have had five hus-
bands, and the man you have now is not
your husband. What you have said is
true." [x]

19 The woman said to him, "Sir, I can see
that you are a prophet. [y] 20 Our ancestors
worshiped on this mountain, * but you say
that the place where people must worship
is in Jerusalem." [z] 21 Jesus told her,

"Believe me, woman,
the hour is coming
when you will worship the Father
neither on this mountain
nor in Jerusalem. [a]
22 You worship what you do not know;
we worship what we do know,
for salvation is from the Jews. [b]
23 "But the hour is coming,
indeed it is already here,
when the true worshipers
will worship the Father
in Spirit and truth. *
Indeed it is worshipers like these
that the Father seeks. [c]
24 God is Spirit,
and those who worship him
must worship in Spirit and truth." [d]

---

o Jn 3:22, 26.—p Mt 10:5; Lk 9:52-55.—q Gen 33:18-19; 48:22; Jos 24:32.—r Gen 24:17; 1 Ki 17:10.—s Sir 50:25-26; Mt 10:5.—t Sir 24:20-21; Isa 44:3; 55:1; Jer 2:13; Zec 14:8.—u Jn 8:53; Mt 12:4.—v Jn 6:35, 58; 7:37-39; Isa 12:3; 44:3; 49:10; Joel 4:18; Rev 7:16; 21:6.—w Jn 6:34.—x 2 Ki 17:24-34.—y Jn 9:17; Hag 1:3; Mt 21:11.—z Deut 11:29; 27:4; Jos 8:33; Ps 122:1-5; Lk 9:53.—a Jn 5:28; Mal 1:11.—b 2 Ki 17:27; Ps 76:2-3; Isa 2:3.—c Jn 5:25; Phil 3:3.—d 2 Cor 3:17.

4:4-30 Jesus converses with a woman, a daughter of Samaria, and therefore belonging to what the Jews considered to be a heretical breed and as accursed as the Gentiles; in addition, she is well known as a sinner. But God's gift is for everyone. Jesus is the living water, and for peoples dwelling on the edge of the wilderness, living water symbolizes life, hope, renewal, and spiritual riches.

Jesus urges the new worship of God as Father "in Spirit and truth." This means to pray to the Father in the Holy Spirit and in Jesus who is the truth. Such worship springs up from the heart; it comes from the Spirit.

4:4 The inhabitants of Samaria were a mixed race, descended from the intermarriage of Israelites and Assyrian colonists. Although they worshiped the same God as the Jews and believed in the Pentateuch, they disowned the Jerusalem temple and priesthood and erected a rival sanctuary on Mount Gerizim in the 4th century B.C. (see 2 Mac 6:2).

4:5 *Sychar* was in the neighborhood of ancient Shechem. See Gen 33:18-20; 48:21f.

4:6 *Noon:* literally, "the sixth hour." See note on Mk 15:25.

4:9 *Samaritan woman:* characterized as ritually unclean by the Jews, who were therefore forbidden to drink from any vessel handled by them.

4:11 *Well is deep:* the depth of the well, which still exists, has not been determined. The estimates given over the centuries range from 240 feet to 150 feet to 75 feet (the most recent).

4:20 *This mountain:* Gerizim (2,849 feet high, south of Sychar).

4:23 *In Spirit and truth:* the *Spirit* is the Holy Spirit and the *truth* is Jesus. For he is the true Son of God.

25 The woman said to him, "I know that
the Messiah is coming, the one who is
called Christ. When he comes, he will
reveal everything to us." *[e] 26 Jesus said to
her, "I am he, * the one who is speaking to
you."[f]

27 At this point, his disciples returned, and
they were astonished to find him speaking
with a woman, but no one asked, "What do
you want from her?" or "Why are you con-
versing with her?" 28 The woman left behind
her water jar and went off to the town, where
she said to the people, 29 "Come and see a
man who told me everything I have ever
done. Could this be the Christ?"[g] 30 And so
they departed from the town and made
their way to see him.

The Time of the Harvest.* 31 Meanwhile, the
disciples urged him, "Rabbi, eat something."
32 But he told them,

"I have food to eat
about which you do not know."[h]

33 Then his disciples said to one another,
"Could someone have brought him some-
thing to eat?" 34 Jesus said to them,

"My food is to do the will
of the one who sent me,
and to accomplish his work.[i]
35 Do you not have a saying,
'Four months more,
and then comes the harvest'?

"I tell you,
open your eyes and look at the fields;
already they are white for the harvest.[j]
36 The reaper is even now receiving his pay;
already he is gathering the crops for
eternal life
so that the sower and the reaper can
rejoice together.[k]
37 "Thus, the saying holds true,
'One sows and another reaps.'[l]
38 I sent you to reap
what you had not worked for.
Others have performed the work,
and you have reaped the benefits of
their labor."[m]

Jesus Is Truly the Savior of the World.*
39 Many Samaritans from that town came to
believe in him because of the woman's testi-
mony, "He told me everything I have ever
done." 40 So when the Samaritans came to
him, they pleaded with him to stay with
them, and he remained there for two days.
41 And many more began to believe in him
because of the words he spoke to them.
42 They said to the woman, "We no longer
believe simply because of what you said, for
we have heard him for ourselves, and we are
convinced that this man is truly the Savior
of the world."[n]

Return to Galilee.* 43 When the two days
were over, Jesus departed for Galilee. 44 He
himself had declared that a prophet is not
treated with honor in his own hometown.[o]
45 When he arrived in Galilee, the Galileans
welcomed him, since they had seen all he
had done in Jerusalem during the feast, hav-
ing been at the feast themselves.[p]

Jesus Heals the Official's Son.* 46 [q] He went
again to Cana in Galilee where he had
changed the water into wine. At Capernaum,
there was a royal official whose son was ill.

---

e Jn 1:41; Deut 18:18-22; Mt 1:16.—f Jn 8:24; 9:37; Isa 52:6.—g Jn 7:26, 31; Mt 12:23.—h Jn 6:27; Mt 4:4.—i Jn 5:30, 36; 6:38; 9:4; 17:4; 19:30.—j Mt 9:37-38; Lk 10:2; Rev 14:15.—k Ps 126:5-6; Am 9:13-14; Rom 1:13.—l Deut 20:6; 28:30; Job 31:8; Mic 6:15.—m Acts 8:14-17.—n 1 Jn 4:14.—o Mt 13:57; Mk 6:4; Lk 4:24.—p Jn 2:23.—q 46-54: Jn 2:1-11; Mt 8:5-13; 15:21-28; Mk 7:24-30; Lk 7:1-10.

4:25 The Samaritan Messiah was called the *Ta'eb.* He revealed the secrets of God to his people. Jesus reveals to us how much God loves us.

4:26 *I am he:* this phrase may also be translated as "I AM," the name Yahweh used for himself in the Old Testament (see note on Mk 6:50). The phrase "I am" is used in the text of this Gospel 23 times (4:26; 6:20, 35, 41, 48, 51; 8:12, 18, 24, 28, 58; 10:7, 9, 11, 14; 11:25; 13:19; 14:6; 15:1, 5; 18:5, 6, 8). In several of these passages, Jesus joins the phrase with seven significant metaphors that express his saving relationship toward the world: "I am the bread of life" (Jn 6:35, 41, 48, 51). "I am the light of the world" (Jn 8:12). "I am the gate of the sheepfold" (Jn 10:7, 9). "I am the good shepherd" (Jn 10:11, 14). "I am the resurrection and the life" (Jn 11:25). "I am the way and the truth and the life" (Jn 14:6). "I am the true vine" (Jn 15:1, 5).

4:31-38 Jesus is not thinking of an ordinary harvest. The arrival of the Samaritans announces the crops of the end time, the harvest in which all will be gathered together by the coming of God. Samaritans wore white robes: they are the harvest.

4:39-42 The personal and prolonged encounter with Jesus allows believers to measure the magnitude of their mission. This Jewish teacher is not only a prophet who announces salvation. He is the Messiah who brings about salvation for the whole world, for all human beings.

4:43-45 Jesus' stay in Galilee and his ministry in his own town will not be crowned by a more satisfactory success than the one in Judea, the heart of Judaism. With this sad reflection, the fourth evangelist confirms a saying of the Lord found in Mt 13:57 and parallels.

4:46-54 Jesus shows the price of faith (believing in the Word) to his unbelieving companions (v. 44) even though they had already seen him at work. Faith, and it alone, is necessary to be saved. To believe is to welcome in Jesus the salvation that God gives. The miracle is first of all a response to faith. Then it sheds light on the man's faith and makes it strong. The cure is reported less to bring a demonstration of faith than to call upon us to believe. This account may be a third version of the cure of the centurion's son (Mt 8:5-13) or servant (Lk 7:1-10).

47 When this man heard that Jesus had come from Judea to Galilee, he went to him and pleaded that he come and heal his son who was near death.

48 Jesus said to him, "Unless you witness signs and wonders, you will not believe."[r] 49 The royal official said to him, "Sir, come down before my child dies." 50 Jesus replied, "Return home. Your son will live."

The man believed what Jesus said to him, and he departed.[s] 51 While he was still on his way, his servants met him saying that his child was going to live. 52 He asked them at what time the boy had begun to recover, and they told him, "The fever left him yesterday at one o'clock in the afternoon." * 53 Then the father realized that was the exact hour at which Jesus had assured him, "Your son will live," and he and his entire household came to believe.

54 This was the second sign that Jesus performed after returning from Judea into Galilee.[t]

III: JESUS RESTORES THE WORK OF GOD*

CHAPTER 5

The Sign Given on a Sabbath.* 1 Some time later, Jesus went up to Jerusalem for one of the Jewish feasts.[u] 2 Now in Jerusalem, by the Sheep Gate, there is a pool that in Hebrew is called Bethesda. * It has five porticos,[v] 3 and in these a large number of invalids used to lie, people who were blind, lame, and paralyzed, waiting for the movement of the water. * [4 For occasionally an angel of the Lord would come down into the pool and stir up the water. The first one into the pool after each such disturbance would be cured of whatever disease he had.] *

5 A man who was there had been an invalid for thirty-eight years.[w] 6 When Jesus saw him lying there and was aware that he had been ill for a long time, he said to him, "Do you want to get well?" 7 The invalid answered him, "Sir, I have no one to put me into the pool when the water is stirred up. While I am still on my way, someone else steps into the pool ahead of me." 8 Jesus said to him, "Rise! Take up your mat and walk!"[x] 9 Immediately, the man was cured, and he took up his mat and began to walk.

Now that day was a Sabbath.[y] 10 Therefore, the Jews said to the man who had been cured, "Today is the Sabbath. It is not lawful for you to carry your mat."[z] 11 He replied, "The man who cured me said to me, 'Take up your mat and walk!' " 12 They asked him, "Who is the man who told you to take it up and walk?" 13 But the man who had been cured did not know who it was, for Jesus had disappeared into the crowd that was there.[a]

14 Later, Jesus found him in the temple and said to him, "See, you have been made well. Do not sin anymore, so that nothing worse happens to you."[b] 15 The man went away and told the Jews that Jesus was the man who had made him well. 16 Therefore, the Jews began to harass Jesus because he was doing such things on the Sabbath.[c] 17 However, Jesus responded to them, saying,

"My Father is still working,
and I am at work as well."[d]

18 For this reason, the Jews became even more determined to kill him, because he was not only breaking the Sabbath but also calling God his own Father, making himself equal to God.[e]

The Work of the Son.* 19 Jesus replied to them, saying,

r Jn 2:18, 23; Wis 8:8; Dan 4:2, 3; Mt 12:38; Acts 2:43; 1 Cor 1:22.—s 1 Ki 17:23.—t Jn 2:11.—u Jn 6:4.—v Jn 19:13; Neh 3:1, 32; 12:39; Acts 21:40; 22:2.—w Deut 2:14.—x Mt 9:6; Mk 2:11; Lk 5:24; Acts 3:6.—y Jn 9:14; Mt 12:1-14; Mk 2:12; Lk 5:25.—z Ex 20:8; Neh 13:15-22; Jer 17:21-27; Mk 3:2; Lk 13:10; 14:1.—a Mt 8:18; 13:36; Mk 4:36; 7:17.—b Jn 8:11; 9:2; Ezek 18:20; Mk 2:5.—c Jn 7:23; 9:4; Mt 12:8.—d Jn 9:4; Ex 20:11; Lk 2:49.—e Jn 7:1, 25; 8:37, 40; 10:33, 36; 14:28; Gen 3:5-6; Wis 2:16; Mt 12:14; 26:4; 2 Thes 2:4.

4:52 *One o'clock in the afternoon:* literally, "the seventh hour." See note on Mk 15:25.

5:1-47 Every Jewish feast is a memorial of what God has done for his people in deeds that manifest his power to create and restore. It is in this setting that the evangelist places an important action of Jesus, which leads to a debate over the meaning of the action: Is God himself at work here?

5:1-18 Jesus, the Son of God, claims a power that belongs to God alone. In addition, by breaking the Sabbath precept, Jesus proclaims the end of the old covenant. The incident is perhaps to be connected with the feast of Pentecost, which, according to Jewish tradition, commemorates the promulgation of the Law on Sinai. This would make Jesus' action even more eloquent.

5:2 *Bethesda,* also called Bethsaida or Bethzatha.

5:3 *Waiting for the movement of the water:* these words appear only in the Caesarean and Western recensions.

5:4 This verse is lacking in many important manuscripts, including the oldest.

5:19-30 The action of Jesus creates scandal and anger among the religious authorities. He has to explain his activity and especially his claim that he and the Father are one. The evangelist deepens this affirmation of Jesus' divinity. What would be seen as blasphemous in anyone else is here a profound reality.

Jesus is one with his Father. All the work of Jesus is God's action among us. Jesus has the power to give or restore life to those who welcome his word as that of God, even if they are victims of sin. To encounter Jesus is to face judgment and to experience eternal life even now. To accept or refuse his work: no decision is more important for us.

"Amen, amen, I say to you,
the Son can do nothing by himself;
he can do only what he sees the Father doing.
For whatever the Father does,
the Son also does.[f]
20 For the Father loves the Son
and shows him everything
that he himself is doing.
And he will show him
even greater works than these,
so that you might be astonished.[g]

21 "Indeed, just as the Father raises the dead
and gives them life,
so does the Son give life
to anyone he chooses.[h]
22 The Father judges no one,
for he has entrusted all judgment to the Son,[i]
23 so that all may honor the Son
as they honor the Father.
Anyone who does not honor the Son
does not honor the Father who sent him.[j]

24 "Amen, amen, I say to you,
whoever hears my words
and believes in the one who sent me
possesses eternal life.
He will not come to judgment
but has passed from death to life.[k]

25 "Amen, amen, I say to you,
the hour is coming,
indeed it is already here,
when the dead will hear
the voice of the Son of God,
and all those who hear it will live.[l]

26 For just as the Father has life in himself,
so also he has granted the Son to have life in himself.[m]
27 And he has also granted him
the power to pass judgment,
because he is the Son of Man.[n]

28 "Do not be astonished at this,
for the hour is coming
when all those who are in their graves[o]
will hear his voice
29 and will come forth from their graves.
Those who have done good deeds
will rise to life,
while those who have done evil
will rise to judgment.[p]

30 "I can do nothing on my own.
As I hear, I judge,
and my judgment is just,
because I seek to do
not my own will
but the will of him who sent me.[q]

A Witness to Jesus

31 [r] * "If I were to testify about myself,
my testimony would not be true.
32 However, there is another who testifies about me,
and I know that his testimony is true,
the testimony he bore concerning me.
33 You sent messengers to John,
and he has testified to the truth.[s]
34 Not that I accept such human testimony,
but I say these things
so that you may be saved.[t]

35 "John was a burning and shining lamp,
and for a time you were willing
to exult in his light.[u]
36 But I have testimony that is greater than John's.
The works that my Father
has given me to accomplish,
the very works that I am doing,
testify about me,
that the Father has sent me.[v]

37 "And the Father who sent me
has himself testified about me.
You have not heard his voice
or seen his form,[w]
38 and you do not have his word
abiding in you,
because you do not believe
him whom he has sent.[x]

39 "Search the Scriptures carefully
because you believe that through them

---

f Jn 3:34; 8:26; 9:4; 10:30; 12:49.—g Jn 3:35; 10:17; 14:12.—h Jn 11:25; Deut 32:39; 1 Sam 2:6; 2 Ki 5:7; Tob 13:2; Wis 16:13; Isa 26:19; Dan 12:2; Rom 4:17; 2 Cor 1:9; Heb 11:19.—i Gen 18:25; Jdg 11:27; Acts 10:42; 17:31.—j Lk 10:16.—k Jn 3:18; 8:51; Mt 10:40; 1 Jn 3:14.—l Jn 4:23; 5:28; 8:51; 11:25-26; Eph 2:1; 5:14; Rev 3:1.—m Jn 1:4; Deut 30:20; Ps 36:10; 1 Jn 5:11.—n Jn 5:22; Dan 7:13; Mt 25:31; Lk 21:36.—o Jn 11:43; 16:2.—p Dan 12:2; Mt 16:27; 25:46; Acts 24:15; 2 Cor 5:10.—q Jn 6:38; Isa 28:6.—r 31-32: Jn 8:13-14, 18.—s Jn 1:19-27; Mt 11:10-11.—t Acts 16:30; Eph 2:8; 1 Jn 5:9.—u Jn 1:8; Ps 132:17; Sir 48:1; Dan 12:3; 2 Pet 1:19.—v Jn 10:25; 14:11.—w Jn 8:18; Deut 4:12, 15; 1 Tim 1:17; 1 Jn 5:9.—x Isa 26:10; 1 Jn 2:14.

5:31-47 The claim made by Jesus has to be confirmed. People cannot testify on their own behalf. There was, of course, John the Baptist's testimony in favor of Christ, but it had already become no more than a remembrance. It is in the works of Jesus that believers recognize the attestation of the Father.

But how could other people accept this recognition, those who are only preoccupied with their rank in the world, with their person, or with their religious role? Victimized by such an attitude, they falsify even the testimony of Scripture to protect themselves. Only those people can come to Jesus who rid themselves of their pretensions, human and even religious, those who are truly inflamed with love for God.

you will gain eternal life.
Even they testify on my behalf.[y]
40 Yet you refuse to come to me
to receive that life.[z]

Unbelief of Jesus' Hearers

41 "I do not accept the praise of men.
42 Moreover, I know that you do not have
the love of God in your hearts.[a]
43 I have come in the name of my Father,
yet you do not accept me.
But if another should come in his own
name,
you will accept him.[b]
44 How can you believe
when you accept praise from one another,
yet you do not seek
the praise that comes from
the only God?[c]

45 "Do not think that I will accuse you
before the Father.
You have placed your hope in Moses,
and he is the one who will accuse you.[d]
46 If you truly believed Moses,
you would have believed in me,
for it is about me that he wrote.[e]
47 But since you do not believe what he
wrote,
how will you believe what I say?"[f]

IV: THE BREAD OF LIFE*

CHAPTER 6

A: Signs of Salvation

Jesus Feeds the Crowds.* 1 [g] After this,
Jesus crossed the Sea of Galilee, also called
the Sea of Tiberias, 2 and a large crowd of
people followed him because they saw the
signs he performed on the sick.[h] 3 Jesus went
up on a mountainside and sat down there
with his disciples. 4 The Jewish feast of
Passover was approaching.[i]

5 When Jesus looked up and saw a large
crowd coming toward him, he said to Philip,
"Where are we to buy bread for them to
eat?"[j] 6 He said this to test him, because
Jesus himself knew what he was going to do.
7 Philip answered him, "Two hundred days'
wages* would not buy enough bread for
each of them to have a small piece."[k] 8 One
of his disciples, Andrew, the brother of
Simon Peter, said to him,[l] 9 "There is a boy
here who has five barley loaves and two fish.
But what help will they be among so
many?"[m]

10 Jesus said, "Have the people sit down."
Now there was plenty of grass in that place,
so the men sat down, about five thousand of
them.[n] 11 Then Jesus took the loaves, and
when he had given thanks, he distributed
them to the people who were sitting there.
He did the same with the fish, as much as
they wanted.[o] 12 When they all had eaten
enough, he said to the disciples, "Gather up
the fragments that are left over, so that nothing
will be wasted." 13 So they gathered them
up and filled twelve baskets with the fragments
of the five barley loaves left by those
who had eaten.

14 When the people saw the sign he had
performed they began to say, "This is indeed
the Prophet who is to come into the world."[p]
15 Then Jesus realized that they were going
to come and carry him off to make him
king, so he again withdrew to the mountain
by himself.[q]

Jesus Walks on the Water.* 16 [r] When evening
came, the disciples went down to the sea,
17 got into a boat, and set out across the sea
to Capernaum. It was already dark, and
Jesus had not yet joined them. 18 The sea
then became rough because a strong wind
had started to blow.

y Jn 12:16; 19:28; 20:9; Lk 24:27, 44; Acts 13:27; Rom 2:17, 18; 1 Pet 1:10.—z Jn 6:44.—a 1 Jn 2:15.—b Mt 24:5, 24.—c Jn 12:43; Rom 2:29; 1 Cor 4:5.—d Jn 9:28; Deut 31:26.—e Jn 5:39; Deut 18:15; Lk 16:31; 24:44; Acts 26:22.—f Lk 16:29, 31.—g 1-13: Mt 14:13-21; Mk 6:32-44; Lk 9:10-17.—h Jn 2:11.—i Jn 2:13; 11:55.—j Jn 1:43; Num 11:13.—k Mt 20:2.—l Jn 1:40.—m 2 Ki 4:42-44.—n Mt 14:21; Mk 6:44.—o Jn 21:13; Mt 14:19.—p Deut 18:15, 18; Mal 3:1; Mt 11:3; Acts 3:22.—q Jn 18:36; Mk 6:46.—r 16-21: Mt 14:22-27; Mk 6:45-52.

6:1-71 The Jewish Passover is near at hand, and with it the days on which unleavened bread is eaten as a sign of renewal; the action also recalls the manna that fed the Hebrews in the wilderness. It is in this context that the evangelist places Jesus' act of feeding the hungry crowd. The whole action is a sign and foreshadowing of a new Passover and a true life-giving food. Jesus himself, in his person, is the bread of life that God offers to humanity. In order to receive this bread that makes a person live forever, one must believe in the Word.

6:1-15 This is one of the rare passages in which all four Gospels are clearly parallel. At this point, John introduces the discourse on the bread of life. The sign of the loaves is seen as a symbol of the food given to mankind in the Word of God and especially in the Eucharist.

6:7 *Two hundred days' wages:* literally: two hundred denarii. A denarius was the average wage for a day's work (see Mt 20:2).

6:16-21 This account is connected with the preceding passage in the oldest tradition. Like the miracle of the loaves, it shows the absolute mastery Jesus exercises over creatures. For the disciples it is an invitation to believe without reserve: with Jesus present, they will lack nothing, and nothing can put them in peril.

19 When they had rowed about three or
four miles, they saw Jesus walking on the sea
and approaching the boat, and they were
terrified.[s] 20 But he said to them, "It is I.*
Do not be afraid!"[t] 21 They were ready to
take him into the boat, but the boat imme-
diately reached the shore toward which they
were heading.

B: Jesus, the Bread of Life for Believers*

Earthly Food and Heavenly Bread.* 22 The
next day, the crowd that had stayed on the
other side of the sea realized that there had
only been one boat there, and that Jesus had
not gone along with his disciples; rather, the
disciples had left by themselves. 23 Then some
boats from Tiberias came near the place
where the people had eaten the bread after
the Lord had given thanks. 24 When the crowd
saw that neither Jesus nor his disciples were
there, they themselves got into the boats and
came to Capernaum looking for Jesus.

25 When the people found him on the other
side of the sea, they said to him, "Rabbi,
when did you come here?"[u] 26 Jesus
answered them,

"Amen, amen, I say to you,
you came looking for me
not because you have seen signs
but because you ate the loaves
and your hunger was satisfied.
27 Do not work for food that perishes
but for the food that endures for eternal life,
which the Son of Man will give you.
For it is on him
that God the Father has set his seal."[v]

28 Then they asked him, "What must we
do if we are to carry out the works of God?"
29 Jesus replied,

"This is the work of God:
to believe in the one whom he has sent."[w]

30 They asked him further, "What sign can
you give us that we can see and come to
believe in you? What work will you do?[x]
31 Our ancestors ate manna in the desert. As
it is written, 'He gave them bread from
heaven* to eat.' "[y] 32 Jesus replied,

"Amen, amen, I say to you,
it was not Moses
who gave you the bread from heaven.
It is my Father
who gives you the true bread from heaven.[z]
33 For the bread of God is
he who comes down from heaven
and gives life to the world."[a]

The Bread of Life.* 34 "Sir," they begged
him, "give us this bread always."[b] 35 Jesus
answered them,

"I am* the bread of life.
Whoever comes to me will never be hungry,
and whoever believes in me will never be thirsty.[c]
36 But I said to you that you have seen me
and yet you do not believe.[d]
37 All that the Father gives me
will come to me,
and anyone who comes to me
I will never turn away.[e]
38 For I have come down from heaven
not to do my own will
but the will of him who sent me.[f]

s Job 9:8; Pss 29:3-4; 77:20; Isa 43:16.—t Mt 14:27.—u Mt 23:7.—v Jn 6:50, 51, 54, 58; Ex 16:20; Isa 55:2; Rom 4:11.—w 1 Jn 3:23.—x Jn 1:21; 2:11; Mt 16:1-4; Lk 11:29-30.—y Ex 16:4, 15; Num 11:7-9; Neh 9:15; Ps 78:24.—z Mt 6:11.—a Jn 3:13, 31.—b Jn 4:15.—c Jn 8:12; Ex 3:14; Isa 55:1-3; Am 8:11-13.—d Jn 20:29.—e Jn 17:2, 6, 9.—f Jn 4:34; Mt 26:39; Heb 10:9.

6:20 *It is I:* literally, "I AM," the formula that reveals the name of the Lord in the Old Testament (see Ex 3:14; Isa 41:4, 10, 14; 43:1-3, 10, 13). Hence, the evangelist is alluding to Jesus as the Son of God. See note on Jn 4:26.

6:22-71 Jesus' gestures and actions are always signs of God; in them is expressed something of the mystery of Christ. Thus, the fourth evangelist places on the lips of Jesus a discourse that unveils the mystery. Here, then, is the deep meaning of the miracle of the loaves: Jesus is the Messenger of God, the true Bread handed over to gain life with God for the whole world.

Thus, it is announced that the words of Jesus are food for people, and that the life of Jesus is given on the cross for the salvation of all. But the Christian addressees of the fourth Gospel could not read this discourse without interpreting it as already announcing the rite inaugurated at the Last Supper (Mt 26:26), the Eucharist, memorial of the body handed over, of the blood shed, of the sacrifice of the cross.

Therefore, this discourse can be read on two levels. The author of the Gospel certainly wanted it so read: the word of God instructs one in the ways of God and the word of God is the bread of life that nourishes the spiritual hunger of God's people.

6:22-33 There is a hunger for everlasting life, a hunger for God! And there is a bread of God, a food that gives everlasting life to those who believe in Jesus. The miracle of the manna was a symbol of this food (Ex 16:4, 13-15).

6:31 *Bread from heaven:* see Ex 14:4, 15, 32-34; Ps 78:24. There was a belief that the manna had been hidden by Jeremiah (see 2 Mac 2:5-8) and would reappear at Passover in Messianic times.

6:34-40 Jesus makes an astonishing affirmation: there is a Bread of God for us, and it is a person. Jesus himself fulfills his Father's plan for us; in Jesus, God is present so that we may have true life. To receive God's Bread is to believe in Jesus and accept him as the Son of God to receive through him the life his Father intends for us. What an astonishing gift! Jesus does not allow himself to be worshiped as a god or a hero; he says of himself that he came to satisfy the hunger of people and to fulfill our life. Every other food is only a diversion for our essential hunger. Jesus is the Bread that satisfies this hunger.

6:35 *I am . . . :* this is the first of seven self-descriptions of Jesus introduced by "I am" (see Jn 8:12; and 9:5; 10:7, 9; 10:11, 14; 11:25; 14:6; 15:1, 5). These echo Ex 3:14 (see notes on Jn 4:26 and 6:20).

39 "And this is the will of him who sent me:
that I should lose nothing
of all that he has given me,
but that I should raise it up
on the last day.[g]
40 This indeed is the will of my Father:
that all who see the Son
and believe in him
may have eternal life,
and I shall raise them up
on the last day."[h]

Faith, a Gift of God.* 41 Then the Jews murmured about him because he said, "I am the bread that came down from heaven." 42 They said, "Is this not Jesus, the son of Joseph? We know his father and mother. How can he say, 'I have come down from heaven'?"[i]

43 "Stop murmuring among yourselves!" Jesus said.[j]

44 "No one can come to me
unless he is drawn by the Father who sent me,
and I will raise up that person on the last day.[k]
45 It is written in the Prophets,
'They will all be taught by God.'
Everyone who has listened to my Father
and learned from him
comes to me.[l]
46 Not that anyone has seen the Father
except the one who is from God;
he has seen the Father.[m]

47 "Amen, amen, I say to you,
whoever believes has eternal life.

My Flesh for the Life of the World*

48 "I am the bread of life.
49 Your ancestors ate the manna in the wilderness,
and yet they died.[n]
50 This is the bread that comes down from heaven,
so that one may eat it and not die.
51 I am the living bread that came down from heaven.
Whoever eats this bread will live forever;
and the bread that I will give
is my flesh, for the life of the world."[o]

52 Then the Jews started to argue among
themselves, saying, "How can this man give
us his flesh to eat?"[p] 53 Jesus said to them,

"Amen, amen, I say to you,
unless you eat the flesh of the Son of Man
and drink his blood,
you do not have life within you.[q]
54 Whoever feeds upon my flesh
and drinks my blood
has eternal life,
and I will raise him up on the last day.
55 For my flesh is real food,
and my blood is real drink.

56 "Whoever feeds upon my flesh and drinks my blood
dwells in me and I dwell in him.[r]
57 Just as the living Father sent me
and I have life because of the Father,
so whoever feeds upon me will live because of me.[s]
58 This is the bread that came down from heaven.
Unlike your ancestors who ate
and nevertheless died,
the one who feeds upon this bread
will live forever."[t]

The Holy One of God.* 59 Jesus said these
things while he was teaching in the synagogue at Capernaum. 60 After hearing his
words, many of his disciples said, "This is a
hard saying. Who can accept it?" 61 Aware of

g Jn 10:28-29; 17:12; 18:9; Isa 27:3; Jer 23:4; Mt 18:14.—h Jn 12:45; 1 Jn 2:25.—i Jn 7:27; Mt 13:54-57; Mk 6:1-4; Lk 4:22.—j Ex 16:2, 7-8; Lk 4:22.—k Mt 16:17.—l Isa 54:13; Jer 31:33-34; 1 Cor 2:13; Heb 8:10.—m Jn 1:18; 7:29; Ex 33:20; 1 Jn 4:12.—n 1 Cor 10:3, 5.—o Mt 26:26-27; Lk 22:19; 1 Cor 11:24; Heb 10:10.—p Jn 7:43; 9:16.—q Mt 8:20.—r Jn 15:4-7.—s Jn 5:26.—t Jn 3:36.

6:41-47 During the period in the wilderness, the Hebrews doubted the Lord and "grumbled" against him; the memory of this had remained as a warning for all time (see Ex 16; Num 11; Ps 106:25).

When the fourth Gospel speaks of "the Jews," the reference is to this mentality, this attitude of rejection, rather than to people as a whole or even to their leaders.

6:48-58 In what sense does Jesus do the Father's will? By giving his life. He does not use the word "sacrifice," but the terms "flesh" and "blood" express that idea in a very realistic way. In this gift, the life of the Father is given to human beings and becomes their everlasting life. That is a strong statement, and yet the objection of the Jews, who take it in the most material sense, does not lead to any toning down of it. On the contrary!

6:59-71 After the success of the multiplication of loaves, scandal arises. The "flesh" (v. 63)—that is, people with their petty desires and thoughts—could not but be shocked by a revelation as absolute as the one they have just heard (that Jesus is the living Bread come down from heaven). Many of his disciples as well as some other people stopped following him, and Judas was already thinking of handing him over.

Only the Spirit gives people the will to believe that the Father speaks in Jesus. It is the Spirit who inspires Peter's profession of faith (see Mt 16:16; Mk 8:29; Lk 9:20). But the Spirit would not be given in fullness until after Jesus' Resurrection (see Jn 7:39).

In regard to Jesus, there is a division among the people. This division and Peter's profession of faith mark a parting of the ways in the life of Jesus. The time of revelation to the disciples has begun and from now on the conflict with the official religion will develop irreconcilably.

the complaints of his disciples, Jesus said to them,

"Does this shock you? [u]
62 What then if you were to behold the Son of Man
ascend to where he was before?
63 It is the spirit that gives life;
the flesh * can achieve nothing.
The words that I have spoken to you
are spirit and life. [v]
64 But there are some among you
who do not believe." [w]

For from the very beginning Jesus knew who did not believe, and who would betray him. 65 He said,

"This is why I told you
that no one can come to me
unless it is granted to him by my Father."

66 After this, many of his disciples turned away and no longer remained with him. 67 Then Jesus said to the Twelve, "Do you also wish to leave?" 68 Simon Peter answered him, "Lord, to whom shall we go? You have the words of eternal life. [x] 69 We have come to believe and know that you are the Holy One of God." [y]

70 Jesus replied, "Did I not choose you twelve? Yet one of you is a devil." [z] 71 He was speaking of Judas, the son of Simon Iscariot. Although he was one of the Twelve, he would be the one who would betray him. [a]

V: THE LIGHT OF THE WORLD*

A: Jesus, Sign of Contradiction

CHAPTER 7

Jesus' Time Has Not Yet Been Fulfilled.* 1 After this, Jesus resumed his travels throughout Galilee. He did not want to go about in Judea because the Jews were seeking to kill him. [b]

2 However, when the Jewish feast of Tabernacles was drawing near, [c] 3 his brethren * said to him, "Depart from here and go into Judea so that your disciples can perceive the works you are doing. 4 No one who wishes to be publicly known acts in secret. Since you are doing these things, reveal yourself to the world." [d] 5 For not even his brethren believed in him. [e] 6 Jesus answered them,

"My time has not yet come,
but your time is always right. [f]
7 The world cannot hate you,
but it does hate me
because I testify against it
that its works are evil. [g]
8 Go up to the feast yourselves.
I am not going to this feast,
because my time has not yet fully come."

9 After he had said this, he stayed behind in Galilee. 10 Later, however, after his brethren had gone up to the feast, he himself also went, not publicly, but in secret.

11 During the feast the Jews were looking for him and asking, "Where is he?" [h] 12 There was widespread murmuring about him among the crowds. Some maintained, "He is a good man," but others insisted, "No, for he is leading the people astray." 13 However, no one spoke openly about him for fear of the Jews. [i]

Do Not Judge by Appearances.* 14 When the feast was half over, Jesus went up into the temple and began to teach. 15 The Jews were astonished, and they wondered, "How has

u Mt 13:57.—v 2 Cor 3:6.—w Jn 13:11.—x Acts 7:38.—y Jn 11:27; Mt 16:16; Mk 1:24; Lk 4:34; 9:20.—z Jn 13:27; 15:16.—a Jn 12:4; 13:2, 27; Mt 26:14.—b Jn 5:18; 8:37, 40; Mk 9:30.—c Ex 23:16; Lev 23:34; Num 29:12; Deut 16:13-16; Zec 14:16-19.—d Jn 14:22.—e Ps 69:9; Mk 3:21.—f Dan 7:22.—g Jn 3:19, 20; 15:18.—h Jn 11:56.—i Jn 9:22; 19:38; 20:19.

6:63 *Flesh:* the human being with its desires and thoughts.

7:1—9:41 The feast of Tabernacles, one of the most important Jewish solemnities, was a harvest festival. There was also a commemoration of the miraculous deeds that God had done for his people in the wilderness, with a joyous feast of lamps, a festival of lights. The feast was the ideal setting in which to present Christ as the Word of God who had come to enlighten and save everyone.

7:1-13 From now on the threat of death hangs over Jesus and creates tension for him. The tension has to be relieved as quickly as possible. A gathering of people in Jerusalem would be a good occasion for rallying them and neutralizing the adversaries. An impressive public manifestation by Jesus would also be helpful; people would at least know what to make of him. So reason the "brethren" of Jesus—that is, the relatives if not the disciples.

But these perspectives of glory have no hold on Jesus. He has come to fulfill God's plan; this is not the same as looking for a temporary success. He also has come to turn back the course of evil, falsehood, and hatred in the world. Jesus overcame the hatred of the world by handing himself over to it.

7:3 *Brethren:* i.e., according to Hebrew idiom, close relatives. See note on Mt 12:46.

7:14-24 Personal success is never the motive for an action of Jesus. His words and his miracles testify that he is the messenger of the Father. Jesus lives by this testimony, of which he is convinced, and does not defend any doctrine of a school or group; one care alone impels him: that the Father's plan for us be recognized and fulfilled.

Only those will understand Jesus who take the Law seriously in its deep inspiration and know the price of fidelity to God. But those who accuse Jesus of violating the Law and take upon themselves the authority to condemn him fail to recognize him.

this man acquired such knowledge when he has never studied?”*[j] 16 Jesus answered them,

“My teaching is not my own;
rather, it comes from him who sent me.
17 Anyone who resolves to do his will
will know whether my teaching comes from God
or whether I am speaking on my own authority.[k]
18 Whoever speaks on his own authority
is simply seeking his own glory,
but whoever seeks the glory
of the one who sent him
is a truthful person,
and there is no dishonesty in him.[l]

19 “Did not Moses give you the Law?
And not one of you keeps the Law.
Why are you trying to kill me?”[m]

20 The crowd shouted, “You are possessed! Who is trying to kill you?”[n] 21 Jesus replied,

“I performed a single work,*
and all of you are astonished.[o]
22 Moses gave you circumcision
—although it did not originate with Moses
but with the patriarchs—
and you circumcise a man on the Sabbath.[p]
23 Now if a man can be circumcised on the Sabbath
so that the Law of Moses may not be broken,
why are you angry with me
for making a man’s entire body
completely healthy on the Sabbath?[q]
24 Do not base your judgment on appearances;
judge according to what is right.”[r]

Where Is Jesus from and Where Is He Going?* 25 Then some of the inhabitants of Jerusalem said, “Is this not the man they are trying to kill? 26 And yet he is speaking publicly, and they say nothing to him! Can it be that the authorities realize that he is the Christ? 27 And yet we know where this man is from. But when the Christ appears, no one will know where he is from.”[s]

28 Then Jesus cried out as he was teaching in the temple,

“You know me,
and you also know where I am from.
Yet I have not come of my own accord,
but he who sent me is true.
You do not know him,[t]
29 but I know him
because I am from him
and it was he who sent me.”[u]

30 So they tried to arrest him, but no one laid a hand on him because his hour had not yet come.[v] 31 Yet many in the crowd believed in him, and they said, “When the Christ comes, will he perform more signs than this man has accomplished?”[w]

32 When the Pharisees overheard the crowd murmuring about him, the chief priests and the Pharisees sent temple guards to arrest him. 33 Jesus then said,

“I will remain with you
only for a short time longer,
and then I shall return
to him who sent me.[x]
34 You will search for me,
but you will not find me,
for where I am you cannot come.”[y]

35 The Jews said to one another, “Where does this man intend to go that we will not be able to find him? Will he go abroad to the people who are dispersed among the Greeks and teach the Greeks?[z] 36 What does he mean when he says, ‘You will search for me, but you will be unable to find me,’ and ‘Where I am you cannot come’?”

---

j Mt 13:54; Lk 2:47; Acts 26:24.—k Jn 6:29; Ps 25:14.—l Ps 92:16.—m Jn 1:17; Deut 32:46; Acts 7:53; Rom 2:17-23.—n Jn 8:48-49; 10:20; Mt 12:24-27.—o Jn 5:1-9.—p Gen 17:10; Lev 12:3.—q Jn 5:2-9, 16; Mt 12:11-12; Lk 14:5.—r Jn 8:15; Lev 19:15; 1 Sam 16:7; Isa 11:3-4; Zec 7:9; 2 Cor 10:7.—s Mt 13:55; Lk 4:22; Heb 7:3.—t Jn 8:14, 19; Mt 11:27.—u Jn 6:46; 8:55.—v Jn 7:44; 8:20; Mt 26:18; Lk 4:29-30.—w Jn 2:11; 8:30; 10:42; 11:45.—x Jn 12:35; 13:33; 16:16.—y Jn 8:21; 12:36; 13:33, 36; 16:5; Deut 4:29; Prov 1:28; Isa 55:6; Hos 5:6.—z Acts 17:4; Jas 1:1.

7:15 The people want to know how Jesus can teach like a rabbi, when he was never trained by one and never quotes his teacher.

7:21 *A single work:* the work of which Jesus speaks may be the cure of the paralytic that is recounted in Jn 5:1-15.

7:25-36 The new prophet intrigues the people. He is one of theirs, yet claims an origin that does not cease to be mysterious. Some of the people are tempted to recognize him as the Messiah. The official authorities rebel against this temptation and want him arrested. In veiled words, Jesus announces his return to the Father (vv. 33-34). The authorities see this as an attempt to flee Palestine.

In all these contrasts there is perhaps some irony. Jesus escapes the people who want to place him in their preconceived ideas, just as he escapes the people who want to lay hands on him. Jesus can be talked about endlessly; it is quite another thing to accept his mystery.

Streams of Living Water.* 37 * On the last and greatest day of the feast, Jesus stood up and cried out,

"If anyone is thirsty,
let him come to me and drink.[a]
38 Whoever believes in me,
as Scripture has said,
'Streams of living water
shall flow from within him.' "[b]

39 Now he was referring here to the Spirit whom those who believed in him were to receive. As yet the Spirit had not been bestowed because Jesus had not yet been glorified.[c]

People Are Divided concerning Jesus.* 40 On hearing these words, some in the crowd said, "This must truly be the Prophet."[d] 41 Others thought, "This is the Christ." But still others retorted, "How can the Christ come from Galilee?[e] 42 Does not Scripture assert that the Christ will be of the seed of David and come from Bethlehem, the city where David lived?"[f] 43 As a result, the crowd was sharply divided because of him.[g] 44 Some of them even wanted to arrest him, but no one laid a hand on him.

45 Then the temple guards went back to the chief priests and the Pharisees, who asked them, "Why did you not arrest him?" 46 The guards answered, "No one has ever spoken as this man has."[h] 47 Then the Pharisees said, "Have you also been deceived? 48 Has any one of the authorities or of the Pharisees come to believe in him?[i] 49 As for this crowd, they do not know the Law—they are cursed."

50 One of them, Nicodemus, who had previously come to Jesus, said to them,[j] 51 "Does our Law allow us to pass judgment on someone without first giving him a hearing to ascertain what he is doing?"[k] 52 They replied, "Are you too a Galilean? Look it up, and you will find that no prophet is to arise from Galilee."[l]

CHAPTER 8

B: Jesus, Savior of Sinners

A Woman Caught in Adultery.* [7:53 Then each of them returned home. 1[m] But Jesus went to the Mount of Olives. 2 At daybreak he entered the temple courts, and all the people gathered around him. He sat down and began to teach them.

3 The scribes and the Pharisees brought in a woman who had been caught in adultery. Forcing her to stand in their midst, 4 they said to him, "Teacher, this woman was caught in the very act of adultery. * 5 Now in the Law Moses commanded us to stone such women. * What do you have to say?"[n]

6 They asked him this question as a test so that they could bring a charge against him. Jesus bent down and started to write on the ground with his finger.[o] 7 When they continued to persist in their question, he straightened up and said to them, "Let anyone among you who is without sin be the first to throw a stone at her." * 8[p] Then he again bent down and wrote on the ground.

9 When they heard his response, they went away one by one, beginning with the elders,

a Lev 23:36; Isa 55:1; Rev 21:6.—b Jn 4:10, 14; 19:34; Isa 12:3; 58:11; Ezek 47:1.—c Jn 16:7; Isa 44:3; Joel 3:1; 1 Cor 10:4.—d Deut 18:15, 18.—e Jn 1:46.—f 2 Sam 7:12-14; Pss 89:3-4; 132:11; Mic 5:2; Mt 2:5-6; Rom 1:3.—g Jn 6:52.—h Mt 7:28.—i Jn 12:42.—j Jn 3:1; 19:39.—k Deut 1:16-17; 17:4; Acts 5:35.—l Jn 1:46; Mt 16:14.—m 1-2: Lk 21:37-38.—n Lev 20:10; Deut 22:22-29; Job 31:11; Ezek 16:38, 40.—o Mt 22:15, 18; Lk 20:20.—p Deut 17:7; Ezek 16:40; Rom 2:1, 22.

7:37-39 The last day was for the pilgrims a festival of water. How many symbolic meanings water evokes! Water had flowed miraculously from the rock in the midst of the wilderness to slake the thirst of the Hebrews (Ex 17:1-7). The Prophets had foretold a spring that would some day open in the midst of the people (Ezek 47:1; Zec 14:8). In all areas affected by drought, water is a sign of life and joy; it is a gift of God. Christians think of Pentecost and Baptism.

7:37-38 An alternative reading and translation is: "If anyone is thirsty, let him come to me, and let him who believes in me drink. As Scripture has said. . . . " In this second reading, the Scripture passage refers to Jesus and not to the believer. See Ps 105:41; Isa 44:3; 48:21; Ezek 36:25; Joel 3:1; etc.

7:40-52 The upper class felt only contempt for the ordinary people. How could one accept a Messiah who came from distant Galilee, where Jews mingled with Gentiles and were cut off from the heart of Jewish life? Some justified their rejection by citing passages of the Law, but there were others who appealed to the spirit of the Law.

7:53—8:11 This story is missing in a number of ancient manuscripts and is inserted at other points in others; it does not seem to be from the author of the fourth Gospel, for it is written in quite a different style. However, it has been accepted by the Church as the work of an inspired author.

We are struck by the portrait of Jesus found herein: his silence, his sober gesture, his refusal to use religion as a pretext to spy on and judge others, and his courage to proclaim his own truth. It is pointless to ask what he wrote on the ground. Let us dwell on what he considered the Law to be: it condemns sin not so that people may judge one another but so that they may feel the need to be saved by God. And it is to this salvation that he bears witness.

8:4 *Caught in the very act of adultery:* Jewish law required witnesses to have seen the act.

8:5 *Stone such women:* stoning was required only if the woman was a betrothed virgin (Deut 22:23-24). The Law also demanded the execution of *both* parties (Lev 20:10; Deut 22:22).

8:7 The Law stipulated that the first stones were to be cast by the witnesses (Deut 17:7).

until Jesus was left alone with the woman standing before him. [10] Then Jesus straightened up and said to her, "Woman, where are they? Has no one condemned you?" [q] [11] She replied, "No one, sir." "Neither do I condemn you," Jesus said. "Go on your way, and sin no more."] [r]

C: The Light Triumphs over Darkness

The Light of the World.* [12] Jesus addressed them once again, saying,

"I am * the light of the world.
The one who follows me
will never walk in darkness.
Rather, he will have the light of life." [s]

[13] On hearing this, the Pharisees said to him, "You are testifying on your own behalf. Your testimony is not true." [14] Jesus replied,

"Even though I testify on my own behalf,
my testimony is true,
because I know where I have come from
and where I am going,
whereas you do not know
where I have come from
or where I am going. [t]
15 You judge by the flesh,
whereas I do not judge anyone. [u]
16 Yet even if I do judge,
my judgment is true
because it is not I alone who judge,
but it is I and the Father who sent me. [v]
17 "In your Law it is written
that the testimony of two witnesses is true. [w]
18 I testify on my own behalf,
and the Father who sent me
also testifies on my behalf." [x]

[19] They continued to question him, saying, "Where is your Father?" Jesus answered,

"You know neither me nor my Father.
If you knew me,
you would know my Father also." [y]

[20] He spoke these words while he was teaching at the treasury of the temple. * However, no one arrested him because his hour had not yet come. [z]

I AM!* [21] Again he said to them,

"I am going away,
and you will search for me
but you will die in your sin.
Where I am going, you cannot come." [a]

[22] Then the Jews wondered, "Is he planning to kill himself—because he was saying, 'Where I am going, you cannot come'?" [23] He continued,

"You belong to what is below,
whereas I belong to what is above.
You belong to this world,
but I am not of this world. [b]
24 That is why I told you
that you would die in your sins.
For if you do not believe
that I AM,
you will die in your sins." [c]

[25] "Who are you then?" they asked him. Jesus answered,

"Just what I have been telling you
from the beginning. [d]
26 I have much to say about you,
and much to condemn.
But the one who sent me is true,
and what I have heard from him
I declare to the world." [e]

[27] They did not understand that he was speaking to them about the Father. [28] Therefore, Jesus said,

"When you have lifted up the Son of Man,
then you will know
that I AM,
that I do nothing on my own authority
and I say nothing except what
the Father has taught me. [f]

q Ezek 33:11.—r Jn 3:17; 5:14; Ps 103:8, 13-14.—s Jn 1:4-5, 9; 12:46; Ex 13:21; Ps 27:1; Prov 4:18; Wis 7:26: Isa 42:6; Zec 14:7.—t Jn 5:31; 13:3.—u Jn 12:47; 1 Sam 16:7.—v Jn 5:30.—w Num 35:30; Deut 17:6; 19:15; Mt 18:16.—x Jn 5:23, 37.—y Jn 7:28; 14:7; 15:21; 16:3.—z Jn 7:30; Mk 12:41.—a Jn 7:34; 13:33; Ezek 3:18; 18:20.—b Jn 3:31; 17:14; 18:36.—c Jn 4:26; Deut 32:39; Isa 43:10.—d Jn 10:24.—e Jn 7:28; 12:44-50.—f Jn 3:14; 12:32, 34.

8:12-20 Here is another symbol, which has the feast of Lights for its setting and enables us to understand more fully the part Jesus intends to play in the life of human beings: he is light. We may think of the luminous cloud during the journey in the wilderness (see Ex 13:21; Wis 18:3), the form in which God was leading his people.

8:12 *I am:* see notes on Jn 6:20 and 6:35.

8:20 *The treasury of the temple:* not the place where the offerings were stored, since this was closed to the public, but the adjacent room where the boxes for the offerings stood (see Mk 12:41; Lk 21:1).

8:21-30 The discussion is continued so that the reader may come into direct contact with the mystery of Jesus. Who then is he? He does not belong to the world of sin but gathers around himself those who believe in him. Without this faith in him, people remain shut up in death, cast off from God. A sudden word is uttered: *I am,* the name by which God revealed himself to Moses (Ex 3:14). Jesus is so closely united to his Father that he can claim the title "Lord" for himself. Jesus will appear as Judge and Lord when he is lifted up on the cross (Jn 3:14; 19:37).

29 He who sent me is with me.
He has not left me alone,
for I always do what pleases him." [g]

30 On hearing these words, many came to
believe in him.

Jesus and Abraham.* 31 Then Jesus said to
those Jews who did believe in him,

"If you remain faithful to my word,
you will truly be my disciples. [h]
32 You will know the truth,
and the truth will set you free." [i]

33 They answered him, "We are descen-
dants of Abraham, and we have never been
slaves to anyone. What do you mean by say-
ing, 'You will be set free'?" [j] 34 Jesus replied,

"Amen, amen, I say to you,
everyone who sins
is a slave of sin. [k]
35 A slave does not remain in a household forever,
but a son remains in it forever. [l]
36 Therefore, if the Son sets you free,
you then will truly be free.

37 "I know that you are descendants of Abraham,
but you seek to kill me
because my word has no place in your heart. [m]
38 I speak of what I have seen
in my Father's presence,
whereas you do what you have heard
from your father." [n]

39 The Jews said to him, "Abraham is our
father." Jesus said to them,

"If you were Abraham's children,
you would be doing the works that Abraham did. [o]
40 But now you seek to kill me,
a man who has told you the truth
that I heard from God.
This is not what Abraham did. [p]
41 You are doing the works of your father!"

They retorted, "We are not illegitimate
children. We have one father—God." [q]
42 Jesus said to them,

"If God were your father,
you would love me,
for I came from God;
neither did I come of my own will,
but he was the one who sent me. [r]
43 Why do you not understand
what I am saying?
It is because you cannot bear
to hear my words.

44 "You are from your father, the devil,
and you choose to carry out your father's desires.
He was a murderer from the beginning,
and he does not abide by the truth,
for there is no truth in him.
When he lies,
he speaks in accord with his own nature,
for he is a liar
and the father of lies. [s]
45 But because I speak the truth
you refuse to believe me. [t]

46 "Which of you can convict me of sin?
If I say what is true,
why do you not believe me? [u]
47 Whoever comes from God
listens to the words of God.
The reason why you refuse to listen
is that you do not belong to God." [v]

48 The Jews answered, "Are we not right in
saying that you are a Samaritan and are
possessed?" [w] 49 Jesus said,

"I am not possessed.
I honor my Father,
but you dishonor me.
50 I do not seek my own glory.
There is one who seeks it,
and he is the judge. [x]
51 Amen, amen, I say to you,
whoever keeps my word
will never see death." [y]

52 The Jews retorted, "Now we are positive
that you are possessed. Abraham died, and
the Prophets are dead. Yet you say, 'Whoever
keeps my word will never taste death.' 53 Are
you greater than our father Abraham? He is
dead, and the Prophets are also dead. Who
do you claim to be?" [z] 54 Jesus answered,

g Jn 16:32; Isa 50:5.—h Jn 15:7; 2 Jn 9.—i Isa 42:7; Rom 8:2; 2 Cor 3:17; Gal 4:31.—j Mt 3:9; Lk 3:18.—k Rom 6:16-17.—l Gen 21:10; Gal 4:30; Heb 3:5-6.—m Mt 21:33-46.—n Jn 5:19, 30.—o Gen 26:5; Rom 4:11-17; Jas 2:21-23.—p Gen 15:6; Mt 12:14.—q Ex 4:22; Deut 32:6; Isa 63:16; Mal 2:10.—r Jn 7:28; 1 Jn 5:1.—s Gen 3:4; 2 Chr 18:21; Pss 5:7; 12:3; Wis 1:13; 2:24; Acts 13:10; 1 Jn 3:8-15.—t Jn 18:37.—u Heb 4:15; 9:14-28; 1 Pet 2:22; 1 Jn 3:5.—v Jn 10:26; 1 Jn 4:6.—w Mk 3:22.—x Jn 5:41; 7:18.—y Jn 5:24-29; 6:40, 47; 11:25-26.—z Jn 4:12.

8:31-59 The Jews can rightly protest that they are not illegitimate children, that is, using the imagery of the time, they have not grown up in idolatry but in faith in the true God. But that is not enough. To oppose Jesus and reject the truth means entering into an agreement with the devil. Jesus says that he is superior even to Abraham, the father of the people.

"If I glorify myself,
that glory is of no value.
It is my Father who glorifies me,
the one about whom you say,
'He is our God,' [a]
55 even though you do not know him.
However, I do know him.
If I would say
that I do not know him,
I would be a liar like you.
But I do know him,
and I keep his word. [b]
56 Your father Abraham rejoiced
that he would see my day.
He saw it and was glad." * [c]

57 The Jews then said to him, "You are not yet fifty years old. How can you have seen Abraham?" 58 Jesus responded,

"Amen, amen, I say to you,
before Abraham was,
I AM." * [d]

59 Then they picked up stones to throw at him, but he hid himself and left the temple. [e]

D: A Sign of the Triumph of the Light*

CHAPTER 9

Jesus Cures a Man Born Blind.* 1 [f] As Jesus walked along, he saw a man who had been blind from birth. 2 His disciples asked him, "Rabbi, who sinned, this man or his parents, that he was born blind?" [g] 3 Jesus answered,

"Neither this man nor his parents
sinned,
but it happened
so that the works of God
might be revealed in him. [h]
4 We must do
the works of him who sent me
while it is still day.
Night is coming when no one can work. [i]
5 While I am in the world,
I am the light of the world." [j]

6 When he had said this, he spat on the ground, made a paste with the saliva, and smeared the paste on the eyes of the blind man. [k] 7 Then he said to him, "Go and wash in the Pool of Siloam." * (The name means "Sent.") The man went forth and washed, and he returned seeing. [l]

That Man Is a Prophet.* 8 His neighbors and those who had seen him begging asked, "Is this not the man who used to sit and beg?" [m] 9 Some were saying, "Yes, this is the same man," but others insisted, "No. It simply is someone who looks like him." He said, "I am the man."

10 Therefore, they asked him, "Then how were your eyes opened?" 11 He replied, "The man called Jesus made a paste and smeared it over my eyes. Then he said to me, 'Go to Siloam and wash.' So I went and washed, and then I was able to see." 12 They asked him, "Where is he?" He replied, "I do not know."

13 They then brought the man who had formerly been blind to the Pharisees. 14 Now it was on a Sabbath day that Jesus had made the paste and opened his eyes. [n]

15 The Pharisees also asked him how he had gained his sight. He said to them, "He put a paste on my eyes. Then I washed, and now I can see."

16 Some of the Pharisees said, "This man cannot be from God, for he does not observe the Sabbath." But others said, "How can a

a Jn 16:14; Heb 5:5.—b Jn 7:28-29.—c Gen 17:17; Mt 13:17; Lk 17:22.—d Jn 1:30; 17:5; Ex 3:14; 6:3.—e Jn 10:31, 39; 11:8; Ex 17:4; Lev 24:16; 1 Sam 30:6; Lk 4:29-30.—f 1-2: Isa 42:7.—g Ex 20:5; Job 21:19; Ezek 18:20; Lk 13:2; Acts 28:4.—h Jn 5:14; 11:4.—i Jn 11:9-10; 12:35-36.—j Jn 1:4; 8:12.—k Jn 5:11; Mk 7:33; 8:23.—l 2 Ki 5:10-14; Isa 35:5; Lk 13:4.—m Acts 3:2, 10.—n Jn 5:9.

8:56 Abraham rejoiced at the promise given to him by the Lord that the future Messiah would come from his descendants (Gen 12:7; 15:2f.; 17:15f; see Gal 3:16). *My day:* that is, the presence of the Messiah, whom Abraham saw and greeted "from a distance" (Heb 11:13).

8:58 *I AM:* see notes on Jn 6:20 and 6:35.

9:1-41 The preceding chapters have made grand statements about Jesus, e.g., that he is the light of the world; in those chapters, however, the evangelist was guiding us through sometimes difficult reasonings. Here, on the other hand, is a lively story that illustrates the teaching that has been given. The man born blind is an image of the catechumen and of Christians, who allow themselves to be enlightened by Jesus. Not only their eyes but their hearts open to the light.

9:1-7 In the view of the ancients, every illness had its origin in some sin, perhaps a secret one. Jesus firmly condemns this mentality. The blind man must take himself to the Pool of "Siloam" (= "Sent"); the evangelist emphasizes the word. Jesus is the one sent by the Father to bring light; it is he who opens the eyes of faith in those who go down into the pool of Baptism.

9:7 *The Pool of Siloam:* it was at the foot of the southern spur of the temple mount.

9:8-23 Who, then, is Jesus? Again there is questioning. Again also Jesus upsets the Pharisees, who have lost the essence of religion in the complexities of their traditions. The care for observances makes them forget that the Sabbath is first of all a testimony of liberty. In the presence of these teachers, the blind man who has been cured declares that Jesus is a prophet. They challenge his attestation and denounce it as a fraud. Thus an inquiry is made to give themselves basis for their treatment of the man. A climate of fear ensues and no one feels free to speak.

man who is a sinner perform such signs?"
Thus, they were divided in their opinions.[o]
17 And so they spoke again to the blind man,
asking, "What do you have to say about him?
It was your eyes that he opened." He replied,
"He is a prophet."[p]

18 However, the Jews refused to believe
that the man had been blind and had
received his sight until they summoned the
parents of the man who had received his
sight[q] 19 and asked them, "Is this your son
who you say was born blind? How then is he
now able to see?" 20 His parents answered,
"We know that this is our son and that he
was born blind, 21 but we do not know how he
is now able to see, nor do we know who
opened his eyes. Ask him. He is of age. He
can speak for himself."

22 His parents responded in this way
because they were afraid of the Jews. For the
Jews had already agreed that anyone who
acknowledged Jesus to be the Christ would
be put out of the synagogue.[r] 23 This is why
his parents said, "He is of age. Ask him."[s]

That Man Is from God.* 24 And so for a sec-
ond time they summoned the man who had
been blind and said to him, "Give glory to
God. We know that this man is a sinner."[t]
25 He answered, "I do not know whether he
is a sinner. But one thing I do know: I was
blind, and now I am able to see." 26 They
then asked him, "What did he do to you?
How did he open your eyes?" 27 He
answered them, "I have told you already
and you would not listen. Why do you want
to hear it again? Do you also want to
become his disciples?"

28 Then they began to taunt him, saying,
"It is you who are his disciple. We are disci-
ples of Moses.[u] 29 We know that God spoke
to Moses, but as for this man, we do not
know where he is from."[v] 30 He answered,
"That is what is so amazing. You do not
know where he comes from, and yet he
opened my eyes. 31 We know that God does
not listen to sinners, but that he does listen
to anyone who is devout and obeys his will.[w]

32 "Never since the world began has it been
heard that anyone opened the eyes of a per-
son born blind. 33 If this man were not from
God, he could not have been able to accom-
plish anything."[x] 34 They answered him,
"You were born in sin and you would teach
us?" Then they threw him out.[y]

Do You Believe in the Son of Man?* 35 When
Jesus heard that they had thrown him out,
he found him and asked, "Do you believe in
the Son of Man?"[z] 36 He replied, "Who is he,
sir, so that I may believe in him?"[a] 37 "You
have seen him," said Jesus, "and he is the one
who is speaking to you."[b] 38 He said, "I do
believe, Lord," and he fell down in worship
before him.

Spiritual Blindness.* 39 Then Jesus said,

"It is for judgment
that I have come into this world,
so that those without sight may see
and those who do see may become
blind."[c]

40 On hearing this, some Pharisees who
were present asked him, "Are we blind
too?"[d] 41 Jesus replied,

"If you were blind,
you would have no guilt;
but since you claim, 'We see,'
your guilt remains.[e]

o Jn 3:2; Mt 12:10-11; Lk 13:10-11; 14:1-4.—p Jn 4:19; Mt 16:14; 21:11.—q Jn 1:19.—r Jn 7:13; 12:42; 16:2; 19:38; Lk 6:22.—s Jn 12:42.—t Jos 7:19; 1 Sam 6:5 LXX.—u Jn 5:45.—v Jn 8:14; Ex 33:11.—w Jn 10:21; Gen 18:23-32; Pss 34:16; 66:18; Prov 15:29; Isa 1:15.—x Jn 3:2.—y Isa 66:5.—z Mt 8:20.—a Rom 10:14.—b Jn 4:26.—c Jn 3:19; Mt 13:33-35; Lk 4:18.—d Mt 15:14; 23:26; Rom 2:19.—e Jn 3:36; 15:22, 24; Mt 23:16.

9:24-34 The miraculously cured individual is interrogated a second time. His questioners bring up Moses to show that Jesus is in contradiction with him. This, they think, cannot be refuted. But it is necessary to recognize here the presence of the same God who spoke to Moses! The man born blind recognizes that Jesus came from God with a special mission. That is too much for them. They throw him out bodily.

9:35-38 This is an encounter with Jesus, who identifies himself as the Son of Man—that is, as a being with a divine prerogative who has come to bring people to the presence of and communion with God. The profession of faith comes to the lips of the man born blind when he encounters Jesus, who is our light.

9:39-41 Human beings cannot remain indifferent or neutral in the presence of Jesus: we must opt either for light or for darkness. In this choice, the divine judgment comes into play with a sentence of life or death—which foretells the division between synagogue and Church. The lot of each person depends on one's attitude of faith or unbelief toward Jesus. Those who realize they are walking along the way of error and open themselves to the light of the Gospel revelation will be saved. Those who delude themselves that they possess the truth and voluntarily close their eyes to the light will be lost.

While the man born blind receives not only his physical sight but also the light of faith, the Jews who claim that they have sight are blind in a spiritual sense, because they refuse the light of revelation brought by Christ. True blindness is not the physical blindness of the blind man but the lack of belief. The Pharisees are convinced that they possess the truth and oppose themselves to the Envoy of God. They deprive themselves of the way to salvation. For they remain slaves of the sin of unbelief.

VI: THE SHEPHERD WHO GIVES UP HIS LIFE*

CHAPTER 10

A: I Am the Good Shepherd*

The Good Shepherd

1[f] "Amen, amen, I say to you,
anyone who does not enter
the sheepfold through the gate
but climbs in some other way
is a thief and a bandit.
2 The one who enters through the gate
is the shepherd of the flock.[g]
3 The gatekeeper opens for him,
and the sheep hear his voice.
He calls his own sheep by name
and leads them out.

4 "When he has brought out all his own,
he goes on ahead of them,
and the sheep follow him
because they know his voice.[h]
5 However, they will never follow a stranger.
Rather, they will run away from him,
because they do not recognize
the voice of strangers."[i]

6 Jesus used this parable to instruct them,
but they did not understand what he was
saying to them. 7 Therefore, Jesus spoke to
them again,

"Amen, amen, I say to you,
I am the gate of the sheepfold.
8 All who came before me
were thieves and bandits,
but the sheep did not listen to them.[j]

9 "I am the gate.
Anyone who enters through me
will be saved.
He will go in and out
and will find pasture.

10 "A thief comes only
to steal and kill and destroy.
I have come
that they may have life,
and have it in abundance.[k]

11 "I am the good shepherd.
The good shepherd
lays down his life for the sheep.[l]
12 The hired hand,
who is not the shepherd
nor the owner of the sheep,
sees the wolf approaching,
and he leaves the sheep and runs away,
while the wolf catches and scatters them.[m]
13 He runs away
because he is only a hired hand
and he has no concern for the sheep.

14 "I am the good shepherd.
I know my own,
and my own know me,[n]
15 just as the Father knows me
and I know the Father.
And I lay down my life for the sheep.[o]

16 "I have other sheep too
that do not belong to this fold.
I must lead them as well,
and they will hear my voice.
Thus, there will only be one flock,
one shepherd.[p]

17 "This is why the Father loves me,
because I lay down my life
in order to take it up again.[q]
18 No one takes it away from me.
I lay it down of my own free will.
And as I have the power to lay it down,
I have the power to take it up again.
This command I have received from my Father."[r]

f 1-5: Gen 48:15; 49:24; Pss 23:1-4; 80:2; Jer 23:1-4; Ezek 34:1-31; Mic 7:14.—g Jn 21:16; Mk 6:34.—h Mt 2:12-13.—i Jn 16:25; Mk 9:32.—j Jer 23:1-2; Ezek 34:2.—k Ps 65:12; Rom 5:17.—l Ps 23:1-4; Isa 40:11; 49:9-10; Ezek 34:11-16; Heb 13:20; Rev 7:17.—m Zec 11:17.—n Ex 33:12.—o Jn 15:13; Mt 11:27; 1 Jn 3:16.—p Jn 11:52; Isa 56:8; Jer 23:3; Ezek 34:23; 37:24; Mic 2:12; Acts 10:34, 35; Eph 2:11-19.—q Heb 10:10.—r Jn 19:11; Mt 26:53; Phil 2:8.

10:1—11:54 The parable of the good shepherd, the feast of the Dedication, and the raising of Lazarus are three passages that describe who Christ is and what he wants to be for us. The ideas of life and unity dominate in these pages. The desire of Jesus is that we have access to the full reality of life. He gives life to the point of giving up his own; he is the life.

Another preoccupation impels him: to gather into one all who believe in him. So the work of God is to overcome the forces of death, destruction, and dispersion, forces that disfigure the world and our existence.

10:1-21 The image of the flock and the shepherd occurs frequently in the Bible to describe the relationship of Israel with God, or simply the relations of the people with their leader (this language came spontaneously to any civilization of antiquity). More than once the Prophets denounced as wicked shepherds those in authority who exploited the people or led them astray: kings, princes, priests, prophets of comfort (see Jer 23; Ezek 34; Zec 11:4-17). In the final analysis (they said), God alone is the shepherd to whom the flock belongs and who can properly lead and feed it. They were longing for a devoted shepherd who would act solely in God's name.

Jesus now dares to describe himself as this Messiah-shepherd, who comes to deliver human beings from those who enslave them for their own profit or to impose upon them their own convictions. There are no other ways of reaching life and the knowledge of God: Jesus is the "gate"; he is the Shepherd who knows and gathers believers into a single flock. The word "know" signifies a mutual exchange, a reciprocal and radical belonging. This is the main assertion of the passage.

19 Once again, these words provoked a division among the Jews.[s] 20 Many of them were saying, "He is possessed and out of his mind. Why should we listen to him?"[t] 21 But others said, "No one possessed by a demon could speak like this. Can a demon open the eyes of the blind?" *[u]

B: I and the Father Are One

Feast of the Dedication.* 22 At that time, the feast of the Dedication was taking place in Jerusalem. It was winter,[v] 23 and Jesus was walking in the temple along the Portico of Solomon. *[w] 24 The Jews gathered around him and asked, "How much longer will you keep us in suspense? If you are the Christ, tell us plainly."[x] 25 Jesus replied,

"I have told you,
but you do not believe.
The works that I do in my Father's name
bear witness to me,[y]
26 but you do not believe
because you are not my sheep.[z]

27 "My sheep listen to my voice.
I know them, and they follow me.[a]
28 I give them eternal life,
and they will never perish.
No one will ever snatch them from my hand.[b]
29 My Father who has given them to me
is greater than all,
and no one can snatch them
out of the Father's hand.[c]
30 I and the Father are one." *[d]

31 Once again, the Jews picked up rocks to stone him,[e] 32 but Jesus said to them, "I have performed in your presence many good works from my Father. For which of these works are you going to stone me?" 33 The Jews answered, "We are not going to stone you for any good work you have done, but for blasphemy. Even though you are a man, you are claiming to be God."[f] 34 Jesus replied,

"Is it not written in your Law, *
'I said: You are gods'?[g]
35 If those to whom
the word of God was addressed
are called 'gods'
—and Scripture cannot be set aside—
36 how can you say, 'You blaspheme,'
to the one whom the Father has consecrated
and sent into the world
for saying, 'I am the Son of God'?[h]

37 "If I am not performing
the works of my Father,
then do not believe me.
38 However, if I am doing them,
then even if you do not believe me,
at least believe my works,
so that you may realize and understand
that the Father is in me
and I am in the Father."[i]

39 They again tried to seize him, but he escaped from their clutches.[j]

The Testimony of John the Baptist.* 40 He went back across the Jordan to the place where John had first been baptizing, and he remained there.[k] 41 Many people came to him, and they were saying, "John performed no sign, but everything that John said about this man was true."[l] 42 And many there came to believe in him.[m]

---

s Jn 7:43; 9:16.—t Jn 7:20; 8:48; 2 Ki 9:11; Jer 29:26.—u Jn 3:2; Ex 4:11.—v 1 Mac 4:54, 59.—w Acts 3:11.—x Jn 16:25; Lk 22:67.—y Jn 5:36; 8:25; 10:38.—z Jn 8:45, 47; Prov 28:5; 1 Cor 2:14.—a Rom 8:33-39.—b Deut 32:39; Isa 66:22.—c Wis 3:1; Isa 43:13.—d Jn 1:1; 12:45; 14:9; 17:21; Deut 6:4.—e Jn 8:59.—f Jn 5:18; 19:7; Lev 24:16; Mt 26:63-66.—g Jn 8:17; Ps 82:6; Rom 3:19.—h Jn 5:18; Jer 1:5.—i Jn 14:10-11, 20.—j Jn 7:30; Lk 4:30.—k Jn 1:28; Mt 19:1.—l Jn 1:26-27.—m Jn 2:23; 7:31; 8:30.

10:21 This is a reference to the incident of the man born blind (in the preceding chapter).

10:22-39 In the fourth Gospel, the trial of Jesus takes place throughout the book, and on each occasion the Lord asserts his oneness with the Father in unequivocal terms. Here we have a new disagreement, connected with the feast of the Dedication of the temple, which was celebrated toward the end of December. It commemorated the historical fact that in 165 B.C. Judas Maccabeus wrested the temple from the pagan king who had profaned it by installing an idol in it. It was thus a celebration of the liberation, purification, and restoration of the holy place and of its worship (see 1 Mac 4:36-39; 2 Mac 1:9-18; 10:1-8).

10:23 *Portico of Solomon:* located on the east side of the temple, and thus sheltered against the winds from the wilderness.

10:30 *I and the Father are one:* this is the most solemn declaration of the passage. Jesus expresses his perfect unity with the Father (literally, "one thing"), so that his power is identified with that of the Father. Trinitarian theology takes its start from this verse. For here Jesus affirms in peremptory fashion his identity of operation and will with the Father. This is clear from the violent reaction of the Jews, who seek to stone him because he is guilty of blasphemy.

10:34 *Your Law:* the term *Law* usually meant the Pentateuch, but it was also used in the sense of the whole Old Testament—as it is in this case. *You are gods:* these words from Ps 82:6 referred to the judges (as well as other leaders or rulers) of Israel whose tasks were appointed by God (see Ex 22:28; Deut 1:17; 16:18; 2 Chr 19:6).

10:40-42 The testimony of John the Baptist is recalled: the Prophet announced a Messiah whose dignity and power were superhuman (see Jn 1:26-34).

C: I Am the Resurrection*

CHAPTER 11

Death of Lazarus.* 1 [n] In Bethany, the village of Mary and her sister Martha, a certain man named Lazarus had fallen ill. [o] 2 This Mary was the woman who had anointed the Lord with ointment and wiped his feet with her hair. It was her brother Lazarus who was ill. [p] 3 And so the sisters sent this message to him, "Lord, the one you love is ill."

4 When Jesus heard this, he said,

"This illness is not to end in death.
Rather, it is for God's glory,
so that by means of it
the Son of Man may be glorified." [q]

5 Jesus loved Martha and her sister and Lazarus. 6 So after learning that Lazarus was ill, he remained for two more days in the place where he was. 7 Then he said to his disciples, "Let us return to Judea." [r] 8 His disciples said to him, "Rabbi, just a short time ago the Jews were trying to stone you. Why do you want to go back there?" [s] 9 Jesus answered,

"Are there not twelve hours of daylight? [t]
If someone walks in the daylight,
he does not stumble,
because he sees by the light of this world. [u]
10 But if he walks at night,
he stumbles,
because he does not have the light."

11 After saying this, he went on to tell them, "Our friend Lazarus has fallen asleep, but I am going there to awaken him." 12 The disciples responded, "Lord, if he has fallen asleep, he will recover." 13 Jesus, however, had been speaking about the death of Lazarus, but they thought that he was speaking of ordinary sleep. [v]

14 Finally, Jesus told them in plain words, "Lazarus is dead. 15 I am glad for your sake that I was not there, so that you may believe. Let us go to him." 16 Then Thomas (who was called "the Twin" *) said to his fellow disciples, "Let us also go so that we may die with him." [w]

The Kingdom and the Promise of the Resurrection.* 17 [x] When Jesus arrived, he learned that Lazarus had already been in the tomb for four days. * 18 Now Bethany was near Jerusalem, about two miles distant, 19 and many of the Jews had come to Martha and Mary to console them * for the loss of their brother. [y]

20 When Martha heard that Jesus was coming, she went forth to meet him, while Mary remained at home. [z] 21 Martha said to Jesus, "Lord, if you had been here, my brother would not have died. [a] 22 But even now I know that God will grant you whatever you ask of him." [b] 23 Jesus said to her, "Your brother will rise again." 24 Martha replied, "I know that he will rise again in the resurrection on the last day." [c] 25 Jesus then said to her,

"I am the resurrection and the life.
Whoever believes in me,
even though he dies, will live, [d]
26 and everyone who lives
and believes in me

n 1-2: Jn 12:1-8; Lk 10:38-42; 16:19-31.—o Mt 21:17.—p Jn 12:3; Mk 14:3.—q Jn 1:14; 2:11; 9:3, 24.—r Jn 10:40.—s Jn 8:59; 10:31; Mt 23:7.—t 9-10: Jn 12:35; 1 Jn 2:10.—u Jn 8:12; 9:4.—v Mt 9:24.—w Jn 14:5, 22; Mt 10:3; Acts 1:13.—x 17-18: Mt 21:17.—y Jn 12:9, 17-18; Job 2:11.—z Lk 10:39.—a Jn 11:32.—b Mk 11:24.—c Jn 5:29; 6:39-40, 44, 54; 12:48; Isa 2:2; Dan 12:2; Mic 4:1; Acts 23:8; 24:15.—d Jn 5:24; 8:51; 14:6; 1 Jn 3:14.

11:1-54 Unceasingly, Jesus attests that he has come to give life. The Resurrection is the sign that shows he came to give life. Death is no longer the last word on the human condition, and life now assumes an unusual stability; it is filled with endless hope.

11:1-16 Death spares no one, not even friends of the Son of God. But unhurriedly and without fear, Jesus confronts it in order to liberate from it those he loves. Death can no longer be the final destination; henceforth, it is simply a passage for which sleep is like a first image.

The Gospel of Luke also speaks of the two sisters, Martha and Mary, but without naming their village (Lk 10:38-42); we know from this passage that it was Bethany, and we also learn that they had a brother. Bethany was on the eastern slope of the Mount of Olives, about two miles from Jerusalem.

One notes the decision of Jesus to accomplish his work without hesitation even to the destiny established by his Father (v. 9); and his light must instill courage into those who follow him (vv. 10-11).

11:16 *Twin,* i.e., *Didymus,* is the Greek translation of the Aramaic *Toma,* which means "twin."

11:17-44 Faced with the death of a friend and the sufferings of the man's relatives, Jesus responds with true humanity and a compassionate heart; by restoring life to Lazarus, he shows himself to be the Son of God, to whom the Father has given everything he asks for. The hope of a resurrection on the last day was shared by many believers, such as Martha; this conviction had been growing for about a century or two in fervent Jewish circles, such as that of the Pharisees (2 Mac 7:9-14, 22f; 12:43-45; Dan 12:1-3; see Wis 2:3—3:9). In the time of Jesus, however, the priestly caste in Jerusalem opposed the belief (Acts 23:6-9) and tried to ridicule it (Mt 22:23-33). Here Jesus not only confirms the hope but also reveals that he is the one who fulfills it.

11:17 *Four days:* the Jews believed that the soul remained near the body for three days after death, giving hope for a return to the body. By the fourth day there was no hope of coming back.

11:19 *To console them:* according to Jewish custom, there were thirty days of mourning: three days of very great mourning, four days of great mourning, and 23 days of lighter mourning.

will never die.
Do you believe this?"[e]
27 "Yes, Lord," she replied. "I believe that
you are the Christ, the Son of God, the one
who is to come into the world."[f]
28 When she had said this, she went back
and took her sister Mary aside, telling her
privately, "The Teacher is here and is ask-
ing for you."[g] 29 As soon as she heard this,
she got up quickly and went to him. 30 For
Jesus had not yet come to the village, but
was still at the place where Martha had
met him. 31 When the Jews who were in the
house consoling her saw Mary get up
quickly and go out, they followed her,
assuming that she was going to the tomb to
weep there.
32 Mary came to the place where Jesus
was, and as soon as she saw him, she fell at
his feet and said to him, "Lord, if you had
been here, my brother would not have
died." 33 When Jesus saw her weeping, and
beheld the Jews who were with her also
weeping, he became deeply moved in spir-
it and angry.[h] 34 He asked, "Where have
you laid him?" They said to him, "Lord,
come and see." 35 Jesus began to weep,[i]
36 causing the Jews to say, "See how greatly
he loved him!" 37 But some of them re-
marked, "He opened the eyes of the blind
man. Why could he not have done some-
thing to prevent this man's death?"[j]
38 Again deeply moved, Jesus came to the
tomb. It was a cave, with a stone closing
the entrance.[k] 39 Jesus said, "Take away the
stone." Martha, the dead man's sister, said
to him, "Lord, by now there will be a
stench, for he has been dead for four days."
40 Jesus replied, "Did I not tell you that if
you have faith you will see the glory of
God?" 41 And so they removed the stone.
Then Jesus looked up and said,

"Father, I thank you for hearing me.[l]
42 I know that you always hear me,
but I have said this
for the sake of the people standing
here,
so that they may believe
that it was you who sent me."[m]

43 When he had said this, he cried out in
a loud voice, "Lazarus, come out!"[n] 44 The
dead man came out, his hands and feet
bound with linen bands, and his face
wrapped in a cloth. Then Jesus said to
them, "Untie him and let him go free."[o]

One Man Must Die for the People.* 45 This
caused many of the Jews who had come to
visit Mary, and had seen what Jesus did, to
believe in him.[p] 46 However, some of them
went to the Pharisees and reported to
them what Jesus had done.
47 As a result, the chief priests and the
Pharisees summoned a meeting of the
Sanhedrin and said, "What are we going to
do? This man is performing many signs.[q]
48 If we let him go on like this, everyone will
start to believe in him, and then the
Romans will come and suppress both our
temple and our nation."
49 [r] However, one of them, Caiaphas, who
was high priest that year,* said to them,
"You know nothing at all.[s] 50 You do not
seem to realize that it is better for us that
one man die for the people rather than the
whole nation be destroyed."
51 He did not say this on his own, but as
the high priest that year he was prophesy-
ing that Jesus was to die for the nation,
52 and not for the nation alone, but to gath-
er into one the dispersed children of God.[t]
53 And so from that day on, they plotted to
kill him.*[u] 54 As a result, Jesus no longer
walked about openly among the Jews. He
withdrew to a town called Ephraim* in the
region bordering the desert, and he
remained there with the disciples.

e Mt 25:46.—f Jn 1:9; 6:69; Lk 2:11.—g Jn 13:13; Mt 26:18.—h Jn 12:27; 13:21.—i Lk 19:41.—j Jn 9:6, 7.—k Jn 20:1; Mt 27:60; Lk 24:2.—l Jn 17:1; Mt 14:19.—m Jn 12:30.—n Isa 49:9; Lk 7:14.—o Jn 19:40.—p Ex 14:31; Lk 16:31.—q Jn 12:19; Mt 26:3-5; Lk 22:2; Acts 4:16.—r 49-50: Jn 18:13-14.—s Mt 26:3; Lk 3:2.—t Jn 10:16; Deut 30:3; Isa 49:6.—u Jn 5:18; 7:1; Mt 12:14.

11:45-54 There is peril for the city and its religion unless they accept the unimaginable: that God no longer needs his temple and henceforth is present through Jesus Christ alone. Because of civic and religious considerations it is necessary to decide the fate of this man, who unsettles the certainties and confronts the institutions and the established power.

Without realizing it, Caiaphas, the high priest who had held this office since A.D. 18 and would continue to hold it until A.D. 36, makes a statement that is at the heart of the Christian Faith: Christ will die for all, so that the entire human family may have life. The temple and Jewish tradition are now transcended by a worship and a salvation that are universal.

11:49 *That year:* i.e., at that time. The Jews believed that the high priest possessed a gift of prophecy, which was at times unknowingly carried out (see v. 51).

11:53 Jesus is placed under a death sentence, which the careful reader will suspect to be illegal because of Nicodemus' question to the authorities in Jn 7:51: "Does our Law allow us to pass judgment on someone without first giving him a hearing to ascertain what he is doing?"

11:54 *Ephraim:* on the edge of the wilderness of Judea, 16 miles north of Jerusalem.

VII: THE TRUE PASSOVER THAT BRINGS ABOUT THE SALVATION OF HUMANKIND*

A: The Hour Has Come*

The Last Passover. 55 * Now the Jewish Passover * was drawing near, and many people went up from the country to Jerusalem before the Passover in order to purify themselves.[v] 56 They kept looking for Jesus, and they asked one another as they stood in the temple, "What do you think? Will he come to the feast or not?"[w] 57 Meanwhile, the chief priests and the Pharisees had given orders that anyone who knew where he was should inform them so that they might arrest him.

CHAPTER 12

The Anointing at Bethany. 1 [x] Six days before the Passover, Jesus came to Bethany, the hometown of Lazarus, whom he had raised from the dead.[y] 2 They gave a dinner there for him. Martha served the meal, and Lazarus was among those at table with him.[z]

3 Mary brought in a pint * of very costly ointment, made from pure nard, anointed Jesus' feet, and dried them with her hair. The house was filled with the fragrance of the ointment.[a] 4 Judas Iscariot, one of his disciples, the one who was about to betray him, said,[b] 5 "Why was this ointment not sold for three hundred denarii * and the money given to the poor?" 6 He said this not because he had any concern for the poor but because he was a thief. He was in charge of the money bag, and he used to steal from it.[c]

7 Jesus said in response, "Leave her alone! Let her keep it for the day of my burial.[d] 8 The poor you will always have with you, but you will not always have me."[e]

9 Meanwhile, a large number of Jews learned that he was there, and they came not only because of Jesus but also because they wanted to see Lazarus, whom he had raised from the dead.[f] 10 The chief priests then decided to put Lazarus to death as well, 11 since it was because of him that many of the Jews were leaving and putting their faith in Jesus.[g]

The Triumphal Entry into Jerusalem.* 12 [h] The next day the great crowd of people who had come for the feast heard that Jesus was on his way to Jerusalem. 13 Thus, they went out

v Jn 2:13; 5:1; 6:4; 18:28; Ex 12:13, 23; Num 9:6-14; 19:12; Deut 16:6; 2 Chr 30:1-3, 15-18; Mt 26:1-2; Mk 14:1.—w Jn 7:11.—x 1-11: Mt 26:6-13; Mk 14:3-9; Lk 7:37-39.—y 1-2: Jn 11:1.—z Lk 10:38-42.—a Jn 11:2; Mk 14:3.—b Mt 10:4.—c Jn 13:29.—d Jn 19:40.—e Deut 15:11.—f Jn 11:19, 43.—g Jn 11:45.—h 12-19: Mt 21:1-16; Mk 11:1-10; Lk 19:28-40.

11:55—21:25 It is the feast of Passover in Jerusalem, a time when faith and hope are reborn in the minds of the people, as they commemorate their deliverance from slavery, the formation of the people, the Covenant, the journey to the mountain of God, and the promised land. Lambs are sacrificed, reproducing the shedding of the blood that had preserved the life of Israel long ago. The feast is full of memories, which are at the same time a promise of a different future. This future is now becoming a reality.

There is now a new Passover, the once-for-all Passover that is accomplished not in a ritual but in an action: Jesus fulfills the former Covenant by bringing to pass that which it had announced and prefigured (Ex 12:1-13, 16); he is the true Lamb who gives his life and whose blood poured out delivers the people from enslavement to evil and sin and opens the way to the true promised land, to the Father, in a communion of life with him.

The last section of the Gospel of John is centered on this mystery of the Passion of Christ.

The fate awaiting Jesus from the first pages of this Gospel is fulfilled; his adversaries have decided to put him to death and are waiting to have the sentence executed. It is the reign of darkness. But the hour of Jesus' death and defeat is another reality, that of triumph and glory; and it will be confirmed by the Resurrection of the Crucified.

The time of the Church will be inaugurated. She will receive the Spirit promised by Jesus and—as is indicated by the last signs (the miraculous catch of fish and the investiture of Peter)—will be established and sent forth to preach everywhere. She is to proclaim salvation and life so as to gather together all believers until the day when Christ will return in his glory as Son of God and Savior of the world.

11:55—12:50 The time for signs has ended. The glory that the signs announced is going to appear. How? It will not be through the deceitful glory of human triumphs; it will be through the presence of God in the action of Jesus and in the transformation of the human condition. Jesus' hour of glory is above all the hour of his death.

11:55—12:11 According to the tradition followed by the fourth Gospel, the woman who pours the perfume on the feet of Jesus is Mary, the sister of Lazarus. With the prodigality of love she expresses her gratitude for the raising of her brother from the dead; but Jesus evokes his own death, and Mary's gesture points ahead to this, anticipating by her anointing the rite of burial: it is an act of veneration.

Wasteful squandering? Only Judas, whose shadow already darkens the picture, thinks so. It is not such veneration of Christ that turns his attention to the poor; it is avarice—at the same time that Jesus is being glorified at Bethany, the plot against him is being laid for civic reasons, as we saw earlier.

11:55-57 This is probably the Passover of the year 30, which was to be Jesus' last. The devout Jews journeyed to Jerusalem to complete the ritual purifications necessary for Passover celebrations (see Ex 19:10-11, 15; Num 9:6-14; 2 Chr 30:1-3, 15-18). Since Jesus had been present in Jerusalem at the feasts of Tabernacles and Dedication, the populace expected him to be there again. A warrant had been issued for his arrest, and anyone who knew his whereabouts had to declare it under penalty of complicity.

12:3 *Pint:* Greek: *litra,* i.e., about a half-liter.

12:5 *Three hundred denarii:* a year's wages, a denarius being a day's wages for a laborer.

12:12-19 To a greater degree than the Synoptics, the fourth Gospel describes this entry as a triumph and stresses above all the theme of the glory of Christ. The raising of Lazarus has provoked the enthusiasm of the crowd, and for the first time Jesus allows himself to be acclaimed "King of Israel"; he lets himself be known as the King-Messiah announced by Zechariah (9:9).

to meet him, carrying branches of palm *
and shouting,

"Hosanna!
Blessed is he who comes in the name of
the Lord,
the King of Israel." [i]

14 Jesus found a young donkey and rode it,
as it is written,

15 "Do not be afraid, daughter of Zion. *
Behold, your King is coming,
riding on a donkey's colt." [j]

16 At first, his disciples did not understand
this, but later, when Jesus had been glorified,
they recalled that these things had been writ-
ten about him and had happened to him. [k]

17 Now the people who had been present
when he called Lazarus out of the tomb and
raised him from the dead continued to testi-
fy about this. * [l] 18 Because the crowd had
heard that he had performed this sign, they
went out to meet him. [m] 19 So the Pharisees
said to one another, "As you see, we are get-
ting nowhere. The entire world has gone
after him." [n]

The Glory of the Cross.* 20 [o] Among those
who had come up to worship at the feast
were some Greeks.* 21 They approached
Philip, who was from Bethsaida in Galilee,
and said to him, "Sir, we would like to see
Jesus." [p] 22 Philip went to tell Andrew of this,
and Philip and Andrew informed Jesus. [q]
23 Jesus answered them,

"The hour has come
for the Son of Man to be glorified. [r]

24 Amen, amen, I say to you,
unless a grain of wheat
falls into the earth and dies,
it remains just a grain of wheat.
However, if it dies,
it bears much fruit. [s]

25 "Anyone who loves his life loses it,
but the one who hates his life in this
world
will preserve it for eternal life. [t]

26 If anyone wishes to serve me,
he must follow me.
Where I am,
there also will my servant be.
If anyone serves me,
my Father will honor that person. [u]

27 "Now my soul is troubled.
Yet what should I say:
'Father, save me from this hour'?
No, it was for this
that I have come to this hour. [v]

28 Father, glorify your name."

Then a voice came from heaven,

"I have glorified it,
and I will glorify it again." [w]

29 The crowd that was present heard this,
and some of them said that it was thunder,
while others asserted, "An angel has spoken
to him." [x] 30 Jesus answered,

"This voice did not come for my sake
but for yours. [y]

31 Now is the judgment on this world.
Now the prince of this world *
will be driven out. [z]

---

i Jn 1:49; Lev 23:40; 1 Mac 13:51; 2 Mac 10:7; Ps 118:25, 26; Rev 7:9.—j Isa 40:9; Zec 9:9.—k Jn 2:22; Mk 9:32.—l Jn 11:42.—m Lk 19:37.—n Jn 11:47-48.—o Acts 10:2; 11:20.—p Jn 1:44.—q Jn 1:40.—r Jn 2:4; 13:32.—s Isa 53:10-12; 1 Cor 15:36.—t Mt 10:39; 16:25; Mk 8:35; Lk 9:24; 14:26; 17:33.—u Jn 14:3; 17:24; Mt 16:24; Mk 8:34; Lk 9:23; 2 Cor 5:8; Phil 1:23.—v Jn 6:38; 11:33; 18:11; Mt 26:38-39; Mk 14:34-36; Lk 22:42; Heb 5:7-8.—w Jn 2:11; 17:5; Dan 4:31, 34; Mt 3:17.—x Ex 9:28; 2 Sam 22:14; Job 37:4; Ps 29:3; Lk 22:43; Acts 23:9.—y Jn 11:42; Ex 19:9.—z Jn 16:11; Lk 10:18; 2 Cor 4:4; Eph 2:2; Rev 12:9.

12:13 *Branches of palm:* customarily used in victory celebrations (see 1 Mac 13:51; 2 Mac 10:7). *Hosanna:* an acclamation meaning "Grant salvation!" The citation is from Ps 118:25. *He who comes in the name of the Lord:* see note on Mt 21:9. *The King of Israel:* a reference to the coming king mentioned by Zep 3:14-15 and Zec 9:9. See also note on Mt 21:9.

12:15 *Daughter of Zion:* see note on Mt 21:5.

12:17 Another reading for this verse is given in some manuscripts: "Then the crowd that was with him began to bear witness that he had called Lazarus out of the tomb and raised him from the dead."

12:20-36 Jesus' single-day success does not divert him from his hour, nor that of his adversaries, and it is his deciding moment. This page with so many themes gives us a glimpse into his thinking.

To the crowd, among whom are sympathetic Gentiles, he proposes the image of a grain of wheat that must die. Conscious of the necessity for his death, he realizes the fruitfulness of his approaching sacrifice for the whole world.

Paradoxically, that death is elevation and glorification: it will show who Jesus is and be the reversal in the fate of human beings. As in the account of the agony in the garden related by the Synoptics (Mt 26:36-46; Mk 14:32-42; Lk 22:39-46), he overcomes his fear in the face of what humans regard as ruin; he dominates the cruel paradox.

His death transforms the fate of the world: it is defeat for the forces of evil and opens up hope for those called to the communion of Jesus, to life.

Here is an unexpected Messiah who completes God's work by his own death; as here, so elsewhere we read constantly of Christ's invitation to his disciples to share his lot (see Mt 16:25; Mk 8:35; Lk 9:24). Believers may fear death but not lose hope, since for Jesus, in whom they believe, the hour of death was the hour in which he conquered the devil, was glorified by the Father, and showed himself to be the light of the world. This beautiful text leaves us the meditation of the ancient Church on the cross of Christ; it has become the glorious cross.

12:20 *Greeks:* not Jews, but adherents of Judaism, although without embracing its practices.

12:31 *Prince of this world:* Satan, who has the ability to control human beings by drawing them away from God (see Jn 14:30; 16:11; 2 Cor 4:4; Eph 2:2; 6:12).

32 And when I am lifted up from the earth,
I will draw all to myself." [a]

33 He said this to indicate the kind of death he was to die. [b]

34 The crowd answered, "Our Law * teaches that the Christ will remain forever. How then can you say that the Son of Man must be lifted up? Who is this Son of Man?" [c]
35 Jesus replied,

"The light will be with you
for only a little longer.
Go on your way
while you still have the light,
so that the darkness
will not overtake you.

"Whoever walks in the darkness
does not know where he is going. [d]
36 While you have the light,
believe in the light
so that you may become children of light."

After Jesus had said this, he departed and hid himself from their sight. [e]

The Choice To Believe in the Light.* 37 [f] Although he had performed so many signs in their presence, they did not believe in him. [g]
38 This was to fulfill the word of the prophet Isaiah,

"Lord, who has believed our preaching?
To whom has the power of the Lord
been revealed?" [h]

39 They therefore could not believe for as Isaiah said,

40 "He has blinded their eyes
and hardened their hearts,
lest they see with their eyes
and understand with their hearts,
and thereby be converted,
so that I could heal them." * [i]

41 Isaiah said this because he saw his glory, and his words referred to him. [j]

42 Nevertheless, there were many, even among the authorities, who believed in him, but because of the Pharisees they did not confess their faith in him, for fear of being banned from the synagogue. * [k]
43 For they valued human glory more highly than the glory that comes from God. [l]

The Choice To Believe in Jesus.* 44 Then Jesus cried out,

"Whoever believes in me
believes not only in me
but in him who sent me. [m]
45 And whoever sees me
sees the one who sent me. [n]
46 I have come into the world as light
so that everyone who believes in me
may not have to remain in darkness. [o]
47 * "But if anyone listens to my words
and fails to observe them,
I will not pass judgment on him,
for I did not come to judge the world
but to save the world. [p]
48 Anyone who rejects me
and does not accept my words
already has a judge. [q]
On the last day,
the word that I have spoken
will serve as his judge.
49 "For I have not spoken on my own,
but the Father who sent me
has himself given me command
about what I am to say
and how I am to speak. [r]
50 I know that his commandment
is eternal life.
Therefore, what I speak
is what the Father has told me to say." [s]

a Jn 3:14; 8:28; Isa 11:10; 52:13.—b Jn 18:32.—c Pss 89:5; 110:4; Isa 9:7; Ezek 37:25; Dan 7:14; Rev 20:1-6.—d Jn 9:4; 11:10; Job 5:14; 1 Jn 1:6.—e Jn 8:59; Jer 13:16; Lk 16:8; Eph 5:8.—f 37-43: Deut 29:2-4; Mk 4:11-12; Rom 9:11.—g Jn 2:11.—h Isa 53:1; Rom 10:16.—i Isa 6:9-10; Mt 13:13-15; Mk 4:12.—j Jn 5:39; Isa 6:1, 4; Lk 24:27.—k Jn 7:48; 9:22.—l Jn 5:44; 1 Sam 15:30; Rom 2:29.—m Jn 13:20; 14:1; Mt 10:40.—n Jn 14:7-9.—o Jn 1:9; 8:12.—p Jn 3:17.—q Jn 5:45; Deut 31:26-29; Lk 10:16; Heb 4:12.—r Jn 14:10, 31; Deut 18:18-19.—s Jn 6:63; Mt 25:46.

12:34 *Law:* taken here as the entire Old Testament (see Jn 10:34), and referring specifically to Pss 89:37; 110:4; Isa 9:7; Dan 7:14. *Son of Man:* see notes on Jn 1:51 and Mt 8:20.

12:37-43 The early Christian generations always remained astonished at Israel's refusal of the light, and they meditated on the text of Isaiah on the blindness of people when faced with an unexpected work of God. To recognize the light is to choose to accept its demands: such a choice turns a life upside down; it is necessary to accept the risk of being marginalized from the usual social and religious milieu.

12:40 This text, like others in the Old Testament, appears to say that hardened hearts and blinded eyes are God's doing. However, the evangelist is simply assuring Christian readers that even though God would give people every opportunity to convert, many would still choose to stay in their sin.

12:42 John is indicating that in the Israel of his time there is, as always, a remnant that believes. But they are not a true People of God because of their fear of being excommunicated by the authorities.

12:44-50 But who is the light? It is Jesus himself, sent by the Father to make known the Father's love and to save believers. All through the Gospel, Christ has testified how deeply aware he is of this mission because of the unity in which he lives with his Father. What Jesus says in these few verses sums up his entire teaching concerning his mission.

12:47-48 This parallels the statement found at the end of the Sermon on the Mount (Mt 7:24-27). Everything hangs upon a person's acceptance or rejection of what Jesus has said.

B: The Testament of the Lord*

CHAPTER 13

Jesus Washes the Feet of the Disciples.* 1 As
the feast of Passover drew near, Jesus was
aware that his hour had come to depart
from this world and to go to the Father. He
had loved his own who were in the world,
and he loved them to the end. [t]

2 The devil had already put it into the
mind of Judas, son of Simon Iscariot, to
betray Jesus. During supper, [u] 3 Jesus, fully
aware that the Father had entrusted all
things into his hands, and that he had come
from God and was returning to God, [v] 4 got
up from the table, removed his outer gar-
ments, and took a towel that he tied around
his waist. [w] 5 Then he poured water into a
basin and began to wash the disciples' feet
and to wipe them with the towel wrapped
around his waist. [x]

6 He came to Simon Peter, who said to
him, "Lord, are you going to wash my feet?"
7 Jesus answered, "You do not understand
now what I am doing, but later you will
understand." [y] 8 Peter said to him, "You shall
never wash my feet." Jesus replied, "Unless I
wash you, you will have no share with me." [z]
9 Simon Peter said to him, "Lord, then wash
not only my feet, but also my hands and my
head."

10 Jesus then said, "Anyone who has
bathed has no need to wash further, except
for his feet, for he is clean all over. You also
are clean, although not every one of you is
clean." [a] 11 He knew the one who was going to
betray him. That is why he added the words,
"Not every one of you is clean." [b]

12 After he had finished washing their feet
and had once again put on his outer
garments, he reclined at table and said to
them,

"Do you understand
what I have done for you?
13 You call me 'Teacher' and 'Lord,'
and rightly so,
for that is what I am. [c]
14 So if I, your Lord and Teacher,
have washed your feet,
you also should wash one another's feet. [d]

15 "I have given you an example.
What I have done for you,
you should also do. [e]
16 Amen, amen, I say to you,
a servant is not greater than his master,
nor is a messenger greater
than the one who sent him. [f]

17 "Now that you know these things,
you will be blessed
if you do them. [g]

Jesus Predicts His Betrayal*

18 "I am not speaking about all of you.
I know those whom I have chosen.
However, what the Scripture says
must be fulfilled,
'The one who ate bread with me
has raised his heel against me.' [h]

19 "I tell you this now,
before it occurs,
so that when it does occur,
you may believe that I am. *
20 Amen, amen, I say to you,
whoever receives the one I send
receives me,
and whoever receives me
receives the one who sent me." [i]

21 [j] After saying this, Jesus was deeply dis-
tressed, and he declared,

t Jn 2:4; 7:30; 8:20; 16:28; Mt 26:17, 45; Mk 14:12, 41; Lk 22:7.—u Jn 6:71; 17:12; Mt 26:20-21; Mk 14:17-18; Lk 22:3.—v Jn 3:35; 8:42.—w Mt 20:28.—x 1 Sam 25:41; Lk 7:44; 12:37.—y Jn 14:26.—z 2 Sam 20:1; 1 Cor 6:11.—a Jn 15:3.—b Jn 6:70; Mt 10:4.—c Jn 11:28; Mt 23:8, 10; 26:18; Acts 10:36; Rom 10:9.—d 1 Pet 5:5.—e Lk 22:27; Phil 2:5, 8; 1 Tim 4:12; 1 Pet 2:21.—f Jn 15:20; Mt 10:24; Lk 6:40.—g Isa 56:2; Mt 7:24; Jas 1:25.—h Jn 15:16; Ps 41:10.—i Mt 10:40; Mk 9:37; Lk 9:48.—j 21-30: Mt 26:21-25; Mk 14:18-21; Lk 22:21-23.

13:1—14:31 This is the first of three parts that can clearly be distinguished in Jn 13:1—17:26. These pages constitute the best known section of the fourth Gospel, which at this point becomes the great book of meditation for Christians. The author develops a lengthy farewell address in the setting of the final meal. On the eve of his death, Christ lets his disciples know the deepest secrets of his love for God.

The other two parts in this lengthy piece are: the community of the witnesses to Christ (15:1—16:33) and the priestly prayer of Jesus (17:1-26). Scholars believe that the three parts probably reflect three redactional stages.

13:1-17 The story of the Last Supper is not told in John, and we shall never know exactly why, but the farewell meal here is described in the same spirit. By washing the feet of his disciples, Jesus performs the action of a slave; love has indeed made him the servant of his friends.

13:18-32 The announcement of the betrayal of Jesus comes in the discourse that follows the washing of the feet. Jesus brings the crisis to a head. The traitor can no longer remain in the intimacy of the Lord, sharing his table and his confidences. The darkness must one day be separated from the light (see v. 30).

Now the drama of the Passion begins; Jesus considers it the hour of his glory. He acts with a knowledge of the events that is the knowledge of God. Jesus is the Lord, as indicated by his title "I AM." This attestation serves to make the faith of the disciples stronger.

For the first time we meet "the disciple whom Jesus loved"; we shall find this unusual "name" three more times: once beneath the cross (Jn 19:26f), and the other two times in connection, once again, with Peter (Jn 20:2-10; 21:20-22). The tradition has always identified this disciple with John.

13:19 See note on Jn 4:26.

"Amen, amen, I say to you,
one of you will betray me." [k]

22 The disciples looked at one another,
puzzled as to which one of them he meant.
23 One of them, the disciple whom Jesus
loved, was reclining at Jesus' side. [l] 24 Simon
Peter signaled to him to ask Jesus which one
he meant.

25 Therefore, leaning back toward Jesus, he
asked, "Lord, who is it?" [m] 26 Jesus answered,
"It is the one to whom I give this piece of
bread after I have dipped it into the dish."
And when he had dipped the piece of bread,
he gave it to Judas, son of Simon Iscariot. [n]

27 As soon as Judas had received the piece
of bread, Satan entered into him. Jesus then
said to him, "Do quickly what you are going
to do." [o] 28 Now no one at the table knew why
he had said this to him. 29 Some thought that
since Judas was in charge of the money bag,
Jesus was telling him to purchase what was
needed for the feast, or to give something to
the poor. [p] 30 As soon as Judas had received
the piece of bread, he immediately departed. It was night. [q]

31 After Judas had departed, Jesus said,

"Now is the Son of Man glorified,
and God is glorified in him. [r]
32 If God is glorified in him,
God will also glorify him in himself,
and he will glorify him at once. [s]

A New Commandment*

33 "My children,
I will be with you
only a short time longer.
You will look for me,
and, as I told the Jews,
so I now say to you,
'Where I am going, you cannot come.' [t]
34 "I give you a new commandment:
love one another.
Just as I have loved you,
so you should also love one another. [u]
35 This is how everyone will know
that you are my disciples:
if you love one another." [v]

Jesus Predicts Peter's Denial.* 36 Simon
Peter said to him, "Lord, where are you
going?" Jesus answered,

"Where I am going,
you cannot follow me now,
but you will follow me later on." [w]

37 Peter said, "Lord, why can I not follow
you now? I will lay down my life for you."
38 Jesus answered, "Will you really lay down
your life for me? Amen, amen, I say to you,
before the cock crows, you will have denied
me three times. [x]

C: The Way, the Truth, and the Life*

CHAPTER 14

Jesus, the Way, Leads to the Father*

1 "Do not let your hearts be troubled.
You place your trust in God. *
Trust also in me. [y]
2 In my Father's house
there are many dwelling places.
If there were not,
would I have told you
that I am going to prepare a place for you? [z]
3 And if I go and prepare a place for you,
I will come again
and will take you to myself,
so that where I am,
you may also be. [a]

k Jn 12:27.—l Jn 19:26; 20:2; 21:7, 20; Mt 10:37.—m Jn 21:20; Mt 26:22.—n Mt 10:4.—o Jn 13:2; Lk 22:3.—p Jn 12:5-6.—q Lk 22:53.—r Jn 7:39; 1 Pet 4:11.—s Jn 17:1-5.—t Jn 7:33; 8:21.—u Jn 15:12-13, 17; Lev 19:18; Mt 19:19; Eph 5:2; 1 Thes 4:9; 1 Pet 1:22; 1 Jn 2:7-10; 3:23; 2 Jn 5.—v Deut 28:9-10; Acts 4:32.—w Jn 16:5; 21:18-19; Mk 14:27; 2 Pet 1:14.—x Jn 18:27; Mt 26:33-35; Mk 14:29-31; Lk 22:33-34.—y Jn 3:15; 14:27; 16:33; Deut 1:21; Ps 4:6.—z Jn 13:33, 36.—a Jn 12:26; 17:24; Mt 16:27; Heb 6:19-20; 1 Jn 2:28.

13:33-35 Jesus is not the first to recommend friendship, mutual service, and brotherly affection. But to love as he loved goes so much further as to become an absolute. It is no doubt for the purpose of underlining this that the fourth Gospel puts the commandment to love in the context of farewells; it likewise makes evident that this law of life is the most original sign of the community's faithfulness to Christ.

To love, to serve to the point of taking the last place and giving one's life, goes beyond human strength. Perhaps the dialogue with Peter is there to say that good feelings are not enough and that it takes the grace given by the death of Christ to have such strength.

13:36-38 Peter's denial is predicted in all four Gospels (Mt 26:33-35; Mk 14:29-31; Lk 22:31-34 and here).

14:1-31 Facing the death of Jesus, or facing our death, we might be shaken by fear. After all, without God is not existence for us a flight from the useless to nothingness? We have, then, to meditate on this chapter 14, where the themes are intermingled too numerously to discern the whole universe of meaning each verse opens to us. Yes, there is fulfillment, but it comes from God; it is abiding in God, truth in God, life from God. The symbols tell us that the fulfillment comes about in the communication of life from the Father, from Jesus, and from the Spirit.

14:1-5 The departure of Jesus ought not to become a time of discouragement amid hostility or uncertainty. The departure opens to all people the possibility of being in communion with God. Jesus gives the disciples the light and the life to enter this communion: he is the way not only through his teaching but also through his presence and his being—but what do we call the way and the goal of life for us?

14:1 *You place your trust in God:* this could also be translated as an imperative: "Place your trust in God!"

4 You know the way
to the place I am going."

5 Thomas said to him, "Lord, we do not
know where you are going. How can we
know the way?" [b]

Jesus, the Truth, Reveals the Father*

6 Jesus replied,

"I am the way, and the truth, and the life.
No one comes to the Father
except through me. [c]
7 If you know me,
then you will know my Father also.
From now on you do know him.
You have seen him." [d]

8 Philip said to him, "Lord, show us the
Father, it will be enough for us." [e] 9 Jesus
answered,

"Have I been with you all this time,
Philip,
and you still do not know me?
Whoever has seen me
has seen the Father.
How can you say,
'Show us the Father'? [f]
10 Do you not believe
that I am in the Father
and the Father is in me?

"The words that I speak to you
I do not speak on my own.
The Father who dwells in me
is doing his works. [g]
11 Believe me when I say
that I am in the Father
and the Father is in me.
But if you do not,
then believe
because of the works themselves. [h]

Jesus, the Life, Communicates the Spirit*

12 "Amen, amen, I say to you,
the one who believes in me
will also do the works that I do,
and indeed will do even greater ones
than these,
because I am going to the Father. [i]
13 Whatever you ask in my name I will do,
so that the Father may be glorified in
the Son. [j]
14 If you ask me for anything in my name,
I will do it. [k]

15 "If you love me,
you will keep my commandments. [l]
16 And I will ask the Father,
and he will give you another Advocate
to be with you forever, [m]
17 the Spirit of Truth
whom the world cannot accept
because it neither sees him nor knows him.
But you know him,
because he dwells with you
and will be in you. [n]

18 "I will not leave you orphans;
I will come to you. [o]
19 In a little while,
the world will no longer see me,
but you will see me.
Because I live,
you also will live. [p]
20 On that day, you will know
that I am in my Father,
and you in me, and I in you. [q]
21 "Anyone who has received my commandments
and observes them
is the one who loves me.
And whoever loves me
will be loved by my Father,
and I will love him
and reveal myself to him." [r]

b Jn 11:16.—c Jn 8:31-47; 10:9; Eph 2:18.—d Jn 1:18; 8:19; 12:45.—e Ex 24:9-10; 33:18.—f Jn 1:18; 10:30; 12:45; Isa 9:6; 2 Cor 4:4; Col 1:15; Heb 1:3.—g Jn 1:1; 10:37-38; 12:49.—h Jn 5:36; 10:38.—i Jn 1:50; 5:20; Mt 21:21.—j Jn 15:7, 16; 16:23-24; Mt 7:7-11.—k Acts 3:16.—l Jn 15:10; Deut 6:4-9; Pss 103:18; 119; Wis 6:18; 1 Jn 5:3; 2 Jn 6; Rev 12:17.—m Jn 15:26; 16:7; Lk 24:49; 1 Jn 2:1.—n Jn 16:13; Mt 28:20; 1 Cor 2:14; 2 Jn 1-2.—o 1 Ki 6:13; Mt 16:27; 28:20.—p Jn 7:33-34; 16:16.—q Jn 10:38; 17:21; Isa 2:17; 4:2-3; Rom 8:10.—r Jn 16:27; Deut 7:13; Prov 8:17; 1 Jn 2:5; 3:24.

14:6-11 We can reflect upon the mystery of God to struggle to develop a better understanding of our life and the meaning of the world. But our power to discern cannot establish any certainties on our own. To know the Father, to discover what he wants for us, and to enter into his communion, we first have to look on Jesus, on his work, and on his love. Only the gift of the Son reveals the love of the Father in its fullness.

14:12-26 Here is a beautiful hymn on what it means to be Christians. They are not nostalgic survivors of a great experience that is past. In daily life, with its insults and interrogations, they remain in true communion with Christ and continue his work—i.e., they bear in his name the testimony of salvation and the testimony of truth. This communion, unceasingly renewed, gives them strength to cope with attacks of despair, falsehood, incomprehension, and nothingness—what John often calls "the world."

In this effort, which is never finished, they are uplifted by a new and constant presence of God: the Spirit. It is the Spirit who gives Christians the power to experience the divine presence in their inmost being, because the Spirit makes them live in the participation of God. It is the Spirit who gives Christians the courage to obey, as Christ did, the will of God, who is love, truth, testimony. It is the Spirit who makes them penetrate the heart of the words and acts of Jesus in the questions and debates of life.

The Spirit is the consoler of Jn 16:5-13. The Greek word *Parakletos* means an advocate, one who aids by his power and advice. In the situations and struggles of living as a Christian, the Spirit supports us so that we may remain united with God and bear witness to him before the world.

[22] Judas (not Judas Iscariot) * asked him, "Lord, why is it that you are revealing yourself to us and not to the world?" [s] [23] Jesus answered him,

"Whoever loves me will keep my word,
and my Father will love him,
and we will come to him
and make our abode with him. [t]
24 Whoever does not love me
does not keep my words.
And the word that you hear
is not my own,
but that of the Father who sent me. [u]
25 "I have told you these things
while I am still with you.
26 However, the Advocate, the Holy Spirit,
whom the Father will send in my name,
will teach you everything
and remind you of all
that I have said to you. [v]

The Peace of Jesus*

27 "Peace I leave with you,
my peace I give to you.
Not as the world gives
do I give it to you.
Do not let your hearts be troubled;
be not afraid. [w]
28 "You have heard me say to you,
'I am going away,
and I will come back to you.'
If you loved me,
you would rejoice
that I am going to the Father,
for the Father is greater than I. * [x]
29 And now I have told you this
before it happens,
so that when it does happen
you may believe. [y]
30 "I will no longer talk at length with you
because the prince of the world is coming.
He has no power over me, [z]
31 but the world must come to understand
that I love the Father
and that I do
just as the Father has commanded me.
Get up! Let us be on our way. [a]

D: The Community of the Witnesses to Christ*

CHAPTER 15

Union with Jesus*

1 "I am the true vine,
and my Father is the vinegrower. [b]
2 He removes every branch
that does not bear fruit,
and every branch that does
he prunes to make it bear even more. [c]
3 You have already been cleansed
by the word I have spoken to you. [d]
4 "Abide in me,
as I abide in you.
Just as a branch cannot bear fruit by itself
unless it abides in the vine,
so you cannot bear fruit
unless you abide in me. [e]
5 "I am the vine,
you are the branches.
Whoever abides in me, and I in him,
will bear much fruit.
Apart from me you can do nothing.
6 Whoever does not abide in me
will be thrown away like a withered branch.

s Jn 7:4; Lk 6:16; Acts 10:40-41.—t Rev 3:20.—u Jn 5:19; 7:16; Deut 18:18.—v Jn 15:26; 16:7, 13-14; Ps 51:12; Isa 63:10; Acts 2:33; 1 Jn 2:20.—w Jn 16:33; 20:19; Num 6:26; Ps 85:9; Mal 2:6; Eph 2:14-18.—x Jn 8:40; 10:29; Mt 16:27.—y Jn 13:19; 16:4.—z Jn 12:31; 13:2.—a Jn 6:38; Mt 26:46.—b Jn 6:35; Ps 80:9-17; Isa 5:1-7; Jer 2:21; Ezek 15:2; 17:5-10; 19:10.—c Ps 92:15; Mt 3:8; Gal 5:22.—d Jn 13:10; Eph 5:26.—e Jn 6:56.

14:22 *Judas (not Judas Iscariot):* Jude Thaddeus (see Mt 13:15).

14:27-31 Christ's departure is imminent. Is the triumph over evil that the Passion effects merely a spectacle? No, this departure expresses Christ's free decision to do the will of the Father and to be at the Father's side, which is his true state of being. Such is God's peace, whose way and meaning are opened for believers. Yes, there is a fulfillment and a happiness for us—it is this that the word "peace" evokes in the Bible. It is not found in the satisfaction of the passions. True peace is a divine gift, to which Christ gives us access in our communion with God.

14:28 *The Father is greater than I:* this does not refer to the trinitarian relation between the Father and the Son. It probably refers to the fact that Jesus was sent by the Father and that the messenger (in the Hebrew mentality) is inferior to the one who sends him.

15:1—16:23 To the Lord's testament (farewell discourse) were added new instructions, as though to complete it. No doubt people did not want to lose other words of the Master, often meditated on, to explain the condition of the Christian community.

It is the life of the community on which these chapters throw light. In this group of texts, chs. 13 to 17, none of our usual words are pronounced; People of God, Body of Christ, Church, congregation. The words preferred are: to abide in, to love, to testify. In ch. 16, an image is used that suggests this mystery: the image of the vine and the branches. In these texts, love is above all a characteristic of the community itself. It is the Spirit who gives these groups the strength to exist as people of love and as witnesses of Christ.

15:1-11 Every reader of the Bible knows that the image of the vine suggests not only the union but also the tragic relationship between God and Israel. The Prophets rebuked the people of the Old Testament for not producing the fruit God expected of them, for being a spouse often unfaithful to her calling to bear witness to God among the nations (see Isa 5:1-7; Jer 2:21; Ezek 19:10-14; Hos 10:1). Jesus is the new Israel, the only vine that the Father has planted. This means that the radical, constitutive reality of the Church is her inclusion in Christ through Baptism, grace, and close attachment, and that any fruitfulness the disciple may have depends on this union with Christ.

Such branches are gathered up,
thrown into the fire, and burned.[f]

7 "If you abide in me
and my words abide in you,
you may ask for whatever you wish,
and it will be done for you.[g]
8 By this is my Father glorified,
that you bear much fruit
and become my disciples.[h]

9 "As the Father has loved me,
so have I loved you.
Remain in my love.[i]
10 If you keep my commandments,
you will remain in my love,
just as I have kept my Father's commandments
and remain in his love.[j]

11 "I have told you these things
so that my joy may be in you
and your joy may be complete.[k]

Love as Jesus Does*

12 "This is my commandment:
love one another
as I have loved you.[l]
13 No one can have greater love
than to lay down his life for his friends.[m]
14 You are my friends
if you do what I command you.[n]

15 "I shall no longer call you servants,
because a servant does not know
what his master is doing.
I have called you friends
because I have revealed to you
everything that I have heard from my Father.[o]

16 "You did not choose me.
Rather, I chose you.
And I appointed you
to go out and bear fruit,
fruit that will remain,
so that the Father may give you
whatever you ask him in my name.[p]
17 The command I give you is this:
love one another.[q]

Witnesses to Jesus in the Face of the World's Hatred*

18 "If the world hates you,
be aware that it hated me
before it hated you.[r]
19 If you belonged to the world,
the world would love you as its own.
But you do not belong to the world
because I have chosen you out of the world,
and therefore the world hates you.[s]

20 "Remember the word that I said to you:
'a servant is not greater than his master.'
If they persecuted me,
they will persecute you.
If they kept my word,
they will keep yours as well.[t]
21 But they will do all these things to you
on account of my name,
because they do not know the one who sent me.[u]

22 "If I had not come
and spoken to them,
they would not be guilty of sin,
but now they have no excuse for their sin.[v]
23 Whoever hates me
hates my Father also.[w]
24 If I had not done works among them
that no one else had ever done,
they would not be guilty of sin.
But now they have seen and hated
both me and my Father.[x]
25 All this was to fulfill the word
that is inscribed in their Law:
'They hated me without cause.'[y]

26 "When the Advocate comes
whom I will send you from the Father,

f Ezek 15:6-7; 19:10-14; Mt 3:10.—g Jn 14:13; Mt 7:7; Mk 11:24; 1 Jn 5:14.—h Jn 8:31; Mt 5:16; 9:8; Rom 7:4.—i Jn 17:23.—j Jn 8:29; 14:15.—k Jn 3:29; 16:22; 17:13.—l Jn 13:34.—m Gen 44:33; Rom 5:6-8; 1 Jn 3:16.—n Ex 33:11; Job 16:20; Prov 18:24; Lk 12:4.—o Jn 8:26; Deut 34:5; Jos 24:29; 2 Chr 20:7; Ps 89:21; Isa 41:8; Rom 8:15; Gal 4:7; Jas 2:23.—p Jn 13:18; 14:13; Deut 7:6; Rom 6:20-23.—q Jn 13:34; 1 Jn 3:23; 4:21.—r Jn 7:7; 14:17; Isa 66:5; Mt 10:22; 24:9; Mk 13:13; Lk 6:22; 1 Jn 3:13.—s Jn 17:14-16; 1 Jn 4:5.—t Jn 13:16; Mt 10:24; 2 Tim 3:12.—u Jn 8:19; 16:3; Isa 66:5; Mt 5:10; Acts 5:41.—v Jn 8:21, 24; 9:41; Ezek 2:5; Rom 1:20.—w Jn 5:23; Lk 10:16; 1 Jn 2:23.—x Jn 3:2; 5:36; 9:32; Deut 4:32-33; Mt 12:24-28.—y Pss 35:19; 69:4; 109:3.

15:12-17 There are many reasons for people to regroup: affinity, interest, defense. But the Christian community has only one reason: Christ and his choice of us. It also has only one way of life: to love like Christ, who went so far as to give his life. To have Christ's love is a gift. Then prayer is not a delusion; then the Christian community's mission can bear fruit. The fruit has already been given, God's love for us. In Christianity all is a gift.

15:18—16:4 The trial of Jesus, which the fourth Gospel unveils all through its pages, will not cease until the Father, to whom he is going, will have rendered justice to him in glorifying him. This drama, which people sometimes would like to conceal through reassuring words and sentiments, will not cease until the end of time. Persecution awaits Jesus, not because of some fatal error but because Christianity is different from what we want and claim it to be.

The early Christians were excluded from the synagogue; hatred and violence were stirred up against them under the guise of religion. Blindness and stubbornness: this is the world in the Johannine sense, the world of the persecutors. The Spirit is the strength and the light that assists the persecuted to hold fast in this affront, which no doubt also comes to pass in the heart of every believer.

the Spirit of Truth who comes from the Father,
he will testify on my behalf. [z]
27 And you also are my witnesses
because you have been with me from the beginning. [a]

CHAPTER 16

1 "I have told you this
to prevent you from falling away. [b]
2 They will expel you from the synagogues.
Indeed the hour is coming
when anyone who kills you
will believe that by doing so
he is serving God. [c]
3 And people will do such things
because they have not known the Father or me. [d]
4 But I have told you this
so that when the hour arrives
you may remember that I forewarned you about them. [e]

The Spirit of Truth, Our Guide to All Truth*

"I did not tell you all this previously
because I was with you.
5 But now I am going away
to the one who sent me.
Not one of you asks me,
'Where are you going?' [f]
6 However, because I have told you this,
you are overcome with grief.

7 "Nevertheless, I am telling you the truth:
it is better for you that I depart.
For if I do not go away,
the Advocate will not come to you,
whereas if I go,
I will send him to you. [g]

8 "And when he comes,
he will prove the world wrong
about sin and righteousness and judgment:
9 about sin,
because they do not believe in me; [h]
10 about righteousness,
because I am going to the Father
and you will see me no longer; [i]
11 about judgment,
because the ruler of this world has been condemned. [j]

12 "I have much more to tell you,
but you would not be able to bear it now. [k]
13 But when the Spirit of Truth comes,
he will guide you into all the truth.
He will not speak on his own authority,
but he will speak what he hears,
and he will declare to you
the things that are coming. [l]
14 He will glorify me,
for he will take what is mine
and communicate it to you.
15 Everything that the Father has is mine.
That is why I said
that he will take what is mine
and communicate it to you. [m]

Triumph of Jesus and the Joy of the Witnesses*

16 "In a little while
you will no longer see me,
and then a short time later
you will see me again." [n]

17 Then some of his disciples said to one
another, "What does he mean by saying to
us, 'In a little while you will no longer see
me, and then a short time later you will see

z Jn 14:16, 26; Mt 10:19-20; 1 Jn 5:7.—a Jn 21:24: Lk 1:2; Acts 1:8.—b Jn 15:18-27; Mt 11:6.—c Jn 9:22; 12:42; Isa 66:5; Mt 10:17; Lk 21:12; Acts 26:11; Rev 6:9.—d Jn 15:21; 1 Jn 3:1.—e Jn 13:19; 14:29; 15:27; Mk 13:23.—f Jn 7:33; 13:36; 14:5.—g Jn 7:39; 14:16-17, 26; 15:26.—h Jn 8:21-24; 15:22.—i Acts 3:14; Rom 1:17; 1 Pet 3:18.—j Jn 12:31.—k Mk 4:33; 1 Cor 3:2.—l Jn 14:17, 26; 15:26; Pss 25:5; 86:11; 143:10; 1 Jn 2:27; Rev 7:17.—m Jn 17:10; Lk 15:31.—n Jn 7:33; 14:19.

16:4b-15 The disciples have to overcome sadness at the departure and absence of Jesus so that they may understand the meaning of the event: passage to glory, gift of the Spirit, and the beginning of a new era in the world. But until the end of history the trial of Jesus will not stop, and the disciples will have to testify to him in a world where unbelief appears unceasingly.

The testimony of Christians can never stop; such testimony does not depend on the intelligence and the strength of people but on the action of the Spirit, who unveils to Christians, in faith, the glory of Christ and the view that history takes of this light (Christ). It is not a matter of a new revelation but of a discovery of what the words, actions, Death, and Resurrection of Jesus mean for each era: the truth of God that denounces the falsehood of sin, the goodness of God that denounces evil, and the condemnation of the forces that enslave people. The Spirit is the Paraclete: defender of Jesus in the heart of believers, defender of believers facing unbelief and refusal of the light—that is, the world in the sense the world is taken here (Jn 15:5-15). The Spirit is strength, support, light (see Jn 14:16).

16:16-33 The departure of Jesus will be a moment of disarray for the disciples; his absence will more than once be a moment of disarray for believers. But that is not the last word. The sufferings, like the pains of giving birth, make a testimony fruitful. Let us rather look at the Death and Resurrection of Christ; they are the definitive events in history. From the cross and Easter a new light is given to believers; a new confidence with God is offered to them. Christ will be the mediator; with him believers will be one with God. This intimacy will be a time of endless joy and peace for people who have believed they are children of God.

What is the return of Christ? Is it the glorious coming at the end of time or the Resurrection manifested in the appearances? The two things go together. The Resurrection will inaugurate a new era, the last times; and the end of time will manifest the glory of the Risen One.

me again,' and 'Because I am going to the
Father'? 18 What is this 'little while'? We
do not know what he means."

19 Jesus knew that they wanted to question
him, so he said to them,

"You are asking one another
what I meant by saying,
'In a little while
you will no longer see me,
and then a short time later
you will see me again.'
20 Amen, amen, I say to you,
you will weep and mourn
while the world rejoices.
You will be sorrowful,
but your grief will turn into joy. [o]

21 "A woman in labor suffers anguish
because her hour has come.
But when her baby is born,
she no longer recalls the suffering
because of her joy
that she has brought a child into the world. [p]
22 In the same way,
you are now in anguish,
but I will see you again,
and your hearts will rejoice,
and no one shall deprive you of your joy. [q]

23 "On that day,
you will not ask me anything further.
Amen, amen, I say to you,
if you ask the Father for anything in my name,
he will give it to you. [r]
24 Until now, in my name,
you have not asked for anything.
Ask and you will receive,
so that your joy may be complete. [s]

25 "I have used figures of speech
to explain these things to you.
The hour is coming
when I will no longer use figures,
but I will tell you about the Father in plain words. [t]
26 When that day comes,
you will make requests in my name.
I do not say
that I will entreat the Father on your behalf. [u]
27 For the Father himself loves you
because you have loved me
and have come to believe
that I came from God. [v]
28 I came from the Father
and have come into the world.
Now I am leaving the world
and returning to the Father." [w]

29 "At last you are speaking plainly," his
disciples said, "and not using figures of
speech. 30 Now we realize that you know
everything and do not need to have anyone
question you. Because of this, we believe that
you came from God." [x] 31 Jesus responded,

"Have you finally come to believe?
32 I tell you, the hour is coming,
indeed it has already come,
when you will be scattered,
each one going to his own home,
and you will leave me alone.
And yet I am not alone
because the Father is with me. [y]

33 "I have told you this
so that in me you may be in peace.
In the world
you will endure suffering.
But take courage!
I have overcome the world." [z]

E: The Priestly Prayer of Jesus*

CHAPTER 17

Knowledge of the Father and the Son.* 1 After
saying this, Jesus raised his eyes to heaven
and said,

"Father, the hour has come.
Glorify your Son,
so that your Son may glorify you, [a]
2 since you have given him authority
over all people,
so that he may give eternal life
to all those you have given him. [b]

o Jn 20:20; Ps 126:6; Mk 16:10; Lk 6:21.—p Isa 26:17-18; Jer 31:13; Mic 4:9; 1 Thes 5:3.—q Jn 14:19; 15:11; 20:20; Isa 66:14; Jer 31:12.—r Jn 14:13, 20.—s Jn 3:29; Mt 7:7.—t Ps 78:2; Ezek 21:5; Mt 13:34-35.—u Jn 14:13.—v Jn 14:21, 23.—w Jn 1:1; 13:13.—x 1 Ki 17:24.—y Jn 8:29; Zec 13:7; Mt 26:31; Mk 14:27.—z Jn 14:27; Rom 8:37; 1 Jn 4:4; Rev 2:7, 11.—a Jn 11:41; 13:31; Mt 26:18; Lk 9:16.—b Jn 3:35; Dan 7:14; Mt 28:18.

17:1-26 The hour has come for Jesus to do the final action that shows how far his union with the Father reaches and how great is the gift he makes of himself to human beings for their salvation. This sublime prayer reveals the ultimate meaning of his sacrifice; the title that has been given to the chapter, the "priestly prayer," is well deserved. But it is also a "missionary" prayer, since at the moment when there seems to be nothing but failure and isolation, Jesus adheres to God's plan. He is entirely the One Sent, who completes the mission given to him by the Father. He thinks only of this mission that his disciples must continue.

17:1-5 The word "glory" speaks of the greatness of God, of his final intervention, of his presence that gives strength, meaning, and fulfillment to people. Paradoxically, this glory is revealed in the destiny of Jesus, glory that is manifested during the Passion. One observes the love that was given to Christ for all eternity, love that became eternal life, shared by believers.

3 And eternal life is this:
to know you,
the only true God,
and the one you have sent,
Jesus Christ.[c]

4 "I have glorified you on earth
by completing the work
that you entrusted to me.[d]
5 So now, Father,
glorify me in your presence
with the glory I had with you
before the world began.[e]

The Son and the Disciples*

6 "I have made your name known
to those whom you gave me from the world.
They were yours,
and you gave them to me,
and they have kept your word.[f]
7 Now they have come to understand
that everything you gave me is from you.
8 For the words you gave to me
I have given to them,
and they have accepted them
and know with certainty
that I have come from you,
and they have believed that you sent me.[g]

9 "It is for them that I pray.
I do not pray for the world,
but for those you gave me
because they are yours.[h]
10 Everything I have is yours,
and everything you have is mine,
and through them I have been glorified.[i]
11 I will remain no longer in the world,
but they will still be in the world
while I will be coming to you.

"Holy Father,
protect by the power of your name
those you have given me,
so that they may be one,
even as we are one.[j]
12 While I was with them
I protected them by your name
that you have given me,
and I kept them safe.
Not one of them was lost,
except the one destined to be lost,*
so that the Scripture might be fulfilled.[k]

13 "Now I am coming to you,
and I say these things
while I am still in the world
so that my joy may come
to full measure in them.[l]
14 I have given them your word,
and the world has hated them
because they do not belong to the world
any more than I belong to the world.[m]
15 I am not asking you
to take them out of the world,
but I do ask you
to protect them from the evil one.[n]
16 They do not belong to the world
any more than I belong to the world.

17 "Consecrate them in the truth.
Your word is truth.[o]
18 As you sent me into the world,
so have I sent them into the world.[p]
19 And for their sakes I consecrate myself,
so that they too may be consecrated in truth.

The Disciples and the Church To Come*

20 "I pray not only on behalf of these,
but also for those who through their word
will come to believe in me.
21 May they all be one.
As you, Father, are in me
and I in you,
may they also be in us
so that the world may believe
that you have sent me.[q]

---

c Jn 1:17; Wis 14:7; 15:3; Jer 24:7; Phil 3:8; 1 Jn 5:20.—d Jn 13:31.—e Jn 1:1-2; 12:28; Phil 2:6, 9-11.—f Jn 1:18; Ex 3:13.—g Jn 3:17; 14:24; Deut 18:8.—h Jn 17:20; Lk 22:32.—i Jn 16:15; 2 Thes 1:10, 12.—j Jn 7:33; 13:1; Ps 133:1.—k Jn 6:70; 13:18; 18:9; Ps 41:10; Mt 26:24; Acts 1:16.—l Jn 3:29; 15:11.—m Jn 8:23; 15:19.—n Mt 5:37; 6:13; 2 Thes 3:3; 1 Jn 5:18.—o 2 Sam 7:28; 1 Ki 17:24; 1 Pet 1:22.—p Jn 20:21-22.—q Jn 10:30; 14:10-11, 20; Jer 32:39.

17:6-19 People who have accepted his word and recognized his truth live in close union with Jesus,which is a wonderful gift from the Father. Jesus calls for their fidelity.

People who have accepted the words of Jesus are no longer trapped in worthlessness, emptiness, and falsehood—in everything that is a denial of God and what is here called "the world." Their future is not in running away but in being insulted and giving testimony. The trial of Jesus continues in these people. May they remain in truth and faith; may they not become a prey of the falsehood, worthlessness, and unbelief that are the face of the Evil One or of Evil.

17:12 *The one destined to be lost* (literally, "The son of perdition"): Judas the traitor (see Jn 13:18). The literal translation reflects a Hebraism, meaning one who is destined for destruction, and this by his own free action. It is by this free choice that the Scripture is fulfilled.

17:20-26 The prayer of Jesus indicates the destiny of his followers for all times and places. He asks what is essential for them: that they live in the bonds of peace and unity that express their union with Christ. Here is the mystery of the Church in the light of the sacrifice of Christ: the Church is anchored in the inexpressible love of the Son and the Father; this is the mystery of communion. Christians testify to this communion when they live in it. Hence, they will discover more and more, in terms of experience, who Christ is and who the Father is: the glory of Christ and the name of the Father will be unveiled to their eyes as the highest realities.

22 "The glory that you have given me
I have given to them,
so that they may be one,
as we are one, [r]
23 I in them and you in me,
that they may become completely one,
and thus the world may know
that you have sent me
and that you have loved them
even as you have loved me. [s]

24 "Father, allow those you have given me
to be with me where I am,
so that they may behold my glory,
which you have bestowed on me
because you loved me
before the foundation of the world. [t]

25 "Righteous Father,
the world has not known you;
I have known you,
and they have known that you have
sent me. [u]
26 I have made your name known to them,
and I will make it known,
so that the love with which you loved me
may be in them, and I in them." [v]

F: The Passion—The Supreme Testimony*

CHAPTER 18

Jesus Gives Himself Up Freely.* 1 After Jesus
had spoken these words, he went out with
his disciples and crossed the Kidron * valley.
He and his disciples entered a garden
there. [w] 2 This place was known to Judas, his
betrayer, because Jesus had often met there
with his disciples. [x] 3 Therefore, Judas went
to that garden with a detachment of sol-
diers, * together with temple guards provid-
ed by the chief priests and the Pharisees,
equipped with lanterns and torches and
weapons. [y]
4 Then Jesus, fully aware of everything that
was going to happen to him, came forward
and asked them, "Whom are you look-
ing for?" [z] 5 They answered, "Jesus the
Nazorean." * Jesus replied, "I am." Judas
who betrayed him was standing with them. [a]
6 When Jesus said to them, "I am," they
drew back and fell to the ground. [b] 7 Again,
he asked them, "Whom are you looking
for?" And they said, "Jesus the Nazorean."
8 Jesus answered, "I have told you that I am.
If you are looking for me, let these men go."
9 This was to fulfill the word he had spoken,
"I did not lose any of those you gave me." * [c]
10 Then Simon Peter, who had a sword,
drew it and struck the high priest's servant,
slicing off his right ear. The servant's name
was Malchus. 11 Jesus said to Peter, "Put
your sword back into its scabbard! Am I
not to drink the cup * that the Father has
given me?" [d]

Jesus and Peter at the Hour of Bearing Witness. 12 * [e] Then the detachment of sol-
diers, their commander, and the Jewish
guards seized Jesus and bound him. 13 They
took him first to Annas, the father-in-law of
Caiaphas who was the high priest that year. [f]
14 It was Caiaphas who had advised the Jews
that it was better for one man to die for the
people. [g]

Peter's First Denial. 15 [h] Simon Peter and
another disciple were following Jesus. That

r Jn 1:14; 14:20; Rom 8:30.—s Jn 16:27; 2 Cor 13:5.—t Jn 14:3; Mt 25:34; 1 Thes 4:17.—u Jn 1:10; 15:21.—v Jn 15:9; Ex 3:13.—w 2 Sam 15:23; Mt 26:30,36; Mk 14:26,32; Lk 22:39.—x Lk 21:37.—y Mt 26:47-51; Mk 14:43-44; Lk 22:47; Acts 1:16.—z Jn 6:64; 12:27; 13:1, 11.—a Mk 1:24.—b Ps 27:2.—c Jn 6:39; 10:28; 17:12.—d Mt 20:22; 26:39; Mk 10:38; Lk 22:42.—e 12-14: Mt 26:57-58; Mk 14:53-54; Lk 22:54-55.—f Mt 26:3; Lk 3:2.—g Jn 11:49-50.—h 15-18: Mt 26:58, 69-70; Mk 14:54, 66-68; Lk 22:54-57.

18:1—19:42 Jesus does not submit passively to what happens; he controls his life and his sufferings; he even wills them and defines their meaning. The fourth Gospel, more than the others, emphasizes his sovereign freedom. Jesus is not, however, only pretending to share the human condition: he is a human being who suffers hostility, violence, and death, and the Passion Narrative demonstrates this. John, no less than the Synoptics, emphasizes the realistic character of the events; in fact, some details are even peculiar to him. In the fourth Gospel, the Passion and cross are an exaltation or uplifting of Jesus, a glorification by the Father, and a manifestation of all his love for humanity. By traveling the way of the cross with full awareness and on his own initiative, Jesus makes the truth of God shine forth.

18:1-11 Fear and disgust have no place in this account of the arrest. From the beginning, Jesus manifests his sovereign liberty to enter upon the Passion; it is his initiative and his destiny. The betrayal by Judas and his wicked cohorts cannot take away the liberty of Jesus, any more than the violence of Peter can defend it. Jesus depends only on his Father; he gives his life willingly.

18:1 *Kidron:* a brook, fed by the rains, divided the hill of Jerusalem from the Mount of Olives.

18:3 *Detachment of soldiers:* this refers to a complement of Roman troops—either 600 (a cohort) or 200 men, hinting at Roman complicity in the plot against Jesus even prior to his trial before Pilate. *Lanterns and torches:* these may stress that the hour of darkness has come.

18:5 *Nazorean:* this is the form found in Mt (2:23 and 26:71) and Acts (e.g., 2:22), not the *Nazarene* of Mark. *I am:* probably intended by John as an expression of divinity (see note on Jn 4:26).

18:9 The citation may refer to Jn 6:39; 10:28; or 17:12.

18:11 *Cup:* symbol of a person's calling and, above all, of his tragic destiny ("lots" were shaken in a cup); here it signifies the bitter hour of the Passion (see Mt 22:39).

18:12-27 In the fourth Gospel, the trial before the Jewish authorities is told in a few swift strokes; throughout his public ministry Jesus has spoken about his ministry and the mission he has undertaken; the trial is already over. Annas, who appears here, was a high priest removed from office by the Romans, but by his influence he controlled Jewish life. *Another disciple* (v. 15): John, the one "whom Jesus loved."

disciple was known to the high priest, so he went with Jesus into the high priest's courtyard, [16] but Peter remained standing outside at the gate. The other disciple who was known to the high priest went out and spoke to the woman who was in charge of the gate, and he brought Peter inside.

[17] The woman said to Peter, "Are you not one of this man's disciples?" He replied, "I am not." [18] Since it was cold, the servants and the guards had made a charcoal fire, and they were standing around it, warming themselves. Peter was also standing there and warming himself. [i]

The Inquiry before Annas. [19] * [j] The high priest questioned Jesus about his disciples and about his teaching. [20] Jesus answered,

"I have spoken openly
for the world to hear.
I have always taught
in synagogues and in the temple
where all the Jews congregate.
I have said nothing in secret. [k]
21 Why do you ask me?
Interrogate those who heard
what I said to them.
They know what I said."

[22] * When he had said this, one of the temple guards standing there struck Jesus with his hand, saying, "Is that any way to answer the high priest?" [l] [23] Jesus replied, "If I have spoken wrongly, testify to my error. But if I have spoken rightly, why did you strike me?" [m] [24] Then Annas sent him bound to Caiaphas, the high priest. [n]

Peter's Second and Third Denials. [25] [o] Meanwhile, as Simon Peter stood warming himself, he was asked, "Are you not also one of his disciples?" He denied it and said, "I am not." [26] Then one of the servants of the high priest, a relative of the man whose ear Peter had sliced off, asked, "Did I not see you in the garden with him?" [27] Again, Peter denied it. And at that very moment, a cock crowed. [p]

Jesus Handed Over to Pilate. [28] * [q] Then they took Jesus from Caiaphas to the praetorium. * It was early in the morning, and they did not enter the praetorium in order to avoid becoming defiled and thus be able to eat the Passover meal. [r]

[29] Therefore, Pilate went out to them and asked, "What charge do you bring against this man?" [30] They answered, "If he were not a criminal, we would not have handed him over to you." [31] Pilate said to them, "Take him yourselves and judge him according to your law." The Jews replied, "We are not allowed to put anyone to death." [s] [32] This was to fulfill what Jesus had said when he indicated the kind of death he was to die. [t]

The First Hearing before Pilate. [33] Then Pilate went back into the praetorium, and having summoned Jesus he asked him, "Are you the King of the Jews?" [u] [34] Jesus answered, "Are you saying this on your own, or have others told you about me?" [35] Pilate said, "Am I a Jew? Your own people and the chief priests have handed you over to me. What have you done?" [v] [36] Jesus replied,

"My kingdom does not belong to this world.
If my kingdom did belong to this world,
my followers would have fought
to prevent me from being handed over to the Jews.

i Jn 21:9; Mk 14:54.—j 19-24: Mt 26:59-66; Mk 14:55-64; Lk 22:66-71.—k Jn 6:59; 7:14, 26; Isa 45:19; 48:16; Mt 26:55; Mk 4:23; Lk 19:47; 22:53.—l Jn 19:3; Mt 16:21; Acts 23:2.—m Mt 5:39; Acts 23:2-5.—n Mt 26:57.—o 25-27: Mt 26:71-75; Mk 14:69-72; Lk 22:58-62.—p Jn 13:38.—q 28-38a: Mt 27:1-2, 11, 25; Mk 15:1-5; Lk 23:1-5.—r Jn 11:55; 19:9.—s Acts 18:15.—t Jn 3:14; 8:28; 12:32-33; Mt 20:19.—u Jn 19:9; Lk 23:3.—v Jn 1:11.

18:19-24 It is not very probable that this nighttime inquiry before Annas, mentioned only by John, is the same as the trial before Caiaphas mentioned by the Synoptics (at night by Mt and Mk and in the morning by Lk).

18:22-23 Jesus remains calm and self-restrained throughout the entire Passion. He responds to the guard's aggressiveness with meekness, but he does not fail to defend the legitimacy of his behavior and to point out the injustice done to him. Hence, Christians' defense of their rights is compatible with meekness and humility (see Acts 22:25).

18:28—19:22 We should try to imagine the scene. A Roman official, Pontius Pilate, had been governor of restless Judea since A.D. 26 (we are now in the year 30). He had two guiding principles: to keep public order at any cost, and not to compromise his own reputation with Emperor Tiberius. The Jewish authorities wanted to rid themselves of Jesus in a legal way, thereby saving their own good name. Jesus himself did not want to disappear in an uprising, but had decided to go forward even to torture and execution on the cross (see Jn 18:32). In seven successive steps, dealing now with the Jews, now with Jesus, the governor is led to seek, find, and proclaim the truth. Jesus is in fact innocent; he claims the title of king, not in order to dominate but in order to give. This man, whose innocence the governor asserts three times and whom he wishes to set free, says that he is Son of God, and explains his present subordination to an earthly authority as a phase in a divinely willed plan over which the imperial official has no power (Jn 19:10-11).

The Gospel notes that this event took place around midday on the day of Preparation for the Passover; it was the hour when they began to slaughter the lambs for the feast. The new Passover, marking God's deliverance of humanity, is at hand; the new Passover Lamb is about to offer the true and final sacrifice.

18:28 *Praetorium:* the residence of the Roman procurator. *Passover meal:* unlike the members of the Sanhedrin, Jesus has already celebrated the Passover supper (Mt 26:20-29).

Matson Photo Service

WAY OF THE CROSS (VIA DOLOROSA) — The location of Pilate's judgment hall in which Jesus was sentenced to death is uncertain. Very probably it was in the fortress Antonia at the northwest angle of the temple area.

Pictured above is the street leading from the ruins of the fortress to the traditional site of Calvary in the Church of the Holy Sepulchre. In the background is the "fifth station," the little chapel of Simon the Cyrenian who helped Jesus carry the cross. (See Jn 19:13-18 and Mt 27:32-34)

R. Kugelman

ANCIENT JEWISH TOMB — The tomb pictured above is located a few miles west of Jerusalem. Note the large circular stone (some stones are said to have weighed one or more tons) used to seal the entrance to the tomb. The tomb in which Jesus was laid was probably similar to this one. (See Jn 19:42)

Matson Photo Service

TOMB OF OUR LORD — A continuous tradition going back to the time of Constantine identifies Calvary and the tomb of Jesus with the site of the Church of the Holy Sepulchre in Jerusalem. The tomb itself is preceded by a vestibule called the Chapel of the Angel to commemorate the angel who rolled back the stone and announced to the women that Jesus had risen as he had said. (See Jn 20:1 and Mt 28:2, 5, 6)

The fact is that my kingdom is not
here."[w]

37 Pilate then said to him, "So you are a king!" Jesus answered,

"It is you who say
that I am a king.
For this was I born,
and for this I came into the world:
to testify to the truth.
Everyone who is of the truth
listens to my voice."[x]

38 Pilate responded, "What is truth?"

Barabbas Preferred to Jesus.[y] Then, having said this, he went out again to the Jews and said, "I find no evidence of a crime in this man.[z] 39 But according to your custom, I release one prisoner to you at Passover. Do you want me to release to you the King of the Jews?" 40 They shouted, "Not this man, but Barabbas!" Now Barabbas was a thief. *

CHAPTER 19

Behold, the Man! 1 [a]Then Pilate ordered that Jesus be scourged. *[b] 2 The soldiers twisted together some thorns into a crown and placed it on his head, and they dressed him in a purple robe. 3 They kept going up to him, saying, "Hail, King of the Jews," while striking him on the face repeatedly.[c]

4 Once again, Pilate went out and said to the Jews, "Look, I am bringing him out to you to let you know that I find no evidence of a crime in him."[d] 5 Then Jesus came out, wearing the crown of thorns and the purple robe. Pilate said to them, "Behold, the man!"[e]

6 When they saw him, the chief priests and the temple guards shouted, "Crucify him! Crucify him!" Pilate said to them, "Take him yourselves and crucify him. I find no evidence of a crime in him."[f] 7 The Jews answered, "We have a Law, and according to that Law he ought to die because he has claimed to be the Son of God."[g]

The Second Hearing before Pilate. 8 Now when Pilate heard this, he was more frightened than ever. 9 Returning to the praetorium, he asked Jesus, "Where are you from?" But Jesus offered no response.[h] 10 Pilate then said to him, "Are you refusing to speak to me? Do you not realize that I have the power to release you and the power to crucify you?" 11 Jesus answered him,

"You would have no authority over me
at all
unless it had been given to you from
above.
Therefore, the one who handed me over
to you
is guilty of a greater sin."[i]

Jesus Is Condemned to Death. 12 From that moment on, Pilate sought to release him, but the Jews kept shouting, "If you release this man, you are no Friend of Caesar. * Everyone who claims to be a king opposes Caesar."[j]

13 When Pilate heard these words, he brought Jesus out and seated him on the judge's bench at a place known as the Stone Pavement * (in Hebrew, "Gabbatha").[k] 14 It was the day of Preparation for the Passover, and it was about noon. * Pilate said to the Jews, "Behold, your King!"[l] 15 They shouted, "Away with him! Away with him! Crucify him!" "Am I to crucify your King?" Pilate asked them. The chief priests replied, "We have no king but Caesar." 16 Then he handed him over to them to be crucified.[m]

Jesus Is Crucified. Then they took him away, 17 [n]and, carrying the cross * by himself, he went out to what is called the Place of the Skull (in Hebrew, "Golgotha").[o] 18 There they crucified him * along with two others, one on either side, with Jesus in the middle.[p]

19 Pilate also had an inscription written and fastened to the cross. It read, "Jesus the

w Jn 1:10; 8:23; Mt 3:2; 26:53.—x Jn 3:32; 8:47; 1 Tim 6:13; 1 Jn 4:6.—y 38b-40: Mt 27:15-26; Mk 15:6-15; Lk 23:18-25; Acts 3:14.—z Lk 23:4.—a 1-16: Mt 27:27-31; Mk 15:16-20; Lk 23:13-25.—b Deut 25:3; Isa 50:6; 53:5.—c Jn 18:22.—d Jn 18:38; Lk 23:4.—e Isa 52:14.—f Jn 18:31; 19:15; Lk 23:4; Acts 3:13.—g Jn 5:18; 10:33-36; Lev 24:16; Mt 26:63-66.—h Jn 7:28; 18:33; Isa 53:7.—i Jn 3:27; 10:18; 18:28-30; Acts 3:13; Rom 13:1.—j Lk 23:2; Acts 17:7.—k Jn 5:2; Mt 27:19.—l Mt 27:62; Mk 15:25.—m Mt 27:26; Mk 15:15; Lk 23:25.—n 17-22: Mt 27:32-37; Mk 15:21-26; Lk 23:26-35.—o Gen 22:6; Lk 14:27.—p Lk 23:32; Isa 53:12.

18:40 *Barabbas . . . thief:* the word for *thief* can also mean *revolutionary* (see note on Mk 15:9).

19:1 Pilate was obviously hoping that a scourging would suffice for the Jews and he could then release Jesus.

19:12 *Friend of Caesar:* an honorific Roman title given to high officials for merit.

19:13 *Stone Pavement:* Greek, *lithostrotos;* it has been identified with the great courtyard of the fortress Antonia, northeast of the temple, and therefore with the praetorium, the place or headquarters mentioned in Jn 18:28.

19:14 *Noon:* literally, the sixth hour. See note on Mk 15:25.

19:17 *Carrying the cross:* see note on Mk 15:21.

19:18 *Crucified him:* see note on Mt 27:35.

Nazorean, King of the Jews." * [q] 20 This
inscription, in Hebrew, Latin, and Greek,
was read by many Jews, because the place
where Jesus was crucified was near the
city. [r] 21 Therefore, the chief priests of the
Jews said to Pilate, "You should not write,
'The King of the Jews,' but rather, 'This man
claimed to be the King of the Jews.' " [s]
22 Pilate responded, "What I have written, I
have written."*

23 * [t] When the soldiers had crucified
Jesus, they took his clothes and divided them
into four shares, one share for each soldier.
[u] They also took his tunic, which was woven
seamless, top to bottom. 24 They said to one
another, "Instead of tearing it, let us cast lots
for it to see who is to get it." In this way, the
Scripture was fulfilled that says,

> "They divided my garments among
> them,
> and for my clothing they cast lots."

And that is what the soldiers did.

Mary and John at the Cross. 25 Standing
near the cross of Jesus were his mother and
his mother's sister, Mary the wife of Clopas,
and Mary Magdalene. [v] 26 When Jesus saw
his mother and the disciple whom he loved
standing beside her, he said to his mother,
"Woman, behold, your son." [w] 27 Then he
said to the disciple, "Behold, your mother."
And from that hour the disciple took her
into his home.

Jesus Dies on the Cross. 28 [x] After this,
aware that everything had now been com-
pleted, and in order that the Scripture
might be fulfilled, Jesus said, "I thirst." [y] 29 A
jar filled with sour wine was standing near-
by, so they soaked a sponge in the wine on a
branch of hyssop and held it up to his lips. [z]
30 When Jesus had taken the wine, he said,
"It is finished."* Then he bowed his head and
gave up his spirit. [a]

The Blood and the Water. 31 It was the day of
Preparation, and the Jews did not want to
have the bodies remain on the cross on the
Sabbath, especially since that Sabbath day
was a great solemnity. Therefore, they
requested Pilate to order that their legs be
broken and the bodies taken down. [b]

32 So the soldiers came and broke the legs
of the first man and then of the other who
had been crucified with him. 33 However,
when they came to Jesus and saw that he
was already dead, they did not break his
legs, 34 but one of the soldiers thrust a lance
into his side, and immediately a flow of
blood and water came forth. [c] 35 An eyewit-
ness has testified to this, and his testimony is
true. He knows that what he says is true, so
that you also may believe. [d]

36 This happened so that the Scripture
might be fulfilled,

> "Not one of his bones will be broken." [e]

37 And again, in another passage Scripture
says,

> "They shall look on the one
> whom they have pierced." [f]

q Mk 1:24.—r Heb 13:12.—s Jn 18:33; Lk 19:14.—t 23-27: Mt 27:38-44; Mk 15:27-32; Lk 23:36-43.—u 23-24: Ps 22:19; Mt 27:35; Mk 15:24; Lk 23:34.—v Jn 20:1, 18; Mt 27:55; Mk 15:40-41; Lk 8:2; 23:49.—w Jn 13:23.—x 28-30: Mt 27:45-56; Mk 15:33-41; Lk 23:44-49.—y Jn 13:1; Ps 22:16.—z Ps 69:22.—a Jn 4:34; 10:18; 17:4; Lk 12:50; 23:46.—b Ex 12:16; Deut 21:23; Jos 8:29.—c Num 20:11; Zec 12:10; 1 Jn 5:6; Rev 1:7.—d Jn 7:37-39; 21:24; Lk 24:48.—e Ex 12:46; Num 9:12; Ps 34:21.—f Num 21:9; Zec 12:10; Rev 1:7.

19:19 The *inscription* is found in all four Gospels under a slightly different form. John gives the most complete form, corresponding to the Latin of the three forms: INRI = *IESU NAZARENUS REX IUDAEORUM* ("Jesus the Nazorean, King of the Jews"). See also note on Jn 18:5.

19:20-22 *What I have written, I have written:* by this statement, Pilate affirms the truth of Jesus' divinity, which is rejected by his opponents. At the same time, Pilate stresses the inscription's public and universal character—for it can be read by Jews *(Hebrew,* i.e., Aramaic), Greeks (*Greek*), and Romans (*Latin*).

19:23-37 To the last moment, Jesus retains a keen awareness that he is completing God's work for the world, the will of God that all of the Scriptures (so frequently cited) proclaim. We see how Jesus' final gestures are symbols of the gifts given to humankind.

In dividing the garments of the crucified man, the soldiers are careful not to tear the seamless tunic. By calling attention to this, John perhaps wishes to signify the unity that Christ leaves as a heritage to those whom he wills to save.

Tradition identifies John with the beloved disciple (see Jn 13:23; 20:2-10; 21:7-20; and compare Jn 1:35-39; 18:15) to whom Jesus entrusts his mother. As she did with the servants at Cana (Jn 2:5), Mary will teach the disciple how to follow the example and teaching of her Son. The passage suggests the maternal vocation of the Mother of Jesus in relation to all believers.

The author bears witness to the fulfillment of the Scriptures. The words "I thirst" recall Ps 69:22: "In my thirst they gave me vinegar to drink." By drinking the sour wine offered to him, Jesus finishes the cup of his suffering (Jn 18:11).

Jesus is pierced by a lance, immolated like the Passover lamb, the bones of which are not broken. From his opened breast spurt blood, the sign of life surrendered, and water, the sign of the Spirit that he gives to believers (see Jn 7:38-39). Spiritual meditation has taken these symbols further; the blood and water are seen as prefigurations of the Eucharist and Baptism, the two Sacraments that form and feed the Church, this new Eve that has come forth from the opened side of the new Adam, Jesus Christ.

All are called to the heart of the Redeemer where they can joyfully draw water from the fountain of salvation (see Isa 12:3). A privileged disciple, doubtless the beloved disciple once again, offers a special guarantee of the truth of the events and the richness of their meaning: in his mind it is a case not of the sad death of a human being but of the fulfillment of God's plan, the shining forth of his love and his glory.

19:30 *It is finished:* this may correspond to the loud cry mentioned in Mt 27:50 and Mk 15:37. Jesus died as a victor, completing what he came to accomplish. *Gave up his spirit:* a description of death that is out of the ordinary—it may suggest an act of will.

Jesus Is Buried.* 38 [g] Shortly thereafter, Joseph of Arimathea, who was a disciple of Jesus, but secretly, because of his fear of the Jews, asked Pilate for permission to remove the body of Jesus. Pilate granted him permission, and so he came and took his body away. [h]

39 Nicodemus, who had first come to Jesus at night, also came, bringing with him a mixture of myrrh and aloes weighing about one hundred pounds.* [i] 40 They took the body of Jesus and wrapped it with the spices in linen cloths, in accordance with the burial custom of the Jews. [j]

41 At the place where Jesus had been crucified there was a garden, and in that garden there was a new tomb in which no one had ever been buried. 42 And so, since it was the Jewish day of Preparation and the tomb was nearby, they laid Jesus there.

G: The Appearances of the Risen One*

CHAPTER 20

The Mystery of the Empty Tomb.* 1 [k] Early on the first day of the week, while it was still dark, Mary Magdalene came to the tomb and saw that the stone had been moved away from the tomb. [l] 2 Therefore, she ran to Simon Peter and the other disciple, the one whom Jesus loved, and said to them, "They have taken the Lord out of the tomb, and we don't know where they have put him." [m]

3 Then Peter and the other disciple set out and made their way toward the tomb. [n] 4 They both were running, but the other disciple outran Peter and reached the tomb first. 5 He bent down and saw the linen cloths lying there, but he did not go in. [o]

6 When Simon Peter caught up with him, he entered the tomb. He saw the linen cloths lying there, [p] 7 and also the cloth that had covered his head not lying with the burial cloths but rolled up in a separate place. [q] 8 Then the other disciple who had reached the tomb first also went inside, and he saw and believed. 9 They still did not understand the Scripture indicating that he must rise from the dead. [r] 10 Then the disciples returned to their homes.

Mary Magdalene Recognizes Jesus.* 11 [s] Mary Magdalene remained weeping outside the tomb. And as she wept, she bent down to look into the tomb, 12 and she saw two angels in white sitting there where the body of Jesus had been, one at the head and the other at the feet. [t] 13 They asked her, "Woman, why are you weeping?" She answered, "They have taken my Lord away, and I do not know where they have put him."

14 As she said this, she turned around and saw Jesus standing there, but she did not realize that it was Jesus. [u] 15 [v] Jesus said to her, "Woman, why are you weeping? Whom are you looking for?" Thinking he was the gardener, she said to him, "Sir, if you have removed him, tell me where you have put him, and I will take him away." 16 Jesus said to her, "Mary!" She turned and said to him in Hebrew, *"Rabbouni!"** (which means "Teacher"). [w]

g 38-42: Mt 27:57-60; Mk 15:42-46; Lk 23:50-54.—h Jn 7:13.—i Jn 3:1-2; 7:50; Ps 45:9.—j Jn 11:44; Lk 24:12.—k 1-10: Mt 28:1-10; Mk 16:1-11; Lk 24:1-12.—l Jn 19:25; Mt 27:60; Lk 8:2.—m Jn 13:23.—n Lk 24:12.—o Jn 19:40.—p Lk 24:12.—q Jn 11:44; 19:40.—r Jn 2:22; Mt 22:29; Acts 2:26-27; 1 Cor 15:4.—s 11-18: Mk 16:9-11.—t Mt 28:2; Mk 16:5; Acts 1:10.—u Jn 21:4; Mk 16:12; Lk 24:16; 1 Cor 15:43-44.—v 15-17: Mt 28:9-10.—w Jn 5:2.

19:38-42 Some disciples, who until now were afraid to declare themselves, proceed to the burial of Jesus. According to Jewish custom, an executed criminal could not be put in a tomb where other people had already been buried; to do so would have brought dishonor on them. But the sepulcher where Jesus is put is new in another sense perhaps—in it lies concealed the source of new life.

19:39 *One hundred pounds:* literally, "a hundred *litrai.*" *Myrrh and aloes:* possibly a fulfillment of Ps 45:9.

20:1—21:25 Here, as in the rest of his work, John is pleased to dwell on some incidents not set down, or at least barely noticed, by the Synoptics; more than once, these are episodes involving the very person who is passing them on to his brethren in the faith. We owe to John the most extensive part of the Easter Gospel. By speaking of the empty tomb, he emphasizes the victory of life over death. When he describes one or other of the appearances, he wants to show how Jesus was recognized by his followers, what his new presence in their midst is like, how we are to believe in Christ, the mission to be carried out in the world in order to bear witness to him, and the gift of the Spirit to all believers. The last chapter, which has every appearance of having been added by disciples to the first edition of John's Gospel, emphasizes and expands the ecclesial perspective: The Resurrection, which ends the earthly career of Jesus, begins the earthly career of the Church.

20:1-10 Why is the body no longer there and why are the linen cloths still there? The beloved disciple, who had come with Peter, becomes the witness of the event and its meaning. Because he looks at the linen cloths with faith, he understands them as belonging to God's plan: the linen cloths mean that Jesus is alive.

The tomb is the symbol of death, but in the presence of this tomb the sign of death is changed. We are here at the beginning of a new life. Death is overcome.

20:11-18 To Mary Magdalene everything has been taken away, even the mortal remains of the One who has just died. But the appearance of the living Christ stands out in bold relief before her. And nothing is as it was before. The time of privileged encounters and sensible presence is past. The joy of Mary will be to announce to the disciples this new Covenant: Jesus lives with the Father, who is our Father too. Believers are brothers and sisters of Jesus. Here lies the mystery of the Church—that is, in the communion with Jesus.

20:16 *Rabbouni* is more solemn than "Rabbi"; it means "My Teacher."

17 Jesus then said to her, "Do not hold on to me, because I have not yet ascended to my Father. But go to my brethren and tell them, 'I am ascending to my Father and your Father, to my God and your God.' "* [x] 18 Mary Magdalene then went and announced to the disciples, "I have seen the Lord," and repeated what he had said to her. [y]

Jesus Appears to the Disciples.* 19 [z] On the evening of that same day, the first day of the week, the doors of the house where the disciples had gathered were locked because of their fear of the Jews. Jesus then came and stood in their midst and said to them, "Peace be with you." [a] 20 After saying this, he showed them his hands and his side.

The disciples were filled with joy when they saw the Lord. [b] 21 "Peace be with you," Jesus said to them again.

"As the Father has sent me,
so I send you." [c]

22 After saying this, he breathed on them and said,

"Receive the Holy Spirit. [d]
23 If you forgive anyone's sins,
they are forgiven.
If you retain anyone's sins,
they are retained." [e]

Jesus Appears to Thomas.* 24 Now Thomas, called the Twin, who was one of the Twelve, was not with the rest when Jesus came. [f] 25 When the other disciples told him, "We have seen the Lord," he replied, "Unless I see the mark of the nails on his hands and put my finger into the place where the nails pierced and insert my hand into his side, I will not believe." [g]

26 Eight days later, the disciples were again in the house, and on this occasion Thomas was with them. Although the doors were locked, Jesus came and stood in their midst, and he said, "Peace be with you." [h] 27 Then he said to Thomas, "Put your finger here and see my hands. Reach out your hand and put it into my side. Do not doubt any longer, but believe." [i] 28 Thomas exclaimed, "My Lord and my God!" [j] 29 Then Jesus said to him,

"You have come to believe
because you have seen me.
Blessed are those who have not seen
and yet have come to believe." [k]

Believe in Order To Live.* 30 Now Jesus performed many other signs in the presence of his disciples that are not recorded in this work. [l] 31 But those written here have been recorded so that you may come to believe that Jesus is the Christ, the Son of God, and that through your belief you may have life in his name. [m]

EPILOGUE

CHAPTER 21

Jesus Appears to Seven Disciples.* 1 Some time later, Jesus once again revealed himself to his disciples at the Sea of Tiberias, in the following manner. [n] 2 Simon Peter, Thomas called the Twin, Nathanael from Cana in Galilee, the sons of Zebedee, and two other disciples were gathered together. [o] 3 Simon Peter said to them, "I am going out to fish." The others replied, "We will go with you." They set off and got into the boat, but that night they caught nothing. [p]

4 Shortly after daybreak, Jesus was standing on the shore, but the disciples did not

x Jn 7:33; Ps 89:27; Acts 1:9.—y Lk 24:10.—z 19-23: Mt 28:16-20; Mk 16:14-18; Lk 24:36-44.—a Jn 7:13; Lk 24:36-39.—b Lk 24:41.—c Jn 3:17; 14:27; 17:18; Mt 28:19; Mk 16:15; Lk 24:47-48.—d Jn 7:39; Gen 2:7; Ezek 37:9; Acts 2:38; 1 Cor 15:45; Gal 3:2.—e Mt 16:19; 18:18.—f Jn 11:16.—g Mk 16:11; 1 Jn 1:1.—h Jn 21:14.—i Lk 24:40.—j Jn 1:1.—k Jn 3:15; 4:48; Lk 1:45; 1 Pet 1:8.—l Jn 21:25; Deut 34:10, 12.—m Jn 3:14, 15; Mt 4:3; Acts 3:16; 1 Jn 5:13.—n Jn 6:1; 20:19; Mt 26:32; 28:7.—o Jn 1:45; 2:1.—p Mt 4:18; Lk 5:4-10.

20:17 Jesus tells Mary Magdalene not to delay. She must immediately go and announce his Resurrection to the disciples, while he will ascend to the Father before returning to manifest himself to them in full possession of all his prerogatives as the firstborn among many brothers. He had foretold that his glorification was necessary in order for the Holy Spirit to be sent. Hence, for John, the Ascension takes place on the same day as the Resurrection. The external and more demonstrative Ascension described in the Acts of the Apostles (1:6-11), forty days after the Resurrection, was only Jesus' sensible and definitive departure from the disciples after the various appearances to sustain and confirm their faith.

20:19-23 This is the first "Sunday" of the Church, the day on which the risen Lord meets his disciples. The season of joy has come (see Jn 15:11; 16:20-24; 17:13). He who comes, alive, into the midst of his followers is the same one who took on himself the suffering of the cross. He will now make them preachers of his mystery and ministers of his forgiveness. He sends the Spirit upon them as the Spirit had been sent on him by the Father at his Baptism, when he was beginning his mission (see also Ezek 37:9; Jn 15:26-27); this marks the beginning of the apostolic mission, which is a continuation of the work of Jesus Christ.

20:24-29 The true happiness of the disciples was not to have seen the Lord but to have understood the meaning of his Passion. The Passion makes known God's love. Blessed are they who believe in this love. Christian generations who have not known the visible Christ will meet him in faith.

20:30-31 The purpose of John's Gospel was to bring people to belief in Jesus: there is life only in communion with him.

These verses undoubtedly constituted the first conclusion of the fourth Gospel.

21:1-14 This miraculous catch is the final "sign" given by Jesus. He does not reveal himself; he remains mysterious, but the true disciple is able to recognize him (see Jn 21:20).

realize that it was Jesus.[q] 5 Jesus called out, "Children, have you caught anything?" When they answered, "No,"[r] 6 he said to them, "Cast the net over the right side of the boat and you will find something." They did so, and they were unable to haul the net on board because of the great number of fish.[s]

7 Then the disciple whom Jesus loved said to Peter, "It is the Lord." When Simon Peter heard him say that it was the Lord, he wrapped his outer garment around him, for he had taken it off, and jumped into the sea.[t] 8 The other disciples came in the boat, towing the net full of fish, for they were not far from land, only about one hundred yards.

9 When they came ashore, they saw a charcoal fire there, with fish on it, and bread.[u] 10 Jesus said to them, "Bring some of the fish you have just caught." 11 Simon Peter went on board and dragged the net ashore, full of large fish, one hundred and fifty-three of them. Even though there were so many, the net was not torn.[v]

12 Jesus then said to them, "Come and have breakfast." None of the disciples dared to ask him, "Who are you?" because they knew that it was the Lord. 13 Jesus then came forward, took the bread, and gave it to them, and likewise the fish.[w] 14 This was now the third time that Jesus revealed himself to his disciples after his resurrection from the dead.[x]

Jesus and Peter.* 15 When they had finished breakfast, Jesus said to Simon Peter, "Simon, son of John, do you love me more than these?" He replied, "Yes, Lord, you know that I love you." Jesus said to him, "Feed my lambs."[y]

16 Jesus said to him again, "Simon, son of John, do you love me?" He replied, "Yes, Lord, you know that I love you." Jesus said to him, "Tend my sheep."[z]

17 Jesus said to him a third time, "Simon, son of John, do you love me?" Peter was hurt that Jesus had asked him a third time, "Do you love me?" "Lord," he said to him, "you know everything. You know that I love you." Jesus said to him, "Feed my sheep.[a]

18 "Amen, amen, I say to you,
when you were young
you used to fasten your own belt
and you would go wherever you wished.
But when you grow old,
you will stretch out your hands,
and someone else will put a belt around you
and take you where you do not wish to go."[b]

19 He said this to indicate the kind of death by which Peter would glorify God. After this, he said to him, "Follow me."[c]

The Beloved Disciple.* 20 Peter looked around and saw the disciple whom Jesus loved following them—the one who had reclined next to Jesus at the supper and had asked, "Lord, who is it that will betray you?"[d] 21 When Peter saw him, he said to Jesus, "Lord, what about him?" 22 Jesus replied, "If it should be my will that he remain until I come, how does that concern you? Follow me!"[e]

23 The saying then spread among the brethren that this disciple would not die. However, Jesus had not said to Peter, "He will not die," but, "If it should be my will that he remain until I come, how does that concern you?"[f]

Signature of the Redactors.* 24 This is the disciple who testifies to these things and has written them, and we know that his testimony is true.[g] 25 But there are also many other things that Jesus did; and if every one of them was recorded, I do not think the world itself could contain the books that would be written.[h]

q Jn 20:14; Mt 28:17; Lk 24:16.—r Lk 24:41.—s Lk 5:4-7.—t Jn 13:23.—u Jn 18:18; Lk 24:41-43.—v 2 Chr 2:16.—w Lk 24:42.—x Jn 20:19,26.—y Jn 13:37; Mt 26:33; Lk 12:32.—z Jn 10:11; 2 Sam 5:2; Ezek 34:2.—a Jn 13:37-38; 16:30; 18:15-18, 25-27; Mt 26:69-75; Mk 14:66-72; Lk 22:55-62.—b Acts 21:11, 14; 2 Pet 1:14.—c Jn 12:33; 13:36; Mt 4:19; 2 Pet 1:14.—d Jn 13:25.—e Mt 4:19; 16:28.—f Acts 1:16.—g Jn 15:27; 19:35.—h Jn 20:30.

21:15-19 In this touching dialogue, Christ makes Peter a sign of his own perennial presence with his followers as their Good Shepherd (see ch. 10). Catholic tradition has seen in this passage the fulfillment of the promise made at Caesarea Philippi: "I will give you the keys of the kingdom of heaven" (Mt 16:17-19; see also Lk 22:31-32). The First Vatican Council made reference to vv. 15-17 in its definition that Jesus appointed Peter supreme shepherd and ruler over the whole flock.

21:20-23 Peter will ultimately make the supreme sacrifice, but what will become of the beloved disciple of whom the fourth Gospel often speaks (Jn 13:23; 19:26-27; 20:2-10; see Jn 1:35-39; 18:15)? The first Christian generations still believed in the imminent return of Christ in glory (2 Thes 2), although they had not begun to experience the time of the Church. We no longer have the same preoccupation. However, the response made by Jesus still holds: what is important is to follow Christ faithfully.

21:24-25 The faith of believers is a grace, but it goes back in history to those who were witnesses: those who saw the deeds and understood their meaning. Nonetheless, the life of Jesus goes beyond everything that can be written or said about him, even in a Gospel. Opening or closing the sacred writing, we are brought back to the encounter with Christ himself.

"Then there appeared to them tongues as of fire, which separated and came to rest on each one of them. All of them were filled with the Holy Spirit" *(Acts 2:3-4)*.

THE ACTS OF THE APOSTLES

The Power of the Gospel and of the Spirit in the World

Christ's work, which the Gospels showed us being carried on in Palestine, was then carried on, and is being carried on today, throughout the entire world.

Those desirous of learning about the first steps taken on that journey have the Book of the Acts of the Apostles, which bears witness to the presence of the good news and of the Spirit in the midst of the nations. It is a book that describes the Church's youth.

The title "Acts of the Apostles" was probably given to this Book many years after the death of the author. In fact, the title corresponds only imperfectly to the contents of the work, since it follows in some detail the story of only two of the apostles: Peter and Paul. Nor does it intend to write their biographies, but simply to hand on to us recollections of the early events in the Church's life.

What it wants to tell us is, above all, the proclamation of a belief: A new age has begun in the history of humankind and the nations, the age of Easter, the age of the Church.

The author singles out the decisive turning points in this Spirit-sustained journey of the Gospel: Pentecost; the first martyrdom, that of Stephen the deacon; the conversion of Paul the persecutor; the acceptance of Gentiles into the Church through the intervention of Peter himself; the persecution in Jerusalem and the scattering of the apostles; and the establishment of Churches in the pagan world, at Antioch, Corinth, Ephesus, and finally Rome.

We must not expect the Book of Acts to tell us everything about the history of the very early Church. Events are reported in connection with some geographical points that mark the entrance of the Gospel into the world and its various cultures: Jerusalem, Antioch, Ephesus, Rome. Only a few of the principal figures appear. Peter and Paul share the pages of the work in almost equal measure, but we are not given their biographies. Both leave the scene of the story without our knowing anything of their further work or their martyrdom.

The Church is God's work, not a project of human beings, however great. There were other apostles, other communities; the author is well aware of this, but he does not mention them in his narrative. He has a different purpose.

In fact, he does not intend to serve as chronicler of the Church's beginnings; rather, as in the third Gospel, of which he is also the author, he intends to remain an evangelist. His guiding principle is to proclaim the great deeds of God that attest to the presence of salvation, to bear witness to the life of the communities, and to tell the signs of the conversion of the world.

Half of the Book is devoted to Paul, but we are told relatively little of the struggles and trials he had to face, or of the conflicts that shook the communities of Corinth and Galatia. Fortunately, Paul's own Letters have preserved lively traces of all these. The author sometimes refers to disagreements among the missionaries, but he does not regard these as important for the structure of his story.

Moreover, the Book ends too abruptly for our taste, when it has barely shown the way of the Gospel being opened throughout the world.

In this Book a lot of space is given to discourses. Ancient historians liked to put their own reflections and interpretations in the mouths of their heroes; by doing so they gave readers an opportunity to pause and reflect as the story moved on. It is not possible to say precisely the same of the author of Acts. Admittedly, he does not claim to be giving us a stenographic report of the discourses, but he does try to report, even if in concentrated form, the Christian preaching that was characteristic from the very beginning, and to show how sermons were developed.

The same author composed the third Gospel and the Book of Acts. There are no valid reasons for rejecting the tradition that this author was Luke.

These pages were composed around A.D. 80–90. Luke makes use of traditions preserved by various Churches that tell of their origin and the work of the first missionaries there, but he is also free to fill in the overall picture according to his own criteria. He recalls very early events, especially those that would inspire the Church of his own day; by the end of the first century, custom had already set a patina on the fervor of the early days.

The text of the Book of Acts has come down to us in two forms or redactions. Alongside the common redaction (the "Oriental" text) that is transmitted in the earliest manuscripts and versions, there existed as early as the second century a somewhat fuller redaction that added, not new events, but details that give the impression of coming from an eyewitness. This text (the "Western") is now regarded by the majority of scholars as an amplification of the first.

The Acts of the Apostles may be divided as follows:

I: At Jerusalem (1:1—12:25)
II: Antioch (13:1—18:22)
III: Ephesus (18:23—20:38)
IV: From Jerusalem to Rome (21:1—28:31)

I: AT JERUSALEM*

A: From Jesus to the Community of the Lord*

CHAPTER 1

Prologue.* 1 In my previous book,
Theophilus,* I wrote of everything that
Jesus did and taught from the beginning[a]
2 until the day he was taken up, after first
giving instructions through the Holy Spirit
to the apostles whom he had chosen.[b]

The Promise of the Spirit.* 3 After his passion
Jesus had presented himself alive to them by
many proofs. He appeared to them during
forty days and spoke to them about the king-
dom of God.[c] 4 When they were gathered
together, he ordered them not to leave
Jerusalem, saying, "Wait there for the
promise of the Father about which you have
heard me speak.[d] 5 For John baptized with
water, but within a few days you will be bap-
tized with the Holy Spirit."[e]

6 As they were all gathered together, they
asked him, "Lord, is this the time when you
are going to restore the kingdom to Israel?"[f]
7 He replied, "It is not for you to know the
dates or the times that the Father has desig-
nated by his own authority.[g] 8 But you will
receive power when the Holy Spirit comes
upon you, and then you will be my witnesses
not only in Jerusalem, but throughout Judea
and Samaria, and indeed to the farthest
ends of the earth."[h]

The Ascension of Jesus.* 9 After he said
this, he was lifted up as they looked on, and
a cloud took him from their sight.[i] 10 While
he was departing as they gazed upward
toward the sky, suddenly two men dressed in
white robes stood beside them,[j] 11 and they
said, "Men of Galilee, why are you standing
there looking up into the sky? This Jesus who
has been taken up from you into heaven will
come back in the same way as you have seen
him going into heaven."[k]

The First Community Waiting for the Spirit.
12 [l]Then they returned to Jerusalem from
the mount called Olivet, which is near
Jerusalem, no farther distant than a Sabbath
day's journey.* 13 When they arrived, they
went to the upper room where they were
staying: Peter and John and James and
Andrew, Philip and Thomas, Bartholomew
and Matthew, James son of Alphaeus and
Simon the Zealot, and Judas son of James.[m]
14 All of these were constantly engaged in
prayer, together with the women and Mary
the mother of Jesus, and with his
brethren.*[n]

a Lk 1:1-4; 3:23.—b Mt 28:19-20; Lk 24:44-49; Jn 13:18; 20:22; 1 Tim 3:16.—c Acts 10:41; 13:31; Mt 28:17; Lk 24:36.—d Ps 27:14; Lk 24:49; Jn 14:16, 17, 26; Eph 1:13.—e Acts 11:16; Mt 3:11; Mk 1:8; Lk 3:16; Jn 1:26; Eph 1:13.—f Acts 3:21; Mt 17:11.—g Deut 29:28; Ps 102:14; Mt 24:36; 1 Thes 5:1-2.—h Acts 2:1-13; 10:39; Isa 32:15; 43:10; Mt 28:19; Lk 24:47-48.—i 2 Ki 2:11; Mk 16:19; Lk 24:51.—j Jn 20:17; Rom 10:6.—k Acts 2:7; Zec 14:4; Lk 24:4, 51; Eph 4:8-10; 1 Pet 3:22; Rev 1:7.—l 12-14: Lk 6:14-16.—m Acts 9:37; 20:8.—n Acts 2:42; 6:4; Lk 23:49; Rom 12:12.

1:1—12:25 In the Gospel of Luke, the life of Jesus takes the form of an ascent to Jerusalem, where through him God will decisively intervene in the destiny of humanity. The Book of Acts allows us to be present at the spread of the Gospel from that center to the ends of the earth. The Holy City is very important as the starting point of evangelization.

The experience of the young Christian community becomes exemplary, as in stories of foundations. Thus in chs. 1—7 everything takes place in Jerusalem, while in chs. 8—12 the city serves as the starting point and point of return of the stories. The Church of Jerusalem, then, is the source of Christianity: it is the mother Church and the inspiration for every other Church and for the whole Church.

1:1-26 The first two chapters of Acts serve a special purpose. In them we move from the risen Jesus to the community that is founded and established in the midst of the Jewish people—the community that is the starting point of the main routes along which the life of the Church develops. For readers of that period, the language used constantly recalls the great traditions of the Old Testament: the entire plan of God is recapitulated in these passages that in turn establish the perspective for what follows.

1:1-2 One author conceived the third Gospel and the Book of Acts as a single whole; the combination is not the result of chance. The first work tells the story of the actions and teachings of Jesus, "beginning from [John's] baptism" (see Acts 1:22; 10:37); the second shows us the life and activity of the risen Lord, which is likewise made visible in the deeds and acts of the various communities.

1:1 *Theophilus:* perhaps a rich and distinguished person who has paid for the publication of the work. He is the same person as in Lk 1:3.

1:3-8 This is the important theme that characterizes the period of the Lord's appearances (the period lasts forty days, between Easter and Pentecost; the number 40, which recurs so often in the Bible, is a symbol of fullness). The story highlights what it means to experience the risen Lord.

It is the Spirit who links the past phase of the life of Jesus with its present phase. This Spirit, often promised by Jesus (Lk 11:13; 24:49), brings to fulfillment all the blessings that the Messiah was to bring (see Joel 4:9; Am 9:11). The day of national restoration is no longer something to be awaited; the decisive moment has already arrived, and the Spirit is beginning to unite the peoples.

1:9-11 The Ascension is not the final act, but the beginning of the time to come. The cloud that hides Jesus from the eyes of the disciples recalls the cloud that covered the people in the wilderness, accompanying them night and day on their journey (Ex 40:36-38); it is a sign of God's presence, of his glory (Lk 9:34f). The risen Jesus reunites earth with heaven, i.e., the world of human beings with the world of God.

1:12 *Sabbath day's journey:* about two-thirds of a mile.

1:14 This is the only place in which the mother of Jesus is mentioned in Acts; the collateral relatives of Jesus, *his brethren,* will later on have an important place in the Jerusalem community (Acts 12:20; 15:13; 21:18; see note on Mt 12:46).

Matson Photo Service

BETHSAIDA–SEA OF GALILEE — View of the Sea of Galilee (which is an expansion of the Jordan River) with the Plain of Gennesaret and the Mount of Beatitudes in the distance. This might have been the scene of the breakfast that Jesus took with his disciples after his resurrection. (See Jn 21:1, 15)

Matson Photo Service

MOUNT OF THE ASCENSION — An overall view of the Mount of Olives and surroundings where Jesus led his disciples before his ascension forty days after his resurrection. The Church of the Ascension rises in the background. There is little doubt that though he described the ascension in physical terms, Luke meant to emphasize our Lord's exaltation. (See Acts 1:11)

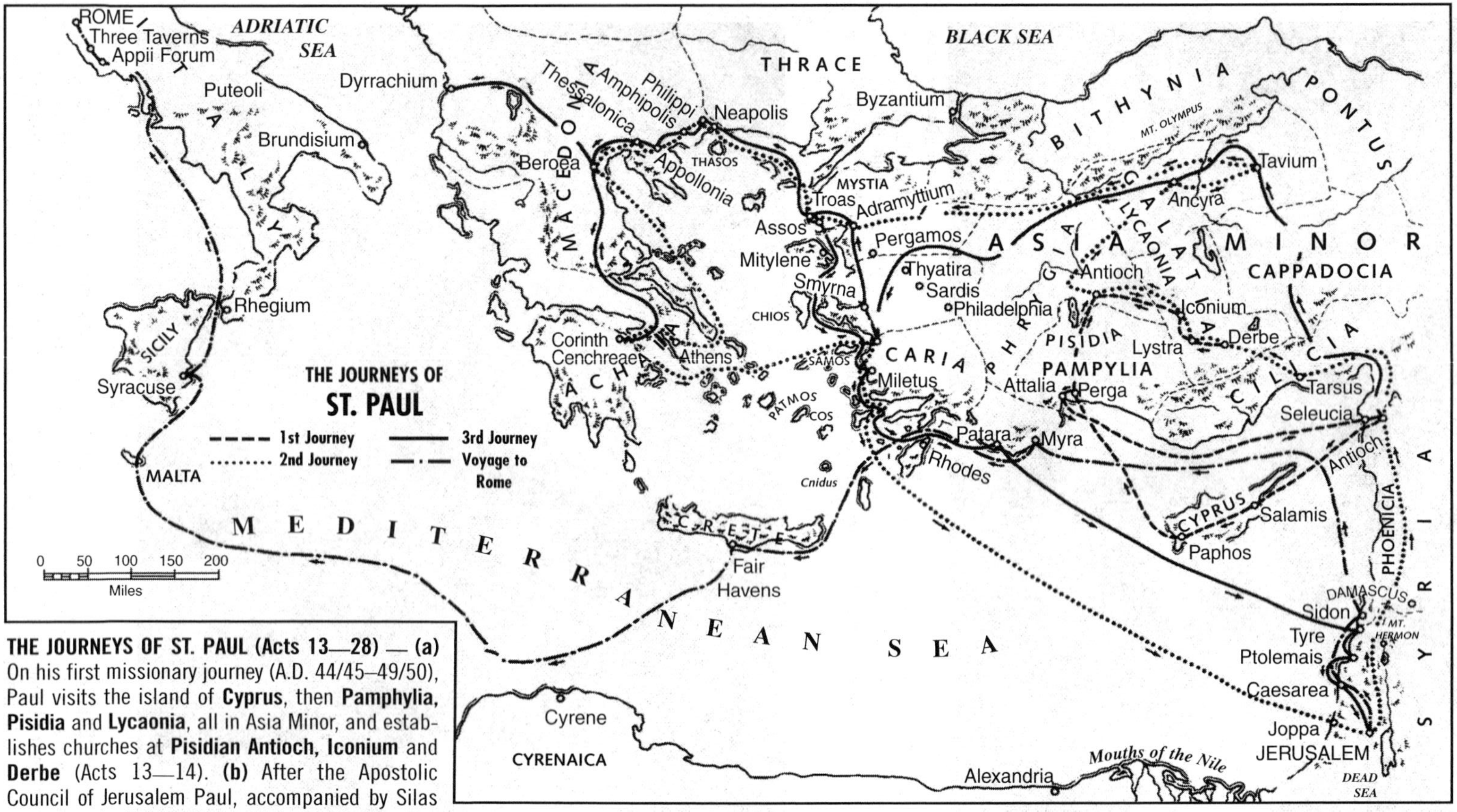

THE JOURNEYS OF ST. PAUL (Acts 13—28) — (a) On his first missionary journey (A.D. 44/45–49/50), Paul visits the island of **Cyprus**, then **Pamphylia, Pisidia** and **Lycaonia**, all in Asia Minor, and establishes churches at **Pisidian Antioch, Iconium** and **Derbe** (Acts 13—14). **(b)** After the Apostolic Council of Jerusalem Paul, accompanied by Silas and later also by Timothy and Luke, makes his second missionary journey (A.D. 50–53), first revisiting the churches previously established by him in **Asia Minor** and then the region of **Galatia** (Acts 16:6). At **Troas** Paul has a vision in which a man from Macedonia invites him to preach the gospel to his countrymen. Paul accordingly sails for **Europe** and preaches the gospel in **Philippi, Thessalonica, Beroea,** and then in **Athens** and **Corinth**. Then he returns to **Antioch** by way of **Ephesus** and **Jerusalem** (Acts 15:36—18:22). **(c)** On his third missionary journey (A.D. 53/54–58) Paul visits nearly the same regions as on the second, but makes **Ephesus**, where he remains nearly three years, the center of his missionary activity. He lays plans also for another missionary journey, intending to leave **Jerusalem** for **Rome** and **Spain**. But persecutions by the Jews hinder him from accomplishing his purpose. After two years of imprisonment at **Caesarea** he finally reaches **Rome,** where he is kept another two years in chains (Acts 18:23—28:31).

The Choice of Judas's Successor.* [15] In those days, Peter stood up before the assembled brothers, numbering about one hundred and twenty, and said, [16] "Brethren, the Scripture had to be fulfilled that the Holy Spirit revealed through the mouth of David concerning Judas, who served as guide for those who arrested Jesus. [o] [17] He was one of our number and was granted a share in this ministry. [p]

[18] "With the money from his traitorous act, this man purchased a plot of land upon which he fell headlong, and he burst open, all of his entrails pouring out. [q] [19] The news about this became known to all the people living in Jerusalem, so that in their own language that plot of land was called 'Hakeldama,' which means 'Field of Blood.' * [20] For it is written in the Book of Psalms,

'May his encampment become deserted,
and may there be no one to dwell in it.'

And again,

'Let another take over his position.' [r]

[21] "Therefore, it is necessary to choose one of the men who have accompanied us during the entire time that the Lord Jesus lived with us, [22] beginning from his baptism by John until the day when he was taken up from us. For he must become a witness with us of his resurrection." [s]

[23] And so they nominated two candidates: Joseph called Barsabbas, who was also known as Justus, and Matthias. [24] Then they prayed, saying, "Lord, you know the hearts of everyone. Show us which one of these two you have chosen [t] [25] to take the place in this apostolic ministry that Judas abandoned to go to his own place." [26] Then they cast lots for them, and the lot fell to Matthias, who was then added to the eleven apostles. [u]

B: Pentecost*

CHAPTER 2

Descent of the Spirit and Birth of the Church.* [1] When the day of Pentecost arrived, they were all assembled together in one place. [v] [2] [w] Suddenly, there came from heaven a sound similar to that of a violent wind, and it filled the entire house in which they were sitting. [3] Then there appeared to them tongues as of fire, which separated and came to rest on each one of them. [x] [4] All of them were filled with the Holy Spirit and began to speak in different languages, * as the Spirit enabled them to do so. [y]

[5] Now staying in Jerusalem there were devout Jews from every nation under heaven. [z] [6] At this sound, a large crowd of them gathered, and they were bewildered because each one heard them speaking in his own language. [a]

[7] They were astounded and asked in amazement, "Are not all these men who are speaking Galileans? [b] [8] How is it then that each of us hears them in his own native language? [9] Parthians, Medes, and Elamites, residents of Mesopotamia, Judea, and Cappadocia, Pontus and Asia, [c] [10] Phrygia and Pamphylia, Egypt and the districts of Libya around Cyrene, visitors from Rome, both Jews and proselytes, * [d] [11] Cretans and Arabs—we hear them speaking in our own languages about the mighty deeds of God." [e]

[12] They were all astounded and perplexed, and they said to one another, "What does all this mean?" [13] However, others said mockingly, "They are filled with new wine." [f]

o Acts 6:3; 11:1; Ps 41:10; Lk 22:47.—p Jn 6:70, 71.—q Mt 27:3-10; Wis 4:19.—r Pss 69:26; 109:8; Jn 17:12.—s Acts 1:8-9; 10:39.—t Acts 6:6; 15:8; 1 Sam 14:41; Jer 11:20; Rev 2:23.—u Acts 2:14; Prov 16:33.—v Acts 20:16; Lev 23:15-21; Deut 16:9-11; 1 Cor 16:8.—w 2-3: Acts 4:31; Jn 3:8.—x Lk 3:16.—y Acts 1:5; 4:31; 8:15, 17; 10:44; 11:15-16; 15:8; 19:6; Ps 104:30; Jn 20:23.—z Acts 8:2; Lk 2:25.—a Gen 11:1-9.—b Acts 1:11.—c Acts 18:2; 1 Pet 1:1.—d Acts 16:6; 18:23.—e Acts 10:46.—f 1 Cor 14:23; Eph 5:18.

1:15-26 The ministry (*diakonia:* service) of the apostle ("one who is sent") appears from the outset as a solidly established institution, and one that is indispensable for the people of God. The apostles are twelve in number, as though to preside over the twelve tribes, i.e., the true Israel (see Acts 26:7), and it is around them that this community of one hundred and twenty (or ten for each apostle) has formed.

1:19 The language spoken is Aramaic.

2:1-47 For the first time, the witnesses come in contact with the crowd, which is made up of persons from all the nations. We are at the center of the world that is the starting point for a universal future.

2:1-13 The gift of the Spirit founds the Church as a living reality; Christ has prepared the way for the Church; the Spirit comes to take possession of her, to animate her, to help her with his charisms. Thus, for every community of believers, Pentecost is the feast of its own birth. The Spirit is "poured out" (see Acts 2:17) like rain, which is the source of life in an arid land; as Jesus had promised, there is a "baptism with the Spirit" (Acts 1:5).

The phenomena that accompany the event are rich in symbolism and also have a biblical meaning: they call to mind the theophanies, i.e., the manifestations of God to his people in order to change their anonymous destiny into a life-giving covenant (see Ex 19:18; Deut 4:9-24, 36; Ps 68).

Pentecost, which occurred fifty days after Passover, was the feast on which the firstfruits of the harvest were offered to God, but it was above all the feast of the covenant and of the gift of the Law.

2:4 *Different languages:* i.e., different from their usual language. The reference may also be to ecstatic language (see Mk 16:17; 1 Cor 14:2-23).

2:10 *Proselytes:* those who had accepted circumcision and the Jewish Law.

Peter Preaches in the Name of the Twelve.*

14 Then Peter stood up with the Eleven and proclaimed to them in a loud voice, "Men of Judea and all you who live in Jerusalem, let this be known to you, and listen carefully to my words. 15 These men are not drunk, as you suppose. It is only nine o'clock in the morning. *[g] 16 Rather, this is what was revealed through the prophet Joel:

17 'It will come to pass in the last days,
God declares,
that I will pour out my Spirit on all flesh.
Your sons and your daughters shall prophesy;
your young men shall see visions,
and your old men shall dream dreams. [h]
18 Indeed, even upon my servants and my handmaids
I shall pour out my Spirit in those days,
and they shall prophesy. [i]
19 I will show portents in the sky above
and signs on the earth below:
blood and fire and billows of smoke. [j]
20 The sun will be turned into darkness
and the moon to blood
before the day of the Lord comes,
that great and glorious day. [k]
21 Then it will come to pass
that everyone who calls on the name of the Lord will be saved.' [l]

22 "Men of Israel, hear these words. Jesus of Nazareth was a man commended to you by God by means of miracles and portents and signs that God worked through him, as you yourselves know. [m] 23 By the set plan and foreknowledge of God, he was handed over into the hands of lawless men. Crucifying him, you killed him. [n] 24 However, God raised him up, releasing him from the pangs of death, because it was impossible for him to be held in its power. [o] 25 [p] For David says of him:

'I saw the Lord always before me;
with him at my right hand I shall not be shaken.
26 Therefore, my heart rejoiced and my tongue exulted;
moreover, my flesh will live in hope.
27 For you will not abandon me to the netherworld
or allow your holy one to suffer corruption. [q]
28 You have made known to me the way of life;
you will fill me with joy in your presence.'

29 "Brethren, I can say to you boldly that our ancestor David both died and was buried, and his tomb is in our midst to this very day. [r] 30 But since he was a prophet and knew that God had sworn an oath to him that one of his descendants would sit on his throne, [s] 31 he foresaw and spoke of the resurrection of the Christ, saying that he was not abandoned to the netherworld and that his flesh did not suffer corruption. [t]

32 "God raised this Jesus to life. Of that we are all witnesses. 33 Exalted at God's right hand, he received from the Father the promise of the Holy Spirit and has poured out what you now see and hear. [u] 34 [v] For David did not ascend to heaven, and yet he said,

'The Lord said to my Lord,
"Sit at my right hand
35 until I make your enemies your footstool." '

36 "Therefore, let the whole house of Israel know with complete certitude that God has made this Jesus whom you crucified both Lord and Christ." [w]

37 When they heard this, they were cut to the heart and said to Peter and to the other apostles, "What are we to do, brethren?" [x] 38 Peter answered, "Repent, and be baptized, every one of you, in the name of Jesus Christ so that your sins may be forgiven, and you will receive the gift of the Holy Spirit. [y] 39 For the promise that was made is for you, for your children, and for all those who are far away, for all those whom the Lord our God will call." [z]

g 1 Thes 5:7.—h Acts 2:33; Num 11:25; Isa 2:2; 44:3; Joel 3:1-5.—i Acts 21:9-12.—j Lk 21:11.—k Mt 24:29.—l Gen 4:26; Ps 105:1; Rom 10:13.—m Acts 10:38; Lk 24:19; Jn 5:36.—n Isa 53:10; Mt 16:21; 1 Thes 2:15.—o Acts 13:34; 17:31; Rom 6:4.—p 25-28: Ps 16:8-11.—q Acts 13:35.—r Acts 7:8, 9; 1 Ki 2:10.—s 2 Sam 7:12; Ps 132:11.—t Acts 13:35; Ps 16:10.—u Acts 1:4-5; Jn 7:39.—v 34-35: Ps 110:1.—w Acts 2:23; 9:22; Rom 10:9; Phil 2:11.—x Lk 3:10.—y Acts 3:19; 8:12; 16:31; Jer 36:3; Lk 3:3; Col 2:12.—z Acts 10:45; Isa 44:3; 57:19; Joel 3:5; Eph 2:17.

2:14-39 The author of Acts does not make up his discourses like the historians of antiquity, who liked to place their own thoughts and reactions on the lips of their subjects. In Luke's view, the Word is decisive for the life of the community.

This sermon is the first; therefore, it has programmatic value in addition to its function in the immediate context. It proclaims the paschal event to all of Israel and even to distant peoples. The same fundamental pattern will recur in the other addresses of the apostles to the Jews.

2:15 *Nine o'clock in the morning:* literally, "the third hour." See notes on Mt 27:35 and Mk 15:25.

Life of the First Community—I.* 40 He offered
further testimony with many other argu-
ments as he exhorted them, "Save your-
selves from this corrupt generation." [a]
41 Those who accepted his message were
baptized, and on that day about three thou-
sand people were added to their number. [b]
42 [c] They devoted themselves to the teaching
of the apostles and to the communal fellow-
ship, to the breaking of bread and to
prayers. [d]

43 A sense of awe was felt by all for many
wonders and signs were performed by the
apostles. [e] 44 All the believers were together
and owned everything in common. [f] 45 They
would sell their property and possessions
and distribute the proceeds to all according
to what each one needed. [g] 46 Every day,
united in spirit, they would assemble togeth-
er in the temple. They would break bread in
their homes and share their food with joyful
and generous hearts [h] 47 as they praised God,
and they were regarded with favor by all the
people. And day by day the Lord added to
those who were being saved. [i]

C: First Encounter with the Authorities in Israel

CHAPTER 3

In the Name of Jesus Christ, Walk!* 1 One
day, Peter and John were on their way to the
temple for the hour of prayer at three
o'clock in the afternoon. * [j] 2 [k] A man who
had been crippled from his birth was car-
ried there every day and laid at the gate of
the temple called the Beautiful Gate * so
that he could beg for alms from those who
entered the temple. [l]

3 When this man saw Peter and John
about to enter into the temple, he asked
them for alms. 4 Peter looked intently at
him, as did John, and said to him, "Look at
us!" 5 He looked at them attentively, expect-
ing to receive something from them. 6 But
Peter said, "I have neither silver nor gold,
but what I have I give you. In the name of
Jesus Christ of Nazareth, stand up and
walk." [m]

7 Then Peter grasped him by the right
hand and helped him to get up. Immediately,
his feet and ankles were strengthened. 8 He
jumped up, stood straight, and began to
walk, and he entered the temple with them,
walking and leaping and praising God. [n]
9 When all the people there saw him walking
and praising God, [o] 10 they recognized him as
the man who used to sit and beg for alms at
the Beautiful Gate of the temple, and they
were filled with wonder and amazement at
what had happened to him.

Peter Speaks to the People.* 11 While he con-
tinued to cling to Peter and John, all the peo-
ple came running in amazement toward
them in Solomon's Portico, as it is called. [p]
12 When Peter saw the people assembling, he
addressed them:

"Men of Israel, why are you so surprised
at this? Why do you stare at us, as though
we had enabled this man to walk by our
own power or holiness? [q] 13 The God of
Abraham, and Isaac, and Jacob, the God of
our ancestors, has glorified his servant *
Jesus whom you handed over and disowned
in the presence of Pilate after he had decid-
ed to release him. [r] 14 You rejected the Holy
and Righteous One and asked that a mur-
derer be released to you. [s] 15 The author of
life * you put to death, but God raised him
from the dead. Of this we are witnesses. [t]

16 "By faith in his name, this man whom
you see here and who is known to you has
been made strong. Faith in him has made

a Deut 32:5; Ps 78:8; Mt 17:17; Lk 9:41; Phil 2:15.—b Acts 2:47; 4:4; 5:14; 6:7; 11:21, 24; 14:1; 16:5; 21:20.—c 42-47: Acts 4:32-35.—d Acts 1:14; 6:4; Mt 28:20.—e Acts 5:12-16.—f Acts 4:32, 34-35.—g Mt 19:21; Lk 12:33.—h Acts 3:1; Lk 24:53.—i Rom 14:18.—j Acts 2:4; Ps 55:18.—k 2-8: Acts 14:8-10.—l Lk 16:20; Jn 9:8.—m Acts 4:10; Mk 1:24.—n Acts 14:10; Isa 35:6; Lk 7:22.—o Acts 4:16, 21.—p Acts 5:12; Lk 22:8; Jn 10:23.—q Acts 14:15.—r Acts 2:23; 5:30; Ex 3:6, 15; Isa 52:13; Lk 23:14-25.—s Acts 4:27; Mt 27:20-21; Mk 15:11; Lk 23:18; Jn 18:40.—t Acts 4:10; 5:31.

2:40-47 Luke offers us three general descriptions of the first community, each depicting their manner of life: here, and in Acts 4:32-35 and 5:12-16.

3:1-10 Peter's action, as he takes the initiative in the first miracle that Acts ascribes to the disciples of the wonder-worker of Nazareth, has special significance: it is done "in the name of Jesus Christ of Nazareth" and aims to show the presence of Christ and his divine activity.

3:1 *Three o'clock in the afternoon:* literally, "the ninth hour." See notes on Mt 27:35 and Mk 15:25.

3:2 The *Beautiful Gate:* it was made of Corinthian bronze and led from the court of the Gentiles to the court of the women, on the side where Solomon's Portico was (v. 11).

3:11-26 The discourse that follows embodies the *kerygma* (i.e., the essentials of Christian preaching) as intended for a Jewish audience.

3:13 *Servant:* the Greek word can also be translated as "son" or "child" (see Acts 3:26; 4:25, 27, 30). However, scholars believe that the word "servant" fits in better with the underlying idea of Jesus as the suffering Servant of the Lord (Isa 52:13—53:12).

3:15 *Author of life:* this may also be rendered as the "prince of life" or the "pioneer of life"—indicating Jesus as the originator of salvation.

him completely well in the presence of all
of you.

17 "Now I am aware, brethren, that you
acted out of ignorance as did your rulers. [u]
18 God fulfilled what he had foretold through
all the Prophets, revealing that his Christ
would suffer. [v] 19 Repent, therefore, and be
converted so that your sins may be wiped
away, [w] 20 that a time of refreshment may
come from the Lord, and that he may send
the Christ appointed for you, that is, Jesus.
21 He must remain in heaven until the time
comes for the universal restoration
announced by God in ages past through his
holy Prophets. [x] 22 For Moses said,

'The Lord your God will raise up for you
a prophet like me
from among your own people.
To him shall you listen
in whatever he tells you. [y]
23 Everyone who refuses to listen to that
prophet
will be cut off from the people.' [z]

24 "Furthermore, all the Prophets who
have spoken, from Samuel onward, predict-
ed these days. [a]

25 "You are the heirs of the Prophets and
of the covenant that God made with your
ancestors when he told Abraham, 'And in
your descendants all the families of the earth
shall be blessed.' [b] 26 When God raised up his
servant, he sent him first to you, to bless you
by turning each one of you from your wicked
ways." [c]

CHAPTER 4

First Phase of the Trial: A Warning.* 1 While
they were still speaking to the people, the
priests, the captain of the temple guard, *
and the Sadducees came over to them, [d]
2 greatly annoyed that they were teaching
and proclaiming to the people the resurrec-
tion of the dead through Jesus. [e] 3 Therefore,
they arrested them and placed them in cus-
tody until the next day, for it was already
evening. [f] 4 However, many of those who had
listened to their message became believers,
their total approaching five thousand.

5 On the next day, their rulers, elders, and
scribes assembled in Jerusalem, [g] 6 with
Annas the high priest, Caiaphas, John, *
Alexander, and all who belonged to the high
priestly family. 7 They then brought the apos-
tles before them and asked, "By what power
or by what name have you done this?" [h]

8 Then Peter, filled with the Holy Spirit,
said to them, "Rulers of the people and
elders, [i] 9 if you are interrogating us today in
regard to a good deed done to someone who
was crippled and how he was healed, [j] 10 let it
be known to you and to all the people of
Israel that it was in the name of Jesus Christ
of Nazareth whom you crucified, and whom
God raised from the dead, that this man
standing before you was cured. 11 This is

'the stone rejected by you, the builders,
that has become the cornerstone.' [k]

12 There is no salvation in anyone else, nor is
there any other name under heaven given to
men by which we can be saved." [l]

13 They were amazed to see the fearless-
ness shown by Peter and John and to discov-
er that they were uneducated ordinary men.
They recognized them as companions of
Jesus, [m] 14 but, when they saw the man who
had been cured standing beside them, they
could not say anything in reply. 15 They
ordered them to stand outside while the
Sanhedrin discussed the matter.

---

u Acts 13:27; 22:5; Lk 23:34; 1 Cor 2:8; 1 Tim 1:13.—v Acts 2:23; 17:2; Lk 18:31.—w Acts 2:38; Ps 51:3; Isa 43:25; 2 Pet 3:11-13.—x Acts 1:11; Mt 17:11.—y Acts 7:37; Deut 18:15, 18; Mt 16:14.—z Lev 23:29; Deut 18:19.—a Lk 24:27.—b Acts 2:39; Gen 12:3; 18:18; 22:18; Sir 44:19-21; Rom 9:4, 5; Gal 3:8-9.—c Acts 13:46; Rom 1:16.—d Acts 5:17; Mt 3:7; Lk 22:4.—e Acts 17:18; 23:6-8; 24:21; 1 Cor 15:20-23.—f Acts 5:18.—g Lk 22:66; 23:13.—h Lk 20:2.—i Mt 10:20; Lk 23:13.—j Acts 3:6, 16.—k Ps 118:22; Isa 28:16; Zec 10:4; Mt 21:42; Mk 12:10; Lk 20:17; Rom 9:33; Eph 2:20; 1 Pet 2:7.—l Acts 2:21; 10:43; Mt 1:21; Jn 14:6; 1 Cor 3:11.—m Mt 11:25; Mk 3:14; Lk 12:11-12.

4:1-22 The religious authorities understand very well the main points of Peter's discourse: Jesus has been raised; therefore, he has entered the sphere of God. Christians are not healers possessed of some secret or magical art; they act and teach with an authority that does not belong to a group of people. They do it in the name of Jesus Christ. When the Jewish authorities ask Peter and John why they are still preaching in the name of Jesus even though they have been told not to do so anymore, Peter and John answer, "You be the judges about whether it is right in the sight of God to listen to you rather than to God. We cannot possibly refrain from speaking about what we have seen and heard." Concerning the name of Jesus, Peter says, "There is no salvation in anyone else, nor is there any other name under heaven given to men by which we can be saved." This is a call to salvation. To act in the name of Jesus, or to invoke him, means that every action of God is done through Jesus. God's role in the last times announced by Joel (3:5) is fulfilled through Jesus alone. If the Jewish authorities accept the fact that the movement of the History of Salvation lies in this new initiative of Jesus, they would signal the failure of their mandate and their institutions. As it is, they seek to escape embarrassment by cutting short the interrogation. But they cannot withstand the assurance of the apostles.

4:1 *Captain of the temple guard:* a priest who oversaw the activities of the police within the temple. *Sadducees:* a religious sect of the Jews that insisted upon human free will but denied immortality, the resurrection, and the existence of angels.

4:6 *John* and *Alexander:* not otherwise known.

16 Then they said, "What are we going to do with these men? Everyone living in Jerusalem is aware that a notable sign has been worked through them, and we clearly cannot deny it.[n] 17 But to stop the news from spreading any further among the people, let us issue them a warning never again to speak to anyone in his name."[o]

18 Therefore, they summoned them back and ordered them not to speak or teach at all in the name of Jesus.[p] 19 However, Peter and John answered them, "You be the judges about whether it is right in the sight of God to listen to you rather than to God.[q] 20 We cannot possibly refrain from speaking about what we have seen and heard."[r]

21 After threatening them once again, they released them, for they could find no way to punish them inasmuch as the people were praising God for what had happened.[s] 22 For the man who had been miraculously healed was over forty years old.

The Community's Prayer for the Apostles.* 23 As soon as they were released, they went back* to the community and reported everything that the chief priests and the elders had said to them. 24 When they heard it, they raised their voices to God with one accord and said, "Lord, maker of heaven and earth and the sea and of everything that is in them,[t] 25 [u] you said by the Holy Spirit through the mouth of our ancestor David, your servant,

'Why do the Gentiles rage
and the peoples devise futile plots?
26 The kings of the earth take their stand,
and the rulers gather together
against the Lord and against his
Anointed.'

27 "Indeed, in this very city both Herod and Pontius Pilate along with the Gentiles and the peoples of Israel plotted against your holy servant Jesus, whom you anointed,[v] 28 to do whatever your hand and your decree had predestined to take place. 29 And now, O Lord, be aware of their threats, and grant that your servants may proclaim your word with all boldness,[w] 30 as you stretch out your hand to heal and as signs and wonders are accomplished through the name of your holy servant Jesus."

31 When they had finished their prayer, the place where they were gathered together shook, and they were all filled with the Holy Spirit and proclaimed the word of God fearlessly.[x]

Life of the First Community—II.* 32 The entire community of believers was united in heart and soul. No one claimed any of his possessions as his own, for everything was held in common.[y] 33 With great power, the apostles bore witness to the resurrection* of the Lord Jesus, and they were all greatly respected. 34 [z] There was never anyone among them in need, because those who were the owners of lands or houses would sell them, bring the proceeds of the sale,[a] 35 and lay them at the feet of the apostles, to be distributed to any who were in need.

Barnabas.* 36 [b] One such instance involved Joseph, a Levite and a native of Cyprus, to whom the apostles gave the name Barnabas, meaning "son of encouragement." 37 He sold a field that belonged to him and then brought the money to the apostles and laid it at their feet.

n Acts 3:6-10; Jn 11:47.—o Acts 5:28.—p Acts 5:40; Am 7:13.—q Acts 5:29-32.—r Job 32:18; Jer 20:9; Am 3:8; 1 Cor 9:16; 2 Cor 13:8.—s Acts 5:26.—t Acts 14:15; Neh 9:6.—u 25-26: Acts 10:38; Ps 2:1-2; Dan 9:25.—v Acts 3:13; Lk 23:12-13.—w Acts 13:46; Ps 138:3; Eph 6:19.—x Acts 2:4.—y Acts 2:44; Jn 17:11, 21; Phil 1:27.—z 34-35: Acts 2:44-45.—a Deut 15:4; Mt 19:21; Lk 12:33.—b 36-37: Acts 9:27; 11:22, 30; 12:25; 13:2; 1 Cor 9:6; Gal 2:1, 9, 13; Col 4:10.

4:23-31 The prayer begins with an invocation of the Creator, embracing the horizon of the world: heaven, earth, and sea. It follows the traditional practice of calling for God's protection of his people. This community is the new people compelled to make a new Exodus; and this people needs strength from God for this departure and this journey. It is rejected by the Jews who act like the pagan nations as these are characterized by the Old Testament. The future of the people is going to be bleak if its authorities refuse to recognize the name of God's holy Servant.

The invocation of the prayer for the apostles is made in the name of Jesus, and all the new people receive the gift of the word as at the first Pentecost, but in a situation of defense and interrogation. Such a prayer is the type of Christian prayer for times of crisis, for a community that must face an uncertain future and an unexpected road.

4:23 *Went back:* probably to the same Upper Room where the apostles had met (Acts 1:13) and where the community may have continued to meet (Acts 12:12).

4:32-35 These verses present a view of the early Church. Luke stresses the internal bonds of the community at the moment of persecution. The picture he paints shows the voluntary sharing of material possessions, an activity connected with Jesus' teaching on detachment and fraternal love (see Lk 8:3; 12:33; 16:9-13). The text does not say that all sold their property—only that they were prepared to do so if a member of the community was in need. The comportment of Barnabas and then that of Ananias and Sapphira demonstrate the right use of property in the Church.

4:33 *Bore witness to the resurrection:* although the death of Christ was a significant event, his Resurrection was the most compelling event of his life, and the apostles could not but proclaim it.

4:36-37 Barnabas is given as an example of the new understanding of property. He will soon play a chief role in the life of the Church (Acts 9:27; 11:22-30; 12:25; 13:1-15, 46; see 1 Cor 9:6; Gal 2; Col 4:10).

CHAPTER 5

The Fraud of Ananias and Sapphira.* 1 There
was a man named Ananias who with his wife
Sapphira sold a piece of property. 2 With the
approval of his wife, he held back some of
the proceeds, and he brought the remainder
to the apostles and laid it at their feet. [c]

3 Then Peter asked, "Ananias, why has
Satan so gained control of your heart that
you lied to the Holy Spirit and retained part
of the sale price of the land? [d] 4 While it
remained unsold, did it not belong to you?
And after it was sold, were not the proceeds
yours? What caused you to contrive this
scheme? You have lied not to men but to
God." [e]

5 When Ananias heard these words, he col-
lapsed and died, and a great sense of fear
seized all who heard about it. [f] 6 The young
men came forward and wrapped up his
body. Then they carried him out and buried
him. [g]

7 After about three hours, his wife came
in, unaware of what had happened. 8 Peter
said to her, "Tell me whether you sold the
land for this much." She replied, "Yes, that
was the price." 9 Then Peter asked her, "Why
did the two of you agree to put the Spirit of
the Lord to the test? Listen! The footsteps of
those who have buried your husband are at
the door, and they will also carry you out." [h]

10 Instantly, she fell down at his feet and
died. When the young men came in, they
found her dead. And so they carried her out
and buried her beside her husband. 11 And a
great sense of fear seized the whole Church *
and all those who heard of this. [i]

Life of the First Community—III.* 12 Many
signs and wonders were done among the
people by the hands of the apostles. They all
used to assemble in Solomon's Portico. [j]
13 No one else dared to join them, but the
people esteemed them highly. [k] 14 More
believers, men and women, were constantly
being added to their ranks. 15 People brought
those who were sick into the streets and
placed them on cots and mats so that when
Peter passed by, his shadow might fall on
some of them. [l] 16 A large number of people
also came from the neighboring towns
around Jerusalem, bringing with them the
sick and those tormented by unclean spirits,
and all of them were cured. [m]

Conclusion of the Trial.* 17 Then the high
priest and his colleagues from the party
of the Sadducees rose up, filled with jeal-
ousy, [n] 18 and they arrested the apostles and
placed them in the public jail. 19 But during
the night the angel of the Lord opened the
prison doors, led them out, and said, [o]
20 "Go, stand in the temple, and tell the
people everything about this new life." [p]
21 Accordingly, they entered the temple at
daybreak and taught the people.

When the high priest and his colleagues
arrived, they convened the Sanhedrin, the
full assembly of the elders of Israel, and sent
to the jail to have them brought in. 22 But
when the temple police went to the prison,

c Acts 4:35; Jos 7:11.—d Deut 23:22-24; Lk 22:3; Jn 13:2, 27.—e Lev 5:21.—f Ps 5:7; Lk 1:12.—g Jn 19:40.—h Acts 15:10; 1 Cor 10:9.—i Acts 2:43; 5:5; 19:17.—j Acts 2:43; 6:8; 14:3; 15:12; Jn 10:23.—k Acts 2:47; 4:21.—l Acts 19:11-12; Mk 6:56.—m Mt 8:16; Lk 4:40.—n Acts 4:1-3, 6; 15:5.—o Acts 12:7-10; 16:25-26; Gen 16:7; Ex 3:2; Ps 34:8; Mt 1:20.—p Jn 6:63, 68.

5:1-11 The sharing of goods is voluntary, but gold has a fascinating power. A couple lies to the community, contrary to the life of the Spirit. They violate the life of the community and undermine it. In the Old Testament (Jos 7:1), such people were to be put to death. Paul would have harsh words on the problem of riches and neglect of the poor when the Christians of Corinth later failed to respect the assembly, the Body of Christ.

5:11 The word *Church* (Greek: *ekklesia,* "assembly called together"), already heard on the lips of Jesus (Mt 16:18), appears for the first time in Acts at the end of this story. In the Greek world, the word denoted an assembly convoked for deliberation; in the Jewish tradition, the *ekklesia* was the assembly of God's people, which God had called together in the wilderness.

5:12-16 These verses show the components of a believing community: its unity, its internal communication, and its worship. Luke emphasizes the difference between this community and the rest of society. In the miracles worked by the apostles, the Spirit of Pentecost shines forth, continuing the work of Jesus, which is so significant of a change in the human condition.

5:17-42 The apostles continue their activity without letting themselves be intimidated. A time in prison is ended with deliverance, described in Old Testament terminology—with angels personifying God's providential intervention as in the Exodus. Luke stresses the positive conclusion of the matter: the Word of God cannot be chained.

Standing in the midst of the Sanhedrin and the party of the Sadducees (who desire to crush the new movement), Peter repeats the message about Jesus. His discourse has the same structure as the previous ones, and the name of Jesus remains at the center of the discussion. Of the life of Jesus, only the trial and death are recalled, but Peter stresses that the God of their ancestors has raised the one who was hung on a gibbet and has exalted him as head of a people capable of introducing them to repentance. The apostles are to bear witness to the Resurrection under the power of the Spirit, and nothing can stifle their testimony.

The suppression of the leaders of this new movement is decreed. They are saved by the intervention of Gamaliel, who was a teacher of Paul (Acts 22:3). He speaks in the manner of a sage of the Old Testament and points out that there have been other uprisings that have come to naught and only time will tell if this enterprise of the followers of Christ is a more serious thing. For their part, the apostles express their joy at suffering everything for Christ. The community has a provisional freedom but looks to the future to bring the good news of the risen Christ to the world.

they did not find them there. So they
returned and announced,[q] 23 "We found the
jail securely locked and the guards stationed
outside the doors, but when we opened the
doors we found no one inside."

24 Now when the captain of the temple
guard and the chief priests heard this report,
they were at a loss to understand what this
would come to.[r] 25 Then someone arrived to
report, "The men whom you imprisoned are
standing in the temple and teaching the peo-
ple." 26 The captain thereupon went with
the temple officers and brought them in,
although without force, for they were afraid
of being stoned by the people.[s]

27 When they had brought them in, they
had them stand before the Sanhedrin. The
high priest questioned them, saying, 28 "Did
we not give you strict orders not to teach in
this name? Yet, despite that, you have filled
Jerusalem with your teaching, and you
appear determined to hold us responsible for
that man's death."[t]

29 Peter and the other apostles replied, "We
must obey God rather than men.[u] 30 The
God of our ancestors raised up Jesus after
you had put him to death by hanging him on
a tree.[v] 31 God exalted him at his right hand
as leader and Savior so that he might grant
repentance and forgiveness of sins to Israel.[w]
32 And we are witnesses to these things, as is
the Holy Spirit whom God has given to those
who obey him."[x]

33 When they heard this, they became
enraged, and they wanted to put them to
death. 34 However, one member of the
Sanhedrin, a Pharisee named Gamaliel who
was a teacher of the law and respected by all
the people, stood up and ordered that the
apostles be sent outside for a little while.[y]

35 Then he addressed them, "Men of Israel,
consider carefully what you intend to do to
these men. 36 Some time ago Theudas*
appeared. He claimed to be someone impor-
tant, and about four hundred men decided
to follow him. He was killed, and all of his fol-
lowers disbanded, and everything came to
naught. 37 After him, Judas the Galilean rose
up at the time of the census. He also con-
vinced people to follow him, but he too was
killed and his followers were dispersed.

38 "Therefore, I advise you to keep away
from these men and let them go. If this
movement is human in origin, it will fail.[z]
39 If, however, it comes from God, you will
never be able to overcome them, but may
find yourselves fighting against God."

His words persuaded them.[a] 40 After they
summoned the apostles once again, they had
them scourged. Then, ordering them not to
speak in the name of Jesus, they released
them.[b] 41 They left the Sanhedrin, rejoicing
that they had been considered worthy to suf-
fer humiliation for the sake of the name.*[c]
42 And every day, both in the temple and at
home, they never stopped teaching and pro-
claiming Jesus as the Christ.[d]

D: Jerusalem, First Center of Diffusion*

CHAPTER 6

Institution of the Seven Deacons.* 1 In those
days, as the number of disciples grew, the
Hellenists made a complaint against the
Hebrews,* asserting that their own widows
were being neglected in the daily distribu-
tion of food.[e] 2 And so the Twelve called
together the entire community of disciples
and said, "It is not right for us to neglect the
word of God in order to wait on tables.

q Acts 12:18, 19.—r Acts 4:1.—s Acts 4:21; Lk 20:19; 22:2.—t Acts 4:18; Mt 27:25.—u Acts 4:19; Ex 1:17.—v Acts 2:23-24; Gal 3:13.—w Acts 2:38; Mk 1:4.—x Lk 24:48; Jn 7:39; 15:26.—y Acts 22:3; Lk 2:46.—z Mt 15:13; Lk 20:4.—a Acts 7:51; 2 Chr 13:12; Isa 46:10.—b Acts 4:17-18; Mt 10:17.—c Mt 5:10-11; Jn 15:21; 1 Cor 4:9; 1 Pet 4:13.—d Acts 2:46; 5:20-21, 25; 8:35; 13:32; 17:3; 18:5, 28; 19:4-5.—e Acts 2:45; 4:34-35; 9:29; 1 Tim 5:3.

5:36 *Theudas:* one of the many agitators of the period. Another agitator was *Judas the Galilean,* who rebelled around the year A.D. 6 and was the leader of the most terrible uprising prior to that of 70. He had a following in the Zealot party. The movements of Theudas and Judas were probably associated—and both occurred in the time of Quirinius.

5:41 *The name:* some manuscripts add "of Jesus." In Judaism, "the Name" signified God himself. Christians immediately took over the term and applied it to Jesus who had been given "the name that is above all other names" (Phil 2:9).

6:1—8:4 The community at Jerusalem lived in the impetus of the Resurrection and of the Spirit. It could not stay by itself and remain sheltered from the threats of religious authorities. Its energy made it go out into the world and tell the good news.

6:1-7 The Church decides on the ministers needed in order to maintain her freedom to pray and preach. The "deacons," all of whom have Greek names, are not limited to an economic function; we also see them in the service of the Gospel, as in the case of Stephen (Acts 6:8) and Philip (Acts 8:6; 21:8), who also baptizes (Acts 8:12-13). The laying on of hands is a sign of the official investiture of those who have been appointed by the choice of the assembly.

6:1 *Hellenists . . . Hebrews:* although the Church at this time was composed of Jews, these were of two types: Hellenists and Hebrews. The Hellenists were Greek-speaking Jews born outside Palestine who followed a Grecian philosophy. Hebrews spoke Aramaic and followed Jewish customs.

3 Therefore, brethren, we direct you to select from among you seven * men of good reputation, men filled with the Spirit and with wisdom, to whom we may assign this task.[f] 4 We will then be able to devote ourselves to prayer and to the ministry of the word."[g]

5 The entire community found this proposal to be acceptable, and they chose Stephen, a man full of faith and the Holy Spirit, together with Philip, Prochorus, Nicanor, Timon, Parmenas, and Nicholas of Antioch who was a convert to Judaism.[h] 6 They then presented these men to the apostles, who prayed and laid hands on them. *[i]

7 The word of God continued to spread ever more widely. The number of the disciples in Jerusalem increased greatly, and a large number of priests became obedient to the faith.[j]

Accusation against Stephen. 8 * Stephen, a man filled with grace and power, began to work great wonders and signs among the people. 9 Then certain members of the so-called Synagogue of Freedmen, people from Cyrene and Alexandria, as well as others from Cilicia and Asia, came forward to debate with Stephen.[k] 10 However, they were unable to refute him because of his wisdom and the Spirit who inspired his speech.[l]

11 So they bribed some men to say, "We heard this Stephen speak blasphemous words against Moses and against God."[m] 12 After this, stirring up the people as well as the elders and the scribes, they seized Stephen, placed him under arrest, and brought him before the Sanhedrin.

13 Then they called forward false witnesses who claimed, "This man never stops speaking against this holy place and the Law.[n] 14 For we have heard him assert that Jesus of Nazareth will destroy this place and change the traditions that Moses handed down to us."[o] 15 All those who sat in the Sanhedrin looked intently at Stephen, and his face appeared like the face of an angel.[p]

CHAPTER 7

Stephen's Discourse. 1 Then the high priest asked him, "Are these things true?" 2 He replied, "Brethren and fathers, listen to me. The God of glory appeared to our ancestor Abraham while he was in Mesopotamia, before he lived in Haran,[q] 3 and said to him, 'Leave your country and your relatives and go to the land that I will show you.'[r]

4 "Therefore, he departed from the land of the Chaldeans and settled in Haran. And after his father died, God led him to the land where you now dwell.[s] 5 He did not give him any of this land as a heritage, not even as little as a foot, but he promised to give it to him as his possession, and to his descendants after him, even though he was childless.[t]

6 [u] "This is what God said: 'His descendants will reside in a country not their own, and they will be enslaved and oppressed for four hundred years.[v] 7 But I will bring judgment on the nation that enslaved them,' God said, 'and after that they will come out and worship me in this place.'[w] 8 Then he gave him the covenant of circumcision. And so, when he became the father of Isaac, he circumcised him on the eighth day, as Isaac did for Jacob, and Jacob did for the twelve patriarchs.[x]

9 "The patriarchs were jealous of Joseph and they sold him into Egypt, but God was with him[y] 10 and rescued him from all his afflictions. He gave Joseph wisdom and the favor of Pharaoh, the king of Egypt, who appointed him governor of Egypt and his entire household.[z]

11 "Then a severe famine struck all of Egypt and Canaan, causing severe affliction, and our ancestors could find no food.[a] 12 However, when Jacob learned that there was grain available in Egypt, he sent our ancestors there on their first visit.[b]

f Ex 18:21; Num 27:16-18; Neh 13:13; 1 Tim 3:8-10.—g Acts 1:14; 2:42.—h Acts 7:55-60.—i Acts 1:24; 13:3; 14:23; 1 Tim 4:14.—j Acts 2:41; 9:31; 12:24; 16:5; 19:20; 28:30-31; Rom 1:5.—k Acts 15:23.—l Acts 1:8; Lk 21:15.—m Acts 21:21; 1 Ki 21:10; Mt 26:59-61; Mk 14:55-58.—n Ex 23:1; Ps 27:12.—o Mt 26:59-61; 27:40; Jn 2:19.—p Lk 4:20.—q Acts 22:1; Gen 11:31; 12:1; Ps 29:3.—r Gen 12:1.—s Gen 12:5; 15:7.—t Gen 12:7; 13:15; 15:2; 16:1; 17:8; Deut 2:5; Heb 11:13.—u 6-7: Gen 15:13-14.—v Ex 1:8-11.—w Ex 3:12.—x Gen 17:10-14; 21:2-4; 25:26.—y Gen 37:11, 28; 39:2, 3, 21, 23; Ps 105:17.—z Gen 41:37-43; Ps 105:21; Wis 10:13-14.—a Gen 41:54-57; 42:5.—b Gen 42:1-2.

6:2-3 *Twelve . . . seven:* the Twelve are representative of the twelve tribes of Israel; the Seven represent the Gentiles dwelling in Canaan (see Acts 13:19; Deut 7:1).

6:6 *Laid hands on them:* the Jewish practice of assigning someone for a task and calling down God's blessing on that person to carry it out (Num 27:18, 23; Deut 34:9).

6:8—7:60 The first Christian martyr has his gaze fixed on Christ in profound attachment to his person (Acts 7:55) and in an interior imitation of Christ's suffering and death. Unlike the Passion of Jesus, however, that of Stephen is accompanied by a lengthy discourse that has as its basic theme God present in the midst of humanity in Jesus Christ. The lengthy interpretation of the history of Israel, made up of citations from the Old Testament, is less a demonstration than an indictment of a religion that is locked into its past.

13 During their second visit, Joseph made himself known to his brothers, and his ancestry became known to Pharaoh.[c] 14 Then Joseph sent for his father Jacob and his entire family, seventy-five people in all.[d]

15 "Jacob migrated to Egypt, and after he and our ancestors had died there,[e] 16 they were brought back to Shechem and placed in the tomb that Abraham had purchased from the sons of Hamor at Shechem for a sum of money.[f]

17 "When the time of the promise that God had pledged to Abraham drew near, our people in Egypt had greatly increased in number.[g] 18 Then a new king came to power who had never heard of Joseph.[h] 19 He dealt treacherously with our people and forced our ancestors to abandon their infants so that they could not survive.[i]

20 "It was at this time that Moses was born, who was pleasing to God. For three months he was nursed in his father's house,[j] 21 but after he had been abandoned, the daughter of Pharaoh adopted him and brought him up as her own son.[k] 22 Moses was trained in all the wisdom of the Egyptians, and he was powerful both in word and in deed.[l]

23 [m] "When he was forty years old, he decided to visit his fellow countrymen, the children of Israel. 24 When he saw one of them being maltreated, he went to his aid and avenged the victim by slaying the Egyptian. 25 He thought that his brethren would realize that God was offering them deliverance through him, but they did not understand.

26 [n] "The next day, he came upon two of them fighting, and he tried to reconcile them, saying, 'Men, you are brethren! Why are you trying to hurt one another?' 27 But the man who had wronged his neighbor pushed him aside, saying, 'Who appointed you to be our ruler and judge?[o] 28 Do you intend to kill me as you killed the Egyptian yesterday?' 29 Moses fled when he heard this, and he dwelt as an alien in Midian and became the father of two sons.[p]

30 [q] "After forty years had passed, an angel appeared to him in the desert near Mount Sinai in the flame of a burning bush. 31 When Moses saw it, he was amazed, and as he approached to examine it, the voice of the Lord said to him, 32 'I am the God of your ancestors, the God of Abraham, Isaac, and Jacob.'

"Moses was terrified and did not dare to look. 33 Then the Lord said to him, 'Take off the sandals from your feet, for the place where you stand is holy ground.[r] 34 I have seen the oppression of my people in Egypt and have heard their sighs, and I have come down to rescue them. Now come! I will send you to Egypt.'

35 "This Moses whom they rejected by saying 'Who appointed you to be our ruler and judge?' God now sent forth as both ruler and liberator through the angel who appeared to him in the bush.[s] 36 It was he who led them out, performing wonders and signs in Egypt, at the Red Sea, and for forty years in the desert.[t] 37 It was this Moses who said to the children of Israel, 'God will raise up for you, from your own people, a prophet like me.'[u] 38 It was he who was in the assembly in the desert with the angel who spoke to him on Mount Sinai and with our ancestors, and who received words of life to hand on to us.[v]

39 "This is the man whom our ancestors refused to obey. Instead they thrust him aside, and in their hearts they turned back to Egypt,[w] 40 saying to Aaron, 'Make gods for us who will lead us on the way. As for this Moses, who led us out of the land of Egypt, we do not know what has happened to him.'[x]

41 "It was then that they made a calf, offered a sacrifice to the idol, and rejoiced over the work of their hands.[y] 42 [z] So God turned away from them and gave them up to worship the host of heaven, as it is written in the book of the Prophets:

'Did you bring me sacrifices and offerings
during those forty years in the desert,
O house of Israel?[a]
43 No, you carried aloft the tent of Moloch
and the star of your god Rephan,
the images that you had made to worship.
And so I shall send you into exile beyond Babylon.'

c Gen 45:3-4, 16.—d Gen 45:9-11, 18-19; 46:27; Ex 1:5 LXX; Deut 10:22.—e Gen 46:5-6; 49:33.—f Gen 23:3-20; 33:19; 49:29-30; 50:13; Jos 24:32.—g Ex 1:7; Ps 105:24.—h Ex 1:8.—i Ex 1:10-22.—j Ex 2:2; Heb 11:23.—k Ex 2:3-10.—l 1 Ki 5:10; Isa 19:11; Lk 24:19.—m 23-24: Ex 2:11-12.—n 26-28: Ex 2:13-14.—o Gen 19:9; Num 16:13; Lk 12:14.—p Ex 2:11-15; 15:21-22; 18:3-4.—q 30-34: Ex 3:2-3.—r Jos 5:15.—s Ex 2:14.—t Ex 7:3, 10; 14:21; Num 14:33; Am 5:25.—u Acts 3:22; Deut 18:15.—v Ex 19:3; 20:1-17; Lev 27:34; Deut 5:4-22; 6:4-25; Jn 1:17; Rom 3:2.—w Num 14:3.—x Ex 32:1, 23.—y Ex 32:4-6; Ps 106:19; Rev 9:20.—z 42-43: Am 5:25-27.—a Jos 24:20; Isa 63:10; Jer 7:18; 8:2; 19:13.

44 "While they were in the desert, our
ancestors had the Tent of Testimony, as God
commanded when he directed Moses to
make it according to the pattern he had
been shown.[b] 45 Our ancestors with Joshua
brought it with them when they dispos-
sessed the nations that God drove out before
our ancestors. It remained there until the
time of David,[c] 46 who found favor with God
and desired to provide a dwelling for the
God of Jacob.[d]

47 "However, it was Solomon who built a
house for him.[e] 48 Yet the Most High does
not dwell in houses made with human
hands.[f] As the prophet says,

49 'Heaven is my throne,
and the earth is my footstool.
What kind of house can you build for
me? asks the Lord.
Where shall my resting place be?[g]
50 Did not my hand make all these
things?'[h]

51 "You stiff-necked people, with uncir-
cumcised hearts and ears! You are always
resisting the Holy Spirit, just as your ances-
tors used to do.[i] 52 Was there ever a prophet
whom your fathers did not persecute? They
killed those who foretold the coming of the
Righteous One, and now you have become
his betrayers and murderers.[j] 53 You
received the Law through God's angels, and
yet you have not observed it."[k]

Stephen's Martyrdom. 54 When they heard
this, they became enraged, and they ground
their teeth at him. 55 [l] But Stephen, filled
with the Holy Spirit, looked up intently to
heaven and saw the glory of God, and Jesus
standing at God's right hand. 56 "Look!" he
cried. "I see the heavens opened and the Son
of Man standing at the right hand of God."[m]

57 On hearing these words, they covered
their ears, cried out loudly, and rushed en
masse against him. 58 Then they dragged
him out of the city and began to stone him.
The witnesses laid their coats at the feet of a
young man named Saul.*[n]

59 While they were stoning Stephen, he
prayed aloud, "Lord Jesus, receive my spir-
it."[o] 60 Then he knelt down and cried out in a
clear voice, "Lord, do not hold this sin
against them." And with these words he fell
asleep.[p]

CHAPTER 8

The Church Becomes Open to the Gentiles.*
1 Saul approved of his death. That day
marked the beginning of a severe persecu-
tion of the Church in Jerusalem, and every-
one except the apostles scattered to the
country districts of Judea and Samaria.[q]
2 Stephen was buried by devout men who
made loud lamentations over him. 3 Saul,
meanwhile, began to inflict great harm on
the Church. He entered house after house,
dragging off men and women and sending
them to prison.[r] 4 Now those who had been
scattered went from place to place pro-
claiming the word.[s]

E: The Mission in Judea and Samaria

Springtime in Samaria.* 5 Philip went down
to a city in Samaria and began proclaiming
the Christ to them.[t] 6 The crowds welcomed
the message proclaimed by Philip because
they had heard and seen the signs he was
doing. 7 For unclean spirits emerged with

b Ex 25:9, 40; Num 1:50; Heb 8:5.—c Jos 3:14-17; 2 Sam 7:5-7; Ps 44:3.—d 2 Sam 7:1-2; 1 Ki 8:17; Ps 132:1-5.—e 1 Ki 6:1; 1 Chr 17:12.—f Acts 17:24; 1 Ki 8:27; Heb 9:11, 24.—g Isa 66:1-2; Mt 5:34-35.—h Isa 66:1-2.—i Lev 26:41; Deut 9:13; Jer 4:4.—j 2 Chr 30:7-8; 36:16; Mt 23:31, 34; 1 Thes 2:15.—k Gal 3:19; Heb 2:2.—l 55-56: Acts 2:34; Mt 26:64; Mk 14:62; Lk 22:69.—m Mt 8:20.—n Acts 22:20; Lev 24:14; Lk 4:29.—o Ps 31:6; Lk 23:46.—p Acts 9:40; Mt 27:46, 50; Mk 15:34; Lk 23:46.—q Acts 7:58; 22:20.—r Acts 9:1, 13; 22:4; 26:9-11; 1 Cor 15:9; Gal 1:13; Phil 3:6; 1 Tim 1:13.—s Acts 11:19; 15:35.—t Acts 6:5; 21:8-9.

7:58 *Saul:* i.e., Paul, the future apostle, who is here mentioned for the first time; see Acts 22:20.

8:1-4 The Hellenist Christians are driven out of Jerusalem. Their dispersion proceeds in an underground manner throughout the narrative until the moment when we will encounter a list of people who emigrate to Cyprus and Antioch. There, for the first time, the Church is opened to Gentiles (Acts 11:9ff). During this period, Luke shows the Gospel spreading to Samaria, Gaza, and the coast as far as Caesarea, Damascus in Syria, and Tarsus. The Gospel is received by many different cultures and people: the Pharisean persecutor, the functionary, the peasant of the plain of Sharon, the notable rich of Joppa, the artisan, the army, and the non-Jewish Greeks of Antioch. Luke presents Paul under the somber traits of persecutor; once he becomes an apostle, Paul will remain marked by the memory of the time when he wanted to obstruct the path of the infant Gospel (see Acts 22:20; 26:10; 1 Cor 15:9; Gal 1:13, 23; Phil 3:6).

8:5-8 Another deacon brings about an opening of the Church to the world. Since their separation, their installation of a worship of their own, and their intermingling with other peoples, the Samaritans who were once brethren in religion with the Jews have come to be regarded by the latter as heretics every bit as evil as the Gentiles. The Gospel is a powerful means of salvation for all human beings, surpassing the ancient religions and political frontiers. Presented here is the first step. The ministry of Philip the deacon is described in the spirit of the Gospels, and Luke stresses the climate of joy that follows in the wake of the good news.

loud shrieks from many people who were possessed, and many others who were paralyzed or crippled were cured.[u] 8 Thus, there was great joy in that city.

The Encounter with Magic. 9 * A man named Simon had been in that city for some time practicing magic and had astounded the people of Samaria, claiming to be someone great.[v] 10 All of them, from the least to the greatest, believed in him, declaring, "This man is the power of God that is called 'The Great One.'" *[w] 11 And they listened to him because for a long time they had been captivated by his magic.

12 However, when the people came to believe Philip as he preached about the kingdom of God and the name of Jesus Christ, they were baptized, both men and women.[x] 13 Even Simon himself became a believer. After his baptism, he was constantly in Philip's company, and he was astonished when he saw the great signs and mighty deeds that were taking place.[y]

The Holy Spirit. 14 When the apostles in Jerusalem heard that Samaria had accepted the word of God, they sent Peter and John to them.[z] 15 When they arrived there, they prayed for them that they might receive the Holy Spirit, 16 for as yet he had not come upon any of them; they had only been baptized in the name of the Lord Jesus.[a] 17 Then they laid hands on them, and they received the Holy Spirit.[b]

Condemnation of Simony. 18 When Simon saw that the Spirit was bestowed by the laying on of the apostles' hands, he offered them money, 19 saying, "Give me this power too so that anyone on whom I lay my hands may receive the Holy Spirit." 20 But Peter said to him, "May your silver perish with you, because you thought that you could obtain God's gift with money.[c] 21 You have no part or share in this, for your heart is not upright in the eyes of God.[d] 22 Repent, therefore, of this wickedness of yours and beg the Lord that if possible you may be forgiven for devising your evil scheme. 23 I see that you are engulfed in the gall of bitterness and the chains of wickedness."[e]

24 Simon said in reply, "Pray for me to the Lord that nothing of what you have spoken about may befall me."[f] 25 Then, after giving their testimony and proclaiming the word of the Lord, they returned to Jerusalem, preaching the good news to many Samaritan villages.

Baptism of a High Official.* 26 Then the angel of the Lord said to Philip, "Get up and head south along the road that leads from Jerusalem down to Gaza, the desert road."[g] 27 Therefore, he got up and set out.

Now there was an Ethiopian eunuch, * an official at the court of the Candace, that is, the queen of the Ethiopians, who was in charge of her entire treasury. He had come to Jerusalem to worship[h] 28 and was now returning home. As he sat in his chariot, he was reading the prophet Isaiah.

29 Then the Spirit said to Philip, "Go up and join that chariot."[i] 30 When Philip ran up, he heard him reading from the prophet Isaiah, and he asked, "Do you understand what you are reading?" 31 He replied, "How can I, unless I have someone to instruct

u Mt 4:24; 8:29; Mk 16:17.—v Acts 5:36; 13:6.—w Acts 14:11; 28:6.—x Acts 1:3; 2:38; 19:8; 28:23, 31.—y Acts 19:11.—z Heb 4:12.—a Acts 1:5; 10:44; Mt 28:19.—b Acts 2:4; 4:31; 10:44-47; 15:8-9; 19:2, 6; 1 Tim 4:14.—c 2 Ki 5:16; Isa 55:1; Dan 5:17; Mt 10:8.—d Ps 78:37; Neh 2:20.—e Prov 5:22; Jer 4:18.—f Ex 8:8; Num 21:7; 1 Ki 13:6.—g Acts 11:13.—h Isa 56:3-5; Ps 68:32; Zep 3:10.—i Acts 10:19; 11:12.

8:9-25 The proclamation of the Gospel is faced with an important problem as in our day. Can human beings own spiritual forces? Under an Eastern influence, personages endowed with the power of performing prodigies circulated throughout the Empire. There were itinerant exorcists or healers (Acts 9:11, 18). Simon has an outstanding reputation in this sphere. Now the magician has come to believe in the word of the Gospel. The community at Jerusalem is troubled to hear of prodigies and conversions in Samaria, a rejected land; an apostolic inspection can only confirm the facts and give them the authentication of the Spirit.

Simon the magician is attracted by the prestige that would be given him by the Spirit, and he wants to have the Spirit at his disposal, as do the apostles. He is even ready to pay well for it (whence the word "simony"). But he receives a stern refusal. Luke wants to set aside the forgeries that one could ascribe to Christ and the Spirit. We have here an example of a faith that becomes deeper, for the author stresses the importance of intercessory prayer for one another in matters of conversion.

8:10 *The Great One:* perhaps a divine title, which Simon has given himself.

8:26-40 In this passage, Luke shows us the encounter of the Church with a new cultural environment. The official in charge of the treasury of the queen of Ethiopia (Candace, like Pharaoh, is a title of a ruler) is interested in a passage of the Old Testament that speaks of a mysterious personage who is overwhelmed by suffering for the salvation of all; the passage is Isa 53, often used by the first community to express the mystery of Christ. The marvelous elements in this story of Philip recall God's freedom of action in the time of the ancient Prophets: angel, Spirit, instantaneous transportation (see 1 Ki 18:12; 2 Ki 2:16; Ezek 3:12, 14; Dan 14:36). We will come across Philip the deacon again later on as the father of four daughters (Acts 21:9).

8:27 *Eunuch:* may be simply a court title; for eunuch in the literal sense, see the prophecy of Isa 56:3-7.

me?" Then he invited Philip to get in and sit beside him.[j]

32 [k] This was the Scripture passage he had been reading:

"Like a sheep he was led to the slaughter;
like a lamb that is silent before its shearer
he did not open his mouth.
33 In his humiliation justice was denied him.
Who will be able to speak of his posterity?
For his life on earth has been taken away."

34 Then the eunuch said to Philip, "Please tell me, about whom is the prophet speaking—about himself or someone else?" 35 And so Philip, starting with this text of Scripture, proceeded to explain to him the good news of Jesus.[l]

36 As they were traveling along the road, they came to some water. The eunuch said, "Look, here is some water. What is to prevent me from being baptized?"[m] [37 And Philip said, "If you believe with all your heart, you may." The eunuch said in reply, "I believe that Jesus Christ is the Son of God."] * 38 Then he ordered the chariot to stop, and Philip and the eunuch both went down into the water, and he baptized him.

39 When they came up out of the water, the Spirit of the Lord snatched Philip away, and the eunuch did not see him again, but he went on his way rejoicing.[n] 40 Philip, however, appeared in Azotus * and continued his journey, proclaiming the good news in every town until he reached Caesarea.[o]

CHAPTER 9

Conversion of Saul on the Road to Damascus. 1 * Now, Saul, * still breathing threats and violence against the Lord's disciples, went to the high priest[p] 2 and asked him for letters to the synagogues at Damascus, * authorizing him to arrest any men or women there who were followers of the Way and bring them back to Jerusalem.[q]

3 While he was drawing near Damascus on his journey, suddenly a light from the sky flashed around him.[r] 4 He fell to the ground and heard a voice saying to him, "Saul, Saul, why are you persecuting me?"[s] 5 He asked, "Who are you, Lord?" The reply came, "I am Jesus, whom you are persecuting.[t] 6 Now get up and go into the city, and you will be told what you have to do."[u]

7 The men who were traveling with him stood there speechless, for they had heard the voice but had seen no one.[v] 8 Saul got up from the ground, but when he opened his eyes he was unable to see. Therefore, they led him by the hand and brought him into Damascus.[w] 9 For three days, he was without sight and neither ate nor drank.

Saul's Baptism. 10 [x] There was a disciple in Damascus named Ananias. In a vision, the Lord said to him, "Ananias." He answered, "Here I am, Lord."[y] 11 The Lord said to him, "Get up and go to the Street called Straight, * to the house of Judas, and ask for a man from Tarsus named Saul. He is praying,[z] 12 and in a vision he has seen a man named Ananias come in and lay his hands on him so that he may regain his sight."

13 Ananias answered, "Lord, I have heard from many people about this man and how much harm he has done to your saints * in Jerusalem.[a] 14 Now he has come here with authority from the chief priests to imprison all who invoke your name."[b]

j Jn 16:13; Rom 10:14.—k 32-33: Isa 53:7-8 LXX; Lk 18:31.—l Acts 17:2; Mt 5:2.—m Acts 10:47.—n 1 Ki 18:12; Ezek 3:12; Lk 24:31-32; 2 Cor 12:2.—o Acts 10:1; 21:8.—p Acts 8:3; 9:13; 22:4; 1 Cor 15:9; Gal 1:13-14.—q Acts 9:14; 26:10; Isa 17:1; Jer 49:23.—r Ezek 1:28; 1 Cor 9:1; 15:8; Gal 1:16.—s Acts 22:6; 26:14; Isa 6:8.—t Acts 22:8; 26:15; Mt 25:40; 1 Cor 8:12.—u Acts 22:10; 26:16; Ezek 3:22.—v Acts 22:9; 26:13-14; Dan 10:7; Jn 12:29.—w Acts 22:11.—x 10-19: Acts 22:12-16.—y 1 Sam 3:4.—z Acts 11:25; 21:39.—a Acts 8:3; 9:1; 26:10; Rom 1:7; Eph 1:1.—b Acts 9:1-2; 26:10; 1 Cor 1:2; 2 Tim 2:22.

8:37 This verse is added by some ancient manuscripts.

8:40 *Azotus* (called Ashdod in the Old Testament as one of the five Philistine cities) was about 25 miles north of Gaza. *Caesarea,* on the coast, was 33 miles north of the modern Tel Aviv, and served as the headquarters for the Roman governors.

9:1-30 The story of Paul's conversion is repeated twice more in this Book, with some variations in details (Acts 22:4-21; 26:9-18).

The heart of the story is the identification of Jesus with the persecuted community of believers: The Lord can no longer be separated from his Church. Saul is given the mission of carrying the name of Jesus to Israel and the rulers of the nations.

9:1 *Saul:* present at the stoning of Stephen (Acts 7:58), he was born in Tarsus and had studied under Gamaliel (Acts 22:3).

9:2 *Damascus:* an important city of the Roman province of Syria with a large Jewish population; it was some 150 miles from Jerusalem and a four-to-six-day journey. *Way:* behavior, a concept of life, the teaching of the Lord, teaching about salvation; in short, Christianity (see Acts 16:17; 18:25-26). The Romans granted the high priest authority in religious matters, even over Jews outside of Palestine.

9:11 *Street called Straight:* one of the oldest streets in the world. In Paul's time, Damascus was laid out in the form of a rectangle intersected by "straight" streets. The longest of them all was the "Street called Straight."

9:13 *Saints:* so named because Christians are consecrated to Christ, the Holy One (Acts 3:14). The word recurs in verses 32 and 41. See also note on Rom 1:7.

15 However, the Lord said to him, "Go, for
this is the man I have chosen as a vessel to
bring my name before the Gentiles and their
kings and before the people of Israel.[c] 16 I
myself will show him how much he will have
to suffer for the sake of my name."[d]

17 And so Ananias went forth and entered
the house. He laid his hands on Saul and
said, "Brother Saul, the Lord Jesus who
appeared to you on your way has sent me so
that you may regain your sight and be filled
with the Holy Spirit."*[e] 18 Immediately,
something like scales fell from his eyes, and
he regained his sight. He got up and was
baptized;[f] 19 then, after taking some food, he
regained his strength.

Saul Preaches in Damascus. For several
days, Saul stayed with the disciples in
Damascus,[g] 20 and he began to preach in the
synagogues that Jesus is the Son of God.[h]
21 All those who heard him were astounded,
and they said, "Is not this the man who in
Jerusalem was persecuting those who
invoked this name? And did he not come
here for the specific purpose of arresting
them so that they might be taken to the chief
priests?" 22 But Saul's strength continued to
increase, and he confounded the Jews who
lived in Damascus by showing that Jesus is
indeed the Christ.[i]

23 After some time had passed, the Jews
devised a plan to kill him, 24[j] but their plot
became known to Saul. They were keeping
watch on the city gates day and night so that
they might kill him,[k] 25 but his disciples took
him one night and let him down in a basket
over the wall.

Saul in Jerusalem and Tarsus. 26[l] When he
arrived in Jerusalem, he tried to join the dis-
ciples, but they were all afraid of him
because they did not believe that he had
become a disciple.[m] 27 However, Barnabas
took him and brought him to the apostles.
He related to them how on his journey Saul
had seen the Lord who had spoken to him,
and how at Damascus he had preached
boldly in the name of Jesus.

28 Saul then moved about with them in
Jerusalem, speaking boldly in the name of
the Lord. 29 He also engaged in debate with
the Hellenists* but they began planning to
kill him.[n] 30 When the brethren learned of
this, they brought him to Caesarea and sent
him off to Tarsus.*[o]

Period of Peace for the Church. 31 * Mean-
while, the Church throughout Judea, Galilee,
and Samaria enjoyed peace, building up
strength and living in the fear of the Lord.
Encouraged by the Holy Spirit,* the Church
grew in numbers.[p]

Peter Heals Aeneas at Lydda. 32 As Peter
traveled throughout the region, he went
down to visit the saints living in Lydda.*
33 While there, he found a man named
Aeneas who had been bedridden for eight
years, for he was paralyzed. 34 Peter said to
him, "Aeneas, Jesus Christ heals you. Get up
and make your bed." He immediately stood
up.[q] 35 All the inhabitants of Lydda and
Sharon saw him, and they turned to the
Lord.[r]

Peter Restores Tabitha to Life. 36 In Joppa,
there was a disciple named Tabitha, or
Dorcas in Greek, whose life was devoted to
performing good works and giving to those
in need.[s] 37 In those days, she became ill and
died. After they had washed her body, they
laid her out in an upper room.*[t] 38 Since
Lydda was near Joppa, the disciples, on
hearing that Peter was there, sent two men
to him with the request, "Please come to us
without delay."

39 Peter immediately set out with them,
and when he arrived, they escorted him to
the upper room. All the widows stood
around him, weeping and showing him the

c Acts 13:2; 22:15; 26:1; 27:24; Gal 1:15.—d Acts 20:23; 2 Cor 6:4-10.—e Acts 28:8; 1 Cor 9:1.—f Tob 11:10-15.—g Acts 26:20.—h Acts 13:5, 14; 14:1.—i Acts 5:42; 17:3.—j 24-25: Jos 2:15; 1 Sam 19:12; 2 Cor 11:32-33.—k Acts 20:3, 19.—l 26-27: Gal 1:18.—m Acts 22:17.—n Acts 6:1; 2 Cor 11:26.—o Acts 11:25.—p 1 Cor 8:1; Eph 4:16.—q Acts 3:6, 16.—r 1 Chr 5:16; Isa 33:9.—s Jos 19:46; Jon 1:3; Tit 3:8.—t Acts 1:13; 20:8.

9:17 It was the resurrected Christ who appeared to Paul. Paul insisted on this point and based his qualifications as an apostle on it (see 1 Cor 9:1; 15:8).

9:29 *Hellenists:* see note on Acts 6:1.

9:30 *Tarsus,* the capital of Cilicia (in Asia Minor), was Paul's native place (Acts 22:3); it is there that Barnabas will go looking for him (Acts 11:25).

9:31-43 Luke gives us a new panoramic picture in which the themes of fervor and growth are stressed. A precarious peace is established, providing the time to contemplate the Church living and animated by the Spirit and planted in the whole land of ancient Israel. In verse 31, Church refers, not to a single Church, as it usually does in Scripture, but to all the communities. Peter visits the various centers, especially those in the area of present-day Tel Aviv. His miracles are recounted in the manner of pages in the Gospels.

9:31 *Encouraged by the Holy Spirit:* this Book stresses the work of the Holy Spirit (see Acts 13:2). Hence, it is sometimes called "The Acts of the Holy Spirit."

9:32 *Lydda:* a town about 12 miles from Joppa.

9:37 The body was washed in preparation for burial.

tunics and other clothes that Dorcas had made while she was with them.[u]

40 Peter sent them all out and knelt down and prayed. Then he turned to the body and said, "Tabitha, get up." She opened her eyes, saw Peter, and sat up.[v] 41 He gave her his hand and helped her up. Then he called the saints and the widows, and he showed her to them alive.[w] 42 It came to be known throughout Joppa, causing many to come to believe in the Lord. 43 Peter stayed on for many days in Joppa at the house of a tanner* named Simon.[x]

F: Baptism of the Centurion Cornelius

CHAPTER 10

The Vision of Cornelius.* 1 [y]In Caesarea, there was a man named Cornelius who was a centurion of the so-called Italian cohort.*[z] 2 He was a devout and God-fearing man, as were all the members of his household. He gave alms generously to the people and prayed constantly to God.[a]

3 One afternoon about three o'clock,* he had a vision in which he clearly saw an angel of God approaching him and calling to him, "Cornelius!"[b] 4 He stared at him in terror and asked, "What is it, Lord?"

The angel said, "Your prayers and acts of charity have ascended as a memorial offering before God.[c] 5 Now send some men to Joppa and summon a man named Simon, who is also called Peter. 6 He is lodging with another Simon, a tanner, whose house is by the sea." 7 When the angel who spoke to him had departed, he summoned two of his servants and a devout soldier on his staff. 8 He told them all that had happened and sent them to Joppa.

The Vision of Peter. 9 *About noon* the next day, as they were on their way and approaching the city, Peter went up on the roof to pray.[d] 10 He became hungry and wanted something to eat, but while it was being prepared, he fell into a trance.[e] 11 [f]He then saw heaven opened and something that looked like a large sheet descending, being lowered to the ground by its four corners. 12 In it were all kinds of four-footed animals as well as reptiles and birds of the air.

---

u Acts 6:1; 1 Tim 5:3.—v Mt 9:25; Mk 5:40-41; Lk 22:41.—w Lk 7:15.—x Acts 10:6.—y 1-8: Acts 10:30-33.—z Lk 7:2, 4-5.—a Acts 13:16, 26.—b Acts 3:1; Ps 55:18.—c Ps 20:4; Lk 18:1; Rev 8:4.—d Jud 8:5.—e Acts 22:17; Dan 6:11.—f 11-20: Acts 11:5-12.

9:43 *A tanner:* one who tans hides of animals and hence is considered unclean by the Law. Peter's stay with him prepares the way for his mission to the Gentiles who were considered to be unclean by the Jews.

10:1—11:18 The moment in which the Christian movement entered into the Gentile world was a major event for the Church. Luke speaks of God's initiative that captures the world through the Resurrection and the Spirit and expresses itself in the dynamism with which the Lord animates the first community. To illustrate it, he elevates an account of conversion to the rank of an historic event and an irreversible theological fact. Indeed, it is the longest account in the Acts of the Apostles.

Cornelius, a Roman official in Caesarea—the city that is the seat of government—is, along with his entire family, a "God-fearing" man, i.e., one who has accepted the beliefs and principal practices of Judaism, though not going so far as to share the Jewish way of life and become part of the people through circumcision.

In his inner righteousness and generosity, Cornelius is recognized by God as suitable to enter into communication with him. However, to find the truth that he desires he must hear the announcement of the facts concerning Jesus from the mouth of eyewitnesses and thus must meet Peter—who is living some 30 miles away. Only then will these Gentiles master the word of Christ and make it their own through the inspiration of the Spirit (Acts 10:40).

Thus, Cornelius is no longer the central figure of our account. Luke wishes to stress a fact: the initiative of God to liberate the Gospel from being shut up in the Jewish world. The community of Jerusalem, still bound by its Jewish ties, opens itself to the outside world by a series of encounters, but it is blocked from doing so by a redoubtable problem. The Jewishness of the first disciples prevents them from frequenting the Gentiles' houses of prayer and from sharing their tables without incurring a legal uncleanness and violating the Law. How then can they live in community and partake in the Eucharist, for example? Must not the Gentiles first be made part of Israel through circumcision? In the face of the gift given by God to the Gentiles "as ... upon us at the beginning" (Acts 11:15), in the face of this Pentecost of the Gentile nations (Acts 10:45), the community of Jerusalem must also be converted and realize that the religious and ritual appurtenances can no longer provide superiority or priority, that these are no longer to be regarded as a wall of separation—finally, that no person can be declared unclean (Acts 10:27).

The text is carefully constructed. Each personage has a vision that presents itself as an enigma. Then it becomes clear in the concrete action, the encounter, and the mutual hospitality. Peter's discourse is the pivotal point of the account. Like its predecessors (Acts 2:14-41; 3:11-26), it relates the major themes of the announcement of Jesus. The Spirit authenticates the word concerning Jesus and inspires Gentiles to become witnesses of the Resurrection.

The concrete problems of the entry of Gentiles into the Church and of contacts between Jews and Gentiles will be definitively regulated at the Council of Jerusalem (Acts 15:10, 19-21), but Paul will struggle all his life against the Judaizing practices and theories that tempt certain communities of Israelite origin (see Gal 2; 5). The encounter of Peter and Cornelius leads to the formation of the first Christian community made up of the two most difficult milieux: the Christian and the Gentile. Henceforth, the Church will no longer be able to shut herself up within her own confines.

10:1 *Italian cohort:* an auxiliary unit of soldiers.

10:3 *Three o'clock:* literally, "about the ninth hour." This time period was a Jewish hour of prayer (see Acts 3:1).

10:9-16 The vision that now occurs makes it possible for Peter to sit down at table and eat with Gentiles without feeling any guilt. Hence, it is clear that at first not even the apostles fully understood the Lord's teaching about the Law. However, with the aid of this vision and the inspiration of the Holy Spirit the apostles ultimately arrive at a fuller understanding.

10:9 *Noon:* literally, "about the sixth hour."

[13] A voice then said to him, "Get up, Peter! Kill and eat!" [14] But Peter said, "Certainly not, Lord. For I have never eaten anything profane or unclean."[g] [15] The voice spoke again to him, for a second time, "What God has made clean, you must not call profane."[h] [16] This happened three times, and then immediately the object was taken up into heaven again.

[17] While Peter was wondering about the meaning of the vision he had seen, suddenly the men who were sent by Cornelius appeared. They had asked for directions to Simon's house, and now they were standing at the entrance [18] and inquiring whether Simon known as Peter was lodging there.

[19] As Peter was still thinking about the vision, the Spirit said to him, "Some men have come to see you.[i] [20] Hurry down and go with them without any hesitation, for I have sent them."[j]

[21] Then Peter went down to the men and said, "I am the one you are looking for. What is the reason you have come?" [22] They replied, "A centurion named Cornelius, who is greatly respected by the entire Jewish nation as an upright and God-fearing man, was directed by a holy angel to summon you to his house and to hear what you have to say."[k] [23] So he invited them in and gave them lodging.

The next day, he set out with them, accompanied by some of the brethren from Joppa. [24] On the following day, they reached Caesarea. Cornelius had been expecting them and had called together his relatives and close friends. [25][l] When Peter arrived, Cornelius came out to meet him and, falling at his feet, did him reverence. [26] But Peter helped him up, saying, "Stand up. I am only a man myself."

[27] While they conversed together, they went inside where a large crowd had gathered. [28] Peter said to them, "You are well aware that Jews are forbidden to associate with or visit a Gentile. However, God has shown me that I should not call anyone profane or unclean.[m] [29] That is why I came without offering any objection when I was summoned. I would like to know exactly why you sent for me."

[30] Cornelius replied, "Four days ago, at this very hour, three o'clock in the afternoon, * I was in my house praying when suddenly I saw a man in shining robes standing before me.[n] [31] He said, 'Cornelius, your prayer has been heard and your almsgiving has not been forgotten by God.[o] [32] Therefore, send to Joppa and ask for Simon, who is also called Peter. He is lodging at the house of Simon the tanner, by the sea.' [33] And so I sent for you immediately, and you have been kind enough to come. Now all of us have assembled here in the presence of God to listen to everything that the Lord has commanded you to say."

Peter's Speech. [34] Then Peter addressed them: "I now understand how true it is that God has no favorites,[p] [35] but that in every nation all those who fear God and do what is right are acceptable to him.[q] [36] He sent his word to the children of Israel and proclaimed the good news of peace through Jesus Christ, who is the Lord of all.[r]

[37] "You are well aware of what was proclaimed all over Judea, beginning in Galilee after the baptism of John,[s] [38] how God anointed Jesus of Nazareth with the Holy Spirit and with power. He went around doing good and healing all those who were oppressed by the devil, for God was with him.[t]

[39] "We are witnesses to everything he did in the Jewish countryside and in Jerusalem. They put him to death by hanging him on a tree,[u] [40] but God raised him to life on the third day and allowed him to be seen [41] not by all the people but by witnesses who were chosen by God in advance—by us who ate and drank with him * after he rose from the dead.[v] [42] He commanded us to preach to the people and to bear witness that he is the one designated by God as Judge of the living and the dead.[w] [43] To him all the Prophets bear witness that everyone who believes in him will receive forgiveness of sins through his name."[x]

g Acts 9:5; Lev 11:1-47; Deut 14:3-20.—h Gen 1:31; 9:3; Mt 15:11; Gal 2:12.—i Acts 9:10; 13:2.—j Acts 15:7-9.—k Acts 11:14; Lk 7:4-5.—l 25-26: Acts 14:13-15; Rev 19:10.—m Acts 11:3; 15:9; Jn 4:9; Gal 2:11-16.—n Acts 3:1.—o Lk 1:13.—p Deut 10:17; 17:2; 2 Chr 19:7; Job 34:19; Wis 6:7; Mk 12:14; Rom 2:11; Gal 2:8; Eph 6:9; Jas 2:1; 1 Pet 1:17.—q Acts 15:9; Rom 10:12.—r Isa 52:7; Nah 2:1; 1 Jn 1:5.—s Mt 4:12; Mk 1:14; Lk 4:14.—t Acts 4:26; Isa 61:1; Lk 4:18.—u Lk 24:48.—v Lk 24:41-43; Jn 14:17, 22.—w Acts 1:8; 3:15; 17:31; Mt 28:19; Lk 24:48; Rom 14:9; 2 Cor 5:10; 2 Tim 4:1.—x Acts 26:22; Isa 53:11.

10:30 *Three o'clock in the afternoon:* literally, "about the ninth hour."

10:41 *Ate and drank with him:* those who shared a table with Jesus after he rose from the dead were given unmistakable evidence of the Lord's bodily Resurrection (see Lk 24:42f; Jn 21:12-15).

The Baptism of Cornelius. 44 While Peter was still speaking, the Holy Spirit descended upon all who were listening to his message.[y] 45 The circumcised believers who had accompanied Peter were astonished that the gift of the Holy Spirit should have been poured out on the Gentiles also.[z] 46 For they heard them speaking in tongues and proclaiming the greatness of God.

Peter said further, 47 "Can anyone withhold the water of baptism from these people who have received the Holy Spirit just as we have?"[a] 48 Then he ordered them to be baptized in the name of Jesus Christ. 49 Afterward, they asked him to stay with them for a few days.

CHAPTER 11

Peter's Explanation of Cornelius' Baptism. 1 The apostles and the brethren in Judea heard that the Gentiles too had accepted the word of God. 2 Therefore, when Peter went up to Jerusalem, the circumcised believers protested to him,[b] 3 saying, "Why did you enter the house of uncircumcised men and eat with them?"[c]

4 Peter replied by explaining the facts to them step by step, saying, 5 [d] "While I was praying one day in the city of Joppa, I fell into a trance and had a vision. I saw something like a large sheet lowered down from heaven by its four corners, and it landed close to me.

6 "I looked into it carefully and observed four-footed animals, wild beasts, reptiles, and birds. 7 I also heard a voice saying to me, 'Get up, Peter! Kill and eat!' 8 But I said, 'Certainly not, Lord. For nothing profane or unclean has ever been in my mouth.' 9 But the voice spoke to me from heaven for a second time, 'What God has made clean, you must not call profane.' 10 This happened three times, and then everything was taken up into heaven again.

11 "At that very moment, three men arrived at the house where we were staying. They had been sent to me from Caesarea. 12 The Spirit instructed me to go with them without any hesitation. These six brethren also went with me, and we entered the man's house.[e] 13 He told us how he had seen an angel standing in his house who said, 'Send to Joppa and ask for Simon who is also called Peter.[f] 14 He will give you a message that will grant salvation to you and your entire household.'[g]

15 "As I began to speak, the Holy Spirit descended upon them just as it had upon us at the beginning,[h] 16 and I remembered the word of the Lord, how he had said, 'John baptized with water, but you will be baptized with the Holy Spirit.'[i] 17 If then God gave them the same gift that he gave to us when we came to believe in the Lord Jesus Christ, who was I to oppose God?"[j]

18 When they heard this, they held their peace, and they praised God, saying, "God has given even to the Gentiles the repentance that leads to life."

A Church at Antioch.* 19 Meanwhile, those who had scattered after the persecution that arose because of Stephen traveled as far as Phoenicia, * Cyprus, and Antioch, preaching the word only to Jews.[k] 20 However, among them there were some natives of Cyprus and Cyrene who went to Antioch where they started preaching also to the Greeks, proclaiming to them the good news of the Lord Jesus.[l] 21 The hand of the Lord was with them, and a great number of them became believers and turned to the Lord.[m]

22 News of this reached the ears of the church in Jerusalem, and they sent Barnabas to Antioch. 23 When he arrived and perceived the grace of God, he rejoiced, and he encouraged them all to remain faithful to the Lord with resolute devotion,[n] 24 for he was a good man, filled with the Holy Spirit and with faith. And a large number of people were added to the Lord.

y Acts 11:15; 15:8.—z Acts 2:33, 38; 11:18.—a Acts 8:36.—b Acts 10:45.—c Acts 10:25; Gal 2:12.—d 5-12: Acts 10:11-20.—e Acts 15:9; Rom 3:22.—f Acts 10:3-5, 30-32.—g Acts 10:36; Jn 4:53; 1 Cor 1:11, 16.—h Acts 10:44.—i Acts 1:5; 19:4; Mk 1:4; Lk 3:16.—j Acts 2:38; 15:8-9; Mt 16:23.—k Acts 8:1-4; 13:1; Gal 2:11.—l Acts 4:36.—m Lk 1:66.—n Acts 13:43; 15:40.

11:19-26 The narrative picks up the story of persecution (see Acts 8:14). But we leave the coast of Palestine for a region some 300 miles further north. A new Church enters the picture, that of Antioch, where Barnabas is encouraging the converts from paganism.

In Antioch, the name *Christian* is used for the first time (v. 26), and it will henceforth be used by all the disciples of the Lord for the community in the service of the Lord.

11:19 *Phoenicia:* a land 15 miles wide and 120 miles long on the northeastern coast of the Mediterranean Sea, with Tyre and Sidon as its principal cities. *Cyprus:* the island home of Barnabas (see Acts 4:36), located in the northeastern Mediterranean, 60 miles from Syria. *Antioch:* the third most important city (after Rome and Alexandria) of the Roman Empire, located in Syria, in the northeast corner of the Mediterranean. It was from the Church of Antioch that Paul's three missionary journeys were launched (see Acts 13:1-4; 15:40; 18:23).

25 Barnabas then went to Tarsus * to look
for Saul, 26 and when he had found him, he
brought him to Antioch. For a whole year
they met with the church and taught a large
number of people. It was in Antioch that the
disciples were first called Christians. [o]

G: Threats against the Church*

A Famine in the World.* 27 During these
days, some prophets * came down from
Jerusalem to Antioch. [p] 28 One of them,
named Agabus, stood up and predicted
through the Spirit that a severe famine
would afflict the entire world. This in fact
occurred during the reign of Claudius. [q]
29 [r] The disciples decided to send relief to the
brethren living in Judea, each according to
his means. [s] 30 This they did, delivering it to
the elders * through Barnabas and Saul. [t]

CHAPTER 12

Persecution, Death, and Imprisonment.* 1 It
was about this period of time that King
Herod * persecuted certain members of the
Church. 2 He had James, the brother of John,
killed with the sword, [u] 3 and when he noted
that this pleased the Jews, he proceeded to
arrest Peter as well. Since this happened
during the feast of Unleavened Bread, [v] 4 he
imprisoned him and assigned four squads of
four soldiers each to guard him, intending to
subject him to a public trial after Passover.
5 While Peter was thus imprisoned, the
Church prayed fervently to God for him. [w]

6 On the night before Herod was to bring
him to trial, Peter, secured by two chains,
was sleeping between two soldiers, while
guards outside the door were keeping watch
over the prison. [x] 7 Suddenly, an angel of the
Lord appeared, and a light flooded the
building. He tapped Peter on the side and
awakened him, saying, "Get up quickly!"
And the chains fell away from his wrists. [y]
8 Next, the angel said to him, "Fasten your
belt and put on your sandals." After he did
so, the angel instructed him, "Wrap your
cloak around you and follow me."

9 Accordingly, Peter followed him out. He
did not realize that the intervention of the
angel was real, thinking that he was seeing a
vision. 10 After passing through the first
guard post and then the second, they
reached the iron gate that led out to the city.
This opened for them of its own accord. They
went outside and had walked the length of
one street when suddenly the angel left him. [z]

11 Then Peter came to his senses and said,
"Now I am positive that the Lord sent his
angel and rescued me from Herod's clutch-
es and from all that the Jewish people were
expecting." [a] 12 As soon as he realized this, he
went to the house of Mary, the mother of
John, also called Mark, * where many had
assembled and were at prayer. [b]

13 When he knocked at the outer door, a
maid named Rhoda came to answer it. [c]
14 Recognizing Peter's voice, she was so over-
joyed that, instead of opening the door, she
ran in with the news that Peter was standing
outside. [d] 15 They said to her, "You are out of
your mind," but she insisted that it was true.
Then they said, "It must be his angel."

---

o Acts 6:1, 2; 26:28; 1 Pet 4:16.—p Acts 13:1; Mt 16:14; 1 Cor 11:4.—q Acts 18:2; 21:10.—r 29-30: Acts 12:25.—s Rom 15:26; 2 Cor 8:1-4.—t Acts 14:23; 1 Tim 5:17; Tit 1:5; Jas 5:14.—u Mt 20:22-23; Mk 10:39.—v Acts 24:27; Ex 12:15.—w Rom 15:30, 31; Eph 6:18; Jas 5:16.—x Acts 21:33.—y Acts 16:26; 1 Ki 19:5-7; Ps 107:14.—z Acts 5:19; 16:26.—a Ps 34:8; Dan 3:95; Lk 15:17.—b Acts 12:25; 13:5; 15:37; Col 4:10; 2 Tim 4:11.—c Jn 18:16-17.—d Lk 24:41.

11:25 *Tarsus:* see note on Acts 9:30.

11:27—12:25 Calamities strike the Church—famine, persecution, political conflicts. This corresponds to the description of the signs of the last times in Luke (21:9-13). As the Gospel says, it is not the time of the end but the time of perseverance. When the signs of crisis are manifested in the world, believers testify to the hope and the effort for a change. The Church emerges from these threats with tranquil joy and humility. This account brings to a close the first twelve chapters of Acts.

11:27-30 A collection is organized in the Church. The action is an application of one of the essential elements of the community: the sharing of goods, which gives a new meaning to economic property. Paul will regard this kind of mutual help as very important (see Rom 15:31; 1 Cor 16:15; 2 Cor 8:4; 9:1, 12-13; Gal 2:10).

11:27 *Prophets:* the first mention of the gift of prophecy in this Book. Prophets are to preach, exhort, explain, or predict (see Acts 13:1; 15:32; 19:6; 21:9f; Rom 12:6; 1 Cor 12:10; 13:2-8).

11:30 *Elders:* collaborators of the apostles, or substitutes for them (see Acts 20:17f).

12:1-19 Death and imprisonment are the fate of the disciple. Jesus has foretold it emphatically. Herod puts James ("the Greater"), the brother of John, to death by the sword. Since this pleases some of the Jews, he intends to put Peter to death, too, and takes him into custody. But Peter is freed from prison by an angel and goes back to the community, which rejoices that he is freed. Peter now departs from Acts without any indication of his further activity and his fate—martyrdom. Luke also leaves us in suspense regarding the end of Paul, on the last page of Acts.

12:1-2 *Herod:* i.e., Herod Agrippa I, ruler of Judea and Samaria from A.D. 41 to 44; he was a nephew of the Herod Antipas whom we meet in the Passion of Jesus. *James* ("the Greater") was the first of the apostles to drink the Lord's cup (Mk 10:39) and give his life for the Master; his brother, *John,* will be the last of the apostles to leave the scene.

12:12 *Mark:* cousin of Barnabas (see Col 4:10); we find Mark in Acts 12:25; 13:5, 13; 15:37-39, and in the service of Paul the prisoner (Col 4:10; Philem 24; 2 Tim 4:11). He was a disciple of Peter (1 Pet 5:13), and tradition considers him to be the author of the second Gospel.

16 Meanwhile, Peter continued to knock, and when they opened the door they saw him and were astounded. 17 He motioned to them with his hand to be silent. After he described to them how the Lord had brought him out of the prison, he said, "Report this to James * and the brethren." Then he left and went to another place. [e]

18 At daybreak, there was a great deal of commotion among the soldiers about what had become of Peter. [f] 19 After instituting a search for him and being unable to find him, Herod interrogated the guards and ordered their execution. Then he left Judea to reside for a while in Caesarea. [g]

Death of Herod Agrippa I.* 20 For a long time, Herod had been very angry with the people of Tyre and Sidon, who now came to him in a body. After gaining the support of Blastus, the king's chamberlain, they asked for peace because their country depended on the king's territory for their food supplies. [h]

21 On the designated day, Herod donned his royal robes and, seated on a throne, delivered a public address to them. 22 They began to acclaim him, shouting, "This is the voice of a god, not a man!" 23 Immediately, the angel of the Lord struck him down because he had not attributed the honor to God. He was eaten away by worms and died. [i]

Return of Barnabas and Saul to Jerusalem.* 24 Meanwhile, the word of God continued to spread and gain more followers. [j] 25 Then, after Barnabas and Saul had completed their mission, they returned to Jerusalem, bringing with them John, also called Mark. * [k]

II: ANTIOCH*

A: Paul's First Missionary Journey*

CHAPTER 13

Barnabas and Paul Sent Out on Mission.* 1 In the Church at Antioch, there were prophets and teachers: Barnabas, Simeon who was called Niger, Lucius of Cyrene, Manaen who had been brought up with Herod the tetrarch, and Saul. [l] 2 On one occasion, while they were worshiping the Lord and fasting, the Holy Spirit said, "Set Barnabas and Saul apart for me to do the work to which I have called them." [m] 3 Then, after completing their fasting and prayer, they laid their hands on them and sent them off. [n]

4 Having been sent on their mission by the Holy Spirit, they went down to Seleucia, * and from there they set sail for Cyprus.

e Acts 13:16.—f Acts 5:22-24.—g Acts 16:27.—h 1 Ki 5:9, 11; 2 Mac 9:5-28; Ezek 27:17.—i 1 Sam 25:38; 2 Ki 19:35; Ezek 28:2.—j Acts 6:7; 19:20.—k Acts 11:29-30.—l Acts 4:36; 11:27.—m Rom 1:1.—n Acts 14:26.

12:17 *James:* this is James the Lesser, a brother of the Lord, i.e., one of Jesus' collateral relatives; we will find him presiding over the Church of Jerusalem (Acts 15; 17). Peter is said, in words surely carefully weighed, to have gone "to another place"; Acts will not speak of him again.

12:20-23 This time again, in the manner of the Old Testament, the intervention of the hand of God is emphasized. The account poses the problem of war: it is a scourge in which the economy is tied to the will for power. Here the war against Tyre and Sidon is put off thanks to a compromise. But the political pride of a leader who takes himself for God is dissipated by a mortal sickness, which popular tradition interprets as a punishment.

The episode accords with the chronology of the time. It inserts Acts into universal history. Herod died, after a great feast, eaten by worms, in A.D. 44.

12:24-25 As in a refrain, Luke again refers to the vital power of the Gospel. With the return of Barnabas and Saul from Antioch, a new page begins.

12:25 *Mark:* see note on Acts 12:12.

13:1—18:22 Under the impulse of the Spirit and the call of events, the community of Jerusalem finds the main points of its internal fire; it has broken out of the Jewish world to spread the Gospel into the Gentile world. New communities have been founded in which the Spirit stirs up the same internal fire and strong missionary initiative. The cycle of Jerusalem ends with the establishment of the Church at Antioch (Acts 11:19-26). In the second cycle in Acts, this young Church is the point of departure and return for all the stories, replacing Jerusalem as the center for the spread of the Gospel. Henceforth, the action takes place outside of Palestine; the Church now exists independently of the temple and of Jewish life in the Holy Land.

According to the historians of the period, Antioch, a main communications center of the Mediterranean world, was a "hotbed of falsehood." Two missionary journeys take off from it: the first to Asia Minor (Acts 13:1—14:28), the second as far as Greece (Acts 15:36—18:23). We shall witness the encounter with quite different environments, from Oriental magic to Greek philosophy.

Paul will soon take the initiative in this missionary activity by means of the first two voyages ordinarily called missionary journeys of the Apostle. The Council of Jerusalem is called upon to officially resolve the problem in the community between converts from the Gentiles and converts from Judaism.

13:1—14:28 A missionary undertaking begins that will reach into the heart of Asia Minor. The story dwells at length on the outward journey; the return is told in a few verses, but makes clear that in the interim some Churches have been born that have their own life and personality. The Gospel will be addressed first of all to Jews and then directly to the Gentiles. Is Christianity a complete novelty or Judaism with a new face?

13:1-5 Events suggest the vitality of the community of Antioch, whose importance is also underlined by the list of people available. Paul and Barnabas are chosen to go on mission. The laying on of hands by the community here is not a communication of powers (as in Acts 6:6) but a confirmation of the inspiration of the Spirit.

13:4 *Seleucia:* this was Antioch's seaport, 16 miles to the west. *Cyprus:* the Gospel had already been preached there (see Acts 11:19f).

5 When they arrived in Salamis,* they pro-
claimed the word of God in the Jewish syna-
gogues, while John served as their assistant.[o]

**At Cyprus Facing a Proconsul and a
Magician.*** 6 When they had traveled through
the whole island as far as Paphos,* they
encountered a magician named Bar-Jesus,
who was a Jewish false prophet.[p] 7 He was
an attendant of the proconsul Sergius
Paulus, a learned man who had summoned
Barnabas and Saul because he wanted to
hear the word of God.[q] 8 However, the magi-
cian Elymas (for that is the translation of his
name) opposed them in an attempt to pre-
vent the proconsul's conversion to the faith.[r]

9 Then Saul, also known as Paul,* filled
with the Holy Spirit, looked intently at
Elymas 10 and said, "You offspring of the
devil, you enemy of righteousness, filled with
every kind of deceit and fraud, will you
never cease to pervert the straight paths of
the Lord?[s] 11 Now take note of how the hand
of the Lord will strike you. You will be blind,
and for a period of time you will not be
able to see the sun." Immediately, he was
enveloped in a dark mist, and he groped
about for someone to lead him by the hand.[t]
12 When the proconsul saw what had hap-
pened, he became a believer, having been
deeply impressed by the teaching of the
Lord.[u]

Paul's Arrival at Antioch in Pisidia. 13 * Paul
and his companions set sail from Paphos
and arrived at Perga* in Pamphylia. There,
John left them and returned to Jerusalem.[v]
14 Then they went on from Perga and
arrived at Antioch* in Pisidia.

On the Sabbath, they went into the syna-
gogue and took their seats.[w] 15 After the
readings from the Law and the Prophets,
the officials of the synagogue sent this mes-
sage to them, "Brethren, if you have any
words of exhortation to offer to the people,
please do so."[x]

Paul's Speech in the Synagogue. 16 Then
Paul stood up, motioned with his hand, and
began to speak, saying, "Listen, men of
Israel and you others who fear God!* 17 The
God of this people Israel chose our ancestors
and made our people great while they were
dwelling as foreigners in Egypt. With uplift-
ed arm, he led them out,[y] 18 and for about
forty years he endured their conduct in the
desert.[z]

19 "After he had destroyed seven nations in
the land of Canaan, he gave their land to his
people as their inheritance[a] 20 at the end of
about four hundred and fifty years.* After
that, he appointed judges for them until the
time of the prophet Samuel.[b]

21 "Then they asked for a king, and God
gave them Saul, son of Kish, a man from the
tribe of Benjamin. He reigned for forty
years,[c] 22 after which God removed him and
raised up David as their king. In commend-
ing him, he said, 'I have found David, the son
of Jesse, to be a man after my own heart. He
will carry out my every wish.'[d]

23 "From this man's descendants, God has
fulfilled his promise by raising up for Israel
a savior, Jesus.[e] 24 Prior to his coming, John
had already proclaimed a baptism of repen-
tance to all the people of Israel.[f] 25 And as
John was nearing the end of his work, he
said, 'I am not the one you believe me to be.
One is coming after me whose sandals I am
not worthy to unfasten.'[g]

o Acts 9:20; Heb 4:12.—p Acts 8:9.—q Acts 18:12; 19:38.—r Acts 8:9; Isa 30:11.—s Hos 14:9; Mt 13:38; Jn 8:44.—t Ex 9:3; 1 Sam 5:6-7; Ps 32:4.—u Lk 4:32.—v Acts 15:38.—w Acts 14:19, 21.—x Acts 15:21.—y Ex 6:6, 7; Deut 7:6-8.—z Ex 16:1, 35; Num 14:34; Ps 95:10.—a Deut 7:1; Jos 14:1-2; Ps 78:55.—b Acts 3:24; Gen 15:13; Jdg 2:16; 1 Sam 3:20.—c 1 Sam 8:5, 19; 9:16; 10:1, 20-21, 24; 11:15.—d 1 Sam 13:14; 16:12-13; Ps 89:20-21; Isa 44:28; Jer 3:15.—e Isa 11:1; Mt 1:21.—f Mt 3:1-2; Mk 1:4-5; Lk 3:2-3.—g Acts 20:24; Mt 3:11; Mk 1:7; Lk 3:16; Jn 1:20, 27.

13:5 *Salamis:* a town on the east coast of Cyprus.

13:6-12 The problem preoccupying some spiritual authorities once again comes to the fore: What is Christianity's relation to magic? Luke once again dissociates the Church from the magical arts practiced at the time (see Acts 8:18-24).

13:6 *Paphos:* a town 100 miles west of Salamis.

13:9 *Known as Paul:* Saul drops his Hebrew name and uses his Roman name, Paul, to show that he has entered fully into his mission to the world of the "nations." Henceforth, he will also be mentioned before Barnabas, his companion in missionary activity.

13:13-52 Christianity came into being within Judaism and brought the history of Israel to its conclusion. Therefore, the proclamation of the word must follow that same order: it is to be addressed first to the Jews, then to the Gentiles (see Acts 11:19-20). Only at the end of Acts will the mission be aimed directly at the Gentiles without first passing through the synagogue (see Acts 28:28). This sermon of Paul is delivered to Jews and follows the pattern of early Christian preaching that has already characterized the discourses of Peter.

13:13 *Perga:* the capital of Pamphylia, which was a province of Asia Minor, 80 miles long and 20 miles wide, between the provinces of Lycia and Cilicia on the southern coast of Asia Minor.

13:14 *Antioch:* a city 110 miles from Perga strategically situated for commerce, which was a Roman colony and had a large Jewish population. *Pisidia:* a district north of Pamphylia that was 120 miles long and 50 miles wide.

13:16 *Others who fear God:* Gentiles who accept the beliefs and moral principles of Judaism without becoming members of the Jewish people by circumcision.

13:20 *Four hundred and fifty years:* this could also refer to the period of the Judges until the time of the prophet Samuel.

26 "Brethren, children of the family of
Abraham, and those others among you who
fear God, we are the ones to whom this mes-
sage of salvation has been sent.[h] 27 The peo-
ple of Jerusalem and their leaders failed to
recognize Jesus or to understand the words
of the Prophets that are read on every
Sabbath, and they fulfilled those prophecies
by condemning him.[i] 28 Even though they
found no basis to justify his execution, they
asked Pilate to have him killed.[j]

29 "When they had carried out everything
that was written about him, they took him
down from the tree and placed him in a
tomb.[k] 30 However, God raised him from the
dead,[l] 31 and over a period of many days he
appeared to those who had come up with
him from Galilee to Jerusalem. These are
now his witnesses before the people.[m]

32 "We have come here to proclaim to you
the good news—what God promised to our
ancestors[n] 33 he has fulfilled for us, their
children, by raising Jesus up as it is written
in the second psalm:

'You are my Son;
this day I have begotten you.'[o]

34 "God raised him from the dead, never
to be subjected to corruption. He declares it
in these words, 'To you I will give the bless-
ings promised to David.'[p] 35 And he also says
in another psalm, 'You will not allow your
Holy One to suffer corruption.'[q] 36 When
David had served God's purposes during his
lifetime, he fell asleep, and he was buried
with his ancestors, and he saw corruption.[r]
37 However, the one whom God raised up did
not see corruption.

38 "You must understand, brethren, that it
is through him that forgiveness of sins is
being proclaimed to you.[s] 39 All those who
believe are justified from all the things from
which they could not be justified by the Law
of Moses.[t] 40 Beware, then, lest what the
Prophets have foretold will happen to you:

41 'Look carefully, you scoffers!
Be amazed and perish!
For I am doing a work in your days
that you will never believe
even if someone tells you.' "[u]

42 As they were leaving the synagogue, the
people urged them to speak further on these
subjects on the following Sabbath. 43 After
the congregation had dispersed, many Jews
and devout converts to Judaism followed
Paul and Barnabas, who spoke to them and
urged them to remain faithful to the grace
of God.[v]

Paul's Speech to the Gentiles. 44 On the next
Sabbath, almost the entire city gathered to
hear the word of the Lord. 45 When the Jews
saw the crowds, they were filled with jeal-
ousy, and with blasphemy they contradicted
whatever Paul said.[w] 46 Then both Paul and
Barnabas spoke out boldly, saying, "It was
necessary that the word of God should be
proclaimed to you first. However, since you
have rejected it and judge yourselves to be
unworthy of eternal life, we now turn to the
Gentiles.[x] 47 For so has the Lord command-
ed us to do, saying,

'I have made you a light for the Gentiles
so that you may bring salvation
to the farthest corners of the earth.' "[y]

48 When the Gentiles heard this, they were
delighted, and they praised the word of the
Lord. All those who were destined for eter-
nal life became believers.[z] 49 Thus, the word
of the Lord continued to spread throughout
the entire region.

50 However, the Jews incited the devout
women of the upper classes and the leading
men of the city. As a result, a campaign of
persecution was stirred up against Paul and
Barnabas, and they were driven out of the
territory. 51 And so they shook the dust from
their feet in protest against them and went
to Iconium.*[a] 52 And the disciples were
filled with joy and with the Holy Spirit.[b]

CHAPTER 14

Jews and Gentiles at Iconium.* 1 In Iconium,
they went into the Jewish synagogue and

h Acts 4:12; 28:28.—i Acts 3:17.—j Acts 3:14; Mt 27:20, 22-23; Mk 15:13-14; Lk 23:4, 14-15, 21-23; Jn 19:4-6, 15.—k Mt 27:59-60; Mk 15:46; Lk 18:31; 23:53; Jn 19:38, 41-42.—l Acts 2:24, 32; 3:15; 4:10; 17:31.—m Acts 1:3, 8; 10:39, 41; Mt 28:8-10, 16-20; Mk 16:9, 12-20; Lk 24:13-53; Jn 20:11-29; 21:1-23.—n Acts 5:42; Isa 40:9; Rom 1:2.—o Ps 2:7.—p Isa 55:3.—q Acts 2:27; Ps 16:10.—r Acts 2:29; 2 Sam 7:12; 1 Ki 2:10.—s Acts 2:38.—t Rom 1:16; 3:20.—u Hab 1:5.—v Acts 11:23.—w Acts 18:6; 1 Thes 2:14; 1 Pet 4:4; Jude 10.—x Acts 3:26; Mt 21:41; Rom 1:16.—y Isa 49:6; Jn 8:12.—z Acts 8:25; 19:10.—a Acts 14:1, 19; Mt 10:14; Mk 6:11; Lk 9:5; 10:11; 2 Tim 3:11.—b Acts 2:46.

13:51 *Iconium:* an important crossroads and center of agriculture in the province of Galatia.

14:1-7 A good number of both Jews and Gentiles accept the Gospel. But the crucial question is this: Since the Gospel is so anchored in the movement of the history of Israel, is it not a perversion to open the Church to the Gentiles? And the answer is: No. It is a new message: that the word of God is for everyone.

spoke so effectively that a great number of both Jews and Greeks became believers. [c] [2] However, the Jews who refused to believe stirred up the Gentiles and poisoned their minds against the brethren. [d] [3] Therefore, they stayed there for a considerable period of time, speaking boldly on behalf of the Lord, who confirmed the message of his grace by enabling them to work signs and wonders. [e]

[4] However, the people in the city were divided, some siding with the Jews, others with the apostles. [f] [5] Eventually, a plot was hatched by both the Gentiles and the Jews, together with their leaders, to attack and stone them. [g] [6] When they became aware of this, they fled to the Lycaonian cities * of Lystra and Derbe and to the surrounding area. [h] [7] There they preached the good news. [i]

At Lystra Paul and Barnabas Are Taken for Gods.* [8] At Lystra, there was a man who was crippled. Lame from birth, he had never once been able to walk. [j] [9] He listened to Paul speaking. Paul looked intently at him, and, seeing that he had the faith to be healed, [k] [10] called out to him in a loud voice, "Stand up on your feet." The man sprang up and began to walk. [l]

[11] * When the crowds saw what Paul had done, they shouted in Lycaonian, "The gods have come down to us in human form!" [m] [12] They called Barnabas Zeus, and since Paul was the chief speaker, they called him Hermes. [n] [13] And the priest of Zeus, who was on the outskirts of the city, brought oxen and garlands to the gates, since he and the people intended to offer sacrifice.

[14] However, when the apostles Barnabas and Paul learned about this, they tore their clothes * and rushed into the crowd, shouting, [15] "Men, why are you doing this? We are only human beings, just like you. We proclaim to you the good news so that you may turn from these idols to the living God who made heaven and earth and the sea and all that is in them. [o]

[16] "In the past, God allowed all the Gentiles to go their own way. [p] [17] However, even then he did not leave you without a witness in doing good, for he sends you rain from heaven and crops in their seasons, and he provides you with food and fills your hearts with joy." [q] [18] Yet, even with these words, they were barely able to prevent the crowds from offering sacrifice to them.

End of the First Mission.* [19] [r] Shortly thereafter, some Jews arrived on the scene from Antioch and Iconium, and they won over the crowds. They stoned Paul and dragged him outside the town, believing that he was dead. [20] But when the disciples gathered around him, he got up and entered the city. On the next day, he and Barnabas departed for Derbe.

[21] After they had proclaimed the good news in that city and gained a considerable number of disciples, they returned to Lystra and then moved on to Iconium and Antioch. [22] They strengthened the disciples and encouraged them to persevere in the faith, saying, "It is necessary for us to undergo many hardships in order to enter the kingdom of God." [s] [23] In each Church, they appointed presbyters for them, and with prayer and fasting they commended them to the Lord in whom they had come to believe. [t]

c Acts 13:5.—d 1 Thes 2:14.—e Mk 16:17-20.—f Acts 17:4-5.—g 2 Tim 3:11.—h Mt 10:23.—i Acts 16:10.—j Acts 3:2.—k Mt 9:28-29.—l Acts 3:8; Ezek 2:1.—m Acts 8:10; 28:6.—n Ex 7:1.—o Acts 3:12; 10:26; Ex 20:11; 1 Sam 12:21; Ps 146:6; 1 Thes 1:9; Rev 14:7.—p Acts 17:30; Ps 81:13; Mic 4:5.—q Deut 11:14; Ps 65:11; Wis 13:1; Rom 1:20.—r 19-20: Acts 13:45; 2 Cor 11:25; 2 Tim 3:11.—s Acts 11:23; Mt 10:22; Jn 16:33; 1 Thes 3:3.—t Acts 20:32.

14:6 *Lycaonian cities:* Lycaonia was a district east of Pisidia, north of the Taurus Mountains, and part of the Roman province of Galatia. *Lystra:* a Roman colony about 20 miles from Iconium and 130 miles from Antioch. *Derbe:* a town about 60 miles from Lystra.

14:8-18 A new problem arises for the Church: the kind of reaction shown here by a crowd of rural Gentiles, who regard the two apostles as divinities. Peter had already raised up Cornelius when the latter knelt before him (Acts 10:25). The sermon here, the first one on the Gospel to Gentiles, is a fragment. It is to be completed in light of the more fully developed discourse in Acts 17:22-31.

When addressed to Gentiles, the *kerygma* was profoundly different than when addressed to Jews. It urged the abandonment of dead idols in order to turn to the living God. Proofs were not taken from Scripture; rather the emphasis was on God manifesting himself to all human beings through the cycles of life and of the world.

14:11-13 The strange reaction of the people of Lystra to the cure performed by Paul is a result of local folklore that told tales of the gods coming to earth without being recognized. Struck by the deed performed, the people believe that the gods—in the guise of Zeus and Hermes—have visited again in the form of these two wonderworkers. Zeus was the chief of the gods and patron of the city, and Hermes was a son of Zeus and messenger of the gods (like the Roman Mercury).

14:14 *Tore their clothes:* an expression of horror and revulsion at someone's blasphemy (see Mt 26:65).

14:19-28 The Gospel of Jesus has been planted in Asia Minor as a force of life. On the return of Paul and Barnabas to Antioch, the first movement of the community is to gather to hear what God has helped them to accomplish, and to give thanks, as was done on Peter's return to Jerusalem (Acts 11:18). The Christian community in Antioch lives the good news of Jesus.

24 Then they passed through Pisidia and
came to Pamphylia. 25 After proclaiming the
word at Perga, they went down to Attalia,*
26 and from there they sailed to Antioch,*
where they had been commended to the
grace of God for the work that they had
completed.[u] 27 When they arrived, they
called the church together and related all
that God had accomplished through them
and how he had opened the door of faith to
the Gentiles.[v] 28 And they stayed there with
the disciples for some time.

CHAPTER 15

B: The Council of Jerusalem*

The Question of Circumcision. 1 [w] Some men
who had come down from Judea were teach-
ing the brethren, "Unless you are circum-
cised in accordance with the tradition of
Moses, you cannot be saved."[x] 2 As a result,
Paul and Barnabas engaged in a lengthy and
acrimonious debate with them, and finally it
was decided that Paul and Barnabas and
some of the others should go up to
Jerusalem to discuss this question with the
apostles and the elders.

3 So the church sent them on their journey;
and as they passed through Phoenicia and
Samaria, they reported how the Gentiles had
been converted, and this news was received
with great joy by all the brethren.[y] 4 When
they arrived in Jerusalem, they were wel-
comed by the Church and by the apostles
and the elders, and they gave a report of all
that God had accomplished through them.
5 But some from the group of Pharisees who
had become believers stood up and declared,
"It is necessary for the Gentiles to be cir-
cumcised and ordered to observe the Law of
Moses."[z]

Salvation through the Grace of Christ. 6 The
apostles and the elders convened to consid-
er this matter. 7 After a long period of
debate, Peter stood up to address them.
"Brethren," he said, "you are well aware that
in the early days God made his choice
among you that it would be through my
mouth that the Gentiles would hear the
message of the gospel and become believ-
ers.[a] 8 And God, who knows the heart, bore
witness by giving to them the Holy Spirit
just as he did to us.[b] 9 He made no distinc-
tion between them and us, for he purified
their hearts by faith.[c]

10 "Therefore, why are you determined to
try God's patience by laying a yoke on the
neck of the disciples that neither we nor our
ancestors have found easy to bear?[d] 11 On
the contrary, we believe that we are saved in
the same way as they are, through the grace
of the Lord Jesus."[e] 12 On hearing this, the
whole assembly fell silent, and they listened
as Barnabas and Paul described all the signs
and wonders that God had worked through
them among the Gentiles.[f]

James on Dietary Law. 13 After they had
finished speaking, James responded,
"Brethren, listen to me.[g] 14 Simon* has
related how God first looked favorably upon
the Gentiles and took from among them a
people for his name.[h] 15 This agrees with the
words of the Prophets, as it is written,

16 [i] 'After this I will return
    and rebuild the fallen tent of David.
From its ruins I will rebuild it
    and raise it up again,

u Acts 13:1-3.—v Acts 15:4, 12; 1 Cor 16:9; Col 4:3.—w 1-4: Gal 2:1-9.—x Gen 17:10; Lev 12:3; Gal 2:12; 5:2.—y Acts 11:19; 14:27.—z Acts 5:17; Mt 3:7.—a Acts 10:27-43.—b Acts 10:44-48.—c Acts 10:34-35; 11:12.—d Acts 5:9; Mt 23:4; Gal 5:1.—e Gal 2:16; 3:11; Eph 2:5-8.—f Acts 14:27; 21:19.—g Acts 12:17; 1 Cor 15:7; Gal 1:19.—h Deut 7:6; Rom 9:26; 2 Pet 1:1.—i 16-18: Am 9:11-12.

14:25 *Attalia:* the finest harbor on the coast of Pamphylia (see note on Acts 13:13).

14:26 *Antioch:* see note on Acts 11:19.

15:1-35 Christian communities have sprung up everywhere and include converts from both Jews and Gentiles. Radical problems have also arisen. The Church is clearly aware that she exists thanks only to the union of the two very contrasting portions of humanity of that time: Jews and Gentiles (Acts 15:14-17); this union should express the true reality of salvation in Jesus Christ. What we see here is an authentically theological inquiry, which consists in interpreting the experience of the apostles' encounters with the Gentiles and shedding light on them from the Scriptures.

As they reflect on the words of the Prophets, the members of the Council realize that the People of God, with which all the prophecies are concerned, exists in its full reality only at the moment when Gentile inquiry meets the original nucleus of Jewish testimonies. However, the practical decisions made are more cautious than the great theological statements. The Council asks for the observance of some elementary precepts that no Jew can abandon and that people know almost everywhere.

They are not to eat meat that has been sacrificed, because this would signify a fellowship with the divinities of the Gentiles (see 1 Cor 10:18-20). They are to avoid illegitimate unions ("unchastity"). They are not to eat flesh with blood in it ("[abstain] from the meat of animals that have been strangled, and from blood" [v. 20]), since according to the mind of the time blood was the sacred principle of life. The last two concern dietary laws (see Gen 9:14; Lev 3:17; Deut 12:16, 23; 1 Sam 14:34; Ezek 33:25).

All agree on these theological principles and their practical consequences. What a staggering sentence we read here for the first time, one that has passed from the Council to our own day: "It is the decision of the Holy Spirit and also our decision"!

15:14 *Simon:* the Greek text has "Simeon." "Simon," the Semitic name of Peter, is unusual but fits well on the lips of James, who was very attached to Jewish culture.

17 so that the rest of mankind may seek
the Lord,
as well as all the Gentiles whom I
have claimed as my own.
Thus says the Lord who is doing this,
18 as he made known from long ago.’ [j]

19 [k] “Therefore, I have come to this deci-
sion. We should not make things more diffi-
cult for the Gentiles who are turning to God.
20 [l] Rather, we should send a letter simply
instructing them to abstain from things that
have been polluted by idols, from unchastity,
from the meat of animals that have been
strangled, and from blood. 21 For in every
town for many generations, Moses has had
those who proclaim him, for he is read aloud
in the synagogues on every Sabbath.” [m]

The Letter of the Apostles. 22 Then the apos-
tles and the elders, with the approval of the
whole Church, decided to choose represen-
tatives from their number and to send them
with Paul and Barnabas to Antioch. They
sent Judas, who was called Barsabbas, * and
Silas, leaders in the community, [n] 23 to deliv-
er the following letter:

The apostles and the elders, your
brethren,
To the brethren in Antioch, Syria, and
Cilicia: [o]

Greetings.

24 It has come to our attention that
some of our number, without having
received any instructions from us, have
upset you with their teachings and dis-
turbed your peace of mind. [p] 25 There-
fore, we have decided unanimously to
choose representatives and send them
to you together with our beloved
Barnabas and Paul, 26 men who have
dedicated their lives to the name of our
Lord Jesus Christ. [q] 27 And so we are
sending Judas and Silas who will con-
firm these things by word of mouth.

28 [r] It is the decision of the Holy Spirit
and also our decision not to lay any fur-
ther burden upon you beyond these
essentials: [s] 29 you are to abstain from
food that has been sacrificed to idols,
from blood, from the meat of animals
that have been strangled, and from
unchastity. If you avoid these, you will
be doing what is right.

Farewell. [t]

Delegates at Antioch. 30 So the men
departed. When they reached Antioch,
they summoned together the entire con-
gregation and delivered the letter. 31 Upon
reading it, the community rejoiced at its
encouragement.

32 Judas and Silas, who were themselves
prophets, spoke at length to strengthen and
encourage the brethren. [u] 33 After they had
spent some time there, they were sent off in
peace by the brethren to return to those who
had sent them. [v] 34 [But Silas decided to
remain there.] * 35 Meanwhile, Paul and
Barnabas remained in Antioch, where,
along with many others, they taught and
proclaimed the word of God. [w]

C: Paul’s Second Missionary Journey*

Paul and Barnabas Separate.* 36 After some
time had passed, Paul said to Barnabas,
“Let us go back and visit the brethren in all
the cities where we proclaimed the word of
the Lord so that we can see how they are
progressing.” [x] 37 Barnabas wanted to take
John, also called Mark, with them, 38 but
Paul was adamant about not taking with
them a man who had deserted them in
Pamphylia and had not continued to share
in their work. [y]

39 As a result, there was such a sharp dis-
agreement that they parted company, and
Barnabas sailed to Cyprus with Mark.
40 However, Paul chose Silas and set out on
his journey, as the brethren commended
him to the grace of the Lord. [z]

j Isa 45:21.—k 19-20: Acts 15:28-29; 21:25.—l Gen 9:4; Lev 3:17; 17:10-14; Deut 12:16, 23; 1 Cor 8:7-13; Rev 2:14, 20.—m Acts 13:15; 2 Cor 3:14, 15.—n Acts 16:19, 25; 1 Pet 5:12.—o Acts 23:25-26; Jas 1:1.—p Gal 1:7; 5:10.—q Acts 9:23-25; 1 Cor 15:30.—r 28-29: Acts 15:19-20.—s Acts 1:8; 5:32.—t Acts 21:25; Gen 9:4; Lev 3:17; 17:10-14.—u Acts 11:27.—v 1 Sam 1:17; Mk 5:34; Lk 7:50.—w Acts 8:4.—x Acts 13:4, 13; 14:1, 6.—y Acts 13:13.—z Acts 11:23; 13:3.

15:22 *Barsabbas:* otherwise unknown. *Silas* is perhaps Paul’s coworker (from Acts 15:40 on).

15:34 This verse is lacking in the better manuscripts.

15:36—18:22 The planned visit to the communities already established turns into the “second missionary journey,” during which the Gospel enters into the daily life and culture of the Greco-Roman world.

15:36-40 The choice of members of the team is not without difficult but normal confrontations. Attitudes toward John Mark lie at the origin of the tension (see Acts 13:5; 13:13). Finally, two teams are formed for two different projects. Barnabas takes John with him, and Paul takes Silas.

Pastoral Visit to Asia Minor.* 41 He traveled through Syria and Cilicia, bringing strength to the churches. [a]

CHAPTER 16

1 He then moved on to Derbe and Lystra where there was a disciple named Timothy, * the son of a Jewish woman who had become a believer, but his father was a Greek. [b] 2 The brethren of Lystra and Iconium regarded him highly, [c] 3 and Paul decided to take him along. Therefore, he had him circumcised, because of the Jews in that region who all knew that his father was a Greek. [d]

4 As they traveled from town to town, they made known to the brethren there the decisions that had been reached by the apostles and the elders in Jerusalem for the people to obey. [e] 5 Day by day, the churches grew strong in the faith and increased in numbers. [f]

6 They traveled through the region of Phrygia * and Galatia because they had been told by the Holy Spirit not to preach the word in the province of Asia. [g] 7 When they approached the border of Mysia, they tried to go into Bithynia, but since the Spirit of Jesus did not allow them to do so, [h] 8 they passed through Mysia and came down to Troas. * [i]

Paul at Philippi.* 9 During the night, Paul had a vision in which a man of Macedonia appeared to him and pleaded with him, saying, "Cross over to Macedonia and help us." [j] 10 Once he had seen this vision, we immediately arranged for passage to Macedonia, convinced that God had summoned us to proclaim the good news to them. [k]

11 We set sail from Troas and made a straight run to Samothrace. * On the following day, we reached Neapolis, 12 and from there we sailed to Philippi, * a leading city in the district of Macedonia and a Roman colony. We spent some time in that city. [l]

13 On the Sabbath, we went outside the city gate alongside the river where we assumed there would be a place of prayer. We sat down and spoke to the women who had gathered there. 14 One of the women, whose name was Lydia, was a worshiper of God. She was from the city of Thyatira and a dealer in purple cloth. As she listened to us, the Lord opened her heart to accept what Paul was saying. [m] 15 When she and her household had been baptized, she urged us insistently, "If you regard me as a believer in the Lord, come and stay at my home." And she won us over. [n]

Paul Imprisoned at Philippi. 16 * On one occasion, as we were on our way to the place of prayer, we were met by a slave girl who was possessed by a spirit of divination and brought large profits to her owners by fortune-telling. [o] 17 She began to follow Paul and the rest of us, shouting, "These men are servants of the Most High God, and they have come to proclaim to you a way of salvation." 18 She kept doing this for many days,

a Acts 6:9; Lk 2:2.—b Acts 14:6; Rom 16:21; 1 Tim 1:2; 2 Tim 1:5.—c Phil 2:20.—d Gal 2:3.—e Acts 15:2.—f Acts 9:31; 14:22.—g Acts 2:10; 18:23; Gal 4:13-15.—h Rom 8:9; Phil 1:19; 1 Pet 1:11.—i Acts 20:5; 2 Cor 2:12.—j Acts 10:9-23; 19:21; 1 Thes 1:7, 8.—k Acts 14:7.—l Acts 20:6; 1 Thes 2:2.—m Lk 24:45; Rev 1:11.—n Acts 10:48.—o Deut 18:11; 1 Sam 28:3, 7.

15:41—16:8 Paul is opposed in principle to the circumcision of Christians of non-Jewish origin, but Timothy is a special case. If he were not circumcised, he could not speak in a synagogue and, in addition, he would have been regarded as an apostate, since his mother was Jewish; in the present missionary program, the first contacts were still taking place in the synagogues. The Spirit mysteriously intervenes to decide which direction the mission is to take. The whole Book of Acts is written in this perspective: the entire spread of the Gospel has been guided by the Spirit (see 1 Pet 1:12).

16:1 *Timothy:* a fellow worker of Paul, to whom the latter will address two Letters.

16:6 *Phrygia:* originally, this was the Hellenistic country of Phrygia, but it had now become part of the Roman provinces of Asia (which was only one-third of Asia Minor) and *Galatia.* Galatian Phrygia contained both Iconium and Antioch. *Asia* included Mysia, Lydia, and Caria in addition to parts of Phrygia.

16:8 *Troas:* a Roman colony and an important seaport 10 miles from the ancient city of Troy. Paul returned to it after his third missionary journey (Acts 20:5-12).

16:9-15 The account shifts to the first person, "we" (v. 10), as Luke will do three more times (Acts 20:5-15; 21:1-18; 27:1—28:16); these passages probably represent personal notes of Luke about events that he himself witnessed (see Lk 1:1). The listeners and different social groups are always addressed according to the same order. One tries at first to make the Jewish community change its mind and accept the fulfillment of the history of its people; then one turns to the Gentiles. At Philippi, Paul encounters some Jews who are influenced by Hellenism and devoted to commerce. The home of Lydia becomes the center of a community.

16:11 *Samothrace:* an island in the northeastern Aegean Sea. *Neapolis:* the seaport for Philippi, ten miles away.

16:12 *Philippi:* a city in eastern Macedonia. Some of its members establish a flourishing Christian community to which one of Paul's Letters will later be addressed.

16:16-40 Even when it is not stirred up by the reaction of the Jews, opposition to the Gospel arises out of a desire for ill-gotten gain. Some Jews at Ephesus claim Christianity advocates customs that as Roman citizens they cannot legally tolerate in the cities of the Empire.

The account of Paul's deliverance is centered above all on the transformation that takes place in the jailer. It is an account of conversion. Paul makes good use of his Roman citizenship to keep the field open for his future missionary activity (see Acts 22:19).

until Paul became very greatly troubled. He
turned and said to the spirit, "I command
you in the name of Jesus Christ to come out
of her." And the spirit came out of her
instantly. [p]

19 When her owners realized that their
hope of making money from her was gone,
they seized Paul and Silas and dragged them
into the marketplace before the authorities. [q]
20 They brought them before the magistrates
and said, "These men are causing a distur-
bance in our city. They are Jews, [r] 21 and they
are advocating practices that it is illegal for
us as Romans to adopt or follow." [s]

22 [t] The crowd joined in the attack against
them, and the magistrates had them
stripped and ordered them to be beaten.
23 After they had inflicted a severe beating on
them, they threw them into prison and
instructed the jailer to guard them closely.
24 Following these instructions, he put them
in the innermost cell and locked their feet in
the stocks. [u]

Paul Set Free. 25 About midnight, Paul and
Silas were praying and singing hymns of
praise to God, and the prisoners were listen-
ing to them. [v] 26 Suddenly, there was such a
huge earthquake that the very foundations
of the prison were shaken. At once, all the
doors flew open, and everyone's chains were
loosened. [w]

27 When the jailer awakened and saw all
the doors of the prison wide open, he drew
his sword, intending to kill himself, since he
assumed that the prisoners had escaped. [x]
28 However, Paul shouted in a loud voice,
"Do not harm yourself, for we are all here."

29 The jailer called for lights and, rushing
in, he threw himself before Paul and Silas,
trembling with fear. 30 Then he brought
them outside and said, "Sirs, what must I do
to be saved?" [y] 31 They answered, "Believe in
the Lord Jesus, and you will be saved, and so
too will your household." 32 After this, they
preached the word of the Lord to him and to
everyone in his house.

33 At that late hour of the night, the jailer
took them and bathed their wounds. Then he
and his entire family were baptized without
delay. [z] 34 Afterward, he brought them into
his house and set a meal before them, and
he and his entire household rejoiced over
their belief in God.

35 When it was daylight, the magistrates
sent police officers with the order, "Let those
men go." 36 The jailer reported the message
to Paul, saying, "The magistrates sent word
to let you go. Now you can come out and
depart in peace." 37 But Paul said to the offi-
cers, "We are Roman citizens. They gave us
a public beating and threw us into prison
without a trial. And now they are going to
release us secretly. Absolutely not! Let them
come in person and escort us out them-
selves." [a]

38 The officers reported Paul's words, and
the magistrates became alarmed when they
learned that those men were Roman citi-
zens. [b] 39 So they came and apologized to
them, then escorted them out and begged
them to leave the city. [c] 40 After emerging
from the prison, they went to Lydia's home,
where they met the brethren and spoke
words of encouragement to them. Then they
departed.

CHAPTER 17

Paul in Thessalonica. 1 * After they had
passed through Amphipolis and Apollonia,
they reached Thessalonica * where there was
a Jewish synagogue. [d] 2 Following his usual
practice, Paul went in, and for three
Sabbaths he argued with them from the
Scriptures, [e] 3 explaining and proving that it
was necessary for the Christ to suffer and
rise from the dead. "And the Christ," he
said, "is this Jesus whom I am proclaiming
to you." [f] 4 Some of them were convinced

p Mk 1:25-26; 16:17.—q Acts 19:25-26; Jas 2:6.—r Acts 17:6.—s Est 3:8.—t 22-23: 2 Cor 6:5; 11:25; Phil 1:30; 1 Thes 2:2.—u Job 13:27; Jer 20:2-3.—v Ps 119:55, 62; Col 3:16.—w Acts 4:31.—x Acts 12:19.—y Acts 2:37.—z Acts 1:5f; 8:36, 38.—a Acts 22:25-29.—b Acts 22:29.—c Mt 8:34; Lk 8:37.—d 1 Thes 2:1-2; 2 Tim 4:10.—e Acts 8:35; 18:28.—f Acts 3:18; Lk 24:25-26, 46.

17:1-15 Jewish groups resent the rise of Christian communities as a rival enterprise and a risk for their peaceful establishment in the cities of the Empire—something that is always precarious. Unless the Jews accept Jesus as the fulfillment of the Scriptures, they can do nothing but be opposed to such communities.

The community of the Thessalonians will later receive the first two Letters written by Paul, which enable us to glimpse the fervor and anxieties of a young Church. The substance of Paul's preaching at Thessalonica is summed up in verse 3: there we find the general structure of the discourses of Acts. A woman once again appears in a new role (Acts 17:12; 18:2) and is even named for her own sake, with no reference to a man (Acts 17:34). Christian lay people suffer in the name of the apostles. The opposition they encounter is on the juridical level. The confrontation with the Roman world will take place on a political level, where Roman culture and civilization are better expressed.

17:1 *Amphipolis . . . Thessalonica:* cities on the so-called Egnatian Way, which ran east and west through Greece and also included Philippi. Thessalonica was the capital of Macedonia with a population of more than 200,000, and it lay about 100 miles from Philippi.

and joined Paul and Silas, as did a great many God-fearing Greeks as well as not a few prominent women.

5 However, the Jews became jealous, and they recruited some ruffians from the marketplace, formed a mob, and soon had the city in an uproar. They stormed Jason's house, intending to bring them out before the crowd.[g] 6 And when they could not find them there, they dragged Jason and some of the brethren before the city magistrates, shouting, "These people who have been causing trouble all over the world have come here also,[h] 7 and Jason has given them shelter. They are all acting in opposition to the decrees of Caesar, claiming that there is another king named Jesus."[i] 8 Upon hearing this, the mob and the magistrates were greatly agitated. 9 They then took a bond from Jason and the others before releasing them.

Paul in Beroea. 10 As soon as it got dark, the brethren sent Paul and Silas away to Beroea. Upon their arrival, they immediately went to the Jewish synagogue.[j] 11 The people there were more receptive than those in Thessalonica. They received the word with great eagerness, and they examined the Scriptures every day to check whether these things were so.[k] 12 Many of them became believers, as did a considerable number of influential Greek women and men.

13 However, when the Jews of Thessalonica learned that the word of God was being proclaimed by Paul in Beroea, they followed him there to cause trouble and stir up the crowds.[l] 14 Therefore, the brethren immediately sent Paul on his way to the coast, while Silas and Timothy remained behind.[m] 15 After Paul's escorts brought him as far as Athens, they returned with instructions for Silas and Timothy to join him as soon as possible.[n]

Paul in Athens.* 16 While Paul was waiting for them in Athens, he was outraged to note that the city was full of idols. 17 Therefore, he debated in the synagogue with the Jews and God-fearing Gentiles, and also in the city square with whoever chanced to be there. 18 Even a few Epicurean and Stoic philosophers* argued with him. Some asked, "What is this man babbling about?" Others said, "Apparently, he is here to promote foreign deities," because he was preaching about Jesus and the resurrection.

19 Therefore, they took him and brought him to the Areopagus* and asked him, "Can you explain to us what this new doctrine is that you are teaching?[o] 20 You are presenting strange ideas to us, and we would like to find out what they all mean."[p] 21 The major pastime of the Athenians and the foreigners living there was to spend their time telling or listening to the latest ideas.

Paul's Speech at the Areopagus. 22 * Then Paul stood before them in the Areopagus and said: "Men of Athens, I have seen how religious you are. 23 For as I walked around, looking carefully at your shrines, I noticed among them an altar with the inscription, 'To an Unknown God.' What, therefore, you worship as unknown, I now proclaim to you.[q]

24 "The God who made the world and everything in it, the Lord of heaven and earth, does not dwell in shrines made by human hands.[r] 25 Nor is he served by human hands as though he were in need of anything.

g Rom 16:21; 1 Thes 2:16.—h Acts 16:20; 24:5.—i Lk 23:2; Jn 19:12-15.—j Acts 20:4.—k Deut 29:28; Jn 5:39.—l Acts 13:50; 14:2.—m 1 Thes 3:1-2.—n Acts 18:1, 5.—o Mk 1:27; 1 Cor 1:22.—p Acts 28:22.—q Jn 4:22.—r Acts 7:48-50; 14:15; Gen 1:1; Deut 10:14; 1 Ki 8:27; Isa 42:5; Mt 11:25.

17:16-21 Paul reaches Athens, which some 500 years before had been at the height of its glory in philosophy, literature, and art. In the twilight of its fame, it still housed a highly regarded university and was a force in philosophical thinking, as evidenced by the Epicureans and Stoics who engage Paul in discussion. He is led to the Areopagus, before a body that functioned in matters pertaining to religion, culture, and education. They evaluate him as the promoter of a new religion.

17:18 *Epicurean and Stoic philosophers:* followers of the two prevailing philosophical systems. The Epicureans follow Epicurus (342–271 B.C.) in abandoning the search for pure truth by reason as hopeless and giving themselves over to present pleasures. The Stoics follow Zeno and Chrysippius (3rd century B.C.) and embrace a philosophy of self-repression because of human self-sufficiency. *What is this man babbling about?:* it seems to be a way of saying that the speaker is an eclectic, gathering ideas from all sources. *Jesus and the resurrection:* the Athenians misconstrue Paul's words, thinking that he is speaking about Jesus and the goddess Anastasis, which means resurrection.

17:19 *Areopagus:* this may refer either to a hill of Ares west of the Acropolis or to the Council of Athens that once met on it.

17:22-31 Paul's speech is a masterpiece of judicious adaptability to the Greek mentality. Yet he and his hearers are on different wave lengths. He preaches a way of life and calls for a faith while the cultured Greeks seek only a truth that satisfies the mind. A crucified and resurrected God can make no impact on them, and they take Paul for a buffoon (v. 14). Others think of him as a fanatic worshiper of new gods: "Jesus" and "Resurrection," his spouse (v. 18). Paul first sets forth his theodicy: there is one God, who is spiritual, personal, and provident (vv. 22-26). Then he cites their poets, interpreting them in a monotheistic fashion (vv. 27-30). Finally, his Christology is very brief (v. 31), because of the uproar provoked by the subject of the resurrection, which was openly rejected by all the Hellenistic schools of philosophy.

Rather, it is he who gives to everyone life and
breath and all other things.[s] 26 From one
ancestor,* he created all peoples to occupy
the entire earth, and he decreed their
appointed times and the boundaries of
where they would live.[t]

27 "He did all this so that people might
seek God in the hope that by groping for him
they might find him, even though indeed he
is not far from any one of us.[u] 28 For 'In him
we live and move and have our being.'* As
even your own poets have said, 'We are all
his offspring.'[v]

29 "Since we are God's offspring, we ought
not to think that the deity is like an image of
gold or silver or stone, fashioned by human
art and imagination.[w] 30 God has over-
looked the times of human ignorance, but
now he commands people everywhere to
repent,[x] 31 because he has fixed a day on
which he will judge the world with justice by
a man whom he has appointed. He has given
public confirmation of this to all by raising
him from the dead."[y]

32 When they heard about the resurrection
of the dead, some scoffed, but others said,
"We should like to hear you speak further on
this subject at another time." 33 After that,
Paul left them. 34 However, some of them
joined him and became believers, including
Dionysius* the Areopagite, and a woman
named Damaris, as well as some others.

CHAPTER 18

Paul in Corinth. 1 * At that point, Paul
departed from Athens and moved on to
Corinth.[z] 2 There he met a Jew named
Aquila, a native of Pontus, who had
recently come from Italy with his wife
Priscilla because Claudius* had ordered
all Jews to leave Rome. He went to visit
them,[a] 3 and because they were tentmak-
ers just as he was, he stayed with them and
they worked together.*[b] 4 Every Sabbath,
he entered into discussions in the syna-
gogue, attempting to convert both Jews
and Greeks.

5 After Silas and Timothy arrived from
Macedonia, Paul devoted all his efforts to
preaching the word, testifying to the Jews
that Jesus was the Christ.[c] 6 When they
opposed him and began to hurl insults, he
shook out his garments in protest and said
to them, "Your blood be on your own heads!
I have a clear conscience. From now on, I
will go to the Gentiles."[d]

7 With that, he left and went to the house of
a man named Titus Justus, a worshiper of
God, who lived next door to the synagogue.[e]
8 Crispus, the leader of the synagogue, became
a believer in the Lord along with his entire
household. Many Corinthians who heard
Paul came to believe and were baptized.[f]

9 [g] One night, the Lord appeared to Paul in
a vision* and said, "Do not be afraid.
Continue with your preaching, and do not
be silent, 10 for I am with you. No one will
attack you or try to harm you, for there are
many in this city who are my people." 11 And
so he remained there for eighteen months,
teaching the word of God to them.

Accusations before Gallio. 12 However, when
Gallio became proconsul of Achaia, the Jews
made a concerted attack on Paul and
brought him before the tribunal,[h] 13 saying,

s Gen 2:7; Ps 50:10-12.—t Deut 32:8; Job 12:23.—u Deut 4:7; Wis 13:6; Isa 55:6; Jer 23:23; Rom 1:19.—v Deut 30:20; Job 12:10; Dan 5:23; Jn 1:12.—w Acts 19:26; Isa 40:18-20; 44:10-17; Rom 1:22-23.—x Acts 14:16; Rom 3:25; Tit 2:11-12.—y Acts 10:42; 24:25; Pss 9:8; 96:13.—z Acts 19:1; 1 Cor 1:2; 2 Tim 4:20.—a Rom 16:3; 1 Cor 16:19.—b Acts 20:34; 1 Cor 4:12; 1 Thes 2:9.—c Acts 15:22; 1 Thes 3:6.—d Acts 13:51; 28:28; 2 Sam 1:16; Neh 5:13; Ezek 33:4; Mt 10:14; 27:24-25; Mk 6:11; Lk 9:5; 10:10-11.—e Acts 13:46-47; 16:14.—f 1 Cor 1:14.—g 9-10: Jer 1:8.—h Acts 13:7, 8; Rom 15:26; 1 Thes 2:14.

17:26 *From one ancestor:* or "from one blood." *Decreed their appointed times:* or "decreed limits to their existence."

17:28 *In him we live and move and have our being:* a citation from the writings of the Cretan poet Epimenides (6th century B.C.). *We are all his offspring:* a citation from the Cilician poet Aratus (c. 315–240) as well as from Cleanthes (331–233 B.C.). Paul also quotes Greek poets in 1 Cor 15:33 and Tit 1:12.

17:34 *Dionysius:* the passage suggests that this individual should be known to the readers. A theologian of the 5th or 6th century published mystical writings under this name. Some claim that this Pseudo-Dionysius (Denis) was the first bishop of Paris in the 3rd century.

18:1-17 These passages deal with one of Paul's most important activities. The great city of Corinth was at that time a cosmopolitan place and had a rather bad reputation due to the erotic cult of the goddess Aphrodite.

With its reference to Gallio in verse 12, the account provides us with a sure chronological clue to the events reported, since an inscription enables us to pinpoint the proconsulate of Gallio, a brother of Seneca, to the years A.D. 51–52 or 52–53.

18:2 *Claudius:* Emperor of Rome from A.D. 41 to 54. He expelled the Jews from Rome because of "their continuous tumults instigated by *Chrestus,*" a common misspelling for "Christ." Needless to say, the tumults were instigated not *by* Christ but by the differing opinions people held *about* him.

18:3 Paul was probably taught the trade of tentmaker in his youth, in accord with the Jewish custom of giving manual training to sons.

18:9 *In a vision:* Paul now glimpses in a vision (see Acts 23:11) the Lord whom he has already seen in a resurrected body at his conversion (see Acts 9:4-6; 1 Cor 15:8) and in the temple in ecstasy (see Acts 22:17-18).

"This man is persuading people to worship God in ways that are contrary to the Law."

[14] Just as Paul was about to refute them, Gallio said to the Jews, "If you were accusing this man of some crime or fraudulent act, O Jews, I would be more than willing to listen to your complaint. [15] But since your argument is about words and names and your own Law, settle it yourselves. I have no intention of making judgments about such matters."[i] [16] With that, he dismissed them from the tribunal. [17] Then they all attacked Sosthenes, the leader of the synagogue, and beat him in front of the tribunal. But Gallio remained unconcerned about their action.[j]

Return to Antioch in Pisidia.* [18] After he remained in Corinth for some considerable time, Paul took leave of the brethren and sailed for Syria, accompanied by Priscilla and Aquila. At Cenchreae, he had his hair cut because he had taken a vow.[k]

[19] When they reached Ephesus,* he left them there. He himself went into the synagogue and had discussions with the Jews.[l] [20] When they asked him to stay longer, he declined, [21] but on taking leave of them he promised, "I will return to you, if God wills." Then he set sail from Ephesus.[m] [22] When he landed at Caesarea, he went up and greeted the Church,* and then he went down to Antioch.

III: EPHESUS*

A: Paul's Third Missionary Journey*

Paul Strengthens the Churches. [23] After spending some time there, he departed and traveled through the regions of Galatia and Phrygia, strengthening all the disciples.[n]

Apollos.* [24] Meanwhile, a Jew named Apollos, a native of Alexandria and an eloquent speaker, came to Ephesus. He was well-versed in the Scriptures,[o] [25] and he had been instructed in the Way of the Lord. Filled with spiritual fervor, he spoke and taught accurately about Jesus, although he had experienced only the baptism of John.[p]

[26] He then began to speak boldly in the synagogue, but when Priscilla and Aquila heard him, they took him aside and explained to him more accurately the Way.[q] [27] And when he expressed a wish to cross over to Achaia, the brethren encouraged him and wrote to the disciples there, asking that they make him welcome. From the time of his arrival, he was of great help to those who by the grace of God had become believers. [28] For he vigorously refuted the Jews in public, establishing from the Scriptures that Jesus is the Christ.[r]

CHAPTER 19

Paul in Ephesus.* [1] While Apollos was in Corinth, Paul traveled through the interior regions and came to Ephesus, where he found some disciples.[s] [2] He said to them, "Did you receive the Holy Spirit when you became believers?" They replied, "No. We have not even heard that there is a Holy

i Acts 23:29; Jn 18:31.—j 1 Cor 1:1.—k Acts 21:24; Num 6:2, 5, 18; Rom 16:1.—l Acts 19:1; Rev 1:11.—m Rom 1:10; 1 Cor 4:19; Jas 4:15.—n Acts 2:10; 16:6.—o Acts 19:1; 1 Cor 1:12.—p Acts 9:2; Rom 12:11.—q Acts 19:3-5.—r Acts 8:35; 9:22.—s Acts 18:24.

18:18-22 After more than two and a half years of labor in Corinth, Paul embarks for Antioch. The Nazirite vow was a special consecration to God, usually lasting 30 days and taking the form of a special way of life (see Num 6:1-21).

Instead of reaching Antioch Paul lands at Ephesus, which will soon become the center of the following cycle of the Book. He leaves Priscilla and Aquila there, who will become the nucleus of a Christian community.

18:19 *Ephesus:* a leading city of Asia Minor and the capital of the province of Asia, where the temple of Artemis (Diana) was located.

18:22 *He went up and greeted the Church:* although this could refer to a congregation in Caesarea, the words "he went up" indicate that it was the Church at Jerusalem, which was about 2500 feet above sea level.

18:23—20:38 According to the author of Acts, Ephesus is the third center for the spread of God's word. The city was a great center of commerce, and in it the cultural and religious currents of the Greco-Roman world and the East came together. Paul remains there for more than two years, and it is thought that he there wrote the Letters to the Corinthians, the Philippians, and perhaps the Galatians. Later on, the Letter to the Ephesians, one of the imprisonment letters, would be addressed to this community.

The early Church was now encountering other religious currents (besides the Judaic), and non-Jewish life was coming to the fore. And the essence of the faith had to be brought out in the face of multiple cultural influences.

18:23—20:6 Paul remains at Syrian Antioch for some time, probably through the spring of 53, and then starts his third missionary journey. Setting out for Ephesus, some 1500 miles to the west, he revisits the Churches around Pisidian Antioch, Iconium, Lystra, and Derbe. The account of this third journey focuses on his work at Ephesus (Acts 19:1—20:1).

18:24-28 Apollos is a talented preacher who knows the Scriptures and instructs in the new Way of the Lord. He speaks and teaches accurately about Jesus, although he knows only of John's baptism. He too begins to express himself fearlessly in the synagogue. When Priscilla and Aquila hear him, they take him home and explain to him God's new Way in greater detail. Some scholars believe that he was the author of the Letter to the Hebrews.

19:1-10 The foundation of the Church of Ephesus takes place in the house of a Greek professor. In all likelihood, during this same period Paul's group established the nearby Churches, such as those of Colossae, Laodicea, and Hierapolis.

Spirit." [t] 3 He asked, "Then how were you baptized?" They answered, "With the baptism of John."

4 Paul said, "John baptized with the baptism of repentance, telling the people to believe in the one who was to come after him, that is, Jesus." [u] 5 On hearing this, they were baptized in the name of the Lord Jesus. [v] 6 When Paul had laid his hands on them, the Holy Spirit came upon them, and they spoke in tongues and prophesied. [w] 7 There were about twelve of them in all.

8 He then entered the synagogue, and during the next three months he spoke out fearlessly and argued persuasively about the kingdom of God. [x] 9 But some remained stubborn in their disbelief and began to malign the Way publicly. So he withdrew from them, taking the disciples with him, and began to hold daily discussions in the hall of Tyrannus. [y] 10 This continued for two years, with the result that all the residents of the province of Asia, both Jews and Greeks, heard the word of the Lord. [z]

New Encounter of the Church with Magic.* 11 So extraordinary were the wonders God worked through Paul [a] 12 that when handkerchiefs or aprons that had touched his skin were brought to the sick, they were cured of their diseases and the evil spirits came out of them. [b]

13 Then some itinerant Jewish exorcists used the name of the Lord Jesus over those possessed by evil spirits, saying, "I adjure you by the Jesus whom Paul proclaims." [c] 14 Seven sons of a Jewish leading priest named Sceva were among those who were doing this. 15 But the evil spirit responded, "Jesus I know, and Paul I know, but who are you?" 16 Then the man with the evil spirit sprang at them, overpowered them, and prevailed over them so violently that they fled out of the house battered and naked.

17 When this became known to all the residents of Ephesus, both Jews and Greeks, everyone was awestruck, and the name of the Lord Jesus came to be held in ever increasing honor. [d] 18 Moreover, many of those who had become believers came forward and openly confessed their deeds, 19 while a great number of those who practiced magic collected their books and burned them publicly. When the value of these books was calculated, it was found to come to fifty thousand silver pieces. * 20 In such ways did the word of the Lord spread ever more widely and successfully. [e]

Paul's Future Plans.* 21 After all this had been accomplished, Paul decided in the Spirit to visit Macedonia and Achaia and then return to Jerusalem. "And after I have been there," he said, "I must also visit Rome." [f] 22 Then he sent two of his assistants, Timothy and Erastus, to Macedonia, while he himself stayed a while longer in the province of Asia. [g]

The Riot of the Silversmiths. 23 About that time, a serious disturbance broke out concerning the Way. [h] 24 A man named Demetrius was a silversmith who crafted silver shrines of Artemis * that provided considerable employment for the craftsmen. 25 He called a meeting of these craftsmen and of those in similar trades, and addressed them: "As you men know, our prosperity depends upon this business. [i] 26 And as you can now see and hear, not only in Ephesus but also throughout most of the province of Asia this Paul has persuaded and turned away a considerable number of people by insisting that gods fashioned by human hands are not gods. [j]

t Jn 7:39.—u Acts 1:5; 11:16; 13:24-25; Mt 3:11; Mk 1:8; Lk 3:16; Jn 1:7.—v Acts 2:38.—w Acts 8:15-17; 10:44-46; 1 Tim 4:14.—x Acts 13:5, 46; 28:13.—y Acts 14:4.—z Acts 20:31.—a Acts 8:13.—b Acts 5:15-16; Lk 8:44-47.—c Mt 12:27; Mk 9:38; Lk 9:49.—d Acts 5:5, 11.—e Acts 6:7; 12:24.—f Acts 20:16, 22; 23:11; Rom 1:13; 15:22-32; 1 Cor 16:1-8.—g Acts 13:5; 2 Tim 4:20.—h Acts 9:2.—i Acts 16:16, 19-20.—j Acts 17:29; Deut 4:28; Ps 115:4; Isa 44:10-20; Jer 10:3-5.

19:11-20 Here we have a new account of miracles analogous to those of Peter (Acts 5:15); the Gospel changes one's life. Then the account becomes picturesque in reporting a new encounter with a milieu influenced by magic. From the Gospels, we know that there were Jewish exorcists (Mt 12:27) and that some even acted in the very name of Jesus (Mk 9:38; Lk 9:49). Those at Ephesus must have moved with ease in this city of superstition where books of magic proliferated. And the feeling is that since there is a new name circulating—that of Paul's Jesus—why not profit from that name so as to be up-to-date! However, once again we see the affirmation of the incompatibility between the magic enterprise and the Christian life. The Gospel will never be a secret act in the hands of sorcerers.

19:19 *Fifty thousand silver pieces* was an enormous sum, representing the wages for 50,000 days of work.

19:21-22 Luke announces the two stages that comprise the last part of Acts (21—28). He presents beforehand each cycle of new events in the course of the one that precedes.

19:24 *Artemis:* the Greek name for the Roman goddess Diana. However, Artemis also had the characteristics of Cybele, the mother goddess of fertility worshiped in Asia Minor. She was one of the most widely worshiped female deities in the Hellenistic world (see Acts 19:27), and her temple at Ephesus was known as one of the seven wonders of the ancient world.

27 “Therefore, we are facing a dangerous situation. Not only may our business be discredited, but it could also happen that the temple of the great goddess Artemis will become an object of scorn, and that she who is worshiped throughout the province of Asia and the entire world will be deprived of her greatness.”

28 When they heard this, they became enraged and began to shout, “Great is Artemis of the Ephesians!” 29 The entire city was in an uproar, and the people all rushed to the theater, dragging along with them Gaius and Aristarchus,* Macedonians who were Paul’s traveling companions.[k] 30 Paul wanted to appear before the crowd, but the disciples would not permit him to do so. 31 Even some officials of the province of Asia who were friendly to him sent him a message urging him not to venture into the theater.*

32 Meanwhile, some were shouting one thing, some another, for the assembly was in an uproar, and most of the people had no idea why they had all come together.[l] 33 Some of the crowd prompted Alexander, whom the Jews had pushed forward. Then Alexander motioned for silence and tried to offer some type of defense.[m] 34 However, as soon as the crowd recognized him to be a Jew, all of them shouted in unison for about two hours, “Great is Artemis of the Ephesians!”

35 Finally, the town clerk quieted the crowd and said, “Citizens of Ephesus, is there anyone who does not know that the city of the Ephesians is the guardian of the temple* of the great Artemis and of her statue that descended from heaven? 36 Since these things cannot be denied, you ought to remain calm and do nothing rash. 37 These men whom you have brought here are not temple robbers, nor have they uttered any blasphemy against our goddess.[n]

38 “Therefore, if Demetrius and his fellow artisans have a complaint against anyone, the courts are open, and proconsuls are available. Let them bring charges there against one another.[o] 39 If there are further charges to present, let these be settled in the lawful assembly. 40 As it is, we are in danger of being charged with rioting today. There is no reason for it, and we will be unable to offer any justification for this commotion.” 41 When he had said this, he dismissed the assembly.

CHAPTER 20

Journey to Macedonia and Greece. 1 * When the uproar was over, Paul sent for the disciples, and after encouraging them, he embraced them and set out on his journey to Macedonia.*[p] 2 As he traveled through those areas, he gave the believers much encouragement. Then he arrived in Greece, 3 where he stayed for three months.

Return to Troas. He was about to set sail for Syria when a plot against him was devised by the Jews, and so he decided to return by way of Macedonia.[q] 4 He was accompanied by Sopater son of Pyrrhus from Beroea, by Aristarchus and Secundus from Thessalonica, by Gaius from Derbe, and by Timothy, as well as by Tychicus and Trophimus from Asia.*[r] 5 They went ahead and were waiting for us in Troas.*[s] 6 We sailed from Philippi after the feast of Unleavened Bread, and five days later we joined them in Troas, where we stayed for seven days.

k Acts 20:4; Col 4:10; Philem 24.—l Acts 21:34.—m Acts 12:17; 13:16.—n Rom 2:22.—o Acts 13:7-8.—p Acts 11:26; 14:22; 1 Cor 16:1.—q Acts 9:23-24; 2 Cor 11:26; 1 Thes 2:14.—r Acts 19:29; Rom 16:21; Eph 6:21; Col 4:7.—s Acts 21:29; 2 Tim 4:20.

19:29 *Aristarchus:* later he traveled with Paul from Corinth to Jerusalem (Acts 20:3f) and again from Jerusalem to Rome (Acts 27:1f; Col 4:10).

19:31 The story mentions the sympathy Paul won from some officials of the province (“asiarchs,” “heads of Asia”). It also underscores the participation of lay believers in the struggle (vv. 29-30).

19:35 *Guardian of the temple:* a title given by Rome to cities that provided a temple for the cult of the Emperor. Ephesus was recognized as the provider of the temple of Artemis and of the cult of the Emperor. The statue of the goddess (425 feet long and 220 feet wide, with 127 marble columns 62 feet high and less than four feet apart) was thought of as having descended from heaven.

20:1-16 This departure constitutes an important moment as indicated by the fact that Luke inserts a list of Paul’s companions. Then he describes three brief journeys: one to Greece, to revisit the communities, especially that of Corinth, which had caused some trouble; the second to Troas; and the third to Miletus, on the return route to Jerusalem.

In connection with these journeys we discover new aspects of the life of the communities. The Eucharist, which had been mentioned at the beginning of Acts (2:46), is clearly referred to here: Christians came together on Sunday (“the first day of the week”) in order to “break bread,” after a lengthy hearing of the Gospel and a communal reflection on it. The raising of the boy is a sign of the presence of the Lord; through his Resurrection, life is possible in its fullness.

20:1 Paul had apparently been seeking to preach in Troas on his way to Macedonia, meet Titus at Troas with a report from Corinth (see 2 Cor 2:12f), and continue collecting the offering for Judea (see Rom 15:25-28; 1 Cor 16:1-4; 2 Cor 8:1—9:15).

20:4 These men have no doubt been assigned to accompany Paul and the collection for the needy in Judea (see 2 Cor 8:23).

20:5 Here begins the second so-called “we-section” of Acts (see note on Acts 16:9-15).

B: Paul's Witness and Testament*

Paul Raises Eutychus to Life. 7 On the first day of the week, when we gathered for the breaking of the bread, Paul spoke to the people, and because he was going to leave on the next day, he continued speaking until midnight.[t] 8 There were many lamps in the upper room where we were assembled,[u] 9 and a young man named Eutychus, who was sitting on the window ledge, became ever more drowsy as Paul talked on and on. Finally, overcome by sleep, he fell to the ground three floors below, and when they picked him up, he was dead.

10 Paul went down, threw himself upon him, and took him in his arms. "Do not be alarmed," he said. "He is still alive."*[v] 11 Then he went back upstairs and broke bread and ate. He went on to converse with them until dawn, at which time he left. 12 Meanwhile, they had taken the boy home, greatly relieved that he was alive.

Journey to Miletus. 13 We went on ahead to the ship and set sail for Assos, where we were to take Paul aboard, since he intended to continue his journey by land. 14 When he met us in Assos, we took him aboard and went to Mitylene.

15 We sailed from there, and on the following day we reached a point opposite Chios. A day later, we reached Samos; and the day after that, we came to Miletus.[w] 16 For Paul had decided to sail past Ephesus in order to avoid spending time in the province of Asia. He was eager to be in Jerusalem, if possible, on the day of Pentecost.

Paul's Farewell Speech at Miletus.* 17 From Miletus, he sent a message to Ephesus, summoning the elders of the Church. 18 When they came to him, he addressed them as follows:

"You yourselves know how I lived among you the whole time from the first day that I set foot in the province of Asia.[x] 19 I served the Lord with all humility and with tears, enduring the trials that befell me as a result of the intrigues of the Jews.[y] 20 I did not hesitate to tell you what was for your benefit as I proclaimed the word to you and taught you publicly as well as from house to house.[z] 21 I have attested to Jews and Gentiles alike about repentance before God and faith in our Lord Jesus.[a]

22 "And now, compelled by the Spirit, I am on my way to Jerusalem without knowing what will happen to me there, 23 except that in every city the Holy Spirit warns me that I will face imprisonment and hardships.[b] 24 As for me, I do not regard my life as of any value, only that I finish the race and complete the mission that I received from the Lord Jesus—to bear witness to the gospel of God's grace.[c]

25 "I have gone among you proclaiming the kingdom, but now I realize that none of you will ever see my face again. 26 Therefore, I solemnly declare to you this day that I am innocent of the blood of all of you,[d] 27 for I did not shrink from proclaiming to you the entire plan of God. 28 Keep watch over yourselves and over all the flock of which the Holy Spirit has made you overseers, and be shepherds of the Church of God that he purchased with the price of his own blood.[e]

29 "I know that after I have gone, savage wolves will come among you and will not spare the flock.[f] 30 Even from your own ranks men will come distorting the truth in order to entice the disciples to follow them.[g] 31 Therefore, be on your guard. Remember

t Acts 2:42; 1 Cor 16:2; Rev 1:10.—u Acts 1:13; 9:37.—v Acts 9:36-42; 1 Ki 17:17-24; 2 Ki 4:30-37; Mt 9:24; Mk 5:39; Lk 8:52.—w 2 Tim 4:20.—x Acts 18:19-21; 1 Thes 1:5.—y Ps 6:7; 2 Cor 1:8-9.—z Ps 40:11; Jer 26:2.—a Acts 18:5; Eph 1:15; Col 2:5.—b Acts 9:16; 21:4.—c Gal 1:1; 2 Tim 4:7; Tit 1:3.—d Ezek 3:17-19.—e Jn 21:15-17; 1 Pet 5:2.—f Ezek 34:5; Mt 7:15; Jn 10:12.—g Mt 7:15; 2 Pet 2:1-3; 1 Jn 2:18-19.

20:7-38 In this chapter, it is no longer a case of proclaiming the word or creating a Church; it is a moment of respite and retreat that clears up Paul's personal destiny and expresses the principal concerns for the development and perseverance of a Church. Paul is aware that he will never return (see Acts 21:14), and he envisages undergoing the same suffering as Christ. The Book of Acts will not recount his martyrdom, no more than it will enlighten us about Peter's martyrdom, for this Book is not intended to be a biography of the apostles. Its purpose is to make known the life of the Churches and the power of the Spirit who animates them, the great realities that ensure their development, their relationships and their unity. The communities are to find themselves devoted to one another, but with the Spirit (v. 28) and the living tradition that carries them along. The atmosphere recalls Christ's discourse after the Last Supper (Jn 14—16). Paul gives his testament.

20:10 Paul's action of throwing himself upon a boy thought to be dead recalls that of Elijah in raising the son of the widow of Zarephath (1 Ki 17:21) and that of Elisha in raising the son of the Shunammite (2 Ki 4:34). Thus, as Peter had raised Tabitha (Acts 9:40), so now Paul raises Eutychus.

20:17-38 This farewell scene is especially important for the history of the Church as an institution. Those whom Paul summons are the "elders" (in Greek: *presbyteroi,* whence our "priests"), whom he describes (v. 28) as "shepherds" and "overseers" (Greek: *episkopoi,* whence our "bishops"; see 1 Pet 2:25), i.e., as responsible for the spiritual nourishment, guidance, and protection of the People of God. This authority they receive not from the assembly of the faithful but from the Spirit.

Here, in substance, is the ecclesial structure in which we live today (although only later would a distinction be made between "presbyters" and "bishops").

that for three years I never ceased night and day to warn every one of you with tears.[h]

32 “And now I commend you to God and to the word of his grace that is able to build you up and give you your inheritance among all who are sanctified.[i] 33 I have never coveted anyone’s silver or gold or clothing.[j] 34 You are aware that I worked with my own hands to support myself and my companions.[k] 35 In all this, I have shown you that by such hard work we must help the weak, keeping in mind the words of the Lord Jesus who himself said, ‘It is more blessed to give than to receive.’ ” *[l]

36 When he had finished speaking, he knelt down and prayed with them.[m] 37 They were all weeping loudly as they embraced Paul and kissed him, 38 for they were deeply distressed at his words that they would never see his face again. Then they escorted him to the ship.[n]

IV: FROM JERUSALEM TO ROME*

CHAPTER 21

A: Last Journey to Jerusalem*

Arrival at Tyre. 1 When we * had finally torn ourselves away from them and set sail, we traveled directly to Cos, and the next day to Rhodes, and from there to Patara.[o] 2 There, we found a ship bound for Phoenicia, so we went on board and set sail.[p] 3 After sighting Cyprus, we passed by it on our left and sailed to Syria, landing at Tyre where the ship was to unload her cargo.

4 We sought out the disciples there and stayed with them for seven days. Through the Spirit, they advised Paul to abandon his plans to move on to Jerusalem.[q] 5 However, when our time with them was ended, we left and continued on our journey. All of them, including women and children, escorted us outside the city. Kneeling down on the beach, we prayed[r] 6 and then bid farewell to one another. Afterward, we boarded the ship and they returned home.

Arrival at Ptolemais and Caesarea. 7 We finished our voyage from Tyre and arrived at Ptolemais, where we greeted the brethren and stayed with them for one day. 8 On the next day, we left and came to Caesarea, where we went to the house of Philip the evangelist, who was one of the Seven, * and stayed with him.[s] 9 He had four unmarried daughters who possessed the gift of prophecy.[t]

10 After we had been there for several days, a prophet named Agabus arrived from Judea.[u] 11 He came up to us, took Paul’s belt, bound his own feet and hands with it, and said, “Thus says the Holy Spirit: ‘In this way the Jews in Jerusalem will bind the owner of this belt, and they will hand him over to the Gentiles.’ ”[v]

12 When we heard this, we joined with the people who lived there in begging Paul not to go up to Jerusalem. 13 Then Paul replied, “What are you doing, weeping and breaking my heart? For I am ready not only to be bound but even to die in Jerusalem for the name of the Lord Jesus.”[w] 14 Since he would not be dissuaded, we finally gave up and said, “The Lord’s will be done.”[x]

B: Various Events and Paul’s Defenses at Jerusalem

Paul Is Welcomed by the Elders.* 15 At the end of our stay, we made preparations and

h Acts 19:10; 1 Thes 2:11.—i Acts 14:23; Col 1:12; Heb 9:15.—j 1 Sam 12:3; 1 Cor 9:12; 2 Cor 2:17.—k 1 Cor 4:12; Eph 2:20-22; 1 Thes 2:9; 2 Thes 3:8.—l Sir 4:31.—m Acts 9:40; Lk 22:41.—n Acts 21:5.—o Acts 16:10.—p Acts 11:19.—q Acts 20:23; 21:11.—r Acts 9:40; Lk 22:41.—s Acts 6:5; 8:5-6; Eph 4:11; 2 Tim 4:5.—t Ex 15:20; Jdg 4:4; Neh 6:14.—u Acts 11:28.—v Acts 11:28; 20:23; 1 Ki 22:11; Isa 20:2-4.—w Acts 19:15-16; 20:24.—x Ru 1:18; Mt 6:10; 26:39; Mk 14:36; Lk 22:42.

20:35 *It is more blessed to give than to receive:* a saying of Jesus that is not found in the canonical Gospels.

21:1—28:31 The period of missionary journeys is over. The new series of events begins in Jerusalem with an address of the elders of the community to Paul (Acts 21:20-26), followed by an address of Paul to the people (Acts 22:1-21). Then follows a series of four trials, of increasing importance, in Jerusalem and in Caesarea (Acts 23:1ff; 24:1ff; 25:1ff; 26:1ff). In this suffering of Paul, which makes him, like every martyr, a sharer in the suffering of Jesus, the basic theme of the discourses, almost their very reason for being, is the resurrection. Finally, there is the journey to Rome. In the capital of the Empire, the decisive turning point comes. Paul henceforth addresses himself to the Gentiles without any longer taking account of the privilege of the Jews to be the first to receive the message (Acts 28:28).

21:1-18 This is the third “we-section” (see note on Acts 16:9-15).

21:1-14 Right from the beginning, the presence of the Spirit is apparent. It is he who urges Paul toward his destiny, and his presence is signified by the prophets who discuss the hour from which all want to save Paul. The assembly takes up the words of our Lord in the Garden of Olives: “The Lord’s will be done” (v. 14).

21:8 *Seven:* see Acts 6:2-4.

21:15-26 The elders extend a cordial but anxious welcome. Paul gives the community of Jerusalem an account of his mission, and the Church offers thanks. In this Jewish city, in a community presided over by James, a relative of Jesus deeply attached to Judaism, Paul accepts to live in the Jewish manner—in accord with his dictum: “I have become all things to all” (1 Cor 9:22). He must also give proof of his good faith: if he does not impose the practices of Judaism on Gentiles, he does not on the other hand wish to turn away those of Jewish origin from those practices.

In fact, Paul does not blame Jewish practices but those who insist on making them the condition of salvation. As a Jew himself, he loyally consents to perform a typically Jewish act of devotion: he joins a group of pilgrims who have taken a Nazirite vow (see Acts 18:18); at the appointed time he will come to be purified in the temple in accord with the prescriptions of the Law (Num 6:1-21) and will even pay the expenses. The Book of Acts does not say anything about Paul bringing the collection of the Churches to this mother community that has fallen in need.

went up to Jerusalem. 16 Some of the disci-
ples from Caesarea accompanied us and
brought us to the house of Mnason of
Cyprus, one of the early disciples, with
whom we were to stay.

17 When we arrived in Jerusalem, the
brethren gave us a warm welcome.[y] 18 On
the next day, Paul paid a visit to James. We
accompanied him, and all the elders were
present. 19 After greeting them, he reported
in detail what God had done among the
Gentiles through his ministry.[z]

20 When they heard this, they gave praise
to God. Then they said to Paul, "You can see,
brother, how many thousands of believers
there are among the Jews, and all of them
are zealous upholders of the Law.[a] 21 They
have been informed in your regard that you
teach all the Jews who live among the
Gentiles to forsake Moses and that you tell
them not to circumcise their children or to
observe their custom.[b] 22 What then is to be
done? They are sure to hear that you have
arrived.

23 [c] "This is what we suggest that you do.
We have four men here who are under a vow.
24 Take these men, go through the rite of
purification with them, and pay the expens-
es involved with the shaving of their heads.
In this way, all will know that there is
nothing in these reports they have been
given about you and that you observe the
Law. 25 As for the Gentiles who have become
believers, we have informed them of our
decision that they must abstain from meat
that has been sacrificed to idols, from blood,
from anything that has been strangled, and
from unchastity."[d]

26 Therefore, on the next day Paul took the
men and purified himself along with them.
He then entered the temple to give notice of
the date when the period of purification
would end and the offerings would be made
for each of them.[e]

Paul's Arrest in the Temple.* 27 When the
seven days were nearly over, the Jews from
the province of Asia saw him in the temple.
Stirring up the whole crowd, they seized
him,[f] 28 shouting, "Men of Israel, help us!
This is the man who is teaching everyone
everywhere against our people, the Law, and
this place. What is more, he has brought
Greeks into the temple and defiled this holy
place."[g] 29 They had previously seen Troph-
imus the Ephesian with him in the city and
assumed that Paul had brought him into the
temple.[h]

30 Thus, the entire city was in turmoil, and
people came running from all directions.
They seized Paul and dragged him out of the
temple, and the gates were then shut.[i]
31 While they were trying to kill him, word
reached the commander of the cohort that
all Jerusalem was in an uproar. 32 Imme-
diately, he took soldiers and centurions with
him and charged down on them.[j]

When the Jews saw the commander and
the soldiers, they stopped beating Paul.
33 Then the commander came forward,
arrested him, and ordered him to be bound
with two chains. Next he asked who he was
and what he had done.[k] 34 Some in the crowd
shouted one thing and some another; and
since the commander could not arrive at the
truth because of the uproar, he ordered that
Paul be taken into the barracks.[l] 35 When he
came to the steps, the violence of the crowd
was so intense that he had to be carried by
the soldiers. 36 The crowd that followed kept
shouting, "Away with him!"[m]

37 Just as he was about to be taken into the
barracks, Paul said to the commander,
"May I say something to you?" The com-
mander replied, "So you speak Greek?
38 Then you are not the Egyptian* who

y Acts 15:4.—z Acts 14:27.—a Mk 7:1-13; Rom 10:2; Gal 1:14; Phil 3:6.—b Acts 15:19-21; 1 Cor 7:18, 19.—c 23-27: Acts 18:18; Num 6:1-21.—d Acts 15:19-20, 28-29.—e Acts 24:18; 1 Cor 9:20.—f Jer 26:8.—g Ezek 44:9; Mt 24:15; Rom 15:31.—h Acts 20:4; 2 Tim 4:20.—i Acts 26:21.—j Acts 23:27.—k Acts 12:6; Eph 6:20.—l Acts 19:32.—m Acts 22:22; Lk 23:18; Jn 19:15.

21:27-40 Now the time for imprisonment and captivity has arrived, sparked by a misunderstanding. The Jews come to believe that Paul is bringing into the temple a non-Jew—someone who is forbidden under penalty of death from entering the inner courts. Hence, a cry of sacrilege rings out. In reality, hatred is about to explode. Judaism has felt the jolt of a nascent Christianity and has reacted defensively to it. This reflexive sentiment has already been at work against Stephen (see Acts 6:11-14), and the same accusations were formulated against Jesus (Mt 26:61; 27:40; Mk 14:58; 15:29). The defensive reaction is a violent, irrational, and almost visceral one. It has to be such in order that the Christian originality may be manifest and that one may know what to hold on to. The commander of the cohort, who watches the temple from the fortress installed at the northwest corner, intervenes to prevent a riot. The soldiers believe they are arresting a nationalist extremist. Luke stresses once more that neither Paul nor Christians have ever been involved in a subversive plot against the Empire.

21:38 *The Egyptian:* in A.D. 54, an Egyptian agitator, Ben Stada, had stirred up the Jewish nationalists to whom reference is made here, as we know from the historian Flavius Josephus. The Roman authorities were forced to put down the riot, and thousands were killed. *Assassins:* literally, *sicarii,* violent nationalists who carried a short dagger, called *sica* in Latin, and did not hesitate to use it.

recently started a revolt and led the four thousand assassins into the desert."[n] [39] Paul asserted, "I am a Jew from Tarsus in Cilicia, a citizen of no mean city. May I have your permission to speak to the people?" [40] When the permission was granted, Paul stood on the steps and raised his hand to the people for silence. As soon as quiet was restored, he started speaking to them in Aramaic. *[o]

CHAPTER 22

Paul's Speech to the People of Jerusalem.* [1] "Brethren and fathers, listen to what I have to say to you in my defense."[p] [2] When they heard him addressing them in Aramaic, they became even more quiet than before.

Then he continued,[q] [3] "I am a Jew, born at Tarsus in Cilicia, but brought up in this city. As a pupil of Gamaliel, I was thoroughly trained in the Law of our ancestors. I have always been zealous toward God, just as all of you are today.[r] [4] I even persecuted the followers of this Way to their death, sending both men and women to prison in chains,[s] [5] as the high priest and the whole council of elders can testify. From them I also received letters to our brethren in Damascus, and I set out to bring prisoners back from there to Jerusalem for punishment.[t]

[6] "While I was on my way and drawing near Damascus, around midday a great light from the sky suddenly shone all around me.[u] [7] I fell to the ground and heard a voice saying, 'Saul, Saul, why are you persecuting me?'[v] [8] I answered, 'Who are you, Lord?' Then he said to me, 'I am Jesus of Nazareth, whom you are persecuting.'[w]

[9] "Now those who were with me saw the light, but they did not hear the voice of the one who was speaking to me.[x] [10] I asked, 'What do you want me to do, Lord?' The Lord said to me, 'Get up and go into Damascus. There you will be told everything that you have been appointed to do.'[y] [11] I could not see because of the brilliance of that light, and so my companions led me by the hand to Damascus.[z]

[12] [a] "A man named Ananias, who was a devout observer of the Law and highly regarded by all the Jews who lived there, [13] came to see me. Standing beside me, he said, 'Brother Saul, regain your sight.' Instantly, I saw him.

[14] "Then he said, 'The God of our ancestors has chosen you to know his will, to see the Righteous One, and to hear him speak.[b] [15] For you will be his witness * to tell all what you have seen and heard.[c] [16] And now, what are you waiting for? Get up, be baptized, and have your sins washed away, calling on his name.'[d]

[17] "After I had returned to Jerusalem, and while I was praying in the temple, I fell into a trance[e] [18] and saw Jesus there. 'Hurry and leave Jerusalem at once,' he said, 'because they will not accept your testimony about me.' [19] But I replied, 'Lord, they themselves know that in every synagogue I used to imprison and scourge those who believe in you.[f] [20] And while the blood of your martyr Stephen was being shed, I myself stood by, giving my approval and guarding the coats of his murderers.'[g] [21] Then he said to me, 'Go! I am sending you far away to the Gentiles.'"[h]

Paul Claims His Roman Citizenship.* [22] Up to this point, the crowd had listened to him, but then they raised their voices and began to shout, "Rid the earth of this man! He should not be allowed to live."[i] [23] And as they were shouting and throwing off their cloaks and flinging dust into the air,[j] [24] the commander ordered that he be brought into the barracks and gave instructions that he be interrogated while being scourged to discover the reason for this outcry against him.

[25] But when they had stretched him out and bound him with thongs, Paul said to the centurion who was standing nearby, "Is it lawful for you to scourge a man who is a

n Acts 5:36-37; Mt 24:26.—o Acts 12:17; 13:16.—p Acts 7:2.—q Acts 21:40.—r Acts 5:34; 21:20; 26:4-5; 1 Ki 19:10; 2 Cor 11:22; Gal 1:13-14; Phil 3:5-6.—s Acts 8:3; 9:1-2; 22:19; 26:9-11; Phil 3:6.—t Lk 22:66.—u Acts 9:3; 26:13; 1 Cor 15:8.—v Acts 9:4; 26:14.—w Acts 9:5; 26:15; Mt 2:23; 25:40; Mk 1:24.—x Acts 9:7; 26:13-14.—y Acts 9:6; 16:30; 26:16.—z Acts 9:8.—a 12-16: Acts 9:10-19.—b Acts 7:52; Mt 13:16.—c Acts 23:11.—d Lev 8:6; Ps 51:4; Ezek 36:25.—e Acts 9:26; Gal 1:18.—f Acts 8:3; 9:1-2; 22:4-5; 26:9-11.—g Acts 7:58; 8:1.—h Acts 2:39; 9:15; Gal 2:7-9.—i Acts 21:36; Lk 23:18; Jn 19:15.—j Acts 7:58.

21:40 *Aramaic:* the language spoken by Jews at this time; Hebrew was no longer spoken or understood by the people after the Babylonian exile (587 B.C.).

22:1-21 Paul refers chiefly to his conversion and explains it. That event dominated his life: the story is told three times in Acts (9:1-19; 22:1-21; 26:9-18). In speaking to Jews, as he does here, Paul mentions a detail that is omitted in the other two accounts: he received his mission in the temple (vv. 17-21).

22:15 *His witness:* Paul is to be a witness to Jesus' Resurrection in the same way that the apostles have been, since he too has seen the risen Lord (see Acts 1:8; 10:39-41; Lk 24:48).

22:22-29 Luke doubtless recalls this fact to emphasize that the Empire has no reason to suspect Christianity of any subversive intent.

Roman citizen and who has not been con-
demned?"[k] 26 When the centurion heard
this, he went to the commander and asked,
"What are you going to do? This man is a
Roman citizen."

27 Then the commander came to him and
inquired, "Tell me, are you a Roman citi-
zen?" And he answered, "Yes." 28 The com-
mander responded, "It cost me a great deal
of money to acquire this citizenship." Paul
replied, "But I was born a citizen." 29 Then
those who were about to interrogate him
withdrew hurriedly, and the commander
himself was alarmed when he realized that
Paul was a Roman citizen and that he had
put him in chains.[l]

Paul's First Trial—before the Sanhedrin.*
30 Since the commander wanted to learn
with certitude what Paul was being accused
of by the Jews, he released him on the fol-
lowing day and ordered the chief priests and
the entire Sanhedrin to meet. Then he
brought Paul down and had him stand
before them.

CHAPTER 23

1 Paul looked intently at the Sanhedrin
and said, "Brethren, to this very day, I have
conducted myself before God with a perfect-
ly clear conscience."[m] 2 At this, the high
priest Ananias * ordered his attendants to
strike him on the mouth.[n]

3 Then Paul said to him, "God will strike
you, you whitewashed wall! How can you sit
there to judge me according to the Law and
then in defiance of the Law order me to be
struck?"[o] 4 The attendants said, "Do you
dare to insult God's high priest?" 5 Paul
replied, "Brethren, I did not realize that he
was the high priest. It is clearly written: 'You
shall not curse the ruler of your people.'"[p]

6 Well aware that some of them were
Sadducees and the others were Pharisees,
Paul called out in the Sanhedrin, "Brethren,
I am a Pharisee and the son of Pharisees. I
am on trial concerning our hope in the res-
urrection of the dead."[q] 7 When he said this,
a dispute ensued between the Pharisees and
the Sadducees, and the assembly was divid-
ed. 8 For the Sadducees hold that there is no
resurrection and that there are no angels or
spirits, while the Pharisees believe in all
three.[r]

9 Then a great uproar arose, and some of
the scribes belonging to the party of the
Pharisees stood up and forcefully stated,
"We find nothing wrong with this man.
What if a spirit or an angel has really spoken
to him?"[s] 10 When a violent dissension
arose, the commander was fearful that Paul
would be torn to pieces. He ordered the sol-
diers to go down, seize him from their
midst, and bring him into the barracks.

11 On the following night, the Lord ap-
peared to Paul and said, "Keep up your
courage! For just as you have borne witness
to me in Jerusalem, so you must also bear
witness in Rome."[t]

A Plot To Kill Paul.* 12 When morning came,
the Jews formed a conspiracy and bound
themselves by an oath * not to eat or drink
until they had killed Paul.[u] 13 There were
more than forty who entered this pact.
14 They went to the chief priests and elders
and told them, "We have bound ourselves by
a solemn oath not to consume any food until
we have killed Paul. 15 You and the Sanhedrin
should make an official request to the com-
mander to bring him down to you on the pre-
text that you want to investigate his case
more thoroughly. We on our part have
arranged to kill him before he arrives."[v]

16 However, the son of Paul's sister learned
of the plot. He thereupon went to the bar-

k Acts 16:37.—l Acts 16:38.—m Acts 24:16; 1 Cor 4:4; Heb 9:14.—n Acts 24:1; Jn 18:22.—o Lev 19:15; Deut 25:1-2; Ezek 13:10-15; Mt 23:27.—p Ex 22:28.—q Acts 24:15, 21; 26:5; 2 Mac 7:9; Phil 3:5.—r Mt 22:23; Lk 20:27; 1 Cor 15:12.—s Jer 26:16; Mk 2:16.—t Acts 19:21; Mt 14:27.—u Acts 9:23; 1 Thes 2:14.—v Acts 22:30.

22:30—23:11 In the last cycle of Acts, each discourse is inserted into a very colorful account. The episode of the affront to the high priest, a man with a poor reputation, is not lacking in irony. In addition, each time there is a "suspense" created that becomes ever more intense. In the present case, the subject of the resurrection stirs discord among the hearers, because it was a matter of dispute within Jewish theology. In fact, belief in the resurrection, with the resultant different fates of the good and the bad, came into existence late in Judaism (2 Mac 7:9, 11, 14, 23, 29, 36; 12:38-46; Dan 12:2f; see Wis 3:1-5, 16). It was accepted by the Pharisees, but the Sadducees tried to combat it, even by ridiculing it (see Mt 22:23-33; Mk 12:18-27; Lk 20:27-38). As is the case with the other discourses, this one also wishes to make clear that Paul and the Churches are innocent of the accusations of the Jews and the suspicions of the Romans. Then the debate, which at first was carried out on the juridical level, is raised to the level of theological realities.

23:2 *Ananias* was high priest from A.D. 47 to 59.

23:12-22 Luke contrasts the correct behavior of the Roman authorities with the blind fanaticism of the Jews: from the outset the Romans realized that there was nothing subversive about Christianity. This is proof of the loyalty of Christians. Note the reference to Paul's sister and nephew; this is the only information we have about his family.

23:12 *Oath:* they call God's curse upon themselves if they fail to carry out the commitment they have assumed.

racks and related the news to Paul. 17 Paul then summoned one of the centurions and said, "Take this young man to the commander, for he has something to report to him." 18 He brought him to the commander and said, "The prisoner Paul called me and requested that I bring this young man to you. He has something to tell you."

19 The commander took him by the hand, drew him aside, and asked him in private, "What is it that you have to report to me?" 20 He replied, "The Jews have agreed to request you to bring Paul down to the Sanhedrin tomorrow on the pretext of inquiring more thoroughly into his case. 21 Do not believe them. More than forty of them are waiting for your consent to their request, for they have sworn an oath not to eat or drink until they have killed him. They are ready now and are waiting only for your consent." 22 The commander dismissed the young man, ordering him, "Tell no one that you have given me this information."

C: Paul's Imprisonment and Defenses at Caesarea

Paul Is Imprisoned at Caesarea.* 23 Then he summoned two of his centurions and said, "Have two hundred soldiers ready to leave for Caesarea by nine o'clock tonight,* along with seventy cavalrymen and two hundred auxiliaries.[w] 24 Also provide mounts for Paul to ride, and deliver him to Felix the governor."[x] 25 He then wrote a letter as follows:

26 Claudius Lysias,

To his Excellency the governor Felix:*

Greetings.[y]

27 This man was seized by the Jews and was about to be killed by them; but when I learned that he was a Roman citizen, I arrived on the scene with my troops and rescued him.[z]

28 Wanting to learn what charge they were making against him, I had him brought before their Sanhedrin. 29 I discovered that the accusation dealt with questions about their Law, but that there was no charge against him that merited death or imprisonment.[a] 30 Now I have been informed of a plot to assassinate this man. I am sending him to you without delay, and I have instructed his accusers to present to you their case against him.[b]

31 Therefore, the soldiers, acting in accordance with their orders, took Paul and escorted him during the night to Antipatris. 32 On the next day, they returned to the barracks, leaving the cavalrymen to escort him the rest of the way. 33 When they arrived in Caesarea, they delivered the letter to the governor and handed over Paul to him.

34 After reading the letter, the governor asked Paul what province he was from, and on learning that he was from Cilicia, 35 he said, "I will hear your case as soon as your accusers arrive." Then he ordered that he be held in custody in Herod's praetorium.[c]

CHAPTER 24

Paul's Second Trial—before Felix.* 1 Five days later, the high priest Ananias came down with some of the elders and an advocate named Tertullus, and they presented charges against Paul to the governor.[d] 2 Then Paul was summoned, and Tertullus began the prosecution.

He said, "Because of you we have enjoyed an unbroken period of peace, and reforms have been made in this nation as a result of your caring concern. 3 We acknowledge this everywhere and in every way with the utmost gratitude, most noble Felix.[e]

4 "But in order not to detain you needlessly, I beg you to be kind enough to listen to a

w Acts 8:40.—x Acts 24:1-3.—y Acts 24:3; Lk 1:3.—z Acts 21:30-34; 22:27.—a Acts 18:14-15; 25:18-19.—b Acts 24:19.—c Acts 25:16.—d Acts 23:2.—e Acts 23:26; Lk 1:3.

23:23-35 The commander cannot risk having a Roman citizen assassinated while in his custody, so he seeks to transfer Paul to the jurisdiction of Felix, the governor of the province of Judea. He also sends a letter to Felix summarizing the events, from the riot in the temple to the commander's discovery of a plot against Paul's life. The most important thing he says is that there is no charge against Paul deserving of death or punishment. Felix then agrees to hear the case himself.

23:23 *Nine o'clock tonight:* literally, "the third hour of the night."

23:26 *Felix:* M. Antonius Felix was governor (procurator) of Judea from A.D. 52 to 60, and he ruled with an iron hand.

24:1-21 The language is that of grave accusations and fine speeches. Once again, Paul dispels the Jewish accusations and the Roman suspicions. He is given a trial, but those who are directly opposed to him, and should be there, are missing, i.e., the Jews of Asia who stirred up more than one riot against him during his missionary journeys. Accusations leveled at him are not backed up by the facts. More profoundly—and herein lies the problem—the first Christians are convinced that their faith is not a perversion of, a secession from, or an opposition to Judaism but the fulfillment of its historical hope. The resurrection is their most ineradicable certitude. But this belief also exists among some people in Israel. More and more in the course of the trial, stress is placed on the subject of the hope of the resurrection.

brief statement. 5 We have found this man to be a troublemaker. He is a fomenter of dissension among Jews all over the world and a ringleader of the sect of the Nazarenes.[f] 6 When he even tried to profane the temple, we placed him under arrest.[g] [7 We would have judged him according to our own Law, but the commander Lysias came and forcibly removed him out of our hands, ordering his accusers to appear before you.] * 8 If you examine him yourself, you will be able to ascertain the validity of all the charges we bring against him." 9 The Jews supported the charge, asserting that these things were true.

10 Then the governor motioned to Paul to speak, and he replied, "I know that you have administered justice to this nation for many years, and therefore I feel confident in presenting my defense. 11 As you can verify for yourself, no more than twelve days have elapsed since I went up to worship in Jerusalem.[h] 12 They did not find me disputing with anyone in the temple or stirring up a crowd either in the synagogues or throughout the city.[i] 13 Nor can they offer you any proof concerning their charges against me.

14 "But this much I will admit to you: it is as a follower of the Way, which they call a sect, that I worship the God of my ancestors, believing everything that is in accordance with the Law or is written in the Prophets.[j] 15 I hold the same hope in God as they do that there will be a resurrection of the righteous and the wicked alike.[k] 16 Accordingly, I strive at all times to have a clear conscience before God and man.[l]

17 "After several years, I came to bring charitable gifts to my people and to offer sacrifices.[m] 18 [n] They found me in the temple after I had completed the rite of purification. There was no crowd with me, nor was I involved in any disturbance.

"However, some Jews from the province of Asia were there, 19 and they are the ones who should have appeared before you to give such evidence if they had any charge against me.[o] 20 At the very least, those who are present here should state what crime they discovered when I was brought before the Sanhedrin, 21 unless it has to do with this one declaration I made when I stood up among them, 'I am on trial on account of the resurrection of the dead.' "[p]

In the Procurator's Hall.* 22 Then Felix, who was well informed about the Way, adjourned the hearing with the comment, "When Lysias the commander comes down, I shall issue a ruling on this case." 23 He also ordered the centurion to keep Paul in custody, but allow him some freedom, and not to prevent any of his friends from caring for his needs.[q]

24 Several days later, Felix came with his wife Drusilla, * who was a Jewess. He sent for Paul and listened to him speak about faith in Christ Jesus.[r] 25 But as Paul discussed justice, self-control, and the coming judgment, Felix became frightened and exclaimed, "Go away for the present. When I have an opportunity, I will send for you."[s] 26 At the same time, he hoped that Paul would offer him a bribe. Therefore he used to send for him quite often and converse with him.

27 After two years had passed, Felix was succeeded by Porcius Festus, * and since he wanted to ingratiate himself with the Jews, Felix left Paul in custody.[t]

CHAPTER 25

Paul's Third Trial—before Festus.* 1 Three days after his arrival in the province, Festus went up from Caesarea to Jerusalem, 2 where the chief priests and the leaders of the Jews informed him about Paul.[u] They urged him 3 as a favor to send for Paul to

f Acts 16:20; 24:14; Mt 2:23; Mk 1:24; Lk 23:2.—g Acts 21:28.—h Acts 11:30; 21:27.—i Acts 25:8.—j Acts 24:5; Mt 5:17; Rom 3:31.—k Dan 12:2; Jn 5:28-29.—l Acts 23:1.—m Acts 11:29-30; Rom 15:25-26; 1 Cor 16:1-4; Gal 2:10.—n 18-19: Acts 21:26-30.—o Acts 23:30.—p Acts 23:6; 24:15.—q Acts 23:35; 28:16.—r Mk 6:17-20.—s Gal 5:23; 1 Thes 5:6; 1 Pet 4:7.—t Acts 25:1, 4, 9.—u Acts 23:12-15; 24:1.

24:7 This verse is lacking in the better manuscripts.

24:22-27 Felix is willing to listen to Christian teaching, but not to take the risk of converting his ways. He governs with complacencies, cruelties, and briberies, and he doubtless will have contributed to stirring up discontent, the precursor of the rebellion that would lead to the destruction of the Jewish State in A.D. 70. He seems to have been sympathetic to Paul, while keeping him in detention beyond the time provided by the Law.

24:24 *Drusilla:* at the age of fifteen, this daughter of Herod Agrippa I had abandoned her first husband, the king of Emesa, in order to become Felix's third wife.

24:27 *Porcius Festus* was an excellent governor and remained in office from A.D. 59 to 62. The "two years" to which reference is made here ran from A.D. 57 to 59.

25:1-12 The governors change, but at Jerusalem the Jewish authorities do not forget Paul. They seek once again to suppress the Apostle by a criminal act, but they appeal to the governor in vain. Since the dispute is religious in theme, why not entrust it to the jurisdiction of the Sanhedrin, while continuing the debates? Paul cannot consent to this for he realizes that he would never receive justice.

bring him to Jerusalem. They were going to kill him in an ambush along the way.

[4] Festus replied that Paul was in custody in Caesarea, and that he himself would be returning there shortly. [5] He said, "Let your authorities come down with me, and if this man has done something improper, they can bring a charge against him."

[6] After staying with them for eight to ten days, Festus went down to Caesarea. On the next day, he took his seat on the tribunal and ordered Paul to be summoned. [7] When he appeared, the Jews who had come down from Jerusalem surrounded him, and they leveled many serious charges against him that they were unable to prove. [v]

[8] Paul said in his defense, "I have committed no offense against the Jewish Law, or against the temple, or against the Emperor." [w] [9] Festus, anxious to ingratiate himself with the Jews, asked Paul, "Do you wish to go up to Jerusalem and stand trial there before me on these charges?"

[10] Paul replied, "I am standing before the tribunal of Caesar, and this is where I should be tried. I have committed no crime against the Jews, as you yourself well know. [11] If I am guilty of any capital crime, I do not ask to be spared death. However, if there is no substance to the charges they are bringing against me, then no one has the right to turn me over to them. I appeal to Caesar." * [x] [12] Then, after Festus had conferred with his advisors, he said, "You have appealed to Caesar. To Caesar you shall go."

Paul's Fourth Trial—before Agrippa.* [13] Some days later, King Agrippa and Bernice arrived in Caesarea to pay their respects to Festus. [14] Since they spent several days there, Festus raised the subject of Paul's case before the king, saying, "There is a man here who was left in custody by Felix. [y] [15] When I was in Jerusalem, the chief priests and the elders of the Jews brought charges against him and requested his condemnation. [16] I told them that it was not the custom of the Romans to hand over anyone before he had met his accusers face to face and had had an opportunity to defend himself against their charges. [z]

[17] "Therefore, when they had come here, I wasted no time; the very next day, I took my seat on the tribunal and ordered the man to be summoned. [18] [a] When the accusers rose, they did not charge him with any of the crimes that I was expecting. [19] Instead, they had certain points of disagreement with him about their own religion and about someone named Jesus, a dead man who Paul asserted was alive. [b]

[20] "Since I did not feel qualified to deal with such questions, I asked him if he would be willing to go to Jerusalem to stand trial on these charges. [21] But Paul appealed to be held in custody for the Emperor's decision, and I ordered him to be held until I could send him to Caesar." [22] Agrippa said to Festus, "I would like to hear this man for myself." He replied, "Tomorrow you will hear him." [c]

[23] On the next day, Agrippa and Bernice arrived with great pomp and entered the audience hall, accompanied by officers of high rank and prominent men of the city. Festus ordered Paul to be brought in. [24] Then he said, "King Agrippa and all of you here present with us, you see this man about whom the entire Jewish community petitioned me, both in Jerusalem and here, shouting loudly that he should not be allowed to live any longer. [d]

[25] "I have found nothing deserving of death, but when he made his appeal to the Emperor, I decided to send him. [e] [26] However, I have nothing definite about him to put in writing for our sovereign. Therefore, I have brought him before all of you, and especially before you, King Agrippa, so that after this examination I may have something to write. [27] For it seems senseless to me

v Mt 26:59; Mk 15:3; Lk 23:2, 10.—w Acts 6:13.—x Acts 26:32.—y Acts 24:27.—z Acts 23:30.—a 18-19: Acts 18:14-15; 23:29.—b Lk 24:5; 2 Cor 13:4.—c Acts 9:15.—d Acts 22:22.—e Acts 23:29.

25:11 A Roman citizen could not be transferred from one jurisdiction to another without his consent. Paul had an unassailable right to appeal to Caesar.

25:13-27 Paul has already appeared in the presence of Drusilla (Acts 24:24); this time, he meets Agrippa and Bernice. The three children of Herod Agrippa I (Acts 12:1) have made his acquaintance. Bernice has also become famous because of her ties to Titus. The meeting takes place in a formal setting. The Roman governor probably thinks that his guests who are Jewish in origin can shed light on the dispute. Before giving a kind of curriculum of life, Paul places into evidence the Christian belief in the resurrection and shows Christianity as the fulfillment of the Jewish hope for the betterment of all human beings.

We now read the third account of Paul's conversion (see Acts 9:1-19; 22:1-21), which puts more emphasis on Paul's mission being in accord with prophetic callings in the Old Testament. It is a splendid Christian biography of Paul, a vision of Christianity as the fulfillment of the destiny of Israel, and a profession of faith in the Resurrection of Jesus being for the salvation of all human beings.

to send on a prisoner without indicating the charges against him."

CHAPTER 26

Paul's Defense before Agrippa. [1] Agrippa said to Paul, "You have permission to speak for yourself." Then Paul stretched out his hand and began to defend himself:[f] [2] "I consider myself fortunate, King Agrippa, that it is before you today that I am to defend myself against all the accusations of the Jews,[g] [3] particularly since you are well acquainted with all our Jewish customs and controversies. Therefore, I implore you to listen to me patiently.

[4] "The Jews all know my way of life from my youth, which I first lived among my own people and in Jerusalem. [5] They have known about me from my youth, and they could testify, if they were willing, that I belonged to the strictest sect of our religion and lived as a Pharisee.[h] [6] [i] But now I am on trial because of my hope in the promise made by God to our ancestors.[j]

[7] "Our twelve tribes worship night and day with intense devotion in the hope of seeing its fulfillment. It is because of this hope that I am accused by the Jews, O king.[k] [8] Why should it seem incredible to any of you that God raises the dead?[l]

[9] [m] "I myself once thought that I had to do everything possible against the name of Jesus of Nazareth.[n] [10] And that is what I did in Jerusalem. With the authorization of the chief priests, I not only sent many of the saints * to prison, but when they were being condemned to death, I cast my vote against them.[o] [11] In all the synagogues, I tried by inflicting repeated punishments to force them to blaspheme, and I was so enraged with fury against them that I even pursued them to foreign cities.

[12] "On one such occasion, I was traveling to Damascus with the authorization and commission of the chief priests. [13] [p] At midday, as I was on my way, O king, I saw a light from the sky, brighter than the sun, shining all around me and my companions.[q] [14] We all fell to the ground, and I heard a voice saying to me in Aramaic, 'Saul, Saul, why are you persecuting me? It is hard for you to kick against the goad.' * [r]

[15] "I asked, 'Who are you, Lord?' The Lord answered, 'I am Jesus, whom you are persecuting.[s] [16] Get up now and stand on your feet, for I have appeared to you for this purpose, to appoint you as my servant and as a witness to what you have seen of me and what you will yet see.[t] [17] I will rescue you from your own people and from the Gentiles to whom I am sending you.[u] [18] You are to open their eyes so that they may turn from darkness to light * and from the power of Satan to God. Thus, they may obtain forgiveness of their sins and an inheritance among those who have been consecrated through faith in me.'[v]

[19] "And so, King Agrippa, I did not disobey the vision from heaven.[w] [20] Rather, I started to preach, first to the people in Damascus, and then in Jerusalem and throughout the countryside of Judea, and also to the Gentiles, calling on them to repent and turn to God and prove their repentance by their deeds.[x] [21] That is why the Jews seized me in the temple and tried to kill me.[y]

[22] [z] "But I have had help from God to this very day, and I stand here and testify to both the lowly and the great. I assert nothing more than what the Prophets and Moses said would occur: [23] that the Christ must suffer, and that, by being the first to rise from the dead, he would proclaim light to the people and to the Gentiles."[a]

Reactions to Paul's Speech. [24] While Paul was still speaking in his own defense, Festus exclaimed, "You are out of your mind, Paul! Too much learning is driving you insane."[b] [25] But he replied, "I am not out of my mind, most excellent Festus. What I am asserting is true and reasonable. [26] The king understands these matters, and to him I now speak freely. I am confident that none of this

f Acts 9:15; 13:16.—g Ps 119:46.—h Acts 22:3; 2 Cor 11:22; Gal 1:13-14; Phil 3:5-6.—i 6-8: Acts 23:6; 24:15, 21; 28:20.—j Rom 15:8.—k 1 Thes 3:10; Jas 1:1.—l 2 Mac 7:9; Dan 12:1-3; Rom 4:17.—m 9-11: Acts 8:3; 9:1-2; 22:19; Phil 3:6.—n Acts 22:5-16; Jn 16:2; 1 Tim 1:13.—o Acts 9:14, 21.—p 13-14: Acts 9:7.—q Acts 9:3; 22:6.—r Acts 9:4; 22:7.—s Acts 9:5; 22:8; Mt 25:40.—t Acts 9:6; 22:10; Ezek 2:1; Dan 10:11; 1 Cor 9:16.—u Jer 1:5-8, 19.—v Isa 42:7, 16; 61:1 LXX; Jn 8:12; Eph 5:8; Col 1:13; 1 Pet 2:9.—w Isa 50:5.—x Acts 9:19-25; Jer 18:11; Mt 3:8.—y Acts 21:31.—z 22-23: Acts 3:18; Lk 24:26-27, 44-47.—a Isa 42:6; 49:6; Lk 2:32; 1 Cor 15:20-23; Rev 1:5.—b Jn 7:15.

26:10 *Saints:* see note on Acts 9:13.

26:14 *It is hard for you to kick against the goad:* a well-known expression in the Greek world to express the futility of opposing the gods.

26:18 *From darkness to light:* a figure used often by Paul (see Rom 13:12; 2 Cor 4:6; Eph 5:8-14; Col 1:13; 1 Thes 5:5).

has escaped his notice, for all this was not done in a corner. * [27] King Agrippa, do you believe the Prophets? * I know that you do."

[28] Then Agrippa said to Paul, "Do you think that in such a brief time you can persuade me to become a Christian?" [c] [29] Paul responded, "Whether in a short time or longer, I pray to God that not only you but also all who are listening to me today may become what I am, except for these chains."

[30] Then the king rose, and with him the governor and Bernice and those who had been seated with them. [d] [31] And as they were leaving, they said to one another, "This man is doing nothing that deserves death or imprisonment." [e] [32] And Agrippa said to Festus, "This man could have been set free if he had not appealed to Caesar." [f]

D: The Journey to Rome*

CHAPTER 27

Paul's Voyage toward Rome. [1] When it was decided that we * should sail for Italy, Paul and some other prisoners were handed over to Julius, a centurion of the Augustan cohort. [g] [2] We embarked on a ship from Adramyttium * that was about to sail to ports in the province of Asia, and we put out to sea, accompanied by Aristarchus, a Macedonian from Thessalonica. [h]

[3] On the next day, we landed at Sidon, * and Julius was considerate enough to allow Paul to visit his friends there and be cared for by them. [i] [4] From there, we put out to sea again and sailed around the sheltered side of Cyprus because of the headwinds. [5] Then, crossing the open sea off the coast of Cilicia and Pamphylia, we reached Myra in Lycia. *

Storm and Shipwreck. [6] There the centurion found an Alexandrian ship * that was bound for Italy and put us on board. [j] [7] For a good many days, we made little headway, and we experienced difficulty in reaching Cnidus. * Then, as the wind continued to pose difficulties, we sailed for the sheltered side of Crete off Salmone. [8] We moved along the coast with difficulty and reached a place called Fair Havens, * near the city of Lasea.

[9] Much time had already been lost, and sailing had now become hazardous, since the time of the Fast * had already gone by. Therefore, Paul gave them this warning, [k] [10] "Men, I can see that this voyage will be fraught with danger and involve heavy losses, not only of the ship and the cargo but also of our lives."

[11] However, the centurion paid more attention to the advice of the captain and of the ship's owner than to what Paul said. [12] Since the harbor was unsuitable for spending the winter, the majority were in favor of putting out to sea from there, in the hope that they could reach Phoenix, * a harbor of Crete facing southwest and northwest, and spend the winter there.

c Acts 11:26.—d Acts 25:23.—e Jn 18:37-38.—f Acts 25:11-12; 28:18.—g Acts 10:1; 16:10; 18:2.—h Acts 19:29; 20:4.—i Acts 24:23; Mt 11:21.—j Acts 28:11.—k Lev 16:29-31; Num 29:7; Mt 8:23-27.

26:26 *Not done in a corner:* a phrase stressing the fact that the Gospel is based on real events lived out in history. The king is bound to confirm the truth of the things Paul says.

26:27 *Do you believe the Prophets?:* this question by Paul puts King Agrippa in a no-win situation. If he says "Yes," Paul will insist that he recognize Jesus as the fulfillment of the Prophets. If he says "No," he will earn the wrath of the devout Jews, who accept the Prophets as God's spokespersons. So Agrippa skirts the question.

27:1—28:15 A journey full of vicissitudes. For 15 days, the ship will drift from the coast of Crete to the island of Malta, without any planned direction because the mariners cannot rely on the stars or the sun, which supplied the only way of determining direction at that time (Acts 27:20). Paul very calmly takes control of the situation; he is used to the sea and has already experienced three shipwrecks (see 2 Cor 11:25).

Paul evidently cannot think of founding a community on Malta, since it is a mere stopover, but he does effect cures. There are three more stopovers: Syracuse, Rhegium, and Puteoli. In the last-named place Paul has the joy of finding *some brothers* (Acts 28:13-14). *In Rome,* he finds a community of Christians of whose origin we know nothing, but which has already received from him the great Letter on salvation in Jesus Christ; the members of this community go to meet Paul at a place over 30 miles from the City (at the Forum of Appius and the Three Taverns, north of Terracina: Acts 28:15-16). He was, therefore, known and expected.

27:1 This begins the final "we-section" in Acts (see note on Acts 16:9-15). *Augustan cohort:* a name identifying the Roman legion to which the centurion belonged.

27:2 *Adramyttium:* a harbor on the west coast of the province of Asia.

27:3 *Sidon:* a city 70 miles north of Caesarea.

27:5 *Myra in Lycia:* an important harbor on the journey from Egypt to Rome as well as a prominent place for storing grain.

27:6 *Alexandrian ship:* a ship traveling from Egypt to Rome with a cargo of grain.

27:7 *Cnidus:* a city at the southeastern part of Asia Minor. A journey from Myra to Cnidus was 170 miles and required 10 to 15 days. *Crete:* an island 160 miles in length. *Salmone:* a promontory on the northeast tip of Crete.

27:8 *Fair Havens:* a city midway on the southern coast of Crete. *Lasea:* a city about five miles from Fair Havens.

27:9 *The Fast:* the fast that was called for on the Day of Atonement, i.e., either late September or early October. The season for sailing lasted from Pentecost (May-June) to Tabernacles (five days after the Fast). Sailing was regarded as hazardous after September 15 and as catastrophic after November 11.

27:12 *Phoenix:* a city with a harbor that provided protection from storms.

[13] When a gentle southerly breeze began to
blow, they thought that they would be able to
achieve their objective. They weighed
anchor and began to sail past Crete, hugging
the shore. [14] But before long a violent wind,
called a northeaster, swept down on them. [l]
[15] Since the ship was caught up in it, we had
to give way to the wind and let ourselves be
driven along.

[16] As we passed along the sheltered side of
a small island called Cauda, * we managed
with some difficulty to secure the ship's
lifeboat. [17] After hoisting it up, they used
cables to undergird the ship. Then, afraid of
running aground on the shallows of Syrtis, *
they lowered the sea anchor and so let them-
selves drift.

[18] We were being pounded so violently by
the storm that on the next day they began to
throw the cargo overboard. [m] [19] Then on the
third day, they threw the ship's gear over-
board with their own hands. [20] For many
days, neither the sun nor the stars could be
seen, and the storm continued to rage until
we finally abandoned all hope of being saved.

[21] When they all had gone without food for
a long time, Paul stood up among them and
said, "Men, you should have listened to me
and not have set sail from Crete. Then you
would have avoided all this damage and loss.
[22] I urge you now to keep up your courage.
There will be no loss of life among you. Only
the ship will be lost.

[23] "Last night an angel of the God to whom
I belong and whom I serve appeared to me, [n]
[24] and he said, 'Do not be afraid, Paul. You
shall appear before Caesar. Furthermore,
for your sake God has granted safety
to all those who are sailing with you.' [o]
[25] Therefore, men, keep up your courage. I
have complete trust in God that what he
told me will be fulfilled. [p] [26] But we will run
aground on some island." [q]

[27] On the fourteenth night, we were still
drifting across the Adriatic Sea. * About
midnight, the sailors began to suspect that
they were nearing land, [28] so they took
soundings and found that the water was
twenty feet deep. A little farther on they
again took soundings and found fifteen feet.

[29] Fearing that we might run aground on
the rocks, they let down four anchors from
the stern and prayed for daylight to come.
[30] The sailors then tried to abandon ship.
They had already lowered the lifeboat into
the sea, on the pretext that they were going
to lower some anchors from the bow. [31] But
Paul said to the centurion and the soldiers,
"Unless these men stay * with the ship, you
cannot be saved." [32] Then the soldiers cut the
ropes of the lifeboat and set it adrift.

[33] Just before daybreak, Paul urged all of
them to take some food, saying, "This is the
fourteenth day that you have been in sus-
pense, going hungry and eating nothing.
[34] Therefore, I beg you to take some food.
You need it to survive. Not one of you will
lose even a hair of his head."

[35] After he had said this, he took bread,
gave thanks to God in front of them all, broke
it, and began to eat. [r] [36] Then they were all
encouraged and began to eat. [37] Altogether,
there were two hundred and seventy-six
persons on board. [38] After they had eaten as
much as they wanted they lightened the ship
by throwing the grain into the sea. [s]

[39] In the morning, they did not recognize
the land, but they sighted a bay with a sandy
beach, and they decided to run the ship
aground on this if they could. [t] [40] And so they
cut loose the anchors and left them in the
sea. At the same time, they loosened the
ropes that held the rudders. Then, hoisting
the foresail to the wind, they made for the
beach. [41] But they struck a reef, and the ves-
sel ran aground. The bow became stuck and
remained unmovable, while the stern was
broken to pieces by the pounding of the
waves. [u]

[42] The soldiers decided to kill the prisoners
lest any of them might swim away and
escape. [43] However, the centurion was deter-
mined to spare Paul's life, and he prevented
them from carrying out their plan. He
ordered those who could swim to jump over-
board first and make for land, [44] while the
rest were to follow either on planks or on
pieces of wreckage from the ship. In this
way, all were brought safely to land.

---

l Mk 4:37.—m Jon 1:5.—n Acts 18:9; Jon 1:9; Rom 1:9; 2 Tim 4:17.—o Acts 23:11.—p Rom 4:20, 21.—q Acts 28:1.—r Mt 15:36; Mk 6:41; 8:6; Lk 22:19; 1 Cor 11:23-34.—s Jon 1:5.—t Acts 28:1.—u 2 Cor 11:25.

27:16 *Cauda:* a city about 23 miles from Crete.

27:17 *Syrtis:* a sandy stretch of land off the coast of Tunis and Tripoli in North Africa.

27:27 *Adriatic Sea:* the name was used generally for the seas between Italy, Greece, and Africa.

27:31 *Unless these men stay:* Paul points out that if the sailors jump ship, the passengers will be unable to bring the vessel to shore by themselves and will perish.

CHAPTER 28

Paul at Malta. 1 Once we had made our way to safety, we learned that the island was called Malta.*[v] 2 The natives* treated us with unusual kindness. Since it had begun to rain and was cold, they lit a bonfire and welcomed all of us around it.

3 Paul had gathered an armful of sticks and put them on the fire when a viper, driven out by the heat, attached itself to his hand. 4 On seeing the snake hanging from his hand, the natives said to one another, "This man must be a murderer. Although he escaped from the sea, Justice* has not allowed him to live."[w]

5 However, he shook off the snake into the fire and suffered no harm.[x] 6 They were expecting him to swell up or drop dead, but after waiting for a long time and seeing nothing unusual happen to him, they changed their minds and began to say that he was a god.[y]

7 In the vicinity of that place there were lands belonging to the leading man of the island, whose name was Publius.* He received us and gave us his hospitality for three days. 8 It so happened that this man's father was sick with a fever and dysentery. Paul visited him and cured him by praying and laying hands on him.[z] 9 After this happened, the rest of the sick people on the island also came and were cured. 10 They honored us with many marks of respect, and when we were about to set sail, they put on board all the supplies we needed.[a]

From Malta to Rome. 11 Three months later,* we set sail on a ship that had wintered at the island. The ship was from Alexandria, with the Dioscuri as its figurehead.[b] 12 We landed at Syracuse* and spent three days there. 13 Then we sailed along the coast and came to Rhegium.* After one day there, a south wind came up, and we reached Puteoli in two days.

14 In Puteoli, we found some brethren, and we were invited to stay with them for seven days. And so we came to Rome. 15 When the brethren there learned of our arrival, they came out to meet us as far as the Forum of Appius* and the Three Taverns. On seeing them, Paul gave thanks to God, and his courage was strengthened.

E: Paul's Activity at Rome*

Meetings with the Jewish Leaders. 16 On his arrival in Rome, Paul was allowed to live by himself, with a soldier guarding him.*[c] 17 Three days later, he called together the leaders of the Jews. When they had assembled, he said to them, "Brethren, although I have done nothing against our people or our ancestral customs, I was arrested in Jerusalem and handed over to the Romans.[d] 18 After they had examined me, the Romans wanted to release me because they had found nothing against me that deserved the death penalty.[e] 19 But the Jews objected, and I was compelled to appeal to Caesar, even though I had no accusation to make against my own nation.[f] 20 This is the reason I have asked to see you and speak with you, for it is because of the hope of Israel that I wear these chains."[g]

21 They replied, "We have received no letters from Judea about you, nor have any of the brethren who arrived here reported or spoken anything evil about you. 22 But we

v Acts 27:26.—w Mk 16:18; Lk 13:2, 4.—x Lk 10:19.—y Acts 14:11.—z Acts 9:40; Lk 4:40; 1 Tim 4:14; Jas 5:14-15.—a Ps 15:4.—b Acts 27:6.—c Acts 24:23; 27:3.—d Acts 21:21; 24:12-13; 25:2, 8.—e Acts 22:24; 23:29; 25:25; 26:31-32.—f Acts 25:11.—g Acts 23:6; 24:15, 21; 26:6-8.

28:1 *Malta:* a port of the province of Sicily, though located 58 miles away from the island itself.

28:2 *Natives:* literally, "barbarians"—which was the name the Greeks attached to all non-Greek speaking people.

28:4 *Justice:* a personification of divine avenging justice.

28:7 *Publius:* this local magistrate was the representative of the praetor of Sicily.

28:11 *Three months later:* the time was probably February of the year 60. *Dioscuri:* i.e., Castor and Pollux, pagan divinities who protected seafarers.

28:12 *Syracuse:* the most important city of Sicily, located on its east coast.

28:13 *Rhegium:* a town of Italy located opposite Messina and close to the narrowest part of the strait that lies between Italy and Sicily. *Puteoli:* the chief port of Rome, located almost 200 miles from Rhegium in the northern part of Naples.

28:15 *Forum of Appius:* a town 43 miles from Rome and known for its uncivilized behavior. *Three Taverns:* a town 33 miles from Rome.

28:16-29 As he has done throughout the Book, Paul first contacts the Jews established in the city. He must clarify his situation with regard to this colony. And he must first of all proclaim the Gospel as the fulfillment of Israel's Scriptures and its hope. The Jews see and hear, as the apostles did, but they choose not to understand because they do not make the connection from the past to the future. Henceforth, the Word will be directly addressed to the Gentiles without passing through the synagogue. Paul's speech is a last appeal and a conclusion.

We conclude from Acts that the movement of the Resurrection and Pentecost now enters freely into the whole universe. The limits of the old Israel have crumbled; the People of God gathers together all humanity.

28:16 Though he lived in a house of his own choice, he was under house arrest during his stay in Rome.

would like to hear from you what you think, for all we know about this sect is that it is denounced everywhere." [h]

23 And so they agreed on a day to meet
with him, and they came to his lodgings in great numbers. From early morning until evening, he presented his case to them, testifying to the kingdom of God and attempting to convince them about Jesus as he argued from both the Law of Moses and the
Prophets. [i] 24 Some were persuaded by what
he had said, but others refused to believe. [j]

25 Having failed to reach an agreement among themselves, they began to leave. Then Paul made his final statement, "How right the Holy Spirit was when he spoke to your ancestors through the prophet Isaiah, saying,

26 'Go to the people and say
You will indeed listen but never understand,
and you will indeed look but never perceive. [k]

27 For this people's heart has become dull,
their ears have been stopped up,
and they have shut their eyes,
lest their eyes might see,
their ears might hear,
and their hearts might understand.
Then they would be converted,
and I would heal them.' [l]

28 "Therefore, let it be known to you that this salvation offered by God has been sent to the Gentiles, and they will listen." [m]
[29 And when he had said this, the Jews departed, arguing vigorously among themselves.] *

Conclusion—But Not an End.* 30 Paul
remained there in his lodgings for two full years at his own expense. He welcomed all
who came to him, 31 and without hindrance
he boldly proclaimed the kingdom of God and taught about the Lord Jesus Christ. [n]

h Acts 24:5,14.—i Acts 17:3; 19:8.—j Acts 14:4.—k Isa 6:9-10; Mt 13:14-15; Mk 4:12; Lk 8:10; Jn 12:40; Rom 11:8.—l Ps 119:70; Isa 6:9-10.—m Acts 13:46; 18:6; Ps 67:2; Isa 40:5 LXX; Lk 2:30; 3:6.—n Acts 4:29; Mt 4:23; Phil 1:12-13.

28:29 This verse is lacking in the oldest manuscripts.

28:30-31 Luke knows that Paul died a martyr in Rome, but he does not speak of it, just as he says nothing of Peter's activity after his deliverance from the hands of Herod. His purpose is not to give us a history of the Church but to show the spread of the Gospel down to the point of its free entry among all the peoples.

According to the most popular view, Paul wrote the Captivity Letters (Ephesians, Colossians, Philippians, and Philemon) during this first Roman imprisonment. One tradition of the early Church also presupposes that Paul was set free after two years. Clement of Rome in his Epistle to the Corinthians (5:5-7) says that Paul went "to the end of the West," i.e., that he carried out the missionary journey to Spain that he had planned (see Rom 15:24). This point is also attested by the Muratorian Fragment (lines 37-38) and by the apocryphal Acts of Peter (chs. 1 and 3).

PAUL, APOSTLE OF CHRIST

The Gospel of the Gentiles

The Gospels are certainly the most important of the New Testament writings, but they were not the first to be composed. As early as the year A.D. 50, some young communities of former Gentiles were receiving Letters from an "apostle," namely, Paul, who had not belonged to the Twelve or to the circle around Jesus. Of the great figures of newborn Christianity, this "first Christian author" is the most remarkable one known to us, and he remains such through the testimony he has left us in his writings.

I. CHRONOLOGICAL ORDER OF THE LETTERS

Modern criticism has come to the following conclusions in this area.

A first series of Letters was written at intervals during the fifties and sixties; there is practically no one who doubts that Paul was their author.

—*1 and 2 Thessalonians:* The first two Christian writings that have come down to us. They were surely written in Corinth between A.D. 50 and 52, in order to encourage a recently founded community and to clarify some points of doctrine (although some scholars have questioned the authorship of 2 Thessalonians).

—*1 and 2 Corinthians:* Two Letters written in A.D. 56, during Paul's time in Ephesus. They contain rather spirited interventions occasioned by disorders and divisions in the community.

—*Philippians:* A Letter that is especially cordial in tone. It is the first Letter that Paul wrote from prison and can be dated to A.D. 56, although others place it with the Letters of Paul's Roman captivity between A.D. 61 and 63. We know that Paul was imprisoned more than once.

—*Galatians:* A fiery Letter to a Church in full crisis; probably written in A.D. 56 or 57.

—*Romans:* A lengthy theological writing, covering at greater length, and in a more serene tone, the same themes the writer had dealt with in the Letter to the Galatians. It may date from A.D. 57 or 58.

A second and later series of texts is known as the Captivity Letters (which may include the Letter to the Philippians, as noted a moment ago). They can be attributed to Paul, although a bit tentatively, and dated from A.D. 61 to 63, the period of his imprisonment in Rome.

—*Colossians:* A Letter that encourages authentic faith and authentic Christian life in face of the commingling of religions and new ideas.

—*Philemon:* A short note of recommendation for a fugitive slave.

—*Ephesians:* A circular Letter inspired by a profound theology and mysticism.

A third series of Letters is addressed no longer to communities but to individuals, pastors of souls, and is lavish with recommendations and guidelines for the exercise of their responsibilities. These are known as the Pastoral Letters and must be dated to A.D. 66 or 67 at the latest, if they are to be attributed to Paul. Some exegetes think the Letters may be the work of disciples and written around the eighties.

—*1 and 2 Timothy:* Two Letters.

—*Titus:* One Letter.

Toward the end of the 1st century a final writing supposedly by Paul was in circulation, but the attribution is most uncertain. It was written by someone else who remains anonymous.

—*Hebrews:* A lengthy piece of theology and exhortation, written either just before the destruction of Jerusalem in A.D. 70 or much later, between A.D. 80 and 90.

II. WHO WAS PAUL?

Until His Conversion

Saul was born around the beginning of the century, in Tarsus, the capital of Cilicia in Asia Minor, a little city but open to cultural influences and commercial exchanges between East and West. He was from a family of Diaspora Jews who belonged to the tribe of Benjamin and were intent on a strict observance of the religion of their forebears. They did not, however, reject all contact with the life and culture of the Empire; in fact, they had acquired Roman citizenship and thereby become the Paulus family.

In about A.D. 36/37 a mysterious event changed the course of Saul's life in an instant. The persecutor of Christians became the most ardent missionary of the Gospel.

On the road to Damascus, he had a vision that changed his life. He saw Christ, who revealed that he was totally one with all who believed in him: "Why are you persecuting me?" (Acts 9:4).

After His Conversion

Paul underwent a radical turnaround. From then on, he did nothing but put into practice the unshakable certitude that he received on that day. His Letters set forth this conviction: Christ is living and reconciles human beings in his Spirit; salvation is given by him to the Gentile world and indeed to all peoples. His entire existence was henceforth seized by this mission. His life and thought were animated by an unconquerable love for Jesus.

Allowing Gentiles to become part of the Christian communities posed theoretical problems. Paul was present at the Council of Jerusalem in A.D. 48/49, which rendered liberating decisions on this point (Acts 15; Gal 2:1-10).

Thereupon Paul traveled to the great urban centers of the Mediterranean world, proclaiming the Gospel of Jesus Christ and establishing churches, i.e., small groups of men and women, free people and slaves, Jews and Greeks, who believed in Christ. His plan was to go to the ends of the known world, possibly as far as the Spanish coast, by way of Rome. All the while, he nurtured the young Churches by his Letters and delegates, recalling the main lines of the Gospel—Jesus Christ is the only Savior.

We have no sure information on the subsequent course and end of Paul's life. He would be executed at Rome on the Ostia Road (Via Ostiensis), probably in A.D. 66/67. Many, especially those who defend the attribution of the Captivity Letters to Paul, think that he had once again regained his freedom, had visited the Churches of Greece and Asia Minor, and perhaps had even gone to Spain. Arrested once again, he endured a harsh imprisonment.

Writings

The traditional order of the Letters, as seen in any Bible, is not based on chronology. Their order is primarily one of length, longest to shortest. In reading them, however, it is advantageous to follow the chronological order.

"The gospel . . . is the power of God" *(Rom 1:16).*

THE LETTER TO THE ROMANS

Human Beings Are Justified through Faith

Paul wanted to visit Rome—the center of the universe in his day—on more than one occasion, but he was prevented from doing so (see Rom 1:13). Now, in the winter of A.D. 56–57, his third missionary journey has been completed, and he has established the Church in the principal Mediterranean urban centers, from Jerusalem to Illyricum (Rom 15:19). In addition, the great crises in Corinth and Galatia seem to have subsided.

Hence, Paul seeks new fields. The West calls to him, and he projects a missionary journey that will take him to the cities along the Spanish coastline. To get there he must pass through Rome (see Rom 15:22-23), and he looks for the welcome and assistance of the Christian community established in the capital.

He will not be a stranger there. The Jewish community at Rome has more than 40,000 members and some fifteen synagogues. Moreover, the seed of the Gospel has already taken root in its midst. We will probably never know who were the first missionaries of Christ there. It may be that pilgrims from Rome were among the witnesses and converts on the day of Pentecost in the year A.D. 30.

In any case, merchants and travelers could surely have encountered the Gospel and the Church on their travels and in their business dealings and could then have become the promoters of a new community at Rome. St. Peter himself was there for a time and eventually suffered martyrdom under the infamous Emperor Nero, but doubtless his coming took place later than the date of this Letter.

The Church of Rome seems to have developed rapidly. In the year A.D. 49 an edict of Emperor Claudius expelled the Jews. Jewish Christians like Priscilla and Aquila were also affected; they found refuge and work in Greece and Asia (see Acts 18:2, 18, 26; 1 Cor 16:19). As a result, converts from paganism became the majority of Christians in Rome. This brought new problems and some difficulties, especially when the exiles returned after two or three years.

In order to announce his coming, Paul dictated a Letter to his secretary, Tertius (Rom 16:22), and entrusted it, apparently, to Phoebe, "a deaconess of the Church at Cenchreae" (Rom 16:1), who was about to travel to Rome. But if he wanted simply to announce his arrival, why did he send so lengthy a Letter? It is probable that his person and ideas were sufficiently well known in Rome and that there was debate over the positions he had taken.

Writing thus to a community, Paul gave free expression to the main concerns that preoccupied him concerning the life of the Church and, above all, concerning faith. To facilitate the reading we can group its themes around three main centers: the necessity of faith, the riches of the faith, the demands of the faith.

We shall discover, contained in these central ideas, the most profound intuitions regarding the realism of the incarnation (Rom 1:3-4), justification and redemption (Rom 3:21-26; 8:2-4), the universality of sin and salvation (Rom 5:12-19), the Paschal Mystery present in Baptism (Rom 6:2-5), the hope of Christians and the future of the universe (Rom 8:19-23), the divine sonship (Rom 8:14-17), the certainty of salvation (Rom 8:28-39), the mystery of Israel and the theology of history (Rom 9—11), spiritual worship (Rom 12:12), and the new priesthood (Rom 15:15-16).

Paul sets forth on a theological level what Jesus himself signified and practiced when he mingled with tax collectors and sinners; he did not condone what they did but he affirmed that justice is a grace of the Father and that it is not acquired by a person's moral, legal, or cultural effort—no matter how scrupulous that might be.

God's love is offered to everyone by God; it is he who sets free, and it is up to each person to embrace this liberation as a source of life. The redemption and salvation of human beings is of another order than that of social, personal, and historical situations. It pertains to a human transformation inaugurated in Jesus.

Hence, if such liberation is given in the mystery of Christ, in Baptism that enables one to participate in it, and in faith in his Gospel, what is the value of the Law and the whole Old Testament and what is the destiny of Israel? This is a question that needs an answer to show the fundamental unity of revelation, of the promise of fulfillment in Christ. Such an answer is even more necessary since non-Jewish Christians ran the risk of ignoring the plan of God inaugurated in Creation and the time of preparation that constitutes the Old Testament and even looking down on Jewish Christians. It is an answer that Paul carefully provides in this Letter (Rom 9:1—11:36).

The Letter presents the essence of Paul's message and his mission. It is regarded as the first formulation of Christian theology. Yet its tranquil tone is far different from the stormy character of the Letter to the Galatians whose themes it amplifies. Nonetheless, we sense herein the stirrings of an impassioned soul, for example beneath some uncalled-for blow (Rom 2:17ff), in the trust of being in God's grace (ch. 8), in the convert's compassion for those of his race (Rom 9:1-15; 10:1; 11:14-16), and in the enthusiasm of the Apostle of Christ (Rom 11:33-36).

The Letter to the Romans also distinguishes itself by its literary variety. In its construction, Paul makes use of liturgical pieces and hymns; he follows the expository style of the rabbis or employs the methods of orators of his day. All of this adds up to an exceptional example of Paul's work.

Did Paul really reach Rome? Yes, but later than he had hoped. In the spring of A.D. 58, he arrived at Jerusalem with the funds collected for the poor Christians of the Mother Church (2 Cor 8—9).

He was arrested in the temple and spent two years in custody at Caesarea before appealing to Caesar as a Roman citizen. In the spring of the year A.D. 60, Paul, apostle and prisoner of Jesus Christ, entered Rome (Acts 28:16) and was welcomed by the Christian community there.

The Letter to the Romans may be divided as follows:

PROLOGUE

CHAPTER 1

Set Apart for the Gospel. 1 Paul, * a servant of Christ Jesus, called to be an apostle and set apart for the service of the gospel [a] 2 that God promised beforehand through his Prophets * in the holy Scriptures, [b] 3 * the gospel concerning his Son who according to the flesh was descended from David, [c] 4 and who according to the Spirit of holiness was proclaimed to be the Son of God in power by his resurrection from the dead: Jesus Christ our Lord. [d]

5 Through him we have received grace and our apostolic commission to proclaim the obedience of faith among all the Gentiles for the sake of his name. [e] 6 And you are among those who are called to belong to Jesus Christ. [f]

7 To all of you who are God's beloved in Rome and called to be saints: * grace to you and peace from God our Father and the Lord Jesus Christ. [g]

Thanksgiving and Prayer.* 8 First of all, I give thanks to my God through Jesus Christ for all of you because your faith has been proclaimed throughout the world. [h] 9 For God, whom I serve with my spirit in the gospel of his Son, is the witness on my behalf that I remember you constantly in my prayers, [i] 10 always asking that by God's will I may somehow be granted my desire of coming to visit you. [j] 11 For I am longing to see you so that I may bestow on you some spiritual gift to strengthen you [k]—12 or, rather, so that we may be mutually encouraged by each other's faith, both yours and mine.

13 I want you to be aware, brethren, * that I have often planned to visit you (although until now I have been prevented from doing so) because it has been my desire to achieve some harvest among you as I have among other Gentiles. [l] 14 I have an obligation to Greeks and non-Greeks * alike, to both the educated and the ignorant. [m] 15 Thus, I am ready to preach the gospel also to you who are in Rome. [n]

a Rom 15:16; Acts 9:15; 13:2; 1 Cor 1:1; Gal 1:10, 15; Phil 1:1; Tit 1:1; Jas 1:1.—b Rom 3:21; 16:25-26; Acts 13:32; Tit 1:2.—c Rom 9:5; 2 Sam 7:12; Mt 1:1; Mk 12:35; Jn 1:14; 7:42; Acts 13:22-23; 2 Tim 2:8; Rev 22:16.—d Rom 10:9; Acts 13:33; Phil 3:10.—e Rom 15:15; 16:26; Acts 2:24; 9:15; 26:16-18; Gal 1:16; 2:7, 9.—f 1 Cor 1:9; Jude 1; Rev 17:14; Num 6:25-26; 1 Cor 1:2-3.—g Rom 8:39; 2 Cor 1:1-2; 1 Thes 1:4.—h Rom 16:19; 1 Cor 1:4; Eph 1:16; 1 Thes 1:8.—i Job 16:19; Jer 42:5; 2 Cor 1:23; Eph 1:16; Phil 1:8; 1 Thes 1:2; 2:5, 10; 2 Tim 1:3.—j Rom 15:23, 32; 1 Sam 12:23; Lk 18:1; Acts 18:21; 1 Cor 4:19; 1 Thes 2:17.—k Rom 15:23; 1 Cor 1:7; 1 Thes 2:17; 3:10.—l Rom 11:25; 15:22; Jn 15:16; Acts 19:21.—m 1 Cor 9:16.—n Rom 15:20; Acts 28:30-31.

1:1 *Paul:* in accord with ancient custom, Paul puts his name at the beginning of the Letter; for information about Paul, see Acts 9:1ff; Phil 3:4-14; and the Introduction to his Letters, pp. 234–235. *Servant:* literally, (1) a "slave," who belongs wholly to his master and is not free to leave, or (2) a "servant," who chooses to serve his master (see Ex 14:31; Ps 18; Isa 41:8-9; 42:1). *Apostle:* one especially commissioned by Christ (see note on Mk 6:30). *Gospel:* see note on Mk 1:1-8. The word Gospel occurs with special frequency in the collection of Paul's Letters (40 times).

1:2 *Prophets:* not just the writers of the Prophetic Books of the Bible but the whole Old Testament, which prophesied about Jesus (see Lk 24:27, 44). *Holy Scriptures:* the Old Testament.

1:3-4 An early Christian profession of faith that proclaims Jesus' sonship as the Messianic descendant of David (see Mt 22:42; 2 Tim 2:8; Rev 22:16) and as the Son of God, as indicated by the Resurrection. Since Jesus is a "life-giving spirit" (1 Cor 15:45), he is able to give the Spirit to those who believe in him.

1:7 *Saints:* the Greek meaning of the word accentuates the idea of "holiness." All Christians are saints insofar as they are "set apart" for God and are being made increasingly "holy" by the Holy Spirit (see 1 Cor 1:2; 1 Thes 4:7). The Christian community regarded its members as made holy through Baptism (Rom 6:22; 15:16; 1 Cor 6:11; Eph 5:26f).

1:8-15 Paul acknowledges that he has no authority over the Church of Rome, which he did not found; he presents himself as a simple Christian who wants to be one in faith with his brothers and sisters through mutual instruction and edification. The word *non-Greeks* (literally, "barbarians") (v. 14) signifies here that the pagans had not received Greek culture.

1:13 *Brethren:* all those (both men and women) who believe in the Gospel are kin of Paul (see Rom 4:3).

1:14 *Greeks and non-Greeks:* literally, "Greeks and barbarians." The "Greeks" were all who spoke Greek or followed the Greek way of life; the "non-Greeks" were all the other Gentiles to whom Paul preached.

The Gospel of God*

Power of Salvation for All Believers. 16 For I am not ashamed of the gospel, since it is the power of God that offers salvation to everyone who has faith—to Jews first, and then to Gentiles as well.[o] 17 In it the righteousness of God is revealed, beginning in faith and established in faith.* As it is written: "The one who is righteous will live through faith."[p]

I: JUSTIFICATION THROUGH FAITH IN JESUS*

A: The World in the Wrath of God*

Exchanging the Truth of God for a Lie. 18 The wrath of God is being revealed from heaven against all the ungodliness and wickedness of those who by their wickedness suppress the truth.[q] 19 [r] For that which can be known about God is clearly evident to them because God has revealed it plainly to them. 20 Ever since the creation of the world the invisible attributes of God's eternal power and divine nature have been clearly understood and perceived through the things he has made.

Therefore, the conduct of these people is inexcusable.[s] 21 Despite knowing God, they refused to honor him as God or give thanks to him. As a result, their speculations became foolish and their uncomprehending hearts became darkened.[t] 22 Although they claimed to be wise, in reality they became fools,[u] 23 exchanging the glory of the immortal God for images fashioned in the likeness of a mortal man or birds or four-footed animals or reptiles.[v]

24 Therefore, God abandoned them in the sinful lusts of their hearts to impurity and the mutual degradation of their bodies.[w] 25 They exchanged the truth of God for a lie and offered worship and service to the creature rather than to the Creator, who is blessed forever. Amen.[x]

26 * That is why God abandoned them to their shameful passions. Their women exchanged natural intercourse for unnatural practices.[y] 27 Likewise, men gave up natural relations with women and were consumed with passion for one another. Men committed shameful acts with men and received in their own persons the fitting penalty for their perversion.[z]

28 Furthermore, since these people did not see fit to acknowledge God, he abandoned them to their depraved way of thinking and to all types of vile behavior. 29 [a] As a result, they are filled with every kind of wickedness, evil, greed, and malice. Reveling in envy, murder, strife, deceit, and malice, they are gossips,[b] 30 slanderers, God-haters, insolent, arrogant, and boastful, as they devise new ways of doing evil and rebel against their parents. 31 They are senseless, faithless, heartless, and ruthless. 32 Although they are fully cognizant of God's decree that those who behave in this way deserve to die, they not only do these things themselves but also praise all those who engage in such conduct.[c]

CHAPTER 2

Judging Is Inexcusable. 1 Therefore, you have no excuse, whoever you may be, when you pass judgment on others. For in judging

o Rom 2:9; Ps 119:46; Acts 3:26; 13:46; 1 Cor 1:18, 24; 2 Tim 1:8.—p Rom 3:21-22; Hab 2:4; Gal 3:11; Phil 3:9; Heb 10:38.—q Rom 2:5, 8-9; Isa 66:15; Jn 3:36; Eph 5:6; Col 3:6; Rev 19:15.—r 19-32: Wis 13:19; Acts 14:15-17; 17:23-29.—s Rom 2:1; Job 12:7-9; Pss 8:4; 19:2; Sir 17:7-9; Isa 40:26; Acts 14:17; 17:25-28.—t Gen 8:21; Jer 2:5; Eph 4:17-18.—u Wis 13:1-9; Isa 5:21; Jer 10:14; Acts 17:29-30; 1 Cor 1:19-21.—v Deut 4:15-19; Ps 106:20; Wis 11:15; 12:24; 13:10-19; Jer 2:11; Acts 17:29.—w Wis 12:25; 14:22-31; Acts 7:41-42; Eph 4:19; 1 Pet 4:3.—x Rom 9:5; Isa 44:20; Jer 13:25-27.—y Eph 4:19; 1 Thes 4:5.—z Lev 18:22; 20:13; Wis 14:26; 1 Cor 6:9, 18; 1 Tim 1:10.—a 29-31: Rom 13:13; Mt 15:19; Mk 7:21-22; Gal 5:19-21; 2 Tim 3:2-4.—b 2 Cor 12:20; Jas 3:2.—c Ps 50:18; Lk 11:48; Acts 8:1; 2 Thes 2:12.

1:16-17 This extremely dense paragraph sums up the entire Letter. When we hear the word "gospel" we should not think of a book, but of the proclamation of salvation through faith. The citation in v. 17 from the prophet Habakkuk (2:4), each word of which here takes on a Christian value, constitutes the theological pivot of the entire Letter.

1:17 *Beginning in faith and established in faith:* literally, "from faith to faith," i.e., by an ever more perfect faith. But other interpretations have been given.

1:18—4:25 In comparison with the liberation brought by the Gospel, humanity apart from Christ and without grace seems to be filled with sin and alienation. Paul begins by sketching a grim picture of the world as a prison and of the darkness in which human beings walk, whether Jews or Gentiles, who have abandoned themselves to their passions and to their own vain efforts (Rom 1:18—3:20). But into this world that is without vitality or a future, the love of God bursts forth and brings liberation. This conviction is central to the section. And this justification is given to whoever believes in Christ (Rom 3:20-31). What does "believe" mean? Paul explains it at length, using what he regards as the magnificent example of Abraham (Rom 4:1-25).

1:18—3:20 Without Christ the world goes astray and cannot reach its goal, which is God. It is under "the wrath of God," an Old Testament phrase that indicates the ineradicable opposition between God and evil (see Isa 9:11-20; 10:4; 30:27). Thus, the world is a victim of corruption, of its useless efforts, of its lack of a sense of sin. Paul is especially sensitive to this situation and paints the dark scene on two panels: an indictment against paganism and a statement on the failure of Judaism. Neither paganism nor Judaism can save human beings.

1:26-27 See note on 1 Tim 1:10.

others you condemn yourself, since you are
doing the same things. [d] 2 We are all aware
that God's judgment on those who commit
such deeds is just. 3 How can you then sup-
pose that you will escape the judgment of
God for doing such things when you are con-
demning those who perform the same
things? [e]

4 How can you despise the riches of God's
kindness and forbearance and patience?
How can you fail to realize that his kindness
is meant to lead you to repentance? [f] 5 By
your obstinate refusal to repent you are stor-
ing up retribution for yourself on the day of
wrath when God's righteous judgment will
be revealed. [g]

6 For God will repay everyone in accor-
dance with what his deeds deserve. * [h] 7 To
those who seek after glory and honor and
immortality by persevering in good works,
he will grant eternal life. [i] 8 But for those who
are slaves to selfish ambition and follow the
path of wickedness and not of truth, wrath
and fury will be their lot. [j]

9 There will be affliction and distress for
everyone who does evil—Jews first and then
Gentiles. [k] 10 However, glory, honor, and
peace await everyone who does good—Jews
first, and then Gentiles. [l] 11 For God shows no
partiality. * [m]

The Law and Conscience.* 12 All those who
have sinned outside the Law will perish out-
side the Law, and all who sinned under the
Law will be judged by the Law. [n] 13 For it is
not those who hear the Law who are justified
by God; rather, it is those who observe the
Law who will be justified. [o] 14 Therefore,
when Gentiles, who do not have the Law, act
by nature in conformity with the Law, they
are a law for themselves, even though they
have no Law. [p] 15 They show that the require-
ments of the Law are inscribed in their
hearts; and their own conscience will also
bear witness for them, since their conflicting
thoughts will accuse or even defend them *
16 on the day when, according to the gospel,
God will judge the thoughts of all through
Jesus Christ. [q]

17 * You call yourself a Jew and rely on the
Law and are proud of your relationship to
God, [r] 18 and you know his will and are able
to distinguish between right and wrong
because you have been instructed in the
Law, [s] 19 and you are confident that you are a
guide to the blind, a light for those in dark-
ness, [t] 20 an instructor of the foolish, and a
teacher of the simple because in the Law you
have the embodiment of knowledge and
truth. [u]

21 You, then, who teach others, do you not
teach yourself? You who preach against
stealing, are you yourself a thief? [v] 22 You
who forbid adultery, are you yourself an
adulterer? You who abhor idols, do you com-
mit sacrilege? [w] 23 You who boast of the Law,
do you dishonor God by breaking it? 24 As it
is written, "Because of you the name of God
is reviled among the Gentiles." [x]

Circumcision and the Heart.* 25 [y] Circum-
cision has value if you obey the Law.
However, if you break the Law, you have
become as if you had never been circum-
cised. [z] 26 In the same way, if one who is not
circumcised keeps the precepts of the Law,
will not his uncircumcision be regarded as
circumcision? [a] 27 Then the man who is not
physically circumcised but nevertheless
observes the Law will condemn you who
have the written code and circumcision but
break the Law. [b]

28 A man is not a Jew who is only one out-
wardly, nor is true circumcision external and
physical. [c] 29 Rather, the Jew is one who is a Jew

d Rom 1:20; Mt 7:1-2.—e Wis 16:15-16.—f Rom 3:25-26; 9:22; Wis 11:23; 15:1; Eph 1:7; Col 2:2; 2 Pet 3:9, 15.—g Ex 33:3; Ps 110:5; Acts 7:51; Rev 6:17; 11:18.—h Ps 62:13; Prov 24:12; Sir 16:14; Mt 16:27; Jn 5:29; 2 Cor 5:10.—i 1 Cor 15:53.—j Ezek 22:31; 2 Thes 1:8.—k Ps 32:10.—l Rom 1:16; 3:9.—m Deut 10:17f; 2 Chr 19:7; Sir 35:12-13; Acts 10:34; Gal 2:6; Eph 6:9; Col 3:25; 1 Pet 1:17.—n Rom 3:19; 1 Cor 9:20; Gal 4:21.—o Mt 7:21; Lk 6:46-49; 8:21; Jas 1:22-25; 1 Jn 3:7.—p Acts 10:35.—q Eccl 12:14; Acts 10:42; 1 Cor 4:4.—r Isa 48:1-2; Jer 8:8; Mic 3:11; Phil 3:4-5.—s Phil 1:10.—t Mt 15:14; Lk 6:39.—u 2 Tim 3:15.—v Ps 50:16-21; Mt 23:3-4.—w Acts 19:31.—x Isa 52:5; Ezek 36:20; 2 Pet 2:2.—y 25-29: Jer 4:4; 9:24-25.—z 1 Cor 7:19; Gal 5:3.—a Rom 8:4; 1 Cor 7:19; Gal 5:6.—b Mt 12:41-42.—c Mt 3:9; Jn 7:24; 8:15, 39; Gal 6:15.

2:6 *Will repay everyone in accordance with what his deeds deserve:* a combination of Ps 62:12 and Prov 24:12 from the Septuagint (the Greek translation of the Old Testament).

2:11 *God shows no partiality:* a basic teaching of both the Old and the New Testament (see Deut 10:17).

2:12-24 This passage is an important one for theology: God speaks to all human beings through the law of conscience; the authentic virtues and the interior resistances of the Gentiles bear witness to this fact.

2:15 Paul takes up and develops the teaching of Jer 31:33 and Wis 17:11.

2:17-20 In the original, the sentence is left incomplete; it has been translated in a way that makes it complete.

2:25-29 For Israel, circumcision was the sign of its covenant with God; to receive it was to belong to the People of God, and the Jews were proud of it. But was the rite enough, when the person did not live the reality that the rite signified? The Prophets had long been criticizing formalism and calling for a religion of the heart (see Jer 4:4; 9:24-25; Lev 26:41; Deut 10:16; 30:6; Sir 35:1-10; Dan 3:36-40; Phil 3:3-7).

inwardly, and true circumcision is of the heart—spiritual, not literal. He receives his praise not from human beings but from God. [d]

CHAPTER 3

The Value of Judaism. 1 Is there any advantage, therefore, in being a Jew? Or what is the value of circumcision? 2 A great deal in every respect. In the first place, they were entrusted with the words of God. [e] 3 What if some were unfaithful? Will their lack of faith nullify the fidelity of God? [f] 4 By no means! God must be true even if every human being is a liar, * as it is written,

"That you may be justified in your words,
and vindicated when you are judged." [g]

5 But if our wickedness serves to confirm the righteousness of God, what are we to say? Is God unjust (I speak of him in human terms) to bring retribution upon us? [h] 6 Of course not! For that would imply that God could not judge the world. [i] 7 But if, as a result of my falsehood, God demonstrates his truthfulness, to his greater glory, why am I still being condemned as a sinner? [j] 8 And why not say, as some people slanderously accuse us of proposing, "Let us do evil so that good may result"? Such people deserve their condemnation. [k]

The Whole World Guilty before God.* 9 Well, then, are we any better? * No, not at all. For we have already charged that both Jews and Gentiles alike are all under the power of sin. [l] 10 [m] As it is written,

"There is no one who is righteous,
not even one.
11 There is no one who has understanding,
there is no one who seeks God.
12 All have turned away;
together they have become worthless.
There is no one who shows kindness,
not even one.
13 Their throats are open graves;
they use their tongues to deceive.
The venom of vipers is on their lips; [n]
14 their mouths are full of cursing and bitterness. [o]
15 [p] Their feet hasten to shed blood;
16 ruin and misery mark their paths.
17 The way of peace they do not know; [q]
18 there is no fear of God before their eyes." [r]

19 Now we know that what the Law says is addressed to those who are under the Law, so that every mouth may be silenced and the entire world may be seen as guilty before God. [s] 20 For no one can be regarded as justified in the sight of God by keeping the Law. The Law brings only the consciousness of sin. [t]

B: The Redemption in Jesus Christ *

God's Righteousness through Faith in Jesus Christ.* 21 But now the righteousness of God that is attested by the Law and the Prophets has been manifested apart from law: [u] 22 the righteousness of God through faith in Jesus Christ for all who believe. No distinction has been made. [v] 23 For all have sinned and thereby are deprived of the glory of God, [w] 24 and all are justified by the gift of his grace that is given freely through the redemption in Christ Jesus. [x]

25 God designated him to be a sacrifice of expiation of sin through faith by the shedding of his blood because in his divine forbearance he allowed to be unpunished the sins previously committed. [y] 26 He thus demonstrated his righteousness in the present time so that he might show himself to be just as the one who justifies anyone who has faith in Jesus.

d Deut 30:6; Jer 4:4; 9:25; Jn 5:44; 1 Cor 4:5; 2 Cor 10:18; Phil 3:3; Col 2:11.—e Rom 9:4; Deut 4:7-8; Pss 103:7; 147:19-20; Acts 7:38.—f Rom 9:6; 11:1, 29; Ps 89:30-37; 2 Tim 2:13; Heb 4:2.—g Pss 51:6; 116:11; Jn 3:33.—h Rom 9:14; Job 34:12-17; Gal 3:15.—i Rom 2:16; Gen 18:25.—j Rom 9:19.—k Rom 6:1.—l Rom 1:18—2:25; 3:23; 1 Ki 8:46; 2 Chr 6:36; Sir 8:5.—m 10-12: Pss 14:1-3; 53:2-4; Eccl 7:20.—n Pss 5:10; 140:4.—o Ps 10:7.—p 15-17: Prov 1:16; Isa 59:7-8.—q Isa 59:7, 8.—r Ps 36:2.—s Rom 2:12; 7:7; Jn 10:14.—t Rom 7:7; Ps 143:2; Acts 13:39; Gal 2:16.—u Isa 46:13; 51:6-8; Jer 23:6; Acts 10:43.—v Rom 1:17; Gal 2:16; Phil 3:9; Col 3:11.—w Rom 3:9; 5:12.—x Rom 4:25; 5:1-2; Jn 1:14; Eph 1:7; 2:6; Tit 3:7.—y Ex 25:17; Lev 16:12-15; Acts 17:31; Heb 2:17; 1 Jn 4:10.

3:4 *Every human being is a liar:* these words are taken from Ps 116:11 LXX; the rest of the verse comes from Ps 51:6 LXX.

3:9-20 To ensure the solidity of his inquiry concerning the universal reign of sin, Paul applies the Biblical proof to it. In the manner of the rabbis, he offers several citations on human corruption from the Psalms and the Book of Isaiah (the references are—in the order of the citations—Pss 14:1-3; 5:9; 140:4; 10:7; Isa 59:7-8; Pss 36:1; 143:21). Paul has led us in this descent into the hell of sin, in which humankind lies impotent, in order to enable us to appreciate the greatness of redemption and the necessity of faith.

3:9 *Are we any better?:* i.e., are Jews better than Gentiles in God's sight?

3:21-31 By dying on the cross, Jesus Christ publicly manifested the justice of God, that is, the faithful fulfillment of what God had promised for the salvation of every human being.

3:21-26 *Sacrifice of expiation* alludes to the cover of the ark, known as the "propitiatory," which played an important role in the Jewish ritual of the Day of Atonement (Lev 16). It was sprinkled with the blood of animals, as though to atone for collective sin. By giving his life, Christ really freed the people from sin and brought them God's forgiveness.

**Justification through Faith Apart from the
Works of the Law.** 27 What reason then does
one have to boast? It is excluded! By works
of the Law? No, rather by the law of faith.[z]
28 For we maintain that one is justified by
faith apart from the works of the Law.[a]

29 Is God the God only of the Jews? Is he
not also the God of the Gentiles? Yes, he is
the God of the Gentiles too,[b] 30 since there is
only one God, and he will justify both the cir-
cumcised and the uncircumcised on the
basis of their faith.[c] 31 Are we thereby nulli-
fying the Law by this faith? By no means! On
the contrary, we are upholding the Law.[d]

C: Abraham Justified through Faith*

CHAPTER 4

Justified through Faith, Not Works.* 1 What
then are we to say about Abraham, our
ancestor according to the flesh?[e] 2 If
Abraham was justified by the works he did,
he has good reason to boast, but not in the
eyes of God.[f] 3 For what does Scripture say?
"Abraham placed his faith in God, and it
was credited to him as righteousness." *[g]

4 Now when a man works, his wages are
not regarded as a gift but as something that
is due to him.[h] 5 However, when someone
who does not work places his faith in one
who justifies the godless, such faith is reck-
oned as righteousness.[i] 6 * In the same way,
David speaks of the blessedness of the one to
whom God attributes righteousness apart
from works:

7 [j] "Blessed are those whose iniquities are
forgiven
and whose sins are blotted out.
8 Blessed is the man
to whom the Lord imputes no guilt."

Justified before Being Circumcised.* 9 Is this
blessedness granted only to the circumcised,
or does it apply to the uncircumcised as
well? We have asserted that Abraham's faith
"was credited to him as righteousness."[k]
10 How was it credited? Was it when he was
circumcised or uncircumcised? Not when he
was circumcised, but when he was uncir-
cumcised.

11 Abraham received the sign of circumci-
sion as a seal of the righteousness that he
had by faith while he was still uncircum-
cised. In this way, he was the father of all
who believe without being circumcised and
who thus have righteousness credited to
them.[l] 12 Therefore, he is the father of the
circumcised who have not only received cir-
cumcision but also follow that path of faith
traversed by Abraham before he was cir-
cumcised.

Justified Apart from the Law.* 13 It was not
through the Law that Abraham and his
descendants received the promise that he
would inherit the world, but through the
righteousness of faith.[m] 14 If those who live
by the Law are the heirs, faith is null and the
promise is void.[n] 15 For the Law produces
only wrath, and where no Law exists, there
cannot be any violation.[o]

16 Therefore, the promise depends on faith,
so that it may be a free gift and the promise
may be guaranteed to all descendants, not
only to the adherents of the Law but also to
those who share the faith of Abraham. For he
is the father of all of us,[p] 17 as it is written, "I

z Rom 8:2; 1 Cor 1:29-31; Eph 2:9.—a Rom 5:1; Acts 13:39; Gal 2:16; Eph 2:9.—b Rom 10:12; Acts 10:34; Gal 3:28.—c Rom 4:11; Deut 6:4; Gal 3:8, 20; Jas 2:19.—d Rom 8:4; Mt 5:17.—e Lk 3:8; Gal 3:6-9.—f 1 Cor 1:31.—g Gen 15:6; Gal 3:6; Jas 2:23.—h Rom 11:6.—i Rom 9:30.—j 7-8: Ps 32:1-2; 2 Cor 5:19.—k Rom 3:30; 4:3.—l Gen 17:10-11; Lk 3:8; Gal 3:6-8.—m Gen 12:7; 18:18; 22:17-18; Sir 44:21; Acts 13:32; Gal 3:16-18, 29.—n Gal 3:18.—o Rom 3:20; 5:13; 7:8; 1 Cor 15:56; 2 Cor 3:7; Gal 3:19.—p Rom 15:8; Sir 44:19; Gal 3:7-9.

4:1-25 There is but one dispensation, that of grace and faith, which excludes all human pride and allows us to receive everything from God with thanksgiving. The story of Abraham is the purest illustration of this truth. Christian faith is present germinally in the faith of the father of believers (see Gal 3:6-8).

4:1-8 The father of believers can do nothing that is of value before God. He is regarded as just, i.e., holy and close to God, because he acknowledges that he is poor and entrusts himself wholly to the Lord. To forgive sins constitutes the gratuitous act par excellence, the act of God (vv. 7-8).

4:3 At first glance, it seems that the Letter of James (2:24) goes against this statement of Paul. However, it is clear from the context in James that the phrase "by works and not by faith alone" does not mean that *genuine* faith is not sufficient for justification but rather that *faith* unaccompanied by works is not *genuine*. Thus, the teaching of James does not conflict with that of Paul.

4:6-8 When a sinner repents, God takes away his unrighteousness by forgiving him when he confesses his sins (see Ps 32:3-5; Ezek 18:23, 27f, 32; 33:14-16.

4:9-12 Abraham became the friend of God (see Gen 15:6) before being circumcised (see Gen 17:19). This means that circumcision is neither the source of nor the condition for being justified; it is simply given as a sign of the promise that God made to Abraham because he believed (Gen 17). Circumcision is the external mark of the Covenant—not the source of righteousness. It is faith that links Christ to the chosen people, who are neither Jews nor Gentiles.

4:13-17 Abraham owes nothing to the Law, for this came into force a long time after him (see Gal 3:17). Moreover, no law can do anything but "lay bare" sin and condemn the sinner (see Gal 3:10). Now, the promise of salvation is something else—it is a grace of God. In Abraham, it is assured to all who believe. Thus, all believers have access to the historic plan of God, and Paul loves to celebrate the universality of faith.

have made you the father of many nations,"[q] in the sight of God in whom he believed, the God who gives life to the dead and calls into being what does not exist.

The Power of Faith.* 18 Though he hoped against hope, he believed that he would become the father of many nations, in fulfillment of the promise, "So shall your descendants be."[r] 19[s] His faith was not shaken when he considered his own body, which was as good as dead (for he was about one hundred years old), and the barren womb of Sarah.[t] 20 Confident in the promise of God, he did not doubt in unbelief; rather, he was strengthened in his faith and gave glory to God,[u] 21 remaining fully convinced that he was able to fulfill his pledge.[v] 22 Therefore, his faith "was credited to him as righteousness."[w]

23 "It was credited to him" was not written with Abraham alone in mind. 24 This was also meant for us as well, to whom it will be credited as righteousness—for us who believe in him who raised from the dead Jesus our Lord[x] 25 who was handed over to death for our sins and who was raised to life for our justification.[y]

II: FAITH, THE RICHES OF LIFE*

CHAPTER 5

A: At Peace with God

Hope Does Not Disappoint. 1 Therefore, now that we have been justified by faith, we are at peace* with God through our Lord Jesus Christ,[z] 2 through whom by faith we have been given access to this grace in which we now live, and we rejoice in the hope of the glory of God.[a] 3 And not only that, but we also glory in our sufferings, because we realize that suffering develops perseverance,[b] 4 and perseverance produces character, and character produces hope.[c] 5 Such hope will not be doomed to disappointment,* because the love of God has been poured into our hearts through the Holy Spirit that has been given to us.[d]

Reconciliation Already Obtained. 6 At the appointed time, while we were still helpless, Christ died for the ungodly.[e] 7 Indeed, it is seldom that anyone will die for a just person, although perhaps for a good person someone might be willing to die. 8 Thus, God proved his love for us in that while we were still sinners Christ died for us.[f]

9 And so, now that we have been justified by Christ's blood, how much more certainly will we be saved through him from divine retribution.*[g] 10 For if, while we were enemies, we were reconciled to God through the death of his Son, how much more certain it is that, having been reconciled, we shall be saved by his life.[h] 11 And not only that, but we now even trust exultantly in God through our Lord Jesus Christ, through whom we have already been granted reconciliation.

B: Adam and Christ—Sin and Grace*

Humanity's Sin through Adam. 12 Therefore, sin entered the world as the result of one man, and death* as a result of sin, and thus death has afflicted the entire human race

q Gen 17:5; Isa 48:13; 1 Cor 1:28; Heb 11:19.—r Gen 15:5.—s 19-20: Gen 17:17; Heb 11:11.—t Gen 18:11.—u 1 Sam 30:6.—v Gen 18:14; Mt 19:26; Lk 1:37.—w Gen 15:6.—x Rom 10:9; Hab 2:2; 1 Cor 9:10; 1 Pet 1:21.—y Rom 8:11; Isa 53:4-5, 12; 1 Cor 15:17; 2 Cor 5:21; 1 Pet 1:3.—z Rom 3:24-28; Lk 2:14; Gal 2:16.—a 1 Cor 15:1; Eph 2:18; 3:12.—b Mt 5:12.—c 2 Cor 12:9-10; Jas 1:2-4; 1 Pet 1:5-7; 4:12-14.—d Rom 8:14-16; Pss 22:5-6; 25:21; Phil 1:20; Heb 3:6.—e Mk 1:15; Gal 4:4.—f Jn 3:16; 1 Pet 3:18; 1 Jn 4:10, 19.—g Rom 1:18; 4:25; 1 Thes 1:10.—h Rom 8:7-8; 2 Cor 5:18; Col 1:21-22; Heb 7:25.

4:18-25 God is the "Master of the Impossible"; he is even powerful enough to bring about the raising of a dead person. It is in such certitude that believers live. Abraham believed in the word of the Lord who announced that two "dead" bodies, i.e., sterile people, himself and Sarah, would give life to Isaac (Gen 15:5). Moreover, circumstances called into question the fulfillment of the promise; yet Abraham—ever the father of believers—never doubted. Thus, he shared the condition of Christians who steadfastly believe in Life because they believe in the risen Jesus, the Son of the Living God. The object of faith is the Passover of Christ.

5:1—11:36 Without faith human beings remain in the night of sin. When they have been justified through Christ and believe in the redemption he gives, they enter into a new life, that of salvation. Paul confronts the believer with a living reality.

First, he speaks of peace and reconciliation (Rom 5:1-11); he must then show how Christ opens for us the way of deliverance from sin (Rom 5:12-21), from death (Rom 6:1-23), and from the Law (Rom 7:1-25); the song of Christian life is a song of the Spirit and of hope. But Paul cannot forget the lot of the Israel that rejects the Gospel; he enters upon a lengthy discussion and asserts again that the love of God is stronger than any human rejection (chs. 9—11).

5:1 *We are at peace:* some manuscripts and Fathers of the Church give: "Let us have peace."

5:5 *Such hope will not be doomed to disappointment:* the hope of believers is more than just an earthly optimism. It is the assurance of our future destiny based on the love of God for us—revealed to us by the Holy Spirit and demonstrated for us by Christ's Death.

5:9 *Saved . . . from divine retribution:* the image expresses the tragic situation of humanity without God, that is, without hope and without an authentic future (see Rom 1:18; 1 Thes 1:10).

5:12-21 The religious history of humanity is here summarized in an incisive synthesis. We should keep our gaze fixed on the luminous heights to which Paul wants to lead us: his vision points to life, grace, and the salvation given in Christ Jesus. The vision is all the more fascinating in that it stands out against the dark background of sin and death.

5:12 *Death:* physical death is the penalty for sin as well as the symbol of spiritual death, the ultimate separation of a human inasmuch as everyone has sinned.[i] [13] Sin was already in the world before there was any Law, even though sin is not reckoned when there is no Law.[j] [14] Nevertheless, death reigned over all from Adam to Moses, even over those who had not sinned by disobeying a command, as did Adam who prefigured the one who was to come.[k]

Grace and Life through Christ. [15] However, the gift is not like the transgression. For if the transgression of one man led to the death of the many, * how much greater was the overflowing effect of the grace of God and the gift of the one man Jesus Christ that has abounded for the many.[l] [16] The gift of God cannot be compared with the sin of the one man. For the one sin resulted in the judgment that brought condemnation, but the gift freely given after many transgressions resulted in justification. [17] For if, because of one man's transgression, death reigned through that man, how much more shall those who receive the abundance of grace and the gift of righteousness come to reign in life through the one man Jesus Christ.[m]

[18] Therefore, just as one man's transgression brought condemnation for all, so one man's righteous act resulted in justification and life for all.[n] [19] For just as through the disobedience of one man the many were made sinners, so by the obedience of one man the many will be made righteous. *[o]

Purpose of the Law. [20] When the Law was added, offenses multiplied; but the increase in sins was far exceeded by the increase in grace.[p] [21] Hence, as sin's reign resulted in death, so the grace of God also might reign through righteousness resulting in eternal life through Jesus Christ our Lord.[q]

C: Death and Life with Christ*

CHAPTER 6

Baptized in Christ Jesus.* [1] What then shall we say? Should we persist in sin in order that grace may abound?[r] [2] Of course not! We have died to sin. How can we live in it any longer?[s] [3] Do you not know that all of us who have been baptized into Christ Jesus were baptized into his death?[t] [4] Through that baptism into his death we were buried with him, so that, just as Christ was raised from the dead by the glory of the Father, * so we too might begin to live a new life.[u]

[5] For if we have been united with him in a death like his, we shall also be united with him in his resurrection.[v] [6] We know that our old * self was crucified with him, so that our sinful body might be destroyed and we might no longer be enslaved to sin.[w] [7] For whoever has died has been freed from sin.[x]

[8] However, if we have died with Christ, we believe that we shall also live with him. *[y] [9] We know that Christ, once raised from the dead, will never die again. Death no longer has power over him.[z] [10] When he died, he died to sin once and for all. However, the life he lives, he lives for God.[a] [11] In the same way, you must regard yourselves as being dead to sin and alive for God in Christ Jesus.[b]

[12] Therefore, do not allow sin to reign over your mortal body and make you obey its desires.[c] [13] Nor should you present any part of your body as an instrument for wickedness leading to sin. Rather, present yourselves to God as having been raised from death to life and the parts of your body to God as instruments for righteousness.[d]

i Gen 2:17; 3:1-19; Wis 2:24; Rom 3:19, 23; 1 Cor 15:21, 22.—j Rom 4:15.—k Gen 3:11-12; 1 Cor 15:21.—l Acts 15:11.—m Jn 10:10.—n Rom 4:25; 1 Cor 15:21-22.—o Rom 3:9; Isa 53:11; Phil 2:8-9.—p Rom 4:15; 7:7-8; Gal 3:19; 1 Tim 1:13,14.—q Rom 6:23; Mt 25:46.—r Rom 3:5-8; 8:31.—s Rom 8:13; Col 3:5; 1 Pet 4:1.—t Mt 28:19; Gal 3:27.—u Acts 2:24; Eph 4:22-24; Col 2:12; 1 Pet 3:21-22.—v 2 Cor 4:10; Eph 2:6; Phil 3:10-11; 2 Tim 2:11.—w Gal 5:24; 6:14; Eph 4:22-23.—x Rom 6:18.—y 1 Thes 4:17.—z Acts 2:24; 13:34; 1 Cor 15:26; 2 Tim 1:10; Rev 1:18.—a Heb 7:27; 9:26-28; 1 Pet 3:18.—b 2 Cor 5:15; 1 Pet 2:24.—c Gen 4:7.—d Rom 12:1; 2 Cor 5:14-15; Eph 2:5; 5:14; Col 3:5.

being from God. *Inasmuch as everyone has sinned:* we start life with a sinful nature (see Gen 8:21; Pss 51:7; 58:4; Eph 2:3).

5:15 *The many:* this has the same meaning as "everyone" in verse 12 (see Isa 53:11; Mk 10:45).

5:19 *Disobedience* is the refusal to acknowledge the primacy of God when it comes to giving life meaning. *Obedience* is the commitment of one's life to the plan and call of God.

6:1-23 Salvation is grace that transcends sin and the power of human beings or even of the Law. This passage urges us to reflect on the meaning of Baptism in the life of a Christian.

6:1-14 In the History of Salvation, there is a unique event: the Death and Resurrection of Jesus; it is the departure for a new life. Through Baptism, the believer enters into this experience of Christ and shares its power. Baptism inaugurates a newness of life that will be brought to completion in the future.

6:4 *Glory of the Father:* God who reveals his power and holiness.

6:6 The adjective *old* has a precise meaning for Paul: it describes the reality of a sinful world that is closed against the new life that has its source in Christ (see 1 Cor 5:7-8; 2 Cor 3:14); the *old self* and the *sinful body* signify the human being as marked by sin (Gal 3:26-29).

6:8 In the experience of Christ, resurrection followed upon death; hence, believers who die with Christ are raised to a new quality of moral life. This resurrection is already a fact, and it exerts itself more and more in the life of believers.

14 For sin is no longer to have any power over
you, since you are not under the Law but
under grace. [e]

A Slave of Righteousness. 15 What then?
Should we sin because we are not under the
Law but under grace? Of course not! [f] 16 [g] Do
you not know that if you offer yourself as an
obedient slave, you are the slave of the one
you obey—either of sin, which leads to
death, or of obedience, which leads to righ-
teousness? [h]

17 Once you were slaves of sin, but, thanks
be to God, you have become obedient in
your heart to that pattern of teaching to
which you have been delivered. [i] 18 Now, hav-
ing been set free from sin, you have become
slaves of righteousness. [j]

19 I am speaking in human terms because
you are still weak human beings. For just as
you once offered your bodies as slaves to
impurity and to lawlessness leading to
greater iniquity, so now present them as
slaves to righteousness for sanctification. [k]

20 When you were slaves of sin, you were
free from the restraints of righteousness. [l]
21 But what advantage did you get then from
the things of which you are now ashamed?
For the end of those things is death. [m]
22 However, now that you have been freed
from sin and bound to the service of God,
the benefit you receive is sanctification, and
the end is eternal life. [n] 23 For the wages of
sin is death, but the gift freely given by God
is eternal life in Christ Jesus our Lord. [o]

D: Christ Has Freed Us from the Law*

CHAPTER 7

The Time of the Law Has Passed.* 1 Are you
aware, brethren (for I am certain that you
are people who have knowledge of the Law),
that a person is bound by the Law only dur-
ing that person's lifetime? [p] 2 For example, a
woman is bound by the Law to her husband
as long as he lives, but if her husband dies,
she is released from her husband in regard
to the Law. [q] 3 Therefore, she will be judged
to be an adulteress if she has relations with
another man while her husband is still alive.
However, if her husband dies, she is free
from that provision of the Law, and if she
then has relations with another man, she is
not an adulteress. [r]

4 In the same way, brethren, through the
body of Christ you have died to the Law and
have been set free to belong to another, that
is, to the one who rose from the dead in
order that we might bear fruit for God. [s]
5 For when we were in the flesh, our sinful
passions were aroused by the Law and at
work in our bodies, and they bore fruit for
death. [t] 6 But now, we are released from the
Law, having died to that which held us cap-
tive, so that we may serve in the new life of
the Spirit in contrast to the old written
code. * [u]

The Function of the Law.* 7 What then
should we say? That the Law is sinful?
Absolutely not! Yet if it had not been for the
Law, I would not have known what sin was. I
would not have known what covet is if the
Law had not said, "You shall not covet." [v]
8 But sin seized the opportunity offered by
the commandment and produced in me all
kinds of covetousness. Apart from the Law,
sin is dead. [w]

9 I lived apart from the Law, but when the
commandment came, sin came to life,
10 and I died. The commandment that was
for life proved to be death for me. [x] 11 For sin,
seizing an opportunity offered by the com-
mandment, deceived me, * and through it
killed me. [y] 12 And so the Law is holy, and the
commandment is holy and just and good. [z]

13 Did what is good, then, cause my death?
By no means! But in order that sin might be

e Gal 5:18; 1 Jn 3:6.—f Rom 5:17, 21.—g 16-18: Jn 8:32-36.—h Jn 8:31-34; 2 Pet 2:19.—i Rom 1:8; 2 Tim 1:13.—j Rom 8:2; 1 Pet 4:1.—k Gal 3:15.—l Jn 8:34.—m Rom 8:6, 13; Prov 12:28; Ezek 16:61, 63.—n Rom 7:25; 1 Cor 7:22; 1 Pet 1:9.—o Gen 2:17; Prov 10:16; Ezek 18:4; Gal 6:7-9; Jas 1:15.—p 1 Cor 1:10; Gal 3:15.—q 1 Cor 7:39.—r Lk 16:18.—s Gal 2:19; Col 1:22.—t Rom 6:21; 7:7-11; 8:6, 13; Gal 5:22.—u Rom 8:2; 2 Cor 3:6.—v Rom 3:20; 8:31; Ex 20:17; Deut 5:21.—w Rom 4:15; 5:13, 20; 1 Cor 15:56.—x Rom 10:5; Lev 18:5; Lk 10:26-28.—y Gen 3:13; Heb 3:13.—z Rom 8:4; Gal 3:21; 1 Tim 1:8.

7:1-25 Human alienation finds expression in three main forms: sin, death, and law. Salvation delivers human beings from this threefold enslavement. The law here is, of course, the Law of Moses, but it is also the command given by God to the first couple and, in the last analysis, every law that is imposed from outside.

7:1-6 Christians have been freed from the Law. This is a way of saying that a new regime, that of the Spirit, henceforth energizes their life.

7:6 *Written code* or "letter" is here the written Law of Moses.

7:7-12 Christ was put to death because he affirmed the priority of the spirit over legalism. In fact, it is sin that falsifies the human condition. Without having the power to neutralize it, the Law unmasks it and then buries human beings under the weight of guilt (see Gal 3:10-14, 19-22).

7:11 *Deceived me:* an allusion to the temptation by the serpent in Gen 3:13.

recognized as such, it brought about my
death through what is good, and therefore
through the commandment sin became
completely sinful. [a]

Sin and Death. 14 We clearly understand
that the Law is spiritual, but I am unspiritu-
al, sold into slavery to sin. [b] 15 I do not under-
stand my own actions. For I do not do what
I want; rather, I do what I hate. [c] 16 Now if I
do what I do not want, then I agree that the
Law is good. * [d] 17 This indicates that it is no
longer I who do it, but sin that dwells in me.
18 For I know that nothing good dwells in
me, that is, in my flesh. I have the desire to
do what is good, but I cannot do what is
good. [e] 19 For I do not do the good I desire;
rather, it is the evil I do not desire that I end
up doing. 20 Now if I do what I do not desire,
it is no longer I who do it, but sin that dwells
in me. [f]

21 I have thus discovered this principle:
when I want to do what is good, evil lies close
at hand. 22 In my innermost self, I delight in
the Law of God, [g] 23 but I perceive in the
members of my body another law at war
with the Law that I cherish in my mind.
Thus, I am made captive to the law of sin
that dwells in my members. [h]

24 What a wretched man I am! Who will
rescue me from this body destined for
death? [i] 25 Thanks be to God through Jesus
Christ our Lord. So then, with my mind I
am a slave to the Law of God, but with my
flesh to the law of sin. [j]

E: The Spirit of God Dwells in Christians*

CHAPTER 8

There Is No Longer Any Condemnation.
1 Hence, there is now no condemnation for
those who are in Christ Jesus. [k] 2 For the law
of the Spirit of life in Christ Jesus has set you
free from the law of sin and death. [l] 3 That
which the Law, weakened by the flesh, was
unable to do, God has done. By sending his
own Son in the likeness of our sinful nature
as a sin offering, he condemned sin in the
flesh [m] 4 so that the righteous requirements
of the Law * might be fulfilled in us who live
not according to the flesh but according to
the Spirit. [n]

**Animated by the Spirit and Rendered
Children of God.*** 5 Those who live according
to the flesh fix their attention on the things
of the flesh, while those who live according
to the Spirit set their thoughts on spiritual
things. [o] 6 The desires of the flesh result in
death, but the desires of the Spirit result in
life and peace. [p] 7 Indeed, the desires of the
flesh will be hostile to God, for they do not
submit to the Law of God, nor could they do
so. [q] 8 Those who live according to the flesh
can never be pleasing to God. [r]

9 You, however, do not live according to
the flesh but according to the Spirit, since
the Spirit of God dwells in you. Anyone who
does not possess the Spirit of Christ cannot
belong to him. [s] 10 But if Christ is in you,
then even though the body is dead as a result
of sin, the Spirit is alive in you because of
righteousness. [t] 11 If the Spirit of him who
raised Jesus from the dead dwells in you,
then the one who raised Christ from the
dead will also give life to your mortal bodies
through his Spirit that dwells in you. * [u]

12 Consequently, brethren, we are not
debtors to the flesh and obliged to live
according to the flesh. [v] 13 If you do live

a Rom 4:15; 5:20; 6:23.—b Rom 6:16; 8:7-8; 1 Ki 21:20, 25; Ps 51:7; 1 Cor 3:1.—c Gal 5:17.—d 1 Tim 1:8.—e Gen 6:5; 8:21; Job 14:4; Gal 5:24; Phil 2:13.—f Rom 7:17; Ps 1:2.—g 2 Cor 4:16; Eph 3:16.—h Rom 6:16; Gal 5:17; Jas 4:1; 1 Pet 2:11.—i Rom 6:6; 8:23.—j Rom 6:22; 1 Cor 15:57; 2 Cor 2:14.—k Rom 16:3.—l Rom 7:23-24; Jn 6:64; 1 Cor 15:45; 2 Cor 3:17.—m Rom 7:18, 19; Jn 3:16-17; Acts 13:38; 15:10; 2 Cor 5:21; Gal 3:13; 4:4; Phil 2:7; Col 1:22; Heb 2:17; 4:15; 1 Jn 4:9.—n Rom 2:26; Gal 5:16-25.—o Mt 16:23; Gal 5:19-21.—p Rom 6:21; 7:5; 8:13; Gal 6:8.—q Rom 5:10; 1 Cor 2:14; Jas 4:4.—r Gal 5:24; 1 Jn 2:16.—s Jn 14:17; 1 Cor 3:16; 6:19; 2 Tim 1:14.—t Ex 29:45; 2 Cor 13:5; Gal 2:20; 1 Pet 4:6.—u Jn 5:21; Acts 2:24.—v Gal 5:24.

7:16 *I agree that the Law is good:* the Holy Spirit reveals to Paul the essential goodness of the Law even when Paul is inclined to rebel against it and disobey it.

8:1-39 In the experience of the love of God there are three dominant elements: the life of the Spirit (vv. 5-13), the sure realization of being children of God (vv. 14-17), and the certainty of future glory (vv. 18-30). This ascending description ends with a triumphant hymn to the unfailing love of the Lord (vv. 31-39).

8:4 *Righteous requirements of the Law:* although the Law is not a means of salvation, it still plays a role in the life of a believer as a moral guide, obeyed out of love for God and by the power of the Holy Spirit. This marks the fulfillment of Jeremiah's prophecy of the New Covenant (Jer 31:33ff).

8:5-17 What is the Christian life in its deepest reality? Paul thinks of all that the Holy Spirit inaugurates in the existence of the believer. He is the Spirit of the Father and of Christ, dwells in every Christian, and is a source of spiritual life for each. We can look upon him as the soul of the Church. He is the power of a progressive transformation, which culminates in the resurrection of the body. In a privileged moment—that of prayer—believers grasp their new state as children of God. Thus, believers escape from the flesh, i.e., an orientation to and a realization of a life without future and without accomplishment (see Gal 5:16-25).

8:11 For the connection between the Resurrection of Christ and that of believers, see 1 Cor 6:14; 15:20, 23; 2 Cor 4:14; Phil 3:21; 1 Thes 4:14.

according to the flesh, you will die. However, if by the Spirit you put to death the deeds of the body, you will live.[w]

[14] * Those who are led by the Spirit of God are children of God.[x] [15] For you did not receive a spirit of slavery leading to fear; rather, you received the Spirit of adoption, enabling us to cry out, "*Abba!* Father!"[y] [16] The Spirit himself bears witness with our Spirit that we are children of God.[z] [17] And if we are children, then we are heirs—heirs of God and joint heirs with Christ, provided that we share his sufferings so that we may also share his glory.[a]

The Future Glory That Shall Be Revealed.* [18] I consider that the sufferings we presently endure are not worth comparing with the glory to be revealed in us.[b] [19] Indeed, creation itself eagerly awaits the revelation of the children of God. [20] For creation was subjected to frustration, not of its own choice but by the will of the one who subjected it, in the hope[c] [21] that creation itself will be freed from its slavery to corruption and share in the glorious freedom of the children of God.[d]

[22] As we know, the entire creation has been groaning in labor pains until now—[e] [23] and not only creation, but we ourselves, who have the firstfruits of the Spirit, groan inwardly as we wait for our adoption as children, the redemption of our bodies.[f] [24] For in hope we were saved. Now to see something does not involve hope. For why should we hope for what we have already seen?[g] [25] But if we hope for what we do not yet see, then we wait for it with patience.[h]

[26] In the same way, even the Spirit helps us in our weakness. For we do not know how to pray as we should, but the Spirit himself intercedes for us with sighs that cannot be put into words.[i] [27] And the one who searches hearts knows the mind of the Spirit, because the Spirit intercedes for the saints in accordance with God's will.[j]

[28] [k] We know that God makes all things work together for good for those who love him * and who are called according to his purpose.[l] [29] For those whom he foreknew he also predestined to be conformed to the image of his Son so that he might be the firstborn among many brethren.[m] [30] Those whom he predestined he also called, and those whom he called he also justified, and those whom he justified he also glorified.[n]

Who Can Separate Us from the Love of Christ? [31] What then can we say in response to all this? If God is for us, who can be against us?[o] [32] He did not spare his own Son but gave him up for all of us. How then can he fail also to give us everything else along with him?[p]

[33] [q] Who will bring any charge against those whom God has chosen? It is God who acquits. [34] Who will condemn? Christ Jesus, who died, or rather rose again, who is at God's right hand and intercedes for us? *[r] [35] Who then can separate us from the love of Christ? Will hardship, or distress, or persecution, or famine, or nakedness, or danger, or the sword?[s] [36] As it is written,

> "For your sake we are being slain all day long;
> we are treated like sheep to be slaughtered."[t]

[37] No, throughout all these things we are conquerors because of him who loved us.[u] [38] [v] For I am convinced that neither death,

w Rom 6:23; Gal 5:24; 6:8; Eph 4:22-24.—x Hos 2:1; Mal 3:17; Mt 5:9; Gal 5:18.—y Mk 14:36; Jn 20:22; Gal 4:5-6; 2 Tim 1:7.—z Jn 1:12; 2 Cor 1:22; Gal 3:26-29.—a Acts 20:32; Gal 4:7; Eph 3:6; 1 Pet 4:13; 5:1.—b 2 Cor 4:17; 1 Pet 4:13.—c Gen 3:17-19.—d Jn 1:12; Acts 3:21; 2 Pet 3:12-13; Rev 21:1.—e Jer 12:4; 2 Cor 5:2-5.—f 2 Cor 1:22; Gal 5:5; Phil 3:21.—g 2 Cor 5:7; 1 Thes 5:8; Tit 3:7; Heb 11:1.—h Ps 37:7.—i Eph 6:18.—j Ps 139:1; 1 Cor 4:5; Rev 2:23.—k 28-29: Eph 1:4-14; 3:11.—l Gen 50:20; Isa 38:17; Jer 29:11.—m Rom 11:2; 1 Cor 15:49; Eph 1:5; 1 Pet 1:2.—n Isa 45:25; Eph 1:5; 2 Thes 2:13-14.—o Rom 4:1; Ex 3:12; Ps 118:6; Heb 13:6.—p Gen 22:13; Jn 3:16.—q 33-34: Isa 50:8.—r Rom 5:6-8; Ps 110:1; Acts 2:29; Heb 7:25; 1 Jn 2:1.—s 1 Cor 4:11.—t Ps 44:23; 1 Cor 4:9; 15:30; 2 Cor 4:11; 2 Tim 3:12.—u 1 Cor 15:57; Gal 2:20; 1 Jn 5:4.—v 38-39: 1 Cor 3:22; Eph 1:21; 1 Pet 3:22.

8:14-17 Because of the Holy Spirit's presence in them, Christians possess a new life as well as a new relationship with God. They have become adopted children of God and heirs through Christ, sharing both in his sufferings and in his glory.

8:18-30 The exalting perspective of salvation is expanded to the dimensions of the universe. Paul takes up a Biblical idea: the cosmos is linked with the fate of humankind, cursed then redeemed. All creation prepares for the new world (v. 22). Paul beautifully sketches the proofs of this movement that is nearing its fulfillment: (1) the presentiment of the universe whose Creator and Lord is Christ (vv. 19-22); (2) the firm hope of believers transformed through Baptism and urged to seize fully that which—even here below—the Spirit inaugurates in them (vv. 23-25); (3) the very prayer by which the Spirit inspires this grand aspiration (vv. 26-27); and finally (4) the will of God, whose love embraces believers in order to associate them with the risen and glorified Christ, so that they may be in the image of his Son, who is himself the perfect image of the Father (see Col 1:15) (vv. 28-30).

8:28 *We know that God makes all things work together for good for those who love him:* some manuscripts have: "We know that all things work together for good to those who love God."

8:34 The reasons why no one can condemn us who are God's elect are three: (1) Christ died for us; (2) Christ is alive and seated at God's right hand, a position of awesome power; and (3) Christ himself makes intercession for us.

nor life, nor angels, nor principalities, nor
present things, nor things to come, nor pow-
ers,[w] 39 nor height, nor depth,* nor any
other creature will be able to separate us
from the love of God in Christ Jesus our
Lord.[x]

F: The Lot of the Jewish People*

CHAPTER 9

Paul's Love for Israel. 1 I am speaking the
truth in Christ—I am not lying, as my con-
science bears witness for me through the
Holy Spirit[y] 2 that I have great sorrow and
unending anguish in my heart. 3 I would
even be willing to be accursed, cut off from
Christ for the sake of my brethren who are
my kinsmen according to the flesh.[z] 4 [a] They
are Israelites* who have the adoption, the
glory, the covenants, the Law, the worship,
and the promises.[b] 5 To them belong the
patriarchs, and from them, according to the
flesh, came the Christ, God forever, who is
over all.* Amen.[c]

The Word of God Has Not Proved False. 6 It is
not as though the word of God has proved
false. For not all who were Israelites truly
belong to Israel,[d] 7 and not all of Abraham's
children are his true descendants. On the
contrary, "It is through Isaac that descen-
dants will bear your name."[e]

8 In other words, it is not through physical
descent that people are regarded as children
of God. Rather, the children of the promise
are those who are counted as descendants.[f]
9 For this is how the promise was worded:
"About this time next year I shall return,
and Sarah will have a son."[g]

10 And not only that, but Rebekah became
pregnant by one man, her husband Isaac.[h]
11 Yet even before her children had been
born or done anything good or bad, in order
that God's purpose of election might pre-
vail,[i] 12 dependent not on human works but
on his call, she was told, "The older shall
serve the younger."[j] 13 As it is written,

> "I loved Jacob,[k]
> but Esau I hated."*

Has God Been Unjust? 14 * What then are
we to say to that? Has God been unjust? Of
course not![l] 15 For he says to Moses,

> "I will have mercy
> on whomever I will have mercy,
> and I will have pity
> on whomever I will have pity."[m]

16 Therefore, it does not depend on any-
one's will or exertion but on God's mercy.[n]
17 For Scripture says to Pharaoh, "I have
raised you up so that I may display my power
in you and that my name may be proclaimed
throughout the earth."[o] 18 Consequently, he
shows mercy to whomever he wills, and he
hardens the hearts of whomever he wills.[p]

w Col 1:16.—x Rom 5:8; 16:3.—y Rom 1:9; 2 Cor 11:31; Gal 1:20; 1 Tim 2:7.—z Ex 32:32; Acts 22:5 1 Cor 12:3.—a 4-5: Rom 3:2; Ex 4:22; Deut 7:6; 14:1-2.—b Gen 17:2; Ex 4:22; Deut 4:13; Ps 147:19; Acts 13:32; Heb 9:5.—c Rom 11:28; Ps 41:14; Mt 1:1-16; Lk 3:23-38; Jn 1:1; Col 2:9.—d Num 23:19; Mt 3:9; Gal 6:16; Heb 4:12.—e Gen 21:12; Gal 3:29; Heb 11:18.—f Rom 8:14; Gal 4:23-28.—g Gen 18:10, 14.—h Gen 25:21.—i Rom 8:28; 9:16.—j Rom 4:17; 11:5-6; Gen 25:23-24.—k Mal 1:2-3.—l Rom 8:31; Deut 32:4; 2 Chr 19:7.—m Ex 33:19; Mt 20:15.—n Eph 2:8; Tit 3:5.—o Ex 9:16; Ps 76:10.—p Rom 11:30-32; Ex 4:21; 7:3; Deut 2:30.

8:39 In the terms *angels . . . principalities . . . height . . . depth* Paul is perhaps speaking of spiritual entities that were considered to be intermediaries between God and humanity.

9:1—11:36 Paul was born a Jew. In his eyes, Christianity was the historical fulfillment of the destiny and hope of Israel, the authentic conclusion of the Old Covenant, which was destined to shine out brightly in the New Covenant that was inaugurated by the Passover of Christ. But reality confronts him with agonizing problems. It had been necessary to make Jewish Christians understand that the salvation given by Jesus Christ caused a break from the Jewish religious system (see 2 Cor 3; Gal; Rom 7). An even more serious problem: Israel had officially rejected Jesus and now rejected the Gospel and the young Church. Paul's reflections are organized in three stages: first, he stresses the fidelity of God (Rom 9:6-29); he then points out Israel's responsibility (Rom 9:31—10:21); finally, with the entire plan of God in view, he insists that the infidelity of Israel is only provisional and partial (Rom 11:1-32). A hymn to the wisdom of God (Rom 11:33-36) ends these difficult pages.

9:4 *Israelites:* descendants of Jacob, who was named Israel by God (see Gen 32:28). The name originally designated the whole nation of Israel (see Jdg 5:7), but after the division into two kingdoms it was given to the northern kingdom alone. In New Testament times, Palestinian Jews used the term "Israelites" to indicate that they were God's chosen people.

Paul shows that God's promises to them are still in effect: *adoption,* i.e., as God's children (see Ex 4:22f; Jer 31:9; Hos 1:1); *glory,* i.e., God's presence among them (see Ex 16:7, 10; Lev 9:6, 23; Num 16:19); *covenants,* e.g., the Abrahamic (see Gen 15:17-21; 17:1-8), the Mosaic (see Ex 19:5; 24:1-10); the Levitical (Num 25:12f; Jer 33:21; Mal 2:4f), the Davidic (see 2 Sam 7; 23:5; Pss 89:4f, 29f; 132:11f), and the New Covenant (prophesied in Jer 31:31-40); and the *promises,* especially those made to Abraham (see Gen 12:7; 13:14-17; 17:4-8; 22:16-18) and the Messianic promises (e.g., 2 Sam 7:12, 16; Isa 9:6f; Jer 23:5; 31:31-34; Ezek 34:23f; 37:24-28).

9:5 *Came the Christ, God forever, who is over all:* another possible translation is: "came the Christ. God who is over all be praised."

9:13 *Hated:* in the Biblical sense of the word, that is, "I preferred Jacob."

9:14-29 Paul thinks with astonishment of the unforeseeable calls of God, who chooses individuals and people from the midst of a sinful world. The image of the potter signifies in the Bible the sovereign freedom of God that defies all expectations. The texts from Hosea (2:25 and 1:10) spoke of the conversion of Israel; Paul interprets them as proclamations of an unprecedented initiative of God: the call of the Gentiles.

19 In response, you will say to me, "Why
then does he still find fault? Who can resist
his will?" [q] 20 [r] But who indeed are you, a
human being, to argue with God? Can some-
thing that is made say to its maker, "Why did
you make me like this?" [s] 21 Surely, the potter
can mold the clay as he wishes. Does he not
have the right to make out of the same lump
of clay one vessel for a noble purpose and
another for ordinary use? [t]

22 What if God, although wishing to show
his wrath and to make known his power, nev-
ertheless with great patience endured the
objects of his wrath * destined for destruc-
tion? [u] 23 He did so in order to make known
the riches of his glory to the recipients of
his mercy whom he prepared long ago for
glory. [v] 24 We are the ones whom he has called
not only from the Jews but also from the
Gentiles. [w]

Witness of the Old Testament. 25 As indeed
he says in Hosea,

"Those who were not my people
  I will call 'my people,'
and her who was not beloved
  I will call 'beloved.' [x]
26 And in the very place
  where it was said to them,
  'You are not my people,'
there they shall be called
  children of the living God." [y]

27 [z] And Isaiah cries out in regard to Israel:

"Though the number of the Israelites
  will be like the sand of the sea,
  only a remnant of them will be saved. [a]
28 For the sentence of the Lord on the
  earth
  will be executed quickly and with
  finality."

29 Isaiah had foretold previously:

"If the Lord of hosts
  had not left us any descendants,
we would have become like Sodom
  and been made like Gomorrah." [b]

A Misguided Zeal. 30 What then shall we say?
That the Gentiles who did not strive for
righteousness have achieved it, that is, righ-
teousness based on faith, [c] 31 but that Israel,
who did strive for righteousness based on the
Law, did not succeed in attaining it? [d] 32 Why
did this happen? Because they did not pur-
sue it by faith but on the basis of works. They
tripped over the stone that causes one to
stumble, [e] 33 as it is written:

"Behold, I am laying in Zion [f]
  a stone that will make people stumble
  and a rock that will cause them to fall.
But the one who trusts in him
  will never be put to shame." *

CHAPTER 10

1 Brethren, my heart's desire and my prayer
to God for them is that they may be saved. [g]
2 I can testify to the zeal that they have for
God, but it is not based on knowledge. [h] 3 For,
being ignorant of the righteousness that
comes from God, and thereby seeking to
establish their own, they have not submitted
themselves to God's righteousness. [i] 4 For
Christ is the fulfillment of the Law for the
justification of all who believe. [j]

The Word Is Near You.* 5 Concerning the
righteousness that comes from the Law,
Moses writes, "The person who does these
things will attain life by them." [k] 6 However,
the righteousness that comes from faith
says, "Do not say in your heart, 'Who will go
up to heaven?' (that is, to bring Christ
down), [l] 7 or 'Who will descend into the
abyss?' (that is, to bring Christ up from the
dead)." * [m] 8 But what does it say?

"The word is near you,
  on your lips and in your heart" [n]

(that is, the word of faith that we proclaim).
9 If you confess with your lips, "Jesus is
Lord," * and believe in your heart that God

q Rom 3:7; 2 Sam 16:10; Wis 12:12; Jas 2:18.—r 20-21: Wis 15:7; Isa 29:16; 45:9; Jer 18:6.—s Job 1:22; Isa 64:8.—t 2 Tim 2:20.—u Rom 2:4; Prov 16:4; Wis 12:20-21; Jer 50:25.—v Rom 8:30; Eph 1:3-13.—w Rom 3:29; 8:28.—x Hos 2:25; 1 Pet 2:10.—y Hos 2:1; Mt 16:16.—z 27-28: Rom 11:5; Isa 10:22-23; 28:22; Hos 2:1.—a Gen 22:17; 2 Ki 19:4.—b Gen 19:24-29; Isa 1:9; Mt 10:15; Jas 5:4.—c Rom 8:31; 10:4, 20; Gal 2:16.—d Rom 10:3; Deut 6:25; Isa 51:1; Heb 11:7.—e Isa 8:14; Lk 2:34; 1 Pet 2:8.—f Isa 28:16; 1 Pet 2:6-8.—g Rom 9:1, 3; Ps 20:5.—h Acts 21:20; 22:3.—i Rom 1:17; 9:31-32; Phil 3:9.—j Acts 13:38-39; 2 Cor 3:14; Gal 3:24; Heb 8:13.—k Lev 18:5; Deut 4:1; Prov 19:16; Gal 3:12.—l Rom 9:30; Deut 9:4; 30:12.—m Deut 30:13; Acts 2:24; 1 Pet 3:19.—n Deut 30:14.

9:22 *Objects of his wrath:* human beings who by sinning incur God's anger.

9:33 This verse uses a combination of two texts from Isaiah that was apparently in common use by the early Christians to defend Christ's Messiahship (see 1 Pet 2:4, 6-8; see also Ps 118:22; Lk 20:17f).

10:5-13 In Jesus God has placed himself at our disposal; we need only acknowledge the risen Christ. This is one of the earliest formulas with which candidates for Baptism professed their faith.

10:7 Paul here combines Deut 30:13 and Ps 107:26.

10:9 *Jesus is Lord:* the word "Lord" occurs some 6,000 times in the Septuagint (the Greek translation of the Old Testament) for "Yahweh," the name of the God of Israel. Here it is applied to Jesus by an early baptismal profession of faith to indicate Christ's divinity.

raised him from the dead, you will be saved.[o] 10 For one believes in the heart and so is justified, and one confesses with the mouth and so is saved.[p] 11 As Scripture asserts, "No one who believes in him will be put to shame."[q] 12 For there is no distinction between Jew and Gentile. The same Lord is Lord of all, and his generosity is manifested to all who call upon him.[r] 13 Indeed, "everyone who calls on the name of the Lord will be saved."[s]

Not All Have Responded to the Good News. 14 But how can they call on him if they have not come to believe in him? And how can they believe in someone about whom they have never heard? And how can they hear without someone to preach to them?[t] 15 And how will there be people to preach if they are not sent? As it is written, "How beautiful are the feet of those who proclaim the good news!"[u]

16 However, not all have accepted the good news. As Isaiah says, "Lord, who has believed our message?"[v] 17 So then, faith comes from what is heard, and what is heard comes through the word of Christ.[w]

18 And so I ask: Have they not heard? Indeed, they have:

"Their voice has gone out all over the world,
and their words to the ends of the earth."[x]

19 Well then, I ask: Is it possible that Israel failed to understand? First Moses says:

"I will make you envious
of those who are not a nation.
I will rouse your anger
against a foolish nation."[y]

20 And Isaiah boldly states:

"I was found by those
who were not looking for me.
I have revealed myself to those
who never asked for me."[z]

21 But regarding Israel, he says:

"All day long I have stretched forth my hands
to a disobedient and rebellious people."[a]

CHAPTER 11

The Remnant of Israel.* 1 [b] I ask, then: Has God rejected his people? Of course not! I too am an Israelite, a descendant of Abraham, of the tribe of Benjamin.[c] 2 God has not rejected his people whom he foreknew. You surely must know what Scripture asserts in the passage about Elijah where he pleads with God against Israel:[d] 3 "Lord, they have killed your Prophets, they have torn down your altars. I alone am left, and they are seeking my life."[e]

4 What was God's response to him? "I have spared for myself seven thousand men who have not knelt before Baal."[f] 5 So too, at the present time, there is a remnant, chosen by grace.[g] 6 But if it is by grace, then it is no longer by works; otherwise grace would no longer be grace.[h]

7 What follows, then? Israel was unable to attain what it was seeking. The elect attained it, but the rest were hardened,[i] 8 as it is written:

"God gave them a spirit of lethargy:
eyes that could not see
and ears that could not hear,
down to this very day."[j]

9 [k] And David says:

"Let their table become a snare and a trap,
a stumbling block and a retribution for them.
10 Let their eyes be darkened so that they cannot see,
and their backs be bent forever."

A Providential Misstep.* 11 And so I ask: Have they stumbled so that they might fall? By no means! However, through their transgression salvation has come to the Gentiles, and this has stirred them to envy.[l] 12 Now if their transgression results in riches for the world, and their loss results in riches for the

o Mt 10:32; Jn 13:13; 1 Cor 12:3.—p Mt 13:15.—q Rom 9:33; Isa 28:16.—r Rom 1:16; 3:22-29; Mt 28:18; Acts 10:34; 15:9, 11; Gal 3:28; Eph 2:14.—s Joel 3:5; Acts 2:21.—t Acts 8:31; Eph 4:21; Tit 1:3.—u Isa 52:7; Nah 2:1; Eph 6:15.—v Isa 53:1; Jn 12:38; Heb 4:2.—w Jn 17:20; Gal 3:2.—x Ps 19:5; Mt 16:15; 24:14; Col 1:6.—y Rom 11:11, 14; Deut 32:21; Tit 3:3.—z Rom 9:30; Isa 65:1.—a Isa 65:2; Jer 35:17.—b 1-2: 1 Sam 12:22; Pss 44:9ff; 94:14.—c Lev 26:44; Jer 31:37; 33:24-26; 2 Cor 11:22; Phil 3:5.—d Rom 8:29.—e 1 Ki 19:10, 14.—f 1 Ki 19:18.—g Rom 3:24; 9:27; Jer 3:14; Zec 13:8.—h Rom 4:4; 9:18; Deut 9:4-5; Gal 3:18.—i Rom 9:31; 2 Cor 3:14; Eph 4:18.—j Deut 29:3; Isa 29:10; Mt 13:13-15; Acts 28:26-27.—k 9-10: Pss 35:8; 69:23-24.—l Rom 5:15-18, 20; 10:19; Deut 32:21; Acts 13:46; 18:6; 28:28.

11:1-10 The threat to "harden" human beings (Isa 29:10) is often cited in the New Testament in censuring seemingly irremediable human blindness (see Mt 13:14; Jn 12:40; Acts 28:26). God is not indifferent to human rejection.

11:11-15 Everything works together to carry out God's plan, which is to save all human beings. The Gospel, poorly accepted by a large part of Israel, has now been announced to the Gentile world. This fact should stir up the envy of the Israelites and make them take more careful notice of Christ. Paul hopes for their conversion and already foresees it as a passage from death to life, like the great resurrection of the people about which Ezekiel speaks in ch. 37.

Gentiles, how much greater riches will their
full participation bring! [m]

13 Now I am addressing you Gentiles.
Inasmuch then as I am the apostle to the
Gentiles, I glory in my ministry [n] 14 in the
hope that it will arouse the jealousy of those
who are of my flesh so that some might be
saved. [o] 15 For if their rejection leads to the
reconciliation of the world, what will their
acceptance be but life from the dead? [p]

The Gentiles' Salvation.* 16 If the firstfruits
are holy, then so is the whole lump of dough.
And if the root is holy, so are the branches. [q]
17 But if some of the branches were broken
off, and you, a wild olive shoot, have been
grafted in their place to share in the rich root
of the olive tree, [r] 18 do not boast over against
the branches! If you start to boast, remem-
ber that it is not you who support the root
but the root that supports you. [s]

19 You will assert, "Branches were broken
off so that I might be grafted in." 20 That is
true. They were broken off because of their
unbelief, but you hold your place only
because of your faith. Therefore, do not rise
up in pride but be filled with awe. [t] 21 For if
God did not spare the natural branches, he
might not spare you either. [u]

22 Therefore, keep in mind the kindness
and the severity of God: his severity toward
those who fell, but his kindness to you pro-
vided that you remain deserving of that
kindness. Otherwise, you also will be cut off, [v]
23 while those who do not persist in their
unbelief will be grafted in, since God has the
power to do so again. [w] 24 For if you have been
cut from what is by nature a wild olive tree
and grafted contrary to nature into a culti-
vated one, how much more easily will these
natural branches be grafted back into their
own olive tree. [x]

All Israel Will Be Saved.* 25 I do not want you
to be unaware of this mystery, brethren, lest
you think yourselves too wise: this hardening
that has afflicted Israel will continue only
until the full number of the Gentiles has
come in. [y] 26 [z] This is how all Israel will be
saved, as it is written,

> "The Deliverer will come out of Zion;
> he will banish godlessness from Jacob. [a]
>
> 27 And this will be my covenant with them
> when I take away their sins." [b]

28 As far as the gospel is concerned, they
are enemies for your sake. However, as
regards election, they are beloved for the
sake of the patriarchs. [c] 29 For the gifts of God
and his calling are irrevocable. [d]

30 Just as you who were at one time disobe-
dient to God have now received mercy as a
result of their disobedience, [e] 31 so they too
have now become disobedient in order that,
through the mercy shown to you, they too
may receive mercy. 32 For God has impris-
oned all in disobedience so that he may show
mercy to all. [f]

The Judgments of God Are Unfathomable.*
33 Oh, the depth of the riches and
wisdom and knowledge of God! How
inscrutable are his judgments and how
unfathomable his ways! [g]

> 34 "For who has known the mind of the Lord,
> or who has been his counselor? * [h]
>
> 35 Or who has given him anything
> in order to receive something in return?" * [i]

m Rom 11:25.—n Rom 1:5; 15:16; Acts 9:15; 26:17.—o 1 Cor 10:33; 1 Thes 2:16.—p Rom 5:10; Lk 15:24.—q Lev 23:10, 17; Num 15:17-21; Ezek 44:30; Neh 10:36-38.—r Jer 11:16; Jn 15:2; Eph 2:11-19.—s Jn 4:22; 1 Cor 1:31.—t Rom 12:16; Prov 28:14; 2 Cor 1:24; 1 Pet 1:17.—u 1 Cor 10:12.—v Jn 15:2, 4; 1 Cor 15:2; Col 1:23; Heb 3:14.—w 2 Cor 3:16.—x Jer 11:16.—y Rom 1:13; 12:16; Prov 3:7; Mk 13:10; Lk 21:24; Jn 10:16; 1 Cor 10:1.—z 26-27: Ps 14:7; Isa 59:20-21.—a Jer 31:34; Mt 23:39; Jn 4:22; Acts 13:23.—b Isa 27:9; 59:20-21; Jer 31:33-34; Heb 8:10.—c Rom 5:10; 15:8; Deut 7:8; 1 Thes 2:15-16.—d Rom 8:28; 9:6; Num 23:19; Isa 54:10; Heb 7:21.—e Eph 2:2; Col 1:21; Tit 3:3.—f Rom 3:9; Gal 3:22; 1 Tim 2:4.—g Job 11:7-8; Ps 139:6, 17-18; Wis 17:1; Isa 55:8-9; Eph 3:10; Col 2:3.—h Job 15:8; Wis 9:13; Isa 40:13; Jer 23:18; 1 Cor 2:11-16.—i Job 35:7; 41:3, 11; Isa 40:14.

11:16-24 As for the Gentile converts who may be tempted to look down on their Jewish brothers, the Apostle recalls their own spiritual origins: the Church was born from the Jewish people; she is the fulfillment of the Remnant of Israel. The Gentiles were grafted like a wild olive shoot onto this olive tree. Each one of them must remember that God has called them out of love and mercy. Even in their rejection of Jesus, the Jews do not lose their quality of belonging to the chosen people.

The lesson is always valid: no one can boast about being saved. Anti-Semitism can be nothing but a scandal in the Christian world: "We are spiritual Semites" (Pope Pius XI). The originality of the Church of Jesus consists in bringing about the unity of humankind, and first of all of the two opposed groups that are the Jews and the Gentiles (Eph 2:14-16).

11:25-32 Prolonging the vision of the Prophets, Paul declares that the chosen people have not been definitively rejected; God does not go back on his choice. The coming of salvation remains open to the People of the Promise. The fate of Israel is not closed off from the salvation that it contributes to bring about for the profit of the Gentiles. In spite of detours of an often tragic history, the Lord continues to guide his people toward a glorious destiny in order to show that he saves his people because he loves them. The entry of the Gentiles cannot signify the exclusion of Israel; God's mercy is for all.

11:33-36 Having arrived at this summit where all humankind is reunited in the salvation of God, Paul cannot refrain from crying out in adoration and admiration.

11:34 This citation is from the Septuagint of Isa 40:13.

11:35 This citation is from an old Greek version of Job 41:3a and does not coincide with the Hebrew text of Job 41:11a.

36 For from him and through him and for
him are all things. To him be glory forever.
Amen.[j]

III: THE NEED FOR FAITH IN DAILY LIFE*

CHAPTER 12

The New Life and the True Worship.
1 Therefore, brethren, I implore you by the
mercies of God to offer your bodies as a liv-
ing sacrifice that is holy and acceptable to
God—a spiritual act of worship.[k] 2 Do not be
conformed to the world, but be transformed
by the renewal of your minds, so that you
will be able to discern the will of God and
to know what is good and acceptable and
perfect.[l]

Right Use of the Gifts of the One Body.
3 Through the grace that God has bestowed
upon me, I advise every one of you not to
think of yourself too highly, but to regard
yourself objectively, based on the measure of
faith that God has granted.[m] 4 [n] For just as in
one body we have many parts, and the parts
do not all have the same function, 5 so we,
though many, make up one body in Christ,*
and individually we are all parts of one
another.[o]

6 [p] We all have different gifts according to
the grace given to us. If it is a gift of prophe-
cy, we should exercise it in proportion to our
faith. 7 If it is a gift of ministry, we should engage
in serving others. If it is a gift of teaching, we
should teach.[q] 8 If it is a gift of exhortation,
we should encourage. Whoever gives alms
should do so generously; whoever leads
should do so conscientiously; whoever
performs acts of mercy should do so
cheerfully.[r]

A Truly Sincere Love. 9 Let your love be sin-
cere. Loathe what is evil and hold fast to
what is good.[s] 10 Love one another with gen-
uine affection. Esteem others more highly
than yourself.[t] 11 Do not be lacking in zeal,
but serve the Lord with spiritual fervor.[u]
12 Be joyful in your hope. Be patient in times
of affliction. Persevere in prayer.[v]

13 Contribute to the needs of the saints,
and practice hospitality.[w] 14 [x] Bless those
who persecute you; bless them and do not
curse them.[y] 15 Rejoice with those who
rejoice; weep with those who weep.[z] 16 Live
in harmony with one another. Do not con-
sider yourself to be better than others, but
associate with the lowly, and never be con-
ceited.[a]

17 Do not repay anyone evil for evil.
Rather, be concerned about doing what is
good in the eyes of all.[b] 18 As much as possi-
ble, and to the extent of your ability, live in
peace with everyone.[c]

19 Dearly beloved, never seek revenge.
Leave that to the time of retribution. For it
is written, "Vengeance is mine, says the
Lord. I will repay."[d] 20 On the contrary,

"If your enemy is hungry, feed him;
 if he is thirsty, give him something to
 drink.
By doing this,
 you will heap burning coals* on his
 head."[e]

21 Do not be conquered by evil, but con-
quer evil with good.

CHAPTER 13

Obedience to Authority.* 1 Let everyone sub-
mit himself to the governing authorities, for
there is no authority except that which
derives from God, and whatever authorities
exist have been instituted by God.[f] 2 Con-
sequently, anyone who resists authority is

j 1 Cor 8:6; Col 1:16-17; 1 Tim 1:17; Heb 2:10; Rev 5:13.—k Rom 6:13; 2 Cor 1:3; 1 Pet 2:5.—l Eph 4:17, 22-23; 5:10, 17; Phil 1:10; 1 Tim 5:4; 1 Pet 1:14.—m Rom 15:15; 1 Cor 12:11; Gal 2:9; Eph 4:7; Phil 2:3.—n 4-5: 1 Cor 12:12, 27; Eph 4:25.—o Jn 17:11; 1 Cor 6:15; Eph 2:16.—p 6-8: 1 Cor 12:4-11, 28-31; 2 Cor 9:7; Eph 4:7-12; 1 Pet 4:10-11.—q 2 Tim 2:15.—r Acts 11:23; 2 Cor 8:2; 1 Tim 5:17.—s Am 5:15; 2 Cor 6:6; 1 Thes 5:21, 22; 1 Tim 1:5; 1 Pet 1:22.—t Ps 133:1; Jn 13:34; Phil 2:3; 1 Thes 4:9; Heb 13:1; 1 Pet 2:17; 2 Pet 1:7.—u Mt 18:32; Acts 18:25.—v Rom 5:2-3; Lk 18:1; Col 4:2; 1 Thes 5:17; Heb 10:32, 36.—w 2 Ki 4:10; Acts 24:17; Heb 13:2; 1 Pet 4:9.—x 14-21: Mt 5:38-48; 1 Cor 4:12; 1 Pet 3:9.—y Lk 6:27-28.—z Job 30:25; Ps 35:13; Sir 7:34; 1 Cor 12:26.—a Rom 11:20; 15:5; Ps 131:1; Prov 3:7; Isa 5:21; Jer 45:5; Phil 2:2-3.—b Prov 3:4; 2 Cor 8:21; 1 Thes 5:15; 1 Pet 3:9.—c Rom 14:19; Mk 9:50; 1 Thes 5:13; Heb 12:14.—d Gen 50:19; Lev 19:18; Deut 32:35; Prov 20:22; Mt 5:39; 1 Cor 6:6-7; Heb 10:30.—e Ex 23:4; Prov 25:21-22; Mt 5:44; Lk 6:27.—f Dan 2:21; Prov 8:15-16; Wis 6:3; Jn 19:11; Tit 3:1; 1 Pet 2:13-17.

12:1—15:13 Following his custom, Paul ends his Letter (before the Epilogue) with a number of ideas and counsels for Christian life in the midst of everyday reality.

12:5 *One body in Christ:* see 1 Cor 12:12-27.

12:20 *Burning coals:* this means that the responsibility of the other is increased, or else that he is given a stimulus to repentance. In any case, the doing of good must not depend on its acknowledgment by the other.

13:1-7 Christians do not keep themselves apart from the city in which they live and normally carry out their duties in the civic community. Society is willed by God as an organized entity. Authority comes from God and is supposed to serve the common good. Paul here gives a practical rule of conduct for Christians. In the face of power, Christians choose neither disinterest nor subversion.

rebelling against what God has appointed, and those who so resist will bring judgment upon themselves.[g]

3 Rulers are a source of fear not to those who do good but rather to those who do evil. Do you wish to be free of fear from someone in authority? Then continue to do what is right and you will receive his approval.[h] 4 For he is acting as God's representative for your welfare. But if you do what is evil, then be afraid for he does not wear a sword for nothing. People in authority are God's servants to mete out punishment to wrongdoers.[i]

5 Therefore, you are obliged to submit, not only because of fear of punishment but also because of conscience.[j] 6 That is why you also pay taxes, for the authorities are God's servants, and they devote themselves to this service.[k] 7 Pay to each person what is rightfully his—taxes to the one to whom taxes are due, tolls to the one to whom tolls are due, respect to the one to whom respect is due, honor to the one to whom honor is due.[l]

Love Is the Fulfillment of the Law.* 8 Owe nothing to anyone except the debt of love you owe one another. The one who loves others has fulfilled the Law.[m] 9 "You shall not commit adultery, You shall not kill, You shall not steal, You shall not covet," and every other commandment are all summed up in this: "You shall love your neighbor as yourself."[n] 10 Love cannot result in any harm to the neighbor; therefore, love is the fulfillment of the Law.[o]

Live Honestly As in the Light.* 11 Do this knowing that the hour has come. It is time for you to awaken from sleep. For our salvation is nearer to us now than it was when we first began to believe.[p] 12 The night is nearly over, and the day is at hand.

Let us therefore cast aside the works of darkness and put on the armor of light.[q] 13 Let us behave honorably as in the day: not in orgies and drunkenness, not in debauchery and licentiousness, not in quarreling and jealousy.[r] 14 Rather, put on the Lord Jesus Christ and allow no opportunity for the flesh to gratify its sinful desires.[s]

CHAPTER 14

The Weak and the Strong in the Community. 1 *[t] Welcome anyone whose faith is weak, but do not get into arguments about doubts.[u] 2 One person may have the faith to eat any kind of food, whereas a weak person may eat only vegetables.[v] 3 The one who eats everything must not look contemptuously on the one who does not, and the one who abstains must not pass judgment on the one who eats, for God has welcomed both.[w] 4 What right do you have to pass judgment on someone else's servant? The master will determine whether that servant will stand or fall. But the servant will be upheld, for the Lord has the power to enable him to stand.[x]

5 One person may consider one day to be more sacred than another, while another may judge all days to be alike. Let everyone be convinced in his own beliefs.[y] 6 Whoever

g Ex 16:8.—h 1 Pet 2:13-14; 3:13.—i Rom 12:19; Deut 1:7; 1 Thes 4:6.—j Prov 24:21-22; Eccl 8:2; 1 Pet 2:19.—k Mt 22:17.—l Mt 22:21; Mk 12:17; Lk 20:25; 23:2.—m Jn 13:34; Gal 5:14; Col 3:14.—n Ex 20:13-17; Lev 19:18; Deut 5:17-21; Mt 5:43-44; 7:12; 19:18-19; 22:39; Mk 12:31; Lk 10:27; Gal 5:14; Jas 2:8.—o Mt 22:40; 1 Cor 13:4-7.—p 1 Cor 7:29-31; Eph 5:8-16; 1 Thes 5:5-7; Jas 5:8.—q Jn 8:12; 2 Cor 6:7; 10:4; Eph 5:11; 6:13-17; 1 Thes 5:4-8; Heb 10:25; 1 Jn 2:8.—r Lk 21:34; Eph 5:18; 1 Pet 4:3.—s Gal 3:27; 5:16; Eph 4:24; 6:11; Col 3:10, 12.—t 1-23: 1 Cor 8:1-13.—u Rom 15:1, 7; 1 Cor 7:9, 11; 9:22.—v Rom 14:14; Gen 1:29; 9:3; 1 Cor 8:1-13; 10:14-33.—w Lk 18:9; Col 2:16.—x Rom 2:1; Mt 7:11; Jas 4:11-12.—y Gal 4:10; Col 2:16.

13:8-10 The fact that love fulfills the whole Law is an essential tenet of Christianity, and Paul shows how it is true in the concrete.

13:11-14 Paul does not say that the end time is near. Rather he affirms that those who have been baptized, and delivered from the grasp of evil, of Satan who is the prince of darkness (Col 1:13), live in a new era. This new state also requires a new way of conduct. As Paul contrasted flesh and spirit, now he contrasts light and darkness—an image that is current to his epoch and self-explanatory. To put on Jesus Christ is to act in accord with the Holy Spirit and his inspirations—in short, to carry out the very meaning of Baptism.

14:1—15:6 Two groups or tendencies are already manifested in the early Christian communities. Some cling, though not without some scruples, to the religious practices in which they have been reared: refusal of sacrificed meats or abstentions from foods on certain days—and these may be termed "the weak." Others, in the same freedom of the Gospel, criticize the former—and these may be termed "the strong." The text evokes a situation like that in Corinth (1 Cor 8:4-13).

Paul has always been categorically opposed to confusing grace with the Law; he has refused to impose either Jewish or Gentile practices on new converts and has declared that all ancient religious practices are excluded as a way to gain justification. He is undoubtedly also aware of the teaching of Jesus concerning what is clean and unclean (Mk 7:1-23). Moreover, he has never refused to allow Christians of Jewish origin to esteem attachment to their religious tradition. He has put clamps on the new freedom only when such freedom turns into provocative pretense and an attitude of superiority.

Freedom is not given to enable someone to criticize others; it does not consist in remonstrating with others about theory or comportment. No principle of freedom can lead to an attitude of scorn or incomprehension. Christians maintain a desire for the salvation of all, and regard everyone as a brother or sister for whom Christ died. They are open to safeguard the relations and exchanges of a varied and pluralist community. Profound respect for the conscience of each person is required, as is the refusal to judge one another. Most important, all must have the freedom to act according to their consciences before God (see Acts 15).

observes the day observes it for the Lord. Also, the one who eats, eats in honor of the Lord, since he gives thanks to God, while the one who abstains, abstains in honor of the Lord and thereby also gives thanks to God.[z]

[7] None of us lives for himself, and none of us dies for himself.[a] [8] If we live, we live for the Lord, and if we die, we die for the Lord. Therefore, whether we live or die, we are the Lord's.[b] [9] It was for this reason that Christ died and came to life again: so that he might be Lord of both the dead and the living.[c]

[10] Why then do you pass judgment on your brother? Or why do you despise your brother? All of us will have to stand before the judgment seat of God.[d] [11] For it is written,

> "As I live, says the Lord,
> every knee shall bow before me,
> and every tongue shall give praise to God."[e]

Consideration for the Weak Conscience. [12] So, then, each one of us will have to give an account of himself to God.[f] [13] Therefore, let us cease passing judgment on one another, but rather judge never to put a stumbling block or hindrance in the way of a brother.[g] [14] I know, and am convinced in the Lord Jesus, that nothing is unclean in itself. However, it is unclean for someone who believes it to be unclean.[h]

[15] If your brother is seriously offended by what you eat, then you are no longer being guided by love. Do not allow the food that you eat to destroy anyone for whom Christ died.[i] [16] Do not let what you think is good to become what others say is evil.[j] [17] For the kingdom of God is not a matter of food and drink but of righteousness, peace, and joy in the Holy Spirit.[k] [18] The one who serves Christ in such things is pleasing to God and respected by others.[l]

[19] Let us * then pursue the ways that lead to peace and mutual edification.[m] [20] [n] Do not destroy the work of God for the sake of food. All food is indeed clean, but it is wrong for you to cause others to fall by what you eat.[o] [21] It is best not to eat meat or drink wine or do anything else that causes your brother to stumble.[p]

[22] Whatever faith you have, keep it between yourself and God. Blessed is the one who has no reason to condemn himself because of what he approves.[q] [23] But whoever has doubts is condemned if he eats, because he does not act from faith. Whatever does not proceed from faith is sin.[r]

CHAPTER 15

Patience and Self-Denial. [1] Those of us who are strong must resolve to put up with the failings of the weak and not please ourselves.[s] [2] Each of us must consider his neighbor's good for the purpose of building him up.[t] [3] Even Christ never sought to please himself, but, as it is written, "The insults of those who insult you have fallen upon me."[u] [4] For everything that was written in the past was written for our instruction, so that by perseverance and the encouragement of the Scriptures, we may continue to have hope.[v]

[5] May the God of perseverance and encouragement grant that you may live in harmony with one another, following in the example of Jesus Christ,[w] [6] so that with one mind and one voice you may glorify the God and Father of our Lord Jesus Christ.[x]

God's Fidelity and Mercy.* [7] Therefore, accept one another for the glory of God, just as Christ has accepted you.[y] [8] For I tell you that Christ became a servant of the circumcised to manifest God's truthfulness by confirming the promises given to the patriarchs[z] [9] and so that the Gentiles might glorify God for his mercy, as it is written:

> "Therefore, I will praise you among the Gentiles
> and sing praises to your name."[a]

z Mt 14:19; 15:36; 1 Cor 10:30-31; 1 Tim 4:3-4.—a 1 Cor 6:19; 1 Pet 4:2.—b Lk 20:38; 2 Cor 5:15; Gal 2:20; Phil 1:20; 1 Thes 5:10.—c Acts 10:42; Rev 1:18; 2:8.—d Mt 7:1; Acts 17:31; 2 Cor 5:10.—e Isa 45:23; 49:18; Phil 2:10-11.—f Mt 12:36; Gal 6:5; 1 Pet 4:5.—g Mt 7:1; 1 Cor 8:9, 13; 2 Cor 6:3.—h Mk 7:5, 20; Acts 10:15; 1 Cor 10:25-27; 1 Tim 4:4.—i 1 Cor 8:11-13; Eph 5:2.—j Rom 2:24; 1 Cor 10:30; Tit 2:5.—k Isa 32:17; 1 Cor 8:8; Gal 5:22.—l Acts 24:16; 2 Cor 8:21.—m Rom 12:18; 15:2; 1 Cor 7:15; 2 Tim 2:22.—n 20-21: 1 Cor 8:11-13; 10:28-29; Tit 1:15.—o Acts 10:15.—p Mt 5:29; 1 Cor 8:13.—q 1 Jn 3:21.—r Rom 14:5; Tit 1:15; Jas 4:17.—s Rom 14:1-2; 1 Cor 9:22; Gal 6:1; 1 Thes 5:14.—t Rom 14:1, 19; 1 Cor 9:19; 10:24, 33; Phil 2:4.—u Ps 69:10; Jn 5:30; Phil 2:5, 8.—v Rom 4:23-24; 1 Mac 12:9; Jer 15:16; 1 Cor 10:11; 2 Tim 3:16.—w Rom 12:16; 1 Cor 1:10; 2 Cor 1:3; 13:11; Eph 4:3; Phil 2:2; 4:2.—x Ps 34:4; Acts 1:14; Rev 1:6.—y Rom 14:1.—z Mt 15:24; Lk 2:21; Acts 3:25; 2 Cor 1:20.—a Rom 11:30; 2 Sam 22:50; Ps 18:50; Mt 9:8.

14:19 *Let us:* some manuscripts and Fathers of the Church have: "We."

15:7-13 It is the unity of believers that glorifies God (Rom 15:6). That is why, despite the fact that Christ himself preached only to the Jews—to the circumcised—he willed that the Gentiles should also be called to salvation and thereby attest that they too are loved by God. In that same love, all Christians should embrace their neighbors.

10 And again it says:
"Rejoice, O Gentiles, with his peo-
ple." * [b]
11 Further it adds:
"Praise the Lord, all you Gentiles,
and let all the peoples praise him." [c]
12 And again Isaiah asserts:
"The root of Jesse shall come,
the one who will arise to rule the
Gentiles;
the Gentiles will hope in him." * [d]
13 May the God of hope fill you with all joy
and peace in believing, so that you may grow
rich in hope by the power of the Holy
Spirit. [e]

EPILOGUE *

Apostle to the Gentiles.* 14 Brethren, I
myself am convinced that you yourselves
are immersed in goodness, filled with all
knowledge, and able to instruct one anoth-
er. [f] 15 Nevertheless, I have written to you
rather boldly to refresh your memory in
some respects because of the grace given to
me by God. [g] 16 He has appointed me to be a
minister of Christ Jesus to the Gentiles in
the priestly service of the gospel of God, in
order that the Gentiles might become an
acceptable offering consecrated by the Holy
Spirit. [h]
17 In Christ Jesus, then, I have reason to
glory in my service of God. [i] 18 I will not dare
to speak of anything except what Christ has
accomplished through me to lead the
Gentiles to obedience to God by word and
deed, [j] 19 by the power of signs and wonders,
through the power of the Spirit of God.
So from Jerusalem * and the surrounding
area, even as far as Illyricum, I have com-
pleted the preaching of the gospel of
Christ. [k] 20 Moreover, I have always striven
to preach the gospel of Christ where the
name of Christ is not known, not wanting
to build on someone else's foundation. [l]
21 Rather, as it is written:
"Those who have never been told of him
shall see,
and those who have never heard of
him shall understand." [m]

Paul's Plans for Traveling—Even to Spain.*
22 That is why I have so often been prevented
from coming to you. [n] 23 But now, since there
is nothing more to keep me in these regions,
and since for a good many years I have
desired to visit you, [o] 24 I hope to see you
when I am on my way to Spain. Then, after I
have enjoyed your company for a while, you
can send me on my way there. [p]
25 Presently, however, I am going to Jeru-
salem to minister to the saints. [q] 26 For
Macedonia and Achaia * have resolved to
make a contribution for the benefit of the
poor among the saints in Jerusalem. [r]
27 They were pleased to do so, and indeed
they are indebted to them, for if the Gentiles
have come to share in their spiritual bless-
ings, they owe it to them to share their mate-
rial blessings with them. [s]

b Deut 32:43; Isa 66:10.—c Ps 117:1.—d Isa 11:10; Mt 12:21; Rev 5:5; 22:16.—e Rom 5:1-2; 1 Cor 2:4; 1 Thes 1:5.—f 2 Cor 8:7; Eph 5:9.—g Rom 1:5; 12:3.—h Rom 11:13; Isa 66:20; Acts 9:15; Phil 2:17.—i Phil 3:3; Heb 2:17.—j Acts 15:12; 2 Cor 12:12.—k Jn 4:48; Acts 19:11.—l Rom 1:15; 2 Cor 10:13-18.—m Isa 52:15.—n Rom 1:13; 1 Thes 2:18.—o Rom 1:10-13; Acts 19:21-22.—p 1 Cor 16:6; Tit 3:13.—q Acts 19:21; 20:22.—r Acts 16:9; 1 Cor 16:1; 2 Cor 8:1-4; 9:2, 12.—s Rom 9:4; 1 Cor 9:11.

15:10 The citation from Deut 32:43 is given in the Septuagint version.

15:12 The citation is based on Isa 11:10 and Rev 5:5; 22:16. *Root of Jesse:* Jesse was the father of David (see 1 Sam 16:5; Mt 1:6), and the Messiah was the "Son of David" (Mt 21:9). *The Gentiles will hope in him:* this prophecy is fulfilled in the evangelization of the Gentiles.

15:14—16:27 *Paul has set forth his main ideas on Christian faith in Christ dead and risen. He now briefly explains his plans and in this context tells his readers in what his ministry consists. The Letter ends with a liturgical hymn that is also a profession of faith.*

15:14-21 Paul regards his apostolic work as a sacred service, as a Liturgy of God in the world of human beings; in fact, it is in the name of God and under the inspiration of the Holy Spirit that the Apostle intervenes to prompt people to belief and to lead the human family to be committed to God. He looks upon this action as the true sacrifice, one that expresses a gift and a love for life itself. It is understood that a community that proclaims the Gospel is also a community that celebrates the Eucharist (see Rom 1:9; 12:1; Phil 2:17).

Paul is conscious that, aided by the power of Christ and the Holy Spirit, he is carrying out a proper task. He makes the Gospel present in the human groups of the Gentile world and rejoices in having accomplished a foundational work.

15:19 *Jerusalem* and *Illyricum,* which borders on Macedonia in the northwest, are the two extremes of Paul's apostolate at this time.

15:22-33 Rome is not to be anything more than a stopover on Paul's journey to Spain. For he plans to travel to the very ends of the West to continue his mission to make the Gospel present where it has not yet been announced. Apparently, he intends to go to Jerusalem to bring to indigent Christians ("saints") of that mother community the fruits of the collection organized by Christians converted from paganism. This will be not only a gesture of mutual aid but a test of unity among Christians of both Gentile and Jewish origin (see 1 Cor 16:14; 2 Cor 8—9; Gal 2:10). A genuine fraternal communion requires a new practice of exchanging goods with one another.

In the wake of the Galatian crisis, the Apostle is justified in thinking that he risks being badly received in Judea. The prayer of the Romans will be a comfort to him. The Book of Acts tells the story of his arrest in Jerusalem (ch. 21) and his journey to Rome (chs. 27—28).

15:26 *Achaia:* the Roman province of southern Greece.

28 Therefore, when I have completed this task and have delivered the fruit of their generosity to them, I will set out for Spain and visit you along the way.[t] 29 And I am sure that when I come, I shall do so with the full measure of the blessing of Christ.[u]

30 Therefore, I exhort you, brethren, by our Lord Jesus Christ and by the love of the Spirit, to join me in my labors by praying to God for me[v] 31 that I may be delivered from the unbelievers in Judea and that my service in Jerusalem may be acceptable to the saints there.[w] 32 In that way, I can come to you in joy, if God so wills, and be refreshed together with you.[x] 33 The God of peace be with you all. Amen.[y]

CHAPTER 16

Recommendation of Phoebe. 1 * I commend to you our sister Phoebe, who is a deaconess * of the Church at Cenchreae.[z] 2 Welcome her in the Lord in a manner worthy of the saints, and help her with whatever she may need from you, for she has been a benefactor of many people, including myself.[a]

List of Greetings. 3 Give my greetings to Prisca and Aquila, my fellow workers in Christ Jesus.[b] 4 They risked their lives for me, and I as well as all the Churches of the Gentiles am grateful to them. 5 Greet also the Church that assembles in their house.

Give my greetings to my beloved friend Epaenetus, who was the first convert to Christ in the province of Asia.[c] 6 Greet Mary, who has worked extremely hard for you. 7 Greet Andronicus and Junia, * my relatives who were in prison with me; they are eminent in the ranks of the apostles and were in Christ before I was.[d]

8 Greet Ampliatus, my beloved in the Lord. 9 Greet Urbanus, our fellow worker in Christ, and my dear friend Stachys.[e] 10 Greet Apelles, * who has proved worthy in the service of Christ, and those who belong to the family of Aristobulus. *[f]

11 Greetings to my kinsman Herodion. Greet those in the Lord who belong to the household of Narcissus. * 12 Greet Tryphaena and Tryphosa * who labor diligently in the Lord's service. Greet my dear friend Persis, who also works hard for the Lord.[g] 13 Give my greetings to Rufus, * one chosen by the Lord, as well as to his mother who has also been a mother to me.[h]

14 Greet Asyncritus, Phlegon, Hermes, Patrobas, Hermas, and the brethren who are with them. 15 Greetings to Philologus and Julia, Nereus and his sister, and Olympas, as well as all the saints who are with them.[i] 16 Greet one another with a holy kiss. All the Churches of Christ send you their greetings.[j]

Beware of Dissenters. 17 I urge you, brethren, to watch out for those who incite dissensions and obstacles in opposition to the teaching that you have learned. Take care to avoid them.[k] 18 For such people are not servants of our Lord Jesus Christ but of their own appetites, and by smooth words

t Rom 15:24.—u Rom 1:10-11.—v 2 Cor 1:11; Gal 5:22; Phil 1:27; Col 1:8; 4:3; 2 Thes 3:1; Heb 13:18.—w Acts 21:17; 2 Cor 1:10; 2 Thes 3:12; 2 Tim 3:11.—x Acts 18:21; 1 Cor 16:18; 2 Cor 7:13; Philem 7.—y Rom 16:20; 2 Cor 13:11; Phil 3:9; 1 Thes 5:23; 2 Thes 3:16; Heb 13:20.—z Acts 18:18; 2 Cor 3:1; 1 Tim 5:10.—a Acts 9:13; Phil 2:29.—b Acts 18:2, 18-26; 1 Cor 16:19; Gal 1:22; Eph 1:13; 2 Tim 4:19.—c Acts 2:9; 1 Cor 16:15, 19; Col 4:15; Philem 2.—d Rom 9:3; Col 4:10; Philem 23.—e Rom 16:3.—f Acts 11:14.—g 1 Thes 5:12.—h Mk 15:21; 2 Jn 1.—i Acts 9:13.—j 1 Cor 16:20; 2 Cor 13:12; 1 Thes 5:26; 1 Pet 5:14.—k Mt 7:15; 1 Cor 5:11; Gal 1:8; Tit 3:10.

16:1-24 Relations between the Churches became closer thanks to the fraternal relations among their members. Many of the persons named here remain unknown to us. *Phoebe,* who exercises a ministry of assistance among poor and sick women in Cenchreae, the port of Corinth, is possibly the bearer of the Letter. *Prisca and Aquila:* since "Prisca" is a variant of "Priscilla," it is obvious that these are the same two people who are placed at Rome, Corinth, and Ephesus by the Book of Acts and Paul's Letters (see Acts 18:2, 18-19, 26; 1 Cor 16:19; 2 Tim 4:19). In the Greek, Roman, and Jewish names, we can assume differences of social condition. Thus, this list testifies to the internal diversity of communities assembled together in the Church of Christ and, at the same time, to the responsibilities held by members of each group, made up of lay people, men or women, celibate or married.

In the midst of these salutations, a severe condemnation is lodged against all those who sow division and scandal. Paul is probably thinking of Judaizing preachers (see Gal 5:7-12; Phil 3:18f) or teachers of religion preoccupied with their profit.

16:1 *Phoebe, who is a deaconess:* this verse seems to allow an office of a woman deacon although Scripture does not define the specific responsibilities of a woman deacon. See also 1 Tim 4:14.

16:7 *Junia:* this name is usually taken to be masculine; others see it as feminine. In fact, some manuscripts have "Julia" in place of "Junia."

16:8-10 *Ampliatus . . . Urbanus . . . Stachys . . . Apelles:* these are all common names of slaves found in the imperial household.

16:10 *Aristobulus:* some think this name refers to the grandson of Herod the Great and the brother of Herod Agrippa I.

16:11 *Narcissus:* sometimes identified with Tiberius Claudius Narcissus, a wealthy freedman of the Roman Emperor Tiberius.

16:12 *Tryphaena and Tryphosa:* may refer to twin sisters who were wont to bear names based on the same root. *Persis:* i.e., a Persian woman.

16:13 *Rufus:* possibly the Rufus mentioned in Mk 15:21 as the son of Simon the Cyrenian, who helped Jesus carry his cross.

and flattery they deceive the minds of the simple.[l] 19 Your obedience has become known to all and has caused me to rejoice greatly over you. However, I want you to be wise in what is good and innocent in what is evil;[m] 20 then the God of peace will soon crush Satan under your feet. The grace of our Lord Jesus Christ be with you.[n]

Greetings from Paul's Companions at Corinth. 21 Timothy, my coworker, sends greetings to you, as do Lucius and Jason * and Sosipater, my kinsmen.[o] 22 I, Tertius, who am writing down this letter, greet you in the Lord.[p] 23 Greetings also from Gaius, * my host and the host to the whole Church, and from Erastus, the city treasurer, and our brother Quartus.[q] [24 The grace of our Lord Jesus Christ be with you all. Amen.] *

Glory to God through Jesus Christ *

25 Now to him who has the power to
strengthen you
in accordance with the gospel that I
preach
and the proclamation of Jesus Christ,
according to the revelation of the
mystery
that was kept secret for long ages[r]
26 but is now revealed,
and through the prophetic writings is
made known to all the nations
according to the command of the eternal God
to bring them to the obedience of
faith—[s]
27 to God who alone is wise,
through Jesus Christ
be glory forever! Amen.[t]

l Rom 14:18; 2 Sam 15:6; Phil 3:18-19; Col 2:4; 2 Pet 2:3.—m Rom 1:8; Jer 4:22; Mt 10:16; 1 Cor 14:20.—n Rom 15:33; Gen 3:15; Mt 4:10; Lk 10:19; 1 Cor 16:23; 2 Cor 13:13; 1 Thes 5:28; 2 Thes 3:18.—o Acts 13:1; 16:1-2; 19:22; 20:4; 1 Cor 4:17; 16:10; Phil 2:19-22; Heb 13:23.—p 1 Cor 16:22; Gal 6:11; Philem 19.—q Acts 19:29; 20:4; 1 Cor 1:14; 2 Tim 4:20.—r Isa 48:6; 1 Cor 2:7; 2 Cor 9:8; Eph 1:9; 3:3-9; Col 1:26; Jude 24.—s Rom 1:2, 5; Eph 3:4-5, 9; 2 Tim 1:10; 1 Pet 1:20; Tit 1:3.—t Rom 11:36; Gal 1:5; Eph 3:20-21; Phil 4:20; 1 Tim 1:17; 2 Tim 4:18; Heb 13:21; 1 Pet 4:11; 2 Pet 3:18; Jude 25; Rev 1:6.

16:21 *Jason:* possibly the person mentioned in Acts 17:5-9. *Sosipater:* some think this is the son of Pyrrhus from Beroea who is called Sopater in Acts 20:4.

16:23 *Gaius:* some think this is the Titus Justus in whose house Paul lodged while in Corinth (see Acts 18:7 and 1 Cor 1:14). *Erastus, the city treasurer:* this may be the same person referred to in Acts 19:22 and 2 Tim 4:20. He may also be the person mentioned in the following Latin inscription recently found on a block of stone at Corinth: "Erastus, commissioner of public works, bore no expense of this pavement."

16:24 This verse is found in some manuscripts (see v. 20).

16:25-27 This fine liturgical hymn expresses the Church's joy at living in a time when the mystery of salvation is being fulfilled. *Mystery:* Paul uses this word to set forth: (1) the Incarnation (see 1 Tim 3:16); (2) Christ's saving Death on the Cross (see 1 Cor 2:1, 7); (3) the restoration of all things in Christ (see Eph 1:9); (4) the change wrought by Christ's Resurrection (see 1 Cor 15:51); and (5) the inclusion of both Jew and Gentile in the Kingdom of God (see v. 25).

"You . . . are the body of Christ, and each of you is a part of it . . . apostles . . . prophets . . . teachers" *(1 Cor 12:27-28).*

THE FIRST LETTER TO THE CORINTHIANS

Communities Making Their Way in the Great Cities

Once again, the Church is born in a large city. In the first century A.D., Corinth was the capital of central and southern Greece. In this important commercial center at the heart of the Mediterranean world, all possible ideas commingled, creating a cultural and religious ferment.

The city was known for its sporting life, but also for the moral corruption that gave it its reputation. "Live like a Corinthian" was a slogan suggesting an environment teeming with criminality and libertinism. Seamen coming ashore in this cosmopolitan port were certainly not the only ones to take advantage of that life. Sacred prostitution flourished in the temple of Aphrodite, the favorite goddess of the city.

"There are many in this city who are my people," the Lord had told Paul in a vision (Acts 18:10).

From the winter of A.D. 50–51 to the summer of A.D. 52, the Apostle laid the foundations of a vital community, whose members he recruited chiefly from among pagans of modest circumstances (Acts 18:1-18).

Two years later, while preaching the Gospel in Ephesus, Paul was informed of the divisions that were agitating his young Greek Church. In addition, two Christians came from Corinth to lay their problems before him. He then wrote the present Letter, which we know as the First Letter to the Corinthians; it had been preceded, however, by another that has been lost (see 1 Cor 5:9).

The outline is a simple one. Serious incidents have been brought to the Apostle's knowledge; these have also raised some concrete questions, of varying degrees of importance; Paul simply deals with the several points one after another.

As a result, this Letter is in no sense a systematic doctrinal treatise. The author follows the list of the situations experienced at Corinth, and this enables him to see the dynamic growth of a young Church, but also its crises.

Nonetheless, this Letter gives us a rather alarming portrait of the community. It shows that the Gospel does not transform a pagan mentality in one day. The newly baptized must review their behavior in the light of the message of Jesus and rectify their judgment, which is permeated by the thinking and morals of their environment.

These Greeks are characteristically prompt to embrace new ideas and can easily regard the Church as simply a philosophical group. Their love of freedom threatens to lead them back to libertinism and turn them into a cause of scandal for those who are weaker or more demanding. In order to exalt the life of the spirit, they look down on what comes from the body and they more easily become its slaves. Like all Christians, they are tempted to choose in the Gospel that which corresponds with their own likes and to neglect the rest.

This Letter is an exceptional document in the history of the early Church. In addition to the internal problems of a community, it also brings before us important issues that are debated: confronting a civilization's currents of ideas and ways of life; dissension in thought and disparity in fortune; discipline within the community; questions of sexuality in the face of an environment wherein eroticism seems to be the rage (Corinth is the capital of dissoluteness); and the problem of marriage and celibacy.

Other issues that it lays bare concern the social relations of Christians with pagans; the attitude toward other religious practices; the types of behavior in the Liturgy; and the demands of the spiritual initiative. Most of all, because of its birth in the midst of a culture, Christianity must question itself, in fact as well as in theory, about its originality and its differences with respect to the life of an age and an environment.

In this context, we are more interested in what inspires the reaction of Paul. Obviously, as a Jew, he would be mistrustful of the cultural and religious agitation of Corinth; if he does not like the rigorist legalism of the scrupulous, he is also without pity for those who confuse freedom with disorder.

Nonetheless, he does not respond simply according to his own religious tastes; in the face of questions posed and dangers encountered, he meditates on the essential points of faith: salvation in the Death and Resurrection of Christ, the mystery of the Church, the presence of the Spirit, the meaning of the Eucharist, the requirements of a faith that wishes to grow and its influence on the behavior of the baptized, and the hope that guides the Christians' existence and colors their view of the world in the light of Easter.

Paul reminds his correspondents that the Gospel is not a philosophical theory to be discussed. He brings them personally into the presence of the dead and risen Christ who gathers together and transforms human beings in the Church—which is his Body—and calls them to a radical renewal of life.

Despite the dangers he must point out and the sufferings they cause him (2 Cor), Paul will always be proud of this community that he has founded in such a pervasive pagan environment. He praises its sincere and active faith, as well as its generosity, which is not without some illusions and a dangerous feverishness; he admires the rich gifts that the Spirit is pouring out on this handful of men and women who live the Gospel and challenge all the cultural pressures brought to bear on them by their environment.

The First Letter to the Corinthians may be divided as follows:

I: Greetings and Thanksgiving (1:1-9)
II: Divisions in the Church of Corinth (1:10—4:21)
III: Deviant Behavior (5:1—6:20)
IV: Marriage and Celibacy among Christians (7:1-40)
V: Christians and Pagan Customs (8:1—11:1)
VI: Liturgical Assemblies and Their Problems (11:2—14:40)
VII: The Resurrection (15:1-58)
VIII: Final Recommendations and Greetings (16:1-24)

I: GREETINGS AND THANKSGIVING

CHAPTER 1

Address to a Church.* 1 Paul, called by the
will of God to be an apostle of Christ Jesus,
and Sosthenes* our brother,[a] 2 to the
Church of God in Corinth,* to those who
have been sanctified in Christ Jesus and
called to be holy together with all those
everywhere who call on the name of our
Lord Jesus Christ, their Lord as well as
ours.[b] 3 Grace to you and peace from God
our Father and the Lord Jesus Christ.[c]

4 I continually give thanks to my God for
you because of his grace that has been
granted to you in Christ Jesus.[d] 5 For
through him you have been enriched in
every way in all facets of speech and knowl-
edge,[e] 6 as our testimony about Christ has
been confirmed in you.[f]

7 Therefore, you do not lack any spiritual
gift as you wait for the revelation of our Lord
Jesus Christ.[g] 8 He will keep you steadfast
until the very end, so that you may be
blameless on the day of our Lord Jesus
Christ.[h] 9 God is faithful, and it is by him
that you have been called into fellowship
with his Son, Jesus Christ our Lord.[i]

II: DIVISIONS IN THE CHURCH OF CORINTH*

The Existence of Factions. 10 Brethren, I
exhort you in the name of our Lord Jesus
Christ to be in full agreement with one
another and not permit any divisions to
arise among you. Be perfectly united in
mind and purpose.[j] 11 For I have heard
reports from Chloe's people, brethren, that
there are quarrels among you.*[k]

12 What I mean is that each of you is
asserting, "I belong to Paul," or "I belong to
Apollos,"* or "I belong to Cephas," or "I
belong to Christ."[l] 13 Has Christ now been
divided? Did Paul die on the cross for you?
Was it in Paul's name that you were bap-
tized?[m]

a Acts 18:17; Rom 1:1; Eph 1:1.—b 1 Cor 10:32; Acts 18:1; Rom 1:7.—c Rom 1:7.—d Rom 1:8.—e 2 Cor 8:7; 9:11.—f 2 Thes 1:10; 1 Tim 2:6; Rev 1:2.—g 1 Cor 12:1-11; Mt 16:27; Lk 17:30; Rom 1:11; Tit 2:13; Jas 5:7-8.—h 1 Cor 5:5; Am 5:18; Phil 1:6; 1 Thes 3:13.—i 1 Cor 10:13; Deut 7:9; Isa 49:7; 1 Jn 1:3.—j 1 Cor 11:18; Phil 2:2.—k 1 Cor 3:3; Acts 1:14.—l 1 Cor 3:4, 22; 16:12; Jn 1:42; Acts 18:24-28.—m Mt 28:19; Acts 2:38.

1:1-9 From the outset Paul emphasizes his calling as an apostle, because if throughout the Letter he teaches, reproaches, and corrects, he does so in the name of the mission he has received from Christ. See note on Mk 6:30.

1:1 *Sosthenes:* perhaps the same person as in Acts 18:17.

1:2 *Church of God in Corinth:* see note on 2 Cor 1:1.

1:10—4:21 The divisions in the Church cannot be regarded simply as a phenomenon inevitable in any form of communal life. The divisions here bear on essentials; they show that the Gospel has not been understood and that people had an erroneous idea of the role of the apostles.

1:11 The name *Chloe* probably identifies a Christian woman of Corinth, some members of whose household have brought the news to Paul.

1:12 *Apollos:* one of the important figures in the beginnings of Christianity, and Paul speaks more than once of his sincerity (see Acts 18:24-29; 1 Cor 3:4-5, 22; 16:12). Some scholars think he may be the author of the Letter to the Hebrews. *Cephas:* the apostle Peter (see Jn 1:42), who may have paid a visit to Corinth.

14 I am thankful that I never baptized any of you, aside from Crispus and Gaius,[n] 15 so that no one can say you were baptized in my name. (16 I also baptized the household of Stephanas. Aside from those I do not know if I baptized anyone else.)[o]

The Message of the Cross and Human Wisdom.* 17 For Christ did not send me to baptize but to preach the gospel—and to do so without words of human wisdom lest the cross of Christ be devoid of its meaning.[p] 18 Indeed, the message of the cross is foolishness to those who are perishing, but to us who are being saved it is the power of God.[q] 19 For it is written,[r]

> "I will destroy the wisdom of the wise,
> and the understanding of the learned
> I will bring to naught." *

20 Where now are the wise ones? Where are the men of learning? Where are the debaters of this present age? Has God not shown the wisdom of the world to be foolish?[s] 21 For since, in the wisdom of God, the world was unable to come to know him through wisdom, he chose, through the folly of preaching, to save those who have faith.[t]

22 Jews demand signs, and Greeks look for wisdom,[u] 23 but we proclaim Christ crucified. This is a stumbling block to Jews and foolishness to Gentiles;[v] * 24 but to those who are called, both Jews and Greeks, Christ is the power of God and the wisdom of God.[w] 25 For the foolishness of God is wiser than human wisdom, and the weakness of God is stronger than human strength.[x]

God Has Chosen Those Who Count for Nothing. 26 Consider, brethren, your calling. Not many of you were wise by human standards, * not many were powerful, not many were of noble birth.[y] 27 Rather, God chose those who were regarded as foolish by the world to shame the wise; God chose those in the world who were weak to shame the strong.[z] 28 God chose those in the world who were lowly and despised, those who count for nothing, to reduce to nothing those who were regarded as worthy,[a] 29 * so that no one could boast in the presence of God.[b]

30 It is through him that you are in Christ Jesus, who became for us wisdom of God, as well as righteousness, sanctification, and redemption.[c] 31 Therefore, as it is written, "If anyone wishes to boast, let him boast in the Lord."[d]

CHAPTER 2

Jesus Christ—and Him Crucified. 1 When I came to you, brethren, I did not proclaim to you the mystery of God * with words of eloquence or wisdom.[e] 2 For I resolved that, while I was with you, I would know nothing except Jesus Christ—and him crucified.[f] 3 I came to you in weakness, in fear, and in great trepidation.[g] 4 My message and my proclamation were not made with persuasive words of wisdom, but in a demonstration of the Spirit and of power,*[h] 5 so that your faith might rest not on human wisdom but on the power of God.[i]

A: The Mysterious Wisdom of God

The Plan of God, True Wisdom. 6 However, to those who are mature, we do speak of wisdom, although not a wisdom of this age or of

n Acts 18:8; 19:29; Rom 16:23.—o 1 Cor 16:15-17; Acts 11:14.—p 1 Cor 2:1, 4, 13; Jn 4:2; Acts 2:38.—q 1 Cor 2:14; Rom 1:16; 2 Cor 2:15.—r Job 5:12-13; Isa 29:14; Mt 11:25.—s 1 Cor 2:6, 8; Job 12:17; Isa 19:12; Gal 1:4.—t 1 Cor 6:2; Rom 11:14.—u Mt 12:38; 16:1; Jn 2:11; Acts 17:18-21.—v 1 Cor 2:2; Lk 2:34; Gal 3:1, 5:11.—w Rom 8:28; Col 2:3.—x 2 Cor 13:4.—y Mt 11:25; Jn 7:48; Rom 8:28.—z 1 Cor 3:18, 19; Jas 2:5.—a Rom 4:17; Jas 2:5.—b Jdg 7:2; Eph 2:9.—c 1 Cor 1:2; Jer 23:5-6; Rom 3:24-26; 4:17; 16:3; 2 Cor 5:21; Eph 1:7; Col 1:14; 1 Thes 5:23.—d Ps 44:9; Jer 9:23; 2 Cor 10:17.—e 1 Cor 1:17; 2:13; 2 Cor 1:12.—f 1 Cor 1:23; Gal 6:14; Col 1:23.—g 1 Cor 4:10; Acts 18:1-18; 2 Cor 11:29-30.—h 1 Cor 4:20; Rom 15:13, 19; 1 Thes 1:5.—i 2 Cor 4:7; 6:7.

1:17-25 The most beautiful construction of the human spirit cannot by itself bring salvation to the human race. This section does not oppose faith and philosophy to one another. It affirms above all that people are saved not by an intellectual theory but by God's intervention in Jesus Christ. Faith does not consist in an ideology.

1:19 The citation is from Isa 29:14, where the Lord denounces the "wise" for their policy of seeking an alliance with Egypt against King Sennacherib of Assyria. *The wise:* the 6th-century B.C. Athenian statesman Aristedes remarked that every street in Corinth had its own so-called wise man, who claimed to have a solution to all the problems of the world.

1:23 Jesus was a stumbling block for the Jews, because they were expecting a Messiah who would perform sensational wonders (see Mt 12:38; Jn 4:48); he was foolishness to Gentiles, because he did not act in accordance with human wisdom.

1:26 *Wise by human standards:* literally, "wise according to the flesh," that is, in the eyes of human beings.

1:29-31 "Boasting" refers to a person's sin in thinking that one is saved by oneself. The truth is that we live only from God and for God. Hence, the only "boasting" possible is "boasting in the Lord."

2:1 *Mystery of God:* God's plan of salvation, which involves Jesus and the cross (see 1 Cor 1:18-25; 2:2, 8-10). Some manuscripts have "testimony" in place of "mystery."

2:4 Paul is not downgrading study and preparation for preachers. He is simply stressing that in addition to such things they also need the Holy Spirit working in their hearts in order for their words to bear fruit.

the rulers of this age * whose end is not far distant.[j] [7] Rather, we speak of the mysterious and hidden wisdom of God, which God decreed before the ages for our glory.[k] [8] None of the rulers of this age comprehended it. If they had, they would not have crucified the Lord of glory. *[l] [9] For as it is written,

> "Eye has not seen, ear has not heard,
> nor has the human heart imagined
> what God has prepared for those
> who love him."[m]

The Spirit Enables Faith To Mature. [10] However, God has revealed these things to us through the Spirit. For the Spirit explores everything, even the depths of God.[n] [11] And just as no human being comprehends any person's innermost being except the person's own spirit within him, so also no one comprehends what pertains to God except the Spirit of God.[o]

[12] We have not received the spirit of the world but the Spirit who is from God, so that we may understand the gifts bestowed upon us by God.[p] [13] And we speak of these things in words taught to us not by human wisdom but by the Spirit, expressing spiritual things in spiritual words. *[q]

[14] An unspiritual person refuses to accept what pertains to the Spirit of God, for to him such things are foolish. He is unable to understand them because they can be discerned only in a spiritual way.[r] [15] A spiritual person * discerns all things, and he is himself subject to no one else's judgment:[s]

> 16 "For who has ever known the mind of
> the Lord?
> Who has ever been his instructor?"

But we possess the mind of Christ.[t]

CHAPTER 3

You Are Still Infants in Christ. [1] Brethren, I could not talk to you as spiritual people, but as worldly, as infants in Christ.[u] [2] I fed you with milk, rather than with solid food that you were not ready to digest. Indeed, even now you are still not ready to receive it,[v] [3] for you are still of the flesh.

As long as jealousy and rivalry continue among you, are you not of the flesh and acting as mere mortals?[w] [4] Whenever someone says, "I belong to Paul," and another asserts, "I belong to Apollos," are you not acting in a merely human fashion?[x]

B: Missionaries and Servants of Christ*

God's Coworkers. [5] What then is Apollos? What is Paul? We are only servants through whom you have come to believe, as the Lord assigned each to accomplish.[y] [6] I planted the seed, and Apollos watered it, but God caused it to grow.[z]

[7] Therefore, neither the one who plants nor the one who waters is of any importance but only God who causes the growth.[a] [8] The one who plants and the one who waters have a common end, and each will be rewarded in accordance with his labor.[b] [9] For we are God's coworkers; you are God's field, God's building.[c]

[10] By the grace that God has given to me, I laid a foundation like a skilled master builder, and someone else is building on that foundation. But each one must be careful how he builds on it.[d] [11] For no one can lay any foundation other than the one that has already been laid, namely, Jesus Christ.[e]

[12] Now if anyone builds on that foundation with gold, silver, and precious stones, or with wood, hay, and straw,[f] [13] the work of each

j Eph 4:13; Phil 3:15; Col 4:12; Heb 5:14.—k Mt 13:35; Rom 16:25; Col 1:27.—l 1 Cor 1:20; Lk 23:34; Acts 13:27; Jas 2:1.—m Isa 64:3; 65:17; Jas 1:12.—n Mt 11:25; 13:11, 16-17; 2 Cor 12:1, 7; Gal 1:12.—o Prov 20:27; Jer 17:9.—p 1 Cor 1:20, 27; Rom 8:15; Jas 2:5.—q 1 Cor 1:17.—r 1 Cor 1:18; Jn 14:17.—s 1 Cor 3:1; Rom 7:14; Gal 6:1.—t Wis 9:13; Isa 40:13; Jn 15:15; Rom 11:34.—u 1 Cor 2:15; 14:20; Rom 7:14.—v Jn 16:12; Heb 5:12-14; 1 Pet 2:2.—w 1 Cor 1:11; Rom 13:13; Gal 5:20; Jas 3:13-16.—x 1 Cor 1:12.—y 1 Cor 4:1; Acts 18:24; 2 Cor 6:4; Eph 3:7.—z 1 Cor 4:15; Acts 18:1-11, 24.—a 2 Cor 12:11; Gal 6:8.—b 1 Cor 9:17; Ps 18:21; Mt 25:21.—c Isa 61:3; Mk 16:20; 2 Cor 6:1; Eph 2:20-22; 1 Pet 2:5.—d Rom 12:3; 15:20; Eph 2:20.—e Isa 28:16; Eph 2:20.—f 1 Cor 4:15.

2:6 *Rulers of this age:* not only the Jewish and Roman leaders under whom Jesus was crucified (see Acts 4:25-28) but also the cosmic powers that were in league with them (see Eph 1:20-23; 3:10).

2:8 Here *the Lord of glory* is Jesus Christ. In the Old Testament, it is a title of God (see Ex 24:16; Pss 24:7; 29:9); Paul is therefore asserting here the divinity of Jesus.

2:13 *Expressing spiritual things in spiritual words:* another possible translation is: "expressing spiritual realities to spiritual people."

2:14-15 *Unspiritual person . . . spiritual person:* an *unspiritual person* is one who follows mere natural human instincts (see Rom 8:9; Jude 19); a *spiritual person* is one who follows the Spirit of God. The former lives according to the "natural" order and the latter according to the "supernatural" order.

3:5—4:21 The apostles are not inventors of foreign mysteries and strange secrets. They are sent to build up the community of God, and are therefore subject to the Lord's judgment. This is one of the main texts in which Paul gives a glimpse of how he understood his personal mission.

person will come to light. For the Day * will disclose it, because it will be revealed with fire, and the fire itself will test the worth of each person's work.[g] 14 If what has been built survives, the builder will be rewarded.[h] 15 If it burns down, that person will suffer loss. The person will be saved, though only by passing through fire. *[i]

You Belong to Christ. 16 Do you not realize that you are God's temple, and that the Spirit of God dwells in you?[j] 17 If anyone destroys God's temple, God will destroy that person. For the temple of God is holy, and you are that temple.[k]

18 Let no one delude himself. If anyone among you considers himself to be wise by worldly standards, he must become a fool in order to be truly wise.[l] 19 For the wisdom of this world is foolishness with God. It is written,

> "He catches the wise in their own craftiness,"[m]

20 and again,

> "The Lord knows the thoughts of the wise, that they are futile."[n]

21 And so, let no one boast about human beings. For everything belongs to you,[o] 22 whether Paul or Apollos or Cephas, the world or life or death, the present or the future. All belong to you,[p] 23 and you belong to Christ, and Christ belongs to God.[q]

CHAPTER 4

Do Not Judge before the Appointed Time. 1 People should regard us as servants of Christ and stewards of the mysteries of God.[r] 2 Now it is required of stewards that they be found trustworthy.[s] 3 It is of no importance to me if I am to be judged by you or by any human court. I do not even judge myself.

4 I personally have nothing on my conscience, but that does not mean that I am innocent. It is the Lord who judges me.[t] 5 Therefore, do not pronounce judgment before the appointed time, until the Lord comes. He will bring to light what is hidden in darkness and will disclose the motives of all hearts. Then each one will receive the proper praise from God.[u]

Fools for Christ. 6 Brethren, I have applied all this to Apollos and myself for your benefit, so that you may learn from us the meaning of the saying, "Do not go beyond what has been written." * None of you should become inflated with pride against anyone else.[v] 7 Who made you so important? What do you have that you did not receive? And if you have received it, why do you boast as though you had not received it?[w]

8 You already have everything! You have already become rich! You have become kings without our help! How I wish that you truly reigned so that we might reign with you! *[x]

9 It seems to me that God has designated us apostles as the last of all, like men sentenced to death, because we have become a spectacle to the world, to angels, and to men.[y] 10 We are fools for the sake of Christ, but you are wise in Christ. We are weak, but you are strong. You are held in honor, but we are in disrepute.[z]

11 To this very hour, we endure hunger and thirst. We are poorly clad and beaten and homeless,[a] 12 and we exhaust ourselves working with our hands. When we are cursed, we bless; when we suffer persecution, we endure it;[b] 13 when we are slandered, we respond gently. We are regarded as the rubbish of the world, the dregs of humanity, to this very day.[c]

The Authority of a Father in Christ. 14 I am writing all this not to make you ashamed but to admonish you as my beloved children.[d]

g 1 Cor 1:8; 4:5; Mt 3:11-12; 2 Thes 1:7-10; 2 Tim 1:12, 18.—h Isa 45:2.—i Jude 23.—j 1 Cor 6:19; 2 Cor 6:16; Eph 2:20-22; Heb 3:6.—k 2 Cor 7:1.—l 1 Cor 1:20; 8:2; Isa 5:21; Gal 6:3.—m 1 Cor 1:20; Job 5:13; Rom 1:22.—n Ps 94:11.—o 1 Cor 4:6; Rom 8:32.—p 1 Cor 1:12; Rom 8:38.—q 1 Cor 15:23; 2 Cor 10:7; Gal 3:29.—r 1 Cor 3:5; 9:17; Rom 16:25; Tit 1:7; 1 Pet 4:10.—s 1 Cor 9:17; Mt 24:45; Lk 19:17.—t Job 9:2; 2 Cor 1:12; 5:10; 10:18; Acts 23:1; Rom 2:16; 1 Jn 3:21.—u 1 Cor 3:13; Job 12:22; Mt 7:1-2; 1 Thes 2:19.—v 1 Cor 1:19, 31; 3:19, 20.—w Jn 3:27; Rom 12:3, 6.—x Rev 3:17-18.—y 1 Cor 15:31; Isa 20:3; Rom 8:36; 2 Cor 4:8-12; 11:23; Heb 10:33.—z 1 Cor 1:18; 2:3; 3:18; Acts 17:18; 26:24; 2 Cor 11:19; 13:9.—a Mt 8:20; Acts 23:2; Rom 8:35; 2 Cor 11:23-27.—b Mt 5:44; Acts 9:6-14; 18:3; 20:34; Rom 12:14; 1 Thes 2:9; 1 Pet 3:9.—c Isa 30:22; Jer 20:18; Lam 3:45.—d 1 Cor 6:5; 15:34; 1 Thes 2:11; 2 Thes 3:14.

3:13 *The Day:* the day of judgment—to the joy of the righteous and the gloom of the wicked. *Fire:* an element that destroys but also purifies.

3:15 Many theologians see in this verse an implicit reference to purgatory.

4:6 *Do not go beyond what has been written:* this proverbial saying was perhaps current in Corinth; there are those, however, who think that this was originally a marginal note and was later inserted into the text. In any case, the meaning seems to be: Do not exaggerate, do not make things complicated.

4:8 Although the Corinthians are only beginners in faith, they act as if they have already reached the level of mature Christians. Paul shows how ludicrous this attitude is in the face of the hardships that the very preachers of the faith encounter and endure day after day.

[15] Even though you have ten thousand tutors in Christ, you do not have many fathers, for I became your father in Christ Jesus through the gospel. [e]

[16] I appeal to you then to be imitators of me. [f] [17] For this reason I have sent you Timothy, who is my beloved and faithful son in the Lord. He will remind you of my ways in Christ, as I teach everywhere in every Church. [g]

[18] Some of you have become arrogant, on the assumption that I am not coming to you. [h] [19] However, I will come to you soon, if it is the Lord's will, and then I will ascertain the actual power of these arrogant people as opposed to their words. [i] [20] For the kingdom of God* is not a matter of words but of power. [j] [21] What would you prefer? Am I to come to you with a whip or with love and a spirit of gentleness? [k]

III: DEVIANT BEHAVIOR*

CHAPTER 5

Reports of Sexual Immorality. [1] There have been widely circulated reports of sexual immorality among you, immorality of such a nature that not even pagans practice—the union of a man with his father's wife. [l] [2] How can you be proud of yourselves? You should rather have been overcome with grief and expelled from the community anyone who acted in such a manner. [m]

[3] I for my part am with you in spirit, even though I am not physically present. I have already passed judgment on the man who did this, as if I were actually present. [n] [4] In the name of our Lord Jesus Christ, when you have all assembled together and I am with you in spirit through the power of our Lord Jesus, [o] [5] you are to hand over this man to Satan to be destroyed in the flesh, so that on the day of the Lord his spirit may be saved. [p]

[6] Your boasting is not good. Do you not know that a small amount of yeast leavens the whole batch of dough? [q] [7] * Throw out the old yeast so that you may become a fresh batch of unleavened dough. And truly you already are, because Christ, our paschal lamb, has been sacrificed. [r] [8] Therefore, let us celebrate the feast, not with the old yeast, the yeast of depravity and wickedness, but with the unleavened bread of sincerity and truth. [s]

[9] In my letter, I wrote to you not to associate with people who are leading immoral lives. * [t] [10] Obviously, I was not referring to contact with people in the world who are immoral or with those who are greedy or thieves or worshipers of false gods, since to do this you would have to leave the world. [u] [11] What I really meant to get across was that you should not associate with any brother or sister who is sexually immoral, greedy, an idolater, a slanderer, a drunkard or a robber. You should not even eat with such a person. [v]

[12] It is no concern of mine to judge those who are outside the fold. * It is your responsibility to judge those who are inside. [w] [13] God will pass judgment on the outsiders. Banish the evil person from your midst. [x]

CHAPTER 6

Avoid Lawsuits against Each Other.* [1] If any of you has a dispute with another, how can you seek judgment before those who are unrighteous * instead of before the saints? [y] [2] Do you not know that the saints will judge the world? And if the world is to be judged

e 1 Cor 9:12, 14, 18, 23; Gal 4:19; Philem 10.—f 1 Cor 11:1; Phil 3:17; 4:9; 1 Thes 1:6; 2 Thes 3:7, 9.—g 1 Cor 16:10; Acts 16:1; 19:22; 1 Tim 1:2.—h Jer 43:2.—i 1 Cor 16:5, 6; Acts 18:21; 2 Cor 1:15, 16.—j 1 Cor 2:4; Rom 14:17; 15:13; 1 Thes 1:5.—k 2 Cor 1:23; 2:1; 10:2; 13:2, 10.—l Lev 18:7-8; 20:11; Deut 23:1; 27:20.—m 2 Cor 7:7-11.—n Col 2:5; 1 Thes 2:17.—o 2 Thes 3:6.—p 1 Cor 1:8; Mt 4:10; 1 Tim 1:20.—q Mt 16:6, 12; Gal 5:9; Jas 4:16.—r Ex 12:1-13; Deut 16:1-2; Mk 14:12; 1 Pet 1:19.—s Ex 12:15-20; 13:7; Deut 16:3.—t 2 Cor 6:14; Eph 5:11; 2 Thes 3:6, 14.—u 1 Cor 10:27; Jn 17:15; Eph 5:5; Col 3:5.—v 1 Cor 10:7, 14; Mt 18:17; Lk 15:2; Rom 7:1; 2 Thes 3:6, 14; 2 Jn 10.—w 1 Cor 6:1-4; Mk 4:11.—x Deut 13:6; 17:7; 19:19; 22:24; Jdg 20:13.—y Mt 18:17.

4:20 *Kingdom of God:* the reign of God in the lives of his people, consisting of a new birth (Jn 3:3-8) and new life in Christ (2 Cor 5:17), which is evinced by dedicated membership in the Church and service to others (Mt 25:40ff).

5:1—6:20 Paul here denounces some behaviors as real scandals. He has confidence, nonetheless, that the power of Christ will transform the lives of the baptized.

5:7-8 These verses have been described as the earliest Easter homily in Christian literature. Paul urges the Corinthians to keep the feast of Unleavened Bread (which followed Passover) by living the Christian life in total dedication to God (see Rom 12:1-2; 1 Pet 2:5). The true Passover is the Death of Christ, which should give rise to a life of newness, purity, and integrity in the same way that during the feast of Unleavened Bread the old bread gave way to unleavened bread.

5:9 This earlier Letter has been lost, although some scholars suggest that a fragment of the original Letter can be found in 2 Cor 6:14—7:1.

5:12 *Those who are outside the fold:* non-Christians. A Jewish expression. See Mk 6:11.

6:1-11 Paul condemns the litigiousness of some members of the Church.

6:1 *Unrighteous:* describes simply those who have not yet been justified by faith, that is, non-Christians, as contrasted with the *saints*, that is, Christians sanctified by God.

by you, how can you consider yourselves as
incompetent to deal with smaller cases? [z]
[3] Do you not realize that we are to judge
angels? * Why then should we not deal with
matters of this life? [a]

[4] Therefore, if you have such matters to
resolve, how can you seek judgment from
those who have no standing in the Church?
[5] I write this to make you ashamed. Is it real-
ly possible that there is no one among you
who is wise enough to mediate a dispute
between brethren? [b] [6] Why should a brother
go to court against another brother, seeking
a decision from unbelievers? [c]

[7] In truth, the very fact that you engage in
lawsuits with one another is a misfortune for
you. Why not prefer to be wronged? Why not
prefer to be defrauded? [d] [8] Instead, you your-
self are guilty of wronging and defrauding
your own brethren. [e]

[9] Are you not aware that wrongdoers will
never inherit the kingdom of God? Do not be
deceived! Fornicators, idolaters, adulterers,
male prostitutes, sodomites, * [f] [10] thieves,
extortioners, drunkards, slanderers, swin-
dlers—none of these will inherit the kingdom
of God. [g] [11] Some of you were once such as
these. However, now you have been washed
clean, you have been sanctified, you have
been justified in the name of the Lord Jesus
Christ and in the Spirit of our God. [h]

All Things Are Lawful for Me!* [12] "All things
are lawful for me," but not all things are ben-
eficial. "All things are lawful for me," but I
will not allow myself to be dominated by
anything. [i] [13] "Food is meant for the stomach
and the stomach is meant for food," but God
will destroy them both. However, the body is
not meant for immorality but for the Lord,
and the Lord for the body. [j] [14] God raised up
the Lord, and he will raise us up also by his
power. [k]

[15] Do you not know that your bodies are
members of Christ? Should I then take
Christ's members and make them members
of a prostitute? Never! [l] [16] Do you not know
that anyone who joins himself to a prostitute
becomes one body with her? For it is said,
"The two shall become one flesh." [m] [17] But
anyone who joins himself to the Lord
becomes one spirit with him. * [n]

[18] Flee from sexual immorality! Every
other sin that a person commits is outside
the body, but the fornicator sins against his
own body. [o] [19] Do you not know that your
body is the temple of the Holy Spirit within
you, whom you have received from God, and
that you are not your own? [p] [20] You have been
purchased at a price. Therefore, glorify God
in your body. [q]

IV: MARRIAGE AND CELIBACY AMONG CHRISTIANS*

CHAPTER 7

Christian Marriage.* [1] Now I will move on to
the matters about which you wrote. Yes, it is

z 1 Cor 5:12; Wis 3:8; Mt 19:28; Lk 22:30; Rev 20:4.—a 2 Pet 2:4; Jude 6.—b 1 Cor 4:14; 15:34; Acts 1:15.—c Rom 7:1; 2 Cor 6:14, 15; 1 Tim 5:8.—d Mt 5:38-42; Rom 12:17-21; 1 Thes 5:15.—e 1 Thes 4:6.—f 1 Cor 15:50; Lev 18:20; Deut 22:22; Job 13:9; Mt 25:34; Gal 5:19-21; Eph 5:5; Jas 1:16.—g 1 Tim 1:10; Rev 21:8; 22:15.—h 1 Cor 1:2; Acts 22:16; Rom 4:25; Eph 2:2; Tit 3:3-7.—i 1 Cor 10:23.—j Rom 12:1; Col 2:22.—k Acts 2:24; Rom 8:11; 2 Cor 4:14; Eph 1:19, 20; 1 Thes 4:16.—l 1 Cor 12:27; Rom 6:12-13; 12:5; Eph 5:30.—m Gen 2:24; Mt 19:5; Mk 10:8; Eph 5:31.—n Jn 17:21-23; Rom 8:9-10; 2 Cor 3:17; Gal 2:20.—o 1 Cor 5:1; 2 Cor 12:21; Gal 5:19; Eph 5:3; 1 Thes 4:3, 4; Heb 13:4.—p 1 Cor 3:16-17; Jn 2:21; Rom 5:5; 14:7-8.—q 1 Cor 7:23; Ps 74:2; Mt 20:28; Acts 20:28; Phil 1:20; Rev 5:9; 14:4.

6:3 *Angels:* here the fallen angels (see Letter of Jude 6).

6:9 *Sodomites:* see note on 1 Tim 1:10.

6:12-20 In this city of Corinth, with its reputation for corruption, some Christians claim that they have the right to free love: "All things are lawful for me!" Paul's response gives us the first intuitions of a Christian reflection concerning what the body is for—a reflection that is totally new in this Greek environment in which the spirit is exalted while the body is denigrated almost to the point of being a slave. The Christian ethic is not locked in on disputes about what is permitted and what is prohibited. Indeed, in its eyes, all the realities of life have a meaning.

A person's behavior cannot be reduced to a physical way of acting (v. 13). It expresses and sheds light on human and spiritual values. And since in this case one must strive to deregulate established pagan customs, Paul stresses this point especially with regard to sexuality. A new conception of the body and sexual life imposes itself on those who live in union with Christ. It concerns their whole being, which has the indwelling of the Holy Spirit and is destined for the resurrection. Freedom does not authorize the corruption of life.

6:17 *One spirit with him:* the spiritual union of believers with Christ is a higher one than the marriage bond and the model of the union that should exist in the marriage relationship.

7:1-40 The Apostle here expounds some basic ideas about marriage; elsewhere he will develop some deeper aspects of it (Eph 5:4-33). His reply is formulated in response to concrete situations. When he speaks of celibacy, he manifests something of his personal conviction resulting from his experience of a life devoted entirely to Christ. This chapter remains one of the major Christian documents for understanding consecrated virginity, but also for keeping alive in the Church the discussion of marriage and celibacy as choices of ways of life.

7:1-11 The call to celibacy is an excellent gift, but conjugal life is also a gift of the Lord and continues to be the normal condition. In speaking of couples, Paul emphasizes their life in common, their mutual belonging, and the reciprocal gift of self. He reminds his readers of the clear Gospel message: the conjugal community is an indissoluble one (see Mt 5:32; 19:9; Mk 10:11-12; Lk 16:18). Spouses may follow calls to a more intense spiritual life, but let them first safeguard the essential realities of their union.

a good thing for a man to refrain from
touching a woman. [r] 2 However, to avoid the
temptation to immorality, each man should
have his own wife and each woman her own
husband. 3 A husband should give to his wife
her conjugal rights, and likewise a wife
should fulfill her conjugal obligations to her
husband. [s] 4 For a wife does not have author-
ity over her own body, but the husband does.
Likewise, a husband does not have authority
over his own body, but the wife does.

5 Do not deprive one another, except per-
haps by mutual consent for a specified time
so as to devote yourselves to prayer. Then
come together again so that Satan may not
tempt you by taking advantage of your lack
of self-control. [t] 6 I suggest this not as a com-
mand but by way of concession. [u] 7 I wish
that all of you would be as I myself am.
However, each person has a particular gift
from God, one having one kind and another
a different kind. [v]

8 To the unmarried and to widows, I say
that it is a good thing for them to remain as
they are, as I do. [w] 9 However, if they are
unable to exercise self-control, they should
marry, for it is better to be married than to
burn with passion. [x]

10 [y] To those who are married, I give this
command, which is not mine but the Lord's:
a wife should not separate from her hus-
band— [z] 11 and if she does separate, she must
either remain unmarried or become recon-
ciled to her husband—and a husband should
not divorce his wife. [a]

Living at Peace with an Unbelieving Spouse.*
12 To the rest, I say this (I, not the Lord): If
any brother has a wife who is an unbeliever,
and she is willing to remain with him, he
should not divorce her. [b] 13 And if any
woman has a husband who is an unbeliever,
and he is willing to remain with her, she
should not divorce him. [c] 14 For the unbeliev-
ing husband is made holy through his wife,
and the unbelieving wife is made holy
through her husband. Otherwise, your chil-
dren would be unclean, whereas in fact they
are holy. [d]

15 However, if the unbelieving partner
chooses to separate, let that person go. The
brother or sister is no longer bound in this
case. God has called you to live in peace. [e]
16 As a wife, how can you be certain that you
will save your husband? As a husband, how
can you be certain that you will save your
wife? [f]

Living Where Christ Calls Us. 17 Everyone
should accept the role in life assigned to
each one by the Lord, continuing as he was
when the Lord called him. This is the rule
that I give to all the Churches. [g] 18 Was a man
called after he had been circumcised? Then
he must remain circumcised. Was a man
uncircumcised when he was called? He
should remain uncircumcised. [h] 19 To be cir-
cumcised is of no importance, and to be
uncircumcised is of no importance. What
matters is keeping God's commandments. [i]
20 Everyone should remain as he was when
he was called. [j]

21 Were you a slave when you were called?
Do not let that concern you. But if you have
an opportunity to gain your freedom, take it.
22 For whoever was called in the Lord as a
slave is a freedman of the Lord, just as who-
ever was free when he was called is a slave of
Christ. [k] 23 You were purchased at a price.
Do not become slaves of men. [l] 24 Therefore,
brethren, everyone should remain before
God in the condition in which he was called.

Virginity—Total Consecration to Christ.* 25 In
regard to virgins, I have received no instruc-
tions from the Lord, but let me offer my own
opinion as one who by the Lord's mercy can
be considered trustworthy. [m] 26 I think that

r 1 Cor 7:8, 26.—s Ex 21:10; 1 Pet 3:7.—t Ex 19:15; 1 Sam 21:5, 6; Mt 4:10.—u 1 Cor 10:40; 2 Cor 8:8.—v 1 Cor 9:5; 12:4, 11; Mt 19:11-12; Rom 12:6.—w 1 Cor 7:1, 26; Acts 26:29; 1 Tim 5:11-16.—x 1 Tim 5:14.—y 10-11: Mt 5:32; 19:9, 14; Rom 11:16.—z Mal 2:14, 16; Lk 16:18.—a 1 Cor 7:39; Mk 10:12; Rom 7:2-3.—b 2 Cor 11:17.—c 2 Cor 6:14.—d Mal 2:15; 1 Pet 3:1.—e 1 Cor 14:33; Rom 14:19.—f Rom 11:14; 1 Pet 3:1.—g 1 Cor 4:17; 14:33; Rom 12:3; 2 Cor 8:18; 11:28.—h 1 Mac 1:15; Acts 15:1-2, 5, 19; Gal 5:2.—i Rom 2:25-29; Gal 5:6; 6:15; Col 3:11.—j 1 Cor 7:24.—k Jn 8:32, 36; Rom 6:22; Eph 6:5-9; Col 3:11; Philem 16.—l 1 Cor 6:20; Lev 25:45, 55; 1 Pet 1:18.—m 2 Cor 4:1; 8:8; 1 Tim 1:13, 16.

7:12-16 What is to be done if one of the spouses is a pagan? The pagan spouse has the right to be free, and if he or she wants to leave the household, the Christian spouse ("the believing partner": v. 15) regains his or her own freedom. This is the so-called Pauline Privilege.

7:25-35 Paul looks for words and ideas to render intelligible the entirely new experience of virginity as the gift of one's life to the Lord. Man and woman are made for one another, but when Christ came into the world, he threw a new light on the realities of the present world: these do not say the final word about the human condition, but represent only a stage (this includes even marriage; see Mt 22:30) on the way to the final fulfillment. We must judge everything in the light of the coming kingdom and give first place to love of the Lord.

Jesus had already stressed the grandeur of celibacy as a radical consecration to God and to the kingdom, but he did not impose it (Mt 19:10-12). Paul gives the same counsel to those Christians of Corinth who are not bound by the state of matrimony.

in this time of stress, a man should remain in his current state.[n] [27] Are you bound to a wife? Do not seek to be free. Are you free of a wife? Then do not look for a wife. [28] However, if you do marry, you do not sin, nor does a virgin sin if she marries. But those who marry will experience hardships in this life,* and from these I would like to spare you.[o]

[29] What I am saying, brethren, is that our time is short. From now on, those who have wives should live as though they had none,[p] [30] and those who mourn as though they were not mourning, and those who rejoice as though they were not rejoicing, and those who buy as though they had nothing, [31] and those who make use of the world as though they had no dealings with it. For the world as we know it is passing away.[q]

[32] It is my wish that you be free of all anxieties. An unmarried man devotes himself to the Lord's affairs and is concerned as to how he can please the Lord.[r] [33] However, a man who is married devotes himself to worldly matters and is concerned about how he can please his wife,[s] [34] and his interests are divided. In the same way, an unmarried woman or a virgin is concerned about the affairs of the Lord and strives to be holy in both body and spirit, whereas the married woman is concerned about worldly matters and how she may please her husband.[t]

[35] I am speaking about this for your own good. I have no intention to impose any restraint upon you, but I wish you to be guided by a sense of propriety, to devote yourself to the Lord free from distraction.[u]

Freedom To Marry.* [36] If a man feels that he is behaving improperly toward his virgin because a critical moment has come * and it seems that something should be done, let him do what he wills. He does not sin if there is a marriage. [37] However, if he stands firm in his resolve and is under no obligation and, being free to carry out his will, decides in his heart to keep his virgin, he also does well. [38] Therefore, the man who gives her in marriage does well, and the one who does not give her in marriage does better.[v]

[39] A wife is bound to her husband as long as he lives. But should the husband die, she is free to marry anyone she wishes, only let it be in the Lord.[w] [40] However, in my opinion she is happier if she remains as she is, and I believe that I too have the Spirit of God.[x]

V: CHRISTIANS AND PAGAN CUSTOMS*

A: The Question of Meat Sacrificed to Idols

CHAPTER 8

An Idol Is Nothing. [1] Now concerning the question of meat that has been sacrificed to idols, we are well aware that all of us possess knowledge. However, while knowledge puffs up, love builds up.[y] [2] Anyone who believes that his knowledge about something is complete will soon discover that his knowledge is flawed,[z] [3] but anyone who loves God is known by him.[a]

[4] Now in regard to the eating of meat sacrificed to idols, we know that idols are nothing in the world and that there is only one God.[b] [5] Indeed, even though there are so-called gods in heaven and on earth—and

n 1 Cor 7:8.—o 1 Cor 7:36.—p Rom 13:11-12.—q Heb 12:27; Jas 1:10; 1 Jn 2:17.—r Mt 6:25; Lk 10:41; 1 Tim 5:5.—s Lk 14:20.—t Lk 2:37; 1 Tim 5:5.—u Ps 86:11; Prov 22:23; Lk 10:39-42.—v Heb 13:4.—w Jn 11:11, 13; Rom 7:2-3; 2 Cor 6:14.—x 1 Cor 7:25; Acts 15:28; 1 Tim 4:8.—y 1 Cor 13:1-13; Rom 14:15, 19; 15:14.—z 1 Cor 3:18; 13:8-9, 12; 1 Tim 6:4.—a Jer 1:5; Rom 8:29; Gal 4:9.—b Ex 34:15; Acts 14:15; Eph 4:6.

7:28 *Hardships in this life:* literally, "tribulations of the flesh," which refer not so much to the difficulties of spouses as to the trials proper to the last times. Those who possess material goods or family in this world will feel more deeply the trial of having to leave them (see Lk 17:26-37). Christians ought to be already living, at least spiritually, in that eschatological era.

7:36-40 It is not clear whether Paul is speaking of a father who has a daughter of marriage age, or of the guardian of an orphan, or simply of fiancés (a Jewish espousal was a real marriage, but not yet consummated). Paul is keeping to his general principle: Answer God's call in the life situation in which we find ourselves.

Another translation could read as follows:

"[36] If a man feels that he is behaving improperly toward his fiancée and he believes that something should be done because he is having difficulty restraining his passions, they should marry as he wishes. There is nothing sinful in that. [37] However, if he stands firm in his resolve and is under no obligation, and, being free to carry out his own will, he decides to respect her virginity, he will do well. [38] Therefore, the man who marries his fiancée does well, and the man who refrains from marriage does better still."

7:36 *A critical moment has come:* this probably refers to the fact that the woman or virgin may soon be beyond the usual age to marry and bear children or the fact that passions are becoming uncontrollable (see 1 Cor 7:9).

8:1—11:1 Paul is clearly convinced that as we do not allow any value to idols, neither do we allow it to meats sacrificed in honor of idols. Christians are therefore free to eat of them. But this principle holds only for a firm and enlightened faith that rises above every danger of contamination by superstition.

there are in fact many gods and many lords—[c] [6] for us there is

one God, the Father,
from whom all things are
and for whom we exist, *
and one Lord, Jesus Christ,
through whom all things are
and through whom we exist. [d]

Do Not Cause a Brother To Fall. [7] However, not everyone possesses this knowledge. There are some who have become so accustomed to idolatry up until now that when they consume meat that has been sacrificed to an idol, their conscience in its weakness is defiled. [e]

[8] Obviously, food cannot bring us closer to God. We do not lack anything if we do not eat, and we have no advantage if we do.[f] [9] Just take care that your freedom does not become a stumbling block to the weak. [g] [10] If someone who regards you as knowledgeable observes you eating in an idol's temple, will he not, burdened by a weak conscience, be influenced to eat food that has been sacrificed to idols? [h]

[11] Therefore, through your knowledge, this weak believer is brought to destruction, the brother for whom Christ died. [i] [12] And when you sin against your brethren and wound their weak consciences, you sin against Christ.[j] [13] Hence, if food can lead my brother to sin, I will never again eat meat lest I cause the downfall of one of my brethren. [k]

CHAPTER 9

B: The Example of Paul's Apostolate

A Missionary's Rights. [1] Am I not free? Am I not an apostle? Have I not seen Jesus our Lord? Are you not my work in the Lord? [l] [2] Although others may not regard me as an apostle, at least I am to you, for you are the seal of my apostleship in the Lord. [m]

[3] To those who seek to pass judgment on me, my defense is this. [4] Do we not have the right to eat and drink? [n] [5] Do we not have the right to be accompanied by a believing wife like the other apostles, the brethren of the Lord, and Cephas? * [o] [6] Are Barnabas * and I the only ones who do not have the right to refrain from working? [p] [7] What soldier would ever serve in the army at his own expense? Who plants a vineyard without eating its fruit? Or who tends a flock without consuming some of its milk? [q]

[8] I am not saying this based simply on human authority, for the Law says the very same thing. [9] In the Law of Moses it is written, "You shall not muzzle an ox while it is treading out the grain." Is it for oxen that God is concerned, [r] [10] or does he not rather say this for our sake? Without question it was written for our sake, for whoever plows should plow in hope and whoever threshes should thresh in hope, both in expectation of a share in the crop. [s] [11] If we have sown a spiritual crop for you, is it unreasonable for us to expect from you a material harvest? [t] [12] If others have this claim on you, do not we?

Despite this, we have never availed ourselves of any such right. On the contrary, we put up with anything rather than place an obstacle to the gospel of Christ. [u] [13] Do you not know that those who perform the temple service receive their food from the temple, and that those who officiate at the altar share in the offerings? [v] [14] In the same way, the Lord ordered that those who preach the gospel should get their living from the gospel. * [w]

I Have Become All Things to All. [15] However, I have never availed myself of any of these rights, and I have not written this to influence you to grant me such treatment; I would rather die first. No one shall deprive me of this boast! [x] [16] If I proclaim the gospel, that is no reason for me to boast, for the

c 2 Thes 2:4.—d 1 Cor 1:2-3; Mal 2:10; Jn 1:3; Rom 11:36; Eph 4:5-6; Col 1:16.—e 1 Cor 10:28; Rom 14:1, 14, 23; 15:1.—f Rom 14:17.—g Rom 14:1, 13, 20-21; 2 Cor 6:3; Gal 5:13.—h 1 Cor 10:27.—i Rom 14:15, 20.—j Mt 18:6; 25:40, 45; Acts 9:4-5.—k Mt 5:29; 18:6; Rom 14:13, 20-21.—l 1 Cor 1:1; 3:6; 4:15; 9:19; 15:8-9; Acts 9:17; 26:16; 2 Cor 12:12.—m 1 Cor 15:8; Acts 9:3, 17; 2 Cor 3:2, 3; 12:1-4.—n 1 Cor 9:14.—o 1 Cor 1:12; 7:7-8; Mt 12:46.—p Acts 4:36-37; 13:1-2; Gal 2:1, 9, 13; Col 4:10.—q 1 Cor 3:6, 8; Deut 20:6; Prov 27:18; 2 Tim 2:3-4.—r Deut 22:1-4; 25:4; Prov 12:10; 1 Tim 5:18.—s Prov 11:25; Rom 4:23-24; 2 Tim 2:6.—t Rom 15:27; Gal 6:6.—u Acts 18:3; 2 Cor 6:3; 11:7-12; 12:13-18; 2 Thes 3:6-12.—v Lev 6:9, 19; Num 18:8, 31; Deut 18:1-5.—w Mt 10:10; Lk 10:7-8; 1 Tim 5:18.—x Acts 18:3; 2 Cor 11:9-10.

8:6 *For whom we exist:* another possible translation is: "toward whom we return." *Through whom all things are:* this is the earliest mention in the New Testament of the role of Jesus in creation.

9:5 *The other apostles, the brethren of the Lord, and Cephas:* i.e., the missionaries or the heads of communities who were related to Jesus. It may be assumed that the married apostles, such as Peter, were accompanied by their wives.

9:6 *Barnabas:* see Acts 4:36-37; 11:25-26; chs. 13—14; 15:36-39.

9:14 *Those who preach the gospel should get their living from the gospel:* see Mt 10:10; Lk 10:7-8. This is one of the rare instances in which Paul expressly cites a saying of the Lord.

obligation to do so has been given to me, and woe to me if I fail to fulfill it.[y]

[17] If I proclaimed the gospel of my own volition, I would deserve a reward; but if I do not do so voluntarily, I am simply discharging the commission that has been given to me.[z] [18] What then is my reward? It is simply that in my preaching I may offer the gospel free of charge and not make use of the rights that the gospel affords me.[a]

[19] Although I am free and belong to no man, I have made myself a slave to all so as to win over as many as possible.[b] [20] To the Jews, I became like a Jew in order to win the Jews. To those under the Law, I became like one under the Law—although I myself am not under the Law—in order to win over those under the Law.[c] [21] To those outside the Law, I became like one outside the Law—although I am not outside the Law of God but am subject to the Law of Christ—in order to win over those outside the Law.[d] [22] To the weak, I have become weak in order to win over the weak. I have become all things to all, so that by every possible means I might save some.[e] [23] I do all this for the sake of the gospel so that I might share it with you.[f]

C: Flee from Idolatry*

Discipline Yourself So As Not To Be Disqualified. [24] You are well aware that while all the runners in the stadium compete in the race, only one wins the prize. Run in such a way as to win the prize.[g] [25] Everyone who seeks a prize submits himself to rigorous self-discipline in every respect. They do so to win a perishable crown, while we seek an imperishable one.[h] [26] Therefore, I do not run without purpose, nor do I fight like a man beating the air.[i] [27] Rather, I discipline my body and bring it under control, for fear that after preaching to others I myself may be disqualified.[j]

CHAPTER 10

The Lesson of Israel's Past.* [1] Brethren, I do not want you to be unaware that our ancestors were all under the cloud and all passed through the sea,[k] [2] and they were all baptized into Moses in the cloud and in the sea.[l] [3] All ate the same spiritual food,[m] [4] and all drank the same spiritual drink—for they drank from the spiritual rock that followed them, and that rock was Christ.[n] [5] Yet God was not pleased with most of them, and they were struck down in the desert.[o]

[6] These events occurred to offer examples for us so that we might not desire evil things as they did.[p] [7] Do not become idolaters, as some of them did. It is written, "The people sat down to eat and drink, and they rose up to engage in revelry."[q]

[8] Let us not indulge in sexual immorality as some of them did, and twenty-three thousand of them died in a single day.[r] [9] Let us not put Christ to the test, as some of them did, and they were destroyed by serpents.[s] [10] And do not complain, as some of them did, and they were slain by the Destroyer.*[t] [11] All these things happened to them to serve as an example, and they have been written down as a warning to us upon whom the end of the ages has come.[u]

[12] Therefore, if you think you are standing securely, take care that you do not fall.[v] [13] No trial has confronted you except what a person can stand. God is faithful, and he will not allow you to be tried beyond your

y Acts 9:15; 26:14-18; Rom 1:14.—z 1 Cor 3:8; 4:1; Gal 2:7; Col 1:25.—a 2 Cor 11:7; 12:13.—b Mt 18:15; 20:26-27; 2 Cor 4:5; Gal 5:13; 1 Pet 3:1.—c Acts 16:3; 21:20-26; Rom 2:12; 11:14.—d Rom 2:12, 14; Gal 6:2.—e 1 Cor 2:3; 10:33; Rom 11:14; 14:1; 15:1; 2 Cor 11:29.—f 1 Cor 10:24; Mk 8:35; Rom 1:16.—g Gal 2:2; 5:7; Phil 2:16; 3:14; Col 2:18; 2 Tim 4:7; Heb 12:1.—h 2 Tim 2:5; 4:7-8; Jas 1:12; 1 Pet 5:4; Rev 2:10; 3:11.—i 1 Cor 14:8; 1 Tim 6:12; Heb 12:4.—j Jer 6:30; Rom 6:19; 8:13; Heb 6:8.—k Ex 13:21-22; 14:19-20, 21-22, 26-30; Pss 66:6; 105:39; Rom 11:25.—l Ex 16:4-35; Rom 6:3; Gal 3:27.—m Ex 16:15,35; Deut 8:3; Jn 6:31.—n Ex 17:1-7; Num 20:7-11; Deut 8:15; Pss 78:15; 105:41.—o Num 14:28-38; Heb 3:17; Jude 5.—p 1 Cor 10:11; Num 11:4, 34.—q Ex 32:4, 6, 19.—r Num 25:1-9.—s Ex 17:2; Num 21:5-9; Pss 78:18; 95:9.—t Ex 12:23; Num 14:2-37; 16:1-35; 1 Chr 21:15; Heb 11:28.—u Rom 4:24; 13:11.—v Rom 11:20; 2 Cor 1:24.

9:24—11:1 To take part in a sacred meal in the temples of idols is to run the risk of being seduced by idolatry. The reader should not play down this danger, which is connected with the danger of scandalizing the weak.

10:1-13 Paul calls to mind the story of the Hebrews in the wilderness, where the people were given all the gifts needed for life: the water and the manna, which symbolize Baptism and the Eucharist.

According to a tradition dear to the rabbis, the rock that Moses struck followed the Hebrews so that they might always have water; Paul uses this interpretation in order to make the point that since the time of the Exodus Christ has been leading the people (see Num 20:8).

If the events in the life of the desert community foreshadow the reality of the Church, the behavior of the Israelites at that time must also serve as a warning that is ever actual: in order to please God, it is not enough to belong to the Church and to receive the Sacraments; Christians must also be committed to an unwavering effort to be faithful, relying on the help of the Spirit.

In this section, Paul is teaching us how to read the Old Testament in a Christian perspective.

10:10 *The Destroyer:* the angel charged with inflicting divine punishments (see Ex 12:21-28).

strength. But together with the trial he will
also provide a way out and the strength to
bear it. [w]

The Eucharist Versus Pagan Sacrifices.*
14 Therefore, my dear friends, avoid idolatry
at all costs. * [x] 15 I am talking to you as sensi-
ble people. Judge for yourselves what I say. [y]
16 The cup of blessing that we bless, is it not
a sharing in the blood of Christ? The bread
that we break, is it not a sharing in the body
of Christ? [z] 17 Because there is one bread, we
who are many are one body, for we all par-
take of the one bread. [a]

18 Consider the people of Israel. * Are not
those who eat the sacrifices participants in
the altar? [b] 19 What then am I implying? That
meat sacrificed to idols is anything, or that
an idol is anything? [c]

20 No, I simply mean that pagan sacrifices
are offered to demons, not to God, and I do
not want you to become partners with
demons. [d] 21 You cannot drink the cup of the
Lord and the cup of demons. You cannot
partake of the table of the Lord and the table
of demons. [e] 22 Do we truly wish to provoke
the Lord to jealous anger? * Are we stronger
than he is? [f]

Concerning Idol Offerings. 23 "All things are
lawful," you may say—but not all things are
beneficial. All things may be lawful—but not
all things are constructive. [g] 24 No one should
seek his own advantage in preference to that
of his neighbor. [h] 25 You may eat whatever
meat is sold in the market without raising
questions on grounds of conscience, [i] 26 for
"the earth and all it contains belong to the
Lord." [j]

27 If an unbeliever invites you to a meal and
you decide to accept, eat whatever is set
before you without raising any questions on
the grounds of conscience. [k] 28 However, if
someone says to you, "This food was offered
in sacrifice," then do not eat it, out of consid-
eration for the one who informed you and for
the sake of conscience— [l] 29 I mean the other
person's conscience, not your own. For why
should my freedom be governed by someone
else's conscience? [m] 30 If I partake of the meal
with thankfulness, why should I be criticized
for eating food for which I give thanks? [n]

Give No Offense. 31 Therefore, whether you
eat or drink, or whatever you do, do every-
thing for the glory of God. [o] 32 Give no
offense to Jews or to Greeks or to the
Church of God, [p] 33 just as I try to please
everyone in everything I do, not seeking my
own good but that of the many, so that they
may be saved. [q]

CHAPTER 11

1 Be imitators of me, as I am of Christ. [r]

VI: LITURGICAL ASSEMBLIES AND THEIR PROBLEMS*

A: Propriety in Worship*

The Question of Head Coverings. 2 I praise
you because you remember me in every-
thing and you maintain the traditions just as
I handed them down to you. [s]

---

w 1 Cor 1:9; Mt 6:13; Jas 1:13-14; 2 Pet 2:9.—x Heb 6:9; 1 Pet 2:11; 1 Jn 2:7; 5:21; Jude 3.—y Mt 7:24; Lk 16:8.—z 1 Cor 11:23-25; Mt 14:19; 26:26-29; Acts 2:42.—a Rom 12:5; Eph 4:4; Col 3:15.—b Lev 7:6; 14:15; Heb 13:10.—c 1 Cor 8:4.—d Lev 17:7; Deut 32:17; Ps 106:37; Rev 9:20.—e Isa 65:11; 2 Cor 6:14-18.—f Deut 32:16, 21; 1 Ki 14:22; Ps 78:58; Eccl 6:10; Isa 45:9; Jer 44:8.—g 1 Cor 6:12.—h 1 Cor 13:5; Rom 15:2; Phil 2:4, 21.—i 1 Cor 8:7; Acts 10:15.—j Ex 9:29; 19:5; Job 41:11; Pss 24:1; 50:12; 1 Tim 4:4.—k Lk 10:7.—l 1 Cor 8:7, 10, 12.—m 1 Cor 9:1, 19; Rom 14:16.—n Rom 14:6; 1 Tim 4:3-4.—o Zec 14:21; Col 3:17; 1 Pet 4:11.—p 1 Cor 1:2; 11:16, 22; Mt 5:29; Acts 20:28; 24:16; 2 Cor 6:3; 1 Tim 3:5, 15.—q 1 Cor 9:22; Rom 11:14; 15:2.—r 1 Cor 4:16; Rom 15:3; Phil 3:17; 1 Pet 2:21.—s 1 Cor 4:17; 15:3; Lk 1:2; 1 Thes 3:6; 2 Thes 2:15.

10:14-22 Taking part in a form of worship means entering into communion with the divinity to which it is offered. Christians, who participate in the Body and Blood of Christ in the Eucharist, are well aware of this. By emphasizing the radical opposition between the Eucharist and pagan cults, Paul makes clear the place that the Eucharistic celebration had in the early Church. This participation gives rise to the Body of Christ that is the Church, but it also requires a serious commitment to live according to the Gospel.

10:14 *Avoid idolatry at all costs:* the Christians of Corinth must do their utmost to avoid idolatry especially since they are surrounded by temples of other gods. They daily come into contact with temples for the worship of Apollo, Asclepius, Demeter, Aphrodite, and other pagan gods and goddesses. The most common temptation was that of the worship of Aphrodite with its many sacred prostitutes (which at one time numbered 1000).

10:18 *The people of Israel:* literally, "Israel according to the flesh," that is, Jews by birth, as distinct from "the Israel of God," to which persons belong by faith (see Rom 2:28-29).

10:22 *Provoke the Lord to jealous anger:* in the Old Testament, this points to the incompatibility of adoring God and worshiping idols.

11:2—14:40 Gatherings of Christians are liturgical assemblies. The members listen to the Word of God, give thanks, break bread, the Lord is present and the Spirit enters their hearts. On more than one point, Christians readily imitated the mode of acting of the Jews, who came together in their synagogues on the Sabbath, but they were more distrustful of the religious customs of the pagans. In any case, through the celebration of the Eucharist and the inspiration of the Holy Spirit, the Christian Liturgy is profoundly original. Paul does not wish to impose laws upon it but insists that it be genuine worship.

11:2-16 In ancient times men went with heads uncovered, while women wore a veil as a sign of modesty and also of dependence on their husbands.

3 But I want you to understand that Christ
is the head of every man, and the husband is
the head of his wife, and God is the head of
Christ.[t] 4 Any man who prays or prophesies
with his head covered brings disgrace on his
head.[u] 5 And any woman who prays or
prophesies with her head unveiled brings
disgrace upon her head, for it is just as
though she had her head shaved.[v] 6 Indeed,
if a woman refuses to wear a veil, then she
might as well have her hair cut off. If it is
disgraceful for a woman to have her hair cut
off or her head shaved, then she should wear
a veil.

7 It is not right for a man to have his head
covered, since he is the image of God and
the reflection of his glory, whereas woman is
the reflection of the glory of man.[w] 8 For
man was not made from woman, but
woman was made from man.[x] 9 Nor was
man created for the sake of woman, but
woman was created for the sake of man.[y]

10 Therefore, a woman should have on her
head a sign* of her dependence, because of
the angels.[z] 11 Nevertheless, in the Lord,
woman is not independent of man, nor is
man independent of woman.[a] 12 Although
woman came from man, so does every man
come from a woman, and all things come
from God.[b]

The Question of Long Hair. 13 Judge for your-
selves. Is it proper for a woman to pray to
God with her head unveiled? 14 Does not
nature itself teach you that if a man has long
hair, he is disgraced, 15 whereas if a woman
has long hair, it is her glory? For her hair was
given to her as a covering. 16 However, if any-
one wishes to argue further on this point, we
have no such custom to do so, nor do any of
the Churches of God.[c]

B: The Lord's Supper, Sign of Unity*

Do You Despise the Church of God? 17 Now
in giving you this instruction I cannot praise
you, because your meetings tend to do more
harm than good. 18 To begin with, when you
come together in your assembly, I hear that
there are divisions among you, and to some
extent I am inclined to believe it.[d] 19 There
must be such factions among you so that it
will become clear to you which groups
should be trusted.[e]

20 * When you do assemble, it is not to eat
the Lord's supper, 21 for each of you goes
ahead with his own supper, and one goes
hungry while another has too much to
drink.[f] 22 Do you not have homes in which
you can eat and drink? Or do you have such
contempt for the Church of God that you
humiliate those who have nothing? What
should I say to you? Should I praise you? In
this matter, I cannot praise you.[g]

You Proclaim the Death of the Lord. 23 * For
what I received from the Lord I handed on
to you: the Lord Jesus, on the night he was
betrayed, took bread,[h] 24 and after giving
thanks he broke it and said, "This is my body
that is for you. Do this in remembrance of
me."[i]

25 In the same fashion, after the supper,*
he also took the cup and said, "This cup is
the new covenant in my blood. Whenever
you drink it, do this in remembrance of
me."[j] 26 And so, whenever you eat this bread
and drink this cup, you proclaim the death
of the Lord until he comes.[k]

---

t 1 Cor 3:23; Gen 3:16; Eph 1:22; 5:23; Col 1:18; 1 Thes 4:1-2.—u Acts 11:27.—v Num 5:18; Deut 21:12; Lk 2:36; Acts 2:9; 13:1.—w Gen 1:26-27; 5:1; Prov 12:4; Jas 3:9.—x Gen 2:21-23; 1 Tim 2:13.—y Gen 2:18.—z Mt 18:10; 1 Tim 5:21.—a Gal 3:27-28.—b 1 Cor 8:6; Rom 11:36.—c 1 Cor 7:17; 10:32; Acts 20:28; 1 Thes 2:14; 2 Thes 1:4.—d 1 Cor 1:10-12; 3:3; Gal 5:20.—e Deut 13:3; Mt 18:7; Acts 20:30; 1 Jn 2:19: 2 Pet 2:1.—f 2 Pet 2:13; Jude 13.—g 1 Cor 10:32; Prov 17:3; Jas 2:1-7.—h 1 Cor 2:3, 15; 10:16-17; Mt 26:26-29; Mk 14:22-25; Lk 22:14-20; Gal 1:12.—i 1 Cor 10:16; Mt 15:36.—j Ex 24:8; Lk 22:20; 2 Cor 3:6; Heb 8:6-13.—k 1 Cor 1:7; Jn 21:22.

11:10 *Sign:* of the presence of the Lord, who demands holiness and propriety (see Deut 23:15).

11:17-34 From the very beginning, the Church has celebrated the Eucharist. She does so by renewing the actions and words of Jesus on the night of the Last Supper, and here we have the most ancient document written about it. The document evokes the celebration itself and expresses its most profound meaning. Nevertheless, Paul does not intend to give an explanation of the subject. He is simply intervening in the face of abuses. He stresses that the Eucharist is not to be celebrated in the same way as one organizes a sacred meal in a temple with one's friends. We are not going to partake passingly in some magical or symbolic food of immortality. Celebrating the Eucharist is a serious action that engages the whole community in the highest reality of its faith: the union with Christ in his Passion, the unity that he imparts to human beings, and the expectation of his coming and its accomplishment for all. Such an action entails exigencies for Liturgy and life.

11:20-22 Before the Eucharist, the Corinthians apparently held an ordinary meal, an early form of the *agape* (see 2 Pet 2:13; Jude 12). Paul condemns the abuses that occurred in it.

11:23-25 This is the earliest written New Testament account of the institution of the Eucharist. The words over the bread and the cup stress the Lord's self-giving, and the words "Do this in remembrance of me" command Christians to repeat his action.

11:25 *After the supper:* i.e., after the Passover supper. The Lord's Supper was first celebrated by Jesus in connection with the Passover meal (see Mt 26:18-30). *The cup:* a symbol of the New Covenant in the blood of Jesus (Lk 22:20; see Jer 31:31-34). The Old Covenant was the Mosaic Covenant (see Ex 24:3-8).

God's Judgment on the Community.* 27 Therefore, anyone who eats the bread or drinks the cup of the Lord in an unworthy manner is guilty of an offense against the body and blood of the Lord. [l] 28 Everyone should examine himself about eating the bread and drinking from the cup. [m] 29 For a person who eats and drinks without discerning the body of the Lord is eating and drinking judgment on himself.

30 That is why many of you are weak and ill, and a number of you have fallen asleep. [n] 31 If we were to examine ourselves, we would not be condemned. [o] 32 However, when we are judged by the Lord, he is disciplining us to save us from being condemned together with the world. [p]

Practical Conclusion. 33 Therefore, brethren, when you come together for the meal, wait for one another. 34 If anyone is hungry, he should eat at home, so that in assembling you may not incur condemnation. As for the other matters, I will resolve them when I come. [q]

C: The Gifts of the Spirit in the Service of the Church*

CHAPTER 12

Discerning the Gifts of the Spirit. 1 Now in regard to the gifts of the Spirit, brethren, I do not want you to be uninformed. [r] 2 You know that when you were still pagans you were constantly being enticed and led astray to the worship of mute idols. [s] 3 Therefore, I wish you to understand that no one speaking under the influence of the Spirit of God says, "May Jesus be cursed." * Likewise, no one can say "Jesus is Lord," except under the influence of the Holy Spirit. [t]

The Spirit Distributes the Gifts for the Common Good. 4 * There are different varieties of gifts, but the same Spirit. [u] 5 There are different kinds of service, but the same Lord. [v] 6 There are different forms of activity, but the same God who produces all of them in everyone. [w]

7 To each of us, the manifestation of the Spirit is given for the common good. [x] 8 To one, is given through the Spirit the utterance of wisdom; and to another, the utterance of knowledge according to the same Spirit. [y] 9 Another by the same Spirit is granted faith, while still another is granted the gift of healing by the same Spirit. [z]

10 To one, is granted the gift of mighty deeds; * to another, the gift of prophecy; and to yet another, the gift to discern spirits. One receives the gift of tongues and another the ability to interpret them. [a] 11 One and the same Spirit works all these things, distributing them individually to each person as he wills. [b]

You Are the Body of Christ.* 12 The body is one, although it has many parts; and all the parts, though many, form one body. So it is with Christ. [c] 13 For in the one Spirit we were all baptized into one body, Jews as well as Greeks, slaves as well as free men, and we were all given the same Spirit to drink. [d]

14 Now the body is one, although it has many parts. [e] 15 If the foot were to say, "Because I am not a hand, I do not belong to the body," it nevertheless still belongs to the body. 16 Or if an ear were to say, "Because I

l Num 9:10, 13; Jn 13:27; Heb 10:29.—m 2 Cor 13:5; Gal 6:4.—n Mt 9:24; 13:25.—o Ps 32:5; Jn 1:9.—p Deut 8:5; Pss 94:12; 118:18; Prov 3:11-12; Heb 12:5-11.—q 1 Cor 4:19.—r 1 Cor 1:7; 14:1, 37; Rom 1:11; 11:25.—s Jer 10:5; Hab 2:18, 19; Eph 2:11-18.—t 1 Cor 16:22; Jn 13:13; Rom 9:3; 10:9; 1 Jn 4:2-3.—u Rom 12:6; Eph 4:7, 11; Heb 2:4.—v Rom 12:7; Eph 4:11.—w Eph 4:6; Phil 2:13.—x 1 Cor 14:12 Rom 12:8; Eph 4:7, 12.—y 1 Cor 1:5; 2:6-13; 2 Cor 8:7.—z 1 Cor 13:2; Mt 10:1; 17:19, 20.—a 1 Cor 14:5, 26-39; Mt 16:17; Acts 2:4; Gal 3:5; Eph 4:11.—b 1 Cor 3:5; 7:7; Jn 3:8; Rom 12:3; Eph 4:7.—c 1 Cor 10:17; Rom 12:4-5; Eph 2:16; Col 3:15.—d Mk 1:8; Jn 7:37-39; Gal 3:28; Eph 2:13-18; Col 3:11.—e 1 Cor 12:12, 20.

11:27-34 In this passage Paul presents a profound teaching: The reception of Christ's Body is a source of life and unity; it also has an effect on the relationships of human beings and on their salvation. But if the fraternal bond created by communion loosens, as at Corinth, the community becomes disunited in spirit and in body.

12:1—14:40 These pages have new relevance today. Such words as "charism" and "prophet" have once again become common in the Church. We are deeply interested in the relationships, undertakings, and inspirations that characterize the life and vitality of communities. God does indeed grant the grace of renewal for the sake of the authentic development of the Christian community. Nevertheless, we should not stop at the visible gifts, but should seek initiatives that help to unite the community and promote true love and the knowledge of the mystery of Christ. Christian experience is not a spectacle but a lived reality. This is a principle for discernment.

12:3 *Cursed:* to say this is to fail to recognize Jesus as the messenger of God (see Jn 8:48f; 9:24).

12:4-6 Note that these verses speak of the intervention of the three divine Persons. The charismatic movement cannot become a competition of visions nor a conflict of claims and a quest for prestige.

12:10 *Mighty deeds:* this phrase refers to actions that cannot be explained by natural means—hence, actions of God intended to show his power and purpose.

12:12-31a The Church, united and in harmony like a physical body, really forms the Body of Christ (1 Cor 10:17; Col 1:8-24; Eph 1:22-23; 5:23), brought into being by participation in his Eucharistic Body and given life by the life of the Spirit. This is one of Paul's major ideas regarding the mystery of the Church.

am not an eye, I do not belong to the body," it nevertheless still belongs to the body.

17 If the whole body were an eye, how would we be able to hear? If the whole body were an ear, how would we exercise a sense of smell? 18 But God arranged each part in the body as he intended.[f] 19 If all the members were identical, where would the body be?

20 As it is, there are many members, but one body.[g] 21 The eye cannot say to the hand, "I do not need you," any more than the head can say to the feet, "I do not need you." 22 On the contrary, those parts of the body that seem to be weaker are in fact indispensable, 23 and those parts of the body that we regard as less honorable we clothe with greater honor, and our less respectable parts are treated with greater propriety, 24 whereas our more respectable members have no need of this.

But God has so designed the body as to give greater honor to the more humble parts, 25 in order that there may be no dissension within the body and each part may have equal concern for all the others.[h] 26 If one member suffers, all suffer together with it. If one member is honored, all the members rejoice together with it.[i]

27 You therefore are the body of Christ, and each of you is a part of it.[j] 28 And those whom God has appointed in the Church are first apostles, second prophets, third teachers; then doers of mighty deeds, those who have the gifts of healing, helping others, administering, and various kinds of tongues.[k] 29 Are all apostles? Are all prophets? Are all teachers? Are all doers of mighty deeds? 30 Do all possess gifts of healing? Do all speak in tongues? Do all interpret?[l] 31 Set your hearts on the greater gifts.[m]

Hymn to Love.* Now I will show you a more excellent way.

CHAPTER 13

1 If in speaking I use human tongues
and angelic as well,
but do not have love, *
I am nothing more than a noisy gong or
a clanging cymbal.[n]
2 If I have the gift of prophecy
and the ability to understand all mysteries and all knowledge,
and have all the faith necessary to move
mountains,
but do not have love,
I am nothing.[o]
3 If I give away everything to feed the poor
and hand over my body to be burned,
but do not have love,
I achieve nothing.[p]

4 Love is patient;
love is charitable.
Love is not envious;
it does not have an inflated opinion of
itself;
it is not filled with its own importance.[q]
5 Love is never rude;
it does not seek its own advantage.
It is not prone to anger;
neither does it brood over setbacks.[r]
6 Love does not rejoice over wrongdoing
but rejoices in the truth.[s]
7 Love bears all things,
believes all things,
hopes all things,
endures all things.[t]

8 Love never fails.
Prophecies will eventually cease,

f 1 Cor 12:11, 28.—g Rom 12:5.—h 1 Cor 1:10; 11:18; Jn 9:16.—i Rom 12:4-5.—j Rom 12:5-8; Eph 1:23; 4:12; 5:30; Col 1:18, 24.—k 1 Cor 10:32; Mk 16:17; Acts 13:1; 20:35; Rom 12:6-8; Eph 2:20; 3:5; 4:11; 1 Tim 5:17; Heb 13:7.—l 1 Cor 12:10.—m 1 Cor 14:1, 39.—n 1 Cor 8:1, 16:14; Mk 16:17; Rom 12:9-10; 13:8-10.—o 1 Cor 1:5; 4:1; 8:1-3; 12:8; 14:2; Mt 17:20; 21:21; Acts 11:27; 2 Cor 8:7; Eph 4:11; Col 2:3.—p Mt 6:2; Lk 19:8; Acts 2:45.—q 1 Cor 4:6, 18; 5:2; 8:1; Eph 4:2; 1 Thes 5:14.—r 1 Cor 10:24, 33; Job 14:16-17; Prov 10:12; Mt 5:22; Phil 2:4, 21; 1 Thes 5:15; 1 Pet 4:8.—s 2 Thes 2:12; 2 Jn 4; 3 Jn 3-4.—t 1 Cor 13:8, 13; Prov 10:12; 1 Pet 4:8.

12:31b—13:13 This may be termed a passage for the ages. The word "love" summarizes for Paul all the newness that Jesus brings to the world. Wherever love exists, something of the eternal and the divine enters into the life and communication of human beings. In comparison to love, every other value is relative and transitory; love is the ultimate meaning.

We should leave aside all the cloying sentiments with which the words "love" and "charity" are often burdened and read these few strophes to rediscover this supreme reality that is so simple, so demanding, and so sublime. What a reversal this emphasis on genuine love is for the Corinthians! All the gifts that they like permit pretense, vanity, and ostentation even in the religious sphere; love is the direct opposite of all that.

Where love is lacking, all the charisms lose their power and meaning, even those that are the most needed and the most fruitful for the mission of the Church. The gifts are all provisional. When humankind attains its completion in the love of God, it will be genuinely and definitively fulfilled. In the fullness of this communion and in the complete vision of the Lord, faith and hope themselves will be left behind. But love alone will remain; it is eternal, for God is love (1 Jn 4:8). Even on earth, love is the reality and the power by which Christians must live.

13:1 *Love:* the Greek term for this word means selfless concern for the welfare of others regardless of whether they are lovable or not. It arises from a willingness to love in obedience to the command of God and a desire to follow Christ's love manifested on the cross (see Jn 13:34f; 1 Jn 3:16).

tongues will become silent,
and knowledge will pass away,[u]
9 for our knowledge is partial
and our prophesying is partial;[v]
10 but when we encounter what is perfect,
that which is imperfect will pass away.[w]
11 When I was a child,
I used to talk like a child,
think like a child,
and reason like a child.
However, when I became a man,
I put all childish ways aside.[x]
12 At the present time we see indistinctly,
as in a mirror;
then we shall see face to face.
My knowledge is only partial now;
then I shall know fully,
even as I am fully known.[y]
13 Thus there are three things that endure:
faith, hope, and love,
and the greatest of these is love.*[z]

CHAPTER 14

Seek the Gifts That Build Up the Community.*

1 Make love your aim, but strive earnestly after the spiritual gifts, especially for that of prophecy.[a] 2 If anyone speaks in tongues, he is speaking not to men but to God, and no one understands him, for he is speaking mysteries in the Spirit.[b] 3 On the other hand, the one who prophesies speaks to men for their building up, their encouragement, and their consolation.[c]

4 Whoever speaks in a tongue builds himself up, but whoever prophesies builds up the Church.[d] 5 I wish that all of you could speak in tongues, but I would much prefer that you could prophesy. For the one who prophesies is greater than the one who speaks in tongues, unless the latter can interpret what he is saying so that the Church may be built up.[e]

6 Now suppose, brethren, that I should come to you and speak in tongues. Of what value would I be to you if you were unable to discern from my words any revelation or knowledge or prophecy or instruction?[f] 7 Even inanimate things produce sound, such as a flute or a harp. If they do not produce distinct notes, how can anyone tell what tune is being played?

8 Or again, if the bugle call is unclear, who will get ready for battle?[g] 9 Similarly, if you speak in tongues and your speech is unintelligible, how will anyone be able to understand what you are saying? For you will be talking to empty air.

10 There are many different languages that are used in the world, and none of them is without meaning. 11 But if I do not comprehend the meaning of the language, I will be a foreigner to the speaker and he will be a foreigner to me.[h] 12 Since you are eager to acquire spiritual gifts, try to excel in those that build up the Church.[i]

13 Therefore, anyone who speaks in tongues should pray for the ability to interpret.[j] 14 For if I pray in a tongue, my spirit is at prayer but my mind derives no benefit.[k] 15 What then should I do? I will pray with my spirit, but I will also pray with my mind. I will sing with my spirit, but I will also sing with my mind.[l]

16 If you are praising only with the spirit, how will the uninstructed person who is present be able to answer "Amen" to your thanksgiving when he does not comprehend what you are saying?[m] 17 Your thanksgiving may be inspiring, but the other person has not been edified.[n]

18 I thank God that I speak in tongues more than any of you, 19 but when I am in the church I would prefer to speak five intelligible words to instruct others rather than ten thousand words in a tongue.[o]

u 1 Cor 13:2.—v 1 Cor 8:2.—w Jn 15:15; Phil 3:12.—x Ps 131:2.—y 1 Cor 8:3; Gen 32:30; Job 19:26; 26:14; 36:26; 2 Cor 5:7; Gal 4:9; 2 Tim 2:19; Heb 11:1; 1 Jn 3:2.—z 1 Cor 16:14; Mt 22:37-40; Rom 5:2-5; Gal 5:5-6; Eph 4:2-5; Col 1:4; 1 Thes 1:3; 5:8; Heb 6:10-12; 1 Jn 4:7-12, 16.—a 1 Cor 12:31; 14:5, 12, 39; 16:14; Eph 4:11.—b 1 Cor 13:2; Mk 16:17.—c 1 Cor 3:9; 8:1, 10; 10:23; 14:4-5, 12, 17, 26.—d 1 Cor 13:2; Mk 16:17.—e 1 Cor 14:10, 12, 28; Num 11:29.—f Acts 2:42; Rom 6:17; 2 Cor 8:7; Eph 1:17.—g Num 10:9; Isa 58:1; Jer 4:19; Ezek 33:3-6; Joel 2:1.—h Gen 11:7; Acts 28:1.—i 1 Cor 12:1.—j 1 Cor 14:5.—k 1 Cor 14:2.—l Eph 5:19; Col 3:16; Jas 5:13.—m Deut 27:15-26; 1 Chr 16:36; Neh 8:6; Jer 11:5; Rev 5:14; 7:12.—n 1 Cor 14:3.—o 1 Cor 14:6.

13:13 *The greatest of these is love:* this conclusion follows from the fact that God is love (1 Jn 4:8) and has communicated his love to us (1 Jn 4:10) and commands us to love one another (Jn 13:34f).

14:1-25 The Corinthians aimed especially at a spectacular gift that Paul calls the gift of tongues. The reference is to a type of ecstatic prayer: the inspired person speaks in the midst of the assembly, using incomprehensible words, in a kind of religious rapture; he or she sings the praises of God, either in foreign languages that an inspired interpreter can translate, or by repeating litanies of hardly articulated words, without any order, in a state of ecstasy.

In v. 14, Paul contrasts "spirit" and "mind": the spirit is the innermost part of the soul, where the Holy Spirit acts in mysterious ways; the mind is the soul insofar as it reflects and analyzes itself; it is the level, that is, of self-consciousness and the communication of thought.

When inspiration disregards the mind, the way is opened to enthusiasm and disorder, instead of fraternal exchanges and communion.

[20] Brethren, do not be childish in your
thinking. Be like infants in regard to evil, but
in your thinking be mature. [p] [21] In the Law *
it is written,

> "By people speaking strange tongues
> and by the lips of foreigners
> I will speak to this people,
> and even so they will not listen to me, [q]
> says the Lord."

[22] Clearly, then, tongues are intended as a
sign not for believers but for unbelievers,
while prophecy is designed not for unbeliev-
ers but for believers. [r]

[23] Therefore, if the whole Church has
assembled and everyone is speaking in
tongues, would not any uninstructed person
or any unbeliever on entering conclude that
you are all out of your minds? [s] [24] However, if
everyone is prophesying and an unbeliever
or uninstructed person should enter, he
would be reproved by all and judged by all,
[25] and the secrets of his heart would be
revealed. Then he would fall down and wor-
ship God, declaring, "God is truly in your
midst." [t]

**Let Everything Be Done Properly and in
an Orderly Fashion.** [26] And so, what then
should be done, brethren? When you assem-
ble, each of you should bring a psalm or
some lesson or a revelation, or speak in a
tongue, or offer an interpretation. Every-
thing should be done with the goal in mind
of building up. [u] [27] If any of you speak in a
tongue, let only two or at most three come
forward, one at a time, and someone must
interpret. [28] If no one is available to inter-
pret, let those who speak in tongues be silent
in the church and speak only to themselves
and to God.

[29] As for the prophets, let two or three
speak, and let the rest weigh their words. [v]
[30] Should a revelation be made to someone
else who is sitting there, let the one who is
speaking stop. [w] [31] You can all prophesy, but
one at a time, so that all may receive
instruction and encouragement. [32] Indeed,
the spirits of the prophets are subject to
their prophets' control, [x] [33] for God is not a
God of disorder but of peace.

As in all the Churches of the saints, [y]
[34] * women are to keep silent at the assem-
blies. For they are not permitted to speak,
since the Law asserts that they are to be sub-
ordinate. [z] [35] If there is anything they wish to
know, they should ask their husbands at
home. It is improper for them to speak in
the church.

[36] Did the word of God originate with you?
Or are you the only ones to whom it has
come? [a] [37] Anyone who claims to be a
prophet or to have spiritual powers must
recognize that what I am writing to you is a
commandment of the Lord. [b] [38] Anyone who
does not acknowledge this should be
ignored.

[39] Therefore, brethren, be eager to proph-
esy and do not forbid speaking in tongues. [c]
[40] But ensure that everything is done prop-
erly and in an orderly fashion. [d]

VII: THE RESURRECTION*

CHAPTER 15

A: The Resurrection of Christ

The Risen Christ, Foundation of Our Faith.*
[1] And now, brethren, I want to remind you of
the gospel I proclaimed to you, which you
received and in which you stand firm. [e]

p Jer 4:22; Mt 10:16; Rom 16:19; Eph 4:14; Heb 5:12-13; 1 Pet 2:2.—q Deut 28:49; Isa 28:11-12; Jn 10:34.—r 1 Cor 14:1.—s Acts 2:6, 13; 17:32.—t 1 Cor 4:5; Isa 45:14; Zec 8:23; Rom 2:16; Heb 4:12; Jn 4:29.—u 1 Cor 12:7-10, 30; 2 Cor 12:19; Rom 7:1; Eph 4:12; 5:19.—v 1 Cor 12:10; 13:2; Job 12:11.—w 1 Thes 5:19-20.—x 1 Jn 4:1.—y 1 Cor 7:17; Acts 9:13; Rom 15:33.—z 1 Cor 11:5; Gen 3:16; Eph 5:22; 1 Tim 2:11-15; 1 Pet 3:1.—a Heb 4:12.—b 1 Cor 2:15; 13:2; Acts 11:27; 2 Cor 10:7; 1 Jn 4:6.—c 1 Cor 12:31; Eph 4:11.—d Col 2:5.—e 1 Cor 3:6; Isa 40:9; Rom 2:16; Gal 1:8.

14:21 *In the Law:* i.e., the Old Testament; see Rom 3:10-19 where Paul cites a number of passages from the Old Testament and then calls them "the Law" in v. 19.

14:34-35 Paul is not against women speaking in church (see 1 Cor 11:5). He is against women speaking in a disorderly manner in church.

15:1-58 According to Greek thought, the soul is imprisoned in the body; it alone is destined for immortality, and death comes to set it free. As heirs of this mentality, the Corinthians are unable to understand why there should be a resurrection of the body. Does Christianity perhaps desire that the soul again become a prisoner? Paul corrects this notion, which is not in accord with the Christian faith. The biblical tradition holds that the human being is one, created by God in body and soul. Death does not constitute the deliverance of the soul, but the unraveling of this unity. It is a violent state produced by sin. In atoning for sin, Christ has conquered death. It is the whole person that is saved and the whole person that is involved in the resurrection. But Paul takes account of the objection that the Greeks can bring up: the resurrection is not a simple return to the earthly condition; the risen body does not limit the aspirations of the spirit. It will be "spiritual," a new creation in the risen Christ.

15:1-11 Paul takes as his starting point a fact: the resurrection of Christ. This is the primordial certainty of the Christian faith. He recalls this teaching of the Church and confirms it by listing the witnesses who had seen the risen Christ. In this passage, we find the main elements of the Christian creed and, at the same time, the earliest written witness to the handing on of the original teaching of the Church and to the appearances of Jesus Christ.

2 Through it you are also being saved,
provided that you are holding fast to what I
proclaimed to you. If not, then you have
believed in vain.[f]

3 * For I handed on to you as of primary
importance what I received: that Christ died
for our sins, in accordance with the
Scriptures,[g] 4 that he was buried and that he
was raised to life on the third day in accor-
dance with the Scriptures,[h] 5 and that he
appeared to Cephas, and later to the
Twelve.[i] 6 Then he appeared to more than
five hundred of the brethren at one time,
most of whom are still alive, although some
have fallen asleep.*[j] 7 After that he appeared
to James,* and then to all the apostles.[k]

8 Last of all, he appeared to me, as to one
born abnormally.[l] 9 For I am the least of the
apostles. I am not worthy to be called an
apostle, because I persecuted the Church of
God.[m] 10 However, by the grace of God I am
what I am, and the grace he has bestowed
upon me has not proved to be fruitless.
Indeed, I have worked harder than any of
them—although that should not be credited
to me but to the grace of God within me.[n]
11 But whether it was I or they, this is what we
preach and what you have come to believe.[o]

B: The Resurrection of the Dead

The Resurrection and Faith.* 12 Now if Christ
is proclaimed as raised from the dead, how
can some of you say that there is no resur-
rection of the dead?[p] 13 If there is no resur-
rection of the dead, then Christ has not been
raised.[q] 14 And if Christ has not been raised,
then our preaching is useless, and so is your
faith. 15 We are even false witnesses to God,
for we testified that he raised Christ when he
did not raise him up, assuming it is true that
the dead are not raised.[r]

16 For if the dead are not raised, then
Christ has not been raised. 17 And if Christ
has not been raised, your faith is without any
foundation, and you are still in your sins.[s]
18 Then those who have fallen asleep in
Christ are utterly lost.[t] 19 If it is for just this
life that we have hoped in Christ, we are the
most pitiable of all men.[u]

Christ, the Firstfruits.* 20 But Christ has
been raised from the dead, the firstfruits of
those who have fallen asleep.[v] 21 For since
death came into the world through a man,
the resurrection of the dead has also come
through a man.[w]

22 Just as in Adam all die, so all will be
brought to life in Christ,[x] 23 but each one in
proper order: Christ the firstfruits; after-
ward, at his coming, those who belong to
Christ.[y] 24 Then comes the end, when he
hands over the kingdom to God the Father,
after he has destroyed every sovereignty and
authority and power.*[z] 25 For he is destined
to reign until he has put all his enemies
under his feet.[a]

26 The last enemy to be destroyed is
death.[b] 27 For he has put all things under his
feet. But when it says "all things are put
under," it is obvious that this excludes the
one who subjected everything to him.[c]
28 When all things are subjected to him, then
the Son himself will also be subjected to the

f Rom 1:16; 11:22.—g 1 Cor 11:23; Isa 53:4-12; Mt 26:24; Lk 24:27; Jn 1:29; Gal 1:12; 1 Pet 2:24; 3:18.—h Ps 16:8-11; Hos 6:1-2; Jon 2:1; Mt 27:59, 60; Jn 2:21, 22; Acts 2:23-24.—i Mt 28:16-17; Mk 16:14; Lk 24:36; Jn 20:19.—j Mt 9:24; 28:17.—k Lk 24:33, 36, 37, 50; Acts 1:3-4; 15:13.—l 1 Cor 9:1; Acts 9:3-6; Gal 1:16.—m 1 Cor 10:32; Acts 8:3; 9:1-2; 2 Cor 12:11; Gal 1:23; Eph 3:8; 1 Tim 1:15.—n Rom 3:24; 12:3; 2 Cor 11:23; Phil 2:13; Col 1:29.—o Gal 2:6.—p Jn 11:24; Acts 17:32; 23:8; 2 Tim 2:18.—q 1 Thes 4:14.—r Acts 2:24; 5:32.—s Rom 4:25.—t Mt 9:24; Jn 11:11, 13.—u 1 Cor 4:9; 2 Tim 3:12.—v Mt 9:24; Acts 26:23; Rom 8:11; Col 1:18; 1 Thes 4:14; 1 Pet 1:3.—w Rom 5:12; 6:23; Jn 11:25.—x 1 Cor 6:14; Gen 3:17-19; Rom 5:12-19.—y 1 Cor 3:23; 1 Thes 2:19; 4:15-17.—z Rom 8:38; Eph 1:22; 2 Pet 1:11.—a Ps 110:1; Isa 9:7; 52:7; Mt 22:44.—b Rom 6:9; 2 Tim 1:10; Rev 20:14; 21:4.—c Ps 8:7; Mt 22:44; 28:18; Eph 1:22; Phil 3:21.

15:3-5 Paul offers two lines of testimony for Christ's Passion and Resurrection: (1) the testimony of the Old Testament (e.g., Ps 16:8-11; Isa 53:5f, 11) and (2) the testimony of eyewitnesses (Acts 1:21f). He lists only six appearances of the risen Christ; the Gospels and Acts offer ten (see note on Mt 28:10).

15:6 *Have fallen asleep:* an image of death. The same expression is used in vv. 18, 20, and 51, and is the usual one in the New Testament. In it, Christians indirectly expressed their faith in the resurrection (in Greek the same verb means both "to awaken" and "to bring back to life"). From this phrase, we also derive our word "cemetery," i.e., literally, a place of sleepers.

15:7 *Appeared to James:* Paul inserts the risen Lord's appearance to James as a kind of transition to his own experience of seeing Christ. Like Paul, James, "the brother of the Lord" (Gal 1:19), had not been a disciple of Jesus (see Acts 1:12f). An account of such an appearance to James is found in the *Gospel of the Hebrews,* an apocryphal Jewish-Christian gospel.

15:12-19 The Resurrection of Jesus, to which the apostles are witnesses, is the basic proof that there is a resurrection of the dead; the Old Testament initially voiced a hope of this (Ps 16:10; Job 19:25; Ezek 37:10) and later taught it explicitly (2 Mac 7:9). The Resurrection of Jesus is thus the very foundation of our faith; Christ is the firstborn of the dead, who will rise in their turn.

15:20-28 Paul contrasts two states of the human race: on the one side, the fallen state of sin, symbolized by Adam; on the other, the state of life and salvation brought about by Christ (see Rom 5:17-21).

15:24 *Sovereignty and authority and power:* these words signify all the forces, angelic and human, that are opposed to the Kingdom of God (see 1 Cor 2:6; Col 2:15).

one who made all things subject to him, so that God may be all in all.[d]

Practical Faith. 29 Otherwise, what will people accomplish when they have themselves baptized for the dead?* If the dead are not raised at all, why should anyone be baptized for them?[e] 30 And why should we be placing ourselves in danger every hour?[f] 31 I face death every day—that is as sure as the pride that I have in you, brethren, through Jesus Christ our Lord.[g]

32 With only human hopes, what would I have gained by fighting those wild beasts at Ephesus? If the dead are not raised,

"Let us eat and drink,
for tomorrow we die."[h]

33 Do not let anyone lead you astray. "Bad company corrupts good morals." 34 Come to your senses and sin no more.[i] For some of you have no knowledge of God. I say this to your shame.[j]

C: The Mode of the Resurrection

The Resurrected Body. 35 Someone may ask, "How are the dead raised? What sort of body will they have when they come back?"[k] 36 This is foolish. What you sow must die before it is given new life,[l] 37 and what you sow is not the body that is to be but a bare grain of wheat or of something else. 38 God gives to it a body that he has chosen, and to each kind of seed its own particular body.[m]

39 Not all flesh is alike. There is one kind for human beings, another for animals, another for birds, and another for fish. 40 There are both heavenly bodies and earthly bodies. The splendor of heavenly bodies is of one kind, and that of earthly bodies is another. 41 The sun has a splendor of its own, the moon another splendor, and the stars still another. Indeed, the stars differ among themselves in splendor.[n]

42 So it is with the resurrection of the dead. What is sown is perishable; what is raised is imperishable.[o] 43 What is sown in dishonor is raised as glorious. What is sown in weakness is raised in power.[p] 44 What is sown is a physical body; what is raised is a spiritual body.[q]

The Natural and the Spiritual Body. If there is a natural body, there is also a spiritual body. 45 As it is written, the first man, Adam, became a living being; the last Adam has become a life-giving spirit.[r] 46 But the spiritual body did not come first. Rather the natural body came first, and then the spiritual.

47 The first man was formed from the dust of the earth; the second man is from heaven.[s] 48 The man formed from dust is the pattern for earthly people; the heavenly man is the pattern for those who are of heaven.[t] 49 Just as we have borne the image of the man formed from dust, so shall we also bear the likeness of the heavenly one.[u]

Where, O Death, Is Your Victory?* 50 What I am asserting, brethren, is that flesh and blood cannot inherit the kingdom of God, nor can the perishable inherit what is imperishable.[v]

51 Listen while I tell you a mystery. We shall not all fall asleep, but we shall all be changed[w] 52 in an instant, in the twinkling of an eye, at the sound of the last trumpet. For the trumpet will sound, and the dead will be raised imperishable, and we will be changed.*[x] 53 For this perishable body must be clothed with the imperishable, and this mortal body must put on immortality.[y]

54 When this perishable body puts on imperishability, and this mortal body puts on immortality, then will the words that are written be fulfilled:

"Death has been swallowed up in victory.[z]
55 Where, O death, is your victory?
Where, O death, is your sting?"[a]

56 The sting of death is sin, and the power of sin is the Law.[b] 57 But thanks be to God

d 1 Cor 3:23; Eph 4:6; Phil 3:21; Col 3:11.—e 2 Cor 1:10.—f 2 Cor 4:8-12; 11:23-27.—g Ps 44:23; Rom 8:36; 1 Thes 2:19.—h 1 Cor 4:9; Wis 2:5-7; Isa 22:13; Lk 12:19; Acts 18:19; 2 Cor 4:10-11.—i 1 Cor 6:19; Prov 22:24, 25.—j 1 Cor 4:14; Mt 22:29; Mk 12:24; Gal 4:8.—k Ezek 37:3; Rom 9:19.—l Lk 11:40; 12:20; Jn 12:24.—m Gen 1:11.—n Pss 8:2-4; 19:5-7.—o Mt 13:43.—p Phil 3:20-21; Col 3:4.—q Wis 7:1.—r Gen 2:7; Jn 5:21-29; Rom 5:14; 8:2; 2 Cor 3:6, 17.—s Gen 2:7; 3:19; Ps 90:3; Jn 3:13.—t Phil 3:20-21.—u Gen 5:3; Rom 8:29; Phil 3:21.—v Mt 25:34; Jn 3:3-6; Eph 6:12; Heb 2:14.—w 1 Cor 13:2; 14:2; Mt 9:24; 2 Cor 5:4; Phil 3:21; 1 Thes 4:14-17.—x Joel 2:1; Zec 9:14; Mt 24:31; Jn 5:25; Rev 11:15-18.—y 2 Cor 5:2-4.—z Isa 25:8; 2 Cor 5:4; 2 Tim 1:10; Heb 2:14-15; Rev 20:14.—a Hos 13:14.—b Rom 4:15; 5:12; 7:7, 13.

15:29-34 *Baptized for the dead* (v. 29) refers to a rite, unknown to us, a type of baptism by proxy. Paul uses the image of *wild beasts* (v. 32) to express the hostility he encountered at Ephesus. In v. 33 he is citing Menander, a Greek comic poet, although by this time the saying may already have become a popular proverb.

15:50-58 Using images traditional in the Bible, Paul describes in a few lines the great day of universal salvation, when humanity reaches its destiny.

15:52 The *trumpet* was part of apocalyptic choreography (see Mt 24:31; 1 Thes 4:16); it symbolized the solemn proclamation of the divine plan (see the seven trumpets of the Book of Revelation: 8:6-11, 19).

who gives us the victory through our Lord Jesus Christ. [c]

58 Therefore, my beloved brethren, stand firm and immovable, devoting yourselves completely to the work of the Lord, knowing that in the Lord your labor is not in vain. [d]

VIII: FINAL RECOMMENDATIONS AND GREETINGS*

CHAPTER 16

The Collection. 1 Now in regard to the collection for the saints, * you should follow the instructions I gave to the churches of Galatia. [e] 2 On the first day of every week, * each of you should set aside and save whatever you can spare, so that when I come to you, no collections will have to be taken. [f] 3 And when I arrive, I shall send those who have been approved by you with letters of recommendation to deliver your gift to Jerusalem. [g] 4 If it seems advisable that I should also go, they will accompany me. [h]

Paul's Plans. 5 I shall come to visit you after passing through Macedonia—for I am going to pass through Macedonia. [i] 6 I may stay for some time with you, perhaps even for the entire winter, and then you can send me forth on my journey, wherever I may be going. [j] 7 I do not want to see you now in passing. If the Lord permits, I hope to spend some time with you. [k] 8 However, I will remain in Ephesus until Pentecost, [l] 9 because a wide door for productive work has been opened for me, although there are also many adversaries to face. [m]

News of Other Missionaries. 10 If Timothy comes, put him at ease, for he is doing the work of the Lord just as I am. [n] 11 Therefore, let no one treat him with disdain. Rather, send him on his way in peace when he leaves you to come to me, for the brethren and I are expecting him. [o]

12 As for our brother Apollos, I urged him strongly to visit you with the others, but he was determined not to go at this particular time. He will come to you when he has the opportunity. [p]

13 Keep alert; stand firm in the faith; be courageous; be strong. [q] 14 Everything that you do should be done in love. [r]

15 As you know, brethren, the members of the household of Stephanas were the first converts in Achaia, and they have devoted themselves to the service of the saints. [s] 16 I urge you to put yourselves at the service of such people and of all those who work and toil with them. [t]

17 I was delighted at the arrival of Stephanas and Fortunatus and Achaicus, because they have made up for your absence. [u] 18 For they have raised my spirits as well as yours. Such men deserve recognition. [v]

Salutations and Best Wishes. 19 The Churches of Asia send you greetings. Aquila and Prisca greet you warmly in the Lord, together with the Church that meets in their house. [w] 20 All the brethren send their greetings. Greet one another with a holy kiss. [x]

21 I, Paul, have written this greeting with my own hand. [y] 22 If anyone does not love the Lord, let him be accursed. * O Lord, come! [z] 23 The grace of the Lord Jesus be with you. 24 My love to you all in Christ Jesus. [a]

c Jn 16:33; Rom 8:37; 2 Cor 2:14; Heb 2:14-15; 1 Jn 5:4.—d 1 Cor 16:10; Isa 65:23; Jer 48:10; Jn 6:28; Gal 6:9; 2 Pet 3:14; Rev 2:26.—e Acts 9:13; 16:6; 24:17; Rom 15:25-32; 2 Cor 8—9; Gal 2:10.—f Bar 1:6; Acts 20:7; 2 Cor 9:4, 5; Rev 1:10.—g Acts 18:27; 2 Cor 3:1; 8:18, 19.—h Acts 19:21; 20:3.—i 1 Cor 4:19; Acts 16:9; 19:21; Rom 15:26; 2 Cor 1:15-16.—j Rom 15:24; Tit 3:13.—k 1 Cor 4:19; Acts 18:21; 2 Cor 1:15, 16.—l 1 Cor 15:32; Acts 2:1; 18:19; 19:1-10.—m Acts 14:27; 19:9, 23; 2 Cor 2:12.—n 1 Cor 4:17; 15:58; Acts 16:1; 19:22; Phil 2:19-23.—o Acts 15:31; 2 Cor 1:16; 1 Tim 4:12; 3 Jn 6.—p 1 Cor 1:12; 3:4-6, 22; Acts 18:24-28.—q 1 Cor 1:8; Mt 24:42; 2 Cor 1:21; Gal 5:1; Eph 6:10; Phil 1:27; 1 Thes 3:8; Tit 1:9.—r 1 Cor 14:1.—s 1 Cor 1:16; Acts 9:13; 18:12; 24:17; Rom 15:31; 16:5.—t 1 Thes 5:12; Heb 13:17.—u 2 Cor 11:9; Phil 2:30; Philem 13.—v 2 Cor 7:13; Rom 15:32; Phil 2:29; 1 Thes 5:12-13; Philem 7.—w Acts 2:9; 18:2, 18, 26; Rom 16:3-5; Col 4:15.—x Rom 16:16; 2 Cor 13:12; 1 Thes 5:26; 1 Pet 5:14.—y Rom 16:22; Gal 6:11; Col 4:16; 2 Thes 3:17; Philem 19.—z 1 Cor 12:3; Rom 9:3; Gal 1:8-9; Eph 6:24; Rev 22:20.—a Rom 16:20.

16:1-23 The collection for the Church of Jerusalem—the "saints"—had an important place in Paul's outlook, because it was a sign of communion between the Churches that originated in the Gentile world and the mother Church that had grown up at the heart of Judaism (see Acts 24:17; Rom 15:25-26; 2 Cor 8—9; Gal 2:10).

16:1 The *saints* in Jerusalem were obviously in dire need—possibly as a result of the famine recorded in Acts 11:28 (about A.D. 44 or 46) or the persecution to which they were subjected (Acts 8:1).

16:2 *On the first day of every week:* i.e., Sunday, the Lord's Day (see Acts 20:7; Rev 1:10). *Each of you should set aside:* each Sunday Christians were to bring what they had set aside for the Lord's work. It was then probably collected at the worship service. Justin Martyr indicates in his *Apology* (1:67-68) that during his day (c. A.D. 150) offerings were brought to the altar on Sundays.

16:22 *Accursed:* = "anathema," separated from the community. *O Lord, come!:* in Aramaic *Marana tha:* a liturgical acclamation in the Aramaic-speaking communities of Palestine.

THE SECOND LETTER TO THE CORINTHIANS

The Drama of the Apostolate

After the First Letter to the Corinthians, some serious disturbances troubled the community of Corinth. Relations between Paul and those he considered his "children" went through a crisis caused by some radical challenges to him. His correspondents were, of course, only too familiar with the facts; therefore, there was no need to describe these to them. As a result, there is a danger that we may not understand this highly emotional Letter. Fortunately, the rather numerous references in the text itself make it possible to sketch a picture of the dark situation.

In A.D. 56, Paul was in Ephesus (Acts 19). He learned that some Jewish Christian intriguers (men who were converts from Judaism) were rousing the Corinthian community against him. He made a lightning visit but was received with coldness; pressed for time, perhaps weary and too personally caught up in the conflict, he settled nothing, and his passage through the community rather increased the disorder. He promised to return later and take all the time needed.

The affair became worse. Passions mounted and intrigues and cabals multiplied. One part of the community categorically rejected Paul's authority and vilified his person. Another part remained silent and let things ride. Some missionaries, claiming a recommendation from the communities of Palestine and boasting of having known Jesus himself, wanted to establish themselves as leaders of the Corinthian community.

They cunningly sought to destroy Paul's reputation, mocking his supposedly authoritarian and jealous character, lack of eloquence, and timidity. They denied his vocation of apostle and went so far as to call into doubt the purity of his Gospel as well as his intentions. These were the people who would soon reproach him for not obliging the Gentile converts to practice the Jewish Law. They were united by a systematic opposition to Paul, and for them all means were good. The Apostle unmasks these agitators in the last two chapters of this Letter.

While Paul waited in Ephesus, he was publicly insulted back in Corinth, probably by one of his closest fellow workers: he speaks of an offense and an offender (2 Cor 2:5; 7:12). Impelled by his feelings, he sent a Letter that would be judged to be too severe (2 Cor 2:3-4, 9-11), and in it he demanded that reparation be made for the offense. Some exegetes regard the last four chapters of Second Corinthians as a fragment of this lost Letter.

A bit later, Paul sent one of his coworkers, Titus, a firm and capable diplomat, to turn the situation around. The community was stabilized and the offender punished (1 Cor 2:6).

But Titus was slow in returning. Paul, who had been forced to leave Ephesus because of the riot of the silversmiths (Acts 19:23-40; 21:1), was unable to bear the waiting any longer and set out on his journey. He encountered Titus in Macedonia and received excellent news. He immediately sent Titus to Corinth to carry out the collection for the penniless mother Church of Jerusalem. A little later, around the year A.D. 56, he dictated this Second Letter to the Corinthians.

The complexity of the situation and Paul's emotions explain the tone of the Letter. Arising from a heart that is overflowing with love yet revolted at the same time, it defies all analysis. Indeed, certain exegetes believe they distinguish portions of at least three different Letters therein. In any case, it is the movements of thought that are important, and they will be brought out in the notes.

After making his point about the sorrowful affair, Paul is led to meditate on the drama of the Christian apostolate: a mystery of human weakness and divine greatness. Then he stresses the ecumenical aspect of the collection: a sign of unity between Christians of Gentile origin and those of Jewish origin.

Finally—resolved to drain the abscess—Paul lays the blame at the feet of those who have calumniated him. He initiates a strong counterattack in order to safeguard the Christian life of the Corinthians, whom he has evangelized at length. In no other place do we feel so concretely the link between the Apostle's faith and his authority.

The Second Letter to the Corinthians is less rich in doctrinal instruction than the first, but it has the great merit of introducing us to the interior life and mysticism of the Apostle. We must look to the psychology and passionate nature of Paul for the unity of these chapters. In order to understand the Apostle, we must continually go back to this ardent Letter, which can be regarded as his personal diary, his "confessions."

Nowhere else in his writings does his personality come through so clearly with its contrasting strength and weakness, its boldness and reserve, its impetuosity and tenderness. We find him to be an organizer and a missionary, a founder and a pastor, a mystic and a man of action. And what a profound awareness he shows of the apostolic mission and its originality! The First Letter to the Corinthians provided a first reflection on the meaning of the apostolate; here we find the experience, mysticism, spirituality, and, at the same time, theology of the apostolate.

The Second Letter to the Corinthians may be divided as follows:

I: Address (1:1-11)
II: Apostle by the Power of Jesus and for Jesus (1:12—7:16)
III: The Collection for the Christians of Jerusalem (8:1—9:15)
IV: Paul's Self-Defense (10:1—13:10)
V: Conclusion (13:11-13)

I: ADDRESS

CHAPTER 1

Greeting to the Church. [1] Paul, an apostle *
of Christ Jesus by the will of God, and
Timothy our brother, to the Church of God
in Corinth, and to all the saints throughout
Achaia: [a] [2] grace to you and peace from God
our Father and the Lord Jesus Christ. [b]

Sufferings and Consolation.* [3] Blessed be
the God and Father of our Lord Jesus
Christ, the Father of mercy and the God of
all consolation. * [c] [4] He consoles us in all our
afflictions and thereby enables us to console

a 2 Cor 1:19; Acts 16:1; Rom 1:7; 1 Cor 1:1-2; 10:32; Eph 1:1; Col 1:1; 2 Tim 1:1.—b Gen 14:20; Rom 1:7.—c Rom 15:5; 1 Cor 15:24; Eph 1:3; 1 Pet 1:3.

1:1 *Apostle:* a person specially commissioned by Christ (see notes on Mk 6:30; 1 Cor 1:1-9; Heb 3:1). *Timothy:* a fellow worker of Paul (see Acts 18:5) and his companion on the second and third missionary journeys. *Brother:* a fellow believer, a brother in Christ (see Acts 9:17; Heb 2:11). *Church of God in Corinth:* the community of believers at Corinth, the local representative of the universal Church. "Church of God" is an expression used only by Paul and solely in Acts 20:28, 1 Cor 1:2, and here. It corresponds to the Old Testament expression "assembly (or community) of the LORD" (see Deut 23:2; see also Num 16:3; 20:4; 1 Chr 28:8). *Saints:* another term for God's people, those who have been set apart as holy to the Lord (see note on Rom 1:7). *Achaia:* Greece as distinct from Macedonia. Although the Letter was written specifically for the situation in Corinth, it was also intended for Christians elsewhere in Greece. Copies would doubtless be made and circulated to them.

1:3-11 The Gospel is the power of liberation not only in time of exaltation when the gifts of the Spirit carry the whole community along but also in the most difficult trials of an apostle's life. Paul has known sickness and the fear of an approaching death, he has suffered persecution, and he has experienced misunderstanding and rejection at the hands of his own communities. Discouraged and weighed down, he discovers the weakness of an apostle, whose evidence is inscribed forever in his life. However, another certitude—one even more profound—imposes itself upon him: the joy of being in the hand of the Lord and imitating Jesus himself!

The word "consolation" occurs in some form ten times in these lines, not as a facile formula but as a term that expresses inner freedom, strength renewed, the reversal of a situation, the experience of being blessed by God who triumphs over evil and death. In addition, the solidarity of Christians is deepened in trials and in joy, for they all belong to the one Body of Christ. Paul's safety serves as a source of comfort for his followers, and their prayer is a means of sustenance for him.

1:3 *Consolation:* i.e., comfort and encouragement.

others in their tribulations, offering them the consolation with which we ourselves are consoled by God. [d]

5 For just as we share abundantly in the sufferings of Christ, so too, through Christ, do we receive our consolation. [e] 6 If we are being afflicted, it is for your consolation and salvation. If we are being consoled, it is to help us to console you and give you the patience and the strength to endure the same sufferings that we endure. [f] 7 Our hope for you is unshaken, because we know that as you share in the sufferings, you also share in the consolations. [g]

8 Brethren, we do not want you to be unaware of the hardships we experienced * in Asia. The burden we endured was far too heavy for us to bear, to such an extent that we even despaired of life itself. [h] 9 Indeed, in our hearts we felt that we were under a sentence of death. This was so that we not put our trust in ourselves but in God who raises the dead. [i]

10 He delivered us from this deadly peril, and he will continue to so deliver us. He on whom we have set our hopes will deliver us again, [j] 11 as you assist us with your prayers, so that thanks may be given by many to God on our behalf for the blessing granted to us through the prayers of so many. [k]

II: APOSTLE BY THE POWER OF JESUS AND FOR JESUS*

A: A Visit Not Made*

You Are Our Boast. 12 Indeed, this is our boast: the testimony of our conscience that in our dealings with the world, and especially with you, we have conducted ourselves with simplicity and godly sincerity, depending not on worldly wisdom but on the grace of God. [l] 13 For we write nothing to you that you cannot read and comprehend. It is my hope that you will come to understand fully, 14 as you have already understood in part, that on the day of the Lord Jesus we will have as much reason to boast of you as you will have reason to boast of us. [m]

Our Language Is Not "Yes" and "No." * 15 So certain am I of this that I had originally intended to come to you first of all and thereby reward you with a double benefit. [n] 16 I planned to visit you on my way to Macedonia, and then to come to you again on my return from Macedonia and have you send me forth to Judea. [o]

17 Since that was my original intention, was I being impulsive, or do you believe that my plans are based on human considerations, ready to say "Yes, Yes" and "No, No" at the same time? [p] 18 As surely as God is faithful, our word to you has not been "Yes" and "No." [q] 19 The Son of God, Jesus Christ, who was proclaimed to you by us, that is, by Silvanus * and Timothy and me, was not a mixture of "Yes" and "No." He was never anything but "Yes." [r]

20 In him is the "Yes" to every one of the promises of God. Indeed, it is through him that we say "Amen" to give glory to God. [s] 21 However, it is God who enables both us and you to stand firm in Christ. He has anointed us [t] 22 and marked us with his seal

d 2 Cor 7:6-7, 13; Isa 49:13; 51:12; 1 Thes 3:6-8; 2 Thes 2:16.—e 2 Cor 4:10; Rom 8:17; Gal 6:17.—f 2 Cor 4:15; 2 Tim 2:10.—g 2 Cor 1:5; Rom 8:27.—h Acts 2:9; 20:18-19; Rom 11:25; 1 Cor 15:32.—i 2 Cor 4:7-11; Jer 17:5; Jn 5:21; Rom 4:17.—j Rom 15:31; 1 Tim 4:10; 2 Tim 4:18.—k 2 Cor 4:15; 9:12; Rom 15:30; Phil 1:19.—l 2 Cor 2:17; Acts 23:1; 1 Cor 1:17; 1 Thes 2:10.—m 1 Cor 1:8; Phil 2:16; 1 Thes 2:19-20.—n Rom 1:11, 13; 1 Cor 4:19.—o Acts 16:9; 19:21; 1 Cor 16:5-9, 11; 3 Jn 6.—p 2 Cor 10:2-3; Mt 5:37; Jas 5:12.—q 1 Cor 1:9; Eph 4:14.—r Mt 4:3; Acts 15:22; 16:1-3; 1 Thes 1:1; 2 Thes 1:1; Heb 13:8.—s Rom 15:8, 9; 1 Cor 14:16; Rev 3:14.—t 1 Cor 16:13; 1 Jn 2:20, 27.

1:8 *We experienced:* throughout the Letter, Paul uses the editorial plural (*we, us, our, ourselves*). These terms should be taken as referring to Paul alone—except where the context demonstrates otherwise. *Asia:* Asia Minor, with its capital at Ephesus, which was a Roman province.

1:12—7:16 Paul recalls recent events. There must be a full understanding between himself and the Corinthians; let them no longer have any doubt of his sincerity and intentions. The preaching of Christ is not a teaching that can be accommodated to each person's taste. The apostle exists only by the power of Jesus and for Jesus, who calls every human being to salvation. To take sides for or against the apostle is to take a position on the Gospel and on Jesus himself. At the same time, Paul describes the way he thinks of his own life: an apostle not only comes in the name of Jesus but is so bound to his Master and his message that he shares the lot and imitates the Death and Resurrection of Jesus.

1:12—2:13 Paul had promised to come to Corinth twice: once from Ephesus before going on to Macedonia in the north and then on his return from Macedonia when going on to Ephesus. However, because of a situation that had arisen, he had canceled one or both of these visits. He has been criticized for this and here gives his explanation.

1:15-22 Paul insists that his dialogue with the Corinthians is not one of "Yes" and "No" at the same time—just as Jesus, the Son of God, did not simultaneously say "Yes" and "No." Indeed, God fulfilled his promises by sending his Son among us, and Christ also did what his Father wanted. Thus, Christ is a "Yes," consenting to the Father's plan. Similarly, we say "Yes" to Christ, first at our Baptism when we receive the first outpouring of the Spirit and then at every Eucharist when we say "Amen" (which means, "Yes, it is true"). When we sin, on the other hand, we say "No" to Christ.

1:19 *Silvanus:* another fellow worker of Paul. The Hebrew name was Silas, but this was romanized to Silvanus (see Acts 18:5).

and given us the Spirit in our hearts, as a down payment of what is to come. [u]

The Delay Was Intended Merely To Spare Them.* [23] I call upon God as a witness that it was only to spare you that I did not come again to Corinth. [v] [24] We do not wish to lord it over your faith, but to work together with you for your joy, because you are standing firm in your faith. [w]

CHAPTER 2

[1] Therefore, I made up my mind not to have you endure another painful visit. [x] [2] For if I cause you pain, then who would be there to cheer me up aside from you whom I offended? [y] [3] And I wrote as I did, so that when I came I would not suffer distress from those who should have made me rejoice. I know all of you well enough to be certain that we both share the same joy. [z] [4] It was with great distress and anguish of heart and many tears that I wrote to you, not to grieve you but to let you know how abundant is the love I have for you. [a]

Forgiveness for the Offender. [5] If anyone has caused distress, he has done so not only to me but to some extent—not to exaggerate—to all of you. [b] [6] The punishment that was imposed by the majority was appropriate. [c] [7] But now you should forgive and encourage him so that he may not be overwhelmed by the burden of his distress. [d] [8] Therefore, I urge you to reassure him of your love.

[9] I wrote to you to test your obedience in all matters. [e] [10] Anyone whom you forgive I forgive as well. Whatever I have forgiven, if I have forgiven anything, I have done for your sake in the presence of Christ, [11] so that we may avoid being outwitted by Satan, for we are not unaware of his schemes. [f]

Paul's Anguish.* [12] When I came to Troas to proclaim the gospel of Christ, and a door of opportunity was opened for me in the Lord, [g] [13] my mind knew no relief because I could not find my brother Titus in that place. And so I said farewell to them and moved on to Macedonia. [h]

B: Greatness and Weakness of the Apostles*

Ambassadors of God. [14] But thanks be to God, for he brings us to victory in Christ and through us he manifests the fragrance of the knowledge of him throughout the world. [i] [15] We are indeed the aroma of Christ to God both among those who are being saved and among those who are perishing: [j] [16] to the latter, the odor of death that leads to death; to the former, a fragrance of life leading to life.

Who is truly qualified for such a task? [k] [17] For we are not like so many others who adulterate the word of God for profit. When we speak, we do so in Christ and in all sincerity, as men sent from God and standing in God's presence. [l]

CHAPTER 3

A Letter from God.* [1] Are we beginning once again to commend ourselves to you? Surely, as is true in some cases, we do not need letters of recommendation to you or from you. [m] [2] You yourselves are our letter, one

u 2 Cor 5:5; Gen 38:18; Ezek 9:4; Rom 5:5; 8:16, 23; Eph 1:13-14; 4:30.—v 2 Cor 1:3; 13:2; Rom 1:9; 1 Cor 4:21.—w Rom 11:20; 1 Cor 15:1; 1 Pet 5:3.—x 2 Cor 1:23; 12:20-21.—y 2 Cor 7:8.—z 2 Cor 7:8, 12; 12:21; Gal 5:10; 2 Thes 3:4; Philem 21.—a 2 Cor 7:8, 12; Acts 20:19.—b 1 Cor 5:1-2; Gal 4:12.—c 2 Cor 7:11; 1 Cor 5:4-5.—d Gal 6:1; Eph 4:32; Col 3:13.—e 2 Cor 7:8, 12, 15; 10:6.—f Mt 4:10; Lk 22:31; Eph 4:27; 1 Pet 5:8-9.—g 2 Cor 4:3-4; Acts 16:8; Rom 1:1.—h 2 Cor 7:5, 6; Gal 2:1, 3; 1 Tim 1:3.—i 2 Cor 9:15; Ezek 20:41; Rom 6:17; 1 Cor 15:57.—j 2 Cor 4:3; Gen 8:21; Ex 29:18; Num 15:3; 1 Cor 1:18.—k 2 Cor 3:5-6; Lk 2:34; Jn 3:36.—l 2 Cor 4:2; Acts 20:33; 1 Cor 5:8; 1 Thes 2:5.—m 2 Cor 5:12; 10:12, 18; Acts 18:27; Rom 16:1; 1 Cor 16:3.

1:23—2:4 Paul explains why he has substituted a severe Letter for the announced visit. The details of the incidents escape us, but we know that Paul was attacked by an agitator who was opposed to the Apostle's coworkers. Paul estimated that an immediate visit would inflame the situation whereas a letter would foster reflection, an examination of conscience, and ultimately peace and harmony. The Letter of which he speaks has been lost; according to some, however, it is to be found in the last chapters of the present Letter.

2:12-13 What Paul is saying about Macedonia is interrupted by what follows, and is picked up again in 2 Cor 7:5.

2:14—6:10 The Corinthian incident seems to have been resolved and good relations to have been established. Difficult as the trial was, it served to clarify and deepen the meaning of the apostolic ministry for Paul, who now has a better grasp of the dimensions of his mission. What force this life attains under the direction of Christ! The power of God is manifested in a person who is weak, ill, and under attack!

3:1-6 Preachers are circulating, exhibiting and collecting their letters of credibility from one Church to another. But how futile are merely human recommendations and written documents! The apostolate is attested by one's life. The existence of the community of Corinth and the Spirit's action in it certify that Paul and his coworkers have been chosen by God. This is the new covenant announced by the Prophets that inserts itself into the lives of individuals and peoples (see Jer 31:31-33; Ezek 11:19; 36:26).

For the first time in Christian literature, the idea of a "New Covenant" and the term itself make their appearance, and a clear distinction is drawn between the two Testaments. Paul has understood that there has been a radical change: from the letter to the Spirit, from the written book to the live hearts of human beings.

that is written on our hearts, so that it may be known and read by all.[n] 3 And you make it clear that you are a letter from Christ entrusted to our care, a letter written not with ink but with the Spirit of the living God, and written not on tablets of stone* but on tablets of the human heart.[o]

4 Such is the complete confidence in God that we have through Christ.[p] 5 Obviously, we are not competent of ourselves to take credit for anything as coming from us.[q] Our competence comes from God 6 who has empowered us to be the ministers of a new covenant, not written but of the Spirit. For the letter kills, but the Spirit gives life.[r]

Ministers of a New Covenant.* 7 Now if the ministry of death, engraved with letters on stone, was so glorious that the Israelites could not fix their glance on the face of Moses because of its glory, a glory that would soon fade,[s] 8 how much greater will be the glory of the ministry of the Spirit?

9 For if the ministry of condemnation was glorious, how much richer in glory will be the ministry of righteousness![t] 10 Indeed, what was once glorious is now without any glory in comparison with the surpassing glory. 11 For if what was destined to fade away was glorious, how much greater will be the glory of that which endures!

The Lord Is the Spirit.* 12 Therefore, since we have such hope, we can act with complete confidence,[u] 13 and not like Moses who put a veil over his face so that the Israelites could not observe the radiance that was fading away.[v] 14 However, their minds were hardened. Even to this very day, the same veil remains unlifted during the reading of the old covenant,* since only in Christ is it set aside.[w] 15 Indeed, to this very day, whenever Moses is read, a veil lies over their hearts.[x]

16 However, when one turns to the Lord, the veil is removed.[y] 17 Now this Lord is the Spirit,* and where the Spirit of the Lord is, there is freedom.[z] 18 And as we gaze upon the glory of the Lord with unveiled faces, all of us are being transformed into that same image from glory to glory, which comes from the Lord, who is the Spirit.[a]

CHAPTER 4

The Gospel of the Glory of Christ.* 1 Therefore, since we are engaged in this ministry through the mercy of God, we do not lose heart.[b] 2 Rather, we have renounced all shameful and hidden ways. We do not engage in deception or falsify the word of God. By stating the truth in an open manner, we commend ourselves to the conscience of everyone in the sight of God.[c]

3 If our gospel is veiled, it is veiled to those who are perishing,[d] 4 those unbelievers whose minds have been blinded by the god of this world to prevent them from seeing

n 1 Cor 9:2.—o Ex 24:12; 31:18; 32:15-19; Prov 3:3; 7:3; Jer 31:33; Ezek 11:19; 36:26-27; Mt 16:16.—p Eph 3:12.—q 2 Cor 2:16; Jn 3:27; 1 Cor 15:10.—r Jer 31:31-34; Lk 22:20; Jn 6:63; Rom 2:29; 7:6; Eph 3:7.—s Ex 34:29-35; Isa 42:21; Rom 4:15.—t Deut 27:26; Rom 1:17; 3:21-22.—u 2 Cor 11:15; Acts 4:29; Rom 5:4-5.—v Ex 34:33.—w 2 Cor 4:4; 7:4; Acts 13:15; Rom 11:7; Eph 6:19.—x Mt 11:25; Rom 11:7-10.—y Ex 34:34; Isa 25:7; Rom 11:23.—z Isa 61:1-2; Jn 8:32; Gal 4:6-7.—a 2 Cor 4:4-6; Jn 17:22; 1 Cor 13:12; 15:49; Rom 8:29-30; 12:2; Gal 4:19; Phil 3:10, 20-21; Col 1:15; 3:9-11; 1 Jn 3:2.—b Isa 40:3; 1 Cor 7:25; 1 Tim 1:13, 16.—c 2 Cor 2:17; Rom 6:21; 1 Cor 4:5; 1 Thes 2:4-7; Heb 4:12.—d 2 Cor 2:12, 15-16; 3:14; 1 Cor 1:18; 2 Thes 2:10.

3:3 *Tablets of stone:* a reference to the Law given on Sinai (see Ex 24:12).

3:7-11 Proceeding in the manner of the rabbis, Paul freely interprets an episode in the life of Moses (see Ezek 34:29-35) in order to assert the superiority of the New Testament. Set down by Moses, the Law denounces sin without giving the power to conquer sin; it thus condemns people without glorifying or saving them. It is not God's definitive gift.

Indeed, Paul dares to compare the ministry of the apostles to that of Moses, which was the most prestigious in the Old Testament. He dares to state that the apostolic ministry is greater than that of the founder of the Jewish people. And he invites everyone to enter fully into this New Covenant so as to surpass definitively the universe of the Old Testament. The Letter to the Romans will later offer a lengthy development of this singularly new vision in that age.

3:12-18 Paul continues to comment in rabbinical fashion on the veil of Moses. The veil is now over the faces of the Jews. He makes clear that they refuse to accept the provisional character of the Old Covenant—they do not truly understand either Moses or the Old Testament, for Christ is the key to both. It is he who established a new and definitive Covenant, which leads to life and is the power of liberation, the source of freedom. The light of the risen Christ is reflected in the life of believers by their transformation in an ever more profound manner.

3:14 *Old covenant,* i.e., "Old Testament": this is the first time that this expression, referring to a collection of Scriptures, appears in a Christian text.

3:17-18 *This Lord is the Spirit:* the "Lord" to whom the Christian turns (v. 16) is the life-giving Spirit of the living God (vv. 6, 8), who is also the Spirit of Christ. This Spirit is the inaugurator of the New Covenant and the ministry.

4:1-6 Paul has been defamed as one who does not impart the authentic teaching of Christ. He responds that, on the contrary, everything he preaches is nothing but authentically Christ's. For Paul, the Gospel is not a narrative of the past but the action of God today. The apostle, qualified for the ministry of this New Covenant, cannot falsify the Gospel in order to seek his own glory. His entire existence is illumined by the light and glory of Christ, the image of God, and the sole image that can take profound hold of a person's life. Illuminated by Christ, the apostle himself becomes a light to irradiate every conscience that refuses to be seduced by the god of this world, i.e., Satan, who personifies the traits of perversion capable of undermining a human existence.

the light of the gospel of the glory of Christ, who is the image of God.[e]

5 We do not proclaim ourselves. Rather we proclaim Jesus Christ as Lord and ourselves as your servants for the sake of Jesus.[f] 6 For the God who said, "Let light shine out of darkness," has enabled his light to shine in our hearts in order to enlighten them with the knowledge of the glory of God in the face of Jesus Christ.[g]

The State of an Apostle.* 7 However, we hold this treasure in earthen vessels so that it may be clear that this immense power belongs to God and does not derive from us.[h] 8 We are afflicted on all sides but not crushed, bewildered but not sunk in despair,[i] 9 persecuted but not abandoned, struck down but not destroyed.[j]

10 We always carry around in our body the death of Jesus, so that the life of Jesus may also be manifested in our body.[k] 11 For in our lives we are constantly being given up to death for Jesus' sake, so that the life of Jesus may be revealed in our mortal flesh.[l] 12 As a result, death is at work in us, but life in you.[m]

13 Therefore, since we have that spirit of faith about which it has been written: "I believed, and therefore I spoke," we also believe, and therefore speak.[n] 14 For we know that the one who raised the Lord Jesus will raise us also with Jesus and bring us side by side with you into his presence.[o] 15 Indeed, everything is for your sake, so that the grace that is abundantly bestowed on more and more people may cause thanksgiving to superabound, to the glory of God.[p]

An Eternal Dwelling in Heaven. 16 Therefore, we do not lose heart. Even though our outer self is continuing to decay, our inner self is being renewed day by day.[q] 17 Our temporary light afflictions are preparing for us an incomparable weight of eternal glory,[r] 18 for our eyes are fixed not on what is seen but rather on that which cannot be seen. What is visible is transitory; what is invisible is eternal.[s]

CHAPTER 5

1 Now we know that if the earthly tent in which we live is destroyed, we have a dwelling prepared for us by God, a dwelling in the heavens, not made with human hands, that will be eternal.[t] 2 While we are in this earthly tent, we groan, longing to be clothed with our heavenly dwelling;[u] 3 for when we have put it on, we will not be naked.*

4 While we are enclosed in this earthly tent we groan, burdened because we do not wish to be stripped naked but rather to be further clothed, so that our mortal state may be swallowed up by immortality.[v] 5 God is the one who has prepared us for this destiny, and he has given us the Spirit as a pledge of this.[w]

6 Therefore, we are always confident, even though we realize that as long as we are at home in the body, we are exiles from the Lord,[x] 7 for we walk by faith, not by sight.[y] 8 Yet we are filled with confidence, even as we long to be exiled from the body and be at home with the Lord.[z]

9 For this reason, whether at home or away, we strive to please him.[a] 10 For all of us must appear before the judgment seat of Christ, so that each one may receive suitable recompense for his conduct in the body, whether good or bad.[b]

Well Known to God. 11 And so, with this fear of the Lord always foremost in our thoughts, we try to persuade others. We ourselves are well known to God, and I hope we are also well known to your consciences.[c] 12 We are not once again commending ourselves to you, but we are rather affording you an opportunity to boast about us. Then you will have an answer to those who boast of external

e 2 Cor 3:14; Jn 12:31-38; 1 Cor 1:20; 1 Tim 1:11.—f Mt 20:27; 1 Cor 1:13, 23; 9:19.—g Gen 1:3; Ps 18:29; Isa 9:1; Jn 8:12; Acts 26:13-23; Gal 1:15-16; Heb 1:3; 2 Pet 1:19.—h Jdg 7:2; Job 4:19; Isa 64:8; 2 Tim 2:20.—i 2 Cor 6:4-10; 7:5; 1 Cor 4:9-13; Gal 4:20.—j Jn 15:20; Rom 8:35; Heb 13:5.—k 2 Cor 1:5; Rom 6:5-6; Col 1:24.—l Rom 8:36; 1 Cor 15:31.—m 2 Cor 13:9.—n Ps 116:10; 1 Cor 12:9.—o Acts 2:24; Rom 4:24-25; 8:11; 1 Cor 6:14; Eph 5:27; 1 Thes 4:14; Jude 24.—p 2 Cor 1:11; 9:11.—q 2 Cor 4:1; Ps 103:5; Rom 7:22; 1 Pet 3:4.—r Isa 54:7; Mt 5:11-12; Rom 8:18; 1 Pet 1:6.—s 2 Cor 5:7; Rom 8:24-25; Heb 11:1, 13.—t Isa 38:12; Mk 14:58; 1 Cor 15:47; Col 2:11; 3:1-4; Heb 9:11, 24; 2 Pet 1:13-14.—u Rom 7:24; 8:23; 1 Cor 15:54.—v Isa 25:8; 38:12; Rom 8:23;1 Cor 15:54; 2 Pet 1:13-14.—w 2 Cor 1:22; Rom 8:23; Eph 1:13, 14.—x Heb 11:13, 14.—y 2 Cor 4:18; 1 Cor 13:12; 1 Pet 1:8.—z Jn 12:26; Phil 1:21-23; 1 Thes 4:17.—a Rom 14:18; Eph 5:10; Col 1:10; 1 Thes 4:1.—b Mt 16:27; 25:31-46; Acts 10:42; Rom 2:16; 14:10-11; Eph 6:8.—c 2 Cor 1:12-14; Job 23:15; Heb 10:31; Jude 23.

4:7-15 In his life, Paul shows the "mystique" of the apostle. He knows that his existence must be identified with that of Christ, that he must enter into Christ's struggle and his agony. Thus, he reproduces in his person and his action the Paschal Mystery, the mystery of death and life, suffering and victory, until the day when he will share fully, with all the saved, in the life of the risen Lord.

5:3 *Naked:* without an earthly tent (body), which is the condition of those who have died.

appearances and not the heart.[d] 13 If, indeed, we are out of our minds, it is for God; if we are rational, it is for your sake.[e]

The Ministry of Reconciliation. 14 For the love of Christ urges us forward, once we conclude that one has died for all, and therefore all have died.[f] 15 And he died for all, so that those who live might no longer live for themselves, but for him who for their sakes died and was raised to life.[g]

16 Therefore, from now on we will not regard anyone according to human standards. Even though we once judged Christ from a human point of view,* we no longer do so.[h] 17 Consequently, anyone united to Christ is a new creation. The old order has passed away. Behold, all has become new.[i]

18 All this has been done by God, who has reconciled us to himself through Christ and entrusted us with the ministry of reconciliation.[j] 19 In other words, God was in Christ, reconciling the world to himself, and not holding people's transgressions against them, and he committed to us the message of reconciliation.[k]

20 Therefore, we are ambassadors for Christ, since God is appealing to you through us. We implore you through Christ to be reconciled to God.[l] 21 He made him who did not know sin to be sin for our sake, so that through him we might become the righteousness of God.*[m]

CHAPTER 6

1 As his coworkers, we urge you not to receive the grace of God in vain.[n] 2 For he says,

"In an acceptable time I have listened to
you,
and on the day of salvation I have
helped you."

Behold, now is the acceptable time; behold, now is the day of salvation.*[o]

Ministers of God. 3 We avoid placing obstacles in anyone's way, so that no fault may be found with our ministry.[p] 4 On the contrary, in everything we do we present ourselves as ministers of God: in steadfast perseverance; in afflictions, hardships, and distress;[q] 5 in floggings, imprisonments, and riots; in labors, sleepless nights, and fasts;[r] 6 in purity, knowledge, patience, and kindness; in holiness of spirit, genuine love,[s] 7 truthfulness, and the power of God.

We wield weapons of righteousness with right hand and left,*[t] 8 in times of honor or dishonor, praise or insult. We are regarded as impostors, and yet we speak the truth;[u] 9 as unknown men, and nevertheless we are well known; as dying, and behold we live on; as scourged, but we are not put to death;[v] 10 as sorrowful, and yet we are always rejoicing; as poor, and yet we make many rich;* as having nothing, and yet we possess everything.[w]

C: Relations Have Been Established*

Paul's Heart Is Wide Open. 11 O Corinthians, we have spoken frankly to you, and we have opened our heart to you.[x] 12 We are not withholding our love from you, but you

d 2 Cor 1:14; 3:1; Phil 1:26.—e 2 Cor 11:1, 16-17; 12:11.—f Rom 6:1-6; Gal 2:20; Col 3:3.—g Rom 4:25; 6:4-11; 14:9; Gal 2:19; Col 3:3-4.—h 2 Cor 10:4; 11:18.—i Isa 43:18-21; Jn 1:13; Rom 16:3; Gal 6:15; Eph 2:15; Rev 21:5.—j Rom 5:10; 11:36.—k Rom 4:8; 5:10-11; Col 1:20.—l 2 Cor 6:1; Isa 27:5; Eph 6:20; Philem 9.—m Isa 53:6-9; Rom 1:17; 3:24-26; 1 Cor 1:30; Gal 3:13; Heb 4:15; 7:26; 1 Pet 2:24; 1 Jn 3:5-8.—n 2 Cor 5:20; 1 Cor 3:9; 1 Thes 3:2.—o Ps 69:14; Isa 49:8; 55:6.—p 2 Cor 8:20-21; Mt 5:29; Rom 14:13, 20; 1 Cor 9:12; 10:32.—q 2 Cor 3:6; 4:8-11; 11:23-27; 1 Cor 4:9-13.—r 2 Cor 11:23-25; Acts 16:23; 1 Cor 4:11.—s Rom 12:9; 1 Cor 2:4; Gal 5:22-23; 1 Thes 1:5.—t 2 Cor 4:2, 7; 10:4; Rom 13:12; Eph 6:11-17.—u Mt 27:63; 1 Cor 4:10, 13.—v 2 Cor 1:8-10; 4:10-11; Rom 8:36.—w 2 Cor 7:4; Mt 5:12; Rom 8:32; 1 Cor 3:21; Phil 2:17; Col 1:24.—x 2 Cor 7:3.

5:16 *We once judged Christ from a human point of view:* literally: "we knew Christ according to the flesh." The literal translation does not mean that Paul met Jesus during the latter's mortal life; it means, rather, that before Paul was converted he had human prejudices regarding Jesus, but now no longer does so.

5:21 This is a splendid summary of the redemption. God made the penalty for sins to fall on Jesus (see Isa 53:6; Gal 3:13). Christ, the only one who is entirely righteous, took our sins upon himself at Calvary and endured the punishment reserved for us, i.e., death and separation from God. He made it possible for us to receive his righteousness and be recommended to God. Yet all this stems from the love of the Father, who prompted Christ by his plan and enabled him to bring it about by his grace.

6:2 This verse does not exclude from grace and salvation those people who lived before Christ's coming. For they received the promises that were later fulfilled in Christ (2 Cor 1:20) and saw and welcomed their fulfillment from a distance (see Jn 8:56; Heb 11:13).

6:7 *Weapons . . . with right hand and left:* with the right hand, offensive weapons (the sword); with the left, defensive weapons (the shield).

6:10 *We make many rich:* i.e., rich toward God, for true wealth does not consist in worldly possessions (see Lk 12:15, 21). Even if believers have none of the world's goods, they possess everything in him who is Lord of all (see 1 Cor 1:4f; 3:21-23; Eph 2:7; 3:8; Phil 4:19; Col 2:3).

6:11—7:16 After the gripping testimony concerning the apostolate and its mystery, the Letter returns to concrete situations of the community of Corinth. Moving appeals, pastoral concern, and profound attachment come to the fore in these lines.

have withheld yours from us.[y] 13 I speak to you as my children. In return, also open wide your hearts to us.[z]

What Relation Can There Be between Righteousness and Iniquity? 14 Do not associate with unbelievers.* For what basis can there be for a partnership between righteousness and lawlessness? What do light and darkness have in common?[a] 15 Can Christ ever be in accord with Beliar? *What does a believer have in common with an unbeliever?[b] 16 Can there be an agreement between the temple of God and idols? For we are the temple of the living God, and for this we have God's word:[c]

"I will live in them and walk among
them.
I will be their God,
and they shall be my people.
17 Therefore, come out from their midst
and separate yourselves from them,
says the Lord.
Do not touch anything unclean,
and I will welcome you.[d]
18 I will be a father to you,
and you shall be my sons and
daughters,
says the Lord Almighty."[e]

CHAPTER 7

1 Since we have these promises, beloved, let us cleanse ourselves from anything that can defile flesh or spirit, and thereby make our holiness perfect in the fear of God.[f]

Trust Reestablished. 2 Make room in your hearts for us. We have wronged no one, we have corrupted no one, we have exploited no one.[g] 3 I do not say this to condemn you, for I have already told you that your place in our hearts is secure, so that we will live together and we will die together.[h] 4 I have great confidence in you, and I boast about you with intense pride. Despite all of our afflictions, I am greatly encouraged and overflowing with joy.[i]

5 *Even when we arrived in Macedonia, we were unable to rest our bodies, for we were afflicted in every way: conflicts on the outside and fears on the inside.[j] 6 But God, who comforts the downcast, encouraged us by the arrival of Titus[k]—7 and not merely by his arrival but also by the encouragement he received from you. He told us of your longing for me, your deep regrets, and your zeal for me, all of which cause me even greater joy.

8 Even if I did cause you sorrow with my letter, I do not regret it. I did regret this letter briefly, but, having come to realize that you were sorrowful only for a short time,[l] 9 I now am able to rejoice, not because you were grieved but because your sorrow led to repentance. For you were sorrowful in a godly way and so received no harm because of us.[m] 10 Such godly sorrow results in repentance that leads to salvation and causes no regret, whereas worldly sorrow produces death.[n]

11 For see what earnestness this godly sorrow has produced for you, what eagerness to repent, what indignation, what fear, what yearning, what zeal, what desire to see justice done. In every way, you have proved your innocence in this matter.[o]

12 Therefore, even though I wrote to you, it was not on account of the one who committed the offense or on account of the one who was wronged, but rather that you should be fully aware of your zeal for us in the sight of God.[p] 13 In this we have been greatly encouraged.

In addition to being encouraged ourselves, we rejoiced still more at the joy of Titus, because his mind has been completely refreshed by all of you.[q] 14 Anything I may have said to him in boasting about you has not caused me to feel ashamed. But just as

y 2 Cor 7:3-4; Mt 5:12; Phil 2:17; Col 1:24.—z 2 Cor 7:2; Gal 4:19; 1 Thes 2:11.—a Gen 24:3; Deut 22:10; 1 Cor 5:9-10; 1 Jn 1:6.—b Acts 5:14; 1 Cor 6:6; 10:21.—c Ex 25:8; 29:45; Lev 26:12; Jer 31:1; 32:38; Ezek 37:27; Mt 16:16; 1 Cor 3:16-17; 6:19; 10:20-21; Rev 21:3.—d Isa 52:11; Ezek 20:34, 41; Rev 18:4; 21:27.—e Ex 4:22; 2 Sam 7:14; 1 Chr 17:13; Ps 2:7; Isa 43:6; Jer 31:9; Rom 8:14; Rev 4:8; 11:17; 15:3; 21:7, 22.—f 2 Cor 6:17-18; 1 Cor 10:14; 1 Thes 4:7.—g 2 Cor 6:12, 13; Acts 20:33.—h 2 Cor 6:11-13; Phil 1:7.—i 2 Cor 6:10; 8:24.—j 2 Cor 2:13; Deut 32:25; Acts 16:9.—k 2 Cor 1:3, 4; 2:13; 7:13-14; 1 Thes 3:6-8.—l 2 Cor 2:2-4; Heb 12:11.—m Joel 2:13; 1 Cor 5:2.—n Prov 17:22; Mt 5:5; Acts 11:18.—o 2 Cor 7:7.—p 2 Cor 2:3, 9; 7:8; 1 Cor 5:1-2.—q 2 Cor 2:13.

6:14 *Do not associate with unbelievers:* Paul is here thinking of the Old Testament prohibition on intermingling (Deut 22:10ff). The false teachers among the Corinthians are servants of Satan; hence, believers should not associate with them, for such association will destroy the harmony and fellowship that unite them in Christ.

6:15 *Beliar:* (= nothingness, uselessness) is a Greek variant of the Hebrew "Belial," which designates idols and Satan, a title used for Satan in the writings of Qumran. This passage may have been taken from another Letter of Paul to the Corinthians. The passage interweaves several citations from the Old Testament (which are in order: Lev 26:11-12; Ezek 37:27; Isa 52:11; Jer 51:45; 2 Sam 7:14; Jer 31:9; Isa 43:6).

7:5ff Paul picks up, after an interruption, the account of events that he had been giving earlier (2 Cor 2:13). *Titus* (v. 6) is not mentioned in the Book of Acts, but he is mentioned in other Letters of Paul (Gal 2:1-3; 2 Tim 4:10), and is the addressee of another.

everything we said to you was true, so our
boasting to Titus has proved equally true.[r]
15 And his affection for you grows even more
as he recalls the obedience of all of you and
how you welcomed him in fear and trem-
bling.[s] 16 I rejoice because I can rely com-
pletely on you.[t]

III: THE COLLECTION FOR THE CHRISTIANS OF JERUSALEM*

CHAPTER 8

Example of Christians of Macedonia. 1 Now
we want you to know, brethren, about the
grace of God that has been bestowed on the
Churches of Macedonia.[u] 2 In a period of
severe affliction, their abundant joy and
their extreme poverty have overflowed in
rich generosity on their part.[v] 3 I can testify
that they contributed to the limit of their
resources, and even beyond,[w] 4 begging us
insistently for the privilege of sharing in this
service to the saints.[x]

5 Far exceeding our expectations, they
gave themselves first to the Lord, and then,
by the will of God, to us. 6 As a result, we
urged Titus that, inasmuch as he had al-
ready begun this work of charity, he should
bring this enterprise to a successful comple-
tion among you.[y]

The Example of Christ. 7 Now, inasmuch as
you excel in everything—in your faith, your
eloquence, your knowledge, your concern
for others, and your love for us*—so we
want you also to excel in this generous
undertaking.[z]

8 I am not saying this to you as a com-
mand, but rather I am testing the genuine
character of your love by the concern you
show for others.[a] 9 For you are well aware of
the grace of our Lord Jesus Christ. Although
he was rich, he became poor for your sake so
that by his poverty you might become
rich.*[b]

10 I will now give you my advice about
what I believe is appropriate in this matter.
Last year, you were the first not only to
engage in this good work but also to do so
willingly.[c] 11 Now finish it, so that your
eagerness may be matched by completing it
according to your means.[d] 12 As long as the
goodwill is present, the gift will be accept-
able according to what one has, not accord-
ing to what one does not have.[e]

13 I am not suggesting that others should
have relief while you are reduced to difficult
straits. Rather, there should be an equitable
balance. 14 Your surplus at the present time
should relieve the needs of others, so that at
another time their surplus may relieve your
needs, and in this way there will be equality.[f]
15 As it is written,

> "The one who gathered much did not
> have too much,
> and the one who gathered less did
> not have too little."[g]

Paul Recommends the Delegates. 16 Thanks
be to God for putting into the heart of
Titus a concern for you that is the equal of
mine.[h] 17 For he not only welcomed our
request, but, because of his great concern,
he is coming to you of his own accord.[i]
18 Together with him, we are sending the
brother who is praised by all the Churches
for his proclamation of the gospel.*[j] 19 In
addition, he has also been appointed by the
Churches to be our traveling companion as
we engage in our charitable work for the
glory of the Lord and to show our eagerness
to be of service.[k]

20 In this way, we want to ensure that no
one will be able to criticize us for our
handling of this generous collection. 21 For

r 2 Cor 7:4, 6.—s 2 Cor 2:9; 10:6; Ps 55:6; 1 Cor 2:3; Phil 2:12.—t 2 Cor 2:3.—u 2 Cor 11:9; Acts 16:9; Rom 15:26.—v 2 Cor 9:11; Ex 36:5; Mk 12:44; Acts 16:20.—w 1 Cor 16:2.—x 2 Cor 9:1; Acts 9:13; 24:17; Rom 15:31.—y 2 Cor 2:13; 7:6-7, 13-14; 8:16, 23; 12:18.—z 2 Cor 9:8; Rom 15:14; 1 Cor 1:5.—a 1 Cor 7:6.—b 2 Cor 6:10; 13:13; Mt 20:28; Rom 3:24; Phil 2:6-8.—c 2 Cor 9:2; 1 Cor 7:25, 40; 16:1-4.—d 2 Cor 8:12, 19; 9:2; Ex 25:2.—e 2 Cor 9:7; Mk 12:43-44.—f 2 Cor 9:12; Acts 4:34.—g Ex 16:18.—h 2 Cor 2:14; Phil 2:13; Rev 17:17.—i 2 Cor 8:8.—j 2 Cor 2:12; 12:18; 1 Cor 7:17.—k 2 Cor 4:15; Acts 14:23; 1 Cor 16:3-4.

8:1—9:15 In the Churches that he establishes among the Gentiles, Paul inculcates a sense of generosity on behalf of the mother Church of Jerusalem, which finds herself in great material distress (see Acts 24:17; Rom 15:25-27; Gal 2:10). For him, this initiative is not something secondary but a sign of the authenticity of his mission. He wishes to attest in deeds, for Jews and Gentiles, that the love of Christ brings down the wall of separation so long standing between them (see Eph 2:13-17). The Corinthians had already decided some time ago that they would take up a collection (see 1 Cor 16:1), but the project had been abandoned because of the disputes that raged among them. Paul relaunches the project.

8:7 *Your love for us:* some manuscripts read: "our love for you."

8:9 Paul now returns to the point, expressed earlier, about Jesus' experience. Instead of using life and death (2 Cor 5:15) or sin and righteousness (2 Cor 5:21), he uses poverty and wealth. This passage has been interpreted by many scholars as referring to Jesus' preexistence with God ("wealth") (see Jn 1:1) and to his Incarnation and Death ("poverty") (see Phil 2:6-8). Others take it to refer to phases of Jesus' earthly existence, i.e., his sense of intimacy with the Father (Jn 10:15, 30; 11:42) and his feeling of estrangement from him in his Death (Mk 15:34).

8:18 *The brother who is praised . . . gospel:* the reference is very likely to Luke.

we intend to do what is honorable not only in the Lord's sight but also in the sight of others.[l]

22 And with them, we are also sending our brother * whose dedication we have tested in many ways and found to be exemplary. Now he is even more dedicated than before because of his great confidence in you.

23 As for Titus, he is my partner and coworker in your service. And as for the others, they are the apostles of the Churches and the glory of Christ.[m] 24 Therefore, show these men, and all the Churches, the proof of your love and the legitimacy of our boasting about you.[n]

CHAPTER 9

Let the Offering Be Ready. 1 In regard to the ministry toward the saints, there really is no necessity for me to write to you.[o] 2 For I am fully aware of your eagerness to help, which has been the subject of my boasting about you to the Macedonians, telling them that Achaia has been ready since last year. Your ardor has excited most of them.[p]

3 Nevertheless, I am sending the brethren to ensure that our boasts about you may not seem to have been offered in vain. I want you to be as prepared as I said you would be.[q] 4 For if I bring some Macedonians with me and they come to the realization that you are not prepared, it would be a source of shame to us—to say nothing of you—because of our confidence in you.[r] 5 Therefore, I thought it necessary to encourage the brethren to go on to you ahead of us and arrange in advance for the gift that you have promised, so that it may be ready as a genuine gift and not as something that has been granted grudgingly.[s]

God Loves a Cheerful Giver. 6 Remember this: if you sow sparingly, you will reap sparingly, and if you sow generously, you will reap generously as well.[t] 7 Each person should give as much as he has decided in his heart, not with reluctance or under compulsion, for God loves a cheerful giver.[u] 8 And God is able to enrich you with an abundance of every grace, so that, with all of your needs provided for, you may be able to produce a surplus of good works.[v] 9 As it is written,

"He scatters abroad his gifts to the poor;
his righteousness lasts forever."[w]

Generosity Will Prompt Thanksgiving. 10 The one who provides seed for sowing and bread for food will supply and multiply your seed and increase the harvest of your righteousness.[x] 11 Enriched in every way, you will be able to practice all your acts of generosity, which, through our intervention, will result in thanksgiving to God.[y]

12 The administering of this public service not only helps to satisfy the needs of the saints but also overflows in countless acts of thanksgiving to God.[z] 13 Through the evidence of such service, you are giving glory to God for your obedient profession of the gospel of Christ and the generosity of your contribution to them and to all others as well.[a] 14 At the same time, their hearts will go out to you in their prayers for you, because of the surpassing grace that God has bestowed upon you. 15 Thanks be to God for his indescribable gift.*[b]

IV: PAUL'S SELF-DEFENSE*

CHAPTER 10

Recommendation from Human Beings or from God?* 1 I myself, Paul, exhort you by the gentleness and the mercy of Christ, I who am "timid" when I am face to face with

l Prov 14:19; Mt 5:16; Rom 12:17; 14:18; Tit 2:14.—m 2 Cor 2:13; Phil 2:25; Philem 17.—n 2 Cor 7:4, 14; 9:2.—o Acts 9:13; 24:17; 1 Thes 4:9.—p 2 Cor 8:10; 12:19; Acts 18:12; Rom 15:26.—q 2 Cor 8:23; 1 Cor 16:2.—r 2 Cor 11:17; Acts 20:4; Rom 15:26.—s 2 Cor 12:17-18; Gen 33:11; Phil 4:17.—t Prov 11:24-25; 22:9; Gal 6:7, 9.—u 2 Cor 8:12; Ex 25:2; Deut 15:10; Prov 22:8 LXX.—v Eph 3:20; Phil 4:19.—w Ps 112:9; Mal 3:10.—x Isa 55:10; Hos 10:12.—y 2 Cor 1:11; 1 Cor 1:5.—z 2 Cor 1:11; 8:14.—a 2 Cor 2:12; 8:4; Mt 9:8; Jn 15:8; Rom 15:31; 1 Tim 6:12; Heb 3:1.—b 2 Cor 2:14; Rom 5:15.

8:22 *Our brother:* not identified.

9:15 *Indescribable gift:* i.e., his own Son (Jn 3:16). It is God who has first given himself to us in the person of his Son; thus, all genuine Christian giving is our response for such a gift (see 2 Cor 8:9; 1 Jn 4:9-11).

10:1—13:10 All at once, the tone of the Letter changes. The text becomes harsh and unyielding. It indicates that some missionaries have slipped into the Corinthian community, probably Jewish Christian in origin, who wish to take over this new Church. Their human and religious pretensions go beyond all measure. They strive to discredit Paul, and many Christians lend a complacent ear to their calumnies and caricatures. Paul rebukes both his attackers and those who failed to defend him, for the Christian life itself is at stake and the authenticity of the Gospel of Jesus is threatened. The Letter is no longer a paternal address to children but a strong indictment.

Some exegetes think that these chapters were part of a stern Letter mentioned earlier (2 Cor 2:3); if so, the text predates the rest of the present Letter.

10:1-18 In order to be accepted and applauded, the false apostles seek their human prestige. They have nothing more than that, for they usurp the work of others. In contrast, Paul and his coworkers are missionaries of the Gospel in the midst of Gentiles and it was they who founded the community of Corinth—that is their recommendation. The work of God has become a reality through their efforts.

you, but "bold" when I am at a distance! [c] 2 I beg you that when I am in your presence I will not have to act with boldness and the self-assurance that I consider necessary when I oppose some of those who accuse us of acting according to human standards. * [d]

3 * Although we are human beings, we do not engage in battle according to human standards. [e] 4 For the weapons of our warfare are not merely human, but they possess the divine power to destroy strongholds. We demolish arguments [f] 5 and every proud pretension against the knowledge of God, and we compel every thought to surrender in obedience to Christ. [g] 6 What is more, once your obedience is complete, we are prepared to punish every disobedience. [h]

7 * Face the facts squarely. If anyone is confident that he belongs to Christ, he should reflect on the fact that we belong to Christ as much as he does. [i] 8 It is possible that I tend to boast a bit too much about our authority, which the Lord has entrusted to us for building you up rather than for tearing you down, but I will not apologize for doing so. [j]

9 Therefore, I do not want to seem to be someone who frightens you with my letters. 10 Some may assert, "His letters are impressive and forceful, but his personal appearance is insignificant, and he cannot speak well." [k] 11 Let them understand that what we are in our letters when we are absent will be the same as what we are in our deeds when we are present. [l]

12 We do not dare to rank ourselves or to compare ourselves with any of those who commend themselves. But when they measure themselves by one another and compare themselves with one another, they only demonstrate their ignorance. [m] 13 In contrast, we will not boast beyond the proper limits. Rather, we will measure ourselves according to the standard that God laid down for us, which enabled us to reach out all the way to you. [n]

14 We are not overreaching ourselves as we would be if we had not come to you; indeed, we came to you with the gospel of Christ. [o] 15 Neither are we boasting immoderately of the labors of others. Our hope is rather that, as your faith increases, our influence among you will be greater than ever, [p] 16 so that we may preach the gospel to regions beyond you, rather than boasting about work already done in someone else's region. [q]

17 If anyone would boast, let him boast in the Lord. * [r] 18 For it is not the one who commends himself who is really approved, but the one whom the Lord commends. [s]

CHAPTER 11

Promised to One Spouse. 1 I hope that you will put up with a little of my foolishness. Please bear with me. [t] 2 For I am jealous of you with a godly jealousy, since I promised all of you to one spouse, to present you as a chaste virgin to Christ. [u]

3 However, I am afraid that, just as the serpent deceived Eve by his cunning, your thoughts may be led astray from a single-hearted fidelity to Christ. [v] 4 For if someone comes and proclaims another Jesus * than the one we proclaimed, or if you receive a different spirit from the one you received, or a different gospel from the one you accepted, you put up with that readily enough! [w]

c Mt 11:29; Gal 5:2; Eph 3:1.—d 2 Cor 13:2, 10; Rom 12:2; 1 Cor 4:21.—e 2 Cor 10:2.—f 2 Cor 6:7; 13:2-3; Jer 1:10; 23:29; 1 Cor 1:25; 2:5; Eph 6:10-14.—g 2 Cor 9:13; Isa 2:11-12; 1 Cor 1:19.—h 2 Cor 2:9; 7:15.—i 2 Cor 5:12; 11:23; Jn 7:24; 1 Cor 1:12.—j 2 Cor 12:6; 13:10; Jer 1:10.—k 2 Cor 11:6; 1 Cor 2:3; Gal 4:13-14.—l 2 Cor 13:1-2.—m 2 Cor 3:1-2; 4:2; 5:12; 6:4; 10:18; 12:11; Prov 20:12.—n Rom 12:3; Gal 1:15; Eph 4:7.—o 2 Cor 2:12; 1 Cor 3:6.—p Rom 15:20; 2 Thes 1:3.—q 2 Cor 2:12; Acts 19:21; Rom 1:1; 15:20-21.—r Pss 34:3; 44:9; Jer 9:22-23; 1 Cor 1:31.—s 2 Cor 13:3-9; Wis 7:14; Rom 2:29; 1 Cor 4:5.—t 2 Cor 5:13; 11:21; 12:11; Mt 17:17.—u 2 Cor 4:14; Hos 2:21-22; Eph 5:26-27.—v Gen 3:1-6; 1 Tim 2:14; Rev 12:9.—w Rom 8:15; 1 Cor 3:11; Gal 1:6-9.

10:2 *Human standards:* literally, "according to the flesh."

10:3-4 Paul is ready to wage war, but his weapons are not those prized by this world and forged by human pride and arrogance. They have "the divine power" (e.g., the Word of God and the Spirit) and can demolish arguments and every pretension put forth against "the knowledge of God" (see Rom 1:18-23). Among the latter are the reasonings by which the false apostles strive to shake the faith of the Corinthian Christians (see 1 Cor 2:13f).

10:7-8 Paul makes use of Jeremiah's description of the purpose of the prophetic power given him by God (see Jer 1:9-10; 12:16f; 24:6). The Apostle's intention is to build up, not to tear down.

10:17 *Let him boast in the Lord:* boasting is not wrong when it is done "in the Lord." Paul boasts of God's work accomplished through him in the community (2 Cor 10:13-16; see 2 Cor 1:12-14). This is his recommendation (2 Cor 3:1-3). See note on 1 Cor 1:29-31.

11:4 *Another Jesus:* the false apostles present Jesus cast in the mold of Judaistic teachings (see 2 Cor 11:22). *Different spirit:* e.g., a spirit of bondage, fear, and worldliness (see Rom 8:15; 1 Cor 2:12; Gal 2:4; 4:24; Col 2:20-23) instead of a Spirit of freedom, love, joy, praise, and power (see 2 Cor 3:17; Rom 14:17; Gal 2:4; 5:1, 22; Eph 3:20; Col 1:11; 2 Tim 1:7). *Different gospel:* i.e., a gospel that is really no gospel at all (see Gal 1:6-9).

5 I do not regard myself as being inferior to these "super-apostles."[x] 6 I may be untrained in the art of speaking, but the same is not true of me in regard to knowledge. In every way and in all respects, we have made this evident to you.[y]

Paul's Apostolate. 7 Did I make a mistake by preaching the gospel of God without charge, humbling myself* so that you might be exalted?[z] 8 I robbed other Churches, accepting support from them in order to serve you.[a] 9 And when I was with you and in need, I did not burden anyone, for the brethren who came from Macedonia supplied my needs.

I refrained, and will continue to refrain, from burdening you in any way.[b] 10 As surely as the truth of Christ is in me, this boast of mine will not be silenced in the regions of Achaia.[c] 11 And why? Because I do not love you? God knows I do.[d]

12 And I shall continue to do just as I am doing at present in order to thwart the efforts of those who are seeking the opportunity to be regarded as my equals in the aspects they boast about.[e] 13 Such people are false apostles, dishonest workers who masquerade as apostles of Christ.[f] 14 And no wonder! Even Satan masquerades as an angel of light.[g] 15 Therefore, it should not be considered unusual that his servants also disguise themselves as ministers of righteousness. Their end will be appropriate to their deeds.[h]

Paul's Boast. 16 I repeat: let no one take me for a fool. However, if you do, then treat me like a fool and let me boast a little.[i] 17 In saying this, I am not speaking according to the Lord but out of foolishness in the conviction that I have something to boast about.[j] 18 Since many boast of their human accomplishments, I will do likewise.[k]

19 Since you are wise yourselves, you gladly put up with fools![l] 20 For you endure it if someone makes slaves of you, or robs you of all you possess, or takes advantage of you, or puts on airs, or slaps you in the face.[m] 21 To my shame, I must admit that we have been too weak for that sort of thing!

But whatever anyone dares to boast of—I am speaking out of foolishness—I also dare to boast of.[n] 22 Are they Hebrews? So am I. Are they Israelites? So am I. Are they descendants of Abraham?* So am I.[o] 23 Are they ministers of Christ?* (I am talking now like a madman.) I am too, having endured far greater labors, far more imprisonments, far harsher scourgings, and far more brushes with death.[p]

24 Five times I received from the Jews forty lashes minus one.*[q] 25 Three times I was beaten with rods; once I was stoned; three times I was shipwrecked; once I was adrift in the open sea for a night and a day.[r] 26 I have traveled continually and faced dangers from rivers, dangers from robbers, dangers from my own people, dangers from Gentiles, dangers in the city, dangers in the desert, dangers at sea, and dangers from false brethren.[s]

27 I have endured toil and hardship, and sleepless nights. I have been hungry and thirsty, and I have often gone without food. I have been cold, and often all but naked.[t]

28 Apart from these external things, I am burdened each and every day with the anxiety of caring for all the Churches.[u] 29 Who is weak, and I am not similarly afflicted? Who is led into sinfulness, and I am not filled with indignation?[v]

---

x 2 Cor 12:11; Gal 2:6.—y 2 Cor 8:7; 1 Cor 1:5, 17; 2:5.—z 2 Cor 12:13-18; Acts 18:3; Rom 1:1; 1 Cor 9:6-18.—a 1 Cor 16:17; 1 Thes 2:7.—b 2 Cor 12:13-14, 16; Phil 4:15, 18.—c Acts 18:12; Rom 9:1; 1 Cor 9:15.—d 2 Cor 12:15; Rom 1:9.—e 2 Cor 8:20-21; 1 Cor 9:12.—f Mt 7:15; Tit 1:10; Rev 2:2.—g Mt 4:10; Gal 1:8.—h Mt 16:27; Phil 3:19.—i 2 Cor 11:13; 12:6.—j 2 Cor 9:4; 1 Cor 7:12, 25.—k 2 Cor 5:16; 10:4; Phil 3:3-4.—l 1 Cor 4:10.—m 2 Cor 7:2; Gal 2:4; 4:9.—n 2 Cor 10:1, 10; Phil 3:4.—o Lk 3:8; Acts 22:3; Rom 9:4; 11:1; Phil 3:5-6.—p 2 Cor 6:5; Acts 16:22-24; Rom 8:36; 1 Cor 3:5; 15:31-32.—q Deut 25:2-3.—r Acts 14:19; 16:22; 27:43-44.—s Acts 20:3; 21:31; Gal 2:4.—t 2 Cor 6:5; Acts 18:3; 1 Cor 4:11; Col 1:29.—u 1 Cor 7:17.—v Mt 5:29; Rom 14:1; 1 Cor 2:3; 9:22.

11:7 *Humbling myself:* apparently Paul's opponents took issue with the fact that he failed to accept payment for his services. This went counter to the practice of first-century traveling philosophers and religious teachers, who exacted payment in proportion to the worth of their performance.

11:22 *Hebrews . . . Israelites . . . descendants of Abraham:* apparently, the false apostles are Jewish Christians who feel superior to Gentile Christians. They want to impose distinctly Jewish practices on Gentile converts. Paul is completely opposed to such a thing (see Rom 2:28f; 1 Cor 12:13; Gal 3:28f; Eph 2:11-18; Col 3:11) and emphasizes that he is everything they are—a Hebrew, an Israelite, and a descendant of Abraham.

11:23 *Ministers of Christ:* Paul states that though the false apostles can claim the title, he can claim it with far greater force because of his unremitting labor and ceaseless endurance of trials. *Far more brushes with death:* a biographical fragment about a dramatic series of sufferings of which Acts says nothing, perhaps because they had been endured in the first decade of Paul's apostolate.

11:24 *Forty lashes minus one:* see Deut 25:3; thirty-nine, in order not to risk going beyond the forty allowed by the Law.

30 If I must boast, I will boast of the things that exhibit my weakness.[w] 31 The God and Father of the Lord Jesus knows—he who is blessed forever—that I am telling the truth.[x] 32 When I was in Damascus, the governor under King Aretas * assigned guards around the city of Damascus in order to arrest me.[y] 33 However, I was let down in a basket through a window in the wall, and I thereby escaped from his clutches.[z]

CHAPTER 12

Caught Up into Heaven.* 1 Although nothing is to be gained by doing so, I must continue to boast. So I will move on to the visions and revelations given me from the Lord.[a]

2 I know a man in Christ who fourteen years ago (whether in the body or out of the body I do not know—God knows) was caught up to the third heaven.[b] 3 And I know that this man (whether in the body or out of the body I do not know—God knows) 4 was caught up into paradise and heard inexpressible things, things that no man may repeat.[c]

5 About this man I am willing to boast, but about myself I will not boast, except as it concerns my weaknesses.[d] 6 Actually, if I were to boast, I would not be a fool, because I would be telling the truth. However, I refrain from doing so in order that no one may regard me more highly than would be evident from what he has seen in me and heard from me.[e]

A Boast of One's Weakness.* 7 Therefore, to keep me from becoming unduly elated by the wondrous nature of these revelations, I was given a thorn in the flesh, a messenger of Satan, to beat me and prevent me from becoming unduly elated.[f] 8 Three times I begged the Lord to have it leave me,[g] 9 but he answered me, "My grace is sufficient for you, for power is made perfect in weakness." Hence, I will boast most gladly of my weaknesses, in order that the power of Christ may dwell within me.[h] 10 For this reason, I rejoice when I endure weaknesses, insults, hardships, persecutions, and distress for the sake of Christ. For it is when I am weak that I am strong.[i]

Characteristic Traits of an Apostle. 11 I have been very foolish, but it was you who drove me to it. I should have been commended by you, for in no way did I prove to be inferior to those super-apostles, even though I am nothing.[j] 12 The traits of a true apostle were evident in what I did in your presence: perseverance, signs, wonders, and mighty deeds.[k] 13 How then have you been less privileged than the other Churches, except that I myself did not place a burden on you? Forgive me for being so unfair![l]

14 Now I am getting ready to come to you for a third time, and I do not intend to be a burden to you. What I want is not your money, but you yourselves. Children are not expected to save up for their parents, but parents for their children.[m] 15 I will be happy to spend and be spent for you. Are you going to love me less because I love you so much more?[n]

16 In any case, let it be assumed that I myself did not prove to be a burden to you. However, you may say that I was crafty and took you in by a trick.[o] 17 Did I take advantage of you through any of those I sent to you?[p] 18 I urged Titus to come to you, and I sent a brother with him. Did Titus take advantage of you? Did not he and I walk in the same Spirit, in the same footsteps?[q]

There Will Be No More Forgiveness. 19 Have you been supposing all this time that we have been defending ourselves before you? Not at all! We have been speaking in Christ and in the presence of God, my dear ones,

w 2 Cor 12:5, 9; 1 Cor 2:3; Gal 6:14.—x Rom 1:25; 9:5.—y 2 Mac 5:8; Acts 9:24.—z Jos 2:15; Acts 9:23-25.—a 2 Cor 11:16, 30; 1 Cor 2:10; Gal 1:12.—b 2 Cor 11:11; Rom 16:3; Eph 4:10; 1 Thes 4:17.—c Lk 23:43; Rev 2:7.—d 1 Cor 2:3.—e 2 Cor 10:8; 11:16, 17.—f Num 33:55; Jos 23:13; Ezek 28:24; Mt 4:10; 1 Cor 2:10.—g Mt 26:39-44.—h 2 Cor 4:7; 1 Ki 19:12; Rom 3:24; 1 Cor 2:3; Phil 4:13.—i 2 Cor 6:4-5; 13:4; Mt 5:12; Rom 5:3; Phil 4:13; 2 Thes 1:4.—j 2 Cor 11:5; Lk 17:10; 1 Cor 15:9-10; Gal 6:3.—k Jn 4:48; Rom 15:19; 1 Thes 1:5.—l 2 Cor 11:9-12; 1 Cor 9:12, 18.—m 2 Cor 13:1; Prov 19:14; 1 Cor 4:14-15.—n 2 Cor 11:11; Phil 2:17; 1 Thes 2:8.—o 2 Cor 11:3, 9, 13.—p 2 Cor 9:5.—q 2 Cor 2:13; 8:6, 16, 23.

11:32 *King Aretas:* Aretas IV, father-in-law of Herod Antipas, who ruled over the Nabatean Arabs from c. 9 B.C. to A.D. 40.

12:1-6 Paul here provides an exceptional testimony. His spirit was elevated to the highest contemplation of the divine mysteries, which no human words can describe. He was caught up to the third heaven, that is, beyond the created world, to the point of losing all awareness of his own bodily life, so greatly was his spirit overwhelmed by this experience. This event occurred around the year A.D. 42, five years after his conversion; at that time, Paul was in Syria or Cilicia, some years still before the beginning of his great missions.

12:7-10 Paul refers to a mysterious trial, possibly an illness, of which Christ did not will to cure him and which increased the difficulties of his apostolic life.

doing all things to build you up.[r] 20 I fear that when I come I may find you different from what I wish you to be, and that you may find me different from what you wish me to be.

I am afraid that this will lead to quarreling, jealousy, anger, factions, slander, gossip, conceit, and disorder.[s] 21 I fear that when I come back my God may humiliate me in your presence and that I may have to mourn over many who previously sinned and have not repented of the impurity, immorality, and licentiousness in which they have indulged.[t]

CHAPTER 13

1 This will be the third visit I am making to you. Every charge must be established on the testimony of two or three witnesses.[u] 2 I warned those who have sinned, as well as everyone else, and I warn them now in my absence as I did when present on my second visit: when I come again, I will spare no one.[v]

3 This will give you the proof you seek that Christ is speaking in me. He is not weak in dealing with you, but he is powerful among you.[w] 4 For he was crucified in weakness, but he is now alive by the power of God. Similarly, we are weak in him, but in dealing with you we will live in the power of God.[x]

Examine Yourselves. 5 Examine yourselves to see whether you are in the faith. Test yourselves. Do you not realize that Jesus Christ is in you? If he is not, then you have failed the test.[y] 6 It is my hope that you will come to the realization that we have not failed. 7 But we pray to God that you may not do anything wrong—not so that we may appear to have passed the test, but so that you may do what is right, even though we may appear to have failed.

8 We have no power to do anything against the truth but only for the truth. 9 We rejoice when we are weak, just as long as you are strong. This is what we desire—that you may become perfect.[z]

10 I am writing this letter prior to my arrival so that when I come I may not have to treat you harshly in exercising the authority that the Lord has given me to build up and not to tear down.[a]

V: CONCLUSION*

Live in Peace. 11 And now, brethren, farewell. Mend your ways. Encourage one another. Be of one mind and live in peace. Then the God of love and peace will be with you.[b] 12 Greet one another with a holy kiss. * All the saints send you greetings.[c]

13 The grace of the Lord Jesus Christ and the love of God and the fellowship of the Holy Spirit be with you all.[d]

---

r 2 Cor 10:8; Rom 9:1; 14:19; 1 Cor 10:14.—s 2 Cor 2:1-4; 1 Cor 1:11; 3:3; 4:21; Gal 5:20.—t 2 Cor 2:1, 4; 13:2; 1 Cor 6:18.—u 2 Cor 12:14; Deut 19:15; Mt 18:16; Jn 8:17; Heb 10:28.—v 2 Cor 1:23; 10:2; 12:21; 1 Cor 4:21.—w Mt 10:20; 1 Cor 5:4.—x Rom 1:4; 6:4; 1 Cor 1:25; Phil 2:7-8; 1 Pet 3:18.—y Lam 3:40; Jn 6:6; Rom 8:10; 1 Cor 11:28.—z 2 Cor 4:12; 1 Cor 2:3; Eph 4:13.—a 2 Cor 1:23; 2:3; 10:8; Tit 1:13.—b Mt 9:50; 1 Thes 4:1; 2 Thes 3:1; 1 Jn 4:16.—c Rom 16:16; 1 Cor 16:20; Phil 4:22; 1 Thes 5:26; 1 Pet 5:14.—d Rom 16:20; 1 Cor 16:23; Phil 4:2.

13:11-13 The final greeting includes the most carefully worded and the richest of the formulas that name the Trinity (v. 13); it has now deservedly found a place in the Liturgy as a greeting to the faithful.

13:12 *Kiss:* a symbol of mutual affection and trust still used in the Near East. It corresponds to the handshake in the West.

"I set before [the acknowledged leaders in Jerusalem] the gospel that I preach to the Gentiles" *(Gal 2:2)*.

THE LETTER TO THE GALATIANS

Christian Freedom

Paul did not impose on Gentile converts either the Law of Moses or circumcision; he did not teach the Law. But was it possible to conceive of humanity being saved apart from the laws God gave to Moses? For some, there was no doubt: apart from the Law and its practices there was no salvation.

These Jewish Christians have been dubbed Judaizers. They taught that Gentiles must first submit to at least part of the Mosaic Law, especially circumcision, before they could become Christians (see Gal 1:7; 4:17, 21; 5:2-12; 6:12, 13). In order to better cancel the authority and revolutionary teaching of Paul, they hinted that he was not a true apostle. The Galatians were perturbed.

Learning of this, Paul wrote a passionate Letter (probably in A.D. 56–57) in which irony vied with logic, in order to reestablish the truth. The issue was not simply his apostolate but the very truth of Christianity. Jesus Christ is the only Savior: True or false? If true, then what connection still exists between the Galatians and a Law that has now been left behind?

The Apostle clearly realized that to bond the Church to the former traditions of Judaism was to make her hateful to Gentiles and to condemn the growth of the Church and her mission as well. Above all, it was to deny the Church's very being.

The Letter to the Galatians informs us of this crisis. The Galatians were probably the descendants of three Gallic tribes that had settled in Cappadocia and Pontus in the second half of the third century B.C. In 25 B.C. this little state, which had expanded through the acquisition of territories from Lycaonia, Phrygia, and Pisidia, had become the Roman province of Galatia. It continued, however, to call itself the "region of Galatia," the land occupied by descendants of the immigrants.

Luke followed this usage when he says that the second (A.D. 49–52) and third (A.D. 53–57) missions of Paul and his companions passed through "the region of Phrygia and Galatia" (Acts 16:6;

18:23). It seems, then, that the Letter sent "to the Churches of Galatia" (Gal 1:2) is addressed precisely to these former Gauls, especially since their character, as it emerges from this document, is strangely like that of the Gauls of whom Julius Caesar speaks: inconstancy and lightness of mind, desire of novelty, love of freedom, very great generosity (The Gallic War IV, 59).

This Letter to "foolish Galatians," who have allowed themselves to be "bewitched" (Gal 3:1), is a burning stream of lava, a torrent of feeling: Paul, with his tender paternal love, is bewildered by such a rapid turnabout in some; the clever deceits of his detractors disgust him; he is terribly upset because the Gospel is being falsified. Then he becomes a pitiless dialectician and a polemicist who uses steely irony and contempt.

In retrospect, this was a happy crisis that allowed Christianity to assert its autonomy and henceforth to travel its own road amid the peoples and for their salvation! It obliged the Church to become a People of God that acknowledges no borders, a people universal in time and space, with a changeless Gospel but at the same time with a life and activity that are continually renewed! Henceforth, the only thing that counts for the salvation of human beings is faith in Christ.

The Letter to the Galatians may be divided as follows:

I: Paul Defends His Apostolate (1:1—2:14)
II: Paul Defends the Freedom of Christians (2:15—6:10)
III: Conclusion (6:11-18)

I: PAUL DEFENDS HIS APOSTOLATE*

CHAPTER 1

A: Address

Paul Commissioned by Christ Himself.
1 * [a] Paul, an apostle *—commissioned not
by human authority or by any human being,
but by Jesus Christ and God the Father who
raised him from the dead— [b] 2 and all the
brethren * who are with me, to the Churches
of Galatia. [c] 3 Grace to you and peace from
God our Father and the Lord Jesus Christ, [d]
4 who gave himself for our sins to deliver us
from the present evil age * in accordance
with the will of our God and Father, [e] 5 to
whom be glory forever and ever. Amen. * [f]

B: One Gospel, One Revelation, One Apostolate*

Loyalty to the Gospel. 6 [g] I am astonished
that you are so quickly deserting the one
who called you by the grace of Christ and

a 1-3: Rom 1:1-7; 1 Cor 1:1-3; 11:23.—b Gal 1:11-12, 15-16; Acts 2:24; 9:15; 20:24; 1 Tim 1:1.—c Acts 16:6; 1 Cor 16:1; Phil 4:21.—d Rom 1:7; 2 Cor 1:2.—e Gal 2:20; Mt 20:28; Rom 4:25; 12:2; 1 Cor 1:20; 15:3; Eph 5:2; Phil 4:20; 1 Tim 2:6; Heb 10:10; 1 Jn 5:19.—f Rom 11:36; 16:27.—g 6-7: Gal 5:8, 10; Acts 15:1, 24; 2 Cor 11:4.

1:1—2:14 Without preliminary, Paul gets right to the point. He distinguishes two problems that his detractors, in order to inflame the conflict, cleverly intermingle: a question of persons and a question of ideas. First of all, Paul furnishes proofs of the authenticity of his apostolate. He specifies that his call comes directly from Christ and the Father. He received his Gospel by an immediate revelation from Christ, began at once to proclaim it without asking for the authorization of any human person, and on coming to Jerusalem interacted on an equal plane with the apostles, who approved his evangelization of the Gentiles. Finally, in the incident at Antioch, he showed his independence of Peter.

This first part of the Letter is one of our best sources of information about the history of the newborn Church and the life of Paul.

1:1-10 Without taking the time for another introduction, Paul tells us how he sees his apostolate in Christ's work of salvation. One must read these lines in order to understand what constitutes a mission of the Church. This Letter will be the "Gospel of the Cross."

In his address, Paul sets forth his name, his mission as apostle, and the name of those to whom he is writing as well as the central teaching of the Christian faith—the Resurrection of Jesus (see Acts 17:18; Rom 1:4; 1 Cor 15:20; 1 Pet 1:3).

1:1 *Apostle:* see note on 1 Cor 1:1-9.

1:2 *Brethren:* i.e., fellow Christians (see Gal 3:15; 4:12; 5:11; 6:18). *Galatia:* probably the Roman province of Galatia and an extended area southward, through which Paul traveled on his first missionary journey (Acts 13:14—14:23).

1:4 *The present evil age:* that is, the age in which sin reigns and Jesus Christ has not been accepted.

1:5 For similar doxologies, see Rom 9:5; 11:36; 16:27; Eph 3:21; 1 Tim 1:17.

1:6-24 Paul stresses that there is only one Gospel, one revelation, and one apostolate—all of which he shares with the original apostles. He discussed this apostolate and what it means first at Jerusalem with Peter (Cephas) and James and then at Antioch with Peter.

are turning to a different gospel.[h] 7 In reali-
ty, there is not another one, but there are
some who are troubling you by perverting
the gospel of Christ.[i] 8 [j]But even if we or an
angel from heaven should preach a gospel to
you other than the one we proclaimed to
you, let him be accursed![k] 9 We have said
this before, and now I repeat it: if anyone
preaches to you a gospel other than the one
you received, let him be accursed! *[l]

10 Does it now appear to you that I am try-
ing to gain the approval of human beings
rather than the approval of God? Am I seek-
ing to please people? If I were still trying to
please people, I would not be a servant of
Christ.[m]

Paul's Gospel Revealed to Him by Christ.
11 *[n] Brethren, I want you to be assured that
the gospel I preached to you is not human in
its origin.[o] 12 I did not receive it from a
human being, nor was I taught it. Rather, I
received it through a revelation of Jesus
Christ.[p]

13 Undoubtedly you have heard about
my former way of life in Judaism,* how I
fiercely persecuted the Church of God and
tried to destroy it.[q] 14 I progressed in
Judaism far beyond many of my contempo-
raries, inasmuch as I was much more
zealous in upholding the traditions of my
ancestors.[r]

Paul's Early Years as a Christian. 15 How-
ever, when God, who had set me apart even
before my birth, called me through his grace
and chose[s] 16 to reveal his Son to me so that
I might proclaim him to the Gentiles, I did
not confer with flesh and blood, *[t] 17 nor did
I go up to Jerusalem to consult with those
who were apostles before me. Rather, I went
off to Arabia, and afterward I returned to
Damascus.[u]

Paul's First Meeting with Peter.* 18 Then after
three years, I did go up to Jerusalem to
become acquainted with Cephas, and I
stayed with him for fifteen days.[v] 19 How-
ever, I did not set eyes on any of the other
apostles, except for James, the brother of the
Lord. *[w] 20 I declare before God that I am
not lying in anything I have written.[x]

21 Afterward, I went into the regions of
Syria and Cilicia. *[y] 22 I was still unknown
by sight to the Churches of Judea that are in
Christ.[z] 23 They had only heard it said, "The
one who was formerly persecuting us is now
preaching the faith that he had once tried to
destroy."[a] 24 As a result, they gave glory to
God because of me.[b]

CHAPTER 2

C: The Council of Jerusalem*

Confirmation of Paul's Gospel and Mission.
1 Fourteen years later, I traveled up to
Jerusalem again, this time with Barnabas,
and I also took along Titus.[c] 2 I went up in
response to a revelation, and I set before
them the gospel that I preach to the
Gentiles—in a private meeting with the

h Gal 4:13; Rom 8:28.—i Jer 23:16, 30; Acts 4:12.—j 8-9: Gal 5:3, 21; 1 Cor 16:22; 2 Cor 13:2.—k Gal 1:11, 16; 2:2; 1 Cor 15:1; 2 Cor 11:4.—l Rom 16:17.—m Rom 2:29; 2 Cor 5:11; 1 Thes 2:4.—n 11-12: Gal 1:1; 1 Cor 15:1; Eph 3:3.—o Rom 2:16.—p 1 Cor 2:10; 11:23.—q Acts 8:1-3; 9:1-2; 1 Cor 10:32; 15:9.—r Mt 15:2; Acts 21:20; 26:4-5.—s Isa 49:1; Jer 1:4; Acts 9:15; Rom 8:28.—t Gal 1:11-12; 2:2, 7, 9; Mt 16:17; Acts 9:3-9, 15; Rom 1:5; 1 Cor 15:20.—u Acts 9:2; 19:22.—v Jn 1:42; Acts 9:22-23, 26-30.—w Gal 2:9; Mt 13:55; Mk 6:3; Acts 12:17; 15:13.—x Rom 1:9; 9:1; 2 Cor 11:31.—y Lk 2:2; Acts 6:9; 9:30.—z Rom 16:3; 1 Thes 2:14.—a Gal 1:13; Acts 6:7; 8:3.—b Mt 9:8.—c Acts 4:36; 15:2; 2 Cor 2:13.

1:9 *Accursed:* "anathema," a term signifying condemnation.

1:11-17 For Paul, everything begins with the event that took place on the road to Damascus. He does not describe it here but expresses its meaning. It was for him the revelation of the risen Lord in all his glory as well as the investiture that established Paul as the prophet of the last times, charged by divine authority to proclaim the mystery of salvation and to introduce the Gentiles into the new world where the Spirit is at work (see Is 49:1; Jer 1:5). This mission is clear; Paul has no need of consulting with "flesh and blood," i.e., to embrace other human considerations or instructions. His destiny is laid out by the Lord himself.

1:13 *Judaism:* i.e., the Jewish faith and way of life that developed during the intertestamental period. The word comes from "Judah," the name of the southern kingdom that existed from the tenth to the sixth century B.C. and ended with the Babylonian Exile.

1:16 *Flesh and blood:* a phrase that in the New Testament always connotes human weakness or ignorance (see Mt 16:17; 1 Cor 15:50; Eph 6:12). Paul's teaching came not from any human person but directly from God.

1:18-24 Paul visited Jerusalem to become acquainted with the head of the apostles (see Acts 9:23-31), whom he calls "Cephas" (Aramaic for "Rock"), the name given to Peter by Jesus himself (see Mt 16:18). He then went to Syria and Cilicia (including his hometown Tarsus) and probably did some evangelizing there. He was known to Christians in Judea only by reputation.

1:19 *James, the brother of the Lord:* i.e., the cousin of Jesus, who was head of the Church of Jerusalem after the scattering of the apostles; see Acts 12:17; 15:13; 21:18.

1:21 For Paul's time in Syria (Antioch) and Cilicia (Tarsus) see Acts 9:30; 11:25-26.

2:1-10 Despite slight differences of detail, the passage speaks of the same assembly in Jerusalem that Acts 15 narrates: the same apostles, the same opponents, the same discussions, the same results in essentials. Paul was with Barnabas, who had an important place in the early stages of his mission (Acts 9:27; 11:25; 13:2; 15:2). When Paul wrote this Letter, about seven years after the events, he was completing the collection for the poor Christians of Jerusalem; this collection was for him a sign of unity (see 1 Cor 16:1; 2 Cor 8—9).

leaders—to ensure that I was not running, or had not run, in vain.[d]

3 Yet not even Titus, who was accompanying me, was compelled to be circumcised, even though he was a Greek.[e] 4 Yet some false brethren were secretly brought in to spy on the freedom we have in Christ Jesus, so that they might reduce us to slavery.[f] 5 But not for a single moment did we submit to them, in order that the truth of the gospel might remain untouched for you.[g]

6 As for those who were regarded as men of importance—whether or not they actually were important makes no difference to me, nor does it matter to God—these men did not add anything further to my message.[h] 7 On the contrary, they realized that I had been entrusted with preaching the gospel to the uncircumcised, just as Peter had been entrusted with preaching the gospel to the circumcised[i] (8 for the one who worked through Peter in his mission to the Jews was also at work in me in my mission to the Gentiles).[j]

9 Therefore, when James and Cephas and John, who were acknowledged as pillars of the community, recognized the grace that had been bestowed upon me, they gave to Barnabas and me the right hand of fellowship, agreeing that we should go to the Gentiles while they concentrated on the Jews.[k] 10 They asked only one thing: that we remember the poor, which is the very thing I was eager to do.[l]

D: Paul Rebukes Peter*

Peter's Inconsistency at Antioch. 11 However, when Cephas came to Antioch, I opposed him to his face, because he was in the wrong.[m] 12 For until some people came from James,* he had been eating with the Gentiles; but when they arrived, he drew back and kept himself apart because he was afraid of the circumcised.[n] 13 And the rest of the Jews* carried out the same pretense that he did, so that even Barnabas was led astray by their pretense.[o]

Paul's Rebuke. 14 But when I saw that their conduct was not in accordance with the truth of the gospel, I said to Peter in front of all of them, "You are a Jew, yet you are living like a Gentile and not like a Jew. How then can you require the Gentiles to live like Jews?"[p]

II: PAUL DEFENDS THE FREEDOM OF CHRISTIANS*

A: It Is Faith That Saves*

Justified by Faith in Christ.* 15 We ourselves are Jews by birth and not Gentile sinners,*[q] 16 yet we know that a man is justified not by the works of the Law but through faith in

d Gal 1:11-12, 16; Acts 15:4, 12; 1 Cor 2:10; Phil 2:16.—e Gal 2:14; 6:12; Acts 16:3; 1 Cor 9:21; 2 Cor 2:13; 7:6-7; 8:16-17; 12:18; Tit 1:4.—f Gal 5:1; Acts 1:16; 15:1, 24; 2 Cor 11:26; Jude 4.—g Gal 2:14; 4:16; Tit 1:14; 2 Jn 1.—h Deut 10:17; Acts 10:34; Rom 2:11; 1 Cor 15:11; Rev 2:23.—i Gal 1:15-16; 2:9, 11, 14; Acts 9:15; 15:12; 22:21; Rom 1:5; 1 Tim 1:11.—j Acts 1:25; 1 Cor 1:1.—k Gal 1:18-19; 2:1, 7, 11, 14; Jn 1:42; Acts 12:17; 15:13; Rom 15:15; 1 Tim 3:15; Rev 3:12.—l Acts 11:29; 24:17; Rom 15:25-28; 1 Cor 16:1-4; 2 Cor 8:9.—m Gal 1:18; 2:7, 9, 14; Acts 11:19-30; 15:1-2.—n Acts 10:15, 28; 11:3; 15:13; 1 Cor 5:11.—o Gal 2:1, 9; Acts 4:36.—p Gal 1:18; 2:3, 5, 9; Mt 18:17; Acts 10:28.—q Lk 24:7; Phil 3:4-5.

2:11-14 The Council of Jerusalem had acknowledged the freedom of Gentile Christians from the Jewish Law, but the question of table fellowship between Jewish Christians and Gentile believers was not yet settled. When Peter came to Antioch, he at first ate with non-Jews, since faith in Christ brings all people together. But when Jewish Christians arrived from Jerusalem, he gave up doing so. Paul rebuked Peter's inconsistency in an important religious matter. Peter's behavior was clearly wrong, and even grievously wrong if the table fellowship in question involved the meal at the Lord's Supper (see 1 Cor 11:17-25). The reason why Jews would not eat with Gentiles was that they were considered to be unclean. If Peter was refusing to eat with Gentile Christians, he was implicitly saying that they were still in sin, which would mean that their Baptism had no effect, which meant that their cross did not redeem them.

2:12 *Some people came from James:* i.e., Jewish Christians who still believed in the Law and in circumcision (Acts 15:1, 5; 21:20f) and either came from James or claimed to be from him. *Circumcised:* i.e., Jewish Christians.

2:13 *Jews:* i.e., Jewish Christians.

2:15—6:10 Paul has explained his view of the apostolate; almost by degrees he now passes on to the defense of freedom for the new converts. He reverses the accusation brought against him. Indeed, one can falsify the Gospel by making the practices of the Jewish Law a prerequisite for becoming Christian. Faith in Christ, and it alone, saves believers and sets them free. Paul sketches his thinking about Baptism and about the indissoluble bond that must exist between faith and the Sacrament.

2:15—4:31 Law or faith: the famous antithesis. Two religious outlooks are opposed: to accept the one is to reject the other. Christianity's purpose is not to produce a better Law but to offer faith. On one side, there is an objective, external norm of good and evil, and even a slavery; on the other side, there is a principle of internal action, a spiritual dynamism, a call, even more the very life of God in the heart of human beings, a freedom.

Christianity cannot shut itself up in a code, no matter how noble; it is a Person, and Christians are those in whom Christ lives (Gal 2:20) and the Spirit acts (Gal 4:6). If there is a moral for Christians, a "law of Christ" (Gal 6:2), it can only be the living and free expression of the love that God inspires in the human heart: "You shall love!"

2:15-21 The baptized must not look elsewhere: Christ has become their very self, and faith lays hold of and permeates their entire life. This statement of Paul is at the same time a self-revelation of a highly mystical nature.

2:15 *Gentile sinners:* a usual formula for describing pagans as opposed to the chosen people. In this passage it has no pejorative meaning; Paul will in fact say that Jews and Gentiles alike are sinners and in need of redemption (see Rom 3:23f).

Jesus Christ. So we too came to believe in
Christ Jesus so that we might be justified by
faith in him and not by the works of the Law,
for no one will be justified by the works of
the Law. [r]

17 But if, in seeking to be justified in
Christ, we ourselves are found to be sinners,
is Christ then a servant of sin? By no
means! [s] 18 However, if I am now rebuilding
what I previously tore down, then I prove
myself to be a transgressor. 19 For through
the Law I died to the Law * so that I might
live to God.

I have been crucified with Christ. [t] 20 And
now it is no longer I who live, but it is Christ
who lives in me. The life I live now in the
flesh I live by faith in the Son of God who
loved me and gave himself up for me. [u] 21 I
do not set aside the grace of God, for if justi-
fication comes through the Law, then Christ
died for nothing. [v]

CHAPTER 3

The Christian Experience. 1 You foolish
Galatians! Who has bewitched you? Before
your very eyes Jesus Christ was clearly pre-
sented as crucified. [w] 2 I only wish you to tell
me this: Did you receive the Spirit by
observing the Law or by believing what you
heard? [x]

3 How can you be so foolish? After having
begun with the Spirit, are you now ending in
the flesh? [y] 4 Is everything you have suffered
to result in absolutely nothing—if indeed it
was for nothing? [z] 5 Does God give you the
Spirit and work mighty deeds among you
because you have kept the Law or because
you believed what you have heard? [a]

The Blessing of Abraham. 6 * Thus Abraham
believed in God, and it was credited to him
as righteousness. [b] 7 You can be assured that
those who have faith are children of
Abraham. [c] 8 Because Scripture foresaw *
that God would justify the Gentiles by faith,
it declared the gospel beforehand to
Abraham, saying, "In you all the nations will
be blessed." [d] 9 For this reason, those who
have faith share the blessing with Abraham,
the faithful one. [e]

The Curse of the Law. 10 In contrast, those
who rely on the works of the Law are under
a curse, for it is written "Cursed is every-
one who does not persevere in doing all the
things that are written in the book of the
Law." [f] 11 Now it is evident that no one is
justified before God by the Law, for the one
who is righteous will live by faith. [g]
12 However, the Law is not based on faith.
On the contrary, whoever does these things
shall live by them. [h]

13 Christ redeemed us from the curse of
the Law by becoming a curse himself for us,
as it is written, "Cursed is everyone who is
hung upon a tree." [i] 14 This is so that the
blessing bestowed upon Abraham might be
extended to the Gentiles through Jesus
Christ so that we might receive the promise
of the Spirit through faith. [j]

The Promise of the Covenant. 15 Brethren,
allow me to give you an everyday example.
Once a human will has been ratified, no one
can make further additions to it or set it
aside. [k] 16 Now the promises were made to
Abraham and his descendant. It does not
say "and to your descendants," as referring
to many, but it says "and to your descen-
dant," that is, to one person, who is Christ. [l]

17 This is what I am saying: the Law, which
came four hundred and thirty years later,
cannot invalidate a covenant that had been
previously ratified by God, so as to nullify the
promise. [m] 18 Obviously, if the inheritance
comes from the Law, it no longer comes
from the promise. However, God bestowed it
on Abraham through a promise. [n]

---

r Gal 3:2, 11; Ps 143:1-2; Rom 3:20, 28; 4:5; 11:6; Eph 2:8-9; Phil 3:9.—s Gal 3:21.—t Gal 5:24; 6:14; Lk 20:38; Rom 6:6, 8, 10; 7:4, 6; 2 Cor 5:15; 1 Thes 5:10.—u Gal 1:4; Mt 4:3; Rom 6:6; 8:10-11; Eph 3:17; Col 3:3-4; 1 Pet 4:2.—v Gal 3:21; 5:2; Heb 7:11.—w Gal 5:7; Lk 24:25; Acts 16:6; 1 Cor 1:23.—x Gal 2:16, 3:5, 10, 14; Jn 20:22; Rom 10:17; Heb 4:2.—y Gal 4:9; 5:16-18; Phil 1:6.—z 1 Cor 15:2; Heb 10:35; 2 Jn 8.—a Gal 2:16; 1 Cor 12:10.—b Gen 15:6; 1 Mac 5:52; Rom 4:3; Jas 2:23.—c Gal 3:29; Sir 44:19-21; Lk 3:8; Rom 4:11-12.—d Gen 12:3; 18:17-19; Acts 3:25.—e Rom 4:18-22.—f Gal 2:16; Deut 27:26; Jer 11:3; Rom 4:15.—g Gal 2:16; Hab 2:4; Rom 1:17; 3:28; 9:30; Heb 10:38.—h Lev 18:5; Rom 10:5.—i Gal 4:5; Deut 21:23; Acts 5:30; Rom 8:3; 2 Cor 5:21.—j Gal 3:2-3, 5; Isa 44:3; Joel 3:1; 3:1-2; Jn 20:22; Acts 2:33; Rom 4:9.—k Rom 3:5; 7:1; Heb 9:16-17.—l Gen 17:19; Ps 132:11; Mic 7:20; Mt 1:1; Lk 1:55; Rom 4:13.—m Gen 15:13-14; Ex 12:40; Acts 7:6.—n Rom 4:14, 16; 11:6.

2:19 *I died to the Law:* the formula is obscure because it is overly concise. Christians have died to the Law because it left them frustrated since it helped them recognize their brokenness but did not liberate them from that brokenness. Only the love of Jesus can do that.

3:6-22 God has a blessing for humankind; it is reserved to faith. The promise made to Abraham was a personal, free, and direct commitment of God, and such it remained and still remains for all human beings; it is this promise that Christ fulfills.

3:8 *Scripture foresaw:* Paul personifies Scripture, thus stressing its divine origin (see 1 Tim 5:18).

The Purpose of the Law. 19 Why then? It was added because of transgressions * until the descendant appeared to whom the promise had been made, and it was promulgated by angels through an intermediary.[o] 20 Now an intermediary is not necessary when there is only one party, and God is one.[p]

21 Is the Law then opposed to the promises of God? Absolutely not! If the Law that had been given had the power to bestow life, then righteousness would have come through the Law.[q] 22 But according to Scripture all things have been confined under sin, so that through faith in Jesus Christ what was promised might be given to those who believe.[r]

The Benefit of Faith. 23 * Now before faith came, we were prisoners of the Law, confined as we waited for the faith that would eventually be revealed.[s] 24 Therefore, the Law was our tutor to bring us to Christ, so that we might be justified by faith. 25 However, now that faith[t] has come, we are no longer under a tutor.[u]

Children of God in Christ. 26 Through faith you are all children of God in Christ Jesus.[v] 27 For all of you who were baptized into Christ have clothed yourselves in Christ.[w] 28 There is no longer Jew or Greek, there is no longer slave or free man, there is no longer male or female. For all of you are one in Christ Jesus.[x] 29 And if you are Christ's, then you are the offspring of Abraham and heirs according to the promise.[y]

CHAPTER 4

Set Free by Christ. 1 What I am saying is that as long as an heir is a minor, he is no different from a slave, even though he is the owner of it all. 2 He remains under the supervision of guardians and trustees until the date designated by the father. 3 This is also true of us. As long as we were children, we were enslaved to the forces of this world.[z]

4 However, when the fullness of time had come, God sent his Son, born of a woman, born under the Law,[a] 5 in order to redeem those who were under the Law, so that we might receive adoption as sons.[b]

6 And because you are sons, God has sent into our hearts the Spirit of his Son, crying out "*Abba!* Father!"[c] 7 Therefore, you are no longer a slave but a son; and if you are a son, then through God you are also an heir.[d]

No Return to Slavery.* 8 Previously, when you did not know God, you were slaves to forces who were not really gods at all.[e] 9 But now that you have come to know God—or rather to be known by God—how can you turn back once again to those powerless and destitute forces? How can you consider becoming enslaved once again?[f] 10 You even observe special days and months and seasons and years.[g] 11 Now I am afraid for you, that I have labored among you in vain.[h]

Appeal To Enter into Freedom from the Law. 12 I beg you, brethren, to be like me, just as I have become like you. You never did me any wrong.[i] 13 As you remember, it was because of illness * that I originally preached the gospel to you.[j] 14 And though my illness was a trial to you, it did not lead to any scorn or revulsion; rather, you welcomed me as an angel of God, as if I were Christ Jesus himself.[k]

15 What has become of your blessedness? For I can testify that, if it had been possible, you would have plucked out your eyes and given them to me. 16 Have I now become your enemy because I have told you the truth?[l]

o Ex 20:19; Deut 5:5; 33:2; Acts 7:38, 53; Rom 4:15; 5:20; 7:7, 13.—p Deut 6:4; 1 Tim 2:5; Heb 8:6; 9:15.—q Gal 2:17, 21; Rom 7:7, 10; 8:2-4.—r Acts 10:43; Rom 3:9-20, 23; 11:32.—s Gal 4:3-5; 5:18; Rom 11:32.—t Gal 2:16; Rom 4:15; 10:4.—u Rom 7:4; 10:4.—v Gal 4:5-7; Jn 1:12; Rom 8:14-17.—w Mt 28:19; Rom 6:3; 13:14; Eph 4:24.—x Gen 1:27; 5:2; Joel 3:2; Jn 10:16; Rom 10:12; 1 Cor 12:13; Eph 2:14, 15; Col 3:11.—y Gal 3:7, 14, 16, 18; 4:1, 7; Lk 3:8; Rom 4:13-14, 16-17; 8:17; 9:7; 1 Cor 3:23; Heb 6:12; Jas 2:5.—z Gal 2:4; 3:23; 4:8-9, 24; Col 2:8, 20.—a Mk 1:15; Lk 2:27; Jn 3:17; Rom 5:6; Eph 1:10.—b Gal 3:13, 26; Jn 1:12; Rom 3:24; 8:14.—c Gal 3:26; Acts 16:7; Rom 5:5; 8:15.—d Gal 3:29; Rom 8:16-17.—e 2 Chr 13:9; Isa 37:19; Rom 1:28; 1 Cor 12:2.—f Gal 4:3; 1 Cor 8:3; Col 2:20.—g Rom 14:5; Col 2:16-20.—h Gal 2:2; 1 Thes 3:5.—i Gal 6:18; Rom 7:1; 1 Cor 11:1.—j Gal 1:6; 1 Cor 2:3.—k Zec 12:8; Mt 10:40; 2 Cor 5:20.—l Gal 2:5; Am 5:10.

3:19 *Because of transgressions:* i.e., in order that transgressions might be brought to light. Where there is no Law, there is no transgression (see Rom 5:13; 7:7).

3:23—4:7 In a few words, Paul provides great affirmations about faith and Baptism. He gives praise to the Person and work of Christ and to the action of the Holy Spirit. He sets forth the new meaning of the condition of human beings, their divine filiation, and their unity. The mystery of Christianity is found in these few lines.

4:8-11 The baptized have suddenly become concerned with the calendar of Jewish feasts or of pagan cults; do they, then, believe themselves to be slaves of the forces that they think rule the world and do they therefore desire to conciliate those forces by rites? God is not to be confused with any force, known or unknown, of this world.

4:13 *Illness:* a sickness, of what kind we do not know, that afflicted Paul during his second missionary journey (see Acts 16:6).

[17] Others are seeking to curry your favor, but they are not sincere. They are attempting to alienate you from us so that you may make them the sole object of your attention. [m] [18] It is good to be made much of for a good purpose at all times, and not just when I am in your presence. [n] [19] You are my children, and I am experiencing the pain of giving birth to you all over again, until Christ is formed in you. [o] [20] I truly wish that I could be with you now and be able to alter my approach to you, because I do not know what to think about you.

Sarah and Hagar Foreshadow the Two Covenants.* [21] And so tell me, you who are so eager to be subject to the Law: why do you not listen to the Law? [p] [22] For it is written that Abraham had two sons, one by a slave woman and one by a free woman. [q] [23] The son by the slave woman was born through the flesh. The son by the free woman was born through a promise. [r]

[24] Now this is an allegory. These women represent two covenants. One covenant is given on Mount Sinai and bears children who are born into slavery; this is Hagar. [s] [25] Hagar stands for Sinai, a mountain in Arabia, and corresponds to the present city of Jerusalem, for she is in slavery together with her children. [26] However, the Jerusalem that is above is the free woman, and she is our mother. [t] [27] For it is written,

> "Rejoice, you barren woman
> who never bore a child;
> break forth in song and shout with joy,
> you who never were in labor.
> For more numerous are the children of
> the deserted wife
> than the children of the one who has
> a husband." [u]

[28] Now you, brethren, are, like Isaac, the children of the promise. [v] [29] But just as in those days the child who was born through the flesh persecuted the child who was born through the Spirit, so is it now also. [w] [30] However, what does Scripture say?

> "Drive out the slave woman and her son!
> For the son of the slave woman shall
> not share the inheritance
> with the son of the free woman." [x]

[31] Therefore, brethren, we are the children not of the slave woman but of the free woman. [y]

B: There Is No Freedom Except in Christ*

CHAPTER 5

Faith Expressing Itself through Love. [1] It was for freedom that Christ set us free. Therefore, stand firm and refuse to submit again to the yoke of slavery. [z]

[2] Listen to me! I, Paul, tell you that if you allow yourselves to be circumcised, Christ will be of no value to you. [a] [3] Once again, I testify that every man who accepts circumcision is under obligation to observe the entire Law. [b] [4] Those of you who seek to be justified by the Law have cut yourselves off from Christ and have fallen away from grace. [c] [5] For it is through the Spirit and by faith that we eagerly hope to attain righteousness, [d] [6] since in Christ Jesus neither circumcision nor lack of circumcision is worth anything. All that matters is faith expressing itself through love. [e]

Against Being Misled. [7] You were running a good race. Who kept you from obeying the truth? [f] [8] This change did not come from the one who called you. [g] [9] A little yeast leavens the entire batch of dough. [h] [10] I am confident of you in the Lord that none of you will think differently, and that anyone who is trying to confuse you will be condemned, no matter who it is. [i]

m Gal 1:7; 2:4, 12; 6:12; Acts 20:30.—n Gal 4:13-14.—o Rom 8:29; 1 Cor 4:14-15; 2 Cor 6:13; Eph 4:13; 1 Thes 2:7-8, 11.—p Rom 2:12.—q Gen 16:15; 19:5, 15; 21:2-3.—r Gal 4:29; Gen 17:16; Jn 1:13; Rom 4:19-20; 9:7-9.—s Gal 3:17; Gen 16:1; Ex 19:20; Deut 33:2; Rom 9:4.—t Heb 12:22; Rev 3:12; 21:2.—u Isa 54:1.—v Gal 3:16, 29; Gen 17:10; Rom 9:8.—w Gal 5:11; Gen 21:9.—x Gen 21:10; Jn 8:35; 1 Pet 3:6.—y Gal 2:4; 3:29; Jn 8:35; Rom 6:18; 7:4.—z Gal 2:4; 4:5, 9; Mt 23:4; Jn 8:32, 36; Rom 7:4; 1 Cor 16:13.—a Gal 2:21; Acts 15:1-29.—b Gal 3:10; Rom 2:25; Jas 2:10.—c Rom 3:28; Heb 12:15; 2 Pet 3:17.—d Rom 8:23, 25.—e Gal 3:28; 6:15; Rom 16:3; 1 Cor 7:19; 1 Thes 1:3; Jas 2:22.—f Gal 3:1; 1 Cor 9:24.—g Gal 1:6; Rom 8:28.—h Mt 16:6; 1 Cor 5:6; Heb 12:15.—i Gal 1:7; 2 Cor 2:3; Phil 3:15.

4:21-31 A famous allegory, but one that is obscure and subtle for the modern reader. Paul wants to show by means of the Old Testament itself that we must go beyond the Law. In this perspective, he gives a free interpretation of an incident in the life of Abraham (see Gen 16:15; 21:2-14). The text explains the meaning of the enmity between two women, two descendants, two cities, two covenants.

5:1—6:10 After an involved argumentation, Paul turns to a more direct style, using shorter sentences, and he becomes more pressing. He calls upon the Galatians to measure the gravity of their about-face. Any compromise is out of the question; they must choose between the Law and Christ.

11 As for me, brethren, if I were still advocating circumcision,* why would I continue to be persecuted? If I were doing that, the cross would no longer be a stumbling block.[j] 12 I wish that those who are confusing you would even castrate themselves!

Proper Use of Freedom. 13 Brethren, you were called to freedom. However, make sure that you do not use your freedom as an opportunity for the flesh. Instead, serve one another in love.[k] 14 For the entire Law can be summed up* in a single commandment: "You shall love your neighbor as yourself."[l] 15 But if you continue biting and tearing one another to pieces, at least be on your guard lest you be consumed by one another.

16 Hence, I advise you to be guided by the Spirit, so that you will not gratify the desires of the flesh.[m] 17 For the desires of the flesh are opposed to the Spirit, and those of the Spirit are opposed to the flesh. They are in conflict with one another, so that you cannot do what you want.[n] 18 But if you are guided by the Spirit, you are not subject to the Law.[o]

19 *[p] Now the works of the flesh are obvious: fornication, impurity, licentiousness, 20 idolatry, sorcery, enmities, strife, jealousy, anger, quarrels, dissensions, factions,[q] 21 envy, drunkenness, carousing, and the like. I warn you, as I warned you previously, that no one who does such things will inherit the kingdom of God.[r]

22 * In contrast, the fruit of the Spirit is love, joy, peace, patience, kindness, generosity, faithfulness,[s] 23 gentleness, and self-control. There is no law against such things.[t] 24 And those who belong to Christ Jesus have crucified the flesh with its passions and desires.[u] 25 If we live by the Spirit, let us also be guided by the Spirit.[v] 26 We should not become conceited, or provoke one another, or be envious of one another.[w]

CHAPTER 6

The Law of Christ.* 1 Brethren, if anyone is detected committing a transgression, you who are spiritual must set him right in a spirit of gentleness. Meanwhile, you should take care so that you yourselves are not tempted.[x] 2 Bear one another's burdens, and in this way you will fulfill the law of Christ.[y]

3 [z] If anyone thinks he is something when in fact he is nothing, he is only deceiving himself.[a] 4 Each person must examine his own work. Then he will have reason to boast with regard to himself alone and not in comparison with someone else.[b] 5 For everyone has his own burden to bear.[c]

6 Anyone who is being taught should give his teacher a share in all his possessions.[d] 7 Do not be deceived; God cannot be mocked. A person will reap only what he sows.[e] 8 The one who sows in his flesh will reap a harvest of corruption, but the one who sows in the Spirit will reap from the Spirit the reward of eternal life.[f]

9 Let us never grow weary in doing what is right, for if we do not give up, we will reap our harvest in due time.[g] 10 Therefore, while we have the opportunity, let us labor for the good of all, but especially for those members of the household of the faith.[h]

---

j Gal 4:29; 6:12, 14; Lk 2:34; 1 Cor 1:23.—k Gal 5:1; Rom 6:18; 1 Cor 8:9; 2 Cor 4:5; Eph 5:21; 1 Pet 2:16.—l Gal 6:2; Lev 19:18; Mt 5:4; 22:39; Rom 13:8-10.—m Gal 5:24-25; Rom 8:5; 2 Cor 5:17.—n Rom 7:15, 23; 8:6.—o Rom 2:12; 6:14; 8:14; 1 Tim 1:9.—p 19-21: Rom 1:29-31; 1 Cor 6:9-10, 18; Col 3:5-6, 8.—q 1 Cor 11:19; Rev 22:15.—r Mt 15:19; Rom 13:13.—s Mal 2:6; Mt 7:16-20; 1 Cor 13:4-7; 2 Cor 6:6; Eph 5:9; Col 3:12; 1 Tim 4:12; 2 Pet 1:6.—t Acts 24:25; 1 Tim 1:9.—u Gal 2:19; 6:8; Rom 6:6; 8:13; Col 2:11.—v Gal 5:16.—w Phil 2:3.—x Mt 18:15; 1 Cor 2:15; 10:12-13; 2 Cor 2:7; Jas 5:19.—y 1 Cor 9:21; Col 3:13; Jas 2:8.—z 3-4: 1 Cor 3:18; 8:2; 2 Cor 12:11.—a Rom 12:3; 1 Cor 8:2.—b 2 Cor 10:12; 13:5.—c Jer 31:30; Rom 14:12.—d 1 Cor 9:11, 14; 1 Tim 5:17-18.—e Prov 22:8; Jer 34:17; Hos 10:12, 13; 1 Cor 6:9.—f Gal 5:24; Job 4:8; Prov 11:18; Rom 8:6, 13; Jas 3:18.—g Job 42:12; 1 Cor 15:58; 2 Cor 4:1; 2 Thes 3:13; Heb 12:1-3; Rev 2:10.—h Prov 3:27; Eph 2:19; 1 Thes 5:15; Tit 2:14; 1 Pet 4:17.

5:11 *Advocating circumcision:* probably an accusation by Paul's opponents that he also had advocated circumcision since he had allowed Timothy (whose mother was Jewish) to be circumcised (Acts 16:1-3). *Cross . . . stumbling block:* see 1 Cor 1:13.

5:14 *Entire Law can be summed up:* the whole spirit and intention of "the Law and the Prophets" is expressed by doing to others what you would want them to do to you (see Mt 7:12).

5:19-21 For other lists of vices, see 1 Cor 6:9f; Eph 5:5; Rev 22:15.

5:22-23 For other lists of virtues, see 2 Cor 6:6; Eph 4:2; 5:9; Col 3:12-15. Paul stresses that justification by faith does not mean advocating libertinism. He stresses that the Holy Spirit brings forth in believers Christian virtues and he lists nine of them. These have come to be known as "the fruits of the Holy Spirit."

The text of the Vulgate originally listed three other fruits, making a total of twelve. This formed the basis for the twelve fruits of the Holy Spirit listed in older catechisms, e.g., the *Baltimore Catechism:* charity, joy, peace, patience, benignity, goodness, long-suffering, mildness, faith, modesty, continence, and chastity. In truth, the three fruits not named in the original Greek are contained in one or other of the nine named: "long-suffering" in *patience,* and "modesty" and "continence" in *self-control.*

6:1-10 To the spiritual urge that leads the believer to live in solidarity with others and in service to them, Paul gives the name *law of Christ* (6:2), *law of faith* (Rom 3:27), and *law of the Spirit of life* (Rom 8:2).

III: CONCLUSION*

The Cross of Christ, Our True Boast.
11 Observe what large letters I make when I
am writing to you in my own handwriting.[i]
12 It is those who want to gain human
approval who are trying to compel you to be
circumcised, their sole purpose being to
escape persecution for the cross of Christ.[j]
13 Even the circumcised do not themselves
obey the Law. They want you to be circum-
cised so that they may boast in your flesh.[k]
14 May I never boast of anything except the
cross of our Lord Jesus Christ, through
which the world is crucified to me and I to
the world.[l] 15 Neither circumcision nor
uncircumcision is important, but only a new
creation.[m]

Blessing and a Plea. 16 May peace and
mercy be given to all who follow this rule,
and to the Israel of God.*[n]
17 In the future, let no one make trouble
for me, for I bear the marks of Jesus brand-
ed on my body.[o]
18 May the grace of our Lord Jesus Christ
be with your spirit, brethren. Amen.[p]

---

i 1 Cor 16:21.—j Gal 5:2, 11; Mt 23:25, 26; Acts 15:1.—k Rom 2:25; Phil 3:3.—l Gal 2:20; Rom 6:2, 6; 1 Cor 2:2; Phil 3:3.—m Gal 5:6; 1 Cor 7:19; 2 Cor 5:17.—n Pss 125:5; 128:6; Rom 2:29; Phil 3:3.—o Isa 44:5; Ezek 9:4; 2 Cor 1:5; 4:10; Rev 13:16.—p Rom 16:20; Phil 4:23; 2 Tim 4:22; Philem 25.

6:11-18 Paul himself underlines the importance of the Letter (v. 11) and for one last time situates the problem of the Galatians before the mystery of the cross. There is an old world, that of circumcisions and human successes, and a new world, in which God calls the new Israel, i.e., all Christians, true children of Abraham. Christians belong to this world. For them, the cross is something to be shared. They agree to suffer for Christ and with him. It involves more suffering than being circumcised, but they have become "new" people (2 Cor 5:17), delivered from the world, i.e., sin. There is no other way of salvation except the cross of Christ, nor any other assurance before God. Paul knows this from experience, for he bears in his body the traces of the blows received in the exercise of his missionary work (2 Cor 6:5; 11:23-27).

6:16 *The Israel of God:* i.e., the Church (see Rom 9:6f) as opposed to Israel according to the flesh (see 1 Cor 10:18).

"He has made known to us the mystery of his will . . . the plan to bring all things, both in heaven and on earth, together in Christ as the head" *(Eph 1:9-10)*.

THE LETTER TO THE EPHESIANS

The Mystery and Life of the Church

The Letters to the Philippians, Philemon, and the Colossians, along with Ephesians, form the group known as the "Captivity Letters." Philippians undoubtedly goes back to an earlier period. The other three make up a well-defined group in the Pauline epistolary.

But are these Letters really Paul's? The style is elevated and almost liturgical. Grandiose themes are treated in a sustained way; it is certainly not easy to recognize in them the pen that wrote, for example, the Letters to the Corinthians and the Letter to the Romans. Some therefore prefer to attribute these Letters to a Pauline school that operated after the death of Paul and was influenced by new ideas coming especially from Essene Judaism. According to others, a secretary of Paul drafted the text in a rather free way, in accordance with a fixed image of the Apostle.

It is possible to go even further: at that time it was not regarded as a forgery to publish, under the name of a famous personage, a text written by someone else in order to promote the work and thought of the former. But these are only hypotheses. How is it possible to prove that Paul did not pass through very different periods in his life? And why cannot the Letter to the Ephesians have been a work of his maturity?

The Letters to the Colossians and the Ephesians have more than one trait in common; we might even say that the latter borrows entire verses from the former. Colossians is more lively and direct; it intervenes at a moment of crisis in a Church. Ephesians takes up the same ideas and perhaps even the same text as the subject of a more serene and elevated contemplation.

This is all the more true since it is very doubtful that the Letter is addressed to a particular Church, that of Ephesus. Paul had stayed for about three years in that very large metropolis, and, while there, had attended to the problems of the Corinthians; that was an important period for his work and his thinking (see Acts 19—20). The addressees of the present Letter seem, however, to be anonymous. This great dogmatic reflection is not linked to any concrete situation and involves no personal connections. It may be said that the writer does not know his correspondents. Furthermore, the mention of "Ephesus" is lacking in some very early manuscripts.

We are led, then, to think that what we have is rather a circular Letter intended for the Churches of the region. Some scholars even think that our Letter to the Ephesians may be the Letter to the Laodiceans mentioned in Col 4:16.

During all the vicissitudes of Paul's mission to the Gentiles, a singular idea has been germinating in his mind: Christ is the sole principle of salvation—and it is this that constitutes his Gospel!

When he is imprisoned at Jerusalem and then placed in house arrest at Rome from A.D. 61 to 63, the Apostle has the time to deepen his understanding of the Christ event, for the crisis that had flared up among the Colossians has been doused. Thus, at fifty-seven years of age, he sets forth in the Letter to the Ephesians the mature fruit of his thought and his life. It is a lengthy theological meditation, a great vision of Christianity.

Contemplating God's entire plan for the salvation of the human race, Paul fixes his gaze on Christ the Lord established in heaven: this is the key to the Letter. Although he is seated at the right hand of his Father, Christ has not distanced himself from the world and human beings. His sovereignty spans all creation. He enables the community of the saved, his Church, to live and grow.

Through and in the Church he pours out his grace and love to the world. Through and in her, the risen Christ gathers human beings together in peace and unity, eliminating all discrimination of race and religious origin. The call of Gentiles to salvation and reconciliation with Jesus in the heart of the new Christian communities was the most beautiful testimony of the universal action of Christ.

The very facts of the life of the Church manifest the unfathomable depths of the riches of the mystery of Christ and the unheard-of newness of God's saving love. Beneath this dynamism, a new world appears—the Church is the first cell of the humanity of the Spirit. Paul contemplates her in the dimensions of the universe. He also describes her with the aid of splendid images: the Church is God's spouse (Eph 5:22-33), body (Eph 1:23; 4:16), and building (Eph 2:19-22). He thus sets forth the intimate as well as the organic bonds by which Christ unites believers in a community with her and leads them to their expansion.

The Letter to the Ephesians is the Letter about the Church and her mystery; Vatican Council II in its treatment of the Church drew extensively upon it.

In section III of the Letter, the author gives the baptized a number of more concrete directives. Concern for unity, charity, and progress in the community is the first requirement of the new life that has been received in Baptism. In this part, there are well-known passages on the organization of the Church and on Christian marriage. The passage on this last-named subject is included among recommendations for personal conduct and family morality. It is also the occasion for a final thought about the Church, described as the spouse of Christ.

This splendid document does not possess the direct and spontaneous qualities of a letter. Its slow and solemn style stems from the majesty of the Liturgy and the fervor of contemplation. It expresses the believer's awe concerning the grace of God given in Christ and manifested in the liturgical and communitarian life of the Church as well as in the development of her mission among the Gentiles.

The Letter to the Ephesians may be divided as follows:

I: Introduction (1:1-2)
II: The Risen Christ, Lord and Savior of the Whole Human Race (1:3—3:21)
III: New Life in the Church (4:1—6:20)
IV: Conclusion (6:21-24)

CHAPTER 1

I: INTRODUCTION

Address and Greeting.* 1 Paul, by the will of God an apostle of Christ Jesus, to the saints who are in Ephesus* and are faithful in Christ Jesus.[a] 2 Grace to you and peace from God our Father and the Lord Jesus Christ.[b]

II: THE RISEN CHRIST, LORD AND SAVIOR OF THE WHOLE HUMAN RACE*

A: God's Glorious Plan of Salvation*

Conceived by the Father

3 Blessed be the God,
and Father of our Lord Jesus Christ,
who has blessed us in Christ
with every spiritual blessing in the heavens.[c]
4 Before the foundation of the world
he chose us in Christ
to be holy and blameless in his sight
and to be filled with love.[d]
5 He predestined us
for adoption as his children
through Jesus Christ,
in accordance with his purpose and pleasure,[e]
6 to the praise of the glory
of his grace
that he so freely bestowed on us
in the Beloved.[f]

Realized by the Son

7 In Christ
and through his blood
we have redemption*
and the forgiveness of our sins.
In accord with the riches of his grace,[g]
8 God lavished on us[h]
all wisdom and insight.
9 He has made known to us
the mystery of his will
in accordance with his good pleasure
that he had predetermined in Christ[i]
10 to be realized when
the fullness of time had been achieved:
namely, the plan to bring all things,
both in heaven and on earth,

a Acts 9:13; 18:19; Rom 1:7; 1 Cor 1:1-2; 2 Cor 1:1.—b Rom 1:7; Col 1:2.—c Eph 2:6; 2 Cor 1:3; 1 Pet 1:3.—d Eph 5:27; Lev 11:44; 2 Sam 22:24; Mt 25:34; Jn 15:16; 17:24; Rom 8:29; 2 Thes 2:13.—e Lk 12:32; Jn 1:12; Rom 8:29-30; 1 Jn 3:1.—f Mt 3:17; Phil 1:11; Col 1:13.—g Eph 2:7-13; Rom 3:24; Col 1:14, 20; Tit 2:14.—h Col 1:9.—i Eph 3:3, 9; Rom 16:25.

1:1-2 For the form used at the beginning of each of Paul's Letters, see note on Rom 1:1.

1:1 *In Ephesus:* omitted in many manuscripts.

1:3—3:21 The style here becomes solemn and liturgical in the manner of the great Jewish blessings, for the Church is celebrating the plan of God. The stages of the divine plan are set forth in a great movement. To God the Father belongs all the initiative to make human beings his children. Everything is realized "in Christ": indeed, the whole movement of the universe is oriented toward Christ as an edifice is built on its cornerstone and held up by it. Christ is at the same time the heart and summit, the movement and purpose of history.

He gathers together the whole of humankind, reuniting in the Church both Gentiles (v. 13) and Jews (vv. 11-12), the two groups whose irreconcilable antagonism is the sign of the broken unity of the human family. And all the forces of the universe—notably the "heavenly forces": i.e., angels or demons, secret powers of fatality or fecundity to whom religions customarily give names—are carried along in this élan of rebirth and accomplishment. The universe is led to peace under the authority of Christ. There is thus a grand meaning to the world and to history!

Henceforth, the gift of the Spirit enables Christians to live by it. Indeed, there is a fulfillment of human beings, an "inheritance," as the Bible says when it wishes to sum up in a word the blessings promised to believers. The Spirit, who is presently at work in the Church, is the pledge of this inheritance. Since the Resurrection of Jesus, this redeemed universe, i.e., a universe delivered from sin and the Law and placed under God's plan, is being built up by the life of the Church, by the dynamism of the Gospel.

However, no one can say that any person is predestined either for salvation or for condemnation. When Paul speaks of choosing and placing apart in advance (vv. 5, 11), he simply wishes to indicate that salvation is a grace for all the People of God, that it is the fulfillment of God's plan.

1:3-14 These verses form a single sentence in the Greek. In it Paul sets forth the blessings that we have from the Father, then those from the Son, and finally those from the Holy Spirit.

1:7 *Redemption:* Paul uses the Greco-Roman practice of redeeming slaves by the payment of ransom to show what Christian redemption means. Christ's death ("his blood") constitutes the ransom necessary to free sinners from the bondage of sin and the curse of the Law (see Gal 3:13).

together * in Christ
as the head.[j]

Fulfilled by the Holy Spirit

11 In Christ we were also chosen,
having been predestined
by the one who accomplishes all things
in accordance with the design of his will,[k]
12 so that we,
who were the first ones
to place our hopes in Christ,
would devote ourselves
to the praise of his glory.[l]
13 In Christ
you also heard the message of truth
and the gospel of your salvation,
and you came to believe in him.
In him,
you were marked with the seal
of the Holy Spirit
who had been promised.[m]
14 That Spirit is the down payment * of our inheritance,
which we shall share
when God has redeemed us
as his own possession,
to the praise of his glory.[n]

B: The Church's Unity with Christ*

Christ, Head of the Church. 15 Having heard
of your faith in the Lord Jesus and of your
love toward all the saints,[o] 16 I therefore
never cease to give thanks to God for you as
I remember you in my prayers.[p] 17 I pray
that the God of our Lord Jesus Christ, the
Father of glory, may give you a spirit of wis-
dom and revelation to know him.[q]
18 I further pray that the eyes of your heart
may be enlightened so that you may know
the hope to which he has called you, how
rich and glorious is his inheritance * in the
saints,[r] 19 and how immeasurably great is
the power that he has exercised toward
those who have faith.[s]

Such was his mighty power 20 that he exhibited in Christ
when he raised him from the dead
and enthroned him
at his right hand in heaven,[t]
21 far above
every principality and authority,
power and dominion,
and every other title
that can be named,
not only in this age
but also in the age to come.[u]
22 He has put all things
under Christ's feet
and has made him
the head of the Church,[v]
23 which is his body,
the fullness of him
who fills the universe
in all its parts.[w]

CHAPTER 2

Christ Brought Us from Death to Life. 1 * You
formerly were dead as a result of your trans-
gressions and sins,[x] 2 which were your way
of life in this worldly era, * obeying the ruler

j Mk 1:15; Rom 5:6; Gal 4:4; Col 1:16, 20.—k Eph 3:11; Isa 46:10; Rom 8:28; Col 1:12; Heb 6:17; Rev 4:11.—l Eph 1:6, 14.—m Eph 4:21, 30; Jn 14:16-17; Acts 2:33; Rom 16:3; Col 1:6-8.—n Acts 20:32; Rom 3:24; 2 Cor 1:22; 5:5.—o Acts 20:21; Col 1:3-4; Philem 4-5.—p Rom 1:8, 10; Col 1:3, 9.—q Eph 3:14, 16; Ex 28:3; Isa 11:2; Jn 20:17; Rom 15:6; Col 1:9-10; 1 Jn 5:20; Rev 1:6.—r Eph 4:4; Job 42:5; Rom 8:28; 2 Cor 4:6; Col 1:12, 27; Heb 6:4.—s Eph 3:7; Isa 40:26; 2 Cor 13:4; Col 1:11; 2:12.—t Ps 110:1; Mk 16:19; Acts 2:24; Heb 1:3.—u Eph 3:10; Mt 12:32; Phil 2:9; Col 1:16; 1 Pet 3:22.—v Eph 4:15; 5:23; Ps 8:7; Mt 22:44; 28:18; 1 Cor 11:3; Col 1:18.—w Eph 3:19; 4:10, 12; Jn 1:16; Rom 12:5; 1 Cor 12:27; Col 1:19.—x Col 1:21; 2:13.

1:10 *Bring . . . together:* i.e., "recapitulate." The Greek verb contains two ideas: to gather together or unite and to place under a rule or head.

1:14 *Down payment:* for "if the Spirit of him who raised Jesus from the dead dwells in you, then the one who raised Christ from the dead will also give life to your mortal bodies through his Spirit that dwells in you" (Rom 8:11).

1:15—2:22 Our spirit is gripped with admiration before the diverse aspects of the mystery of Christ: Resurrection, Ascension, universal Kingship, mysterious and activating presence in the Church. The power of God is present in this mystery and sweeps away every other force. And with Christ rises the Church, the community of those called.

Paul clearly distinguishes the glorified Christ reigning in heaven and his mystical body developing on earth. We cannot confuse the Church and the Lord. But they are intimately connected. The community of those called is realized and grows under the impulsion of the life that Christ gives it. This community is the "fullness" of God, for in it everything must be reunited to be filled with God's presence and love. The Church is the mystery of grace and charisms, of unity and growth (see Rom 12:4f; 1 Cor 12:12; Col 1:18).

The Apostle then goes on to describe the sinful state of humankind, in the grip of the power of evil (Eph 2:1-10), and the new state of humankind in which Gentiles and Jews now form a single new person, created in Christ and reconciled to one another and to God (Eph 2:11-22).

1:18 *Inheritance:* a Biblical word signifying what God promised to the chosen people. This was initially identified with the land and the blessings connected with it. But as revelation progressed, the true meaning of the "inheritance" was increasingly understood, until its definitive content was revealed in the New Testament: the inheritance is the state of the risen Jesus himself, communicated to those who believe in him.

2:1-7 In Greek, these verses comprise a single sentence.

2:2 *This worldly era:* i.e., synonymous with "rulers of this world." It may also refer to the first of the two ages of the world—the present evil age and the age to come (see 1 Cor 3:19; 5:10; 7:31; Gal 1:4; Tit 2:12).

of the kingdom of the air, the spirit that is
now at work among the children of rebel-
lion.[y] 3 We too were all numbered among
them at one time. We were ruled by our sin-
ful nature, succumbing to the temptations of
the flesh and desires. And like all others, we
were by nature children of wrath.[z]

4 But God is rich in his mercy, and because
he had such great love for us,[a] 5 he brought
us to life with Christ when we were already
dead through sin—it is by grace that you
have been saved.[b] 6 He raised us up in union
with Christ Jesus and enthroned us with him
in the heavens,[c] 7 so that in the ages to come
he might show the immeasurable riches of
his grace evidenced by his mercy to us in
Christ Jesus.[d]

8 * For it is by grace that you have been
saved through faith. This has not come from
you but from the gift of God.[e] 9 It does not
come from works, so that no one can boast.[f]
10 For we are God's handiwork, created in
Christ Jesus for a life of good works that God
had prepared for us to do.[g]

Jews and Gentiles Reconciled in the Church.*
11 Therefore, do not forget that at one time
you were Gentiles in the flesh, called the
uncircumcised by those who refer to them-
selves as the circumcised because of a phys-
ical rite.[h] 12 Remember that you were at that
time separated from Christ, excluded from
the community of Israel, and foreigners to
the covenants * of promise. You were in the
world without hope and without God.[i]

13 But now in Christ Jesus, you who once
were far off have been brought near through
the blood of Christ.[j]

14 For he is our peace,
who has made the two into one,
by breaking down the barrier of hostility.[k]
In his flesh
15 he has abolished the Law
with its commandments and ordinances,
so that he might create in himself
a single new person * out of the two,
thereby making peace,[l]
16 and that he might reconcile both groups
to God in one body
through the cross,
thereby putting that enmity to death.[m]
17 Therefore, Jesus came
and proclaimed peace
to you who were far away
and peace to those who were near.[n]
18 For through him
we both have access to the Father
in the one Spirit.[o]

19 As a result, you are no longer strangers
and foreigners. Rather, you are fellow citi-
zens of the saints and members of the
household of God,[p] 20 built upon the founda-
tion of the apostles and prophets, with
Christ Jesus himself as the cornerstone.[q]
21 Through him the entire structure is joined
together and grows into a holy temple in the
Lord.[r] 22 In him you are also being built
together into a dwelling place for God in the
Spirit.[s]

C: Paul's Commission To Preach the Mystery*

CHAPTER 3

The Mystery Made Known. 1 [t] This is the rea-
son why I, Paul, a prisoner of Christ Jesus for
the sake of you Gentiles— * 2 For you surely
must have heard of the mystery of God's

y Eph 5:6; 6:12; Jn 12:31; Rom 11:30; 1 Cor 6:11; Col 1:13; Tit 3:3; 1 Pet 1:4.—z Gal 5:24; Col 3:6-7.—a Jn 3:16; Tit 3:5.—b Jn 5:24; Acts 15:11; Rom 5:8; 6:13; Col 2:13.—c Eph 1:3, 20; Rom 6:5; 8:10-11; Phil 3:20; Col 2:20.—d Eph 1:7; Rom 2:4; Tit 3:4.—e Rom 3:24; 9:30; Gal 2:16.—f Deut 9:5; Rom 4:2; 1 Cor 1:29; 2 Tim 1:9; Tit 3:5.—g Eph 4:24; Isa 29:23; 43:7; Tit 2:14.—h Rom 2:20; Col 2:11.—i Isa 14:1; Rom 9:4; Gal 3:17; Col 1:21, 27; 1 Thes 4:13.—j Eph 2:17; Isa 57:19; Acts 2:39; Rom 3:25; Col 1:20.—k Eph 3:6; Jn 14:27; 1 Cor 12:13; Gal 3:28.—l 2 Cor 5:17; Gal 3:28; Col 2:14.—m 2 Cor 5:18; Col 1:20, 22.—n Isa 57:19; Zec 9:10; Lk 2:14.—o Eph 3:12; 1 Cor 12:13; Col 1:12.—p Gal 6:10; Phil 3:20; Heb 12:22-23.—q Eph 4:11; Isa 28:16; Mt 16:18; Acts 4:11; 1 Cor 3:9-11; Rev 21:14.—r Eph 4:15; 1 Cor 3:16-17; Col 2:19.—s 1 Cor 3:16; 1 Pet 2:5.—t 1-2: Eph 4:1; 6:20; Acts 23:18; Phil 1:7, 13; Col 1:24-29; 4:18; 2 Tim 2:9; Philem 1:9.

2:8-9 We are saved by God's gift, not by the works of the Law (see Rom 3:20-21).

2:11-22 On the esplanade of the Jewish temple a wall separated Gentiles from Jews, symbolizing the deep division within humanity. Gentiles seemed definitively excluded from any call of God. The death of Jesus radically alters the situation: Jews and Gentiles alike have access to God; God's plan embraces the entire human race.

2:12 *The covenants:* i.e., those made with Abraham, with Moses, and with David (see note on Rom 9:4).

2:15 *A single new person:* i.e., a new humanity made up of Jews and Gentiles in the Christian community.

3:1-21 No one could have foreseen the call and reconciliation of the Gentiles. It is now a fact in the fraternal life of communities and in the spread of the Gospel, announcing the joy of salvation to all peoples. It shows that the mystery of God is being revealed, for in Christ all human beings can now approach God. Since his conversion on the road to Damascus, Paul has had no other desire but to proclaim and manifest this mystery.

The Apostle finally completes the prayer that he started several times previously. He asks that God himself may enable believers to comprehend the inexpressible riches of the mystery. This is true not only for the initiated but also for all the "saints," i.e., all those who have been baptized and called.

3:1 The sentence breaks off and is continued in v. 14.

grace that was entrusted to me on your behalf,[u] 3 and how the mystery was made known to me by a revelation, as I have briefly written.[v] 4 Reading this, you will be able to perceive my understanding of the mystery of Christ.[w]

5 It was not disclosed to human beings in previous generations, but now it has been revealed to his holy apostles and prophets by the Spirit,[x] 6 namely that the Gentiles have become coheirs, members of the same body, and sharers of the promise in Christ Jesus through the gospel.[y]

Mission to the Gentiles. 7 I became its minister by God's grace bestowed on me through the working of his power.[z] 8 Although I am the very least of all the saints, this grace was given me: to proclaim to the Gentiles the unfathomable riches of Christ[a] 9 and to enlighten all concerning the administration of the mystery that had been kept hidden throughout the ages in God, the creator of all things.[b]

10 In this way, the wisdom of God in its infinite variety might be made known through the Church to the principalities and powers in the heavens.[c] 11 This was in accordance with the eternal purpose that he has carried out in Christ Jesus our Lord,[d] 12 in whom we have free access to God in boldness and confidence because of our faith in him.[e] 13 Therefore, I beg you not to lose heart over my sufferings for you. Truly, they are your glory.[f]

Prayer for a Deeper Faith. 14 This is the reason why I kneel in prayer before the Father,[g] 15 from whom every family * in heaven and on earth takes its name.[h] 16 I ask that from the riches of his glory he may grant through his Spirit that you be strengthened with power in your inner being[i] 17 and that Christ may dwell in your hearts through faith.

And I pray that, rooted and grounded in love,[j] 18 you may have the power to comprehend with all the saints its breadth and length and height and depth,[k] 19 and know Christ's love even though it is beyond knowledge, so that you may be filled with all the fullness of God.[l]

20 To him who in all things is able
through the power
that is at work within us
to accomplish abundantly far more
than all we can ask or imagine,[m]
21 to him be glory in the Church
and in Christ Jesus
through all generations,
forever and ever. Amen.[n]

III: NEW LIFE IN THE CHURCH

A: For Christians in General*

CHAPTER 4

Christian Unity and Maturity.* 1 Therefore, as a prisoner for the Lord, I implore you to behave in a manner worthy of the calling you have received,[o] 2 with all humility, gentleness, and patience, bearing with one another in a spirit of love.[p] 3 Make every possible effort to preserve the unity of the Spirit through the bond of peace.[q]

4 There is one body and one Spirit, as well as one hope to which you have been called by your vocation,[r] 5 one Lord, one faith, one baptism,[s] 6 one God and Father of all, who is over all and through all and in all.[t]

u Eph 1:10; 1 Cor 9:17; Col 1:25.—v Eph 1:9-10; Rom 16:25; 1 Cor 2:10; Col 1:26.—w 2 Cor 11:6; Col 4:3.—x Eph 4:11; Rom 16:26; Col 1:26.—y Eph 2:13, 18-19; Ezek 47:22; Acts 15:9; Rom 8:17.—z Eph 1:19; Rom 15:15; 1 Cor 3:5; Col 1:25-29.—a Acts 9:15; Rom 2:4; 1 Cor 15:8-10; Gal 1:16; 2:7-9.—b Rom 16:25; Col 1:26-27.—c Eph 1:21; 6:12; Rom 11:33; 1 Cor 2:7; 1 Pet 1:12.—d Eph 1:11.—e Eph 2:18; Rom 5:1-2; 2 Cor 3:4; Heb 4:16.—f Col 1:22-24; 2 Tim 2:10; 1 Jn 2:28; 3:21.—g Phil 2:10.—h Eph 1:21.—i Eph 6:10; Rom 2:4; 7:22; 2 Cor 4:16; Phil 4:13; Col 1:11.—j Jn 14:23; Rom 8:10; Col 1:23; 2:7.—k Eph 1:15; Job 11:8-9; Col 2:2.—l Eph 1:23; Phil 4:7; Col 2:3, 9.—m 1 Ki 3:13; Rom 16:25-27; 2 Cor 9:8; Col 1:29; Jude 24.—n Rom 11:36.—o Eph 3:1; Rom 8:28; Phil 1:27; Col 1:10; 1 Thes 2:12.—p Eph 1:4; Acts 20:19; Rom 12:10; Col 3:12-13.—q Rom 15:5; Col 3:14-15.—r Eph 2:18; Rom 12:5; 1 Cor 10:17; 12:12-13.—s Zec 14:9; 1 Cor 8:6; Gal 3:27, 28.—t Deut 6:4; Zec 14:9; Rom 11:36; 1 Cor 12:6.

3:15 *Every family:* in this case, the family of the human race.

4:1—5:20 Christians must conduct themselves in a manner that befits their calling. First of all, they must have unity in the one body of the Church. Unity requires humility as a preliminary condition and meekness and loving patience in bearing with one another. The chief gifts that Paul has in mind are those that Christ communicates to us after the Ascension.

The Spirit of Christ allots to each Christian the measure of Christ needed to fulfill the function of each. This entails a change from one's old self to a new self in Christ. In this connection, six vices are specified to be avoided: lying, anger, stealing, bad language, uncurbed temper, and lust. Although Paul singles out lying to be described as unbecoming for fellow-members of the body of Christ, the same could be said of all vices.

4:1-16 The plan of God, which Paul has just revealed, is a vision of unity. To explain this, Paul follows rabbinical practice in taking a passage from Ps 18 and commenting on the two words that strike him: "ascended" and "gave." In his interpretation, the text announces the Ascension of Christ, who had first descended in the Incarnation on earth and even down to the subterranean regions, the place of the shadowy survival of the dead (see 1 Pet 3:9); the text then proclaims the sovereignty of Christ over all powers; finally, it speaks of the outpouring of the Spirit on Pentecost.

7 But each of us was given grace according to the measure in which Christ allotted it. [u] 8 Therefore, it is written,

"When he ascended to the heights,
he took prisoners into captivity
and gave gifts to men." [v]

9 Now the word "ascended" implies that he also descended into the lower regions of the earth. [w] 10 The one who descended is also the one who ascended far above all the heavens, so that he might fill all things. [x]

11 It was he who established some as apostles, some as prophets, some as evangelists, and some as pastors and teachers, *[y] 12 to equip the saints for the work of ministry in building up the body of Christ, [z] 13 until all of us attain to the unity of faith and the knowledge of the Son of God, to full maturity, as measured by the full stature of Christ. [a]

14 In this way, we will no longer be like children, tossed back and forth by the waves and swept along by every new wind of teaching, emanating from human cunning and craftiness and leading people into error. [b] 15 Rather, professing truth and love, we will in all things grow into him who is the head, Christ. [c] 16 From him, the entire body, joined and held together by every ligament, continues to grow and to build itself up in love, as each part performs its particular function. [d]

The Newness of the Christian Life. 17 Therefore, I declare and attest in the Lord that you must no longer live as the Gentiles do, in the futility of their minds. [e] 18 They are darkened in their understanding and alienated from the life of God because of their ignorance and their hardness of heart. [f] 19 Having lost all sensitivity, they have abandoned themselves to vice, committing every kind of impurity in growing excess. [g]

20 That is not how you learned Christ. 21 Clearly, you were told about him and were taught what the truth is in Jesus. [h] 22 You were taught to cast aside the old self of your former way of life that had been corrupted by its captivating desires. [i] 23 You are to be renewed in the spirit of your minds, [j] 24 and to clothe yourselves with the new self created in God's image, in the way of uprightness and holiness that belong to the truth. [k]

A Life Based on Love. 25 Therefore, cease your lying and speak the truth to each other, for we are all members of one another. [l] 26 If you are angry, do not sin. Do not let the sun set on your anger, [m] 27 and do not give the devil an opening. [n] 28 Anyone who has been stealing must no longer do so; rather, let him labor, performing some honest work with his own hands, so that he may have something to share with those in need. [o]

29 Let no foul word ever pass your lips. Say only what is useful for edification, so that your words may benefit your listeners. [p] 30 And do not grieve the Holy Spirit of God who has marked you with his seal for the day of redemption. [q] 31 Remove all forms of bitterness and wrath and anger and shouting and slander, as well as all malice from your lives. [r] 32 Rather, be kind to one another and compassionate, and forgive one another as God has forgiven you in Christ. [s]

CHAPTER 5

1 Hence, be imitators of God, as beloved children, [t] 2 and walk in love, as Christ loved us and gave himself up for us as a sacrificial offering whose fragrance is pleasing to God. [u]

Sins To Avoid. 3 Indeed, fornication and impurity of any kind, as well as greed, should not even be mentioned among you. Such talk is not fitting for saints. [v] 4 You should never engage in any obscene or foolish or suggestive conversation. All this is completely out of

u Mt 25:15; Rom 3:24; 12:3, 6; 1 Cor 12:28.—v Ps 68:19; Col 2:15.—w Isa 44:23; Jn 3:13.—x Eph 1:23; Prov 30:1-4; Mk 16:19; Heb 4:14.—y Eph 2:20; 3:5; Acts 11:27; 1 Cor 12:28; 2 Pet 3:2; Jude 17.—z Rom 14:19; 1 Cor 12:27.—a Eph 1:23; Jn 1:16; 1 Cor 2:6; Phil 3:8; Col 1:28.—b Eph 6:11; Isa 57:20; 1 Cor 14:20; Col 2:4, 8; Heb 13:9; Jas 1:6.—c Eph 1:4, 22; 1 Cor 11:3; Col 1:18; 2:19.—d Eph 1:4; 1 Cor 12:7; Col 2:19.—e Eph 2:2; Rom 1:21; Col 2:18; 1 Thes 4:5.—f Eph 2:12; Deut 29:4; Rom 1:21; Col 1:21; 1 Pet 1:14.—g Rom 1:24; Col 3:5; 1 Tim 4:2; 1 Pet 4:3.—h Eph 1:13; Col 2:7.—i Jer 17:9; Rom 8:13; Gal 6:6; Col 3:9; Heb 3:13; Jas 1:21.—j Rom 12:2; Col 3:10.—k Eph 2:10; Gen 1:26-27; Rom 13:14; Col 3:10.—l Lev 19:11; Zec 8:16; Col 3:9.—m Deut 24:15; Ps 4:5 LXX; Mt 5:22.—n 2 Cor 2:11; Jas 4:7.—o Acts 20:35; Gal 6:10; 1 Thes 4:11.—p Eph 5:14; Mt 12:36; Rom 14:19; Col 3:16; 4:6.—q Eph 1:13; Isa 63:10; 2 Cor 1:22; 1 Thes 5:19.—r Col 3:8; 1 Pet 2:1.—s Mt 6:14; Col 3:12-13; 1 Pet 3:8.—t Mt 5:45, 48; Lk 6:36; Jn 1:12; 13:15.—u Ex 29:18; Ps 40:7; Jn 13:34; Rom 14:15; Gal 2:20; Heb 7:27; 1 Jn 3:16.—v 1 Cor 6:18; Gal 5:19; Col 3:5.

4:11 Other lists of ministers in the Church are found in Rom 12:6-8 and 1 Cor 12:28. *Apostles:* mentioned here because of their role in establishing the Church (see Eph 2:20). In a broader sense, the term "apostle" is also applied to Paul (see Eph 1:1). *Prophets:* those who brought a message from God appropriate to their people's situation. *Evangelists:* missionary preachers (see Acts 2:8 and 2 Tim 4:5), not the writers of the Gospels. *Pastors and teachers:* those who have pastoral care of the people and feed them with the food of the Scriptures.

place. Instead, you should rather be engaged in offering thanks to God.[w]

5 You can be absolutely certain that no immoral or impure person or one who is greedy—that is, an idolater—will have any inheritance in the kingdom of Christ and of God.[x]

6 Let no one deceive you with worthless arguments. These are the very things that bring down the wrath of God on those who are disobedient.[y] 7 Do not associate with them.

Christians Are Children of Light. 8 Once you were darkness, but now you are light in the Lord. Live as children of light,[z] 9 for light produces all goodness and righteousness and truth.[a] 10 Discern what the Lord finds pleasing.[b] 11 Take no part in the fruitless deeds of darkness, but rather seek to expose them.[c]

12 For it is shameful even to speak of what deeds people do in secret. 13 However, everything that is exposed by the light is made visible,[d] 14 and whatever is made visible is light. Therefore, it is said, *

"Awake, O sleeper!
Rise from the dead,
and Christ will shine on you."[e]

15[f] Therefore, take care to live as intelligent people, and do not be like those who are senseless. 16 Make the most of the present time, for this is a wicked age.[g] 17 Do not be foolish, but recognize what is the will of the Lord.[h] 18 Do not get drunk on wine, which can lead to debauchery.

Rather, be filled with the Spirit,[i] 19 as you sing psalms and hymns and spiritual songs with one another. Sing and chant to the Lord in your hearts,[j] 20 giving thanks to God the Father at all times and for everything in the name of our Lord Jesus Christ.[k]

B: Christ and Christian Spouses*

Be Subject to One Another in Christ. 21 Be subject to one another out of reverence for Christ.[l] 22 Wives, be subject to your husbands as you are to the Lord.[m] 23 For the husband is the head of the wife, just as Christ is the head of the Church, the body of which he is the Savior.[n] 24 Just as the Church is subject to Christ, so also wives must be subject to their husbands in everything.[o]

Love One Another in Christ. 25 Husbands, love your wives, just as Christ loved the Church and gave himself up for her[p] 26 in order to sanctify her by cleansing her with water and the word,*[q] 27 in order to present the Church to himself in splendor, without spot or wrinkle or any such flaw, but holy and without the slightest blemish.[r]

28 In the same way, husbands should love their wives as they do their own bodies. The man who loves his wife loves himself. 29 For no one ever hates his own body; rather, he nourishes it and cares for it, even as Christ does for the Church, 30 because we are members of his body.[s]

31 For this reason
a man shall leave his father and mother
and be joined to his wife,
and the two shall become one flesh.[t]

32 This is a great mystery. Here I am applying it to Christ and the Church.[u] 33 However, each one of you should love his wife as he loves himself, and the wife should respect her husband.[v]

w Eph 4:29; Rom 1:28; Col 3:8; Philem 8.—x Mt 25:34; Acts 20:32; 1 Cor 8:9-10; Gal 5:21; Col 3:5.—y Eph 2:2; Mk 13:5; Rom 1:18; Col 2:4, 8.—z Eph 2:2, 11-13; Lk 16:8; Jn 12:36; Acts 26:18; Col 1:12-13.—a Mt 7:16-20; Rom 15:14; Gal 5:22.—b Rom 12:2; 1 Tim 5:4.—c Rom 13:12; 2 Cor 6:14.—d Jn 3:20-21.—e Isa 26:19; 60:1; Mal 3:20; Jn 5:25; Rom 13:11.—f 15-16: Prov 15:21; Col 4:5.—g Eph 6:13.—h Rom 12:2; Col 1:9; 1 Thes 4:3.—i Lev 10:9 Prov 23:31 LXX; Isa 28:7; Lk 21:34; Rom 13:13.—j Ps 33:2-3; Acts 16:25; 1 Cor 14:15, 26; Col 3:16.—k Job 1:21; Col 3:17; Heb 13:15.—l Gal 5:13; 1 Pet 5:5.—m Eph 6:5; Gen 3:16; 1 Cor 14:34; Col 3:18–4:1; 1 Tim 2:12; 1 Pet 3:1.—n Eph 1:22; 1 Cor 11:3; Col 1:18.—o Tit 2:9.—p Col 3:19; 1 Tim 2:6.—q Jn 17:19; Acts 22:16; Rom 6:4; Heb 2:11; Tit 3:5-7.—r Eph 1:4; 2 Cor 4:14; 11:2; Col 1:22.—s Rom 12:5; 1 Cor 6:15; 12:27.—t Gen 2:24; Mt 19:5; Mk 10:7-8; 1 Cor 6:16.—u Rev 19:7.—v 1 Pet 3:2, 6.

5:14 *It is said:* the text cited was probably taken from an early Christian liturgical hymn (see also Isa 26:19; 60:1).

5:21—6:9 Christianity promotes, in community and in family, a new kind of relationship that is marked by humility and mutual submission. Here is a practical essay on the subject. The Old Testament had a lofty idea of marriage and liked to use the image of spouses to suggest God's faithful love for his people (Ps 45; Song 1:3; Isa 54:4, 8; 62:4-5; Ezek 16; Hos 1:3). In the same tradition, Christians compare the relationship of Christ and the Church with a marriage (Mt 9:15; 22:2-4; 25:1-13; Jn 3:29; 2 Cor 11:2; Rev 19:7; 21:2-9). Here Paul goes even further: marriage as such is related to the mystery of Christ and the Church; the reciprocal love of Christ and the Church becomes the foundation and model for the life of spouses, who ought to be a sign and manifestation of that reciprocal love. There is a profound connection between the oneness of marriage and the oneness of Christ with the Church; the former reveals the ultimate intention of the creator when he created the human couple: an intention that the first generation of Christians saw in the text of Gen 2:24 (see Mt 19:5; Mk 10:8; 1 Cor 6:16-17). Chapter 5 of the Letter to the Ephesians, following the same theological line of thought, gives us one of the finest passages on the mystery of the Church and the spirituality of marriage. Paul's ideas on marriage may be completed by a reading of 1 Cor 7:1-14 and Col 3:18-19.

5:26 *Cleansing her with water and the word:* a reference to Baptism (pouring of water and sacramental formula). Perhaps Paul had in mind the Oriental practice in the purification of a wife.

CHAPTER 6

C: Christ and the Members of the Household*

Children and Parents. [1] Children, obey your parents in the Lord, for it is only right that you should do so. [w] [2] [x] "Honor your father and your mother." This is the first commandment that is connected with a promise: [3] "that it may go well with you and that you may have a long life on earth."

[4] Fathers, do not provoke your children to anger, but bring them up in the discipline and instruction of the Lord. [y]

Slaves and Masters. [5] Slaves, be constant in your unwavering obedience to your earthly masters with fear and trembling and with the same heartfelt sincerity that you show to Christ. [z] [6] Do this not just when they are watching you, as if you only had to please human beings, but as slaves of Christ, wholeheartedly carrying out the will of God. [a] [7] Do your work willingly, as for the Lord and not for human beings, [b] [8] knowing that whatever good we may do, whether as slaves or as free men, we will be repaid by the Lord. [c]

[9] And masters, treat your slaves fairly. Stop threatening them. Remember that both of you have the same Master in heaven, and he shows no favoritism. [d]

D: The Christian Warfare*

Put On the Armor of God. [10] Finally, find your strength in the Lord and in his mighty power. [e] [11] Put on the armor of God so that you will be able to stand firm against the deceit of the devil. [f] [12] For we are not struggling against flesh and blood, but against the principalities, the powers, and the cosmic rulers of this present darkness, and against the spirits of evil in the heavens. [g]

[13] Therefore, put on the armor of God, so that you will be able to hold fast on the evil day and to hold your ground with all your strength. [h] [14] Stand firm, then, with the belt of truth fastened around your waist, with the breastplate of righteousness clothing you, [i] [15] and with your feet shod in zeal to proclaim the gospel of peace. [j]

[16] In all circumstances, hold in your hand the shield of faith with which you will be able to quench all the flaming arrows of the evil one. [k] [17] And take the helmet of salvation as well as the sword of the Spirit, which is the word of God. [l]

Be Vigilant in Prayer. [18] In all of your prayers and entreaties, pray always in the Spirit. To that end, keep alert and always persevere in supplication for all the saints. [m] [19] Pray also for me, so that whenever I open my mouth, I may be given the proper words to make known with boldness the mystery of the gospel, [n] [20] for which I am an ambassador in chains. Pray that I may proclaim it fearlessly, as is my duty. [o]

IV: CONCLUSION*

A Personal Message. [21] So that you may know how I am and what I am doing, Tychicus, my beloved brother and a faithful minister in the Lord, will keep you informed. [p] [22] I am sending him to you for this specific purpose, so that you will know how we are and that your hearts may be encouraged. [q]

Final Greeting. [23] May God the Father and the Lord Jesus Christ grant peace and love with faith to all the brethren. [r]

[24] Grace be with all who love our Lord Jesus Christ with undying devotion. [s]

---

w Prov 1:8; 6:20; Sir 3:1-6; Col 3:20.—x 2-3: Ex 20:12; Deut 5:16.—y Gen 18:19; Deut 6:7; Prov 13:24; Col 3:21-22; 2 Tim 3:15.—z Eph 5:22; Col 3:22-25; 1 Tim 6:1-2; Tit 2:9-10; 1 Pet 2:18.—a Rom 6:22; 1 Pet 2:18.—b Col 3:23.—c Mt 16:27; Gal 3:28; Col 3:24.—d Job 31:13-14; Acts 10:34; Col 4:1.—e Eph 1:19; 2 Sam 10:12; Hag 2:4; 1 Cor 16:13; 2 Tim 2:1.—f Rom 13:12; 2 Cor 6:7; 10:4; 1 Thes 5:8; Jas 4:7.—g Eph 1:21; 2:2; Rom 8:38; 1 Cor 15:50; Col 1:13; Heb 2:14.—h Rom 13:12; 2 Cor 6:7.—i Wis 5:17-20 Isa 11:5; 59:17; Lk 12:35; 1 Thes 5:8.—j Isa 52:7; Rom 10:15.—k Mt 5:37; 1 Pet 5:9; 1 Jn 5:4.—l Isa 59:17; 1 Thes 5:8; Heb 4:12.—m Mt 26:41; Lk 18:1; Acts 1:14; Rom 8:26-27; Col 4:2-3.—n Acts 4:29; Rom 16:25; Col 4:3; 1 Thes 5:25; 2 Thes 3:1.—o Acts 21:33; 2 Cor 5:20; Col 4:4.—p Acts 20:4; Col 2:2; 4:7; 2 Tim 4:12; Tit 3:12.—q Col 4:8.—r Gal 5:6; 6:16; 2 Thes 3:16; 1 Pet 5:14.—s 1 Cor 16:22; 1 Pet 1:8; 5:14.

6:1-9 Christian life also gives a new meaning to relations between children and parents. In an age less attentive than ours to the lot of little children, Paul was already emphasizing the responsibility of parents, without denying the duties of the young. The atmosphere he suggests is one of dialogue.

As for slavery, Paul does not pass judgment on the social structure of his age (see 1 Cor 7:21-22; Col 3:22-25; 1 Tim 6:1-2; Tit 2:9-10; Philem), but he does foretell new relations between master and slave, since all are equal before God, whatever the differences in their roles and social obligations.

6:10-20 Christ's triumph over evil and the devil must be appropriated by individual Christians in the human sphere through a kind of spiritual warfare against the malevolent spirits in the heavens. For this, Christians need to be clothed with the armor of God (see Isa 11:5; 59:17; see also Wis 5:17-20)—a spiritual armor. They must strive to counter the forces of evil by relying on the Gospel and prayer.

6:21-24 Paul issues a personal message and a final blessing. He sends Tychicus, his coworker, to carry the Letter personally to the addressees and to be his surrogate. He then offers final greetings. The fact that he does not give any personal references such as can be found in his Letters seems to indicate that the Letter was a circular one, not sent to the Ephesians alone.

"At the name of Jesus every knee should bend" *(Phil 2:10)*.

THE LETTER TO THE PHILIPPIANS

Christian Joy

Philippi was a well-known city, founded by Philip of Macedon, father of Alexander the Great, in 358/357 B.C. It was also the site where Marc Antony defeated Brutus and Cassius in 31 B.C. In Paul's time, the city was the capital of the region of Macedonia and a center of trade because of its location on the Egnatian Way that linked Rome with the East. It was also a colony of military people, whose citizens enjoyed the full rights of those living in Italy.

The time was A.D. 49–50 and Europe was waiting for the Gospel. The moment constituted a turning point in the life of Paul and in the missionary efforts of the young Church. Philippi was the first European city in which Paul proclaimed Jesus Christ and founded a community of Christians. The Acts of the Apostles (16:11-40) has preserved the memory of that mission and of a visit of Paul, who retained a special affection for that community, as he did for the nearby one of Thessalonica (see 1 Thes 1—2). It was perhaps the only community from which he accepted any financial aid.

Paul began his preaching in Philippi at a "place of prayer" by the riverside. His exorcism of a slave girl resulted in his arrest, scourging, and imprisonment. After an earthquake during the night, Paul refused to escape and revealed his Roman citizenship (Acts 16:12-40).

The community seems to have been made up predominantly of Gentiles and to have had leading roles for women right from the start, especially Lydia, a "worshiper of God" (Acts 16:14f, 40), Euodia, and Syntyche (Phil 4:2f).

In order to ease Paul's imprisonment, the Christians of Philippi had recently sent Epaphroditus with a generous offering (Phil 4:10-18). Paul was in fact a prisoner, perhaps in Rome (see the final greeting in Phil 4:22); we would then be in the years A.D. 62–63. However, Paul was imprisoned more than once, although the Book of Acts does not record this fact (see 2 Cor 11:23).

He may also have written this Letter from Ephesus, which was closer and where he spent difficult days (see 1 Cor 15:32; 2 Cor 1:8; 4:8-10; 6:9). If so, the Letter can be dated A.D. 56-57, and the tone of closeness becomes more intelligible. Trust, surrender, and cordiality are the characteristics of this Letter from prison. It is, above all, a letter of joy and of fellowship in joy.

The absence of any grave problems to be treated enables Paul to carry on this heart-to-heart discourse. He injects in it something about his lot as a prisoner but he does not forget his fundamental preoccupation with the unity of Christians in the internal relations of the community. He goes on to pass quickly from one idea to another—leading some scholars to consider this writing as an amalgam of several Letters.

The Apostle offers personal news and is also aware that internal or external influences lead to the temptation to establish antagonistic groups. However, the desire for unity brings with it the refusal of all personal pretense. He emphasizes this point by setting forth Christ as an example—which results in our having the wonderful hymn to the Lord Jesus (Phil 2:6-11).

In contrast to the temptation to follow the easy way of life, Paul depicts the Christian life as a journey and even as a course to run, as the project of a life united with Christ so that—with him and through him—one may ultimately enter the city of God.

The Letter to the Philippians may be divided as follows:

- *I: Introduction (1:1-11)*
- *II: News and Instructions (1:12—3:1a)*
- *III: Warning against False Teachers (3:1b—4:1)*
- *IV: Counsels and Thanksgiving (4:2-9)*
- *V: Acknowledgment of the Community's Gift (4:10-20)*
- *VI: Conclusion (4:21-23)*

CHAPTER 1

I: INTRODUCTION

Address.* 1 Paul and Timothy, servants of
Christ Jesus, to all the saints in Christ Jesus
at Philippi, together with their bishops and
deacons:[a] 2 grace to you and peace from
God the Father and our Lord Jesus Christ.[b]

Joyful Prayer for the Philippians.* 3 I give
thanks to my God every time I think of you.[c]
4 I always pray for you, interceding for you
with joy[d] 5 because of your sharing in the
gospel from the first day until now.[e] 6 I am
confident of this: that the one who began a
good work in you will bring it to completion
on the day of Christ Jesus.*[f]

7 It is only right for me to feel this way
toward you, because I hold you in my heart,
for you have all shared with me in God's
grace, both during my imprisonment and in
the defense and confirmation of the gospel.[g]
8 Indeed, God is my witness how I long for all
of you with the affection of Christ Jesus.[h]

9 And for this I pray: that your love may
increase ever more and more in knowledge
and full insight[i] 10 to enable you to discover
what is really important, so that on the day

a Acts 9:13; 16:1; Rom 1:1; 2 Cor 1:1; 1 Thes 1:1; 1 Tim 3:1-13; Philem 1.—b Rom 1:7; 1 Cor 1:3; Gal 1:3; Philem 3.—c Rom 1:8; 1 Cor 1:4; Eph 1:16; 1 Thes 1:2.—d Rom 1:10.—e Phil 4:15; Acts 2:42: 16:12-40.—f Phil 1:10; 2:13, 16; Ps 138:8; 1 Cor 1:8; 1 Thes 5:24.—g Acts 21:33; 2 Cor 7:3; 2 Pet 1:13.—h Rom 1:9, 11; 2 Cor 1:23; 1 Thes 2:5.—i Eph 1:17; 3:14-19; Col 1:9-10; 1 Thes 3:12.

1:1-2 While writing to all of the baptized—"the saints"—the author thinks in particular of the responsibility of the "bishops" (literally, "overseers"), that is, of those who, under the higher authority of the apostles and with the help of deacons (literally, "assistants"), lead and encourage the community (see 1 Tim 3:1; 5:17; Tit 1:5-9).

1:3-11 This prayer, filled with confidence and thanksgiving, gives us a glimpse of the deep attachment held by Paul, the prisoner, for the living community of Philippi that shares his concerns and his initiatives. He regards the action and life of Christians as a project that must be ceaselessly developed until the encounter with Christ at his Second Coming. Hence, he prays that believers might have the spiritual sense that will enable them to take hold of the essential, i.e., the very will of the Lord, in any situation: faith and love will help discern what is the best thing for them to do.

1:6 *The day of Christ Jesus:* the Second Coming of the Lord in all his glory, when the faithful will be with him and will share in eternal glory (see 1 Cor 1:8; Phil 1:10; 2:16; 3:20f; 1 Thes 4:17; 5:10; 2 Thes 1:10).

of Christ you may be pure and blameless,[j] 11 filled with the fruits of righteousness that comes through Jesus Christ for the glory and praise of God.[k]

II: NEWS AND INSTRUCTIONS

To Live Is Christ.* 12 [l] Brethren, I want you to know that what has happened to me has actually helped spread the gospel, 13 for my imprisonment has become known not only throughout the praetorium * but to everyone else as well.[m] 14 And the majority of the brethren having taken encouragement in the Lord from my imprisonment, dare more than ever to proclaim the word without fear.[n]

15 It is true that some are proclaiming Christ out of envy and rivalry, but others are doing so with goodwill.[o] 16 These latter ones do so out of love, aware that I have been put here for the defense of the gospel.[p] 17 The former proclaim Christ out of selfish ambition, not in sincerity, but in an effort to increase my suffering while I am in chains.[q] 18 But what does it matter, as long as in every way, with false motives or true, that Christ is proclaimed? And in that I rejoice.

Yes, and I will continue to rejoice,[r] 19 for I know that through your prayers and with the help of the Spirit of Jesus Christ this will result in deliverance for me.[s] 20 It is my firm expectation and hope that I will not be put to shame in any way, but will act with complete fearlessness, now as always, so that Christ will be exalted in my body, whether by my life or by my death.[t]

21 For to me, to live is Christ and to die is gain. *[u] 22 But if I continue living in the body, that will mean fruitful work for me. Hence, I do not know which I should choose.[v] 23 I am pulled in opposite directions. My desire is to depart and to be with Christ, for that is far better,[w] 24 but, it is a more urgent need for you that I remain in the body.

25 Since I am convinced of this, I know that I shall remain and continue with all of you to ensure your progress and joy in the faith.[x] 26 Thus, you will rebound with joy in Christ Jesus when I return to be with you once again.

Striving and Suffering for Christ.* 27 Only live in a manner worthy of the gospel of Christ. Then, whether I come and see you or simply hear news of you from a distance, I will know that you are standing firm and united in spirit, striving together for the faith of the gospel,[y] 28 and being in no way intimidated by those who oppose you.

This will be a clear sign to them of their forthcoming destruction as well as of your salvation. All of this is in accord with God's design.[z] 29 For it has been granted you not only to believe in Christ but also to suffer for him.[a] 30 You are taking part in the same struggle that you have seen in me and that you now hear I am experiencing. *[b]

CHAPTER 2

Unity and Humility.* 1 Therefore, if there is any consolation in Christ, any comfort in love, any fellowship in the Spirit, any com-

j Phil 1:6; Rom 2:18; 12:2; 1 Cor 1:8.—k Jn 15:8; Jas 3:18.—l 12-13: Eph 3:1; 6:20; 2 Tim 2:9; Philem 9.—m Phil 4:22; Acts 21:33.—n Acts 4:29, 31.—o 2 Cor 11:13.—p Acts 9:15; 1 Cor 9:17.—q Phil 2:3.—r Phil 4:10.—s Job 13:16; Acts 16:7; 2 Cor 1:11; Gal 3:5; Philem 22.—t Rom 8:19; 14:8; 1 Cor 6:20; 1 Pet 4:16.—u Gal 2:20.—v Rom 1:13.—w Jn 12:26; 2 Cor 5:8; 2 Tim 4:6.—x Phil 2:24; Acts 20:25; Rom 15:13.—y Phil 4:3; 1 Cor 16:13; Eph 4:1; Col 1:10; 1 Thes 2:12; Jude 3.—z Lk 2:34; 1 Cor 1:23-24.—a Mt 5:10-12; 10:35; Mk 8:34; Acts 5:41; 14:22.—b Phil 1:13; Acts 16:19-40; 1 Thes 2:2; Heb 10:32.

1:12-26 Little concerned for his own fate, the prisoner is interested only in the progress of the Good News of Christ. Certain missionaries, jealous of his success among the Gentiles, profit from his captivity to gain influence at his expense (see 1 Cor 1). Far from taking offense, Paul is able to rejoice in this: for it means that Christ is better known and loved.

Never before has he let his readers discern the profound bond that unites him to Jesus, a bond inaugurated by Baptism and sealed by the Eucharist but a bond that is lived in the whole initiative of his existence. He has already attained his spiritual maturity, and all his desire is fixed on Christ. As in the Second Letter to the Corinthians (5:6-8), he lets us glimpse his eager longing for an immediate meeting with the Savior. There is a part of him that can no longer wait for the day of the resurrection. This striking text constitutes one of the highest points of Christian mysticism.

1:13 *Praetorium:* this may refer to the praetorian guard in the city of Paul's imprisonment or to the governor's residence in a Roman province (see Mk 15:16; Acts 23:35).

1:21 Paul has reached the highest level of spiritual growth.

1:27-30 At Philippi itself, Paul quickly encountered persecution (see Acts 16:19-40; 1 Thes 2:2). His mission was plagued by unceasing threats and perils (see 2 Cor 11:24—12:10). The life and activity of Christians partakes of the Lord's Passion (see Mt 5:12; Acts 5:41).

1:30 This verse refers to the Apostle's earlier imprisonment in Philippi (Acts 16:29-34; 1 Thes 2:2) and to his present situation in chains.

2:1-5 For those who live by faith, united to Christ and the Holy Spirit, communion is the most precious of goods. It demands a complete turnaround extending to true humility. This means a generous abnegation that makes one prefer the interests of others rather than one's own. Paul presses ahead on this subject and suddenly, gripped by the shining example of Christ, he then chants the hymn of the incredible abasements of God.

passion and sympathy,[c] 2 make my joy com-
plete by being of the same mind, having the
same love for one another, and united in
thought.[d] 3 Do nothing out of selfish ambi-
tion or vanity, but humbly regard others as
better than yourselves.[e] 4 Be concerned not
only with your own interests but also with
those of others.[f]

5 Let your attitude be identical to that of
Christ Jesus.[g]

The Humbled and Exalted Christ*

6 Though he was in the form of God,
he did not regard equality with God
as something to be grasped.[h]

7 Rather, he emptied himself, *
taking the form of a slave,
being born in human likeness.

Being found in appearance as a man,[i]
8 he humbled himself,
and became obedient to death,
even death on a cross.[j]

9 Because of this, God greatly exalted him
and bestowed on him the name
that is above all other names,[k]
10 so that at the name of Jesus
every knee should bend
of those in heaven and on earth and
under the earth,[l]
11 and every tongue should proclaim
to the glory of God the Father:
Jesus Christ is Lord. *[m]

Innocence of the Children of God.*

12 [n] Therefore, my beloved, just as you have
always been obedient when I am present,
you must be so all the more now when I am
absent, as you work out your salvation in
fear and trembling. * 13 For it is God who is
at work in you, enabling you both to desire
and to act for his chosen purpose.[o]

14 Do everything without grumbling or
arguing,[p] 15 so that you may show yourselves
blameless and beyond reproach, children of
God without spot in the midst of an evil and
depraved generation, among which you
shine like lights in the world[q] 16 as you hold
fast tenaciously to the word of life. Then I
will have cause to boast of you on the day of
Christ that I did not run in vain or labor to
no purpose.[r]

17 But even if my blood is to be poured out
as a libation upon the sacrifice and the offer-
ing of your faith, I rejoice, and I share my joy
with all of you.[s] 18 In the same way, you too
must rejoice and share your joy with me.[t]

Timothy Commended. 19 * I hope, in the
Lord Jesus, to send Timothy to you soon, so
that I may be cheered by hearing news of
you.[u] 20 I have no one else like him in his
genuine concern for your welfare.[v] 21 All the
others serve their own interests more than
those of Jesus Christ.[w]

---

c 2 Cor 13:13; Col 3:12.—d Phil 4:2; Jn 3:29; Rom 15:5; 1 Cor 1:10.—e Rom 12:3, 10; Gal 5:26; 1 Pet 5:5.—f 1 Cor 10:24, 33; 13:5.—g Mt 11:29; Rom 8:5; Col 3:1-2.—h Jn 1:1-2; 5:18; 17:5; Col 2:9; Heb 1:3.—i Isa 53:3, 11; Mt 20:28; Jn 1:14; Rom 8:3; 2 Cor 8:9; Gal 4:4; Heb 2:14, 17.—j Mt 26:39; Jn 10:17; Rom 5:19; 1 Cor 1:23; Heb 5:8; 12:2.—k Isa 52:13—53:12; Mt 23:12; Acts 2:33; Eph 1:20-21; Heb 1:3-4; 2:9.—l Ps 95:6; Isa 45:23; Mt 28:18; Jn 5:23; Rom 14:11; Eph 1:10; Col 1:20; Rev 5:13.—m Jn 13:13; Acts 2:36; Rom 10:9; 1 Cor 12:3.—n 12-18: Ps 2:11; 1 Cor 2:3; 2 Cor 7:15.—o Phil 1:6; 1 Cor 12:6; 15:10; 2 Cor 3:5; Gal 2:8; Eph 1:5; Heb 13:21.—p 1 Cor 10:10; 1 Pet 4:9.—q Deut 32:5; Dan 12:3; Mt 5:14, 16, 45, 48; 10:16; Acts 2:40; Eph 5:1, 8; 1 Thes 3:13.—r Isa 49:4; 65:23; 1 Cor 1:8; 9:24; Gal 2:2; 1 Thes 2:19.—s Rom 15:16; 2 Cor 6:10; 12:15; 2 Tim 4:6.—t Phil 3:1; 4:4.—u Acts 16:1-3; 17:14-15; 1 Cor 4:17; 16:10.—v 1 Cor 16:10.—w 1 Cor 10:24; 13:5; 2 Tim 3:2; 4:10.

2:6-11 The full breadth of the mystery of Christ is expressed in this hymn, which was either written by Paul himself or perhaps taken from the Liturgy of another community. The mystery is celebrated in two of its major aspects: descent and return, which form a curve whose two ends meet.

During his stay on earth, Jesus was deprived of the glory that belonged to him, so that he might receive it again from the Father as a reward for his supreme sacrifice. He descended into the ultimate depths of abasement; then the movement was reversed: the Father glorified him, made the universe subject to him, and gave him the supreme prerogative, the regal and Divine title of "Lord."

In the background here, Paul was thinking of the pride shown by created beings who want to be equal to God (the desire of Adam); he contrasts with this the self-giving and self-denial of Christ. But the hymn reminds us even more clearly of the songs of the Servant of God (especially Isa 53), which echoed strongly in the preaching of Jesus and in the teaching and Liturgy of the very early Church.

It is the whole mystery of the incarnate Son of God that Paul here chants with such clarity and depth: his preexistence, his abasement, and his exaltation. And the Apostle does so in order to exhort some Christians to live the demands of their Baptism!

2:7 *He emptied himself:* this means, not that Jesus ceased to be equal to God, but rather that in his humanity he stripped himself of the Divine glory, manifesting this only at the Transfiguration (Mt 17:1-8), and subsequently received it again from the Father (v. 8).

2:11 *Jesus Christ is Lord:* a common acclamation used by the early Christians (see Rom 10:9; 1 Cor 12:3).

2:12-18 Christians are touched by the Lord to the very depths of their being. Their conduct, their plans, and their testimony are the authentic expression of this in their life. Using the religious language of the time, Paul regards his role as apostle and the surrender of his life as an offering and sacrifice, a true worship of God (see Rom 1:9; 15:16).

2:12 *Fear and trembling:* an expression common in the Old Testament to indicate awe and devotion in God's service (see Ex 15:16; Jud 2:28; Ps 2:11; Isa 19:16).

2:19—3:1a Paul announces to the Philippians that he is sending them his most trusted coworker—Timothy, whom they already know (see Acts 16:1-15). He also hopes to visit them himself upon being released. And he will send Epaphroditus back to them when he is well. The last line (v. 1a) seems to be the beginning of a conclusion to the Letter.

[22] His reputation is well known to you. Like a son helping his father, he has worked with me in the service of the gospel.[x] [23] I hope to send him to you as soon as I see how things will go with me. [24] And I am confident in the Lord that I myself shall also come before long.[y]

Epaphroditus Praised. [25] I have also decided that it is necessary to send you Epaphroditus, my brother and coworker and fellow soldier, who was your messenger and ministered to my needs.[z] [26] He has missed all of you and been greatly distressed because you heard that he was ill.[a] [27] And indeed he was dangerously ill and close to death. However, God had mercy on him—and not merely on him but on me as well, so that I would not have to endure one sorrow on top of another.

[28] Therefore, I am all the more eager to send him in order that you may rejoice on seeing him again and I may thereby feel less anxious. [29] Receive him joyfully in the Lord, and value people like him very highly.[b] [30] For he came perilously close to death for the work of Christ, risking his life to render me those services that you were unable to provide.[c]

CHAPTER 3

[1] Finally, my brethren, rejoice in the Lord.[d]

III: WARNING AGAINST FALSE TEACHERS

Worship by the Spirit.* I do not mind writing the same things to you again; it is for your safety.

x 1 Cor 4:17; 1 Tim 1:2.—y Phil 1:25; Philem 22.—z Phil 4:10-11, 15-16, 18; Rom 16:3, 9; 2 Cor 8:23; Col 4:11; Philem 2.—a Phil 1:8.—b Rom 16:2; 1 Cor 16:18; 1 Tim 5:17.—c Acts 20:24; 1 Cor 16:17.—d Phil 2:18; 4:4; 1 Thes 5:16.—e Ps 22:17, 21; 2 Cor 11:13; Gal 5:6, 12; Rev 22:15.—f Rom 2:28-29; 15:17; Gal 6:14-15; Col 2:11.—g 2 Cor 11:18, 21-23.—h Lk 1:59; 2:21; Acts 22:3; 23:6; 26:5; Rom 11:1; 2 Cor 11:22.—i Acts 8:3; 21:20; 22:4; 26:9-11; Rom 10:5.—j Mt 13:44-46; Lk 14:33.—k Jer 9:23-24; Jn 17:3; Eph 4:11; 2 Pet 1:2.—l Jer 13:16; Rom 3:21-22; 10:5.

3:1b-3 In a Letter that seemed to be coming to an end, a new subject is introduced. Paul is opposing the Jews or Jewish Christians who regard the practice of certain rites as indispensable, notably circumcision, even for those who believe in Christ. Christianity is total union with Christ in the greatest spiritual freedom. It cannot consist—like Judaism—in meticulous practices that lead to formalism. There is no salvation except in Jesus Christ, as the Letters to the Romans and to the Galatians demonstrate at length. Anything else is a human practice that pertains to the order of the flesh.

[2] Beware of the dogs!* Beware of evildoers! Beware of those who mutilate the flesh![e] [3] For we are the circumcision,* we who worship by the Spirit of God and who boast in Christ Jesus and do not place any confidence in the flesh—[f] [4] even though I too have reason for confidence in the flesh.

Joyous Sacrifice of All Things for Christ.* If anyone thinks that he has reasons to be confident in the flesh, I have more![g] [5] I was circumcised on the eighth day of my life. I was one of the people of Israel, the tribe of Benjamin.* I am a Hebrew and the son of Hebrews. In regard to the Law, I was a Pharisee;[h] [6] in regard to religious zeal, I was a persecutor of the Church; in regard to righteousness under the Law, I was without fault.[i]

[7] All these I once regarded as assets, but now I have come to regard them as losses because of Christ.[j] [8] Even more than that, I count everything as loss because of the supreme good of knowing Christ Jesus my Lord. For his sake, I have suffered the loss of all other things, and I regard them as so much rubbish, in order that I may gain Christ[k] [9] and be found in him.

I do not wish to have any righteousness of my own based on the Law, but one that comes through faith in Christ, the righteousness given by God in response to faith.[l]

If the word "circumcision" must be used, it can refer only to the circumcision of the heart; if there is need to speak of worship, it can only be a spiritual worship. Christ has now become the sole focus of Paul's interest; his entire life will be dedicated to knowing Christ, the Lord and Savior of the world, and making him known to others.

3:2 *Dogs:* this is the name given to Gentiles by Jews (see Mt 15:26); here it is applied ironically to the Judaizers (see Gal 5:12). *Those who mutilate the flesh:* i.e., the Judaizers who insist that the Gentile Christians must agree to submit to circumcision (see Gal 5:12).

3:3 *We are the circumcision:* Christians are the true People of God and offspring of Abraham (see Gal 3:7, 29; 6:15).

3:4b-11 Paul had everything needed to forge for himself a brilliant career in Judaism, and he dreamed about it. He was a Jew of the most elite tribe and the most rigorous sect as well as a zealous advocate and defender of his religion. His encounter with Jesus on the road to Damascus—a Jesus who identified himself totally with his followers and who loved him unconditionally—turned everything upside down for Paul.

Henceforth, Christ becomes his sole interest. His very existence will be the knowledge of the Lord Jesus, that is, communion in his Paschal Mystery of dying and rising to new life, and participation in his work for the salvation of the world. One thing is evident for Paul: human beings can become fully realized only by giving themselves to Christ without reservation.

3:5 *The tribe of Benjamin* was descended from the one son of Jacob who was born in Palestine (Gen 35:16f), and it had always been faithful to the Davidic dynasty. The Jerusalem temple was in the territory of Benjamin.

10 All I want is to come to know Christ and the power of his resurrection and to share in his sufferings by becoming conformed to his death,[m] 11 so that I may attain the resurrection from the dead.[n]

Racing toward the Goal.* 12 It is not that I have already attained this or have yet reached perfection. But I press on to take hold of that for which Christ once took hold of me.[o] 13 Brethren, I do not claim to have taken hold of it as yet. Only this one thing: forgetting what is behind and straining forward to what lies ahead,[p] 14 I press on toward the finishing line to win the heavenly prize to which God has called me in Christ Jesus.[q]

15 Those of us who are mature should adopt this same attitude. If on any matter you have a different point of view, this too God will make clear to you.[r] 16 Only let us hold fast in our conduct to what we have already attained.[s]

Our Citizenship Is in Heaven.* 17 Brethren, join in imitating me, * and take note of those who conduct themselves in accord with the model you have in us.[t] 18 As I have told you before, and now remind you with tears, many live as enemies of the cross of Christ.[u] 19 Their end is destruction. Their god is their stomach. Their glory is in their shame. Their minds are set on earthly things.[v]

20 But our citizenship is in heaven, * and from there we await our Savior, the Lord Jesus Christ.[w] 21 He will transform our lowly bodies so that they will be conformed to his glorified body by the power that also enables him to make all things subject to himself.[x]

CHAPTER 4

1 Therefore, my brethren, whom I love and for whom I long, my joy and crown: stand firm in the Lord, beloved.[y]

IV: COUNSELS AND THANKSGIVING

Christian Concord.* 2 I exhort both Euodia and Syntyche to come to a mutual understanding in the Lord.[z] 3 I also ask you, my loyal companion Syzygus, to help these women, for they have struggled alongside me in the work of the gospel, together with Clement and the rest of my fellow workers, whose names are in the book of life.[a]

Rejoice without Ceasing.* 4 Rejoice in the Lord always. Again I say: Rejoice![b] 5 Let your kindness be known to everyone. The Lord is near.[c] 6 Do not worry about anything, but present your needs to God in prayer and petition, with thanksgiving.[d] 7 Then the peace of God, which is beyond all understanding, will guard your hearts and your minds in Christ Jesus.[e]

All That Is Truly Human Is Christian.* 8 Finally, brethren, let your minds be filled with whatever is true, whatever is honorable, whatever

m Rom 6:3-5; 8:17; 2 Cor 1:5; Gal 6:17.—n Jn 11:23-26; Acts 4:2; Rom 6:5; Rev 20:5-6.—o Acts 9:5, 6; 1 Cor 13:10; 1 Tim 6:12, 19.—p Lk 9:62; Heb 12:1.—q Rom 8:28; 1 Cor 9:24-25; 2 Tim 4:7; Heb 6:1.—r 1 Cor 2:6; Gal 5:10; Eph 1:17; 1 Thes 4:9.—s Gal 6:16.—t 1 Cor 4:16; 11:1; 1 Thes 1:7; 1 Tim 4:12; 1 Pet 5:3.—u Acts 20:11; 1 Cor 1:17, 23; Gal 6:12.—v Ps 73:18; Rom 8:5-6; 16:18; Col 3:2; Jude 13.—w 1 Cor 1:7; Eph 2:6, 19; Col 3:1-3; Heb 12:22.—x Rom 8:23, 29; 1 Cor 15:27-28, 42-57; 2 Cor 3:18; 5:1-5; Eph 1:19; Col 3:4.—y Phil 1:8; 1 Cor 16:13; 1 Thes 2:19-20.—z Phil 2:2; 2 Cor 13:11.—a Phil 2:25; Ex 32:32-33; Ps 69:29; Dan 12:1; Lk 10:20; Rev 3:5; 13:8; 17:8; 20:12, 15; 21:27.—b Phil 2:18; 3:1; Hab 3:18; Mt 5:12; Rom 12:12.—c Pss 119:151; 145:18; Tit 3:2; Heb 10:37; Jas 5:8-9.—d Mt 6:25-34; Eph 6:18; Col 4:2; 1 Tim 2:1; 1 Pet 5:7.—e Isa 26:3; Jn 14:27; Eph 3:19; Col 3:15.

3:12-16 Grasped by Christ on the road to Damascus, Paul strains toward him with his whole being, and this aim of his life energizes all his forces. The Christian life is inner growth, deepening, and development, and Paul loves to describe it as a course to be run. Once anyone has begun the race, there cannot be any stopping: "If you say 'Enough,' you are already dead" (St. Augustine). Those who have already "reached perfection" are Christians whose faith can be termed "mature."

3:17—4:1 Paul stresses that the Christian life is carried along by a profound hope. We turn that hope away from its goal when we fix its fulfillment in the realities of earth and even more when we polarize it on failed religious practices. Paul was probably thinking of the Jewish dietary customs and the circumcision that some Jewish-Christian preachers wanted to impose on new communities.

3:17 *Join in imitating me:* since Paul's wholehearted imitation of Christ is well known to his readers (1 Cor 4:6; 11:1; Phil 4:9; 1 Thes 1:6; 2 Thes 3:7, 9), he encourages them to follow his example in that respect.

3:20 *Our citizenship is in heaven:* Christians are, as it were, aliens in this world, for their real home is heaven. They are not of the world but fully involved in it (see Jn 17:14-16; 1 Cor 7:29-31; 1 Pet 2:11).

4:2-3 Lines of communication are established in all the new communities, and women play an important role in their life and apostolate. Doubtless, members at times experience the difficulty of living and working together, as is the case between *Euodia* and *Syntyche.* Paul is confident that these two good women will be reconciled to one another. *Clement:* it is possible, but not certain, that this is Clement, the first Roman Pope. *Book of life:* an image current at the time to evoke the collectivity of the saved (see Ex 32:32; Ps 69:29; Isa 4:3; Dan 12:1; Rev 3:5).

4:4-7 Joy is the great secret of Christians, the sign that faith has triumphed over all fears, the normal fruit of a spiritual life that progresses. The peace of God is more profound than any kind of peace that the human spirit can attain solely by its own effort.

4:8-9 Radically detached from earthly goods, a purified heart is able to recognize the gifts of Christ through all human values. In these verses, Etienne Gilson saw "the eternal charter of Christian humanism."

is just, whatever is pure, whatever is pleasing, whatever is commendable, whatever is excellent, whatever is worthy of praise.[f] 9 Do the things that you have learned, received, and heard from me and that you saw me doing. Then the God of peace will be with you.[g]

V: ACKNOWLEDGMENT OF THE COMMUNITY'S GIFT*

Contentment in Any Circumstances. 10 I rejoice greatly in the Lord that now at last you have renewed your concern for me. You were, of course, concerned about me, but you had no opportunity to show it.[h] 11 [i]I do not say this because I have been in need, for I have learned to be content with whatever I have.[j]

12 I know how to live with little, and I know how to live with plenty. In any and all circumstances, I have learned the secret of being well fed and of going hungry, of having plenty and of being in need. 13 I can do all things in him who strengthens me.[k]

Philippian Generosity. 14 Even so, it was kind of you to share my difficulties.[l] 15 You Philippians are aware that in the early days of the gospel* when I set out from Macedonia, not a single Church other than yours shared with me in giving and receiving.[m] 16 Even when I was in Thessalonica, you sent me something for my needs on more than one occasion.[n]

17 Do not think that it is the gift that I value most. What I desire is for the interest to mount up in your account.[o] 18 I have been paid in full and have more than enough. I am satisfied now that I have received from Epaphroditus the gifts you sent. They are a fragrant offering, an acceptable sacrifice pleasing to God.*[p] 19 And my God will fully supply all your needs out of the riches of his glory in Christ Jesus.[q]

Doxology. 20 To our God and Father be glory forever and ever. Amen.[r]

VI: CONCLUSION

Final Greetings.* 21 Give my greetings to every one of the saints in Christ Jesus. The brethren who are with me send their greetings to you,[s] 22 as do all the saints here, especially those in the emperor's service.[t]

Benediction.* 23 The grace of our Lord Jesus Christ be with your spirit.[u]

f Rom 12:17.—g Rom 15:33; 16:20; 1 Cor 4:16; 14:33; 1 Thes 4:1; 5:23.—h Phil 1:18; 2:25; 1 Cor 12:25; 2 Cor 11:9.—i 11-12: 1 Cor 4:11; 2 Cor 6:10; 11:27; 12:9-10.—j 1 Tim 6:6, 8; Heb 13:5.—k 2 Cor 12:9; Eph 3:16; Col 1:11, 29; 1 Tim 1:12; 2 Tim 4:17.—l Phil 1:7; Rev 1:9.—m Phil 1:5; Acts 16:9; 2 Cor 11:8-9.—n Acts 17:1; 2 Cor 8:1-5.—o 1 Cor 9:11-12.—p Phil 2:25; Gen 8:21; Ex 29:18; 2 Cor 2:14; Eph 5:2; Heb 13:16.—q Ps 23:1; Rom 2:4; 2 Cor 9:8; 1 Thes 3:11, 13.—r Rom 11:36; 16:27; Gal 1:4; Eph 5:20; 1 Thes 1:3; 3:11, 13.—s Gal 1:2.—t Phil 1:13; Acts 9:13; Rom 16:11; 2 Cor 13:13.—u Rom 16:20; Gal 6:18.

4:10-20 Even when in need, Paul did not want to depend on the communities for material help (see 1 Cor 9:14, 18; 2 Cor 11:7-10; 12:13-18; 1 Thes 2:5-9; 2 Thes 3:7-9), and he made no exception except for the Christians of Philippi with whom he had especially cordial ties. Like a true poor person, he remains free in any situation, enriched or deprived, ready to accept whatever will come—for the important thing is to serve the Gospel.

4:15 *Early days of the gospel:* during Paul's second missionary journey, when he first preached the Gospel in Europe at Philippi (Acts 16:9ff).

4:18 *A fragrant offering, an acceptable sacrifice pleasing to God:* Paul sees the Philippians' gift to him in terms of the Old Testament sacrifice of thanksgiving and praise (see Lev 7:12-15; Rom 12:1; Eph 5:2; Heb 13:15f).

4:21-22 Paul mentions especially those who in some way ensure the service of the emperor: dignitaries and soldiers, freedmen or slaves. Hence, Christians are also part of these circles.

4:23 Paul adds a typical closing benediction. *Your spirit:* i.e., the whole person viewed from his inner side (see Gal 6:18; 2 Tim 4:22; Philem 25).

"He is the head of the body, that is, the Church" *(Col 1:18).*

THE LETTER TO THE COLOSSIANS

The Mystery of Christ

The Letters to the Ephesians and the Colossians are like twin sisters. They were entrusted to the same messenger: Tychicus; the style is the same, as is the thought. Furthermore, half of the Letter to the Ephesians is to be found in the Letter to the Colossians, which was certainly written first. The Letter to the Ephesians thus seems to be a deeper reflection on the same subject after the crisis in the Colossian community.

Some exegetes are reluctant to ascribe these two Letters to Paul. The tone and the subject are new; a different vision inspires the author when he speaks of Christ, the Church, and Baptism. And at that time, when people were much less scrupulous than today about literary ownership, some disciples could have written these Letters, in their master's name, in order to further his apostolic work. This position is not impossible. But why could not Paul's ideas develop, due partly to deeper experience, partly to the influence of new problems that he may have met? It is therefore not unjustified to think that these Letters were written in Rome in A.D. 62–63, toward the end of Paul's imprisonment.

Colossae was at that time a little city in the interior of Asia Minor, about 80 miles northeast of Ephesus. Paul probably never went there in person, but some new converts and missionaries had scattered from Ephesus to the other cities of the province; among these was Epaphras, to whom Paul here gives his apostolic approval.

The Greeks were once enamored of the image of a harmonious cosmos, but that is no longer the idea of the universe possessed by Paul's contemporaries. They often feel that they are in the grip of an existence without purpose, prisoners of obscure forces working in the world. So they seek to master these forces by means of practices and cults. This religious ferment, stemming from a civilization's malaise, influences even certain Jewish circles. These current troubles lend fuel to the crisis at Colossae.

In fact, the error that threatens the youthful Church bears the earmarks of an intermingling of the Jewish religion with Eastern influences and recalls the concepts of the Essene sect of Qumran. In an atmosphere of religious fear, its adherents make salvation depend on a multitude of human practices, observances, and rites. At the same time, to explain the laws of the world and history, which do not cease to astonish and frighten, they contrive a clever system of spirits, intermediaries between God and creatures, that preside over the life of the cosmos and the destiny of the world.

They give the imagination free rein to speculate about the role and place of mythological forces. In every age, human beings find reasons to avoid their responsibilities by believing that they are the playthings of anonymous forces and offering sacrifice to them!

Made aware that such a situation is present at Colossae, Paul immediately sees the danger. It is the very sovereignty of Christ that is being attacked. In its place, futile powers, impotent lords, and vain ideologies are erected as masters of our destiny. Until now, Paul has contemplated the presence of Christ in the life of Christians; this time, he contemplates Christ's place in the destiny of the cosmos.

He clearly affirms that Christ dominates everything. He is the author and head of the universe—set over human beings and over the cosmic forces. He is the Risen One living in full glory—set over all the faithful. He rules over his earthly Church in which he acts in meaningful ways so that she may develop and gradually succeed in crossing to his side.

Christians believe in this total primacy of Christ; they do not seek to join their existence to other forces, but they know that their existence is profoundly united with Jesus through Baptism, and they strive to develop this aspect of personal union even here below. Thus, their existence unfolds in the light, power, and love of Easter.

The Letter to the Colossians is the Easter letter par excellence. But Paul is too much of a realist to separate mysticism from ethical requirements. The human beings with a new self are those who never cease to model themselves on Christ; new values transform their activity and their life situation.

The Apostle's insights are developed in an ample style with an almost liturgical rhythm. They are far removed from the sparkling but choppy style of the early Letters. The author of the Letters to the Colossians and Ephesians repeatedly contemplates the Paschal Mystery of Christ in order to reflect on the meaning of life and on the destiny of the universe.

In the process, he forges a more highly developed Christology than that of the major Letters, but it comes from themes developed in them. The teachings (1) that Christ has created everything (Col 1:16), (2) that in him all things hold together (Col 1:17), and (3) that everything in heaven and on earth has been reconciled by his death (Col 1:20) flow from developing the ideas of 1 Cor 8:6; 10:4; and 2 Cor 5:19. And when Paul states that by the work of the Redemption Christ has subdued the principalities and powers (Col 2:15), he is expanding on Rom 8:38ff; Gal 4:3, 9; and Phil 2:10ff.

The Letter to the Colossians may be divided as follows:

I: Introduction (1:1-14)
II: The Supremacy of Christ (1:15—2:5)
III: Instruction about Errors That Are Circulating (2:6-23)
IV: Exhortation To Live as Christians (3:1—4:6)
V: Conclusion (4:7-18)

CHAPTER 1

I: INTRODUCTION

Address. 1 Paul, an apostle of Christ Jesus by the will of God, and Timothy our brother,[a] 2 to the saints * and faithful brethren in Christ in Colossae. May God our Father grant you grace and peace.[b]

A Community Pervaded by the Gospel.* 3 In all our prayers for you we always give thanks to God, the Father of our Lord Jesus Christ,[c] 4 because we have heard of your faith in Christ Jesus and of the love that you have for all the saints[d] 5 because of the hope that is stored up for you in heaven. You had learned of this hope through the word of truth, the gospel, *[e] 6 that has come down to you.

Just as it is bearing fruit and growing throughout the entire world, so it has been bearing fruit among you, ever since the day when you heard it and came to understand the grace of God in truth.[f] 7 You learned this from Epaphras, * our beloved fellow servant and a faithful minister of Christ on your behalf.[g] 8 He was also the one who made known to us your love in the Spirit.[h]

9 That is why, ever since the day we first heard about it, we have not ceased to pray for you and to ask that you may be filled with the knowledge of God's will through all spiritual wisdom and understanding.[i] 10 And we ask this so that you may live in a manner worthy of the Lord and become fully pleasing to him, bearing fruit in every good work and continuing to grow in the knowledge of God.[j]

11 May you be fortified with the strength that comes from his glorious power, and may you be granted patience and endurance, while joyfully[k] 12 giving thanks to the Father who has enabled you to share in the inheritance of the saints in light. *[l] 13 He has rescued us from the power of darkness and brought us into the kingdom of his beloved Son,[m] 14 in whom we have redemption, the forgiveness of sins.[n]

II: THE SUPREMACY OF CHRIST

In Christ, through Him, and for Him *

15 He is the image of the invisible God,
the firstborn of all creation.[o]
16 For in him were created all things
in heaven and on earth,
whether visible or invisible,
whether thrones or dominions or rulers
or powers—
all things were created through him and
for him.[p]

a Acts 16:1; 1 Cor 1:1; 2 Cor 1:1; Eph 1:1.—b Col 4:18; Rom 1:7.—c Rom 1:8; Eph 1:15-16; Philem 4-5.—d Acts 9:13; Gal 5:6; Eph 1:15; Philem 5.—e Eph 1:13, 18; 1 Thes 5:8; 2 Tim 2:15; Tit 1:2; 1 Pet 1:4.—f Jn 15:16; Rom 10:18.—g Col 4:12; Philem 23.—h Rom 15:30.—i Col 2:2; Rom 1:10; Eph 1:8, 15-17; 5:17; Phil 1:9.—j 2 Cor 5:9; Eph 2:10; 4:1.—k Eph 4:2; Phil 4:13.—l Col 3:17; Jn 8:12; Acts 20:32; 26:18; Eph 5:20; 1 Tim 6:16; 1 Pet 2:9.—m Mt 3:17; Acts 26:18; 2 Pet 1:11.—n Rom 3:24; Eph 1:7.—o Ps 89:28; Jn 1:3, 18; 14:9; 2 Cor 4:4; 1 Tim 1:17; Heb 11:27.—p Jn 1:3; Rom 11:36; 1 Cor 8:6; Eph 1:10, 21.

1:2 *Saints:* Christians are called *saints* because through Baptism they have been consecrated to God and are called to live accordingly.

1:3-14 The power of the Gospel to live and spread is extraordinary; it is God's grace and action among human beings. In the vitality of a young Church, Paul recognizes this work of the Lord, and he prays that it will develop in all its richness. Thanksgiving and prayer succeed each other in this introduction and indicate the principal features of an authentic Christian life: to accept the truth of the Gospel; to grow in faith, love, and hope; and to know God more in order to be more faithful in the concrete.

Nonetheless, the initiative comes from the Lord. It is he who changes our life; it is he who frees us from the bondage of sin and leads us into a new world, the kingdom of Christ. Now he is extending to all the Gentiles the salvation formerly reserved for Israel—"the inheritance of the saints." Such a text gives us the echo of what might have been the mystique of Baptism and the joy of the Christian in the early Church.

1:5 This verse refers to the three theological virtues of faith, hope, and love, which also appear in Rom 5:2-5; 1 Cor 13:13; Gal 5:5f; 1 Thes 1:3; 5:8; Heb 10:22-24. For the special nuance mentioned here, that hope gives rise to faith and love, see Tit 1:2.

1:7 *Epaphras:* a Colossian and founder of the Church of Colossae, who is now with Paul.

1:12 *Light:* this term is used to symbolize glory (Isa 60:1-3; 1 Tim 6:16), life (Jn 1:4), holiness (Mt 5:14; 6:23; Acts 26:18; 1 Jn 1:5), love (Jas 1:17; 1 Jn 2:9f), and truth (Pss 36:9; 119:105, 130; 2 Cor 4:6). Thus, the character of light is found in God (1 Jn 1:5), Christ (Jn 8:12), and Christians (Eph 5:8).

1:15-20 This great hymn to Christ and his universal primacy was probably a baptismal hymn. It draws upon the most beautiful motifs of the Old Testament on Divine wisdom (see Prov 8:1-9, 12; Wis 7:21—8:12; Sir 24). In the perspective Paul adopts here, he contemplates Christ as the image of the invisible God and clearly asserts his Divine preexistence (see 2 Cor 4:4; Phil 2:6; Heb 1:3).

Christ is before all and above all; whether we consider the universe or the History of Salvation, he is both the reason for being and the explanation of everything in them. If we seek the origin of, the rationale for, or the end of creation, he is the one we must name. All the heavenly forces and hierarchies so prized in certain Jewish or Christian circles in Colossae—in a word, everything that claims to rule the universe—are subject to him as the Creator.

He alone is Lord of the world. He alone is the power giving life to the Church, that is, his Body. He alone is the Mediator who reconciles all beings with one another and with God. We experience a universe disordered by sin; it is re-created and transformed in him. Hence, for the Christian, history has a movement and a meaning: it is oriented toward Christ, directed by him, and consummated in him.

Paul wants to enunciate a hope that is infinitely more than merely human, a hope founded in faith (see Rom 8:19-22; 1 Cor 15:22-28; Phil 3:21): the risen Christ is the center in whom two worlds are united, the Divine and the created.

17 He exists before all things,
and in him all things hold together. [q]
18 He is the head of the body,
that is, the Church.
He is the beginning,
the firstborn from the dead,
so that in every way
he should be supreme. [r]
19 For in him
it pleased God
to make all fullness dwell, * [s]
20 and through him
to reconcile all things for him,
whether on earth or in heaven,
by making peace through his blood of
the cross. [t]

Christ among the Gentiles. 21 * You your-
selves were once alienated and hostile in
your intent because of your evil deeds. [u]
22 But now, through Christ's death in his
body of flesh, God has reconciled you to
himself so that you may stand holy, blame-
less, and irreproachable in his presence. [v]

23 However, you must persevere in the
faith, firmly grounded and steadfast in your
belief, and never allowing yourselves to drift
away from the hope of the gospel that you
accepted and that has now been proclaimed
to every creature under heaven, the gospel
of which I, Paul, have become a servant. [w]

Christ's Suffering in His People. 24 I find
great joy at present in suffering for you, and
in my own body I am completing the suffer-
ings that still must be undergone by Christ
for the sake of his body, the Church. * [x] 25 I
was made a minister of that Church, with
the commission given to me by God to make
fully known to you the word of God, [y] 26 the
mystery that has been hidden throughout
the ages and from past generations but that
now has been revealed to his saints. [z]

27 To these God chose to make known how
rich is the priceless glory that this mystery
brings to the Gentiles—Christ in you, your
hope of glory. * [a] 28 It is he whom we pro-
claim, admonishing and instructing every-
one in all wisdom so that we may present
everyone to Christ in a state of perfection. [b]
29 For this I labor and struggle with all his
energy working within me mightily. [c]

CHAPTER 2

Closely United in Love.* 1 I want you to real-
ize how greatly I am struggling for you as
well as for those in Laodicea * and all the
others who have never seen me face to
face. [d] 2 I want their hearts to be encouraged
and united in love so that they may grow
rich in their complete understanding as they
come to the knowledge of the mystery of
God, that is, Christ, [e] 3 in whom are hidden
all the treasures of wisdom and knowledge. [f]

4 I am telling you all this so that no one
may deceive you with deceptive argu-
ments. [g] 5 Even if I am not physically present
to you, I am with you in spirit, and I rejoice
to see your unity and the resolute firmness
of your faith in Christ. [h]

---

q Jn 1:2.—r Ps 89:27; Acts 26:23; Rom 8:29; 1 Cor 11:3; 12:12, 27; 15:20; Eph 1:22-23; Heb 1:6; Rev 1:5.—s Col 2:9; Jn 1:16; Eph 1:5.—t Lk 2:14; Rom 5:10; 2 Cor 5:18; Eph 1:10; 2:13.—u Rom 5:10; Eph 2:3, 14-16.—v Rom 5:10; 7:4; 2 Cor 4:14; Eph 1:4.—w Rom 11:22; 1 Cor 3:5; Eph 3:17.—x 1 Cor 12:27; 2 Cor 1:5; 6:10.—y Rom 15:19; 1 Cor 3:5; Eph 3:2; Heb 4:12.—z Rom 16:25-26; 1 Cor 2:7; Eph 3:3, 9.—a Col 2:2; 3:4; Mt 13:11; Rom 8:10.—b Col 3:16; Mt 5:48; 1 Cor 2:6; Eph 4:13.—c Col 2:1; 4:12; 1 Cor 15:10; 2 Cor 11:23; Eph 1:19; Phil 4:13.—d Col 1:29; 4:12-13; Eph 1:19; 3:7; Rev 1:11.—e Col 1:26-27; 4:8; Rom 16:25; Eph 3:18-19; 6:22.—f Prov 2:4-5; Isa 11:2; 45:3; Jer 23:5; Rom 11:33; 1 Cor 1:30.—g Rom 16:18; Eph 4:14.—h Acts 20:21; 1 Cor 5:3; 14:40; Phil 1:27; 1 Thes 2:7; 1 Pet 5:9.

1:19 *All fullness (plêrôma):* the fullness of deity (see Col 2:9) or, better, the universe full of the creative and redemptive presence of God. According to Paul, the risen Christ rules the whole of creation, what has been raised from sinfulness to salvation.

1:21-29 By dying on the cross, Christ has accomplished the reconciliation of all human beings. The Gospel changes their condition before God, provided that they accept it with faith. Paul rejoices in suffering to announce such a message, for he knows that the ordeal of a missionary is united with the Passion of Christ and contributes to the life and growth of the Church. He is captivated by the "mystery" of God. This term frequently means, depending on the context, Christ as prophesied, Christ who has come into this world, Christ continuing his work in the Church, Christ in his triumphal return. Here, in this grand perspective of unity, Paul focuses his attention on the present aspect of the mystery. Today, Jews and Gentiles are admitted into the same inheritance, they are members of the same body, and they benefit from the same promise; today, even the multitudes of the Gentiles whom Israel regarded as excluded from the Covenant are called to the embrace of the Church. This is the wonderful mystery that the Apostle is charged to reveal.

1:24 *For the sake of his body, the Church:* nothing is lacking in the sufferings of Christ, but believers who form a single reality with him (his body) prolong and complete his Paschal Mystery of Death and Resurrection by their trials and sufferings.

1:27 Christ dwells in us when we are regenerated (see Eph 3:17). We partake of the divine nature by feeding on him (Jn 6:56) and by having his word abide in us, and we grow in grace and bear fruit as we abide in him (Jn 15:5f).

2:1-5 The Apostle draws his strength from faith, and believers draw their unity from that same faith: i.e., knowledge of the mystery of God, whose riches love will never cease uncovering. It is not a case of speculating about abstract ideas or empty words, but of recognizing the action of God in history and in the hearts of human beings—today as yesterday—so as to save them.

2:1 *Laodicea:* a town about 11 miles away from Colossae; the Letter was to be read there too (Col 4:16).

III: INSTRUCTION ABOUT ERRORS THAT ARE CIRCULATING

Walk in Christ. 6 * Therefore, just as you received Christ Jesus the Lord, continue to walk in him.[i] 7 Be rooted and built up in him, and remain established in the faith as you were taught, overflowing with thanksgiving.[j] 8 Make sure that no one leads you astray with an empty and deceitful philosophy that depends on human tradition * and worldly principles, and not on Christ.[k]

God Has Given You Life in Christ. 9 For it is in him that the entire fullness of deity dwells in bodily form, *[l] 10 and you share this fullness in him who is the head of every ruler and power.[m] 11 In him also you were circumcised, not with a physical circumcision but with a spiritual stripping away of the old nature with the circumcision of Christ.[n]

12 When you were buried with him in baptism, you were also raised with him through faith in the power of God who raised him from the dead.[o] 13 And even when you were dead in your sins and your flesh was uncircumcised, God gave you new life along with him. He has forgiven us all our sins,[p] 14 erasing the record against us * with its decrees that are hostile to us. He set this aside, nailing it to the cross.[q] 15 Disarming the rulers and powers, he made a public spectacle of them, parading them in his triumphal procession.[r]

The Reality Is Christ.* 16 Therefore, do not allow anyone to pass judgment on you in regard to what you eat or drink, or about the observance of Festivals, New Moons, or Sabbaths. *[s] 17 These are only a shadow of what is to come. The reality is Christ.[t]

18 Do not allow yourself to be declared disqualified by those who revel in false humility and worship angels and visions, their vanity foolishly inflated by a human way of thinking.[u] 19 They are not united with the head, from whom the whole body, supported and held together by its ligaments and sinews, achieves the growth that comes from God.[v]

20 Since you died with Christ to the elemental principles of this world, why are you living in the world as if you were subject to it?[w] 21 "Do not handle!" "Do not taste!" "Do not touch!"[x] 22 All this refers to things that perish as they are used. They are simply human commands and teachings.[y] 23 Rules of this type indeed appear to be wise in promoting self-imposed piety, false humility, and harsh treatment of the body, but they are of no value in combating the flesh.[z]

IV: EXHORTATION TO LIVE AS CHRISTIANS

CHAPTER 3

Seek the Things That Are Above.* 1 Therefore, since you have been raised with Christ, seek the things that are above, where Christ

i Col 1:10; Jn 13:13; 1 Pet 5:9.—j Eph 2:20-22; 3:17; 4:21.—k Gal 4:3; Eph 5:6; 1 Tim 6:20.—l Col 1:19; Jn 1:16; Eph 3:19.—m Mt 28:18; Eph 1:22.—n Col 1:22; Jer 4:4; Rom 2:25-29; Gal 5:24; Phil 3:3.—o Mt 28:19; Acts 2:24; Rom 6:3-4.—p Eph 2:1, 5; 4:32.—q Eph 2:14-15; 1 Pet 2:24.—r Col 1:16, 20; Mt 12:29; Lk 10:18; Jn 12:31; 2 Cor 2:14; Eph 1:21; 6:12.—s Lev 23:2; Num 28:11; Mk 7:19; Rom 14:3-4, 17; Gal 4:10; 1 Tim 4:3.—t 1 Cor 10:6, 11; Heb 8:5; 10:1.—u Col 2:23; Mt 24:4; 1 Cor 9:24; Phil 3:14.—v 1 Cor 12:27; Eph 1:22; 2:21-22; 4:16.—w Rom 6:6; Gal 4:3, 9.—x Acts 10:15; 1 Tim 4:3.—y Isa 29:13; Mt 15:9; 1 Cor 6:12; Tit 1:14.—z Rom 13:14; 1 Tim 4:8.

2:6-15 Paul states that human laws, even the Law of Moses, could forbid sin but not overcome it; they drive human beings to sin and are like a sentence of death. We could imagine all sorts of hidden forces that might rule the world, but they can only add to the alienation of humans. Christ has liberated believers from this tyranny of observances and myths. In his Resurrection, he is the sole master through whom human beings are raised, and all the imaginable forces are subjected to him. For Christians, the conception of the world and life has changed; having been baptized, they share in the very life of God. This is a much more profound turnaround than the ancient circumcision. Why then do the Colossians insist on seeking salvation in material observances, human theories, and myths?

2:8 *Human tradition:* literally, "philosophy," a word that occurs only here in the New Testament. In this context, it refers not to systematic thought but to religious speculations.

2:9 *The entire fullness of deity dwells in bodily form:* i.e., in the risen and glorified body of Christ.

2:14 *Record against us:* the reference is perhaps to the Mosaic Law. The latter pointed out the way of the commandments but did not give the power to observe; as a result, it became the source of indictment.

2:16-23 Certain Colossian Christians of Jewish extraction minutely observed the customs of the Jewish religion, others were partial to visions and revelations, and still others gave themselves over to ascetical practices. All of them acted as if their method was necessary for salvation. But wasn't it Christ who saved them and who enabled his Church to live as a new seed in the world? To believe is to be set free and to dedicate oneself entirely to the Lord. What can human rites, exercises, usages, and theories do in this respect?

2:16 *Observance of Festivals, New Moons, or Sabbaths:* observances that were in vogue on a yearly, monthly, or weekly basis. These were usually reckoned according to heavenly bodies, sun, moon, and stars (see Col 2:8).

3:1-4 It is not a question here of having contempt for earthly realities but of a new movement by which Christians must let themselves be grasped. Seemingly, Baptism has changed nothing for them, but in reality they live henceforth united to Christ in an even more mysterious manner. They have entered the world of the Resurrection. It is a certitude that transforms the idea that they have of their existence. At the same time, it is an impatient longing for the return of the Lord, when this change in their lives will be made complete.

is, sitting at God's right hand.[a] 2 Fix your thoughts on things that are above, not on things that are on the earth,[b] 3 for you have died, and your life is hidden with Christ in God.[c] 4 When Christ, who is your life, appears, then you also will appear with him in glory.[d]

A New Self.* 5 And so you should put to death everything in your nature that is earthly: sexual immorality, impurity, passion, evil desires, and greed (which is idolatry).*[e] 6 Because of these practices, the wrath of God will fall on those who are disobedient.[f] 7 In the life you formerly lived, you used to do these things.[g] 8 But now you must cast them all aside—anger, rage, malice, slander, and foul language out of your lips.[h]

9 Do not lie to one another, since you have stripped off the old self with its practices[i] 10 and have put on the new self that is being renewed in knowledge after the image of its creator.[j] 11 Now there is no longer Greek and Jew, circumcised and uncircumcised, barbarian and Scythian,* slave and free man. Rather, Christ is all and in all.[k]

Characteristics of Life in Common.* 12 As God's chosen ones, holy and beloved, put on compassion, kindness, humility, gentleness, and patience.[l] 13 Bear with one another, and forgive one another if anyone has reason to be offended with another. You must forgive just as the Lord has forgiven you.[m]

14 Over all these put on love, which is the bond of perfection.[n] 15 And let the peace of Christ reign in your hearts, because it was for this that you were called together in one body. Always be thankful.[o]

16 Let the word of Christ* with all its richness dwell in you. Teach and admonish one another in all wisdom, singing psalms, hymns, and spiritual songs to God with gratitude in your hearts.[p] 17 And whatever you do in word or deed, do everything in the name of the Lord Jesus, giving thanks to God the Father through him.[q]

The Christian Family. 18 *Wives, be subject to your husbands, as is fitting in the Lord.[r] 19 Husbands, love your wives and do not treat them harshly.[s] 20 Children, obey your parents in everything, for this is pleasing to the Lord.[t] 21 Fathers, do not provoke your children lest they lose heart.[u]

Slaves and Masters. 22 Slaves, obey your earthly masters in everything, not only when you are being observed or in order to please them, but wholeheartedly, out of reverence for the Lord.[v] 23 Whatever you do, do it wholeheartedly, as if you were doing it for the Lord and not for others,[w] 24 since you know that you will receive from the Lord an inheritance as your reward for you are serving the Lord Christ.[x] 25 But anyone who does wrong will be repaid for what he has done. There will not be any favoritism shown.[y]

---

a Col 2:12; Ps 110:1; Mk 16:19; Rom 6:5; Eph 2:6; Phil 3:20.—b Mt 16:23; Rom 8:5; Phil 3:19-20.—c Rom 6:2, 5; 2 Cor 5:14.—d 1 Cor 1:7; Gal 2:20; 1 Pet 1:13; 1 Jn 3:2.—e Mt 15:19; Rom 1:29-30; 6:2; 1 Cor 6:18; Gal 5:19-21, 24; Eph 4:22; 5:3, 5.—f Mt 3:7; Rom 1:18.—g Eph 2:2, 11.—h Eph 4:22, 25, 31.—i Col 2:11; Rom 6:4, 6; Eph 4:22-25; Heb 12:1; 1 Pet 2:1; 4:2.—j Gen 1:26-27; Rom 6:4; 12:2; 2 Cor 4:16; Eph 2:10; 4:23.—k Rom 10:12; 1 Cor 12:13; Gal 3:27-28; Eph 1:23.—l 2 Cor 6:6; Gal 3:22-23; Eph 4:1-2, 32; Phil 2:3; 1 Thes 5:15.—m Mt 6:14; 18:21-35; Eph 4:32.—n Jn 17:23; Rom 13:8-10; 15:5; 1 Cor 13:1-13; Eph 4:3.—o Jn 14:27; Rom 12:5; 1 Cor 12:12; Eph 2:16; 4:3-4; Phil 4:7.—p Col 1:28; Rom 10:17; Eph 5:19-20.—q 1 Cor 10:31; Eph 5:20.—r 1 Cor 7:24; Eph 5:22; Tit 2:5; 1 Pet 3:1.—s Eph 4:31.—t Eph 6:1.—u Eph 6:4.—v Eph 6:5; 1 Tim 6:1; Tit 2:9-10; 1 Pet 2:18.—w Gal 1:10; 1 Thes 2:4.—x Mt 16:27; Acts 20:32; 1 Cor 7:22.—y Acts 10:34; Rom 2:11.

3:5-11 This is a Christian endeavor, something that expresses the reality of life and the transformation of Baptism, and something that enables believers to become each day a bit more what they in fact are, i.e., living members of the risen Christ. Morality is then no longer a list of recommended reactions but a thrust that opposes sin and degradation, a growth in an ever more profound affinity with the Lord. United with Christ, Christians are new persons who no longer identify themselves by cultural references or by ethical and religious differences. Union with Christ basically destroys all divisions (see Gal 3:28).

3:5, 8 See Rom 1:29-31 and Gal 5:19-21 for other lists of vices.

3:11 *Scythian:* the Scythians lived on the steppes of Asia and were regarded as barbarians par excellence.

3:12-17 The Church is a community of persons bound together by love to give testimony to love. Without ceasing, models must be invented to express this truth. As a community united with the Lord, the Church lives in peace and joy. She lives in faith and mutual pardon, and she puts forth her deepest sentiments in prayer and thanksgiving.

3:16 *Word of Christ:* principally Christ's teaching, which was transmitted orally at that time but which also includes the Old Testament and the New. *Hymns:* these set forth some of the most important doctrines and have been preserved for us only in Paul's Letters (e.g., Col 1:15-20; Eph 5:14; Phil 2:6-11; 1 Tim 3:16).

3:18—4:1 Husbands and wives, parents and children, masters and slaves were accustomed in ancient society to live in accord with links of superiority and submission. Paul does not reverse this social structure. However, neither is he content simply to enumerate the rights of husbands, parents, and masters so as to oppose them with the duties of wives, children, and slaves. He stresses a reciprocity of duties and preaches a Christian attachment—"in the Lord"—an appeal to conscience. He does not call upon slaves to revolt but gives them another way to look upon themselves—the fact that they belong to the Lord takes precedence over their dependence on their human masters. And in a near contradiction of terms, slaves are regarded as heirs of the Lord.

This short list of precepts of family morality was developed at length in the Letter to the Ephesians (5:21—6:9).

CHAPTER 4

1 Masters, be just and fair in your treat-
ment of your slaves, knowing that you too
have a Master in heaven. [z]

Assiduous Prayer.* 2 Persevere in prayer,
with alert minds and thankful hearts. [a] 3 At
the same time, pray for us too, so that God
may open a door to us to proclaim the word,
the mystery of Christ, for which I am in
prison. [b] 4 Pray that I may proclaim it as
clearly as I should.

Christian Behavior.* 5 Conduct yourselves
wisely toward outsiders, making the most of
your opportunity. [c] 6 Let your speech always
be gracious and seasoned with wisdom, so
that you will know how to respond properly
to all. [d]

V: CONCLUSION

Tychicus and Onesimus. 7 * Tychicus will
tell you all the news about me. He is a
beloved brother, a faithful minister, and a
fellow servant in the Lord. [e] 8 I am sending
him to you for this very purpose, so that
you will know how we are and that he may
cheer your hearts. [f] 9 He will be accompa-
nied by Onesimus, our trustworthy and
beloved brother, who is one of you. They
will tell you about everything that has hap-
pened here. [g]

Paul's Coworkers. 10 Aristarchus, * my fel-
low prisoner, sends you his greetings, as does
Mark, the cousin of Barnabas. (You have
received instructions about him; if he comes
to you, make him welcome.) [h] 11 And Jesus
who is called Justus also greets you. Of all
those who are of the circumcision, these are
the only ones who are working with me for
the kingdom of God, and they have been a
great comfort to me. [i]

12 Epaphras sends you greetings. He is one
of you, a servant of Christ Jesus, and he is
always pleading earnestly in his prayers on
your behalf so that you may seek perfection
and fulfill the will of God. [j] 13 I can testify for
him that he has worked tirelessly for you
and those in Laodicea and Hierapolis. * [k]
14 Luke, * the beloved physician, and Demas
send you greetings. [l]

Notes for the Laodiceans. 15 Give my greet-
ings to the brethren in Laodicea, and to
Nymphas * and the Church in her house. [m]
16 Then when this letter has been read to
you, see to it that it is also read to the
Church at Laodicea; and I ask you in turn to
read my letter that is coming from
Laodicea. [n] 17 Also tell Archippus: * "See that
you carry out fully the ministry that you
received in the Lord." [o]

Paul's Signature.* 18 I, Paul, write this
farewell in my own hand. Remember my
chains. Grace be with you. [p]

---

z Lev 25:39-42, 53.—a Col 2:7; Lk 18:1; Rom 12:12; Eph 6:18-20; 1 Thes 5:17.—b Acts 14:27; 21:33; Rom 15:30; 16:25; 1 Cor 2:12; 16:9; Eph 6:19; 2 Thes 3:1; Rev 3:8.—c Mk 4:11; Eph 5:15-16; 1 Thes 4:1, 11f.—d Mk 9:50; Eph 4:19, 29; 1 Pet 3:15.—e Col 1:7; Acts 20:4; Eph 6:21-22; Phil 1:12.—f Col 2:12; Eph 6:21-22.—g Philem 10-11, 16.—h Acts 12:12, 25; 13:13; 15:37-40; 19:29; 20:4; 27:2; Rom 10:7; 2 Tim 4:11; Philem 24; 1 Pet 5:13.—i Acts 1:23; 11:2; Phil 2:25; Philem 7.—j Col 1:7 Rom 15:30; 1 Cor 2:6; Philem 23.—k Col 2:1.—l Acts 16:21; 2 Tim 4:10-11; Philem 24.—m Col 2:1; Rom 16:5.—n 2 Thes 3:14; 1 Tim 4:13.—o 1 Tim 4:14; 2 Tim 1:6; 4:5; Philem 2.—p Acts 21:33; 1 Cor 16:21; Gal 6:11; Eph 3:1-2; 2 Thes 3:17; 1 Tim 6:21; 2 Tim 4:22; Tit 3:15; Heb 13:3, 25.

4:2-4 Prayer keeps the conscience watchful and revives the concern for the apostolate.

4:5-6 The behavior of Christians must serve as a sign to those who do not share their faith. The present period is the time of the Church, which must be regarded as a final time of grace, both short (see 1 Cor 7:29) and perilous (see Eph 5:16), in which human beings can open themselves to salvation while waiting for Christ's Second Coming (see Gal 6:10).

4:7-17 *Tychicus* is assigned to carry the Letter to the Colossians. *Onesimus,* his companion, is the slave whom Paul has converted and is now sending back to Colossae, while recommending him to his former owner (Letter to Philemon). Also named are *Mark,* who was for a short time Paul's associate in the apostolate and is generally regarded as the author of the Second Gospel; then *Luke,* to whom we owe the Third Gospel and the Book of Acts; and finally *Epaphras,* founder of the Church of Colossae. The Letter to the Laodiceans (v. 16) may be the Letter to the Ephesians, which probably circulated in the communities of the region.

4:10 *Aristarchus:* a native of Thessalonica and companion of Paul at Ephesus and on the journey to Macedonia (see Acts 19:29; 20:4).

4:13 *Hierapolis:* a town six miles from Laodicea and 14 miles from Colossae. Its Church may have been founded during Paul's stay at Ephesus (Acts 19) but probably not by Paul himself (see Col 2:1).

4:14 *Luke:* this is the only place where the author of the Third Gospel is described as a medical doctor; see Philem 24 and 2 Tim 4:11. *Demas:* a Christian who later deserted Paul (2 Tim 4:10).

4:15 *Nymphas:* probably a Laodicean in whose house Christians met for church services. The early Church had no buildings of its own and so Christians were accustomed to meeting at the homes of individuals for instruction and services, e.g., Prisca and Aquila (Rom 16:5; 1 Cor 16:19), Philemon (Philem 2), and Mary the mother of John Mark (Acts 12:12).

4:17 *Archippus:* perhaps the son of Philemon (Philem 2); he was to take care of the Church of Colossae in the absence of Epaphras.

4:18 Paul ordinarily dictated his Letters, but added to them a few words in his own hand (1 Cor 16:21; Gal 6:11; 2 Thes 3:17).

"God gave us the courage to declare the gospel of God to you" *(1 Thes 2:2)*.

THE FIRST LETTER TO THE THESSALONIANS

The Gospel of Hope

A few pages, dealing with a particular need of a young community, written in Corinth in the winter of A.D. 50-51, twenty years after Christ's Death and Resurrection: such is the first written document of Christianity.

During his Second Missionary Journey, Paul left Philippi in haste under the pressure of persecution (see Acts 16:19-40). He still showed the signs of this when he reached Thessalonica (today: Salonika), the first great European metropolis he encountered on his journey. The city was the capital of the Roman province of Macedonia and housed a great Mediterranean naval base.

The city was immense; commerce at the port was constant; ideas circulated; the teachers of thought and religion were in search of clients and their own prosperity. All this made it an important focus for missionary activity. Paul and his team spent only a short time there (from three weeks to three months—see Acts 17:2).

Paul could not but proclaim to many people the joyous message that inspired him; it was heard by a few dozen, perhaps a few hundred men and women, out of a countless population (estimated at 200,000). Persecution began (organized by a hostile Jewish population), and the Apostle's work was violently interrupted; there he was, a fugitive once again (see Acts 17:1-8). What was left of his hastily founded community? He was uneasy.

From Athens he had sent Timothy and Silas, his fellow workers, to gain information about this community now shaken by persecution. They rejoined him in Corinth, and their report was a good one. The community, which one would have thought to be so weak, was in fact growing; it was animated by an unexpected spirit of hope, faith, and love. Paul was surprised, even after fifteen years of missionary work, and gave utterance to his joy: the Gospel is God's work in the midst of a pagan world! This was the Apostle's constantly repeated experience.

In this first Letter of Paul, then, we will not look for a clear plan or lengthy trains of thought; what abound are marks of thoughtfulness and moving memories. The Letter is first of all a message of encouragement, gratitude, and affection. It is still a refreshing testimony to the birth of a community that is animated by the Gospel amid the turmoil of a great city.

Certainly, there are shadows. In a first preaching, Paul could not explain all aspects of the Christian message. And he regarded it as necessary to clarify some points that remained questionable or misunderstood.

One point especially holds his attention, for it preoccupies the new believers—the question of the parousia or Second Coming of Christ. Every one of the five chapters of the Letter ends with a reference to the Second Coming (1:9-10; 2:19-20; 3:13; 4:13-18; 5:23-24), with chapter 4 according it major consideration. Hence, the Second Coming of Christ may be regarded in some respect as the Letter's principal theme.

Among the Thessalonians, the Second Coming is thought to be imminent. Yet some believers have already died. Will they be absent from God's great convocation?

Paul's thought from this first writing is already firm. It is completely oriented toward the end of history when the dead and the living will be reunited with the risen Jesus, the universal victor, so as to live with him for eternity. The Christian hope, founded on the great event of Easter morning, will not prove deceptive. All believers will participate in Christ's triumph over evil and death.

In the Apostle's eyes, the Christian life is an active waiting for the Lord: a waiting that builds up the Church in love; a waiting that makes Christians turn their eyes to heaven, even while fully involving believers, along with all other human beings, in the realities of this world, such as marriage and work; finally, a waiting that ceaselessly strengthens fidelity to and union with the Lord. Why? Because heaven will be simply the marvelous flowering of the friendship entered into here below; we will be with the Lord forever.

Another characteristic of the Letter is Paul's affirmation of the divinity of Christ. First he links together Christ and God the Father as the common source of divine blessings and as the object of prayer (1:1; 3:11). Then he identifies Christ as "the Lord" in the Old Testament phrase "Day of the Lord" (5:2).

The First Letter to the Thessalonians may be divided as follows:

- *I: Salutation (1:1)*
- *II: Evangelization Is the Work of the Spirit (1:2—3:13)*
- *III: God Wills Your Sanctification (4:1—5:11)*
- *IV: Building Up the Community (5:12-22)*
- *V: Conclusion (5:23-28)*

CHAPTER 1

I: SALUTATION

Address and Greeting. 1 Paul, Silvanus, * and Timothy to the Church of Thessalonians in God the Father and the Lord Jesus Christ: grace to you and peace. [a]

II: EVANGELIZATION IS THE WORK OF THE SPIRIT*

A Model for All Believers.* 2 We always give thanks to God for all of you and mention you in our prayers. [b] 3 We constantly remember before our God and Father your work of faith and your labor of love and your perseverance in hope * in our Lord Jesus Christ. [c]

4 Brethren, beloved by God, we know that he has chosen you, [d] 5 because our gospel * came to you not merely in words alone but also in power and in the Holy Spirit and with profound conviction. And you are fully aware what sort of people we proved to be when we were among you for your sake. [e]

6 And you in turn became imitators * of us and of the Lord, for despite great suffering you received the word with joy in the Holy Spirit, [f] 7 so that you became a model for all the believers in Macedonia and Achaia. * [g]

8 Not only has the word of the Lord rung forth from you in Macedonia and Achaia, but also your faith in God has become known everywhere. Therefore, we do not have the need to speak about it. [h] 9 For the people themselves report what kind of reception we had from you, and how you turned to God from idols to serve the living and true God [i] 10 and await his Son from heaven whom he raised from the dead—Jesus, who will deliver us from the wrath that is to come. [j]

CHAPTER 2

Paul's Loving Treatment of the Thessalonians.* 1 You yourselves are well aware, brethren, that our visit to you has not been in vain. [k] 2 Although we had suffered and

a Acts 15:22, 40; 16:1-3, 19; 17:14-15; Rom 1:7; 2 Cor 1:19; 2 Thes 1:1-2; 1 Pet 5:12.—b Gen 43:23; 1 Mac 12:11; Mt 10:12-13; Rom 1:8; Eph 5:20; 2 Thes 1:3.—c 1 Cor 13:13; Gal 5:6; Phil 4:20; 2 Thes 1:11; Jas 2:14-26.—d Col 3:12; 2 Thes 2:13; 2 Pet 1:10.—e Acts 13:52; 17:1-9; Rom 1:16; 2 Cor 2:12; 2 Thes 2:14.—f Acts 17:5-10; 1 Cor 4:16; 2 Cor 6:10.—g 1 Thes 2:14; Acts 16:9; 1 Cor 4:16; 11:1; Phil 3:17; 2 Thes 1:4; 1 Tim 4:12.—h Rom 1:8; Col 1:6, 23; 2 Thes 3:1.—i Mt 16:16; Acts 14:15; 1 Cor 12:2; Gal 4:8.—j 1 Thes 5:9; Acts 2:24; Rom 1:18; 2:1-16; 5:9; 13:4; 1 Cor 1:7.—k 1 Thes 1:5, 9; Acts 17:2-4; 2 Thes 1:10; 3:7.

1:1 *Silvanus:* the Roman form of the Hebrew name "Silas"; this man, along with Timothy, was a fellow worker with Paul in the Macedonian apostolate (see Acts 16—18). *Church: ekklesia* in Greek, it was originally used of the People of God in the Old Testament; it designates here the Messianic gathering convoked by Jesus. The term Church is further defined as those who are "in God the Father and the Lord Jesus Christ." Being *in union* with these two persons of the Deity means a new sphere of life, on an infinitely higher plane. *Grace* and *peace:* i.e., Messianic blessings that find their basis in both persons, the Father and Jesus Christ, Lord, as the basis for the community's existence.

1:2—3:13 This is a magnificent passage in which Paul describes his experience as a missionary in an important pagan city. He has had faith in the efficacy of the Gospel and its universal power. He has not hesitated to seek out pagans, those who were once thought to be excluded from God's kingdom. The Spirit of Pentecost breathes everywhere.

1:2-10 In the announcement of the Gospel and the success of his preaching, Paul recognizes the work of the Spirit. He rejoices at the vitality of this young Church. It is God who gives her the power to break away from the pagan life. What a radical change of life conversion entails for the converts! It means turning away from idols, i.e., from all that deceives, and toward the true God to serve him and to await the coming of Jesus Christ. In this very first passage of Christian literature the three divine Persons are named; also listed are the three characteristic virtues of the Christian life: faith, hope, and love.

Behind the term *wrath* in v. 10 there is a whole theology of history (see Rom 1:18—4:25): all human beings are sinners; sin degrades and destroys the person who rejects love and justice. Punishment is a manifestation of God who judges. But by redeeming humanity from sin, Jesus has delivered it from the wrath; he takes away sin and death and gives life—this is the Christian certainty.

1:3 *Faith . . . love . . . hope:* together with 1 Thes 5:8, this is the earliest mention of the three so-called theological virtues (see 1 Cor 13:13). The accent here is on eschatological hope in accord with the Letter's emphasis on the Second Coming of Christ (see 1 Thes 1:10; 2:12, 19; 3:13; 4:13—5:11; 5:23).

1:5 *Our gospel:* this is the Gospel of God the Father (1 Thes 2:8) who originated it and of Christ (1 Thes 3:2) who brought it forth by his atoning death. Paul, Silas, and Timothy had received it through faith and preached it to others. *Power:* a power residing in the Gospel itself (see Rom 1:16) and also coming from the Holy Spirit (see Rom 15:13, 18f; 1 Cor 2:4f), which delivered the Thessalonians from spiritual bondage.

1:6 *Imitators:* all Christians are to imitate God (see Eph 5:1) and Christ (see 1 Cor 11:1) as well as their spiritual leaders (see 2 Thes 3:7, 9; 1 Tim 4:12; Tit 2:7; 1 Pet 5:3) and their fellow Christians (see 1 Thes 2:14; 1 Cor 4:6; 11:1), for all believers are one in Christ.

1:7 *In Macedonia and Achaia:* the two Roman provinces in Greece. The phrase amounts to saying "in all Greece."

2:1-12 In the quest for disciples, fame, and profit, the teachers of thought and of religion seek to found schools in this city where all currents came together at the time. Paul sketches for himself another portrait, that of messenger of Christ. Fearlessness, openness, and authenticity are the mark of the apostle seized by the Gospel. The missionary fervor takes root in God and in Jesus Christ and transforms human hearts. It then creates ties that are as strong as those of parenthood.

Paul always wanted to combine evangelization with manual work; this was doubtless to earn his own living and not be a burden on anyone, but also to reach out to human beings where they were living their lives (see Acts 20:33-35; 2 Cor 11:7-20; 12:13-18; 2 Thes 3:7-9). But he was also able to devote himself entirely to preaching (see Acts 18:3-5).

been shamefully mistreated at Philippi, as you surely recall, God gave us the courage to declare the gospel of God to you despite great opposition. [l]

[3] The exhortation we impart does not spring from deceit or impure motives or trickery. [m] [4] God has judged us worthy to be entrusted with the gospel. Therefore, when we speak, our intention is not to please human beings but to please God who tests our hearts. [n]

[5] As you are also aware, and as God is our witness, we have never resorted to flattering words or to your sense of greed. [o] [6] Neither did we seek praise from human beings, whether from you or from others. [p]

[7] As apostles of Christ, we could have imposed our will on you,* yet we were as gentle in our treatment of you as a mother nursing and caring for her own children. [q] [8] Our affection for you was so great that we were determined to share with you not only the gospel of God but also our very lives, because you had become so dear to us. [r]

[9] You surely remember, brethren, our toil and drudgery as we worked night and day so that we would not be a burden to anyone while we proclaimed the gospel of God to you. [s] [10] You are witnesses, as is God, that our treatment of you who believed has been devout, upright, and blameless. [t]

[11] As you are well aware, we treated each one of you as a father treats his children, [u] [12] urging and encouraging you and pleading with you to lead lives worthy of God who calls you into his kingdom and glory. [v]

The Word of God Is at Work.* [13] We also unceasingly give thanks to God because, when we handed on the word of God to you, you accepted it not as a human word but as what it truly is, the word of God, which is at work in you who believe. [w] [14] Indeed, brethren, you have become imitators of the Churches of God that are in Judea in Christ Jesus. For you have suffered the same treatment from your own countrymen as they did from the Jews, [x] [15] who killed both the Lord Jesus and the Prophets and also persecuted us.

They displease God and have become enemies of the entire human race [y] [16] by trying to prevent us from speaking to the Gentiles so that they may be saved. In this way, they constantly reach the full measure of their sins. The wrath of God has begun to overtake them at last. [z]

The Glory and Joy of the Apostles.* [17] Brethren, when we were separated from you for a brief time—in body but not in heart—we had an intense longing to see you again face to face. [a] [18] Therefore, we were determined to come to visit you—I, Paul, on more than one occasion—but Satan thwarted us. * [b] [19] For what is our hope or our joy or our crown of honor in the presence of our Lord Jesus upon his return? Is it not you yourselves? [c] [20] You truly are our glory and our joy. * [d]

l Acts 14:19; 16:19—17:10; Phil 1:30.—m 2 Cor 2:17; 4:2.—n Rom 2:29; Gal 1:10; 2:7; 1 Tim 1:11; Rev 2:23.—o Acts 20:33; Rom 1:9.—p Jn 5:41-44; 1 Cor 10:31; 2 Cor 4:17; 11:7-11.—q 1 Thes 2:11; Mt 18:23; 1 Cor 9:1-2, 14-15.—r Rom 1:1; 2 Cor 12:15; 1 Jn 3:16.—s Acts 18:3; 20:34; 1 Cor 4:12; 9:3-18; 2 Cor 11:9; 2 Thes 3:7-9.—t 1 Thes 1:5; Rom 1:9; 2 Cor 1:12.—u 1 Thes 2:7; Acts 20:31; 1 Cor 4:14; Gal 4:19; 1 Tim 1:2; Philem 10.—v 1 Thes 4:7; Rom 8:28; Eph 4:1; 2 Thes 2:14; 1 Pet 5:10.—w 1 Thes 1:2; Rom 1:8; Heb 4:12.—x 1 Thes 1:6; Acts 17:5; Gal 1:22; 2 Thes 1:4.—y Mt 5:12; Lk 24:20; Acts 2:23; 7:52.—z Gen 15:16; 2 Mac 6:14; Mt 23:32; Acts 13:45, 50; 17:5; Rom 1:18; 2:5-6.—a 1 Thes 3:10; Rom 1:10-11; 1 Cor 5:3; Col 2:5.—b Mt 4:10; Rom 1:13; 15:22.—c 1 Thes 3:13; Prov 16:31; Isa 62:3; Mt 16:27; Lk 17:30; 1 Cor 1:7; 4:5; 2 Cor 1:14; Phil 2:16; 4:1; Rev 1:7.—d 2 Cor 1:14.

2:7 *We could have imposed our will on you:* another possible translation is: "we could have been a burden to you." It was accepted among the early Christians that apostles are entitled to the support of the Churches (see 1 Cor 9:3-14; 2 Cor 11:7-11). Paul insisted on this right although he did not always make use of it.

2:13-16 It is the Word of God that is at work in the preaching of the apostles. Heard and accepted, then recognized as coming from God, it deploys its energy in the life of human beings. It prompts pagan converts to imitate Christ with the same ardor possessed by Christians of the mother Church of Jerusalem. Hence, the converts are not second-class believers. The beautiful title "you who believe" immediately designated those who accepted the Gospel.

We are amazed by the violent indictment leveled by Paul at his compatriots, for on several occasions he states his pride in belonging to the Jewish people (see 2 Cor 11:22; Phil 3:4-6) and proclaims his love for his racial brothers and sisters (see Rom 9:3-5; 10:2—11:2). His reaction here flows from the persecution that the Jewish colony carried out against him at each stage of his mission, whereas in his view the people of the Promise should discover in the Gospel the fulfillment of their historic mission.

Paul reprises the vehement diatribe of the Prophets against the blindness of the chosen people and calls down the wrath of God and his judgment (see 1 Thes 1:10). This threat is addressed against all who oppose the call of salvation that awaits them (see Rom 2:8) and especially against those who hinder others from responding to that call. When Paul paints a picture of the pagan life, he gives hardly more than a nuance of it. Hence, this passage cannot be used to justify any anti-Semitism (see Rom 1:18-22).

2:17-20 Paul perceives the hand of Satan—i.e., the forces hostile to God and to the fulfillment of human beings—behind everything that paralyzes his missionary action.

2:18 *But Satan thwarted us:* we do not know how this occurred. Concerning Satan as enemy of the Gospel, (see Rom 16:20; 1 Cor 7:5; 2 Cor 11:14; Eph 6:11-13; 1 Tim 3:6). Hence, he has already been defeated (see Col 2:15), and Christians should not feel overwhelmed by him (see Eph 6:16). His final overthrow is certain (Rev 20:10).

2:20 *You truly are our glory and our joy:* this is true now (see Phil 4:1) as well as at the Second Coming of the Lord.

CHAPTER 3

Standing Firm in the Lord. 1 * Therefore, when we * could not stand it any longer, we decided to remain alone in Athens. [e] 2 We sent Timothy, our brother and coworker for God * in the gospel of Christ, to confirm and encourage you in your faith, [f] 3 so that no one might be troubled by these hardships.

You yourselves realize that we were destined to endure such afflictions. [g] 4 In fact, when we were with you, we warned you beforehand that we could suffer persecution, and that is what has now come to pass, as you are well aware. [h] 5 For this reason, when I could bear it no longer, I sent to learn of your faith, lest the tempter might have put you to the test and all our labor might have been for naught. [i]

6 But Timothy has just now returned to us from you and brought us the joyful news of your faith and love. He tells us that you always speak fondly of us and long to see us just as much as we long to see you. * [j] 7 For this reason, brethren, in the midst of our distress and hardship we have been reassured by your faith. [k] 8 For now we live inasmuch as you stand firm in the Lord. [l]

Plea for Growth in Holiness. 9 How can we possibly give thanks to God for all the joy we feel in the presence of our God because of you? [m] 10 We pray fervently day and night that we will be allowed to see you face to face once again and complete whatever may be lacking in your faith. [n]

11 May our God and Father himself and our Lord Jesus prepare the way to you. [o] 12 May the Lord * cause your love to increase and overflow for one another and for everyone else, just as our love does for you. [p] 13 May he so strengthen your hearts in holiness that you may stand blameless before our God and Father at the coming of our Lord Jesus with all his holy ones. * [q] [Amen.]

III: GOD WILLS YOUR SANCTIFICATION*

CHAPTER 4

Respect for the Body.* 1 Finally, brethren, you learned from us how you ought to live so that you may be pleasing to God—and as you are indeed doing. Now we ask and exhort you in the Lord Jesus to do so even more. [r] 2 For you know what instructions we gave you by the authority of the Lord Jesus.

3 It is the will of God that you should lead a life of sanctity. You must refrain from sexual immorality. [s] 4 Each of you must learn to acquire a wife from pure and honorable motives, [t] 5 not to gratify passion * like the Gentiles who do not know God. [u] 6 No one is ever to wrong or take advantage of a brother in this regard.

As we have previously instructed you and solemnly warned you, the Lord is the avenger in all this. [v] 7 For God has called us

---

e 1 Thes 3:5; Acts 17:14-15.—f Acts 16:1-2; 1 Cor 3:5-9; 2 Cor 2:12; Phil 2:19.—g Mk 4:17; Jn 16:33; Rom 5:3; 2 Tim 3:12.—h 1 Thes 2:14; Acts 14:22; 2 Thes 2:5-7; 2 Tim 3:12.—i Mt 4:3; Gal 2:2; Phil 2:16.—j 1 Thes 1:3; 2:17-18; Acts 16:1; 18:5.—k 2 Cor 1:4; 2 Thes 1:4.—l 1 Cor 6:13; 16:13.—m 1 Thes 1:2; 2:19-20.—n 1 Thes 2:17; 2 Tim 1:3.—o Gal 1:4; Phil 4:20; 2 Thes 3:5.—p 1 Thes 4:1, 9-10; Phil 1:9; 2 Thes 1:3.—q 1 Thes 5:23; Ps 15:2; Zec 14:5; Mt 25:31; 1 Cor 1:8; Phil 2:15; 1 Tim 6:14; 2 Pet 3:14.—r 2 Cor 5:9; 13:11; Eph 4:1; Col 1:10; 2 Thes 3:1.—s Rom 6:19; 1 Cor 6:18; Eph 5:17.—t 1 Cor 7:2, 9.—u Ps 79:6; Jer 10:25; Rom 1:26; Gal 4:8; Eph 4:17; 2 Thes 1:8; 1 Pet 3:7.—v Lev 25:17; Deut 32:35; Ps 94:1; Rom 2:5-11; 1 Cor 6:8; Heb 10:30-31.

3:1-13 Persecution has ravaged the small community. Sent to these new Christians, Timothy reassures Paul. In the Apostle's thanksgiving and in his prayer for the continual progress of the community, we divine his deep attachment for Christians that he has evangelized. The missionary's action must be pervaded by prayer—both private and liturgical.

3:1 *We:* in this First Letter Paul uses the first person plural extensively. That is not true of the later letters.

3:2 *Coworker for God:* see also 1 Cor 3:9. *Gospel of Christ:* see notes on 1 Thes 1:5 and Mk 1:1. *Confirm:* literally, "build you up."

3:6 Paul is rendered joyful because of their "faith" (i.e., their right attitude toward God), their "love" (i.e., their right attitude toward others), and their longing "to see" him (i.e., their right attitude toward the Apostle).

3:12 *Lord:* in Paul's usage this word is usually applied to Jesus, not the Father (see, e.g., Rom 10:9; 1 Cor 1:2; Phil 2:11).

3:13 *Holy ones:* usually translated as "saints," referring to all Christians.

4:1—5:11 Conversion to Christ involves a total rejection of the values and the way of life that one previously led. Speaking of sanctification and holiness in Biblical language, we are conscious of being in the presence of the Lord. This gives new value to the destiny, action, and relationships of human beings—nothing is any longer lost in insignificance. In his correspondence, Paul always underlines some important traits for one's way of life, in keeping with the needs of the community. He does so usually by way of a warm exhortation, but sometimes also by way of a warning. The Christian life is a journey toward a goal: union with God in Christ.

4:1-8 In the language of the period, two interpretations are possible: that each person should take a spouse in order to live honorably (see 1 Cor 7:2); or that each should exercise self-control and self-respect. In either case, and in light of the dissolute morals of the period, the affirmation of marriage and of sexual morality was a rejection of a meaningless and sordid existence. Paul has a high idea of human beings, for he views them in the call of God addressed to him. The effort of Christians arises from living ties with the divine Persons.

4:5 *Acquire a wife . . . gratify passion:* another possible translation is: "control your own body in a way that is holy and honorable and not to succumb to lustful passion."

to holiness, not to impurity.[w] 8 Therefore,
anyone who rejects these instructions*
rejects not human authority but the God
who also gives his Holy Spirit to you.[x]

An Honorable Life.* 9 In respect to brother-
ly love, there is no necessity to write to you
about that, for you yourselves have been
taught by God to love one another.[y] 10 And
indeed you have shown your love to all the
brethren throughout Macedonia. However,
we urge you, brethren, to make even greater
progress in this regard.[z]

11 Strive to live quietly, to attend to your
own affairs, and to work with your hands, as
we instructed you.*[a] 12 In this way, you will
earn the respect of outsiders and not have to
be dependent on anyone.[b]

The Dead and the Living at the Lord's Coming.* 13 We do not wish you to be uncer-
tain, brethren, about those who have fallen
asleep.* You should not grieve as do those
who have no hope.[c] 14 For we believe that
Jesus died and rose again, and so too do we
believe that God will bring forth with Jesus
those who have fallen asleep in him.[d]

15 Indeed, we can assure you, on the word
of the Lord himself, that we who are still
alive at the coming of the Lord will not have
any advantage over those who have fallen
asleep.*[e] 16 When the command is given, at
the sound of the archangel's voice and the
call of God's trumpet, the Lord himself will
descend from heaven, and those who have
died in Christ will be the first to rise.[f]

17 Then those of us who are still alive and
are left will be caught up* together with
them on clouds in the air to meet the Lord.
And so, we will be with the Lord forever.[g]
18 Therefore, comfort one another* with
these words.[h]

CHAPTER 5

The Christian Life Is One Long Vigil.* 1 In
regard to specific dates and times,*
brethren, it is not necessary to write you.[i]
2 For you yourselves are fully aware that
the Day of the Lord* will come like a thief

w Lev 11:44; 1 Pet 1:15.—x Ezek 36:27; Lk 10:16; Rom 5:5; 2 Cor 1:22; Gal 4:6.—y 1 Thes 5:1; Jn 6:45; 13:34; Rom 12:10; 1 Jn 2:20-21, 27; 4:7.—z 1 Thes 3:12; Acts 16:9; 2 Thes 3:6-12.—a Eph 4:28; 2 Thes 3:10-12.—b Mk 4:11; Col 4:5.—c Mt 9:24; Rom 11:25; Eph 2:12.—d Rom 14:9; 1 Cor 15:3-4, 12, 20; 2 Cor 5:15.—e 1 Cor 1:7; 7:10, 25; 15:51; Rev 14:13; 20:4-6.—f Mt 16:27; 24:31; 1 Cor 15:23, 52; 2 Thes 2:1; Jude 9; Rev 14:13.—g Jn 12:26; Acts 1:9; 8:39; 1 Cor 15:52; Rev 1:7; 11:12.—h 1 Thes 5:11.—i 1 Thes 4:9; Mt 24:36-45; Acts 1:7.

4:8 *Instructions:* this word does not necessarily refer to the sayings of Jesus but rather to guidelines set forth in the Holy Spirit.

4:9-12 God pours the Spirit into the hearts of believers and that Spirit guides them in God's ways. However, other questions remain: certain Christians, awaiting the imminent coming of the Lord, experience a crisis of laziness (see 2 Thes 3:6-12); they must be seriously reminded of the personal and social life, without which love is but a futile word.

4:11 The early Church strongly believed in the need of Christians to earn their living. However, some of the converts—possibly as a result of their belief in Christ's imminent return (see 2 Thes 3:11)—were not working and so were letting others support them.

4:13-18 We are now at the heart of the Letter. Some Christians of Thessalonica have a few difficulties. One or other believer has died, and they cannot shake the image of those beautiful cemeteries built at the edge of cities like "high places" of despair. Christ must appear; this definitive coming mobilizes the hope of all; but will not Christians who have died be deprived of this grand and triumphant coming?

In speaking of this resurrection, Paul uses the images and symbols of the Jewish apocalypses, just as in describing the return of Christ he compares it to the "parousias" or official visits of the emperors to the great cities, where the people escorted them in a lengthy procession. The scene has its grandeur, but the essential is to be found elsewhere: the solid conviction of believers that they are with Christ forever. These words sum up the final message of Christian hope.

4:13 *Those who have fallen asleep:* sleep was an especially apt metaphor for death, since the finality and horror of death disappear in the assurance of the resurrection.

4:15 Here Paul seems to be hoping that the parousia would take place within his own lifetime. We can say that while entertaining the possibility of his own death (see 2 Tim 4:6-8) and not wanting to go against Christ's teaching about the date of the parousia (see Mt 24:48; 25:5; Lk 19:11-27), Paul (and all the first Christians) reckoned on the prospect of remaining alive until Christ's return (Rom 13:11; 1 Cor 7:26, 29; 10:11; 15:51-52; 16:22; Phil 4:5). *The word of the Lord:* this may refer to a special revelation or simply be a general reference to the teachings of Jesus.

4:17 *Will be caught up:* literally, "will be carried away," which in the Vulgate is translated by *rapiemur.* This Latin word has given birth to the idea of the "Rapture," i.e., that believers will be carried away from the troubles of this world. It simply means that those who are alive on the Last Day will not have to die; they will be transformed.

4:18 *Comfort one another:* vv. 13-18 are not primarily intended to provide a chronology of future events but rather to urge the Thessalonians to comfort one another.

5:1-11 The Old Testament announced unceasingly the Day of Yahweh, which would be one of judgment, liberation, gathering of the people, and sometimes of all humankind (see Am 5:18-20). The image is taken over by Christians. In this framework, Paul reprises the teaching of Christ. God alone is the master of time, but human beings must keep vigil in the expectation of God (see Mt 24:36-44; Lk 17:26-37; 21:34-36; Acts 1:7).

Indeed, there is a greater difference between being a Christian and not being one than between day and night. Christians are those who can see clearly, even in the daily conduct of their existence. The Gospel of Jesus, light of the world, becomes in the very practice of life a new way of seeing that goes to the heart of the real and of human destiny.

5:1 *Dates and times:* a well-known phrase describing the end time (see Acts 1:16f). Apparently, the Thessalonians had already been instructed about the basic features of the Second Coming when Paul had visited them.

5:2 *Day of the Lord:* the Old Testament uses this phrase as a time of God's judgment (see Isa 2:12-21; Joel 2:1, 11; Am 5:18; Zep 1:7, 14; Mal 3:23-24) but also of his blessing (see Am 5:18ff; Isa 13; Joel 3:4; 4:16-20). The New Testament uses the phrase in other same sense (see Rom 2:5; 2 Pet 2:9) but also utilizes it in other ways: e.g., the "day of redemption" (Eph 4:30); the "Day of God" (2 Pet 3:12) or "of Christ" (1 Cor 1:8; Phil 1:6); and "that Day" (2 Thes 1:10). That *Day* is the culmination of all things prefigured by signs (see 2 Thes 2:3), but its coming will be like a thief in the night (see Mt 24:43f; Lk 12:39f; 2 Pet 3:10; Rev 3:3; 16:15).

in the night.[j] 3 When people are saying,
"Everything is peaceful and secure,"
instant destruction * will overwhelm them,
in the manner that labor pains suddenly
come upon a pregnant woman, and there
will be no means of escape.[k]

4 However, brethren, you do not live in
darkness, and therefore that Day will not
catch you unawares like a thief.[l] 5 For all of
you are children of the light * and children
of the day. We do not belong to the night or
to the darkness.[m] 6 So we must not fall
asleep as the others do, but we must stay
alert and sober.[n]

7 Those who sleep do so at night, and
those who get drunk do so at night.[o] 8 But
since we belong to the day, let us be sober,
arming ourselves with faith and love as our
breastplate and the hope of salvation as
our helmet. *[p] 9 * For God has not destined
us to suffer wrath, but to achieve salvation
through our Lord Jesus Christ.[q] 10 He died
for us so that, whether we are awake or
asleep, we may live together with him.[r]
11 Therefore, encourage one another and
strengthen one another, as indeed you are
doing.[s]

IV: BUILDING UP THE COMMUNITY*

Show Respect for Leaders. 12 * Brethren, we
beg you to respect those whose duty it is to
labor among you as your leaders in the Lord
and to admonish you.[t] 13 Show the highest
esteem for them in love because of their
work. Be at peace with one another.[u]

14 * We also exhort you, brethren, to
admonish those who are idle, encourage
those who are afraid, support those who are
weak, and be patient with everybody.[v]
15 Make sure that no one pays back evil for
evil. Rather, always aim to achieve what is
best for each other and for everyone.[w]

16 * Rejoice always;[x] 17 pray continually;[y]
18 give thanks in all circumstances; for this is
the will of God for you in Christ Jesus.[z]

Do Not Extinguish the Spirit.* 19 Do not
quench the Spirit.[a] 20 Do not despise
prophecies. *[b] 21 Test everything, and hold
fast to what is good.[c] 22 Avoid every form of
evil.[d]

j Lk 12:39; 2 Cor 1:8; 2 Pet 3:10.—k Job 15:21; Isa 29:5; Jer 4:10; 6:14; Ezek 13:10.—l Acts 26:18; Eph 5:8-9; 1 Jn 2:8.—m Lk 16:8; Eph 5:8; Phil 2:15.—n Mt 24:42; 25:13; Acts 24:25; Rom 13:12-13; 1 Pet 5:8.—o Acts 2:15; Rom 13:13; 2 Pet 2:13.—p Isa 59:17; Rom 8:24; 13:11-14; Eph 6:11, 14-17.—q 1 Thes 1:10; 2 Thes 2:13-14; Heb 10:39.—r Rom 6:11; 14:9; 2 Cor 5:15; 2 Tim 2:11.—s 1 Thes 1:7; 4:18; Rom 15:2; 1 Cor 8:13; 14:12, 26; Eph 4:29.—t Rom 16:6, 12; 1 Cor 15:10; 1 Tim 5:17; Heb 13:17.—u Mk 9:50; Rom 12:18; 14:19.—v Rom 14:1; 1 Cor 8:7-12; 2 Thes 3:6, 7, 11.—w Prov 20:22; Mt 5:38-42; Rom 12:17; Eph 4:32; 1 Pet 3:9.—x Phil 4:4.—y Lk 18:1; Rom 12:2.—z Eph 5:20; Col 4:2.—a Mt 12:20; 1 Cor 14:39; Eph 4:30.—b 1 Cor 14:1-40.—c Job 34:4; Rom 12:9; 1 Cor 14:29; 1 Jn 4:1.—d 2 Mac 6:21.

5:3 *Destruction:* this does not mean annihilation but exclusion from the presence of the Lord (see 2 Thes 1:9), i.e., ruination of one's life and accomplishments. And it will be a ruin that occurs in an instant. *Labor pains:* the stress here is not on the pains so much as their suddenness and inevitability. *No means of escape:* literally, "They will not escape."

5:5 *Children of the light:* in Semitic languages, to be "children of [something]" meant to be characterized by it. Christians not only live in the light but are characterized by light.

5:8 Paul makes use of a metaphor of armor that he also utilizes in Rom 13:12; 2 Cor 6:7; 10:4; and Eph 6:13-17. However, he does not affix a particular virtue to the same piece of armor.

5:9-10 These verses provide a summary of the primitive preaching, which was wholly focused on the deliverance of humanity in Jesus Christ and on a life in union with him. *Whether we are awake or asleep:* i.e., whether we are alive or dead.

5:12-22 In this section Paul gives brief but cogent instructions in building a community. He especially lists the responsibilities of Christians toward leaders (vv. 12-13), toward all (vv. 14-15), toward themselves (vv. 16-18), and toward public worship (vv. 19-22).

5:12-13 Christians must show respect for their leaders, just as those same leaders must show caring leadership for their people. The leaders were undoubtedly the "bishops" and "presbyters" of 1 Tim 3:1-2; 5:17; Tit 1:5. Christians must hold these leaders in the highest esteem and render them wholehearted support in a spirit of love.

5:14-15 Christians must warn the recalcitrant, such as those who are lazy and do not pull their weight at Thessalonica. They must also encourage the fainthearted, like those troubled about their friends who had died before the Second Coming of Christ (1 Thes 4:13) and confused about what that event meant for themselves (1 Thes 5:1-11). They must also help those afflicted with moral or spiritual weakness in the face of persecution (1 Thes 3:3-5) or temptation (1 Thes 4:3-8) or the like. Finally, they should show patience with everyone. Above all, they should never pay back evil for evil in accord with the words of Christ (see Mt 5:38-42).

5:16-18 In order to carry out the regulations given in vv. 12-15, Christians need personal communion with God. They are to be joyful always (see Mt 5:11-12; Acts 5:41; 16:25; Phil 1:18; 4:4). Indeed, they are to be "sorrowful, and yet . . . always rejoicing" (2 Cor 6:10). However, this Christian joy does not depend on earthly circumstances or feelings. It stems from what Jesus has done for us supernaturally, which never goes away.

At the same time, Christians are to be constant in prayer. It is vital for them to lift the heart to God while being occupied with their duties. Concerning prayer, see 1 Thes 1:3; 2:13; Rom 1:9-10; Eph 6:18; Col 1:3; 2 Tim 1:3.

Finally, Christians are to give thanks in all circumstances. Regardless of their human situation, they know that God has called them to eternal salvation and gives them the grace to attain it. Therefore, no matter what the circumstances may be, they can remain in a state of thankfulness (see Eph 5:20).

5:19-22 Paul now speaks about the responsibilities in communal worship. Christians must never extinguish the Spirit (v. 19). He is probably referring to curbing the charisms in any way. Guiding the charisms is necessary, but overcontrol is detrimental. In particular, the gift of prophecy must be esteemed properly and all charismatic manifestations must be duly tested. Any evil that tries to mask itself as a genuine representation of the Spirit must be discarded. Only then can worship be true.

5:20 *Prophecies:* the reference is not to the Old Testament Prophets but to those who exhorted the Christian communities (see 1 Cor 12:10-29; 13:2; 14:3).

V: CONCLUSION*

Final Prayer. 23 May the God of peace himself grant you the gift of perfect sanctity, and may you—spirit and soul and body*—be preserved blameless for the coming of our Lord Jesus Christ.[e] 24 The one who calls you is faithful, and he will accomplish this.[f]

Final Greeting. 25 Pray for us, brethren.[g] 26 Greet all the brethren with a holy kiss.[h] 27 I charge you before the Lord to have this letter read to all the brethren.[i]

28 The grace of our Lord Jesus Christ be with you.[j]

e 1 Thes 2:19; 3:13; Rom 15:33; 2 Thes 3:16; Tit 2:12; Heb 4:12; 2 Pet 3:14.—f Num 23:19; Rom 8:28; 1 Cor 1:9; Phil 1:6; 2 Thes 3:3.—g Eph 6:19; Col 4:3; 2 Thes 3:1.—h Rom 16:16.—i Col 4:16; 2 Thes 3:14; 1 Tim 4:13.—j Rom 16:20.

5:23-28 This Letter concludes like a liturgy: blessing, kiss of peace, request to have the apostolic Letter read publicly, and final wish.

5:23 *Spirit and soul and body:* i.e., the whole Christian person. The spirit is that which is open to the influence of grace; it is also the source of divine life with the Christian (see Rom 5:5). This is the only place in Paul that refers to this tripartite division.

THE SECOND LETTER TO THE THESSALONIANS

Christian Realism

Paul's First Letter to the Thessalonians was so clear and encouraging that it sufficed to reassure the community as a whole. However, persecution continued to afflict the new believers. Naturally, then, the thought arose in the minds of some of them: was this the necessary and immediate prelude to the end of time? Indeed, whatever the reason, the expectation of the Lord was passing through a serious crisis. Some, belonging perhaps to the lazy folk to whom Paul has alluded earlier (1 Thes 4:11; 5:14), claimed that the Day of the Lord was imminent. They caused a kind of panic or feverish expectation.

At the same time, they no longer engaged in work but roamed around as beggars and thus became an embarrassment to the community (2 Thes 3:6-15). They even seem to have circulated spurious letters for the purpose of authenticating their ideas, or at least Paul thinks that they did (2 Thes 2:2), and he attaches his genuine signature to the present Letter (2 Thes 3:17).

To counter their teaching and cut short any type of undisciplined straying, Paul dictated this Second Letter to the Thessalonians. He seems to have written it from Corinth in the year A.D. 51. He first had to correct the doctrinal error of those who were convinced of the imminence of the Second Coming (2 Thes 2:1-12), then the practical error to which these same believers were led: they were overly anxious to rid themselves of earthly things and to neglect their duties (2 Thes 2:13—3:15).

The Apostle shows that it is not by abandoning the world but by courageously facing up to it that Christians make their way to the Lord and are a sign to those who do not share their faith. They must put aside every type of bizarre speculation and evasion and instead pitch in to build the future in the journey toward God.

This Letter remains a lesson in realism for Christians at the very moment when the Church found herself buffeted by the crisis of a civilization, and it offers us a dramatic vision of human history.

Some scholars have questioned Paul's authorship of the Letter because of close similarities in subject matter and phrasing. Yet who but Paul could sound more like himself!

Others see contradictory ecclesiologies (teachings about the end time) in the two Letters. They claim the First Letter speaks of an imminent return of Christ while the Second indicates that before Christ comes there are certain events that must take place.

However, the First Letter does not rule out intervening events but merely mentions the unexpected character of the Second Coming. The intervening events mentioned in Second Thessalonians can fit nicely into the previous teaching, and at the same time they rebut the new misunderstanding at Thessalonica that the Day of the Lord had already come.

The Second Letter to the Thessalonians may be divided as follows:

I: Salutation (1:1-2)

II: Perseverance in Faith (1:3-12)

III: The Day of the Lord (2:1-12)

IV: Never Weary of Doing Good (2:13—3:15)

V: Conclusion (3:16-18)

CHAPTER 1

I: SALUTATION*

Address and Greeting. 1 Paul, Silvanus, and Timothy to the Church of Thessalonians in God our Father and the Lord Jesus Christ: [a]
2 Grace to you and peace from God our Father and the Lord Jesus Christ. [b]

II: PERSEVERANCE IN FAITH*

A Word of Praise. 3 Brethren, we must always give thanks to God for you, and it is only right that we do so. For your faith grows ever more, and the love that all of you have for one another continues to increase. [c]
4 Therefore, we boast incessantly of you to the Churches of God for your steadfastness and faith despite all the persecutions and tribulations that you have had to endure. [d]

Judgment and the Coming of the Lord. 5 All this is proof of God's just judgment, and it shows that you are worthy of the kingdom of God, for the sake of which you are suffering. [e] 6 It is only just that God will repay with suffering those who make you suffer [f] 7 and grant relief to you who are suffering, and to us as well. This will take place when the Lord Jesus is revealed from heaven with his mighty angels. [g]

8 He will come in blazing fire to inflict punishment on those who do not know God and do not obey the gospel of our Lord Jesus. [h]
9 They will suffer the penalty of eternal destruction, excluded from the presence of the Lord and from the majesty of his power [i]
10 on that Day when he comes to be glorified by his holy ones and to be adored by all believers, among whom you will be present since you believed the testimony we offered to you. [j]

Prayer for the Community. 11 Therefore, we always pray for you, asking that our God will make you worthy of his call and by his power bring to fulfillment every good resolve and every work of faith. [k] 12 In this way, the name of our Lord Jesus may be glorified in you, and you in him, according to the grace of our God and Lord Jesus Christ. * [l]

a Acts 15:22; 16:1; 17:1; 1 Thes 1:1.—b Rom 1:7.—c Rom 1:8; 1 Cor 1:4; Eph 5:20; 1 Thes 1:2-3, 12.—d 2 Cor 7:14; 1 Thes 1:3, 6; 2:14.—e Mt 22:8; Lk 20:35; 21:30; Acts 5:41; Phil 1:28; 1 Thes 2:12.—f Lk 18:7-8; Rom 12:19; Col 3:25; Rev 6:10.—g Lk 17:30; Heb 10:27; 2 Pet 3:7; Rev 1:14.—h Ps 79:5-6; Isa 66:15; Jer 10:25; Rom 2:8; 2 Cor 2:12; Gal 4:8.—i 2 Thes 2:8; Isa 2:10, 19, 21; Phil 3:19; 1 Thes 5:3.—j Ps 89:8; Dan 7:18-22, 27; Jn 17:10; 1 Cor 3:13; 1 Thes 3:13.—k Rom 1:10; 8:28; 1 Thes 1:2-3.—l Isa 24:15; 66:5; Phil 2:9, 11.

1:1-2 The salutation is identical to that of First Thessalonians (1:1) except for two additions: (1) God is called "our" Father (v. 1), the Father of Christians—his Fatherhood of Jesus is expressed in other Letters (e.g., 2 Cor 1:3; Eph 1:3; 1 Pet 1:3). (2) The phrase "from God our Father and the Lord Jesus Christ" is added to v. 2 to identify the sources of "grace and peace." Paul regards Jesus as the Deity *in the fullest sense* since he names him on a par with the Father as coauthor of the favor and the relationship promised in the blessing.

1:3-12 Paul thanks God for the progress made by his valiant community in their faith, love, courage, and good name. All this will be manifested and judged at the Lord's Coming, which Paul describes once more by utilizing the dramatic scenario current among the Jews of his day. Woe to those who oppose God, for they will be immediately distanced from the Lord. But what glory there will be for those who believe!

The concept of revelation, or apocalypse, that emerges in this passage represents an essential idea of the Old and New Testaments: our religion is, above all else, something that precedes and transcends time. In history God is constantly manifesting himself as the Savior of humanity. To illustrate it, one can have recourse to the grand imaginative visions of the judgments set forth in Isa 24—27; Dan 7—12; Mt 24—25; Mk 13; and Lk 17:22-37; 19:11-27; see also introduction to the Book of Revelation.

1:12 *The grace of our God and Lord Jesus Christ:* another translation possible is: "The grace of our God and of the Lord Jesus Christ."

CHAPTER 2

III: THE DAY OF THE LORD*

Has the Day of the Lord Already Come?* 1 As to the coming of our Lord Jesus Christ and our being gathered to him, we beg you, brethren:[m] 2 do not become too easily thrown into confusion or alarmed, either by something spiritual or by a statement or by a letter claiming to come from us, alleging that the Day of the Lord is already here.*[n] 3 Let no one deceive you in any way.

The Adversary and the Obstacle.* That Day cannot come* before the final rebellion occurs and the lawless one is revealed, the son of destruction.[o] 4 He is the adversary who sets himself in opposition to, and exalts himself above, every so-called god or object of worship, and who even seats himself in the temple of God, declaring himself to be God.[p]

5 Do you not remember that I told you these things when I was still with you?[q] 6 And you also know what is now restraining him,* so that he may not be revealed before his time comes.[r] 7 For the mystery of lawlessness is already at work, but the one who restrains it will continue to do so until he is removed.[s]

The Two Comings.* 8 Then the lawless one will be revealed, and the Lord Jesus will slay him by the breath of his mouth and destroy him by the splendor of his coming.[t]

9 His coming will be the work of Satan made manifest in all power and signs and wonders of falsehood,[u] 10 and in every wicked deception designed for those who are perishing because they refused to accept the love of the truth* and thereby gain salvation.[v]

11 For this reason, God imposes on them a powerful delusion. They believe what is false,[w] 12 so that all who have not believed the truth but instead have taken pleasure in wickedness will be condemned.[x]

IV: NEVER WEARY OF DOING GOOD*

Call To Remain Steadfast. 13 *However, we must always give thanks to God for you,

m Mk 13:27; 1 Thes 2:19; 4:13-17.—n 2 Thes 3:17; Mt 24:6; 1 Cor 1:8; 14:26, 32-33; 1 Thes 5:1-2; 2 Tim 2:18.—o Mt 24:10, 12; Mk 13:5; Rev 13:5-6.—p Isa 14:13-14; Ezek 28:2; Dan 11:36-37; 1 Cor 8:5.—q 1 Thes 3:4.—r 2 Thes 2:7.—s 2 Thes 2:6; Mt 13:36-43; Acts 20:29; Gal 5:10; 2 Pet 2:1; Rev 22:11.—t Job 4:9; Isa 11:4; Lk 17:30; Rev 2:16; 19:15.—u Mt 4:10; 24:24; Jn 4:48; Rev 13:13.—v Prov 4:6; Jn 3:17, 19; 1 Cor 1:18.—w Mt 24:5; Mk 13:5; Rom 1:28.—x 2 Thes 1:3; Rom 1:32; 2:8; 1 Thes 1:2-4.

2:1-12 Paul uses the style and manner of apocalypses, but he speaks first and foremost as an apostle. He employs images and symbols to express where he is going and where he is leading the faithful. From the very beginning of Biblical history, God and Satan (i.e., the forces of evil) are involved in an implacable combat in which human beings are at the same time the terrain and the stakes. Christ is the conqueror of these evil forces. His victory, obtained on the cross, will be manifested on the great Day of his majestic return. We must prepare for this Coming.

2:1-3a Paul indicates that a problem has arisen concerning the circumstances surrounding the Day of the Lord. In times of crisis, there are always falsehood-mongers to whom the faithful give willing ear—but whom they should avoid altogether. So the Apostle intends to set forth certain features of the Day in order to correct what is being falsely claimed.

2:2 *Is already here:* Paul insists that the Day of the Lord has not already come, for the final days have not begun and their completion is not imminent.

2:3b-12 Making use of images borrowed from the Prophets and from the authors of apocalypses, Paul brings on stage the forces of evil and the true witnesses of God: they constitute respectively the adversary and the obstacle. The portrait of the adversary gathers together in one personage all the doers of evil who are based on the historical enemies of God's people in the Old Testament—especially Antiochus IV Epiphanes (see Dan 11:36) who in his supreme folly wanted to make himself a god.

The obstacle, which was doubtlessly well known to the Thessalonians, stands for a more obscure reality for us; it could refer to the ensemble of believers who work to bring about the Kingdom of God (see also note on 2:6 below). Even though their victory is to be awaited, it is no less assured. This victory is based upon the Paschal Mystery with its twofold aspect of Death and Resurrection. Throughout the centuries, the forces of death and the People of God never cease to confront one another in the life of the world, in the heart of each person.

2:3b-4 *That Day cannot come:* these words have been supplied in the text in order to bring out more clearly Paul's meaning; the original sentence is incomplete. *The lawless one . . . the son of destruction . . . the adversary:* the leader of the rebellion, who will also come to be called "the Antichrist" (1 Jn 2:18; 4:3; 2 Jn 7).

2:6 *What is now restraining him:* some suggestions about the identity of this obstacle (in addition to the one mentioned in note 2:3b-12 above) are: the Roman State and its emperor; the principle of law embodied in the state; the Holy Spirit through the Church; and the preaching of the Gospel (possibly by Paul himself), for the end could not come until the Gospel was preached to all nations (see Mk 13:10).

2:8-12 Paul describes what will precede the Lord's coming. He glimpses, toward the end of human history, a spectacular offensive launched by the forces of evil under the instigation of Satan. A great apostasy will follow (see Mt 24:10-12; Lk 18:8; 21:12-19; 1 Tim 4:1). *The lawless one* is both anti-God and anti-Christ, but he will not have the last word. On the day, when he thinks he has conquered, he will be confronted with the dazzling manifestation of Christ and completely overcome.

2:10 *Love of the truth:* one of Paul's most felicitous expressions, it refers to love of the Gospel, the acceptance of this unprecedented gift that comes from the Father, Christ, and the Spirit. To refuse it is to exclude oneself from love forever.

2:13—3:15 Paul is thankful that he and his coworkers can look forward to salvation for themselves and for their converts. The beneficiaries of God's saving work cannot rest on their laurels, however. They must be ever active in good works and keep the teachings (traditions) of the Church. The Apostle goes on to ask the converts to pray for him and his coworkers and calls down God's grace on them.

He also sets forth the proper solution for idlers. The Thessalonians must admonish idlers yet deal charitably with their mistakes. Such persons are not to be cast out of the community, but to be given frequent warnings.

2:13—3:5 Here we find the same advice as was given in the First Letter. Christian life unfolds in the love of the three divine Persons; fidelity to the authentic tradition that the apostles have transmitted in writing or by living word; prayer; and constancy of effort.

brethren beloved by the Lord, because God chose you from the beginning to be saved through sanctification by the Spirit and through belief in the truth.*[y] 14 It was for this purpose that he called you through our gospel so that you might come to share in the glory of our Lord Jesus Christ.[z]

15 Therefore, stand firm, brethren, and hold fast to the traditions* that you have been taught, whether by word of mouth or by a letter of ours.[a] 16 And may our Lord Jesus Christ himself and God our Father, who loved us and through his grace gave us unending encouragement and a sure hope,*[b] 17 comfort your hearts and strengthen you in every good deed and word.[c]

CHAPTER 3

Request for Prayers. 1 Finally, brethren, pray for us, so that the word of the Lord may spread rapidly and be glorified, as it was with you.[d] 2 Pray too that we may be rescued from wicked and evil people, for not all have faith.[e]

3 However, the Lord is faithful. He will strengthen you and protect you from the evil one.[f] 4 And we are confident in the Lord that you are doing and will continue to do all that we direct you to do.[g] 5 May the Lord guide your hearts to the love of God and the steadfastness of Christ.[h]

Christian Value of Work.* 6 In the name of our Lord Jesus Christ, brethren, we command you to keep your distance from any of the brethren who are living an idle existence and who disregard the tradition you received from us.[i] 7 For you yourselves know how you should follow our example. We were not idle when we were with you.[j] 8 We did not ever accept food from anyone, but with toil and drudgery we worked night and day so that we would not burden any of you.[k] 9 We did so, not because we have no right to accept such help, but to present ourselves as a model for you to imitate.[l]

10 In fact, even when we were with you, we charged that anyone who was unwilling to work should not eat.[m] 11 Now we have been told that some among you are living a life of idleness, not working but acting as busybodies.[n] 12 We command and urge such people in the name of the Lord Jesus Christ to do their work quietly and earn their own living.[o]

13 Brethren, never grow weary of doing what is right.[p] 14 If anyone refuses to obey our instructions in this letter, take note of him and have nothing to do with him so that he may be put to shame.[q] 15 However, do not treat him as an enemy, but admonish him as a brother.[r]

V: CONCLUSION*

Final Prayer. 16 May the Lord of peace himself give you peace at all times and in every way. The Lord be with all of you.[s]

Final Blessing. 17 I, Paul, write this greeting in my own hand. It is the distinguishing mark of every letter of mine.[t] 18 The grace of our Lord Jesus Christ be with you all.[u]

---

y Rom 1:8; Eph 1:4; 1 Thes 2:13; 5:9; 1 Pet 1:2.—z 2 Thes 3:6; Rom 5:1-10; 8:29-30; 1 Cor 10:13; 1 Thes 1:5; 4:7; 5:9.—a 1 Cor 11:2; 16:13; 1 Jn 4:10; Rev 1:5.—b Jn 3:16; Phil 4:20; 1 Pet 5:10.—c 2 Thes 3:3; 1 Thes 3:2.—d Eph 6:19; Col 4:3; 1 Thes 4:1; 5:25.—e Rom 15:31.—f Mt 5:37; 6:13; 1 Cor 1:9; 16:13; 1 Thes 5:24.—g 2 Cor 2:3; 7:16; 1 Thes 4:1-2.—h 1 Chr 29:18.—i Rom 16:17; 1 Cor 5:4; 11:2.—j 1 Cor 4:16; 1 Thes 1:6; 5:14.—k Acts 18:3; Eph 4:28; 1 Thes 2:9.—l Mt 10:10; 1 Cor 4:16; 9:4-14; Phil 3:17.—m Gen 3:19; 1 Thes 3:4; 4:11.—n 1 Thes 5:14; 1 Tim 5:13; 1 Pet 4:15.—o Eph 4:28; 1 Thes 4:1, 11.—p 1 Cor 15:58; Gal 6:9-10.—q Rom 16:17; 1 Cor 4:14.—r 2 Cor 2:7; Gal 6:1; 1 Thes 5:14; Philem 16.—s Jn 14:27; Rom 2:4; 15:33; Eph 6:23; 1 Thes 5:25.—t 2 Thes 2:2; 1 Cor 16:21; Gal 6:11.—u Rom 16:20.

2:13-14 These two verses show the harmonious working of all three Persons of the Trinity in the divine plan of salvation: God the Father chooses and calls his people; God the Son shares his glory with his own; and God the Holy Spirit imparts his sanctifying grace. *From the beginning:* another translation possible is: "as the firstfruits."

2:15 *Traditions:* i.e., the teachings contained in tradition; they are both oral and written (see 2 Thes 2:5; 3:6; 1 Cor 11:2), just as was the case with rabbinic law (see note on Mt 15:2ff).

2:16 Jesus is here named before the Father; despite the double subject, the verbs in the Greek text are in the singular number. Could the unity of Father and Son be better expressed?

3:6-15 In putting work at the service of the community, Paul places it under the sign of love for God, for one's brothers and sisters, and for the Church. To eat one's own bread constitutes the primary dignity of a person (v. 10). By demanding exemplary conduct from Christians, Paul remains in line with Jesus and the primitive Church (see Mt 18:15-18; 1 Cor 5:1-13).

3:16-18 In order to discourage forgeries of his letters (see 2 Thes 2:2), Paul takes care to authenticate the letters that he dictates and causes to be set down—he writes out a few words with his own hand (see also 1 Cor 16:21 and Col 4:18). In the cases of Galatians and Philemon, it appears that Paul wrote more than just the concluding phrases (see Gal 6:11 and Philem 19).

"As for you, man of God, . . . pursue righteousness, godliness, faith, love, fortitude, and gentleness" *(1 Tim 6:11).*

THE FIRST LETTER TO TIMOTHY

Guidelines for Pastors of the Church

The Letters to Timothy and Titus form a group apart in the literature attributed to Paul. They are addressed not to communities but to individuals, Timothy and Titus, that is, men who were responsible for the government, instruction, and behavior of communities. Because the Letters give guidelines for pastors of the Church, they are called the Pastoral Letters.

A very ancient tradition has placed these Letters among those of Paul; today, however, there are doubts about this attribution, doubts stronger than in the case of the Letters to the Colossians and the Ephesians. In these Pastoral Letters we do not see the vehemence of the Letter to the Galatians or the sensitivity of those to the Corinthians. The tone is weightier, the style more opaque, the vocabulary very different.

Certainly, numerous ideas dear to Paul are presented in their pages, but they lack much of the mystical Pauline aspect. The newness of the faith appears less dazzling. They place a great deal of emphasis on piety, good conduct, and an honorable life, while listing lengthy moral recommendations. The life of communities is also different. We no longer find the previous animation stemming from countless charisms and ministries, such as prophecies; leaders appear to be invested with a regular and stable office, and the Letters speak primarily to them. Doctrine itself is no longer affirmed as such, in opposition to Judaism or paganism and in its fresh and vibrant newness. There is a tradition to maintain and to renew, a teaching to conserve and to deepen.

We thus have the image of a Church seeking to organize her life and functions. A very great crisis threatens her, possibly very much like the Church we encountered at Colossae. The new Christian doctrine is set forth in answer to a heretical movement that mixes together Jewish ideas and Eastern speculations. This movement was important at the end of the first century and the beginning of the second. In the face of these new currents, Christianity had to make precise its teaching and its identity.

Not a few critics are therefore inclined to date the Pastoral Letters toward the end of the first century. But without reaching that conclusion, regarding which various difficulties can be raised, it would be enough to imagine a Paul advanced in years, who makes use of secretaries and is writing in rather difficult practical circumstances. Since he is addressing individuals, it is not surprising that he no longer has the same enthusiasm as when he was writing to entire communities. On the other hand, the problems are new, and so too, therefore, are the answers.

It is of little importance, however, whether these Letters were from Paul himself or from the Pauline tradition. The directions they give are precious because of their reflections on fidelity, on Christian behavior, on the effort to live continually in faith, and on organizing the responsibilities and relationships in the Church. They provide us with important concerns for the thought and life of communities. We can, however, assign them to the last period of Paul's life, the years to which the Book of Acts makes no reference.

After the Apostle was set free in A.D. 63/64, there is reason to believe that he undertook a Fourth Missionary Journey (not recorded in Acts 28). This belief is based on (1) Paul's expressed intention to travel to Spain (see Rom 15:24, 28); (2) the implication by the early Church historian Eusebius that Paul was released after his first Roman imprisonment; and (3) early attestations by Clement of Rome and the Canon of Muratori that he preached the Gospel in Spain. The places Paul may have visited are indicated by statements of intent to do so in his earlier Letters and by their mention in the Pastoral Letters.

After this last visit, Paul left Titus in Crete and Timothy in Ephesus. This was the period that ended with a new arrest of Paul: he would be condemned to death and executed on the Via Ostiensis about the year A.D. 67.

Timothy was Paul's chief fellow worker; he was often with Paul when the latter wrote his Letters, so much so that more than one of them are described as written by Paul and Timothy. The Book of Acts (16:1-2) tells us of a man, though in poor health (1 Tim 5:23). From that point on he was a traveling companion of Paul (see Acts 17:14-15; 18:5; 24:4; 2 Cor 1:19) and carried out rather difficult missions for him in Macedonia (see Acts 19:22) and in the tumultuous community of Corinth (see 1 Cor 4:17; 16:10).

If the Second Letter to Timothy was written in Rome, almost on the eve of Paul's martyrdom, the first may have been written some time earlier, around A.D. 64 or 65, after a mission in Macedonia. Paul, to whom God had entrusted the care of the Churches among the pagans, insists, in the First Letter, that Timothy exercise, firmly and courageously, the office he received from Christ in the rite of the laying on of hands, which entails the proclamation of the truth, the organization of worship, and the guidance of the People of God and their varied groups. This last is the starting point for a theological and spiritual reflection on ministry in the Church.

The First Letter to Timothy may be divided as follows:

I: Salutation (1:1-2)
II: Timothy, Champion of the Truth (1:3-20)
III: Qualities of Public Worship and Church Leaders (2:1—3:16)
IV: General Regulations (4:1-16)
V: Specific Regulations for Various Groups (5:1—6:2a)
VI: Final Charge (6:2b-19)
VII: Conclusion (6:20-21)

CHAPTER 1

I: SALUTATION*

Address. 1 Paul, an apostle of Christ Jesus by command of God our Savior * and Christ Jesus our hope, [a] 2 to Timothy, my loyal child in the faith: grace, mercy, and peace to you from God the Father and Christ Jesus our Lord. [b]

II: TIMOTHY, CHAMPION OF THE TRUTH*

On Holding Fast to Sound Doctrine. 3 When I was setting out for Macedonia, * I urged you to stay on in Ephesus to instruct certain people that they are not to teach erroneous doctrines [c] 4 and not to concern themselves with myths and endless genealogies. These promote controversies and do not produce godly edification in faith. [d]

5 The aim of this instruction is love that derives from a pure heart, a good conscience, and a sincere faith. [e] 6 Some people have departed from these and turned to empty speculation, [f] 7 desiring to be teachers of the Law; but they understand neither the words they are using nor the matters about which they make such confident assertions. [g]

Purpose of the Law. 8 We are well aware that the Law is good, provided that one uses it properly, [h] 9 recognizing that laws are not designed for the upright. They are for the lawless and insubordinate, for the godless and sinful, for the unholy and irreligious; they are for those who slay their fathers and mothers, for murderers, [i] 10 for those who are fornicators, sodomites, * slave traders, liars, perjurers, and for whatever else is contrary to the sound teaching [j] 11 that conforms to the glorious gospel of the blessed God, which has been entrusted to me. [k]

Called To Preach the Gospel. 12 I am grateful to Christ Jesus our Lord who has given me strength, because he judged me trustworthy and appointed me to his service, [l] 13 even though in the past I was a blasphemer, a persecutor, and an insolent man. However, I have been treated with mercy because I had acted out of ignorance and unbelief. [m] 14 As a result, the grace of our Lord overflowed for me with the faith and the love that are in Christ Jesus. [n]

15 This saying can be trusted and merits complete acceptance: * Christ Jesus came into the world to save sinners. I myself am the greatest of these. [o] 16 But for that very reason I was treated mercifully, so that in me Jesus Christ might exhibit his inexhaustible patience, making me an example for those who would come to believe in him for eternal life. [p] 17 To the King of the ages, immortal, invisible, the only God, * be honor and glory forever and ever. Amen. [q]

Never Falsify the Gospel. 18 To you, Timothy, my child, I am giving these instructions in accordance with those prophecies once

a 1 Tim 2:3; Lk 1:47; 2 Cor 1:1; Col 1:27; Tit 1:3; 2:10.—b Acts 16:1; Rom 1:7; 1 Cor 4:17; 1 Thes 2:11; 2 Tim 1:2; Tit 1:1.—c 1 Tim 6:3; Acts 16:9; 18:19; 20:1; Gal 1:6-7.—d 1 Tim 4:7; 2 Tim 4:4; Tit 1:14; 3:9; 2 Pet 1:16.—e 1 Tim 4:2; Acts 23:1; Rom 13:10; Gal 5:6; 2 Tim 2:22.—f 1 Tim 6:4, 20; 2 Tim 2:18; Tit 1:10.—g 1 Tim 6:4; Job 38:2; Eph 4:11; Col 2:18.—h Rom 7:12, 16.—i Gal 3:19; 5:23.—j 1 Tim 4:6; 6:3; 2 Tim 1:13; 4:3; Tit 1:9; 2:1.—k Gal 2:7; 1 Thes 2:4; Tit 1:3.—l Acts 9:15, 22; 1 Cor 4:2; Gal 1:15-16; Phil 4:13; 2 Tim 4:17.—m Acts 8:3; 9:1-2; 26:9; 1 Cor 15:7, 9; Gal 1:13.—n Rom 5:20; 2 Cor 4:15; 1 Thes 1:3; 2 Tim 1:13.—o 1 Tim 3:1; 4:9; Mk 2:17; Lk 15:2; 19:10; Jn 3:17; 2 Tim 2:11; Tit 3:8.—p Mt 25:46; Jn 3:15; Rom 2:4.—q 1 Tim 6:16; Rom 16:27; Col 1:15; Jude 25; Rev 15:3.

1:1-2 The majority of Paul's Letters were sent to Churches, but four were addressed to individuals: Timothy (two Letters), Titus, and Philemon. Titus and Timothy were not apostles but evangelists (see 2 Tim 4:5). Timothy (whose father was Greek and his mother a Jewish Christian) had been converted by Paul's preaching (see Acts 16:1-3) and so was Paul's "loyal child in the faith."

1:1 *Savior:* this title, given to both the Father and Jesus, is characteristic of the later Letters of Paul, perhaps in reaction to the pagan environment in which the gods were "saviors" and the emperor was worshiped as a god. *Jesus our hope* is one of Paul's finest descriptions.

1:3-20 In writing to the Colossians, Paul had already denounced the infatuation with hazardous theories that characterized some Christians of Jewish origins in the region of Ephesus. Once again, fanciful theologies, hollow ideas, and obscure mythologies are being given free rein in Ephesus. Some converts from Judaism—who are familiar with the new Greek mythological currents as well as the play of Biblical genealogies—give themselves up to speculations without end or purpose, and they abandon the essence of faith and love.

They claim to be teachers of the Law, but they preach nonsense. Hence, they must be reminded that the Law is primarily a discipline of life rather than an object of speculation (see Rom 7:12-16; Gal 3:19); above all, the importance of a sane doctrine that fixes one's thoughts and guides one's life must be inculcated in them. In the midst of an anarchic agitation, Christians must always come back to the profound meaning of the Gospel, exemplified by Paul's life and vocation.

1:3 *When I was setting out for Macedonia:* an event not mentioned in Acts; hence, it probably occurred after Acts 28 between Paul's first and second Roman imprisonment. He had founded the Church at Ephesus on the Third Missionary Journey some eight years earlier (see Acts 19:1—20:1).

1:10 *Sodomites:* adult males who have relations with boy prostitutes. The latter are also known as *catamites* after the Latin name (*Catamitus*) of Ganymede, the cupbearer of the gods in Greek mythology. See also Rom 1:26f and 1 Cor 6:9. *Slave traders:* literally, "dealers in men," who included slaves but also men destined to be thrown into the arena or to serve unmentionable vices.

1:15 *This saying can be trusted and merits complete acceptance:* a formula that corresponds to the Aramaic expression in the Gospels: "Amen, I say to you." It is found only in the Pastoral Letters—here and in four other places: 1 Tim 3:1; 4:9; 2 Tim 2:11; Tit 3:8. (In the first, third, and fourth of these it is abbreviated.)

1:17 *Immortal, invisible, the only God:* here again Paul gives the true God titles used in pagan worship; see vv. 1 and 11.

made about you, * so that by following them
you may fight the good fight [r] 19 with faith
and a good conscience. Some people have
spurned their conscience and destroyed
their faith. [s] 20 Among them are Hyme-
naeus * and Alexander whom I have handed
over to Satan so that they may learn not to
blaspheme. [t]

III: QUALITIES OF PUBLIC WORSHIP AND CHURCH LEADERS*

CHAPTER 2

Prayer for Those in Authority.* 1 I urge then,
first of all, that supplications, prayers, inter-
cessions, and thanksgivings be offered for
everyone, [u] 2 for kings and for all those who
hold positions of authority, so that we may
be able to lead a tranquil and quiet life with
all possible devotion and dignity. [v] 3 To do so
is right and acceptable to God our Savior, [w]
4 who desires everyone to be saved and to
come to full knowledge of the truth. [x]

5 * For there is one God,
and there is one mediator between God
and man,
Christ Jesus, himself a man, [y]
6 who gave himself as a ransom for all. [z]

This was the testimony he offered at the
appointed time. 7 And I was made a herald
and an apostle of it (I am telling the truth; I
am not lying), a teacher of the Gentiles in
faith and truth. [a]

Positions at Public Worship.* 8 I desire, then,
that in every place the men should pray, lift-
ing up their hands reverently in prayer with-
out anger or argument. [b] 9 I also ask that the
women should dress themselves modestly
and decently in suitable clothing. They
should be adorned not with braided hair or
with gold or pearls or expensive clothes,* [c]
10 but with good works, as is fitting for wo-
men who profess their reverence for God. [d]

11 [e] Women are to learn in silence with
complete submission. [f] 12 I do not allow a
woman to teach or to hold authority over a
man. She should keep silent. [g] 13 For Adam
was formed first, and Eve afterward. [h]
14 Furthermore, Adam was not deceived; it
was the woman who was deceived and fell
into sin. [i] 15 However, women will be saved
through the bearing of children, provided
that they continue to persevere in faith, love,
and holiness, marked by modesty. [j]

---

r 1 Tim 4:14; 6:12; 1 Cor 9:7; 2 Cor 10:4; 2 Tim 2:3; 4:7; Jude 3.—s 1 Tim 3:9; 6:2; Acts 23:1; 2 Tim 2:18.—t 1 Cor 5:5; 2 Tim 2:17; 4:14.—u Eph 6:18; Phil 4:6-7.—v 1 Tim 3:16; 4:7-8; Rom 13:1; 2 Tim 3:5; Tit 1:1.—w 1 Tim 1:1; 4:10; 5:4; Lk 1:4.—x 1 Tim 4:10; Ezek 18:23, 32; 33:11; Jn 3:17; Rom 11:14; 2 Tim 3:7; 2 Pet 3:9.—y Deut 6:4; Rom 3:29-30; 5:15; 1 Cor 8:6; Gal 3:20; Heb 8:6; 9:15; 12:24.—z 1 Tim 6:15; Mt 20:28; Mk 10:45; 1 Cor 1:6; Gal 1:4; 2:20; Eph 5:25; Tit 2:14.—a Acts 9:15; Rom 9:1; 1 Cor 9:1; Gal 2:7-8; 2 Tim 1:11.—b Pss 24:4; 63:5; 134:2; 141:2; Lk 24:50.—c Isa 3:18-23; 1 Pet 3:3-5.—d 1 Tim 5:10; Prov 31:13; 1 Pet 3:1.—e 11-12: 1 Cor 14:34-35.—f 1 Pet 3:1, 3-4.—g Eph 5:22; Tit 2:5.—h Gen 1:27; 2:7, 22; 1 Cor 11:8-9.—i Gen 3:1-6, 13; 2 Cor 11:3.—j 1 Tim 1:14; 5:14; Gal 4:4.

1:18 *Prophecies . . .about you:* Timothy received his investiture as an apostle in the presence of prophets, that is, charismatic individuals who had the gift of guiding the faithful along their way to God or of calling men to the missionary apostolate (see 1 Cor 12:28-29; Acts 13:1-3; Eph 3:5).

Fight the good fight: the Christian life is one long struggle against (1) Satan (see 2 Cor 2:11; Eph 6:11-12); (2) the flesh (see Rom 7:23; Gal 5:17; 1 Pet 2:11); (3) the world (see Jn 16:33; 1 Jn 5:4f); and (4) death (see 1 Cor 15:26; Heb 2:14f). Christians are called upon to be filled with faith and to use the armaments of faith (see Eph 6:14-18), and to be vigilant (see 1 Pet 5:8). Through Christ, they will attain the final victory with its eternal rewards (see Rom 16:20; 2 Tim 4:8; Rev 2:17; 3:5; 21:7).

1:20 *Hymenaeus:* see 2 Tim 2:17f. *Alexander:* possibly the same person as in 2 Tim 4:14. *Handed over to Satan:* these individuals were probably excluded from the community and abandoned "to Satan." This excommunication was inflicted for the purpose of correcting them and making them come to their senses as they rediscovered their desire for salvation and the Gospel (see 1 Cor 5:5).

2:1—3:16 This section instructs Timothy about the public worship of the community and lists some qualifications that bishops and deacons must possess. In the process, it bestows on the Church two time-hallowed titles: "the Church of the living God" and "the pillar and bulwark of the truth."

It then concludes by stressing the universality of Jesus' role in his Resurrection visitation to angels as well as humans and in his enthronement as Lord of the Church. Hence, the belief in Christ's Paschal Mystery is shown to be one of the basic aspects of the faith of the Church.

2:1-7 Nero was in power, and Paul perhaps had a presentiment of a dark future for Christians. He therefore urges them to include all human beings in their intercession. Liturgical prayer must be universal prayer, for it is carried along by a conviction: God has sent his Son to bear witness that the Father wills the salvation of the whole world. It is the mission of Paul and ultimately of the Church to make this truth well known.

2:5-6a This text was probably part of a very early creed. Some scholars regard it as a Christian version of the Jewish *shema:* "Hear, O Israel, the LORD, our God, is LORD alone . . ." (Deut 6:4f). The Letter to the Hebrews gives a lengthy development of this central affirmation of the Christian faith.

2:8-15 First of all, Paul describes the attitude of prayer, stressing that it must arise from a heart filled with love (see Mt 6:14; Mk 11:25). Then he issues recommendations for different groups and states of life. In keeping with the custom of the time, women were excluded from official roles in worship (see 1 Cor 14:34-35).

We see a teaching already in existence concerning style of dress, a teaching that has often been renewed in the Church: Christians should endeavor *to be* rather than *to appear*. The New Testament several times recognizes the value of virginity (see 1 Cor 7:8, 25); but here, in opposition to heretics who forbade marriage (1 Tim 4:3), Paul emphasizes the point that the vocation of women is to give life.

2:9 This verse does not place a total ban on wearing jewelry or expensive clothes or braiding one's hair. These things are singled out here because in the society of Paul's day they were signs of unconscionable extravagance and self-importance.

CHAPTER 3*

Qualifications of Bishops. 1 [k] This saying can be trusted: Whoever wants to be a bishop desires a noble task. [l] 2 Therefore, a bishop must be above reproach, the husband of only one wife, temperate, self-controlled, respectable, hospitable, and a good teacher. [m] 3 He must not be a drunkard, not violent but gentle, not prone to quarreling, not greedy. [n]

4 He must manage his own household well and ensure that his children are submissive and respectful in every way. 5 For if someone does not know how to manage his own family, how can he take care of the Church of God? [o] 6 He should not be a recent convert so that he will not become conceited and incur the same condemnation as the devil. [p] 7 He must also enjoy a good reputation among outsiders so that he may not fall into disgrace and into the devil's snare. [q]

Qualifications of Deacons. 8 Similarly, deacons must exhibit a sense of dignity, not indulging in double-talk or excessive consumption of wine, and not being greedy. [r] 9 They must hold fast to the mystery of the faith with a clear conscience. [s] 10 Let them first be tested. They can be appointed as deacons only if they are beyond reproach. [t]

11 Women * must likewise exhibit a sense of dignity and not be given to spreading slander. They must be temperate and faithful in all things. [u]

12 Deacons must have only one wife and be able to manage their children and their own households. [v] 13 Those deacons whose work is exemplary will achieve a high standing and gain great assurance in their faith in Christ Jesus. [w]

Greatness of the Divine Majesty. 14 While I am hoping to come to you soon, I am writing to you about these matters 15 so that if I am delayed, you will know how to regulate your conduct in God's household—that is, in the Church of the living God, the pillar and bulwark of the truth. [x] 16 Without any doubt, the mystery of our religion is great:

He was made visible in the flesh,
vindicated by the Spirit, *
seen by angels,
proclaimed to the Gentiles,
believed in throughout the world,
taken up in glory. [y]

IV: GENERAL REGULATIONS*

CHAPTER 4

False Asceticism. 1 The Spirit clearly says that during the last times some will abandon the faith. They will run after deceitful spirits and demonic doctrines, [z] 2 through the hypocrisy of liars whose consciences have been branded as with a burning iron. [a] 3 They forbid marriage and require abstinence from foods * that God created to be

k 1-7: Tit 1:6-9.—l 1 Tim 1:15; Acts 20:28; Phil 1:1.—m Rom 12:13; 2 Tim 2:24; Tit 1:6-8.—n 1 Tim 6:10; Lk 16:14; Tit 1:7; Heb 13:5; 1 Pet 5:2.—o 1 Cor 10:32.—p 1 Tim 6:4; 2 Tim 3:4; 2 Pet 2:4.—q 1 Tim 5:10; 6:9; Mk 4:11; 2 Cor 8:21; 2 Tim 2:26.—r Acts 6:3; Phil 1:1; Tit 1:7.—s 1 Tim 1:19; Acts 23:1.—t 1 Tim 5:22.—u 2 Tim 3:3; Tit 2:3, 10.—v 2 Tim 3:2, 4.—w Mt 25:21, 23; Lk 19:17.—x Mt 16:16; 1 Cor 10:32; Eph 2:19-22; 2 Tim 2:23; Heb 3:6.—y 1 Tim 2:2; Mk 16:19; Jn 1:14; Rom 1:3-4; 16:25; Col 1:23; 1 Pet 1:20; 1 Jn 1:2.—z Mk 13:5; Jn 16:13; Acts 8:29; 1 Cor 2:10; 2 Tim 3:1; 4:3; 2 Pet 3:3; Jude 18.—a Rom 1:25; Eph 4:19; 2 Pet 2:1.

3:1-16 Christian communities have multiplied and grown; the Church needs organization. Bishops ("overseers") or presbyters ("elders") preach, lead liturgical meetings, and govern the local Churches under the more or less close supervision of the Apostle or his delegates (Timothy at Ephesus, Titus in Crete). These authorities, who are carefully chosen, are aided by deacons, who are appointed to help the apostles in material matters (see Acts 6:1-6) and also in their missionary work (see Acts 8:5-13, 38): to take upon themselves the management of the organization and to bring help to the poor and the sick. It seems that some women, too, may have had similar tasks (v. 11; see Rom 16:1).

Thus, Paul sketches a hierarchy of the Church. To serve the Church, Paul demands solid human qualities on the part of candidates. People cannot proclaim the mystery of faith, i.e., announce that God saves the world through Jesus Christ, unless they live that faith. A fragment from a hymn of the time is used to celebrate this mystery: Incarnation, Resurrection, Mission, Ascension.

3:11 *Women:* this word could refer either to women deacons or to women who were the wives of deacons. Scholars usually opt for the first reference since there is no possessive (e.g., "their") and since they are introduced by the same word as in v. 8 ("similarly . . . likewise"), indicating that women too could possess the ministry of deacon. See note on Rom 16:1, in which verse Paul sends greetings to "our sister Phoebe, who is a deaconess of the Church at Cenchreae."

3:16 *He was . . . vindicated by the Spirit:* the holiness and divinity of Christ were made known in the Resurrection (see Rom 1:4). These six lines are regarded as a fragment of a hymn of the time.

4:1-16 The time left to announce salvation to the whole world is limited; it is the end time, an age of crisis. In fact, troubled spirits jumble religious ideas together, seeking salvation in a pseudo-asceticism. But true Christians know how to celebrate creation and its realities in a positive way. Such an outlook in matters of doctrine rejects anything that is disordered and inconsistent; it endorses godliness, i.e., the worship of God and the desire to seek his will; attentiveness to the great virtues; love for the public reading of Sacred Scripture (v. 13); and teaching. An apostle finds the strength to persevere in this line of thought by ceaselessly renewing the gift that was given to him through the laying on of hands, i.e., when the community consecrated him for his office, in the name of the Lord.

4:3 *They forbid marriage and require abstinence from foods:* this asceticism was not from the Bible but from the erroneous belief that the material world was evil, which was a principal tenet of Gnosticism.

accepted with thanksgiving by those who believe and who know the truth.[b] [4]For everything created by God is good, and nothing is to be rejected, provided that it is received with thanksgiving,[c] [5]for it is made holy by the word of God and by prayer.*[d]

The Benefits of Godliness. [6]If you offer these instructions to the brethren, you will prove to be a good servant of Christ Jesus, nourished on the truths of the faith and of the good teaching that you have followed.[e] [7]Have nothing to do with profane myths and old wives' tales; rather, train yourself in godliness.[f]

[8]While physical training has some value, the benefits of godliness are unlimited, since it holds out promise not only for this life but also for the life to come.[g] [9]This saying can be trusted and merits complete acceptance.[h] [10]For this is why we toil and struggle, because we have placed our hope in the living God, who is the Savior of all, especially of all those who believe.[i]

Pastoral Duties. [11]These are the things you must insist upon in your teaching.[j] [12]Let no one regard you with contempt because of your youth, but serve as an example to the believers in your speech and conduct, in your love, your faith, and your purity.[k]

[13]Until I arrive, devote yourself to reading,* to exhortation, and to teaching.[l] [14]Do not neglect the gift that was bestowed upon you when, as a result of prophecy, the elders laid their hands on you.*[m]

[15]Meditate on these things and put them into practice so that your progress may be evident to everyone.[n] [16]Be conscientious about your life and your teaching. Persevere in both of these tasks, for by doing so you will save both yourself and your listeners.[o]

V: SPECIFIC REGULATIONS FOR VARIOUS GROUPS*

CHAPTER 5

Different Age Groups.* [1]Never speak harshly to an older man; rather, appeal to him as if he were your father. Treat younger men as brothers,[p] [2]older women as mothers, and younger women as sisters, with the greatest purity.

Widows.* [3]Give proper consideration to those widows who are truly in need.[q] [4]If a widow has children or grandchildren, these should learn first of all to carry out their religious duty to their own family and repay their debt to their parents, for this is pleasing in the eyes of God.[r]

[5]However, a widow who is truly in need and is alone in the world places all her trust in God and never ceases her prayers and supplications night and day.[s] [6]But the widow who is interested solely in pleasure is dead even while she lives.[t]

[7]Insist upon these things, so that people may be beyond reproach.[u] [8]And whoever does not provide for relatives, especially for those who are living with him, has disowned the faith and is worse than an unbeliever.[v]

---

b Gen 9:3; Rom 14:6; 1 Cor 10:30-31; Col 2:16; Heb 13:4.—c Gen 1:10, 12, 31; Mk 7:18-19; Acts 10:15; Rom 14:14-18.—d Tob 8:4-10; Heb 4:12.—e 1 Tim 1:10; 2 Tim 3:15.—f 1 Tim 2:2; 4:2; 2 Tim 2:16; Tit 1:14.—g 1 Tim 6:6; Prov 22:4; Mt 6:33; Mk 10:29-30.—h 1 Tim 1:15; 2 Tim 2:11; Tit 3:8.—i 1 Tim 2:4; Mt 16:16; Lk 1:47; Tit 2:11.—j 1 Tim 5:7; 6:2.—k 1 Tim 1:14; 1 Cor 16:11; Phil 3:17; 1 Thes 1:7; 2 Tim 1:7; Tit 2:15.—l 1 Tim 3:14; Lk 4:16; Acts 13:14-16; Col 4:16.—m 1 Tim 1:18; 5:22; Acts 6:6; 8:17; 2 Tim 1:6.—n Rom 14:18.—o Ezek 33:9; Acts 20:28; Rom 11:14.—p Lev 19:32; Tit 2:2, 6.—q 1 Tim 5:5, 16.—r 1 Tim 2:3; Rom 12:2; Eph 5:10; 6:1-2.—s 1 Tim 5:3, 16; Jer 49:11; Lk 2:37; 18:7; Rom 1:10; 1 Cor 7:34; 1 Pet 3:5.—t Lk 15:24; Jas 5:5; Rev 3:1.—u 1 Tim 4:11; 6:2.—v Gal 6:10; 2 Tim 3:5; 2 Pet 2:1; Jude 4.

4:5 *It is made holy by the word of God and by prayer:* another possible translation is: "it is made holy by the invocation of God in prayer."

4:13 *Reading:* i.e., the public reading of Scripture.

4:14 *Laid their hands on you:* an action that had various meanings in the Old Testament, among which was the transmission of authority (e.g., from Moses to Joshua: see Num 27:18-23; Deut 34:9). In the New Testament it symbolizes (1) the bestowal of blessings and benediction (see Mt 19:13, 15; Lk 24:50); (2) the restoration of health (see Mt 9:18; Acts 9:12, 17); (3) the imparting of the Holy Spirit (see Acts 8:17, 19; 19:6); and (4) the gifts and rights of an office (as in this verse and in Acts 6:6; 13:3; 2 Tim 1:6).

5:1—6:2a Paul sets forth the attitude that Timothy should have toward various groups in his Church: the old and the young, widows, presbyters, and slaves. With reference to slavery, one should note that the New Testament does not attack the institution directly but attacks the principle of slavery. For Christian slaves are freedmen of the Lord and their owners are slaves of the Lord (1 Cor 7:21-23). In Christ Jesus there is no distinction between slave and free; all are baptized in one Spirit and form one body (see 1 Cor 12:13; Gal 3:28; Col 3:11). Ultimately, the principle of Christian love prevented Christians from regarding other human beings as slaves.

5:1-2 The apostle must have an attitude of respect and closeness for the different categories of the faithful.

5:3-16 In reading this passage, the circumstances of the period and concrete conditions in the community must be taken into account. Different types of widows are discussed. Some have a family; in their case, the accent is placed upon a true exchange on the family level. Other widows are all alone; they can serve the Church and are taken into her care.

When he speaks of young widows, the author cannot resist injecting a caricatural trait; he refuses to let them engage in the exclusive service of Christ and the Church out of fear that later events in their existence may take away their initial enthusiasm. It seems that some communities had the bad experience of premature vows. (1 Corinthians 7:9, 40 exhibited much less distrust in such cases.) It is interesting to note the existence of organized groups of widows in the community.

9 A woman should not be enrolled as a widow if she is not at least sixty years old. In addition, she must have been married only once,[w] 10 and have a reputation for good works by bringing up her children, offering hospitality to strangers, washing the feet of the saints,* helping those in distress, and being active in all kinds of good work.[x]

11 However, refuse to enroll younger widows, for when their passions distract them from the service of Christ, they will want to marry again 12 and will incur condemnation for having broken their original vow.[y] 13 In addition, they fall into the habit of being idle, as they go around from house to house, and also become gossips and busybodies, saying things that would better be left unsaid.[z]

14 Therefore, I think younger widows should marry again, bear children, and manage their households, so as not to give our enemies any occasion to revile us.[a] 15 Indeed, some have already turned away to follow Satan.[b]

16 If any woman believer has relatives who are widows, she must assist them herself. The Church should be free of such burdens and consequently able to assist those who are widows in the true sense.[c]

Presbyters.* 17 Presbyters who do their duty well should be considered deserving of a double honor,* especially those who labor at preaching and teaching.[d] 18 For Scripture says, "You shall not muzzle an ox while it is treading out the grain," and "A worker deserves his wages."*[e]

19 Never accept any accusation brought against a presbyter except on the evidence of two or three witnesses.[f] 20 As for those who persist in sin, rebuke them publicly, so that the others may also be afraid.[g]

21 In the presence of God and Christ Jesus and the chosen angels,* I charge you to follow these rules impartially and without being influenced by any favoritism.[h] 22 Do not lay hands on others too hastily or you may find yourself regarded as an accomplice in the sins of others. Keep yourself pure.[i]

23 Stop drinking nothing but water. Take a little wine for the sake of your stomach and your frequent ailments.[j]

24 The sins of some people are so flagrant that they are publicly known before judgment, while the sins of others will only become known later on. 25 In the same manner, good works are often easily recognized, but even if they are not, they cannot remain hidden forever.[k]

CHAPTER 6

Slaves.* 1 All those who are under the yoke of slavery must regard their masters as worthy of complete respect, so that the name of God and our teaching may not be brought into disrepute.[l] 2 Those whose masters are believers must not despise them because they are brethren. On the contrary, they should serve them more, since those who receive the benefits of their services are believers and beloved brethren.[m]

VI: FINAL CHARGE*

False Teaching about Wealth. These are the things you should teach and recommend.

w 1 Tim 3:2.—x 1 Tim 6:18; Lk 7:44; Jn 13:14; Acts 9:36; Rom 12:13; Heb 13:2; 1 Pet 2:12.—y Rev 2:4.—z 1 Tim 3:11; Rom 1:29; 2 Thes 3:11.—a 1 Tim 4:3; 6:1; 1 Cor 7:9; Tit 2:5.—b 1 Tim 1:20; Mt 4:10.—c 1 Tim 5:3, 5; Jn 1:27.—d Acts 11:30; 1 Cor 16:18; Phil 2:29; 1 Thes 5:12.—e Deut 24:14-15; 25:4; Mt 10:10; Lk 10:7; 1 Cor 9:8.—f Deut 17:6; 19:15; Mt 18:16; Acts 11:30; 2 Cor 13:1.—g Deut 13:11; Gal 2:14; Eph 5:11; 2 Tim 4:2; Tit 1:9, 13; 2:15.—h 1 Tim 6:13; 2 Tim 4:1.—i 1 Tim 4:14; Acts 6:6; Eph 5:11; 2 Tim 1:6.—j 1 Tim 3:8; Jdg 9:13.—k Prov 10:9; Mt 10:26.—l 1 Tim 5:14; Eph 6:5; Tit 2:5, 8, 9-10.—m 1 Tim 4:11; Philem 16.

5:10 *Washing the feet of the saints,* i.e., the faithful, was a ritual of hospitality (see Lk 7:44; Jn 13:1ff). It was necessary because the roads were dusty and the footwear consisted of sandals.

5:17-25 Presbyters do not seem to be on the same level as the bishops (i.e., "overseers") mentioned earlier (1 Tim 3:1-7), although they preside at the Liturgy and explain the Scriptures. This fact seems to pave the way for the monarchical episcopate that developed in the Church during the second and third centuries. The poverty required of his ministers by Christ does not prevent the Gospel workers from earning a living by their labor, even though Paul himself has always refused to accept any assistance. But anyone who has the desire to serve the Church must have shown to be a serious Christian. The responsibility for the community must not be conferred lightly on anyone.

Paul then places his full attention on his favorite disciple (v. 23).

5:17 *Double honor:* i.e., respect and an honorarium for their labor.

5:18 Both citations (Deut 25:4 and Lk 10:7) are called "Scripture." This shows that whatever portions of the New Testament were available at the time were already regarded as equal to the Old Testament in authority.

5:21 *The chosen angels:* in contrast to the fallen angels (see 2 Pet 2:4; Jude 6).

6:1-2b Paul speaks on more than one occasion of the lot of slaves (see 1 Cor 7:21-24; Gal 3:28; Eph 6:5-9; Col 3:22-25; Tit 2:9-10; Philem 10-17; 1 Pet 2:18-20). What he speaks of here is not about the social institution of the time but about fidelity and relationships within a de facto institution.

6:2c-19 The final instruction to Timothy concerns combating false teaching about wealth, fighting the good fight of the faith, and amassing true riches in place of earthly wealth. In order to understand the kind of disastrous teaching we are dealing with here, it suffices to examine the portrait of a false teacher. He is a man who gives in to every snare, chasing after reputation, emotional satisfaction, and money without paying any real attention to the faith. The true teacher, on the other hand, knows how to embrace suffering and live according to the truth. He is a man who professes the faith and fights for it while totally enveloped by the mystery of Christ that is evoked in the beautiful final hymn in 1 Tim 6:14-16.

[3] Whoever teaches something different and
does not agree with the wholesome instruc-
tion of our Lord Jesus Christ and with the
godly teaching [n] [4] is a conceited person who
understands nothing and who has an
unhealthy enthusiasm to engage in argu-
ments and to dispute the meaning of words.
From these come envy, dissension, slander,
base suspicions, [o] [5] and unending disputes
among people whose minds are corrupted
and who are deprived of truth, supposing
that godliness is a means of gain. [p]

[6] Godliness produces great gain, but only
to those who are content. [q] [7] For we brought
nothing into this world, and we can take
nothing out. [r] [8] If we have food and clothing,
let us be content with these. [s]

[9] However, those who want riches fall into
temptations and are trapped into many
senseless and harmful desires that plunge
them into ruin and destruction. [t] [10] The love
of money is the root of all evils, and in their
desire for it some have wandered away from
the faith and pierced themselves with many
serious wounds. * [u]

Fight the Good Fight. [11] But as for you, man
of God, * you must shun all this. Rather, pur-
sue righteousness, godliness, faith, love, for-
titude, and gentleness. [v] [12] Fight the good
fight of faith. Take hold of the eternal life to
which you were called when you made your
noble confession * of faith in the presence of
many witnesses. [w]

[13] In the sight of God, who gave life to all
things, and before Jesus Christ, who himself
made that noble confession of faith in his
testimony before Pontius Pilate, I charge
you [x] [14] to obey the commands of God with-
out fault or failure until the appearance of
our Lord Jesus Christ, [y] [15] which he will
make manifest at the proper time—he who
is the blessed and only ruler of all, the King
of kings and the Lord of lords. [z] [16] He alone is
immortal and dwells in unapproachable
light. No one has seen him or is able to do so.
To him be honor and everlasting power.
Amen. [a]

Right Use of Riches.* [17] Instruct those who
are rich in this world's goods that they
should not be proud, nor should they trust in
the uncertainty of riches but rather in God
who richly provides us with everything we
need for our enjoyment. [b] [18] Tell them to do
good and to be rich in good works, to be gen-
erous in giving and ready to share. [c] [19] In this
way, they will acquire the treasure of a
good foundation for the future so that they
will be able to grasp the life that is true life. [d]

VII: CONCLUSION*

Admonition to Timothy. [20] My brother
Timothy, guard carefully what has been
entrusted to you. * Avoid the profane chat-
ter and the contradictions of what is wrong-
ly considered to be knowledge. [e] [21] By pro-
fessing it some people have strayed far from
the faith. [f]

Farewell. Grace be with all of you. *

n 1 Tim 1:3, 10; Gal 1:6-9; 2 Tim 1:13.—o 1 Tim 3:6; 2 Tim 2:14; 3:4.—p 2 Tim 3:8; 4:4; Tit 1:14.—q 1 Tim 4:8; Phil 4:11-12; Heb 13:5.—r Job 1:21; Eccl 5:14.—s Gen 28:20; Prov 30:8; Heb 13:5.—t 1 Tim 3:7; Prov 15:27; 23:4; 28:22.—u 1 Tim 3:3; Jos 7:21; Jas 5:19.—v 1 Tim 1:14; 2:2; 6:3, 5-6; 2 Tim 2:22; 3:17.—w 1 Tim 1:18; Mt 25:46; 1 Cor 9:26; Phil 3:12; 2 Tim 4:7; Heb 3:1.—x 1 Tim 5:21; Jn 18:36-37; 19:11; 2 Tim 4:1.—y 1 Cor 1:7; 1 Thes 3:13; 2 Tim 1:10.—z 1 Tim 1:11; 2:6; Deut 10:17; 2 Mac 13:4; Tit 1:3; Rev 17:14.—a 1 Tim 1:17; Ex 33:20; Ps 104:2; Jn 1:18.—b 1 Tim 4:10; Jer 49:4; Ps 62:11; Lk 12:20-21; Acts 14:17.—c 1 Tim 5:10; Rom 12:8, 13; Eph 4:28.—d Mt 6:20; Phil 3:12.—e 1 Tim 4:7; 1 Cor 2:7-8; 2 Tim 1:14.—f 1 Tim 1:6; Col 4:18; 2 Tim 2:18.

6:10 Money in itself is neither good nor bad. It is *the love of money* that is evil, and indeed the root of all types of evil. Therefore, it is not wrong for believers to be well off—so long as they do not take pride in their riches but use them "to do good."

6:11 *Man of God:* a well-known title that had been applied to Moses and the Prophets in the Old Testament (see Deut 33:1; 1 Sam 2:27). It highlights the spiritual power possessed by leaders of the Church.

6:12 *Confession:* perhaps the profession of faith that Timothy made when consecrated to the ministry.

6:17-19 This passage calls for Christians to cast off the quest for riches that permeated their society and to change their attitude toward them.

6:20-21 Once again one of the major themes of the Letter is highlighted in this Conclusion: guard the deposit of faith that has been entrusted to you.

6:20 *What has been entrusted to you:* literally, "the deposit," that is, sacred doctrine, the authentic Gospel (see 1 Tim 1:10-11; 2 Tim 1:13-14). *Wrongly considered to be knowledge:* the ensemble of doctrines that were taught by heretics and that on many points foreshadowed the Gnosticism of the second century.

6:21 *All of you:* the plural indicates that this Letter was intended to be read to the whole community.

THE SECOND LETTER TO TIMOTHY

The Good Fight

This document presents itself as a last testament. Is it a letter of Paul? We accept it as such based on the reasons given in the Introduction to the First Letter to Timothy.

The Apostle is again a prisoner in Rome in A.D. 67. Conditions in prison are harsh, quite different from those of his previous imprisonment, when he preached freely in the house of his internment (see Acts 28:16). Now he languishes in a cold dungeon and wears the chains of a common criminal.

He feels terribly alone. No one has defended him in court, and only Luke is with him. His days are numbered, and he is preparing for the supreme sacrifice.

Timothy was at Ephesus when Paul sent his First Letter to him (1 Tim 1:3), and he is still there at the writing of this Second Letter. Paul is disturbed by what is going on in the developing communities: every new and alien idea is finding supporters; everyone who makes claims or calls himself enlightened is successful, to the detriment of the Gospel, of unity, and of the Church's mission.

The Apostle is also worried about the welfare of the Churches during this time of persecution under Nero. He sees it as a time to strengthen the internal character of the Church, to seek out and confirm new leaders, to clarify the faith of the developing communities, and to remain rooted in the tradition.

Paul has had experience of fighting for Jesus, and he urges his correspondent to endure the struggle with the same courage. He calls for fidelity and boldness: fidelity to the Gospel that Christ has entrusted to his Church; boldness in trying to have people live in accordance with the Gospel.

Aware that Timothy is fully versed in the apostolic teaching, Paul does not instruct him further on doctrine. He makes allusion to several important doctrines, including salvation by God's grace, the person of Christ, and perseverance. Finally, he lays special stress on the divine inspiration of Sacred Scripture.

This is a letter of farewell, a testament, the testimony of a man who regrets nothing. Despite his abandonment, the misunderstandings, the torments, and his imminent execution, thanksgiving flows from his heart. He has trusted only in the Christ who rose from the dead, and he has not been deceived.

Before dying, however, Paul wants to see his "beloved child," Timothy, once again and at least to strengthen him in his mission. He urges Timothy to come before winter (2 Tim 4:21) and to bring the warm cloak Paul left at Troas. Timothy is also to bring the Apostle's scrolls and parchments, possibly to enable Paul to do some further reading and writing (2 Tim 4:13).

The Second Letter to Timothy may be divided as follows:

I: Salutation (1:1-5)
II: The Endurance of a Man of God (1:6-18)
III: The Exemplars of a Man of God (2:1-26)
IV: The Tasks of a Man of God (3:1-17)
V: The Preaching of a Man of God (4:1-5)
VI: The Triumphs of a Man of God (4:6-18)
VII: Conclusion (4:19-22)

CHAPTER 1

I: SALUTATION*

Address. [1] Paul, an apostle of Christ Jesus by the will of God, whose promise of life is fulfilled in Christ Jesus, [a] [2] to Timothy, my beloved child: grace, mercy, and peace from God the Father and Christ Jesus our Lord. [b]

Thanksgiving and Prayer. [3] I am grateful to God—whom I worship with a clean conscience as did my ancestors—when I remember you constantly in my prayers night and day. [c] [4] As I recall your tears, * I long to see you again so that my joy may be complete. [d] [5] I also remember your sincere faith, a faith that first came to life in your grandmother Lois and in your mother Eunice, and that I am convinced also dwells in you. * [e]

II: THE ENDURANCE OF A MAN OF GOD*

Revive the Gift of God. [6] For this reason, I remind you to stir up the gift of God that is within you through the laying on of my hands. * [f] [7] For God did not give us a spirit of timidity but rather a spirit of power and of love and of wisdom. [g] [8] Therefore, you should never be ashamed of bearing witness to our Lord, nor of me because I am imprisoned for his sake. Rather, you should utilize the strength that comes from God to share in my hardships for the sake of the gospel. [h]

[9] God saved us and called us to a life of holiness, not because of our works but according to his own purpose and the grace that has been bestowed upon us in Christ Jesus from all eternity. * [i] [10] That grace has now been revealed by the appearance * of our Savior Jesus Christ. He has abolished death and brought life and immortality to light through the gospel, [j] [11] for which I have been appointed a herald and an apostle and a teacher. * [k]

Guard the Treasure Entrusted to Us. [12] That is the reason why I am undergoing my present sufferings. However, I am not ashamed, for I know the one in whom I have placed my trust, and I am confident that he is able to guard until that Day * what he has entrusted to me. [l] [13] Follow the pattern of sound teaching that you heard from me, with faith and love that are in Christ Jesus. [m] [14] With the help of the Holy Spirit who dwells in us, guard the treasure that has been entrusted to us. [n]

Comfort Those in Suffering. [15] As you are well aware, everyone in Asia has deserted me, including Phygelus and Hermogenes. * [o] [16] May the Lord be merciful to the household of Onesiphorus, * because he has often been a comfort to me in my troubles, and he has never been ashamed of my chains. [p] [17] When he arrived in Rome, he concentrated on searching for me until he found me.

---

a 1 Cor 1:1; 2 Cor 1:1; Eph 3:6; 1 Tim 6:10; Tit 1:2.—b Acts 16:1; Rom 1:7; 1 Tim 1:2.—c Acts 23:1; Rom 1:8; Phil 3:5; 1 Tim 3:9.—d 2 Tim 4:9; Acts 20:37.—e 2 Tim 3:15; Acts 16:1; 1 Tim 1:5.—f Acts 6:6; 8:17; 1 Thes 5:19; 1 Tim 4:14; 5:22.—g Isa 11:2; Jer 42:11; Rom 5:5; 8:15; 1 Cor 2:4; 16:10-11; 1 Tim 4:12.—h 2 Tim 1:12, 16; 2:3, 15; Mk 8:38; Rom 1:1; Eph 3:11.—i Rom 8:28; 11:14; Eph 1:4; 2:8-9; Tit 1:2; 3:5.—j Rom 16:26; 1 Cor 15:26, 53-55; Eph 1:9; Phil 3:20; 1 Tim 6:14; Tit 1:4; 2:13; Heb 2:14; 1 Pet 1:20; 2 Pet 1:11.—k Acts 9:15; 1 Tim 2:7.—l 2 Tim 1:8, 16; 4:8; Mk 8:38; 1 Tim 1:10-11; 6:20; 1 Pet 4:16.—m 2 Tim 2:2; Rom 6:17; 1 Thes 1:3; 1 Tim 1:14; Tit 1:9.—n Rom 8:9, 11; 1 Tim 6:20.—o 2 Tim 4:10, 16; Acts 2:7.—p 2 Tim 1:8, 12; 4:19; Mk 8:38; Acts 21:33.

1:1-5 Paul begins his Letter with a salutation that is similar to the one found in 1 Timothy, adding to it the words "whose promise of life is fulfilled in Christ Jesus." He calls Timothy his "beloved child," and the actual greeting is the same as that of 1 Timothy, showing that everything we have comes to us from God through Christ. As in most of his Letters (the exceptions are Gal, 1 Tim, and Tit), Paul then follows his salutation with a section thanking God for the recipients of the Letter. He focuses on his relationship with Timothy and his confidence in Timothy's faith.

1:4 *Your tears:* those shed by Timothy when Paul was leaving Ephesus (see 1 Tim 1:3).

1:5 According to Acts 16:1, Timothy's mother (Eunice) was a Jewish Christian while his father was a Greek and apparently an unbeliever. Here we learn that his grandmother (Lois) was also a Christian.

1:6-18 Paul warns that self-interest and discouragement must not get the best of the apostle's ardor and determination. Rather, he must rely upon the graces that were given him when he received the ministry and was gripped by the Spirit at his missionary sending forth (see 1 Tim 4:14). He must once again place himself at the service of the Gospel, which is the announcement of the coming of Christ and the salvation that he gives. There is no missionary life without spiritual renewal.

The last seven verses go on to give examples of men of God who have endured: Paul and Onesiphorus.

1:6 *Laying on of . . . hands:* see note on 1 Tim 4:14.

1:9 Paul insists that redemption from sin and the call to holiness are freely given to human beings in accord with God's plan (see Eph 1:4).

1:10 *Appearance:* the reference here is to the Incarnation.

1:11 *Teacher:* most manuscripts read: "teacher of the nations," which scholars regard as a gloss based on 1 Tim 2:7.

1:12 *That Day:* the day of judgment and crowning. *What he has entrusted to me:* i.e., the deposit of faith (see 1 Tim 6:20). Another possible translation is: "what I have entrusted to him," i.e., the fruits of his ministry.

1:15 Paul is deeply disappointed that he has been deserted by Christians from Asia, including two upon whom he was counting—Phygelus and Hermogenes. Some scholars believe that Phygelus was the leader of lapsed Christians in Rome (see Phil 1:15f).

1:16 *Onesiphorus:* a helper of Paul—probably during his first Roman imprisonment (see v. 8)—whose household was in Ephesus and who is not mentioned elsewhere (see 2 Tim 4:19).

18 May the Lord grant that he will find mercy
from the Lord * on that Day. He also helped
me in many ways at Ephesus, as you are well
aware. [q]

III: THE EXEMPLARS OF A MAN OF GOD*

CHAPTER 2

Accept Your Share of Sufferings.* 1 As for
you, my child, take strength from the grace
that is in Christ Jesus. [r] 2 And the things you
learned from me in the presence of many wit-
nesses you must pass on to trustworthy peo-
ple who will be capable of teaching others. [s]

3 Together with me, bear your share of suf-
ferings like a good soldier of Christ Jesus. [t]
4 A soldier does not become involved in
everyday affairs, for his task is to obey his
commanding officer. [u] 5 In a similar vein, no
athlete can receive the winner's crown unless
he has competed according to the rules. [v]
6 Again, the farmer who does the hard work
should have the first claim on the crops. [w]
7 Think about what I am saying, for the Lord
will help you to understand it perfectly. [x]

Remember That Jesus Christ Is Risen.*
8 Remember the gospel that I preach: Jesus
Christ, a descendant of David, was raised
from the dead. [y] 9 It is because of this that I
have endured great suffering, even to the
point of being chained like a criminal. But
the word of God cannot be chained. [z]
10 Therefore, I endure everything for the
sake of those who are chosen, so that they
too may obtain the salvation that is in Christ
Jesus, with eternal glory. [a]

11 This saying can be trusted:

If we have died with him,
we shall also live with him. [b]
12 If we endure,
we shall also reign with him.
If we deny him,
he will also deny us. [c]
13 If we are unfaithful,
he will remain faithful,
for he cannot deny himself. [d]

A True Servant of the Lord.* 14 Remind peo-
ple of these things, and warn them before
God * that they must stop arguing over
words. This does no good and only causes
harm to those who are listening. [e] 15 Make
every effort to present yourself before God
as one who is worthy of his approval, a work-
er who has no need to be ashamed, but who
imparts the word of truth without any alter-
ation. [f]

16 Avoid idle and worldly chatter, for those
who indulge in it will become more and
more ungodly, [g] 17 and their teaching will
spread like a plague. Included among these
are Hymenaeus * and Philetus, [h] 18 who have
gone astray from the truth. They claim that
the resurrection has already taken place,
and they damage the faith of some. [i]
19 However, the foundation that God has
sealed * remains firm, and it bears this inscrip-

q Acts 18:19; Heb 6:10; Jude 21.—r Eph 6:10; 1 Tim 1:2.—s 2 Tim 1:13; 1 Tim 6:12.—t 2 Tim 1:8; 4:5; 1 Tim 1:18; Philem 2.—u 1 Cor 9:6; 2 Pet 2:20.—v 2 Tim 4:8; 1 Cor 9:25.—w 1 Cor 9:7; Heb 6:7.—x Prov 2:6; Col 1:27; 1 Jn 2:20-21.—y Mt 1:1; Acts 2:24; Rom 1:3; 2:16; 16:25; 1 Cor 15:4, 20; Gal 1:11; 2:2.—z Acts 9:16; 21:33; Phil 1:12-14; Heb 4:12.—a 2 Cor 1:6; Col 1:24; 1 Tim 1:15; Tit 1:1.—b Rom 6:2-11; 1 Tim 1:15.—c Mt 10:22, 33; Lk 12:9; Rom 8:17; 1 Pet 4:13.—d Num 23:19; Rom 3:3-4; 1 Cor 1:9; 10:13; Tit 1:2.—e 1 Tim 1:4; 6:4; Tit 3:9.—f 2 Tim 1:8; 2 Cor 6:7; Eph 1:13; Col 1:5; Jas 1:18.—g 1 Tim 4:7; 6:20; Tit 3:9.—h 1 Tim 1:20.—i 2 Thes 2:2; 1 Tim 1:19; 6:21.

1:18 *Lord . . . Lord:* the first "Lord" doubtless refers to Christ and the second to the Father.

2:1-26 The author then goes on to enumerate eight exemplars that a man of God can follow in some way: Paul (vv. 1-2), a soldier (vv. 3-4), an athlete (v. 5), a farmer (vv. 6-7), Jesus (vv. 8-13), a worker (vv. 14-19), a vessel (vv. 20-23), and a servant (vv. 24-26).

2:1-7 The apostolate requires a person's complete commitment. He bears and transmits the message entrusted by God to the Christian community.

2:8-13 Another heading for this section would read "Be a memorial of Jesus Christ," i.e., be a person whose whole being and action recalls the Resurrection of Christ and renders it present to those he meets, while announcing to them that its fullness will take place at the time of the Lord's return. This is the finest picture one could give of the life of Paul.

Verses 11b-13 are probably from a baptismal hymn; to be baptized meant that one should live out, throughout one's days, the mystery of Christ's Death and Resurrection (see Rom 6:8; 1 Cor 15:31; Gal 6:14; Phil 3:10; Col 3:3-5).

2:14-26 In the portrait of a true missionary, a certain number of virtues must be present: honesty, respect for and acceptance of everyone, courage in persecution, truthfulness without alteration, and rejection of faddish witticisms. The author once more condemns the errors being propagated in the region of Ephesus; they have the look not of a new religion but of a feverish and babbling emotionalism. The Greek mind had difficulty in accepting the resurrection of the body (see Acts 17:32; 1 Cor 15:22), and some avoid the problem by saying that the resurrection has already taken place at Baptism but that it is solely a case of a spiritual resurrection.

They forget above all that the faith is founded on the word of God, which provides the initiative and that believers have merely to respond. It is the quality of their faith that classifies believers in the Church, not the abundance of their opinions. Yet leaders must be very kind and not condemn any of the members of the community.

2:14 *Before God:* many manuscripts read: "before the Lord."

2:17 *Hymenaeus:* see 1 Tim 1:20. His punishment has not helped him.

2:19 *Foundation . . . sealed:* the foundations of buildings in antiquity were sealed and adorned with inscriptions. As inscriptions Paul uses Scripture texts that complement one another: Num 16:5 (God cares for those he loves) and Num 16:26; Isa 26:13; 52:11 (these must lead upright lives).

tion: "The Lord knows those who are his own,"
and "Everyone who calls on the name of the
Lord must turn away from wickedness."[j]

20 In every large house, there are utensils
not only of gold and silver but also of wood
and clay—some for noble purposes and
some for ordinary purposes.[k] 21 If someone
avoids these things I have mentioned, he will
be regarded as a vessel of special value, ded-
icated and useful for the master of the house,
and ready to perform any good work.[l]

22 Turn away from youthful passions and
pursue righteousness, faith, love, and peace,
together with those who call on the Lord*
with a pure heart.[m] 23 Avoid foolish and stu-
pid speculations, for you are well aware that
they only result in quarrels.[n]

24 A servant of the Lord should not engage
in quarrels but should be kind to everyone.
He should be a good teacher and patient,[o]
25 correcting with gentleness those who
oppose him. For God may grant them
repentance so that they may come to recog-
nize the truth[p] 26 and regain their senses,
enabling them to escape the snare of the
devil who had held them captive and sub-
jected them to his will.[q]

IV: THE TASKS OF A MAN OF GOD*

CHAPTER 3

Repulse the Onslaughts of False Teachers.
1 You must realize that there will be great
distress in the last days.[r] 2 [s] People will love
nothing but themselves and money. They
will be boastful, arrogant, abusive, disobedi-
ent to their parents, ungrateful, irreligious,[t]
3 and devoid of natural affection. They will
be implacable, slanderous, licentious, bru-
tal, and haters of everything that is good.
4 They will be treacherous, reckless, conceit-
ed, and lovers of pleasure rather than lovers
of God[u] 5 as they maintain the appearance
of godliness * but deny its power. Avoid per-
sons like that![v]

6 They are the type who insinuate them-
selves into households and gain control of
the women there who are burdened by their
sins and obsessed with their desires,[w] 7 and
who are always seeking to be taught but
unable to ever arrive at a knowledge of the
truth.[x]

8 Just as Jannes and Jambres opposed
Moses, so these men, with their depraved
minds and their deceitful pretense of faith,
also oppose the truth.[y] 9 But they will not
succeed in their efforts. As was the case with
those men, their folly will become obvious to
everyone.[z]

Remain Faithful in Persecution. 10 As for you,
however, you have followed my teaching, my
way of life, my aims, my faith, my patience,
my love, my perseverance,[a] 11 my persecu-
tions, my sufferings—the things that I faced
in Antioch, Iconium, and Lystra and that I
endured. Yet the Lord brought me out safely
from all of them. *[b]

12 Indeed, persecution will afflict all who
want to lead a godly life in Christ Jesus,[c]
13 while wicked people and impostors will
grow ever worse, deceiving others and being
themselves deceived.[d] 14 But as for you,
stand by what you have learned and firmly
believed, because you know from whom you
have learned it. *[e]

Gain Wisdom from the Inspired Scriptures.
15 Also remember that from the time you
were a child you have known the sacred
Scriptures. From these you can acquire the
wisdom that will lead you to salvation

j Ex 33:12; Num 16:5; Isa 26:13; Jn 10:14; 1 Cor 3:10-15; Gal 4:9.—k Rom 9:21; 1 Cor 1:12.—l 2 Tim 3:17; 2 Cor 9:8; Eph 2:10.—m Acts 2:21; Rom 10:13; 1 Cor 1:2; Gal 5:22; 1 Tim 1:14; 6:11.—n 2 Tim 2:14; 1 Tim 1:4; 4:7; 6:4; Tit 3:9.—o 1 Tim 3:2-3; 6:11; 1 Pet 3:6.—p 2 Tim 3:7; 4:2; Prov 22:15; Gal 6:1; 1 Tim 2:4.—q 1 Tim 3:7; 6:9.—r Mt 24:9-12; 1 Tim 4:1; 2 Pet 3:3; Jude 18.—s 2-4: Rom 1:29-31.—t Phil 2:21; 1 Tim 3:3; 2 Pet 2:10-12.—u Phil 3:18, 19; 1 Tim 3:6; 6:4.—v Mt 7:15, 21; Rom 2:20-22; 16:17; 1 Tim 2:2; Tit 1:16.—w Mt 23:14; Tit 1:11; Jude 4.—x 2 Tim 2:25; 1 Tim 2:4.—y Ex 7:11, 22; Acts 13:8; 1 Tim 6:5.—z Ex 7:12; 8:18; 9:11; Lk 6:11.—a Phil 2:20; 1 Tim 4:6.—b 2 Tim 4:17, 18; Ps 34:20; Acts 13:14, 50; 14:5, 19; Rom 15:31; 2 Cor 11:23-27.—c Jn 15:20; Acts 14:22; 2 Cor 12:10.—d 2 Tim 2:16; Mk 13:5; 1 Tim 4:1; Rev 22:11.—e 2 Tim 1:13; 2:2; 1 Tim 4:6.

2:22 *Those who call on the Lord:* i.e., Christians (see Acts 19:14ff; Rom 10:12f).

3:1-17 For the last times, Jesus had already announced somber perspectives: false messiahs would be preached to mislead people into doctrines of perversion (see Mt 24:4-5, 24). For his part, Paul too has evoked this revival of evil for the end of history (see 2 Thes 2:3-12; see also 1 Jn 2:18-24; 4:3; 2 Jn 7). Undoubtedly, magicians practiced their wiles at Ephesus; in fact, according to Jewish legend, *Jannes* and *Jambres* were leading sorcerers who opposed Moses before Pharaoh (see Ex 7:8ff). Like Paul, everyone who announces the Gospel must accept persecution (see Mt 5:10-11; 10:22; Jn 15:19-20; Acts 13:1—14:28). It is a call for strength and firmness.

The important thing for the envoy of God and the Church is to remain faithful to the word of God as reported in Scripture. He is assured of finding therein nourishment for his faith and help for his ministry. This text is often referred to as bearing witness to the inspiration of Scripture.

3:5 *Godliness:* i.e., true religion (see 1 Tim 4:7).

3:11 Lystra was Timothy's native place; for the persecutions, see Acts 13:50; 14:5-19.

3:14 *From whom you have learned it:* Timothy had been instructed by his Jewish grandmother and mother (see 1 Tim 1:5).

through faith in Christ Jesus.[f] 16 All Scrip-
ture is inspired by God and is useful for
teaching, for refutation, for correction, and
for training in uprightness, *[g] 17 so that the
man of God may be proficient and equipped
for good work of every kind.[h]

CHAPTER 4

V: THE PREACHING OF A MAN OF GOD*

The Charge To Preach. 1 In the presence of
God and of Christ Jesus, who is to judge the
living and the dead, * and by his appearing
and his kingdom, I charge you:[i] 2 preach the
message; be persistent in doing so, whether
in season or out of season; convince,
reprove, and encourage, but with great
patience and instruction.[j]

The Need for Preaching. 3 For the time is
coming when people will not accept sound
doctrine, but they will follow their own
desires and accumulate teachers who will
preach to their itching ears.[k] 4 They will shut
their ears to the truth and be captivated by
myths.[l] 5 As for you, always be sober. Endure
hardships, do the work of preaching the
gospel, and carry out your ministry to the
fullest extent. *[m]

VI: THE TRIUMPHS OF A MAN OF GOD*

Reward for Fidelity. 6 As for me, I am
already being poured out as a libation, and
the time has come for my departure.[n] 7 I
have fought the good fight; I have finished
the race; I have kept the faith.[o] 8 Now wait-
ing for me is the crown * of righteousness,
which the Lord, the righteous judge, will
award to me on that Day—and not only to
me, but to all those who have eagerly longed
for his appearance.[p]

Comfort in Trial. 9 Make every effort to come
to me as soon as possible.[q] 10 Because of his
love of worldly pursuits, Demas * has desert-
ed me and gone off to Thessalonica.
Crescens has gone to Galatia, and Titus has
left for Dalmatia.[r] 11 No one but Luke *

f 2 Tim 1:5; Deut 4:6; Jn 5:39.—g Deut 29:29; Rom 4:23-24; 15:4; 2 Pet 1:19-21.—h 2 Tim 2:21; Lk 6:20; 1 Tim 6:11.—i Acts 10:42; Rom 14:9-10; 1 Thes 4:15-16; 1 Tim 5:21; 6:14; 1 Pet 4:5.—j Acts 20:20, 31; Gal 6:6; 1 Tim 4:13; 5:20; Tit 1:13; 2:15.—k Isa 30:10; 1 Tim 1:10; 4:1.—l 1 Tim 1:4; 4:1, 7; Tit 1:14.—m 2 Tim 1;8; 2:3, 9; Acts 21:8; Eph 4:11.—n Num 15:1-12; 28:7, 24; Phil 2:17.—o Acts 20:24; 1 Cor 9:24; 1 Tim 1:18; 6:12; Heb 12:1; Jude 3.—p 2 Tim 1:12; 2:5; Wis 5:16; 1 Cor 9:25; Phil 3:14; Col 1:5; 1 Tim 6:14; Jas 1:12; 1 Pet 5:4; Rev 2:10.—q 2 Tim 4:21; Tit 3:12.—r Acts 16:6; 17:1; 2 Cor 2:13; 7:6-7; 8:23; Gal 2:3; Col 4:14; Tit 1:4; Philem 24; 1 Jn 2:15.

3:16 The verse gives clear witness to the inspiration of Scripture. The Jews of that day believed in the inspiration of the three parts of the Old Testament. However, they ascribed the highest type of inspiration to the *Pentateuch* or Five Books attributed to Moses (also known as the "Torah" or Law), a lower type to the *Prophets*, and an even lower one to the *Writings*.

The sacred writers of the New Testament cited the Old Testament about 350 times in such a way as to show that Christians shared the belief of the Jews in the divine origin of the sacred books. In addition, the New Testament speaks of inspiration in the Old Testament Scriptures explicitly here and in 2 Pet 1:19-21, and of the New Testament writings implicitly in 2 Pet 3:14-16.

In the *Constitution on Divine Revelation*, Vatican II says: "Holy Mother Church, relying on the belief of the apostles, holds that the Books of both the Old and the New Testament in their entirety, with all their parts, are sacred and canonical because, written under the inspiration of the Holy Spirit, they have God as their Author" (no. 11).

However, this does not mean that God used the sacred author as a secretary to whom he dictated. Nor did he simply reveal to the human author the contents of the Book and the way in which this should be expressed. Rather, the human author is a living instrument endowed with reason who under the divine impulse brings his faculties and powers into play in such a way that all can easily gather from the Book produced by his work his distinctive genius and his individual characteristics and features. In other words, the sacred author, like every author, makes use of all his faculties—intellect, imagination, and will—to consign to writing whatever God wanted written, and no more.

By virtue of the *divine condescension*, things are presented to us in the Bible in a manner that is in common use among human beings. For as the substantial Word of God made himself like human beings in all things except sin (see Heb 4:15), so God's words, spoken by human tongues, have taken on all the qualities of human language except error.

4:1-5 Apostles, missionaries, and pastors are first of all men of the Gospel and evangelization. The project that animates their existence is to awaken human beings to the true worship of the living God. This is a much more pressing task when a swarm of vain ideas sows confusion. Such a time has come, says Paul.

4:1 *Living and the dead:* Christ will return to judge both the living and the dead (see Mt 25:31; Jn 5:26-29; 1 Thes 4:15-17). This was doubtless an early teaching (see Acts 10:42; 1 Pet 4:5) and it became part of the Creed.

4:5 At the end of this verse, the Vulgate adds the words "Be sober."

4:6-18 In these last moments Paul affirms that his blood is about to be shed as a sacrifice to God (it was Jewish practice to pour oil or wine on a burnt offering: see Ex 29:40; Phil 2:17). He then uses images from sports to express his certainty of having remained steadfast in the faith. Although his fate had recently been a sad one and he was abandoned and betrayed, his gaze remains fixed on the Lord to announce the Gospel of salvation to the very end and to enter into his Kingdom.

4:8 *Crown:* probably a reference taken from the laurel wreath that was accustomed to be placed on the head of a winning athlete or a victorious soldier (see 2 Tim 2:5; 1 Cor 9:25).

4:10 *Demas* had been with Paul during the latter's first imprisonment in Rome (see Col 4:14; Philem 24). *Crescens* is mentioned only here in the New Testament. *Galatia* here means Gaul, according to the terminology used at that time by writers of Greek. *Dalmatia* is equivalent to present-day Albania and part of the former Yugoslavia; it is also called Illyricum in the New Testament (see Rom 15:19).

4:11 *Luke:* the "beloved physician," mentioned in Col 4:14 and Philem 24, who accompanied Paul throughout much of his Second and Third Missionary Journeys (see note on Acts 16:9-15). *Mark:* the same person who had left Paul and Barnabas in the midst of the First Missionary Journey (see Acts 13:13). Paul's refusal to take him along on the Second Missionary Journey caused Barnabas to separate himself from the Apostle and take Mark with him on a mission to Cyprus (see Acts 15:36-41). However, Mark later proved himself to Paul and was present with him during the first Roman imprisonment (see Col 4:10; Philem 24).

is with me. Get Mark and bring him with you, for he has been helpful to me in my ministry.[s]

[12]I have sent Tychicus* to Ephesus.[t] [13]When you come, bring along with you the cloak* that I left with Carpus in Troas, and also the scrolls, particularly the parchments.[u]

[14]Alexander the coppersmith* has done me a great deal of harm. The Lord will repay him for his deeds.[v] [15]Be on guard yourself against him, for he has been strongly opposed to our teaching.

[16]At the first hearing of my case, no one came to court to support me. Every one of them deserted me. May it not be held against them![w] [17]But the Lord stood at my side* and gave me strength so that through me the message might be fully proclaimed and all the Gentiles might hear it.

Thus was I rescued from the lion's jaws.[x] [18]The Lord will rescue me from every evil attack and bring me safely into his heavenly kingdom. To him be glory forever and ever. Amen.*[y]

VII: CONCLUSION*

Final Greetings. [19]Greet Prisca and Aquila,* and the household of Onesiphorus.[z] [20]Erastus* remained in Corinth, while I left Trophimus ill in Miletus.[a] [21]Do your best to get here before winter. Eubulus sends greetings to you, as do Pudens and Linus and Claudia and all the brethren.*[b]

Farewell. [22]The Lord be with your spirit. Grace be with all of you.*[c]

---

s 2 Tim 1:15; Acts 12:12; Col 4:10, 14; Philem 24.—t Acts 18:19; 20:4; Eph 6:21; Col 4:7.—u Acts 16:8; 20:6.—v 2 Sam 3:39; Pss 28:4; 62:12; Prov 24:12; Acts 19:33; Rom 2:6; 12:19; 1 Tim 1:20.—w 2 Tim 1:15; Acts 7:60.—x 1 Sam 17:27; 1 Mac 2:60; Ps 22:22; Dan 6:23; Acts 9:13; 23:11; 27:23; 1 Cor 15:32; Phil 4:13.—y Rom 11:36; 16:27; 2 Cor 1:10; 2 Pet 2:9.—z 2 Tim 1:16; Acts 18:2; Rom 16:3; 1 Cor 16:19.—a Acts 19:22; 20:4, 15, 17; 21:29.—b 2 Tim 4:9; Tit 3:12.—c Gal 6:18; Phil 4:23; Col 4:18; 1 Tim 6:21; Tit 3:15; Philem 25.

4:12 *Tychicus:* a fellow worker of Paul (see Acts 20:3-5; Eph 6:21; Col 4:7).

4:13 *Cloak:* probably a long-sleeved traveling garment that Paul could use to keep warm during his imprisonment. *Carpus:* possibly the Apostle's host at Troas, but nothing is known for certain about him. *Scrolls:* undoubtedly some type of printed documents. *Parchments:* perhaps leather scrolls of Old Testament Books.

4:14 *Alexander the coppersmith:* this seems to be the same Alexander mentioned in 1 Tim 1:20; he may have testified against Paul in court. *The Lord will repay:* citation from Pss 28:4; 62:13; and Prov 24:12.

4:17 *The Lord stood at my side:* Paul's ultimate strength lay in his total dependence on the one who commissioned him (see 2 Cor 12:9-10; Phil 4:11-13).

4:18 It is noteworthy that this doxology is centered on Christ the Savior and Redeemer (see Rom 16:25; Gal 1:5).

4:19-22 This conclusion gives a series of short requests, instructions, and greetings.

4:19 *Prisca and Aquila:* Prisca (see Rom 16:3; 1 Cor 16:19) is the diminutive form of Priscilla (see Acts 16:2, 18f, 26). She and her husband Aquila were Jewish Christians who had met Paul on his first visit to Corinth during the Second Missionary Journey. They had come to Corinth from Rome, and like Paul they were tentmakers (see Acts 16:2f). Later they went with Paul to Ephesus (see Acts 18:18f), where their house became a Christian meeting place for several years before they returned to Rome (Rom 16:3f; 1 Cor 16:19). They had now gone back to Ephesus (see 1 Tim 1:3). *Onesiphorus:* see note on 2 Tim 1:16.

4:20 *Erastus:* see note on Rom 16:23. *Trophimus:* a Christian from Ephesus (see Acts 21:29), who accompanied Paul to Jerusalem (see Acts 20:4) and was thought by the Jews to have entered the temple, thus leading to the riot that resulted in Paul's arrest (see Acts 21:29ff) and first imprisonment at Rome. *Miletus:* a seaport on the coast of Asia Minor about 50 miles from Ephesus.

4:21 Nothing is known for certain about *Eubulus* and *Pudens.* There is a western tradition that *Linus* was the successor of Peter as Bishop of Rome, and that *Claudia* was his mother.

4:22 Some manuscripts add the words "Jesus Christ" after "Lord" and "Amen" at the end of the verse. The first "you" in the Greek (translated as "your") is singular, indicating that the Letter was addressed to Timothy alone; the second is plural ("all of you"), indicating that it was intended to be read aloud to the community.

"Exhort the younger men to exercise self-control" *(Tit 2:6)*.

THE LETTER TO TITUS

Lead an Upright Life

The Gospel has been preached and communities established for several decades; it is now that the first real problems begin. Some Christians, doubtless of Jewish origin, are mingling with the Gospel some theories propagated by rather marginal Jewish groups. The relaxed morals of paganism are also infiltrating the communities. It has become necessary to remind people that Christian salvation has been brought by the coming of Christ. It has also become necessary to sketch the main lines of proper behavior in everyday private and social life. Finally, it has become necessary to provide the Churches with an organization.

The First Letter to Timothy and the Letter to Titus deal with the same problems. The tone is sometimes peremptory in reminding people that Christian convictions must be translated into practical behavior.

If we accept the attribution of this Letter to Paul, it would date from A.D. 64 or 65 and be addressed to Titus, Paul's personal delegate on the island of Crete. Paul relies on Titus to give the communities a solid organization and to combat those who are falsifying the word of God.

Titus was a Gentile Christian converted by Paul (see Tit 1:4) who became one of his most helpful coworkers. The Apostle took him along to Jerusalem when he went there to meet the leaders of the Church and discuss his Gospel (see 2 Tim 2:8). The leaders accepted Titus as a Christian without imposing circumcision on him, thereby vindicating Paul's teaching (see Gal 2:3-5).

There is no reference in Acts to Titus, but he is mentioned 13 times in the rest of the New Testament. Titus worked with Paul at Ephesus on his Third Missionary Journey and possibly his

Fourth (see Introduction to First Timothy). From there the Apostle sent him to assist the Church at Corinth (see 2 Cor 2:12f; 7:5f; 8:6), where he courageously and tactfully carried out his mission of reconciliation (see 2 Cor 7:6-16).

Upon Paul's release from his first Roman imprisonment, he and Titus worked in Crete (see Tit 1:5). When Paul departed, he left Titus behind to continue the work (Tit 1:5; 2:15; 3:12f).

In the present Letter, Paul asks Titus to bring his ministry in Crete to a close. To do so, Titus must organize the churches (Tit 1:5-9), oppose the false teachers (Tit 1:10-14; 3:9-11), and instruct the churches on genuine Christian conduct (Tit 2:1—3:8). When his replacement arrives, Titus is to meet Paul at Nicopolis on the west coast of Greece (Tit 3:12).

The last we hear of Titus is that he went on mission to Dalmatia (see 2 Tim 4:10).

The Letter to Titus may be divided as follows:

I: Salutation (1:1-4)
II: Church Organization (1:5-16)
III: Proper Conduct for Christians (2:1—3:11)
IV: Conclusion (3:12-15)

CHAPTER 1

I: SALUTATION*

Address.
1 Paul, a servant of God * and an apostle of Jesus Christ, to further the faith of those whom God has chosen and their knowledge of religious truth, [a]
2 with its hope of eternal life that God, who does not lie, promised before the beginning of time, [b]
3 and who now at his appointed time has revealed his word through the proclamation with which I was entrusted by the command of God our Savior, [c]
4 to Titus, my loyal child in the faith we share: * grace and peace from God the Father and Christ Jesus our Savior. * [d]

II: CHURCH ORGANIZATION

A Bishop Must Be Blameless.*
5 The reason I left you behind in Crete was so that you could finish up the work that remained to be done and appoint presbyters in every town as I directed you. [e]
6 Each man must be blameless and the husband of only one wife, with children who are believers and free from any suspicion of licentious or rebellious behavior. [f]

7 For in his role as God's steward a bishop * must be blameless. He must not be arrogant or quick-tempered or prone to drunkenness or violent or avaricious. [g]
8 Rather, he must be hospitable, a lover of goodness, prudent, upright, devout, and self-controlled. [h]
9 In addition, he must hold firmly to the authentic message he has been taught, so that he may be able both to exhort with sound doctrine and to refute those who contradict it. [i]

a Rom 1:1; 1 Cor 1:1; 1 Tim 2:4; 4:3; 2 Tim 2:25; 3:7; Heb 10:26; Jas 1:1.—b Tit 3:7; Num 23:19; 2 Tim 1:1, 9; Heb 6:18; 1 Jn 2:25.—c Tit 2:10; 3:4; Ps 24:5; Lk 1:47; 2 Cor 1:1; 1 Tim 1:1; 2:3; 4:10; 2 Tim 1:10; Jude 25.—d Tit 2:13; 3:6; Rom 1:7; 2 Cor 2:13; Phil 3:20; 1 Tim 1:2; 2 Tim 1:10; 2 Pet 1:1, 11; 2:20; 3:2, 18.—e Acts 11:30; 27:7; 1 Tim 1:3; 2 Tim 2:2.—f 1 Thes 3:13.—g 1 Cor 4:1; 1 Tim 3:1; 1 Pet 4:10.—h Tit 2:2, 5-6, 12; Rom 12:13; 2 Tim 3:3.—i Tit 1:13; 2:1-2, 8; 1 Cor 16:13; 1 Tim 1:10, 19; 6:3; 2 Tim 1:13; 4:3.

1:1-4 In this beautiful salutation the author highlights the centrality of the Letter's salvation theme in two ways. (1) He defines the role of an apostle—to tell all people of God's plan to lead them to eternal life. (2) He specifically mentions Christ's role as Savior, which he does in no other salutation.

1:1 *Servant of God:* this is the only place Paul applies the phrase to himself; elsewhere he calls himself "servant of Christ" (see Rom 1:1; Gal 1:10; Phil 1:1). *Apostle:* see note on Mk 6:30.

1:3-4 *God our Savior . . . Christ Jesus our Savior:* the term "Savior" is applied three times to God the Father (here and Tit 2:10; 3:4; see also 1 Tim 1:1; 2:3; 4:10) and three times to Jesus (Tit 1:4; 2:13; 3:6; see also 2 Tim 1:10).

1:4 *My loyal child in the faith we share:* Titus is Paul's true child because he accepts and will proclaim the faith that Paul preaches. This links Titus with the developing chain of tradition.

1:5-9 The young communities remain under the direct supervision of the Apostle or his delegate. But the latter establishes a group of people entrusted with its day-to-day operation and regular instruction. Such delegates are given various names in the New Testament: *presbyters, bishops,* and *pastors.* Each one seems to be responsible for the community.

After the disappearance of the Apostles and their immediate delegates, the situation will evolve; the community will be led by a *bishop,* who presides over the college of *priests* and the group of *deacons.* At the time of this Letter, the leaders possess an authority linked to that of the Apostle. They must truly imitate his manner of life and also fulfill the primary task of preaching the word of God.

1:7 *Bishop:* (i.e., "overseer") this term could replace *presbyter* (i.e., "elder": vv. 5-6) because the two were equivalent at that time (see Acts 20:17, 28).

For the Pure All Things Are Pure.* 10 For there are also many rebellious people, especially among the Jewish converts,* who deceive others with their empty talk.[j] 11 It is essential to silence them, since they are ruining whole households by teaching for dishonest gain what it is not right to teach.[k] 12 It was one of their very own prophets, a man from Crete, who said,

> "Cretans have always been liars, vicious
> beasts, and lazy gluttons."[l]

13 This testimony is true. Therefore, rebuke them sharply so that they may be restored to a sound faith,[m] 14 rather than paying attention to Jewish myths or to the commandments of those who turn away from the truth.[n]

15 To the pure all things are pure, but to those who are corrupt and without faith nothing is pure. *Their very minds and their consciences have been corrupted.[o] 16 They profess to know God, but they deny him by their deeds. They are detestable and disobedient, totally unfit for any good work.[p]

III: PROPER CONDUCT FOR CHRISTIANS

CHAPTER 2

Teach What Is Consistent with Sound Doctrine.* 1 As for you, teach what is consistent with sound doctrine.[q] 2 Exhort the older men to be temperate, dignified, self-controlled, and sound in faith, in love, and in perseverance.[r]

3 Similarly, exhort the older women to be reverent in their behavior, not to be slanderous or slaves of drink, and eager to teach what is good.[s] 4 They can then instruct the younger women to love their husbands and their children,[t] 5 to be self-controlled and chaste, to be diligent homemakers, to be agreeable, and to respect the authority of their husbands so that the word of God may not be derided.[u]

6 Likewise, exhort the younger men to exercise self-control.[v] 7 Show yourself to them in all respects as a model of good works, while in your teaching exhibit integrity and dignity[w] 8 and a soundness of speech that cannot be criticized. Then any opponent will be put to shame when he can find nothing evil to say about us.[x]

9 Exhort slaves to be submissive to their masters and to give them satisfaction in every respect. They are not to talk back to them,[y] 10 nor are they to steal from them. Rather, they should show themselves to be completely trustworthy so that in every way they may add luster to the doctrine of God our Savior.[z]

The Grace of God Has Appeared.* 11 For the grace of God has appeared bringing salvation to the entire human race.[a] 12 It teaches us to reject godless ways and worldly desires, and in the present age to lead lives that are temperate, just, and godly,[b] 13 while we await our blessed hope, the appearance of the glory of our great God and Savior Jesus Christ.*[c] 14 He gave himself for us in

j Acts 10:45; 11:2; 1 Tim 1:6.—k 1 Tim 5:13; 2 Tim 4:2.—l Acts 2:11; 17:28; 1 Cor 15:33.—m Tit 1:9; 2:2; 1 Tim 5:20.—n Tit 3:9; Col 2:22; 1 Tim 1:4; 4:7; 2 Tim 4:4; 2 Pet 1:16.—o Mt 15:10-11; Mk 7:14-23; Acts 10:9-16; Rom 14:14-23; Col 2:20-22; 1 Tim 6:5.—p Jer 5:2; 12:2; Hos 8:2-3; 2 Tim 3:5, 8; 1 Jn 2:4.—q Tit 1:9, 13; 2:8; 1 Tim 1:10; 6:3; 2 Tim 1:13; 4:3.—r Tit 1:8, 13; 2:5-6, 12; 1 Tim 3:2; 5:1.—s 1 Tim 2:9, 12; 3:8, 11.—t 1 Tim 5:2.—u Tit 1:8; 2:2, 6, 12; 1 Cor 11:3; 14:34; Eph 5:22-24; Col 3:18; 1 Tim 2:11-15; Heb 4:12; 1 Pet 3:1-6.—v Tit 1:8; 2:2, 5, 12; 1 Tim 5:1.—w Tit 2:14; 1 Tim 4:12.—x 1 Tim 5:14; 1 Pet 2:12.—y 1 Cor 7:21-22; Eph 6:5-8; Col 3:22-25; 1 Tim 6:1-2; 1 Pet 2:18.—z Tit 1:3; 3:4; Ps 24:5; Mt 5:16; Lk 1:47; 1 Tim 1:1; 2:3; 4:10; Jude 25.—a Rom 3:24; 1 Tim 2:4; 4:10; 2 Tim 1:10.—b Tit 1:8; 2:2, 5-6; 3:3; 2 Tim 3:12.—c Tit 1:4; 3:6; 1 Cor 1:7; Phil 3:20; 1 Thes 1:10; 1 Tim 6:14; 2 Tim 1:10; 2 Pet 1:1, 11; 2:20; 3:2, 18.

1:10-16 There will always be troublemakers who profit from fables and practices that they propagate; they monopolize religion instead of entering into the Gospel. The important thing, Jesus had declared (see Mk 7:1-23), was not to wash one's hands or to forbid foods but to give oneself to God with an upright and sincere heart (see Mt 5:8). The author sternly reminds the Cretans of their now firm reputation as liars, and he does not miss the opportunity to cite (in v. 12) a saying (which had become a veritable proverb) of one of their poets, Epimenides of Cnossos, who lived in the sixth century B.C.

1:10 *Jewish converts:* literally, "those of the circumcision." These individuals (who have come to be called "Judaizers") had two basic characteristics: (1) the belief that Christians had to be circumcised and also keep the Jewish ceremonial law (see notes on Gal, ch. 2); (2) a fondness for unscriptural Jewish myths and genealogies (see note on 1 Tim 1:3-20).

1:15 This is a proverb that takes on a Christian meaning (see Mt 15:10-20; Rom 14:14-23). Christians have been purified by the sacrificial Death of Christ. Hence, to them "everything created by God is good, and nothing is to be rejected, provided that it is received with thanksgiving" (1 Tim 4:4). On the other hand, to those who are corrupt and without faith, nothing is pure. They set up man-made prohibitions against certain foods, marriage, and the like (see Mt 15:10-11, 16-20; Mk 7:14-19; Acts 10:9-16; Rom 14:20).

2:1-10 The moral rules set forth here could also have been voiced by a Stoic philosopher of the time. The author does not criticize the social climate of his day, but he wants the Christian communities to be models of honesty and dignity. He describes a new spirit: charity. Christians of all ages and all conditions who form the Church must show by their most ordinary actions that they live for God. On these matters, see Eph 5:21—6:9; Col 3:18-21.

2:11-14 Here, at the center of the Letter, is a beautiful passage for Christmastime. The manifestation (or epiphany) of God must change our way of knowing and living. Christians are on the way to an event; they are hastening toward the final manifestation of Christ in glory. Hence, this text is also a valuable testimony to the faith of the early Christians in the divinity of Christ (v. 14).

2:13 *Of our great God and Savior Jesus Christ:* this is a clear statement of the divinity of Christ (see also Rom 9:5). Some, however, offer another translation that does not possess that same clarity: "of the great God and of our Savior Jesus Christ."

order to deliver us from all iniquity and to purify for himself a people as his own who are eager to do good. [d]

The Goodness of God Our Savior.* 15 These are the things you should expound. Exhort and reprove with all authority. Let no one disregard you. [e]

CHAPTER 3

1 Remind everyone to be subject to rulers and authorities, to obey them, to be ready to
perform any honorable task, * [f] 2 to slander
no one, to avoid quarrels, to be gentle, and to be gracious to everyone. [g]

3 For we ourselves were once foolish, disobedient, led astray, and enslaved by various passions and pleasures, passing our days in malice and envy. We ourselves were hateful, and we hated one another. [h]

4 But when the goodness and loving kindness
of God our Savior appeared, [i]
5 * not because of any righteous deeds on our part
but because of his mercy,
he saved us through the bath of rebirth
and renewal by the Holy Spirit, [j]
6 whom he lavished on us abundantly
through Jesus Christ our Savior, [k]
7 so that we might be justified by his grace
and become heirs in hope of eternal life. [l]

8 This saying can be trusted.

Be Devoted to Good Works.* I want you to stress these points, so that those who have come to believe in God will be determined to devote themselves to good works. All this
is right and beneficial for people. [m] 9 But
avoid foolish arguments, genealogies, dissensions, and quarrels about the Law, for they are unprofitable and futile. [n]

10 Warn a heretic once or twice, but after-
ward reject him. [o] 11 You may be sure that
such a person is perverted and sinful and stands self-condemned. [p]

IV: CONCLUSION*

Final Message. 12 As soon as I have sent
Artemas * or Tychicus to you, do your best to come to me at Nicopolis, where I intend to
spend the winter. [q] 13 Send Zenas the lawyer
and Apollos * on their way, and see to it that
they lack nothing. [r] 14 Meanwhile, our people
must be taught to devote themselves to good works in order to meet urgent needs * so that they will not be unfruitful. [s]

Farewell. 15 All those with me send you greetings. Greetings to those who love us in the faith.

Grace be with all of you. * [t]

d Ex 19:5; Deut 4:20; Ps 130:8; Mt 1:21; 20:28; Gal 1:4; 2:20; Eph 5:2, 25; 1 Tim 2:6; Heb 1:3; 1 Pet 1:18-19; 1 Jn 1:7.—e Tit 1:13; 1 Tim 4:12; 5:20.—f Tit 2:14; Rom 13:1-7; 1 Tim 2:1-2; 2 Tim 2:21; 1 Pet 2:13-14.—g Eph 4:31.—h Rom 6:16; 1 Cor 6:9-11; Eph 2:1-3; 5:6; Col 3:5-7; 1 Pet 4:3; 2 Pet 2:19.—i Tit 1:3; 2:10; Ps 24:5; Lk 1:47; Eph 2:7; 1 Tim 1:1; 2:3; 4:10; Jude 25.—j Deut 9:5; Rom 11:14; Eph 2:4-5, 8-9; 2 Tim 1:9; 1 Pet 1:3.—k Tit 1:4; 2:13; Rom 5:5; Phil 3:20; 2 Tim 1:10; 2 Pet 1:1, 11; 2:20; 3:2, 18.—l Tit 1:2; Mt 25:46; Rom 3:24; 2 Tim 1:1; 1 Jn 2:25.—m Tit 1:10-16; 2:14; 1 Tim 1:15; 3:1; 4:9; 2 Tim 2:11.—n 1 Tim 1:4; 4:7; 2 Tim 2:14, 16, 23.—o Mt 18:15-18; Rom 16:17; 1 Cor 5:11; 2 Thes 3:6, 14-15; 2 Tim 2:25, 26.—p Mt 16:16; Jn 3:10.—q Acts 20:4; Eph 6:21; Col 4:7; 2 Tim 4:9, 12.—r Acts 18:24-26; 1 Cor 1:12; 3:4-6, 22; 4:6; 16:12.—s Tit 2:14; 3:8; Mt 7:19; Heb 10:24; 1 Pet 3:13; 2 Pet 1:8.—t Gal 6:10; Col 4:18; 1 Tim 1:2; 2 Tim 4:22; Heb 13:25.

2:15—3:8a The fact that someone's life is no longer ruled by passion, egoism, and wickedness is always surprising. It is the sign that such a person is marked by the idea of God's goodness. With these practical recommendations, the author knows how to evoke in a few words the major aspects of the Christian mystery: love of God; salvation through grace; Baptism; the gift of the Spirit; and the expectation of fulfillment in the end time.

3:1 *To be ready to perform any honorable task:* another possible translation is: "to be open to every good enterprise."

3:5-7 The effects of Baptism are delineated: rebirth, forgiveness of sins by Christ, reception of the Holy Spirit, and the right to eternal life (of which the indwelling Spirit is a pledge—see 2 Cor 1:22).

3:8b-11 The act of believing is not something pertaining only to one's spirit; it engages one's whole life. The author shows himself to be severe toward those who spend their time and their understanding on idle discussions and on speculations whose object is no longer the sincere search for truth. Here, for the first time, is enunciated the idea of the seditious person, the "heretic," a word borrowed from the philosophical schools of the time. In a Christian setting, he is a person who chooses the elements of the faith that suit him and is ready to deny essentials and divide the community.

3:12-15 Paul takes the opportunity to stress one more time that Christians should do what is good (see Tit 3:1, 8, 14). This will ensure that their lives will not be "unfruitful." The practice of doing good is above all the concrete mutual help among those who are disenfranchised.

3:12 *Artemas:* apparently one of Paul's coworkers, who is mentioned nowhere else. *Tychicus:* a trusted coworker of Paul who on several occasions seems to be traveling with the Apostle or for him (see Acts 20:4; Eph 6:21f; Col 4:7f; 2 Tim 4:12). *Nicopolis:* a city in the Roman province of Epirus on the west coast of Greece.

3:13 *Zenas . . . Apollos:* almost certainly the bearers of this Letter. Zenas is a coworker of Paul mentioned nowhere else. Apollos is the well-known Alexandrian Jewish convert who was fully instructed at Ephesus and worked effectively in the Church of Corinth (see Acts 18:24-28; 19:1; 1 Cor 1:12; 3:4-6; 16:12).

3:14 *Urgent needs:* another possible translation is: "practical needs."

3:15 *Grace be with all of you:* some manuscripts have: "The grace of the Lord [or 'of God'] be with all of you. Amen." *All of you:* the plural form indicates that Paul intended the Letter to be read to the whole Church (see 1 Tim 6:21; 2 Tim 4:22).

THE LETTER TO PHILEMON

Let the Slave Become a Brother

Paul entrusted his Letter to the Colossians to Tychicus and assigned him as a companion "Onesimus, our trustworthy and beloved brother" (Col 4:9). Onesimus was perhaps a lazy slave and a thief, who had run away from Colossae. He had reached one of the larger cities—Caesarea or Rome—where outlaws could hide. When did he meet Paul? We do not know. The Apostle accepted him, instructed him in the Gospel, and grew fond of him. But he also had to regulate the situation of this man whose owner could have hunted him down and even put him to death; in addition, Paul risked being accused of complicity, a serious crime during that age.

Since the slave belonged to a rich Christian of Colossae, named Philemon, whom the Apostle himself had converted to the faith, probably during his stay at Ephesus, Paul sends the slave back to his master with a letter of recommendation. He hopes that Philemon will free Onesimus and allow yesterday's slave to become his fellow worker in the apostolate. This subtle and skillful Letter gives us a glimpse of Paul's warmth and his boundless respect for a less circumspect human being but one redeemed by the blood of Jesus Christ.

Paul does not take a position on the social structures of his time that divided human beings into slave and free (see 1 Cor 7:20-24; Eph 6:5-9; Col 3:22—4:1). But for believers there is no division between Jew and Greek or between slave and free; they know that all are equal in God's sight, and they believe that all are brothers and sisters in the Church. Without directly attacking social structures, Paul does, in a concrete case, propose a new attitude for Christians. Slaves are no longer regarded as things; they are persons and, more than that, they are brothers and sisters in the Lord. The Apostle expects Philemon to give spontaneous and concrete witness to this new manner of conceiving the relationships among human beings and actually living them.

The present Letter is reminiscent of similar letters of recommendation written in the Greco-Roman world of the time. It begins with a salutation, is followed by expressions of thanksgiving and petition, discusses the principal subject matter, and ends with a conclusion and farewell. It stresses Christian love for others, which, if followed out to its rightful conclusion, will eliminate the scourge of slavery in the world. The Letter is also dominated by the theme of forgiveness, which is found throughout the New Testament (see, e.g., Mt 6:12-15; 18:21-35; Eph 4:32; Col 3:13). Although Paul does not use the word, he exemplifies the Biblical definition of forgiveness.

The Letter to Philemon may be divided as follows:

Salutation (1-3)
Thanksgiving and Prayer (4-7)
Plea for Onesimus (8-20)
Conclusion (21-25)

Salutation.* 1 Paul, a prisoner of Christ Jesus, and Timothy* our brother, to Philemon, our beloved friend and fellow worker, [a]
2 to Apphia our sister, to Archippus* our fellow soldier, and to the Church that meets in

a Philem 9, 23; Acts 16:1; 2 Cor 1:1; Eph 3:1; 4:1; Phil 1:7, 13; 2:25.

1-3 The salutation indicates that a group of Christians meets together in Philemon's house and should aid him to decide Onesimus' fate. These include Apphia, thought to be his wife, and Archippus, thought to be his son, who is also a pastor like Paul ("fellow soldier [of Christ]"). Under the circumstances, Philemon would have had to be an extremely strong-minded individual to resist the eloquent plea of Paul and his protégé Timothy.

1 *Timothy:* see Introduction to First Timothy.

2 *Archippus:* the apostolic worker mentioned in Col 4:17. *Fellow soldier:* the only other use of this phrase in the New Testament is in Phil 2:25 concerning Epaphroditus. It exemplifies Paul's use of military terms to symbolize the service of a Christian (see Rom 6:13; 13:12; 2 Cor 10:3f; Eph 6:10).

your house: [b] 3 grace to you and peace from
God our Father and the Lord Jesus Christ. [c]

Thanksgiving and Prayer.* 4 [d] I always give
thanks to my God when I remember you in
my prayers, 5 because I hear of the love and
faith that you have for the Lord Jesus and for
all the saints. * [e] 6 I pray that the sharing of
your faith may become even more effective
so that you may come to perceive all the
blessings we have in Christ. [f] 7 Your love has
given me much joy and encouragement
because the hearts * of the saints have been
refreshed by you, my brother. [g]

Plea for Onesimus.* 8 Therefore, although I
am confident that in Christ I have the right
to command you to do your duty, [h] 9 I would
rather appeal to you on the basis of love. I,
Paul, an old man, and now also a prisoner
for Christ Jesus, [i] 10 am appealing to you on
behalf of my child, * Onesimus, whom I have
fathered during my imprisonment. [j]

11 He was formerly useless to you, but now
he is indeed useful both to you and to me.
12 Therefore, I am sending him back to you,
that is, I am sending my very own heart. * 13 I
wanted to keep him with me so that he might
be of service to me on your behalf during my
imprisonment for the gospel, [k] 14 but I did
not want to do anything without your knowl-
edge, so that your good deed might be volun-
tary and not compelled. [l]

15 Perhaps this is the reason he was sepa-
rated from you for a while, so that you might
have him back forever, * [m] 16 no longer as a
slave, but as more than a slave: as a brother.
He is beloved especially to me, but even more
so to you, both as a man * and in the Lord. [n]

17 * Therefore, if you consider me to be a
friend, welcome him as you would welcome
me. [o] 18 If he has wronged you in any way or
owes you anything, charge that to my
account. [p] 19 I, Paul, am writing this with my
own hand: I will repay it. I say nothing about
the fact that you owe me your very self. [q]
20 Yes, my brother, grant me some benefit * in
the Lord. Set my heart at rest in Christ. [r]

Conclusion.* 21 I have written to you confi-
dent of your acceptance, and in fact I am cer-
tain that you will do even more than I ask. [s]
22 At the same time, please prepare a guest
room for me, for I am hoping through your
prayers to be restored to you. [t]

23 Epaphras, * my fellow prisoner in Christ
Jesus, sends you greetings, [u] 24 and so do
Mark, Aristarchus, Demas, and Luke, * my
fellow workers. [v]

25 The grace of the Lord Jesus Christ be
with your spirit. * [w]

---

b Rom 16:5; Phil 2:25; Col 4:17.—c Rom 1:7; Gal 1:3; Phil 1:2.—d 4-5: Rom 1:8-9; Eph 1:15-16.—e Acts 20:21; Col 1:4; 1 Thes 3:6.—f Mt 5:16; Phil 1:9; Col 1:9.—g Rom 15:32; 1 Cor 16:18; 2 Cor 7:4, 13.—h Eph 5:4; 6:20.—i Philem 1, 23; 1 Cor 1:10; Eph 3:1; 4:1; Phil 1:7, 13.—j Acts 21:33; 1 Cor 4:14-15; Gal 4:19; Col 4:9; 1 Thes 2:11.—k Philem 10; Acts 21:33; Phil 2:30.—l 2 Cor 9:7; 1 Pet 5:2.—m Gen 45:5, 8; 50:20.—n Mt 23:8; Acts 1:16; 1 Cor 7:22; 1 Tim 5:1f.—o 2 Cor 8:23.—p Gen 43:9.—q 1 Cor 16:21; Gal 6:11; 2 Thes 3:17.—r Philem 7; 1 Cor 16:18.—s 2 Cor 2:3.—t 2 Cor 1:11; Phil 1:23; Heb 13:19.—u Philem 1; Rom 16:7; Col 1:7; 4:12-13.—v Philem 1; Acts 12:12; 13:13; 15:37-39; 19:29; 20:4; 27:2; Col 4:10, 14; 2 Tim 4:10-13.—w Rom 16:20; Gal 6:18.

4-7 Recalling his friend's love and faith, Paul prays that Philemon's active participation in the Christian faith will be increased as a result of the latter's perception of God's great goodness to both of them. He is implying what he makes specific elsewhere—that good works are the result of a mature knowledge of the faith (see Col 1:9f). In this case, Philemon's Christian maturity will lead to the beneficial treatment of Onesimus at his hands.

5 *Saints:* all the faithful are "saints" in virtue of their consecration to Christ.

7 *Hearts:* literally, "intestines," the part of the body that was considered to house the emotions of pity and love (see vv. 12, 20).

8-20 With a touch of humor, Paul utilizes a double play on words. He plays with the meaning of the name "Onesimus," which is "useful," and with the meaning of another Greek word, *chrestos,* which is part of *achrestos,* the word for "useless," and *euchrestos,* the word for "useful." In the background is the point that *chrestos* sounds like *Christos,* which means "Christ."

Paul also takes the responsibility to relieve any financial burden that Philemon may have incurred in the affair, but he ends up saying that it is Philemon who is more indebted to the Apostle himself! Indeed, the slave's flight may turn out to be a grace—it offers Philemon the chance to acknowledge him as a "brother" in Christ.

10 *My child:* Paul became a father to Onesimus by converting him (see 1 Cor 4:15; Gal 4:19).

12 *My very own heart:* a wonderful description at a time when slaves were regarded as things.

15 Paul reasons that since he has found Christ, Onesimus is returning to Philemon as a beloved brother in Christ rather than as just a slave. Master and slave are now both brothers in Christ. Hence, for Philemon to treat Onesimus solely as a runaway slave would be entirely unfitting with his Christian witness.

16 *As a man:* literally "in the flesh."

17-19 Paul is doing the same thing for Onesimus with Philemon that Christ did for us with God the Father.

20 *Benefit:* the Greek for this word is another play on the name Onesimus: what Paul wishes to get out of the master is Onesimus himself; he wants to be able to make use of the Useful One.

21-25 The Apostle is confident not only that his request will be more than fully granted but also that he will soon have the joy of being reunited with Philemon. He thus sees hope for a quick release from imprisonment.

23 *Epaphras:* founder of the Church at Colossae, who may have been a tenant in the house in which Paul lived as a prisoner (see Acts 28:30).

24 *Mark, Aristarchus, Demas, and Luke:* see notes on Col 4:7-17; 4:10; and 4:14; also notes on 2 Tim 4:10; 4:11.

25 See note on Phil 4:23.

"The blood of Jesus has given us confidence to enter the sanctuary by the new and living way" *(Heb 10:19f)*.

THE LETTER TO THE HEBREWS

Christ, the One True Priest

A tradition going back at least to the end of the second century describes this important writing as the Letter of St. Paul to the Hebrews. But the correctness of these data—genre of the work, author, addressees—is challenged by critics nowadays. Is it a letter? Only the last section is in the epistolary style. At the beginning there is no greeting to the readers nor is there subsequently any direct dialogue with a community, nor are there any references to concrete events. The pages seem rather to be a sermon throughout.

Is it by Paul? At more than one point the thought may recall that of the Apostle, but the tone, the choice of main themes, the atmosphere, and the manner of arguing force us to look for a different author. The author is certainly of Jewish origin, since he is completely at home with the Bible. In addition, he has quite a gift of eloquence. His faith is complete and deep, he is highly educated, he is devoted to teaching and familiar also with the work of Philo, a famous philosopher of Alexandria. Among the various possible authors that fit this picture the favorite is Apollos, of whom Luke speaks admiringly in the Acts of the Apostles (18:24-28), but this is, and will always remain, simply a guess.

As for the addressees—Jews—the author is seeking to revive the faith and courage of converts of long standing, who in all probability were of Jewish origin. In debating with them the author continually cites the Scriptures and ceaselessly recalls the most important ideas and realities of the Jewish religion. These individuals know Jewish tradition, its great personages, its worship, and its Law. Persecution has dispersed them, and they live in poverty, uprooted and excluded from their former religious activities. The modest and youthful Church of Christ crucified does not seem to them to bear comparison with Judaism, which benefits from a long and often glorious past and the splendor of its worship.

In response, the Letter begins by emphasizing the grandeur of the mystery of Christ's Death and Resurrection for all human beings. It stresses the superiority of Christ, who is the express image of God, superior to Moses, to Aaron, to the angels, and to any other thing. A brother to humans and a sharer in their misery and anguish, he is also the Son of God. Believers must not look with nostalgia to the past but press on toward heaven where the human condition will find its fulfillment in eternity. Secondly, the author states that the old dispensation has gone and a new dispensation is here—the New Covenant. Now people can come to Christ wherever they are, not by way of Jerusalem—except in a figurative way, through the heavenly Jerusalem. Thirdly, the author highlights the glorious priesthood of Christ in contrast to the superseded priesthood of Jerusalem. Jesus is now at God's right hand, pleading for us eternally. Since he knows what it is like to be human, he can plead with full understanding. Hence, we can go to the throne of grace with full confidence of being heard.

The author emphasizes the need for perseverance. His addressees must not quit and fall like their ancestors in the wilderness. And such a sorrowful event will never take place if they stand fast and do not become discouraged. To help them stand fast, the author sets before them the glories of faith and a series of personages who have possessed it in abundance. He preaches a wonderful sermon on those who used faith in God to endure even the greatest of trials.

Along the way, the author insists on the internal dynamism of God's Revelation. It has only one goal: the Redemption of the world in Christ. It is a movement toward a fullness and an accomplishment. And the Scriptures are what enable people to be gripped by its power and its teaching. The realities of the Old Testament are there like a sketch, figure, or shadow of a greater reality. They are of the terrestrial order in order to announce a heavenly and eternal order: the unique supremacy of the work of Christ. The Biblical meditation is developed and deepened in order to better express the mystery of Christ. Hence, this Letter introduces us to the Christian reading of the Old Testament. It utilizes some thirty-three citations from the Old Testament as well as fifty-three reminiscences or allusions. All the citations are attributed to God himself, most often introduced by the anonymous formula "he said." The author then passes from theological reflection to moral exhortation. The appeals are multiplied: live in faith and hope for the things to come, and in constancy amid trials.

As far as the date in which this Letter was written, it was certainly completed by the year A.D. 90 since it is cited by Clement of Rome. One is tempted to situate it around A.D. 67, just before the destruction of the temple. For the cessation of the worship at Jerusalem would certainly have been echoed in this writing that speaks so much about sacrifices and sanctuaries; yet a reading gives the impression that these realities are still functioning. However, such a reasoning is not decisive, for in speaking of the temple, the author hardly describes what is taking place in the ostentatious sanctuary built by Herod. He is more acquainted with the ideal images, set forth in the Pentateuch, concerning the tabernacle of the desert at the time of Moses.

The Letter to the Hebrews may be divided as follows:

- *I: Prologue (1:1-4)*
- *II: The Son of God, Superior to the Angels (1:5—2:18)*
- *III: A High Priest for Humanity (3:1—5:10)*
- *IV: Christ, the One True Priest (5:11—10:18)*
- *V: Perseverance in Faith (10:19—12:29)*
- *VI: Conclusion (13:1-25)*

CHAPTER 1

I: PROLOGUE*

1 In previous times, God spoke to our ancestors
in many and various ways
through the Prophets, * [a]
2 but in these last days he has spoken to us through his Son,
whom he appointed heir of all things
and through whom he created the universe. [b]
3 He is the reflection of God's glory
and the perfect expression of his very being, *
sustaining all things by his powerful word.
Achieving purification from sins,
he took his seat at the right hand of the Majesty on high. [c]
4 So he became as far superior to the angels
as the name he has inherited is superior to theirs. [d]

II: THE SON OF GOD, SUPERIOR TO THE ANGELS*

Messianic Enthronement.* 5 For to which of the angels did God ever say,

"You are my Son;
this day I have begotten you"?

Or again,

"I will be his Father,
and he will be my Son"? * [e]

6 And again, when he brings his firstborn into the world, he says,

"Let all the angels of God pay him homage." [f]

7 Of the angels he says,

"He makes his angels winds,
and his servants flames of fire." [g]

8 But of the Son he says,

"Your throne, O God, is forever and ever,
and a righteous scepter is the scepter of your kingdom. [h]
9 You have loved righteousness and detested wickedness;
therefore God, your God, has anointed you
with the oil of gladness far above your companions." [i]

10 [j] He also says,

"In the beginning, O Lord, you laid the foundations of the earth,
and the heavens are the work of your hands. [k]
11 They will perish, but you remain;
they will all wear out like a garment. [l]

---

a Heb 2:2-3; 4:8; 12:28; Gen 9:29; Num 12:6, 8; Lk 1:70; Acts 2:30.—b Heb 3:6; 5:8; 9:26; Deut 4:30; Prov 8:30; Wis 7:22; Isa 2:2; Jer 23:20; Ezek 38:16; Dan 10:14; Mt 3:17; 11:27; Jn 1:3; 3:17; Rom 8:3; 1 Cor 8:6; Gal 4:4; Col 1:16; 1 Pet 1:20.—c Heb 7:27; 8:1; 10:12; 12:2; Wis 7:26; Mk 16:19; Jn 1:14; 14:19; Acts 2:33; 7:55-56; Rom 8:34; 2 Cor 4:4; Eph 1:20; Col 3:1; 4:4; Tit 2:14; 1 Pet 3:22.—d Heb 8:6; Eph 1:21; Phil 2:9-11.—e Ps 2:7; 2 Sam 7:14; Mt 3:17.—f Heb 10:5; Deut 32:43 LXX; Ps 97:7; Jn 3:16; Col 1:18.—g Ps 104:4 LXX.—h Ps 45:7-8; Lk 1:33.—i Isa 61:1, 3; Phil 2:9.—j 10-12: Ps 102:26-28.—k Zec 12:1.—l Heb 12:27; Isa 34:4.

1:1-4 From the opening words to the final "Amen" (Heb 13:21), readers are to keep their gaze fixed on Christ. In this magisterial sentence, "God ... has spoken to us through his Son" (Heb 1:2), which is one of the most tightly packed and beautiful of the entire New Testament, the essence of the Letter is expressed.

God has spoken definitively in Christ, who is his real, living Word. Everything that can be said about the plan of God is made fully real in Christ. Using expressions taken from Alexandrian thought, the author says that the Son, born of the Father, is in every respect equal to him; the glorified Christ is far superior to the world of the angels, and he gives existence and salvation to every creature.

Thus, seven great theological themes are set forth: (1) *Theism:* God exists; (2) *Revelation:* God has revealed himself through the Prophets and through his Son; (3) *Incarnation:* God became man in Jesus Christ; (4) *Creation:* God created all things through Christ; (5) *Providence:* God upholds all things by his almighty word; (6) *Redemption:* by his mediatorship and his suffering Christ made salvation possible; and (7) *Ascension:* the Lord Jesus has ascended into heaven and sits at the right hand of the Father.

1:1 *Through the Prophets:* this refers not only to the Prophets but to all the writers of the Old Testament, for they constituted the preparation for the coming of Christ.

1:3 *Perfect expression of his very being:* that is, there is an identity of nature (see Wis 7:25-26).

1:5—2:18 How can God, who is inaccessible and transcendent, communicate with human beings? Are not intermediaries needed to establish the link between the heavenly world and the terrestrial one? This was a question that preoccupied many Jewish circles after the Exile. In reply they insisted on the role and importance of beings who were neither human nor divine: angels. They even imagined that the intervention of the angels was needed to bring the Law to Moses (see Heb 2:2; Gal 3:19). However, if it is necessary to multiply intermediaries between God and humans, does not this mean that humanity remains decisively distant from the Lord? The perspective is completely reversed when one speaks of Christ.

No one is like him in intimacy with God, neither is anyone like him in proximity to humans. The link between heaven and earth is established in his very Person. It is the principal aim of the Letter to the Hebrews to hold to these two aspects of Christ: he is united through and through with God, and he is completely one with human beings. In this first part of the Letter, he is presented as Son of God and brother to human beings.

1:5-14 In Christ God has spoken in a definitive way (Heb 1:2), and the author sees this truth already proclaimed in the Old Testament. He cites a series of passages, almost all of which were regarded in the Jewish tradition as announcements of the Messiah. What are angels? Merely subordinates, mediators, and messengers ever being replaced. But the Son is the Firstborn. This is the title of honor reserved for Christ that includes a priority over creatures (see Col 1:15). He receives adoration, is enthroned, and partakes unceasingly in the status of God.

1:5 *I will be his Father,/and he will be my Son:* before the coming of Christ, this text from 2 Sam 7:14 and the text of Ps 2 were acknowledged to be Messianic.

12 You will roll them up like a cloak;
like a garment they will be changed.
But you are ever the same,
and your years will have no end." [m]

13 But to which of the angels has he ever said,

"Sit at my right hand
until I make your enemies your footstool"? [n]

14 Are not all angels ministering spirits sent forth to serve for the sake of those who will inherit salvation? [o]

CHAPTER 2

The Oneness of Christian Salvation.* 1 Therefore, we should pay much closer attention to what we have heard so that we do not drift away. [p] 2 For if the message delivered by angels proved to be so valid that every transgression and disobedience brought a proper punishment, [q] 3 how shall we escape if we ignore so great a salvation?

It was first announced by the Lord and then confirmed for us by those who heard him. [r] 4 God also testified to it by signs and wonders and various miracles, and by gifts of the Holy Spirit distributed according to his will. [s]

Christ Our Brother.* 5 For it was not to angels that God subjected the world to come, about which we are speaking. [t] 6 But someone has offered this testimony somewhere:

"What is man that you are mindful of him,
or the son of man that you care for him? [u]
7 You made him a little lower than the angels,
yet crowned him with glory and honor [v]
8 and put everything under his feet."

Now in putting everything under his feet, he left nothing that is not subject to his control. Right now we do not yet see everything under his feet. [w] 9 However, we do see Jesus, who was made a little lower than the angels, now crowned with glory and honor because he suffered death, so that by the grace of God he might taste death for everyone. [x]

10 In bringing many sons to glory, it was completely fitting that he, for whom and through whom everything exists, should make the author of their salvation perfect through sufferings. [y] 11 Both the one who sanctifies and those who are sanctified all proceed from one Father. That is why Jesus is not ashamed to call them brethren, [z] 12 saying,

"I will proclaim your name to my brethren; *
in the midst of the assembly I will praise you." [a]

13 And again,

"I will put my trust in him."

And again,

"Here I am,
together with the children God has given me." [b]

14 Therefore, since the children are all made of flesh and blood, * Jesus likewise shared in the same flesh and blood, so that by his death he might destroy the one who has the power of death—that is, the devil— [c]
15 and set free those who throughout their lives had been held in slavery by the fear of death. [d]

16 For clearly he did not come to help angels but rather he came to help the descendants of Abraham. [e] 17 Therefore, he had to be made like his brethren in every way in order that he might become a com-

m Heb 13:8.—n Heb 10:13; Jos 10:24; Ps 110:1; Mt 22:44; Mk 16:19.—o Heb 2:3; 3:9; 9:28; Ps 91:11; Dan 7:10; Mt 25:34; Mk 10:17; Acts 20:32; Rom 11:14.—p Rom 11:22.—q Heb 1:1; 10:28; Deut 33:2; Acts 7:38-53; Gal 3:19.—r Heb 1:2; 10:29; 12:25; Lk 1:2.—s Mk 16:20; Jn 4:48; Acts 14:3; 19:11; 1 Cor 12:4; Eph 1:5.—t Heb 6:5.—u Heb 4:4; Job 7:17; Ps 8:5-7.—v Lk 20:36.—w Mt 22:44; 28:18; 1 Cor 15:25-28; Eph 1:20-23; Phil 3:21; 1 Pet 3:22.—x Heb 2:7; Acts 3:13; 2 Cor 5:15; Phil 2:6-11.—y Heb 5:8-9; 12:2; Isa 53:4; Lk 24:26; Rom 11:36; 1 Cor 8:6.—z Heb 13:12; Mt 28:10; Eph 5:26.—a Ps 22:23.—b Isa 8:17-18; Jn 10:29.—c Gen 3:15; Isa 25:8; Hos 13:14; Jn 1:14; 12:31; Rom 6:9; 1 Cor 15:54-55; Eph 6:12; 2 Tim 1:10; 1 Jn 3:8; Rev 12:10.—d Rom 8:15; 2 Tim 1:7.—e Isa 41:8; Lk 3:8.

2:1-4 The Law of Sinai, which according to rabbinic tradition was communicated by angels, binds humanity to live in a certain way. Much greater is the authority of the voice of Christ transmitted to the Church by the Apostles with the evident guarantee of the Spirit (see Mt 10:1; Mk 16:20; Acts 1:8). This is the first of five warnings scattered throughout the Letter (the other four are: Heb 3:7—4:13; 5:11—6:12; 10:19-39; and 12:4-29).

2:5-18 The Son of God, who became a human being and was crucified, is Lord of the universe (see Phil 2:6-11); all human beings have been brought into solidarity with him. To throw light on this destiny of Christ, the author gives a free interpretation of Ps 8:5-7. Angels and institutions are incapable of establishing a bond between God and humanity; in Christ humanity is given one of its own, but one who is the true high priest (v. 17) and capable of being its guarantor in heaven. The principal theme of the Letter is here announced.

2:12 *I will proclaim your name to my brethren:* a quotation from Ps 22:23, a psalm that describes the sufferings of the Servant of God. The key phrase is "my brethren" (i.e., the Septuagint text; the Hebrew has "the community"), which is spoken by the triumphant Messiah.

2:14 *Flesh and blood:* i.e., the human condition.

passionate and faithful high priest before God and expiate the sins of the people.[f] 18 Because he himself was tested by suffering, he is able to help those who are being tested.[g]

III: A HIGH PRIEST FOR HUMANITY*

CHAPTER 3

Christ's Fidelity Is Superior to That of Moses.* 1 Therefore, holy brethren, who share in a heavenly calling, concentrate your thoughts on Jesus, the apostle and the high priest of our profession of faith.[h] 2 He was faithful to the one who appointed him, just as Moses was faithful in God's household.[i]

3 However, he is deserving of a greater glory than Moses, just as the builder of a house is more honored than the house itself.[j] 4 For every house is built by someone, but the builder of all is God.[k]

5 Now Moses was faithful as a servant in God's household, testifying to the things that would later be revealed,[l] 6 whereas Christ was faithful as a son watching over his house. And we are that house if we hold firm to our confidence and take pride in our hope.[m]

The "Today" of God. 7 *[n] Therefore, as the Holy Spirit says,

"Today, if you hear his voice,[o]
8 harden not your hearts as at the rebellion,
in the day of testing in the desert,[p]
9 where your ancestors tried me and tested me
though they had seen what I could do[q]
10 for forty years.[r]
As a result I became angered with that generation,
and I said, 'Their hearts have always gone astray,
and they do not know my ways.'
11 Therefore, I swore in my anger,
'They will never enter into my rest.' "[s]

12 Take care, brethren, that none of you will ever have an evil and unbelieving heart that will cause you to forsake the living God.[t] 13 Rather, encourage each other every day, as long as it is today, so that none of you will become hardened by the deceitfulness of sin.[u]

14 For we will become partners with Christ only if we maintain firmly until the end the confidence we originally had,[v] 15 as it is said,

"Today, if you hear his voice,
harden not your hearts as at the rebellion."[w]

16 [x] Who were those who heard and yet rebelled? Were they not all those whom Moses had led out of Egypt? 17 And with whom was he angered for forty years? Was it not with those who had sinned and whose corpses lay in the wilderness?[y] 18 And to whom did he swear that they would never enter into his rest, if not to those who disobeyed?[z] 19 So we see clearly that they were unable to enter because of their refusal to believe.[a]

CHAPTER 4

The Sabbath Rest of God's People.* 1 Therefore, since the promise of entering

f Heb 2:14; 3:1; 4:14, 15; 5:1-3; Rom 3:28; Phil 2:7.—g Heb 4:15; Lk 22:28.—h Heb 2:11, 17; 4:14; Rom 8:28; 1 Tim 6:12.—i Heb 3:5; Num 12:7.—j Deut 34:12; 2 Cor 3:7-8.—k Gen 1:1; Eph 2:10; 3:9.—l Heb 3:2; Ex 14:31; Num 12:7.—m Heb 1:2; 3:14; 10:21; Rom 11:22; 1 Cor 3:16; Eph 2:19; 1 Tim 3:15; 1 Pet 4:17.—n 7-11: Ps 95:7-11.—o Heb 9:8; 10:15; Acts 28:25.—p Heb 3:15; 4:7.—q Ex 17:7; Num 14:33; 20:2-5; Deut 1:3; Acts 7:36.—r Acts 7:36.—s Heb 4:3, 5; Deut 1:34-35.—t Mt 16:16; Lk 8:13; 1 Tim 4:1.—u Heb 10:24-25; Jer 17:9; Eph 4:22.—v Heb 3:6; Rom 8:17; Eph 3:12.—w Heb 3:7, 8; 4:7; Ps 95:7-8.—x 16-19: Num 14:1-38; Deut 1:19-40.—y Num 14:29; 1 Cor 10:6.—z Heb 4:6; Num 14:22-23; Deut 1:34, 35.—a Heb 4:6; Jn 3:36.

3:1—5:10 The Covenant with Israel was entered into in the wilderness. Two great figures stood out: Moses and Aaron—the two mediators of the Law and sacrifice, of authority and worship. But when the work of Christ becomes known, all of that proves to have been provisional. And to speak of Christ the author develops two ideas: fidelity to God and solidarity or sympathy with humans. In between these two developments he inserts a long exhortation to serious Christians.

3:1-6 The fidelity of Jesus is greater than that of Moses. Both were "apostles," sent by God to the people, and "priests," i.e., representatives of the people before God. But Moses acted in the world as a servant who carries out a limited mandate. Christ accomplishes his work personally, in his own name, like a Son. This work belongs to him; and it is the community of believers that he establishes in the world of God.

3:7—4:11 Like Israel of the Exodus, the Church is on the march, on earth, certain of the promise of God but exposed to temptation. Since the Jewish people love to cling to the great epoch in the wilderness, the author invites them to profit from the lesson of that time—which is one of fidelity—offering them a commentary on Ps 95. His argument, which follows the exegetical methods of the time, may seem somewhat complicated. The generation of Hebrews delivered from Egypt did not enter the promised land because it rebelled against God (see Ex 17:1-7; Num 14:28-35). The memory of that rebellion remained alive in the Jewish tradition (see 1 Cor 10:1-11). Ps 95, which at that period was attributed to David, was written long after the Exile, when the perspective was no longer the conquest of Canaan, which had been accomplished by Joshua. The promise to enter into the rest of God has not become something distant: it is deeply involved with the fulfillment of creation, with sharing today in the divine life by following Christ along the way he has opened up (Heb 4:14).

4:1-11 The first "rest" in Scripture was the one that God took on the seventh day of creation (see Gen 2:3). The second "rest" was the one God promised to the Israelites in Canaan, but which they were not allowed to enter because of their lack of faith (see v. 2 and Ps 95:11). The third "rest" was the one Jesus took upon entering the eternal sphere after completing the work of Redemption (see Eph 1:20; 2:6; 4:8). These "rests" foreshadow the ultimate "rest" that awaits all Christians (v. 11), provided they have a living faith in the person and work of Jesus.

into his rest endures, we must take care that none of you be judged to have fallen short. [b] 2 For we too have received the good news just as they did, but the message they heard was of no benefit to them because those who listened did not combine it with faith. [c] 3 For we who have faith enter into that rest, just as God has said:

"Therefore, I swore in my anger,
'They will never enter into my rest.' "

Yet God's work had been finished at the beginning of the world. [d] 4 For somewhere he says in reference to the seventh day, "And God rested on the seventh day from all his works." [e] 5 And in this passage it says, "They will never enter into my rest." [f]

6 Seeing, therefore, that some will enter into that rest, and since those who first had received the good news failed to enter because of their refusal to believe, [g] 7 God once more set a day—"today"—when long afterward he spoke through David, as already quoted:

"Today, if you hear his voice,
harden not your hearts." [h]

8 Now if Joshua had given them rest, God would not have spoken afterward of another day. [i] 9 Therefore, a Sabbath rest still remains for the people of God, 10 since those who enter into God's rest also cease from their own labors as God did from his. [j] 11 Let us then make every effort to enter into that rest, so that no one may fall by following that example of refusing to believe. [k]

The Word of God Is Living.* 12 Indeed, the word of God is living and active. Sharper than any two-edged sword, it pierces to the point where it divides soul and spirit, joints and marrow; it judges the thoughts and the intentions of the heart. [l] 13 Nothing in creation is hidden from his sight. Everything is uncovered and exposed to the eyes of the one to whom we must all render an account. [m]

A Compassionate High Priest.* 14 Therefore, since we have a great high priest who has passed through the heavens, Jesus, the Son of God, let us hold fast to our profession of faith. [n] 15 For we do not have a high priest who is unable to sympathize with our weaknesses, but one who has been tested in every respect as we are, but without sinning. [o] 16 Let us then approach the throne of grace with confidence so that we may receive mercy and find grace when we are in need of help. [p]

CHAPTER 5

1 Every high priest is taken from among men to represent them in their dealings with God, to offer gifts and sacrifices for sins. * [q] 2 He is able to deal patiently with those who are ignorant and misguided, since he himself is subject to weakness. [r] 3 And as a result of this, he must make sin offerings for himself as well as for the people. [s] 4 Moreover, one does not assume this position of honor on his own initiative, but only when called by God, just as Aaron was. [t]

5 Even Christ did not confer upon himself the glory of becoming a high priest. Rather, he was appointed by the one who said to him:

"You are my Son;
this day I have begotten you." [u]

6 And he says in another place:

"You are a priest forever,
according to the order of Melchizedek." [v]

7 During the course of his earthly life, Jesus offered up prayers and petitions with loud cries and tears to the one who had the power to save him from death, and he was

b Heb 12:15.—c 1 Thes 2:13.—d Heb 3:11; Deut 1:34-35; Ps 95:11; Mt 25:34; Lk 11:50.—e Gen 2:2-3; Ex 20:11.—f Heb 4:3; Ps 95:11.—g Heb 3:18; 4:11.—h Heb 3:7-8, 15; Ps 95:7-8.—i Heb 1:1; Deut 31:7; Jos 22:4; Acts 7:45.—j Heb 4:4; Lev 23:3; Rev 14:13.—k Heb 3:12, 18; 4:6.—l Wis 18:15-16; Isa 49:2; Mk 4:14; Lk 5:1; 11:28; Jn 10:35; Acts 12:24; Eph 6:17; 1 Thes 2:13; Rev 1:16; 2:12.—m Job 34:21-22; Pss 90:8; 139:2-4; Jer 16:17; 23:24; Dan 2:22.—n Heb 2:17; 6:20; 8:1; 9:11, 24; Mt 4:3.—o Heb 2:17-18; 5:2; 2 Cor 5:21.—p Heb 7:19; 8:1; 10:19, 22, 35; 12:2; Eph 3:12.—q Heb 2:17; 7:27; 8:3; 9:9.—r Heb 2:18; 4:15; 7:28; Isa 29:24.—s Heb 7:27; 9:7; Lev 9:7; 16:15-17, 30, 34.—t Ex 28:1; Num 14:40; 18:7.—u Heb 1:1; 2:17; Ps 2:7; Mt 3:17; Jn 8:54.—v Heb 5:10; 6:20; 7:1-22; Gen 14:18; Ps 110:4.

4:12-13 The word of God is living and effective. It pierces into the most inner part of believers who open themselves completely to it. This dynamic word of God appears in both the Old and the New Testament (see Pss 107:20; 147:18; Isa 40:8; 55:11; Gal 3:8; Eph 5:26; Jas 1:18; 1 Pet 1:23).

4:14—5:10 Trait by trait, the portrait of the high priest is developed. It is fully verified only in Christ; moreover, we are now beyond the priesthood of Aaron and the earthly liturgy. Christ has set free his own; the Risen One who now lives forever expresses that compassion for humans to which he bore witness in his Passion. This priest is more one with human beings than Aaron was. He is established by God to perform more than a passing service for them. As Son and according to the order of Melchizedek (who will be spoken about later) he is engaged with all his person in his supplication and his sacrifice. The Passion is the most solemn prayer of intercession, the greatest act of obedience at the heart of humanity.

5:1 *To offer gifts and sacrifices for sins:* on the Day of Atonement (which the author is here envisioning), atonement was made for the sins of the Israelites (see Lev 16:34).

heard because of his godly fear. [w] 8 Although he was a Son, he learned obedience through his sufferings, [x] 9 and when he had been made perfect, he became the source of eternal salvation for all who obey him, [y] 10 and he was designated a high priest by God according to the order of Melchizedek. [z]

IV: CHRIST, THE ONE TRUE PRIEST*

Deepen the Christian Life.* 11 We have much to say about this subject, but it is difficult to explain because you have been slow in learning. [a] 12 By this time you should have been teachers, yet you still need to have someone explain to you the basic elements of God's words.

You need milk, not solid food. [b] 13 Anyone who lives on milk is still an infant and is ignorant of the word of righteousness. [c] 14 But solid food is for adults whose faculties have been trained by practice to distinguish between good and evil. [d]

CHAPTER 6

1 * Therefore, let us leave behind the basic teaching about Christ and advance toward maturity. We must not be forever laying the foundation: repentance for actions that lead to death, faith in God, [e] 2 instruction about baptisms and the laying on of hands, the resurrection of the dead, and eternal judgment. [f] 3 And we will do so, if God permits. [g]

4 * For when people have once been enlightened and have experienced the heavenly gift, and have shared in the Holy Spirit, [h] 5 and have tasted the goodness of the word of God and the powers of the age to come, [i] 6 and then in spite of all this have fallen away, it is impossible to restore them again to repentance. For they are crucifying the Son of God for themselves once again and are holding him up to contempt. [j]

7 When the soil drinks in the rain that repeatedly falls on it and produces a crop that is useful to those for whom it was cultivated, it receives a blessing from God. [k] 8 However, if it brings forth thorns and thistles, it is worthless, and a curse hangs over it. It will end by being burned. [l]

9 But, beloved, in spite of what we have just said, we are convinced that your status is far superior as you proceed to salvation. [m] 10 For God would not be so unjust as to ignore your work and the love that you have shown for his name by the services you have rendered to the saints and still continue to render. [n]

11 However, we desire that each one of you will show the same diligence until you have achieved the ultimate fulfillment of your hope. [o] 12 We do not want you to allow yourselves to become sluggish; rather, we want you to become imitators of those who through faith and patience are now heirs of the promises. [p]

w Mt 26:38-44; 27:46, 50; Mk 14:34-40; Lk 22:41-46; Jn 12:27.—x Heb 1:2; Rom 5:19; Phil 2:8.—y Heb 2:10; 7:24-25, 28.—z Heb 2:17; 5:5, 6; 6:20; Ps 110:4.—a Isa 6:10; Mt 13:15; 2 Pet 3:16.—b Heb 6:1; 1 Cor 3:1-3; 1 Pet 2:2.—c 1 Cor 3:1; 14:20; 1 Pet 2:2.—d Isa 7:15; 1 Cor 2:6.—e Heb 5:12; 9:14; Phil 3:12-14.—f Heb 9:10; Mk 7:4; Jn 3:25; Acts 2:24; 6:6; 8:17; 13:3; 17:18, 32; 19:6; 1 Tim 4:14; 5:22; 2 Tim 1:6.—g Acts 18:21; 1 Cor 16:7.—h Heb 10:26, 32; Ps 34:6; 2 Cor 4:6; Gal 3:2; Eph 2:8.—i Heb 4:12; Mk 10:30; 1 Pet 2:3.—j Mt 4:3; 2 Pet 2:21; 1 Jn 5:16.—k Gen 1:11-12; Deut 11:11.—l Gen 3:17-18; Isa 5:6; 27:4; Mt 7:16; 13:7; Mk 4:7; Lk 8:7.—m 1 Cor 10:14.—n Mt 10:40, 42; 1 Thes 1:3.—o Heb 3:6, 14; Rom 5:2-5.—p Heb 5:11; 13:7; Gal 3:14; Eph 1:13-14; 2 Thes 1:4; Jas 1:3; Rev 13:10.

5:11—10:18 This is the central part of the letter. Its themes center around a single great idea: Christ, "high priest of the good things that have come" (Heb 9:11), or "that are to come." The vision starts with the past and with a reflection on all the religious situations already experienced, then leaves them and focuses on their fulfillment: the future of humanity with God, in and with Christ. Proofs are piled up to show that this new priesthood transcends all the ancient institutions, brings them to fulfillment, and renders them things of the past.

The word "priest" is taken here in the sense used by the Old Testament and by religions of the time: the man of worship, the man who represents his brothers and sisters in ritual actions that will enable them to be purified and have access to the divinity. Jesus Christ appears as the only one who is the presence of the forgiveness of God, the one who gives access to God, the representative of all that humanity expects from God. Every other priesthood and all other sacrifices are only a sketch, sign, shadow, prefiguration, and expectation. They are now surpassed. The ancient words and hopes are evoked to say more than they could have suggested without the faith in Christ.

5:11—6:12 The author warns his readers against regressing spiritually and morally. They must become "perfect"—what we would call "adults" or "mature." That is, they must not be content with the rudiments of faith but must deepen their faith by reflection. Six basic teachings are enumerated and apostasy is condemned. Finally, a note of hope is given. A life marked by love cannot be insignificant; and this love has a concrete expression: the service of the saints (Heb 6:10), i.e., the sustenance of the poor of the Jerusalem community (see Rom 15:25-31; 2 Cor 8:4; 9:1-15).

6:1-2 Six basic teachings are mentioned. (1) *Repentance:* turning away from the darkness of sin and useless rituals. (2) *Faith in God:* i.e., turning to the light of God. (3) *Instruction about baptisms:* e.g., Jewish initiation rites for proselytes, John the Baptist's baptism, and the Baptism commanded by Jesus. (4) *Laying on of hands:* a rite connected with ordaining or commissioning (see Acts 6:6; 13:3; 1 Tim 5:22; 2 Tim 1:6), with healing the sick (see Mk 6:5; 16:18; Lk 4:40; Acts 28:8), and with bestowal of blessings (see Mt 19:13-15). (5) *Resurrection of the dead:* the resurrection of all people in the end time (see Jn 5:25-29). (6) *Eternal judgment:* the lot of those who reject God.

6:4-8 The author asserts that repentance for apostates is impossible. However, he may be using hyperbole to impress on his readers that abandoning Christ is most serious.

Cling Tightly to Hope.* [13] When God made his promise to Abraham, since he had no one greater by whom to swear, he swore by himself,[q] [14] saying, "I will surely bless you and multiply your descendants."[r] [15] And so, after waiting patiently, he obtained the promise.[s]

[16] Human beings swear by someone greater than themselves, and the oath given as confirmation puts an end to all argument.[t] [17] Likewise, when God desired to show even more clearly to the heirs of his promise the unalterable nature of his purpose, he confirmed it by an oath.[u]

[18] Therefore, by these two unchangeable acts in which it was impossible for God to lie, we who have taken refuge in his protection have been strongly encouraged to grasp firmly the hope that has been held out to us.[v] [19] We have this hope as the anchor of the soul, a hope that enters the sanctuary behind the veil,*[w] [20] where Jesus has entered as a forerunner on our behalf, having become a high priest forever according to the order of Melchizedek.[x]

A: A Different Kind of High Priest*

CHAPTER 7

Melchizedek.* [1] This Melchizedek, the king of Salem and a priest of God Most High, met Abraham as he was returning from his defeat of the kings, and he blessed him.[y] [2] Abraham gave him a tenth of everything. His name first means "king of righteousness," and then "king of Salem," that is, "king of peace." [3] Without father, or mother, or genealogy, and without beginning of days or end of life, thus bearing a resemblance to the Son of God, he remains a priest forever.[z]

[4] Just consider now how great this man must have been for the patriarch Abraham to give him a tenth of his spoils.[a] [5] The descendants of Levi who succeed to the priestly office are required by the Law to collect tithes from the people, that is, from their fellow countrymen, although they too are descended from Abraham.[b] [6] However, Melchizedek, who was not of the same ancestry, received tithes from Abraham and blessed him who had received the promises.[c]

[7] It is indisputable that a lesser person is blessed by one who is greater. [8] In the one case, it is ordinary mortal men who receive tithes; in the other, the recipient is one of whom it is attested that he is alive.[d] [9] One could even say that Levi himself, who receives tithes, actually paid tithes through Abraham, [10] inasmuch as he was still in his father's loins when Melchizedek met Abraham.

Another High Priest according to the Order of Melchizedek.* [11] If perfection was therefore achieved through the Levitical priesthood, on the basis of which the Law was given to the people, what need would there have been for another priest to arise according to the order of Melchizedek rather than one according to the order of Aaron?[e] [12] For when there is any change in the priesthood, there must also be a change in the Law.

[13] Now the one about whom these things were said belonged to a different tribe, from which no one has ever served at the altar.[f] [14] For it is clear that our Lord was descend-

q Gen 22:16f; Lk 1:73.—r Gen 22:17.—s Heb 6:12; Gen 21:5; Rom 4:20.—t Ex 22:11.—u Heb 6:12, 18; 11:9; Rom 4:16.—v Heb 3:6; Num 23:19; 1 Sam 15:29; Jn 8:17; 2 Tim 2:13; Tit 1:2.—w Heb 3:7; 9:2; 10:20; Ex 26:31-33; Lev 16:2.—x Heb 2:17; 4:14; 5:6, 10; Ps 110:4.—y Heb 7:8; Gen 14:17-20; Mk 5:7.—z Heb 4:14; 6:6; 7:6; 10:29; Mt 4:3.—a Gen 14:20; Acts 2:29.—b Gen 35:11; Num 18:21, 26.—c Gen 14:19; Rom 4:13.—d Heb 5:6; 6:20; 7:17; Lk 24:5; Jn 6:57.—e Heb 5:6; 7:18-19; 8:7; 10:1; Ps 110:4; Gal 2:21.—f Heb 7:11, 14.

6:13-20 In the beginning, before any law and any institution of worship, there were two immutable realities: God's promise and his oath. There were also two figures: Abraham and Melchizedek. The author wishes to stress one solid point: God committed himself radically to the future and salvation of human beings, a future and a salvation that become realities forever through Christ—as the following chapters will explain.

6:19 The veil separated the two most sacred parts of the Jewish temple.

7:1-28 A mysterious figure made his appearance in the story of Abraham: Melchizedek (see Gen 14:17-20), and Ps 110—which held a special place in Israel's meditation on the Messiah—speaks of a mysterious priesthood of the kind exercised by Melchizedek (v. 4). The Letter to the Hebrews says that those passages foretell the priesthood of Christ. Yet the priesthood of Christ cannot be measured by the same standard as the Jewish priesthood, because it renders the latter obsolete.

7:1-10 The figure of Melchizedek is full of symbols. His name means "king of righteousness"; his reign was one of "peace." Most unusually, the Bible gives us no chronological or genealogical information about him, naming neither his ancestors nor his descendants. His priesthood does not seem to be connected in any way with a hereditary line of priests, but only with his own person, as though it were something everlasting. And Abraham, to whom is given all the power to bless and the promises for Israel, receives a blessing from Melchizedek and offers him a tithe. All the more, then, does this priest stand above all the descendants of the Patriarch, and especially Levi, from whom descends all the Jewish priests whose standing the people acknowledge by paying them a tithe (see Lev 27:30-33; Num 18:21f). In the person of Abraham, they all bowed down to the mysterious priesthood of Melchizedek, who prefigured Jesus.

7:11-25 Jesus Christ, foretold by the person of Melchizedek, does not have a place in the priestly genealogies that were set up after Moses; his priesthood is based on the commitment of God himself, on the divine oath (vv. 20-22). He is the definitive mediator between God and humanity.

ed from Judah, a tribe about which Moses said nothing in regard to priests.[g]

[15] This becomes even more obvious now that another priest has arisen, one like Melchizedek, [16] who was one not through a legal requirement concerning physical descent, but by the power of an indestructible life. [17] For it is attested of him:

"You are a priest forever,
according to the order of Melchizedek."[h]

[18] The earlier commandment is abrogated because of its weakness and ineffectiveness,[i] [19] since the Law brought nothing to perfection. On the other hand, a better hope is introduced through which we draw nearer to God.[j]

[20] This was confirmed by an oath. When others became priests, no oath was required, [21] but this one became a priest with the swearing of an oath by the one who said to him,

"The Lord has sworn, and he will not repent:
'You are a priest forever.' "[k]

[22] Accordingly, Jesus has also become the guarantee of a better covenant.[l]

[23] Furthermore, the former priests were many in number, because they were prevented by death from remaining in office. [24] However, Jesus holds a perpetual priesthood because he remains forever.[m] [25] Therefore, he has the full power to save those who approach God through him, since he lives forever to intercede for them.[n]

The High Priest That We Needed.* [26] It was fitting that we should have such a high priest—holy, innocent, undefiled, separated from sinners, and raised high above the heavens.[o] [27] Unlike the other high priests, he has no need to offer sacrifices day after day, first for his own sins and then for those of the people. He accomplished this once for all when he offered himself.[p] [28] The Law appoints as high priests those who are subject to weakness, but the word of the oath, which came later than the Law, appointed the Son who has been made perfect forever.[q]

B: A New Kind of Priesthood*

CHAPTER 8

Another Sanctuary.* [1] The main point of what we have been saying is this: we have such a high priest. He has taken his seat at the right hand of the throne of the Majesty in heaven,[r] [2] and he is a minister of the sanctuary and of the true tabernacle established by the Lord and not by human beings.[s]

[3] Every high priest is appointed to offer gifts and sacrifices, and so it is necessary for this one also to have something to offer.[t] [4] Actually, if he were on earth, he would not be a priest at all, since there are already others who offer gifts according to the Law,*[u] [5] although the sanctuary in which they offer worship is only a shadow and a reflection of the heavenly one. This is the reason why, when Moses was about to erect the tabernacle, he was warned, "See to it that you make everything according to the pattern that was shown you on the mountain."[v]

g Gen 49:10; Isa 11:1; Mt 1:1-2, 16, 20; 2:6; Lk 1:27; 2:4; 3:33; Rom 1:3; Rev 5:5.—h Heb 5:6; 7:21; Ps 110:4.—i Heb 10:1; Rom 8:3.—j Heb 7:11; 9:9-10; Rom 3:20; Gal 3:21; Jas 4:8.—k Num 23:19; 1 Sam 15:29; Ps 110:4; Mal 3:6; Rom 11:29.—l Heb 8:6-10; 9:15-20; 10:29; 12:24; 13:20; Lk 22:20.—m Heb 5:6; 7:28; 13:8.—n Heb 7:19; Rom 8:34; 11:14; 1 Jn 2:1; Rev 1:18.—o Heb 2:17; 4:14-15; 2 Cor 5:21.—p Ex 29:38-39; Lev 16:6, 11, 15-17; Num 28:3-4; Isa 53:10; Rom 6:10; Eph 5:2; 1 Pet 3:18.—q Heb 1:2; 2:10; 5:1-2, 9.—r Heb 1:3; 2:17; 4:14; 7:26-28; Mk 16:19.—s Heb 9:11; Ex 33:7; Num 24:6 LXX.—t Heb 2:17; 5:1; 9:9, 14.—u Heb 5:1; 7:13; 9:9.—v Heb 9:23; 10:1; 11:7; 12:25; Ex 25:40; Acts 7:44; Col 2:17.

7:26-28 A first conclusion rises as a chant of freedom and a beautiful hymn to Christ. Perishable offerings are no longer anything but a symbol of self-giving already completed in reality: Christ alone can commit himself completely to God, become an offering, and in his very person be the representative of human beings before God. *The Son who has been made perfect forever:* Jesus, the Son, is God, and he shares the divine attributes, e.g., holiness (see v. 26; Jn 8:46; 2 Cor 5:21); eternity (see Mic 5:2; Jn 1:1; 8:58; 17:5, 24; Col 1:17); omnipotence (see Heb 1:3; Mt 28:18; Rev 1:8); omniscience (see Mt 9:4; Jn 6:64; 16:30; Col 2:3); immutability (see Heb 1:11f; 13:8); omnipresence (see Mt 28:20; Jn 3:13; Eph 1:23); creative power (see Heb 1:8, 10; Jn 1:3; 1 Cor 8:6; Col 1:16f); power to forgive sins (see Mk 2:5, 7-10; Lk 24:47; Jn 1:29; Acts 10:43; 1 Jn 1:7); the right to be worshiped (see Mt 8:2; Phil 2:10).

8:1—10:18 Speaking about a high priest means speaking about worship, the Covenant, the sanctuary, and sacrifices. Point by point, the author describes the practices of Jewish worship; in doing so his aim is to draw a radical contrast between them and the immense newness of Christ. Jesus not only excelled the Levitical priests in dignity; he also accomplished the true worship that surpasses all prestige from the ceremonial codified in the Law of Moses.

8:1-5 The author recalls some passages of the Bible (Ps 110:1-4; Num 24:6; Ex 25:40) to show that both the sanctuary in the wilderness and the sanctuary in Jerusalem were signs pointing to true worship, which consists in having access to God. As priest, Jesus acts at that level of reality and not at the level of signs.

8:4 By his human birth Jesus belonged to the tribe of Judah (see Heb 7:12-14), whereas priests were taken from the tribe of Levi (see Deut 18:1). Some scholars take the present tense of the verb "offer" as an indication that the temple was still standing in Jerusalem and so the Letter must have been written before A.D. 70 when the temple was destroyed by the Romans.

Another Covenant.* 6 But Jesus has now
received a ministry that is far superior, for he
is the mediator of a far better covenant that
has been established on better promises.[w]
7 For if that first covenant had been faultless,
there would have been no necessity to estab-
lish a second one to replace it.[x] 8 * However,
God finds fault with his people, and he says,

"Behold, the days are coming, says the
Lord,
when I will establish a new covenant
with the house of Israel
and with the house of Judah.[y]
9 It will not be like the covenant
that I made with their ancestors
on the day when I took them by the hand
to lead them out of the land of Egypt.
For they did not remain faithful to my
covenant,
and therefore I abandoned them, says
the Lord.[z]
10 This is the covenant that I will make
with the house of Israel
after those days, says the Lord.
I will plant my laws in their minds
and inscribe them on their hearts.
I will be their God,
and they will be my people.[a]
11 And they shall not teach one another,
each saying to his neighbor and his
brother,
'Know the Lord.'
For they shall all know me,
from the least of them to the greatest.[b]
12 I shall forgive them for their wicked
deeds,
and I shall remember their sins no
more."[c]

13 By calling this covenant "new," he has
made the first one obsolete. And anything
that is obsolete and aging will shortly disap-
pear.[d]

CHAPTER 9

The Ancient Worship.* 1 Now the first
covenant also had regulations for worship
and an earthly sanctuary.[e] 2 For a tabernacle
was constructed. In the outer section, called
the Holy Place, were located the lampstand,
the table, and the consecrated bread.[f]

3 Behind the second veil was the taberna-
cle called the Holy of Holies[g] 4 in which
stood the gold altar of incense and the ark of
the covenant overlaid on all sides with gold.
In that ark were the gold jar containing the
manna, and Aaron's staff that had sprouted
buds, and the tablets of the covenant.[h]
5 Above it were the cherubim of glory over-
shadowing the place of atonement (but we
cannot discuss these things in detail now).[i]

6 With these arrangements for worship
having been made, the priests continually
enter the first tabernacle to carry out their
ritual duties.[j] 7 However, the high priest
alone enters the second tabernacle, and he
can do so only once a year, and not without
the blood that he offers for himself and for
the errors that the people had committed.[k]

8 By this the Holy Spirit reveals to us that
as long as the first tabernacle remains
standing, the way into the sanctuary has not
been disclosed.[l] 9 This is a symbol of the
present time, during which the gifts and sac-
rifices that are offered are unable to cleanse
the conscience of the worshiper.[m] 10 They
deal only with food and drink and various

w Heb 7:22; 8:8, 13; 9:15; Lk 22:20; Gal 3:20.—x Heb 7:11; 10:1.—y Heb 8:6, 13; Jer 31:31-34; Lk 22:20.—z Ex 19:5-6; 20:1-17.—a Heb 10:16-17; Ezek 11:20; Zec 8:8; Rom 11:27; 2 Cor 3:3.—b Isa 54:13; Jn 6:45.—c Heb 10:17; Jer 31:31-34.—d Heb 8:6, 8; Lk 22:20; Rom 10:4; 2 Cor 5:17.—e Heb 8:2; Ex 25:8.—f Ex 25:8-9, 23-30; 26:33-34; Lev 24:5-8.—g Ex 26:31-34.—h Ex 16:32-34; 25:10, 16, 21; 30:1-10; 31:18; 32:15; Lev 16:12-13; Num 17:2-7, 16-26.—i Ex 25:16-22; 26:34; 37:6-9; Lev 16:2, 14-15.—j Ex 27:21; 30:7; Lev 24:8; Num 28:3.—k Heb 5:2, 3; 9:2-3; Ex 30:10; Lev 16:1-14.—l Heb 3:7; 10:19-20; Jn 14:6.—m Heb 5:1; 7:19; 8:3; 10:1.

8:6-13 Israel was known as the people of the Covenant, the Covenant that was expressed in the Law and in worship. A text had been in circulation since the time of Jeremiah that was critical of the past and full of hope for a new future: it was the prophecy of the New Covenant, with which everyone was familiar (see Jer 31:31-34). The author cites it in its entirety (vv. 8-12). In this New Covenant the relationship between God and human beings will no longer be based on laws and institutions, but will have as its basis the person of Jesus Christ, mediator of a life-giving relationship with God (see 1 Tim 2:5).

The priesthood of Christ has given rise to the ministerial or hierarchical priesthood and the common priesthood of the faithful, which differ from one another in essence and not only in degree, and each of which is a participation in the royal priesthood of Christ: "The ministerial priest, by the sacred power he enjoys, teaches and rules the priestly people; acting in the person of Christ, he makes present the Eucharistic Sacrifice, and offers it to God in the name of all the people. But the faithful, in virtue of their royal priesthood, join in the offering of the Eucharist. They likewise exercise that priesthood in receiving the Sacraments, in prayer and thanksgiving, in the witness of a holy life, and in self-denial and active charity" (Vatican II: *The Church,* no. 10).

8:8-12 The New Covenant is superior to the old because of the following: (1) God's laws are inner principles (v. 10a) enabling his people to carry out his will (see Ezek 36:26f; Rom 8:2-4). (2) God and his people enjoy an intimate fellowship (v. 10b). (3) There will nevermore be sinful ignorance of God (v. 11). (4) Forgiveness of sins will last forever (v. 12).

9:1-10 Once a year, on the Day of Atonement (see Lev 16:2-19; Ex 30:10), the high priest entered alone into the innermost part of the temple, the Holy of Holies. He poured blood on the altar to obtain forgiveness of sins. (For more details on the worship in the temple, see Ex 25—31 and 35—40.)

ceremonial washings, regulations in regard
to the body that are imposed until the com-
ing of the new order. [n]

Christ Has Come.* 11 But now Christ has
arrived as the high priest of the good things
that have come. He has passed through the
greater and more perfect tabernacle not
made by human hands, that is, not a part of
this creation, [o] 12 and he has entered once for
all into the sanctuary not with the blood of
goats and calves but with his own blood,
thus obtaining eternal redemption. [p]

13 The blood of goats and bulls and the
sprinkling of ashes of a heifer sanctify those
who have been defiled and restore bodily
purity. [q] 14 How much more, then, will the
blood of Christ, who through the eternal
Spirit offered himself without blemish to
God, purify our conscience from acts that
lead to death so that we may worship the liv-
ing God. [r]

A Covenant Sealed with the Blood of Christ.*
15 For this reason, he is the mediator of a
new covenant, so that those who have been
called may receive the promised eternal
inheritance, since his death has served to
redeem the sins that were committed under
the first covenant. [s]

16 Now when a will is involved, it is obliga-
tory to prove the death of the one who made
it. [t] 17 For a will takes effect only at death,
since it has no force while the one who made
it is still alive.

18 Hence, not even the first covenant was
inaugurated without blood. [u] 19 For when all
the commandments of the Law had been
proclaimed by Moses to all the people, he
took the blood of calves and goats, together
with water and scarlet wool and hyssop, and
sprinkled both the book itself and all the
people, [v] 20 saying, "This is the blood of the
covenant that God has commanded you to
observe." [w]

21 And in the same way, he sprinkled with
blood both the tabernacle and all the liturgi-
cal vessels. [x] 22 Indeed, under the Law almost
everything is purified by blood, and without
the shedding of blood there is no forgive-
ness. [y]

23 Therefore, it was necessary for the
copies of the heavenly things to be purified
with these rites, but the heavenly things
themselves required still greater sacrifices. [z]

Once and for All.* 24 For Christ did not enter
a sanctuary made by human hands, a mere
copy of the true one, but he entered into
heaven itself, so that he now appears in the
presence of God on our behalf. [a]

25 Nor was it his purpose to offer himself
again and again, as the high priest enters into
the sanctuary year after year with the blood
that is not his own. [b] 26 For then he would have
had to suffer over and over again since the
creation of the world. But as it is, he has
appeared once and for all at the end of the
ages to abolish sin by sacrificing himself. [c]

27 And just as human beings are destined
to die but once, and after that to face judg-
ment, [d] 28 so Christ, having been offered once
to take away the sins of many, will appear a
second time, not to deal with sin but to bring
salvation to those who are eagerly waiting
for him. [e]

CHAPTER 10

C: A Unique Sacrifice*

The Law Was a Shadow. 1 The Law contains
little more than a shadow of the good things

n Heb 7:16; 13:9; Lev 11; 14:8; Num 6:3; 19:11-21; Col 2:16.—o Heb 2:17; 4:14; 8:2; 9:24; 10:1, 20; Jn 2:19.—p Heb 7:27; 9:19; Lev 16:6, 15; Mt 26:28; Rom 3:25.—q Heb 10:4; Lev 16:6-16; Num 19:9, 14-21.—r Heb 10:10; Jer 33:8; Zec 13:1; Mt 16:16; Rom 5:9; Eph 5:2; 1 Tim 3:9; Tit 2:14; 1 Pet 1:18-19; 1 Jn 1:7; Rev 1:5.—s Heb 6:15; 10:36; Lk 22:20; Acts 20:32; Rom 8:28; Gal 3:20; 1 Tim 2:5.—t Gal 3:15.—u Ex 24:6-8; Mt 26:28.—v Heb 1:1; 9:12-13; Ex 24:6-8.—w Ex 24:3-8; Mt 26:28; Mk 14:24.—x Heb 9:8, 15; Ex 40:9; Lev 8:15-19.—y Ex 29:21; Lev 8:15; 17:11.—z Heb 8:5; Job 15:15.—a Heb 4:14; 7:25; 8:2; 9:12; 1 Jn 2:1.—b Heb 9:7-8; 10:19.—c Heb 4:3; 7:27; Jn 1:29; Gal 4:4; 1 Jn 3:5.—d Gen 3:19; 2 Cor 5:10.—e Heb 5:9; 7:27; 10:10; Isa 53:12; Mt 16:27; 1 Cor 1:7; 1 Pet 2:24.

9:11-14 The whole of Jewish hope, which was revived on the Day of Atonement, now finds its definitive fulfillment in the Passover of Christ. His is the true sacrifice. This time, a human being sheds his own blood, i.e., willingly gives his life to God for the benefit of his brothers and sisters; this time, a human being purifies the human conscience from within by his obedience; this time, a human being has access to God. The risen Christ remains in this relationship of giving and presence, once and for all, definitively and eternally. There is no longer any other sacrifice to perform. This is the future, filled with "the good things that have come" (v. 11).

9:15-23 In the Jewish mind sacrifice and blood were reminders of atonement and Covenant (see Ex 24). The New Covenant is accomplished by the Paschal Mystery of Christ. In Greek, the word *diathêkê* signified both "covenant" and "testament"; it was easy to move from the one meaning to the other, as the author does in vv. 15 and 16.

9:24-28 Everything that could envisage priesthood, rites, and cults, without in fact obtaining them, is now a reality in Christ: sin is forgiven, access to God is available, reconciliation is realized, and the Paschal event is living, efficacious, and eternal. Christ, who offered himself, is at God's right hand for the benefit of human beings. There is no need of new sacrifices, and so he will not return for that but for the complete fulfillment of his promise of life and love.

10:1-18 The great, endless act of self-giving that extends through the entire existence of Christ is the authentic priestly act, the authentic sacrifice of Christ. He takes away sin and restores the bond with God in his own person, in his own living experience. He founds the New Covenant, the new people who have access to God.

to come and not the true image of them. These sacrifices that are offered year after year can never bring the worshipers to perfection.[f] 2 If they could, those sacrifices would no longer be offered, for the worshipers would have been cleansed once for all and would no longer feel guilty for sins.[g]

3 However, in these sacrifices sins are brought to mind year after year,[h] 4 because sins cannot be taken away by the blood of bulls and goats.[i]

One Sacrifice for Sins. 5 [j] That is why, when Christ came into the world, he said,

"Sacrifice and offering you did not desire,
but a body you have prepared for me.[k]
6 You took no delight
in holocausts and sin offerings.
7 Then I said, 'As it is written of me in the scroll,
behold, I have come to do your will, O God.' "[l]

8 First he says, "Sacrifices and offerings, holocausts and sin offerings, you neither desired nor delighted in," even though they are offered according to the Law.[m] 9 Then he adds, "Behold, I have come to do your will." He thus abolishes the first to establish the second.[n] 10 And it was by this "will" that we have been consecrated through the offering of the body of Jesus Christ once for all.[o]

11 * Day after day every priest stands to perform his ministry, offering over and over again the same sacrifices that can never remove sins.[p] 12 [q] But Jesus offered one sacrifice for sins for all time, and then took his seat at the right hand of God,[r] 13 where he now waits until his enemies are made his footstool.[s] 14 Therefore, by a single offering he has made perfect forever those who are being sanctified.[t]

15 The Holy Spirit also testifies to us about this. For he first says,[u]

16 "This is the covenant that I will make with them
after those days, says the Lord.
I will place my laws in their hearts
and inscribe them on their minds."[v]

17 Then he also asserts,

"Their sins and their lawless acts
I will remember no more."[w]

18 When these have been forgiven, there are no longer any offerings for sins.

V: PERSEVERANCE IN FAITH*

A: The Need To Stand Firm

Let Us Approach with Sincerity of Heart.* 19 Therefore, brethren, the blood of Jesus has given us confidence to enter the sanctuary[x] 20 by the new and living way that he has opened for us through the veil, that is, through his flesh.[y] 21 Since we have a great priest over the household of God,[z] 22 let us approach with sincerity of heart and the full assurance of faith, with hearts sprinkled clean from an evil conscience and bodies washed in pure water.[a]

23 Let us remain firm in the confession of our hope without wavering, for the one who made the promise is trustworthy.[b] 24 And let us consider how to spur one another to love and good works.[c] 25 Do not neglect to attend your assemblies, as some do, but rather encourage one another, especially since you can see the Day * approaching.[d]

f Heb 7:19; 8:5; 9:11, 23; Col 2:17.—g Heb 9:9.—h Heb 9:7; Lev 16:21, 34; Num 5:15 LXX.—i Heb 9:12-13; 10:1, 11; Isa 1:11; Mic 6:6-8.—j 5-7: Ps 40:7-9; Mk 12:33.—k Heb 1:6; 2:14; 1 Pet 2:24.—l Jer 36:2; Mt 26:39.—m Heb 10:5-6; Ps 40:7; Mk 12:33.—n Heb 10:7; Ps 40:8; Mt 26:39; Mk 14:36; Lk 22:42; Jn 6:38.—o Heb 2:14; 7:27; 9:12, 14; Eph 5:26; 1 Pet 2:24.—p Heb 5:1; 7:27; 10:1, 4; Deut 10:8; 18:7.—q 12-13: Ps 110:1.—r Heb 5:1; Mk 16:16.—s Heb 1:13; Jos 10:24.—t Heb 9:28; 10:1; Eph 5:26.—u Heb 3:7.—v Heb 8:10; Jer 31:33-34.—w Heb 8:12; Jer 31:34.—x Heb 3:6; 4:16; 6:19-20; 9:8; Lev 16:2; Eph 1:7; 2:18; 3:12.—y Heb 6:19-20; 9:3, 8, 11-12; Mt 27:51; Mk 15:38; Lk 23:45; Jn 14:6.—z Heb 2:17; 3:6; 4:14; Zec 6:11-12.—a Heb 7:19; 9:13-14; 10:1; 12:24; Ezek 36:25; Acts 22:16; 1 Cor 8:11; Eph 5:12; Tit 3:5; 1 Pet 1:2; 3:21.—b Heb 3:1, 6; 4:14; 11:11; 1 Cor 10:13; 2 Cor 1:9.—c Heb 3:13; Tit 2:14.—d Heb 3:13; Acts 2:42; Rom 13:12; 1 Cor 3:13.

10:11-12 *Every priest stands to perform his ministry . . . Jesus . . . took his seat:* members of the Levitical priesthood always "stood" because their work was never finished; Jesus "took his seat" because his work was completed.

10:19—12:29 A definitive event has been realized for the world: the Death and Resurrection of Christ. The Letter to the Hebrews makes us aware of this by presenting it as the act of the authentic priesthood, the authentic sacrifice, while at the same time downgrading the status of the preceding religious regime, although that too had been established by God. So too faith in Christ is a decisive step forward in the life of a human being. The believer is henceforth engaged in a march toward the full encounter with the Lord. In the midst of temptations, fears, and risks, the Christian life is not a simple fidelity to a past but a thrust forward toward the future, toward God. These chapters are a pressing invitation not to let such perspectives be obscured.

10:19-25 The path that leads to God is a person, Christ recognized under the characteristics of a high priest. Once baptized, Christians are associated with the Son of God. They must strengthen their conviction and the links of mutual love. May the signs of crises be a call for them to prepare for the return of the Lord.

10:25 *The Day:* this refers to the Day of the Lord at the end of time.

Apostasy Remains Unforgiven.* 26 If we
deliberately persist in sin after having
received the knowledge of the truth, then
there no longer remains any sacrifice for
sins.[e] 27 There is only a terrifying expecta-
tion of judgment and of a fierce fire that will
consume the adversaries.[f]

28 Anyone who violates the Law of Moses
is put to death without mercy on the testi-
mony of two or three witnesses.[g] 29 How
much more punishment do you think is
deserved by the one who has contempt for
the Son of God, profanes the blood of the
covenant by which he was sanctified, and
insults the Spirit of grace?[h] 30 For we know
the one who said,

> "Vengeance is mine; I will repay,"

and

> "The Lord will judge his people."[i]

31 It is a dreadful thing to fall into the
hands of the living God.[j]

Do Not Abandon Your Assurance.*
32 Remember the days gone by when, after
you had been enlightened,* you endured a
difficult struggle filled with suffering.[k]
33 Sometimes you were publicly exposed to
abuse and persecution, and sometimes you
were companions of those who were treated
in the same way.[l] 34 You not only had compas-
sion upon those who were in prison but also
cheerfully accepted the confiscation of your
property, because you realized that you pos-
sessed something better and more lasting.[m]

35 Therefore, do not lose your confidence
now, since your reward will be so great.[n]
36 You need to be steadfast if you want to do
the will of God and receive what he has
promised.[o]

37 "For, after a little while,
he who is to come will do so,
and he will not delay.[p]
38 My righteous one shall live by faith,
but if he shrinks back,
I will not be pleased with him."[q]

39 But we are not among those who draw
back and are lost. Rather, we are among
those who have faith and are saved.

B: The People of Faith*

CHAPTER 11

What Faith Is. 1 Faith is the assurance of
what we hope for and the conviction about
things that cannot be seen.*[r] 2 Indeed, it
was because of it that our ancestors were
commended.[s]

3 By faith we understand that the universe
was created by the word of God, so that what
is seen came into being from the invisible.[t]

The Faith of the Early Patriarchs. 4 * By faith
Abel* offered to God a better sacrifice than
that of Cain. Because of this he was attested
as righteous, God himself bearing witness
to his gifts. Although he is dead, he continues
to speak through it.[u]

5 By faith Enoch* was taken up so that he
did not see death. He was found no more,

e Heb 3:12; 5:2; 6:4-8; Ex 21:14; Num 15:30; 1 Tim 2:4; 2 Pet 2:20.—f Heb 9:27; 12:29; Isa 26:11 LXX; Zep 1:18; 2 Thes 1:7.—g Heb 2:2; Deut 17:6; Mt 15:16.—h Heb 6:6; Mt 4:3; 26:28; 1 Cor 6:11; Eph 4:30; Rev 1:5.—i Deut 32:35f; Rom 12:19.—j Heb 10:27; Mt 10:28; Lk 12:4-5; 2 Cor 5:11.—k Heb 6:4; Phil 1:29-30.—l 1 Cor 4:9; Phil 4:14; 1 Thes 2:14.—m Heb 11:16; 13:3; Mt 6:19-20; Lk 12:33-34; 1 Pet 1:4-5.—n Heb 4:16; Eph 3:12.—o Heb 12:1; Lk 21:19; Rom 5:3; Jas 1:3-4.—p Isa 26:20; Hab 2:3; Mt 11:3; Rev 22:20.—q Hab 2:3f; Acts 20:20; Rom 1:17; Gal 3:11.—r Heb 1:3; 3:6, 14; Rom 8:24; 2 Cor 4:18.—s Heb 11:4, 39; Mt 15:2.—t Heb 1:2; Gen 1:3; Ps 33:6; Wis 9:1; Jn 1:3; 2 Pet 3:5.—u Heb 11:2, 39; 12:24; Gen 4:4, 10; Mt 23:35; Jn 3:12.

10:26-31 Once again the author repeats this somber warning (see Heb 6:1-8; Mt 12:31). Those who rebel against Christ exclude themselves from Christ's forgiveness, from his life, and from his grace. Let them, therefore, meditate on the threats of God's vengeance about which the Bible speaks, and especially the texts cited here (see Ex 24:8; Deut 17:6; 32:35f; Isa 26:11).

10:32-39 As soon as they were baptized and enlightened, believers sacrificed everything for Christ and confronted all difficulties. Now is not the time for them to be discouraged. The Lord will come and he is the recompense for all who do not weaken. Faith is the courageous commitment to Christ.

10:32 *Been enlightened:* an ancient phrase for "been baptized"; "enlightenment" or "illumination" was an ancient term for Baptism (see Heb 6:4; Eph 5:14).

11:1-40 Before exhorting his readers to serve Christ, the author shows the importance and power of faith throughout sacred history. This is a magnificent chapter of Biblical theology that should inspire the courage of believers and urge them to read the Old Testament in order to give new vigor to the impulse of faith.

11:1 Theologians have often cited this sentence. Faith establishes human beings in the invisible and orients them toward the future, toward the fulfillment. The spiritual writer Charles Péguy affirmed: "The faith that I love most, says God, is hope."

11:4-40 Christian faith has firm roots in the Old Testament. Note v. 6, in which theologians have seen an assertion of the irreplaceable necessity of faith for salvation: the belief that God exists and has a personal relationship with human beings. The references to Biblical personages and the Old Testament citations are mainly from the Book of Genesis, from Exodus when speaking of Moses, and from Joshua and the following Books when speaking of the others. But the author adds non-Biblical details, such as the fate that legend attributed to Isaiah (v. 37). A similar list of heroes is found in Sirach (44:1—50:21).

11:4 *Abel:* see Gen 4:1-15. Christ himself referred to the righteousness of Abel (see Mt 23:35).

11:5 *Enoch:* see note on Gen 4:25—5:32 (last paragraph).

because God had taken him, and before he was taken up he was attested to have pleased God.[v] 6 But without faith it is impossible to please him, for whoever comes to God must believe that he exists and that he rewards those who seek him.[w]

7 By faith Noah,* having been warned by God about things not yet seen, took heed and built an ark to save his household. Through his faith he condemned the world and inherited the righteousness that derives from faith.[x]

The Faith of Abraham and His Descendants. 8 By faith Abraham* obeyed when he was called to set out for a place that he was to receive as an inheritance. He went forth without knowing where he was going.[y] 9 By faith he sojourned in the promised land as in a foreign country, dwelling in tents with Isaac and Jacob, who were heirs with him of the same promise.[z] 10 For he was looking forward to a city with firm foundations, whose architect and builder is God.[a]

11 By faith Abraham also received the power of procreation, even though he was well past the age—and Sarah herself was barren*—because he believed that the one who had made the promise would be faithful in fulfilling it.[b] 12 Therefore, from one man, himself as good as dead, came forth descendants as numerous as the stars of heaven and as innumerable as the grains of sand on the seashore.[c]

13 All these died in faith without having received what had been promised, but from a distance they saw far ahead how those promises would be fulfilled and welcomed them, and acknowledged themselves to be strangers and foreigners on the earth.[d] 14 People who speak in this way make it clear that they are looking for a country of their own. 15 If they had been thinking of the land that they had left behind, they would have had the opportunity to return.[e] 16 But in fact they were longing for a better country, a heavenly one. Therefore, God is not ashamed to be called their God, for he has prepared a city for them.[f]

17 By faith Abraham, when put to the test, offered up Isaac. He who had received the promises was ready to offer up his only son,[g] 18 of whom he had been told, "Through Isaac descendants shall bear your name."[h] 19 For he reasoned that God was able even to raise someone from the dead, and in a sense he was given back Isaac from the dead.*[i]

20 By faith Isaac* gave his blessings to Jacob and Esau for the future.[j]

21 By faith Jacob,* as he was dying, blessed each one of the sons of Joseph and bowed in worship, leaning on his staff.[k]

22 By faith Joseph,* near the end of his life, mentioned the Exodus of the Israelites and gave instructions about his burial.[l]

23 By faith Moses* was hidden by his parents for three months after his birth, because they saw that he was a beautiful child, and they did not fear the king's edict.[m]

24 [n] By faith Moses, when he had grown up, refused to be called a son of Pharaoh's daughter. 25 He preferred to be ill-treated along with the people of God rather than to enjoy the fleeting pleasures of sin.[o] 26 He considered that abuse suffered for the sake of the Messiah was a more precious gift than all the treasures of Egypt, for he was looking ahead to the final reward.[p]

27 By faith Moses departed from Egypt, unafraid of the wrath of the king; he persevered as if he could see the one who is invisible.[q]

28 By faith he kept the Passover and sprinkled the blood so that the Destroyer would not harm the firstborn of Israel.[r]

v Gen 5:21-24; Sir 44:16.—w Heb 7:19; Wis 4:10; Jer 29:12-14.—x Heb 11:1; Gen 6:8-22; Ezek 14:14, 20; Sir 44:17-18; Mt 24:37-39; Lk 17:26-27; Rom 9:30; 1 Pet 3:20; 2 Pet 2:5.—y Gen 12:1-4, 7; 15:7-21; Sir 44:19-22; Acts 7:2-8; Rom 4:16-22.—z Heb 6:17; Gen 12:8; 13:12; 18:1-9; 23:4; 26:3; 35:27; Acts 7:5.—a Heb 11:16; 12:22; 13:14; Rev 21:10-22.—b Gen 17:19; 18:11-14; 21:2; Rom 4:19-21; 1 Cor 1:9; 10:13.—c Gen 15:5; 22:17; 32:13; Ex 32:13; Deut 10:22; Dan 3:36; Rom 4:19.—d Heb 11:39; Gen 23:4; Lev 25:23; Ps 39:13; Mt 13:17.—e Gen 24:6-8; 28:2.—f Heb 13:14; Gen 26:24; Ex 3:6, 15; Mk 8:38; 2 Tim 4:18.—g Gen 22:1-10; Sir 44:20; 1 Mac 2:52; Mt 25:34; Jn 14:2; Jas 2:21.—h Gen 21:12 LXX; Rom 9:7.—i Jn 5:21; Rom 4:16-22.—j Gen 27:27-40.—k Gen 27:38-40; 47:31 LXX; 48:1, 15-16.—l Gen 50:24-25; Ex 13:19; Jos 24:32.—m Ex 1:16-22; 2:2; Acts 7:20.—n 24-25: Ex 2:10-15; Acts 7:23-29.—o Heb 11:37.—p Heb 10:35; 13:13; Lk 14:33.—q Ex 2:15; 12:50-51; Acts 7:29.—r Ex 12:21-23; Wis 18:25; 1 Cor 10:10.

11:7 *Noah:* see Gen 5:28—9:29; Ezek 14:14.

11:8 *Abraham:* see Gen 11:27—25:11. The New Testament refers to this Patriarch as the exemplar of those who live by faith and as the father of all believers (see Rom 4:11f, 16; Gal 3:7, 9, 29).

11:11 *Sarah herself was barren:* probably refers to the fact that she was past the age of childbearing (see Gen 18:11f).

11:19 Isaac, who was to be sacrificed, was saved and came back from the dead, so to speak (see Gen 22); in this respect, he prefigured Jesus crucified and risen.

11:20 *Isaac:* see Gen 27:1—28:5.

11:21 *Jacob:* see Gen 47:28—49:33. *Each one of the sons:* both of Joseph's sons, Ephraim and Manasseh, received a blessing from Jacob; hence two tribes descended from Joseph whereas only one tribe descended from each of his brothers.

11:22 *Joseph:* see Gen 37:1—50:26.

11:23-28 *Moses:* see Ex 1—15; Acts 7:17-36.

The Faith of the Israelites and Rahab. 29 By
faith the people crossed the Red Sea as
though it were dry land. However, when the
Egyptians attempted to do so, they were
drowned. [s]

30 By faith the walls of Jericho * fell when
the people had marched around them for
seven days. [t]

31 By faith Rahab * the prostitute did not
perish with those who were disobedient, for
she had received the spies in peace. [u]

The Faith of the Judges and Prophets.
32 What more shall I say? Time is too short
for me to speak of Gideon, Barak, Samson,
and Jephthah, of David and Samuel and the
Prophets, * [v] 33 who by faith conquered king-
doms, administered justice, and obtained
the promises. They closed the mouths of
lions, * [w] 34 quenched raging fires, * and es-
caped the edge of the sword. Their weakness
was turned into strength as they became
mighty in battle and put foreign armies to
flight. [x]

35 Women received their dead * back
through resurrection. Others who were tor-
tured refused to accept release in order to
obtain a better resurrection. [y] 36 Still others
were mocked and scourged, even to the
point of enduring chains and imprison-
ment. [z]

37 They were stoned, * or sawed in two, or
put to death by the sword. They went about
in skins of sheep or goats—destitute, perse-
cuted, and tormented. [a] 38 The world was not
worthy of them. They wandered about in
desert areas and on mountains, and they
lived in dens and caves of the earth. [b]

39 Yet all these, even though they were
commended for their faith, did not receive
what was promised. [c] 40 For God had made
provision for us to have something better,
and they were not to achieve perfection
except with us. * [d]

C: Let Us Run with Eyes Fixed on Jesus*

CHAPTER 12

**You Have Not Yet Resisted to the Point of
Bloodshed.** 1 Therefore, since we are sur-
rounded by such a great cloud of witness-
es, * let us throw off everything that weighs
us down and the sins that so easily distract
us and with perseverance run the race that
lies ahead of us, [e] 2 with our eyes fixed on
Jesus, the author and perfecter of our faith.
For the sake of the joy that lay before him, he
endured the cross, ignoring its shame, and is
now seated at the right hand of the throne of
God. [f]

3 Reflect on how he endured such great
hostility from sinners so that you may not
grow weary and lose heart. [g] 4 In your strug-
gle against sin, you have not yet resisted to
the point of shedding your blood. [h]

God Is Treating You as His Children.* 5 [i] You
have forgotten the exhortation that address-
es you as children:

s Ex 14:22-28.—t Jos 6:12-21; 2 Mac 12:15.—u Jos 2:1-21; 6:22-25; Jas 2:25.—v Jdg 4:5-22; 6:8, 11; 8:32; 11:1—12:7; 1 Sam 16:1, 13, 20.—w 2 Sam 8:1-3; Dan 6:23.—x Ez 18:4; Jdg 15:8; Dan 3:22-25, 49-50.—y 1 Ki 17:17-24; 2 Ki 4:18-37; 2 Mac 6:18—7:42.—z Gen 39:20; 2 Chr 36:16; Jer 20:2; 37:15.—a 1 Ki 19:10; 2 Ki 1:8; 2 Chr 24:21; Jer 26:23.—b 1 Ki 18:4; 19:9; 1 Mac 2:28-30.—c Heb 10:36; 11:2, 4, 13.—d Heb 2:10; Rev 6:11.—e Heb 10:36; 1 Cor 9:24.—f Heb 2:10; 13:13; Ps 110:1; Mk 16:19; Phil 2:6-8.—g Gal 6:9; Rev 2:3.—h Heb 10:32-34; 13:13.—i 5-6: Deut 8:5; Prov 3:11-12; 1 Cor 11:32.

11:30 *Jericho:* see Jos 6. The Israelites did not conquer the city through military action but merely followed God's instructions in faith (see 2 Cor 10:4).

11:31 *Rahab:* see Jos 2:1-24; 6:22-25; Mt 1:5; Jas 2:25.

11:32 All those mentioned in this verse held positions of power (Judges, Prophets, and one King) but none is praised for anything but faith in God. They are given in pairs and out of chronological order, with the more important person mentioned first. *Gideon:* see Jdg 6—9; *Barak:* see Jdg 4—5. *Samson:* see Jdg 13—16; *Jephthah:* see Jdg 11—12. *David:* King (see 1 Sam 13:14; 16:1, 12; Acts 13:22) and Prophet (see Heb 4:7; 2 Sam 23:1-3; Mk 12:36); *Samuel and the Prophets:* Samuel was the last of the Judges and the first of the Prophets (see 1 Sam 7:15; Acts 3:24; 13:20); he anointed David as King (see 1 Sam 16:13) and was renowned as a man of intercessory prayer (see 1 Sam 12:19, 23; Jer 15:1).

11:33 *Mouths of lions:* e.g., Daniel in the lions' den (see Dan 6).

11:34 *Quenched raging fires:* e.g., Daniel's friends, Shadrach, Meshach, and Abednego, in the fiery furnace (see Dan 3).

11:35 *Their dead:* allusion to the two miracles worked by Elijah and Elisha (1 Ki 17:23; 2 Ki 4:36). *Tortured:* e.g., the Maccabean patriots of the second century B.C. (see 2 Mac 7).

11:37 *They were stoned:* e.g., Zechariah, the son of Jehoiada the priest, who was put to death for stating the truth (see 2 Chr 24:20-22; Lk 11:51). *Sawed in two:* an ancient Jewish tradition said that Isaiah was killed in this way by order of King Manasseh.

11:40 The saints of the Old Testament were able to reach the perfection of life with God only through Christ, who is "the resurrection and the life" (Jn 11:25f).

12:1-29 Christians have only one person on whom to keep their eyes as the object of faith and salvation: Christ (see Heb 11:26f; Acts 7:55f; Phil 3:8). They look to the Crucified Lord to understand how to behave at all times, and especially in difficulties and persecution.

12:1 *Surrounded by such a great cloud of witnesses:* the author may be thinking of an athletic contest in a large amphitheater wherein the heroes just mentioned are inspiring examples for us, urging us on to stand firm in the faith and even to martyrdom if need be.

12:5-13 God treats us as his sons and daughters. And the trials that we must withstand in order to make progress in the faith is another sign of this point for us. Hence, we must take heart.

"My son, do not scorn the discipline of
the Lord
or lose heart when you are punished
by him.[j]
6 For the Lord disciplines those whom he
loves,
and he chastises every son whom he
acknowledges."[k]

7 Endure the trials you receive as a form of
discipline. God is treating you as sons. For
what son is there who is not disciplined by
his father?[l] 8 If you have not received the
discipline in which all share, then you are
illegitimate and not true sons.[m]

9 In addition, we have all received disci-
pline from our earthly fathers, and we
respected them. Should we not then be even
more willing to submit to the Father of spir-
its and live?[n] 10 They disciplined us for a
short time as they thought best, but he does
so for our benefit so that we may share his
holiness.[o]

11 At the time that discipline is received, it
always seems painful rather than pleasant,
but afterward it yields a harvest of peace
and uprightness to those who have been
trained by it.[p] 12 Therefore, strengthen your
drooping hands and your weak knees,[q]
13 and make straight paths for your feet, so
that your weakened limbs may not be dis-
abled but rather may be healed.[r]

Seek Peace and Sanctification.* 14 Seek
peace with everyone, as well as the holiness
without which no one will ever see the
Lord.[s] 15 See to it that no one is deprived of
the grace of God, and that no root of bitter-
ness may spring up and cause trouble,
resulting in the defilement of many.[t]

16 Do not be like Esau, an immoral and
worldly-minded person who sold his birth-
right for a single meal.[u] 17 Afterward, as you
know, when he sought to inherit the blessing,
he was rejected. Even though he sought it
with tears, he found no possibility for repen-
tance.[v]

Listen to the One Who Is Speaking.* 18 You
have not come to something that can be
touched: a blazing fire, or complete dark-
ness, or gloom, or a storm,[w] 19 or the sound
of a trumpet, or a voice speaking words that
made those who heard them beg that noth-
ing more be said to them.[x] 20 For they could
not bear to hear the command that was
given, "If even an animal touches the moun-
tain, it must be stoned to death."[y] 21 Indeed,
so terrifying was the sight that Moses cried
out, "I am terrified and trembling."[z]

22 But you have come to Mount Zion and
to the city of the living God, the heavenly
Jerusalem. You have come to myriads of
angels in joyful gathering,[a] 23 and to the
assembly of the firstborn * whose names are
written in heaven, and to God the judge of
all, and to the spirits of the righteous who
have been made perfect.[b] 24 You have come
to Jesus the mediator of a new covenant and
to the sprinkled blood that speaks more
powerfully than even the blood of Abel.[c]

25 See that you do not reject the one who is
speaking. For if those did not escape when
they rejected the one who warned them on
earth, how much more is this true of us if we
turn away from the one who is from heav-
en?[d] 26 At that time, his voice shook the
earth, but now he has promised, "Once
more I will shake not only the earth but
heaven as well."[e]

27 The words "once more" indicate the
removal of what can be shaken—that is, all
created things—so that what cannot be
shaken may remain.[f] 28 Therefore, since we
are receiving a kingdom that cannot be
shaken, let us give thanks, offering to God a
worship that is pleasing to him.[g] 29 For our
God is a consuming fire.[h]

j Heb 12:3.—k Rev 3:19.—l Deut 8:5; 2 Sam 7:14; Prov 13:24; Sir 30:1.—m 1 Pet 5:9.—n Num 16:22; 27:16 LXX; Isa 38:16; Rev 22:6.—o 2 Pet 1:4.—p Isa 32:17; 2 Cor 4:17; Phil 1:11; Jas 3:18.—q Job 4:3-4; Sir 25:24; Isa 35:3.—r Prov 4:26 LXX; Gal 6:1.—s Mt 5:8; Rom 6:22; 12:18; 14:19.—t Heb 3:12; 4:1; Deut 29:18 (17 LXX); Gal 5:4.—u Gen 25:33; 1 Cor 6:18.—v Gen 27:34-38.—w Ex 19:12-22; Deut 4:11; 5:22-23.—x Ex 19:16-19; 20:18-19; Deut 4:12; 5:5.—y Ex 19:12-13.—z Ex 19:16; Deut 9:19; Rev 14:1.—a Heb 11:10; 13:14; Isa 24:23; Mt 16:16; Gal 4:26; Rev 14:1; 21:2.—b Gen 18:25; Ex 4:22; Lk 10:20; Rev 5:11; 20:12.—c Heb 7:22; 8:6; 9:15; 11:4; Gen 4:10; Gal 3:20; 1 Pet 1:2.—d Heb 1:1; 3:12; Ex 20:19; Deut 18:19.—e Ex 19:18; Jdg 2:6; 5:4-5; Ps 68:9; Hag 2:6.—f Isa 34:4; 54:10; 66:22; Mt 24:35; Mk 13:31; Lk 21:33; 1 Cor 7:31; 2 Pet 3:10.—g Heb 13:15; Dan 7:14, 18; Mal 2:5; 3:20; Rom 1:9.—h Ex 24:17; Deut 4:24; Isa 33:14; 2 Thes 1:7.

12:14-17 Once again the author places their responsibilities before his hearers. They must not revert to the past by returning to Judaism. This would be tantamount to dishonoring the gift of salvation and perverting the atmosphere of the community.

12:18-29 The author alludes to the Covenant of Sinai, which was a fascinating and terrifying spectacle in the history of Israel (see Ex 19—20; Deut 4:11; 9:19). The New Covenant is a celebration of peace and festivity. Israel's way of life was only a figure for the conduct of the Church. Once people are gripped by the Covenant of grace, they cannot turn back toward an insufficient religion of yesteryear—that would be to show disdain for God. The Lord is "a consuming fire": the image evokes all at once his holiness, his demands, his judgment to the very depths of a being, and his hold that burns one's existence.

12:23 *Assembly of the firstborn:* either all the elect or the angels as the first creatures.

VI: CONCLUSION

CHAPTER 13

Aspects of the Christian Life.* 1 Let mutual
love continue,[i] 2 and do not forget to offer
hospitality to strangers, for by doing this
some have entertained angels without
knowing it. *[j] 3 Be mindful of those who are
in prison, as though you were imprisoned
with them, and of those who are being mal-
treated, since you too are in the body.[k]

4 Let marriage be held in honor by all, and
the marriage bed kept undefiled, for those
who are immoral and adulterers will have to
face God's judgment.[l] 5 Do not succumb to
the love of money, but be content with what
you have, for God has said, "I will never for-
sake you or abandon you."[m] 6 Therefore, we
can say with confidence:

> "The Lord is my helper;
> I will not be afraid.
> What can anyone do to me?"[n]

Let Us Seek the City That Is To Come.*
7 Remember your leaders who spoke the
word of God to you. Keep in mind the out-
come of their way of life and imitate their
faith.[o] 8 Jesus Christ is the same yesterday,
today, and forever.[p]

9 Do not be led astray by all kinds of
strange doctrines. It is good for us to have
our hearts strengthened by grace, and not
by ceremonial foods, which have not benefit-
ed those who partake of them.[q]

10 We have an altar * from which those who
serve the tabernacle have no right to eat.[r]
11 For the bodies of those animals whose
blood is brought into the sanctuary by the
high priest as a sin offering are burned out-
side the camp. *[s] 12 Therefore, Jesus also suf-
fered outside the city gate in order to sancti-
fy the people by his own blood. *[t]

13 Let us then go to him outside the camp *
and bear the abuse he endured.[u] 14 For here
we have no lasting city, but we are seeking
the one that is to come.[v] 15 Through him let
us continually offer up to God a sacrifice of
praise, * that is, the fruit of lips that confess
his name.[w]

16 * Do not neglect to do good works and to
share with others what you have, for these
are the kind of sacrifices that please God.[x]
17 Obey your leaders and submit to them, for
they watch over your souls and will have to
render an account in that regard. Make this
a joy for them to do rather than a grief, for
that would be of no advantage to you.[y]

18 Pray for us. We are sure that our own
conscience is clear, and our desire is to act
honorably in everything we do.[z] 19 I especial-
ly ask you to do this that I may be restored
to you as soon as possible.[a]

Final Doxology. 20 * May the God of peace—
who brought back from the dead our Lord

i Rom 12:10; 1 Tim 4:9; 2 Pet 1:7.—j Gen 18:3; 19:2-3; Jdg 6:11-22; Tob 5:4; Job 31:32; Mt 25:35; Rom 12:13.—k Heb 10:24; Mt 25:36; Col 4:18.—l Deut 22:22; Mal 2:15; 1 Cor 5:13; 7:38; Eph 5:5; 1 Tim 4:3; Rev 22:13.—m Deut 31:6, 8; Jos 1:5; Phil 4:11; 1 Tim 3:3; 6:6, 8.—n Pss 27:1-3; 118:6.—o Heb 4:12; 13:17, 24; 1 Cor 16:16.—p Heb 1:12; 7:24; Jn 6:58; Rev 1:17.—q Heb 9:10; Rom 14:17; 1 Cor 8:8; Eph 4:14; Col 2:7, 16.—r Heb 8:5; 1 Cor 9:13; 10:18.—s Ex 29:14; Lev 4:12; 16:27.—t Mt 21:39; Mk 12:8; Lk 20:15; Jn 19:17; Rom 3:25; Eph 5:26.—u Heb 11:26; Lk 9:23.—v Heb 11:10, 14; 12:27; Phil 3:20.—w Isa 57:19; Hos 14:3; 1 Pet 2:5.—x Rom 12:13; Phil 4:18.—y Heb 13:7, 24; Isa 62:6; Acts 20:28.—z Acts 23:1; 1 Thes 5:25.—a Philem 22.

13:1-6 The Letter's conclusion opens with a series of recommendations concerning the conduct and attitude of Christians.

13:2 *Some have entertained angels without knowing it:* e.g., Abraham (see Gen 18), Gideon (see Jdg 6), and Manoah (see Jdg 13).

13:7-15 The remembrance of leaders, who perhaps confronted martyrdom, is a call to fidelity. It provides the author with the opportunity to insert a new development in the Letter. Christians must cling to the teaching received from their leaders and not to the doctrines of Judaism. They should, therefore, look to Christ; only in him and nowhere else will believers find what can evoke the altar or the sacrifice. If Christ suffered outside of Jerusalem and not in the temple, was that not perhaps a sign that the worship of Mosaic times must be replaced by the definitive worship, which is spiritual? Note three important verses in this section: v. 8, a splendid profession of faith in Christ; v. 14, the thrust toward the future and the realities that endure; and v. 15, life as praise of God (see Ps 50:14, 23; Hos 14:3).

13:10 *Have an altar:* an allusion to Eucharistic worship and sacrifice, compared with the Levitical worship and sacrifices of the Old Testament ("the tabernacle").

13:11 *Camp:* here, as in v. 9, the author uses the great Jewish rite of atonement as a point of comparison (see Lev 16:27).

13:12 Christ's death outside Jerusalem symbolized the removal of sin in the same way that the removal of the bodies of sacrificed animals outside the camp of Israel had done.

13:13 *Let us then go to him outside the camp:* this is a call to separate from Judaism. Just as Christ died in disgrace outside the city, so Christians should be willing to face scorn by leaving Judaism for Christ.

13:15 *Sacrifice of praise:* "sacrifice" here means an offering to God (see Rom 12:1; Phil 4:18). There is no longer need for animal sacrifices.

13:16-19 Christians will have to facilitate the task of the leaders of the community and to put their preoccupations in prayer, even when these leaders believe themselves obliged to remind them of the difficult demands of fidelity.

13:20-25 The author artfully summarizes his ideas and his concerns. The news that he gives seems to indicate that he is waiting for Timothy in order to visit Palestine with him. The mention of "those from Italy" can indicate that he is in a port in Italy or simply that he is surrounded by Italians in some city of the Empire.

Jesus, the great shepherd of the sheep, by the blood of the eternal covenant—[b] 21 make you perfect in every respect so that you may do his will. And may he enable us to achieve what is pleasing to him through Jesus Christ, to whom be glory forever and ever. Amen.[c]

News and Farewell. 22 I urge you, brethren, to listen to my words of exhortation; that is why I have written to you only a short letter.[d] 23 I want to let you know that our brother Timothy has been set free.* If he arrives in time, he will be with me when I see you.[e]

24 My greetings to all your leaders and to all the saints.* Those from Italy send you their greetings as well.[f]

25 Grace be with all of you.[g]

b Gen 9:16; 17:7; Isa 55:3; 61:8; 63:11; Ezek 37:26; Zec 9:11; Mt 26:28; Jn 10:11; Acts 2:24; Rom 15:33.—c Rom 11:36; 2 Cor 9:8; Phil 2:13; 1 Jn 3:22.—d 1 Pet 5:12.—e Acts 16:1; 1 Thes 3:2; 2 Tim 4:9.—f Heb 13:7, 17; Acts 18:2.—g Col 4:18; Tit 3:15.

13:23 *Timothy has been set free:* the event to which the author is referring is unknown to us.

13:24 *Saints:* a term in use among the early Church for God's people, those who have been set apart as holy to the Lord (see note on Rom 1:7).

THE CATHOLIC LETTERS

There are seven New Testament Letters that have this in common: they are in the form of letters, but no one has ever thought of attributing them to Paul. These are: The Letter of James, The First Letter of Peter, The Second Letter of Peter, The First Letter of John, The Second Letter of John, The Third Letter of John, and The Letter of Jude.

Most of these Letters are not addressed to specific communities but deal with general questions that are relevant to a very wide circle of readers. For this reason, they certainly deserved to be grouped together, as they have been since the fourth century, under the title of "Catholic Letters," i.e., General or Universal Letters, Letters intended for the Church as a whole. The particular destination of the brief Second and Third Letters of John could be a problem in this regard. However, it is very likely that their brevity caused them to be annexed to the First Letter of John as simple appendices that had little effect on the overall title.

These seven Letters gradually acquired authority throughout the Church, all the more so since they carried the signatures of important men: James, Peter, John, and Jude. However, critics disagree widely both as to these attributions and as to the dates of the Letters.

The Catholic Letters do not form a homogeneous group, but they do possess some common traits. We are no longer involved in the great struggles of Paul to affirm—against Jewish claims and pagan illusions—that salvation has been given in Christ Jesus and him alone. We find in these documents a Christianity that is no longer in the early years after its formation; the communities are already more firmly established and have acquired their habitual ways.

The problem the Letters deal with is perhaps that of keeping communities from yielding to wear and tear and becoming lax, of keeping them from losing their taste for essentials and returning to alien ideas.

We have the impression of entering a world that is less familiar to us and of hearing questions that are somewhat alien to us, if not downright bizarre.

These Letters deal with problems that occupied Christianity, or at least parts of it, at the time they were written: e.g., certain false doctrines—a form of Gnosis in Asia Minor (1 John); Gnostic-Antinomian tendencies (2 Peter; Jude); the non-occurrence of the Second Coming (2 Peter); severe sufferings and persecutions of the Christian communities (1 Peter).

At the same time, these Letters do not have a uniform literary form. James, Peter, and Jude have written real pastoral Letters, destined for an entire region of the Christian world. With the circle of addressees increasing, their message turns easily into an impersonal treatise and into the general considerations of a homily or of an episcopal mandate. On the other hand, the Third Letter of John is a private missive, addressed to a benefactor of Christian missionaries.

The first two Letters of John lend themselves to discussion: the First because of its lack of all epistolary structure, and the Second because of the ambiguous way in which it designates its addressees. However, scholars view them as real Letters addressed to a community or communities that the author knows intimately and precisely and that are within the radius of his customary apostolic solicitude. The First Letter of John thus fits the genre of the Letters of James, Peter, and Jude, while the Second is a more intimate communication.

The theology of these Letters is a faithful reproduction of the preaching of Jesus. The sacred authors repeat the teachings of their Master with complete fidelity. Hence, Christian love holds the greatest importance in them, especially in James and above all in John.

The Letters also endow their authors with well-defined personalities. James is a Christian well versed in the sapiential and prophetic schools who masterfully dispenses austere moral teaching. Peter is a pastor of souls who harmoniously unites doctrinal and moral teaching, exhortation and warning. John is the disciple of love who takes on a polemical ardor in the face of attempted deviations from Christianity. Jude is a disciple rooted in a rich apocalyptic foundation who writes as the implacable foe of error.

Comparing the contents of these Letters with the other writings of the New Testament, we find that they contain some doctrinal points that are exclusive to them: the Sacrament of the Anointing of the Sick (James), Christ's descent to the netherworld (1 Peter), and the final conflagration (2 Peter).

At the same time, these Letters are filled with incisive passages on authentic Christianity. They are replete with reminders to let the Gospel be the life-giving activity that it should be rather than something tasteless due to boastful theories.

"Have you not shown favoritism among yourselves and judged by wrongful standards?" *(Jas 2:4)*.

THE LETTER OF JAMES

Faith Active in Works

Without the first verse, this writing would have no resemblance at all to a letter. In it we find moral exhortations, striking aphorisms, and finely etched portraits succeeding one another in no discernible order. We also find themes such as courage in trials, concern for true wisdom, and critique of social conditions, which make us think of the great sapiential writings of the Old Testament with their didactic bent. This type of thinking was thus still active in the first Christian generations.

We also find here all the vigor of prophetic invective to denounce abuses and injustice. Jewish, Greek, and Christian ideas all seem to meld together. And though the name of Christ is cited only in an occasional manner, this pressing sermon is an application of the Beatitudes. It is preoccupied with the authenticity of the Christian faith.

In these recommendations that follow one another in rapid succession, we can discern a few prophetic and evangelical concerns.

The Letter of James will always be cited for its concern for the weak and the afflicted, its understanding of poverty and distrust of wealth, its lively attack on social injustice, and its warnings to businessmen.

Apparently, for many Christians of that time, faith seems to have been an occasion for fine discourses or gratuitous considerations apart from any life commitment. James retaliated against such a way of thinking. This has led some to suppose that the author was opposed to the great Pauline teaching concerning salvation by faith alone in Jesus Christ (see Rom 3:28).

However, the reality is that Paul and James were speaking of the same thing from different viewpoints. For Paul, faith is an incontestable change and commitment of life; James knows people for whom faith is nothing more than discourses, discussions, and doctrinal debates, without any impact on their existence. For Paul, works are the observances prescribed by the Law on which one would like to make salvation depend by attributing it to people's merits instead of God's grace. But it is not in this sense that James speaks of works; for him, they express the commitment to faith, a Christianity in action. In order to understand Paul and James, we must pinpoint the concrete problems that each of them is addressing; they are not the same for each.

The problems of the liturgical assembly hold a large place in the Letter of James. There are references to listening to the word of God, songs of praise, the confession of sins followed by prayer, and the Anointing of the Sick. The author goes even farther. He criticizes the assemblies of worship that follow the style of social gatherings and provide the wealthy with the occasion to pursue their ambition and their success. For him, as well as for the Prophets and for Christ, authentic worship commits one to a fraternal life, and it is above all the sum total of the Christian life that is the true spiritual worship. Outside of this, every Liturgy is only so much ornamentation. True religion is the care of widows, orphans, the sick, and the disenfranchised.

This piece of writing circulated under the name of "James." Christian tradition has identified this person with James, who, like Jude and Simon, was a "brother of the Lord" (Mt 13:55; Mk 6:3). He was perhaps the son of Alphaeus who is named in all the lists of the Twelve. He had a very important place in the mother community of Jerusalem. Paul mentions him among the witnesses of the Resurrection (see 1 Cor 15:7). He is also found at the Upper Room with the first group of Christians (see Acts 1:12-14).

When Peter left prison, he was concerned to get news of his deliverance to James immediately (see Acts 12:17). After his conversion, Paul got in touch with him (see Gal 1:18-19). James played a decisive role in the Council of Jerusalem; though his mentality was Jewish, he showed himself conciliatory toward and receptive to converts coming from paganism (see Acts 15:13-29).

Beginning with the first scattering of the Apostles in A.D. 36/37, James seems to have taken responsibility for the mother Church; the elders gathered around him; he welcomed Paul when the latter brought the collection taken up in the Churches (see Acts 21:18-26), shortly before Paul's arrest in the temple (Pentecost, A.D. 58). James died a martyr around A.D. 62. If the present Letter is from that James, it must be dated to around A.D. 60. But Hellenistic influences and an affinity with other Christian writings of a later date prevent too certain an attribution.

The Letter is addressed to "the twelve tribes of the Dispersion," which is another way of saying that it is addressed to the Church scattered throughout the world, to the true Israel (see Rom 2:29; 9:6; Gal 6:16; Phil 3:3). The term "Dispersion" (in Greek diaspora*) signified all the Jews living outside of Palestine (see Jud 5:19; Ps 147:2; Jer 15:7). Here the reference is to Christians of Jewish origin, who are scattered throughout the Greco-Roman world.*

Whatever be the case with the author, the date, and the addressees, this document—recognized as inspired—is a strong warning against a purely verbal Christianity and is a call to a faith that has the courage to change lives.

The Letter to James may be divided as follows:

- *I: Salutation (1:1)*
- *II: Exhortation To Practice Patience (1:2-18)*
- *III: Exhortation To Practice Faith (1:19—2:26)*
- *IV: Exhortation To Practice Christian Living (3:1—5:18)*
- *V: Conclusion (5:19-20)*

CHAPTER 1

I: SALUTATION

Greeting.* 1 James, a servant of God and of the Lord Jesus Christ, to the twelve tribes of the Dispersion: greetings. [a]

II: EXHORTATION TO PRACTICE PATIENCE

Trials—the Test of a Faith in Progress.* 2 My brethren, consider it a cause of great joy whenever you endure various trials, [b] 3 for you know that the testing of your faith will develop perseverance. [c] 4 And let perseverance complete its work so that you may become perfect and complete, and not be deficient in any respect. [d]

A Believer's Prayer.* 5 If someone among you lacks wisdom, he should ask God, who gives to all generously and without finding fault, and it will be given to him. [e] 6 But he is to ask with faith, without doubting, for the one who doubts is like a wave of the sea that is driven and tossed about by the wind. [f] 7 A man like that should not think that he will receive anything from the Lord, 8 since he is of two minds and inconsistent in everything he does. [g]

Rich and Poor.* 9 The brother who is in modest circumstances should take pride in being raised up. [h] 10 Likewise, the one who is rich should glory in being brought low, for he will disappear like a flower of the field. [i] 11 Once the sun comes up with its scorching rays and withers the grass, its flower droops and its beauty vanishes. So too the rich man will fade away in the midst of his affairs. [j]

Trials and Temptations. 12 Blessed is the man who perseveres when he is tempted, for when he has been proven, he will receive the crown of life that the Lord has promised to those who love him. * [k]

13 * While experiencing temptation, no one should say, "God is tempting me." For God cannot be tempted by evil, and he himself tempts no one. [l] 14 Rather, temptation occurs when someone is attracted and seduced by his own desire. [m] 15 Then the desire conceives and gives birth to sin, and that sin, when it reaches full growth, gives birth to death. [n]

Light and Life.* 16 Do not be deceived, my beloved brethren. [o] 17 Every good act of giving and every perfect gift are from above, coming down from the Father of all light. With him there is no alteration or shadow caused by change. [p] 18 By his own choice he gave us birth through the way of truth so that we may be a kind of firstfruits of all his creation. [q]

III: EXHORTATION TO PRACTICE FAITH

Living by God's Word.* 19 Remember this, my beloved brethren: everyone should be quick to listen but slow to speak and slow to anger. [r] 20 For human anger does not bring about the righteousness of God. [s] 21 Therefore, rid yourselves of everything sordid and of every wicked excess, and welcome in all humility the word that is implanted in you and is able to save your souls. [t]

22 Be doers of the word and not just hearers who only deceive themselves. [u] 23 For anyone who listens to the word and fails to do it is like someone who looks at his face in a mirror. 24 After seeing his reflection, he goes off and immediately forgets what he

a Deut 32:26; Jn 7:35; Acts 15:13; Rom 1:1; Tit 1:1; 1 Pet 1:1.—b Mt 5:12; Rom 5:3-5; Heb 10:34; 12:11; 1 Pet 1:6; 4:13-16.—c Heb 10:36; 1 Pet 1:7.—d Mt 5:48; 1 Cor 2:6; 1 Thes 5:23.—e 1 Ki 3:9-10; Prov 2:2-6; Wis 9:4, 9-12; Mt 7:7.—f Mt 7:7; 21:21; Mk 11:24.—g Jas 4:8; 2 Pet 2:14; 3:16.—h Jas 2:5; Mt 23:12.—i Job 14:2; Isa 40:6-7; 1 Cor 7:11; 1 Pet 1:24.—j Isa 40:6-8; Mt 20:12.—k Jas 1:2; 2:5; 5:11; Gen 22:1; Ex 20:6; 1 Cor 9:25; 2 Tim 4:8; 1 Pet 5:4; Rev 2:10.—l Sir 15:11-20; 1 Cor 10:13.—m Prov 19:3; Rom 7:7-8.—n Gen 3:6; Job 15:35; Isa 59:4; Rom 5:12; 6:23.—o Jas 1:19; 2:5; 1 Cor 6:9.—p Jas 3:15; Gen 1:16; Num 23:19; Mal 3:6; Jn 3:27; 1 Jn 1:5.—q Jer 2:3; Jn 1:12-13; 2 Tim 2:15; 1 Pet 1:23; Rev 14:4.—r Jas 1:16; 2:5; Prov 14:17; Sir 5:11.—s Mt 5:22; Eph 4:26.—t Eph 1:13; 4:22; Col 3:8.—u Jas 2:19-20; Mt 7:26; Rom 2:13.

1:1 Only this verse gives the writing the form of a letter. Concerning the author and the addressees, see the Introduction. *Servant:* see note on Rom 1:1. *Twelve tribes:* they prefigured the new People of God (see Acts 26:7; Rev 7:4).

1:2-4 The Christian is exposed to the opposition of society. *Joy . . . various trials:* a teaching based on the words of Jesus (see Mt 5:10-12; Jn 10:11).

1:5-8 A believer's prayer requires lucidity and courage to pursue a Christian way of life—that is, wisdom.

1:9-11 In becoming Christians, the rich lose their privileged position in society and the poor wait to be enriched by God. Both of them must live in the spirit of the poor of the Bible (see Ps 72:4, 12; Mt 5:3; Lk 1:52).

1:12 Those who bear trials patiently will go from distress to sharing the joy and life of the Lord.

1:13-15 The passage from trials to temptations reveals the depths of a person—and is one more reason to be vigilant.

1:16-18 Light and life are opposed to sin and death. They are the grace of the new birth through the Gospel and Baptism.

1:19-27 It costs nothing to place oneself among the distracted listeners and let oneself go to the demon of words for the sake of words. Hearing the Gospel for the sake of putting it into practice obliges one to notice the sufferings of others, to be concerned with truth, to cling to the Christian originality in the face of current mentalities and morals.

looked like. 25 However, the one who looks
intently at the perfect law of freedom and
perseveres—not forgetting what he has
heard but putting it into practice—will be
blessed in everything he does. [v]

26 If anyone thinks that he is religious but
does not restrain his tongue, he is deceiving
himself, and his religion is worthless. [w]
27 Religion that God our Father accepts as
pure and undefiled is this: to come to the aid
of orphans and widows in their hardships
and to keep oneself untarnished by the
world. [x]

CHAPTER 2

Rich and Poor in the Christian Assembly.*
1 My brethren, since you are believers in our
glorious Lord Jesus Christ, you must never
practice favoritism. [y] 2 Suppose a man wear-
ing a gold ring and expensive clothes comes
into your assembly as well as a poor man
dressed in shabby clothes. 3 If you lavish spe-
cial attention on the one wearing the expen-
sive clothes and say, "Please sit in this good
seat," while to the poor man you say, "Stand
over there," or "Sit on the floor at my feet," [z]
4 have you not shown favoritism among
yourselves and judged by wrongful stan-
dards? [a]

5 Listen to me, my beloved brethren. Did
not God choose those who are poor * in the
world to be rich in faith and to be heirs of the
kingdom that he promised to those who love
him? [b] 6 But you have humiliated the poor
man. Furthermore, is it not the rich who
oppress you? Are they not the ones who drag
you into court? [c] 7 Is it not they who blas-
pheme the noble name that was invoked
over you? [d]

8 You will be doing well if you truly observe
the sovereign law enjoined in Scripture,
"You shall love your neighbor as yourself." [e]
9 However, if you show partiality, you are
committing a sin and stand convicted by the
law as lawbreakers. [f] 10 For whoever observes
the whole Law but trips up on a single point
is held guilty of breaking all of it. [g]

11 The one who said, "You shall not commit
adultery," also said, "You shall not kill." Now
if you do not commit adultery but you
do kill, you have become a lawbreaker. [h]
12 Therefore, always speak and act as those
who will be judged by the law of freedom. [i]
13 For judgment will be without mercy to the
one who has not shown mercy, but mercy tri-
umphs over judgment. [j]

True Faith Is Proved by Works.* 14 What good
is it, my brethren, if someone claims to have
faith but does not have good works? Can
such faith save him? [k] 15 * Suppose a brother
or sister is naked and lacks his or her daily
food. [l] 16 If one of you says to such a person,
"Go in peace; keep warm and eat well," but
does not take care of that person's physical
needs, what is the good of that? [m] 17 In the
same way, faith by itself is dead if it does not
have works. [n]

18 But perhaps someone will say, "You
have faith and I have works." Show me your
faith without works, and by works I will
show you my faith. [o] 19 You believe that there
is one God. You do well to assert that. But
even the demons believe and tremble. [p]

20 You fool! Do you want proof that faith
without works is futile? [q] 21 Was not
Abraham our father justified by works when
he offered his son Isaac on the altar? [r]
22 Thus, you can see that his faith and his

v Jas 2:12; Ps 19:8; Jn 8:32; 13:17; Rom 8:2.—w Jas 3:2; Ps 34:14; 1 Pet 3:10.—x Jas 4:4; Ex 22:21; Deut 14:29; Job 31: 16-17, 21; Isa 1:17, 23; Mt 25:36; Rom 12:2; 2 Pet 1:4.—y Lev 19:15; Deut 1:17; Prov 24:23; Acts 7:2; 1 Cor 2:8.—z Prov 18:23.—a Jn 7:24.—b Jas 1:12, 16, 19; Job 34:19; Mt 25:34; Lk 12:21; 1 Cor 1:26-28; Rev 2:9.—c Acts 8:3; 16:19; 1 Cor 11:22.—d Acts 18:6; 1 Pet 4:4.—e Lev 19:18; Mt 5:43; 22:39; Rom 13:9.—f Jas 2:1; Deut 1:17.—g Jas 3:2; Mt 5:19; Gal 3:10; 5:3.—h Ex 20:13-14; Deut 5:17-18.—i Jas 1:25; Mt 16:22; Rom 8:1.—j Mt 5:7; 6:14-15; 9:13; 18:32-35; Lk 6:37.—k Jas 1:22-25; Mt 7:26; 25:31-46; Gal 5:6.—l Mt 25:35-36.—m Lk 3:11; 1 Jn 3:17-18.—n Jas 2:20, 26; Gal 5:6.—o Jas 3:13; Mt 7:16-17; Rom 3:28; Heb 11.—p Deut 6:4; Mt 8:29; Mk 12:29; Lk 4:34; 1 Cor 8:4-6.—q Jas 2:17, 26.—r Gen 22:9-12; Heb 11:17.

2:1-13 Remaining impartial is the most difficult as well as the most significant demand of the Bible and the Gospel. But even in the liturgical assembly notables are often honored because of their fortune and their culture, while the poor are sometimes put down. The Gospel cannot stand for such discrimination. On the contrary, it calls for all to be poor.

2:5 *Poor:* the poor of the Lord, who relied on God alone and were in turn loved by God and under his protection (see Ps 35:10; Isa 61:1; Mt 5:3; 11:5; Lk 6:20; 1 Cor 1:17-20).

2:14-26 The main concern of the Letter is expressed in this passage. The author attacks a faith that is satisfied with words and ideas that do not lay hold of one's existence and do not find expression in charity and prayer. Paul had said that salvation comes only through faith in Jesus Christ, but this is a faith that unsettles and transforms one's life (see Rom 3:28; Gal 2:16). Like him, James too gives Abraham, the model for believers, as an example, but at first sight the two writers seem to draw contrary conclusions. In fact, however, James regards Abraham's action as a gesture and expression of his faith; in this context, Paul speaks rather of the fruits of the Spirit (see Rom 12—14; 1 Cor 13:1; 4:20; Gal 5:13; 6:10). The two writers both cite Rahab, of whom the Book of Joshua speaks. The Letter of James by no means minimizes faith; rather it demands an authentic life.

2:15-16 These verses illustrate a faith that is faulty similar to the way 1 Jn 3:17 illustrates a love that is faulty. What is needed is a faith that is genuine, i.e., operative.

works were active together; his faith was brought to completion by works. [s]

23 Thus, the words of Scripture were fulfilled that say, "Abraham believed God, and it was credited to him as righteousness," and he was called the friend of God. [t] 24 You can see, then, that a man is justified by works and not by faith alone.

25 Likewise, Rahab the prostitute,* was she not also justified by works when she welcomed the messengers and sent them away by a different road? [u] 26 For just as the body is dead without a spirit, so faith without works is also dead. [v]

IV: EXHORTATION TO PRACTICE CHRISTIAN LIVING

CHAPTER 3

Avoid Faults of the Tongue.* 1 My brethren, not many of you should become teachers, for you know that we will face a more severe judgment. [w] 2 For all of us fall short in many ways. Anyone who never makes a mistake in speech has reached perfection* and is able to control every part of his body. [x]

3 When we put a bit into a horse's mouth to make it obey us, we also guide its entire body. 4 Or think of ships. Even though they are large and are driven by strong winds, they are steered by a very small rudder on whatever course the helmsman chooses. 5 In the same way, the tongue is a small member but its pretensions are great.

Consider how a small fire can set ablaze a great forest. 6 And the tongue is also a fire, a world of evil that infects the entire body. It sets afire the entire course of our existence and is itself set on fire by Gehenna. [y]

7 For every species of beast and bird, of reptile and sea creature, can be tamed and has been tamed by man, 8 but no one can tame the tongue. It is a restless evil, full of deadly poison. [z] 9 With it we bless the Lord and Father, and with it we curse people who are made in the likeness of God. * [a]

10 Out of the same mouth flow blessings and curses. This should not be so, my brethren. 11 Does a spring pour forth from the same opening both fresh and salt water? 12 Can a fig tree, my brethren, produce olives or can a grapevine produce figs? Neither can salt water yield fresh water. [b]

True Wisdom and Its Opposite.* 13 Who among you is wise and understanding? Prove by your good life that your works are done with the humility that comes from wisdom. [c] 14 But if your hearts are filled with bitter envy and selfish ambition, do not be boastful in defiance of the truth. [d]

15 Such wisdom does not come down from above, but is earthly, unspiritual, and demonic. [e] 16 For where there is envy and selfish ambition, there will also be disharmony and every type of wickedness. [f]

17 However, the wisdom that comes from above is first of all pure, then peaceable, gentle, and considerate, full of mercy and good fruits, without any trace of partiality or hypocrisy. [g] 18 And a harvest of righteousness is sown in peace by those who are peacemakers. [h]

s 1 Thes 1:3; Heb 11:17.—t Gen 15:6; 2 Chr 20:7; Isa 41:8; Rom 4:3; Gal 3:6.—u Jos 2:1-21; Heb 11:31.—v Jas 2:17, 20.—w Mt 7:1; Rom 2:21; Eph 4:11.—x Jas 1:26; 2:10; 1 Ki 8:46; Prov 13:3; 10:19; Sir 28:12, 26; Mt 12:37; Rom 3:9-20; 1 Pet 3:10.—y Mt 15:11, 18, 19; Prov 16:27.—z Ps 140:4; Rom 3:13.—a Gen 1:26-27; 1 Cor 11:7.—b Mt 7:16-17; Lk 6:44.—c Jas 2:18; Eph 4:1-2; 1 Pet 2:12.—d Jas 3:16; 5:19; 2 Cor 12:20.—e Jas 1:17; 3:17.—f Jas 3:14; Gal 5:20-21.—g Jas 1:17; Wis 7:22-23; Lk 6:36; Rom 12:9; 1 Cor 2:6; Heb 12:11.—h Prov 11:18; Isa 32:17; Hos 10:12; Mt 5:9; Rom 14:19; Phil 1:11.

2:25 *Rahab the prostitute:* the author of the Letter is not intending to approve Rahab's occupation but simply to commend the faith she showed in helping the spies (see Jos 2; see also Heb 11:31).

3:1-12 What is more beautiful and what more ugly than the tongue? All the wisdoms of the world repeat it, and the sages of the Old Testament more than once issued denunciations against inconsiderate words (see Prov 10:9; 13:3; 15:1-4; 18:21; 21:23; Sir 5:11—6:1). Christ had spoken of the evil that comes forth from the mouth of man (see Mk 7:21-23). There is a kind of passionate outburst of words that disfigures society; with a word one can disrupt an assembly, with a lie break a friendship or unleash a rivalry—in short, destroy the world's harmony. We might say that an infernal power is at work; "Gehenna" was the cursed spot around Jerusalem that became a symbol for hell. The author is speaking especially to those who have the responsibility to teach in the assemblies. What a perversion it is to announce God's praise yet do harm to one's neighbor.

3:2 *Perfection:* so difficult is the tongue to control that those who are successful gain control of themselves in all other areas of life as well.

3:9 *In the likeness of God:* human beings are made in the likeness of God (see Gen 1:26f); hence, to curse them is tantamount to cursing God (see Gen 9:6).

3:13-18 There is a way of life and a concept of relationships that are inspired by a sense of God. There is another that is nothing more than the uncontrolled expression of passions. The Old Testament thus opposed wisdom and folly (see Prov 2:6; 8:22-31; Wis 7:22—8:1; Sir 1:1-4; 24:3-22). Paul distinguished between the fruits of the flesh and the fruits of the Spirit (see Gal 5:22-25). The Christian faith is transmitted by mildness, conciliation, goodness, and peace.

CHAPTER 4

The Need To Control Passions.* 1 What is the
source of these conflicts and quarrels
among you? Are they not the result of your
passions * that are at war within you? [i] 2 You
want something that you cannot have, so
you commit murder. And you covet some-
thing but cannot obtain it, so you engage in
quarrels and fights. You do not have because
you do not ask. [j] 3 When you ask, you do not
get what you want because you do not ask
for it with the proper motives, seeking
rather to indulge your passions. [k]

4 Adulterers! Do you not know that love
of the world results in enmity with God?
Therefore, whoever wishes to be a lover of
the world makes himself an enemy of God. [l]
5 Or do you suppose that it is without reason
that Scripture says, "He yearns jealously for
the Spirit that he sent to live in us"? * [m] 6 But
he has bestowed an even stronger grace.
Therefore, it says,

"God resists the proud,
but he gives grace to the humble." [n]

7 Hence, be subject to God. Resist the devil,
and he will flee from you. [o] 8 Draw near to
God, and he will draw near to you. Cleanse
your hands, you sinners, and purify your
hearts, you waverers. [p] 9 Be sorrowful, lament,
and weep. Let your laughter turn to mourning
and your joy to gloom. [q] 10 Humble yourselves
before the Lord, and he will exalt you. [r]

Do Not Judge Others.* 11 Do not slander one
another, my brethren. Whoever speaks ill of a
brother or passes judgment on a brother
speaks ill of the Law and passes judgment on
the Law. But if you judge the Law, you are not
keeping it but passing judgment upon it. [s]
12 There is only one Lawgiver and Judge, the
one who is able to save or to destroy. Who then
are you to pass judgment on a neighbor? [t]

A Warning against Presumption.* 13 Come
now, you who say, "Today or tomorrow we
shall head off to this or that town and spend
a year doing business there and making
money." [u] 14 Yet you do not know what
tomorrow will bring.

What is your life, after all? For you are like
a mist that appears for a brief time and then
vanishes. [v] 15 Instead, what you ought to say
is, "If it is the Lord's will, we shall live to do
this or that." [w] 16 But instead you boast in
your arrogance, and all such boasting is
evil. [x] 17 Anyone who knows the right thing to
do and fails to do it commits a sin. [y]

CHAPTER 5

Woe to the Rich.* 1 Come now, you who
are rich. Lament and weep over the miseries
that will soon overwhelm you. [z] 2 Your riches
have rotted. Your clothes are all moth-eaten. [a]
3 Your gold and silver have corroded. Their
corrosion will serve as a witness against you

i Rom 7:23; Tit 3:9; 1 Pet 2:11.—j Jas 5:6; Mt 5:21-22; 1 Jn 3:15.—k Mt 7:7; 1 Jn 3:22; 5:14.—l Jas 1:27; Isa 54:5; Jer 3:20; Hos 2:2-5; 3:1; Mt 6:24; Lk 16:13; Rom 8:7; 1 Jn 2:15-16.—m 1 Cor 6:19.—n Job 22:29; Prov 3:34; Mt 23:12; 1 Pet 5:5.—o Eph 4:27; 6:11; 1 Pet 5:8-9.—p Jas 1:8; Isa 1:16; Jer 4:14; Zec 1:3; Mal 3:7; Heb 7:19.—q Lk 6:25.—r Jas 4:6; Job 5:11; Mt 23:12; Lk 14:11; 18:14; 1 Pet 5:6.—s Jas 1:22; 2:8; Mt 7:1; Rom 1:30; 2 Cor 12:20; 1 Pet 2:1.—t Jas 5:9; Isa 33:22; Mt 7:1; 10:28; Rom 2:1; 14:4.—u Jas 5:1; Prov 27:1; Lk 12:18-20.—v Job 7:7; Ps 39:6-7; Prov 27:1; Isa 2:22.—w Acts 18:21.—x 1 Cor 5:6.—y Lk 12:47; Jn 9:41.—z Jas 2:2-6; 4:13; Isa 13:6; Ezek 30:2; Lk 6:24; 1 Tim 6:9.—a Job 13:28; Isa 50:9; Mt 6:19-20.

4:1-10 Troubles, unjust and murderous confrontations, and wars are the scourges of social life, and Christians share in them. Murderous passions are given free rein even in the community, creating antagonisms and divisions. The desire to possess and to monopolize things seems to be without limits and takes over the human heart. Hence, let all Christians question themselves about their innermost affiliation and choice. Do they really opt for God or do they live under the weight of their evil passions? When someone became unfaithful to God in the concrete, the Old Testament as well as Christ designated it as adultery (see Hos 3:1; Mt 12:39; 16:4). All these evils are the result of a failure to pray. True prayer is a drawing near to God, and it requires a reversal of mentality.

4:1 *Passions:* literally, "pleasures." The author is not saying that pleasures are evil in themselves; the evil consists only in the way they are used.

4:5 *He yearns jealously for the Spirit that he sent to live in us:* two other translations are possible (because James is citing a passage that does not appear in any extant Bible manuscript): "The Spirit he caused to live in us envies intensely" and "The Spirit he caused to live in us longs jealously." The meaning of the translation in the text is that God jealously longs for our fidelity and love (see Jn 4:4). The meaning of the first alternative translation is that because of the fall the spirit of man that was put in us at the Creation (see Gen 2:7) envies intensely—however, God's grace is able to overcome that envy (see Ex 20:5). The meaning of the second alternative translation is that it is the Holy Spirit who longs jealously for our full devotion.

4:11-12 Nothing is more current in the thoughts and conversations of human beings than passing judgment on others and slandering them. This is a usurpation. Only God can pass judgment, and it is he who has established a law—the law of love (see Lev 19:16-18; Mt 7:1-5).

4:13-17 This is a warning to those people who live only for the glory of their projects, the exploitation of others, and the lure of gain (see Mk 8:36). It reproduces the theme of human weakness (see Pss 39:5-7, 11; 102:3; Wis 2:4; 5:9-14), which obliges people to put their trust solely in God and not in self.

5:1-6 Here, we hear again the cries of the Prophets denouncing the injustice and inhumanity of riches (see Isa 5:8-10; Jer 5:26-30; Am 8:4-8); we also hear the voice of Christ placing us on guard against the danger of riches (see Lk 6:24; 18:24-27). The Bible has always seen the accumulation of goods as tarnished by some injustice. It instinctively feels how riches give birth to a type of person whose sense of his own human condition becomes warped and who loses sight of the proper relationship of fraternity and justice in regard to others.

and consume your flesh like a fire. You have hoarded wealth for the last days. [b]

4 Behold, the wages you fraudulently withheld from the laborers who harvested your fields are crying out, and the cries of those harvesters have reached the ears of the Lord of hosts. [c] 5 You have lived on earth in luxury and self-indulgence. You have gorged yourselves as on the day of slaughter. [d] 6 You have condemned the righteous man and murdered him, even though he offered you no resistance. [e]

Patience, for the Lord's Coming Is Near.* 7 Therefore be patient, brethren, until the coming of the Lord. Think of how patiently a farmer awaits the precious crop from his fields until they have received the early and the late rains. [f] 8 You too must be patient. Take courage, for the coming of the Lord is near. * [g]

9 Brethren, do not raise complaints against one another lest you yourselves be brought to judgment. Behold, the Judge is standing at the gates. [h]

10 As an example of patience in enduring hardship, brethren, consider the Prophets who spoke in the name of the Lord. [i] 11 Indeed, those who had perseverance are the ones we call blessed. You have heard of the perseverance of Job and have come to understand the Lord's purpose in this respect, because the Lord is merciful and compassionate. [j]

Do Not Swear. 12 Above all, my brethren, do not swear, either by heaven or by earth, or use any oaths at all. Let your "Yes" mean "Yes" and your "No" mean "No." Otherwise you may be condemned. * [k]

Anointing of the Sick. 13 * Is anyone among you suffering? He should pray. Is anyone cheerful? He should sing songs of praise. [l] 14 Is anyone among you sick? He should send for the presbyters of the Church so that they may pray over him and anoint him with oil in the name of the Lord. [m] 15 The prayer of faith will save the sick person, and the Lord will raise him up. And if he has committed any sins, he will be forgiven. [n]

Confession and Intercession. 16 Therefore, confess your sins to one another and pray for one another, so that you may be healed. The prayer of a righteous man is powerful and effective. [o]

17 Elijah was a man like us. Yet when he prayed fervently that it might not rain for three and a half years, it did not rain on the earth. [p] 18 Then he prayed again, and the heavens gave forth rain, and the earth once again brought forth its harvest. [q]

V: CONCLUSION

The Peace of Fraternal Love.* 19 My brethren, if one of you should stray from the truth and another succeeds in bringing him back, [r] 20 remember this: A person who brings back a sinner from erring ways will rescue his soul from death and cover a multitude of sins. [s]

b Jas 5:7-8; Jud 16:17; Ps 21:10; Prov 11:4.—c Lev 19:13; Deut 24:14-15; Jer 22:13; Mal 3:5; Rom 9:29.—d Jer 12:3; Ezek 16:4-9; Am 6:1; Lk 16:19-25.—e Jas 4:2; Wis 2:10-20; Heb 10:38.—f Deut 11:14; Jer 5:24; Joel 2:23; 1 Cor 1:7; Gal 6:9.—g Lk 21:19; Rom 13:11; 1 Cor 1:7; Heb 10:25, 36; 1 Pet 4:7.—h Jas 4:11-12; Mt 24:33; 1 Pet 4:5.—i Mt 5:12.—j Ex 34:6; Num 14:18; Job 1:21-22; Ps 103:8; Mt 5:10; Heb 10:36.—k Ex 20:7; Mt 5:34-37.—l Col 3:16.—m Isa 1:6; Mk 6:13; Lk 10:34; Acts 11:30.—n Jas 1:6.—o Mt 3:6; Jn 9:31; Acts 19:18; Heb 12:13; 1 Pet 2:24.—p 1 Ki 17:1; Lk 4:25; Acts 14:15.—q 1 Ki 18:41-45.—r Jas 3:14; Mt 18:15; Gal 6:1.—s Prov 10:12; Rom 11:14; 1 Pet 4:8.

5:7-11 For the Old Testament as well as for the New, the life of believers tends toward the final encounter with the Lord. The future of human beings does not rest in any terrestrial value in an absolute manner. It rests in God.

5:8 The expectation of the Lord's Second Coming (see 1 Cor 15:23) is the ultimate basis for Christian patience (see Jas 1:2—4:12; 1 Thes 3:13; 1 Pet 4:7; 5:10).

5:12 The Sermon on the Mount gives us the same recommendation in the same terms (see Mt 5:34-37).

5:13-18 The Church was to pay special attention to the sick. Catholic tradition sees in this passage a testimony to the Sacrament of the Anointing of the Sick. It was with an appeal to it that Pope Innocent I (in his Letter of March 19, 416, to Decentius, Bishop of Gubbio) justified the rite used in the Church and declared it to be a "Sacrament"; this doctrine was later solemnly defined by the Council of Trent despite the opposition of the Protestants (Session 14, November 25, 1551).

The reference to prayer ends with the example of Elijah. The Jewish tradition was familiar with several examples of Prophets who had interceded for the people (see Gen 18:22-32; Ex 32:11-14, 30-32). Elijah was a very popular figure both in Jewish tradition and in the early Christian tradition (which identified the coming Elijah with John the Baptist).

5:19-20 James regards the return of a straying brother to the truth as a real rescue from death (see Mt 18:12-13; 1 Jn 5:16). It would seem that the sins "covered," i.e., forgiven, are those of the brother who had gone astray (see 1 Pet 4:8) rather than those of the brother who brings him back to the truth (see Ezek 3:20-21; 1 Tim 4:16). In speaking of a "multitude of sins" James is perhaps including the sins of both (see Jas 2:13).

"He himself bore our sins in his body on the cross" *(1 Pet 2:24).*

THE FIRST LETTER OF PETER

Witnesses to Hope

Grave threats darken the horizon for the Churches located in Asia Minor. For the most part, these communities have been founded by Paul and his coworkers. They bring together in one assembly, one faith, and one conception of life Jews and Gentiles who have become Christian. Such a union could appear strange to people on the outside. In addition, these men and women have broken away from the ways of life and thought of those who surround them. Christians are thus suspected of subversive behavior and morals.

If persecution has not struck as yet, it is just around the corner. We can think of the Emperor Nero, who gave rise to the first persecutions in A.D. 64. We have the impression that for the moment Christians are being subjected mainly to pressures, vexations, scorn, and suspicions, and they are despised and ostracized from the social life of their area.

In such circumstances, could Christians forget that, according to the Old Testament and the Gospel, the onset of opposition announces the last times and that Christ has promised persecution as an advance sign of his return (see Mt 5:11f; 10:22; Lk 21:12-19)? Believers must not be frozen in fear. The moment must inspire a renewal of hope. They must remain filled with courage, joy, simplicity, and loyalty, keeping their eyes on the future, the great future of the encounter with Jesus (see 1 Pet 1:5, 13, 20; 2:12; 4:5, 13, 17; 5:1-4, 10). This is not a case of minimizing the judgment that is also coming, for Christians regard it with hope, not fear.

The First Letter of Peter seems to be an excellent example of catechesis as practiced around the sixties of the first century. Here and there, the author seems to have read Paul, the discourses in Acts, or passages of the Gospels; we have in this document part of the patrimony of Christian initiation and instruction.

In addition to giving us a theology of Baptism, a teaching about the baptismal life, this document is also one of the texts best suited for conveying an understanding of the mystery of the Church, the community that carries out God's plan in the midst of the world, the new human race that is maturing in Christ. The theology of the Church is in this case a spirituality of joy.

In this Christian milieu one places the Gospel into evidence when one speaks of salvation, hope, and the time of God for humanity. One must focus on the mystery of Christ: the innocent, humble, and suffering Christ, in whose footsteps believers must walk, exposed to all kinds of attacks (see 1 Pet 2:9, 21-23).

Appeal is always made to this Letter when the topic is Christ's descent to the netherworld (see 1 Pet 3:19f; 4:6). The theme can receive diverse interpretations, among which it is difficult to navigate. It certainly stresses Christ's sovereignty over all humanity from its origin as well as his sovereignty over the universe, and it demonstrates the universal efficacy of his redemptive work.

This Letter presents the Christian life as something simple and right, without any complicated rule of life but with the sense of love and loyalty. When they are threatened by persecution and when they live in a perspective of the end of the world, these Christians do not construct any new project for society. They accept the structures and conditions of life that form part of their world. However, in this real context, they want to bear witness to righteousness, loyalty, and the meaning of human duties. It is in this sense that we must read the passage concerning slaves, women, and public officials (see 1 Pet 2:13—3:7). In the face of persecution, they reflect on the meaning of suffering and on the Beatitudes. They must remember that the servant is not greater than the Master, as Christ declared (see Mt 10:24).

A very ancient tradition, the first attestations of which go back to the end of the first century, attributes this Letter to Peter, the head of the Apostles. Critical studies often cast doubt on the attribution because of the difficulties it raises, but good arguments for it are not lacking. The text is written in simple and correct Greek; Peter was linked with the family of Zebedee, which ran a fishing business in Galilee, and so would have known the language. Moreover, in its final redaction, the Letter may have been fine-tuned by the writer's secretary, Silvanus or Silas, a Greek by birth and found more than once in the company of Paul (see Acts 15:22; 17:4; 2 Cor 1:19).

Peter would have written this Letter from "Rome," which was the most current interpretation of "Babylon" (1 Pet 5:13). For in Judaism this name signified the power that from time to time oppressed the Jewish faith and scattered the people, and from the first century B.C. onward that power was Rome.

In a more dramatic context, the Book of Revelation (18:2, 10, 21) uses the same image for the public authority that persecutes. On the other hand, we also know that Peter was martyred in Rome, under Nero, in A.D. 64 or 67.

The First Letter of Peter may be divided as follows:

I: Salutation (1:1-2)
II: The Privileges and Responsibilities of Salvation (1:3—2:10)
III: God's People in a Hostile World (2:11—3:12)
IV: Christian Conduct in Suffering and Persecution (3:13—5:11)
V: Conclusion (5:12-14)

CHAPTER 1

I: SALUTATION*

To the Faithful in the Dispersion. 1 Peter, * an
apostle of Jesus Christ, to all the exiles of the
Dispersion who are now living in Pontus,
Galatia, Cappadocia, Asia, and Bithynia, [a]
2 chosen * in the foreknowledge of God the
Father, through sanctification by the Spirit,
to be obedient to Jesus Christ and to be
sprinkled with his blood: may grace and
peace be yours in abundance. [b]

II: THE PRIVILEGES AND RESPONSIBILITIES OF SALVATION*

The Song of the New Life.* 3 Blessed be the
God and Father of our Lord Jesus Christ. In
his great mercy he has given us a new birth
to a living hope through the resurrection of
Jesus Christ from the dead [c] 4 and to an
inheritance that is imperishable, undefiled,
and unfading. It is reserved in heaven for
you [d] 5 who because of your faith are being
protected by God's power until the salvation
that is ready to be revealed at the end of
time. * [e]
6 This is a reason for you to rejoice, even if
now for a little while you must suffer trials of
many kinds. [f] 7 Thus, the genuine quality of
your faith—which is more valuable than gold
that is perishable even if it has been tested by
fire—may be proved worthy of praise, glory,
and honor when Jesus Christ is revealed. [g]
8 Although you have not seen him, you love
him; and even though you do not see him
now, you believe in him and are filled with a
joy that is indescribable and glorious. [h] 9 For
you are achieving the goal of your faith, that
is, the salvation of your souls. [i]
10 This salvation was the subject of intense
scrutiny and investigation by the Prophets *
who spoke about the grace that you were to
receive. [j] 11 They were searching out the time
and the circumstances to which the Spirit of
Christ * within them was pointing when it
testified in advance to the sufferings that
Christ would endure and the glories that
would then follow. [k]
12 It was revealed to them that they were
serving not themselves but you when they
spoke of the things that have now been
announced to you through those who pro-
claimed the good news to you by the Holy
Spirit sent from heaven. Even the angels
long to catch a glimpse of such things. [l]

a Mt 24:22; Acts 2:9; 18:2; Heb 11:12; Jas 1:1; 2 Pet 1:1.—b Rom 1:7; 8:29; 2 Thes 2:1; Heb 10:22.—c 1 Pet 1:23; Jn 1:13; 2 Cor 1:3; Eph 1:3; Tit 3:5; Heb 3:6.—d 1 Pet 5:4; Mt 6:19-20; Acts 20:32; Rom 8:17; Col 1:5; 2 Tim 4:8.—e 1 Sam 2:9; Jn 10:28; Rom 11:14.—f 1 Pet 4:12; 5:10; Rom 5:2; Jas 1:2-3.—g Job 23:10; Prov 17:3; Isa 48:10; 1 Cor 3:13; 2 Cor 4:17.—h Jn 20:29; 2 Cor 5:6-7.—i Rom 6:22.—j Mt 13:17; 26:24.—k Isa 52:13—53:12; Dan 9:24; Mt 26:24; 2 Pet 1:21.—l 1 Pet 1:25; Lk 24:49; Rom 4:24.

1:1-2 Christians regarded themselves as the true Israel and made use of the term Dispersion, which designated the Jews who had been dispersed and awaited the reunion of their people (see Jas 1:1). By divine choice, they are the New Covenant, evoked by the mention of the Blood of Christ (see Ex 24:3-8; Heb 9:12-14). Related to the three divine Persons, the Church is born of the Trinity. This is an extremely dense salutation.

1:1 *Peter:* see notes on Mt 16:18; 16:19; Jn 1:42. *Apostle:* see notes on Mk 6:30; Rom 1:1; Heb 3:1-6. *Exiles:* literally, "strangers" or "pilgrims," because the homeland and inheritance of the children of God are in heaven (see 1 Chr 29:15; Ps 39:13; Heb 13:14). *Living in Pontus . . . Bithynia:* Jewish and Gentile Christians living in Asia Minor.

1:2 *Chosen:* see note on Eph 1:3—3:21. *Father . . . Spirit . . . Jesus Christ:* all three persons of the Trinity are involved in the redemption of the Elect. *To be sprinkled with his blood:* in the Old Testament, the blood of a sacrificial animal was sprinkled on the altar and the benefit of the sacrifice descended on the offerer. The sprinkled blood of Christ brings us these benefits: (1) justification (see Rom 5:19); (2) sealing with God's Covenant promise represented for us in the Eucharist (see Lk 22:20); (3) cleansing of all sin (see 1 Jn 1:7); and (4) empowerment to become citizens of the Kingdom of heaven (see Heb 10:19).

1:3—2:10 The author stresses the privileges and responsibilities that come with salvation (the Greek word means "deliverance" or "preservation"). Salvation was prophesied in the past and achieved by God in Christ, and it calls for a life of holiness and love on the part of Christians, including the true worship of God, for they are a "nation of priests."

1:3-12 Adversity can do nothing in the face of the joyous certitude of believers. May they relive the fundamental experience of faith described in this grand praise. In Christ, the mercy of God gives human beings an inviolable faith that has no common measure with all human projects. The rebirth of Baptism opens another life and another history; a promise of salvation is on the way to being fulfilled. How then can Christ's personal love fail to take hold of hearts? The plan of God is not a theory but a reality in the life of each person. Today, the goal toward which all the expectations of the Prophets were directed, has become a reality and it brings about the joy of angels.

In this great passage of praise the fundamental experience of faith is described.

1:5 *The end of time:* i.e., the time of salvation, which is close at hand in the sense that it is certain; the glorious coming of Christ is the only really new thing to be awaited.

1:10 *This salvation was the subject of intense scrutiny and investigation by the Prophets:* the inspiration of the Prophets is attributed to the universal effectiveness of Christ, which works retroactively. The unity of the two Testaments is here highlighted.

1:11 *The Spirit of Christ:* the Holy Spirit is called thus because Christ sent him (see Jn 16:7) and ministered through him (see Lk 4:14, 18). *The sufferings that Christ would endure and the glories:* this is a theme found throughout the Bible (see Ps 22; Isa 52:13—53:12; Zec 9:9f; 13:7; Mt 16:21-23; 17:22; 20:19; Lk 24:26, 46; Jn 2:19; Acts 3:17-22; 4:12-16; 5:1, 4, 9f). Those who are united with Christ in everything, including suffering, will also be united with him in glory. And in the midst of their present sufferings they will benefit from the fact that he has already entered into his glory (see 1 Pet 2:3, 8, 21; 3:21f).

Convictions for Living.* 13 Therefore, pre-
pare your minds for action. Be calm and fix
your hopes completely on the grace that you
will be granted at the revelation of Jesus
Christ.[m] 14 Like obedient children, do not
yield to the evil desires you had in your for-
mer ignorance.[n] 15 He who called you is holy.
Therefore, be holy yourselves in all your
conduct.[o] 16 For Scripture says, "Be holy, for
I am holy."[p]

17 If you address as Father the one who
judges everyone impartially on the basis of
each person's deeds, live in reverent fear
during the time of your exile here.[q] 18 For
you are aware that you were ransomed from
your futile way of life inherited from your
ancestors not with perishable things like sil-
ver or gold,[r] 19 but with the precious blood of
Christ, * a lamb without blemish or defect.[s]

20 He was chosen before the foundation of
the world, but in this final age he has been
revealed for your sake.[t] 21 Through him you
have come to believe in God, who raised him
from the dead and gave him glory, so that
your faith and your hope are fixed on God.[u]

22 Now that you have purified your souls
by your obedience to truth so that you have
genuine love for your brethren, love one
another intensely with all your heart.[v] 23 You
have been born anew, not of perishable but
of imperishable seed, through the living and
enduring word of God. *[w] 24 For:

All flesh is like grass,
and all its glory like the flower of the field.
The grass withers, and the flower fades,[x]
25 but the word of the Lord endures forever.

It is this word that has been proclaimed to
you.[y]

CHAPTER 2

1 [z] Rid yourselves, therefore, of all mal-
ice, and all deceit, hypocrisy, and envy, and
all slander.[a] 2 Like newborn infants, long for
pure spiritual milk, so that by it you may
advance on the path to salvation,[b] 3 now
that you have tasted that the Lord is good.[c]

The Mystery of the Church.* 4 Come to
him, a living stone, rejected by men but
chosen by God and precious.[d] 5 You, too,
are like living stones, being built up into a
spiritual temple and a holy priesthood * to
offer spiritual sacrifices acceptable to God
through Jesus Christ.[e] 6 For it states in
Scripture,

"See, I am laying a stone in Zion,
a cornerstone chosen and precious.
Whoever believes in it
will not be put to shame."[f]

7 Therefore, it is precious to you who
believe. However, for those who do not
believe,

"The stone that the builders rejected
has become the cornerstone,"[g]

8 and

"A stone that makes them stumble,
and a rock that makes them fall."

m Acts 24:25; 1 Cor 1:7; Heb 3:6.—n Rom 12:2; Eph 4:18.—o Isa 35:8; Mt 5:48; 1 Thes 4:7; 1 Jn 3:3.—p Lev 11:44; 19:2; 20:7.—q 1 Pet 2:11; Mt 6:9; 16:27; Acts 10:34.—r Isa 52:3; Mt 20:28; 1 Cor 6:20; Gal 4:3.—s Ex 12:5; Jn 1:29; Rom 3:25; Heb 9:14.—t Mt 25:34; Eph 1:4; Heb 9:26.—u Acts 2:24; Rom 4:24; 10:9; Phil 2:7-9; Heb 2:9; 3:6.—v Jn 13:34; Rom 12:10; Jas 4:8.—w Jn 1:13; Heb 4:12; 1 Jn 3:9.—x Isa 40:6-8; Jas 1:10-11.—y Isa 40:6-8; Jas 1:10-11.—z 1-2: Jas 1:21.—a Jn 4:11; Eph 4:22.—b 1 Pet 3:18; 1 Cor 3:2; Heb 5:12, 13.—c Ps 34:9; Heb 6:5.—d 1 Pet 2:7; Ps 118:22; Isa 42:1; Mt 21:42; Acts 4:11.—e Ex 19:6; Prov 9:1; Isa 61:6; 1 Cor 3:9; Eph 2:21-22; 1 Tim 3:15; Rev 1:6.—f Isa 28:16; Rom 9:32-33; 10:11; Eph 2:20.—g 1 Pet 2:4; Ps 118:22; Mt 21:42; Lk 20:17; Acts 4:11; 2 Cor 2:16.

1:13—2:3 An existence given over to passions and inclinations is without meaning or real purpose. But Christians are delivered from insignificance; it is God who becomes their reason for living and its accomplishment. This is translated by a profound reversal of sentiments and behavior. Believers have a sense of God and his holiness, and they bear something of God's absoluteness in their existence. A life saved by the gift of Christ is an Easter. From then on, fraternal love becomes the goal. Thus, the Christian life is something new, a new birth, and a new destiny. It is developed by coming to maturity in one's reflection upon the word of God.

1:18-19 *Ransomed . . . with the precious blood of Christ:* i.e., bought back or redeemed in the way laid out in the Scriptures (see Ex 13:13; 21:30). Our need for being ransomed comes from our bondage to Satan and sin (see Jn 8:34; Rom 6:17, 23). Jesus has bought our freedom by paying not silver or gold but his own blood (see Eph 1:7; Rev 5:9), i.e., his Death (see Mt 20:28; Mk 10:45; Heb 9:15) or Christ himself (see Gal 3:13).

1:23 *Born anew . . . through the . . . word of God:* the Christian's new birth results from the action of the Holy Spirit (see Tit 3:5), but the word of God also plays an important part therein (see Jas 1:18). The latter presents the Gospel to us and summons us to repent and believe in Christ (see v. 25). *The living and enduring word of God:* another possible translation is: "the word of the living and enduring God."

2:4-10 The following terms—*spiritual temple, chosen race, royal priesthood, holy nation, a people claimed by God as his own possession*—were coined by the Old Testament to express Israel's awareness of itself as a people called upon to carry out God's plan. The Church regards herself as chosen by God and called to act in such a way that human life itself becomes a worship of God. This passage can be more profoundly understood by reflecting upon 1 Cor 3:16; Eph 2:20-22. In verses 9 and 10 citations from the Old Testament occur in this order: Isa 43:20-21; Ex 19:5-6; Hos 1:6-9; 2:23-24. These are reminiscences more than citations.

2:5 *Holy priesthood:* all who are united with Christ by faith share in the priesthood of Christ (see note on Heb 8:6-13).

They stumble because they disobey the
word—for this they were born. *[h]
9 But you are "a chosen race, a royal priest-
hood, a holy nation, a people claimed by God
as his own possession," so that you may pro-
claim the praise of him who called you out of
darkness into his marvelous light. [i]

10 Once you were not a people,
but now you are God's people.
Once you had not received mercy,
but now you have received mercy. [j]

III: GOD'S PEOPLE IN A HOSTILE WORLD*

Lead a Good Life amidst Pagans.* 11 Beloved,
I urge you as aliens and exiles not to suc-
cumb to the desires of the flesh that wage
war against the soul. [k] 12 Conduct yourselves
honorably among the Gentiles so that,
although they now malign you as evildoers,
they may observe your good works and glo-
rify God on the day of visitation. [l]

Christianity Is Not a Subversive Group.*
13 For the Lord's sake, submit to every
human institution, whether of the emperor
as supreme [m] 14 or of governors as sent by
him to punish those who do wrong and to
commend those who do good works. [n] 15 For
it is the will of God that by doing right you
should silence the ignorant talk of fools. [o]
16 As servants of God, behave as free peo-
ple, but do not use your freedom as a means
to cover up wrongdoing. [p] 17 Give due honor
to everyone. Love your fellow believers. Fear
God. Honor the emperor. [q]

Recommendations for Slaves.* 18 Slaves,
submit to your masters with due respect,
not only to those who are kind and forbear-
ing but also to those who are harsh. [r] 19 It is a
sign of grace if you endure the pain of unjust
suffering because of your awareness of God. [s]
20 What credit do you deserve if you are
patient when you are beaten for doing
wrong? However, if you are patient when
you do what is right and suffer for it, you
have earned merit with God. [t]
21 * This, in fact, is what you have been
called to do, because Christ himself suffered
for you and left an example for you to follow
in his footsteps. [u]

22 He committed no sin, *
and no deceit was found on his lips. [v]

23 When he was abused, he did not retali-
ate. When he suffered, he made no threats,
but he placed his trust in the one who judges
justly. [w] 24 He himself bore our sins in his
body on the cross, so that we might die to sin
and live in righteousness.
By his wounds you have been healed. [x]
25 For you were like sheep who had gone
astray, but now you have returned to the
shepherd and guardian of your souls. *[y]

h Isa 8:14; Lk 2:34; Rom 9:33.—i Ex 19:6; Deut 10:15; 1 Sam 12:22; Isa 61:6; Acts 20:18; Tit 2:14; Rev 1:6; 20:6.—j Hos 1:6, 9; 2:25; Rom 9:25, 26.—k Rom 13:14; 1 Cor 10:14; Gal 5:24; Heb 11:13; Jas 4:1.—l 1 Pet 3:16; Mt 9:8; Phil 2:15; Tit 2:8, 14.—m Rom 13:1-7; Tit 3:1.—n Rom 13:3, 4.—o 1 Pet 3:17; 4:19.—p Jn 8:32; Rom 6:22; Gal 6:13.—q Prov 24:21; Mt 22:21; Rom 12:16; 13:7.—r Eph 6:5; Jas 3:17.—s 1 Pet 3:14, 17.—t 1 Pet 3:17.—u Mt 11:29; 16:24; Acts 14:22; Rom 8:28; Phil 1:29.—v Isa 53:9; 2 Cor 5:21.—w 1 Pet 3:9; Isa 53:7; Mt 5:39; Lk 23:46; Heb 12:3.—x Deut 32:39; Isa 53:4-5, 12; Acts 5:30; Rom 6:2; Heb 9:28; Jas 5:16.—y Job 10:12; Isa 53:6; Jn 10:11.

2:8 *For this they were born:* the author states that by rejecting the Gospel, the people of the former Covenant have lost their prerogatives, which have now been given to the people of the New Covenant, i.e., Christians. The Scripture references in vv. 6-10 reflect the concern of early Christianity to explain Israel's unbelief in light of the Old Testament itself.

2:11—3:12 The author sets forth a few practical implications of what it means to be God's people in a hostile world. Christians are to be submissive to others—to civil authority, to masters, and to spouses in imitation of Christ's submissiveness. He ends up citing five virtues from Christ's life that should be of help to all.

2:11-12 Christians are to be on their best behavior in the midst of pagans even if for a time they are greeted with criticism and hostility because they do not accept the morals of the age. On the day of the Lord's arrival, everything will be made clear. While they wait for that day, Christians are on earth as a pilgrim people, i.e., they do not put their stamp of approval on any society and any culture.

2:13-17 Christianity is not subversive and does not oppose the organization of society on principle. The first persecutions were based on such accusations, and it is one more reason to stress their loyalty but also their sense of freedom. Political power has its ultimate foundation in God the Creator of human society, and not in the personality of those who govern (see Rom 13:1-7; Tit 3:1). In the Book of Revelation, the Christian attitude toward the imperial power will be less serene.

2:18-25 The first generations of Christians have above all the concern to spread the Gospel as the response to desire for salvation on the part of all people. The believers are only a handful. It would be a mistake to attribute to them the plan to develop a critique of the structures of society. But they themselves model new human and social relations. Many of them are slaves; in the Church, they are recognized as full Christians. This is one more reason not to lay oneself open to the accusation of insubordination that is leveled at these new communities. Hence, for the present moment, here is a way of living with service, even in conditions of injustice. The example of Christ imposes itself; it is interpreted here in magnificent terms by means of one of the great texts about the Servant of God (Isa 53:5-12). We should not interpret this text as presenting a doctrine of resignation. It calls for an attitude that refuses to respond to injustice with hatred or duplicity (see Eph 6:5-9; Col 3:22-25; 1 Tim 6:1-2; Tit 2:9-10).

2:21-25 The example of Christ is obvious; it is here interpreted in grandiose terms by means of the great text on the Servant of God in Isa 53:5-12.

2:22 *He committed no sin . . .:* Christ was absolutely sinless (see Acts 3:14; 2 Cor 5:21; Heb 4:15; 7:26; 1 Jn 3:5).

2:25 *The shepherd and guardian of your souls:* the sheep had wandered from their shepherd (Christ), but now they have returned to him. Thus, the Suffering Servant, vindicated in the Resurrection (see Isa 52:13; 53:11), becomes the Good Shepherd (see Jn 10:11; 13:10). For "shepherd" in the Old Testament, see Ps 23; Isa 40:11; Ezek 37:24.

CHAPTER 3

Recommendations for Spouses.* 1 In the same way, you who are wives should accept the authority of your husbands. Then, even if they do not believe the word, they may be won over without words simply by the conduct of their wives[z] 2 as they observe your reverence and your chaste behavior.[a]

3 * Do not seek to adorn yourself externally—by the braiding of your hair and the wearing of gold jewelry or fine clothing.[b] 4 Rather, let your adornment be of your inner self, the imperishable beauty of a gentle and quiet spirit, which is precious in the sight of God.[c]

5 It was in this way that the holy women who placed their hope in God long ago used to adorn themselves and be submissive to their husbands.[d] 6 Thus, Sarah obeyed Abraham and called him her "lord." You are now her daughters as long as you live good lives and never allow fears to alarm you.[e]

7 Likewise, you who are husbands must show consideration for your wives in your life together. Treat your wife with respect, for even though she is the weaker partner, she is also an equal heir of God's gift * of life. Thus, your prayers will not be hindered in any way.[f]

Mutual Love.* 8 Finally, all of you should be united in spirit, sympathetic, filled with love for one another, compassionate, and humble.[g] 9 Do not repay evil with evil or abuse with abuse. On the contrary, repay with a blessing. This is what you were called to do, so that you might inherit a blessing.[h] 10 For:

"If anyone wishes to love life[i]
and to experience good days,
he must restrain his tongue from evil
and his lips from deceitful speech.
11 He must turn away from evil and do good,
seek peace and pursue it.
12 For the eyes of the Lord are on the righteous
and his ears are attentive to their prayer.
However, the face of the Lord
is set against those who do evil."

IV: CHRISTIAN CONDUCT IN SUFFERING AND PERSECUTION

The Blessings of Suffering for Righteousness.* 13 Now who is going to harm you if you are eager to do what is right?[j] 14 Yet even if you should suffer for doing what is right, you are thereby blessed. Have no fear of others, and refuse to be intimidated by them.[k] 15 Rather, revere Christ as Lord in your hearts.

Always be prepared to offer an explanation to anyone who asks you to justify the hope that is in you. However, do so with gentleness and respect[l] 16 and with a clean conscience so that those who slander you for your good behavior in Christ may be put to shame.[m] 17 For it is better to suffer for doing what is right, if such is the will of God, than for doing what is wrong.[n]

Christ's Victory and Descent to the Netherworld, and Christian Baptism.* 18 For Christ

z 1 Pet 2:18; 1 Cor 7:16; 9:19; Eph 5:22.—a 1 Cor 7:12-16; Eph 5:22-24; Col 3:18; 1 Tim 2:9-15.—b Isa 3:18-23; 1 Tim 2:9-10.—c Rom 2:29; 7:22; Eph 3:16.—d Est 2:15; 1 Tim 5.5.—e Gen 18:12; Prov 3:25.—f Eph 5:25-33; Col 3:19; 1 Thes 4:4.—g 1 Pet 5:5; Rom 12:10; 15:5.—h 1 Pet 2:23; Mt 5:44; Lk 6:28; Rom 8:28; 12:14; 1 Thes 5:15; Heb 6:14.—i 10-12: Ps 34:13-17.—j Tit 2:14.—k 1 Pet 2:19, 20; Isa 12:13.—l Isa 8:12; Col 4:6; Heb 3:6.—m 1 Pet 2:12, 16; Acts 23:1.—n 1 Pet 2:15, 20.

3:1-7 How does one's Christianity affect the way that one lives family life? The main problem is the difficult one of the wife who converts but is not followed by her husband. Let her not seek to put pressure on him, but let her give him the witness of a Christian wife whose gentleness and silence are in contrast to agitation and vanity.

A Christian husband is asked to regard his wife as a believing Christian in all respects, to understand feminine psychology, and to show great sensitivity of heart (see 1 Cor 7:12-15; Eph 5:32-33; Col 3:19).

3:3-5 The author does not prohibit the use of jewelry and other adornments but stresses the fact that the greatest adornments are spiritual ones.

3:7 *An equal heir of God's gift:* both spouses in a marriage have received the same gift from God. Hence, there should be mutual respect and love between them (see Eph 5:33; Col 3:19).

3:8-12 Mutual love of Christians is expressed in a new type of social relations and inner attitudes that lead up to evangelical behavior (see Lk 6:28; Rom 12:9-20).

3:13-17 Persecution must not come as a surprise to believers; it is their lot according to one of the Beatitudes of the Gospel (see Mt 5:10), almost repeated here word for word. Thus, Christians follow the example of Christ, ready to justify their hope but refusing to retaliate with hatred and violence. They are not enemies of society or other people, a crime that has apparently already been leveled at them.

3:18—4:6 The author presents the vision of a new world. Christ's Death and Resurrection have been victorious over sin; the risen Lord dominates the universe and all the good or evil forces in it, e.g., angels, dominations, and powers. Christ truly died and was in the sojourn of the dead, as the New Testament more than once attests (see Mt 12:40; Acts 2:31; Rom 10:7; Eph 4:8-10).

The intent of this passage is probably to say that nothing human or cosmic can be excluded from the Redemption that Christ effected. It is in this sense that we are to understand the article of the Creed that speaks of Christ "descending into hell." The story of Noah (see Gen 6:1—7:4) is interpreted as a saving of the righ-teous and a destruction of sin; it seems to be taken as a symbolic anticipation of Baptism, which at the time was received by immersion.

also suffered for our sins once for all, the
righteous for the unrighteous, in order to
bring you to God. He was put to death in the
flesh but raised to life in the spirit. [o]
19 In the spirit * also he went to preach to
the spirits in prison, [p] 20 those who had
refused to obey long ago while God waited
patiently in the days of Noah during the
building of the ark. In it only a few persons,
eight in all, were saved through water. [q]
21 This water prefigured Baptism, which
now saves you. It does so not by the washing
away of dirt from the body but by the pledge
of a good conscience given to God through
the resurrection of Jesus Christ. [r] 22 He has
entered heaven and is at the right hand of
God, with angels, authorities, and powers
made subject to him. [s]

CHAPTER 4

1 Therefore, since Christ suffered in the
flesh, you should arm yourselves also with
the same intention. For anyone who has suf-
fered in the flesh has finished with sin [t] 2 and
for the remainder of life on earth must be
ruled not by human passions but by the will
of God. [u]
3 You have already spent enough time in
doing what the Gentiles like to do, pursuing
a life of debauchery, licentiousness, drunk-
enness, orgies, carousing, and sacrilegious
idolatry. [v] 4 They are surprised that you no
longer join them in a life of dissipation, and
they revile you as a result. [w] 5 However, they
will have to render an account to him who
stands ready to judge * the living and the
dead. [x]
6 And this is the reason why the gospel was
preached even to the dead, so that, although
they might be judged in the flesh like men,
they might enjoy the life of God in the spirit. [y]

**Qualities of a Christian Community Waiting
for Christ.*** 7 The end of all things is near.
Therefore, lead disciplined lives and be
watchful in prayer. [z] 8 Above all, maintain
the fervor of your love for one another,
because love covers a multitude of sins. [a]
9 Be hospitable to one another without
complaining. [b] 10 Like good stewards of the
varied graces of God, use whatever gift each
one of you has received to serve one an-
other. [c]
11 Whoever speaks should do so as one
who is speaking the very words of God.
Whoever serves should do so with the
strength that God provides. In all things, let
God be glorified through Jesus Christ, for to
him belong all glory and power forever and
ever. Amen. [d]

Courage and Joy in Suffering.* 12 Beloved, do
not be surprised that you are being tested by
a fiery ordeal, * as though it were something
extraordinary. [e] 13 But rejoice insofar as you
are sharing in the sufferings of Christ, so
that your joy will be without limit when his
glory is revealed. [f]
14 If you are reviled for the name of Christ,
consider yourself blessed, for upon you rests
the Spirit of glory * and of God. [g] 15 * How-
ever, let none of you suffer as a murderer, a
thief, or any other kind of criminal, or as one
who meddles in another person's business. [h]

---

o 1 Pet 2:21; Rom 5:2; 1 Cor 15:45; Col 1:22; Heb 7:27.—p 1 Pet 4:6; Isa 42:7; 45:9; 61:1.—q Gen 5:13-14; 6:3; 7:7, 17; Rom 2:4; Heb 11:7; 2 Pet 2:5.—r 1 Pet 1:3; Acts 22:16; 23:1; Eph 5:26; Heb 10:22.—s Mt 8:18; Mk 16:19; Rom 8:36; Eph 1:20-21; Heb 4:14.—t 1 Pet 2:21; Rom 6:18.—u 1 Pet 1:14; Rom 6:2.—v Rom 13:13; Eph 2:2-3; 4:17-19; Col 3:7; Tit 3:3.—w 1 Pet 2:12; 3:16; Acts 10:42; 1 Cor 5:10; 2 Tim 4:1; Jas 5:9.—x Mt 12:36.—y 1 Pet 3:19.—z Acts 24:25; Rom 13:11.—a 1 Pet 1:22; Prov 10:12; Jas 5:20.—b Rom 12:13; Phil 2:14; Heb 13:2.—c Rom 12:6-8; 1 Cor 4:2; 12:4-11.—d Rom 11:36; 1 Cor 10:31; Eph 6:10; 1 Thes 2:4.—e 1 Pet 1:6-7; 3:14, 17.—f 1 Pet 1:7; Mt 5:12; Rom 5:3-5; 8:17; 2 Cor 1:5; Phil 3:10; 2 Tim 2:12.—g Isa 11:2; Mt 5:11; Jn 15:21; Acts 5:41.—h Lk 23:31; 1 Thes 2:12; 2 Thes 1:8.

3:18-19 *In the spirit. . . . In the spirit:* another translation possible is: "by the Spirit . . . through which."

4:5 *Him who stands ready to judge:* the New Testament assigns judgment to both the Father and the Son on the last day (see Jn 5:27; Acts 17:31). *The living and the dead:* i.e., those who are alive as well as those who have died when the last day arrives.

4:7-11 Living in expectation of the Lord's Second Coming, Christian communities are characterized by a serious atmosphere, by relationships of responsibility and fraternity, and by concern for prayer and the Liturgy.

4:12-19 Hostility seems to be unleashed against the communities. We will always be astounded by the conviction of the first Christian generations in the face of persecution. They do not regard it as a strange fate but as something that indicates the arrival of a new age, that of the last times of history. It announces a change in the course of the things of the world. The destiny of Christ is not only an example to consider but a mystery to share in these conditions. However, the persecution in question must be a real one against the faith and not a reaction against the abuses committed by Christians themselves. Concerning the necessity of persecution and the meaning of the announcement of a change, see Mt 5:11-12; Lk 6:22-23; 21:12-19.

4:12 *Fiery ordeal:* literally, "fire for testing." Suffering is a source of purification.

4:14 *Spirit of glory:* because the Spirit bestows glory after trials.

4:15ff There is suffering that believers bring down upon themselves by their own sins and weaknesses and suffering that God allows to afflict them. In both instances, they should entrust themselves to God and offer their sufferings to him.

16 Let it be because you are a Christian, * not
considering it a disgrace, but glorifying God
because you bear this name. [i]
17 The time has come for the judgment of
the household of God to begin. If it begins
with us, how will it end for those who refuse
to obey the gospel of God? [j]
18 And:

"If it is hard for the righteous to be
saved,
what will become of the godless and
those who are sinners?" [k]

19 And so, those who suffer in accordance
with God's will entrust their souls to a faith-
ful Creator, while continuing to do good. [l]

CHAPTER 5

Faithful and Humble Leadership.* 1 I now
exhort the presbyters * among you, as a fel-
low presbyter myself and a witness to the suf-
ferings of Christ, and as one who has shared
in the glory that is to be revealed. [m] 2 Be shep-
herds of the flock of God that has been
entrusted to your care. Watch over it, not as a
duty, but willingly in accord with the will of
God, not for sordid gain, but because you are
eager to do so. [n]
3 Do not lord it over those in your charge,
but be examples to the flock. [o] 4 Then, when
the chief Shepherd appears, you will receive
the crown of glory that never fades away. [p]

Humility and Firm Faith. 5 * In the same way,
you who are younger must be submissive to
those who are older. And all of you should
clothe yourselves with humility in your rela-
tionships with one another, for

"God opposes the proud,
but he gives grace to the humble." [q]

6 Therefore, humble yourselves under the
mighty hand of God, so that at the proper
time he may exalt you. [r] 7 Cast all your anx-
iety on him, because he cares about you. [s]
8 Remain sober and alert, for your enemy the
devil is on the prowl like a roaring lion, looking
for someone to devour. [t] 9 Resist him and be
firm in your faith, for you are well aware that
your brethren throughout the world are under-
going the same kinds of suffering. [u]

Promise of Strength and Vindication.
10 After you have suffered for a brief period,
the God of all grace, who has called you to
his eternal glory in Christ, will himself
restore, confirm, strengthen, and support
you. [v] 11 All power belongs to him forever
and ever. Amen. [w]

V: CONCLUSION

Final Greetings.* 12 I have written this brief
letter to you through Silvanus, whom I
regard as a faithful brother, in order to
exhort you and to testify that this is the true
grace of God. Stand firm in it. [x]
13 Your sister Church * in Babylon sends
you greetings, as does my son Mark. [y]
14 Greet one another with a loving kiss. *
Peace to all of you who are in Christ. [z]

---

i Acts 5:41.—j Jer 25:29; Ezek 9:6; Am 3:2; 2 Thes 1:8; 1 Tim 3:16.—k Prov 11:31 LXX; Lk 23:31.—l 1 Pet 2:15; 3:17; Lk 23:36; 2 Tim 1:12.—m 1 Pet 1:5, 7; Lk 24:48; Acts 11:30; Rev 1:9.—n Jn 21:16; Acts 20:28; 2 Cor 9:7; Tit 1:7; Philem 14.—o Ezek 34:4; Mt 20:25-28; 1 Tim 4:12.—p 1 Pet 1:4; Jn 10:11; Wis 5:15-16; 1 Cor 9:25; 2 Tim 4:8; Jas 1:12.—q 1 Pet 3:8; Prov 3:34; Mt 23:12; Eph 5:21.—r Job 5:11; 22:29; Jas 4:10.—s Ps 55:23; Mt 6:25-33; Lk 12:22-31; Phil 4:6; Heb 13:5.—t Job 1:7; Acts 24:25; 1 Thes 5:6; 2 Tim 4:17.—u Acts 14:22; Col 2:5; Jas 4:7.—v 1 Pet 1:6; Rom 8:18; 2 Cor 4:17; 2 Thes 2:17; 2 Tim 2:10.—w Rom 11:36; 1 Cor 8:6; 10:13; Col 1:16f.—x Acts 15:22; 1 Cor 16:13; Heb 13:22.—y Acts 12:12.—z Rom 16:16; 1 Cor 16:20; 2 Cor 13:12; Eph 6:23.

4:16 *Christian:* this word occurs only here and in Acts 11:26; 26:28 in the New Testament.

5:1-4 The presbyters (or elders) exercise responsibilities in the life of communities (see 1 Tim 5:17; Tit 1:5-9). However, authority always experiences the temptation to exercise power for its own profit. This should not be the case in a Christian group. We might recall the word of Jesus: "I am in your midst as one who serves" (Lk 22:27). On this subject, we could also read Paul's reflection to the elders of the region of Ephesus (see Acts 20:28-35).

5:1 *Presbyters:* the official teachers of the Christian community (see 1 Tim 5:17f; Tit 1:5-8; Jas 5:14). *Witness to the sufferings of Christ:* Peter had been a witness of all the phases and aspects of Christ's ministry, including his suffering (see Mt 26:58; Mk 14:54; Lk 22:60-62; Jn 18:10-11, 15-16).

5:5-11 Nothing is more opposed to the Gospel than pretense and pride; hence this Letter insists on attitudes of submissiveness. It also recommends that Christians remain steadfast in the spiritual combat—which is more difficult to do in this context of threats—in order to achieve true victory. It is from God himself that believers await the courage. *You who are younger:* these may simply be the faithful distinguished from their leaders.

5:12-14 The Letter is doubtless written at Rome, the "Babylon" of the age (see Introduction). *Silvanus:* one of Paul's coworkers (see 1 Thes 1:1; 2 Thes 1:1; 2 Cor 1:19) also known by the name of "Silas" (see Acts 15:22; 17:4).

5:13 *Your sister Church:* literally, "Your chosen sister." *Mark:* an occasional companion of Paul (see Acts 12:25; 2 Tim 4:11) and probably the author of the second Gospel.

5:14 *Kiss:* on the liturgical kiss, see 1 Cor 16:20. *Peace to all of you who are in Christ:* in concluding, the author stresses a basic theme of the Letter—the union of believers with Christ.

THE SECOND LETTER OF PETER

Awaiting the Day of the Lord

With this Letter we find ourselves already at the beginning of the second century. The Church is experiencing a difficult transition from the primitive stage to the post-apostolic stage. For several decades her members have lived the newness of the Christian Faith and, so to speak, sung its praises; the coming of Jesus remained near and his return was thought to be imminent.

Now these two poles are disappearing from view, the former in the past and the latter in a future that is more and more out of focus. A distance is being established with respect to the immediate experience of Christianity's beginnings. A new climate must be forged for remaining in the faith and practicing the Christian life in everyday existence.

Such a transformation is not achieved without crisis. It bears the visage of uncertainty as well as anxiety.

The first point that comes under attack is orthodoxy. The most diverse religious ideas and the most varied Gnostic currents are unfurled within the Empire, often accompanied by immorality. Will Christianity simply vanish in the wake of this maelstrom of competing ideas and morals?

The delay of the Parousia, or Return of Christ, has already disquieted spirits. Now there is danger that Christians will resign themselves to this delay to the detriment of a fundamental aspect of the Christian symmetry and conscience. Will the tension toward fulfillment and the perspective of being confronted with a judgment be lost in out-of-focus ideas that have no impact on life?

In order of time, this writing was probably the last of the New Testament and thus of the entire Bible. It is a spirited exhortation to discouraged spirits; even more vigorously it attacks the spreaders of dangerous doctrines that sow disorder. It does not lack power when it evokes the final devastation of the world, but it also teaches patience, the sense of living under the judgment of God, and progress in faith and in grace.

In defending the essentials of the faith, the Letter emphasizes the word of God as transmitted by the Prophets and the Apostles, and it already cites the Letters of Paul as forming a literary whole well known in the Church. This passage bears witness to the awareness of Biblical inspiration and also to the conviction that Scripture must be interpreted within the Church.

To get his meaning across, the author imitates a literary genre current in the Judaism of the time: the testament of the ancestors—in other words, the practice of placing one's own exhortations and advice in the mouths of Patriarchs who are about to die. Our author has thought of the man who took first place in the origins of Christianity, namely, Peter, who speaks in Jesus' name (see 1 Tim 1:14-15). St. Jerome tells us that many denied Peter was the author of the document.

This Letter seems strange to us by reason of its many expressions and its very style. But it contains an important lesson for Christianity, which must be able to accept ongoing history, even while refusing to settle down calmly in it. The Letter claims to be a continuation of the First Letter of Peter (see 2 Pet 3:1), but in fact it is to be connected rather with the Letter of Jude, from which it takes various themes and explains them more fully. (See Introduction to Jude.)

The Second Letter of Peter may be divided as follows:

- *I: Salutation (1:1-2)*
- *II: Exhortation to Growth in Christian Virtues (1:3-21)*
- *III: Warning against False Teachers (2:1-22)*
- *IV: The Fact of Christ's Return (3:1-16)*
- *V: Conclusion (3:17-18)*

CHAPTER 1

I: SALUTATION

Address.* 1 Simon Peter,* a servant and
apostle of Jesus Christ, to those who have
received a faith as precious as ours through
the righteousness of our God and Savior
Jesus Christ:[a] 2 may grace and peace be
yours in abundance through the knowl-
edge* of God and of Jesus our Lord.[b]

II: EXHORTATION TO GROWTH IN CHRISTIAN VIRTUES

Strengthen Your Vocation.* 3 His divine
power has bestowed on us everything that is
necessary for life and for devotion through
our knowledge of him who called us by his
own glory and virtue.[c] 4 By these he has
given us his precious promises, great beyond
all price, so that through them you may
escape from the corruption with which evil
desires have infected the world and thereby
may come to share in the divine nature.*[d]

5 *[e] In view of all this, you should make
every effort to supplement your faith with
virtue, and virtue with knowledge,[f] 6 and
knowledge with self-control, and self-control
with endurance, and endurance with piety,[g]
7 and piety with mutual affection, and mutu-
al affection with love.[h]

8 If you possess these qualities and they
increase in abundance, they will prevent
your knowledge of our Lord Jesus Christ
from being ineffective and unfruitful.[i] 9 For
anyone who lacks them is near-sighted or
blind, since he has forgotten how his past
sins were washed away.*[j]

10 Therefore, brethren, be diligent in pro-
viding a firm foundation for your call and
election. If you do this, you will never stum-
ble,[k] 11 and you will receive a glorious wel-
come into the eternal kingdom of our Lord
and Savior Jesus Christ.*[l]

The Witness of an Apostle.* 12 Therefore, I
will continue to emphasize these things
repeatedly, even though you already know

a Rom 1:1; 3:21-26; Tit 2:13; 1 Pet 1:1.—b 2 Pet 1:3, 8; 2:20; 3:18; Rom 1:7; Phil 3:8.—c 2 Pet 1:2; Rom 8:28; 2 Cor 4:6; 1 Pet 1:5; 2:9.—d 2 Pet 2:18-20; 2 Cor 7:1; Eph 4:24; Heb 12:10; Jas 1:27; 1 Jn 2:15.—e 5-7: Gal 5:22-23.—f 2 Pet 1:2; Col 2:3.—g 2 Pet 1:3; Jas 1:3; Heb 10:36.—h Rom 12:10; 1 Thes 3:12.—i 2 Pet 1:2; Jn 15:2; Col 1:2; Tit 3:14.—j Mt 1:21; Eph 5:26; 1 Jn 2:9, 11.—k 2 Pet 3:17; Rom 8:28; Jude 24.—l 2 Pet 2:20; 3:18; 2 Tim 4:18.

1:1-2 From the very first words, the author addresses believers, those who have received salvation or righteousness. He insists on faith and on knowledge of the Lord, the Christ.

1:1 *Simon Peter:* see notes on Mt 16:18; 16:19; Jn 1:42. *Servant:* see note on Rom 1:1. *Apostle:* see notes on Mk 6:30; Rom 1:1; Heb 3:1-6. *To those:* probably the same addressees as in 1 Pet 1:1.

1:2 *Knowledge:* a key theme of the Letter (see 2 Pet 1:3, 5, 8; 2:20; 3:18), probably to combat the claims of the Gnostics.

1:3-11 Christianity is not just another religious theory among those that are actually in vogue. To believe is to place oneself personally under the very action of God and to know that the destiny of human beings is accomplished in his eternal Kingdom. Christians live in communion with God; the earthly dimension does not suffice for them. And these great realities are not mere words; they demand a radical change in the manner of conceiving one's destiny and conducting one's existence. Thus, regardless of the historical distance from the time of its foundation, the Christian life constitutes a new state of existence.

1:4 *Share in the divine nature:* an expression found only here in the Bible. The author uses it to express the fullness of divine life in Christ (see Jn 1:12; 14:20; 15:4f; Rom 6:5; 1 Cor 1:9f; 1 Jn 1:3b).

1:5-9 The author lists the virtues that are needed for a genuine Christian life.

1:9 This is similar to the warning in the Johannine Letters against the Gnostics (see 1 Jn 1:8f), who claimed to know God without keeping the commandments.

1:11 *Kingdom of . . . Christ:* it is also the Kingdom of the Father (see Eph 5:5; 2 Tim 4:1; Rev 11:15).

1:12-18 The testimony of an Apostle has a greater value than any arbitrary Gnostic speculation.

To emphasize this point, the author presents his work as a testament of Peter, who reminds the readers that the Lord had told him of his proximate death (see Jn 21:18-19) and insists above all on the fact that he had been a witness of the Transfiguration (see Mt 17:1-13; Mk 9:2-13; Lk 9:28-36), an event that bore witness to the glory of Christ and thereby guaranteed his glorious Return, which was being challenged at this time.

them and are well grounded in the truth you possess.[m] [13] For I think it is right, to refresh your memory as long as I remain in this body,*[n] [14] since I know that my death* will come soon, as our Lord Jesus Christ made clear to me.[o] [15] And I shall also make every effort to ensure that you will always recall these things after my departure.[p]

[16] We did not rely upon cleverly concocted myths when we made known to you the power and coming of our Lord Jesus Christ. Rather, we had beheld his majesty with our own eyes.[q] [17] For he received honor and glory from God the Father when a voice came to him from the transcendent Majesty, saying, "This is my beloved Son in whom I am well pleased."[r] [18] We ourselves heard this voice that came down from heaven, when we were with him on the sacred mountain.[s]

Pay Close Attention to the Message of the Prophets.* [19] This confirms the message of the Prophets more fully for us. You would do well to pay close attention to it, as to a lamp shining in a dark place, until the day dawns and the morning star rises in your hearts.[t]

[20] First of all, however, you must understand that no prophecy of Scripture is a matter of private interpretation.[u] [21] No prophecy ever came from human initiative. Rather, when people spoke as messengers of God, they did so under the inspiration of the Holy Spirit.*[v]

III: WARNING AGAINST FALSE TEACHERS*

CHAPTER 2

False Teachers Will Arise. [1] Just as there were false prophets who arose among the people, so there will be false teachers among you. They will introduce their disruptive views and even deny the very Master who redeemed them, thus bringing swift destruction on themselves.[w]

[2] Many will be seduced by their licentious ways, and because of these teachers the way of truth will be brought into disrepute.[x] [3] In their greed they will exploit you with concocted stories.

The Condemnation of False Teachers. However, their condemnation has been hanging over them for a long time, and the destruction awaiting them does not slumber.[y] [4] For God did not spare the angels who sinned, but he cast them into the dark abyss to be chained, where they are being held until the judgment.*[z] [5] Nor did he spare the ancient world,* even though he saved Noah, a herald of righteousness, one of eight, when he brought a flood upon the world with its godless people.[a]

[6] God also reduced the cities of Sodom and Gomorrah to ashes, thereby condemning them to total ruin and making them an example of what awaited the ungodly.[b] [7] However, he rescued Lot, an upright man who was sickened by the licentiousness of the lawless society in which he lived,[c] [8] for

m Phil 3:1; 1 Jn 2:21; 2 Jn 2; Jude 5.—n 2 Pet 3:1; Isa 38:12; 2 Cor 5:1, 4.—o Isa 38:12; Jn 13:36; 21:18-19; 2 Tim 4:6.—p Lk 9:31.—q Mt 17:1-8; Mk 13:26; 14:62; Lk 9:28-36; Jn 1:14.—r Ps 2:7; Mt 3:17; 17:4-6.—s Ex 3:5; Isa 5:15; Mt 17:6.—t Lk 1:78-79; 2 Cor 4:6; 1 Pet 1:10-11; Rev 2:28; 22:16.—u 2 Pet 3:3.—v 2 Sam 23:2; Acts 1:16; 3:18; 2 Tim 3:16; 1 Pet 1:11.—w Deut 13:1; Jer 6:13; Mt 7:15; 24:11, 24; 1 Cor 6:20; 1 Tim 4:1; Jude 4.—x Isa 52:5; Jude 4.—y 2 Pet 2:14; Rom 16:18; 2 Cor 2:17; 1 Thes 2:5.—z Gen 6:1-4; 1 Tim 3:6; Jude 6; Rev 20:1-2.—a 2 Pet 3:6; Gen 6:5; 8:15-19; Heb 11:7; 1 Pet 3:20.—b Gen 19:24-25; Num 26:10; Mt 10:15; Rom 9:29; Jude 7.—c 2 Pet 3:17; Gen 19:16.

1:13 *Body:* literally, "tent."

1:14 *My death:* literally, "the time for laying aside this tent."

1:19-21 While awaiting the great Day of fulfillment, Scripture constitutes the light on the human journey. It cannot be handed over to the arbitrary interpretations of teachers of fortune who construe it in their own peculiar way; the inspiration of the Spirit must be respected.

1:21 *Under the inspiration of the Holy Spirit:* see note on 2 Tim 3:16. Both God and the authors were active in producing Scripture: God was the source of the content, but the writers used all their talents to set that message down.

2:1-22 The portrait of the false teachers is drawn in living colors. They deny Christ and his salvation, disfigure the Gospel's grand ideas about life, and seek their own profit and personal success. They "are not afraid to insult celestial beings" (v. 10)—either the angels or the evil powers whom they claim the right to judge although this right belongs to the Lord. The teachings of the Gnostics multiply theories about the heavenly beings. But these lofty speculations do not prevent them from being propagators of immorality; the author likens them to Balaam, who at this time had become the prototype of the false, venal, and corrupting teacher (see Num 22:2—24:25; Deut 23:5; Rev 2:14-15); all of their preaching focuses only on false freedom, enslavement, and degeneracy. Despite all this, these teachers of falsehood call themselves Christians.

The notice of their fate is severe. The author recalls the great chastisements of the past, the fall of the heavenly beings, the Flood, the unforgettable cursed cities of Sodom and Gomorrah, and the story of Balaam. These illustrations are taken from ancient Biblical accounts (see Gen 6:1-2; 6:5—8:22; 19:1-29; Num 22:2—24:25). Above all, the author wishes to exhort the believers to stand firm in their faith so that they will be spared on the day of judgment, as were Noah and Lot. Once in a while people have need of such efficacious admonition in order to take stock of their spiritual life.

2:4 The Bible gives no details on the sin of the angels. *The dark abyss* or Tartus: the term used by the Greeks for the place where the most wicked spirits were imprisoned.

2:5 *The ancient world:* the world before the Flood.

that man was greatly tormented in his righteous soul by the crimes that he saw and about which he was told day after day. [d]

9 Therefore, the Lord knows how to rescue the godly from their trials and to hold the wicked for punishment until the Day of Judgment. [e] 10 Above all, he will punish those who succumb to the desires of their corrupt human nature and show no respect for authority.

The Ways of False Teachers. Bold and headstrong, they are not afraid to insult celestial beings, [f] 11 whereas angels, despite their superior strength and power, do not bring slanderous accusations against such men in the Lord's presence. * [g] 12 These men are like wild beasts, mere creatures of instinct born to be caught and killed.

They pour abuse on things they do not understand, and in their corruption they also will be destroyed, [h] 13 receiving the penalty * for doing wrong. They regard it as a pleasure to carouse in broad daylight. While they share your table, they are ugly blots and blemishes, reveling in their pleasures. [i]

14 They have eyes that are always on the trail of adultery, insatiable in their desire for sinful pursuits. They seduce unstable people, and their hearts are fixed on greed. Truly, they are an accursed brood. * [j] 15 They have abandoned the straight path and have gone astray, following in the steps of Balaam, the son of Beor, * who loved to receive payment for wrongdoing. [k] 16 However, he received a rebuke for his crime when a mute donkey spoke with a human voice and put a stop to the prophet's madness. [l]

17 Such people are waterless springs and mists driven by a storm. For them the gloom of darkness has been reserved. [m]

18 They speak boastful words devoid of meaning, and by arousing licentious desires of the flesh they entice people who are just escaping from living in error. [n]

19 They promise them freedom, although they themselves are slaves of depravity. * For people are slaves of whatever has mastered them. [o] 20 If they have escaped the world's defilements through coming to know our Lord and Savior Jesus Christ and then again become entangled and are overpowered, they are worse off in this latter state than they were before. [p]

21 It would have been better for them never to have known the way of righteousness than, having known it, to turn back and abandon the holy commandment that was handed on to them. [q] 22 What happened to them manifests the truth of the proverbs:

> "The dog returns to its own vomit," * [r]

and

> "The washed sow returns to wallowing
> in the mud."

CHAPTER 3

IV: THE FACT OF CHRIST'S RETURN

The Day of the Lord Will Come.* 1 Beloved, this is now the second letter I have written to you. In both of them I have tried to stir up your memories for a clear understanding [s]
2 so that you might remember the words spoken in the past by the holy Prophets and by the apostles at the command of our Lord and Savior. [t]

d Heb 11:4.—e Mt 10:15; Rom 15:31; 1 Cor 10:13; Rev 3:10.—f 2 Pet 3:3; Jude 8, 16, 18.—g Jude 9.—h Ps 49:13-15.—i Rom 13:13; 1 Cor 11:20-21; 1 Thes 5:7; Jude 12.—j 2 Pet 2:18; 3:16; Eph 2:3; Jas 1:8.—k Num 22:4-20; 31:16; Deut 23:4; Jude 11; Rev 2:14.—l Num 22:28-33.—m Jer 2:13; Jude 12-13.—n 2 Pet 1:4; 2:20; Jude 16.—o Jn 8:34; Rom 6:16-17.—p 2 Pet 1:2, 11; 3:18; Mt 12:45.—q Ezek 3:20; 18:24; Heb 6:4-6; 10:26, 27.—r Prov 26:11.—s 2 Pet 1:13; 1 Cor 10:14.—t Lk 1:70; Acts 3:21; Eph 4:11; Jude 17.

2:11 *In the Lord's presence:* some manuscripts have: "from the Lord."

2:13 *Receiving the penalty:* some manuscripts have: "receiving a reward." *In their pleasures:* some manuscripts have: "in their love feasts."

2:14 *Accursed brood:* literally, "children of a curse."

2:15 *Balaam, the son of Beor:* see Num 22—24. Even though God had forbidden Balaam to curse Israel, Balaam was intent on doing it because he wanted the money he had been promised by Balak. In the same way, the false teachers wanted to extract money from those who listened to them.

2:19 *Freedom . . . depravity:* the "scoffers" use "freedom" to divest themselves of the moral law. But it is faith in Christ that leads to good behavior and true freedom (see Rom 6:15; Jas 1:25; 1 Pet 2:16).

2:22 *The dog . . . vomit:* see Prov 26:11. *The washed . . . mud:* its source is unknown. The dog that returns to its own vomit and the sow that is washed portray people who have made a religious profession or outward change without an inner change that affects their nature. They soon return to their true nature.

3:1-10 We know the spectacle of an immutable universe; the days fly by and the seasons return. Could the fate of the world change someday? Christians of that day are loath to think of it and quick to deny it. To eliminate this uncertainty, the author first of all recalls the teaching of the Prophets, the Apostles, and Christ himself about the end of the world. Furthermore, in the Bible there are two or three passages that make us reflect: the manner in which the cosmos rises in the midst of the initial disorder as well as the drowning of everything at the Flood; hence, our world does not have the promises for eternity.

What then is the reason for the long delay? There are two reasons: first, the Lord does not count time as we do; above all, his mercy is immense and he awaits the conversion of everyone. But the announcement of the end remains such as was taught by the Gospels (see Mt 24:43; Lk 12:39-40; 1 Thes 5:2). In the face of the unforeseeable character of history and the unforeseeable plan of God, there is the temptation to take refuge in the name of the perpetuity of the cosmos.

3 First of all, you must understand that in the last days scoffers will appear who have led lives of indulgence.[u] 4 They will say, "Where is this 'coming' that was promised? Ever since our ancestors * died, everything has remained just as it was from the beginning of creation."[v]

5 * These people deliberately ignore the fact that by the word of God the heavens existed long ago, and that the earth stands out of water and in water.[w] 6 Furthermore, by these waters also the world of that time was deluged and destroyed.[x] 7 By the same word, the present heavens and earth have been reserved for fire, being kept for the Day of Judgment and the destruction of sinners.[y]

8 But do not ignore this one fact, beloved: with the Lord one day is like a thousand years, and a thousand years are like one day.[z] 9 The Lord does not delay in keeping his promise, as some think in terms of delay, but he is patient with you. It is not his wish that any should perish but rather that all should be brought to repentance.[a]

10 However, the Day of the Lord will come like a thief. The heavens will disappear with a mighty roar, * and the elements will be dissolved in flames, and the earth and all that it contains will be disclosed.[b]

Wait for and Speed the Day of God.* 11 Since everything is to be destroyed in this way, consider what sort of people you ought to be, living holy and saintly lives.[c] 12 Wait for and speed the coming of the Day of God, * on which the heavens will be set ablaze and all the elements will melt because of the intense heat.[d] 13 We eagerly await the promised new heavens and a new earth * in which righteousness dwells.[e]

14 Therefore, beloved, in expectation of all this, do everything possible to lead blameless lives that are above reproach so that he will find you at peace.[f] 15 Think of our Lord's patience as your opportunity to be saved; * our beloved brother Paul told you this when he wrote to you with the wisdom that was given to him,[g] 16 speaking of it * in all his letters. In them, there are some things that are difficult to understand, which the ignorant and the unstable distort in the same way that they distort the other Scriptures, to their own destruction.[h]

V: CONCLUSION

Guard against Error and Grow in Grace. 17 Therefore, beloved, you have been forewarned about this. Take care that you are not led astray by the errors of unprincipled people and thus lose your secure position.[i] 18 Rather, grow in the grace and the knowledge * of our Lord and Savior Jesus Christ.

Doxology. To him be glory both now and for all eternity. Amen.[j]

---

u 2 Pet 2:10; 1 Tim 4:1; 2 Tim 3:1; Jude 18.—v Isa 4:19; Ezek 12:22; Mt 24:48; Mk 10:6; Lk 17:30.—w Gen 1:2, 6, 8; Ps 24:2; Heb 11:3.—x 2 Pet 2:5; Gen 7:21.—y 2 Pet 3:10, 12; Isa 51:6; Mt 3:12; 10:15; 2 Thes 1:7.—z Ps 90:4.—a Ezek 18:23; Hab 2:3; Rom 2:4; 1 Tim 2:4; Heb 10:37; Rev 2:21.—b 2 Pet 3:7, 12; Isa 34:4; 66:15-16; Mt 24:29, 35; Lk 12:39; 2 Thes 1:7; Heb 12:27; Rev 21:1.—c Acts 3:19-21.—d 2 Pet 3:10; Isa 34:4; 1 Cor 1:7; Heb 10:27.—e Isa 65:17; 66:22; Rom 8:21; Rev 21:1, 27.—f 1 Cor 15:58; Phil 1:10; 1 Thes 3:13; 5:23.—g 2 Pet 3:9; Rom 2:4; 8:19; Eph 3:3; Jude 24.—h 2 Pet 2:14; 3:2; Jer 23:36; Jas 1:8.—i 2 Pet 2:7, 18; Mk 13:5; 1 Cor 10:12; Heb 2:1; Rev 2:5.—j 2 Pet 1:2, 11; 2:20; Rom 3:24; 11:36; 16:27.

3:4 *Our ancestors:* the faithful of the first Christian generation.

3:5-7 God created the world by his word, and that word will be just as active in the final conflagration.

3:10 *The Day of the Lord . . . a mighty roar:* this "Day" is also mentioned in Acts 2:20, 1 Cor 5:5, and 1 Thes 5:2 and refers to Christ's Second Coming, repeating the sayings of the Prophets (e.g., Joel 2:1; Zeph 1:7). This coming is certain, but the time is known only to the Father (see Mk 13:32). It will arrive suddenly, unexpectedly, and without warning (see 1 Thes 5:1-3), ushering in the solemn judgment (see Acts 17:31). *The heavens will disappear with a mighty roar:* this is apocalyptic, figurative language like that of the Books of Daniel and Revelation.

3:11-16 What is it that is delaying the coming of the Messiah? The sins of human beings. This is what many thought among the Jewish circles, and our author shared that conviction. He wishes above all to encourage Christians to stand fast and make progress in the faith. Their eyes are not fixed on a hazy horizon; rather, they live from the promise of an unimaginable renewal of humankind and the world through the Christ who comes.

3:12 *Day of God:* synonymous with "Day of the Lord." The idea of a final conflagration, found only here in the New Testament, was common in apocalyptic writings and in Greco-Roman thought.

3:13 *New heavens and a new earth:* promised by Isaiah (65:17; 66:22) and confirmed by Revelation (21:1).

3:15 *Your opportunity to be saved:* literally, "salvation."

3:16 *Speaking of it:* the teaching just set forth in this Letter, which is also found in Paul: God's saving will (see Rom 2:4; 9:22f; 1 Cor 1:7f); Christ's return (see 1 Thes 4:16f; 1 Cor 15:23-52); getting ready for the judgment (see Col 1:22f; Eph 1:4-14; 4:30; 5:5-14); God's just judgment (see Rom 2:5-9); and God's forbearance as time to repent (see Rom 2:4). *Other Scriptures:* this comparison of Paul's Letters with the rest of Scripture indicates that Christian writings are on a par with the Old Testament Books (see 2 Pet 1:21; 2 Tim 3:16).

3:18 *Grow in . . . knowledge:* the author closes by stressing knowledge once more (see note on 2 Pet 1:2). *To him be glory:* this doxology corresponds to the one in 1 Pet 5:11.

"Anyone who hates his brother is a murderer" *(1 Jn 3:15).*

THE FIRST LETTER OF JOHN

To Live in Love

At the end of the first century, several currents of religious thought described as "Gnostic" were beginning to circulate; their spokesmen emphasized a special religious "knowledge" (Greek: gnosis*), from which they expected salvation. Among them certain themes were constantly repeated, but in a radically dualistic perspective: light and darkness, truth and falsehood, life and death.*

Against these innovators, four ideas had to be developed: knowledge of God, the person of Jesus, the reality of sin, and fraternal love.

Knowledge of God, who is light and love, brings Christians their happiness. This knowledge comes not from an inspiration from on high nor from the searching of our minds; it is given in Jesus Christ, in whom we touch, as it were, the self-manifestation of God, a point that is emphasized at the beginning of the Letter. Christian faith goes back to the direct testimony of those who were with the Lord.

Jesus is the Son of God. But he had a real body, really gave his blood, suffered, and rose from the dead. If the coming of Christ in the flesh is rejected (see 1 Jn 4:2), Christianity in its entirety collapses. There is no longer any redemption or any knowledge of God.

Christ saves from sin. Therefore, sin exists. We must acknowledge this and accept our being saved from it. This realism does not open the way to discouragement, but on the contrary is a prerequisite for hope.

Finally, God is love, communion. He first loves, and Jesus bears witness to this love. To believe in God means to enter into this relationship of love.

Never has it been made so clear that fraternal love is so essential to faith. Faith is not a form of abstract speculation, but a participation with God in the victory over evil, which is here called "the world."

The way of entering into the themes, repeating them, enriching them, and advancing in a spiral fashion is characteristic of this document, as it already was of the Gospel of John. We cannot regard the work as an occasional Letter; rather it is a long-matured effort to respond to the crisis that was agitating the communities.

Let us think of it, therefore, as a circular Letter, a meditation rather than a treatise, a text for preaching and teaching.

Where did it come from?

So great is its affinity in thought and form with the fourth Gospel that it evidently came, if not directly from the author of that work, then at least from circles close to him. The document was probably written toward the end of the first century, in Asia Minor (perhaps at Ephesus), and for the Churches of that province.

The First Letter of John may be divided as follows:

Prologue (1:1-4)
I: Walk in the Light (1:5—2:28)
II: Children of God (2:29—4:6)
III: Remain in Love (4:7-21)
IV: Believe in the Son of God (5:1-12)
Epilogue (5:13-21)

CHAPTER 1

PROLOGUE*

An Authentic Communion of Life

1 This is what we proclaim to you:
what existed from the beginning,
what we have heard,
what we have seen with our own eyes,
what we have looked at
and touched with our hands—
we are speaking of the Word of life. * [a]

2 That life was made visible;
we have seen it and bear witness,
proclaiming to you the eternal life *
that was with the Father
and was revealed to us. [b]

3 What we have seen and heard
we declare to you
so that you may have fellowship * with us.

a 1 Jn 2:13; 4:14; Jn 1:1, 14; 20:20, 25, 27; Lk 24:48; Acts 4:20; 2 Pet 1:16.—b 1 Jn 3:5, 8; Mt 25:46; Jn 1:1-4; 11:25; 15:27; 17:5; 1 Tim 3:16; 1 Pet 1:20.

1:1-4 An identical movement of life is transmitted from the Father to the Son, from the Son to his witnesses, and from his witnesses to believers. And the authenticity of this sharing is guaranteed by the real contact of the witnesses with the Son of God, the Word of Life (see Jn 1:1), the Messiah who is truly man. The Christian faith starts from a fact, an event, an experience. Thus, everything appears as a movement from God and a striving toward him, a fellowship of life. Without such an insertion in the bonds of the Church and this link with a real testimony, it would be vain speculation.

This Prologue deals with the same themes and makes use of the same words as the Prologue to John's Gospel (*beginning, Word, life*).

1:1 The Word of God was the source of life (see Deut 4:1; 32:47; Mt 4:4; Phil 2:16). John gives the title "Word" to the Son of God become man with whom the Apostles lived. Thus, they became eyewitnesses of his glory. They touched him and knew he was real. They heard him with their ears as he spoke the words of life. Everything they preached and wrote about him was based on fact.

1:2 *That life . . . the eternal life:* i.e., Christ. He is called "life" because he is the living one who has life in himself (see Jn 11:25; 14:6). He is also the source of life and sovereign over life (1 Jn 5:11). This Letter begins and concludes (1 Jn 5:11) with the theme of eternal life.

1:3 *Fellowship* (or communion): the word expresses one of the most important themes in Johannine mysticism: the unity of the Christian community, based on the oneness of each believer with God in Christ. This unity is described in the figures of the vine and the branches (see Jn 15:1-5) and the body and the head (see 1 Cor 12:12; Col 1:18). It also finds expression in various formulations: Christians "abide in God and God in them"; "they are born of God"; "they belong to God"; "they know God." Such a union with God is manifested in faith and fraternal love.

For our fellowship is with the Father
and with his Son Jesus Christ. [c]
4 We are writing this
so that our joy may be complete. [d]

I: WALK IN THE LIGHT

God Is Light*

5 This is the message
that we have heard from him
and that we declare to you:
God is light,
and there is no darkness * at all in him. [e]
6 If we claim that we have fellowship with him
while we continue to live in darkness,
we are lying and do not live in the truth. [f]
7 However, if we live in the light
as he himself is in the light,
then we have fellowship with one another,
and the blood of Jesus his Son
purifies us from all sin. [g]

Deliverance from Sin*

8 If we claim that we are sinless,
we are only deceiving ourselves,
and the truth is not in us. [h]
9 However, if we confess our sins,
he who is faithful and just
will forgive our sins
and cleanse us from all wrongdoing. [i]
10 If we say that we have never sinned,
we make him out to be a liar,
and his word is not in us. [j]

CHAPTER 2

1 My dear children,
I am writing this to you
so that you may avoid committing sin.
However, if anyone does sin,
we have an Advocate with the Father,
Jesus Christ, the Righteous One. [k]
2 He is himself the sacrifice for our sins—
and not only for our sins
but also for the sins of the whole world. [l]

The Commandment of Love*

3 Now we may be certain that we know him
if we obey his commandments. [m]
4 Whoever says, "I know him,"
but does not keep his commandments,
is a liar,
and the truth is not in him. * [n]
5 However, the love of God is truly perfected
in the one who obeys his word.
This is how we can be certain
that we are in union with him: [o]
6 whoever claims to abide in him
must live just as he himself lived. [p]

7 Beloved,
I am not writing a new commandment * for you,
but an old commandment
that you have had from the beginning.
The old commandment is the word
that you have heard. [q]

c 1 Jn 1:1; Jn 17:21; Acts 4:20; 1 Cor 1:9.—d 1 Jn 2:1; Jn 3:29; 15:11; 2 Jn 12.—e 1 Jn 3:11; Lk 22:53; 1 Tim 6:16.—f 1 Jn 2:11; Jn 3:19-21; 12:35; 2 Cor 6:14; Eph 5:8.—g Isa 2:5; Mt 26:28; Rom 3:24-25; Heb 9:14; Rev 1:5; 7:14.—h 1 Jn 2:4; 2 Chr 6:36; Prov 20:9; Jer 2:35; Jn 8:44; Rom 3:9-19; Jas 3:2.—i 1 Jn 1:7; Prov 28:13; Mic 7:18-20; Heb 10:22; Jas 5:16.—j 1 Jn 1:8; 2:14; 5:10; Jn 5:38.—k 1 Jn 2:12-13, 28; Jn 3:7, 18; 4:4; 14:16; Rom 8:34; 1 Thes 2:11; 1 Tim 2:5; Heb 7:25.—l 1 Jn 4:10; Mt 1:21; Jn 3:17; Rom 3:25.—m 1 Jn 2:5; 3:24; 4:13; Jn 14:15; 15:10.—n 1 Jn 2:3; 3:6; 4:20; Tit 1:16.—o 1 Jn 2:3; 4:12; Jn 14:23.—p Mt 11:29; 1 Pet 2:21.—q 1 Jn 2:24; 3:11; Deut 6:5; Mt 22:37-40; 1 Cor 10:14; 2 Jn 5-6.

1:5-7 There is no fellowship with God in the absence of faith or love. Christians do not achieve fellowship with God the Light (see Jn 8:12) by giving themselves over to Illuminism or by some magical rite; they do so by believing in the Redemption brought about by Christ's Passion and by living in the truth (see Jn 3:31), i.e., by entering into a life experience that keeps the commandments of the Gospel in a concrete manner.

1:5 *Light . . . darkness:* light represents all that is good, true, and holy, whereas darkness stands for all that is evil and false (see Jn 3:19-21).

1:8—2:2 Christians do not live in some superior spiritual sphere far removed from our daily lives on earth. We must in all honesty acknowledge that sin is present in our lives with all its weight. If we do not do so, we oppose the whole experience attested by Scripture and render insignificant the voluntary sacrifice that Christ made of himself so that human beings might have life. Deliverance from sin is obtained not by evasion but by the act of God who forgives and justifies us in the very depths of our being.

2:3-11 Gnostics claimed to possess a special revealed "knowledge." But John stresses that there is a real and living knowledge of God, a true light, an authentic truth, and it is expressed in a life that is lived in accord with the commandments of God. Its great characteristic is love. New doctrines are being put forth. Christian teaching is a commandment of Jesus, which in this sense is old. Yet it is also new because it is revealed in Jesus as a fact as well as in the life of believers. In the face of everything that is without purpose or sense, faith is a ray of light, a victory over darkness, a bright dawn for the world.

2:4 John reiterates the testimony of Paul and James about faith and works. James said that faith without works is dead (see note on Jas 2:14-26). Paul indicated that rewards would be based on good and bad deeds (see 2 Cor 5:10; see also note on Rom 4:3). John says that Christians who do not keep the commandments of Jesus are liars and the truth is not in them. For faith in Christ without good deeds, i.e., keeping the commandments, is not authentic.

2:7-8 *New commandment:* see Jn 13:34f. The Biblical commandment to love was old (see Lev 19:18; also Mt 22:39-40). However, its newness is seen in (1) the new illustration of love on the Cross; (2) Christ's exposition of the Old Testament law (see Mt 5), which appeared to be new to those who heard it; and (3) the everyday experience on the part of believers as they grow in mutual love.

8 And yet I am writing you a new commandment,
whose truth is in him and in you,
because the darkness is passing away
and the true light is already shining. [r]
9 Whoever says, "I am in the light,"
yet hates his brother,
is still in the darkness. [s]
10 Whoever loves his brother lives in the light,
and there is nothing in him
to make him stumble. [t]
11 Whoever hates his brother is in the darkness,
and he walks about in darkness.
He does not know where he is going
because the darkness has blinded him. [u]

The Concupiscences of the World*

12 I am writing to you, dear children,
because your sins have been forgiven
on account of his name. [v]
13 I am writing to you, fathers,
because you have known him
who has existed from the beginning.
I am writing to you, young people,
because you have conquered the evil one. [w]
14 I am writing to you, dear children,
because you have known the Father.
I am writing to you, fathers,
because you have known him
who has existed from the beginning.
I am writing to you, young people,
because you are strong,
and the word of God abides in you,
and you have overcome the evil one. [x]

15 Do not love the world
or what is in the world.
If anyone does love the world,
the love of the Father is not in him. [y]
16 For everything that is in the world—
the concupiscence of the flesh,
the concupiscence of the eyes,
and the pride of life—
comes not from the Father
but from the world. * [z]
17 And the world with all its enticements
is passing away,
but whoever does the will of God
abides forever. [a]

Behold the Antichrist*

18 Dear children,
this is the last hour.
You have heard that the Antichrist was coming,
and now many antichrists have already come. *
Thus, we know
that it is the final hour. [b]
19 They went out from us,
but they never really belonged to us.
If they had belonged to us,
they would have remained with us.

r Ezek 5:8; Jn 1:5; 13:34; Rom 13:12; 1 Thes 5:5; Heb 10:25.—s 1 Jn 2:11; 3:10, 15-16; Lev 19:17; Jn 8:12.—t 1 Jn 2:11; 3:14; Eccl 2:14; Jn 11:10.—u 1 Jn 2:9.—v 1 Jn 2:1; 3:23; 1 Cor 6:11.—w 1 Jn 1:1; 2:1; Mt 5:37; Jn 1:1; 16:33.—x 1 Jn 1:10; 2:13; Jn 1:1; 5:38; Eph 6:10; Heb 4:12.—y Rom 8:7-8; 12:2; Jas 4:4; 2 Pet 1:4.—z Gen 3:6; Prov 27:20; Rom 13:14; Eph 2:3.—a Isa 40:8; Mt 7:21; 12:50; 1 Cor 7:31; 1 Pet 4:2.—b 1 Jn 2:22; 4:1, 3; Rom 13:11; 1 Tim 4:1; 2 Jn 7.

2:12-17 The author addresses all with affection: "Dear children," as he says. He wants to answer every one of them—the old as well as the young. He recalls that Christians are set free from sin, that they are the vanquishers of the power of evil, personified in the Bible as the devil, "the evil one." This victory is attained by the action of God and not by adhering to the speculations that are being spread about. Adhering therein is the "world"—a term that refers to all that is opposed to God. The fourth Gospel had already accustomed us to this language that opposes God to the world and light to darkness. The author wishes to speak thereby of all the limitations of the human, e.g., unregulated desires, the need to possess, and the satisfaction of extravagance. In the face of this seduction that troubles every existence, believers can stand fast only by a life marked profoundly by the word of God.

2:16 The author here defines three great sins of worldliness: *the concupiscence of the flesh, the concupiscence of the eyes, and the pride of life.* The first has to do with inordinate desire for sensuality (see Eph 2:3; 1 Pet 2:11; 2 Pet 2:10, 18). The second has to do with covetousness, which springs from the eyes and has to do with the desire for things (see Job 31:1; Ezek 23:12-17; Mt 5:27ff). The third has to do with worldly ambition, ostentation, pride and arrogance, independence of God (see Ps 10:4; Prov 16:5; Isa 13:11; Lk 1:51-52; Jas 4:6, 10; 1 Pet 3:8; 5:5).

2:18-28 New teachers have arisen proclaiming a message different from that of the Gospel of Jesus. Is this not a sign that the end is near? The circumstances that Jesus had described in this respect (see Mk 13:22; see also 2 Thes 3:4; Rev 13:12-15) suddenly appear to be present. It is at least a time of crisis. The false teachers refuse to acknowledge either Christ or the Father, and they do away with the Gospel. The author is quick to set these teachers straight: those who do not accept the Gospel are no longer in the Church in spite of all appearances. Believers should cling to the teaching they originally received, i.e., to the great ideas of Christian initiation, for what is at issue is the Word of Jesus. They have been *anointed by the Holy One,* that is, they are penetrated by the word and the grace of Jesus. Let them not be concerned with new words and new teachings but be alert to await the Lord's coming.

2:18 Scripture distinguishes the *Antichrist* from many *antichrists* and from *the spirit of the Antichrist* (1 Jn 4:3). Here John is speaking of all who follow the Antichrist and imitate his evil spirit. He assumes that his readers know that a great enemy of his people will arise before Christ's return. This enemy is the *Antichrist,* "the man of lawlessness" (see notes on 2 Thes 2:3b-12 and 2:3b-4) and "the beast" (Rev 13:1-10). But before his coming there will be many antichrists characterized by (1) denial of Christ's Incarnation (see 1 Jn 4:2; 2 Jn 7) and Divinity (see 1 Jn 2:22); (2) denial of the Father (see 1 Jn 2:22); (3) nonpossession of the Father (see 1 Jn 2:23); (4) falsehoods (see 1 Jn 2:22), deceptions (see 2 Jn 7); (5) many in number (see 1 Jn 2:18); (6) nothing in common with believers (see 1 Jn 2:19).

By departing from us,
they made it clear
that none of them belonged to us. [c]
20 However, you have been anointed
by the Holy One, *
and you all have knowledge. [d]
21 I write to you
not because you do not know the truth
but because you do know it,
and because no lie can come from the truth. [e]
22 Who is the liar
but the one who denies that Jesus is the Christ?
The antichrist is
anyone who denies both the Father
and the Son. [f]
23 Whoever denies the Son
does not have the Father,
but whoever acknowledges the Son
has the Father also. [g]

24 Let what you heard from the beginning
remain in you.
If what you heard from the beginning
remains in you,
then you will remain in the Son
and in the Father. [h]
25 And this is the promise he made to us:
eternal life. [i]
26 I write these things to you
in reference to those
who seek to lead you astray. [j]
27 But as for you,
the anointing you received from him
remains in you,
and therefore you do not need anyone
to teach you.
This same anointing
teaches you everything
and is true and not false,
so abide in him just as he taught you. [k]
28 And now, dear children,
abide in him,
so that when he appears
we may have confidence
and not be put to shame by him
at his coming. [l]

II: CHILDREN OF GOD

Everyone Whose Life Is Righteous Has Been Born of God*

29 If you know that he is righteous,
you also know that everyone whose life is righteous
is born of him. [m]

CHAPTER 3

1 See what love
the Father has bestowed on us,
enabling us to be called the children of God,
and that is what we are.
If the world does not recognize us,
that is because it did not know him. [n]
2 Beloved,
we are God's children now.
What we shall be
has not yet been revealed.
However, we do know that when he appears
we shall be like him,
for we shall see him as he really is. [o]
3 Everyone who has this hope in him
keeps himself pure,
just as he is pure. [p]

The Rupture with Sin*

4 Everyone who sins breaks the law,
for sin is lawlessness. [q]
5 You know that he appeared
in order to take away sins,
and that there is no sin in him. [r]

c Acts 20:30; 1 Cor 11:19.—d 1 Jn 2:27; Jer 31:34; Mt 3:11; Mk 1:24; Jn 14:26; 2 Cor 1:21.—e 1 Jn 3:19; 2 Pet 1:12; Jude 5.—f 1 Jn 4:3; 2 Thes 2:4; 2 Jn 7.—g 1 Jn 4:15; 5:1; Jn 8:19; 14:7-9; 2 Jn 9.—h 1 Jn 1:3; 2:7; Jn 14:23; 2 Jn 9.—i Mt 25:46; Jn 5:24; 10:28; 17:2.—j 1 Jn 3:7; 2 Jn 7.—k 1 Jn 2:20; Jn 15:4; 1 Cor 2:12.—l 1 Jn 2:1; 3:2; Eph 3:12; Col 3:4; 1 Thes 2:19.—m 1 Jn 3:7; Jn 1:13.—n 1 Jn 3:2, 10; Jn 1:12; 3:16; 15:21; 17:25; Eph 1:5.—o 1 Jn 3:1, 10; Jn 1:12; Rom 8:29; 1 Cor 10:14; Phil 3:21; Col 3:4.—p 1 Jn 2:6; 2 Cor 7:1; 2 Pet 3:13-14.—q 1 Jn 5:17.—r 1 Jn 3:8; Isa 53:9; Jn 1:29; 8:46; 2 Cor 5:21; 1 Pet 2:22.

2:20 *Anointed by the Holy One:* reference to the Spirit who has been given to the Messiah (see Isa 11:2; 61:1), and then conferred by the Messiah on believers (see 1 Jn 3:24; 4:13; 2 Cor 1:21) so as to teach them about all things (see 1 Jn 2:27; Jn 16:13f; 1 Cor 2:10, 15). As a result, the words of Jesus are "spirit and life" (Jn 6:63).

2:29—3:3 The author takes ideas already expressed and develops them in new ways. In ch. 1:5-7 he used the phrase "God is light"; now he expresses the new theme that "God is righteous." God forgives human beings, bestowing upon them a condition in which they can stand before him. Here, too, it is not a question of abstract ideas but of life practices. What a bold affirmation about the Divine Sonship, what a dizzying perspective of a faith that must one day go beyond itself in the full vision of God!

3:4-10 Breaking away from sin does not take place by delighting in sublime thoughts but by the action of God in Jesus Christ. For it is Christ alone who is without sin (see Jn 8:26). And it is not words but deeds that bear witness to this liberation. To what options or influences does our life cling? Is it in the grip of the devil or does it cling to the word of God? Certainly, sin is part of the daily life of believers (1 Jn 1:8-10), but we are speaking about the fundamental and general choice between sin and righteousness. Which do we choose?

6 Whoever remains in him does not sin, *
and whoever sins has not seen him
nor known him. [s]
7 Dear children,
do not let anyone deceive you.
Everyone who does what is right is righteous,
just as he is righteous. [t]
8 Everyone who sins comes from the devil,
for the devil has been a sinner
from the very beginning.
The Son of God appeared for this very purpose:
to destroy the work of the devil. [u]
9 Whoever is born of God
does not sin,
because his seed * remains in him.
He cannot sin
because he is begotten by God. [v]
10 This is what distinguishes
the children of God from the children of the devil:
anyone who fails to live righteously
does not belong to God;
neither does anyone who fails to love a brother. [w]

The Message of Love*

11 For from the beginning
you have heard the message
that we should love one another, [x]
12 unlike Cain who was from the evil one
and slew his brother.
And why did he slay him?
Because his own deeds were evil
while those of his brother were righteous. [y]
13 Do not be surprised, my brethren,
if the world hates you. [z]
14 We know that we have passed
from death to life
because we love our brethren.
Whoever does not love remains in death. [a]
15 Anyone who hates his brother
is a murderer,
and you know that no murderer
has eternal life abiding in him. [b]
16 This is how we know what love is:
he laid down his life for us,
and we in turn must be prepared
to lay down our lives for our brethren. [c]
17 If anyone is rich in worldly possessions
and sees a brother in need
but refuses to open his heart,
how can the love of God abide in him? [d]
18 Dear children,
let us love not in word or speech
but in deed and truth. * [e]
19 This is how we know
that we belong to the truth
and reassure our hearts in his presence
20 even if our hearts experience a sense of guilt.
For God is greater than our hearts,
and he knows everything.
21 Beloved,
if our hearts do not condemn us,
we can approach God with confidence [f]
22 and receive from him whatever we ask,
because we obey his commandments
and do whatever is pleasing to him. * [g]
23 And this is his commandment:
that we should believe
in the name of his Son, Jesus Christ,
and love one another just as he commanded us. * [h]
24 All those who keep his commandments
abide in him,
and he abides in them.

s 1 Jn 2:4; 3:9; 5:18; Jn 3:17; 3 Jn 11.—t 1 Jn 2:1, 26, 29.—u 1 Jn 3:10; Jn 8:44; 12:31-32.—v 1 Jn 3:6; 5:18; Mt 4:3; Jn 1:13; Heb 2:14; 1 Pet 1:23.—w 1 Jn 3:1-2, 8; 4:8; Jn 1:12.—x 1 Jn 1:5; 2:7; Jn 13:34; 15:12, 17; 2 Jn 5.—y Gen 4:8; Prov 29:10; Mt 5:37; Jude 11.—z Mt 24:9; Jn 15:18; 17:14.—a 1 Jn 2:9; Lev 19:17; Jn 5:24.—b 1 Jn 2:9; Mt 5:21-22; Jn 8:44; Gal 5:20-21.—c Mt 20:28; Jn 10:11; 15:13; Phil 2:17; 1 Thes 2:8.—d 1 Jn 4:20; Deut 15:7, 11; Jas 2:15-16.—e 1 Jn 2:1; Ezek 33:31; Rom 12:9; Jas 1:22.—f 1 Jn 5:14; Ezek 3:12; 1 Cor 10:14.—g 1 Jn 5:15; Mt 7:7-11; Jn 8:29; 14:13-14; Heb 13:21.—h 1 Jn 5:13; Lk 24:47; Jn 1:12; 3:18; 6:29; 13:34; 15:17; 1 Cor 6:11.

3:6 *Whoever remains in him does not sin:* the author is not speaking about sinless perfection (see 1 Jn 1:8—2:1). He is simply asserting that the life of believers is dominated not by sin but by doing the right thing.

3:9 *His seed:* a reference to Christ (see 1 Jn 5:18; Gal 3:16) or to the Holy Spirit (see 1 Jn 2:20-27) or to the seed of Divine life that God introduced into us.

3:11-24 There are two attitudes toward life—hate and love, murder and the offering of one's life. Cain is the Biblical prototype of all the homicidal impulses that arise in the human heart (see Gen 4; Heb 11:4); these come together in what the author's language terms "the world." This symbolizes death. Christian behavior—which is life, love, and offering of self—draws us away from the world. Christ gives us both the power to do so and the example to follow in the concrete reality of his Passion. Believers must do likewise. They can count on God's mercy. Verse 23, which expresses the whole intent of the Letter, brings out clearly the mind of the author in regard to the growing Gnosticism.

3:18 Like James, John insists on the value of good works. Love is not a mere matter of lip service; it must be seen and known in actions. Beautiful words are meaningless if they are not accompanied by good deeds.

3:22 Believers who have a good conscience desire nothing that is contrary to God's honor and glory. They will trust in God, who will give them the good things they request (see Ps 84:12).

3:23 This commandment has two parts: (1) belief in Christ (see Jn 6:29) and (2) love for one another (see Jn 13:34f). The Letter develops part one in 4:1-6 and the second part in 4:7-12.

And the proof that he abides in us
is the Spirit that he has given us. [i]

CHAPTER 4

The Spirit of the Antichrist in the World*

1 Beloved,
do not trust every spirit,
but test the spirits
to see whether they are from God.
For many false prophets
have gone out into the world. [j]
2 This is how you can recognize the Spirit of God:
every spirit that acknowledges
that Jesus Christ has come in the flesh *
is from God, [k]
3 and every spirit that does not acknowledge Jesus
is not from God.
This is the spirit of the Antichrist,
about whose coming you have been told,
and that it is already in the world. [l]
4 Dear children,
you are from God *
and you have conquered them,
for the one who is in you is greater
than the one who is in the world. [m]
5 They are from the world;
therefore, what they say is from the world,
and the world listens to them. [n]
6 We are from God.
Anyone who knows God listens to us,
while anyone who is not from God
refuses to listen to us.
This is how we can distinguish
the spirit of truth from the spirit of falsehood. * [o]

III: REMAIN IN LOVE*

What Love Is

7 Beloved,
let us love one another,
because love is from God. *
Everyone who loves is born of God
and knows God. [p]
8 Whoever does not love
does not know God,
because God is love. [q]
9 God's love was revealed to us
in this way:
God sent his only-begotten Son into the world
so that we might have life through him. [r]
10 This is what love is:
not that we have loved God,
but that he loved us
and sent his Son as expiation for our sins. * [s]
11 Beloved,
since God loved us so much,
we should love one another. [t]
12 No one has ever seen God,
but if we love one another,

i 1 Jn 2:3, 6; 4:13; Jn 14:21-23; 1 Thes 4:8.—j 1 Jn 2:18; Jer 29:8; Mt 7:15; 24:24; 1 Cor 10:14; 2 Thes 2:2.—k 1 Jn 2:23; Jn 1:14; 1 Cor 12:3; 1 Thes 5:21.—l 1 Jn 1:22; 2:18, 22; 2 Jn 7.—m 1 Jn 2:1; 2 Ki 6:16; Jn 12:31; 16:33; Rom 8:31.—n Jn 15:19; 17:14, 16.—o Mk 13:5; Jn 8:17; 10:16; 14:17.—p 1 Jn 2:4; 3:11; Jn 1:13.—q 1 Jn 4:7, 16; 2 Cor 13:11.—r 1 Jn 5:11; Jn 1:18; 3:16.—s Rom 3:25; 5:8, 10.—t 1 Jn 3:11; Jn 3:16; 1 Cor 10:14.

4:1-6 We must learn to discern the thoughts of human beings—the "spirits." Among the teachers and theorists that had appeared at this time there were those who did not acknowledge Jesus as the Lord and Savior and wished to impose their views on the Christian communities. John says that this is perversion, the appearance of false christs of the end times (see 1 Jn 2:18-22). He strengthens believers by telling them that they do not belong to the world, i.e., this universe that delights in its limitations and its own insignificances. They must believe in the Gospel of God proclaimed by the witnesses who have been sent, among whom he places himself by saying "We are from God" (v. 6).

4:2 *Jesus Christ has come in the flesh:* see note on 1 Jn 1:1. John excludes the Gnostics, especially those known as Cerinthians, who taught that the Divine Christ came upon the human Christ at his Baptism and left him at the Cross—thus claiming that only the man Jesus died.

4:4 *From God:* another expression for "born of God" (1 Jn 2:29; 3:9). *The one who is in the world:* the devil (see Jn 12:31; 16:11).

4:6 *Spirit of truth . . . spirit of falsehood:* this refers to the theme of the two spirits, which is similar to the theme of the two ways (see Deut 11:26; Mt 7:13-14). Confronted by two worlds, those who live on earth choose one or the other by partaking of the spirit of either one (see 1 Jn 3:8, 19). However, those who choose the right one (*the spirit of truth*) will attain certain victory (see 1 Jn 2:13f; 4:4; 5:4f).

4:7-21 There are splendid pages in the Bible that speak of what love is—for example, Paul's hymn on love (1 Cor 13) and this text. The whole theology of love is developed in these verses, which give us the deepest understanding of Christianity as a great movement of life and experience, and not an abstract speculation. Love is reality: i.e., in God; it is witnessed to in an experience: i.e., in Christ; and it is expressed in the reality of fraternal love: i.e., among believers.

God and love: the two words go together, just as do knowledge of God and fraternal love. The living discovery of God does not take place in plumbing the most compelling ideas but in becoming like Christ, in the experience of fraternal love. Without this, no fellowship with God is possible. Fraternal love and faith in Christ go together; and this experience enables us to verify the value of every religion and every spirituality. Nothing else can deliver human beings from the fear of judgment.

4:7-8 *Love is from God:* hence, those who love God show that they are born of God. *God is love:* i.e., he is loving in his essential nature and in all his actions. The Gospel of John also affirms that God is spirit (see Jn 4:24) and light (see Jn 1:5) as well as true and just, powerful, holy, and faithful.

4:10 It was God who first loved us when we had no love for him or even for ourselves (see Rom 5:6-10). He showed his love by sending his Son to atone for our sins (see 1 Jn 2:2). This is the motive for our love for one another.

God abides in us,
and his love is made complete in us. [u]
13 This is how we can be certain
that we abide in him
and that he abides in us:
he has given us a share in his Spirit. * [v]
14 Moreover, we have seen for ourselves
and can testify
that the Father has sent the Son
as the Savior of the world. [w]
15 God abides in anyone who acknowledges
that Jesus is the Son of God,
and that person abides in God. [x]
16 We have come to know
and to believe in
the love that God has for us. [y]
God is love,
and whoever abides in love
abides in God,
and God in him.
17 This is how love is made perfect in us,
enabling us to have confidence
on the Day of Judgment,
because even in this world
we have become like him. [z]
18 In love there is no fear;
indeed, perfect love casts out fear,
because fear has to do with punishment,
and whoever fears
has not yet achieved perfection in love. [a]
19 Therefore, we love because he first loved us. [b]
20 If someone says, "I love God,"
but at the same time hates his brother,
he is a liar.
For whoever does not love the brother
whom he has seen
cannot love God
whom he has not seen. [c]
21 This is the commandment
we have received from him:
whoever loves God
must also love his brother. [d]

CHAPTER 5

IV: BELIEVE IN THE SON OF GOD*

Faith Conquers the World

1 Everyone who believes
that Jesus is the Christ
is born of God,
and everyone who loves the parent
loves the one begotten of him as well. [e]
2 This is how we know
that we love the children of God:
by loving God and obeying his commandments. [f]
3 For the love of God is this:
that we keep his commandments.
And his commandments are not burdensome, [g]
4 for everyone born of God
conquers the world.
And the victory that conquers the world
is our faith. [h]
5 Who indeed conquers the world
except the one who believes
that Jesus is the Son of God? [i]
6 This is the one
who came by water and blood,
Jesus Christ—
not by water alone,
but by water and blood.
And to this the Spirit bears witness,
for the Spirit is truth. * [j]
7 Thus, there are three * witnesses, [k]

u 1 Jn 2:5; 4:17; Jn 1:18; 1 Tim 6:16.—v 1 Jn 2:3; 3:24.—w Lk 2:11; Jn 3:17; 15:27.—x 1 Jn 2:23; 3:24; 5:5.—y 1 Jn 3:24; 4:8, 12, 13.—z 1 Jn 2:5, 28; 4:12; Mt 10:15; Eph 3:12.—a Rom 8:15.—b 1 Jn 4:10.—c 1 Jn 1:6; 2:4, 9; 3:17; 4:12; Jn 1:16.—d 1 Jn 2:7, 9; Mt 5:43; Jn 13:34; 14:15, 21; 15:17.—e 1 Jn 2: 22-23; 4:2.—f 1 Jn 2:3; 3:14.—g Mt 11:30; 23:4; Jn 14:15.—h Jn 1:13; 16:33.—i 1 Jn 2:23; 5:1; 1 Cor 15:57.—j 1 Jn 5:8; Jn 14:17; 15:26; 19:34.—k Deut 17:6; 19:15; Mt 18:16; Jn 15:26.

4:13 *A share in his Spirit:* this is the Spirit promised for the Messianic Age (see Acts 2:17-21, 33); he has been poured out into our hearts (see Rom 5:5; 1 Thes 4:8) and brings forth in us the inner certainty that the Apostles proclaimed outwardly (see 1 Jn 5:6f; Acts 5:32)—in this case about the Divine adoption of Christians (see Rom 8:15f; Gal 4:6).

5:1-12 In opposition to the fantasies spread about by the false teachers, John insists that there is no knowledge of God without an acknowledgment of his Son and acceptance of his commandments and his Gospel. There is no victory over the world (the forces of evil and human limitations) without adherence to Christ. There is no finding God except through the testimony in which he makes himself present: in Jesus Christ who offers his life for the world. Baptism and the Spirit are nothing if the blood is forgotten, for Redemption, the Paschal Mystery, and the Eucharist are the heart of faith. God's self-revelation includes the entire life of Jesus from his Baptism to his Cross: the water and the blood (see Jn 19:34). Hence, there is no knowledge of God that does not transform itself into faith in his Son and in the acknowledgment of other human beings as brothers and sisters because they are God's children.

5:6 John is answering the false teachers who claimed that Jesus was born only a man, then at his Baptism the Son of God descended on him, but he left Jesus before the latter's death on the Cross; therefore, it was only the man Jesus who died. In keeping with his teaching throughout the Letter that Jesus is God as well as man (1 Jn 1:1-4; 4:2; 5:5), John emphasizes that Jesus was Son of God all the time. This is a key point because if Jesus had died only as a man, his atonement would not have been enough to take away the sins of human beings.

5:7 *Three:* the Scriptures required three witnesses (see Deut 17:6; 19:15; 1 Tim 5:19). In many manuscripts the text has been amplified; thus the post-Tridentine Vulgate has: "There are three witnesses *in heaven: the Father, the Word, and the Spirit, and these three are as one: there are three witnesses on earth:* the Spirit, the water, and the blood, and these three are as one." The words in *italics* are not found in any of the early Greek manuscripts or translations, or in the best manuscripts of the Vulgate. They are almost universally regarded as a gloss.

8 the Spirit, the water, and the blood,
and these three are as one.* [l]
9 If we accept human testimony,
the testimony of God is greater.
For it is the testimony of God,
the testimony that he has given about his Son. [m]
10 Whoever believes in the Son of God
has this testimony in himself,
but those who do not believe in God
have made him out to be a liar
by refusing to believe the testimony
that God has given about his Son. [n]
11 And this is the testimony:
God gave us eternal life,
and this life is in his Son. [o]
12 Whoever possesses the Son
possesses life;
whoever does not possess the Son of God
does not possess life. [p]

EPILOGUE*

So That You May Know*

13 I write these things to you
who believe in the name of the Son of God
so that you may know
that you have eternal life. [q]

Prayer for Sinners*

14 And thus we can have confidence in him
that if we ask anything
that is in accordance with his will,
he hears us. [r]
15 And if we know that he hears us
in regard to whatever we ask him,
we may be sure
that all we ask of him will be ours. [s]
16 If anyone sees a brother commit a sin
that does not lead to death,
he should intercede for him,
and God will grant him life—
provided that the sin is not deadly.
There is a sin that leads to death,
and I do not say
that you should pray about it.* [t]
17 All wrongdoing is sinful,
but not all sins are deadly. [u]

The Great Certitudes*

18 We know that one born of God does not continue to sin,
because he who is born of God protects him,
and the evil one has no power over him. [v]
19 We know
that we are from God
and that the entire world
lies under the power of the evil one. [w]
20 We also know
that the Son of God has come
and given us understanding
so that we can know the one who is true.
And we are in the one who is true,
since we are in his Son Jesus Christ.
He is the true God and eternal life. [x]
21 Dear children,
keep away from idols. [y]

l Jn 5:32, 36; 15:26.—m Mt 3:16-17; Jn 5:32, 37; 8:17-18.—n 1 Jn 1:10; Jn 3:33; Rom 8:16; Gal 4:6.—o 1 Jn 1:2; Mt 25:46; Jn 1:4; 5:21, 26; 17:3.—p Jn 3:15-16, 36.—q 1 Jn 3:23; 5:11; Mt 25:46; Jn 1:12; 20:31.—r 1 Jn 3:21-22; Mt 7:7; Jn 14:13-14; Eph 3:12.—s 1 Jn 5:18-20; 1 Ki 3:12.—t Ex 23:21; Jer 7:16; 14:11; Mt 12:31; Heb 6:4-6; 10:26; Jas 5:15.—u 1 Jn 2:1; 3:4; 5:16.—v Mt 5:37; Jn 1:13; 14:30.—w 1 Jn 4:6; Jn 12:31; 14:30; 17:15.—x 1 Jn 5:5, 11; Jer 24:7; Mt 25:46; Lk 24:45; Jn 17:3.—y 1 Jn 2:1; 1 Cor 10:14; 1 Thes 1:9.

5:8 The three witnesses converge; blood and water join the Spirit (see 1 Jn 2:20, 27; Jn 3:5; 4:14) in testifying (see Jn 3:11f) to the mission of the Son who gives life (v. 11; Jn 3:15).

5:13-21 Believers can be certain of partaking of the life of God; this whole Letter has given them the criteria that allow them to be sure of it.

5:13 This summary of the Letter is reminiscent of the Epilogue of John's Gospel (20:30f).

5:14-17 Believers are not perfect; they all have their weaknesses. However, these failures are not to be confused with refusal of Christ, which is refusal of fellowship with God. The Bible speaks to us about Abraham and Moses, who could intervene for the sins of human beings. In the Church, all members can intercede for their brethren. The author does not include in his prayer those who pervert the faith.

5:16 In general, the words *There is a sin that leads to death* refer not to just any sin that causes the loss of sanctifying grace (the "life of the soul"), but to an especially serious sin, such as apostasy, that causes the loss not only of grace but of faith as well. The distinction is intended to underscore the danger in which those who abandon the Christian fellowship ("are excommunicated") place themselves, and to instill a salutary fear into them.

5:18-21 The great certitudes that the speculations of the false teachers would like to shake are affirmed one last time, like a cry of victory. The community of God's children, adhering to Christ, overcomes the forces of evil, truly knows God, and shares his life. To seek anything else is idolatry. The *idols* to be avoided are either paganism or the false gods of the heart that can turn believers away from faith and love.

THE SECOND LETTER OF JOHN

The Way of Truth

New teachers have been preaching an alien type of knowledge (gnosis)*; they are enthusiasts for a profound spiritual knowledge that has no need of faith in Jesus or of his Gospel of love.*

A community—the "chosen Lady and . . . her children," as it is called here—is exposed to the danger of losing what is the very heart of the faith and of Christian life. A "presbyter" (or elder) intervenes, whose authority is so great that the community must accept it, for he is a witness from the earliest time, a witness of Christ.

This person is certainly the one whose voice resounds in the fourth Gospel and in the First Letter of John.

This Second Letter is even older than the preceding one; the threat to the Churches has hardly shown its face; the response to it is as yet only sketched, but in a lively and direct way. The First Letter, on the other hand, will go more deeply into the threat and give a much fuller reply. We must refer to that Letter in order to understand the concern in the present document, which is from the same period (toward the end of the first century) and addressed to a Church of Asia Minor.

The Second Letter of John may be divided as follows:

Salutation (1-3)
The Commandment of Love (4-6)
Warning against False Teachers (7-11)
Conclusion (12-13)

Salutation. 1 The Presbyter * to the chosen
Lady and to her children whom I love in the
truth—and not I alone but also all who know
the truth—[a] 2 because of the truth that
abides in us and will be with us forever. [b]
3 Grace, mercy, and peace will be with us
from God the Father and from Jesus Christ,
the Son of the Father, in truth and love. [c]

The Commandment of Love.* 4 It was a cause
of great joy to me to discover that some of
your children have been walking in the
truth * just as we have been commanded by
the Father. [d] 5 * But now, Lady, I am making
this request of you, not as though I were writ-
ing you a new commandment but simply
one that we have had from the beginning: let
us love one another. [e] 6 And this is love: when
we walk according to his commandments. *
This is the commandment that you have
heard from the beginning, and you must fol-
low it. [f]

Warning against False Teachers.* 7 Many
deceivers have gone forth into the world,
those who refuse to acknowledge that Jesus
Christ has come in the flesh. Any such per-
son is the Deceiver * and the Antichrist. [g]

a 2 Jn 3, 13; Jn 8:32; Acts 11:30; Rom 16:13; 1 Tim 2:4; 1 Pet 5:13; 3 Jn 1.—b Jn 14:17; 2 Pet 1:12; 1 Jn 1:8.—c Rom 1:7; 1 Tim 1:2; 2 Tim 1:2.—d 3 Jn 3-4.—e Jn 13:34; 15:12; 1 Jn 2:7; 4:7.—f Jn 13:34; 14:15; 1 Jn 2:5, 7; 5:3.—g Jn 1:14; 1 Jn 2:18, 22; 4:2.

1 *Presbyter:* i.e., a term (which may also be translated as "elder") used to designate a leader in the early Church (see notes on Tit 1:5-9 and 1:7). *Chosen Lady* (or "Sovereign Lady"): reference to one of the local churches of the time, which was under the leadership of the Presbyter and was confused by the advent of false teachers among her members.

4-6 For more details, see 1 Jn 2:3-11; 3:11-14; 4:7-21.

4 *Walking in the truth:* i.e., leading a specifically Christian way of life (see 1 Jn 1:6f; 2:6, 11; 3 Jn 3).

5-6 John stresses the truth that words and deeds go together. Love means keeping the commandments of Jesus. And when Christians keep them, they are leading a life of faith.

6 *His commandments:* see 1 Jn 2:7f; 3:23; 4:21.

7-11 The false teachers are under the sign of the Antichrist (see 1 Jn 2:18-26; 4:1-3). They want to "go beyond" the teaching of Christ, thus adulterating Christ, the Gospel, and Love. This seems to be the Gnostic teaching attacked in the First Letter of John—that the Son of God did not become flesh (see Jn 1:14) but came upon the man Jesus temporarily at his Baptism and left before the crucifixion (see note on 1 Jn 5:6).

7 *Deceiver:* another title of the Antichrist or of those associated with him (see 1 Jn 2:18f, 22; 4:2f). *Antichrist:* see note on 1 Jn 2:18.

8 Be on your guard that you do not lose what
we have worked to accomplish so that you
will receive your reward in full. * [h]
9 Anyone who fails to remain faithful to
the teaching of Christ but goes beyond * it
does not have God. Only the one who
remains faithful to the teaching possesses
both the Father and the Son. [i] 10 If anyone
comes to you and does not impart this
teaching, do not receive him into your house
or welcome him. * [j] 11 For anyone who wel-
comes him has a share in his evil deeds. [k]

Conclusion. 12 I have much to write to you,
but I do not think it prudent to do so with
paper and ink. * Instead, I hope to visit you
and to talk with you face to face so that our
joy may be complete. [l]
13 The children of your sister, the chosen
one, * send you greetings. [m]

h Mt 10:42; Mk 10:29-30; 1 Cor 3:8; Heb 10:35, 36; 11:26.—i Jn 8:31; 1 Jn 2:23; 4:15.—j Rom 16:17; 2 Thes 3:6.—k 1 Tim 5:22.—l Jn 3:29; 15:11; 1 Jn 1:4; 3 Jn 13-14.—m 2 Jn 1.

8 The author stresses that a future reward awaits those who work faithfully on earth (see Mk 9:41; 10:29f; Lk 19:16-19; Heb 11:26). *We:* some manuscripts have "you."

9 *Goes beyond:* a reference to the Gnostics' claim that they had advanced far beyond the teaching of the Apostles; they were, in effect, teaching pure speculation as apostolic doctrine (see 2 Tim 2:16; Tit 3:9).

10-11 The author warns against feeding and housing the false teachers, for that would be sharing in their evil deeds and tantamount to public approval.

12 The Presbyter is well aware that some things are better spoken face to face than written. So he hopes to visit the Church soon. *Paper and ink:* paper came from papyrus reeds, which were easily acquired. Ink was made by mixing carbon, water, and gum. *Our joy:* or "your joy."

13 *Your sister, the chosen one:* most likely, another local church (perhaps that of Ephesus), which was also under the leadership of the Presbyter. Just as Christians are "brothers [and sisters]," the churches are "sisters."

THE THIRD LETTER OF JOHN

Personal and Doctrinal Problems

This is a letter of encouragement that deals with the problems of individuals. Above all, it has to do with the life of a local Church in which communication has become difficult, probably because of the appearance there of the Gnostic initiates, of whom we have already spoken in the Introduction to the First Letter of John. They were spreading false teachings, agitating Churches, and destroying the true Gospel.

Let us review the situation. Diotrephes, head of a local Church and probably involved in the new Gnostic currents of thought, has refused to communicate with the "Presbyter," who is certainly a witness of Jesus and in charge of all the Churches of the region; in all likelihood, he is John the Apostle. The man locally in charge rejects the itinerant missionaries, whose task it was to proclaim the Gospel and establish and develop Churches.

However, in this community there is a steadfast man, Gaius, who must be supported in his behavior and his undertakings; he is a man who courageously receives and supports the missionaries.

A third person comes on the scene: Demetrius, who likewise deserves to be supported and encouraged.

This Letter was written about the same time as the other two Letters of John.

The Third Letter of John may be divided as follows:

Salutation (1-2)
Commendation of Gaius (3-8)
Condemnation of Diotrephes (9-10)
Exhortation to Gaius (11)
Example of Demetrius (12)
Conclusion (13-15)

Salutation. 1 The Presbyter* to my be-
loved Gaius, whom I love in the truth. [a]
2 Beloved, I pray that everything is going
well with you and that your bodily health is
equal to that of your soul. *

Commendation of Gaius. 3 I rejoiced greatly
when some of the brethren* arrived and
related how faithful you are to the truth, and
that you continue to walk in the truth. [b]
4 Nothing gives me greater joy than to hear
that my children are walking in the truth. [c]

5 * Beloved, you have been faithful in
everything you do for the brethren, especial-
ly to strangers. [d] 6 They have testified before
the Church to your love. Please continue to
help them on their journey in a manner wor-
thy of God. [e] 7 For they began their journey
for the sake of the Name,* and they have
refused to accept any support from non-
believers. [f] 8 Therefore, we ought to show
hospitality to such people so that we may be
collaborators in the truth. [g]

Condemnation of Diotrephes. 9 I have previ-
ously written something to the Church, but
Diotrephes,* who enjoys being in a position
of leadership, refuses to acknowledge our
authority. [h] 10 Therefore, if I come, I shall
draw attention to what he is doing. He has
circulated false charges against us. And not
content with that, he not only refuses to wel-
come the brethren but interferes with those
who want to do so and expels them from the
Church. [i]

Exhortation to Gaius. 11 Beloved, do not imi-
tate what is evil; rather, imitate what is good.
Whoever does what is good is from God.
Whoever does what is evil has never seen
God. * [j]

Example of Demetrius. 12 Everyone has spo-
ken favorably about Demetrius,* and so has
the Truth itself. We also will vouch for him,
and you are well aware that our testimony is
true. [k]

Conclusion. 13 * I have much to write to
you, but I do not think it prudent to do so
with pen and ink. [l] 14 Instead, I hope to visit
you in the very near future, when we can talk
together face to face. [m]

15 Peace be with you. The friends* send
you their greetings. Greet each of our
friends there by name. [n]

---

a Jn 3:18; Acts 11:30; 2 Jn 1.—b 3 Jn 5, 10; Acts 1:16; Gal 6:10; 2 Jn 4.—c 3 Jn 3; 1 Thes 2:11-12; 1 Tim 1:2; 2 Tim 1:2; 1 Jn 2:1; 2 Jn 4.—d 3 Jn 3; Rom 12:13; Gal 6:10; Heb 13:2.—e Acts 15:3; 1 Cor 16:11; 2 Cor 1:16; Eph 4:1; Col 1:10; 1 Thes 2:12.—f Jn 15:21; Acts 5:41; 20:33, 35.—g Mt 10:41.—h 2 Jn 10.—i 3 Jn 5, 14; Jn 9:22, 34; 2 Jn 12.—j Isa 1:16-17; 1 Jn 2:29; 3:6, 9-10.—k Jn 19:35; 21:24; 1 Tim 3:7.—l 2 Jn 12.—m Jn 10:3; Rom 1:7; Eph 6:23; 2 Jn 12.—n Jn 20:19, 21, 26; Eph 6:23; 1 Pet 5:14.

---

1 *Presbyter:* see note on 2 Jn 1. *Gaius:* a loyal member of one of the churches in the province of Asia, who bears a common Roman name—one mentioned in four other places in the New Testament (Acts 19:29; 20:4; Rom 16:23; 1 Cor 1:14).

2 John wishes Gaius well both spiritually and physically, for he knows that grace and health are two of the greatest gifts of God.

3 *Brethren:* most likely itinerant missionaries to whom Gaius showed Christian hospitality. *Walk in the truth:* i.e., practice true Christian living.

5-6 Apparently, the early Church provided hospitality and support for missionaries because they had given up their means of livelihood in order to preach the faith to others and deserved some kind of compensation (see 1 Cor 9:3-12).

7 *Name:* of Jesus Christ (see note on Acts 5:41), which expresses the mystery of his divinity (see Phil 2:9; Jas 2:7; 1 Jn 2:12; 3:23; 5:13.

9 *Diotrephes:* a leader of the local church who overstepped his boundaries. He not only failed to give allegiance to the Presbyter but also refused to offer hospitality and support to the missionaries who came to his church.

11 John exhorts Gaius to keep on doing good and not be swayed by the un-Christian behavior of Diotrephes.

12 *Demetrius:* possibly the bearer of the Letter. He may have been an important member of the community or one of the missionaries. *Spoken favorably . . . and so has the Truth itself:* most likely, John is referring to the Truth of the Gospel in Demetrius' life. Like Gaius, Demetrius is "walking in the truth." He lives the life of love.

13-14 See 2 Jn 12-13 for a similar conclusion.

15 *Friends:* probably those who oppose Diotrephes and are loyal to the Presbyter.

THE LETTER OF JUDE

Contending for the Faith

The Letter of Jude, which consists of only twenty-five verses, is a strange and surprising document, in which many of the details escape us. One thing is clear, however: there was a need to defend the essentials of the faith handed down by the Apostles and to warn people against erroneous currents of thought that combined immorality and mysticism in an odd way.

Some groups were tearing the communities apart, right in the midst of the community gatherings. These people, who thought of themselves as spiritual, went on inventing classes and hierarchies of celestial beings, to the point of dissolving the lordship of Christ and of insulting the angels.

Although the Letter does not indicate for whom it was specifically intended, it was most likely aimed at the Jews of the Dispersion (i.e., those living throughout the Roman empire) who had accepted Christ as their Savior. If such were not the case, it would be difficult to understand the reason for the use of such obscure personages in Jude's Old Testament illustrations and for the citations from apocryphal books that would have meant very little to a Gentile audience.

We are here in the final period of the apostolic age, toward the end of the first century. The author, who speaks so vehemently in the name of truth, writes under the name of Jude, a brother of James (the most representative person of the Jerusalem Church: see Gal 1:19; 2:9; Acts 15:13-21; James: Introduction) and therefore perhaps also a relative of Jesus (see Mt 13:55; Mk 6:3).

It is possible, though not necessary, to identify this Jude with the apostle of the same name: Jude Thaddeus (see Mt 10:3; Mk 3:18; Lk 6:16; Jn 14:22; Acts 1:13). Perhaps this person filled some office after the death of his brother James in A.D. 62. He may have exhorted the faithful to fight for the true faith against a distortion of the Gospel.

Whoever the author was, he wrote in some of the best Greek of the New Testament. Furthermore, he shows great acquaintance with Jewish writings of his time, the texts of apocalypses that he cites and that he approximates in his writing. His energetic and picturesque style is also reminiscent of the early Prophets of the Old Testament.

His violent intervention must have had some success, for in fact it is picked up in the Second Letter of Peter, but with some revisions (see, for example, verses 17-18 cited almost verbatim in 2 Pet 3:3).

We should not be surprised that the author is not afraid to employ abusive formulas; these are formulas often already in use in the religious literature of the time. We should attend rather to the author's deeper concern: not to let the Christian mystery be enfeebled.

Indeed, the Letter opens with a salutation and a splendid expression of the awareness of being a Christian (1-4). It goes on to warn against false teachers (5-19). Then it provides a capsule program of the Christian life encompassing faith, prayer, love, mutual assistance, and avoidance of corruptors of the faith (20-23). It concludes with one of the most beautiful doxologies of the New Testament, noting that we must stand one day before the living God, who gives us strength to persevere and make progress (24-25).

The Letter of Jude may be divided as follows:

Salutation (1-2)
Benefits of Being a Christian (3-4)
Character and Doom of the False Teachers (5-16)
Appeal to the Faithful (17-19)
A Program of the Christian Life (20-23)
Doxology (24-25)

Salutation. 1 Jude, a servant of Jesus Christ,
and the brother of James,* to those who
have been called, who are dear to God the
Father and have been kept safe by Jesus
Christ:[a] 2 may mercy, peace, and love be
granted you in abundance.[b]

Benefits of Being a Christian. 3 Beloved, I
was just at the point of writing to you about
the salvation we share, when it became nec-
essary for me to write and urge you to fight
earnestly for the faith that was once and for
all entrusted to the saints.*[c] 4 For certain
men have infiltrated your ranks, people who
long ago were designated for condemna-
tion.* These godless persons pervert the
grace of our God into an excuse for
immorality and disown our only Master and
Lord, Jesus Christ.[d]

Character and Doom of the False Teachers.*
5 Although you already know all this, allow
me to remind you that the Lord, who once
delivered the people out of the land of Egypt,
afterward destroyed those who refused to
believe.*[e] 6 Remember also that the angels,
who were dissatisfied with the dominion
that had been assigned to them and aban-
doned their proper dwelling place, have
been kept bound by him in darkness with
eternal chains until the judgment of the
great Day.*[f] 7 And do not fail to remember
Sodom and Gomorrah and the neighboring
cities, which in a similar way indulged in
sexual immorality and perversion. They
serve as an example of those who undergo
the punishment of eternal fire.*[g]

8 In the same way, these dreamers defile
their bodies, make light of authority, and
insult celestial beings.*[h] 9 Even the arch-
angel Michael, when he engaged in an argu-
ment with the devil about the body of Mo-
ses, did not dare to bring a slanderous
accusation against him, but instead said:
"May the Lord rebuke you!"*[i] 10 However,

a Mt 13:55; Mk 6:3; Jn 14:22; 17:12; Acts 1:13; 12:17; Rom 1:1, 6-7.—b Rom 1:7; Gal 6:16; 1 Tim 1:2; 2 Pet 1:2.—c Jude 17, 20; Acts 6:7; 9:13; 1 Cor 10:14; 1 Tim 6:12; Tit 1:4.—d Gal 2:4; 2 Tim 3:6; Tit 1:16; 2 Pet 2:1; 1 Jn 2:22.—e Num 14:35; Deut 1:32; 2:15; 1 Cor 10:5; Heb 3:16-17; 2 Pet 1:12-13; 1 Jn 2:20.—f Mt 25:41; Acts 17:31; 2 Thes 1:9; 2 Pet 2:4, 9.—g Deut 29:22-24; Mt 10:15; 25:41; 2 Thes 1:8-9.—h 2 Pet 2:10.—i Deut 34:6; Dan 10:21; 12:1; Zec 3:2; 1 Thes 4:16; Rev 12:7.

1 *Jude . . . the brother of James:* see Introduction. *Servant:* see note on Rom 1:1. *Kept safe by Jesus Christ:* he holds the universe together (see Col 1:17; Heb 1:3) and will ensure that Christians persevere in the faith and reach their eternal inheritance (see Jn 6:37-40; 17:11f; 1 Pet 1:3-5).

3 Those who possess the true faith must defend it zealously against all error. But this defense of the truth must always be carried out in a lawful manner. *Saints:* see note on Rom 1:7.

4 *Long ago were designated for condemnation:* the author may be referring to Old Testament denunciations of godless men or to Enoch's prophecy (see vv. 14-15) or he may mean that condemnation has long ago been ready to overtake them because of their sin (see 2 Pet 2:3).

5-16 The fate of those who pervert faith in Christ and the Christian life is sketched out, in the eyes of the author, in that which overtook the most infamous evildoers of the Bible and which the Jewish literature of the period readily recounts. Thus, a few Biblical scenes are strung together: the people rebelling in the wilderness (Num 14:26-35; see 1 Cor 10:5); the fall of the mysterious heavenly beings that are likened to angels (Gen 6:1-3); the chastisement of the wicked cities (Gen 19:1-29); the punishment of Cain (Gen 4:1-24); the error of Balaam (Num 22:2—24:25; 31:16); the revolt of Korah (Num 16:1-35). Upon those whom he regards as liars, the author calls down the prophecy of judgment that is placed on the lips of Enoch, that ancestor whose mysterious destiny is scrutinized in Jewish literature (see Gen 5:18-24; Wis 4:10f; Lk 3:32-38; Heb 11:5).

Who, then, are these men who pervert the Gospel? They are people who delight in bizarre speculations, who go so far as to deny the lordship of Christ and forget his Person, his role, and his unique work. They insult celestial beings; they doubtless misunderstand the angels or want to judge their merits and their respective roles. Even the archangel Michael—according to the apocryphal book entitled *The Assumption of Moses*—left to God alone the task of condemning the devil (see Zec 3:2). They are spiritual in discourse but lax in morals and corruptors.

5 The first of three examples of divine punishment formerly meted out is that which befell those who had been saved but failed to keep the faith (see Num 14:28f).

6 The second example is taken from Gen 6:1-4 as elaborated in the apocryphal *Book of Enoch* (see Jude 14). Enoch says that the celestial beings let themselves be seduced by the "daughters of men." But in Jude as in 2 Pet 2:4, the statement that the angels sinned is not accompanied by any details.

7 The third example is taken from Gen 19:1-25. The townsmen of Sodom lusted not after human beings but after the strangers who were angels. The apocryphal *Testament of the Twelve Patriarchs,* like Jude 6-7, also compares the sin of the angels with that of the Sodomites.

8 The false teachers are undeterred by the punishment of the fallen angels (vv. 6-7). Yet they themselves, by their crime and punishment, are like those who were chastised in the Old Testament.

9 This is a reference to an incident recorded in the apocryphal *Assumption of Moses,* in which Michael the archangel has a dispute with the devil concerning who can claim Moses' body after his death. Jude argues that if an archangel refrained from reviling even the devil, mere human beings are certainly wrong to revile angels (*celestial beings*—v. 8).

these people pour abuse on anything they do
not understand, and the very things that they
know by instinct, like irrational animals, lead
to their destruction.[j]

11 Woe to them! They have followed in the
footsteps of Cain; they have abandoned
themselves to the error of Balaam for the
sake of gain; and they have perished in the
rebellion of Korah. *[k] 12 * They are blemish-
es at your love feasts, eating with you with-
out fear. They are shepherds who feed only
themselves. They are like clouds blown
about by winds without giving rain, or like
trees in autumn barren and uprooted and so
twice dead.[l] 13 They are like wild sea waves
whose foam reflects their shameless deeds,
or like wandering stars for whom the gloom
of darkness is stored up forever.[m]

14 *[n] Enoch, in the seventh generation
from Adam, also prophesied against them
when he said, "Behold, the Lord is coming
with tens of thousands of his saints,[o] 15 to
pronounce judgment on humanity and to
convict all the ungodly for all the godless
deeds that each has impiously committed
and for all the defiant words spoken against
him by godless sinners."[p] 16 These are grum-
blers and fault-finders. They indulge their
own passions, * and their mouths are full of
bombastic talk as they flatter others in order
to achieve their own ends.[q]

Appeal to the Faithful. 17 But you, dear
friends, must remember the predictions
made by the apostles of our Lord Jesus
Christ. *[r] 18 For they said to you, "In the final
age there will be scoffers who will follow
their own ungodly passions." *[s] 19 It is these
people who create divisions, who follow their
natural instincts and do not possess the
Spirit.[t]

A Program of the Christian Life.* 20 How-
ever, you, dear friends, must build yourselves
up in your most holy faith and pray in the
Holy Spirit.[u] 21 Keep yourselves in the love of
God as you await our Lord Jesus Christ in his
mercy, who will grant you eternal life.[v]

22 Have compassion for those who are
wavering.[w] 23 Save others by snatching them
out of the fire. And for still others have com-
passion mixed with fear, hating even the
tunic defiled by their bodies.[x]

Doxology.* 24 Now to him who is able to
keep you from falling and to bring you safe-
ly to his glorious presence, unblemished and
rejoicing,[y] 25 to the only God, our Savior,
through Jesus Christ, our Lord, be glory,
majesty, power, and authority, before all
time, now, and forevermore. Amen.[z]

---

j 2 Pet 2:12.—k Gen 4:8-16; Num 16:19-35; 31:15-16; 2 Pet 2:15; 1 Jn 3:12; Rev 2:14.—l Prov 25:14; Ezek 34:2, 8, 10; Mt 15:13; 1 Cor 11:20; Eph 4:14; 2 Pet 2:13, 17.—m Isa 57:20; Phil 3:19; 2 Pet 2:17.—n 14-15: Mt 16:27; Heb 12:22-23.—o Gen 5:18, 21-24; Deut 33:2; Zec 14:5.—p 1 Tim 1:9; 2 Pet 2:6-9.—q Jude 18; 1 Cor 10:10; 2 Pet 2:10, 18.—r Eph 4:11; Heb 2:3; 2 Pet 3:2.—s Jude 16; 1 Tim 4:1; 2 Tim 3:1-5; 2 Pet 3:3.—t 1 Cor 2:14; Jas 3:15.—u Jude 2-3; Eph 6:18; Col 2:7; 1 Thes 5:11.—v Mt 25:46; Tit 2:13; Heb 9:28; 2 Pet 3:12.—w 2 Tim 4:16.—x Am 4:11; Zec 3:2-5; 1 Cor 3:15; Rev 3:4.—y Rom 16:25; 2 Cor 4:14; Col 1:22; 1 Pet 4:13.—z Jn 5:44; Rom 11:36; 1 Tim 1:17; Heb 13:8.

---

11 The author gives three Old Testament personalities who each in some way illustrate the character of the false teachers: (1) *footsteps of Cain:* selfishness and hatred for a brother (see Gen 4:3f); (2) *error of Balaam:* surrendering integrity as a spiritual leader because of consuming greed (see note on 2 Pet 2:15); (3) *rebellion of Korah:* rebelling against God's appointed leadership (see Num 16). Thus, the false teachers are loveless, greedy, and insubordinate—and destruction is sure to overtake them.

12-13 Jude now characterizes the false teachers by the use of six graphic metaphors: (1) *blemishes at your love feasts:* see notes on 1 Cor 11:17-34; 11:27-34; and 2 Pet 2:13; (2) *shepherds who feed only themselves:* instead of caring for their sheep (see Ezek 34:8-10; Jn 10:12f); (3) *clouds blown about by winds without giving rain:* the false teachers promise much but give nothing; (4) *trees in autumn barren and uprooted and so twice dead:* once again, a figure of empty promises; (5) *wild sea waves whose foam reflects their shameless deeds:* their product is like the foam or scum at the seashore; (6) *wandering stars:* as these provide no guidance for navigation, neither do the false teachers give any reliable guide to the Christian life.

14-15 Cited from the noncanonical *Book of Enoch* 1:9, probably from memory. *Enoch, in the seventh generation from Adam:* cited from Enoch 60:8; this refers to the Enoch in the line of Seth (Gen 5:18-24; 1 Chr 1:1-3), not the one in the line of Cain (Gen 4:17). The *Book of Enoch* was highly respected by many Jews and Christians of that time.

16 *These are . . . passions:* suggested by Enoch 5:5.

17 This is a reference to the apostolic preaching received through tradition, to which Jude alluded in v. 3.

18 Right from the start, the apostolic catechesis had announced that Christians should not be astonished at the appearance of men full of delirium (see Acts 20:29-30). *In the final age . . . ungodly passions:* this does not seem to be an exact Scripture citation, but see Acts 20:29-31; 1 Tim 4:1; 2 Tim 3:1-5; 4:3; 2 Pet 3:3; see also Mt 24:24; Mk 13:22.

20-23 Jude now tells Christians how to contend for the faith. (1) They must build themselves up in their faith, which is the orthodox body of truth and practice received from the Apostles (see Acts 2:42; Rom 6:17; Gal 1:23); they do so by having fellowship with the Lord and his people, by continuing in the Gospel and in the Word of God, and by worshiping in spirit and truth—especially the Eucharist. (2) They must be a praying people (see Lk 18:1), praying in the Holy Spirit (see Rom 8:26-27; Gal 4:6; Eph 6:18) that God's Kingdom may come and his will may be done (see Mt 6:10-11). (3) They are to remain in God's love by imitating Jesus (Mt 16:24) and by mutual love and support (see 1 Jn 5:1-4). (4) They are to wait expectantly for the Second Coming and to keep their eyes on the mercy of Jesus that leads to eternal life (see v. 3). (5) They are to tend to those who waver, snatching others from the judgment, and maintain an attitude of pity and concern but keep their distance from the corruptors.

24-25 One of the greatest doxologies of the New Testament concludes this brief Letter. Remaining in the presence of the living God gives Christians the power to persevere and make progress. All this is due to Jesus Christ, who sums up in himself the majesty, the power, and the authority of God.

VISIONS OF HOPE

"And behold, I am with you always, to the end of the world" (Mt 28:20). Each of the Gospels ends with a chapter that leads into the time of the Church. The Acts of the Apostles and the Letters, especially those of Paul, attest to the spread of the Good News, the presence of the Lord in the life of the communities, and the action of the Spirit. True enough, the Christian message ran into many difficulties and much opposition; but these enabled Christians to understand better the originality of their faith and the urgency of missionary work. Besides, had not Jesus often predicted persecution for his disciples?

At some moments, however, persecution took the form of a systematic political plan that was well organized and efficiently carried out throughout the vast empire subject to Rome. The aim was to exterminate the Christian movement everywhere and completely.

Would Christianity be able to weather the storm? How were people not to waver? What was to be thought of these events, and, above all, how were Christians to be steadfast in their faith in the face of oppression?

Here, in the Book of Revelation or the Apocalypse, we have a first effort to interpret the signs of a difficult time. In hours of crisis the need is to revive profound convictions; this Book sets forth these convictions in its own vigorous way, which takes the form of visions.

"A white horse appeared. Its rider was called 'Faithful and True' . . . 'King of kings and Lord of lords' " *(Rev 19:11-16).*

THE BOOK OF REVELATION

The Age of the Martyrs

The resistance of Christians to worship of the emperor was a sure sign to the Roman authorities that they were trying to draw people away from it! The result was persecution: it had already occurred at the end of Nero's reign (the burning of Rome, A.D. 64), but now, and most especially, under Domitian (A.D. 81-96).

Was Christianity destined to disappear due to persecution by the public authorities? Or, at least, would not many Christians abandon the struggle? The time for protestations of loyalty to the Roman state was past (see Rom 13:1-7; Tit 3:1; 1 Pet 2:13-17); now it was necessary to resist, even to the acceptance of martyrdom.

A man, or group of people, experienced this anguish. Here he gives free rein to his protest against oppression and cries out a message of encouragement, and this on a grandiose stage: an enormous catastrophe strikes the earth, the present world disappears under the judgment of God, and a new world begins, the age of joy and God's salvation.

The author uses images we find bewildering, for in them the substance and the details change continually, and the most glaring colors are set in contrast; there are numerical sayings, each of which is thick with hidden meanings: everything is symbolical.

This is the kind of literature that is born in periods of disturbance. It is at such times that people speak of "apocalypses." The word means the act of revealing, of removing the veil. The author speaks on the basis of a vision that comes to him from above; the vision aims at unveiling the reality hidden in the future and the true meaning of what is coming, a meaning known only to God.

Understood in this way, an apocalypse is a special kind of prophecy. It is a reclusive literature because it is addressed to initiates and uses a mysterious language; it seeks to escape the surveillance of oppressors and of censors. It is a protest of conscience against intolerable pressures, a claim to a different vision of society and the world, a call to resistance in the midst of torment. The apocalyptic current entered the Bible beginning in the second century B.C.; at that time we find it especially in the Book of Daniel, in the Book of Joel, and in some passages of Isaiah (see chs. 24—27) and of Zechariah (chs. 9—11).

Furthermore, we must not forget the extraordinary descriptions given by Ezekiel. In the Jewish world all this material would be used in order to draw from it extremely subtle new constructs. We may recall the apocalypse in the Synoptic Gospels (Mk 13; Mt 24:10-36; Lk 17:22-37; 21:5-33) and certain passages of Paul (1 Thes 4:15-17; 2 Thes 2:1-12).

In this literary genre our Book of Revelation is a prime example. It was written at a difficult time, at the end of the first century, and aims, first, at quickening the life of the community in the face of internal crises (chs. 1—3).

Its primary purpose is to encourage these communities to stand up to the persecution that is inflicted on Christians when they refuse to offer sacrifice to the emperor (Rev 13:12-18; 14:9-13).

The author of this work calls himself "John" (Rev 1:1, 4, 9; 22:8) and describes himself to his readers as their "brother and partner in the suffering" (Rev 1:9), who has been exiled to the island of Patmos because of his faith.

He certainly belongs to the category of individuals whom the New Testament calls prophets (Rev 1:1-20; 22:9), and he enjoys great authority in the churches in the region of Asia Minor.

He does not, however, claim to be John the Apostle, son of Zebedee, with whom tradition has identified him; in fact, he never describes incidents of which he was an eyewitness, as the author of the fourth Gospel does.

There are undoubtedly many similarities with the Johannine writings, but the differences are even greater: the language is different; above all, the theological setting is different.

We do not, therefore, know anything specific about the author, whom the readers of his own time must have known. If we judge by the detailed knowledge and skill with which he handles the apocalyptic genre, he was, in all probability, of Jewish descent.

The Christian Apocalypse is not simply a song of God's power, but a splendid praise of Christ, who brings to fulfillment the destiny of the world through a breaking off of history.

It is also a book about the Church. In this new People of God, who are characterized by attachment to Christ, fidelity, and resistance, the most fascinating figures that emerge are the martyrs.

The Book of Revelation may be divided as follows:

Prologue (1:1-20)

I: Letters to the Churches (2:1—3:22)

II: Celestial Visions about What Is To Come (4:1—22:5)

Epilogue (22:6-21)

PROLOGUE

CHAPTER 1

The Revelation or Apocalypse of Jesus Christ.* 1 The revelation of Jesus Christ, which God entrusted to him so that he might show his servants what must soon take place. He made it known by sending his angel to his servant John, [a] 2 who has borne witness to the word of God and to the testimony of Jesus Christ by reporting everything that he has seen. [b]

3 Blessed * is the one who reads the words of this prophecy, and blessed are those who keep what is written in it, for the appointed time is near. [c]

He Is, He Was, and He Will Return.* 4 John, to the seven Churches * in Asia: grace to you and peace from him who is, who was, and who is to come, and from the seven spirits before his throne, [d] 5 and from Jesus Christ, the faithful witness, * the firstborn from the dead and the ruler of the kings of the earth. He loves us and has washed away our sins with his blood [e] 6 and made us to be a kingdom and priests to serve his God and Father—to him be glory and power forever and ever. Amen. *[f]

7 Behold, he is coming with the clouds;
every eye will see him,
even those who pierced him.
All the peoples of the earth will mourn him.
So shall it be. Amen. [g]

8 "I am the Alpha and the Omega," says the Lord God, "the one who is, and who was, and who is to come, the Almighty." [h]

"I Am the First and the Last."* 9 I, John—your brother and partner in the suffering and the kingdom and the patient endurance that are ours in Jesus—was on the island of

a Rev 1:19; 4:9; 19:10; 22:6-8, 20; Dan 2:28-29; Jn 12:49; 17:8.—b Rev 1:9; 6:9; 12:17; 19:10; 1 Cor 1:6; Heb 4:12.—c Rev 22:7; Lk 11:28; Rom 13:11.—d Rev 1:8, 11, 20; 3:1; 4:5, 8; 5:6; 11:17; 16:5; Ex 3:14; Isa 11:2; Rom 1:7.—e Rev 3:14; Isa 55:4; Jn 18:37; Rom 3:25; 8:37; 1 Cor 15:20; Col 1:18; 1 Tim 6:15; Heb 9:14; 1 Pet 1:19; 1 Jn 1:7.—f Rev 5:10; 20:6; Ex 19:6; Rom 11:36; 15:6; 1 Pet 2:5, 9.—g Dan 7:13; Zec 12:10; Mt 16:27; 24:30; Lk 17:10; Jn 19:37; 1 Cor 1:7; 1 Thes 2:19; 4:16-17.—h Rev 1:17; 4:8; 15:3; 19:6; 21:6; 22:13; Isa 41:4; 44:6; 48:12.

1:1-3 Christians are living in the last period of history. They are facing difficult times, and God's plan is questioned. More than ever, faithfulness to his plan is required. Here then is a vision of faith concerning what is happening. The one who attests to it, in the Name of Christ, is prepared to give testimony for it even by shedding his blood.

1:3 *Blessed:* this is the first of seven beatitudes that appear in the book (see Rev 14:13; 16:15; 19:9; 20:6; 22:7; 22:14). The word "blessed" is more all-encompassing than "happy"; it indicates the favorable conditions in which God has placed a person (see Ps 1:1; Mt 5:3). *Prophecy:* i.e., any word from God, whether it foretells the future, commands, instructs, or sets forth history.

1:4-8 The greeting and the address introduce the work as a letter. *[He] who is:* this is how God revealed himself to Moses at the burning bush (Ex 3:14); this time, the divine name embraces the past, present, and future of humankind and is turned to the future, to the immediate fulfillment of all things: God, he *who is to come.* God is also described with the first and last letters of the Greek alphabet, *Alpha and . . . Omega*; he is *the Beginning and the End*, the origin and the completion (a proper name of God according to Isa 44:6; 48:12). In addition, he is the master of all historical events, including the pres-ent ones, which, according to the author, are decisive. And Christ will appear in all the glory of his Resurrection and in the grandeur of the work accomplished to save humankind, comprising the body of the Church (see 1 Pet 2:5, 9), in the imminence of his coming to *judge the world.*

In order to speak of him, the author here multiplies Biblical reminiscences (Ex 19:6; Ps 89:28, 38; Isa 55:3). The seven spirits before the throne (v. 4) represent the Holy Spirit in the many ways that the Spirit manifests himself in the world (e.g., Isa 11:2, 5).

1:4 *Seven Churches:* the Churches (named in v. 11) formed a circle in the province of Asia and were separated from one another by some fifty miles.

1:5 *Faithful witness:* the Messiah is the witness to the promise the Lord made to David (2 Sam 7:1; Ps 89; Isa 55:3-4; Zec 12:8) in his person as well as in his work. He also fulfills this promise and is thus the efficacious Word, God's Yes (see Rev 3:14; 19:11, 13; 2 Cor 1:20). He is the heir of David (see Rev 5:5; 22:16) but also the firstborn from the dead because of his Resurrection (see Col 1:18) who will rule the universe after his enemies have been overcome (see Rev 19:6; Dan 7:14).

1:6 Those who follow Christ will be part of a kingdom, because they will rule over all the nations (see Isa 54:11-17; Dan 7:22, 27; Zec 12:1-3; see Rev 2:26; 5:10; 20:6; 22:5). They will also be priests because like Jesus the Priest they offer up the sacrifice of their own lives as a burnt offering of love.

1:9-20 The author describes himself as a Christian who has been exiled to a little island that lay off the coast of Miletus and Ephesus and was known as a prison island. Before his eyes the risen Christ appears. The majestic description derives its images from the portrait of the Son of Man in chs. 7 and 10 of the Book of Daniel. The description of his stance and clothing suggests majesty and power; this being who is master of life possesses the secret of all things and holds even the realm of death subject to him (v. 18).

The netherworld, or the lower world (Hebrew: *Sheol;* not to be confused with hell, the place of eternal damnation), is a localization of the realm of death, where, it is imagined, the dead dwell, deprived of the ability to perform any existential act. Another term for it is *Hades.* Christ has the power to release souls from the netherworld (see Jn 5:26-28).

The very figure of Christ shows the judgment to be imminent. But he is also present in the life of the Churches, and the author lists seven of them (seven is the number symbolizing universality).

The text speaks of the angels of the Churches; according to the religious vision of the world at that time, some heavenly representatives presided over the destinies of cities, peoples, and Churches. The seer might be speaking of the earthly persons in charge of the Churches. However, the Churches are also in the power of Christ and under his protection.

What is happening now, and what will take place afterward (v. 19): these words anticipate the two main parts of the work.

Patmos* because I had proclaimed the word of God and given testimony to Jesus.[i] 10 On the Lord's day, I was caught up in the spirit,* and I heard behind me a loud voice, like the sound of a trumpet,[j] 11 that said, "Write down on a scroll* what you see and send it to the seven Churches: to Ephesus, Smyrna, Pergamum, Thyatira, Sardis, Philadelphia, and Laodicea."[k]

12 Then I turned to see whose voice it was that had spoken to me, and when I turned I beheld seven gold lampstands.[l] 13 * And in the midst of the lampstands I saw one like a son of man,* dressed in a robe that reached down to his feet and with a golden breastplate around his chest.[m] 14 His head and his hair were white with the whiteness of wool, like snow, and his eyes were like a burning flame.[n] 15 His feet were like burnished bronze refined in a furnace, and his voice was like the sound of rushing waters.[o] 16 In his right hand he held seven stars. From his mouth there protruded a sharp, two-edged sword, and his face shone like the sun in all its brilliance.[p]

17 When I saw him, I fell at his feet as though dead, but he laid his right hand on me and said, "Do not be afraid. I am the First and the Last. I am the Living One.[q] 18 I was dead, but now I am alive forevermore, and I hold the keys to death and the netherworld.[r]

19 "Now write down what you have seen, what is happening now, and what will take place afterward.[s] 20 The mystery of the seven stars that you saw in my right hand, and of the seven gold lampstands, is this: the seven stars are the angels of the seven Churches, and the seven lampstands are the seven Churches themselves.[t]

I: LETTERS TO THE CHURCHES*

CHAPTER 2

To Ephesus.* 1 "To the angel of the Church in Ephesus,* write:

"'These are the words of the one who holds the seven stars in his right hand and who walks in the midst of the seven lampstands:[u]

2 "'"I know your deeds, your hard work, and your endurance. I know that you cannot tolerate wicked people, and how you have put to the test those who claim to be apostles but are not, and have found them to be impostors.[v] 3 I am also aware of your perse-

i Rev 1:1-2, 6; Acts 14:22; 2 Cor 1:7; Phil 4:14; 2 Tim 2:12; Heb 4:12.—j Rev 4:2; 17:3; 21:10; Ex 20:18; Acts 20:7.—k Rev 1:4, 19, 20; 2:8, 12, 18, 24; 3:1, 7, 14; Acts 16:14; 18:19; Col 2:1.—l Rev 1:20; 2:1; Ex 25:31-40; Zec 4:2.—m Rev 2:1; 4:14; 15:6; Isa 6:1; Ezek 1:26; Dan 7:13; 10:5, 16.—n Rev 2:18; 19:12; Dan 7:9.—o Rev 2:18; 14:2; 19:6; Ezek 1:7; 43:2.—p Rev 1:20; 2:1, 12, 16; 3:1; 19:15; Jdg 5:31; Isa 1:20; 49:2; Mt 17:2; Heb 4:12.—q Rev 1:8; 2:8; 22:13; Isa 41:4; 44:6; Ezek 1:28; Dan 8:18.—r Rev 2:8; 4:9-10;10:6; 15:7; 20:1; Deut 32:40; Rom 6:9.—s Rev 1:11; Hab 2:2.—t Rev 1:4, 12, 16; Mt 5:14-15.—u Rev 1:12-13, 16; Acts 18:19.—v Rev 2:19; 3:1, 8, 15; 2 Cor 11:13; 1 Jn 4:1.

1:9 *Patmos:* a small island in the Aegean Sea about 50 miles from Ephesus. According to the third-century Church historian Eusebius, John the Apostle was released from Patmos under the emperor Nerva (A.D. 96-98).

1:10 *In the spirit:* i.e., in a state of spiritual ecstasy (see also Rev 4:2; 17:3; and 21:10). *The Lord's day:* Sunday. In the Old Testament the expression "Day of the Lord" signifies some special intervention of God in history. For Christians, the eschatological age is the last times that have begun with the Resurrection of Christ; to celebrate the Lord's day means therefore to commemorate his Paschal victory and to hasten his return (see Acts 20:7; 1 Cor 11:26; 2 Pet 3:12; see also the present-day liturgical acclamations after the consecration of the Eucharist).

1:11 *Scroll:* pieces of papyrus or parchment sewn together and rolled up. The book form came into use some time in the second century.

1:13-15 Jesus appears in garments that are priestly (the habit or long tunic) and royal (the golden breastplate). The white hair is a symbol of eternity; the flaming eyes signify omniscience, and the bronze feet, immutability. He is also a Judge, prepared to sentence those who are unfaithful (see Rev 2:16; 19:15; Isa 49:2; Eph 6:17; Heb 4:12). One or other of his attributes as Judge is used by the author at the beginning of each of the seven letters to indicate the circumstances of the Church addressed.

1:13 *Son of man:* see note on Mt 8:20.

2:1—3:21 Christian communities at the end of the first century found themselves faced with difficulties that were substantially the same as those faced by the Church in every age, from the Passover of Christ to the end of history. The real struggle was and would be that of fidelity in the midst of constant renewal. The letters here are addressed to seven Churches of Asia Minor; the number seven is symbolic, in the sense that these communities represent all the Churches with their difficulties and problems, their efforts to be faithful, and their undertakings.

Each letter follows the same pattern: Christ comes on the scene bearing one of the symbols listed in the great vision of Rev 1:9-20; he judges the communities according to their deficiencies, their fidelity, and their constancy; then he concludes with the promise of final victory.

In every age each community and each believer will read these letters in order to submit to the Lord's judgment and to hear once again his call. Addressed as they are to angels who, according to the religious thinking of the time, were regarded as presiding over the destiny of a community, they envisage first of all the leaders of the communities.

2:1-7 Under the pretext of Christian spirituality and freedom, a sect that, certainly without justification, claims reliance on one of the first deacons, Nicholas (see Acts 6:5), allows itself the most serious moral deviations and takes part very freely in pagan worship. (A similar group at Pergamum holds the teaching of Balaam [vv. 14-15], and a third at Thyatira follows the woman Jezebel [v. 20]. All three groups are usually termed Nicolaitans.)

The community of Ephesus does resist the danger that threatens it, but unfortunately in its effort to be faithful it has become judgmental. It has lost its charity. The time has come for it to be renewed. Otherwise, the community will lose its place. What a perspective is thus opened for fidelity! A new access to the tree of life militates against succumbing to sin (see Gen 2:9; 3:22-24); expressed in Jewish language, it is the hope of an unending life.

2:1 *Ephesus:* see introduction to the Letter to the Ephesians.

verance and how you have toiled for my
name without becoming weary. [w]

4 “ ‘ “However, I have this complaint
against you: you have lost the love you had at
first. [x] 5 Remember from where you have
fallen. Repent and do as you did originally.
Otherwise, unless you repent, I will come to
you and remove your lampstand from its
place. [y] 6 Nonetheless, this may be said in
your favor: you detest the works of the
Nicolaitans, which I also hate. [z]

7 “ ‘ “Whoever has ears should listen to
what the Spirit says * to the Churches. To
anyone who is victorious, I will give the
right to eat from the tree of life that is in the
paradise of God.” ’ [a]

To Smyrna.* 8 “To the angel of the Church
in Smyrna, * write:

“ ‘These are the words of the First and
the Last, who was dead and came to life
again: [b]

9 “ ‘ “I know of your hardships and your
poverty, but in reality you are rich. I am
aware of the slander of those who claim to
be Jews but are actually members of the syn-
agogue of Satan. [c] 10 Do not be frightened
when thinking about the sufferings that you
will have to endure. The devil will throw
some of you into prison so that you may be
tested, and you will endure affliction for ten
days. Remain faithful until death, and I will
give you the crown of life. [d]

11 “ ‘ “Whoever has ears should listen to
what the Spirit says to the Churches.
Anyone who is victorious will not be
harmed by the second death.” ’ [e]

To Pergamum.* 12 “To the angel of the
Church in Pergamum, * write:

“ ‘These are the words of the one who has
the sharp double-edged sword: [f]

13 “ ‘ “I know that you live in the place
where Satan is enthroned. Yet you have
remained firm in support of my name, and
you did not deny your faith in me even at
the time when Antipas, * my faithful wit-
ness, was put to death among you, where
Satan lives. [g]

14 “ ‘ “Nevertheless, I have a few things
against you. Some of you are holding to the
teaching of Balaam, * who instructed Balak
to place temptations in the path of the
Israelites, encouraging them to eat food sac-
rificed to idols and to engage in fornication. [h]
15 Likewise, there are some of you
who follow the teaching of the Nicolaitans. [i]
16 Therefore, repent. If you do not do so, I will
come to you quickly and attack them with
the sword of my mouth. [j]

17 “ ‘ “Whoever has ears should listen to
what the Spirit says to the Churches. To any-
one who is victorious I will give some of the
hidden manna. I will also give him a white
stone, upon which will be inscribed a new
name, known only to the person who
receives it.” ’ [k]

---

w Jn 15:21.—x Jer 2:2; Mt 24:12.—y Rev 1:20; 2:16, 22; 3:3, 19.—z Rev 2:15.—a Rev 2:11, 17, 29; 3:6, 13, 22; 13:9; 22:2, 14, 19; Gen 2:9; 3:22-24; Mt 11:15; Lk 23:43; Jn 16:33.—b Rev 1:11, 17-18.—c Rev 2:13, 24; 3:9; Mt 4:10; 2 Cor 6:10; Jas 2:5.—d Rev 2:13; 3:10; 17:14; Mt 10:22; 1 Cor 9:26.—e Rev 2:7; 20:6, 14; 21:8.—f Rev 1:11, 16; 2:16.—g Rev 1:5; 2:9, 24; 11:3; 14:12; Mt 4:10.—h Rev 2:20; Num 22—24; 25:1-3; 31:16; Acts 15:20; 1 Cor 6:13; 2 Pet 2:15; Jude 11.—i Rev 2:6.—j Rev 1:16; 2:5; 2 Thes 2:8.—k Rev 2:7; 19:12; Isa 62:2; 65:15; Jn 6:49, 50; 16:33.

2:7 *Whoever has ears should listen to what the Spirit says . . . :* this formula concludes each of the seven letters and stresses the role of the Spirit in Christ's relation with his Church. *Anyone who is victorious:* i.e., anyone who clings to the faith in the face of persecution. *Right to eat from the tree of life:* a right lost by our first parents but now restored by Christ who abrogated the decree that excluded human beings from the tree of life. God and humans are restored to the perfect fellowship that existed before the advent of sin.

2:8-11 Those Jews who did not acknowledge Christ as the one who fulfilled their hope, nor the Church as the true Israel, slandered the Christian community. They were regarded as partisans of the forces of opposition represented by Satan. However, the Christians must take courage, for the trial will last only for ten days, i.e., it will be of short duration—the reward for a life in God is near. Believers will escape the second death, i.e., defeat and definitive perdition at the judgment of God.

2:8 *Smyrna:* a city closely aligned with Rome that housed a large Jewish population hostile to Christians (see Acts 14:2, 19; 17:5, 13). One of the most famous early martyrs, Polycarp, was bishop of Smyrna.

2:12-17 In this city, a main center of emperor worship, the presence of Satan is visible. Deviant heresies, like that of the Nicolaitans, glorify participation in pagan forms of worship and in the moral disorders they represent, which in the eyes of the Old Testament is tantamount to prostitution. The episode of Balaam is evoked to stigmatize these wanderings of the conscience of believers (see Num 25:3; 31:16). The reward is illustrated by two symbols: the *manna,* i.e., the food of life (see Ps 78:24f), evokes all the blessings God bestows on those who remain faithful to him, blessings of which the Eucharist is the sign (see Ex 16:32-34; 2 Mac 2:4-8; Heb 9:4); the *white stone* probably recalls the stones upon which Greeks wrote the names of the candidates for whom they were voting in elections. God chooses us.

2:12 *Pergamum:* the ancient capital of Asia, built on a hill. Its name means "citadel" in Greek and is the origin of the word "parchment." It was the center of emperor worship in Asia.

2:13 *Antipas:* the first martyr of Asia, who was put to death under the emperor Domitian.

2:14 *Teaching of Balaam:* Balaam counseled the Midianite women on how to lead the Israelites astray (see Num 25:1-2; 31:16; see also Jude 11); thus he is the exemplar of teachers who lead the faithful into becoming completely worldly-minded.

To Thyatira.* 18 “To the angel of the Church
in Thyatira, * write:

“ ‘These are the words of the Son of God
who has eyes like a burning flame and feet
like burnished bronze: [l]

19 “ ‘ “I know your deeds—your love, your
faithfulness, your service, and your
endurance—and that you are doing greater
works than you did at first. [m] 20 Neverthe-
less, I have this against you, that you toler-
ate that woman Jezebel, who calls herself a
prophetess and who by her teaching is lur-
ing my servants into acts of fornication and
encouraging them to eat food that has been
sacrificed to idols. [n]

21 “ ‘ “I have given her time to repent, but
she refuses to repent of her fornication. [o]
22 So I will cast her onto a bed of pain, and all
those who commit adultery with her will
suffer intensely unless they renounce her
practices. [p] 23 I will also strike her children
dead. Thereby all the Churches will be
shown that I am the one who searches
minds and hearts and I will give to each of
you what your works deserve. [q]

24 “ ‘ “And I say to the rest of you in
Thyatira who have not accepted this teach-
ing and who have no knowledge of what are
designated as the deep secrets of Satan, * I
shall not impose any further burden on you, [r]
25 but hold firmly to what you have until I
come. [s]

26 “ ‘ “To anyone who is victorious
and perseveres in doing my works
until the end,
I will give authority over the nations, [t]
27 the same authority that I received
from my Father,
to rule them with an iron rod
and shatter them like clay pots. [u]

28 And to such a person I will also give the
morning star. [v]

29 “ ‘ “Whoever has ears should listen to
what the Spirit says to the Churches.” ’ [w]

CHAPTER 3

To Sardis.* 1 “To the angel of the Church in
Sardis, * write:

“ ‘These are the words of the one who has
the seven spirits of God and the seven
stars: [x]

“ ‘ “I know your deeds. You have a reputa-
tion for being alive, but you are dead. 2 Be
on guard and strengthen what remains and
is at the point of death. For I have not found
any of your deeds perfect in the sight of my
God. [y] 3 Therefore, remember the teaching
that you have received and heard. Hold on
to it and repent. If you do not wake up, I
will come like a thief, and you will never
know at what hour I will come upon you. [z]

4 “ ‘ “However, there are still a few in
Sardis who have not soiled their robes, and
they will walk with me dressed in white, for
they are worthy. [a] 5 Anyone who is victorious
will be dressed like these in white robes, and
I shall not blot his name from the book of
life. * Rather, I shall acknowledge it in the
presence of my Father and his angels. [b]

6 “ ‘ “Whoever has ears should listen to
what the Spirit says to the Churches.” ’ [c]

l Rev 1:11, 14, 15; 2:18; Mt 4:3; Acts 16:14.—m Rev 2:2.—n Rev 2:14; 1 Ki 16:31; 21:2; 2 Ki 9:7; Acts 15:20.—o Rev 9:20; 16:9, 11; Rom 2:4; 2 Pet 3:9.—p Rev 17:2; 18:9.—q 1 Sam 16:7; 1 Ki 8:39; Prov 21:2; Jer 11:20; 17:10; Mt 16:27; Lk 16:15; Rom 8:27.—r Rev 22:12; Acts 15:28; 1 Cor 2:10.—s Rev 3:11; Mt 16:27.—t Rev 12:5; Ps 2:8-9; Mt 10:22; Jn 16:33.—u Rev 12:5; 19:15; Isa 30:14; Jer 19:11.—v Rev 22:16.—w Rev 2:7.—x Rev 1:4, 11, 16; 2:2; 1 Tim 5:6.—y Rev 16:15; Mt 24:42-43; 1 Thes 5:2; 2 Pet 3:10.—z Rev 2:5; Mt 24:14; Mk 13:33; Lk 12:39; 1 Thes 5:2; 2 Pet 3:10.—a Rev 3:5, 18; 4:4; 6:11; 7:13-14; Jude 23.—b Rev 3:4; 20:12; Ps 69:29; Dan 12:1; Mt 10:32; Jn 16:33.—c Rev 2:7.

2:18-29 A prophetess, who is compared to Jezebel of sad memory in the Books of the Kings of Israel (see 1 Ki 16:31; 2 Ki 9:22), is inciting Christians to take part in idolatrous worship. Some, who are doubtless Nicolaitans, believed that they could obtain a deeper religious knowledge through a mysterious initiation. Believers cling to Christ. He will be at their side on the Day of Judgment, according to the classic images of Psalm 2. The *morning star* is the symbol of the Resurrection and its power—for Jesus rose from the dead just before dawn, the time when the morning star is visible.

2:18 *Thyatira:* a military outpost noted for its trade guilds.

2:24 *The deep secrets of Satan:* perhaps the esoteric teaching of the Nicolaitans.

3:1-6 This community seems to be dead! Hence, it is urged to change and become spiritually alive. From now on people must align themselves with Christ (see Mt 10:32). Those who truly follow Jesus will one day be clad in a white garment, which recalls the white garment worn by Jesus at the Transfiguration and Resurrection. It was the garment already being given at Baptism.

3:1 *Sardis:* capital of the ancient kingdom of Lydia, it was a wealthy and famous city.

3:5 Those who are victorious are promised three things: (1) they will receive white garments like those Christ will give to the faithful Sardinians; (2) their names will never be blotted out of the book of life; and (3) their names will be acknowledged by Christ in the presence of the Father and his angels.

White garments symbolize God’s righteousness, victory, and glory (see Rev 3:18; 6:11; 7:9, 13f; 19:14). The *book of life* is a reference to the divine register in which the names of the redeemed are written (see Rev 13:8; 17:8; 20:12, 15; 21:27; Dan 12:1; Phil 4:3). Christians who were loyal to Christ were continually threatened with being stripped of their citizenship in cities they inhabited, i.e., having their names blotted out of the city’s register. Christ’s acknowledgment of them in heaven offers an eternal, safe citizenship in his eternal Kingdom (see Mt 10:32; Lk 12:8).

To Philadelphia.* 7 "To the angel of the
Church in Philadelphia, * write:

" 'These are the words of the holy one,
the true one,
who has the key of David,
who opens the door,
and no one can shut it;
who closes the door,
and no one can open it: [d]

8 " ' "I know your deeds. I have set before
you an open door * that no one will be able
to close. I know that your strength is limit-
ed, yet you have kept my word and have
not disowned my name. [e] 9 Behold, I will
make those of the synagogue of Satan who
claim to be Jews but are not, for they are
lying—I will make them come and fall
down at your feet and recognize that I have
loved you. [f]

10 " ' "Because you have kept my word to
endure patiently, I will keep you safe during
the time of trial that is going to come upon
the whole world to put the inhabitants of the
earth to the test. [g] 11 I am coming soon. Hold
fast to what you already have so that no one
may rob you of your crown. [h]

12 " ' "Anyone who is victorious I will make
into a pillar in the temple of my God, and
never again will he depart from it. I will
inscribe on him the name of my God and the
name of the city of my God, the new
Jerusalem, which is coming down out of
heaven from my God, as well as my own new
name.* [i]

13 " ' "Whoever has ears should listen to
what the Spirit says to the Churches." ' [j]

To Laodicea.* 14 "To the angel of the
Church in Laodicea, * write:

" 'These are the words of the Amen, the
faithful and true witness, the source of God's
creation: [k]

15 " ' "I know your deeds, that you are nei-
ther cold nor hot. I wish you were either hot
or cold. [l] 16 As it is, since you are lukewarm,
neither cold nor hot, * I will spit you out of
my mouth. 17 For you say, 'I am rich; I have
prospered; I have everything I want,' never
realizing that you are wretched, pitiable,
poor, blind, and naked. * [m]

18 " ' "I advise you to buy from me gold
that has been refined by fire so that you will
be truly rich, and white robes to clothe you
so that you may keep the shame of your
nakedness from being seen, and ointment to
smear on your eyes so that you may see. [n] 19 I
reprove and discipline all those whom I
love. * Therefore, be sincere in your desire to
repent. [o]

20 " ' "Behold, I am standing at the door,
knocking. If one of you hears my voice and
opens the door, I will come in and dine with
that person and that person with me. [p] 21 To
anyone who is victorious, I will give the right
to sit with me on my throne, as I myself
overcame and sat with my Father on his
throne. [q]

22 " ' "Whoever has ears should listen to
what the Spirit says to the Churches." ' " [r]

d Rev 1:11; 6:10; 19:11; Isa 22:22; Mt 6:19; Mk 1:24; 1 Jn 5:20.—e Rev 2:2, 13; Acts 14:27.—f Rev 9:2; Isa 45:14; 49:23; 60:14; Rom 8:37.—g Rev 2:10; 6:10; 8:13; 11:10; 13:8, 14; 17:8; Mt 24:14; 2 Pet 2:9.—h Rev 2:25; 22:7, 20; Mt 16:27; 1 Cor 9:25.—i Rev 14:1; 21:2-3; 22:4; Ezek 48:35; Jn 16:33; Gal 2:9; 4:26.—j Rev 2:7, 11, 17; 2:29; 3:6, 13, 22; 21:2, 10; 22:16.—k Rev 1:5, 11; Col 1:16, 18; 2:1; Jn 1:3; 18:37.—l Rev 2:2; Rom 12:11.—m Prov 13:7; Hos 12:8; Lk 12:21; 1 Cor 4:8.—n Rev 3:4; 16:15; 1 Pet 1:7.—o Rev 2:5; Deut 8:5; Prov 3:11-12; 1 Cor 11:32; Heb 12:5-11.—p Mt 24:33; Lk 12:36; Rom 8:10; Jas 5:9.—q Rev 5:5; Mt 19:28; Lk 22:28-30; Jn 16:33.—r Rev 2:7; 3:6.

3:7-13 The Messiah, Son of David—who holds all power over the lot of the People of God, according to the image of Isa 22:22—addresses himself to the community of Philadelphia. Like the Church of Smyrna, it was suffering persecution, but it remained faithful. The reward of those who are faithful is evoked in symbolic terms: they will live in God's dwelling and meet God; they will be members of Christ's Body, bearing his name and sharing his lot.

3:7 *Philadelphia:* the gateway to the central plateau in the province of Asia. *The holy one, the true one:* see Rev 6:10 and Isa 40:25; Hab 3:2-3; Mk 1:24. *Key of David:* Christ is the Davidic Messiah empowered to control entrance into the Kingdom (see Isa 22:22; Mt 16:19).

3:8 The open door may refer to the missionary apostolate.

3:12 *Inscribe on him . . . my own new name:* this may be a name that characterizes his redemptive work and will not be known until the Second Coming or the name "the Word" (see Rev 19:13).

3:14-22 Christ cannot bear lukewarmness, since he is the "Amen," the one who commits himself completely (see 2 Cor 1:19-20). By his love he urges people to change their lives. He stands at the door and knocks, i.e., his coming is imminent (see Mk 13:29; Lk 12:35; 22:16). This may seem to be a threat, but it is above all a wonderful invitation—the invitation to share the most lovable intimacy with Christ, of which the Eucharistic Banquet is the inauguration. He invites us to be at his side when the Judgment and the destiny of the world are fulfilled.

3:14 *Laodicea:* a very wealthy city known for its banks, medical school, and textile industry as well as its lack of sufficient water, to each of which the letter alludes. *Amen:* a divine title (see Isa 65:16) applied to Christ (see 2 Cor 1:20). *Source of God's creation:* a concept that is found in Jn 1:3; Col 1:16f; Heb 1:2; see also Prov 8:22-31; Wis 9:1f.

3:16 *Lukewarm, neither cold nor hot:* i.e., complacent, self-satisfied, and indifferent to the real issues of faith in Christ—hence, lacking in zeal and useless.

3:17 *Never realizing that you are . . . naked:* the spiritual wretchedness of the community of Laodicea in contrast to its material prosperity. The Laodiceans may have interpreted their material wealth as a blessing from God and were thus deceived into thinking that their spiritual state was better than it truly was.

3:19 *I . . . discipline all those whom I love:* see Job 5:17; Ps 94:12; Prov 3:11f; 1 Cor 11:32; Heb 12:5-11.

II: CELESTIAL VISIONS ABOUT WHAT IS TO COME*

A: Christ, Lord of History*

CHAPTER 4

Vision of the Throne.* 1 Following this, I had
a vision of heaven with an open door, and I
heard the voice like a trumpet that I had
heard speaking to me before, saying, "Come
up here, and I will show you what must take
place after this." [s] 2 [t] At once I was caught up
in the spirit, * and there in heaven I beheld a
throne. [u] 3 Seated upon the throne was one
whose appearance was similar to that of
jasper and carnelian, and surrounding it was
a rainbow that looked like an emerald. [v]

4 Encircling the throne were twenty-four
thrones, and seated on them were twenty-
four elders, * dressed in white with gold
crowns on their heads. [w] 5 Emanating from
the throne were flashes of lightning and
rumblings and peals of thunder. Burning in
front of the throne were seven flaming
lamps, the seven spirits of God, [x] 6 and in
front of the throne there was something like
a sea of glass as transparent as crystal.

In the center of the throne and around it
there were four living creatures, * and they
were covered with eyes in front and in
back. [y] 7 The first living creature resembled a
lion, the second resembled an ox, the third
had a human face, and the fourth resembled
an eagle in flight. [z] 8 Each of the four living
creatures had six wings, and all of them
were covered with eyes all around and
underneath their wings. Day and night they
never stop saying:

"Holy, holy, holy
is the Lord God, the Almighty,
who was, and who is, and who is to
come." [a]

9 And whenever the living creatures give
glory and honor and thanks to the one who

s Rev 1:10, 19; 11:12; 22:6; Mt 3:16.—t 2-3: Isa 6:1; Ezek 1:26-28.—u Rev 1:10; 4:9-10; 20:11; 1 Ki 22:19.—v Rev 10:1; 21:11, 19.—w Rev 3:4-5; 4:10; 5:6, 8, 14; 11:16; 19:4; Isa 24:23.—x Rev 1:4; 8:5; 11:16; 16:18.—y Rev 4:8, 9; 5:6; 6:1; 7:11; 15:2; 19:4; Ex 24:10.—z Ezek 1:10; 10:14.—a Rev 1:4, 8, 11, 17; 4:6; 14:11; 16:5; Isa 6:2-3; Ezek 1:18.

4:1—22:5 In antiquity, books took the form of large scrolls. Thus, the most important and difficult part of the Book of Revelation is presented to us as a well-sealed scroll; the seals must be broken and, as they are, the visions unfold one after the other. In their main lines these visions intersect according to the classic plan of an apocalypse. After a grandiose inaugural vision (chs. 4 and 5), there is the prelude of events to come (Rev 6:1—11:9): it is the history of Israel, whose fall under the blows of the Roman armies is regarded as a judgment of God on his people. Then follow the trials and confrontations of the decisive moment (Rev 12:1—20:15): the nations come before us, slaves to the powers of evil that oppose the plan of God, who wants to save human beings. The Roman empire is certainly in the forefront. The Judgment will be even more terrible than that of Jerusalem if they remain hostile to Christ the Lord, to his Gospel, and to his Church. In any case, the great battle between God and the wicked powers will end with the extermination of these powers. Then, the drama can be resolved in the final accomplishment (Rev 21:1—22:15): God creates a new world reserved for his Elect.

But must we read, in this succession of numberless visions, the sketches of a mysterious calendar, a succession of events to come? The whole would then appear terribly supercharged, badly ordered, and—in a nutshell—incoherent. Doubtless, one can imagine that the elements of two different apocalypses—each redacted according to a similar movement—have been poorly coordinated, in a single book. But the author multiplies images and explanations to such an extent as to disconcert and baffle us. Yet, these events are described in such an ambiguous manner that they could be applied to all times. These things are always happening; we should always be ready for the end.

4:1—5:14 This is a view of history imparted by faith. The Book suggests it by immediately transporting us to the throne of God where the destinies of the universe are decided. Images are multiplied to suggest in advance and to represent the hidden meaning of history. This inaugural vision places the readers in the worship of God; it confirms the role of Christ as Master of the history of the world.

4:1-11 Emperors are entertained like gods and are thought to have power over the world's destiny. The truth is far different. Who indeed can open the door of the true God's dwelling and express the greatness of his life and plan? Here are innumerable symbols orchestrated like a brilliant symphony. Everything is inaccessible greatness: the peace of the light, the dread of the All-powerful, the power that dominates the universe, the perfect knowledge of all things. All this is what is proclaimed in these images.

Already present around God are the fathers, those great ancestors whose sacred history faith proclaims (see Sir 44—50; Heb 10—12); for he is the God of the living and not of the dead, the God of Abraham, Isaac, and Jacob, as Jesus attests in the Gospel (see Mk 12:26-27). The great manifestations (or epiphanies) of God depicted in the Old Testament are an invitation to adore God, and the author was inspired by them. We recognize the themes of Isaiah in the temple (see Isa 6) and especially the images of Ezekiel (see Ezek 1 and 10). In this way, the Jews were wont to express God's domination over the universe.

Thus, the sea, always felt to be a savage and hostile power, was itself tamed by the all-powerful God. All the forces of heaven that can be imagined—for example, those to which are attributed the government of the seasons and the rhythm of time, the four living creatures that represent the best of creation—are at the service of God. All these symbols form a great hymn to the Creator.

4:2 *In the spirit:* see note on Rev 1:10.

4:4 The *elders* exercise a priestly and royal role: they praise and adore God, offer him the prayers of the faithful, assist him in governing the world, and share in his power. The number twenty-four corresponds perhaps to the twenty-four classes or divisions of priests in 1 Chr 24:1-9, or to the twelve patriarchs plus the twelve apostles. They thus represent salvation history.

4:6 The *four living creatures* represent the created world that reveals God's goodness and power. Their many eyes symbolize the universal knowledge and providence of God. They continue to give glory to God through their work in creation. Their forms (*lion, ox, human, eagle*) represent what is noblest, strongest, wisest, and most agile in the created world. Ever since St. Irenaeus, Christian tradition had seen in them symbols of the evangelists Mark, Luke, Matthew, and John, respectively.

sits on the throne, who lives forever and
ever,[b] 10 the twenty-four elders prostrate
themselves before him who is seated on the
throne and worship the one who lives for-
ever and ever. As they lay down their crowns
in front of the throne, they cry out:[c]

11 "Worthy are you, O Lord our God,
to receive glory and honor and power,
for you created all things;
by your will they were created
and have their being."[d]

CHAPTER 5

Vision of the Lamb.* 1 Then I saw in the
right hand of the one who was seated on the
throne a scroll with writing on both sides
and sealed with seven seals.[e] 2 And I beheld
a mighty angel who proclaimed in a loud
voice, "Who is worthy to open the scroll and
break its seals?"[f] 3 But there was no one in
heaven or on earth or under the earth who
was able to open the scroll and examine it.

4 I began to weep bitterly because no one
was found worthy to open the scroll and
examine it. 5 Then one of the elders said to
me, "Do not weep. The Lion of the tribe of
Judah, the Root of David, has triumphed,
and thus has won the right to open the scroll
and its seven seals."[g]

6 Then I saw, standing in the center of the
throne, encircled by the four living creatures
and the elders, a Lamb that had been slain.
He had seven horns and seven eyes, which
are the seven spirits of God sent forth into
the entire world.[h] 7 He came forward and
took the scroll from the right hand of the one
who was seated on the throne.[i]

8 When he had taken the scroll, the four
living creatures and the twenty-four elders
prostrated themselves before the Lamb.
Each of the elders was holding a harp, and
they had gold bowls filled with incense,
which are the prayers of the saints.[j] 9 They
sang a new song: *

"You are worthy to receive the scroll
and to open its seals,
for you were slain,
and with your blood you purchased for
God
people of every tribe and language,
nation and race.[k]
10 You have made them to be a kingdom
and priests to serve our God,
and they will reign on earth."[l]

11 In my vision, I heard the voices of a mul-
titude of angels who surrounded the throne
and the living creatures and the elders.
These angels numbered thousands upon
thousands and ten thousand times ten thou-
sand of them.[m] 12 And they cried out with a
loud voice:

"Worthy is the Lamb that was sacrificed
to receive power and riches, wisdom
and strength,
honor and glory and praise."[n]

13 Then I heard every creature in heaven
and on earth and under the earth and in the
sea, and all that is in them, saying:

"To the one seated on the throne
and to the Lamb
be blessing and honor and glory and
might
forever and ever."[o]

---

b Rev 1:18; 4:2; 5:1.—c Rev 4:2, 4; 5:8, 14; 7:11; 11:16.—d Rev 1:6; 5:12; 10:6; Ps 33:9-11; Acts 14:15; Rom 4:17.—e Rev 4:2, 9; 5:7, 13; 6:16; Isa 29:11.—f Rev 10:1; 18:21.—g Rev 22:16; Gen 49:9; Isa 11:1, 10; Rom 15:12; Heb 7:14.—h Rev 1:4; 4:4, 6; 5:8-9, 12-13; Zec 4:10; Jn 1:29.—i Rev 5:1.—j Rev 4:4, 6; 8:3-4; 14:2; 15:2.—k Rev 4:11; 13:7; 14:3-4.—l Rev 1:6; 3:21; 20:4; Ex 19:6; Isa 61:6.—m Rev 4:4, 6; Dan 7:10; Heb 12:22; Jude 14-15.—n Rev 1:6; 4:11; 5:9, 13.—o Rev 5:3, 6-7; 6:16; 17:10; 1 Chr 29:11; Mal 1:6; 2:2; Rom 11:36; Phil 2:10.

5:1-14 As we have seen, the whole universe sings of the limitless power of the Creator. But he is also the Master of the universe, and the book he holds in his hand represents the destiny of the world. The book is held closed by seven seals, i.e., it contains the totality of the events of history, though in a hidden fashion, which no one can unveil.

However, a mediator of the Revelation does exist. He is the Messiah, who is designated here by the titles foretold of him in the Old Testament: the lion of Judah (see Gen 49:9) to whom victory is promised (see Isa 11:1, 10; see also 2 Sam 7), the Messiah King, shoot of the stock from which David was descended.

It is Christ in the power of his Resurrection who receives the mastery over the destinies of the entire universe. He is represented in his glory after the manner of a Lamb slain but standing (the figure of the Paschal Lamb is the main title for Christ in this Book, used twenty-eight times). This unusual expression is intended to recall Passover, the passover lamb, and the sacrificial Death of Christ for the redemption of the human race, but also to assert that he is ever living and the conqueror of death. The seven horns symbolize an infinite power.

The one with infinite power is the Redeemer who has acquired the people by his Blood. The Creator ratifies this and places in Christ's hands the succession of events until their fulfillment. Then the angels, the elders, and all the great figures in heaven that can be imagined will each come in turn to render the worship due to the Master of time, and the entire universe unites to acclaim the risen one. Indeed, the coming of Christ is a capital turning point, and a new song is required to celebrate it (see Phil 2).

5:9 *New song:* a song that celebrates a new act of divine deliverance (see Rev 14:3; Pss 33:3; 96:1; 144:9; Isa 42:10). *With your blood you purchased for God people:* the theme of Christ's sacrificial Death (see Mk 10:45; 1 Cor 6:20).

14 The four living creatures said, "Amen,"
and the elders prostrated themselves in wor-
ship.[p]

B: Prelude to the End of Times: Israel and the Church*

CHAPTER 6

The First Four Seals and the Horsemen.*
1 Then, in my vision, I saw the Lamb break
open the first of the seven seals, and I heard
one of the four living creatures shout in a
voice like thunder, "Come!"[q] 2 I looked, and
before my eyes I saw a white horse, and its
rider was holding a bow. He was given a
crown, and he rode forth as a victor to
amass still further conquests.[r]

3 When he broke open the second seal, I
heard the second living creature shout,
"Come!"[s] 4 And another horse came forth;
it was red. Its rider was empowered to take
away peace from the earth so that people
would slay each other. He was given a large
sword.*[t]

5 When he broke open the third seal, I
heard the third living creature shout,
"Come!" I looked, and there was a black
horse, and its rider was holding a pair of
scales* in his hand.[u] 6 Then I heard what
sounded like a voice emanating from the
midst of the four living creatures, saying, "A
quart of wheat costs a day's wages, and three
quarts of barley cost a day's wages. But do
not damage the olive oil or the wine."[v]

7 When he broke open the fourth seal, I
heard the voice of the fourth living creature
shout, "Come!"[w] 8 I looked, and there was a
pale green horse. Its rider was named
Death, and Hades* followed close behind.
They were given authority over a fourth of
the earth, to kill with sword, famine, and
plague, and by means of wild beasts.[x]

The Fifth Seal: Vision of the Martyrs.* 9 When
he broke open the fifth seal, I saw under-
neath the altar the souls of those who had
been slain on account of the word of God
and for witnessing to it.[y] 10 They shouted in
a loud voice, "How long is it to be, holy and
true Master, before you judge the inhabi-
tants of the earth* and avenge our death?"[z]

11 Each of them was given a white robe,*
and they were instructed to be patient for a
little longer until the roll was completed of
their fellow servants and brethren who were
still to be killed as they themselves had been.[a]

---

p Rev 4:4, 6, 9-10.—q Rev 4:6-7; 5:1, 6; 14:2; 19:6.—r Rev 14:14; 19:11-12; Zec 1:8-10; 6:1-3, 11.—s Rev 4:7; 14:2; 19:6.—t Ezek 21:14-16; Zec 1:8; 6:2; Mt 10:34.—u Rev 4:7; Zec 6:2.—v Rev 4:6-7; 7:1, 3; 9:4; Lev 26:26; Ezek 4:16-17.—w Rev 4:7.—x Rev 1:18; 20:13-14; Jer 15:2-3; Ezek 5:12, 17; 14:12; Hos 13:14; Zec 6:3.—y Rev 14:18; 16:7; 20:4; Ex 29:12; Lev 4:7; Rom 1:2; Heb 4:12.—z Rev 3:7, 10; Deut 32:43; 2 Ki 9:7; Zec 1:12; Lk 2:29; 2 Pet 2:1.—a Rev 3:4; Heb 11:40.

6:1—11:19 The book of destiny is probably not a scroll in the classical sense. It is a document that is folded and then sealed, folded and sealed, etc., seven times. It resembles a Roman legal document. Thus, as each seal is broken, part of the document becomes legible. When the seventh seal is broken (Rev 8:1), the hour is going to sound; but we are still living in suspense: trumpets will sound, one after another until the seventh one; then the great act will be played out (Rev 11:15).

Nonetheless, the unfurling of the wrath is not described to frighten believers; the author wants to strengthen them, to announce to them that the destiny of the world has been turned around and God's plan is on the way to being fulfilled. In accord with the perspectives of the prophecies and the Gospel, a Remnant will be saved, the community of Christ and the true People of God (Rev 7). All the chapters that follow seem to interpret the history of the world in the perspective of the destiny reserved for the Jewish people. Yet the end of Jerusalem and its destruction are not the end of history; they are only a turning point (Rev 10:1—11:13)—then the time of the nations can truly begin (Rev 12:1—19:10).

6:1-8 The first secrets are unveiled. Already the images are terrifying. The colors of the horses suffice to create fright. Three horsemen sow war, famine, and pestilence, those great scourges in which the ancients see God's judgment on proud and indifferent ages and on unjust people (see, e.g., Lev 26:21-26; Deut 32:34; Ezek 5:17; 6:11f; 7:14f; 12:16; 14:13-21; 33:27; Jer 15:2-4; Mt 24:6f). Hades follows in the wake of the last horseman to swallow the victims into its gloomy abode.

There is some doubt about the figure of the first horseman, crowned and mounted on a white horse. Is it Christ, or a false Messiah, or simply another scourge, the well-known scourge of the voracious beasts who decimate travelers? The allegory of the four horses and horsemen who ride out into the four quarters of the world is taken from Zechariah (1:8-10; 6:1-8).

6:4 *A large sword:* symbol of war.

6:5-6 *Scales:* symbol of hunger: food is rationed and sold at very high prices. The rider with the scales probably represents social injustice. *A day's wages:* literally, "a denarius."

6:8 *Hades:* personification of the abode of the dead, i.e., the netherworld (see notes on Rev 1:9-20 and Mt 16:18).

6:9-11 Persecution is unleashed. The victims, as though immolated in sacrifice, are all reunited around God and already clothed in the garment of joy. This presence of the victims attests that oppression has been lifted on earth. For the people of the Bible possess too great a sense of justice to imagine that such violent injustices as persecutions constitute an indifferent thing in the eyes of God and that they can go unpunished forever. They are like a challenge to God (see Lk 18:7). God must intervene, and bloody persecutions are among the signs of the end (see Mk 13:9-13).

6:10 *Inhabitants of the earth:* i.e., humankind in its hostility to God (see Rev 3:10; 8:13; 11:10; 13:8, 12; 17:2, 8).

6:11 *White robe:* symbol of the joy and triumph of the Resurrection (see Rev 3:5, 18; 11:10; 13:8, 12; 17:2, 8). *Until the roll was completed of their fellow servants and brethren who were still to be killed:* there was an apocalyptic idea in the air—sparked by noncanonical literature—that God rules the world according to a predetermined time schedule (see 2 Esdras 4:35-37) and that the death of a certain number of the righteous must occur before the end takes place (see 1 Enoch 47:4).

The Sixth Seal: the Universe Disturbed.* 12 In
my vision, when he broke open the sixth seal,
there was a violent earthquake. The sun
turned as black as coarse sackcloth, the
moon became as red as blood, [b] 13 and the
stars in the sky fell to earth like unripe figs
dislodged from a tree when shaken by a
strong wind. [c] 14 The heavens were torn apart
like a scroll being rolled up, and every moun-
tain and island was dislodged from its
place. [d]

15 Then the kings of the earth, the nobles,
and the commanders, the rich and the pow-
erful, and the whole population, both slaves
and free, hid themselves in caves and among
the rocks of the mountains. [e] 16 They shouted
to the mountains and the rocks, "Fall on us
and hide us from the face of the one who sits
on the throne, and from the wrath of the
Lamb. [f] 17 For the great day of their wrath
has come, and who can endure it?" [g]

CHAPTER 7

An Immense Crowd before God's Throne.*
1 After this I saw four angels standing at the
four corners of the earth, holding back the
four winds of the earth so that no wind could
blow on land or on the sea or on any tree. [h]
2 Then I saw another angel rising from the
east, bearing the seal of the living God. He
cried out in a loud voice to the four angels
who had been given the power to ravage the
land and the sea, [i] 3 "Do not damage the
land or the sea or the trees until we have set
the seal on the foreheads of the servants of
our God." [j]

4 Then I heard how many had been marked
with the seal—one hundred and forty-four
thousand from all the tribes of Israel: [k]

5 From the tribe of Judah,* twelve thousand,
from the tribe of Reuben, twelve thousand,
from the tribe of Gad, twelve thousand,
6 from the tribe of Asher, twelve thousand,
from the tribe of Naphtali, twelve thousand,
from the tribe of Manasseh, twelve thousand,
7 from the tribe of Simeon, twelve thousand,
from the tribe of Levi, twelve thousand,
from the tribe of Issachar, twelve thousand,
8 from the tribe of Zebulun, twelve thousand,
from the tribe of Joseph, twelve thousand,
from the tribe of Benjamin, twelve thousand.

9 After this, in my vision, I witnessed a vast
throng that no one could count, from every
nation, race, people, and language. They
were standing before the throne and before
the Lamb, dressed in white robes and hold-
ing palm branches in their hands. [l] 10 They
cried out in a loud voice:

"Salvation belongs to our God,
who sits on the throne,
and to the Lamb." [m]

11 All the angels who were standing
around the throne, and around the elders
and the four living creatures, prostrated
themselves before the throne and worshiped
God, [n] 12 saying:

"Amen. Praise and glory,
wisdom and thanksgiving,
honor and power and might,

b Rev 8:5; 11:13; 16:18; Isa 29:6; Ezek 38:19; Joel 3:4; Mt 24:29.—c Rev 8:10; 9:1; Isa 34:4; Mt 24:29.—d Rev 16:20; 20:11; 21:1; Isa 34:4; Jer 4:24; 2 Pet 3:10.—e Rev 19:18; Isa 2:10; 19:21.—f Rev 5:1; Isa 2:19; Hos 10:8; Lk 23:30.—g Rev 16:14; Joel 1:15; 2:1-2, 11; 3:4; Zep 1:14-15; Mal 3:2.—h Isa 11:12; Jer 49:36; Ezek 37:9; Zec 6:5; Mt 24:31.—i Rev 7:1; 9:4; Mt 16:16.—j Rev 6:6; 9:4; 14:1; 22:4; Ex 12:7-14; Ezek 9:4; 2 Cor 1:22; Eph 1:13; 4:30.—k Rev 9:16; 14:1, 3.—l Rev 3:4; 7:15; 13:7.—m Rev 5:1; 12:10; 19:1.—n Rev 4:4, 6, 10.

6:12-17 The cosmic destruction announces the Day of the Lord (see Isa 34:4; Mk 13:6, 24f). It is an astonishing spectacle that this firmament will be rolled up like a large scroll. The cosmos enters a phase of distortion and convulsion. The threat hangs over everyone; no one escapes the paralyzing fear. The author uses to great advantage many of the images of the Old Testament (see Isa 2:10, 19; 34:4; Hos 10:8; Joel 2:11; 3:4).

7:1-17 In 587 B.C., on the eve of the destruction of Jerusalem, the survivors were, so to speak, marked to be preserved from the catastrophe (see Ezek 9). The great fear is not for the community of the persecuted. The calamities that will overtake the world will not touch them. Thus, God gathers together his Elect. They may go through the trial of the years A.D. 66 to 70 and finally the history of the world, which is that of the sufferings of the Church. But they will not fall prey to condemnation. This people that is gathered together is first of all the Remnant of Israel. From each of the twelve tribes there will be twelve thousand survivors: this is a symbolic number meaning fullness and perfection. Then the vision is enlarged: the Remnant becomes a multitude without number, gathered together from amid all the nations of the earth. From all sides come forth the martyrs and all those who endured trials: the whole Church. This is a grandiose celebration of happiness and triumph. In a striking foreshortening, the author sketches a tableau of the Church in the grip of tribulations and persecutions, assisted by Christ, her Shepherd, and led toward her heavenly victory, which anticipates the splendid final vision of the new Jerusalem (Rev 21:1—22:5).

7:5-6 Judah is placed first because of Christ, who is "the Lion of the tribe of Judah" (Rev 5:5). *Manasseh:* one of the two halves of the tribe of Joseph that are both cited (the other being Ephraim but called "Joseph" in v. 8)—doubtless in order to make up twelve tribes. Daniel is omitted probably because of a late tradition that the Antichrist was to arise from that tribe.

be to our God forever and ever.
Amen." [o]

13 Then one of the elders spoke to me and
inquired, "Who are these people, all dressed
in white robes, and where have they come
from?" [p] 14 I replied, "My lord, you are the
one who knows." Then he said to me, "These
are the ones who have survived the great
tribulation. They have washed their robes
and made them white in the blood of the
Lamb. [q]

15 "That is why they stand before the
throne of God
and worship him day and night in his
temple,
and the one who sits on the throne will
shelter them. [r]
16 They will never again experience hunger
or thirst,
nor will the sun or any scorching heat
cause them discomfort. [s]
17 For the Lamb who is at the center of the
throne
will be their shepherd.
He will guide them to springs of living
water, *
and God will wipe away every tear
from their eyes." [t]

CHAPTER 8

The Seventh Seal.* 1 When the Lamb broke
open the seventh seal, there was silence in
heaven for about half an hour. [u] 2 And I saw
that seven trumpets were given to the
seven angels who stand in the presence of
God. [v]

3 Another angel came forward with a gold
censer and stood at the altar. * He was given
a large quantity of incense to offer, with the
prayers of all the saints, on the gold altar
that stood before the throne. [w]

4 The smoke of the incense together with
the prayers of the saints rose before God
from the hand of the angel. [x] 5 Then the
angel took the censer, filled it with fire from
the altar, and emptied it upon the earth.
Immediately, there came peals of thunder,
rumblings, flashes of lightning, and an
earthquake. [y]

6 The seven angels who held the seven
trumpets now made ready to blow them. [z]

The First Four Trumpets.* 7 When the first
angel blew his trumpet, there was a storm of
hail and fire, mixed with blood, and it fell
upon the earth. * A third of the earth was
burned up, as well as a third of the trees and
all the green grass. [a]

8 * When the second angel blew his trum-
pet, something that looked like a huge
mountain ablaze with fire was hurled into
the sea. A third of the sea turned into
blood, [b] 9 a third of the creatures living in the
sea died, and a third of the ships were
destroyed. [c]

10 When the third angel blew his trumpet,
a great star fell from the sky, burning like a
torch. It came down on a third of the rivers
and on the springs of water. [d] 11 This star was
called "Wormwood," and a third of the
waters turned to wormwood. * Great num-
bers of people died from the waters that had
become bitter. [e]

12 When the fourth angel blew his trum-
pet, a third of the sun was struck, a third of
the moon, and a third of the stars. As a
result, a third of their light was darkened,
and the day lost its illumination for a third of
the time, and so did the night. * [f]

The Cry of the Eagle.* 13 In my vision, I
heard an eagle cry out in a loud voice as it

o Rev 5:12-14; Rom 11:36.—p Rev 3:4; Ezek 37:3.—q Rev 12:11; 22:14; Mt 24:21; Heb 9:14; 1 Jn 1:7.—r Rev 5:1; 7:9; 11:19; 21:3; 22:3; Isa 4:5-6.—s Isa 49:10; Jn 6:35.—t Rev 21:4; Isa 25:8; 35:10; 51:11; Jn 4:10; 10:11.—u Rev 6:1; Hab 2:20; Zep 1:7; Zec 2:17.—v Rev 4:5; 8:6-13; 9:1, 13; 11:15; Tob 12:15; Mt 24:31.—w Rev 5:8; 7:2; 8:5; 9:13; Ex 30:1-6; Tob 12:12; Ps 141:2; Heb 9:4.—x Ps 141:2.—y Rev 4:5; 6:12; 11:19; 16:18; Lev 16:12; Ezek 10:2; Ps 11:6.—z Rev 8:2; 16:1-21.—a Rev 8:2, 7-12; 9:4, 15; Ezek 38:22.—b Rev 8:7; 16:3; Ex 7:20; Jer 51:25.—c Rev 8:7.—d Rev 6:13; 9:1; 14:7; 16:4; Isa 14:12.—e Rev 8:7; Jer 9:14; 23:15.—f Rev 6:12-13; 8:7; Ex 10:21-23; Ezek 32:7.

7:17 *Springs of living water:* i.e., the grace of God, which flows from Christ (see Rev 21:6; 22:1, 17; Jn 4:10, 14).

8:1-6 We are now at the great Day of God's Coming. Everything is unmoving in a solemn silence. It is the hour when the prayer of those persecuted—which is symbolized by the incense—is going to be heard (see Rev 6:9-11). Calamities arise to jostle the earth. At the sound of the trumpets, which are part of the scene for the Coming of God (see 1 Thes 4:16), seven tableaus will pass before our eyes in a dramatization without let-up.

8:3 The *altar* is the altar of incense in the Jewish sanctuary; the *gold censer* is the thurible or fire-shovel used to carry the burning coals from the altar of holocausts to the altar of incense.

8:7-12 The earth, sea, streams, sources, and stars—everything is disfigured. The universe becomes chaos and lays itself waste. The author amplifies images taken from the Book of Exodus (chs. 7—10).

8:7 See the seventh plague of Egypt (Ex 9:23f) and Joel 3:3.

8:8-11 See the first plague of Egypt (Ex 7:20f).

8:11 *Wormwood:* a bitter-tasting plant that is a metaphor for calamity, sorrow, and death (see Prov 5:3f; Jer 9:15; Lam 3:19).

8:12 See the darkness that occurred for three days during the ninth plague of Egypt (Ex 10:21-23).

8:13 After the universe, the human race will itself be struck. The eagle announces the three calamities.

flew high overhead, "Woe! Woe! Woe to the inhabitants of the earth because of the other trumpet blasts that the three angels have not yet blown!" [g]

CHAPTER 9

The Fifth Trumpet: the First Woe.* 1 Then the fifth angel blew his trumpet, and I saw a star that had fallen from the sky to the earth. He was given the key to the shaft leading down to the abyss. [h] 2 When he unlocked the shaft of the abyss, smoke rose up from the abyss like smoke from a huge furnace, so that the sun and the sky were darkened by the smoke from the abyss. [i] 3 And out of the smoke locusts dropped down onto the earth, and they were given the same powers that scorpions have on the earth. [j] 4 They were commanded not to damage the grass or the earth or any plant or tree, and they were told to attack only those people who did not have God's seal on their foreheads. [k]

5 They were given permission to torture these people for five months, but they were not allowed to kill them, and the torment they were to inflict was to be like that of a scorpion when it stings someone. [l] 6 During that time, these people will seek death but will not find it; they will long to die, but death will elude them. [m]

7 In appearance the locusts were like horses equipped for battle. On their heads they wore what appeared to be gold crowns. Their faces were like human faces, [n] 8 and their hair was like women's hair. Their teeth were like lions' teeth, [o] 9 and their chests were like iron breastplates. The sound of their wings was like the rumble of many horses and chariots rushing into battle. [p]

10 These locusts had tails and stings like those of scorpions, and in their tails they had the power to torment people for five months. [q] 11 They had as their king the angel of the abyss, whose name in Hebrew is Abaddon, and in Greek, Apollyon. [r]

12 The first woe has passed, but two more are still to come. [s]

The Sixth Trumpet: the Second Woe.* 13 Then the sixth angel blew his trumpet, and I heard a voice * emanating from the horns of the gold altar that stood in the presence of God. [t] 14 It said to the sixth angel who was holding the trumpet, "Release the four angels who are bound at the great river Euphrates." [u]

15 And so the four angels, who had been held in readiness for this very hour, day, month, and year, were released to kill a third of mankind. * [v] 16 The number of their cavalry troops was two hundred million. This was the number I heard. [w]

17 This is how I saw the horses and their riders in my vision. The riders wore breastplates in shades of red, blue, and yellow. The heads of the horses were like heads of lions, and issuing forth from their mouths were fire, smoke, and sulfur. [x] 18 By these three plagues of fire, smoke, and sulfur that poured forth from their mouths, a third of mankind was killed. [y] 19 The power of the horses was in their mouths and in their tails. Their tails were like serpents, with heads that inflicted harm.

20 However, the rest of mankind who survived these plagues did not repent of the work of their hands or cease their worship of demons * and of idols of gold, silver, bronze, stone, and wood, which can neither see nor hear nor walk. [z] 21 Nor did they repent of

g Rev 3:10; 9:12; 11:14; 12:12; 14:6; 19:17.—h Rev 1:18; 8:10; 9:2, 11; 20:1; Lk 8:31.—i Rev 9:1, 11; Gen 19:28; Ex 19:18; Joel 2:2, 10; Lk 8:31.—j Rev 9:5, 10; Ex 10:12-15; Wis 16:9.—k Rev 6:6; 7:2-3; 8:7.—l Rev 9:3, 10.—m Rev 6:16; Job 3:21; 7:15; Jer 8:3.—n Num 3:17; Joel 1:6.—o Joel 1:6.—p Job 39:21-25; Jer 8:6; Joel 2:5.—q Rev 9:3, 5, 19.—r Rev 9:1-2; 16:16; Job 26:6; 28:22; 31:12; Lk 8:31.—s Rev 8:13.—t Rev 8:3; Ex 30:1-3.—u Rev 7:1; 16:12; Gen 15:18; Deut 1:7; Jos 1:4; Isa 11:15.—v Rev 8:7; 9:8; 20:7.—w Rev 5:11; 7:4.—x Rev 9:18; 11:5; 14:10; 19:20; Job 41:10-13; Isa 30:33; Ezek 38:22.—y Rev 8:7; 9:15, 17.—z Rev 2:21; Deut 4:28; 31:29; Ps 135:15-17; Isa 17:8; Jer 1:16; Dan 5:4; Mic 5:13; Acts 7:41; 1 Cor 10:20.

9:1-12 A fallen star, doubtless Satan himself, opens the door of the abyss, which is regarded as the prison in which the evil spirits are held while awaiting their final punishment. An army of strange locusts escapes (see the eighth and ninth plagues of Egypt—Ex 10:12-15, 21-23—as well as the invasion of locusts in Joel 1:4—2:10). These do not devour the harvest, as one would expect, but attack humans. It is an invasion of a fierce army, led by a satanic being, whose name in Hebrew is *Abaddon*, meaning perdition or ruin, and in Greek *Apollyon*, meaning destroyer. The writer has not resisted the enticing pleasure of giving this being a name that is a caricature of the great Greek god Apollo. Job 3:21 is cited in v. 6.

9:13-21 These ancient monsters seem to have had an appointment to meet on the banks of the Euphrates, to be then unleashed as a savage horde on the people. The visionary is undoubtedly thinking of the four corps of the military that invaded Judea from Syria for the second phase of the Jewish War in an expedition that was particularly destructive and murderous. The event was always supposed to be a sign that jump-started consciences. Alas, it merely leads to bewilderment and decomposition!

9:13 *I heard a voice:* to show that the punishment inflicted on the pagans was the result of the prayer of the martyrs, described in Rev 6:9-10.

9:15 For the day of the divine wrath, see Rev 6:17.

9:20 *Demons:* spiritual beings allied with Satan and wielding an evil influence on human beings (see Deut 4:28; Ps 115:5-7; 1 Cor 10:20).

their murders, their sorcery, their sexual immorality, or their thefts. [a]

CHAPTER 10

A Small Scroll: Sweet and Bitter.* 1 Then I
saw another mighty angel coming down
from heaven. He was wrapped in a cloud,
with a rainbow over his head. His face was
like the sun, his legs were like pillars of fire, [b]
2 and his hand held a small scroll that had
been opened.

Placing his right foot on the sea and his
left foot on the land, [c] 3 the angel gave forth a
great shout like the roar of a lion. And when
he shouted, the seven thunders spoke. [d]
4 After the seven thunders had spoken, I was
preparing to write when I heard a voice
from heaven say, "Seal up what the seven
thunders have spoken, but do not write it
down." [e]

5 Then the angel whom I had seen standing
on the sea and on the land raised his right
hand to heaven [f] 6 and swore by him who lives
forever and ever and who created heaven
and earth and the sea and everything that is
in them: "There will be no further delay. [g]
7 When the time comes for the seventh angel
to sound his trumpet, the mysterious purpose of God* will be fulfilled, just as he
announced to his servants the Prophets." [h]

8 Then I again heard the voice that had
spoken to me from heaven, and it said, "Go
and take that open scroll from the hand of
the angel who is standing on the sea and on
the land." [i] 9 Therefore, I went to the angel
and asked him to give me the small scroll.
He replied, "Take it and eat it. It will turn
your stomach sour, but in your mouth it will
taste as sweet as honey." [j]

10 I took the small scroll from the angel's
hand and ate it. In my mouth it did taste as
sweet as honey, but when I had eaten it my
stomach turned sour. [k] 11 Then I was told,
"You must prophesy once again about many
peoples, nations, languages, and kings." [l]

CHAPTER 11

The Two Witnesses and the Fate of Jerusalem.* 1 I was next given a staff to use as
a measuring rod, and I was told, "Go forth

a Rev 2:21; 17:2, 5; 18:23; Isa 47:9, 12.—b Rev 1:16; 4:3; 5:2; 18:1; 20:1; Ezek 1:28; Mt 17:2.—c Rev 5:1; 10:5, 8-10.—d Rev 4:5; Ps 29:3-9; Jer 25:30; Hos 11:10; Am 3:8.—e Rev 1:11, 19; 10:8; 22:10.—f Rev 10:1-2; Deut 32:40.—g Rev 1:18; 4:11; 16:17; Gen 14:22; Ex 6:8; Num 14:30; Deut 32:40; Ezek 12:28; Dan 12:7.—h Am 3:7; Mt 24:31; Rom 16:25.—i Rev 10:2, 4.—j Jer 15:16; Ezek 2:8; 3:3.—k Rev 10:9; Ezek 3:1-3.—l Rev 13:7; Ezek 37:4, 9.

10:1-11 The large scroll, whose seven seals are being broken one after another, is said to contain the entire History of Salvation, which unfolds from Christ's Death and Resurrection to the day of the final judgment. This history is brought to mind from the viewpoint of the destiny of the Jewish people, but the last episode in this history includes the judgment and salvation of the nations, which are here set forth.

An angel brings forth and unrolls another text; the messenger dominates heaven and the sea, i.e., his announcement concerns the whole universe. The scroll that the angel is holding here contains the story of clashes between the Church and the forces that control the pagan world. It is a small scroll, because the events told in it are connected with the history of Israel, in which the end of Jerusalem introduces the era of the nations.

There will be no more delay. Everything remains secret, yet everything will be played out between the sixth and the seventh trumpet. The scene of the scroll that is eaten was inspired by an account of Ezekiel (2:8—3:3). The revelation is sweet and bitter: sweet because it is a word of salvation and makes known the final triumph of Christ and his faithful; bitter because it announces the trials and tribulations that in so many texts of the Bible precede the judgment of God. The Gospel speaks of the joy of the woman giving birth in sorrow (Jn 16:21).

10:7 *The mysterious purpose of God:* literally, "the mystery of God," i.e., the end of the present age when the power of evil will be overcome (see Rev 17:1—19:4, 11-21; 20:7-10; Rom 16:25f; 2 Thes 2:6-12) and the Kingdom of God is established and all creation is renewed (see Rev 21:1—22:5).

11:1-13 The holy city is crushed under the blows of Titus, but in the Church, the new Israel, everything that the temple, the altar, and the worshipers represent will not cease; true worship will continue. In a hostile world, the witnesses of Christ will continue to spread the Word of God, despite persecutions, until the Second Coming.

Let us try to see a bit more clearly into the details of the symbols used by the author to impart this certitude to believers subjected to torture. Measuring Jerusalem calls to mind—since Ezekiel (40:3) and Zechariah (2:5-6)—protection and reconstruction. But only the reserved part of the temple is spared, i.e., while the Church will be persecuted and even give forth martyrs, the saints will never be harmed. While the bodies of the holy ones (represented by the exterior of the temple) are crushed, their souls (represented by the interior of the temple) are safe in God's hands.

The two witnesses—perhaps Peter and Paul—combine the traits of several persons, especially Moses and Elijah (of whom Judaism of that time mentions the ascension: v. 11) and one of whom changed water into blood (Ex 7:17; 10:11), while the other predicted a drought (1 Ki 17:1). The Gospel places both at the side of Christ during the Transfiguration (Mk 9:2-8).

Next come two mysterious personalities who, according to Zechariah (4:3, 14) cited in v. 4 of our text, represent the priesthood and the Kingdom uniting their efforts to guide the people of God. These are also Christian figures, of Christ first and then of the apostles—tradition names Peter and Paul, the two champions of the early Church, who died at Rome under Nero in A.D. 64 or 67.

Finally, these mysterious figures stand for the whole Church bearing witness to her faith and suffering for the sake of the Gospel even until martyrdom. It is not permitted to put their bones in the grave (v. 9), i.e., the testimony of the martyr Church cannot disappear into oblivion.

Just as the dry bones of the people of the Old Testament came to life in the eyes of the Prophet Ezekiel (37:5, 10), so the Christian martyrs are destined for resurrection and glorification.

The great city is symbolic of the high places of infidelity according to the Bible. In Rev 16:19; 17:18; 18:10, it is Rome; here, it is Rome or Jerusalem or any other city that makes itself omnipotent.

The beast cited in v. 7 (see Dan 7:21) represents the imperial power, destructive power, that claimed to be divine. Speaking of survivors (v. 13), the author thinks, perhaps, as did Paul (Rom 11:13-27), of a conversion of the Jewish people preceding Christ's Return.

and measure the temple of God and the
altar, and count the people who are wor-
shiping there.[m] 2 However, exclude the outer
court of the temple from your measure-
ments, because it has been handed over to
the Gentiles and they will trample on the
holy city for forty-two months.*[n] 3 I will
grant my two witnesses authority to proph-
esy for those twelve hundred and sixty days,
wearing sackcloth."[o]

4 These are the two olive trees and the two
lampstands that stand in the presence of the
Lord of the earth.[p] 5 If anyone tries to harm
them, fire pours forth from their mouths
and consumes their enemies. Anyone who
attempts to harm them will surely be killed
in this manner.[q] 6 They have the power to
shut up the sky so that it does not rain dur-
ing the time they are prophesying. They also
have the power to turn water into blood and
to afflict the earth with every type of plague
as often as they desire.[r]

7 When they have completed their testi-
mony, the beast that comes up from the
abyss will wage war against them and over-
power and kill them.[s] 8 Their corpses will lie
in the street of the great city, known by the
symbolic names of Sodom and Egypt, where
their Lord was crucified.[t]

9 People of every race, tribe, nation, and
language will gaze at their corpses for three
and a half days and refuse to allow them to
be buried.[u] 10 The inhabitants of the earth
will gloat over them as they celebrate and
exchange gifts, because these two prophets
had been a source of torment to them.[v]

11 However, after the three and a half days,
the breath of life from God entered them,
and when they rose to their feet, great terror
filled those who saw them.[w] 12 Then I heard
a loud voice from heaven say to them,
"Come up here," and while their enemies
were watching, they went up to heaven in a
cloud.[x]

13 At that very hour there was a violent
earthquake, and a tenth of the city was
destroyed. Seven thousand people were
killed during the earthquake. Those who
survived were overcome with fear and gave
glory to the God of heaven.[y]

14 The second woe has passed, but the
third will come quickly.[z]

The Seventh Trumpet: the Third Woe.* 15 The
seventh angel blew his trumpet, and voices
in heaven were heard crying loudly:

"The kingdom of the world belongs
to our Lord and his Messiah,
and he will reign forever and ever."[a]

16 Then the twenty-four elders who sit on
their thrones in the presence of God pros-
trated themselves and worshiped God,[b]
17 saying:

"We give you thanks, Lord God Almighty,
who are and who were.
For you have taken your great power
and have begun to reign.[c]
18 The nations rose in rage,
but now your wrath has come.
It is the time for judging the dead
and for rewarding your servants the Prophets,
as well as the saints who revere your name,
both small and great,
and for destroying those who destroy the earth."[d]

19 Then God's temple in heaven was
opened, and the ark of his covenant* was
seen within his temple. There followed flash-

m Rev 21:15; Ezek 40:3-5; Zec 2:5-9.—n Rev 11:3; 12:6; 21:2; Ezek 40:17, 20; Lk 21:24.—o Rev 1:5; 2:13; 11:2; Gen 37:34; 2 Sam 3:31; Neh 9:1.—p Jer 11:16; Zec 4:3, 14.—q Rev 9:17, 18; Num 16:29, 35; 2 Sam 22:9; 2 Ki 1:10; Jer 5:14.—r Rev 8:8; 11:3; Ex 7:17; Lk 4:25.—s Rev 13:1-4, 7; Dan 7:21; Lk 8:31.—t Rev 16:19; Isa 1:9; Jer 23:14; Ezek 16:46.—u Rev 13:7.—v Rev 3:10; Neh 8:10, 12; Est 9:19, 22.—w Rev 11:9; Gen 2:7; Ezek 37:5, 9, 10, 14.—x Rev 4:1; 12:5; 2 Ki 2:11; Acts 1:9.—y Rev 6:12; 14:7; 16:9, 11; 19:7.—z Rev 8:13.—a Rev 12:10; 16:17; 19:1; Mic 4:7; Zec 14:9; Lk 1:33.—b Rev 4:4, 10.—c Rev 1:4, 8; 19:6.—d Rev 10:7; 19:5; 20:12.

11:2-3, 11 *Forty-two months . . . twelve hundred and sixty days . . . three and a half days . . . a year, two years, and a half year* (12:14): symbolic durations, designating typical periods of persecution according to Dan 7:25.

11:15-19 The seventh trumpet sounds to announce the definitive restoration of the Kingdom of God and Christ. With the resurrection of the dead, Israel sees the completion of its promises of salvation: there will be reward for true worshipers and condemnation for rebels. The thanksgiving of the elders can rise before the throne of God.

According to a Jewish tradition, allusions to which are found in the Second Book of Maccabees (2:5-8), the Ark of the Covenant, which was destroyed by the fire in the temple in 587 B.C., was to reappear in the last times; the hour for this has come.

A new Sinai arises in heaven forever. The hour of judgment is, in the final analysis, the judgment of the definitive and perfect Covenant. Certainly, the earthly temple is destroyed, but the true and complete worship takes place in heaven.

11:19 *Ark of his covenant:* the ark of the Old Testament was a chest of acacia wood (see Deut 10:1f) that symbolized God's throne and his presence among his people. It was probably destroyed during Neburazadan's destruction of the temple in Jerusalem (see 2 Ki 25:8-10). The New Testament writers use it to symbolize God's faithfulness to the Covenant made with his people.

es of lightning, rumblings, peals of thunder,
an earthquake, and a violent hailstorm. [e]

CHAPTER 12

C: The Great Confrontation: Pagan Rome and the Church*

Two Signs in Heaven: the Woman and the
Dragon.* 1 A great sign appeared in heaven: a
woman clothed with the sun, with the moon
beneath her feet, and a crown of twelve stars
on her head. [f] 2 She was with child and about
to give birth, crying aloud in the anguish of
her labor. [g]

3 Then another sign appeared in heaven: a
huge red dragon with seven heads and ten
horns, and seven diadems crowning his
heads. [h] 4 His tail swept away a third of the
stars in the sky and hurled them to the earth.

The dragon stood in front of the woman
who was about to give birth, so that it might
devour her child as soon as it was born. [i]
5 She gave birth to a son, a male child who is
destined to rule all the nations with an iron
rod. And her child was taken up directly to
God and to his throne. [j] 6 The woman herself
fled into the wilderness where she would be
looked after for twelve hundred and sixty
days * in a place prepared for her by God. [k]

7 Next, war broke out in heaven, with
Michael * and his angels in combat against
the dragon. The dragon and his angels
fought back, [l] 8 but they were defeated, and
they lost their place in heaven. 9 The great
dragon—the ancient serpent who is called
the devil, or Satan, the deceiver of the whole
world—was hurled down to earth, and his
angels were cast down with him. [m]

10 Then I heard a loud voice in heaven say:

"Now have come the salvation and the
power
and the kingdom of our God
and the authority of his Messiah.
For the accuser * of our brethren has
been cast out,
the one who accused them day and
night before our God. [n]
11 They have conquered him
by the blood of the Lamb
and by the word of their testimony;
even in the face of death
they did not cling to life. [o]
12 Therefore rejoice, you heavens,
and you who dwell in them!
But woe to you, earth and sea,
because the devil has come down to you.
He is filled with rage,
for he knows that his time is short." [p]

e Rev 4:5; 16:21; 15:5, 8; Ex 25:10-22; 2 Chr 5:7; Heb 9:4.—f Rev 11:19; 12:3; 15:1; Gen 37:9.—g Isa 26:17; Gal 4:19.—h Rev 12:1, 9; 13:16; 15:1; 17:1; 19:12; Dan 7:7.—i Rev 8:7; Dan 8:10; Mt 2:16.—j Rev 2:27; 19:15; Ps 2:9; Isa 66:7; Acts 8:39.—k Rev 11:2; 12:14; 2 Cor 12:2.—l Rev 12:3; Mt 25:41; Jude 9.—m Rev 12:15; 20:2, 3, 8, 10; Gen 3:1-4; Mt 4:10; 25:41; Lk 10:18; Jn 12:31.—n Rev 7:10; 11:15; Job 1:9-13; Zec 3:1; 1 Pet 5:8.—o Rev 6:9; 7:14; 15:2; Lk 14:26; Jn 16:33.—p Rev 8:13; 10:6; 18:20; Isa 44:23.

12:1—15:4 The animosity exhibited by the public authorities against Christian communities has become persecution. Now the grand declarations of loyalty toward the power are ended (see Rom 13:1-7; Tit 3:1; 1 Pet 2:13-17). The time has come, not to organize some armed defense or subversion but to resist every pressure and to stand fast in fidelity to Christ even to the shedding of blood. At this point, the Roman empire comes on the scene as the instrument used by all the forces hostile to Christ, his Kingdom, and his faithful. The Roman empire is a symbol of all earthly empires with their claim to impose their own ideas and purposes as a religion. The struggle will end with the victory of the risen Christ and those who have put their trust in him.

Here then is the time of the nations or the pagans. In the previous chapters, which envisaged the last times from the viewpoint of Israel's destiny, its place had already been marked out in anticipation (Rev 10:1—11:13). This is the scene itself. The structure of the chapters that follow is less clear; however, we find once again the same procedure as in the seven visions and the seven bowls.

12:1-17 Two types play a role in this inaugural vision. The ancient prophecy of Genesis (3:15) is fulfilled: a struggle in which there is no truce opposes the posterity of the chosen people and the forces of evil. The woman who gives birth personifies first of all the chosen people, from which the Messiah is to be born; there is certainly a reference to him in v. 5, which cites some classic Messianic texts: Isa 66:7 and Ps 2:9.

A long-standing Christian tradition also identifies the woman with the Virgin Mary, an exemplar of the chosen people. Modern exegetes rarely support so explicit an interpretation, but do not deny that the role of the one called "woman" in the fourth Gospel (Jn 2:4; 19:26) may have indirectly inspired, at least partially, this description in the Book of Revelation.

The dragon (see Dan 7; 8:10) has all the characteristics of the power that rises up against God: seven heads, ten horns, behavior capable of destroying the order of the universe (v. 4, citing Dan 8:10). The dragon is Satan, the eternal accuser of human beings before God (see Job 1:6-11; 2:1-17). After this "the rest of her [the woman's] offspring" (v. 17)—i.e., the faithful followers of Christ—suffer a period of struggles and trials in "the wilderness" (v. 6), i.e., on the earthly journey of the Church. In these trials the Church will not lack the strength given by the manna (see v. 6), an evident reference to the Eucharist.

Hell can launch against the Church all the forces unleashed by the Roman political authorities. In this scene there is also a struggle between Michael and the dragon (v. 7), which illustrates the victory of Christ; the description draws its inspiration from the Book of Daniel.

12:6 *Twelve hundred and sixty days:* see note on Rev 11:2-3, 11.

12:7 *Michael:* i.e., God's champion according to Jewish tradition (see Dan 10:12-21; 12:1); his name means "Who can compare with God?"

12:10 *Accuser:* the translation for the Hebrew word "Satan" (see 1 Chr 21:1; Job 1—2; Zec 3:1). In Hebrew scripture, Satan is a type of district attorney who accuses people of their sins at the Last Judgment.

13 When the dragon realized that he had
been hurled down to earth, he pursued the
woman who had given birth to the male
child.[q] 14 But the woman was given the two
wings of the great eagle so that she could fly
away from the serpent into the wilderness,
to the place where she was to be looked after
for a year, two years, and a half year.*[r]

15 Then from his mouth the serpent
spewed out water like a river after the
woman to sweep her away with the flood.[s]
16 However, the earth came to the rescue of
the woman: it opened its mouth and swallowed the river spewed from the dragon's
mouth.

17 Then the dragon became enraged at the
woman and went off to wage war on the rest
of her offspring, those who keep God's commandments and bear witness to Jesus.[t]

A Beast Rises from the Sea.* 18 Meanwhile, I
took my position* on the seashore.

CHAPTER 13

1 Then I saw a beast rising out of the sea.
It had ten horns and seven heads. On its
horns were ten diadems, and on its heads
were blasphemous names.[u] 2 The beast that
I saw resembled a leopard, but it had feet
like those of a bear, and its mouth was like
the mouth of a lion. The dragon conferred
on the beast his own power and his throne,
as well as great authority.[v]

3 One of his heads appeared to me to have
been mortally wounded, but its mortal
wound had been healed. The whole world
then became fascinated with the beast,[w]
4 and they worshiped the dragon because he
had conferred authority on the beast. They
also worshiped the beast, saying, "Who can
compare with the beast? Who can fight
against it?"[x]

5 It was allowed to mouth its haughty and
blasphemous words, and it was granted permission to exercise its authority for forty-two months.*[y] 6 It opened its mouth to utter
blasphemies against God, as well as against
his name and his dwelling and all those who
live in heaven.[z]

7 The beast was also allowed to wage war
on the saints and conquer them, and it was
given authority over every tribe, people, language, and nation.[a] 8 All the inhabitants of
the earth will worship it, all those whose
names have not been written from the creation of the world* in the book of life belonging to the Lamb who was slain.[b]

9 Whoever has ears should listen to these
words:[c]

10 "If anyone is to go into captivity,
into captivity he will go.
If anyone is destined to be slain by the sword,
by the sword he must be slain."

This demands patient endurance and
faithfulness on the part of the saints.[d]

A Beast Rises from the Earth.* 11 Then I saw
another beast, this one rising up out of the
earth. It had two horns like those of a lamb,
but it spoke like a dragon.[e] 12 It wielded all
the authority of the first beast on its behalf,
and it forced the earth and all its inhabitants to worship the first beast, whose mor-

q Rev 12:3, 5; Gen 3:15.—r Rev 11:2; Ex 19:4; Dan 7:25; 12:7.—s Rev 12:9.—t Rev 1:2; 11:7; 13:7; Gen 3:15; Jn 14:15.—u Rev 12:3; 15:2; 16:13; 17:3; 2 Thes 2:3-12.—v Rev 2:13; 16:10; Dan 7:3-6.—w Rev 13:12, 14; 17:8.—x Rev 13:8; Ex 15:11; 2 Thes 2:4.—y Rev 11:2; Dan 7:8, 11, 25; 8:14; 9:27; 11:36; 12:7; 2 Thes 2:4.—z Rev 12:12.—a Rev 5:9; 7:9; 10:11; 11:7; 17:15; Dan 7:21.—b Rev 3:5, 10; 13:12, 14; 17:8; 20:12; Mt 25:34; Jn 1:23.—c Rev 2:7; Mt 13:9.—d Rev 14:12; Jer 15:2; 43:11; Heb 6:12.—e Rev 13:1-2; 16:13.

12:14 *A year, two years, and a half year:* see note on Rev 11:2.

12:18—13:10 This beast that is possessed of extraordinary power (seven heads and ten horns) personifies the Roman empire. Its historical success is a blasphemous parody of the Christian mystery; the emperors have themselves acclaimed with divine titles, while for Christians only God and the Lamb have a right to the title "Lord" (*Kyrios*). The head that was wounded and then healed probably refers to Nero who was forced to commit suicide (by pushing a sword into his head) and was said to have risen from the dead (again, a blasphemous parody of Jesus' Death and Resurrection).

12:18 *I took my position . . . :* another translation is: "he took his position . . ."—which would join v. 18 to the preceding paragraph.

13:5 *Forty-two months:* see note on Rev 11:2-3, 11.

13:8 *Written from the creation of the world:* some place these words at the very end of the sentence (after the word "slain"). *Book of life belonging to the Lamb:* see note on Rev 3:5.

13:11-18 The beast comes probably from Asia, because it was the East that gave rise to so many religious currents of thought that promoted emperor worship. The time has come when pressures are brought to bear and people are seduced. This picture fits in very well with the reign of Domitian, who banished Christians from the empire for refusing to practice emperor worship, the new sign of civic submission. The majority of believers resist, despite pressures and seductions of every kind.

The number of the beast has always been a snare for those who seek, by way of abstruse calculations, to identify the Antichrist with some figure of their own time. The number probably conceals the name of some personage known to readers of that time; the letters of the Greek alphabet and those of the Hebrew alphabet also stood for numbers, as is still the case with the Roman alphabet to some extent. Using gematria, a procedure for interpreting numbers, it was certainly possible to discern in the number 666 the words "Emperor Nero" in Hebrew. If we read "616" instead of "666," as some manuscripts do, it could be "Emperor Nero" in Greek.

tal wound had been healed.[f] 13 It performed
great signs, even making fire come down
from heaven to earth in the sight of all.[g]

14 By the signs it was allowed to perform
on behalf of the beast, it deceived the inhab-
itants of the earth, persuading them to erect
an image for the beast that had been wound-
ed by the sword and yet lived.[h] 15 It was per-
mitted to give life to the beast's image so
that it could even speak and cause all those
to be put to death who would not worship
the image of the beast.[i]

16 It also forced all the people, both small
and great, both rich and poor, both free and
slave, to be branded on the right hand or on
the forehead.[j] 17 No one could buy or sell
anything except one who has been branded
with the name of the beast or with the num-
ber of its name.[k]

18 There is wisdom here. Let anyone who
has understanding calculate the number of
the beast, for it is the number of a person.
The number is six hundred and sixty-six.[l]

CHAPTER 14

The Song of the Martyrs.* 1 Next in my
vision, I saw the Lamb standing on Mount
Zion, and with him were one hundred and
forty-four thousand* people who had his
name and his Father's name written on their
foreheads.[m] 2 I heard a sound from heaven
like that of a mighty torrent or a loud peal of
thunder. It was like the sound of harpists
playing their harps.[n]
3 They were singing a new song* before
the throne and before the four living crea-
tures and the elders. No one could learn this
song except the one hundred and forty-four
thousand who had been redeemed from the
earth.[o] 4 These are the ones who have not
defiled themselves with women.* They are
virgins, and they follow the Lamb wherever
he goes. They have been redeemed as the
firstfruits of mankind for God and for the
Lamb.[p] 5 No lie was found on their lips. They
are irreproachable.[q]

The Nearness of the Judgment.* 6 Then I saw
another angel flying in midair, with an eter-
nal gospel to proclaim to all those who live
on the earth, to every nation, race, language,
and people.[r] 7 He said in a loud voice, "Fear
God and give him glory, for the time has
come for his judgment. Worship him who
made heaven and earth, the sea and the
springs of water."[s]

8 A second angel followed him, saying:

"Fallen, fallen is Babylon the great.
She has made all the nations drink
the wine of the wrath of her immo-
rality."[t]

9 A third angel followed them, crying out
in a loud voice, "Anyone who worships the
beast or its image and receives its mark on
his forehead or hand[u] 10 will also drink the
wine of God's wrath, poured undiluted into
the cup of his wrath.* Such people will be
tormented in burning sulfur in the presence
of the holy angels and of the Lamb.[v] 11 The
smoke of their torment will rise forever and
ever. There will be no respite day or night for
those who worship the beast or its image or
for those who receive the mark of its
name."[w]

f Rev 13:3-4; 14:9, 11, 13; 16:2; 19:20.—g Rev 20:9; Deut 13:2-4; 1 Ki 18:38; 2 Ki 1:10; Mt 24:24; Lk 9:54; 2 Thes 2:9-10.—h Rev 3:10; 12:9; 13:3, 12; 2 Thes 2:9-10.—i Rev 13:12; Dan 3:5-7, 15.—j Rev 7:3; 14:9; 16:2; 19:5, 20; 20:4.—k Rev 13:18; 14:9, 11; 15:2.—l Rev 15:2; 17:9; 21:17.—m Rev 3:12; 5:6; 7:4; 14:3; 22:4; Joel 3:5; Ob 17; Acts 2:21; Heb 12:22.—n Rev 1:15; 5:8; 6:1; 15:2.—o Rev 4:4, 6; 5:9; 14:1; Pss 33:3; 96:1; 98:1; Isa 42:10.—p Rev 3:4; 5:9; 7:17; Jer 2:2; 2 Cor 11:2; Jas 1:18.—q Zep 3:13; Jn 1:47; Eph 5:27; 1 Pet 2:22.—r Rev 3:10; 8:13; 13:7; 19:17.—s Rev 2:10; 8:10; 10:6; 11:13; 15:4; Mt 10:28.—t Rev 2:4; 16:19; 17:5; 18:2-3; Isa 21:9; 51:17; Jer 25:15-17; 51:8.—u Rev 13:12, 14, 16.—v Rev 9:17; 18:6; Isa 51:17; Jer 25:15; 51:7.—w Rev 4:8; 13:12, 17; 14:9; 19:3; Isa 34:10.

14:1-5 The great hopes of the Prophets (e.g., Isa 2:1-5) are here realized; the new chosen people, in a full and perfect number, gather at Zion, the mount of definitive encounter with God. The martyrs sing the new song of deliverance and victory (see Ex 15:1-18; Pss 33:1-3; 98:1). It expresses the virginal joy of those who have remained faithful to God, those who have not committed falsehood, adultery, and fornication—i.e., in the language of the Bible, those who have not succumbed to the worship of false gods. They have not followed the emperor but only Christ. They have been, as it were, espoused to Christ (see Rev 19:9; 21:2; 2 Cor 11:2).

14:1 *One hundred and forty-four thousand:* that is, twelve thousand from each tribe.

14:3 *New song:* see note on Rev 5:9.

14:4 *The ones who have not defiled themselves with women:* this probably refers to those who avoided defiling relationships with the pagan world. *Follow the Lamb:* as disciples (see Mt 19:21; Mk 8:34). *Firstfruits:* a word used to refer to the first converts in a region (see Rom 16:5) and the first to rise from the dead (see 1 Cor 15:20). The author of this Book regards believers as choice offerings to God and the Lamb.

14:6-13 In the Old Testament, Babylon had become a symbol of every empire that was hostile to the People of God.

14:10 *Cup of his wrath:* the Old Testament commonly portrays the wrath of God by a cup of wine to be drunk (see Ps 75:9; Isa 51:17; Jer 25:15). *Burning sulfur:* this figured prominently in the destruction of Sodom and Gomorrah (see Gen 19:24), and Ps 11:6 speaks of a similar fate awaiting the wicked. The figure is also found elsewhere in the Old Testament and in the final chapters of Rev (19:20; 20:10; 21:8).

12 This demands patient endurance on the part of the saints who keep the commandments of God and remain faithful to Jesus.[x]

13 Then I heard a voice from heaven say, "Write: Blessed* are those who die in the Lord from now on."

"Yes," says the Spirit, "they will find rest from their labors, for their deeds go with them."[y]

One Like a Son of Man.* 14 Now in my vision, I saw a white cloud, and seated on the cloud was one "like a son of man,"* with a gold crown on his head and a sharp sickle in his hand.[z] 15 Another angel then came out of the temple and called out in a loud voice to the one seated on the cloud, "Use your sickle and reap, for the time to reap has come, because the harvest of the earth is fully ripe."[a] 16 So the one who was seated on the cloud swept over the earth with his sickle, and the earth was harvested.

17 Another angel came out of the temple in heaven, and he too had a sharp sickle.[b] 18 Then from the altar came forth still another angel who was in charge of the fire, and he cried out in a loud voice to the one who had the sharp sickle, "Take your sharp sickle and gather the clusters from the vines of the earth, for her grapes are ripe."[c]

19 So the angel swung his sickle over the earth and gathered in its vintage, which he then cast into the great winepress of God's wrath.[d] 20 The winepress was trodden outside the city, and blood flowed from the winepress to the height of a horse's bridle for a distance of two hundred miles.[e]

CHAPTER 15

The Seven Angels and the Seven Plagues.* 1 Then I saw in heaven another great and wondrous sign: seven angels with the seven plagues, the last plagues of all, for through them the wrath of God is completed.[f]

The Song of Moses and the Song of the Lamb.* 2 I saw something that looked like a sea of glass mixed with fire. Standing beside the sea of glass and holding the harps that God had given them were those who had been victorious over the beast and its image and over the number of its name. They were holding harps given them by God[g] 3 and singing the song of Moses, the servant of God, and the song of the Lamb:

"How great and wonderful are your works,
 Lord God Almighty!
Just and true are your ways,
 O King of the nations![h]
4 Who shall not fear you, O Lord,
 and bring glory to your name?
 For you alone are holy.
All nations will come
 and worship before you,
 for your acts of justice have been revealed."[i]

D: The Justice and Triumph of God*

Vision of the Temple. 5 After this, in my vision, the temple, that is, the tabernacle of the Testimony,* was opened in heaven,[j] 6 and

x Rev 12:17; 13:16; Jn 14:15; Heb 6:12.—y Rev 2:7; 22:17; Mt 11:28-29; 1 Cor 15:18; 1 Thes 4:16; 2 Thes 1:7; Heb 4:10.—z Rev 1:7, 13; Dan 7:13; Mt 17:5.—a Rev 11:19; 14:17, 18; Jer 51:33; Joel 4:13; Mt 13:36-43; Mk 4:29.—b Rev 14:15.—c Rev 6:9; 8:5; 14:15; 16:7.—d Rev 19:15; Isa 63:1-6.—e Rev 11:8; 14:19; 19:15; Gen 49:11; Isa 63:3; Joel 4:13; Heb 13:12.—f Rev 12:1, 3; 15:6-8; 16:1; 17:1; Lev 26:21.—g Rev 4:6; 5:8; 7:9, 14; 12:11; 13:1, 15-18; 14:2.—h Rev 1:8; 5:9; Ex 15:1; Deut 32:4; Jos 1:1; Pss 92:6; 98:1; 145:17.—i Rev 19:8; Ps 86:9-10; Isa 66:23; Jer 10:7.—j Rev 11:19; Ex 38:21; Num 1:50; Mt 3:16.

14:13 *Blessed:* the second beatitude (see note on Rev 1:3).

14:14-20 "You will see the Son of Man seated at the right hand of the Power and coming with the clouds of heaven," Jesus had declared in the presence of the high priest who condemned him (Mk 14:62, inspired by Dan 7:13). The Judgment is near; the time of vintage and harvest is its classic image in the Bible, evoking the reaping or storing of fruits as well as the harsh plundering of the terrain and the relentless gathering of the produce.

The winepress, in which the grapes are crushed, is an image of a battle aimed at savage extermination (see Isa 63:23); as such, it yields blood and not juice. Here the entire earth is involved; the *two hundred miles*, literally, "1600 stadia" (4 x 4 x 100), indicate this universality. The Judgment takes place outside Jerusalem—the author wants to indicate that those condemned are excluded from the assembly united around God.

14:14 *Son of man:* see note on Mt 8:20.

15:1 These constitute the decisive sign of the Judgment, whose execution will be set forth later.

15:2-4 Those who have resisted are like the Hebrews after their crossing of the Red Sea. Here the mass of water, so terrifying to the ancients, seems marvelously tamed. It is the turn of the martyrs to chant the song of liberation (see Ex 15:1-8), playing on instruments far superior to any earthly musical instruments.

15:5—19:10 Will heaven be mute in the presence of oppression by political authorities or by a civilization that turns human beings into slaves and claims to pass as God? Are the sufferings and martyrdom of victims a cry that is perhaps useless and fades away in the history of the world? The conscience of believers protests against this possibility. But it is necessary to determine in what God's Judgment consists: it will unmask the imposture and recognize the courage of those who have resisted this perversion. Here some scenes of this Judgment flash before our eyes.

15:5 *The temple, that is, the tabernacle of the Testimony:* i.e., the heavenly sanctuary. The phrase conflates the tabernacle of Moses and the temple of Solomon. The Old Testament had described in blazing images the God who mysteriously took possession of the temple. In the same images (see 1 Ki 8:10) we here contemplate the true temple of heaven, the manifestation of God. It is a description of the Judgment.

from the temple emerged the seven angels
with the seven plagues. They were robed in
clean, shining linen, and breastplates of gold
were fastened around their chests.[k]
7 Then one of the four living creatures
gave to the seven angels seven gold bowls full
of the wrath of God, who lives forever and
ever.[l] 8 The temple was filled with the smoke
from the glory of God and from his power, so
that no one could enter the temple until the
seven plagues of the seven angels were com-
pleted.[m]

CHAPTER 16

The Seven Bowls of the Wrath of God.*
1 Then I heard a loud voice from the tem-
ple say to the seven angels, "Go forth and
pour out on the earth the seven bowls of
the wrath of God."[n]
2 The first angel went forth and poured
out his bowl on the earth. Immediately, foul
and malignant sores broke out on those who
had the mark of the beast and who wor-
shiped its image.*[o]
3 * The second angel poured out his bowl
on the sea. It turned to blood, like the blood
of a dead person, and every living thing in
the sea died.[p]
4 The third angel poured out his bowl on
the rivers and the springs of water, and they
turned to blood.[q] 5 Then I heard the angel in
charge of the waters say:

"You are just, O Holy One,
who are and who were,
in these your judgments.[r]
6 For they have shed the blood
of the saints and the Prophets,
and you have given them blood to drink,
as they deserve."[s]

7 And I heard the altar respond:

"Yes, Lord God Almighty,
true and just are your judgments."[t]

8 The fourth angel poured out his bowl on
the sun, and the sun was allowed to burn
people with its flames.[u] 9 They were
scorched by the fierce heat, and they cursed
the name of God who had the power to
inflict those plagues, but they refused to
repent and pay him homage.[v]
10 The fifth angel poured out his bowl on
the throne of the beast, and its kingdom was
plunged into darkness. * People gnawed their
tongues in agony[w] 11 and cursed the God of
heaven because of their pains and sores,
instead of repenting for what they had done.[x]
12 The sixth angel poured out his bowl on
the great river Euphrates, and its water was
dried up to prepare the way for the kings
from the East.[y] 13 I saw three unclean spirits
like frogs * come forth from the mouth of
the dragon, from the mouth of the beast,
and from the mouth of the false prophet.[z]
14 These are demonic spirits with the
power to work miracles. They were sent to
the kings of the entire world to assemble
them for battle on the great day of God the
Almighty.[a]
15 * "Behold, I am coming like a thief!
Blessed is the one who stays awake and
keeps his clothes close by so that he will not
have to go naked and be exposed to
shame."[b] 16 These spirits then assembled the
kings at the place that in Hebrew is called
Armageddon.*[c]
17 The seventh angel poured out his bowl
into the air, and a loud voice came out of the
temple from the throne, saying, "It is
done!"[d] 18 Then there followed flashes of
lightning, rumblings, peals of thunder, and a

k Rev 1:13; 14:15; 15:1; 19:8; Ezek 9:2.—l Rev 1:18; 4:6; 15:1.—m Ex 40:34-35; 1 Ki 8:10-11; 2 Chr 5:13-14; Isa 6:4.—n Rev 11:19; 15:1; 16:2-21; Zep 3:8.—o Rev 8:7; 13:15-17; 16:11; Ex 9:9-11; Deut 28:35.—p Rev 8:8, 9; 11:6; Ex 7:17-21.—q Rev 8:10; Ex 7:14-24.—r Rev 1:4; 6:10; 15:3-4.—s Rev 17:6; 18:24; Isa 49:26; Ezek 35:6; Mt 23:34-35; Lk 11:49-51.—t Rev 1:8; 6:9; 14:18; 15:3; 19:2; Tob 3:2; Dan 3:27.—u Rev 6:12; 8:12; 14:18.—v Rev 2:21; 11:13; 16:11, 21; Am 4:6.—w Rev 8:12; 9:2; 13:2; Ex 10:21-23; Isa 8:22.—x Rev 2:21; 11:13; 16:9, 21; Ex 9:8-11; Jer 5:3.—y Rev 9:14; Isa 11:15, 16; 41:2; 46:11.—z Rev 12:3; 13:1-2; 19:20; 20:10; Ex 8:2-3.—a Rev 6:17; 17:14; 19:19; 20:8; Mt 24:14, 24; 1 Cor 1:8; 1 Tim 4:1.—b Rev 3:17, 18; Mt 24:42-44; Lk 12:37, 39.—c Rev 9:11; 16:14; Jdg 5:19; 2 Ki 23:29-30; Zec 12:11.—d Rev 11:15; 14:15; 21:6; Isa 66:6; Eph 2:2.

16:1-21 The story of the plagues in Egypt (Ex 7—12) remained deeply inscribed in the imagination of the Jews; once again, as in chapters 8—10 (vision of the trumpets), that story here inspires the description of the final cataclysm of the universe and of the lives of its peoples and nations. The desolating picture shows all the hostile forces united at Armageddon (the Megiddo of the Bible, where King Josiah died with his troops); it became a place of sinister memory, and an omen and symbol of military defeat and even annihilation (see 2 Ki 23:29-30; Zec 12:11). The great city Babylon, i.e., Rome, is collapsing.

16:2 Similar to the sixth plague of Egypt (see Ex 9:8-11).

16:3-4 Similar to the first plague of Egypt (see Ex 7:20f).

16:10 Similar to the ninth plague of Egypt (see Ex 10:21-23).

16:13 *Frogs:* an allusion to the second plague of Egypt (see Ex 7:26—8:11).

16:15 This verse interrupts the text. It fits in better in the literary atmosphere of the letters to the Churches, especially Rev 3:3-4, 18. *Blessed:* the third beatitude (see note on Rev 1:3).

16:16 *Armageddon:* i.e., the "mountain of Megiddo," the site of many battles in antiquity (see Jdg 5:19f; 2 Ki 9:27; 2 Chr 35:20-24); it symbolized the final defeat of the powers of evil.

violent earthquake—so violent that there
has never been one like it since the human
race has inhabited the earth.[e]

19 The great city was split into three parts,
and the cities of the nations collapsed in
ruin. Babylon the Great was also remem-
bered by God, as he made her drink the cup
filled with the wine of his fury and wrath.[f]
20 Every island vanished, and no mountains
were to be found.[g] 21 Huge hailstones, each
weighing about one hundred pounds, fell
from the sky on the people, and they cursed
God on account of the plague of hail that
turned out to be so terrible.[h]

CHAPTER 17

Babylon the Great, the Infamous Harlot.*
1 One of the seven angels who held the seven
bowls approached me and said, "Come here
and I will show you the judgment on the
great harlot who is enthroned over many
waters.[i] 2 The kings of the earth have com-
mitted fornication with her, and the inhabi-
tants of the earth have become drunk on the
wine of her harlotry."[j]

3 Then he carried me away in the spirit*
into the wilderness, and I saw a woman seat-
ed on a scarlet beast that had seven heads
and ten horns and was covered with blas-
phemous names.[k] 4 The woman was clothed
in purple and scarlet and adorned with gold
and jewels and pearls. In her hand she held
a gold cup filled with accursed things and
the impurities of her harlotry.[l]

5 On her forehead was written a mysteri-
ous name: "Babylon the Great, the mother
of harlots and of every abomination on the
earth."[m] 6 And I noticed that the woman
was drunk with the blood of the saints and
the blood of those who had borne witness to
Jesus.[n]

When I saw her, I was utterly astounded.
7 But the angel said to me, "Why are you
astounded? I will explain to you the mystery
of the woman and of the beast with the
seven heads and the ten horns that carries
her.[o] 8 The beast that you saw was once alive
but is now alive no longer. It is about to
ascend from the abyss and go to its destruc-
tion. All the inhabitants of the earth whose
names have not been written in the book of
life since the foundation of the world will be
astonished when they see the beast, because
it was once alive but is now alive no longer,
and yet it is still to come.[p]

9 "This calls for a mind with wisdom. The
seven heads represent seven hills upon
which the woman is seated. They also repre-
sent seven kings.[q] 10 Five have already fallen,
one is still living, and the other has not yet
come. When he does come, he must remain
only for a short while. 11 As for the beast that
was alive but is now alive no longer, it is at
the same time the eighth and one of the
seven, and it is headed for destruction.[r]

12 "The ten horns that you saw are ten
kings who have not yet begun to reign. They
will have royal authority for only a single
hour together with the beast.[s] 13 They are all
of the same mind and will confer their
power and authority on the beast.[t] 14 They
will wage war against the Lamb, but because
the Lamb is Lord of lords and King of
kings,* he will overcome them—he and
those who are with him, the called, the cho-
sen, and the faithful."[u]

15 The angel continued, "The waters that
you saw, where the harlot sits, represent peo-
ples, multitudes, nations, and languages.[v]

e Rev 4:5; 6:12; Mt 24:21; Mk 13:19.—f Rev 14:8,10; 17:18; 18:5.—g Rev 6:14; 20:11.—h Rev 8:7; 11:19; 16:9,11; Ex 9:22-26; Ezek 13:13; 38:22.—i Rev 15:1,7; 16:19; 17:5,15-16; 19:2; Isa 23:17; Jer 50:38; 51:13.—j Rev 14:8; Jer 51:7.—k Rev 1:10; 12:6; 13:1; 14:3; 18:12, 16.—l Rev 14:8; 17:2; 18:6, 16; Jer 51:7; Ezek 28:13.—m Rev 1:2; 14:8; 17:7.—n Rev 16:6; 18:24.—o Rev 12:3; 17:3, 5.—p Rev 3:5; 13:3-4, 8; 20:12; Lk 8:31.—q Rev 13:18; 17:3.—r Rev 17:8.—s Rev 12:3; 18:10, 17, 19; Dan 7:24.—t Rev 17:17.—u Rev 16:14; 19:11-21; 2 Mac 13:4; Mt 22:14; Jn 16:33; Rom 1:6; 1 Tim 6:15; 1 Pet 2:9; Jude 1.—v Rev 13:7; 17:1; Isa 8:7; Jer 47:2.

17:1-18 *Harlot* and *mother of harlots:* such is Babylon because it is the wellspring of idolatry, especially by imposing emperor worship; and for the people of the Bible an idol is an abomination, and idolatry is prostitution (Ezek, chs. 16 and 23). The woman on the beast is named Babylon, a name that stands for all oppressions and all sufferings; the real reference is to imperial Rome, the famous city on the seven hills (v. 9), the center of the great empire that has enslaved the peoples of the Mediterranean basin (vv. 1, 15). She will drink the blood of Christians, especially during the terrible persecutions of Nero and Domitian.

The beast that once was and now is not, but is returning—a parody of God who is described as "him who is, who was, and who is to come" (Rev 1:4)—is probably Nero (A.D. 54–68), whose resurrection was predicted in some popular legends. And if the seven kings need to be identified (vv. 9-11), the list is as follows: Augustus, Tiberius, Caligula, Claudius, Nero, Vespasian, and Titus (omitting Galba, Otho, and Vitellius, interim emperors, who ruled in quick succession in A.D. 68–69, after the death of Nero). The eighth emperor acts as people would expect Nero to act if he returned to life, i.e., as a beast; we can give him a name: Domitian (A.D. 81–96), during whose reign the Book of Revelation was probably composed. The other ten kings (v. 12) lead peoples subject to the empire. Empires and governors waste the political and cultural patrimony of Rome (v. 16): tyranny and bullying will be the cause of its destruction.

17:3 *In the spirit:* see note on Rev 1:10.

17:14 *Lord of lords and King of kings:* a title that stresses the Lamb's supreme sovereignty (see Deut 10:17; Ps 136:2-3; Dan 2:47; 1 Tim 6:15).

[16] The ten horns that you saw and the beast
will hate the harlot. They will render her des-
olate and naked; after they devour her flesh,
they will burn her up with fire. [w]
[17] "For God has influenced their hearts to
carry out his purpose by agreeing to confer
their royal powers upon the beast until the
words of God will be fulfilled. [x] [18] The
woman you saw is the great city that has
authority over the kings of the earth." [y]

CHAPTER 18

The Fall of Babylon the Great.* [1] After this I
saw another angel coming down from heav-
en. He had great authority, and his splendor
illumined the earth. [z] [2] He cried out in a
mighty voice:

"Fallen, fallen is Babylon the Great!
She has become a dwelling place for demons,
a haunt for every unclean spirit
and for every filthy and loathsome bird. [a]
3 For all the nations have drunk
the wine of the wrath of her harlotry.
The kings of the earth have committed fornication with her,
and the merchants of the earth have grown rich
from her wealth and luxury." [b]

[4] Then I heard another voice from heaven
saying:

"Depart from her, my people,
so that you will not take part in her sins
and share in her plagues. [c]
5 For her sins are piled up as high as the heavens,
and God has remembered her crimes. [d]
6 Pay her back as she has done to others,
and repay her double for her deeds;
mix her a double portion of her own poison. [e]
7 Give her torment and grief
to equal the measure of her glory and luxury.
In her heart she says,
'I rule as a queen.
I am not a widow,
and I will never experience grief.' [f]
8 Therefore, in a single day
her plagues will come upon her:
pestilence and mourning and famine.
And she will be consumed by fire,
for mighty is the Lord God who judges her. [g]

Funereal Ode over Rome.* [9] "The kings of
the earth who committed fornication with
her and shared in her luxury will weep and
mourn over her when they behold the smoke
of her immolation. [h] [10] In terror at her tor-
ment, they will keep their distance and say:

" 'Woe, woe, O great city,
mighty city of Babylon.
In one hour your judgment has come.' [i]

[11] "The merchants of the earth will weep
and mourn over her, since no one buys their
cargo anymore: [j] [12] their cargo of gold, silver,
precious stones, and pearls; purple and scar-
let cloth, silks, and fine linens; all sorts of fra-
grant wood and all kinds of objects of ivory,
all kinds of objects of expensive wood,
bronze, iron, and marble; [k] [13] cinnamon and
spices; incense, myrrh, and frankincense;
wine and olive oil; fine flour and wheat;
cattle and sheep; horses and chariots; and
slaves, that is, human lives. [l] They will say:

14 " 'The fruit you longed for
is no longer available to you.
All your riches and splendor are gone,
and you will never find them again.' [m]

[15] "The merchants of these things who
made a fortune from her will stand far off,
weeping and mourning aloud, and terrified
as they behold her torment: [n]

16 " 'Woe, woe, O great city,
clothed in fine linen and purple and scarlet,
adorned with gold, jewels, and precious stones! [o]
17 Within one hour
all this wealth has been destroyed.'

w Rev 12:3; 17:1; 18:8, 17, 19; 19:18; Ezek 16:37-41; 23:25-29.—x Rev 10:7; 17:13; Jer 39:16; 2 Cor 8:10.—y Rev 16:19; 18:10, 18-19, 21.—z Rev 1:20; 3:10; 17:1; Ezek 43:2.—a Rev 14:8; 16:13; Isa 13:21-22; Isa 21:9; Jer 50:2-3; 51:8.—b Rev 14:8; 17:2; 18:7, 9, 11, 15, 23; Jer 51:7; Ezek 27:9-25.—c Gen 19:15; Isa 48:20; Jer 50:8; 2 Cor 6:17.—d Rev 16:19; Gen 28:9; Jer 51:9; Ezek 9:6.—e Rev 14:10; 16:19; 17:4; Isa 40:2; Jer 16:18; 50:15.—f Isa 47:8-9; Ezek 28:2-8; Zep 2:15.—g Rev 17:16; 18:10; Isa 9:13; 47:9; Jer 50:31-32.—h Rev 14:8; 17:2-4; 18:3, 7, 18; Jer 51:8; Ezek 26:16-19.—i Rev 16:19; 17:12; 18:15.—j Rev 18:3, 15, 19; Ezek 27:27, 31.—k Rev 17:4; Ezek 27:12, 22.—l Ezek 27:13; 1 Tim 1:10.—m Hos 10:5; Am 6:7.—n Rev 18:3, 10-11, 17, 19; Ezek 27:31.—o Rev 17:4; 18:10, 19.

18:1-8 The fall of Rome is described as if the empire were already collapsing.

18:9-24 Drawing upon the laments of Ezekiel over the fall of Tyre (Ezek 26—28), the author greets the fall of Rome as already complete. This satire on the ruins of the empire also harbors, in its final lines, a tone of poignant complaint. The tableau nicely sketches the maritime grandeur of Rome, the development of commercial exchanges—without forgetting the traffic in slaves and prostitutes (v. 13)—and the extraordinary accumulation of riches.

"All the ship captains and voyagers, all the
sailors and those who make their living by
trading upon the sea, will stand far off[p]
18 and exclaim as they see the smoke caused
by her immolation, 'Has there ever been a
city to compare with this great city?'[q]
19 Then they will throw dust on their heads
and with mourning and weeping cry out:

" 'Woe, woe, O great city,
where all who had ships at sea
became rich through her wealth!
Within one hour
she has been brought to ruin.[r]
20 Rejoice over her, O heaven,
you holy ones, apostles, and prophets!
For God has passed judgment on her for
you.' "[s]

21 Then a mighty angel picked up a stone
the size of a large millstone and threw it into
the sea, saying:

"This is how
the great city of Babylon will be
thrown down,
never to be found again.[t]
22 The sound of harpists and minstrels,
flute players and trumpeters,
will never be heard in you again.
Craftsmen of every trade
never will be found in you again.
The sound of a millstone
will never be heard in you again.[u]
23 The light from a lamp
will never be seen in you again.
The voices of a bridegroom and bride
will never be heard in you again.
Since your merchants were the world's
great men,
all the nations were led astray by your
enticements.[v]
24 In you* was found the blood of the
Prophets,
of the saints,
and of all who have been slain on the
earth."[w]

CHAPTER 19

**Song of Victory and Wedding Day of the
Lamb.*** 1 After this I heard what sounded like
the roar of a great multitude in heaven,
shouting:

"Alleluia! *
Salvation and glory and power belong to
our God,[x]
2 for true and just are his judgments.
He has condemned the great harlot
who corrupted the earth with her harlotry.
And he has paid her back
for the blood of his servants."[y]

3 Once again they shouted:

"Alleluia!
Her smoke will rise
forever and ever."[z]

4 The twenty-four elders and the four liv-
ing creatures threw themselves to the
ground and worshiped God who was seated
on the throne, and they cried:

"Amen. Alleluia!"[a]

5 Then a voice came from the throne, saying:

"Praise our God,
all you his servants,
and all who fear him,
small and great alike."[b]

6 And I heard what seemed to be the
sound of a vast multitude, like the sound of
a torrential stream or of great peals of thun-
der, crying out:

"Alleluia.
The reign of the Lord our God,
the Almighty, has begun.[c]
7 Let us rejoice and be glad
and give him glory.
For the wedding day of the Lamb has
come,
and the bride has made herself ready.[d]

---

p Rev 16:15; 17:12; 18:10; Ezek 27:28-30.—q Rev 13:4; 17:18; 18:19; 19:3; Ezek 27:32.—r Rev 17:16, 18; 18:10-11, 15-16; Jos 7:6; Ezek 27:27-32.—s Rev 12:12; 19:1-2; Deut 32:43; Jer 51:4-8.—t Rev 5:2; 17:18; Jer 51:63-64; Ezek 26:21.—u Isa 24:8; Jer 25:10; Ezek 26:13.—v Rev 18:3; Isa 23:8; Jer 7:34; 16:9; 25:10.—w Rev 16:6; 17:6; Jer 51:49.—x Rev 4:11; 7:10, 12; 11:15; 12:10; 19:3-4, 6.—y Rev 6:10; 16:7; 17:1; Jer 51:48-49; Dan 3:27.—z Rev 14:11; 19:1, 4, 6; Isa 34:10.—a Rev 4:4, 6, 10; 19:3, 6.—b Rev 11:18; 13:16; 19:18; 20:12; Ps 115:13.—c Rev 1:8, 15; 11:15; 19:1, 3-4.—d Rev 11:13; 19:9; 21:2, 9; 22:17; Mt 22:9; Eph 5:27.

18:24 *You:* the Greek has "her."

19:1-10 No other image could better evoke the fulfillment of all the expectations of believers than this vast heavenly liturgy and the vision of the wedding feast (see Mt 22:1-14; 25:1-13).

The plea of the martyrs (see Rev 6:9) has been heard; the immense throng, along with the twenty-four elders and the four living beings, makes up the entire Church, reunited at last. The Kingdom of God reveals itself in all its reality. It is described as Christ's marriage to the Church and as the complete manifestation of the Covenant, which is God's ardent, jealous love for his people (see Isa 54:1-8; Hos 2:16-18) and Christ's nuptial love for his Church (see Eph 5:23, 25, 32; see also Jn 3:29).

19:1, 3, 4, 6 *Alleluia:* an important exclamation of praise in the Psalms that is found only here in the New Testament. It is derived from two Hebrew words meaning "Praise the Lord."

8 She has been permitted to wear
a bright and clean garment of fine
linen."

(The fine linen represents the righteous
deeds of the saints.)[e]

9 Then the angel said to me, "Write:
'Blessed* are those who are invited to the
wedding banquet of the Lamb.'" And he
added, "These are the true words of God."[f]

10 I fell at his feet to worship him, but he
said to me, "You must not do that! I am a
fellow servant with you and with your
brethren who have given witness to Jesus.*
Worship God! For the witness to Jesus is the
spirit of prophecy."[g]

E: Recapitulative Visions of the History of Salvation*

The White Horse and the King of Kings.*
11 Now I saw heaven opened, and a white
horse appeared. Its rider was called
"Faithful and True," for with righteousness
he judges and wages war.[h] 12 His eyes were
like fiery flames, and on his head were many
crowns. The name inscribed on him was
known to no one but himself.[i]

13 He was clothed in a robe dipped in
blood, and he was known by the name The
Word of God.[j] 14 The armies of heaven were
following him, riding on white horses and
dressed in fine linen, white and clean.[k]

15 Coming out of his mouth was a sharp
sword with which to strike down the nations.
He will rule them with an iron scepter, and
he will tread the winepress* of the fury of the
wrath of God the Almighty.[l] 16 On his robe
and on his thigh* he had a name inscribed:
"King of kings and Lord of lords."[m]

The Great Booty.* 17 Then I saw an angel
standing in the sun, and with a loud voice he
cried out to all the birds flying in midair,
"Come here! Gather together for the great
supper of God,[n] 18 to eat the flesh of kings,
the flesh of commanders, and the flesh of
warriors, the flesh of horses and their riders,
the flesh of all, both free and slave, both
small and great."[o]

The Beast and the False Prophet.* 19 Next I
saw the beast and the kings of the earth and
their armies gathered together to wage war
against the one upon the horse and against
his army.[p] 20 The beast was captured, and
with it the false prophet who in its presence
had performed the signs by which he had
deluded those who had received the mark of
the beast and those who had worshiped its
image.

These two were thrown alive into the fiery
lake of burning sulfur.[q] 21 The rest were
killed by the sword that came forth from the
mouth of the rider on the horse, and all the
birds gorged themselves on their flesh.[r]

CHAPTER 20

The Dragon.* 1 Then I saw an angel coming
down from heaven, with the key to the abyss

e Rev 15:4, 6; 19:14; Isa 61:10; Ezek 44:17; Zec 3:4; Mt 22:11-12.—f Rev 1:19; 19:10; 21:5; 22:6; Mt 8:11; Lk 14:15.—g Rev 1:2; 22:8-9, 18; Lk 10:22; Acts 10:25-26.—h Rev 3:14; 6:2; 19:19, 21; Ex 15:3; Isa 11:4; Mt 3:10.—i Rev 1:14; 2:17; 6:2; 12:3; 19:16.—j Isa 63:1-2; Jn 1:1.—k Rev 3:4; 15:6; 19:8.—l Rev 1:16; 2:27; 12:5; 14:20; 19:21; Isa 11:4; 63:3; 2 Thes 2:8.—m Rev 17:14; 19:12; 2 Mac 13:4; 1 Tim 6:15.—n Rev 8:13; 14:6; 19:21; Isa 34:6; Jer 12:9; 46:10; Ezek 39:17.—o Rev 6:15; 19:5; Ezek 39:17-20.—p Rev 13:1; 16:14, 16; 19:11, 21.—q Rev 9:17; 13:12, 14-16; 14:10, 15; 16:13; 20:10; 21:8; Mt 24:24.—r Rev 1:16; 19:11, 15, 17, 19.

19:9 *Blessed:* the fourth beatitude (see note on Rev 1:3).

19:10 *Witness to Jesus:* the proclamation that the predictions of the Prophets have been truly fulfilled.

19:11—20:15 There now follows a new series of six tableaus, which the imagination projects onto the destiny of the world. Is it necessary then to foresee a new series of events in an ever more distant future? And is the history of God's judgments something that is forever beginning again? The author has no intention of setting forth an indefinite series of calendars of the future. But before sketching the tableau of the new heaven and the new earth, he wishes one last time to interpret the drama of the world; for he has at hand other materials, some of which greatly resemble those that he has already used. He organizes them to compose this rapid sequence: a powerful summary of the whole History of Salvation. It begins with Jesus and takes us well beyond the fall of Rome to the resurrection of the dead and the last judgment—a kind of tragic prelude whose contrast heightens the dazzling joy that will later inform the grand symphony of the heavenly Jerusalem.

19:11-16 To describe the victory of Christ, the author uses the classic images of the warrior Messiah who establishes justice (Isa 11:4), annihilates hostile powers (Isa 63:3), subjects the nations (Ps 2:9), and traverses the world as the efficacious Word of God (see Wis 18:14-18). Through him justice reigns upon the world. He is the truthful and faithful one who fulfills God's promise and makes his justice a reality.

19:15 *Will tread the winepress:* the image was commonplace in the Prophets for symbolizing God's destruction of the enemies of his people on the great day of his wrath (see Gen 49:9-12; Isa 63:1-6; Jer 25:30; Joel 4:13); the wine is the blood of the enemies.

19:16 *Thigh:* this should probably be "standard"; the two words are quite similar in Hebrew and can be confused. *King of kings and Lord of lords:* see note on Rev 17:14.

19:17-18 In a final, gigantic combat, the forces of destruction will be annihilated (see Rev 14:6-13). This is the terrible sacrifice of which Ezekiel speaks (39:2, 17-20).

19:19-21 The beast and the false prophet are thrown into the fiery lake and destroyed. The vision sums up in a single scene all the tableaus of the fall of Rome, and corresponds to that in Rev 14:14-20. The beast, the false prophet, and the entire campaign aimed at imposing emperor worship are described in ch. 13.

20:1-3 The dragon is enchained for a thousand years in the abyss, the dwelling of the powers of evil (see Rev 9:2). This refers to Satan's defeat when Jesus died and rose from the dead. The thousand year period means "for a long time." Satan's power is limited (as if he is imprisoned for a long time). Yet he still tempts the holy ones on the earth during this period.

and a great chain in his hand.[s] 2 He seized
the dragon, that ancient serpent, who is the
devil, or Satan, and chained him up for a
thousand years.[t] 3 He threw him into the
abyss and locked and sealed it over him, so
that he would not again deceive the nations
until the thousand years were ended. After
that he must be released, but only for a short
time.[u]

The Reign of the Martyrs: Return and Destruction of Satan.* 4 Next, I saw thrones on
which were seated those who had been given
the authority to judge. I also saw the souls of
those who had been beheaded for bearing
witness to Jesus and the word of God. They
had not worshiped the beast or its image
and had not received its mark on their fore-
heads or their hands. They lived and reigned
with Christ for a thousand years. *[v]

5 The rest of the dead did not come to life
until the thousand years were ended. This is
the first resurrection.[w] 6 Blessed * and holy
are those who share in the first resurrection.
The second death has no power over them.
They will be priests of God and of Christ,
and they will reign with him for a thousand
years.[x]

7 When the thousand years are ended,
Satan will be released from his prison[y] 8 and
will emerge to lead astray the nations in
the four corners of the earth—Gog and
Magog—in order to gather them for battle.
They are as numerous as the sands of the
sea. *[z]

9 They marched across the breadth of the
earth * and laid siege to the camp of the
saints and the beloved city. However, fire
came down from heaven and devoured
them.[a] 10 The devil who had led them astray
was thrown into the fiery lake of burning sul-
fur, where the beast and the false prophet
had been flung to be tormented day and
night forever and ever.[b]

Preparation for the Judgment.* 11 Then I saw
a great white throne, and the one who was
seated upon it. The earth and the sky fled so
far from his presence that they could no
longer be found.[c]

The Resurrection and Judgment.* 12 And I
saw the dead, great and small, standing
before the throne, and the scrolls were
opened. Then another scroll was opened, the
book of life, and the dead were judged
according to their deeds, as were recorded
in the scrolls.[d]

13 The sea gave up all the dead who were
in it, and Death and Hades gave up the
dead that were in them. The dead were
judged according to their deeds.[e] 14 Then

---

s Rev 1:18; 9:1; 10:1; 18:1; Lk 8:31.—t Gen 3:1; Isa 24:22; Mt 4:10.—u Rev 12:9; 20:1, 8, 10; Mt 27:66.—v Rev 1:2; 3:21; 6:9; 13:12; 22:5; Mt 19:28; Heb 4:12; 2 Pet 2:4.—w Rev 20:6; Lk 14:14; Phil 3:11; 1 Thes 4:16.—x Rev 2:11; 14:13; 20:4; 22:5; 1 Pet 2:5.—y Rev 20:2; Ezek 38:2, 7-9.—z Rev 7:1; 12:9; 20:3, 10; Isa 11:12; Ezek 7:2; 38:2, 9, 16; Heb 11:12.—a Rev 13:13; Ezek 38:9, 22.—b Rev 9:17; 12:9; 14:10-11; 16:13; 19:20; 20:3, 8.—c Rev 4:2; 6:14; 2 Pet 3:7, 10, 12.—d Rev 19:5; 20:15; Ex 32:32; Deut 29:20; Jer 17:10; Mal 3:16; Lk 10:20; Rom 2:6.—e Rev 1:18; 6:8; Isa 26:19; Mt 16:27.

20:4-10 While waiting for the History of Salvation to be completed, the witnesses to Christ's love already reign with Jesus when they take up their crosses and follow Jesus. However, before the final triumph arrives—the great Judgment that one imagines must complete history—evil unleashes a last terrible assault on the Church, as envisaged by Ezekiel (chs. 36—39) and Paul (2 Thes 2). Then will be fulfilled the prophecy of Genesis (3:15) that in advance sketched the profound link of the drama of history and its end: the annihilation of the serpent, the personification of evil.

A reign of a thousand years? This passage has served as the basis of all the millenniarist interpretations, which await the coming of a political kingdom of Christ on earth. Must we at least imagine a first earthly accomplishment of the Kingdom of God before the final and eternal transformation? But the author does not speak of a return of Christ in earthly conditions. He wants to affirm above all that those who have died as witnesses of Jesus are not separated from him while awaiting the full resurrection (vv. 11-13); he also wishes to suggest that from now on believers have access to the tree of life in heaven—of which the figure "one thousand" may be a symbol—hence that they partake in the communion of God. In any case, the thousand-year reign is a symbolic representation, which thus prohibits all speculation. At best it evokes a length of time and a life of the Church beyond persecutions. But we must not forget that for God a thousand years are like one day (see Ps 90:4).

20:4 *A thousand years:* early tradition took this verse literally: after a first real resurrection, that of the martyrs, Christ would return to earth and reign there for a thousand years. The Church has rejected this literal millenniarism.

20:6 *Blessed:* the fifth beatitude (see note on Rev 1:3). *The second death:* eternal death, or damnation, which cannot be followed by a resurrection.

20:8 Ezekiel speaks of "Gog, king of Magog." Here the two names symbolize the pagan nations gathered together against the Church at the end of the world.

20:9 The *earth* is Palestine; the *beloved city* is Jerusalem, a symbol of the Church.

20:11 The earth and the sky disappear; the first creation is abolished. Human beings alone remain, responsible toward God.

20:12-15 This is a grandiose final sequence. As in Daniel (12:1-7) and Matthew (25:31-36), all human beings appear before the tribunal of God and are judged according to their choices and life commitments. (This principle of judgment according to one's works is also found in Ps 62:12; Jer 17:10; Rom 2:6; 1 Pet 1:17 and elsewhere.) Everything is laid bare before the Lord—the same idea expressed in the symbol of books in Daniel (7:10). There is another book—that of Life; it contains the names of those who have resolutely chosen Christ in the face of idolatry and are now destined for glory (see Rev 13:8; 17:8). When one knows all that is represented by the concept of the netherworld, the sojourn of death and the power of death personified in the Bible, verse 14 announces the end of the anguish and fear that have weighed heavily on humankind throughout history.

Death and Hades were hurled into the fiery lake. This fiery lake is the second death. *[f] 15 Anyone who was not found written in the book of life was thrown into the fiery lake.[g]

F: The New Jerusalem
A New World and a New People*

CHAPTER 21

The New Heaven and the New Earth. 1 Then I saw a new heaven and a new earth. For the first heaven and the first earth had passed away, and there was no longer any sea. *[h] 2 And I saw the holy city, the new Jerusalem, coming down out of heaven from God, like a bride adorned and ready for her husband.[i] 3 And I heard a loud voice proclaim from the throne:

"Behold, God's dwelling is with mankind;
he will dwell with them.
They will be his people,
and he will be their God,
God-with-them. *[j]
4 He will wipe every tear from their eyes,
and there will no longer be death.
Neither will there be any mourning or crying or pain,
for the old order has passed away."[k]

5 The one seated on the throne then said, "Behold, I am making all things new." He also said, "Write this down, for these words are trustworthy and true."[l] 6 Then he said to me, "It is done. I am the Alpha and the Omega, the Beginning and the End.* To those who are thirsty I will give to drink without cost from the spring of life-giving water.[m]

7 "The one who is victorious will inherit these things, and I will be his God and he will be my son. *[n] 8 But as for the cowardly, the faithless, the depraved, the murderers, the sexually immoral, the sorcerers, the idolaters, and liars of every kind, their place is the fiery lake of burning sulfur, which is the second death." *[o]

The New Jerusalem. 9 One of the seven angels who had the seven bowls filled with the seven final plagues came forward and said to me, "Come, and I will show you the bride, the wife of the Lamb."[p] 10 Then he carried me away in the spirit * to the top of a very high mountain and showed me the holy city Jerusalem coming down out of heaven from God.[q] 11 It possessed the glory

f Rev 2:11; 19:20; 20:13; 1 Cor 15:26, 54-55.—g Rev 20:12.—h Rev 6:14; Isa 65:17; 66:19-23; 2 Pet 3:13.—i Rev 3:12; 11:2; 19:7-9; 21:10; 22:19; Neh 11:18; Isa 52:1; Heb 11:10.—j Ex 25:8; 2 Chr 6:18; Ezek 37:27; Zec 2:10; 2 Cor 6:16.—k Rev 7:17; 20:14; Isa 25:8; 35:10; 1 Cor 15:26; 2 Cor 5:17.—l Rev 4:9; 19:9; 20:11; 21:4; 22:6; Isa 43:19; 2 Cor 5:17.—m Rev 1:8; 16:17; 22:13, 17; Ps 36:8-9; Isa 55:1; Jn 4:10.—n Rev 21:3; 2 Sam 7:14; Jn 16:33; Rom 8:14; 2 Cor 6:16.—o Rev 2:11; 9:17; 21:27; 22:15; Rom 1:29-32; Heb 12:14.—p Rev 15:1, 6-7; 19:7.—q Rev 1:10; 17:3; 21:2; Ezek 40:2.

20:14 *The second death*, in which death itself is swallowed up, is the definitive failure, the condemnation from which no resurrection can rescue (Rev 2:11; 20:6; 21:8).

21:1—22:5 A new city for human beings descends from heaven, as beautiful as a new bride; a new universe replaces the old; life gushes up in floods, and an endless feast begins. How can we interpret these marvelous images? We must let ourselves be captivated by the poetic evocation, by the incantation of this exciting symphony. We must project all the attention of people and the Church toward this meeting and this reconciliation, which we regard as the sole definitive condition for humankind—creating a mystical impetus toward Christ, a hope without frontiers.

Let us then strive to highlight some themes that this vision overlaps on one another. At the end of the work of salvation, it is a new creation that God accomplishes (v. 1), surpassing all the images of paradise. Gone are all things that constrained, all limits, imperfections, implacable necessities, evil: the sea, the sun and moon, and the night. Streams spring forth more attractive than those of Eden, for they are a share in the unfathomable life of God; the tree of life finds its power multiplied to infinity (Rev 22:2).

For human beings, this work of salvation is essentially the gathering of the People of God for a definitive Covenant with the Lord. It is presented as a wedding feast in which is realized—in unimaginable fullness—the love of God and human beings, of Christ and the Church, which in keeping with beautiful Biblical texts is expressed as a wedding (see Isa 54:5; 62:4; Mt 9:15; Jn 3:29; 2 Cor 11:2; Rev 19:1-10).

Dreams of the restoration of Jerusalem haunted the Jewish people, and the Prophets wrote about its spectacular resurrection like an image of the coming of God and the salvation of the people (see Ezek 40—48; Isa 65—66; Zec 14); the chant of Jerusalem is a crown-jewel in the Bible (see Pss 87; 122; 137; Isa 33:17-23). One day this movement finds its accomplishment far beyond all warrior or political images. We can think of inexpressible repatriation of human beings in the friendship of God, joy, and happiness. The future city of God's elect is no longer built up by force of arms—it is a gift and grace coming from on high; it is nothing less than splendor (Rev 21:15-21).

There is no more need of institutions and signs for worship—the temple itself is surpassed: the risen Jesus is the sole place where may be found the joy of really and directly encountering God (see Heb 9:11; Jn 2:21). What extraordinary and joyous celebration in the eternal face-to-face vision of the Lord!

21:1 The sea, the usual dwelling of the dragon and a symbol of evil, will disappear before the victorious march of the new Israel, as it did in the days of the Exodus, but this time for good.

21:3 This verse contains a combination of the classic formula of the Covenant ("You will be my people, and I will be your God") and the name Immanuel ("God-with-us"), which was regarded as a name of the Messiah (Mt 1:28)—a fine assertion of the divinity of Christ, who is God and man. The complete and definitive Covenant between God and humankind will be accomplished at the end of time (see Isa 12:6; Joel 4:17, 21; Zep 3:15-17; Zec 2:14).

21:6 *Alpha, Omega, Beginning, End:* on these divine titles see note on Rev 1:4-8. *Spring of life-giving water:* see note on Rev 7:17.

21:7 *He will be my son:* this expression is reserved in the Old Testament for the King Messiah (2 Sam 7:14). Jesus reveals its full meaning by proclaiming his own divine sonship. Believers now share in this state of Christ.

21:8 *Second death:* see note on Rev 20:6.

21:10 *In the spirit:* see note on Rev 1:10.

of God and had the radiance of some priceless jewel, like jasper, clear as crystal.[r]

12 Its wall was of a great height, with twelve gates,* and at the gates there were twelve angels. On the gates were written the names of the twelve tribes of Israel.[s] 13 There were three gates to the east, three to the north, three to the south, and three to the west.[t] 14 The city wall had twelve foundation stones, and on them were the names of the twelve apostles of the Lamb.[u]

15 The angel who was speaking to me was carrying a gold measuring rod to measure the city,* its gates, and its wall.[v] 16 The city was laid out like a square, with its length and its width identical. He measured the city with his measuring rod: it was fifteen hundred miles* in length and width, and equal in height.[w]

17 Then he measured its wall, and it was one hundred and forty-four cubits* high by human measurements, which the angel employed.[x] 18 * The wall was built of jasper, while the city itself was of pure gold, as bright as clear glass.[y]

19 The foundations of the city wall were adorned with precious stones of every kind. The first of the foundation stones was jasper, the second sapphire, the third turquoise, the fourth emerald,[z] 20 the fifth onyx, the sixth carnelian, the seventh chrysolite, the eighth beryl, the ninth topaz, the tenth chrysoprase, the eleventh jacinth, and the twelfth amethyst.[a] 21 The twelve gates were twelve pearls, each of the gates fashioned from a single pearl, and the street of the city was pure gold, like transparent glass.[b]

22 I did not see any temple there, for the Lord God Almighty and the Lamb are its temple.[c] 23 And the city had no need for the sun or the moon to shine on it, for it was lit by the glory of God, and its lamp was the Lamb.[d] 24 * The nations will walk by its light, and to it the kings of the earth will bring their treasures.[e]

25 The gates of the city will never be shut during the day—and there will be no night there.[f] 26 The nations will come into it bringing their treasures and wealth.[g] 27 However, nothing unclean will ever enter it, nor will anyone who does abominable or deceitful things, but only those who are written in the Lamb's book of life.*[h]

CHAPTER 22

1 Then the angel showed me the river of the water of life, bright as crystal, flowing from the throne of God and of the Lamb*[i] 2 down the middle of the street. On either side of the river was the tree of life* with its twelve crops of fruit, yielding fruit each month. The leaves of the trees are for the healing of the nations.[j]

3 Nothing accursed will be found there anymore. The throne of God and of the Lamb will be in it, and his servants will worship him.[k] 4 They will see his face,* and his name will be on their foreheads.[l] 5 And there will be no more night. They will have no need for light from a lamp or from the sun,

r Rev 21:18-19, 23; Isa 60:1-2; Ezek 43:2; Heb 11:10.—s Rev 21:15, 21, 25; 22:14; Ezek 48:30-34.—t Ezek 48:31-35.—u Acts 1:26; Eph 2:20; Heb 11:10.—v Rev 11:1; 21:12; Ezek 40:3.—w Ezek 43:16; 48:16, 17.—x Rev 13:18; 21:9; Deut 3:11.—y Rev 21:11, 21.—z Rev 21:11; Ex 28:17-20; Isa 54:11-12; Ezek 28:13.—a Rev 4:3.—b Rev 21:12, 18; Isa 54:12.—c Rev 1:8; 5:6; Jn 2:19-20; 4:21, 23.—d Rev 5:6; 21:11; 22:5; Isa 24:23; 60:1-2, 19-20.—e Rev 21:26; Isa 60:3, 5, 11.—f Rev 21:12; 22:5; Isa 60:11; Zec 14:7.—g Rev 21:24.—h Rev 3:5; 20:12; Isa 35:8; 52:1; Joel 4:17; Zec 13:2.—i Rev 4:6; 22:17; Ezek 47:1-12; Zec 14:8; Jn 4:10.—j Rev 2:7; Ezek 47:12.—k Rev 2:15; Zec 14:11.—l Rev 7:3; Mt 5:8.

21:12 *Twelve gates:* see Ezek 48:30-35. The number twelve here most likely stresses that the Church of the New Testament is a continuation of the People of God of the Old Testament. See v. 14, in which the twelve foundation stones bear the names of the twelve apostles.

21:15 *Measure the city:* see Ezek 40—41. The measuring in Rev 11 was to ensure protection; here it is done to indicate the size and symmetry of the eternal dwelling place of God's people.

21:16 *Fifteen hundred miles:* literally, "twelve hundred stadia," about twelve thousand furlongs. In the mind of the ancients the square was the perfect form. When the number twelve, which symbolizes the new Israel, is multiplied by 1000, it signifies supreme perfection. The city possesses the symmetrical dimensions of a perfect cube, which is akin to its earthly counterpart, the inner sanctuary in the tabernacle and temple (see 1 Ki 6:20).

21:17 *One hundred and forty-four cubits:* a cubit measured about eighteen inches in length.

21:18-20 The materials used show that this is not an earthly city. The twelve foundation stones of the wall are decorated with twelve precious stones, which correspond to the twelve stones on the high priest's breastplate (see Ex 28:39). The gems form a magnificent kaleidoscope of colors symbolizing the ineffable glory of God.

21:24ff The author is alluding to Isa 60:1-20, which foretells the entrance of the nations into the People of God. The open gates are a sign of an everlasting feast.

21:27 *Book of life:* see notes on Rev 3:5 and 20:12-15.

22:1 An allusion to the Trinity, since "the river of the water of life" symbolizes the Spirit (see Jn 7:37-39). See also note on Rev 7:17.

22:2 *Tree of life:* see Gen 2:9; 3:22; Ezek 47:12.

22:4 *See his face:* no human could see God's face and live (Ex 33:20-23). This was in keeping with the custom in ancient times whereby criminals were banished from the king's presence (see Est 7:8; see also 2 Sam 14:24). However, the residents of heaven will look on God without harm because they are now holy (see Mt 5:8; Jn 1:18; 1 Cor 13:12; 1 Tim 6:16; 1 Jn 3:2).

for the Lord God will give them light, and they will reign * forever and ever. [m]

EPILOGUE: MY RETURN IS NEAR*

Worship God Alone. 6 The angel said to me, "These words are trustworthy and true, for the Lord God who inspires the prophets has sent his angel to show his servants what soon must take place. [n]

7 " 'Behold, I am coming soon!' * Blessed is the one who observes the words of prophecy contained in this book." [o]

8 I, John, am the one who heard and saw these things. And when I had heard and seen them, I knelt at the feet of the angel who had shown them to me to worship him. [p] 9 However, he said to me, "You must not do that. I am a fellow servant of you and of your brethren the prophets and of those who observe the words of this book. Worship God!" [q]

The Great Separation.* 10 Then he said to me, "Do not seal up the words of prophecy that are in this book, for the time is near. [r] 11 Let the wicked persist in acting wickedly, and let the vile continue in their vileness, but let the righteous persevere in righteousness, and let the holy continue to be holy." [s]

12 " 'Behold, I am coming soon, and I will bring with me my reward to repay everyone as his deeds deserve. [t] 13 I am the Alpha and the Omega, the First and the Last, the Beginning and the End.' [u]

14 "Blessed * are those who wash their robes clean so that they will be free to eat from the tree of life and may enter the city by the gates. [v] 15 Others must remain outside: the dogs, * the sorcerers, the sexually immoral, the murderers, the idolaters, and everyone who loves and practices deceit. [w]

"Come, Lord Jesus!"* 16 " 'I, Jesus, sent my angel to you with this testimony for the churches. I am the Root and the Offspring of David, * the bright Morning Star.' " [x]

17 The Spirit and the bride say, "Come!" Let each listener say, "Come!" Let everyone who thirsts come forward, and let the one who desires it receive the gift of life-giving water. [y]

18 I warn everyone who hears the words of prophecy in this book: if anyone adds to them, God will add to him the plagues written about in this book; [z] 19 if anyone takes away from the words in this book of prophecy, God will take away his share in the tree of life and in the holy city, which are written about in this book. [a]

20 The one who gives this testimony says, "Yes, I am coming soon."

Amen. Come, Lord Jesus! * [b]

21 The grace of the Lord Jesus be with you all. [c]

---

m Rev 20:4; 21:23, 25; Isa 50:20; Zec 14:7.—n Rev 1:1; 21:5; 22:16; 1 Cor 14:32; Heb 12:9.—o Rev 1:3; 16:15; 22:12, 20; Mt 16:27.—p Rev 1:1; 19:10; Mt 4:10; Acts 10:20.—q Rev 19:10; 22:10, 18-19.—r Rev 10:4; 22:7, 18-19; Rom 13:11.—s Wis 6:11; Ezek 3:27.—t Rev 22:7, 20; Ps 62:12; Isa 40:10; 62:11; Mt 16:27; 2 Tim 4:14.—u Rev 1:8, 17; 21:6; Isa 41:4; 44:6.—v Rev 2:7; 7:14-15; 21:12, 27; 22:2.—w Rev 21:8; Deut 23:18; Rom 1:29-32; 1 Cor 6:9-10; Gal 5:19-21; Col 3:5-6.—x Rev 1:1, 4, 11-12; 2:28; 5:5; 22:6; Mt 7:1; 2 Pet 1:19.—y Rev 2:7; 14:13; 19:7; 21:6; Isa 55:1; Jn 4:10.—z Rev 22:7, 10, 19; Deut 4:2; 13:1; Prov 30:6.—a Rev 2:7; 22:7, 10, 18; Deut 4:2; 13:1; Prov 30:6.—b Rev 1:2; 22:7, 12; Mt 16:27; Acts 3:20-21; 1 Cor 10:22; 15:23; 16:22.—c Rom 16:20.

22:5 *They will reign:* see Rev 5:10; 20:6; Dan 7:18, 27.

22:6-21 The Epilogue is a series of disparate propositions in which we find: statements of Christ and John that authenticate the Book (vv. 6-9, 16); a notification from Christ about the coming fulfillment of the prophecy (vv. 10-15); a warning from Christ to falsifiers of the Scripture (vv. 18-19); the word of Christ's promise and the word of the Christians' faith (v. 20); and the epistolary greeting (v. 21).

These serve to exhort the readers to take this whole revelation seriously. They should realize that they are living at the decisive moment and so fix their attention on the Lord who is coming!

22:7 *I am coming soon:* the speaker is Christ. *Blessed:* the sixth beatitude (see note on Rev 1:3).

22:10-15 The history of humankind continues up to the return of Christ. We must take his part and be polarized by the idea of a definitive lot, by the expectation of Life and Light, by the joyous certitude of the Elect. The author draws here on Ps 62:13 and Isa 40:10; 41:4; 44:6.

22:14 *Blessed:* the seventh beatitude (see note on Rev 1:3).

22:15 *Dogs:* they were regarded as despicable creatures; when the term was applied to people it referred to all types of ceremonially unclean persons and also to people of low moral character: e.g., male prostitutes (Deut 23:18) and unfaithful leaders (Isa 56:10).

22:16-21 At its beginning, the Book of Revelation took the form of a letter (Rev 1:4). Now it ends with the classic salutation of a letter—but a salutation preceded by a threat to forgers, who would otherwise be at ease in the exploitation of apocalyptic writings.

22:16 *The Root and the Offspring of David:* see note on Rev 1:5; see also Isa 11:1, 10; Rom 1:3. *The bright Morning Star:* a beautiful title for Christ, already used in Rev 2:28 to signify his power.

22:20 *Come, Lord Jesus!:* this is the ardent plea of those who, in the midst of persecutions and trials, await the return of Christ (see note on 1 Cor 16:22). The Church should ceaselessly strive to recover this fervent expectation for the one in whom she has placed her faith, her hope, and her love, the one from whom she awaits all things.

The New Testament is not a book that one can close upon itself. It is the charter of the Covenant, the Good News from which one must live. It remains open toward its fulfillment: on the last page we have the beautiful and ancient liturgical prayer of Christians: "Come, Lord Jesus!"

BIBLE DICTIONARY

ABEL. The religious and just son of Adam and Eve whose sacrifice pleased God, yet aroused the murderous envy of his brother Cain. He was a shepherd and offered the firstlings of his flock to the Lord (Gen 4: 2-8).

ABRAHAM. "Father of believers." At God's command he left his home in Ur of the Chaldees about 2000 B.C. and settled in Palestine. God made a covenant with him and promised him a great posterity. In his old age his wife Sarah bore him a son (Isaac) in fulfillment of God's promise (Gen 11—25).

ABYSS. In the Old Testament this word refers to the primordial ocean of the ancient Semitic cosmogony. After God's creative activity this vast body forms the saltwater seas (Gen 1:9f); part of it is the fresh water under the earth (Ps 33:7), which wells forth on the earth as springs and fountains (Gen 7:11). Part of it, "the upper waters" (Ps 148:4), is held up by the dome of the sky (Gen 1, 6f), from which rain descends on the earth (Gen 7:11). In the New Testament this word is used to describe the depths of the earth, variously considered the abode of the dead (Rom 10:7) or of the demons (Lk 8:3; Rev 9:1ff; 11:7; 17:8; 20:1. 3). Sheol, Pool of Fire, Gehenna and the netherworld are similar conceptions.

ADONAI. One of the names of God. It is a plural of majesty and signifies "my lord." In Jewish tradition, it is the word which designates God and replaces the "ineffable Name" (YHWH), which no one was permitted to pronounce. *See* LORD. NAME. YAHWEH.

ALLELUIA. Triumphal acclamation signifying: "Praise God," which is often found at the beginning or the end of certain psalms (105—107; 135; Rev 19:1). It has passed over untranslated into the Catholic liturgy.

ALPHA AND OMEGA. The first and last letters of the Greek alphabet. The Hebrews used these two letters to symbolize the fullness, the eternity of God. The Christians inherited this tradition and used alpha and omega to express their belief that in Jesus, the Son of God, is to be found all grace and truth (Rev 1:8; 21:6; 22:13).

ALTAR. A stone or pile of stones, or any structure or place on which sacrifices were burned or incense was offered to God. In the temple at Jerusalem there was an altar of bronze. Solomon had a special altar constructed for burning incense (2 Chr 4:1).

AMEN. A Hebrew word meaning, "certainly, truly," used to give assent to a statement, a curse, a blessing, a prayer, or the like; in this sense of "so be it," the term came to be employed in Jewish worship and as such the Christian liturgy also uses it after prayers and blessings. In the Gospels, Jesus uses it to give force to his statements (Mt 5:18, 26). However, the present translation does not reproduce "Amen" but translates it according to the sense of the context.

ANANIAS. Three persons bear this name in the New Testament: (1) the husband of Sapphira (Acts 5); (2) a Christian who received Paul after his conversion (Acts 9 and 22); (3) a high priest who ordered St. Paul to be slapped (Acts 23) and was later assassinated (66 A.D.).

ANATHEMA (DOOMED). In Hebrew: *herem,* which originally signified some thing (or person) set aside from profane use and made sacred to the Lord (Deut 12:12ff; Jos 11:11, 14). Hence, it could not be appropriated by anyone; in a good number of cases, the obligation existed to destroy it. This often barbaric custom expressed God's absolute rights over every creature. In the course of time, the term was softened and came to refer to nothing more than objects offered to God (Lev 27:28; Ezek 44:27; Mk 7:11). The Greek term *anathema* in the New Testament is used in the sense of "cursed," "separated from God." Later Christianity used this word in the sense of "excommunication" (1 Cor 12:3: "let a curse be upon him").

ANCIENTS. The forebears of Israel, whose traditions were supposed to be the authority for the unwritten law (Mt 5:27-33; 15:2). *See* ELDER.

ANGEL OF THE LORD. Someone who has received a divine delegation, through whom God reveals himself, says, or does something (Jdg 6:11ff). In numerous biblical texts, the word designates the visible manifestation of God (Gen 16:7-13; Zec 3:1ff). In the New Testament, *angels* are heavenly spirits (Heb 1:7).

ANGER (WRATH) OF GOD. This expression is to be compared with other similar expressions: repentance, jealousy, hand, and arm of God. It is an "anthropomorphism," a figure of speech, an image. Seeking to explain the external phenomena supposedly produced by God (storms, floods, earthquakes, catastrophes), we attribute to him sentiments or attitudes which would be found in similar circumstances among men (Ps 78; Deut 32:15ff; Isa 1:18-20; Lk 13:3-5).

ANTICHRIST. This word, which is found only in the Letters of St. John (1 Jn 2:18-22; 4:3; 2 Jn 7), designates a personage who is at once both an enemy of Christ and his evil-doing imitator. The idea stems from the Jewish writers of the age preceding Christianity. These described the Messiah as having to appear at the end of times to renew all things, but as having to take part in a very violent struggle against a mysterious Adversary. This idea is found throughout the New Testament. Paul calls him "the lawless one," "the one doomed to perdition" (2 Thes 2:3, 8). Matthew, Mark, and Revelation seem to refer to a collectivity of persons (Mt 24:23f; Mk 13:14-20; Rev 13:17; 17:7-14).

ANTIOCH. Capital of the Roman province of Syria, it was the most active center of early Christianity (Acts 11:26).

APOCRYPHA. Religious books used by both Jews and Christians which were not included in the collection of inspired writings. In the Protestant Church, this term designates the books of Tobit, Judith, 1 and 2 Maccabees, Wisdom, Sirach, and Baruch as well as parts of Esther and Daniel, which were introduced rather late into the collection of the Bible. Catholics call them "deuterocanonical" books.

APOSTLES. Twelve men chosen by Christ to enjoy special jurisdiction and to teach. They are: Peter, Andrew, James, John, Philip, Bartholomew, Thomas, Matthew, James the Less, Jude, Simon the Zealot, and Judas, who was replaced by Matthias. Within the circle of Jesus' disciples, the Twelve were given a privileged position. They alone were present with him at the Last Supper (Mk 14:17). Later they exercised leadership over the primitive community in Jerusalem (Acts 1:26; 2:14; 5:20f), and were responsible for the information about Jesus that developed into the gospel tradition (Acts 6:2, 4). Paul and Barnabas are also called apostles (Gal 2:7ff), which means literally "one who is sent" (Lk 24:35, 48; Mt 28:19-20).

ARK OF THE COVENANT. Wooden chest, overlaid with gold, fashioned by Moses, which contained the two tablets of the law (Ex 25: 10-16; 37:1-5). It was the symbol of the covenant and God's presence among his people. God was pictured as resting his feet on its golden lid (called "propitiatory"). The ark was placed in the sanctuary of the temple (1 Ki 8:1-9) in Jerusalem and disappeared in its ruin at the destruction of the city by the Chaldeans in 586 B.C. (2 Ki 25:1-21).

ARMOR. Leather or metal covering which was worn by warriors. It included a helmet, breastplate, and shield (Eph 6:13-17).

ASIA. In the New Testament, used of the Roman Province of Asia, which included only the western third of what is now Asia Minor. Ephesus was its capital, and of its other important cities and districts many are mentioned in the New Testament. The evangelization of the province was accomplished by St. Paul on his third missionary journey (Acts 18—21), St. Peter addressed the churches of Asia (1 Pet 1:7), and the Book of Revelation conveys messages to each of its most important cities the "seven churches" (Rev 1:4ff).

ASSYRIA. A country occupying the northern and middle part of Mesopotamia, including Babylonia and Chaldea. The Assyrians were probably of Semitic origin, descendants of Asshur, one of the sons of Shem (Gen 10:22). An independent kingdom began about the seventeenth century B.C. In 605 B.C. Nineveh was destroyed by the Medes and Babylonians, and Assyria became a province of these countries.

ASTARTE. Phoenician goddess of fertility often associated with Baal. Her cult experienced great success in Palestine and her attraction frequently led the Hebrews into idolatry (Jdg 2:13; 10:6; 2 Ki 17:16).

AZYMES. Unleavened bread which was the only kind permitted during the week of the Jewish Passover. They recalled at the same time the agricultural feast of the barley harvest and the exodus from Egypt, when the Hebrews in their haste were unable to have their dough leavened (Ex 34:25; 23:18).

BAAL. This Hebrew word is translated as master, lord. It designates the chief god of the Canaanites and the Phoenicians. His cult was preserved by the Hebrews in Palestine, in spite of the efforts of the prophets (1 Ki 16:31-33). The word Baal also designates small local gods (Jdg 2:11).

BABYLON. Capital of Babylonia, to which many Jewish captives were deported after the fall of Jerusalem in 586 B.C.; this is known as the Babylonian Captivity (2 Ki 25:7ff). The name was then applied to any nation hostile to God (Rev 14; 17; etc.).

BALANCES. Scales for weighing money and other items. The moral necessity of a just balance and true weights and the iniquity of false ones are frequently emphasized by the prophets (Am 8:5; Mi 6:11).

BAPTISM. The baptism of John the Baptist (Mt 3:1) is thought to stem from the rabbinical custom of baptizing proselytes who had converted to the faith of Israel (Mt 21:25). This seems to be a remembrance of the baptism the Jewish people received in crossing the sea (1 Cor 10:1-2) to acquire the law at Sinai and to attain the promised land. The events of the Exodus foreshadowed the imminent coming of the Lord. Jesus himself underwent baptism to inaugurate his mission (Mt 3:13ff; Jn 1:32). He thus became one with the Jewish people and took personal charge of them (Isa 53). In this sense, baptism was a preparation for the cross (Mk 10:38; Lk 12:50). After the Redemption, baptism became a sacrament for entering a new state of grace (Mt 28:19; Acts 2:38-41), the way of regeneration to the divine life.

BEELZEBUL (BAALZEBUB). Name of the god of the nation of Canaan. In the Old Testament it appears under the form *Baalzebub* "Baal (Lord) of Flies." Later association with the Aramaic *beeldebaba*, "enemy," gave the ancient name its connotation of "devil," and the New Testament uses Beelzebul to refer to the prince of demons (Mt 10:25; 12:24; Lk 11:15).

BETHEL. In Hebrew: house of God. This town was originally called Luz. It is there that Abraham established one of the first sanctuaries and that Jacob had the famous vision of the ladder (Gen 12:8; 13:3 and 28:10). King Jeroboam established the idol of the golden calf here after the schism of the northern tribes (1 Ki 12:26-30). The prophets saw therein the symbol of idolatry and gave it the surname of *Bethaven*, house of iniquity (Hos 4:15).

BISHOP. Greek word signifying "overseer." From the beginning, it has designated the heads of the Christian communities, also called "presbyters" or "elders" (1 Tim 3: 1-7).

BLESSING. The word *bless* changes its meaning according to whether its subject is God or man. Man blesses God by his acts of adoration and thanksgiving (Ps 103:1, 2), men bless other men by wishing them well or happiness (Mt 5:44). The ancient Hebrews believed that such wishes were always efficacious (belief in magic) just as they did in the case of maledictions which are the opposite of blessings.

God blesses men by giving them material or spiritual benefits (Gen 24:1).

Finally, man pronounces blessings on objects, on nourishment, to consecrate them to God (1 Cor 10:16) or on persons, to sanctify them (Gen 49).

BLOOD. According to the ancients, blood is the seat and sign of life over which only God has power and so must be respected (Gen 9:4). It is forbidden to consume it in the various offerings (Lev 1—7). This abstention was extended to the consummation of all fleshly nourishment. In the solemn sacrifice of the Day of Atonement, the blood of the victim was spilled over the ark of the covenant. Hence, the blood of Christ, who died for men, has in the eyes of Christians taken on an expiatory value (Heb 9:28).

BREAD. In an extended sense, this often designates all that is necessary for subsistence. In the Gospels, we find the expression "bread of life," and "living bread" (Jn 6:31-35), an image by which Jesus affirms that he is the principle of eternal life; at the same time it suggests the use of the Eucharist. Bread of heaven refers first of all to manna and secondly to the sacrament of the Eucharist.

In the Acts of the Apostles, the rite of breaking bread designates the Eucharist (Acts 2:42).

BREAK BREAD. Among the Jews, the person who presided at the repast would break bread and distribute it to those at table. This is what Jesus did at the multiplication of the loaves (Mt 14:19) and the Last Supper (Mt 26:26).

BROTHERS OF THE LORD. Persons who formed part of Jesus' entourage. Among them are James, Joseph, Jude, and Simon. They are "relatives" of Jesus. For Greek-speaking Semites used the terms *adelphos* and *adelphe* not only in the ordinary sense of blood brother and sister but also for nephew, niece, half-brother, half-sister, and cousin. Since, according to tradition, Jesus was Mary's only child, this expression is understood in the sense of "cousin," as belonging to the same blood (Mk 6:1-6).

CAIAPHAS. High priest functioning at Jerusalem from the year A.D. 18 to 36. He was the son-in-law of the former high priest Annas and involved in the conspiracy to destroy Jesus (Jn 11:49; Mt 26:57). He was deposed by the legate of Syria, Vitellius, after the recall of Pontius Pilate in 36 A.D.

CALENDAR. (1) The civil *day* was reckoned from sunset to sunset, and hence Jewish Sabbaths and feasts began with the setting of the sun. (2) The *hours* of the day were twelve, beginning at about our 6:00 A.M. and ending at 6:00 P.M. The third, sixth, ninth, and twelfth hours were specially sacred to prayer. The night was divided into four watches, the evening watch beginning at 6:00 P.M., the midnight watch at 9:00, "cockcrow" at 12:00, the morning watch at 3:00 A.M. (3) The *week* contained seven days ending in the sabbath, or "Rest." The "first day of the week" became sacred for Christians because of Christ's Resurrection (Jn 20:19; Acts 20:7). (4) The *year* consisted of twelve lunar months of twenty-nine or thirty days—i.e., 354 days. The month began with the new moon, and this first day was observed as a holy day. To preserve the proper relation between the lunar and solar calendars, an extra lunar month was intercalated every two or three years. The first month, Nisan, always began on the new moon nearest to and preceding the vernal equinox, March 21.

CANAANITE. Inhabitant of the country of Canaan situated east of the Jordan River (Mt 15:22). At the time of Jesus, a variant of this word ("Cananean," translated from the Greek as "Zealot") signified a political party which laid claim to national independence. The apostle Simon was a member of this movement (Mt 10:4-11).

CAPTIVITY. This word denotes the exile and deportation of the northern kingdom into Babylonia in 721 (2 Ki 17—18) and more especially of the southern kingdom in 586 (2 Ki 25). After the latter date, Israel continually asks God for deliverance from her slavery, the return of the exiles, and the restoration of the chosen people. In 539 Cyrus the Great conquered Babylonia and allowed the Israelites to return home (Ezr 1:1-4). From then on the Babylonian captivity became a symbol of man's state after Adam's sin from which Jesus has delivered him (Heb 2:14-15).

CENTURION. Officer in charge of a century (originally 100 men), sixtieth part of the Roman legion. Legionnaires in Palestine were recruited locally, but officers were Roman (Mt 8: 5-13).

CHALICE-CUP. These words are often taken in a figurative sense. For a cup contains either a bitter beverage, symbol of trial (the cup of the divine wrath, for example) (Rev 15:7) or a sweet beverage, symbol of divine blessing (Rev 5:8). Since the Last Supper, in which it contained Christ's blood, it has become the expression for the eucharistic mystery (1 Cor 10:21). In another sense, the word signifies man's destiny, fixed by God. Indeed, in an apportionment the lots to be drawn were in a cup (Ps 16:5-6).

CHARISM. Word copied from the Greek. It designates, in the Letters of St. Paul, certain extraordinary spiritual gifts, enabling Christians to collaborate fruitfully in the building up of the mystical body of Christ. For example, the gifts of healing, preaching, and teaching (1 Cor 13).

CHARITY. Word taken from the Latin *caritas* but translating the Greek term *agape*. It designates a very elevated and pure love similar to the love of God for humankind and the love of Christians for God and others. This word is not to be confused with the sense of almsgiving, or charitable work. The fraternal meals of the first Christians often followed by the Eucharist received the name *agape* (Jude 12; 2 Pet 2:13, note) translated by "love feasts" in this Bible.

CHRIST. This word, derived from the Greek, signifies "anointed" and translates the Hebrew word for *Messiah*. The Hebrew king was anointed with holy oil; so was the high priest (2 Sam 12:7; Ex 29:21). In the Bible, it is the title given to the one who, in the future, will come to restore Israel (Dan 9:25-26). Jesus presents himself as the expected Messiah (Mk 14:62). St. Paul and the first Christians gave him the name *Christos* (past participle of the verb) which quickly became a proper name: Jesus Christ, Christ Jesus, or simply Christ (Acts 17:3). *See* JESUS.

CHRISTIAN. This word is derived from *Christ*. It was used for the first time at Antioch around A.D. 35 to designate the disciples of Jesus Christ who until then had been called *Nazoreans* (Acts 11:26).

CHURCH. (1) Among the Hebrews, this word designates the sacred assembly of the Israelites (cf Jdg 21:8 where it is translated "assembly"). (2) In the New Testament, it refers first to the assembly of the Christians of Jerusalem (Acts 5:11). Later, the word was applied to each of the communities founded by St. Paul (1 Cor 1:2). Finally, it designates the totality of Christians and that ideal Church which will be fully realized only at the end of times. In this sense, the Church is the body of Christ (Mt 16:18).

CIRCUMCISION. Removal of the prepuce. It is a very ancient ethical practice which the Hebrews converted into a religious rite. Abraham received it as a sign of the covenant (Gen 17:10ff). Later, the prophets stressed the fact that this bodily mark has no value unless it is accompanied by an "internal circumcision" signifying moral purity (Jer 9:25f).

COMING. Translation of the Greek word *parousia*. This word designates the second coming of Christ for the last judgment (Mt 24:3; 1 Thes 4:15). The belief in a twofold messianic coming distinguishes the Christian mentality from Jewish messianism.

COMMUNION. State in which the faithful is united to God, is close to God, and enjoys his intimacy. Christianity has as its object to place us in communion with the Father and the Son through the action of the Holy Spirit, that is, to give us a share in the divine life (Jn 15). In the Bible, the word never signifies sacramental communion in the Eucharist.

CONSECRATE. Withdrawal of an object or person from secular use so as to transfer it into the domain of God and keep it there (Ex 13:1; 30:29).

CONVERSION. This word is frequently associated with other terms of repentance and penitence. It signifies changing one's life. In their preaching, the apostles ask that their hearers be converted (repent) and be baptized (Acts 2:38). In the Bible, the word conversion is never used in the sense of "changing one's religion."

COVENANT. Man has always sought to place himself in contact with the divinity. In sacred history, this contact has taken the form of a kind of contract between God and the people of Israel. But there had already been a personal covenant between God and Noah (Gen 6:18-22), and between God and Abraham (with the sign of circumcision: Gen 17:10-14). This covenant is made by God without the opinion of the other party being asked. It is therefore gratuitous. But it is bilateral by reason of the promises of the contracting parties: the people promise to observe the law, and God promises to reward fidelity (Ex 19:4-8; Deut 5:1-21).

Unfortunately, the people were often unfaithful. It is then that the prophets promise (for the messianic times) a new covenant in which the union between God and humankind will no longer be solely in a national religion but in an interior and spiritual piety (Jer 31:31-34; 11:1-17).

This hope is realized by the Gospel in Jesus Christ, in whom Christians receive the grace promised (Mt 26:28; Heb 10:9-18).

Hence, the two parts of the Bible were designated by the first Christians with the terms Old Covenant, New Covenant. However, since the Greek word *diatheke* (covenant) also signifies testament, the custom arose (we do not know why) in Latin and the modern languages of using this latter word, even though the meaning is almost incomprehensible.

CREATION. This notion is at the basis of the faith of Israel. It is presented not only as an abstract notion (2 Mac 7:28), but also as the corollary to the existence of an active Creator, present in the world (Ps 104; Job 38). It expresses itself in popular cosmological descriptions of the time (Gen 1—3) and establishes the fundamental relation between man and God in the Judaeo-Christian religion. The revelation and redemption of the Messiah sometimes appears as a re-creation "new world," "new heaven" (Isa 45:8), reestablishing the order and first destiny of things and of men, lost through sin.

CROSS. This instrument of Roman torture reserved for slaves was particularly infamous. It was known to Jesus who preached a type of detachment to his disciples which would go as far as this humiliation of the cross (Mt 10:38). He himself followed this way of self-denial out of love and obedience (Phil 2:8). The death on the cross of the Messiah, Son of God, is a scandal, the paradox which will become the most incontestable historical and spiritual center of the work of salvation accomplished by Jesus (1 Cor 1:18-23). By his abasement on the cross which paid humankind's debt to sin and crushed the devil (1 Cor 2:8; Col 2:14) Jesus is elevated (2 Cor 13:4), and the wood of infamy has become a tree of life (Rev 2:7). Crucified with Christ through baptism and the life of faith (Gal 2:19; Rom 6:6), the Christian must glory only in the cross of Jesus (Gal 6:12-15).

DAGON. Word derived from the root *dag*: fish. It is the name originally of a Mesopotamian deity who became the principal god of the Philistines. His body was half-man and half-fish (Jdg 16:23).

DAMASCUS. Capital of Syria, destroyed in 732 B.C. (2 Ki 16:9), which had a large Jewish population. It was the scene of Paul's conversion (Acts 9:1-27).

DARKNESS. Absence of light. In the Bible God, who is eternal truth, is considered the true light and the source of all light (Isa 10:17); therefore darkness becomes a symbol of estrangement from God. Jesus said that those who followed him would not walk in darkness (Jn 8:12), i.e., he would show them clearly the truth.

DAY OF THE LORD (JUDGMENT). This is the day on which God will judge. The judgment is often conceived of as a punishment. The "day of the Lord" was announced by the prophets as affecting chiefly the pagan nations, who were guilty of attacking and enslaving the people of God (Isa 2:12-22). Later, the same prophets will affirm that the judgment will also touch Israel (Zep 1:7, 14-18) and, at the end of times, all mankind (Zec 14:1-7). In the New Testament this idea persists, and it is toward this glorious manifestation of Christ that the whole of Christian hope tends (1 Cor 1:8; 1 Thes 5:2, 4).

DEACON. This word signifies: server, assistant. It has taken on a particular meaning with the institution of the deacons in the early church to serve the poor and assist the apostles (Acts 6:1-6).

DEMON. The Jews recognized the existence of destructive evil spirits, wicked powers dedicated to doing harm. These are the demons, enslaved by Satan, who dwell within and stir up those who are possessed (Mt 8:28-32).

DESERT. This word holds a major place in biblical thought: It is in the desert that the people experienced divine intimacy (Ex 19). The desert symbolizes the desolate sojourn of the times of trial. Jesus withdraws to the desert before beginning his ministry (Mt 4:1).

DIASPORA (DISPERSION). This word designates the Jews scattered throughout the pagan regions of the Roman Empire (Jn 7:35).

DIVORCE. The Bible presents marriage as a union of the natural order, indissoluble and allowable once for each couple, in order to assure the mutual complement of man and woman (Gen 2:24). Moses, for reasons of "hardness of heart" and in order to limit the abuses of polygamy, codified the custom of repudiation then in use, exacting a tribute, that is, a written piece of paper which the married man had to give his wife signifying that her freedom was restored. He was not allowed to take her back again (Deut 24:1-4). Our Lord, in bringing the law of charity and a higher moral order, renewed the natural precept of Gen 2:24, and gave marriage its original unity and indissolubility (Mt 19:3; 5:32; Mk 10:2; Lk 16:18).

ELDER. In the Old Testament the word refers to an official class having both civil and religious jurisdiction (Ex 3:16; 24:1). In the New Testament it refers to an official of the early Christian Church, such as a bishop or priest (Acts 20:17, 28; Jas 5:14).

ELECT, ELECTION. This refers to the divine choice. (1) Abraham is chosen and taken from his family and country. This election culminates in the election of Israel (Gen 12:1-7; Ex 19:1-9). (2) Certain persons are said to be chosen (David, the Messiah) (2 Sam 7:14ff). (3) Jesus is called the elect ("chosen one") of God (Lk 23:35). (4) Christ chooses his apostles (Mt 10:2-4). (5) All Christians are the object of a divine election (Rom 1:6).

ELOHIM. Ordinary Hebrew word for God. It is the plural of majesty. Elohim ordinarily designates God in his action on the world in contrast to Yahweh which is used of the God of the covenant (Ex 3:14).

ESSENES. The Dead Sea Scrolls have indicated that the Essenes ranked in importance with the Pharisees and Sadducees. There were about 4000 Essenes although only 200 lived in Qumran, their most important center. A member had to undergo a one-year "postulancy" and a three-year "novitiate." He then vowed to be reverent, just, hate sinners, help the just, obey his superiors, tell the truth, share his property, and keep Essene teaching secret. Meals and ritual baths were of great importance. Some think that John the Baptist was a member of this sect (Lk 1:80; 3:1-21).

ETERNAL. This corresponds to the Hebrew word *olam*, signifying a long period of time; these terms indicate primarily something that perdures throughout the centuries (Gen 17:8); then something that has neither beginning nor end, like God (Gen 21:33); and finally something outside of time (1 Jn 5:11-12).

EXPIATION-PROPITIATION. Translation of the Hebrew *Kippur* signifying pardon or suppression of sin. Jesus is called "expiation" because he assures pardon of all sins (Rom 3:25).

FAITH. In the Old Testament, faith is rarely mentioned. Its essential component is trust in God. Thus, Abraham's trust becomes the type of true faith (Gal 3:6). In the New Testament, faith holds a predominant place: Jesus requires faith in himself which presupposes the acceptance of his message and trust in the person of the Master (Jn 6:29-40). In St. Paul, faith is the chief element of his teaching and the key to salvation (Rom 1:16).

FASTS. The chief Jewish fast was that of the Day of Atonement known as "the (autumn) fast" (Acts 27:9). The especially devout customarily fasted on the second and fifth days of the week (Mt 9:14; Lk 18:12). Our Lord's great fast (Mt 4:2) was foreshadowed by those of Moses (Ex 24:18) and Elijah (1 Ki 19:8).

FEAR OF GOD. (1) Feeling experienced before any kind of divine manifestation: dread, fear, dismay (Ex 20:18ff). (2) The same word also serves to denote the service of God, religion (Deut 4:10). (3) The term *God-fearer* was used of a pagan who had adopted Jewish religious practices, without however belonging completely to the religion of Israel (Acts 10:1).

FEASTS. In memory of the rest of God after the work of creation, the Jews kept as sacred the seventh day or sabbath, the seventh month, the seventh or sabbatical year, and the fiftieth or jubilee year (Gen 2:1-3; Lev 25:1-22).

The weekly sabbath was observed by special sacrifices, by rest from servile work, and by attendance at religious instruction (Ex 20:8-11; Lev 23:2f).

The first day of the month, the New Moon, was a holy day on which special offerings were made (Num 28:11-15; Col 2:16).

The three major feasts of the year, on which male Israelites were required to go to the temple, were Passover, in March or April, Pentecost, fifty days later, and Tabernacles, toward the end of September.

Passover began on the evening of the fourteenth Nisan with the eating of the lamb. On the fourteenth, after all leaven had been removed from the house, the lamb was sacrificed at the temple, and then brought home for cooking. It was eaten with herbs and unleavened bread in memory of the going out of Israel from Egypt (Lev 23:5f; Heb 41:27-29). The following week was known as the days of the Unleavened Bread (Lev 23:6-8). The eve of the sabbath within this week was the Preparation Day (Mt 27:62). During this week the firstfruits of the barley harvest were presented as the opening of the seven weeks of harvest.

Pentecost recalled the giving of the law, and it offered in thanks the firstfruits of the wheat harvest (Lev 23:15-22). At Pentecost the Holy Spirit came upon the apostles and the others gathered in the Upper Room (Acts 2:1ff).

Tabernacles was celebrated in the month of Tishri. The first day of that month was the feast of Trumpets, the civil New Year. On the tenth fell the Day of Atonement, a day of fast and of expiatory sacrifices, when the high priest entered the holy of holies to sprinkle blood (Lev 16; 23:23-36; Num 29:7-11). From the fifteenth to the twenty-first of the month the feast of Tabernacles (Booths) was celebrated. It recalled the wanderings of the

Israelites in the desert. This week marked the end of the harvest of fruit, wine, and oil (Lev 23:39-43). The last day of the feast was a day of rest on which were observed the ceremonies of water libation and the lighting of the four great golden candelabra (Jn 7:37; 8:12).

Two minor feasts were kept during the winter, Dedication and Purim (Lots). The former was held in our December, and was a joyous commemoration of the rededication of the temple by Judas Maccabeus (1 Mac 4:56-59). It was also known as the feast of Lights, since during it the temple was illuminated (Jn 10:22). Purim, held at the close of winter, recalled the rescue of the Jews by Esther when Haman cast lots to determine the day on which they should be destroyed (Est 9:20-32; 2 Mac 15:36).

FIGURE (TYPE). A person, event, or object which in God's intention signifies or foreshadows something else. Many realities of the Old Testament foreshadowed those of the New (Heb 7:1-22).

FIRE. This is used as a symbol to express the divinity which radiates and consumes at the same time, with a joyous or terrifying aspect: God present in the fire on Mt. Sinai, in a storm (Ex 19:18). On the altar of the temple, there was a perpetual fire (Lev 6:5; 2 Chr 4:1). God, a devouring fire, consumes Sodom and Gomorrah (Gen 19:24-25). Jesus is said to baptize "with fire," that is, with the Holy Spirit (Mt 3:11).

FIRSTBORN. By right, every firstborn male must be reserved for God. He must be either immolated or (since infant-sacrifice was abolished by the Hebrews) redeemed (Ex 13:2; Num 3:11-13). The title "firstborn" could be given to the boy even if he had no brother or sister. And it entailed the privilege of "birthright," entitling him to a position of honor in the family and to a double share in the possessions inherited from the father (Ex 25:31). Jesus is called the firstborn of creation because of his position as the head of mankind (Heb 1:6).

FIRSTFRUITS. The first fruits of the season, which out of obligation were offered to God (Ex 23:19). Paul calls Jesus "the firstfruits" of the dead, showing that his resurrection will be followed by theirs (1 Cor 15:20, 23).

FLESH. (1) First meaning: the flesh of an animal in contrast to the blood and bones (Gen 9:3ff). (2) Everything that has life (Gen 6:13). (3) Man in contrast to God by reason of his weakness; hence, the person, human nature (Mt 26:41). (4) Especially in St. Paul's Letters, natural man, without grace, with his weaknesses and tendencies toward sin, in contrast to the "spirit" which designates the faculty that enables one to share in the Holy Spirit through the new birth of baptism (Rom 7:14).

FOREIGNERS. Term reserved for those who were not of Hebrew stock, the Gentiles (Ex 12:44).

GALILEE. The most northerly region of Palestine and the most favored by nature. Among its flourishing towns were Cana, Chorazin, Nazareth, Capernaum, Bethsaida, Tiberias. The population was predominantly Jewish, but there was a noticeable Galilean dialect (Mt 26:73). The Galileans were very loyal to their religion and nation, though regarded by the Judeans as ignorant and lawless (Jn 7:41; Mk 14:70). Our Lord was reared in Galilee, he spent most of his time preaching there, and all but one of his apostles were from Galilee.

GALILEE, SEA OF. A lake which formed the eastern boundary of Galilee. It was also called the Lake of Gennesaret, from the plain on its northwest corner (Lk 5:1), and the Sea of Tiberias, from the city of this name, the residence of Herod Antipas (Jn 6:11). The lake is about thirteen miles long and six broad.

GEHENNA. This comes from the Hebrew "Valley of Hinnom," a place near Jerusalem where ritual infant-sacrifices had been practiced (2 Chr 28:3). This place was later used as a depot for refuse. The word became synonymous with place of malediction (Jer 7:31) and then in the New Testament with the abode of the damned, a place of torment, unquenchable fire and the consuming worm (Mt 5:29; 10:28; 18:8f; Mk 9:44ff). *See* SHEOL.

GETHSEMANE. This word, which signifies "oil press," became the name for a plantation of olive trees located opposite the temple of Jerusalem, east of the torrent of Kidron. This is the "mount of Olives," scene of Christ's agony and betrayal (Mt 26:36-56).

GLORY. A very important notion in biblical theology. In Hebrew *(kabod)*, the word designates "to be heavy," "to be illustrious." It often denotes the radiant manifestation of God in his grandeur (Ezek 1:28). This divine glory is possessed by Jesus (Jn 1:14). According to St. Paul, every Christian shares in this divine glory already here below (Phil 3:21).

GOEL. *See* KIN, NEXT OF.

GOLGOTHA. Aramaic word signifying "skull place." It was the name of a little hill located northwest of the city of Jerusalem. Those condemned were executed there, and it was here that Jesus suffered crucifixion (Mt 27:33). The Latin rendering of this word is *Calvaria* which is the origin of our "Calvary."

GOOD NEWS. *See* GOSPEL.

GOSPEL. In Greek, this word signifies good news, and specifically the good news of the Kingdom of God (Heb 4:2; Mt 4:23). St. Paul uses the word to indicate his preaching; later, the same word will be applied to the accounts of Christ's life (1 Cor 9:16; Rom 1:3).

GRACE. This word (in Greek: *doxa*) has a great variety of meanings: favor, benevolence, benefit. Hence, it signifies God's gratuitous love which makes the creature its acceptable beneficiary (Rom 11:5, 6). The grace par excellence is salvation, justification (Eph 2:5). In the plural—graces—it signifies the supernatural gifts and helps given to each one by the Holy Spirit.

HASIDEANS. This word is derived from the Hebrew word *hasidim*, "pious ones," and designates the faithful servants of God. They are mentioned in the Book of Proverbs (2:8) and in the Psalms (40:5; 50:5; 148:14). They played a leading part during the resistance directed by Judas Maccabeus (1 Mac 2:42 and 7:6; 2 Mac 14:6). They are undoubtedly at the origin of the Essenes, the brotherhood established in the monastery of Qumran which left us the famous Dead Sea Scrolls.

HEART. The Hebrews regarded the heart as the seat not only of emotions but also of thoughts and voluntary acts. Thus, the heart represents the whole person (Joel 2:13; 1 Pet 3:4).

HEAVEN. This word has several meanings: (1) the firmament in which the stars are perceived (Gen 1:14-17); (2) the region of the atmosphere where the birds fly (Deut 4:17); (3) the place of God's residence, the throne-room where the Everlasting One is seated surrounded by the angels (Mt 5:12; 24:36). Jewish tradition had imagined several heavens or firmaments superimposed on one another populated with various kinds of angels. It is in this sense that they spoke of the "heavenly host" and that St. Paul spoke of having been caught up in ecstasy "to the third heaven" (2 Cor 12:2).

HELL. The place of eternal punishment, also called Gehenna. *See* GEHENNA. SHEOL.

HELLENIST. A Jew, or a Jew turned Christian, living in a foreign land and speaking Greek (Acts 6:1).

HERITAGE. *See* INHERITANCE.

HEROD. The Herodian family, though Jewish in religion, was Idumean in origin. Herod "the Great" (B.C. 62 to 4) was appointed by Rome as king of Judea in B.C. 40, to the exclusion of the native Hasmonean line. He rebuilt the temple, and was in general an efficient ruler, but his cruelties made him odious. He slaughtered the infants at Bethlehem (Mt 2:16-18). Four of his children are mentioned in the New Testament: Archelaus, Antipas and two named Philip.

Archelaus, ethnarch of Judea (4 B.C.-A.D. 6), was deposed on account of his cruelty and exiled to Vienne in Gaul.

Antipas, tetrarch of Galilee and Perea, was deposed in A.D. 39. He divorced his wife, the daughter of King Aretas, and married Herodias, the wife of his brother Philip, who resided in Rome. He imprisoned and later beheaded John the Baptist (Mt 14:1ff). He was present in Jerusalem at the time of our Lord's trial (Lk 23:7-12).

Philip, tetrarch of Trachonitis (4 B.C.-A.D. 34) unlike his brothers, was a moderate and peaceful ruler.

Two other descendants of Herod are also mentioned in the New Testament. Herod Agrippa I, grandson of Herod the Great, was king of all Palestine from A.D. 41 to 44. He was a strict observer of Judaism, and a persecutor of Christianity (Acts 12:1ff). His death is mentioned in Acts 12:23. His son Agrippa II, ruled in Trachonitis until his death in A.D. 100. This Agrippa and his sister Bernice heard St. Paul's defense (Acts 25—26). Another sister, Drusilla, was married to the procurator Felix (Acts 24:24).

HERODIANS. These were partisans and courtiers of the reigning dynasty of the Herods. Though they were Jews in religion, their spirit was Gentile. They conspired with their enemies the Pharisees against Christ (Mt 22:16).

HERODIAS. Daughter of Aristobulus and granddaughter of Herod the Great and Mariamme. She was the wife of Philip but left him to marry Antipas. Her daughter Salome (who has unfortunately achieved some notoriety) resulted from the first marriage (Mt 14:6-10).

HIGH PLACES. In Hebrew *bamoth* designates the sanctuaries ordinarily built on the heights by the inhabitants of Canaan (Num 33:52) as well as the Hebrews before the temple was built (1 Ki 3:2). However, later they became the symbol of idolatry for Israel, a symbol to which the ancient Jewish people constantly returned, in spite of the prohibition of Deuteronomy (12:4ff), and the constant condemnations of the prophets (Ezek 6:3-6).

HIGH PRIEST. The chief of the sacred ministers among the Jews. He was supreme in religious matters, and to him was reserved the exclusive right of offering the great sacrifice of expiation and of entering the holy of holies (Heb 9:7). Through him at times God announced things to come (Jn 11:51). He was a member of the Sanhedrin and ordinarily presided over its deliberations (Mt 26:57; Acts 4:5f; 5:27; etc.). Induction into this high priesthood was by anointing or by investiture in the precious robes of the office. The dignity descended at first by primogeniture from Aaron and the elder branch of Aaron's family and was held for life. But in the days of Christ the high priests were appointed and removed at will by the Herods and the Roman procurators. During the lifetime of our Lord some fifteen different individuals held the office, the most noted of whom were Annas (A.D. 5-6) and his son-in-law Caiaphas (A.D. 18-36). Annas and Caiaphas, often named together, judged Christ (Jn 18:13, 24), Peter and John (Acts 4:6), then all the apostles (Acts 5:17ff) and St. Stephen (Acts 6:12ff), while Ananias acted against Paul (Acts 23:2; 24:1).

HOLOCAUST. In the ancient sacrifices only the blood and certain parts of the victim were offered to God; the rest was divided among the priest and faithful who had offered it (Lev 7:11-21). A holocaust (from the Greek "wholly burned") was a sacrifice in which an entire animal except its hide was consumed in the fire on the altar, with the primary purpose of rendering glory to God (Lev 1:1ff).

HOLY (SANCTIFY). The term "holy" is applied to anything that is consecrated to God, and hence withdrawn from all (secular) human use. In this sense, holy or sacred implies that no one can touch the object, for such contact would entail an "impurity" (1 Ki 8:4). God is "holy," because he is completely apart from any contact with the universe; but also because he possesses moral perfection. The people of Israel was to be "holy" in order to resemble God (Lev 20:7, 26). Christians are "holy" because they have been consecrated to God by baptism. They are thus called to achieve moral perfection (Rom 6:3ff). To *sanctify* means to consecrate something or someone to the service of God (Heb 13:12). God shows himself to be holy by manifesting his justice (Isa 5:16).

HOPE. The messianic hope is at the center of the life of Israel, the source of all its unity, its action, and influence on others. The Hebrew terms which designate it express the tension of a bow ready to shoot its arrow to infinity (Zec 9:13-14); this hope thus represents a search, an absolute confidence and a concentration of all one's energy flowing from God's covenant with Israel. It does not rest on human resources and initiative, but on the all-powerful Presence of God (Ps 18:7). It is unshakable in spite of all the vicissitudes of the history of Israel (Mic 7:7-9; Ps 22:5-6; Jer 30:7). It is the constant on which many of the words of the prophets are predicated (Mic 4—5; Isa 40ff; Jer 30—33; Ezek 40ff). This hope was confirmed and reinforced by the coming of the Messiah, the incarnation and redemption of Christ. Christian hope takes its character from this absolute witness of love and God's fidelity to his promises. It brings the gospel to the far corners of the world as well as souls to a more complete assurance of salvation (Rom 5:1-11; Heb 6:18-20) until the end of time (1 Pet 1:3-5).

HORNS. These are the symbol of power and strength (1 Sam 2:1). The Bible often speaks of the horns of the altar, ornaments jutting out over the four corners of the altar of the temple of Jerusalem (1 Ki 1:50).

HOSANNA. Hebrew expression signifying: "may God save," used in the course of Jewish feasts (Ps 118:25f). It served as an acclamation during Christ's entrance into Jerusalem, in the sense of "Long live," and it is always chanted during the course of the Catholic liturgy (Mt 21:9).

HOSTS. Translation of the Hebrew word *sabaoth* which signifies armies. These armies are either a warrior grouping (material sense) (Ex 14:17) or the multitude (such as an army) of stars (Ps 33:6) or angelic beings that express God's glory (Job 25:3).

IMPOSITION OF HANDS. The customary Jewish way of designating a person for a task and invoking upon him the divine blessing and power to perform it (Num 8:10-11). Jesus used it when healing (Mk 6:5). By the imposition of hands, the apostles conferred the Holy Spirit (Acts 8:17), the diaconate (Acts 6:6), and the priesthood (1 Tim 4:14).

INHERITANCE. The corresponding Greek indicates a portion (of a share) as the result of drawing lots. This word designates the various parts of the promised land chosen for each Israelite tribe (Jos 15:1). The word is retained in the New Testament in reference to Jesus who has been constituted by God as the heir of all things (Heb 1:2); and in reference to Christians, sons and heirs of God through Jesus Christ (Rom 4:13-16; 8:17).

ISRAEL. Proper name signifying "one who struggles with God." The popular explanation of this glorious surname recalling Jacob's struggle (Gen 32:9) then passes on to his posterity and designates the People of the Promise (Ex 3:16).

JEALOUS (GOD). This is the translation used for a Hebrew verb which contains the concept of ardor: it can characterize the divine justice as ardent, zealous, and prompt to chastise sinners (Ex 20:5). God is also termed jealous because since he is unique he cannot allow man not to render single-minded worship to him (Ex 34:14).

JERUSALEM. In Hebrew, *Yerushalaim*, vision of peace. But the origin of the name seems to be *Ursalim* which signifies "foundation of Salem," a Canaanite divinity. The city was a citadel of the Jebusites (Jdg 1:8). It was conquered by David who made it his capital (2 Sam 5; 6). Destroyed in 586 B.C., it was rebuilt by the Jews who returned from the exile in the fifth century before the Christian era (2 Ki 25:1-21; Ezr 3—6). It was besieged and destroyed for the second time by the emperor Titus in A.D. 70. At the time of Christ, Jerusalem was the chief city of Palestine and the religious center of Judaism. Situated on a plateau, its walls looked down into deep ravines, the Kidron on the east and the Valley of Hinnom on the south and west. Within the walls the city was divided by the Valley of the Tyropoean, and sloped gradually toward the southeast.

The northeastern part of the city rested on Mount Moriah and was occupied chiefly by the temple and the fortress Antonia. North of the temple were the Sheep Gate and the Pool of Bethesda (Jn 5:2). The Golden Gate, in the eastern wall of the city, opened on the road to Gethsemane, Mount Olivet, Bethany, and Jericho. On its western side the temple had a bridge that led over the Tyropoean to the Upper City. The southeastern section of the city was the ancient city of David, whose walls contained the tower of Siloam (Lk 13:4) and the various gates that led to the fountains outside the walls. This part of the city was inhabited largely by priests. The southwestern section of the city contained the business districts, the palaces of Annas and Caiaphas, of Herod and of the Hasmoneans. To the east of it was the Pool of Siloam (Jn 9:7), and to the south the Valley of Hinnom (a place for refuse) and Akeldama ("Blood Field") (Mt 27:8; Acts 1:19).

Another section of the city lay to the northwest, across from the temple. Beyond its walls were fields, gardens, and places of burial. The Ephraim Gate which opened here on the highway to Jaffa was not far from the place of the Crucifixion, which lay just outside the city (Jn 19:17-20; Heb 13:12).

JESUS. This name, which was common in Israel, signifies "God saves." It was bestowed by God (Lk 1:31) on the son of the Virgin Mary—who was truly man (Acts 2:22, 32) and later recognized as Lord (Phil 2:11) and Savior (2 Tim 1:10)—in consequence of his mission (Mt 1:21).

But before being recognized as the Messiah and Son of God, Jesus of Nazareth is taken for the son of Joseph and Mary, and he appears in history at the moment when John the Baptist is preaching repentance in Judea (Lk 3:1ff). Jesus wins the admiration of the crowds by his preaching and healing, proclaiming the good news of the kingdom of God and doing good. He is soon followed by numerous disciples and like John his precursor becomes a sign of contradiction for the Judaism of his time (Mt 10:34; Lk 4:15; 11:27). He speaks with authority in the synagogues and is called Teacher and Rabbi. He criticizes the formalism of certain religious practices (the sabbath, ablutions), questions the worship tied down to the perdurance of the temple, and overturns social barriers (publicans and sinners draw near to him). He allows himself to be called Messiah and Son of David by the enthusiastic crowds. However, Jesus knows that this is an ambiguous messianism and so he reveals his true identity to a few of those chosen for their faith (Mt 16:16; Jn 6:67-70).

Jesus is condemned as a blasphemer by those who hand him over to the Roman authority to be crucified (Mt 26:65). Under the Roman procurator Pontius Pilate (A.D. 26-36) he is put to death for the crime of having made himself "King of the Jews."

All the direct testimonies about Jesus and his work (the New Testament) concern firstly his resurrection and the divine character of his person. Foretold by the prophets and all the Scriptures (Lk 18:31; 24:25-27; Heb 1:1ff), Jesus can be known only in the light of the Spirit of God. He will be understood only after his resurrection when he has sent forth this Spirit to the witnesses of his work, chosen by him. They will then recognize him as the Suffering Servant (Mt 3:17; Phil 2:7), the Son of David (Jn 7:41-42), the High Priest and Mediator of the new Covenant (Jn 16:26; Heb 3:1; 8:6), the Son of Man manifested as the savior at the time willed by God (1 Tim 1:1-5), the Lord, image and Son of God, and God himself (Acts 2:36; 11:20; Rom 8:29; 9:5; Phil 2:11; Heb 1:3); the one who has come from God in the humility of the flesh (Jn 1; 7:15-16, 27; 8:14; Phil 2:6-7) and after his death, has been exalted by the Father whom he has revealed (Jn 3:14; 12:32).

All these titles—Word, Elect, or Holy One of God, Lamb of God, Rabbi, Messiah, Son of God, Son of Man, King of Israel—are gathered together by John in the introduction accorded Jesus in the first chapter of his Gospel. But his name Jesus is henceforth above every name (Phil 2:9). Lord of the universe and head of the Church he is the salvation which he brings to us (Lk 1:71); thus the one who believes in him will desire to be worthy to die for his name (Acts 15:26; 21:13).

JORDAN. The foremost river of Palestine. From the Lebanons to the Dead Sea it covers a distance of 125 miles, though with its meanderings the stream itself is more than double that. The width varies from 80 to 150 feet, and the depth in summer from 4 to 12 feet. The river is generally hidden by a thick growth of willow. There are many fords which allow passage from the one bank to the other (Jos 2:7; Mt 3:13).

JUBILEE. Year of joy and amnesty, celebrated at the end of each 49-year period, in the course of which one's debts must be remitted and slaves set free (Lev 25:8-55).

JUDGMENT. In the Old Testament, judgment is related to the covenant. Judges and kings were established to maintain or reestablish the faithfulness to the covenant in the midst of national difficulties and in matters concerning the observation of the law (1 Ki 3:6). They represented the supreme Judge (Isa 11:3-5). Referring to God, judgment designates divine intervention, sometimes to assure his people victory or deliverance and at other times to condemn and punish them after an infidelity (Deut 32:36; Jer 30:11ff).

In the Psalms Yahweh appears as the supreme Judge above all in the great deeds of the "Day of the Lord" *(see this term)* and his power extends over all the earth. Among the prophets this perspective becomes more and more connected with the eschatological plane (Zec 14; Dan 7:12).

In the New Testament, judgment is connected with the work of Christ, accepted by the faithful or rejected by the unbelievers. It is already present and marks a difference between groups of people (Jn 3:17-21; 8:15; 12:31). Hence, it is necessary to be on one's guard, because judgment is coming. It will be made evident at the last day, which will be marked by the definitive triumph of Christ (Mt 25:31; 1 Thes 4:16; 2 Thes 2:3-10).

JUST (JUSTICE). The just man is one who is virtuous, faithful to God and to the law of Moses (Mt 19:17-20). In the New Testament the "just" man is one who does the will of God (Mt 7:21). In the teachings of St. Paul, the terms justice and justification appear often: God makes man "just," free from sin and pleasing to God through grace (grace attested by faith) (Rom 3:20-30).

KIN (NEXT OF), AVENGER OF BLOOD, GOEL. *See* LEVIRATE.

KINGDOM (REIGN) OF GOD. The Kingdom will be established by the Messiah, over Israel first (Zep 3:14-15), and then over all the nations of the earth (Zec 14:9). "Kingdom" signifies a state of things in which God is recognized as King to whom everything must be submitted: Kingdom of God and Kingdom of heaven are equivalent. The Kingdom is proclaimed by John the Baptist (Mt 3:2), inaugurated by Jesus (Mt 12:25-28), continued in the Church (Mt 10:7; 16:19), and will be definitively accomplished in the glory of Christ's return (Mt 24:26-31). The members of the Kingdom are children of God and even in this life enjoy that eternal life which will be completely expanded in the future world (Jn 3:15-16; Rev 22:2).

KISHON. Name of a brook flowing at the foot of Mt. Tabor. It witnessed several violent scenes and battles (Jdg 4:13; 1 Ki 18:40).

KITTIM. This name referred originally to inhabitants of Kiti, capital of the isle of Cyprus, then to any Cypriots (Gen 10:4; Isa 23:1; Jer 2:10), later to Greeks in general (Num 24:24), and finally even to Romans (Dan 11:30).

KNOW. God knows everything, since he is the Creator (Job 37:16). He knows his people, since he has chosen it (Gen 18:19). On his part, man seeks to know God in faith (Deut 29:3; Jer 31:31-34). The word "know" has a third meaning in the Bible: man "knows" his wife; he has carnal relations with her (Gen 4:1).

LAW OF MOSES. The law, respected by all Jews as from God, consisted of the five books of Moses. These formed the basis of the Scripture reading and instruction in the synagogue services. In addition the Pharisees observed a traditional law, the *Mishna*, which they taught also had its author in Moses. Our Lord observed the Mosaic law and promulgated for his followers its essential element, the Ten Commandments (Mt 5:17). He criticized the Pharisees for their neglect of it in favor of their traditions (Mt 15:2-9).

LEBANON. Mountainous chain north of Palestine. Its name, derived from *laban* which signifies "to be white," alludes to its tops covered with permanent snows (Jer 18:14).

LEVIATHAN. A mythological sea monster symbolizing the chaos that existed in the beginning of creation. Also used for a crocodile or a whale (Ps 74:14). *See* RAHAB.

LEVIRATE. This word derived from the Latin *levir* (brother-in-law) designates an ancient Israelite custom (Gen 38:8ff), codified in the Bible: when a man dies without leaving a male child, the closest relative of the deceased—generally, his brother—must marry the widow who is his sister-in-law and thus perpetuate the line. The first son born of this union would be considered the son and heir of the dead man (Deut 25:5-10).

LEVITES. Sacred ministers of lowest rank among the Jews. Unlike the priests, they were members of the tribe of Levi who did not belong to the house of Aaron. While on duty they wore a distinctive linen dress, but they entered only the inner court and not the holy place of the temple. The higher levites assisted the officiating priests, others had charge of the music during the services, and still others acted as doorkeepers and overseers of the temple (1 Chr 23:4-6).

LIGHT. Has various meanings in Scripture: (1) material sense of outward light or daybreak (Gen 1, 3); (2) symbol of God (showing his incorporeal, pure and holy nature) (1 Jn 1:5); (3) symbol of Christ (Jn 8:12); (4) Christians are children of light because they have received the spiritual light of truth and grace, and are to radiate it in the world by their good example (Mt 5:14; Eph 5:8).

LORD. Originally, this title signified nothing more than "sir." From the 3rd century B.C. onward, the Jews re-placed the ineffable name *Yahweh* with *Adonai* (Lord) in reading the Bible. Applied to Jesus by the first Christians, the name "Lord" was thus equivalent to an affirmation of his divinity (Acts 2:36). *See* ADONAI. NAME. YAHWEH.

LOVE. In the Old Testament, the love of God expresses itself in his many interventions of creation (Gen 1:3; Job 38ff) and the history of Israel (Deut 4:37; Ps 41:12). It is a freely-given elective love (Deut 7:7) working for the salvation of mankind, ever merciful in the face of human infidelity (Hos 11:1-4).

The New Testament explores these first glimmerings more fully. The love of God is historical because God has not spared his own Son and has delivered him to death in order to save us (Jn 3:16). It is also freely-given and elective by the work of Christ, which was in perfect correspondence with the will of the Father and which made the faithful the beloved ones of God (Jn 5:20-25; Col 3:12). Finally, this love in action is merciful, as shown above all by the cross and explained in the parables (Jn 15:13; Lk 15:11-32).

The love of man for God is thus a love which is returned. It must be sealed by a total obedience to the Commandments, a fidelity to the covenant. In the New Testament it must respond without limit to the prior love of God and Christ (1 Jn 3:1-16; 4:10-19).

MAGI. In the texts of the Old Testament magi are often associated with sorcerers and diviners. They seem to have been a Persian religious caste of royal advisers (Jer 39:2: "princes"), and were regarded as wise men, astrologers. In the Gospel of Matthew, many think it refers to learned men from Babylon who had contact with Jewish Messianism (cf Dan 2:2). In the Acts of the Apostles, the word is taken in the pejorative sense in the case of a magician who sets himself up as an adversary of Paul the apostle (Acts 8:9).

MEDIATOR. In its primary sense, the word signifies an intermediary, a third person who intervenes between other parties to bring them together or reconcile them. Moses was thus a mediator between God and the people (Num 14:13-20). Applied to Jesus, the term takes on an even more profound meaning, for Jesus is at the same time God and man; he belongs, at once, to the two parties. Through Christ we have access to the Father, and through Christ the Father gives himself to mankind (Heb 9:11-25; 12:24).

MERCY. This word is found in both Testaments, but retains all the primitive value of the Hebrew word *hesed*, which suggests love more than pity (Jas 2:1-13).

MERIBAH. This Hebrew word, which signifies "the (place of the) quarreling," served to designate the same place as Massah (Ex 17:7). *See* MASSAH.

MESSIAH. Hebrew word signifying "one who has been anointed." The kings of Israel were anointed in the name of God (1 Sam 9:16). The term Messiah later was used to designate a "future king" who would make all things new (Dan 9:25-26). This son of David, expected by the Jewish nation, was the Messiah par excellence (Mk 10:47-48), a term that has been rendered in Greek by *Christos*. This was a common name that ultimately became a title for Jesus the Savior (Rom 1:1). *See* CHRIST. JESUS.

MIRACLES. This word corresponds to two biblical words: sign and wonder. In the sense of "sign," a miracle is an unaccustomed and unexpected event which serves as a motive for credibility by manifesting the power of Christ, and leads the spectator to believe in his person (Jn 2:11).

MISSION. Out of love the Father sends his only Son into the world. Jesus speaks in this way of his "mission" which is to save men by giving them Life (Jn 16:27-28). Then, just as the Father has sent the Son into the world, so Jesus sends the apostles into the world (Jn 20:21). This second mission is a prolongation of the former one.

MONEY. In the time of our Lord the coins current in Palestine were Roman, Greek, Syrian, and Jewish. The Jews might issue coins only in bronze.

1) Large sums were expressed in *talents* and *minas*. The talent equaled about $1920.00 in United States currency. The mina was one-sixtieth of a talent, or about $32.00. The units of Luke 19:13ff were minas.

2) Silver coins mentioned in the New Testament are: the Syrian *stater* (51 cents), the Roman *denarius* (about 17 cents), the Greek *drachme*, equivalent to the denarius. The stater was accepted as equal to the Jewish *shekel*, one-fiftieth of a mina (about 64 cents), the temple tax for two persons (Mt 17:26). The denarius was the usual day's wage for a laborer in the field, and it was the coin of the tax to the Emperor (Mt 20:2; 22:19).

3) Bronze coins referred to are the Roman *assarion* (one cent) and *quadrans* (one-fourth of a cent), the Jewish *perutah* or *lepton* (one-eighth of a cent), the coin of the "widow's mite" (Mt 10:29; 5:26; Mk 12:42).

It should be remembered that the coin values here given are only approximate, and that the purchasing power of money was much greater in ancient times than today.

MOUNTAIN (MOUNT). A mountain is regarded as the dwelling place of divinity. Sanctuaries were set up on a good many mounts. It was on mountains that God chose to give his revelations (Sinai, Tabor) (Deut 33:2; Mt 17:1ff). Zion is called the "mountain God has chosen" (Ps 68:17).

MUSICAL INSTRUMENTS. The Hebrews were devoted to music and used it for both secular and religious purposes. Various types of instruments are mentioned in the Bible—stringed, wind, and percussive instruments (Ps 150:3-5).

MYSTERY. The origin of this word is Greek. It signified first of all the place where religious ceremonies took place which were reserved only to those who had been "initiated." In the plural, it signified the rites themselves. In a derived sense, the word is synonymous with divine secret. St. Paul uses it in the sense of divine plan (inaccessible to man, secret, but revealed by Jesus Christ), having the salvation of men as its object (Rom 16:25-26). In Scripture it must never be taken in the sense (to which the catechism has accustomed us) of revealed truth incomprehensible to the human intelligence (for example, the mystery of the Blessed Trinity).

NAME. According to the conception of the ancients, the Name designates more than the external person; it tends to express his basic character, his personality (Gen 21:3ff). We might say it is an emanation of the person himself. Change of vocation entailed changing one's name (Mt 16:16-19). In the ancient texts of the Bible, to name or give a name can signify "to have power over" (Gen 2:19-21). The "name of God" thus signifies God himself. Hence, we find the expressions: God acting for his name's sake—to glorify and sanctify his name (Ezek 20:14; Isa 29:23). In the same way sin profanes the name of God (Lev 18:21). Among the Israelites, the veneration which came to be accorded to the name of God approached superstition. The Israelites did not dare pronounce this name and forbade even the use of the name *Yahweh*. In place of this word whose consonants were written out, the reader had to read *Adonai* (Lord). This custom continues to exist in present-day Judaism. Hence, the first Christians surrounded the name of Jesus with great veneration and the expressions: "in the name of Jesus" and "for the name of Jesus" occur frequently in the sense of: "acting in such an intention in dependence on Jesus" and "by authority of Jesus" (Col 3:17). In John's Gospel, we are urged to pray "in the name of Jesus" (Jn 14:13). Moreover, this manner of speaking has been retained until our own day; for example, we say: "In the name of the Father, and of the Son, and of the Holy Spirit." In the Our Father, the expression: "Hallowed be thy name," signifies that we pray for God's holiness to be acknowledged and adored by all men.

NATIONS. The Israelites distinguished themselves from foreign peoples. They designated the latter by the Hebrew term *goiim*; this word, which includes a certain nuance of scorn, is often translated in our modern languages as "nations" or "Gentiles" (Isa 49:6). *See* FOREIGNERS.

NAZIRITE. This term stems from the Hebrew word nazir, meaning "set apart as sacred dedicated, vowed." The nazirite vow could be either for a limited period or for life. Those bound by this vow had to abstain from all the products of the grapevine, from cutting or shaving their hair, and from contact with a corpse. They were regarded as men of God like the prophets; cf Am 2:11f. Examples of lifelong nazirites were Samson (Jdg 13:4f, 7; 16:17), Samuel (1 Sam 1:11), and John the Baptist (Lk 1:15). At the time of Christ the practice of taking the nazirite vow for a limited period seems to have been quite common even among the early Christians; cf Acts 18:18; 21:23f, 26.

NAZOREAN. A title of Jesus that the Gospel derives from the name of the town of Nazareth (Mt 2:23). The Christians were called Nazoreans for a long time (Acts 24:5). In Hebrew this word has a certain resemblance with the word *nezer* which signifies "shoot." Primitive Christian tradition thus saw in this an allusion to a passage of Isaiah (11:10) in which the Messiah is presented as the shoot par excellence of David, son of Jesse.

NUMBERS. In the Bible, numbers often have a symbolic value. For example 7 (seven days, seven angels, seven lights . . .); 12 (tribes, apostles); 40 (days of rain, days of prayer on Sinai, days of fast, period before the Ascension), 144,000 (the elect, in the Book of Revelation). It must also be noted that in the ancient accounts numbers must be regarded in accord with Oriental custom, and they are subject to poetic approximation: *thousand* can signify a group or family. In the military accounts, most numbers are considerably exaggerated (Deut 32:30).

PARACLETE. (ADVOCATE). Word derived from the Greek. It is used only in John's Gospel and signifies "advocate or defender." This word is applied either to Christ, who fulfilled this role toward his disciples, or to the Holy Spirit, who continues to exercise it with Christ himself (Jn 14:16).

PARADISE. Word of Persian origin, which passed over into Hebrew and then Greek, used to designate a garden; in particular, the garden of Eden (Gen 2:15). Later, it signified the eternal abode of the just (Lk 23:43).

PASSOVER. *See* FEASTS.

PASTOR. *See* SHEPHERD.

PEACE. This word is used in the Bible to express two ideas: (1) peace with God, reestablished by the covenant, often a synonym for reconciliation, and (2) peace between individuals and peoples.

The promises of the messianic covenant are often accompanied by the announcement of peace. Thus the Messiah will be called the "Prince of Peace" (Isa 9:5). The word "peace" is contained in the literal translation of the word Jerusalem (Salem) (Heb 7:2). Peace demands faithfulness to the covenant and justice among men (Ps 72:3-7) so often invoked by the prophets. Christ came to bring peace (Lk 2, 14) and to render it effective by a reconciliation of mankind to God (Jn 14:27; Eph 2:14-17). The extension of the peaceful reign of Christ is thus for the true Christian the condition and source of true peace and true justice between individuals and between nations.

PEOPLE OF GOD. This is how Israel is designated throughout the Bible. God has gratuitously chosen her, and she is his own possession (Deut 7:6). God dwells in her midst (Ex 25:8). The people is thus holy and set apart from other peoples (Lev 20:24). In its turn, Christianity is also called the People God claims for his own, but it rejects any kind of national particularism (1 Pet 2:9).

PERFECT. In the ancient text, this word indicates someone who avoids sin and practices the law. The passage in which Jesus says: "Be perfected as your heavenly Father is perfect" (Mt 5:48) signifies—according to its context —that one must imitate the divine mercy and impartiality. In a single passage (Mt 19:21) Jesus speaks of the perfection of the disciple who goes beyond his ordinary duties. St. Paul uses the term perfect of the "spiritually mature" Christians who know true wisdom and want all men to be perfect in Christ (1 Cor 2:6ff).

PHARISEES. A religious sect of the Jews that numbered about 6000 in the time of Christ. Originating in the days of the Greek conquest of Palestine, they sought above all to preserve the Jews from the contamination of foreign religion, and to this end insisted upon strict separation from the Gentiles. They insisted also on strict loyalty to the Scriptures and to the traditions of the rabbis. Among many Pharisaic hedges about the law, ceremonial purity and payment of religious dues were emphasized. In doctrine the Pharisees were inclined to fatalism, but on the other hand they strongly upheld the resurrection and the future life. By the time of Christ their primitive zeal had degenerated into fanaticism and hypocrisy. They took a leading part in the opposition to Christ, and he scathingly rebuked their insincerity (Mt 23:25; Lk 11:39; 18:9-14). That they were not all bad is evidenced by such men as Gamaliel (Acts 5:34).

PHILADELPHIA. A city of Lydia in Asia Minor, founded by Attalus II Philadelphus, king of Pergamum. The Book of Revelation alludes to it twice (1:11 and 3:7).

PHILISTINES. Non-Semitic invaders who gave their name to all of Palestine although they occupied only its southwestern plains. They were subdued by David (2 Sam 5:17-25), but became practically independent under the separated kingdom and disappeared as a people after the time of the Maccabees.

PIETY. In Hebrew as in English, account must be taken of the relationship between this word *piety* and *pity* (in the sense of goodness). God is called pious, that is, good (Isa 1:4). Men are termed pious, that is, faithful, just, and devoted to God (Acts 10:7).

POOR. Originally, this word had merely an economic and social meaning. Gradually, it took on the meaning of humble, modest, small, the little people often oppressed by the rich and powerful but who remained faithful to God (Am 2:6-7). It was in this sense that Jesus said: "Blessed are the poor in spirit" (Mt 5:3).

PRESBYTERS. *See* ELDER.

PRIESTS, JEWISH. Sacred ministers, whose duty it was to offer sacrifice at the altar of holocausts, and to enter morning and evening into the holy place to burn incense at the golden altar (Heb 7:27; 10:11). They also had care of the loaves of proposition (Mt 12:4) and certified the cure of lepers (Lk 17:13f). They were divided into twenty-four classes, each of which in turn officiated for a week at the temple (Lk 1:5). During the three great feasts all the classes ministered together. Their dress comprised a long linen tunic, ornamented sash, and turban. The priesthood was hereditary by descent from the tribe of Levi through the younger branch of Aaron's family (Heb 7:5). For their support the priests received tithes and other offerings.

PROMISE. This term of Greek origin is employed only in the New Testament. It designates and interprets the meaning of all the previous prophetic history of the chosen people in their messianic mission. The Old Testament gave promise of Christ. But it is in Christ that all this preparatory and figurative history finds its perfect fulfillment (Mt 5:17; Acts 13:32-33; Rom 15:8; 2 Cor 1:20; Gal 3:14). An analogous relationship exists between Christ's work of the Redemption and his second coming which, at the end of time will assure the glorious consummation of all things (Acts 1:4-5; 2:16-21) and fulfill the promise of Christ's work.

PROPHET. One who speaks to another on the part of God (Deut 18:18). Prophets are also called "seers" by reason of their gift of reading thoughts. *Prophet* does not necessarily signify that one foretells the future and there were prophets in the first Christian communities (1 Cor 12:28ff).

PUBLICANS. Management of imperial taxation was farmed by the Roman government to the highest bidders, who in turn entrusted the collection in the provinces to native agents by whom the privilege had been purchased with advance payments. These agents are the "publicans." They were often guilty of merciless extortion, and were universally hated as plunderers of their own people. Among the Jews they were also considered as disloyal to their religion since they cooperated with Gentiles and exacted tribute from the race that God had made free (Jn 8:33; Mt 22:17). Like the Baptist, our Lord condemned the injustice of the publicans, but did not reject those who were sincerely repentant (Mt 5:46; 21:31f). Two publicans are distinguished in the Gospels, Zacchaeus (Lk 19:2) and Matthew (Mt 10:3), who became an apostle and evangelist.

PURITY (RITUAL). State of the man who fulfills the conditions imposed by the Mosaic law on every one of the faithful who appeared for worship (Lev 7:19-21). Certain bodily functions, contact with forbidden animals, and with corpses forbade participation in worship; anyone who was guilty of such things was "impure" or "unclean" (Num 19:1-10). "Purity" could be recovered by various rites: sacrifices, washings, aspersions, etc. (Num 19:19). There is no relation between this term and what we call "purity" in the sense of chastity.

REDEMPTION. This word comes from the Latin *redimere* which signifies to buy back or redeem. The corresponding Hebrew term was used in the Bible for the first time with reference to the exodus from Egypt (Ex 15:13). God has redeemed his people from the bondage of Egypt, gratuitously, just as a master sets free his slave (Lev 19:20). In the New Testament, it signifies that God through Jesus Christ (gratuitously), redeems his people in order to establish his kingdom (Rom 3:24).

REMNANT. An expression often used by the prophets. It designates the survivors of great catastrophes: the flood, the exile (Gen 7:1f; Isa 6:13). God reserves this remnant for himself to help in the restoration (Isa 37:31). It is they who are and will remain the depositories of the promise (Mic 4:6-7). In the New Testament, the Church is presented as fulfilling the function of the faithful Remnant, and the "Israel according to the flesh" is contrasted with the "Israel of God" which is the Church (Rom 9:27; 1 Cor 10:18; Gal 6:16); and this interpretation follows the teaching of the Old Testament.

RESURRECTION. The Bible does not have this unique and specific term. It uses the verbs to awake, to raise up, to cure, or the intransitive verbs, to get up, to appear, to show (one's self) sometimes as an act showing the power of God, sometimes as a manifestation of the victory of life over death. In the Old Testament, the idea is made known little by little at first in the perspective of the entire people (Ezek 37:1, 14), then for the Servant of Yahweh (Isa 53) but always in a very limited fashion (Pss 16:10ff; 49:16; 73:26; 17:15). In the New Testament, this idea takes on an elemental importance through the resurrection of Jesus, which became the fundamental historical fact, the principal witness of his divinity (1 Cor 15:4, 12). The Resurrection is also the divine judgment which has ordered the defeat of death and pledges salvation and resurrection to all the faithful (Rom 4:25; Col 2:12ff; Eph 2: 1-7). This resurrection in grace is the prelude to the final and glorious resurrection (1 Cor 15:20ff; 1 Thes 4:14ff).

SACRED. The same Hebrew word has both the active meaning of "holy," that is, keeping oneself free from profane impurities, and the passive meaning of "sacred," that is, set apart from what is profane and therefore treated with religious reverence (Lev 21:6).

SACRIFICE. The supreme form of divine worship, by which some creature is offered to God and used in adoration as an acknowledgment of his majesty and the creature's subjection. True sacrifices were offered in the Old Law (Heb 9:1ff), but they were only preparations for the perfect sacrifice of Christ on the cross (Heb 9:11).

SADDUCEES. A religious sect of the Jews, less numerous than their rivals the Pharisees, but very influential on account of the many noble and wealthy persons who belonged to their ranks (Acts 4:1; 5:17). They set aside traditions and even rejected truths taught in the Sacred Books themselves. They insisted upon human free will, but denied immortality, the resurrection, and the existence of angels (Mt 22:23; Mk 12:18; Lk 20:27; Acts 23:8). They were denounced by John the Baptist (Mt 3:7) and by our Lord (Mt 16:6). Though less prominent in their opposition to Christ than the Pharisees, they nevertheless sought to entrap him (Mt 16:1; 22:23), and through their representatives joined in his condemnation by the Sanhedrin. They also strongly opposed the early Church because the apostles proclaimed our Lord's Resurrection (Acts 4:1f; etc.).

SALVATION, SAVIOR. Inasmuch as the terms express redemption (*see* REDEMPTION) and appear as a cause of salvation, the Hebrew uses one word: *Yacha*, which means to be generous, to deliver from slavery or from distress. This term in the Old Testament expresses the Work of God, assuring the deliverance of his people as a whole (Hos 5:13; Isa 31:1; Ps 33:16-17) and then personal salvation (Ps 51:14)—the whole bound up in the messianic and eschatological perspective. This term provides the substantive "*machia*," translated as Savior (Isa 45:21). In the New Testament, the term is employed very frequently for a cure, the health of the body, but often, in connection with faith, of the soul (Mk 5:34; Lk 8:48; 18:42). Thus, the work of the New Testament even in its temporal action is entirely oriented toward the work of spiritual salvation, of remission of sins (Lk 17:19) and the liberation from the servitude that sin brings to man (Mt 1:21; Lk 1:77; Acts 5:31; etc.) and leading the Christian to their highest destiny (Rom 1:16; 5:9-10; 1 Cor 15:2; Jas 1:21). This work will be definitively manifested at the last judgment (Rom 8:22-25).

SAMARITANS. The inhabitants of Samaria were a mixed race, descended from intermarriage of Israelites and Assyrian colonists. The enmity between the Jews and the Samaritans was so great that travelers between Galilee and Judea often had to cross the Jordan into Perea for safety. In religion the Samaritans acknowledged the Pentateuch, Joshua, and Judges, but not the additional revelation or Jewish traditional doctrine. They looked for the Messiah who would teach all truth (Jn 4:25f). In practice they worshiped the same God as the Jews, and in such matters as sabbaths and feasts, circumcision and worship, they did not dissent. But though vying with the Jews in the strict observance of Mosaic regulations, they disowned the Jerusalem temple and priesthood. The rival sanctuary of Gerizim they revered as their holy place (Jn 4:20). Our Lord passed through their country more than once, and preached and worked miracles among the people. He also spoke well of them (Lk 10:30-37) defended them (Lk 9:51-56), and commanded that the gospel be preached to them. This was done with success, and a Christian community was early formed among the Samaritans (Acts 8:4-17; 9:31; 15:3).

SANHEDRIN. Literally *session*, a council, national or local, endowed with authority to pass on cases ecclesiastical or civil.

1) The national Sanhedrin, or Great Council, of the Jews met at Jerusalem. The high priest himself seems to have presided as a rule. The full membership was seventy-two, representing equally the three groups of priests, scribes, and elders. This council took cognizance of grave matters of a doctrinal, judicial, or administrative character affecting the Jewish religion and nation. The Romans acknowledged the decrees of the Sanhedrin, and guards attended the meetings to fulfill the orders of the judges (Mt 26:58). Sentence of death, however, was reserved to the Roman authority (Jn 18:31).

2) Local tribunals, subordinate to the supreme Sanhedrin, were found in the towns of Palestine. Their membership varied from three to twenty-three, according to the size of the male population of the place. The "Sanhedrin" of Mt 5:22 probably refers to one of these lower tribunals.

SAVIOR. Exact translation of the word *Yehoshua* which has become "Jesus" (Lk 1:31ff). *See* SALVATION.

SCRIBES. Literally this title means a writer, but in the New Testament the reference is to the learned class among the Jews, the official authorities on the written law and oral traditions. One who had made successful studies became a scribe at the age of thirty by receiving imposition of hands with the delivery of a tablet and key.

As the function of the priests was ritualistic, that of the scribes was doctrinal. These latter were interpreters of the Scriptures (Mt 2:4; 17:10; Mk 12:35), but our Lord condemned them for their burdensome additions to the divine law (Mt 23). They taught by quoting the celebrated doctors of the past (Mk 1:22). In our Lord's day the chief rival schools among the scribes were those of the liberal Hillel and the severe Shammai. Generally the scribes opposed the Sadducees (Lk 20:39) and upheld the Pharisees (Mk 7:1ff). Like the Pharisees, the scribes were noted for hypocrisy, pride, and contradiction of Christ (Mt 23:2ff; Mk 12:28-30; Lk 20:46; Mt 9:3). But there were noble and sincere characters among them (Mt 8:19), especially Nicodemus and Gamaliel (Jn 3; Acts 5:34).

SCRIPTURES. (1) The inspired books, the work of the Holy Spirit. They were customarily divided into three series: the Law, the Prophets, and the Writings. (2) Christianity added its own writings: the Gospels and the Letters of the apostles.

SEPTUAGINT. Translation into Greek of the Hebrew and Aramaic Old Testament (including the deuterocanonical books) made in Egypt by various authors during the period between 250 B.C. and 100 B.C. Its name comes from the fact that legend ascribes the work to a group of seventy-two scholars and it is designated by the Roman numerals LXX. It is by far the most important ancient version of the Old Testament and until recently was our sole witness for the state of the original text of the Hebrew Old Testament before the Christian era. The Septuagint was the version used by the Hebrews in Christ's time, by the apostles and New Testament writers, and by the Greek Fathers of the Church; it is still the official text of the Greek Church.

SHEOL. The ancient concept of the abode of the dead (*the netherworld,* in Hebrew, *Sheol*) supposed no activity or lofty emotion among the deceased, who were pictured as surrounded by the darkness of oblivion (Num 16:30ff; Ps 6:6). The Hebrews shared in this common idea almost to the time of Christ, when God revealed a clearer notion of the hereafter (Wis 3). It is at this time that belief in the resurrection of the dead was introduced (Dan 12:2). Some (for example, the Sadducees) refused to believe it; but the people embraced it like some great revelation. In the New Testament, the whole concept is transfigured in the light of Christ's resurrection. His body did not see corruption in Hades; he has the keys of death and the netherworld (Rev 1:18). The word "Gehenna" (hell) is used of the netherworld when punishment is involved (Mt 5:29; 10:28). *See* GEHENNA.

SIN. In the Old Testament sin is not so much a wrong action in one's conscience as something which disrupts the order of the world wished by God, and particularly the covenant fixed by the law. Thus the Israelite did not search himself for deep causes or establish its relationship with original sin; it is necessary to wait for the Book of Wisdom to find such an allusion (2:24). The New Testament describes sin as relating to original sin and tells of the universal sorrow because of sin (Rom 1—5) erased by the Redemption (Rom 5—8). It describes responsibility for it. This conception of sin thus became linked with the ideas of faith and love which gave life to Christians (Rom 13:8ff; 1 Cor 5:9; 13:4ff).

SON. In Hebrew, this word is used to designate diverse relations or dependencies: (1) relations of direct descendence (Ex 1:1-5); (2) relations of disciples to their master (Prov 1:8); (3) relations of origin or analogy (Job 1:3; 42:13); (4) moral relations (Jos 7:19).

SON OF MAN. An enigmatic title. Jewish apocryphal tradition (1 Enoch, 2 Esdras, 2 Baruch) uses it to describe a unique religious personage, a messiah with extraordinary spiritual endowments. Jesus' use of it seems to derive from Ezek 2, where it is a title of humility and Dan 7:13f, where it indicates a clearly messianic figure. It expresses for him his twofold destiny, of suffering (Mk 8:31; 9:11, 31; 10:33; 12:31; 14:21) and of glory (Mk 8:38; 12:36; 14:62). Peter, along with the other disciples, fails (despite his confession) to grasp the association of suffering and death with the office of Messiah. Only after the resurrection does the Christian community endow it with its messianic meaning (Acts 7:56; Rev 1:3).

SOUL. In its first sense, the Hebrew word *nephesh* signifies breath, life, the principle of animal life (Gen 1:20). It was only much later (toward the beginning of the Christian era) that the Hebrews adopted the distinction (of Greek philosophy) of soul and body (Rev 6:9; 20:4).

SPIRIT. Literally, breath. It is an element with as little materiality as possible; it is the innermost part of man, more subtle than his soul. The Old Testament attributes to the Spirit of God both external and internal actions that surpass human powers (Num 11:24-29). The Spirit is a person distinct from the Father and the Son (Jn 14:26). Each Christian possesses the Spirit. He is the principle of life and a pledge of resurrection (Rom 8:2, 11).

SYNAGOGUES. Minor places of religious assembly among the Jews, used also as schools libraries, and halls of judgment. The central place of worship was the temple, the one national sanctuary and the only place of sacrifice. The synagogue served local communities or separate congregations for less solemn religious functions. Every considerable Jewish community, whether in or out of Palestine, had at least one synagogue. The building, commonly rectangular, was erected on the plan of the temple. There was a gallery reserved for women, another space for men, and the worshipers faced toward Jerusalem and the holy of holies. In front was a platform on which stood the holy ark containing the Scriptures and an eight-branch candlestick burning before it. Nearest the platform were the chief seats, where sat the leading men facing the congregation (Mt 23:6; Mk 12:39; Lk 11:43; 20:46). Among these leading men were the ruler of the synagogue and the elders, and various functionaries whom they appointed.

TEMPLE. The sacred place of worship on Mount Moriah, including all buildings and courts. The first temple was built by Solomon, in 967 to 964 B.C., but was destroyed by the Chaldeans in 586 B.C. The second was erected by Zerubbabel in 515 B.C., but was profaned in 167 B.C. by the Syrians. Herod the Great began a magnificent restoration of this temple. It is his structure that is the temple referred to in the time of our Lord. In a more restricted sense the term applies only to the "House" in which were the holy place and the holy of holies, or to the immediate precincts of this "House." The space covered by the temple and its courts was about 585 by 6100 feet.

The temple proper (Naos) measured 30 feet north to south, and 90 feet east to west. The innermost part of this building was the holy of holies, set apart from the outer room, the holy place, by a double curtain (Mt 27:51). The holy of holies contained the stone on which once rested the ark of the covenant. It was entered once a year by the high priest (Heb 9:3-5). The holy place had within it the golden altar of incense (Lk 1:11), and the table of loaves (Mt 12:4). About the Naos ran an uncovered court reserved to the priests. In front of the entrance to the holy place stood the altar of holocausts (Ex 27:1-8). The lay Israelite might approach this altar only to bring his sacrifice to the priests (Mt 5:23).

Outside this court of the priests, toward the east, was the court of the Israelites, where the laity could assist at the services. Beyond this was an outer court known as the court of the women, since to it women were admitted. This court was surrounded by rooms one of which was the treasury with thirteen boxes for contributions (Lk 21:1ff). To these courts only Jews were admitted, inscriptions warning non-Jews not to enter under pain of death (Acts 21:28). By a staircase of fifteen steps one descended to the outer court which was known as that of the Gentiles. This outside court was surrounded by walls with high towers. The court of the Gentiles was open to all, and it was used for buying and selling (Mk 11:15). Against the walls of this court on the interior were porches or colonnades where the people listened to religious teachers (Lk 2:46; Mt 26:55). The porch attached to the eastern wall was known as Solomon's (Jn 10:23; Acts 3: 11; 5:12). At its northwestern corner this court was adjacent to the fortress Antonia, whose garrison was ready to keep order among the crowds (Acts 21:30ff). But the Jews had also their own temple police, with captains and officers, who patrolled the whole area day and night (Lk 22:52; Acts 4:1).

TIME. In Hebrew, *olam* designates a very long and indefinite period. In Greek, this word has been translated by two terms: "world" and "age" which are often taken for one another. Hence, one says: this world, the next world, or the ages to come. In the plural ages is practically equivalent to eternity (Mt 12:32; Eph 2:7).

TONGUES (SPEAK IN). Two passages of the New Testament speak of the *gift of tongues* (Acts 2 and 1 Cor 14). In the first, we find the mention of the miracle by which the apostles suddenly began to speak in tongues foreign to them—or by which their auditors each understand in their own language what the apostles said to them in the apostles' tongue. In the second, it is a case of a phenomenon that is difficult to describe and analyze: this was a manner of expressing oneself in inarticulate sounds or cries, proper to certain states of mystical exaltation.

TRUTH. This word, in Hebrew *emeth*, designates something firm and solid, hence something faithful. The adjective "true" signifies not only what is true and authentic but also what is the principle of this truth and this authenticity (Gen 32:10; Ps 12:1-2).

VULGATE. The official Latin translation of the Bible which was prepared almost entirely by St. Jerome from 382 to 405 A.D. Jerome borrowed heavily from Origen in translating the Psalter and took Ecclesiasticus, Baruch, and both books of Maccabees from Old Latin texts. He translated everything else from the existing Hebrew, Aramaic, or Greek manuscripts. The Council of Trent declared the Vulgate to be "authentic in public readings disputations, preachings, and exposition" because it conforms to the original texts and contains no errors in faith or morals. The Benedictine Order has, at the request of St. Pius X, published a revised edition of the modern Vulgate text to make it conform as closely as possible to the text of St. Jerome.

YAHWEH. The proper personal name of the God of Israel signifying "I am who am" (Ex 3:14-15). It is commonly explained in reference to God as the absolute and necessary Being. It may be understood of God as the Source of all created beings. Out of reverence for this name, the term *Adonai*, "my Lord," was later used as a substitute. The word LORD in the present version represents this traditional usage. The word "Jehovah" arose from a false reading of this name as it is written in the current Hebrew text. *See* ADONAI. NAME.

DOCTRINAL BIBLE INDEX

Other subjects will be found in the Bible Dictionary, pp. 436-453.

Absolution, the power promised and given to the pastors of the church, Mt 16:19; 18:18; Jn 20:22f.

Abstinence, from food: God forbids Adam to eat the fruit of a certain tree, Gen 2:17; 3:11; □ from flesh with its blood, forbidden, Gen 9:4; Deut 12:16; Acts 15:29; □ paschal lamb not to be eaten raw, or boiled, Ex 12:9; □ leaven forbidden, Ex 13:7; □ ox that has killed a man not to be eaten, Ex 21:28; □ observed by St. John the Baptist, Lk 1:15; □ even permitted food to be abstained from, so as not to scandalize others, 2 Mac 6:24; 7:1f; Rom 4:20f; 1 Cor 8:13.

Almsgiving, Ex 22:24; 23:11; Lev 19:10; 23:22; 25:34; Deut 15:7, 10; 24:19; 1 Ki 17:10; Neh 8:10; Mt 6:3; 10:42; 19:21; 25:35, 42; Lk 3:11; 6:35; 11:41; 12:33; 14:13.

Angels, they have a charge over us, Mt 18:10; Heb 1:14. See also Ex 23:20f; Ps 91:11f. □ pray for us, Rev 8:4; Zec 1:12; □ communion with, Heb 12:22; □ fall of, Job 4:18; Isa 14:12; Lk 10:18; Jude 6; Rev 12:4; 20:9.

Anger, Pss 4:5; 37:8; Prov 15:18; 26:21; 27:3f; 29:22; Sir 8:16; 25:13; 27:30; 28:3-11; Mt 5:22; Eph 4:26, 31; Jas 1:19f.

Apostles, chosen from the disciples, Lk 6:13; □ sent to announce the kingdom of God in Judea, Mt 10; □ sent to evangelize the whole world, Mt 18:19; Mk 16:15; Lk 24:46; Jn 15:16, 27; 20:21; Acts 1:8; 10:42.

Apostolical Traditions, 1 Cor 11:2; 2 Thes 2:15; 3:6; 2 Tim 1:13; 2:2; 3:14. See also Deut 32:7; Pss 44:2; 78:3.

Avarice, Pss 39:7; 119:36; Prov 15:27; 28:16; 29:4; Eccl 5:9, 14; Sir 10:9f; 14:3; Isa 5:8; 57:17; Heb 2:9; Lk 12:15-21; 1 Cor 5:11; 6:9f; Eph 5:3, 5; Col 3:5; 1 Tim 6:9; Heb 13:5.

Beatitudes, Mt 5:3-11; Lk 6:20-23.

Bishop, at Ephesus, Acts 20:28; □ at Philippi, Phil 1:1; □ qualities required of, 1 Tim 3:1-7; Tit 1:6-9.

Blessings, by which creatures are consecrated and sanctified, Ex 28:2; 29:6, 27; Lev 21:10; 22:2; 27:28-30; Num 5:17; 31:6; Jos 6:24; Jdg 17:3; 2 Sam 21:5; 1 Chr 18:11; 1 Tim 4:5; Heb 19:2f; □ temporal, promised to Israel, Ex 15:26; Lev 26:4-12; Deut 4:1; 5:29; □ conditions for these blessings, Deut 15:5; □ spiritual blessings: salvation, Ps 91:16; Acts 4:12; presence of God, Ex 33:14-17; Mt 28:20; strength, Col 1:11; help, Heb 2:18; joy, Ps 40:4; Acts 13:52; peace, Jn 14:27; Phil 4:7; □ of praise, Gen 24:48; Ps 68:27; 1 Cor 1:9.

Body, of Christian is temple of Holy Spirit, 1 Cor 3:16, 17; 2 Cor 6:16; and member of Christ, 1 Cor 6:15; 12:27; □ Church is body of Christ, Eph 1:22, 23; Col 3:15; 1 Cor 10:17; □ of man will be raised up, Job 19:26, 27; Mt 22:23-32; 1 Cor 15:12-57; □ Word of God received a human body, Mt 1:18-23; Jn 1:14; Heb 10:5; □ which was crucified, Jn 19:17-18, 33; and raised again, 1 Cor 15:3-8.

Charity, a virtue more excellent than faith, Prov 10:12; Mt 22:38; 1 Cor 13:13; □ fraternal, Gen 13:8; Lev 19:18; Deut 22:1; 1 Sam 18:1; Sir 25:2; Ps 133:31; Prov 10:12; Mt 7:3; 19:19; 23:38; Jn 13:14, 34; 15:12; Rom 12:10; 13:9; 1 Cor 13; Gal 5:14; Eph 4:15; 5:2; Phil 2:2; Col 3:13f; 1 Thes 4:9; 1 Tim 1:5; Heb 13; 1 Pet 4:8; 1 Jn 3:23; 4:7; □ toward our enemies, Ex 23:4; 1 Sam 24:5, 7; 26:5; 30:11; 2 Sam 19:19; 2 Ki 6:21; Job 31:29; Prov 25:21; Mt 5:44; Lk 6:27, 35; 23:33; Acts 7:60; Rom 12:20; □ produced by the Holy Spirit, Col 1:8; □ exemplified by Jesus, Jn 13:1 □ 16:34; 15:12; Eph 5:2, 25; Rev 1:5.

Chastity, praised, Tob 6:16; Jdg 15:11; 16:26; Prov 22:11; Wis 3:13; 4:1; 6:20; Sir 6:28; 26:20; Isa 5:14; Zec 9:17; □ virginity preferable to marriage, Ps 45:15; Wis 6:20; Mt 22:30; □ evangelical perfection, Mt 19:12; 1 Cor 7:25; □ recommended to ministers of the church, 1 Tim 3:2, 8; □ recommended to women, Tit 2:5.

Children, of Hebrews, drowned by Pharaoh, Ex 1:22; □ firstborn of Egyptians struck dead, Ex 11:5; □ devoured by bears, 2 Ki 2:24; □ massacred by Herod, Mt 2:16; □ blessed by our Lord, Mt 10:16; Lk 18:17; □ duty to parents, Gen 9:23; 28:7; 37:14; Ex 20:12; 21:17; Lev 19:3; Deut 21:18; 27:16; Jdg 14:1; 1 Sam 2:22; 18:5; 1 Ki 2:19; 2 Ki 2:23; Sir 3:2; 6:18; 7:27; 8:9; 22:3; 23:14; 25:7; Tob 14:5; Job 8:4; Prov 1:8; 4:1; 6:20; 10:1; 13:1; 15:20; 19:26; 23:19; 28:24; 30:17; Jer 35:16; Mt 10:35; 19:19; Mk 10:19; Lk 2:51; Acts 7:14; Col 3:20; 1 Pet 5:5.

Christ, Jesus, foretold in the Old Testament, Gen 3:15; 49:10; Num 24:17; Deut 18:15; 2 Sam 7:12-16; Ps 2:1-9; Isa 7:14; 9:6; 11:1; 49:1; 50:4; 52:13; Jer 23:5; Ezek 34:23-24; Dan 7:13; Mic 5:2; Zec 6:12; 9:9; Mal 3:1; □ Son of Man, Mt 9:6; 26:64; Mk 8:31; Lk 19:10; Jn 3:13-14; 5:27; Acts 7:55; □ Son of David, Mt 1:1; 9:27; Jn 7:42; □ Son of Mary, Mt 1:21; Lk 2:7; Jn 19:25; Acts 1:14; □ Son of God, Mt 3:17; 4:3; 14:33; 16:16; Mk 1:1; Lk 1:32; Jn 1:34; 10:36; Rom 1:3; □ the same God with his Father and equal to Him, Jn 5:18, 19, 23; 10:30; 14:1, 9; 16:14f; 17:10; Phil 2:5f; □ true God, Isa 9:6; 35:4f; Mt 1:23; Lk 1:16f; Jn 1:1; 20:28f; Acts 20:25; Rom 9:5; Tit 2:13; 1 Jn 5:20; Heb 1:8; □ Creator of all things, Jn 1:3, 10f; Col 1:16f; Heb 1:2, 10-12; 3:4; □ the Lord of glory, 1 Cor 2:8; □ the King of kings and Lord of lords, Rev 17:14; 19:16; □ the Alpha and Omega, the beginning and the end, Rev 1:7f, 17f; 2:8; 22:12f; □ circumcised, Lk 2:21; □ baptized in the Jordan, Mt 3:16; Mk

Devil, always seeks to injure men, Gen 3:1; 1 Chr 21:1; Job 1:11; Zec 3:1; Lk 8:12; Acts 13:8; Eph 6:11; Rev 2:10; 12:9; □ tempts our Lord, Mt 4:1-11; □ transforms himself into an angel of light, 2 Cor 11:14; □ his empire destroyed by Christ, Mt 12:25-29; Lk 10:18; 11:20-22; Jn 12:31; Col 1:13; 2 Tim 1:10; Heb 2:14; 1 Jn 3:8; Rev 20:9.

Divorce, allowed in the Old Law, Deut 24:1-4; □ forbidden in the New Law, Mt 5:31f; 19:3-9; Mk 10:2-12; Lk 16:18; 1 Cor 7:10-13.

Ecumenism, Mt 7:21-23; Jn 17:9-11, 20-23; Eph 4:3-16; 1 Cor 10:17; 12:12-27; Rom 12:5; 9:6-8.

Elect, Christ, Lk 23:35; 1 Pet 2:4, 6 (Isa 42:1); □ Israel, Deut 14:2; Isa 14:1; Ps 105:6, 43; □ the Church, Mt 24:22, 24, 31; Lk 18:7; Rom 8:33; 2 Tim 2:10; 1 Pet 1:2; 2:9.

Enemies, attitude toward, Ex 23:4f; Deut 23:35; 1 Ki 3:11; Job 31:29; Mt 5:24, 38f; Lk 6:29; Rom 12:17ff; □ God saves from enemies, 1 Sam 12:11; Ezr 8:31; Pss 18:47-49; 59:1-5; Acts 16:19-40; □ punishment for enemies of God, Ex 15:6f; Deut 32:41; Ps 68:2f; 2 Thes 1:6-9; Rev 21:8.

Envy, Ps 37:1; Prov 3:31; 14:30; Wis 2:24; 6:23; Sir 30:24; 40:5; Mt 27:18; Acts 5:17; Phil 1:15.

Eucharist, real presence of the body and blood of Christ, Mt 26:26-28; Mk 14:22-24; Lk 22:19f; Jn 6:51f; 1 Cor 10:16; 11:24f, 27, 29.

Excommunication, used by the apostles, 1 Cor 5:3-5, 9-13; 2 Thes 3:6, 14; 1 Tim 1:20; Tit 3:10f; □ of the Pharisees, Jn 9:22, 34; 12:42; 16:2.

Expiation, effected under the Old Law, Lev 1; 4; 5; 16; Heb 9:7, 13; □ effected by Christ, Lk 19:22; Jn 1:29, 36; Rom 5:6-10; 1 Cor 1:30; Gal 4:5; Eph 2:13-18; Heb 9:12, 14, 28; 1 Pet 3:8.

Faith, necessary to salvation, Mk 16:16; Acts 2:44-47; 4:12; Heb 11:6; □ without good works is dead, Jas 2:14, 17, 20; □ alone, does not justify, Jas 2:24; □ working with charity, Gal 5:6; □ does not imply an absolute assurance of our being in grace; much less of our eternal salvation, Rom 11:20-22; 1 Cor 9:27; 10:12; Phil 2:12; Rev 3:11.

Fasting, commended in Scripture, Joel 2:12; □ practiced by God's servants, Ezr 8:23; Neh 1:4; Dan 10:3; □ moves God to mercy, Jon 3:5, 10; □ of great efficacy against the devil, Mt 9:15; Mk 2:20; Lk 5:35; See also Acts 13:3; 14:22; 2 Cor 6:5; 11:27; □ the obligation of, Joel 2:12; Tob 12:8; Mt 6:16; Mk 2:20; Lk 2:36f; 5:35; Acts 13:2f; 14:22; Rom 13:13f; 2 Cor 6:5; 11:27; Eph 5:18; 1 Thes 5:6; 1 Pet 1:13; 5:8; □ merits of, 1 Sam 31:13; 2 Sam 1:12; Jer 35:14, 19; Jon 3:7, 9f; Jud 4:8; 8:6; Mt 6:17; Lk 2:37; □ Christ fasting for forty days, Mt 4:2;

Fear of God, and keep him always before our eyes, Ex 20:20; Deut 4:10; 6:2, 13; 10:12; 13:5; Jos 24:14; 2 Ki 17:36; 2 Chr 19:7; Pss 27:1; 33:8; Mt 10:28; Lk 12:5; 1 Pet 2:17; Rev 14:7; □ is the beginning of wisdom, Prv 9:10; □ is the source of life, Prv 14:27; □ surpasses all else, Sir 25:11; □ fruit of the fear of God and his praise, Gen 20:11; Deut 6:24; Job 28:28; Pss 103:17; 111:5; 112:1; Prov 8:13; 10:27; 14:26; 16:6; Sir 1:9-18; 40:26; Acts 9:31; □ not opposed to faith, Eccl 9:1; Sir 2:8; Rom 11:20; Heb 3:14; 4:1.

Fornication, provokes God's anger, Deut 22:21; Jer 5:7; Hos 4:14; 1 Cor 6:9; Heb 13:4; □ occasions of, to be avoided, Sir 9:4; 42:12; □ desire of, forbidden, Ex 20:17; Mt 5:28; □ idolatry so called, Deut 31:16.

Free-will, Gen 4:7; Deut 30:19; Sir 15:14; □ often resists the grace of God, Prov 1:24; Isa 5:4; Ezek 18:23, 31f; 33:11; Mt 23:37; Lk 13:34; Acts 7:51; Heb 12:15; 2 Pet 3:9; Rev 20:4.

Gentiles, conversion of, Gen 49:10; Num 24:17; Pss 2:8; 68:33; 82:8; 87:4; Isa 2:2; 11:10; Jer 9:24; Hos 2:1; Mic 4:2; Zep 3:8f; Zec 2:11; Mt 8:11; Jn 10:16; Acts 8:26f; 1 Cor 12:12f.

Gifts of God, Jesus, Jn 3:16; 2 Cor 9:15; □ the Holy Spirit, Lk 11:13; Acts 2:38; □ salvation, Eph 2:8; □ eternal life, Jn 10:28; Rom 6:23; 1 Jn 5:11; □ grace and glory, Ps 84:12; Jas 4:6; □ various spiritual gifts, 1 Cor 1:7; 12:1-11; Jas 1, 17.

Glory, of God, to be sought in all things, Jos 7:19; Ps 115:1; Mt 6:9; Jn 17:4; Acts 3:13; 12:23; 1 Cor 6:20; 10:31; Phil 1:20; Col 3:17; Tit 2:10.

Gluttony, Gen 25:29, 34; Prov 21:17; 23:20f; Sir 37:26-30; Heb 12:16f.

God, a pure spirit and self-existent, Ex 3:14, 16; 6:2; Jn 4:24; □ He is one, Deut 6:4; 32:39; Wis 12:13; Isa 43:10; 44:6; 45:6; Eph 4:5f; □ there are three persons in one God, the Creator □ Elohim (plural), Gen 1:1, 2, 26; the Son, Heb 1:8-10; the Spirit of God, Job 33:4; revealed at the baptism of Jesus, Mt 3:16f; at the transfiguration, Lk 9:28-35; by Jesus, Mt 28:19; Jn 3:16; 5:21-23; 14:16f; □ he is infinite, Job 36:26; Ps 145:3; Wis 11:23; □ eternal, Job 36:26; Pss 90:2; 102:25; Isa 57:15; Dan 7:14; □ unchangeable, Num 23:19; Ps 102:26; Mal 3:6; Jas 1:17; □ omniscient, 2 Chr 16:9; Est 14:14; Job 21:22; 28:24; 34:21; Ps 139:1-6, 16; Prov 16:2; Sir 39:20; Dan 13:42; 1 Cor 2:10; Heb 4:13; 1 Jn 3:20; □ almighty, Gen 17:1; Job 9:13; 11:10; 23:13; Prov 21:30f; Wis 11:22f; 16:13, 15; Sir 43; Isa 44:24; □ Creator of all things, Gen 1:1, 31; 2:4; Pss 33:6f; 74:16f; 148:4-6; Isa 37:16; 45:18; Jn 1:3; Acts 17:24; Col 1:16; Heb 3:4; 11:3; Rev 4:11; □ his fidelity, Deut 7:9, 12; 32:4; Ps 100:5; Isa 49:7; 1 Cor 1:9; 2 Thes 3:3; Heb 10:23; 1 Jn 1:9; □ his justice, Deut 32:4; 1 Sam 26:23; Job 34:10, 12, 19; Pss 11:7; 119:75, 137, 142; Eccl 7:14; 12:14; Sir 35:12, 16; Acts 10:34f; Rom 11:22, 33; □ his mercy, Ex 20:6; 34:6; Num 14:18; Pss 25:10; 33:5; 103:8, 11, 17; 118:1; 136; 145:9; Sir 18:11f; Isa 30:18; Lam 3:32; Heb 3:2; Lk 1:50; Jas 2:13; □ his grace, Ps 33:22; Lk 2:40; Acts 13:43; 20:24; Rom 9:15; 2 Cor 12:9; 1 Pet 5:10; □ loves all men, Wis 11:23f, 26; 12:2; Jer 31:3; Hos 11:4; Jn 3:16; 16:27; Rom 5:8f; 8:32; 1 Tim 2:4; □ wills all to be saved, Wis 1:13; Ezek 18:32; Mt 23:37; Jn 6:39f; 1 Tim 2:4.

Good Works, meritorious, Gen 4:7; 22:16, 18; Pss 18:21, 23-25; 19:8, 11; Mt 5:11f; 10:42; 16:27; 1 Cor 3:8; 2 Tim 4:8.

Gospel, the preaching of, Gen 3:15; Isa 53:1; 55:5; 61:1; Mt 1:21; 11:28; 28:19f; Mk 16:15; Lk 2:10; 24:46f; Jn 3:16; 6:35; 8:12; 10:9; 12:46; Rom 1:16; 3:21, 24f; 8:3; 1 Cor 1:17, 23; 4:15; 15:1; 2 Cor 5:18; Gal 1:6, 11; Eph 1:13; 1 Tim 1:15; 2 Tim 1:8; 2:8; 1 Pet 4:17.

Grace, spoken of in Scripture as a favor, Gen 6:8; 18:3; 19:19; 39:21; Ex 12:36; Ru 2:20; 2 Sam 2:6; 15:20; Tob 3:13; Est 2:17; Prov 13:15; Dan 1:9; Acts 2:47; 25:9; □ as a reward expected from God, Prov 1:9; 12:2; 2 Mac 12:46; Lk 6:33; 1 Pet 2:19; □ as a supernatural gift, Ps 84:12; Lk 1:28; 2:40; Jn 1:16; Rom 1:7; 1 Cor 16:23; 2 Cor 1:12; Gal 5:4f; Heb 13:9; Jas 4:6; □ before and after meals, Deut 8:10; 1 Sam 9:13; Isa 62:9; Mt 14:19; 15:36; 26:26; Mk 6:41; 8:6; 14:22; Lk 9:16; Jn 6:11. 23; Acts 27:35; Rom 14:6; 1 Cor 10:30; 1 Tim 4:3.

Gratitude, recommended, Num 15:18-20; Deut 4:9; 2 Chr 15:11; Sir 7:21; Acts 4:21; Eph 5:19f; Phil 4:6; Col 2:7; 3:15.

Happiness, condition for, Deut 4:40; 5:29, 33; Pss 32:1f; 40:5; 84:6, 13; 128:1; Prov 3:13; 29:18; Isa 56: 1f; Mt 5:1-12; Lk 11:28; Jn 13:17; Rom 4:7f.

Heaven, joys of, Ps 16:11; Dan 12:3; Mt 5:12; 13:43; Jn 12:26; 14:3; 17:24; 1 Cor 13:12; Rev 7:16; □ those who will attain it, Pss 15:2; 24:3f; Mt 5:8; 25:33-40; Rom 8:17; Phil 4:3; Heb 12:23; Rev 3:5; □ new heaven, Isa 65:17; 66:22; 2 Pet 3:13; Rev 21:1.

Hell, pains of, Deut 32:22; Job 24:19; Pss 21:10; 112:10; Sir 21:10; Isa 33:14; 34:9; Jer 9:15; Mal 4:1; Mt 8:12; Lk 13:28; Rev 14:10; □ proportioned to sins, Wis 11:16; Lk 16:25; Rev 18:7; □ endless, Isa 66:24; Mt 25:41; 2 Thes 1:9.

Holy Scripture, divinely inspired, 2 Tim 3:16f; 2 Pet 1:21; □ purpose of, to instruct, Deut 6:6-9; Ps 19:8, 12; Rom 15:4; □ give spiritual nourishment, Deut 8:3; Mt 4:4; 1 Pet 2:2; □ lead to faith, Jn 20:31; □ sanctify, Jn 17:17; Eph 5:26; □ edify, Acts 20:32; 2 Tim 3:16f; □ fulfilled by Christ, Mt 5:17; Lk 24:25-27; Jn 19:30; □ explained by the apostles, Acts 2:16-21, 25-36; Rom 3:10-18; □ danger of rejecting Scriptures, Jn 12:48; Heb 2:2-4; 10:28-31.

Holy Spirit, his divinity, Acts 5:3f; 28:25f; 1 Cor 2:10f; 6:11, 19f. See also Mt 12:31f; Acts 13:2; 20:28; 2 Cor 13:13; □ and the solemn form of baptism, Mt 28:19f; □ proceeds from the Father and the Son, Jn 15:26; □ his works, Gen 1:2; Job 33:14; Ps 104:30; Jn 3:3-8; 6:63; 14:16f, 26; 16:12-14; Rom 5:5; 8:14, 26; Gal 5:18; Eph 6:18; Phil 3:3; □ governs the work of the Church, Acts 13:2, 4; 20:22, 28; □ dwells within the followers of Christ, Jn 14:16f.

Hope, in God, Pss 31:25; 71:5; Isa 8:17; Jer 14:22; Acts 24:15; 1 Tim 4:10; □ in Christ, Acts 28:20; Rom 15:13; 1 Cor 15:19; 1 Tim 1:1; □ effects of, Rom 5:5; 12:12; 2 Cor 3:12; Heb 3:6; 1 Jn 3:3.

Hospitality, commended, Tob 4:7; Lk 14:13; Rom 12:13; 1 Tim 3:2; 3 Jn 5; □ examples of, Gen 18; 19; 24; Jdg 13:15; 1 Ki 17:10-16; □ want of, punished, Jdg 8:5-9; 19:18; 1 Sam 25; Wis 19:13.

Idolatry, folly and sin of, Wis 13-15; Jer 10:1-16; Isa 46:1; □ forbidden, Ex 20:4; □ punished, Ex 32:27f, 35; Wis 14:30.

Ignorance, dangers of, Acts 3:17; 17:29-31; Eph 4:18f; 1 Pet 1:14; □ mercy of God for the ignorant, Ps 19:13; Acts 17:30; 1 Tim 1:13; Heb 5:2.

Image, man created in God's, Gen 1:26f; 1 Cor 11:7; □ Christ is image of God, 2 Cor 4:4; Phil 2:6; Col 1:15; Heb 1:3.

Immortality, of God, 1 Tim 1:17; 6:16; 2 Tim 1:10; □ of men, Rom 2:7; 1 Cor 15:53.

Jews, their reprobation announced by St. Paul, Rom 10:1; □ persecute the apostles, Acts 5:18; □ three thousand converted, Acts 2:41; □ five thousand converted, Acts 4:4; □ Greek Jews murmur as to alms, Acts 6:1; □ rise against St. Stephen, Acts 7; □ gospel preached to, Acts 11:19; □ resist St. Paul, Acts 13:45; □ abandoned for the Gentiles, Acts 13:46; □ persecute St. Paul, Acts 13:50; □ do themselves what they condemn, Rom 2:1; □ their privileges over the Gentiles, Rom 3:1; □ their salvation excites St. Paul's zeal, Rom 9:1, 3; □ their fall does not make void God's promises, Rom 9:6; □ zeal of the ignorant Jews, Rom 10:2; □ their incredulity opposed, Rom 10:21; □ their future recall, Rom 11:26; □ Christ promised to them, Rom 15:5; □ the cross a scandal to them, 1 Cor 1:23; □ Jews in tutelage under the law, Gal 4:2; □ their union with the Gentiles, Eph 2:19; □ true Jews, Rom 2:28f.

Joy, of the People of God, 1 Ki 1:40; Ezr 6:16; Ps 149:2; Isa 35:1f; Heb 3:18; Mt 2:10; Jn 15:11; Acts 2:46; Rom 14:17; 2 Cor 8:2; □ follows afflictions, Pss 30:5f; 126:5f; Isa 35:10; 66:10-14; Jn 16:20-22; Jas 1:2-4; □ sources of, 2 Chr 20:27; Ps 89:16f; Isa 60:10; Lk 10:20f; Acts 2:28; Rom 15:13; □ in heaven over repentant sinners, Lk 15:7, 10; □ vanity of human joys, Eccl 2; 12:1f; Isa 16:10.

Judgment, men should examine before judging, after the example of God, Gen 3:9-19; 11:5; 18:21; Ex 3:7f; 23:2; Deut 13:4; 17:9; 19:18; Jos 7:19; 23:12f; Jdg 20:3, 12; Prov 18:13; Sir 11:7-9; 1 Mac 7:7; □ we must not judge rashly, Mt 7:1; 12:7; Lk 7:33f; Jn 7:24; 9:16; Acts 28:3-6; Rom 14:4, 13; 1 Cor 4:5; 1 Tim 5:21; □ last judgment an-nounced by our Lord, and reserved to him alone, Jn 5:22; □ last judgment described, Mt 25:31-46; Rev 6:14-17; 7; 8:9; □ particular judgment, Wis 3:1f; Eccl 8:6-8; 11:9; 12:14; Sir 11:28f; 16:13-22; 2 Mac 12:13-46; Lk 16:19-31; Heb 9:27; 10:31.

Justification, through faith, Acts 13:39; Rom 1:17; 3:20-30; 4; 5; Gal 3:11.

Kingdom, of God, 1 Chr 29:11; Isa 24:23; Dan 2:44; Mt 6:10; Lk 11:2; Acts 1:3; □ of Christ, Isa 2:1-5; 29:17-24; 61:4-9; Mt 26:29; Jn 18:36f; □ of heaven, Mt 3:2; 5:19; 7:21; 23:13; □ parables of, Mt 13:1-52; 20:1-16; 22:2-14; 25.

Law, the first, given, Gen 2:16; □ the first, violated, Gen 3:4-6; □ of the ten commandments given to Moses, Ex 20; Deut 5; □ tablets, of the, given, Ex 31:18; Deut 5:22; □ tablets, of the, broken, Ex 32:19; Deut 9:17; □ other tablets, of the, given, Ex 34:27; Deut 10:1; □ the

Old and the New, Rom 3:20; 4:15; 5:20; 7:1-7; Gal 3:19; 1 Tim 1:8; Heb 7:18-27; □ the natural, Rom 1:18-23; 2:12-16; □ ceremonies of the, abrogated by Christ, Mt 15: 1-20; Mk 15:38; Acts 13:38; 15:11; Rom 6:14; 7:4; 8:3; Gal 3:13; 4:5; Eph 2:13; Col 2:14; 1 Pet 1:11-19.

Lepers, healed, 2 Ki 5:14; Mt 8:2f; Mk 1:40-42; Lk 17:12-14.

Liberty, evangelical, Jn 8:32; Rom 6:18; 8:2, 21; Gal 5:13; 1 Pet 1:18; 2:16; 2 Pet 2:19; □ evil and condemned liberty, Jer 34:14ff.

Light, Jesus Christ is the light of the world, Isa 9:2; 49:6; 60:1, 19; 62:1; Jn 1:5; 8:12; 9:5; 12:36, 46; 1 Jn 1:5; 2:8; □ how Christians are, Prov 4:19; Mt 5:14; Rom 2:19; Phil 2:15.

Man, creation and dignity, Gen 1:26f; 2:7; Deut 4:32; Eccl 7:29; Isa 43:7; 45:12; 1 Cor 11:7; □ his fall, Gen 3; 2 Cor 11:3; □ his sinful state, Ps 51:1-6, 9-12; Rom 3:13-18; 7:18; 1 Jn 1:8; □ his weakness, Job 14:1-12; Pss 39:5-14; 103:14-16; Eccl 12:4-10; Mt 6:27; 1 Cor 3:7; □ his redemption, Rom 5; 1 Cor 1:30; Gal 3:14; Eph 3; Col 1:12-29; Heb 2:9-18; 1 Pet 1:18f; □ lot of wicked man, Job 18:5-21; 8:11-15; □ of the child of God, Ps 31:16; Acts 13:48; 22:14; 1 Thes 3:5; 1 Pet 1:3-5.

Mary, mother of God, foretold and prefigured, Gen 3:15; Pss 45:10; 46:5; 85:2; 87:3; 132:8; Prov 31:10-31; Song; Sir 24; Isa 7:14; 11:1; 19:1; 45:8; Jer 31:22; □ called mother of our Lord, Lk 1:43; □ mother of Jesus, Mt 2:13; □ the angel Gabriel sent to, Lk 1:26; □ visits St. Elizabeth, Lk 1:39f; □ composes her canticle, the Magnificat, Lk 1:46; □ gives birth to our Savior, Mt 1:16; Lk 2:7; □ presents Jesus in the temple, Lk 2:22; □ sorrows prophesied to her, Lk 2:34f; □ flees into Egypt, Mt 2:13f; □ returns to Nazareth, Mt 2:20-23; □ loses Jesus in the temple, Lk 2:42-51; □ at the foot of the cross, Jn 19:25; □ St. John given to her as a son, Jn 19:26f; □ remains with the apostles, Acts 1:14.

Mass, sacrifice of, prefigured, Gen 14:18; 22:13; □ foretold, Mal 1:10f; □ instituted by Christ, Lk 22:19f; □ attested, 1 Cor 10:16, 18-21; Heb 13:10. See Eucharist.

Messiah, he is promised to Adam, Gen 3:15; □ promised to Abraham, Gen 12:3; 21:12; 22:18; □ he will have a precursor, Mal 3:1; 4:5f; □ his birth miraculously announced, Isa 7:14; Jer 23:5f; □ time of his coming revealed to Daniel, Dan 9:24ff; □ place of his birth designated, Mic 5:2. 5; □ his reign described, Jer 23:5; □ his presence in the second temple, Hag 2:8; □ his abode among men, Isa 12:6; □ he will be rejected by his people, Ps 22:7; Isa 49:7; □ called the Christ, Mt 26:63f; Jn 1:41; 4:25; 7:41; 11:27; Acts 17:3; 18:28; □ he is the Lamb of God, Jn 1:29, 36; □ his passion prefigured and foretold; his birth, life, works and death. *See* Christ.

Name, of God, to be venerated, Deut 5:11; Lev 18:21; Ps 111:9; Ezek 36:20f; Mic 4:5; 1 Tim 6:1; Lk 1:49; □ of Christ, to be confessed, Acts 9:15, 28; 19:17; 2 Thes 1:12; 2 Tim 2:19; □ actions done in Christ's name, Mt 28:19; Mk 9:41; Jn 14:13; 16:23f; Acts 3:6; 4:10; 1 Cor 5:4f; Eph 5:20; Col 3:17; Heb 13:15; □ salvation in Christ's name, Acts 2:21; Rom 10:13; 1 Cor 6:11; 1 Jn 3:23; 5:13.

Neighbor, duties toward, Ex 2:13; 20:16; 22:26; Lev 19:18; Deut 15:2; 27:17; Prov 3:28; 24:28; 25:8, 17; Lk 10:25-37; Rom 3:9; Gal 5:14; Jas 2:8.

Obedience, Prov 25:12; Rom 6:16; 13:5; 1 Pet 1:22; □ to God, Deut 11:27f; 30:19f; 1 Sam 15:22f; Eccl 4:17; Jer 43:7; Acts 4:19; □ to parents, Ex 20:12; 21:15, 17; Lev 19:3; Deut 5:16; Tob 4:3f; Prov 19:26; 30:17; Sir 3:1-16; 23:14; Mt 15:4; 19:19; Mk 7:10; Eph 6:1-4; 2 Tim 3:2; Heb 12:7; □ to masters and those in authority, Eph 6:5-9; Heb 13:17; □ of Christ, Lk 2:51; Phil 2:8; Heb 5:8f.

Original Sin, Job 14:4; 15:14; Ps 51:7; Sir 8:5; Rom 3:9, 23; 5:12; □ its effects, Gen 8:21; Rom 5:12, 17; 6:23; 8:6-8, 11, 13, 17; Gal 5:17.

Pardon, granted by God alone, Ps 51:6; Mk 2:7; Lk 5:21; □ granted in virtue of Christ's blood, Mt 26:28; Eph 1:7; Heb 9:12, 22; 1 Pet 1:18f; □ as a result of faith in Jesus, Acts 10:43; 26:18; □ in Christ, Eph 4:32; Col 1:14; after repentance, Mk 1:4; Lk 3:3; 24:47; Acts 5:31; □ through baptism, Acts 2:38; □ power to pardon granted by Jesus to disciples, Jn 20:23; □ happiness of those pardoned, Ps 32:1; Rom 4:7; □ pardon one another, Mt 6:14f; 18:23-35; Mk 11:25f; Lk 6:37; 2 Cor 2:7; Eph 4:32; Col 3:13; Jas 2:13.

Parents, their duties, Gen 18:19; 21:19; 24:2; 25:6; 34:4ff; 49; Ex 10:2; 12:26; 13:14; 21:9f; Lev 19:29; Num 30:6; Deut 4:9; 6:7; 11:19; 21:19; 22:15; 32:46; Jos 4:21; 1 Sam 2:23; 3:13; 1 Ki 2:1; Tob 1:10; 4; 10:12f; 14:5, 12; Job 1:5; Ps 78:5; Prov 1:8; 4:1; 5:7; 11:29; 13:24; 19:18; 20:7; 22:6, 15; 23:13; 29:17; Sir 4:23; 7:23; 8:9; 25:7; 30:1-13; 42:5, 9-14; Dan 13:3; 1 Mac 2:49ff; 2 Mac 6:24, 28; 7:20-29; Mt 10:37; Eph 6:4; Col 3:21; 2 Tim 3:15; Tit 2:4.

Peace, of God, Lev 26:6; Prov 16:7; Job 11:18f; Rom 1:7; 2 Cor 1:2; Phil 4:7; □ of Christ, Lk 7:50; 8:48; Jn 14:27; Rom 5:1; 1 Cor 1:3; Gal 1:3; 2 Thes 3:16; □ fruit of the Spirit, Rom 8:6; Gal 5:22; Eph 2:17; □ peace with God, Isa 27:5; Acts 10:34-36; Rom 5:1; 2 Cor 5:18-20; Eph 2:12-18; □ no peace for the wicked, Isa 48:22; 57:21; 59:8; Jer 12:12; 16:5; Rom 3:17; Rev 6:4.

Penance, satisfaction for sins, Ps 6:7; Mt 3:8; Lk 3:8; Acts 2:38; 8:22; 2 Cor 7:7-10; □ is preached, Jer 7:3; Mt 3:2, 4, 8; Lk 3:3, 8; 13:3; 24:47; Acts 2:38; 3:19; 8:21; 17:30; 20:21; 26:20; □ examples of true, Jdg 10:15; 2 Sam 12:13; 24:10-17; 2 Chr 12:6f; 33:12; Jud 4:7-9; Jon 3; Mt 26:75; Lk 7:37-44; 15:18; 18:13; 19:8; 22:62; 23:41; Acts 2:37-41; □ examples of false, Gen 4:13; 27:38; Ex 8:4-11; 9:27; 10:16; Jos 7:20; Jdg 1:7; 1 Sam 15:24, 30; 24:19; 1 Ki 13:6; 21:27; Wis 5:3; 1 Mac 6:12; 2 Mac 9:12; Mt 27:4; Acts 8:13-23; Heb 12:17.

People of God, privileges and blessings, Deut 32:9; 33; 2 Sam 7:23f; Pss 3:9; 149:4; Lk 1:17; Rom 11; 1 Pet 2:9; Rev 21:3-7; □ belongs to God, Ps 103:3; Tit 2:14; Heb 8:10; □ saved, Mt 1:21; Rev 5:9; □ happiness of, Ps 144:15; □ will never be abandoned, 1 Sam 12:22; Ps 94:14; □ the rest of God, Heb 4:9-11.

Perseverance, exhortations to, Mt 10:22; 24:13; Lk 9:62; Acts 13:43; 1 Cor 15:58; Eph 6:18; Heb 3:6, 13; 10:23, 28; 2 Pet 3:17; □ rewarded, Isa 56:4-7; Lk 8:15; Rom 2:7; 15:4; Heb 6:15; Jas 1:25; □ examples of, Acts 1:14; 2:42; 1 Cor 15:1; Rev 1:9.

Poor, not to be oppressed, Ex 22:25; Deut 24:10-17; Isa 3:14f; Prov 14:31; 28:3; Eccl 5:7; Am 2:6f; 4:1f; 5:11f; Zec 7:10; Jas 2:2-6; □ duties toward, Ex 23:11; Lev 19:10; Deut 1:17; 15:7-10; Pss 82:3f; 112:9; Prov 21:13; 24:23; 29:7; Isa 58:7; Jer 22:3; Mt 5:42; Lk 3:11; Gal 2:10; Eph 4:28; 1 Tim 6:18; 1 Jn 3:17; □ equal to the rich before God, Ex 30:15; Job 31:15; 34:19; Ps 49:2f; Prv 22:2; □ promises of God for, Job 5:15; Pss 9:19; 72:7; 132:15; Zep 3:12; 2 Cor 8:9; □ to be consoled by the Church, Acts 6:1; 11:29f; 1 Cor 16:1; 2 Cor 8:1-3; 9:11-13; Gal 2:10; Heb 13:16; □ blest are the poor in spirit, Mt 5:3; Lk 6:20; Isa 66:2.

Pope, or chief bishop, St. Peter, by Christ's ordinance, was raised to this dignity, Mt 16:18f; Lk 22:31f; Jn 21:15; 17. See also Mt 10:2; Acts 5:29; Gal 2:7f.

Prayer, Gen 18:27; Ex 17:11; Tob 4:20; 12:8; Jud 4:12; Ps 141:2; Prov 28:9; Wis 16:28; Sir 2:10; 7:10, 14; 35:12-18; Isa 29:13f; Mt 6:5-13; 7:7-11; 18:19f; Mk 14:24-26; Lk 11:2-13; 18:1; Jn 14:13f; 15:7; 16:23f; Rom 8:26f; Eph 6:18; Phil 4:6; Col 4:2; 1 Thes 5:17; 1 Tim 2:1-3; Jas 4:3; 5:16-18; 1 Jn 3:22; 5:14f; □ the Lord's, Mt 6:9-13; Lk 11:2-4; □ of Christ for his disciples, Jn 17; □ of the apostles, Acts 4:24-30.

Prayers for the Dead, 2 Mac 12:43.

Preaching, of repentance, Jon 3; Mt 3:1-12; 4:17; 12:41; Mk 1:4-8, 14; Lk 3:3-20; □ of the gospel, by Jesus, Mt 4:23; 5; 6; 7; Mk 1:14; Lk 4:18-27; by the apostles, Mt 28:19f; Mk 16:15; Lk 24:47; Acts 2:14-40; 3:12-26; 4:8-12; 10:34-48; 13:16-41; 17:22-31; 26:1-19.

Promises, of God, inviolable, Num 23:19; Deut 7:8f; Jos 23:14; Ps 89:3; 1 Ki 8:56; 2 Cor 1:20; Heb 6:17f; □ obtained by faith and perseverance, Heb 6:12; 10:36; Rom 4:13; Lk 1:45; □ of a celestial inheritance, 1 Pet 1:3f; □ of the reestablishment of Israel, Isa 43:5f; Jer 31:4; Hos 14:4-8; Zec 10:6-12; □ made to the poor and orphans, Deut 10:18; Ps 9:19; Prov 15:25; Jer 49:11; Hos 14:3; □ made to Abraham, Gen 12:2, 3, 7; 13:14-17; 15; 17; 18:10, 14; 22:15-18; □ made to David and Solomon, 2 Sam 7:11-16; 1 Ki 3:12-14; 9:2-9; □ of Christ, to his disciples, Mt 6:4, 6, 18; 7:7-10; 16:8, 19, 25, 28; Lk 11:9f; 12:31f; Jn 14:15; 16; 20:21-23; □ about his return, Mt 24:30, 44; Mk 13:26; Lk 12:40; 21:27; Jn 14:3; Acts 1:11.

Prophecy, gift of God, Isa 44:7; 45:21; Lk 1:70; □ of the Spirit, 1 Cor 12:9f; 1 Pet 1:21; □ of Jesus, Eph 4:11; Rev 1:1; 11:3; □ how to receive it, Lk 24:25; 1 Thes 5:20; 2 Pet 1:19; Rev 1:3; 22:7; □ prophecies concerning Jesus the Messiah and their fulfillment:

Gen 12:3; 18:18 □ Acts 3:25f
Deut 18:15, 18 □ Acts 3:22f
Ps 2:1f □ Acts 4:25-28
Ps 2:7 □ Acts 13:33; Heb 1:5
Ps 22:2 □ Mt 27:46; Mk 15:34
Ps 22:19 □ Mt 27:35; Jn 19:23
Ps 69:22 □ Mt 27:34, 48
Isa 7:14 □ Mt 1:18-23
Isa 8:23 □ Mt 4:15f
Isa 53:12 □ Mk 15:27f; Lk 23:33f
Mic 5:1 □ Mt 2:1, 5f
Zec 9:9 □ Mt 21:1-9
Zec 11:13 □ Mt 27:3-10
Zec 13:7 □ Mt 26:31, 56
Mal 3:1 □ Mt 11:7-10
Mal 4:5f □ Mt 11:13f; 17:10

Prophecies, pronounced by Jesus about his death and resurrection, Mt 12:40; 17:22f; 20:18f; Jn 2:19-22; 12:32f; □ about Judas' betrayal, Mt 26:21-25; Jn 6:70f; 13:18f; □ about Peter's denial, Mt 26:34; Jn 13:38; □ about the sending of the Holy Spirit, Jn 14:16; Lk 24:49; Acts 1:5, 8; □ about the preaching of the gospel, Mt 24:14; 26:13; Mk 13:10; □ about persecutions, Mt 10:17-25; Jn 16:2, 32f; □ about destruction of Jerusalem, Mt 24; Mk 13; Lk 19:43f; 21.

Prudence, described, Prov 12:16, 23; 13:16; 14:8; 15:5, 18; 16:21-23; 22:3; Am 5:13; □ exhortations to, Mt 24:45; 25:13; 26:41; Lk 12:35; 21:36; 1 Cor 10:12; 1 Thes 5:6; 2 Tim 4:5; 1 Pet 4:7; 5:8.

Purgatory, or a middle state of souls suffering for a time on account of their sins, is shown by those many texts of Scripture which affirm that God will render to every man according to his works, so that such as die in lesser sins shall not escape without punishment, 2 Mac 12:43-46; Mt 5:25f; 12:32; Lk 12:58f; 1 Cor 3:15; 1 Pet 3:18-20; 1 Jn 5:16; Rev 5:3, 13.

Redemption, Job 19:25; Pss 31:6; 49:16; 71:23; 111:9; 130:7f; Isa 63:16; Hos 13:14; Lk 21:28; Rom 3:24; 1 Cor 6:20; 7:23; 15:55; 2 Cor 5:15; 1 Tim 2:5f; 2 Tim 1:9; Tit 2:14; Heb 9:11f; 1 Pet 1:18f; Rev 1:5; 5:9.

Relics, miraculous, 2 Ki 13:21; Mt 9:20f; Acts 19:11f.

Repentance, preached by John the Baptist, Mt 3:2; 8:11; Mk 1:4; Lk 3:3, 8, 19; □ preached by Jesus, Mt 4:17; Mk 1:15; Lk 15; 24:27; □ preached by the disciples, Mk 6:12; Acts 2:38; 3:19; 17:30; □ exhortations to, Hos 1:4; Zep 2:1-3; Zec 1:3f; Mal 3:7; Mt 3:3; 4:17; Rev 2:5, 16, 21; 3:3, 19.

Revelation, communications to man of hidden things, Deut 29:29; Isa 21:2; Jer 33:3; Dan 2:19; Am 3:7; Mt 11; 25; Rom 8:18; 1 Cor 2:9f; 1 Pet 1:5, 12; Rom 16:25; Col 1:26; □ God the author of, Isa 22:14; 53:1; Jer 33:3; Dan 2:22f, 28; Mt 16:17; □ through the Spirit, 1 Cor 2:10; Eph 3:5; □ depositaries of, chosen by God and Christ, Mt 11:25-27; Lk 10:22; Jn 11:38-40; Gal 1:15f; □ Jesus reveals God, Mt 11:27; Lk 10:22; Jn 1:18; Col 1:15; □ his justice, Rom 8:19; □ his love, 1 Jn 4:9; Jn 3:16.

Reward, promised to the just, Pss 19:10, 12; 58:12; Prov 11:18; 25:22; Isa 61:8; Mt 10:41f; Lk 6:35; □ promised to those unjustly persecuted, Mt 5:11f; □ promised to each according to his works, 1 Cor 3:8; Col 3:23f; 2 Jn 8; Rev 22:12.

Riches, dangers of, Deut 8:13ff; 32:15; Job 31:24f; Ps 62:11; Prov 11:28; 18:23; 30:8f; Eccl 5:12; Jer 9:23; Hos 12:9; Mic 6:12; Mt 6:19; Lk 12:15; 1 Tim 6:9. 17; Jas 2:6; □ evils brought on by, Neh 9:25f; Mt 10:22f; 13:22; 19:23f; Mk 10:22; 1 Tim 6:10; □ true riches, Isa 45:3; Mt 6:20; Lk 12:33; Rom 11:33; Col 3:1f; 1 Tim 6:19; Rev 2:9; 3:18; □ duties imposed by, Deut 8:18; 1 Chr 29:3-5, 12f; Job 31:16-20; Mt 19:21; 1 Tim 6:18f; 1 Jn 3:17.

Sacraments, they produce Grace, Jn 6:57ff; Acts 2:37f; 19:5; 8:17; 1 Pet 3:20f;

BAPTISM, commanded by Christ, Mt 28:19; Mk 16:16; Jn 3:5; □ taught and administered by the apostles, Acts 2:38, 41; 8:12, 38; 9:18; 10:48; 16:15, etc.; □ the laver of regeneration, 1 Pet 2:21; Tit 3:5; □ takes away all sin, Mk 1:4; 16:16; Lk 3:3; Jn 3:5; 1:33; Acts 2:38; 8:12f; 16:33; Rom 6:3-6; Gal 3:27; 1 Cor 6:11; Eph 5:26; Col 2:12-14; Heb 10:22; □ not to be repeated, Eph 4:5; Heb 6:4-6; 10:26; □ signifies passion or suffering, Mk 10:38; Lk 12:50; □ to be administered to children, Mt 18:14; 19:13f; Mk 10:13-16; Lk 18:15, 17; Jn 3:5; Acts 2:39; 16:15, 33; 1 Cor 1:16; 15:22; □ persons baptized receive the Holy Spirit, Acts 2:38; 19:5f; □ the baptized put on Christ, Gal 3:27; □ Christians are baptized in Christ's death, Rom 6:3; □ are baptized in one body, 1 Cor 12:13, 27;

CONFIRMATION, Acts 8:17; 19:6, 20; Heb 6:2; 2 Cor 1:21f; Eph 1:13;

HOLY EUCHARIST, prophesied, Mal 1:11; □ prefigured, Ex 16:15; □ promised, Jn 6:32-60; □ instituted, Mt 26:26-28; Mk 14:22-24; Lk 22:19f; 1 Cor 10:16; 11:23-27, 29; □ should be frequently received, Ps 78:24f; Prov 9:2f; Wis 16:20; Acts 2:42; 20:7; □ Eucharist under one kind, Lk 24:30f; Jn 6:29, 33, 38, 51, 52, 58; Acts 2:42; 20:7; 1 Cor 11:27;

PENANCE, Mt 18:18; 16:19; Jn 20:22f; 2 Cor 5:18-20.

ANOINTING OF THE SICK, Mk 6:12f; Jas 5:14f;

HOLY ORDERS, instituted by Christ, Lk 22:19; Jn 20:22f; □ conferred by imposition of hands, Acts 6:6; 13:3; 14:22; □ give grace, 1 Tim 4:14; 2 Tim 1:6.

MATRIMONY, Mt 19:5; Mk 10:7; Eph 5:25, 31f; 1 Thes 4:4; 1 Tim 2:15.

Saints, departed, assist us by their prayers, Lk 16:9; 1 Cor 12:12, 20f; Rev 5:8; □ we have a communion with them, 1 Cor 12:26; Heb 12:22f; □ they have power over nations, Rev 2:26f; 5:10; □ they are with Christ in heaven, before the general resurrection, 2 Cor 5:1, 6-8; Phil 1:23f; Rev 4:4; 6:9; 7:9, 14, 15; 14:1, 3f; 19:1, 4-6, 20:4; □ their invocation, consult the texts quoted above with relation to angels, and such as testify to the great power which the prayers of God's servants have with him, and which authorize us to call for their prayers. For which see Ex 32:11, 14; 1 Sam 7:8-10; Job 42:7f; Rom 15:30; Eph 6:18f; 1 Thes 5:25; Heb 13:18; Jas 5:16.

Sinner, prayer of, for pardon, 2 Sam 19:18-20; 24:10, 17; Ezr 9:6-15; Neh 1:5-11; 9:7-37; Jud 9:16f; Pss 6; 32; 38; 51; 102; 130; 143; Isa 59:12f; 64:8f; Jer 17:14; Mt 8:2; Lk 15:17-19; 18:13.

Spouses, relations with each other, Gen 2:23f; Mt 19:4-6; Mk 10:6-9; 1 Cor 7:3-5; Eph 5:22-24; Col 3:18; 1 Pet 3:7; □ fidelity owed each other, Ex 20:14; Deut 5:18; Mk 10:12; Lk 18:20; Rom 7:2f; □ love one another, Eph 5:25-33; Col 3:19; □ figure of Christ and the Church, Mt 9:15; 25:1-13; 2 Cor 11:2; Eph 5:23, 24; Rev 19:7.

Trinity, prefigured and declared, Gen 1:26; 18:2; Ex 3:6, 15f; 4:5; Ps 33:6; Isa 6:3; 34:16; 48:16; 61:1; Mt 3:16; 10:20; 17:5; 28:19; Lk 4:18; Jn 3:34f; 14:16, 26; 1 Jn 5:7.

Will of God, Mt 7:21; 12:50; Mk 3:36; Jn 6:39; Rom 12:2; Eph 5:17; Col 1:9; 1 Thes 4:3; 1 Tim 2:4; 1 Jn 2:17.

Women, beauty of, Gen 12:4; Song 1:8; 4:1-7; 5:9; Sir 36:22; □ celebrated in salvation history, Gen 11:29; 24:15-67; 35:19f; Num 20:1; Jdg 4:1; 5:32; 1 Sam 25:3-39; 2 Sam 11:21; Jud 15:13; Mt 1:1-17; Lk 2:36f; 1 Pet 3:5; □ complement man, Gen 1:27; 2:23; 3:12; 5:2; Mt 19:4; 1 Cor 11:7; □ condition of, 1 Cor 14:34; Eph 5:22; Col 3:18; 1 Tim 2:12; □ emancipation of, Lk 10:38; 24:22; Acts 1:14; 16:13; 3:28; □ gift of God, Gen 2:22; Prov 19:14; Sir 26:14f; □ helpmate for man, Sir 36:24; 40:19ff; □ ideal wife, Prov 31:10-31; □ love for, Sir 7:19, 26; Mk 10:7f; □ as poets, Hannah: 2 Sam 1–2; Elizabeth: Lk 1:42-45; Mark: Lk 1:46-55; □ as prophets, Miriam: Ex 15:20-21; Deborah: Jdg 4:5-14; Anna: Lk 2:36-38; Philip's daughters: Acts 21:9; □ religious privileges of, Acts 1:14; 12:12f; 1 Cor 11:5; 14:34; 1 Tim 2:11; □ rules for dress of Christian, 1 Tim 2:9f; 1 Pet 3:3f; □ saw risen Christ first, Mk 16:9; Jn 20:14-18; □ sold for husband's debts, Mt 18:25; □ standing at the Cross, Mt 27:55f; Mk 15:40f; □ strength of, Jdg 5:29; 9:10f; 11:21; 13:18; Song 4:1-5; 7:2-10.

Works, of God, Job 9:1-20; 37 □ 41; Pss 8; 19; 89:6-15; 104; 111; 145; Eccl 8:17; Jer 10:12-16; □ inadequacy of works of law, Rom 3:20; Gal 2:16; Eph 2:9; □ demonstrate faith, Acts 26:20; Jas 2:14-26; □ exhortations to good works, Mt 5:16; Acts 9:36; 2 Cor 8:9; Eph 2:10; Phil 2:12; 1 Thes 4:11f; 2 Thes 2:17; 3:7-13; Heb 10:24; 1 Pet 2:12.

Worship, to be offered to God alone, Ex 20:3-5; Deut 5:7-9; Mt 4:10; Lk 4:8; Acts 10:26; □ manner of offering, Lev 10:3; Eccl 5:1-6; Ps 100; Jn 4:23f; Eph 5:19; Col 3:16.

THE SUNDAY GOSPELS (3-Year Cycle)

See p. 464 for feasts of the year that displace the Mass of Sunday.

2020 — A	2024 — B	2028 — C	2032 — A	2036 — B	2040 — C
2021 — B	2025 — C	2029 — A	2033 — B	2037 — C	2041 — A
2022 — C	2026 — A	2030 — B	2034 — C	2038 — A	2042 — B
2023 — A	2027 — B	2031 — C	2035 — A	2039 — B	2043 — C

Year A

Year B

ADVENT

CHRISTMAS TIME

LENT

SACRED PASCHAL TRIDUUM AND EASTER TIME

SOLEMNITIES OF THE LORD DURING ORDINARY TIME

ORDINARY TIME

Year C

ADVENT

CHRISTMAS TIME

LENT

SACRED PASCHAL TRIDUUM AND EASTER TIME

SOLEMNITIES OF THE LORD DURING ORDINARY TIME

ORDINARY TIME

Major Feasts of the Year